2000

Acronyms, Initialisms & Abbreviations Dictionary

ISSN 0270-4404

Acronyms, Initialisms & Abbreviations Dictionary

A Guide to Acronyms, Abbreviations,
Contractions, Alphabetic Symbols, and Similar Condensed Appellations

Covering: Aerospace, Associations, Banking, Biochemistry, Business, Data Processing,
Domestic and International Affairs, Economics, Education, Electronics, Genetics,
Government, Information Technology, Internet, Investment, Labor, Law, Medicine, Military Affairs,
Pharmacy, Physiology, Politics, Religion, Science, Societies, Sports, Technical
Drawings and Specifications, Telecommunications, Trade, Transportation, and Other Fields

27th Edition

Volume 1

Part 3
P-Z

Mary Rose Bonk,
Editor

Pamela Dear,
Associate Editor

GALE GROUP

Detroit
San Francisco
London
Boston
Woodbridge, CT

Editor: Mary Rose Bonk

Associate Editor: Pamela Dear
Assistant Editor: Phyllis Spinelli

Data Capture Manager: Ronald D. Montgomery
Project Administrator: Gwendolyn S. Tucker
Data Capture Specialists: Beverly Jendrowski, Constance Wells

Manufacturing Manager: Dorothy Maki
Buyer: Nekita McKee

Graphic Services Manager: Barbara J. Yarrow
Graphic Artist: Gary Leach

Manager, Technical Support Services: Theresa A. Rocklin
Programmer: Charles Beaumont

Library of Congress Catalog Card Number 84-643188
ISBN 0-7876-2857-3 (Volume 1 Complete)
ISBN 0-7876-2858-1 (Part 1: A-F only)
ISBN 0-7876-2859-X (Part 2: G-O only)
ISBN 0-7876-2860-3 (Part 3: P-Z only)
ISSN 0270-4404

Printed in the United States of America

Contents

Gale's publications in the acronyms and abbreviations field include:

Acronyms, Initialisms & Abbreviations Dictionary series:

Acronyms, Initialisms & Abbreviations Dictionary (Volume 1). A guide to acronyms, initialisms, abbreviations, and similar contractions, arranged alphabetically by abbreviation.

Acronyms, Initialisms & Abbreviations Dictionary Supplement (Volume 2). An interedition supplement in which terms are arranged alphabetically both by abbreviation and by meaning.

Reverse Acronyms, Initialisms & Abbreviations Dictionary (Volume 3). A companion to Volume 1 in which terms are arranged alphabetically by meaning of the acronym, initialism, or abbreviation.

Acronyms, Initialisms & Abbreviations Dictionary Subject Guide series:

Computer & Telecommunications Acronyms (Volume 1). A guide to acronyms, initialisms, abbreviations, and similar contractions used in the field of computers and telecommunications in which terms are arranged alphabetically both by abbreviation and by meaning.

Business Acronyms (Volume 2). A guide to business-oriented acronyms, initialisms, abbreviations, and similar contractions in which terms are arranged alphabetically both by abbreviation and by meaning.

International Acronyms, Initialisms & Abbreviations Dictionary series:

International Acronyms, Initialisms & Abbreviations Dictionary (Volume 1). A guide to foreign and international acronyms, initialisms, abbreviations, and similar contractions, arranged alphabetically by abbreviation.

Reverse International Acronyms, Initialisms & Abbreviations Dictionary (Volume 2). A companion to Volume 1, in which terms are arranged alphabetically by meaning of the acronym, initialism, or abbreviation.

Periodical Title Abbreviations series:

Periodical Title Abbreviations: By Abbreviation (Volume 1). A guide to abbreviations commonly used for periodical titles, arranged alphabetically by abbreviation.

Periodical Title Abbreviations: By Title (Volume 2). A guide to abbreviations commonly used for periodical titles, arranged alphabetically by title.

User's Guide

The following examples illustrate possible elements of entries in *AIAD:*

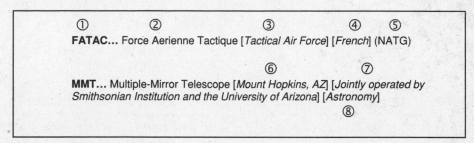

①   Acronym, Initialism, or Abbreviation

②   Meaning or Phrase

③   English Translation

④   Language (for non-English entries)

⑤   Source code (Allows you to verify entries or find additional information. Decoded in the List of Selected Sources)

⑥   Location or Country of origin (Provides geographic identifiers for airports, colleges and universities, libraries, military bases, political parties, radio and television stations, and others)

⑦   Sponsoring organization

⑧   Subject category (Clarifies entries by providing appropriate context)

The completeness of a listing is dependent upon both the nature of the term and the amount of information provided by the source. If additional information becomes available during future research, an entry is revised.

Arrangement of Entries

Acronyms, initialisms, and abbreviations are arranged alphabetically in letter-by-letter sequence. Spacing, punctuation, and capitalization are not considered. If the same term has more than one meaning, the various meanings are subarranged in word-by-word sequence.

Should you wish to eliminate the guesswork from acronym formation and usage, a companion volume could help. *Reverse Acronyms, Initialisms and Abbreviations Dictionary* contains essentially the same entries as *AIAD,* but arranges them alphabetically by meaning, rather than by acronym or initialism.

List of Selected Sources

Each of the sources included in the following list contributed at least 50 terms. It would be impossible to cite a source for every entry because the majority of terms are sent by outside contributors, are uncovered through independent research by the editorial staff, or surface as miscellaneous broadcast or print media references.

For sources used on an ongoing basis, only the latest edition is listed. For most of the remaining sources, the edition that was used is cited. The editors will provide further information about these sources upon request.

Unless further described in an annotation, the publications listed here contain no additional information about the acronym, initialism, or abbreviation cited.

(AABC)   *Catalog of Abbreviations and Brevity Codes.* Washington, DC: U.S. Department of the Army, 1981. [Use of source began in 1969]

(AAEL)   *Common Abbreviations and Acronyms in Electronics.* By Gunham Kaytaz. <http://www.seas.smu.edu/~kaytaz/menu.html> (27 April 1999)

(AAG)   *Aerospace Abbreviations Glossary.* Report Number AG60-0014. Prepared by General Dynamics/Astronautics. San Diego, CA: 1962.

(AAGC)   *Acronyms and Abbreviations in Government Contracting.* 2d ed. By Patricia A. Tobin and Joan Nelson Phillips. Washington, DC: George Washington University, 1997.

(AAMN)   *Abbreviations and Acronyms in Medicine and Nursing.* By Solomon Garb, Eleanor Krakauer, and Carson Justice. New York, NY: Springer Publishing Co., 1976.

(ABBR)   *Abbreviations: The Comprehensive Dictionary of Abbreviations and Letter Symbols.* Vol. 1 C. By Edward Wall. Ann Arbor, MI: The Pierian Press, 1984.

(AC)   *Associations Canada 1995/96.* Edited by Ward McBurney. Toronto, Canada: Canadian Almanac & Directory Publishing Co. Ltd., 1995.

(ACII)   *"Acronym and Initials Index."* 7 February 1996. <http://www.ioi.ie/~readout/cl.html> (7 November 1996)

(AD)   *Abbreviations Dictionary.* 8th ed. By Ralph De Sola. Boca Raton, FL: CRC Press, 1992.

(ADA)   *The Australian Dictionary of Acronyms and Abbreviations.* 2nd ed. Compiled by David J. Jones. Leura, NSW, Australia: Second Back Row Press Pty. Ltd., 1981.

(ADDR)   *Army Dictionary and Desk Reference.* By Tim Zurick. Harrisburg, PA: Stackpole Books, 1992.

(AEBS)   *Acronyms in Education and the Behavioral Sciences.* By Toyo S. Kawakami. Chicago, IL: American Library Association, 1971.

(AEE)   *American Educators' Encyclopedia.* By Edward L. Dejnozka and David E. Kapel. Westport, CT: Greenwood Press, 1991.

(AEPA)   U.S. Environmental Protection Agency. *ACCESS EPA*. 1995/96 ed. Washington, DC: Office of Information Resources Management, 1996.

(AF)   *Reference Aid: Abbreviations in the African Press*. Arlington, VA: Joint Publications Research Service, 1979.

(AFIT)   *Compendium of Authenticated Systems and Logistics*. Washington, DC: Air Force Institute of Technology, 1984.

(AFM)   *Air Force Manual of Abbreviations*. Washington, DC: U.S. Department of the Air Force, 1975. [Use of source began in 1969]

(AIA)   *Aviation Insurance Abbreviations, Organisations and Institutions*. By M.J. Spurway. London, England: Witherby & Co. Ltd., 1983.

(AIE)   *Acronyms and Initialisms in Education*. 6th ed. Compiled by John Hutchins. Norwich, England: Librarians of Institutes and Schools of Education, 1995.

(AL)   *"Acronyms & Abbreviations."* American Library Association. <http://www.ala.org/> (2 December 1997)

(ANA)   *"Abbreviations" - U.S. Navy Dictionary*. 3rd revision. Washington, DC: DCP, 1989.

(APTA)   *Australian Periodical Title Abbreviations*. Compiled by David J. Jones. Leura, NSW, Australia: Second Back Row Press Pty. Ltd., 1985.

(ARC)   *Agricultural Research Centres: A World Directory of Organizations and Programmes*. 2 vols. Edited by Nigel Harvey. Harlow, Essex, England: Longman Group, 1983.
    A world guide to official, educational, industrial, and independent research centers which support research in the fields of agriculture, veterinary medicine, horticulture, aquaculture, food science, forestry, zoology, and botany.

(ARCH)   *Dictionary of Architecture and Construction*. Edited by Cyril M. Harris. New York, NY: McGraw-Hill, Inc., 1975.

(ASF)   *Guide to Names and Acronyms of Organizations, Activities, and Projects*. By Food and Agriculture Organization of the United Nations. Fishery Information, Data, and Statistics Service and U.S. National Oceanic and Atmospheric Administration. Aquatic Sciences and Fisheries Information System Reference Series, Number 10, 1982. n.p.

(BABM)   *Bailliere's Abbreviations in Medicine*. 5th ed. By Edwin B. Steen. London, England: Bailliere Tindall, 1984.

(BARN)   *The Barnhart Abbreviations Dictionary*. Edited by Robert K. Barnhart. New York, NY: John Wiley & Sons, Inc., 1995.

(BCP)   *BCP Guidebook*. <http://www.dtic.dla.mil/environdod/> (Fall 1995)

(BI)   *British Initials and Abbreviations*. 3rd ed. By Ian H. Wilkes. London, England: Leonard Hill Books, 1971.

(BIB)   *Bibliotech*. Ottawa, Canada: National Library of Canada, 1988-89.

(BJA)	*Biblical and Judaic Acronyms*. By Lawrence Marwick. New York, NY: Ktav Publishing House, Inc., 1979.
(BRI)	*Book Review Index*. 1997 Cumulation. Edited by Beverly Baer. Detroit, MI: Gale Research, 1998.
(BROA)	*Broadcasting and Cable Yearbook 1998*. 2 vol. New Providence, NJ: Reed Elsevier, Inc., 1998.
(BTTJ)	*Breaking Through Technical Jargon: A Dictionary of Computer and Automation Acronyms*. By Mark S. Merkow. New York, NY: Van Nostrand Reinhold, 1990.
(BUAC)	*Buttress's World Guide to Abbreviations of Organizations*. 11th ed. Revised by L.M. Pitman. London, England: Blackie Academic and Professional, 1997.
(BUR)	*Computer Acronyms and Abbreviations Handbook*. Tokyo, Japan: Burroughs Co. Ltd., 1978.
(BYTE)	*Byte: The Small Systems Journal*. Peterborough, NH: McGraw-Hill Information Systems, Inc., 1987-89.
(CAAL)	*CAAL COMOPTEVFOR Acronym and Abbreviation List*. Norfolk, VA: (CAAL-U) Operational Test and Evaluation Force, 1981.
(CB)	*Centres & Bureaux: A Directory of Concentrations of Effort, Information and Expertise*. Edited by Lindsay Sellar. Beckenham, Kent, England: CBD Research Ltd., 1987. A guide to British organizations which include the words "centre" or "bureau" in their names. Entries include name and address; telephone and telex numbers; chief official; and a description of the purposes, activities, and services of the organization.
(CDAI)	*Concise Dictionary of Acronyms and Initialisms*. By Stuart W. Miller. New York, NY: Facts on File Publications, 1988.
(CDE)	*The Computer Desktop Encyclopedia*. By Alan Freedman. New York, NY: AMACOM, 1996.
(CDI)	*The Cancer Dictionary*. By Roberta Altman and Michael Sarg, M.D. New York, NY: Facts on File, 1992.
(CED)	*Current European Directories*. 2nd ed. Edited by G.P. Henderson. Beckenham, Kent, England: CBD Research, 1981.
(CET)	*Communications-Electronics Terminology*. AFM 11-1. Vol. 3. U.S. Department of the Air Force, 1973.
(CINC)	*A CINCPAC Glossary of Commonly Used Abbreviations and Short Titles*. By Ltc. J.R. Johnson. Washington, DC: 1968.
(CIST)	*Computer & Information Science & Technology Abbreviations & Acronyms Dictionary*. Edited by David W. South, ed. Boca Raton, FL: CRC Press, Inc., 1994.
(CMD)	*Complete Multilingual Dictionary of Computer Terminology*. Compiled by Georges Nania. Chicago, IL: National Textbook Co., 1984. Computer-related terms in Spanish, French, Italian, Portuguese, and English. Indexes in French, Italian, Spanish, and Portuguese are also provided.

(CNC)   *American National Standard Codes for the Representation of Names of Countries, Dependencies, and Areas of Special Sovereignty for Information Interchange.* U.S. National Bureau of Standards. Washington, DC: Government Printing Office, 1986. [Use of source began in 1977]

> These standard codes, approved by the International Organization for Standardization and the American National Standards Institute, are used in the international interchange of data in many fields.

(COE)   *Cooper's Comprehensive Environmental Desk Reference.* Edited by Andre R. Cooper. New York, NY: John Wiley & Sons, 1990.

(CPH)   *The Charles Press Handbook of Current Medical Abbreviations.* 3rd ed. Philadelphia, PA: The Charles Press Publishers, Inc., 1991.

(CRD)   *Computer-Readable Databases: A Directory and Data Sourcebook.* 6th ed. Edited by Kathleen Young Marcaccio. Detroit, MI: Gale Research, 1990.

> A guide to online databases, offline files available in various magnetic formats, and CD-ROM files. Entries include producer name, address, telephone number, description of coverage, vendors, and contact person.

(CROSS) *Cross-Border Links: A Directory of Organizations in Canada, Mexico, and the United States.* Edited by Ricardo Hernandez and Edith Sanchez. Albuquerque, NM: Inter-Hemispheric Education Resource Center, 1992.

(CSR)   *Computer Science Resources: A Guide to Professional Literature.* Edited by Darlene Myers. White Plains, NY: Knowledge Industry Publications, Inc., 1981:

> Covers several types of computer-related literature including journals, technical reports, directories, dictionaries, handbooks, and university computer center newsletters. Five appendices cover career and salary trends in the computer industry, user group acronyms, university computer libraries, and trade fairs and shows.

(CTT)   *Corporate TrendTrac.* Edited by A. Dale Timpe. Detroit, MI: Gale Research, 1988-89.

> Covers mergers and acquisitions, stock exchange listings and suspensions, company name changes, bankruptcies, liquidations, and reorganizations.

(DA)   *Dictionary of Aviation.* By R. J. Hall and R. D. Campbell. Chicago, IL: St. James Press, 1991.

(DAS)   *Dictionary of Abbreviations and Symbols.* By Edward Frank Allen. London, England: Cassell and Co. Ltd., 1949.

(DAVI)   *The Davis Book of Medical Abbreviations: A Deciphering Guide.* By Sarah Lu Mitchell-Hatton. Philadelphia, PA: F. A. Davis Co., 1991.

(DB)   *Dictionary of Biomedical Acronyms and Abbreviations.* 2nd ed. By Jacques Dupayrat. New York, NY: John Wiley & Sons, 1990.

(DBA)   *Directory of British Associations.* Edited by G. P. Henderson and S. P. A. Henderson. Beckenham, Kent, England: CBD Research, Ltd., 1990.

(DBQ)   *A Dictionary of British Qualifications.* London, England: Kogan Page Ltd., 1985.

(DCTA)   *Dictionary of Commercial Terms and Abbreviations.* By Alan E. Branch. London, England: Witherby & Co. Ltd., 1984.

(DD)   *The Financial Post Directory of Directors 1997*. Toronto, Canada: The Financial Post, 1996.

(DDC)   *The International Dictionary of Data Communications*. By Robert A. Saigh. Chicago, IL: The Glenlake Publishing Company, Ltd., 1998.

(DDSO)   *D & D Standard Oil Abbreviator*. 4th ed. Compiled by the Association of Desk and Derrick Clubs. Tulsa, OK: PennWell Books, 1994.

(DEN)   *Dictionary of Electronics and Nucleonics*. By L.E.C. Hughes, R.W.B. Stephens and L. D. Brown. New York, NY: Barnes & Noble, 1969.

(DET)   *Dictionary of Educational Terms*. Edited by David Blake and Vincent Hanley. Brookfield, VT: Ashgate Publishing Co., 1995.

(DFIT)   *Dictionary of Finance and Investment Terms*. 4th ed. Edited by John Downes and Jordan Elliot Goodman. Hauppauge, NY: Barron's Educational Series, 1995.

(DGA)   *Dictionary of Graphic Arts Abbreviations*. By L. W. Wallis. Rockport, MA: Rockport Publishers, Inc., 1986.

(DHP)   *Dictionary of Abbreviations and Acronyms in Helping Professions*. By John W. Hollis. Muncie, IN:
Accelerated Development, Inc., 1987.

(DHSM)   *Dictionary of Health Services Management*. 2nd ed. By Thomas C. Timmreck. Owings Mills, MD: Rynd Communications, 1987.

(DI)   *The Dictionary of Initials--What They Mean*. Compiled and edited by Harriette Lewis. Kingswood, Surrey, England: Paper Fronts Elliot Right Way Books, 1983.

(DICI)   *The Dictionary of Initials*. By Betsy M. Parks. Secaucus, NJ: Citadel Press, 1981.

(DIT)   *Dictionary of Informatics Terms in Russian and English*. By G.S. Zhdanov, E.S. Kolobrodov, V.A. Polushkin, and A.I. Cherny. Moscow: Nauka, 1971.

(DLA)   *Bieber's Dictionary of Legal Abbreviations*. 3rd ed. By Mary Miles Prince. Buffalo, NY: William S. Hein & Co., 1988.

(DMA)   *Dictionary of Military Abbreviations: British, Empire, Commonwealth*. By B.K.C. Scott. Hastings, East Sussex, England: Tamarisk Books, 1982.

(DMAA)   *Dictionary of Medical Acronyms and Abbreviations*. 3rd ed. Edited by Stanley Jablonski. Philadelphia, PA: Hanley & Belfus, Inc., 1998.

(DMC)   *Webster's New World Dictionary of Media and Communications*. Revised ed. By Richard Weiner. New York, NY: Macmillan, 1996.

(DNAB)   *Dictionary of Naval Abbreviations*. 3rd ed. Compiled and edited by Bill Wedertz. Annapolis, MD: Naval Institute Press, 1984.

(DOAD)   *The Dictionary of Advertising*. Edited by Laurence Urdang. Lincolnwood, IL: NTC Business Books, 1986.

(DOG)   *A Dictionary of Genetics*. 5th ed. By Robert C. King and William D. Stansfield. New York, NY: Oxford University Press, 1997.

(DOGT)   *"List of Acronyms."* <http://www.em.doe.gov/rtc1994/loa.html> (5 March 1997)

(DOM)   *The Dictionary of Multimedia: Terms & Acronyms.* By Brad Hansen. Wilsonvillee, OR: Franklin, Beedle & Associates, 1997.

(DOMA)   *Dictionary of Military Abbreviations.* By Norman Polmar, Mark Warren, and Eric Wertheim. Annapolis, MD: Naval Institute Press, 1994.

(DS)   *Dictionary of Shipping International Trade Terms and Abbreviations.* 3rd ed. By Alan E. Branch. London, England: Witherby & Co. Ltd., 1986.

(DSA)   *Dictionary of Sigla and Abbreviations to and in Law Books before 1607.* By William Hamilton Bryson. Charlottesville, VA: University Press of Virginia, 1975.

(DSUE)   *A Dictionary of Slang and Unconventional English.* 8th ed. By Eric Partridge. New York, NY: Macmillan Publishing Co., 1984.

(DUND)   *Directory of United Nations Databases and Information Services.* 4th ed. Compiled by the Advisory Committee for the Coordination of Information Systems. New York, NY: United Nations, 1990.
> A guide to computerized databases and information systems/services. Entries include sponsoring organization, year established, type, scope, coverage, timespan, and contact information.

(DWSG)   *Defense Weapon Systems Glossary.* By David Trotz. Piscataway, NJ: Target Marketing, 1992.

(EA)   *Encyclopedia of Associations.* 34th ed. Vol. 1, National Oranizations of the U.S. Edited by Christine Maurer and Tara E. Sheets. Farmington Hills, MI: Gale Group, 1999.
[Use of source began in 1960]
> A guide to trade, professional, and other nonprofit associations that are national and international in scope and membership and that are headquartered in the United States. Entries include name and address; telephone and telex number; chief official; and a description of the purpose, activities, and structure of the organization.

(EAAP)   *Encyclopedia of Associations: Association Periodicals.* 3 vols. Edited by Denise M. Allard and Robert C. Thomas. Detroit, MI: Gale Research, 1987.
> A directory of publications issued by all types of national nonprofit organizations in the United States. Entries include title and organization name, address, telephone number; description of periodical, frequency of publication, and price.

(EAIO)   *Encyclopedia of Associations: International Organizations.* 29th ed. Edited by Linda Irvin. Detroit, MI: Gale Research, 1995. [Use of source began in 1985]
> A guide to trade, professional, and other nonprofit associations that are national or international in scope and membership and that are headquartered outside the United States. Entries include name and address; principal foreign language name; telephone and telex number; chief official; and a description of the purpose, activities, and structure of the organization.

(EBF)   *Encyclopedia of Banking and Finance.* 10th ed. Edited by Charles J. Woelfel. Chicago, IL: Probus Publishing Co., 1994.

(ECED)   *The European Communities Encyclopedia and Directory 1992.* London, England: Europa Publications Ltd., 1991; distributed in U.S. by Gale Research, Detroit, MI.

A comprehensive guide to the European Communities. Entries explain widely-used acronyms and include address, telephone, telex, fax numbers and chief officers for EC-level organizations.

(ECII)   *Electronics, Computers and Industrial Instrumentation Abbreviations and Acronyms.* Edited by Sergio Sobredo. Miami, FL: Sergio Sobredo Technical Services, 1986.

(ECON)   *The Economist.* London, England: The Economist Newspaper Ltd., 1997. [Use of source began in 1988]

(EDAC)   *Dictionary of Educational Acronyms, Abbreviations, and Initialisms.* 2nd ed. Edited by James C. Palmer and Anita Y. Colby. Phoenix, AZ: Oryx Press, 1985.

(EDCT)   *Encyclopedic Dictionary of Chemical Technology.* By Dorit Noether and Herman Noether. New York, NY: VCH Publishers, Inc., 1993.

(EE)   *Eastern Europe and the Commonwealth of Independent States 1992.* London, England: Europa Publications Ltd., 1992; distributed in U.S. by Gale Research, Detroit, MI.

(EECA)   *Dictionary of Electrical, Electronics, and Computer Abbreviations.* By Phil Brown. London, England: Buttersworth, 1985.

(EES)   *A Dictionary of Ecology, Evolution and Systematics.* 2nd edition. Edited by Roger Lincoln, Geoff Boxshall and Paul Clark. New York, NY: Cambridge University Press, 1998.

(EFIS)   *Corporate Acronym Resource Guide, 1800s-1995.* Seattle, WA: Environmental Financial Information Services, Inc. (EFIS), 1996.

(EG)   *Environmental Glossary.* 4th ed. Edited by G. William Frick and Thomas F.P. Sullivan. Rockville, MD: Government Institutes, Inc., 1986.

(EGAO)   *Encyclopedia of Governmental Advisory Organizations.* 9th ed. Edited by Donna Batten. Detroit, MI: Gale Research, 1994-95 (and supplement, 1995). [Use of source began in 1975]
> A reference guide to permanent, continuing, and ad hoc U.S. presidential advisory committees, interagency committees, and other government-related boards, panels, task forces, commissions, conferences, and other similar bodies serving in a consultative, coordinating, advisory, research, or investigative capacity. Entries include name and address, telephone number, designated federal employee, history, recommendation and findings of the committee, staff size, publications, and subsidiaries. Also includes indexes to personnel, reports, federal agencies, presidential administration, and an alphabetical and keyword index.

(EMRF)   *The St. James Encyclopedia of Mortgage & Real Estate Finance.* By James Newell, Albert Santi, and Chip Mitchell. Chicago, IL: St. James Press, 1991.

(EPA)   *Glossary of EPA Acronyms.* Washington, DC: Environmental Protection Agency, 1987.

(ERG)   *Environmental Regulatory Glossary.* 5th ed. Edited by G. William Frick and Thomas F.P. Sullivan. Rockville, MD: Government Institutes, Inc., 1990.

(EY)   *The Europa World Year Book 1992.* London: Europa Publications Ltd., 1992. distributed in U.S. by Gale Research, Detroit, MI.
> An annual survey containing detailed information about the political, economic, statistical, and commercial situation of the regions and countries covered.

(FAAC)   *Contractions Handbook*. Changes. U.S. Department of Transportation. Federal Aviation Administration, 1993. [Use of source began in 1969]

(FAAL)   *Location Identifiers*. U.S. Department of Transportation. Federal Aviation Administration. Air Traffic Service, 1982.

(FEA)   *The Far East and Australasia 1987*. 18th ed. London, England: Europa Publications Ltd., 1986; distributed in U.S. by Gale Research, Detroit, MI.
           An annual survey containing detailed information about the political, economic, statistical, and commercial situation of the regions and countries covered.

(FFDE)   *The Facts on File Dictionary of Environmental Science*. By L. Harold Stevenson and Bruce Wyman. New York, NY: Facts on File, 1991.
           Defines terms from disciplines as diverse as biology, chemistry, geology, physics, engineering, meteorology, social science, medicine, and economics.

(GAAI)   *"Glossary of Abbreviations, Acronyms, and Initialisms."*
           <http://www.em.doe.gov/idb97/acropdf.html> (17 February 1998)

(GAVI)   *"Glossary of Aviation Acronyms and Abbreviations."*
           <http://olias.arc.nasa.gov/AFO_Acronyms_.html> (5 March 1997)

(GEA)   *Government Economic Agencies of the World: An International Directory of Governmental Organisations Concerned with Economic Development and Planning*. A Keesing's Reference Publication. Edited by Alan J. Day. Harlow, Essex, England: Longman Group Ltd., 1985.
           Covers over 170 countries and territories. Two introductory sections for each area cover economic data and prevailing economic and political conditions. Individual entries provide title, address, and names of chief officials of each agency. Current activities and financial structure of each agency are also detailed. An index of agency officials is provided.

(GFGA)   *Guide to Federal Government Acronyms*. Edited by William R. Evinger. Phoenix, AZ: The Oryx Press, 1989.

(GNE)   *The Green Encyclopedia.* By Irene Franck and David Brownstone. New York, NY: Prentice Hall General Reference, 1992.

(GPO)   *Style Manual*. Washington, DC: Government Printing Office, 1984.[Terms are included in Chapter 24, Foreign Languages]

(GRD)   *Government Research Directory*. 8th ed. Edited by Joseph M. Palmisano. Detroit, MI: Gale Research, 1994. (and supplement, 1994).
           A descriptive guide to U.S. government research and development centers, institutes, laboratories, bureaus, test facilities, experiment stations, data collection and analysis centers, and grants management and research coordinating offices in agriculture, business, education, energy, engineering, environment, the humanities, medicine, military science, and basic applied sciences.

(HCT)   *Health Care Terms.* 2nd ed. By Vergil N. Slee and Debora A. Slee. St. Paul, MN: Tringa Press, 1991.

(HGAA)   *The Handy Guide to Abbreviations and Acronyms for the Automated Office*. By Mark W. Greenia. Seattle, WA: Self-Counsel Press, Inc., 1986.

(HGEN)   *Human Genome Acronym List.* <http://www.ornl.gov/hgmis/acronym.html> (2 December 1998)

(HRG)   *The Human Resources Glossary: The Complete Desk Reference for HR Executives, Managers, and Practitioners.* 2nd ed. By William R. Tracey. Boca Raton, FL: St. Lucie Press, 1998.

(IAA)   *Index of Acronyms and Abbreviations in Electrical and Electronic Engineering.* Compiled by Buro Scientia. New York, NY: VCH Publishers, 1989.

(IBMDP)   *IBM Data Processing Glossary.* 6th ed. White Plains, NY: IBM Corp., 1977.

(ICAO)   *Aircraft Type Designators.* 13th ed. International Civil Aviation Organization, August, 1981.

(ICDA)   *Designators for Aircraft Operating Agencies, Aeronautical Authorities and Services.* 49th ed. International Civil Aviation Organization, June, 1982.
          Document also includes telephony designators and postal and telegraphic addresses of government civil aviation authorities.

(ICLI)   *Location Indicators.* 51st ed. International Civil Aviation Organization, February, 1987.
          Document also contains addresses of flight information centers.

(IDOE)   *The Illustrated Dictionary of Electronics.* 6th ed. By Stan Gibilisco. New York, NY: TAB Books, 1994.

(IEEE)   *IEEE Standard Dictionary of Electrical and Electronics Terms.* Edited by Frank Jay. New York, NY: The Institute of Electrical and Electronics Engineers, Inc., 1977, 1984.
          Includes definitions for thousands of electrical and electronics terms. Each entry includes a numeric source code.

(IGQR)   *The Internet Glossary & Quick Reference Guide.* By Alan Freedman, Alfred Glossbrenner and Emily Glossbrenner. New York, NY: AMACOM, 1998.

(IIA)   *Index of Initials and Acronyms.* Compiled by Richard Kleiner. New York, NY: Auerbach Publishers, 1971.

(IID)   *Information Industry Directory.* 15th ed. Edited by Annette Novallo. Detroit, MI: Gale Research, 1995. (and supplement, 1995).
          An international guide to computer-readable databases, database producers, and publishers, online vendors and time-sharing companies, telecommunications networks, and many other information systems and services. Entries include name and address, telephone number, chief official, and a detailed description of the purpose and function of the system or service.

(ILCA)   *Index to Legal Citations and Abbreviations.* By Donald Raistrick. Abingdon, Oxfordshire, England: Professional Books Ltd., 1981.

(IMH)   *International Marketing Handbook.* 2nd ed. Edited by Frank Bair. Detroit, MI: Gale Research, 1985.
          An in-depth guide to commercial and trade data on 142 countries of the world. Features include a list of European trade fairs and a report on growth markets in Western Europe.

(INF)   *Infantry.* Fort Benning, GA: U.S. Army Infantry Training School, 1996. [Use of source began in 1983]

(IRC)   *International Research Centers Directory 1992-93.* 6th ed. Edited by Annette Piccirelli. Detroit, MI: Gale Research, 1991.
> A world guide to government, university, independent, nonprofit, and commercial research and development centers, institutes, laboratories, bureaus, test facilities, experiment stations, and data collection and analysis centers, as well as foundations, councils, and other organizations which support research.

(IRUK)   *Industrial Research in the United Kingdom.* 12th ed. Harlow, Essex, England: Longman Group UK Ltd., 1987.
> A guide to all groups conducting or funding research relevant to British industrial development. Entries include name, address, telephone and telex numbers; chief officials; and scope of activities.

(IT)   *Information Today: The Newspaper for Users and Producers of Electronic Information Services.* Medford, NJ: Learned Information, Inc., 1988-89.

(ITD)   *International Tradeshow Directory.* 5th ed. Frankfurt, Germany: M + A Publishers for Fairs, Exhibitions and Conventions Ltd., 1989.
> A guide to trade fairs and exhibitions throughout the world. Entries include event name, dates, frequency, location, description of purpose, profile of exhibitors and attendees.

(IYR)   *The 1989-92 International Yacht Racing Rules.* London, England: International Yacht Racing Union, 1989.

(KSC)   *A Selective List of Acronyms and Abbreviations.* Compiled by the Documents Department, Kennedy Space Center Library, 1971, 1973.

(LAIN)   *Latest Intelligence: An International Directory of Codes Used by Government, Law Enforcement, Military, and Surveillance Agencies.* By James E. Tunnell. Blue Ridge Summit, PA: TAB BOOKS, 1990.

(LCCP)   *MARC Formats for Bibliographic Data.* Appendix II. Washington, DC: Library of Congress, 1982.

(LCLS)   *Symbols of American Libraries.* 14th ed. Edited by the Enhanced Cataloging Division. Washington, DC: Library of Congress, 1992. [Use of source began in 1980]

(LWAP)   *Legal Words and Phrases: Speed Abbreviations.* By Joel Larus. Boston, MA: Aurico Publishing, 1965.

(MAE)   *Medical Abbreviations and Eponyms.* By Sheila B. Sloane. Philadelphia, PA: W.B. Saunders Co., 1985.

(MAH)   *Medical Abbreviations Handbook.* 2nd ed. Oradell, NJ: Medical Economics Co., Inc., 1983.

(MCD)   *Acronyms, Abbreviations, and Initialisms.* Compiled by Carl Lauer. St. Louis, MO: McDonnell Douglas Corp., 1989. [Use of source began in 1969]

(MDG)   *Microcomputer Dictionary and Guide.* By Charles J. Sippl. Champaign, IL: Matrix Publishers, Inc., 1975.
> A listing of definitions for over 5,000 microelectronics terms. Seven appendices.

(ME)   *The Marine Encyclopaedic Dictionary.* 5th ed. By Eric Sullivan. London, England: LLP Ltd., 1996.

(MEC)   *Macmillan Encyclopedia of Chemistry.* Vol. 1. Edited by Joseph J. Lagowski. New York, NY:

Macmillan Reference USA, 1997.

(MED)   *McGraw-Hill Electronic Dictionary.* 5th ed. Edited by John Markus and Neil Sclater. New York, NY: McGraw-Hill, Inc., 1994.

(MEDA)   *Medical Acronyms.* 2nd ed. By Marilyn Fuller Delong. Oradell, NJ: Medical Economic Books, 1989.

(MELL)   *Melloni's Illustrated Dictionary of Medical Abbreviations.* By John Melloni and Ida G. Dox. Pearl River, NY: Parthenon Publishing Group, Inc., 1998.

(MENA)   *The Middle East and North Africa 1987.* 33rd ed. London, England: Europa Publications Ltd., 1986; distributed in U.S. by Gale Research, Detroit, MI.
        An annual survey containing detailed information about the political, economic, statistical, and commercial situation of the regions and countries covered.

(MHDB)   *McGraw-Hill Dictionary of Business Acronyms, Initials, and Abbreviations.* By Jerry M. Rosenberg. New York, NY: McGraw-Hill, Inc., 1992.

(MHDI)   *McGraw-Hill Dictionary of Information Technology and Computer Acronyms, Initials, and Abbreviations.* By Jerry M. Rosenberg. New York, NY: McGraw-Hill, Inc., 1992.

(MHDW)   *McGraw-Hill Dictionary of Wall Street Acronyms, Initials, and Abbreviations.* By Jerry M. Rosenberg. New York, NY: McGraw-Hill, Inc., 1992.

(MSA)   *Military Standard Abbreviations for Use on Drawings, and in Specifications, Standards, and Technical Documents.* MIL-STD-12D. U.S. Department of Defense, 1981. [Use of source began in 1975]

(MSC)   *Annotated Acronyms and Abbreviations of Marine Science Related Activities.* 3rd ed. Revised by Charlotte M. Ashby and Alan R. Flesh. Washington, DC: U.S. Department of Commerce. National Oceanographic and Atmospheric Administration. Environmental Data Service. National Oceanographic Data Center, 1976, 1981.

(MUGU)   *The Mugu Book of Acronyms and Abbreviations.* Missile Range, CA: Management Engineering Office, 1963, 1964.

(MUSM)   *Dictionary of Modern United States Military.* By S.F. Tomajczyk. Jefferson, NC: McFarland and Co., Inc., 1996.

(NADA)   *The New American Dictionary of Abbreviations.* By Mary A. De Vries. New York, NY: Signet, 1991.

(NAKS)   *"NASA/KSC Aronym List."* <http://www.ksc.nasa.gov/facts/acronyms.html> (27 May 1999)

(NASA)   *Space Transportation System and Associated Payloads: Glossary, Acronyms, and Abbreviations.* Washington, DC: U.S. National Aeronautics and Space Administration, 1985.

(NATG)   *Glossary of Abbreviations Used in NATO Documents.* AAP 15(B), n.p., 1979. [Use of source began in 1976]

(NCC)   *NCC The National Centre for Information Technology. Guide to Computer Aided Engineering, Manufacturing and Construction Software.* Manchester, England: NCC Publications, The National Computing Centre Ltd., 1985.

Includes software classifications and descriptions, names and addresses of suppliers, processor manufacturers, and operating systems.

(NFD)   *The NSFRE Fund-Raising Dictionary.* Edited by Barbara R. Levy. New York, NY: John Wiley & Sons, Inc., 1996.

(NFPA)   *Standard for Fire Safety Symbols/NFPA170.* Quincy, MA: National Fire Protection Association, 1994.

(NG)   *NAVAIR Glossary of Unclassified Common-Use Abbreviated Titles and Phrases.* NAVAIRNOTE 5216 AIR-6031, n.p., July, 1969.

(NGC)   *Catalogue of the National Gallery of Canada.* Compiled by National Gallery of Canada. Ottawa, Canada: National Gallery of Canada, 1998.

(NHD)   *The New Hacker's Dictionary.* Edited by Eric Raymond. Cambridge, MA: MIT Press, 1991.

(NITA)   *Dictionary of New Information Technology Acronyms.* 2nd ed. By Michael Gordon, Alan Singleton, and Clarence Rickards. London, England: Kogan Page, Ltd., 1986.

(NLC)   *Symbols of Canadian Libraries.* 12th ed. National Library of Canada. Minister of Supply and Services Canada, 1987.

(NOAA)   *NOAA Directives Manual.* 66-13 Acronyms. 1977.

(NQ)   *NASDAQ Company Directory.* New York, NY: National Association of Securities Dealers, Inc., 1990. [Use of source began in 1983]

(NRCH)   *A Handbook of Acronyms and Initialisms.* Washington, DC: U.S. Nuclear Regulatory Commission. Division of Technical Information and Document Control, 1985.

(NTCM)   *NTC's Mass Media Dictionary.* R. Terry Ellmore. Lincolnwood, IL: National Textbook Co., 1991.

(NTPA)   *NTPA '97: National Trade and Professional Associations of the United States.* 32nd ed. Edited by John J. Russell. Washington, DC: Columbia Books, Inc., 1997.

(NUCP)   *A Dictionary of Nuclear Power and Waste Management with Abbreviations and Acronyms.* Foo-Sun Lau. Letchworth, England: Research Studies Press Ltd., 1987.

(NUMA)   *The Numa Dictionary of Derivatives Acronyms.* <http://www.numa.com/ref/acronym.html> (24 February 1999)

(NVT)   *Naval Terminology.* NWP3. Rev. B. U.S. Department of the Navy. Office of the Chief of Naval Operations, 1980. [Use of source began in 1974]

(OA)   *Ocran's Acronyms: A Dictionary of Abbreviations and Acronyms Used in Scientific and Technical Writing.* By Emanuel Benjamin Ocran. London, England: Routledge & Kegan Paul Ltd., 1978.

(OAG)   *Official Airline Guide Worldwide Edition.* Oak Brook, IL: Official Airlines Guide, Inc., 1984. [Use of source began in 1975]

(OCD)   *Oxford Classical Dictionary.* 2nd ed. Edited by N.G. Hammond and H.H. Scullard. London, England: Oxford University Press, 1970.

(OCLC)   *OCLC Participating Institutions Arranged by OCLC Symbol.* Dublin, OH: OCLC, 1981.

(ODBW)   *The Oxford Dictionary for the Business World.* New York, NY: Oxford University Press, Inc., 1993.

(ODCC)   *The Oxford Dictionary of the Christian Church.* Edited by F.L. Cross and E.A. Livingstone. New York, NY: Oxford University Press, 1997.

(OICC)   *Abbreviations and Acronyms.* Des Moines, IA: Iowa State Occupational Information Coordinating Committee, 1986.

(OLDSS)   *Online Database Search Services Directory.* 2nd ed. Edited by Doris Morris Maxfield. Detroit, MI: Gale Research, 1988.
           Provides detailed descriptions of the online information retrieval services offered by libraries, private information firms, and other organizations in the United States and Canada. Entries include name and address, telephone number, and key contact, as well as online systems accessed, frequently searched databases, and access hardware.

(OPSA)   *"Official Postal Service Abbreviations."* <http://www.usps.gov/ncsc/lookups/abbr_suffix.txt> (17 December 1996)

(OSI)   *OSI Standards and Acronyms.* 3rd ed. Compiled by Adrian V. Stokes. United Kingdom: Stokes, 1991.

(OTD)   *Official Telecommunications Dictionary.* Edited by Thomas F.P. Sullivan. Rockille, MD: Government Institutes, Inc., 1997.

(PA)   *Planning Acronyms.* <http://www.planning.org/info/acronyms/html> (24 February 1999)

(PAZ)   *Parenting A to Z.* By Irene M. Franck and David M. Brownstone. New York, NY: HarperCollins Publishers, Inc., 1996.

(PCM)   *PC Magazine.* New York, NY: Ziff-Davis Publishing Co., 1997. [Use of source began in 1987]

(PD)   *Political Dissent: An International Guide to Dissident, Extra-Parliamentary, Guerrilla and Illegal Political Movements.* A Keesing's Reference Publication. Compiled by Henry W. Degenhardt. Edited by Alan J. Day. Harlow, Essex, England: Longman Group, 1983.
           Includes the history and aims of approximately 1,000 organizations, with details of their leaderships.

(PDAA)   *Pugh's Dictionary of Acronyms and Abbreviations: Abbreviations in Management, Technology and Information Science.* 5th ed. By Eric Pugh. Chicago, IL: American Library Association, 1987.

(PGP)   *Peterson's Graduate Programs in the Humanities, Arts & Social Sciences.* 31st ed. Princeton, NJ: Peterson's 1997.

(PHSD)   *1998/1999 Public Human Services Directory.* Vol 59. Washinton, DC: American Public Human Services Association, 1998.

(PPE)   *Political Parties of Europe.* 2 vols. Edited by Vincent E. McHale. The Greenwood Historical Encyclopedia of the World's Political Parties. Westport, CT: Greenwood Press, 1983.
           One of a series of reference guides to the world's significant political parties. Each guide provides concise histories of the political parties of a region and attempts to detail the evolution of ideology, changes in organization, membership, leadership, and each party's impact upon society.

(PPW)   *Political Parties of the World*. 2nd ed. A Keesing's Reference Publication. Compiled and edited by Alan J. Day and Henry W. Degenhardt. Harlow, Essex, England: Longman Group, 1980, 1984.
    Covers historical development, structure, leadership, membership, policy, publications, and international affiliations. For each country, an overview of the current political situation and constitutional structure is provided.

(PS)   *Popular Science*. New York, NY: Times-Mirror Magazines, Inc., 1995. [Use of source began in 1992]

(PSS)   *Peterson's Sports Scholarships & College Athletic Programs*. 3rd ed. Edited by Ron Walker. Princeton, NJ: Peterson's, 1998.

(RCD)   *Research Centers Directory*. 19th ed. Edited by Thomas J. Cichonski. Detroit, MI: Gale Research, 1994. [Use of source began in 1986]
    A guide to university-related and other nonprofit research organizations carrying on research in agriculture, astronomy and space sciences, behavioral and social sciences, computers and mathematics, engineering and technology, physical and earth sciences and regional and area studies.

(RDA)   *Army RD and A Magazine*. Alexandria, VA: Development, Engineering, and Acquisition Directorate, Army Materiel Command, 1997. [Use of source began in 1979]

(REAL)   *Abbreviations*. <http://www.reboc.on.ca/abbreviations.html> (24 February 1999)

(ROG)   *Dictionary of Abbreviations*. By Walter T. Rogers. London, England: George Allen & Co. Ltd., 1913; reprinted by Gale Research, 1969.

(SAA)   *Space-Age Acronyms, Abbreviations and Designations*. 2nd ed. By Reta C. Moser. New York, NY: IFI/Plenum, 1969.

(SAG)   *Stock Abbreviation Guide*. New York, NY: Associated Press. [Database]

(SDI)   *Report to the Congress on the Strategic Defense Initiative*. U.S. Department of Defense. Strategic Defense Initiative Organization, April, 1987.

(SEIS)   *Seismograph Station Codes and Characteristics*. Geological Survey. Circular 791. By Barbara B. Poppe, Debbi A. Naab, and John S. Derr. Washington, DC: U.S. Department of the Interior, 1978.

(SG)   *Standard & Poor's Stock Guide*. New York, NY: Standard & Poor's, 1999.

(SLS)   *World Guide to Scientific Associations and Learned Societies/Internationales Verzeichnis Wissenschaftlicher Verbande und Gesellschaften*. 4th ed. Edited by Barbara Verrel. New York, NY: K.G. Saur, 1984.
    A directory of more than 22,000 societies and associations in all fields of science, culture, and technology. International, national, and regional organizations from 150 countries are also included.

(SPSG)   *Security Owner's Stock Guide*. New York, NY: Standard & Poor's Corp., 1994. [Use of source began in 1988]

(SRA)   *State and Regional Associations of the United States*. 9th ed. Edited by Tracey E. Chirico, Buck J. Downs and John J. Russell. Washington, DC: Columbia Books, Inc., 1997.

(SSD)   *Space Station Directory and Program Guide*. Edited and compiled by Melinda Gipson, Jane Glass, and Mary Linden. Arlington, VA: Pasha Publications, Inc., 1988.

(STED)   *Stedman's Abbreviations, Acronyms and Symbols*. Edited by William R. Hensyl. Baltimore, MD: Williams & Wilkins, 1992.

(TAD)   *The AIDS Dictionary*. By Sarah Barbara Watstein and Karen Chandler. New York, NY: Facts on File, Inc., 1998.

(TAG)   *Transportation Acronym Guide 1996*. U.S. Department of Transportation. Washington, DC: Bureau of Transportation Statistics, 1996.

(TBD)   *Thomson Bank Directory*. Skokie, IL: Thomson Financial Publishing, 1991.

(TDOB)   *The Dictionary of Banking*. By Charles J. Woelfel. Chicago, IL: Probus Publishing Company, 1994.

(TEL)   *Telephony's Dictionary*. 2nd ed. By Graham Langley. Chicago, IL: Telephony Publishing Corp., 1986.
          Includes definitions for U.S. and international telecommunications terms. Ten appendices.

(TELE)   *List of Libraries Abbreviations Encountered in the Context of EU R&D*.
          <http://www2.echo.lu/libraries/en/acronym.html> (24 February 1999)

(TES)   *Tests: A Comprehensive Reference for Assessments in Psychology, Education, and Business*. 3rd ed. Austin, TX: PRO-ED, Inc., 1991.

(TMMY)   *The Thirteenth Mental Measurements Yearbook*. Edited by James C. Impara and Barbara S. Plake. Lincoln: NE: The Buros Institute of Mental Measurements of the University of Nebraska-Lincoln, 1998.

(TNIG)   *Telecommunications, Networking and Internet Glossary*. By George S. Machovec. Chicago, IL: American Library Association, 1993.

(TOCD)   *The Official Catholic Directory 1997*. New Providence, NJ: P.J. Kennedy & Sons, 1997.

(TSPED)   *Trade Shows and Professional Exhibits Directory*. 2nd ed. Edited by Robert J. Elster. Detroit, MI: Gale Research, 1987. [Use of source began in 1986]
          A guide to scheduled events providing commercial display facilities including conferences, conventions, meetings, fairs and festivals, etc. Entries include name of trade show; sponsor name, address, and telephone number; attendance figures; principal exhibits; special features; publications; and date and location of shows.

(TSSD)   *Telecommunications Systems and Services Directory*. 4th ed. (and supplement). Edited by John Krol. Detroit, MI: Gale Research, 1989. [Use of source began in 1985]
          An international descriptive guide to telecommunications organizations, systems, and services. Entries include name and address, telephone number, chief official, and a description of the purposes, technical structure, and background of the service or system.

(USDC)   *"Glossary of Acronyms."* U.S. Department of Commerce.
          <http://www.pmel.noaa.gov/pubs/acronym.html> (5 March 1997)

(USGC)   *"U.S. Government Commonly Used Abbreviations and Acronyms."*
          <http://www.fed.gov/hptext/infohwy/gov_acro.html> (5 March 1997)

(USMO)   *The Military Online: A Directory for Internet Access to the Development of Defense.* Edited by
          William M. Arkin. Washington, DC: Brassey's, 1997.

(VERA)   *VERA-Virtual Entity of Relevant Acronyms.*
          <http://www/thphy.uni~duesseldorf.de/~gnu/info/VERA/vera_2.html#SEC3> (1 December
          1998)

(VNW)   *Words of the Vietnam War.* By Gregory R. Clark. Jefferson, NC: McFarland and Co., Inc., 1990.

(VRA)   *VRA Special Bulletin. No. 2, 1987: Standard Abbreviations for Image Descriptions for Use in Fine
          Arts Visual Resources Collections.* Compiled by Nancy S. Schuller. Austin, TX: Visual Resources
          Association, 1987.

(WDAA)   *Webster's New World Dictionary of Acronyms and Abbreviations.* By Auriel Douglas and Michael
          Strumpf. New York, NY: Webster's New World, 1989.

(WDMC)   *Webster's New World Dictionary of Media and Communications.* Revised and updated ed. By
          Richard Weiner. New York, NY: Webster's New World, 1996.

(WGA)   *Webster's Guide to Abbreviations.* Springfield, MA: Merriam-Webster, Inc., 1985.

(WPI)   *Selected Acronyms and Abbreviations for Wood Products, Forest Industry and
          Governmental Affairs.* <http://www.ari.net/awpi/acronyms.html> (3 March 1999)

(WYGK)   *HR Words you Gotta Know!* By William R. Tracey. New York, NY: AMACOM, 1994.

P
By Acronym

P .... Aircraft [*Wind triangle problems*]
P .... All India Reporter, Patna [*A publication*] (DLA)
P .... Armour Pharmaceutical Co. [*Research code symbol*]
P .... Assistant in Private Practice [*Chiropody*] [*British*]
P .... Asta Werke AG [*Germany*] [*Research code symbol*]
P .... Bristol Laboratories [*Research code symbol*]
P .... cis-Platinum [*Cisplatin*] [*Also, cis-DDP, CDDP, CPDD, CPT, DDP*] [*Antineoplastic drug*]
P .... Dainippon Pharmaceutical Co. [*Japan*] [*Research code symbol*]
P .... Democratic People's Republic of Korea [*Aircraft nationality and registration mark*] (FAAC)
p .... Density [*Heat transmission symbol*]
P .... Departure
p .... Difficulty [*of a test item*] [*Psychology*]
P .... Electric Dipole Moment (BARN)
P .... Farbenfabriken Bayer [*Germany*] [*Research code symbol*]
P .... Farmitalia [*Italy*] [*Research code symbol*]
P .... Faulty Punctuation [*Used in correcting manuscripts, etc.*]
P .... Force of Concentrated Load
P .... Games [*or Matches*] Played [*Sports statistics*]
P .... Hole P-Type Semiconductor Material
P .... Indian Law Reports, Patna Series [*A publication*] (DLA)
P .... Law Reports, Probate, Divorce, and Admiralty [*Since 1890*] [*England*] [*A publication*] (DLA)
P .... Lepetit [*Italy*] [*Research code symbol*]
P .... Mainsail Hoist Lenght [*IOR*]
p .... Momentum [*Symbol*] [*IUPAC*]
P .... Office of Personnel [*Coast Guard*]
p .... On Probation [*Navy British*]
P .... Orbital Period [*of a comet*] [*In years*]
P .... Pacer
P .... Pacific Coast Stock Exchange [*Later, PSE*]
p----- .... Pacific Ocean [*MARC geographic area code Library of Congress*] (LCCP)
P .... Pacific Reporter [*A publication*] (DLA)
P .... Pack [*JETDS*]
P .... Packed Lunches [*School meals*] [*British*]
P .... Pad (SAA)
P .... Paddington Railway Station (ROG)
P .... Paddle (DS)
P .... Page
P .... Paid This Year [*In stock listings of newspapers*]
P .... Pain [*Medicine*]
P .... Pair (IAA)
P .... Paired [*for or against*] [*Votes in Congress*]
P .... Paise [*Monetary unit*] [*India*]
P .... Palace (ROG)
P .... Pale (ADA)
P .... Pallet [*Spacelab*] [*NASA*] (NASA)
p .... Pallet (NAKS)
P .... Pamphlet
P .... Pancuronium [*A muscle relaxant*]
P .... Pandects [*A publication Authority cited in pre-1607 legal work*] (DSA)
P .... Panel (NFPA)
P .... Papa [*Phonetic alphabet*] [*International*] (DSUE)
P .... Papa [*Pope*] [*Latin*]
P .... Paper
P .... Paperback (WGA)
P .... Papilla [*Optic*] [*Medicine*]
P .... Papillate [*A type of seed*] [*Botany*]
p .... Para [*Chemistry*]
P .... Para [*Monetary unit*] [*Former Yugoslavia*]
P .... Parachutist [*Army skill qualification identifier*] (INF)
P .... Paragraph (ADA)
P .... Paralegal Program [*Association of Independent Colleges and Schools specialization code*]
P .... Parallax
P .... Parallel
P .... Paramecin [*A protozoan toxin*]
P .... Parashah (BJA)
P .... Pardon (ADA)
P .... Parenchyma [*Botany*]
P .... Parent (CPH)
P .... Parental
P .... Parietal Electrode Placement in Electroencephalography [*Medicine*] (DMAA)

P .... Parish (ROG)
P .... Parity [*Atomic physics*]
P .... Parity [*Obstetrics*] (DAVI)
P .... Park
P .... Parking Place [*Traffic sign*] [*British*]
P .... Parlophone [*Record label*] [*Great Britain, Italy, Australia, etc.*]
P .... Parous (STED)
P .... Parson
P .... Part
p .... Part (WDMC)
P .... Parthian [*Language, etc.*]
P .... Partial [*Astronomy*]
P .... Partial Pressure (MAE)
P .... Partial Tension [*Medicine*] (DAVI)
P .... Participle [*Grammar*]
P .... Partim [*In Part*]
P .... Partnership
P .... Party
P .... Parve [*or Pareve*] [*In food labeling, indicates food is kosher and can be used with either meat or dairy products*]
P .... Passed [*Examination*]
P .... Passing Showers [*Meteorology*]
P .... Past
p .... Past (WDMC)
P .... Paste
P .... Pasteboard (DGA)
P .... Pasteurella [*Genus of bacteria*]
P .... Pastor
P .... Patent
P .... Pater [*Father*] [*Latin*]
P .... Paternal (STED)
P .... Paternally Contributing [*Genetics*] (DAVI)
P .... Patient
P .... Patrol [*Designation for all US military aircraft*]
P .... Patrol Service Gunnery Instructor [*Officer's rating*] [*British Royal Navy*]
P .... Patron
P .... Pattern
P .... Paulus de Liazaris [*Deceased, 1356*] [*Authority cited in pre-1607 legal work*] (DSA)
P .... Paused Program [*Computer science*]
P .... Paved Surface [*Aviation*] (DA)
P .... Pavilion (ROG)
P .... Pawn [*Chess*]
P .... Pax [*Peace*] [*Latin*]
P .... Pay
P .... Payee
P .... Paymaster [*Military*] (ROG)
p .... P-Doped Semiconductor [*Photovoltaic energy systems*]
P .... Peak
P .... Peat (ROG)
P .... Pebbles [*Quality of the bottom*] [*Nautical charts*]
P .... Pectoral [*Anatomy*] (ROG)
p .... Peculiar [*Astronomy*]
P .... Pedal (WDAA)
P .... Pedestrian (WDAA)
P .... Peg [*Telecommunications*] (IAA)
P .... Pelagius [*Deceased, 1232*] [*Authority cited in pre-1607 legal work*] (DSA)
P .... Pelvis (STED)
P .... Pen [*Sports*]
p .... Pence [*Monetary unit*] [*British*]
P .... Pencil Tube (MDG)
P .... Pengo [*Monetary unit in Hungary until 1946*]
P .... Penicillin
p .... Penni(a) [*Penny or Pence*] [*Monetary unit*] [*Finland*] (GPO)
P .... Pennsylvania (DLA)
P .... Pennsylvania State Library, Harrisburg, PA [*Library symbol Library of Congress*] (LCLS)
P .... Penny
p .... Penny (ODBW)
P .... Pentachlorophenol [*Also, PCP*] [*Wood preservative*] [*Organic chemistry*] (TEL)
P .... Pentode [*Electronics*] (OA)
P .... Peony [*Horticulture*]
P .... People

P	Pepper *(DICI)*
P	Per
p	Per *(WDMC)*
P	Percent *(STED)*
P	Percentile
P	Perceptual
P	Perceptual Speed *[A factor ability]* *[Psychology]*
P	Perch
P	Perchloroethylene *[Also, TCE]* *[Dry cleaning]*
P	Percussion
P	Pere *[Father]* *[French]*
P	Perforateur Honeywell Bull *(IAA)*
P	Perforation
P	Performance *[Army]* *(INF)*
P	Performer
P	Perfusionist *[Medicine]* *(DAVI)*
P	Perianth
P	Pericardium *[Medicine]*
P	Perimeter
P	Period
p	Period *(NAKS)*
P	Peripheral *(DAVI)*
P	Perishable
P	Permanent *[Inks]* *(DGA)*
P	Permanent Stay *[in hospital]* *[British]*
P	Permeability *(STED)*
P	Permeance *(IDOE)*
P	Permutation *(NITA)*
P	Perpetuus *[Uninterrupted]* *[Latin]*
p	Perseverate *[Psychology]*
P	Persian *(DLA)*
P	Persimmon
P	Persistence *[Medicine]*
P	Person
P	Personal *(DA)*
P	Personality Organization and Stability *[Eysenck]* *[Psychology]*
P	Personnel
P	Person to Person *[Telecommunications]* *(TEL)*
P	Perstetur *[Continue]* *[Pharmacy]* *(ROG)*
P	Persuasion *[Novel by Jane Austen]*
P	Peseta *[Monetary unit]* *[Spain and Latin America]*
P	Pesewa *[Monetary unit]* *[Ghana]*
P	Pesher *(BJA)*
P	Peshitta *(BJA)*
P	Peso *[Monetary unit]* *[Spain and Latin America]*
P	Peta *[A prefix meaning multiplied by 10^{15}]* *[SI symbol]*
P	Peter *[Phonetic alphabet]* *[World War II]* *(DSUE)*
P	Peter *[New Testament book]*
P	Peters' United States Supreme Court Reports *[26-41 United States]* *[A publication]* *(DLA)*
P	Petiole *[Botany]*
P	Petite *(WGA)*
P	Petrol *[British Waterways Board sign]*
P	Petrus Hispanus *[Authority cited in pre-1607 legal work]* *(DSA)*
P	Peyote
P	Pfizer, Inc. *[Research code symbol]*
P	Pharmacopoeia
P	Pharmacy *(WDAA)*
P	Phenacetin *(STED)*
P	Phencyclidine *[An anesthetic]*
P	Phenolphthalein *[Chemical indicator]*
P	Philadelphia *[Pennsylvania]* *[Mint mark, when appearing on US coins]*
P	Philadelphia Stock Exchange, Inc.
P	Phillips Petroleum *[NYSE symbol]* *(TTSB)*
P	Phillips Petroleum Co. *[NYSE symbol]* *(SPSG)*
P	Phoenician *(BJA)*
P	Phon *[Unit of loudness level]*
P	Phone *(IAA)*
p	Phosphate *[One-letter symbol]* *[Biochemistry]*
p	Phosphoric Residue *[As substituent on nucleoside]* *[Biochemistry]*
P	Phosphorus *[Chemical element]*
P	Photographic Reconnaissance Capability *[When suffix to Navy aircraft designation]*
P	Phototropism *[Botany]*
P	Phrase Structure Rule *[Linguistics]*
P	Physics *[Secondary school course]* *[British]*
P	Physiology *[Medical Officer designation]* *[British]*
P	Phytophthora *[A fungus]*
P	Piaggio Rinaldo *[Industria Aeronautiche & Meccaniche SpA]* *[Italy ICAO aircraft manufacturer identifier]* *(ICAO)*
P	Pianissimo *[Very Softly]* *[Music]*
P	Piano *[Softly]* *[Music]*
p	Piano *(WDAA)*
P	Piano *[Softly]* *[Music]* *(WA)*
P	Piaster *[Monetary unit]* *[Spain, Republic of Vietnam, and some Middle Eastern countries]*
p	Pica *[Typography]* *[Also, P]* *(WDMC)*
P	Pick *(IAA)*
P	Pickering's Massachusetts Reports *[18-41 Massachusetts]* *[A publication]* *(DLA)*
p	Pico *[A prefix meaning divided by one trillion]* *[SI symbol]*
P	Picot *[Crochet]* *(ROG)*
P	Pie
P	Pied *[Foot]* *[French]*

P	Pierced *[Quilting]*
P	Pigs *(ROG)*
P	Pilaster *[Technical drawings]*
P	Pillar *[Buoy]*
P	Pilot
p	Pilot *(NAKS)*
P	Pink
P	Pinnule
P	Pint
P	Pip *[Phonetic alphabet]* *[Pre-World War II]* *(DSUE)*
P	Pipe
P	Pipe Rolls *[British]*
P	Pique; Inclusions *[Diamond clarity grade]*
P	Pitch *[Technical drawings]*
P	Pitch *[or Pitcher]* *[Baseball]*
p	Pitch *(NAKS)*
P	Pitch *(IDOE)*
P	Pith *[Botany]*
P	Pitman Examination Institute *[British]*
P	Pitman-Moore Co. *[Research code symbol]*
P	Pius *[Dutiful]* *[Latin]*
P	Placebo *[Medicine]*
P	Placentinus *[Deceased, 1192]* *[Authority cited in pre-1607 legal work]* *(DSA)*
P	Placitum *[or Placita]* *[Agreeable, Agreed Upon]* *[Latin]* *[Legal term]* *(DLA)*
P	Plaintiff *[Legal shorthand]* *(LWAP)*
P	Plan *(CPH)*
P	Planed
P	Planning
P	Plasma
P	Plasmodium *[Biology]* *(MAE)*
P	Plastid *[Botany]*
P	Plate *[Electron tube]* *[Technical drawings]*
P	Platform *(DCTA)*
P	Players League *[Major league in baseball, 1890]*
P	Pleasant
P	Pleinsbachian *[Geology]*
P	Plotter *[British military]* *(DMA)*
P	Plug
P	Plus *[More]*
P	Poco *[Somewhat]* *[Music]*
P	Point *[Lacrosse position]*
P	Point *(IDOE)*
P	Point-to-Point Radio *[FAA designator]* *(CET)*
P	Poise *[Unit of dynamic viscosity]*
P	Poison
P	Polar Distance *[Navigation]*
P	Polarization
P	Pole
p	Pole *(NAKS)*
P	Political Division *[Geography]*
P	Polka *[Music]*
P	Pollen *[Botany]*
P	Polymorphic *[Biology]*
P	Polymyxin *[An antibiotic]* *(DAVI)*
P	Polyneuropathy *[Medicine]*
P	Polynomial Time *(IAA)*
P	Polyphagous *[Biology]*
P	Polytechnic *(AIE)*
P	Pond *[Maps and charts]*
P	Pondere *[By Weight]* *[Latin]*
p	Pondus *[Weight]* *[Latin]* *(MAE)*
P	Ponendum *[To Be Placed]* *[Latin]*
P	Pontifex *[Bishop]* *[Latin]*
P	Pool
P	Poop *[Portion of a ship]*
P	Poorly Organized, Unstable Personality *[Eysenck]* *[Psychology]*
P	Poor Skiing Conditions
P	Pope
P	Popular Response *[Rorschach]* *[Psychology]*
P	Population
P	Populus *[People]* *[Latin]*
P	Porcelain
P	Porphyrin *[Medicine]* *(DAVI)*
P	Port *[Maps and charts]*
P	Portable *[JETDS nomenclature]*
P	Portion
P	Portland *[Diocesan abbreviation]* *[Oregon]* *(TOCD)*
P	Portugal *[IYRU nationality code]*
P	Position
p	Positive *[Crystal]*
P	Positive *(IAA)*
P	Positive Conducting *[Electronics]* *(IAA)*
P	Post *[After]* *[Latin]*
P	Post *[Surgery laboratory work]* *(DAVI)*
P	Postage
P	Posten *[Sentry]* *[German military]*
P	Posterior
P	Postpartum *[Medicine]*
P	Pouce *[Inch]* *[French]*
P	Pound *(IDOE)*
P	Pounds *[As measurement of total stress]* *[Aerospace]* *(AAG)*
P	Pour *[For]* *[French]*
P	Power *[Symbol]* *[IUPAC]*

P...............	Poynting Vector [Electromagnetism] (DEN)
P...............	Practical
P...............	Practical Intelligence
P...............	Pre-1920 [Deltiology]
P...............	Preceding
P...............	Precipitation Static
P...............	Precise Code [Computer science] (RDA)
P...............	Predators Present [Ecology]
P...............	Predicate
P...............	Predictor [British military] (DMA)
P...............	Prednisolone [Endocrinology]
P...............	Prednisone [Also, PDN, Pr, Pred, Pro] [Endocrinology] [Antineoplastic drug]
P...............	Preferred
P...............	Prefix [Indicating a private radiotelegram]
P...............	P-Register [Computer science]
P...............	Preliminary
P...............	Premolar [Dentistry]
P...............	Presbyopia [Ophthalmology]
P...............	Presbyterian
P...............	Prescribing
P...............	Present
P...............	Present BIT [Binary Digit] [Computer science]
P...............	Preset
P...............	President
P...............	Press [Publishing]
P...............	Pressure [or p] [Symbol IUPAC]
p...............	Pressure (NAKS)
P...............	Pressurized Tank [Liquid gas carriers]
P...............	Preview
P...............	Prey [Zoology]
P...............	Price [Economics]
P...............	Pridie [The Day Before] [Latin]
P...............	Priest
P...............	Priestly Source [Biblical scholarship]
P...............	Prilled
P...............	Primary
p...............	Primary (NAKS)
P...............	Primary [or Push] Wave [Earthquakes]
p...............	Prime (NAKS)
P...............	Primipara [Woman bearing first child] [Medicine] (MAE)
P...............	Primitive
P...............	Primus [First] [Latin]
P...............	Prince
P...............	Princeps [First Edition] [French]
P...............	Princess (ROG)
P...............	Principal
P...............	Print
P...............	Priority [Telecommunications] (TEL)
P...............	Priory
P...............	Prismatic Joint (IAA)
P...............	Prisoner [Military]
P...............	Private
P...............	Private Trust [Includes testamentary, investment, life insurance, holding title, etc.] [Legal term] (DLA)
P...............	Private Venture
P...............	Privy (ROG)
P...............	Pro [For] [Latin]
P...............	Probability [or Probability Ratio] [Statistics]
P...............	Probate
P...............	Probe (MSA)
P...............	Probucol [Anticholesteremic]
P...............	Procarbazine [Also, PC, PCB, Pr] [Antineoplastic drug]
P...............	Procedure
P...............	Proceedings (IAA)
P...............	Processor [Computer science]
P...............	Proconsul
P...............	Producer [Films, television, etc.]
P...............	Product
P...............	Production [of Energy]
P...............	Profession
P...............	Professional [Civil Service employees designation]
P...............	Proficiency
P...............	Profit
P...............	Progesterone [A hormone]
P...............	Program (KSC)
P...............	Programmable
P...............	Progressive
P...............	Prohibited Area [Followed by identification]
P...............	Proliferation [Biology]
P...............	Proline [One-letter symbol; see Pro]
P...............	Promoter [Genetics]
P...............	Prompt [i.e., the right side] [A stage direction]
P...............	Proof [Philately]
P...............	Prop (DS)
P...............	Propagation Distribution [Broadcasting]
P...............	Propionic [Bacteriology] (DAVI)
P...............	Proportional (IAA)
P...............	Proportion in a Specific Class
P...............	Propulsion (AAG)
P...............	Protein
P...............	Proteinuria [Clinical chemistry]
P...............	Protestant
P...............	Protet [Protest] [French]
P...............	Proteus [Genus of bacteria] (MAE)
P...............	Proto [Linguistics]
p...............	Proton [A nuclear particle]
P...............	Protoplasmic [Freeze etching in microscopy]
P...............	Prototroch
P...............	Prototype (AAG)
P...............	Provisional
p...............	Proximum [Near] [Latin] (MAE)
P...............	Psychiatry
P...............	Psychometrist [Psychology]
P...............	Public (AL)
P...............	Publications
P...............	Public Houses [Public-performance tariff class] [British]
P...............	Public Safety [FCC] (NTCM)
P...............	Pudding [Phonetic alphabet] [Royal Navy World War I] (DSUE)
P...............	Pugillus [A Handful] [Pharmacy] (ROG)
P...............	Pula [Monetary unit] (ODBW)
P...............	Pull (NFPA)
P...............	Pulled Up [Horse racing]
P...............	Pulse
P...............	Pump (AAG)
P...............	Punch
P...............	Punctum Proximum [Near Point of vision] [Ophthalmology] (DAVI)
P...............	Punic (BJA)
P...............	Punkt [Point] [German military]
P...............	Punter [Football]
P...............	Pupil
P...............	Purchased (AAG)
P...............	Purified [Animal breeding]
P...............	Purinethol [Mercaptopurine] [Also, M, MP] [Antineoplastic drug]
P...............	Purkinje Cell [Neuroanatomy]
P...............	Purl [Knitting]
P...............	Purple
P...............	Purpure [Purple] [Heraldry]
P...............	Pursuit [Airplane designation]
P...............	Put [In options listings of newspapers]
P...............	Pya [Monetary unit] [Myanmar]
p...............	Pyranose [One-letter symbol] [Biochemistry]
P...............	Pyroxene Subgroup [Acmite, sodium metasilicate, potassium metasilicate, diopside, wollastonite, hypersthene] [CIPW classification Geology]
P...............	RADAR [JETDS nomenclature]
P...............	Reproducing [JETDS nomenclature]
P...............	Single Paper [Wire insulation] (AAG)
P...............	Soft Pad [Missile launch environment symbol]
P...............	Warner-Lambert Pharmaceutical Co. [Research code symbol]
P$_1$...............	Inorganic Phosphate [Chemistry] (DAVI)
p-1...............	Page 1 [Also, P-1] (WDMC)
P-1...............	Page One [Broadcasting] (WDMC)
p1...............	Para 1 [Unipara - having borne one child] (DAVI)
P$_1$...............	Parental Generation (MAE)
P1...............	Pershing 1 [Missile] (GFGA)
P$_1$...............	Pulmonic First Heart Sound [Medicine] (DAVI)
P$_1$...............	Pulmonic First Sound [Medicine] (MEDA)
P1a...............	Pershing 1a [Missile] (GFGA)
P1E...............	Planed One Edge [Technical drawings] (DAC)
P1MG...........	P1 [Code] for Multigroup [Method] [Nuclear energy] (NRCH)
P1S...............	Planed One Side [Technical drawings] (DAC)
P1S2E...........	Planed One Side and Two Edges [Technical drawings] (DAC)
P2...............	Papua New Guinea [Aircraft nationality and registration mark] (FAAC)
P-2...............	Propaganda Due [Secret Italian Masonic organization, allegedly tied to the Roman Catholic church]
P$_2$...............	Pulmonic Second Sound [Medicine]
P2...............	Second Parental Generation (EES)
P2...............	Second Pilot [Aviation] (AIA)
P2d...............	Pacific Reporter, Second Series [West] [A publication] (AAGC)
P2I...............	Planned Product Improvement
p2NBC2...........	Physiological and Psychological Effects of NBC [Nuclear, Biological, and Chemical Warfare] and Extended Operations [Army study project] (INF)
P3...............	Industry Composites and Polymer Processing Program [Massachusetts Institute of Technology] [Research center] (RCD)
P3...............	Phillips Post Processor
P3...............	Portable Plotting Package [Nuclear energy] (NRCH)
P/3...............	Proximal Third [of bone] [Orthopedics] (DAVI)
P3FE...........	Polytrifluoroethylene (EDCT)
P$_3$I...............	Planned Program Product Improvement [Army]
P^{3}I...............	Preplanned Product Improvement [DoD]
P3P...............	Platform for Privacy Preferences Project [Computer science]
P4...............	Aruba [Aircraft nationality and registration mark] (FAAC)
P4...............	Production Process Prove-Out Program
P4P...............	Pagans for Peace Network [Canada] (EAIO)
P4S...............	Planed Four Sides [Technical drawings] (DAC)
P4SR...........	Predicted Four Hour Sweat Rate (PDAA)
P6ROC...........	P6 Rover Owners Club (EAIO)
P 14...............	Pattern 14 Rifle [Made in the US for Great Britain, beginning in 1914]
P 32...............	Radioactive Phosphorus (DAVI)
P$_{50}$...............	Partial pressure of oxygen at 50% hemoglobin saturation [Medicine]
P-55...............	Hydroxypregnanedione [Endocrinology] (DAVI)
P-88/ARA...........	Project '88: Americans for the Reagan Agenda [Defunct] (EA)
P$_A$...............	Alveolar Pressure [Medicine] (DAVI)
PA...............	B. F. Jones Memorial Library, Aliquippa, PA [Library symbol Library of Congress] (LCLS)
PA...............	Office of Public Affairs [DoD]
PA...............	Packet Adapter [Telecommunications] (IAA)
PA...............	Pad Abort [NASA] (KSC)

PA	Paging and Area Warning (MCD)
Pa	Paine's United States Circuit Court Reports [*A publication*] (DLA)
PA	Paintmakers Association [*British*] (DBA)
PA	Paired Associates [*Psychometrics*]
PA	Pakistan Army
PA	Paleopathology Association
PA	Palestine Affairs [*New York*] [*A publication*] (BJA)
PA	Palestinian Authority [*Political movement*] (ECON)
PA	Palladium [*Chemical element*] (ROG)
PA	Panama [*ANSI two-letter standard code*] (CNC)
PA	Pan American World Airways, Inc. [*See also PAA, PAN-AM, PN*] [*ICAO designator*] (MCD)
P-A	Pan-Atlantic Steamship Corp. (MHDW)
PA	Panatlas Energy, Inc. [*Toronto Stock Exchange symbol*]
PA	Panic Attack [*Medicine*] (MEDA)
PA	Pantothenic Acid [*Biochemistry*] (DB)
PA	Paper (WGA)
pa	Paper (VRA)
PA	Paper Advance (BUR)
PA	Para-Amps (EA)
Pa	Parachutist [*British military*] (DMA)
PA	Paralysis Agitans
PA	Parametric Amplifier
PA	Par Amitie [*By Favor*] [*French*]
Pa	Paranoia [*Psychology*]
PA	Parapsychological Association (EA)
PA	Parathion (LDT)
PA	Par Autorite [*By Authority*] [*French*]
PA	Parental Advisory (WDMC)
PA	Parents Anonymous (EA)
PA	Parents' Association
PA	Parish
Pa	Paris Stock Exchange [*France*]
PA	Parti Affectae [*To the Affected Part*] [*Pharmacy*]
PA	Partial Application [*Military*] (AFIT)
P$_A$	Partial Pressure in Arterial Blood [*Medicine*] (DAVI)
PA	Participating Activity [*Responsible for standardization efforts*] [*DoD*]
PA	Participial Adjective [*Grammar*]
PA	Particular Average
PA	Parti de l'Action [*Party of Action*] [*Morocco*] [*Political party*] (PPW)
PA	Partido Andalucista [*Spain*] [*Political party*] (ECED)
PA	Partido Arnulfista [*Panama*] [*Political party*] (EY)
PA	Partners of the Americas (EA)
Pa	Pascal [*Symbol*] [*SI unit of pressure*]
PA	Passenger Address System [*Aviation*] (DA)
PA	Passenger Agent
PA	Passenger Ship
PA	Passive Aggressive (DMAA)
PA	Patent Assignee (NITA)
PA	Patents (NITA)
PA	Pathfinder Association (EAIO)
PA	Pathology (AAMN)
PA	Patient
PA	Patient's Advocate [*Medicine*] (DMAA)
PA	Patrol Aircraft (NATG)
PA	Pattern Analysis [*Test*]
PA	Paying Agent [*Legal term*] (DLA)
P/A	Payment Authority [*Business term*]
PA	Peak Amplitude [*Medicine*] (DMAA)
PA	Pedestrians Association [*British*] (DBA)
PA	Pending Availability
PA	Pendulous Axis [*Accelerometer*] (IEEE)
PA	Pennsylvania [*Postal code*]
Pa	Pennsylvania (ODBW)
Pa	Pennsylvania Reports [*A publication*] (AAGC)
PA	Pennsylvania Supreme Court Reports [*1845-date*] [*A publication*] (DLA)
PA	People's Alliance [*Althydubandalag*] [*Iceland*] [*Political party*] (PPW)
P-A	Peptide Absorption
PA	Per Abdomen
PA	Per Adresse [*Care Of*] [*German*]
PA	Per Annum [*By the Year*] [*Latin*]
pa	Per annum (EBF)
PA	Per Auguri [*Used on visiting cards to express congratulations, birthday wishes, etc.*] [*Italian*]
PA	Percentage Activity [*Measurement*] (DAVI)
PA	Performance Alertness (AEBS)
PA	Performance Analysis
PA	Performance Appraisal Required [*Civil Service*]
PA	Performance Assessment (DOGT)
PA	Performing Arts [*US Copyright Office class*]
PA	Periapical [*Anatomy*] (DAVI)
PA	Periarteritis [*Medicine*] (DMAA)
PA	Peridural Artery [*Medicine*] (DMAA)
PA	Periodic Acid [*Inorganic chemistry*]
pA	Periplanone A [*Biochemistry*]
PA	Permanent Abeyance [*FDA*]
PA	Permanent Address (ROG)
PA	Permanent Appointment
PA	Permanently Associated [*Telecommunications*] (TEL)
PA	Pernicious Anemia [*Hematology*]
PA	Personal Accident [*Insurance*] (AIA)
P/A	Personal Account (WDAA)
PA	Personal Affairs (AFM)
PA	Personal Appearance

PA	Personal Assistant [*British*]
PA	Personal Audit [*Psychological testing*]
PA	Personnel Administrator [*American Society for Personnel Administration*] [*A publication Information service or system*]
PA	Personnel Area (NRCH)
PA	Pfizer, Inc. [*Research code symbol*]
PA	Phakic-Aphakic [*Ophthalmology*] (MAE)
PA	Pharmacology, Clinical [*Medical specialty*] (DHSM)
PA	Phase Angle (IAA)
PA	Phenol Alcohol [*Chemistry*] (DAVI)
PA	Phentolamine [*Antiadrenergic*]
PA	Philippine Army
PA	Philippine Association (EA)
PA	Phonocardiogram Amplifier [*Cardiology*]
PA	Phosphatidic Acid [*Biochemistry*]
PA	Phosphoarginine [*Biochemistry*]
PA	Phosphoric Acid (ECON)
PA	Photoallergenic [*Response*] [*Medicine*]
PA	Photodiode Amplifier
PA	Photoinduced Anisotropy [*Physics*]
PA	Phthalic Anhydride [*Organic chemistry*]
PA	Physical Activity (MCD)
PA	Physician Advisor (HCT)
PA	Physician's Assistant
PA	Physics Abstracts [*Institution of Electrical Engineers*] [*Information service or system A publication*] (CRD)
PA	Phytoalexin [*Plant pathology*]
PA	Piaster [*Monetary unit*] [*Spain, Republic of Vietnam, and some Middle Eastern countries*]
PA	Picatinny Arsenal [*New Jersey*] [*Later, Armament Development Center*] [*Army*]
pA	Picoampere [*One trillionth of an ampere*]
PA	Pierre Allain [*Lightweight rock-climbing boot named after its designer*]
PA	Pierre Arpels [*Jewelry designer*]
PA	Pills Anonymous [*Later, DA*] [*An association*] (EA)
PA	Pilot Approval [*Automotive project management*]
P/A	Pilotless Aircraft
PA	PIMCO Advisors'A' [*NYSE symbol*] (TTSB)
PA	Pimco Advisors Ltd. [*NYSE symbol*] (SAG)
PA	Pipeline Authority [*Australia*]
PA	Piper Aircraft Corp. [*ICAO aircraft manufacturer identifier*] (ICAO)
PA	Pirke Avot (BJA)
PA	Pitch Angle
PA	Pituitary-Adrenal [*Endocrinology*] (DAVI)
P/A	Planetary Atmosphere (SAA)
PA	Planning Assistance (EA)
PA	Plasma Adsorption [*Medicine*] (DMAA)
PA	Plasma Aldosterone [*Endocrinology*]
PA	Plasminogen Activator [*Biochemistry*]
PA	Platelet Adhesiveness [*Hematology*]
PA	Platelet-Associated (DB)
PA	Platform Assembly (MCD)
PA	Podiatry Association [*British*] (DBA)
PA	Point of Aim [*Military*]
PA	Points Against [*Football*]
PA	Polar Atlantic [*American air mass*]
PA	Polarization Approximation [*Physical chemistry*]
PA	Polarographic Analyzer
P/A	Polar to Analog (KSC)
PA	Police Academy
PA	Police Agent (WDAA)
PA	Policy Analyst (GNE)
PA	Polyacetal [*Organic chemistry*]
PA	Polyacrylate (EDCT)
PA	Polyacrylic [*Organic chemistry*]
PA	Polyamide [*Organic chemistry*]
PA	Polyanhydride [*Organic chemistry*]
PA	Polyarteritis [*Medicine*]
PA	Polyarthritis [*Medicine*] (DMAA)
PA	Polymer Adhesive
PA	Port Agency [*Army*]
PA	Port Authority [*Western Australia*]
PA	Position Angle [*Astronomy*]
PA	Position Approximate [*Nautical charts*]
PA	Positive Addiction [*Self-improvement method developed by William Glasser, MD*]
PA	Positive Attitude
PA	Post Adjutant
PA	Postal Assistant (DCTA)
PA	Post Amplifier
PA	Post-Aural [*Medicine*] (DMAA)
PA	Posterior Anterior [*Medicine*]
PA	Posterior Aorta
PA	Postmortem Aging [*of meat*]
PA	Potato Agar [*Microbiology*]
PA	Potsmokers Anonymous (EA)
PA	Power Amplifier
PA	Power Approach [*Aerospace*]
PA	Power of Attorney
P/A	Power of Authority
PA	Practice Amendment (AAG)
PA	Prealbumin [*Biochemistry*]
PA	Preamplifier
PA	Preapproved
PA	Prearm

PA..............	Preavailability
PA..............	Precision-Acrobatics (DOMA)
PA..............	Precision Angle (IAA)
PA..............	Precision Architecture [Hewlett-Packard Co.] [Computer science]
PA..............	Precomputed Altitude
PA..............	Predictive Accuracy [Medicine] (DMAA)
PA..............	Predictive Analyzer [Computer science] (DIT)
PA..............	Prefect-Apostolic [Roman Catholic]
PA..............	Pregnancy-Associated [Gynecology] (MAE)
PA..............	Preliminary Acceptance (KSC)
PA..............	Preliminary Amplifier (IAA)
PA..............	Preliminary Assessment (ERG)
PA..............	Preparing Activity [Responsible for Federal document and study projects]
P/A..............	Presence or Absence
PA..............	Present Again (ADA)
PA..............	Preservation Action (EA)
PA..............	Presidents Association [New York, NY] (EA)
PA..............	Press Agency (WDAA)
PA..............	Press Agent
PA..............	Press Association Ltd. (IID)
PA..............	Pressure Actuated [Switch]
PA..............	Pressure Alarm [Nuclear energy] (NRCH)
PA..............	Pressure Altitude [Aviation]
PA..............	Pressure Angle (MSA)
PA..............	Pressure Area [Medicine]
PA..............	Price Analyst
PA..............	Primary Aerospace Vehicle [or Aircraft]
PA..............	Primary Amenorrhea [Gynecology] (MAE)
PA..............	Primary Anemia [Medicine]
PA..............	Prince Albert Coat [Slang]
PA..............	Principal Assistant (NOAA)
PA..............	Principal Axes
PA..............	Principle of Adding [New math]
PA..............	Priority A (MCD)
PA..............	Priority Aggregate
PA..............	Prior to Admission [Medicine]
PA..............	Prison Auxiliary (WDAA)
PA..............	Privacy Act
PA..............	Privacy Act of 1974 (COE)
PA..............	Private Account [Banking]
PA..............	Private Architect [British]
Pa..............	Proactinium (IDOE)
PA..............	Proactivator [Medicine]
PA..............	Pro Anno [For the Year] [Latin]
PA..............	Proanthocyanidin (Assay) [Analytical chemistry]
PA..............	Pro Applicatione [To Be Applied] [Pharmacy] (ROG)
PA..............	Probability of Acceptance (KSC)
PA..............	Probability of Acquisition [Military]
P/A..............	Problem Analysis (NASA)
PA..............	Probleme der Agyptologie [A publication] (BJA)
PA..............	Procainamide [Cardiac depressant]
PA..............	Process Allocator [Telecommunications] (TEL)
PA..............	Process Automation (CMD)
PA..............	Procurement Agency (MCD)
PA..............	Procurement Appropriations [Army] (AABC)
PA..............	Procurement, Army
PA..............	Procurement Authorization
PA..............	Procuring Activity [Military]
PA..............	Product Acceptance [Automotive engineering]
PA..............	Product Administration (HCT)
PA..............	Product Analysis (IEEE)
PA..............	Product Assortment (MHDB)
PA..............	Product Assurance (NASA)
PA..............	Production Adjustment
PA..............	Production Agency (COE)
PA..............	Production Assistant
PA..............	Professional Administrator [Australia A publication]
PA..............	Professional Agent [Professional Insurance Agents] [A publication]
PA..............	Professional Association [Telecommunications]
PA..............	Profile Analysis [Medicine]
PA..............	Profile Angle (MSA)
PA..............	Program Access
PA..............	Program Account (NG)
PA..............	Program Address
PA..............	Program Administrator (MCD)
PA..............	Program Agent (OICC)
PA..............	Program Aid [A publication]
PA..............	Program Amount (NITA)
PA..............	Program Analysis [Computer science]
PA..............	Program Application Instructions [Telecommunications] (TEL)
PA..............	Program Assessment (MCD)
PA..............	Program Attention [Computer science] (IAA)
PA..............	Program Attention Key [Computer science]
PA..............	Program Authorization (AFM)
PA..............	Program for the Aging (OICC)
PA..............	Programmable Automation
PA..............	Programmed Arithmetic (IAA)
PA..............	Progressive Alliance [Defunct] (EA)
PA..............	Project Administration (MCD)
PA..............	Project Analysis (MHDB)
PA..............	Project Authorization
PA..............	Proliferating Angioendotheliomatosis
PA..............	Prolonged-Action [Pharmacy]
PA..............	Prolotherapy Association (EA)
PA..............	Property Administrator [DoD]
PA..............	Prophylactic Antibiotic
PA..............	Propionic Acid (DMAA)
PA..............	Proponent Agency [Army]
PA..............	Proportional Action (AAG)
PA..............	Proposal Authorization
PA..............	[The] Proprietary Association [Later, NDMA] (EA)
PA..............	Propulsion Assistance (DS)
PA..............	Prosecuting Attorney
PA..............	Prospecting Authority [Australia]
PA..............	Prostitutes Anonymous (EA)
Pa..............	Protactinium [or Protoactinium] [Chemical element]
PA..............	Protected Area [Nuclear energy] (NRCH)
PA..............	Protective Action (COE)
PA..............	Protective Antigen
PA..............	Protestant Alliance [British] (DBA)
PA..............	Prothonotary Apostolic
Pa..............	Protocatinium (LDT)
PA..............	Proton Affinity [Surface ionization]
PA..............	Protrusio Acetabuli [Medicine] (DMAA)
PA..............	Provisional Allowance.
PA..............	Pseudoaneurysm [Medicine]
PA..............	Pseudo-Astronomy
PA..............	Pseudomonas aeruginosa [Bacterium]
PA..............	Psoriasis Association [Australia]
PA..............	Psychiatric Aide (DAVI)
PA..............	Psychoanalyst
PA..............	Psychogenic Aspermia [Medicine]
PA..............	Psychological Age
PA..............	Public Accountant
PA..............	Public Act
PA..............	Public Address [Amplification equipment] [Communications]
PA..............	Public Address System (WDMC)
PA..............	Public Administration
PA..............	Public Advocate (EA)
PA..............	Public Affairs
PA..............	Public Agent (WDAA)
PA..............	Public Archives [of Canada]
PA..............	Public Assistance
PA..............	Publication Announcement
PA..............	Publicity Agent (WDAA)
PA..............	Publishers' Alliance [Defunct] (EA)
PA..............	Publishers' Association [London, England] (DIT)
PA..............	Pull and Adjust [Brace] [Medicine]
PA..............	Pulmonary Angiography [Medicine]
PA..............	Pulmonary Artery [Medicine]
PA..............	Pulmonary Atresia [Medicine]
PA..............	Pulpoaxial [Dentistry]
PA..............	Pulsating Arc (IAA)
PA..............	Pulse Amplifier
PA..............	Puppeteers of America (EA)
PA..............	Purchasing Agent
PA..............	Purge Alarm [Nuclear energy] (NRCH)
PA..............	Puromycin Aminonucleoside [Biochemistry] (OA)
PA..............	Purpose and Activities (NITA)
PA..............	Put Away [Papers] [British]
PA..............	Puumala [Vole virus]
PA..............	Pyro Ammonia (ROG)
PA..............	Pyrrolizidine Alkaloid [Toxicology]
PA..............	Pythium aphanidermatum [A fungus]
PA0$_2$..........	Arterial Oxygen Pressure (MAE)
PAA..............	Pa-An [Myanmar] [Airport symbol] (OAG)
PAA..............	Pacific Arts Association (EA)
PAA..............	Pan Am Corp. [AMEX symbol] (SAG)
PAA..............	Pan American Minerals Corp. [Toronto Stock Exchange symbol Vancouver Stock Exchange symbol]
PAA..............	Pan American World Airways, Inc. [See also PA, PAN-AM, PN]
PAA..............	Pancretan Association of America (EA)
PAA..............	Pancyprian Association of America [Defunct] (EA)
PAA..............	Panguna [Solomon Islands] [Seismograph station code, US Geological Survey] (SEIS)
PAA..............	Paper Agents Association [British] (DBA)
paa	Papuan-Australian [MARC language code Library of Congress] (LCCP)
PAA..............	Para-Azoxyanisole [Organic chemistry]
PAA..............	Parke, Davis & Co. [Research code symbol]
PAA..............	Parti Affectae Applicandus [Apply to the Affected Part] [Pharmacy]
PAA..............	Partial Agonist Activity (DB)
PAA..............	Patriot Airlines, Inc. [ICAO designator] (FAAC)
PAA..............	Pay Adjustment Authorization
PAA..............	Peracetic Acid [Organic chemistry]
PAA..............	Peruvian American Association (EA)
PAA..............	Petroleum Administration Act [Canada]
PAA..............	Phased Array Antenna
PAA..............	Phenanthrene Amino Alcohol [Organic chemistry]
PAA..............	Phenanthrylacetamide [Organic chemistry]
PAA..............	Phenylacetic Acid [Organic chemistry]
PAA..............	Phonetic Alphabet Association (DGA)
PAA..............	Phosphonoacetic Acid [Antiviral compound]
PAA..............	Photographers Association of America [Later, Professional Photographers of America]
PAA..............	Photon Activation Analysis
PAA..............	Pi Alpha Alpha (EA)
PAA..............	Pill Addicts Anonymous (EA)
PAA..............	Planar Array Antenna

PAA............ Plasminogen Activator Activity [Biochemistry]
PAA............ Platelet Associated Activity [Pharmacology]
PAA............ Polish Association of America [Later, NFLI] (EA)
PAA............ Polocrosse Association of Australia
PAA............ Polyacrylamide [Also, PAAM, PAM] [Organic chemistry]
PAA............ Polyacrylic Acid [Organic chemistry]
PAA............ Polyaspartic Acid [Biochemistry]
PAA............ Polycyclic Aromatic Amine [Organic chemistry]
PAA............ Population Association of America (EA)
PAA............ Port Autonome d'Abidjan [The Ivory Coast] (EY)
PAA............ Post Award Action
PAA............ Potato Association of America (EA)
PAA............ Power Amplifier Assembly
PAA............ Pre-Apprenticeship Allowance
PAA............ Primary Aircraft Authorized [Air Force]
PAA............ Primary Auxiliary Area [Nuclear energy] (NRCH)
PAA............ Print Advertising Association [Defunct] (EA)
PAA............ Priority Abatement Areas [Environment] (GNE)
PAA............ Procurement Appropriation, Army (MCD)
PAA............ Procurement of Ammunition, Army (AABC)
PAA............ Professional Apparel Association
PAA............ Professional Archers Association (EA)
PAA............ Programme d'Aide aux Athletes [Athlete Assistance Program] [Canada]
PAA............ Purchasing Agents Association (NADA)
PAA............ Pyridineacetic Acid [Organic chemistry]
P/AA3.......... Probationary Aircraft Artificer 3rd Class [British military] (DMA)
PAAA......... Premium Advertising Association of America [Later, PMAA] (EA)
P/AAA2 .... Probationary Aircraft Artificer, Acting, 2nd Class [British military] (DMA)
PAAB .... PERSCOM [Personnel Command] Acquisition Accession Board [Army] (INF)
PAABA .... Para-Acetamidobenzoic Acid [Biochemistry]
PAABS .... PanAmerican Association of Biochemical Societies (EA)
PAAC .... Pacific and Asian Affairs Council
PAAC .... Pennsylvania Athletic Conference (PSS)
PAAC .... Program Analysis Adaptable Control [Computer science]
PAACE .... Precision Aircraft Armament Control Experiment (RDA)
PAACS .... Prior Active Army Commissioned Service
PAACT .... Patient Advocates for Advanced Cancer Treatments
PAADAR....... Passive Airborne Detection and Ranging (MSA)
PAADC .... Principal Air Aide-de-Camp [RAF] [British]
PA Admin Bull... Pennsylvania Bulletin [A publication] (DLA)
PA Admin Code... Pennsylvania Administrative Code [A publication] (DLA)
PAAECI .... Pan American Association of Educational Credit Institutions [See also APICE] (EAIO)
PAAES .... Prior Active Army Enlisted Service
PAAES .... Publications. American Archaeological Expedition to Syria [A publication] (BJA)
PAAFB .... Patrick Auxiliary Air Force Base [Florida] (SAA)
PAAFCS........ Prior Active Air Force Commissioned Service
PAAFES........ Prior Active Air Force Enlisted Service
PAAGE .... Panel on Alternate Approaches to Graduate Education (EA)
PAAH .... Polyacrylamide-Hydrazide [Organic chemistry]
PAAHA......... Para-Acetamidohippuric Acid [Biochemistry]
PAAM.......... Physicians Association for Anthroposophical Medicine (EA)
PAAM.......... Polyacrylamide [Also, PAA, PAM] [Organic chemistry]
PAAM.......... Projective Assessment of Aging Method [Personality development test] [Psychology]
P/AAMHRC... Pacific/Asian American Mental Health Research Center [University of Illinois at Chicago] [Research center] (RCD)
PAAN .... Product Assurance Alert Notice (MCD)
PA & E........ Program Analysis and Evaluation
PA & F........ Percussion, Auscultation, and Fremitus [Medicine]
PA & I .... Planning, Analysis, and Integration
PA & T........ Product Assurance and Test
PAANG........ Pennsylvania Air National Guard (MUSM)
PAANS .... Pan African Association of Neurological Sciences (EAIO)
PAANSW...... Prisoners' Aid Association of New South Wales [Australia]
PAAO .... Pan-American Association of Ophthalmology (EA)
P(A-a)O2 ...... Alveolar-Arterial Pressure Difference [For A-aDO2] [Medicine] (DAVI)
PAAORLBE... Pan-American Association of Oto-Rhino-Laryngology and Broncho-Esophagology [Mexico City, Mexico] (EAIO)
PAAP .... Peaceful Alternatives to the Atlantic Pact
PAAP .... Provisional Algal Assay Procedure [Test measuring impact of chemicals on algal growth]
PAAQ .... Palmer [Alaska] [ICAO location identifier] (ICLI)
PAAR .... Precision Approach Airfield RADAR [Aviation] (IAA)
PAAS .... Pan American Allergy Society (EA)
PAAS .... Performance Assessment and Appraisal System
PAAS .... Phased Array Analysis System
PAAS .... Phased Array Antenna System
PAASF .... Pan American Silver Corp. [NASDAQ symbol] (SAG)
PAASF .... Pan Amer Silver [NASDAQ symbol] (TTSB)
PAAT .... Parent as a Teacher Inventory [Psychology]
PAAT .... Personnel and Administrative Assistance Team [Navy] (NVT)
PAAT .... Personnel Assistance and Audit Team [Military]
PAAT .... Professional Association of Alexander Teachers [British] (DBA)
PAAT .... Programmer Analyst Aptitude Test
PAAT .... Public Affairs Assist Team [Hazardous substance emergency response]
PAATI.......... Phased Array Antenna Technology Investigation
PAATLANT ... Personnel and Administration Assistance Team, Atlantic [Navy] (DNAB)

PAATPAC ..... Personnel and Administration Assistance Team, Pacific [Navy] (DNAB)
PAAWA .... Pakistan Australia Association of Western Australia
PAAWA .... Progressive Axemen's Association of Western Australia
P(A-awo) ..... Pressure Gradient from Alveolus to Airway Opening [Medicine] (DAVI)
PAAWWW... Pacific Asian American Women Writers West (EA)
PAAXOP....... Pan-Dodecanesian Association of America "Xanthos O Philikos" (EA)
PAb............. Abington Free Library, Abington, PA [Library symbol Library of Congress] (LCLS)
PAB............. Cabrini College, Library, Radnor, PA [OCLC symbol] (OCLC)
PAB............. PAB Bankshares, Inc. [AMEX symbol] (SAG)
PAB............. Pacific Air Boats Ltd. [Canada ICAO designator] (FAAC)
PAB............. Panair do Brasil, SA
PAB............. Para-Aminobenzoate (DB)
PAB............. Para-Aminobenzoic Acid [Also, PABA] [Biochemistry]
PAB............. Paramaribo [Suriname] [Geomagnetic observatory code]
PAB............. Parti des Paysans, Artisans, et Bourgeois [Farmers', Artisans', and Burghers' Party] [Switzerland Political party] (PPE)
PAB............. Patent Abstracts Bibliography [NASA]
PAB............. Patrick Air Force Base [Florida]
PAB............. Peanut Advisory Board (EA)
PAB............. Pedro Afonso [Brazil] [Airport symbol] (AD)
PAB............. Pension Appeals Board [Canada]
PAB............. Performance Assesment Battery [Medicine] (DMAA)
PAB............. Personal Address Book [MAPI - Mail Applications Program Interface] [Microsoft Corp.] [Computer science]
PAB............. Petroleum Administrative Board [Terminated, 1936]
PAB............. Pharmacologic Autonomic Block [Medicine] (DMAA)
PAB............. Plastic Assault Boat [Navy]
PAB............. Plumbing Advisory Board [South Australia]
PAB............. Police Administration Building
PAB............. Police Appeal Board [South Australia]
PAB............. Policies Allotment Board [Navy] (DNAB)
PAB............. Polyclonal Antibody [Immunochemistry]
P/AB............ Port Side Abreast (DNAB)
PAB............. Potter & Brumfield, Inc. (IAA)
PAB............. Poultry Advisory Board [Queensland, Australia]
PAB............. Power-Assisted Brakes
PAB............. Prealbumin [Biochemistry]
PAB............. Precision Aneroid Barometer (DNAB)
PAB............. Preliminary As-Built [Nuclear energy] (NRCH)
PAB............. Premature Atrial Beat [Cardiology] (AAMN)
PAB............. Price Adjustment Board
PAB............. Price Agreement Bulletin
PAB............. Primary Auxiliary Building [Nuclear energy] (NRCH)
PAB............. Priorities Allotment Board
PAB............. Priority Assignment Base (MCD)
PAB............. Private Activity Bond (AAGC)
PAB............. Product Application Bulletins [A publication] (EAAP)
PAB............. Program Advisory Board (MCD)
PAB............. Programmer Aptitude Battery [Terence R. Taylor] (TES)
PAB............. Promotions Appeal Board [Victoria, Australia]
PAB............. Psychiatric Attitudes Battery [Psychology]
PAB............. Psychology of Addictive Behaviors [An association] (EA)
PAB............. Pulmonary Artery Banding [Cardiology]
PAB............. Pulsed Adsorption Bed [Process]
PAB............. Pulsed Air Blast
PAB............. Purple Agar Base [Media] [Microbiology]
PABA........... Barter Island [Alaska] [ICAO location identifier] (ICLI)
PABA........... Para-Aminobenzoic Acid [Also, PAB] [Biochemistry]
PA BA .... Pennsylvania Bar Association. Reports [A publication] (DLA)
PABA........... Pro-Am Bowfishing Association
PABA........... Progressive Angus Breeders Association
PAB Bk .... PAB Bankshares, Inc. [Associated Press] (SAG)
PA B Brief ... Pennsylvania Bar Brief [A publication] (DLA)
PABC........... Pacific Bancorp (EFIS)
PABC........... Pan American Basketball Confederation [See also CPB] (EAIO)
PABD........... Precise Access Block Diagram
PABE........... Bethel [Alaska] [ICAO location identifier] (ICLI)
PABE........... Program and Budget Estimate (MCD)
PABF........... Precision Air-Bearing Floor (SSD)
PABFSA....... Pediatric Association of Black French-Speaking Africa (EAIO)
PABG........... Big Delta [Alaska] [ICAO location identifier] (ICLI)
PABI............ Delta Junction/Allen Army Air Field [Alaska] [ICAO location identifier] (ICLI)
PA Bk Cas ... Pennsylvania Bank Cases [A publication] (DLA)
PABLA......... Problem Analysis by Logical Approach
PABLE......... Payable (ROG)
PABLI.......... Pages Bleues Informatisees [Commission of the European Communities] [Information service or system] (CRD)
PABLOS....... Program to Analyse the Block System [Computer science] (PDAA)
PABM.......... Big Mountain Air Force Station [Alaska] [ICAO location identifier] (ICLI)
PABMI.......... Performing Arts Biography Master Index [A publication]
PABN .... Pacific Capital Bancorp [NASDAQ symbol] (SAG)
PABP .... Poly(A)-Binding Protein
PABP .... Pulmonary Artery Ballon Pump [Medicine] (DMAA)
PAB-PTC ..... Promotion Appeal Board, Postal and Telecommunications Commission [Australia]
PAB(Q)........ Poultry Advisory Board (Queensland) [Australia]
PABR.......... Barrow [Alaska] [ICAO location identifier] (ICLI)
PABR.......... Planning Appeals Board. Reports [A publication]
P Abr .... Pulton's Abridgment of the Statutes [A publication] (DLA)
PA Browne (PA)... Browne's Reports (Pennsylvania) [A publication] (DLA)

PA Browne R... Browne's Reports [*Pennsylvania*] [*A publication*] (DLA)
PABRX .... Phoenix-Engemann Balanced Return Cl.A [*Mutual fund ticker symbol*] (SG)
PABS .... Pan-American Biodeterioration Society (EA)
PABS .... Para-Aminobenzensulfonamide [*Antibiotic*]
PABST........... Primary Adhesively Bonded Structural Technology [*Aviation*]
PABT............ Bettles [*Alaska*] [*ICAO location identifier*] (ICLI)
PABV .... Percutaneous Aortic Balloon Valvuloplasty [*Medicine*] (HCT)
PABV .... Pyroactuated Ball Valve
PABX .... Private Automatic Branch Exchange [*Telecommunications*] (DEN)
PAC............. cis-Platinum [*Cisplatin*], Adriamycin, Cyclophosphamide [*Antineoplastic drug regimen*]
Pac .... Pacific [*Record label*] [*France*]
PAC............. Pacific (AFM)
Pac .... Pacifica: Australian Theological Studies [*A publication*] (APTA)
PAC............. Pacific Air Command [*Air Force*]
PAC............. Pacific Command [*Military*] (GFGA)
PAC............. Pacific Ocean
PAC............. Pacific Region [*USTTA*] (TAG)
Pac .... Pacific Reporter [*A publication*] (DLA)
PAC............. Pacific Telesis Group [*NYSE symbol*] (SPSG)
PAC............. Pacific Telesis Group Financing I [*NYSE symbol*] (SAG)
PAC............. Pacific Telesis Group Financing II [*NYSE symbol*] (SAG)
PAC............. Package Attitude Control [*NASA*]
PAC............. Packaged Assembly Circuit
PAC............. Packard Automobile Classics (EA)
PAC............. Packed Memory [*Computer science*] (IAA)
PAC............. Packet Autopiloted Cruiseway
PAC............. Pacto de Alianza de Centro [*Chile*] [*Political party*] (EY)
PAC............. Pak-Man Resources, Inc. [*Vancouver Stock Exchange symbol*]
PAC............. Palestine Affairs Center (EA)
PAC............. Palo Alto - Branner [*California*] [*Seismograph station code, US Geological Survey Closed*] (SEIS)
PAC............. Pan-Africanist Congress [*South Africa*]
PAC............. Panama City [*Panama*] Paitilla Airport [*Airport symbol*] (OAG)
PAC............. Pan American College [*Texas*]
PAC............. Pan-American Congress
PAC............. Papular Acrodermatitis of Childhood
PAC............. Para-Aminoclonidine [*Biochemistry*]
PAC............. Para-Aminosalicylic Acid Calcium Salt [*Pharmacology*]
PAC............. Parachute and Cable Defence [*British military*]
PAC............. Parallel Alternate Curriculum (EDAC)
PAC............. Parametric Amplifier Converter
P-A-C .... Parent-Adult-Child [*Transactional analysis*]
PAC............. Parent Advisory Committee [*Migrant education*] (AEE)
PAC............. Parent Advisory Council (EDAC)
PAC............. Parker Aircraft Corp. (MCD)
PAC............. Partido Autentico Constitucional [*Authentic Constitutional Party*] [*El Salvador*] [*Political party*]
PAC............. Parts Allocation Chart (MCD)
PAC............. Pascagoula, MS [*Location identifier FAA*] (FAAL)
PAC............. Passed the Final Examination of the Advanced Class [*Military College of Science*] [*British*]
PAC............. Passive Acoustic Classification (NVT)
PAC............. Patents Advisory Committee [*British*]
PAC............. Patient Airlift Center [*Aeromedical evacuation*]
PAC............. Patriot Advanced Capability [*Missile technology*] [*Military*] (PS)
PAC............. Patriot Antimissile Capability [*Army*]
PAC............. Payment after Closing [*Insurance*]
PAC............. Peace Action Center [*Defunct*] (EA)
PAC............. Pedagogic Automatic Computer (IEEE)
PAC............. Pediatric AIDS [*Acquired Immune Deficiency Syndrome*] Coalition (EA)
PAC............. Penal Affairs Consortium (WDAA)
PAC............. Penalty Assessment Criteria [*Environmental Protection Agency*]
PAC............. Penetration Aids Deployment Concept (SAA)
PA C .... Pennsylvania Commonwealth Court Reports [*A publication*] (DLA)
PAC............. People Against Cancer
PAC............. People's Army Congress
PAC............. Peptide Acid [*Organic chemistry*]
PAC............. Performance Analysis and Control
PAC............. Performance Assured Certification
PAC............. Peripheral Autonomous Control (NITA)
PAC............. Personal Access Code
PAC............. Personal Analog Computer
PAC............. Person in Addition to Crew [*Sailing*]
PAC............. Personnel Action Center [*Army*] (INF)
PAC............. Personnel Action Code
PAC............. Personnel and Administration Center [*Army*] (AABC)
PAC............. Personnel Assistance Center [*Military*] (INF)
PAC............. Perturbed Angular Correlation
PAC............. Pesticides Advisory Committee [*Tasmania, Australia*]
PAC............. Petroleum Advisory Committee [*of Organization for Economic Cooperation and Development*] [*Terminated, 1976*] (EGAO)
PAC............. Pharmaceutical Advertising Council [*New York, NY*] (EA)
PAC............. Phenacetin [*Acetophenetidin*], Aspirin, Caffeine [*Pharmacology*]
PAC............. Photoacoustic [*Spectroscopy*]
PAC............. Photoactive Compound [*Chemistry*]
PAC............. Photo Aperture Card (SAA)
PAC............. Phototypesetting Automatic Controller (DGA)
PA-C .... Physician's Assistant-Certified (WGA)
PAC............. Pilotless Aircraft [*Navy*] (IAA)
PAC............. Piper Aircraft Corp.
PAC............. Place Complement of Address in Index Register (SAA)
PAC............. Planned Amortization Class [*Investment term*] (DFIT)

PAC............. Planned-Amortization-Class Bond [*Investment term*]
PAC............. Planned Amortization Credit [*Investment term*] (ECON)
PAC............. Planned Availability Concept (MHDI)
PAC............. Planning Advisory Committee (OICC)
PAC............. Plasma Aldosterone Concentration [*Hematology*] (DMAA)
PAC............. Plasma Arc Chamber
PAC............. Plasma Arc Cutting [*Welding*]
PAC............. Platelet-Associated Complement [*Medicine*] (DMAA)
PAC............. Platinol [*Cisplatin*], Adriamycin, Cyclophosphamide [*Antineoplastic drug regimen*]
PAC............. Plowshare Advisory Committee [*AEC*]
PAC............. Pneumatic Analog Computer
PAC............. Pneumatic Auxiliary Console (AAG)
PAC............. Pod Air Conditioner (AAG)
PAC............. Poisons Advisory Committee [*Australia*]
PAC............. Polar Air Cargo, Inc. [*FAA designator*] (FAAC)
PAC............. Policy Advisory Center
PAC............. Policy Advisory Committee [*National Cancer Institute*] [*Department of Health and Human Services*] (GFGA)
PAC............. Policy Advisory Committee [*Office of Economic Opportunity*]
PAC............. Polish American Congress (EA)
PAC............. Political Action Caucus [*Superseded by LPAC*] (EA)
PAC............. Political Action Committee [*Generic term*]
PAC............. Polled Access Circuit
PAC............. Pollution Abatement and Control
PAC............. Polyaluminum Chloride [*Inorganic chemistry*]
PAC............. Polyanionic Cellulose [*Organic chemistry*]
PAC............. Polycyclic Aromatic Compound [*Organic chemistry*]
PAC............. Population Action Council (EA)
PAC............. Porterfield Airplane Club (EA)
PAC............. Post-Adoption Centre [*British*] (CB)
PAC............. Post Award Conference (MCD)
PAC............. Post Award Contract
PAC............. Powdered Activated Carbon [*Adsorbent*]
PAC............. Pre-Action Calibration [*Gunnery*] (NVT)
PAC............. Pre-Admission Certification [*Medicine*] (MEDA)
PAC............. Preauthorized Check Plan [*Insurance*]
PAC............. Pre-Authorized Chequing [*Canada*]
PAC............. Premature Atrial Contraction [*Medicine*]
PAC............. Premature Auricular Contraction [*Cardiology*] (AAMN)
PAC............. Preservation and Conservation [*IFLA Core Program*]
PAC............. Presidents' Athletic Conference (PSS)
PAC............. Pressure Alpha Center (MCD)
PAC............. Primary Address Code (AFM)
PAC............. Prime [*or Principal*] Associate Contractor (MCD)
PAC............. Principal Associate Contractor (MCD)
PAC............. Printing Accountants Club (EA)
PAC............. Priority Area Children (AIE)
PAC............. Privacy Act Coordinator [*Navy*] (DNAB)
PAC............. Probe Aerodynamic Center [*NASA*]
PAC............. Problem Action Center [*NASA*] (NASA)
PAC............. Process Analytical Chemistry
PAC............. Procurement and Contract (IAA)
PAC............. Production Acceleration Capacity [*Manufacturing*]
PAC............. Product of Ambulatory Care [*Medicine*] (HCT)
PAC............. Professional Activities Survey [*Medicine*]
PAC............. Program Acquisition Cost (MCD)
PAC............. Program Address Counter [*Computer science*] (FECA)
PAC............. Program Adjustment Committee
PAC............. Program Advisory Committee
PAC............. Program Allocation Checker
PAC............. Program Application Code (DNAB)
PAC............. Program Assembly Card (NITA)
PAC............. Program Authorized Credentials [*Computer science*]
PAC............. Programmable Analogical Controller (NITA)
PAC............. Programmable Automatic Comparator
PAC............. Programme Activity Center [*Advisory Committee on Pollution of the Sea*]
PAC............. Progress Assessment Chart [*Psychology*]
PAC............. Project Advisory Committee (EGAO)
PAC............. Project Analysis and Control (IAA)
PAC............. Promoting Achievement through Communications [*Education*]
PAC............. Protect America's Children [*An association*] (EA)
PAC............. Protection Auxiliary Cabinet [*Nuclear energy*] (NRCH)
PAC............. Prudential Assurance Co. Ltd. [*Australia*]
PAC............. Public Access Catalogue (ADA)
PAC............. Public Access Control
PAC............. Public Accounts Committee [*British government*]
PAC............. Public Affairs Committee [*Defunct*] (EA)
PAC............. Public Affairs Coordinator [*Nuclear energy*] (NRCH)
PAC............. Public Affairs Council (EA)
PAC............. Public Archives of Canada
PAC............. Public Authority Contribution [*Australia*]
PAC............. Public Awareness Committee [*American Library Association*]
PAC............. Publishers' Ad Club [*New York, NY*] (EA)
PAC............. Pulmonary Artery Catheter [*Medicine*]
PAC............. Purchasing and Contracting [*Army*] (IAA)
PAC............. Pure and Applied Chemistry [*IUPAC*]
PAC............. Pursuant to Authority Contained In [*Army*]
PAC............. Put and Call [*Stock exchange term*]
Pac 2d .... Pacific Reporter, Second Series [*A publication*] (DLA)
PAC-3 .... Patriot Advanced Capability-3 [*Army*]
PAC-10 .... Pacific 10 Conference (EA)
Pac A........... Pacific Affairs [*A publication*] (BRI)
PACA .... Perishable Agricultural Commodities Act, 1930

PACA .... Picture Agency Council of America (EA)
PACA .... Principal Assistant County Architect [British]
PACA .... Propulsion and Control Assembly
PACA .... Proyecto Ambiental para Centro America [Environmental Project for Central America] [Spanish] (ECON)
PACAACS .... Pacific Area Airways and Air Communications (IAA)
PacA & E ... Pacific Aerospace & Electronics, Inc. [Associated Press] (SAG)
PACADIV ..... Pacific Fleet Advance Headquarters Division (DNAB)
PACADV ...... Pacific Fleet Advance Headquarters [Guam]
PACAF .... Pacific Air Forces
PACAFBASECOM... Pacific Air Forces Base Command
PACAF-OA.... Pacific Air Forces Operations Analysis
PACAF-OA.... Pacific Air Forces Operations Analysis Office [Hickam Air Force Base, HI]
PACAH .... Pitch Attitude Command/Attitude Hold [Aviation] (MCD)
PacAni .... Pacific Animated Imaging Corp. [Associated Press] (SAG)
PACAP .... Pituitary Adenylate Cyclase Activating Polypeptide [Biochemistry]
PACAP .... Pituitary Adenylyl Cyclase-Activating Polypeptide [Endocrinology]
Pacar .... PACCAR, Inc. [Associated Press] (SAG)
PacAS .... Pacific American Income Shares, Inc. [Associated Press] (SAG)
PACAS .... Patient Care System [Army] (AABC)
PA Cas .... Pennsylvania Supreme Court Cases (Sadler) [A publication] (DLA)
PACAS .... Personnel Access Control Accountability System [NASA] (MCD)
PACAS .... Psychological Abstracts Current Awareness Service (IID)
PACB .... Pan-American Coffee Bureau [Defunct] (EA)
PACB .... Pennsylvania Association of Community Bankers (TBD)
PACB .... Poppy Advisory and Control Board [Tasmania, Australia]
PACBAR ...... Pacific Barrier RADAR (MCD)
PacBB .... Pacific Basin Bulk Shippers Ltd. [Associated Press] (SAG)
PacBBS .... Pacific Basin Bulk Shippers Ltd. [Associated Press] (SAG)
PacBio .... Pacific Biometrics, Inc. [Associated Press] (SAG)
PacBiom ..... Pacific Biometrics, Inc. [Associated Press] (SAG)
PACC .... Pacific Coast [Railroad] (MHDB)
PA CC .... Pennsylvania County Court Reports [A publication] (DLA)
PACC .... PERT [Program Evaluation and Review Technique] Associated Cost Control [Computer science] (IAA)
PACC .... Portable Arm Control Console (KSC)
PACC .... Primary Ambulatory Care Center [Medicine] (DMAA)
P(ACC) .... Probability of Acceptance
PACC .... Problem Action Control Center [NASA] (NASA)
PACC .... Product Administration and Contract Control (IAA)
PACC .... Products Administration Contract Control
PACC .... Professional Association of Custom Clothiers (EA)
PACC .... Programmable Array Combinatorial Circuit (NITA)
PACC .... Promoting Aphasics' Communicative Competence [Medicine] (DMAA)
PACC .... Propulsion and Auxiliary Control Console [NASA] (DNAB)
PACC .... Protected Air-Cooled Condenser [Nuclear energy] (NRCH)
PACC .... Protein A Immobilized in Collodion Charcoal (DAVI)
PACC .... Public Arts Advisory Council (NADA)
PACCA .... Policy Alternatives for the Caribbean and Central America (EA)
PACCALL ..... Pacific Fleet Calls [Radio call signs]
PacCapB ...... Pacific Capital Bancorp [Associated Press] (SAG)
PACCAR ...... Pacific Car and Foundry
PACCE .... Providing Professional Development, Assessment, and Coordination of Competency-Based Education Project [Illinois] (EDAC)
PACCIOS ..... Pan American Council of International Committee of Scientific Management
PACCO .... Cisplatin, Adriamycin, Cyclophosphamide, CCNU [Lomustine], Oncovin [Vincristine] [Antineoplastic drug regimen]
Pac Coast Int... Pacific Coast International [A publication] (ILCA)
Pac Coast LJ... Pacific Coast Law Journal [A publication] (DLA)
PACCOM ...... Pacific Command [Military]
PACCOM ...... Pacific Communications Network [Computer science] (TNIG)
PACCOM ...... Pacific Fleet Communications Instructions
PACCOMOPCONCEN... Pacific Fleet Command Operational Control Center (DNAB)
PA CCR .... Pennsylvania County Court Reports [A publication] (DLA)
PA CC Reps.. Pennsylvania County Court Reports [A publication] (DLA)
PacCrst .... Pacific Crest Capital [Associated Press] (SAG)
PACCS .... Pan American Cancer Cytology Society [Defunct] (EA)
PACCS .... Post-Attack Command and Control System [Military]
PACCS/ADA... Post-Attack Command and Control System/Airborne Data Automation [Military]
PACCSq .... Post-Attack Command Control Squadron [Air Force]
PACCT .... PERT [Program Evaluation and Review Technique] and Cost Correlation Technique
PACCT .... Political Action Committee for Cable Television (NTCM)
PACD .... Cold Bay [Alaska] [ICAO location identifier] (ICLI)
PACD .... Pacific Division [Military]
PACD .... Parachute and Cable Defence [British military] (DMA)
PACDA .... Personnel and Administration, Combat Development Activity [Army] (AABC)
PA C Dec WCC... Pennsylvania Courts, Decisions in Workmen's Compensation Cases [A publication] (DLA)
PACDIV .... Pacific Division [Military]
PacDunl .... Pacific Dunlop Ltd. [Associated Press] (SAG)
PACE .... Ampace Corp. [NASDAQ symbol] (SAG)
PACE .... Pacific Agricultural Cooperative for Export [Corte Madera, CA] (EA)
PACE .... Pacific Alternate Command Element (CINC)
PACE .... Pacific America Container Express (MHDB)
PACE .... Pacific Atoll Cratering Experiment [Military] (DNAB)
PACE .... Packaged CRAM [Card Random-Access Memory] Executive [NCR Corp.] [Computer science]
PACE .... Package for Architectural Computer Evaluation (PDAA)

PACE .... Packet of Accelerated Christian Education [Educational material marketed by fundamentalist company, Accelerated Christian Education]
PACE .... Parental Alliance for Choice in Education (AIE)
PACE .... Parents and Children's Equality [An association] (PAZ)
PACE .... Passive Attitude Control Experimental [Satellite]
PACE .... Patient Advise and Consent Encounter
PACE .... Patrol Airship Concept Evaluation
PACE .... People with Arthritis Can Exercise [Medical program]
PACE .... Performance Advantage with Cummins Electronics [Automotive engineering]
PACE .... Performance and Cost Evaluation
PACE .... Performing Arts, Culture, and Entertainment [Proposed cable television system]
PACE .... Peripheral Automatic Channel Emulator [Computer science]
PACE .... Personalized Aerobics for Cardiovascular Enhancement
PACE .... Petroleum Association for Conservation of the Canadian Environment
PACE .... Phased Array Control Electronics
PACE .... Physics and Chemistry Experiment
PACE .... Planetary Association for Clean Energy (EA)
PACE .... Plan for Action by Citizens in Education
PACE .... Planned Action with Constant Evaluation [Computer science]
PACE .... Planning and Control Made Easy (PDAA)
PACE .... Plant Acquisition and Construction Equipment [Nuclear energy] (NRCH)
PACE .... Plant and Capital Equipment (MCD)
PACE .... Plasma-Assisted Chemical Etching [Metallurgy]
PACE .... Platinol [Cis-Platinum] [Antineoplastic drug regimen] (DAVI)
PACE .... Police and Criminal Evidence Act [1964] [British]
PACE .... Policy Analysis for California Education [Research center] (RCD)
PACE .... Political Action for Candidate Election [National Association]
PACE .... Pollution Abatement Capital Expense (EDCT)
PACE .... Portable Acoustic Collection Equipment (MCD)
PACE .... Precision Analog Computing Equipment
PACE .... Preflight Acceptance Checkout Equipment
PACE .... Prelaunch Automatic Checkout Equipment [NASA]
PACE .... Priority Access Control Enabled [Telecommunications]
PACE .... Priority Activities in Cancer Education
PACE .... Prisoners Accelerated Creative Exposure [An association]
PACE .... Procedural Approach to the Composition of Essays [In book title]
PACE .... Processing and Control Element [Computer science] (IAA)
PACE .... Producers of Associated Components for Electronics (IAA)
PACE .... Professional Activities for Continuing Education [AEC]
PACE .... Professional and Administrative Career Examination [Formerly, FSEE] [Civil Service]
PACE .... Professional Application Creation Environment (NITA)
PACE .... Professional Association of Christian Educators (EA)
PACE .... Professional Association of Consulting Engineers
PACE .... Program Analysis Control and Evaluation [Computer science] (IAA)
PACE .... Program for Acquiring Competence in Entrepreneurship (EDAC)
PACE .... Program for Afloat College Education [Navy] (NVT)
PACE .... Programmable Autonomously-Controlled Electrode [Instrumentation]
PACE .... Programmed Automatic Communications Equipment
PACE .... Programming Analysis Consulting Education (IEEE)
PACE .... Program of All-Inclusive Care for the Elderly
PACE .... Progressive Aerobic Circuit Exercise [Fitness training]
PACE .... Project for the Advancement of Church Education
PACE .... Projects to Advance Creativity in Education [HEW]
PACE .... Promoting Aphasics Communicative Effectiveness [Australia]
PACE .... Providing Avenues for Continuing Encouragement [Scholarship awarded by Fraternity of Recording Executives]
PACE .... Provisioning Action Control Evaluation [Military] (AFIT)
PACE .... Public Affairs Council Education [An association] [Canadian] (NFD)
PACE .... Public Affairs Council for Education [Canada]
PACE .... Pulse-Synthesized Advanced Conversion Equipment
P/ACEA2 ..... Probationary Control Electrical Artificer, Acting, 2nd Class [British military] (DMA)
PACED .... Program for Advanced Concepts in Electronic Design
PACEE .... Propulsion and Auxiliary Control Electronic Enclosure (DNAB)
PaceHlt .... Pace Health Management Systems, Inc. [Associated Press] (SAG)
PACE/LV ..... Preflight Acceptance Checkout Equipment-Launch Vehicle
PACEMAKER... Public Agency Career Employment Maker [OEO project]
PACEN .... Public Affairs Center [Navy] (DNAB)
PACENLANT... Public Affairs Center, Atlantic [Navy] (DNAB)
PACENPAC... Public Affairs Center, Pacific [Navy] (DNAB)
PACENS ...... Patient Census
PacEnt .... Pacific Enterprises [Associated Press] (SAG)
PACEO .... Professional Application Creation Environment (HGAA)
PACER .... Parent Advocacy Coalition for Educational Rights [Minnesota] (EDAC)
PACER .... Part and Component Evaluation Report [NASA]
PACER .... Planning Automation and Control for Evaluating Requirements
PACER .... Portable Aircraft Condition Evaluator Recorder
PACER .... Postadoption Center for Education and Research
PACER .... Postoperational Analysis Critique and Exercise Report [Military] (CAAL)
PACER .... Prescriptive Analysis for Curriculum Evaluation [Vocational guidance]
PACER .... Priority for Allocation/Application of COMSEC Equipment Resources (MCD)
PACER .... Private Access to Court Electronic Records (AAGC)
PACER .... Process Assembly Case Evaluator Routine [Computer science]
PACER .... Professional Association of Comics Entertainment Retailers (NTPA)
PACER .... Program-Assisted Console Evaluation and Review [Air Force]
PACER .... Programmed Automatic Circuit Evaluator and Recorder
PACER .... Program of Active Cooling Effects and Requirements

PACER	Public Access to Court Electronic Records
PACERS	Pacing and Cardiac Electrophysiology Retrieval System [*Intermedics, Inc.*] [*Information service or system*] (IID)
PACES	Parent Attitude Toward Child Experssiveness Scale (EDAC)
PACES	Patient as Customer Evaluation Survey
PACES	Political Action Committee for Engineers and Scientists
PACE-S/C	Preflight Acceptance Checkout Equipment for Spacecraft
Pace U	Pace University (GAGS)
PAC-EX	Canadian National Packaging Exposition [*Packaging Association of Canada*] (TSPED)
PACEX	Pacific Exchange [*System*] [*Military*] (AFM)
PACF	Pacific
Pacf	PacifiCorp [*Associated Press*] (SAG)
PACF	Partial Autocorrelation Function [*Statistics*]
PAC-FACS	Programmed Appropriation Commitments - Fixed Asset Control System (PDAA)
PACFAST	Pacific Forward Area Support Team (DNAB)
PACFASTDET	Pacific Forward Area Support Team Detachment (DNAB)
PACFASTREP	Pacific Forward Area Support Team Representative (DNAB)
PacFIN	Pacific Fishery Information Network [*Database*] [*National Marine Fisheries Service*]
PACFLAP	Pacific Fleet Augmentation Plan [*Navy*] (NVT)
PACFLT	Pacific Fleet
PACFLTCOM	Pacific Fleet Command
PACFLTMOPHOTOU	Pacific Fleet Mobile Photographic Unit (MUGU)
PACFLTPROPEXAMBD	Pacific Fleet Propulsion Examining Board (DNAB)
PACFORNET	Pacific Coast Forest Research Information Network [*Later, WESTFORNET*] [*Forest Service*] (IID)
PACFW	President's Advisory Committee for Women [*Terminated, 1980*] (EGAO)
PacGate	Pacific Gateway Properties [*Associated Press*] (SAG)
PACGCS	Prior Active Coast Guard Commissioned Service
PacGE	Pacific Gas & Electric Co. [*Associated Press*] (SAG)
PACGEEIA	Pacific Area Ground Environment Electronic Installation Agency (CINC)
PACGES	Prior Active Coast Guard Enlisted Service
PACGO	President's Advisory Committee on Government Organization [*Abolished, 1961*]
PACGSR	Pan American Center for Geographical Studies and Research [*See also CEPEIGE*] (EAIO)
PacGul	Pacific Gulf Properties, Inc. [*Associated Press*] (SAG)
PacGulf	Pacific Gulf Properties [*Associated Press*] (SAG)
PACH	Performing Arts Center for Health [*New York University/Bellevue Hospital, New York, NY*] [*Superseded by Center for Dance Medicine -CDM*]
PACH	Pipers to After Coming Head [*Obstetrics*] (DAVI)
PACH	Public Administration Clearing House [*1931-1956*]
PACH	Publishers' Accounts Clearing House [*British*] (BI)
PACHACH	Partizanim-Chayalim-Chalutzim (BJA)
PACHEDPEARL	Pacific Headquarters, Pearl Harbor, Hawaii [*Navy*]
PACHG	Program Advisory Committee on the Human Genome (HGEN)
PACI	Partnerships for Advanced Computational Infrastructure [*National Science Foundation*]
PACIA	Particle Counting Immunoassay
PACICOM	Pacific Coastal Marine Productivity [*Marine science*] (OSRA)
PACIF	Pacific
Pacif	PacifiCorp [*Associated Press*] (SAG)
PacifBnk	Pacific Bank NA [*Associated Press*] (SAG)
PacifC	PacifiCare Health Systems, Inc. [*Associated Press*] (SAG)
PacifCp	PacifiCorp [*Associated Press*] (SAG)
Pacif Defence Reporter	Pacific Defence Reporter [*A publication*]
Pacific CLJ	Pacific Coast Law Journal [*San Francisco*] [*A publication*] (DLA)
Pacific Law Mag	Pacific Law Magazine [*A publication*] (DLA)
Pacific Rep	Pacific Reporter [*A publication*] (DLA)
Pacif Is Mon	Pacific Islands Monthly [*A publication*]
Pacif Rep	Pacific Reporter [*A publication*] (DLA)
PACIFY	Parents and Alumni Committee Involved for Youth [*Brown University*]
PACIMS	Passive Chemical Ionization Mass Spectrometry
PACINTCEN	Pacific Intelligence Center (DNAB)
PacIntl	Pacific International Services Corp. [*Associated Press*] (SAG)
PACIR	Practical Approach to Chemical Information Retrieval
PACIT	Passive and Active Interface Test [*Electronic warfare*]
PACK	Gibraltar Packaging Group [*NASDAQ symbol*] (TTSB)
PACK	Gibraltar Packaging Group, Inc. [*NASDAQ symbol*] (SAG)
PACK	Packing and Allocation for a COMPOOL [*Communications Pool*] Kaleidoscope (SAA)
PACK	Parents and Cataract Kids [*An association*] (PAZ)
PACK	Pontoon Air Cushion Kit [*Army*] (RDA)
PACKAGE	Planned Aids for Cross-Culture Knowledge, Action and Growth in Effectiveness
PackRs	Packaging Research Corp. [*Associated Press*] (SAG)
PackRsh	Packaging Research Corp. [*Associated Press*] (SAG)
PACL	Clear [*Alaska*] [*ICAO location identifier*] (ICLI)
Pac Law Mag	Pacific Law Magazine [*A publication*] (DLA)
Pac Law Reptr	Pacific Law Reporter [*San Francisco*] [*A publication*] (DLA)
Pac Leg N	Pacific Legal News [*A publication*] (DLA)
Pac Luth U	Pacific Lutheran University (GAGS)
PACM	Parts and Componenets Manual (IAA)
PACM	Passive Countermeasures (MSA)
PACM	Pulse Amplitude Code Modulation [*Electronics*]
PACMD	Philadelphia Contract Management District (SAA)
PACMETNET	Pacific Meteorological Network (AAG)
PACMI	President's Advisory Committee on Management Improvement [*Terminated, 1973*]
PACMISCEN	Pacific Missile Center [*Marine science*] (DNAB)

PACMISRAN	Pacific Missile Range [*Later, WTR*] (MUGU)
PACMISRANFAC	Pacific Missile Range Facility [*Obsolete*]
PACMISRANFACDET	Pacific Missile Range Facility Detachment [*Obsolete*] (DNAB)
PACMISRANFACREP	Pacific Missile Range Facility Representative [*Obsolete*] (DNAB)
PACMISTESTCEN	Pacific Missile Test Center [*Navy*]
PACMISTESTCEN LO	Pacific Missile Test Center Liaison Office [*Navy*] (DNAB)
PACMS	Psycho-Acoustical Measuring System (PDAA)
PA Cmwlth	Pennsylvania Commonwealth Court Reports [*A publication*] (DLA)
PACN	Pacific Area Communicatios Network (SAA)
PACNAVCONSTFOR	Pacific Naval Construction Force (DNAB)
PACNAVFACENGCOM	Pacific Division Naval Facilities Engineering Command
PACNCF	Pacific Naval Construction Force (DNAB)
PACNCO	Personnel Assistance Center Noncommissioned Officer (INF)
PACNET	OCLC Pacific Network [*Claremont, CA*] [*Information service or system*] (IID)
PACNET	Plymouth Audioconferencing Network [*Plymouth Polytechnic*] [*Plymouth, England*] [*Telecommunications*] (TSSD)
PACNET	POCC [*Payload Operations Control Center*] Automated Computer Network
PACNY	Pawnbrokers' Association of the City of New York (EA)
PACO	Accounting Policy Division (AAGC)
PacO	Pacific Ocean
PACO	Peak Aboriginal Community Organisation [*Australia*]
PACO	Pivot Ambulating Crutchless Orthosis [*Medicine*]
PACO	Polaris Accelerated Change Operation [*Missiles*]
PACO	Primary Administrative Contracting Officer [*Military*] (AFIT)
PACO	Principal Administrative Contracting Officer (AAGC)
PACO_2	Alveolar Carbon Dioxide Pressure [*in blood gases*] [*Medicine*] (DAVI)
Paco$_2$	Arterial Carbon Dioxide Pressure, Tension [*Medicine*] (MAE)
PACOB	Propulsion Auxiliary Control Box (AAG)
PA Co Ct	Pennsylvania County Court Reports [*A publication*] (DLA)
PA Co Ct R	Pennsylvania County Court Reports [*A publication*] (DLA)
PACOM	Pacific Command [*Military*]
PACOM	Pacific Communications Group
PACOMBPO	Pacific Command Blood Program Office [*Military*] (DNAB)
PACOMDET	Pacific Command Detachment [*Military*] (DNAB)
PACOMEP	Pacific Command Emergency Procedures (CINC)
PACOMEW	Pacific Command Electronic Warfare (CINC)
PACOMINTS	Pacific Command Intelligence School (CINC)
PACOMJRO	Pacific Command Joint Medical Regulating Office (DNAB)
PA Commw	Pennsylvania Commonwealth Court Reports [*A publication*] (DLA)
Pa Commw	Pennsylvania Commonwealth Reports [*A publication*] (AAGC)
PA Commw Ct	Pennsylvania Commonwealth Court Reports [*A publication*] (DLA)
PA Com Pl	Pennsylvania Common Pleas Reporter [*A publication*] (DLA)
PA Cons Stat	Pennsylvania Consolidated Statutes [*A publication*] (DLA)
PA Cons Stat Ann	Pennsylvania Consolidated Statutes, Annotated [*A publication*] (DLA)
PA Cons Stat Ann (Purdon)	Pennsylvania Consolidated Statutes, Annotated (Purdon) [*A publication*] (DLA)
PACOPS	Pacific Air Combat Operations Staff
PACOPS	Pacific Air Force Operations (MCD)
PACOR	Passive Correlation and Ranging
PACOR	Passive Correlation and Ranging Station (IAA)
PACORE	Parabolic Corner Reflector
PACORNALOG	Pacific Coast Coordinator of Naval Logistics
PA Corp	Pennsylvania Corp. Reporter [*A publication*] (DLA)
PA Corp R	Pennsylvania Corp. Reporter [*A publication*] (DLA)
PA Corp Rep	Pennsylvania Corp. Reporter [*A publication*] (DLA)
PACOS	Package Operating System (PDAA)
PA County Ct	Pennsylvania County Court Reports [*A publication*] (DLA)
PA CP	Pennsylvania Common Pleas Reporter [*A publication*] (DLA)
PACP	Photo Aperture Card Program (SAA)
PACP	Propulsion Auxiliary Control Panel [*NASA*] (KSC)
PACP	Pulmonary Artery Counter-Pulsation [*Cardiology*] (MAE)
PacPhy	Pacific Physician Services, Inc. [*Associated Press*] (SAG)
PACPIP	Public Advocate - Coalition of Public Interest Professionals (EA)
PACPrT	Pac Telesis Fin I 7.56%'TOPrS' [*NYSE symbol*] (TTSB)
PACQI	Probability of Acquisition [*Military*]
Pac R	Pacific Reporter [*Commonly cited as P*] [*A publication*] (DLA)
PA CR	Pennsylvania County Court Reports [*A publication*] (DLA)
PACR	Performance and Compatibility Requirements
PACR	Perimeter Acquisition RADAR (MSA)
PACRAD	Practical Absolute Cavity Radiometer (PDAA)
PacR & E	Pacific Research & Engineering Corp. [*Associated Press*] (SAG)
PACRAO	Pacific Association of Collegiate Registrars and Admission Officers
PACRED	Pacific Area Cooperative Renewable Energy Development [*University of Hawaii*]
PacRehab	Pacific Rehabilitation & Sports Medicine, Inc. [*Associated Press*] (SAG)
Pac Rep	Pacific Reporter [*Commonly cited as P*] [*A publication*] (DLA)
PACREP	Port Activities Report [*Navy*]
PACREPCOMNAVSURFRES	Pacific Representative for Commander Naval Surface Reserve Force (DNAB)
PACREPNAVRES	Pacific Representative of the Chief of Naval Reserve (DNAB)
Pac Repr	Pacific Reporter [*A publication*] (DLA)
PACRESFLT	Pacific Reserve Fleet
PacRim	Pac Rim Holding Corp. [*Associated Press*] (SAG)
PACS	Cape Sarichef Air Force Station [*Alaska*] [*ICAO location identifier*] (ICLI)
PACS	Pacific Area Communications System (MCD)
Pac S	Pacific Studies [*A publication*] (BRI)
PACS	Pan America Climate Studies [*Marine science*] (OSRA)
PACS	Particle Analysis Cameras for the Shuttle [*NASA*]

PACS .... Patient Accounting, Census, and Statistics
PACS .... Patient Care and Services (DMAA)
PACS .... Peace and Common Security [*Defunct*] (EA)
PACS .... Photo Aperture Card System (SAA)
PACS .... Physics and Astronomy Classification Scheme
PACS .... Picture Archival and Communication System
PACS .... Pitch Augmentation Control System (PDAA)
PACS .... Plant Automation Communication System [*IBM Corp.*]
PACS .... Pointing and Attitude Control System [*Aerospace*] (NASA)
PACS .... Post-Attack Communication System
PACS .... Principal Appreciation Conversion Security [*Finance*]
PACS .... Process Automation & Computer Systems
PACS .... Program Authorization Control System (MCD)
PACS .... Programmable Armament Control Set (DOMA)
Pa CSA ...... Pennsylvania Consolidated Statutes, Annotated [*A publication*] (DLA)
PACSAT ...... Packet Satellite [*Telecommunications*]
PACSAT ...... Passive Communications Satellite
PA/CSC .... Payload Accommodation/Carrier Support Center [*NASA*] (SSD)
PACSCAT ..... Pacific Ionospheric Scatter (CINC)
PacSci .... Pacific Scientific Co. [*Associated Press*] (SAG)
PACS DB..... Picture Archiving and Communication System Data Base (DMAA)
PacSen .... Pacific Sentinel Gold Corp. [*Associated Press*] (SAG)
PACSUBDSEC... Pacific Submarine Direct Support Element Coordinator (DNAB)
PacSun .... Pacific Sunwear of California, Inc. [*Associated Press*] (SAG)
PacT .... Pacific Telesis Group Financing I [*Associated Press*] (SAG)
PacT .... Pacific Telesis Group Financing II [*Associated Press*] (SAG)
PACT........... Pan American Commission of Tampa (EA)
PACT........... Pandick Computerized Typesetting (NITA)
PACT........... Papillary Carninoma of Thyroid [*Medicine*] (DMAA)
PACT........... Parents, Children, and Teachers (AIE)
PACT........... Participating and Assertive Consumer Training [*Health education*]
PACT........... Paved Concrete Track [*Railways*]
PACT........... Pay Actual Computer Time
PACT........... PCTE Added Common Tools (NITA)
PACT........... Performing Arts for Crisis Training [*In association name, PACT Training*] (EA)
PACT........... Perturbed-Anisotropic-Chain Theory [*Chemistry*]
PACT........... Phased Control Technique (PDAA)
PACT........... Philadelphia Association for Clinical Trials (DAVI)
PACT........... Philco Automatic Circuit Tester
PACT........... Plan of Action for Challenging Times (EA)
PACT........... Portable Aircraft Calibration Tracker [*NASA*]
PACT........... Poseidon Automatic Cable Tester [*Missiles*] (DNAB)
PACT........... Powdered Activated Carbon Treatment [*For wastewater*] [*E. I. Du Pont De Nemours & Co., Inc.*]
PACT........... Precision Aircraft Control Technology (MCD)
PACT........... Precordial Acceleration Tracing [*Medicine*] (DMAA)
PACT........... Predictive Analysis and Crash Testing [*Automotive safety research*]
PACT........... Prepaid Accountable Care Term [*Medicine*] (DMAA)
PACT........... Print Active Computer Tables (SAA)
PACT........... Private Agencies Collaborating Together (EA)
PACT........... Processing and Communications Terminal (MCD)
PACT........... Production Action Control Technique (SAA)
PACT........... Production Analysis Control Technique [*Navy*]
PACT........... Professional Association of Canadian Theatres
PACT........... Program for Automatic Coding Techniques [*Computer science*]
PACT........... Programmable Asynchronous Clustered Teleprocessing
PACT........... Programmed Analysis Computer Transfer (KSC)
PACT........... Programmed Automatic Circuit Tester
PACT........... Progress in Advanced Component Technology (IAA)
PACT........... Project for the Advancement of Coding Techniques
PACT........... Protective Action for Children's Television (NTCM)
PACT........... Provide Addict Care Today [*Later, NADAP*]
PACT........... Public Action Coalition on Toys [*Opposes sexist toys*]
PACTA .... Packed Tape Assembly
PACTCU ...... Pacific Area Communications Message Traffic Control Unit (IAA)
PacTec......... Pacer Technology [*Associated Press*] (SAG)
PACTEL .... Pacific Telesis (NITA)
PacTel .... Pacific Telesis Group [*Associated Press*] (SAG)
PACTEL .... PA Computers & Telecommunications [*Information service or system*] (IID)
PACTEL....... Planning Associates for Computers and Telecommunications (NITA)
PACTEX....... Pacific-Texas [*Pipeline*]
PACTIV .... Principos Activos [*Ministerio de Sanidad y Consumo*] [*Spain Information service or system*] (CRD)
PACTO .... Professional, Administrative, Clerical, Technical, and Other (BARN)
PACTOA ...... Pacific Technical Operations Area [*Military*]
PacTOP....... Pacific Tsunami Observation Program [*Marine science*] (OSRA)
PACTS .... Parents, Administrators, Community, Teachers, and Students [*School-community groups*]
PACTS .... Programmer Aptitude Competence Test System
PACTS .... Public Access Cordless Telephone Service [*Australia*]
PACTT......... Planning the Australian Capital Territory Together
Pac U.......... Pacific University (GAGS)
PACU.......... Post-Anesthesia Care Unit (MEDA)
PACUIT .... Packet + Circuit (MHDI)
Pac Union C... Pacific Union College (GAGS)
PACUSA...... Pacific Air Command, United States Army
PACV .... Cordova [*Alaska*] [*ICAO location identifier*] (ICLI)
PACV .... Patrol Air-Cushion Vehicle [*Also called Hovercraft*] [*Navy*]
PACV .... Personnel Air-Cushion Vehicle
PACV .... Post-Accident Containment Venting [*Nuclear energy*] (NRCH)
PACVD........ Plasma-Assisted Chemical Vapor Deposition [*Coating technology*]
PACVIS .... Pathological Cardiovascular Ischemic States [*Medicine*] (DB)
PACWP .... Pulmonary Arterial Capillary Wedge Pressure [*Medicine*] (DMAA)

PACX .... Private Automatic Computer Exchange [*Telecommunications*]
PACZ........... Cape Romanzof Air Force Station [*Alaska*] [*ICAO location identifier*] (ICLI)
PAD .... Accounting Policy Division (AAGC)
PAD .... Anthropology of Development Programme [*McGill University*] [*Canada Research center*] (RCD)
PAD .... Packet Assembler/Disassembler [*Switching technique*] [*Computer science*]
PAD .... Packet Assembly Disassembly (NITA)
PAD .... Padder [*Capacitor*] [*Electronics*]
PAD .... Paderborn [*Germany Airport symbol*] (OAG)
PAD .... Padova [*Italy*] [*Seismograph station code, US Geological Survey*] (SEIS)
PAD .... Padstow [*Town in England*]
PAD .... Paducah Gaseous Diffusion Plant [*Department of Energy*] [*Paducah, KY*] (GAAI)
PAD .... Palestine Arab Delegation (EA)
PAD .... Partido Accion Democratica [*Democratic Action Party*] [*El Salvador*] [*Political party*]
PAD .... Partido de Accion Democrata [*Democratic Action Party*] [*Spain Political party*] (PPW)
PAD .... Passenger Airbag Disable
PAD .... Passive Acoustic Detection [*Military*] (CAAL)
PAD .... Passive Air Defense [*British*]
PAD .... Patriot Arm Decoy [*Weaponry*] (DWSG)
PAD .... Payable after Death [*Insurance*] (ADA)
PAD .... Pedagogischer Austauschdienst [*Pedagogical Exchange Service*] [*German*]
PAD .... Penetration Aids Deployment [*Weaponry*] (DWSG)
PAD .... People Against Displacement (NADA)
PAD .... Percutaneous Abscess Drainage [*Surgery*] (DAVI)
PAD .... Percutaneous Automated Diskectomy [*Neurology*] (DAVI)
PAD .... Performance Analysis and Design [*Nuclear energy*] (NRCH)
PAD .... Performing Arts Directory [*A publication*]
PAD .... Peripheral Arterial Disease [*Medicine*]
PAD .... Permissible Accumulated Dose
PAD .... Personal Articulation Device [*Facetious term for pre-word-processing equipment*]
PAD .... Perturbed Angular Distribution [*Nuclear physics*]
PAD .... Peters' United States District Court Reports, Admiralty Decisions [*A publication*] (DLA)
PAD .... Petroleum Administration for Defense [*Abolished, 1954*]
PAD .... Phenacetin [*Acetophenetidin*], Aspirin, Deoxyephedrine [*Pharmacology*]
PAD .... Phi Alpha Delta [*An association*] (NTPA)
PAD .... Phonological Acquisition Device (DAVI)
PAD .... Photon Absorption Densitometry [*Medicine*] (DMAA)
pad .... Photoshop File [*Computer science*]
PAD .... Pilotless Aircraft Division [*Navy*]
PAD .... Pitch Angle Distribution
PAD .... Pitch Axis Definition
PAD .... Pitless Adapter Division of Water Systems Council (EA)
PAD .... Planning Action Directive [*Military*] (AFIT)
PAD .... Planning and Analysis Division [*Environmental Protection Agency*] (GFGA)
PAD .... Player Assessment Device
PAD .... Polar and Auroral Dynamics [*Meteorology*]
PAD .... Polyaperture Device [*NASA*] (KSC)
PAD .... Pontoon Assembly Depot (NVT)
PAD .... Pontoon Assembly Detachment
PAD .... Poor Acquisition Data (AAG)
PAD .... Port of Aerial Debarkation [*Air Force*]
PAD .... Positioning Arm Disk
PAD .... Post-Activation Diffusion (IEEE)
PAD .... Post Alloy Diffusion (IAA)
PAD .... Potential Area of Danger [*Navigation*]
PAD .... Power Amplifier Device [*or Driver*]
PAD .... Preadvisory Data (KSC)
PAD .... Pre-Authorized Debit (EBF)
PAD .... Precise Access Diagram
PAD .... Preferred Arrival Date (AFM)
PAD .... Preliminary Advisory Data (MCD)
PAD .... Presence and Amplitude Detector
PAD .... Pressure Anomaly Difference (PDAA)
PAD .... Preventive Aggressive Device [*Restraint*] [*Medicine*]
PAD .... Primary Aeronautical Designation (DNAB)
PAD .... Primary Affective Disorder [*Psychiatry*] (DAVI)
PAD .... Primary Afferent Depolarization [*Electrophysiology*]
PAD .... Procurement Acquisition Directive
PAD .... Product Assembly Document
PAD .... Product Assembly Drawing [*Automotive project management*]
PAD .... Product Assurance Directorate [*Armament, Munitions, and Chemical Command*] [*Army*]
PAD .... Professional Administrative Development [*Medicine*]
PAD .... Professional Express Courier Service, Inc. [*ICAO designator*] (FAAC)
PAD .... Program Action Directive (AFM)
PAD .... Program Analysis Division (AAGC)
PAD .... Program Analysis for Documentation [*Computer science*]
PAD .... Program Approval Document [*NASA*] (KSC)
PAD .... Project Approval Document [*NASA*]
PAD .... Propellant Acquisition Device (NASA)
PAD .... Propellant-Actuated Device
PAD .... Provisional Acceptance Date (NATG)
PAD .... Psychoaffective Disorder [*Psychiatry*] (DAVI)
PAD .... Public Affairs Division [*Military*] (AABC)

PAD .... Public Assistance Director [*Federal disaster planning*]
PAD .... Pueblo Army Depot [*Colorado*]
PAD .... Pulmonary Artery Diastolic [*Pressure*] [*Cardiology*]
PAD .... Pulsatile Assist Device [*Cardiology*]
PAD .... Pulse Averaging Discriminator
PAD .... Pulsed Activation Doppler (MCD)
PAD .... Pulsed Amperometric Detection [*Electroanalytical chemistry*]
PADA .... Payroll Automation for Department of Agriculture
PADA .... Pharmacists Against Drug Abuse (EA)
PADA .... Poly(adipicanhydride) [*Organic chemistry*]
PADA .... Prespin Automatic Dynamic Alignment
PADA .... Public Address Assembly [*Ground Communications Facility, NASA*]
PADA .... (Pyridylazo)dimethylaniline [*Organic chemistry*]
PADAC .... Professional Art Dealers Association of Canada
PADAF .... Pacific Command Air Defense Analysis Facility (CINC)
PADAL .... Pattern for Analysis, Decision, Action, and Learning
PA D & C .... Pennsylvania District and County Reports [*A publication*] (DLA)
PA D & C 2d... Pennsylvania District and County Reports, Second Series
 [*A publication*] (DLA)
PA D & C 3d... Pennsylvania District and County Reports, Third Series
 [*A publication*] (DLA)
PA D & C Rep... Pennsylvania District and County Reports [*A publication*] (DLA)
PADAR......... Passive Airborne Detection and Ranging
PADAR......... Passive Detection and Ranging [*Electronics*] (IAA)
PADAR......... Program Approval Disposal and Redistribution [*Army*] (AABC)
PADAT .... Psychological Abstracts Direct Access Terminal
PADC .... Pennsylvania Avenue Development Corp. [*Washington, DC*] [*Federal
 corporatio n*]
PADC .... Piccole Apostole della Carita [*Ponte Lambro, Italy*] (EAIO)
PADCP .... Paul Andrew Dawkins Children's Project (EA)
PADD .... Passive Antidrown Device (DWSG)
PADD .... Petroleum Administration for Defense District [*Department of Energy*]
PADD .... Planned Active Duty Date [*Military*]
PADD .... Portable Acoustic Doppler Detector
PADDS .... Procurement Automated Data Document System [*Military*] (RDA)
PADE .... Pad Automatic Data Equipment (PDAA)
PADEL .... Pattern Description Language
PA Dep L & I Dec... Pennsylvania Department of Labor and Industry Decisions
 [*A publication*] (DLA)
PA Dep Rep... Pennsylvania Department Reports [*A publication*] (DLA)
PADER........ Pennsylvania Department of Environmental Resources
PADF .... Driftwood Bay Air Force Station [*Alaska*] [*ICAO location identifier*]
 (ICLI)
PADF .... Pan American Development Foundation (EA)
PADGEM...... Platelet Activation-Dependent Granulocyte External Membrane
 Protein [*Biochemistry*]
PADGERC .... PACOM [*Pacific Command*] Air Defense Ground Environment
 Requirements Committee (CINC)
PADGT .... Past Assistant Deputy Grand Treasurer [*Freemasonry*]
PADI .... Parti pour l'Avancement de la Democratie en Ituri [*Party for
 Democratic Advancement in Ituri*] [*Political party*]
PADI .... Professional Association of Diving Instructors (EA)
PADIA .... Patrol Diagnosis (NITA)
PADIE .... Prevention and Detection of Illegal Entry [*Military*] (DNAB)
PADIL .... Patriot Air Defense Information Language [*Army*]
Padin .... Partido de Integracion Nacional [*National Integration Party*] [*Peru*]
 [*Political party*] (PPW)
PADIS .... Pan-African Documentation and Information System [*Economic
 Commission for Africa*] [*United Nations*] (IID)
PA Dist .... Pennsylvania District Reporter [*A publication*] (DLA)
PA Dist & Co R... Pennsylvania District and County Reports [*A publication*] (DLA)
PA Dist & Co Repts... Pennsylvania District and County Reports [*A publication*]
 (DLA)
PA Dist & C Rep... Pennsylvania District and County Reports [*A publication*] (DLA)
PA Dist R..... Pennsylvania District Reporter [*A publication*] (DLA)
PA Dist Rep... Pennsylvania District Reports [*A publication*] (DLA)
PADK .... Adak/Davis [*Alaska*] [*ICAO location identifier*] (ICLI)
PADL .... Dillingham [*Alaska*] [*ICAO location identifier*] (ICLI)
PADL .... Part and Assembly Description Language [*Computer science*]
PADL .... Parts and Design Language (NITA)
PADL .... Performing and Captive Animals Defence League [*British*] (BI)
PADL .... Personal Activities of Daily Living (DMAA)
PADL .... Pilotless Aircraft Development Laboratory [*Navy*]
PADLA .... Programmable Asynchronous Dual Line Adapter
PADLOC...... Passive Active Detection and Location (IEEE)
PADLOC...... Passive Detection and Location [*Air Force*] (IAA)
PADLOC...... Passive Detection and Location of Countermeasures [*Air Force*]
PADLOCC..... Passive Detection and Location of Countermeasures [*Air Force*]
 (IAA)
PAdm......... Professional Administrator (DD)
PADMIS ...... Patient Administration Information System [*Army*] (AABC)
PADO .... Proposed Advanced Development Objective [*Army*] (AABC)
PADOC........ Pay Adjustment Document [*Army*]
PADP .... Physicians Against the Death Penalty (EA)
PADP .... Proposal for Advanced Development Program
PADP .... Pulmonary Artery Diastolic Pressure [*Cardiology*] (AAMN)
PADQ .... Kodiak [*Alaska*] [*ICAO location identifier*] (ICLI)
PADR .... Parts and Data Record System (MCD)
PA DR .... Pennsylvania District Reports [*A publication*] (DLA)
PADR .... Production Administration Deficiency Report [*DoD*]
PADRA .... Pass to Air Defense RADAR [*Aviation*] (FAAC)
PADRE .... Particle Analysis and Data Reduction [*Environmental Protection
 Agency*] (GFGA)
PADRE .... Particulate Data Reduction (EPA)
PADRE .... Patient Automatic Data Recording Equipment (IEEE)

PADRE........ Portable Automatic Data Recording Equipment
PADS ......,.... Parametric Array Doppler SONAR (PDAA)
PADS .... Passive-Active Data Simulation
PADS .... Passive Advanced Sonobuoy
PADS .... Pen Application Development System [*Computer software*] [*Slate
 Corp.*] (PCM)
PADS .... People Against Dioxins in Sanitary Products [*An association
 Australia*]
PADS .... Performance Analysis and Design Synthesis [*Computer program*]
 [*NASA*]
PADS .... Performance Analysis Display System (NITA)
PADS .... Peroxylaminedisulfonate [*Organic chemistry*]
PADS .... Personnel Automated Data System [*TIMMS*] [*Navy*]
PADS .... Planned Arrival and Departure System [*FAA*] (TAG)
PADS .... Plant Alarm and Display System [*Nuclear energy*] (NRCH)
PADS .... Point Air Defense System
PADS .... Position and Azimuth Determining System [*Aviation*]
PADS .... Precision Aerial Delivery System
PADS .... Precision Aerial Display System
PADS .... Precision Antenna Display System (IAA)
PADS .... Professional Application Development System [*Slate*] [*Computer
 science*]
PADS .... Programmer Advanced Debugging System [*Computer science*]
PADT .... Postalloy Diffusion Technique (IAA)
PADT .... Postalloy Diffusion Transistor
PADU .... Dutch Harbour [*Alaska*] [*ICAO location identifier*] (ICLI)
PADUA........ Progressive Augmentation by Dilating the Urethra Anterior
 [*Medicine*] (DMAA)
PADUD........ Program of Advanced Professional Development, University of
 Denver College of Law (DLA)
PADWSS...... Pulsed Acoustic Doppler Wind Shear Sensing System (PDAA)
PAE............ Everett, WA [*Location identifier FAA*] (FAAL)
PAE............ Paea [*Society Islands*] [*Seismograph station code, US Geological
 Survey*] (SEIS)
PAE............ Paisajes Espanoles SA [*Spain ICAO designator*] (FAAC)
PAE............ Parachutust Adjustable Equipment Bag [*Army*] (VNW)
P AE.......... Partes Aequales [*Equal Parts*] [*Pharmacy*]
PAE............ Passed Assistant Engineer [*British*]
PAE............ Payload Accomodations Equipment [*NASA*] (SSD)
PAE............ Payload Attach Equipment [*NASA*] (SSD)
PAE............ Peoria & Eastern Railway [*Absorbed into Consolidated Rail Corp.*]
 [*AAR code*]
PAE............ Personal Arms and Equipment [*Army*] (ADDR)
PAE............ Phase Angle Error
PAE............ Photo-Anodic Engraving (PDAA)
PAE............ Phthalic Acid Esters [*Organic chemistry*]
PAE............ Physical Aptitude Examination (AFM)
PAF........... Planning and Estimating (IAA)
PAE............ Polyarylether [*Organic chemistry*]
PAE............ Polyaspartic Ester [*Organic chemistry*]
PAE............ Port of Aerial Embarkation [*Air Force*]
PAE............ Post-Accident Environment [*Nuclear energy*] (IEEE)
PAE............ Preliminary Airworthiness Evaluations
PAE............ Preliminary Army Evaluation (MCD)
PAE............ Preventive Action Engineer (NASA)
PAE............ Problem Assessment Engineering (NASA)
PAE............ Projets pour une Agriculture Ecologique [*Ecological Agriculture
 Projects - EAP*] [*Sainte Anne De Bellevue, PQ*] (FAIO)
PAE............ Public Affairs Event (NVT)
PAEAC .... Parliamentary Association for Euro-Arab Cooperation (EA)
PAEC.......... Pakistan Army Education Corps [*British military*] (DMA)
PAECI.......... Pan American Association of Educational Credit Institutions [*Bogota,
 Colombia*] (EAIO)
PAECT........ Pollution Abatement and Environmental Control Technology [*Army*]
 (AABC)
PAED .... Anchorage/Elmendorf Air Force Base [*Alaska*] [*ICAO location
 identifier*] (ICLI)
PAED .... Paediatric [*or Paediatrics*]
PAED .... Plans, Analysis, and Evaluation Division [*Army*] (MCD)
PAEDP .... Pulmonary Artery End-Diastolic Pressure [*Cardiology*]
PAEF.......... Peace Action Education Fund (EA)
PAEG .... Prueba de Admisiones para Estudios Graduados (GAGS)
PAEH .... Cape Newenham Air Force Station [*Alaska*] [*ICAO location
 identifier*] (ICLI)
PAEI............ Fairbanks/Eielson Air Force Base [*Alaska*] [*ICAO location identifier*]
 (ICLI)
PAEI............ Periscope Azimuth Error Indicator
PAEI............ Purchasing Agents of the Electronic Industry [*Rosedale, NY*] (EA)
PAEK........... Polyaryletherketone [*Organic chemistry*]
PAEL........... Preliminary Allowance Equipage List [*Military*] (CAAL)
PAEM.......... Program Analysis and Evaluation Model (IEEE)
PAEN .... Kenai [*Alaska*] [*ICAO location identifier*] (ICLI)
PAEP .... Preliminary Annual Engineering Plan [*Military*] (AFIT)
P AEQ .... Partes Aequales [*Equal Parts*] [*Pharmacy*]
PAES........... Phenyl(aminoethyl)sulfide [*Biochemistry*]
PAES........... Planning Analysis Evaluation System
PAET........... Planetary Atmosphere Experimental [*or Experiments*] Test [*NASA*]
PAEW.......... Personnel and Equipment Working [*Aviation*] (FAAC)
PAEWCC...... Peace Activists East and West Coordinating Committee (EA)
PAF........... Pacific Air Forces
PAF........... Pacific Aqua Foods Ltd. [*Toronto Stock Exchange symbol*]
PAF........... Page Address Field
PAF........... Panaf Airways Ltd. [*Gambia*] [*ICAO designator*] (FAAC)
PAF........... Pan American Foundation [*Defunct*] (EA)
PAF........... Paraburdoo [*Western Australia*] [*Airport symbol*] (AD)

PAF	Paroxysmal Atrial [or Auricular] Fibrillation [Medicine] (MAE)
PAF	Partitive Analytical Forecasting (PDAA)
PAF	Payload Attachment Fitting [NASA]
PAF	Peak Annual Funding (NASA)
PAF	Pediatric AIDS Foundation (PAZ)
PAF	Performing Arts Foundation (EA)
PAF	Peripheral Address Field
PAF	Permanent Air Force [Australia]
PAF	Peroxisome Assembly Factor [Biochemistry]
PAF	Personal Achievement Formula [Test] (TES)
PAF	Personal Ancestry File [Computer science] (PCM)
PAF	Personal Article Floater [Air baggage insurance]
PAF	Philippine Air Force
PAF	Phosphodiesterase-Activating Factor [Medicine] (DMAA)
PAF	Photoactivated Fluorescence Molecules [Analytical biochemistry]
PAF	Platelet-Activating Factor [Hematology]
PAF	Platelet Aggregation Factor [Hematology]
PAF	Polaris Accelerated Flight [Chamber] [Missiles]
PAF	Pollen Adherence Factor [Immunology] (DMAA)
PAF	Portable Arc Furnace
PAF	Port-Aux-Francais [Kerguelen Islands] [Seismograph station code, US Geological Survey Closed] (SEIS)
PAF	Portuguese Air Force
PAF	Postcode Address File [Computer science] (TELE)
PAF	Posterior Auditory Field
PAF	Preadmission Assessment Form [Health Care Financing Administration]
PAF	Prearranged Fire
PAF	Preatomized Fuel [Trademark] [Petroferm product]
PAF	Premature Anti-Fascist [World War II designation used by Army Counterintelligence Department]
PAF	Price Analysis File (AFIT)
PAF	Printed and Fired Circuit
PAF	Pro-American Forum [Defunct] (EA)
PAF	Production Assembly Facility [Manufacturing]
PAF	Pseudoamniotic Fluid [Gynecology]
PAF	Pseudo-Archaic Forgery
PAF	Psychoanalytic Assistance Fund (EA)
PAF	Public Agenda Foundation (EA)
PAF	Public Art Fund (EA)
PAF	Publication Authority Form (AAG)
PAF	Pulmonary Arteriovenous Fistula [Medicine]
PAF	Pulse-Air Feeder [Automotive engineering]
PAFA	Fairbanks/International [Alaska] [ICAO location identifier] (ICLI)
PAFA	Pakistan Australia Friendship Association [Australia]
PAFA	Pan-American Festival Association (EA)
PAFA	Pennsylvania Academy of the Fine Arts
PAFA	Presidential Academic Fitness Award [Department of Education] (GFGA)
PAFA	Priority Based Assessment of Foot Additives [Medicine] (DMAA)
PAFAM	Performance and Failure Assessment Monitor (MCD)
PAFAMS	Pan American Federation of Associations of Medical Schools [See also FEPAFEM] [Caracas, Venezuela] (EAIO)
PAFATU	Pan-African Federation of Agricultural Trade Unions (EA)
PAFB	Fairbanks/Wainwright Army Air Field [Alaska] [ICAO location identifier] (ICLI)
PAFB	Patrick Air Force Base [Florida]
PAFC	Paul Anka Fan Club (EA)
PAFC	Phase-Locked Automatic Frequency Control [Telecommunications]
PAFC	Phosphoric Acid Fuel Cell [Energy source]
PAFCOMNET	Pacific Air Forces Communications Network (SAA)
PAFCS	Prior Active Foreign Commissioned Service
PAFD	Percutaneous Abscess and Fluid Drainage [Medicine] (DMAA)
PAFDEFNET	Pacific Air Forces Defense Network (SAA)
PAFE	Place Accepted for Enlistment
PAFEC	Program for Automatic Finite Element Calculation (IAA)
PAFES	Prior Active Foreign Enlisted Service (DNAB)
PAFI	Platelet-Aggregation Factor Inhibitor [Medicine] (DMAA)
PAFIB	Paroxysmal Atrial [or Auricular] Fibrillation [Medicine] (MAE)
PA Fid	Pennsylvania Fiduciary Reporter [A publication] (DLA)
PA Fiduc	Pennsylvania Fiduciary Reporter [A publication] (DLA)
PAFMECSA	Pan African Freedom Movement for East, Central, and Southern Africa [Superseded in 1963 by the liberation committee of the Organization of African Unity] (PD)
PAFP	Photochemical Aerosol-Forming Potential of Polluted Air [Environmental chemistry]
PAFP	Pre-Achilles Fat Pad [Medicine] (DMAA)
PAFR	Fort Richardson/Bryant Army Air Field [Alaska] [ICAO location identifier] (ICLI)
PAFS	Primary Air Force Specialty
PAFSC	Primary Air Force Specialty Code
PAFT	Polish American Folk Theatre
PAFT	Programme for Alternative Fluorocarbon Toxicity Testing [British]
PA-FTIR	Photoacoustic Fourier Transform Infrared Spectroscopy (AAEL)
PAFTT	Program for Alternative Fluorocarbon Toxicity Testing [Environmental science]
PAFU	Patriot Arm Fire Unit [Weaponry] (MCD)
PAFU	Propulsion Arming and Firing Unit [Military]
PAFVA	Polish Air Force Veterans Association (EA)
PAFW	Farewell [Alaska] [ICAO location identifier] (ICLI)
PAG	I Pagliacci [Opera] (DSUE)
PAG	Pacific Gulf Properties [AMEX symbol] (TTSB)
PAG	Pacific Gulf Properties, Inc. [AMEX symbol] (SAG)
PAG	Pagadian [Philippines] [Airport symbol] (OAG)

Pag	Page's Three Early Assize Rolls, County of Northumberland [Surtees Society Publications, Vol. 88] [A publication] (ILCA)
PAG	Paget Resources Ltd. [Vancouver Stock Exchange symbol]
Pag	Pagoda
PAG	Panagjuriste [Bulgaria] [Geomagnetic observatory code]
PAG	Panjim [India] [Airport symbol] (AD)
PAG	Pariaqueductal Grey Matter [Neurology] (DAVI)
PAG	Parts Acquisition Group
PAG	Party for the Autonomy of Gibraltar [Political party] (PPW)
PAG	Pentaacetylglucose [Laundry bleach activator]
PAG	Periaqueductal Gray Matter [Brain anatomy]
PAG	Perimeter Aviation Ltd. [Canada ICAO designator] (FAAC)
PAG	Pesticide Assessment Guideline [Environmental Protection Agency]
PAG	Photoacid Generator
Pag	Piper [Airplane code]
PAG	Polyacrylamide Gel [Analytical chemistry]
PAG	Polyalkylene Glycol [Organic chemistry]
PAg	Poultry-Related Antigens [Immunology]
PAG	Poverty Advisory Group
PAG	Prealbumin Globulin [Biochemistry] (OA)
PAG	Precision Alignment Gyrocompass
PAG	Precursor Active Galaxies
PAG	Pregnancy-Associated alpha-Glycoprotein [Gynecology]
PAG	Preliminary Analysis Group (NATG)
PAG	Prince Albert's Guard [British military] (DMA)
PAG	Professional Activities Group
PAg	Professional Agrologist (DD)
PAG	Professional Auto Group, Inc.
PAG	Program Assessment Guide [Department of Labor] (OICC)
PAG	Progress Analysis Group [Navy] (MCD)
PAG	Project Advisory Group [Army]
PAG	Property Advisory Group [British] (DCTA)
PAG	Protective Action Guide [Nuclear energy]
PAG	Protein Advisory Group [United Nations]
pAg	Protein A-Gold Technique [Medicine] (DMAA)
PAG	Public Affairs Guidance [Environmental science] (COE)
PAG	Spring Garden College, Philadelphia, PA [OCLC symbol] (OCLC)
PAGA	Galena [Alaska] [ICAO location identifier] (ICLI)
PAGA	Pan American Grace Airways, Inc. [Also, PANAGRA]
PAGA	Proliferation-Associated Gene A (DMAA)
PAGAD	People Against Gangsterism and Drugs [South Africa]
PAGAN	Pattern Generation Language [Computer science]
PAGAN	People Against Goodness & Normalcy (WDAA)
PAGB	Proprietary Association of Great Britain
PAGDC	Past Assistant Grand Director of Ceremonies [Freemasonry] (ROG)
PAGE	Page Generation [or Generator] (PDAA)
Page	Page's Three Early Assize Rolls, County of Northumberland [Surtees Society Publications, Vol. 88] [A publication] (DLA)
PAGE	Paging Network [NASDAQ symbol] (SPSG)
PAGE	PERT [Program Evaluation and Review Technique] Automated Graphical Extension (KSC)
PAGE	Philatelic Association of Government Employees
PAGE	Piston Arrestment Gas Entrapment System [SPRINT launch cell] [Army] (AABC)
PAGE	Polyacrylamide Gel Electrophoresis [Analytical chemistry]
PAGE	Preliminary Automated Ground Environment
PAGE	Preview and Graphics Editing [Computer science] (MHDI)
PAGE	Program for Automated Gated Evaluation [Cardiology] (DAVI)
PAGE	Publish Australia Group Enterprise
PageAm	Page America Group, Inc. [Associated Press] (SAG)
Page Contr	Page on Contracts [A publication] (DLA)
Page Div	Page on Divorce [A publication] (DLA)
PAGEL	Priced Aerospace Ground Equipment List
PAGEOS	Passive Geodetic Earth-Orbiting Satellite [NASA]
Pages	Pages, Inc. [Associated Press] (SAG)
PAGES	Past Global Changes [Marine science] (OSRA)
PAGES	Program Affinity Grouping and Evaluation System
PAGI	Penn America Group [NASDAQ symbol] (SAG)
PAGICEP	Petroleum and Gas Industry Communications Emergency Plan [FCC]
PAGIF	Polyacrylamide Gel Isoelectric Focusing (DB)
Paging	Paging Network, Inc. [Associated Press] (SAG)
Paging	Paging Partners Corp. [Associated Press] (SAG)
PagingN	Paging Network Inc. [Associated Press] (SAG)
PagingP	Paging Partners Corp. [Associated Press] (SAG)
PAGIS	Performance Assessment of Geological Isolation System [Nuclear energy] (NUCP)
Pag Jud Puz	Paget's Judicial Puzzles [A publication] (DLA)
PAGK	Gulkana [Alaska] [ICAO location identifier] (ICLI)
PAGL	Pulsed Argon Gas LASER
PAGM	Permit Applicants Guidance Manual (COE)
PAGMK	Primary African Green Monkey Kidney [Cells]
PAGN	Pagnall [England]
PAGS	Parti de l'Avant-Garde Socialiste [Socialist Vanguard Party] [Algeria] [Political party] (PD)
PAGS	Polish-American Guardian Society (EA)
PAGTU	Pan-American Ground Training Unit
PAGZ	Pages, Inc. [NASDAQ symbol] (SAG)
PAH	Paducah [Kentucky] [Airport symbol] (OAG)
PAH	Pahoa [Hawaii] [Seismograph station code, US Geological Survey Closed] (SEIS)
PAH	Panorama Air Tour, Inc. [ICAO designator] (FAAC)
PAH	Para-Aminohippurate [Clearance Test] [Urology] (DAVI)
PAH	Para-Aminohippuric [Biochemistry]
PAH	Parts Application Handbook
PAH	Pathtechnics Ltd. [Vancouver Stock Exchange symbol]

PAH	Patriot Amer Hospitality [*NYSE symbol*] (TTSB)
PAH	Patriot American Hospitality, Inc. [*NYSE symbol*] (SAG)
PAH	Payload Accommodations Handbook [*NASA*] (NASA)
PAH	Phase Adjusting Hub
PAH	Phenylalanine Hydroxylase [*An enzyme*]
Pah	Piper Pressurised Prop-Jet [*Airplane code*]
PAH	Pitch Attitude Hold [*Aviation*] (MCD)
PAH	Polyaromatic Hydrocarbon (EDCT)
PAH	Polycyclic [*or Polynuclear*] Aromatic Hydrocarbon [*Organic chemistry*]
PAH	Polycyclic Aromatic Hydrocarbons [*Automotive emissions*] [*Organic chemistry*]
PAH	Pulmonary Artery Hypertension [*Medicine*]
PAH	Pulmonary Artery Hypotension [*Cardiology*] (DAVI)
PAH	Push and Hold [*Push button*]
PAHA	Para-Aminohippuric Acid
PAHA	Polish American Historical Association (EA)
PAHA	Procainamide-Hydroxylamine (DMAA)
PAHBAH	Para-Hydroxybenzoic Acid Hydrazide [*Organic chemistry*]
PAHC	Pan American Highway Congresses (EA)
PAHC	Pontifical Association of the Holy Childhood (EA)
PAHCOM	Professional Association of Health Care Office Managers
PAHEF	Pan American Health and Education Foundation (EA)
PAHEL	Pay Records and Health Records
PAHEO	Particle Accelerators in High Earth Orbit [*Proposed*]
PAHEP	Plasma and High Energy Physics (IAA)
PAHF	Pan American Hockey Federation [*Winnipeg, MB*] (EAIO)
PAHL	Pressure Alarm, High-Limit [*Nuclear energy*] (NRCH)
PAHO	Homer [*Alaska*] [*ICAO location identifier*] (ICLI)
PAHO	Pan American Health Organization (EA)
PAHR	Post-Accident Heat Removal [*Nuclear energy*]
PAHS	Passive Annual Heat Storage [*Housing technology*]
PAHVC	Pulmonary Alveolar Hypoxic Vasoconstriction [*Medicine*] (STED)
PAI	Kitty Hawk Aircargo, Inc. [*ICAO designator*] (FAAC)
PAI	Pacific Aerospace Index (DIT)
PAI	Pacific American Income Shares, Inc. [*NYSE symbol*] (SPSG)
PAI	Pacific American Institute (EA)
PAI	Pacific Am'n Inc. Shrs [*NYSE symbol*] (TTSB)
PAI	Pacoima, CA [*Location identifier FAA*] (FAAL)
Pai	Paige's New York Chancery Reports [*A publication*] (DLA)
Pai	Paine's United States Circuit Court Reports [*A publication*] (DLA)
PAI	Pair Attraction Inventory [*Premarital, marital, and family counseling test*] [*Psychology*]
PAI	Parachute Association of Ireland (EAIO)
PAI	Paradise Airways, Inc. [*FAA designator*] (FAAC)
PAI	Parti Africain de l'Independance [*African Independence Party*] [*Senegal*] [*Political party*] (PPW)
PAI	Partido Aragones Independiente [*Spain Political party*] (EY)
PAI	Parts Application Information [*Manufacturing*]
PAI	Passive-Aggressive Index [*Psychology*]
PAI	Patient Assesment Instrument [*Medicine*] (DMAA)
PAI	Percent Adherence Index
PAI	Performance Audit Inspection [*Environmental Protection Agency*] (GFGA)
PAI	Personal Accident Insurance
PAI	Personal Adjustment Inventory [*Psychology*]
PAI	Personnel Accreditation Institute (EA)
PAI	Phosphate Adsorption Index [*Analytical chemistry*]
PAI	Photographic Administrators, Inc. (EA)
PAI	Piedmont Aviation, Inc. [*Air carrier designation symbol*]
PAI	Piping and Instrumentation [*Nuclear energy*] (IAA)
PAI	Pirchei Agudath Israel (EA)
PAI	Place Accumulator in Indicators (IAA)
PAI	Plasminogen-Activator Inhibitor [*Biochemistry*]
PAI	Platelet Accumulation Index (STED)
PAI	Plunger Actuated Indexer
PAI	Poale Agudath Israel of America (EA)
PAI	Polish Assistance, Inc. (EA)
PAI	Polyamide-Imide [*Organic chemistry*]
PAI	Prearrival Inspection
PAI	Precise Angle Indicator
PAI	Primary Aerospace Vehicle [*or Aircraft*] Inventory
PAI	Process Analytical Instrument
PAI	Process Automation Interface (IAA)
PAI	Processed Apples Institute (EA)
PAI	Production Acceptance Inspection (IAA)
PAI	Production Adjustment Index [*Word processing*]
PAI	Professional Athletes International [*Later, NFLPA*] (EA)
PAI	Programmer Appraisal Instrument [*Computer science*] (IEEE)
PAI	Project Assignment Instruction (MCD)
PAI	Property Agents International
PAI	Protocol Addressing Information [*Telecommunications*] (OSI)
PAI	Public Affairs Information, Inc. [*Sacramento, CA*] [*Database producer*] [*Information service or system*]
PAI	Public Affairs Institute [*Defunct*] (EA)
PAI	Public Assistance Information [*A publication*]
PAIA	Pan American Implant Association (EA)
PAIAW	Philadelphia Association of Intercollegiate Athletics for Women (PSS)
PAIB	Polish-American Information Bureau [*Later, PATIB*] (EA)
PAIC	Persia and Iraq Command [*World War II*]
PAIC	Personal Attribute Inventory for Children (EDAC)
PAIC	Procedures, Alternatives, Indications, and Complications [*Medicine*] (DMAA)
PAIC	Public Address Intercom System (NRCH)
PAICC	Professional Association of the Interstate Commerce Commission
Pai Ch	Paige's New York Chancery Reports [*A publication*] (DLA)

PAID	Pacific Animated Imaging [*NASDAQ symbol*] (TTSB)
PAID	Pacific Animated Imaging Corp. [*NASDAQ symbol*] (SAG)
PAID	Pan African Institute for Development (EAIO)
PAID	Parked Aircraft Intrusion Detector (PDAA)
PAID	Personnel and Accounting Integrated Data [*System*] [*Veterans Administration*]
PAID	Piping and Instrumentation Diagram [*or Design*] [*Nuclear energy*] (IAA)
PAID	Price and Item Display [*British*]
PAID	Problem Areas in Diabetes [*Scale*] [*Medicine*] (DMAA)
PAID	Programmers Aid in Debugging [*Computer science*] (MHDI)
PAIDS	Paralyzed Academic Investigator's Disease Syndrome [*Medicine*] (DMAA)
PAIDS	Pediatric Acquired Immune Deficiency Syndrome [*Medicine*]
PAIDS	Pediatric Acquired Immunodeficiency Syndrome [*Medicine*] (STED)
PAIF	Persia and Iraq Force [*World War II*]
PAIFORCE	Persia and Iraq Force [*World War II*] (DMA)
PAIg	Platelet-Associated Immunoglobulin [*Hematology*]
PAIGC	Partido Africano da Independencia da Guine e do Cabo Verde [*African Party for the Independence of Guinea and Cape Verde*] [*Political party*] (PPW)
Paige	Paige's New York Chancery Reports [*A publication*] (DLA)
Paige Ch	Paige's New York Chancery Reports [*1828-45*] [*A publication*] (DLA)
Paige Ch Rep...	Paige's New York Chancery Reports [*A publication*] (DLA)
Paige's Ch ...	Paige's New York Chancery Reports [*A publication*] (DLA)
PAIgG	Platelet-Associated Immunoglobulin G [*Hematology*]
PAIGH	Pan American Institute of Geography and History [*Research center Mexico*] (IRC)
PAII	Professional Association of Innkeepers International (NTPA)
PAIL	Iliamna [*Alaska*] [*ICAO location identifier*] (ICLI)
PAIL	Post-Attack Intercontinental Link
PAILS	Projectile Airburst and Impact Location System
PAILS	Publication Automated Information Locator System [*Army*]
PAIM	Indian Mountain Air Force Station [*Alaska*] [*ICAO location identifier*] (ICLI)
PAIM	Parti Africain pour l'Independance des Masses [*African Party for the Independence of the Masses*] [*Senegal*] [*Political party*] (PPW)
PAIM	Primary Air Inlet Muffler (MCD)
PAIMEG	Pan American Institute of Mining, Engineering, and Geology [*Defunct*]
PAIN	Parents Against Injustice (WDAA)
PAIN	Prisoners' Advice & Information Network (WDAA)
Paine	Paine's United States Circuit Court Reports [*A publication*] (DLA)
Paine & D Pr...	Paine and Duer's Practice [*A publication*] (DLA)
Paine CC	Paine's United States Circuit Court Reports [*A publication*] (DLA)
Paine CCR ...	Paine's United States Circuit Court Reports [*A publication*] (DLA)
Paine Cir Ct R...	Paine's United States Circuit Court Reports [*A publication*] (DLA)
PAINT	Painting (ROG)
PAINT	Post-Attack Intelligence
PainWeb	PaineWebber Group, Inc. [*Associated Press*] (SAG)
PainWP	Paine Webber Premier Tax Free Income [*Associated Press*] (SAG)
PAIP	Preverbal Assessment-Intervention Profile [*Test*]
PAIP	Production Acceleration Insurance Program
PAIP	Public Affairs and Information Program [*Atomic Industrial Forum*] (NRCH)
PAIR	Pairgain Technologies [*NASDAQ symbol*] (SAG)
PAIR	Performance Accountability and Improvement Report
PAIR	Performance and Improved Reliability
PAIR	Performance and Integration Retrofit
PAIR	Performance Assessment in Reading [*Educational test*]
PAIR	Personal Assessment of Intimacy in Relationships (STED)
PAIR	Precision Approach Interferometer RADAR (MCD)
PAIR	Preliminary Assessment Information Rule [*Environmental Protection Agency*]
PAIR	Procurement Automated Integrated Requirements (MCD)
PAIR	Psychological Audit for Interpersonal Relations [*Psychology*]
PAIR	Pulse-Air Injection Reactor [*Automotive engineering*]
PAIRC	Polish American Immigration and Relief Committee (EA)
PAIRMEM	Paired Word Memory Task (TES)
PAIRS	Parent Assisted Instruction in Reading and Spelling (AIE)
PAIRS	Private Aircraft Inspection Reporting System (PDAA)
PAIRS	Product Assurance Information Retrieval System [*Boeing*]
PAIRS	Program for the Analysis of Infrared Spectra [*Computer program*] [*Analytical chemistry*]
PairTch	Pairgain Technologies [*Associated Press*] (SAG)
PAIS	Padre Island National Seashore [*National Park Service designation*]
PAIS	Partido Amplio de Izquierda Socialista [*Chile*] [*Political party*] (EY)
PAIS	Partido Autentico Institucional Salvadoreno [*Salvadoran Authentic Institutional Party*] [*Political party*] (PPW)
PAIS	Personnel Authentication Identification System (MCD)
PAIS	Petroleum Abstracts Information Services [*University of Tulsa*] [*Oklahoma*] [*Information service or system*] (IID)
PAIS	Project Analysis Information System [*Agency for International Development*]
PAIS	Prototype Advanced Indicator System (MCD)
PAIS	Psychological Abstracts Information Services [*American Psychological Association*]
PAIS	Psychosocial Adjustment to Illness Scale [*Personality development test*] [*Psychology*]
PAISA	Partido Autentico Institucional Salvadoreno [*Salvadoran Authentic Institutional Party*] [*Political party*] (EY)
PAIS FLI	PAIS Foreign Language Index (NITA)
PAIT	Program for Advancement of Industrial Technology [*Canada*]
PAIVS	Pulmonary Atresia with Intact Ventricular Septum [*Cardiology*] (DAVI)
PAIX	Pacific Alaska Airlines [*Air carrier designation symbol*]

PAJ	Kansas City, MO [*Location identifier FAA*] (FAAL)
PAJ	Paralysis Agitans Juvenilis [*Medicine*] (DMAA)
PAJ	Performing Arts Journal [*A publication*]
PAJA	Parachute Jumping Activities [*Aviation*] (FAAC)
PAJAR	Parti Rakyat Jati Sarawak [*Sarawak Native People's Party*] [*Malaysia*] [*Political party*] (PPW)
PAJES	Parents of Adult Jewish Singles
PAJN	Juneau [*Alaska*] [*ICAO location identifier*] (ICLI)
PAK	Hanapepe, HI [*Location identifier FAA*] (FAAL)
PAK	Pacific Alaska Airlines [*ICAO designator*] (FAAC)
PAK	Pakistan [*ANSI three-letter standard code*] (CNC)
Pak	Pakistan (VRA)
PAK	Panzer Abwehr Kanone [*Cannon Against Armor*] [*German antitank gun*]
PAK	Performance Advantage Kit [*Personal computers*]
PAK	Polycyclic Aromatic Ketone [*Organic chemistry*]
PAK	Power Amplifier Klystron
PAK	Program Attention Key [*Computer science*] (BUR)
PAK	Pseudomonas Aeruginosa Strain K (DB)
Pak Bar J	Pakistan Bar Journal [*A publication*] (DLA)
Pak Crim LJ	Pakistan Criminal Law Journal [*A publication*] (DLA)
PAKEX	International Packaging Exhibition [*British*] (ITD)
PakisInv	Pakistan Investment Fund, Inc. [*Associated Press*] (SAG)
Pak LR	Pakistan Law Reports [*India*] [*A publication*] (DLA)
Pak L Rev	Pakistan Law Review [*A publication*] (DLA)
PAKN	King Salmon [*Alaska*] [*ICAO location identifier*] (ICLI)
Pak Sup Ct Q	Pakistan Supreme Court Law Quarterly [*Lahore, Pakistan*] [*A publication*] (DLA)
PAKT	Ketchikan [*Alaska*] [*ICAO location identifier*] (ICLI)
PAL	Allegheny County Law Library, Pittsburgh, PA [*OCLC symbol*] (OCLC)
PAL	Pacific Aeronautical Library
PAL	Pacific Air Lines
pal	Pahlavi [*MARC language code Library of Congress*] (LCCP)
PAL	Paired-Associates Learning [*Task*] [*Psychology*]
PAL	Palace
Pal	Palamedes [*of Gorgias*] [*Classical studies*] (OCD)
pal	Palate (DMAA)
PAL	Palatine [*or Palatinate*] [*Genealogy*]
PAL	Paleography (ROG)
PAL	Paleontology
PAL	Paleozoic [*Period, era, or system*] [*Geology*]
PAL	Palestine
pal	Palette (VRA)
PAL	Palisades [*New York*] [*Seismograph station code, US Geological Survey*] (SEIS)
PAL	Pallor (KSC)
Pal	Palmer's Assizes at Cambridge [*England*] [*A publication*] (DLA)
Pal	Palmer's English King's Bench Reports [*1619-29*] [*A publication*] (DLA)
Pal	Palmer's Reports [*53-60 Vermont*] [*A publication*] (DLA)
PAL	Paloma Petroleum Ltd. [*Toronto Stock Exchange symbol*]
PAL	Paradox Application Language [*ANSA*] [*Computer science*]
PAL	Parcel Air Lift [*US Postal Service*]
PAL	Parents Anonymous Lifeline [*British*] (DI)
PAL	Parser Assembly Language [*Computer science*]
PAL	Parts and Assemblies Locator [*ADP/CES*]
PAL	Parts Authorization List (KSC)
PAL	Passive Activity Loss [*Investment term*] (DFIT)
PAL	Patent Associated Literature
PAL	Pathology Laboratory [*Test*]
PAL	Pectin Acid Lyase [*An enzyme*]
PAL	Pedagogic Algorithmic Language [*Computer science*]
PAL	People Against Chlordane (EA)
PAL	People-Animals-Love (EA)
PAL	Peptidyl-Alpha-Hydroxyglycine Alpha-Amidating Lysine Phase Alteration Plane [*Medicine*] (DMAA)
PAL	Perceptual Alternatives Laboratory [*University of Louisville*] [*Research center*] (RCD)
PAL	Performance Assessment Logic
PAL	Peripheral Access Lattices
PAL	Permanent Artificial Lighting (IEEE)
PAL	Permissive Action Link [*Army*]
PAL	Permissive Arming Line [*or Link*]
PAL	Peroxide Assisted Leach [*Ore processing*]
PAL	Personal Assets Line
PAL	Personnel Accounting Level [*Air Force*] (AFM)
PALS	Personnel Address Listing (SAA)
PAL	Personnel Airlock [*Nuclear energy*] (NRCH)
PAL	Personnel Augmentation List [*Military*]
PAL	Phase Alternate Line (NITA)
PAL	Phase Alternation Line [*West German color television system*]
PAL	Phase-Alternation System [*A color TV format*] [*Also, phase alternate each line*] (WDMC)
PAL	Phenylalanine Ammonia-Lyase [*An enzyme*]
PAL	Philippine Air Lines
PAL	Philippine Air Lines, Inc. [*ICAO designator*] (FAAC)
PAL	Philips Assembler Language (IAA)
PAL	Physical Activity Level (WDAA)
PAL	Pipe Analysis Log [*Gas well*]
PAL	Point, Area, and Line Source Air Quality Model [*Environmental Protection Agency*] (GFGA)
PAL	Police Athletic League
PAL	Police Attendance Line
PAL	Poly-DL-alanine Poly-L-lysine [*Biochemical analysis*]

PAL	Positive Arming Link [*Military*] (DNAB)
PAL	Postal Answer Line [*US Postal Service automated telephone information service*]
PAL	Posterior Axillary Line [*Medicine*]
PAL	Power and Light (IAA)
PAL	Power Assist Lathe
PAL	Pre-Academic Learning Inventory [*Child development test*]
PAL	Preapproved Loan [*Business term*]
PAL	Precision Artwork Language [*Computer science*]
PAL	Preliminary Allowance List [*Military*] (DNAB)
PAL	Premier Automobiles Ltd. [*India*]
PAL	Prescribed Action Link [*DoD*]
PAL	Present Atmospheric Level
PAL	Price and Availability List (CINC)
PAL	Princeton Accelerator Laboratory
PAL	Princeton Air Link
PAL	Prisoner-at-Large
PAL	Privileged Architecture Library Code
PAL	Problem Action Log (AAG)
PAL	Process Assembler Language
PAL	Process Audit List (MCD)
PAL	Process Automation Language [*Computer science*] (AAEL)
PAL	Production and Application of Light (MCD)
PAL	Product of Activated Lymphocyte [*Medicine*] (DB)
PAL	Product of Activated Lymphocytes [*Medicine*] (DMAA)
PAL	Profile Automobile League (EA)
PAL	Profile of Aptitude for Leadership [*Test*] (TMMY)
PAL	Programmable Algorithm Machine Assembly Language [*Computer science*]
PAL	Programmable Array Logic [*Computer science*] (IEEE)
PAL	Programmed Application Library [*IBM Corp.*]
PAL	Programmed Audit Library
PAL	Programmer Assistance and Liaison [*Computer science*] (NRCH)
PAL	Progressive Alliance of Liberia [*Political party*] (PPW)
PAL	Prototype Application Loop [*Nuclear energy*] (NRCH)
PAL	Psycho-Acoustic Laboratory [*Harvard University*] (MCD)
PAL	Public Archives of Canada Library [*UTLAS symbol*]
PAL	Publications Allowance List [*Military*] (CAAL)
PAL	Pulmonary Air Leak [*Medicine*] (DB)
PAL	Pulsed Argon LASER
PAL	Push and Latch [*Push button*]
PAL	Pyogenic Abscess of the Liver [*Medicine*] (DMAA)
PALA	N-(Phosphoacetyl)-L-aspartate [*Biochemistry*]
pala	Palace (VRA)
pala	Palazzo (VRA)
Pala	Partido Laborista [*Labor Party*] [*Panama*] [*Political party*] (PPW)
PALA	Partition Affinity Ligand Assay [*Analytical microbiology*]
PALA	Passenger Acceptance and Load Accumulation [*Aviation*]
PALA	Phosphonoacetyl-L-Aspartate [*Biochemistry*]
PALA	Polish American Librarians Association (EA)
PALA	Prison Atheist League of America (EA)
PALACE	Profiling ALACE [*Autonomous Lagrangian Circulation Explorer*] [*Marine science*] (OSRA)
PALAEOB	Palaeobotany
PALAEOG	Palaeography
PALAEONT	Palaeontology
Pal Ag	Paley on Principal and Agent [*3rd ed.*] [*1833*] [*A publication*] (DLA)
PALASM	Programmable Array Logic Assembler [*Computer science*] (IEEE)
PA Law J	Pennsylvania Law Journal [*A publication*] (DLA)
PA Law Jour	Pennsylvania Law Journal [*Philadelphia*] [*A publication*] (DLA)
PA Laws	Laws of the General Assembly of the Commonwealth of Pennsylvania [*A publication*] (DLA)
PA Law Ser	Pennsylvania Law Series [*A publication*] (DLA)
PALC	Palace
PALC	Passenger Acceptance and Load Control [*Aviation*]
PALC	Point Arguello Launch Complex
PALC	Precastable Autoclaved Lightweight Concrete [*Residential construction*]
PAL-C	Profile of Adaptation to Life - Clinical [*Personality development test*] [*Psychology*]
PALCO	Pacific Lumber Co. (EFIS)
PALCO	Pan American Liaison Committee of Women's Organizations (EA)
PALCON	Pallet-Size Container (MCD)
Pal Conv	Paley on Summary Convictions [*10th ed.*] [*1953*] [*A publication*] (DLA)
PALCR	Propulsion Auxiliaries Local Control Rack (DNAB)
PALCRU	Pay and Allowances Accrue From [*Air Force*]
PALCS	Permissive Action Link Cypher System (MCD)
PAL-D	Phase Alternation Line Delay (IEEE)
PALDS	Point, Area, and Line Source with Deposition and Settling of Pollutants [*Air quality model*] [*Environmental Protection Agency*] (GFGA)
Pale	Palestine (VRA)
PALE	Pelvis and Legs Elevating [*Pilot seat*]
PA Leg Gaz	Legal Gazette (Pennsylvania) [*A publication*] (DLA)
PA Leg Gaz	Legal Gazette Reports (Campbell) [*Pennsylvania*] [*A publication*] (DLA)
PA Legis Serv	Pennsylvania Legislative Service (Purdon) [*A publication*] (DLA)
paleob	Paleobotany (BARN)
PALEOECOL	Paleoecologic
paleog	Paleography
PALEOGEOG	Paleogeographic
Paleol	Paleolithic (VRA)
paleon	Paleontology
PALEONT	Paleontologic

PALEX......... Pacific Armies Look Exercise
Paley Ag...... Paley on Principal and Agent [*A publication*] (DLA)
Paley Princ & Ag... Paley on Principal and Agent [*3rd ed.*] [*1833*] [*A publication*] (DLA)
Palfed......... PALFED, Inc. [*Associated Press*] (SAG)
PA LG......... Legal Gazette (Pennsylvania) [*A publication*] (DLA)
PA LG......... Legal Gazette Reports (Campbell) [*Pennsylvania*] [*A publication*] (DLA)
Palg Ch....... Palgrave's Proceedings in Chancery [*A publication*] (DLA)
Palgrave..... Palgrave's Proceedings in Chancery [*A publication*] (DLA)
Palgrave..... Palgrave's Rise and Progress of the English Commonwealth [*A publication*] (DLA)
Palg Rise & Prog... Palgrave's Rise and Progress of the English Commonwealth [*1832*] [*A publication*] (DLA)
Palg Rise Etc... Palgrave's Rise and Progress of the English Commonwealth [*A publication*] (DLA)
PAL-H........ Profile of Adaptation to Life - Holistic [*Personality development test*] [*Psychology*]
PALI........... Pacific and Asian Linguistics Institute [*University of Hawaii*]
Pali............ Partido Liberal [*Nicaragua*] [*Political party*] (EY)
PALI........... Prince Albert's Light Infantry [*Military unit*] [*British*]
PALIKA ...... Parti de Liberation Kanak [*New Caledonia*] [*Political party*] (EY)
PALINET..... Pennsylvania Area Library Network
PALINET/ULC... PALINET and Union Library Catalogue of Pennsylvania [*Philadelphia, PA*] [*Library network*]
PALIS........ Property and Liability Information System
PA LJ........ Pennsylvania Law Journal [*A publication*] (DLA)
PA LJ........ Pennsylvania Law Journal Reports [*1842-52*] [*A publication*] (DLA)
PA LJR....... Clark's Pennsylvania Law Journal Reports [*A publication*] (DLA)
PALL......... Pallet [*Freight*]
PallCp........ Pall Corp. [*Associated Press*] (SAG)
PALLNIC ...... Palladium-Nickel (EECA)
PALM........ PALFED, Inc. [*NASDAQ symbol*] (NQ)
Palm......... Palmer's Assizes at Cambridge [*England*] [*A publication*] (DLA)
Palm......... Palmer's English King's Bench Reports [*1619-29*] [*A publication*] (DLA)
Palm......... Palmer's Reports [*53-60 Vermont*] [*A publication*] (DLA)
PALM........ Palmistry (ADA)
Palm......... Palmyrene (BJA)
PALM........ Philips Automated Laboratory Management System (NITA)
PALM........ Precision Altitude and Landing Monitor [*Aircraft location*]
Palm Comp L... Palmer's Company Law [*22nd ed.*] [*1976*] [*A publication*] (DLA)
Palm Comp Prec... Palmer's Company Precedents [*17th ed.*] [*1956-60*] [*A publication*] (DLA)
Palmer........ Palmer's Assizes at Cambridge [*England*] [*A publication*] (DLA)
Palmer........ Palmer's English King's Bench Reports [*A publication*] (DLA)
Palmer........ Palmer's Reports [*53-60 Vermont*] [*A publication*] (DLA)
Palmer Co Prec... Palmer's Company Precedents [*16 eds.*] [*1877-1952*] [*A publication*] (DLA)
Palmer Pr Comp... Palmer's Private Companies [*41st ed.*] [*1950*] [*A publication*] (DLA)
PALMES....... Pulsed Appendage Large Mobile Electromagnetic-Pulse Simulator (PDAA)
PalmHH ...... Palm Harbor Homes, Inc. [*Associated Press*] (SAG)
PALMNET .... Protocol for Automotive Local Area Network
Palm Pr Lords... Palmer's Practice in the House of Lords [*1830*] [*A publication*] (DLA)
PalmrMd...... Palomar Medical Technologies [*Associated Press*] (SAG)
PALMS....... Propulsion Alarm and Monitoring System (PDAA)
PALMS....... Provisioning Automated Logistics Material System (MCD)
Palm Sh ...... Palmer's Shareholders [*34th ed.*] [*1936*] [*A publication*] (DLA)
Palm Wr ...... Palmer's Law of Wreck [*1843*] [*A publication*] (DLA)
PALN .... Para-Aortic Lymph Node [*Anatomy*] (DAVI)
PALO .... Phosphonoacetyl-L-Ornithine [*Biochemistry*]
PALO .... Port Amenities Liaison Officer [*British*] (DSUE)
PALOS .... Pacific Logistic Operations - Streamline [*Army*]
PALP......... Palpable [*Medicine*]
palp .... Palpation [*Medicine*] (DMAA)
palp .... Palpitation [*Cardiology*] (DAVI)
PALP......... Pyridoxal Phosphate [*Also, PLP*] [*Biochemistry*]
PALPI......... Palpitation [*Medicine*]
palpit......... Palpitation [*Medicine*]
PALR .... Permissive Action Link Report [*Army*] (AABC)
PA L Rec ..... Pennsylvania Law Record [*A publication*] (DLA)
PALS......... Paediatric Advanced Life Support [*Medicine*] (WDAA)
PALS......... Paired Associate Learning Subtest [*Speech and language therapy*] (DAVI)
PALS......... Patient Advocacy Legal Service [*An association Defunct*] (EA)
PA LS .... Pennsylvania Law Series [*A publication*] (DLA)
PALS......... People Against Lenient Sentences [*An association Australia*]
PALS......... People Against Loneliness [*British*] (DI)
PALS......... Periarteriolar Lymphocyte Sheath (AAMN)
PALS......... Permissive Action Link System [*Army*]
PALS......... Phase Alternation Line Simple [*TV decoding system*]
PALS......... Photo Area and Location System (NASA)
PALS......... Point Arguello Launch Site (AAG)
PALS......... Positioning and Locating System [*Aviation*] (PDAA)
PALS......... Precision Approach and Landing System (NASA)
PALS......... Precision Approach Lighting System [*Aviation*] (FAAC)
PALS......... Prestaged Ammunition Loading System [*Army*] (RDA)
PALS......... Principle of the Alphabet Literacy System [*Software*] [*IBM Corp.*]
PALS......... Principles of Adult Learning Scale (EDAC)
PALS......... Prison-Acquired Lymphoproliferative Syndrome [*Medicine*] (DMAA)
PALS......... Protection Against Limited Strikes [*Military defence system*]
PA L Ser...... Pennsylvania Law Series [*A publication*] (DLA)

PALS-G....... Passive Artillery Locating System - Ground Based (MCD)
PALSG .... Personnel and Logistics Systems Group [*Army*] (AABC)
PA-LS-ID...... Pernicious Anemia-Like Syndrome and Immunoglobulin Deficiency [*Hematology*] (AAMN)
PALST......... Picture Articulation and Screening Test
PAlt........... Altoona Area Public Library, Altoona, PA [*Library symbol Library of Congress*] (LCLS)
PALT........... Procurement Administrative Lead Time
PALU .... Cape Lisburne Air Force Station [*Alaska*] [*ICAO location identifier*] (ICLI)
PALU .... Progressive Arbeiders- en Landbouwersunie [*Progressive Workers' and Farm Laborers' Union*] [*Surinam*] [*Political party*] (PPW)
Palud......... Paludonus [*Pierre de la Palu*] [*Deceased, 1342*] [*Authority cited in pre-1607 legal work*] (DSA)
PALV......... Passiflora Latent Virus [*Plant pathology*]
PALW......... Plasma Arc-augmented Laser Welding
PALX......... Private Automatic Loudspeaking Exchange [*Telecommunications*] (IAA)
PAM .... Pacific Armies Management
PAM .... Palermo [*California*] [*Seismograph station code, US Geological Survey*] (SEIS)
PAM .... Pamida Holdings [*AMEX symbol*] (TTSB)
PAM .... Pamida Holdings Corp. [*AMEX symbol*] (SPSG)
PAM .... Pamour, Inc. [*Toronto Stock Exchange symbol*]
Pam .... Pampa [*Record label*] [*Brazil*]
PAM .... Pamphlet (AFM)
pam .... Pamphlet (WDMC)
PAM .... PAM Transportation Services, Inc. [*Associated Press*] (SAG)
PAM .... Panama City, FL [*Location identifier FAA*] (FAAL)
PAM .... Panel Monitor (MHDI)
PAM .... Panoramic
PAM .... Panvalet Access Method (IAA)
PAM .... Parameter Adjusting Mechanism
PAM .... Parametric Amplifier (NATG)
PAM .... Parents Against Molesters (EA)
PAM .... Partial Mobilization Expansion Plan [*Army*] (GFGA)
PAM .... Partitioned Access Method [*Computer science*]
PAM .... Payload Assist Module [*NASA*] (MCD)
PAM .... Penetration Augmented Munition
PAM .... Penicillin Aluminum Monostearate [*Antibiotic*]
PAM .... People's Action Movement [*Nevis*] [*Political party*] (PPW)
PAM .... People's Anti-War Mobilization (EA)
PAM .... Performance Analysis Model (MCD)
PAM .... Performance Assessment Monitoring (MCD)
PAM .... Performing Arts Medicine
PAM .... Peripheral Adapter Module
PAM .... Personal Accounting Management
PAM .... Personal Applications Manager [*Hewlett-Packard Co.*]
PAM .... Personnel Action Memorandum [*Military*]
PAM .... Personnel Availability Model (PDAA)
PAM .... Phase-Amplitude Modulation
PAM .... Phased Array Module
PAM .... Phenylalanine Mustard (AAMN)
PAM .... Philosophies, Ancient and Modern [*A publication*]
PAM .... Phoenix Airborne Missile
PAM .... Phoenix Air Service GmbH [*Germany ICAO designator*] (FAAC)
PAM .... Pittsburgh, Allegheny & McKees Rocks Railroad Co. [*AAR code*]
PAM .... Planning, Activation, Modification [*Army reorganization*]
PAM .... Plasma-Arc Machining [*Manufacturing term*]
PAM .... Pledged Account Mortgage
PAM .... Pole Amplitude Modulation (IEEE)
PAM .... Polyacrylamide [*Also, PAA, PAAM*] [*Organic chemistry*]
PAM .... Portable Alpha Monitor
PAM .... Portable Automated Mesonet [*Meteorology*]
PAM .... Position and Altitude Monitor (MCD)
PAM .... Postacceptance Modification
PAM .... Post-Accident Monitoring [*Nuclear energy*] (NRCH)
PAM .... Postauricular Myogenic [*Medicine*] (DMAA)
PAM .... Potential Acuity Meter [*Instrumentation*]
PAM .... Power Assist Module [*NASA*]
PAM .... Pozzolan Aggregate Mixture (OA)
PAM .... Pralidoxime [*Pharmacology*] (DAVI)
PAM .... Pralidoxime Chloride [*Pharmacology*] (DAVI)
PAM .... Pralidoxime Methiodide [*Biochemistry*]
PAM .... Presbyterian Association of Musicians (EA)
PAM .... Pressure-Acoustic-Magnetic [*Minesweeping system*] (DNAB)
PAM .... Primary Access Method [*Sperry UNIVAC*]
PAM .... Primary Acquired Melanosis [*Oncology*]
PAM .... Primary Amoebic Meningitis [*or Meningoencephalitis*] [*Medicine*]
PAM .... Primary Auxiliary Memory [*Unit*] [*Computer science*] (MCD)
PAM .... Priorities and Allocations Manual [*Army*] (AABC)
PAM .... Process Application Module (AAEL)
PAM .... Process Automation Monitor [*Texas Instruments, Inc.*]
PAM .... Processor and Memory [*Computer science*]
PAM .... Procurement Aids Man [*Marine Corps*]
PAM .... Procurement of Aircraft and Missiles
PAM .... Profit Analysis Model (MHDI)
PAM .... Program Analysis Memorandum (MCD)
PA-M .... Program Authorization - Map [*Military*] (AFIT)
PAM .... Program Automated Method [*Computer science*]
PAM .... Programmable Algorithm Machine [*Computer science*]
PAM .... Propulsion Assistance Module (MCD)
PAM .... Protopan Chloride [*Medicine*] (BARN)
PAM .... Pulmonary Alveolar Macrophage [*Attacks inhaled particles*]
PAM .... Pulmonary Alveolar Microlithiasis [*Medicine*] (MAE)

PAM............ Pulse-Address MODEM
PAM............ Pulse Amplifier Modulation (NAKS)
PAM............ Pulse Amplitude Modulation [*Electronics*]
PAM............ Pyridine Aldoxime Methiodide [*Biochemistry*]
PAM............ Pyridine Aldoxime Methyl [*Pharmacology*]
PAM............ University of Pennsylvania, School of Medicine, Philadelphia, PA [*OCLC symbol*] (OCLC)
PAm............ Wissahickon Valley Public Library, Ambler, PA [*Library symbol Library of Congress*] (LCLS)
PAM-A .... PAM [*Payload Assist Module*] Atlas-Centaur Class Spacecraft (NASA)
PAMA........... Pan American Medical Association [*Also known as Association Medica Pan Americana*] (EA)
PAMA........... Para-Dimethylaminophenylazopyridine [*An indicator*] [*Chemistry*]
PAM-A .... Payload Assist Module - Atlas Class Spacecraft (MCD)
PAMA........... Polish Alma Mater of America (EA)
PAMA........... Polyalkylmethacrylate (IAA)
PAMA........... Pre-Assigned Multiple Access [*Telecommunications*] (LAIN)
PAMA........... Press Advertisement Managers' Association (DGA)
PAMA........... Professional Aviation Maintenance Association (EA)
PAMA........... Pulse-Address Multiple Access [*Satellite communications*]
PAMAC .... Parts and Materials Accountability Control
PAMAD .... Parents Against Middle-Aged Discrimination [*British*] (DI)
PAMAI .... Program of Action for Mediation, Arbitration, and Inquiry [*American Library Association*]
PAMAM .... Polyamidoamine [*Organic chemistry*]
PAMB........... Pressure Ambient (NASA)
PAmbT.......... Trinity Episcopal School, Ambridge, PA [*Library symbol*] [*Library of Congress*] (LCLS)
PAMC........... McGrath [*Alaska*] [*ICAO location identifier*] (ICLI)
PAMC........... Pakistan Army Medical Corps
PAMC........... Provident American Corp. [*Norristown, PA*] [*NASDAQ symbol*] (NQ)
PAMC........... Provisional Acceptable Means of Compliance (MCD)
PAMC........... Pterygoarthromyodysplasia Congenital [*Medicine*] (DMAA)
PAmC........... Temple University, Ambler Campus, Ambler, PA [*Library symbol Library of Congress*] (LCLS)
PAMCCS ...... Prior Active Marine Corps Commissioned Service
PAMCES .... Prior Active Marine Corps Enlisted Service
PAMCI .... Pyridinealdoxime Methochloride [*Organic chemistry*]
PAMCS .... Phoenix Airborne Missile Control System
PAM-D .... PAM [*Payload Assist Module*] Delta Class Spacecraft (NASA)
PAMD .... Parallel Access Multiple Distribution (PDAA)
PAM-D .... Payload Assist Module - Delta Class Spacecraft (MCD)
PAMD .... Periodic Acid Mixed Diamine (OA)
PAMD .... Price and Management Data
PAMD .... Primary Adrenocortical Micronodular Dysplasia [*Medicine*] (DMAA)
PAM/D .... Process Automation Monitor/Disc Version (NITA)
PAMD .... Process Automation Monitor/Disk Version [*Texas Instruments, Inc.*]
PAMD .... Public Access Machine Readable Documents (NITA)
PAMDS .... Price and Management Data Section [*of a stock list*] [*Navy*]
PAME........... Pandemokratiki Agrotikon Metapon Ellados [*Pan-Democratic Agrarian Front of Greece*] [*Political party*] (PPE)
PAME........... Primary Amoebic Meningoencephalitis [*Medicine*]
P/AMEA2...... Probationary Marine Engineering Artificer, Acting, 2nd Class [*British military*] (DMA)
PAMETON .... Paracetamol and Methionine [*Pain-relief drug*]
PAMF........... Portable Arc Melting Furnace
PAMF........... Programmable Analogue Matched Filter (PDAA)
PAM-FM .... Pulse Amplitude Modulation - Frequency Modulation [*Electronics*]
PAmh........... Amherst Papyri [*A publication*] (OCD)
PamHld......... Pamida Holdings Corp. [*Associated Press*] (SAG)
PAMI........... Personnel Accounting Machine Installation
PAMI........... Prairie Agricultural Machinery Institute [*Canada*]
PAMI........... Primary Angioplasty in Myocardial Infarction [*Cardiology study*]
PAMI........... Professional Arts Management Institute (EA)
PAMIE......... Physical and Mental Impairment of Function Evaluation [*Medicine*] (DMAA)
PAMIF......... Physical and Mental Impairment-of-Function [*Scale*] [*Medicine*] (DB)
PAMII......... Protection and Advocacy for Mentally Ill Individuals Act [*1986*]
PAMIRASAT... Passive Microwave Radiometer Satellite (PDAA)
PAMIRASAT... Primary Afferent Depolarization (PDAA)
PAMIS .... Processing and Manufacturing in Space [*European Space Agency*]
PAMIS .... Psychological Operations Automated Management Information System (MCD)
PA Misc....... Pennsylvania Miscellaneous Reports [*A publication*] (DLA)
PAMLPU ...... Pianoforte Action Makers' Labour Protection Union [*British*]
PAMN.......... Procurement Aircraft and Missiles, Navy [*An appropriation*]
PAMNET ...... Public Affairs Management Network [*Air Force*]
PAMO .... Pacific Airlift Management Office [*Military*]
PAMO .... Port Air Materiel Office
PAMP.......... Pampero [*River Plate gale*] [*Nautical term*] (DSUE)
PAMP.......... Pulmonary Artery Mean Pressure [*Medicine*] (MEDA)
PAMPA .... Pacific Area Movement Priority Agency [*Military*]
PAMPA .... Precision Aerobatics Model Pilots Association (EA)
PamPAC ...... Pamela's Political Action Committee [*Nickname of "Democrats for the '80's," a committee founded by Pamela Harriman*]
PAMPER ...... Practical Application of Mid-Points for Exponential Regression
PAMPH .... Pamphlet [*Freight*]
Pamph Laws... Pamphlet Laws, Acts [*A publication*] (DLA)
Pamphl Laws... Pamphlet Laws, Acts [*A publication*] (DLA)
PAMPS .... Poly(Acrylamidomethyl Propane) Sulphonic Acid [*Organic chemistry*]
PAMPUS ...... Photons for Atomic and Molecular Processes and Universal Studies [*Physics*]
PAMR .... Anchorage/Merrill Field [*Alaska*] [*ICAO location identifier*] (ICLI)
Pamrapo....... Pamrapo Bancorp, Inc. [*Associated Press*] (SAG)

PAMRF .... Palo Alto Medical Research Foundation [*Research center*] (RCD)
PAMRS .... Parameter Adaptive Model Reference System
PAMS.......... Pacific Advanced Media Studies [*Australia*]
PAMS.......... Pacific Armies Management Seminar
PAMS.......... Pad Abort Measuring System [*NASA*] (KSC)
PAMS.......... Paging Area Memory Space [*Computer science*] (IAA)
PAMS.......... Plan Analysis and Modeling System (MHDB)
PAMS.......... Portable Acoustic Monitoring System
PAMS.......... Post-Accident Monitoring System [*Nuclear energy*] (NRCH)
PAMS.......... Predictive Aircraft Maintenance System
PAMS.......... Preselected Alternate Master-Slave [*Telecommunications*] (TEL)
PAMS.......... Printing Advisory and Management Service (DGA)
PAMS.......... Procurement Action Management System (MCD)
PAMS.......... Public Access Message System
PAMTGG ...... Pan Am Makes the Going Great [*Title of ballet choreographed by George Balanchine, taken from Pan American World Airways' slogan*] [*Pronounced "pam-ti-guh-guh"*]
PAMUSA...... Post-Attack Mobilization of the United States Army
PAMUX .... Parallel Addressable Multiplexer [*Telecommunications*] (IAA)
PAMV.......... Petunia Asteroid Mosaic Virus [*Plant pathology*]
PAMWA .... Pan American Medical Women's Alliance (EA)
PAMX.......... Pancho's Mexican Buffet [*NASDAQ symbol*] (TTSB)
PAMX.......... Pancho's Mexican Buffet, Inc. [*NASDAQ symbol*] (NQ)
PAN............ National Action Party [*Mexico Political party*] (PD)
PAN............ Pagans Against Nukes [*British*] (DI)
PAN............ Paladin Fuel Technology [*Vancouver Stock Exchange symbol*]
PAN............ Panama [*ANSI three-letter standard code*] (CNC)
Pan............ Panama (VRA)
pan .... Panchromatic [*Photography*] (WDMC)
PAN............ Panchromatic (DEN)
pan .... Pancreas (STED)
Pan............ Panegyricus [*of Pliny the Younger*] [*Classical studies*] (OCD)
PAN............ Paneled (WGA)
PAN............ Panimavida [*Chile*] [*Seismograph station code, US Geological Survey Closed*] (SEIS)
PAN............ Panis [*Bread*] [*Pharmacy*] (ROG)
pan .... Panjabi [*MARC language code Library of Congress*] (LCCP)
PAN............ Panoramic (MSA)
Pan............ Panormitanus [*Nicholas de Tudeschis*] [*Deceased, 1445*] [*Authority cited in pre-1607 legal work*] (DSA)
Pan............ Pantheon [*Record label*] [*France, etc.*]
PAN............ Pantry (MSA)
PAN............ Partido de Accion Nacional [*Nicaragua*] [*Political party*] (EY)
PAN............ Pattani [*Thailand*] [*Airport symbol*] (OAG)
PAN............ Peace Action Network (EA)
PAN............ Pennsylvania Animal Network [*Coalition operated by Trans-Species Unlimited*]
PAN............ Pennsylvania Association of Notaries (EA)
PAN............ Percussion Actuated Nonelectric [*An explosive disrupter*]
PAN............ Performing Artists Network [*Electronic network*]
PAN............ Periarteritis Nodosa [*Also, PN*] [*Medicine*]
PAN............ Periodic Alternating Nystagmus [*Ophthalmology*]
PAN............ Peroxyacetyl Nitrate [*Lacrimator*]
PAN............ Personal Area Network [*Computer science*]
PAN............ Pesticides Action Network (EA)
PAN............ Polled Access Network
PAN............ Pollution Abatement Notice [*Environmental science*] (COE)
PAN............ Polska Akademia Nauk [*Polish Academy of Sciences*] [*Also, an information service or system*] (IID)
PAN............ Polyacrylonitrile [*Organic chemistry*]
PAN............ Polyarteritis Nodosa [*Medicine*]
PAN............ Positional Alcohol Nystagmus [*Physiology*]
PAN............ Primary Account Number [*Business term*]
PAN............ Project Authorization Notice (MCD)
PAN............ Propodial Anlage [*Zoology*]
PAN............ Publications Account Number [*DoD*]
PAN............ Puromycin Aminonucleoside [*Medicine*] (DMAA)
PAN............ Pyridylazonaphthol [*An indicator*] [*Chemistry*]
PAN............ Switchboard Panel [*Telecommunications*] (TEL)
PA$_{N20}$...... Mean Alveolar Nitrous Oxide Tension [*Medicine*] (DAVI)
PANA .... Panaco, Inc. [*NASDAQ symbol*] (SAG)
PANA .... PanAfrican News Agency (EAIO)
PANA .... Pan-Asia News Agency Ltd. [*Also, PANASIA*] [*Hong Kong*]
PANA .... Pan-Asian Newspaper Alliance [*Also, PANANEWS*] (NADA)
PANA .... Panorama (VRA)
PANA .... Polish-American Numismatic Association (EA)
PANABANK.... Banco Panamericano [*Panama*] (EY)
PanaBev ...... Panamerican Beverages [*Commercial firm Associated Press*] (SAG)
Panaco .... Panaco, Inc. [*Associated Press*] (SAG)
PANAFTEL ... Pan-African Telecommunications (BARN)
PANAFTEL ... Pan-African Telecommunications Network (TELE)
PANAGRA ... Pan American Grace Airways, Inc. [*Also, PAGA*]
PANAIR....... Panama Air Lines
PANAL .... Papuan National Alliance [*Political party*] (PPW)
PANALU ...... Parti National Lumumba [*Lumumba National Party*] [*Political party*]
PAN-AM ...... Pan American World Airways, Inc. [*See also PA, PAA, PN*]
PANAMAC.... Pan American World Airways Communications System
PanAmC....... Pan Am Corp. [*Associated Press*] (SAG)
PanAmSat.... Pan American Satellite [*Greenwich, CT*] [*Telecommunications service*] (TSSD)
Pan-Am TS... Pan-American Treaty Series [*A publication*] (DLA)
PANANEWS... Pan-Asian Newspaper Alliance [*Also, PANA*] (NADA)
PANAR........ Panoramic RADAR
PANASIA..... Organization of Pan Asian American Women (EA)
PANASIA..... Pan-Asia News Agency Ltd. [*Also, PANA*] [*Hong Kong*]

PanASlv......	Pan American Silver Corp. [*Associated Press*] (SAG)
Panax........	Panax Pharmaceutical Co. Ltd. [*Associated Press*] (SAG)
PanaxP......	Panax Pharmaceutical Co. Ltd. [*Associated Press*] (SAG)
PANB.........	Panic Bolt
PANC..........	Anchorage/International [*Alaska*] [*ICAO location identifier*] (ICLI)
PANC..........	Power Amplifier Neutralizing Capacitor (DEN)
P-ANCA......	Perinuclear Anti-Neutrophilic Cytoplasmic Antibody [*Medicine*] (DMAA)
PANCAN......	[*The*] Panama Canal
PANCANCO...	Panama Canal Co. [*Superseded by Panama Canal Commission*]
PANCAP......	Practical Annual Capacity [*FAA*]
panchr........	Panchromatic (VRA)
PancMx.......	Pancho's Mexican Buffet, Inc. [*Associated Press*] (SAG)
PANCO........	Procurement Aids Noncommissioned Officer [*Marine Corps*]
Pand...........	[*The*] Pandects [*A publication*] (DLA)
PAND..........	Pandering [*FBI standardized term*]
PAND..........	Passive Air Navigation Device
PAND..........	Performing Artists for Nuclear Disarmament (EA)
PAND..........	Primary Adrenocortical Nodular Dysplasia [*Endocrinology*] (DMAA)
P & A..........	Page and Adams' Code [*1912*] [*A publication*] (DLA)
P & A..........	Pay and Allowances
P & A..........	Pennsylvania & Atlantic Railroad Co. (IIA)
P & A..........	Percussion and Auscultation [*Medicine*]
PANDA........	Performance and Demand Analyser (PDAA)
P & A..........	Personnel and Administration [*Army*] (AABC)
P & A..........	Pioneer and Ammunition
P & A..........	Plans and Analysis
PANDA........	Portable Array for Numerical Data Acquisition [*Instrumentation*]
P&A..........	Precision and Accuracy (COE)
P&A..........	Prediction and Allocation
PANDA........	Prestel Advanced Network Design Architecture
P & A..........	Price and Availability
P & A..........	Pricing and Acceptability Claims Processing System [*Health insurance*] (GHCT)
P & A..........	Print and Advertising [*Marketing*] (ECON)
P & A..........	Priorities and Allocations (MUGU)
P&A..........	Prizes and Awards Committee (ACII)
P & A..........	Procedures and Analysis
P & A..........	Procurement and Assignment
P & A..........	Professional and Administrative (AAG)
PANDA........	Programmers' Analysis 'N' Development Aid (NITA)
P & A..........	Protection and Advocacy [*System*] [*To protect the rights of developmentally disabled persons*]
PandaPrj....	[*The*] Panda Project, Inc. [*Associated Press*] (SAG)
P & AR........	Pacific & Arctic Railway (MHDB)
P & AW.......	Paging and Area Warning
P&B..........	Pain & Burning [*Medicine*] (DMAA)
P & B..........	Phenobarbital and Belladonna [*A drug regimen*]
P & B..........	Planning and Budgeting [*Military*] (AFIT)
P & B..........	Price and Budgeting (MCD)
P & B..........	Printing and Binding [*Publishing*]
P & B..........	Pugsley and Burbridge's New Brunswick Reports [*A publication*] (DLA)
P & C..........	Parge and Core [*Construction*]
P & C..........	Performance and Control (SSD)
P & C..........	Physical and Chemical (AAG)
P & C..........	Prideaux and Cole's English Reports [*4 New Sessions Cases*] [*A publication*] (DLA)
P & C..........	Prism and Cover (Test) [*Ophthalmology*]
P & C..........	Procurement and Contracting (AFM)
P & C..........	Purchasing and Contracting
P & C..........	Put and Call [*Stock exchange term*]
P & CA........	Paying and Collecting Area (AFM)
P & CO........	Plans and Combat Operations
P & CP........	Plate and Cylinder Production (DGA)
P & CR........	Performance and Compatibility Requirements
P & CR........	Planning and Compensation Reports [*British*]
P & CR........	Property and Compensation Reports [*A publication*] (DLA)
P & CYC......	Police and Citizens' Youth Club [*Australia*]
P & D..........	Law Reports, Probate and Divorce [*England*] [*A publication*] (DLA)
P & D..........	Perry and Davison's English Queen's Bench Reports [*1834-44*] [*A publication*] (DLA)
P & D..........	Pick Up and Delivery [*Business term*]
P & D..........	Pioneer and Demolition Section [*Army*]
P&D..........	Plug and Display [*Computer science*]
P & D..........	Pressing and Distribution (WDMC)
P & D..........	Probate and Divorce [*Legal*] [*British*]
P & D..........	Procurement and Distribution [*Military*]
P & D..........	Promote and Develop Fishery Products Pertaining to American Fisheries Account [*National Oceanic and Atmospheric Administration*] (GFGA)
P & DD........	Plumbing and Deck Drain (MSA)
P & DR........	Price and Delivery Request
P & DSEC.....	Pioneer and Demolition Section [*Army*]
P & E..........	Pike and Eel [*A pub at Cambridge University*] [*British*] (DSUE)
P & E..........	Planning and Estimating (AAG)
P & E..........	Privileges and Elections Subcommittee [*US Senate*]
P & E..........	Procurement and Expedition
P & E..........	Propellants and Explosives [*Military*] (AABC)
P & E..........	Pyrotechnical and Explosive [*NASA*] (KSC)
Pandect Flor...	Pandectae Florentinae [*A publication*] (DSA)
P & EE........	Proof and Experimental Establishments (RDA)
P & EML......	Personnel and Equipment Modification List [*Air Force*]
P & ESI.......	Physical and Engineering Sciences Division [*Army Research Office*]
P & F..........	P & F Industries, Inc. [*Associated Press*] (SAG)

P & F.........	Petroleum and Fuel
P & F.........	Pike and Fischer's Administrative Law [*A publication*] (DLA)
P & F..........	Pike and Fischer's Federal Rules Service [*A publication*] (DLA)
P & F..........	Pike and Fischer's OPA Price Service [*A publication*] (DLA)
P & F..........	Planning and Forecasting (MCD)
P & F..........	Plant and Facilities
P&FA..........	Program and File Analysis [*Computer science*] (CIST)
Pand Flo......	Pandectae Florentinae [*A publication*] (DSA)
P & FM........	Programs and Financial Management [*Navy*]
P & FS.........	Particles and Fields Subsatellite [*NASA*] (KSC)
P & G.........	Post and Girder [*Lumber*] (DAC)
P & G........	Procter & Gamble Co.
P & G News...	Plants and Gardens News [*A publication*]
P & H.........	Patton, Jr., and Heath's Reports [*Virginia Special Court of Appeals*] [*A publication*] (DLA)
P&H..........	Postage and Handling (WDMC)
P & I..........	Passenger and Immigration Lists [*A publication*]
P & I..........	Performance and Interface [*Specification*] [*NASA*] (NASA)
P & I..........	Piping and Instrumentation [*Nuclear energy*] (NRCH)
P & I..........	Postage and Insurance
P&I..........	Principal and Interest [*Finance*] (DFIT)
P & I..........	Privileges and Immunities [*Legal shorthand*] (LWAP)
P & I..........	Properties and Installations
P & I..........	Protection and Indemnity [*Insurance*]
P & ID.........	Piping and Instrumentation Diagram [*or Design or Drawing*] [*Calcomp Ltd. Software package*] [*Nuclear energy*] (NRCH)
P & ID.........	Process and Instrumentation Diagram [*Engineering*] (NRCH)
P&II..........	Personalization and Identification Institute (NTPA)
P & J..........	Plaza y Janes [*Publisher*] [*Spain*]
P&J..........	Protection and Indemnity (EBF)
P & K..........	Perry and Knapp's English Election Cases [*1833*] [*A publication*] (DLA)
P & KI.........	Promisel & Korn, Inc. [*Information service or system*] (IID)
P & L.........	Paul and Lisa (EA)
P & L.........	Points and Lines [*Military*] (CAAL)
P & L.........	Power and Lighting (MSA)
P & L.........	Pratt & Lambert, Inc.
P & L.........	Profit and Loss [*Accounting*]
P&L..........	Profit and Loss Statement [*Finance*] (DFIT)
PANDLCHAR...	Pay and Allowances Chargeable
P & L Dig Laws...	Pepper and Lewis' Digest of Laws [*Pennsylvania*] [*A publication*] (DLA)
P & LERR....	[*The*] Pittsburgh & Lake Erie Railroad Co.
P & L Laws...	Private and Local Laws [*A publication*] (DLA)
P & M.........	Law Reports, Probate and Matrimonial Cases [*England*] [*A publication*] (DLA)
P & M.........	Pollock and Maitland's History of English Common Law [*A publication*] (DLA)
P & M.........	Probate and Matrimonial [*Legal*] [*British*]
P & M.........	Processes and Materials (NASA)
P & MHEL...	Pollock and Maitland's History of English Common Law [*A publication*] (DLA)
P & MP.......	Paris & Mount Pleasant Railroad (IIA)
P & N.........	Piedmont and Northern Railroad (AD)
p & n.........	Psychiatry and Neurology (AD)
P & N.........	Psychiatry and Neurology
P & O.........	Paints and Oil
p & o.........	Paints and Oil (AD)
P & O.........	Parasites and Ova [*Gastroenterology*] (DAVI)
P & O.........	Peninsular & Occidental Steamship Co. (AD)
P&O..........	Peninsular & Oriental (WDAA)
P & O.........	Peninsular & Oriental Steam Navigation Co. [*Steamship line*]
P & O.........	Performance and Operational [*Test or reports*]
P & O.........	Pickled and Oiled
p & o.........	Pickled and Oiled (AD)
P & O.........	Planning and Operations
P & O.........	Planning and Organization
P & O.........	Plans and Operations Division [*War Department*] [*World War II*]
P & O.........	Portland & Ogdensburgh Railroad
P & O.........	Positioning and Orientation
P&O..........	Prosthetic and Orthotic [*Health insurance*] (GHCT)
P & OC........	Peninsular & Oriental (Steam Navigation) Co. Ltd. (ROG)
P & O Div...	Planning and Operations Division [*Military*]
p & oo........	Pianistic and Orchestral Orgasm [*Music*] (AD)
PANDORA....	Passive and Active Signal Digital Correlator Analyzer (MCD)
P & OSCC....	Plans and Operations for the Safeguard Communications Command [*Army*] (RDA)
P & OSNCo...	Peninsular & Oriental Steam Navigation Co. [*Steamship line*]
P&OT..........	Physical & Occupational Therapy (CMD)
P & P.........	Packing and Preservation
P & P.........	Pam and Peter Fisher [*Commercial firm British*]
p & p.........	Parsimonious and Penurious (AD)
P&P..........	Pay & Privileges (WDAA)
p&p..........	Payments and Progress (AD)
P and P......	Payments and Progress Committee [*NATO*] (NATG)
P & P.........	Peace and Prosperity Issue [*Politics*]
P & P.........	Pins and Plaster [*Orthopedics*] (DAVI)
P & P.........	Plans and Policies
P & P.........	Plans and Programs
P & P.........	Postage and Packing [*Shipping*]
p&p..........	Postage & Packing (WDAA)
P & P.........	Pride and Prejudice [*Novel by Jane Austen*]
P & P.........	Procurement and Production [*Military*]

P & P............ Production and Procurement [*Military*]
P & P/CT .... Prothrombin and Proconvertin Control [*Hematology*] (DAVI)
P & PD .... Percussion and Postural Drainage
P & PM....... Packing and Packaging Manual (MCD)
P & PP .... Pull and Push Plate
p & pp .... Pull and Push Plate (AD)
P & PU .... Peoria and Pekin Union [*Railroad*] (AD)
P & PW .... Publicity and Psychological Warfare
P & Q .... Peace and Quiet
p & q .... Peace and Quiet (AD)
P and Q ...... Prime Quality [*Slang*]
p & r........... Parallax and Refraction (AD)
P&R .... Parks & Recreation [*A publication*] (BRI)
P & R .... Pelvic and Rectal [*Medicine*]
P & R .... Performance and Resources (NASA)
P & R .... Philadelphia & Reading Railway
P & R .... Picture and Resume [*Theatre slang*]
P & R .... Pigott and Rodwell's Reports in Common Pleas [*1843-45*] [*A publication*] (DLA)
P & R .... Planning and Review (MCD)
P & R .... Post and Rail
P & R .... Pulse and Respiration [*Medicine*]
P and RD..... Decisions of the Department of the Interior, Pension and Retirement Claims [*United States*] [*A publication*] (DLA)
P & RT .... Physical and Recreational Training [*Navy British*]
P & S .... Packers and Stockyards
P & S .... Pain and Suffering (DAVI)
P & S .... Paracentesis and Suction [*Medicine*]
P & S .... Pay and Supply [*Coast Guard*]
P & S .... Perkins & Squier [*Paper manufacturer*]
P & S .... Physicians and Surgeons (DAVI)
P & S .... [*The*] Pittsburg & Shawmut Railroad Co.
P & S .... Planking and Strutting [*Construction*]
P&S .... Planning and Scheduling (CIST)
P & S .... Port and Starboard
PANDS........ Print and Search Processor [*Computer science*]
P & S .... Purchase and Sale [*Business term*]
P & SA .... Packers and Stockyards Administration [*Department of Agriculture*]
P & SF....... Panhandle & Santa Fe Railway Co.
P & SI .... Pay and Supply Instruction [*Coast Guard*]
P & SM....... Procurement and Subcontract Management [*NASA*] (NASA)
P & SNP...... Pay and Subsistence of Naval Personnel [*Budget appropriation title*]
P & T.......... Permanent and Total [*Disability*] [*Medicine*]
P & T.......... Personnel and Training [*Military*] (MUGU)
P & T.......... Pharmacy and Therapeutics
P & T.......... Plans and Training [*Military*] (IIA)
P & T.......... Posts and Timbers [*Technical drawings*]
P & T.......... Professional and Technology [*Category*] [*British*]
P & T.......... Pugsley and Trueman's New Brunswick Reports [*A publication*] (DLA)
P & T.......... Purge-and-Trap [*Technique*] [*Environmental Protection Agency*]
P & TD .... Parts and Tool Disposition (SAA)
P & T Div ... Plans and Training Division [*Military*]
P&U .... Pharmacia & Upjohn AB [*Commercial firm*] [*Sweden*]
P & V .... Percuss and Vibrate [*Medicine*] (DAVI)
P & V .... Pyloroplasty and Vagotomy [*Medicine*]
P & VE........ Propulsion and Vehicle Engineering [*A Marshall Space Flight Center laboratory*] (MCD)
P & VE-ADM... Propulsion and Vehicle Engineering - Administrative [*Marshall Space Flight Center Laboratory*] (SAA)
P & VE-DIR... Propulsion and Vehicle Engineering - Director [*Marshall Space Flight Center Laboratory*] (SAA)
P & VE-E..... Propulsion and Vehicle Engineering - Vehicle Engineering [*Marshall Space Flight Center Laboratory*] (SAA)
P & VE-F ..... Propulsion and Vehicle Engineering - Advanced Flight Systems [*Marshall Space Flight Center Laboratory*] (SAA)
P & VE-M .... Propulsion and Vehicle Engineering - Engineering Materials [*Marshall Space Flight Center Laboratory*] (SAA)
P & VE-N..... Propulsion and Vehicle Engineering - Nuclear Vehicle Projects [*Marshall Space Flight Center Laboratory*] (SAA)
P & VE-P..... Propulsion and Vehicle Engineering - Propulsion and Mechanics [*Marshall Space Flight Center Laboratory*] (SAA)
P & VE-PC... Propulsion and Vehicle Engineering - Program Coordination [*Marshall Space FlightCenter Laboratory*] (SAA)
P & VE-REL... Propulsion and Vehicle Engineering - Reliability [*Marshall Space Flight Center Laboratory*] (SAA)
P & VE-S ..... Propulsion and Vehicle Engineering - Structures [*Marshall Space Flight Center Laboratory*] (SAA)
P & VE-TS ... Propulsion and Vehicle Engineering - Technical and Scientific Staff [*Marshall Space Flight Center Laboratory*] (SAA)
P & VE-V ..... Propulsion and Vehicle Engineering - Vehicle Systems Integration [*Marshall Space Flight Center Laboratory*] (SAA)
P & VIR....... Pure and Vulcanized Rubber Insulation
P & W .... Penrose and Watts' Pennsylvania Reports [*1829-32*] [*A publication*] (DLA)
P & W .... Pension and Welfare (WDMC)
P & W .... Post and Wire (ADA)
P & W .... Pratt & Whitney [*Aircraft*]
P & WA .... Pratt & Whitney Aircraft (KSC)
P & WV .... Pittsburgh & West Virginia Railroad
P&Z .... Planning and Zoning (PA)
PANE .... Performance Analysis of Networks, Electrical
PanEC........ Panhandle Eastern Corp. [*Associated Press*] (SAG)
Paneg .... Panegyricus [*of Isocrates*] [*Classical studies*] (OCD)
panendo ...... Panendoscopy [*Medicine*]

PANES .... Prior Active Navy Enlisted Service
PANES .... Program for Analysis of Nonlinear Equilibrium and Stability [*NASA*]
PANESS....... Physical and Neurologic Examination for Soft Signs (STED)
PANF .... Plan Account Number File [*IRS*]
PANFI .... Precision Automatic Noise Figure Indicator
PANFX........ Phoenix-Engemann Nifty Fifty Cl.A [*Mutual fund ticker symbol*] (SG)
PANGCS...... Prior Active National Guard Commissioned Service
PANGES...... Prior Active National Guard Enlisted Service
PANGIS........ Pan-African Network for a Geological Information System [*UNESCO*] (DUND)
PANGLOSS... Parallel Architecture for Networking Gateways Linking OSI Systems (NITA)
PANH .... Panhandling [*FBI standardized term*]
PANH .... Picolinaldehyde Nicotinoylhydrazone [*Reagent*]
PANHONLIB... Panama, Honduras, and Liberia [*Acronym used to refer to merchant ships operating under "flags of convenience"*]
PANI .... Patriarch Athenagoras National Institute (EA)
PANIC .... Planned Attack on Nine Inner Cities [*to build education parks*]
Panj C .... Panjab Code [*India*] [*A publication*] (DLA)
Pank Jur ..... Pankhurst's Jurisprudence [*A publication*] (DLA)
PAnL........... Lebanon Valley College, Annville, PA [*Library symbol Library of Congress*] (LCLS)
PANL .... Universal Display [*NASDAQ symbol*] (TTSB)
PANL .... Universal Display Corp. [*NASDAQ symbol*] (SAG)
PANLAR ...... PanAmerican League Against Rheumatism [*Canada*] (EAIO)
PANLIBHON... Panama, Liberia, and Honduras [*Acronym used to refer to merchant ships operating under "flags of convenience"*]
PANLIBHONCO... Panama-Liberia-Honduras-Costa Rica
PANLW .... Universal Display Wrrt [*NASDAQ symbol*] (TTSB)
PANMV .... Panicum Mosaic Virus [*Plant pathology*]
PANN .... Professional Association of Nursery Nurses [*British*] (DBA)
PAN NA....... Pesticides Action Network, North America (GNE)
PANNAP...... Panavia New Aircraft Project (MCD)
PANNA RC... Pesticide Action Network North America Regional Center (EA)
PANNDA ..... Precedent Analysis by Nearest Neighbor Discriminant Analysis
PANNR .... Previous Applicants Need Not Reapply [*Civil Service*]
PANOR........ Panoramic (IAA)
Panor .... Panormitanus [*Nicholas de Tudeschis*] [*Deceased, 1445*] [*Authority cited in pre-1607 legal work*] (DSA)
PANOS........ Panos Institute [*An association*] (EA)
PA NP......... Brightly's Pennsylvania Nisi Prius Reports [*A publication*] (DLA)
PANPA........ Pacific Area Newspaper Publishers Association (EAIO)
PANPRA...... Parti Nationaliste Progressiste Revolutionnaire [*Haiti*] [*Political party*] (EY)
PANPUB...... Panel Publishers (DLA)
PANR .... Panhandle Royalty Co. [*NASDAQ symbol*] (SAG)
PANRA........ Panhandle Rty [*NASDAQ symbol*] (TTSB)
PanRoyl...... Panhandle Royalty Co. [*Associated Press*] (SAG)
PANS .... Pest Articles News Summaries [*Commonwealth Mycological Institute*] [*Kew, England*] [*A publication*]
PANS .... Positioning and Navigation System
PANS .... Pretty Amazing New Services (NITA)
PANS .... Priority Admission to Nursery Schools (AIE)
PANS .... Procedures for Air Navigation Services [*ICAO*]
PANS .... Programmable Augmented Noise Source [*Military*] (CAAL)
PANS .... Puromycin Aminonucleoside [*Biochemistry*]
PANSDOC .... Pakistan National Scientific and Documentation Center [*Later, PASTIC*]
PANSDOC .... Pakistan National Scientific and Technology Documentation Centre (NITA)
PANSEAFRON... Panama Sea Frontier
PANSMET .... Procedures for Air Navigation Services - Meteorology (IEEE)
PANSS........ Positive and Negative Syndrome Scale [*Medicine*] (DMAA)
PANSW .... Playgroup Association of New South Wales [*Australia*]
PANSW .... Police Association of New South Wales [*Australia*]
PANSY........ Program Analysis System (PDAA)
PANT .... Annette Island [*Alaska*] [*ICAO location identifier*] (ICLI)
PANT .... Pantex Plant [*Department of Energy*] [*Amarillo, TX*] (GAAI)
PANT .... Pantograph (KSC)
pant .... Pantomine
PANT .... Police Association of the Northern Territory [*Australia*]
Pantch .... Panatech Research & Development Corp. [*Associated Press*] (SAG)
Pantex .... Pantex Site
Pantex EIS... Pantex Site Environmental Impact Statement
PANTHEON... Public Access by New Technology to Highly Elaborate Online Networks [*Computer science*] (PDAA)
PANTIES ...... Passive Automatic Nighttime Tracking Investigation and Evaluation Studies [*DoD*]
PAntin........ [*The*] Antinoe Papyrus of Theocritus [*Classical studies*] (OCD)
PAntinoop.... Antinoopolis Papyri [*A publication*] (OCD)
PantiP......... Peroxidase-Antiperoxidase [*Immunochemistry*]
PANTO........ Pantomime
panto.......... Pantomime [*British*] [*Slang*] (WDMC)
pantrop....... Pantropical [*Botany*]
PANTS .... Pantaloons (DSUE)
PANX .... Panax Pharmaceutical [*NASDAQ symbol*] (TTSB)
PANX .... Panax Pharmaceutical Company Ltd. [*NASDAQ symbol*] (SAG)
PANXU .... Panax Pharmaceutical Unit [*NASDAQ symbol*] (TTSB)
PANXW .... Panax Pharmaceutical Wrrt [*NASDAQ symbol*] (TTSB)
PANY .... Platinumsmiths Association of New York (EA)
PANY .... Port Authority of New York [*Later, PANYNJ*]
PANYNJ...... Port Authority of New York and New Jersey [*Formerly, PANY*]
Pao .... Ascending Aortic Pressure [*Medicine*] (STED)
PAO .... Palo Alto, CA [*Location identifier FAA*] (FAAL)

PAO .... Paotow [*Republic of China*] [*Seismograph station code, US Geological Survey*] (SEIS)
PAO .... Paragon Group [*NYSE symbol*] (TTSB)
PAO .... Paragon Group, Inc. [*NYSE symbol*] (SAG)
PAO .... Paramount Resources, Inc. [*Vancouver Stock Exchange symbol*]
PaO .... Paranoia Obvious [*Psychology*]
PAO .... Parts Assembly Order (IAA)
PAO .... Peacetime Acquisition Objective [*DoD*] (AFIT)
PAO .... Peak Acid Output [*Physiology*]
PAO .... Penalty Appeals Officer [*IRS*]
PA/O .... Performing Arts/Omaha [*Nebraska*]
PAO .... Peripheral Airway Obstruction [*Medicine*] (DMAA)
PAO .... Phenylarsine Oxide
PAO .... Pinellas Area Office [*Energy Research and Development Administration*]
PAO .... Plasma Amine Oxidase [*Hematology*] (DMAA)
PAO .... Polyalkyleneoxide [*Organic chemistry*]
PAO .... Polyalphaolefin [*Organic chemistry*]
PAO .... Polyamine Oxidase (STED)
PAO .... Polynesian Airline Operations Ltd. [*Western Samoa*] [*ICAO designator*] (FAAC)
PAO .... Primary Action Office [*or Officer*] [*Army*]
PAO .... Prince Albert's Own [*Military unit*] [*British*]
PAO .... Principal Administrative Officer
PAO .... Pro Athletes Outreach (EA)
PAO .... Procurement Assistance Office (AAGC)
PAO .... Product Activity/Operational Code (MCD)
PAO .... Product Assurance Operations [*Army*]
PAO .... Program Action Officer [*Navy*] (CAAL)
PAO .... Project Action Officer [*Air Force*] (AFIT)
PAO .... Project Administration Officer [*Military*] (AFIT)
PAO .... Property Action Order
PAO .... Public Affairs Office [*NASA*]
PAO .... Public Affairs Officer [*Embassies*]
PAO .... Pulmonary Artery Occlusion [*Medicine*] (DMAA)
PAO .... Pulsed Avalanche Diode Oscillator [*Telecommunications*] (IEEE)
PAO .... Pustulotic Arthroosteitis [*Medicine*] (DMAA)
PAO2 .... Alveolar Oxygen Pressure (WDAA)
PAO2 .... Arterial Oxygen Pressure (WDAA)
PaO₂ .... Arterial Partial Pressure of Oxygen [*Medicine*] (DAVI)
pAO₂ .... Oxygen Pressure on Room Air [*Medicine*] (DAVI)
PAOA .... Pan American Odontological Association (EA)
PAOC .... Pakistan Army Ordnance Corps [*British military*] (DMA)
PAOC .... Pan-African Ornithological Congress
PAOC .... Pentacostal Assemblies of Canada
PAOC .... Pollution Abatement Operations Center (MCD)
PAOC .... Principal Administrative Officers Committee [*Chiefs of Staff*] [*World War II*]
PAOD .... Peripheral Arteriosclerotic Occlusive Disease [*Medicine*] (MAE)
P/AOEA2 ..... Probationary Ordnance Electrical Artificer, Acting, 2nd Class [*British military*] (DMA)
PA of W ...... Pentecostal Assemblies of the World (EA)
PAOI .... Peak Acid Output Insulin-Induced (STED)
PAOL .... Poly-alpha-olefin [*Organic chemistry*]
PAOM .... Nome [*Alaska*] [*ICAO location identifier*] (ICLI)
PAOP .... Pulmonary Artery Occlusion Pressure [*Cardiology*]
PAOR .... Northway [*Alaska*] [*ICAO location identifier*] (ICLI)
PAOT .... Kotzebue [*Alaska*] [*ICAO location identifier*] (ICLI)
PAOT .... Persons at One Time
PAP .... Asia Pulp & Paper ADS [*NYSE symbol*] (TTSB)
PAP .... Asia Pulp and Paper Co. Ltd. [*NYSE symbol*] (SAG)
PAP .... Langtry Flying Group Ltd. [*British*] [*FAA designator*] (FAAC)
PAP .... Pacific Automation Products (IAA)
P/AP .... Painter/Apprentice Painter (AAG)
PAP .... Pancreatitis-Associated Protein [*Medicine*] (DMAA)
PAP .... Papain [*An enzyme*]
PAP .... Papanicolaou [*Diagnosis, smear, stain, or test*] [*Medicine*]
PAP .... Paper (DSUE)
PAP .... Paper Bound [*Books*] (ROG)
pap .... Papilla [*Medicine*]
Pap .... Papua [*New Guinea*] (BARN)
pap .... Papyrus (VRA)
Pap .... Papyrus (BJA)
PAP .... Para-Aminophenol [*Organic chemistry*]
PAP .... Parallel Applications Programme [*British*]
PAP .... Participatory Anthropic Principle [*Term coined by authors John Barrow and Frank Tipler in their book, "The Anthropic Cosmological Principle"*]
PAP .... Parti d'Action Paysanne [*Farmers Actions Party*] [*Burkina Faso*] [*Political party*]
PAP .... Partido Accion Popular [*Popular Action Party*] [*Ecuador*] [*Political party*]
PAP .... Partido Accion Popular [*Popular Action Party*] [*Peru*] [*Political party*]
PAP .... Password Authentication Protocol [*Computer science*] (PCM)
PAP .... Patient Assesment Program [*Medicine*] (DMAA)
PAP .... Patrol Amphibian Plane
PAP .... Paulin [*H.*] & Co. Ltd. [*Toronto Stock Exchange symbol*]
PAP .... Payload Activity Planner [*NASA*]
PAP .... Peak Airway Pressure [*Physiology*]
PAP .... Pension Administration Plan [*Insurance*]
PAP .... Pentyl-alpha-pyrone [*Organic chemistry*]
PAP .... People's Action Party [*Singapore*] [*Political party*] (PPW)
PAP .... People's Action Party [*Malaya*] [*Political party*]
PAP .... People's Action Party [*Papua New Guinea*] [*Political party*] (EY)
PAP .... People's Alliance Party [*Solomon Islands*] [*Political party*] (PPW)

PAP .... Periphery Access Processor [*Computer science*] (IAA)
PAP .... Peroxidase-Antibody to Peroxidase (DB)
PAP .... Peroxidase-Antiperoxidase [*Immunochemistry*]
PAP .... Personal Auto Policy [*Insurance*]
PAP .... Personnel Allocation Plan [*Navy*]
PAP .... Personnel Assistance Point [*Army*] (AABC)
PAP .... Phase Advance Pulse
PAP .... Phenolphthalein in Paraffin [*Emulsion*]
PAP .... Phenyl Acid Phosphate [*Organic chemistry*]
PAP .... Philippine Aid Plan
PAP .... Phosphoadenosine Phosphate [*Biochemistry*]
PAP .... Photodiode Array Processing (MCD)
PAP .... Photonic Array Processor [*Device for manipulating light beams in an optical computer*]
PAP .... Physics and Astronomy Programs [*NASA*]
PAP .... Phytolacca Americana Protein (DB)
PAP .... Pierced Aluminum Plank [*Technical drawings*]
PAP .... Pilotless Aircraft Program (NG)
PAP .... Placental Alkaline Phosphatase (DB)
PAP .... Plant Air Package (IAA)
PAP .... Platelet Aggregation Profiler [*Hematology*]
PAP .... Platelet Alkaline Phosphatase [*An enzyme*]
P a P .... Poco a Poco [*Little by Little*] [*Music*]
PAP .... Pokeweed Antiviral Protein [*Immunochemistry*]
PAP .... Political Asylum Project [*Defunct*] (EA)
PAP .... Politiki Aneksartitos Parataksis [*Independent Political Front*] [*Greek Political party*] (PPE)
PAP .... Polska Agencja Prasowa [*Polish Press Agency*]
PAP .... Poly(acryloylpyrrolidine) [*Organic chemistry*]
PAP .... Poly-a-polymerase [*An enzyme*]
PAP .... Port-Au-Prince [*Haiti*] [*Airport symbol*] (OAG)
PAP .... Positive Airway Pressure (MAE)
PAP .... Prearranged Payments [*Business term*]
pAP .... Presynaptic Action Potential [*Neurochemistry*]
PAP .... Primary Atypical Pneumonia [*Medicine*]
PAP .... Printer Access Protocol (BYTE)
PAP .... Prison-Ashram Project (EA)
PAP .... Procurement and Production (AFIT)
PAP .... Product Assurance Plan [*Army*] (AABC)
PAP .... Production Allocation Program
PAP .... Project Aerospace Plane (AAG)
PAP .... Projected Average Progress (NG)
PAP .... Prostatic Acid Phosphatase [*An enzyme*]
PAP .... Proton Attenuation Procedure
PAP .... Public Affairs Program [*of the American Friends Service Committee*] (EA)
PAP .... Public Assistance Program
PAP .... Public Awareness Program
PAP .... Pulmonary Alveolar Proteinosis [*Medicine*]
PAP .... Pulmonary Arterial [*or Artery*] Pressure [*Medicine*]
PAP .... Purple Acid Phosphatase [*An enzyme*]
PAPA .... Back Bay Restaurant Group, Inc. [*NASDAQ symbol*] (SAG)
PAPA .... Back Bay Restaurant Grp [*NASDAQ symbol*] (TTSB)
PAPA .... Parallax Aircraft Parking Aid (PDAA)
PAPA .... Philippines Alien Property Administration
PAPA .... Pizza and Pasta Association [*British*] (DBA)
PAPA .... Pollution Abatement and Prevention Analysis [*Environmental science*] (RCP)
PAPA .... Polyazelaic Polyanhydride (EDCT)
PAPA .... Probabilistic Automatic Pattern Analyzer [*Computer science*]
PAPA .... Programmer and Probability Analyzer [*Computer science*] (IEEE)
PAPA .... Psychiatrists Against Psychiatric Abuse [*Canada*] (EAIO)
PapaJohn ...... Papa Johns International, Inc. [*Associated Press*] (SAG)
Pap & Disc Vic Inst Eng... Papers and Discussions. Victorian Institute of Engineers [*Australia A publication*]
Pap & Proc Roy Soc Tas... Papers and Proceedings. Royal Society of Tasmania [*A publication*]
PAPAS .... Pin and Pellet Assay System [*Nuclear energy*] (NRCH)
PAPAV .... Papaver Poppy [*Botany*] (ROG)
PAPB .... Point Barrow [*Alaska*] [*ICAO location identifier*] (ICLI)
PAPC .... Processed Apple and Pear Committee [*Victoria, Austrial*]
PAPCA .... Pan-American Progressive Consumers Alliance [*Later, NPCA*] (EA)
PAPCAPS..... Publicly Available Price Cap Agreements (AAGC)
PapclS .... Paperclip Imaging Software, Inc. [*Associated Press*] (SAG)
PAPCNY...... Portuguese American Progressive Club of New York (EA)
PAPE .... Photoactive Pigment Electrophotography (IEEE)
PAPER .... Prairie Association of Publishers Education Representatives [*Canada*]
PAPERCHEM... Paper Chemistry [*Institute of Paper Chemistry*] [*Appleton, WI Bibliographic database*]
PAPERMAN... Payroll and Accounting, Personnel Management, Manpower Utilization [*Air Force*]
PAPF .... Platelet Adhesiveness Plasma [*Hematology*] (DMAA)
PAPH .... (Pyridinealdehyde)pyridylhydrazone [*Organic chemistry*]
Papi .... Papi [*Aemilius*] Papinianus [*Deceased, 212*] [*Authority cited in pre-1607 legal work*] (DSA)
Papi .... Papirius Justus [*Flourished, 2nd century*] [*Authority cited in pre-1607 legal work*] (DSA)
PAPI .... Polymethylene Polyphenyl Isocyanate (EDCT)
PAPI .... Precision Approach Path Indicator [*FAA*] (TAG)
PAPI .... Professional Association of Pet Industries (EA)
PapJohn ...... Papa Johns International, Inc. [*Associated Press*] (SAG)
PaPL .... Pennsylvania Power & Light Co. [*Associated Press*] (SAG)
PAPL .... Preliminary Allowance Parts List [*Military*] (CAAL)

PaPL............ W. and F. Pascoe Proprietory Ltd., Milsons Point, NSW, Australia [*Library symbol*] [*Library of Congress*] (LCLS)
PAPM.......... Passed Assistant Paymaster [*British*]
PAPM.......... Port Moller Air Force Station [*Alaska*] [*ICAO location identifier*] (ICLI)
PAPM.......... Pulse Amplitude and Phase Modulation (PDAA)
PAPMOP...... Product Assurance Program Management Operations Plan (MCD)
PAPMV........ Papaya Mosaic Virus [*Plant pathology*]
Papo .... Partido de Accion Popular [*Popular Action Party*] [*Panama*] [*Political party*] (PPW)
PAPOC........ Parents' Alliance to Protect Our Children (EA)
PAPOILA..... Pacis Amico, Persecutionis Osore, Joanne Lockio Anglo [*Pseudonym used by John Locke*]
PAPOVA...... Papilloma Virus, Polyoma Virus, Vacuolating Virus
PAPP .... Pappenheimer Bodies [*Hematology*] (DAVI)
PAPP .... Para-Aminopropiophenone [*Pharmacology*]
PAPP .... Parametric Aircraft Performance Program (MCD)
PAPP .... Pregnancy-Associated Plasma Protein
PAPP .... Pull and Push Plate (IAA)
PAPPA .... Pulp and Paper Prepackaging Association [*Later, SSI*] (EA)
PAPPGM...... Preliminary Army Planning and Program Guidance Memorandum (MCD)
PAPR .... Powered Air Purifying Respirator (ERG)
PA Prac ...... Standard Pennsylvania Practice [*A publication*] (DLA)
PAPRICAN ... Pulp and Paper Research Institute of Canada [*McGill University*] [*Research center*] (RCD)
Paps .... Papillomas [*Medicine*] (DMAA)
PAPS .... Performance Analysis and Prediction Study (PDAA)
PAPS .... Periodic Acid-Schiff with Phenylhydrazine Interposition [*A stain*]
PAPS .... Periodic Armaments Planning System (MCD)
PAPS .... Periodic Arrays of Pinning Sites [*Solid state physics*]
PAPS .... Permissive Arming and Protection System [*AEC*]
PAPS .... Phosphoadenosine Diphosphosulfate [*Phosphoadenosyl-Phosphosulfate*] [*Biochemistry*] (DAVI)
PAPS .... Phosphoadenosine Phosphosulfate [*Also, APPS*] [*Biochemistry*]
PAPS .... Phosphoadenylyl Sulfate [*Biochemistry*]
PAPS .... Procurement and Production Status System
PAPS .... Public Assistance Processing System
PA/PS .... Pulmonary Atresia/Pulmonary Stenosis [*Cardiology*] (DAVI)
PAPSB .... Patent Attorneys' Professional Standards Body [*Australia*]
PA PSC ...... Pennsylvania Public Service Commission Annual Report [*A publication*] (DLA)
PA PSC Dec... Pennsylvania Public Service Commission Decisions [*A publication*] (DLA)
PAPSI .... Pregnancy-Associated Prostaglandin Synthetase Inhibitor [*Endocrinology*]
PAPT............ Palladium Print (VRA)
PAPTC .... Pakistan Army Physical Training Corps [*British military*] (DMA)
PAPTC .... Paper Tape Controller (NITA)
PAPTE......... President's Advisory Panel on Timber and the Environment
PAPUFA ...... Physiologically Active Polyunsaturated Fatty Acid [*Nutrition*]
Pa-Pv.......... Pulmonary Arterial Pressure-Pulmonary Venous Pressure [*Medicine*] (STED)
PAPVC .... Partial Anomalous Pulmonary Venous Connection (MAE)
PAPVR........ Partial Anomalous Pulmonary Venous Return
PAPW .... Papworth [*England*]
PAPW .... Posterior Aspect of the Pharyngeal Wall [*Medicine*] (STED)
Papy .... Papy's Reports [*5-8 Florida*] [*A publication*] (DLA)
PAQ .... Palmer, AK [*Location identifier FAA*] (FAAL)
PAQ .... Partially Allocated Quotas [*Ocean fishery management*]
PAQ .... Personal Attributes Questionnaire
PAQ .... Port Authorities Queensland [*Australia*]
PAQ .... Position Analysis Questionnaire
PAQ .... Preliminary Allowance Quantity [*Military*] (CAAL)
PAQ .... Process Average Quality
PAQAB .... President's Air Quality Advisory Board [*Environmental Protection Agency*]
PAQR .... Polyacenequinone Radical [*Organic chemistry*]
PAQS .... Pacific Association of Quantity Surveyors [*Australia*]
PAR .... Coastcast Corp. [*NYSE symbol*] (SPSG)
Par .... Guiraudus Pargues [*Authority cited in pre-1607 legal work*] (DSA)
PAR .... Pacific-Antarctic Ridge [*Geology*]
PAR .... Page Address Register
PAR .... Panama Canal Commission Acquisition Regulation (AAGC)
PAR .... Parabolic Aluminized Reflector [*Lamp*]
PAR .... Paracel Islands [*ANSI three-letter standard code*] (CNC)
PAR .... Parachute
PAR .... Paraffin (STED)
par .... Paraffin [*Chemistry*] (DAVI)
PAR .... Paragon Resources Ltd. [*Vancouver Stock Exchange symbol*]
PAR .... Paragraph (AAG)
par .... Paragraph (WDMC)
Par.............. Paraguay
Par.............. Parah (BJA)
PAR .... Paralipomenon [*Old Testament book*] [*Douay version*]
PAR .... Parallax
PAR .... Parallax and Refraction (IAA)
PAR .... Parallel (KSC)
par .... Parallel (WDMC)
PAR .... Parallelogram [*Geometry*] (ADA)
PAR .... Parameter
PAR .... Parametric Amplifier
Par.............. Paranoid [*Psychiatry*] (DAVI)
PAR .... Paraphrase (ADA)
PAR .... Parcel
PAR .... Parenthesis

par.............. Parenthesis (WDMC)
Par.............. Parents Magazine [*A publication*] (BRI)
PAR .... Paris [*France*] [*Airport symbol*] (OAG)
PAR .... Parish
PAR .... Paris - Parc St. Maur [*France*] [*Seismograph station code, US Geological Survey*] (SEIS)
PAR .... Parity (ADA)
Par.............. Parker's English Exchequer Reports [*A publication*] (DLA)
Par.............. Parker's New York Criminal Reports [*A publication*] (DLA)
PAR .... Parochial
PAR .... Parole Assessment Report (WDAA)
PAR .... Parole Services for Adults [*Public human service program*] (PHSD)
Par.............. Parsons' Reports [*65-66 New Hampshire*] [*A publication*] (DLA)
par.............. Part (BARN)
PAR .... Partheite [*A zeolite*]
PAR .... Participating [*Health insurance*] (GHCT)
Par.............. Participating Provider [*Insurance*]
PAR .... Participating Provider [*Health insurance*] (DMAA)
PAR .... Participation-Achievement-Reward (PDAA)
PAR .... Partido Aragones Regionalista [*Aragonese Regional Party*] [*Spain Political party*] (PPW)
PAR .... Partito Anti-Reformista [*Anti-Reform Party*] [*Malta*] [*Political party*] (PPE)
PAR .... Parts Approval Request (MCD)
PAR .... Passive Avoidance Reaction [*Medicine*] (DMAA)
PAR .... Payload Adapter Ring
PAR .... [*The*] Payment Analysis Report [*Dun & Bradstreet Credit Services*] [*Information service or system*] (CRD)
PAR .... Peacetime Airborne Reconnaissance (AFM)
PAR .... Peak Accelerometer Recorder (IEEE)
PAR .... Peak Area Ratio [*Chromatographic analysis*]
PAR .... Peak-to-Average Ratio [*Telecommunications*]
PAR .... Pennsylvania Advanced Reactor
PAR .... People Against Racism [*Civil rights organization*]
PAR .... People Against Rape (EA)
PAR .... Per Acre Rental (WDAA)
PAR .... Perennial Allergic Rhinitis [*Medicine*]
PAR .... Performance Analysis and Review
PAR .... Performance Analysis Routine [*Computer science*]
PAR .... Performance Appraisal Report [*Nuclear energy*] (NRCH)
PAR .... Performance Assessment Report [*Small Cities Community Development Block Grant*] [*Department of Housing and Urban Development*] (GFGA)
PAR .... Performance Augmentation Ring (MCD)
PAR .... Perimeter Acquisition RADAR [*Army*]
PAR .... Perimeter Array RADAR (MCD)
PAR .... Personnel Activity Report [*Office of Management and Budget*]
PAR .... Personnel Activity Request
PAR .... Personnel Advancement Requirement [*Navy*] (NVT)
PAR .... PERT [*Program Evaluation and Review Technique*] Analysis Report (KSC)
PAR .... Phased Array RADAR
PAR .... Phosphoric Acid-Resistant
PAR .... Photosynthetically Active Radiation
PAR .... Photosynthetically Active Range
PAR .... Physical Activity Ratio (WDAA)
PAR .... Physiological Aging Rate
PAR .... Pilot Action Request
PAR .... Plain Abdominal Radiograph [*Medicine*] (DMAA)
PAR .... Planed All Round (DAC)
PAR .... Planning Action Request [*NASA*] (MCD)
PAR .... Planning Activity Report
PAR .... Platelet Aggregate Ratio [*Hematology*]
PAR .... Police Accident Report [*NHTSA*] (TAG)
PAR .... Pollen Accumulation Rate [*Botany*]
PAr.............. Polyarteritis (STED)
PAR .... Polyarylate [*Resin*]
PAR .... Population at Risk (FFDE)
PAR .... Positive Acknowledgment and Retransmission [*Telecommunications*] (IAA)
PAR .... Positive Attitudinal Reinforcement [*In George Lee Walker novel "The Chronicles of Doodah"*]
PAR .... Post Adjudicative Review [*Social Security Administration*] (OICC)
PAR .... Postanesthesia [*or Postanesthetic*] Room [*Medicine*]
PAR .... Postanesthetic Recovery [*Medicine*]
PAR .... Post Attach Requirements (AAG)
PAR .... Potassium-Adsorption-Ratio
PAR .... Power Analysis Report [*Automobile testing*]
PAR .... Preadmission Review (WYGK)
PAR .... Precedent, Action, and Result
PAR .... Precision Aerotech (EFIS)
PAR .... Precision Aircraft Reference
PAR .... Precision Approach RADAR [*Aviation*]
PAR .... Preferential Arrival Route [*Aviation*] (DA)
PAR .... Preparedness Assessment Report [*Environmental science*] (COE)
PAR .... Price-Adjusted Rate Preferred [*Investment term*] (MHDW)
PAR .... Prime Assets Ratio
PAR .... Princeton Applied Research Corp. [*Princeton University*]
PAR .... Print Area Reader (DGA)
PAR .... Priority Action Report (AAG)
PAR .... Priority Action Request (AAG)
PAR .... Probabilistic Analysis of Risk (KSC)
PAR .... Probable Allergic Rhinitis [*Medicine*] (DAVI)
PAR .... Problem Accountability Record (NASA)
PAR .... Problem Action Record (KSC)

PAR .... Problem Action Request (NASA)
PAR .... Problem Analysis and Resolution
PAR .... Problem Analysis and Response Program (IAA)
PAR .... Problem Analysis Report (MCD)
PAR .... Process Action Request
PAR .... Product Acceptance & Research [Commercial firm] (WDMC)
PAR .... Product Acceptance Review (NASA)
PAR .... Production Acceptance Review
PAR .... Production Action Request (MCD)
PAR .... Production Analysis Report
PAR .... Production, Augmentation, and Reliability (NG)
PAR .... Production Automated Riveting
PAR .... Product of Antigenic Recognition [Immunochemistry]
PAR .... Professional Abstracts Registries [Database Innovations, Inc.]
PAR .... Profile of Average Reflectivity
PAR .... Program Action Request (SSD)
PAR .... Program Activity Recording [Computer science] (IAA)
PAR .... Program Address Register
PAR .... Program Adjustment Request [Navy]
PAR .... Program Administrator's [Progress] Report [DoD]
PAR .... Program-Aid Routine [Computer science]
PAR .... Program Allocation and Reimbursements (AFIT)
PAR .... Program Analysis and Review
PAR .... Program Appraisal and Review (IEEE)
PAR .... Program Appraisal Report
PAR .... Program Assessment Report [or Review] (MCD)
PAR .... Program Audience Rating
PAR .... Program for Alcohol Recovery
PAR .... Progressive Aircraft Repair [or Rework]
PAR .... Project Audit Report
PAR .... Project Authorization Request (IAA)
PAR .... Projected Automation Requirement
PAR .... Proposal Analysis Report (AAGC)
PAR .... Propulsion and Aeroballistics Research (SAA)
PAR .... Protease-Activated Receptor [Hematology]
PAR .... Protective Action Recommendation (COE)
PAR .... Proximal Alveolar Region [Medicine] (DMAA)
PAR .... Pseudoautosomal Region [Genetics]
PAR .... Psychological Assessment Resources, Inc. (DHP)
PAR .... Public Administration Review [A publication] (BRI)
PAR .... Public Affairs Research Council [Research center] (RCD)
PAR .... Publication Analysis Report (SAA)
PAR .... Pulmonary Arteriolar Resistance [Medicine] (MAE)
PAR .... Pulse Acquisition RADAR [Military] (NG)
PAR .... Purchasing Approval Request (NRCH)
PAR .... Push and Release [Push button]
PAR .... (Pyridylazo)resorcinol [Organic chemistry]
PAR .... Spair [Russian Federation] [ICAO designator] (FAAC)
PARA .... Parabolic (IAA)
para .... Paracentesis [Medicine] (MAF)
PARA .... Parachute
PARA .... Paragraph (AFM)
PARA .... Paraguay
PARA .... Parallel (WDAA)
PARA .... Paramount Financial [NASDAQ symbol] (TTSB)
PARA .... Paramount Financial Corp. [NASDAQ symbol] (SAG)
para .... Paraphrase (BARN)
para .... Paraplegic
para .... Parathy Roidectomy [Medicine] (DMAA)
para .... Parity [Gynecology and obstetrics] (DAVI)
para .... Parquet (BARN)
PARA .... Particle Aiding Replication of Adenovirus [Virology]
PARA .... Policy Analysis and Resource Allocation [Department of State]
PARA .... Polyarylamid [Organic chemistry]
PARA .... Problem Analysis and Recommended Action (IAA)
PARA .... Professional Audiovideo Retailers Association (EA)
Para 1 .... Unipara [Having borne one child] [Gynecology and obstetrics] (DAVI)
Para-A .... Paratyphoid A [Medicine] (DAVI)
PARAB .... Parabola [Mathematics] (IAA)
Para-B .... Paratyphoid B [Medicine] (DAVI)
PARABAT ...... Parachute Battalion [Army]
PARABOL ...... Parabolic (IAA)
Para-C .... Paratyphoid C [Medicine] (DAVI)
Paracels .... Paracelsus Healthcare Corp. [Associated Press] (SAG)
paracent .... Paracentesis [Medicine]
PARACOMPT... Parameter Analysis of Respiration Agents Considering Operations Motivation Protection and Time Model (MCD)
PARACS ...... Perimeter Acquisition RADAR Attack Characterization System (MCD)
PARADA ...... Preparatory Academy for the Royal Academy of Dramatic Art [British] (BI)
PARADE ...... Passive-Active Range Determination
Paradl ...... Paradise, Inc. [Associated Press] (SAG)
PARADISE... Phased Array RADAR and Divers Integrated Semiconductor Elements (PDAA)
Par Adm ...... Parsons on the Law of Shipping and Admiralty [A publication] (DLA)
PARADROP... Airdrop by Parachute
PAR AFF ...... Pars Affecta [The Part Affected] [Pharmacy]
PARAFRAG... Parachute Fragmentation Bomb [Air Force]
PARAG ...... Paraguay [or Paraguayan] (WDAA)
ParagGg ...... Paragon Group, Inc. [Associated Press] (SAG)
ParagGp ...... Paragon Group, Inc. [Associated Press] (SAG)
ParagTr ...... Paragon Trade Brands [Associated Press] (SAG)
Para II .... Bipara [Having borne two children] [Gynecology and Obstetrics] (DAVI)

Para III .... Tripara [having borne three children] [Gynecology and obstetrics] (DAVI)
PARAKU ...... Pasokan Rakyat Kalimantan Utara [North Kalimantan People's Forces] [Malaya]
PARAM .... Parameter (KSC)
ParaMed ...... Paradigm Medical Industries, Inc. [Associated Press] (SAG)
Parameters... Parameters: US Army War College Quarterly [A publication] (BRI)
PARAMI ...... Parsons Active Ring-Around Miss Indicator
PARAMIS ..... Parsons Passive Miss Distance Indicating System (SAA)
Par Am Law... Parsons' Commentaries on American Law [A publication] (DLA)
Par Am Law Comm... Parsons' Commentaries on American Law [A publication] (DLA)
Paramnt .... Paramount Financial Corp. [Associated Press] (SAG)
PARAMP ...... Parametric Amplifier
ParamrkE ...... Paramark Enterprises, Inc. [Associated Press] (SAG)
Paramt .... Paramount Financial Corp. [Associated Press] (SAG)
PARAN .... Perimeter Array Antenna (PDAA)
Par & Fonb Med Jur... Paris and Fonblanque's Medical Jurisprudence [A publication] (DLA)
Par Ant .... Parochial Antiquities [A publication] (DLA)
PARAPSYCH... Parapsychology
PARAQUAD... Paraplegic and Quadriplegic Association of New South Wales [Australia]
PARARESCUE... Rescue by Individuals Parachuted to Distressed Persons [Air Force]
PARAS .... Parasitic (IAA)
PARASEV ..... Paraglider Research Vehicle [NASA]
parasit .... Parasitology [Medicine] (DMAA)
PARASITOL... Parasitology
parasym .... Parasympathetic [Division of autonomic nervous system] [Neurolgoy] (DAVI)
parasym div... Parasympathetic Division [of autonomic nervous system] [Neurology] (DAVI)
PARASYN .... Parametric Synthesis [Computer science]
PARATHORMONE... Parathyroid Hormone [Endocrinology]
PARATROOPS... Parachute Infantry [Military]
para VIII ...... Octipara [Having borne eight children] [Gynecology and obstetrics] (DAVI)
Paravnt .... Paravant Computer Systems, Inc. [Associated Press] (SAG)
PARAW .... Paramount Financial Wrrt [NASDAQ symbol] (TTSB)
PARB .... Perimeter Acquisition RADAR Building [Army] (AABC)
PARB .... Public Accountants Registration Board [Australia]
PARBICA ...... Pacific Regional Branch of the International Council on Archives (EAIO)
Par Bills & N... Parsons on Bills and Notes [A publication] (DLA)
PARC .... Pacific Air Rescue Center [or Command] (CINC)
PARC .... Pacific-Asia Resources Center [Japan] (EAIO)
PARC .... Palo Alto Research Center [Xerox Corp.]
PARC .... Pan-African Resource Center (EA)
PARC .... Pan-African Rinderpest Campaign [Organization of African Unity]
PARC .... Parcelas
parc .... Parchment (VHA)
PARC .... Pennsylvania Association for Retarded Children (EDAC)
PARC .... Pericardial Fluid [Cardiology] (DAVI)
PARC .... Periodic Aircraft Reconditioning Cycle (DNAB)
PARC .... Predator and Rodent Control [US Fish and Wildlife Service] (IIA)
PARC .... President's Appalachian Regional Commission
PARC .... Princeton Applied Research Corp.
PARC .... Principal Assistant Responsible for Contracting [Army]
PARC .... Profile Analysis and Recording Control (PDAA)
PARC .... Progressive Aircraft Reconditioning [or Repair] Cycle
PARCA .... Pan American Railway Congress Association
PARCA .... Patient Access to Responsible Care Act
PARCH .... Parchment (ADA)
Par Ch .... Parents' Choice [A publication]
PARCHM .... Parchment (ROG)
PARCHT ...... Parchment
PaRCL .... Parsec Research Control Language [Pronounced "parkul"] [Parsec Reseach Robotics]
Parcls .... Paracelsian, Inc. [Associated Press] (SAG)
Parclsn .... Paracelsian, Inc. [Associated Press] (SAG)
PARCOM .... Paris Commission [See also CP] (EAIO)
Par Cont .... Parsons on Contracts [A publication] (DLA)
Par Costs.... Parsons on Costs [A publication] (DLA)
PARCP .... PEMARS [Procurement of Equipment and Missiles, Army Management and AccountingReporting System] Accounting and Reporting Control Point [Army]
ParcPplce ...... Parcplace Systems, Inc. [Associated Press] (SAG)
PARCS .... Perimeter Acquisition RADAR Attack Characterization System [Army]
PARCS .... Pesticide Analysis Retrieval and Control System (NITA)
PARD .... Parts Application Reliability Data (IEEE)
PARD .... Periodic and Random Deviation
PARD .... Personnel Actions and Records Directorate [Military Personnel Center] (AABC)
PARD .... Pilot Airborne Recovery Device [A balloon-parachute]
PARD .... Pilotless Aircraft Research Division [Later, Applied Materials and Physics Division] [Langley Research Center]
PARD .... Post-Accident Radioactivity Depletion [Nuclear energy] (NRCH)
PARD .... Precision Annotated Retrieval Display [System] [Computer science]
PARD .... Project Activities Relationship Diagram (PDAA)
PARD .... Protect as Restricted Data (COE)
PARDAC .... Parallel Digital-to-Analog Converter
Par Dec .... Parsons' Decisions [2-7 Massachusetts] [A publication] (DLA)
PARDENTL... Paradental
Pardgm .... Paradigm Technology, Inc. [Associated Press] (SAG)

Pard Lois Mar... Pardessus' Lois Maritimes [*A publication*] (DLA)

PARDON ...... Pastors' Anonymous Recovery-Directed Order for Newness [*Rehabilitation program for troubled clergymen*] [*Defunct*]

PARDOP .... Passive Ranging Doppler

PARDP .... Perimeter Acquisition RADAR Data Processor [*Army*] (AABC)

PARDS .... Phased Array RADAR Detection System (PDAA)

Pard Serv ...... Pardessus' Traites des Servitudes [*A publication*] (DLA)

PARE .... People Against Racism in Education

PARE .... Price Adjusted Rates of Exchange [*Monetary conversion rate*] (ECON)

PARE .... Program Analysis and Resouces Evaluation (IAA)

P/AREA .... Probationary Acting Radio Electrical Artificer [*British military*] (DMA)

PAREC .... Pay Record

PA Rec .... Pennsylvania Record [*A publication*] (DLA)

PAREN .... Parenthesis [*or Parentheses*] (AFM)

paren .... Parenthesis (WDMC)

PAREN .... Progressive Aircraft Engine Repair

PARENS ...... Parentheses (NTCM)

PARENT ...... Parenteral

PARENTS ..... People of America Responding to Educational Needs of Today's Society (EA)

Parents Cit Guide... Parents and Citizens Guide [*A publication*]

PARENTSQ.... Parent Squadron Base [*Military*] (NVT)

PA Rep .... Pennsylvania Reports [*A publication*] (DLA)

Par Eq Cas. .... Parsons' Select Equity Cases [*1842-51*] [*Pennsylvania*] [*A publication*] (DLA)

Par Eq Cases... Parsons' Select Equity Cases [*Pennsylvania*] [*A publication*] (DLA)

PARESEV ..... Paraglider Research Vehicle [*NASA*] (MCD)

Par Ess .... Parsons' Essays on Legal Topics [*A publication*] (DLA)

PARET .... Parallel Architecture Research and Evaluation Tool [*Computer science*]

PAREX .... Programmed Accounts Receivable Extra Service [*Computer science*]

Parexel .... Parexel International Corp. [*Associated Press*] (SAG)

PARF .... Paradise, Inc. [*NASDAQ symbol*] (SAG)

PARF .... Polymorphic Amplifiable Restriction (Endonuclease) Fragment [*Genetics*]

PARF .... Practical Allergy Research Foundation (EA)

PARFAS ...... Passive Radio Frequency Acquisition System

PARFR .... Program for Applied Research on Fertility Regulation [*Northwestern University*] [*Research center*]

PARG .... Polytechnic Academic Registrars' Group (AIE)

Pargs .... Guiraudus Pargues [*Authority cited in pre-1607 legal work*] (DSA)

PARGS .... Parks and Recreation Girls Service

PARI .... Parent Attitude Research Instrument [*A questionnaire*]

PARIET .... Parietal Cell Antibody [*Immunology*] (DAVI)

PARIF .... Program for Automation Retrieval Improvement by Feedback (NITA)

PARIS .... Passenger Routing and Information System [*FTA*] (TAG)

PARIS .... Persantin/Aspirin Reinfarction Study [*Medicine*] (DB)

PARIS .... Pictorial and Artifact Retrieval and Information System [*Canadian Heritage Information Network*] [*Information service or system*]

PARIS .... Planning Aid for Retail Information System [*IBM Corp.*]

PARIS .... Portable Automated Remote Inspection System [*Failure Analysis Associates*] (RDA)

PARIS .... Postal Address Reader Indexer System (PDAA)

PARIS .... Pour l'Amenagement et le Renouveau Institutionel et Social [*France Political party*]

PARIS .... Pulse Analysis-Recording Information System

ParisBu .... Paris Business Forms, Inc. [*Associated Press*] (SAG)

PARK .... Park [*Postal Service standard*] (OPSA)

PARK .... Parkerized [*Metallurgy*] [*Tradename*]

Park .... Parker's English Exchequer Reports [*1743-67*] [*A publication*] (DLA)

Park .... Parker's New Hampshire Reports [*A publication*] (DLA)

Park .... Parker's New York Criminal Cases [*1823-68*] [*A publication*] (DLA)

PARK .... Parking

PARK .... Premier Parks [*NASDAQ symbol*] (TTSB)

PARK .... Premier Parks, Inc. [*NASDAQ symbol*] (SAG)

PARKA .... Pacific Acoustic Research Kaneohe-Alaska [*Navy*]

Park Arb ...... Parker on Arbitration [*1820*] [*A publication*] (DLA)

Park Ch. ...... Parker's Practice in Chancery [*A publication*] (DLA)

Park CR .... Parker's New York Criminal Reports [*A publication*] (DLA)

Park Cr Cas... Parker's New York Criminal Cases [*A publication*] (DLA)

Park Crim L... Parker's New York Criminal Reports [*A publication*] (DLA)

Park Crim (NY)... Parker's New York Criminal Cases [*A publication*] (DLA)

Park Crim R... Parker's New York Criminal Reports [*A publication*] (DLA)

Park Crim Rep... Parker's New York Criminal Reports [*A publication*] (DLA)

Park Cr Rep... Parker's New York Criminal Reports [*A publication*] (DLA)

Park Dig ...... Parker's California Digest [*A publication*] (DLA)

Park Dow. .... Park. Dower [*1819*] [*A publication*] (DLA)

ParkDrl .... Parker Drilling Co. [*Associated Press*] (SAG)

ParkEl .... Park Electrochemical Corp. [*Associated Press*] (SAG)

Parker .... Parker on the Laws of Shipping and Insurance [*England*] [*A publication*] (DLA)

Parker .... Parker's English Exchequer Reports [*A publication*] (DLA)

Parker .... Parker's New Hampshire Reports [*A publication*] (DLA)

Parker .... Parker's New York Criminal Reports [*6 vols.*] [*A publication*] (DLA)

Parker Cr Cas... Parker's New York Criminal Reports [*A publication*] (ILCA)

Parker Cr Cas (NY)... Parker's New York Criminal Reports [*A publication*] (ILCA)

Parker Cr R... Parker's New York Criminal Reports [*A publication*] (ILCA)

Parker Cr R (NY)... Parker's New York Criminal Reports [*A publication*] (ILCA)

Parker's Crim R... Parker's New York Criminal Reports [*A publication*] (DLA)

Parker's Crim Rep (NY)... Parker's New York Criminal Reports [*A publication*] (DLA)

Parker's Cr R... Parker's New York Criminal Reports [*A publication*] (DLA)

Park Exch .... Parker's English Exchequer Reports [*1743-67*] [*A publication*] (DLA)

Park Hist Ch... Parkes' History of Court of Chancery [*1828*] [*A publication*] (DLA)

ParkHn .... Parker-Hannifin Corp. [*Associated Press*] (SAG)

Park Ins .... Parker's Insurance [*8 eds.*] [*1787-1842 England*] [*A publication*] (DLA)

ParkMed ...... Park Meditech, Inc. [*Associated Press*] (SAG)

ParkNatl ...... Park National Corp. [*Associated Press*] (SAG)

Park NH ...... Parker's New Hampshire Reports [*A publication*] (DLA)

ParkOh .... Park Ohio Industries [*Associated Press*] (SAG)

ParkOh .... Park-Ohio Industries, Inc. [*Associated Press*] (SAG)

ParkPar .... Parker & Parsley Petroleum [*Associated Press*] (SAG)

Park Pr Ch ... Parker's Practice in Chancery [*A publication*] (DLA)

Park Rev Cas. ... Parker's English Exchequer Reports (Revenue Cases) [*A publication*] (DLA)

Parkrvsn ...... Parkervision, Inc. [*Associated Press*] (SAG)

PARKS .... Parks [*Commonly used*] (OPSA)

ParkvF .... Parkvale Financial Corp. [*Associated Press*] (SAG)

PARKWAY .... Parkway [*Commonly used*] (OPSA)

PARKWAYS .. Parkways [*Commonly used*] (OPSA)

PARKWY ...... Parkway [*Commonly used*] (OPSA)

Parkwy .... [*The*] Parkway Co. [*Associated Press*] (SAG)

PARL .... Parallel

PARL .... Parliament

PARL .... Parlux Fragrances [*NASDAQ symbol*] (TTSB)

PARL .... Parlux Fragrances, Inc. [*NASDAQ symbol*] (NQ)

Par L .... Parsons' Law by Hughes [*A publication*] (DLA)

PARL .... Prince Albert RADAR Laboratory

PARLARS ..... Particulars

Par Laws Bus... Parsons' Laws of Business [*A publication*] (DLA)

PARLB .... Parliamentary Borough

Parl Cas ...... Parliamentary Cases [*House of Lords Reports*] [*A publication*] (DLA)

Parlex .... Parlex Corp. [*Associated Press*] (SAG)

Parl Hist Eng... Parliamentary History of England [*Pre-1803*] [*A publication*] (DLA)

PARLIGAES... Parliamentary Liaison Group for Alternative Energy Strategies [*British*]

PARLIKDER... Partiya Litsom k Derevne [*The Party Face to Face with the Countryside*] [*Given name popular in Russia after the Bolshevik Revolution*]

PARLO .... Parlando [*Music*] (ROG)

parl proc ...... Parliamentary Procedure [*British*] (WDAA)

Parl Reg .... Parliamentary Register [*England*] [*A publication*] (DLA)

PARLT .... Parliament

PARLTY .... Parliamentary

Parlux .... Parlux Fragrances, Inc. [*Associated Press*] (SAG)

PARLV .... Parsley Latent Virus [*Plant pathology*]

PARLY .... Parliamentary

PARM .... Parallelogram [*Geometry*] (ROG)

PARM .... Parameter [*Computer science*]

PARM .... Participating Manager

PARM .... Partido Autentico de la Revolucion Mexicana [*Authentic Party of the Mexican Revolution*] [*Political party*] (PPW)

PARM .... Persistent Antiradiation Missile (MCD)

PARM .... Post-Attack Resource Management System (MCD)

PARM .... Precision Anti-Radiation Missile [*Military*] (PDAA)

PARM .... Program Analysis for Resource Management

PARMA .... Program for Analysis, Reporting, and Maintenance [*Computer science*]

PARMA .... Public Agency Risk Managers Association [*San Jose, CA*] (EA)

Par Mar Ins... Parsons on Marine Insurance and General Average [*A publication*] (DLA)

Par Mar L .... Parsons on Maritime Law [*A publication*] (DLA)

ParMd .... Paradigm Medical Industries, Inc. [*Associated Press*] (SAG)

PARMEDL .... Paramedical

Par Merc Law... Parsons on Mercantile Law [*A publication*] (DLA)

ParmTch ...... Parametric Technology Corp. [*Associated Press*] (SAG)

PARMV .... Parsnip Mosaic Virus [*Plant pathology*]

Par N & B ... Parsons' Notes and Bills [*A publication*] (DLA)

Parnassus .... Parnassus: Poetry in Review [*A publication*] (BRI)

PARO .... Patent Royalties (AAGC)

PAROCH ...... Parochial (ROG)

Paroch Ant... Kennett's Parochial Antiquities [*A publication*] (DLA)

Parod Epic Gr Rel... Parodorum Epicorum Graecorum Reliquiae [*A publication*] (OCD)

PAROS .... Passive Ranging on Submarines [*Navy*]

PAROS .... Programmed Automated Replenishment Ordering System (IAA)

PAROSS ...... Passive/Active Reporting Ocean Surveillance System [*Navy*] (NVT)

PAROX .... Paroxysmal [*Medicine*]

PARP .... Partially Acidulated Rock Phosphate (OA)

PARP .... Procyclic Acidic Repetitive Protein [*Biochemistry*]

PARP .... Production Assistance Report to Pricing [*DoD*]

Par Part .... Parsons on Partnership [*1889*] [*A publication*] (DLA)

ParPet .... Parallel Petroleum Corp. [*Associated Press*] (SAG)

ParPf2 .... Partners Preferred Yield II [*Associated Press*] (SAG)

ParPf3 .... Partners Perferred Yield III [*Associated Press*] (SAG)

ParPfd .... Partners Preferred Yield [*Associated Press*] (SAG)

PARPRO ...... Peacetime Aerial Reconnaissance Program [*Military*] (NVT)

PARQ .... ParcPlace-Digitalk [*NASDAQ symbol*] [*Formerly, ParcPlace Systems*] (SG)

PARQ .... Parcplace Systems, Inc. [*NASDAQ symbol*] (SAG)

PARQ .... Parental Acceptance-Rejection Questionnaire [*Psychology*]

PARR .... Bullet Sports International, Inc. [*NASDAQ symbol*] (SAG)

PARR .... Bullet Sports Intl [*NASDAQ symbol*] (TTSB)

PARR .... Pakistan Atomic Research Reactor

Par R .... Parsons' Select Equity Cases [*Pennsylvania*] [*A publication*] (DLA)

PARR .... Performance Analysis Reliability Reporting (DNAB)

PARR .... Post-Accident Radioactivity Removal [*Nuclear energy*] (NRCH)

PARR .... Postanesthesia Recovery Room [*Medicine*] (DAVI)

PARR.......... Procurement Authorization and Receiving Report [*NASA*] (KSC)
PARR.......... Program Analysis and Resources Review
PARR.......... Program Assessment Review Report [*Military*] (GFGA)
PARRC........ Pacific Aerospace Rescue and Recovery Center [*Air Force*]
Par Rights Cit... Parsons on the Rights of a Citizen of the United States [*A publication*]
PARRS........ Postal Analysis Response and Reporting System [*Computer system designed to track mail through the US Postal Service*] [*R. R. Donnelley & Sons Co.*]
PARRS........ Psychological Abstracts Reference Retrieval System [*Syracuse University*]
PARS.......... Paging and Radiotelephone Service [*Telecommunications*] (OTD)
PARS.......... Parachute Altitude Recognition System (MCD)
Pars.......... Parsons' Select Equity Cases [*1842-51*] [*Pennsylvania*] [*A publication*] (DLA)
PARS.......... Passenger Airlines Reservation System
PARS.......... Patrol Analysis Recording System [*British*]
PARS.......... Pedestrians Association for Road Safety [*British*] (DI)
PARS.......... Perimeter Acquisition RADAR [*Characterization*] System (MCD)
PARS.......... Pershing Audio Reproduction System (PDAA)
PARS.......... Personal Adjustment and Role Skills Scale [*Medicine*] (DMAA)
PARS.......... Pharmos Corp. [*NASDAQ symbol*] (SAG)
PARS.......... Photoacoustic Raman Spectroscopy
PARS.......... Pilotless Aircraft Research Station [*NASA*]
PARS.......... Precision and Accuracy Reporting System [*Environmental Protection Agency*] (GFGA)
PARS.......... Preservation & Reformatting Section [*Association for Library Collections and Technical Services*] [*American Library Association*]
PARS.......... Prisoner Aid and Rehabilitation Society (NADA)
PARS.......... Private Aircraft Reporting System [*FAA*] (PDAA)
PARS.......... Procurement Accounting and Reporting System [*Navy*] (NVT)
PARS.......... Program Analysis and Review System (EDAC)
PARS.......... Programmed Airline Reservation System
PARS.......... Property Accountability Record System (NASA)
PARS.......... Provincial Archives and Records Service [*Canada*]
PARSA........ Parasitological Society of Southern Africa (EAIO)
PARSA........ Postgraduate and Research Students' Association [*Australian National University*]
PARSAC...... Particle Size Analog Computer (IAA)
PARSAC...... Particle Size Analogue Computer (PDAA)
Pars Ans..... Parsons' Answer to the Fifth Part of Coke's Reports [*A publication*] (DLA)
PARSAVAL... Pattern Recognition System Application Evaluation (IAA)
Pars Bills & N... Parsons on Bills and Notes [*A publication*] (DLA)
Pars Cont..... Parsons on Contracts [*A publication*] (DLA)
Pars Dec...... Parsons' Decisions [*2-7 Massachusetts*] [*A publication*] (DLA)
PARSEC...... Parallax Second [*Unit of interstellar-space measure*]
PARSEC...... Parser and Extensible Compiler [*Programming language*] (CSR)
PARSECS.... Program for Astronomical Research and Scientific Experiments Concerning Space
Pars Eq Cas... Parsons' Select Equity Cases [*1842-51*] [*Pennsylvania*] [*A publication*] (DLA)
PARSET...... Precision Askania Range System of Electronic Timing (MUGU)
PARSEV...... Paraglider Research Vehicle [*NASA*] (KSC)
Par Sh & Adm... Parsons on the Law of Shipping and Admiralty [*A publication*] (DLA)
PARSIM...... Perimeter Acquisition RADAR Simulation [*Missile system evaluation*] (RDA)
PARSIM...... Plant Appropriation Request Simulation (IAA)
PARSIP....... Point Arguello Range Safety Impact Predictor (MUGU)
Pars Mar Ins... Parsons on Marine Insurance [*A publication*] (DLA)
Pars Mar Law... Parsons on Maritime Law [*A publication*] (DLA)
Pars Merc Law... Parsons on Mercantile Law [*A publication*] (DLA)
Parsons'...... Parsons' Select Equity Cases [*Pennsylvania*] [*A publication*] (DLA)
PARSQ........ Pararescue
Pars Sel Eq Cas (PA)... Parsons' Select Equity Cases [*Pennsylvania*] [*A publication*] (DLA)
Pars S Eq Cas... Parsons' Select Equity Cases [*Pennsylvania*] [*A publication*] (DLA)
Pars Shipp & Adm... Parsons on Shipping and Admiralty [*A publication*] (DLA)
PARSYM...... Partial Symmetry
PARSYN...... Parametric Synthesis [*Computer science*]
PART.......... Pan American Round Tables in the USA [*Defunct*] (EA)
PART.......... Partial (MSA)
part.......... Partial (VRA)
PART.......... Participate (AABC)
Part.......... Participating (EBF)
PART.......... Participle [*Grammar*]
PART.......... Particle (IAA)
PART.......... Particular
PART.......... Partis [*A Part*] [*Pharmacy*]
PART.......... Partition [*Ballistics*]
PART.......... Partner (ADA)
PART.......... Parts Allocation Requirements Technique
PART.......... People Against Racist Terror (EA)
PART.......... Performing Arts Repertory Theater
PART.......... Production Allocation and Requirements Technique (MHDB)
PART.......... Professional Audit Review Team (AAGC)
PARTAC...... Precision Askania Range Target Acquisition and Control (MUGU)
PART AEQ... Partes Aequales [*Equal Parts*] [*Pharmacy*]
PART AEQUAL... Partes Aequales [*Equal Parts*] [*Pharmacy*] (ROG)
Part An...... De Partibus Animalium [*of Aristotle*] [*Classical studies*] (OCD)
ParTch........ PAR Technology Corp. [*Associated Press*] (SAG)
PART DOLENT... Partes Dolentes [*Painful Parts*] [*Pharmacy*]

PARTEI........ Purchasing Agents of the Radio, Television, and Electronics Industries [*An association*] (IAA)
PARTES....... Piece-Wise Application of Radiation through the Electromagnetic-Pulse Simulator (PDAA)
Parth.......... Parthenius [*First century BC*] [*Classical studies*] (OCD)
PARTIAL..... Participation in Architectural Layout (PDAA)
parti bd........ Particle Board (VRA)
Partic.......... Participating [*or Participation*] (DLA)
PARTIC....... Participial [*Grammar*]
PARTIC....... Particle
PARTIC....... Particular
PARTICO...... Parti d'Interets Congolais [*Party for Congolese Interests*] [*Political party*]
Partidas....... Moreau-Lislet and Carleton's Laws of Las Siete Partidas in Force in Louisiana [*A publication*] (DLA)
PARTIE........ People's Alliance to Reform, Transform and Improve Everything (EA)
PARTN........ Partnership (ADA)
PARTNER..... Proof of Analog Results through a Numerical Equivalent Routine [*Computer science*]
PartnerR...... PartnerRe Ltd. [*Associated Press*] (SAG)
Part Or........ Partitiones Oratoriae [*of Cicero*] [*Classical studies*] (OCD)
PARTR........ Particular (ROG)
PARTS........ Parts Assembly and Reuse Tool Set [*Computer software*] [*Digitalk, Inc.*] (PCM)
PARTS........ Precision Approach RADAR Training System (MCD)
PARTS........ Price Analysis and Review Technique for Spares
PARTSHIP.... Partnership [*Legal shorthand*] (LWAP)
PartsS........ Parts Source, Inc. (The) [*Associated Press*] (SAG)
PART VIC.... Partitis Vicibus [*In Divided Parts*] [*Pharmacy*]
PARU.......... Personnel Applied Research Unit [*Canadian military*]
PARU.......... Photographic and Reproduction Unit
PARU.......... Police Aerial Reinforcement [*or Resupply*] Unit [*Thailand*] (CINC)
PARU.......... Postanesthetic Recovery Unit [*Medicine*]
PARV.......... Paravane [*Anti-moored-mine device*] (KSC)
PARV.......... Parvus [*Small*] [*Pharmacy*]
PARV3........ Parsnip Virus 3 [*Plant pathology*]
ParVec........ Purdue Center for Parallel and Vector Computing [*Purdue University*] [*Research center*] (RCD)
Parvnt........ Paravant Computer Systems, Inc. [*Associated Press*] (SAG)
PARVSTRCRA... Paravane and Stores Crane [*Engineering*]
PARW.......... Professional Association of Resume Writers (EA)
Par WC........ Parish Will Case [*A publication*] (DLA)
Par Wills..... Parsons on Wills [*1854*] [*A publication*] (DLA)
PAS.......... National Postsecondary Agriculture Student Organization (EA)
PAS.......... Palestine Aid Society of America (EA)
PAS.......... Para-Aminosalicylic [*Acid*] [*Organic chemistry*]
PAS.......... Parametric Amplifier System
PaS.......... Paranoia Subtle [*Psychology*]
PAS.......... Parent Attitude Scale
PAS.......... Paros [*Greece*] [*Airport symbol*] (OAG)
PAS.......... Partido de Accion Socialista [*Socialist Action Party*] [*Costa Rica*] [*Political party*] (PPW)
PAS.......... Parti Islam se Malaysia [*Islamic Party of Malaysia*] [*Political party*] (PPW)
PAS.......... Partito do Azione do Sardogna [*Sardinian Action Party*] [*Italy Political party*] (PPW)
PAS.......... Pasadena [*California*] [*Seismograph station code, US Geological Survey*] (SEIS)
PA S.......... Pascal Second
PAS.......... Pascal Source File [*Computer science*]
PAS.......... Passage (AABC)
PAS.......... Passed to the Adjacent Sector
PAS.......... Passing Aid System (IAA)
Pas.......... Passipoverus [*Flourished, 13th century*] [*Authority cited in pre-1607 legal work*] (DSA)
PAS.......... Passive (WDAA)
PAS.......... Patent Applicant Service (NITA)
PAS.......... Patient Administration System [*British*]
PAS.......... Patient Appointments and Scheduling [*Medicine*] (DMAA)
PAS.......... Patients' Aid Society
PAS.......... Payload Accommodations Studies [*NASA*] (NASA)
PAS.......... Pelita Air Service PT [*Indonesia*] [*ICAO designator*] (FAAC)
PA S.......... Pennsylvania Superior Court Reports [*A publication*] (DLA)
PAS.......... Percussive Arts Society (EA)
PAS.......... Performance Abatement Services, Inc. (EFIS)
PAS.......... Perigee-Apogee Satellite [*Aerospace*]
PAS.......... Perigee-Apogee Stage [*Aerospace*]
PAS.......... Perigee-Apogee System [*Aerospace*]
PA/S.......... Periodic Acid/Schiff [*A stain*]
PAS.......... Peripheral Anterior Synechia [*Ophthalmology*]
PAS.......... Persistent Atrial Standstill [*Medicine*] (DMAA)
PAS.......... Personal Acquaintance Service
PAS.......... Personal Attitude Survey (EDAC)
PAS.......... Personnel Accounting Symbol [*Air Force*] (AFM)
PAS.......... Personnel Accounting System [*Marine Corps*]
PAS.......... Personnel Activity Sequence (AAG)
PAS.......... Personnel Administration Section [*Library Administration Division of ALA*]
PAS.......... Personnel Assignment Survey (MCD)
PAS.......... Phase Address System
PAS.......... Phase Array System
PAS.......... Philanthropic Advisory Service
PAS.......... Phosphoric Acid-Sensitive
PAS.......... Photoabsorption Spectroscopy [*Chemistry*]
PAS.......... Photoacoustic Spectrometry [*Also, OAS*]

PAS.............. Physician-Assisted Suicide
PAS.............. Physicians for Automotive Safety [Defunct] (EA)
PAS.............. Pierce-Arrow Society (EA)
PAS.............. Pilots Advisory Service
PAS.............. Pilot's Attack Sight [British]
PAS.............. Pioneer America Society (EA)
PAS.............. Planning Advisory Service (GNE)
PAS.............. Plant Alarms Sum (ECII)
PAS.............. Plasma Arc System
PAS.............. Plessey Assessment Services (NITA)
PAS.............. Pneumatic Air Saw
PAS.............. Policy Analysis Staff [Environmental Protection Agency] (GFGA)
PAS.............. Polish Academy of Sciences
PAS.............. Polish Astronautical Society [See also PTA]
PAS.............. Poly(alkyl Sulfone) [Organic chemistry]
PAS.............. Polyaminosiloxane [Organic chemistry]
PAS.............. Polyarylsulfone [Organic chemistry]
PAS.............. Positron Annihilation Spectroscopy (MCD)
PAS.............. Post Abortion Syndrome
PAS.............. Postacoustic Spectroscopy
PAS.............. Posterior Airway Space [Medicine] (DMAA)
PAS.............. Posterior Area of [Loose] Skin
PAS.............. Postponed Accounting System [Banking]
PAS.............. Power Apparatus and Systems (MCD)
PAS.............. Power-Assisted Steering [Automotive feature]
PAS.............. Power-Assist System [Motorcycle steering]
PAS.............. Pre-Admission Screening [Medicine] (MEDA)
PAS.............. Preaward Survey [To determine a contractor's capability] [DoD]
PAS.............. Precise Acquisition System
PAS.............. Preconscious Activity Scale (EDAC)
PAS.............. Pregnancy Advisory Service [British]
PAS.............. Premature Atrial Stimulus [Medicine] (DMAA)
PAS.............. Presidential Appointee Subject
PAS.............. President's Advisor for Science
PAS.............. Pressure-Assisted Sintering [Forging] [Automotive engineering]
PAS.............. Pressurized Air Subsystem
PAS.............. Price Analysis Sheet
PAS.............. Primary Alerting System
PAS.............. Primary Ascent System [Aerospace] (NASA)
PAS.............. Principal Assistant Secretary
PAS.............. Prisoners' Advice Service (WDAA)
PAS.............. Prisoners' Aid Society [Australia]
PAS.............. Privacy Act Statement (NRCH)
PAS.............. Problem Appraisal Scales [Personality development test] [Psychology]
PAS.............. Processed Array Signal
PAS.............. Procurement Action System (MCD)
PAS.............. Procurement Appropriation, Secondary (MCD)
PAS.............. Product Acceptance Standard [Automotive engineering]
PAS.............. Product Assurance Survey
PAS.............. Product Availability Search (MCD)
PAS.............. Professional Activity Study [Later, CPHA]
PAS.............. Professional Advancement Series [National Court Reporters Association]
PAS.............. Professor of Aerospace Studies [Air Force] (AFIT)
PAS.............. Professor of Air Science [Air Force]
PAS.............. Program Activity Structure
PAS.............. Program Address Storage (IEEE)
PAS.............. Program Allowance Schedule
PAS.............. Program Alternative Simulation (IAA)
PAS.............. Program of Advanced Studies
PAS.............. Progressive Accumulated Stress [Psychiatry]
PAS.............. Propulsion and Auxiliary Systems Department [David W. Taylor Naval Ship Research and Development Center]
PAS.............. Psychopathological Assessment Scale (DB)
PAS.............. Public Address System
PAS.............. Public Administration Service (EA)
PAS.............. Pulmonary Artery Stenosis [Medicine]
PAS.............. Pulsating Air System [Automotive engineering]
PAS.............. Pump Actuator Set
PAS.............. Pyrotechnics Arming Switch
Pas .... Terminus Paschae [Easter Term] [Latin Legal term] (DLA)
PASA .... Pacific American Steamship Association [Later, AIMS]
PASA .... Para-Aminosalicylic Acid [Organic chemistry]
PASA .... Participating Agency Service Agreement (GNE)
PASA .... PCR [Polymerase Chain Reaction] Amplification of Specific Alleles [Genetics]
PASA .... Personnel Administrative Services Agency [Army]
PASA .... Pioneers' Association of South Australia
PASA .... Pipelines Authority of South Australia
PASA .... Playgroup Association of South Australia
PASA .... Police Association of South Australia
PASA .... Primary Acquired Sideroblastic Anemia [Medicine]
PASA .... Proximal Articular Set Angle [Orthopedics] (DAVI)
PASA .... Quepass.com, Inc. [NASDAQ symbol]
PASAR .... Psychological Abstracts Search and Retrieval
PASARR...... Preadmission Screening and Annual Resident Review [Medicare]
PASAT .... Particle Accelerator Science and Technology (IAA)
PASAT .... Poppleton-Allen Sales Aptitude Test
PASB .... Pan American Sanitary Bureau
PASB .... Perpetual Savings Bank FSB (MHDW)
PASb .... Predneaziatskii Sbornik Voprosy Khattologii i Khurritologii [A publication] (BJA)
P-as-B .... Program as Broadcast [Radio] (DEN)

PASB .... Public Authorities Superannuation Board [New South Wales, Australia]
PASBI .... Palo Alto Social Background Inventory [Psychology]
PASC .... Deadhorse [Alaska] [ICAO location identifier] (ICLI)
PASC .... Pacific Area Standards Congress [American National Standards Institute]
PASC .... Palestine Armed Struggle Command (PD)
PASC .... Pan American Sanitary Conference
PASC .... Pan American Standards Commission [See also COPANT] (EAIO)
PAS-C .... Para-Aminosalicylic Acid Crystallized with Ascorbic Acid [Organic chemistry] (MAE)
Pasc............ Paschal [Easter Term] [Legal term] (DLA)
Pasc............ Paschal's Reports [25, 28-31 Texas] [A publication] (DLA)
PASC .... Precision Adaptive Sub-Band Coding [Electronics]
PASC .... Primitive Art Society of Chicago (EA)
PASCA .... Positron Annihilation Spectroscopy for Chemical Analysis
PASCAL ...... Philips Automatic Sequence Calculator
PASCAL ...... Program Applique a la Selection et a la Compilation Automatique de la Litterature [Centre National de la Recherche Scientifique-Informascience] [Bibliographic database]
PASCALS ..... Projected Antisubmarine Classification and Location System (DNAB)
PASCH .... Pascha [Easter] [Church calendars] (ROG)
Pasch.......... Paschal [Easter Term] [Legal term] (DLA)
Paschal........ Paschal's Reports [28-31 Texas] [Supplement to Vol. 25] [A publication] (DLA)
Paschal's Ann Const... Paschal's United States Constitution, Annotated [A publication] (DLA)
Pasch Dig.... Paschal's Texas Digest of Decisions [A publication] (DLA)
PASCOSS.... Passive and Active Control of Space Structures
PASCT .... Pan American Society for Chemotherapy of Tuberculosis [See also SAQT] [Buenos Aires, Argentina] (EAIO)
PASD .... After Diastase Digestion [Biochemistry] (DAVI)
p'ase .... Alkaline Phosphatase [Biochemistry] (DAVI)
PASE.......... Post-Apollo Space Electrophoresis [European Space Agency]
PASE.......... Power-Assisted Storage Equipment (IEEE)
PASE.......... Product Acceptance Exceptions
PASE.......... Programs in the Arts for Special Education Project (EDAC)
PASEP .... Passed Separately [Military]
PASES .... Performance Assessment of Syntax: Elicited and Spontaneous [Educational test]
Pas Ex .... Passive Exercise [Physical Therapy] (DAVI)
PASF.......... Photographic Art and Science Foundation (EA)
PASFIS .... Philippines Aquatic Sciences and Fisheries Information System [Marine science] (OSRA)
PASG .... Patent Abstracts Section, Official Gazette [Federal government] [A publication]
PASG .... Pneumatic Antishock Garment [Roentgenology]
PASG .... Pulse Amplifier/Symbol Generator
PASG .... Pulse Analyzer Signal Generator
PASGT .... Personnel Armor System for Ground Troops (RDA)
PASGX .... Phoenix-Engemann Growth Cl.A [Mutual fund ticker symbol] (SG)
PASI.......... Pikunas Adult Stress Inventory [Psychology]
PA/SI .... Preliminary Assessment and Site Inspection [Environmental Protection Agency] (FFDE)
PASI.......... Professional Associate, Chartered Surveyors' Institution [Later, ARICS]
PASI.......... Psoriasis Area and Severity Index [Medicine]
PASI.......... Sitka [Alaska] [ICAO location identifier] (ICLI)
PASIC .... Percussive Arts Society International Convention [Percussive Arts Society]
PasifSat...... Pasifik Satelit Nusantara (PT) [Associated Press] (SAG)
PAS-INAH .... Para-Aminosalicylic Acid and Isonicotinic Acid Hydrazide (BARN)
PASITAM ..... Program of Advanced Studies of Institution Building and Technical Assistance Methodologies [MUCIA]
PASL.......... Polish Americans for the Statue of Liberty [Defunct] (EA)
PASLA .... Programmable Asynchronous Line Adapter
PASLIB .... Pakistan Association of Special Libraries (NITA)
Pas Lux ...... Pasicrisie Luxembourgeoise [Luxembourg Law Reports] [A publication] (ILCA)
PASM.......... Partitionable SIMD/MIMD [Single Instruction, Multiple Data/Multiple Instruction, Multiple Data] (MCD)
PASM.......... Periodic Acid - Silver Methenamine [Biological stain]
PASM.......... Preaward Survey Monitor [DoD]
PASMA .... Prefabricated Aluminium Scaffold Manufacturers Association [British] (DBA)
PASN.......... St. Paul Island [Alaska] [ICAO location identifier] (ICLI)
PASO .... Pan American Sanitary Organization
PASO .... Pan American Sports Organization [See also ODEPA] [Mexico City, Mexico] (EAIO)
PA/SO .... Port Antisubmarine Officer [Navy]
PASO .... Principal Armament Supply Officer [British military] (DMA)
PASOC .... Partido de Accion Socialista [Party of Socialist Action] [Spain Political party] (PPW)
PASOCO...... Parti Socialiste des Comores [Socialist Party of Comoros] [Political party] (EY)
PASOH .... Partido de Accion Socialista de Honduras [Political party] (EY)
PASOH .... Partido Socialista de Honduras [Honduran Socialist Party] [Political party]
PASOK .... Panellinion Sosialistikon Kinema [Pan-Hellenic Socialist Movement] [Greek Political party] (PPE)
PASOLS ...... Pacific Area Senior Officer Logistics Seminar (MCD)
PASP .... Pancreas-Specific Protein [Medicine] (DMAA)
PASP .... Port Autonome de San Pedro [The Ivory Coast] (EY)
PA/SP .... Positioner Antenna and Solar Panel [NASA]
PASP .... Price Adjusting Sampling Plan (PDAA)

PASP .... Pulmonary Artery Systolic Pressure [*Medicine*] (DMAA)
PAS(PR) ...... Principal Assistant Secretary (Priority)
PAS procedure... Periodic Acid Schiff Procedure (DOG)
P-as-R .... Program as Recorded [*Radio*] (DEN)
PASRB .... Preaward Survey Review Board [*DoD*]
PASS .... Panic Attack Sufferers' Support Groups (EA)
PASS .... Parents Against Subliminal Seduction [*Defunct*] (EA)
PASS .... Parked Aircraft Security System (PDAA)
PASS .... Parts Analysis Summary Sheet
PASS .... Pass [*Postal Service standard*] (OPSA)
Pass............ Passage (DD)
PASS .... Passage [*Maps and charts*] (KSC)
PASS .... Passenger (KSC)
PASS .... Passenger Automated Selection System (ADA)
PASS .... Passim [*Everywhere*] [*Latin*]
PASS .... Passivate [*Metallurgy*] (IAA)
PASS .... Passive
PASS .... Passive-Active Surveillance System (MCD)
Pass........... Passover (BARN)
PASS .... Patrol Advanced Surveillance System (MCD)
PASS .... Pay/Personnel Administrative Support System (NVT)
PASS .... Penetration Aids/Strike System (NG)
PASS .... Performance Analysis Subsystem [*Military*] (CAAL)
PASS .... Personal Access Satellite System [*NASA*] (CIST)
PASS .... Personalized Automotive Security System [*In product name, PASS-Key*] [*Delco Electronics*] [*Automotive engineering*]
PASS .... Petroleum Abstracts Search Service [*Online information service*]
PASS .... Phased Array Sector Scanner [*Instrument for measuring ultrasound*] [*Trademark of General Electric Co.*]
PASS .... Phoenix Ability Survey System [*Test*]
PASS .... Pilot Aerial Survival System (PDAA)
PASS .... Pirelli Active Safety System
PASS .... Planning and Scheduling Session
PASS .... Planning and Scheduling System (NASA)
PASS .... Policyowner Attitude Survey Service [*LIMRA*]
PASS .... Polymeric Aluminum Silicate Sulfate [*Inorganic chemistry*]
PASS .... Pooled Analytical Stereoplotter System (PDAA)
PASS .... Portable Assisted Study Sequence Program [*California*] (EDAC)
PASS .... Positioning and Surveying System (MCD)
PASS .... Post-Accident Sampling Systems [*Nuclear energy*]
PASS .... Precision Autocollimating Solar Sensor
PASS .... Pressurized Air Starter System (MCD)
PASS .... Price Adjusted Single Sampling (PDAA)
PASS .... Primary Academic Sentiment Scale [*Child development test*]
PASS .... Primary Avionics Software System (NASA)
PASS .... Private Alarm Signalling System
PASS .... Private Automatic Switching System [*Telecommunications*]
PASS .... Procurement Aging and Staging System [*Army*] (AABC)
PASS .... Procurement Automated Source System [*Small Business Administration*] [*Washington, DC Information service or system*] (IID)
PASS .... Production Automated Scheduling System (IEEE)
PASS .... Professional Accounting System for Schools (AIE)
PASS .... Professional Airways Systems Specialists (EA)
PASS .... Professional Amateur Sports Systems [*Cable-television network*]
PASS .... Professional Association of Secretarial Services [*Later, NASS*] (EA)
PASS .... Program Aid Software Systems [*Computer science*] (IEEE)
PASS .... Program Alternative Simulation System (KSC)
PASS .... Program Analysis of Service Systems [*Procedure to evaluate human service programs*]
PASS .... Programmed Access/Security System [*Card Key Systems*]
PASSA .... Pacific American Steamship Association [*Later, AIMS*] (EA)
PASSAGE.... Passage [*Commonly used*] (OPSA)
PASSAT ...... PASCAL Subset for Application in Test Computers (NITA)
PASSEX ...... Passing Exercise (DOMA)
PASSIM ...... President's Advisory Staff on Scientific Information Management
PASS-IN-REVIEW... Priority Aircraft Subsystem Suitability Intensive Review (MCD)
PASSION...... Program for Algebraic Sequences Specifically of Input-Output Nature [*Computer science*]
PASSMAN... Pay/Personnel Administrative Support System Manual (DNAB)
PASSR........ Passenger (DCTA)
PASSWD...... Password [*Computer science*]
PAST........... Pasteurella [*Genus of bacteria*]
PAST........... Pastillus [*A Lozenge, Troch, Pastil*] [*Pharmacy*] (ROG)
Past........... Pastoral Epistles (BJA)
PAST........... Pastorate
PA St .... Pennsylvania State Reports [*A publication*] (DLA)
PAST........... Periodic Acid-Schiff Technique [*Medicine*] (DMAA)
PAST........... Portable Arming System Trainer (MCD)
PAST........... Process Accessible Segment Table
PAST........... Professor of Air Science and Tactics
PAST........... Propulsion and Associated Systems Test (MCD)
PA Stat Ann... Pennsylvania Statutes, Annotated [*A publication*] (DLA)
PA Stat Ann (Purdon)... Pennsylvania Statutes, Annotated (Purdon) [*A publication*] (DLA)
PA State ...... Pennsylvania State Reports [*A publication*] (DLA)
PA State R... Pennsylvania State Reports [*A publication*] (DLA)
PASTIC .... Pakistan Scientific and Technological Information Center [*Formerly, PANSDOC*] [*Quaid-I-Azan University Campus Islamabad, Pakistan*]
PAstO........... Our Lady of Angels College, Aston, PA [*Library symbol Library of Congress*] (LCLS)
PA St R....... Pennsylvania State Reports [*A publication*] (DLA)
PASTRAM... Passenger Traffic Management System [*Army*]
PA St Tr...... Pennsylvania State Trials (Hogan) [*A publication*] (DLA)

PASU .... Pan-African Socialist Union [*Southern Rhodesia*]
PASU .... Patrol Aircraft Service Unit
PASU .... Performing Arts Study Unit (EA)
PASU .... Polyarylsulfone [*Organic chemistry*]
PASU .... Preliminary Approval for Service Use [*Military*]
PASU .... Provisional Approval for Service Use [*Navy*] (NVT)
PA Summary... Summary of Pennsylvania Jurisprudence [*A publication*] (DLA)
PA Super .... Pennsylvania Superior Court Reports [*A publication*] (DLA)
PA Super Ct... Pennsylvania Superior Court Reports [*A publication*] (DLA)
PA Superior Ct... Pennsylvania Superior Court Reports [*A publication*] (DLA)
PASUS .... Pan American Society of the United States (EA)
PASV .... Pangola Stunt Virus [*Plant pathology*]
PASV .... Sparrevohn Air Force Station [*Alaska*] [*ICAO location identifier*] (ICLI)
PASW .... Personal Assistance Service Worker [*Medicine*] (DMAA)
PASW .... Pure Atria [*NASDAQ symbol*] [*Formerly, Pure Software*] (SG)
PASW .... Pure Atria Corp. [*NASDAQ symbol*] (SAG)
PASWEPS .... Passive Antisubmarine Warfare Environmental Protection System [*Navy*] (NATG)
PASY .... Shemya Air Force Base [*Alaska*] [*ICAO location identifier*] (ICLI)
PAt............. Allentown Public Library, Allentown, PA [*Library symbol Library of Congress*] (LCLS)
Pat............. All India Reporter, Patna Series [*A publication*] (ILCA)
PAT............. Athenaeum of Philadelphia (EA)
PAT............. Athenaeum of Philadelphia, Philadelphia, PA [*OCLC symbol*] (OCLC)
Pat............. Indian Law Reports, Patna Series [*A publication*] (DLA)
Pat............. Indian Rulings, Patna Series [*A publication*] (DLA)
PAT............. International Brotherhood of Painters and Allied Trades
PAT............. National Patents Appeal Tribunal [*England*] (DLA)
PAT............. Palleted Automated Transport (PDAA)
PAT............. Parametric Artificial Talker
PAT............. Paroxysmal Atrial [*or Auricular*] Tachycardia [*Medicine*]
PAT............. Parts Accountability Technique (MCD)
PAT............. Passive Acoustic Target [*Military*]
PAT............. Passive Acoustic Torpedo [*Military*]
PA t............. Passive Angle Track (NVT)
pa t............. Past Tense [*Grammar*] (BARN)
pat............. Patella (STED)
pat............. Patent (STED)
Pat............. Patent (AAGC)
PAT............. Patent (KSC)
PAT............. Patent Rolls [*British*]
pat............. Paternal Origin [*Medicine*] (DMAA)
PAT............. Paterson [*Diocesan abbreviation*] [*New Jersey*] (TOCD)
Pat............. Paterson's Scotch Appeals, House of Lords [*A publication*] (DLA)
Pat............. Pathe [*Record label*] [*France*]
PAT............. Patient
pat............. Patina (VRA)
PAT............. Patio
PAT............. Patna [*India*] [*Airport symbol*] (OAG)
Pat............. Paton's Scotch Appeal Cases, House of Lords [*A publication*] (DLA)
PAT............. Patras [*Greece*] [*Seismograph station code, US Geological Survey*] (SEIS)
PAT............. Patriarch [*Greek Church*] (ROG)
PAT............. Patrick Air Force Base [*Florida*] (KSC)
PAT............. Patrol
PAT............. Patten Corp. [*NYSE symbol*] (SPSG)
PAT............. Pattern
PAT............. Pattern Analysis Test [*Army*]
PAT............. People's Action Team [*South Vietnam*]
PAT............. Performance Acceptance Test (SAA)
PAT............. Performance Appraisal Team [*Nuclear energy*] (NRCH)
PAT............. Peripheral Allocation Table (NITA)
PAT............. Peripheral Assignment Table (CMD)
PAT............. Permit Assistance Team [*Environmental Protection Agency*] (GFGA)
PAT............. Personalized Array Translator (IEEE)
PAT............. Personnel Assistance Team [*Military*]
PAT............. Personnel Authorization Table [*Air Force*]
PAT............. Pesticide Applicator Training [*Environmental Protection Agency*] (AEPA)
PAT............. Pets as Therapy (WDAA)
PAT............. Phenylaminotetrazole [*Psychology*]
PAT............. Phosphinothricin Acetyl Transferase [*An enzyme*]
PAT............. Photo Articulation Test
PAT............. Physics Achievement Test
PAT............. Picric Acid Turbidity Test
PAT............. Picture Arrangement Test
PAT............. Plasma Arc Tunnel
PAT............. Plastic Apply Template (MCD)
PAT............. Platoon Anti-Tank (SAA)
PAT............. Plenum Air Tread [*Army amphibian vehicle*]
PAT............. Plutonium Air Transportable [*Nuclear energy*] (NRCH)
PAT............. Point after Touchdown [*Football*]
PAT............. Polar Adjectives Test (AEBS)
PAT............. Polar Auxin Transport [*Botany*]
PAT............. Polaris Acceleration Test [*Military*] (SAA)
PAT............. Police Association of Tasmania [*Australia*]
PAT............. Political Action Teams
PAT............. Polyamine Acetyltransferase (DB)
PAT............. Polyaminotriazole [*Organic chemistry*]
PAT............. Polyarlterephthalate [*Organic chemistry*]
PAT............. Position Adjusting Type
PAT............. Postavailability Trials
PAT............. Power Ascension Testing (IEEE)
PAT............. Preadmission Screening and Assessment Team [*Medicine*] (DB)
PAT............. Preadmission Testing

PAT .... Prearranged Transfers
PAT .... Precision Aim Technique [for helicopters] [Army] (RDA)
PAT .... Prediction Analysis Techniques
PAT .... Pregnancy at Term [Gynecology]
PAT .... Preliminary Acceptance Trials [Navy]
PAT .... Prescription Athletic Turf [Trademark for an artificial turf]
PAT .... Pressure Assembled Thyristor
PAT .... Printer Action Table [Computer science] (HGAA)
PAT .... Prioirty Access Timer [Telecommunications] (OSI)
PAT .... Priority Air Transport [Army] (FAAC)
PAT .... Priority Air Travel [Army]
PAT .... Prism Adaptation Test [Ophthalmology]
PAT .... Problem Action Team [NASA] (NASA)
PAT .... Procedure for Automatic Testing (IAA)
PAT .... Procedures Authorized Task (MCD)
PAT .... Process Action Team [Army] (RDA)
PAT .... Process-Activation Table [Computer science]
PAT .... Process Analysis Team
PAT .... Product Acceptance Test [Advertising] (DOAD)
PAT .... Production Acceptance Test [NASA] (KSC)
PAT .... Production Assessment Test
PAT .... Professional, Administrative, and Technical (OICC)
PAT .... Professional Association of Teachers [British]
PAT .... Proficiency Analytical Testing [National Institute on Occupational Safety and Health]
PAT .... Program Analysis Team (KSC)
PAT .... Program Attitude Test (IEEE)
PAT .... Programmable Actuator-Transducer [Automotive engineering]
PAT .... Programmed Activity Transmission (MCD)
PAT .... Programmer Aptitude Test
PAT .... Progressive Achievement Test of Listening Comprehension (TMMY)
PAT .... Project Action Team [Acquisition Reform] (AAGC)
PAT .... Property and Accounting Technician [Navy]
PAT .... Proportional to Absolute Temperature (IAA)
PAT .... Pseudoadder Tree [Computer science]
PAT .... Psychoacoustic Testing
PAT .... PSYOP [Psychological Operation] Automated Terminal (RDA)
PAT .... Public Administration Times [A publication] (EAAP)
PAT .... Public Affairs Team (COE)
PAT .... Pulsed Amplifier Tube
PAT .... Pump Algebra Tutor [Computer program]
PaT .... Purge-and-Trap [Technique] [Environmental Protection Agency]
PAtA .... Air Products & Chemicals, Inc., Allentown, PA [Library symbol Library of Congress] (LCLS)
PATA .... Pacific American Tankship Association [Defunct] (EA)
PATA .... Pacific Area Travel Association [San Francisco, CA]
PATA .... Pacific Asia Travel Association (EA)
PATA .... Patagonia [Region of South America] (ROG)
PATA .... Plenum Air Tread, Amphibious [Army vehicle]
PATA .... Pneumatic All-Terrain Amphibian (IEEE)
PATA .... Professional Aeromedical Transport Association (EA)
PATA .... Proprietary Articles Trade Association [British] (BI)
PATA .... Tanana [Alaska] [ICAO location identifier] (ICLI)
Pat Abr .... Paterson's Abridgment of Poor Law Cases [1857-63] [A publication] (DLA)
PAT & E ...... Product Acceptance Testing and Evaluation [Marketing] (MCD)
Pat & H ...... Patton, Jr., and Heath's Reports [Virginia Special Court of Appeals] [A publication] (DLA)
Pat & Mr .... Paterson and Murray's Reports [1870-71] [New South Wales] [A publication] (DLA)
Pat App .... Craigie, Stewart, and Paton's House of Lords Appeals from Scotland [1726-1857] [A publication] (DLA)
Pat App Cas... Paterson's Scotch Appeal Cases [A publication] (DLA)
Pat App Cas... Paton's Scotch Appeal Cases [Craigie, Stewart, and Paton] [A publication] (DLA)
PATAS .... Portable Air-Launched Missile Telemetry Acquisition System (MCD)
PATASWDEVGRU... Patrol Antisubmarine Warfare Development Group
PATBOMRON... Patrol-Bombing Squadron
PATBX .... Private Automatic Telegraph Branch Exchange [Telecommunications]
PATBX .... Private Automatic Telex Branch Exchange (NITA)
PATC .... Cedar Crest College, Allentown, PA [Library symbol Library of Congress] (LCLS)
PATC .... Paroxysmal Atrial [or Auricular] Tachycardia [Medicine]
PATC .... PATCLASS [Pergamon ORBIT InfoLine, Inc.] [No longer available online] [Information service or system] (CRD)
PATC .... Pioneer Automobile Touring Club
PAT-C .... Position, Attitude, Trajectory-Control [Aerospace] (AAG)
PATC .... Potomac Appalachian Trail Club (EA)
PATC .... Professional, Administrative, Technical, and Clerical [Bureau of Labor Statistics survey]
PATC .... Tin City Air Force Station [Alaska] [ICAO location identifier] (ICLI)
PATCA .... Panama Air Traffic Control Area
PATCA .... Phase Lock Automatic Tuned Circuit Adjustment [Telecommunications]
PATCA .... Printing and Allied Trades Christian Association (DGA)
PATCA .... Professional and Technical Consultants Association (EA)
Pat Cas .... Reports of Patent, Design, and Trade Mark Cases [England, Scotland, Ireland] [A publication] (DLA)
PATCENT .... Patching Central [Army] (AABC)
PATCH .... People Against Toxic Chemical Hazards [An association Australia]
PATCH .... Planned Approach to Community Health
PA-TCH-SP... Periodic Acid-Thiocarbohydrazide-Silver Proteinate [Test] [Cytology]
PATCO .... Prednisone, ara-C [Cytarabine], Thioguanine, Cyclophosphamide, Oncovin [Vincristine] [Antineoplastic drug regimen]

PATCO .... Professional, Administrative, Technical, Clerical, and Other [Bureau of Labor Statistics survey] (DNAB)
PATCO .... Professional Air Traffic Controllers Organization [Defunct] (EA)
PATCOM ...... Patriot Communications Model (MCD)
Pat Comp .... Paterson's Compendium of English and Scotch Law [A publication] (DLA)
PATD .... Parts and Tool Disposition (IAA)
PATD .... Patented
Pat Dec .... Decisions of the Commissioner of Patents [A publication] (DLA)
Pat Des & TM Rev... Patent, Design, and Trade Mark Review [India] [A publication] (DLA)
Pat Dig .... Pattison's Missouri Digest [A publication] (DLA)
PATDPA ...... Deutsche Patent Datenbank [German Patent Database] [German Patent Office] [Information service or system] (IID)
PATE .... Programmed Automatic Telemetry Evaluator
PATE .... Programmed Automatic Test Equipment
PATE .... Psychodynamics and Therapeutic Education
PATE .... Pulmonary Artery Thromboembolectomy [Cardiology] (DAVI)
Pate .... Pulmonary Artery Thromboembolism [Medicine] (STED)
PATEC .... Pacific Technica Corp. (EFIS)
PATEFA News... Printing and Allied Trades Employers' Federation. News [A publication]
PATELL .... Psychological Abstracts Tape Edition Lease or Licensing
PatEng .... Patterson Energy, Inc. [Associated Press] (SAG)
Pater .... Paterson's New South Wales Reports [A publication] (DLA)
Pater .... Paterson's Scotch Appeal Cases [A publication] (DLA)
Pater Ap Cas... Paterson's Scotch Appeal Cases [A publication] (DLA)
Pater App .... Paterson's Scotch Appeal Cases [A publication] (DLA)
Paters App... Paterson's Appeal Cases [A publication] (ILCA)
Paters Comp... Paterson's Compendium of English and Scotch Law [A publication] (DLA)
Paterson ...... Paterson on the Game Laws [A publication] (DLA)
Paterson ...... Paterson on the Liberty of the Subject [A publication] (DLA)
Paterson ...... Paterson's Compendium of English and Scotch Law [A publication] (DLA)
Paterson ...... Paterson's Law and Usages of the Stock Exchange [A publication] (DLA)
Paterson ...... Paterson's Scotch Appeal Cases [A publication] (DLA)
Paterson Sc App Cas... Paterson's Scotch Appeal Cases [A publication] (DLA)
PATF .... Program Activation Task Force [Military] (AFIT)
PATF .... Property Accountability Task Force [Army] (MCD)
PATFOR ...... Patrol Force
Pat Game L... Paterson on the Game Laws [1861] [A publication] (DLA)
PATGC .... Purge-and-Trap Gas Chromatography [Environmental Protection Agency]
PATH .... Partnership Approach to Health (MEDA)
PATH .... Path [Postal Service standard] (OPSA)
path .... Pathogen (STED)
path .... Pathology (STED)
PATH .... Pathology (AABC)
PATH .... Peer Attitudes Toward the Handicapped Scale [Psychology] (EDAC)
PATH .... Performance Analysis and Test Histories (KSC)
PATH .... Physicians at Teaching Hospitals [Program]
PATH .... Pituitary Adrenotrophic Hormone [Endocrinology]
PATH .... Port Authority Trans-Hudson [New York]
PATH .... Preserve American Patriotic Holidays Committee (EA)
PATH .... Program for Appropriate Technology in Health (EA)
PATH .... Program on Advanced Technology for the Highway
PATH .... Prospectors and Treasure Hunters Guild (EA)
PATHAT ...... Precision Aim-Technique Heliborne Antitank [Gun system concept] [Ballistic Research Laboratory] (RDA)
PATHE .... Positive Action Through Holistic Evaluation Program (EDAC)
Pat HL Sc ... Paterson's Scotch Appeal Cases [A publication] (DLA)
Pat HL Sc ... Paton's Scotch Appeal Cases [A publication] (DLA)
PathoG .... PathoGenesis Corp. [Associated Press] (SAG)
PATHOL ...... Pathological (MSA)
PATHS .... Pacific Transport of Heat and Salt [Canada-Japan-USA] [Marine science] (OSRA)
PATHS .... Path [Commonly used] (OPSA)
PATHS .... Peer Attitudes Toward the Handicapped Scale [Educational testing]
PATHS .... Precursor above the Horizon Sensor [Strategic Defense Initiative]
PATI .... Passive Airborne Time-Difference Intercept [Navy]
PATI .... Patient Infosystems, Inc. [NASDAQ symbol] (SAG)
PATIA .... Pacific Area Trading and Investment Area
Patiala .... Indian Law Reports, Patiala Series [A publication] (DLA)
PATIB .... Polish-American Travel Information Bureau (EA)
PATINA .... Potomac Antique Tools and Industries Association (EA)
PatInfo .... Patient Infosystems, Inc. [Associated Press] (SAG)
Pat Ins .... Paton on Insurance [1962] [A publication] (DLA)
Pat J .... Patent Journal, Including Trademarks and Models [South Africa] [A publication] (DLA)
PATK .... Patrick Indus [NASDAQ symbol] (TTSB)
PATK .... Patrick Industries, Inc. [NASDAQ symbol] (NQ)
PATK .... Talkeetna [Alaska] [ICAO location identifier] (ICLI)
PAtL .... Lehigh County Historical Society, Allentown, PA [Library symbol Library of Congress] (LCLS)
PATL .... Tatalina Air Force Station [Alaska] [ICAO location identifier] (ICLI)
PATLAW ...... Patent Law (NITA)
Pat Law Rev... Patent Law Review [A publication] (DLA)
PATLC .... Progessive Achievement Tests of Listening Comprehension (STED)
Patlex .... Patlex Corp. [Associated Press] (SAG)
Pat Licens ... Paterson's Licensing Acts Annual [A publication] (DLA)
Pat LJ .... Patna Law Journal [India] [A publication] (DLA)
Pat LR .... Patent Law Review [A publication] (DLA)
Pat LR .... Patna Law Reports [India] [A publication] (DLA)

Pat L Reptr... Patna Law Reporter [India] [A publication] (DLA)
Pat L Rev .... Patent Law Review [A publication] (DLA)
Pat LT.......... Patna Law Times [India] [A publication] (DLA)
Pat LW......... Patna Law Weekly [A publication] (DLA)
PAtM............ Muhlenberg College, Allentown, PA [Library symbol Library of Congress] (LCLS)
PAT MED ..... Patent Medicine (WDAA)
pat med........ Patent Medicine (STED)
PATMI.......... Powder Actuated Tool Manufacturers' Institute (EA)
PATMKG ...... Patternmaking (WGA)
Pat Mort ...... Patch on Mortgages [1821] [A publication] (DLA)
PATMRG....... PACOM [Pacific Command] Air Target Materials Review Group (CINC)
PATN .... Pattern (MDG)
PATNT .... Patent
PATNT .... Playgroup Association of the Northern Territory [Australia]
PATO .... Pacific-Asian Treaty Organization (NADA)
PATO .... Partial Acceptance and Takeover Date [Telecommunications] (TEL)
PATO .... Pattetico [Pathetically] [Music] (ROG)
PATO .... Principal Ammunition Technical Officer [British military] (DMA)
Pat Off........ Patent Office (DLA)
Pat Off J ...... Patent Office Journal [India] [A publication] (DLA)
Pat Off Rep... Patent Office Reports [A publication] (DLA)
PATOLIS ...... Patent Online Information System [Database] [Japan]
Paton........... Craigie, Stewart, and Paton's Scotch Appeal Cases [1726-1821] [A publication] (DLA)
Paton App Cas... Paton's Scotch Appeal Cases [A publication] (DLA)
Paton Sc App Cas... Paton's Scotch Appeal Cases [A publication] (DLA)
PATOOMB.... Phage and the Origins of Molecular Biology
PATOS .... Patent-Online-System [Bertelsmann Datenbankdienste GmbH] [Database]
PATP........... Poets and the Pub [Programme] [Australia]
PATP........... Preliminary Authority to Proceed (NASA)
PATP........... Production Acceptance Test Procedure (MCD)
PATP........... (Pyridylcarbonylamino)tetrahydropyridine [Biochemistry]
PATPEND..... Patent Pending
PAT-PTR....... US Patent Data Base - Patent Technology Reports [Patent and Trademark Office] [Database]
PATR .... Patriarch
PATR .... Patriotic (ROG)
PATR .... Patron
PATR .... Production Acceptance Test Requirement (MCD)
PATRA .... Printing, Packaging, and Allied Trades Research Association
PATRA .... Professional and Technical Role Analyses [Occupational therapy]
PatrAH .... Patriot American Hospitality, Inc. [Associated Press] (SAG)
PATRDL....... Pan American Tung Research and Development League [Defunct] (EA)
Patr Elect Cas... Patrick's Election Cases [1824-49] [Upper Canada] [A publication] (DLA)
PATRIC .... Pattern Recognition and Information Correlations [Police crime-detection computer]
PATRIC .... Pattern Recognition Interpretation and Correlation (CET)
PATRIC........ Position and Time-Resolved Ion Counting [Detector]
PATRICIA..... Practical Algorithm to Receive Information Coded in Alphanumeric [Information retrieval]
Patrick El Cas... Patrick's Election Cases [Canada] [A publication] (DLA)
PATRIOT...... Pesticide Assessment Tool for Rating Investigations for Transport [Environmental Protection Agency] (AEPA)
PATRIOT...... Phased Array Tracking to Intercept of Target [Air defense system unit] [Army] (RDA)
PatriotB .... Patriot Bank Corp. (PA) [Associated Press] (SAG)
PatrInd........ Patrick Industries, Inc. [Associated Press] (SAG)
PatrNBk .... Patriot National Bank CT [Associated Press] (SAG)
PATROL....... Program for Administrative Traffic Reports On-Line [Computer program] [Bell System]
PatrolGr....... Patrologia Graeca (BJA)
PatrolLat...... Patrologia Latina (BJA)
PATRON....... Patrol Squadron
PATS........... Payload Avionics Test Station [NASA] (SSD)
PATS........... Payment and Telecommunication Services Corp. [New York, NY Telecommunications Defunct] (TSSD)
PATS........... People Against Tobacco Smoke (EA)
PATS........... Personnel Assistance Teams [Military]
PATS........... Personnel in an Awaiting Training Status [Air Force] (AFM)
PATS........... Plant Action Tracking System [Environmental science] (COE)
PATS........... Portable Acoustic Tracking System for Divers (MCD)
PATS........... Preacademic Training Student [Military]
PATS........... Preauthorized Automatic Transfer Scheme [Banking]
PATS........... Precise Automated Tracking System (PDAA)
PATS........... Precision Altimeter Techniques Study
PATS........... Precision Automated Tracking System [FAA] (TAG)
PATS........... Predicasts Abstract Terminal System [Computer science]
PATS........... Primary Aircraft Training System (MCD)
PATS........... Priority Activity Tracking System (DB)
PATS........... Program for Analysis of Time Series (NASA)
PATS........... Programmatic and Technical Support [Army]
PATS........... Propulsion Analysis Trajectory Simulation [Computer program] [NASA]
PATSEARCH... Patent Search [Computer science]
PATSEARCH... Patent Search System (NITA)
Pat Ser........ Indian Law Reports, Patna Series [A publication] (DLA)
PA-T-SP...... Periodic Acid-Thiocarbohydrazide-Silver Proteinate (STED)
Pat St Tr...... Paton on Stoppage in Transitu [1859] [A publication] (DLA)
PATSU .... Patrol Aircraft Service Unit
PATSY .... Parametric Test Synthesis [Computer science]

PATSY .... Picture Animal Top Star of the Year [or Performing Animal Television Star of the Year] [American Humane Association award]
PATSY .... Programmer's Automatic Testing System
PATSY .... Pulse-Amplitude Transmission System (PDAA)
PATT .... Partial Automatic Translation Technique
pat T .... Patellar Tenderness [Medicine] (STED)
PATT........... Patent (ROG)
PATT........... Pattern (AAG)
PATT........... Programmable Automatic Transistor Tester (PDAA)
PATT........... Project for the Analysis of Technology Transfer [NASA]
Patt & H ...... Patton, Jr., and Heath's Reports [Virginia] [A publication] (DLA)
Patt & Heath R... Patton, Jr., and Heath's Reports [Virginia] [A publication] (DLA)
Patt & H (VA)... Patton, Jr., and Heath's Reports [Virginia] [A publication] (DLA)
PattDntl .... Patterson Dental Co. [Associated Press] (SAG)
Patten.......... Patten Corp. [Associated Press] (SAG)
PATTERN ..... Planning Assistance Through Technical Evaluation of Relevance Numbers [RAND Corp.]
PATTH .... People Against Telephone Terrorism and Harassment (EA)
PATTI .... Precise and Accurate Time and Time Interval [An experiment aboard the Spacelab] [NASA] (PDAA)
PATTI .... Prompt Action to Telephone Inquiries (SAA)
PAT/TM....... Patient's Time (DAVI)
Pat TM & Copyr J of R & Educ... Patent, Trademark, and Copyright Journal of Research and Education [A publication] (DLA)
Patton & H... Patton, Jr., and Heath's Reports [Virginia Special Court of Appeals] [A publication] (DLA)
Patton & Heath... Patton, Jr., and Heath's Reports [Virginia] [A publication] (DLA)
Patton & H (VA)... Patton, Jr., and Heath's Reports [Virginia Special Court of Appeals] [A publication] (DLA)
Pat Trademark & Copyright J (BNA)... Patent, Trademark, and Copyright Journal (Bureau of National Affairs) [A publication] (DLA)
PATU .... PanAfrican Telecommunications Union (EAIO)
PATU .... Pan American Taekwondo Union (EA)
PATWA .... Playgroup Association of Western Australia
PATWA .... Professional and Technical Workers Aliyah [British] (BI)
PATWAS ...... Pilots Automatic Telephone Weather Answering Service
PATWING...... Patrol Wing [Later, Fleet Air Wing]
PATWINGDET... Patrol Wing [Later, Fleet Air Wing] Detachment (DNAB)
PATWINGLANTFLT... Patrol Wing [later, Fleet Air Wing] Atlantic Fleet
PATWINGSCOFOR... Patrol Wing [later, Fleet Air Wing] Scouting Force
PATX........... Private Automatic Telegraph Exchange (PDAA)
PATX........... Private Automatic Telex Exchange (NITA)
PAU .... Pacific Command Frequency Allocation and Uses (CINC)
PAU .... Pan American Union [Central organ and permanent secretariat of the OAS]
PAU .... Pattern Articulation Unit [Computer science]
PAU .... Pauk [Myanmar] [Airport symbol] (OAG)
PAU .... Paulingite [A zeolite]
Pau............ Paulus de Liazaris [Deceased, 1356] [Authority cited in pre-1607 legal work] (DSA)
PAU .... Pauzhetka [Former USSR Seismograph station code, US Geological Survey] (SEIS)
pau............ Pennsylvania [MARC country of publication code Library of Congress] (LCCP)
PAU .... Phenol-Acetic Acid-Urea [Medicine] (DMAA)
PAU .... Pilotless Aircraft Unit
PAU .... Portable Annotation Unit [Military] (CAAL)
PAU .... Position Analog Unit [Manufacturing term]
PAU .... Precision Approach - UNICOM [Aviation]
PAU .... Present Address Unknown
PAU .... Probe Aerodynamic Upper [NASA] (MCD)
PAU .... Production Assurance Unit (MCD)
PAU .... Programmes Analysis Unit [British] (MCD)
PAU .... University of Pennsylvania, Philadelphia, PA [OCLC symbol] (OCLC)
PAUBM .... Pan American Union of Baptist Men [Defunct] (EA)
PAUC........... Program Acquisition Unit Cost (AAGC)
PAUCA........ Providence Association of Ukrainian Catholics in America (EA)
Pau de Cast... Paulus de Castro [Deceased, 1441] [Authority cited in pre-1607 legal work] (DSA)
Pau de La.... Paulus de Liazaris [Deceased, 1356] [Authority cited in pre-1607 legal work] (DSA)
Pau de Montep... Paulus Ruinus de Montepico [Flourished, 15th century] [Authority cited in pre-1607 legal work] (DSA)
PAUDGET..... Photometer, Automated Universal Distribution Gonielectric Type
PAUH .... Harris [Paul] Stores [NASDAQ symbol] (SAG)
PAUH .... Paul Harris Stores [NASDAQ symbol] (SAG)
Pau Hunga... Paulus Hungarus [Deceased, 1242] [Authority cited in pre-1607 legal work] (DSA)
Pau Hungar... Paulus Hungarus [Deceased, 1242] [Authority cited in pre-1607 legal work] (DSA)
PAUKO........ Pan-American Union of Karatedo Organizations [Later, PUKO] (EA)
PAUL .... Paullum [A Little] [Pharmacy]
Paul de Cast... Paulus de Castro [Deceased, 1441] [Authority cited in pre-1607 legal work] (DSA)
Paul de Castr... Paulus de Castro [Deceased, 1441] [Authority cited in pre-1607 legal work] (DSA)
Pau Leon..... Paulus Leonius [Flourished, 16th century] [Authority cited in pre-1607 legal work] (DSA)
Paul Liaz..... Paulus de Liazaris [Deceased, 1356] [Authority cited in pre-1607 legal work] (DSA)
PAULS .... Pennsylvania Union List of Serials
Paulson........ Paulson Capital Corp. [Associated Press] (SAG)
PaulSon....... Paul-Son Gaming Corp. [Associated Press] (SAG)
Paulus .... Julius Paulus. Sententiae Receptae [A publication] (DLA)
PAUMV........ Potato Aucuba Mosaic Virus [Plant pathology]

PAUN .... Peoples Assembly for the United Nations (EA)
PAUN .... Unalakleet [Alaska] [ICAO location identifier] (ICLI)
PAUP .... Phylogenic Analysis Using Parsimony [Biology]
Paus .... Pausanias [Second century AD] [Classical studies] (OCD)
PAUS .... Piedmontese Association of the United States (EA)
PAUS .... Planning and Analysis for Uncertain Situations (MHDI)
PAUS .... Public Advocate of the United States (EA)
PAUSE .... People Against Unconstitutional Sex Education
PAUT .... Pennsylvania & Atlantic Railroad Co. [Absorbed into Consolidated Rail Corp.] [AAR code]
PAUX .... Pauxillum [A Little] [Pharmacy]
P/AV .... Particular Average
PaV .... Pathe-Vox [Record label] [France]
PAV .... Paulo Afonso [Brazil] [Airport symbol] (OAG)
PAV .... Pavia [Italy] [Seismograph station code, US Geological Survey] (SEIS)
PAV .... Pavilion
Pav .... Pavo [Constellation]
PAV .... Pay Adjustment Voucher [Military]
PAV .... Personnel Allotment Voucher [Army]
PAV .... Phase Angle Voltmeter
PA(V) .... Police Association (Victoria) [Australia]
PAV .... Position and Velocity
PAV .... Position and Velocity Tracking (IAA)
PAV .... Poste-Avion [Airmail] [French]
PAV .... Potential Acquisition Valuation Method [Management]
PAV .... Potential AIDS [Acquired Immune Deficiency Syndrome] Victim
PAV .... Pressure-Actuated Valve (NASA)
PAV .... Pressure Altitude Variation [Aviation]
PAV .... Propellant-Actuated Valve
PAV .... Public Access Videotex
PAV .... Public Against Violence [Former Czechoslovakia] [Political party]
PAV .... Puella Americana Vallensis [Valley Girl] [Teenaged girl who follows the fads, fashions, and slang originated among teenagers in California's San Fernando Valley]
PAVA .... Polish Army Veterans Association of America (EA)
PAVAS .... Performing and Visual Arts Society (EA)
PAVD .... Valdez [Alaska] [ICAO location identifier] (ICLI)
PAVE .... Parents Active for Vision Education [An association] (EA)
PAVE .... Paving
PAVE .... Performance-Based Adult Vocational Education (EDAC)
PAVE .... Position and Velocity Extraction
PAVE .... Preparing for AIDS/HIV Vaccine Evaluation [National Institutes of Health project]
PAVE .... Primary Auditory Visual Experience [National Visitor Center]
PAVE .... Principles and Applications of Value Engineering
PAVe .... Procarbazine, Alanine Nitrogen Mustard [L-Phenylanine mustard, L-PAM], Velban [Vinblastine] [Antineoplastic drug regimen]
PAVE .... Professional Audiovisual Education Study
PAVE .... Programmed Analysis for Value Engineers
PAVE PAWS... Precision Acquisition of Vehicle Entry Phased Array Warning System
PAVF .... Pulmonary Arteriovenous Fistula [Medicine]
PAVFC .... Princeton Azimuthally-Varying-Field Cyclotron
PAVG .... Prince Albert's Volunteer Guards [British military] (DMA)
PAVGX .... One Group: Value Growth Cl.A [Mutual fund ticker symbol] (SG)
pavl .... Pavilion (VRA)
PAVLA .... Papal Volunteers for Latin America [Defunct]
PAVM .... Patrons of the Arts in the Vatican Museum (EA)
PAVM .... Phase Angle Voltmeter
PAVM .... Proximity Automatic Vehicle Monitoring (PDAA)
PAVM .... Pulmonary Arteriovenous Malformation [Medicine] (DMAA)
PAVMT .... Pavement
PAVN .... People's Army of Vietnam
PAVO .... Prince Albert Victor's Own [British military] (DMA)
PAVOC .... Prince Albert Victor's Own Cavalry [British military] (DMA)
PA/VR .... Public Assistance/Vocational Rehabilitation
PAVS .... Pulmonary Arterial Vasconstrictor Substance [Medicine]
PA/VSI .... Preliminary Assessment and Visual Site Inspection [Environmental science] (BCP)
PAVT .... Position and Velocity Tracking
PAW .... Pambwa [Papua New Guinea] [Airport symbol] (OAG)
PAW .... Panel of American Women (EA)
PAW .... Peak Airway Pressure [Medicine] (DAVI)
PAW .... Pentecostal Assemblies of the World (EA)
PAW .... People for the American Way (EA)
PAW .... Percussive Arc Welder
PAW .... Performance Analysis Workstation [Computer science]
PAW .... Peripheral Airways [Medicine] (DMAA)
PAW .... Petroleum Administration for War [World War II]
PAW .... Plant-Available Water [Botany]
PAW .... Plasma Arc Welding
PAW .... Poetic Allusion Watch
PAW .... Port Angeles Western Railroad (IIA)
PAW .... Powered All the Way
Paw .... Pressure in the Airway [level to be specified] (DAVI)
PAW .... Primary Affective Witzelsucht [Medicine] (CPH)
PAW .... Protect Appalachian Wilderness [An association] (WPI)
PAW .... Public Administered Whipping [Slang]
PAW .... Pulmonary Artery Wedge [Pressure] [Cardiology] (DAVI)
PAW .... Pulmonary Artery Wedge Pressure [Cardiology]
PAWA .... Pan American Women's Association (EA)
PAWA .... Pan-American World Airways (NADA)
PAWA .... Power and Water Authority [Northern Territory, Australia]
PAWAF .... Polish American Workmen's Aid Fund (EA)

PAWBP .... Pension and Welfare Benefit Programs [Labor-Managment Services Administration] (IAA)
PAWC .... Pacific West Conference (PSS)
PAWC .... Pan-American Weightlifting Confederation (EA)
PA WC Bd Dec... Pennsylvania Workmen's Compensation Board Decisions [A publication] (DLA)
PA WC Bd Dec Dig... Digest of Decisions, Pennsylvania Workmen's Compensation Board [A publication] (DLA)
PA WC Bd (Dep Rep Sup)... Workmen's Compensation Supplement to Department Reports of Pennsylvania [A publication] (DLA)
PAWD .... Kodiak/Municipal [Alaska] [ICAO location identifier] (ICLI)
PAWE .... Program for Analysis of the World Ecosystem
PAWES .... Performance Assessment and Workload Evaluation (GAVI)
PAWLC .... Pan-American Weightlifting Confederation (EA)
PAWN .... First Cash [NASDAQ symbol] (TTSB)
PAWN .... First Cash, Inc. [NASDAQ symbol] (SAG)
PAWN .... Photon Adjoint with Neutron (PDAA)
PAWN .... Poole, Aberley, Worthington, and Nolen [Four early residents of Pawn, Oregon. The city derives its name from the initial letters of their surnames]
PAWNW .... First Cash Wrrt [NASDAQ symbol] (TTSB)
PAWO .... Pan-African Women's Organization [Commercial firm] (NADA)
Pawo .... Pressure at the Airway Opening [Medicine] (DAVI)
PAWOB .... Passenger Arriving Without Baggage
PAWOS .... Portable Automatic Weather Observing Station (MCD)
PAWP .... Pulmonary Artery Wedge Pressure [Medicine]
PAWS .... Parachute Altitude Wind Sensor
PAWS .... Performing Animal Welfare Society (EA)
PAWS .... Pet Animal Welfare Scheme [British] (DI)
PAWS .... Pets Are Worth Safeguarding [An association]
PAWS .... Phased Array Warning System
PAWS .... Polar Automatic Weather Station (NG)
PAWS .... Portable Acoustic Wave Sensor (AAEL)
PAWS .... Portable Automatic Weather Station (MUGU)
PAWS .... Pro-Active World Suspension [Automotive engineering]
PAWS .... Programmed Automatic Welding System
PAWS .... Progressive Animal Welfare Society (GNE)
PAWT .... Wainwright [Alaska] [ICAO location identifier] (ICLI)
PAWW .... Wildwood [Alaska] [ICAO location identifier] (ICLI)
PAX .... OPTEVFOR [Operational Test and Evaluation Force] Detachment, Patuxent River, MD [Navy] (CAAL)
PAX .... Pan Air, Inc. [ICAO designator] (FAAC)
PAX .... Pan Central Explorations Ltd. [Toronto Stock Exchange symbol]
PAX .... Parallel Architecture Extended [Computer science]
PAX .... Passenger (AFM)
PAX .... Patuxent River [Maryland] (MCD)
PAX .... Paxson [Alaska] [Seismograph station code, US Geological Survey] (SEIS)
Pax .... Paxton [Record label] [Great Britain]
PAX .... Person-to-Person Accelerated Xerography [Office technology] [British]
PAX .... Photoemission of Adsorbed Xenon [Physics]
PAX .... Physical Address Extension
PAX .... Place Address in Index Register (SAA)
PAX .... Private Automatic Exchange [Telecommunications]
Paxar .... Paxar Corp. [Associated Press] (SAG)
PAXCON ...... Passenger Airlift Contract [Military]
PaxsnC .... Paxson Communications Corp. [Associated Press] (SAG)
PAXWX .... Pax World Fund [Mutual fund ticker symbol] (SG)
PAY .... Pamol [Malaysia] [Airport symbol] (OAG)
PAY .... SPS Transaction Services [NYSE symbol] (SAG)
PAYA .... Yakutat [Alaska] [ICAO location identifier] (ICLI)
PAYABL .... Payable
Pay & Iv Carr... Payne and Ivamy's Carriage by Sea [10th ed.] [1976] [A publication] (DLA)
PAYC .... Payco American Corp. [NASDAQ symbol] (NQ)
Paychx .... Paychex, Inc. [Associated Press] (SAG)
Payco .... Payco American Corp. [Associated Press] (SAG)
PAYCOM ...... Payload Command [NASA] (MCD)
PayCsh .... Payless Cashways, Inc. [Associated Press] (SAG)
PAYDAT ...... Payload Data [NASA] (MCD)
PAYE .... Pay As You Earn
PAYE .... Pay As You Enter
PAYE .... Pitch and Yaw Engine (MCD)
PAYERS ...... Program Accomplishment Year to Date Evaluation Reviews
PAYES .... Program for Assessing Youth Employment Skills [Vocational guidance test]
PAYG .... Pay-As-You-Go
PAYGO .... Pay as You Go [US Congress]
PAYLD .... Payload
PaylSh .... Payless ShoeSource, Inc. [Associated Press] (SAG)
PAYM .... Pan African Youth Movement (BUAC)
PAYM .... Paymaster [Military British] (ROG)
PAYMARCORPS... Paymaster, Marine Corps
PAYMR .... Paymaster
PAYMT .... Payment
PAYMTR ...... Paymaster [Military British] (ROG)
PAYR .... Paymaster (WGA)
PAYS .... Patriotic American Youth Society
PAYSOP ...... Payroll-Based Stock Option Plan [Human resources] (WYGK)
PAYSOP ...... Payroll/Stock Ownership Plan
PAYSU .... P'Eylim-American Yeshiva Student Union (EA)
PAYT .... Payment
Payt .... Payment (EBF)
payt .... Payment (WDAA)

PAYX	Paychex, Inc. [*NASDAQ symbol*] (NQ)	
PAZ	Palaeozoic Axial Zone [*Geophysics*]	
PAZ	Partial Annealing Zone [*Geology*]	
PAZ	PM Air, Inc. [*ICAO designator*] (FAAC)	
PAZ	Poza Rica [*Mexico*] [*Airport symbol*] (OAG)	
PAZA	Anchorage [*Alaska*] [*ICAO location identifier*] (ICLI)	
PAZA	Pan American Zebu Association [*Later, IZBA*] (EA)	
PAZA	Press Association of Zambia (BUAC)	
PAZF	Fairbanks [*Alaska*] [*ICAO location identifier*] (ICLI)	
PB	Air Burundi [*ICAO designator*] (AD)	
PB	Bachelor of Philosophy (WDAA)	
PB	Barometric Pressure [*Medicine*] (STED)	
PB	Bethlehem Public Library, Bethlehem, PA [*Library symbol Library of Congress*] (LCLS)	
PB	Dr. Karl Thomae GmbH [*Germany*] [*Research code symbol*]	
Pb	Lead	
PB	Lead [*BTS*] (TAG)	
P/B	Pad and Boom [*Refueling*] [*Aerospace*] (MSA)	
PB	Page Buffer (NITA)	
PB	Painted Base (AAG)	
PB	Panama Basin	
PB	Panamerican Beverages [*NYSE symbol*] (SPSG)	
PB	Panamerican Beverages 'A' [*NYSE symbol*] (TTSB)	
PB	Panic Bar [*Technical drawings*]	
PB	Paperback (CDAI)	
PB	Paper Base (MSA)	
PB	Paperboard Industries Corp. [*Toronto Stock Exchange symbol*]	
PB	Papua Besena [*Papua New Guinea*] [*Political party*] (FEA)	
PB	Paraffin Bath [*Medicine*]	
PB	Paris Bourse [*The French stock exchange*]	
PB	Parity BIT [*Binary Digit*] [*Data communications*] (IAA)	
PB	Parke-Bernet [*Later, SPB*] [*Manhattan art auction house*]	
PB	Parliamentary Bill [*British*] (ROG)	
PB	Parole Board [*Australian Capital Territory*]	
PB	Particle-Beam Weapon	
PB	Parts Breakdown	
PB	Passbook [*Banking*]	
PB	Passed Ball	
PB	Patrol Base [*Army*] (VNW)	
PB	Patrol Boat [*Navy symbol*]	
PB	Patrol Bomber	
PB	Paul-Bunnell [*Test*] [*Immunology*] (AAMN)	
PB	Pawnbroker	
PB	Pay Board	
PB	Peaceful Beginnings (EA)	
PB	Peanut Butter [*Brand name of the Red Wing Co.*]	
PB	Pennsylvania Ballet	
PB	Pentaborane [*Rocket fuel*]	
PB	Pentobarbital [*Organic chemistry*]	
PB	Peribrachialis [*Anatomy*]	
PB	Peripheral Blood [*Medicine*] (AAMN)	
PB	Peripheral Buffer	
PB	Permanent Ballast (DS)	
PB	Permanent Bunkers	
PB	Permanently Blind	
PB	Peroneus Brevis [*Muscle*] [*orthopedics*] (DAVI)	
PB	Petrus Brito [*Flourished, 13th century*] [*Authority cited in pre-1607 legal work*] (DSA)	
PB	Phalangeal Bracket [*i.e., cup handle*] [*Slang*]	
PB	Pharmacopoeia Britannica [*British Pharmacopoeia*]	
PB	Phenobarbital [*A drug*]	
Pb	Phenobarbital (STED)	
PB	Philosophiae Baccalaureus [*Bachelor of Philosophy*]	
PB	Phonetically Balanced [*With reference to word lists*]	
PB	Phosphate Buffer	
PB	Phosphoribosyl	
PB	Photon Barrier [*Astrophysics*]	
PB	Physics Briefs [*Physikalische Berichte*] [*American Institute of Physics Database*] [*Information service or system*] (IID)	
PB	Physiotherapists Board [*Australian Capital Territory*]	
PB	Picket Boat [*Navy*]	
PB	Piebald	
PB	Piggyback (IAA)	
PB	Pilotless Bomber [*Air Force*]	
PB	Pinchbeck [*Jewelry*] (ROG)	
PB	Pinch Biopsy [*Medicine*] (MEDA)	
PB	Pine Bark	
PB	Pink Bollworm [*Cotton pest*]	
PB	Pipe Break [*Nuclear energy*] (NRCH)	
PB	Piperonyl Butoxide [*Organic chemistry*]	
PB	Pit Border [*Paleobotany*]	
PB	Pitney-Bowes, Inc.	
PB	Planning Board	
PB	Plasminogen Binding [*Hematology*]	
PB	Plate Block [*Philately*]	
PB	Playback (KSC)	
PB	Plot Board (KSC)	
PB	Plugboard	
PB	Plugging Back [*Computer science*] (IAA)	
Pb	Plumbum [*Lead*] [*Chemical element*]	
PB	Plymouth Brethren (ROG)	
PB	Pocket Book	
PB	Police Burgh	
PB	Policy Board (OICC)	
PB	Polished Buckram (DGA)	

PB	Pollen Body [*Botany*]	
PB	Polybenzene [*Organic chemistry*]	
PB	Polybutylene [*Organic chemistry*]	
PB	Polymyxin B [*An antibiotic*]	
PB	Polystyrene Base (DGA)	
PB	Pony Baseball (EA)	
PB	Poop and Bridge [*of a ship*] (DS)	
PB	Population Biology	
PB	Ports and Beaches (NATG)	
PB	Powder Bed (DAVI)	
PB	Powder Board (DAVI)	
PB	Power Boiler	
PB	Power Box (IAA)	
PB	Power Brakes [*Automotive engineering*]	
PB	Power Builder [*Computer software*] (CDE)	
PB	Prayer Book	
PB	Preburner [*NASA*] (NASA)	
PB	Preliminary Breakdown	
PB	Premature Beat [*Medicine*] (CPH)	
PB	Premium Bond (ODBW)	
Pb	Presbyopia [*Ophthalmology*]	
PB	Presentation Brothers [*See also FPM*] (EAIO)	
PB	President's Budget (DOMA)	
PB	Presiding Bishop [*Episcopal Church*]	
PB	Pressure Breathing	
PB	Primary Buffer [*Chemistry*]	
PB	Primary Bus [*Computer science*] (CAAL)	
PB	Primitive Baptist	
PB	Printed Board (AAEL)	
PB	Prisoners' Barracks (ADA)	
PB	Private Business [*Slang British*]	
PB	Privately Bonded	
Pb	Probability (PCM)	
Pb	Probenecid (STED)	
PB	Process Basic (ECII)	
PB	Process Bulletin	
PB	Production Base (MCD)	
PB	Professional Books Ltd. (ILCA)	
PB	Profile Block (MCD)	
PB	Program Baseline (DOMA)	
PB	Program Block (IAA)	
PB	Program Breakdown	
PB	Program Budgeting (ADA)	
PB	Property Book [*Army*] (AABC)	
PB	Proportional Band	
PB	Protein-Binding (MAE)	
PB	Protein-Bound [*Clinical chemistry*] (DAVI)	
PB	Provisional Battalion [*Military A publication*] (ROG)	
PB	Pseudoterminal Bud [*Botany*]	
PB	Ptychodiscus brevis [*An alga, the cause of the red tide*]	
PB	Public (DSUE)	
PB	Publications (NITA)	
PB	Publications Board [*Later, CFSTI, NTIS*]	
PB	Publications Bulletin	
PB	Publisher (NITA)	
PB	Publishers' Binding (DGA)	
PB	Publisher's Name [*Online database field identifier*]	
PB	Pull Back (NTCM)	
PB	Pull Box (AAG)	
PB	Pulse Beacon (KSC)	
PB	Purl into Back of Stitch [*Knitting*] (WDAA)	
PB	Purplish Blue	
PB	Push Button	
PB4	Plate Block of Four [*Philately*]	
PBa	Academy of the New Church, Bryn Athyn, PA [*Library symbol Library of Congress*] (LCLS)	
Pba	Brachial Arterial Pressure [*Medicine*] (MAE)	
PBA	Pacific Broadcasting Association (EAIO)	
PBA	Paid by Agent [*Business term*] (DCTA)	
PBA	Partido Barrientista Autentico [*Bolivia*] [*Political party*] (PPW)	
PBA	Patrol Boat, Air Cushion (MCD)	
PBA	Patrolmen's Benevolent Association	
PBA	Pencil Beam Antenna	
PBA	Percutaneous Bladder Aspiration [*Urology*] (DAVI)	
PBA	Permanent Budget Account	
PBA	Phenylboronate Agarose [*Biochemistry*] (DAVI)	
PBA	Phenylboronic Acid [*Organic chemistry*]	
PBA	Phenylbutyric Acid [*Organic chemistry*]	
PBA	Physical Blowing Agent [*Plastics technology*]	
PBA	Pill Box Antenna	
PBA	Pine Bluff Arsenal [*Army*] (AABC)	
PBA	Plant Breeding Abstracts [*A publication*]	
PbA	Plasmodium Berghei Anka [*Bacteriology*]	
PBA	Plastic Bag Association (EA)	
PBA	Polar Bear Association (EA)	
PBA	Polish Beneficial Association (EA)	
PBA	Polybenzamide [*Organic chemistry*]	
PBA	Polybutyl Acrylate [*Organic chemistry*]	
PBA	Polyclonal B Cell Activator [*Hematology*]	
PBA	Port Blair [*Andaman Islands*] [*Seismograph station code, US Geological Survey*] (SEIS)	
PBA	Port of Bristol Authority [*British*]	
PBA	Poultry Bowling Association	
PBA	Poultry Breeders of America (EA)	
PBA	Power-Book Army [*Computer science*]	

PBA............ Powered Battle Armor [*A computer game*] (PCM)
PBA............ Prescott Builders Association (EA)
PBA............ President of the British Academy
PBA............ Pressure Breathing Assister [*Medicine*] (STED)
PBA............ Pressure Breathing Assistor [*Medicine*]
PBA............ Principal Business Activity (GFGA)
PBA............ Printed Board Assembly (IAA)
PBA............ Printing Brokerage Association (EA)
PBA............ Production Base Analysis (MCD)
PBA............ Professional Bookmen of America [*Later, Pi Beta Alpha*] (EA)
PBA............ Professional Bowlers Association of America (EA)
PBA............ Prolactin-Binding Assay (STED)
PBA............ Provincetown-Boston Airlines, Inc.
PBA............ Prune Belly Anomaly [*Medicine*] (DMAA)
PBA............ Public Buildings Administration [*Functions transferred to PBS, 1949*]
PBA............ Pulpobuccoaxial [*Dentistry*]
PBA............ Pyrenebutyric Acid [*Organic chemistry*]
PBAA.......... Periodical and Book Association of America (EA)
PBAA.......... Poly(butadiene-acrylic acid) [*Organic chemistry*]
PBAA.......... Polybutadiene Acrylic Acid Copolymer (EDCT)
PBAA.......... Private Businesses Association of Australia
PBAC.......... Pacific Bantam Austin Club (EA)
PBAC.......... Peach Belt Athletic Conference (PSS)
PBAC.......... Program Budget Advisory Committee [*Army*]
PB-AESRS.... Property Book - Army Equipment Status Reporting System (AABC)
PBAL.......... Protected Bronchoalveolar Lavage [*Medicine*] (DMAA)
PBAN.......... Pheromone Biosynthesis-Activating Neuropeptide [*Biochemistry*]
PBAN.......... Poly(butadiene-acrylonitrile) [*Organic chemistry*]
PBAN.......... Polybutadiene Acrylonitrile Copolymer (EDCT)
PB&D.......... Piano, Bass & Drums (WDAA)
PB and J..... Peanut Butter and Jelly
PBAPRS....... Program/Budget Accounting and Progress Reporting System [*Proposed*] [*Navy*]
PBAPS........ Peach Bottom Atomic Power Station (NRCH)
PBAPS........ Pipe Break Air Piping System (IEEE)
PBAPS........ Pipe Break Automatic Protective System (IEEE)
PBAR.......... Baker Island Army Air Field [*Baker Island*] [*ICAO location identifier*] (ICLI)
PBAS.......... Program Budget Accounting System [*Military*] (GFGA)
PBAT.......... Pyro Battery (KSC)
PBATS......... Professional Baseball Athletic Trainers Society (EA)
PBAV.......... Percutaneous Balloon Aortic Valvuloplasty [*Cardiology*] (CPH)
PBAV.......... Power Boat Association of Victoria [*Australia*]
PBB............ Bloomsburg State College, Bloomsburg, PA [*OCLC symbol*] (OCLC)
PBB............ Parallel by Bit
PBB............ Paranaiba [*Brazil*] [*Airport symbol*] (OAG)
PBB............ Parti Pesaka Bumiputera Bersatu Sarawak [*United Bumiputra Party*] [*Malaysia*] [*Political party*] (FEA)
PBB............ Polybrominated Biphenyl [*Flame retardant, toxic chemical*]
PBB............ Posterior Basal Body [*Botany*]
PBB............ Private Boxes and Bags
PBB............ Program Plan Budgeting (TDOB)
PBB............ Project Blue Book [*An association*] (EA)
PBBA.......... Printing Brokerage Buyers Association (NTPA)
PBBA.......... Pro-Bessarabia and Bukovina Association [*Romania*] (BUAC)
PBBATU....... Pastrycooks, Bakers, Biscuitmakers, and Allied Trades Union [*Australia*]
PBBCAS....... Program-Based Budget Classification and Analysis System [*Pronounced "pib-kaz"*] [*Office of Management and Budget*]
PBbCHi....... Columbia County Historical Society, Bloomsburg, PA [*Library symbol Library of Congress*] (LCLS)
PBBFI......... Pearl S. Buck Birthplace Foundation, Inc. (EA)
PBBH.......... Peter Bent Brigham Hospital [*Boston*]
PBbS.......... Bloomsburg State College, Bloomsburg, PA [*Library symbol Library of Congress*] (LCLS)
PBBS.......... Pertubuhan Bumiputera Bersatu Sarawak [*United Sarawak National Association*] [*Malaysia*] [*Political party*] (FEA)
PBBs.......... Polybromated Biphenyls [*Organic chemistry*] (DAVI)
PBBSF........ Pacific Basin Bulk [*NASDAQ symbol*] (TTSB)
PBBSF........ Pacific Basin Bulk Shippers Ltd. [*NASDAQ symbol*] (SAG)
PBBWF....... Pacific Basin Blk Shipng Wrrt [*NASDAQ symbol*] (TTSB)
PBBWF....... Pacific Basin Bulk Shippers Ltd. [*NASDAQ symbol*] (SAG)
PBC............ Columbia/Mt. Pleasant, TN [*Location identifier FAA*] (FAAL)
PBC............ Pacific Bible College [*California*]
PBC............ Packed by Carrier
PBC............ Pakistan Broadcasting Corp. (IMH)
PBC............ Panamerican Badminton Confederation (EAIO)
PBC............ Parallel by Character
PBC............ Parent Behavior Checklist [*Test*] (TMMY)
PBC............ Pedal Branch of Columellar [*Muscle*]
PBC............ Pen and Brush Club (EA)
PBC............ People's Bank of China (ECON)
PBC............ People's Bicentennial [*later, Business*] Commission
PBC............ Periodic Bond Chain (IAA)
PBC............ Peripheral Blood Cells [*Medicine*]
PBC............ Peripheral Bus Computer [*Bell System*]
PBC............ Personnel/Burden Carrier Manufacturers Association [*Defunct*] (EA)
PBC............ Plain Bond Copier [*Pitney Bowes*]
PBC............ Planning and the Black Community (EA)
PBC............ Point of Basal Convergence
PBC............ Practice Bomb Contained
PBC............ Prebed Care [*Medicine*] (MAE)
PBC............ Pregnancy and Birth Complications (STED)
PBC............ Presbyterians for Biblical Concerns (EA)
PBC............ Primary Biliary Cirrhosis [*Medicine*]

PBC............ Progestin-Binding Complement (STED)
PBC............ Program Booking Center [*Telecommunications*] (TEL)
PBC............ Program Budget Committee [*Military*]
PBC............ Psychometric Behavior Checklist [*Psychology*]
PBC............ Public Buildings Commission [*Functions transferred to PBA, 1939*]
PBCA.......... Pacific Bible College of Azusa [*California*]
PBCA.......... Paperboard Butter Chip Association
PBCA.......... Professional Business Colleges of Australia
PBCB .... Pierce-Blank Die (Class B) (MCD)
PBCB .... Professional Boxing Control Board [*Victoria, Australia*]
PBCC .... Packard Bell Computer Corp. (IAA)
PBCC .... Pitney Bowes Credit Corp.
PBCCH........ Pentabromochlorocyclohexane [*Flame retardant*] [*Organic chemistry*]
PBCE.......... Pine Bluff Cotton Exchange [*Defunct*] (EA)
PBCF.......... Prudential-Bache Capital Funding
PBCI.......... Pamrapo Bancorp [*NASDAQ symbol*] (TTSB)
PBCI.......... Pamrapo Bancorp, Inc. [*NASDAQ symbol*] (NQ) .
PBCLS .... Palm Beach County Library System [*Florida*]
PBCMO........ Poly(bis(chloromethyl)oxetane) [*Organic chemistry*]
PBCO.......... Praseodymium Barium Copper Oxide [*Inorganic chemistry*]
PB/COC....... Plymouth Barracuda/Cuda Owners Club (EA)
PbCoNA....... Publishing Co. of North America, Inc. (The) [*Associated Press*] (SAG)
PBCP.......... Political Bureau of the Communist Party (BUAC)
PBCS.......... Persian Bicolor and Calico Society (EA)
PBCS.......... Post Boost Control System [*Aerospace*]
PBCT.......... People's Bank [*Bridgeport, CT*] [*NASDAQ symbol*] (NQ)
PBCT.......... Proposed Boundary Crossing Time [*Aviation*]
PBCTP........ People's Bank 8.5% Cv 'A' Pfd [*NASDAQ symbol*] (TTSB)
PBCU.......... Predominately Black Colleges and Universities
PBC-USA..... Polar Bear Club - USA (EA)
PBC-WS...... Polar Bear Club - Winter Swimmers [*Later, PBC-USA*] (EA)
PBD............ Pacific Basin Development Corp. [*Vancouver Stock Exchange symbol*]
PBD............ Paperboard (MSA)
PBD............ Parallel Blade Damper (OA)
PBD............ Particle Board [*Technical drawings*]
PBD............ Paul-Bunnell-Davidsohn [*Test*] [*Immunology*]
PBD............ Payload Bay Door [*NASA*] (NASA)
PBD............ Percutaneous Biliary Drainage [*Gastroenterology*] (DAVI)
PBD............ Phenylbiphenylyloxadiazole [*Analytical biochemistry*]
PBD............ Pierce-Blank Die (MCD)
PBD............ Place Bearing/Distance [*Way point*] (GAVI)
PBD............ Plasterboard
PBD............ Plenum Bleed Duct [*Hovercraft*]
PBD............ Polybutadiene [*Organic chemistry*]
PBD............ Porbandar [*India*] [*Airport symbol*] (OAG)
PBD............ Postburn Day [*Medicine*] (DMAA)
PBD............ Power Building (NATG)
PBD............ Prayer Book Dictionary [*A publication*] (ODCC)
PBD............ Precise Block Diagram
PBD............ Pressboard (MSA)
PBD............ Professional Building Designer [*Accreditation from the American Institute of Building Designers*]
PBD............ Program Budget Decision [*DoD*]
PBD............ Program Budget Directive (MCD)
PBD............ Program Budget Document (MCD)
PBD............ Programmer Brain Damage [*Computer hacker terminology*] (NHD)
PBD............ Proliferative Breast Disease [*Medicine*]
PBDB.......... Provisional Base Defense Battalion [*Marine Corps*] (VNW)
PBDC.......... Pacific Basin Development Council (EA)
PBDE.......... Polybrominated Diphenyl Ether [*Flame retardant*]
PBDF.......... Payload Bay Door Forward [*NASA*] (MCD)
PBDG.......... Push-Button Data Generator (IEEE)
PBDI .... Position Bearing and Distance Indicator (MCD)
PBDM......... Payload Bay Door Mechanism [*NASA*] (NASA)
PBDMA....... Poly(butadiene-malic Acid) [*A polymer*]
PBDS.......... Parti Bansa Dayak Sarawak [*Malaysia*] [*Political party*] (FEA)
PBDU.......... Pancreaticobiliary Ductal Union [*Anatomy*]
PBe............ Beaver Memorial Library, Beaver, PA [*Library symbol Library of Congress*] (LCLS)
PBE............ Paint, Body, and Equipment [*Automotive engineering*]
PBE............ Paschen-Back Effect [*Spectroscopy*]
PBE............ Pemberton Exploration [*Vancouver Stock Exchange symbol*]
PBE............ Perlsucht Bacillary Emulsion [*Medicine*]
PBE............ Piggyback Experiment
PBE............ Poison-Boltzmann Equation [*Physical chemistry*]
PBE............ Polybutene [*Organic chemistry*]
PBE............ Present-Barrel-Equivalent
PBE............ Prompt Burst Experiments [*Nuclear energy*] (NRCH)
PBE............ Prompt-by-Example [*Computer science*]
PBE............ Proton Balance Equation
PBE............ Proton Binding Energy
PBE............ Puerto Berrio [*Colombia*] [*Airport symbol*] (OAG)
PBE............ Pulsed Bridge Element [*Telecommunications*] (OA)
PBEA.......... Paint, Body, and Equipment Association (EA)
PBEB.......... Pentabromoethylbenzene [*Flame retardant*] [*Organic chemistry*]
PBeC.......... Beaver County Court House, Beaver, PA [*Library symbol Library of Congress*] (LCLS)
PBEC.......... Pacific Basin Economic Council (FEA)
PBEC.......... Public Broadcasting Environment Center [*Corporation for Public Broadcasting*]
PBECL........ Performance-Based Exposure Control Limit [*Environmental science*]
PBEI.......... Performance-Based Evaluation Instrument (EDAC)
PBEIST........ Planning Board European Inland Surface Transport [*Army*] (AABC)

PBel............. Centre County Library, Bellefonte, PA [*Library symbol Library of Congress*] (LCLS)
PBelC........... Centre County Court House, Bellefonte, PA [*Library symbol Library of Congress*] (LCLS)
PBEM........... Play by Electronic Mail [*Computer science*]
PBER .... Program Budget Execution Review [*Army*]
PBerol .... Berlin Papyri [*A publication*] (OCD)
PBET............ Performance-Based Equipment Training (AAEL)
PBf............... Carnegie Free Library, Beaver Falls, PA [*Library symbol Library of Congress*] (LCLS)
PBF.............. Fast Patrol Boat [*Ship symbol*] [*NATO*] (NATG)
PBF.............. Patriotic Burmese Forces [*World War II*]
PBF.............. Patrol Boat, Fast [*British military*] (DMA)
PBF.............. Peribronchial Fibrosis [*Medicine*]
PBF.............. Pilot Bypass Filter (IAA)
PBF.............. Pine Bluff [*Arkansas*] [*Airport symbol Obsolete*] (OAG)
PBF.............. Plastic Bottle Feeder
PBF.............. Plates for Beam Forming (DEN)
PBF.............. Poop, Bridge, and Forecastle [*of a ship*] (DS)
PBF.............. Portal Blood Flow [*Physiology*]
PBF.............. Potential Benefit Factor (OA)
PBF.............. Power Burst Facility [*Nuclear energy*]
PBF.............. Pulmonary Blood Flow [*Medicine*]
PBFA........... Particle Beam Fusion Accelerator
PBFA........... Provincial Booksellers' Fairs Association [*British*] (DI)
PBFC........... Peter Breck Fan Club (EA)
PBFC........... Pierce Brosnan Fan Club (EA)
PBFD .... Pierce Bland and Form Die (MSA)
PBFE........... Peroxisomal Bifunctional Enzyme (DMAA)
PB-Fe.......... Protein-Bound Iron (MAE)
PBfG .... Geneva College, Beaver Falls, PA [*Library symbol Library of Congress*] (LCLS)
PBFG .... Guided Missile Fast Patrol Boat [*Ship symbol*] (NATG)
PBFG .... Patrol Boat, Fast, Guided Weapon [*British military*] (DMA)
PBFI............ Paris Business Forms, Inc. [*Burlington, NJ*] [*NASDAQ symbol*] (NQ)
PBFI............ Paris Corp. [*NASDAQ symbol*] (TTSB)
PBFL........... Planning for Better Family Living [*UN Food and Agriculture Organization*]
PBFP........... Provisioning Budget Forecast Procedure (MCD)
PBF/WR ...... Presiding Bishop's Fund for World Relief (EA)
PBG .... Phenylbiguanide [*Biochemistry*]
PBG .... Photonic Bandgap [*Physics*]
PBG .... Plattsburgh, NY [*Location identifier FAA*] (FAAL)
PBG .... Poly(benzyl Glutamate) [*Organic chemistry*]
PBG .... Porphobilinogen [*Clinical chemistry*]
PBG .... Powszechny Bank Gospodarczy [*Poland*]
PBG .... Program and Budget Guidance [*Army*]
PBGA........... Plastic Ball Grid Arrays
PBGC........... Pension Benefit Guaranty Corp. [*Government agency*]
PBGD .... Porphobilinogen Deaminase [*An enzyme*] (MCD)
PBGI .... Piedmont BankGroup, Inc. [*NASDAQ symbol*] (NQ)
PBG-QN ...... Porphobilinogen - Quantitative [*Genetics*] (DAVI)
PBG-S .... Porphobilinogen Synthase [*Medicine*] (DMAA)
PBH .... Partial Bulkhead (DS)
PBH .... Patrol Boat, Hydrofoil (MCD)
PBH .... Phillips, WI [*Location identifier FAA*] (FAAL)
PBH .... Post Biblical Hebrew [*Language, etc.*] (BJA)
PBH .... Primordial Black Hole [*Astrophysics*]
PBH .... Pulling Boat Hands (DMAA)
PBHB .... Poly-Beta-Hydroxybutyrate (DMAA)
PBHF .... President Benjamin Harrison Foundation (EA)
PBHGX........ PBHG Growth Fund [*Mutual fund ticker symbol*] (SG)
PBHP .... Pounds per Brake Horsepower
PB-HTGR ..... Peach Bottom High-Temperature Gas-Cooled Reactor
PBI.............. Palm Beach International Airport [*FAA*] (TAG)
PBI.............. Paper Bag Institute (EA)
PBI.............. Parental Bonding Instrument
PBI.............. Partial Background Investigation [*Army*]
PBI.............. Partial Bony Impaction [*Orthopedics*] (DAVI)
PBI.............. Paving Brick Institute
PBI.............. Peace Brigades International (EA)
PBI.............. Pen and Brush, Inc. (EA)
PBI.............. Penile-Brachial Index [*Medicine*] (DAVI)
PBI.............. Phenformin [*An oral hypoglycemic*] [*Obsolete*] (DAVI)
PBI.............. Philadelphia Bible Institute [*Pennsylvania*]
PBI.............. Phillips Business Information, Inc. (IID)
PBI.............. Pitch Boundary Indicator (MCD)
PBI.............. Pitney Bowes [*NYSE symbol*] (TTSB)
PBI.............. Pitney-Bowes, Inc. [*NYSE symbol*] (SPSG)
PBI.............. Plant Biological Institute [*University of Saskatchewan*] [*Canada*]
PBI.............. Plant Biotechnology Institute [*National Research Council of Canada*] [*Research center*] (RCD)
PBI.............. Plant Breeding Institute [*British*]
PBI.............. Plastic Bottle Institute (EA)
PBI.............. Plumbing Brass Institute [*Later, PMI*] (EA)
PBI.............. Polybenzimidazole [*Organic chemistry*] (NATG)
PBI.............. Poly(phenylenebibenzimidazole) [*Organic chemistry*]
PBI.............. Poor Bloody Infantry [*British military slang*]
PBI.............. Post, Buckley International
PBI.............. Power Base Inventory [*Test*] (TMMY)
PBI.............. Process Branch Indicator
PBI.............. Programme Biologique Internationale [*International Biological Program - IBP*] (MSC)
PBI.............. Projected Books, Inc. [*Defunct*] (EA)
PBI.............. Prophylactic Brain Irradiation [*Oncology*]

PBI.............. Protein-Bound Iodine [*Clinical chemistry*]
PBI.............. Public Benevolent Institution [*Australia*]
PBI.............. Pupil Behavior Inventory [*Psychology*]
PBI.............. Push Button Indicator (NAKS)
PBI.............. Puzzle Buffs International (EA)
PBI.............. West Palm Beach [*Florida*] [*Airport symbol*]
PBIB............ Partially-Balanced Incomplete Block (PDAA)
PBIC............ Plant Breeding International Cambridge (BUAC)
PBIC............ Poly(butyl Isocyanate) [*Organic chemistry*]
PBIC............ Programmable Buffer Interface Card [*Computer science*] (NASA)
PBICSGH...... Permanent Bureau of International Congresses for the Sciences of Genealogy and Heraldry (EA)
PBIF............ Pacific Bible Institute of Fresno [*California*]
PBIL............ Polybenzimidazolone [*Organic chemistry*]
PBIM........... Programmable Buffer Interface Module (MCD)
PBIO............ PerSeptive Biosystems [*NASDAQ symbol*] (TTSB)
PBIO............ PerSeptive Biosystems, Inc. [*NASDAQ symbol*] (SAG)
PBIOZ.......... PerSeptive Biosystems Wrrt [*NASDAQ symbol*] (TTSB)
PBIP............ Paperbound Books in Print [*A publication*]
PBIP............ Pulse Beacon Impact Predictor (AAG)
PBIPr .... Pitney Bowes $2.12 Cv Pref [*NYSE symbol*] (TTSB)
PBIS............ Performance-Based Incentive System (AAGC)
PBISTP .... Peter Burwash International Special Tennis Programs (EA)
PBIT............ Parity BIT [*Binary Digit*] [*Data communications*]
PBI-USA...... Peace Brigades International-United States of America (EA)
PB/IWT .... Ports and Beaches and Inland Waterways Transports [*Military*] (NATG)
PBIX............ Patriot Bank [*NASDAQ symbol*] (TTSB)
PBIX............ Patriot Bank Corp. (PA) [*NASDAQ symbol*] (SAG)
PBJ............. Paper-Braided Jute (IAA)
PBJ............. Peanut Butter and Jelly
PBJ............. Peanut Butter and Jelly Sandwich (TAG)
PBJ............. Presa Benito Juarez [*Mexico*] [*Seismograph station code, US Geological Survey*] (SEIS)
PBJC........... Palm Beach Junior College [*Lakeworth, FL*]
PBK............. Palm Beach, Inc. (EFIS)
PBK............. Paperback
PBK............. Payload Bay Kit [*NASA*] (NASA)
PBK............. Phi Beta Kappa [*Honorary society*]
PB (k) .... Phonetically Balanced (Kindergarten) [*Speech and language therapy*] (DAVI)
PBK............. Phosphorylase B Kinase [*An enzyme*] (MAE)
PBK............. Poncebank [*NYSE symbol*] (SAG)
PBKAL .... Paris, Brussels, Koln [*Cologne*], Amsterdam, London [*High-speed rail network*] (ECON)
PBKB .... Peoples Bancshares, Inc. [*NASDAQ symbol*] (SAG)
PBKB .... People's Savings Bank of Brockton [*Brockton, MA*] [*NASDAQ symbol*] (NQ)
PBKC........... Premier Bankshares [*NASDAQ symbol*] (TTSB)
PBKC........... Premier Bankshares Corp. [*NASDAQ symbol*] (NQ)
PBKS........... Provident Bankshares [*NASDAQ symbol*] (TTSB)
PBKS........... Provident Bankshares Corp. [*NASDAQ symbol*] (NQ)
PBKTOA....... Printing, Bookbinding, and Kindred Trades' Overseers Association [*British*] (BI)
PBL............. Bethlehem Public Library, Bethlehem, PA [*OCLC symbol*] (OCLC)
PBL............. Blairsville Public Library, Blairsville, PA [*Library symbol Library of Congress*] (LCLS)
PBL............. Lehigh University, Bethlehem, PA [*Library symbol Library of Congress*] (LCLS)
PBL............. Parachute-Braked Landing [*Military*] (IAA)
PBL............. Payload Bay Liner [*NASA*] (MCD)
PBL............. Peripheral Blood Leukocyte [*or Lymphocyte*] [*Hematology*]
PBL............. [*The*] Philadelphia Belt Line Railroad Co. [*AAR code*]
PBL............. Photo Butt Line (MSA)
PBL............. Planetary Boundary Layer [*Aerospace*]
PBL............. Poly-Buffered Local Oxidation of Silicon (AAEL)
PBL............. Potential Binding Level [*Of natural waters for metal ions*]
PBL............. Problem Based Learning [*Education*]
PBL............. Product Baseline (MCD)
PBL............. Prune Brownline [*Plant pathology*]
PBL............. Public Broadcasting Laboratory (NTCM)
PBL............. Public Broadcast Laboratory
pbl............. Publisher [*MARC relator code*] [*Library of Congress*] (LCCP)
PBL............. Pueblo [*Diocesan abbreviation*] [*Colorado*] (TOCD)
PBL............. Puerto Cabello [*Venezuela*] [*Airport symbol*] (OAG)
PBlbM.......... Montgomery County Community College, Blue Bell, PA [*Library symbol Library of Congress*] (LCLS)
PBLD........... Progressive Base Line Dimensioning (SAA)
PBLG .... Polybenzyl-L-glutamate [*Biochemistry*]
PBLI............ Premature Birth, Live Infant [*neonatology*] (DAVI)
PBIP............ Blairsville Public Library, Blairsville, PA [*Library symbol*] [*Library of Congress*] (LCLS)
PBLS........... Production Baseline Set (MCD)
PBLSHNG .... Publishing
PBm............ Bryn Mawr College, Bryn Mawr, PA [*Library symbol Library of Congress*] (LCLS)
PBM............ Paramaribo [*Surinam*] [*Airport symbol*] (OAG)
PBM............ Patrol Search Plane [*Navy designation for Mariner aircraft*]
PBM............ Peak Bone Mass [*Medicine*] (DMAA)
PBM............ Performance-Based Management (AAGC)
PBM............ Performance Based Method [*Environmental Protection Agency*] [*Analytical chemistry*]
PBM............ Peripheral Basement Membrane [*Medicine*] (DMAA)
PBM............ Peripheral Blood Mononuclear [*Cells*] [*Hematology*]
PBM............ Permanent Bench Mark

PBM .... Pharmaceutical Benefit Manager [*or Management*] [*Managed health care*]
PBM .... Pharmacy Benefit Managers (ECON)
PBM .... PIXEL Block Mode [*Computer science*] (BYTE)
PBM .... Placental Basement Membrane [*Medicine*] (DMAA)
PBM .... Portable BIT [*Binary Digit*] Map [*Computer science*]
PBM .... Potential Barrier Method (IAA)
PBM .... Pressure Bias Modulation (MCD)
PBM .... Principal Beach Master [*RAF*] [*British*]
PBM .... Probability Based-Matched [*Database search techniques*]
PBM .... Production Base Modernization (MCD)
PBM .... Program Budget Manager (MCD)
PBM .... Program Business Management (NASA)
PBM .... Pulse Burst Modulation (IAA)
PBmA .... American College of Life Underwriters, Bryn Mawr, PA [*Library symbol Library of Congress*] (LCLS)
PBMA .... Peanut Butter Manufacturers Association [*Later, PBNPA*] (EA)
PBMA .... Plastic Bath Manufacturers Association [*British*] (DI)
PBMA .... Plumbers and Builders Merchants Association [*Australia*]
PBMA .... Polybutyl Methacrylate [*Organic chemistry*]
PBMA .... Pressed Brick Makers' Association Ltd. [*British*] (BI)
PBMASA ...... Paper Bag Manufacturers' Association of South Australia
PBMC .... Moravian College and Theological Seminary, Bethlehem, PA [*Library symbol Library of Congress*] (LCLS)
PBMC .... Peripheral Blood Mononuclear Cells [*Hematology*]
PBMCA .... Archives of the Moravian Church, Bethlehem, PA [*Library symbol Library of Congress*] (LCLS)
PBMCHRC .... Pacific Basin Maternal and Child Health Resource Center [*Guam*] (BUAC)
PBME .... Physiology and Biomedical Engineering [*Program*] (DAVI)
PBME .... Physiology and Biomedical Engineering Program (BABM)
PBMI .... Pacific Biometrics, Inc. [*NASDAQ symbol*] (SAG)
PBmL .... Ludington Public Library, Bryn Mawr, PA [*Library symbol Library of Congress*] (LCLS)
PBMNC .... Peripheral Blood Monomuclear Cell [*Hematology*] (DAVI)
PBMR .... Pennsylvania Bureau of Municipal Research (MCD)
PBMR .... Provisional Basic Military Requirements (NATG)
PBMS .... Parcel Business Machine System (NITA)
PBMS .... Performance-Based Measurement System [*Environmental Protection Agency*]
PBMS .... Photonburst Mass Spectrometry
PBMS .... Pitney Bowes Management Services
PBM/STIRS... Probability Based Matching and Self-Trained Interpretive and Retrieval Systems [*Database*] [*John Wiley & Sons, Inc.*] [*Information service or system*] (CRD)
PBMW .... Moravian College, Bethlehem, PA [*Library symbol Library of Congress*] (LCLS)
PBN .... Northampton County Area Community College, Bethlehem, PA [*Library symbol Library of Congress*] (LCLS)
PBN .... Paralytic Brachial Neuritis [*Medicine*] (MAE)
PBN .... PE Ben Oilfield Services Ltd. [*Toronto Stock Exchange symbol*]
PBN .... Peribrachialis Nuclei [*Neurology*]
PBN .... Phenyl(butyl)nitrone [*Organic chemistry*]
PBN .... Physical Block Number
PBN .... Pilatus Britten-Norman Ltd. [*British ICAO designator*] (FAAC)
PBN .... PointCast Business Network
PBN .... Polymixin-B Sulfate/Bacitracin/Neomycin [*Antibacterial regime*]
PBN .... Porto Amboin [*Angola*] [*Airport symbol*] (OAG)
PBN .... Primary Block Number [*Computer science*]
PBN .... Pyrolytic Boron Nitride [*Inorganic chemistry*]
PBNA .... Partial Body Neutron Activation [*Radiology*]
PBNA .... Phenyl-beta-naphthylamine [*Organic chemistry*]
PBNB .... People's Savings Financial Corp. [*Formerly, People's Savings Bank New Britain*] [*NASDAQ symbol*] (NQ)
PBNB .... Peoples Svgs Finl [*NASDAQ symbol*] (TTSB)
PBNE .... Philadelphia, Bethlehem & New England Railroad Co. [*AAR code*]
PBNI .... PacBell Networking Integration
PBNM .... Parallel Bar Noise Maker [*Antiacoustic torpedo device*]
PBNP .... Phipps Bend Nuclear Plant (NRCH)
PBNP .... Point Beach Nuclear Plant (NRCH)
PBNP .... Porcine Brain Natriuretic Peptide [*Biochemistry*]
PBNPA .... Peanut Butter and Nut Processors Association (EA)
PBNSW .... Pharmacy Board of New South Wales [*Australia*]
PBNSW .... Police Board of New South Wales [*Australia*]
PBNT .... Parole Board of the Northern Territory [*Australia*]
PBO .... Packed by Owner
PBO .... Paleobioclimatic Operator
PBO .... Paraburdoo [*Australia Airport symbol*] (OAG)
PBO .... Pauling Bond Order [*Physical chemistry*]
PBO .... Penicillin in Beeswax [*Medicine*] (DMAA)
PBO .... Penicillin in Beeswax and Oil [*Medicine*] (DMAA)
PBO .... Performance-Based Organization
PBO .... Personal Banking Officer (TBD)
P Bo .... Petrus Boaterius [*Flourished, 1285-1321*] [*Authority cited in pre-1607 legal work*] (DSA)
pbo .... Placebo [*Medicine*]
PBO .... Plotting Board Operator (MUGU)
PBO .... Poly(p-phenylene Benzobisoxazole) (RDA)
PBO .... Poor Bloody Observer [*British World War I military slang*] (DSUE)
PBO .... Print Business Opportunities [*A publication*] (EAAP)
PBO .... Projected Benefit Obligation (TDOB)
PBO .... Property Book Officer [*Army*] (AABC)
PBO .... Push-Button Operation
PBoC .... People's Bank of China
PBOCST .... Poly(butoxycarbonyloxystyrene) [*Organic chemistry*]

PBOD .... Phytoplankton Biochemical Oxygen Demand [*Oceanography*]
PBOI .... Public Board of Inquiry
PBOIP .... Preliminary Basis of Issue Plan [*Military*] (MCD)
PBOS .... Planning Board for Ocean Shipping [*Army NATO*]
PBOT .... Philadelphia Board of Trade (NUMA)
PBP .... [*The*] Paper Bag Players (EA)
PBP .... Para-(Benzyloxy)phenol [*Organic chemistry*]
PB/P .... Particleboard/Plywood
PBP .... Pay-Back Period [*Finance*]
PBP .... Pay by Phone [*Business term*]
PBP .... Peak Blood Pressure [*Cardiology*] (DAVI)
PBP .... Pellin-Broca Prism [*Physics*]
PBP .... Penicillin-Binding Protein [*Biochemistry*]
PBP .... Performance-Based Pay
PBP .... Periplasmic Binding Protein [*Biochemistry*]
PBP .... Person Before Place [*Library cataloguing*] (DGA)
PBP .... Pheromonebinding Proteins [*Biochemistry*]
PBP .... Phosphate-Binding Protein [*Biochemistry*]
PBP .... Picnic Basket Porphyrin [*Organic chemistry*]
PBP .... Picture-by-Picture [*Television technology*] (PS)
PBP .... Play-by-Play (WDMC)
PBP .... Plotting Board Plot (MUGU)
PBP .... Point by Point
PBP .... Porphyrin Biosynthetic Pathway [*Biochemistry*] (AAMN)
PBP .... Power Bias Panel
PBP .... Pregnenolone Binding Protein [*Endocrinology*]
PBP .... Private Brand Proneness [*Marketing*]
PBP .... Production Base Plan (MCD)
PBP .... Program and Budget Planning
PBP .... Program Board Panel
PBP .... Progressive Bulbar Palsy [*Medicine*] (MEDA)
PBP .... Provider Based Physician
PBP .... Pulse Burst Period (PDAA)
PBP .... Purified Brucella Protein [*Biochemistry*] (DAVI)
PBP .... Push-Button Panel
PBPA .... Pharmaceutical Benefits Pricing Authority [*Australia*]
PBPB .... Para-bromophenacyl Bromide [*Organic chemistry*]
PBPB .... Pyridinium Bromide Perbromide [*Inorganic chemistry*]
PBPC .... Passenger and Baggage Processing Committee [*IATA*] (DS)
PBPE .... Population Biology/Physiological Ecology [*Program*] [*National Science Foundation*]
PBPITMT ..... Production Base Productivity Improvement through Manufacturing Technology (MCD)
PBPK .... Physiologically Based Pharmacokinetics [*Biochemistry*]
PBPM .... Poultry Byproduct Meal
PBPS .... Painting Brushmakers' Provident Society [*A union*] [*British*]
PBPS .... Paulist Bible Pamphlet Series [*Glen Rock, NJ*] [*A publication*] (BJA)
PBPS .... Performance-Based Payment System
PBPS .... Post-Boost Propulsion System [*Aerospace*]
PBPTC .... Palm Beach Psychotherapy Training Center (EA)
PBPV .... Percutaneous Balloon Pulmonary Valvuloplasty [*Medicine*] (DMAA)
PBQ .... Pharmacy Board of Queensland [*Australia*]
PBQ .... Physiotherapists' Board of Queensland [*Australia*]
PBQ .... Podiatrists' Board of Queensland [*Australia*]
PBQ .... Poste De La Baleine [*Quebec*] [*Seismograph station code, US Geological Survey*] (SEIS)
PBQ .... Preschool Behavior Questionnaire
PBr .... Carnegie Public Library, Bradford, PA [*Library symbol Library of Congress*] (LCLS)
PBR .... Pabst Blue Ribbon [*Beer*]
PBR .... Packed Bed Reactor
PBR .... Particle Bed Reactor [*Department of Energy*]
PBR .... Patapsco & Back Rivers Railroad Co. [*AAR code*]
PBR .... Patrol Boat, River [*Navy symbol*]
PBR .... Patrol Boat Roadstead [*Navy*]
PBR .... Payment by Results [*Payment system*]
PBR .... Pebble-Bed Reactor [*Nuclear energy*]
PBR .... Pembroke, NH [*Location identifier FAA*] (FAAL)
PBR .... Pencil Beam RADAR
PBR .... Permit by Rule [*Pollution control*]
PBR .... Pigment-Binder Ratio [*Weight*]
PBR .... Pittsburgh Byzantine [*Diocesan abbreviation*] [*Pennsylvania*] (TOCD)
PBR .... Plant Breeders' Rights
PBR .... Plum Brook Reactor [*Nuclear energy*]
PBR .... Pole Broken [*Telecommunications*] (TEL)
PBR .... Power Breeder Reactor (AAG)
PBR .... Precision Bombing Range [*Army*]
PBR .... Pressurized Ballistic Range [*NASA*]
PBR .... Price-to-Book Value Ratio [*Investment term*] (DFIT)
PBR .... Procedure Base Register (IAA)
PBR .... Procion Brilliant Red (DB)
PBR .... Professional Bull Riders [*An association*]
PBR .... Puerto Barrios [*Guatemala*] [*Airport symbol*] (AD)
PBR .... Pyridine-Butadiene Rubber
PBra .... Carnegie Free Library, Braddock, PA [*Library symbol Library of Congress*] (LCLS)
PBRA .... Practical Bomb Rack Adapter (NG)
PBRA .... Professional Bicycle Racers Association [*Defunct*] (EA)
PBracAL ...... Allegheny International, Inc., Brackenridge, PA [*Library symbol Library of Congress*] (LCLS)
Pb-RBC .... Lead Red Blood Count [*For lead poisoning*] [*Medicine*] (DAVI)
PBRE .... Pebble-Bed Reactor Experiment [*Nuclear energy*]
PBRERP .... Permanent Board for Review of the Enlisted Retention Program
PBRERS .... Permanent Board for Review of the Enlisted Rating Structure
PBRESD .... Polar Branch, Research Environmental Science Division [*Army*]

PBRF	Plant Breeding Research Forum [*Defunct*] (EA)
PBRF	Plum Brook Reactor Facility [*Lewis Research Center*]
PBriR	Rohm & Haas Co., Bristol, PA [*Library symbol Library of Congress*] (LCLS)
P/BRK	Power Brake [*Automotive engineering*]
PBroGS	Church of Jesus Christ of Latter-Day Saints, Genealogical Society Library, Philadelphia Branch, Broomall, PA [*Library symbol Library of Congress*] (LCLS)
PBRS	Polybromostyrene [*Organic chemistry*]
PBRS	Pupil Behavior Rating Scale [*Psychology*]
PBRS	Push-Button Rotary Switch
PBRV	Potato Black Ringspot Virus [*Plant pathology*]
PBS	Bethlehem Steel Corp., Charles H. Herty, Jr., Memorial Library, Bethlehem, PA [*Library symbol Library of Congress*] (LCLS)
PBS	Pacific Biological Station [*Department of Fisheries and Oceans*] [*Canada Research center*] (RCD)
PBS	Palestine Broadcasting Service (BJA)
PBS	Parenchymatous Bundle Sheath [*Botany*]
PBS	Parimutuel Betting System
PBS	Parti Bersatu Sabah [*Malaysia*] [*Political party*] (ECON)
PBS	Particulate Biogenic Silica [*Environmental science*]
PBS	Parts Breakdown Structure
PBS	Peninsular Base Section [*Military*]
PBS	Periscope Bombsight Stabilizer
PBS	Personal Bibliographic Software, Inc. [*Information service or system*] (IID)
PBS	Peterborough Board of Education [*UTLAS symbol*]
PBS	Philippine Broadcasting Service (NADA)
PBS	Philips Business Systems (NITA)
PBS	Phosphate-Buffered Saline
PBS	Phosphate-Buffered Sodium (MAE)
PBS	Photon Backscattering (AAEL)
PBS	Phycobilisome [*Biochemistry*]
PBS	Picture Building System (NITA)
PBS	Pigeon Bay [*South Carolina*] [*Seismograph station code, US Geological Survey*] (SEIS)
PBS	Pilgrim Amer Bk & Thrift [*NYSE symbol*] (TTSB)
PBS	Pilgrim American Bank & Thrift Fund, Inc. [*NYSE symbol*] (SAG)
PBS	Pilgrim Regional Bank Shares, Inc. [*NYSE symbol*] (SPSG)
PBS	Place Before Subject [*Library cataloguing*] (DGA)
PBS	Plettenberg Bay [*South Africa*] [*Airport symbol*] (AD)
PBS	Podiatry Bibliographical Society [*Defunct*] (EA)
PBS	Polarization Beam Splitter
PBS	Poly(butenesulfone) [*Organic chemistry*]
PBS	Polysteel Building Systems Ltd. [*Toronto Stock Exchange symbol*]
PBS	Potere Battericida del Sangue [*Bactericidal Property of the Blood*] [*Medicine*]
PBS	Poverty Budget Share [*Bureau of the Census*] (GFGA)
PBS	Power Breakfast Syndrome [*Suffered by late-risers forced to attend breakfast meetings*]
PBS	Prayer Book Society [*British*] (DBA)
PBS	Prefabricated Bituminous Surfacing
PBS	Press-Button Signalling (PDAA)
Pbs	Pressure at the Body Surface [*Medicine*] (DAVI)
PBS	Pressure Boundary Subsystem [*Nuclear energy*] (NRCH)
PBS	Primer Binding Site [*Genetics*]
PBS	Production Base Support [*Army*] (AABC)
PBS	Professional Bibliographic System [*Database manager package*] [*Personal Bibliographic Software, Inc. Ann Arbor, MI*]
PBS	Professional Bowhunters Society (EA)
PBS	Program and Budgeting System (OICC)
PBS	Program Board Stowage
PBS	Program Breakdown Structure [*Nuclear energy*]
PBS	Program Buffer Storage (IAA)
PBS	Project Breakdown Structure [*Nuclear energy*] (NRCH)
PBS	Protective Breathing System (NAKS)
PBS	Protestant Big Sisters
PBS	Prune Belly Syndrome [*Medicine*] (DMAA)
PBS	Public Brand Software (PCM)
PBS	Public Broadcasting Service [*Facetious translation: Primarily British Shows*] (EA)
PBS	Public Broadcasting System
PBS	Public Buildings Service [*of General Services Administration*]
PBS	Push-Button Switch
PBSA	Parole Board of South Australia
PBSA	Pastoral Board of South Australia
PBSA	Pharmacy Board of South Australia
PBSA	Phosphate-Buffered Saline Azide [*Culture medium*]
PBSA	Phylloxera Board of South Australia
PBSA	Physiotherapists' Board of South Australia
PBSAA	Partially Blinded Soldiers' Association of Australia
PBSC	Panelized Building Systems Council (EA)
PBSC	Performance-Based Service Contracting (AAGC)
PBSC	Peripheral-Blood Stem-Cell [*Biochemistry Medicine*]
PBSCMA	Peanut Butter Sandwich and Cookie Manufacturers Association [*Later, PBNPA*] (EA)
PBSE	Philadelphia-Baltimore Stock Exchange [*Later, Philadelphia-Baltimore-WashingtonStock Exchange*]
PBSF	Pacific Bank NA [*NASDAQ symbol*] (SPSG)
PBshBrc	Peoples Bancshares, Inc. [*Associated Press*] (SAG)
PBSM	Plastic Bonded Starter Mix
PBSP	Prognostically Bad Sign During Pregnancy [*Obstetrics*] (MAE)
PBSR	Permanent Building Societies Registrar [*New South Wales, Australia*]
PB SRAM	Pipeline Burst SRAM [*Static Random-Access Memory*] [*Computer science*]

PbSt9	Public Storage Properties IX [*Associated Press*] (SAG)
PbSt 10	Public Storage Properties X, Inc. [*Associated Press*] (SAG)
PbSt 11	Public Storage Properties XI, Inc. [*Associated Press*] (SAG)
PbSt 12	Public Storage Properties XII, Inc. [*Associated Press*] (SAG)
PbSt14	Public Storage Properties XIV, Inc. [*Associated Press*] (SAG)
PbSt15	Public Storage Properties XV, Inc. [*Associated Press*] (SAG)
PbSt16	Public Storage Properties XVI, Inc. [*Associated Press*] (SAG)
PbSt17	Public Storage Properties XVII, Inc. [*Associated Press*] (SAG)
PbSt18	Public Storage Properties XVIII, Inc. [*Associated Press*] (SAG)
PbSt19	Public Storage Properties XIX, Inc. [*Associated Press*] (SAG)
PbSt20	Public Storage Properties XX, Inc. [*Associated Press*] (SAG)
PBSTA	Push-Button Station (IAA)
PBSteel	Bethlehem Steel Corp., Charles M. Schwab Memorial Library, Bethlehem, PA [*Library symbol Library of Congress*] (LCLS)
PBSU	Portable Beacon and Scoring Unit (MCD)
PBSW	Push-Button Switch
PBT	Pacific Ballet Theatre
PBT	Para-Bandit Target
PBT	Parity BIT [*Binary Digit*] Test
PBT	Party of Businessmen and Tradesmen [*Czech Republic*] (BUAC)
PBT	Passband Tuning
PBT	Peoria Board of Trade (EA)
PBT	Permeable Base Transistor [*Electronics*]
PBT	Permian Basin Royalty Trust [*NYSE symbol*] (SPSG)
PBT	Permian Basin Rty Tr [*NYSE symbol*] (TTSB)
PBT	Persistent, Bioaccumulative, and Toxic [*Chemistry*]
PBT	Philippine Ballet Theater (ECON)
PBT	Pierce-Blank Tool (MCD)
PBT	Piggyback Tape [*or Twistor*] [*Computer science*]
PBT	Pittsburgh Ballet Theatre
PBT	Polybay Tier
PBT	Polybenzothiazole [*Organic chemistry*]
PBT	Polybutylene Terephthalate [*Organic chemistry*]
PBT	Preferred Body Temperature [*Physiology*]
PBT	Preliminary-Breath-Test [*Device used by police to determine whether or not a driver is legally intoxicated*]
PBT	Professional Billiards Tour [*An association*]
PBT	Profile-Based Therapy [*Medicine*] (DB)
PBT	Profit before Tax [*Finance*] (WDAA)
PBT	Push-Button Telephone
PBT	Red Bluff, CA [*Location identifier FAA*] (FAAL)
PBT4	Protein-Bound Thyroxine [*Endocrinology*] (DAVI)
PBTC	Peoples Banctrust [*NASDAQ symbol*] (TTSB)
PBTC	Peoples BancTrust Company Inc. [*NASDAQ symbol*] (SAG)
PBTC	Postal Business Training Centre [*British*]
PBTE	Performance-Based Teacher Education (OICC)
PBTF	Pump Bearing Test Facility [*Nuclear energy*]
PBTI	Pancreatic Basic Trypsin Inhibitor (DB)
P/BTN	Push Button [*Automotive engineering*]
PBTP	Polybutylene Terephthalate [*Organic chemistry*]
PBTS	Proton Beam Transport System
PBTX	Ptychodiscus brevis Toxin [*Florida red-tide toxin*]
PBU	Air-Burundi [*ICAO designator*] (FAAC)
PBU	Bucknell University, Lewisburg, PA [*OCLC symbol*] (OCLC)
PBU	Pali Buddhist Union (BUAC)
PBU	Palm Beach County Utility Corp. [*Toronto Stock Exchange symbol*]
PBU	Perry Basin [*Utah*] [*Seismograph station code, US Geological Survey*] (SEIS)
PBU	Premature Baby Unit [*National Health Service*] [*British*] (DI)
PBU	Push Button Unit (NITA)
PBU	Putao [*Myanmar*] [*Airport symbol*] (OAG)
PBUP	Perforated Backup Plate
PBUS	Professional Bail Agents of the United States (NTPA)
PBut	Butler Public Library, Butler, PA [*Library symbol Library of Congress*] (LCLS)
PButV	United States Veterans Administration Hospital, Butler, PA [*Library symbol Library of Congress*] (LCLS)
PBV	English Prayer Book Version (BJA)
PBV	Pedal Blood Vessel
PBV	Pharmacy Board of Victoria [*Australia*]
PBV	Platinol [*Cisplatin*], Bleomycin, Vinblastine [*Antineoplastic drug regimen*]
PBV	Post Boost Vehicle [*Missiles*] (AFM)
PBV	Predicted Blood Volume [*Medicine*]
PBV	Proportioning and Bypass Valve
PBV	Pulmonary Blood Volume [*Medicine*]
PBVM	Presentation of the Blessed Virgin Mary [*Roman Catholic women's religious order*]
PBVM	Presentation of the Blessed Virgin Mary Sisters (TOCD)
PBVM	Sisters of the Presentation of the B.V.M. (TOCD)
PBVM	Union of the Sisters of the Presentation of the Blessed Virgin Mary (TOCD)
PBVP	Post Boost Vehicle Propulsion [*Missiles*] (MCD)
PBVR	[*The*] Port Bienville Railroad [*AAR code*]
PBvu	Andrew Bayne Memorial Library, Bellevue, PA [*Library symbol Library of Congress*] (LCLS)
PBW	Particle-Beam Weapon
PBW	Parts by Weight (IEEE)
PBW	Percussive Butt Welder
PBW	Pink Bollworm [*Cotton pest*]
PBW	Posterior Bite Wing [*Dentistry*]
PBW	Power by Wire [*Flight control*]
PBW	Proportional Bandwidth (MCD)
PBW	Pulse Burst Wave
PBWA	Plasma Beat Wave Accelerator [*Physics*]

PBWA	Plasma Beta-Wave Accelerator [*Plasma physics*]
PBWA	Professional Basketball Writers Association (NTPA)
PBWAA	Professional Basketball Writers' Association of America (EA)
PBWEE........	Pilot Boll Weevil Eradication Experiment [*Department of Agriculture*]
PBWF..........	Pulse Burst Waveform
PBWG	Pakistan Bibliographical Working Group (BUAC)
PBWSE	Philadelphia-Baltimore-Washington Stock Exchange [*Later, Philadelphia Stock Exchange*]
PBWT..........	Parts by Weight (WDAA)
PBX............	PBX Resources [*Vancouver Stock Exchange symbol*]
PBX............	Plastic Bonded Explosive
PBX............	Private Branch Exchange [*Telecommunications*]
PBXFS	Private Branch Exchange Final Selector [*Telecommunications*] (IAA)
PBY............	Kayenta, AZ [*Location identifier FAA*] (FAAL)
PBY............	Patrol Bomber [*Navy designation for Catalina aircraft*]
PBY............	Pearl Air Services (U) Ltd. [*Uganda*] [*ICAO designator*] (FAAC)
PBY............	Pep Boys-Man,Mo,Ja [*NYSE symbol*] (TTSB)
PBY............	Pep Boys - Manny, Moe & Jack [*NYSE symbol*] (SPSG)
PBY............	Pillars Bay [*Alaska*] [*Airport symbol*] (AD)
PBYP	Play-By-Play Toys&Novelties [*NASDAQ symbol*] (TTSB)
PBYP	Play By Play Toys & Novelties, Inc. [*NASDAQ symbol*] (SAG)
PBZ............	Khortitsa-Air Ltd. [*Ukraine*] [*FAA designator*] (FAAC)
PBZ............	Peoples Bank of Zanzibar [*Tanzania*] (BUAC)
PBZ............	Phenoxybenzamine [*Also, POB*] [*Adrenergic blocking agent*]
PBZ............	Phenylbutazone [*Anti-inflammatory compound*]
PBZ............	Plettenberg [*South Africa*] [*Airport symbol*] (OAG)
PBZ............	Pyribenzamine [*Antihistamine*] [*Trademark*]
PBzN	Peroxybenzoyl Nitrate [*Lacrimator*]
PBZT	Poly-P-Phenylene Benzobesthiazole
PC.............	All India Reporter, Privy Council [*1914-50*] [*A publication*] (DLA)
PC.............	British and Colonial Prize Cases [*A publication*] (DLA)
PC.............	Civilian Personnel Division [*Coast Guard*]
PC.............	Coastal Escort [*Ship symbol*] (NATG)
PC.............	Communist Party [*Peru*] [*Political party*] (PD)
PC.............	Fiji Air [*ICAO designator*] (AD)
PC.............	Indian Rulings, Privy Council [*1929-47*] [*A publication*] (DLA)
PC.............	J. Lewis Crozer [*Chester Public*] Library, Chester, PA [*Library symbol Library of Congress*] (LCLS)
PC.............	Judicial Committee of the Privy Council (DLA)
PC.............	Pacific Coast Railroad [*AAR code Terminated*]
PC.............	Pacific Command [*Department of Defense*] (BARN)
PC.............	Package Control [*or Controller*]
PC.............	Packed Cell [*Hematology*] (MAE)
PC.............	Pad Coordinator [*NASA*]
PC.............	Paired Comparisons [*Education*] (EDAC)
PC.............	Palmitoyl Carnitine [*Biochemistry*]
PC.............	[*The*] Panama Canal
Pc	Pancuronium [*A muscle relaxant*]
PC.............	Panoramic Camera
PC.............	Paper Chromatography
PC.............	Paper Copy
PC.............	Paper Core (IAA)
PC.............	Paper or Cloth [*Freight*]
PC.............	Paracortex (DMAA)
PC.............	Paracortical Hyperplasia [*Oncology*]
PC.............	Parallax Second [*Unit of interstellar-space measure*]
PC.............	Parameter Checkout [*Computer science*] (IAA)
PC.............	Parametric Cubic [*Computer science*] (OA)
PC.............	Parental Control [*Channel lockout*] [*Video technology*]
PC.............	Parent Care (EA)
PC.............	Parent Cells
PC.............	Parents' Charter (AIE)
PC.............	Parish Church [*British*] (ROG)
PC.............	Parish Council
PC.............	Parish Councillor (WDAA)
PC.............	Parity Check [*Computer science*] (IAA)
PC.............	Parliamentary Cases [*A publication*] (DLA)
PC.............	PARSEC [*Parallax Second*] [*Unit of interstellar-space measurement*]
pc	Parsec (IDOE)
PC.............	Part Card [*Computer science*] (IAA)
PC.............	Participation Certificate
PC.............	Parti Communiste [*Communist Party*] [*Luxembourg*] [*Political party*] (PPW)
PC.............	Particulate Component (DMAA)
PC.............	Partido Colorado [*Colorado Party*] [*Uruguay*] [*Political party*] (PPW)
PC.............	Partido Conservador [*Conservative Party*] [*Nicaragua*] [*Political party*] (EY)
PC.............	Partido Conservador [*Conservative Party*] [*Ecuador*] [*Political party*] (PPW)
PC.............	Partition Coefficient
PC.............	Parts Catalog (KSC)
PC.............	Passenger Certificate [*Shipping*] (DS)
PC.............	Past Commander
PC.............	Patent Cases [*A publication*] (DLA)
PC.............	Patent Classification (NITA)
PC.............	Patent Committee (MCD)
PC.............	Patentee/Company Code (NITA)
PC.............	Path Control [*Computer science*] (IBMDP)
PC.............	Path Controller (NITA)
PC.............	Patient Cancellation [*Medicine*] (DHP)
PC.............	Patres Conscripti [*Senators*] [*Latin*]
PC.............	Patrol Car [*British military*] (DMA)
PC.............	Patrol Craft
PC.............	Patrol Vessel, Submarine Chaser [*Navy symbol*]
PC.............	Pay Clerk

PC.............	Paymaster-Captain [*Navy British*]
PC.............	Paymaster-Commander [*Navy British*]
PC.............	Payment Center (MHDB)
PC.............	Peace Commissioner [*Ireland*]
PC.............	Peace Corps (EA)
PC.............	Peak Capacity
PC.............	Peg Count [*Telecommunications*] (TEL)
PC.............	Penal Code [*A publication*] (DLA)
PC.............	Penetrating Cell
Pc	Penicillin (STED)
PC.............	Penn Central Transportation Co. [*Subsidiary of Penn Central Corp.*] [*Absorbed into Consolidated Rail Corp.*] [*AAR code*]
PC.............	Penny Cyclopoedia [*British A publication*] (ROG)
PC.............	Penske Car [*Racing model*]
PC.............	Pentose Cycle [*Biochemistry*] (MAE)
PC.............	People for a Change [*An association Defunct*] (EA)
PC.............	People's Conference [*India*] [*Political party*] (PPW)
PC.............	Percent [*or Percentage*] (IAA)
pc	Percent (WDMC)
PC.............	Percent Correct
pc	Per Centum [*In the Hundred*] [*Latin*] (WA)
PC.............	Per Centum [*By the Hundred*] [*Latin*]
PC.............	Perciconia circinata [*A toxin-producing fungus*]
PC.............	Per Compass (IAA)
PC.............	Per Condoglianza [*Used on visiting cards to express condolence*] [*Italian*]
PC.............	Percutaneous Cholecystostomy [*Medicine*]
PC.............	Perfins Club (EA)
PC.............	Performance Code
PC.............	Performance Contract (OICC)
PC.............	Pericarditis [*Avian pathology*]
PC.............	Pericentral
PC.............	Pericynthion [*Perilune, or low point, in lunar orbit*]
PC.............	Period Contract
PC.............	Peripheral Cell
PC.............	Peripheral Control (BUR)
PC.............	Peripheral Controller (NITA)
PC.............	Peritoneal Cell (DMAA)
PC.............	Permeance Coefficient (IAA)
PC.............	Perpetual Curate
PC.............	Personal Call (OA)
PC.............	Personal Care
PC.............	Personal Computer
pc	Personal Computer (WDMC)
PC.............	Personal Copier [*In product name, PC-10*] [*Canon Inc.*]
PC.............	Personal Corporation (BARN)
PC.............	Personal Correction
PC.............	Personnel Carrier [*A vehicle*]
PC.............	Perspective control [*Photography*]
PC.............	Petro-Canada
PC.............	Petty Cash
pc	Petty Cash (WDMC)
PC.............	Pharmacology [*Medicine*] (DMAA)
PC.............	Pharmacy Corps [*Army*]
PC.............	Phase-Change [*Physics*]
PC.............	Phase Code (NITA)
PC.............	Phase Coherent (CET)
PC.............	Phase Control (IAA)
PC.............	Phenol Coefficient (IIA)
PC.............	Pheochromocytoma [*Oncology*]
PC.............	Philco Corp. (IAA)
PC.............	Philosophical Classics [*A publication*]
P-C............	Phlogistic Corticoid (STED)
PC.............	Phobia Clinic (EA)
PC.............	Phosphate Cycle [*Chemistry*] (MAE)
PC.............	Phosphatidylcholine [*Lecithin*] [*Biochemistry*]
PC.............	Phosphocholine [*Biochemistry*]
PC.............	Phosphocreatine [*Also, PCr*] [*Creatine phosphate; see CP*] [*Biochemistry*]
PC.............	Phosphorylcholine [*Biochemistry*]
PC.............	Photocell
PC.............	Photoconductor
PC.............	Photocounting
Pc	Phthalocyanine [*Organic chemistry*]
PC.............	Phycocyanin (DB)
PC.............	Physicians's Corporation [*Medicine*] (DMAA)
PC.............	Physocyanin [*Biochemistry*]
PC.............	Phytophthora Cinnamoni [*A fungus*]
PC.............	Pica [*Typography*] (WDMC)
PC.............	Pick Up Cargo (AFM)
pC.............	Picocoulomb [*One trillionth of a coulomb*]
pc.............	Picocurie [*Also, pCi*] [*One trillionth of a curie*]
pc	Picocurie (IDOE)
PC.............	Picture (MDG)
PC.............	Piece (AAG)
pc	Piece (VRA)
pc	Pied Carre [*Square Foot*] [*French*]
pc	Pied Cube [*Cubic Foot*] [*French*]
PC.............	Pierre Cardin [*Fashion designer*]
PC.............	Pill Counter [*Medicine*] (DMAA)
PC.............	Pilotage Charts [*Air Force*]
PC.............	Pioneer Clubs (EA)
PC.............	Pioneer Conference (PSS)
PC.............	Pioneer Corps [*British military*] (DMA)
PC.............	Piriform Cortex (DMAA)

pc .... Pitcairn [*MARC country of publication code Library of Congress*] (LCCP)
PC .... Pitch Channel
PC .... Pitch Circle [*Technical drawings*]
PC .... Pitch Control (KSC)
PC .... Pitch Cycle (DNAB)
PC .... Pitting Corrosion (PDAA)
PC .... Pittsburgh Commerce Institute
PC .... Plaid Cymru [*Welsh national liberation party*] [*Political party*]
P/C .... Plane Captain (MUGU)
PC .... Plane Change (MCD)
PC .... Plane Commander
PC .... Planetary Citizens (EA)
PC .... Planned Commitment (COE)
PC .... Planning Card (AAG)
PC .... Planning Commission (PA)
PC .... Planning Concept (MCD)
PC .... Plant Computer (NRCH)
PC .... Planting Council (EA)
PC .... Plasma Cell [*Oncology*]
PC .... Plasma Chromatography
PC .... Plasma Cortisol (DB)
PC .... Plasmacytoma [*Medicine*]
PC .... Plastic Core
Pc .... Plastocyanin
PC .... Plate Circuit (DEN)
PC .... Platelet Concentrate [*Hematology*]
PC .... Platelet Count [*Hematology*]
PC .... Platform/Crane (DCTA)
PC .... Pleas of the Crown [*A publication*] (DLA)
P/C .... Pledges/Cost (WDMC)
p/c .... Pledges/Cost [*Fundraising*] (WDMC)
PC .... Plenum Chamber
PC .... Plug Care [*Computer science*] (IAA)
PC .... Plug Cock (AAG)
PC .... Plug Compatible [*Computer science*] (BUR)
PC .... Pneumotoxic Center (AAMN)
PC .... Pocket Computer
PC .... Poetry Criticism [*A publication*]
PC .... Point Contact (IDOE)
PC .... Point of Curve [*Technical drawings*]
PC .... Polar Component [*Food science*]
PC .... Polar Continental [*American air mass*]
PC .... Polar Crane [*Nuclear energy*] (NRCH)
P-C .... Polar to Cartesian
P-C .... Pole Cell [*Insect embryology*]
P/C .... Police Car
PC .... Police Commissioner (WGA)
PC .... Police-Constable [*Scotland Yard*]
PC .... Police Court [*British*] (ROG)
PC .... Policy Control (ADA)
PC .... Polish Council [*Czech Republic*] (BUAC)
PC .... Political Code [*A publication*] (ILCA)
PC .... Political Correctness
PC .... Politically Correct
P/C .... Polizza di Carico [*Bill of Lading*] [*Shipping*] [*Italian*]
PC .... Pollution Control (MHDD)
PC .... Polycarbonate [*Organic chemistry*]
PC .... Polycarbosilane [*Organic chemistry*]
PC .... Polymer-Concrete (KSC)
PC .... Polyposis Coli [*Medicine*] (DMAA)
PC .... Pondus Civile [*Civil (Avoirdupois) Weight*] [*Pharmacy*] (ROG)
PC .... Poni Curavit [*Caused to Be Placed*] [*Latin*]
PC .... Poor Clares [*Roman Catholic women's religious order*]
PC .... Poor Classes [*British*] (DSUE)
P/C .... Poor Condition [*Medicine*] (DMAA)
PC .... Poor Coordination [*Medicine*] (DMAA)
pc .... Pop Corn [*Crochet*]
PC .... Popular Coalition (BUAC)
PC .... Popular Cult
PC .... Population Census
PC .... Population Communication (EA)
PC .... Population Concern [*British*] (EAIO)
PC .... Population Council (EA)
PC .... Portable Computer
PC .... Portacaval [*Medicine*]
PC .... Portal Cirrhosis [*Medicine*] (DB)
PC .... Port Call [*Army*]
PC .... Port Committee (NATG)
PC .... Port Control [*Telecommunications*] (TEL)
PC .... Portion Control [*Food service*]
PC .... Portland Cement
PC .... Position Classification (GFGA)
PC .... Positive Column (IAA)
PC .... Positive Control
Pc .... Positive Wave in Children [*Neurophysiology*]
PC .... Postal Clerk [*Navy rating*]
PC .... Postcard
pc .... Postcard (ODBW)
PC .... Post-Chlorinated (IAA)
PC .... Post Cibos [*After Meals*] [*Latin*] [*Pharmacy*] (DAVI)
PC .... Post Cibum [*After Meals*] [*Pharmacy*]
PC .... Postcode (ADA)
PC .... Postcoital [*Medicine*]
PC .... Post Commander [*Military*]

PC .... Post Consulatum [*After the Consulate*] [*Latin*]
PC .... Posterior Cervical [*Medicine*] (DMAA)
PC .... Posterior Chamber [*Ophthalmology*]
PC .... Posterior Circumflex [*Artery*] [*Anatomy*] (DAVI)
PC .... Posterior Commissure [*Neuroanatomy*]
PC .... Posterior Cortex [*Medicine*] (DMAA)
PC .... Postinflammatory Corticoid [*Medicine*]
PC .... Potential Complications [*Medicine*] (DMAA)
pc .... Pottery Cache (BJA)
PC .... Pour Condoler [*To Offer Sympathy*] [*French*]
PC .... Power Cartesian (IAA)
PC .... Power Circuit (IAA)
PC .... Power Component (IAA)
PC .... Power Contactor
PC .... Power Control [*System*] (NG)
P-C .... Power Conversion (CET)
pc .... Power Cord (BARN)
PC .... Practice Cases [*A publication*] (DLA)
PC .... Precarrier
PC .... Precast
PC .... Precaution Category [*For clinical laboratories*]
PC .... Precedents in Chancery [*A publication*] (DLA)
PC .... Pre-Chamber [*Automotive engineering*]
PC .... Precision Control [*Computer programming*] (BYTE)
PC .... Preconditioning [*Medicine*] (DMAA)
PC .... Precordia [*Anatomy*]
PC .... Pre-Emphasis Circuit (OA)
PC .... Preliminary Commitment (IMH)
PC .... Prenatal Care [*Medicine*] (DMAA)
PC .... Preparatory Commission
PC .... Preparatory Committee
PC .... Present Complaint [*Medicine*]
PC .... Presidents Club [*Commercial firm*] (EA)
PC .... Press Club (NTCM)
PC .... Press Council [*British*]
PC .... Pressure Chamber (NAKS)
PC .... Pressure Controller [*Nuclear energy*]
PC .... Prestressed Concrete (BARN)
PC .... Previous Convictions (WDAA)
pc .... Price (WDAA)
PC .... Price Commission [*Cost of Living Council*]
PC .... Price Control Cases [*A publication*] (DLA)
P/C .... Price/Cost
PC .... Pricellular Corp. [*AMEX symbol*] (SAG)
PC .... PriCellular Corp. 'A' [*AMEX symbol*] (TTSB)
PC .... Price per Copy [*of books*]
PC .... Prices Current
pc .... Prices Current (WDMC)
PC .... Priest Confessor
PC .... Primary Center
PC .... Primary Circuit (MCD)
PC .... Primary Closure [*Medicine*] (DMAA)
PC .... Primary Code
PC .... Primary Contributor
PC .... Primary Control (MCD)
PC .... Prime Contractor
PC .... Prime Cost
PC .... Prince Consort (IIA)
PC .... Prince Edward Island Provincial Library, Charlottetown, Prince Edward Island [*Library symbol National Library of Canada*] (NLC)
PC .... Principal Chaplain (ADA)
PC .... Principal Component
PC .... Print Club (EA)
PC .... Print Command [*Computer science*] (IAA)
PC .... Print Contrast (DGA)
PC .... Print Cycle [*Computer science*] (IAA)
PC .... Printed Card (IAA)
PC .... Printed Circuit
PC .... Printer Control
PC .... Printing Cylinder (DGA)
PC .... Printmakers' Council (BUAC)
PC .... Print of Curve (IAA)
PC .... Prisoner of Conscience (BJA)
PC .... Privacy Commission
PC .... Private Concerns [*An association Defunct*] (EA)
PC .... Private Contract [*Tea trade*] (ROG)
PC .... Private Corporation
PC .... Privatization Council [*New York, NY*] (EA)
PC .... Privilege Car [*on a train*] [*Theatre slang*]
PC .... Privileged Character [*A favored student*] [*Teen slang*]
PC .... Privy Council [*or Councillor*] [*British*]
PC .... Prize Court (DLA)
PC .... Probable Cause [*Legal term*]
PC .... Probate Court [*British*] (ROG)
PC .... Procaer SpA [*Italy ICAO aircraft manufacturer identifier*] (ICAO)
PC .... Procarbazine [*Also, P, PCB, Pr*] [*Antineoplastic drug*]
PC .... Procerebral Lobe [*Neuroanatomy*]
PC .... Process Chemistry
PC .... Process Computer (NRCH)
PC .... Process Control (DEN)
PC .... Processing Center [*Telecommunications*] (TEL)
PC .... Processing Conditions [*Food*] (DICI)
PC .... Processor Controller [*Computer science*] (MDG)
PC .... Procollagen [*Medicine*] (DMAA)
PC .... Procurement Command [*Army*]

PC	Procurement Communication [Military]
PC	Producers' Council [Later, CPMC] (EA)
PC	Product Code (NITA)
PC	Production Certificate (MCD)
PC	Production Company [Films, television, etc.]
PC	Production Control (MCD)
PC	Production Costs
PC	Productive Cough [Medicine] (DMAA)
PC	Professional Communication (MCD)
PC	Professional Corporation
PC	Professors of Curriculum (EA)
PC	Profile Component (DET)
PC	Profit Center (MHDB)
PC	Program Card [Computer science] (IAA)
PC	Program Change
PC	Program Check [Computer science] (IAA)
PC	Program Committee [UN Food and Agriculture Organization]
PC	Program Communications [Military] (AFIT)
PC	Program Control
PC	Program Controller (NITA)
PC	Program Coordination (IEEE)
PC	Program Counter
PC	Programmable Computer
PC	Programmable Controller (ACII)
PC	Programmable Logic Control [Computer science] (IAA)
PC	Programmable Machine Control (IAA)
PC	Programmed Check (AAG)
PC	Progressive Conservative [Canada Political party]
PC	Progressive Conservative Party [Canada] [Political party] (BUAC)
PC	Prohormone Convertase [Medicine] (DMAA)
PC	Project Censored (EA)
PC	Project Children (EA)
PC	Project Control (NASA)
PC	Project Coordinator (NG)
PC	Project Cuddle [An association] (EA)
PC	Projector Charge
PC	Prompt Corner (WDAA)
PC	Proof Coins [Numismatics]
P/C	Property/Casualty [Insurance]
P-C	Prophlogistic Corticoid (LDT)
PC	Proportional Counter [Instrumentation]
PC	Proposed Change
PC	Propositional Calculus [Logic]
PC	Propulsive Coefficient
PC	Propylene Carbonate [Organic chemistry]
PC	Prospectors Club [Later, PCI]
PC	Prostatic Carcinoma [Medicine] (DB)
PC	Prosthetics Center [Veterans Administration]
PC	Protective Climate [Solar heating]
PC	Protective Cover (MCD)
PC	Protein C [Medicine] (DMAA)
PC	Protein Convertase [Medicine] (DMAA)
PC	Proto-Canaanite (BJA)
PC	Protocol Converter (MCD)
PC	Provincial Commissioner [British government]
PC	Provisional Costs
PC	Provisional Cut [Television] (NTCM)
PC	Provocative Concentration [Immunology]
PC	Pseudocode (AAG)
PC	Pseudoconditioning Control [Neurophysiology]
PC	Psychodevelopment Checklist [Psychology] (DAVI)
PC	Publications in Climatology (MCD)
PC	Public Citizen (EA)
PC	Public Contract
PC	[The] Publishers' Circular [A publication] (ROG)
PC	Pubococcygeus [Muscle] [Anatomy]
PC	Pull Chain [Technical drawings] (DAC)
PC	Pulmonary Capillary [Medicine]
PC	Pulmonic Closure [Medicine] (MAE)
PC	Pulsating Current
PC	Pulse Cleaned [Dust filtration]
PC	Pulse Code [Telecommunications] (IAA)
PC	Pulse Comparator (AAG)
PC	Pulse Compression
PC	Pulse Controller
PC	Pulse Counter [Computer science] (MDG)
PC	Pulverized Coal [Fuel technology]
PC	Punch Card (NITA)
PC	Punched Card [Computer science]
PC	Punjab Cavalry [British military] (DMA)
PC	Puns Corps (EA)
PC	Purchase Card
PC	Purchasing and Contracting [Army]
PC	Pure Clairvoyance [Psychical research]
PC	Purified Concentrate
PC	Purkinje Cell [Neuroanatomy]
PC	Pyrrolinecarboxylic Acid [Biochemistry]
PC	Pyruvate Carboxylase [An enzyme] (MAF)
PC	Single Paper Single Cotton [Wire insulation] (AAG)
PC	Submarine Chaser [173 foot] [Navy symbol Obsolete]
PC	Sumitomo Chemical Co. [Japan] [Research code symbol]
PC	Veterans of the US Posse Comitatus (EA)
pc1	Platelet Count Pretransfusion [Medicine] (STED)
PC1	Postal Clerk, First Class [Navy rating]
PC1	Power Control One [Hydraulic] (MCD)
pc2	Platelet Count Posttransfusion [Medicine] (STED)
PC2	Postal Clerk, Second Class [Navy rating]
PC2	Power Control Two [Hydraulic] (MCD)
PC3	Postal Clerk, Third Class [Navy rating]
PCA	Acts of the Privy Council [England] [A publication] (DLA)
PCA	Calgon Corp., Pittsburgh, PA [OCLC symbol] (OCLC)
PCA	Pacific Communications Area [Air Force] (MCD)
PCA	Packaging Council of Australia (BUAC)
PCA	Panama Canal Authority
PCA	Paper Converters Association [Defunct] (EA)
PCA	Paperweight Collectors' Association (EA)
PCA	Papillon Club of America (EA)
PCA	Para-Chloramphetamine (STED)
PCA	Para-Chloroaniline [Organic chemistry]
PCA	Parachute Club of America [Later, USPA] (EA)
PCA	Para-Coumaric Acid [Organic chemistry]
PCA	Parietal Cell Antibodies [Immunology]
PCA	Parietal Cell Antibody (DB)
PCA	Parliamentary Candidates Association (BUAC)
PCA	Parliamentary Commissioner for Administration [British]
PCA	Parochial Clergy Association [British] (DBA)
PCA	Parti Communiste Algerien [Algerian Communist Party] [Political party]
PCA	Partido Comunista de Argentina [Communist Party of Argentina] [Political party] (PD)
PCA	Parts Control Area [NASA] (KSC)
PCA	Party of the Civic Alliance [Romania] [Political party] (EY)
PCA	Passive Cutaneous Anaphylaxis [Immunochemistry]
PCA	Patient Care Aide [or Assistant] (DAVI)
PCA	Patient Care Audit (HCT)
PCA	Patient-Controlled Analgesia
PCA	Patient Support Associate [Medicine]
PCA	Patriotic Catholic Association [Name given to nationalized Catholic Church in China]
PCA	Peak Clipping Amplifier
PCA	Pekingese Club of America (EA)
PCA	Pentachloraniline [Organic chemistry]
PCA	Pentachloroanisole [Organic chemistry]
PCA	Percent Cortical Area [Neurology]
PCA	Perchloric Acid [Inorganic chemistry]
PCA	Percutaneous Carotid Arteriogram [Medicine] (MAE)
PCA	Percutaneous Coronary Agioplasty (STED)
PCA	Pericruciate Association [Cortex, of cat]
PCA	Period Contract Acceptance
PCA	Peripheral Circulatory Assist [Medicine]
PCA	Peritoneal Carcinomatosis [Oncology]
PCA	Permanent Change of Assignment [Army]
PCA	Permanent Court of Arbitration [See also CPA] [Hague, Netherlands] (EAIO)
PCA	Personal Care Aide [or Assistant or Attendant]
PCA	Personal Cash Allowance
PCA	Pest Control Association (NADA)
PCA	Petro-Chemical Associates, Inc. (EFIS)
PCA	Phenylcarboxylic Acid [Chemistry] (DAVI)
PCA	Photocontact Allergic (STED)
PCA	Photon Counting Array [Instrumentation]
PCA	Physical Configuration Audit [Military, NASA]
PCA	Physicians Corp. of America (ECON)
PCA	Pinnacle [Alaska] [Seismograph station code, US Geological Survey] (SEIS)
PCA	Pitcairn Cierva Autogiro [Aeronautics]
PCA	Pitch Control Assembly (MCD)
PCA	Plane Circular Aperture
PCA	Plasma Catecholamine [Biochemistry]
PCA	Plasma Catecholamine Concentration (STED)
PCA	Plasma-Covered Antenna
PCA	Plate Count Agar [Microbiology]
PCA	Pneumatic Control Assembly (NASA)
PCA	Point of Closest Approach
PCA	Polar Cap Absorption
PCA	Polarizer-Compensator-Analyzer (PDAA)
PCA	Police Complaint Authority [British]
PCA	Policy Certification Authority
PCA	Polish Community in Australia
PCA	Pollution Control Agency (COE)
PCA	Polycrystalline Alumina
PCA	Poodle Club of America (EA)
PCA	Pool Critical Assembly [Nuclear reactor]
PCA	Popular Culture Association (EA)
PCA	Pork Council of Australia
PCA	Porous-Coated Anatomical [Prosthesis]
PCA	Porsche Club of America (EA)
PCA	Portacaval Anastomosis [Animal model of chronic liver disease]
PCA	Portage Creek [Alaska] [Airport symbol] (OAG)
PCA	Port Communications Area [Telecommunications] (TEL)
PCA	Portland Cement Association (EA)
PCA	Ports Canada
PCA	Positive Control Area
PCA	Positive Controlled Airspace
PCA	Postconstruction Availability (NVT)
PCA	Posterior Cerebral Artery [Brain anatomy]
PCA	Posterior Communicating Artery [Anatomy]
PCA	Posterior Cricoarytenoid [A muscle of the larynx]
PCA	Potash Co. of America, Inc. [Toronto Stock Exchange symbol]
PCA	Potato Carrot Agar [Culture Media]

PCA............ Potentially Contaminated Area (DNAB)
PCA............ Poultrymen's Cooperative Association (EA)
PCA............ Power Conditioning Assembly
PCA............ Power Control Assembly (NASA)
PCA............ Precipitation with a Compressed Fluid Antisolvent [Chemical engineering]
PCA............ Precision Clearing Agent (DNAB)
PCA............ Pre-Conditioned Air System [Aviation] (DA)
PCA............ Precontractual Authorization
PCA............ Prescribed Concentration of Alcohol (ADA)
PCA............ Presidency of Civil Aviation [Saudi Arabia] (BUAC)
PCA............ President's Council on Aging [Inactive]
PCA............ Prestressed Concrete Association [British] (DBA)
PCA............ Primary Carbon Assimilation [Botany]
PCA............ Primary Control Assembly [Nuclear energy] (NRCH)
PCA............ Primary Coolant Activity [Nuclear energy] (NRCH)
PCA............ Prime Candidate Alloy (MCD)
PCA............ Prime Condition Aircraft
PCA............ Principal Component Analysis
PCA............ Principal Control Authority (NATG)
PCA............ Prindle Class Association (EA)
PCA............ Print Council of America (EA)
PCA............ Printed Circuit Assembly [Telecommunications] (TEL)
PCA............ Printed Circuit Association (BUAC)
PCA............ Printer Communications Adapter
PCA............ Printers' Costing Association [British] (BI)
PCA............ Printing Corp. of America
PCA............ Private Communications Association [Later, NCA]
PCA............ Process Control Analyzer
PCA............ Pro-Choice Alliance (BUAC)
PCA............ Procoagulant Activity
PCA............ Procrastinators' Club of America (EA)
PCA............ Producers Commission Association (EA)
PCA............ Production Code Administration (BARN)
PCA............ Production Compliance Audit [Automotive emissions standards]
PCA............ Production Credit Association (BUAC)
PCA............ Professional Chess Association (EA)
PCA............ Professional Comedians' Association (EA)
PCA............ Professional Cycling Association [British] (DBA)
PCA............ Program Calibration Area [Computer science] (DOM)
PCA............ Program Change Analysis [DoD]
PCA............ Program Coupler Assembly (KSC)
PCA............ Program Cumulative Audience [Advertising] (DOAD)
PCA............ Programmable Communications Adapter [Computer science]
PCA............ Progress Change Authority
PCA............ Progressive Citizens of America
PCA............ Progressive Cultural Association (BUAC)
PCA............ Proprietary Crematoria Association [British] (DBA)
PCA............ Protective Clothing Arrangement [Telecommunications] (TEL)
PCA............ Protective Connecting Arrangement [Telecommunications] (TEL)
PCA............ Prototype Protein O Activator [Biochemistry]
PCA............ Public Archives, Charlottetown, Prince Edward Island [Library symbol National Library of Canada] (NLC)
PCA............ Puli Club of America (EA)
PCA............ Pulp Chemicals Association (EA)
PCA............ Pulse Code Adaptor (NITA)
PCA............ Pulse Counter Adapter
PCA............ Putnam California Investment Grade Municipal [AMFX symbol] (SPSG)
PCA............ Putnam Cal Inv Grade Muni [AMEX symbol] (TTSB)
PCA............ Pyrotechnic Control Assembly [NASA]
PCA............ Pyrrolidonecarboxylic Acid [Organic chemistry]
PCAA .... Pancretan Association of America (EA)
PCAA .... Particulate Combined Amino Acid [Marine biology]
PCaab .... Parietal Cell Autoantibody [Immunology]
PcA&E .... Pacific Aerospace & Electronics, Inc. [Associated Press] (SAG)
PCAC .... Partially Conserved Axial Current [Electronics] (IAA)
PCAC .... Partially Conserved Axial-Vector Current
PCAC .... Poultry Costings Advisory Council (BUAC)
PCAC .... Private College Admissions Center [Later, NAAPHE]
PCAC .... Professional Classes Aid Council (AIE)
PC Act .... Probate Court Act [A publication] (DLA)
PCAD .... Package Computer-Aided Design [Computer science]
PCAD .... Program Change Approval Document (DOMA)
PCADS........ Panoramic Control and Display System (MCD)
PCAE.......... Polar Cap Absorption Event
PC-AEO .... Personal Computer - Annual Energy Outlook Forecasting Model [Department of Energy] (GFGA)
PCAG .... Pentobarbital-Chlorpromazine-Alcohol Group [Medicine]
PCAG .... Petroleum Conservation Action Group [India] (BUAC)
PCAG .... Research Station, Agriculture Canada [Station de Recherches, Agriculture Canada] Charlottetown, Prince Edward Island [Library symbol National Library of Canada] (NLC)
PCAI.......... Parliamentary Commissioner for Administrative Investigations [Western Australia]
PCAI.......... PCA International, Inc. [NASDAQ symbol] (NQ)
PCAI.......... PCA Intl [NASDAQ symbol] (TTSB)
PCAI.......... Personal Care Assessment Instrument [Australia]
PCA Int .... PCA International, Inc. [Associated Press] (SAG)
P Cal .... Petrus Calvelli [Flourished, 14th century] [Authority cited in pre-1607 legal work] (DSA)
PCalS........ California State College, California, PA [Library symbol Library of Congress] (LCLS)
PCAM.......... Partitioned Content Addressable Memory
PCAM.......... Physician Corp. of Amer [NASDAQ symbol] (TTSB)

PCAM.......... Physician Corp. of America [NASDAQ symbol] (SAG)
PCAM.......... Punched Card Accounting Machine [Computer science]
PCamA........ Alliance College, Cambridge Springs, PA [Library symbol Library of Congress] (LCLS)
PCAMIC ...... People Concerned about MIC [Methyl Isocyanate] (EA)
PCAMP .... Protective Coatings and Metalizing Process (DNAB)
PCAN .... Program Change Action Notice (DNAB)
PC & A .... Project Control and Administration [NASA]
PC & B .... Personnel Compensation and Benefits (GFGA)
PC & D .... Priest, Confessor, and Doctor (ROG)
PC & H .... Packing, Crating, and Handling [Shipping] (AFM)
PC & IC ...... Polaris Control and Information Center [Missiles]
PC & OR ...... Procurement, Commitment, and Obligation Record [Navy]
PC & S .... Posts, Camps, and Stations [Military]
PC & S .... Preliminary Command and Sequencing [Viking lander mission] [NASA]
PCANSW...... Pest Control Association of New South Wales [Australia]
PCAO .... President's Commission on Americans Outdoors
PCAP .... Physical Correlation Analysis Program [Military]
P-CAP .... Physically-Challenged Assistance Program [Chrysler Motors Corp.] [Detroit, MI] [Information service or system] (IID)
PCAP .... Post Commercial Action Plan [International Trade Administration]
PCAP .... Programmer Capacity
PC App .... Law Reports, Privy Council, Appeal Cases [England] [A publication] (DLA)
PCAPS .... Production Control and Planning System (MCD)
PCAQ .... Pony Club Association of Queensland [Australia]
PCAR .... PACCAR, Inc. [NASDAQ symbol] (NQ)
PCAR .... Parent-Child Activity Rating Scale [Education] (EDAC)
PCAR .... Process Characterization Analysis Package (MHDI)
P (Card)....... Personal Card [Containing person's name, address, age, description, job, habits, haunts, movements] [Used in Belfast, Northern Ireland]
PCarl .... Bosler Free Library, Carlisle, PA [Library symbol Library of Congress] (LCLS)
PCarlA .... United States Army War College, Carlisle Barracks, PA [Library symbol Library of Congress] (LCLS)
PCarlD .... Dickinson College, Carlisle, PA [Library symbol Library of Congress] (LCLS)
PCarlD-L...... Dickinson School of Law, Sheeley-Lee Law Library, Carlisle, PA [Library symbol Library of Congress] (LCLS)
PCarlH .... Cumberland County Historical Society and Hamilton Library Association, Carlisle, PA [Library symbol Library of Congress] (LCLS)
PCarlMH ...... United States Army, Military History Research Collection, Carlisle Barracks, PA [Library symbol Library of Congress] (LCLS)
PCarlPL ...... United States Army, Carlisle Barracks Post Library, Carlisle Barracks, PA [Library symbol Library of Congress] (LCLS)
PCARR........ Philippines Council for Agricultural Resources and Research (BUAC)
PCARS .... Point Credit Accounting and Reporting System (AFM)
PCAS.......... Patient Care Algorithm System [Medicine] (DMAA)
PCAS .... Persistent Chemical Agent Stimulant
PCAS .... Polytechnics Central Admissions System [British] (DET)
PCAS .... Possible Carotid Artery System [Medicine]
PCAS .... Primary Central Alarm Station [Nuclear energy] (NRCH)
P Cas.......... Prize Cases [1914-22] [England] [A publication] (DLA)
P Cas.......... Prize Cases (Trehearn and Grant) [England] [A publication] (DLA)
PCAS .... Punch Card Accounting System [Computer science]
PCASA .... Pony Club Association of South Australia
PCAS/CADS... Persistent Chemical Agent Stimulant/Chemical Agent Disclosure Solution [Army]
PCASP .... Passive-Cavity Aerosal Spectrometer Probe [Meteorology]
PCASS .... Parts Control Automated Support System [Database]
PCAST .... President's Council of Advisers on Science and Technology [1989]
PCAT .... Pharmacy College Admissions Test (GAGS)
PCAT .... Pharmacy College Admission Test
pCAT.......... Plasmid Chloramphenicol Acetyltransferase [An enzyme]
PCAT .... Procedures for the Control of Air Traffic (SAA)
PCAU .... Parachute Course Administrative Unit [Military British] (INF)
PCAU .... Philippine Civil Affairs Unit [Army unit which supplied emergency subsistence after end of Japanese dominance] [World War II]
PCAV .... Pony Club Association of Victoria [Australia]
PCAV .... Principal Component Analysis with Varimax Rotation
PCAWA .... Pony Club Association of Western Australia
PCB............ Central Pennsylvania District Library Center, Bellefonte, PA [OCLC symbol] (OCLC)
PcB............ Near Point of Convergence [Ophthalmology]
PCB............ Page Control Block [Computer science] (IBMDP)
PCB............ Pancuronium Bromide [A muscle relaxant] (DAVI)
PCB............ Paracervical Block [Anesthesiology]
PCB............ Parti Communiste de Belgique [Communist Party of Belgium] [See also KPB] [Political party] (PPE)
PCB............ Partido Comunista de Bolivia [Communist Party of Bolivia] [Political party] (PPW)
PCB............ Partido Comunista do Brasil [Communist Party of Brazil] [Pro-Albanian] [Political party] (PPW)
PCB............ Parts Control Board
PCB............ Patent Compensation Board [Energy Research and Development Administration]
PCB............ Percutaneous Biopsy [Medicine] (CPH)
PCB............ Petty Cash Book [Business term]
PCB............ Planning Change Board (AAG)
PCB............ Plenum Chamber Burning
PCB............ Polychlorinated Biphenyl [Organic chemistry]
PCB............ Polychlorobenzene

PCB	Portacaval Bypass [*Cardiology*] (DMAA)
PCB	Port Check BIT [*Binary Digit*] [*Telecommunications*] (TEL)
PCB	Postcoital Bleeding [*Medicine*] (DMAA)
PCB	Power Circuit Breaker (MSA)
PCB	Power Control Box (NASA)
PCB	Precambrian Shield Resources Ltd. [*Toronto Stock Exchange symbol*]
PCB	Premier Commercial Bank Ltd. [*Nigeria*]
PCB	Primary Carpet Backing
PCB	Printed Circuit Board (MCD)
pcb	Printed-Circuit Board (IDOE)
PCB	Prix de Cession de Base [*Basic Wholesale Price*] [*French*]
PCB	Procarbazine [*Also, P, PC, Pr*] [*Antineoplastic drug*]
PCB	Process Control Block
PCB	Processor Command Bus (NITA)
PCB	Product Configuration Baseline (NASA)
PCB	Program Communication Block
PCB	Program Control Block [*Computer science*] (BUR)
PCB	Project Change Board (AAG)
PCB	Project Control Branch [*Social Security Administration*]
PCB	Projected Control Board
PCB	Property Control Branch [*of Allied Military Government*] [*Post-World War II*]
PCB	Proposed Committee Bill (WPI)
PCB	Proprietor of Copyright on a Work by a Corporate Body
PCB	Propulsion [*Ground*] Control Box (AAG)
PCB	Public Coin Box [*Telecommunications*] (TEL)
PCB	Publisher's Central Bureau
PCBA	Para-Chlorobenzoic Acid [*Organic chemistry*]
PCBA	Pepsi-Cola Bottlers Association (EA)
PCBA	Pioneer Citizens Band Association (IAA)
PCBA	Polyclonal B Cell Activation [*Hematology*]
PCBA	Printed Circuit Board Assembly (MCD)
PCBB	Power Conditioning Brass Board (MCD)
PCBB	Primary Commercial Blanket Bond [*Insurance*]
PCBC	Para-Chlorobenzyl Chloride [*Organic chemistry*]
PCBC	Partially Conserved Baryon Current (IEEE)
PCBC	Perry County Financial [*NASDAQ symbol*] (TTSB)
PCBC	Perry County Financial Corp. [*NASDAQ symbol*] (SAG)
PCBC	Polk County Biomedical Consortium [*Library network*]
PCBC	Progressive Conservative Broadcasting Corp. [*Fictional version of the Cana dian Broadcasting Corp.*]
PCBCI	Pedigree Cattle Breeders' Council of Ireland (BUAC)
PCBCL	Printed Circuit Board Configuration List (MCD)
PCBD	Polychlorinated Benzodioxin [*Organic chemistry*]
PCBDA	Put and Call Brokers and Dealers Association [*Inactive*] (EA)
PCBG	Primary Care Block Grant
PCB-ML	Partido Comunista Marxista-Leninista de Bolivia [*Marxist-Leninist Communist Party of Bolivia*] [*Political party*] (PPW)
PC-BMP	Phosphorylcholine-Binding Myeloma Protein [*Medicine*] (DMAA)
PCBN	Para-Chlorobenzonitrile [*Organic chemistry*]
PCBN	Pentachlorobenzonitrite (EES)
PCBN	Polycrystalline Cubic Boron Nitrite
PCBPA	Personal Computer Board Panel Assembly (DWSG)
PCBR	Printed Circuit Board Repair (MCD)
PC/BRD	Printed Circuit Board [*Automotive engineering*]
PCBS	Plastic Connector Backing Shell
PCBS	Positive Control Bombardment System [*Air Force*]
PCBS	Printed Circuit Board Socket
PCBS	Pupil Classroom Behavior Scale
PCBTF	Para-Chlorobenzotrifluoride [*Organic chemistry*]
PCBTS	Portable Cesium Beam Time Standard
PCC	Acts of the Privy Council, Colonial Series [*A publication*] (DLA)
PCC	Chief Postal Clerk [*Navy rating*]
PCC	Order of St. Clare (TOCD)
PCC	Pacific Coast Conference (PSS)
PCC	Pacific Conference of Churches (BUAC)
PCC	Pacific Cruise Conference [*Formerly, TPPC*] [*Defunct*] (EA)
PCC	Package Carrier Committee (EA)
PCC	Pad Control Center [*NASA*] (NASA)
PCC	Paid Circulation Council [*Later, ASCMP*]
PCC	Palestine Liberation Organisation's Central Council
PCC	Palestinian Ceramic Chronology [*200BC-70AD*] [*A publication*] (BJA)
PCC	Panama Canal Co. [*Superseded by Panama Canal Commission*]
PCC	Panama Canal Commission [*Independent government agency*]
PCC	Panamerican Cultural Circle (EA)
PCC	Parent and Child Center [*Project Head Start*]
PCC	Parklawn Health Library Computer Center [*Department of Health and Human Services*] (GFGA)
PCC	Parochial Church Council [*Church of England*]
PCC	Partial Crystal Control (IEEE)
PCC	Partido Comunista Chileno [*Communist Party of Chile*] [*Political party*] (PD)
PCC	Partido Comunista Cubano [*Communist Party of Cuba*] [*Political party*] (PPW)
PCC	Partido Conservador Colombiano [*Conservative Party of Colombia*] [*Political party*] (PPW)
PCC	Party of Catalan Communists [*Political party*] (PPW)
PCC	Pasadena City College [*California*]
PCC	Patient Care Coordinator [*Medicine*]
PCC	Payload Control and Checkout [*NASA*] (NASA)
PCC	Peak Cathode Current
PCC	Penn Central Corp. (EFIS)
PCC	People's Caretakers' Council [*Rhodesian*]
PCC	People's Christian Coalition [*Later, Sojourners*] (EA)
PCC	Pepper Community [*Later, IPC*]
PCC	Per-Command Course (MCD)
PCC	Per Copia Conforme [*True Copy*] [*Italian*]
PCC	Performance Certification Component [*SQT*] (MCD)
PCC	Performance Criteria Categories (MCD)
PCC	Peripheral Control Computer
PCc	Periscopic Concave [*Ophthalmology*]
PCC	Permanent Consultative Committee
PCC	Personal Care Clinic (DAVI)
PCC	Personal Code Calling (NITA)
PCC	Personal Communications Controller (NITA)
PCC	Personal Computer Coprocessor
PCC	Personnel Control Center [*Air Force*] (AFM)
PCC	Personnel Coordination Center [*Army*]
PCC	Pertec Computer Corp. (EFIS)
PCC	Perth Chamber of Commerce [*Western Australia*]
PCC	Peters' United States Circuit Court Reports [*A publication*] (DLA)
PCC	Phaeochromocytoma [*Medicine*] (BABM)
PCC	Phenylchlorocarbene [*Organic chemistry*]
PCC	Pheochromocytoma [*Oncology*]
PCC	Philippine Christian College (AEBS)
PCC	Philippine Cotton Corp. (BUAC)
PCC	Philips Consumer Communications
PCC	Phosphate Carrier Compound
PCC	Photoelectric Counter Chronometer (IAA)
PCC	Physical Coal Cleaning [*Fuel technology*]
PCC	Pilarcitos Creek [*California*] [*Seismograph station code, US Geological Survey*] (SEIS)
PCC	Pilot Control Console
PCC	Piperidinocyclohexanecarbonitrile [*Organic chemistry*]
PCC	Planning Coordination Conference [*NATO*] (NATG)
PCC	Plastics in Construction Council [*Later, CCS*]
PCC	Platform Control Center [*NASA*] (SSD)
PCC	Platoon Command Center [*Army*]
PCC	Plug Compatible Computer (ADA)
PCC	Plutonium Concentrator Concentrate [*Nuclear energy*] (NRCH)
PCC	PMC Commercial Tr [*AMEX symbol*] (TTSB)
PCC	PMC Commercial Trust [*AMEX symbol*] (SAG)
PCC	Pointe Claire Public Library [*UTLAS symbol*]
PCC	Point of Compound Curve (KSC)
PCC	Poison Control Center
PCC	Polarity Coincidence Correlator
PCC	Policy Coordination Council (USDC)
PCC	Political Consultative Committee [*Warsaw Pact*]
PCC	Political Consultative Council [*Russia*] (BUAC)
PCC	Polycore Composite Construction [*Automotive engineering*]
PCC	Polymer-Cement Concrete (KSC)
PCC	Polynesian Cultural Center (EA)
PCC	Pontifical Council for Culture [*Vatican City*] (EAIO)
PCC	Poor Clares of St. Colette [*Roman Catholic women's religious order*]
PCC	Population Action International [*An association*] (EA)
PCC	Population Crisis Committee (EA)
PCC	Portable Cable Checker
PCC	Portland Cement Concrete
PCC	Positive Control Communication
PCC	Postal and Courier Communications [*British*]
PCC	Postal Concentration Center [*Army*]
PCC	Pour Copie Conforme [*Certified True Copy*] [*French*]
PCC	Power Control Console [*Diving apparatus*]
PCC	Precast Concrete [*Technical drawings*]
PCC	Precipitated Calcium Carbonate [*Inorganic chemistry*]
PCC	Pre-Command Course [*Military*]
PCC	Precompressor Cooling (MCD)
PCC	Pregnancy Crisis Centre [*Australia*]
PCC	Premature Chromosome Condensation [*Genetics*]
PCC	Prematurely Condensed Chromosome (DB)
PCC	Prerogative Court of Canterbury [*English court previously having jurisdiction over wills*]
PCC	Presbyterian Charismatic Communion [*Later, PRR*] [*An association*] (EA)
PCC	President of the Canteen Committee [*Military British*]
PCC	President's Conference Committee
PCC	Press Complaints Commission (ECON)
PCC	Price Control Council (NADA)
PCC	Primary Care Center [*Health care*] (HCT)
PCC	Primary Care Clinic (DAVI)
PCC	Primary Category Code (NITA)
PCC	Primary Component Cooling (COE)
PCC	Primary Control Center (COE)
PCC	Print Collectors' Club [*British*] (DBA)
PCC	Printed Circuit Card
PCC	Printed Circuit Conference
PCC	Printers' Charitable Corp. (DGA)
PCC	Private Carrier Conference [*of ATA*] (EA)
PCC	Privy Council Cases [*British*]
PC(C)	Privy Councillor (Canada)
PCC	Problem Control and Contact Unit [*IRS*]
PCC	Process Chemistry Cell (NRCH)
PCC	Process Control Computer
PCC	Processor Control Cards [*Computer science*] (IAA)
PCC	Processor Control Console [*Telecommunications*] (TEL)
PCC	Product Control Center [*DoD*]
PCC	Production Compression Capability
PCC	Productivity Communication Center [*Defunct*] (EA)
PCC	Program Control Card (IAA)

PCC............. Program Control Counter
PCC............. Program-Controlled Computer (DIT)
PCC............. Program Coordination Committee (SSD)
PCC............. Program for Cooperative Cataloging [American Library Association]
PCC............. Progress Control Clerk [DoD]
PCC............. Project Control Center
PCC............. Project Coordination Centre [Defence Research Board] [Canada]
PCC............. Propionyl CoA Carboxylase [An enzyme]
PCC............. Protein-Conducting Channel [Biochemistry]
PCC............. Prothrombin Complex Concentrates [Hematology]
PCC............. Protocol Converter Concentrator [Telecommunications] (IAA)
PCC............. Provincial Congress Committee
PCC............. Provisioning Control Code [Military] (AFIT)
PCC............. Psychometric Colorimeter Chamber (MCD)
PCC............. Puerto Rico [Colombia] [Airport symbol] (AD)
PCC............. Pulse Counter Chain
PCC............. Pulverized Coal Combustion [or Combustor]
PCC............. Pure Car Carrier [Shipping] (DS)
PCC............. Pyridinium Chlorochromate [Organic chemistry]
PCC............. Pyroconvective Cooling
PC(C).......... Submarine Chaser (Control) [173 foot] [Navy symbol Obsolete]
PCCA .... Confederation Art Gallery and Museum, Charlottetown, Prince
　　　　　　 Edward Island [Library symbol National Library of Canada] (NLC)
PCCA .... Pacific Class Catamaran Association (EA)
PCCA .... Pattern-Contingent Chromatic Aftereffects
PCCA .... Pewter Collectors Club of America
PCCA .... Pipe Collectors Club of America [Defunct] (EA)
PCCA .... Playing Card Collectors' Association (EA)
PCCA .... Police Car Collectors Association (EA)
PCCA .... Polymerized Crystalline Colloidal Array [Materials science]
PCCA .... Portable Computer and Community Association
PCCA .... Postcard Collector's Club of America [Defunct] (EA)
PCCA .... Power and Communication Contractors Association (EA)
PCCA .... Professional Compounding Centers of America
PCCA .... Promotion of Community and Cultural Awareness [Australia]
PCCADS....... Panoramic Cockpit Control and Display System (MCD)
PCCAF........ Procedure Change Control Action Form (AAG)
PCCAF........ Procedure Committee Change Authorization Form (AAG)
PcCAp........ Pacific Coast Apparel Co., Inc. [Associated Press] (SAG)
PcCap........ Pacificorp Capital [Associated Press] (SAG)
PCCAP........ Physicians' Continued Competence Assessment Program
　　　　　　 [Medicine] (DMAA)
PcCApp....... Pacific Coast Apparel Co., Inc. [Associated Press] (SAG)
PCCB .... Payload Configuration Control Board [NASA] (MCD)
PCCB .... Program Configuration Control Board [NASA] (NASA)
PCCB .... Project Configuration Control Board [Army] (AABC)
PCCC .... Pacific Coast Collegiate Conference (PSS)
PCCC .... Pakistan Central Cotton Committee (BUAC)
PCCC .... Participating College Correspondence Course (MUGU)
PCCC .... Penang Chinese Chamber of Commerce [Malaysia] (BUAC)
PCCC .... Polytechnics and Colleges Computer Committee (AIE)
PCCD .... Peristaltic Charge-Coupled Device (IEEE)
PCCDS........ Patrol Craft Combat Direction System [Navy] (SAA)
PCCE.......... Pacific Coast Coin Exchange
PCCE.......... Payload Common Communication Equipment [NASA] (NASA)
PCCEI......... Permanent Charities Committee of the Entertainment Industries (EA)
PCCEMRSP... Permanent Commission for the Conservation and Exploitation of the
　　　　　　 Maritime Resources of the South Pacific
PCCES .... Planning and Coordinating Committee for Environmental Studies
　　　　　　 [National Research Council]
PCCF.......... Plan Case Control File [IRS]
PCCF.......... Prostate Cancer Cure Foundation Ltd.
PCCF.......... Protein C Cofactor (DMAA)
PCCG .... PCC Group [NASDAQ symbol] (TTSB)
PCCG .... PCC Group, Inc. [NASDAQ symbol] (SAG)
PCCG .... Protestant Cinema Critics Guild [Later, PCG] (EA)
PCCGB........ Photographic Collectors Club of Great Britain (DBA)
PCC Gp ...... PCC Group, Inc. [Associated Press] (SAG)
PCCh.......... Partido Comunista de Chile [Chilean Communist Party] [Political
　　　　　　 party] (EY)
PCCH .... Pentachlorocyclohexene [Organic chemistry]
PCCI........... Pacific Crest Capital [NASDAQ symbol] (SAG)
PCCI........... Paper Cup and Container Institute [Later, SSI] (EA)
PCCI........... President's Committee on Consumer Interests [Terminated, 1971]
PCCL.......... People's Community Civic League (EA)
PCCL.......... Precontract Cost Letter [Navy] (NG)
PCCLAS....... Pacific Coast Council on Latin American Studies (BUAC)
PCCM.......... Master Chief Postal Clerk [Navy rating]
PCCM.......... Pediatric Critical Care Medicine (DMAA)
PCCM.......... Portuguese Cultural Centre of Melbourne [Victoria, Australia]
PCCM.......... Primary Care Case Management [Medicine] (DMAA)
PCCM.......... Primary Care Case Manager [Medicine] (DMAA)
PCCM.......... Private Circuit Control Module [Telecommunications] (TEL)
PCCM.......... Program Change Control Management (NASA)
PCCM.......... Program Control Contract Manager (MCD)
PCC (M-L) ... Parti Communiste Canadien (Marxiste-Leniniste) [Marxist-Leninist
　　　　　　 Communist Party of Canada] [Political party]
PCCN .... Part Card Change Notice (KSC)
PCCN .... Port Call Control Number [Army] (AABC)
PCCN .... Preliminary Configuration Control Number (AAG)
PCCN .... Provisioning Contract Control Number (NASA)
PCCNA........ Pentecostal Charismatic Churches of North America (EA)
PCCNL........ Pacific Coast Coordinator of Naval Logistics
PCCO .... Plant Clearance Contracting Officer [DoD]

PCCOA........ Coles Associates Ltd., Charlottetown, Prince Edward Island [Library
　　　　　　 symbol National Library of Canada] (NLC)
PCCP .... Canadian Pension Commission [Commission Canadienne des
　　　　　　 Pensions], Charlottetown, Prince Edward Island [Library symbol
　　　　　　 National Library of Canada] (BIB)
PCCP .... Preliminary Contract Change Proposal [NASA] (KSC)
PCCP .... Private Child Care Provider (EDAC)
PCCPS .... Pacific Coast Canned Pear Service (EA)
PCCR .... Procurement Code Change Request (IAA)
PCCR .... Publishing Center for Cultural Resources [Defunct] (EA)
PCCS .... Parti Conservateur Chretien-Social [Conservative Christian-Social
　　　　　　 Party] [Switzerland Political party] (PPE)
PCCS .... Photographic Camera Control System (KSC)
PCCS .... Ported Coax Cable Sensor [Military] (DWSG)
PCCS .... Positive Control Communications System
PCCS .... Primate Captive Care Society (BUAC)
PCCS .... Processor Common Communications System
PCCS .... Program and Cost Control System [Army] (RDA)
PCCS .... Program Change Control System (NG)
PCCS .... Project Cost Control System
PCCS .... Publications Contract Coverage Schedule (MCD)
PCCS .... Senior Chief Postal Clerk [Navy rating]
PCCT .... Percept and Concept Cognition Test [Psychology]
PCCU .... Post-Coronary Care Unit [Medicine] (STED)
PCCU .... President's Commission on Campus Unrest (EA)
PCCU .... Psychiatric Criminal Care Unit (WDAA)
PCCU .... Punched Card Control Unit [Computer science] (AABC)
PCCW .... Price/Costco, Inc. [NASDAQ symbol] (SPSG)
PCCW .... Public Citizens Congress Watch (COE)
PCD .... Democratic Conservative Party [Nicaragua] [Political party] (PD)
PCD .... Pacific Car Demurrage Bureau, San Francisco CA [STAC]
PCD .... Pacific Communications Division [Military]
PCD .... Panama Canal Department
PCD .... Papillary Collecting Duct [Medicine] (DMAA)
PCD .... Paroxysmal Cerebral Dysrhythmia [Medicine] (STED)
PCD .... Parti Communiste du Dahomey [Communist Party of Dahomey]
　　　　　　 [Benin] [Political party]
PCD .... Partido Comunista Dominicano [Dominican Communist Party]
　　　　　　 [Dominican Republic] [Political party] (PPW)
PCD .... Party of Christian Democrats [Poland] [Political party] (BUAC)
PCD .... Patriotic Coalition for Democracy [Political group] [Guyana]
PCD .... PCD, Inc. [Associated Press] (SAG)
PCD .... Perceptual-Communicative Disorder [Education] (EDAC)
PCD .... Personal Communication Device [FTA] (TAG)
PCD .... Phenylchlorodiazirine [Organic chemistry]
PCD .... Phosphate-Citrate-Dextrose Polycystic Disease (MAE)
PCD .... Photo Compact Disk [Eastman Kodak Co.] (PCM)
PCD .... Photoconductive Decay [Semiconductor material]
PCD .... Pine Channel Gold [Vancouver Stock Exchange symbol]
PCD .... Pitch Circle Diameter [Technical drawings] (IAA)
PCD .... Planned Commercial Development (PA)
PCD .... Planned Completion Date (TEL)
PCD .... Plasma Cell Dyscrasia [Medicine]
PCD .... Plasma-Coupled Device
PCD .... Plutonium Concentrator Distillate [Nuclear energy] (NRCH)
PCD .... Pneumatic Control Distributors (KSC)
PCD .... Polar Cap Disturbance (DNAB)
PCD .... Polychlorinated Dibenzo (BARN)
PCD .... Polycrystalline Diamond (ECON)
PCD .... Polycystic Disease [of kidneys] [Medicine]
PCD .... Polymeric Carrier Delivery System [Nuclear energy] (NUCP)
PCD .... Port Control Diagnostic [Telecommunications] (TEL)
PCD .... Positive Control Document (MCD)
PCd .... Post Card [Philately]
Pcd .... Postcard (BJA)
PCD .... Posterior Corneal Deposit [Ophthalmology] (MAE)
PCD .... Postmortem Cesarean Delivery (STED)
PCD .... Pounds per Capita per Day (AAG)
PCD .... Power Control and Distribution
PCD .... Power Control Device [Nuclear energy] (NRCH)
PCD .... Power Conversion Distributor
PCD .... Precision Course Direction [Aerospace] (MCD)
PCD .... Pressure Control Distributor (KSC)
PCD .... Primary Ciliary Dyskinesia [Medicine]
PCD .... Primary Current Distribution [Electroplating]
PCD .... Problem Control and Display
PCD .... Procedural Change Directive (KSC)
PCD .... Proceed [ICAO designator] (FAAC)
PCD .... Procurement and Contracts Division [NASA]
PCD .... Procurement Control Document [NASA] (MCD)
PCD .... Product Configuration Documentation (AAGC)
PCD .... Production Common Digitizer
PCD .... Program Change Decision [Army]
PCD .... Program Control Display System [NATO Air Defense Ground
　　　　　　 Environment] (NATG)
PCD .... Program Control Document (KSC)
PCD .... Programmed Cell Death [Cytology]
PCD .... Project Control Drawing (AAG)
PCD .... Projected Charge Density (PDAA)
PCD .... Prolonged Contractile Duration (STED)
PCD .... Protocatechuatedioxygenase [An enzyme]
PCD .... Pulmonary Clearance Delay [Medicine]
PCDA .... Post Card Distributors Association
PCDA .... Professional Currency Dealers Association (EA)
PCDA .... Protective Clothing Distributors Association [British] (DBA)

PCDANA...... Post Card Distributors Association of North America (NTPA)
PCDB .... Poison Control Data Base [Database]
PCDC .... Diagnostic Chemicals Ltd., Charlottetown, Prince Edward Island [Library symbol National Library of Canada] (NLC)
PCDC .... Plasma Clot Diffusion Chamber [Medicine] (DMAA)
PCDC .... Plutonium Canister Decontamination Cell [Nuclear energy] (NRCH)
PCDD .... Pentachlorodioxin [Organic chemistry]
PCDD .... Polychlorinated Dibenzodioxin [Organic chemistry]
PCDD .... Polychlorinated Dibenzodioxins [Automotive emissions] [Organic chemistry]
PCDDS........ Private Circuit Digital Data Service [Telecommunications] (TEL)
PCDE .... Parent Council for Deaf Education [Australia]
PCDESIG..... Plane Captain Designated [or Designation] (DNAB)
PCDF .... Polychlorinated Dibenzofuran [Organic chemistry]
PCDF .... Polychlorinated Dibenzofurans [Automotive emissions] [Organic chemistry]
PCDH .... Polychlorinated Diaromatic Hydrocarbon [Organic chemistry]
PCDHi......... Delaware County Historical Society, Chester, PA [Library symbol Library of Congress] (LCLS)
PCDI .... PCD, Inc. [NASDAQ symbol] (SAG)
PCDI .... Per Capita Disposable Income [Economics]
PCDI .... Pierce Die
PCDI .... Printed Circuit Design Interface (NITA)
PCDJ .... Pakistan Committee for Democracy and Justice [Defunct] (EA)
PCDL .... Pro-Choice Defense League (EA)
PCDMA .... Personal Computer Direct Marketers Association (BUAC)
PCdoB.......... Partido Comunista do Brasil [Communist Party of Brazil] [Political party] (PPW)
PC DOCS ..... PC DOCS Group International [Associated Press] (SAG)
PC-DOS....... Personal Computer-Disk Operating System (DOM)
PCDP .... Parti Comorien pour la Democratie et le Progres [Political party] (EY)
PCDP .... Pilot Control and Display Panel
PCDP .... Punched Card Data Processing
PCDPPP...... Pan Caribbean Disaster Preparedness and Prevention Project (BUAC)
PCD-PRP ..... Pueblo, Cambio, y Democracia - Partido Roldosista Popular [People, Change, and Democracy - Popular Roldosista Party] [Ecuador] [Political party] (PPW)
PCDR .... Procedure (AAG)
PCDS .... Payload Command Decoder Subunit [NASA] (KSC)
PCDS .... Power Conversion and Distribution System
PCDS .... Procurement Congressional Descriptive Summary [Army] (RDA)
PCDS .... Project Control Drawing System (AAG)
PCDU .... Payload Command Decoder Unit [NASA] (NASA)
PCDUS......... Plasma Cell Dyscrasias of Unknown Significance [Medicine]
PCE............ Page Communications Engineers, Inc. [Canada] (MCD)
PCE............ Painter Creek, AK [Location identifier FAA] (FAAL)
PCE............ Palm Island [Queensland] [Airport symbol] (AD)
PCE............ Parameter Checkout Engineer [Computer science] (IAA)
PCE............ Partido Comunista de Espana [Communist Party of Spain] [Political party] (PPE)
PCE............ Partido Comunista Ecuatoriano [Communist Party of Ecuador] [Political party] (PPW)
PCE............ Passenger Car Equivalence [TRB] (TAG)
PCE............ Patrol Escort [Patrol Craft Escort] [Navy symbol]
PCE............ Pedco Energy Ltd. [Vancouver Stock Exchange symbol]
PCE............ Perchloroethylene [Organic chemistry]
PCE............ Peripheral Control Element
PCE............ Peripheral Controller Enclosure (NITA)
PCE............ Personal Consumption Expenditure
PCE............ Petrozavodsk Commodity Exchange [Russian Federation] (EY)
PCE............ Photocell Emitter (IAA)
PCE............ Physical Capacities Evaluation [Test of hand skills]
PCE............ Piece [Numismatics]
PCE............ Plasma Chamber Evacuation Subsystem (MCD)
PCE............ Platinol [Cis-Platinum] Cyclophosphamide, Vindesine [Antineoplastic drug regimen] (DAVI)
PCE............ Plug Compatible Ethernet
PCE............ Pollution Control Equipment (GFGA)
PCE............ Polyarthrite Chronique Evolutive [Chronic Evolutive Polyarthritis] [Medicine French]
PCE............ Polychloroethylene (BARN)
PCE............ Polymer-Coated Erythromycin [An antibiotic] (DAVI)
PCE............ Ponce [Diocesan abbreviation] [Puerto Rico] (TOCD)
PCE............ Pool Control Error (IAA)
PCE............ Positive Continuous Engagement [Automotive engineering]
PCE............ Potentially Compensable Event (DICI)
PCE............ Power Conditioning Equipment
PCE............ Power Conversion Equipment (DNAB)
PCE............ Pressure to Clutch Engage [Aerospace] (AAG)
PCE............ Prince Edward Island Department of Education, Charlottetown, Prince Edward Island [Library symbol National Library of Canada] (NLC)
PCE............ Privy Councillor, England (ROG)
PCE............ Process [or Processor] Control Element [Computer science] (IAA)
PCE............ Production Check Equipment (MCD)
PCE............ Professional Continuing Education (DOMA)
PCE............ Program Cost Estimate (AFM)
PCE............ Prohormone-Converting Endopeptidase
PCE............ Pseudocholinesterase [Same as ACAH] [An enzyme]
PCE............ Pulmocutaneous Exchange
PCE............ Punch Card Equipment [Computer science] (AFM)
PCE............ Pyrometric Cone Equivalent [Refractory industry]
PCE............ Submarine Chaser Escort
PCEA.......... Pacific Coast Electrical Association
PCEA.......... Patient-Controlled Epidural Analgesia

PCEA........... Phosphate Chemicals Export Association (EA)
PCEA........... Presbyterian Church of Eastern Australia
PCEA........... Professional Construction Estimators Association of America (NTPA)
P/CEA3........ Probationary Control Electrical Artificer 3rd Class [British military] (DMA)
PCEAA........ Professional Construction Estimators Association of America (EA)
PCE(C)........ Patrol Vessel, Escort (Control) [180 feet] [Navy symbol Obsolete]
PCEDURE..... Procedure (ROG)
PCEEDGS..... Proceedings (ROG)
PCEEO........ President's Committee on Equal Employment Opportunity [Later, OFCCP] [Department of Labor]
PCEH........... President's Committee on Employment of the Handicapped [Washington, DC]
PCEI........... Prime Contract End Item (MCD)
PCEM........... Parliamentary Council of the European Movement
PCEM........... Process Chain Evaluation Model (IEEE)
PCEM........... Program Committee on Education for Mission (EA)
PCEM........... Propulsion Contamination Effects Module (NASA)
PcEn........... Pacific Enterprises [Associated Press] (SAG)
PCEN........... Paracentesis Fluid [Medicine] (DAVI)
PCEO........... Personal Computer Enhancement Operation [Intel Corp.] (CIST)
PCEQ........... President's Commisssion on Environmental Quality (GNE)
PCE-R......... Partido Comunista de Espana - Reconstituido [Reconstituted Spanish Communist Party] [Political party] (PD)
PCER .... Patrol Rescue Escort [Patrol Craft Escort Rescue] [Navy symbol]
P Cert Ed .... Professional Certificate in Education
PCES........... Pace Health Management Systems, Inc. [NASDAQ symbol] (SAG)
PCES........... PACE Health Mgmt [NASDAQ symbol] (TTSB)
PCES........... President's Committee on Economic Security [New Deal]
PCET........... Personal Computer Extended Technology
PCETF......... Power Conversion Equipment Test Facility [Nuclear energy]
PCEU .... Partido Comunista de Espana Unificado [Unified Communist Party of Spain] [Political party] (PPW)
PCEU .... Pulse Compression/Expansion Unit
PCF............ Pacific Air Express [ICAO designator] (FAAC)
PCF............ Pacific Ridge Resources [Vancouver Stock Exchange symbol]
PCF............ Pacificulture Foundation (EA)
PCF............ Palliative Care Foundation [Canada] (EAIO)
PCF............ Parents' Choice Foundation (EA)
PCF............ Parliamentary Christian Fellowship [British] (WDAA)
PCF............ Parti Communiste Francais [French Communist Party] [Political party] (PPW)
PCF............ Patrol Craft (Fast) [Navy symbol]
PCF............ Payload Control Facility [NASA] (MCD)
PCF............ Peace Centers Foundation [Later, UDC] (EA)
PCF............ Pentagon Counterintelligence Force
PCF............ Peripheral Circulatory Failure [Medicine] (DMAA)
PCF............ Personal Card File
PCF............ Personnel Control Facility [Army] (AABC)
PCF............ Pharyngoconjunctival Fever [Medicine]
PCF............ Plan Characteristics File [IRS]
PCF............ Polycationized Ferritin [Biochemistry]
PCF............ Postcard Club Federation [Defunct] (EA)
PCF............ Posterior Carotid Foramen [Anatomy]
PCF............ Posterior Cranial Fossa [Anatomy] (MAE)
PCF............ Potential Conflict Forecasts [Army]
PCF............ Potentially Critical Failures
PCF............ Pounds per Cubic Foot
pcf............ Pounds per Cubic Foot (WPI)
PCF............ Power Cathode Follower
PCF............ Power per Cubic Foot
PCF............ Prairie Chicken Foundation (EA)
PCF............ Primary Checkpoint File
PCF............ Probability of Consequence Factor
PCF............ Processed Citation File
PCF............ Program Change Factor
PCF............ Program Characteristics File [Medicaid] (GFGA)
PCF............ Program Checkout Facility
PCF............ Program Complex File [Computer science] (MHDI)
PCF............ Program Control Facility
PCF............ Programmed Cryptographic Facility [Computer science]
PCF............ Prothrombin Conversion Factor [Hematology]
PCF............ Public Concern Foundation (EA)
PCF............ Pulse Compression Filter
PCF............ Pulse-to-Cycle Fraction
PCF............ Pulverized Coal-Fired Plant
PCF............ Putnam High Income Convertible & Bond Fund [NYSE symbol] (SPSG)
PCF............ Putnam Hi Income Cv/Bd Fd [NYSE symbol] (TTSB)
PCFA........... Pin, Clip, and Fastener Association [Later, PCFS] (EA)
PCFA........... Polytechnics and Colleges Funding Council (BUAC)
PCFA........... Precast Concrete Frame Association [British] (DBA)
PCFC........... Phil Collins Fan Club (EA)
PCFC........... Pioneer Commercial Funding Corp. [NASDAQ symbol] (SAG)
PCFC........... Polytechnics and Colleges Funding Council [British]
Pcfcp25....... Pacificorp [Associated Press] (SAG)
Pcfcp35....... Pacificorp [Associated Press] (SAG)
PCFE........... Polytrifluorochloroethylene [Organic chemistry]
PCFE........... Prime Contractor Furnished Equipment (MCD)
PCFFA........ Pacific Coast Federation of Fishermen's Associations (EA)
PC/FGD....... Pulverized Coal / Flue Gas Desulfurization [Energy technology]
PCFIA......... Particle Concentration Fluorescence Immunoassay
PCFM........... Production Control File Manager (IAA)
PCFN .... PC Financial Network (PCM)
PCFO........... Position Classification Field Office

PCFP.......... Predicted Comparative Failure Probability
PCFR .... Programmatic Center for Fire Research [*National Institute of Standards and Technology*]
PCFRE .... Professional Council of Religious Education [*British*] (DBA)
PCFS.......... Pin, Clip, and Fastener Services (EA)
PCFT.......... Information Centre, Prince Edward Island Food Technology Centre, Charlottetown [*Library symbol National Library of Canada*] (BIB)
PCG .... Guided Missile Coastal Escort [*Ship symbol*] (NATG)
PCG .... Pacific Gas & Elec [*NYSE symbol*] (TTSB)
PCG .... Pacific Gas & Electric Co. [*NYSE symbol*] (SAG)
PCG .... Pacific Gas & Electric Co. [*AMEX symbol*] (SPSG)
PCG .... Paracervical Ganglion [*Anatomy*]
PCG .... Parti Communiste de Guadeloupe [*Communist Party of Guadeloupe*] [*Political party*] (PPW)
PCG .... Period Costume Group (BUAC)
PCG .... PezCorona Gold Corp. [*Vancouver Stock Exchange symbol*]
PCG .... PG & E Capital I [*AMEX symbol*] (SAG)
PCG .... PG & E Corp. Holdings Co. [*NYSE symbol*] (SAG)
PCG .... Phonocardiogram [*Cardiology*]
pcg........... Picogram [*Measurement*] (DAVI)
P/CG .... Pilot Controller Glossary [*Aviation*] (FAAC)
PCG .... Plain Clothes Gratuity [*British military*] (DMA)
PCG .... Plains Cotton Growers (EA)
PCG .... Planning and Control Guide
PCG .... Planning Career Goals [*Vocational guidance test*]
PCG .... Policy Coordination Group (DOGT)
PCG .... Power Conditioning Group (MCD)
PCG .... Primate Chorionic Gonadotropin [*Medicine*] (DMAA)
PCG .... Printed Circuit Generator
PCG .... Programmable Character Generator
PCG .... Protestant Cinema Guild [*Formerly, PCCG*] [*Defunct*]
PCG .... Pubococcygeus [*Muscle*] [*Anatomy*] (DAVI)
PCG .... Pulsed Coaxial Gun
PCG2 .... Preconditioned Conjugate Gradient
PCGD .... Pollution Control Guidance Document
PCGF .... Protein Crystal Growth Facility (SSD)
PCGG .... Philippine Commission on Good Government (BUAC)
PCGG .... Primary Care Group in Gynaecology (BUAC)
PCGM .... Pacific Coast Garment Manufacturers [*Later, AAMA*] (EA)
PCGN .... Permanent Committee of Geographical Names [*Later, BGN*]
PCGOV .... Port Charges Paid by Foreign Government (DNAB)
PCGPrA....... Pacific Gas & El 6% Pfd [*AMEX symbol*] (TTSB)
PCGPrB....... Pacific Gas & El 5 1/2% Pfd [*AMEX symbol*] (TTSB)
PCGPrC....... Pacific Gas & El 5% Pfd [*AMEX symbol*] (TTSB)
PCGPrCA..... PG&E Cap I 7.90%'QUIPS' [*AMEX symbol*] (TTSB)
PCGPrD....... Pacific Gas & El 5% Pfd [*AMEX symbol*] (TTSB)
PCGPrE....... Pac G&E 5%cmRed1stA Pfd [*AMEX symbol*] (TTSB)
PCGPrG....... Pacific Gas & El 4.80% Pfd (TTSB)
PCGPrH....... Pacific Gas & El 4.50% Pfd [*AMEX symbol*] (TTSB)
PCGPrI....... Pacific Gas & El 4.36% Pfd [*AMEX symbol*] (TTSB)
PCGPrQ....... Pacific Gas & El 7.44% Pfd [*AMEX symbol*] (TTSB)
PCGPrU....... Pacific Gas & El 7.04% Pfd [*AMEX symbol*] (TTSB)
PCGPrX....... Pacific Gas & El 6.875% Pfd [*AMEX symbol*] (TTSB)
PCGPrY....... Pacific Gas & El 6.57% Pfd [*AMEX symbol*] (TTSB)
PCGPrZ....... Pacific Gas & El 6.30% Pfd [*AMEX symbol*] (TTSB)
PCGRIDS ..... Personal Computer Gridded Interactive Display and Diagnostic System [*Marine science*] (OSRA)
PCGRX........ Pioneer Capital Growth Cl.A [*Mutual fund ticker symbol*] (SG)
PCGS .... Professional Coin Grading Service (BARN)
PCGS .... Protein Crystal Growth System
PCGU .... Protein Crystal Growth Unit (SSD)
PCGVB........ Pairwise Correlated Generalized Valence Bond [*Physics*]
PCH .... Cheyney State College, Cheyney, PA [*OCLC symbol*] (OCLC)
PCH .... Packing, Crating, and Handling [*Shipping*]
PCH .... Paper Clearing House (TBD)
PCH .... Parent Compound Handbook [*Later, Ring Systems Handbook*] [*American Chemical Society*]
PCH .... Pari-Cachoeira [*Brazil*] [*Airport symbol*] (AD)
PCH .... Paroxysmal Cold Hemoglobinuria [*Medicine*]
PCH .... Partido Comunista de Honduras [*Communist Party of Honduras*] [*Political party*] (PD)
PCH .... Patrol Craft (Hydrofoil) [*Navy symbol*]
PCH .... PCH Post Career [*Vancouver Stock Exchange symbol*]
PCh .... Phosphocholine [*Biochemistry*]
PCH .... Physicochemical Hydrodynamics [*A publication*]
PCH .... Pitch
PCH .... Polycyclic Hydrocarbon (DMAA)
PCH .... Polycyclic Hydrocarbons (DB)
PCH .... Porch (WGA)
pch........... Porch (VRA)
PCH .... Porous Clay Heterostructure [*Materials science*]
PCH .... Positive Channel [*Telecommunications*] (IAA)
PCH .... Potlatch Corp. [*Formerly, PFI*] [*NYSE symbol*] (SPSG)
PCH .... Prepare Chassis
PCH .... Presbyterian Church House [*British*] (BI)
PCH .... Prince Charles Hospital [*Australia*]
Pch .... Principal Chaplain [*Navy British*]
PCH .... Punch (KSC)
PCH .... Purchase (DCTA)
PCH & T ...... Packaging, Crating, Handling, and Transportation [*Shipping*] (CINC)
PCHAR........ Printing Character [*Computer science*]
PCHBD........ Patchboard (MSA)
PCHC .... Holland College, Charlottetown, Prince Edward Island [*Library symbol National Library of Canada*] (NLC)
PCHC .... People's Center for Housing Change (EA)

PChCo......... Conococheague District Library, Chambersburg, PA [*Library symbol Library of Congress*] (LCLS)
PCHCY .... Parents Campaign for Handicapped Children and Youth (EA)
PCHD .... Purchased (ROG)
PCHE .... Poor Clare Nuns of the Holy Eucharist [*Roman Catholic religious order*]
PC HE .... Pseudocholinesterase [*An enzyme*] (DAVI)
PCHE .... Purchase (ROG)
PCheS .... Cheyney State College, Cheyney, PA [*Library symbol Library of Congress*] (LCLS)
PCHG .... Punching
PCHIS .... Population Clearing House and Information System (NITA)
PCHK .... Parity Check [*Data communications*] (TEL)
PCHL .... Pacific Coast Hockey League [*Later, Western Hockey League*] (EA)
PCHLT .... Pressurized Cabin Hydraulic Leakage Tester (DWSG)
PCHM .... PharmChem Laboratories [*NASDAQ symbol*] (SPSG)
PCHMOS...... Positive-Channel Metal-Oxide Semiconductor [*Electronics*] (IAA)
PCHN .... Programmed Course, Home Nursing [*Red Cross*]
PCHR .... Panamanian Committee for Human Rights (EA)
PCHR .... Paraguay Committee for Human Rights [*British*]
PCHR .... Pentecostal Coalition for Human Rights [*Defunct*] (EA)
PCHR .... Purchaser (ROG)
PCHRG........ Public Citizen Health Research Group (EA)
P Chr N....... Post Christum Natum [*After the Birth of Christ*] [*Latin*]
PCHS .... Purchase (WGA)
PCHSR........ Purchaser
PCHT .... Packaging, Crating, Handling, and Transportation [*Shipping*] (AABC)
PCHT .... Parchment (MSA)
PChW.......... Wilson College, Chambersburg, PA [*Library symbol Library of Congress*] (LCLS)
PCI............. Packet Communications, Inc.
PCI............. Panel Call Indicator
PCI............. Pantone Color Institute (EA)
PCI............. Paramount Communications (EFIS)
PCI............. Parti Communiste Internationaliste [*Internationalist Communist Party*] [*France Political party*] (PPE)
PCI............. Partito Comunista Italiano [*Italian Communist Party*] [*Political party*]
PCI............. Paterson Candy International [*British*]
PCI............. Pattern Correspondence Index
PCI............. Pattern of Cockpit Indication
PCI............. Pavement Condition Index [*Aviation*] (DA)
PCI............. Pax Christi International (EAIO)
PCI............. PCL Industries Ltd. [*Toronto Stock Exchange symbol*]
PCI............. Pellet Clad Interaction [*Nuclear energy*] (NRCH)
PCI............. Per Column Inch [*Publishing*]
PCI............. Periodic Conformance Inspection (MCD)
PCI............. Peripheral Command Indicator
PCI............. Peripheral Component Interconnect [*Telecommunications*] (PCM)
PCI............. Peripheral Component Interface (PCM)
PCI............. Peripheral Controller Interface
PCI............. Personal Computer Interface [*Varitronics Systems, Inc.*]
PCI............. Photographic Credit Institute (EA)
PCI............. Physical Configuration Inspection (AFIT)
PCI............. Physical Configuration Item [*Military*]
Pci............. Phytophthora Citricola [*A fungus*]
pCi............. Picocurie [*Also, pC*] [*One trillionth of a curie*]
PCI............. Pilot Club International (EA)
PCI............. Pilot Controller Integration (IEEE)
PCI............. Pilots for Christ International (EA)
PCI............. Pipe Collectors International [*Later, PCCA*] (EA)
PCI............. Planning Card Index (AAG)
PCI............. Plant Control Interface
PCI............. Pneumatic Circuit Indicator
PCI............. Pneumatosis Cystoides Intestinorum [*Medicine*] (AAMN)
PCI............. Polar Circulation Index [*Climatology*]
PCI............. Political Campaign Institute [*Commercial firm*] (EA)
PCI............. Polycrystal Isolation (IAA)
PCI............. Population Communications International [*An association*] (EA)
PCI............. Population Council of India (BUAC)
PCI............. Portable Cesium Irradiator
PCI............. Portable Compass Indicator
PCI............. Possible Criminal Informant
PCI............. Potato Chip Institute, International [*Later, PC/SFA*] (EA)
PCI............. Powder Coating Institute (EA)
PCI............. Precast/Prestressed Concrete Institute (NTPA)
PCI............. Pre-Chamber Ignition [*Automotive engineering*]
PCI............. Precision Components, Inc. [*Addison, IL*] [*Telecommunications service*] (TSSD)
PCI............. Pre-Combat Inspection (INF)
PCI............. Pre-Counseling Inventory [*Psychology*]
PCI............. Premarital Communication Inventory [*Psychology*] (DHP)
PCI............. Presentation Context Identifier [*Computer science*] (TNIG)
PCI............. Press Control, Inc.
PCI............. Press Council of India (BUAC)
PCI............. Prestressed Concrete Institute (EA)
PCI............. Price Cap Index (OTD)
PCI............. Prime Ceiling Incentive
PCI............. Private Citizen, Inc. [*An association*] (EA)
PCI............. Privy Council Decisions [*India*] [*A publication*] (DLA)
PCI............. Privy Councillor, Ireland (ROG)
PCI............. Process Control Interface
PCI............. Product Change Information
PCI............. Product Configuration Identification (KSC)
PCI............. Product Cost Index

2464 Acronyms, Initialisms & Abbreviations Dictionary • 27th Edition

PCI	Production Control Information [*Software supplier*] [*Sheffield, England*] (NCC)
PCI	Program Check Interruption [*Computer science*] (MDG)
PCI	Program Control Input (NASA)
PCI	Program-Controlled Interruption [*Computer science*] (IBMDP)
PCI	Program in Correctional Institutions (OICC)
PCI	Programmable Communications Interface
PCI	Project Concern International (EA)
PCI	Prophylactic Cranial Irradiation [*Oncology*]
PCI	Proportional Change Index [*Occupational therapy*]
PCI	Prospectors Club International [*Defunct*] (EA)
PCI	Protein C Inhibitor [*Organic chemistry*]
PCI	Prothrombin Consumption Index (PDAA)
PCI	Protocol Computers Inc. (NITA)
PCI	Protocol Control Information [*Telecommunications*]
PCI	Pupil Control Ideology Form [*Education*] (EDAC)
PCIA	Personal Communications Industry Association (DDC)
PCIA	Person Communications Industry Association (NTPA)
PCIAC	Petro-Canada International Assistance Corp.
PCIAOH	Permanent Commission and International Association on Occupational Health (EAIO)
PCIB	Personal Computer Instruments Bus (NITA)
PCIC	Poison Control Information Center
PCICP	Primary Control Inventory Control Point [*Navy*]
PCICS	Permanent Council of the International Convention of Stresa on Cheeses (EAIO)
PCID	Pontifical Council for Inter-Religious Dialogue (BUAC)
PCIE	President's Council on Integrity and Efficiency (AAGC)
PCIE	President's Council on Integrity and Efficiency in Government (EPA)
PCIEC	Permanent Committee for International Eucharistic Congresses (EA)
PCIF	Printed Circuit Interconnection Federation [*British*] (DBA)
PCIFC	Patsy Cline International Fan Club (EA)
PCIFC	Permanent Commission of the International Fisheries Convention
PCIJ	Permanent Court of International Justice (BUAC)
PCIJ	Permanent Court of International Justice Cases [*A publication*] (DLA)
PCIJ Ann R	Permanent Court of International Justice Annual Reports [*A publication*] (DLA)
pCi/L	Picocuries per Liter [*Measure of radioactivity*]
PCIL	Pilot-Controlled Instrument Landing [*Aviation*] (NASA)
PCILO	Perturbative Configuration Interaction [*Based on*] Localized Orbitals [*Quantum mechanics*]
PCIM	Packet Channel Interface Module [*Telecommunications*]
PCIM	Parti du Congres de l'Independance de Madagascar [*Party of the Congress for Malagasy Independence*]
PCIMP	President's Commission on Income Maintenance Programs (EA)
PCIMR	Centre for Information and Technical Assistance, Institute of Man and Resources,Charlottetown, Prince Edward Island [*Library symbol National Library of Canada*] (NLC)
PCIMS	Positive Chemical Ionization Mass Spectroscopy
PCIN	Program Change Identification Number (NASA)
PCIN	Program Change Integration (NASA)
PCI/O	Program-Controlled Input-Output
PC-IOC	Posterior Chamber - Intraocular Lens [*Ophthalmology*]
PCIOL	Posterior Chamber Intraocular Lens [*Ophthalmology*] (DAVI)
PCIOMR	Preconditioning Interim Operating Management Recommendation [*Nuclear energy*] (NRCH)
PCIOS	Processor Common Input/Output System [*Computer science*]
PCIP	Personal Computer, Instrument Product
PCIP	Poseidon [*Missile*] Communication Improvement Program [*Navy*]
PCIPI	Permanent Committee on Industrial Property [*World Intellectual Property Organization*] [*Switzerland Information service or system*] (IID)
PCIR	Post-Contract Implementation Report (AAGC)
PCIRI	Paint and Coatings Industry Research Institute [*China*] (BUAC)
PCIRO	Preparatory Commission for International Refugee Organization
PCIS	Canton Island [*Phoenix Islands*] [*ICAO location identifier*] (ICLI)
PCIS	Patient Care Information System (IID)
PCIS	PCI Services [*NASDAQ symbol*] (TTSB)
PCIS	PCI Services, Inc. [*NASDAQ symbol*] (SAG)
PCIS	Period Cottage Improvement Society (BUAC)
PCIS	Personal Computer Information Service (NITA)
PCIS	Primary Containment Isolation System [*Nuclear energy*] (NRCH)
PCIS	Processed Commodities Inventory System [*Department of Agriculture*] (GFGA)
PCIS	Production Control Information System (NVT)
PCIS	Professional Career Information Service [*Department of Labor*]
PCI Sv	PCI Services, Inc. [*Associated Press*] (SAG)
PCIU	Programmable Communications Interface Unit
PC/IX	Personal Computer / Interactive Executive (HGAA)
PCIYRA	Pacific Coast Intercollegiate Yacht Racing Association
PCIZC	Permanent Committee of International Zoological Congresses (BUAC)
PCJ	Pax Christi Institute (TOCD)
PCJ	Peoples Jewellers Ltd. [*Toronto Stock Exchange symbol*]
PCJ	Petroleum Corporation of Jamaica (BUAC)
PCJ	Pontifical College Josephinum [*Worthington, OH*]
PCJ	Pontifical College Josephinum, Worthington, OH [*OCLC symbol*] (OCLC)
PCJ	Pulsed Combustion Jet
PCJ	Sisters of the Poor Child Jesus [*Roman Catholic religious order*]
PCJC	Pakistan Central Jute Committee (BUAC)
PCJC	Parliamentary Criminal Justice Committee [*Queensland, Australia*]
PCJE	Program on Criminal Justice and the Elderly (DICI)
PCJILMCC	Philip C. Jessup International Law Moot Court Competition (EAIO)
PCjr	Personal Computer-Junior (NITA)

PC Judg	Privy Council Judgments [*India*] [*A publication*] (DLA)
pck	Peacock [*Philately*]
PCK	Peacock H.E. and Son (Thorney) Ltd. [*British*] [*FAA designator*] (FAAC)
PCK	Peck (IAA)
PCK	Phase Control Keyboard
PCK	Polycystic Kidney [*Medicine*] (DMAA)
PCK	Porcupine Creek, AK [*Location identifier FAA*] (FAAL)
PCK	Premarital Counseling Kit [*Psychology*]
PCK	Primary Chicken Kidney [*Cell line*]
PCK	Printed Circuit Keyboard
PCK	Printed Control Keyboard [*Computer science*] (CIST)
PCK	Processor Controlled Keying [*Computer science*] (DCTA)
PCKB	Printed Circuit Keyboard
PCKD	Polycystic Kidney Disease [*Medicine*]
PCKT	Printed Circuit [*Computer science*] (CIST)
PCL	Alberta Attorney General, Provincial Court Libraries [*UTLAS symbol*]
PCl	Clarion Free Library, Clarion, PA [*Library symbol Library of Congress*] (LCLS)
PCL	Confederation Centre Library, Charlottetown, Prince Edward Island [*Library symbol National Library of Canada*] (NLC)
PCL	Pachaco Lake [*California*] [*Seismograph station code, US Geological Survey*] (SEIS)
PCL	Pacific Coast League [*Baseball*]
PCL	Pallet Coolant Loop (NASA)
PCL	Parallel Communications Link
PCL	Parcel
PCL	Paroxysmal Choreathetois Dystonia [*Medicine*]
PCL	Parti Communiste de Luxembourg [*Communist Party of Luxembourg*] [*Political party*] (PPE)
PCL	Parti Communiste Libanais [*Lebanese Communist Party*] [*Political party*] (PPW)
PCL	Pencil (MSA)
PCL	Permissible Contamination Limits [*Nuclear energy*] (NRCH)
PCL	Persistent Corpus Luteum [*Medicine*]
PCL	Personnel Security Clearance
P CI	Petrus Calvelli [*Flourished, 14th century*] [*Authority cited in pre-1607 legal work*] (DSA)
PCL	Philippine Cultural League [*Australia*]
PCL	Phillips Cables Ltd. [*Toronto Stock Exchange symbol*]
PCL	Pilot Controlled Lighting [*Aviation*] (FAAC)
PCL	Planning and Conservation League (EA)
PCL	Planning Configuration List
PCL	Planning Consultancy Ltd. (NITA)
PCL	Plasma Cell Leukemia [*Oncology*]
PCL	Playboy Club of London
PCL	Plum Creek Timber Co., Inc. [*NYSE symbol*] (SPSG)
PCL	Plum Creek Timber L.P. [*NYSE symbol*] (TTSB)
PCL	Plutonium-Contaminated Liquid [*Nuclear energy*] (NUCP)
PCL	Pocket Checklist (MCD)
PCL	Polycaprolactone [*Organic chemistry*]
PCL	[*The*] Polytechnic of Central London
PCL	Pontifical Council for the Laity (BUAC)
PCL	Positive Control Line
PCL	Post Conference List
PCL	Posterior Chamber Lens [*Ophthalmology*] (DAVI)
PCL	Posterior Cruciate Ligament [*Anatomy*]
PCL	PostScript and LASERJet-Type [*LASER printer*]
PCL	Power Control Lever (DNAB)
PCL	Power Control List (MCD)
PCL	Preliminary Change Letter [*Navy*] (NG)
PCL	Premier Cruise Lines
PCL	Primary Coolant Line (NASA)
PCL	Primary Coolant Loop (NASA)
PCL	Print Control Language (NITA)
PCL	Printed Circuit Lamp
PCL	Printer Command Language [*Hewlett Packard*] [*Computer science*]
PCL	Printer Control Language
PCL	Procedural Control Language [*1971*] [*Computer science*] (CSR)
PCL	Process Capability Laboratory
PCL	Process Communications Link (ECII)
PCl	Process Control Language [*Texas Instruments, Inc.*] [*Computer science*] (IAA)
PCL	Programming Checklist (MCD)
PCL	Programming Control Language [*Computer science*] (PCM)
PCL	Project Control Ledgers [*Navy*] (NG)
PCL	Pseudocleistogamous [*Botany*]
PCL	Pucallpa [*Peru*] [*Airport symbol*] (OAG)
PCL	Pulse Compression Loop
PCL	Purkinje Cell Layer [*Cytology*]
PCLA	Polish Canadian Librarians Association
PCLA	Power Control Linkage Assembly
PCLA	Process Control Language [*Texas Instruments, Inc.*]
PCLA	Project Coordination and Liaison Administration (OICC)
PCLC	Pest Control Licensing Committee [*New South Wales, Australia*]
PCLD	Dependent Political Entity [*Board on Geographic Names*]
PCLDI	Prototype Closed-Loop Development Installation [*Nuclear energy*] (NRCH)
PCLE	Pinnacle Systems [*NASDAQ symbol*] (TTSB)
PCLE	Pinnacle Systems, Inc. [*NASDAQ symbol*] (SAG)
PCLFC	Projected Consequences of Less Than Full Control (COE)
PCLG	Public Citizen Litigation Group (EA)
PCLI	Independent Political Entity [*Board on Geographic Names*]
PCLI	Parti de la Convergence pour les Libertes et l'Integration [*Burkina Faso*] [*Political party*] (EY)

PCLI............ Plasma Cell Labeling Index [*Medicine*] (DMAA)
PC-LITE....... Processor, Laptop Imagery Transmission Equipment (DOMA)
PCLJ........... Pacific Coast Law Journal [*A publication*] (DLA)
PCLK........... Pay Clerk
PCLK........... Program Clock [*Computer science*] (CIST)
PCLLG .... Ollennu's Principles of Customary Land Law in Ghana [*A publication*] (DLA)
PCLLRC .... Post-Colonial Literatures and Languages Centre [*Macquarie University*] [*Australia*]
PCLMP......... President's Advisory Committee on Labor-Management Policy [*Abolished, 1973*]
PCLN .... Personalcomputer Literaturnachweis [*Datendienst Weiss*] [*Database*]
PC-LNIM ...... Personal Computer Local Network Interface Module (TSSD)
PCLO .... Passenger Control Liaison Office [*or Officer*] [*Army*] (AABC)
PCLP .... PaperClip Imaging Software [*NASDAQ symbol*] (TTSB)
PCLP........... Paperclip Imaging Software, Inc. [*NASDAQ symbol*] (SAG)
PCLPW .... Paperclip Imaging Softw'r Wrrt [*NASDAQ symbol*] (TTSB)
PCLR .... Parallel Communications Link Receiver (NITA)
P Cl R .... Parker's New York Criminal Reports [*A publication*] (DLA)
PCLR .... PR [*Public Relations*] Committee for Licensing and Registration (EA)
P Cl R .... Privy Council Reports [*A publication*] (DLA)
PCIS........... Clarion State College, Clarion, PA [*Library symbol Library of Congress*] (LCLS)
PCLS........... Law Society of Prince Edward Island, Charlottetown, Prince Edward Island [*Library symbol National Library of Canada*] (NLC)
PCLS........... People's Committee for Libyan Students (EA)
PCLS........... Prototype Closed-Loop System [*Nuclear energy*] (NRCH)
PCLST......... Polychlorstyrene [*Organic chemistry*]
PCLT........... Portable Coded LASER Target
PCLT........... Prototype Closed-Loop Test [*Nuclear energy*] (NRCH)
PCLU .... Pioneer Civil Labour Unit [*British*]
PClvU .... Ursinus College, Collegeville, PA [*Library symbol Library of Congress*] (LCLS)
PCLW.......... Platinum Compensating Lead Wire (PDAA)
PCLX........... Section of Independent Political Entity [*Board on Geographic Names*]
PCM .... Coastal Escort Medium [*200-500 tons*] [*Ship symbol*] (NATG)
PCM .... Pacific Comox Resources [*Vancouver Stock Exchange symbol*]
PCM .... Parabolic Collimator Mirror
PCM .... Paragraph Completion Method [*Education*] (EDAC)
PCM .... Parallel Cutter Mechanism
PCM .... Parity Check Matrix (MCD)
PCM .... Parti Communiste Marocain [*Moroccan Communist Party*] [*Political party*]
PCM .... Parti Communiste Martiniquais [*Communist Party of Martinique*] [*Political party*] (PPW)
PCM .... Parti des Classes Moyennes [*Middle Class Party*] [*Luxembourg*] [*Political party*] (PPE)
PCM .... Partido Comunista Mexicano [*Mexican Communist Party*] [*Political party*] (PPW)
PCM .... Passive Countermeasure
PCM .... Patient Care Manager
PCM .... Patient Management Category (HCT)
PCM .... Penalty Cost Model
PCM .... Pending Contractual Matters (NRCH)
PCM .... Per Calendar Month [*Business term*] (ADA)
pcm .... Per Calendar Month [*Business term*] (ODBW)
PCM .... Percentage of Completion Method (AAGC)
PCM .... Percent Milli (NRCH)
PCM .... Peregrine Capital Myanmar
PCM .... Performance Capability Measure (IAA)
PCM .... Pericentriolar Material [*Biochemistry*]
PCM .... Phase Change Material
PCM .... Phase Change Materials [*Solar energy*]
PCM .... Phase Conjugate Mirror
PCM .... Phase Contrast Microscopy
PCM .... Philippine Campaign Medal
PCM .... Photochemical Machining [*Desktop manufacturing*]
PCM .... Photoformed Ceramic Modules [*Du Pont process for making microconductors*]
PCM .... PIMCO Commercial Mortgage Security Trust [*NYSE symbol*] (SPSG)
PCM .... PIMCO Comml Mtg Sec Tr [*NYSE symbol*] (TTSB)
PCM .... PIPES Buffer with Calcium and Magnesium
PCM .... Pitch Control Motor
PCM .... Planning and Control Memorandum [*Army*]
PCM .... Plug Compatible Mainframe [*Computer science*]
PCM .... Plug Compatible Manufacturer [*Computer science*]
PCM .... Plug Compatible Memory
PCM .... Plug Compatible Module [*Computer science*] (IAA)
PCM .... Plutonium Contaminated Material
PCM .... Police Court Mission [*British*] (ROG)
PCM .... Polyimide Composite Material
PCM .... Portable Conformable Mask [*Microlithography*]
PCM .... Port Command Area [*Telecommunications*] (TEL)
PCM .... Postal [*Service*] Contracting Manual [*A publication*] (AAGC)
PCM .... Post Column Method [*Chromatography*]
PCM .... Postgraduate Committee in Medicine [*Australia*]
PCM .... Postmammillary Caudal Magnocellular Nuclei [*Neuroanatomy*]
PCM .... Power Control Mission (NASA)
PCM .... Power-Cooling Mismatch [*Nuclear energy*]
PCM .... Powertrain Control Module [*Automotive engineering*]
PCM .... Precision Condenser Microphone
PCM .... President's Certificate of Merit [*Military decoration*] (AFM)
PCM .... Primary Care Manager (HCT)
PCM .... Primary Code Modulation [*Computer science*] (IAA)
PCM .... Process Communication Monitor [*Telecommunications*] (IAA)

PCM .... Process Control Module [*Telecommunications*] (TEL)
PCM .... Productive Cost Management (ADA)
PCM .... Profiling Current Meter [*Oceanography*] (MSC)
PCM .... Program Configuration Manager
PCM .... Program Continuity Memorandum [*Military*]
PCM .... Program Cost Management (MCD)
PCM .... Project Cost Model [*Project Software Ltd.*] [*Software package*] (NCC)
PCM .... Protein-Calorie Malnutrition [*Medicine*]
PCM .... Protein-Carboxyl Methylase [*Biochemistry*] (DAVI)
PCM .... Pulse Code Modulation [*Telecommunications*] (OSI)
PCM .... Pulse Code Modulator (NAKS)
PCM .... Punch Card Machine [*Computer science*]
PCM .... Pyrotechnic Countermeasure [*Military*] (SDI)
PCM .... WestAir Industries, Inc. [*ICAO designator*] (FAAC)
PCMA .... Pennsylvania Coal Mining Association (EA)
PCMA .... Personal Computer Management Association [*Orange, CA*] [*Commercial firm Information service or system*] (EA)
PCMA .... Phenylcyclopropanemethylamine [*Organic chemistry*]
PCMA .... Plaited Cordage Manufacturers Association [*British*] (BI)
PCMA .... Plastic Crate Manufacturers Association (BUAC)
PCMA .... Post Card Manufacturers Association [*Defunct*] (EA)
PCMA .... Potato Chip Manufacturers [*British*] (DBA)
PCMA .... Potato Chips Manufacturers Association (BUAC)
PCMA .... Power Cooling Mismatch Accident [*Nuclear energy*] (NUCP)
PCMA .... Precision Chain Manufacturers Association (BUAC)
PCMA .... Prince Edward Island Department of Municipal Affairs, Charlottetown, Prince Edward Island [*Library symbol National Library of Canada*] (NLC)
PCMA .... Professional Convention Management Association [*Birmingham, AL*] (EA)
PCMA .... Provincial Carters' and Motormen's Association [*A union*] [*British*]
PCMANSW... Precast Concrete Manufacturers' Association of New South Wales [*Australia*]
PCMAV .... Precast Concrete Manufacturers' Association of Victoria [*Australia*]
PCMB.......... Para-Chloromercuribenzoate [*Organic chemistry*]
PCMC.......... Para-Chloro-meta-cresol [*Organic chemistry*]
PCMC.......... Postal [*Service*] Contracting Manual Circular (AAGC)
PCMC.......... Primary Children's Medical Center (STED)
PCMC.......... Provided Chief of Mission Concurs [*Army*]
PCMCIA ...... People Can't Memorize Computer Industry Acronyms (PS)
PCMCIA ...... Personal Computer Memory Card International Association (PCM)
PCMCIA ...... Personal Comuter Memory Card Interface Adapter (DDC)
PCMCIA ...... Portable Computer Memory Card Industry Association (DOM)
PCMD .... Particle Count Monitoring Device (KSC)
PCMD .... Passive Count Monitoring Device (KSC)
PCMD .... Procurement and Contracts Management Division [*Environmental Protection Agency*] (GFGA)
PCMD .... Pulse Code Modulation, Digital
PCMDHS...... Pulse Code Modulation Data Handling System [*Telecommunications*] (IAA)
PCMDI .... Program for Climate Model Diagnosis and Intercomparison [*Department of Energy*]
PCME .... Pulse Code Modulation Event
PCMF .... Perceptual Cognitive Motor Function (STED)
PCMF .... Phi Chi Medical Fraternity (EA)
PCM-FM ...... Pulse Code Modulation - Frequency Modulation
PCM/FSK/AM... Pulse Code Modulation/Frequency Shift Keying/Amplitude Modulation (SAA)
PCMGS .... Pulse Code Modulated Ground Station
PCMH .... Para-Cresol Methylhydroxylase [*An enzyme*]
PCMH .... Postgraduate Center for Mental Health (EA)
PCMI .... Photo-Chemical Machining Institute (EA)
PCMI .... Photochromic Microimage [*Microfiche*]
PCMI .... Photochromic Microimage System (IAA)
PCMI .... Plastic Container Manufacturers Institute [*Defunct*] (EA)
PCMI .... President's Council on Management Improvement [*Executive Office of the President*] (GFGA)
PCMIA .... Pittsburgh Coal Mining Institute of America (EA)
PCMIP .... Pontifical Commission for Migrants and Itinerant Peoples [*See also PCMT*] [*Vatican City, Vatican City State*] (EAIO)
PCMK .... Piece Mark
PC-ML .... Marxist-Leninist Communist Party [*Bolivia*] [*Political party*] (PPW)
PCML.......... Parti Communiste Marxiste-Leniniste [*Marxist-Leninist Communist Party*] [*France Political party*] (PPW)
PCML.......... Partito Comunista Marxista-Leninista [*Marxist-Leninist Communist Party*] [*San Marino*] [*Political party*] (PPE)
PCML.......... President's Committee on Migratory Labor [*Terminated, 1964*]
PCMLF......... Parti Communiste Marxiste-Leniniste Francais [*French Marxist-Leninist Communist Party*] [*Dissolved, 1978*] [*Political party*] (PPW)
PC(ML)I .... Partito Comunista (Marxista-Leninista) de Italia [*Communist Party of Italy (Marxist-Leninist)*] [*Political party*] (PPE)
PCMM......... Plug Compatible Mainframe Manufacturer (NITA)
PCMMU ...... PCM [*Punch Card Machine*] Master Unit [*Computer science*] (GFGA)
PCMMU ...... Pulse Code Modulation Master Unit [*Electronics*] (NASA)
PCMNA .... Provisions for Carbon Monoxide Nonattainment Areas [*Environmental science*] (COE)
PCM/NRZ..... Pulse Code Modulation/Nonreturn to Zero (KSC)
PCMO .... Passenger Car Motor Oil
PCMO .... Principal Clinical Medical Officer [*British*]
PCMO .... Principal Colonial Medical Officer [*British*]
PCMOD........ Personal Computer Modification Program
PCMP.......... Packed Computational (IAA)
PCMP.......... Pennsylvania Comprehensive Mathematics Plan (EDAC)
PCMP.......... (Phenylcyclohexyl)methylpiperidine [*Organic chemistry*]

PCMP......... Post Chemical-Mechanical Polishing (AAEL)
PCMP......... Preliminary Configuration Management Plan (MCD)
PCMPM....... Pulse Code Modulation-Phase-Modulation (IAA)
PCMPN....... Pulse Code Modulation Pseudonoise [*Telecommunications*] (IAA)
PCMPS....... Para-Chloromercuriphenylsulfonic Acid [*Organic chemistry*]
PCM-PS...... Pulse Code Modulation - Phase-Shift
PCMR......... Patient Computer Medical Record
PCMR......... Photochromic Microreproduction (DIT)
PCMR......... President's Committee on Mental Retardation [*Washington, DC*]
PCMS......... Para-Chloromercuriphenyl Sulfonate [*or Sulfonic Acid*] [*Organic chemistry*]
PCMS......... Pattern Card Makers' Society [*British*] (BI)
PCMS......... P-Com, Inc. [*NASDAQ symbol*] (SAG)
PCMS......... Photographic Cabinet Makers' Society [*A union*] [*British*]
PCMS......... Plasma Chemistry Monte-Carlo Simulation (AAEL)
PCMS......... Plasma Chromatography Mass Spectroscopy
PCMS......... Production Control Monitoring System (NVT)
PCMS......... Pulse Code Modulation Shared (MCD)
PCMS......... Punch Card Machine System [*Computer science*]
PCMT......... Pontificia Commissione Migrazioni e Turismo [*Pontifical Commission for Migrants and Itinerant Peoples - PCMIP*] [*Vatican City, Vatican City State*] (EAIO)
PCMTE....... Pulse Code Modulation and Timing Equipment (KSC)
PCMTEA...... Pulse Code Modulation and Timing Electronics Assembly
PCMTS....... Pulse Code Modulation Telemetry System (AAG)
PCMU........ Physico-Chemical Measurements Unit [*British*]
PCMU........ Propellant Calibration Measuring Unit (KSC)
PCMV......... Porcine Cerebral Microvascular [*Cell line*]
PCMX......... Para-Chloro-meta-xylenol [*Organic chemistry*]
PCN .... Pacific Communications Network [*Air Force*] (IAA)
PCN .... Package Control Number
PCN .... Page Change Notice (MCD)
PCN .... PanCana Minerals [*Toronto Stock Exchange symbol*]
PCN .... Parent Country National (PDAA)
PCN .... Part Control Number (AAG)
PCN .... Partido Comunista de Nicaragua [*Communist Party of Nicaragua*] [*Political party*] (PD)
PCN .... Partido Conservador Nicaraguense [*Nicaraguan Conservative Party*] [*Political party*] (PPW)
PCN .... Partido de Conciliacion Nacional [*National Reconciliation Party*] [*El Salvador*] [*Political party*] (PPW)
PCN .... Parts Change Notice (MCD)
PCN .... Pavement Classification Number [*Aviation*] (DA)
PCN .... Penicillin [*Antibiotic*]
PCN .... Percutaneous Nephrostomy (DAVI)
PCN .... Permanent Control Number (MCD)
PCN .... Personal Communications Network [*British*]
PCN .... Personal Computer Network [*Telecommunications*]
PCN .... Personal Computer News (NITA)
PCN .... Piacenza [*Italy*] [*Seismograph station code, US Geological Survey Closed*] (SEIS)
PCN .... Pitcairn Islands [*ANSI three-letter standard code*] (CNC)
PCN .... Planning Change Notice
PCN .... PointCast Network [*Internet news service*]
PCN .... Point Comfort & Northern Railway Co. [*AAR code*]
PCN .... Polychlorinated Naphthalene [*Organic chemistry*]
PCN .... Position Control Number (AFM)
PCN .... Post Christum Natum [*After the Birth of Christ*] [*Latin*] (ROG)
PCN .... Potato Cyst Nematode [*Plant pathology*]
PCN .... Pregnenolone Carbonitril [*Pharmacology*] (DAVI)
PCN .... Prelaunch Channel Number [*NASA*] (IAA)
PCN .... Primary Care Network [*Medical insurance*]
PCN .... Primary Care Nursing
PCN .... Princeton Aviation Corp. [*ICAO designator*] (FAAC)
PCN .... Procedure Change Notice
PCN .... Processing Control Number
PCN .... Procurement Control Number (AFM)
PCN .... Product Control Number (AFM)
PCN .... Production Change Number (KSC)
PCN .... Program Change Notice (MCD)
PCN .... Program Composition Notation [*Computer science*]
PCN .... Program Control Number (AFM)
PCN .... Project Control Number (AAG)
PCN .... Proposal Control Number (AAG)
PCN .... Publication Change Notice (MCD)
PCN .... Public Convenience and Necessity [*Department of Transportation*]
PCN .... Pulse Compression Network
PCNA......... Palestine Congress of North America [*Defunct*] (EA)
PCNA......... Porsche Cars North America, Inc.
PCNA......... Proliferating Cell Nuclear Antigen [*Cytology, immunology*]
PCNA......... Publishing Co. North Amer [*NASDAQ symbol*] (TTSB)
PCNA......... Publishing Co. of North America, Inc. (The) [*NASDAQ symbol*] (SAG)
PCNAC....... Professionals Coalition for Nuclear Arms Control (EA)
PCNB........ Pentachloronitrobenzene [*Agricultural fungicide*]
PCNB........ Permanent Control Narcotics Board
PCNC......... Projected Consequences of No Control [*Environmental science*] (COE)
PCNE........ Protocol Converter for Native Equipment [*Telecommunications*] (IAA)
PCNET........ Personal Computer Network
PCNF......... Pacific Central NOTAM [*Notice to Airmen*] Facility [*Military*]
PCN(Fr.)..... Physics, Chemistry & Natural Science-France (CMD)
PCNI......... Physician Computer Network [*NASDAQ symbol*] (SPSG)
PCNI......... Physician Computer Ntwk [*NASDAQ symbol*] (TTSB)
PCNI......... Physicians Computer Network [*NASDAQ symbol*] (SAG)

PCNM .... Polymer-Immobilised Clusters of the Noble Metals [*Catalytic chemistry*]
PCNP .... Personal Computer Network Program (HGAA)
PCNR .... Part Control Number Request (AAG)
PCNR .... Planning Change Notice Request
PCNS .... Polar Coordinates Navigation System
PCNSL .... Polymerised Cashew Nut Shell Liquid (PDAA)
PCNV .... Postchemotherapy Nausea and Vomiting [*Medicine*] (STED)
PCNV .... Provisional Committee on Nomenclature of Viruses (DAVI)
PCNY .... Proofreaders Club of New York (EA)
P$_{co}$ .... Carbon Monoxide Tension (DAVI)
PCO .... Conococheague District Library, Chambersburg, PA [*OCLC symbol*] (OCLC)
PCO .... Pacific Coastal Airline [*Canada ICAO designator*] (FAAC)
PCO .... Parcel Concentration Office [*British*]
PCO .... Parliamentary Counsel's Office [*Australia*]
PCO .... Passport Control Officer [*British*]
PCO .... Patient Complains Of [*Medicine*]
PCO .... Peacetime Contingency Operation [*Army*] (ADDR)
PCO .... Pest Control Operator
PCO .... Philadelphia College of Osteopathy [*Pennsylvania*]
PCO .... Phoenix Canada Oil Co. Ltd. [*Toronto Stock Exchange symbol*]
PCO .... Photocatalytic Oxidation (AAEL)
PCO .... Photosynthetic Carbon Oxidation [*Plant metabolism*]
PCO .... Picture Control Oscilloscope (IAA)
PCO .... Pittston Co. (EFIS)
PCO .... Placement Contracting Officer [*Army*] (AABC)
PCO .... Plant Clearance Officer [*DoD*]
PCO .... Plant Clearance Order
PCO .... Playcore, Inc. [*AMEX symbol*] [*Formerly, Swing-N-Slide Corp.*]
PCO .... Point of Control and Observation [*Telecommunications*] (OSI)
PCO .... Police Commissioner's Office
PCO .... Polycarbonate (EDCT)
PCO .... Polycystic Ovary [*Gynecology*]
PCO .... Ponca City [*Oklahoma*] [*Seismograph station code, US Geological Survey*] (SEIS)
PCO .... Post Checkout
PCO .... Postcheckout Operations
PCO .... Potassium Channel Opener [*Vasodilator*]
PCO .... Predicted Cardia Output [*Medicine*] (DMAA)
PCO .... Primary Communications-Oriented (IAA)
PCO .... Primary Contracting Officer (MCD)
PCO .... Prime Contracting Officer (SAA)
PCO .... Prince Consort's Own [*Military unit*] [*British*]
PCO .... Principal Careers Officer (AIE)
PCO .... Principal Coast Officer [*Customs*] [*British*] (ROG)
PCO .... Principal Contracting Officer [*Air Force*]
PCO .... Printer Control Option (SAA)
PCO .... Printing Control Officer [*Air Force*] (AFM)
PCO .... Prison Custody Officer (WDAA)
PCO .... Privy Council Office [*British*]
PCO .... Procurement Change Order (MCD)
PCO .... Procurement Contracting Officer (AAGC)
PCO .... Procuring Contracting Office [*or Officer*] [*Military*]
PCO .... Procuring Contrast Offer
PCO .... Procytoxid (STED)
PCO .... Professional Conference Organizer
PCO .... Program Comparator
PCO .... Program-Controlled Output (NASA)
PCO .... Program Coordination Office (AAG)
PCO .... Project Control Office (MCD)
PCO .... Property Control Office [*of Allied Military Government*] [*Post-World War II*]
PCO .... Proposed Change Order (AFIT)
PCO .... Prospective Commanding Officer [*Navy*]
PCO .... Provisioning Contracting Officer [*Military*] (AFIT)
PCO .... Publications Control Officer [*DoD*]
PCO .... Public Call Office (DAS)
PCO .... Public Communications Office
PCO .... Purchase Change Order (MCD)
PCO$_2$ .... Carbon Dioxide Tension [*in blood gases*] (DAVI)
pCO$_2$ .... Partial Pressure of Carbon Dioxide (AAMN)
pCO$_2$ .... Pressure of Carbon Dioxide (HGAA)
PCoA........ Principal Co-Ordinates Analysis
PCOAS .... Permanent Council of the Organization of American States
P Coast LJ... Pacific Coast Law Journal [*A publication*] (DLA)
PCOB .... Permanent Central Opium Board [*United Nations*] (BUAC)
PCOB(UN)... Permanent Central Opium Board (United Nations)
PCOC .... Partit Comunista Obrero de Catalunya [*Communist Workers' Party of Catalonia*] [*Political party*] (PPW)
PCOC .... Primary Care Organization Consortium [*Health insurance*] (DMAA)
PCOCA....... Parti-Colour Oriental Cat Association (BUAC)
PCOD .... Permanent Change of Duty [*Navy*] (DNAB)
PCOD .... Polycystic Ovarian Disease [*Medicine*]
PCOE .... Partido Comunista Obrero de Espana [*Communist Workers' Party of Spain*] [*Political party*] (PPW)
PCOF .... Probable Cause of Failure (MCD)
PC of E ...... Presbyterian Church of England
PCOGA....... Pacific Coast Oyster Growers Association (EA)
PCOI .... Preconstruction Operating Instruction [*Environmental Protection Agency*]
PCOIT .... Putnam Convertible Opportunities & Income Trust [*Associated Press*] (SAG)
PCOL .... Protocol Systems [*NASDAQ symbol*] (TTSB)
PCOL .... Protocol Systems, Inc. [*NASDAQ symbol*] (SAG)

PCOLA	Pulse-Coded Optical Landing Aid [*Aviation*] (PDAA)
P-Com	P-Com, Inc. [*Associated Press*] (SAG)
PCOM	Philadelphia College of Osteopathic Medicine
PCOM	Photocomm, Inc. [*NASDAQ symbol*] (NQ)
PCOM	Posterior Communicating [*Artery*] [*Medicine*] (DMAA)
PCON	Para-Chloro-ortho-nitroaniline [*Also, PCONA*] [*Organic chemistry*]
PCON	Personnel Continuity
PCON	Platelet Concentration [*hematology*] (DAVI)
PCON	Potential Contractor (COE)
PCON	Primary Care Organization Network [*Health insurance*] (DMAA)
PCONA	Para-Chloro-ortho-nitroaniline [*Also, PCON*] [*Organic chemistry*]
P Contr LJ ...	Public Contract Law Journal [*A publication*] (AAGC)
PCOP	Pharmacopeia Inc. [*NASDAQ symbol*] (TTSB)
PCOP	Port Charges Operator (DNAB)
PCOP	Port Charges Paid by Commercial Operator (DNAB)
PCOP	President's Commission on Obscenity and Pornography (DGA)
PCOPF	President's Council on Physical Fitness [*Later, PCPFS*] (KSC)
PCOR	Pressure Compensator Over-Ride (PDAA)
PCOR	Profit Commission on Renewal [*Insurance*] (AIA)
PCOR	PSICOR, Inc. [*NASDAQ symbol*] (NQ)
PCoR	Robert Morris College, Coraopolis, PA [*Library symbol Library of Congress*] (LCLS)
PCORN	Perpetual Convertible or Redeemable Note [*Economics*]
PCOS	Polycystic Ovarian Syndrome [*Also, POS*] [*Gynecology*]
PCOS	Primary Communications-Oriented System (IEEE)
PCOS	Process Control Operating System
PCOS	Project Concern's Options Service (EA)
P-COSWA	Pugwash Conferences on Science and World Affairs
PCOT	Payload Center Operations Team [*NASA*] (MCD)
PCOTES	Prototype Carrier Operational Test and Evaluation Site [*Military*] (CAAL)
PCOUNT.......	Parameter Count [*Computer science*]
PCOV	Precombustor Oxidizer Valve (KSC)
P(COV)	Probability of No Covariate Effect [*Statistics*]
PCOYO	President's Council on Youth Opportunity [*Defunct*] (EA)
PCP	Centre for Personal Construct Psychology [*British*] (CB)
PCP	Paired Cone Pigments [*Vision physiology*]
PCP	Palestinian Communist Party [*Political party*] (PD)
PCP	PanCanadian Petroleum [*TS, Exchange Symbol*] (TTSB)
PCP	PanCanadian Petroleum Ltd. [*Toronto Stock Exchange symbol Vancouver Stock Exchange symbol*]
PCP	Para-Chlorophenol [*Organic chemistry*]
PCP	Paraguayan Communist Party
PCP	Parallel Cascade Processor (IEEE)
PCP	Parallel Circular Plate (IEEE)
PCP	Parliamentary Conservative Party [*British*] (BARN)
PCP	Partido Comunista Paraguayano [*Paraguayan Communist Party*] [*Political party*] (PD)
PCP	Partido Comunista Peruano [*Peruvian Communist Party*] [*Political party*] (PPW)
PCP	Partido Comunista Portugues [*Portuguese Communist Party*] [*Political party*] (PPE)
PCP	Partido Comunista Puertorriqueno [*Puerto Rican Communist Party*] [*Political party*] (PPW)
PCP	Passenger Control Point [*Army*] (AABC)
PCP	Past Chief Patriarch [*Freemasonry*]
PCP	Patient Care Publications
PCP	Payload Control Processor [*NASA*]
PCP	Peace Corps Physician
PCP	Pentachlorophenate [*A topical antibacterial*] (DAVI)
PCP	Pentachlorophenol [*Wood preservative*] [*Organic chemistry*]
PCP	Peptidyl Carrier Protein [*Biochemistry*]
PCP	Peridinin-Chlorophyll-Protein [*Botany*]
PCP	Peripheral Control Program
PCP	Peripheral Control Pulse [*Computer science*]
PCP	Peripheral Coronary Pressure [*Cardiology*] (AAMN)
PCP	Personal Communications Programme [*British*]
PCP	Peter Collins Publishing [*British*]
PCP	Phencyclidine Palmitate [*Organic chemistry*] (DAVI)
PCP	(Phenylcyclohexyl)piperidine [*or Phencyclidine*] [*Anesthetic A street drug*]
PCP	Philadelphia College of Pharmacy and Science, Philadelphia, PA [*OCLC symbol*] (OCLC)
PCP	Phosphor Coated Paper
PCP	Photon-Coupled Pair (IEEE)
PCP	Pilot Control Panel
PCP	Planar Combat Problem
PCP	Plastic Clad Plastic [*Materials science*]
PCP	Platoon Command Post [*Military*] (RDA)
PCP	Plug Compatible Peripheral [*Computer science*] (EECA)
PCP	Pneumatics Control Panel (AAG)
PCP	Pneumocystic Pneumonia [*Medicine*] (DAVI)
PCP	Pneumocystis Carinii Pneumonia [*Microbiology*]
PCP	Polaroid Color Pack Camera
PCP	Polychloroprene [*Organic chemistry*]
PCP	Poorly Characterized Phase [*Mineralogy*]
PCP	Portable Code Processor
PCP	Portuguese Communist Party
PCP	Post-Construction Permit [*Nuclear energy*] (NRCH)
PCP	Posted County Price [*Agriculture*]
PCP	Postgraduate Center for Psychotherapy [*Later, Postgraduate Center for Mental Health*] (EA)
PCP	Potential Contractor Program (MCD)
PCP	Power Control Panel [*Aerospace*] (AAG)
PCP	Preassembled Cable in Pipe
PCP	Precision Castparts [*NYSE symbol*] (TTSB)
PCP	Precision Castparts Corp. [*NYSE symbol*] (SPSG)
PCP	Preliminary Cost Proposal (MCD)
PCP	Pressurization Control Panel [*NASA*] (KSC)
PCP	Primary Care Physician
PCP	Primary Command Point [*Military*] (CAAL)
PCP	Primary Control Program [*Computer science*]
PCP	Primary Coolant Pump [*Nuclear energy*] (NRCH)
PCP	Primary Cross-Connection Point (NITA)
PCP	Principal Care Provider [*For a patient*] (DAVI)
PCP	Printed Circuit Patchboard
PCP	Process Control Processor (IEEE)
PCP	Process Control Program [*Nuclear energy*] (NRCH)
PCP	Processor Control Program
PCP	Procollagen Peptide (DB)
PCP	Product Change Proposal (MCD)
PCP	Product Chassis Package
PCP	Production Change Point
PCP	Program Change Procedure
PCP	Program [*or Project*] Change Proposal
PCP	Program Control Plan (AAG)
PCP	Program Control Procedure [*Nuclear energy*] (NRCH)
PCP	Programmable Communication Processor
PCP	Progressive Conservative Party [*Canada Political party*] (PPW)
PCP	Progressive Conservative Party [*Australia Political party*]
PCP	Progressive Constitutionalist Party [*Malta*] [*Political party*] (PPE)
PCP	Progressive Constitutional Party [*Malta*] [*Political party*] (BUAC)
PCP	Project Change Proposal (NAKS)
PCP	Project Control Plan (IEEE)
PCP	Project Cost Plan (NASA)
PCP	Prototype Communications Processor
PCP	Psilcybin [*Medicine*] (MEDA)
PCP	Pulmonary Capillary Pressure [*Medicine*] (CPH)
PCP	Pulse Comparator
PCP	Pulse Cytophotometry [*Hematology*]
PCP	Punched Card Punch [*Computer science*] (IEEE)
PcP	Reflected P Wave [*Earthquakes*]
PCPA	Pacific Conservatory of the Performing Arts
PCPA	Panel of Consultants for the Performing Arts [*of CFC*]
PCPA	Para-Chlorophenoxyacetic Acid [*Organic chemistry*]
PCPA	Para-Chlorophenylacetic Acid [*Organic chemistry*]
PCPA	Para-Chlorophenylalanine [*Biochemistry*]
PCPA	Poor Clares of Perpetual Adoration [*Roman Catholic women's religious order*]
PCPA	Protestant Church-Owned Publishers Association (EA)
PCPAC	Parker-Coltrane Political Action Committee [*Defunct*] (EA)
PCPAV	Pensioners-Combined Pensioners Association of Victoria [*Australia*]
PCPBMA	Pacific Coast Paper Box Manufacturers' Association (EA)
PCPC	Power Conversion Products Council [*Later, PCPCI*] (EA)
PCPCA	Pairpoint Cup Plate Collectors of America (EA)
PCPCI	Power Conversion Products Council International (FA)
PCPCN	Part Card Procurement Change Notice (KSC)
PCPCU	Pontifical Council for Promoting Christian Unity (BUAC)
PCPE	Partido Comunista de los Pueblos de Espana [*Communist Party of the Peoples of Spain*] [*Political party*] (EY)
PCPF	President's Council on Physical Fitness [*Later, PCFO*]
PCPFS	President's Council on Physical Fitness and Sports (EGAO)
PCPG	Primary Clock Pulse Generator
PCPI	Parent Cooperative Pre-Schools International (EA)
PCPI	Permanent Committee on Patent Information [*World Intellectual Property Organization*] [*Information service or system*] (IID)
PCPI	President's Commission on Personnel Interchange [*Later, President's Commission on Executive Exchange*]
PCPJ	Peoples Coalition for Peace and Justice [*Defunct*]
PCPL	Government Services Library, Charlottetown, Prince Edward Island [*Library symbol National Library of Canada*] (NLC)
PCPL	Planning Library, Charlottetown, Prince Edward Island [*Library symbol National Library of Canada*] (NLC)
PCPL	Production Control Priority List (MCD)
PCPL	Proposed Change Point Line [*NASA*] (KSC)
PCPL	Pulmonary Capillary Protein Leakage [*Medicine*] (DMAA)
PCPM	Per Contract per Month
PCPM	PERT [*Program Evaluation and Review Technique*] Cost Performance Measurement
PCP M-L	Partido Comunista de Portugal, Marxista-Leninista [*Marxist-Leninist Communist Party of Portugal*] [*Political party*] (PPE)
pcpn	Precipitation (DAVI)
PCPP	(Para-Chlorophenoxy)propionic Acid [*Organic chemistry*]
PCPP	Peace Corps Partnership Program (EA)
PCPS	Percutaneously-Introduced Cardiopulmonary Support System [*Medicine*]
PCPS	Philadelphia College of Pharmacy and Science [*Pennsylvania*]
PCPS	Pool Cooling and Purification System [*Nuclear energy*] (NRCH)
PCPS	Private Companies Practice Section
PCPS	Proceedings of the Cambridge Philological Society [*A publication*] (OCD)
PCPS	Program Change Package (IAA)
PCPS	Pulse-Coded Processing System
PCPS	Pulverized-Coal Power System [*Environmental science*] (COE)
PCPT	Para-Chlorophenylthio [*Organic chemistry*]
PCPT	Perception
PCPT	Physical Combat Proficiency Test [*Army*]
PCPT	Post Conference Provisioning Tape (MCD)
PCPV	Partido Comunista del Pais Valenciano [*Spain Political party*] (EY)
PCPV	Point-Contact Photo-Voltaic [*Solar cells*]

PCPV	Prestressed Concrete Pressure Vessel
PCQ	Pacificorp [*NYSE symbol*] (SAG)
PCQ	PacifiCorp 8.375% 'QUIDS' [*NYSE symbol*] (TTSB)
PCQ	Production Control Quantometer
PCQ	Productivity Criteria Quotient
PCQ	Professional Capabilities Questionnaire [*Jet Propulsion Laboratory, NASA*]
PCQ	Yuma, AZ [*Location identifier FAA*] (FAAL)
PCQEH	Queen Elizabeth Hospital, Charlottetown, Prince Edward Island [*Library symbol National Library of Canada*] (NLC)
PCQT	Paper-Core Quad Trunk (PDAA)
PCQT	Personal Computer Query Tool [*Military software package*] (INF)
PC Quote	PC Quote, Inc. [*Associated Press*] (SAG)
PCR	Pacific Amber Resources [*VS, Exchange Symbol*] (TTSB)
PCR	Page Control Register
PCR	Parker's Criminal Reports [*New York*] [*A publication*] (DLA)
PCR	Partial Carriage Return (IAA)
PCR	Parti Communiste Reunionnais [*Communist Party of Reunion*] [*Political party*] (PPW)
PCR	Partido Comunista Revolucionario [*Revolutionary Communist Party*] [*Peru*] [*Political party*] (PPW)
PCR	Partidul Comunist Roman [*Romanian Communist Party*] [*Political party*] (PPE)
PCR	Pass Card Reader [*Telecommunications*] (TEL)
PCR	Patient Charge Ratio
PCR	Patient Contact Record [*Medicine*] (DMAA)
PCR	Payload Certification Review (SSD)
PCR	Payload Changeout Room [*NASA*] (NASA)
PCR	Payload Checkout Room [*NASA*] (NASA)
P Cr	Paymaster-Commander [*Navy British*] (DMA)
PCR	PC Resource [*A publication*]
PCR	Pearson Aviation Corp. [*ICAO designator*] (FAAC)
PCR	Peer Code Review (IAA)
PCR	Peninsular Chemresearch [*Calgon Corp.*]
PCR	Pennsylvania Corp. Reporter [*A publication*] (DLA)
PCR	Pennsylvania County Court Reports [*A publication*] (DLA)
PCR	Per Call Rate [*Telecommunications*] (IAA)
PCR	Perini Corp. [*AMEX symbol*] (SPSG)
PCR	Period Contract Request
PCR	Periodic Current Reversal [*Electrochemistry*]
PCR	Peripheral Control Routine (CMD)
PCR	Personal Care Residence (DAVI)
PCR	Personal Communications Report [*FutureComm Publications, Inc.*] [*Information service or system Defunct*] (CRD)
PCr	Phosphocreatine [*Also, CP, PC*] [*Biochemistry*]
PCR	Photoconductive Relay (IEEE)
PCR	Photoconductive Resonance [*Physics*]
PCR	Photosynthetic Carbon Reduction [*Plant metabolism*]
PCR	Physician Contingency Reserve
PCR	Pine Creek Railroad [*An association*] (EA)
PCR	Planned Component Replacement [*Predictive maintenance schedule*]
PCR	Planning Change [*or Check*] Request (AAG)
PCR	Plant Control Room [*Nuclear energy*] (IAA)
PCR	Plasma Clearance Rate [*Medicine*] (DMAA)
Pcr	Plasma Creatinine (DAVI)
PCR	Pneumatic Checkout Rack (KSC)
PCR	Pneumatic Control Regulator (KSC)
PCR	Pollution Control Report [*Navy*]
PCR	Pollution Control Revenue
PCR	Polychromatic Color Removal [*Printing technology*]
PCR	Polymerase Chain Reaction [*Genetics*]
PCR	Population Census Report (OICC)
PCR	Positive Control Route [*Aviation*] (OA)
PCR	Post-Compression Remodeling [*Medicine*] (DMAA)
PCR	Post-Consumer Recycle [*or Reclaim*] [*Plastics industry*]
PCR	Post-Consumer Resin [*Plastic recycling*]
PCR	Postconviction Remedy
PCR	Powell Cycle Registry (EA)
PCR	Power Change Request [*NASA*] (NASA)
PCR	Power Control Room [*Nuclear energy*] (IAA)
PCR	Power Conversion Room
PCR	Pressure Check Range
PCR	Prestressed Ceramic RADOME
PCR	Preventative Cyclic Retransmission [*Telecommunications*] (TEL)
PCR	Primary Chemotherapy-Radiotherapy [*Oncology*]
PCR	Primary Cosmic Radiation
PCR	Principal Components Regression
PCR	Print Command Register
PCR	Probable Causal Relationship [*Medicine*] (MEDA)
PCR	Procedure Change Request [*NASA*]
PCR	Procurement Center Representative [*Small Business Administration*]
PCR	Production & Casting Report (WDAA)
PCR	Production Capability Review [*Army*]
PCR	Production Change Request (MCD)
PCR	Production Control Record [*NASA*] (KSC)
PCR	Program Change Request [*DoD*]
PCR	Program Control Register
PCR	Program Control Report
PCR	Program Counter [*Computor science*] (IAA)
PCR	Programmer in Charge of Records [*Computer science*] (IAA)
PCR	Program to Combat Racism [*British*] (DI)
PCR	Progress Curve Report
PCR	Project Control Room [*NASA*] (NASA)
PCR	Project Cost Record [*or Report*] [*NASA*] (KSC)
PCR	Project on Corporate Responsibility (EA)
PCR	Protein Catabolic Rate [*Biochemistry*] (DAVI)
PCR	Proven Commercial Registration [*Advertising*] (WDMC)
PCR	Publication Change Request (MCD)
PCR	Publication Contract Requirements
PCR	Puerto Carreno [*Colombia*] [*Airport symbol*] (OAG)
PCR	Pulse Compression RADAR
PCR	Punched Card Reader [*Computer science*] (BUR)
PCR	Punched Card Requisition [*Computer science*] (MCD)
PCRA	Phantom Class Racing Association (EA)
PCRA	Poland China Record Association (EA)
PCRAM	Page Composition Random Access Memory (NITA)
PCR & A	Picked Cold, Rolled, and Annealed [*Metallurgy*] (ROG)
PCRAP	Personal Computer Response Analysis Program
PCRB	Personnel and Control Room Building [*Nuclear energy*] (NRCH)
PCRB	Pollution Control Revenue Bond [*Environmental Protection Agency*]
PCRB	Program Change Review Board [*NASA*]
PCRC	Pacific Concerns Resource Center (EA)
PCRC	Paraffined Carton Research Council [*Later, Paperboard Packaging Council*]
PCRC	Perinatal Clinical Research Center [*Case Western Reserve University*] [*Research center*] (RCD)
PCRC	Poor Clergy Relief Corp. [*British*] (BI)
PCRC	Primary Communications Research Centre [*University of Leicester*] [*Canada*]
PCRCA	Pickled, Cold-Rolled, and Close-Annealed [*Metal*]
PCRD	Primary Control Rod Driveline [*Nuclear energy*] (NRCH)
PCRDM	Primary Control Rod Drive Mechanism [*Nuclear energy*] (NRCH)
PC Rep	English Privy Council Reports [*A publication*] (DLA)
PCRF	Paralysis Cure Research Foundatlon (EA)
PCRF	Parker Chiropractic Resource Foundation (EA)
PCRH	Provincial Cities and Rural Highways Program [*Australia*]
PCRI	Papanicolaou Cancer Research Institute [*University of Miami*] [*Research center*]
PCRI	Parent-Child Relationship Inventory [*Test*] (TMMY)
PCRM	Physicians Committee for Responsible Medicine (EA)
PCRM	Primary Certified Reference Material [*Nuclear energy*] (NRCH)
PCRMGPS....	Poor Clerks Regular of the Mother of God of the Pious Schools [*Rome, Italy*] (EAIO)
PCRML	Parti Communiste Revolutionnaire - Marxiste-Leniniste [*Revolutionary Marxist-Leninist Communist Party*] [*France Political party*] (PPW)
PCRMSL.......	Pacific Coast Rocky Mountain Shooting League (PSS)
PC-ROM	Personal Computer Read-Only Memory
PCRP	Pennsylvania Comprehensive Reading Program (EDAC)
Pcr/Pi	Phosphocreatine to Inorganic Phosphate Ratio
PCRPr..........	Perini Corp. Dep Cv Exch Pfd [*AMEX symbol*] (TTSB)
PCRPS	Program for Collaborative Research in the Pharmaceutical Sciences [*University of Illinois at Chicago*] [*Information service or system*] (IID)
PCRR	Pennsylvania Central Railroad (ROG)
PCRS	Poor Clergy Relief Society [*British*]
PCRS	Precision Chiropractic Research Society [*Also known as Spinal Stress Research Society*] (EA)
PCRS	Primary Control Rod System [*Nuclear energy*] (NRCH)
PCRS	Primary CRITICOMM [*Critical Intelligence Communications System*] Relay Station (CET)
PCR test	Polymerase Chain Reaction Test [*Medicine*] (TAD)
PCRV	Poinsettia Cryptic Virus [*Plant pathology*]
PCRV	PowerCerv Corp. [*NASDAQ symbol*] (SAG)
PCRV	Pressurized Concrete Reactor Vessel [*Nuclear energy*]
PCRV	Prestressed Concrete Reactor Vessel [*Nuclear energy*]
PCS	IEEE Professional Communication Society (EA)
PCS	Pace Car Society [*Defunct*] (EA)
PCS	Pacific Command Ship
PCS	Palliative Care Service
PCS	Paracas [*Peru*] [*Seismograph station code, US Geological Survey Closed*] (SEIS)
PCS	Parents' Confidential Statement [*Education*]
PCS	Parti Chretien-Social [*Christian Social Party*] [*Luxembourg*] [*Political party*] (PPW)
PCS	Particle Counting System
PCS	Parti Communiste Suisse [*Communist Party of Switzerland*] [*Political party*] (PPE)
PCS	Particulates, Condensables, and Solubles [*In gases*]
PCS	Partido Comunista Salvadoreno [*Salvadoran Communist Party*] [*Political party*] (PPW)
PCS	Partito Comunista Sammarinese [*Communist Party of San Marino*] [*Political party*] (PPE)
PCS	Parts, Components, Subassemblies
PCS	Parts Control System [*DoD*]
PCS	Passive Containment System [*Nuclear energy*] (NRCH)
PCS	Patient Care System
PCS	Patrol Vessel, Submarine Chaser (Control) [*136 feet*] [*Navy symbol Obsolete*]
PCS	Patterns of Care Study [*Roentgenography*]
PCS	Paul Claudel Society (EA)
PCS	Payless Cashways [*NYSE symbol*] (TTSB)
PCS	Payless Cashways, Inc. [*NYSE symbol*] (SPSG)
PCS	Payload Checkout System [*NASA*] (NASA)
PCS	Payload Control Supervisor [*NASA*] (MCD)
PCS	Pergamon Compact Solution [*CD-ROM publisher*] (IT)
PCS	Periodical Control System [*Libraries*]
PCS	Peripheral Computer System (IAA)
PCS	Permanent Change of Station [*Army*]
PCS	Permanent Cruiser Service [*British military*] (DMA)

PCS............. Permit Compliance System [*Environmental Protection Agency*] (GFGA)
PCS............. Personal Care Subsidy [*Australia*]
PCS............. Personal Communications Service [*Provided by Personal Communications Network*]
PCS............. Personal Communications Services [*Telecommunications*]
PCS............. Personal Communications System
PCS............. Personal Composition System (DGA)
PCS............. Personal Computing System
PCS............. Personal Conferencing Specification [*Telecommunications*] (CDE)
PCS............. Personnel Capabilities System [*Jet Propulsion Laboratory, NASA*]
PCS............. Personnel Change of Station
PCS............. Personnel Consultancy Services Ltd. [*British*]
PCS............. Petrochemical Corp. of Singapore
PCS............. Pharmaceutical Card System (MCD)
PCS............. Pharmacogenic Confusional Syndrome [*Medicine*] (DMAA)
PCS............. Phase Combining System [*Trademark*] [*A solubilizer in scintillation counting*]
PCS............. Phase Compensator System
PCS............. Philippine Collectors Society (EA)
PCS............. Philips Car Systems
PCS............. PhonoCardioScan [*Cardiology*]
PCS............. Photoformed Ceramic Substrates [*Du Pont process for making microconductors*]
PCS............. Photon Correlation Spectroscopy
PCS............. Physical-Chemical System (SAA)
PCS............. Physical Control System
PCS............. Physically Controlled Space [*Military*] (GFGA)
PCS............. Pictorial Cancellation Society [*Defunct*] (EA)
pcs............. Picture File [*Computer science*]
PCS............. Pieces
pcs............. Pieces (EBF)
PCS............. Piezoelectric Crystal Sensor (DB)
PCS............. Pilot Control System (MCD)
PCS............. Pitch Control System (MCD)
PCS............. Planning Control Sheet
PCS............. Plant Computer System (NRCH)
PCS............. Plant Control System [*Nuclear energy*] (NRCH)
PCS............. Plastic-Clad Silica [*Optics*]
PCS............. Plastic Coated Silica (NITA)
PCS............. Plastic Connector Shell
PCS............. Platoon Combat Skills [*Army*] (INF)
PCS............. Plausible Conflict Situations [*Army*]
PCS............. Pluto-Charon System [*Planetary science*]
PCS............. Pneumatic Control System [*Gas chromatography*]
PCS............. Pointing-Control System [*Aerospace*]
PCS............. Polycarbosilane (EDCT)
PCS............. Polymer-Clad Silica [*Chemistry*]
PCS............. Portable Communications System
PCS............. Portacaval Shunt [*Medicine*]
PCS............. Port Command Store [*Telecommunications*] (TEL)
PCS............. Port Control Store [*Telecommunications*] (TEL)
PCS............. Port Control System [*Telecommunications*] (TEL)
PCS............. Position Classification Standard [*Civil Service*]
PCS............. Position Control System
PCS............. Position, Course, and Speed
PCS............. Positive Concatenation Structures [*Mathematics*]
PCS............. Postal Church Service
PCS............. Postal Commemorative Society (EA)
PCS............. Postcardiotomy Syndrome [*Medicine*]
PCS............. Postcaval [*or Portacaval*] Shunt [*Medicine*]
PCS............. Posterior Concave Side
PCS............. Posts, Camps, and Stations [*Military*]
PCS............. Potash Corp. of Saskatchewan [*Canada*]
PCS............. Power Conditioning System
PCS............. Power Conversion System
PCS............. Powered Causeway Section [*Military*] (CAAL)
PCS............. Practical Computer Solutions (NITA)
PCS............. Precedence Charting System (IAA)
PCS............. Precision Casting Standard (MCD)
PCS............. Preconscious
Pcs............. Preconscious [*Medicine*] (STED)
PCS............. Preferred Capital Stock [*Investment term*]
PCS............. Pregnancy Counselling Service [*Australia*]
PCS............. Preliminary Component Specification
PCS............. Press Computer System (DGA)
PCS............. Pressure Control System
PCS............. Pressure Cycling Switch [*Automotive engineering*]
PCS............. Primary Calibration System
PCS............. Primary Cancer Site [*Oncology*]
P c/s .... Primary Cesarian Section (STED)
PCS............. Primary Conditioning Solution
PCS............. Primary Control Ship [*Navy*]
PCS............. Primary Coolant System (MSA)
PCS............. Prime Compatible Set (PDAA)
PCS............. Principal Clerk of Session
PCS............. Principal Coordinating Scientist [*NASA*] (KSC)
PCS............. Print Contrast Scale (IEEE)
PCS............. Print Contrast Signal [*Computer science*]
PCS............. Print Contrast System (BUR)
PCS............. Probability of Command Shutdown (MCD)
PCS............. Probability of Correct Selection [*Statistics*]
PCS............. Probability of Crew Survival (AAG)
PCS............. Procedure Completion Sheet [*NASA*] (MCD)
PCS............. Process Communication Supervisor (IAA)

PCS............. Process Computer System (NRCH)
PCS............. Process Control Sheet [*Nuclear energy*] (NRCH)
PCS............. Process Control System
PCS............. Pro Computer Services (NITA)
PCS............. Production Control Section
PCS............. Production Control System (BUR)
PCS............. Production Cost Savings (AAEL)
PCS............. Professional Careers Sourcebook [*A publication*]
PCS............. Professional Car Society (EA)
PCS............. Program Coordination Staff [*Environmental Protection Agency*] (GFGA)
PCS............. Program Cost Status [*Report*] (MCD)
PCS............. Program Counter Store
PCS............. Programmable Communications Subsystem
PCS............. Project Control Sheet [*Computer science*]
PCS............. Project Control System [*Computer science*]
PCS............. Project Coordination Staff [*NASA*] (KSC)
PCS............. Property Consultants Society [*British*] (DBA)
PCS............. Property Control System
PCS............. Proprietary Computer Systems, Inc. [*Information service or system*] (IID)
PCS............. Prostate Cancer Society (WDAA)
PCS............. Provision Coordinate Schedule (MCD)
PCS............. Pseudotumor Cerebri Syndrome [*Medicine*] (DMAA)
PCS............. Publication Control Sheet (MCD)
PCS............. Public Choice Society (EA)
PCS............. Pump Control Sensor
PCS............. Punch Card System (NITA)
PCS............. Punched Card System [*Computer science*]
PCS............. Pyrotechnics Circuit Simulator
PCS............. Sabah Chinese Party [*Malaysia*] [*Political party*] (FEA)
PCS............. Submarine Chaser
PCS............. Sun Shipbuilding & Dry Dock Co., Chester, PA [*Library symbol Library of Congress*] (LCLS)
PCSA .... Palm and Cycad Societies of Australia
PCSA .... Patrol Craft Sailors Association (EA)
PCSA .... Personal Computing Systems Architecture
PCSA .... Power Crane and Shovel Association (EA)
PCSA .... Seaman Apprentice, Postal Clerk, Striker [*Navy rating*]
PCS(A)........ Submarine Chaser (Air Cushion) (MCD)
PCSAS .... Policy Committee for Scientific Agricultural Society (BUAC)
PCsB............ Baptist Bible College of Pennsylvania, Clarks Summit, PA [*Library symbol Library of Congress*] (LCLS)
PCSC .... Control Submarine Chaser [*136 feet*] [*Navy symbol Obsolete*]
PCSC .... Pacific Coast Swimming Conference (PSS)
PCSC .... Plant Cell Suspension Cultures [*Biotechnology*]
PCSC .... Power Conditioning, Switching, and Control
PCSC .... Principal Commonwealth Supply Committee [*World War II*]
PCS-CSS...... Parents' Confidential Statement of the College Scholarship Service [*Education*] (IIA)
PCSD .... Partido Cristao Social Democratico [*Christian Social Democratic Party*] [*Portugal Political party*] (PPE)
PCSD .... Polychloro(chloromethylsulfonamido)diphenyl Ether [*Insectproofing agent for wool*]
PCSD .... President's Council on Sustainable Development [*1993*]
PCSDC........ Pacific Collegiate Swim/Dive Conference (PSS)
PCSE........... Pacific Coast Stock Exchange [*Later, PSE*] (EA)
PCSE........... President's Committee on Scientists and Engineers [*Expired, 1958*]
PCSE........... Printed Circuit Soldering Equipment
PC/SFA .... Potato Chip/Snack Food Association [*Formerly, NPCI, PCI*] [*Later, SFA*]
PCSFSK....... Phase Comparison Sinusoidal Frequency Shift Keying
PCSG .... Public Cryptography Study Group [*Defunct*] (EA)
PCSH .... Pierce Shell
PCS(H)........ Submarine Chaser (Hydrofoil) (MCD)
PCSIG .... Personal Computer-Software Interest Group (EA)
PCSIR .... Pakistan Council of Scientific and Industrial Research
PCSJ........... All-Party Parliamentary Committee for the Release of Soviet Jewry (EAIO)
PCSM.......... Percutaneous Stone Manipulation [*Medicine*]
PCSN .... PC Satellite Network
PCSN .... Precision Standard [*NASDAQ symbol*] (TTSB)
PCSN .... Precision Standard, Inc. [*NASDAQ symbol*] (NQ)
PCSN .... Private Circuit-Switching Network [*Telecommunications*] (OSI)
PCSN .... Seaman, Postal Clerk, Striker [*Navy rating*]
PCSP .... Permanent Commission for the South Pacific (WDAA)
PCSP .... Programmed Communications Support Program [*Air Force*] (AFM)
PCSPS .... Principal Civil Service Pension Scheme [*British*]
PCSS .... PC Service Source [*NASDAQ symbol*] (TTSB)
PCSS .... PC Service Source, Inc. [*NASDAQ symbol*] (SAG)
PCSS .... Platform Check Subsystem
PCSS .... Princess (ROG)
PCST .... Pakistan Council for Science and Technology (BUAC)
PCST .... Precision Castparts Corp. (MHDW)
PCST .... President's Committee on Science and Technology
PC Svc .... PC Service Source, Inc. [*Associated Press*] (SAG)
PCSW .... Police Chiefs Spouses - Worldwide [*An association*] (EA)
PCSW .... President's Commission on the Status of Women
PCT............. Pacific Coast Tariff Bureau, San Francisco CA [*STAC*]
PCT............. Pacific Crest Trail
PCT............. Paper Crepe Tape
PCT............. Para-Chlorotoluene [*Organic chemistry*]
PCT............. Parti Communiste Tunisien [*Tunisian Communist Party*] [*Political party*] (PD)

PCT............. Parti Congolais du Travail [*Congolese Labor Party*] [*Political party*] (PPW)
PCT............. Partido Conservador Tradicional [*Traditionalist Conservative Party*] [*Nicaragua*] [*Political party*]
PCT............. Patent Cooperation Treaty [*World Intellectual Property Organization, 1978*]
PCT............. Peace Air Togo [*ICAO designator*] (FAAC)
PCT............. Peak Centerline Temperature [*Nuclear energy*] (NRCH)
PCT............. Peak Cladding Temperature [*Nuclear energy*] (NRCH)
PCT............. Percent [*or Percentage*]
PCT............. Percentage [*Used instead of "average"*] [*Baseball*]
PCT............. Perfect Crystal Technology (IAA)
PCT............. Performance Correlation Technique
PCT............. Periodic Confidence Test
PCT............. Peripheral Control Terminal
PC/T............ Personal Computer/Technology (HGAA)
PCT............. Personality Completion Test [*Psychology*]
PCT............. Pharmacy and Chemistry Technician [*Navy*]
PCT............. Philadelphia College of Textiles and Science, Philadelphia, PA [*OCLC symbol*] (OCLC)
PCT............. Photoinduced Charge Transfer [*Electrochemistry*]
PCT............. Photon-Coupled Transistor [*IEEE*]
PCT............. Physical Correlate Theory [*Psychophysics*]
PCT............. Physiognomic Cue Test [*Psychology*] (STED)
PCT............. Picrotoxin [*Biological stimulant*]
PCT............. Picture
PCT............. Pitch Centering Torquer (SAA)
PCT............. Planning and Control Techniques
PCT............. Plasma Clotting Time [*Medicine*] (STED)
PCT............. Plasmacrit Test [*Medicine*]
PCT............. Plasmacytoma [*Medicine*]
PCT............. Platelet Count [*Hematology*]
PCT............. Platelet Hematocrit (STED)
PCT............. Point-Contact Transistor [*Electronics*] (IAA)
PCT............. Polychemotherapy [*Oncology*]
PCT............. Polychlorinated Terphenyl [*Pesticide*]
PCT............. Polychlorinated Triphenyl (STED)
PCT............. Polychloroterphenyl [*Organic chemistry*]
PCT............. Porcine Calcitonin [*Biochemistry*] (AAMN)
PCT............. Porphyria Cutanea Tarda [*Disease*] [*Medicine*]
PCT............. Portable Camera-Transmitter
PCT............. Portable Conference Telephone [*Bell Laboratories*]
PCT............. Portacaval Transportation (STED)
PCT............. Portacaval Transposition [*Medicine*] (MAE)
PCT............. Positron Computed Tomography
PCT............. Postcoital Test [*Medicine*] (DAVI)
PCT............. Potato Curly Top Disease [*Plant pathology*]
PCT............. Potential Current Transformer
PCT............. Precinct
PCT............. Preliminary Change Transmittal (AAG)
PCT............. Pressure Concentration Temperature
PCT............. Prime Contract Termination (AAG)
PCT............. Princeton [*New Jersey*] [*Airport symbol Obsolete*] (OAG)
PCT............. Prism Cover Test [*Ophthalmology*] (CPH)
PCT............. Private Communications Technology [*Microsoft Corp.*] [*Computer science*]
P Ct............. Probate Court (DLA)
PCT............. Process Change Teams (AAEL)
PCT............. Production Confirmatory Test (MCD)
PCT............. Progestin Challenge Test (STED)
PCT............. Programa de Cooperacion Tecnica [*Program of Technical Cooperation - PTC*] [*Organization of American States*] [*Washington, DC*]
PCT............. Program Control Table [*Computer science*]
PCT............. Program Counter Timer (IAA)
PCT............. Project Control Tool (BUR)
PCT............. Property Capital Trust [*AMEX symbol*] (SPSG)
PCT............. Property Cap Tr [*AMEX symbol*] (TTSB)
PCT............. Prothrombin Consumption Time [*Hematology*] (DAVI)
PCT............. Proximal Convoluted Tubule [*of a nephron*]
PCT............. Puangchon Chao Thai [*Thai Mass Party*] [*Thailand*] [*Political party*]
PCT............. Pulmonary Care Team Medicine (STED)
PCT............. Pulse Compression Tube
PCT............. Pulse Count [*Telecommunications*] (TEL)
PCT............. Wesman Personnel Classification Test
PCTA.......... Pentachlorothioanisole [*Organic chemistry*]
PCTB.......... Pacific Coast Tariff Bureau
PCTC.......... Penn Central Transportation Co.
PCTC.......... Pure Car Truck Carrier [*Shipping*] (DS)
PCTC.......... Pyrotechnic Circuit Test Console (KSC)
PCTDS........ Problem and Change Tracking Directory System
PCTE.......... Portable Commercial Test Equipment (NASA)
PCTE.......... Portable Common Test Environment [*British*]
PCTE.......... Portable Common Tools Environment (IAA)
PCTF.......... Plant Component Test Facility [*Nuclear energy*]
PCTF.......... Power Conversion Test Facility (SAA)
PCTFE........ Polychlorotrifluoroethylene [*Organic chemistry*]
PCTFE........ Polymonochlorotrifluorethyle [*Organic chemistry*] (IAA)
PCT-GF...... Plasmacytoma Growth Factor [*Oncology*]
PCTH......... Pacific Aerospace & Electronics, Inc. [*NASDAQ symbol*] (SAG)
PCTH......... PCT Holdings [*NASDAQ symbol*] (TTSB)
PCTH......... PCT Holdings, Inc. [*NASDAQ symbol*] (SAG)
PCTHold...... PCT Holdings, Inc. [*Associated Press*] (SAG)
PCTIS........ Preston Commercial and Technical Information Service (NITA)
PCTL.......... Picture Tel Corp. [*NASDAQ symbol*] (TTSB)

PC/TM........ Performance Criteria and Test Methods Task
PCTM......... Pulse-Count Modulation (MSA)
PCTO .... Payload Cost Tradeoff Optimization [*NASA*] (NASA)
PCTP......... Partido Comunista dos Trabalhadores Portugueses [*Portuguese Workers' Communist Party*] [*Political party*] (PPW)
PCTP......... Pierce Template
PCTR......... Pad Connection Terminal Room [*NASA*] (NAKS)
PCTR......... Physical Constant Test Reactor [*Nuclear energy*]
PCTR......... Program Counter
PCTR......... Property Control Transaction Report
PCTR......... Pulsed Column Test Rig [*Chemical engineering*]
PCTS......... Pentagon Consolidated Telecommunications System (MCD)
PCTS......... Portable Cesium Time Standard
PCTS......... President's Committee for Traffic Safety (EA)
PCTT......... Precommit Track Time [*DoD*]
PCTUULAW... Permanent Congress of Trade Union Unity of Latin American Workers [*See also CPUSTAL*] [*Mexico City, Mexico*] (EAIO)
PCTV......... People's Choice TV [*NASDAQ symbol*] (TTSB)
PCTV......... Peoples Choice TV Corp. [*NASDAQ symbol*] (SAG)
PCTV......... Private Channel Television
PCtvL......... Lukens Steel Co., Coatesville, PA [*Library symbol Library of Congress Obsolete*] (LCLS)
PCtvVA...... United States Veterans Administration Hospital, Medical Library, Coatesville, PA [*Library symbol Library of Congress*] (LCLS)
PCTWin...... PC [*Personal Computer*] Tools for Windows (PCM)
PCTY......... Party City [*NASDAQ symbol*] (TTSB)
PCTY......... Party City Corp. [*NASDAQ symbol*] (SAG)
PCU.......... Packet Communications Unit
PCU.......... Paging Control Unit [*Telecommunications*] (TEL)
PCU.......... Pain Control Unit
PCU.......... Palliative Care Unit [*Medicine*] (CPH)
PCU.......... Partido Conservador Unido [*Chilean Catholic political party*]
PCU.......... Passenger Control Unit (MCD)
PCU.......... Patient Care Unit (HCT)
PCU.......... Payload Checkout Unit [*NASA*] (MCD)
PCU.......... Peripheral Control Unit (CMD)
PCU.......... Picayune, MS [*Location identifier FAA*] (FAAL)
pcu.......... Platinum Cobalt Unit [*Water analysis*]
PCU.......... Pneumatic Checkout Unit (AAG)
PCU.......... Pod Cooling Unit (AAG)
PCU.......... Portable Checkout Unit
PCU.......... Portable Computer Unit
PCU.......... Portuguese Continental Union of the United States of America (EA)
PCU.......... Post-Coronary Care Unit [*Cardiology*] (DAVI)
PCU.......... Pound Centigrade Unit
PCU.......... Power Conditioning Unit
PCU.......... Power Control Unit
PCU.......... Power Conversion Unit (IEEE)
PCU.......... Pressure Control Unit (MCD)
PCU.......... Price [*Utah*] [*Seismograph station code, US Geological Survey*] (SEIS)
PCU.......... Primary Care Unit [*Medicine*] (DMAA)
PCU.......... Primary Control Unit (IAA)
PCU.......... Print Control Unit (SAA)
PCU.......... Printed Control Unit [*Military*] (GFGA)
PCU.......... Prisoner Casework Unit (WDAA)
PCU.......... Process Control Unit (NAKS)
PCU.......... Processor Control Unit
PCU.......... Product Co-Ordination Unit [*British Overseas Trade Board*] (DS)
PCU.......... Program Control Unit [*Computer science*]
PCU.......... Progress Control Unit (KSC)
PCU.......... Progressive Care Unit [*Medicine*]
PCU.......... Propellant Control Unit (SAA)
PCU.......... Protective Care Unit [*Medicine*]
PCU.......... Protein-Calorie Undernutrition [*Medicine*]
PCU.......... Pulmonary Care Unit [*Medicine*] (DMAA)
PCU.......... Punched Card Unit (NITA)
PCU.......... Punched Card Utility [*Computer science*]
PCU.......... Southern Peru Copper [*NYSE symbol*] (TTSB)
PCU.......... Southern Peru Copper Corp. [*NYSE symbol*] (SAG)
PCU.......... University of Prince Edward Island, Charlottetown, Prince Edward Island [*Library symbol National Library of Canada*] (NLC)
PCUA .... Power Controller Unit Assembly (IEEE)
PCUA .... Pressure Control Unit, Atlas (MCD)
PCUA .... PROFIT Control Users Association (EA)
PCUC .... Positive Continuous Ullage Control
PCU/HDR ... Primary Control Unit, Hydraulics (AAG)
PCUI .... Partito Comunista Unificado di Italia [*Unified Communist Party of Italy*] [*Political party*] (PPE)
PCUR .... Pulsating Current
PCUS .... Peace Corps of the United States (EA)
PCUS .... Port Charges Paid by United States Army, Navy, or Air Force (DNAB)
PCUS .... Propeller Club of the United States (EA)
PC-USA ...... Pax Christi - USA (EA)
PCUSAW...... Pen Center USA West (EA)
PCUSEQ...... Pressure Control Unit Sequencer (AAG)
pcut .... Percutaneous [*Medicine*] (AAMN)
PCUUS ...... Polish Council of Unity in the United States [*Defunct*] (EA)
PCV.......... Pacific Concord Resources Corp. [*Vancouver Stock Exchange symbol*]
PCV.......... Packed Cell Volume [*Hematology*] (CPH)
PCV.......... Parietal Cell Vagotomy [*Medicine*] (AAMN)
PCV.......... Partido Comunista Venezolana [*Venezuelan Communist Party*] [*Political party*] (PPW)
PCV.......... Passenger Carrying Vehicle [*Military*] (GFGA)

PCV	Passenger Control Vehicle (WDAA)
PCV	Peace Corps Volunteer
PCV	Peanut Clump Virus [Plant pathology]
PCV	Penciclovir [Antiherpetic]
PCV	Petty Cash Voucher (MCD)
PCV	Phenetic Coefficient of Variation
PCV	Pneumatic Control Valve
PCV	Pollution Control Valve (IEEE)
PCV	Polycythemia Vera [Also, PV] [Hematology]
PCV	Porcine Cirovirus
PCV	Positive Crankcase Ventilation [For automotive antipollution systems]
PCV	Postcapillary Venule [Medicine] (DMAA)
PCV	Precheck Verification [NASA] (NASA)
PCV	Pressure [or Pressurizer] Control Valve (AAG)
PCV	Pressure-Control Ventilation [Medicine] (DMAA)
PCV	Primary Containment Vessel
PCV	Primary Control Vessel (DNAB)
PCV	Primate Calicivirus
PCV	Procarbazine, CCNU [Lomustine], Vincristine [Antineoplastic drug regimen] (DAVI)
PCV	Proportioning Control Valve [Automotive brakes]
PCV	Protocol Converter [Electronics] (ECII)
PCV	Pump Control Valve [Hydraulics]
PCV	Purge Control Valve (NASA)
PCV	Putnam Convertible Opportunities & Income Trust [NYSE symbol] (SAG)
PCV	Putnam Cv Opp Inc. Tr [NYSE symbol] (TTSB)
PCV	Pyrocatechol Violet [Also, PV] [An indicator Chemistry]
PCV	Veterans Affairs, Canada [Affaires des Anciens Combattants Canada] Charlottetown, Prince Edward Island [Library symbol National Library of Canada] (NLC)
PCvA	Allentown College of Saint Francis De Sales, Center Valley, PA [Library symbol Library of Congress] (LCLS)
PCVB	Pyro Continuity Verification Box [NASA] (NASA)
PCVC	Partially Conserved Vector Current (IAA)
PCVC	Public Citizens Visitors Center [An association Defunct] (EA)
PCVD	Plasma Chemical Vapor Deposition
PCVL	Pilot Controlled Visual Landing [Aviation] (NASA)
PCV-M	Myeloid Metaplasia with Polycythemia Vera [Hematology] (MAE)
PCVN	Precracked Charpy V-Notch (PDAA)
PCW	Personal Computer World Show [Montbuild Ltd.] (TSPED)
PCW	Plate Control Wedge [Printing technology]
PCW	Point Calculation Worksheet [Army] (INF)
PCW	PortaCom Wireless [VS, Exchange Symbol] (TTSB)
PCW	Port Clinton, OH [Location identifier FAA] (FAAL)
PCW	Post Consumer Waste (EG)
PCW	Previously Complied With
PCW	Primary Cooling Water [Reactor]
PCW	Princess Charlotte of Wales [Military unit] [British]
PCW	Principal Conductor of the Works [Freemasonry]
PCW	Program Control Word
PCW	Proprietor of Copyright on a Composite Work
PCW	Pulmonary Capillary Wedge [Medicine]
PCW	Pulsed Continuous Wave (IEEE)
PCW	Widener College, Chester, PA [Library symbol Library of Congress] (LCLS)
PCWA	Pharmaceutical Council of Western Australia
PCWBS	Preliminary Contract Work Breakdown Structure (MCD)
PCWCA	Poured Concrete Wall Contractors Association (EA)
PC-WNIM	Personal Computer Wide Area Network Interface Module (TSSD)
PCWO	Production Control Work Order (MCD)
PCWP	Pulmonary Capillary Wedge Pressure [Medicine]
PCWPC	Permanent Committee of the World Petroleum Congress (BUAC)
PCWTU	Philippine Woman's Christian Temperance Union (BUAC)
PCWU	Port Commissioners Workers' Union [India]
PCX	Pacificorp [NYSE symbol] (SAG)
PCX	PacifiCorp 8.55%'QUIDS' [NYSE symbol] (TTSB)
PCx	Periscopic Convex [Ophthalmology]
PCX	Plasma Confinement Experiment [Physics]
PCX	Process Control Executive (MHDI)
PCXR	Portable Chest X-Ray (CPH)
PCY	Aquila Air, Inc. [ICAO designator] (FAAC)
PCY	Pacific Cypress Minerals Ltd. [Vancouver Stock Exchange symbol]
PCY	Pittsburgh, Chartiers & Youghiogheny Railway Co. [AAR code]
PCY	Plastocyanin
PCY	Prerogative Court of York [English court previously having jurisdiction over wills]
PCYC	Pharmacyclics, Inc. [NASDAQ symbol] (SAG)
PCYF	President's Council on Youth Fitness (EA)
PCYF	Progressive Conservative Youth Federation of Canada
PCZ	Canal Zone [ANSI three-letter standard code Obsolete] (CNC)
PCZ	Panama Canal Zone [Panama] [Airport symbol] (AD)
PCZ	Paracomp Technology, Inc. [Vancouver Stock Exchange symbol]
PCZ	Petro-Canada [NYSE symbol] (SAG)
PCZ	Petro-Canada Variable Vtg [NYSE symbol] (TTSB)
PCZ	Physical Control Zone (NASA)
PCZ	Positive Control Zone (DNAB)
PCZ	Procarbazine [Antineoplastic drug] (DAVI)
PCZ	Prochlorperazine [Antiemetic]
PCZ	Waupaca, WI [Location identifier FAA] (FAAL)
PCZPP	Petro-Canada Installm't Vtg [NYSE symbol] (TTSB)
PD	Democratic Party [Ecuador] [Political party] (PD)
PD	Doctor of Pedagogy
PD	Doctor of Pharmacy
PD	Doctor of Philosophy (WDAA)

Pd	Dorsal Pressure Neuron [of a leech]
PD	Dublin Pharmacopoeia
PD	Interpupillary Distance
PD	Law Reports, Probate, Divorce, and Admiralty Division [1875-90] [England] [A publication] (DLA)
p/d	Packs per Day [Cigarettes] [Medicine]
PD	Pad (MCD)
PD	Paget's Disease [Medicine]
PD	Paid
Pd	Paid (EBF)
pd	Paid (ODBW)
PD	Palisade Diabase [Geology]
Pd	Palladium [Chemical element]
PD	Pancreatic Divisum [Medicine]
PD	Pancreatic Duct [Anatomy]
PD	Pants Down [At a disadvantage] [Slang] (DSUE)
pd	Papilla Diameter [Medicine]
PD	Papillary Distance
PD	Paralyzing Dose [Pharmacology] (DAVI)
PD	Parental Ditype [Genetics]
PD	Parke-Davis [Commercial firm] (DAVI)
PD	Parkinsonism Dementia [Medicine]
PD	Parkinson's Disease [Medicine]
PD	Pars Distalis [Medicine]
PD	Part Damaged (ROG)
PD	Partial Discharge [High-voltage testing] (IEEE)
PD	Particle-Density [Forensic science]
PD	Parti Democratique [Democratic Party] [Luxembourg Political party] (EAIO)
PD	Partido Democrata [Democratic Party] [Costa Rica] [Political party] (PPW)
PD	Partido Democrata [Democratic Party] [Chile] [Political party]
PD	Passed
pd	Passed (ODBW)
PD	Passive Detection [Electronics]
PD	Past Due
PD	Paste-Down [Album] [Photography] (ROG)
PD	Patent Ductus [Cardiology] (MAE)
PD	Pay Department [Army British] (ROG)
PD	Pay Dirt
PD	Payload Diameter
PD	Peak Detector
PD	Pedestal (IAA)
PD	Pediatric [or Pediatrics]
Pd	Pediatrics (DMAA)
PD	Pem Air [ICAO designator] (AD)
P/D	Penetration Diameter [Military]
PD	People's Democracy [Ireland] [Political party]
PD	Pepper Dust [An adulterating element]
PD	Percutaneous Drain [Surgery] (DAVI)
pd	Per Diem [By the day] [Latin] (WDMC)
PD	Per Diem [By the Day] [Latin]
PD	Per Diliquium [By Deliquescence] [Pharmacy] (ROG)
PD	Perfect Diffuser [Optics]
PD	Performance Demonstration (MCD)
PD	Performer Diploma (PGP)
PD	Periderm [Botany]
PD	Period (AABC)
PD	Periodic Duty (IAA)
PD	Peripheral Device (BUR)
PD	Periscope Depth (IAA)
PD	Peritoneal Dialysis [Medicine]
PD	Permanent Deactivation
PD	Permits Division [Environmental Protection Agency] (GFGA)
PD	Personnel Department
PD	Personnel Development
PD	Personnel Distribution [Army]
PD	Pharmacy Director
PD	Pharmacy Dispenser [British military] (DMA)
PD	Phase Discriminator
PD	Phelps Dodge [NYSE symbol] (TTSB)
PD	Phelps Dodge Corp. [NYSE symbol] (SPSG)
PD	Phenyldichlorarsine [A war gas]
PD	Philosophiae Doctor [Doctor of Philosophy]
PD	Phosphate Dehydrogenase
PD	Phosphate Dextrose (DAVI)
PD	Phosphodiester [Organic chemistry]
PD	Photodiode
PD	Photo Ditector (EECA)
PD	Photosensitivity Dermatitis [Medicine] (DMAA)
PD	Phyllis Dorothy James White [In name P. D. James] [Author]
PD	Physical Damage [Insurance]
PD	Physical Development (IAA)
PD	Physical Disabilities
PD	Physical Distribution (ADA)
PD	Physics Department
PD	Picknick Dam [TVA]
P/D	Pickup and Deposit
PD	Pictorial Display (MCD)
PD	Pierce's Disease [Plant pathology]
PD	Pilot Dogs (EA)
PD	Piskei Din Shel Bet ha-Mishpat ha-'Elyon le-Yisrael (BJA)
PD	Pitch Circle Diameter [Technical drawings] (IAA)
PD	Pitch Diameter
PD	Pitch Down (MCD)

PD	Pivoted Door (AAG)
PD	Plane Disagreement [*Telecommunications*] (TEL)
PD	Planned Derating [*Electronics*] (IEEE)
PD	Planning Directive (NG)
PD	Planning Document
PD	Plans Division [*Military*]
PD	Plasma Defect [*Hematology*] (DAVI)
PD	Plasma Deposited (IAA)
PD	Plasma Desorption [*of ions for analysis*]
PD	Plasma Display
PD	Plasmodesmata [*Botanical cytology*]
PD	Plate Dissipation
PD	Platelet Deaggregation [*Hematology*]
PD	Plausible Deniability
PD	Plotting Display (IAA)
PD	Point Defense
PD	Point Delay Fuze [*Army*]
PD	Point Detonating [*Projectile*]
PD	Polar Distance [*Navigation*]
PD	Police Department
PD	Policy Determination (GNE)
pd	Pond [*Pound*] [*Monetary unit*] [*Afrikaans*]
PD	Pontoon Dock
PD	Pool Density [*Pisciculture*]
PD	Poorly Differentiated [*Medicine*]
PD	Population Density (NRCH)
PD	Population Distribution (NRCH)
PD	Population Doubling
PD	Porak-Durante [*Disease*] [*Medicine*] (DB)
PD	Pore Diameter
PD	Porphobilinogen Deaminase [*Clinical chemistry*] (MAE)
PD	Port Director
PD	Port Du [*Carriage Forward*] [*French*]
PD	Port Dues
PD	Port of Debarkation [*Navy*]
PD	Position Description
PD	Position Document
PD	Position Doubtful [*Nautical charts*]
PD	Positive Displacement
PD	Positives and Deposition (DGA)
PD	Postage Due
PD	Postal District
PD	Post Dated (WDAA)
PD	Post Diluvium [*After the Flood*] [*Latin*] (ROG)
PD	Postdoctorate
PD	Posterior Deltoid [*Myology*]
PD	Posterior Digestive [*Gland*]
PD	Postnasal Drainage [*Medicine*]
PD	Postural Drainage [*Medicine*] (MAE)
PD	Potential Difference [*Electricity*]
pd	Potential Difference
PD	Pound (ROG)
PD	Power Distribution
PD	Power Divider (IAA)
PD	Power Doubler (IAA)
PD	Power Driven (IAA)
PD	Precision Device [*British military*] (DMA)
PD	Precision Drilling (1987) Ltd. [*Toronto Stock Exchange symbol*]
PD	Predeployment
P/D	Predicted [*NASA*] (KSC)
PD	Predilute
PD	Preference for Duty
PD	Pregnanediol [*Biochemistry*]
PD	Preliminary Design
PD	Prescription Drug
PD	Presidential Determination
PD	Presidential Directive
PD	Press Division [*Environmental Protection Agency*] (GFGA)
PD	Pressor Dose [*Medicine*]
Pd	Pressure, Diastolic [*Cardiology*]
PD	Pressure Distillate (IAA)
PD	Pressure Drop (KSC)
PD	Presumptive Disability [*Title XVI*] [*Social Security Administration*] (OICC)
PD	Pretty Disgusting (WDAA)
PD	Prevention Detention [*Scotland Yard*]
PD	Preventive Dentistry (DAVI)
pd	Prime Driver
PD	Principal Distance [*Graphic arts*] (OA)
PD	Printer Driver
PD	Printer's Devil (ROG)
PD	Priority Designator [*Army*]
PD	Priority Directive
PD	Prism Diopter
PD	Prisoner's Dilemma [*Psychology*]
PD	Privatdozent [*Tutor*] [*German*]
PD	Private Detective
PD	Probability Density [*Statistics*] (IAA)
PD	Probability of Damage (MCD)
PD	Probability of Death [*Biology*]
PD	Probability of Detection
PD	Problem Definition [*Army*]
PD	Procedures Description (COE)
PD	Process Data (NITA)
PD	Process Descriptor [*Telecommunications*] (IAA)
PD	Process Diagnostic [*Interpersonal skills and attitudes test*]
PD	Procurement Data
PD	Procurement Directive [*Army*]
PD	Procurement District [*Air Force*] (AFIT)
PD	Procurement Division
PD	Procurement Document (NASA)
PD	Procurement Drawing
pd	Pro Defendente [*On Behalf of Defendant*] [*Latin Legal term*] (DLA)
PD	Product Design [*Phase*]
P/D	Product Development
PD	Production and Deployment Phase [*Military*] (MCD)
PD	Production Department
PD	Production Director (NTCM)
PD	Professional Development (ADA)
PD	Professional Digital [*Recording*] (NTCM)
PD	Professional Diploma [*Education*] (AEE)
PD	Profile Descent (GAVI)
PD	Programa Democratico [*Democratic Program*] [*Spain Political party*] (PPE)
PD	Program Deceleration (KSC)
PD	Program Decoder
PD	Program Directive (NG)
PD	Program Director [*Television*]
PD	Progression of Disease [*Medicine*]
PD	Progressive Democrats [*Ireland*] [*Political party*]
PD	Project Directive (NASA)
PD	Project Document
PD	Projected Decision Date (NRCH)
PD	Projected Display
PD	Promotion Director
PD	Propellant Dispersal (NAKS)
PD	Propellant Dispersion (KSC)
PD	Property Damage
PD	Property Disposition [*FHA*] (EMRF)
PD	Proportional Derivative (IAA)
PD	Proportional Plus Derivative (IAA)
PD	Proposal Development (AAG)
PD	Prostatodynia [*Medicine*]
PD	Protective Device (BUR)
PD	Protein Diet (DMAA)
PD	Prototype Demonstration
PD	Provisioning Document
PD	Provocation Dose [*Medicine*] (MEDA)
PD	Proximity Detector
PD	Prussian Dollar [*Monetary unit*] (ROG)
PD	Pseudohomogeneous Axial Dispersion Model [*Fluid dynamics*]
PD	Psychodynamic
Pd	Psychopathic Deviate [*Psychology*]
PD	Psychotic Depression [*Medicine*]
PD	Psychotic Deviate [*Psychiatry*] (DAVI)
PD	Publication Date [*Online database field identifier*]
PD	Public Defender [*Australia*]
PD	Public Domain
PD	Publisher's Directory [*Formerly, BPD*] [*A publication*]
PD	Pulley Drive (IAA)
PD	Pulmonary Disease [*Medicine*]
PD	Pulpodistal [*Dentistry*]
PD	Pulse Detector [*Spectroscopy*]
PD	Pulse Doppler
PD	Pulse Driver
PD	Pulse Duration
P-D	Punch-Die (MSA)
PD	Punch Driver
pd	Pupillary Distance [*Medicine*]
PD	Purchase Description
PD	Pyloric Dilator [*Neuron*]
PD	Pyramidal Decussation [*Neuroanatomy*]
PD1	Portable Dictionary 1 [*English/Japanese electronic dictionary*] [*Sanyo Electric*]
PDA	Pacific Dance Association (EA)
PDA	Pacific Dermatologic Association (EA)
PDA	Packaging Distributors Association [*British*] (DBA)
PDA	Panhellenic Dental Association (BUAC)
PDA	Parallel Data Adapter
PDA	Parallel Drive Array [*Computer science*] (CIST)
PDA	Parametric Design Analysis (RDA)
PDA	Parenteral Drug Abuser (STED)
PDA	Parenteral Drug Association (EA)
PdA	Partei der Arbeit [*Labor Party*] [*Switzerland Political party*] (PPE)
PDA	Parti Democratico da Angola [*Democratic Party of Angola*] [*Political party*]
PDA	Partido Democratico Arubano [*Democratic Party of Aruba*] [*Political party*] (EY)
PDA	Parti Dolonti Applicandum [*Apply to Painful Part*] [*Pharmacy*] (ROG)
PDA	Partit Democrata d'Andorra [*Andorran Democratic Party*] [*Political party*] (PPW)
Pd'A	Partito d'Azione [*Action Party*] [*Italy Political party*] (PPE)
PDA	Parts Disposal Area (MCD)
PDA	Party of Democratic Action [*Bosnia-Herzegovina*] [*Political party*] (EY)
PDA	Party of Democratic Action [*Serbia*] [*Political party*] (BUAC)
PDA	Pasadena Energy [*Vancouver Stock Exchange symbol*]
PDA	Patent Ductus Arteriosus [*Cardiology*]
PDA	Patient Data Automation
PDA	Patient Distress Alarm (STED)

PDA	Payroll Deduction Authorization (MCD)
PDA	Peak Distribution Analyzer
PDA	Pediatric Allergy
PdA	Pediatric Allergy [Medicine] (DMAA)
PDA	Pentadecanoic Acid [Organic chemistry]
PDA	Percent Defective Allowable (MHDB)
PDA	Permanent Duty Assignment [Air Force] (AFM)
PDA	Personal Data Assistant
PDA	Personal Deposit Account [Banking]
PDA	Personal Digital Assistant [Computer science]
PDA	Petrol Dealers' Association [British]
PDA	Phenylenediamine [Chemistry]
PDA	Philadelphia Dance Alliance
PDA	Phorbol Diacetate [Organic chemistry]
PDA	Photodiode Array [Instrumentation]
PDA	Photographic Dealers' Association [British] (BI)
PDA	Photon Detector Assembly (MCD)
PDA	Physical Device Address [Computer science] (IBMDP)
PDA	Piperidinedicarboxylic Acid [Organic chemistry]
PDA	Pisatin Demethylase [An enzyme]
PDA	Point Density Analysis [Mathematics]
PDA	Point Director Array
PDA	Pointing Device Adapter [Computer science]
PDA	Poise Distribution Amplifier (AFM)
PDA	Polarization Diversity Array
PDA	Polydiacetylene [Organic chemistry]
PDA	Poly(dimethylacrylamide) [Organic chemistry]
PDA	Ponta Delgada [Azores] [Seismograph station code, US Geological Survey] (SEIS)
PDA	Population and Community Development Association [Thailand] (BUAC)
PDA	Population Drainage Area [Civil Defense]
PDA	Portable Diagnostic Analyzer (SSD)
PDA	Post Acceleration (IAA)
PDA	Post-Deflection Accelerator (DEN)
PDA	Post-Delivery Availability [Military] (NVT)
PDA	Post-Design Analysis
PDA	Posterior Descending Artery [Anatomy] (DAVI)
PDA	Potato Dextrose Agar [Culture media]
PDA	Pour Dire Adieu [To Say Farewell] [On visiting cards] [French]
PDA	Power Distribution Assembly (KSC)
PDA	Precision Drive Axis (KSC)
PDA	Predelivery Acceptance Test [NASA]
PDA	Predialyzed Human Albumin [Medicine] (MAE)
PDA	Predicted Drift Angle [Navigation]
PDA	Predocketed Application (NRCH)
PDA	Pregnancy Discrimination Act [An amendment to Title VII of the Civil Rights Act of 1964] (PAZ)
PDA	Pregnancy Discrimination Act of 1978 (WYGK)
PDA	Preliminary Design Acceptance (NRCH)
PDA	Preliminary Design Activity (LAIN)
PDA	Preliminary Design Approval [or Authorization] (NRCH)
PDA	Preliminary Design Assessment [Nuclear energy] (NRCH)
PDA	Present Duty Assignment Option [Military]
PDA	Principal Decision Authority (DOMA)
PDA	Principal Deputy for Acquistion [Army] (RDA)
PDA	Principal Development Activity [Navy]
PDA	Principal Development Authority (MCD)
PDA	Principal Diagonal Artery [Anatomy] (DAVI)
PDA	Principal DOD Executive (AAGC)
PDA	Private Doctors of America [Defunct] (EA)
PDA	Probabilistic Decision Algorithm [Artificial intelligence job performance aid] [Army]
PDA	Probability Discrete Automata (IEEE)
PDA	Probability Distribution Analyzer [Statistics]
PDA	Probably Disappointed Again (PCM)
PDA	Probate, Divorce, and Admiralty [British] (DLA)
PDA	Problem Determination Aid (EECA)
PDA	Processor and Distribution Assembly [Viking lander analysis equipment] [NASA]
PDA	Procurement Defense Agencies [DoD]
PDA	Product Departure Authorization
PDA	Professional Designers' Association (BUAC)
PDA	Professional Drivers Association
PDA	Program Developing Agency [Military] (CAAL)
PDA	Prolonged Depolarizing Afterpotential [Neurophysiology]
PDA	Propanediamine [Organic chemistry]
PDA	Propellant Drain Area (NASA)
PDA	Property Disposal Account [Military] (NG)
PDA	Property Disposal Agent [Military] (NG)
PDA	Property Disposition Authorization
PDA	Proposed Development Approach [Navy]
PDA	Propylenediamine [Organic chemistry]
PDA	Prospectors' and Developers' Association [Canada]
PDA	Prototype Development Associate
PDA	Public Display of Affection [Slang]
PDA	Puerto Inirida [Colombia] [Airport symbol] (OAG)
PDA	Pulmonary Disease Anemia [Medicine] (STED)
PDA	Pulse Demodulation Analysis
PDA	Pulse Distribution Amplifier
PDA	Pump Distributors Association [British] (DBA)
PDA	Pump Distributors Association of Great Britain (BUAC)
PDA	Pump Drive Assembly
PDA	Pushdown Automation [Computer science] (HGAA)
PDAAP	Plume Data Analysis of Advanced Propellants (MCD)

PDAB	Para-(Dimethylamino)benzaldehyde [Organic chemistry]
PDAB	Physical Disability Appeals Board [Military] (AFM)
PDAC	Professional Development Advisory Committee [American Occupational Therapy Association]
PDAC	Prospectors and Developers Association of Canada (EAIO)
PDAD	Photodiode Array Detector [Spectrophotometry]
PDAD	Probate, Divorce, and Admiralty Division [Legal] [British] (ROG)
PDAFSC	Projected Duty Air Force Specialty Code (AFM)
PDAID	Problem Determination Aid [Computer science] (MDG)
PDAK	Party of Democratic Action for Kosovo [Serbia] [Political party] (BUAC)
PDA-KM	Party of Democratic Action of Kosovo-Metohija [Serbia] [Political party] (EY)
PDalCM	College Misericordia, Dallas, PA [Library symbol Library of Congress] (LCLS)
PDAM	Periodontal Disease-Associated Microbiotae [Dentistry]
PD & C	Postural Drainage and Clapping [Medicine] (DAVI)
PD & D	Product Design & Development [Radnor, PA] [A publication]
PD & E	Provisioning Documentation and Effort [Military] (AFIT)
PD & P	Postural Drainage and Percussion [Medicine] (DAVI)
PD&P	Project Definition and Planning (CIST)
PD & PL	Property Damage and Public Liability [Insurance] (IIA)
PD & R	Policy Development and Research
PD & RS	Payload Deployment and Retrieval Subsystem [NASA] (NASA)
PDanMHi	Montour County Historical Society, Danville, PA [Library symbol Library of Congress] (LCLS)
PDanSH	Danville State Hospital, Danville, PA [Library symbol Library of Congress] (LCLS)
PDAP	Palmer Drug Abuse Program (DMAA)
PDAP	Programmable Digital Autopilot (MCD)
PDAP	Provincial Development Assistance Program [Agency for International Development]
PDAP	Publication Design and Ad Placement (DGA)
PDAR	Parts Drawing Approval Request (MCD)
PD/AR	Photosensitivity Dermatitis and Actinic Reticuloid Syndrome [Medicine] (DMAA)
PDAR	Preferential Departure [Aviation] (DA)
PDAR	Preferential Departure and Arrival Route [FAA] (TAG)
PDAR	Producibility Design Analysis Report (AAG)
PDARR	Program Description and Requirements [NASA] (NASA)
PDARR	Production Drawing and Assembly Release Record (AAG)
PDA-S	Party of Democratic Action of the Sandjak [Serbia] [Political party] (EY)
PDAS	Photo Data Analysis System [Navy]
PDAS	Photodiode Array Spectrophotometer [Marine science] (OSRA)
PDAS	Plant Data Acquisition System (NRCH)
PDAS	[A] Popular Dictionary of Australian Slang [A publication]
PDAS	Portable Data Acquisition System (MCD)
PDAS	Process Design Analysis System (CIST)
PDAS	Programmable Data Acquisition System (IDOE)
PDASD	Principal Deputy Assistant Secretary of Defense
PDate	Pay Date
PDATE	Production Date [Computer science]
PDAV	Parkinson's Disease Association of Victoria [Australia]
P (Day)	Production Day [Army] (AABC)
Pd B	Bachelor of Pedagogy
PDB	Packard Data Bank (EA)
PDB	Para-Dichlorobenzene [Insecticide for moths, etc.]
PDB	Partei der Deutschsprachigen Belgier [Party of German-Speaking Belgians] [Political party] (PPW)
PDB	Pedro Bay [Alaska] [Airport symbol] (OAG)
PDB	Pee Dee Belemnite [An isotopic standard for oxygen and carbon]
PDB	Pentadecylbenzene [Organic chemistry]
PDB	Performance Data Base (GAVI)
PDB	Performance Data Book (NASA)
PDB	Periodical Directories and Bibliographies [A publication]
PDB	Personality Data Base
PDB	Phorbol Dibutyrate [Also, PDBu] [Organic chemistry]
PDB	Phosphorus-Dissolving Bacteria [Microbiology]
PDB	Piedmont Bancorp [AMEX symbol] (TTSB)
PDB	Piedmont Bancorp, Inc. [AMEX symbol] (SAG)
PDB	Pierce's Disease Bacterium [Plant pathology]
PDB	Plant Damage Bin [Environmental science] (COE)
PDB	Plasma Diagnostic Base
PDB	Police Discipline Board [New South Wales, Australia]
PDB	Positive Displacement Blower
PDB	Potato Dextrose Broth [Microbiology]
PDB	Power Distribution Box (NASA)
PDB	President's Daily Brief
PDB	Price Decontrol Board [Post-World War II]
PDB	Primary Data Bus [Computer science]
PDB	Process Descriptor Base [Telecommunications] (TEL)
PDB	Process Display Data Base [Computer science] (ECII)
PDB	Program Definition Block (NITA)
PDB	Project Development Brochure [Military]
PDB	Protein Data Bank [Brookhaven National Laboratory] [Information service or system] (CRD)
PDB	Psychic Detective Bureau (EA)
PDBA	Personnel Database Application (MCD)
PDBA/SIPM	Personnel Database Application / Student Instructor Performance Module (DNAB)
PDBH	Production Broach (AAG)
PDBIN	Processor Data Bus In (MHDI)
PDBM	Pulse Delay Binary Modulation (MCD)
PDBMI	Periodical Directories and Bibliographies Master Index [A publication]

PDBP .... Powered Disposal Bomb Pod (AAG)
PDBR .... Page-Directory Base Register [Computer science] (BYTE)
PDBU .... Pesticides Documentation Bulletin
PDBu .... Phorbol Dibutyrate [Also, PDB] [Organic chemistry]
PDBz .... Phorbol Dibenzoate [Organic chemistry]
PDC .... Community College of Philadelphia, Philadelphia, PA [OCLC symbol] (OCLC)
PDC .... Mueo [New Caledonia] [Airport symbol] (OAG)
PDC .... Pacific Defense College (CINC)
PDC .... Package Design Council [New York, NY] (EA)
PDC .... Pacte Democratica per Catalunya [Democratic Pact for Catalonia] [Spain Political party] (PPE)
PDC .... Page Description Communications [Microsoft Corp.] (PCM)
PDC .... Paper Distribution Centers
PDC .... Paper Distribution Council (EA)
PDC .... Parallel Data Communicator (AAG)
PDC .... Parallel Data Controller
PDC .... Parametric Defense Coverage
PDC .... Parti Democrate Chretien [Christian Democratic Party] [Burundi] [Political party]
PDC .... Parti Democrate-Chretien Suisse [Christian Democratic Party of Switzerland] [Political party] (PPE)
PDC .... Parti des Democrates Camerounais [Political party] (EY)
PDC .... Partido da Democracia Cristao [Christian Democratic Party] [Portugal Political party] (PPW)
PDC .... Partido Democracia Cristiana [Christian Democratic Party] [Guatemala] [Political party] (PPW)
PDC .... Partido Democrata Cristiano [Christian Democratic Party] [Peru] [Political party] (PPW)
PDC .... Partido Democrata Cristiano [Christian Democratic Party] [Paraguay] [Political party] (PPW)
PDC .... Partido Democrata Cristiano [Christian Democratic Party] [Costa Rica] [Political party] (PPW)
PDC .... Partido Democrata Cristiano [Christian Democratic Party] [Honduras] [Political party] (PPW)
PDC .... Partido Democrata Cristiano [Christian Democratic Party] [Bolivia] [Political party] (PPW)
PDC .... Partido Democrata Cristiano [Christian Democratic Party] [Panama] [Political party] (PPW)
PDC .... Partido Democrata Cristiano [Christian Democratic Party] [El Salvador] [Political party] (PPW)
PDC .... Partido Democrata de Confianza Nacional [Nicaragua] [Political party] (EY)
PDC .... Partido Democratico Cristao [Christian Democratic Party] [Brazil Political party]
PDC .... Partido Democratico Cristiano [Christian Democratic Party] [Chile] [Political party] (PPW)
PDC .... Partido Democratico Cristiano [Christian Democratic Party] [Argentina Political party] (PPW)
PDC .... Partisan Defence Committee (BUAC)
PDC .... Partito della Democrazia Cristiana [Christian Democratic Party] [Italy Political party]
PDC .... Partners for Democratic Change [An association] (EA)
PDC .... Passive Data Collection
PDC .... Pediatric Cardiology [Medical specialty] (DHSM)
PDC .... Pentadecylcatechol [An allergen]
PDC .... Per Diem, Travel and Transportation Allowance Committee for Departments of the Army, Navy, and Air Force
PDC .... Performance Data Computer
PDC .... Personnel Data Card
PDC .... Personnel Distribution Command
PDC .... Peru Debt Campaign (BUAC)
PDC .... Petroleum Development Corp. (EFIS)
PDC .... Philosophy Documentation Center (EA)
PDC .... Photo-Data Card [Trademark] [Computer science]
PDC .... Photonuclear Data Center [National Institute of Standards and Technology]
PDC .... Pieve Di Cadore [Italy] [Seismograph station code, US Geological Survey Closed] (SEIS)
PDC .... Piston-Driven Compaction (MCD)
PDC .... Plastic Dielectric Capacitor
PDC .... Pneumatic Damping Control
PDC .... Polaris Documentation Control [Missiles]
PDC .... Policy Determination Committee (AAG)
PDC .... Polycrystalline Diamond Compact [Well drilling technology]
PDC .... Polycrystalline Diamond Compact Drill Bit
PDC .... Polystyrene Dielectric Capacitor
PDC .... Population Documentation Center [Food and Agriculture Organization] [United Nations Information service or system] (IID)
PDC .... Portable Data Carrier
PDC .... Portable Data Communications [British]
PDC .... Position Depth Charge
PDC .... Power Distribution and Control
PDC .... Power Distribution Cubiale (NATG)
PDC .... Practice Depth Charge
PDC .... Prairie Du Chien, WI [Location identifier FAA] (FAAL)
PDC .... Predecessors and Defunct Companies (NITA)
PDC .... Predefined Command (MCD)
PDC .... Predeparture Check [Aviation] (AIA)
PDC .... Pre-Departure Clearance [FAA] (TAG)
PDC .... Predetection Combining (IAA)
PDC .... Predocketed Construction (NRCH)
PDC .... Preliminary Diagnostic Clinic
PDC .... Premission Documentation Change [NASA] (KSC)

PDC .... Premium and Dispersion Credits [Insurance]
PDC .... Prescott Development Corp. [Vancouver Stock Exchange symbol]
PDC .... Presely Cos. 'A' [NYSE symbol] (TTSB)
PDC .... Presley Co. [NYSE symbol] (SPSG)
PDC .... Pressure Die Casting [Commercial firm British]
PDC .... Prevention of Deterioration Center [Defunct] (EA)
PDC .... Price Decontrol Board [Post-World War II] [A publication] (DLA)
PDC .... Private Diagnostic Clinic
PDC .... Probability of Detection and Conversion [Military]
PDC .... Procurement Document Change (NASA)
PDC .... Production Decision Criteria
PDC .... Production Drawing Control
PDC .... Productivity and Development Center [Philippines] (BUAC)
PDC .... Proficiency Data Card [Army]
PDC .... Program Data Cards (OICC)
PDC .... Program Data Coordinator (MCD)
PDC .... Program Development Computer (COE)
PDC .... Programmable Digital Controller (PDAA)
PDC .... Programmes Directorate Committee [British]
PDC .... Project Data Card
PDC .... Project Data Control (MCD)
PDC .... Prolonged Detention Care (CPH)
PDC .... Prosthetic Distribution Center [Veterans Administration]
PDC .... Psychodevelopment Checklist [Psychology] (DAVI)
PDC .... Publications Distribution Center [Military] (AFM)
PDC .... Public Dividend Capital (PDAA)
PDC .... Public Documents Commission [Government agency]
PDC .... Publishers' Data Center, Inc.
PDC .... Pulse-Duration Commutator
PDC .... Pure Direct Current [Electronics] (IAA)
PDC .... Pyridinium Dichromate [Organic chemistry]
PDC .... Pyrotechnic Devices Checker
PDC .... Pyruvate Decarboxylase [An enzyme]
PDC .... Pyruvate Dehydrogenase Complex [Also, PDHC] [Biochemistry]
PDC .... Single Paper Double Cotton [Wire insulation] (AAG)
PDCA .... Painting and Decorating Contractors of America (EA)
PDCA .... Pile Driving Contractors Association (NTPA)
PDCA .... Pioneer Dairymen's Club of America (EA)
PDCA .... Plan-Do-Check-Act [Medicine] (DMAA)
PDCA .... Pug Dog Club of America (EA)
PDCA .... Purebred Dairy Cattle Association (EA)
PDCA .... United States Professional Diving Coaches Association (EA)
PDCAU .... Pete Duel - Clube da Amizade do Universo [Pete Duel Universal Friendship Club - PDUFC] (EAIO)
PDCC .... Print and Drawing Council of Canada [1976] (NGC)
PDCD .... Primary Degenerative Cerebral Disease [Medicine] (DMAA)
PDCG .... Partido Democracia Cristiana Guatemalteca [Guatemalan Christian Democratic Party] [Political party] (PPW)
PDCH .... Parti Democratique Chretien d'Haiti [Political party] (EY)
PDCI .... Parti Democratique de la Cote-D'Ivoire [Democratic Party of the Ivory Coast] [Political party] (PPW)
Pdck .... Probability of Detection Conversion and Kill [for an interceptor system] [Military]
PDCL .... Provisioning Data Check List [NASA] (KSC)
PDCN .... Partido Democratico de Cooperacion Nacional [Democratic Party of National Cooperation] [Guatemala] [Political party]
PDCN .... Public Data Communications Network [Library science]
PDCO .... Patterson Dental [NASDAQ symbol] (TTSB)
PDCO .... Patterson Dental Co. [NASDAQ symbol] (SAG)
PDCO .... Property Disposal Contracting Officer [Military]
PDCP .... Pilot's Display Control Panel
PDCP .... Private Development Corp. of the Philippines
PDCPD .... Polydicyclopentadiene [Organic chemistry]
PDCR .... Project Data Compliance Report (MCD)
PDCR .... Proprietary Data Control Record (NASA)
PDCRC .... Periodontal Disease Clinical Research Center [State University of New York at Buffalo] [Research center] (RCD)
PDCS .... Parallel Digital Computing System
PDCS .... Partito Democratico Cristiano Sammarinese [Christian Democratic Party of San Marino] [Political party] (PPE)
PDCS .... Performance Data Computer System (MCD)
PDCS .... Power Distribution and Control System [or Subsystem] [NASA] (NASA)
PDCS .... Processing Distribution and Control System
PDCS .... Programmable Data Collection System [Military] (CAAL)
PDCS .... Propellant Development & Characterization Subcommittee [Joint Army, Navy, NASA, Air Force]
PDCS .... Prototype Die Casting Service
PD-CSE .... Pulsed Doppler Cross-Sectional Echocardiography [Medicine] (DMAA)
PDCU .... Plotting Display Control Unit
PDCU .... Power Distribution and Control Unit
Pd D .... Doctor of Pedagogy
PDD .... Package Designation and Description File (DOMA)
PDD .... Pancreatic Dorsal Duct [Anatomy]
PDD .... Participacion Democratica de Tzquierda [Chile] [Political party] (EY)
PDD .... Past Due Date
PDD .... Pervasive Developmental Disorder [Medicine]
PDD .... Phenyldodecane [Organic chemistry]
PDD .... Phorbol Didecanoate [Organic chemistry]
PDD .... Physical Damage Division [Navy]
PDD .... Physical Defense Division [Army]
PDD .... Platinum Diamminodichloride [Cisplatin and cis-platinum] [Antineoplastic drug] (DAVI)
PDD .... Plotting Data Distributor (MCD)

PDD .... Post Dialing Delay [Telecommunications] (TEL)
PDD .... Precision Depth Digitizer [Oceanography]
PDD .... Preferred Delivery Date (AFM)
PDD .... Preliminary Design and Development (MCD)
PDD .... Premenstrual Dysphoric Disorder [Proposed psychiatric diagnosis]
PDD .... Premodulation Processor - Deep Space - Data
PDD .... Presidential Decision Directive
PDD .... Primary Degenerative Dementia [Medicine]
PDD .... Principal Distribution Depot [DoD]
PDD .... Priority Delivery Date (AFM)
PDD .... Probability Density Distribution [Statistics]
PDD .... Procurement Description Data [DoD]
PDD .... Professional Development Division [American Occupational Therapy Association]
PDD .... Program Description Document [Military] (CAAL)
PDD .... Program Design Data
PDD .... Program Dimension Drawing (MCD)
PDD .... Program Directive Document (RDA)
PDD .... Projected Data Display
PDD .... Projected Decision Date (NRCH)
PDD .... Prospective Decision Date (NRCH)
PDD .... Provisioning Description Data
PDD .... Public Documents Department [Government Printing Office]
PDD .... Pulse Delay Device
PDD .... Puy-De-Dome [France] [Seismograph station code, US Geological Survey Closed] (SEIS)
PDD .... Pyridoxine-Deficient Diet (MAE)
PDDA .... Power Driver Decontamination Apparatus (NATG)
PDDAIO .... Parts for Direct Discrete Analog Input/Output (MCD)
PDDB .... Phenododecinium [or Phenoxyethyldimethyl-dodecylammonium] Bromide [Antiseptic]
PDDB .... Product Definition Database (MCD)
PDDC .... Proceed Directly on Course [Aviation] (FAAC)
PDDD .... Program Demonstration and Development Division [ACTION]
PDDF .... Propargyl(dideaza)folic Acid [Biochemistry]
PDDGM ...... Past District Deputy Grand Master [Freemasonry]
PDDI .... Product Definition Data Interface (MCD)
PD Div'l Ct... Probate, Divorce, and Admiralty Divisional Court [England] (DLA)
PDDL .... Perpendicular Diffraction Delay Line (PDAA)
PDDLS .... Post D-Day Logistic Support [Army] (AABC)
PDDM .... Disciples of the Divine Master [Roman Catholic women's religious order]
PDDM .... Pious Disciples of the Divine Master (TOCD)
PDD/NOS .... Pervasive Developmental Disorder, Not Otherwise Specified
PDD/RDD .... Priority Delivery Date/Required Delivery Date (AFM)
PDDS .... Parasitic Disease Drug Service (MAE)
PDDS .... Program Definition Data Sheet
PDE .... Page-Directory Entry [Computer science] (BYTE)
PDE .... Pandie Pandie [Australia Airport symbol Obsolete] (OAG)
PDE .... Parade
Pde .... Parade [Record label]
PDE .... Paroxysmal Dyspnea on Exertion [Medicine]
PDE .... Partei fuer Deutschland und Europa [Party for Germany and Europe] [Germany Political party] (PPW)
PDE .... Partial Differential Equation
PDE .... Paste Down Ends [Graphic arts] (DGA)
PDE .... Pediatric Endocrinology [Medical specialty] (DHSM)
PDE .... Personnel Development and Education (MCD)
PDE .... Phosphatidyl(dimethyl)ethanolamine [Biochemistry]
PDE .... Phosphodiesterase [An enzyme]
PDE .... Pilot's Discrete Encoder
PDE .... Plain Deckle Edges [Graphic arts] (DGA)
PDE .... Position-Determining Equipment
PDE .... Preliminary Determination of Epicenter [Seismology]
PDE .... Pride Resources Ltd. [Vancouver Stock Exchange symbol]
PDE .... Principal DOD [Department of Defense] Executive
PDE .... Producers' Durable Equipment (GFGA)
PDE .... Production Design Engineers
PDE .... Professional Development Education [Military] (RDA)
PDE .... Professional Development in Education (WDAA)
PDE .... Projectile Development Establishment [British]
PDE .... Propellant Disposition Effects
PDE .... Prospective Data Element [Army] (AABC)
PDE .... Pulsed Doppler Echocardiography [Medicine] (DMAA)
PDEA .... Phenyldiethanolamine [Organic chemistry]
P de Ancha... Petrus de Ancharano [Deceased, 1416] [Authority cited in pre-1607 legal work] (DSA)
P de B .... Petrus de Bellapertica [Deceased, 1308] [Authority cited in pre-1607 legal work] (DSA)
P de Bp .... Petrus de Bellapertica [Deceased, 1308] [Authority cited in pre-1607 legal work] (DSA)
PDECS .... Portable Detector and Cueing System
PDED .... Partial Double Error Detecting (NITA)
PDED .... Partial Double Error Detection
PDED .... Program Development and Evaluation Division [Environmental Protection Agency] (GFGA)
PDEI .... Phosphodiesterase Inhibitor [Biochemistry]
PDEL .... Partial Differential Equation Language [Computer science]
P de L .... Paulus de Liazaris [Deceased, 1356] [Authority cited in pre-1607 legal work] (DSA)
PDELAN ...... Partial Differential Equation Language [Computer science] (CSR)
PDELB .... Plumbers and Drainers' Examination and Licensing Board [Queensland, Australia]
PDEM .... Personal Dust Exposure Monitor (PDAA)

P de Orfi...... Petrus de Orfila [Deceased, 1307] [Authority cited in pre-1607 legal work] (DSA)
PDEP .... Preliminary Draft Equipment Publication (MCD)
PDEQ .... Profile of DARCOM Environmental Quality (MCD)
PDES .... Phase Image of Poly(diethylsiloxane) [Organic chemistry]
PDES .... Preliminary Draft Environmental Statement (NRCH)
PDES .... Product Data Exchange Specification (NITA)
PDES .... Product Data Exchange using STEP [Sequentially Timed Events Plotting]
PDES .... Product Definition Exchange Specification [Army]
PDES .... Pulse-Doppler Elevation Scan (PDAA)
P de Sal ..... Petrus de Salinis [Flourished, 13th century] [Authority cited in pre-1607 legal work] (DSA)
P de Sam ... Petrus de Sampsone [Flourished, 1246-58] [Authority cited in pre-1607 legal work] (DSA)
P de Samp... Petrus de Sampsone [Flourished, 1246-58] [Authority cited in pre-1607 legal work] (DSA)
P Det .... Port Detachment [British military] (DMA)
PDET.......... Post-Diapause Eclosion Time [Entomology]
PDET.......... Probability of Detection, Evaluation, and Transfer (MCD)
PDEX .... Pro-Dex, Inc. [NASDAQ symbol] (NQ)
PDF............ Hancock [John] Patriot Premium Dividend Fund I [NYSE symbol] (SAG)
PDF............ John Hancock Patr Prem Dv Fd [NYSE symbol] (TTSB)
PDF............ LAR Transregional, Linhas Aereas Regionais SA [Portugal ICAO designator] (FAAC)
PDF............ Pacific Dentistry Association (BUAC)
PDF............ Paget's Disease Foundation (EA)
PDF............ Pair Distribution Function [Physical chemistry]
PDF............ Pakistan Democratic Front
PDF............ Panama Defense Forces [Later, Public Forces]
PDF............ Parkinson's Disease Foundation (EA)
PDF............ Particle Distribution Function
PDF............ Parti Democrate Francais [French Democratic Party] [Political party] (PPW)
PDF............ Passive Direction Finding
PDF............ Pavement Depth Factor (ADA)
PDF............ Peace Development Fund (EA)
PDF............ Pele Defense Fund (EA)
PDF............ People's Democratic Force [The Bahamas] [Political party] (EY)
PDF............ Peritoneal Dialysis Fluid [Medicine] (DMAA)
PDF............ Planar Deformation Feature [Geology]
PDF............ Planet Drum Foundation (EA)
PDF............ Plant Design Factor [Nuclear energy] (NRCH)
PDF............ Plant Design Flood [Nuclear energy] (GFGA)
PDF............ Platform Independent File Format [Computer science]
PDF............ Point Detonating Fuse (IAA)
PDF............ Point Detonating Fuze [Army]
PDF............ Pooled Development Funds [Economics]
PDF............ Popular Defence Forces [Sudan] [Political party]
PDF............ Popular Democratic Front [Jordan] [Political party]
PDF............ Porsche Dual-Function Transmission [Automotive engineering]
PDF............ Portable Document File [Computer science] (PCM)
PDF............ Portable Document Format [Computer science]
pdf............ Portable Document Format [Computer science]
PDF............ Post Defense Force
PDF............ Post Detection Filter [Telecommunications] (TEL)
PDF............ Powder Diffraction File (DICI)
PDF............ Power Diffraction File (NITA)
PDF............ Primordial Density Fluctuation [Cosmology]
PDF............ Principal Direction of Fire [Military]
PDF............ Probability Density Function [Statistics]
PDF............ Probability Distribution Function [Statistics]
PDF............ Processor Defined Function
PDF............ Production and Distribution of Foodstuffs [British]
PDF............ Program Data File
PDF............ Program Data Form [Army]
PDF............ Program Development Facility [Computer science] (MHDI)
PDF............ Project Design Flood (NRCH)
PDF............ Protected Difference Fat (OA)
PDF............ Pyruvate Dehydrogenase (DMAA)
PDFC .... Premature Dead Female Child (DAVI)
PDFCS .... Pennsylvania Dutch Folk Culture Society (EA)
PDFD .... Predemonstration Fusion Device
PDFD .... Pulsed Doppler Frequency Diversity (NG)
PDFES .... Pitch-Synchronous Digital Feature Extraction System (PDAA)
PDFG .... Planar Distributed Function Generator (PDAA)
PDFG .... Platelet-Derived Growth Factor [Endocrinology] (DAVI)
PDFLP .... Popular Democratic Front for the Liberation of Palestine
PDFM.......... Phillips and Drew Fund Management [England] [British]
PDFRR........ Program Directors Flight Readiness Review [NASA] (KSC)
PDFWPR...... Physical Disabilities Fieldwork Performance Report [Occupational therapy]
PDG .... Padang [Indonesia] [Airport symbol] (OAG)
PDG .... Padding
PDG .... Parachute Drop Glider
PDG .... Paradigm (WGA)
PDG .... Parkinsonism-Dementia Complex of Guam [Medicine] (DMAA)
PDG .... Parti Democratique de Guinee [Democratic Party of Guinea] [Political party] (PPW)
PDG .... Parti Democratique Gabonais [Gabonese Democratic Party] [Political party] (PPW)
PDG .... Passive Defense Group (MUGU)
PDG .... Patent Documentation Group (DIT)
PDG .... PDG Remediation, Inc. [Associated Press] (SAG)

PDG .... Personalistic Discussion Group - Eastern Division (EA)
PDG .... Phosphate-Dependent Glutaminase (STED)
PDG .... Phosphogluconate Dehydrogenase [*Organic chemistry*] (MAH)
PDG .... Placer Dome, Inc. [*NYSE symbol Toronto Stock Exchange symbol Vancouver Stock Exchange symbol*] (SPSG)
PDG .... Precision Drop Glider [*Army*]
PDG .... Pregnanediol Glucuronide [*Endocrinology*]
PDG .... President Directeur General [*President Director General*] [*French*]
PDG .... Pretty Damn Good
PDG .... Production Development Group (IAA)
PDG .... Professional Dyers Guild [*Defunct*]
PDG .... Program Documentation Generator [*Computer science*] (MHDI)
PDG .... Programs Development Group (MUGU)
PDG .... Proposal Development Group [*Aerospace*] (AAG)
PDG .... Pyruvate Dehydrogenase (DB)
PDGA .... Professional Disc Golf Association
PDGA .... Pteroyldiglutamic Acid [*Pharmacology*]
PDGDL .... Plasma Dynamics and Gaseous Discharge Laboratory [*MIT*] (MCD)
PDGE .... Partido Democratico de Guinea Ecuatorial [*Democratic Party of Equatorial Guinea*] [*Political party*] (EY)
PDGE .... PDG Environmental [*NASDAQ symbol*] (TTSB)
PDGE .... PDG Environmental, Inc. [*NASDAQ symbol*] (SAG)
PDG En .... PDG Environmental, Inc. [*Associated Press*] (SAG)
PDGF .... Platelet-Derived Growth Factor [*Genetics*]
PDGFA .... Platelet-Derived Growth Factor [*Medicine*] (DMAA)
PDGFR .... Platelet-Derived Growth Factor Receptor [*Genetics*]
PDGMS .... Peabody Developmental Gross Motor Scale
PDGS .... PDG Remediation [*NASDAQ symbol*] (TTSB)
PDGS .... PDG Remediation, Inc. [*NASDAQ symbol*] (SAG)
PDGS .... Precision Delivery Glider System
P-DGs .... Presidents-Directeurs Generaux
PDGS .... Probe Drill Guidance System
PDGS .... Product Design Graphics System [*Prime Computer Ltd.*] [*Software package*] (NCC)
PDGSW .... PDG Remediation Wrrt [*NASDAQ symbol*] (TTSB)
PDGW .... Principle Directorate of Guided Weapons [*British*] (SAA)
PDGXT .... Predischarge Graded Exercise Test [*Cardiology*] (DAVI)
PDH .... Packaged Disaster Hospital [*Public Health Service*]
PDH .... Passive Defense Handbook [*Navy*] (MCD)
PDH .... Past Dental History
PDH .... Phosphate Dehydrogenase (MAE)
PDH .... Planned Derated Hours [*Electronics*] (IEEE)
PDH .... Pocket Dosimeter High (NAKS)
PDH .... Pyruvate Dehydrogenase [*An enzyme*]
PDH & DS ... Plant Data Handling and Display System [*Nuclear energy*] (NRCH)
PDHC .... Pyruvate Dehydrogenase Complex [*Biochemistry*]
PDHF .... Postdilution Hemofiltration [*Medicine*]
PDHL .... Peak Design Heat Loss (PDAA)
PdHO .... Pediatric Hematology-Oncology (STED)
PDHV-RDA ... Parti Democratique de la Haute Volta-Rassemblement Democratique Africain [*Democratic Party of Upper Volta-African Democratic Rally*]
PDI .... Pain Disability Index [*Medicine*] (DMAA)
PDI .... Palmer Drought Index
PDI .... Panel Data Interface [*Computer science*] (IAA)
PDI .... Paradise Island Airlines, Inc. [*ICAO designator*] (FAAC)
PDI .... Partai Demokrasi Indonesia [*Indonesian Democratic Party*] [*Political party*] (PPW)
PDI .... Partial Delivery Injection [*Materials science*]
PDI .... Parti Democratique de l'Independance [*Democratic Independence Party*] [*Morocco*] [*Political party*]
PDI .... Partito Democratica Italiana [*Italian Democratic Party*] [*Political party*] (PPE)
PDI .... Payload Data Interleaver [*NASA*] (NASA)
PDI .... Percentage Difference Index
PDI .... Perfect Digital Invariant (OA)
PDI .... Periodontal Disease Index [*Dentistry*] (DMAA)
PDI .... Personal Disposable Income [*Economics*]
PDI .... Pictorial Deviation Indicator (AAG)
PDI .... Picture Description Instruction [*Telecommunications*]
PDI .... Pilot Direction Indicator [*Electronic communications*]
PDI .... Plan-Do Intergration [*Medicine*] (DMAA)
PDI .... Plastic Drum Institute (NTPA)
PDI .... Plumbing and Drainage Institute (EA)
PDI .... Porto D'Ischia [*Italy*] [*Seismograph station code, US Geological Survey Closed*] (SEIS)
PDI .... Post Detection Integration (MCD)
PDI .... Potential Determining Ions
PDI .... Power Dissipation Index (IAA)
PDI .... Powered Descent Initiation [*Aerospace*]
PDI .... Pre-Delivery Inspection (DCTA)
PDI .... Predeployment Inspection [*Navy*] (NVT)
PDI .... Premdor, Inc. [*Toronto Stock Exchange symbol*]
PDI .... Preschool Development Inventory [*Test*] (TMMY)
PDI .... Privately Developed Item (AAGC)
PDI .... Professional Development Institute [*Canada*]
PDI .... Program Design, Inc. [*Commercial firm*]
PDI .... Program with Developing Institutions (EA)
PDI .... Project Data Index [*Jet Propulsion Laboratory, NASA*]
PDI .... Protein Dispersibility Index [*Analytical chemistry*]
PDI .... Protein Disulfide-Isomerase [*An enzyme*]
PDI .... Psychiatric Diagnostic Interview [*Personality development test*] [*Psychology*]
PDI .... Psychological Distress Inventory [*Student personality test*]

PDI .... Psychomotor Development Index [*Bayley Scales of Infant Development*]
PDI .... Public Debt Interest (ADA)
PDI .... Public Demographics, Inc. (IID)
PDI .... Putnam Dividend Income [*NYSE symbol*] (SPSG)
Pdi .... Transdiaphragmatic [*Pressure*]
PDIAL .... Public Dialup Internet Access List [*Computer science*] (CDE)
PDIC .... Periodic (AFM)
PDIC .... Professional Driver Improvement Course
PDIE .... Phosphodiesterase (DMAA)
PDIF .... Putnam Dividend Income Fund [*Associated Press*] (SAG)
PDII .... Pusat Dokumentasi dan Informasi Ilmiah [*Indonesian Center for Scientific Documentation and Information*] [*Information service or system*] (IID)
PDIIS .... Priority Defense Items Information System
PDIL .... Power-Dependent Insertion Limit [*Nuclear energy*] (NRCH)
PDIN .... Pusat Dokumentasi Ilmiah Nasional (NITA)
PDIO .... Parallel Digital Input/Output
PDIO .... Photodiode
P-DIOL .... Pregnanediol [*Biochemistry*]
PDIP .... Plastic Dual In-Line Packaging (AAEL)
PDIP .... Preflight Data Insertion Program (NVT)
PDIP .... Program Development Increment Package [*Military*]
PDIR .... Priority Disassembly and Inspection Report
PDIR .... Program Directive
PDIS .... Parts Dissection Information System
PDIS .... Payload Data Interleaver System [*NASA*] (MCD)
PDIS .... Pressure Differential Switch (IAA)
PDIS .... Product Description Information Standards [*or System*]
PDISCH .... Pump Discharge
PDISPL .... Positive Displacement [*Engineering*]
PDIT .... Provision for Deferred Income Tax
PDIUM .... Partito Democratico Italiano di Unita Monarchica [*Italian Democratic Party of Monarchical Unity*] [*Political party*] (PPE)
P Div .... Law Reports, Probate Division [*England*] [*A publication*] (DLA)
PDIWT .... Planning and Design Institute for Water Transportation [*China*] (BUAC)
PDJ .... Plaine Des Jarres [*South Vietnam*]
PDJ .... Precision Drill Jig
PDJB .... Precision Drill Jig Bushing
PD/JV .... Project Definition/Joint Validation (MCD)
PDK .... Atlanta [*Georgia*] De Kalb/Peachtree Airport [*Airport symbol Obsolete*] (OAG)
PDK .... Party of Democratic Kampuchea [*Cambodia*] [*Political party*] (BUAC)
PDK .... PDK Labs, Inc. [*Associated Press*] (SAG)
PDK .... Phase-Delay Keying [*Computer science*]
PDK .... Phi Delta Kappa [*Fraternity*]
PDK .... Phileleftheron Demokratikon Kendron [*Liberal Democratic Union*] [*Greek*] (PPE)
PDK .... Phileleftheron Demokratikon Komma [*Liberal Democratic Party*] [*Greek Political party*] (PPE)
PDK .... Poop Deck [*Naval engineering*]
PDK .... Promenade Deck [*of a ship*] (DS)
PDK .... Science Foods, Inc. [*AMEX symbol*] (SAG)
PDKL .... PDK Labs [*NASDAQ symbol*] (TTSB)
PDKL .... PDK Labs, Inc. [*NASDAQ symbol*] (SAG)
PDKLM .... PDK Labs Wrrt'C' [*NASDAQ symbol*] (TTSB)
PDKLP .... PDK Labs $0.49 Cv'A' Pfd [*NASDAQ symbol*] (TTSB)
PDL .... Page Description Language [*Computer graphics*]
PDL .... Partido Democrata Liberal [*Liberal Democratic Party*] [*Spain Political party*] (EY)
PDL .... Parts Deletion List (MSA)
PDL .... Parts Difference List (MCD)
PDL .... Parts Documentation List (MCD)
PDL .... Party of Democratic Left [*Slovakia*] [*Political party*] (BUAC)
PDL .... Pass Down the Line [*Book*] [*Navy*] (MUGU)
PDL .... Patent Depository Library [*Designated by the Patent and Trademark Office*]
PDL .... People's Democracy of Laos [*Political party*] (VNW)
PDL .... Periodontal Ligament [*Dentistry*]
PDL .... Permanent Duty Location
PDL .... Photodissociation Dye LASER
PDL .... Picture Description Language [*Computer science*] (MHDI)
PDL .... Placer Development Ltd. [*Toronto Stock Exchange symbol Vancouver Stock Exchange symbol*]
PDL .... Pocket Dosimeter-Low (MCD)
PDL .... Polarization Diversity LIDAR
PDL .... Ponce De Leon
PDL .... Ponta Delgada [*Portugal*] [*Airport symbol*] (OAG)
PDL .... Poorly Differentiated Lymphocytic [*Oncology*]
PDL .... Population Doubling Level [*Cytology*]
PDL .... Portable Data Loader [*Aviation*]
pdl .... Poundal [*Unit of force*]
PDL .... Poverty Datum Line
PDL .... Precision Delay Line
PDL .... Presidential Realty Corp. [*AMEX symbol*] (SPSG)
PDL .... Print Definition Language [*Computer science*] (EECA)
PDL .... Procedure Definition Language [*Computer science*] (BUR)
PDL .... Procedure Distribution List (MCD)
PDL .... Process Design Language [*Computer science*] (MHDI)
PDL .... Procurement Data List
PDL .... Product Disaster Loans [*Small Business Administration*]
PDL .... Professional Development League (EA)
PDL .... Program Description Language (MCD)
PDL .... Program Design Language (NASA)

PDL............. Program Device Librarian [Computer science]
PDL............. Programmable Data Language (NITA)
PDL............. Programmed Digital Logic
PDL............. Project Document List
PDL............. Protocol Description Language [Telecommunications] (IAA)
PDL............. Publishers' Databases Ltd. [Publishing consortium] [British]
pdl............. Pudendal [Anatomy] (MAE)
PDL............. Pulsed Dye LASER
PDL............. Pumped Dye LASER
PDL............. Push Down List [Computer science] (MHDI)
PDL A......... Presidential Rlty Cl'A' [AMEX symbol] (TTSB)
PD(LAO)...... Public Defender (Legal Aid Office) [Australia]
PDL B......... Presidential Rlty Cl'B' [AMEX symbol] (TTSB)
PDLC.......... North American Palladium [NASDAQ symbol] (SAG)
PDLC.......... Partido Liberal de Cataluna [Liberal Democratic Party of Catalonia]
          [Political party] (PPW)
PDLC.......... Polymer Dispersed Liquid Crystal [Physical chemistry]
PDLC.......... Poorly Differentiated Lung Cancer [Medicine] (DMAA)
PDLCF........ North Amer Palladium [NASDAQ symbol] (TTSB)
PDLD......... Poorly Differentiated Lymphocytic-Diffuse [Oncology] (DMAA)
PDLF......... Pakistan Democratic Labour Federation (BUAC)
PDL/FT²...... Poundals per Square Foot
PDLI........... Protein Design Labs [NASDAQ symbol] (TTSB)
PDLI........... Protein Design Labs, Inc. [NASDAQ symbol] (SAG)
PDLL.......... Poorly Differentiated Lymphatic [or Lymphocytic] Lymphoma
          [Oncology]
PDLM......... Periodic Depot Level Maintenance
PDLM......... Planned Depot Level Maintenance (MCD)
PDLM......... Programmed Depot Level Maintenance [Air Force]
PDLN......... Poorly Differentiated Lymphocytic-Nodular [Oncology] (DMAA)
PDLP......... Pacific Dunlop Ltd. [NASDAQ symbol] (NQ)
PDLPY....... Pacific Dunlop Ltd. (MHDW)
PDLPY....... Pacific Dunlop Ltd. ADR [NASDAQ symbol] (TTSB)
PDLS......... Party of the Democratic Left of Slovakia [Former Czechoslovakia]
          [Political party] (EY)
PDL S/FT²... Poundal Seconds per Square Foot
PDLT......... P-Channel Depletion-Load Triode Inverter
PD/LT........ Program Design and Learning Tool (NITA)
Pd M......... Master of Pedagogy
PDM........... Partial Descriptive Method
PDM........... Parti Democratique Malgache [Malagasy Democratic Party]
PDM........... Partido de los Democratas Melillenses [Spanish North Africa]
          [Political party] (MENA)
PDM........... Patient Data Management
PDM........... Pendant Drop Method
PDM........... People's Democratic Movement [Papua New Guinea] [Political
          party] (FEA)
PDM........... People's Democratic Movement [Guyana] [Political party] (EY)
PDM........... People's Democratic Movement [Turks and Caicos Islands] [Political
          party] (PPW)
PDM........... Percent Deviation from the Median
PDM........... Phase Displacement (IAA)
PDM........... Physical Distribution Management
PDM........... Physiological Data Monitor
PDM........... Pilot Decision Making [Aviation] (DA)
PDM........... Pinch Design Method [Heat exchange design]
PDM........... Pitt-DesMoines Inc. [AMEX symbol] (TTSB)
PDM........... Pittsburgh - Des Moines, Inc. [AMEX symbol] (SPSG)
pdm........... Podium (VRA)
PDM........... Point Distribution Model (DMAA)
PDM........... Polynomial Discriminant Method (PDAA)
PDM........... Portable Differential Magnetometer
PDM........... Power Density Meter
PDM........... Power Density Monitor [Environmental science] (COE)
PDM........... Practical Data Manager [Hitachi Ltd.] [Japan]
PDM........... Precedence Diagraming Method (MCD)
PDM........... Predictive Maintenance
PDM........... Preliminary Development Model
PDM........... Preliminary Draft Manuscript
PDM........... Presidential Decision Memorandum [Jimmy Carter Administration]
PDM........... Print Down Module
PDM........... Processor Data Monitor (NASA)
PDM........... Product Data Management
PDM........... Product Development Manual [Automotive project management]
PDM........... Production Decision Criteria Matrix
PDM........... Program Data Manager (MCD)
PDM........... Program Decision Memorandum [Military]
PDM........... Programmed Depot Maintenance (MCD)
PDM........... Progres et Democratie Moderne [Progress and Modern Democracy]
          [France Political party] (PPE)
PDM........... Project Design Memo
PDM........... Protected Difference Milk (OA)
PDM........... Publications Distribution Manager [Military] (AFM)
PDM........... Pulse Data Modulation [Computer science] (IAA)
PDM........... Pulse Delay Mechanism [British military] (DMA)
PDM........... Pulse Delta Modulation (IEEE)
PDM........... Pulse Duration Modulation [Data transmission]
PDM........... Pursuit Deterrent Munition
PDM........... Push Down Memory [Computer science]
PDMA......... Peninsula Drafting Management Association
PDMA......... Pipelined Direct Memory Access [Computer science] (CIST)
PDMA......... Prescription Drug Marketing Act [1987]
PDMA......... Product Development and Management Association [Indianapolis,
          IN] (EA)
PDMAC........ Prescription Drug Maximum Allowable Cost

PDMAMS..... Product Design Minuteman Airborne Mechanical System (SAA)
PDMC......... Premature Dead Male Child (DAVI)
PDMC......... Princeton Dental Management Corp. [NASDAQ symbol] (SAG)
PDMC......... Princeton Dental Mgmt [NASDAQ symbol] (TTSB)
PDMCW...... Princeton Dental Mgmt Wrrt [NASDAQ symbol] (TTSB)
PDME.......... Pendant-Drop Melt Extraction [Metal fiber technology]
PDME.......... Pendant-Drop Melt-Extraction Process (EDCT)
PDME.......... Precision Distance Measuring Equipment (MCD)
PDM-FM...... Pulse-Duration Modulation - Frequency Modulation (CET)
PDMLR........ Post-Development Maintainability Logistics Review (MCD)
PDMM........ Push Down Memory MODEM [Computer science]
PDMMS...... Product Design Minuteman Mechanical System (IAA)
PDMNT....... Piedmont
PDMO......... Production Mold (AAG)
PDMP......... Positive Displacement Mechanical [or Metering] Pump
PDM/PM...... Pulse-Duration Modulation on Phase Modulation (MED)
PDMPO........ Polydimethyl Phenylene Oxide [Organic chemistry]
PDMR......... Provisioning Data Master Record (MCD)
PDMS......... Particle Desorption Mass Spectrometry
PDMS......... Patient Data Management Systems [Medical records] (DAVI)
PDMS......... Pesticide Document Management System [Environmental Protection
          Agency] (GFGA)
PDMS......... Pharmacokinetic Drug Monitoring Services [Medicine] (DMAA)
PDMS......... Photodissociation Mass Spectrometry
PDMS......... Physiological Data Monitoring System
PDMS......... Plant Design and Management System [Computer Aided Design
          Centre] [Software package] (NCC)
PDMS......... Plasma Desorption Mass Spectroscopy
PDMS......... Point Defense Missile System [NATO] (NATG)
PDMS......... Polydimethylsiloxane [Organic chemistry]
PDMS......... Postal Direct Marketing Service (WDAA)
PDMS......... Power-Plant and Process Design Management System [Computer
          science]
PDMS......... Program Definition and Management System (MCD)
PDMT......... Predominant [National Weather Service] (FAAC)
PDMU......... Passive Data Memory Unit
PDMU......... Production Mock-Up (AAG)
PDMV......... Pressure Differential Monitoring Valve
PDN........... Packet Data Network [Computer science] (IGQR)
PDN........... Partido Democratico Nacional [National Democratic Party] [Chile]
          [Political party]
PDN........... Partido Democratico Nacional [National Democratic Party]
          [Venezuela Political party]
PDN........... Partito Democratico Nazionalista [Democratic Nationalist Party
          (1921-1926)] [Malta] [Political party] (PPE)
PDN........... Partnerships Data Net [Defunct] (EA)
PDN........... Petition Denied
PDN........... Port Heiden, AK [Location identifier FAA] (FAAL)
PDN........... Power Dividing Network [Telecommunications] (LAIN)
PDN........... Prednisone [Also, P, Pr, Pred, Pro] [Endocrinology] [Antineoplastic
          drug]
PDN........... Premises Distribution Network [Computer science] (IGQR)
PDN........... Private Duty Nurse (DAVI)
PDN........... Problem Documentation Number (AAG)
PDN........... Production (AFM)
PDN........... Properly Driven Net
PDN........... Public Data Network [Packet-switching network] [British
          Telecommunications Ltd. London]
PDN........... Putnam Diversified Premium (EFIS)
PDNC......... Presidents' Day National Committee (EA)
PDNES........ Pulse-Doppler Non-Elevation Scan (PDAA)
PDNF......... Prime Disjunctive Normal Form (PDAA)
PD/NSC...... Presidential Directives/National Security Council
PDO........... Pacific Decadal Oscillation [Climatology]
PDO........... Petroleum Development Oman (BUAC)
PDO........... Philips & Du Pont Optical Co. [Wilmington, DE]
PDO........... Phthalate Dioxygenase [An enzyme]
PDO........... Portable Distributed Objects [Next]
PDO........... Port Dry Out [Nuclear energy] (NUCP)
PDO........... Postman's Delivery Office (DCTA)
PDO........... Prado [Brazil] [Airport symbol] (AD)
PDO........... Printer Direction Optimizer (BUR)
PD-O.......... Program Directive - Operations (KSC)
PDO........... Property Disposal Office [Environmental science] (BCP)
PDO........... Property Disposal Officer [Army]
PdO........... Psychopathic Deviate Obvious [Psychology]
PDO........... Publications Distribution Officer [Military]
PDO........... Public Defender's Office (LAIN)
PDoB.......... Bucks County Free Library, Doylestown, PA [Library symbol Library
          of Congress] (LCLS)
PDoBHi........ Bucks County Historical Society, Doylestown, PA [Library symbol
          Library of Congress] (LCLS)
PDOC......... Particulate and/or Dissolved Organic Carbon [Chemistry]
PDOD......... Phytoplankton Dissolved Oxygen Deficit [Oceanography]
PDOF......... Principal Direction of Force [Mechanical engineering]
PDOIS........ People's Democratic Organisation for Independence and Socialism
          [Senegambia] [Political party]
PDOL......... Publishers Discount Option List
PDoN......... Delaware Valley College of Science and Agriculture, Doylestown, PA
          [Library symbol Library of Congress] (LCLS)
PDOP......... Position Dilution of Position [Navigation systems]
PDOP......... Position Dilution of Precision
PDOP......... Prospective Designated Overhaul Point (MCD)
PDOS.......... Parent Diabetes Opinion Survey [Test]

PDowN .... Newcomen Society in North America, Downingtown, PA [*Library symbol Library of Congress*] (LCLS)
P/DOZ .... Per Dozen (WDAA)
PDP .... Packaging Development Plan
PDP .... Pakistan Democratic Party [*Political party*] (PD)
PDP .... Parallel Data Processing [*Computer science*]
PDP .... Parallel Detection Polychromator [*Instrumentation*]
PDP .... Parallel Distributed Processing [*A simulation of mental processes*]
PDP .... Parker & Parsley Petrol [*NYSE symbol*] (TTSB)
PDP .... Parker & Parsley Petroleum [*NYSE symbol*] (SAG)
PDP .... Parliamentary Democratic Party [*Myanmar*] [*Political party*]
PDP .... Parti Democrate Populaire [*Popular Democratic Party*] [*France Political party*] (PPE)
PDP .... Partido da Direita Portuguesa [*Party of the Portuguese Right*] [*Political party*] (PPE)
PDP .... Partido Democrata Popular [*Popular Democratic Party*] [*Spain Political party*] (PPW)
PDP .... Partido Democrata Popular [*Popular Democratic Party*] [*Dominican Republic*] [*Political party*] (PPW)
PDP .... Partido Democratico para o Progresso [*Democratic Progressive Party*] [*Guinea-Bissau*] [*Political party*] (EY)
PDP .... Partito Democratico Populare [*Popular Democratic Party*] [*San Marino*] [*Political party*] (PPE)
PDP .... Party for Democratic Prosperity [*Macedonia*] [*Political party*]
PDP .... Passive Driving Periscope [*Military*] (PDAA)
PDP .... Pattern Disruption Point [*Medicine*] (DMAA)
PDP .... Payload Distribution Panel [*NASA*] (MCD)
PDP .... Payload Distribution Plan
PDP .... Pentadecylphenol [*Organic chemistry*]
PDP .... People's Democratic [*Saint Christopher and Nevis*] [*Political party*] (EY)
PDP .... People's Democratic Party [*South Korea Political party*] (EY)
PDP .... People's Democratic Party [*Sudan*] [*Political party*]
PDP .... People's Democratic Party [*Netherlands Antilles*] [*Political party*] (EY)
PDP .... People's Democratic Party [*Sierra Leone*] [*Political party*] (EY)
PDP .... People's Democratic Party [*Uzbekistan*] [*Political party*] (BUAC)
PDP .... People's Democratic Party [*Montenegro*] [*Political party*] (BUAC)
PDP .... Personal Development Program (MCD)
PDP .... Pesticide Data Program [*Environmental Protection Agency*]
PDP .... Phenyl-Dichlorophosphine (PDAA)
PDP .... Phi Delta Phi [*An association*] (NTPA)
PDP .... Philadelphia, PA [*Location identifier FAA*] (FAAL)
PDP .... Philippine Democratic Party [*Pilipino Lakas Ng Bayan*] [*Political party*] (PPW)
PDP .... Pilot District Project [*Office of Economic Opportunity*] [*Defunct*] (EA)
PDP .... Piperidino-Pyrimidine [*Biochemistry*] (MAE)
PDP .... Pitch-Depitch (AAG)
PDP .... Planning Development Program (OICC)
PDP .... Plasma Diagnostics Package [*NASA*]
PDP .... Plasma Display Panel [*Computer science*]
PDP .... Plasma Display Processor [*Computer science*]
PDP .... Polysilicon Dielectric Polysilicon [*Organic chemistry*] (IAA)
PDP .... Popular Democratic Party [*Puerto Rico*] [*Political party*]
PDP .... Positive Displacement Pump
PDP .... Post Detection Processor [*Military*] (CAAL)
PDP .... Post-Drug Potentiation
PDP .... Post-Insertion Deorbit Preparation [*NASA*] (MCD)
PDP .... Power Distribution Panel
PDP .... Power Drain Protection [*Automotive engineering*]
PDP .... Preliminary Definition Plan (NASA)
PDP .... Preliminary Design Phase
PDP .... Preliminary Design Proposal (MCD)
PDP .... Preprototype Demonstration
PDP .... Prescription Drug Plan [*Insurance*] (WYGK)
PDP .... Prescription Drug Program [*Health insurance*] (GHCT)
PDP .... Present-Day Primers [*A publication*]
PDP .... Pressure Distribution Panel (AAG)
PDP .... Principal Display Panel [*Packaging*]
PDP .... Procedure Definition Processor [*Computer science*]
PDP .... Process Data Processing (IAA)
PDP .... Process Development Pile [*Nuclear energy*]
PDP .... Procurement Data Package [*Military*] (AABC)
PDP .... Product Development Process [*Automotive engineering*]
PDP .... Product Development Protocol [*U.S. Food and Drug Administration*]
PDP .... Production Data Package (MCD)
PDP .... Professional Development Program [*Military*]
PDP .... Program Decision Package [*Military*]
PDP .... Program Definition Phase [*Army*]
PDP .... Program Development Paper (MCD)
PDP .... Program Development Plan [*NASA*]
PDP .... Programmable Data Processor (IAA)
PDP .... Programmed Data Processor
PDP .... Programmed Digital Processor
PDP .... Progressive Democratic Party [*Montserrat*] [*Political party*] (PPW)
PDP .... Progressive Democratic Party [*St. Vincent*] [*Political party*] (PPW)
PDP .... Progressive Democratic Party [*Romania*] [*Political party*] (BUAC)
PDP .... Project Definition Phase (NRCH)
PDP .... Project Development Plan
PDP .... Punta Del Este [*Uruguay*] [*Airport symbol*] (OAG)
PDPA .... People's Democratic Party of Afghanistan [*Political party*] (PPW)
PDPA .... Production Pattern (AAG)
PDPC .... Position Display Parallax Corrected
PDPC .... Post Detection Pulse Compression [*Military*] (CAAL)
PDP-CVS ...... Positive Displacement Pump-Constant Volume Sampler (ERG)

PDPD .... Prolonged-Dwell Peritoneal Dialysis [*Medicine*] (DMAA)
PDPF .... Packet Data Processing Facility (MCD)
PDPGM .... Past Deputy Provincial Grand Master [*Freemasonry*]
PDPH .... Postdural Puncture Headache [*Medicine*] (DMAA)
PDPI .... Primer-Dependent Deoxynucleic Acid Polymerase Index [*Medicine*] (DMAA)
PDPIC .... Professional Development Program Improvement Center (EDAC)
PDPL .... Property Damage, Personal Liability [*Insurance*]
PDPM .... Preliminary Draft Presidential Memo
PDPOA .... Proposal Directive Plan of Action (MCD)
PDPR .... Present-Day Preachers [*A publication*]
PDPS .... Parts Data Processing System [*Bell Telephone*]
PDPS .... Problem Driver Pointer System [*NHTSA*] (TAG)
PDPS .... Program Data Processing Section (AAG)
PDPS .... Program Data Processing System (IAA)
PDPS .... Program Definition Phase Studies [*Navy*]
PDPS .... Project Data Processing System (MCD)
PDPT .... Parti Democratique des Populations Togolaises [*Togolese Democratic People's Party*] [*Political party*]
PDPUB .... Pedicel Pubescence [*Botany*]
PDPVF .... Presidential and Democratic Party Victory Fund (EA)
PDQ .... Packages Delivered Quick [*Allegheny Airlines service*]
PDQ .... Parallel Data Query [*Computer science*] (CDE)
PDQ .... Parental Diagnostic Questionnaire [*Speech evaluation test*]
PDQ .... Parodies Done Quirkily [*Humorous translation of Peter Schickele's PDQ Bach*]
PDQ .... PDQ Air Service, Inc. [*ICAO designator*] (FAAC)
PDQ .... Permanent Durable Quality [*Paper*]
PDQ .... Personal Description Questionnaire
PDQ .... Pertinent Data Quest (MCD)
PDQ .... Photo Data Quantizer
PDQ .... Physician's Data Query [*NIH*]
PDQ .... Please Draw Quickly [*Initialism used as title of TV series*]
PDQ .... Point, Digital, Qualifier [*In automobile name Opel PDQ*]
PDQ .... Prescreening Developmental Questionnaire [*Child development test*]
PDQ .... Pretty Damn Quick
PDQ .... Pretty Darn Quick (TAG)
PDQ .... Price and Delivery Quotations
PDQ .... Prime Hospitality [*NYSE symbol*] (SPSG)
PDQ .... Programmed Data Quantizer
PDQ .... Protocol Data Query [*Database*] [*National Institutes of Health*]
PDQC .... Physicians Data Query: Cancer Information File [*Database*]
PDQD .... Physicians Data Query: Directory File [*Database*]
PDQP .... Physicians Data Query: Protocol File [*Database*]
PDR .... Page Data Register
PDR .... Parent Daily Telephone Report [*Education*] (EDAC)
PDR .... Particulate Data Reduction (EPA)
PDR .... Parti Democratique Progressif [*Algeria*] [*Political party*] (EY)
PDR .... Party of Democratic Reform [*Slovenia*] [*Political party*] (EY)
PDR .... Pattern Delayed-Response [*Ophthalmology*]
PDR .... Peak Dose Rate [*Radiation*] (AAG)
PDR .... Pediatric Radiology [*Medical specialty*] (DHSM)
PDR .... Periscope Depth Range [*SONAR*]
PDR .... Periscope Detection RADAR (NG)
PDR .... Pharma-Dokumentationsring [*Pharma Documentation Ring*] [*Information service or system*] (IID)
PDR .... Phase Data Recorder (KSC)
PDR .... Phase Delay Rectifier
PDR .... Philippine Defense Ribbon [*Military decoration*]
PDR .... Photodissociation [*or Photodominated*] Region [*Galactic science*]
PDR .... Physicians' Desk Reference [*Also, an information service or system A publication*]
PDR .... Pilot's Display Recorder
PDR .... Piskei Din Shel Batei ha-Din ha-Rabaniyim be-Yisrael (BJA)
PDR .... Plasma-Developed Resist Processing [*Lithography*]
PDR .... Polarization Differential Reflectance (AAEL)
PDR .... Position Distribution Report [*DoD*]
PDR .... Pounder (MSA)
PDR .... Powder
PDR .... Power Directional Relay
PDR .... Precision Depth Recorder
PDR .... Predetection Recording
PDR .... Predetermined Demand Rate
PDR .... Pre-Determined Route [*Aviation*] (DA)
PDR .... Preferential Departure Route [*FAA*] (TAG)
PDR .... Preliminary Data Report
PDR .... Preliminary Data Requirements (NASA)
PDR .... Preliminary Design Report (NRCH)
PDR .... Preliminary Design Review (NASA)
PDR .... Pressurized Deuterium Reactor [*Nuclear energy*]
PDR .... Price Description Record [*Computer science*] (IBMDP)
PDR .... Price-Dividend Ratio (WDAA)
PDR .... Primary Demographic Report [*A. C. Nielsen Co.*] (NTCM)
PDR .... Priority Data Reduction
PDR .... Process Dynamics Recorder
PDR .... Processed Data Recorder
PDR .... Processing Data Rate (IEEE)
PDR .... Procurement Data Reference
PDR .... Product Design Review [*Army*]
PDR .... Program Design Review (MCD)
PDR .... Program Director's Review [*NASA*] (NASA)
PDR .... Program Discrepancy Report (IEEE)
PDR .... Program Document Requirement (BUR)
PDR .... Program Drum Recording
PDR .... Proliferative Diabetic Retinopathy [*Ophthalmology*]

PDR	Publications Data Request
PDR	Public Document Room (NRCH)
PDR	Pulse Doppler RADAR
PDR	Pulse Duty Ratio
PDR	Purchase of Development Rights (PA)
PDRA	Professional Drag Racing Association (EA)
PDRB	Permanent Diability Rating Board (DMAA)
PDRC	Clinical Research Center for Periodontal Disease [*University of Florida*] [*Research center*] (RCD)
PDRC	Personnel Despatch and Reception Centre [*British military*] (DMA)
PDRC	Peter Duel Remembrance Club (EA)
PDRC	Poultry Disease Research Center [*University of Georgia*] [*Research center*] (RCD)
PDRC	Preliminary Design Review Commercial (MCD)
PDRC	Pressure Difference Recording Controller
PDRC	Professional Development and Recruitment Career Program [*Military*]
PDRC	Program Development Review Committee [*Navy*] (CAAL)
PDRD	Procurement Data Requirements Document (NASA)
PDRD	Program Definition and Requirements Document (SSD)
PDRE	People's Democratic Republic of Ethiopia
PDRF	Passive Defense Recovery Force (MUGU)
PDRF	Presbyterians for Democracy and Religious Freedom (EA)
PDRH	Partido Democratico Revolucionario Hondureno [*Revolutionary Democratic Party of Honduras*] [*Political party*]
PdRK	Pesikta de-Rav Kahana (BJA)
PDRL	Permanent Disability Retired List
PDRL	Procurement Data Requirements List (NASA)
PDRM	Payload Deployment and Retrieval Mechanism [*NASA*]
PDRM	Post-Depositional Remanent Magnetization [*Geophysics*]
PDRM	Postdetrital Remanent Magnetization [*Geophysics*]
PDRMA	Portable Drilling Rig Manufacturers Association [*Defunct*] (EA)
PDRP	Program Data Requirement Plan [*Nuclear Regulatory Commission*] (NRCH)
PDRS	Payload Data and Retrieval System [*NASA*] (NAKS)
PDRS	Payload Deployment and Retrieval System [*NASA*] (NAKS)
PDRSS	Payload Deployment and Retrieval System Simulation [*NASA*] (SSD)
PDRSS	Payload Development and Retrieval System Simulator [*NASA*] (NAKS)
PDRSTA	Payload Deployment and Retrieval System Test Article [*NASA*] (NASA)
PDRY	People's Democratic Republic of Yemen [*Political party*]
PDS	Auburn/Lewiston, ME [*Location identifier FAA*] (FAAL)
PDS	Pacific Data System (IAA)
PDS	Package Data System (NASA)
PDS	Packet Data Satellites [*Telecommunications*] (TSSD)
PDS	Paid-during-Service [*Billing*]
PDS	Pain Dysfunction Syndrome [*Medicine*] (AAMN)
PDS	Parkinson's Disease Society [*British*]
PDS	Paroxysmal Depolarizing Shift [*Physiology*]
PDS	Partei des Demokratischen Sozialismus [*Party of Democratic Socialism*] [*Germany Political party*] (EAIO)
PDS	Parti Democratique Senegalais [*Senegalese Democratic Party*] [*Political party*] (PPW)
PDS	Partido Democrata Socialista [*Socialist Democratic Party*] [*Panama*] [*Political party*] (PPW)
PDS	Partitioned Data Set [*or System*] [*Computer science*] (NASA)
PDS	Partito Democratico della Sinistra [*Democratic Party of the Left*] [*Formerly, Italian Communist Party*] [*Political party*] (EY)
PDS	Partito di Democrazia Socialista [*Socialist Democracy Party*] [*San Marino*] [*Political party*] (PPW)
PDS	Party of Democratic Socialism [*Germany Political party*]
PDS	Passive Detection System (NVT)
PDS	Patient Data System [*Pharmacology*] (DAVI)
PDS	Patient Decontamination Site [*Army*] (INF)
PDS	Pediatric Surgery [*Medical specialty*] (DHSM)
PdS	Pediatric Surgery [*Medicine*] (DMAA)
PDS	Penultimate Digit Storage [*Telecommunications*] (TEL)
PDS	Performer Design Sheet
PDS	Perimeter Defense System (MCD)
PDS	Periodicals Data System (NITA)
PDS	Peritoneal Dialysis System [*nephrology*] (DAVI)
PDS	Permanent Duty Station [*Air Force*] (AFM)
PDS	Perry Drug Stores, Inc. (EFIS)
PDS	Personal Data System (NITA)
PDS	Personal Decision Series (HGAA)
PDS	Personal Development Study [*Psychology*]
PDS	Personnel Daily Summary [*Army*] (AABC)
PDS	Personnel Data System [*Air Force*]
PDS	Personnel Decontamination Station (MCD)
PDS	Personnel Delivery System
PDS	Petroleum Data System [*University of Oklahoma*] [*Databank*] (IID)
PDS	Pharma-Dokumentations-Service [*Pharma Documentation Service*] [*Information service or system*] (IID)
PDS	Phased Development Shuttle [*NASA*] (KSC)
PDS	Phot Document Sensor [*Electronics*] (IAA)
PDS	Photo-Digital Store
PDS	Photodischarge Spectroscopy (MCD)
PDS	Photothermal Deflection Spectroscopy (MCD)
PDS	Piedras Negras [*Mexico*] [*Airport symbol*] (AD)
PDS	Planning Data Sheet (KSC)
PDS	Planning Data Systems [*Information service or system*] (IID)
PDS	Plant Data System [*Nuclear energy*] (NRCH)
PDS	Plasma-Derived Serum
PDS	Plasma Display (MCD)
PDS	Plotter Display System (DNAB)

PDS	Pneumatic Distribution System
PDS	Polydimethylsiloxane [*Organic chemistry*]
PDS	Polydioxanone [*Organic chemistry*]
PDS	Portable Data System (MCD)
PDS	Portable Document Software [*Computer science*] (DDC)
PDS	Portable Duress Sensor (MCD)
PDS	Position-Determining System
PDS	Post Design Services [*British*] (RDA)
PDS	Power Density Spectra (IEEE)
PDS	Power Distribution Specification (IAA)
PDS	Power Distribution System [*or Subsystem*]
PDS	Power Drive System
PDS	Preadsorb-Dilute-Shake [*Phage growth method*]
PDS	Precision Drilling Corp. [*NYSE symbol*] (SAG)
PDS	Predialyzed Human Serum [*Medicine*] (MAE)
PDS	Predocketed Special Project (NRCH)
PDS	Premises Distribution System [*AT & T Corp.*]
PDS	Priority Decision System (NITA)
PDS	Priority Distribution System [*Military*] (AFM)
PDS	Prison Disciplinary System (WDAA)
PDS	Prisoner Detention System
PDS	Private Database Service (NITA)
PDS	Probability Distribution Subprogram [*Computer science*] (BUR)
PDS	Problem Data System (MCD)
PD/S	Problem Definition/Solution
PDS	Problem Descriptor System
PDS	Procedures Development Simulator (KSC)
PDS	Processor Direct Slot [*Computer science*]
PDS	Procurement Data Sheet
PDS	Product Design Standard
PDS	Production Data Sheet (MCD)
PDS	Professional Development School
PDS	Professional Development Seminar (HGAA)
PDS	Professional Development System [*PC software*] [*Microsoft, Inc.*] (PCM)
PDS	Program Data Sheets [*Army*] (AABC)
PDS	Program Data Source (BUR)
PDS	Program Design Specification (CAAL)
PDS	Program Development Specialist
PDS	Program Development System [*Computer science*]
PDS	Program Distribution System
PDS	Programmable Data Station [*or System*]
PDS	Programming Documentation Standards [*Computer science*] (WDAA)
PDS	Progressive Deterioration Scale
PDS	Propellant Delivery System
PDS	Propellant Dispersion System (MCD)
PDS	Protected Distribution System [*Military*] (GFGA)
PDS	Proximity Defense Systems [*Military*] (INF)
PdS	Psychiatric Deviate, Subtle (DAVI)
PdS	Psychopathic Deviate Subtle [*Psychology*]
PDS	Pulse Doppler Seeker
PDS	Punch Driver Selectric
PDS	Purchasing Department Specification (MSA)
PDS	Pyrotechnic Devices Simulator (SAA)
PDSA	People's Dispensary for Sick Animals [*British*]
PDSA	Peroxydisulfuric Acid (AAEL)
PDS-A	Personnel Data System - Airmen [*Air Force*]
PDSA	Predesign and Systems Analysis [*NASA*] (KSC)
PDSA	Private Doctors' Society of South Australia
PDS-A(I)	Personnel Data System - Airmen (Interim) [*Air Force*] (AFM)
PDSC	PACOM [*Pacific Command*] Data Systems Center (MCD)
PDSC	Parti Democrate et Social Chretien [*Zaire*] [*Political party*] (EY)
PDS-C	Personnel Data System - Civilian [*Air Force*] (AFM)
PDSC	Pressure Differential Scanning Calorimetry [*Analytical technique*]
PDSC	Publishers Data Service Corp. [*Monterey, CA*]
PDSD	Point Detonating Self-Destroying [*Projectile*]
PDSDD	Plotting Display Subchannel Data Distributor (MCD)
PDSE	Production Sample (AAG)
PDSF	PDS Financial [*NASDAQ symbol*] (TTSB)
PDSF	PDS Financial Corp. [*NASDAQ symbol*] (SAG)
PDS Fin	PDS Financial Corp. [*Associated Press*] (SAG)
PDSI	Palmer Drought Severity Index [*Meteorology*]
PDSI	Performance Data Services, Inc. [*Falls Church, VA*] [*Software manufacture r*]
PDSI	Portable Digital Strain Indicator
PDSK	Petroleum Distribution System - Korea [*Army*] (MCD)
PDSM	Powder Diffraction Search-Match System [*International Data Center*]
PDS/MAGEN	Problem Descriptor System/Matrix Generation [*Programming language*] [*1965*] (CSR)
PDSMS	Point Defense Surface Missile System
PDSMS	Power Diffraction Search and Match System (PDAA)
PDS-O	Personnel Data System - Officers [*Air Force*] (AFM)
PDSOF	Public Domain Software on File [*Facts on File, Inc.*] [*Information service or system*] (IID)
PDSOR	Positive Definitive Successive Over-Relaxation (PDAA)
PDSP	Personnel Data System - Planning [*Air Force*] (AFM)
PDSPI	Polyurethane Division, Society of the Plastics Industry (EA)
PDSQ	Point Detonating Super-Quick Fuze (NATG)
PDS-R	Parti Democratique Senegalais - Renovation [*Senegalese Democratic Party - Reform*] [*Political party*]
PDSS	Particle Doppler Shift Spectrometer (PDAA)
PDSS	Physical Disabilities Special Interest Section [*American Occupational Therapy Association*]
PDSS	Post-Deployment Software System (MCD)
PDST	Pacific Daylight Saving Time (KSC)

pdstl	Pedestal (VRA)
PDSTT	Pulse Doppler Single Target Track [*Military*] (CAAL)
PD Supp	Per Diem Supplement (AAGC)
PDT	Hancock [*John*] Patriot Premium Dividend, Inc. II [*NYSE symbol*] (SPSG)
PDT	John Hancock Patr Prem Dv II [*NYSE symbol*] (TTSB)
PDT	Pacific Daylight Time
PDT	Panoramic Design Technique
PDT	Parallel Data Transmission
PdT	Parti du Travail [*Labor Party*] [*Switzerland Political party*] (PPE)
PDT	PDT, Inc. [*Associated Press*] (SAG)
PDT	Pendleton [*Oregon*] [*Airport symbol*] (OAG)
PDT	Performance Demonstration Test
PDT	Peripheral Data Transfer [*Telecommunications*] (IAA)
PDT	Peripheral Device Type (CIST)
PDT	Personal Data Transmitter [*From the movie "Aliens"*]
PDT	Phenyldimethyltriazine [*Organic chemistry*] (AAMN)
PDT	Photodynamic Therapy [*Oncology*]
PDT	Physical Device Table (NITA)
PDT	Picture Description Test (PDAA)
PDT	Piedmont Airlines, Inc. [*ICAO designator*] (FAAC)
PDT	Planned Data to Transportation [*DoD*]
PDT	Plasma Display Terminal [*Computer science*]
PDT	Pollable Data Terminal [*Bell System*]
PDT	Population Doubling Time [*Cytology*]
PDT	Post Alloy Diffused Transistor [*Electronics*] (IAA)
PDT	Posting Data Transfer [*Air Force*] (AFM)
PDT	Power Distribution Trailer (NATG)
PDT	Predelivery Test (MCD)
PDT	Predictor Display Technique
PDT	President Mines [*Vancouver Stock Exchange symbol*]
PDT	Processed Directional Transmission [*Military*] (NVT)
PDT	Product Development Team [*Automotive project management*]
PDT	Programmable Data Terminal [*Digital Equipment Corp.*] (IEEE)
PDT	Published Data Tape [*A. C. Nielsen Co.*] [*A publication*] (WDMC)
PDT	Pulse Delay Time
PDT	Pushdown Transducer (CIST)
PDT	(Pyridyl)diphenyltriazine [*Analytical chemistry*]
PDT-1	Picatinny Arsenal Detonation Trap Number 1 [*Army*] (AABC)
PDTA	Production Tape (AAG)
PDTA	Professional Dance Teachers Association (EA)
PDTA	Propylenediaminetetraacetic Acid [*Organic chemistry*]
PDT & T	Post-Delivery Test and Trials [*Military*] (CAAL)
PDTC	Philadelphia Depository Trust Co.
PDTF	Program Development and Test Facility [*Social Security Administration*]
PDTI	PDT, Inc. [*NASDAQ symbol*] (SAG)
PDTMR	Phalloidin Tetramethylrhodamine [*Biochemistry*]
PDTP	Plasma Display Touch Panel [*Computer science*]
PDTRST	Podiatrist
PDTS	Procurement Document Tracking System (MCD)
PDTS	Program Development Tracking System [*Computer science*]
PDTS	Programmable Data Terminal Set [*Military*] (CAAL)
PDTTT	Post-Delivery Test and Trial Team (MCD)
PDU	Pacific Democrat Union (EAIO)
PDU	Parti Dahomeen de l'Unite [*Dahomean Unity Party*] [*Benin*] [*Political party*]
PDU	Parti Democrate Unifie [*Unified Democratic Party*] [*Name replaced by Section Voltaique de Rassemblement Burkina Faso*] [*Political party*]
PDU	Paysandu [*Uruguay*] [*Airport symbol*] (OAG)
PDU	Phase Demodulation Unit
PDU	Photomultiplier Detector Unit (KSC)
PDU	Pilot's Display Unit (MCD)
PDU	Positive Displacement Unit [*Mechanical pumps*]
PDU	Power Distribution Unit (AAG)
PDU	Power Drive Unit (MCD)
PDU	Pressure Distribution Unit
PDU	Process Demonstration Unit [*Chemical engineering*]
PDU	Process Development Unit [*Chemical engineering*]
PDU	Production Distribution Unit (AAG)
PDU	Programmable Delay Unit
PDU	Programmable Diagnostic Unit [*TACOM*] [*Army*] (RDA)
PDU	Project Development Unit [*Chemical engineering*]
PDU	Projection Display Unit
PDU	Protocol Data Unit [*Telecommunications*]
PDU	Pulsed Doppler Ultrasonography [*Radiology*] (DAVI)
PDU	Pulse Detection Unit (NASA)
PDUFA	Prescription Drug User Fee Act
PDUFC	Pete Duel Universal Friendship Club (EAIO)
PdUP	Partito di Unita Proletaria per il Comunismo [*Democratic Party of Proletarian Unity for Communism*] [*Italy Political party*] (PPE)
PDur	Papyri Durani (BJA)
PDUR	Predischarge Utilization Review [*Medicine*]
PDUS	Primary Data User Station [*Computer science*] (PDAA)
PDV	Parcel Delivery Van
PDV	Phocine Distemper Virus
PDV	Polyhedra Derived Virus
PDV	Ponderosa Ventures, Inc. [*Vancouver Stock Exchange symbol*]
PDV	Premodulation Processor - Deep Space - Voice
PDV	Pressure Disconnect Valve (MCD)
PDV	Probability of Detection and Verification [*Military*] (CAAL)
PDV	Prune Dwarf Virus
PDV Supp	Pyrotechnic Development Vehicle (PDAA)
PDVC	Phase-Dependent Voltage Contrast (AAEL)

PDVN	Power-Driven
PDVOR	Precision Doppler VHF Omni-Range (PDAA)
PDW	Evansville, IN [*Location identifier FAA*] (FAAL)
PDW	Partially Delactosed Whey (OA)
PDW	Personal Defense Weapon [*Army*] (INF)
PDW	Personal Design Workstation (DGA)
PDW	Platelet Distribution Width [*Hematology*]
PDW	Priority Delayed Weather [*NWS*] (FAAC)
PDWHF	Platelet-Derived Wound-Healing Factor [*Biochemistry*]
PDWP	Partially Delactosed Whey Powder (OA)
PDWR	Primary Drinking Water Regulation (COE)
PDX	Passive Dosimeter Experiment (KSC)
PDX	Place Decrement in Index
PDX	Poloidal Divertor Experiment [*Princeton University*]
PDX	Portland [*Oregon*] [*Airport symbol*] (OAG)
PDX	Prado Explorations Ltd. [*Toronto Stock Exchange symbol*]
PDX	Private Digital Exchange
PDX	Probable Diagnosis (DAVI)
PDX	Program Development Executive (MHDI)
PDY	Piccadilly Resources Ltd. [*Vancouver Stock Exchange symbol*]
PDY	Principal Duty [*Military*]
PDYN	Prodynorphin [*Biochemistry*]
PDZ	Ontario, CA [*Location identifier FAA*] (FAAL)
PDZ	Pedernales [*Venezuela*] [*Airport symbol*] (OAG)
PE	British Aircraft Corp. Ltd. [*ICAO aircraft manufacturer identifier*] (ICAO)
PE	Easton Area Public Library, Easton, PA [*Library symbol Library of Congress*] (LCLS)
PE	Edinburgh Pharmacopoeia [*British*] (DAVI)
PE	Ice Pellets [*Meteorology*]
PE	Pacific Electric Railway [*AAR code*]
PE	Page-End Character [*Computer science*]
PE	Paper Electrophoresis [*Medicine*] (MAE)
PE	Parabolic Equation
PE	Parity Error
PE	Partes Aequales [*Equal Parts*] [*Pharmacy*]
PE	Patrol Vessel, Eagle [*Eagle boat*] [*Navy symbol Obsolete*]
PE	Peacetime Establishment [*Military*] (NATG)
Pe	Peclet Number [*IUPAC*]
PE	PECO Energy [*Formerly, Philadelphia Electric Co.*] [*NYSE symbol*] (SPSG)
PE	Pectinesterase [*Also, PME*] [*An enzyme*]
PE	Pediatrics (DAVI)
Pe	Pelagius [*Deceased, 1232*] [*Authority cited in pre-1607 legal work*] (DSA)
PE	Pel-Ebstein [*Disease*] [*Medicine*] (DB)
pe	Pen (VRA)
PE	Penile Erection [*Medicine*] (DMAA)
PE	Pentaeythrol (IAA)
Pe	Pentyl [*Biochemistry*]
PE	People Express [*ICAO designator*] (AD)
PE	Pericardial Effusion [*Cardiology*] (DAVI)
PE	Period Ending
PE	Periodic (AAG)
PE	Peripheral Equipment (AAG)
PE	Periscope
PE	Peritoneal Exudate [*Medicine*]
PE	Perkin Elmer Corp.
PE	Permanent Echo [*RADAR*]
PE	Permanent Error (IAA)
PE	Permissible Error (ADA)
PE	Perry Ellis [*Fashion designer, 1940-86*]
PE	Persistent Estrus [*Endocrinology*]
PE	Personal Effects
PE	Personal Equipment
PE	Personnel, Enlisted [*or Enlisted Personnel Division*] [*Coast Guard*]
PE	Personnel Equipment [*Air Force*] (AFM)
PE	Personnel Equivalent [*DoD*]
PE	Peru [*ANSI two-letter standard code*] (CNC)
pe	Peru [*MARC country of publication code Library of Congress*] (LCCP)
Pe	Perylene [*Organic chemistry*] (AAMN)
PE	Peterborough [*Postcode*] (ODBW)
PE	Petroleum Economist [*London*] [*A publication*] (BJA)
PE	Petroleum Engineer
Pe	Petrus de Bellapertica [*Deceased, 1308*] [*Authority cited in pre-1607 legal work*] (DSA)
Pe	Petrus Hispanus [*Authority cited in pre-1607 legal work*] (DSA)
PE	Phakoemulsification [*Ophthalmology*] (DAVI)
PE	Pharmacopaeia Edinensis [*Edinburgh Pharmacopoeia*] [*A publication*] (ROG)
PE	Pharyngoesophageal [*Medicine*]
PE	Phase Encoding [*Magnetic tape recording*] [*Computer science*] (MDG)
PE	Phenylephrine
PE	Philadelphia Stock Exchange (CDAI)
PE	Phosphatidylethanolamine [*Biochemistry*]
PE	Photoelectric
PE	Photoelectron (IAA)
PE	Photoemission [*Physics*]
PE	Photographic Effect (MAE)
PE	Photon Echo [*Spectroscopy*]
PE	Phycoerythrin [*Biochemistry*]
PE	Physical Education
PE	Physical Evaluation [*Medicine*] (MAE)
PE	Physical Examination

PE	Physiological Ecology
PE	Pictorial Eleven [*Later, PES*] [*An association*] (EA)
PE	Piezoelectric (AAEL)
PE	Pigment Epithelium [*of the retina*]
PE	Pilot Equalizer (IAA)
PE	Pilot Error
PE	Pinion End
PE	Pistol Expert
PE	Plain Edges [*Graphic arts*] (DGA)
PE	Plain End [*Lumber*] (DAC)
PE	Planetary Explorer [*NASA*]
PE	Planification de l'Emploi [*Canadian Jobs Strategy - CJS*]
P/E	Planning Economics Group, Boston [*Information service or system*] (IID)
PE	Planning Estimate
PE	Plant Engineering (AAG)
PE	Plant Equipment (MCD)
PE	Plant Extrusion (OA)
PE	Plasma Emission [*Spectrophotometry*]
PE	Plasma Exchange [*Medicine*]
PE	Plastic Explosive (NATG)
PE	Plating Efficiency (DB)
PE	Pleural Effusion [*Medicine*]
PE	Pneumatic Equalization [*Tube*] [*Otorhinolaryngology*] (DAVI)
PE	Pocket Edition (WDAA)
PE	Pollen Equivalent [*Immunology*]
PE	Polyelectrolyte [*Organic chemistry*]
PE	Polyethylene [*Organic chemistry*]
PE	Population Equivalent (FFDE)
PE	Porcelain Enamel [*Technical drawings*]
PE	Portable Executable
PE	Portable Executable File [*Computer science*]
PE	Port Engineer (DNAB)
PE	Port of Embarkation [*Military*]
PE	Position Effect [*Parapsychology*]
PE	Position Error
PE	Positive Expulsion (SAA)
PE	Positives and Etching (DGA)
PE	Post Engineer [*Army*] (AABC)
PE	Post Exchange [*Marine Corps*]
PE	Postexposure [*Medicine*]
PE	Potato Eaters (EA)
PE	Potential Energy
PE	Potential Evapotranspiration (DICI)
PE	Potential Excess [*of stock*] [*DoD*]
PE	Powdered Extract [*Pharmacy*]
PE	Power Equipment [*Military*] (IAA)
PE	Practical Exercise
P-E	Precipitation-Evaporation
PE	Pre-Eclampsia [*Medicine*]
PE	Pre-Emption [*Telecommunications*] (TEL)
PE	Preliminary Evaluation
PE	Preliminary Exploitation (MCD)
PE	Prepaid Expense [*Finance*] (MHDW)
PE	Presidential Exemption [*Environmental Protection Agency*]
PE	Presiding Elder
PE	Pressure Enclosure (MCD)
PE	Pressure Equalization [*Tube*] [*Otorhinolaryngology*] (DAVI)
PE	Pressure Equalizing [*Tube*] [*Otorhinolaryngology*] (DAVI)
Pe	Pressure on Expiration [*Medicine*]
PE	Priced Exhibit (MCD)
P/E	Price [*or Profit*]/Earnings Ratio [*Relation between price of a company's stock and its annual net income*]
PE	Price Earnings Ratio [*Investment term*] (DFIT)
PE	Primary Education (AIE)
PE	Primary Electricity
PE	Prime Equipment
PE	Primitive Endoderm [*Cytology*]
PE	Primitive Equation
PE	Prince Edward Island [*Canadian province*] [*Postal code*]
PE	Principal Engineer (AAG)
PE	Printer's Error
pe	Printer's Error (WDAA)
PE	Probable Error [*Statistics*]
PE	Procedures Evaluation [*DoD*]
PE	Processing Element [*of central processing unit*]
PE	Procurement Executive [*British*]
PE	Production Engineering
PE	Production Engineering Division [*Frankford Arsenal*] [*Philadelphia, PA*]
PE	Production Executive [*British*]
P/E	Professional and Executive [*Employment register*] [*British*]
PE	Professional Education (AFM)
PE	Professional Engineer
PE	Program Element (AFM)
PE	Program Evaluation (OICC)
PE	Programmed Exciter
PE	Project Engineer
PE	Project Equality (EA)
PE	Prometheus-Europe [*Paris, France*] (EAIO)
PE	Proponent Evaluation (MCD)
PE	Protected Environment
PE	Protect Enable [*Computer science*] (PCM)
PE	Protein Electrophoresis [*Biochemistry*] (DAVI)
PE	Protestant Episcopal

PE	Proteus Engine [*Hovercraft*]
PE	Proton Event
PE	Pseudomonas Exotoxin [*Bacterial toxin*]
PE	Public Eye [*Internet Site*]
PE	Pulley End
PE	Pulmonary Edema [*Medicine*]
PE	Pulmonary Effusion [*Medicine*]
PE	Pulmonary Embolism [*Medicine*]
PE	Pulse Echo [*Materials research*]
PE	Pulse Encoding [*Computer science*]
PE	Purchased Equipment
PE	Pyroelectric
Pe	Warner-Lambert Pharmaceutical Co. [*Research code symbol*]
PE2	Secondary Plating Efficiency (STED)
PEA	Palmitylethanolamide [*Organic chemistry*]
PEA	Pan Europeenne Air Service [*France ICAO designator*] (FAAC)
PEA	Papillary Eccrine Adenoma [*Oncology*]
PEA	Parking Enforcement Aide (ECON)
PEA	Pattern Error Analysis
PEA	Patterson Experimental Array (MCD)
PEA	Payload Enclosure Assembly (MCD)
Pea	Peake's English Nisi Prius Reports [*1790-1812*] [*A publication*] (DLA)
PEA	Pella, IA [*Location identifier FAA*] (FAAL)
PEA	Penneshaw [*Australia Airport symbol*] (OAG)
PEA	Pennsylvania Electric Association
PEA	Phenethyl Alcohol [*Organic chemistry*]
PEA	Phenylethanolamine [*Organic chemistry*]
PEA	Phenylethylamine [*Biochemistry*]
PEA	Phosphoethanolamine [*Organic chemistry*]
PE(A)	Physical Education (Association) [*British*]
PEA	Pilot's Employment Agency
PEA	Pitch Error Amplifier
PEA	Plant Engineering Agency
PEA	Plastics Engineers Association [*Defunct*] (EA)
PEA	Platform Electronics Assembly (KSC)
PEA	Polish Ex-Servicemen's Association [*Australia*]
PEA	Poly(ethyl Acrylate) [*Organic chemistry*]
PEA	Polysaccharide Egg Antigen (STED)
PEA	Portuguese East Africa [*Mozambique*]
PEA	Potash Export Association (EA)
PEA	Poultry Education Association [*British*] (BI)
PEA	Power Excursion Accident [*Nuclear energy*] (NUCP)
PEA	Preliminary Environmental Assessment (MCD)
PEA	Primary Expense Account
PEA	Private Employment Agency (OICC)
PEA	Process Environmental Analysis
PEA	Process Equipment Accessory (MCD)
PEA	Procurement Executives Association (AAGC)
PEA	Program Element Administrator [*Navy*] (NG)
PEA	Progressive Education Association [*Defunct*]
PEA	Proposal Expansion Award (TELE)
PEA	Public Education Association
PEA	Push Effective Address [*Computer science*] (IEEE)
PEA	Pyridylethylamine [*Organic chemistry*]
Pea (2)	Peake's Additional Cases Nisi Prius [*170 English Reprint*] [*1795-1812*] [*A publication*] (DLA)
PEAA	Program Elements Activity Accounts (MCD)
P/EA(A)3	Probationary Electrical Artificer (Air) 3rd Class [*British military*] (DMA)
Pea Add Cas	Peake's English Nisi Prius Reports [*Vol. 2*] [*A publication*] (DLA)
Peab L Rev	Peabody Law Review [*A publication*] (DLA)
Peabody Inst	Peabody Institute of The Johns Hopkins University (GAGS)
PEAC	Pharmaceutical Education Advisory Committee [*Australia*]
PEAC	Photoelectric Alignment Collimator (IAA)
PEAC	Photoelectric Auto Collimator
PEAC	Photoelectroanalytical Chemistry
PEAC	Police Education Advisory Council [*New South Wales, Australia*]
PEACE	People Emerging Against Corrupt Establishments [*Underground military newspaper*]
PEACE	Plan for Excellence in a Collaborative Environment [*School project*]
PEACE	Project Evaluation and Assistance, Civil Engineering [*Air Force*]
PEACESAT	Pan-Pacific Editing and Communication Experiment by Satellite (NITA)
PEACESAT	Pan-Pacific Educational and Cultural Exchange by Satellite Program [*University of Hawaii, Manoa*] [*Research center*] (RCD)
PEACESAT	Pan-Pacific Education and Communication Experiments by Satellites [*University of Hawaii*] [*NASA*]
PEACH	Preschool Evaluation and Assessment for Children with Handicaps (STED)
PEACU	Plastic Energy Absorption in Compression Unit (IEEE)
PEAD	Presidential Emergency Action Document
PEADS	Presidential Emergency Action Direction System (MCD)
PEAI	Physical Education Association of Ireland (EAIO)
PEAK	Peak Technologies Group, Inc. [*NASDAQ symbol*] (SAG)
PEAK	Peak Technologies Grp [*NASDAQ symbol*] (TTSB)
Peake	Peake's Cases [*1790-1812*] [*A publication*] (DLA)
Peake Add Cas	Peake's Additional Cases Nisi Prius [*1795-1812*] [*A publication*] (DLA)
Peake Ev	Peake on the Law of Evidence [*A publication*] (DLA)
Peake NP	Peake's English Nisi Prius Cases [*170 English Reprint*] [*A publication*] (DLA)
Peake NP Add Cas	Peake's Additional Cases Nisi Prius [*170 English Reprint*] [*England*] [*A publication*] (DLA)
Peake NP Add Cas (Eng)	Peake's Additional Cases Nisi Prius [*170 English Reprint*] [*England*] [*A publication*] (DLA)

Peake NP Cas...   Peake's English Nisi Prius Cases [*170 English Reprint*] [*1790-1812*] [*A publication*]   (DLA)

Peake NP Cas (Eng)...   Peake's English Nisi Prius Cases [*170 English Reprint*] [*A publication*]   (DLA)

PeakTch......   Peak Technologies Group, Inc. [*Associated Press*]   (SAG)

PEAM.......   Personal Electronic Aid for Maintenance [*Military*]

Pea MS.......   Peachey on Marriage Settlements [*1860*] [*A publication*]   (DLA)

PEAMUSE ....   Peabody Museum of Archaeology and Ethnology [*Harvard University*] [*Research center*]   (RCD)

PE & M.......   Plant Engineering and Maintenance   (MCD)

PEAO ....   Phenylethylamine Oxidase   (STED)

PEAP...........   Pad Emergency Air Pack [*NASA*]   (KSC)

PEAP...........   Personal Egress Air Pack   (NAKS)

PEAP...........   Pesticide Education and Action Project   (EA)

PEAP...........   Positive End-Airway Pressure [*Medicine*]   (DMAA)

PEAP...........   Principal Error Axis for Position

PEAP...........   Program Evaluation Analysis Plan   (MCD)

PEAQ...........   Personal Experience and Attitude Questionnaire   (STED)

PeAR...........   Die Provinzeinteilung des Assyrischen Reiches [*A publication*]   (BJA)

Pearce CC ...   Pearce's Reports in Dearsley's English Crown Cases [*A publication*]   (DLA)

PEARL ....   Committee for Public Education and Religious Liberty   (EA)

PEARL ....   Performance Evaluation of Amplifiers from a Remote Location

PEARL ....   Periodical Enquiry Acquisition and Registration Locally   (NITA)

PEARL ....   Periodicals Automation, Rand Library

PEARL ....   Personal Equipment and Rescue/Survivable Lowdown   (MCD)

PEARL ....   Personnel Expertise and Resource Listing   (COE)

PEARL ....   Process and Experiment Automation Real-Time Language [*Computer science*]

PEARL ....   Program for EPS [*Electrical Power System*] Analysis and Rapid Look-Ahead [*NASA computer program*]

PEARL ....   Programmed Editor and Automated Resources for Learning

PEARLA ......   Pupils Equal and React to Light and Accomodation [*Medicine*]

Pears ....   Pearson's Reports [*1850-80*] [*Pennsylvania*] [*A publication*]   (DLA)

Pearson......   Pearson's Common Pleas [*Pennsylvania*] [*A publication*]   (DLA)

Pears (PA)...   Pearson's Reports [*1850-80*] [*Pennsylvania*] [*A publication*]   (DLA)

PEART ....   Passive Electronic Advanced Receiver   (MCD)

pearwd ....   Pear Tree Wood   (VRA)

PEAS...........   Pacific's Electronics Acquisition Service   (NITA)

PEAS...........   Physical Estimation and Attraction Scales

PEAS...........   Policy and External Affairs Staff [*Environmental Protection Agency*]   (GFGA)

PEAS...........   Practical Engineering Applications Software   (NITA)

PEAS...........   Presbyterian Educational Association of the South [*Defunct*]   (EA)

Pease ....   Pease Oil & Gas Co. [*Associated Press*]   (SAG)

PeaseOG......   Pease Oil & Gas Co. [*Associated Press*]   (SAG)

PEAT...........   Phenylethanolaminotetralin [*Organic chemistry*]

PEAT...........   Pricing Evaluation for Audit Technique [*Finance*]

PEAT...........   Programme Elargi d'Assistance Technique [*Expanded Program of Technical Assistance*] [*United Nations*]

PEAT...........   Programmer Exercised Autopilot Test   (AAG)

PEAV...........   Principal Error Axis for Velocity

PE B...........   Bachelor of Pedagogy   (ROG)

Pe B...........   Bachelor of Pediatrics

PEB.............   Parametric Empirical Bayes [*Statistics*]

PEB.............   Party Election Broadcast [*British*]   (BARN)

PEB.............   PCIA Expansion Bus [*Computer science*]

PEB.............   Pebble [*Jewelry*]   (ROG)

PEB.............   Pebble Gold Resources [*Vancouver Stock Exchange symbol*]

PEB.............   Pensioners' Employment Bureau [*British*]

PEB.............   Performance Evaluation Board [*NASA*]   (MCD)

PEB.............   Phosphate Ester Base   (PDAA)

PEB.............   Phototype Environment Buoy   (PDAA)

PEB.............   Phycoerythrobilin [*Biochemistry*]

PEB.............   Physical Evaluation Board [*Military*]

PEB.............   Plasma Electron Beam   (PDAA)

PEB.............   Population-Environment Balance   (EA)

PEB.............   Porcelain Enamel Bath [*Classified advertising*]   (ADA)

PEB.............   Positive Expulsion Bladder

PEB.............   Postexposure Baking [*Microlithography*]

PEB.............   Pre-Expanded Bin   (DNAB)

PEB.............   Presidential Emergency Board

PEB.............   Production Efficiency Board [*British World War II*]

PEB.............   Program Element Breakdown [*Computer science*]   (IAA)

PEB.............   Propulsion Examining Board [*Navy*]   (NVT)

PEB.............   Prototype Environmental Buoy [*Marine science*]   (MSC)

PEB.............   Psycho-Educational Battery [*Educational test*]

PEB.............   Pulmonary Ectopic Beat [*Cardiology*]

PEB.............   Pulsed Electron Beam   (IEEE)

PEBA...........   Polyether Block Amide [*Plastics technology*]

PEBA...........   Pulsed Electron Beam Annealer [*Photovoltaic energy systems*]

PEBA...........   Purified Extract of Brucella abortus

PEBAB........   Para-(Ethoxybenzylidene)aminobenzonitrile [*Also, EBCA*] [*Organic chemistry*]

PEB & B......   Porcelain Enamel Bath and Basin [*Classified advertising*]   (ADA)

PEBB..........   Public Employees Blanket Bond

PEBBLE.......   Probe Encapsulated by BioListic Embedding [*Biosensor*]

PeBcCH......   Peoples Bancorp, Inc. (Ohio) [*Associated Press*]   (SAG)

PEBCO........   Program Evaluation and Budget Committee [*American Library Association*]

PEBD..........   Pay Entry Base Date

PEBES........   Personal Earning and Benefit Estimate Statement [*Social Security Administration*]

PEBG ....   Phenethylbiguanide [*Same as PEDG*] [*Antidiabetic compound*]

PEBH ....   Physical Evaluation Board Hospital [*Military*]

PEBK..........   Peoples Bank [*Catawba, NC*] [*NASDAQ symbol*]   (NQ)

PEBL..........   Port Everglades Belt Line Railway [*AAR code Obsolete*]

PEBLO........   Physical Evaluation Board Liaison Officer [*Air Force*]   (AFM)

PEBO..........   Peoples Bancorp [*NASDAQ symbol*]   (TTSB)

PEBO..........   Peoples Bancorp, Inc. (Ohio) [*NASDAQ symbol*]   (SAG)

PEBP..........   Patient Escorted by Police   (DMAA)

PEBS..........   Pulsed Electron Beam Source   (MCD)

PEBV..........   Pea Early-Browning Virus [*Plant pathology*]

PEBW.........   People's Bancorp Worcester   (EFIS)

PEC...........   American Irish Political Education Committee   (EA)

PEc...........   Ellwood City Area Public Library, Ellwood City, PA [*Library symbol Library of Congress*]   (LCLS)

PEC...........   IEEE Power Electronics Council   (EA)

PEC...........   Pacific Command Electronic Intelligence Center   (MCD)

PEC...........   Pacific East Asia Cargo Airline, Inc. [*Philippines*] [*ICAO designator*]   (FAAC)

PEC...........   Pacific Economic Community   (FEA)

PEC...........   Packaged Electronic Circuit [*Computer science*]   (IAA)

PEC...........   Palestine Economic Commission

PEC...........   Panasonic Energy Corp. [*Vancouver Stock Exchange symbol*]

PEC...........   Panel Electronic Circuit   (EECA)

PEC...........   Passive Equipment Cabinet [*Military*]   (CAAL)

PEC...........   Patient Evaluation Center   (DAVI)

PEC...........   Peak Electrode Current

PEC...........   PEC Israel Economic Corp. [*Associated Press*]   (SAG)

PEC...........   Pectoral [*Lungs and Chest*] [*Medicine*]   (ROG)

PEC...........   Pedal Excretory Cell

PEC...........   Peduncle of Cerebrum   (DB)

PEC...........   Pelican [*Alaska*] [*Airport symbol*]   (OAG)

PEC...........   Penelec Capital Ltd. [*NYSE symbol*]   (SAG)

PEC...........   Perfil de Evaluacion del Comportamiento [*Standardized test of elementary through high school students' behavior at school, at home, and with peers*]

PEC...........   Peritoneal Exudate Cells [*Hematology*]

PEC...........   Perkin-Elmer Corp.   (MCD)

PEC...........   Perris [*California*] [*Seismograph station code, US Geological Survey*]   (SEIS)

PEC...........   Persistent Early Curvature

PEC...........   Personal Education Counseling   (DNAB)

PEC...........   Personal Effects Coverage [*Insurance*]

PEC...........   Petro-Canada

PEC...........   Phenylene Ether Copolymer [*Organic chemistry*]

PEC...........   Photoelectric Cell

PEC...........   Photoelectrochemical Cell [*Energy conversion device*]

PEC...........   Photoelectrochromic [*Chemistry*]

PEC...........   Physics, Engineering, and Chemistry   (AAG)

PEC...........   Pigmented Emulsified Creosote

PEC...........   Pigmented Epithelial Cell [*Ophthalmology*]

PEC...........   Pilot Error Correction   (IAA)

PEC...........   Plain English Campaign [*British*]   (DBA)

PEC...........   Planetary Entry Capsule [*Aerospace*]

PEC...........   Plant Equipment Codes [*DoD*]

PEC...........   Platform Electron Card [*Electronics*]   (OA)

PEC...........   Political Education Committee [*American Ireland Education Foundation*]   (EA)

PEC...........   Polyestercarbonate [*Organic chemistry*]

PEC...........   Position Error Correction   (DA)

PEC...........   Positive Engagement Clutch

PEC...........   Potasse et Engrais Chimiques

PEC...........   Potential Enviromental Concentration [*Pollution technology*]

PEC...........   Power Electronics Council   (NTPA)

PEC...........   Predicted Environmental Concentration   (DCTA)

PEC...........   Pre-Existing Condition [*Health Insurance*]

PEC...........   Presbyterian Evangelical Coalition   (EA)

PEC...........   Previous Element Coding

PEC...........   Production Equipment Code [*Military*]

PEC...........   Production Executive Committee

PEC...........   Program Element Code   (AFM)

PEC...........   Program Environment Control

PEC...........   Program Evaluation Center [*Navy*]   (AFIT)

PEC...........   Propulsion Environmental Chamber

PEC...........   Protestant Episcopal Church   (WDAA)

PEC...........   Prova Elementi Combustibili [*An Italian fast reactor*]

PEC...........   Pugwash Etudiant du Canada

PEC...........   Pyridylethylcysteine [*Biochemistry*]

PEC...........   Pyrogenic Exotoxin C [*Medicine*]

PECA ....   Petroleum Equipment Contractors Association   (EA)

Peca ....   Petrus de Bellapertica [*Deceased, 1308*] [*Authority cited in pre-1607 legal work*]   (DSA)

PECA ....   Process Engineers and Constructors' Association [*Australia*]

PECAM.......   Platelet-Endothelial Cell Adhesion Molecule [*Cytology*]

PECAN ....   Pulse Envelop Correlation Air Navigation

PE CARD ....   Production Estimate Card   (MSA)

PECBI........   Professional Engineers Conference Board for Industry   (EA)

PECC.........   Pacific Economic Cooperation Conference   (DOMA)

PECC.........   Panel of Experts on Climatic Change [*WMO*]   (MSC)

PECC.........   Precanceled Envelope Collectors Club   (EA)

PECC.........   Product Engineering Control Center [*Telecommunications*]   (TEL)

PECDAR......   Palestine Economic Council for Development and Reconstruction   (ECON)

PECDS........   Professional Engineering Career Development Series [*Book series*]

PECE..........   Proposed Engineering Change Estimate

PECF..........   Pseudoextracellular Fluid [*for biocompatibility testing*]

PECFA........   Presidential Election Campaign Fund Act of 1966

Pecho ....   Prostatic Echogram [*Medicine*]   (AAMN)

PECI............ Preliminary Equipment Component Index [or Inventory]
PECI............ Productivity Enhancing Capital Investment [DoD]
PECIACESC... Permanent Executive Committee of the Inter-American Council for Education, Science, and Culture
PECIAECOSOC... Permanent Executive Committee of the Inter-American Economic and Social Council
PECIP........... Productivity Enhancing Capital Investment Program (MCD)
Peck............ Peck's Reports [7 Tennessee] [1921-24] [A publication] (DLA)
Peck............ Peck's Reports [24-30 Illinois] [A publication] (DLA)
Peck............ Peckwell's English Election Cases [1802-06] [A publication] (DLA)
Peck El Cas... Peckwell's English Election Cases [A publication] (DLA)
Peck Elec Cas... Peckwell's English Election Cases [1802-06] [A publication] (DLA)
Peck (Ill) ..... Peck's Reports, Illinois Supreme Court Reports [11-22, 24-30] [A publication] (DLA)
Peck (Tenn)... Peck's Reports [7 Tennessee] [A publication] (DLA)
Peck Tr....... Peck's Trial (Impeachment) [A publication] (DLA)
Peckw......... Peckwell's English Election Cases [A publication] (DLA)
PECL........... Preliminary Engineering Configuration List
PECM.......... Passive Electronics Countermeasures [Military] (NG)
PECM.......... Preliminary Engineering Change Memorandum [Air Force] (CET)
PECO .... Pays d'Europe Centrale et Orientale (ECON)
PECO .... PECO Energy [Associated Press] (SAG)
PECO .... Pecos National Monument
PECO₂......... Mixed Expired Carbon Dioxide Tension [Medicine] (DAVI)
PECOS .... Pays D'Europe Centrale et Orientale
PECOS .... Pentagon Computer Operations Support (MCD)
PECOS .... Program Environment Checkout System
PECOS .... Project Evaluation and Control System (MCD)
PECOS .... Project Evaluation and Cost Optimization System (IAA)
PECP........... Preliminary Engineering Change Proposal
PECPrZ........ Penelec Capital L.P. 'MIPS' [NYSE symbol] (TTSB)
PECR........... Program Error Correction Report
Pe Cri .... Petrus Crispanus [Authority cited in pre-1607 legal work] (DSA)
PECS........... Plant Engineering Check Sheet (AAG)
PECS........... Portable Environmental Control System [NASA]
PECS........... Printers' Estimating and Costing System (DGA)
PECSS .... Presorted Emergency Cooling System Sampling [Environmental science] (COE)
PECT........... Pectori [To the Chest] [Pharmacy]
PECTFE........ Polyethylene-Chlorotrifluoroethylene [Organic chemistry]
PECUL......... Peculiar (ROG)
PECUS .... Personal Engineering Computer User's Society [Defunct] (EA)
PECUSA ...... Presidential Ethics Commission (NADA)
PECUY .... Pecuniary (ROG)
PECVD .... Plasma-Enhanced Chemical Vapor Deposition [Coating technology]
PECWBS ...... Proposed Extended Contract Work Breakdown Structure [Military]
PECWG .... Piaster Expenditure Control Working Group [Military]
PED............ Doctor of Physical Education (PGP)
PED............ Parole Eligibility Date (WDAA)
PED............ Patient Examined by Doctor (DMAA)
PED............ Pedagogue
PED............ Pedal
PED............ Peddler [or Peddling] [FBI standardized term]
PED............ Pedestal (AAG)
PED............ Pedestrian
PED............ Pediatric Emergency Department (DMAA)
PED............ Pediatrician
PED............ Pediatrics (AABC)
PED............ Pedlary (ROG)
PED............ Pedro Aguirre Cerda [Antarctica] [Seismograph station code, US Geological Survey Closed] (SEIS)
PED............ Period End Date (MCD)
PED............ Personal Equipment Data [Computer science] (IAA)
PED............ Personnel Equipment Data [Army] (IAA)
PED............ Phosphorus Enhanced Diffusion (IAA)
PED............ Photoemission Diode
PEd............ Physical Education
PED............ Pink-Eyed Dilution [Medicine] (DMAA)
PED............ Polymer Engineering Directive (WDAA)
PED............ Positive Expulsion Device
PED............ Production Eligibility Date (MUGU)
PED............ Production Engineering Division [University of Wisconsin - Madison] [Research center] (RCD)
PED............ Program Element Description
PED............ Program Element Directive
PED............ Program Evaluation Division [Environmental Protection Agency] (GFGA)
PED............ Program Execution Directive (AAG)
PED............ Promotion Eligibility Date [Military]
PED............ Proton-Enhanced Diffusion
PED............ Public Employee Department (of AFL-CIO) (EA)
PEd............ Pulmonary Edema [Medicine]
PED............ Pulse Edge Discrimination (OA)
PED............ Pure Edge Dislocation
PED............ Pyramid Element Designator
PED............ Springfield, TN [Location identifier FAA] (FAAL)
PEDA .... Pedal Artery
PEDA .... Personnel Equipment Data Analysis
Ped B .... Bachelor of Pedagogy
PED B .... Bachelor of Pediatrics (WDAA)
PEDB .... Page Element Data Base [Printing] (DGA)
PEDB .... Payload Engineering Data Base [NASA] (SSD)
PEDB .... Planning and Execution Data Base (COE)
PEDB .... Process Engineering Database
PEDC .... Personal Effects Distribution Center

PEDC .... Professional Educational Development Corp. [An association] (EA)
PEDCUG ...... Planning Engineers Desktop Computer Users Group (EA)
Ped D .... Doctor of Pedagogy
PEDD .... Program Element Descriptive Data (CAAL)
PEddyB .... Baldwin Locomotive Works, Eddystone, PA [Library symbol Library of Congress Obsolete] (LCLS)
Pe de Ancar... Petrus de Ancharano [Deceased, 1416] [Authority cited in pre-1607 legal work] (DSA)
Pe de Anch... Petrus de Ancharano [Deceased, 1416] [Authority cited in pre-1607 legal work] (DSA)
Pe de Ancha... Petrus de Ancharano [Deceased, 1416] [Authority cited in pre-1607 legal work] (DSA)
Pe de Bel ... Petrus de Bellapertica [Deceased, 1308] [Authority cited in pre-1607 legal work] (DSA)
Pe de Belper... Petrus de Bellapertica [Deceased, 1308] [Authority cited in pre-1607 legal work] (DSA)
Pe de Bepe... Petrus de Bellapertica [Deceased, 1308] [Authority cited in pre-1607 legal work] (DSA)
Pe de Blpti... Petrus de Bellapertica [Deceased, 1308] [Authority cited in pre-1607 legal work] (DSA)
Pe de Pal .... Pierre de la Palu [Deceased, 1342] [Authority cited in pre-1607 legal work] (DSA)
Pe de Sal ... Petrus de Salinis [Flourished, 13th century] [Authority cited in pre-1607 legal work] (DSA)
Pe de Samp... Petrus de Sampsone [Flourished, 1246-58] [Authority cited in pre-1607 legal work] (DSA)
PEDET......... Pedetemptim [Gradually] [Pharmacy]
PEDF........... Pigment Epithelium-Derived Factor [Medicine] (DMAA)
PEDF........... Potential-Energy Distribution Function [Physical chemistry]
PEDG .... Phenethyldiguanide [Same as PEBG] [Antidiabetic compound]
PEDI........... Pediatrics [Medicine] (DHSM)
Pediatric ..... Pediatric Services of America, Inc. [Associated Press] (SAG)
PEDIN .... National Petroleum Exploration Database [Australia]
PEDIN .... Peapod Dinghy
PE Dir......... Director of Physical Education (PGP)
PE Dir......... Physical Education Director
PEdiS.......... Edinboro State College, Edinboro, PA [Library symbol Library of Congress] (LCLS)
PEDL.......... Pedicel Length [Botany]
Ped M......... Master of Pedagogy
pedm .... Pediment (VRA)
PEDMAN ...... PACFLT [Pacific Fleet] Enlisted Personnel Distribution Manual (CINC)
PEDMS .... Portable and Extensible Data Management System (IAA)
PEDN .... Planned Event Discrepancy Notification [NASA] (KSC)
PEDOL .... Pedology
PEDP .... Pacific Energy Development Program [Fiji] [United Nations]
PEDRA......... Palestine Economic Development and Reconstruction Agency (ECON)
PEDRO......... Pneumatic Energy Detector with Remote Optics
PEDRO......... Pride, Efficiency, Dedication, Reliability, and Order (DNAB)
PEDRTC .... Pediatric
PEDS .... Packaging Engineering Data System (AFM)
PeDS .... Pediatric Drug Surveillance [Program] (DAVI)
PeDS .... Pediatric Drug Surveillance Program (BABM)
PEDS .... Pediatrics
PEDS .... Peltier Effect Diffusion Separation [Physical chemistry]
PEDS .... Philips Engineering and Development System (NITA)
PEDS D .... Pilgrim Edward Doty Society (EA)
PEDS .... Plasma-Enhanced Deposition System (AAEL)
PEDS .... Program Element Descriptive Summary (CAAL)
PEDS .... Protective Equipment Decontamination Section [Nuclear energy] (NRCH)
PEDSTL....... Pedestal [Freight]
PEDT.......... Pendant [Jewelry] (ROG)
PEDT.......... Peridot [Jewelry] (ROG)
PEDTRC ...... Pediatric
PEDUC......... Professeurs d'Economie Domestique des Universites Canadiennes [Canadian University Teachers of Home Economics - CUTHE]
PEDX .... Pediatrix Medical Group [NASDAQ symbol] (TTSB)
PEDX .... Pediatrix Medical Group, Inc. [NASDAQ symbol] (SAG)
PEE............ Phosphate-Eliminating Enzyme (DMAA)
PEE............ Photoelectron Emission [Also, OSEE]
PEE............ Photoemission Effect
PEE............ Pressure Environmental Equipment (NVT)
PEE............ Program Estimating Equation
PEE............ Proof and Experimental Establishment [British]
PEE............ Talkeetna, AK [Location identifier FAA] (FAAL)
PEEA........... (Phenyl)(ethyl)ethanolamine [Organic chemistry]
PEEC........... Personnel Emergency Estimator Capability
PEEC........... Programmable Electronic Engine Control [Automotive engineering]
PEEC........... Project for an Energy-Enriched Curriculum [Department of Energy]
PEECP......... Pilot Expedited Environmental Cleanup Program (BCP)
PEEIC......... Programme des Economies d'Energie dans l'Industrie Canadienne
PEEK.......... Peekskill Financial [NASDAQ symbol] (TTSB)
PEEK.......... Peekskill Financial Corp. [NASDAQ symbol] (SAG)
PEEK.......... People for the Enjoyment of Eyeballing Knees [Group opposing below-the-knee fashions introduced in 1970]
PEEK.......... Periodically Elevated Electronic Kibitzer
PEEK.......... Polyetheretherketone (DMAA)
PEEK.......... Polyetherketone [Organic chemistry]
PEEKK......... Poly Ether Ether Ketone Ketone (EDCT)
Peekskill...... Peekskill Financial Corp. [Associated Press] (SAG)
PEELS .... Parallel [Detection] Electron Energy Loss Spectroscopy
PEEM.......... Panel of Experts on Environmental Management (GNE)

PEEM .... Photoemission Electron Microscope
PEEM .... Photoemission Electron Microscopy (MCD)
PEEP .... Panel of Experts on Environmental Pollution [*WMO*] (MSC)
PEEP .... Pilot's Electronic Eyelevel Presentation [*British*]
PEEP .... Porous Electrode Electrostatic Precipitation
PEEP .... Positive End Expiratory Pressure [*Medicine*]
PEEP .... Production Electronic Equipment Procurement Status Report
Peeples & Stevens... Peeples and Stevens' Reports [*80-97 Georgia*] [*A publication*] (DLA)
PEER .... Pediatric Examination of Educational Readiness [*Child development test*]
Peer .... Peerless [*Record label*] [*USA, Mexico*]
PEER .... Planned Experience for Effective Relating
PEER .... Price Escalation Estimated Rates
PEER .... Program of Equal Employment Opportunity Evaluation Reports
PEER .... Project Engineer Evaluation Report (HGAA)
PEER .... Project on Equal Education Rights [*Defunct*] (EA)
PEERAMID ... Pediatric Examination of Educational Readiness at Middle Childhood [*Child development test*] [*Psychology*]
PEERC .... Production Engineering Education and Research Center
Peere Wms... Peere-Williams' English Chancery and King's Bench Cases [*1695-1736*] [*A publication*] (DLA)
PeerMf........ Peerless Manufacturing Co. [*Associated Press*] (SAG)
PEET .... Partnerships for Enhancing Expertise in Taxonomy [*National Science Foundation*]
PEET .... Printing Equipment Education Trust [*British*]
PEETPACK ... Process Engineering Evaluation Techniques Package (PDAA)
PEETSA........ Parents, Educators and Environmentalists to Save Anchoives [*An association*]
PEEX .... Pediatric Early Elementary Examination [*Child development test*] [*Psychology*]
PEF .... Pacific-Euro Growth Fund (EFIS)
PEF .... Packaging Education Foundation (EA)
PEF .... Palestine Endowment Funds [*Later, PEF Israel Endowment Funds*] (EA)
PEF .... Palestine Exploration Fund
PEF .... Pathway-Exposure Factor [*Environmental chemistry*]
PEF .... Peak Expiratory Flow [*Pulmonary function*]
PEF .... PEF Israel Endowment Funds [*An association*] (EA)
PEF .... Performance Efficiency Factor (AFIT)
PEF .... Personal Effects Floater [*Insurance*]
PEF .... Personality Evaluation Form [*Psychology*]
PEF .... Phil Esposito Foundation [*Defunct*] (EA)
PEF .... Physical Electronics Facility (MCD)
PEF .... Plastics Education Foundation (EA)
PEF .... Polyethylene Foam
PEF .... Potential-Energy Function [*Physical chemistry*]
PEF .... Powerhouse Exhaust Facility (IAA)
PEF .... Prediction Error Filter [*Wave frequency and phase modifier*]
PEF .... Presbyterian Evangelistic Fellowship [*Defunct*] (EA)
PEF .... Pro Ecclesia Foundation (EA)
PEF .... Program Estimating Factor (AFM)
PEF .... Proposal Evaluation Form (AAG)
PEF .... Psychiatric Evaluation Form [*Psychology*]
PEF .... Pulmonary Edema Fluid [*Medicine*] (DMAA)
PEF .... Pulsed-Electric-Field
PEF .... Pulse Eliminating Filter (IAA)
PEFC .... Private Export Funding Corp. (IMH)
PEFCO .... Private Export Funding Corp.
Pe Fi .... Petrus Filipi [*Authority cited in pre-1607 legal work*] (DSA)
Pe Fili .... Petrus Filipi [*Authority cited in pre-1607 legal work*] (DSA)
PEF/NET...... Public Education Fund Network (EA)
PEFO........... Payload Effects Follow-On Study [*NASA*] (NASA)
PEFO........... Petrified Forest National Park
PEFOS .... Program Evaluation and Field Operations Staff [*Environmental Protection Agency*] (GFGA)
PEFQS .... Palestine Exploration Fund. Quarterly Statement [*London*] [*A publication*] (BJA)
PEFQST....... Palestine Exploration Fund. Quarterly Statement [*London*] [*A publication*] (BJA)
PEFR........... Peak Expiratory Flow Rate
PEFR/PIFR ... Peak Expiratory Flow/Peak Inspiratory Flow Rate [*Medicine*] (DAVI)
PEFSR........ Partial Expiratory Flow-Static Recoil Curve [*Physiology*] (MAE)
PEFT .... Peripheral Equipment Functional Test (CAAL)
PEFT .... Preschool Embedded Figures Test [*Child development test*]
PEFTOK....... Philippine Expeditionary Force to Korea [*United Nations*]
PEFTP......... Parent Education Follow Through Program (EDAC)
PEFU.......... Panel of Experts on Fish Utilization [*FAO*] (ASF)
PEFV.......... Partial Expiratory Flow-Volume [*Physiology*]
PEG............ General Aniline & Film Co., General Research Laboratory, Easton, PA [*Library symbol Library of Congress Obsolete*] (LCLS)
PEG .... Pac Engo Materials [*Vancouver Stock Exchange symbol*]
PEG .... Pacific Environmental Group [*Marine science*] (MSC)
PEG .... Patient Evaluation Grid [*Medicine*] (DMAA)
Peg............ Pegasus [*Constellation*]
PEG............ Pelangi Air Sdn. Bhd. [*Malaysia*] [*FAA designator*] (FAAC)
PEG............ Percutaneous Endoscopic Gastrostomy [*Medicine*] (CPH)
PEG............ Performance Evaluation Group (CINC)
PEG............ Petrochemical Energy Group (EA)
PEG............ Photo Exploitation Group
PEG............ Pneumatic Explosion Generator
PEG............ Pneumoencephalogram [*Medicine*]
PEG............ Polyethylene Glycol [*Organic chemistry*]
PEG............ Powered Explicit Guidance (NAKS)
PEG............ Previous Endorsement(s) Guaranteed [*Banking*]

PEG............ Principle of the Equivalent Generator
PEG............ Prior Endorsement Guaranteed (HGAA)
PEG............ Priorities Exploitation Group
PEG............ Priorities for ELINT Guidance (MCD)
PEG............ Process Evaluation Guide [*Graphic Communications Association*]
PEG............ Production Entitlement Guarantee [*International Agricultural Trade Research Consortium*] (ECON)
PEG............ Professional Emphasis Group [*National Audience Board*] (NTCM)
PEG............ Program Evaluation Group [*Air Force*]
PEG............ Project Engineering Guide (MCD)
PEG............ Protected Employee Group [*Program*]
PEG............ Protection Engineers Group [*United States Telephone Association*] [*Telecommunications*]
PEG............ PSE & G Capital Trust [*NYSE symbol*] (SAG)
PEG............ Public, Educational, Government [*Cable television access channels*] (NTCM)
PEG............ Public Service Elec & Gas Co. [*NYSE symbol*] (SAG)
PEG............ Public Service Electric & Gas Co. (CDAI)
PEG............ Public Service Enterprise Group, Inc. [*NYSE symbol*] (SPSG)
PEG............ Public Svc Enterpr [*NYSE symbol*] (TTSB)
PEG............ Pyrotechnic Electron Generator (MCD)
PEGA .... Pegasystems, Inc. [*NASDAQ symbol*] (SAG)
PEGA .... Polyethylene Glycol Adipate [*Organic chemistry*]
PegaCm........ Pegasus Communications Corp. [*Associated Press*] (SAG)
PEG-ADA....... Polyethylene Glycol-Adenosine Deaminase [*A modified enzyme*]
PEGASUS..... People, Goods, and Services Urban System [*Texas*] [*FHWA*] (TAG)
Pegasys....... Pegasystems, Inc. [*Associated Press*] (SAG)
PEGDE .... Pentaethylene Glycol Dodecyl Ether [*Organic chemistry*]
PEGE........... Program for Evaluation of Ground Environment
PEG-ELS....... Polyethylene Glycol and Iso-Osmolar Electrolyte Solution (STED)
PegGld........ Pegasus Gold, Inc. [*Associated Press*] (SAG)
PEGLN .... Petiole Gland Pairs, Number Of [*Botany*]
PEGPrA .... Pub Sv E&G 4.08% Pfd [*NYSE symbol*] (TTSB)
PEGPrC .... Pub Sv E&G 4.30% Pfd [*NYSE symbol*] (TTSB)
PEGPrD .... Pub Sv E&G 5.05% Pfd [*NYSE symbol*] (TTSB)
PEGPrE .... Pub Sv E&G 5.28% Pfd [*NYSE symbol*] (TTSB)
PEGPrG .... Pub Sv E&G 6.80% Pfd [*NYSE symbol*] (TTSB)
PEGPrI .... Public Sv E&G 7.40% cm Pfd [*NYSE symbol*] (TTSB)
PEGPrJ .... Pub Sv E&G 7.52% Pfd [*NYSE symbol*] (TTSB)
PEGPrV .... Pub Sv E&G 7.44% Pfd [*NYSE symbol*] (TTSB)
PEGPrW .... Pub Sv E&G 5.97% Pfd [*NYSE symbol*] (TTSB)
PEGPrX .... Public Svc E&G Cap 8.00%'MIPS' [*NYSE symbol*] (TTSB)
PEGPrY .... Pub Sv E&G 6.75% Pfd [*NYSE symbol*] (TTSB)
PEGPrZ .... Public Svc E&G Cap 9.375% 'MIPS' [*NYSE symbol*] (TTSB)
PEGR .... Proportional Exhaust Gas Recirculation [*Engines*]
Pegs .... Pegasus [*Constellation*]
PEGS .... Polyethylene Glycol Succinate [*Organic chemistry*]
PEGS .... Project Engineering Graphics System [*Computer Aided Design Centre*] [*Software package*] (NCC)
PEGS .... Project Engineering System
PEH............ Pehpei [*Republic of China*] [*Seismograph station code, US Geological Survey*] (SEIS)
PEH............ Pehuajo [*Argentina*] [*Airport symbol*] (OAG)
PEH............ Periods of European History [*A publication*]
PEH............ Planning Estimate Handbook (SAA)
PEHA .... Pentaethylenehexamine [*Organic chemistry*]
PEHA .... Pony Express Historical Association (EA)
PEHD .... Polyethylene-High Density [*Organic chemistry*]
PEHi........... Northampton County Historical and Genealogical Society, Mary Illick Memorial Library, Easton, PA [*Library symbol Library of Congress*] (LCLS)
Pe His .... Petrus Hispanus [*Authority cited in pre-1607 legal work*] (DSA)
PEI............ Patriotic Education, Inc. (EA)
PEI............ Peine [*Chile*] [*Seismograph station code, US Geological Survey Closed*] (SEIS)
pe/I........... Pen and Ink (VRA)
PEI............ Penna RE Inv Tr SNI [*AMEX symbol*] (TTSB)
PEI............ Pennsylvania Real Estate Investment Trust [*AMEX symbol*] (SPSG)
PEI............ Pereira [*Colombia*] [*Airport symbol*] (OAG)
PEI............ Petrocel Industries, Inc. [*Vancouver Stock Exchange symbol*]
PEI............ Petroleum Equipment Institute (EA)
PEI............ Phosphate Excretion Index [*Biochemistry*] (DAVI)
PEI............ Phosphorous Excretion Index [*Medicine*] (MEDA)
PEI............ Phosphorus Excretion Index [*Biochemistry*] (DAVI)
PEI............ Physical Education Instructor (WDAA)
PEI............ Physical Efficiency Index [*Medicine*] (DMAA)
PEI............ Physical Efficiency Indx [*Medicine*] (DAVI)
PEI............ Planning Executives Institute [*Later, PF*]
PEI............ Plant Engineering Inspection (AAG)
PEI............ Playboy Enterprises, Inc.
PEI............ Polyetherimide
PEI............ Polyethylenimine [*Organic chemistry*]
PEI............ Porcelain Enamel Institute (EA)
PEI............ Postejaculatory Interval [*Physiology*]
PEI............ Precipitation-Efficiency Index
PEI............ Preliminary Engineering Inspection [*NASA*] (KSC)
PEI............ Prince Edward Island [*Canadian province*]
PEI............ Prince Edward Island Provincial Library [*UTLAS symbol*]
PEI............ Prince Edward Island Reports (Haviland's) [*A publication*] (DLA)
PEI............ Professional Engineers in Industry
PEI............ Pupil Evaluation Inventory [*Education*] (EDAC)
PEI-A .... Personal Experience Inventory for Adults [*Test*] (TMMY)
PEIA.......... Poultry and Egg Institute of America (EA)
PEIAS........ Phenylephrine-Activated Isolated Aortic Strip (DB)
PEIC.......... Periodic Error Integrating Controller

PEID............ Program Element Identifier [*Military*] (AFIT)
PEIF............ Productivity Enhancing Incentive Fund (DNAB)
PEILS.......... PACOM [*Pacific Command*] Executive Intelligence Summary (MCD)
PEIP............ Presidential Executive Interchange Program [*Federal government*]
PEIR............ Performance Evaluation and Information Reduction (IAA)
PEIR............ Problem Equipment Indicator Reports (MCD)
PEIR............ Process Evaluation and Information Reduction (IAA)
PEIR............ Project Equipment Inspection Record [*NASA*] (KSC)
PEI Rep ...... Prince Edward Island Reports (Haviland's) [*1850-1914*] [*A publication*] (DLA)
PEI Rev Stat... Prince Edward Island Revised Statutes [*Canada*] [*A publication*] (DLA)
PEIS........... Polyethylene Isopthalate [*Organic chemistry*]
PEIS........... Programmatic Environmental Impact Statement (NRCH)
PEI Stat ...... Prince Edward Island Statutes [*Canada*] [*A publication*] (DLA)
PEITA......... Professional Equestrian Instructors and Trainers Association [*Defunct*] (EA)
PEITV......... Preliminary Encapsulated Inert Test Vehicle (MCD)
PEJ .... Percutaneous Endoscopic Jejunostomy [*Medicine*] (DMAA)
PEJ .... Premolded Expansion Joint [*Technical drawings*]
Pe Ja .... Petrus Jacobi [*Flourished, 14th century*] [*Authority cited in pre-1607 legal work*] (DSA)
PEJO.......... Plant Engineering Job Order (AAG)
PEK............ Beijing [*China*] [*Airport symbol*] (OAG)
PEK............ Jacksonville, FL [*Location identifier FAA*] (FAAL)
PEK............ Peak Aviation, PLC [*British*] [*FAA designator*] (FAAC)
PEK............ Peking [*China*] [*Airport symbol*] (AD)
PEK............ Peking [*Republic of China*] [*Seismograph station code, US Geological Survey*] (SEIS)
PEK............ Pekoe [*Tea trade*] (ROG)
PEK............ Phase-Exchange Keying [*Computer science*] (IEEE)
PEK............ Phi Epsilon Kappa [*Fraternity*]
PEK............ Polyetherketone [*Organic chemistry*]
PEKK.......... Polyetherketoneketone [*Materials science*]
PEL............ Aeropelican Air Services Pty Ltd. [*Australia ICAO designator*] (FAAC)
Pel............ Elastic Recoil Pressure of Lung [*Medicine*] (STED)
PEL............ Lafayette College, Easton, PA [*Library symbol Library of Congress*] (LCLS)
PEL............ Paid Educational Leave (AIE)
PEL............ PanEnergy Corp. [*NYSE symbol*] [*Formerly, Panhandle Eastern*] (SG)
PEL............ Panhandle Eastern Pipe Line Co. [*NYSE symbol*] (SPSG)
Pel............ Pelagius [*Deceased, 1232*] [*Authority cited in pre-1607 legal work*] (DSA)
PEL............ Pelaneng [*Lesotho*] [*Airport symbol*] (OAG)
PEL............ Peldehue [*Chile*] [*Seismograph station code, US Geological Survey*] (SEIS)
Pel............ Pelopidas [*of Plutarch*] [*Classical studies*] (OCD)
PEL............ Peritoneal Exudate Lymphocytes [*Hematology*]
PEL............ Permissible Exposure Level
PEL............ Permissible Exposure Limit [*OSHA*]
PEL............ Personal Effectiveness Inventory (AIE)
PEL............ Personal Exposure Level [*or Limit*]
PEL............ Personnel Licensing and Training [*ICAO*] (AIA)
PEL............ Philatelic Esperanto League [*See also ELF*] [*Solna, Sweden*] (EAIO)
PEL............ Photoelectron Layer
PEL............ Picture Element [*Single element of resolution in image processing*] (IBMDP)
PEL............ Precision Elastic Limit
PEL............ Priests Eucharistic League (EA)
PEL............ Primary Effusion Lymphoma [*Oncology*]
PEL............ Production Error Log (NITA)
PEL............ Professional Education Libraries [*UTLAS symbol*]
PEL............ Proportional Elastic Limit
PEL............ Public Exposure Limit (MCD)
PEIC........... Elizabethtown College, Elizabethtown, PA [*Library symbol*] [*Library of Congress*] (LCLS)
PELC.......... Professional Engineers' Legislative Committee
PELEC........ Photoelectric (MSA)
PEleph........ Elephantine Papyri [*A publication*] (OCD)
PELG.......... Pelger Muet Anomaly [*Laboratory science*] (DAVI)
PELG.......... Poly(ethyl L-Glutamate) [*Organic chemistry*]
PELI........... Production, Engineering and Logistics Information (AAGC)
PELISA........ Paper Enzyme-Linked Immunosorbent Assay (STED)
PELL.......... Papers on English Language and Literature [*A publication*]
PELR.......... Peeler
PELR.......... Pelsart Resources NL [*NASDAQ symbol*] (NQ)
PELRV .... Pea Leafroll Virus [*Plant pathology*]
PELRY .... Pelsart Resources ADR [*NASDAQ symbol*] (TTSB)
PELS.......... Precision Emitter Location System [*Air Force*] (MCD)
PELS.......... Propionyl Erythromycin Lauryl Sulfate [*Antimicrobial agent*]
Pelsart....... Pelsart Resources NL [*Associated Press*] (SAG)
PELSS......... Precision Emitter Location Strike System [*Air Force*]
Pelt........... Peltier's Orleans Appeals [*1917-23*] [*A publication*] (DLA)
PELT.......... Princeton American [*NASDAQ symbol*] (TTSB)
PELT.......... Princeton Electronic Products, Inc. [*NASDAQ symbol*] (NQ)
PELTS......... Personal Emergency Locator Transmitter Service [*Telecommunications*] (CIST)
PELV.......... Pepino Latent Virus [*Plant pathology*]
PEM........... Parametric Earth Model [*Geodynamics*]
PEM........... Parasitic Encephalitis Meningitis [*Medicine*]
PEM........... Particle Environmental Monitor (MCD)
PEM........... Partido Ecologista Mexicano [*Political party*] (EY)
PEM........... Payload Ejection Mechanism
PEM........... PEM-AIR Ltd. [*Canada ICAO designator*] (FAAC)

PEM........... Pembrokeshire [*County in Wales*] (ROG)
PEM........... Performance Evaluation Model
PEM........... Peritoneal Exudate Macrophage [*Hematology*]
PEM........... Perrot Memorial Library, Old Greenwich, CT [*OCLC symbol*] (OCLC)
PEM........... Personal-E Mailbox [*Computer software*] (PCM)
PEM........... Personal Exposure Monitor [*Environmental chemistry*]
PEM........... Petite Ensemble Model (MCD)
PEM........... Petrox Energy & Mineral Corp. [*Toronto Stock Exchange symbol*]
PEM........... Phased Equipment Modernization [*Army*] (AABC)
PEM........... Philco Electronic Module
PEM........... Photoelastic Modulator [*Instrumentation*]
PEM........... Photoelectromagnetic
PEM........... Photoelectron Microscopy
PEM........... Photoemission Microscope
PEM........... Photographic Equipment and Materials (NATG)
PEM........... Plant Engineering and Maintenance (NASA)
PEM........... Plant Engineer Mechanical (AAG)
PEM........... Plastic-Encapsulated Microcircuit [*Telecommunications*]
PEM........... Polaris Evaluation Missile
PEM........... Polyethylene Matrix (DB)
PEM........... Polymer Electrolyte Membrane [*Fuel technology*]
PEM........... Position Encoding Module (CAAL)
PEM........... Precordial Electrocardiographic Mapping (STED)
PEM........... Prescription-Event Monitoring
PEM........... Primary Enrichment Medium [*Microbiology*]
PEM........... Privacy-Enhanced Mail [*Software package*]
PEM........... Probable Error of Measurement
PEM........... Process Execution Module (NITA)
PEM........... Processing Element Memory [*Computer science*]
PEM........... Processing Element Module [*Computer science*] (IAA)
PEM........... Product Effectiveness Manual
PEM........... Production Engineering Measure [*Army*] (MCD)
PEM........... Production Evaluation Missile [*Military*] (CAAL)
PEM........... Program Element Manager (MCD)
PEM........... Program Element Monitor (AFM)
PEM........... Program Endorsement Memorandum (AAGC)
PEM........... Project Engineering Memorandum
PEM........... Proposal Evaluation Manager
PEM........... Protein Energy Malnutrition [*Medicine*]
PEM........... Proton Exchange Membrane [*Fuel technology*] (PS)
PEM........... Puerto Maldonado [*Peru*] [*Airport symbol*] (OAG)
PEM........... Pulmonary Embolus [*Medicine*] (DAVI)
PEMA......... Pheny(ethyl)malonamide [*Organic chemistry*]
PEMA......... Polyethyl Methacrylate [*Organic chemistry*]
PEMA......... Process Equipment Manufacturers Association (EA)
PEMA......... Procurement Equipment Maintenance, Army (MCD)
PEMA......... Procurement, Equipment, Missiles, Army
PEMA......... Procurement of Equipment and Munition Appropriations [*Military*] (AABC)
PEMA......... Production-Equipment-Missile Agency [*Army*]
PEMAP........ President's Environmental Merit Award Program [*Environmental Protection Agency*]
PEMARS ...... Procurement of Equipment and Missiles, Army Management and Accounting Reporting System (AABC)
PEMB......... Pembroke College [*Oxford and Cambridge Universities*] (ROG)
PEMB......... Pembrokeshire [*County in Wales*]
Pemb Eq...... Pemberton's Practice in Equity by Way of Revivor and Supplement [*1867*] [*A publication*] (ILCA)
Pemb Judg... Pemberton's Judgments and Orders [*A publication*] (DLA)
PEMBS........ Pembrokeshire [*County in Wales*]
PEMCONS.... Photographic Equipment Management Control System
PEMD......... Program Evaluation and Methodology Division [*General Accounting Office*] [*Federal government*] (GFGA)
PEMD......... Program for Export Market Development [*Canada*]
PEME......... Pulsed Electromagnetic Energy [*Diathermy*] (CPH)
PEMF......... Pulsating Electromagnetic Field
PEMFC........ Proton Exchange Membrane Fuel Cell [*Energy source*]
PEMISA....... Proficiency Battery in English and Mathematics for Indian South Africans (TES)
PEMN......... Program Engineering Management Network [*Computer science*] (RDA)
Pe Mo........ Petrus Morini [*Authority cited in pre-1607 legal work*] (DSA)
PEMO......... Plant Engineering Maintenance Order
PEMO......... Production Engineering and Manufacturing Organization (AAG)
PE-MOCVD... Plasma-Enhanced Metalorganic Chemical Vapor Deposition [*Coating technology*]
Pe Mori...... Petrus Morini [*Authority cited in pre-1607 legal work*] (DSA)
PEMOV ...... Peanut Mottle Virus [*Plant pathology*]
PEMRam...... Precision Electromagnetic Ram [*Denne Developments*] (PS)
PEMS......... Pesticide Enforcement Management System (NITA)
PEMS......... Physical, Emotional, Mental, Safety [*Model for charting procedure*] [*Medicine*]
PEMS......... Porcelain-Enamelled Metal Substrate (EECA)
PEMS......... Portable Environmental Measuring System
PEMS......... Predictive Emission Monitoring System [*Environmental science*]
PEMS......... Professional Education of the Media Specialist
PEMS......... Propulsion Energy Management Study (MCD)
PEMT......... Phosphatidylethanolamine Methyltransferase [*An enzyme*]
PEMV......... Pea Enation Mosaic Virus [*Plant pathology*]
PeMV......... Pepper Mottle Virus
PEM-West... Pacific Exploratory Mission-West [*Western Pacific Tropospheric Chemistry Experiment*] [*Marine science*] (OSRA)
Pem Yeo...... Pembroke Yeomanry [*British military*] (DMA)
PEN............ Astoria, OR [*Location identifier FAA*] (FAAL)

PEN............. International PEN [*Official name; PEN, never spelled out in use, is said to stand for poets, playwrights, editors, essayists, novelists*] (EAIO)
PEN............. Pacific Exchange Network [*Marine science*] (OSRA)
PEN............. Parenteral and Enteral Nutrition [*Gastroenterology*] (DAVI)
PEN............. Peace Education Network (EA)
PEN............. PEN American Center (EA)
PEN............. Penang [*Malaysia*] [*Airport symbol*] (OAG)
PEN............. Pendeli [*Greece*] [*Geomagnetic observatory code*]
PEN............. Penetration (AFM)
PEN............. Penicillin [*Antibiotic*]
Pen............. Penicillin [*Medicine*] (DMAA)
PEN............. Peninsula [*Maps and charts*]
PEN............. Peninsula Airways, Inc. [*ICAO designator*] (FAAC)
PEN............. Penitent
PEN............. Penitentiary (WDAA)
Pen............. Pennewill's Delaware Reports [*A publication*] (DLA)
Pen............. Pennington's New Jersey Reports [*2, 3 New Jersey*] [*A publication*] (DLA)
PEN............. Pensacola [*Florida*] [*Seismograph station code, US Geological Survey Closed*] (SEIS)
PEN............. Pentazocine [*An analgesic*]
PEN............. Pentobarbital [*Sedative*]
PEN............. Pentode (DEN)
PEN............. Permanent Entry Number [*Computer science*]
PEN............. Pharmacology Equivalent Name
PEN............. Pharmacy Equivalent Name [*Medicine*] (DMAA)
PEN............. Physicians Education Network (EA)
PEN............. Poets, Playwrights, Editors, Essayists, and Novelists [*AccountingPANANEWS*] (NADA)
PEN............. Polyethylene Naphthalate [*Organic chemistry*]
PEN............. Professional Enrichment News [*Portuguese*] (BJA)
PEN............. Program Element Number [*Computer science*] (KSC)
PEN............. Program Error Note [*Computer science*]
PEN............. Public Electronic Network [*Information service or system*] (IID)
PEN............. Purchasing Electronic Notebook (HGAA)
PENA............. Primary Emission Neuron Activation (IEEE)
PENAID........ Penetration Aid [*Weaponry*]
Pen & W...... Penrose and Watts' Pennsylvania Reports [*1829-32*] [*A publication*] (DLA)
PENB .... Poultry and Egg National Board [*Later, AEB*] (EA)
PENBASE .... Peninsular Base Section [*Military*]
Pen C .... Penal Code [*A publication*] (DLA)
PENC .... Pen Interconnect [*NASDAQ symbol*] (TTSB)
PENC .... Pen Interconnect, Inc. [*NASDAQ symbol*] (SAG)
Penchk........ Pennichuck Corp. [*Associated Press*] (SAG)
PENCIL .... Pictorial Encoding Language [*Computer science*] (IEEE)
PENCIL .... Portable Encoder/Illustrator [*Facetious term for pre-word-processing equipment*]
PENCIL .... Public Education Needs Civic Involvement in Learning
Pencp .... Penncorp Financial Group [*Associated Press*] (SAG)
PencpFn ...... Penncorp Financial Group [*Associated Press*] (SAG)
PENCPR....... PEN [*Poets, Playwrights, Essayists, Editors, and Novelists*] Club of PuertoRico (EA)
PENCW .... Pen Interconnect Wrrt [*NASDAQ symbol*] (TTSB)
pend .... Pendant (VRA)
Pend .... Pendant (ROG)
PEND .... Pendens [*Weighing*] [*Pharmacy*]
PEND .... Pending
Pen Dec....... Pension Decisions [*Department of the Interior*] [*A publication*] (DLA)
PENDORF .... Penetrate Dorfman [*FBI investigation of Teamster leader Allen Dorfman*]
Penedrm...... Penedrm, Inc. [*Associated Press*] (SAG)
Penelc .... Penelec Capital Ltd. [*Associated Press*] (SAG)
PenEM .... Penn Engineering & Manufacturing Corp. [*Associated Press*] (SAG)
PenEMA...... Penn Engineering & Manufacturing Corp. [*Associated Press*] (SAG)
P/E NEWS... Petroleum/Energy Business News Index [*American Petroleum Institute*] [*New York, NY Bibliographic database*]
PenG........... Penicillin G [*Antibacterial agent*]
PenG........... Pennsylvania Gas & Water Co. [*Associated Press*] (SAG)
PENG .... Photo-Electro-Nystagmography [*Medicine*]
PENG .... Prima Energy [*NASDAQ symbol*] (TTSB)
PENG .... Prima Energy Corp. [*NASDAQ symbol*] (NQ)
PEng........... Professional Engineer
PEng........... Registered Professional Engineer (DD)
PENGEM ...... Penetrate Gray Electronics Markets [*FBI "sting" operation, 1982, where employees of Japanese computer firms were caught trying to obtain proprietary information illegally from IBM Co.*]
PENIC .... Penicillin [*Antibiotic*]
Penic Cam... Penicillum Camelinum [*A Camel's-Hair Brush*] [*Pharmacy*]
penin .... Peninsula
PenInt......... Pen Interconnect, Inc. [*Associated Press*] (SAG)
PenInter...... Pen Interconnect, Inc. [*Associated Press*] (SAG)
PeninTst ...... Peninsula Trust Bank, Inc. [*Associated Press*] (SAG)
PENIT.......... Penitentiary
PENJERDEL.. Pennsylvania, New Jersey, Delaware
PENK.......... Proenkephalin [*Biochemistry*]
Penn .... Pennewill's Delaware Reports [*A publication*] (DLA)
Penn .... Pennington's New Jersey Reports [*A publication*] (DLA)
PENN .... Penn National Gaming [*NASDAQ symbol*] (TTSB)
PENN .... Penn National Gaming, Inc. [*NASDAQ symbol*] (SAG)
Penn .... Pennsylvania
Penn .... Pennsylvania (ODBW)
PENN .... Pennsylvanian [*Period, era, or system*] [*Geology*]
Penn .... Pennsylvania State Reports [*A publication*] (DLA)

Penn........... Pennypacker's Unreported Pennsylvania Cases [*A publication*] (DLA)
PENNA........ Pennsylvania
Penna........ Pennsylvania (ODBW)
Penna Law Journal... Pennsylvania Law Journal [*A publication*] (DLA)
Penna LJ ..... Pennsylvania Law Journal [*A publication*] (DLA)
PennAm...... Penn America Group [*Associated Press*] (SAG)
Penna R ..... Pennsylvania State Reports [*A publication*] (DLA)
Penna SR .... Pennsylvania State Reports [*A publication*] (DLA)
Penna St..... Pennsylvania State Reports [*A publication*] (DLA)
Penna State Rep... Pennsylvania State Reports [*A publication*] (DLA)
PennBc........ PennFirst Bancorp [*Associated Press*] (SAG)
PennBcp...... PennFirst Bancorp [*Associated Press*] (SAG)
Penn Co Ct Rep... Pennsylvania County Court Reports [*A publication*] (DLA)
Penn C Opt... Pennsylvania College of Optometry (GAGS)
Penn Corp Rep... Pennsylvania Corporation Reporter [*A publication*] (DLA)
Penn Del ..... Pennewill's Delaware Reports [*A publication*] (DLA)
Penn Dist & Co Rep... Pennsylvania District and County Reports [*A publication*] (DLA)
Penn Dist Rep... Pennsylvania District Reports [*A publication*] (DLA)
Penne .... Pennewill's Delaware Reports [*17-23 Delaware*] [*1897-1909*] [*A publication*] (DLA)
PennEn........ Penn Enterprises, Inc. [*Associated Press*] (SAG)
Pennew....... Pennewill's Delaware Reports [*A publication*] (DLA)
Pennewill .... Pennewill's Delaware Supreme Court Reports [*1897-1909*] [*A publication*] (DLA)
Penney .... Penney [*J. C.*] Co., Inc. [*Associated Press*] (SAG)
PennFed ...... PennFed Financial Services, Inc. [*Associated Press*] (SAG)
PenNGm ...... Penn National Gaming, Inc. [*Associated Press*] (SAG)
Penning ...... Pennington's New Jersey Reports [*2, 3 New Jersey*] [*A publication*] (DLA)
Pen NJ......... Pennington's New Jersey Reports [*2, 3 New Jersey*] [*A publication*] (DLA)
Penn Law Jour... Pennsylvania Law Journal [*A publication*] (DLA)
Penn LG ..... Pennsylvania Legal Gazette [*A publication*] (DLA)
Penn LG ..... Pennsylvania Legal Gazette Reports (Campbell) [*A publication*] (DLA)
Penn LJ ..... Pennsylvania Law Journal [*A publication*] (DLA)
Penn LJR.... Pennsylvania Law Journal Reports, Edited by Clark [*1842-52*] [*A publication*] (DLA)
Penn L Rec... Pennsylvania Law Record [*Philadelphia*] [*A publication*] (DLA)
Penn L Rev.. Pennsylvania Law Review [*A publication*] (DLA)
PennOct...... Penn Octane Corp. [*Associated Press*] (SAG)
PENNORTH... Pennyworth [*British*] (ROG)
Penn R ...... Pennsylvania State Reports [*A publication*] (DLA)
Penn Rep..... Pennsylvania State Reports [*A publication*] (DLA)
Penn Rep..... Penrose and Watts' Pennsylvania Reports [*A publication*] (DLA)
Penn St...... Pennsylvania State Reports [*A publication*] (DLA)
PENNSTAC... Penn State University Automatic Digital Computer
Penn Stat..... Pennsylvania State Reports [*A publication*] (DLA)
Penn State Rep... Pennsylvania State Reports [*A publication*] (DLA)
Penn St R .... Pennsylvania State Reports [*A publication*] (ILCA)
Penn St Rep... Pennsylvania State Reports [*A publication*] (DLA)
Penn St U .... Pennsylvania State University (GAGS)
Penn St U Harrisburg... Pennsylvania State University at Harrisburg (GAGS)
Penn Super... Pennsylvania Superior Court Reports [*A publication*] (DLA)
PENNTAP..... Pennsylvania Technical Assistance Program [*Pennsylvania State University*] [*University Park, PA*]
PennTr......... Penn Traffic Co. [*Associated Press*] (SAG)
PennTrty ..... Penn Treaty American [*Associated Press*] (SAG)
PennVa....... Penn Virginia Corp. [*Associated Press*] (SAG)
Pennwd....... Pennwood Savings Bank [*Associated Press*] (SAG)
PENNX........ Pennsylvania Mutual [*Mutual fund ticker symbol*] (SG)
Penny .... Pennypacker's Pennsylvania Colonial Cases [*A publication*] (DLA)
Penny .... Pennypacker's Unreported Pennsylvania Cases [*A publication*] (DLA)
Penny Col Cas... Pennypacker's Pennsyulvania Colonial Cases [*A publication*] (DLA)
Pennyp .... Pennypacker's Unreported Pennsylvania Cases [*A publication*] (DLA)
Pennyp Col Cas... Pennypacker's Pennsylvania Colonial Cases [*A publication*] (DLA)
Pennyp (PA)... Pennypacker's Unreported Pennsylvania Cases [*A publication*] (DLA)
Pennzol....... Pennzoil Co. [*Associated Press*] (SAG)
PEN-O......... Penner Serotype-O [*Laboratory science*] (DAVI)
Penob......... Penobscot Shoe Co. [*Associated Press*] (SAG)
PENOL........ Penology
Pen P.......... Penault's Prerosti de Quebec [*A publication*] (DLA)
PENR........... Penryn [*England*]
PENRAD....... Penetration RADAR
Penr Anal .... Penruddocke's Short Analysis of Criminal Law [*2nd ed.*] [*1842*] [*A publication*] (DLA)
Penr & W .... Penrose and Watts' Pennsylvania Reports [*1829-32*] [*A publication*] (DLA)
PenRE......... Pennsylvania Real Estate Investment Trust [*Associated Press*] (SAG)
Pen Ref ...... Penal Reformer [*1934-39*] [*A publication*] (DLA)
Pen Ref League M Rec... Penal Reform League Monthly Record [*1909-12*] [*A publication*] (DLA)
Pen Ref League Q Rec... Penal Reform League Quarterly Record [*1912-20*] [*A publication*] (DLA)
PENREP........ Penetration Report [*National Security Agency*]
Penril......... Penril Corp. [*Associated Press*] (SAG)
PENS .... Partido Espanol Nacional Sindicalista [*Political party*] [*Spain*]
PENS .... Percutaneous Epidural Nerve Stimulator [*neurology*] (DAVI)
PENS .... Polymer Ejection for Noise Suppression
PENSAM ..... Penetration Survivability Assessment Model (MCD)

Pens & Profit Sharing (P-H)... Pension and Profit Sharing (Prentice-Hall, Inc.) [*A publication*] (DLA)
PensCr........ Pensamiento Cristiano. Tribuna de Exposicion del Pensamiento Evangelico [*Cordoba, Argentina*] [*A publication*] (BJA)
Pension Rep... Pension Reporter [*Bureau of National Affairs*] [*A publication*] (DLA)
PenskeM...... Penske Motorsports, Inc. [*Associated Press*] (SAG)
Pens Rep (BNA)... Pension Reporter (Bureau of National Affairs) [*A publication*] (DLA)
PenST........ Penicillin Skin Test [*Immunology*]
Pen St R...... Pennsylvania State Reports [*A publication*] (DLA)
PENT........... Penetrate (AABC)
PENT........... Pentagon
PENT........... Pentameter
Pent........... Pentateuch (BJA)
PENT........... Pentecost
PENT........... Pentode (AAG)
Pent........... Pentothal [*Anesthetic*] (AAMN)
PENT........... Phenylethanolamine N-Methyltransferase (DMAA)
Penta......... Pentachlorophenol [*Wood preservative*] (WPI)
PENTAC...... Penetration for Tactical Aircraft [*Air Force*]
PENTAFLUX... Fifth Flux Experiment (USDC)
Pentair........ Pentair, Inc. [*Associated Press*] (SAG)
Pentch........ Pentech International, Inc. [*Associated Press*] (SAG)
PENTE........ Pentecostal
PENTENG..... Pentagon English [*Pseudotechnical language*]
Pentl........... Pentelic (VRA)
PenTrt......... Penn Treaty American Corp. [*Associated Press*] (SAG)
pentu......... Pentateuch (VRA)
PENV .... Philip Environmental [*NASDAQ symbol*] (SAG)
PENVAL ...... Penetration Evaluation [*Military*] (NVT)
Pen VK .... Penicillin V Postassium [*An antibiotic*] (DAVI)
PENW .... Penetrating Wound
PENW .... PENWEST Ltd. [*Bellevue, WA*] [*NASDAQ symbol*] (NQ)
PENW .... Penwith [*England*]
Penwst......... PENWEST Ltd. [*Associated Press*] (SAG)
PENZ......... Penzance [*City in England*] (ROG)
PEO............. Pankypria Ergatiki Omospondia [*Pancyprian Federation of Labour*] [*The "Old Trade Unions" Cyprus*]
PEO............. Patrol Emergency Officer [*Nuclear energy*] (NRCH)
PEO............. People
PEO............. Peoria [*Diocesan abbreviation*] [*Illinois*] (TOCD)
peo .... Persian, Old [*MARC language code Library of Congress*] (LCCP)
PEO............. Petroleum & Resources [*NYSE symbol*] (TTSB)
PEO............. Petroleum & Resources Corp. [*NYSE symbol*] (SPSG)
PEO............. Petrolia Oil & Gas [*Vancouver Stock Exchange symbol*]
PEO............. Philanthropic and Educational Organization [*Facetious translation "Pop Eats Out"*]
PEO............. Planners for Equal Opportunity [*Defunct*] (EA)
PEO............. Plant Engineering Order
PEO............. Plant Equipment Operator [*Nuclear energy*] (NRCH)
PEO............. Poly(ethylene oxide) [*Acronym is trade name owned by Seitetsu Kagaku Co.*]
PEO............. President's Export Council (AAGC)
PEO............. Principal Executive Officer [*Civil Service*] [*British*]
PEO............. Process Engineering Order
PEO............. Product Engineering Office
PEO............. Production Engineering Order
PEO............. Program Enrichment Office (COE)
PEO............. Program Evaluation Office [*Army*]
PEO............. Program Executive Office [*or Officer*]
PEO............. Progressive External Ophthalmoplegia
PEO............. Propulsion Engineering Officer (MCD)
PEO............. Prospective Engineer Officer
PEO............. Protect Each Other [*An association*] (NADA)
PEO............. Public Employment Office [*State Employee Security Agency*] (OICC)
PEO-ASM...... Program Executive Office - Armored Systems Modernization [*Army*] (RDA)
PeoBkIN....... Peoples Bank Corp. Indianapolis [*Associated Press*] (SAG)
PEOC.......... Publishing Employees Organizing Committee [*AFL-CIO*]
PEO-FAS...... Program Executive Office - Field Artillery System [*Army*] (RDA)
PEO-GPALS... Program Executive Officer, Global Protection Against Limited Strikes [*Army*] (RDA)
PEO-IEW...... Program Executive Office - Intelligence and Electronic Warfare [*Army*] (RDA)
Peo L Adv.... People's Legal Advisor [*Utica, NY*] [*A publication*] (DLA)
PEO-MD....... Program Executive Office - Missile Defense [*Military*] (RDA)
Peop.......... People's (AL)
PeopBcp...... Peoples Bancorp [*Dekalb County*] [*Associated Press*] (SAG)
PeopBcT...... Peoples BancTrust Co. [*Associated Press*] (SAG)
PeopBk....... Peoples Bank [*Catawba, NC*] [*Associated Press*] (SAG)
PeopChc...... Peoples Choice TV Corp. [*Associated Press*] (SAG)
PeopCT....... Peoples Bank [*Bridgeport, CT*] [*Associated Press*] (SAG)
PeopEn....... Peoples Energy Corp. [*Associated Press*] (SAG)
PeopFin...... Peoples Financial Corp. [*Associated Press*] (SAG)
PeopFst....... People First Corp. [*Associated Press*] (SAG)
PeopHld...... Peoples Holding Co. [*Associated Press*] (SAG)
PeopHrt....... People's Heritage Financial Group, Inc. [*Associated Press*] (SAG)
Peoples .... Peoples' Reports [*77-97 Georgia*] [*A publication*] (DLA)
PeopleTel .... Peoples Telephone Co. [*Associated Press*] (SAG)
Peopsft....... Peoplesoft, Inc. [*Associated Press*] (SAG)
PeopTel ...... People's Telephone Co., Inc. [*Associated Press*] (SAG)
PEOS .... Propulsion and Electrical Operating System (IEEE)
PeoSvFn...... People's Savings Financial Corp. [*Associated Press*] (SAG)
PEOX .... Polyethyleneoxide [*Organic chemistry*]

PEP............. All India Reporter, Patiala and East Punjab States Union Series [*A publication*] (ILCA)
PEPCr........ Charlotte, NC [*Location identifier FAA*] (FAAL)
PEP............. Cyclophosphamide, VM-26 Prednisolone [*Antineoplastic drug regimen*] (DAVI)
PEP............. Packet Exchange Protocol [*Computer science*] (CDE)
PEP............. Packetized Ensemble Protocol [*Computer science*]
PEP............. Paperless Electronic Payment [*Business term*]
PEP............. Paperless Entry Processing User Group [*Defunct*] (CSR)
PEP............. Parenting, Education, and Political Involvement [*Jack and Jill of America*]
PEP............. Parti Ecologiste pour le Progres [*Burkina Faso*] [*Political party*] (EY)
PEP............. Parti Evangelique Populaire [*Popular Protestant Party*] [*Switzerland Political party*] (PPE)
PEP............. Partitioned Emulation Program [*Computer science*] (BUR)
PEP............. Patent Examining Procedure (IAA)
PEP............. Pauli Exclusion Principle [*Physics*]
PEP............. Peak Effective Power
PEP............. Peak Energy Product
PEP............. Peak Envelope Power [*Telecommunications*]
PEP............. Peer Evaluation Program [*College of American Pathologists*]
PEP............. People for Energy Progress [*Defunct*] (EA)
PEP............. Pepitilla [*Race of maize*]
PEP............. Peppermint (DSUE)
PEP............. PepsiCo Inc. [*NYSE symbol*] (SPSG)
Pep............. Peptidase (DB)
PEP............. Peptide [*Biochemistry*]
PEP............. Performance Effectiveness [*or Evaluation*] Program [*Navy*]
PEP............. Performance Evaluation Procedure [*Joint Commission on Accreditation of Hospitals*] (DHSM)
PEP............. Peripheral Event Processor [*Computer science*]
PEP............. Perkin-Elmer Processor [*Computer*]
PEP............. Personal Employee Profiling [*Information service or system*] (IID)
PEP............. Personal Empowerment Program (WDAA)
PEP............. Personal Equity Plan [*Finance*]
PEP............. Personal Exemption Phase-Out [*Income tax*]
PEP............. Personal Exercise Programmer
PEP............. Personality-Profile Exam
PEP............. Personnel Exchange Program [*Military*] (NVT)
PEP............. Pfizer, Inc., Research Center Library, Easton, PA [*Library symbol Library of Congress*] (LCLS)
PEP............. Phenethyl Propionate [*Insect attractant*] [*Organic chemistry*]
PEP............. Phosphoenolpyruvate [*Biochemistry*]
PEP............. Photoelectric Potential
PEP............. Photoelectrophoresis
PEP............. Photographic Exploitation Products (MCD)
PEP............. Physical Education Program
PEP............. Physiological Evaluation of Primates
PEP............. Pictorial End-Papers [*Publishing*]
PEP............. Pipeline Expanding Polymer
PEP............. Piping Efficiency Program
PEP............. Planar Epitaxial Passivated
PEP............. Planetary Ephemeris Program (IEEE)
PEP............. Planetary Exploration Plan [*NACA*]
PEP............. Plant Equipment Package [*DoD*]
PEP............. Platform Electronic Package
PEP............. Platform Evaluation Program
PEP............. Plessey Electronic Payroll (DEN)
PEP............. Plume Exposure Pathway [*Nuclear emergency planning*]
PEP............. Point, Edge, Polygon [*Computer science*]
PEP............. Political and Economic Planning [*A British organization*] [*Later, Policy Studies Institute*]
PEP............. Polyestradiol Phosphate [*Endocrinology*]
PEP............. Polyethylene Powder
PEP............. Polynominal Error Protection (MCD)
PEP............. Pool Exercise Program [*Arthritis Foundation*]
PEP............. Porsche Experimental Prototype [*Automotive engineering*]
PEP............. Portable Energy Provision (SSD)
PEP............. Portfolio Evaluation Plan [*Australia*]
PEP............. Positive Energy [*Vancouver Stock Exchange symbol*]
PEP............. Positron-Electron Project [*High-energy accelerator*]
PEP............. Positron Electron Proton [*Physics*]
PEP............. Postal Efficiency Plan (SAA)
PEP............. Postencephalitic Parkinsonism [*Medicine*] (DB)
PEP............. Postexposure Prophylaxis [*Medicine*]
PEP............. Power Evaluation Program
PEP............. Power Extension Package (MCD)
PEP............. Power Extension Plant (MCD)
PEP............. Practical Engineering Paperwork
PEP............. Pratt & Whitney Engine Program [*Aviation*] (NG)
PEP............. Preamplifier Extension Plug
PEP............. Pre-Ejection Period [*Cardiology*]
PEP............. Pre-Employment Program
PEP............. Preferred Equipment Package [*Automotive retailing*]
PEP............. Preschool Education Program [*Sesame Street TV program*]
PEP............. President's Economy Program
PEP............. Preventive Enforcement Patrol [*New York City police*]
PEP............. Primary Education Program [*Child development test*]
PEP............. Primary Entry Point System (OTD)
PEP............. Primate Equilibrium Platform
PEP............. Princeton Electronic Products, Inc. (IAA)
PEP............. Princeton Experiment Package [*NASA*]
PeP............. Principal of Pedagogy [*Academic degree*]
PEP............. Printer-Emulation Package [*Software*]
PEP............. Priority Energy Policy [*Environmental Protection Agency*]

PEP............ Processing Enhancing Protein [*Biochemistry*]
PEP............ Procurement Evaluation Panel [*Air Force*] (MCD)
PEP............ Procytox [*Cyclophosphamide*], Epipodophyllotoxin Derivative , Prednisolone [*VM-26*] [*Antineoplastic drug regimen*]
PEP............ Producibility Engineering and Planning [*Army*] (AABC)
PEP............ Product Engineering and Production (MCD)
PEP............ Production EAGLE [*Elevation Angle Guidance Landing Equipment*] Package
PEP............ [*The*] Production Engineering and Productivity Exhibition and Conference [*British*] (ITD)
PEP............ Production Engineering Planning
PEP............ Production Equipment Package
PEP............ [*The*] Productivity Effectiveness Program [*Title of a pamphlet by Robert Gedaliah that describes sedentary exercises for desk-bound workers*]
PEP............ Professional Enhancement Project [*American Occupational Therapy Association*]
PEP............ Professional Experience Program [*Australia*]
PEP............ Proficiency Examination Program (MCD)
PEP............ Program Element Plan (AFIT)
PEP............ Program Evaluation Procedure [*Air Force*]
PEP............ Program Evaluation Program [*Air Force*] (IAA)
PEP............ Programmable Extension Package (IAA)
PEP............ Progressive Exercise Program
PEP............ Projects and Exports Policy [*Board of Trade*] [*British*]
PEP............ Prolyl Endopeptidase
PEP............ Promoting Enduring Peace (EA)
PEP............ Promotion Evaluation Pattern
PEP............ Propellant, Explosive, and Pyrotechnic
PEP............ Property Estimation Program [*Utah Water Research Laboratory*]
PEP............ Proposal Equipment Packages (MCD)
PEP............ Proposal Evaluation Panel (MCD)
PEP............ Proposal Evaluation Plan [*or Program*] (MCD)
PEP............ Proposal Exploitation Product
PEP............ Propulsion Evaluation Plan
PEP............ Protection in Evaluation Procedures
PEP............ Protein Electrophoresis [*Medicine*] (DMAA)
PEP............ Proton Electron Positron Colliding Beams (IAA)
PEP............ Proton-Electron-Proton [*Nuclear physics*]
PEP............ Psychiatric Evaluation Profile [*Psychology*] (MAE)
PEP............ Psychoeducational Profile [*Test for autistic children*]
PEP............ Psychoepistemological Profile [*Student personality test*]
PEP............ Public Employment Program (EBF)
PEP............ Pulse Echo Pattern
PEP............ Pulse Effective Power [*Telecommunications*] (IAA)
PEPA.......... Peptidase A [*An enzyme*]
PEPA.......... Per Employee per Annum
PEPA.......... Petroleum Electric Power Association [*Later, EUIPA*] (EA)
PEPA.......... Pitch Fibre Pipe Association of Great Britain (BI)
PEPA.......... Polyether-Polyamide Block Copolymer (EDCT)
PEPA.......... Protected Environment plus Prophylactic Antibiotics [*Oncology*]
PEPA.......... Pulse Echo Pattern Analyzer
PEPAE........ Permanent Entry Permit After Entry
PEPAG........ Physical Electronics and Physical Acoustics Group [*MIT*] (MCD)
PEPAOP...... (Phenylethyl)phenylacetoxypiperidine [*Organic chemistry*]
PEPAS........ WHO [*World Health Organization*] Western Pacific Regional Centre for the Promotion of Environmental Planning and Applied Studies (EAIO)
PEPBNC...... Peninsula Enrichment Program for Bright Needy Children [*Queensland, Australia*]
PepBoy........ Pep Boys-Manny, Moe & Jack [*Associated Press*] (SAG)
PEPC.......... Peptidase C [*An enzyme*]
PEPC.......... Phosphoenolpyruvate Carboxylase [*An enzyme*]
PEPC.......... Polynomial Error Protection Code [*Computer science*]
PEPC.......... Postsecondary Education Planning Commission [*Florida*] (EDAC)
PEPC.......... Potomac Electric Power Co.
PEPCK........ Phosphoenolpyruvate Carboxykinase [*An enzyme*]
PEPCK........ Phosphoenolpyruvate Carboxykinase [*An enzyme*]
PEPCO........ Potomac Electric Power Co.
PEPCOM...... Pacific Engineering Production Company (AAGC)
PEPCOM...... Pepsi-Cola Bottling Companies (EFIS)
PEPD.......... Peptidase D [*An enzyme*]
PEPE.......... Parallel Element Processing Ensemble [*Burroughs Corp.*] (BUR)
PEPE.......... People Persecuted by Pablo Escobar [*Colombia*] (ECON)
PEPE.......... Prolonged Elevated-Pollution Episode [*Environmental Protection Agency*]
PEP/EP........ Pre-Ejection Period to Ejection Period [*Cardiology*] (DAVI)
PEPES......... People Persecuted by Pablo Escobar
PEPG.......... Piezoelectric Power Generation
PEPG.......... Port Emergency Planning Group [*NATO*] (NATG)
PEPI.......... Physical Education Public Information [*Film*]
PEPI.......... Post-Menopausal Estrogen and Progestin Intervention [*Medicine*] (BARN)
PEPI.......... Postmenopausal Estrogen/Progestin Interventions
PEPI.......... Pre-Ejection Period Index [*Cardiology*]
PEPL.......... Preliminary Engineering Parts List
PEPLAN....... Polaris Executive Plan [*British*]
PEP/LVET..... Pre-Ejection Period/Left Ventricular Ejection Time [*Medicine*] (MEDA)
PEPMC........ Printing Estimators and Production Men's Club [*New York, NY*] (EA)
PEPMIS....... Plant Equipment Packages Management Information System (MCD)
PEPMOV...... Pepper Mottle Virus [*Plant pathology*]
PEPMV........ Pepino Mosaic Virus [*Plant pathology*]
PEPP.......... Permanent-Equity Pension Plan [*Human resources*] (WYGK)
PEPP.......... Planetary Entry Parachute Program [*NASA*]
PEPP.......... Positive Expiratory Pressure Plateau [*Medicine*] (MAE)

PEPP.......... Professional Engineers in Private Practice
PEPPA........ Preparedness for Emergency Plant Pest Action [*In Animal and Plant Health Inspection Service publication PEPPA Pot*]
PEPPARD..... Propellant, Explosive, Pyrotechnic Pollution Abatement Research and Development (DNAB)
PEPPER....... Photo-Electric Portable Probe Reader (PDAA)
Pepper & L Dig... Pepper and Lewis' Digest of Laws [*Pennsylvania*] [*A publication*] (DLA)
Pepper & L Dig Laws... Pepper and Lewis' Digest of Laws [*Pennsylvania*] [*A publication*] (DLA)
Pepperdine U... Pepperdine University (GAGS)
PEPPRE....... Photo Electric Portable Probe Reader (IAA)
PEPR .... Precision Encoding and Pattern Recognition Device [*Computer science*]
PEP-R .... Psychoeducational Profile-Revised (TES)
PEPrA......... PECO Energy, $3.80 Pfd [*NYSE symbol*] (TTSB)
PEPrB......... PECO Energy, $4.30 Pfd [*NYSE symbol*] (TTSB)
PEPrC......... PECO Energy, $4.40 Pfd [*NYSE symbol*] (TTSB)
PEPrD......... PECO Energy, $4.68 Pfd [*NYSE symbol*] (TTSB)
PEPrF......... PECO Energy Dep Pfd [*NYSE symbol*] (TTSB)
PEPrY......... PECO En Cap Tr I 8.72% 'TOPrS' [*NYSE symbol*] (TTSB)
PEPrZ......... PECO Energy L.P. MIPS'A' [*NYSE symbol*] (TTSB)
PEPS.......... National Committee on Public Employee Pension Systems (EA)
PEPS.......... Peperomia and Exotic Plant Society (EA)
PEPS.......... Peptidase S [*An enzyme*]
PEPS.......... Pesticide Enforcement Policy Statement [*Environmental Protection Agency*]
PEPS.......... Primary Earnings per Share (TDOB)
PEPS.......... Primary Environmental Prediction System
PEPS.......... Primary Environmental Processing Systems [*Navy*] (GFGA)
PEPS.......... Production Engineering Productivity System [*Camtek Ltd.*] [*Software package*]
PEPS.......... Productivity Environmental Preference Survey [*Test*]
PEPS.......... Program Element Plan Supplement
PEP-SEP ..... Peptide Separation [*Biochemistry*]
PEPSI......... Plasma Electron Profiles, Symmetric Integrals (MCD)
PepsiC........ PepsiCo, Inc. [*Associated Press*] (SAG)
PEPSICO...... Pepsi-Cola Co. (EFIS)
PepsiPR....... Pepsi Cola Puerto Rico Bottling [*Associated Press*] (SAG)
PEPSS........ Preschool and Early Primary Skills Survey [*Child development test*]
PEPSS........ Programmable Equipment for Personnel Subsystem Simulation
PEPSU........ All India Reporter, Patiala and East Punjab States Union [*1950-57*] [*A publication*] (DLA)
PEPSU........ Patiala and East Punjab States Union
PEPSY........ Precision Earth-Pointing System (MCD)
PEPTP........ (Phenylethyl)Phenyltetrahydropyridine [*Organic chemistry*]
PEP/USA..... Parkinson's Educational Program - USA (EA)
PEPUSL....... Pepperdine University School of Law (DLA)
PEpW.......... Westinghouse Electric Corp., East Pittsburgh, PA [*Library symbol Library of Congress*] (LCLS)
PEQ............ Pecos City, TX [*Location identifier FAA*] (FAAL)
PEQ............ Personal Experience Questionnaire [*Psychology*]
PEQ............ Petroquin Resources Ltd. [*Vancouver Stock Exchange symbol*]
PEQ............ Potomac Edison [*NYSE symbol*] (SAG)
PEQ............ Potomac Edison 8.00% 'QUIDS' [*NYSE symbol*] (TTSB)
PEQIX......... Pioneer Equity-Income Cl.A [*Mutual fund ticker symbol*] (SG)
PEQUA........ Production Equipment Agency [*Army*]
PEQUOD ...... Pacific Equatorial Ocean Dynamics [*Project*] [*USA*] [*Marine science*] (OSRA)
PEr............ Erie Public Library, Erie, PA [*Library symbol Library of Congress*] (LCLS)
PER............ For Each (DAVI)
PER............ Packed Encoding Rules (ACII)
PER............ Par Exchange Rate [*Business term*]
PER............ Parity Error Rate
PER............ Parole Evidence Rule [*Legal shorthand*] (LWAP)
PER............ Partido Estadista Republicano [*Puerto Rico*] [*Political party*]
PER............ Path Extension Ratio (MCD)
PER............ Peak Ejection Rate [*Cardiology*]
PER............ Peak Expiration Rate [*Medicine*]
Per............ Pediatric Emergency Room (DAVI)
Pe R .... Pennewill's Delaware Reports [*A publication*] (DLA)
per............ Perennial [*Botany*]
Per............ Perera's Select Decisions [*Ceylon*] [*A publication*] (DLA)
PERD.......... Per Exchange Rate [*Finance*] (MHDW)
PER............ Performance (DA)
PER............ Performance Evaluation Report [*DoD*]
PER............ Perhaps (ROG)
Per............ Pericles [*Shakespearean work*]
Per............ Pericles [*of Plutarch*] [*Classical studies*] (OCD)
PER............ Perigee (KSC)
per............ Perineal [*Gynecology*] (MAE)
Per............ Periochae [*of Livy*] [*Classical studies*] (OCD)
PER............ Period
Per............ Period [*Record label*]
per............ Period (VRA)
per............ Periodic (AAMN)
PER............ Periodical (ROG)
Per............ Periodical (AL)
per............ Periodicity (DMAA)
PER............ Periodogram (DMAA)
PER............ Permission (AABC)
Per............ Perseus [*Constellation*]
PER............ Persia [*Obsolete*]
Per............ Persia (VRA)

per .... Persian, Modern [*MARC language code Library of Congress*] (LCCP)
PER .... Person
per .... Person (WDMC)
PER .... Personnel (KSC)
PER .... PERT [*Program Evaluation and Review Technique*] Event Report
PER .... Perth [*Australia Seismograph station code, US Geological Survey Closed*] (SEIS)
PER .... Perth [*Australia Airport symbol*] (OAG)
PER .... Peru [*ANSI three-letter standard code*] (CNC)
PER .... Pharmaceutical Evaluation Report [*Australia*]
PER .... Phase Engineering Report
PER .... Physical Examination Rate [*Military*] (AFM)
PER .... Planning, Evaluation, and Reporting [*Education-improvement system*]
PER .... Pominex Ltd. [*Toronto Stock Exchange symbol*]
PER .... Ponca City, OK [*Location identifier FAA*] (FAAL)
PER .... Port Everglades Railway [*AAR code*]
PER .... Postelectrophoresis Relaxation
PER .... Post Engineer Request
PER .... Post-Execution Reporting (MHDI)
PER .... Potential Excess Report
PER .... Preedited Region [*Genetics*]
PER .... Pre-Emptive Right (MHDW)
PER .... Preliminary Engineering Report (KSC)
PER .... PressNet Environmental Reports [*Information service or system*] (IID)
PER .... Price Earnings Ratio [*Relation between price of a company's stock and its annual net income*]
PER .... Printing Executive Register (DGA)
PER .... Probable Error Radial [*Statistics*] (IAA)
PER .... Product Engineering Recommendation [*Automotive engineering*]
PER .... Production Engine Remanufacturers Program [*Automotive engineering*]
PER .... Professional and Executive Recruitment Service [*British*]
PER .... Professional Employment Register [*British*] (ODBW)
PER .... Proficiency Evaluation Review
PER .... Program Error Report (MHDI)
PER .... Program Event Recording [*Computer science*] (MDG)
PER .... Program Execution Request
PER .... Proposal Evaluation Report (MCD)
PER .... Protein Efficiency Ratio [*Nutrition*]
PER .... Public Employees Roundtable (EA)
PER .... Pyrotechnical Evaluation Range [*Army*] (RDA)
PERA ..... Planning and Engineering for Repair and Alteration [*Navy*]
PERA .... Production Engineering Research Association [*Research center British*] (IRC)
PERA .... Production Engine Remanufacturers Association (EA)
PERA .... Production Equipment Rental Association (NTPA)
Per A J .... Performing Arts Journal [*A publication*] (BRI)
PERAM .... Personnel Action Memorandum [*Military*]
PER AN .... Per Annum [*By the Year*] [*Latin*]
Per & Dav ... Perry and Davison's English King's Bench Reports [*1838-41*] [*A publication*] (DLA)
Per & Kn .... Perry and Knapp's English Election Reports [*1838*] [*A publication*] (DLA)
PER ANN ..... Per Annum [*By the Year*] [*Latin*]
per ann......... Per Annum (EBF)
PERA system... Project Engineering Research Association system (NITA)
P/E ratio ..... Price/Earnings Ratio (WDAA)
Pe Rave....... Petrus Ravennas [*Flourished, 1468-1508*] [*Authority cited in pre-1607 legal work*] (DSA)
PERB .... Public Employment Relations Board (EDAC)
PERC .... Parents Educational Resource Center
PERC .... Peace on Earth Research Center
PERC .... Perclose, Inc. [*NASDAQ symbol*] (SAG)
PERC .... Percolator (DSUE)
PERC .... Percussion (AAG)
perc .... Percussion (WDAA)
PERC .... Pittsburgh Energy Research Center [*Later, PETC*] [*Energy Research and Development Administration*]
PERC .... Political & Economic Risk Consultancy [*Commercial firm*] [*Hong Kong*]
PERC .... Political Economy Research Center [*Research center*] (RCD)
PERC .... Private Enterprise Research Center (EA)
PERC .... Processor Emergency Recovery Circuit [*Bell System*]
PERC .... Professional Engineering and Research Consultants
PERC .... Psoriasis Education and Research Centre [*University of Toronto*] [*Canada Research center*] (RCD)
PERC .... Public Employment Relations Commission (EDAC)
PERC .... Public Enterprises Reform Commission [*Sri Lanka*]
PERCAM ..... Performance and Cost Analysis Model (MCD)
Per Cap ...... Per Capita [*By the Individual*] [*Latin*]
Per cap....... Per Capita (EBF)
PERCAP....... Persian Gulf Requirements and Capabilities [*Military*]
PERCASREPT... Personnel Casualty Report [*Military*] (NVT)
PERCENT..... Per Centum [*By the Hundred*] [*Latin*]
PERCHLOR... Perchloride [*Chemistry*] (ROG)
PERCI .... Personnel Contamination Instrumentation
Perclose...... Perclose, Inc. [*Associated Press*] (SAG)
PERCOM ..... Personnel Command [*Army*] (MCD)
PERCOMP.... Personal Computing Conference (MHDI)
PERCOMPASIA... South East Asian Personal Computer Hardware and Software Show
Percon......... Percon, Inc. [*Associated Press*] (SAG)
Per con........ Per Contra [*On the Other Side*] [*Latin*]
PERCOS....... Performance Coding System

Percptr......... Perceptron, Inc. [*Associated Press*] (SAG)
Per CS........ Perrault's Conseil Superieur [*Canada*] [*A publication*] (DLA)
PERCS .... Preference Equity Redemption Cumulative Stock (ECON)
PERCUSS..... Percussion [*Medicine*] (DAVI)
PERCUSS & AUSC... Percussion and Ausculation [*Medicine*] (DHSM)
PERD .... Perdendo [*or Perdendosi*] [*Softer and Slower Music*]
PERD .... Periodic (MSA)
PERD .... Perused (ROG)
PERDA......... Per Diem [*By the Day*] [*Latin*] (NOAA)
PERDDiMS... Personnel Deployment and Distribution Management System [*Military*] (AABC)
PERDEN...... Perdendo [*or Perdendosi*] [*Softer and Slower Music*]
PERDEX...... Permuted Formula Index [*Molecular formula indexing*]
PerDia .... Personal Diagnositics, Inc. [*Associated Press*] (SAG)
PEREF......... Personal Effects
PEREF......... Propellant Engine Research Environmental Facility
Pereg......... Peregrinus Fabius [*Authority cited in pre-1607 legal work*] (DSA)
PERF.......... Peak Expiratory Flow Rate [*Medicine*] (DMAA)
PERF.......... Perfect
perf........... Perfect (WDAA)
PERF.......... PerfectData Corp. [*NASDAQ symbol*] (NQ)
PERF.......... Perforate [*or Perforator*]
PERF.......... Perforation (DSUE)
perf........... Perforation (WDMC)
perf........... Performance (VRA)
PERF.......... Performance (KSC)
PERF.......... Perfusionist [*Medicine*] (HCT)
PerF.......... Perma Fix Environmental Services [*Associated Press*] (SAG)
PERF.......... Planetary Entry Radiation Facility [*Langley Research Center*] [*NASA*] (PDAA)
PERF.......... Police Executive Research Forum (EA)
PERFCE...... Performance
PERFD .... Performed (ROG)
Perfdta........ PerfectData Corp. [*Associated Press*] (SAG)
PERFINS...... Perforated Insignia [*Philately*]
PERFM........ Perform (ROG)
PerFood...... Performance Food Group [*Commercial firm Associated Press*] (SAG)
PERFORM... Performance
PERFR....... Perforator (IAA)
PERF RM .... Perfect Ream (DGA)
PerfSys....... Performance Systems International, Inc. [*Associated Press*] (SAG)
PerfTech...... Performance Technologies, Inc. [*Associated Press*] (SAG)
Perfum........ Perfumania, Inc. [*Associated Press*] (SAG)
PERFW .... Perforating Wound
PErG .... Gannon University, Erie, PA [*Library symbol Library of Congress*] (LCLS)
PERG .... Pergola [*Classified advertising*] (ADA)
PERG .... Production Emergency Redistribution Group
PERG .... Production Equipment Redistribution Group [*Army*]
PERGO........ Project Evaluation and Review with Graphic Output (IEEE)
PERGRA...... Permission Granted [*Military*]
PERH .... Perhaps
PerHi .... Erie County Historical Society, Erie, PA [*Library symbol Library of Congress*] (LCLS)
PERI........... Pea Ridge National Military Park
PERI........... Perigee
PERI........... Perimeter (AABC)
peri........... Perineal [*Anatomy*] (DAVI)
PERI........... Periodical
PERI........... Periphonics Corp. [*NASDAQ symbol*] (SAG)
PERI........... Periscope
PERI........... Peritoneal Fluid (DAVI)
PERI........... Platemakers Educational and Research Institute [*Later, IAP*]
PERI........... Production Equipment Redistribution Inventory [*Army*]
PERI........... Production Equipment Reserve Inventory [*Navy*] (NG)
PERI........... Protein Engineering Research Institute [*Japanese governmental and industrial consortium*] [*Later, BERI*]
PERI........... Psychiatric Epidemiology Research Interview
PERIAP .... Periapical [*Dentistry*]
peric .... Pericope (VRA)
Pericom....... Pericom Semiconductor Corp. [*Associated Press*] (SAG)
PERIF......... Peripheral
perig.......... Perigee (BARN)
Pe Rigal ..... Petrus Rigaldi [*Flourished, 14th century*] [*Authority cited in pre-1607 legal work*] (DSA)
PERIM .... Perimeter (KSC)
PERI/M .... Perimortem (DAVI)
PeriniC .... Perini Corp. [*Associated Press*] (SAG)
PERINTREP... Periodic Intelligence Report (NATG)
PERINTREPT... Periodic Intelligence Report
PERINTSUM... Periodic Intelligence Summary [*Army*] (AABC)
perio.......... Periodontist [*Dentistry*] (DAVI)
PERIPH....... Periphery (KSC)
Periphn....... Periphonics Corp. [*Associated Press*] (SAG)
Peripl M Eux... Periplus Maris Euxini [*of Arrian*] [*Classical studies*] (OCD)
PERIS .... Periscope (KSC)
PERJ.......... Perjury [*FBI standardized term*]
PERJY .... Perjury (ROG)
PERK .... Payroll Earnings Record Keeping
Perk........... Perkins on Conveyancing [*A publication*] (DLA)
Perk........... Perkins on Pleading [*A publication*] (DLA)
Perk........... Perkins' Profitable Book (Conveyancing) [*A publication*] (DLA)
PERK .... Perquisite
PERK .... Prospective Evaluation of Radial Keratotomy [*Protocol*] [*Ophthalmology*] (DAVI)

PERKARA..... Parti Perdapuan Kebangsaan Ra'ayat Brunei [*Brunei People's National United Party*] [*Political party*] (EY)
PerkEl......... Perkin-Elmer Corp. [*Associated Press*] (SAG)
PerkF........... Perkins Family Restaurants Ltd. [*Associated Press*] (SAG)
Perk Pr Bk... Perkins' Profitable Book (Conveyancing) [*A publication*] (DLA)
perks........... Perquisites (MHDB)
PERL........... Pathologically Eclectic Rubbish Lister
PERL........... Perkin-Elmer Robot Language
PERL........... Perle Systems Ltd. [*Scarborough, ON*] [*NASDAQ symbol*] (NQ)
PERL........... Perusal (ROG)
PERL........... Pictorial Engineering and Research Laboratory
PERL........... Portable Electronic Runway Lighting (PDAA)
Perl............ Practical Extraction and Report Language [*Computer science*]
PERL........... Practice Extraction and Report Language [*Facetious translation: Pathologically Eclectic Rubbish Lister*] [*Computer science*] (NHD)
PERL........... Prepositioned Equipment Requirements List [*Navy*] (MCD)
PERL........... Public Employee Relations Library [*of International Personnel Management Association*]
PERL........... Pupils Equal and Reactive to Light (DAVI)
PERL........... Pupils Equal, Regular, and Reactive to Light (DAVI)
PERLA......... Pupils Equal, React to Light and Accommodation [*Medicine*]
PERLA......... Pupils Equal, Regular and Reactive to Light and Accommodation (DAVI)
PerleSys...... Pearle Systems Ltd. [*Associated Press*] (SAG)
PERLF......... Perle System [*NASDAQ symbol*] (TTSB)
PERLS........ Principal Exchange-Rate-Linked Securities [*Investment term*]
PERM.......... Permanent
PERM.......... Permanent Bancorp [*NASDAQ symbol*] (SAG)
PERM.......... Permanent Employee (DSUE)
PERM.......... Permeability
PERM.......... Permian [*Period, era, or system*] [*Geology*]
PERM.......... Permission (MSA)
PERM.......... Permutation (DSUE)
PERM.......... Pre-Embossed Rigid Magnetic [*Electronics*] (AAEL)
PERM.......... Pre-Embossed Rigid Magnetic Media [*Computer science*]
PERM.......... Program Evaluation for Repetitive Manufacture (IEEE)
PERMACAP... Personnel Management and Accounting Card Processor [*Military*]
PERMACAPS... Personnel Management and Accounting Card Processing System (MCD)
PERMAFROST... Permanent Frost
PERMAS ..... Persatuan Rakyat Malaysian Sarawak [*Political party*] (EY)
PERMAS ..... Personnel Management Assistance System [*Military*] (AABC)
PERMB .... Permeability
PermBcp...... Permanent Bancorp [*Associated Press*] (SAG)
PErMC .... Mercyhurst College, Erie, PA [*Library symbol Library of Congress*] (LCLS)
PerMdw ...... Perpetual Midwest Financial, Inc. [*Associated Press*] (SAG)
PERME......... Propellants, Explosives, and Rocket Motors Establishment [*British Ministry of Defense*] [*Research center*] (RDA)
PermF......... Perma Fix Environmental Services [*Associated Press*] (SAG)
PermFix...... Perma Fix Environmental Services [*Associated Press*] (SAG)
PERMIC ...... Personnel Management Information Center [*Navy*] (NVT)
PERMINVAR... Permeability Invariant
PERMIXT..... Permixtus [*Mixed*] [*Pharmacy*] (ROG)
PERMLY ...... Permanently
PERMR .... Permanent Residence
PERMREP ... Permanent Representation to North Atlantic Council [*NATO*] (NATG)
PERMS .... Personnel Electronic Record Management System [*Army*] (RDA)
PERMS .... Process and Effluent Radiological Monitoring System [*Nuclear energy*] (NRCH)
PERMSS ..... Process and Effluent Radiological Monitoring and Sampling System [*Nuclear energy*] (NRCH)
PERMT........ Permanent (ROG)
PERMU .... Permanent Magnet Users Association [*Defunct*] (EA)
PernC.......... Perini Corp. [*Associated Press*] (SAG)
PERNOGRA... Permission Not Granted [*Military*]
PERO .... President's Emergency Relief Organization (NADA)
PER OP EMET... Peracta Operatione Emetici [*When the Operation of the Emetic is Finished*] [*Pharmacy*] (ROG)
Per Or Cas... Perry's Oriental Cases [*Bombay*] [*A publication*] (DLA)
PEROX......... Peroxidase Stain [*Biochemistry*] (DAVI)
PEROX........ Peroxide
PERP .... Pan-Ethnic Republican Party of Australia [*Political party*]
PERP .... Peak Effective Radiated Power [*Telecommunications*] (OTD)
PERP .... Perpendicular (AAG)
perp........... Perpendicular (VRA)
PERP .... Perpetrator (WDAA)
PERP .... Perpetual (ADA)
Perp........... Perpetual (EBF)
Per P .... Perrault's Prevoste de Quebec [*A publication*] (DLA)
PERP .... Personnel Processing (MUGU)
perpad........ Perineal Pad [*Gynecology*] (MAE)
PerpBnk...... Perpetual Bank Federal Savings Bank [*Associated Press*] (SAG)
Perpet......... Perpetual (DLA)
Per Pro .... Per Procuration (EBF)
per pro .... Per Procurationem [*By Proxy, By the Action Of*] [*Legal term*] [*Latin*] (BARN)
PER PROC .. Per Procurationem [*By Proxy, By the Action Of*] [*Legal term Latin*]
PerpSB........ Petpetual State Bank [*North Carolina*] [*Associated Press*] (SAG)
Per Psy....... Personnel Psychology [*A publication*] (BRI)
PERR .... Patter-Evoked Retinal Response [*neurology and ophthalmology*] (DAVI)
PERR .... Premature Engine Removal Rate (AAG)
Perrault....... Perrault's Conseil Superieur [*Canada*] [*A publication*] (DLA)
Perrault....... Perrault's Prevoste de Quebec [*A publication*] (DLA)

Perrault........ Perrault's Quebec Reports [*A publication*] (DLA)
Perrigo .... Perrigo Co. [*Associated Press*] (SAG)
PERRL .... Pupils Equal, Round and Reactive to Light (DAVI)
PERRL .... Pupils Equal, Round, Regular and Reactive to Light (DAVI)
PERRLA ...... Pupils Equal, Round, React to Light and Accommodation [*Medicine*]
PERRLA ...... Pupils Equal, Round, Regular, and Reactive to Light and Accommodation (DAVI)
PERRLA (DC)... Pupils Equal, Round, and Reactive to Light and Accommodation (Directly and Consensually) (DAVI)
Perry........... Perry's Oriental Cases [*Bombay*] [*A publication*] (DLA)
Perry & D .... Perry and Davison's English King's Bench Reports [*A publication*] (DLA)
Perry & D (Eng)... Perry and Davison's English King's Bench Reports [*A publication*] (DLA)
Perry & K ... Perry and Knapp's English Election Cases [*A publication*] (DLA)
Perry & Kn... Perry and Knapp's English Election Cases [*A publication*] (DLA)
PerryCF...... Perry County Financial Corp. [*Associated Press*] (SAG)
Perry Ins..... Perry's English Insolvency Cases [*1831*] [*A publication*] (DLA)
Perry OC..... Perry's Oriental Cases [*Bombay*] [*A publication*] (DLA)
PERS .... Patient Evaluation Rating Scale [*Medicine*] (DMAA)
PERS .... Performance Evaluation Reporting System [*DoD*]
PERS .... Periodical Source Index [*A publication*]
Pers........... Persae [*of Aeschylus*] [*Classical studies*] (OCD)
Pers........... Perseus [*Constellation*]
PERS .... Persia [*Obsolete*]
PERS .... Persian Leather [*Bookbinding*] (DGA)
Pers........... Persius [*34-62AD*] [*Classical studies*] (OCD)
PERS .... Person
PERS .... Personal
Pers........... Personal (TBD)
pers........... Personal (WDMC)
PERS .... Personal Emergency Response System [*Telecommunications*]
PERS .... Personnel (AFM)
Pers........... Personnel (AL)
pers........... Personnel (DD)
PERS .... Personnel Squadron
pers........... Persons (WDMC)
PERS .... Perspective (WDAA)
PERS .... Preliminary Engineering Reports (MUGU)
PERS .... Program for Evaluation of Rejects and Substitutions [*Computer science*] (IAA)
PERS .... Public Employees Retirement System (DICI)
PERSACLIT... Peritus in Sacred Liturgy [*Roman Catholic*]
PERSACS..... Personnel Structure and Accounting System [*Army*]
PERSACS..... Personnel Structure and Composition System [*Military*]
PERS & TRACOMD... Personnel and Training Command
PERSC .... Public Education Religion Studies Center [*Defunct*] (EA)
PERS CASREP... Personnel Casualty Report [*Navy*] (ANA)
PERSCEN ..... Personnel Center
PERSCO ...... Personnel Support of Contingency Operations [*Military*]
PersCom...... Personnel Command [*Army*] (INF)
PERSCON .... Personnel Control [*Military*]
PERSD .... Personnel Department [*Marine Corps*]
PERSDEP .... Personnel Deployment Report [*Military*]
PerSep........ PerSeptive Technologies II Corp. [*Associated Press*] (SAG)
PERSEP ...... Pershing Survivability Evaluation Program [*Military*] (MCD)
PERSEPCOMD... Personnel and Separation Command (DNAB)
PERSERVDEPSERVS... Personal Services and Dependents' Services Support System [*Navy*] (DNAB)
PERSET....... Personnel Standardization and Evaluation Team [*Military*]
PERSEVCE... Perseverance (ROG)
PERSEXP .... Personal Expense Money [*Army*]
PersGp........ Personnel Group of America [*Associated Press*] (SAG)
PERSH .... Perishable (WGA)
Pershad ...... Privy Council Judgments [*1829-69*] [*India*] [*A publication*] (DLA)
PERSIL .... Peroxide Silicate [*Detergent and bleach*]
Pers Inj Comment'r... Personal Injury Commentator [*A publication*] (DLA)
Pers Inj LJ... Personal Injury Law Journal [*A publication*] (DLA)
PERSINS...... Personnel Information System [*Army*]
PERSINSCOM... Personnel Information Systems Command [*Army*] (AABC)
PERSINSD ... Personnel Information Systems Directorate [*Military Personnel Center*] (AABC)
PERSIR .... Personnel Inventory Report [*Army*] (AABC)
PERSIS .... Personnel Information System (MHDB)
PERSL .... Personal
Persl........... Personnel (TBD)
Pers Man.... Personnel Management [*A publication*]
PERSMAR..... Personnel Manning Assistance Report (DNAB)
PERSNET ..... Personnel Network [*Army*]
PersnMg...... Personnel Management, Inc. [*Associated Press*] (SAG)
PERSO .... Personnel Officer [*Air Force*]
PERSOF ...... Personnel Officer [*Navy*]
PERSON....... Personnel Simulation On-Line [*Department of State*] [*Computer program*]
Persp.......... Perspective [*Record label*]
PERSP .... Perspective (MSA)
persp .... Perspective (VRA)
PERSPAY..... Personnel and Pay [*Project*] [*Navy*]
Pers Prac B... Personnel Practice Bulletin [*A publication*]
PERSPROC... Personnel Processing [*Army*]
Pers PS ...... Perspectives on Political Science [*A publication*] (BRI)
PerSptv....... PerSeptive Biosystems, Inc. [*Associated Press*] (SAG)
PERSRSCHSYSTM... Personnel Management and Training Research Statistical Data System [*Navy*] (DNAB)
PERSRU....... Personnel Reporting Unit

PERSSEPCENT... Personnel Separation Center
PERSSO...... Personnel System Staff Officer
PERSTAT ..... Personnel Status Report [*Military*]
PERSTATREP... Personnel Status Report [*Military*]
PERSTRAN... Personal Transportation [*Navy*]
PERT............ Patients Experience of the Relationship with the Therapist Method
PERT............ Performance Evaluation Review Technique
PERT............ Perpetual Bank Federal Savings Bank [*NASDAQ symbol*] (SAG)
PERT............ Pertain (AABC)
PERT............ Pertussis [*Whooping cough*]
PERT............ Phenol Enhanced Reassociation Technique [*Clinical chemistry*]
PERT............ Program Estimation Revaluation Technique [*Computer science*] (IAA)
PERT............ Program Evaluation and Review Technique [*Computer science*]
PERT............ Program Evaluation Research Task (IEEE)
PERT............ Project Evaluation and Review Technique (DAC)
PERTCO....... Program Evaluation and Review Technique with Cost
PERT/CPM ... Program Evaluation and Review Technique/Critical Path Method
    [*Computer science*] (DOM)
PERT-CS ..... Program Evaluation and Review Technique - Cost System (DNAB)
PERTHS .... Perthshire [*County in Scotland*]
PERT-NAP.... Program Evaluation and Review Technique - Network Automatic
    Plotting (SAA)
PERTO .... Pertaining To (NVT)
Per Tr .... Perry on Trusts [*A publication*] (DLA)
PERTRAN..... Perturbation Transport [*NASA*]
PERTSIM ..... Program Evaluation and Review Technique Simulation [*Game*]
PERT-TAM ... Program Evaluation and Review Technique Task, Action, and
    Milestone Items
PERT/TIME... Program Evaluation and Review Technique/Time Analyzer [*Sperry
    UNIVAC*]
PERU .... Production Equipment Records Unit (IEEE)
PERUG........ Perusing (ROG)
PERUSA........ Perspectives - United States of America [*History course*]
PERUV .... Peruvian
PERV .... Pervert [*or Perverted*] [*FBI standardized term*]
PERV .... Porcine Endogenous Provirus
PERV .... Porcine Endogenous Retrovirus [*Medicine*]
PErV............ United States Veterans Administration Hospital, Erie, PA [*Library
    symbol Library of Congress*] (LCL3)
PErVM .... Villa Maria College, Erie, PA [*Library symbol Library of Congress*]
    (LCLS)
PERYLENE ... Peri-Dinaphthalene [*A fluorophore*] [*Organic chemistry*]
Pes .... Esophageal Pressure [*Used to estimate intrapleural pressure*] (DAVI)
PES............. IEEE Power Engineering Society (EA)
PES............. Pacific Environmental Services, Inc. (EFIS)
PES............. Paid Educational Services [*British*]
PES............. Pan European Survey [*A publication*]
PES............. Paraendocrine Syndrome [*Endocrinology*]
PES............. Parent Egg Seed
PES............. Partial Energy Service [*Electric power*]
PES............. Partido Ecuatoriano Socialista [*Ecuadorean Socialist Party*] [*Political
    party*]
PES............. Parts Engineering Support
PES............. Passive Electromagnetic System (IAA)
PES............. Patent Examining System
PES............. Pecos Resources [*Vancouver Stock Exchange symbol*]
Pes .... Pesahim (BJA)
PES............. Peshawar [*Pakistan*] [*Seismograph station code, US Geological
    Survey Closed*] (SEIS)
PES............. Philosophy of Education Society (EA)
PES............. Photoelectric Scanner
PES............. Photoelectric Scanning [*Electronics*] (ECII)
PES............. Photoelectron Spectroscopy
PES............. Photoemission Spectroscopy
PES............. Photojet Edge Sensor
PES............. Physicians Equity Services
PES............. Pictorial Eleven Society [*Formerly, PE*] [*PCS*] [*Absorbed by*] (EA)
PES............. Planning and Evaluation Staff (COE)
PES............. Pointing Error Sensor (MCD)
PES............. Polyethersulfone [*Organic chemistry*]
PES............. Polyethylene Sodium Sulfonate [*Anticoagulant*]
PES............. Post-Enumeration Survey [*Bureau of the Census*]
PES............. Postextrasystolic Potentiation [*Cardiology*]
PES............. Potential Energy Source [*Physiology*]
PES............. Potential-Energy Surface [*Chemical kinetics*]
PES............. Poultry and Egg Situation
PES............. Power Engineering Society
PES............. Power Engineering Specification
PES............. Preexcitation Syndrome [*Cardiology*]
PES............. Preparedness Evaluation System (COE)
PES............. Preschool Evaluation Scale [*Test*] (TMMY)
Pes .... Pressure, End-Systole [*Cardiology*]
PES............. Pressure Equalization System [*Nuclear energy*] (NUCP)
PES............. Private Express Statutes (DICI)
P(ES) .... Probability of Equal Regressive Slopes [*Statistics*]
PES............. Probe Entry Site [*Instrumentation*]
PES............. Problem-Etiology-Signs [*or Symptoms*] [*Nursing*]
PES............. Processed Eucheuma Seaweed
PES............. Processor Enhancement Socket [*Computer science*] (PCM)
PES............. Production Engineering Service
PES............. Production Engineering Specification (NG)
PES............. Professional Examination Service
PES............. Program Element Summary
PES............. Program Emphasis Statement [*US Employment Service*] [*Department
    of Labor*]

PES............. Program Execution System
PES............. Programmable Electronic System [*Engineering*]
PES............. Programmed Electrical Stimulation [*Neurophysiology*]
PES............. Projected Engagement Scheduler [*Military*] (CAAL)
PES............. Public Expenditure Survey [*British*]
PESA........... Petroleum Electric Supply Association [*Defunct*] (EA)
PESA........... Petroleum Equipment Suppliers Association (EA)
PESA........... Propellant Expulsion and Storage Assembly
PESA........... Proton Elastic-Scattering Analysis
PESABC .... Permanent Executive Secretariat of the Andres Bello Convention
    [*See also SECAB*] (EAIO)
PESc .... Poly Ethylene Succinate (EDCT)
PESC........... Pool Energy Services [*NASDAQ symbol*] (TTSB)
PESC........... Pool Energy Services Co. [*NASDAQ symbol*] (SAG)
PESC........... Public Expenditure Survey Committee [*British*] (ODBW)
PESD .... Pacific Electronic Security Division [*Military*]
PESD .... Postsecondary Education Statistics Division [*Department of
    Education*] (GFGA)
PESD .... Private and Executive Secretary's Diploma (AIE)
PESD .... Program Element Summary Data [*DoD*]
PESD .... Program Execution Subdirective (AABC)
PESDC .... Properties of Electrolyte Solutions Data Center [*National Institute of
    Standards and Technology*]
PESDS .... Program Element Summary Data Sheet [*DoD*]
PESGB .... Petroleum Exploration Society of Great Britain
Pesh .... Peshitta [*Syriac translation of the Bible*] (BJA)
Peshawar ... All India Reporter, Peshawar [*1933-50*] [*A publication*] (DLA)
Peshawar ... Indian Rulings, Peshawar Series [*1933-47*] [*A publication*] (DLA)
PESI........... Perma Fix Environmental Services [*NASDAQ symbol*] (SAG)
PESI........... Perma Fix Enviro Svcs [*NASDAQ symbol*] (TTSB)
PESIA.......... Postal Employees Salary Increase Act of 1960
PESIC.......... Parti du Progres Economique et Social des Independants Congolais
    Luluabourg [*Party for Economic and Social Progress of the
    Congolese Independents in Luluabourg*] [*Political party*]
Pesik .... Pesikta de-Rav Kahana (BJA)
Pesikt .... Pesikta de-Rav Kahana (BJA)
PesiktR .... Pesikta Rabbati (BJA)
PESIS .... Photo-Electron Spectroscopy of Inner-Shell (PDAA)
PESIW .... Perma-Fix Envir'l Svcs Wrrt [*NASDAQ symbol*] (TTSB)
PESIZ.......... Perma-Fix Envir'l Svcs Wrrt'B' [*NASDAQ symbol*] (TTSB)
PESM........... Photoelectron Spectromicroscope
PeSMoT .... Penn State Microoxidation Test [*Analytical chemistry*]
PESO .... Participation Enriches Science, Music, and Art Organizations
    [*Orlando, Florida*]
PESO .... Performance Evaluation Support Office
PESO .... Plant Engineering Shop Order (AAG)
PESO .... Product Engineering Services Office [*DoD*]
PESOS .... Perkin-Elmer Solvent Optimization System [*Chemistry*]
PESOS .... Photo-Electron Spectroscopy of Outer-Shell (PDAA)
PESOS .... Prepare, Explain, Show, Observe, Supervise [*Formula*] [*LIMRA*]
PESP........... Postextrasystolic Potentiation [*Medicine*] (DMAA)
PesR .... Pesikta Rabbati (BJA)
PESR .... Planning Element System Report (NATG)
PESR .... Precision Echo Sounder Recorder
PESR .... Pseudoequivalent Service Rounds [*Military*] (NVT)
PEsS .... East Stroudsburg State College, East Stroudsburg, PA [*Library
    symbol Library of Congress*] (LCLS)
PESS........... Pessus [*Pessary*] [*Pharmacy*]
PESS........... Problem, Etiology, Signs, and Symptoms [*Medicine*] (DMAA)
PESSO .... Personnel System Staff Officer
PEST........... Parameter Entity Symbol Translator [*Elstree Computing Ltd.*]
    [*Software package*] (NCC)
PEST........... Parameter Estimation by Sequential Testing [*Computer*]
PEST........... Patterned Elicitation Syntax Test [*Educational test*]
PEST........... Pesticide Evaluation Summary Tabulation
PEST........... Political, Environmental, Social, and Technological [*Business term*]
    (ODBW)
PEST........... Pressure for Economic and Social Toryism [*Tory Reform Group*]
    [*British*] (DI)
PEST........... Production Evaluation Surveillance Test
PESTAB....... Pesticides Abstracts (NITA)
PESTAN ...... Pesticide Analytical Model Version [*Environmental Protection
    Agency*] (AEPA)
PESTDOC..... Pest Control Literature Documentation [*Derwent Publications Ltd.*]
    [*Bibliographic database*] [*Information service or system*] (IID)
PESTDOC.... Pesticide Documentation (NITA)
PESTF .... Proton Event Start Forecast [*Solar weather information*]
PESTIC........ Pesticide
PESU .... Polyethersulfone [*Organic chemistry*]
PESV........... Pea Streak Virus [*Plant pathology*]
PESY........... Pheripheral Exchange Synchronization (IAA)
PET............. Aeropetrel [*Chile*] [*ICAO designator*] (FAAC)
PET............. Pacific Enterprises [*NYSE symbol*] (SPSG)
PET............. Pacific Enterprises [*AMEX symbol*] (SAG)
PET............. Panel on Educational Terminology [*Office of Education*]
PET............. Panel on Education and Training [*COSATI*]
PET............. Paper Equilibrium Tester (BARN)
PET............. Parent Effectiveness Training [*A course of study*]
PET............. Particle Electrostatic Thruster
PET............. Patterned Epitaxial Technology (IEEE)
PET............. Pelotas [*Brazil*] [*Airport symbol*] (OAG)
PET............. Pentaerythritol [*Organic chemistry*]
PET............. Pentaerythritol Tetranitrate [*Also, PETN*] [*Explosive, vasodilator*]
PET............. Penthouse Entertainment Network [*Cable television system*]

PET .... Performance Efficiency Test [*Employee screening and placement test*]
PET .... Performance Evaluation Team [*Nuclear energy*] (NRCH)
PET .... Performance Evaluation Test
PET .... Periodic Environmental Test
PET .... Periodic Evaluation Test
PET .... Peripheral Equipment Tester [*Computer science*] (BUR)
PET .... Personal Effectiveness Training (MCD)
PET .... Personal Electronic Transaction Computer (NITA)
PET .... Personal Electronic Transactor [*Computer*] [*Commodore Business Machines*]
PET .... Personal Employee Time (DHSM)
Pet .... Peter [*New Testament book*]
Pet .... Peters' Prince Edward Island Reports [*1850-72*] [*Canada*] [*A publication*] (DLA)
Pet .... Peters' United States Circuit Court Reports [*A publication*] (DLA)
Pet .... Peters' United States District Court Reports, Admiralty Decisions [*A publication*] (DLA)
Pet .... Peter's United States Reports [*1828-42*] [*A publication*] (AAGC)
Pet .... Peters' United States Supreme Court Reports [*26-41 United States*] [*A publication*] (DLA)
Pet .... Petihta (BJA)
Pet .... Pet, Inc., Corporate Information Center, St. Louis, MO [*OCLC symbol*] (OCLC)
PET .... Petition
PET .... Petrine [*Of, or relating to, Peter the Apostle or Peter the Great*]
PET .... Petrolatum (WGA)
PET .... Petroleum
Pet .... Petroleum (DD)
PET .... Petropavlovsk [*Kazakhstan*] [*Seismograph station code, US Geological Survey*] (SEIS)
PET .... Petrotech, Inc. [*Toronto Stock Exchange symbol*]
Pet .... Petrus [*Authority cited in pre-1607 legal work*] (DSA)
Pet .... Petrus de Bellapertica [*Deceased, 1308*] [*Authority cited in pre-1607 legal work*] (DSA)
PET .... Phase Elapsed Time (NASA)
PET .... Philco Epoxy Transistor (IAA)
PET .... Photoelectric Transducer (PDAA)
PET .... Photoemission Tube
PET .... Photoinduced Electron Transfer
PET .... Phototropic Energy Transfer
PET .... Physical Equipment Table
PET .... Pierre Elliott Trudeau [*Canadian prime minister*] [*Acronymic designation considered derogatory*]
PET .... Point of Equal Time [*Aviation*]
PET .... Polyester
PET .... Polyethylene [*Organic chemistry*] (IAA)
PET .... Poly(ethylene Terephthalate) [*Organic chemistry*]
PET .... Portable Earth Terminal [*NASA*]
PET .... Portable Electronic Telephone
PET .... Portable Electronic Translator
PET .... Position-Event-Time
PET .... Positron-Emission Tomography
PET .... Post-Etch Treatment (AAEL)
PET .... Potential Evapotranspiration
PET .... Potentially Exempt Transfer (ODBW)
PET .... Prediction Error Transform (PDAA)
PET .... Pre-Eclamptic Toxemia [*Medicine*]
PET .... Pre-Employment Training (OICC)
PET .... Preliminary Evaluation Team
PET .... Preliminary Examination Team [*NASA*]
PET .... Preprimary Evaluation and Training
PET .... Pressure Equalization [*Tubes or Equalizing*] [*Otorhinolaryngology*] (DAVI)
PET .... Pressurization Events Trainer
PET .... Prisoner's Education Trust (WDAA)
PET .... Probe Ephemeris Tape
PET .... Process Evaluation Tester
PET .... Producibility Evaluation Task [*Army*] (RDA)
PET .... Production Environmental Tests
PET .... Production Evaluation Test
PET .... Production Experimental Test (SAA)
PET .... Program Evaluation Team
PET .... Program Evaluator and Tester [*Computer science*]
PET .... Property Enterprise Trust [*Investment term British*] (ECON)
PET .... Propulsion Experimental Test (SAA)
PET .... Prototype Evaluation Test
PET .... Psychiatric Emergency Team
PET .... Pulsed Electrothermal (MCD)
PET .... Pupil Evaluation Team [*Education*]
PETA .... Pentaerythritol Triacrylate [*Organic chemistry*]
PETA .... People for the Ethical Treatment of Animals (EA)
PETA .... Performance Evaluation and Trend Analysis (NASA)
PETA .... Plutonium Equipment Transfer Area [*Nuclear energy*] (NRCH)
PETA .... Portable Electronic Traffic Analyzer [*British*]
Pet Ab ...... Petersdorff's Abridgment [*A publication*] (DLA)
Pet Abr ...... Petersdorff's Abridgment [*1660-1823*] [*A publication*] (DLA)
Pet Ad .... Peters' United States District Court Reports, Admiralty Decisions [*A publication*] (DLA)
Pet Ad Dec... Peters' United States District Court Reports, Admiralty Decisions [*A publication*] (DLA)
Pet Adm ...... Peters' United States District Court Reports, Admiralty Decisions [*A publication*] (DLA)
Pet Adm App... Peters' United States District Court Reports, Admiralty Decisions (Appendix) [*A publication*] (DLA)

Pet Ad R...... Peters' United States District Court Reports, Admiralty Decisions [*A publication*] (DLA)
PET & S...... Performance Evaluation, Test, and Simulation [*Air Force*]
Pet Aret...... Petrus Aretinus [*Flourished, 1088-91*] [*Authority cited in pre-1607 legal work*] (DSA)
PETAT.......... Periodic Inspection Turn-Around Time [*Military*] (AFIT)
Pet Bail ...... Petersdorff on Bail [*1824*] [*A publication*] (DLA)
Pet Br .... Bellewe's Cases Tempore Henry VIII [*Brooke's New Cases*] [*England*] [*A publication*] (DLA)
Pet Br .... Brooke's New Cases (Petit Brooke) [*1515-58*] [*A publication*] (DLA)
PETC.......... Parent Effectiveness Training Course [*Australia*]
PETC.......... Petco Animal Supplies [*NASDAQ symbol*] (SAG)
PETC.......... Pittsburgh Energy Technology Center [*Formerly, PERC*] [*Department of Energy Pittsburgh, PA*] (GRD)
PETC.......... Polyethylene Tetrachloride [*Organic chemistry*] (IAA)
PETC.......... Portable Equipment Test Chamber (MCD)
Pet CC ...... Peters' United States Circuit Court Reports [*A publication*] (DLA)
Pet Cir CR ... Peters' Condensed United States Circuit Court Reports [*A publication*] (DLA)
PetcoAn...... Petco Animal Supplies [*Associated Press*] (SAG)
Pet Cond...... Peters' Condensed Reports, United States Supreme Court [*A publication*] (DLA)
Pet Cond Rep... Peters' Condensed United States Circuit Court Reports [*A publication*] (DLA)
PETD.......... Petroleum Development [*NASDAQ symbol*] (TTSB)
PETD.......... Petroleum Development Corp. [*NASDAQ symbol*] (NQ)
Pet de Anch... Petrus de Ancharano [*Deceased, 1416*] [*Authority cited in pre-1607 legal work*] (DSA)
Pet de Bel ... Petrus de Bellapertica [*Deceased, 1308*] [*Authority cited in pre-1607 legal work*] (DSA)
Pet de Bellap... Petrus de Bellapertica [*Deceased, 1308*] [*Authority cited in pre-1607 legal work*] (DSA)
Pet de Belper... Petrus de Bellapertica [*Deceased, 1308*] [*Authority cited in pre-1607 legal work*] (DSA)
Pet de Mont... Petrus Piccoli de Monteforte [*Flourished, 14th century*] [*Authority cited in pre-1607 legal work*] (DSA)
Pet de Sam... Petrus de Sampsone [*Flourished, 1246-58*] [*Authority cited in pre-1607 legal work*] (DSA)
Pet de Samp... Petrus de Sampsone [*Flourished, 1246-58*] [*Authority cited in pre-1607 legal work*] (DSA)
Pet Dig ...... Peters' United States Digest [*A publication*] (DLA)
Pet Dig ...... Peticolas' Texas Digest [*A publication*] (DLA)
PetDv.......... Petroleum Development Corp. [*Associated Press*] (SAG)
PETE .... Parliamentary Education for Teacher Education [*Australia*]
PETE .... Partnership for Environmental Technology Education [*Nonprofit organization of 400 community colleges*]
PETE .... Petersburg National Battlefield
PETE .... Pneumatic End to End
PETE .... Portable Educational Tools Environment (AIE)
PETE .... Portable Electronics Test Equipment (DNAB)
PETE .... Portable Emergency Thermal Environment
PETE .... Primary Bank [*NASDAQ symbol*] (SAG)
PETE .... Product Engineering Tribute to Excellence
PETE .... Proof and Experimental Test Establishment [*Canada*] (MCD)
PETEOS...... Plasma-Enhanced Tetraethylosilicate (AAEL)
Peter.......... Analysis and Digest of the Decisions of Sir George Jessel, by A. P. Peter [*England*] [*A publication*] (DLA)
Peters.......... Haviland's Prince Edward Island Chancery Reports, by Peters [*1850-72*] [*Canada*] [*A publication*] (DLA)
Peters.......... Peters' United States Supreme Court Reports [*26-41 United States*] [*A publication*] (DLA)
Peters' Ad ... Peters' United States District Court Reports, Admiralty Decisions [*A publication*] (DLA)
Peters Adm... Peters' United States District Courts Reports, Admiralty Decisions [*A publication*] (DLA)
Peters' Adm Dec... Peters' United States District Court Reports, Admiralty Decisions [*A publication*] (DLA)
Peters' Admiralty Dec... Peters' United States District Court Reports, Admiralty Decisions [*A publication*] (DLA)
Peters' Adm R... Peters' United States District Court Reports, Admiralty Decisions [*A publication*] (DLA)
Peters Adm Rep... Peters' United States District Court Reports, Admiralty Decisions [*A publication*] (DLA)
Peters CC .... Peters' United States Circuit Court Reports [*A publication*] (DLA)
Petersd Ab... Petersdorff's Abridgment [*A publication*] (DLA)
Petes .... Petes Brewing Co. [*Associated Press*] (SAG)
PETFE.......... Polyethylenetetrafluoroethylene [*Organic chemistry*]
PETFEM...... Postsecondary Education Task Force on Energy Management [*Canada*]
PetFood ...... Pet Food Warehouse [*Commercial firm Associated Press*] (SAG)
PETG.......... Phenylethyl(thiogalactoside) [*Organic chemistry*]
Petg Pr & Ag... Petgrave's Principal and Agent [*1857*] [*A publication*] (DLA)
Pet Greg...... Petrus Gregorius [*Deceased, 1617*] [*Authority cited in pre-1607 legal work*] (DSA)
PETH.......... Pink-Eyed, Tan-Hooded Rat [*Medicine*] (DMAA)
Peth Dis ...... Petheram's Discovery by Interrogations [*1864*] [*A publication*] (DLA)
PETI.......... Portable Electronic Typewriter Interface [*Applied Creative Technology, Inc.*]
PETIA.......... Particle Enhanced Turbidometric Immunoassay [*Clinical chemistry*]
Petit Br ...... Petit Brooke, or Brooke's New Cases, English King's Bench [*1515-58*] [*A publication*] (DLA)
PETITN........ Petition
PETLES........ Peritoneal Exudate T-Lymphocyte-Enriched System (DB)
Pet L Nat.... Petersdorff's Law of Nations [*A publication*] (DLA)
PETM.......... Petsmart, Inc. [*NASDAQ symbol*] (SAG)

PETMA........ Portable Electric Tool Manufacturers' Association [*British*] (BI)
Pet M & S ... Petersdorff's Master and Servant [*1876*] [*A publication*] (DLA)
PETMS........ Phenethyltrimethoxy Silane [*Organic chemistry*]
PETN.......... Pentaerythritol Tetraniconitate [*Niceritrol*] [*Pharmacology*] (DAVI)
PETN.......... Pentaerythritol Tetranitrate [*Also, PET*] [*Explosive, vasodilator*]
PETN.......... Petaerythrite Tetranitrate (NAKS)
PETN.......... Petition
PETNR........ Petitioner
PETP.......... (Phenylethyl)phenyltetrahydropyridine [*Organic chemistry*]
PETP.......... Poly(ethylene Terephthalate) [*Organic chemistry*]
PETP.......... Preliminary Engineering Technical Proposal
Pet Peck Zir... Petrus Peckius (Ziricaeus) [*Deceased, 1589*] [*Authority cited in pre-1607 legal work*] (DSA)
Pet PM .... Petersen's Photographic Magazine [*A publication*] (BRI)
PETPrA....... Pacific Ent $4.36 Pfd [*AMEX symbol*] (TTSB)
PetPrac....... [*The*] Pet Practice, Inc. [*Associated Press*] (SAG)
PETPrB....... Pacific Ent $4.40 Pfd [*AMEX symbol*] (TTSB)
PETPrC....... Pacific Ent $4.50 Pfd [*AMEX symbol*] (TTSB)
PETPrD....... Pacific Ent $4.75 Pfd [*AMEX symbol*] (TTSB)
PetPRO....... Pet Professional Retailers Organization [*Defunct*] (EA)
PETQI......... Patient Education Total Quality Improvement [*Medicine*] (DMAA)
PETR.......... Petitioner
PETR.......... PetroCorp [*NASDAQ symbol*] (TTSB)
PETR.......... Petrocorp, Inc. [*NASDAQ symbol*] (SAG)
petr .... Petroleum [*Chemistry*] (DAVI)
PETRA .... Positron-Electron Tandem Ring Accelerator [*Nuclear*]
PETRA .... Program for the Vocational Training of Young People and their Preparation for Adult and Working Life [*EC*] (ECED)
PETRA .... Project for Evaluation and Treatment of Radioactive Waste [*Nuclear energy*] (NUCP)
Petr Bellug... Petrus Belluga [*Flourished, 1446-68*] [*Authority cited in pre-1607 legal work*] (DSA)
Petr de Benint... Petrus de Benintendis [*Flourished, 16th century*] [*Authority cited in pre-1607 legal work*] (DSA)
PETREL....... Professional Education and Training for Research Librarianship Program (EDAC)
PETRES...... Petroleum Reserves [*Navy*]
PETRESO... Petroleum Reserves Office [*or Officer*]
petrgly........ Petroglyph (VΠA)
Petr Greg.... Petrus Gregorius [*Deceased, 1617*] [*Authority cited in pre-1607 legal work*] (DSA)
PETRIBURG... Petriburgensis [*Signature of the Bishops of Peterborough*] [*Latin*] (ROG)
Petrie.......... Petrie Stores Corp. [*Associated Press*] (SAG)
PETRL......... Petroleum (AABC)
Petrl.......... Petroleum (TBD)
PetrlGeo..... Petroleum Geo Services [*Associated Press*] (SAG)
PetrLng...... Petersburg Long Distance [*Commercial firm Associated Press*] (SAG)
Petrlte......... Petrolite Corp. [*Associated Press*] (SAG)
Petrmn........ Petrominerals Corp. [*Associated Press*] (SAG)
Petr Nuni .... Petrus Nunius de Avendano [*Flourished, 16th century*] [*Authority cited in pre-1607 legal work*] (DSA)
PETRO .... Petroleum
PetroC .... Petro-Canada [*Associated Press*] (SAG)
PetroC2....... Petro-Canada [*Associated Press*] (SAG)
PETROCH.... Rock Chemical Database [*Ontario Geological Survey*] [*Canada Information service or system*] (CRD)
Petrocp........ Petrocorp, Inc. [*Associated Press*] (SAG)
PETRODEG... Petroleum Degrading [*Agent*]
PETROEX..... Petroleum Products Exchange Data Clearing House (NITA)
PETROG....... Petrographic
PETROGAL... Petroleos de Portugal, EP [*Portuguese Petroleum Co.*]
PETROGR .... Petrography
PETROL....... Petroleum
PETROL .... Petrology
PETROMIN... General Petroleum & Mineral Organization [*Saudi Arabia state-owned oil company*]
Petromt........ Petromet Resouces Ltd. [*Associated Press*] (SAG)
Petron......... Petronius [*First century AD*] [*Classical studies*] (OCD)
PETRONET... Petroleum Network [*Distribution and interdiction model*] (MCD)
Petron Satyric... Petronius' [*Titus*] Arbiter, Satyricon, Etc. [*A publication*] (DLA)
PETROPHIL... Petroleum Philatelic Society International (EAIO)
PETROPOL... Petropolis [*St. Petersburg*] [*Imprint*] [*Latin*] (ROG)
PetroUn .... Petro Union, Inc. [*Associated Press*] (SAG)
Petr Rave .... Petrus Ravennas [*Flourished, 1468-1508*] [*Authority cited in pre-1607 legal work*] (DSA)
PetRs.......... Petroleum & Resources Corp. [*Associated Press*] (SAG)
PETS.......... Pacific Electronics Trade Show
PETS.......... Payload Environmental Transportation System [*NASA*] (NASA)
PETS.......... Peripheral Equipment Test Set
PETS.......... P/L Experiment Test System [*NASA*] (GFGA)
PETS.......... POCC [*Payload Operations Control Center*] Experiments Timeline System [*Ground Data Systems Division and Spacelab*] [*NASA*] (NASA)
PETS.......... Polaris Engineering Technical Service [*Missiles*]
PETS.......... Portable Engine Test Stand (MCD)
PETS.......... Positions Equipment Task Summary (AAG)
PETS.......... Prior to Expiration of Term of Service [*Reenlistments*] [*Military*]
PETS.......... Procedures for Evaluating Technical Specifications Program (COE)
PETS.......... Programmed Extended Time Sharing [*Computer science*]
PETS.......... Proximity Effect Tunneling Spectroscopy (MCD)
Pet SC .... Peters' United States Supreme Court Reports [*26-41 United States*] [*A publication*] (DLA)
PET scan .... Positron Emission Transaxial Tomography [*Also, PETT*] (PAZ)
PETSEC........ Petroleum Section [*Allied Force Headquarters*]

PetsMrt........ Petsmart, Inc. [*Associated Press*] (SAG)
Pet Suppl..... Supplement to Petersdorff's Abridgment [*A publication*] (DLA)
PETT .... Pendular Eye-Tracking Test [*Medicine*] (DMAA)
PETT .... Phototropic Energy Transfer Technique
PETT .... Positron Emission Transaxial [*or Transverse*] Tomography [*Roentgenography*]
PETT .... Purkinje Fiber [*Medicine*] (DMAA)
PETT .... Purpura Fulminans [*Medicine*] (DMAA)
PETT .... Push Fluids [*Medicine*] (DMAA)
PETV .... Planar Epitaxial Tuning Varactor
PETV .... Process Evaluation Test Vehicle
PEU .... Paneuropa-Union [*Paneuropean Union*] (EAIO)
PEU .... Plasma Equivalent Unit [*Medicine*] (DMAA)
PEU .... Polyether Urethane (STED)
PEU .... Port Expander Unit
PEU .... Protected Environment Unit [*Medicine*]
PEUA......... Pelvic Exam under Anesthesia [*Medicine*]
PEURX........ Pioneer Europe Cl.A [*Mutual fund ticker symbol*] (SG)
PEUU......... Polyether Polyurethane Urea [*Organic chemistry*]
pev........... Peak Electron Volt (STED)
peV........... Peak Electron Volts
PEV .... Peak Envelope Voltage [*Telecommunications*] (TEL)
PEV .... Peak Expiratory Velocity [*Medicine*] (DMAA)
PeV .... Peripheral Vein [*Medicine*] (STED)
PEV .... Permanent Entry Visa
PEV .... Philip Environmental [*NYSE symbol*] (SAG)
PEV .... Pleasant Valley [*California*] [*Seismograph station code, US Geological Survey*] (SEIS)
PEV .... Position-Effect Variegation [*Genetics*] [*Botany*]
PEV .... Positive Expected Value
PEV .... Propeller-Excited Vibration (PDAA)
PEV .... Pulmonary Extravascular Fluid Volume [*Medicine*] (STED)
PEV .... Pyroelectric Vidicon (PDAA)
PEVCV........ Petunia Vein Clearing Virus [*Plant pathology*]
PEVE......... Post Experience Vocational Education (AIE)
PEVE......... Prensa Venezolana [*Press agency*] [*Venezuela*]
PEVI.......... Perry's Victory and International Peace Memorial National Monument
PEVL.......... Polyethylene Expanded Video Longitudinal Cable (MCD)
PEVM........ Personal'naia Elektronnaia Vychislitel'naia Mashina [*Personal Computer*] [*Russian*]
PEVM........ Professional'naia Elektronnaia Vychislitel'naia Mashina [*Professional Computer*] [*Russian*]
PEVN .... Periventricular Nucleus (STED)
PEVR .... Power-Enrichment Vacuum Regulator [*Automotive engineering*]
PEW .... Passive Electronics Warfare (NG)
PEW .... Percussion Welding
PEW .... Peshawar [*Pakistan*] [*Airport symbol*] (OAG)
pew.......... Pewter (VRA)
PEW .... Pulmonary Extravascular Water [*Medicine*] (DMAA)
PEWO........ Plant Engineering Work Order (MCD)
PEWR .... Plant Engineering Work Release (AAG)
PEWS........ Parts Early Warning System (IAA)
PEWS........ Platoon Early Warning System (RDA)
PEWS........ Plutonium Equipment Warm Shop [*Nuclear energy*] (NRCH)
PEWV........ Pulmonary Extravascular Water Volume [*Physiology*]
Pex.......... Peak Exercise (DMAA)
PEX .... Per Example
PEX .... Phenazine Ethosulfate [*Biochemistry*]
PEx .... Physical Examination (MAE)
PEX .... Private Electronic Exchange [*Telecommunications*] (IAA)
PEX .... Pronto Explorations Ltd. [*Vancouver Stock Exchange symbol*]
PEX .... World Aircraft Flight Operation, Inc. [*ICAO designator*] (FAAC)
PEXA .... Pre-Edge X-Ray Absorption [*For study of solids*]
PEXAFS....... Photoelectron Extended X-Ray Absorption Fine Structure
PEXRA .... Programmed Electronic X-Ray Automatic Diffractometer (IAA)
PEXRAD...... Programmed Electronic X-Ray Automatic Diffractometer
PEY .... Pengelly Mines Ltd. [*Vancouver Stock Exchange symbol*]
PEY .... Photoelectric Yield
PEYS......... Photoelectron Yield Spectroscopy (MCD)
PEZ .... Pezgold Resource Corp. [*Vancouver Stock Exchange symbol*]
PEZ .... Pleasanton, TX [*Location identifier FAA*] (FAAL)
PEZV .... Prime Equities International [*NASDAQ symbol*] (SAG)
PEZVF........ Prime Equities Intl [*NASDAQ symbol*] (TTSB)
PF .... Amer First Prep Fd 2 L.P. [*AMEX symbol*] (TTSB)
PF .... American First PREP [*Preferred Real Estate Participation*] Fund 2 Ltd. [*AMEX symbol*] (SPSG)
PF .... Frankford Public Library, Frankford, PA [*Library symbol Library of Congress*] (LCLS)
PF .... French Polynesia [*ANSI two-letter standard code*] (CNC)
PF .... L-Phenylalanine Mustard and 5-Fluorouracil [*Antineoplastic drug regimen*] (DAVI)
PF .... Pacifica Foundation (EA)
PF .... Package Freighter [*Shipping*]
PF .... Packing Factor (EECA)
PF .... Packing Fraction (EECA)
PF .... Paderewski Foundation [*Defunct*] (EA)
PF .... Page Fault (IAA)
PF .... Page Footing (BUR)
PF .... Page Formatter (MDG)
PF .... Pair Feeding (DMAA)
PF .... Paling Fence
PF .... Panchromatic Film (ADA)
PF .... Paper and Foil [*Capacitor*] (DEN)
pf .... Paracel Islands [*MARC country of publication code Library of Congress*] (LCCP)

PF .... Parachute Facility (NASA)
PF .... Parachute Flare (NVT)
PF .... Parafascicular Nucleus [*Neuroanatomy*]
PF .... Parallel Fiber [*Neuroanatomy*]
PF .... Parallel Fold
PF .... Paramount Funding Corp. [*Toronto Stock Exchange symbol*]
PF .... Parapsychology Foundation (EA)
PF .... Partial Function (IAA)
PF .... Partition Factor (NRCH)
PF .... Passage Free (ROG)
P/F .... Pass-Fail [*System*] (MAE)
PF .... Patellofemoral Joint [*Anatomy*] (DAVI)
PF .... Path Finder [*British military*] (DMA)
PF .... Pathfinder Fund (EA)
PF .... Patriotic Front [*Zimbabwe*] [*Political party*] (PPW)
PF .... Patrol Vessel, Frigate [*Navy symbol*]
P/F .... Pattern Flight [*Also, P/FLT*] (MUGU)
PF .... Paved Flume (COE)
PF .... Payload Forward [*NASA*] (MCD)
PF .... Payload Function [*NASA*] (MCD)
PF .... Peace and Freedom Party [*Political party*] (DLA)
PF .... Peak Flow [*Medicine*]
PF .... Peak Frequency
PF .... Peanut Flour
PF .... Pedal Furrow
PF .... Penetration Fracture (IAA)
PF .... Pen Friends [*Defunct*] (EA)
PF .... Pension Fund
PF .... Peregrine Fund (EA)
PF .... Perfect
pf .... Perfect (WDAA)
PF .... Performance Factor
PF .... Perfusion Fixation [*Histology*]
PF .... Perfusion Fluid [*Medicine*] (DMAA)
PF .... Pericardial Fluid [*Medicine*] (DMAA)
PF .... Periosteal Fibroblast [*Medicine*] (DMAA)
PF .... Peritoneal Fluid [*Medicine*] (MAE)
PF .... Permanent Fireman
PF .... Permanent Force [*Canadian Militia before 1940*]
PF .... Permeability Factor
pf .... Perofskite [*CIPW classification*] [*Geology*]
PF .... Personal Fouls [*Basketball*]
PF .... Personality Factor
PF .... Personal Security File Number [*British Secret Service*]
Pf .... Pfeifferella [*Genus of bacteria*]
PF .... Pfennig [*Penny*] [*Monetary unit*] [*German*]
PF .... Phenol-Formaldehyde [*Organic chemistry*]
PF .... Phenylalanine and Methotrexate [*Antineoplastic drug regimen*] (DAVI)
PF .... Philatelic Foundation (EA)
PF .... Photogrammetric Facility [*Army*]
PF .... Physicians Forum (EA)
PF .... Pianoforte [*Soft, then Loud*] [*Music*]
pf .... Pianoforte (WDAA)
pF .... Picofarad
PF .... Picture Frustration [*Study*] (MAE)
PF .... Pilgrim Fellowship (EA)
PF .... Pilot Flying (GAVI)
PF .... Pilot Stop Filter (IAA)
PF .... Pininfarina [*Automotive coachworks*]
PF .... [*The*] Pioneer & Fayette Railroad Co. [*AAR code*]
PF .... Piu Forte [*A Little Louder*] [*Music*]
PF .... Plain Face [*Construction*]
PF .... Plane Frame [*Camutek*] [*Software package*] (NCC)
PF .... Planning Forum (EA)
PF .... Plantar Fasciaitis [*Medicine*]
PF .... Plantar Flexion [*Medicine*]
PF .... Plasma Factor (DMAA)
PF .... Plasticity Index [*Soil*] (DICI)
PF .... Platform (SSD)
PF .... Platelet Factor [*Hematology*]
PF .... Plentiful Foods [*Department of Agriculture*] [*A publication*]
PF .... Pleural Fluid [*Medicine*] (DB)
PF .... Plot Function [*Computer science*]
PF .... Pneumatic Float
PF .... Poco Forte [*Rather Loud*] [*Music*]
PF .... Poe Foundation (EA)
PF .... Point Foundation (EA)
PF .... Point of Frog [*Electronics*] (MSA)
PF .... Points For [*Football*]
PF .... Polar Front [*Climatology*]
PF .... Pole Fittings [*JETDS nomenclature*] [*Military*] (CET)
PF .... Police Forces [*British*]
PF .... Police Foundation (EA)
PF .... POLISARIO [*Frente Popular para la Liberacion de Saguia El Hamra y Rio De Oro*] [*Popular Front for the Liberation of Saguia El Hamra and Rio De Oro Morocco*] (PD)
P/F .... Poll/Final [*Computer science*] (TNIG)
PF .... Poloidal Field (MCD)
PF .... Polyurethane Foam
PF .... Pool Frequency [*Pisciculture*]
PF .... Poop and Forecastle [*of a ship*] (DS)
PF .... Popular Forces [*ARVN*]
PF .... Popular Forces [*South Vietnam*]
PF .... Pore Free (IAA)
PF .... Por Favor [*Please*] [*Portuguese*]

PF .... Portal Fibrosis [*Medicine*]
PF .... Portfolio [*A publication*]
PF .... Position Failure
PF .... Position Finder [*British military*] (DMA)
PF .... Postage Free (ROG)
PF .... Posterior Fontanelle [*Anatomy*] (DAVI)
P/F .... Post Flight (AFIT)
PF .... Postman's Federation [*A union*] [*British*]
PF .... Posture Foundation [*Initialism is used in brand of sneaker shoe, PF Flyers*]
PF .... Potency Factor (GNE)
PF .... Powered Flight (NASA)
PF .... Power Factor [*Radio*]
pf .... Power Factor (IDOE)
PF .... Power Focus [*Photography*]
PF .... Power Frame [*Telecommunications*] (TEL)
P/F .... Practical Factors
PF .... Precursor Fluid [*Medicine*] (MEDA)
PF .... Preference
PF .... Preferred
PF .... Prefetch [*Computer science*]
PF .... Preflight
PF .... Presbyterian Foundation [*Australia*]
PF .... Pressure Fan (AAG)
PF .... Preterm Foundation [*Australia*]
PF .... Primary Fibrinolysin [*Medicine*] (DMAA)
PF .... Prime Function (NASA)
PF .... Prison Fellowship Ministries (EA)
PF .... Probability of Failure (NASA)
PF .... Procurator Fiscal
PF .... Pro Female [*International Bowhunting Organization*] [*Class Equipment*]
PF .... Profile (KSC)
pf .... Pro Forma [*As a Matter of Form*] [*Latin*] (WGA)
Pf .... Pro Forma (EBF)
PF .... Program Function [*Computer science*] (IBMDP)
PF .... Programmable Format [*Perforating keyboard*]
PF .... Programmable Function (NITA)
PF .... Progressive Foundation (EA)
PF .... Project Friend (EA)
PF .... Projectile Fragment
P/F .... Proof
PF .... Prop Forward
PF .... Proposed Finding [*Nuclear energy*] (NRCH)
PF .... Prostatic Fluid [*Medicine*] (DMAA)
PF .... Protection Factor
PF .... Protein-Free
PF .... Protoplasmic Fracture [*Freeze etching in microscopy*]
PF .... Proximity Fuze [*Bomb, rocket, or shell*]
PF .... PsychoHistory Forum (EA)
PF .... Psynetics Foundation (EA)
P/F .... Pteropod/Foramifera [*Ratio in coastal waters*]
PF .... Public Funding [*Finance*] (WDAA)
PF .... Pulmonary Blood-Flow [*Medicine*] (DB)
PF .... Pulmonary Factor [*Medicine*]
PF .... Pulmonary Function [*Medicine*] (DMAA)
PF .... Pulse Feedback [*Telecommunications*] (IAA)
PF .... Pulse Frequency
PF .... Pulverized Fuel
P F .... Pump-Out Facilities [*Nautical charts*]
PF .... Punch Off [*Computer science*] (BUR)
PF .... Purge Fan [*Nuclear energy*] (NRCH)
PF .... Purkinje Fibers [*Cardiology*] (DAVI)
PF .... Purple Finch [*Ornithology*]
PF .... Purpura Fulminans (DB)
PF .... Pygmy Fund (EA)
PF .... Trans Pennsylvania Airlines [*ICAO designator*] (AD)
PF3a .... Platelet Factor 3 Availability [*Hematology*] (DAVI)
PFA .... Pacific Football Alliance (PSS)
PFA .... Palmdale Final Assembly [*NASA*] (NASA)
PFA .... Panarcadian Federation of America (EA)
PFA .... Papermakers Felt Association (EA)
PFA .... Para-Fluorophenylalanine [*Biochemistry*]
PFA .... Participating Field Activity [*DoD*]
PFA .... Parti de la Federation Africaine [*African Federation Party*] [*Political party*]
PFA .... Pedorthic Footwear Association (NTPA)
PFA .... Pellet-Fired Appliance [*Heating system*]
PFA .... Pension Fund Association [*Japan*] (ECON)
PFA .... Perfluoroalkoxy [*Organic chemistry*]
PFA .... Personnel Functional Assessment [*Of the Army Acquisition Corps*] (RDA)
PFA .... Petroflame International [*Vancouver Stock Exchange symbol*]
PFA .... Phosphonoformic Acid [*Antiviral compound*]
PFA .... Pianists Foundation of America [*Defunct*] (EA)
PFA .... Pierce Ferry [*Arizona*] [*Seismograph station code, US Geological Survey Closed*] (SEIS)
PFA .... Pierre Fauchard Academy (EA)
PFA .... Pioneer Fraternal Association (EA)
PFA .... Pitch Follow-Up Amplifier
PFA .... Plan for Action (MCD)
PFA .... Polish Falcons of America (EA)
PFA .... Polyfurfuryl Alcohol [*Organic chemistry*]
PFA .... Polymeric Fatty Acid [*Food science*]
PFA .... Polyurethane Foam Association (EA)

PFA............ Pontius Family Association (EA)
PFA............ Popular Flying Association [*British*]
PFA............ Post Flight Analysis
PFA............ Power Fastenings Association [*British*] (DBA)
PFA............ Prescription Footwear Association (EA)
PFA............ Presidential Families of America (EA)
PFA............ Printer Font ASCII [*Computer science*] (CDE)
PFA............ Prison Families Anonymous (EA)
PFA............ Prison Fellowship of Australia
PFA............ Probability of False Alarm [*DoD*]
PFA............ Production Flow Analysis (PDAA)
PFA............ Professional Farmers of America (EA)
PFA............ Professional Fishermen's Association [*Tasmania, Australia*]
PFA............ Professional Footballers' Association [*British*] (BI)
PFA............ Professional Fraternity Association (EA)
PFA............ Profunda Femoris Artery [*Anatomy*] (DAVI)
PFA............ Program and File Analysis
PFA............ Proportional Fluid Amplifier
PFA............ Pulverized Fuel Ash (IEEE)
PFA............ Pure Fluid Amplification
PFAA.......... Phelps Family Association of America (EA)
PFAA.......... Prairie Farm Assistance Act
PFAB.......... Prefabricated
PFAC.......... Panepirotic Federation of America and Canada [*Later, PFACA*] (EA)
PFAC.......... People for a Change (EA)
PFACA........ Panepirotic Federation of America, Canada, and Australia (EA)
P/FACCTL .... Pad Facility Controls [*Aerospace*] (AAG)
PFACP .... Pro-Fac Co-op 'A' Pfd [*NASDAQ symbol*] (TTSB)
PFACP .... Pro-Fac Cooperative, Inc. [*NASDAQ symbol*] (SAG)
PFAD.......... Palm Fatty Acid Distillate [*Organic chemistry*]
PFAE.......... Perfluoroalkyl Ether [*Organic chemistry*]
PFAM.......... Programmed Frequency Amplitude Modulation
PFANZ........ Police Federation of Australia and New Zealand
PFAP.......... Poly(fluoroalkoxyphosphazene) [*Organic chemistry*]
PFAR.......... Popular Front for Armed Resistance [*Pakistan*]
PFAR .... Power Fail Automatic Restart [*Computer science*]
PFAR .... Preliminary Failure Analysis Report [*NASA*] (KSC)
PFAS.......... Performic Acid-Schiff Reaction [*Medicine*] (MAE)
PFAS.......... President of the Faculty of Architects and Surveyors [*British*] (DBQ)
PFASC .... PATRIOT [*Phased Array Tracking to Intercept Target*] Field Army Suppor t Center [*Army*]
PFAT.......... Pre-First Article Test
PFAT.......... Preliminary Flight Appraisal Test (MCD)
PFAT.......... Private Forestry Association of Tasmania [*Australia*]
PFATS......... Professional Football Athletic Trainers Society (NTPA)
PFAVC........ Pacific Fleet Audio-Visual Command (DNAB)
PFAW.......... People for the American Way (EA)
PFAWA .... Parents and Friends Association of Western Australia
PFAWA .... Poultry Farmers' Association of Western Australia
PFB............ Parallel Filter Bank (CIST)
PFB............ Partei Freier Buerger [*Free Citizens' Party*] [*Germany Political party*] (PPW)
PFB............ Passo Fundo [*Brazil*] [*Airport symbol*] (OAG)
PFB............ Payload Feedback [*NASA*] (MCD)
PFB............ Payload Forward Bus [*NASA*] (MCD)
PFB............ Pentafluorobenzyl [*Organic radical*]
PFB............ Pentafluorobenzyl Bromide [*Organic chemistry*]
PFB............ Photo Flash Battery
PFB............ Plasti-Fab Ltd. [*Toronto Stock Exchange symbol*]
PFB............ Pneumatic Float Bridge
PFB............ Position Feedback (MCD)
PFB............ Prefabricated [*Technical drawings*]
PFB............ Prefetch Buffer (CIST)
PFB............ Preformed Beams [*SONAR*]
PFB............ Pressure Fed Booster (NASA)
PFB............ Pressurized Fluid-Bed [*Chemical engineering*]
PFB............ Printer Font Binary [*Computer science*] (CDE)
PFB............ Provisional Frequency Board [*ITU*]
PFB............ Pseudofollicutitis Barbae [*Medicine*]
PFBA.......... Poly(perfluorobutyl Acrylate) [*Organic chemistry*]
PFBC.......... Pentaflurobenzoyl Chloride [*Organic chemistry*]
PFBC.......... Pressurized Fluidized-Bed Combustion
PFBHA .... Pentafluorobenzylhydroxylamine Hydrochloride [*Analytical biochemistry*]
PFBI........... Premier Financial Bancorp, Inc. [*NASDAQ symbol*] (SAG)
PFBI........... Premier Finl Bancorp [*NASDAQ symbol*] (TTSB)
PFBRG........ Pneumatic Float Bridge
PFBV.......... Pelargonium Flower Break Virus [*Plant pathology*]
PFC............ Pacific City, OR [*Location identifier FAA*] (FAAL)
PFC............ Parallel-Flow Condenser [*Air conditioning systems*]
PFC............ Parti Feministe du Canada
PFC............ Passed Flying College [*British*]
PFC............ Passenger Facility Charge [*Airports*]
PFC............ Pathfinder Industries Ltd. [*Formerly, Pathfinder Financial Corporation*] [*Toronto Stock Exchange symbol*]
PFC............ Patient Focused Care [*Medicine*]
PFC............ Peak Follower Circuit
PFC............ Peculiar Facility Change (AAG)
PFC............ Pelvic Flexion Contracture [*Orthopedics*] (DAVI)
PFC............ Pen Fancier's Club (EA)
PFC............ Pennsylvania Public Library Film Center, University Park, PA [*OCLC symbol*] (OCLC)
PFC............ Perfluorocarbon [*Organic chemistry*]
PFC............ Perfluorochemical [*Organic chemistry*]
PFC............ Perfluorocompound (AAEL)

PFC............ Performance Flight Certification [*NASA*] (NASA)
PFC............ Permanent Families for Children [*Defunct*] (EA)
PFC............ Persistent Fetal Circulation [*Medicine*]
PFC............ Personal Finance Center [*Information service or system*]
PFC............ Physicians for Choice (EA)
PFC............ Plan Filing Cabinet
PFC............ Plaque-Forming Cell [*Immunochemistry*]
PFC............ Plow-Furrow-Cover [*Waste*] (DICI)
PFC............ Pneumatic Function Controller
PFC............ Point Focusing and Centering [*Optics*]
PFC............ Police Forces [*British*]
PFC............ Positive Feedback Circuit
PFC............ Postflight Checklist (MCD)
PFC............ Power Factor Capacitor [*Radio*] (IAA)
PFC............ Power Factor Corrector (MCD)
PFC............ Prairie Fiction Collection, Alberta Culture [*UTLAS symbol*]
PFC............ Praying for Corporal [*Private First Class desirous of promotion, or female in wartime desirous of a boyfriend*]
PFC............ Preflight Console (MCD)
PFC............ Prefrontal Cortex [*Anatomy*]
PFC............ Preliminary Flight Certification [*NASA*]
PFC............ Presley-ites Fan Club (EA)
PFC............ Pressure Function Controller
PFC............ Primary Flight Control
PFC............ Priority Foreign Country [*International trade*] (ECON)
PFC............ Private, First Class [*Army*]
PFC............ Private Forestry Council [*Australia*]
PFC............ Privately Financed Consumption (MHDW)
PFC............ Processing Figure Channel [*Electronics*] (ECII)
PFC............ Programmed Fuel Computer [*Automotive engineering*]
PFC............ Progreso y Futuro de Ceuta [*Political party*] (EY)
PFC............ Pulsed Flame Combustor
PFC............ Pulse-Flow Coulometry
PFCA.......... Performance Ford Club of America (EA)
PFCA.......... Plastic Food Container Association [*Defunct*]
PFCC.......... Power Factor Corrector Capacitor [*Radio*] (IAA)
PFCCG .... Pacific Fleet Combat Camera Group (DNAB)
PFCD.......... Primary Flight Control Display
PFCE.......... Performance (WGA)
PFCE.......... Preface (ROG)
PFCE.......... Preference (AAG)
PFCF.......... Payload Flight Control Facility [*NASA*] (MCD)
PFCF.......... Producer Fixed Capital Formation (MCD)
PFCH .... Prefilled Clutch Hydraulic Actuation [*Automotive Products, Inc.*] [*Automotive engineering*]
PFCM.......... Pittsburgh Festival of Contemporary Music [*Record label*]
PFCO .... Position Field Classification Officer
PFCO .... Principal Fire Control Officer (WDAA)
PFCP.......... Primary Familial and Congenital Polycythemia [*Medicine*]
PFCR.......... Plaque-Forming Cell Response [*Immunochemistry*] (OA)
PFCRA........ Program Fraud Civil Remedies Act
PFCRN........ Partido del Frente Cardenista de Reconstruccion Nacional [*Mexico Political party*] (EY)
PFCS.......... Primary Flight Control System [*NASA*] (MCD)
PFCS.......... Primary Flow Control System [*Nuclear energy*] (NRCH)
PFCS.......... Program and Funds Control System (MCD)
PFCT.......... Pre-Flight Certification Test
PFCU.......... Power Flying Control Unit [*Aviation*] (DA)
PFCV.......... Patriotic Funds Council of Victoria [*Australia*]
PFCWTS ..... Pogo Fan Club and Walt Kelly Society (EA)
PFD............ Particle [*or Proton*] Flux Density
PFD............ Partnership for Democracy [*An association*] (EA)
PFD............ Perfluorodecalin [*Organic chemistry*]
PFD............ Personal, Fatigue, and Delay [*Work measurement factors*]
PFD............ Personal Flotation Device [*Life jacket*]
PFD............ Phase Frequency Distortion [*Telecommunications*] (IAA)
PFD............ Planned Flight Data [*Aviation*] (DA)
PFD............ Planning Factors Development (MCD)
PFD............ Policy Formulation Division (AAGC)
PFD............ Polyostotic Fibrous Dysplasia [*Medicine*] (DMAA)
PFD............ Position Fixing Device (ADA)
PFD............ Power Flux Density [*Telecommunications*] (TEL)
PFD............ Preferred (AAG)
PFD............ Preferred Income Fund [*NYSE symbol*] (SPSG)
PFD............ Preferred Stock [*Investment term*] (DFIT)
PFD............ Preliminary Functional Description (CINC)
PFD............ Present for Duty
PFD............ Primary Flash Distillate [*Chemical technology*]
PFD............ Primary Flight Display
PFD............ Probability of Failure on Demand (ACII)
PFD............ Process Flow Diagram (NRCH)
PFD............ Pseudoinflammatory Fundus Disease [*Medicine*] (DMAA)
PFD............ Puffed [*Freight*]
PFD............ Pulse-Frequency Diversity [*Electronics*] (NG)
PFDA.......... Perfluorodecanoic Acid [*Organic chemistry*]
PFDA.......... Post Flight Data Analysis
PFDA.......... Precision Frequency Distribution Amplifier
PFDA.......... Pulse-Frequency Distortion Analyzer
PFDBAD ...... Pathfinder Badge [*Military decoration*] (GFGA)
PFDC .... Peoples Bancorp (Dekalb County) [*NASDAQ symbol*] (SAG)
PFDC .... Peoples Bancorp(IN) [*NASDAQ symbol*] (TTSB)
PFDC .... Peoples Federal Savings Bank of DeKalb City [*NASDAQ symbol*] (NQ)
PFDCCA .... Prodemca: Friends of the Democratic Center in the Americas [*Defunct*] (EA)

PFDF	Pacific Fisheries Development Foundation [Defunct] (EA)
PFDI	Preferred Funeral Directors International (NTPA)
PfdInco	Preferred Income Fund [Associated Press] (SAG)
PFDJ	People's Front for Democracy and Justice [Formerly, EPLF] [Eritrea] [Political party] (ECON)
PFDJ	Popular Front for Democracy and Justice [Eritrea]
PFDM	Preliminary Final Draft Manuscript
PFDR	Pathfinder [Aircraft]
PfdrBad	Pathfinder Badge [Military decoration] (AABC)
PFDS	Pergamon Financial Data Services [Pergamon Orbit Infoline Ltd.] [British Information service or system] (IID)
PFD SP	Preferred Spelling (WDAA)
PFDTM	Preliminary Flightweight Demonstration Test Motor (MCD)
PFE	Pacific Fruit Express Co. [AAR code]
PFE	Partido Feminista de Espana [Feminist Party of Spain] [Political party] (PPW)
PFE	Pelvic Floor Exercise (DMAA)
PFE	Performance Fitness Examination [Military] (DNAB)
PFE	Pfizer, Inc. [NYSE symbol] (SPSG)
PFE	Photoferroelectric Effect [Physics]
PFE	Physics of Failure in Electronics [A publication] (MCD)
PFE	Plenum Fill Experiment [Nuclear energy] (NRCH)
PFE	Popular Front of Estonia [Political party]
PFE	Post Fire Evaluation [Military] (CAAL)
PFE	Post Flight Evaluation
PFE	Pressure Feedback Exhaust [Automotive engineering]
PFE	Priests for Equality (EA)
PFE	Primary Feedback Element (IAA)
PFE	Process Fuel Equivalent (MCD)
PFE	Pulsed Field Electrophoresis [Analytical biochemistry]
PFE	Purchaser Furnished Equipment (NATG)
PFEAAC	Posterior Fossa Extra-Axial Arachnoid Cyst [Medicine] (DAVI)
PFEC	Philatelic Friends Exchange Circuit (EA)
PFEFES	Pacific and Far East Federation of Engineering Societies
PfeifVac	Pfeiffer Vacuum Technology AG [Associated Press] (SAG)
PFEL	Pacific Far East Line
PFEP	Programmable Front-End Processor [Computer science]
PFES	Pan American Federation of Engineering Societies
PFES	Proposed Final Environmental Statement [Department of Energy]
PFES	Pure Fluid Encoder System
PFET	P-Channel Junction Field-Effect Transistor (IDOE)
PFF	Page Fault Frequency [Computer science] (MHDI)
PFF	Pathfinder Force [British RADAR designation which became overall synonym for RADAR] [Military]
PFF	Permanent Family File [Navy] (NG)
PFF	Phenolfurfural [Organic chemistry]
PFF	Planning Factors File (MCD)
PFF	Plaque-Forming Factor (PDAA)
PFF	Pluto Fast Flyby [NASA] (PS)
PFF	Police Field Force (CINC)
PFF	Porcine Follicular Fluid [Endocrinology]
PFF	Precast Flooring Federation [British] (DBA)
PFF	Pre-Formed Fragmentation (MUSM)
PFF	Presbyterian Frontier Fellowship (EA)
PFF	Primary Focus Feed [Satellite communications]
PFF	Prisoners' Families & Friends (WDAA)
PFF	Proposed Fabric Flammability Standard [Consumer Product Safety Commission]
PFF	Protein Fat-Free [Food technology]
PFF	Punjab Frontier Force [British military] (DMA)
PFFB	PFF Bancorp [NASDAQ symbol] (TTSB)
PFFB	PFF Bancorp, Inc. [NASDAQ symbol] (SAG)
PFFBcp	PFF Bancorp, Inc. [Associated Press] (SAG)
PFFC	Parallel-Flow Film Cooling
PFFC	Peoples Financial Corp. [NASDAQ symbol] (SAG)
PFFC	Philadelphia Flyers Fan Club (EA)
PFFD	Proximal Femoral Focal Deficiency [Orthopedics] (DAVI)
PFF Inc	Police-FBI Fencing, Incognito [Phony fencing ring operated by Washington, DC, law enforcement agents during 1976 to identify and arrest area thieves]
PFFX	Profiling Fixture
PFG	Pacific Rim Mining Corp. [Vancouver Stock Exchange symbol]
PFG	Paeoniflorigenone [Biochemistry]
PFG	Paper Flow Group [Nuclear Regulatory Commission] (GFGA)
PFG	Peak Flow Gauge [Medicine] (AAMN)
PFG	PennCorp Financial Group [NYSE symbol] (SPSG)
PFG	Pfennig [Penny] [Monetary unit] [German]
PFG	Piping and Filter Gallery [Nuclear energy] (NRCH)
PFG	Primary Frequency Generator
PFG	Pulsed-Field Gel Electrophoresis (DMAA)
PFG	Pulsed Field Gradient [Electroanalytical chemistry]
PFG	Purple Flower Gang (EA)
PFGC	Parameters from Group Contribution [Equation of state]
PFGC	Performance Food Group [NASDAQ symbol] (SAG)
PFGE	Pulsed Field Gel Electrophoresis
PFGE	Pulsed-Field Gel Electrophresis (HGEN)
PFGE	Pulsed Field Gradient Gel Electrophoresis
PFGI	Provident Financial Group [NASDAQ symbol] [Formerly, Provident Bancorp.] (SG)
PFGM	Guided Missile Patrol Escort [Ship symbol] (NATG)
PFGPr	PennCorp Finl $3.375 Pfd [NYSE symbol] (TTSB)
PFGX	Pacific Fruit Growers Express
PFH	Hudson, NY [Location identifier FAA] (FAAL)
PFHInco	Pafco Financial Holdings Ltd. [Toronto Stock Exchange symbol]
PFH	Perifornical Hypothalamus (DB)

PFH	Pressurized Fluidized-Bed Hydroretorting [Chemical engineering]
PFHA	Paso Fino Horse Association (EA)
PFHM	Protein-Free Hybridoma Medium
PFHS	Precipitation from Homogeneous Solution [Catalyst preparation process]
PFI	Pacific Forest Industries (EA)
PFI	Pack File Indexer (NITA)
PFI	People First International (EA)
PFI	Pet Food Institute (EA)
PFI	Photo Finishing Institute [Defunct] (EA)
PFI	Photon Flow Integrating (IAA)
PFI	Photon Flux Integration (IAA)
PFI	Physical Fitness Index
PFI	Picture and Frame Institute [Defunct] (EA)
PFI	Pie Filling Institute [Defunct] (EA)
PFI	Pipe Fabrication Institute (EA)
PFI	Police Foundation Institute (NADA)
PFI	Port Fuel Injector [Automotive engines]
PFI	Position Finding Instrument (DS)
PFI	Power Factor Indicator (IAA)
PFI	Power Failure Indicator [NASA] (KSC)
PFI	Prison Fellowship International (EA)
PFI	Private Finance Initiative [British]
PFIA	Police and Firemen's Insurance Association (EA)
PFIA	Prevention of Fraud Investments Act [British]
PFIAB	President's Foreign Intelligence Advisory Board (AFM)
PFI & R	Part Fill In and Ram [Construction]
PFIB	Pentafluoroiodosylbenzene [Organic chemistry]
PFIB	Perfluoroisobutene [Organic chemistry]
PFIB	Perfluoroisobutylene [Organic chemistry] (MAE)
PFIC	Passive Foreign Investment Company [IRS]
PFIC	Processed Food Industry Council [Australia]
PFIEP	Perfluorinated Ion-Exchange Polymer [Organic chemistry]
PFIM	Pure Fluid Impact Modulator
PFIMF	Preferred Income Management Fund, Inc. [Associated Press] (SAG)
PFIN	P & F Industries, Inc. [NASDAQ symbol] (NQ)
PFINA	P&F Indus'A' [NASDAQ symbol] (TTSB)
PFINP	P & F Ind $1 Pfd [NASDAQ symbol] (TTSB)
PFIU	Plot File Import Utility [IBM Corp.]
Pfizer	Pfizer, Inc. [Associated Press] (SAG)
PFJ	Patreksfjordur [Iceland] [Airport symbol] (OAG)
PFJ	Polar Front Jet Stream (ADA)
PFJR	Patellofemoral Joint Reaction [Physiology]
PFK	Payload Function Key [NASA] (MCD)
PFK	Perfluorokerosene [Heat transfer agent]
PFK	Phosphofructokinase [An enzyme]
PFK	Programmed Function Key (NITA)
PFK	Programmed Function Keyboard [Computer science]
PFKM	Phosphofructokinase, Muscle Type [Medicine] (DMAA)
PFKY	People First Corp. [NASDAQ symbol] (SAG)
PFKY	Peoples First [NASDAQ symbol] (TTSB)
PFL	Fort Sill, OK [Location identifier FAA] (FAAL)
PFL	Pacific Cassiar Ltd. [Toronto Stock Exchange symbol]
PFL	People for Life (EA)
PFL	Pharmacists for Life (EA)
PFL	Pioneer Football League (PSS)
PFL	Pol-Fly [Poland ICAO designator] (FAAC)
PFL	Pounds per Lineal Foot [Technical drawings]
PFL	Primary Freon Loop (NASA)
PFL	Propulsion Field Laboratory
PFL	Public Facility Loans
PFLA	Popular Front for the Liberation of Ahvaz [Iran]
P-FLAG	Federation of Parents and Friends of Lesbians and Gays (EA)
PFLAG	Parents, Families, and Friends of Lesbians and Gays [An association] (EA)
PFLF	People, Food and Land Foundation (EA)
PFLI	Pharmacists for Life International (EA)
PFLL	Phase and Frequency Locked Loop [Telecommunications] (IAA)
P Flo	Pandectae Florentinae [A publication] (DSA)
PFLO	Popular Front for the Liberation of Oman [Political party] (PD)
PFLOAG	Popular Front for the Liberation of Oman and the Arabian Gulf [Political party] (PD)
PFLOAG	Popular Front for the Liberation of the Occupied Arabian Gulf
PFLOLS	Portable Fresnel-Lens Optical-Landing System (NG)
P Florent	Pandectae Florentinae [A publication] (DSA)
PFLP	Popular Front for the Liberation of Palestine [Political party] (PD)
PFLP-GC	Popular Front for the Liberation of Palestine - General Command [Political party] (PD)
PFLT	Paint Filter Liquids Test [Environmental science] (FFDE)
P/FLT	Pattern Flight [Also, P/F] (MUGU)
PFLT	People's Front of the Liberation Tigers [Sri Lanka] [Political party] (EY)
PFLTS	Parquet Floor Layers' Trade Society [A union] [British]
PFLV	Pressure Fed Launch Vehicle [NASA] (KSC)
PFM	Little Franciscan Sisters of Mary [Roman Catholic religious order]
PFM	Pacific Minesearch Ltd. [Vancouver Stock Exchange symbol]
PFM	Patriots of Fort McHenry (EA)
PFM	Peak Flow Meter [Medicine] (AAMN)
PFM	Physiological Flow Model [For simulating medical conditions]
PFM	Pitch Follow-Up Motor
PFM	Plan for Maintenance [Navy]
PFM	Planning Factors Management (MCD)
PFM	Platform (NASA)
PFM	Political Freedom Movement [British]
PFM	Porcelain Fused to Metal [Dentistry]

PFM	Porsche Flug Motor [*Automotive engineering*]
PFM	Potato Futures Market [*Finance*]
PFM	Poultry Feather Meal [*Fisheries*]
PFM	Power Factor Meter
PFM	Precision Frequency Multivider (KSC)
PFM	Predictor Frame Memory
PFM	Preferred Income Management Fund [*NYSE symbol*] (SPSG)
PFM	Preferred Income Mgmt Fund [*NYSE symbol*] (TTSB)
PFM	Preliminary Flight Motor (MCD)
PFM	Pressure Flow Meter
PFM	Printer Font Metrics [*Computer science*] (CDE)
PFM	Prison Fellowship Ministries (EA)
PFM	Pulse-Forming Machine
PFM	Pulse-Frequency Modulation [*RADAR*] [*Telecommunications*]
P/FM	Pylon/Fin Movement
PFM	University of Pittsburgh, Falk Library - Health Professions, Pittsburgh, PA [*OCLC symbol*] (OCLC)
PFMA	Pet Food Manufacturers Association [*British*] (DBA)
PFMA	Phenolic Foam Manufacturers Association [*British*] (DBA)
PFMA	Pipe Fittings Manufacturers Association [*Later, APFA*] (EA)
PFMA	Plumbing Fixture Manufacturers Association [*Defunct*] (EA)
PFMA	Pressed Felt Manufacturers' Association [*British*] (BI)
PFMAA	Pet Food Manufacturers' Association of Australia
PFMC	Pacific Fishery Management Council (EA)
PFMO	Planning Factors Management Office
PFMPG	Pacific Fleet Mobile Photographic Group (DNAB)
PFMR	Pasadena Foundation for Medical Research [*California*]
PFMR	Plug-Flow Membrane Reactor [*Chemical engineering*]
PFMR	Project Funds Management Record (MCD)
PFN	Panama City [*Florida*] [*Airport symbol*] (OAG)
PFN	Pantyffynnon [*British depot code*]
PFN	Partially Functional Neutrophil (DMAA)
PFN	Parti des Forces Nouvelles [*New Forces Party*] [*France Political party*] (PPW)
PFN	Passamaquoddy Ferry & Navigation Co. [*AAR code*]
PFN	Permanent File Name
PFN	Plasma Fibronectin [*Biochemistry*]
PFN	PMC Corp. [*Toronto Stock Exchange symbol*]
PFN	Prefinished [*Technical drawings*]
PFN	Profilin (DMAA)
PFN	Pulse-Forming Network
PFNA	Pentecostal Fellowship of North America (EA)
PFNA	Pulsed Fast Neutron Analysis [*for detection of explosives*] (PS)
PFNC	Progress Financial Corp. [*Plymouth Meeting, PA*] [*NASDAQ symbol*] (NQ)
PFNC	Progress Finl [*NASDAQ symbol*] (TTSB)
PFNP	Partido Federalista Nacionalista Popular [*Panama*] [*Political party*] (EY)
PFNS	Position Fixing Navigation System (AABC)
PFNT	Police Force of the Northern Territory [*Australia*]
PFNT	Preferred Networks [*NASDAQ symbol*] (TTSB)
PFNTU	Pathfinder Navigation Training Unit [*Military*]
PFO	Paphos [*Cyprus*] [*Airport symbol*] (OAG)
PFO	Partly Filled Out [*Questionnaire*]
PFO	Patent Foramen Ovale [*Cardiology*]
PFO	Personal Freedom Outreach (EA)
PFO	Physical Fitness Officer [*British military*] (DMA)
PFO	Pitch Follow-Up Operation
PFO	Pomona Public Library, Pomona, CA [*OCLC symbol*] (OCLC)
PFO	Postal Finance Officer [*Army*]
PFO	Preferred Income Opportunity Fund [*NYSE symbol*] (SAG)
PFO	Preferred Income Oppt Fd [*NYSE symbol*] (TTSB)
PFO	Procurement Field Office
PFO	Pyrolysis Fuel Oil [*Petroleum refining*]
PFO	Pyruvate: Ferredoxin Oxidoreductase [*An enzyme*]
PFO	Spofford, TX [*Location identifier FAA*] (FAAL)
PFOA	Perfluorooctanoic Acid [*Organic chemistry*]
PFOB	Perfluorocytylbromide (DMAA)
PFOBA	Paso Fino Owners and Breeders Association [*Later, PFHA*] (EA)
PFOD	Presumed Finding of Death [*DoD*]
PFol	Ridley Township Public Library, Folsom, PA [*Library symbol Library of Congress*] (LCLS)
PFouad	Les Papyrus Fouad I [*A publication*] (OCD)
PFP	Partnership for Peace [*An organization of non-member countries which have established military cooperation with NATO*] (ECON)
PFP	Partnership for Productivity International (EA)
PFP	Peace and Freedom Party (EA)
PFP	Pensions for Professionals, Inc.
PFP	Pentafluoropropionate [*or Pentafluoropropionyl*] [*Organic chemistry*]
PFP	Personal Financial Planning (ADA)
PFP	Pet-Facilitated Psychotherapy [*Psychiatry*]
PFP	Platelet-Free Plasma [*Hematology*]
PFP	Pleiades Foundation for Peace [*Later, PFPSE*] (EA)
PFP	Plutonium Finishing Plant
PFP	Policy-Framework Paper (ECON)
PFP	Popular Front Party [*Ghana*] [*Political party*] (PPW)
PFP	Pore Forming Protein [*Biochemistry*]
PFP	Postage Forward Parcels [*Shipping*]
PFP	Post Flight Processor
PFP	Premier Farnell PLC [*NYSE symbol*] (SAG)
PFP	Premier Farnell PLC ADS [*NYSE symbol*] (TTSB)
PFP	Primary Failed Part (DNAB)
PFP	Probability of Failure, Performance [*NASA*] (SAA)
PFP	Products for Power [*Automotive components manufacturer*]
PFP	Program File Processor

PFP	Program Financial Plan (NASA)
PFP	Program Forecast Period [*Military*] (AFIT)
PFP	Programmable Function Panel (NASA)
PFP	Progressiewe Federale Party [*Progressive Federal Party*] [*South Africa*] [*Political party*] (PPW)
PFP	Proton Flare Project (PDAA)
PFP	Proving for Production (MCD)
PFP	Publishers for Peace [*An association*]
PFPA	Pentafluoropropionic Anhydride [*Organic chemistry*]
PFPA	Pro-Family Press Association [*Defunct*] (EA)
PFPC	Passenger Form and Procedures Committee [*IATA*] (DS)
PFPDBRD	Paget Foundation for Paget's Disease of Bone and Related Disorders [*Formerly, Paget's Disease Foundation (PDF)*] (PAZ)
PFPE	Perfluorinated Polyether [*Organic chemistry*]
PFPE	Polyfluorinated Polyether [*Lubricants, polymers*]
PFP EIS	Plutonium Finishing Plant Environmental Impact Statement
PFPH	Pentafluorophenylhydrazine [*Organic chemistry*]
PFPI	Partnership for Productivity International (EA)
PFPI	Pentafluoropropionyl Imidazole [*Organic chemistry*]
PFPM	Production Flight Procedures Manual (MCD)
PFPPr	Premier Farnell $1.35 Pref ADS [*NYSE symbol*] (TTSB)
PFPS	Patellofemoral Pain Syndrome [*Medicine*] (DMAA)
PFPS	Potential for Foster Parenthood Scale [*Psychology*]
PFPS	Progressive French Polishers' Society [*A union*] [*British*]
PFPSE	Pleiades Foundation for Peace and Space Education (EA)
PFPUT	Pension Fund Property Unit Trust [*British*]
PFQ	Personality Factor Questionnaire (MAE)
PFQ	Preflight Qualification
PFr	Franklin Public Library, Franklin, PA [*Library symbol Library of Congress*] (LCLS)
PFR	Parotid Flow Rate [*otorhinolaryngology*] (DAVI)
PFR	Part Failure Rate
PFR	Patriot Field Report [*Army*]
PFR	Peak Flow Rate [*or Reading*] [*Medicine*]
PFR	Perforator (DEN)
PFR	Pericardial Friction Rub [*Medicine*] (MEDA)
PFR	Perkins Family Restaurants Ltd [*NYSE symbol*] (SPSG)
PFR	Perkins Family Rest L.P. [*NYSE symbol*] (TTSB)
PFR	Permanent Factory Repairable (MCD)
PFR	Permitted Flying Route [*Aviation*] (DA)
PFR	Persistent Fat Retention [*Syndrome*]
PFR	Personal Financial Record [*Army*] (AABC)
PFR	Pfarrer [*Pastor*] [*German*] (EY)
PFR	Phase Failure Relays [*Environmental science*] (COE)
PFR	Photoflash Relay
PFR	Pike Fry Rhabdovirus
PFR	Planning for Results [*A publication*]
PFR	Plug-Flow Reactor [*Engineering*]
PFR	Polarized Field Frequency Relay (IAA)
PFR	Polarized Frequency Relay
PFR	Portable Foot Restraint (NASA)
PFR	Port Francqui [*Zaire*] [*Airport symbol*] (AD)
PFR	Post-Fielding Review [*DoD*]
PFR	Power Fail Recovery System [*Computer science*] (MDG)
PFR	Power Fail/Restart
PFR	Power Failure Release
PFR	Precision Fathometer Recorder [*Raytheon Co.*]
PFR	Preferred Resources, Inc. [*Vancouver Stock Exchange symbol*]
PFR	Preflight Review [*NASA*] (KSC)
PFR	Preheating, Falling-Film, Rising-Film [*Sections of a concentrator*] [*Chemical engineering*]
PFR	Preliminary Flight Rating [*Air Force*]
PFR	Problem/Failure Report
PFR	Programmed Film Reader [*System*]
pfr	Proofreader [*MARC relator code*] [*Library of Congress*] (LCCP)
PFR	Prototype Fast Reactor
PFR	Pulmonary Blood Flow Redistribution [*Medicine*]
PFR	Pulmonary Flow Rate [*Medicine*] (DAVI)
PFR	Pulse Frequency (MDG)
PFR	Punch Feed Read (CMD)
PFRA	Percent of Females Reproductively Active [*Ecology*]
PFRA	Prairie Farm Rehabilitation Administration [*Canada*]
PFRA	Problem-Focused Research Applications [*of ASRA*] [*National Science Foundation*]
PFRA	Professional Football Referees Association (EA)
PFRA	Professional Football Researchers Association (EA)
PFRB	Publications and Films Review Board [*Western Australia*]
PFRC	Pacific Forest Research Centre [*Canada*] (ARC)
PFRD	Preferred Stock [*Investment term*]
PFredY	Joseph A. Yablonski Memorial Clinic, Fredericktown, PA [*Library symbol Library of Congress*] (LCLS)
PFRMG	Performing (ROG)
PFRS	Portable Field Recording System [*NASA*] (KSC)
PFRT	Preliminary Flight Rating Test
PFRT	Preliminary Flight Readiness Test [*NASA*] (KSC)
PFS	Parallel Filter System
PFS	Particles and Fields Subsatellite [*NASA*]
PFS	Path Fault Secure (MHDI)
PFS	Pay for Skills [*Human resources*] (WYGK)
PFS	Percent Full Scale (KSC)
PFS	Performance Funding System [*Department of Housing and Urban Development*] (GFGA)
PFS	Peripheral Fixed Shim [*Nuclear energy*] (NRCH)
PFS	Personal and Family Survival [*Civil Defense*]

PFS............ Personal Filing System [Data-base program] [Software Publishing Corp.]
PFS............ Personal Financial Specialist
PFS............ Photofragment Spectroscopy
PFS............ Physical File System (IAA)
PFS............ Pioneer Financial Services, Inc. [NYSE symbol] (SPSG)
PFS............ Pioneer Financial Svcs [NYSE symbol] (TTSB)
PFS............ Pitch Follow-Up System
PFS............ Pittsburgh, PA [Location identifier FAA] (FAAL)
PFS............ Plasterers' Friendly Society [A union] [British]
PFS............ Platform Functional Specification [Computer science]
PFS............ Porous Friction Surface [Airfield pavement]
PFS............ Positive Fuel Stop
PFS............ Prairie Flying Service (1976) Ltd. [Canada ICAO designator] (FAAC)
PFS............ Precision Frequency Source
PFS............ Preflight School [Military]
PFS............ Press Fit Socket
PFS............ Primary Fibromyalgia Syndrome [Medicine] (DMAA)
PFS............ Primary Flight System (NASA)
PFS............ Primary Frequency Supply [Telecommunications] (TEL)
PFS............ Probability of Failure, Stress [NASA] (SAA)
PFS............ Pro-Forma Statement (MHDI)
PFS............ Programmable Frequency Standard
PFS............ Propellant Feed System
PFS............ Propellant Field System
PFS............ Pulmonary Function Score [Physiology]
PFS............ Pure Fluid System
PFSB.......... PennFed Financial Services, Inc. [NASDAQ symbol] (SAG)
PFSB.......... PennFed Financial Svcs [NASDAQ symbol] (TTSB)
PFSh.......... Partia Fashismit e Shqiperise [Fascist Party of Albania] [Political party] (PPE)
PFSH.......... Porcine Follicle Stimulating Hormone [Endocrinology]
PFSL.......... Pocahontas Federal Savings & Loan Association [NASDAQ symbol] (SAG)
PFSL.......... Pocahontas Fed Svg& L A Ark [NASDAQ symbol] (TTSB)
PFSO.......... Postal Finance and Supply Office (AFM)
PFSP.......... Polyfactorial Study of Personality [Psychology] (AEBS)
PFS/PRS ..... Patent Family Service/Patent Register Service [Database] [International Patent Documentation Center] [Information service or system] (CRD)
PFSR.......... Program Financial Status Report (AAG)
PFSS.......... Particles and Fields Subsatellite [Telecommunications] (OA)
PFSS.......... Patellofemoral Stress Syndrome [Medicine]
PFSS.......... Pesticide Farmworker Safety Staff [Office of Pesticides and Toxic Substances] (COE)
PFT............ Pacific Asia Tech [Vancouver Stock Exchange symbol]
PFT............ Pacific Fisheries Technologists [An association]
PFT............ Page Frame Table (BUR)
PFT............ Pancreatic Function Test [Medicine]
PFT............ Paper, Flat Tape
PFT............ Parafascicular Thalamotomy [Medicine]
PFT............ Parallel Fourier Transform (MCD)
PFT............ Permanent Full-Time (GFGA)
PFT............ Pet-Facilitated Therapy [Psychiatry]
PFT............ Phenylalanine mustard [Melphalan], Fluorouracil, Tamoxifen [Antineoplastic drug regimen]
PFT............ Physical Fitness Test
PFT............ Pittsburgh, Fort Wayne & Chicago Railway Co. (IIA)
PFT............ Plastic Fuel Tank
PFT............ Portable Flame Thrower [Army]
PFT............ Positive Flight Termination (MUGU)
PFT............ Posterior Fossa Tumor [Anatomy] (MAE)
PFT............ Preflight Team [Air Force] (AFM)
PFT............ Preflight Tool (MCD)
PFT............ Prime Factor Transform (IAA)
PFT............ Professional Football Trainers (EA)
PFT............ Program Flying Training [Air Force] (AFM)
PFT............ Projective Field Theory
PFT............ Pulmonary Function Test [Medicine]
PFT............ Pulse Fourier Transform
PFTA.......... Payload Flight Test Article [NASA] (MCD)
PFTA.......... Post-Fielding Training Analysis
PFTB.......... Preflight Test Bus (MCD)
PFTBE........ Progressive Form of Tick-Borne Encephalitis [Medicine] (DMAA)
PFTC.......... Pestalozzi-Froebel Teachers College [Illinois]
PFTE.......... Permanent Full-Time Equivalent (GFGA)
PFTE.......... Pianoforte [Soft, then Loud] [Music]
pfte........... Pianoforte (WDAA)
PFTE.......... Polytetrafluoroethylene [Teflon]
PFTE.......... Portable Field Trainer/Evaluator (MCD)
PFTEA........ Post-Fielding Training Effectiveness Analysis
PFTM.......... Preliminary Flight Test Memo
PFTQ.......... Partnering for Total Quality (AAEL)
PFTR.......... Preliminary Flight Test Report
PFTS.......... Permanent Field Training Site
PFU............ Passive Filtration Unit
PFU............ Physical Fitness Uniform [Army] (INF)
PFU............ Plan for Use (DNAB)
PFU............ Plaque-Forming Unit [Immunochemistry]
PFU............ Please Follow Up
PFU............ Pock-Forming Unit
PFU............ Preparation for Use
PFUA.......... Pitch Follow-Up Amplifier
PFUEI......... Prime Focus Universal Extragalactic Instrument [Astronomy]
PFUM.......... Pitch Follow-Up Motor

PFUO.......... Pitch Follow-Up Operation
PFUO.......... Prolonged Fever of Unknown Origin [Medicine] (DMAA)
PFUS.......... Pitch Follow-Up System
PFV............ Peak Flow Velocity [Cardiology]
PFV............ Peak Forward Voltage (IAA)
PFV............ Pestalozzi-Froebel-Verband [Pestalozzi-Froebel Association]
PFV............ Philippine Forces, Vietnam
PFV............ Physiological Full Value
PFV............ Probability of Failure, Vehicle [NASA] (SAA)
PFVEA........ Professional Film and Video Equipment Association (EA)
PFW............ Power, Fulcrum, Weight
PFW............ Predicted Fire Weapon
PFW............ Progressive Free Wave
PFWA.......... Pet Food Warehouse [NASDAQ symbol] (SAG)
PFWA.......... Professional Football Writers of America (EA)
PFwB.......... Budd Co., Fort Washington, PA [Library symbol Library of Congress] (LCLS)
PFWOAD...... Place from Which Ordered to Active Duty [Military]
PFwR.......... William H. Rorer, Inc., Fort Washington, PA [Library symbol Library of Congress] (LCLS)
PFWS.......... Predicted Fire Weapon System [Army]
PFX............ Pilgrim American Capital [NYSE symbol]
PFX............ Prefix (ROG)
PFX............ Proflex Ltd. [Vancouver Stock Exchange symbol]
PFY............ Prior Fiscal Year (AFIT)
PFYA.......... Predicted First-Year Average [Law school]
PFZ............ Polar Front Zone [Marine science] (MSC)
PFZ............ Potassium Hexafluorozirconate [Inorganic chemistry]
PFZ............ Precipitate-Free Zone (MCD)
PF-ZAPU ..... Patriotic Front - Zimbabwe African People's Union [Political party] (PD)
PG............ Florida Commuter [ICAO designator] (AD)
PG............ Glycerate-3-Phosphate [Biochemistry] (DAVI)
pg............ Page (WDMC)
PG............ Page [or Pagination] [Online database field identifier]
PG............ Paper Gain (MHDW)
PG............ Papua New Guinea [ANSI two-letter standard code] (CNC)
PG............ Paralysie Generale [General Paralysis] [Medicine French]
PG............ Paregoric [Slang]
PG............ Parental Guidance [Pediatrics] (DAVI)
PG............ Parental Guidance Suggested [Formerly, GP] [Some material may not be suitable for preteenagers Movie rating]
PG............ Paris Granite
PG............ Paris Group [See also GP] [France] (EAIO)
PG............ Parotid Gland [Medicine] (DMAA)
PG............ Partial Gum [Philately]
PG............ Parti Quebecois [Canada] [Political party] (WDAA)
PG............ Paste Grain [Bookbinding]
PG............ Past Grand [Freemasonry]
PG............ Patrol Combatant [Gunboat] [Navy symbol]
PG............ Patrol Gunboat, Motorized [Navy symbol] (VNW)
PG............ Patrologiae Cursus. Series Graeca [A publication] (OCD)
PG............ Pay Grade
PG............ Pay Group
PG............ Paying Guest
PG............ PEACE [Program for Emergency Assistance, Cooperation, and Education] for Guatemala (EA)
PG............ Pedal Ganglion
PG............ Pedal Groove
PG............ Pelham Grenville Wodehouse [British humorist, 1881-1975]
PG............ Pentagastrin (DMAA)
Pg............ Pentagram [One billion metric tons]
PG............ Pepsinogen [Medicine] (MEDA)
PG............ Peptidoglycan [Biochemistry]
PG............ Permanent Glow [Telecommunications] (TEL)
PG............ Permanent Grade
PG............ Persian Gulf (MCD)
PG............ Pharmacopoeia Germanica [German Pharmacopoeia]
PG............ Phosphatidylglycerol
PG............ Phosphogluconate [Biochemistry]
PG............ Phosphogypsum [Inorganic chemistry]
PG............ Photogrammetry
pg............ Picogram [One trillionth of a gram]
PG............ Pilot Generator (IAA)
PG............ Pine Grosbeak [Ornithology]
PG............ Pipers Guild (EA)
PG............ Pituitary Gonadotropin [Endocrinology] (MAE)
PG............ Placebo Group [Medicine]
PG............ Planning Group [DoD]
PG............ Planning Guide [HUD]
PG............ Plant Genome (HGEN)
PG............ Plasma Gastrin [Endocrinology] (AAMN)
PG............ Plasma Glucose [Hematology]
PG............ Plasma Triglyceride [Hematology] (DAVI)
PG............ Plate Glass
PG............ Plate-Glazed [Paper]
PG............ Pointer Game (AEBS)
PG............ Pollen Grain [Botany]
PG............ Polyethylene Glycol [Organic chemistry]
PG............ Polygalacturonase [An enzyme]
PG............ Polyglycine [Biochemistry]
PG............ Polypropylene Glycol (EDCT)
PG............ Pontius Guillelmi [Authority cited in pre-1607 legal work] (DSA)
PG............ Port Group [Telecommunications] (TEL)
PG............ Portugal

Pg	Portugal (ODBW)
Pg	Portuguese (ODBW)
PG	Portuguese [Language, etc.]
pg	Portuguese Guinea [Guinea-Bissau] [MARC country of publication code Library of Congress] (LCCP)
PG	Position Guide (MCD)
P/G	Postagram [British military] (DMA)
PG	Postgraduate [Refers to courses or students] [Slang]
PG	Power Gain
PG	Power Gate [Electronics] (OA)
PG	Power Generation (MCD)
PG	Preacher General
PG	Precision Ground [Electronics] (IAA)
PG	Predicted Grade [IRS]
PG	Pregnanediol Glucuronide [Endocrinology]
PG	Pregnant
pg	Pregnant (DMAA)
PG	Pregnant Guppy [Reference to Boeing 377 aircraft] (SAA)
PG	Press Gallery [US Senate]
PG	Pressure Gauge (KSC)
PG	Priority Group
PG	Prisonnier de Guerre [Prisoner of War - POW] [French]
PG	Processed Gas (COE)
PG	Procter & Gamble [NYSE symbol] (TTSB)
PG	Procter & Gamble Co. [NYSE symbol] (SPSG)
PG	Proctor & Gamble [Commercial firm] (NADA)
PG	Procureur Generaal [Public Attorney] [Dutch] (ILCA)
PG	Producers Group (EA)
PG	Professional Geologist
PG	Professional Group (MCD)
PG	Pro-German [Prisoner of war term] [World War I] (DSUE)
PG	Program [Telecommunications]
PG	Program Generator (IAA)
PG	Program Generic [Computer science] (TEL)
PG	Program Guidance
PG	Programmer (AAG)
PG	Programmer Group (IAA)
PG	Project Group
PG	Proof Gallon [Wines and spirits]
PG	Propylene Glycol
PG	Propyl Gallate [Antioxidant] [Organic chemistry]
PG	Prostaglandin [Also, Pg] [Biochemistry]
PG	Protective Ground [Electronics] (IAA)
PG	Protein Granule
PG	Proteoglycan [Biochemistry]
PG	Prothoracic Gland [Insect anatomy]
PG	Province Guard [Cambodia] (CINC)
PG	Proving Ground [Army]
P-G	Prudential Grace Lines [Steamship] (MHDB)
PG	Public Gaol [British]
PG	Pulse Gate
PG	Pulse Generator
PG	Pure Gum [of envelopes]
PG	Pyoderma Gangrenosum [Medicine]
PG	Pyrolytic Graphite (MCD)
PG	Pyrotechnic Gyro (AAG)
PG-13	Parental Guidance Suggested [Now: Parents Strongly Cautioned. Some material may be inappropriate for children under 13] [Movie rating]
PGA	Page [Arizona] [Airport symbol] (OAG)
PGA	Paragould [Arkansas] [Seismograph station code, US Geological Survey] (SEIS)
PGA	Parliamentarians for Global Action [An association] (EA)
PGA	Pega Capital Resources Ltd. [Toronto Stock Exchange symbol]
PGA	Pendulous Gyro Accelerometer
PGA	Pepsinogen A (DMAA)
PGA	Personnel Group of America [NYSE symbol] (SAG)
PGA	PGI, Inc. [AMEX symbol] (SPSG)
PGA	Phosphoglyceric Acid [Biochemistry]
PGA	Pin-Grid-Array [Motorola, Inc.]
PGA	Pin-Grid Arrays
PGA	Pin Grip Array [Computer science] (DDC)
PGA	Pistachio Growers' Association [Australia]
PGA	Plate Glass Association [British] (BI)
PGA	Polyglandular Autoimmune Syndrome [Medicine] (DMAA)
PGA	Polyglycolic Acid [Organic chemistry] (RDA)
PGA	Poly(L-glutamic Acid) [Organic chemistry]
PGA	Port of Geelong Authority [Victoria, Australia]
PGA	Portugalia, Companhia Portuguesa de Transportes Aeros SA [Portugal ICAO designator] (FAAC)
PGA	Potato Growers of Australia
PGA	Power Gain Antenna
PGA	Power Generating Assembly (KSC)
PGA	Pressure Garment Assembly
PGA	Prison Governors' Association [British] (WDAA)
PGA	Producers Guild of America (EA)
PGA	Professional Golfers Association (NADA)
PGA	Professional Golfers' Association of America (EA)
PGA	Professional Graphics Adapter [IBM Corp.]
PGA	Professional Group Audio
PGA	Programmable Gain Amplifier (MCD)
PGA	Programmable Gate Array
PGA	Prostaglandin A [Biochemistry]
PGA	Prostaglandin Analog [Biochemistry]
PGA	Pteroylglutamic Acid (WDAA)

PGA	Pteroylmonoglutamic Acid [Folic acid] [Also, FA, PteGlu] [Biochemistry]
PGA	Puppetry Guild of Australia
PGA	Purchased Gas Adjustment
PGA	Pure Grain Alcohol
PGA	Pyrolysis Gas Analysis
PGA	Upjohn Co. [Research code symbol]
PGAA	Professional Guides Association of America (EA)
PGAA	Prompt Gamma-Ray Activation Analysis
P-GABA	Phenyl-gamma-aminobutryic Acid [Tranquilizer]
PGAC	Guam/Taguac [Mariana Islands] [ICAO location identifier] (ICLI)
PG-AC	Phenylglycine Acid Chloride [Biochemistry] (AAMN)
PGAC	Professional Group - Automatic Control
PGAH	Pineapple Growers Association of Hawaii (EA)
PGAM	Phosphoglyceromutase [An enzyme]
PG & E	Pacific Gas and Electric [Rock music group]
PG & E	Pacific Gas & Electric Co.
PG & E Cp	PG & E Corp. Holdings Co. [Associated Press] (SAG)
PGANE	Professional Group on Aeronautical and Navigational Electronics
PGA-NOC	Permanent General Assembly of National Olympic Committees
PGANSW	Potato Growers' Association of New South Wales [Australia]
PGAP	Pilot Geriatric Arthritis Program [Medicine] (DMAA)
PGAP	Professional Group - Antennas and Propagation
PGAPL	Preliminary Group Assembly Parts List
PGAR	Provisional Government of the Algerian Republic
PGAS	Persisting Galactorrhea-Amenorrhea Syndrome [Medicine] (DMAA)
PGase	Polygalacturonase [An enzyme]
PGAWA	Pastoralists and Graziers' Association of Western Australia
PGAWA	Potato Growers' Association of Western Australia
Pg B	Bachelor of Pedagogy
PGB	Patrol Gunboat [Navy symbol] (NATG)
PGB	Personal Guidance Base (AIE)
PGB	Phoenix Global [Vancouver Stock Exchange symbol]
PGB	Portland General Electric Co. [NYSE symbol] (SAG)
PGB	Portland Genl Elec 8.25% 'QUIDS' [NYSE symbol] (TTSB)
PGB	Prostaglandin B [Biochemistry]
PGB	Protestant Guild for the Blind (EA)
PGB	Pyrographalloy Boron
PGBA	Piece Goods Buyers Association [Defunct] (EA)
PGBA	Possum Growers and Breeders Association (EA)
PGBBX	PaineWebber Global Income Cl.B [Mutual fund ticker symbol] (SG)
PGBD	Pegboard [Freight]
PGBM	Pulse Gate Binary Modulation (MCD)
PGbSH	Seton Hill College, Greensburg, PA [Library symbol Library of Congress] (LCLS)
PGBTR	Professional Group - Broadcast and Television Receivers
PGBTS	Professional Group - Broadcast Transmission Systems
PGbU	University of Pittsburgh at Greensburg, Greensburg, PA [Library symbol Library of Congress] (LCLS)
PGC	Geneva College, Beaver Falls, PA [OCLC symbol] (OCLC)
PGC	Gettysburg College, Gettysburg, PA [Library symbol Library of Congress] (LCLS)
PGC	Pacific Geoscience Centre [Research center] (RCD)
PGC	Pagurian Corp. [Toronto Stock Exchange symbol]
PGC	Parents of Galactosemic Children [An association]
PGC	Past Grand Commander [Freemasonry] (ROG)
PGC	Percentage of Goblet Cells (STED)
PGC	Per Gyro Compass [Navigation]
PGC	Persian Gulf Command [World War II]
PGC	Phillips Gas [NYSE symbol] (SPSG)
PGC	Policy Guidance Council (DOMA)
PGC	Polynomial Generator Checker (IAA)
PGC	Pontine Gaze Center [Eye anatomy]
PGC	Poorly Graphitized Carbon [Physical chemistry]
PGC	Port Group Control [Telecommunications] (TEL)
PGC	Post-Graduate Certificate (PGP)
PGC	Potassium Gold Cyanide [Inorganic chemistry]
PGC	Potential Gas Committee
PGC	Primordial Germ Cell
PGC	Process Gas Chromatography
PGC	Process Gas Consumers Group (EA)
PGC	Professional Graphics Controller [IBM Corp.]
PGC	Program Generation Center [Military] (CAAL)
PGC	Programmable Guidance Controller [Military]
PGC	Programmed Gain Control
PGC	Prostaglandin C [A prostoglandin endoperoxide] [Biochemistry] (DAVI)
PGC	Proving Ground Command [Air Force]
PGC	Pulsed Gas Crymotography
PGC	Pure Glycollide (DB)
PGC	Pyrolysis Gas Chromatography
PGCA	Patent Glazing Contractors Association [British] (DBA)
PGcC	Grove City College, Grove City, PA [Library symbol Library of Congress] (LCLS)
PGCC	Power Generation Control Complex [Nuclear energy] (NRCH)
PGCE	Post Graduate Certificate of Education
PGCh	Past Grand Chaplain [Freemasonry]
PGCML	Prince George's County Memorial Library [Maryland]
PGCOA	Pennsylvania Grade Crude Oil Association (EA)
PGCP	Professional Group - Component Parts
PGCPr	Phillips Gas 9.32% Pfd [NYSE symbol] (TTSB)
PGCRA	Professional Golf Club Repairmen's Association (EA)
PGCS	Professional Group - Communications Systems
PGCT	Professional Group - Circuit Theory
PGCU	International Printing and Graphic Communications Union

PGCVS	Postgraduate Committee in Veterinary Science [*Australia*]
PGD	Hancock [*John*] Patriot Global Dividend Fund [*NYSE symbol*] (SPSG)
PGD	John Hancock Patr Gl Div Fd [*NYSE symbol*] (TTSB)
PGD	Pango Gold Mines Ltd. [*Toronto Stock Exchange symbol*]
PGD	Past Grand Deacon [*Freemasonry*]
PGD	Phosphogluconate Dehydrogenase [*Also, PGDH*] [*An enzyme*]
PGD	Phosphoglyceraldehyde Dehydrogenase [*An enzyme*] (MAE)
PGD	Pikwitonei Granulite Domain [*Geology*]
PGD	Pinion Gear Drive
PGD	Planar Gas Discharge (MCD)
PGD	Planetary Gear Drive
PGD	Policy and Grants Division [*Environmental Protection Agency*] (GFGA)
PGD	Preimplantation Genetic Diagnosis [*For in vitro fertilization*] [*Medicine*]
PGD	Program for Geographical Display (IAA)
PGD	Prostaglandin D [*Biochemistry*]
PGD	Pulse Generator Display
PGD	Punta Gorda [*Florida*] [*Airport symbol*] (OAG)
PGDA	Piercing Pagoda [*NASDAQ symbol*] (TTSB)
PGDA	Piercing Pagoda, Inc. [*NASDAQ symbol*] (SAG)
PGDB	Propylene Glycol Dibenzoate [*Organic chemistry*]
PGDC	Provincial Grand Director of Ceremonies [*Freemasonry*]
PGDCS	Power Generation, Distribution, and Control Subsystem (MCD)
PGDF	Pilot Guide Dog Foundation (EA)
PGDH	Phosphogluconate Dehydrogenase [*Also, PGD*] [*An enzyme*]
PGDip	Postgraduate Diploma [*Australia*]
PGDipA	Postgraduate Diploma in Arts [*Australia*]
PGDipAgrSc...	Postgraduate Diploma in Agricultural Science [*Australia*]
PGDipDevTech...	Postgraduate Diploma in Development Technology [*Australia*]
PGDipEdSt...	Postgraduate Diploma in Educational Studies [*Australia*]
PGDipForSc...	Postgraduate Diploma in Forest Science [*Australia*]
PGDipIEM	Postgraduate Diploma in Irrigation Engineering Management [*Australia*]
PGDipMath & MathEd...	Postgraduate Diploma in Mathematics and Mathematics Education [*Australia*]
PGDipMgtSt...	Postgraduate Diploma in Management Studies [*Australia*]
PGDipPhysio...	Postgraduate Diploma in Physiotherapy [*Australia*]
PGDipSc	Postgraduate Diploma in Science [*Australia*]
PgDn	Page Down [*Computer science*] (CDE)
PGDN	Propylene Glycol Dinitrate [*Organic chemistry*]
PGDP	Paducah Gaseous Diffusion Plant
PGDR	Plasma-Glucose Disappearance Rate [*Hematology*] (MAE)
PGDRB	Plumbers, Gasfitters, and Drainers Registration Board [*Victoria, Australia*]
PGDS	Pioneer Ground Data System
PGDS	Pulse Generator Display System
PGE	Pacific Gas & Electric Co. [*Associated Press*] (SAG)
PGE	Pacific Great Eastern Railway Co. [*Nicknames: Prince George Eventually, Please Go Easy*] [*Later, British Columbia Railway*] [*AAR code*]
PGE	Page Petroleum Ltd. [*Toronto Stock Exchange symbol*] (SPSG)
PGE	Phenyl Glycidyl Ether [*Organic chemistry*]
PGE	Platelet Granule Extract [*Hematology*] (MAE)
PGE	Platinum Group Element [*Chemistry*]
PGE	Polyglycerol Esters of Fatty Acids
PGE	Population Growth Estimation
PGE	Pore Gradient Electrophoresis
PGE	Portland General Electric Co., Library, Portland, OR [*OCLC symbol*] (OCLC)
PGE	Portland Grain Exchange (EA)
PGE	Posterior Gastroenterostomy (STED)
PGE	Precision Gimbal Experiment
PGE	Prime Group Engineer (AAG)
PGE	Professional Group - Education
PGE	Prostaglandin E [*Biochemistry*]
PGE	Provisional Government of Eritrea
PGE	Purge (NASA)
PGEC	Professional Group on Electronic Computers [*IEEE*]
PGECap	PG & E Capital I [*Associated Press*] (SAG)
PGECP	Professional Group Electronic Component Parts (IAA)
PGED	Professional Group - Electronic Devices
PGEM	Professional Group - Engineering Management
PGEM	Prostaglandin E Metabolite (STED)
PGEner	PG Energy, Inc. [*Associated Press*] (SAG)
P-generation...	Parental Generation (WDAA)
PGGeol	Professional Geologist (DD)
PGeoph	Professional Geophysicist (DD)
PGEWS	Professional Group on Engineering Writing and Speech [*Institute of Radio Engineers; now IEEE*]
PGEX	Pacific Gateway Exchange, Inc. [*NASDAQ symbol*] (SAG)
PGF	Pacific Gamefish Foundation (EA)
pgf	Paternal Grandfather (STED)
PGF	Paternal Grandfather (STED)
PGF	Pengrowth Gas Income Fund Trust Units [*Toronto Stock Exchange symbol*]
PGF	Peptide Growth Factor [*Biochemistry*]
PGF	Perpignan [*France*] [*Airport symbol*] (OAG)
PGF	Plerocercoid Growth Factor [*Endocrinology*]
PGF	Portugal Fund [*NYSE symbol*] (SPSG)
PGF	Postglacial Fault [*Biology*]
PGF	Presentation Graphic Feature [*Computer science*]
PGF	Prostaglandin F [*Biochemistry*]
PGFC	Periodical Guide for Computerists [*Applegate Computer Enterprises*] [*Information service or system Defunct*] (IID)

PGFEL	Preliminary Government-Furnished Equipment List (MCD)
PGFM	Prostaglandin F and its Metabolite [*Dihydro-keto-prostaglandin*] [*Medicine*] (BABM)
PGFR	Power-Generating Fusion Reaction
PGFVS	Postgraduate Federation in Veterinary Science [*Australia*]
PGFW	Guam [*Mariana Islands*] [*ICAO location identifier*] (ICLI)
PGG	Page America Group, Inc. [*AMEX symbol*] (SPSG)
PGG	Petrogold Financial Corp. [*Vancouver Stock Exchange symbol*]
PGG	Pneumatic Ground Group
PGG	Polyclonal Gamma Globulin [*Medicine*] (STED)
PGG	Power Generation Group [*Nuclear Regulatory Commission*] (NRCH)
PGG	Prostaglandin G [*A prostaglandin endoperoxide*] [*Biochemistry*]
PG/GAG........	Proteoglycans/Glyosaminoglyans
PGGO	Prescribed Goods (General) Order
PGH	Pantnagar [*India*] [*Airport symbol*] (AD)
PGH	Patrol Gunboat (Hydrofoil) [*Navy symbol*]
PGH	Phosphoglycolohydroxamate [*Biochemistry*]
PGH	Pituitary Growth Hormone [*Endocrinology*]
PGH	Plasma Growth Hormone [*Hematology*] (MAE)
PGH	Polymer Group [*NYSE symbol*] (TTSB)
PGH	Polymer Group, Inc. [*NYSE symbol*] (SAG)
PGH	Porcine Growth Hormone [*Biochemistry*]
PGH	Port Group Highway [*Telecommunications*] (TEL)
PGH	Prostaglandin H [*A prostaglandin endoperoxide*] [*Biochemistry*]
PGHA	Park Gallatin Hereford Association (EA)
PGHFE	Professional Group - Human Factors in Electronics
Pgh Leg Journal...	Pittsburgh Legal Journal [*Pennsylvania*] [*A publication*] (DLA)
PGHM	Payload Ground Handling Mechanism [*NASA*] (MCD)
PGHS	Prostaglandin Hydrogen Synthase [*An enzyme*]
PGHS	Public-General Hospital Section [*American Hospital Association*] (EA)
PGHTS	Port Group Highway Timeslot [*Telecommunications*] (TEL)
PGI	Chitato [*Angola*] [*Airport symbol Obsolete*] (OAG)
PGI	General Information Programme [*UNESCO*] [*Acronym is based on foreign phrase*]
PGI	Panagra Airways, Inc. [*FAA designator*] (FAAC)
PGi	Paragigantocellularis [*Neuroanatomy*]
PGI	Parameter Group Identifier [*Computer science*] (TNIG)
PGI	Paris Gestion Informatique [*Paris Informatics Administration*] [*France*] [*Information service or system*] (IID)
PGI	Peripheral Graphics, Inc.
PGI	Personalized Gift Institute (NTPA)
PGI	Phosphoglucoisomerase [*An enzyme*]
PGI	Ply-Gem, Inc. [*NYSE symbol*] (SAG)
PGI	Ply Gem Industries Inc. [*NYSE symbol*] (TTSB)
PGI	Polar Geophysical Institute [*Murmansk Region*] [*Russia*]
PGI	Port Group Interface [*Telecommunications*] (TEL)
PGI	Potassium, Glucose, and Insulin (MAE)
PGI	Professional Group - Instrumentation
PGI	Project Group, Inc. [*Advertising agency*] [*Acronym now used as official n ame of agency*]
PGI	Prostaglandin I [*Biochemistry*]
PGI	Provigo, Inc. [*Toronto Stock Exchange symbol*]
PGI	Purge Gas Inlet (AAEL)
PGI	Pyrotechnics Guild International (EA)
PGIA	Pendulous Gyro Integrating Accelerometer (IAA)
PGIA	Programmable Gain Instrumentation Amplifier (IAA)
PGIE	Professional Group - Industrial Electronics
PGiess	Griechische Papyri im Museum des Oberhessischen Geschichtsvereins zu Giessen [*A publication*] (OCD)
P-GILD	Projection Gas Immersion LASER Doping (AAEL)
PGIM	Professional Group on Instrumentation and Measurement [*National Bureau of Standards*]
PGIP	Polygalacturonase-Inhibiting Protein [*Biochemistry*]
PGIP	Post Graduate Intelligence Program (DOMA)
PGIS	Project Grant Information System
PGIT	Professional Group - Information Theory
PGJ	Pipeline Girth Joint
PGJD	Past Grand Junior Deacon [*Freemasonry*]
PGJN	Pomegranate Guild of Judaic Needlework (EA)
PGJW	Past Grand Junior Warden [*Freemasonry*] (ROG)
PGK	Pangkalpinang [*Indonesia*] [*Airport symbol*] (OAG)
PGK	Phosphoglycerate Kinase [*An enzyme*]
PGl	Glenside Free Library, Glenside, PA [*Library symbol Library of Congress*] (LCLS)
PGL	Lutheran Theological Seminary, Gettysburg, PA [*Library symbol Library of Congress*] (LCLS)
PGL	Paraglossa of Labium [*Entomology*]
PGL	Pascagoula, MS [*Location identifier FAA*] (FAAL)
PGL	Peoples Energy [*NYSE symbol*] (TTSB)
PGL	Peoples Energy Corp. [*NYSE symbol*] (SPSG)
PGL	Persistent Generalized Lymphadenopathy [*Medicine*]
PGL	Phenolic Glass Laminate
PGL	Phosphoglycolipid
PGL	Polyglutaraldehyde [*Organic chemistry*]
PGL	Portable Gas LASER
PGL	Professional Graphics Language [*Software*] [*IBM Corp.*] (BYTE)
PGL	Provincial Grand Lodge [*Freemasonry*]
PGL	Pulsed Gas LASER
PGladM	Mary J. Drexel Home, Gladwyne, PA [*Library symbol Library of Congress Obsolete*] (LCLS)
PGLAX	One Group: Louisiana Municipal Cl.A [*Mutual fund ticker symbol*] (SG)
PGIB	Beaver College, Glenside, PA [*Library symbol Library of Congress*] (LCLS)
PGLC	Pyrolysis Gas Liquid Chromatography

PGLD	Phoenix Gold International, Inc. [*NASDAQ symbol*] (SAG)
PGLD	Phoenix Gold Intl [*NASDAQ symbol*] (TTSB)
PGL-Hi	Lutheran Historical Society, Gettysburg, PA [*Library symbol Library of Congress*] (LCLS)
PGIL	Glenside Free Library, Glenside, PA [*Library symbol*] [*Library of Congress*] (LCLS)
PGLN	Page and Line (IAA)
PGlyM	Phosphoglyceromutase (DB)
PGM	Messiah College Learning Center, Grantham, PA [*OCLC symbol*] (OCLC)
PGM	Palenque [*Mexico*] [*Airport symbol*] (AD)
PGM	Papyri Graecae Magicae [*A publication*] (OCD)
PGM	Past Grand Master [*Freemasonry*]
PGM	Paternal Grandmother (MEDA)
PGM	Patrol Vessel, Motor Gunboat [*Navy symbol Obsolete*]
PGM	Perron Gold Mines [*Vancouver Stock Exchange symbol*]
PGM	Persatuan Geologi Malaysia [*Geological Society of Malaysia*] (EAIO)
PGM	Phosphoglucomutase [*An enzyme*]
PGM	Planetary Gearhead Motor [*Aerospace*]
PGM	Planning Guidance Memorandum (DOMA)
PGM	Plant Genetic Materials
PGM	Platinum Group Metal [*In meteorites*]
PGM	Poly-Gel Mitigator
PGM	Portable Greymap [*Image format*] (AAEL)
PGM	Port Graham, AK [*Location identifier FAA*] (FAAL)
PGM	Precision Guided Missile
PGM	Precision-Guided Munition (MCD)
PGM	Program
PGM	Program Guidance Memorandum
PGM	Putnam Investment Grade Municipal Trust [*NYSE symbol*] (SPSG)
PGM	Putnam Inv Grade Muni Tr [*NYSE symbol*] (TTSB)
PGMA	Phosphoglycerate Mutase A (DMAA)
PGMA	Poly(glyceryl Methacrylate) [*Organic chemistry*]
PGMA	Private Grocers' Merchandising Association [*British*] (BI)
PGMA	Public Golf Management Association (NTPA)
PGMA	Pulsed Gas Metal Arc (KSC)
PGMA-EA	Polyglycidal Methacrylate-Ethyl Acrylate [*Organic chemistry*] (PDAA)
PGMARV	Precision Guided Maneuvering Re-Entry Vehicle (PDAA)
PGMB	Phosphoglycerate Mutase B (DMAA)
PGMC	Primary Glass Manufacturers Council (NTPA)
PGME	Professional Group - Medical Electronics
PGMEA	Propylene Glycol Monomethyl Ether Acetate [*Organic chemistry*]
PGM-FI	Programmed Fuel Injection [*Automotive engineering*]
PGMIL	Professional Group - Military Electronics (MUGU)
PGMILE	Professional Group - Military Electronics (AAG)
PGML	Precision Graphics Markup Language [*Computer science*]
PGMM	Precision Guided Mortar Munition
PGMOT	Pollution Generation Multiplier from Output Table (PDAA)
PGMP	Preliminary Guaranteed Minimum Price
PGMS	Professional Grounds Management Society (EA)
PGMS	Stillwater Mining [*NASDAQ symbol*] (TTSB)
PGMS	Stillwater Mining Co. [*NASDAQ symbol*] (SAG)
PGMSJ	Professional Group of Mathematical Symbol Jugglers (MUGU)
PGMT	Pigment (MSA)
PGMTT	Professional Group - Microwave Theory and Techniques
PGMV	Pea Green Mottle Virus [*Plant pathology*]
PGN	Paragon Health Network [*NYSE symbol*] [*Formerly, Living Centers of America*] (SG)
PGN	Paragon Petroleum Ltd. [*Toronto Stock Exchange symbol*]
PGN	Perigeniculate Nucleus [*Anatomy*]
PGN	Phi Gamma Nu [*Fraternity*]
PGN	Pigeon (ADA)
PGN	Platinum Group Nugget [*In meteorites*]
PGN	Portland General Corp. [*NYSE symbol*] (SPSG)
PGN	Portland Genl Corp. [*NYSE symbol*] (TTSB)
PGN	Proliferative Glomerulonephritis [*Medicine*]
PGN	Pulse Generator
PGNAA	Prompt Gamma Neutron Activation Analysis [*Analytical chemistry*]
PGNCS	Primary Guidance, Navigation, and Control System [*or Subsystem*] [*Apollo*] [*NASA*] (MCD)
PGND	Propaganda (AABC)
PGNS	PathoGenesis Corp. [*NASDAQ symbol*] (SAG)
PGNS	Primary Guidance and Navigation System [*Apollo*] [*NASA*]
PGNS	Professional Group - Nuclear Science
PGNT	Sabanettan, Tinian Island [*Mariana Islands*] [*ICAO location identifier*] (ICLI)
PGNW	Ritidian Point, Guam Island [*Mariana Islands*] [*ICAO location identifier*] (ICLI)
PGO	Pagecorp, Inc. [*Toronto Stock Exchange symbol*]
PGO	Page, OK [*Location identifier FAA*] (FAAL)
PGO	Past Grand Orient [*Freemasonry*] (ROG)
PGO	Peroxidase-Glucose Oxidase [*Also, GOD-POD*] [*Enzyme mixture*]
PGO	Ponto-Geniculate-Occipital [*Electroencephalography*]
PGO	Positive Grid Oscillator
PGOC	Payload Ground Operations Contractor [*NASA*] (SSD)
PGOR	Payload Ground Operation Requirements [*NASA*] (NASA)
PGORS	Payload Ground Operation Requirements Study [*NASA*] (MCD)
PGP	Pacific Gateway Prop [*AMEX symbol*]
PGP	Pacific Gateway Properties [*Formerly, Perini Investment Properties, Inc.*] [*AMEX symbol*] (SPSG)
PGP	Parti Gabonais du Progres [*Political party*] (EY)
PGP	Peace Garden Project [*Later, NPG*] (EA)
PGP	Phagocyte Glycoprotein [*Biochemistry*]
PGP	Phosphoglycolate Phosphatase [*An enzyme*]
PGP	Pico Glass Pellet
PGP	Planning Grant Program
PGP	Postgamma Proteinuria [*Medicine*] (MAE)
PGP	Precision Gas Products [*Commercial firm*]
PGP	Prepaid Group Practice [*Insurance*]
PGP	Pretty Good Privacy [*Telecommunications*]
PGP	Programmable Graphics Processor
PGP	Project on Government Procurement (EA)
PGP	Prostaglandin Production
PGP	Puerta Galera [*Philippines*] [*Seismograph station code, US Geological Survey*] (SEIS)
PGP	Pulsed Glide Path (IAA)
PGP	University of Southern Maine at Portland, Portland, ME [*OCLC symbol*] (OCLC)
PGPEP	Professional Group - Product Engineering and Production
PGPH	Peptidylglutamyl-Peptide Hydrolyzing [*Biochemistry*]
PGPI	Protein Grain Products International (EA)
PGPR	Plant-Growth-Promoting Rhizobacteria
PGPS	Packaged Gas Pressure System
PGPT	Professional Group - Production Techniques
PGQC	Professional Group-Quality Control (IAA)
PGR	Paragould, AR [*Location identifier FAA*] (FAAL)
PGR	Parental Guidance Recommended [*Movie rating*] [*Australia*]
PGR	Paternal Grandfather (DAVI)
PGR	Peregrine Petroleum [*Vancouver Stock Exchange symbol*]
PGR	Petition Granted (DNAB)
PGR	PGR. Press Gallery Report [*A publication*] (ADA)
PGR	Plant Growth Regulator
PGR	Polymerized Grass Extract [*Immunology*]
PGR	Population Growth Rate
PGR	Precision Graphic Recorder
PgR	Progesterone Receptor [*Endocrinology*]
PGR	Progressive Corp. [*NYSE symbol*] (SPSG)
PGR	Progressive Corp., Ohio [*NYSE symbol*] (TTSB)
PGR	Psychogalvanic Reflex [*or Response*] [*Psychology*]
PGR	Pyrogallol Red [*Also, PR*] [*An indicator Chemistry*]
PGR	Spacelab Planning and Ground Rule [*NASA*] (NAKS)
PGraM	Messiah College, Grantham, PA [*Library symbol Library of Congress*] (LCLS)
PGRC	Plant Gene Resources of Canada [*See also RPC*]
PGRC	Privacy Global Resource Center (EA)
PGRC	Program Guidance and Review Committee [*Army*] (AABC)
PGrev	Greenville Area Public Library, Greenville, PA [*Library symbol Library of Congress*] (LCLS)
PGrevT	Thiel College, Greenville, PA [*Library symbol Library of Congress*] (LCLS)
PGRF	Pacific Gamefish Research Foundation [*Later, PORF*] (EA)
PGRF	Pulse Group Repetition Frequency
PGRFI	Professional Group - Radio Frequency Interference
PGRM	Parti Gerakan Rakyat Malaysia [*People's Action Party of Malaysia*] [*Political party*] (PPW)
P-GRN	Progranulocytes [*Hematology*] (DAVI)
PGRO	Pea Growing Research Organisation Ltd. [*British*] (BI)
PGRO	Processors and Growers Research Organisation [*British*] (IRUK)
PGRO	Rota/International [*Mariana Islands*] [*ICAO location identifier*] (ICLI)
PGRQC	Professional Group - Reliability and Quality Control
PGRS	Pergerakan Guerilja Rakyat Sarawak [*Sarawak People's Guerrilla Forces*] [*Malaya*]
PGRS	Plume Groundwater Recovery System [*Environmental science*] (BCP)
PGRSA	Plant Growth Regulator Society of America (EA)
PGRT	Petroleum Gas and Revenue Tax [*Canada*]
PGRTRC	Professional Group-Radio Telemetry and Remote Control (IAA)
PGRV	Photogravure (VRA)
PGRV	Precision Guided Reentry Vehicle
PGRVT	Precisely Guided Reentry Test Vehicle (SAA)
PGRWG	Payload Ground Requirements Working Group [*NASA*] (NASA)
PGS	Naval Postgraduate School
PGS	Pagosa Springs [*Colorado*] [*Seismograph station code, US Geological Survey Closed*] (SEIS)
PGS	Papergram System [*Military*] (CAAL)
PGS	Parallel Gap Soldering
PGS	Passive Geodetic Satellite [*NASA*]
PGS	Passive Gravity Stabilization
PGS	Peach Springs, AZ [*Location identifier FAA*] (FAAL)
PGS	Pennsylvania German Society [*Later, TPGS*] (EA)
PGS	Pikunas Graphoscopic Scale [*Personality development test*] [*Psychology*]
PGS	Plane Grating Spectrograph
PGS	Plant Growth Substance
PGS	Plasma Generator System
PGS	Polish Genealogical Society (EA)
PGS	Polymer Glass Sealant
PGS	Portable Ground Station
PGS	Power Generation Satellite (HGAA)
PGS	Power Generation System [*or Subsystem*]
PGS	Power Generator Section (KSC)
PGS	Practical Guide Series (ACII)
PGS	Precision Gunnery System [*Army training device*] (INF)
PGS	Predicted Ground Speed [*Navigation*]
PGS	President of the Geographical Society [*British*] (ROG)
PGS	President of the Geological Society [*British*]
PGS	Pressed Glassmakers Society [*British*] (DBA)
PGS	Pressure-Gradient Single-Ended [*Microphone*] (DEN)
PGS	Pretty Good Signature [*Computer science*]
PGS	Pretty Good Stuff [*Liquor*]

PGS	Primary Guidance Subsystem (MCD)
PGS	Professional Guidance Systems, Inc. [*Information service or system*] (IID)
PGS	Progenitor Genealogical Society (EA)
PGS	Program Generation System [*Computer science*] (MDG)
PGS	Propellant Gauging System
PGS	Prostaglandin Synthase [*An enzyme*]
PGS	Provincial Grand Secretary [*Freemasonry*]
PGS	Public Service Co. North Carolina [*NYSE symbol*] (SAG)
PGS	Public Svc No Car [*NYSE symbol*] (TTSB)
PGS	Tauranga Aero Club, Inc. [*New Zealand*] [*ICAO designator*] (FAAC)
PGSA	Petroleum Geo Services [*NASDAQ symbol*] (SAG)
PGSA	Polish Genealogical Society of America (EA)
PGSAY	Petroleum Geo-Svcs A/S ADS [*NASDAQ symbol*] (TTSB)
PGSB	Past Grand Sword Bearer [*Freemasonry*] (ROG)
PGSB	Provincial Grand Sword-Bearer [*Freemasonry*]
PGSC	Payload and General Support Computer [*NASA*]
PGSC	Persian Gulf Service Command
PGSCOL	Naval Postgraduate School
PGSD	Past Grand Senior Deacon [*Freemasonry*]
PGSE	Payload Ground Support Equipment [*NASA*] (MCD)
PGSE	Peculiar Ground Support Equipment [*DoD*]
PGSE	Pulsed Field Gradient Spin-Echo
PGSE	Pulsed Gradient Spin Echo [*Physics*]
PGSEL	Priced Ground Support Equipment List (AAG)
PGSET	Professional Group on Space Electronics and Telemetry (AAG)
PGSF	Public Good Science Fund [*New Zealand*]
PGSGX	One Group: Small Cap. Cl.A [*Mutual fund ticker symbol*] (SG)
PGSI	Prostaglandin Synthetase Inhibitor (DMAA)
PGSN	Saipan Island (Obyan)/International [*Mariana Islands*] [*ICAO location identifier*] (ICLI)
PGSR	Psychogalvanic Skin Resistance [*Otolaryngology*]
PGSS	Paget-Gorman Sign System (AIE)
PGSTAP	Pressure, Gas, Start, Turbine, Auxiliary Pump-Drive Assembly [*Pronounced "pigstap"*]
PGSU	Propellant [*or Propulsion*] Gas Supply Unit
PGSW	Past Grand Senior Warden [*Freemasonry*]
PGT	Page Table [*Computer science*] (IBMDP)
PGT	Partido Guatemalteco del Trabajo [*Guatemalan Labor Party*] [*Political party*] (PD)
PGT	Past Grand Treasurer [*Freemasonry*]
PGT	Pegasus Hava Tasimaciligi AS [*Turkey*] [*ICAO designator*] (FAAC)
PGT	Per Gross Ton [*Shipping*]
PGT	Photo Glow Tube
PGT	Pigtail (MSA)
PGT	Planned Giving Today [*A publication*]
PGT	Platoon Gunnery Trainer (DOMA)
PGT	Pollen Grain Trajectory [*Botany*]
PGT	Polymer Grid Triode [*Imaging technology*]
PGT	Porangatu [*Brazil*] [*Airport symbol*] (AD)
PGT	Potato Extract-Glucose-Thiamine Hydrochloride [*Growth medium*]
PGT	Power Grid Tube
PGT	Princeton Gamma Tech (AAEL)
PGT	Program Global Table (CIST)
PGT	Putnam Intermediate Government Income [*NYSE symbol*] (SPSG)
PGT	Putnam Interm Gvt Income [*NYSE symbol*] (TTSB)
PGTO	Portuguese Government Trade Office (EA)
PGTR	Plasma-Glucose Tolerance Rate [*Hematology*] (MAE)
PGTRC	Professional Group-Telemetry and Remote Control (IAA)
PGTS	Precision Gunnery Training System [*Army*] (INF)
PGTSND	Puget Sound (FAAC)
PGTT	Prednisolone Glucose Tolerance Test [*Medicine*] (DMAA)
PGTTT	Precision Gear Train Tools and Test
PGTV	Pegasus Communications Corp. [*NASDAQ symbol*] (SAG)
PGTW	Guam [*Mariana Islands*] [*ICAO location identifier*] (ICLI)
PGTZ	Praegitzer Industries [*NASDAQ symbol*] (TTSB)
PGTZ	Praegitzer Industries, Inc. [*NASDAQ symbol*] (SAG)
PGU	Gannon University, Nash Library, Erie, PA [*OCLC symbol*] (OCLC)
PGU	Pegasus Gold [*AMEX symbol*] (TTSB)
PGU	Pegasus Gold, Inc. [*AMEX symbol Toronto Stock Exchange symbol*]
PGU	Plant Growth Unit [*NASA*] (MCD)
PGU	Postgonococcal Urethritis [*Medicine*]
PGU	Power Generator Unit (IAA)
PGU	Pressure Gas Umbilical (KSC)
PGU	Propulsion Gas Umbilical
PGUA	Andersen Air Force Base, Guam Island [*Mariana Islands*] [*ICAO location identifier*] (ICLI)
PGUE	Professional Group - Ultrasonic Engineering
PGUM	Agana Naval Air Station, Guam Island [*Mariana Islands*] [*ICAO location identifier*] (ICLI)
PgUp	Page Up [*Computer science*] (BARN)
PGUT	Phosphogalactose Uridyltransferase [*Known as Galactose-1-phosphate Uridyl yltransferase*] [*An enzyme*]
PGV	Greenville [*North Carolina*] [*Airport symbol*] (OAG)
PGV	Proximal Gastric Vagotomy [*Medicine*]
PGVC	Professional Group - Vehicular Communications
PGW	Parallel Gap Welding
PGW	Past Grand Warden [*Freemasonry*]
PGW	Practice Guided Weapon (MCD)
PGW	Pressure Gas Welding
PGW	Pressurized Stone Groundwood [*Pulp and paper technology*]
PGW	United Plant Guard Workers of America
PGWA	Pottery and Glass Wholesalers Association (NADA)
PGWB	Psychological General Well Being [*Index*] (DMAA)
PGWC	Pennsylvania Gas & Water Co. [*NASDAQ symbol*] (SAG)

PGWC	PG Energy, Inc. [*NASDAQ symbol*] (SAG)
PGWCX	PIMCO: Growth Cl.C [*Mutual fund ticker symbol*] (SG)
PGWCZ	P G Energy $2.25 Dep Pfd [*NASDAQ symbol*] (TTSB)
PGWD	Pesticides in Ground Water Database [*Environmental Protection Agency*]
PGWG	Parliamentary Group for World Government
PGWG	Particles and Gases Working Group [*NASA*] (NASA)
PGWR	Pressurised Gas-Cooled Water Reactor [*Nuclear energy*] (NUCP)
PGWS	P. G. Wodehouse Society (EA)
PGWT	Peipeinimaru, Tinian Island [*Mariana Islands*] [*ICAO location identifier*] (ICLI)
PGwvG	Gwynedd-Mercy College, Gwynedd, PA [*Library symbol Library of Congress*] (LCLS)
PGX	Prostaglandin X [*or Prostacyclin*] [*Biochemistry*]
PGY	Global Yield Fund, Inc. [*NYSE symbol*] (SPSG)
PGY	Postgraduate Year
PGY	San Diego, CA [*Location identifier FAA*] (FAAL)
PGYE	Peptone, Glucose Yeast Extract [*Medium*] [*Biochemistry*] (DAVI)
PGZ	Ponta Grossa [*Brazil*] [*Airport symbol*] (OAG)
PG/ZD	Group Propagate / Zero Detect (MHDI)
PH	Czechoslovakia [*License plate code assigned to foreign diplomats in the US*]
pH	Hydrogen Ion Concentration (MAE)
Ph	[*The*] New Testament in Modern English [*1958*] [*J. B. Phillips*] [*A publication*] (BJA)
PH	Page Heading (BUR)
PH	Pan Head [*Screw Head*] (ECII)
PH	Parathyroid Hormone (STED)
PH	Parker-Hannifin [*NYSE symbol*] (TTSB)
PH	Parker-Hannifin Corp. [*NYSE symbol*] (SPSG)
PH	Parotid Hormone [*Biochemistry*]
PH	Partially Hepatectomized (DB)
PH	Passive Hemagglutination (STED)
PH	Past History [*Medicine*]
PH	Pearl Harbor, Hawaii
PH	Peliosis Hepatitis (STED)
PH	Penthouse
pH	Percent Hydrogen (SSD)
PH	Performance History
PH	Per Hour (IAA)
PH	Period Hours (IAA)
PH	Persistent Hepatitis [*Medicine*]
PH	Personal History [*Medicine*] (AAMN)
PH	Personal Hygiene (MCD)
PH	Perth [*Postcode*] (ODBW)
Ph	Phallacidin [*Biochemistry*]
PH	Phantom (IAA)
PH	Phantom Circuit [*Telecommunications*] (TEL)
Ph	Pharmacia AB [*Sweden*] [*Research code symbol*]
Ph	Pharmacopeia (STED)
Ph	Pharmacopoeia
PH	Phase (KSC)
ph	Phase (WDMC)
Ph	Phenanthrene [*Organic chemistry*] (AAMN)
Ph	Phenyl [*Organic chemistry*]
PH	Phenylalanine Hydroxylase (STED)
PH	Phiala [*Bottle*] [*Pharmacy*]
Ph'	Philadelphia [*Chromosome*]
PH	Philadelphia [*Diocesan abbreviation*] [*Pennsylvania*] (TOCD)
PH	Philadelphia Stock Exchange [*Pennsylvannia*]
PH	Philharmonic Hall (NADA)
Ph	Philippians [*New Testament book*] (BJA)
ph	Philippines [*IYRU nationality code*] [*MARC country of publication code Library of Congress*] (LCCP)
PH	Philippines [*ANSI two-letter standard code*] (CNC)
Ph	Philippus [*Flourished, 13th century*] [*Authority cited in pre-1607 legal work*] (DSA)
Ph	Phillimore's English Ecclesiastical Reports [*A publication*] (DLA)
Ph	Phillips' English Chancery Reports [*1841-49*] [*A publication*] (DLA)
Ph	Phillips' English Election Cases [*1780-81*] [*A publication*] (DLA)
PH	Phillips Head (DAC)
PH	Phone (MDG)
Ph	Phosphate
PH	Phot [*Electronics*] (DEN)
PH	Photographer's Mate [*Navy rating*]
PH	Photography Program [*Association of Independent Colleges and Schools specialization code*]
Ph	Photoreceptor
PH	Photostat (BJA)
PH	Phrase (ADA)
Ph	Physica [*of Aristotle*] [*Classical studies*] (OCD)
Ph	Physically Handicapped (OICC)
Ph	Phytane [*Organic chemistry*]
PH	Piano Type Hinge
PH	Picohenry [*One trillionth of a henry*]
P/H	Pier to House [*Classified advertising*] (ADA)
Ph	Pilot-Helicopter [*Navy British*]
Ph	Pilot House
PH	Pinch Hitter [*Baseball*]
PH	Pin Hole [*Eye examination*] (CPH)
PH	Plane Handler [*Navy*]
PH	Plant Height [*Botany*]
PH	Pleckstrin-Homology [*Domain*] [*Biochemistry*]
PH	Polynesian Airlines [*Airline code*] [*Australia*]
PH	Poor Health (DAVI)

PH............... Porphyria Hepatica (STED)
PH............... Porta Hepatis [Anatomy]
PH............... Porter House [Initials often used as a pattern on clothing designed by this firm]
P/H.............. Postage and Handling [Shipping]
PH............... Posterior Hypothalamus (STED)
PH............... Post History (STED)
pH............... Potential Hydrogen (WDAA)
pH............... Pouvoir Hydrogene [Hydrogen Power] [Negative logarithm of effective H ion concentration Chemistry]
PH............... Powerhouse
PH............... Power of Hydrogen (IAA)
PH............... Practitioner's Handbooks [A publication]
PH............... Precipitation Hardening
P-H............. Prentice-Hall, Inc. [Publishers]
PH............... Presidential Medal of Honour [Botswana]
PH............... Previous History [Medicine]
PH............... Primary Hyperparathyroidism
PH............... Private Hotel
PH............... Probability of Hit [Military] (MCD)
PH............... Professional Hydrologist
PH............... Project Handclasp (EA)
PH............... Prolyl Hydroxylase (STED)
PH............... Prospect Hill [Vole virus]
PH............... Prostatic Hypertrophy [Medicine] (MAE)
PH............... Public Health
PH............... Public Holiday (DA)
PH............... Public House [A drinking establishment] [British]
PH............... Pulmonary Hypertension [Medicine] (MAE)
PH............... Punctate Hemorrhage [Medicine] (STED)
PH............... Purple Heart [Given to personnel wounded in military service] [Military decoration]
PH............... Purpura Hyperglobulinemia [Medicine] (DAVI)
pH₁.............. Isoelectric Point [Chemistry] (DAVI)
PH1.............. Phase I Environmental Inspection (COE)
Ph¹............. Philadelphia Chromosome (MAE)
PH1.............. Photographer's Mate, First Class [Navy rating]
Ph¹c........... Philadelphia Chromosome
PH2.............. Phase II Environmental Inspection (COE)
PH2.............. Photographer's Mate, Second Class [Navy rating]
Ph₂0........... Partial Pressure of Water Vapor [Chemistry] (DAVI)
PH3.............. Phase III Environmental Inspection (COE)
PH3.............. Phosphine (AAEL)
PH3.............. Photographer's Mate, Third Class [Navy rating]
PHA............. Arterial pH [Hydrogen ion concentration] [Medicine] (DAVI)
PHA............. Chicago, IL [Location identifier FAA] (FAAL)
PHa............. Hazelton Public Library, Hazelton, PA [Library symbol Library of Congress] (LCLS)
PHA............. Pachena Industries Ltd. [Vancouver Stock Exchange symbol]
PHA............. Pacific Pharmaceuticals [AMEX symbol] [Formerly, Xytronyx, Inc.] (SG)
PHA............. Palomino Horse Association (EA)
PHA............. Parts per Hundred of Asphalt [Chemical technology]
PHA............. Passive Hemagglutination [Immunology]
PHA............. Peripheral Hyperalimentation (Solution) [Medicine]
PHA............. Peruvian Heart Association (EA)
PHA............. Phenylalanin [An amino acid] (DAVI)
PHA............. Phenylalanine [Medicine] (MEDA)
PHA............. Phytohemagglutinin [Immunology]
PHA............. Phytohemagglutinin Antigen [A skin test for cellular based immunity] (DAVI)
PHA............. Polyhydroxyalkanoate [Organic chemistry]
PHA............. Poly(hydroxystearic Acid) [Organic chemistry]
PHA............. Port Heiden [Alaska] [Seismograph station code, US Geological Survey Closed] (SEIS)
PHA............. Poultry Husbandry Adviser [Ministry of Agriculture, Fisheries, and Food] [British]
PHA............. Preferred Hotels Association [Also known as Preferred Hotel Worldwide] (EA)
PHA............. Prelaunch Hazard Area (MUGU)
PHA............. Preliminary Hazard Analyses (NASA)
PHA............. Preliminary Hazards Assessment [Environmental science] (COE)
PHA............. Primary Human Amnion [Biology] (BARN)
PHA............. Pritikin Health Association of Australia
PHA............. Process Hazard Analysis [Environmental science]
PHA............. Process Hazard Analysis [Engineering]
PHA............. Process Hazards Analysis [Chemical engineering]
PHA............. Professional Hairdressers' Association [Australia]
PHA............. Professional Handlers Association (EA)
PHA............. Professional Horsemen's Association of America (EA)
PHA............. Programmable Host Access [Computer science] (IAA)
PHA............. Pseudohypoaldosteronism [Medicine]
PHA............. Public Health Act (DAS)
PHA............. Public Health Agency (DMAA)
PHA............. Public Housing Administration [or HHFA; disbanded 1965]
PHA............. Public Housing Agencies (USGC)
PHA............. Public Housing Agency [Department of Housing and Urban Development] (GFGA)
PHA₁............ Pulse Height Analysis [Spectroscopy]
PHA₁............ State Library of Pennsylvania, Harrisburg, PA [OCLC symbol] (OCLC)
PHAA........... Airman Apprentice, Photographer's Mate, Striker [Navy rating]
PHAA........... Percheron Horse Association of America (EA)
PHAA........... Photographer's Airman Apprentice [Navy]
PHAA........... Positive High-Angle of Attack

PHAA.......... Professional Horsemen's Association of America [Later, PHA] (EA)
PHAABO....... Purebred Hanoverian Association of American Breeders and Owners (EA)
PHAB.......... Physically Handicapped and Able Bodied [Charitable organization] [British]
PHABSIM..... Physical Habitat Simulation Model [Ecology]
PHABY........ Pharmacia AB [Commercial firm] (MHDW)
PHADA........ Public Housing Authorities Directors Association (EA)
PHADS........ Phoenix Air Defense Sector (SAA)
phaeo........ Phaeochromocytoma [Pheochromocytoma] [Endocrinology] (DAVI)
PHAID......... Positive Hostile Aircraft Identification
PHAL.......... Phalange (WDAA)
PHAL.......... Phalanx (WDAA)
PHAL.......... Phytohemagglutinin-Stimulated Lymphocyte [Medicine] (DMAA)
Phal CC....... Phalen's Criminal Cases [A publication] (DLA)
PHALCM...... Phytohemagglutinin Stimulated Leukocyte Conditioned Medium
PHALSE....... Phreakers, Hackers, and Laundry Service Employees [East Coast group of computer trespassers raided by the FBI]
PHAM......... Phamis, Inc. [NASDAQ symbol] (SAG)
PHAM......... Phase Amplitude Monopulse (PDAA)
PHA-M........ Phytohemagglutinin M [Immunology] (MAE)
PHAM......... Project: Hearts and Minds [An association] (EA)
Phamis....... Phamis, Inc. [Associated Press] (SAG)
P-H Am Lab Arb Awards... American Labor Arbitration Awards (Prentice-Hall, Inc.) [A publication] (DLA)
P-H Am Lab Cas... American Labor Cases (Prentice-Hall, Inc.) [A publication] (DLA)
PHAMOS...... Promote Hemodynamics and Metabolism in an Orbiting Satellite (KSC)
PHAN.......... Airman, Photographer's Mate, Striker [Navy rating]
PH and P..... Peace, Health, and Prosperity
PHANT........ Phantom-Glass [Theater term] (DSUE)
PHAOMU..... Pianoforte, Harmonium, and American Organ Makers' Union [British]
PHAP.......... Palmitoyl Hydrolyzed Animal Protein [Organic chemistry]
PHAP.......... Provincial Health Assistance Program [Vietnam]
PHAQ.......... Private Hospitals' Association of Queensland [Australia]
PHAR.......... Pharmaceutical (WDAA)
PHAR.......... Pharmacology
PHAR.......... Pharmacopoeia (ROG)
PHAR.......... Pharmacy [or Pharmacist] (MSA)
phar........... Pharmacy (WDAA)
PHaR.......... Photosynthetically Active Radiation (EES)
PHarA......... AMP, Inc., Harrisburg, PA [Library symbol Library of Congress] (LCLS)
Phar B........ Pharmaciae Baccalaureus [Bachelor of Pharmacy]
PHarC......... Harrisburg Area Community College, Harrisburg, PA [Library symbol Library of Congress] (LCLS)
PharC......... Pharmaceutical Chemist [British]
PHarD......... Dauphin County Library System, Harrisburg, PA [Library symbol Library of Congress] (LCLS)
Phar D........ Pharmaciae Doctor [Doctor of Pharmacy]
PHARE........ Poland and Hungary Assistance for Economic Restructuring [EC] (ECED)
PHARE........ Program for Harmonized ATC [Air Traffic Control] Research in Europe (GAVI)
PharER-T.... Pennsylvania Department of Environmental Resources, Bureau of Topographic and Geologic Survey, Harrisburg, PA [Library symbol] [Library of Congress] (LCLS)
Phar G........ Graduate in Pharmacy (AAMN)
PHarH......... Pennsylvania Historical and Museum Commission, Harrisburg, PA [Library symbol Library of Congress] (LCLS)
PHarH-Ar..... Pennsylvania Historical and Museum Commission, Division of Archives and Manuscript, Harrisburg, PA [Library symbol] [Library of Congress] (LCLS)
PharLb........ Pharmchem Laboratories, Inc. [Associated Press] (SAG)
PHARM....... Pharmaceutical
Phar M........ Pharmaciae Magister [Master of Pharmacy]
PHARM....... Pharmacist [or Pharmacy]
PHARM....... Pharmacology
PHARM....... Pharmacy
Pharm........ Pharmacy (DD)
PHARMAC... Pharmacology
PHARMACOL... Pharmacological (MSA)
Pharmacol & Toxicol... Pharmacology and Toxicology (MEC)
Pharm C..... Pharmaceutical Chemist (MEDA)
PHARM CHEM... Pharmaceutical Chemistry (WDAA)
PHARMCL... Pharmaceutical
PharmD...... Doctor of Pharmacology [Canada] (ASC)
PharmD...... Doctor of Pharmacy
Pharm D...... Doctor of Pharmacy
Pharm G..... Graduate in Pharmacy (MEDA)
PHARML..... Pharmaceutical
Pharm M..... Master of Pharmacy
PharMor...... Phar-Mor, Inc. [Associated Press] (SAG)
PharmoS..... Pharmos Corp. [Associated Press] (SAG)
PharmP...... Pharmaceutical Product Development, Inc. [Associated Press] (SAG)
PHAROS..... Phased Array RADAR Operational Simulation [Army] (AABC)
PHAROS..... Plan Handling and RADAR Operating System [Aviation] (DA)
PHarP........ Harrisburg Polyclinic Hospital, Harrisburg, PA [Library symbol Library of Congress] (LCLS)
PHarris....... Paul Harris Stores [Associated Press] (SAG)
PharUpj...... Pharmacia & Upjohn, Inc. [Associated Press] (SAG)
PHAS......... Pollution Hazard Assessment System [Environmental science]
PHAS......... Pulse Height Analyzer System
PHASE....... Pre-Hospital Arrest Survival Evaluation [Cardiology study]

PHASR .... Personnel Hazards Associated with Space Radiation [*Satellite*]
PHatfB .... Biblical School of Theology, Hatfield, PA [*Library symbol Library of Congress*] (LCLS)
PHatU .... Union Library Co., Hatboro, PA [*Library symbol Library of Congress Obsolete*] (LCLS)
PHav .... Haverford Township Free Library, Havertown, PA [*Library symbol Library of Congress*] (LCLS)
PHAV .... Private Hospitals' Association of Victoria [*Australia*]
PHAWA .... Private Hospitals' Association of Western Australia
Ph B .... Bachelor of Pharmacy
PhB .... Bachelor of Philosophy (DAVI)
Ph B .... Bachelor of Physical Culture
PhB .... British Pharmacopoeia (DAVI)
PHB .... Para-Hexadecylaminobenzoate [*Clinical chemistry*]
PHB .... Para-Hydroxybenzoate [*Organic chemistry*]
PHB .... Parahydroxy Benzoic Acid (EDCT)
PHB .... Parliament House Book [*Scotland*] [*A publication*] (DLA)
PHB .... Parnaiba [*Brazil*] [*Airport symbol*] (OAG)
Ph B .... Philosophiae Baccalaureus [*Bachelor of Philosophy*]
PHB .... Photochemical Hole Burning [*Spectrometry*]
PHB .... Photographic Bulletin (MCD)
PHB .... Pioneer Hi-Bred International [*NYSE symbol*] (SAG)
PHB .... Pioneer Hi-Bred Intl [*NYSE symbol*] (TTSB)
PHB .... Poly(hydroxybenzoate) [*Organic chemistry*]
PHB .... Polyhydroxybutyrate [*Organic chemistry*]
PHB .... Pre-Homeobox [*Genetics*]
PHB .... Preventive Health Behavior [*Medicine*] (DMAA)
PHB .... Public Health Bibliography
PHB .... Public Health Service Building
PHBA .... Palomino Horse Breeders of America (EA)
PHBA .... Para-Hydroxybenzoic Acid [*Organic chemistry*]
PHBB .... Propylhydroxybenzyl Benzimidazole [*Organic chemistry*] (MAE)
Ph BD .... Doctor of Bible Philosophy
PHBH .... Para-Hydroxybenzoate Hydroxylase [*An enzyme*]
Ph B in Arch... Bachelor of Philosophy in Architecture
Ph B in Com... Bachelor of Philosophy in Commerce
Ph B in Ed ... Bachelor of Philosophy in Education
PhBJ .... Bachelor of Philosophy in Journalism (NADA)
PHBK .... Barking Sands, Kauai Island [*Hawaii*] [*ICAO location identifier*] (ICLI)
PHBK .... People's Heritage Financial Group, Inc. [*NASDAQ symbol*] (NQ)
PHBK .... Peoples Heritage Finl Gr [*NASDAQ symbol*] (TTSB)
PHBLX .... Phoenix Balanced [*Mutual fund ticker symbol*] (SG)
PHB/PHBV ... Poly-3-Hydroxybutyric Acid
PHBRZ .... Phosphor Bronze
PhBSp .... Bachelor of Philosophy in Speech (NADA)
PHBV .... Hydroxy Butyric Valeric Acid [*Polymer*]
PHBV .... Poly(hydroxybutyrate-Valerate) [*Organic chemistry*]
ph bz .... Phosphor Bronze (BARN)
PHC .... Chief Photographer's Mate [*Navy rating*]
PHC .... Children's Hospital of Pittsburgh, Pittsburgh, PA [*OCLC symbol*] (OCLC)
PHC .... Haverford College, Haverford, PA [*Library symbol Library of Congress*] (LCLS)
PHC .... Pacific Holding Corp. (EFIS)
PHC .... Pacific Hurricane Centers [*National Weather Service*]
PHC .... Palmitoyl Homocysteine [*Biochemistry*]
PHC .... Panhandle Conference (PSS)
PHC .... Pathonic Network, Inc. [*Toronto Stock Exchange symbol*]
PHC .... Personal Health Costs [*Medicine*] (DMAA)
PHC .... Personal Holding Company [*Generic term*]
PHC .... Perturbed-Hardness Chain [*Molecular thermodynamics*]
Ph C .... Pharmaceutical Chemist
PHC .... PHC, Inc. [*Associated Press*] (SAG)
Ph C .... Philosopher of Chiropractic
PHC .... Photographic Change (MCD)
PHC .... Population Housing Census (OICC)
PHC .... Port Harcourt [*Nigeria*] [*Airport symbol*] (OAG)
PHC .... Port Hardy [*British Columbia*] [*Seismograph station code, US Geological Survey*] (SEIS)
PHC .... Posthospital Care [*Medicine*]
PHC .... [*A*] Prairie Home Companion [*National Public Radio program*]
PHC .... Pratt Hotel Corp. [*AMEX symbol*] (SPSG)
PHC .... Premature Hereditary Canities [*Medicine*]
PHC .... Premolar Hypodontia, Hyperhidrosis, Canities Prematura [*Syndrome*] [*Medicine*] (DMAA)
PHC .... Primary Health Care
PHC .... Primary Health Centre [*British*]
PHC .... Primary Hepatic Carcinoma [*Medicine*]
PHC .... Primary Hepatocellular Carcinoma [*Oncology*] (DAVI)
PHC .... Principal Hazardous Constituent (GNE)
PHC .... Proliferative Helper Cells [*Immunology*]
PHCA .... Philippine Heart Center for Asia (PDAA)
PHCA .... Pig Health Control Association [*British*]
PHCA .... Pleasure Horse Club of America (EA)
PHCAA .... Public Health Cancer Association of America [*Defunct*] (EA)
P-H Cas .... American Federal Tax Reports (Prentice-Hall, Inc.) [*A publication*] (DLA)
PHCC .... Patients Encountered at [*Primary*] Health Care Centers
P-HCC .... Piston-Hand Control Clutch (DNAB)
PHCC .... Primary Hepatocellular Carcinoma [*Medicine*] (DMAA)
PHCC .... Punjab High Court Cases [*India*] [*A publication*] (DLA)
Ph Ch .... Phillips' English Chancery Reports [*1841-49*] [*A publication*] (DLA)
PHCIB .... Plumbing-Heating-Cooling Information Bureau (EA)
PHC Inc .... PHC, Inc. [*Associated Press*] (SAG)

PHCLIS .... Protected Home Circle Life Insurance Society (EA)
PHCM .... Master Chief Photographer's Mate [*Navy rating*]
PHCM .... Phone.com, Inc. [*NASDAQ symbol*]
PHCO .... Peoples Holding [*NASDAQ symbol*] (TTSB)
PHCO .... Peoples Holding Co. [*NASDAQ symbol*] (SAG)
PHCONST .... Phase Constant (IAA)
P-H Corp ...... Corporation [*Prentice-Hall, Inc.*] [*A publication*] (DLA)
PHCP .... Prehospital Care Provider [*Health insurance*] (DMAA)
PHCS .... Private Healthcare Systems
PHCS .... Senior Chief Photographer's Mate [*Navy rating*]
PHCSC .... Piers-Harris Children's Self-Concept Scale [*Child development test*] [*Psychology*]
PHCT .... Perturbed Hard Chain Theory [*Equation of state*]
PHCV-SD ..... Phase Conversion and Step-Down (MSA)
PHD .... Chesapeake Biological Laboratories, Inc. [*AMEX symbol*] (SAG)
PHD .... Dixmont State Hospital, Sewickley, PA [*OCLC symbol*] (OCLC)
Ph D .... Doctor of Pharmacy
PH D .... Doctor of Philosophy
PhD .... Doctor of Philosophy (GAGS)
PHD .... Doctor of Public Health [*British*] (DAS)
PHD .... Duncan Aviation, Inc. [*ICAO designator*] (FAAC)
PHD .... New Philadelphia, OH [*Location identifier FAA*] (FAAL)
PHD .... Parallel Head Disk
PhD .... Perfect Hard Disk [*Century Data Systems*] [*Computer science*]
Phd .... Phaedo [*of Plato*] [*Classical studies*] (OCD)
PhD .... Pharmaciae Doctor [*Doctor of Pharmacy*] (DAVI)
PHD .... Phase-Shift Driver (CET)
Ph D .... Philosophiae Doctor [*Doctor of Philosophy*] [*Facetious translation: Piled Higher and Deeper*]
PHD .... Photoelectron Diffraction [*Spectroscopy*]
PHD .... Photohydrodynamic [*Astrophysics*]
PHD .... Pilot's Horizontal Display [*Aviation*] (CAAL)
PHD .... Poly Harnstoff Dispersion [*Organic chemistry*]
PHD .... Port Hueneme Division [*Naval Surface Warfare Center*]
PHD .... Port Huron & Detroit Railroad Co. [*AAR code*]
PHD .... Positioning-Head Drum (DNAB)
PHD .... Precision High Dose
PH D .... Pre-Pearl Harbor Dad [*A humorous wartime degree*]
PHD .... Pride, Hustle, and Drive
PHD .... Public Health Department
PHD .... Public Health Director
PHD .... Public Housing Development [*Department of Housing and Urban Development*] (GFGA)
PHD .... Pulsed Holograpy Development [*Department of Energy*]
PHD .... Pulse Height Discrimination
PHDAN .... Physically Dangerous (DNAB)
PHDD .... Personal History of Depressive Disorders (MEDA)
PHDDS .... PSRO [*Professional Standards Review Organization*] Hospital Discharge Data Set
PHDE .... Poly(heptadiester) [*Organic chemistry*]
PHDEA .... Public Housing Drug Elimination Act [*1988*]
PHD.EC .... Chesapeake Bio Labs 'A' [*ECM, Symbol*] (TTSB)
PhDEd .... Doctor of Philosophy in Education [*British*] (ADA)
PHDH .... Dillingham Air Force Base, Oahu Island [*Hawaii*] [*ICAO location identifier*] (ICLI)
PHDI .... Palmer Hydrological Drought Index
PhD(Med) .... Doctor of Philosophy (Medicine) (ADA)
PhDMH .... Doctor of Philosophy in Mechanics and Hydraulics
PhD Otol ...... Doctor of Philosophy in Otolaryngology (PGP)
PhDPM Rehab... Doctor of Physical Medicine and Rehabilitation (PGP)
PHDr .... Doctor of Philosophy
Phdr .... Phaedrus [*of Plato*] [*Classical studies*] (OCD)
PHDR.......... Preliminary Hardware Design Review
PhD(RCA) .... Doctor of Philosophy (Royal College of Art) [*British*] (DBQ)
PHDS .... Post-Harvest Documentation Service [*Kansas State University*] (IID)
PhD Surg ..... Doctor of Philosophy in Surgery (PGP)
PHE .... Aviation POL [*Petroleum, Oil, and Lubrication*] Handling Equipment (NATG)
PHE .... Eastern State School and Hospital, Trevose, PA [*OCLC symbol*] (OCLC)
PHE .... Pawan Hans Ltd. [*India*] [*ICAO designator*] (FAAC)
PHE .... Periodic Health Examination
PHE .... Petroleum Handling Equipment (MCD)
Phe .... Phenylalanine [*Also, F*] [*An amino acid*]
phe .... Phenylalanine [*Also, F*] [*An amino acid*] (DOG)
PHE .... Phenylephrine [*Medicine*] (DMAA)
PHE .... Pheophytin [*Biochemistry*]
Phe .... Phoenix [*Constellation*]
PHE .... Photo Engravers & Electrotypers Ltd. [*Toronto Stock Exchange symbol*]
PHE .... Plate Heat Exchanger [*Chemical engineering*]
PHE .... Port Hedland [*Australia Airport symbol*] (OAG)
PHE .... Post-Heparin Esterase [*Medicine*] (MAE)
PHE .... Preflight Heat Exchanger [*NASA*] (KSC)
PHEA .... Public Health Engineering Abstracts [*A publication*]
PHEAA .... Pennsylvania Higher Education Assistance Agency (EDAC)
Phear Wat .... Phear's Rights of Water [*1859*] [*A publication*] (DLA)
PHEEM .... Photoelectron-Emission Microscopy (AAEL)
PhEEM .... Photoemission Electron Microscopy [*Medicine*] (DMAA)
PHEI .... Penetrator, High-Explosive, Incendiary (MCD)
PHEL .... Petroleum Helicopters, Inc. [*NASDAQ symbol*] (NQ)
PHEL .... Petroleum Helicopters (Vtg) [*NASDAQ symbol*] (TTSB)
PHELK .... Petroleum Helicopters [*NASDAQ symbol*] (TTSB)
PhelpD......... Phelps Dodge Corp. [*Associated Press*] (SAG)

PHeM............ Hershey Medical Center, Hershey, PA [*Library symbol Library of Congress*] (LCLS)
PHEM............ Primitive Helium Mantle [*Geology*]
PHEMA .... Poly(hydroxyethyl Methacrylate) [*Organic chemistry*]
pHEMT......... Psedomorphic High Electron Mobility Transistor [*Electronics*] (AAEL)
phen .... o-Phenanthroline [*Organic chemistry*]
PHEN .... Phenolic (AAG)
PHEN .... Phenotype [*Microbiology*] (DAVI)
Pheney Rep... Pheney's New Term Reports [*England*] [*A publication*] (DLA)
PHENG......... Photoengraving (VRA)
PH Eng .... Public Health Engineer
PHENO......... Phenobarbital [*A drug*]
pheno .... Phenotype
PHENO......... Precise Hybrid Elements for Nonlinear Operation (IEEE)
PHENOB...... Phenobarbital [*A Drug*] (DAVI)
phenobarb.. Phenobarbital [*A drug*] (DAVI)
phenom .... Phenomenon (BARN)
PHENOS...... Precise Hybrid Elements for Nonlinear Operations (IAA)
PHENTH ...... Phenothiazine [*A drug*] (DAVI)
PHENYL ...... Phenylpropanol [*A drug*] (DAVI)
PHEO .... Pheochromocytoma [*Oncology*]
PHER .... Photographic Mechanical Equipment Repair [*Course*] (DNAB)
PHER .... Plate Heat Exchanger [*Chemical Engineering*] (DNAB)
PHERMEX .... Pulsed High-Energy Radiographic Machine Emitting X-Rays
PHET............ Photoetching (VRA)
Ph Ev .... Phillips on Evidence [*A publication*] (DLA)
PHEWA .... Presbyterian Health, Education, and Welfare Association (EA)
PHF............... Fairview State Hospital, Waymart, PA [*OCLC symbol*] (OCLC)
PHF............... Newport News [*Virginia*] [*Airport symbol*] (OAG)
PHF............... Paired Helical Filaments [*Neuroanatomy*] [*Term coined by Dr. Robert Terry to describe the components of neurofibrillary tangles in the brains of Alzheimer's Disease patients*]
PHF............... Patrick Henry Foundation [*Liberty, NY*] (EA)
PHF............... Patrol Hydrofoil [*Missile*] (HGAA)
PHF............... Payload Handling Fixture [*NASA*] (NAKS)
PHF............... Peak Hour Factor [*Transportation*]
PHF............... Peanut Hull Flour
PHF............... Pergamon Holding Foundation [*Liechtenstein*]
PHF............... Personal Hygiene Facility [*NASA*] (NASA)
PHF............... Phoenix House Foundation (EA)
PHF............... Plug Handling Fixture (NRCH)
PHF............... Potomac Horse Fever [*Veterinary science*] (DB)
PHF............... Procedure History File (COE)
PHF............... Process Holding Fixture (MCD)
PHF............... Procurement History File [*DoD*]
PHF............... Public Health Foundation [*Information service or system*] (IID)
PHF............... USF&G Pacholder Fd [*AMEX symbol*] (TTSB)
PHF............... USF & G Pacholder Fund, Inc. [*AMEX symbol*] (CTT)
PHFA .... Potomac Horse Fever Agent
PHFC .... Pittsburgh Home Fin1 [*NASDAQ symbol*] (TTSB)
PHFE........... Pulsed High Frequency Electroporation [*Analytical biochemistry*]
P-H Fed Taxes... Federal Taxes (Prentice-Hall, Inc.) [*A publication*] (DLA)
PHFF............. Oahu [*Hawaii*] [*ICAO location identifier*] (ICLI)
PHFG........... Primary Human Fetal Glial [*Cytology*]
PHFPrA........ USF&G $4.10cm Cv Exch A Pfd [*NYSE symbol*] (TTSB)
PHFTX .... Prentice-Hall Federal Taxes [*Database*] (IT)
Ph G .... Graduate in Pharmacy
PhG .... Pharmacopoeia Germanica [*German Pharmacopeia*] (MAE)
PHG .... Phenate-Hexamine Goggle [*British World War I anti-poison-gas helmet*]
PHG .... Philips Electronics NV [*Formerly, Philips NV*] [*NYSE symbol*] (SPSG)
PHG .... Phillipsburg, KS [*Location identifier FAA*] (FAAL)
PHG .... Phosphatidylglycerol [*Test used to determine fetal lung maturity*] (DAVI)
Phg.............. Phytophthora Megasperma Glycinea [*A fungus*]
PHG .... Postman, Higher Grade [*British*] (DI)
PHG .... Prototype Hydrofoil Gunboat
PHG .... Scranton State General Hospital, Scranton, PA [*OCLC symbol*] (OCLC)
PHGA .... Pteroylhexaglutamylglutamic [*or Pteroylheptaglutamic*] Acid [*Biochemistry*]
PhGABA ...... Phenyl-gamma-aminobutyric Acid [*Tranquilizer*]
PHGLTF .... Physiological Training Flight [*Air Force*]
Phgly .... Phenylglycine [*An amino acid*]
PHGM .... Patrol Hydrofoil Guided Missile [*Navy*] (DNAB)
Phgn .... Physiognomonica [*of Aristotle*] [*Classical studies*] (OCD)
PHGNDWG... Photogenic (VRA)
PHGRM .... Photogram (VRA)
P HGT .... Package Height [*Freight*]
PHH .... Andrews, SC [*Location identifier FAA*] (FAAL)
PHH .... Haverford State Hospital, Haverford, PA [*OCLC symbol*] (OCLC)
PHH .... Peterson, Howell & Heather, Inc. (EFIS)
PHH .... Phan Thiet [*South Vietnam*] [*Airport symbol*] (AD)
PHH .... PHH Corp. [*NYSE symbol Toronto Stock Exchange symbol*] (SPSG)
PHH .... Phillips Head [*Screw*]
PHH .... Posthemorrhagic Hydrocephalus [*Neurology*] (DAVI)
PHH .... Puu Huluhulu [*Hawaii*] [*Seismograph station code, US Geological Survey Closed*] (SEIS)
PHHA .... Pearl Harbor History Associates (EA)
PHHC .... Programmable Hand-Held Calculator (RDA)
PHHI .... Persistent Hyperinsulinemic Hypoglycemia of Infancy [*Medicine*]
PHHI .... Wheeler Air Force Base, Oahu Island [*Hawaii*] [*ICAO location identifier*] (ICLI)
PHHM .... Palm Harbor Homes [*NASDAQ symbol*] (TTSB)
PHHM .... Palm Harbor Homes, Inc. [*NASDAQ symbol*] (SAG)

PHHN .... Hana, Maui Island [*Hawaii*] [*ICAO location identifier*] (ICLI)
PHHSA......... Protestant Health and Human Services Assembly (EA)
PHi.............. Historical Society of Pennsylvania, Philadelphia, PA [*Library symbol Library of Congress*] (LCLS)
PhI.............. International Pharmacopoeia
PHI.............. Passive Hemagglutination Inhibitor (DB)
PHI.............. Permanent Health Insurance [*British*]
PHI.............. Petroleum Helicopters, Inc. (MCD)
PHI.............. Pharmacopoeia Internationalis [*International Pharmacopoeia*] (DAVI)
PHI.............. Philadelphia [*Pennsylvania*] [*Seismograph station code, US Geological Survey Closed*] (SEIS)
PHI.............. Philippine Long Distance Telephone Co. [*NYSE symbol*] (SAG)
PHI.............. Philippine Long D Tel ADS [*NYSE symbol*] (TTSB)
Phi.............. Philippus [*Flourished, 13th century*] [*Authority cited in pre-1607 legal work*] (DSA)
Phi.............. Philips [*Holland & International*] [*Record label*]
PHI.............. Philips Aviation Services [*Netherlands ICAO designator*] (FAAC)
PHI.............. Philipsburg State General Hospital, Philipsburg, PA [*Inactive*] [*OCLC symbol*] (OCLC)
PHI.............. Phillipsite [*A zeolite*]
PHI.............. Philosophie Informationsdienst [*Philosophy Information Service*] [*University of Dusseldorf*] [*Information service or system*] (IID)
PHI.............. Philosophy (WGA)
PHI.............. Phosphine (LDT)
PHI.............. Phosphohexose Isomerase [*An enzyme*]
Phi.............. Physeptone [*A narcotic substitute*]
PHIA .... Physiological Hyaluronidase Inhibitor [*Biochemistry*]
PHI.............. Polarity Health Institute (EA)
PHI.............. Position and Homing Indicator
PHI.............. Prentice-Hall International [*Publisher*]
PHI.............. Programme Hydrologique International [*International Hydrological Program - IHP*] [*UNESCO*] (MSC)
PHI.............. Provincial House, Inc. (EFIS)
PHI.............. Public Health Inspector [*British*]
PHIA .... Pharmaceutical Ingredients Asia [*Conference*]
PHIA .... Phenylalanine (MAE)
PHIAL .... Phiala [*Bottle*] [*Pharmacy*]
PHIB .... Amphibious
PHib .... Hibeh Papyri [*A publication*] (OCD)
PHIBB .... Project for Historical Biobibliography [*A publication*]
PHIBCB ...... Amphibious Construction Battalion [*Also, ACB*] (NVT)
PHIBCORPAC... Amphibious Corps, Pacific Fleet [*Marine Corps*]
PHIBCORPS... Amphibious Corps [*Marine Corps*]
PHIBDET ...... Amphibious Detachment
PHIBDETIND... Amphibious Detachment, India
PHIBEU .... Amphibious Forces, Europe
PHIBEX .... Amphibious Exercise [*NATO*]
PHIBFOR...... Amphibious Forces
PHIBGROUP... Amphibious Group
PHIBGRU ..... Amphibious Group
PHIBLANT.... Amphibious Forces, Atlantic Fleet
PHIBLEX ..... Amphibious Landing Exercise [*Navy*] (NVT)
PHIBNAW .... Amphibious Forces, Northwest African Waters
PHIBOPS..... Amphibious Operations [*Navy*] (NVT)
PHIBPAC..... Amphibious Forces, Pacific Fleet
PHIBRAIDEX... Amphibious Raid Exercise [*Navy*] (NVT)
PHIBRECONEX... Amphibious Reconnaissance Exercise [*Navy*] (NVT)
PHIBREFTRA... Amphibious Refresher Training [*Navy*] (CAAL)
PHIBRFT...... Amphibious Refresher Training [*Navy*] (NVT)
PHIBRON ..... Amphibious Squadron [*Army*]
PHIBSEU ..... Amphibious Forces, Europe
PHIBSFORPAC... Amphibious Forces, Pacific Fleet
PHIBSKDN ... Amphibious Ship Shakedown Cruise [*Navy*] (NVT)
PHIBSLANT... Amphibious Forces, Atlantic Fleet
PHIBSPAC... Amphibious Forces, Pacific Fleet
PHIBSS .... Amphibious Schoolship [*Navy*] (NVT)
PHIBSTRAPAC... Training Command Amphibious Forces, US Pacific Fleet
PHIBSUKAY... Amphibious Bases, United Kingdom
PHIBTF .... Amphibious Task Force [*Navy*] (NVT)
PHIBTRA...... Training Command Amphibious Forces
PHIBTRABASE... Amphibious Training Base [*Navy*]
PHIBTRAEX... Amphibious Training Exercise [*Navy*] (NVT)
PHIBTRAINLANT... Training Command Amphibious Forces, US Atlantic Fleet
PHIBTRAINPAC... Training Command Amphibious Forces, US Pacific Fleet
PHIBTRALANT... Training Command Amphibious Forces, US Atlantic Fleet
PHIBTRANS... Amphibious Transport [*Navy*]
PHIBTRAPAC... Training Command Amphibious Forces, US Pacific Fleet
PHIBTRBASE... Amphibious Training Base [*Navy*]
PHIBUF .... Performance Buffet Limit (GAVI)
PHIBWARTRACEN... Amphibious Warfare Training Center [*Navy*]
PHIC .... Poly(hexyl Isocyanate) [*Organic chemistry*]
PHICB .... Putnam High Income Convertible & Bond Fund [*Associated Press*] (SAG)
PHICT .... Philips Inventory Control Technique [*Computer science*] (IAA)
Phi D .... Doctor of Philanthropy
PHID .... Positive Hostile Identification Device [*Air Force*]
Phi Dex....... Phi Delta Chi [*An association*] (NTPA)
PHIGS .... Programmers Hierarchical Interactive Graphics Standards (NITA)
PHIGS .... Programmers Hierarchical Interactive Graphics System [*IBM Corp.*]
PHII .... Planet Hollywood International, Inc. [*NASDAQ symbol*] (SAG)
PHII .... Planet Hollywood Intl'A' [*NASDAQ symbol*] (TTSB)
PHIK .... Honolulu/Hickam Air Force Base, Oahu Island [*Hawaii*] [*ICAO location identifier*] (ICLI)
Phil............. Orationes Philippicae [*of Cicero*] [*Classical studies*] (OCD)
PHIL............ Philadelphia [*Pennsylvania*]

Phil............. Philadelphia (ODBW)
PHIL............. Philadelphia Exchange (EBF)
Phil............. Philadelphia Reports [*A publication*] (DLA)
Phil............. Philemon [*New Testament book*]
Phil............. Philharmonia [*Record label*]
PHIL............. Philharmonic
Phil............. Philippians [*New Testament book*]
Phil............. Philippine Island Reports [*A publication*] (DLA)
PHIL............. Philippines (AFM)
Phil............. Philippines (VRA)
Phil............. Phillimore's English Ecclesiastical Reports [*A publication*] (DLA)
Phil............. Phillips' English Chancery Reports [*1841-49*] [*A publication*] (DLA)
Phil............. Phillips' English Election Cases [*1780-81*] [*A publication*] (DLA)
Phil............. Phillips' Illinois Reports [*152-245 Illinois*] [*A publication*] (DLA)
Phil............. Phillips' North Carolina Law Reports [*A publication*] (DLA)
Phil............. Phillips' Treatise on Insurance [*A publication*] (DLA)
Phil............. Philoctetes [*of Sophocles*] [*Classical studies*] (OCD)
PHIL............. Philology
Phil............. Philopoemen [*of Plutarch*] [*Classical studies*] (OCD)
PHIL............. Philosophy
Phil............. Philosophy (DD)
PHIL............. Potential Host Institutes List [*European Commission*]
PHIL............. Programmable Algorithm Machine High-Level Language [*Computer science*]
PHILA............. Philadelphia [*Pennsylvania*]
Phila............. Philadelphia Reports [*Pennsylvania*] [*A publication*] (DLA)
Phila C Pharmacy... Philadelphia College of Pharmacy and Science (GAGS)
Philad............. Philadelphia Reports [*Pennsylvania*] [*A publication*] (DLA)
PHILADA............. Philadelphia (ROG)
Philada R ... Philadelphia Reports [*Pennsylvania*] [*A publication*] (DLA)
Philada Rep... Philadelphia Reports [*Pennsylvania*] [*A publication*] (DLA)
PHILADEL............. Philadelphia (ROG)
Philadelphia Leg Int... Philadelphia Legal Intelligencer [*Pennsylvania*] [*A publication*] (DLA)
Philadelphia Rep... Philadelphia Reports [*Pennsylvania*] [*A publication*] (DLA)
PHILAGRP ... Philadelphia Group (DNAB)
Phila Leg Int... Philadelphia Legal Intelligencer [*Pennsylvania*] [*A publication*] (DLA)
Phila LJ....... Philadelphia Law Journal [*A publication*] (DLA)
PHILAMCHAM... Philippine-American Chamber of Commerce (NTPA)
philan .... Philanthropical (BJA)
PHILANTHR... Philanthropic (ROG)
Phila (PA)..... Philadelphia Reports [*Pennsylvania*] [*A publication*] (DLA)
Phila Reports... Philadelphia Reports [*Pennsylvania*] [*A publication*] (DLA)
philat........... Philately
Philbro......... Philipp Brothers Ltd. [*Commercial firm*]
Phil C .... Philosophy in Chiropractic
PHILCAG...... First Philippine Civic Action Group [*Deployed in 1964 to assist South Vietnam*] (VNW)
Phil Civ & Can Law... Phillimore's Civil and Canon Law [*A publication*] (DLA)
PHILCOM..... Philippine Global Communications, Inc. [*Manila*] [*Telecommunications*]
PhilCon....... Philadelphia Consolidated Holding [*Commercial firm Associated Press*] (SAG)
PHILCON..... Philippine Contingent [*Military*]
Phil Cop ...... Phillips' Law of Copyright Designs [*A publication*] (DLA)
Phil D .... Philosophiae Doctor [*Doctor of Philosophy*] [*See also Ph D*] [*Latin*]
PHILDANCO... Philadelphia Dance Company
Phil Dec ...... Philippus Decius [*Deceased circa 1537*] [*Authority cited in pre-1607 legal work*] (DSA)
Phil Dom ..... Phillimore's Law of Domicil [*A publication*] (DLA)
Phil Ecc ...... Phillimore's Ecclesiastical Judgments [*A publication*] (DLA)
Phil Ecc ...... Phillimore's English Ecclesiastical Law [*2 eds.*] [*1873, 1895*] [*A publication*] (DLA)
Phil Ecc ...... Phillimore's English Ecclesiastical Reports [*1809-21*] [*A publication*] (DLA)
Phil Ecc Judg... Phillimore's Ecclesiastical Judgments [*1867-75*] [*A publication*] (DLA)
Phil Ecc Law... Phillimore's English Ecclesiastical Law [*2 eds.*] [*1873, 1895*] [*A publication*] (DLA)
Phil Ecc R ... Phillimore's English Ecclesiastical Reports [*1809-21*] [*A publication*] (DLA)
Phil El Cas... Phillips' English Election Cases [*1780-81*] [*A publication*] (DLA)
Philem......... Philemon [*New Testament book*]
PhilEnv........ Philip Environmental [*Commercial firm Associated Press*] (SAG)
Phil Eq......... Phillips' North Carolina Equity Reports [*A publication*] (DLA)
Phil Ev......... Phillips on Evidence [*A publication*] (DLA)
Phil Ev Cow & H & Edw Notes... Phillips on Evidence, Notes by Cowen, Hill, and Edwards [*A publication*] (DLA)
PHILEX......... Philadelphia Stock Exchange
Phil Fam Cas... Phillipps' Famous Cases in Circumstantial Evidence [*A publication*] (DLA)
Phil Grand ... Phillips' Grandeur of the Law (DLA)
PHILI I......... Philippine Islands (WDAA)
Phili Fran .... Philippus Francus [*Deceased, 1471*] [*Authority cited in pre-1607 legal work*] (DSA)
Phil ILJ........ Philippine International Law Journal [*A publication*] (DLA)
Phil Ins........ Phillips on Insurance [*A publication*] (DLA)
Phil Insan.... Phillips on Lunatics [*1858*] [*A publication*] (DLA)
Phil Int Law... Phillimore's International Law [*A publication*] (DLA)
Phil Int LJ .. Philippine International Law Journal [*A publication*] (DLA)
Phil Int Rom Law... Phillimore's Introduction to the Roman Law [*A publication*] (DLA)
Philip........... Philippines

Philip Fran... Philippus Franchus [*Deceased, 1471*] [*Authority cited in pre-1607 legal work*] (DSA)
Philipp......... Philippines (BARN)
Philippine.... Philippine Reports [*A publication*] (DLA)
Philippine Co... Philippine Code [*A publication*] (DLA)
Philippine Internat LJ... Philippine International Law Journal [*Manila, Philippines*] [*A publication*] (DLA)
Philippine Int'l LJ... Philippine International Law Journal [*A publication*] (DLA)
Philippine LJ... Philippine Law Journal [*A publication*] (DLA)
Philippine L Rev... Philippine Law Review [*A publication*] (DLA)
PhilipsEI...... Philips Electronics NV Holding Co. [*Associated Press*] (SAG)
Phil Jud....... Phillimore's Ecclesiastical Judgments [*1867-75*] [*England*] [*A publication*] (DLA)
Phil Judg..... Phillimore's Ecclesiastical Judgments [*1867-75*] [*A publication*] (DLA)
Phill............ Phillips' English Chancery Reports [*1841-49*] [*A publication*] (DLA)
Phill............ Phillips' English Election Cases [*1780-81*] [*A publication*] (DLA)
Phill............ Phillips' Illinois Reports [*152-245 Illinois*] [*A publication*] (DLA)
Phill............ Phillips' North Carolina Equity Reports [*A publication*] (DLA)
Phill............ Phillips' North Carolina Law Reports [*A publication*] (DLA)
Phil Lab Rel J... Philippine Labour Relations Journal [*A publication*] (DLA)
Phil Law...... Phillips' North Carolina Law Reports [*A publication*] (DLA)
Phill Ch ...... Phillips' English Chancery Reports [*1841-49*] [*A publication*] (DLA)
Phill Ch (Eng)... Phillips' English Chancery Reports [*1841-49*] [*A publication*] (DLA)
Phil LD .... Doctor of Lithuanian Philology
Phill Ecc Judg... Phillimore's Ecclesiastical Judgments [*1867-75*] [*A publication*] (DLA)
Phill Ecc R... Phillimore's English Ecclesiastical Reports [*1809-21*] [*A publication*]
Phill Eq (NC)... Phillips' North Carolina Equity Reports [*A publication*] (DLA)
Phil Lic........ Licentiate of Philosophy [*British*]
Phillim......... Phillimore's English Ecclesiastical Reports [*1809-21*] [*A publication*] (DLA)
Phillim Dom... Phillimore's Law of Domicil [*A publication*] (DLA)
Phillim Eccl... Phillimore's Ecclesiastical Judgments [*1867-75*] [*A publication*] (DLA)
Phillim Eccl... Phillimore's English Ecclesiastical Reports [*1809-21*] [*A publication*] (DLA)
Phillim Ecc Law... Phillimore's English Ecclesiastical Law [*A publication*] (DLA)
Phillim Int Law... Phillimore's International Law [*A publication*] (DLA)
Phill Ins...... Phillips on Insurance [*A publication*] (DLA)
Phillips........ Phillips' English Chancery Reports [*1841-49*] [*A publication*] (DLA)
Phillips........ Phillips' English Election Cases [*1780-81*] [*A publication*] (DLA)
Phillips........ Phillips' Illinois Reports [*152-245 Illinois*] [*A publication*] (DLA)
Phillips........ Phillips' North Carolina Equity Reports [*A publication*] (DLA)
PhillipS....... Phillips' North Carolina Law Reports [*A publication*] (DLA)
Phillips U .... Phillips University (GAGS)
Phil Lit R .... Philatelic Literature Review [*A publication*]
Phil LJ........ Philippine Law Journal [*Manila*] [*A publication*] (DLA)
Phill L (NC)... Phillips' North Carolina Law Reports [*A publication*] (DLA)
Phil L Rev ... Philippine Law Review [*A publication*] (DLA)
Phil Lun...... Phillips on Lunatics [*1858*] [*A publication*] (DLA)
Philly.......... Philadelphia
PhilM.......... Master of Philosophy (GAGS)
Phil Mech Liens... Phillips on Mechanics' Liens [*A publication*] (DLA)
PhilMr .... Philip Morris Companies, Inc. [*Associated Press*] (SAG)
philn .... Philanthropy
Phil NC .... Phillips' North Carolina Law Reports [*A publication*] (DLA)
Philo........... Philo Judaeus [*First century AD*] [*Classical studies*] (OCD)
philo........... Philology (WDAA)
Philol.......... Philologus [*A publication*] (OCD)
PHILOL .... Philology
Philol Suppl... Philologus. Supplement [*A publication*] (OCD)
PHILOM .... Philomathes [*Lover of Learning*] (ROG)
PHILOMATH... Philomathematicus [*Lover of Mathematics*] (ROG)
PHILOS........ Philosophy (EY)
Philostr....... Philostratus [*Second century AD*] [*Classical studies*] (OCD)
Phil (PA)...... Philadelphia Reports [*Pennsylvania*] [*A publication*] (DLA)
Phil Pat ...... Phillips on Patents [*A publication*] (DLA)
PhilPet....... Phillips Petroleum Co. [*Associated Press*] (SAG)
PHILPUC..... Philippine Presidential Unit Citation Badge [*Military decoration*]
PHILQA........ Philips Question Answering System (NITA)
Phil R .... Philadelphia Reports [*Pennsylvania*] [*A publication*] (DLA)
Phil R .... Philosophical Review [*A publication*] (BRI)
Phil Rep ..... Philadelphia Reports [*Pennsylvania*] [*A publication*] (DLA)
PhilRH........ Phillips [*R.H.*], Inc. [*Associated Press*] (SAG)
Phil Rom Law... Phillimore's Private Law among the Romans [*A publication*] (DLA)
PHILSEAFRON... Philippine Sea Frontier
PHIL SOC..... Philharmonic Society (WDAA)
PHILSOM..... Periodical Holdings in the Library of the School of Medicine [*Washington University School of Medicine*] [*Library network*]
Phil St Leg R... Phillips' Studii Legalis Ratio [*A publication*] (DLA)
Phil St Tr.... Phillipps' State Trials [*Prior to 1688*] [*A publication*] (DLA)
PhilSub....... Philadelphia Suburban Corp. [*Associated Press*] (SAG)
Phil Unters... Philologische Untersuchungen [*A publication*] (OCD)
Phil US Pr ... Phillips' United States Practice [*A publication*] (DLA)
Phil Wochenschr... Philologische Wochenschrift [*A publication*] (OCD)
Phil Yb Int'l L... Philippine Yearbook of International Law [*Manila, Philippines*] [*A publication*] (DLA)
PHIM .... Posthypoxic Intention Myoclonus [*Medicine*] (DMAA)
PHIN .... Position and Homing Inertial Navigator
PHIND......... Pharmaceutical and Healthcare Industries News Database [*PJB Group Publications Ltd.*] [*Information service or system*] (IID)
P-H Ind Rel Lab Arb... Industrial Relations, American Labor Arbitration (Prentice-Hall, Inc.) [*A publication*] (DLA)

P-H Ind Rel Union Conts... Industrial Relations, Union Contracts, and Collective Bargaining (Prentice-Hall,Inc.) [A publication] (DLA)
PHINet........ Prentice-Hall Information Network [Prentice-Hall Information Services] [Information service or system] (IID)
Phip............ Phipson's Digest, Natal Reports [South Africa] [A publication] (DLA)
Phip............ Phipson's Reports, Natal Supreme Court [South Africa] [A publication] (DLA)
Phip Ev....... Phipson on Evidence [12th ed.] [1976] [A publication] (DLA)
PHIPrA........ Philippine L-D Tel Pfd GDS [NYSE symbol] (TTSB)
PHIPS......... Professional Hi-Resolution Image Processing System [TerraVision, Inc.] (PCM)
Phipson .... Reports of Cases in the Supreme Court of Natal [A publication] (DLA)
PHIRB......... Public Health Inspectors' Registration Board [British] (BI)
PHIS .... Physically Handicapped in Science (BABM)
PHIS .... Program Hardware Interface Specification (CAAL)
PHITAP........ Predesigned [or Priority] High-Interest Tactical Air Prediction [Acoustic forecast] (MCD)
PHITAR....... Predesignated High-Interest Tactical Area [Navy] (NVT)
PhIUS .... Pharmaceutical Ingredients U.S.
PHJ............. Danville State Hospital, Danville, PA [OCLC symbol] (OCLC)
PHJC........... Penn Hall Junior College [Pennsylvania] [Closed, 1973]
PHJC........... Poor Handmaids of Jesus Christ [Ancilla Domini Sisters] [Roman Catholic religious order]
PHJC........... Port Huron Junior College [Michigan]
PH/JO .... Photojournalist (DNAB)
PHK .... Pahokee, FL [Location identifier FAA] (FAAL)
PHK .... Personal Hygiene Kit (MCD)
PHK .... Phosphorylase Kinase [An enzyme]
PHK .... Platelet Phosphohexokinase (MAE)
PHK .... Postmortem Human Kidney [Cells]
PHKO .... Kona/Ke-Ahole, Hawaii Island [Hawaii] [ICAO location identifier] (ICLI)
PHKP .... Kaanapali, Maui Island [Hawaii] [ICAO location identifier] (ICLI)
PHKU .... Kunia [Hawaii] [ICAO location identifier] (ICLI)
PHKW .... Powerhouse Resources, Inc. [NASDAQ symbol] (SAG)
PHKWE .... Powerhouse Resources [NASDAQ symbol] (TTSB)
PHL............. Allentown State Hospital, Allentown, PA [OCLC symbol] (OCLC)
Ph L............ Licentiate in Philosophy
Ph L............ Licentiate of Pharmacy
PHL............. Periodical Holdings List [Libraries]
PHL............. Philadelphia [Pennsylvania] [Airport symbol]
PHL............. Philippines [ANSI three-letter standard code] (CNC)
PHL............. Phillips Michigan City Flying Service, Inc. [ICAO designator] (FAAC)
PHL............. Pressure to Horizontal Locks [Missiles] (AAG)
PHL............. Public Health Law
PHLA .... Plasma Postheparin Lipolytic Activity [Clinical chemistry]
PHLA .... Postheparin Lipolytic Activity [Medicine] (DMAA)
PHLAG .... Philips Load and Go (NITA)
PHLAG .... Phillips Petroleum Load and Go [System]
PHLAGS ...... Phillips Petroleum Load and Go System (DNAB)
Phlb............ Philebus [of Plato] [Classical studies] (OCD)
Phld............ Philodemus [First century BC] [Classical studies] (OCD)
PHLEGM ...... People's Hayfever Listener Examiner Gazette Magazine [A publication] (WDAA)
PHLH .... Phillips Head [Screw]
PHLI............ Lihue, Kauai Island [Hawaii] [ICAO location identifier] (ICLI)
PHLITHO...... Photolithographic (VRA)
PhILD.......... Philippine Long Distance Telephone Co. [Associated Press] (SAG)
Phlm .... Philemon [New Testament book]
PHLO .... Phloretin [Biochemistry]
PHLODOT .... Phase Lock Doppler Tracking [System] (MUGU)
PhlpGs .... Phillips Gas [Associated Press] (SAG)
PHLS .... Public Health Laboratory Service [British]
PHLSB .... Public Health Laboratory Service Board [British]
PhIVH .... Phillips-Van Heusen Corp. [Associated Press] (SAG)
PHLX .... Philadelphia Stock Exchange
PHLY .... Philadelphia Consol Hldg [NASDAQ symbol] (TTSB)
PHLY .... Philadelphia Consolidated Holding [NASDAQ symbol] (SAG)
Ph M........... Master in Pharmacy
Ph M........... Master of Philosophy
PHM............ Mayview State Hospital, Bridgeville, PA [OCLC symbol] (OCLC)
PHM............ Patrol Hydrofoil Missile [Navy symbol]
PHM............ Patterson-Harker Method [Physics]
PHM............ Per Hundred Million (NASA)
PHM............ Petroleum Helicopters, Inc. [ICAO designator] (FAAC)
PHM............ Phantom (MSA)
PhM............ Pharmaciae Magister [Master of Pharmacy] (DAVI)
PHM............ Pharmacist's Mate [Navy rating]
PHM............ Phase Meter
PHM............ Phase Modulation [Radio data transmission] (DEN)
Phm............ Philemon [New Testament book] (BJA)
PhM............ Philips Minigroove [Record label]
PHM............ Posterior Hyaloid Membrane [Eye anatomy]
PHM............ Post-Holiday Movie
PHM............ Power Hybrid Microcircuit
PHM............ Pulmonary Hyaline Membrane [Syndrome] [Medicine] (DB)
PHM............ Pulte Corp. [NYSE symbol] (SPSG)
PHM............ Pulte Home Corp. (EFIS)
PHMA .... Plastic Houseware Manufacturers Association
PHMA .... Polyhexyl Methacrylate [Organic chemistry]
PHMA .... Professional Housing Management Association (NTPA)
Phm B .... Bachelor of Pharmacy
PHMB.......... Para-Hydroxymercuribenzoate [Biochemistry]
PHMC .... Probe Heater Motor Controller [NASA] (MCD)

Phmcyc........ Pharmacyclics, Inc. [Associated Press] (SAG)
PHMD.......... Pseudohypertrophic Muscular Dystrophy (CPH)
PHMDP........ Pharmacist's Mate, Dental Prosthetic Technician [Navy rating]
Phm G .... Graduate in Pharmacy
PHMK .... Molokai, Molokai Island [Hawaii] [ICAO location identifier] (ICLI)
PHMO .... Partially Hydrogenated Menhaden Oil [Food science]
PhMor......... Phar-Mor, Inc. [Associated Press] (SAG)
PHMOV........ Phleum Mottle Virus [Plant pathology]
PHMP .... Primordial Hot Mantle Plume (PDAA)
PhmRes....... Pharmaceutical Resources, Inc. [Associated Press] (SAG)
PHMS .... Para-Hydroxymercuriphenylsulfonate [Organic chemistry]
PHMS .... Patrol Hydrofoil Missile Ship [Navy/NATO]
PHMS .... Polish Historical Military Society (EA)
PHMU .... Waimea-Kohala, Kamuela, Hawaii Island [Hawaii] [ICAO location identifier] (ICLI)
PhMV .... Phleum Mottle Virus
PHMV .... Physalis Mosaic Virus [Plant pathology]
PHMWO....... Prospect Hill Millimeter Wave Observatory [Waltham, MA] [Air Force]
PHMX .... PhyMatrix Corp. [NASDAQ symbol] (SAG)
PHN .... Norristown State Hospital, Norristown, PA [OCLC symbol] (OCLC)
PHN .... Passive Heymann Nephritis [Medicine] (DMAA)
PHN .... Phoenix Resource Companies, Inc. [AMEX symbol] (SAG)
PHN .... Phone (KSC)
PHN .... Port Huron [Michigan] [Airport symbol] (AD)
PHN .... Port Huron, MI [Location identifier FAA] (FAAL)
PHN .... Postherpetic Neuragia [Medicine]
PHN .... Postherpetic Neuralgia [Medicine] (DAVI)
PHN .... Public Health Network [Information service or system] (IID)
PHN .... Public Health Nurse
PHNA .... Barbers Point Naval Air Station, Oahu Island [Hawaii] [ICAO location identifier] (ICLI)
PHNC .... Pearl Harbor, Oahu Island [Hawaii] [ICAO location identifier] (ICLI)
PHNG .... Kaneohe Bay Marine Corps Air Station, Oahu Island [Hawaii] [ICAO location identifier] (ICLI)
PHNL .... Honolulu/International, Oahu Island [Hawaii] [ICAO location identifier] (ICLI)
PHNS .... Pearl Harbor Naval Shipyard
PHNX .... Phoenix Shannon Ltd. [NASDAQ symbol] (SAG)
PhnxRs .... Phoenix Resource Companies, Inc. [Associated Press] (SAG)
PhnxShn ..... Phoenix Shannon Ltd. [Associated Press] (SAG)
PhnxTc........ Phoenix Technologies Ltd. [Associated Press] (SAG)
PHNXY .... Phoenix Shannon plc ADR [NASDAQ symbol] (TTSB)
PHNY .... Lanai City, Lanai Island [Hawaii] [ICAO location identifier] (ICLI)
PHNY .... Pearl Harbor Navy Yard [Later, Pearl Harbor Naval Shipyard]
P-H NYETR... Prentice-Hall New York Estate Tax Reports [A publication] (DLA)
PHO .... Pediatric Hematology-Oncology [Medical specialty] (DHSM)
PHO .... Peoples Telephone Co. [AMEX symbol] (SAG)
PHO .... Phenolic Heavy Oil
PHO .... Philco Houston Operations (SAA)
PHO .... Phoenix Airways (Pfy) [South Africa] [FAA designator] (FAAC)
Pho .... Photographer [British military] (DMA)
PHO .... Physician-Hospital Organization [Information service or system] (HCT)
PHO .... Point Hope [Alaska] [Airport symbol] (OAG)
PHO .... Polk State School and Hospital, Polk, PA [OCLC symbol] (OCLC)
PHO .... Port Health Officer
PHO .... Potentially Hazardous Object
PHO .... Principal House Officer [Australia]
PHO .... Public Hazard Office [Environmental science] (COE)
PHO .... Public Hazards Office (NADA)
PHO .... Puu Honuaula [Hawaii] [Seismograph station code, US Geological Survey] (SEIS)
PHOAC........ Photographer's Mate, Combat Aircrewman [Navy rating Obsolete]
Phob........... Previous Highroller, on a Budget [Lifestyle classification]
PHOBOS ...... Photometric Instrument for Biological Optical Sections
PHOC.......... Photo Control [NASDAQ symbol] (TTSB)
PHOC.......... Photo Control Corp. [NASDAQ symbol] (NQ)
PHOC.......... Photocopy (MSA)
PHOCAS...... Photo Optical Cable Controlled Submersible (PDAA)
PHOCIS....... Photogrammetric Circulatory Survey (PDAA)
PHOD.......... Philadelphia Ordnance Depot [Military] (AAG)
PHODEC...... Photometric Determination of Equilibrium Constants [Computer science]
Phoe .... Phoenix [Constellation]
Phoen .... Phoenician (BJA)
Phoen .... Phoenissae [of Euripides] [Classical studies] (OCD)
PHOENIX..... Plasma Heating Obtained by Energetic Neutral Injection Experiment (IEEE)
PHOFEX....... Photofragment Excitation [Spectroscopy]
PHOFL .... Photoflash (AAG)
PHOG.......... Kahului, Maui Island [Hawaii] [ICAO location identifier] (ICLI)
PHOM.......... Photographer's Mate [Navy rating Obsolete]
PHON........... Phoenician
PHON........... Phonetics
PHON........... Phonogram (ROG)
PHON........... Phonograph (AAG)
PHONCON..... Telephone Conversation [or Conference]
PHONE........ Telephone (NTCM)
PHONET....... Phonetics (ROG)
Phonetel ..... Phonetel Technologies [Commercial firm Associated Press] (SAG)
P HONG ...... Ponchong [Tea trade] (ROG)
Phono......... Phonocardiogram [Cardiology] (DAVI)
PHONO .... Phonograph (MSA)
PHONOG...... Phonography
PHONOL ...... Phonology

phonol	Phonology (WDAA)
PHOPT	Pseudohypoparathyroidism [*Endocrinology*]
Phorm	Phormio [*of Terence*] [*Classical studies*] (OCD)
PHOS	Phosphate (KSC)
PHOS	Phosphorescent (KSC)
PHOS	Phosphorus [*Chemical symbol is P*]
PhosBro	Phosphor Bronze
PHOSCHEM	Phosphate Chemicals Export Association (EA)
PHOSI	Preliminary Handbook of Operations and Service Instructions
PHOSIAC	Photographically Stored Information Analog Comparator
PHosp	Post Hospital [*Army*]
PHOS-S	Phosphorus Spot [*Urine Test*] [*Chemistry*] (DAVI)
PHOST	Poly(hydroxystyrene) [*Organic chemistry*]
Phot	Photius [*Ninth century AD*] [*Classical studies*] (OCD)
PHOT	Photograph
PHOT	Photographer [*Navy rating British*]
PHOTABS	Photographic Abstracts [*Pergamon*] [*Database*]
PHOTAC	Phototypesetting and Composing [*AT & T*]
Photcm	Photocomm, Inc. [*Associated Press*] (SAG)
PHOTINT	Photographic Intelligence [*Military*]
photmur	Photo Mural (VRA)
photo	Photograph (VRA)
PHOTO	Photograph (AAG)
Photo	Photogravure [*Philately*]
PhotoC	Photo-Control Corp. [*Associated Press*] (SAG)
Photochem Photobiol	Photochemistry and Photobiology (MEC)
PHOTOG	Photographic
PHOTOGR	Photographer
PHOTOGR	Photography
PHOTOLITH	Photolithographic
PHOTOM	Photometry
photomon	Photomontage (VRA)
Photon	Photon Dynamics, Inc. [*Associated Press*] (SAG)
PHOTOTRIGULANT	Photographic Triangulation Group, Atlantic [*Military*] (DNAB)
PHOTOTRIGUPAC	Photographic Triangulation Group, Pacific [*Military*] (DNAB)
PhotrIn	Photronic Labs [*Associated Press*] (SAG)
PHOTRIPART	Photo Triangulation Party [*Military*]
PHOTRON	Photographic Squadron [*Navy*]
PHOTUB	Phototube (KSC)
PHO/TY	Photo Type [*Deltiology*]
PHP	Pacific Hawaiian Products Co. [*Later, PHP Co.*]
PHP	Packing-House Products [*Food industry*]
PHP	Parents Helping Parents [*An association*] (EA)
PHP	Parts, Hybrids, and Packaging (MCD)
PHP	Passive Hyperpolarizing Potential [*Neurochemistry*]
PHP	Payload Handling Panel [*NASA*] (MCD)
PHP	Pennhurst State School and Hospital, Spring City, PA [*OCLC symbol*] (OCLC)
PHP	Personal Handy Phone [*Telecommunications*]
PHP	Petroleum Heat & Power (EFIS)
PHP	Philip, SD [*Location identifier FAA*] (FAAL)
PHP	Phillip Resources, Inc. [*Vancouver Stock Exchange symbol*]
PHP	Philosophia Patrum [*A publication*] (BJA)
PHP	PHP Healthcare Corp. [*Associated Press*] (SAG)
PHP	Physician's Health Plan
PHP	Pinane Hydroperoxide [*Organic chemistry*]
PHP	Planetary Horizon Platform [*Aerospace*]
PHP	Post-Heparin Phospholipase [*Medicine*] (MAE)
PHP	Postheparin Plasma (DAVI)
PHP	Post-Hostilities Planning Subcommittee of the Chiefs of Staff Committee [*World War II*]
PHP	Pounds per Horsepower
PHP	Prentice Hall Press [*Publisher*]
PHP	Prepaid Health Plan [*Insurance*]
PHP	Presbyterian Hunger Program (EA)
PHP	Primary Hyperparathyroidism (MAE)
PHP	Propeller Horsepower
PHP	Pseudohyperbolic Particle [*Astrophysics*]
PHP	Pseudohypoparathyroidism [*Endocrinology*]
PHP	Pump Horsepower
PHPA	Pacific Herring Packers Association (EA)
PHPA	Partially-Hydrolyzed Polyacrylamide [*Well drilling technology*]
PHPC	Post-Hostilities Planning Committee [*Navy World War II*]
PHPG	Poly(hydroxypropylglutamine) [*Organic chemistry*]
PHPHB	P-heptyl-p-hydroxy Benzoate [*A preservative used in the making of American and British beer*]
PHPK	Probability of Hit to Probability of Kill (INF)
PHPL	Parallel Hardware Processing Language [*1977*] [*Computer science*] (CSR)
PHPO	Private Health Plan Option [*Medicare*] (GFGA)
PHPS	Post-Hostilities Planning Staff [*World War II*]
PHPT	Portable High-Potential Tester
PHPT	Primary Hyperparathyroidism
pHPT	Primary Hyperparathyroidism [*Medicine*] (STED)
PHPT	Pseudohypoparathyroidism [*Medicine*] (DB)
PHPV	Persistent Hyperplastic Primary Vitreous [*Ophthalmology*]
PHQ	Personnel History Questionnaire (MHDB)
PHQ	Phenylhydroquinone [*Organic chemistry*]
PHQ	Postal Headquarters [*British*]
PHR	Pacific Harbour [*Fiji*] [*Airport symbol*] (OAG)
PHR	Pacific Historical Review [*A publication*] (BRI)
PHR	Parts per Hundred of Rubber [*Chemical technology*]
PHR	Payload Hazardous Report (NASA)
PHR	Peak Heart Rate [*Cardiology*]
PHR	Peak Height Ratio

PHR	Phorbol [*Organic chemistry*]
PHR	Photographic Reconnaissance
PHR	Photoreactivity (DMAA)
PHR	Phrase
Phr	Phrenomena: an Annual Review [*A publication*] (APTA)
PHR	Physical Record [*Computer science*]
PHR	Physicians for Human Rights (EA)
PHR	Pound-Force per Hour (MCD)
PHR	Pounds per Hour (AAG)
PHR	Preheater (KSC)
PHR	Process Hazardous Review [*Environmental science*]
PHR	Process Heat Reactor Program [*Nuclear Regulatory Commission*]
PHR	Public Health Reports [*A publication*]
PHR	Pulse-Height Resolution [*By photomultiplier tubes*]
PHR	Retreat State Hospital, Hunlock Creek, PA [*OCLC symbol*] (OCLC)
PHRACT	Print-Handicapped Radio, Australian Capital Territory
PHRC	Palestine Human Rights Campaign (EA)
PHRED	Public Health Risk Evaluation Data [*Environmental Safety*]
PHREN	Phrenology
Ph Rep	Philadelphia Reports [*Pennsylvania*] [*A publication*] (DLA)
PHRF	Performance Handicap Racing Fleet [*Boating*]
PHRF	Performance Handicap Racing Formula [*Sailing*]
PHRG	Park Home Residents Guild [*British*] (DBA)
PHRG	Parliamentary Human Rights Group (EAIO)
PHRHD	Pump, Hydraulic Ram, Hand-Driven (MSA)
PHRI	Public Health Research Institute (NADA)
PHRI	Public Health Research Institute of the City of New York, Inc. [*Research center*] (RCD)
PHRIC	Palestine Human Rights Information Center (EA)
PHRK	Power and Heat Rejection Kit [*NASA*]
PhRMA	Pharmaceutical Research and Manufacturers of America (NTPA)
Phrmhse	Pharmhouse Corp. [*Associated Press*] (SAG)
PhrmMkt	Pharmaceutical Marketing Services, Inc. [*Associated Press*] (SAG)
PHRMST	Pharmacist
PHRR	Parenchymal Hepatic Resection Rate [*Medicine*]
PHRS	Portable Heat Rejection System
PHRT	Procarbazine, Hydroxyurea, Radiotherapy Protocol (DAVI)
PHRW	Preferred Hotels and Resorts Worldwide (NTPA)
PHS	Packaging, Handling, and Storage (MCD)
PHS	Pallottine House of Studies
PHS	Pan Head Steel (IAA)
PHS	Partial Hospitalization Program (STED)
PHS	Paternal Half Sister (OA)
PHS	Pathological Human Serum [*Serology*]
PHS	Patient-Heated Serum (STED)
PHS	Payload Handling Station [*NASA*] (MCD)
PHS	Personal Handyphone System [*Telecommunications*]
PHS	Personal Health Survey [*Psychology*]
PHS	Personal Hygiene Subsystem [*NASA*] (KSC)
PHS	Phenylalanine Hydroxylase Stimulator (STED)
PhS	Philosophical Society [*British*] (DBA)
PHS	Phitsanuloke [*Thailand*] [*Airport symbol*] (OAG)
PHS	Photographic Historical Society (EA)
PHS	Physicians Health Services
PHS	Physicians' Health Study
PHS	Police History Society [*British*] (DBA)
PHS	Polyhydroxystyrene [*Also, PHOST*] [*Organic chemistry*]
PHS	Pooled Human Serum [*Hematology*] (DMAA)
PHS	Postal History Society (EA)
PHS	Postcard History Society (EA)
PHS	Posthypnotic Suggestion [*Psychology*]
PHS	Precision Hover Sensor (PDAA)
PHS	Prepared Hessian Surfacing [*Air Force*]
PHS	Presbyterian Historical Society (EA)
PHS	Price History System (MCD)
PHS	Printing Historical Society [*British*]
PHS	Printing House Square (DGA)
PHS	Probability of Having a Space
PHS	Progressive Hongkong Society [*Political party*]
PHS	Prostaglandin H Synthase [*An enzyme*] (GNE)
PHS	Public Health Service [*Department of Health and Human Services*]
PHS	Pumped Hydro Storage [*Power source*]
PHS	Somerset State Hospital, Somerset, PA [*OCLC symbol*] (OCLC)
PHSA	Pearl Harbor Survivors Association (EA)
PHSA	Polyhydroxystearic Acid [*Organic chemistry*]
PHSA	Polymerized Human Serum Albumin [*Biochemistry*]
PHSA	Provincial Hospital Services Association [*British*] (DBA)
PHSA	Public Health Service Act (GFGA)
PHS & T	Packaging, Handling, Storage, and Transportation [*Shipping*]
PhSAP	Physical Service Access Point [*Telecommunications*] (OSI)
PHSAR	Public Health Service Acquisition Regulations [*Department of Health and Human Services*] (GFGA)
PHSBG	Preventive Health Services Block Grant [*Public human service program*] (PHSD)
PHSC	Pluripotent Hematopoietic Stem Cells [*Cytology*]
PHSC	Postal History Society of Canada (EA)
PHSC	Private Hospital Supplementary Charges (ADA)
PHSCS	Pier-Harris Self-Concept Scale (EDAC)
PHSE	Pharmhouse Corp. [*NASDAQ symbol*] (SAG)
PHSE	Phase [*Computer science*]
PHSE	Piedmont Health Survey of the Elderly [*Department of Health and Human Services*] (GFGA)
PHSF	Bradshaw Field, Hawaii Island [*Hawaii*] [*ICAO location identifier*] (ICLI)
PHSF	Payload Hazardous Servicing Facility [*NASA*] (NAKS)

PHSG .... Postal History Study Group (EA)
PHSI .... Plant Health and Seeds Inspectorate [*Ministry of Agriculture, Fisheries, and Food*] [*British*]
PHSIG .... Pan Hellenic Society Inventors of Greece in USA [*Defunct*] (EA)
PHSKX .... Phoenix Aggressive Growth Cl.A [*Mutual fund ticker symbol*] (SG)
PHSNZ .... Postal History Society of New Zealand [*Auckland*] (EA)
PHSO .... Partially Hydrogenated Soybean Oil [*Cooking fat*]
PHSO .... Postal History Society of Ontario [*Later, PHSC*] (EA)
PHSOC .... Photographical Historical Society of Canada
P-H Soc Sec Taxes... Social Security Taxes (Prentice-Hall, Inc.) [*A publication*] (DLA)
PHS of A..... Postal History Society of the Americas (EA)
PHSP .... Phase-Splitter (MSA)
PHSP .... Public Health Service Publications
PHSPS .... Preservation, Handling, Storage, Packaging, and Shipping (NRCH)
PHSS .... Physician Support Systems [*NASDAQ symbol*] (TTSB)
PHSS .... Physician Support Systems, Inc. [*NASDAQ symbol*] (SAG)
PHST .... Packaging, Handling, Storage, and Transportation [*Shipping*]
Ph St Tr..... Phillipps' State Trials [*A publication*] (DLA)
PHSV .... Physicians Health Services, Inc. [*NASDAQ symbol*] (SAG)
PHSV .... Physicians Health Svcs'A' [*NASDAQ symbol*] (TTSB)
PHSY .... PacifiCare Health Systems, Inc. [*Cypress, CA*] [*NASDAQ symbol*] (NQ)
PHSYA .... PacifiCare Health Sys'A' [*NASDAQ symbol*] (TTSB)
PHT .... Managed High Yield Fd [*NYSE symbol*] (TTSB)
PHT .... PaineWebber Premium High Income [*NYSE symbol*] (SPSG)
PHT .... Paired Hands Test [*Education*] (EDAC)
PHT .... Paris, TN [*Location identifier FAA*] (FAAL)
PHT .... Passive Hemagglutination Technique [*Immunology*]
PHT .... Peak Hour Traffic (PA)
PHT .... Peak Hour Trips (PA)
PHT .... Peroxide Hemolysis Test [*Medicine*] (STED)
PHT .... Phenylhydantoin [*Pharmacology*] (CPH)
PhT .... [*The*] Phoenix and the Turtle [*Shakespearean work*]
pht .... Photographer [*MARC relator code*] [*Library of Congress*] (LCCP)
PHT .... Phototube
Pht .... Phthaloyl [*Also, Phth*] [*Organic chemistry*]
PHT .... Physical Therapy Technician [*Navy*]
PHT .... Pitch, Hit, and Throw [*Youth competition sponsored by professional baseball*]
PHT .... Poly-Hexylthiophene [*Organic chemistry*]
PHT .... Portal Hypertension [*Medicine*]
PHT .... Preheat
PHT .... Primary Hyperthyroidism [*Medicine*] (STED)
PHT .... Pulmonary Hypertension [*Cardiology*] (CPH)
PHT .... Putting Hubby Through [*College "degree" earned by some wives*]
PHT .... Pyridohomotropane [*Organic chemistry*]
PHT .... Torrance State Hospital, Torrance, PA [*OCLC symbol*] (OCLC)
PHTab .... President's Hundred Tab [*Military decoration*] (AABC)
PHTAT .... Para-Hydroxytriamterene [*Biochemistry*]
PHTATS ...... Para-Hydroxytriamterene Sulfate [*Biochemistry*]
P-H Tax ...... Federal Taxes (Prentice-Hall, Inc.) [*A publication*] (DLA)
P H Tax Ct Mem... Tax Court Memorandum Decisions (Prentice-Hall, Inc.) [*A publication*] (DLA)
P-H Tax Ct Rep & Mem Dec... Tax Court Reported and Memorandum Decisions (Prentice-Hall, Inc.) [*A publication*] (DLA)
PHTBX .... Phoenix Tax Exempt Bond [*Mutual fund ticker symbol*] (SG)
PHTC .... Pneumatic Hydraulic Test Console (KSC)
PHTC .... Pulse Height to Time Converter (OA)
PhTD .... Physical Therapy Doctor
PHTF .... Pearl Harbor Training Facility [*Navy*]
Phth .... Phthaloyl [*Also, Pht*] [*Organic chemistry*]
PHTN .... Photon Dynamics [*NASDAQ symbol*] (TTSB)
PHTN .... Photon Dynamics, Inc. [*NASDAQ symbol*] (SAG)
PHTN .... Public Health Training Network
PHTO .... Hilo/General Lyman Field, Hawaii Island [*Hawaii*] [*ICAO location identifier*] (ICLI)
PHTS .... Primary Heat Transport System [*Nuclear energy*] (NRCH)
PHTS .... Psychiatric Home Treatment Service (DAVI)
PHU .... Philadelphia Ukrainian [*Diocesan abbreviation*] [*Pennsylvania*] (TOCD)
PHU .... Pressure, Hydraulic Unit
PHuJ .... Juniata College, Huntingdon, PA [*Library symbol Library of Congress*] (LCLS)
P-H Unrep Tr Cas... Prentice-Hall Unreported Trust Cases [*A publication*] (DLA)
Phus Plu...... Philippus Puldericus [*Authority cited in pre-1607 legal work*] (DSA)
PHV .... Pahlavi [*Iran*] [*Airport symbol*] (AD)
PHV .... Parallel Hybrid Vehicle
PHV .... Paramount Home Video
PHV .... Peak Height Velocity (DMAA)
PHV .... Persistent Hypertrophic Vitreous [*Ophthalmology*] (DAVI)
PHV .... Phase Velocity
PHV .... Pro Haec Vice [*For This Turn*] [*Latin*] (ROG)
PHV .... Prospect Hill Virus [*Medicine*] (DMAA)
PHV .... Wernersville State Hospital, Wernersville, PA [*OCLC symbol*] (OCLC)
PHVA .... Plasma Homovanillic Acid [*Biochemistry*]
PHVPS .... Primary High-Voltage Power Supply
PHW .... Pemberton Houston Willoughby Investment Corp. [*Toronto Stock Exchange symbol Vancouver Stock Exchange symbol*]
PHW .... Phalaborwa [*South Africa*] [*Airport symbol*] (OAG)
PHW .... Philatelic Hobbies for the Wounded (EA)
PHW .... Prime Hard Wheat
PHW .... Warren State Hospital, Warren, PA [*OCLC symbol*] (OCLC)
PHWA .... Professional Hockey Writers' Association (EA)
PHWA .... Protestant Health and Welfare Assembly [*Later, PHHSA*] (EA)

PHWC .... Polish Helsinki Watch Committee (EAIO)
PHWFJD ...... Partners in Harmony, World Family of John Denver (EA)
PHWR .... Hickam United States Air Force Automatic Weather Switch, Oahu Island [*Hawaii*] [*ICAO location identifier*] (ICLI)
PHWR .... Pressurized Heavy Water-Moderated and Cooled Reactor [*Nuclear energy*] (IAA)
PHWR .... Pressurized Heavy Water Reactor [*Nuclear energy*]
PHX .... Partial Hepectomy [*Medicine*]
PHx .... Past History [*Medicine*] (MAE)
Phx .... Pharynx [*Anatomy*] (DAVI)
PHX .... Phoenix [*Arizona*] [*Airport symbol*] (OAG)
PHX .... Phoenix 2000 Airtaxi Ltd. [*Hungary ICAO designator*] (FAAC)
PHX .... Phoenix Network [*AMEX symbol*] (TTSB)
PHX .... Phoenix Network, Inc. [*AMEX symbol*] (SPSG)
PHX .... Woodville State Hospital, Carnegie, PA [*OCLC symbol*] (OCLC)
PhxDffP...... Phoenix Duf & Phelps Corp. [*Associated Press*] (SAG)
PhxDfP....... Phoenix Duff & Phelps Corp. [*Associated Press*] (SAG)
PhxDuffP..... Phoenix Duff & Phelps Corp. [*Associated Press*] (SAG)
PhxGold...... Phoenix Gold International, Inc. [*Associated Press*] (SAG)
PhxNet....... Phoenix Network, Inc. [*Associated Press*] (SAG)
PHY .... C. Howard Marcy State Hospital, Pittsburgh, PA [*OCLC symbol*] (OCLC)
PHY .... Norman, OK [*Location identifier FAA*] (FAAL)
PHY .... Pharyngitis
Phy .... Physalaemin [*Biochemistry*]
PHY .... Physical
PHY .... Physical Layer (AAEL)
PHY .... Physician
PHY .... Physics
PHY .... Physiology (DMAA)
PHY .... Phytohemagglutinin [*Immunology*] (AAMN)
PHY .... Prospect Street High Income Portfolio, Inc. [*NYSE symbol*] (SPSG)
PHY .... Prospect Street Hi Income [*NYSE symbol*] (TTSB)
PHYC .... PhyCor, Inc. [*NASDAQ symbol*] (SPSG)
PHYCOM ...... Physicians Communications Service [*Fisher-Stevens, Inc.*] [*Merged into BRS/COLLEAGUE*]
PhyCor........ PhyCor, Inc. [*Associated Press*] (SAG)
PhyCpt....... Physicians Computer Network [*Associated Press*] (SAG)
PHYCUS...... Physical Custody [*of Records*] (MHDB)
PHY ED....... Physical Education (WGA)
PHYL .... Physiological
PHYLIP .... Phylogeny Inference Package [*Botany*]
PHYLIS .... Physics Online Information System [*Computer science*] (PDAA)
PHYM .... Putnam High Yield Municipal Trust [*Associated Press*] (SAG)
PhyMatr...... PhyMatrix Corp. [*Associated Press*] (SAG)
PHYN .... Physician Reliance Network [*NASDAQ symbol*] (TTSB)
PHYN .... Physician Reliance Network, Inc. [*NASDAQ symbol*] (SAG)
PHYS .... Physical (AFM)
PHYS .... Physician
Phys .... Physician (CMD)
PHYS .... Physicist [*or Physics*] (ADA)
Phys .... Physics (DD)
PHYS .... Physio-Control Intl [*NASDAQ symbol*] (TTSB)
PhyS .... Physiological Saline [*Pharmacology*] (DAVI)
PHYS .... Physiology
PhySale...... Physician Sales & Service, Inc. [*Associated Press*] (SAG)
PHYSB .... PacifiCare Health Sys'B' [*NASDAQ symbol*] (TTSB)
PHYSBE ...... Physiological Simulation Benchmark Experiment
Phys Chem... Physiological Chemistry and Physics (MEC)
PHYSCL ...... Physical
PhysCpA...... Physician Corp. of America [*Associated Press*] (SAG)
Phys Dis .... Physical Disability (CPH)
PHYSEC ...... Physical Security (MCD)
PHYS ED...... Physical Education
Phys Eng .... Physical Engineer
PHYSEXAM... Physical Examination
Phys Hndcpd... Physically Handicapped (AL)
PhysicHlt.... Physicians Health Services, Inc. [*Associated Press*] (SAG)
Physik Chem... Physikalisch-Chemische Trenn- und Messmethoden (MEC)
PhysIn .... Physicians Insurance Co. of Ohio [*Associated Press*] (SAG)
Physio .... Physiology (DAVI)
PHYSIO....... Physiotherapy [*Medicine*]
physio........ Physiotherapy [*Medicine*] (DMAA)
PHYSIOG ..... Physiognomy [*Slang*] (DSUE)
PHYSIOG ..... Physiographic
PHYSIOL..... Physiographic
PHYSIOL..... Physiological (MSA)
PHYSIOL..... Physiology (ROG)
PHYSL .... Physiological (AFM)
Phys Med ... Physical Medicine (CPH)
Physmet ..... Physiometrix, Inc. [*Associated Press*] (SAG)
PHYSN .... Physician
PHYSOG ...... Physiognomy [*Slang*] (DSUE)
PhysPRC..... Physician's Payment Review Commission (HCT)
PHYSQUAL... Physical Disqualification [*Military*] (DNAB)
PhysRel...... Physician Reliance Network, Inc. [*Associated Press*] (SAG)
Phys Rev .... Physiological Review (MEC)
Phys Rev A... Physical Review A (MEC)
Phys Rev C.. Physical Review C: Nuclear Physics (MEC)
Phys Rev Lett... Physical Review Letters (MEC)
PhysRs .... Physician Resources Group, Inc. [*Associated Press*] (SAG)
PHYS SC ..... Physical Science (WDAA)
PhysSup...... Physician Support Systems, Inc. [*Associated Press*] (SAG)
PHYST .... Physicist
PHYSTER..... Physical Therapy (AABC)
Phys Ther .... Physical Therapist (DMAA)

Phys Today...	Physics Today [*A publication*] (BRI)
PHYSY	Physiology
Phytogeog ...	Phytogeography (BARN)
PHYTOPATH...	Phytopathology
PHYX............	Physiometrix, Inc. [*NASDAQ symbol*] (SAG)
PHZ..............	Ashland State General Hospital, Ashland, PA [*OCLC symbol*] (OCLC)
PHZ..............	Phenylhydrazine (LDT)
PHZH	Honolulu Air Traffic Control Center [*Hawaii*] [*ICAO location identifier*] (ICLI)
pI.................	Isoelectric Point (MAE)
PI..................	Pacing Impulse [*Cardiology*] (DAVI)
PI..................	Pacing Item (MCD)
PI..................	Package Insert [*Instructional leaflet distributed with certain prescription drugs*] [*Also, PPI*]
PI..................	Packaging Institute [*Later, PI/USA*] (EA)
PI..................	Paducah & Illinois Railroad [*AAR code*]
PI..................	Palmaris Longus (DMAA)
PI..................	Pancreatic Insufficiency [*Gastroenterology*]
PI..................	Pancreatic Lipase [*Medicine*] (DMAA)
PI..................	Pandectae (Pisanae) Florentinae [*A publication*] (DSA)
PI..................	Panel Input
PI..................	Pansophic Institute [*Defunct*] (EA)
PI..................	Pantera International (EA)
PI..................	Paper Insulated
PI..................	Paracel Islands [*ANSI two-letter standard code*] (CNC)
PI..................	Parallel Importation (DB)
PI..................	Parallel Input [*Computer science*] (BUR)
PI..................	Parameter Identifier [*Computer science*] (TNIG)
PI..................	Parametric Industry (IAA)
PI..................	Paranoid Ideation (DAVI)
PI..................	Parental Generation [*Medicine*] (DMAA)
PI..................	Parental Investment [*Biology*]
PI..................	Parity Index [*EEO*]
PI..................	Particle Integration (CAAL)
PI..................	Partido Independiente [*Independent Party*] [*Costa Rica*] [*Political party*]
PI..................	Partido Intransigente [*Intransigent Party*] [*Argentina Political party*] (PD)
PI..................	Parti Independantiste [*Quebec*]
PI..................	Passeport International [*International Passport*] [*An association France*] (EAIO)
PI..................	Pathfinder International (EA)
PI..................	Patient's Interests [*Medicine*]
PI..................	Patrol Inspector [*Immigration and Naturalization Service*]
PI..................	Payload Interrogator [*NASA*] (MCD)
PI..................	Payload Interrogator [*NASA*] (NAKS)
PI..................	Pen and Ink (NAKS)
PI..................	Pen and Ink
PI..................	Penetration Index (IAA)
PI..................	Pepsin Inhibitor (OA)
PI..................	Peptide Inhibitor (DB)
PI..................	Perceptions, Inc. (EA)
PI..................	Perceptual Isolation
PI..................	Perfect Initials [*Philately*]
PI..................	Performance Improvement
PI..................	Performance Index
PI..................	Performance Indicator (MCD)
PI..................	Performance Intensity (MAE)
PI..................	Perinatal Injury [*Neonatology*] (DAVI)
pi..................	Per Inquiry (WDMC)
PI..................	Per Inquiry [*Advertising*]
PI..................	Periodical Index Term (NITA)
PI..................	Periodicals Institute (EA)
PI..................	Periodic Inspection [*Military*] (AFM)
PI..................	Peripheral Interface [*Computer science*] (PCM)
pi..................	Peripheral Iridectomy [*Medicine*]
PI..................	Perlite Institute (EA)
PI..................	Permaculture International [*Australia*]
PI..................	Permeability Index [*Clinical chemistry*]
PI..................	Personal Identification
PI..................	Personal Income
PI..................	Personal Injury [*Insurance*]
PI..................	Personal Injury Accident [*British police term*]
PI..................	Personal Investment [*A publication*] (ADA)
PI..................	Personality Inventory [*Psychology*]
PI..................	Petroleum Information Corp. (IID)
PI..................	Petrol Injection [*British*]
PI..................	Pharmacopoeia Internationalis [*International Pharmacopoeia*]
PI..................	Phase-In
PI..................	Phenanthroimidazole [*Organic chemistry*]
PI..................	Phenyl Isocyanate [*Organic chemistry*]
PI..................	Phosphate, Inorganic [*Chemistry*]
PI..................	Phosphatidylinositol [*Also, PtdIns*] [*Biochemistry*]
P-I...............	Photogrammetric Instrumentation (AAG)
PI..................	Photographic Interpreter
PI..................	Photo International [*Defunct*] (EAIO)
PI..................	Photointerpretation [*or Photointerpreter*]
PI..................	Photointerpreter (IAA)
PI..................	Photoionization [*Physical chemistry*]
PI..................	Physical Inventory (NRCH)
PI..................	Physically Impaired
PI..................	Physics International
PI..................	Piaster [*Monetary unit*] [*Spain, Republic of Vietnam, and some Middle Eastern countries*]
pi..................	Pica [*Typesetting*] [*Also called pie*] (WDMC)
PI..................	Piedmont Aviation, Inc. [*ICAO designator*] (OAG)
PI..................	Pigeon Trainer [*Navy*]
PI..................	Pig Iron
PI..................	Pillius Medicinensis [*Flourished, 1165-1207*] [*Authority cited in pre-1607 legal work*] (DSA)
PI..................	Pilot International (EA)
PI..................	Pilot Item (MCD)
PI..................	Pilotless Intercepter [*Air Force*]
PI..................	Pineal Body (DB)
PI..................	Pinedale [*Wyoming*] [*Seismograph station code, US Geological Survey Closed*] (SEIS)
PI..................	Pink (ROG)
PI..................	Pipe [*Freight*]
PI..................	Plant Introduction [*Botany*]
PI..................	Plaque Index [*Dentistry*]
PI..................	Plasma Iron [*Hematology*]
PI..................	Plastics Institute (NADA)
PI..................	Plastochron Index [*Botany*]
PI..................	Plug-In Instrument (IAA)
PI..................	Pneumatosis Intestinalis [*Medicine*]
PI..................	Point Initiating
PI..................	Point Insulating
PI..................	Point of Impact (AFM)
PI..................	Point of Interception [*Navigation*]
PI..................	Point of Intersection
PI..................	Poison Ivy [*Campers' slang*]
PI..................	Polyimide [*Organic chemistry*]
PI..................	Polyisoprene [*Organic chemistry*]
PI..................	Polymer International (NS), Inc. [*Toronto Stock Exchange symbol*]
PI..................	Pompeiiana, Inc. (EA)
PI..................	Ponderal Index [*Measurement*] (DAVI)
PI..................	Poni Iussit [*Ordered to Be Placed*] [*Latin*]
PI..................	Popcorn Institute (EA)
PI..................	Population Institute (EA)
PI..................	Porch Index [*Psychiatry*] (DAVI)
PI..................	Portfolio Insurance [*Finance*]
PI..................	Position Indicator [*Army*]
PI..................	Positive Identification Feature
PI..................	Positive Intelligence (LAIN)
PI..................	Positive Interlace [*Television*]
PI..................	Postal Instruction (IAA)
PI..................	Postimpressionist Movement [*Art*]
PI..................	Postinfection [*Medicine*] (DB)
PI..................	Postinoculation [*Medicine*]
PI..................	Postischemic [*Medicine*]
PI..................	Potash Institute [*Later, PPI*] (EA)
PI..................	Potomac Institute [*Defunct*] (EA)
PI..................	Power Indicator (IAA)
PI..................	Power Injection
PI..................	Power Input
PI..................	Power Interlock (IAA)
PI..................	Precision Instrument (NVT)
PI..................	Predicted Impact (MCD)
PI..................	Pregnancy Induced [*Gynecology*]
PI..................	Preinduction [*Medicine*]
PI..................	Preliminary Incubation (OA)
PI..................	Preliminary Injunction [*Legal term*] (HGAA)
PI..................	Preliminary Inspection (MCD)
PI..................	Preliminary Investigation (NASA)
PI..................	Preliminary Investigation (NAKS)
PI..................	Preliminary Issue
PI..................	Premdor, Inc. [*NYSE symbol*] (SPSG)
PI..................	Preparatory Interval [*Psychometrics*]
PI..................	Prepositioned Instruction [*DoD*]
PI..................	Present Illness [*Medicine*]
PI..................	Pressure Indicator [*Nuclear energy*]
PI..................	Pressure of Inspiration [*Medicine*]
PI..................	Primacord Interstage
PI..................	Primary Infarction [*Medicine*]
PI..................	Primary Input (IAA)
PI..................	Prime Interest Rate [*Banking*]
PI..................	Principal Investigator (MCD)
PI..................	Principal Investigator (NAKS)
PI..................	Printer [*Navy*]
PI..................	Print Image (IAA)
PI..................	Printing Impressions [*A publication*] (DGA)
PI..................	Priority Interrupt (IEEE)
PI..................	Private Institution [*British*]
PI..................	Private Investigator
PI..................	Priviledged Information (SAA)
PI..................	Proactive Inhibition [*Psychology*]
PI..................	Proactive Interference (EDAC)
PI..................	Problem Input (SAA)
PI..................	Process Image (NITA)
PI..................	Process Instrumentation [*Nuclear energy*] (NRCH)
PI..................	Processor Interface [*Computer science*] (IAA)
PI..................	Procurement Inspection (MCD)
PI..................	Procurement Item (NASA)
PI..................	Prodigy Internet
PI..................	Product Improvement (MCD)
P/I................	Production Illustration (MSA)
PI..................	Production Interval
PI..................	Productivity Index (IEEE)
PI..................	Professional Indemnity [*Insurance*]
pi..................	Professional Indemnity [*Insurance*] (ODBW)

PI	Program Indicator (IEEE)
PI	Program Information
PI	Program Innovations (ADA)
PI	Program Instruction [Computer science] (BUR)
PI	Program Integrator [Military] (RDA)
PI	Program Interrupt
PI	Program Introduction
PI	Program Introduction (NAKS)
PI	Program Issuances [Assistance Payments Administration, HEW]
PI	Programmed Information [Computer science]
PI	Programmed Instruction
PI	Programmed Introduction (MCD)
PI	Program of Instrumentation (MUGU)
PI	Project Inform (EA)
PI	Project Intrex [Massachusetts Institute of Technology] (EA)
PI	Prolactin Inhibitor [Endocrinology]
PI	Property Index [British police term]
PI	Propidium Iodide [Fluorescent dye]
PI	Proportional Integral (AAEL)
PI	Proportional-Plus Integral [Digital control]
PI	Proprietary Information (SAA)
PI	Propyl Isome (OA)
PI	Protamine Insulin
PI	Protease Inhibitor
PI	Proteinase Inhibitor [Biochemistry]
PI	Protocol Internationale
PI	Psychiatric Institute
PI	Psychosynthesis Institute (EA)
PI	Publication Instructions
PI	Public Information
PI	Puebla Institute (EA)
PI	Pulmonary Incompetence [Medicine]
PI	Pulmonary Indices [Medicine]
PI	Pulmonary Infarction [Medicine]
PI	Pulmonary Intervertebral Disc [Medicine]
PI	Pulse Induction (ADA)
PI	Purge Isolation [Nuclear energy] (NRCH)
PI	Pyritization Index [Geoscience]
PI	Sunshine Airlines [Airline code] [Australia]
PI1	State Correctional Institute at Camp Hill, Camp Hill, PA [OCLC symbol] (OCLC)
PI2	State Correctional Institute at Dallas, Dallas, PA [OCLC symbol] (OCLC)
PI3	State Correctional Institute at Grateford, Grateford, PA [OCLC symbol] (OCLC)
PI4	State Correctional Institute at Huntingdon, Huntingdon, PA [OCLC symbol] (OCLC)
PI5	State Correctional Institute at Muncy, Muncy, PA [OCLC symbol] (OCLC)
PI6	State Correctional Institute at Pittsburgh, Pittsburgh, PA [OCLC symbol] (OCLC)
PI7	State Regional Correctional Facility, Greensburg, PA [OCLC symbol] (OCLC)
PIA	Municipal Prem Income Tr [NYSE symbol] (TTSB)
PIA	Municipal Premium Income Trust [Formerly, Allstate Municipal Premium Fund] [NYSE symbol] (SPSG)
PIA	National Association of Professional Insurance Agents (NTPA)
PIA	Pacific Islands Association (EA)
PIA	Packaged Ice Association (EA)
PIA	Paid in Advance (WDMC)
PIA	Pakistan International Airlines Corp. [ICAO designator] (FAAC)
PIA	Panel-Information-Air Operation
PIA	Parapsychology Institute of America (EA)
PIA	Particle Impact Analyzer [Astrophysics]
PIA	Partitioning Industry Association [British] (DBA)
PIA	Passive Immunological Agglutination
PIA	Payload Interface Adapter [NASA] (SSD)
PIA	Peoria [Illinois] [Airport symbol] (OAG)
PIA	Perfumery Importers Association [Defunct] (EA)
PIA	Peripheral Interface Adapter [Computer science]
PIA	Personal Information Appliance [Telecommunications] (PCM)
PIA	Personal Investment Authority [British] (ECON)
PIA	Personnel Inventory Analysis [Army]
PIA	Perspective Inversion Algorithm [Computer science]
PIA	Petervin Information Associates [Also, an information service or system] (IID)
PIA	Petroleum Incentives Administration [Canada]
PIA	Phenylisopropyladenosine [Biochemistry]
PIA	Phosphoroimmunoassays
PIA	Photoelectric Intravenous Angiography [Medicine] (DMAA)
PIA	Photographic Importers Association [British] (BI)
PIA	Piano [Softly] [Music]
PIA	Pilots International Association (EA)
PIA	Pitten [Austria] [Seismograph station code, US Geological Survey] (SEIS)
PIA	Place Indicator in Accumulators (SAA)
PIA	Plasma Insulin Activity [Clinical chemistry]
PIA	Plastics Industries Association [Ireland]
PIA	Plastics Institute of America (EA)
PIA	Plug-In Amplifier
PIA	Polycultural Institution of America
PIA	Positive Ion Accelerator
PIA	Positron Intensity Accumulator (MCD)
PIA	Postal Inspectors' Association [A union] [British]
PIA	Potentiometric Immunoassay [Clinical chemistry]

PIA	Predominant Interest Agency (AAGC)
PIA	Preferential Trade Area (EBF)
PIA	Preinfarction Angina [Cardiology] (DMAA)
PIA	Pre-Inspection Acceptance (SAA)
PIA	Preinstallation Acceptance
PIA	Pressure Indicating Alarm [Engineering]
PIA	Primary Inspection Agency [Federal Manufactured Housing Construction and Safety Standards] [Department of Housing and Urban Development] (GFGA)
PIA	Primary Insurance Account [Social Security Administration] (OICC)
PIA	Primary Insurance Amount
PIA	Principal Industry Activity [IRS]
PIA	Printing Industries of America (EA)
PIA	Production Inventory Analysis (AAG)
PIA	Professional Insurance Agents [Alexandria, VA] (EA)
PIA	Program Initiation Agreement (SSD)
PIA	Programmable Interconnect Array [Computer science] (CIST)
PIA	Project Impact Analysis (NASA)
PIA	Project Interface Adapter (SSD)
PIA	Proprietary Industries Association (AAGC)
PIA	Psychiatric Institute of America [For-profit network of private psychiatric hospitals] (EA)
PIA	Public and International Affairs [USCG] (TAG)
PIA	Public Information Act
PIA	Public Information Adviser [NATO] (NATG)
PIA	Public Intoxication Act [Australia]
PIA	Pumice Institute of America (EA)
PIA	Purified Isophthalic Acid
PIA	White Haven Center, White Haven, PA [OCLC symbol] (OCLC)
PIAA	Physician Insurers Association of America
PIAA	Pre-Arrangement Interment Association of America [Later, PAA] (EA)
PIAC	Partido de Integracion de America Central [Nicaragua] [Political party] (EY)
PIAC	Peak Instantaneous Airborne Count (DA)
PIAC	Permanent International Altaistic Conference (EA)
PIAC	Petroleum Industry Advisory Committee [British]
PIAC	Problem Identification and Correction [DoD] (AFIT)
PIACCS	Pacific Integrated Automatic Command and Control System [Military] (DNAB)
PIACS	Pacific Integrated Automatic Communications Systems [Military]
PIACT	Program for the Introduction and Adaptation of Contraceptive Technology (EA)
PIADC	Plum Island Animal Disease Center [Formerly, PIADL]
PIADL	Plum Island Animal Disease Laboratory [of ARS, Department of Agriculture] [Later, PIADC]
PIAGET	Promoting Intellectual Adaptation Given Experiential Transforming Project (EDAC)
PIAM	PIA Merchandising Services, Inc. [NASDAQ symbol] (SAG)
PIAM	PIA Merchandising Svcs [NASDAQ symbol] (TTSB)
PIAMA	Professional Institute for the American Management Association (OICC)
PIA Mer	PIA Merchandising Services, Inc. [Associated Press] (SAG)
PIANC	Permanent International Association of Navigation Congresses [Brussels, Belgium] (EAIO)
PIand	Papyri Iandanae [A publication] (OCD)
PIANG	Piangendo [Plaintive] [Music]
PIANISS	Pianissimo [Very Softly] [Music]
PIAP	Psychologists Interested in the Advancement of Psychotherapy [Later, APA] (EA)
PIAPACS	Psychophysiological Information Acquisition, Processing, and Control System
PIAR	Problem Identification and Analysis Report [Military] (CAAL)
PIAR	Project Impact Analysis Report (MCD)
PIARC	Permanent International Association of Road Congresses [See also AIPCR] [Paris, France] (EAIO)
PIAS	Photographic Inventory and Accountancy System
PIAS	Piaster [Monetary unit] [Spain, Republic of Vietnam, and some Middle Eastern countries]
PIAS	Prague Institute of Advanced Studies
PIAS	Precision Intelligence Augmentation System
PIAS	Pressure Indicating Alarm Switching [Engineering]
PIAS	Program Impact Analysis Scenario
PIASA	Polish Institute of Arts and Sciences of America (EA)
PIASS	Paris International Aviation and Space Salon (MCD)
PIAT	Peabody Individual Achievement Test [Education]
PIAT	Platoon Infantry Anti-Tank (WDAA)
PIAT	Project Integrity Assurance Team (WDAA)
PIAT	Projector Infantry, Antitank [British shoulder-controlled weapon]
PIAT	Public Information Assist Team [Environmental Protection Agency] (ERG)
PIAT-R	Peabody Individual Achievement Test-Revised (TES)
PIAVA	Polydactyly-Imperforate Anus-Vertebral Anomalies [Syndrome] [Medicine] (DMAA)
PIB	George Junior Republic, Grove City, PA [OCLC symbol] (OCLC)
PIB	Laurel/Hattiesburg [Mississippi] [Airport symbol] (OAG)
PIB	Pacific Inland Tariff Bureau, Portland OR [STAC]
PIB	Papuan Infantry Battalion
PIB	Parachute Infantry Battalion [Army]
PIB	Partial Ileal Bypass [Medicine]
PIB	Partido Indio de Bolivia [Political party]
PIB	Payload Integration Bay [NASA] (KSC)
PIB	Pender Island [British Columbia] [Seismograph station code, US Geological Survey] (SEIS)
PIB	Periodic Information Briefing (MCD)
PIB	Personal Information Briefing [of returning POW's] [Air Force]

PIB............	Petroleum Information Bureau
PIB............	Photo Intelligence Brief (AFM)
PIB............	Photo Interpretation Brief (MCD)
PIB............	Plug-In Blank
PIB............	Polar Ionospheric Beacon
PIB............	Polyisobutylene [Organic chemistry]
PIB............	Polytechnic Institute of Brooklyn [Later, PINY] (MCD)
PIB............	Pre-Flight Information Bulletin [Aviation] (DA)
PIB............	Preliminary Instruction Book
PIB............	Prices and Incomes Board [British]
PIB............	Processor Interface Buffer [Telecommunications] (TEL)
PIB............	Product Improvement Bulletin
PIB............	Program Information Block (IAA)
PIB............	Program Information Briefing
PIB............	Programmable Input Buffer
PIB............	Propellant Inspection Building [NASA] (KSC)
PIB............	Publishers Information Bureau [New York, NY] (EA)
PIB............	Pulse Interference Blanker
PIB............	Pyrotechnic Installation Building [NASA] (KSC)
PIBA..........	Primary Industry Bank of Australia Ltd. (ADA)
PIBAC........	Permanent International Bureau of Analytical Chemistry of Human and Animal Food
PIBAL.........	Pilot Balloon Observation
PIBAL.........	Polytechnic Institute of Brooklyn Aeronautical Laboratory (MCD)
PIBALS	Pilot Balloon Soundings
PIBC..........	Pacific Institute of Bio-Organic Chemistry
PIBC..........	Percutaneous Intraaortic Balloon Counterpulsation [Catheter] [Medicine] (DMAA)
PIBD	Point Initiating, Base Detonating Projectile [Army]
PIBD	Portable Interface Bond Detector (IAA)
PIBL..........	PEMA Item Baseline List [Army] (AABC)
PIBMM........	Permanent International Bureau of Motorcycle Manufacturers
PIBMRI........	Polytechnic Institute of Brooklyn, Microwave Research Institute (IEEE)
PIBO	Poly Isobutylene Oxide (EDCT)
PIBOL	Pilot Back Up Control
PIBOL	Pilot in Booster Loop (SAA)
PIBOR	Paris Interbank Offered Rank (ODBW)
PIBS..........	Permanent Interest-Bearing Shares [Finance] (WDAA)
PIBS..........	Polar Ionospheric Beacon Satellite [NASA]
PIBUC........	Pilot Back Up Control
PIC............	Calverton, NY [Location identifier FAA] (FAAL)
PIC............	Craig House Technoma Workshop, Pittsburgh, PA [OCLC symbol] (OCLC)
PIC............	Pacific Airlines Holding Co. [Vietnam] [ICAO designator] (FAAC)
PIC............	Pacific Insurance Conference
PIC............	Pacific Intelligence Center (MCD)
PIC............	Paid-In Capital [Finance] (MHDW)
PIC............	Paired-Ion Chromatography
PIC............	Para-iodoclonidine [Biochemistry]
PIC............	Parent Indicator Code (DNAB)
PIC............	Partially Incinerated Compound [Furnace technology]
PIC............	Particle in Cell [Gas solid]
PIC............	Partners in Change Program [Department of Labor]
PIC............	Payload Integration Center [NASA] (MCD)
PIC............	Payload Integration Committee [NASA] (NASA)
PIC............	Payload Integration Contractor (MCD)
PIC............	Peak Identification Computer
PIC............	People's Involvement Corp. (EA)
PIC............	Performance Incentive Contracting (AAGC)
PIC............	Periodic Inspection Control [Military] (IAA)
PIC............	Peripheral Interface Controller [Computer science]
PIC............	Peripherie Controller [Computer science] (IAA)
PIC............	Pershing Instant Comment [Donaldson, Lufkin & Jenrette] [Database]
PIC............	Personal Identification Code [Banking]
PIC............	Personal Intelligent Communicator [Computer science] (PCM)
PIC............	Personal Internet Connection [Fee-based accounts]
PIC............	Personality Inventory for Children [Psychology]
PIC............	Personnel Investigations Center
PIC............	Pesticides Information Center [National Agricultural Library] [Terminated, 1969]
PIC............	Petrochemical Investing Corp.
PIC............	Phosphoinositidase C [An enzyme]
PIC............	Photographic Industry Council [Defunct] (EA)
PIC............	Photographic Interpretation Center (MCD)
PIC............	Photo Interpretation Console (IAA)
PIC............	Piccadilly Cafeterias [NYSE symbol] (TTSB)
PIC............	Piccadilly Cafeterias, Inc. [NYSE symbol] (SPSG)
PIC............	Piccadilly Saloon [London] (DSUE)
PIC............	Piccolo [Music] (ROG)
pic............	Piccolo (WDAA)
PIC............	[The] Pickens Railroad Co. [Later, PICK] [AAR code]
PIC............	Picos [Brazil] [Airport symbol] (AD)
Pic	Picrotoxin [Biochemistry]
Pic	Pictor [Constellation]
PIC............	Pictorial (WDAA)
PIC............	Picture (AABC)
PIC............	Picture File Format [Computer science] (BTTJ)
PIC............	Picture Interactive Computer System (IAA)
pic............	Pictures [Slang] (WDMC)
PIC............	Pig Improvement Co. [British] (ECON)
PIC............	Pilot in Command [Navy] (DOMA)
PIC............	Pilot-Integrated Cockpit (AAG)
PIC............	Pine Cay [British West Indies] [Airport symbol Obsolete] (OAG)
PIC............	Pitch Impregnation Carbonization (MCD)
PIC............	Planned Insurance Coverage
PIC............	Plasma Insulin Concentration [Clinical chemistry]
PIC............	Plastic Igniter Cord (IAA)
PIC............	Plastic Insulated Cable (IAA)
PIC............	Plastic Insulated Conductor
PIC............	Policy Information Center [Department of Health and Human Services Information service or system] (IID)
PIC............	Polyethylene Insulated Conductor [Telecommunications]
PIC............	Polymer-Impregnated Concrete (KSC)
PIC............	Polymorphism Information Content [Medicine] (DMAA)
PIC............	Portable Imaging Computer
PIC............	Position Independent Code [Telecommunications] (TEL)
PIC............	Positive Immittance Converter (PDAA)
PIC............	Positive Impedance Converter (IAA)
PIC............	Positive Ion Chamber
PIC............	Postinflammatory Corticoid [Medicine]
PIC............	Potential Icing Category [Meteorology] (DA)
PIC............	Power Information Center [Interagency Advanced Power Group] [DoD Washington, DC]
PIC............	Power Integrated Circuit [Computer science]
PIC............	Predicted Intercept Contour
PIC............	Preinitiation Complex [Genetics]
PIC............	Preinstallation Calibration (KSC)
PIC............	Preinstallation Checkout (NASA)
PIC............	Presbyterian Interracial Council (EA)
PIC............	Pressure Indicator Controller
PIC............	Primary Interexchange Carrier [Telecommunications] (OTD)
PIC............	Primate Information Center [University of Washington] [Seattle, WA]
pic............	Prince Edward Island [Canada MARC country of publication code Library of Congress] (LCCP)
PIC............	Printer Interface Cartridge [Epson America, Inc.]
PIC............	Prior Informed Consent [For use of pesticides]
PIC............	Priority Interrupt Controller
PIC............	Private Industry Council [Generic term for group that helps provide job training]
PIC............	Procedures for Instrument Calibration
PIC............	Process Interface Control
PIC............	Processor Input Channel (NVT)
PIC............	Processor Interconnection Channel (NITA)
PIC............	Procurement Information Center
PIC............	Procurement Information Circular (AAGC)
PIC............	Procurement Information for Contracts [AFSC]
PIC............	Product Information Center [AgriData Resources, Inc.] [Information service or system]
PIC............	Production Inventory Control (MHDI)
PIC............	Product of Incomplete Combustion [Environmental Protection Agency] (ERG)
PIC............	Professional Image Computer (NITA)
PIC............	Professional Instrument Course [Aeronautics]
PIC............	Professional Interfraternity Conference [Later, PFA] (EA)
PIC............	Program for Improved Contract Management [Military] (AFIT)
PIC............	Program Identification Code (MUGU)
PIC............	Program Information Center
PIC............	Program Initiations and Commitments (AAG)
PIC............	Program Instruction, Calibration [Marine Corps]
PIC............	Program Interrupt Control [Computer science]
PIC............	Programmable Industrial Controller (NITA)
PIC............	Programmable Interrupt Controller [Computer science]
PIC............	Programmable Interval Clock (NASA)
PIC............	Project Information Center
PIC............	Prolonged Illness Coverage [Insurance] (PAZ)
PIC............	Promotion Industry Club (EA)
PIC............	Promotion Industry Council (NTPA)
PIC............	Proton Induced Cascade [Physics]
PIC............	Prudential Insurance Co. of America (EFIS)
PIC............	Pseudolsocyanine [Organic chemistry]
PIC............	Pseudo-Isocytidine [Antineoplastic compound]
PIC............	Public Information Center [Nuclear energy] (NRCH)
PIC............	Public Information Committee [of the NATO Military Committee] (NATG)
PIC............	Publishers' Information Card [Later, IBIS] [British]
PIC............	Pulsed Ionization Chamber
PIC............	Purpose Identification Code
PIC............	Pursuant to Instructions Contained In (MUGU)
PIC............	Pyro Initiator Controller [NASA] (NAKS)
PIC............	Pyrotechnic Ignition Control [NASA]
PIC............	Pyrotechnic Initiator Capacitor (NASA)
PIC............	Pyrotechnic Initiator Controller (NASA)
PICA..........	Palestine Israelite Colonisation Association
PICA..........	Participating Interest Contingency Agreement
PICA..........	Police Insignia Collectors Association [British] (DBA)
PICA..........	Porch Index of Communicative Ability [Psychology]
PICA..........	Posterior Inferior Cerebal Artery [Cardiology] (DAVI)
PICA..........	Posterior Inferior Cerebellar Artery [Anatomy]
PICA..........	Posterior Inferior Communicating Artery [Cardiology] (DAVI)
PICA..........	Posterior Internal Cerebral Artery [Cardiology] (DAVI)
PICA..........	Power Industry Computer Applications (MCD)
PICA..........	Press Independence and Critical Ability (NTCM)
PICA..........	Primary Inventory Control Activity (MCD)
PICA..........	Printing Industry Computer Associates, Inc.
PICA..........	Private Investment Co. for Asia SA
PICA..........	Procedures for Inventory Control Afloat [Navy]
PICA..........	Professional Insurance Communicators of America (EA)
PICA..........	Programming Interpersonal Curricula for Adolescents [Learning model] [Education]

PICA............ Project for Integrated Catalogue Automation [*Royal Netherlands Library*] [*Cataloging cooperative*] (IID)

PICA............ Property Services Agency Information on Construction and Architecture [*Property Service Agency Library Service*] [*British Information service or system*]

PICA............ Public Interest Computer Association (EA)

PICAC .... Porch Index of Communicative Ability in Children [*Psychology*]

PICAC .... Power Industry Computer Applications Conference (MCD)

PICADAD...... Place Identification/Characteristics and Area/Distance and Direction [*Bureau of the Census*]

PICAO .... Provisional International Civil Aviation Organization [*Later, ICAO*]

PICASO .... Picture Algorithms-Subroutine Orientated (NITA)

PICASSO...... Pen Input to Computer and Scanned Screen Output [*Computer science*] (PDAA)

PICB............ Peabody Institute of the City of Baltimore [*Maryland*]

PICC............ Parts for Import Cars Coalition [*Defunct*] (EA)

PICC............ Peripherally-Inserted Central Catheter [*Medicine*]

PICC............ Philadelphia International Convention Center [*Pennsylvania*]

PICC............ Piccolo

PICC............ Plastics in Construction Council [*Later, CCS*] (EA)

PICC............ Professional Institutions Council for Conservation [*British*]

PICC............ Provisional International Computation Center

PICCA......... Positive Ion Cluster Composition Analyzer [*Instrumentation*]

PicCafe .... Piccadilly Cafeterias, Inc. [*Associated Press*] (SAG)

PICCED .... Pratt Institute Center for Community and Environmental Development [*Research center*] (RCD)

PICCO .... Pennsylvania Industrial Chemical Corp. [*Trademark*]

PICD .... Preliminary Interface Control Drawing

PICD .... Primary Irritant Contact Dermatitis [*Medicine*] (DMAA)

PICDG......... Polar Icebreaker Canadian Design Group

PICE............ Product Improved Compatibility Electronics (MCD)

PICE............ Programmable Integrated Control Equipment

PICEE.......... President's Interagency Committee on Export Expansion [*Absorbed by President's Export Council in 1979*] (EGAO)

PICE/PIA ...... Printing Industry Credit Exchange/PIA [*of the Printing Industries of America*] [*Defunct*] (EA)

PICES.......... North Pacific Marine Science Organization (USDC)

PICESP .... Put It in Corporate Executives' Swimming Pools [*Waste management slang*]

PICFS.......... Postinfective Chronic Fatigue Syndrome [*Medicine*] (DMAA)

PICG .... Pig Industry Consultative Group [*Queensland, Australia*]

PICG .... Programme International de Correlation Geologique [*International Geological Correlation Programme - IGCP*] (EAIO)

PICGC .... Permanent International Committee for Genetic Congresses

PicGPA .... Picrylated Guinea Pig Albumin [*Immunochemistry*]

PICK............ Part Information Correlation Key

PICK............ [*The*] Pickens Railroad Co. [*Formerly, PIC*] [*AAR code*]

Pick .... Pickering's Massachusetts Supreme Judicial Court Reports [*1822-39*] [*A publication*] (DLA)

Pickle .... Pickle's Reports [*85-108 Tennessee*] [*A publication*] (DLA)

PICKLE........ Preserving Individual Cultures and Knowledge in Lands Everywhere [*An association*]

PICKLE........ President's Intelligence Checklist [*Daily report prepared by CIA*]

Pick (Mass)... Pickering's Massachusetts Reports [*18-41 Massachusetts*] [*A publication*] (DLA)

Pick Stat...... Pickering's English Statutes [*A publication*] (DLA)

PICKUP .... Professional, Industrial and Commercial Updating [*Vocational training*] [*British*]

PICM........... Master Chief Precision Instrumentman [*Navy rating*]

PICM........... Permanent International Committee of Mothers

PICM........... Picom Insurance [*NASDAQ symbol*] (TTSB)

PICM........... PICOM Insurance Co. [*NASDAQ symbol*] (SAG)

PICM........... Professional Group [*NASDAQ symbol*] [*Formerly, Professionals Insurance Co. Management Group*]

PICM........... Professionals Insurance Co. Management Group [*NASDAQ symbol*] (SAG)

PICM Gp ...... Professionals Insurance Co. Management Group [*Associated Press*] (SAG)

PIC-MOD...... Purpose Identification Code - Month and Calendar Year of Detachment (DNAB)

PIC-NF .... Picroindigocarmine-Nuclear Fast Red [*A biological stain*]

PICO .... Pacific Islands Contact Office (COE)

PICO .... Partido Independiente de la Clase Obrera [*Panama*] [*Political party*] (EY)

PICO .... Person in Column One [*1980 census*]

PICO .... Physicians Insurance Co. of Ohio [*NASDAQ symbol*] (NQ)

PICO .... PICO Holdings, Inc. [*NASDAQ symbol*] (SAG)

PICO .... Polar Ice Core Drilling Office [*National Science Foundation*] (MSC)

PICO .... Portable Interactive Computing Object

PICO .... Product Improvement Control Office (AFM)

Pico .... Progressive Tools and Industries Co.

PICO .... Purchasing Internal Change Order (MCD)

PICOA......... Physicians Insur Ohio [*NASDAQ symbol*] (TTSB)

PICODE........ Program Indicator-Code [*Computer science*] (ECII)

PICOE.......... Programmed Initiations, Commitments, Obligations, and Expenditures [*AFSC*]

PICO Hld...... PICO Holdings, Inc. [*Associated Press*] (SAG)

PICOM......... PICOM Insurance Co. [*Associated Press*] (SAG)

PICOMM...... Potter Instrument Coordinated Measuring Machine

PICON......... Process Intelligent Control [*A data processing system from LISP Machine, Inc.*]

PicoPd........ Pico Products, Inc. [*Associated Press*] (SAG)

PICORNAVIRUS... Pico Ribonucleic Acid Virus

PICOS .... Purchased Input Concept Optimization with Suppliers [*Auto industry quality and cost management program*]

PICOST .... Probability of Incurring Estimated Costs [*Military*] (MCD)

PICP............ Prime Inventory Control Point (DNAB)

PICP............ Program Interface Control Plan (NASA)

PICPAB .... Phenomena Induced by Charged Particle Beams

PICPSA .... Permanent International Commission for the Proof of Small-Arms (EAIO)

PICRC .... Pesticide and Industrial Chemicals Research Center [*Public Health Service*] (GRD)

PICRS .... Program Information Control and Retrieval System (NASA)

PICRS .... Program Information Coordination and Review Service [*NASA*] (NASA)

PICS............ Permit Imprint Collectors Society (EA)

PICS............ Perpetual Inventory Control System

PICS............ Personnel Information Communication [*or Control*] System [*Computer science*]

PICS............ Pharmaceutical Information Control System (DIT)

PICS............ Photographic Information Condensing System (DNAB)

PICS............ Photography in Community Self-Development [*Program of Master Photo Dealers and Finishers Association*]

PICS............ Photo Index and Cataloging System (NASA)

PICS............ Pioneer Image Converter System [*NASA*]

PICS............ Plastid Isolation Column System [*Analytical chemistry*]

PICS............ Platform for Internet Content Selection [*Computer science*]

PICS............ Platform for Internet Content Specification [*Computer science*]

PICS............ Platform for Internnet Content Selection [*Computer science*]

PICS............ Plug-In Inventory Control System [*Bell System*]

PICS............ Predefined Input Control Sequence (MCD)

PICS............ Procurement Information Control System [*NASA*]

PICS............ Production Information and Control System [*IBM Corp.*] [*Software package*]

PICS............ Production Inventory Control System

PICS............ Productivity Improvement and Control System (BUR)

PICS............ Program Information and Control System (MCD)

PICS............ Protocol Implementation Conformance Statement [*Computer science*] (TNIG)

PICS/DCPR... Plug-In Inventory Control System/Detailed Continuing Property Record [*Telecommunications*] (TEL)

PICSEC .... Picture per Second (IAA)

PICSO .... Pressure-Controlled Intermittent Coronary Sinus Occlusion [*Medicine*] (DMAA)

PICT............ Perceived Instrumentality of the College Test

PICT............ Philips Inventory Control Technique [*Computer science*] (IAA)

Pict............ Pictor [*Constellation*]

PICT............ Pictorial (ROG)

pict .... Pictorial (WDAA)

Pict............ Picture (AL)

PICT............ Picture File Format [*Computer science*] (BTTJ)

PICT............ Project on the Improvement of College Teaching

Pict Dict Rome... Pictorial Dictionary of Ancient Rome [*A publication*] (OCD)

PicTel .... PictureTel Corp. [*Associated Press*] (SAG)

PICTEL........ Picture Telephone [*Telecommunications*] (EECA)

pictg .... Pictograph (VRA)

PICTOMAP... Photographic Image Conversion by Tonal Masking Procedures (MCD)

PICTS.......... Photo-Induced Current Transient Spectroscopy (AAEL)

PICU .... Parallel Instruction Control Unit

PICU .... Pediatric Intensive Care Unit [*Medicine*]

PICU .... Priority Interrupt Control Unit [*Computer science*] (MDG)

PICU .... Pulmonary Intensive Care Unit [*Medicine*]

PICUTPC...... Permanent and International Committee of Underground Town Planning and Construction

PIC(WA)....... Potato Industry Council (Western Australia)

PID.............. D. T. Watson Home for Crippled Children, Leetsdale, PA [*OCLC symbol*] (OCLC)

PID.............. Pain Intensity Differences [*Medicine*]

PID.............. Parameter Identification [*Communications*]

PID.............. Partial Initial Decision [*Nuclear energy*] (NRCH)

PID.............. Partido de Integracion Democrata [*Democratic Integration Party*] [*Argentina Political party*] (PPW)

PID.............. Partido Izquierda Democratica [*Democratic Left Party*] [*Political party*] (EAIO)

PID.............. Passenger Information Display

PID.............. Patrol Input Device (MCD)

PID.............. Payload Insertion Device (NASA)

PID.............. Pelvic Inflammatory Disease [*Medicine*]

PID.............. Perfect-Gas Isentropic Decompression [*Engineering*]

PID.............. Peripheral Interface Device [*Computer science*] (EECA)

PID.............. Personal Identification Device (MHDI)

PID.............. Personality and Individual Differences [*A publication*]

PID.............. Personnel Identification Device [*Navy*] (IAA)

PID.............. Personnel Inquiry/Death/Occupational Illness [*Report*] (DNAB)

PID.............. Phenindione [*or Phenylindandione*] [*Anticoagulant*]

PID.............. Photointerpretation Department [*Military*]

PID.............. Photoionization Detector

PID.............. Photon-Induced Dissociation [*For spectral studies*]

PID.............. Pictorial Information Digitizer [*Computer science*] (DIT)

PID.............. Pilot-Induced Deceleration

PID.............. Plan Identification Number (DOMA)

PID.............. Planned Industrial Development (PA)

PID.............. Plasma-Iron Disappearance [*Hematology*] (MAE)

PID.............. Political Intelligence Department [*British World War II*]

PID.............. Port Identification [*Telecommunications*] (TEL)

PID.............. Primary Immunodeficiency Disease [*Medicine*]

PID............... Prime Item Development (MCD)
PID............... Process & Instrument Design (ACII)
PID............... Process Identifier [*Computer science*] (PCM)
PID............... Procurement Information Digest (AFM)
PID............... Procurement Item/Identification Description [*DoD*]
PID............... Product Innovation and Design
PID............... Program Information Document [*NASA*] (MCD)
PID............... Program Introduction Document (NASA)
PID............... Project Implementation Directive [*Air Force*]
PID............... Prolapsed Intervertebral Disc [*Medicine*]
PID............... Proportional-Integral Derivative [*Engineering*]
PID............... Proportional Integral Differential [*Digital control-algorithm*] (IAA)
PID............... Proportional-Plus Integral-Plus Derivative [*Digital control algorithm*]
PID............... Protruded Intervertebral Disc [*Medicine*]
PID............... Pseudo Interrupt Device
PID............... Public Information Division [*Army*]
PIDA .... Payload Installation and Deployment Aid [*NASA*] (NASA)
PIDA .... Pet Industry Distributors Association (EA)
PIDA .... Phenylindane Dicarboxylic Acid (EDCT)
PIDA .... Pig Industry Development Authority [*British*] (BI)
PIDAS .... Portable Instantaneous Display and Analysis Spectrometer
PIDC .... Philadelphia Industrial Development Corp.
PIDC .... Procurement Intern Development Center (DNAB)
PIDC .... Prototype International Data Centre [*For evaluating seismic signals*]
PIDCOM....... Process Instruments Digital Communication System [*Beckman Industries*]
PIDD .... Passive Identification/Detection and Direction (MCD)
PIDD .... Planned Inactivation or Discontinued Date [*Environmental science*] (COE)
PI/DE .... Passive Identification/Direction Finding Equipment (MCD)
PI/DE .... Positive Identification and Direction Equipment
PIDEP .... Preinterservice Data Exchange Program
PIDP .... Pacific Islands Development Program [*East-West Center*] [*Research center*] (RCD)
PIDP .... Pilot Information Display Panel
PIDP .... Programmable Indicator Data Processor [*Military*] (CAAL)
PIDR .... Product Inspection Discrepancy Report (MCD)
PIDRA .... Portable Insulin Dosage-Regulating Apparatus [*Medicine*]
PIDRS......... Photographic Instrumentation Data Recording System (MCD)
PIDS .... Parameter Inventory Display System (DNAB)
PIDS .... Physical Intrusion Detection System (DWSG)
PIDS .... Portable Image Display System (NASA)
PIDS .... Primary Immunodeficiency Syndrome [*Medicine*] (DMAA)
PIDS .... Prime Item Development Specification
PIDS .... Public Investment Data System (MHDW)
PIDSA......... Population Information Documentation System for Africa
PIDT........... Plasma-Iron Disappearance Time [*Hematology*] (MAE)
PIE............... Air South West [*British*] [*FAA designator*] (FAAC)
PIE............... Clearwater-St. Petersburg [*Florida*] [*Airport symbol*] (AD)
PIE............... Elwyn Institute, Elwyn, PA [*OCLC symbol*] (OCLC)
PIE............... Pacific Information Exchange [*Information service or system*] (IID)
PIE............... Pacific Islands Ecosystems [*Springfield, VA*] [*Department of the Interior No longer available online*] [*Information service or system*]
PIE............... Pacing Item Evaluation (MCD)
PIE............... Paedophile Information Exchange [*British*] (ILCA)
PIE............... Parallel Instruction Execution [*Computer science*] (BUR)
PIE............... Parallel Interface Element
PIE............... Patent Information Exploitation [*Canadian Patent Office*]
PIE............... Payload Integration Equipment [*NASA*] (MCD)
PIE............... Payroll Audit, Indexing, and Expiration
PIE............... Period of Interruption of Employment (WDAA)
PIE............... Peripheral Interface Element [*Computer science*] (IAA)
PIE............... Personal Interactive Electronics [*Apple Computer Inc.*]
PIE............... Photo-Induced Electrochromism
PIE............... Pietermaritzburg [*South Africa*] [*Seismograph station code, US Geological Survey Closed*] (SEIS)
PIE............... Pipestone Petroleums, Inc. [*Toronto Stock Exchange symbol Vancouver Stock Exchange symbol*]
PIE............... Plug-In Electronics
PIE............... Plug-In Extension
PIE............... Plume Interaction Experiment [*Army*] (RDA)
PIE............... Pocket Internet Explorer [*Microsoft Corp.*] [*Computer science*]
PIE............... Poly(iminoethylene) [*Organic chemistry*]
PIE............... Portable Information Evaluation
PIE............... Post-Irradiation Examination [*Nuclear energy*] (NRCH)
PIE............... Post-Irradiation Experiment [*Nuclear energy*] (NRCH)
PIE............... Preimplantation Embryo
PIE............... Price in Effect [*Military*]
PIE............... Primary Industry and Energy
PIE............... Program for Increased Education [*Military*]
PIE............... Program Interrupt Element [*Computer science*] (IAA)
PIE............... Program Interrupt Entry [*Computer science*]
PIE............... Programming and Instrumentation Environment [*Computer science*]
PIE............... Prolog Inference Engine [*Computer science*]
PIE............... Proposal Information Exchange [*Military*]
PIE............... Proto-Indo-European [*Language*] (BARN)
PIE............... Publications Indexed for Engineering [*A publication*]
PIE............... Public Interest Economics Foundation [*Defunct*] (EA)
PIE............... Pulmonary Infiltration with Eosinophilia [*Medicine*]
PIE............... Pulmonary Interstitial Edema [*Medicine*] (DAVI)
PIE............... Pulmonary Interstitial Emphysema [*Medicine*]
PIE............... Pulse Interference Eliminator [*RADAR*]
PIE............... Pulse Interference Emitting (MCD)
PIE............... St. Petersburg [*Florida*] [*Airport symbol*] (OAG)

PIEA............. Pencil Industry Export Association [*Defunct*] (EA)
PIEA............. Petroleum Industry Electrical Association [*Later, ENTELEC*] (EA)
PIEA............. Petroleum Industry Electrotechnical Association (IAA)
PIEA............. Pre-Arrangement Interment Exchange of America [*Later, PIAA*]
PIE-C .... Public Interest Economics Center (EA)
PIECOST...... Probability of Incurring Estimated Costs [*Military*]
PIECP......... Preliminary Impact Engineering Change Proposal (MCD)
PIED............ Piedmont Mining Co., Inc. [*NASDAQ symbol*] (NQ)
PiedBcp...... Piedmont Bancorp, Inc. [*Associated Press*] (SAG)
PiedBGp...... Piedmont Bancgroup [*Associated Press*] (SAG)
PiedmBc...... Piedmont Bancorp, Inc. [*Associated Press*] (SAG)
PiedMg....... Piedmont Managment Co., Inc. [*Associated Press*] (SAG)
PiedMn....... Piedmont Mining Co., Inc. [*Associated Press*] (SAG)
PiedNG ...... Piedmont Natural Gas Co., Inc. [*Associated Press*] (SAG)
PIE-F........... Public Interest Economics Foundation [*Defunct*] (EA)
Piemnt........ Piemonte Foods, Inc. [*Associated Press*] (SAG)
PIEP........... Peripheral Infarct Epicardium [*Medicine*] (DB)
PIEP........... Primary Irritation Evaluation Program
PIER........... Product Inventory Electronically Recorded (PDAA)
Pier 1 .... Pier 1 Imports, Inc. [*Associated Press*] (SAG)
Pierce RR.... Pierce on Railroad Law [*A publication*] (DLA)
PiercPag..... Piercing Pagoda, Inc. [*Associated Press*] (SAG)
PIERS .... Port Import/Export Reporting Service [*Journal of Commerce, Inc.*] [*Information service or system*]
PIES........... Packaged Interchangeable Electronic System
PIES........... Penning Ionization Electron Spectroscopy
PIES........... Pollution Prevention Information Exchange System [*Environmental science*]
PIES........... Procurement and Inventory of Equipment System (DNAB)
PIES........... Project Independence Evaluation System [*Energy policy*]
PIESA........ Parasite-Induced Erythrocyte Surface Antigen [*Immunology*]
PIF............... Insured Muni Income Fd [*NYSE symbol*] (TTSB)
PIF............... Package Information Form (IAA)
PIF............... PaineWebber Premium Insured Municipal Income [*NYSE symbol*] (SPSG)
PIF............... Pakistan Islamic Front [*Pakistan*] [*Political party*] (ECON)
PIF............... Paper Industry Federation (NADA)
PIF............... Partners in Friendship (EA)
PIF............... Payload Integration Facility [*NASA*] (KSC)
PIF............... Peak Inspiratory Flow [*Medicine*] (AAMN)
PIF............... Perpetual Inventory File (DNAB)
PIF............... Personnel Identification Feature [*Navy*] (NVT)
PIF............... Phase Inversion Formulation [*Chemistry*]
PIF............... Pilot Information File [*Army*]
PIF............... Place in Inactive File [*Army*]
PIF............... Point Initiating Fuze
PIF............... Positive Identification Feature (MCD)
PIF............... Predictive Influence Function [*Statistics*]
PIF............... Preparer Inventory File [*IRS*]
PIF............... Privatization Investment Fund Trust Units [*Toronto Stock Exchange symbol*]
PIF............... Productivity Investment Fund [*Program*] [*Air Force*]
PIF............... Program Information File
PIF............... Proinsulin-Free [*Medicine*] (DB)
PIF............... Project in Foreign Language Pedagogy (AIE)
PIF............... Prolactin Inhibiting Factor [*Endocrinology*] (DAVI)
PIF............... Prolactin-Release Inhibiting Factor [*Also, PRIH*] [*Endocrinology*]
PIF............... Proliferation Inhibitory Factor [*Immunochemistry*]
PIF............... Provision of Industrial Facilities [*Army*] (AABC)
PIF............... Pseudo-Identification Feature (MCD)
PIF............... Punjab Irregular Force [*British military*] (DMA)
PIFA............ Packaging and Industrial Films Association [*British*] (DBA)
PIFAL......... Program Instruction Frequency Analyzer [*Telecommunications*] (IAA)
PIFCM........ Pitch Integrated Flight Control Module (MCD)
PI-FET........ Piezoelectric Field-Effect Transistor (PDAA)
PIFEX........ Programmable Image Feature Extractor [*to provide real-time machine vision for the Martian Rover robot*] [*Jet Propulsion Laboratory*] (BYTE)
PIFF........... Punjab Irregular Frontier Force [*British military*] (DMA)
PIFG........... Poor Intrauterine Fetal Growth (STED)
PIFI............ Piedmonte Foods [*NASDAQ symbol*] (TTSB)
PIFI............ Piemonte Foods, Inc. [*NASDAQ symbol*] (NQ)
PIFI............ Pressure-Induced Intracranial Focal Ischemia [*Medicine*]
PIFL........... Pipe Flow (PDAA)
PIFOV .... Planet in Field of View [*NASA*]
PIFR........... Peak Inspiratory Flow Rate [*Medicine*]
PIFR........... Program Interrupt Flag Register [*Computer science*] (IAA)
PIFS........... Plume-Induced Flow Separation
PIFS........... Post Infection Fatigue Syndrome [*Medicine*]
PIFS........... Prime Item Fabrication Specification
PIFT........... Platelet Immunofluorescence Test [*Analytical biochemistry*]
PIFUA........ Powerplant and Industrial Fuel Use Act of 1978
PIG............... Glenn Mills School, Glenn Mills, PA [*OCLC symbol*] (OCLC)
PIG............... Pacific Institute of Geography
PIG............... Passive-Income Generator [*Investment term*]
PIG............... Pendulous Integrating Gyro
PIG............... Penning Ionization Gauge (IAA)
PIG............... Pertussis Immune Gobulin [*Medicine*] (STED)
PIG............... Phillips Ionization Gauge
PIG............... Phosphatidylinositol Glycan [*Biochemistry*]
PIG............... Photo-Island Grid
pig............... Pigment (BARN)
Pig............... Pigmentation (STED)
Pig............... Pigott's Common Recoveries [*3 eds.*] [*1739-92*] [*A publication*] (DLA)
PIG............... Plasmatron Inert Gas (SAA)

PIG............ Polymeric Immunoglobulin [*Medicine*] (DMAA)
PIG............ Pride, Integrity, Guts [*Police alternative for the appellation applied to police by radical groups*]
PIG............ Process Ink Gamut [*Printing technology*]
PIG............ Production Image Generator (MCD)
PIG............ Production Installation Group [*Military*] (CAAL)
PIG............ Program Implementation Guideline (EG)
PIG............ Pulse Inert Gas
PIGA............ Pendulous Integrating Gyro Accelerometer
Pig & R....... Pigott and Rodwell's English Registration Appeal Cases [*1843-45*] [*A publication*] (DLA)
PIGDX.......... Pioneer Gold Shares Cl.A [*Mutual fund ticker symbol*] (SG)
PIGI............ Pregnancy-Induced Gluclose Intolerance (STED)
PIGIT.......... Putnam Intermediate Government Income Trust [*Associated Press*] (SAG)
Pig Judg...... Pigott's Foreign Judgments [*3rd ed.*] [*1908-09*] [*A publication*] (DLA)
PIGLET........ Purchase Information, Gifts, Loans, Exchanges Tracking [*Suggested name for the Library of Congress computer system*]
pigm............ Pigment (STED)
PIGM............ Pigmentum [*Paint*] [*Pharmacy*]
PIGM............ Putnam Investment Grade Municipal Trust [*Associated Press*] (SAG)
PIGMA.......... Pressurized Inert Gas Metal Arc (KSC)
PIGME.......... Programmed Inert Gas Multi-Electrode (PDAA)
PIGMI.......... Pion Generator for Medical Irradiation [*Radiology*]
PIGMI.......... Position Indicating General Measuring Instrument
PIGMT2........ Putnam Investment Grade Municipal Trust II [*Associated Press*] (SAG)
PIGMT3........ Putnam Investment Grade Multiple Sectors III [*Associated Press*] (SAG)
PIGPA.......... Pyruvate, Inosine, Glucose Phosphate, Adenine (AAMN)
PIGR............ Polymeric Immunoglobulin Receptor [*Biochemistry*]
Pig Rec........ Pigott's Recoveries [*England*] [*A publication*] (DLA)
PIGS............ PAFEC Interactive Graphics System [*PAFEC Ltd.*] [*Software package*] (NCC)
PIGS............ Passive Infrared Guidance System [*DoD*]
PIGS............ Pesticides in Groundwater Strategy [*Environmental Protection Agency*] (GFGA)
PIGS............ Poles, Italians, Greeks, and Slavs
PIGS............ Portable Inertial Guidance System
PIGS............ Procedures, Information, Guidance & Standards (WDAA)
PIGU............ Pendulous Integrating Gyro Unit
PIH............ Passive Immune Hemolysis (PDAA)
PIH............ Permanent Income Hypothesis [*Economics*]
PIH............ Pheniprazine (LDT)
PIH............ Phenylisopropylhydrazine [*Pharmacology*]
PIH............ Pin in Hole (AAEL)
PIH............ Pipeline Induction Heat [*Industrial firm*] [*British*]
PIH............ Pocatello [*Idaho*] [*Airport symbol*] (OAG)
PIH............ Pork Industry Handbook [*A publication*]
PIH............ Pregnancy-Induced Hypertension [*Gynecology*]
PIH............ Primary Intracerebral Hemorrhage (CPH)
PIH............ Prolactin-Inhibiting Hormone (STED)
PIH............ Prolactin-Release Inhibiting Hormone [*Endocrinology*]
PIH............ Public and Indian Housing [*HUD*]
PIH............ St. Gabriel's Hall, Phoenixville, PA [*OCLC symbol*] (OCLC)
PIHC............ PHC, Inc. [*NASDAQ symbol*] (SAG)
PIHC............ PHC Inc.'A' [*NASDAQ symbol*] (TTSB)
PIHCA.......... Polyisohexylcyanoacrylate [*Antibacterial*]
PIHCW.......... PHC Inc. Wrrt [*NASDAQ symbol*] (TTSB)
PIHH............ Postinfluenza-Like Hyposmia and Hypogeusia (STED)
PIHM............ Polish Institute of Hydrology and Meteorology
PIHSMP........ Protocol Relating to Intervention on the High Seas in Cases of Marine Pollution by Substances other than Oil [*Environmental science*] (COE)
PII............ Fairbanks, AK [*Location identifier FAA*] (FAAL)
PII............ Pershing II [*Army*]
PII............ Phantom II [*Model of automobile*]
PII............ Plasma Inorganic Iodine [*Clinical chemistry*] (MAE)
PII............ Polaris Industries [*NYSE symbol*] (TTSB)
PII............ Polaris Industries, Inc. [*NYSE symbol*] (SAG)
PII............ Positive Immittance Inverter (IEEE)
PII............ Predominant Interest Installation (AAGC)
PII............ Primary Irritation Index [*Medicine*] (STED)
PII............ Primary Irritation Indices [*for skin*]
PII............ Printing Industry Institute [*A graphic arts training school*]
PII............ Procurement Instrument Identification (NG)
PII............ Sleighton School, Darling, PA [*OCLC symbol*] (OCLC)
PIIC............ Pergamon International Information Corp. [*Information service or system*] (IID)
PIIC............ Public Interest Immunity Certificate [*British*] (ECON)
PIID............ Prediction Interval Initiation Date (DNAB)
PIIF............ Proteinase Inhibitor Inducing Factor [*Biochemistry*]
PIII............ plasma Immersion Ion Implantation (AAEL)
PIIM............ Planned Interdependency Incentive Method
PIIN............ Procurement Instruction Identification Number [*Army*] (AABC)
PIIN............ Procurement Instrument Identification Number [*Military*]
PI/INT'L....... Packaging Institute International [*Later, IoPP*] (EA)
PIIO............ Poultry Industry Investigation Officer [*Australia*]
PIIP............ Potable Insulin Infusion Pump [*Medicine*] (STED)
PIIS............ Posterior Inferior Iliac Spine [*Medicine*] (STED)
PIJ............ Pickled-in-Jar [*Food technology*]
PIJAC.......... Pet Industry Joint Advisory Council (EA)
PIJR............ Product Improvement Joint Review [*Military*]
PIK............ Glasgow-Prestwick [*Scotland*] [*Airport symbol*] (OAG)
PIK............ Pay in Kind Preferred Stock (TDOB)
PIK............ Payment in Kind
PIK............ Pic Prospectors [*Vancouver Stock Exchange symbol*]
PIK............ Portable Injection Kit
PIK............ Prestwick [*Scotland*] [*Airport symbol*] (AD)
PIK............ Programmer's Imaging Kernel [*Computer science*] (BTTJ)
PIKE............ Pike [*Postal Service standard*] (OPSA)
Pike............ Pike's Reports [*1-5 Arkansas*] [*A publication*] (DLA)
Pike & F Adm Law... Pike and Fischer's Administrative Law [*A publication*] (DLA)
Pike & F Fed Rules Service... Pike and Fischer's Federal Rules Service [*A publication*] (DLA)
Pike & Fischer Admin Law... Pike and Fischer's Administrative Law [*A publication*] (DLA)
Pike H of L... Pike's History of the House of Lords [*A publication*] (DLA)
PIKES.......... Pike [*Commonly used*] (OPSA)
Pikeville...... Pikeville National Corp. [*Associated Press*] (SAG)
PIK Securities... Payment-in-Kind Securities [*Investment term*] (DFIT)
PIL............ Brazos Santiago, TX [*Location identifier FAA*] (FAAL)
PIL............ Pair Inter Langues [*Bourg La Reine, France*] (EAIO)
PIL............ Parti de l'Independance et de la Liberte [*Party for Independence and Liberty*] [*Congo*] [*Political party*]
PIL............ Patient Information Leaflet [*Pharmacy*]
PIL............ Payment in Lieu
PIL............ Percentage Increase in Loss [*Statistics*]
PIL............ Pest Infestation Laboratory [*Agricultural Research Council*] (PDAA)
PIL............ Pilar [*Argentina*] [*Seismograph station code, US Geological Survey*] (SEIS)
pil............ Pilaster (VRA)
PIL............ Pilot (WGA)
PIL............ Pilula [*Pill*] [*Pharmacy*]
Pil............ Pilula [*Pill*] [*Pharmacology*] (DAVI)
PIL............ Pistol Petroleum [*Vancouver Stock Exchange symbol*]
PIL............ Pitt Interpretive Language [*Computer science*] (DIT)
PIL............ Pittsburgh Interpretive [*or Interactive*] Language [*Computer science*] (IAA)
PIL............ Plastic Impregnated Laminate
PIL............ Practice Instrument Landing (ADA)
PIL............ Precision In Line [*Electronics*] (EECA)
PIL............ Preferred Item List (RDA)
PIL............ Processing Information List [*Computer science*]
PIL............ Procurement Information Letter (MCD)
PIL............ Publications International Ltd.
PIL............ Publishing Interchange Language [*Computer science*] (CDE)
PIL............ Purple Indicating Light (MSA)
PIL............ Purpose in Life [*Personality development test*] [*Psychology*]
PILA............ Power Industry Laboratory Association [*Defunct*] (EA)
PILAC.......... Pulsed Ion Linear Accelerator
PILAR.......... Petroleum Industry Local Authority Reporting (PDAA)
PILB............ Passenger and Immigration Lists Bibliography [*A publication*]
PILC............ Paper-Insulated, Lead-Covered Cable [*Telecommunications*]
PILC............ Pillared Interlayered Clays [*Catalysis technology*]
PILC............ Pregnancy and Infant Loss Center (EA)
PILCX.......... PIMCO: International Cl.C [*Mutual fund ticker symbol*] (SG)
PILE............ Product Inventory Level Estimator (PDAA)
PilgAmer........ Pilgrim American Bank & Thrift Fund, Inc. [*Associated Press*] (SAG)
PilgAPr.......... Pilgrim America Prime Rate Trust [*Associated Press*] (SAG)
PilgPr............ Pilgrims Pride Corp. [*Associated Press*] (SAG)
PilgPrm.......... Pilgrim Prime Rate Trust [*Associated Press*] (SAG)
Pilgr............ [*The*] Passionate Pilgrim [*Poetry*] (BARN)
Pilgr............ [*The*] Pilgrim's Progress [*Bunyan*] (BARN)
PilgRg.......... Pilgrim Regional Banc Shares, Inc. [*Associated Press*] (SAG)
PILI............ Passenger and Immigration Lists Index [*A publication*]
PILL............ Newport Dock [*British depot code*]
PILL............ Pilgrim League (PSS)
PILL............ Programmed Instruction Language Learning [*Computer science*]
PILL............ ProxyMed, Inc. [*NASDAQ symbol*] (SAG)
PILL............ Proxymed Pharmacy [*NASDAQ symbol*] (SAG)
PILLS.......... Particulate Instrumentation by LASER Light Scattering (PDAA)
PILM............ Pillared Interlayered Montmorillonite [*Catalysis technology*]
PILMS.......... Precision Insertion Loss Measurement Set (IAA)
PILO............ Public Information Liaison Officer [*Military*]
PILOH.......... Pay in Lieu of Holiday (WDAA)
PILOT.......... Paton Lyall Tosh [*Rock music group*]
PILOT.......... Payment in Lieu of Taxes
PILOT.......... Permutation Indexed Literature of Technology (IEEE)
PILOT.......... Piloted Low-Speed Test [*Aerospace*]
PILOT.......... Printing Industry Language for Operations of Typesetting
PILOT.......... Programmed Inquiry, Learning or Teaching [*Computer science*]
PILOT.......... Programmed Instruction Learning on Teaching [*A simplified programming language for computer-assisted instruction*] (EDAC)
Pilowtex........ Pillowtex Corp. [*Associated Press*] (SAG)
PILP............ Parametric Integer Linear Program [*Computer science*]
PILP............ Program of Industry/Laboratory Projects [*National Research Council of Canada*]
PILP............ Pseudoinfinite, Logarithmically Periodic
PILS............ Payload Integration Library System [*NASA*] (SSD)
PILS............ Pilsener Lager (DSUE)
PILS............ Precision Instrument Landing System
PIL STA........ Pilot Station [*Nautical charts*]
PILT............ Payment in Lieu of Taxes Program [*Department of the Interior*]
PILTA.......... Payment in Lieu of Taxes Act
PIM............ Grey Nuns - Partners in Ministry (EA)
PIm............ Immaculata College, Immaculata, PA [*Library symbol Library of Congress*] (LCLS)
PIM............ Pacem in Maribus [*Secondary name for the International Ocean Institute*] (MSC)

PIM............ Pacific Rim Energy [*Vancouver Stock Exchange symbol*]
PIM............ Parallel Inference Machine [*Computer science*]
PIM............ Partners-in-Mission [*Church of England*]
PIM............ Penalties in Minutes [*Hockey*]
PIM............ Penicillamine-Induced Myasthenia (STED)
PIM............ Peripheral Interface Module
PIM............ Personal Illumination Marker [*Military*] (INF)
PIM............ Personal Information Manager [*Computer science*]
PIM............ Phosphatidylinositol Mannoside [*Biochemistry*]
Pi M.......... Pillius Medicinensis [*Flourished, 1165-1207*] [*Authority cited in pre-1607 legal work*] (DSA)
PIM............ Pilot Machine (NITA)
PIM............ Pine Mountain, GA [*Location identifier FAA*] (FAAL)
PIM............ Planned Incremental Modernization (DOMA)
PIM............ Plan of Intended Movement (MUGU)
PIM............ Plated Interconnecting Matrix
PIM............ Plug-In Module (MCD)
PIM............ Point Indicating Machine (IAA)
PIM............ Point of Intended Movement [*Military*]
PIM............ Polyphase Induction Motor
PIM............ Position and Intended Movement [*or Maneuver*] (NATG)
PIM............ Position in Miles (MCD)
PIM............ Powder Injection Molding [*Metallurgy*]
PIM............ Precision Indicator of the Meridian
PIM............ Precision Instrument Mount
PIM............ Presa Del Infiernillo [*Mexico*] [*Seismograph station code, US Geological Survey Closed*] (SEIS)
PIM............ Presbyterian Inland Mission
PIM............ Pricing Instructions Memorandum (MCD)
PIM............ Processor in Memory [*Computer science*]
PIM............ Processor Interface Module
PIM............ Product Information Memoranda
PIM............ Program Initialization Module [*Computer science*] (ECII)
PIM............ Program Integration Manual
PIM............ Program Interface Module
PIM............ Pro Independence Movement [*Puerto Rico*]
PIM............ Provincial Institute of Mining
PIM............ Public Information Meeting (COE)
PIM............ Pulse Intensity Modulation
PIM............ Pulse Interval Modulation
PIM............ Putnam Master Intermediate Income Trust [*NYSE symbol*] (SPSG)
PIM............ Putnam Master Interm Income [*NYSE symbol*] (TTSB)
PIM............ South Mountain Restoration Center, South Mountain, PA [*OCLC symbol*] (OCLC)
PiMA............ Ateneo de Manila University, Manila, Philippines [*Library symbol Library of Congress*] (LCLS)
PIMA............ Paper Industry Management Association (EA)
PIMA............ Photographic Industry Marketing Association [*Australia*]
PIMA............ Plug-In Module Assembly (MCD)
PIMA............ Polyisocyanurate Insulation Manufacturers Association (EA)
PIMA............ Portable Intelligence Maintenance Aid [*Army*] (DOMA)
PIMA............ Prime Intermediate Maintenance Activity
PIMA............ Printing Industry Management Association (DGA)
PIMA............ Professional Insurance Mass-Marketing Association [*Bethesda, MD*] (EA)
PIMCC .... Packards International Motor Car Club (EA)
PIMCO .... Pacific Investment Management Co.
PIMCO .... Physicians Insurance Medical Co. (DAVI)
PIMCO .... Poultry Industry Manufacturers Council [*Defunct*] (EA)
PimcoAd...... Pimco Advisors Ltd. [*Associated Press*] (SAG)
PimCom...... Pimco Commercial Mortgage [*Associated Press*] (SAG)
pime .... Pontifical Institute for Foreign Missions (TOCD)
PIME.......... Pontifical Institute for Foreign Missions (TOCD)
PIME.......... Pontifical Institute for Mission Extension [*Roman Catholic men's religious order*]
PIMI.......... Preinactivation Material Inspection [*Military*] (NVT)
PIMIA.......... Potentiometric Ionophore Modulated Immunoassay [*Electrochemistry*]
PIMIS.......... Portable Integrated Maintenance Information System
PIMK.......... Portable Injection Molding Kit
PIML.......... Polynomial Propogation Time Immediate Language [*Computer science*] (MHDI)
PIMMA........ Professional Insurance Mass-Marketing Association [*Bethesda, MD*] (EA)
PIMNY........ Printing Industries of Metropolitan New York
PIMO .... Presentation of Information for Maintenance and Operation [*DoD*]
PIMOS........ Parallel Inference Multiprocessor Operating System [*Computer science*]
PIMP.......... Permissible Individual Maximum Pressure (SAA)
PIMP.......... Peroxisomal Integral Membrane Protein [*Biochemistry*]
PIMP.......... Pimperne [*England*]
PIMP.......... Program for Interactive Multiple Process Simulation (PDAA)
PIMRA........ Pirmasens Missile Repair Activity [*Germany Army*]
PIMRIS .... Pacific Islands Marine Resources Information System [*Marine science*] (OSRA)
PIMS.......... Peacekeeper in Minuteman Silos (DWSG)
PIMS.......... Personnel Inventory Management System [*AT & T*]
PIMS.......... Photoionization Mass Spectrometry
PIMS.......... Pontifical Institute of Mediaeval Studies [*Canada*] (IRC)
PIMS.......... Preform In-Mold Surfacing [*Plastics technology*]
PIMS.......... Printers Integrated Management System (DGA)
PIMS.......... Profit Impact of Marketing Strategy
PIMS.......... Programmable Implantable Medication System
PIMSA........ Prensa Independiente Mexicana Sociedad Anonima [*Press agency*] [*Mexico*]
PIMT.......... Protein Isoaspartyl Methyltransferase [*An enzyme*]

Pim Ten...... Pim on Feudal Tenures [*A publication*] (DLA)
PIMV.......... Plantago Mottle Virus [*Plant pathology*]
PIN............ Jasper, TX [*Location identifier FAA*] (FAAL)
PIN............ Pacific Island Network [*Marine science*] (OSRA)
PIN............ Page and Item Number
PIN............ Parallel Input
PIN............ Parintins [*Brazil*] [*Airport symbol*] (AD)
PIN............ Patriots Information Network [*Defunct*] (EA)
PIN............ Pennsylvania School for the Deaf, Philadelphia, PA [*OCLC symbol*] (OCLC)
PIN............ People in Need [*Food program sponsored by family of kidnapped heiress, Patricia Hearst, 1974*]
PIN............ Personal Identification Name (NITA)
PIN............ Personal [*or Private*] Identification Number [*Banking*]
PIN............ Personal Information Network [*Indesys, Inc.*] [*Telecommunications service*] (TSSD)
PIN............ Personal Injury Notice (AAG)
PIN............ Personnel Increment Number (DOMA)
PIN............ Pesticide Information Network [*Environmental Protection Agency*] (AEPA)
PIN............ Phase Inversion nanoencapsulation [*Materials science*]
PIN............ Piece Identification Number
PIN............ Pinedale [*Wyoming*] [*Seismograph station code, US Geological Survey Closed*] (SEIS)
PIN............ Pinion (MSA)
Pin............ Pinney's Wisconsin Supreme Court Reports [*1839-52*] [*A publication*] (DLA)
PIN............ Plan Identification Number (AFM)
PIN............ Plant Information Network [*Fish and Wildlife Service*] [*Ceased operation*] (IID)
PIN............ Plastics Industry Notes [*Later, CIN*]
PIN............ Police Information Network [*San Francisco Bay area, California*]
PIN............ Position Indicator
PIN............ Positive-Intrinsic-Negative [*or P-Type Intrinsic N-Type*]
PIN............ Power Information Network [*Computer science*]
PIN............ Preliminary Imagery Nomination File (MCD)
PIN............ Private Intelligent Networker (NITA)
PIN............ Processor Independent NetWare [*Computer science*]
PIN............ Procurement Information Notice [*Environmental Protection Agency*] (ERG)
PIN............ Product Identification Number
PIN............ Product Information Network [*McGraw-Hill Information Systems Co.*] [*Information service or system*] (IID)
PIN............ Program Identification Number (MUGU)
PIN............ Program Integrated Network
PIN............ Property Inheritance Network Computer
PIN............ Proposal Identification Number (AAG)
PIN............ Protein Inhibitor of nNOS [*Neuronal Nitric Oxide Synthase*] [*Neuroscience*]
PIN............ PSI Energy, Inc. [*NYSE symbol*] (SPSG)
PIN............ P-Type/Insulator/N-Type [*Electronics*] (AAEL)
PIN............ P-Type Intrinsic N-Type [*or Positive-Intrinsic-Negative*]
PIN............ Publication Identification Number [*Military*] (INF)
P IN^2............ Parts per Square Inch (WDAA)
P IN^3............ Parts per Cubic Inch (WDAA)
PINA.......... Pacific Islands News Association [*Australia*]
PINA.......... Parallax in Altitude [*Navigation*]
P in A............ Parallax in Altitude [*Navigation*]
PINA.......... Parenting in a Nuclear Age (EA)
PINA.......... Potash Institute of North America [*Later, PPI*] (EA)
PinBG .... Pinnacle Bank Group, Inc. [*Associated Press*] (SAG)
P-in-C......... Priest-in-Charge [*Church of England*]
PINC.......... Property Income Certificate [*Investment term British*]
PINCCA........ Price Index Numbers for Current Cost Accounting [*Service in Information and Analysis*] [*British Information service or system*] (IID)
PinclF......... Pinnacle Financial Services, Inc. [*Associated Press*] (SAG)
PinclFn........ Pinnacle Financial Services [*Associated Press*] (SAG)
PinclM........ Pinnacle Micro, Inc. [*Associated Press*] (SAG)
PinclMic....... Pinnacle Micro, Inc. [*Associated Press*] (SAG)
PIND.......... Particle Impact Noise Detection
Pind.......... Pindar [*518-438BC*] [*Classical studies*] (OCD)
PINE.......... Passive Infrared Night Equipment (MCD)
PINE.......... Pine [*Commonly used*] (OPSA)
PINELLAS .... Pinellas Plant [*Department of Energy*] [*Largo, FL*] (GAAI)
PINES .... Pines [*Commonly used*] (OPSA)
PINES .... Public Information on Nuclear Energy Service [*American Nuclear Society*]
PING .... Packet Internet Groper [*Computer program*] (PCM)
ping .... Packet Internet Groper [*Computer science*] (IGQR)
ping .... Pinguis [*Fat, Grease*] [*Latin*] (DAVI)
Ping Chat Mortg... Pingrey's Treatise of Chattel Mortgages [*A publication*] (DLA)
PINGO......... Public Interest Nongovernmental Organization
PINGP......... Prairie Island Nuclear Generating Plant (NRCH)
PINH.......... Pyridoxal Isonicotinoylhydrazone [*Biochemistry*]
PINI.......... Positive Ion Neutral Injector [*Nuclear energy*] (NUCP)
Pinktn .... Pinkerton's, Inc. [*Associated Press*] (SAG)
PINN.......... Pinnacle Banc Group [*NASDAQ symbol*] (TTSB)
PINN.......... Pinnacle Banc Group, Inc. [*NASDAQ symbol*] (SAG)
PINN.......... Pinnacles National Monument
Pinn.......... Pinney's Wisconsin Reports [*A publication*] (DLA)
PINN.......... Proposed International Nonproprietary Name [*Drug research*]
PinnclBk...... Pinnacle Bank [*Associated Press*] (SAG)
Pinney .... Pinney's Wisconsin Reports [*A publication*] (DLA)
Pinney (sv)... Pinney's Wisconsin Reports [*A publication*] (DLA)

PinnSyst ...... Pinnacle Systems, Inc. [Associated Press] (SAG)
PINO .... Positive Input - Negative Output [Computer science]
PINPrB .... PSI Energy, 4.16%cmPfd vtg [NYSE symbol] (TTSB)
PINPrC .... PSI Energy, 4.32% Pfd [NYSE symbol] (TTSB)
PINPrD .... PSI Energy, 7.15% Pfd [NYSE symbol] (TTSB)
PINPrJ .... PSI Energy, 6.875% Pfd [NYSE symbol] (TTSB)
PINPrK .... PSI Energy, 7.44% Pfd [NYSE symbol] (TTSB)
PinptRtl ...... Pinpoint Retail Solutions [Associated Press] (SAG)
PINS .... Palletized Inertial Navigation System [Military] (LAIN)
PINS .... Personnel Information System [Army] (AABC)
PINS .... Persons in Need of Supervision [Classification for delinquent
                  children]
PINS .... Point-in-Space (MCD)
PINS .... Political Information System [Databank of political strategist Richard
                  Wirthlin]
PINS .... Portable Inertial Navigation System
PINS .... Precise Integrated Navigation System [Offshore Systems of
                  Vancouver]
PINS .... Precise Integrated Navigation System [Navy] (DOMA)
PINS .... Professional International Network Society (NTPA)
PINSAC .... PINS [Portable Inertial Navigation System] Alignment Console
PINSTD .... Preinserted
PINSTECH .... Pakistan Institute of Nuclear Science and Technology
PINT .... Power Intelligence (DNAB)
PINT .... Purdue Interpretive Programming and Operating System (MCD)
PINTE .... Processor Interrupts Enabled [Computer science] (MHDI)
PINTS .... Ported-Coax Intrusion Sensor [Military] (INF)
PInU .... Indiana University of Pennsylvania, Indiana, PA [Library symbol
                  Library of Congress] (LCLS)
PINV .... Post-Imperative Negative Variation [Medicine] (DMAA)
Pin (Wis) .... Pinney's Wisconsin Reports [A publication] (DLA)
Pin Wis R .... Pinney's Wisconsin Reports [A publication] (DLA)
PINWOR ...... Pinworm [Gastroenterology] (DAVI)
PinWst .... Pinnacle West Capital Corp. [Associated Press] (SAG)
PINX .... Pinxit [He, or She, Painted It] [Latin]
pinx .... Pinxit (WDAA)
PINXT .... Pinxit [He, or She, Painted It] [Latin] (ROG)
PINY .... Polytechnic Institute of New York
PIO .... Palestine Information Office (EA)
PIO .... Parallel Input/Output
PIO .... Peripheral Input/Output (NITA)
PIO .... Peripheral Input-Output Controller [Computer science] (CIST)
PIO .... Pheniminooxazolidinone [Pharmacology]
PIO .... Photocomposition Input Option (NITA)
PIO .... Photo Interpretation Officer [Air Force]
PIO .... Physical Input-Output [Computer science] (IAA)
PIO .... Pielago [Ship's rigging] (ROG)
PIO .... Pilot-Induced Oscillation
PIO .... Pilot Information Office
PIO .... Pinon, NM [Location identifier FAA] (FAAL)
PIO .... Pi Omicron National Sorority (EA)
PIO .... Pioneer Airlines, Inc. [ICAO designator] (FAAC)
PIO .... Pioneer Electron ADR [NYSE symbol] (TTSB)
PIO .... Pioneer Electronic Corp. [NYSE symbol] (SPSG)
PIO .... Poets International Organisation [Bangalore, India] (EAIO)
PIO .... Position Iterative Operation
PIO .... Precision Interactive Operation [Computer science]
PIO .... Precision Iterative Operation (IAA)
PIO .... Preliminary Inquiry Officer (DNAB)
PIO .... Private Input/Output [Telecommunications] (TEL)
PIO .... Process Input-Output [Computer science] (ECII)
PIO .... Processor Input-Output [Computer science] (MDG)
PIO .... Programmed Input/Output
PIO .... Provisioned Item Order (MCD)
PIO .... Public Information Office [or Officer]
PIO .... Western Pennsylvania School for the Deaf, Pittsburgh, PA [OCLC
                  symbol] (OCLC)
PIOB .... President's Intelligence Oversight Board (DOMA)
PIOBX .... Pioneer Bond Fund [Mutual fund ticker symbol] (SG)
PIOC .... Program Input-Output Cassette [Computer science] (IAA)
PIO/C .... Project Implementation Order/Commodity [Agency for International
                  Development]
PIOCC .... Province Intelligence and Operations Coordination Center [Vietnam]
                  (VNW)
PIOCS .... Parallel Input/Output Control System (NITA)
PIOCS .... Physical Input-Output Control System [Computer science] (BUR)
PIODCA .... Peruvian Inca Orchid Dog Club of America (EA)
PIODX .... Pioneer Fund Cl.A [Mutual fund ticker symbol] (SG)
PIOFA .... Petroleum Ether Insoluble Oxidized Fatty Acid [Food science]
PIOG .... Pioneer Group [NASDAQ symbol] (TTSB)
PIOG .... [The] Pioneer Group, Inc. [NASDAQ symbol] (NQ)
pion .... Pi-Meson (BARN)
PION .... Pioneer (AABC)
PIONA .... Pioneer Companies, Inc. [NASDAQ symbol] (SAG)
PIONA .... Pioneer Cos. 'A' [NASDAQ symbol] (TTSB)
PionCos ...... Pioneer Companies, Inc. [Associated Press] (SAG)
PioneerC ...... Pioneer Commercial Funding Corp. [Associated Press] (SAG)
PionF .... Pioneer Financial Services, Inc. [Associated Press] (SAG)
PionFS .... Pioneer Financial Services, Inc. [Associated Press] (SAG)
PionGp .... [The] Pioneer Group, Inc. [Associated Press] (SAG)
PionHiB .... Pioneer Hi-Bred International [Associated Press] (SAG)
PionInt .... Pioneer Interest Shares [Associated Press] (SAG)
PionrC .... Pioneer Commercial Funding Corp. [Associated Press] (SAG)
PionrEl .... Pioneer Electronic Corp. [Associated Press] (SAG)
PionStd .... Pioneer Standard Electronics [Associated Press] (SAG)

PionStd .... Pioneer-Standard Electronics, Inc. [Associated Press] (SAG)
PIOP .... Pharmacists in Ophthalmic Practice (EA)
PIOPED .... Prospective Investigation of Pulmonary Embolism Diagnosis
                  [Medicine]
PIOPIC .... Protection and Indemnity of Oil Pollution Indemnity Clause
                  [Insurance] (DS)
PioRail .... Pioner Railcorp [Associated Press] (SAG)
PIOS .... Pioneer-Standard Electronics, Inc. [NASDAQ symbol] (NQ)
PIOS .... Pioneer Std Electr [NASDAQ symbol] (TTSB)
PIOSA .... Pan-Indian Ocean Science Association (NOAA)
PIOSP .... Process Input-Output Subroutine Package [Computer science]
                  (MHDI)
PIO/T .... Project Implementation Order/Technical [Agency for International
                  Development]
PIOTA .... Post-Irradiation Open Test Assembly [Nuclear energy] (NRCH)
PIOTA .... Proximity Instrumented Open Test Assembly [Nuclear energy]
                  (NRCH)
PIOTX .... Pioneer II Cl.A [Mutual fund ticker symbol] (SG)
PIOU .... Parallel Input-Output Unit [Computer science] (IEEE)
PIOUS .... Peripheral Integrated Off-Line Utility System (SAA)
PIP .... 6-Mercaptopurin, Vincristine, Methotrexate, Citrovorum Factor
                  [Chemotherapy] (DAVI)
PIP .... Package Irradiation Plant [Nuclear energy] (NUCP)
PIP .... Pan-Iranist Party [Political party] (PPW)
PIP .... Paper Impact Printing (HGAA)
PIP .... Para-Isothiocyanatephenethylamine [Biochemistry]
PIP ....i... Paralytic Infantile Paralysis [Medicine] (DB)
PIP .... Parental Involvement Project (AIE)
PIP .... Participant Instrumentation Package
PIP .... Participating Irredeemable Preference [Shares]
PIP .... Participation Interest Purchase [FNMA] (EMRF)
PIP .... Partido Independentista Puertorriqueno [Puerto Rican Independence
                  Party] [Political party] (PPW)
PIP .... Partners in Progress [Government] [Civil rights]
PIP .... Pasuquin [Philippines] [Seismograph station code, US Geological
                  Survey] (SEIS)
PIP .... Path Independent Protocol
PIP .... Payload Integration Plan [NASA] (NASA)
PIP .... Payload Interface Plan [NASA] (NASA)
PIP .... Payment in Part [Business term]
PIP .... Peak Inspiratory Pressure [Medicine] (DAVI)
PIP .... Periodic Interim Payment Program [Medicare] (GFGA)
PIP .... Peripheral Interchange Program [Computer science]
PIP .... Peripheral Interface Programmer [Circuit] [Computer science]
PIP .... Persistent Internal Polarization
PIP .... Personal Identification Project [Computer science]
PIP .... Personal Innovation Program
PIP .... Personnel Interface Processor (MCD)
PIP .... Pesticide Information Profiles (GNE)
PIP .... Petroleum Incentives Program [Canada]
PIP .... Phosphatidylinositol Phosphate [Biochemistry]
PIP .... Photo Image Processor (MCD)
PIP .... Photo Interpretive Program (BUR)
PIP .... Picture-In-a-Picture [Multi-Vision Products] [Video technology]
PIP .... Pilot Point [Alaska] [Airport symbol] (OAG)
PIP .... Piperacillin [An antibiotic]
PIP .... Plant-in-Place
PIP .... Plant Instrumentation Program
PIP .... Policy Improvement Program
PIP .... Policy Integration Program
PIP .... Pollution Information Project (NITA)
PIP .... Population Information Program [Later, CCP] (EA)
PIP .... Portable Instrumentation Package [Military] (CAAL)
PIP .... Position Indicating Probe (IEEE)
PIP .... Postal Instant Press (EFIS)
PIP .... Postinspiratory Pressure [Medicine] (DAVI)
PIP .... Power Input Panel
PIP .... Prearrival Inspection Procedure
PIP .... Precise Installation Position
PIP .... Predicted Impact Point [Aerospace] (AAG)
PIP .... Predicted Intercept Point
PIP .... Preliminary Information Pamphlet
PIP .... Preparatory Investment Protection [For the consortia which invested
                  in deep sea mining]
PIP .... Preparedness and Industrial Planning
PIP .... Pretty Important Person
PIP .... Primary Indicating Position (IAA)
PIP .... Primary Indicating Position Data Logger (IEEE)
PIP .... Prior Immobilization and Positioning [Roentgenology]
PIP .... Probabilistic Information Processing
PIP .... Problem Identification Program (MCD)
PIP .... Problem Input Preparation [Computer science] (BUR)
PIP .... Procedural Information Pamphlet
PIP .... Proceedings in Print [A bibliographic publication]
PIP .... Process-Induced Particles (AAEL)
PIP .... Product Improvement (MCD)
PIP .... Product Improvement Plan
PIP .... Product Improvement Program [Military]
PIP .... Product Improvement Proposal (MCD)
PIP .... Product Introductory Presentation
PIP .... Production Implementation Program (AAG)
PIP .... Production Improvement Program [Navy] (NG)
PIP .... Production Instrumentation Package (NASA)
PIP .... Productivity Improvement Program [Office of Management and
                  Budget] (GFGA)

PIP.............. Productivity Improvement Program [*Department of Labor*]
PIP.............. Profile Ignition Pick-Up [*Automotive engineering*]
PIP.............. Profit Improvement Program
PIP.............. Program Implementation Plan (MCD)
PIP.............. Program Information Package (AAGC)
PIP.............. Program in Process [*Computer science*] (BUR)
PIP.............. Program in Progress [*Computer science*] (IAA)
PIP.............. Program Integrating Plan [*Computer science*] (IAA)
PIP.............. Program Integration Plan
PIP.............. Programmable Integrated Processor (IEEE)
PIP.............. Programmable Interconnect Point [*Computer science*]
PIP.............. Programmed Individual Presentation (IAA)
PIP.............. Programs for the Improvement of Practice [*Washington, DC Department of Education*] (GRD)
PIP.............. Progressive Independent Party [*South Africa Political party*] (EY)
PIP.............. Progressive Inspection Plan [*Navy*] (NG)
PIP.............. Projected Impact Point [*Aviation*]
PIP.............. Project Implementation Plan
PIP.............. Project Implementation Profile [*Test*] (TMMY)
PIP.............. Project Initiation Period
PIP.............. Project Instrumentation Plan [*NASA*] (GFGA)
PIP.............. Project on Information Processing (IEEE)
PIP.............. Proof in Print
PIP.............. Proposal Instruction Package (MCD)
PIP.............. Proprietary Information Protection
PIP.............. Prototypic Inlet Piping [*Nuclear energy*] (NRCH)
PIP.............. Provabilistic Information Processing [*Computer science*] (IAA)
PIP.............. Prove in Plan (MCD)
PIP.............. Proximal Interphalangeal [*Joint*]
PIP.............. Psychotic Inpatient Profile [*Psychology*]
PIP.............. Public and Institutional Property [*Insurance*]
PIP.............. Public Involvement Program (GNE)
PIP.............. Puerto Rican Independence Party [*Political party*] (PD)
PIP.............. Pulse Input Proportional [*Electro-optical system*]
PIP.............. Pulse Integrating Pendulum
PIP.............. Western Psychiatric Institute and Clinic, University of Pittsburgh, Pittsburgh, PA [*OCLC symbol*] (OCLC)
PIPA.............. Pacific Industrial Property Association (EA)
PIPA.............. Pulse Integrating Pendulum Accelerometer
PIPA.............. Pulse Integrating Pendulum Assembly (NASA)
PIPACE.......... Peacetime Intelligence Plan, Allied Central Europe [*NATO*]
Pip & C Mil L... Pipon and Collier's Military Law [*3rd ed.*] [*1865*] [*A publication*] (DLA)
PI-PB .... Performance Versus Intensity Function for Phonetically Balanced Words (MEDA)
PIPCST .... Piping Cost and Weight Analysis Program (DNAB)
PIPE........... Consolidated Stainless [*NASDAQ symbol*] (TTSB)
PIPE........... Consolidated Stainless, Inc. [*NASDAQ symbol*] (SAG)
PIPE........... Persistent Interstitial Pulmonary Emphysema [*Medicine*] (DMAA)
PIPE........... Pipestone National Monument
PIPE........... Plumbing Industry Progress and Education Fund
PIPECO........ Photoion-Photoelectron Coincidence [*Spectroscopy*]
PIPER .... Pulsed Intense Plasma for Exploratory Research
PiperJaf....... Piper Jaffray, Inc. [*Associated Press*] (SAG)
PIPES........... Piperazinediethanesulfonic Acid [*A buffer*]
PIPES........... Program on International Politics, Economics, and Security [*University of Chicago*]
PIPICO .... Panel on International Programs and International Cooperation in Oceans Affairs [*Department of State*] (NOAA)
PIPICO .... Panel on International Programs and International Organizations [*US State Department*] (USDC)
PIPIDA .... N-Para-Isopropylacetanilide-Iminodiacetic Acid [*Scan*] [*Radiology*] (DAVI)
PIPIDA .... Para-Isopropylphenyl(iminodiacetic Acid)
PIPIT........... Peripheral Interface and Program Interrupt Translator (PDAA)
PIPJ........... Proximal Interphalangeal Joint [*Anatomy*]
PIPLC.......... Phosphatidylinositol-Specific Phospholipase C [*Biochemistry*]
PIPO........... Parallel-In Parallel-Out [*Telecommunications*] (TEL)
PIPO .... Phase-In, Phase-Out (MCD)
PIPPAP........ Pile for Producing Power and Plutonium [*Nuclear energy*] (NRCH)
PIPPS .... Publication Information Processing and Printing System
Pippy .... Person Inheriting Parents' Property [*Lifestyle classification British*]
PIPQUIC....... Program Integration Project Queries Use in Interactive Command (COE)
PIPR .... Plant-in-Place Records
PIPR .... Polytechnic Institute of Puerto Rico
PIPR .... Public Interest Public Relations (EA)
PIPRS .... Ping Intercept Passive Ranging SONAR [*Military*]
PIPS........... Paperless Item Processing System [*Banking*]
PIPS........... Patient-Identified Physicians Survey [*Department of Health and Human Services*] (GFGA)
PIPS........... Pattern Information Processing System
PIPS........... Peabody Intellectual Performance Scale [*Education*]
PIPS........... Plans Integration Partitioning System (COE)
PIPS........... Postinjection Propulsion Subsystem [*NASA*]
PIPS........... Preschool Interpersonal Problem Solving Test
PIPS........... Production Information Processing System (IAA)
PIPS........... Professional Improvement Points Program [*Louisiana*] (EDAC)
PIPS........... Professional Institute of the Public Service of Canada [*See also IPFP*]
PIPS........... Properties of Irregular Parts System (MCD)
PIPS........... Pulsed Integrating Pendulums [*NASA*] (QAA)
PIPS........... Science and Technology Policies Information Exchange Programme [*SPINES*] [*UNESCO*] [*Superseded by*] [*Information service or system*] (IID)

PIPSAR .... Pipe Sizing Program - Air (DNAB)
PIPSCR .... Philippine Islands Public Service Commission Reports [*A publication*] (DLA)
PIPSPK .... Pipe Sizing Program - Sprinkling (DNAB)
PIPSST .... Pipe Sizing Program - Steam (DNAB)
PIPTA .... Panel on International Procurement in the Technology Age (AAGC)
PIPUCR........ Philippine Islands Public Utility Commission Reports [*A publication*] (DLA)
PIQ.............. Parallel Instruction Queue
PIQ.............. Performance Intelligence Quotient [*Psychology*] (DMAA)
PIQ.............. Program Idea Quotient [*Home testing measurement*] (NTCM)
PIQ.............. Property in Question
PIQ.............. State Regional Correctional Facility at Mercer, Mercer, PA [*OCLC symbol*] (OCLC)
PIQA.......... Procurement Integration Quality Assurance (AAGC)
PIQA.......... Proofing, Inspection, and Quality Assurance [*Military*]
PIQSY .... Probes for the International Quiet Solar Year [*OSS*]
PIR.............. Packaging Information Record (MCD)
PIR.............. Parachute Infantry Regiment [*Military*]
PIR.............. Paragnostic Information Retrieval [*Parapsychology*]
PIR.............. Parallel Injection Readout (IAA)
PIR.............. Partido de la Izquierda Revolucionaria [*Party of the Revolutionary Left*] [*Bolivia*] [*Political party*] (PPW)
PIR.............. Passive Infrared
PIR.............. Past in Review (EA)
PIR.............. Peak Intensity Ratio [*Spectroscopy*]
PIR.............. Pennsylvania International Raceway [*Auto racing*]
PIR.............. Pennsylvania Rehabilitation Center, Johnstown, PA [*OCLC symbol*] (OCLC)
PIR.............. Periodic Incremental Release [*Physiology*]
PIR.............. Periodic Intelligence Report
PIR.............. Periodic Intelligence Review [*Supreme Allied Commander, Atlantic*] (NATG)
PIR.............. Personal Interview Record
PIR.............. Personnel Information Roster [*Military*]
PIR.............. Pesticide Ingredient Review Program [*Chemical Specialties Manufacturers Association*]
PIR.............. Petrolite Irradiation Reactor
PIR.............. Philippine Independence Ribbon [*Military decoration*]
PIR.............. Phoenix International Raceway
PIR.............. Photographic Intelligence Report [*Military*]
PIR.............. Photo Interpretation Report [*Air Force*] (AFM)
PIR.............. Pier 1 Imports [*NYSE symbol*] (SPSG)
PIR.............. Pierre [*South Dakota*] [*Airport symbol*] (OAG)
PIR.............. Pilot Request (SAA)
PIR.............. Piriform (DB)
PIR.............. Pirmasens [*Federal Republic of Germany*] [*Seismograph station code, US Geological Survey*] (SEIS)
PIR.............. Plug-In Relay
PIR.............. Post Implementation Review
PIR.............. Postinhibitory Rebound [*Physiology*]
PIR.............. Precision Inspection Request (IAA)
PIR.............. Precision Instrumentation RADAR
PIR.............. Predicted Intercept Range [*Military*] (CAAL)
PIR.............. Prematriculation Immunization Requirement
PIR.............. Pressure Ignition Rocket (NATG)
PIR.............. Pressure Indicator Recorder (ECII)
PIR.............. Prim-Air Aps [*Denmark ICAO designator*] (FAAC)
PIR.............. Primary Intelligence Requirement [*Military*] (INF)
PIR.............. Priority Information Requirement [*Military intelligence*] (INF)
PIR.............. Priority Intelligence Requirement [*Military*] (INF)
PIR.............. Prisoner-Initiated Review
PIR.............. Process and Indoctrinate Recruits
PIR.............. Procurement Initiation Request (MCD)
PIR.............. Product Improvement Review
PIRJ.......... Product Information Release
PIR.............. Production Inspection Record
PIR.............. Professional Investor Report [*A publication*] (IT)
PIR.............. Program Incident Report
PIR.............. Program Information Report [*Head Start Program*] [*Department of Health and Human Services*] (GFGA)
PIR.............. Program Interrupt Register [*Computer science*] (IAA)
PIR.............. Project Independence Report
PIR.............. Protein Identification Resource [*National Biomedical Research Foundation*] [*Georgetown University Medical Center*] [*Information service or system*] (IID)
PIR.............. Protein Information Resource (HGEN)
PIR.............. Protocol-Independent Routing [*Computer science*]
PIR.............. Publication Information Register (IAA)
PIR.............. Pure India Rubber [*Cables*]
PIRA.......... Paper Industries Research Association (NADA)
PIRA.......... Photographic Instrument Repairing Associates [*British*] (DBA)
PIRA.......... Printing and Packaging Research Association
PIRA.......... Printing Industry Research Association (NADA)
PIRA.......... Prison Industries Reorganization Administration [*Terminated, 1940*]
PIRA.......... Provisional Irish Republican Army
PIRA.......... Research Association for the Paper and Board, Printing and Packaging Industries [*Research center*] (IRC)
PIRAD.......... Proximity Information, Range, and Disposition
PIRAI .... PIRA International [*British*] (EAIO)
PIRAMID....... Project: Individualized Reading and Mathematics Inter-District (EDAC)
PIRAS.......... Polarized Infrared Absorption Spectroscopy
PIRATA .... Pilot Research Moored Array in the Tropical Atlantic [*Proposed project*] [*Marine science*] (OSRA)
PIRATE .... Public Information in Rural Areas Technical Experiment (NITA)

PIRATE	Public Information in Rural Areas Technology Experiment [*British Library*] (PDAA)
PIRAZ	Positive Identification RADAR Advisory Zone (NVT)
PIRB	Position Indicating Radio Beacon
PIRC	Portable Inflatable Recompression Chamber (MCD)
PIRC	Pressure Indicator Recorder Controller (ECII)
PIRC	Preventive Intervention Research Center for Child Health [*Yeshiva University*] [*Research center*] (RCD)
PIRC	Protocol Implementation Review Committee [*National Institutes of Health*]
PIRCS	Passive Infrared Confirming Sensor (MCD)
PIRD	Program Instrumentation Requirements Document [*NASA*]
PIR databases	Protein Information Resource Databases (DOG)
PIRE	Pacific Institute for Research and Evaluation [*Research center*] (RCD)
PI Rep	Philippine Island Reports [*A publication*] (DLA)
PIREP	Pilot Report [*Pertaining to meteorological conditions*] [*FAA*]
PIREPS	Pilot Reports [*Marine science*] (OSRA)
PIRETS	Pittsburgh Retrieval System (NITA)
PIRF	Perimeter-Insulated Raised Floor [*Residential construction*]
PIRF	Petroleum Industry Research Foundation (NADA)
PIRFC	Pilot Requests Forecast [*Aviation*] (FAAC)
PIRG	Public Interest Research Group [*Formed by consumer-advocate Ralph Nader*]
P-IRI	Plasma Immunoreactive Insulin [*Hematology*] (MAE)
PIRI	Psychologists Interested in Religious Issues (EA)
PIRID	Passive Infrared Intrusion Detector (NVT)
PIRINC	Petroleum Industry Research Foundation (EA)
PIRL	PRISM [*Personnel Record Information System for Management*] Information RetrievalLanguage [*Computer science*] (PDAA)
PIRN	Preliminary Interface Revision Notice [*NASA*] (KSC)
PIRO	People, Ideas, Resources, Objectives [*Management strategy*] (DHSM)
PIRO	Pictured Rocks National Lakeshore [*National Park Service designation*]
PIRP	Provisional International Reference Preparation
PIRR	Parts Installation and Removal Record [*NASA*] (KSC)
PIRR	Prepositioned War Reserve Interrogation and Readiness Reporting (MCD)
PIRR	Problem Investigation and Repair Record [*NASA*] (KSC)
PIRR	PWRS [*Prepositioned War Reserve Stock*] Interrogation and Readiness Reporting System [*Navy*]
PIRRB	Photo Intelligence Requirements Review Board [*Military*]
PIRS	Passive Infrared Seeker
PIRS	Personal Information Retrieval System
PIRS	Philosopher's Index Retrieval System (NITA)
PIRS	Philosopher's Information Retrieval System [*Bowling Green State University*]
PIRS	Plasma Immunoreactive Secretion [*Medicine*] (DMAA)
PIRS	Pollution Incident Reporting System [*Coast Guard*]
PIRS	Poseidon Information Retrieval System [*Missiles*]
PIRS	Project Information Retrieval System [*HEW*]
PIRT	Precision Infrared Tracking
PIRT	Precision Infrared Triangulation
PIRT	Pretreatment Implementation Review Task Force [*Environmental Protection Agency*] (EPA)
PIRU	Public Information Reference Unit [*Environmental Protection Agency*] (GFGA)
Pis	In Pisonem [*of Cicero*] [*Classical studies*] (OCD)
PIS	Parts Identification Service
PIS	Passenger Information System
PIS	Passive Infrared System
PIS	Patent Inventor Service (NITA)
PIS	Penning Ionization Spectroscopy (PDAA)
PIS	Photographic Interpretation Section
PIS	Pisa [*Italy*] [*Seismograph station code, US Geological Survey Closed*] (SEIS)
PIS	Piscivorous
PIS	Poitiers [*France*] [*Airport symbol*] (OAG)
PIS	Polyisobutylene (EDCT)
PIS	Position Indicator System
PIS	Positive Ion Source
PIS	Postal Inspection Service
PIS	Preinfarction Syndrome [*Cardiology*]
PIS	Preinsert Sequencing
PIS	Pressure-Indicating Switch [*Nuclear energy*] (NRCH)
PIS	Prime Implicant Solution (IAA)
PIS	Process Instrumentation System [*Nuclear energy*] (NRCH)
PIS	Process Instrument Sheet
PIS	Product Information Specialist
PIS	Provisional International Standard
PIS	Public Information Specialist (COE)
PIS	Pulsed Illumination Source
PIS	Pulse Integration System
PIS	Stevens Trade School, Lancaster, PA [*OCLC symbol*] (OCLC)
PISA	Persistent Information Space Architecture [*Computer science*]
PISA	Phase Invariant Signature Algorithm [*Chemistry*] (DAVI)
PISA	Polish Independent Student Association (EA)
PISA	Public Interest Satellite Association [*Defunct*] (EA)
PISAB	Pulse Interference Separation and Blanking [*RADAR*]
PISAL	Periodicals in South African Libraries (NITA)
PISB	People's Institute for Survival and Beyond (EA)
PISC	Pacific International Services Corp. [*NASDAQ symbol*] (NQ)
PISC	Parris Island, South Carolina [*Marine Corps*]
PISC	Petroleum Industry Security Council (EA)

Pisc	Pisces [*Constellation*]
PISCES	Percutaneously Inserted Spinal Cord Electrical Stimulation [*Medicine*] (DMAA)
PISCES	Production Information Stocks and Cost Enquiry System (MHDB)
PISE	No Pilot Balloon Observation Due to Unfavorable Sea Conditions [*NWS*] (FAAC)
PISE	Pnuematically-Impacted Stabilized Earth
PISG	Pitcairn Islands Study Group (EA)
PISGA	Palestinian Interim Self-Government Authority [*Proposed*] (ECON)
PISH	Program Instrumentation Summary Handbook [*NASA*] (KSC)
PISMV	Plantago Severe Mottle Virus [*Plant pathology*]
PISO	No Pilot Balloon Observation Due to Snow [*Meteorology*] (FAAC)
PISO	Parallel-In Serial-Out [*Telecommunications*] (TEL)
PISP	Pipe Springs National Monument
PISSC	Programme International sur la Securite des Substances Chimiques [*International Programme on Chemical Safety*] (EAIO)
PIST	Piston [*Automotive engineering*]
Pist	Piston's Mauritius Reports [*A publication*] (DLA)
Piston	Piston's Mauritius Reports [*A publication*] (DLA)
PISU	Polyimidesulfone [*Organic chemistry*]
PISUKI	Pacific Islands Society of the United Kingdom and Ireland (EAIO)
PISW	Process Interrupt Status Word
PISW	Program Interrupt Status Word (NITA)
PIT	Pacific Investment Trust [*Finance*] [*British*]
PIT	Panair International SRL [*Italy ICAO designator*] (FAAC)
PI/T	Parallel Interface/Timer [*Motorola, Inc.*]
PIT	Parameter Input Tape (IAA)
PIT	Participate in Archeology
PIT	Parti de l'Independance et du Travail [*Party of Independence and Labor*] [*Senegal*] [*Political party*] (PPW)
PIT	Parti Ivoirien des Travailleurs [*Ivorian Workers' Party*] [*The Ivory Coast*] [*Political party*] (EY)
PIT	Partners in Transition [*Poland, Czechoslovakia, and Hungary*] (ECON)
PIT	Part-Time, Intermittent, Temporary [*Nuclear energy*]
PIT	Passive Immunotherapy [*Medicine*] (TAD)
PIT	Passive Integrated Transponder
PIT	Patellar Inhibition Test [*Neurology*] (DAVI)
Pit	Pateller Inhibition Test (STED)
PIT	Performance Improvement Tests
PIT	Peripheral Input Tape [*Computer science*]
PIT	Peripheral Interface Tests (MCD)
PIT	Permanent Income Theory [*Econometrics*]
PIT	Personal Income Tax
PIT	Phase Inversion Temperature [*Physical Chemistry*]
PIT	Photographic Interpretation Technique
PIT	Physical Inventory Taking (MHDB)
PIT	Picture Identification Test [*Psychology*]
PIT	Picture Impressions Test [*Psychology*]
PIT	Pilot Instructor Training [*Aviation*] (FAAC)
PIT	Pirates Gold Corp. [*Vancouver Stock Exchange symbol*]
Pit	Pitocin [*Trademark of Parke, Davis & Co. for Oxytocin, a labor-inducing drug*]
Pit	Pitressin [*Trademark of Parke, Davis & Co. for Vasopressin, an antidiuretic hormone*]
PIT	Pittsburgh [*Pennsylvania*] [*Seismograph station code, US Geological Survey Closed*] (SEIS)
PIT	Pittsburgh [*Pennsylvania*] [*Airport symbol*]
PIT	Pituitary [*Endocrinology*] (AAMN)
pit	Pituitary (STED)
PIT	Plasma Iron Transport [*Hematology*]
PIT	Plasma Iron Turnover [*Hematology*] (DAVI)
PIT	Polar Ionospheric Trough
PIT	Polaris Industrial Team [*Missiles*]
PIT	Pre-Induction Training
PIT	Preinstallation Test [*NASA*] (KSC)
PIT	Prevailing-In Torque [*Automotive engineering*]
PIT	Print Illegal and Trace
PIT	Printing and Information Technology Division (NITA)
PIT	Processing of Indexing Terms
PIT	Product Improvement Test
PIT	Program Instruction Tape [*Computer science*] (IEEE)
PIT	Programmable Interval Timer
PIT	Programmed Instruction Text
PIT	Projected Inactive Time [*Computer science*]
PIT	Property Income Trust [*Investment term*]
PIT	Provincial Institute of Textiles
PIT	Psychological Insight Test [*Psychometrics*]
PIT	University of Pittsburgh, Pittsburgh, PA [*OCLC symbol*] (OCLC)
PITA	Pacific International Trapshooting Association (EA)
PITA	Pain in the Ass
PITA	Paper Industry Technical Association [*British*] (EAIO)
PITA	Provincial Institute of Technology and Art
PITB	Pacific Inland Tariff Bureau
PITB	Push Commercial Division [*An association*] (EA)
PITB	PUSH [*People United to Save Humanity*] International Trade Bureau (EA)
Pitblado Lect	Isaac Pitblado's Lectures on Continuing Legal Education [*A publication*] (DLA)
PITC	Phenylisothiocyanate [*Organic chemistry*]
PITC	Photoinduced Tunnel Current
Pitc	Pitcairn's Criminal Trials [1488-1624] [*Scotland*] [*A publication*] (DLA)
PITC	Pittencrieff Communic [*NASDAQ symbol*] (TTSB)
PITC	Pittencrieff Communications [*NASDAQ symbol*] (SAG)
Pitc Crim Tr	Pitcairn's Ancient Criminal Trials [*Scotland*] [*A publication*] (DLA)

PITCOM .... Parliamentary Information Technology Committee [*Political communications*] [*British*]
Pitc Tr .... Pitcairn's Criminal Trials [*3 Scotland*] [*A publication*] (DLA)
PitDsm .... Pittsburgh-Des Moines Corp. [*Associated Press*] (SAG)
PITE .... Project on Information Technology and Education [*Defunct*] (EA)
Pitencr .... Pittencrieff Communications [*Commercial firm Associated Press*] (SAG)
PITF .... Poultry Industry Trust Fund [*Australia*]
PITFC .... Potato Industry Trust Fund Committee [*Western Australia*]
PITG .... Payload Integration Task Group [*NASA*] (NASA)
PITHX .... Pioneer Mid Cap Cl.A [*Mutual fund ticker symbol*] (SG)
PITI .... Principal, Interest, Taxes, Insurance [*Real estate*]
Pitisc Lex ... Pitisci's Lexicon [*A publication*] (DLA)
Pitm Prin & Sur... Pitman on Principal and Surety [*A publication*] (DLA)
PITN .... Polyisothianaphthene [*Organic chemistry*]
PitnB .... Pitney-Bowes, Inc. [*Associated Press*] (SAG)
PitnyBw ...... Pitney-Bowes, Inc. [*Associated Press*] (SAG)
PITP .... Phosphatidylinositol Transfer Protein [*Biochemistry*]
PITP .... Pseudoidiopathic Thrombocytopenic Purpura (STED)
PITR .... Plasma Iron Transport [*or Turnover*] Rate [*Hematology*]
PITS .... Parent-Infant Traumatic Stress (DAVI)
PITS .... Partners In Transition [*Poland, Czech, Hungary - called the Visegrad Trio*]
PITS .... Passive Intercept Tracking System
PITS .... Patriot Integration and Test System [*Army*]
PITS .... Payload Integration Test Set [*NASA*] (MCD)
PITS .... Photoinduced Transient Spectroscopy
PITS .... Primary Influent Treatment System
PITS .... Project Information Tracking System [*Environmental Protection Agency*] (GFGA)
PITS .... Propellant Injector Tube Simulator (MCD)
PITS .... Propulsion Integration Test Stand
PitstnMn ...... [*The*] Pittston Co. [*Associated Press*] (SAG)
PitstnSvc .... [*The*] Pittston Co. [*Associated Press*] (SAG)
Pit Sur .... Pitman on Principal and Surety [*1840*] [*A publication*] (DLA)
Pitt .... Pittsburgh, PA (DLA)
PITT .... Polaris Integrated Test Team [*Missiles*]
Pitt Bank .... Pitt's Bankruptcy Acts [*A publication*] (DLA)
PITTC .... Philips International Telecommunications Training Center (IAA)
Pitt CC Pr ... Pitt's County Court Practice [*A publication*] (DLA)
Pitt LJ .... Pittsburgh Legal Journal [*A publication*] (DLA)
Pitts .... Pittsburgh, PA (DLA)
Pitts .... Pittsburgh Reports [*A publication*] (DLA)
Pittsb .... Pittsburgh, PA (DLA)
Pittsb .... Pittsburgh Reports [*A publication*] (DLA)
Pittsb Leg J... Pittsburgh Legal Journal [*Pennsylvania*] [*A publication*] (DLA)
Pittsb Leg J NS... Pittsburgh Legal Journal, New Series [*Pennsylvania*] [*A publication*] (DLA)
Pittsb Leg J (OS)... Pittsburgh Legal Journal, Old Series [*A publication*] (DLA)
Pittsb Leg J (PA)... Pittsburgh Legal Journal [*Pennsylvania*] [*A publication*] (DLA)
Pittsb LJ ...... Pittsburgh Legal Journal [*Pennsylvania*] [*A publication*] (DLA)
Pittsb L Rev... Pittsburgh Law Review [*A publication*] (DLA)
Pittsb R (PA)... Pittsburgh Reporter [*Pennsylvania*] [*A publication*] (DLA)
Pittsburgh Leg J... Pittsburgh Legal Journal [*Pennsylvania*] [*A publication*] (DLA)
Pittsburgh Leg Journal... Pittsburgh Legal Journal [*Pennsylvania*] [*A publication*] (DLA)
Pittsburg St U... Pittsburg State University (GAGS)
Pitts Leg J... Pittsburgh Legal Journal [*Pennsylvania*] [*A publication*] (DLA)
Pitts Leg J (NS)... Pittsburgh Legal Journal, New Series [*Pennsylvania*] [*A publication*] (DLA)
Pitts Leg Jour... Pittsburgh Legal Journal [*Pennsylvania*] [*A publication*] (DLA)
Pitts LJ .... Pittsburgh Legal Journal [*A publication*] (DLA)
Pitts LJ (NS)... Pittsburgh Legal Journal, New Series [*A publication*] (DLA)
Pitts R .... Pittsburgh Reports [*Pennsylvania*] [*A publication*] (DLA)
Pitts Rep .... Pittsburgh Reports [*A publication*] (DLA)
Pitts Rep (PA)... Pittsburgh Reports [*Pennsylvania*] [*A publication*] (DLA)
Pittway .... Pittway Corp. [*Associated Press*] (SAG)
Pittwy .... Pittway Corp. [*Associated Press*] (SAG)
PittwyA .... Pittway Corp. [*Associated Press*] (SAG)
PITU .... Pipe or Tubing [*Freight*]
PitWVa .... Pittsburgh & West Virginia Railroad [*Associated Press*] (SAG)
PITY-EM ..... Principal, Interest, Taxes, Energy, and Maintenance [*Real estate*]
PITYP .... Pinatype (VRA)
PIU .... East Pennsylvania Psychiatric Institute, Philadelphia, PA [*OCLC symbol*] (OCLC)
PIU .... Path Information Unit [*Computer science*]
PIU .... Pathological Internet Use
PIU .... Photographic Interpretation Unit [*Marine Corps*]
PIU .... Pilot Indicator Unit [*Aviation*] (IAA)
PIU .... Pilot Information Utilization
PIU .... Piura [*Peru*] [*Airport symbol*] (OAG)
PIU .... Plug-In Unit
PIU .... Polymerase-Inducing Unit
PIU .... Power Integration Unit (SSD)
PIU .... Power Intercept Unit [*Military*] (CAAL)
PIU .... Power Interface Unit (MCD)
PIU .... Private Islands Unlimited (EA)
PIU .... Process Input Unit [*Computer science*] (BUR)
PIU .... Process Interface Unit
PIU .... Programmer Interface Unit (MCD)
PIU .... Pyrotechnic Initiator Unit (MCD)
PiU .... University of the Philippines, Quezon City, Philippines [*Library symbol Library of Congress*] (LCLS)
PIUG .... Parti Independantiste de l'Unite Guyanaise [*Pro-Independence Party of Guyanese Unity*] [*Political party*] (PPW)

PIUMP .... Plug-In Unit Mounting Panel
PIUS .... Process Inherent Ultimately Safe [*Nuclear reactor*]
PI/USA .... Packaging Institute, United States of America [*Later, PI/INT'L*] (EA)
PIV .... Parainfluenza Virus
PIV .... Peak Inverse Voltage [*RADAR*]
PIV .... Peripheral Intravenous [*Line*] [*Pharmacology*] (DAVI)
PIV .... Personal Indentification Verification
PIV .... Pick Inverse Voltage [*Electronics*] (ECII)
PIV .... Piva [*Solomon Islands*] [*Seismograph station code, US Geological Survey Closed*] (SEIS)
PIV .... Pivot [*Automotive engineering*]
PIV .... Planet in View [*NASA*]
PIV .... Plug-In Valve
PIV .... Positive Infinitely Variable
PIV .... Post Indicator Valve
PIV .... Product Inspection Verification
PIV .... Propellant Isolation Valve
PIV .... Scotland School for Veterans' Children, Scotland, PA [*OCLC symbol*] (OCLC)
PIV4 .... Plantago Virus 4 [*Plant pathology*]
PIVAD .... Product Improvement Vulcan Air Defense (MCD)
PIVADS .... Product Improved Vulcan Air Defense System (MCD)
PIVD .... Protruded Intervertebral Disc [*Medicine*]
PIVED .... Plasma-Injection Vacuum Energy Diverter
PIVKA .... Protein-Induced by Vitamin K Antagonist (DB)
PIVKA .... Protein in Vitamin K Absence (AAMN)
PIVN .... Public Interest Video Network/New Voices Radio (EA)
PIVOT .... Planning and Implementing Vocational Readiness in Occupational Therapy
PIVR .... Pacemaker-Induced Ventricular Rate [*Cardiology*] (CPH)
PIVS .... Particle-Induced Visual Sensations
PIVT .... Production Improvement Verification Test
PIVX .... Plantain Virus X [*Plant pathology*]
PIW .... Period of Incapacity for Work (DI)
PIW .... Plastic Insulated Wire
PIW .... Ports and Inland Waterways
PIW .... Program Interrupt Word
PIW .... Woodhaven Center, Philadelphia, PA [*OCLC symbol*] (OCLC)
PIWC .... Petroleum Industry War Council
PIWG .... Product Improvement Working Group [*Military*] (AFIT)
PIWI .... No Pilot Balloon Observation Due to High, or Gusty, Surface Wind [*NWS*] (FAAC)
PIWWC .... Planetary Initiative for the World We Choose (EA)
PIX .... Parallel Interface Extender [*Computer science*] (IAA)
PIX .... Pico Island [*Azores*] [*Airport symbol*] (OAG)
PIX .... Picture
PIX .... Picture Rocks, PA [*Location identifier FAA*] (FAAL)
PIX .... Pinxit [*He, or She, Painted It*] [*Latin*] (ROG)
PIX .... Proton-Induced X-Ray Analysis
PIX .... Youth Development Center, Loysville, Loysville, PA [*OCLC symbol*] (OCLC)
Pix Aud .... Pixley on Auditors [*8th ed.*] [*1901*] [*A publication*] (DLA)
PIXE .... Particle [*or Proton*]-Induced X-Ray Emission
PIXEL .... Picture Element [*Single element of resolution in image processing*]
PIXES .... Particle-Induced X-Ray Emission Spectroscopy (EDCT)
PIXR .... Pixar [*NASDAQ symbol*] (TTSB)
PIXT .... PixTech, Inc. [*NASDAQ symbol*] (SAG)
PixTech ...... PixTech, Inc. [*Associated Press*] (SAG)
PIY .... Pembroke Imperial Yeomanry [*British military*] (DMA)
PIY .... Personality Inventory for Youth [*Test*] (TMMY)
PIY .... Youth Development Center, New Castle, New Castle, PA [*OCLC symbol*] (OCLC)
PIZ .... Pizazz European [*British*] [*FAA designator*] (FAAC)
PIZ .... Point Lay [*Alaska*] [*Airport symbol*] (OAG)
PIZ .... Point Lay, AK [*Location identifier FAA*] (FAAL)
PIZ .... Youth Development Center, Waynesburg, Waynesburg, PA [*OCLC symbol*] (OCLC)
PIZZ .... Pizzicato [*Plucked*] [*Music*]
pizz .... Pizzicato [*Plucking*] [*Italian*] [*Music*] (WDAA)
PizzaInn ..... Pizza Inn, Inc. [*Associated Press*] (SAG)
PJ .... Air St. Pierre [*ICAO designator*] (AD)
PJ .... Bombay High Court Printed Judgments [*1869-1900*] [*India*] [*A publication*] (DLA)
PJ .... Netherlands Antilles [*International civil aircraft marking*] (ODBW)
PJ .... Pajamas
PJ .... Panel Jack
PJ .... Parnelli Jones [*Race car driver*]
PJ .... Parteijargon [*Party Language*] [*German*]
PJ .... Participating Jurisdiction
PJ .... Peripheral Jet (AAG)
PJ .... Petajoule (ADA)
PJ .... Peutz-Jeghers [*Syndrome*] [*Medicine*] (DB)
PJ .... Picojoule [*Logic gate efficiency measure*] (MDG)
PJ .... Plasma Jet (AAG)
PJ .... Plastic Jacket
PJ .... Police Justice
PJ .... Possible Jobs [*Test*] [*Psychology*]
PJ .... Presiding Judge
PJ .... Presiding Probate Judge [*British*] (ROG)
PJ .... Prince of Jerusalem [*Freemasonry*]
PJ .... Probate Judge
PJ .... Procurement Justification [*Navy*]
PJ .... Project Jonah [*Defunct*] (EA)
PJ .... Puisne Judge [*Australia*]
PJ .... Pulsejet

PJ	Purchases Journal [Accounting]
PJA	Abington Library Society, Jenkintown, PA [Library symbol Library of Congress Obsolete] (LCLS)
PJA	Pipe Jacking Association [British] (DBA)
PJA	Proper Job Analysis (COE)
PJAFC	P. J. Allman Fan Club (EA)
PJAL	Progressive Jewish Activism List [An association]
PJAIG	Alverthorpe Gallery, Rosenwald Collection, Jenkintown, PA [Library symbol Library of Congress] (LCLS)
PJAM	PJ America, Inc. [NASDAQ symbol] (SAG)
PJ Amer	PJ America, Inc. [Associated Press] (SAG)
PJB	Pad Journal Bearing
PJB	Premature Junctional Beat [Cardiology]
PJBD	Permanent Joint Board on Defense [US, Canada]
PJC	Jean Coutu Group (PJC), Inc. [Toronto Stock Exchange symbol]
PJC	Paducah Junior College [Kentucky]
PJC	Paris Junior College [Texas]
PJC	Pensacola Junior College [Florida]
PJC	Perkinston Junior College [Mississippi]
PJC	Piper Jaffray Companies [NYSE symbol] (SPSG)
PJC	Piper Jaffray Cos. Inc. [NYSE symbol] (TTSB)
PJC	Post Junior College [Connecticut]
PJC	Poteau Junior College [Oklahoma]
PJC	Pratt Junior College [Kansas]
PJC	Premature Junctional Contractions [Cardiology] (DMAA)
PJC	University of Pittsburgh, Johnstown, Johnstown, PA [OCLC symbol] (OCLC)
PJCTL	Projectile (MSA)
Pjctvs.	Projectavision, Inc. [Associated Press] (SAG)
Pjctvsn.	Projectavision, Inc. [Associated Press] (SAG)
PJD	Pedro Dome [Alaska] [Seismograph station code, US Geological Survey Closed] (SEIS)
PJE	Parachute Jumping Exercise
PJE	Private Jet Expeditions, Inc. [ICAO designator] (FAAC)
PJE	Project Engineer
PJE	Pulse Jet Engine
PJES	Photojet Edge Sensor
PJF	Peripheral Jet (Flat-Bottom)
PJF	Pharmaceutical Journal Formulary (ROG)
PJF	Pin Jointed Framework
PJFS	Philip Jose Farmer Society (EA)
PJG	Panjgur [Pakistan] [Airport symbol] (OAG)
PJG	Potts Junction [Guam] [Seismograph station code, US Geological Survey] (SEIS)
PJH	Piper, Jr., H. E., Philadelphia PA [STAC]
PJH	PLRS/JTIDS [Position Location Reporting System/Joint Tactical Information Distribution System] Hybrid (MCD)
PJHI	PLRS/JTIDS [Position Location Reporting System/Joint Tactical Information Distribution System] Hybrid Interface
PJI	Parachute Jump Instructor [Military British] (INF)
PJI	Pattern Jury Instructions [A publication]
PJI	Personnel Journal Index [Personnel Journal] [Information service or system] (CRD)
PJI	Point Judith, RI [Location identifier FAA] (FAAL)
PJI	Proper Job Instruction (COE)
PJILMCC	Philip C. Jessup International Law Moot Court Competition (EA)
PJIT	Parts Just in Time
P JI	Pharmaceutical Journal [A publication] (ROG)
PJL	Printer Job Language [Computer science]
PJLB	Lower Burma Printed Judgments [A publication] (DLA)
PJM	Pennsylvania-Jersey-Maryland [Electric power pool]
PJM	Polymer Jell Material
PJM	Positive Joint Mobilization [Medicine] (DMAA)
PJM	Postjunctional Membrane
PJM	Power Jets Memorandum
PJM	Project Manager [Military]
PJN	Fort Lauderdale, FL [Location identifier FAA] (FAAL)
PJo	Cambria County Library System, Johnstown, PA [Library symbol Library of Congress] (LCLS)
PJO	Pioneer Jupiter Orbit [NASA]
PJON	Johnston Island/Johnston Atoll [Johnston Island] [ICAO location identifier] (ICLI)
PJOP	Preliminary Joint Operation Procedure (KSC)
PJoU	University of Pittsburgh at Johnstown, Johnstown, PA [Library symbol Library of Congress] (LCLS)
PJP	Pancreatic Juice Protein [Medicine] (DMAA)
PJPC	Plug/Jack Patch Cord
PJR	Peoria, IL [Location identifier FAA] (FAAL)
PJR	Peterson, J. Robert, New York NY [STAC]
PJR	Philadelphia Journalism Review [A publication]
PJR	Pipe Joint Record (DNAB)
PJR	Port Jersey [AAR code]
PJR	Power Jets Report
P Jr & H	Patton, Jr., and Heath's Reports [Virginia Special Court of Appeals] [A publication] (DLA)
PJS	Jet Aviation, Business Jets AG [Switzerland ICAO designator] (FAAC)
PJS	Newport News, VA [Location identifier FAA] (FAAL)
PJ's	Pajamas [Slang]
PJ's	Paramedic Jumpers
PJS	Peripheral Jet (Skegs)
PJS	Peritoneojugular Shunt [Medicine] (DB)
PJS	Peutz-Jeghers Syndrome [Oncology]
PJ's	Physical Jerks [Exercise] [Slang British] (DSUE)
PJS	Piezojunction Sensor

PJS	Plug and Jack Set
PJS	Production Job Sheet
PJSS	PACAF [Pacific Air Forces] Jungle Survival School (AFM)
PJT	Paroxysmal Junctional Tachycardia [Cardiology]
PJT	Practical Job Training (MCD)
PJT	Pulse Jitter Tester
PJTN	Projection (MSA)
PJTR	Projector (MSA)
PJTV	Projectavision, Inc. [NASDAQ symbol] (SAG)
PJTVP	Projectavision $0.40 Cv'B'Pfd [NASDAQ symbol] (TTSB)
PJTVW	Projectavision Inc. Wrrt [NASDAQ symbol] (TTSB)
PJU	Juniata College, Huntingdon, PA [OCLC symbol] (OCLC)
PJU	Physician's Journal Update [Television program]
PJV	Pump Jet Vehicle
PJVT	Paroxysmal Junctional-Ventricular Tachycardia [Medicine] (MEDA)
PK	Central Parking [NYSE symbol] (TTSB)
PK	Central Parking Corp. [NYSE symbol] (SAG)
pK	Dissociation Constant [Chemistry] (DAVI)
pK'	Negative Log of the Dissociation Constant [Medicine]
PK	Pack (AAG)
PK	Package [Shipping] (MCD)
pk	Pakistan [IYRU nationality code] [MARC country of publication code Library of Congress] (LCCP)
PK	Pakistan [ANSI two-letter standard code] (CNC)
PK	Park [or Parking]
pk	Park (VRA)
PK	Park (DD)
PK	Parrot-Kaufmann (DB)
PK	Paterson-Kelly [Syndrome] [Medicine] (DB)
PK	Peak [Valve] (NAKS)
PK	Peak [Maps and charts]
pK	Peak Value [Computer science]
PK	Peck (AAG)
pk	Peck (DMAA)
PK	Penetrating Keratoplasty [Ophthalmology] (DAVI)
PK	Pericardial Knock [Medicine] (DB)
PK	Peter King [Afro-jazz band]
PK	Pharmacokinetic
PK	Phileleftheron Komma [Liberal Party] [Greek Political party] (PPE)
PK	Pig Kidney [Medicine] (DMAA)
PK	Pike
PK	Piringer-Kuschinka [Syndrome] [Medicine] (DB)
P$_K$	Plasma Potassium [Biochemistry] (DAVI)
PK	Pokhvala Knige [A publication]
PK	Pole Cat [Slang]
PK	Polyketone (EDCT)
PK	Position Keeper
PK	Posta Kutusu [Postbox] [Turkish] (EY)
PK	Prausnitz-Kuestner [Reaction] [Immunology]
PK	Prausnitz-Kunstner [Reaction or Transfer Test] [Medicine] (DAVI)
PK	Preacher's Kid [Slang]
PK	Pridie Kalendas [The Day before the Calends] [Latin]
PK	Primary Key [Computer science] (PCM)
PK	Principal Keeper [Slang for a warden]
PK	Probability of Kill (MCD)
PK	Prophets and Kings (BJA)
PK	Protein Kinase [Also, PKase] [An enzyme]
PK	Psychokinesis
PK	Psychokinetic (DB)
PK	Pyruvate Kinase [An enzyme]
PK	West Irian [Aircraft nationality and registration mark] (FAAC)
P-K4	Pawn to King Four [Standard opening to a game of chess. Pawn is moved to the fourth square in front of the king]
PKA	Equator Airlines Ltd. [Kenya] [ICAO designator] (FAAC)
PKA	Napaskiak [Alaska] [Airport symbol] (OAG)
PKA	Napaskiak, AK [Location identifier FAA] (FAAL)
pKa	Negative Log of Dissociation Constant [Medicine] (DAVI)
PKA	Paul Kagan Associates, Inc. [Information service or system Telecommunications] (IID)
PKA	Pi Kappa Alpha [Fraternity]
PKA	Polk Audio [AMEX symbol] (SAG)
PKA	Primary Knock-on-Atom (MCD)
PKA	Professional Karate Association [Defunct] (EA)
PKA	Prokininogenase [An enzyme] (MAE)
PKA	Protein Kinase A [An enzyme]
PKA	Public Key Algorithm [Computer science]
PkAF	Pakistani Air Force
PKAFA	PKA [Professional Karate Association] Fighters Association [Defunct] (EA)
PKAR	Protein Kinase Activation Ratio [Medicine] (DMAA)
PKAS	Parti Kadazan Asli Sabah [Malaysia] [Political party] (FEA)
PKase	Protein Kinase [Also, PK] [An enzyme]
PKAWA	Pocket Knife Ancillary Workers' Association [A union] [British]
PKB	Parkersburg [West Virginia] [Airport symbol] (OAG)
PKB	Parkersburg, WV [Location identifier FAA] (FAAL)
PKB	Photoelectric Keyboard
PKB	Portable Keyboard
PKB	Protein Kinase B [An enzyme]
PKBS	Preschool and Kindergarten Behavior Scales [Test] (TMMY)
PKC	Cocoa, FL [Location identifier FAA] (FAAL)
PKC	Peckham Road [California] [Seismograph station code, US Geological Survey] (SEIS)
PKC	Phuket [Thailand] [Airport symbol] (AD)
PKC	Position Keeping Computer
PKC	Problem-Knowledge Coupler (DMAA)

PKC.............. Protein Kinase C [An enzyme]
PKC.............. Public Key Cryptography
PKCS .... Public Key Cryptography Standards [Telecommunications service]
PKD .... Pac Ed Systems Corp. [Vancouver Stock Exchange symbol]
PKD .... Packed (IAA)
PKD .... Parker Drilling [NYSE symbol] (TTSB)
PKD .... Parker Drilling Co. [NYSE symbol] (SPSG)
PKD .... Park Rapids, MN [Location identifier FAA] (FAAL)
PKD .... Partially Knocked Down [Consignment] [Shipping] (DS)
PKD .... Philip K. Dick [Science fiction writer]
PKD .... Pi Kappa Delta [Society]
PKD .... Polycystic Kidney Disease [Medicine]
PKD .... Programmable Keyboard and Display [Computer science] (NASA)
PKD .... Proliferative Kidney Disease [Medicine] (DMAA)
PKDB .... Partai Kebang-Saan Demokratik Brunei [Brunei National Democratic Party] [Political party] (EY)
PKDG .... Professional Knitwear Designers Guild
PKDOM........ Pack for Domestic Use
PKD PDR .... Packed Powder (WGA)
PKDS .... Philip K. Dick Society [Defunct] (EA)
PKE .... Pacific Kenridge [Vancouver Stock Exchange symbol]
PKE .... Park Electrochemical [NYSE symbol] (TTSB)
PKE .... Park Electrochemical Corp. [NYSE symbol] (SPSG)
PKE .... Parker, CA [Location identifier FAA] (FAAL)
PKE .... Parkes [Australia Airport symbol] (OAG)
PKE .... Public-Key Encryption [Microcomputer technology]
PKF .... Pakistan Investment Fd [NYSE symbol] (TTSB)
PKF .... Pakistan Investment Fund [NYSE symbol] (SPSG)
PKF .... Park Falls, WI [Location identifier FAA] (FAAL)
PKF .... Parkfield Array [California] [Seismograph station code, US Geological Survey] (SEIS)
PKF .... Phagocytosis and Killing Function [Immunology] (AAMN)
PKF .... Phosphofructokinase (DB)
PKF .... Polarity Correlation Function (IAA)
PKF .... Primary Kidney Fold
PKFC .... Princess Kitty Fan Club (EA)
PKG .... Package
pkg.............. Package (WDMC)
Pkg .... Packing (DS)
PKG .... Parking (KSC)
PKG .... Phonocardiogram [Cardiology]
PKGD .... Packaged (IAA)
PKGE .... Package
pkge.............. Package (WDMC)
Pkg instr...... Packing Instruction (DS)
PKGNG........ Packaging
PKG-POL.... Packaged POL [Petroleum, Oils and Lubricants] (DOMA)
Pkgs............. Packages (EBF)
PKH .... Park Hill [California] [Seismograph station code, US Geological Survey] (SEIS)
PKH .... Probability of a Kill Given a Hit [Military] (DNAB)
PKHOW....... Pack Howitzer [Marine Corps]
PKI.............. Parkland Industries Ltd. [Toronto Stock Exchange symbol]
PKI.............. Partai Katolik Indonesia [Catholic Party of Indonesia] [Political party]
PKI.............. Partai Komunis Indonesia [Communist Party of Indonesia] [Political party]
PKI.............. Partai Kristen Indonesia [Christian Party of Indonesia] [Political party]
PKI.............. Potato Kallikrein Inhibitor [Medicine] (DMAA)
PKI.............. Protein Kinase Inhibitor [Biochemistry]
PKI.............. Pyruvate Kinase, Liver Type [Medicine] (DMAA)
PKK .... Kurdish Workers' Party [Turkey Political party] (PD)
PKK .... Kurdistan Workers' Party
PKK .... Pakokku [Myanmar] [Airport symbol] (OAG)
PKK .... Porkkala [Finland] [Seismograph station code, US Geological Survey] (SEIS)
PKK .... Protein Kinase K [An enzyme]
PKKP .... Pakistan National Scientific and Documentation Center, Karachi, Pakistan [Library symbol Library of Congress] (LCLS)
PKL .... Parklane Technologies, Inc. [Vancouver Stock Exchange symbol]
PKL............. Pi Kappa Lambda [Society]
PK-LT.......... Psychokinesis on Living Targets
PKM .... Packmaster [Army] (WGA)
PKM .... Perigee Kick Motor (MCD)
PKMA.......... Eniwetok [Marshall Islands] [ICAO location identifier] (ICLI)
PK-MB......... Psychokinetic Metal-Bending [Parapsychology]
PKMJ .... Majuro [Marshall Islands] [ICAO location identifier] (ICLI)
PKMKCMD ... Perhaps...Kids Meeting Kids Can Make a Difference (EA)
Pkmr............. Packmaster [Army]
PKMS........... Pertubohan Kebangsaan Melayu Singapura [Singapore Malays' National Organization] [Political party] (FEA)
PKN .... Aspen, CO [Location identifier FAA] (FAAL)
PKN .... Pangkalanbuun [Indonesia] [Airport symbol] (OAG)
PKN .... Parkinsonism [Medicine] (DMAA)
PKN .... Pauken [Kettledrums]
PKN .... Perkin-Elmer [NYSE symbol] (TTSB)
PKN .... Perkin-Elmer Corp. [NYSE symbol] (SPSG)
PKNG HSE.. Packing House [Freight]
PKO .... Parakou [Benin] [Airport symbol] (OAG)
PKO .... Peace-Keeping Operation (MCD)
PKO .... Perdant par Knockout [Losing by a Knockout] [French]
PKOH .... Park-Ohio Indus [NASDAQ symbol] (TTSB)
PKOH .... Park Ohio Industries [NASDAQ symbol] (SAG)
PKOH .... Park-Ohio Industries, Inc. [NASDAQ symbol] (NQ)
PKP............. Palestiner Komunistische Partei [Palestine Communist Party] [Political party] (BJA)

PKP............. Partido Komunista ng Pilipinas [Communist Party of the Philippines] [Political party] (PPW)
PKP............. Penetrating Keratoplasty [Ophthalmology]
PKP............. Perustuslaillinen Kansanpuolue [Constitutional People's Party] [Finland Political party] (PPE)
PKP............. Phi Kappa Phi [Honor society] (AEE)
PKP............. Polskie Koleje Panstwowe [Polish State Railways]
PKP............. Preknock Pulse
PKP............. Pukapuka [French Polynesia] [Airport symbol] (OAG)
PKP............. Purple-K-Powder
PKPA .... Parental Kidnapping Prevention Act (BARN)
PK/PK .... Peak-to-Peak (MCD)
PKpP .... Pennwalt Corp., King Of Prussia, PA [Library symbol Library of Congress] (LCLS)
PKPS .... [The] Poughkeepsie Savings Bank FSB [Poughkeepsie, NY] [NASDAQ symbol] (NQ)
PKPS .... Poughkeepsie Svgs Bank [NASDAQ symbol] (TTSB)
PKQ .... Dallas-Fort Worth, TX [Location identifier FAA] (FAAL)
PKR .... Packer (WGA)
PKR .... Phased Knee Rehabilitation (DMAA)
PKR .... Picker
PKR .... P. K. Le Roux Dam [South Africa] [Seismograph station code, US Geological Survey] (SEIS)
PKR .... Pokhara [Nepal] [Airport symbol] (OAG)
PKR .... Polycystic Kidney Research Foundation (PAZ)
PKRDD........ Pravitel'stvennaya Komissiya po Raketam Dalnego Deistviya [State Commission for the Study of the Problems of Long-Range Rockets] [Former USSR]
PKs .... Bayard Taylor Memorial Library, Kennett Square, PA [Library symbol Library of Congress] (LCLS)
PKS .... Packs of Cigarettes Smoked
PKS .... Parti Kongres Sarawak [Malaysia] [Political party] (EY)
PKS .... Phi Kappa Sigma [Fraternity]
PKS .... Polyketide Synthase [An enzyme]
PKSEA .... Pack for Overseas
PKSh........... Partia Komuniste e Shqiperise [Communist Party of Albania] [Later, PPSh] [Political party] (PPE)
PKsL........... Longwood Gardens Library, Kennett Square, PA [Library symbol Library of Congress] (LCLS)
PKSS .... Probability of Kill Single Shot (MCD)
PKT .... Packet
PKT .... Phase Keying Technique
PKT .... Phi Kappa Tau [Fraternity]
PKT .... Pittsburgh Theological Seminary, Pittsburgh, PA [OCLC symbol] (OCLC)
PKT .... Pocket (MSA)
PKTN .... Pinkerton's, Inc. [NASDAQ symbol] (SAG)
PKU .... Pekanbaru [Indonesia] [Airport symbol] (OAG)
PKU .... Phenylketonuria [Congenital metabolism disorder] [Medicine]
PKU .... Pianoforte Keymakers' Union [British]
PKU-P......... PKU [Phenylketonuria] Parents (EA)
PKuS........... Kutztown State College, Kutztown, PA [Library symbol Library of Congress] (LCLS)
PKV .... Killed Poliomyelitis Vaccine [Immunology] (MAE)
PkV .... Peak Kilovolts
PKV .... Port Lavaka, TX [Location identifier FAA] (FAAL)
PKVL .... Pikeville National [NASDAQ symbol] (TTSB)
PKVL .... Pikeville National Corp. [NASDAQ symbol] (NQ)
PKW .... Kenosha, WI [Location identifier FAA] (FAAL)
PKW .... Personenkraftwagen [Automobile] [German]
PKW .... Selebi-Phikwe [Botswana] [Airport symbol] (OAG)
PKWA .... Kwajalein [Marshall Islands] [ICAO location identifier] (ICLI)
PKWAY .... Parkway (MSA)
PKWY .... Parkway (KSC)
Pkwy .... Parkway (ASC)
PKWY .... [The] Parkway Co. [NASDAQ symbol] (NQ)
PKWYS .... Parkways [Commonly used] (OPSA)
PKX............. Pohang Iron & Steel ADS [NYSE symbol] (TTSB)
PKX............. Pohang Iron & Steel Co., Ltd. [NYSE symbol] (SAG)
PKY .... Pak Lay [Laos] [Airport symbol] (AD)
PKY .... Palangkaraya [Indonesia] [Airport symbol] (OAG)
PKY .... Parkway (MCD)
Pky .... Parkway (DD)
PKY .... Pecky (WGA)
Pky .... Pecky (WPI)
PKZ .... Pakse [Laos] [Airport symbol] (AD)
PKZ .... Pensacola, FL [Location identifier FAA] (FAAL)
PL .... Aero Peru [ICAO designator] (AD)
PL .... Front Line [Revolutionary group] [Italy]
PL .... Lancaster County Library, Lancaster, PA [Library symbol Library of Congress] (LCLS)
PL .... Packing List
PL .... Padlock (AAG)
PL .... Pail
PL .... Palm Leaf [Reaction] [Medicine]
PL .... Pamphlet Laws [A publication] (DLA)
PL .... Panel Left [Nuclear energy] (NRCH)
PL .... Paperleg [A favored student] [Teen slang]
PL .... Paper Life Ltd. [British]
PL .... Paper Loss (MHDW)
PL .... Parish Line R. R. [AAR code]
PL .... Partial Loss [Insurance]
PL .... Partido Liberal [Liberal Party] [Paraguay] [Political party] (PPW)
PL .... Partido Liberal [Liberal Party] [Honduras] [Political party]
PL .... Partido Liberal [Liberal Party] [Colombia] [Political party] (EY)

PL	Partido Liberal [*Liberal Party*] [*Portugal Political party*] (PPE)
PL	Partido Liberal [*Liberal Party*] [*Peru*] [*Political party*] (EY)
PL	Partido Liberal [*Liberal Party*] [*Panama*] [*Political party*] (PPW)
PL	Partido Liberal [*Liberal Party*] [*Spain Political party*] (PPE)
PL	Partido Libertador [*Liberating Party*] [*Brazil Political party*]
PL	Parti Liberal [*Liberal Party (1974-1979)*] [*Belgium Political party*] (PPE)
PL	Parting Line [*Castings*] (AAG)
PL	Parts List
PL	Passenger Liability [*Insurance*] (BARN)
PL	Patent Location (NITA)
PL	Path Loss [*Communications*]
PL	Patriot League (PSS)
PL	Patrol Land [*Aviation*]
PL	Patrologiae Cursus. Series Latina [*A publication*] (OCD)
Pl	Paul (BJA)
PL	Paulist League (EA)
PL	Payload [*NASA*] (KSC)
PL	Paymaster-Lieutenant [*Navy British*]
PL	Peak Loss (IAA)
PL	Peanut Leafspot [*Plant pathology*]
PL	Pectate Lyase [*An enzyme*]
Pl	Pelagius [*Deceased, 1232*] [*Authority cited in pre-1607 legal work*] (DSA)
PL	Pelusium Line [*Nile delta*] [*Geology*]
pl	Pencil (VRA)
PL	People for Life (EA)
PL	People's Lobby (EA)
PL	Perceived Level [*Noise*]
PL	Perception of Light
PL	Peroneus Longus [*Muscle*] [*Orthopedics*] (DAVI)
P/L	Personal Lines
PL	Personnel Laboratory [*Air Research and Development Command*] [*Air Force*] (AAG)
PL	Petro-Lewis Corp. (EFIS)
PL	Petty Larceny
PL	Phase Line
PL	Philosophical Library [*A publication*]
PL	Phone Line
PL	Phospholipid [*Biochemistry*]
PL	Photoconductor Lamp (IAA)
PL	Photolettering (DGA)
PL	Photolocator (MCD)
PL	Photoluminescence
pl	Piazza (VRA)
pl	Picoliter [*One trillionth of a liter*] (MAE)
PL	Pilatus Flugzeugwerke AG [*Switzerland ICAO aircraft manufacturer identifier*] (ICAO)
PL	Pile
PL	Pipeline
PL	Pipe Lines Act [*Town planning*] [*British*]
PL	Piping Load [*Nuclear energy*] (NRCH)
PL	Pitch Line (MSA)
Pl	Place
Pl	Place (TBD)
pl	Place (VRA)
PL	Placebo [*Medicine*]
PL	Placental Lactogen [*Endocrinology*]
Pl	Plagioclase [*Lunar geology*]
PL	Plain (MSA)
PL	Plain Language [*As opposed to coded message*] [*Military*]
PL	Plans
PL	Plantagenet [*Genealogy*] (ROG)
PL	Plantar [*Related to the sole of the foot*] (DAVI)
pl	Plasma
Pl	Plasmodium [*The malarial parasite*] [*Infectious diseases*] (DAVI)
PL	Plaster (WGA)
PL	Plastic Laboratory [*Princeton University*] (MCD)
PL	Plastic Limit (IEEE)
PL	Plastic Surgery [*Medicine*]
pl	Plastid [*Botany*]
PL	Plate (KSC)
PL	Plateau Length
PL	Plated (IAA)
pl	Platelet [*Hematology*] (MAE)
PL	Platelet Lactogen [*Hematology*] (DMAA)
PL	Platinum [*Chemistry*] (ROG)
Pl	Plato [*Fourth century BC*] [*Classical studies*] (OCD)
PL	Platoon (NATG)
PL	Platoon Leader [*Military*] (INF)
PL	Platz [*Square*] [*German*] (EY)
pl	Platz (VRA)
PL	Players League [*Major league in baseball, 1890*]
pl	Plaza (VRA)
PL	PLC Capital LLC, Inc. [*NYSE symbol*] (SAG)
PL	Pleadings [*Legal shorthand*] (LWAP)
PL	Pleasure (ROG)
PL	[*The*] Plessey Co. Ltd. (MCD)
pl	Pleural [*Medicine*] (MAE)
PL	Plimsoll Line [*Shipping*] (DAS)
PL	Ploshchad [*Square*] [*Russian*] (EY)
Pl	Plowden's English King's Bench Commentaries [*or Reports*] [*1550-80*] [*A publication*] (DLA)
PL	Plug (AAG)
PL	Plume [*Numismatics*]

PL	Plural
pl	Plural (ODBW)
PL	Plymouth [*Postcode*] (ODBW)
PL	Poet Laureate
PL	Poetry London [*A publication British*]
Pl	Poiseuille [*Unit of dynamic viscosity*]
PL	Poland [*ANSI two-letter standard code*] (CNC)
pl	Poland [*MARC country of publication code Library of Congress*] (LCCP)
PL	Polarized Light
PL	Policy Loan
PL	Poly-L-lysine [*Also, PLL*] [*Biochemical analysis*]
PL	Poor Law [*A publication*] (DLA)
PL	Portable Low-Power [*Reactor*] (NRCH)
PL	Port Line [*Steamship*] (MHDW)
PL	Position Line [*Navigation*]
PL	Position Location [*DoD*]
PL	Post Landing [*NASA*] (KSC)
PL	Post Laundry [*Army*]
PL	Power Line (IAA)
PL	Power Loading (IAA)
PL	Power Locks (BARN)
PL	Prayers for Life (EA)
PL	Prelaunch (NASA)
PL	Preliminary Leaf [*Bibliography*]
P/L	Presentation Label [*Publishing*]
PL	Presley Labs [*Vancouver Stock Exchange symbol*]
PL	Pressurizer Level (IEEE)
PL	Price Level [*Economics*]
PL	Price List
PL	Primary Leading [*Photography*] (DGA)
PL	Primrose League [*British*] (DI)
PL	Prince Line [*Steamship*] (MHDW)
PL	Princess Louise's Sutherland and Argyll Highlanders [*Military British*] (ROG)
PL	Private Label [*Business term*]
PL	Private Line
PL	Procedural Language (PCM)
PL	Procedure Library [*Computer science*]
PL	Production Language
PL	Production List (AAG)
PL	Product Liability [*Insurance*]
PL	Product License
P/L	Profit and Loss [*Accounting*]
PL	Program Level (IAA)
PL	Program Library [*Computer science*]
PL	Program Logic [*Computer science*] (TEL)
PL	Programming Language [*Computer science*]
PL	Progressive Labor [*A faction of Students for a Democratic Society*]
PL	Projection Lens [*Microscopy*]
PL	Project Leader
PL	Project Lighthawk [*Later, LH*] (EA)
PL	Project Local [*Defunct*] (EA)
PL	Prolymphocytic Leukemia [*Also, PLL*] [*Oncology*]
PL	Promotion List (DICI)
PL	Propagation Loss
PL	Propellant Loading [*NASA*] (KSC)
Pl	Property Line [*Real estate*] (MSA)
PL	Proportional Limit
P/L	Proprietary Limited (ADA)
PL	Propulsion Laboratory [*Army*] (GRD)
PL	Prospective Loss
PL	Protected Location [*Shipping*] (DS)
PL	Protective Life Corp. [*NYSE symbol*] (SPSG)
PL	Protectively Located [*Plant layout*]
PL	Provisioning List (MCD)
PL	Pseudolumina [*Anatomy*]
PL	Psychological Laboratory (MCD)
PL	Public Law [*An act of Congress*]
PL	Public Liability [*Business term*]
PL	Public Library
Pl	Pulmonary Venous Pressure [*Medicine*] (MAE)
PL	Pulpolingual [*Dentistry*]
PL	Pulsatility Index [*Medicine*]
PL	Pulse Length (NVT)
P/L	Purchased Labor (NASA)
PL	Pyridoxal [*Also, Pxl*] [*Biochemistry*]
PL	Radio Positioning Land Station [*ITU designation*] (CET)
P_L	Transpulmonary Pressure [*Cardiology*] (DAVI)
PL/1	Programming Language, Version One [*Computer science*] (MCD)
PLA	Pakistan Liberation Army (PD)
PLA	Palau [*Palau Islands*] [*Seismograph station code, US Geological Survey Closed*] (SEIS)
PLA	Palestine Liberation Army
PLA	Parachute Location Aid (MCD)
PLA	Para Legal Association [*British*] (DBA)
PLA	Parlamento Latinoamericano [*Latin American Parliament - LAP*] [*Bogota, Colombia*] (EAIO)
PLA	Parlar Resources Ltd. [*Vancouver Stock Exchange symbol*]
PLA	Partido Laborista Agrario [*Panama*] [*Political party*] (EY)
PLA	Partido Liberal Autentico [*Panama*] [*Political party*] (EY)
PLA	Party of Labor of Albania [*Political party*] (PPW)
PLA	Passengers' Luggage in Advance [*Railway*] (ROG)
PLA	Patriotic Liberation Army [*Myanmar*] (PD)
PLA	Pedestrian League of America [*Later, APA*] (EA)

Pla	Pelagius [*Deceased, 1232*] [*Authority cited in pre-1607 legal work*] (DSA)
PLA	Pennilane Development [*Vancouver Stock Exchange symbol*]
PLA	People's Liberation Army [*India*] (PD)
PLA	People's Liberation Army [*National Liberation Front*] [*North Vietnam*] (VNW)
PLA	People's Liberation Army [*China*]
PLA	Pet Lovers Association (EA)
PLA	Phase Locked Arrays [*Physics*]
PLA	Philatelic Literature Association [*Later, APRL*] (EA)
PLA	Phospholipase A [*An enzyme*] (DAVI)
PLA	Physiological Learning Aptitude (KSC)
PLA	Pitch Lock Actuator (MCD)
PLA	Place (ADA)
PLA	Placebo [*Medicine*]
Pla	Placentinus [*Deceased, 1192*] [*Authority cited in pre-1607 legal work*] (DSA)
PLA	Placita
PLA	Placitum [*or Placita*] [*Agreeable, Agreed Upon*] [*Latin*] [*Legal term*] (DLA)
PLA	Plain Language Address [*Telecommunications*] (TEL)
PLA	Planned Labor Application [*Military*] (AFIT)
PLA	Planned Landing Area [*NASA*]
PLA	Plan of Launch Azimuth [*Aerospace*] (AAG)
pla	Plaster (VRA)
PLA	Platelet Antigen (DB)
PLA	Playboy Enterprises CI'B' [*NYSE symbol*] (TTSB)
PLA	Playboy Enterprises, Inc. [*NYSE symbol*] (SPSG)
PLA	Plaza (ADA)
PLA	Poetry League of America (EA)
PLA	Polylactic Acid [*Organic chemistry*] (RDA)
PLA	Poly-L-arginine [*Biochemistry*]
PLA	Polynesian Air-Ways [*ICAO designator*] (FAAC)
PLA	Popular Library of Art [*A publication*]
PLA	Port of London Authority [*British*]
PLA	Posterior Left Atrial Wall [*Cardiology*]
PLA	Potential Leaf Area [*Botany*]
PLA	Potentially Lethal Arrhythmia [*Medicine*] (DMAA)
PLA	Power Lever Angle
PLA	Practice Landing Approach [*Aviation*]
PLA	Price-Level-Adjusted Accounting (ADA)
PLA	Print Load Analyzer
PLA	Private Libraries Association [*British*]
PLA	Product License Application [*FDA*]
PLA	Professional Legal Assistants (EA)
PLA	Program-Length Advertising [*Broadcasting*] (WDMC)
PLA	Programmable Line Adapter
PLA	Programmable Logic Array [*Computer science*]
PLA	Programmed Logic Array (NITA)
PLA	Project Labor Agreement (AAGC)
PLA	Proton Linear Accelerator
PLA	Psycholinguistic Age [*Education*]
PLA	Psychological Learning Aptitude (MCD)
PLA	Public Library Association (EA)
PLa	Pulpolabial [*Dentistry*]
PLA	Pulpolinguoaxial [*Dentistry*]
PLA	Pulsed LASER Annealing [*Semiconductor technology*]
PLA	Pulverized Limestone Association (EA)
PLA	University of Pittsburgh, Law School, Pittsburgh, PA [*OCLC symbol*] (OCLC)
PLA₂	Phospholipase A₂ [*An enzyme*]
PLAA	Playboy Enterprises'A'(vtg) [*NYSE symbol*] (TTSB)
PLAA	Positive Low Angle of Attack
PLA AEPS	PLA [*Public Library Association*] Alternative Education Programs Section
PLAAF	People's Liberation Army Air Force
PLA AFLS	PLA [*Public Library Association*] Armed Forces Library Section
PLAAR	Packaged Liquid Air-Augmented Rocket (MCD)
PLAAS	Plasma Atomic Absorption System [*Spectrometry*]
PLA AV	PLA [*Public Library Association*] Audiovisual
PLA AVC	PLA [*Public Library Association*] Audiovisual Committee
PLAB	Party-Line Adapter Board [*Telecommunications*] (MHDI)
PLAB	Photronics, Inc. [*NASDAQ symbol*] (NQ)
PLAB	Professional and Linguistic Assessment Board (AIE)
PLAC	Placebo [*Medicine*]
Plac	Placentinus [*Deceased, 1192*] [*Authority cited in pre-1607 legal work*] (DSA)
PLAC	Post-Launch Analysis of Compliance [*NASA*]
Plac Abbrev	Placitorum Abbreviatio [*Latin A publication*] (DLA)
Plac Ang Nor	Bigelow's Placita Anglo-Normanica [*A publication*] (DLA)
PLACE	Place [*Commonly used*] (OPSA)
PLACE	Positioner Layout and Cell Evaluator [*Robotics*]
PLACE	Position Location and Aircraft Communication Equipment
PLACE	Position Location and Communications Experiment [*NASA*]
PLACE	Post-LANDSAT Advanced Concept Evaluation (MCD)
PLACE	Programa Latinoamericano de Cooperacion Energetica [*Latin American Energy Cooperation Program*] (EAIO)
PLACE	Programming Language for Automatic Checkout Equipment
PlacerD	Placer Dome, Inc. [*Associated Press*] (SAG)
Plac Gen	Placita Generalia [*Latin A publication*] (DLA)
PLACID	Payload Aboard, Caution in Descent [*NASA*]
PLA CIS	PLA [*Public Library Association*] Community Information Section
PLACO	Planning Committee [*International Organization for Standardization*] (IEEE)
PLAD	Parachute Low-Altitude Delivery [*Air Force*]
PLAD	Plain Language Address Directory
PLAD	Price-Level-Adjusted Deposit
PLAD	Public Lands Appreciation Day [*A joint effort of Times Mirror Magazines and the Bureau of Land Management*] (PS)
PLADS	Parachute Low-Altitude Delivery System [*Military*]
PLADS	Pulsed LASER Airborne Depth Sounding System [*Naval Oceanographic Office*]
PLAF	People's Liberation Armed Forces [*National Liberation Front*] [*North Vietnam*] (VNW)
PLAFB	Plattsburgh Air Force Base [*New York*] (AAG)
PLAFSEP	Processing Libraries - Anecdotes, Facetia, Satire, Etc., Periodicals [*A publication*]
Plag	Plagioclase [*Lunar geology*]
PLAGM	Placid, Louisiana Land and Exploration, Amerada Hess, Getty, and Marathon [*Oil-and gas-holding bloc in Alaska*]
PLAI	Preschool Language Assessment Instrument [*Child development test*]
PLAIC	Purdue Laboratory for Applied Industrial Control [*Purdue University*] [*Research center*] (RCD)
PLAID	Professional Library Access and Information Delivery [*Information service or system*] (IID)
PLAID	Programmed Learning Aid
PLAIL	Public Libraries and Independent Learners (TELE)
PLAIN	Plain [*Commonly used*] (OPSA)
PLAINES	Plains [*Commonly used*] (OPSA)
PLAINS	Plains [*Commonly used*] (OPSA)
Plaintr	Plaintree Systems, Inc. [*Associated Press*] (SAG)
PLAL	Pro-Life Action League (EA)
PLA LC	PLA [*Public Library Association*] Legislative Committee
PLAM	Plastic Laminate [*Technical drawings*]
PLAM	Practice Limpet Assembly Modular [*Navy*] (CAAL)
PLAM	Price-Level-Adjusted Mortgage
PLAME	Propulsive Left Landing with Aerodynamic Maneuvering Entry (PDAA)
PLAMED	Plantas Medicinales [*Ministerio de Sanidad y Consumo*] [*Spain Information service or system*] (CRD)
PLA MLS	PLA [*Public Library Association*] Metropolitan Libraries Section
PLA MPLSS	PLA [*Public Library Association*] Marketing of Public Library Services Section
PLAN	Open Plan Systems [*NASDAQ symbol*] (TTSB)
PLAN	Open Plan Systems, Inc. [*NASDAQ symbol*] (SAG)
PLAN	Parts Logistics Analysis Network
PLAN	Payload Local Area Network [*NASA*] (SSD)
PLAN	People's Liberation Army Navy
PLAN	People's Liberation Army of Namibia [*Political party*] (PPW)
PLAN	Personal LAN (NITA)
PLAN	Personal Local Area Network [*Telecommunications*] (OSI)
PLAN	Planned Lifetime Advocacy Network
Plan	Planning (DLA)
PLAN	Planning
PLAN	Positive Locator Aid to Navigation
PLAN	Prevent Los Angeles Now
PLAN	Problem Language Analyzer [*Computer science*]
PLAN	Professional Local Area Network (NITA)
PLAN	Program for Learning in Accordance with Needs [*Westinghouse Learning Corp.*]
PLAN	Program Language Analyzer [*Computer science*] (IEEE)
PLAN	Programming Language Nineteen-Hundred [*Computer science*]
PLAN	Protect Life in All Nations (EA)
PLAN	Public Libraries Automation Network [*California State Library*] [*Sacramento, CA*]
Plan & Comp	Planning and Compensation Reports [*British A publication*] (DLA)
PlanarSy	Planar Systems [*Commercial firm Associated Press*] (SAG)
PLANAT	North Atlantic Treaty Regional Planning Group
Planc	Pro Plancio [*of Cicero*] [*Classical studies*] (OCD)
PLANCODE	Planning, Control, and Decision Evaluation System [*IBM Corp.*]
PLand	Professional Landman [*Canada*] (DD)
PL & PD	Public Liability and Property Damage [*Insurance*]
Pl & Pr Cas	Pleading and Practice Cases [*1837-38*] [*England*] [*A publication*] (DLA)
PL & R	Postal Laws and Regulations [*Later, Postal Manual*]
PLANES	Programmed Language-Based Enquiry System
PLANES	Programmed Language Enquiry System (NITA)
PLANET	Planned Logistics Analysis and Evaluation Technique [*Air Force*]
PLANET	Planning Evaluation Technique (MCD)
PLANET	Private Local Area Network [*Racal LAN Systems, Inc.*] [*Boca Raton, FL*] (TSSD)
PLANET	Probing Lensing Anomalies Network [*Astronomy*]
PLANEX	[*The*] Planning Exchange Database [*Pergamon InfoLine*] [*Database*] [*Information service or system*] (IID)
PLANEX	Planning Exercise [*Military*] (NVT)
Pl Ang-Norm	Placita Anglo-Normannica Cases (Bigelow) [*A publication*] (DLA)
Plan Higher Ed	Planning for Higher Education [*A publication*]
PlanHlly	Planet Hollywood International, Inc. [*Associated Press*] (SAG)
PLANIT	Programming Language for Interaction and Teaching [*1966*] [*Computer science*]
PLANMAN	Planned Maintenance [*Contract Data Research*] [*Software package*] (NCC)
PLANN	Plant Location Assistance Nationwide Network
PLANNET	Planning Network
PLANS	Position Location and Navigation System
PLANS	Program Logistics and Network Scheduling System (IEEE)
PLANS	Programming Language for Allocation and Network Scheduling [*1975*] [*Computer science*] (CSR)
PlanSci	Planning Sciences International [*Associated Press*] (SAG)
Plant	De Plantatione [*Philo*] (BJA)

PLANT	Program for Linguistic Analysis of Natural Plants (IEEE)
PLANT	Programming Language for Interactive Teaching [*Computer science*] (IAA)
PLANTFACTS...	Steel Plants Information System [*German Iron and Steel Engineers Association*] [*Dusseldorf*] [*Information service or system*] (IID)
plant-flex....	Plantar Flexion [*Orthopedics*] (DAVI)
Plantron......	Plantronics, Inc. [*Associated Press*] (SAG)
PLANY	Protestant Lawyers Association of New York (EA)
PLAO	Parts List Assembly Order (MCD)
PLAP	Placental Alkaline Phosphatase [*An enzyme*]
PLAP	Power Lever Angle Position (MCD)
PLAP	Prelaunch, Launch, and Ascent Procedures [*NASA*] (IAA)
Pla Par	Placita Parliamentaria [*Latin A publication*] (DLA)
PLapK	Keystone Junior College, La Plume, PA [*Library symbol Library of Congress*] (LCLS)
PLA PLSS ...	PLA [*Public Library Association*] Public Library Systems Section
PLAR	Postal Laws and Regulations (IAA)
PLARA	Packaged Liquid Air-Augmented (IAA)
PLARS	Position Location and Reporting System [*Military*] (INF)
PLAS	Plaster (AAG)
PLAS	Plastic
plas	Plastic (VRA)
PLas	Premier Laser Systems, Inc. [*Associated Press*] (SAG)
PLAS	Private Line Assured Service [*Telecommunications*] (TEL)
PLAS	Professional Library Automation System (TELE)
PLAS	Program Logical Address Space
PLAS	Programmable Link Adaptation System (MCD)
PLASCAMS...	Plastics: Computer Aided Materials Selector [*Rapra Technology Ltd.*] [*Information service or system*] (CRD)
PLASI	Pulsating Visual Approach Slope Indicator [*Aviation*] (FAAC)
PLASI	Pulse Light Approach Slope Indicator (PDAA)
PLASMA	Parents League of American Students of Medicine Abroad [*Defunct*] (EA)
PLASMA	Plant Services Maintenance (PDAA)
Plasma	Plasma & Materials Technologies, Inc. [*Associated Press*] (SAG)
PLASMEX	International Plastics Exhibition
PLA SMLS ...	PLA [*Public Library Association*] Small and Medium-Sized Libraries Section
PLAST	Propellant Loading and All Systems Test [*NASA*] (KSC)
PLASTEC......	Plastics Technical Evaluation Center [*Dover, NJ*] [*Army*]
PLASTEUROTEC...	Groupement Europeen des Fabricants de Pieces Techniques Plastiques [*European Group of Fabricators of Technical Plastics Parts*] (EAIO)
PlasThrm.....	Plasma-Therm, Inc. [*Associated Press*] (SAG)
PlastLn......	Plasti-Line, Inc. [*Associated Press*] (SAG)
PLAT	Pilot-LOS [*Line of Sight*] Landing Aid Television (NG)
plat	Plate (VRA)
PLAT	Plateau [*Board on Geographic Names*]
PLAT	Platelet [*Hematology*]
PLAT	Platform (KSC)
PLAT	Platinum [*Chemical symbol is Pt*] (AAG)
PLAT	Platinum Technology [*NASDAQ symbol*] (SPSG)
PLAT	Platonic
PLAT	Platoon
plat	Platoon (WDAA)
PLAT	Platt National Park
PLATF	Platform (AAG)
PLATL	Platelets [*Hematology*] (DAVI)
PLATLDR	Platoon Leader [*Military*]
PLATN	Platinum [*Chemistry*] (ROG)
platn	Platinum [*Metal*] (VRA)
PLATO	Pennzoil Louisiana and Texas Offshore [*Oil industry group*]
PLATO	Platform Observables Subassembly
PLATO	Pollution Liability Agreement Among Tanker Owners [*Insurance*] (DS)
PLATO	Programmed Logic for Automated Learning Operation [*Computer science*] (IAA)
PLATO	Programmed Logic for Automatic Teaching [*or Training*] Operations [*University of Illinois*] [*Programming language*]
PLATR	Pawling Lattice Test Rig [*United Nuclear Co.*]
PLATS	Pilot Landing and Takeoff System (IIA)
PLATS	Precision Location and Tracking System (PDAA)
PLatS	Saint Vincent College, Latrobe, PA [*Library symbol Library of Congress*] (LCLS)
PlatSoft.....	Platinum Software Corp. [*Associated Press*] (SAG)
PLATT	Page Level Availability Time Test [*Computer science*]
Platt	Platt on Leases [*A publication*] (DLA)
Platt	Platt on the Law of Covenants [*1829*] [*A publication*] (DLA)
PlatTc	Platinum Technology, Inc. [*Associated Press*] (SAG)
Platt Cov.....	Platt on the Law of Covenants [*A publication*] (DLA)
Platt Leas...	Platt on Leases [*1847*] [*A publication*] (DLA)
PLAT/VLA	Pilot Landing Aid Television / Visual Landing Aid [*System*] (DNAB)
Plaut	Plautus [*Third century BC*] [*Classical studies*] (OCD)
PLAV	Polish Legion of American Veterans (NADA)
PLAV	Polish Legion of American Veterans, USA (EA)
PLAVA	Polish Legion of American Veterans, USA , Ladies Auxiliary (EA)
PLAVLA......	Polish Legion of American Veterans, USA, Ladies Auxiliary (EA)
PLAWM Trough...	Pockels Langmuir Adam Wilson McBain Trough [*Surface film balance*]
Plaxton	Plaxton's Canadian Constitutional Decisions [*A publication*] (DLA)
PLAY	Players International [*NASDAQ symbol*] (TTSB)
PLAY	Players International, Inc. [*NASDAQ symbol*] (NQ)
PLAY	Providing Lifetime Activity for Youth
Playby	Playboy Enterprises, Inc. [*Associated Press*] (SAG)
PlayBy	Play By Play Toys & Novelties, Inc. [*Associated Press*] (SAG)

PlaybyA	Playboys Enterprises [*Associated Press*] (SAG)
PlaybyB	Playboys Enterprises [*Associated Press*] (SAG)
PlayCo	Play Co. Toys [*Associated Press*] (SAG)
Play Co	Play Co. Toys & Entertainment Corp. [*Associated Press*] (SAG)
Players	Players International Corp. [*Associated Press*] (SAG)
PlaytxPd	Playtex Products, Inc. [*Associated Press*] (SAG)
PLAZA	Plaza [*Commonly used*] (OPSA)
PLB	Payload Bay [*NASA*] (NAKS)
PLB	Per Pound [*Freight*]
PLB	Personal Locator Beacon [*Military*] (AFM)
PLB	Phopholipase B [*An enzyme*] (DAVI)
PLB	Phospholamban [*Biochemistry*]
PLB	Picture Level Benchmark [*Computer science*] (CDE)
PLB	Plattsburgh [*New York*] [*Airport symbol*] (OAG)
PLB	Plattsburgh, NY [*Location identifier FAA*] (FAAL)
PLB	Plumbing Mart [*Vancouver Stock Exchange symbol*]
PLB	Poor Law Board
PLB	Porous Layer Bead [*Chromatography*] (DB)
PLB	Prior-Lien Bond [*Business*] (MHDB)
PLB	Proctolin-Like Bioactivity [*Neurobiology*]
PLB	Public Light Bus [*British*]
PLB	Publisher's Library Binding
PLB	Pullbutton (AAG)
PLBB	Patent Licensing Bulletin Board [*U.S. Department of Commerce*] (BARN)
PLBD	Payload Bay Door [*NASA*] (MCD)
PLBD	Plugboard (MSA)
PLBG	Plumbing (WGA)
PLBK	Playback (NASA)
PL-BLK	Plate Block [*Philately*]
PLBLK	Pillow Block
PLBOL	Position Launch/Bearing Only Launch
PLBR	Plumber (WGA)
PLBR	Prototype Large Breeder Reactor [*Also, NCBR*] [*Nuclear energy*]
PLC	Pacific Logging Congress (EA)
PLC	Packaged Laboratory Chemicals (COE)
PLC	Palomares Road [*California*] [*Seismograph station code, US Geological Survey*] (SEIS)
PLC	Parti de la Liberte du Citoyen [*Belgium Political party*] (EY)
PLC	Partido Liberal Constitucionalista [*Constitutionalist Liberal Party*] [*Nicaragua*] [*Political party*] (PPW)
PLC	Patrice Lumumba Coalition (EA)
PLC	Paymaster-Lieutenant-Commander [*Navy British*]
PLC	Periventricular Leukomalacia Complex [*Medicine*]
PLC	Perry-Link Cubmarine [*A submersible vehicle*]
PLC	Phospholipase C [*An enzyme*]
PLC	Phospholysine C [*Biochemistry*]
PLC	Pilot Laboratories Corp. [*Vancouver Stock Exchange symbol*]
PLC	Placer Development Ltd. [*AMEX symbol*] (SPSG)
PI C	Placita Coronae [*Pleas of the Crown*] [*Latin Legal term*] (DLA)
PLC	Planar Chromatography
PLC	Planeta Rica [*Colombia*] [*Airport symbol*] (AD)
PLC	Platform Control
PLC	Platoon Leader's Class [*Army*]
PLC	PLC Capital LLC, Inc. [*Associated Press*] (SAG)
PLC	PLC Systems [*AMEX symbol*] (SPSG)
PLC	Pneumatic Lead Cutter
PLC	Poet Laureatus Caesareus [*Imperial Poet Laureate*] [*Latin*] (ROG)
PLC	Point Loma College [*California*]
PLC	Police
PLC	Police Aviation Services [*British ICAO designator*] (FAAC)
PLC	Poor Law Commissioners [*British*]
PLC	Power Lever Control (MCD)
PLC	Power Line Carrier
PLC	Power Line Communications
PLC	Power Loading Control (IAA)
PLC	Predictive Linguistic Constraint
PLC	Preparative Layer Chromatography
PLC	Presbyterian Lay Committee (EA)
PLC	Primary Leadership Course [*Army*]
PLC	Primary Location Code [*Computer science*]
PLC	Prime Level Code
PLC	Private Line Carrier [*Telecommunications*] (IAA)
PLC	Process Liquid Chromatography
PLC	Production Line Configured [*Military*] (CAAL)
PLC	Product Life Cycle (ODBW)
PLC	Products List Circular [*Patents*]
PLC	Program-Length Commercial [*Television*]
PLC	Program Level Change Tape [*Computer science*] (IBMDP)
PLC	Programmable Line Controller (NITA)
PLC	Programmable Logic Control [*Computer science*]
PLC	Programmable Logic Controller
PLC	Programming Language Committee [*CODASYL*]
PLC	Proinsulin-Like Compound [*Endocrinology*]
PLC	Provisional Legislative Council [*Hong Kong*]
PLC	Pseudolymphocytic Choriomeningitis [*Medicine*] (DMAA)
PLC	Pseudophase Liquid Chromatography
PLC	Public Lands Council (EA)
PLC	Public Liability Company (DFIT)
PLC	Public Lighting Commission
PLC	Public Limited Co. [*British*]
PLC	Public Utility Company (EBF)
PLCA	Parallel Line Communication Adaptor (NITA)
PLCa	Pipe Line Contractors Association (EA)
PLCAA	Professional Lawn Care Association of America (EA)

PLCAI............ Pipe Line Contractors Association, International (EA)
PLCB............. Planetary Liquid-Cooled Brake [Off-highway equipment]
PLCB............. Pseudoline Control Block [Computer science]
PLCC............. Paulson Cap [NASDAQ symbol] (TTSB)
PLCC............. Paulson Capital Corp. [NASDAQ symbol] (SAG)
PLCC............. Plastic Chip Carrier (NITA)
PLCC............. Plastic Leaded Chip Carrier [Computer science]
PLCC............. Plastic Leadless Chip Carrier [Computer technology] (PCM)
PLCC............. Power Line Carrier Communication (PDAA)
PLCC............. Primary Liver Cell Cancer [Oncology]
PLCC............. Propulsion Local Control Console (DNAB)
PLCCE........... Preliminary Life-Cycle Cost Estimate
PLCCE........... Program Life-Cycle Cost Estimate [Army]
PLCD............ Product Liability Common Defense [Later, PLPD] [An association] (EA)
PLCDR.......... Private Line Carrier Divided Ringing [Telecommunications] (IAA)
PLCEA.......... Part-Length Control Element Assembly [Nuclear energy] (NRCH)
PLCEDM ...... Part-Length Control Element Drive Mechanism [Nuclear energy] (NRCH)
PLCH .... Kiritimati Island [Christmas Islands] [Kiribati] [ICAO location identifier] (ICLI)
PLCL............. Phase-Locked Control Loop [NASA] (IAA)
PLCL............. Polyclonal Gammopathy Identified [Immunology] (DAVI)
PLCLAS........ Propagation Loss Classification System [Navy] (NVT)
PL-CLP......... Plantelet Clumps [Hematology] (DAVI)
PLCM........... Polycom, Inc. [NASDAQ symbol] (SAG)
PLCM........... Propellant Loading Control Monitor [NASA] (KSC)
PLCMC........ Public Library of Charlotte and Mecklenburg County [North Carolina]
PLCN .... Parts List Change Notice (MCD)
PLCO............ Play Company Toys [NASDAQ symbol] (SAG)
PLCO............ Play Co. Toys & Entertainment Corp. [NASDAQ symbol] (SAG)
PLCO............ Play Co. Toys & Entmt [NASDAQ symbol] (TTSB)
PLCO............ Postoperative Low Cardiac Output [Medicine] (DMAA)
Pl Com .... Plowden's English King's Bench Commentaries [or Reports] [1550-80 England] [A publication] (DLA)
PL Com......... Poor Law Commissioner [A publication] (DLA)
PLCOP .... Prelaunch Checkout Plan [NASA] (KSC)
PLCOW......... Play Co. Toys & Entmt Wrrt [NASDAQ symbol] (TTSB)
PLCP............ Photochromic Liquid Crystal Polymer [Organic chemistry]
PLCP............ Physical Layer Convergence Procedure (CIST)
Pl Cr Con Tr... Plowden's Criminal Conversation Trials [A publication] (DLA)
PlcrD............ Placer Dome [Associated Press] (SAG)
PLCS............ Propellant Loading Control System [NASA] (AAG)
PLC Sys....... PLC Systems [Associated Press] (SAG)
PLCU............ Propellant Level Control Unit [NASA] (KSC)
PLCU............ Propellant-Loading Control Unit [NASA] (IAA)
PLCURR........ Plate Current [Electronics] (IAA).
PLCV............ Pelargonium Leaf Curl Virus [Plant pathology]
PLCWTWU ... Power Loom Carpet Weavers' and Textile Workers' Union [British]
PLCY............ Policy
Plcy .... Policy (TBD)
PlcyMg .... Policy Management Systems [Associated Press] (SAG)
PLD.............. All Pakistan Legal Decisions [A publication] (ILCA)
PLD.............. Paid Land Diversion Program [Department of Agriculture] (GFGA)
PLD.............. Partial Line Down (NITA)
PLD.............. Partial Lipodystrophy [Medicine]
PLD.............. Partido de la Liberacion Dominicana [Dominican Liberation Party] [Dominican Republic] [Political party] (PPW)
PLD.............. Parti Liberal-Democrate [Cameroon] [Political party] (EY)
PLd.............. Path Loss, Downlink [Communications]
PLD.............. Payload [NASA]
PLD.............. Peripheral Light Detection (DMAA)
PLD.............. Permanently Lubricated Drivetrain
PLD.............. Personnel Letdown Device
PLD.............. Phase Lock Demodulator
PLD.............. Phase-Locked Detector (IAA)
PLD.............. Phase-Locked Discriminator (IAA)
PLD.............. Phospholipase D [An enzyme]
PLD.............. Physical Logical Description (MHDI)
PLD.............. Plaid (ADA)
PLD.............. Plated (MSA)
PLD.............. Platelet Defect [Hematology] (MAE)
PLD.............. Played Matches [Cricket] (ROG)
PLD.............. Policy Liaison Division (AAGC)
PLD.............. Polycystic Liver Disease [Medicine] (DMAA)
PLD.............. Polymer-Linked Ligand Dimer [Biochemistry]
PLD.............. Portland, IN [Location identifier FAA] (FAAL)
PLD.............. Posterior Latissimus Dorsi [Anatomy]
PLD.............. Posterolateral Dendrite [Neurology]
PLD.............. Potentially Lethal Damage [Medicine]
PLD.............. Precision LASER Designator (RDA)
PLD.............. Pregnancy, Labor and Delivery (DAVI)
PLD.............. Primary Layer Depth [Military] (CAAL)
PLD.............. Principle of Limit Design
PLD.............. Probable Line of Deployment [Army] (AABC)
PLD.............. Procurement Legal Division [Later, Office of General Counsel] [Navy]
PLD.............. Product Line Development
PLD.............. Program Listing Document (MCD)
PLD.............. Programmable Logic Device
PLD.............. ProLogis Trust [NYSE symbol] [Formerly, Security Capital Industries Trust]
PLD.............. Protective LASER Devices (MCD)
PLD.............. Pulsed LASER Deposition [Coating technology]
PLD.............. Pulse-Length Discriminator (IEEE)
PLD.............. Pulse Level Detector (MCD)

PLdaC.......... Calvary Baptist School of Theology, Lansdale, PA [Library symbol Library of Congress] (LCLS)
PLDAL .... Pro-Life Direct Action League (EA)
PLDC .... Preliminary List of Design Changes
PLDC .... Primary Leadership Development Course [Army] (INF)
PLDC .... Primary Long-Distance Carrier [Telephone service]
PLDD .... Poorly Differentiated Lymphoma, Diffuse [Oncology and pathology] (DAVI)
PLDD .... Profiled Lightly Doped Drains (NITA)
PLDF .... Pseudo Load Factor (IAA)
PLDG .... Portuguese Language Development Group [Modern Language Association of America] (AEBS)
PLDH .... Plasma Lactic Dehydrogenase [An enzyme] (AAMN)
PLDI .... Payload Data Interleaver [NASA] (MCD)
PLDI .... Petersburg Long Distance [NASDAQ symbol] (SAG)
PLDI .... Plastic Die [Tool] (AAG)
PLDI .... PLD Telekom, Inc. [NASDAQ symbol] (SAG)
PLDIF.......... Petersburg Long Distance [NASDAQ symbol] (TTSB)
PLDIF.......... PLD Telekom [NASDAQ symbol] [Formerly, Petersburg Long Distance] (SG)
PLDIS .... Public Library Development Incentive Scheme [British]
PLDISS .... Plate Dissipation [Electronics] (IAA)
PLDK .... Peabody Language Development Kits [Education]
PLDK-P .... Peabody Language Development Kit: Preschool (EDAC)
PLDM .... Payload Management [NASA] (MCD)
PLDMI .... Precise LASER Distance Measuring Instrument
PLDP .... Parti Liberal Democrate et Pluraliste [Belgium Political party] (PPW)
PLDP .... Public Library Development Plan [American Library Association, Public Library Association]
PLD-PACOM... Petroleum Logistical Data - Pacific Command (CINC)
PLDR .... Potentially Lethal Damage Repair [Medicine]
PLDS .... Payload Support [NASA] (MCD)
PLDS .... Public Library Data Service
PLDT .... Philippine Long Distance Telephone Co.
PLD Tele ..... PLD Telekom, Inc. [Associated Press] (SAG)
PLDTS .... Propellant Loading Data Transmission System [NASA] (KSC)
PL DYL .... Placidyl [Ethchlorvynol] [A hypnotic and sedative] (DAVI)
PLE.............. Encyclopedia of Pennsylvania Law [A publication] (DLA)
PLE.............. Painfully Long Extension (MUSM)
PLE.............. Panlobular Emphysema [Medicine] (STED)
PLE.............. Personal Level Encryption [Computer science]
PLE.............. Phased Loading Entry [Computer science]
PLE.............. Photoluminescence Excitation [Physics]
PLE.............. Pinnacle Bank [AMEX symbol] (TTSB)
PLE.............. Pipeline Element (NITA)
PLE.............. [The] Pittsburgh & Lake Erie Railroad Co. [AAR code]
PLE.............. Planned Life Extension [Pershing] (MCD)
Ple.............. Pleiade [Record label] [France]
PLE.............. Plesetsk [Satellite launch complex] [Former USSR]
PLE.............. Preliminary Logistics Evaluation
PLE.............. Primary Loss Expectancy [Insurance]
PLE.............. Product Limit Estimator (MHDB)
PLE.............. Professional Land Economist [Canada] (DD)
PL/E............ Programming Language / Edit [Computer science] (MHDI)
PLE.............. Protein-Losing Enteropathy [Gastroenterology] (DAVI)
PLE.............. Prudent Limit of Endurance (NVT)
PLE.............. Pseudolupus Erythematosus [Syndrome] (STED)
PLE.............. Pulsed LASER Experiment
PLE.............. Pulse Length Error (MCD)
PLEA............ Pacific Lumber Exporters Association (EA)
PLEA............ Poverty Lawyers for Effective Advocacy
PLEA............ Prototype Language for Economic Analysis [Computer science] (IID)
PLEAD .... Place of Last Entered Active Duty [Military]
PLEADGS..... Pleadings [Legal term] (ROG)
PLEASE........ Parolees, Law-Enforcement Assist Student Education [Project to reduce drug abuse among junior and senior high school students in California]
PLeB............ Bucknell University, Lewisburg, PA [Library symbol Library of Congress] (LCLS)
PLEB............ Plebeian (WGA)
PLEB............ Plebiscitum [A Decree of the People] [Latin] (DLA)
PLebHi......... Lebanon County Historical Society, Lebanon, PA [Library symbol Library of Congress] (LCLS)
PLebV.......... United States Veterans Administration Hospital, Lebanon, PA [Library symbol Library of Congress] (LCLS)
PLED........... Periodic Lateralized Epileptiform Discharge [Medicine] (MAE)
PLEDM......... Phase-State Low Electron-Hole-Number Drive Memory
P Leg J .... Pittsburgh Legal Journal [Pennsylvania] [A publication] (DLA)
P Leg Jour... Pittsburgh Legal Journal [Pennsylvania] [A publication] (DLA)
PLEI............. Public Law Education Institute (EA)
PLEM .... Pipeline End Manifold (PDAA)
PLEN........... Plenipotentiary
PLEN........... Plenum Publishing [NASDAQ symbol] (TTSB)
PLEN........... Plenum Publishing Corp. [NASDAQ symbol] (NQ)
PLEN........... Public Leadership Education Network (EA)
PLENAPS..... Plans for the Employment of Naval and Air Forces of the Associated Powers in theEastern Theatre in the Event of War with Japan
PLENCH ...... Pliers and Wrench [Combination tool]
PLENG .... Physical Record Length [Computer science] (MHDI)
Plenum .... Plenum Publishing Corp. [Associated Press] (SAG)
PLES........... Parallel-Line Equal Space [Medicine] (DMAA)
PLES........... Parallel-Line Equal Spacing (STED)
PLESA......... Programs for Persons with Limited English-Speaking Ability [Department of Labor]
PLEU........... Pleural Fluid [Medicine] (DAVI)

Pleur Fl ...... Pleural Fluid [Medicine] (MAE)
PLEURO .... Pleuropneumonia [Veterinary medicine] (DSUE)
PLEVA .... Pityriasis Lichenoides et Varioliformis Acuta [Dermatology] (MAE)
PLEX .... Plant Experimentation (PDAA)
PLEX .... Programming Language Extension [Computer science] (CIST)
plexg .... Plexiglass (VRA)
Plexus .... Plexus Corp. [Associated Press] (SAG)
PLEYA .... Public Library Entrepreneur of the Year Award [Sponsored by Geac
                Computers Ltd.]
PLF .... Franklin and Marshall College, Lancaster, PA [Library symbol Library
                of Congress] (LCLS)
PLF .... Free Library of Philadelphia, Philadelphia, PA [OCLC symbol]
                (OCLC)
PLF .... Pacific Legal Foundation (EA)
PLF .... Page Length Field
PLF .... Pala [Chad] [Airport symbol] (AD)
PLF .... Palestine Liberation Front [Political party] (PD)
PLF .... Parachute Landing Fall [Military]
PLF .... Pastel Food [Vancouver Stock Exchange symbol]
PLF .... Patient Load Factor (AFM)
PLF .... People's Liberation Forces [Ethiopia] [Political party] (AF)
PLF .... Perilymphatic Fistula [Medicine] (DMAA)
PLF .... Perilymph Fistula [Medicine]
PLF .... Phase Lock Frequency
PLF .... Phone Line Formatter
PLF .... Plaintiff
PLF .... Pohjanmaan Lento OY [Finland ICAO designator] (FAAC)
PLF .... Polar Lipid Fraction [Biochemistry]
PLF .... Positive Lock Fastener
PLF .... Posterior Lung Fiber [Medicine] (DMAA)
plf .... Pounds per Foot (WPI)
PLF .... Power for Level Flight [Aeronautics]
PLF .... Private Line Telephone
PLF .... Proliferin [Biochemistry]
PLF .... Proposition Letter Formula
PLF .... Public Lands Foundation (EA)
PLFA .... Phospholipid Fatty Acids (COE)
PLFA .... Polar Lipid Fatty Acid [Biochemistry]
PLFA .... Primary Level Field Activity [Defense Supply Agency]
PLFA .... Tabueran Island [Fanning Islands] [Kiribati] [ICAO location
                identifier] (ICLI)
PLFC .... Premature Living Female Child [Neonatology] (DAVI)
PLFC .... Pulaski Furniture [NASDAQ symbol] (TTSB)
PLFC .... Pulaski Furniture Corp. [NASDAQ symbol] (NQ)
PLFC & A .... Peggy Lee Fan Club and Archives [Later, OOPLFC & A] (EA)
PLFE .... Presidential Life [NASDAQ symbol] (TTSB)
PLFE .... Presidential Life Corp. [NASDAQ symbol] (NQ)
PLFP .... Plaintiff
PLFP .... Pity Large Family Present-Buyers
PLFS .... Perilymphatic Fistula Syndrome [Medicine] (DMAA)
PLFTR .... Please Furnish Transportation Requests (NOAA)
PLFUR .... Please Furnish (NOAA)
PLG .... Piling (MSA)
PLG .... Place Resources Corp. [Toronto Stock Exchange symbol]
PLG .... Plane Guard (NVT)
PLG .... Plasminogen [An enzyme] (DAVI)
PLG .... Pleural Ganglion [Medicine]
PLG .... Plug (AAG)
PLG .... Poetae Lyrici Graeci [A publication] (OCD)
PLG .... PolyGram NV [NYSE symbol] (SPSG)
PLG .... Polygyros [Greece] [Seismograph station code, US Geological
                Survey] (SEIS)
PLG .... Poor Law Guardian [British]
PLG .... Private-Label and Generic Brands
PLG .... Progressive Librarians Guild [American Library Association]
PLG .... Prolyl(leucyl)glycinamide [Biochemistry]
PLG .... Pulsed Light Generator
PLGA .... Polylacticco-Glycolic Acid [Organic chemistry]
PLGC .... Presbyterians for Lesbian/Gay Concerns (EA)
PLGL .... Plasminogen-Like [Medicine] (DMAA)
PLGL .... Plate Glass
PLGM .... NYC Parents of Lesbians and Gay Men (EA)
PLGR .... Plunger (MSA)
PLGR .... Precision Lightweight Global-Positioning-Satellite Receiver
PLGR .... Precision Lightweight GPS [Global Positioning System] Receiver
                [Navigation systems]
PLGS .... Partita Liberale Giovani Somali [Somali Liberal Youth Party] [Political
                party]
PLGSS .... Payload Ground Support Systems [NASA] (NASA)
PLGT .... Prototype Lunar Geologist Tool
P-LGV .... Psittacosis-Lymphogranuloma Venereum [Medicine]
PLH .... Hamilton Watch Co., Lancaster, PA [Library symbol Library of
                Congress Obsolete] (LCLS)
PLH .... Palaemontes-Lightening Hormone
PLH .... Paroxysmal Localized Hyperhidrosis [Dermatology] (DAVI)
PLH .... Partido Liberal de Honduras [Liberal Party of Honduras] [Political
                party] (PPW)
PLH .... Payload Handling [NASA] (NASA)
PLH .... Placental Lactogenic Hormone (DB)
PLH .... Plaser Light [Vancouver Stock Exchange symbol]
PLH .... Plymouth [England] [Airport symbol] (OAG)
PLH .... Punjab Light Horse [British military] (DMA)
PLHi .... Lancaster County Historical Society, Lancaster, PA [Library symbol
                Library of Congress] (LCLS)
PLHR .... Power Line Harmonic Radiation

PLhS .... Lock Haven State College, Lock Haven, PA [Library symbol Library
                of Congress] (LCLS)
PLI .... Empresa de Transporte Aereo del Peru [ICAO designator] (FAAC)
PLI .... Ltd. Systems [Vancouver Stock Exchange symbol]
pli .... Pali [MARC language code Library of Congress] (LCCP)
PLI .... Panarea [Lipari Islands] [Seismograph station code, US Geological
                Survey] (SEIS)
PLI .... Partido Liberal Independiente [Independent Liberal Party]
                [Nicaragua] [Political party] (PPW)
PLI .... Partito Liberale Italiano [Italian Liberal Party] [Political party] (PPW)
PLI .... Passenger and Immigration Lists Index [A publication]
PLI .... Payload Interrogator [NASA] (MCD)
PLI .... Phone Line Interface [IBM Corp.] (PCM)
PLI .... Pilot Location Indicator
PLI .... Polyvision Corp. [AMEX symbol] (SAG)
PLI .... Power Level Indicator
PLI .... Practising Law Institute (EA)
PLI .... Preload Indicating
PLI .... Private Line Interface
PLI .... Proctolin-Like Immunoactivity [Neurobiology]
PLI .... Professional Liability Insurance (DMAA)
PLI .... Public Lands Institute (EA)
PLI .... Pulsed LASER Interferometry
PLIA .... Pollution Liability Insurance Association [Defunct] (EA)
PLIANT .... Procedural Language Implementing Analog Techniques [Computer
                science] (IEEE)
PLIB .... Pacific Lumber Inspection Bureau (EA)
PLIB .... Program Library [Computer science]
PLIC .... Procedural Language for Integrity Constraints [Computer science]
                (MHDI)
PLICK .... Pride, Loyalty, Integrity, Capability, Knowledge (DNAB)
PLIE .... Phase Linear Interferometer Experiment (MCD)
PLIF .... Planar Laser Induced Fluorescence
PLI F .... Polo Laico Liberali-Repubblicani Federalisti [Italy] [Political party]
                (ECED)
PLIF .... Postlumbar Interbody Fusion [Neurology] (DAVI)
PLIM .... Post Launch and Instrumentation Message [NASA] (IAA)
PLIM .... Post Launch Information Message [NASA] (KSC)
PLIMC .... Pipe Line Insurance Managers Conference [Defunct] (EA)
PLIMS .... Programming Language for Information Management System
                [Computer science] (MHDI)
PLimT .... Tyler Arboretum, Lima, PA [Library symbol Library of Congress]
                (LCLS)
PLIN .... Power Line Impedance Network
PLINK .... American People/Link [American Design and Communication]
                [Information service or system] (IID)
PLIP .... Preamplifier Limited Infrared (IAA)
PLIRRA .... Pollution Liability Insurance and Risk Retention Act (GFGA)
PLIS .... Preclinical Literature Information System [Computer science]
PLIS .... Public Libraries in the Information Society (TELE)
PLISN .... Parts List Item Sequence Number (MCD)
PLISN .... Provisioning List Item Sequence Number (NASA)
PLISSIT ...... Permission, Limited Information, Specific Suggestions, and Intensive
                Therapy [Occupational therapy]
PLIT .... Petrolite Corp. [NASDAQ symbol] (NQ)
PLITTY .... Private Line Teletypewriter Service [Telecommunications] (TEL)
PLIUN .... Partido Liberal Independiente de Unidad Nacional [Nicaragua]
                [Political party] (EY)
PLIW .... Preload Indicating Washer
PLJ .... Pacific Law Journal [A publication] (ILCA)
PLJ .... Parliamentary Lobby Journalists [British]
PLJ .... Pass Lake Resources Ltd. [Vancouver Stock Exchange symbol]
PLJ .... Patna Law Journal [India] [A publication] (ILCA)
PLJ .... Pennsylvania Law Journal [A publication] (DLA)
PLJ .... Permanent Loop Junctor (NITA)
PLJ .... Philippine Law Journal [A publication] (ILCA)
PLJ .... Pittsburgh Legal Journal [Pennsylvania] [A publication] (DLA)
PLJ .... Punjab Law Reporter [India] [A publication] (DLA)
PLJ .... Pure Lemon Juice
PLJ NS .... Pittsburgh Legal Journal, New Series [Pennsylvania] [A publication]
                (DLA)
PLK .... Branson, MO [Location identifier FAA] (FAAL)
PLK .... Phi Lambda Kappa [Fraternity]
PLK .... Plank (AAG)
PLK .... Ploecker-Lee-Kesler [Equation of state]
PLK .... Plucky Little King [Used by Western diplomats in Amman in reference
                to King Hussein of Jordan]
PLK .... Poincare-Lighthill-Kuo [Method]
PLK .... Salomon, Inc. [AMEX symbol] (SAG)
PLK .... Salomon Inc. 6.125% PRI 'ELKS' [AMEX symbol] (TTSB)
PLKR .... Peacoat Locker
PLL .... Pall Corp. [NYSE symbol] (SAG)
PLL .... Pallet [Building construction]
PLL .... Parts Load List (MCD)
PLL .... Passenger Legal Liability [Insurance] (AIA)
PLL .... Peripheral Light Loss
PLL .... Permanent Logical Link [Telecommunications]
PLL .... Phase-Locked Loop [NASA]
PLL .... Pilgrim Lacrosse League (PSS)
PLL .... Plasma Lockload (AAEL)
PI L .... Platt on Leases [1841] [A publication] (DLA)
PLL .... Polo, IL [Location identifier FAA] (FAAL)
PLL .... Poly-L-lysine [Also, PL] [Biochemistry]
PLL .... Positive Logic Level
PLL .... Prescribed Load List [Vehicle maintenance operation] [Army]

PLL.............	Pressure Length Loop (DB)
PLL.............	Prince Line Ltd. [*Steamship*] (MHDW)
PLL.............	Prolymphocytic Leukemia [*Also, PL*] [*Oncology*]
PLL.............	Pseudoalcoholic Liver Lesions [*Medicine*]
PLLDF..........	Phase-Locked Loop with Decision Feedback [*NASA*] (IAA)
PLLE	Prueba de Lectura y Lenguaje Escrito [*Standardized test of reading and writing in Spanish for students in grades 3 through 10*]
PLLL...........	Parallel Petroleum [*NASDAQ symbol*] (TTSB)
PLLL...........	Parallel Petroleum Corp. [*NASDAQ symbol*] (NQ)
PLLL...........	Posterior Lateral Line Lobe [*Of electric fishes*]
PLLR...........	Phase Lock Loop Receiver
PLLRC	Public Land Law Review Commission [*Terminated, 1970*]
PLLS...........	Portable Landing Light System (PDAA)
PLLT...........	Pallet (NATG)
PLLTN..........	Pollution
PLLVM..........	Pennsylvania Farm Museum of Landis Valley, Lancaster, PA [*Library symbol Library of Congress*] (LCLS)
PLM.............	Pacific Law Magazine [*A publication*] (DLA)
PLM.............	Packaged Liquid Missile
PLM.............	Pakistan Liberation Movement [*Political party*] (PD)
PLM.............	Palembang [*Indonesia*] [*Airport symbol*] (OAG)
PLM.............	Palomar [*California*] [*Seismograph station code, US Geological Survey*] (SEIS)
PLM.............	Passive Line Monitor [*Datapoint*]
PLM.............	Passive Lunar Marker
PLM.............	Payload Management [*NASA*] (NASA)
PLM.............	Payload Monitoring [*NASA*] (NASA)
PLM.............	People's Liberation Movement [*Montserrat*] [*Political party*] (PPW)
PLM.............	Percent Labeled Mitosis [*Cytology*]
PLM.............	Periodic Leg Movement (DMAA)
PLM.............	Phleomycin [*Biochemistry*]
PLM.............	Phospholemman [*Biochemistry*]
PLM.............	Planetary Rotation Machine (IAA)
PLM.............	Plasma Level Monitoring [*Medicine*] (DMAA)
PLM.............	Plastic Laminating Mold (MCD)
PLM.............	PLM International [*AMEX symbol*] (TTSB)
PLM.............	PLM International, Inc. [*AMEX symbol*] (SPSG)
PLM.............	Plymouth Financial [*Vancouver Stock Exchange symbol*]
PLM.............	Poetae Latini Minores [*A publication*] (OCD)
PLM.............	Polarized Light Microscopy
PLM.............	Polymer-Linked Ligand Monomer [*Biochemistry*]
PLM.............	Poor Law Magazine [*A publication*] (DLA)
PLM.............	Power Line Modulation (AABC)
PLM.............	Prelaunch Monitor [*NASA*] (KSC)
PLM.............	Preliminary (KSC)
PLM.............	Private Label Merchandiser [*USCG*] (TAG)
PLM.............	Production Line Maintenance [*Air Force*]
PLM.............	Production Line Manufacturing
PLM.............	Product Line Manager
PL/M...........	Programming Language for Microprocessors (NITA)
PL/M...........	Programming Language/Microcomputers [*Intel Corp.*] [*1973*] [*Computer science*] (CSR)
PLM.............	Programming Logic Manual
PLM.............	Progressive Labor Movement (BARN)
PLM.............	Pulse-Length Modulation
PLMA...........	Private Label Manufacturers Association (EA)
PLMA...........	Producers Livestock Marketing Association [*Later, IPLA*] (EA)
PL Mag........	Poor Law Magazine [*1858-1930*] [*Scotland*] [*A publication*] (DLA)
PLMATH	Procedure Library Mathematics [*Computer science*] (IAA)
PLMB...........	Plumbing (AAG)
PLMBR..........	Plumber
PLMC...........	Premature Living Male Child [*Neonatology*] (DAVI)
PLMD...........	Payload Mating Dolly [*NASA*]
PLME...........	Peak Local Mean Error (MCD)
PLMES..........	Planning, Measurement, and Evaluation Section [*PLA*] (AL)
PLMES..........	Planning, Measurements & Evaluation Section [*Public Library Association*] [*American Library Association*]
PLMG...........	Plumbing (WGA)
PLMG...........	Publishers' Library Marketing Group [*Defunct*] (EA)
PLMHi.........	Lancaster Mennonite Conference Historical Society, Lancaster, PA [*Library symbol Library of Congress*] (LCLS)
PLMN...........	Partido Marxista Leninista de Nicaragua [*Political party*] (EY)
PLMP...........	Program Logistic Management Plan (MCD)
PLMPA..........	Permanent Labourers' Mutual Protective Association [*A union*] [*British*]
PLMR...........	Paris, Lyons, and Mediterranean Railway (ROG)
PLMR...........	Post Launch Memorandum Report
PlmrW	Palmer Wireless [*Associated Press*] (SAG)
PLMS...........	Palms
PLMS...........	Partitioned Libraries Management System (MHDI)
PLMS...........	Plastic Master [*Tool*] (AAG)
PLMS...........	Preservation of Library Materials Section [*Resources and Technical Services Division*] [*American Library Association*]
PLMS...........	Program Logistics Master Schedule [*NASA*] (NASA)
PLMS...........	Public Land Mobile Service Data Base [*Comp Comm, Inc.*] [*Information service or system*] (CRD)
PlmSSB	Palm Springs Savings Bank [*Associated Press*] (SAG)
PLMT...........	Plasmacytoid Lymphocyte [*Hematology*] (DAVI)
PLMV...........	Posterior Leaf Mitral Valve [*Cardiology*] (DMAA)
PLMX...........	PL/M Extended [*Programming language*] (CSR)
PLN.............	Flight Plan [*Aviation code*]
PLN.............	Partido de Liberacion Nacional [*National Liberation Party*] [*El Salvador*] [*Political party*] (EY)
PLN.............	Partido Liberacion Nacional [*National Liberation Party*] [*Costa Rica*] [*Political party*] (PPW)
PLN.............	Partido Liberal Nacionalista [*Nationalist Liberal Party*] [*Nicaragua*]
PLN.............	Pellston [*Michigan*] [*Airport symbol*] (OAG)
PLN.............	Pellston, MI [*Location identifier FAA*] (FAAL)
PLN.............	Pelvic Lymph Node [*Gynecology*] (DAVI)
PLN.............	Peripheral Lymph Node [*Medicine*] (DB)
PLN.............	Phospholamban [*Biochemistry*]
PLN.............	Plain
PLN.............	Plan (NASA)
PLN.............	Plane (MSA)
Pln.............	Platoon [*British military*] (DMA)
PLN.............	Plauen [*German Democratic Republic*] [*Seismograph station code, US Geological Survey*] (SEIS)
PLN.............	Polnippon [*Poland ICAO designator*] (FAAC)
PLN.............	Popliteal Lymph Node [*Anatomy*]
PLN.............	Posterior Lip Nerve (DAVI)
PLN.............	Potassium Lithium Niobate (PDAA)
PLN.............	Primary Learning Network [*Computer science*] (IAA)
PLN.............	Program Line Number [*DoD*]
PLN.............	Program Logic Network (NASA)
PLN.............	Proteoliaisin [*Biochemistry*]
PLN.............	Pump-Line-Nozzle
PLNAG..........	Public Libraries Networking Advisory Group [*British*] (TELE)
PLNAP	Pro-Life Nonviolent Action Project (EA)
PLNASG........	Public Libraries Network Awareness Steering Group [*British*] (TELE)
plnd	Planned (DA)
PLNG...........	Planning
Plng...........	Planning (TBD)
PLNN...........	Planning (MCD)
PLNR...........	Planar (MSA)
PLNR...........	Planar Systems [*NASDAQ symbol*] (SAG)
PLNR...........	Planner
PlnRsc........	Plains Resources, Inc. [*Associated Press*] (SAG)
PLNS...........	Plains
PLNS...........	Planning Sciences International [*NASDAQ symbol*] (SAG)
PLNSTD........	Planned Standard Equipment [*Navy*] (AFIT)
PLNSY	Planning Sciences ADS [*NASDAQ symbol*] (TTSB)
PLNT...........	Planet (MSA)
PLNT...........	Plant
PLNTY	Planetary (MSA)
PLO.............	Pacific Launch Operations [*NASA*]
PLO.............	Palestine Liberation Organization [*Political party*] (PD)
PLO.............	Parliamentary Liaison Officer (ADA)
PLO.............	Partial Lunar Orbit [*Planetary science*]
PLO.............	Parts List Only (MCD)
PLO.............	Passenger Liaison Office [*Military*] (AABC)
PLO.............	Payload Officer [*NASA*] (MCD)
PLO.............	Pentagon Liaison Office (MCD)
PLO.............	Peoples Liberation Organization (NADA)
PLO.............	Phase-Locked Oscillator
PLO.............	Plans Officer
PLO.............	Polycystic Lipomembranous Osteodysplasia [*Medicine*] (DMAA)
PLO.............	Poly-L-ornithine
PLO.............	Poor Law Office (ROG)
PLO.............	Port Liaison Officer
PLO.............	Port Lincoln [*Australia Airport symbol*] (OAG)
PLO.............	Presidential Libraries Office (NADA)
PLO.............	Price-Lifting Operation [*Business term*] (ECON)
PLO.............	Probability of Leakage through Overlay
PLO.............	Product Line Organization
PLO.............	Program Line Organization
PLO.............	Programmed Local Oscillator
PLO.............	Project Line Organization
PLO.............	Public Land Order [*Interior*]
PLO.............	Public Limit Order [*British*] (NUMA)
PLO.............	Pulsed LASER Oscillator
PLO.............	Pulsed Locked Oscillator
PLOA	Proposed Letter of Agreement (MCD)
PLOB	Patrol Log Observations [*Aviation*] (DSUE)
PLOB	Place of Birth
PLOB	Public Limit Order Board [*British*] (NUMA)
PLOC	Payload Operations Contractor [*NASA*] (SSD)
PLOCAP........	Post Loss-of-Coolant Accident Protection [*Nuclear energy*] (NRCH)
PLOCSA........	Personnel Liaison Officer, Chief of Staff, Army (AABC)
PLOD	Periodic List of Data [*Computer science*]
PLOD	Planetary Orbit Determination (IEEE)
PLOKTA........	Press Lots of Keys to Abort [*Computer term*]
P Lom.........	Petrus Lombardi [*Flourished, 1154-59*] [*Authority cited in pre-1607 legal work*] (DSA)
PLOM..........	Prescribed Loan Optimization Model [*Army*] (AABC)
PLOME.........	Poor Little Old Me Syndrome [*British*]
PLondon.......	Greek Papyri in the British Museum [*A publication*] (OCD)
PLONEF........	Plates on Elastic Foundations [*Structures & Computers Ltd.*] [*Software package*] (NCC)
PLONG.........	Present Longitude [*Aviation*] (FAAC)
PLOO	Pacific Launch Operations Office [*NASA*]
PLOP	Planetary Landing Observation Package [*Aerospace*]
PLOP	Pressure Line of Position [*Air Force*]
PLor..........	Saint Francis College, Loretto, PA [*Library symbol Library of Congress*] (LCLS)
PLOS	Primary Line of Sight [*Sextants*]
PLOT	People's Liberation Organization of Tamil Eelam [*Sri Lanka*] [*Political party*]
PLOT..........	Piagetian Logical Operations Test (EDAC)

PLOT............	Plotting
PLOT............	Porous Layer, Open Tubular Column [Gas chromatography]
PLOT............	Probability of Launch on Time (MCD)
Plot............	Vita Plotini [of Porphyry] [Classical studies] (OCD)
PLOTE..........	People's Liberation Organization of Tamil Eelam [Sri Lanka] [Political party]
PLOW	Petunia Lovers of the World
Plow	Plowden's English King's Bench Commentaries [or Reports] [A publication] (DLA)
Plowd	Plowden's English King's Bench Commentaries [or Reports] [A publication] (DLA)
PLOYREP....	Unit Deployment Report (CINC)
PLP.............	La Palma [Panama] [Airport symbol] (OAG)
PLP.............	Packet Layer Protocol [Computer science] (TNIG)
PLP.............	Packet Level Procedure [or Protocol] [Computer programming] (PCM)
PLP.............	Palo [Philippines] [Seismograph station code, US Geological Survey] (SEIS)
PLP.............	Palpus [Arthropod anatomy]
PLP.............	Parliamentary Labour Party [British]
PLP.............	Parti de la Liberte et du Progres [Party of Liberty and Progress] [See also PVV] [Belgium] (PPE)
PLP.............	Partido de los Pobres [Poor People's Party] [Mexico Political party] (PD)
PLP.............	Parti Liberal Progressiste [Liberal Progressive Party] [Morocco] [Political party] (PPW)
PLP.............	Parti pour la Liberation du Peuple [People's Liberation Party] [Senegal] [Political party] (PPW)
PLP.............	Partners for Livable Places (EA)
PLP.............	Parts List Page (KSC)
PLP.............	Passive Low Pass (IAA)
PLP.............	Pattern Learning Parser
PLP.............	People's Liberation Party [Pakistan]
PLP.............	Periodate Lysine-Paraformaldehyde
PLP.............	Personal LASER Printer [Computer science]
PLP.............	Phillips Petroleum Co. [Toronto Stock Exchange symbol]
PLP.............	Phoenix Aviation [British ICAO designator] (FAAC)
PLP.............	Photolithographic Process (IAA)
PLP.............	Plastic-Lined Pipe
PLP.............	Polyoma-Like Particle [Genetics]
PLP.............	Polystyrene Latex Particles (DB)
PLP.............	Post Launch Phase
PLP.............	Preferred Lenders Program [Small Business Administration]
PLP.............	Preformed Line Product (IAA)
PLP.............	Presentation Level Protocol [AT & T Videotex System]
PLP.............	Principal Locating Point [Automotive engineering]
PLP.............	Prison Link Project (WDAA)
PLP.............	Procedural Language Processor
PLP.............	Process Layup Procedure
PLP.............	Product Liability Prevention [Conference]
PLP.............	Progressive Labor Party (EA)
PLP.............	Progressive Labour Party [Saint Lucia] [Political party] (EAIO)
PLP.............	Progressive Liberal Party [Bahamas] [Political party] (PPW)
PLP.............	Prolactin-Like Protein [Biochemistry]
PLP.............	Proteolipid [Biochemistry]
PLP.............	Proteolipid Protein [Biochemistry]
PLP.............	Pyridoxal Phosphate [Also, PALP] [Biochemistry]
PLPA...........	Pageable Link-Pack Area
PLPA...........	Palmyra, Palmyra Island [Line Islands] [ICAO location identifier] (ICLI)
PLPA...........	Permissive Low-Pressure Alarm (IEEE)
Pl Par.........	Placita Parliamentaria [Latin A publication] (DLA)
PLPB...........	Petroleum Labor Policy Board [Abolished, 1936]
PLPBD	Pulpboard
PLPD...........	Product Liability Prevention and Defense [An association] (EA)
PLP FOR.....	Foramen of Labial Palpus [Arthropod anatomy]
PLPG	Publishers' Library Promotion Group [Later, PLMG] (EA)
PLP GRNDG...	Pulp Grinding [Freight]
PLPH	Post-Lumbar Puncture Headache [Medicine] (DMAA)
PLPI...........	Product Licence Parallel Importation (DB)
PlPolyT.......	Planet Polymer Technologies, Inc. [Associated Press] (SAG)
PLPP...........	Position Location Post Processor (MCD)
PLPrM	PLC Capital LLC 'A' 'MIPS' [NYSE symbol] (TTSB)
PLPS...........	Packaged Liquid Propellant System
PLPS...........	Propellant Loading and Pressurization System [NASA]
PLPT...........	Presentation Level Protocol [Computer science]
PLPV...........	Pelargonium Line Pattern Virus [Plant pathology]
PLQ............	Plaque (MSA)
PLQ............	Tallahassee, FL [Location identifier FAA] (FAAL)
PLR............	LaRoche College, Pittsburgh, PA [OCLC symbol] (OCLC)
PLR............	Northwestern Air Lease Ltd. [Canada ICAO designator] (FAAC)
PLR............	Pacific Law Reporter [A publication] (DLA)
PLR............	Pakistan Law Reports [A publication] (DLA)
PLR............	Pakistan Law Review [A publication] (DLA)
PLR............	Parlake Resources Ltd. [Toronto Stock Exchange symbol]
PLR............	Partido Liberal Radical [Radical Liberal Party] [Paraguay] [Political party] (PPW)
PLR.:..........	Partido Liberal Radical [Radical Liberal Party] [Ecuador] [Political party] (PPW)
PLR............	Patent Law Review [A publication] (DLA)
PLR............	Patent Log Reading [Navigation]
PLR............	Patna Law Reporter [India] [A publication] (DLA)
PLR............	Pell City, AL [Location identifier FAA] (FAAL)
PLR............	Pennsylvania Law Record [Philadelphia] [A publication] (DLA)
P-LR	Pennsylvania Legislative Reference Bureau, Harrisburg, PA [Library symbol Library of Congress] (LCLS)
PLR............	Periodic Logistical Report
PLR............	Philippine Liberation Ribbon [Military decoration]
PLR............	Pillar (MSA)
PLR............	Pliers (MSA)
PLR............	Plymouth Rubber Co., Inc. [AMEX symbol] (SPSG)
plr.............	Poplar (VRA)
PLR............	Portable LASER Range-Finder
PLR............	Power Line Radiation [Radioscience]
PLR............	Presentation Loss Rate (MCD)
PLR............	Pressure Level Recorder
PLR............	Primary Language Record [Education] (AIE)
PLR............	Primary Loss Retention [Insurance]
PLR............	Private Legislation Reports [Scotland] [A publication] (DLA)
PLR............	Product Licence of Right (DB)
PLR............	Program Life Requirement (NG)
PLR............	Program Lock-in Register (NITA)
PLR............	Prolactin Receptor [Biochemistry]
PLR............	Pronation/Lateral Rotation [Fracture] [Orthopedics] (DAVI)
PLR............	Psychological Laboratories [Harvard University] (KSC)
PLR............	Public Law Review [A publication]
PLR............	Public Lending Right [Royalty for books borrowed from public libraries] [British]
PLR............	Puller (MSA)
PLR............	Pulse Link Relay [Telecommunications] (TEL)
PLR............	Pulse Link Repeater [Telecommunications] (TEL)
PLR............	Punjab Law Reporter [India] [A publication] (DLA)
PLRA	Partido Liberal Radical Autentico [Authentic Liberal Radical Party] [Paraguay] [Political party] (PD)
PLRA	Pennsylvania Learning Resources Association (EDAC)
PLRA	Photo-Litho Reproducers' Association [British] (BI)
PLR. A........	Plymouth Rubber 'A'vtg [AMEX symbol] (TTSB)
PLRACTA	Position Location, Reporting, and Control of Tactical Aircraft [Military]
PLR.B.........	Plymouth Rubber Cl'B' [AMEX symbol] (TTSB)
PLRB	Property Loss Research Bureau (EA)
PLRC	Pulsed LASER Remote Crosswind Sensor (MCD)
PLRCAE	Radio Corp. of America, Electron Tube Division, Engineering Section, Lancaster, PA [Library symbol Library of Congress Obsolete] (LCLS)
PLRD	Payload Requirements Document (NASA)
PLRD	Polaroid (VRA)
PLRD	Procurement, Logistics, and Readiness Division (AAGC)
PLRD	Pull Rod
PLR Dacca..	Pakistan Law Reports, Dacca Series [A publication] (DLA)
PLRE..........	Program on Long-Range Forecasting Research [Marine science] (OSRA)
PLRF...........	Pediatric Liver Research Foundation [Defunct] (EA)
pLRF...........	Placental Luteinizing Hormone-Releasing Factor [Endocrinology]
PLRF...........	Planer Fixture
PLRG	Public Libraries Research Group [British] (TELE)
PLRI...........	Posterolateral Rotation Instability [Sports medicine]
PLRJ & K....	Punjab Law Reporter, Jammu and Kashmir Section [India] [A publication] (DLA)
PLR Kar......	Pakistan Law Reports, Karachi Series [1947-53] [A publication] (DLA)
PLR Lah	Pakistan Law Reports, Lahore Series [1947-55] [A publication] (DLA)
PLRPF	Personnel Loss Rate Planning Factors (MCD)
PLRS	Pelorus
PLRS	Phase Lock Receiving System
PLRS	Position Location Reporting System [Military]
PLRS/TIDS...	Position Location Reporting System/Tactical Information Distribution Systems [Military] (RDA)
PLRSTN	Pelorus Stand
PLRT..........	Polarity (MSA)
PLRV	Payload Launch Readiness Verification [NASA] (MCD)
PLRV	Potato Leafroll Virus
PLRWP	Pakistan Law Reports, West Pakistan Series [A publication] (DLA)
pls.............	Isoelectric Point (STED)
PLS............	Page Layout System [Graphic arts] (DGA)
PLS............	Palio Air Service [Italy ICAO designator] (FAAC)
PLS............	Palletized Load System [Army] (RDA)
PLS............	Palomar-Leiden Survey
PLS............	Papillon-Lefevre Syndrome [Medicine] (DMAA)
PLS............	Paracelsus Healthcare Corp. [NYSE symbol] (SAG)
PLS............	Parcels (MSA)
PLS............	Parent Locator Service [A service of the Office of Child Support Enforcement (OCSE)] (PAZ)
PLS............	Parsons Language Sample
PLS............	Partial Least Squares
PLS............	Parti Liberal Suisse [Liberal Party of Switzerland] [Political party] (PPE)
PLS............	Patrol Locator System [Army]
PLS............	Payload Systems [NASA] (MCD)
PLS............	Peerless Tube Co. [AMEX symbol] (SPSG)
PLS............	Peninsula Library System [Belmont, CA] [Library network]
PLS............	People's Law School [Defunct] (EA)
PLS............	Peralto Resources Corp. [Vancouver Stock Exchange symbol]
PLS............	Periodic Log System
PLS............	Personal Library Software [Commercial firm]
PLS............	Physical Signalling (NITA)
PLS............	Pitch Limit Switch
PLS............	Plaisance [Mauritius] [Geomagnetic observatory code]
PLS............	Plasma Light Source
PLS............	Plates [Classical studies] (OCD)

PLS.............. Please (AFM)
PLS.............. Plugging Switch (IEEE)
PLS.............. Pneumatic Limit Switch
PLS.............. Polson, MT [Location identifier FAA] (FAAL)
PLS.............. Polynomial Solution (IAA)
PLS.............. Polystyrene Latex Sphere
PLS.............. Popular Low-Power Schottky [Electronics] (MCD)
PLS.............. Portable Laboratory Salinometer
PLS.............. Position Location System [Army]
PLS.............. Post Landing and Safing [NASA] (NASA)
PLS.............. Postsecondary Longitudinal Studies Program [Department of Education] (GFGA)
PLS.............. Precautions, Limitations, and Setpoints [Nuclear energy] (NRCH)
PLS.............. Preliminary Landing Site (NASA)
PLS.............. Preschool Language Scale [Child development test]
PLS.............. President of the Linnaean Society [British]
PLS.............. Primary Landing Site (MCD)
PLS.............. Primary Lateral Sclerosis [Medicine] (DMAA)
PLS.............. Private Line Service
PLS.............. Product Line Simulator
PLS.............. Professional Legal Secretary [National Association of Legal Secretaries] [Designation awarded by]
PLS.............. Profit-and-Loss-Sharing Account [Banking] (IMH)
PLS.............. Program Liaison Staff (COE)
PLS.............. Programmable Logic Sequencer [Computer science]
PLS.............. Programming Language for System [Computer science] (IAA)
PLS.............. Progressive Learning Systems [Potomac, MD] (TSSD)
PLS.............. Projection of Latent Structures (AAEL)
PLS.............. Propellant Loading Sequencer (AAG)
PLS.............. Propellant Loading System
PLS.............. Prostaglandin-Like Substance [Biochemistry] (MAE)
PLS.............. Providenciales [British West Indies] [Airport symbol] (OAG)
PLS.............. Publishers Licensing Society (DGA)
PLS.............. Pulse (MSA)
PLS.............. Pulsed LASER System
PLS.............. Pulsed Light Source
PLS.............. Purnell Library Service [Commercial firm]
PLSC............ Project Level Steering Committee (HGAA)
PLSD .... Post Hoc Least Significant Difference [Statistics]
PLSD .... Promotion List Service Date [Air Force]
PLSD .... Protected Least Significant Difference (DMAA)
PLSFC......... Part Load Specific Fuel Consumption [Gas turbine]
PLSGT .... Platoon Sergeant [Marine Corps]
PLSHD........ Polished [Freight]
PLSI............ Premier Laser Systems, Inc. [NASDAQ symbol] (SAG)
PLSIA.......... Premier Laser Systems 'A' [NASDAQ symbol] (TTSB)
PLSIW .... Premier Laser Systems Wrrt 'A' [NASDAQ symbol] (TTSB)
PLSIZ .... Premier Laser Systems Wrrt 'B' [NASDAQ symbol] (TTSB)
PLSL........... Propellants and Life Support Laboratory [NASA] (NASA)
PLSN .... Pulsation (MSA)
PL/SNSR..... Payload Sensor [NASA] (GFGA)
PLSNT .... Pleasant
PLSO .... Propellant Life Support and Ordnance [NASA] (KSC)
PLSP........... Payload Signal Processor [NASA] (NAKS)
PLSP........... Prelaunch Survival Probability (CINC)
PLSPS .... Performance Levels of a School Program Survey [Teacher evaluation test]
PLSR .... Pulsator (MSA)
PLSS........... Payload Support Structure [NASA] (SSD)
PLSS........... Portable Life Support System [or Subsystem] [NASA]
PLSS........... Post-Landing Survival System [NASA]
PLSS........... Precision Location Strike System [Air Force]
PLSS........... Prelaunch Status Simulator
PLSS........... Primary Life Support System [or Subsystem] (NASA)
PLSS........... Public Library Systems Section [Public Library Association]
PLSSRS ...... Plant and Soil Science Research Station [Southern Illinois University at Carbondale] [Research center] (RCD)
PLSSU .... Portable Life Support Stretcher Unit [Military] (CAAL)
PLST........... Palletized Load System Truck [Military]
PLST........... Plastering
PLSTC......... Plastic (AAG)
PLSTR......... Plasterer (ADA)
PLSTRER .... Plasterer (WGA)
PLSV........... Propellant Latching Solenoid Valve
PLT............. Columbus, NE [Location identifier FAA] (FAAL)
PLT............. Lancaster Theological Seminary of the United Church of Christ, Lancaster, PA [Library symbol Library of Congress] (LCLS)
PLT............. Lutheran Theological Seminary, Philadelphia, PA [OCLC symbol] (OCLC)
PLT............. Page Layout Terminal [Graphic arts] (DGA)
PLT............. Pallet (AABC)
Plt............. Parliament
PLT............. Partido Liberal Teete [Teete Liberal Party] [Paraguay] [Political party] (PPW)
PLT............. Patna Law Times [India] [A publication] (DLA)
Plt............. Peltier's Orleans Appeals Decisions [Louisiana] [A publication] (DLA)
PLT............. Photoluminescent Thermometer
PLT............. Pi Lambda Theta [An association] (NTPA)
PLT............. Pilot (AFM)
PLT............. Pilot Knob [California] [Seismograph station code, US Geological Survey] (SEIS)
PLT............. Pipeline Time [Army]
PLT............. Plaint [Legal term] (ROG)
PLT............. Planar Tube
PLT............. Plant

PLT............. Plantronics, Inc. [NYSE symbol] (SPSG)
PLT............. Plate
PLT............. Platelet [Hematology]
PLT............. Platoon [Military] (AABC)
PLT............. Port Light
PLT............. Post Loading Test (NG)
PLT............. Power Line Transient (IEEE)
PLT............. Primed Lymphocyte Typing [Hematology]
PLT............. Princeton Large Torus [Nuclear reactor]
PLT............. Private Line Telephone
PLT............. Private Line Teletypewriter
PLT............. Procurement Lead Time [Army]
PLT............. Production Lead Time
PLT............. Program Library Tape [Computer science] (IEEE)
PLT............. Programmed Learning Textbook
PLT............. Progressive Lowering of Temperature
PLT............. Project Learning Tree (WPI)
PLT............. Psittacosis-Lymphogranuloma Venereum Trachoma [Microbiology]
PLT............. Pulsed Light Theodolite
PLT............. Punjab Law Times [India] [A publication] (DLA)
PLT............. South Carolina Aeronautics Commission [FAA designator] (FAAC)
PLTC........... Partnership for Long Term Care
PLTC........... Port Liner Terms Charges [Shipping] (DS)
PLTC........... Propellant Loading Terminal Cabinet (AAG)
PLTD........... Plated
PLTF........... Par Leadership Training Foundation [Defunct] (EA)
PLTF........... Plaintiff [Legal term] (ROG)
PLTF........... Purple Loosestrife Task Force [Defunct] (EA)
PLTFF .... Plaintiff
PLTFM .... Platform
PLT-G......... Giant Platelet [Hematology] (DAVI)
PLTG........... Plating
PLT GL .... Plate Glass [Freight]
PLTHS .... Pilothouse
PLT LT........ Pilot Light (MSA)
PLTN........... Platoon
Plt Off......... Pilot Officer [British military] (DMA)
PLTP........... Phospholipid Transfer Protein [Biochemistry]
PLTR........... Plan for Long-Range Technical Requirements
PLTR........... Plotter (MSA)
PLTR........... Procurement Lead Time Requirement
Pltrsq.......... Plateresque (VRA)
PLTRY .... Poultry [Freight]
PLTS........... Precision LASER Tracking System (NASA)
PLTTNG ...... Pilot Training [Air Force]
PLTTNGSq .. Pilot Training Squadron [Air Force]
PLTTY .... Private Line Teletypewriter [Telecommunications] (IAA)
PLTTY .... Private Line Teletypewriter Service (NITA)
PLTV........... Percentage Local Thickness Variation (AAEL)
PLTXAU...... Public Telex Access Unit [Telecommunications] (OSI)
PLTY........... Poultry
PLTYP......... Plumbeotype (VRA)
PLTZC......... Pulitzer Publishing Co. (MHDW)
PLU............. Partial Line Up (NITA)
PLU............. Partido Liberal Unificado [Unified Liberal Party] [Paraguay] [Political party] (PPW)
PLu............. Path Loss, Uplink [Communications]
PLU............. People Like Us (IIA)
PLU............. PERT [Program Evaluation and Review Technique] Life Cycle Unified System (IAA)
PLU............. Phi Lambda Upsilon [Fraternity]
PLU............. Platoon Leaders Unit [Marine Corps]
PI U............ Plowden on Usury [A publication] (DLA)
PLU............. Pluggable Unit (SAA)
PLU............. Plural
plu............. Plural (WDMC)
PLU............. Plutonium [Chemical symbol is Pu] (AAG)
PLU............. Poor Law Union [British]
PLU............. Pratt & Lambert United, Inc. [NYSE symbol] (SAG)
PLU............. Preservation of Location Uncertainty [Strategy for protecting missiles] [Military]
PLU............. Pressure Lubrication Unit
PLU............. Price Look-Up (IAA)
PLU............. Primary Logical Unit [Computer science] (CIST)
PLU............. Probability of Leakage through Underlay
PLU............. Propellant Loading and Utilization (AAG)
PLUCON....... Plutonium Decontamination Emergency Team [Army]
PLUG........... Propellant Loading and Utilization Group (AAG)
PLUGE......... Picture Line-Up Generator [Television]
PLuL........... Lincoln University, Lincoln University, PA [Library symbol Library of Congress] (LCLS)
PLUM........... Payload Launch Module
PLUM........... Payload Umbilical Mast (NASA)
PLUM........... Priority Low-Use Minimal
PLUM........... Programmes Library Update and Maintenance (PDAA)
PLUM........... Programming Language for Users of MAVIS [Microprocessor-Based Audio Visual Information System] (PDAA)
PLUMB .... Plumbum [Lead] [Pharmacy]
Plum Contr... Plumptre on Contracts [2nd ed.] [1897] [A publication] (DLA)
PlumCrk..... Plum Creek Timber Co., Inc. [Associated Press] (SAG)
PLUNA........ Primeras Lineas Uruguayas de Navegacion Aerea [Uruguayan National Airlines]
PLund .... Papyri Lundenses [A publication] (OCD)
PLUOT .... Parts Listing Used On-Line Technique [Computer science] (IAA)
PLUP .... Pluperfect [Grammar]

PLUPF .... Pluperfect [Grammar]
PLUR .... Jarvis Island [Line Islands] [ICAO location identifier] (ICLI)
PLUR .... Photo Lab Usage Reporting (MCD)
PLUR .... Plural
PLUS .... Parent Loans to Undergraduate Students [Later, ALAS] [Department of Education]
PLUS .... PERT [Program Evaluation and Review Technique] Lifecycle Unified System
PLUS .... Portable Lightweight Upper Air Sounding System (MCD)
PLUS .... Potential Long Supply Utilization Screening (NATG)
PLUS .... Precision Loading and Utilization System (AAG)
PLUS .... Prima Leben und Sparen [Quality Living and Saving] [Brand name and discount store chain in West Germany and US]
PLUS .... Procedures for Long Supply Assets Utilization Screening [DoD]
PLUS .... Professional Liability Underwriting Society (NTPA)
PLUS .... Program Language for User's System (NITA)
PLUS .... Program Library Update System
PLUS .... Programmed Learning under Supervision
PLUS .... Programming Language for UNIVAC [Universal Automatic Computer] Systems [Computer science] (CSR)
PLUS .... Project Literacy US [Joint project of American Broadcasting Co. and Public Broadcasting Service]
PLUS .... Prudent Laboratory Use System [Health insurance] (GHCT)
PLUS .... Room Plus, Inc. [NASDAQ symbol] (SAG)
Plut .... Plutarch [First century AD] [Classical studies] (OCD)
PLUT .... Plutchnik [Geriatric rating scale] (DMAA)
Plut .... Plutus [of Aristophanes] [Classical studies] (OCD)
PLUTHARCO... Plutonium, Uranium, Thorium Assembly Reactivity Code
PLUTO .... Pipeline under the Ocean [British project] [World War II]
PLUTO .... Plutonium [Loop-Testing] Reactor [British] (DEN)
PLUVUE ...... Plume Visibility Model [Environmental Protection Agency] (GFGA)
PLUZ .... Policy Land Use Zone [Australian Capital Territory]
PLV .... Live Poliomyelitis Vaccine [Immunology] (MAE)
PLV .... Panleukopenia Virus [Medicine] (MAE)
PLV .... Peak Left Ventricular [Pressure] [Cardiology]
PLV .... Phenylalanine-Lysine-Vasopressin (MAE)
PLV .... Phu-Lien [Kien-An] [Vietnam] [Seismograph station code, US Geological Survey] (SEIS)
PLV .... Polaravia OY [Finland ICAO designator] (FAAC)
PLV .... Posterior Left Ventricle [Anatomy] (DAVI)
PLV .... Posterior Left Ventricular Wall [Cardiology]
PLV .... Postlanding Vent [or Ventilation] [Apollo] [NASA]
PLV .... Power Limiting Valve
PLV .... Presentation Level Video (PCM)
PLV .... Production Level Video
PLVC .... Post-Landing Vent Control [NASA] (KSC)
PLVL .... Present Level [Aviation] (FAAC)
PLVRZD .... Pulverized (MSA)
PLW .... Palau [ANSI three-letter standard code] (CNC)
PLW .... Palu [Indonesia] [Airport symbol] (OAG)
PLW .... Patna Law Weekly [India] [A publication] (DLA)
PLW .... Plastic Engine Technology Corp. [Toronto Stock Exchange symbol]
PLW .... Plow Snow [NWS] (FAAC)
PLW .... Preload Washer
PLWA .... People Living with AIDS [Acquired Immunodeficiency Syndrome] [Medicine] (TAD)
PL/WA .... Plain Washer [Automotive engineering]
PLWA .... Primary Light Water Addition (COE)
plwd .... Plywood (BARN)
PLWG .... Photographic Laboratories Working Group [Range Commanders Council] [White Sands Missile Range, NM]
PLWHA .... People Living With HIV/AIDS [Human Immunodeficiency Virus / Acquired Immune Deficiency Syndrome] [Australia]
PLWS .... Prader-Labhart-Willi Syndrome [Medicine] (DMAA)
PLX .... Parallax Developments [Vancouver Stock Exchange symbol]
PLX .... Plains Resources [AMEX symbol] (TTSB)
PLX .... Plains Resources, Inc. [AMEX symbol] (SPSG)
PLX .... Plexus [Medicine]
PLX .... Position Launch [Search mode wherein X signifies the launch mode number] (MCD)
PLX .... Propellant Loading Exercise (MCD)
PLX .... Robinson, IL [Location identifier FAA] (FAAL)
PLXS .... Plexus Corp. [NASDAQ symbol] (NQ)
PLY .... Photoluminescence Yield [Spectroscopy]
Ply .... Plymouth [Record label]
PLY .... Plywood
ply .... Plywood (VRA)
PLY .... Polaris Energy [Vancouver Stock Exchange symbol]
PLY .... Polyphase Corp. [AMEX symbol] (SPSG)
PLY .... Prune Extract Lactose Yeast Medium [Microbiology]
plyc .... Polychrome (VRA)
plyes .... Polyester (VRA)
PlyGem .... Ply-Gem, Inc. [Associated Press] (SAG)
PLYINST ...... Command Comply Current Instructions
PLYM .... Plymouth [England]
plym .... Polymer (VRA)
P-LYM .... Prolymphocyte [Hematology] (DAVI)
PLYMCHAN... Plymouth Subarea Channel [NATO] (NATG)
Plymouth St C... Plymouth State College (GAGS)
PLYMP .... Plympton [England]
PLYMT .... Plymtree [England]
PLYPASSPORT... Application for Passport for Self and/or Dependents Accordance BUPERS Manual [Navy]
plypt .... Polyptic (VRA)
PlyR .... Plymouth Rubber Co., Inc. [Associated Press] (SAG)

plyst .... Polystyrene (VRA)
plyur .... Polyurethane (VRA)
plyvn .... Polyvinyl (VRA)
PLYWD .... Plywood
PLZ .... Phenelzine (DMAA)
Plz .... Plaza (AD)
PLZ .... Plaza (MCD)
PLZ .... Please
PLZ .... Polarize (MSA)
PLZ .... Port Elizabeth [South Africa] [Airport symbol] (OAG)
PLZ .... Programming Languages for the Zilog [Computer science] (CSR)
PLZA .... Plaza [Commonly used] (OPSA)
PLZF .... Promyelocytic Leukaemia Zinc-Finger [Protein]
PLZN .... Polarization (MSA)
PLZT .... Pb-based Lanthanum-doped Zirconate Titanates
PM .... [The] Chesapeake & Ohio Railway Co. (Pere Marquette District) [AAR code]
PM .... Cold Press Molding
PM .... Ha-Po'el ha-Mizrahi (BJA)
PM .... Pacemaker [Medicine] (DMAA)
PM .... Pacific Mail (ROG)
P/M .... Pacific Molasses (AD)
PM .... Pacific Mutual Life Insurance Co. (EFIS)
PM .... Pad Mechanic [Aerospace]
PM .... Painting Machine
PM .... Pak [or Phak] Mai [New Party] [Political party]
PM .... Pamphlet
PM .... Panel Maintenance (IAA)
PM .... Panel Meter (IEEE)
pm .... Papier Mache (VRA)
PM .... Papillary Muscle [Medicine] (DB)
PM .... Papular Mucinosis (DB)
PM .... Parachute Mine [British military] (DMA)
PM .... Parameter [Computer science]
pm .... Paramilitary (AD)
Pm .... Paratid Midle [Band protein] (DMAA)
PM .... Paraxial Magnification (SAA)
P/M .... Parent-Metabolite Ratio [Medicine] (MEDA)
PM .... Parlor Maid
PM .... Partial Remission [Medicine] (CDI)
PM .... Particulate Matter
PM .... Partito Monarchico [Monarchist Party] [Italy Political party] (PPE)
P/M .... Parts per Million (IEEE)
PM .... Passed Midshipman
PM .... Passed Motion
PM .... Past Master [Freemasonry]
PM .... Patriotic Majority [An association] (EA)
PM .... Patriotikon Metopon [Patriotic Front] [Greek Cyprus] [Political party] (PPE)
PM .... Patternmaker [Navy rating]
PM .... Payload Management [NASA] (NASA)
PM .... Payload Midbody [NASA] (MCD)
PM .... Paymaster
PM .... Peabody Museum (AD)
PM .... Peace Museum (EA)
PM .... Pectoralis Major [Anatomy]
PM .... Peculiar Meter
PM .... Pelizaeus-Merbacher [Disease] [Medicine] (DB)
PM .... Penalty Minutes [Hockey]
PM .... Pension Mortgage [British]
PM .... People Meter [TV ratings measuring device] [Advertising]
PM .... Pere Marquette Railroad
PM .... Perfect Master [Freemasonry]
PM .... Performance Monitor [NASA] (NASA)
PM .... Periodic Maintenance (AFM)
PM .... Peritoneal Macrophage [Immunology] (AAMN)
PM .... Permanent Magnet [Loudspeaker]
p-m .... Permanent Magnet (AD)
PM .... Per Million
PM .... Per Minute (IAA)
PM .... Per Month
p/m .... Per Month (WDAA)
Pm .... Petameter (IDOE)
PM .... Petit Mal [Epilepsy]
PM .... Petroleos Mexicanos [Spanish] (AD)
PM .... Petroleum Marketers, Inc. (EFIS)
PM .... Phased Maintenance (MCD)
PM .... Phase Match (IAA)
p-m .... Phase Modulation [Radio data transmission]
p-m .... Phase Modulation (AD)
PM .... Philip Morris, Inc.
PM .... Phorbol Monomyristate [Organic chemistry]
PM .... Phosphoramide Mustard [Antineoplastic drug]
PM .... Photo Marketing Magazine [A publication] (EAAP)
PM .... Photo Master (MCD)
PM .... Photomultiplier
PM .... Phyllosticta maydis [A toxin-producing fungus]
P/M .... Physical Medicine [Medical officer designation] [British]
PM .... Piae Memoriae [Of Pious Memory] [Latin]
pm .... Picometer [One trillionth of a meter]
pM .... Picomoler [One trillionth of a mole] (AAMN)
PM .... Pilgrim Airlines [ICAO designator] (AD)
PM .... Pilot Motor (MSA)
PM .... Pioneer Ministries (EA)
PM .... Pitching Moment [Physics]

PM	Pitch Mark [Shipfitting]
PM	Pit Membrane [Paleobotany]
PM	Planetary Mission [NASA] (NASA)
PM	Plasmalemma [Cytology]
PM	Plasma Membrane [Cytology]
PM	Plaster Master (MSA)
PM	Plastic Mold (MCD)
PM	Platelet Microsome [Medicine] (DMAA)
P/M	Player/Missile [Atari computers]
PM	Plus Minus [More or less]
PM	Pneumomediastinum [Medicine] (AAMN)
pm	Poids Moliculaire [Molecular Weight] [French] (AD)
PM	Polarization-Maintaining [Optical Film]
PM	Polarization Modulation (MCD)
PM	Police Magistrate
PM	Police Mutual Assurance Society [British]
PM	Policy Memorandum [Military]
PM	Poliomyelitis [Medicine]
PM	Pollen Mass [Botany]
PM	Pollution Minimum
PM	PolyMedica Industries [AMEX symbol] (TTSB)
PM	PolyMedica Industries, Inc. [AMEX symbol] (SAG)
PM	Polymeric Membrane
PM	Polymethacrylic [Organic chemistry]
PM	Polymorph [Hematology]
PM	Polymorphonuclear [Leukocyte] [Hematology] (DAVI)
PM	Polymyositis [Medicine]
PM	Pondus Medicinale [Medicinal Weight] [Pharmacy] (ROG)
PM	Pontifex Maximus [Supreme Pontiff] [Latin]
PM	Poor Metabolism [Medicine]
PM	Pope and Martyr [Church calendars]
PM	Popular Movement Against the European Community (ECON)
PM	Portable Magnetometer [NASA]
PM	Portable Medium Power Plant [Nuclear energy] (NRCH)
PM	Postal Manual
PM	Posterior Mitral Leaflet [Cardiology]
PM	Postmark [Deltiology]
PM	Postmaster
PM	Postmenopausal [Gynecology] (DAVI)
pm	Post Meridiem [Afternoon] [Latin] (WDMC)
PM	Post Meridiem [After Noon] [Latin]
PM	Postmodernist [Architecture]
PM	Post Mortem [After Death] [Latin]
pm	Post Mortem (AD)
PM	Potentiometer (DEN)
PM	Potting Mold (MCD)
PM	Pounds per Minute
PM	Powder Metallurgy
PM	Power Management (NAKS)
PM	Power Module (MCD)
PM	Powlesland & Mason [Railway] [Wales]
PM	Precious Metal
PM	Preincubation Mixture
PM	Premium
pm	Premium (AD)
pm	Premolar [Dentistry] (AD)
PM	Premolar [Dentistry]
PM	Prenegotiation Memorandum (AAGC)
PM	Preparation Meetings [Quakers]
PM	Prepared Message
PM	Presbyterian Men (EA)
PM	Presentation Manager [Computer science]
PM	Presidential Memo
PM	Pressure, Manifold
PM	Pressure Multiplier [Nuclear energy] (NRCH)
PM	Pressurized Module (SSD)
PM	Presystolic Murmur [Cardiology]
pm	Presystolic Murmur [Medicine] (AD)
PM	Pretibial Myxedema [Medicine] (DMAA)
PM	Preventive Maintenance
pm	Preventive Maintenance (AD)
PM	Preventive Material
PM	Preventive Medicine [Also, PVNTMED] (AFM)
PM	Priest and Martyr [Church calendars]
PM	Primary Market [Investment term]
PM	Primary Motivation [Psychology] (DAVI)
PM	Primary Munition
PM	Prime Minister
PM	Prime Mover (MCD)
PM	Primitive Methodists (ROG)
PM	Principal Matron [Navy British]
PM	Principle of Multiplying [New math]
PM	Printing Mechanism (IAA)
PM	Print Matrix (IAA)
PM	Prize Money
PM	Procedures Manual (IEEE)
PM	Processing Modflow [Computer program] [Scientific Software Group]
PM	Processing Module [Computer science]
PM	Process Manager (USDC)
PM	Process Manual
PM	Processor Module (NITA)
PM	Procurement and Material
PM	Procurement Manual [US Postal Service] [A publication] (AAGC)
PM	Production [or Product] Manager
PM	Production Mode

PM	Production Monitor (IAA)
p/m	Professional/Managerial (WDMC)
PM	Profit Margin (TDOB)
PM	Profit Motivated [Housing]
PM	Program (NG)
PM	Program Manager [or Management] (MCD)
pm	Program Manager (AD)
PM	Program Memorandum (MCD)
PM	Program Method [Computer science] (IAA)
PM	Program Milestone [NASA] (NASA)
PM	Program Monitoring (MUGU)
PM	Project Magic (EA)
PM	Project Manager [Military]
PM	Pro Memoria [In Remembrance] [Latin]
PM	Pro Mense [Per Month] [Latin]
Pm	Promethium [Chemical symbol]
PM	Pro Mille [Per Thousand] [Latin]
PM	Propellant Management (KSC)
PM	Proper Motion [Astronomy] (BARN)
PM	Property Management (OICC)
PM	Propulsion Memorandum
PM	Propulsion Module [NASA] (KSC)
PM	Prostatic Massage [Medicine]
PM	Protein Methylesterase (DB)
PM	Protocol Machine [Computer science] (TNIG)
PM	Provost Marshal [Army]
PM	Puberal Macromastia [Medicine] (DMAA)
PM	Publicity Man [Slang]
pm	Publicity Man (AD)
PM	Pulmonary Macrophages [Medicine]
PM	Pulpomesial [Dentistry]
PM	Pulse Code Modulation [Telecommunications] (IAA)
PM	Pulse Modulation
pm	Pulse Modulation (AD)
PM	Pulse Modulator (IDOE)
pm	Pumice (AD)
Pm	Pumice [Quality of the bottom] [Nautical charts]
PM	Punjabi Muslim [Pakistan]
PM	Purchase Memo (MCD)
pm	Purchase Money Morgage, Premium (EBF)
PM	Purchase-Money Mortgage [Real estate]
PM	Purchase Money Mortgage, Premium (EBF)
PM	Purchasing Manager
PM	Purple Membrane [Protein] (DB)
PM	Purpose-Made [Construction]
PM	Push Money [Sales incentive]
P/M	Put of More [Stock exchange term]
PM	Pyridoxamine [Also, Pxm] [Biochemistry]
PM	Sisters of the Presentation of Mary [Roman Catholic religious order]
PM	St. Pierre and Miquelon [ANSI two-letter standard code] (CNC)
PM1	Patternmaker, First Class [Navy rating]
PM2	Patternmaker, Second Class [Navy rating]
PM3	Patternmaker, Third Class [Navy rating]
PM10	Particulate Matter [Less than 10 microns]
PM10	Particulate Matter, 10 Millimeters and Less (COE)
PM-10	Particulate Matter of 10 Microns in Diameter or Smaller [BTS] (TAG)
PM15	Particulate Matter, 15 Millimeters and Less (COE)
PMA	Allegheny College, Meadville, PA [Library symbol Library of Congress] (LCLS)
PMA	Pacific Maritime Association (EA)
PMA	Pan-Macedonian Association (EA)
PMA	Pan Malaysian Air Transport [ICAO designator] (FAAC)
PMA	Panorama Resources Ltd. [Vancouver Stock Exchange symbol]
PMA	Papillary, Marginal, Attached [With reference to gingivae] [Dentistry]
PMA	Paramethoxyamphetamine
pma	Paramethoxyamphetamine (AD)
PMA	Parts Manufacturer Approval [FAA] (MCD)
PMA	Parts Manufacturing Associates (AD)
PMA	Peat Moss Association (EA)
PMA	Pemba Island [Tanzania] [Airport symbol] (OAG)
PMA	Pencil Makers Association (EA)
PMA	Performance Management Association (EAIO)
PMA	Performance Monitor Annunciator [NASA] (MCD)
PMA	Permanent Magnet Association (IAA)
PMA	Permanent Mailing Address
PMA	Personal Managers Association [British] (DBA)
PMA	Personal Money Allowance
PMA	Personnel Management Advisor (NOAA)
PMA	Personnel Management Assistance
PMA	Perth Market Authority [Australia]
PMA	Perth Muslim Association [Australia]
PMA	Petroleum Monitoring Agency [Ministry of Energy, Mines, and Resources] [Canada]
PMA	Pharmaceutical Manufacturers Association (EA)
PMA	Phased Maintenance Availability [Navy] (DOMA)
PMA	Phenylmercuric Acetate [Also, PMAC] [Herbicide and fungicide]
PMA	Philadelphia Museum of Art (AD)
PMA	Philadelphia Musical Academy
PMA	Philippine Mahogany Association [Defunct] (EA)
PMA	Phonograph Manufacturers Association (EA)
PMA	Phorbol Myristate Acetate [Also, PTA, TPA] [Organic chemistry]
PMA	Phosphomolybdic Acid [Organic chemistry]
PMA	Photo Marketing Association (AD)
PMA	Photo Marketing Association International (EA)
PMA	Photonic Multichannel Analyzer

PMA	Physical Medium Attachment [*Telecommunications*] (OSI)
PMA	Physical Memory Address
PMA	Pianoforte Manufacturers' Association Ltd. [*British*] (BI)
PMA	Pine Manor College, Chestnut Hill, MA [*OCLC symbol*] (OCLC)
PMA	Planetary Microbiological Assay [*Aerospace*]
PMA	Plasma Membrane Adenosinetriphosphatase (DB)
PMA	Plastic Mock-Up Assembly
PMA	Plumbers' Merchants Association [*British*] (BI)
PMA	PMI Group [*NYSE symbol*] (TTSB)
PMA	PMI Group, Inc. [*NYSE symbol*] (SAG)
PMA	Pole-Mounted Amplifier
PMA	Police Management Association [*Defunct*] (EA)
PMA	Police Marksman Association (EA)
PMA	Polish Museum of America (EA)
PMA	Politico-Military Affairs [*U.S. Department of State*] (BARN)
PMA	Poly(methyl Acrylate) [*Organic chemistry*]
PMA	Polyurethane Manufacturers Association (EA)
PMA	Portable Maintenance Aid [*Army*]
PMA	Port Moller [*Alaska*] [*Seismograph station code, US Geological Survey*] (SEIS)
PMA	Positive Mental Attitude
pma	Positive Mental Attitude (AD)
PMA	Potato Marketing Authority [*Australia*]
PMA	Potato Merchants' Association [*Australia*]
PMA	Power Marketing Administration [*Department of Energy*]
PMA	Preamplifier Module Assembly
PMA	Precious Metal Adder (Cost) (MCD)
PMA	Precious Metal Anode
PMA	Precision Measurements Association (EA)
PMA	Precision Metalforming Association (EA)
PMA	Premarket Approval Application [*Food and Drug Administration*]
PMA	Prevalence of Gingivitis [*Dentistry*] (DAVI)
PMA	Preventive Maintenance Agreement
PMA	Primary Market Area
PMA	Primary Mental Abilities [*Test*] [*Education*]
PMA	Prime Macro-Assembler (NITA)
PMA	Prinzmetal's Angina [*Cardiology*] (DAVI)
PMA	Priority Memory Access
PMA	Priority Memory Address (NITA)
PMA	Prison Mission Association (EA)
PMA	Probability of Mission Abort [*Navy*] (ANA)
PMA	Probationary Medical Assistant [*British military*] (DMA)
PMA	Procurement and Management Assistance [*Small Business Administration*]
PMA	Procurement Methods Analyst (AFM)
PMA	Produce Marketing Association [*Newark, DE*] (EA)
PMA	Production and Marketing Administration [*Department of Agriculture*] [*Functions dispersed, 1953*]
PMA	Professional Managers Association (EA)
PMA	Professional Manufacturers' Agents (EA)
PMA	Professional Mariners Alliance [*Defunct*] (EA)
PMA	Programa Mundial de Alimentos [*World Food Program*] [*Spanish*] (AD)
PMA	Progressive Muscular Atrophy [*Medicine*]
PMA	Project Manager, Air Systems Command [*Navy*]
PMA	Project Military Adviser (NATG)
PMA	Property Management Association of America (EA)
PMA	Property Market Analysis [*Consulting firm*] [*British*]
PMA	Prorated Mental Age [*Psychology*]
PMA	Protected Memory Address
PMA	Publishers Marketing Association (EA)
PMA	Pulpomesioaxial [*Dentistry*]
PMA	Pump-Motor Assembly
PMA	Purchase Methods Analyst
PMA	Pyridylmercuric Acetate [*Fungicide*] [*Organic chemistry*]
PMA	Pyromellitic Acid [*Organic chemistry*]
PMAA	Paper Makers Advertising Association (EA)
PMAA	Petroleum Marketers Association of America (EA)
PMAA	Promotion Marketing Association of America [*New York, NY*] (EA)
PMAA	Property Management Association of America (EA)
PMAA	Proprietary Medicines Association of Australia
PM-AAH	Project Manager, Advanced Attack Helicopter [*Military*]
PMA/ARR	Probable Missed Approach per Arrival [*Aviation*] (PDAA)
PMAC	Parallel Memory Address Counter [*Computer science*]
P-MAC	Perceptual-Motor Assessment for Children (TES)
PMAC	Phamaceutical Manufacturers Association of Canada
PMAC	Pharmaceutical Manufacturers Association of Canada
PMAC	Phenylmercuric Acetate [*Also, PMA*] [*Herbicide and fungicide*]
PMAC	PMA Communications, Inc. [*Boston, MA*] (TSSD)
PMAC	Polymethoxy Acetal (EDCT)
PMAC	Preliminary Maintenance Allocation Chart (MCD)
PMAC	Proprietary Medicines Advisory Committee [*Australia*]
PMAC	Provisional Military Administrative Council [*Ethiopia*] [*Political party*] (PD)
PMAC	Purchasing Management Association of Canada
PMACODS	Project Manager, Army Container Oriented Distribution System (MCD)
PM ACS	Product Manager, Army Communications System
PMACS	Project Management and Control System (CIST)
PMAD	Performance Monitor Annunciation Driver [*NASA*] (MCD)
PMAD	Personnel Management Authorization Document [*Army*]
PMAD	Power Management and Distribution (NASA)
PMadW	Westinghouse Electric Corp., Waltz Mill Site Library, Madison, PA [*Library symbol Library of Congress*] (LCLS)
PMAE	Peabody Museum of Archeology and Ethnology (AD)
PMAESA	Port Management Association of Eastern and Southern Africa (EA)
PMAF	Pharmaceutical Manufacturers Association Foundation (IAA)
PMAF	Polaris Missile Assembly Facility
PMAFS	Public Members Association of the Foreign Service (EA)
PMAG	Program Manager Assistance Group [*Military*] (MCD)
PMAG	Provisional Military Advisory Group
PMA-I	Photo Marketing Association-International (NTPA)
PMAI	Piano Manufacturers Association International (EA)
P/Maj	Pipe-Major [*British military*] (DMA)
PMALS	Prototype Miniature Air-Launched System
PMAN	Piedmont Management Co., Inc. [*NASDAQ symbol*] (NQ)
PMAN	Polymethacrylonitrile (EDCT)
PM & ACS	Procurement Management and Acquisition Control System [*Social Security Administration*]
PM & C	Plant Monitoring and Control [*IBM Corp.*]
PM & C-HI	Plant Monitoring and Control - Host Interface [*IBM Corp.*]
PM & OA	Printers' Managers and Overseers Association (AD)
pm & r	Physical Medicine and Rehabilitation (AD)
PM&R	Physical Medicine and Rehabilitation
PManM	Mansfield State College, Mansfield, PA [*Library symbol Library of Congress*] (LCLS)
PMANY	Pattern Makers Association of New York (EA)
PMAP	Performance Monitor Annunciation Panel [*NASA*] (MCD)
PMAP	Photomap
PMAR	Page Map Address Register
PMAR	Precious Metals Area Representative [*DoD*] (AFIT)
PMAR	Preliminary Maintenance Analysis Report [*Aerospace*] (AAG)
PMarhSO	Sun Oil Co., Marcus Hook, PA [*Library symbol Library of Congress*] (LCLS)
PMARP	Peacetime Manpower Allocation Requirements Plan (CINC)
PMARS	Performance Management and Recognition System (MCD)
PMAS	Police Mutual Assurance Society [*British*]
PMAS	Purdue Master Attitude Scales [*Psychology*]
PMASA	Printers' Medical Aid and Sanatoria Association [*British*] (BI)
PM-ASE	Project Manager, Aircraft Survivability Equipment [*Military*]
PM-ASH	Project Manager, Advanced Scout Helicopter [*Military*]
PM-ASI	Program Management Office for Armored Systems Integration [*Army*] (RDA)
PMAT	Page Map Address Table [*NASA*] (NASA)
PMAT	Plasma & Materials Technologies [*NASDAQ symbol*] (TTSB)
PMAT	Plasma & Materials Technologies, Inc. [*NASDAQ symbol*] (SAG)
PMAT	Portable Maintenance Access Terminal [*Computer science*]
PMAT	Primary Mental Abilities Test [*Education*]
PMAT	Purdue Mechanical Adaptability Test
PMATA	Paint Manufacture and Allied Trades' Association [*British*] (BI)
PMATA	Paper Makers' Allied Trades Association [*British*] (DBA)
PMax	Peak Inspiratory Pressure [*Medicine*] (DAVI)
PMB	Canadian Print Measurement Bureau (NITA)
PMB	Cis-Platinum, Methotrexate, Bleomycin [*Antineoplastic drug regimen*] (DAVI)
PMB	Pacific Motor Tariff Bureau, Inc., Oakland CA [*STAC*]
PMB	Palm Beach [*Diocesan abbreviation*] [*Florida*] (TOCD)
PMB	Para-Hydroxymercuribenzoate [*Biochemistry*] (MAE)
PMB	Paranormal Metal Bending
PMB	Pembina, ND [*Location identifier FAA*] (FAAL)
PMB	Performance Measurement Baseline (MCD)
PMB	Physical Metallurgy Branch
PMB	Pilot Make Busy (IEEE)
PMB	Plastic Media Blasting [*Coating technology*]
PMB	Polychrome Methylene Blue
PMB	Polymethylbenzene [*Organic chemistry*]
PMB	Polymorphonuclear Basophilic [*Leucocytes*] [*Hematology*]
PMB	Polymyxin B (DB)
pmb	Post-Menopausal Bleeding [*Medicine*] (AD)
PMB	Postmenopausal Bleeding [*Medicine*]
PMB	Potato Marketing Board [*British*]
PMB	Practice Multiple Bomb (MCD)
PMB	Precision Manned Bomber
PMB	Premier Bancshares [*NYSE symbol*]
PMB	Print Measurement Bureau [*Founded in 1971*] [*Also the name of a database*] [*Canada*]
PMB	Private Mail Bag
PMB	Program Management Board (AFM)
PMB	Project Management and Budgeting
PMB	PROM [*Programmable Read-Only Memory*] Memory Board
PMBA	Professional Master of Business Administration (PGP)
PMBC	Pacific Motor Boat Club (AD)
PMBC	Phuket Marine Biological Center [*Marine science*] (MSC)
PMBC	Portland Motor Boat Club [*Oregon*] (AD)
PMBC	Process-Model Based Controller (ACII)
PMBIAS	Percentage Median Bias [*Statistics*]
pmbo	Participative Management by Objectives (AD)
PMBOK	Project Management Body of Knowledge
PMBR	Practice Multiple Bomb Rack (NG)
PMBS	Pelican Man's Bird Sanctuary (EA)
PMBU	Personal Member of the Baptist Union [*British*]
PMBX	Private Manual Branch Exchange [*Communications*]
pmbx	Private Manual Branch Exchange (AD)
PMC	Carnegie-Mellon University, Pittsburgh, PA [*OCLC symbol*] (OCLC)
PMC	Chief Patternmaker [*Navy rating*]
PMC	Little Missionary Sisters of Charity [*Roman Catholic religious order*]
PMC	Pacific Marine Center [*National Oceanic and Atmospheric Administration*]
PMC	Pacific Medical Center (BABM)
PMC	Pacific Missile Center [*Marine science*] (MSC)

PMC	Pan Metal [*formerly, Patton Morgan*] Corp. [*Ammunition manufacturer*]
PMC	Parents of Missing Children [*Australia*]
PMC	Parents of Murdered Children [*Later, POMC*] (EA)
PMC	Partially Mission Capable [*Maintenance and supply*] (MCD)
PMC	Patient Management Categories [*Medicine*] (MEDA)
PMC	Patrol/Mine Countermeasure Craft [*British*]
PMC	Payload Monitoring and Control [*NASA*] (NASA)
PMC	Penguin Modern Classics [*Book publishing*]
PMC	Pennsylvania Military Academy (AD)
PMC	Pennsylvania Military College
PMC	Pentamethyl(hydroxy)chromane [*Organic chemistry*]
PMC	People's Mandate Committee (EA)
PMC	Percent Modern Carbon [*In atmosphere*]
PMC	Performance Management Computer (PDAA)
PMC	Peripheral Mononuclear Cell [*Cytology*]
PMC	Peritoneal Mast Cell
PMC	Permanently Manned Capability (SSD)
PMC	Personnel Management Centre [*British*] (ODBW)
PMC	Personnel Mobilization Center [*Military*]
PMC	Phased Maintenance Checklist (MCD)
PMC	Phenolic Molding Compound
PMC	Phenylmercuric Chloride [*Antiseptic*]
PMC	Philatelic Music Circle (EA)
PMC	Piperidinomethylcyclohexane [*Organic chemistry*]
PMC	Planning Ministers' Conference [*Australia*]
PMC	Plaster-Molded Cornice [*Construction*]
PMC	Plutona-Molybdenum CERMET [*Ceramic Metal Element*] (NASA)
PMC	PMC Capital [*AMEX symbol*] (TTSB)
PMC	PMC Capital, Inc. [*AMEX symbol*] (SPSG)
PMC	Pollen Mother Cell [*Botany*]
PMC	Polymer Matrix Composite [*Materials science*]
PMC	Posterior Medial Corner of Knee [*Sports medicine*]
PMC	Post Maintenance Check (MCD)
PMC	Post Manufacturing Checkout (KSC)
PMC	Post Master's Certificate (PGP)
PMC	Powdered Metal Cathode
PMCV	Power-Mate Corp. (IAA)
PMC	Precision Machining Commercialization (MCD)
pmc	Precision Mirror Calorimeter (AD)
PMC	Predictive Multisensor Correlation
PMC	Pre-Mission Calibration (PDAA)
PMC	Premium Merchandising Club of New York (EA)
PMC	Premotor Cortex [*Neuroanatomy*]
PMC	President of the Mess Committee [*Military British*]
PMC	President's Management Council (AAGC)
PMC	Pressurized Membrane Container
pmc	Preventive Maintenance Contract (AD)
PMC	Primary Mesenchyme Cell [*Cytology*]
PMC	Prime Mover Control [*Valve*]
PMC	Princeton Microfilm Corp.
PmC	Princeton Microfilm Corporation, Princeton, NJ [*Library symbol Library of Congress*] (LCLS)
PMC	Private Mailing Card [*Deltiology*]
PMC	Private Medical Communication
PMC	Private Meter Check [*Telecommunications*] (TEL)
PMC	Processed Meats Committee [*Later, DPMC*] (EA)
PMC	Process Module Controller (AAEL)
PMC	Procurement Committee (MCD)
PMC	Procurement Management Code [*Military*] (AFIT)
PMC	Procurement, Marine Corps [*An appropriation*]
PMC	Procurement Method Coding [*DoD*]
PMC	Professional and Managerial Class [*British*] (DI)
PMC	Professional Musicians' Club [*Australia*]
PMC	Programmable Machine Controller (NRCH)
PMC	Programmable Machine Tool Controller (IAA)
PMC	Programmable Matrix Controller (IAA)
PMC	Program Management Control
PMC	Program Management Course [*Army*] (RDA)
PMC	Program Marginal Checking
PMC	Project Management Committee (AD)
PMC	Project Management Course [*Army*]
PMC	Project Manufacturing Controller (MCD)
PMCA	Pro Maria Committee (EA)
PMC	Propellant Monitor and Control (AFM)
PMC	Pseudo Machine Code [*Computer science*] (BUR)
PMC	Pseudomembranous Colitis [*Medicine*]
PMC	Public Media Center (EA)
PMC	Puerto Montt [*Chile*] [*Airport symbol*] (OAG)
PMC	Pumice (MSA)
pMc	Pure Mexican Cocaine (AD)
PMCA	Purple Martin Conservation Association (EA)
PM-CAWS	Project Manager for Cannon Artillery Weapon Systems (RDA)
PMCB	Partially Mission Capable Both [*Maintenance and supply*] (MCD)
P/MCB	Project/Miscellaneous Change Board (MCD)
PMCC	Paper Machine Clothing Council (NTPA)
PMCC	Peerless Motor Car Club
PMCC	Pensky-Martens Closed Cup [*Flash point test*]
PMCC	Platform Mission Control Center [*NASA*]
PMCC	Post Mark Collectors Club (EA)
PMCC	Product-Moment Correlation Co-Efficient (DMAA)
PMC CT	PMC Commercial Trust [*Associated Press*] (SAG)
PMCD	Post Mortem Core Dump [*Computer science*]
PMCD	Process Measurement & Control Division (ACII)
PMCD	Program Module Connection Diagram (MHDI)

PMCF	Partial Mission Capability Factor
PMCF	Post Maintenance Check Flight (MCD)
PMCH	Pro-Melanin-Concentrating Hormone (DMAA)
PMCHI	Crawford County Historical Society, Meadville, PA [*Library symbol Library of Congress*] (LCLS)
PMCHL	Pro-Melanin-Concentrating Hormone-Like (DMAA)
PMCI	Phosphate Mining Corp. of Christmas Island (EY)
PMC INC	Precision Management of Concordville, Inc. [*Media, PA*] (TSSD)
PMck	Carnegie Free Library of McKeesport, McKeesport, PA [*Library symbol Library of Congress*] (LCLS)
PMCL	Posterior Medial Collateral Ligament [*Anatomy*]
PMCL	Proposed MAPAD Change Letter (AAGC)
PMCL	Proposed MILSTRIP Change Letters
PMCM	Master Chief Patternmaker [*Navy rating*]
PMCM	Partially Mission Capable Maintenance [*Maintenance and supply*] (MCD)
PMCM	Permanent Mold Casting Mold (MCD)
PMCM	Pulse Morse Code Modulation (OA)
PMCP	Prime Capital Corp. [*NASDAQ symbol*] (SAG)
PMCQ	Paper Marketing Council of Queensland [*Australia*]
PMCS	Partially Mission Capable Supply [*Maintenance and supply*] (MCD)
PMCS	Patient Management Computer Stimulation (DMAA)
PMCS	PMC-Sierra, Inc. [*NASDAQ symbol*] [*Formerly, Sierra Semiconductor*] (SG)
PMCS	Preventive Maintenance Checks and Services [*for Army vehicles*] (INF)
PMCS	Process Monitoring and Control System
pmcs	Process Monitoring and Control Systems (AD)
PMCS	Professional Military Comptroller School
PMCS	Program [*or Project*] Management Control System [*Army*]
PMCS	Pulse-Modulated Communications System
PMCS	Senior Chief Patternmaker [*Navy rating*]
PMCT	PAL [*Permissive Action Link*] Management Control Team [*Army*] (AABC)
PMCTF	Prime Minister's Country Task Force [*Australia*]
PMCU	Personal Member of the Congregational Union [*British*]
PMCU	Predominately Minority Colleges and Universities
PMCV	Programmed Multichannel Valve [*Chromatography*]
PMD	Palmdale, CA [*Location identifier FAA*] (FAAL)
PMD	Palmdale/Lancaster [*California*] [*Airport symbol*] (OAG)
PMD	Palmer Industries Ltd. [*Vancouver Stock Exchange symbol*]
PMD	Panel-Mounted Display (MCD)
PMD	Part Manufacturing Design
PMD	Payload Mating Dolly [*NASA*]
PMD	Payload Module Decoder [*NASA*]
PMD	Pelizaeus-Merzbacher Disease [*Medicine*]
PMD	Personnel Management Division [*Environmental Protection Agency*] (GFGA)
PMD	Pharmaco-Medical Documentation, Inc. [*Information service or system*] (IID)
PMD	Physical Medium Dependent [*Computer science*]
PMD	Physical Medium Dependent Layer [*Telecommunications*] (OSI)
PMD	Planning and Management Division [*Environmental Protection Agency*] (GFGA)
PMD	Pontiac Motor Division [*General Motors Corp.*]
Pmd	Portmadoc (AD)
PMD	Post-Mortem Debugger [*Computer science*] (PCM)
PMD	Post Mortem Dump [*Computer science*]
pmd	Post-Mortem Dumps (AD)
PMD	Preventive Maintenance, Daily (MCD)
PMD	Preventive Maintenance Division [*Air Force*]
PMD	Primary Myeloproliferative Disease [*Medicine*]
PMD	Primary Myocardial Disease [*Medicine*]
PMD	Private Management Domain [*Computer science*] (TNIG)
PMD	Private Medical Doctor (DAVI)
PMd	Private Physician
PMD	Processing, Marketing, and Distribution
PMD	Program for Management Development [*Harvard Business School*] (DD)
PMD	Program Management Directive [*Air Force*]
PMD	Program Management Documentation [*Army*]
PMD	Programmed Multiple Development [*Analytical chemistry*]
PMD	Program Module Dictionary
PMD	Program Monitoring and Diagnosis
PMD	Progressive Muscular Dystrophy [*Medicine*]
PMD	Projected Map Display
pmd	Projected Map Display (AD)
PMD	Project Manager Development (MCD)
PMD	Psychemedics Corp. [*AMEX symbol*] (SAG)
PMD	Psychiatric Military Duty
PMDA	Photographic Manufacturers and Distributors Association (EA)
PMDA	Pianoforte Manufacturers and Distributors Association [*British*] (DBA)
PMDA	Plastics Machinery Distributors Association [*British*] (EAIO)
PMDA	Pyromellitic Dianhydride [*Organic chemistry*]
PMDAMT	Pacific Mobile Depot Activity Maintenance Team (CINC)
PMDB	Program Management Decision Brief [*Defense Systems Management College*] (DOMA)
PMD/BMI	Project Management Division/Batelle Memorial Institute (AD)
PMDC	Pakistan Minerals Development Corp. (AD)
PMDC	Project for Mathematical Development of Children [*National Science Foundation*]
PMDC	Project Manager Development Course [*Military*] (RDA)
PMDD	Personnel Management Development Directorate [*Military Personnel Center*] (AABC)
PMDD	Premenstrual Dysphoric Disorder [*Gynecology*] (DMAA)

PMDF	Project Master Data File [*For spacecraft*]
PMDG	Pentamethylene Diguanidine [*Organic chemistry*]
PMDI	Polymeric Methylene Diphenylene Isocyanate (EDCT)
PMDL	Palmdale, CA (NASA)
PMDL	Post M-Day Deployment List [*Military*] (AABC)
PMDL	Provisional Military Demarcation Line (CINC)
PMDM	Polyhedra Molecular Demonstration Model
PMDM	Poly(mellitic Dianhydride Methacrylate) [*Organic chemistry*]
PM/DM	Polymyositis/Dermatomyositis [*Rheumatology*] (DAVI)
PMDO	Phased Maintenance During Overhaul
PMDP	Pavement Marking Demonstration Program [*Federal Highway Administration*]
PMDP	Project Manager Development Program [*Army*] (RDA)
PMDR	Parametric Monotone Decreasing Ratio [*Statistics*]
PMDR	Phosphorescence-Microwave Double Resonance
PMDR	Provisioning Master Data Record
PM-DRG	Pediatric-Modified Diagnosis-Related Group (HCT)
PMDRMU	Paper Mould and Dandy Roll Makers' Union (DGA)
PMDS	Peristent Muellerian Duct Syndrome [*Medicine*] (DMAA)
PMDS	(Phenylmercury)dodecenyl Succinate [*Antimicrobial agent*]
PMDS	Pilot Map Display System
PMDS	Point Missile Defense System (DNAB)
PMDS	Portable Diver Monitoring System
PMDS	Primary Myelodysplastic Syndrome [*Medicine*] (DMAA)
PMDS	Process Monitoring and Display Software [*Computer science*] (ECII)
pmds	Projected Map Display Set (AD)
PMDS	Projected Map Display System
PMDS	Property Management and Disposal Service [*Abolished, 1973*] [*General Services Administration*]
PMDT	Park Meditech, Inc. [*NASDAQ symbol*] (SAG)
PMDT	Pentamethyldiethylenetriamine [*Organic chemistry*]
PMDTF	Park Meditech [*NASDAQ symbol*] (TTSB)
PMDU	Projected Map Display Unit (DNAB)
PMDY	Midway Naval Station [*Henderson Field*], Sand Island [*Midway Islands*] [*ICAO location identifier*] (ICLI)
PME	Allstate Corp. [*NYSE symbol*] (SAG)
PME	Allstate Cp 6.76% Exch Nts '98 [*NYSE symbol*] (TTSB)
PME	Caltech Political Military Exercise [*International relations simulation game*]
PME	Paramagnetic Meissner Effect [*Physics*]
PME	Passive Microelectronic Element
PME	Peace Movement of Ethiopia (EA)
PME	Pectin Methylesterase [*Also, PE*] [*An enzyme*]
PME	Pedal Mode Ergometer
PME	Performance Management and Evaluation
pme	Performance-Measuring Equipment (AD)
PME	Performance Monitoring Equipment (NVT)
PME	Personnel Management Evaluation [*Marine science*] (OSRA)
PME	Personnel Management for Executives [*Military*] (RDA)
PME	Phosphatidylmonomethylethanolamine [*Biochemistry*]
PME	Phosphomonoester [*Biochemistry*]
PME	Phosphorylated Monester [*Organic chemistry*]
PME	Photomagnetoelectric
PME	Photomagnetoelectric Effect (IAA)
PME	Pinosylvin Methyl Ether [*Organic chemistry*]
pme	Planning, Management, Evaluation (AD)
PME	Polymorphonuclear Eosinophile [*Hematology*]
P Me	Portland, Maine (AD)
PME	Portsmouth [*England*] [*Airport symbol*] (AD)
PME	Postmenopausal Estrogen Therapy [*Gynecology*] (CPH)
PME	Precision Measuring Equipment (AFM)
PME	Primary Mission Equipment
PME	Prime Ministers of England [*A publication*]
PME	Process and Manufacturing Engineering (NRCH)
PME	Processor Memory Enhancement
PME	Professional Management for Executives [*Army*]
PME	Professional Military Education (AFM)
PME	Professional Military Ethic (MCD)
PME	Progressive Myoclonus Epilepsy [*Medicine*] (STED)
PME	Project Management Engineering, Inc. (EFIS)
PME	Project Manager, Electronics System Command [*Navy*]
PME	Protective Multiple Earthing [*Electricity*]
pme	Protective Multiple Earthing (AD)
PMEA	(Phenyl)(methyl)ethanolamine [*Organic chemistry*]
PMEA	Phosphonylmethoxyethyladenine [*Antiviral*]
PMEA	Powder Metallurgy Equipment Association (EA)
P/MEA	Probationary Marine Engineering Artificer [*British military*] (DMA)
PMEA	Production and Maintenance Engineering Agent (MCD)
PMEA	Publishing Manufacturers Executive Association (EA)
PMEAR	Preliminary Maintenance Engineering Analysis Requirement (MCD)
PMEC	Postgraduate Medical Education Committee [*University of Queensland, Australia*]
PMEC	Pseudomembranous Enterocolitis [*Medicine*] (STED)
PMED	Paradigm Medical Industries, Inc. [*NASDAQ symbol*] (SAG)
PMedS	Delaware County Institute of Science, Media, PA [*Library symbol Library of Congress*] (LCLS)
PMEE	Prime Mission Electronic Equipment [*NASA*] (KSC)
PMEF	Petroleum Marketing Education Foundation (EA)
PMEG	Perforated Metal Export Groups [*British*] (DBA)
PMEL	Pacific Marine Environmental Laboratory [*Seattle, WA*] [*National Oceanic and Atmospheric Administration*] (GRD)
PMEL	Precision Measurements Equipment Laboratory [*NASA*]
PMEL	Precision Measuring Equipment Laboratory (AD)
PMEL	Precision Mechanics and Electronics Laboratory (COE)
PMEM	Piezoelectric Micro Electro Mechanical (AAEL)
PMEM	Processor Memory [*Computer science*] (CIST)
PM-ENDOR	Polarization Modulated Electron Nuclear Double Resonance [*Spectroscopy*]
PMEP	Pumping Mean Effective Pressure [*Automotive engine testing*]
PMer	Mercer Free Library, Mercer, PA [*Library symbol Library of Congress*] (LCLS)
PMES	Personnel Management Evaluation System [*Department of Labor*]
PMES	Productivity Measurement and Evaluation System (MCD)
PMES	Proposed Material Erection Schedule (MCD)
PMEST	Personality, Matter, Energy, Space, Time [*Colon classification, S. R. Ranganathan*] [*Library science*]
pmest	Personality, Matter, Energy, Space, Time (AD)
pmet	Painted Metal (AD)
PMET	Painter Metal (AAG)
PMEV	Panel-Mounted Electronic Voltmeter
PMEXPO	Property Management Exposition [*Bachner Communications*] (TSPED)
PMF	L-Phenylalanine Mustard, 5-Fluorouracil, Methotrexate [*Antineoplastic drug regimen*] (DAVI)
PMF	Parts Master File (MCD)
PMF	Patriot Maintenance Facility [*Army*]
PMF	Performance Measurement Facility (IAA)
PMF	Performance Monitor Function [*NASA*] (NASA)
PMF	Perigee Motor Firing [*Aerospace*] (MCD)
PMF	Permanent Magnetic Field
PMF	Permanent Military Force (ADA)
PMF	Personnel Master File [*Army*] (AABC)
PMF	Pilot Mortar Fire
PMF	Polaris Missile Facility [*Military*] (IAA)
PMF	Presidential Medal of Freedom (AD)
PMF	Price Master File (MCD)
PMF	Principle Management Facility (MCD)
PMF	Probability Mass Function (IAA)
PMF	Probable Maximum Flood [*Nuclear energy*] (NRCH)
pmf	Probable Maximum Flooding (AD)
PMF	Processed Message File (MCD)
PMF	Product Measurement Facility (IAA)
PMF	Professional Medical Film (AABC)
PMF	Programmable Matched Filter (IAA)
PMF	Program Management Facility [*NASA*] (MCD)
PMF	Progressive Massive Fibrosis
pmf	Progressive Massive Fibrosis [*Medicine*] (AD)
PMF	Project Management File (MCD)
PMF	Pro Male Fingers [*International Bowhunting Organization*] [*Class equipment*]
PMF	Pro Media Foundation (EA)
PMF	Proton Motive Force [*Physics*]
PMF	Pterygomaxillary Fossa (STED)
PMFA	Fireman Apprentice, Patternmaker, Striker [*Navy rating*]
PM-FAC	Prednisone, Methotrexate, Fluorouracil, Adriamycin, Cyclophosphamide [*Antineoplastic drug regimen*]
PMFC	Pacific Marine Fisheries Commission [*Later, PSMFC*] (EA)
PMFC	Pacific Marine Fisheries Compact (COE)
PMFC	Patsy Montana Fan Club (EA)
PMFG	Peerless Manufacturing Co. [*NASDAQ symbol*] (NQ)
PMFG	Peerless Mfg [*NASDAQ symbol*] (TTSB)
PMFI	Perpetual Midwest Financial [*NASDAQ symbol*] (TTSB)
PMFI	Perpetual Midwest Financial, Inc. [*NASDAQ symbol*] (SAG)
PM/FL	Performance Monitor/Fault Locator [*Military*] (CAAL)
PMFLT	Pamphlet (MSA)
PMFN	Fireman, Patternmaker, Striker [*Navy rating*]
PMFPAC	Polaris Missile Facility, Pacific Fleet
PMFS	Pulsed Magnetic Field System
PMFWCMA	Paper Mill Fourdrinier Wire Cloth Manufacturers Association [*Later, FWC*] (EA)
PMG	Pall Mall Gazette [*A publication*]
PMG	Paymaster General [*Navy*]
PMG	Permanent Magnet Generator
PMG	Phase Modulation Generator
PMG	Photographic Materials Specialty Group (NTPA)
PMG	Physiological Measurement Group
PMG	Phytophthora Megasperma F. Sp. Glycinea [*A fungus*]
PMG	Pinto Malartic [*Vancouver Stock Exchange symbol*]
PMG	Polymethylgalacturonase [*An enzyme*]
PMG	Ponta Pora [*Brazil*] [*Airport symbol*] (OAG)
PMG	Port Moresby [*Papua New Guinea*] [*Seismograph station code, US Geological Survey*] (SEIS)
PMG	Postmaster General
PmG	Postmaster General (AD)
PMG	Poultry Marketing Guide
PMG	Power Metal Grid (PDAA)
PMG	Prediction Marker Generator
PMG	Primary Medical Group [*Insurance*] (DMAA)
PMG	Propodial Mucus Gland [*Zoology*]
PMG	Provisional Military Government [*Ethiopia*]
PMG	Provost Marshal General [*Army*]
PMG	Putnam Investment Grade Municipal Trade II [*NYSE symbol*] (SPSG)
PMG	Putnam Inv Grade Muni Tr II [*NYSE symbol*] (TTSB)
PMGCT	Primary Mediastinal Germ-Cell Tumor [*Medicine*] (DMAA)
PMGDINYC	Production Men's Guild of the Dress Industry of New York City (EA)
PMGFEL	Preliminary Master Government-Furnished Equipment List (MCD)
PMGI	Prime Management Group, Inc. [*NASDAQ symbol*] (SAG)
PMGI	Princeton Media Group, Inc. [*NASDAQ symbol*] (SAG)
PMGM	Program Manager's Guidance Memorandum
PMGO	Office of the Provost Marshal General [*Army*]

PM-GPV ...... Project Manager, General Purpose Vehicle (SAA)
PMgr............ Professional Manager (DD)
PMGS .... Predictable Model Guidance Scheme (OA)
PMGS .... Provost Marshal General's School, United States Army
PMGW .... Primary Mission Gross Weight
PMH............ Past Medical History
pmh .... Past Medical History (AD)
PMH............ Per Man Hour (WDAA)
PMH............ Phenylmercuric Hydroxide [Organic chemistry]
PMH............ Portsmouth, OH [Location identifier FAA] (FAAL)
PMH............ Postermedial Hypothalamus (DB)
PMH............ Posteromedial Hypothalamus [Medicine] (DMAA)
pmh .... Probable Maximum Hurricane (AD)
PMH............ Probable Maximum Hurricane [Nuclear energy] (NRCH)
PMH............ Production per Man-Hour
PMH............ Programmed Medical History (STED)
PMH............ Putnam Tax-Free Health Care Fund [NYSE symbol] (SPSG)
PMH............ Putnam Tax-Free Hlth Care Fd [NYSE symbol] (TTSB)
PMHC.......... Pyridinylmethylethylene(hydrazinecarbothioamide) [Organic chemistry]
PMHL.......... Preferred Measurement Hardware List [NASA] (NASA)
PMH/M .... Productive Man-Hours per Month [Navy] (NG)
PMHP .... Para-Menthane Hydroperoxide [Organic chemistry]
PMHP .... Primary Mental Health Project (AD)
PMHR .... Predicted Maximum Heart Rate [Medicine] (DMAA)
PMHRON ..... Patrol Combatant Missile Hydrofoil Squadron (DNAB)
PMHRON MLSG... Patrol Combatant Missile Hydrofoil Squadron Mobile Logistics Support Group (DNAB)
PMHS .... Polymethylhydrosiloxane [Organic chemistry]
PMHS .... Poly(methyl-Hydrostyrene) [Organic chemistry]
PMHSA........ Polish Military History Society of America (EA)
PMHx.......... Past Medical History (DAVI)
PMHYT .... Putnam Managed High Yield Trust [Associated Press] (SAG)
PMi............. Milton Public Library, Milton, PA [Library symbol Library of Congress] (LCLS)
PMI............. Palma [Mallorca Island] [Airport symbol] (OAG)
PMI............. Palma de Mallorca Balearic Islands, Spain (AD)
PMI............. Parmac Mines [Vancouver Stock Exchange symbol]
PMI............. Partai Muslimin Indonesia [Indonesian Muslim Party] [Political party] (AD)
PMI............. Past [or Previous] Medical Illness
PMI............. Patient Medication Instruction
PMI............. Pearlitic Malleable Iron (MCD)
PMI............. Pennsylvania Muscle Institute [University of Pennsylvania] [Research center] (RCD)
PMI............. Pensions Management Institute [British] (EAIO)
PMI............. Perioperative Myocardial Infarction [Medicine] (DMAA)
PMI............. Permanent Manufacturing Information (MSA)
PMI............. Personnel Management Information (IAA)
PMI............. Pesticide Monitoring Inventory [Environmental Protection Agency] (AEPA)
PMI............. Petroleum Monitoring, Inc. (EFIS)
PMI............. Phase Measuring Interferometer (AAEL)
PMI............. Phenylmethylisoxazole [Organic chemistry]
PMI............. Phosphomannose Isomerase [An enzyme] (MAE)
pmi .... Photographic Micro-Image (AD)
PMI............. Photographic Microimage Master [Reprography]
PMI............. Plant Manager Instruction [Nuclear energy] (NRCH)
PMI............. Plasma-Materials Interactions (MCD)
PMI............. Plumbing Manufacturers Institute (EA)
PMI............. Point of Maximal Impulse [Medicine]
pmi .... Point of Maximum Impulse (AD)
PMI............. Point of Maximum Intensity
PMI............. Polymethacrylimide (EDCT)
PMI............. Posterior Myocardial Infarction [Medicine] (DMAA)
PMI............. Post Mortem Interval [Forensics] [Medicine]
PMI............. Postmyocardial Infarction [Syndrome] [Medicine]
PMI............. Power Management Inventory [Test]
PMI............. Precision Monolithics Inc (NITA)
PMI............. Preliminary Maintenance Inspection (MCD)
PMI............. Pre-Marital Inventory (AD)
PMI............. Premark International, Inc. [NYSE symbol] (SPSG)
PMI............. Premark Intl [NYSE symbol] (TTSB)
PMI............. Prescriptive Math Inventory
PMI............. Present Medical Illness
PMI............. Presidential Management Incentives [Office of Management and Budget]
PMI............. Pressed Metal Institute [Later, AMSA]
PMI............. Preventive Maintenance Inspection (AFM)
PMI............. Preventive Maintenance Instruction (NASA)
PMI............. Previous Medical Illness (CPH)
PMI............. Primary Measurement Instrument
PMI............. Principal Maintenance Inspector (NASA)
PMI............. Private Mortgage Insurance [Insurance of mortgages by private insurers]
pmi .... Private Mortgage Insurance (AD)
PMI............. Probe Ministries International (EA)
PMI............. Processor Monitoring Instrument [Computer science] (ADA)
PMI............. Programmable Machine Interface (MCD)
PMI............. Programmable Memory Interface [Computer science]
PMI............. Programmable MODEM Interface [Computer science] (MCD)
PMI............. Program Management Instruction
PMI............. Project Management Institute (EA)
PMI............. Proposed Military Improvement (CAAL)
PMI............. Pseudomatrix Isolation

PMI............. Purchased Materials Inspection
PMIA............ Parallel Multiplexer Interface Adapter (MCD)
PMIA............ Powder Metal Industries Association [Australia]
PMIA............ Presidential Management Improvement Award
PMIC............ Parallel Multiple Incremental Computer
PMIC............ Payload Mission Integration Contract (MCD)
PMIC............ Periodic Maintenance Information Cards (MCD)
PMIC............ Personnel Management Information Center [Air Force] (AFM)
PMIC............ Poultry Meat Industry Committee [New South Wales, Australia]
PMIC............ Precious Metal Indicator Code
PMIC............ President's Management Improvement Council (AD)
PMIF............ Powder Metal Industries Federation
PMIG............ Political-Military Interdepartmental Group (AD)
PMIG............ Programmers Minimal Interface to Graphics (MCD)
PMI Gp .... PMI Group, Inc. [Associated Press] (SAG)
PMIIT........... Putnam Master Intermediate Income Trust [Associated Press] (SAG)
PMIJ............ Pulse-Modulated Infrared Jammer
PMilan.......... Papiri Milanesi [A publication] (OCD)
PMilS........... Millersville State College, Millersville, PA [Library symbol Library of Congress] (LCLS)
PMI/MO .... Precedence Manual In / Manual Out (DNAB)
PMIP............ Paleoclimate Modeling Intercomparison Project [Marine science] (OSRA)
PMIP............ Pan Malayan Islamic Party
PMIP............ Postmaintenance Inspection Pilot
PMIP............ Presidential Management Intern Program [Executive Office of the President] (GFGA)
PMIPK.......... Poly(methyl Isopropenyl Ketone) [Organic chemistry]
PMIR............ Program Manager's Integration Review [NASA] (NASA)
PMIR............ Psi-Mediated Instrumental Response [Parapsychology]
PMIRD.......... Passive Microwave Intercept Receiver Display
PMIS............ Passive Microwave Imaging System [NASA]
PMIS............ Patient Medical Information System (OA)
PMIS............ Personal Management Information System [Computer science] (IAA)
PMIS............ Personnel Management Information System
PMIS............ Planning Management Information System (AD)
PMIS............ Plant Management Information System
PMIS............ Plant Monitoring and Information System [Nuclear energy] (NRCH)
PMIS............ Postmyocardial Infarction Syndrome [Medicine] (DMAA)
PMIS............ Precision Mechanisms in Sodium [Nuclear energy] (NRCH)
PMIS............ Premis Corp. [NASDAQ symbol] (SAG)
PMIS............ Printing Management Information Systems
PMIS............ Process Management Information System (ACII)
PMIS............ Product Management Information System (AD)
PMIS............ Program Management Information System [Army]
PMIS............ Program Measurement Information System [Computer science] (IAA)
PMIS............ Projects Management Information System [UNESCO] (DUND)
PMIS............ PSRO [Professional Standards Review Organization] Management Information System (DHSM)
PMIT............ Putnam Master Income Trust [Associated Press] (SAG)
PMITS........... Post Mobilization Individual Training and Support (MCD)
PMJ............. Porto Murtinho [Brazil] [Airport symbol] (AD)
PMJ............. Pulse-Modulated Jammer
PMJC .... Pine Manor Junior College (AD)
PMJEG .... Performance Measurement Joint Executive Group (DOMA)
PMJI............ Pardon My Jumping In [E-Mail discussion]
PMK............ Palair Macedonian [Yugoslavia] [ICAO designator] (FAAC)
PMK............ Panel Marking Kit
PMK............ Pitch Mark [Shipfitting] (AAG)
pmk .... Pitch Mark (AD)
PMK............ Pointe Molloy [Kerguelen Islands] [Seismograph station code, US Geological Survey] (SEIS)
PMK............ Portable Molding Kit
PMK............ Postmark
pmk .... Postmark (AD)
PMK............ Primark Corp. [NYSE symbol] (SPSG)
PMK............ Primary Monkey Kidney [Physiology]
PMK............ Primary Rhesus Monkey Kidney (AAMN)
PMKM.......... Past Master, Knights of Malta [Freemasonry] (ROG)
PMKY.......... Pittsburgh, McKeesport & Youghiogheny [AAR code]
PML............ Pacific Micronesian Line (AD)
PML............ Pakistan Muslim League [Political party]
PML............ Parts Material List
PML............ Pattern Makers' League of North America (EA)
PML............ Phoenix Mutual Life Insurance Co. (EFIS)
PML............ Physical Memory Level
PML............ Physical Memory Loss [Computer science] (CIST)
PML............ PI Edit's Macro Language [Iliad Group] [Computer science]
PML............ [The] Pierpont Morgan Library (BJA)
PML............ Plymouth Marine Laboratory [Natural Environment Research Council] [British Information service or system] (IID)
PML............ Polymer Microdevice Laboratory [Case Western Reserve University] [Research center] (RCD)
PML............ Polymorphonuclear Leukocyte [Hematology]
PML............ Port Moller [Alaska] [Airport symbol] (OAG)
PML............ Port Moller, AK [Location identifier FAA] (FAAL)
PML............ Posterior Mitral Leaflet [Cardiology]
PML............ Preliminary Materials List [NASA]
PML............ Probable Maximum Loss [Insurance]
pml .... Probable Maximum Loss (AD)
PML............ Programmable Macro Logic (NITA)
PML............ Progressive Multifocal Leukoencephalopathy [Oncology]
PML............ Promotion Management List [Pronounced "pemell"] [Air Force]
PML............ Promyelocytic Leukaemia Protein [Biochemistry]
PML............ Promyelocytic Leukemia [Medicine]

PML............ Putnam Investment Grade Multiple Sectors III [*AMEX symbol*] (SPSG)
PML............ Putnam Inv Grade Muni Tr III [*AMEX symbol*] (TTSB)
PML............ University of Windsor, Paul Martin Law Library [*UTLAS symbol*]
pmla............ Parmelia (AD)
PMLA............ Production Music Libraries Association (EA)
PMLA............ Publication of the Modern Language Association of America (AD)
PMLC............ Pooled Mixed Lymphocyte Culture [*Clinical chemistry*]
PMLC............ Programmed Multiline Controller
PMLD............ Profound and Multiple Learning Difficulties (AIE)
PMLE............ Polymorphous Light Eruption [*Medicine*]
PMLF............ Project Marketing Loan Facility [*Australia*]
PMLG............ Poly(methyl L-Glutamate) [*Organic chemistry*]
PMLM............ Photosensitive Membrane Light Modulator
PMLO............ Philippine Military Liaison Officer (DNAB)
PMLO............ Principal Military Landing Officer (AD)
PMLO............ Principal Military Landing Offices [*British*]
PMLPC............ Permanent Mass Layoffs and Plant Closings Program [*Bureau of Labor Statistics*]
PM-LSM...... Polarization-Modulation Laser-Scanning Microscopy
PMLV............ Permanent Magnet Latch Valve
PMM............ Military Morale Division [*Coast Guard*]
PMM............ Partial Matrix Multiply (IAA)
PMM............ Peace Mission Movement (EA)
PMM............ Peat Marwick McLintock [*Accounting firm*] [*British*]
PMM............ Pedestal-Mounted Manipulator [*Nuclear energy*] (NRCH)
PMM............ Penobscot Marine Museum (EA)
PMM............ Permanent Magnet Motor (IAA)
PMM............ Personnel Management Manual [*A publication*] (ADA)
PMM............ Petroleum Marketing Management [*Petroleum Marketers Association of America*] [*A publication*]
PMM............ Petroleum Marketing Monthly [*Department of Energy Information service or system*] (CRD)
PMM............ Physical Memory Manager [*Computer science*] (PCM)
PMM............ Phytophthora Megasperma F.Sp Medicaginia [*A fungus*]
PMM............ Poly(methyl Methacrylate) [*Also, PMMA*] [*Organic chemistry*]
PMM............ Pool Maintenance Module [*Telecommunications*] (TEL)
PMM............ Portavideo [*Vancouver Stock Exchange symbol*]
PMM............ Post Mast Message (IAA)
PMM............ Presa Malpaso [*Mexico*] [*Seismograph station code, US Geological Survey*] (SEIS)
PMM............ Primitive Martian Mantle [*Planetary science*]
PMM............ Process Monitoring Modules (ACII)
PMM............ Procom Emerald [*Vancouver Stock Exchange symbol*]
PMM............ Professional Music Men, Inc. (EA)
PMM............ Profile Milling Machine
PMM............ Programmable Microcomputer Module
PMM............ Property Management Manual [*NASA*] (MCD)
PMM............ Protoplast Maintenance Medium (DB)
PMM............ Pullman, MI [*Location identifier FAA*] (FAAL)
PMM............ Pulse Mode Multiplex
pmm............ Pulse Mode Multiplex (AD)
PMM............ Purchase-Money Mortgage [*Real estate*]
PMM............ Putnam Managed Municipal Income [*NYSE symbol*] (SPSG)
PMM............ Putnam Managed Muni Income [*NYSE symbol*] (TTSB)
PMMA............ Pere Marquette Memorial Association (EA)
PMMA............ Poly(methyl Methacrylate) [*Also, PMM*] [*Organic chemistry*]
pmma............ Polymethylmethacrylate (AD)
PMMA............ Poly Methyl Methacrylate Association [*European Council of Chemical Manufacturers Federations*] [*Brussels, Belgium*] (EAIO)
PMMAP............ Poly(methyl Methacrylate Peroxide) [*Organic chemistry*]
PMMAPA...... Poly Methyl Methacrylate Producers Association [*Belgium*] (EAIO)
PMMB............ Parallel Memory-to-Memory Bus
PMMC............ Permanent Magnetic Movable Coil
PM-MCD...... Project Manager for Mines, Countermine, and Demolitions [*Army*] (RDA)
PM-MEP...... Project Manager - Mobile Electric Power [*DoD*]
PMMF............ Precious Metals Master File [*DoD*] (AFIT)
PMMI............ Packaging Machinery Manufacturers Institute (EA)
PMMI............ Polypyromellitimide (EDCT)
PMMI............ Putnam Managed Municipal Income Trust [*Associated Press*] (SAG)
PMMM............ Pall Mall Money Management [*Investment group*] [*British*]
PMMO............ Particulate Methane Monooxygenase [*Biochemistry*]
PMMP............ Preventive Maintenance Management Program
PMMR............ Panel-Mounted Microfilm Reader
PMMR............ Passive Multichannel Microwave Radiometer [*NASA*]
PMMS............ Phrenicon Metabolic Monitoring System
PMMS............ Plainsong and Mediaeval Music Society (EA)
PMMS............ Program Master Milestone Schedule (MCD)
PMMU............ Paged Memory Management Unit [*Computer chip*] (BYTE)
pmmu............ Paged Memory-Management Unit (AD)
PMMV............ Pea Mild Mosaic Virus [*Plant pathology*]
PMN............ Pacific Mountain Network [*Television*]
PMN............ Pahute Mesa [*Nevada*] [*Seismograph station code, US Geological Survey Closed*] (SEIS)
PMN............ Permian Resources Ltd. [*Vancouver Stock Exchange symbol*]
PMN............ Phenylmercuric Nitrate [*Antiseptic*]
PMN............ Polymorphonuclear [*Hematology*]
pmn............ Polymorphonuclear Neutrophil (AD)
PMN............ Polymorphonuclear Neutrophilic [*Hematology*]
PMN............ Polymorphonucleocyte [*Hematology*] (CPH)
PMN............ Postman (DCTA)
PMN............ Premanufacture Notification [*Environmental Protection Agency*]
PMN............ Pre-Manufacturing Notice [*Government regulations*]

PMN............ Premarket Notification [*Requirement for introducing new chemicals into the EEC*]
pmn............ Producto Material Neto [*Net Material Product*] [*Spain*] (AD)
PMN............ Program Management Network (MCD)
PMN............ Proposed Material Need (MCD)
PMN............ Pumani [*Papua New Guinea*] [*Airport symbol*] (OAG)
PMN............ Putnam New York Investment Grade Municipal [*AMEX symbol*] (SPSG)
PMN............ Putnam NY Inv Grade Muni [*AMEX symbol*] (TTSB)
PMNA............ Pacific Mountain Network Association (AD)
PMNA............ Parkers Marsh Natural Area [*Virginia*] (AD)
PM-NAVCON... Project Manager, Navigation and Control [*Military*]
PMNC............ Peripheral Blood Mononuclear Cell [*Medicine*] (DMAA)
PMNC............ Pharmaceutical Multinational Company (DB)
PMNF............ Premanufacture Notification Form [*Environmental Protection Agency*] (GFGA)
PMNG............ Polymorphonuclear Granulocyte [*Hematology*] (DAVI)
PMNH............ Peabody Museum of Natural History (NADA)
pmnl............ Polymorphonuclear Leukocyte (AD)
PMNL............ Polymorphonuclear Leukocyte [*Hematology*]
PMNN............ Polymorphonuclear Neutrophil (DB)
PMNP............ Platform-Mounted Nuclear Plant (NRCH)
PMNR............ Periadenitis Mucosa Necrotica Recurrens [*Medicine*]
pmnr............ Periadenitis Mucosa Necrotica Recurrens (AD)
PMNR............ Porter McLeod National Retail [*NASDAQ symbol*] (SAG)
PMNR............ Porter McLeod Natl Retail [*NASDAQ symbol*] (TTSB)
PMN/SFS...... People's Music Network for Songs of Freedom and Struggle (EA)
PMNT............ Permanent (IAA)
PM-NUC...... Project Manager for Nuclear Munitions [*Army*] (RDA)
PMNV............ Project Manager, Night Vision (RDA)
PM NV/RSTA... Project Manager for Night Vision/Reconnaissance Surveillance and Target Acquisition [*Military*] (RDA)
PMo............ Monessen Public Library, Monessen, PA [*Library symbol Library of Congress*] (LCLS)
PMO............ Palermo [*Italy*] [*Airport symbol*] (OAG)
PMO............ Palermo Resources, Inc. [*Vancouver Stock Exchange symbol*]
pmo............ Palomar Mountain Observatory (AD)
PMO............ Perroni, Martin, O'Reilly [*Commercial firm*]
PMO............ Personnel Management Officer [*Army*] (INF)
PMO............ Perturbation Molecular Orbital [*Theory*]
PMO............ Pianissimo [*Very Softly*] [*Music*] (ROG)
pmo............ Pianissimo [*Very Softly*] [*Italian*] [*Music*] (AD)
PMO............ Pine Mountain Observatory
PMO............ Polaris Material Office [*Missiles*]
PMO............ Polaris Missile Office
PMO............ Pomariorio [*Tuamotu Archipelago*] [*Seismograph station code, US Geological Survey*] (SEIS)
PMO............ Port Meteorological Office [*National Weather Service*]
PMO............ Postal Money Order [*Military*]
PMO............ Postmenopausal Osteoporosis [*Medicine*]
PMO............ Prime Minister's Office
PMO............ Principal Medical Officer
pmo............ Printed Matter Only (AD)
PMO............ Product Manager's Office (RDA)
PMO............ Product Manufacturing Organization
PMO............ Profit Making Organization
PMO............ Program Management Office [*NASA*] (KSC)
PMO............ Program Management Office [*Environmental Protection Agency*] (GFGA)
PMO............ Program Management Office [*Army*]
PMO............ Project Management Office [*Army*] (AABC)
PMO............ Property Movement Order
PMO............ Provisional [*Program Management*] Office [*Army*]
PMO............ Provost Marshal's Office
PMO............ Psychiatric Military Officer
PMO............ Putnam Municipal Opportunities Trust [*NYSE symbol*] (SPSG)
PMO............ Putnam Muni Opport Tr [*NYSE symbol*] (TTSB)
PMOA............ Programmatic Memorandum of Agreement (COE)
PMOA............ Prospectors and Mine Owners Association (EA)
PMOC............ Pioneer Mission Operations Center [*NASA*]
PMODA............ Phenyl(mercapto)oxadiazole [*Reagent*]
PMOF............ Presidential Medal of Freedom [*Military decoration*] (GFGA)
PM of F....... Presidential Medal of Freedom [*Military decoration*] (AABC)
PMOG............ Plutonium Maintenance and Operating Gallery [*Nuclear energy*] (NRCH)
PMOG............ Proposed Material Ordering Guide (MCD)
pmol............ Picomole [*One trillionth of a mole*] (WGA)
PMOLANT..... Polaris Material Office, Atlantic Fleet [*Missiles*]
pmole............ Picomole [*One trillionth of a mole*] (DAVI)
PMOM............ Performance Management Operations Manual [*NASA*] (NASA)
PMON............ Performance Management Operations Network [*NASA*] (NASA)
P-MONO...... Promonocytes [*hematology*] (DAVI)
PMOPAC...... Polaris Material Office, Pacific Fleet [*Missiles*]
PMOR............ Phar-Mor, Inc. [*NASDAQ symbol*] (SAG)
P Mor............ Port Moresby (AD)
PMORW........ Phar-Mor Wrrt [*NASDAQ symbol*] (TTSB)
PMOS............ Permanent Manned Orbital Station (AAG)
PMOS............ Physical Movement of Spacecraft (SAA)
PMOS............ Positive-Channel Metal-Oxide Semiconductor [*Telecommunications*] (TEL)
PMOS............ Primary Military Occupational Specialty [*Army*]
PMOS............ Program Management and Operations Staff [*Environmental Protection Agency*] (GFGA)
PMOSC........ Primary Military Occupational Code (AD)
PMOSC........ Primary Military Occupational Specialty Code [*Army*] (AABC)

PMOT............	Putnam Municipal Opportunities Trust [*Associated Press*] (SAG)
PMP............	Pacific Magazines and Printing Ltd. [*Commercial firm Australia*]
PMP............	Packed Main Parachute
PMP............	Pain Management Program [*Neurology*] (DAVI)
PMP............	Parallel Microprogrammed Processor [*Computer science*]
PMP............	Parent Mass Peak
PMP............	Parents' Magazine Press
PMP............	Partido ng Masang Pilipino [*Political party*] (EY)
PMP............	Parti du Mouvement Populaire de la Cote Francaise des Somalis [*Popular Movement Party of French Somaliland*] [*Political party*]
PMP............	Partito Monarchico Popolare [*Popular Monarchist Party*] [*Italy Political party*] (PPE)
PMP............	Parts, Materials, and Packaging (MCD)
PMP............	Parts, Materials, and Processes (MCD)
PMP............	Passive Measurement Program
PMP............	Past Menstrual Period [*Medicine*]
PMP............	Patient Management Problem [*Gerontology*]
PMP............	Patient Medication Profile (STED)
PMP............	Performance Management Package [*NASA*] (NASA)
PmP............	Pergamon Press, Inc., Fairview Park, Elmsford, NY [*Library symbol Library of Congress*] (LCLS)
PMP............	Permanent Manned Presence (SSD)
pmp............	Per-Member Payment (AD)
PMP............	Persistent Mentoposterior [*A fetal position*] [*Obstetrics*]
PMP............	Peter Miller Apparel Group, Inc. [*Toronto Stock Exchange symbol*]
PMP............	Phenyl(methyl)pyrazolone [*An organic pigment*]
PMP............	Piecewise Markov Process (PDAA)
PMP............	Pimaga [*Papua New Guinea*] [*Airport symbol*] (OAG)
PMP............	Planar Metallization with Polymer (IAA)
PMP............	Planned Maintenance Plan (MCD)
PMP............	Poly(metal Phosphinate) [*Organic chemistry*]
PMP............	Poly(methylpentene) [*Organic chemistry*]
PMP............	Pompano Beach, FL [*Location identifier FAA*] (FAAL)
PMP............	Pompeii [*Italy*] [*Seismograph station code, US Geological Survey Closed*] (SEIS)
PMP............	Pontifical Mission for Palestine (EA)
PMP............	Position Management Program
PMP............	Powdered Metal Part
PMP............	Powder Melting Process [*Physics*]
PMP............	Power Management Profile [*Test*]
pmp............	Precious Metal Plating (AD)
PMP............	Preliminary Management Plan (AD)
PMP............	Preliminary Mission Profile (MCD)
PMP............	Premodulation Processor
PMP............	Preoperational Maintenance Plan
PMP............	Preoperational Monitoring Program [*Nuclear energy*] (NRCH)
PMP............	Pressure Measurement Package
PMP............	Prevention, Mitigation and Preparedness [*Office of U.S. Foreign Disaster Assistance*]
PMP............	Preventive Maintenance Plan (KSC)
PMP............	Preventive Maintenance Procedure [*Nuclear energy*] (NRCH)
PMP............	Previous Menstrual Period [*Medicine*]
pmp............	Previous Menstrual Period [*Medicine*] (AD)
PMP............	Prime Mission Project [*Military*]
PMP............	Prime Motor Inns L.P. [*NYSE symbol*] (TTSB)
PMP............	Prime Motor Inns Ltd. [*NYSE symbol*] (SPSG)
PMP............	Prior Menstrual Period [*Gynecology*] (DAVI)
PMP............	Prism-Mirror-Prism [*For electron microscopy*]
PMP............	Probable Maximum Precipitation [*Nuclear energy*] (NRCH)
PMP............	Procurement Methods and Practices (AD)
PMP............	Product and Marketing Planning (IAA)
PMP............	Professor of Moral Philosophy
PMP............	Profit-Maximizing Price (MHDW)
PMP............	Program Management Plan [*NASA*]
PMP............	Program Monitor Panel
PMP............	Progressive Merger Procedure [*Econometrics*]
PMP............	Project Management Professional
PMP............	Project Master Plan [*Army*]
PMP............	Project on Military Procurement [*Later, PGP*] (EA)
PMP............	Property Management Plan [*Australia*]
PMP............	Protective Mobilization Plan
PMP............	Psychotropic Medication Plan (STED)
PMP............	Pulmonary Mean Pressure [*Medicine*]
PMP............	Pulsed Microwave Power
PMP............	Pump (KSC)
PMP............	Pyridoxamine Phosphate [*Biochemistry*]
PMPA............	Permanent Magnet Producers Association [*Later, MMPA*] (EA)
PMPA............	Petroleum Marketing Practices Act
PMPA............	(Phosphonylmethoxypropyl)adenine [*Antiviral*]
PMPA............	Precision Machined Products Association (NTPA)
PMPA............	Proximal Main Pulmonary Artery [*Anatomy*]
PMPE............	Punch Memory Parity Error [*Computer science*] (IAA)
PMPEA............	Professional Motion Picture Equipment Association [*Later, PFVEA*] (EA)
PMPFR	Program Manager's Preflight Review [*NASA*] (KSC)
PMPG	Pumping
PMPH	Pamphlet (DLA)
PMPL	Preferred Mechanical Parts List [*NASA*] (NASA)
PMPM	Per Member per Month
PMPM	Perpetual Motion Poetry Machine
PMPM	Phase Margin Performance Measure [*Manual control system*]
PMPM	Programmable Multiple Position Machine (MCD)
PMPM	Pulse Mode Performance Model (KSC)
PMPMA	Plastic and Metal Products Manufacturers Association (EA)
PMPO	Postmenopausal Palpable Ovary [*Gynecology*]
PMPP............	Program Management Phase-Out Plan [*Military*] (AFIT)
PMPPI	Polymethylenepolyphenyl Polyisocyanate [*Organic chemistry*]
PMPQ	Professional and Managerial Position Questionnaire [*Test*]
PMPR	Program Management and Performance Review
PMPS	Postmastectomy Pain Syndrome [*Medicine*] (DMAA)
PMPS	Program Management Planning and Scheduling [*Military*] (DNAB)
PMPY	Per Member per Year
PMQ	Perito Morono [*Argentina*] [*Airport symbol*] (OAG)
PMQ	Permanent Married Quarters [*Canadian Forces*]
PMQ	Phytylmenaquinone [*Vitamin K*] [*Also, K*] [*Biochemistry*]
PMQ	Prime Minister's Question [*British*] (BARN)
PMQ	Primitive Methodist Quarterly Review [*A publication*] (ROG)
PMR	Pacific Missile Range [*Later, WTR*]
PMR	Palmer [*Alaska*] [*Seismograph station code, US Geological Survey*] (SEIS)
PMR	Palmerston North [*New Zealand*] [*Airport symbol*] (OAG)
PMR	Parabolic Microwave Reflector
PMR	Paramagnetic Resonance (IAA)
PMR	Partido Mariateguista Revolucionario [*Peru*] [*Political party*] (EY)
PMR	Partidul Muncitoresc Roman [*Romanian Workers' Party*] [*Political party*]
PMR	Parts Material Requirements File
PMR	Patient Medical Record (DB)
PMR	Payload Mass Ratio
PMR	Paymaster
Pmr	Paymaster (AD)
PMR	Performance Measurement Report [*NASA*] (NASA)
PMR	Performance Monitoring Receiver
PMR	Perinatal Mortality Rate [*Medicine*]
PMR	Periodic Medical Review (STED)
PMR	Physical Medicine and Rehabilitation (STED)
PMR	Planned Maintenance Requirements
PMR	Point of Minimum Radius (IAA)
PMR	Polise-Air [*Russian Federation*] [*ICAO designator*] (FAAC)
PMR	Pollutant Mass Rate [*Environmental science*] (GFGA)
PMR	Polymerization of Monomer Reactants [*Organic chemistry*]
PMR	Polymorphic Reticulosis [*Ophthalmology*] (DAVI)
PMR	Polymyalgia Rheumatica [*Medicine*]
PMR	Portable Microfiche Reader [*DASA Corp.*]
PMR	Posteromedial Release [*Orthopedics*] (DAVI)
PMR	Postmaster (DCTA)
PMR	Potential Military Relevance
PMR	Power Monitor Relay
PMR	Preliminary Materials Review
P/M/R	Premakeready [*Graphic arts*] (DGA)
pmr	Pressure-Modulated Radiometer (AD)
PMR	Pressure Modulation Radiometer
PMR	Preventive Maintenance and Repair [*Aviation*] (MCD)
PMR	Primary Mission Readiness
PMR	Prime Resources Corp. [*Vancouver Stock Exchange symbol*]
PMR	Priority Monitor Report
PMR	Prior Medical Record (DB)
PMR	Procurement Management Review [*DoD*]
PMR	Profoundly Mentally Retarded
PMR	Program Management Responsibility (MCD)
PMR	Program Manager's Review [*NASA*] (NASA)
PMR	Programmed Mixture Ratio (KSC)
PMR	Projection Microradiography (IAA)
PMR	Project Management Report
PMR	Pro Male Release [*International Bowhunting Organization*] [*Class equipment*]
PMR	Propellant Mass Ratio (SAA)
PMR	Property Management Regulation (AAGC)
PMR	Property Movement Request (MCD)
PMR	Proportionate Morbidity Ratio [*Statistics*] (DAVI)
PMR	Proportionate Mortality Rate [*or Ratio*]
PMR	Protein Magnetic Resonance [*Medicine*] (MAE)
PMR	Proton Magnetic Resonance
PMR	Provisioning Master Record (MCD)
PMR	Psychomotor Retardation (STED)
PMR	Public Mobile Radio (WDMC)
PMR	Pulsational Magnetic Radiation [*Astronomy*]
PMRA	Percent of Males Reproductively Active [*Ecology*]
PMRA	Projected Manpower Requirements Account [*Navy*]
PMRAFNS....	Princess Mary's Royal Air Force Nursing Service [*British*]
PMRB	Preliminary Materials Review Board
PMRC	Pakistan Medical Research Council
PMRC	Parents' Music Resource Center (EA)
PMRC	Prepositioned Material Receipt Card [*DoD*]
PMRC	Proctor Maple Research Center [*University of Vermont*] [*Research center*] (RCD)
PMR Cp	PMR Corp. [*Associated Press*] (SAG)
PMRD	Prepositioned Material Receipt Documents (MCD)
PMRDET	Pacific Missile Range Detachment [*Obsolete*] (MUGU)
PMRF	Pacific Missile Range Facility [*Military*] (MUSM)
PMRFAC	Pacific Missile Range Facility [*Obsolete*] (MUGU)
PMRG	Preliminary Materials Review Group [*NASA*] (KSC)
PMRI	Porous Media Research Institute [*University of Waterloo*] [*Research center*] (RCD)
PMRI	Posteromedial Rotation Instability [*Sports medicine*]
PMRL	Pulp Manufacturers' Research League
PMRM	Periodic Maintenance Requirements Manual [*Navy*]
PMRMO	Protectable Mobilization Reserve Materiel Objective [*Army*] (AABC)
PMRMR	Protectable Mobilization Reserve Materiel Requirements [*Army*]
PMRN	Parents' Music Resource Network (EA)

PMR/NMC....	Pacific Missile Range / Naval Missile Center (SAA)
PMRO	Popular Magazine Review Online [EBSCO Subscription Services] [Information service or system]
PMRP	Petroleum Material Requirements Plan (MCD)
PMRP	PMR Corp. [NASDAQ symbol] (SAG)
PMRP	Precious Metals Recovery Program [DoD] (AFIT)
PM-RPV......	Project Manager, Remotely Piloted Vehicle [Military]
PMRR	Pacific Missile Range Representative [Obsolete] (MUGU)
PMRR	Pre-Mate Readiness Review [NASA] (KSC)
PMRS	Parachute Medical Rescue Service (EA)
PMRS	Performance Management and Recognition System
PMRS	Physical Medicine and Rehabilitation Service
PMRSG	Pacific Missile Range Study Group [Obsolete]
PMRT.........	Peabody Mathematics Readiness Test [Educational test]
PMRT.........	Program Management Responsibility Transfer (MCD)
PMRT.........	Progressive Muscle Relaxation Training [Psychology]
PMRTD	Program Management Responsibility Transfer Date (AFIT)
PMRTF.......	Pacific Missile Range Tracking Facility [Obsolete] (MUGU)
PMRTP	Program Management Responsibility Transfer Plan (AFIT)
PMRX	Pharmaceutical Marketing Services [NASDAQ symbol] (SPSG)
PMRX	Pharmaceutical Mktg Svcs [NASDAQ symbol] (TTSB)
PMRY	Pomeroy Computer Resources [NASDAQ symbol] (TTSB)
PMRY	Pomeroy Computer Resources, Inc. [NASDAQ symbol] (SAG)
PMRY	Presidio of Monterey [Military] (AABC)
PMS............	Chorionic Gonadotropin in Pregnant Mare's Serum [Veterinary medicine] (DAVI)
PMS............	Palmer - Arctic Valley [Alaska] [Seismograph station code, US Geological Survey] (SEIS)
PMS............	Pantone Matching System [Printing]
PMS............	Paper Manifesting System
PMS............	Parallel Mass Spectrometer
PMS............	Para-Methylstyrene [Organic chemistry]
PMS............	Partial Metric System (MCD)
PMS............	Particle Measuring Systems [Aerosol measurement device]
PMS............	Partido Mexicano Socialista [Political party] (EY)
PMS............	Pavement Management System [Australia]
PMS............	Peabody Museum of Salem (AD)
PMS............	Pedestal-Mounted Stinger [Army]
PMS............	People's Medical Society (EA)
PMS............	People's Message System [For Apple II computers] [Electronic bulletin board]
PMS............	Performance Management Software (IAA)
PMS............	Performance Measurement System [Nuclear Regulatory Commission] (MCD)
PMS............	Performance Measurement System (NAKS)
PMS............	Performance Monitoring System [Fort Belvoir, VA] [Army] (NASA)
PMS............	Periodical Management System [Library science] (TELE)
PMS............	Permanent Magnet Speaker
PMS............	Permanent Manual System (AD)
PMS............	Personal Mailing System (HGAA)
PMS............	Personnel Management Series [Civil Service Commission]
PMS............	Personnel Management Specialist (GFGA)
PMS............	Personnel Management System [Air Force] (AFM)
PMS............	Phenazine Methosultate [Biochemistry]
pms	Phenazine Methosulphate (AD)
PMS............	Phoenix Missile System
PMS............	Physiological Monitoring System (SAA)
PMS............	Phytophthora Megasperma Var. Sojae [A fungus]
PMS............	Piccola Missione per il Sordomuti [Little Mission for the Deaf-Mute - LMDM] [Rome, Italy] (EAIO)
PMS............	Picturephone Meeting Service [AT & T]
PMS............	Pitch Microwave System
PMS............	Planemasters Services, Inc. [ICAO designator] (FAAC)
PMS............	Planned Maintenance System [SNMMS]
PMS............	Planned Missile System
PMS............	Plant Monitoring System [Nuclear energy] (NRCH)
PMS............	Plasmid Maintenance Sequence [Genetics]
PMS............	Plastic to Metal Seal
PMS............	P-Methylstyrene [Plastics]
PMS............	PM Industries, Inc. [Vancouver Stock Exchange symbol]
PMS............	Polaris Missile System
PMS............	Polar Meteorological Satellite (SSD)
PMS............	Policy Management Systems [NYSE symbol] (SPSG)
PMS............	Policy Mgmt Systems [NYSE symbol] (TTSB)
PMS............	Pollution Monitoring Satellite
pms	Pollution-Monitoring Satellite (AD)
PMS............	Polymethylstyrene [Organic chemistry]
PMS............	Poor Miserable Soul [Medical slang]
pms	Poor Miserable Soul (AD)
PMS............	Popular Music and Society [A publication] (BRI)
PMS............	Portable Monitoring Set (MCD)
PMS............	Post-Marketing Surveillance
PMS............	Postmeiotic Segregation [Genetics]
PMS............	Postmenopausal Syndrome [Medicine]
pms	Post-Menopausal Syndrome [Medicine] (AD)
PMS............	Post-Merger Syndrome [Business term]
PMS............	Postmitochondrial Supernatant [Medicine] (MAE)
PMS............	Post-Mortem Survival [Parapsychology]
PMS............	Power Management System
PMS............	Prang-Mark Society (EA)
PMS............	Predicted Manning System [Military]
PMS............	Pregnant Mare's Serum [Endocrinology]
pms	Pregnant Mare's Serum (AD)
PMS............	Premature Start [Yacht racing] (IYR)
PMS............	Premenstrual [Stress] Syndrome [Medicine]

pms	Pre-Menstrual Syndrome [Medicine] (AD)
PMS............	Pre-Midshipmen School
PMS............	President of the Meteorological Society [British]
PMS............	President of the Miniature Society [British] (DI)
PmS	Preston Microfilming Services Ltd., Toronto, ON, Canada [Library symbol Library of Congress] (LCLS)
PMS............	Preventive Maintenance System
PMS............	Probability of Mission Success [Aerospace] (AAG)
PMS............	Probable Maximum Surge [Nuclear energy] (NRCH)
PMS............	Process Measurement Systems Ltd. (NITA)
PMS............	Processor Memory Switch [Computer science] (ECII)
PMS............	Processors, Memories, and Switches [Programming language] (CSR)
p-m-s........	Processors-Memories-Switches (AD)
PMS............	Production Management System [Safe Computing Ltd.] [Software package] (NCC)
PMS............	Product Management System
PMS............	Professor of Military Science
PMS............	Program Management Staff (COE)
PMS............	Program Management Support [Army]
PMS............	Program Management System [Computer science]
PMS............	Program Master Schedule (MCD)
PMS............	Programmed Mode Switch (IAA)
PMS............	Projected Map System (OA)
PMS............	Project Management System [IBM Corp.] [Computer science]
PMS............	Project Manager, Ships
PMS............	Proposal Management System
PMS............	Public Management Sources [A publication]
PMS............	Public Message Service [Western Union Corp.]
PMS............	Publisher Management System (NITA)
PMS............	Pureed, Mechanical, Soft [Diet] (DAVI)
PMSA.........	Office of the Project Manager Selected Ammunition [DoD]
PMSA.........	Pacific Merchant Shipping Association (AD)
PMSA.........	Paddy's Market Stallholders' Association [Australia]
PMSA.........	PM [Product Management] Materiel Systems Assessment (RDA)
PMSA.........	Posterior Middle Suprasylvian Area [Anatomy]
PMSA.........	Primary Metropolitan Statistical Area [Census Bureau]
PMSA.........	Professional Master of Science in Accounting (PGP)
P/MSA.......	Project/Major Subcontractor Affected (MCD)
PMSA.........	Project Manager for Selected Ammunition
PMSA.........	Project Manager's System Assessment
PMS & T.....	Professor of Military Science and Tactics
PMSAT.......	Pre-Medical Student Assessment Test (EDAC)
PMSC.........	Pediatric Medical Special Care (DMAA)
PMSC.........	Pluripotent Myeloid Stem Cell [Cytology] (MAE)
PMSC.........	Prime Minister's Science Council [Australia]
PMSD	Parti Mauricien Social-Democrate [Mauritian Social Democratic Party] [Political party] (PPW)
PMSD	Program Management and Support Division [Environmental Protection Agency] (GFGA)
PMS/DOD	Performance Measurement System/Department of Defense
PMSE.........	Percentage Mean Squared Error [Statistics]
PMSE.........	Permanent Memory with Semi-Elastic Range (MCD)
PMSE.........	Program Management Simulation Exercise [Aerospace]
PMSF.........	Phenylmethylsulfonyl Fluoride [Analytical chemistry]
PMSFN	Planetary Manned Space Flight Network [Aerospace] (MCD)
PMSG	Peace Movement Study Group [Colgate University] (EA)
PMSG	Pregnant Mare's Serum Gonadotrophin [Endocrinology]
pmsg	Pregnant Mare's Serum Gonadotrophin (AD)
PMSGT	Paymaster Sergeant [Marine Corps]
PMSI..........	Prime Medical Services [NASDAQ symbol] (TTSB)
PMSI..........	Prime Medical Services, Inc. [NASDAQ symbol] (NQ)
PMSI..........	Prime Medics [NASDAQ symbol] (SAG)
PMSN	Permission (FAAC)
PMSO	Project Management Staff Officer [Military] (AFIT)
PMSO	Project Management Support Office [Army] (RDA)
PMSP.........	Parallel Modular Signal Processor
PMSP.........	Photon-Counting Microspectrophotometer
PMSP.........	Plant Modelling System Program (PDAA)
PMSP.........	Preliminary Maintainability and Spare Parts
pm specialists...	Paramilitary Specialists (AD)
PMSPS.......	Project Management Staffing Practices Study [Navy] (NG)
PMSR	Patternmaker, Ship Repair [Navy rating]
PMSR	Physical, Mental, Social, Religious ["Fourfold Life" symbol of American Youth Foundation]
PMSRC	Pittsburgh Mining and Safety Research Center [Bureau of Mines]
PMSRP	Physical and Mathematical Sciences Research Paper (IEEE)
PMSS.........	Personnel Mobility Support System [Military]
PMSS.........	Policy and Management Support Staff (COE)
PMSS.........	Precision Measuring Subsystem (KSC)
PMSS.........	Preventive Maintenance Scheduling System (CIST)
PMSS.........	Program Management Support Staff [Environmental Protection Agency] (GFGA)
PMSS.........	Program Manager's Support System [Defense Systems Management College] [Fort Belvoir, VA] (RDA)
PMSSMS	Planned Maintenance System for Surface Missile Ships (AD)
PMST..........	Professor of Military Science and Tactics (MUGU)
PMSV.........	Pilot-to-Metro Service
PMSX.........	Processor Memory Switch Matrix
PMT............	Medical Photography Technician [Navy]
PMT............	Page Map Table [NASA] (HGAA)
PMT............	Para-Methoxytoluene [Organic chemistry]
PMT............	Partido Mexicano de los Trabajadores [Mexican Workers' Party] [Political party] (PPW)
PMT............	Passenger-Miles Traveled [DOE] (TAG)
PMT............	Payment (AFM)

pmt	Payment (AD)
PMT	Pennsylvania Motor Truck Association, Inc., Harrisburg PA [STAC]
PMT	Perceptual Maze Test [Psychology]
PMT	Perceptual Memory Task (TES)
PMT	Performance Measuring Tool (MCD)
PMT	Periodic Maintenance Team
PMT	Permanent Magnet Tester [Memory] [Bell Laboratories] (IAA)
PMT	Permanent Magnet Twistor [Memory] [Bell Laboratories]
PMT	Permit (FAAC)
PMT	Person-Miles of Travel [FHWA] (TAG)
PMT	Personnel Management Team
PMT	Phase-Modulated Transmission
PMT	Philip Michael Thomas [Co-star in TV series "Miami Vice"]
PMT	Photomechanical Transfer [Negative paper] [Eastman Kodak]
PMT	Photomultiplier Tube [Electronics]
pmt	Photomultiplier Tubes (AD)
PMT	Physical Master Tape (IAA)
PMT	Physical Message Type [Communications]
PMT	Pine Mountain [Oregon] [Seismograph station code, US Geological Survey] (SEIS)
PMT	Planning/Management Team [NASA] (MCD)
PMT	PMC Technologies Ltd. [Vancouver Stock Exchange symbol]
PMT	Polaromicrotribrometry [Analytical chemistry]
PMT	Portable Magnetic Tape
PMT	Porteus Maze Test [Medicine] (MAE)
PMT	Portsmouth Marine Terminal
pmt	Positive Matte Technique (AD)
PMT	Post-Maastricht Tension [European community] (ECON)
PMT	Post-Market Trading
PMT	Potteries Motor Traction Co. [British]
PMV	Power Microwave Tube
PMT	Precious Metal Tip (IAA)
PMT	Pre-Determined Motion-Time [Management] (PDAA)
PMT	Premenstrual Tension [Medicine]
pmt	Premenstrual Tension [Medicine] (AD)
PMT	Premillennial Tension
PMT	Preparatory Marksmanship Training [Military] (INF)
PMT	Prepare Master Tape
PMT	Preventive Maintenance Time (MCD)
PMT	Production Monitoring Test (NG)
PMT	Products, Marketing, and Technology [Bank Administration Institute] [A publication]
PMT	Program Master Tape
PMT	Programmed Math Tutorial [National Science Foundation]
pmt	Programs, Materials, Techniques (AD)
PMT	Project Management Team (ODBW)
PMT	Pulse-Modulator Tube
PMT	Pure Milk Tablet (IIA)
PMT	Putnam Master Income Tr [NYSE symbol] (TTSB)
PMT	Putnam Master Income Trust [NYSE symbol] (SPSG)
PMTA	Page Map Table Address Register [NASA] (HGAA)
PMTA	Phosphomolybdic-Phosphotungstic Acid Mixture (EDCT)
PMTAS	Pre-Menstrual Tension Advisory Service [British]
PMTB	Pacific Motor Tariff Bureau (AD)
PMTC	Pacific Missile Test Center [Point Mugu, CA] [Navy]
PMTC	Parametric Technical [NASDAQ symbol] (TTSB)
PMTC	Parametric Technology Corp. [NASDAQ symbol] (NQ)
PMTC	Pittsburgh Mining Technology Center [Department of Energy] (GRD)
PMTD	Post Mortem Tape Dump [Computer science]
PMTE	Page Map Table Entry [NASA] (IAA)
PMT-EM	Project Manager, Training Devices Engineering Management [Orlando, FL] [Army]
PMTF	Product Management Task Force (AAEL)
PMTHP	Project Mercury Technical History Program [NASA]
PMTI	Palomar Medical Technologies [NASDAQ symbol] (SAG)
PMTI	Palomar Med Tech [NASDAQ symbol] (TTSB)
PM TMDS	Program Manager - Test, Measurement, and Diagnostic Systems [Army]
PMTO	Project Manager Test Offices [Military]
PMTP	Production Missile Test Program
P/MTR	Potentiometer [Automotive engineering]
PM TRADE	Office of the Project Manager for Training Devices [Military] (RDA)
PMTS	PMT Services [NASDAQ symbol] (SAG)
PMTS	Precision Missile Tracking System [Military] (IAA)
PMTS	Predetermined Motion Time Standards [Management] (IAA)
PMTS	Predetermined Motion Time Systems [Management]
PMTS	Premenstrual Tension Syndrome [Medicine]
PMT Svc	PMT Services [Associated Press] (SAG)
PMTT	Phase-Modulated Telemetry Transmission
PMTT	Pulmonary Mean Transit Time [Medicine] (MAE)
PMTV	Potato Mop-Top Virus [Plant pathology]
PMU	Paimiut, AK [Location identifier FAA] (FAAL)
PMU	Pattern Makers Union (AD)
pmu	Performance Monitor Unit (AD)
PMU	Performance Monitor Unit [Communications]
PMU	Permanently Medically Unfit
PMU	Physical Mock-Up
pmu	Physical Mockup (AD)
PMU	Pierce Mountain [Vancouver Stock Exchange symbol]
PMU	Plant Makeup [Nuclear energy] (NRCH)
PMU	Pontifical Missionary Union [Later, PMUPR] [See also OPM] (EA)
PMU	Population Management Unit (WDAA)
PMU	Portable Memory Unit [Computer science]
PMU	Power Management Unit [Computer science] (CIST)
PMU	Pregnant Mare's Urine [Veterinary medicine] (BARN)
PMU	Pressure Measuring Unit (KSC)
PMU	Preventive Medicine Unit [Navy] (NVT)
pmu	Productive Man Work Unit (AD)
PMU	Program Management Unit [Computer science] (IAA)
PMU	Pulse Modulation Unit (NASA)
PMUB	Presbyterian, Methodist, and United Board [British military] (DMA)
PMUPR	Pontifical Missionary Union of Priests and Religious (EA)
PMUS	Permanently Mounted User Set [Computer science] (ADA)
PMUSAOAS	Permanent Mission of the United States of America to the Organization of American States (AD)
PM-UTTAS	Project Manager, Utility Tactical Transport Aircraft System [Military]
PMUX	Programmable Multiplex [Computer science] (TEL)
PMUX	Propulsion Multiplexer
PMv	Monroeville Public Library, Monroeville, PA [Library symbol Library of Congress] (LCLS)
PMV	Panicum Mosaic Virus
PMV	Papaya Mosaic Virus
PMV	Paramyxovirus
PMV	Parcel Mail Vans [British railroad term]
PMV	Passenger Motor Vehicle
PMV	Peanut Mottle Virus
PMV	Plasma Membrane Vesicle [Cytology]
PMV	Plate-Motion Vector [Geology]
PMV	Plattsmouth, NE [Location identifier FAA] (FAAL)
PMV	Politically Motivated Violence (ADA)
PMV	Porlamar [Venezuela] [Airport symbol] (OAG)
PMV	Prime Mission Vehicle (MCD)
PMV	Private Market Value [Investment term] (DFIT)
PMV	Private Motor Vehicle (DNAB)
PMV	Prolapsing Mitral Valve [Cardiology]
PMV	Pro Mundi Vita [Brussels, Belgium] [Defunct] (EAIO)
PMvAC	Community College of Allegheny County, Boyce Campus, Monroeville, PA [Library symbol Library of Congress] (LCLS)
PMVB	Pocono Mountain Vacation Bureau (AD)
pmvi	Periodic Motor Vehicle Inspection (AD)
PMVI	Periodic Motor Vehicle Inspection (PDAA)
PMvK	Koppers Co., Inc., Research Department, Monroeville, PA [Library symbol Library of Congress] (LCLS)
PMVL	Posterior Mitral Valve Leaflet [Anatomy] (AAMN)
PMV-LATA	Passenger Motor Vehicle Labour Adjustment Training Arrangements [Australia]
PMVMP	Passenger Motor Vehicle Manufacturing Plan [Australia]
pmvp	Precio Maximo de Venta al Publico [Maximum Price Charged the Public] [Spanish] (AD)
p mvr	Prime Mover (AD)
PMVR	Prime Mover [Technical drawings]
PMvS	United States Steel Corp., Research Center Library, Monroeville, PA [Library symbol Library of Congress] (LCLS)
PMW	Pacemaker Wire [Cardiology] (DAVI)
PMW	Parts Manufacturing Workmanship
PMW	Pole Mountain [Wyoming] [Seismograph station code, US Geological Survey Closed] (SEIS)
PMW	Preventive Maintenance Welding (PDAA)
PMW	Private Microwave [System]
PMW	Progressive Mine Workers of America
PMW	Project Magic Wand [Military] (MCD)
PMW	Project Management Work-Bench (NITA)
PMW	Prompt Mobilization Designation Withdrawn
PMW	Pulse-Modulated Wave [Telecommunications] (IAA)
PMWCMA	Paper Mill Wire Cloth Manufacturers' Association (DGA)
PMWIN	Processing MODFLOW for Windows
PMWP	Probable Maximum Winter Precipitation [Nuclear energy] (NRCH)
PMX	Packet Multiplexer
PMX	Palmer, MA [Location identifier FAA] (FAAL)
PMX	Pamorex Minerals, Inc. [Toronto Stock Exchange symbol]
PMX	Petroleos Mexicanos [Mexico ICAO designator] (FAAC)
PMX	Physical Modelling Extension (NITA)
PMX	Private Manual Exchange
pmx	Private Manual Exchange (AD)
PMX	Protected Message Exchange
PMyE	Evangelical Congregational School of Theology, Myerstown, PA [Library symbol Library of Congress] (LCLS)
PMYOB	Please Mind Your Own Business
pmyob	Please Mind Your Own Business (AD)
PMZ	Palmar [Costa Rica] [Airport symbol] (AD)
PMZ	Plymouth, NC [Location identifier FAA] (FAAL)
PN	Coastal Airways [ICAO designator] (AD)
PN	Nacionalista [Nationalist Party] [Spain] [Political party] (AD)
Pn	North Celestial Pole (AD)
pn----	North Pacific [MARC geographic area code Library of Congress] (LCCP)
PN	North Pole [Also, NP]
PN	Pacific Communications Net [Air Force]
PN	Pacific Northern [Airline] (AD)
PN	Pakistan Navy
PN	Palus Nebularum [Lunar area]
pn	Panama [MARC country of publication code Library of Congress] (LCCP)
PN	Pan-American World Airways [Stock exchange symbol] (AD)
PN	Papillary or Nodular Hyperplasia [Medicine]
PN	Parenteral Nutrition [Medicine]
PN	Partenavia Construzioni Aeronautiche SpA [Italy ICAO aircraft manufacturer identifier] (ICAO)
PN	Particulate Nitrogen [Chemistry]
PN	Partido Nacional [National Party] [Honduras] [Political party] (PPW)

PN............... Partido Nacional [*National Party*] [*Uruguay*] [*Political party*] (PPW)
PN............... Partido Nacional [*National Party*] [*Dominican Republic*] [*Political party*]
PN............... Partido Nacional [*National Party*] [*Spain*] [*Political party*] (AD)
PN............... Parti Nationaliste [*Canada*]
Pn............... Partition (WGA)
pn............... Partition (AD)
PN............... Partit Nazzjonalista [*Nationalist Party*] [*Malta*] [*Political party*] (EAIO)
PN............... Part Number
pn............... Part Number (AD)
PN............... Party Notified (IAA)
PN............... Patent Number (NITA)
PN............... Pennaco Energy [*AMEX symbol*]
PN............... Perceived Noise
PN............... Percussion Note [*Physiology*]
pn............... Percussion Note (AD)
PN............... Performance Number
PN............... Periarteritis [*or Polyarteritis*] Nodosa [*Also, PAN*] [*Medicine*]
PN............... Perigean Range
Pn............... Perigean Range (AD)
PN............... Peripheral Nerve [*Anatomy*]
PN............... Peripheral Neuropathy [*Medicine*]
PN............... Peroxide Number [*Hydrocarbon fuel specifications*]
PN............... Personal Name (NITA)
PN............... Personal Names from Cuneiform Inscriptions of the Cassite Period [*A publication*] (BJA)
PN............... Personnelman [*Navy rating*]
PN............... Personnel Navigant
PN............... Phase Name (NITA)
PN............... Phenolic Nylon
PN............... Philippine Navy
PN............... Phon [*Unit of loudness level*] (IAA)
P/N............... Phonogram [*British military*] (DMA)
pN............... Piconewton [*Unit of force*]
PN............... Piedmont & Northern Railway Co. [*AAR code*]
PN............... Pilot Navigator (IAA)
pn............... Pine (VRA)
P/N............... Pin Number (AAG)
PN............... Pitcairn Islands [*ANSI two-letter standard code*] (CNC)
PN............... Place-Name
PN............... Place of Publication Class Number (NITA)
PN............... Planetary Nebulae [*Astrophysics*]
PN............... Planners Network (EA)
PN............... Plant Normal [*Nuclear energy*] (NRCH)
PN............... Plaque Neutralization [*Dentistry*] (DMAA)
PN............... Plasticity Number (AAG)
PN............... Please Note
pn............... Please Note (AD)
P/N............... Please Note [*Copyediting*] (WDMC)
PN............... Pneumatic
PN............... Pneumonia [*Medicine*]
PN............... Point of No Return (AD)
PN............... Polish Notation [*Mathematics*]
PN............... Polyarteritis Nodosa [*Rheumatology*] (DAVI)
PN............... Polyneuritis (DB)
PN............... Pontine Nuclei [*Neuroanatomy*]
P/N............... Porter/Novelli [*A public relations firm*] [*New York, NY*] (WDMC)
PN............... Position (WGA)
pn............... Position (AD)
PN............... Positional Nystagmus [*Physiology*] (MAE)
PN............... Position Number (ADA)
PN............... Position Pennant [*Navy British*]
P/N............... Positive/Negative
PN............... Postal Note (ADA)
PN............... Postnasal [*Otorhinolaryngology*] (DAVI)
PN............... Postnatal [*Medicine*]
PN............... Practical Nurse
PN............... Preliminary Notification (NRCH)
PN............... Press Night
PN............... Princeton Aviation [*ICAO designator*] (AD)
PN............... Processing Negativity [*Computer science*]
PN............... Procurement Notice [*NASA*] (AAGC)
Pn............... Production [*Economics*]
PN............... Production Notice (KSC)
PN............... Product Name (NITA)
PN............... Programmable Network
PN............... Program Notice (KSC)
PN............... Program Number [*Horse racing*]
PN............... Progress note [*Medical records*] (DAVI)
PN............... Projection Neurons [*Neuroanatomy*]
PN............... Project Note
PN............... Project Number [*Online database field identifier*] [*Computer science*]
PN............... Promissory Note [*Business term*]
pn............... Promissory Note (AD)
PN............... Pronuclei [*Embryology*]
PN............... Proportional Navigation (IAA)
PN............... Pseudonoise
PN............... Pseudo-Random Noise (NAKS)
PN............... Pseudorandom Number
PN............... Psychiatric Nurse
pn............... Psychiatry-Neurology (AD)
PN............... Psychoneurologist
PN............... Psychoneurotic [*Cases, patients, etc.*]
PN............... Public Network [*Telecommunications*]
PN............... Publisher's Name [*Online database field identifier*]

PN............... Pulse Network (KSC)
PN............... Punch On
pn............... Punch-On [*Computer science*] (AD)
PN............... Pupil Nurse [*British*] (DI)
PN............... Putative Neurotransmitter [*Biochemistry*]
PN............... Pyelonephritis [*Medicine*] (MAE)
PN............... Pyridine Nucleotide [*Medicine*] (DMAA)
PN............... Pyridoxine [*or Pyridoxol*] [*Also, Pxn*] [*Biochemistry*]
PN............... Pyrrolnitrin [*Antifungal antibiotic*]
PN............... Regular Pending Transaction [*IRS*]
PN1............... Personnelman, First Class [*Navy rating*]
P_{N2}............... Partial Pressure of Nitrogen [*Medicine*] (DAVI)
PN2............... Personnelman, Second Class [*Navy rating*]
PN3............... Personnelman, Third Class [*Navy rating*]
Pn6............... Partenavia [*Airplane code*]
PNA............... Nomina Anatomica (Paris) [*Anatomical Nomenclature*] (DAVI)
PNA............... Pacific/North American [*Sector*] [*Marine science*] (OSRA)
PNA............... Pacific North Atlantic [*Marine science*] (OSRA)
PNA............... Pacific Northern Airlines (AD)
PNA............... Packet Network Adaptor (NITA)
PNA............... Pakistan National Alliance (PD)
PNA............... Palestinian National Authority [*Political party*] (ECON)
PNA............... Pamplona [*Spain*] [*Airport symbol*] (OAG)
PNA............... Panna [*India*] [*Airport symbol*] (AD)
PNA............... Pa-O National Army [*Myanmar*] [*Political party*] (EY)
PNA............... Paper Napkin Association
PNA............... Parallel and Novel Architectures [*British*]
PNA............... Para-Nitroaniline [*Organic chemistry*]
PNA............... Parenting in a Nuclear Age (EA)
PNA............... Parisiensis Nomina Anatomica [*Paris Anatomical Nomenclature*] [*Medicine*]
PNA .... Partacoona [*Australia Seismograph station code, US Geological Survey*] (SEIS)
PNA .... Parti Nationale Africain [*African National Party*] [*Chad*] [*Political party*]
PNA .... Passed, but Not Advanced
PNA............... Peanut Agglutinin [*Immunology*]
PNA............... Pentosenucleic Acid [*Biochemistry*]
PNA............... People's News Agency [*An association*] (EA)
PNA............... Peptide Nucleic Acid [*Biochemistry*]
PNA............... Philippines News Agency (AD)
PNA............... Pinedale, WY [*Location identifier FAA*] (FAAL)
PNa............... Plasma Sodium [*Organic chemistry*] (DAVI)
PNA............... Polish National Alliance of the United States of North America (EA)
PNA............... Polish Nobility Association (EA)
PNA............... Polyamide Nucleic Acid [*Biochemistry*]
PNA............... Polynuclear Aromatic [*Organic chemistry*]
PNA............... Price Not Available (DNAB)
PNA............... Processing Terminal Network Architecture [*Computer science*] (BUR)
PNA............... Professional Numismatists' Association [*British*] (BI)
PNA............... Project Network Analysis
PNA............... Universal Airlines, Inc. [*ICAO designator*] (FAAC)
PNAB............... Percutaneous Needle Aspiration Biopsy [*Medicine*]
PNAC............... Pacific Northwest Athletic Conference (PSS)
PNAC............... President's National Advisory Committee (NADA)
PNAC............... Psychiatric Nurses' Association of Canada
PNAF .... Plan Name and Address File [*IRS*]
PNAF............... Potential Network Access Facility
PNAF............... Primary Nuclear Airlift Force
PNAH............... Polynuclear Aromatic Hydrocarbon [*Environmental chemistry*]
PNAI .... Provincial Newspapers Association of Ireland (AD)
PNAMBIC.... Pay No Attention to the Man Behind the Curtain [*Computer hacker terminology*] (NHD)
PNAP .... Pro-Life Nonviolent Action Project (EA)
PNAS............... Palletized Night Attack System
PNAS............... Prudent No Added Salt [*Diet*] (DAVI)
PNASA............... Para-Nitroaniline-o-sulfonic Acid [*Organic chemistry*]
PnASat........... PanAmSat Corp. [*Associated Press*] (SAG)
P-NAV .... Personal Navigation
PNAV .... Precise Navigation
PNAV............... Precision Navigation Ambiguity Resolution
PNAV .... Proportional Navigation
PNAvQ .... Positive-Negative Ambivalent Quotient [*Psychology*]
pnavq............... Positive-Negative Ambivalent Quotient (AD)
PNazMHi...... Moravian Historical Society, Nazareth, PA [*Library symbol Library of Congress*] (LCLS)
PNB .... North Platte, NE [*Location identifier FAA*] (FAAL)
PNB .... Pacific Northwest Ballet
PNB .... Particle/Neutral Beam (MCD)
PNB .... Partido ng Bayan [*Party of the Nation*] [*Philippines*] [*Political party*]
PNB .... Permodalan Nasional Bank [*Malaysia*]
PNB .... Personal Needs Break (WDAA)
PNB .... Philippine National Bank (AD)
PNB .... Pomio [*New Britain*] [*Seismograph station code, US Geological Survey Closed*] (SEIS)
PNB .... Porto Nacional [*Brazil*] [*Airport symbol*] (AD)
PNB .... Premature Nodal Beat [*Cardiology*] (DAVI)
PNB .... Premier National Bancorp [*AMEX symbol*] [*Formerly, Hudson Chartered Bancorp*]
pnb .... Producto Nacional Bruto [*Gross National Product*] [*Spanish*] (AD)
PNB .... Produto Nacional Bruto [*Gross National Product*] [*Portugal*] (AD)
PNB .... Prostatic Needle Biopsy [*Oncology*] (DAVI)
PNBA .... Pacific Northwest Booksellers Association (AD)
PNBAS .... ((Para-Nitrophenyl)azo)salicylic Acid [*A dye*] [*Organic chemistry*]

PNBB	Parc National de la Boucle du Baoule [*Baoule River Bend National Park*] [*French*] [*Mali*] (AD)
PNBC	Pacific Northwest Bibliographic Center [*Library network*]
PNBC	Princeton National Bancorp [*NASDAQ symbol*] (SAG)
PNBC	Princeton Natl Bancorp [*NASDAQ symbol*] (TTSB)
PNBF	Peak Nucleate Boiling Flux
PNBK	Patriot National Bank CT [*NASDAQ symbol*] (SAG)
PNBK	Patriot Natl Bk [*NASDAQ symbol*] (TTSB)
PNBMS	Pacific Northwest Bird and Mammal Society [*Later, SNUB*] (EA)
PNBP	Parc National de la Boucle de la Pendjari [*Penjari River Bend National Park*] [*French*] [*Dahamey*] (AD)
PNBS	Pyridinium(nitro)benzenesulfonate [*Organic chemistry*]
PNBT	Para-Nitroblue Tetrazolium
PNC	Chief Personnelman [*Navy rating*]
PNc	New Castle Free Public Library, New Castle, PA [*Library symbol Library of Congress*] (LCLS)
PNC	Northampton County Area Community College, Bethlehem, PA [*OCLC symbol*] (OCLC)
PNC	Pakistan National Congress [*Political party*]
PNC	Palestine National Council (PD)
PNC	Parity Nonconservation [*Physics*]
PNC	Parque Nacional Canaima [*Canaima National Park*] [*Venezuela*] (AD)
PNC	Partido Nacional Ceuti [*Ceuta National Party*] [*Political party*] (PPW)
PNC	Partido Nacional Conservador [*Nicaragua*] [*Political party*] (EY)
PNC	Partido Nacional Cristiano [*National Christian Party*] [*Colorado Political party*] (EY)
PNC	Partido Nacionalista Ceuti [*Political party*] (EY)
PNC	Partidual Nationale Crestine [*National Christian Party*] [*Romania*] [*Political party*] (PPE)
PNC	Parti National Caledonien [*Caledonian National Party*] [*Political party*] (PPW)
PNC	Passenger Name Check-In (MCD)
pnc	Pencillin (AD)
PNC	Pencrude Resources, Inc. [*Vancouver Stock Exchange symbol*]
PNC	Penicillin
PNC	People's National Congress [*Guyana*] (PD)
PNC	Peripheral Nerve Conduction [*Neurology*] (DAVI)
PNC	Peripheral Nucleated Cell (AAMN)
PNC	Personal Number Calling [*Telecommunications*]
PNC	Philatelic-Numismatic Combination [*or Commemorative*]
PNC	Phosphonitrilic Chloride [*Inorganic chemistry*]
PNC	Physitest Normalise Canadien [*Canadian Standardized Test of Fitness - CSTF*]
PNC	Pine Canyon [*California*] [*Seismograph station code, US Geological Survey*] (SEIS)
PNC	Place Names Committee [*Victoria, Australia*]
PNC	Plate Number Coil [*Philately*]
pnc	Plate Number Coil (AD)
PNC	PNC Bank Corp. [*NYSE symbol*] (TTSB)
PNC	Pneumotaxic Center [*Medicine*] (DAVI)
PNC	Police National Computer [*British*]
PNC	Ponca City [*Oklahoma*] [*Airport symbol*] (OAG)
PNC	Ponca City, OK [*Location identifier FAA*] (FAAL)
PNC	Postnatal Clinic
PNC	Power Reactor and Nuclear Fuel Development Corp. [*Japan*] (PDAA)
PNC	Premature Nodal Contraction [*Cardiology*]
pnc	Premature Nodal Contraction (AD)
PNC	Prenatal Care [*Obstetrics*] (DAVI)
PNC	Prenatal Clinic [*Obstetrics*] (DAVI)
PNC	Prenodal Contraction [*Cardiology*] (DAVI)
PNC	PRIMENET Node Controller (NITA)
PNC	Programmed Numerical Control
PNC	Prohibition National Committee (EA)
PNC	Provident National Financial Corp. (EFIS)
PNC	Pseudonurse Cells [*Cytology*]
PNCB	Pakistan Narcotics Control Board
PNCB	Para-Nitrochlorobenzene [*Organic chemistry*]
PNCC	Pacific Northwest College Conference (PSS)
PNCC	Partial Network Control Center
PNCC	President's National Crime Commission (AD)
PNCE	Private New Capital Expenditure
PNCEA	Paulist National Catholic Evangelization Association (EA)
PNCFN	Permanent Nordic Committee on Food and Nutrition [*Copenhagen, Denmark*] (EAIO)
PNCH	Partido Nacional Conservador de Honduras [*National Conservative Party of Honduras*] [*Political party*]
PNCH	Punch
pnch	Punch (AD)
PNCK	Pancake
PNCL	Pinnacle Micro [*NASDAQ symbol*] (TTSB)
PNCL	Pinnacle Micro, Inc. [*NASDAQ symbol*] (NQ)
Pncla	Pensacola, Florida (AD)
PNCM	Master Chief Personnelman [*Navy rating*]
PNCOC	Primary Noncommissioned Officer Course [*Army*] (INF)
PNCPrC	PNC Bank Cp $1.60 Cv C Pfd [*NYSE symbol*] (TTSB)
PNCPrD	PNC Bank Cp $1.80 Cv D Pfd [*NYSE symbol*] (TTSB)
PNCS	Private Network Communication Systems (MCD)
PNCS	Senior Chief Personnelman [*Navy rating*]
PNCU	Police National Computer Unit [*British*]
Pnd	Pandjang (AD)
pnd	Paroxysmal Noctural Dyspnoea (AD)
pnd	Paroxysmal Nocturnal Dyspnea [*Medicine*]
PND	Parti des Nationalistes du Dahomey [*Dahomean Nationalists Party*] [*Political party*]
PND	Partido Nacional Democratico [*National Democratic Party*] [*Costa Rica*] [*Political party*] (PPW)
PND	Partido Nacional Democratico [*National Democratic Party*] [*Dominican Republic*] [*Political party*]
PND	Partidul National-Democratic [*National Democratic Party*] [*Romania*] [*Political party*] (PPE)
PND	Parti National Democrate [*Morocco*] [*Political party*] (EY)
PND	Passive Navigation Device
PND	Pending
PND	Pictorial Navigation Display (OA)
PND	Postnasal Drainage [*or Drip*] [*Medicine*]
pnd	Postnasal Drip [*Medicine*] (AD)
PND	Postnatal Days
PND	Postnatal Depression [*Medicine*] (ECON)
pnd	Pound (MAE)
PND	Preliminary Number Deflator [*Empirical mathematics*] (ECON)
PND	Premodulation Processor - Near Earth Data (KSC)
PND	Prenatal Diagnosis [*Medicine*]
PND	Present Next Digit
PND	Pressed Notch Depth (PDAA)
PND	Primary Navigation Display (GAVI)
PND	Principal Neutralizing Determinant [*Immunology*]
PND	Principal Neutralizing Domain [*Medicine*]
PND	Program Network Diagram [*Telecommunications*] (TEL)
PND	Pronatriodilatin (DB)
PND	Pseudonyms and Nicknames Dictionary [*A publication*]
PND	Punta Gorda [*Belize*] [*Airport symbol*] (OAG)
PNDA	Panda Project [*NASDAQ symbol*] (TTSB)
PNDA	[*The*] Panda Project, Inc. [*NASDAQ symbol*] (SAG)
PNDA	People for Nuclear Disarmament Australia [*An association*]
PNDB	Pelerinage a Notre Dame de Beauraing [*An association*] (EAIO)
PNdB	Perceived Noise Decibels
pndb	Perceived Noise Decibels (AD)
PNDC	Parallel Network Digital Computer (IEEE)
PNDC	Partido Nacional de Democracia Centrista [*Chile*] [*Political party*] (EY)
PNDC	Progressive Neuronal Degeneration of Childhood [*Medicine*]
PNDC	Provisional National Defence Council [*Ghana*] (PD)
PNDD	Parti National pour la Democratie et le Developpement [*Benin*] [*Political party*] (EY)
PNDG	Pending (AFM)
pndg	Pending (AD)
PNDI	Pennsylvania Natural Diversity Inventory [*Bureau of Forestry*] [*Harrisburg*] [*Information service or system*] (IID)
PNDL	Pentland Group plc [*LO Symbol*] (TTSB)
P-N-D-L-R	Park-Neutral-Drive-Low-Reverse (AD)
PNDLR	Pendular
PNDM	Project Nondesign Memo
pndnt	Pendentive (VRA)
PNDO	Partial Neglect of Differential Overlap [*Physics*]
Pndo	Pinedo (AD)
PNDP	Para-Nitrophenyl Diphenyl Phosphate [*Organic chemistry*]
PNDR	Ponder Industries [*NASDAQ symbol*] (TTSB)
PNDR	Ponder Industries, Inc. [*NASDAQ symbol*] (SAG)
PNDT	Parti Nationale pour la Developpement du Tchad [*National Party for the Development of Chad*]
PNE	Pacific National Exchange Vancouver [*Vancouver*] (AD)
PNE	Pacific National Exhibition [*Vancouver*] (AD)
PNE	Pacific National Exhibition Home Show [*Southex Exhibitions*] (TSPED)
PNE	Paine College, Warren A. Candler Library, Augusta, GA [*OCLC symbol*] (OCLC)
PNE	Panhandle Eastern Corp. [*Toronto Stock Exchange symbol*]
PNE	Peaceful Nuclear Explosion
pne	Peaceful Nuclear Explosion (AD)
PNE	Philadelphia [*Pennsylvania*] North Philadelphia [*Airport symbol*] (OAG)
PNE	Philadelphia, PA [*Location identifier FAA*] (FAAL)
PNE	PINE [*Postal Service standard*] (OPSA)
PNE	Plasma Norepinephrine [*Medicine*] (DMAA)
PNE	Pneumoencephalography [*Medicine*] (CPH)
PNe	Pointe Noire (AD)
pne	Practical Nurse's Education (AD)
PNE	Practical Nurse's Education
PNEA	Parque Nacional El Avila [*El Avila National Park*] [*Spanish*] (AD)
PNEC	Predicted No Effect Concentration [*Environmental technology*]
PNEC	Primary Navy Enlisted Classification [*Code*]
PNed	Pharmacopeia Nederlandsche [*Netherlands Pharmacopoeia*]
PNEDC	Programme National D'etude de la Dynamique du Climat [*France*] [*Marine science*] (OSRA)
PNEDC	Programme National d'Etudes de la Dynamique du Climat (USDC)
PNEM	Paraneoplastic Encephalomyelitis [*Medicine*] (DMAA)
PNEM-APROME	Partido Nacionalista Espanol de Melilla - Asociacion pro Melilla [*Spanish North Africa*] [*Political party*] (MENA)
PNERL	Pacific Northwest Environmental Research Laboratory [*Environmental Protection Agency*] (MSC)
PNES	Pines
Pnes	Pines (AD)
PNET	Peaceful Nuclear Explosions Treaty [*Officially, Treaty on Underground Nuclear Explosions for Peaceful Purposes*]
PNET	Peripheral Neuroepithelioma [*Medicine*] (DMAA)
PNET	Primitive Neuroectodermal Tumor [*Oncology*]
PNET	ProNet, Inc. [*NASDAQ symbol*] (NQ)
PNEU	Parents' National Educational Union [*British*]
PNEU	Pneumatic (AAG)

pneu	Pneumatic (AD)
pneu	Pneumonia [Medicine] (MAE)
PNEUG	Pneumatic Pressure Generator (MCD)
PNEUM	Pneumatic
PNEUM	Pneumonia (WDAA)
PNEUMO	Pneumothorax [Medicine]
pneumoccon...	Pneumocconiosis [Medicine] (AD)
pneumog	Pneumograph (AD)
pneumonoultra...	Pneumonoultra-Microscopicsilicovolcanoconiosis [Medicine] (AD)
PNEUROP	European Committee of Manufacturers of Compressors, Vacuum Pumps, and Pneumatic Tools (EA)
PNF	Pacific National Financial Corp. [Toronto Stock Exchange symbol Vancouver Stock Exchange symbol]
PNF	Palestine National Front [Political party] (PD)
PNF	Partito Nazionale Fascista [National Fascist Party] [Italy Political party] (PPE)
PNF	Peierls-Nabarro Force [Physics]
PNF	Penn Traffic [NYSE symbol] (TTSB)
PNF	Penn Traffic Co. [NYSE symbol] (SAG)
PNF	Phosphonitrilic Fluoroelastomer [Synthetic rubber]
PNF	Pilot Not Flying (GAVI)
PNF	Positive Neutral Finder [Automotive engineering]
PNF	Postnuclear Fraction [Biochemical tissue analysis]
PNF	Prenex Normal Form [Logic]
PNF	Proprioceptive Neuromuscular Facilitation [Neurology]
pnf	Proprioceptive Neuromuscular Facilitation (AD)
pnfd	Present Not for Duty (AD)
PNFD	Present Not for Duty [Military]
PNFI	Petawawa National Forestry Institute [Canadian Forestry Service] [Research center] (RCD)
PNFI	Pinnacle Financial Services, Inc. [NASDAQ symbol] (NQ)
PNFI	Pinnacle Financial Svcs [NASDAQ symbol] (TTSB)
PNFS	Peak and Northern Footpaths Society [British] (DBA)
PNFSO	Primary Nonferrous Smelter Order [Environmental Protection Agency]
PNG	Pacific Northern Gas Ltd. [Toronto Stock Exchange symbol Vancouver Stock Exchange symbol]
PNG	Papua New Guinea [ANSI three-letter standard code] (CNC)
PNG	Papua New Guinea Banking Corp.
PNG	Papua Nueva Guinea [Papua New Guinea] [Spanish] (AD)
PNG	Paranagua [Brazil] [Airport symbol] (OAG)
PNG	Parque Nacional Guatopo [Guatopo National Park] [Venezuela] [Spanish] (AD)
PNG	Partido Nacional Guevarista [Ecuador] [Political party] (PPW)
PNG	Passive Night Goggles [Military] (WDAA)
Png	Penang (AD)
PNG	Penghu [Hokoto] [Republic of China] [Seismograph station code, US Geological Survey] (SEIS)
PNG	Penicillin G [Medicine] (DMAA)
PNG	Persona Non Grata [Unacceptable Person] [Latin]
png	Persona Non Grata [An Unacceptable Person] [Latin] (AD)
PNG	Philippine Natural Gum
PNG	Plant Nitrogen in Grain [Harvest nitrogen index]
PNG	Popondetta [New Guinea] [Airport symbol] (AD)
PNG	Portable Network Graphic [Computer science] (PCM)
PNG	Portable Network Graphics [Computer science] (PCM)
PNG	Professional Numismatists Guild (EA)
PNG	Pseudonoise Generator
PNG	Puerto Rico Air NAtional Guard [FAA designator] (FAAC)
PNGCS	Primary Navigation, Guidance and Control System (KSC)
PNGFA	Pacific Northwest Grain and Feed Association (EA)
PNGI	Papua New Guinea Institute of Chemistry
PNGL	Papua New Guinea Line (AD)
PNGS	Primary Navigation System
PNGV	Partnership for a New Generation of Vehicles [Collaboration of government and industry]
PNH	North Hills School District Instructional Materials Center, Pittsburgh, PA [OCLC symbol] (OCLC)
PNH	Pan Head [Design engineering]
PNH	Paroxysmal Nocturnal Hemoglobinuria [Medicine]
pnh	Paroxysmal Nocturnal Hemoglobinuria (AD)
PNH	Partido Nacional Hondureno [Honduran National Party] [Political party]
PNH	Parti National d'Haiti [National Party of Haiti] [Political party]
PNH	Phnom Penh [Cambodia] [Airport symbol] (OAG)
PNH	Pitcher Mountain [New Hampshire] [Seismograph station code, US Geological Survey] (SEIS)
PNH	Polynuclear Hydrocarbon (DMAA)
PNHA	Physicians National Housestaff Association [Defunct]
PNHDL	Panhandle
PNHP	Parque Nacional Henri Pittier [Henri Pittier National Park] [Venezuela] [Spanish] (AD)
PNHP	Phsyicians for a National Health Program (EA)
PNHS	Pacific Northwest Heather Society [Later, NAHS] (EA)
PNI	Aerovias de Poniente SA de CV [Mexico ICAO designator] (FAAC)
PNI	Parque Nacional Iguazu [Iguazu National Park] [Spanish] (AD)
PNI	Partai Nasionalis Indonesia [Nationalist Party of Indonesia] [Political party]
PNI	Participate but Do Not Initiate [Investment term]
PNI	Partido Nacional Independiente [National Independent Party] [Costa Rica] [Political party] (PPW)
PNI	Part Number Index (MCD)
PNI	Pascoe Nally International [British]
PNI	Peer Nomination Inventory [Psychology]
PNI	Peripheral Nerve Injury [Medicine]
PNI	Pharmaceutical News Index [UMI/Data Courier] [Information service or system A publication]
PNI	Pictorial Navigation Indicator [Aviation] (DA)
PNI	Picture Network International, Ltd.
PNI	Picture Network International [Commercial firm Information service or system]
PNI	Pinerola [Italy] [Seismograph station code, US Geological Survey] (SEIS)
PNI	Ponape [Caroline Islands] [Airport symbol] (OAG)
PNI	Positive Noninterfering [Alarm system]
pni	Positive Noninterfering (AD)
PNI	Postnatal Infection [Medicine]
PNI	Principal Neo-Tech, Inc. [Toronto Stock Exchange symbol]
PNI	Prognostic Nutrition Index [Dietetics] (DAVI)
PNI	Protease Nexin I [Biochemistry]
PNI	Psychoneuroimmunology
pni	Psychoneuroimmunology (AD)
pni	Pulsed Neutron Interrogation (AD)
PNI	Pulsed Neutron Interrogation (PDAA)
PNIC	Pleasure Navigation International Joint Committee [See also CINP] [The Hague, Netherlands] (EAIO)
P Nic	Port Nicholson (AD)
PNID	Peer Nomination Inventory of Depression [Child development test] [Psychology]
P-NID	Precedence Network In-Dialing [Telecommunications] (TEL)
PNID/NOD ...	Priority Network In-Dial / Network Out-Dial (DNAB)
PNIE	Priority National Intelligence Estimate [CIA] (LAIN)
PNII	Prentiss Normal and Industrial Institute [Mississippi]
PNII	Protease Nexin II [Biochemistry]
PNIO	Priority National Intelligence Objectives (MCD)
PNIP	Positive-Negative-Intrinsic-Positive [Electron device] (MSA)
PNIPAAM	Poly-N-isopropylacrylamide [Organic chemistry]
PNIPAM	Poly-N-Isopropylacrylamide [Organic chemistry]
PNITC	Pacific Northwest International Trade Council (AD)
PNJ	Paterson [New Jersey] [Airport symbol] (AD)
PNJ	Paterson, NJ [Location identifier FAA] (FAAL)
PNJ	Polar Night Jet Stream (ADA)
PNJALBB	Peter Noone Just a Little Bit Better Promotion Club (EA)
PNK	Pink [Electrical wiring]
PNK	Pinkham Creek [Montana] [Seismograph station code, US Geological Survey Closed] (SEIS)
PNK	Pink Pages Publication [Vancouver Stock Exchange symbol]
PNK	Polynucleotide Kinase [An enzyme]
PNK	Pontianak [Indonesia] [Airport symbol] (OAG)
PNK	Pyridoxine Kinase (DMAA)
PNkA	Aluminum Co. of America, ALCOA Research Laboratories Library, New Kensington, PA [Library symbol Library of Congress] (LCLS)
PNKA	Protein Induced by Vitamin K Absence and Antagonists (PDAA)
pnksh	Pinkish [Philately]
PNL	Aero Personal SA de CV [Mexico ICAO designator] (FAAC)
PNL	Instrument Panel [Automotive engineering]
PNL	Pacific Naval Laboratories (AD)
PNL	Pacific Northwest Laboratory [Department of Energy] [Richland, WA]
PNL	Pakistan National League [Political party]
PNL	Panel (KSC)
pnl	Panel (AD)
PNL	Pantelleria [Italy] [Airport symbol] (OAG)
PNL	Partidul National Liberal [National Liberal Party] [Romania] [Political party] (PPE)
PNL	Parti National Liberal [National Liberal Party] [Lebanon] [Political party] (PPW)
PNL	Passenger Name List [Travel industry]
PNL	Peanut Lectin [Immunochemistry]
PNL	Peninsula [Alaska] [Seismograph station code, US Geological Survey] (SEIS)
PNL	Perceived Noise Level
PNL	Philippine National Line (AD)
PNL	Pine Bell Mines [Vancouver Stock Exchange symbol]
PNL	Polytechnic of North London, School of Librarianship, London, England [OCLC symbol] (OCLC)
PNL	Prescribed Nuclear Load [Military] (AABC)
PNL	Pressure Noise Level (MCD)
PNL	Pulsed Neodymium LASER
PNLA	Pacific Northwest Library Association
PNLA	Pacific Northwest Loggers Association (EA)
PNLA	Percutaneous Needle Lung Aspiration [Medicine] (DMAA)
PNLAADA	Programme National de Lutte Contre l'Abus de l'Alcohol et des Drogues chez les Autochtones [Canada]
pnlbd	Panelboard [National Electrical Code] (IEEE)
PNLBRG	Panel Bridge (MUGU)
PNLG	Phase Nulling LASER Gyroscope
PNL/I	Provisioning Numerical Listing/Index
PNLM	Palestine National Liberation Movement [Political party] (BJA)
PNLO	Principal Naval Liaison Officer [British]
PNLRM	Preferred National Land Rights Model [Australia]
PNLT	Perceived Noise Level, Tone Corrected
PNM	Pan-Somali Nationalist Movement [Political party]
PNM	Partido Nacionalista de Mexicano [Nationalist Party of Mexico] [Political party]
PNM	Partito Nazionale Monarchico [National Monarchist Party] [Italy Political party] (PPE)
PNM	People's National Movement [Trinidad and Tobago] [Political party] (PD)
PNM	Perinatal Mortality [Medicine]
PNM	Peripheral Nerve Myelin (STED)

PNM............. Phenolic Nylon with Microballoon
PNM............. Pinnacles National Monument [California] (AD)
PNM............. Postneonatal Mortality (STED)
PNM............. Price Negotiation Memorandum (MCD)
PNM............. Public Service Co. of New Mexico [NYSE symbol] (SPSG)
PNM............. Public Svc New Mexico [NYSE symbol] (TTSB)
PNM............. Pulse Number Modulation
PNM-Aprome Partido Nacionalista de Melilla - Asociacion Pro Melilla [Political party] (EY)
PNMC .... Phenyl Methylcarbamate [Organic chemistry]
PNMF......... Pseudo Noise Matched Filter (IAA)
PNMG .... Persistent Neonatal Myasthenia Gravis [Medicine] (DAVI)
PNMO .... Provided No Military Objection Exists [Army]
PNMT .... Phenylethanolamine N-Methyltransferase [An enzyme]
PNMT .... Positive-Negative Metal Transistor [Electronics] (IAA)
PNN .... Penn Engineering & Manufacturing Corp. [AMEX symbol] (SPSG)
PNN .... Penn Engr & Mfg [AMEX symbol] (TTSB)
PNN .... Pinnacle Mountain [Alaska] [Seismograph station code, US Geological Survey] (SEIS)
PNN .... Princeton, ME [Location identifier FAA] (FAAL)
PNN.A......... Penn Engr & Mfg'A' [AMEX symbol] (TTSB)
PN-NAIPC .... Patriot Network - National Association of Independent Patriot Clubs (EA)
pn nb .... Piano Nobile (VRA)
PNNCF........ Pacific Northern Naval Coastal Frontier
PNNL .... Pacific Northwest National Laboratory
PNNT .... Pennant (MSA)
PNNW .... Pennichuck Corp. [NASDAQ symbol] (SAG)
PNo............. Montgomery County-Norristown Public Library, Norristown, PA [Library symbol Library of Congress] (LCLS)
PNO .... Nashville, TN [Location identifier FAA] (FAAL)
PNO .... Pancontinental Oil Ltd. [Toronto Stock Exchange symbol]
PNO .... Pa-O National Organization [Myanmar] [Political party] (EY)
PNO .... Parque Nacional Ordesa [Ordesa National Park] [Spanish] (AD)
PNO .... Parti Nationaliste Occitan [Occitanian Nationalist Party] [France Political party] (PPE)
PNO .... Party for National Order [Turkey Political party Defunct] (MENA)
PNO .... Pendleton [Oregon] [Seismograph station code, US Geological Survey] (SEIS)
pno .... Pergamino [Parchment] [Spanish] (AD)
pno .... Piano (AD)
PNO .... Piano
pno .... Pianoforte (WDAA)
PNO .... Port of New Orleans (AD)
PNO .... Preliminary Notification [Nuclear energy] (NRCH)
PNO .... Premium Notice Ordinary [Insurance]
PNO .... Principal Naval Overseer [British]
PNO .... Principal Nursing Officer
PNOA .... Para-Nitro-ortho-anisidine [Organic chemistry]
pnob .... Pencil Note on Back [Philately]
PNOC .... Philippine National Oil Co. (AD)
PNOC .... Proposed Notice of Change
PNO-CI .... Pair Natural Orbital Configuration Interaction [Atomic physics]
PNoH .... Norristown State Hospital, Norristown, PA [Library symbol Library of Congress] (LCLS)
PNohM........ Mary Immaculate Seminary, Northampton, PA [Library symbol Library of Congress] (LCLS)
PNOK .... Primary Next of Kin [Army] (AABC)
PNOM .... Procedural Nomenclature (MCD)
PNOPO .... Parliament National Organisations and Public Offices [British]
PNortHi........ Historical Society of Montgomery County, Norristown, PA [Library symbol Library of Congress Obsolete] (LCLS)
PNOT .... Para-Nitro-ortho-toluidine [Organic chemistry]
PNOT .... Para-Nitro-o-toluidine [Organic chemistry]
PNP .... Pakistan National Party [Political party] (PD)
PNP .... Panache Resources, Inc. [Vancouver Stock Exchange symbol]
PNP .... Para-Nitrophenol [or Nitrophenyl] [Organic chemistry]
PNP .... Para-Nitrophenyl-Beta-Galactosidase [An enzyme] (DAVI)
PNP .... Partido Nacionalista del Pueblo [Bolivia] [Political party] (PPW)
PNP .... Partido Nacionalista ng Pilipinas [Philippine Nationalist Party] [Political party] (EY)
PNP .... Partido Nacionalista Popular [Popular Nationalist Party] [Panama] [Political party] (PPW)
PNP .... Partido Nashonal di Pueblo [National People's Party] [Netherlands Antilles] [Political party] (EY)
PNP .... Partido Nuevo Progresista [New Progressive Party] [Puerto Rico] [Political party] (PPW)
PNP .... Partidul National Poporului [National People's Party] [Romania] [Political party] (PPE)
PNP .... Parti National du Progres [National Progress Party] [Congo] [Political party]
PNP .... Parti National Populaire [National Popular Party] [Canada Political party] (PPW)
PNP .... Parti National Progressiste [Haiti] [Political party] (EY)
PNP .... Peake's English Nisi Prius Cases [1790-1812] [A publication] (DLA)
PNP .... Peak Negative Pressure [Medicine] (DAVI)
PNP .... Pearl Necklace Polymer [Organic chemistry]
PNP .... Pediatric Nephrology [Medical specialty] (DHSM)
PNP .... Pediatric Nurse Practitioner
PNP .... Penuelas [Puerto Rico] [Seismograph station code, US Geological Survey] (SEIS)
PNP .... People's National Party [Jamaica] [Political party] (PPW)
PNP .... People's National Party [Ghana] [Political party] (PPW)
PNP .... Peripheral Neuropathy [Medicine]
PNP .... Platelet Neutralization Procedure [Medicine] (MEDA)

PNP .... Platt National Park [Oklahoma] (AD)
PNP .... Plug and Play [Microsoft Corp.] [Computer auto-configuration system] (PCM)
PnP .... Plug and Play (PCM)
PNP .... Polyneuropathy [Medicine] (STED)
PNP .... Popondetta [Papua New Guinea] [Airport symbol] (OAG)
PNP .... Popular Nationalist Party [Panama] [Political party] (PD)
PNP .... Positive-Negative-Positive [Transistor]
pnp .... Positive Negative Positive (AD)
PNP .... Precision Navigation Project
PNP .... Preliminary Network Plan (SSD)
PNP .... Prenegotiation Position (MCD)
PNP .... Private Non-Profit
PNP .... Progressive National Party [Turks and Caicos Islands] [Political party] (PPW)
PNP .... Progressive Nuclear Palsy [Neurology] (DAVI)
PNP .... Prototype Nuclear Process
PNP .... Psychogenic Nocturnal Polydipsia [Medicine]
PNP .... P-Type, N-Type, P-Type Transistor (NITA)
PNP .... Purine-Nucleoside Phosphorylase [An enzyme]
PNP .... Purine Nucleotide Phosphorylase [An enzyme] (DAVI)
PNP .... Pyridoxine Phosphate [Biochemistry]
PNPA .... Para-Nitrophenyl Acetate [Organic chemistry]
PNPB .... Positive-Negative Pressure Breathing [Medicine] (STED)
PNPDPP...... Para-Nitrophenyl Diphenyl Phosphate [Organic chemistry]
PNPF .... Piqua Nuclear Power Facility
PNPG .... Para-Nitrophenylglycerine [Biochemistry]
PNPG .... Parti National Populaire Guyanais [French Guiana] [Political party] (EY)
PNPG .... P-Nitrophenyl-B-Galactoside [Chemistry] (MAE)
PNPH .... Parti National Progressiste d'Haiti [National Progressive Party of Haiti] [Political party]
PNPL .... Para-Nitrophenyl Laurate [Organic chemistry]
PNPLS .... Progress at NPL [National Priorities List] Sites [A publication] [EPA]
PNPN .... Positive-Negative-Positive-Negative [Transistor] (MUGU)
pnpn .... Positive-Negative Positive-Negative (AD)
P-NPNN ...... Para-Nitrophenyl Nitronyl Nitroxide
PNPP .... Para-Nitrophenyl Phosphate [Organic chemistry]
PNPP .... Perry Nuclear Power Plant (NRCH)
PNPR .... Positive-Negative Pressure Respiration
pnpr .... Positive-Negative Pressure Respiration (AD)
PNPS .... Palisades Nuclear Power Station (NRCH)
P-NPS........ Para-Nitrophenylsulfate [Pharmacology] (DAVI)
PNPS .... Plant Nitrogen Purge System (IEEE)
PNPS .... Plant Nuclear Protection System (IAA)
PNQ .... Pine Crest Resources [Vancouver Stock Exchange symbol]
PNQ .... Poona [India] [Airport symbol] (OAG)
PNR .... Panair [Spain ICAO designator] (FAAC)
PNR .... Partido Nacionalista Renovador [Nationalist Renewal Party] [Guatemala] [Political party] (PPW)
PNR .... Partido Nacionalista Revolucionario [Revolutionary Nationalist Party] [Ecuador] [Political party] (PPW)
PNR .... Partido Nacional Republicano [National Republican Party] [Portugal Political party] (PPE)
PNR .... Partido Nacional Republicano [National Republican Party] [Paraguay] [Political party]
PNR .... Partido Nacional Revolucionario [National Revolutionary Party] [Venezuela Political party]
PNR .... Partij Nationalistische Republiek [Nationalist Republic Party] [Surinam] [Political party] (PPW)
PNR .... Passenger Name Record [Airlines]
PNR .... Pennant Resources Ltd. [Toronto Stock Exchange symbol]
PNR .... Penrod [Nevada] [Seismograph station code, US Geological Survey Closed] (SEIS)
PNR .... Pentair, Inc. [NYSE symbol] (TTSB)
PNR .... Philippine National Railways (DS)
PNR .... Pioneer
Pnr............. Pioneer (AD)
PNR .... Pittsburgh Naval Reactor (AD)
PNR .... Pittsburgh Naval Reactors Office [Energy Research and Development Administration]
PNR .... Pointe Noire [Congo] [Airport symbol] (OAG)
PNR .... Point of No Return [Aviation]
pnr............. Point of No Return (AD)
PNR .... Popular News and Review [A publication]
PNR .... Preliminary Negotiation Reports
PNR .... Primary Navigation Reference (AAG)
PNR .... Prior Notice Required (AFM)
pnr............. Prior Notice Required (AD)
PNR .... Prisoner
PNR .... Proved Name Registraton [Advertising] (DOAD)
PNR .... Proximal Negative Response
PNR .... Pulletop Nature Reserve [New South Wales] (AD)
PNR .... Pulse Nuclear Radiation (AAG)
PNRBC....... Pacific Northwest River Basin Commission
PNRC .... Pacific Northwest Regional Commission [Department of Commerce]
PNRC .... Potomac Naval River Command (MCD)
PNRC .... Projet National de Coordination des Ressources dans le Domaine de la Statistiques et de l'Information Judiciaires [Canada]
PNRE .... Pan Atlantic Re, Inc. (MHDW)
PNRG .... Prime Energy [NASDAQ symbol] (SAG)
PNRG .... PrimeEnergy Corp. [NASDAQ symbol] (SPSG)
PNRHSL ..... Pacific Northwest Regional Health Science Library [Library network]
PNRL .... Penril DataComm Ntwks [NASDAQ symbol] (TTSB)
PNRL .... Penril Data Communication Networks [NASDAQ symbol] (SPSG)

PNRO........... Pittsburgh Naval Reactors Office [*Department of Energy*] [*West Mifflin, PA*] (GAAI)
PNRP........... Philadelphia Pulmonary Neoplasm Research Project (AD)
PNRS........... Preliminary Natural Resources Survey (GNE)
PNRS........... Project Notification and Review System [*Department of Labor*]
PNRSV........ Prunus Necrotic Ringspot Virus
PNS............. Pacific Navigation Systems (AD)
PNS............. Pakistan Naval Ship (AD)
PNS............. Parabolized Navier-Stokes Modeling (MCD)
PNS............. Paraneoplastic Neurodegenarative Syndrome [*Medicine*]
PNS............. Parasympathetic Nervous System
pns............. Parasympathetic Nervous System (AD)
PNS............. Park-Neutral Switch [*Automotive engineering*]
PNS............. Partial Niche Separation
PNS............. Partial Nonprogressing Stroke (CPH)
PNS............. Part Number Specification (MCD)
PNS............. Peculiar and Nonstandard Items (AAG)
PNS............. Penas [*Bolivia*] [*Seismograph station code, US Geological Survey*] (SEIS)
PNS............. Pennington's Stores Ltd. [*Toronto Stock Exchange symbol*]
PNS............. Pensacola [*Florida*] [*Airport symbol*] (OAG)
Pns............. Pension (TBD)
PNS............. People's News Service [*British*]
PNS............. Peripheral Nerve Stimulator [*Medicine*] (MAE)
PNS............. Peripheral Nervous System [*Medicine*]
pns............. Peripheral Nervous System (AD)
PNS............. Perkins Nuclear Station (NRCH)
PNS............. Philadelphia & Norfolk Steamship [*AAR code*]
PNS............. Philadelphia Naval Shipyard (AD)
PNS............. Philippines News Service
PNS............. Pic'N'Save Corp. (EFIS)
PNS............. Plate Number Society [*Defunct*] (EA)
PNS............. Polynucleotide Sequence (DB)
PNS............. Pooled Normal Serum (PDAA)
PNS............. Portable Navigation System
PNS............. Portsmouth Naval Shipyard [*New Hampshire*]
PNS............. Positive-Negative Selection [*Genetic engineering technique*]
PNS............. Posterior Nasal Spine [*Medicine*] (DMAA)
PNS............. Post Nickel Strike (PDAA)
PNS............. Postnuclear Supernatant
PNS............. Practical Nursing Student (DAVI)
PNS............. Prescribed Nuclear Stockage [*Military*] (AABC)
PNS............. Principal Nursing Sister (WDAA)
PNS............. Probability of Not Having a Space
PNS............. Professionals for National Security [*Defunct*] (EA)
PNS............. Professor of Naval Science
PNS............. Project of National Significance
PNS............. Publishers Newspaper Syndicate
PNS............. Survey Udara (Penas) PT [*Indonesia*] [*ICAO designator*] (FAAC)
PNSA.......... Pacific Northwest Ski Association (EA)
PNSA.......... Peanut and Nut Salters Association [*Later, PBNPA*] (EA)
PNSA.......... Seaman Apprentice, Personnelman, Striker [*Navy rating*]
PNS & T...... Professor of Naval Science and Tactics [*Naval ROTC*]
PNSC.......... Packet Network Service Centre (NITA)
PNSCP........ Plan for Navy Satellite Communications Plan
PNSD.......... Parti National pour la Solidarite et le Developpement [*Algeria*] [*Political party*] (EY)
PNSI........... Polhemus Navigational Sciences, Inc. (MCD)
PNSN.......... Parque Nacional Sierra Nevada [*Sierra Nevada National Park*] [*Venezuela*] [*Spanish*] (AD)
PNSN.......... Pension
PNSN.......... Seaman, Personnelman, Striker [*Navy rating*]
PNSO.......... Pull Next Stitch Over [*Knitting*] (BARN)
PNSP.......... Penicillin-Nonsusceptible S. Pneumoniae [*Clinical chemistry*]
PNSQ.......... Porter Need Satisfaction Questionnaire (EDAC)
PNSS.......... Pediatric Nutrition Surveillance System [*Centers for Disease Control*] (DAVI)
PNSTDC....... Pakistan National Scientific and Technical Documentation Center (AD)
PNSUS........ Placename Survey of the US (EA)
PNSY.......... Portsmouth Naval Shipyard [*New Hampshire*]
PNt............. Newtown Library Co., Newtown, PA [*Library symbol Library of Congress Obsolete*] (LCLS)
PNT............. Paint (MSA)
pnt............. Paint (AD)
Pnt............. Panart [*Record label*] [*Cuba, USA*]
PNT............. Para-Nitrotoluene [*Organic chemistry*]
PNT............. Paroxysmal Nodal Tachycardia [*Cardiology*]
PNT............. Parque Nacional Tijuca [*Tijuca National Park*] [*Brazil*] [*Portuguese*] (AD)
PNT............. Partial Nodular Transformation (DMAA)
PNT............. Partido Nacionalista de los Trabajadores [*Argentina Political party*] (EY)
PNT............. Parti National du Travail [*Benin*] [*Political party*] (EY)
PNT............. Parti National du Travail [*Haiti*] [*Political party*] (EY)
PNT............. Patient (AABC)
PNT............. Penna Enterprises [*NYSE symbol*] (TTSB)
PNT............. Penn Enterprises, Inc. [*NYSE symbol*] (SAG)
PNT............. Pentagon
Pnt............. Pentagon (AD)
PNT............. Penticton [*British Columbia*] [*Seismograph station code, US Geological Survey*] (SEIS)
PNT............. Percutaneous Nephrostomy Tube [*Nephrology*] (DAVI)
PNT............. Petromet Resources Ltd. [*Toronto Stock Exchange symbol*]
PNT............. Point

PNT............. Pontiac, IL [*Location identifier FAA*] (FAAL)
PNT............. Position-Navigation-Time
PNT............. Project Network Technique (EECA)
PNTA.......... Pacific Northwest Trade Association
PNTA.......... Pentair, Inc. [*NASDAQ symbol*] (NQ)
Pnt Anx....... Pentagon Annex (AD)
PNtB........... Bucks County Community College, Newtown, PA [*Library symbol Library of Congress*] (LCLS)
PNTB.......... Peninsula Trust Bank [*NASDAQ symbol*] (TTSB)
PNTB.......... Peninsula Trust Bank, Inc. [*NASDAQ symbol*] (SAG)
PNTBT........ Partial Nuclear Test Ban Treaty (AD)
PNtC........... Council Rock High School, Newtown, PA [*Library symbol Library of Congress*] (LCLS)
PNTC.......... Panatech Res & Dev [*NASDAQ symbol*] (TTSB)
PNTC.......... Panatech Research & Development Corp. [*NASDAQ symbol*] (NQ)
PNTCENS.... Patient Census Report
PNTD.......... Painted
pntd............ Painted (AD)
PNTD.......... Personnel Neutron Threshold Detector (IEEE)
PN/TDMA.... Pseudo Noise/Time Division Multiple Access (MCD)
PNtE........... Ellis College, Newtown, PA [*Library symbol Library of Congress Obsolete*] (LCLS)
PNTG.......... Petromet Resources Ltd. [*NASDAQ symbol*] (NQ)
PNTG.......... Printing (ROG)
PNTGF........ Petromet Resources [*NASDAQ symbol*] (TTSB)
PNTGN........ Pentagon (MSA)
PNTK.......... Pentech International [*NASDAQ symbol*] (TTSB)
PNTK.......... Pentech International, Inc. [*NASDAQ symbol*] (NQ)
PNTL.......... Phonetel Technologies [*NASDAQ symbol*] (TTSB)
PNTL.......... Phonetel Technologies, Inc. [*NASDAQ symbol*] (NQ)
PNTO.......... Portuguese National Tourist Office (EA)
PNTO.......... Principal Naval Transport Officer [*British military*] (DMA)
PNTOS........ Para-Nitrotoluene-ortho-sulfonic Acid [*Organic chemistry*]
pntr............ Painter (AD)
PNTR.......... Painter
PNTR.......... Pointer (MCD)
PNTRY........ Pantry
PNts........... Newtown Public Library, Newtown Square, PA [*Library symbol Library of Congress*] (LCLS)
PNTYP........ Panno Type (VRA)
PNU........... Panguitch [*Utah*] [*Airport symbol*] (OAG)
PNU........... Peasants' National Unity [*Afghanistan*] [*Political party*] (EY)
PNU........... Personennamen der Texte aus Ugarit [*A publication*] (BJA)
PNU........... Pharmacia & Upjohn [*NYSE symbol*] (TTSB)
PNU........... Pharmacia & Upjohn, Inc. [*NYSE symbol*] (SAG)
PNU........... Platinum Communication System [*Vancouver Stock Exchange symbol*]
PNU........... Pneumatic Scale Corp. [*Stock exchange symbol*] (AD)
PNU........... Protein Nitrogen Units [*Clinical chemistry*]
PNUA.......... Partito Nazionale Unito Africa [*National Party of United Africans*] [*Somalia*] [*Political party*]
PNUA.......... Polish National Union of America (EA)
PNUD.......... Programa de las Naciones Unidas para el Desarrollo [*United Nations Development Program - UNDP*] [*Spanish*] (MSC)
PNUMA....... Programa de las Naciones Unidas para el Medio Ambiente [*United Nations Environmental Programme Regional Office for Latin America*] (EAIO)
PNUT.......... Portable Nursing Unit Terminal
PNUT.......... Possible Nuclear Underground Test
pnutbutsan... Peanut-Butter Sandwich (AD)
p-nut butter... Peanut-Butter Sandwich (AD)
pnutbutwich... Peanut-Butter Sandwich (AD)
PNUTS........ Possible Nuclear Test Site [*Pronounced "peanuts"*] [*Air Force intelligence*]
PNV........... National Velasquista Party [*Ecuador*] [*Political party*] (PPW)
PNV........... Panavia SA [*ICAO designator*] (FAAC)
PNV........... Partido Nacionalista Vasco [*Basque Nationalist Party*] [*Spain Political party*] (PPE)
PNV........... Partido Nacional Velasquista [*National Velasquista Party*] [*Ecuador*] [*Political party*] (PPW)
PNV........... Parti National Voltaique [*Voltaic National Party*] [*Political party*]
PNV........... Patino N. V. [*Toronto Stock Exchange symbol*]
PNV........... Potential Natural Vegetation (GNE)
PNV........... Prenatal Vitamins (DAVI)
PNV........... Present Net Value (WPI)
PNVAL........ Previously Not Available [*Army*] (AABC)
PNVD.......... Passive Night Vision Devices [*Army*] (AABC)
PNVS.......... Pilot Night Vision System [*Army*] (MCD)
PNVS.......... Pilot's Night Vision Sensor
PNVTS........ Pyrotechnics No-Voltage Test Set
PNW.......... Pacific Northwest
PNW.......... Pacific Northwest Outpost [*MTMC*] (TAG)
PNW.......... Pinnacle West Capital [*NYSE symbol*] (TTSB)
PNW.......... Pinnacle West Capital Corp. [*NYSE symbol*] (SPSG)
PNW.......... [*The*] Prescott & Northwestern Railroad Co. [*AAR code*]
PNWC......... Pacific Northwest Writers' Conference
PNwC......... Westminster College, New Wilmington, PA [*Library symbol Library of Congress*] (LCLS)
PNWCSC..... Pacific Northwest Canadian Studies Consortium [*University of Oregon*]
PNWD/BMI.. Pacific Northwest Division/Battelle Memorial Institute (AD)
PNWL......... Pacific Northwest Laboratory [*AEC*]
PNWR......... Piedmont National Wildlife Refuge [*Georgia*] (AD)
PNWR......... Presquile National Wildlife Refuge [*Virginia*] (AD)
PNWR......... Pungo National Wildlife Refuge [*North Carolina*] (AD)

PNWRBC......	Pacific Northwest River Basins Commission [*Water Resources Council*] [*Terminated, 1981*] (NOAA)
PNX	Imperial Airways, Inc. [*ICAO designator*] (FAAC)
PNX	Pneumothorax [*Medicine*]
pnx	Pneumothorax [*Medicine*] (AD)
pnxt	Pinxit [*He or She Painted It*] [*Latin*] (AD)
PNXT	Pinxit [*He, or She, Painted It*] [*Latin*]
PNY	Camp Parks, CA [*Location identifier FAA*] (FAAI)
PNY	Penny
PNY	Piedmont Natl Gas [*NYSE symbol*] (TTSB)
PNY	Piedmont Natural Gas Co., Inc. [*NYSE symbol*] (SPSG)
PNY	Plattsburgh [*New York*] [*Seismograph station code, US Geological Survey*] (SEIS)
PNY	Portuguese Navy
PNYA	Port of New York Authority [*Later, PANYNJ*]
PNYCTC	Pennsylvania New York Central Transportation Co. (AD)
PNZ	Pennzoil Co., Exploration Library, Houston, TX [*OCLC symbol*] (OCLC)
Pnz.............	Penzance (AD)
PNZ	Petrolina [*Brazil*] [*Airport symbol*] (OAG)
PO	Aeropelican Intercity Commuter Air Services [*ICAO designator*] (AD)
po----	Oceanica [*MARC geographic area code Library of Congress*] (LCCP)
PO	Officer Personnel Division [*Coast Guard*]
PO	Oil City Library, Oil City, PA [*Library symbol Library of Congress*] (LCLS)
PO	Oscillopolarograph
PO	Paarieto-Occipital [*Medicine*] (DMAA)
PO	Pacific Ocean
PO	Palomar Capital [*Vancouver Stock Exchange symbol*]
PO	Parallel Output [*Computer science*] (BUR)
P:O	Parent Offspring [*Genetics*]
PO	Parieto-Occipital [*Anatomy*] (AAMN)
PO	Parity Odd
PO	Parking Orbit [*NASA*]
PO	Parliamentary Officer [*Australia*]
PO	Parole Officer
PO	Partial Pressure of Oxygen (DAVI)
P/O	Part Of (KSC)
p/o	Part of (AD)
PO	Passport Office [*Department of State*]
PO	Patent Office [*Later, PTO*] [*Department of Commerce*]
PO	Patrologia Orientalis [*A publication*] (ODCC)
PO	Performance Objectives (OICC)
PO	Performing Organization (NITA)
PO	Period of Onset [*Medicine*]
PO	Perioperative [*Medicine*] (DMAA)
PO	Permit Office [*British*] (ROG)
PO	Per Order (WDMC)
PO	Per Os [*By Mouth*] [*Pharmacy*]
po	Per Os [*By Mouth*] [*Latin*] (AD)
PO	Peroxidase [*Also, POD*] [*An enzyme*]
PO	Personnel Office [*Kennedy Space Center Directorate*] (NASA)
PO	Personnel Officer
PO	Pesticides Office [*Environmental Protection Agency*]
PO	Petty Officer [*Navy*]
PO	Phase-Out
PO	Phenoxy (EDCT)
PO	Philharmonic Orchestra [*Music*]
P/O	Phone Order [*Medicine*]
P/O	Phosphate to Oxygen (BARN)
PO	Phymatotrichum omnivorum [*A fungus*]
PO	Pilot Officer
P/O	Pitch Over
PO	Planetary Office (IAA)
PO	Planetary Orbit
PO	Planned Obsolescence (MHDB)
PO	Planning Objectives
PO	Poco [*Somewhat*] [*Music*]
po	Poetry (AD)
PO	Point (WGA)
PO	Polarity (AAG)
po	Polarity (AD)
PO	Pole [*Unit of measurement*]
PO	Police Officer
PO	Political Officer [*NATO*]
P/O	Pollen/Ovule Ratio [*Botany*]
Po	Polonium [*Chemical element*]
PO	Polskie Zaklady Lotnicze [*Poland ICAO aircraft manufacturer identifier*] (ICAO)
PO	Polymerizable Oligomer (OA)
PO	Polyolefin [*Organic chemistry*]
Po	Poly Propylene Oxide (EDCT)
Po	Polyzoa [*Quality of the bottom*] [*Nautical charts*]
PO	Por Orden [*By Order*] [*Spanish*]
PO	Portal (DB)
PO	Port Flag [*Navy British*]
P:O	Portland Oregonian [*A publication*] (AD)
PO	Port Officer
PO	Portugal [*NATO*]
po	Portugal [*MARC country of publication code Library of Congress*] (LCCP)
Po	Portuguese [*Language, etc.*] (DLA)
PO	Position Offered
Po	Possible
PO	Postal Officer (DCTA)
PO	Postal Order
PO	Posterior (MAE)
PO	Post Flight Inspection [*Air Force*]
PO	Post Office
po	Post Office (WDMC)
PO	Post Office Department [*Canada*]
PO	Postoperative [*Medicine*]
p-o	Postoperative (AD)
PO	Post Orbit [*NASA*]
PO	Postpay Coin Telephone [*Telecommunications*] (TEL)
PO	Potential Officer [*British military*] (DMA)
PO	Power-Operated
po	Power-Operated (AD)
po	Power Oscillator (AD)
PO	Power Oscillator [*Electronics*]
PO	Power Output
PO	Pre-Authorization Order
PO	Predominating Organism (AAMN)
PO	Preoperational (MCD)
PO	Preoptic [*Area of the brain*]
PO	Presbyteri Oratorii [*Oratorians*] [*Roman Catholic religious order*]
PO	Presbyterorum Ordinis [*Decree on the Ministry and Life of Priests*] [*Vatican II document*]
PO	Pressure Oscillation (IAA)
PO	Preventive Officer [*British*] (ROG)
PO	Previous Orders [*Military*]
po	Previous Orders (AD)
PO	Primary Output (IAA)
PO	Principal Officer [*Foreign Service*]
PO	Principal Only (EBF)
PO	Principal Only Strip [*Mortgage security*]
PO	Printout
PO	Privately Owned (AFM)
PO	Private Office [*Documents issued by the Secretary General, NATO*] (NATG)
PO	Probation Officer
PO	Processing Office [*Bureau of the Census*] (GFGA)
PO	Procurement Objective (NVT)
PO	Production Offset (AABC)
PO	Production Order (KSC)
PO	Professional Officer
PO	Professor Ordinarius [*Ordinary Professor*] [*Latin*] (ROG)
PO	Programmed Oscillator
PO	Program Objective
PO	Program Office [*Air Force*] (CET)
PO	Program Operations (COE)
PO	Program Originator (AFM)
PO	Project Office [*or Officer*] [*Military*]
PO	Project Officer (COE)
PO	Project ORBIS (EA)
PO	Project Order [*DoD*]
PO	Project Overcome (EA)
PO	Proposals Outstanding
PO	Proposition One [*Defunct*] (EA)
PO	Propylene Oxide [*Organic chemistry*]
PO	Province of Ontario [*Canada*]
PO	Provisioning Order (AFM)
PO	Pseudoadiabatic Operation [*Chemical engineering*]
PO	Psychological Operation [*Military*] (CINC)
PO	Public Offering [*Investment term*]
PO	Public Office [*British*] (ROG)
PO	Public Official
PO	Pull Out (IAA)
PO	Pulmonary Valve Opening [*Cardiology*]
PO	Pulsed Carrier without Any Modulation Intended to Carry Information (IEEE)
PO	Pulse Oscillator (IAA)
PO	Pulse Output
PO	Punch Out [*Computer science*] (IAA)
PO	Punted Over [*Boating*] [*British*] (ROG)
PO	Purchase Order
PO	Purchasing Office [*DoD*] (AFIT)
PO	Putout [*Baseball*]
P-0	Pyrenees-Orientales (AD)
PO	Radio Positioning Mobile Station [*ITU designation*] [*Telecommunications*] (CET)
PO1	Petty Officer, First Class [*Navy*]
PO 1/C	Petty Office First Class [*Military*] (AD)
pO2	Oxygen Pressure (DAVI)
PO_2	Partial Pressure of Oxygen (AAMN)
PO2	Petty Officer, Second Class [*Navy*]
PO 2/C	Petty Office Second Class [*Military*] (AD)
PO3	Petty Officer, Third Class [*Navy*]
PO 3/C	Petty Office Third Class [*Military*] (AD)
POA	Le Point Air [*France ICAO designator*] (FAAC)
POA	Pacific Ocean Area [*World War II*]
POA	Pahoa, HI [*Location identifier FAA*] (FAAL)
POA	Pancreatic Oncofetal Antigen [*Immunochemistry*]
POA	Panel of Americans [*Defunct*] (EA)
POA	Parallel Overlap Assembly [*Computer science*]
POA	Pay-on-Answer [*Telecommunications British*]
POA	Peacetime Operating Assets [*DoD*] (AFIT)
POA	Petroleum Operating Agreement (CINC)
POA	Petty Officer Airman [*British military*] (DMA)
POA	Phalangeal Osteoarthritis [*Medicine*]

POA .... Phenoxyacetic Acid [*Organic chemistry*]
POA .... Place of Acceptance [*Business term*] (DCTA)
poa .... Place of Acceptance (AD)
POA .... Plan of Action (NASA)
POA .... Point Of Action (EECA)
POA .... Point of Application [*Medicine*] (MAE)
POA .... Polarized Orbital Approximation (PDAA)
POA .... Police Officers' Association [*British*] (BI)
POA .... Pontifica Opera di Assistenza [*Pontifical Relief Organization*]
POA .... Pony of the Americas
PoA .... Pony of the Americas Club (NTPA)
POA .... Portland Opera Association [*Oregon*] (AD)
POA .... Porto Alegre [*Brazil*] [*Airport symbol*] (OAG)
POA .... Port of Arrival
POA .... Power of Attorney
PoA .... Power of Attorney (AD)
POA .... Power Open Association [*Computer science*] (CDE)
POA .... Preoptic Area [*of the brain*]
POA .... Price on Application [*Business term*] (ADA)
POA .... Primary Optic Afferents
poa .... Primary Optical Area (AD)
POA .... Primary Optic Atrophy
POA .... Prison Officers' Association [*A union*] [*British*] (DCTA)
POA .... Privately Owned Automobile
POA .... Privately-Owned Open Air-Braked [*Railway wagons*] (PDAA)
POA .... Probability of Acceptance (IAA)
POA .... Program Office Approvals (COE)
POA .... Proof of Accounts
POA .... Property Owners Association (NTPA)
POA .... Provisional Operating Authorization [*for nuclear power plant*]
POA .... Public Order Act
POA .... Purchased on Assembly (KSC)
POA .... Purchase Order Authorization (SAA)
POA .... Purgeable Organic Analyzer
POAA .... Planetary Operations Analysis Area [*NASA*]
POAA .... Post Office Agents' Association [*Australia*]
POAA .... Property Owners Association of America [*Defunct*] (EA)
POA & M ..... Plan of Action and Milestones (NVT)
POAC .... Peace Officers Association of California (AD)
POAC .... Pony of the Americas Club (EA)
POAC .... Port and Ocean Engineering Under Arctic Conditions International
  Committee (EAIO)
POAC .... Post Office Advisory Committee [*British*]
POAC .... Post Office Advisory Council (AD)
POAC .... Post Office Ambulance Centre [*British*] (DI)
POACH .... Prednisone, Oncovin [*Vincristine*] Cytosine Arabinoside,
  Cyclophospham ide, and Adriamycin [*Antineoplastic drug
  regimen*] (DAVI)
POACMN ...... Petty Officer Aircrewman [*British military*] (DMA)
POACS .... Prior Other Active Commissioned Service [*Military*]
POADS .... Portland Air Defense Sector (SAA)
POAE .... Port of Aerial Embarkation [*Air Force*]
POAE .... Principal Officer of Aircraft Equipment [*Ministry of Aircraft Production*]
  [*British World War II*]
POAES .... Prior Other Active Enlisted Service [*Military*]
POAF .... Petty Officer Air Fitter [*British military*] (DMA)
POAG .... Peace Officers Association of Georgia (AD)
POAG .... Primary Open-Angle Glaucoma [*Ophthalmology*]
POA-HA .... Preoptic Anterior Hypothalamic Area [*Medicine*] (DMAA)
POAHEDPEARL... Pacific Ocean Areas Headquarters Pearl Harbor
POALS .... Petty Officers Advanced Leadership School [*Navy*] (MUGU)
POAM .... Polar Ozone Aerosol Measurement
POAN .... Procurement of Ordnance and Ammunition - Navy
PO & CS .... Post Office and Civil Service Committee [*US Senate*] [*Obsolete*]
POANSW ..... Property Owners' Association of New South Wales [*Australia*]
POAQ .... Property Owners' Association of Queensland [*Australia*]
POAR .... Postal Laws and Regulations [*Later, Postal Manual*] (IAA)
POAR .... Problem-Objective-Approach-Response [*System of planning patient
  care*] [*Medicine*]
POAR .... Project Order Action Request [*Navy*] (NG)
poas-- .... American Samoa [*MARC geographic area code Library of
  Congress*] (LCCP)
POAS .... Pankypria Omospondia Anexartiton Syntechnion [*Pancyprian
  Federation of Independent Trade Unions*] [*Cyprus*]
POAS .... Psychological Operations Automated System (COE)
POASP .... Plans and Operations Automated Storage Program [*Military*]
POAT .... Psychological Operations Assessment Team (COE)
POATSC ...... Pacific Overseas Air Technical Service Command
POAU .... Protestants and Other Americans for Separation of Church and
  State (NADA)
POAU .... Protestants and Other Americans United [*for Separation of Church
  and State*]
POB .... Fayetteville, NC [*Location identifier FAA*] (FAAL)
POB .... Paris Opera Ballet
POB .... Parti Ouvrier Belge [*Belgian Workers' Party*] [*Later, Belgian Socialist
  Party*] [*Political party*] (PPE)
POB .... Penicillin, Oil, Beeswax [*Medicine*]
POB .... Perfluorooctyl Bromide [*Organic chemistry*]
POB .... Persons on Board [*Aviation*]
pob .... Persons on Board (AD)
POB .... Phenoxybenzamine [*Later, PBZ*] [*Adrenergic blocking agent*]
pob .... Pilot on Board (AD)
POB .... Place of Birth
pob .... Poblacion [*Population*] [*Spanish*] (AD)
pob .... Point of Beginning (AD)

POB .... Point of Beginning
POB .... Point of Business
PoB .... Port of Baltimore (AD)
POB .... Postal Bulletin [*A publication*]
POB .... Post Office Box
POB .... Power Outlet Box
POB .... Prevention of Blindness [*Medicine*] (MAE)
pob .... Prevention of Blindness (AD)
POB .... Public Oversight Board
POB .... Push-Out Base (IAA)
POB .... Servicios Aereos Poblanos, SA de CV [*Mexico*] [*FAA designator*]
  (FAAC)
POB[2] .... Prepped Out Beyond Belief [*Book title*]
POBA .... Patent Office Board of Appeals (IAA)
POBA .... Plain Old Balloon Angioplasty [*Cardiology*] [*Facetious*]
PO Bag ...... Post Office Bag (ASC)
POBAL .... Powered Balloon [*System*]
POBATO ...... Propellant on Board at Takeoff
POBCOST.... Probabilistic Budgeting and Forward Costing (MCD)
POBE .... Profile of Out-of-Body Experiences (STED)
POBN .... (Pyridyloxide)butylnitrone [*Organic chemistry*]
POBN .... Pyridyl Oxide-N-tert-butylnitrone [*Organic chemistry*]
pobp-- .... British Solomon Islands [*MARC geographic area code Library of
  Congress*] (LCCP)
POBR .... Poe & Brown [*NASDAQ symbol*] (SAG)
POBR .... Problem-Oriented Basic Research [*National Science Foundation*]
pobra .... Pony and Zebra (AD)
POBS .... Portsmouth Bank Shares [*NASDAQ symbol*] (TTSB)
POBS .... Portsmouth Bank Shares, Inc. [*NASDAQ symbol*] (NQ)
POBSP .... Pacific Ocean Biological Survey Program [*Smithsonian Institution*]
  (GFGA)
POBY .... Prior Operating Budget Year [*Military*] (AFIT)
POC .... Clarion State College, Oil City, PA [*Library symbol Library of
  Congress*] (LCLS)
POC .... La Pocatiere [*Quebec*] [*Seismograph station code, US Geological
  Survey*] (SEIS)
POC .... La Verne, CA [*Location identifier FAA*] (FAAL)
Po/C .... Ocular Pressure (STED)
POC .... Packaged Optimization Control [*Engineering*]
POC .... Parallel Optical Computer
POC .... Parent-Offspring Conflict
POC .... Particulate Organic Carbon
POC .... Particulate Organic Concentration [*Environmental science*]
POC .... Particulate Organic Matter
POC .... Parti d'Opposition Congolais [*Congolese Opposition Party*] [*Political
  party*]
POC .... Patch Output Converter (IAA)
POC .... Payload Operations Center [*NASA*] (NASA)
Poc .... Payload Operations Center [*NASA*] (NAKS)
POC .... Performance Optimization Code
POC .... Personnel Operations Center
POC .... Peugeot Owners' Club (EA)
POC .... Physics of Control (IAA)
POC .... Pick Off, Circuit
POC .... Pittsburgh Opera Co. (AD)
POC .... Planning Objective Coordinator
POC .... Platoon Operations Center [*Army*]
POC .... Plymouth Owners Club (EA)
POC .... Pocono Airlines, Inc. [*ICAO designator*] (FAAC)
POC .... Poco Petroleums Ltd. [*Toronto Stock Exchange symbol*]
POC .... Poculum [*Cup*] [*Pharmacy*]
POC .... Point of Care [*Medicine*]
POC .... Point of Compliance (FFDE)
POC .... Point of Contact (AABC)
poc .... Point of Contact (AD)
POC .... Policy Oversight Committee [*Library Science*] (TELE)
POC .... Porsche Owners Club (EA)
POc .... Porte-Oceane [*Record label*] [*France*]
POC .... Port of Call
POC .... Post Office Corps [*British military*] (DMA)
POC .... Post Office Counters Ltd. [*British*]
POC .... Post of the Corps
POC .... Postoperative Care [*Medicine*]
POC .... Postoral Ciliary [*Gland*]
POC .... Potential Officer Cadet (WDAA)
POC .... Potential Operated Channel (DB)
POC .... Power Control
POC .... Power on Clear (MHDI)
POC .... Precision Oscillator Crystal
POC .... Preliminary Operational Capability [*Military*] (AFIT)
POC .... Preservation of Capital [*Investment term*]
POC .... Principal Operating Component
poc .... Principal Operating Component (AD)
POC .... Prisoners of Conscience [*File of persons imprisoned for political or
  religious beliefs kept by Amnesty International*]
POC .... Prison Officer's Club (AD)
poc .... Privately Owned Conveyance (AD)
POC .... Privately Owned Conveyance [*Army*]
POC .... Procarbazine, Oncovin [*Vincristine*], CCNU [*Lomustine*]
  [*Antineoplastic drug regimen*]
POC .... Proceeding on Course [*Aviation*] (FAAC)
POC .... Process Operator Console
POC .... Production Office Coordinator (WDMC)
POC .... Production Operational Capability
POC .... Production Order Change (KSC)

POC	Products of Combustion (DICI)
POC	Products of Conception [Medicine] (MEDA)
POC	Professional Officer Course [AFROTC] (AFM)
POC	Program Office Contacts (COE)
POC	Programs of Cooperation (MCD)
POC	Proof of Concept [Army]
POC	Proopiocortin [Biochemistry]
POC	Public Oil Co. (AD)
Poc	Purchase Order Closeout (NAKS)
POC	Purchase Order Closeout (NASA)
POC	Purchase Order Contract
POC	Purgeable Organic Carbon [Chemistry]
POCA	Association of Psychiatric Outpatient Centers of America [Psychiatric Out patient Centers of America] [Acronym is based on former name,] (EA)
POCA	Petty Officer Caterer [British military] (DMA)
POCA	Post Office Clerks' Association [A union] [Northern Ireland]
POCA	Prednisone, Oncovin [Vincristine], Cytarabine, Adriamycin [Antineoplastic drug regimen]
POCA	Public Offender Counselors Association [Later, IAAOC] (EA)
POCAL	Pre-Operational Common Age List
PO Cas	Perry's Oriental Cases [Bombay] [A publication] (DLA)
POCASEA	Protection of Children Against Sexual Exploitation Act of 1977
POCB	Plain Ol' Country Boy
POCC	Payload Operations Control Center [NASA] (NASA)
POCC	Penn Octane [NASDAQ symbol] (TTSB)
POCC	Penn Octane Corp. [NASDAQ symbol] (SAG)
POCC	Procarbazine, Oncovin [Vincristine], Cyclophosphamide, CCNU [Lomustine] [Antineoplastic drug regimen]
POCC	Program Operation Control Center [Space science]
Poc Costs	Pocock on Costs [1881] [A publication] (DLA)
POCE	Pantone Open Color Environment [Joint venture between Pantone, Inc. and LightSource Computer Images] [Computer science] (PCM)
POCE	Proof-of-Concept Experiment [Solar thermal conversion]
POCEL	Petty Officer Control Electrician [British military] (DMA)
POCET	Proof-of-Concept Experiment Testbed [Solar thermal conversion] (MCD)
POCH	Progressiven Organisationen der Schweiz [Progressive Organizations of Switzerland] [Political party] (PPE)
PochFdl	Pocahontas Federal Savings & Loan Association [Associated Press] (SAG)
poci--	Caroline Islands [MARC geographic area code Library of Congress] (LCCP)
POCI	Pontiac-Oakland Club International (EA)
POCI	Precision Optics Corp. [NASDAQ symbol] (SAG)
POCI	Precision Optics Mass [NASDAQ symbol] (TTSB)
POCIBO	Polar Circling Balloon Observatory
POCIL	Pocillum [Little Cup] [Pharmacy] (ROG)
Pocill	Pocillum [Little Cup] [Pharmacy]
POCK	Petty Officer Cook [British military] (DMA)
pock	Pocket (AD)
Pocket Bks	Pocket Books (AD)
POCL	Power on Clear [Navy Navigation Satellite System] (DNAB)
POCL	Project Office Change Letter
POCM	Partido Obrero y Campesino de Mexico [Mexico Political party]
POCM	Postal Contracting Manual [Postal Service]
POCN	Purchase Order Change Notice
POCN	Purchase Order Change Number
POCO	European Political Cooperation [EC] (ECED)
POCO	Physiology of Chimpanzees in Orbit [NASA]
Poco	Politically Correct
POCO	Position Computer (IAA)
POCO	Power On - Clock On [Aerospace]
POCO	Purchase Order Change Order (AAG)
POCO	Purchase Order Closeout (AAG)
POCOA	Post Office Controlling Officers' Association [A union] [British]
pocp--	Canton and Enderbury Islands [MARC geographic area code Library of Congress] (LCCP)
POCP	Program Objectives Change Proposal
POCR	Program Objectives Change Request [DoD]
POCS	Patent Office [later, PTO] Classification System
POCSC	Penn-Ohio Collegiate Swimming Conference (PSS)
Po Ct	Police Court (DLA)
POCTA	Prevention of Cruelty to Animals Society Member (DSUE)
POCUL	Poculum [Cup] [Pharmacy] (ROG)
pocw--	Cook Island [MARC geographic area code Library of Congress] (LCCP)
POCY	Postoperative Chronologic Year (STED)
POD	Pacific Ocean Division [Army Corps of Engineers]
pod	Paid on Delivery (AD)
POD	Parent Organization Designator (MCD)
POD	Parents of Diabetics
POD	Payable on Death [Insurance]
pod	Payable on Death (AD)
POD	Payload Operations Division [NASA] (MCD)
POD	Pay on Delivery [Shipping]
POD	Period of Disability [Social Security Administration] (DHP)
POD	Permissible Operating Distance [Army] (AFIT)
POD	Peroxidase [Also, PO] [An enzyme]
POD	Personal Orientation Dimensions [Personality development test] [Psychology]
POD	Piece of Data [Computer science] (NHD)
POD	Place of Death (MAE)
POD	Place of Delivery [Shipping] (DS)

POD	Place of Discharge
POD	Plan of the Day
POD	Pneumatically Operated Disconnect (KSC)
POD	Pocket Oxford Dictionary [A publication]
POD	Podiatry (DAVI)
POD	Podkamennaya [Former USSR Geomagnetic observatory code]
POD	Podor [Senegal] [Airport symbol] (OAG)
POD	Point of Departure
POD	Point of Discharge (GFGA)
POD	Point-of-Origin Device (IEEE)
pod	Point-of-Origin Device (AD)
POD	Points of Domination [Military]
POD	Polycystic Ovarian Disease [Medicine]
POD	Port of Debarkation [Military]
pod	Port of Debarkation (AD)
POD	Port of Delivery [Shipping]
pod	Port of Departure (AD)
POD	Port of Destination [MARAD] (TAG)
POD	Port of Discharge [Navy]
POD	Post of Duty
POD	Post Office Department [Later, United States Postal Service]
POD	Post Office Directory
POD	Postoperative Day [Medicine]
POD	Potential Ozone Depleter
POD	Pounds-Out-the-Door [Measure of industrial production]
POD	Precision Orbit Determination (MCD)
POD	Preflight Operation Division [NASA]
POD	Price on Delivery (EBF)
pod	Probability of Detection (AD)
POD	Probability of Detection (USDC)
pod	Process-Oriented Design (AD)
POD	Professional and Organizational Development [In association name Professional and Organizational Development Network in Higher Education] (EA)
POD	Programmed Operational Date (AFIT)
POD	Program Objectives Document (AAGC)
POD	Program Office Directive
POD	Program Operation Description
POD	Project Operations Director (BARN)
POD	Proof of Debt [Business term] (DCTA)
POD	Proof of Delivery [Shipping] (DS)
POD	Proof of Deposit [Banking]
POD	Proof of Design (MCD)
POD	Prosthetics and Orthotics Database [University of Strathclyde] [Glasgow, Scotland] [Information service or system] (IID)
POD	Protective Oceanic Device
POD	Proton Omnidirectional Detector (USDC)
POD	Proximity Optical Device (NASA)
POD	Pulse Omission Detector (MCD)
POD	Purchase Order Deviation (KSC)
PO'd	Put Out [i.e., angry] [Bowdlerized version]
PODA	Piloting of Office Documentation Architecture (NITA)
PODA	Priority Oriented Demand Assignment [Computer science Telecommunications]
PODAF	Post Operation Data Analysis Facility
PODAF	Power Density Exceeding a Specified Level over an Area with an Assigned Frequency Band (IEEE)
PoDAG	Polar DAAC [Distributed Active Archive Center] Advisory Group [Marine science] (OSRA)
PODAPS	Portable Data Processing System
PODAS	Portable Data Acquisition System
PODBCA	Post Office Department Board of Contract Appeals (AFIT)
PODCC	Plan, Organize, Direct, Coordinate, Control [Principles of management]
Pod D	Doctor of Podiatry
PODE	Pacific Ocean Division Engineers (CINC)
podex	Photographic Exercise (AD)
PODF	Post of Duty File
podia	Podiatrist (AD)
PODIM	Poseidon Design Information Memo [Missiles]
PODM	Preliminary Orbit Determination Method [Computer] [NASA]
POD Network	Professional and Organizational Development Network in Higher Education (NTPA)
PODO	Profit on Day One [Classification for new newspaper]
PODRS	Patent Office [later, PTO] Data Retrieval System [Department of Commerce]
PODS	Parents of Children with Down Syndrome [An association] (EA)
PODS	Parents of Down's Syndrome (EA)
PODS	Perceptions of Developmental Skills Profile [Education] (EDAC)
PODS	Pilot Ocean Data System (MCD)
PODS	Portable Data Store [Computer science] (PDAA)
PODS	Postoperative Destruct System (MCD)
PODSC	Parents of Down's Syndrome Children (EA)
PODUC	Provided [Following Named] Officers Have Not Departed Your Command [Amend Assignment Instructions as Indicated] [Army] (AABC)
PODx	Postoperative Diagnosis [Medicine]
PODx	Preoperative Diagnosis [Medicine]
POE	Fort Polk [Louisiana] [Airport symbol] (OAG)
POE	Fort Polk, LA [Location identifier FAA] (FAAL)
POE	Pacific Orient Express (WDAA)
POE	Panel on the Environment [of President's Science Advisory Committee]
POE	Payment Option Election (MCD)
POE	Peace on Earth [Australia Political party]

POE............. People of the Earth [Also, RAN] (EA)
POE............. Pilot Operational Equipment (MCD)
POE............. Plank-on-Edge
POE............. Pneumatically Operated Equipment (AAG)
POE............. Point of Entry [Accounts]
POE............. Point of Exposure [Environmental Protection Agency] (ERG)
POE............. Polyolefin Elastomers [Plastics]
POE............. Polyoxyethylene [Organic chemistry]
poe............. Polyoxyethylene (AD)
POE............. Port of Embarkation (DFIT)
POE............. Port of Entry [Shipping]
POE............. Post-Occupancy Evaluation
POE............. Post-Operations Evaluation (MCD)
POE............. Postoperative Endophthalmitis [Ophthalmology]
POE............. Postoperative Exercise [Medicine] (DAVI)
POE............. Power Open Environment [Computer science]
POE............. Predicted Operational Environment [Military] (CAAL)
POE............. Pretesting Orientation Exercises [US Employment Service] [Department of Labor]
POE............. Primary Organization Element (NOAA)
POE............. Print Out Effect
POE............. Projected Operational Environment (NVT)
POE............. Proof of Eligibility [Medicine] (DMAA)
POE............. Pull-Over Enrichment [Automotive engineering]
POE............. Pulsar Energy/Resources [Vancouver Stock Exchange symbol]
POE............. Pulse Oriented Electrophoresis [Analytical biochemistry]
poea--......... Easter Island [MARC geographic area code Library of Congress] (LCCP)
POEA .... Philippines Overseas Employment Administration (PDAA)
POEA .... Protection of Offshore Energy Assets [Navy] (NVT)
P/OEA3 .... Probationary Ordnance Electrical Artificer 3rd Class [British military] (DMA)
POEAS .... Planetary Orbiter Error Analysis Study Program
poe buoy ..... Plank-on-Edge Buoy (AD)
PoeBwn .... Poe & Brown [Commercial firm Associated Press] (SAG)
poecrit........ Poetry Criticism (AD)
POED .... Post Office Engineering Department (IAA)
POED .... Program Organization for Evaluation and Decision
PO'ed.......... Put Out [i.e., angry] [Bowdlerized version]
POEE.......... Post Office Electrical Engineer (IAA)
POEER .... Pacific Oceanographic Equipment Evaluation Range (NOAA)
POEF.......... Post Office Engineering Federation [A union] [British]
POEIT.......... Provisional Organization for European Inland Transportation [World War II]
POEL(A)....... Petty Officer Electrician (Air) [British military] (DMA)
POEL(AW).... Petty Officer Electrician (Air Weapon) [British military] (DMA)
POEMS .... Plasma Cell Dyscrasia with Polyneuropathy, Organomegaly, Endocrinopathy, Monoclonal Protein [M-protein], Skin changes [Medicine] (DAVI)
POEMS .... Polyneuropathy Associated with Organomegaly Endocrine Disorders, Myeloma, and Skin Modifications
POEMS .... Polyoxyethylene Monostearate [Organic chemistry]
POENIT........ Poenitentia [Penance] [Latin] (ADA)
POEOP........ Polyoxyethyleneoxypropylene [Organic chemistry]
Poe Pl .... Poe on Pleading and Practice [A publication] (DLA)
POES .... Polar Operational Environmental Satellite (USDC)
POES .... Polar Orbiting Environmental Satellite
POES .... Polar-Orbiting Operational Environmental Satellite (USDC)
POESID .... Position of Earth Satellite in Digital Display (MCD)
Poet........... De Poetis [of Suetonius] [Classical studies] (OCD)
POET........... Petty Officer Enroute Training [Navy] (NVT)
Poet........... Poetica [of Aristotle] [Classical studies] (OCD)
poet--......... Poetical (AD)
Poet........... Poetry [A publication] (BRI)
POET........... Portable Optic-Electronic Tracker (PDAA)
POET........... Portable Orders Entry Terminal (IAA)
POET........... Primed Oscillator Expendable Transponder [Military] (CAAL)
POET........... Program Operation and Environment Transfer (SAA)
POET........... Psychological Operations Exploitation Team [Vietnam]
POET........... Pulse Oximeter/End Tidal [Carbon Dioxide] [Medicine] (DAVI)
Poetics T ..... Poetics Today [A publication] (BRI)
Poet Mel Gr.. Poetae Melici Graeci [A publication] (OCD)
POETRI .... Programme on Exchange and Transfer of Information (NITA)
POETRI .... Programme on Exchange and Transfer of Information on Community Water Supply and Sanitation [International Reference Center for Community Water Supply and Sanitation] [Information service or system] (IID)
Poet Rom Vet... Poetarum Romanorum Veterum Reliquiae [A publication] (OCD)
POETS .... Phooey on Everything, Tomorrow's Saturday [Bowdlerized version]
POETS .... Push Off Early, Tomorrow's Saturday [Bowdlerized version]
POEU .... Post Office Engineering Union [British]
POF............. American Jurisprudence Proof of Facts [A publication]
POF............. Philharmonic Orchestra of Florida (AD)
POF............. Pillar of Fire Church (IIA)
POF............. Pinhole Occulter Facility (SSD)
POF............. Planned Outage Factor [Electronics] (IEEE)
POF............. Plastic Optical Fiber [Automotive electronics]
pof............. Please Omit Flowers (AD)
POF............. Point-of-Failure [Computer science] (IBMDP)
POF............. Police Officer, Female
POF............. Polymer Optical Fiber [Telecommunications]
POF............. Poplar Bluff [Missouri] [Airport symbol] (OAG)
POF............. Poplar Bluff, MO [Location identifier FAA] (FAAL)
POF............. Positive Opening Fin (MCD)
POF............. Postovulatory Follicle [Endocrinology]

POF............. Primary Ovarian Failure [Gynecology] (DMAA)
POF............. Priority of Fire [Military] (INF)
POF............. Privately Owned Firearm (MCD)
POF............. Prolific Resources [Vancouver Stock Exchange symbol]
POF............. Pyruvate Oxidation Factor [Biochemistry]
POFA........... Programmed Operational Functional Appraisal [Navy]
PofB........... Ponies of Britain [An association] (DBA)
P of E .... Portal of Entry [Bacteriology]
P of E .... Port of Embarkation [Military]
PofE .... Port of Entry [Immigration] (DAVI)
P of H......... Patron of Husbandry
POFI........... Pacific Oceanic Fisheries Investigations (NOAA)
pofj--......... Fiji [MARC geographic area code Library of Congress] (LCCP)
P of L .... Port of London (ROG)
POFOOGUSA.. Protection of Foreign Officials and Official Guests of the United States Act
pofp........... French Polynesia [MARC geographic area code Library of Congress] (LCCP)
PO-FY .... Program Objectives for Fiscal Year (DNAB)
POG .... Pacific Oceanographic Group [British Columbia] (AD)
POG .... Parents of Gays (EA)
POG .... Patina Oil & Gas [NYSE symbol] (TTSB)
POG .... Petty Officer's Guide [A publication Navy]
POG .... Piping Instrumentation and Operating Gallery [Nuclear energy] (NRCH)
POG .... Plant Operating Guide (DNAB)
Pog .... Pogonion (DMAA)
POG .... Polymyositis Ossificans Generalisata (DB)
POG .... Port Gentil [Gabon] [Airport symbol] (OAG)
POG .... Position of Germany [British World War II]
POG .... Post Office Guide [Book of regulations] [British]
POG .... Project Officer's Group
POG .... Propulsion Operating Guide (DNAB)
POG .... Provisional Ordnance Group [Military]
POG .... Psychological Operations Group (DOMA)
POGASIS...... Planetary Observation Geometry and Science Instrument Sequence Program [Aerospace]
POGaz......... Post Office Gazette [British A publication] (DCTA)
POGE .... Planning Operational Gaming Experiment [Game]
pogg--......... Galapagos Islands [MARC geographic area code Library of Congress] (LCCP)
pogn--......... Gilbert and Ellice Islands [Tuvalu] [MARC geographic area code Library of Congress] (LCCP)
POGO .... Pennzoil Offshore Gas Operators (AD)
POGO .... Personal Objectives and Goals (MCD)
Pogo .... Pogonomyrinex Occidentalis [A genus of ants]
POGO .... Polar Orbiting Geophysical Observatories [Marine science] (OSRA)
POGO .... Polar Orbiting Geophysical Observatory [NASA]
POGO .... Pop Your Seat Belt, Open the Window, Get Out [Automobile safety]
POGO .... Pre-Oxidation Gettering of the Other Side (PDAA)
POGO .... Prime's Online Graduate Opportunities (NITA)
POGO .... Privately Owned/Government Operated (GFGA)
POGO .... Programmer-Oriented Graphics Operation (IEEE)
POGO .... Program Optimizer (IAA)
POGO .... Project on Government Oversight (EA)
PogoPd........ Pogo Producing Co. [Associated Press] (SAG)
POGPr......... Patina Oil & Gas 7.125% Pfd [NYSE symbol] (TTSB)
POGR .... Poplar Grove National Cemetery
POGS .... National Association of Post Office and General Service Maintenance Employees [Later, APWU] [AFL-CIO]
POGSI......... Policy Group on Scientific Information [Marine science] (MSC)
POGT.......... Power-Operated Gun Turret
pogu--......... Guam [MARC geographic area code Library of Congress] (LCCP)
POG.WS ...... Patina Oil & Gas Wrrt [NYSE symbol] (TTSB)
pOH........... Hydroxyl Concentration [Organic chemistry] (MAE)
POH........... Path Overhead [Telecommunications] (ITD)
POH........... Pilot's Operating Handbook [Aviation] (DA)
POH........... Placed off Hire
POH........... Planned Outage Hours [Electronics] (IEEE)
POH........... Pocahontas, IA [Location identifier FAA] (FAAL)
Poh........... Pohang
POH........... Pull-Out Harness
poh........... Pull Out of Hole (AD)
Pohang........ Pohang Iron & Steel Co., Ltd. [Associated Press] (SAG)
POHC.......... Principal Organic Hazardous Constituent [Environmental chemistry]
POHI.......... Physically or Otherwise Health Impaired
POHM......... Page-Oriented Holograph Memory [Computer science]
POHMA....... Project for the Oral History of Music in America
POHS.......... Presumed Ocular Histoplasmosis Syndrome [Ophthalmology]
POHWARO... Pulsated, Overheated, Water Rocket [Swiss space rocket]
POI............. Parking Orbit Injection [NASA]
POI............. Parti Oubanguien de l'Independance [Ubangi Independence Party] [Political party]
POI............. Period of Interest (MCD)
POI............. Personal Orientation Inventory [Psychology]
POI............. Personal Outlook Inventory [Employment test]
POI............. Plan of Instruction
POI............. Point of Impact
POI............. Point of Interception (GNE)
POI............. Point of Interface [Telecommunications]
POI............. Poison
POI............. Potosi [Bolivia] [Airport symbol] (AD)
POI............. Pre-Overhaul Inspection (MCD)
POI............. Pressure-Operated Initiator (MCD)
POI............. Probability Of Intercept (LAIN)

POI.............. Product of Inertia (MCD)
POI.............. Program of Instruction
POI.............. Public Office of Information (MCD)
POI.............. Purchase Order Item (KSC)
POIC............ Petty Officer in Charge [*Navy*] (NVT)
POIC............ Poly(octyl Isocyanate) [*Organic chemistry*]
POID............ Post Office Investigation/Intelligence Department [*British*] (DI)
POIF............ Plan Organization Index File [*IRS*]
poik .... Poikilocyte [*or Poikilocytosis*] [*Medicine*] (MAE)
POIL............ Power Density Imbalance Limit (IAA)
POINT .... Pasadena Online Information Network [*Pasadena Public Library*] (OLDSS)
POINT .... Point [*Commonly used*] (OPSA)
POINT .... Pursuing Our Italian Names Together (EA)
POINTER...... Particle Orientation Interferometer [*ASD*]
POINTER...... Pre-University Orbital Information Tracker Equipment and Recorder (PDAA)
POINTERM... Appointment Will Be Regarded as Having Terminated upon This Date
Point Loma C... Point Loma Nazarene College (GAGS)
POINTMAIL... Letter Appointment in Mail
POINTS........ Points [*Commonly used*] (OPSA)
POIP............ Potential Offender Identification Program
POIPCD........ Patent Office and Industrial Property and Copyright Department [*British*]
POIQT .... Performance-Oriented Infantry Qualification Test (INF)
POIR............ Project Officers Interim Report [*Air Force*] (MCD)
POIS............ Parkland On-Line Information Systems [*Computer science*] (DMAA)
POIS............ Poison (AAMN)
pois .... Poison (AD)
POIS............ Poisoning [*FBI standardized term*]
POIS............ Post Office Insurance Society [*British*] (DI)
POIS............ Procurement Operations Information System (MCD)
POIS............ Prototype On-Line Instrument System [*Computer science*] (NRCH)
POIS............ Purchase Order Information System (MCD)
POISE .... Panel on Inflight Scientific Experiments [*NASA*]
POISE .... Photosynthetic Oxygenation Illuminated by Solar Energy
POISE .... Pointing and Stabilization Platform Element [*Army*] (MCD)
POISE .... Preoperational Inspection Services Engineering (IAA)
POIT............ Power of Influence Test [*Psychology*]
POJ............. Patent Office Journal [*India*] [*A publication*] (DLA)
POJ............. Selma, AL [*Location identifier FAA*] (FAAL)
poji--.......... Johnston Atoll [*MARC geographic area code Library of Congress*] (LCCP)
POK .... Sacramento, CA [*Location identifier FAA*] (FAAL)
poki--.......... Kermadec Islands [*MARC geographic area code Library of Congress*] (LCCP)
POKMV ...... Pokeweed Mosaic Virus [*Plant pathology*]
POL............. Pacific Oceanographic Laboratories [*Later, Pacific Marine Environmental Laboratory*]
POL............. Pair Orthogonalized Lowdin [*Physics*]
POL............. Parents of Large Families
POL............. Patent Office Library (AD)
POL............. Paul Otchakovsky-Laurens [*Publishing imprint, named for imprint editor*]
POL............. Pemba [*Mozambique*] [*Airport symbol*] (OAG)
POL............. Petroleum, Oil, and Lubricants [*Military*]
pol.............. Petroleum-Oil-and-Lubricants (AD)
POL............. Philips Optical Language (IAA)
POL............. Physician-Owned Laboratory (HCT)
POL............. Physician's Office laboratory
POL............. Pola [*Yugoslavia*] [*Seismograph station code, US Geological Survey Closed*] (SEIS)
POL............. Polacca [*Ship's rigging*] (ROG)
POL............. Poland [*ANSI three-letter standard code*] (CNC)
Pol.............. Poland (VRA)
pol.............. Polar (AD)
POL............. Polar International Airlines, Inc. [*ICAO designator*] (FAAC)
POL............. Polarity [*or Polarize*] (KSC)
Pol.............. Polen [*Poland*] [*Norwegian*] (AD)
POL............. Police
Pol.............. Police (WDAA)
POL............. Policy
pol.............. Polish [*MARC language code Library of Congress*] (LCCP)
POL............. Polish (AAG)
pol.............. Polished (VRA)
POL............. Polish Ocean Lines (AD)
POL............. Polite
Pol.............. Politica [*of Aristotle*] [*Classical studies*] (OCD)
POL............. Political
POL............. Political Section [*Foreign service*]
POL............. Politician
Pol.............. Pollexfen's English King's Bench Reports [*1669-85*] [*A publication*] (DLA)
POL............. Polling (IAA)
POL............. Pollution
POL............. Polonium [*Chemical symbol is Po*] (AAG)
Pol.............. Polydor & Deutsche Grammophon [*Record label*] [*Germany, Europe, etc.*]
POL............. Polymerase [*An enzyme*]
Pol.............. Polyphon [*Record label*] [*Denmark, etc.*]
POL............. Porto Amelia [*Mozambique*] [*Airport symbol*] (AD)
POL............. Port of Loading [*Shipping*]
POL............. Practical Quantification Limit [*Metallurgy*]
POL............. Premature Onset of Labor [*Obstetrics*] (DAVI)
POL............. Problem-Oriented Language [*Computer science*]

pol.............. Problem-Oriented Language (AD)
POL............. Procedure-Oriented Language [*Computer science*]
POL............. Process-Oriented Language [*Computer science*] (IEEE)
POL............. Program Oriented Language [*Computer science*] (ECII)
POL............. Proudman Oceanographic Laboratory [*UK*] [*Marine science*] (OSRA)
POL............. Provisional Operating License [*for nuclear power plant*]
POL............. Public Opinion Laboratory [*Northern Illinois University*] [*Research center*] (RCD)
p-ola .... Payola (AD)
POLA .... Polymerase Alpha (DMAA)
POLA .... Port of London Authority [*England*] (WDAA)
POLA .... Project on Linguistic Analysis
POLA .... Prostitutes of Los Angeles [*An association*] (AD)
POLAC .... Problem-Oriented Language for Analytical Chemistry [*Computer science*] (PDAA)
POLAD .... Political Adviser
Pol Ad .... Political Adviser (AD)
polad .... Political Adviser (AD)
Polam LJ...... Polamerican Law Journal [*A publication*] (DLA)
POLANG ...... Polarization Angle [*Telecommunications*]
polang .... Polarization Angle (AD)
polar........... Polarity (AD)
POLAR .... Polarity [*or Polarize*] (IAA)
POLAR .... Production Order Location and Reporting [*NASA*] (NASA)
POLAR .... Projected Operational Logistics Analysis Requirements
Polar BEAR... Polar Beacon Experiments and Auroral Research (AD)
PolarE......... Polar Express Corp. [*Associated Press*] (SAG)
Polaris........ Polaris Industries, Inc. [*Associated Press*] (SAG)
POLARIS...... Polar-Motion Analysis by Radio Interferometric Surveying [*Geodetic measuring facilities*]
Polaroid....... Polaroid Corp. [*Associated Press*] (SAG)
POLARS....... Pathology On-Line Logging and Reporting System [*Computer science*] (PDAA)
POL BKM..... Polished Buckram (DGA)
Pol C .... Political Code [*A publication*] (DLA)
POLCAP....... Petroleum, Oils, and Lubricants Capabilities (MCD)
POLCATS...... Pollution Characterization by Absorption on Spectroscopy (SSD)
POLCOD....... Police Code [*INTERPOL*]
Pol Code..... Political Code [*A publication*] (DLA)
Pol Col .... Police College (AD)
Pol Com ...... Police Commissaire [*Interpol*] [*British*] (AD)
Pol Com ...... Police Commissioner (AD)
pol com....... Political Committee (AD)
Pol Cont ..... Pollock on Contracts [*A publication*] (DLA)
polcrit......... Political Critic (AD)
POLD .... Professional and Occupational Licensing Directory [*A publication*]
POLDAM...... POL [*Petroleum, Oil, and Lubricants*] Installations Damage Report (NATG)
poldamr....... Petroleum, Oil, and Lubrication Installation Damage Report (AD)
POLDER....... Polarization and Directionality of the Earth's Reflectances [*Instrumentation*]
Pol Dig Part... Pollock's Digest of the Laws of Partnership [*A publication*] (DLA)
POLDPS....... Pioneer Off-Line Data-Processing System [*NASA*]
POLE........... Point-of-Last-Environment [*Computer science*] (IBMDP)
POLE........... Prednisolone, Oncovin [*Vicristine*], L-Asparaginase [*Antineoplastic drug regimen*] (DAVI)
POL/ECO...... Political/Economic Section [*Foreign service*]
pol econ...... Political Economy (AD)
polem.......... Polemic (AD)
POLEX .... Polar Experiment
POLEX .... Political Exercise [*International relations game*]
POLEX-NORTH... Polar Experiment in the Northern Hemisphere (MSC)
POLEX-SOUTH... Polar Experiment in the Southern Hemisphere (MSC)
polf............ Parents of Large Families (AD)
POLF.......... Parents of Large Families
Pol Fed....... Police Federation [*London*] (AD)
Pol Fedn Newsl... Police Federation Newsletter [*A publication*] (DLA)
POLFER .... Polizia Ferroviaria [*Railroad Police*] [*Italian*] (AD)
Pol Found.... Police Foundation [*Washington, D.C.*] (AD)
POLGEN....... Problem-Oriented Language Generator [*Computer science*] (BUR)
poli............ Politician (AD)
POLIC .... Petroleum Intersectional Command [*Army*] (AABC)
Police Fedn Newsl... Police Federation Newsletter [*A publication*] (ILCA)
Police J Ct... Police Justice's Court [*A publication*] (ILCA)
Police LQ..... Police Law Quarterly [*A publication*] (ILCA)
POL IND ...... Pollen Index (WDAA)
pol ind .... Pollen Index (AD)
pol in the pen... Politician in the Penitentiary (AD)
polio.......... Poliomyelitis [*Medicine*] (AD)
POLIO......... Poliomyelitis [*Medicine*]
POLIS .... Parliamentary On-Line Information System [*House of Commons Library*] [*Bibliographic database*] [*Information service or system*] [*British*] (IID)
POLIS .... Petroleum Intersectional Service [*Army*]
POLIS .... Political Institutions Simulation [*Game*]
POLISARIO... Popular Front for the Liberation of Saguiet el Hamra and Rio de Oro [*Morocco*]
poli sci ...... Political Science
PolishTel..... Polish Telephones & Microwave Corp. [*Associated Press*] (SAG)
POLIT.......... Political (EY)
polit........... Political (AD)
Polit........... Political (TBD)
Polit........... Politics [*A publication*]
polit........... Politics (WDAA)
POLITBUREAU... Political Bureau [*of USSR*]

POLITBURO... Politicheskoe Byuro [*Political Bureau of USSR*]
Politburo...... Politicheskoe Byuro [*Political Bureau of the Central Committee*] [*Russian*] (AD)
Pol J .... Police Journal [*A publication*] (ILCA)
POLK .... Polk Audio [*NASDAQ symbol*] (TTSB)
POLK .... Polk Audio, Inc. [*Baltimore, MD*] [*NASDAQ symbol*] (NQ)
POLKA .... Periodical On-Line Keyword Access [*Computer science*] (PDAA)
PolkAu .... Polk Audio, Inc. [*Associated Press*] (SAG)
PolkAud ...... Polk Audio [*Associated Press*] (SAG)
POLK of A.... Polka Lovers Klub of America (EA)
Poll............ Pollack's Ohio Unreported Judicial Decisions Prior to 1823 [*A publication*] (ILCA)
POLL.......... Pollex [*An Inch*] [*Pharmacy*]
Poll............. Pollexfen's English King's Bench Reports [*1669-85*] [*A publication*] (ILCA)
poll .... Pollution (AD)
POLL........... Public Opinion Location Library [*The Roper Center for Public Opinion Research*] [*Information service or system*] (CRD)
POL/LAB ..... Political and Labor Section [*Foreign service*]
Pol Law of Nat... Polson's Law of Nations [*1848*] [*A publication*] (DLA)
Poll CC Pr ... Pollock's Practice of the County Courts [*A publication*] (ILCA)
Poll Contr Guide... Pollution Control Guide [*A publication*] (DLA)
Pollex .... Pollexfen's English King's Bench Reports [*1669-85*] [*A publication*] (ILCA)
Pollexf .... Pollexfen's English King's Bench Reports [*1669-85*] [*A publication*] (ILCA)
Pollexfen .... Pollexfen's English King's Bench Reports [*1669-85*] [*A publication*] (ILCA)
Pollock & Maitl... Pollock and Maitland's History of English Common Law [*A publication*] (DLA)
PolloTrp...... Pollo Tropical [*Commercial firm Associated Press*] (SAG)
Poll Prod ..... Pollock on the Production of Documents [*A publication*] (DLA)
Pol LQ .... Police Law Quarterly [*A publication*] (DLA)
POLLS .... Parliamentary On-Line Library Study [*Atomic Energy Authority*] [*British*]
POLLUT .... Pollution
Pollution Cont Guide (CCH)... Pollution Control Guide (Commerce Clearing House) [*A publication*] (DLA)
Pol Mil Dig... Poland's Digest of the Military Laws of the United States [*A publication*] (DLA)
poln--.......... Central and Southern Line Islands [*MARC geographic area code Library of Congress*] (LCCP)
poln .... polnisch [*Polish*] [*German*] (AD)
POLO .... Pacific Command Operations Liaison Office [*Army*] (AABC)
POLO .... Plant and Office Layout (MCD)
POLO .... Polar Orbiting Lunar Observatory [*Satellite*]
POLO .... Problem-Oriented Language Organizer [*Computer science*] (PDAA)
POLO .... Procurement Online Ordering System (MCD)
Polon .... Polonais [*Polish*] [*French*] (AD)
POLOPS...... Polynomial Operations [*Air Force*]
Pol Part....... Pollock's Digest of the Laws of Partnership [*A publication*] (DLA)
Pol Prod Doc... Pollock on the Power of Courts to Compel the Production of Documents [*A publication*] (DLA)
POLPS .... Polymorphonuclear Leukocytes [*Hematology*] (DAVI)
POLR .... Polar Express Corp. [*NASDAQ symbol*] (SAG)
POLREG ...... Polynomial Regression (IAA)
POLREP ...... Pollution Report (GNE)
Pol Res Q .... Political Research Quarterly [*A publication*] (BRI)
PolrEx......... Polar Express Corp. [*Associated Press*] (SAG)
PolRs........... Pollution Research and Control Corp. [*Associated Press*] (SAG)
POLRW .... Polar Express Wrrt'B' [*NASDAQ symbol*] (TTSB)
Pol Rze Lud... Polaska Rzeczpospolita Ludowa [*Polish People's Republic*] (AD)
pols .... Political Prisoners (AD)
pols .... Politicians (AD)
PolSc........... Political Science (DD)
pol sci .... Political Science (AD)
Pol Sci Quar... Political Science Quarterly [*A publication*] (ILCA)
POLSG........ Polishing
Pols Nat ...... Polson's Law of Nations [*1848*] [*A publication*] (DLA)
POLSTRADA... Polizia Stradale [*Highway Police*] [*Italian*] (AD)
Pol Stud J ... Policy Studies Journal [*A publication*] (BRI)
PolTel......... Polish Telephones & Microwave Corp. [*Associated Press*] (SAG)
POLTHN ...... Polyethylene [*Organic chemistry*]
POLTL......... Political (AFM)
POLTN .... Pollution
Pol Tr Mar... Poland's Law of Trade Marks [*A publication*] (DLA)
POLUT .... Pollution
PolutRs........ Pollution Research and Control Corp. [*Associated Press*] (SAG)
POLWAR...... Political Warfare
polwar .... Political Warfare (AD)
POLWARADDIR... Political Warfare Advisory Directorate
POLX .... Polydex Pharmaceuticals Ltd. [*NASDAQ symbol*] (NQ)
POLXF .... Polydex Pharmaceuticals [*NASDAQ symbol*] (TTSB)
POLY .... Planet Polymer Technologies [*NASDAQ symbol*] (TTSB)
POLY .... Planet Polymer Technologies, Inc. [*NASDAQ symbol*] (SAG)
Pol'y .... Policy (DLA)
poly .... Polydipsia [*Medicine*] (DAVI)
POLY .... Polyester
POLY .... Polyethylene (DEN)
poly .... Polyethylene (AD)
POLY .... Polygamy [*FBI standardized term*]
poly .... Polymer (AD)
POLY .... Polymorphonuclear Leukocyte [*Hematology*]
poly J .... Polymorphonuclear Neutrophil Granulocyte [*Hematology*] (DAVI)
Poly .... Polynesia (AD)

poly .... Polyphagia [*Medicine*] (DAVI)
poly .... Polytechnic (AD)
POLY .... Polytechnic
poly .... Polyuria [*Medicine*] (DAVI)
poly .... Polyvinyl (AD)
PolyA .... Polyadenylated
poly(A)........ Polyadenylic Acid [*Biochemistry*] (MAE)
Polyb .... Polybius [*Second century BC*] [*Classical studies*] (OCD)
Pol YB Int'l L... Polish Yearbook of International Law [*Warsaw*] [*A publication*] (DLA)
Pol Yb of Internat L... Polish Yearbook of International Law [*Warsaw*] [*A publication*] (DLA)
poly bot...... Polyethylene Bottle (AD)
POLYC .... Polychromasia [*Hematology*] (DAVI)
poly-C......... Polycytidylic Acid [*Biochemistry*] (DMAA)
Polycom ...... Polycom, Inc. [*Associated Press*] (SAG)
Polydex....... Polydex Pharmaceuticals Ltd. [*Associated Press*] (SAG)
POLYDOC .... Polytechnical Documentation (NITA)
POLYDOP .... Polystation Doppler Tracking System (MCD)
POLYEST .... Polyester
polyg .... Polygraph (AD)
poly-G......... Polyguanylic Acid [*Biochemistry*] (DMAA)
POLYGON .... Oceanographic Experiment in the North-East Atlantic [*Former USSR*] [*Marine science*] (OSRA)
PolyGp........ Polymer Group, Inc. [*Associated Press*] (SAG)
Polygr......... PolyGram NV [*Associated Press*] (SAG)
poly-I......... Polyinosinic Acid [*Biochemistry*] (DMAA)
poly I:C....... Polyinosinic Polycytidylic Acid (BARN)
Polym .... Polymusic [*Record label*]
POLYMAT .... Polymer Materials [*Deutsches Kunststoff-Institut*] [*Germany Information service or system*] (CRD)
Polymed ...... PolyMedica Industries, Inc. [*Associated Press*] (SAG)
Polym Lett Ed... Polymer Letters Edition of the Journal of Polymer Science (MEC)
POLYMODE... Polygon-MODE [*Mid-Ocean Dynamics Experiment*] [*Soviet-US cooperative undersea weather exploration*]
polymorph ... Polymorphonuclear [*Leukocyte*] [*Hematology*] (DAVI)
polymorph ... Polymorphous (AD)
POLYN .... Polynesia
Polyn .... Polynesia (VRA)
POLYOX....... Poly(ethylene Oxide) [*Trademark*]
Polyph .... Polyphase Instrument Corp. [*Associated Press*] (SAG)
PolyRs........ Polymer Research Corp. of America [*Associated Press*] (SAG)
poly sci....... Political Science (AD)
polysex........ Polysexual (AD)
polys (segs)... Polymorphonuclear Segmented Neutrophils [*Hematology*] (DAVI)
poly-T......... Polythymidylic Acid [*Biochemistry*] (DMAA)
polytech....... Polytechnical (BARN)
POLYTRAN... Polytranslation Analysis and Programming (IEEE)
Poly U .... Polytechnic University (GAGS)
poly(U) .... Polyuridylic Acid [*Biochemistry*] (MAE)
Polyvisn...... Polyvision Corp. [*Associated Press*] (SAG)
Polyvsn....... Polyvision Corp. [*Associated Press*] (SAG)
polywater ... Polymerized Water (AD)
POLY-WRI ... Polytechnic Institute of New York Weber Research Institute [*Farmingdale, NY*]
POM............ Aurelio y Gustavo Pompa Estrella [*Mexico*] [*FAA designator*] (FAAC)
POM............ Operation: Peace of Mind [*Later, Runaway Hotline*] [*An association*] (EA)
POM............ Pain on Motion (STED)
POM............ Pallet-Only Mode [*NASA*] (NASA)
POM............ Particulate Organic Matter [*Environmental chemistry*]
POM............ Pennsylvania-Ohio-Maryland League [*Old baseball league*]
POM............ Peritronics Med [*Vancouver Stock Exchange symbol*]
POM............ Personal Opinion Matrix [*Test*] (TES)
POM............ Personal Opinion Message [*Western Union*] (IIA)
POM............ Personnel, Operations, Maintenance (MCD)
POM............ Phase of the Moon [*Astronomy*] (NHD)
POM............ Phenomenon of Man [*Project*] (EA)
POM............ Polarizing Optical Microscopy
POM............ Police Officer, Male
POM............ Polycyclic Organic Matter
pom............ Polycyclic Organic Matter (AD)
POM............ Polyformaldehyde (EDCT)
POM............ Polymerized and Oxidized Material [*Food science*]
POM:........... Polynuclear Organic Matter (FFDE)
POM............ Polyoxometalate [*Organic chemistry*]
POM............ Poly(oxymethylene) [*Organic chemistry*]
pom............ Polyoxymethylene (AD)
pom............ Pomeranian (AD)
POM............ Pomeranian Dog (DSUE)
pom............ Pomeridiano [*Afternoon*] [*Italian*] (AD)
Pom............ Pommy [*British*] (ODBW)
pom............ Pomological (AD)
POM............ Pomona [*California*] [*Seismograph station code, US Geological Survey Closed*] (SEIS)
POM............ Pomona, CA [*Location identifier FAA*] (FAAL)
pom............ Pom-Pom (AD)
Pom............ Pompon [*Horticulture*]
POM............ Pool Operational Module [*Telecommunications*] (TEL)
POM............ Port Moresby [*Papua New Guinea*] [*Airport symbol*] (OAG)
PoM............ Port of Miami (AD)
POM............ Position Modulator (NRCH)
POM............ Potential Officer Material [*British military*] (DMA)
POM............ Potomac Electric Power Co. [*NYSE symbol*] (SPSG)
POM............ Potomac Electric Pwr [*NYSE symbol*] (TTSB)

POM.......... Preobservational Mean [*Statistics*]
pom.......... Preparation for Overseas Movement (AD)
POM.......... Preparation for Overseas Movement [*Military*]
POM.......... Prescription Only Medicine [*British*]
POM.......... Printer Output Microfilm
POM.......... Print on Metal (DGA)
POM.......... Printout Microfilm (NITA)
POM.......... Priority of Movements [*Military British*]
POM.......... Prior to Overseas Movement [*DoD*]
POM.......... Professional or Managerial (WDMC)
POM.......... Professionals, Owners, and Managers [*A. C. Nielsen Co.*] [*Demographic category*] (NTCM)
POM.......... Program Objectives Memorandum [*Military*]
POM.......... Program Operation Mode
POM.......... Project Office Memo
POM.......... Project Officers Meeting
POM.......... Public Order Member (NUMA)
POMA .... Petty Officer Medical Assistant [*British military*] (DMA)
POMA .... Petty Officer's Military Academy [*Navy*]
POMA .... Polyoctyl Methacrylate [*Organic chemistry*]
POMAR...... Position Operational, Meteorological Aircraft Report
POMAR...... Preventive Operational Maintenance and Repair [*Military*] (NVT)
POMAS...... Procurement Office for Military Automotive Supplies
pomato ...... Potato-Tomato (AD)
POMBA...... Parents of Multiple Births Associations of Canada
POM/BES...... Program Objective Memorandum/Budget Estimate Submission (MCD)
POMC...... Parents of Murdered Children (EA)
POMC .... Pro-Opiomelanocortin [*Endocrinology*]
Pom Code Rem... Pomeroy on Code Remedies [*A publication*] (DLA)
Pom Const Law... Pomeroy's Constitutional Law of the United States [*A publication*] (DLA)
Pom Contr ... Pomeroy on Contracts [*A publication*] (DLA)
pomcus...... Prepositioned Material Configured in Unit Sets (AD)
POMCUS..... Prepositioning of Materiel Configured to Unit Sets [*Army*] (AABC)
POMD...... Program Operation Mode (IAA)
pome--...... Melanesia [*MARC geographic area code Library of Congress*] (LCCP)
POME...... Principal Ordnance Mechanical Engineer [*British military*] (DMA)
POME.......... Prisoner of Mother England [*Nineteenth-century convict in penal colony of Australia, now a nickname for any Australian*]
POME...... Problems-Objectives-Methods-Evaluation [*Planning method*]
POMEM...... Petty Officer Marine Engineering Mechanic [*British military*] (DMA)
Pom Eq Jur... Pomeroy's Equity Jurisprudence [*A publication*] (DLA)
Pom Eq Juris... Pomeroy's Equity Jurisprudence [*A publication*] (DLA)
POMERID...... Pomeridianus [*In the Afternoon*] [*Pharmacy*]
Pomeroy...... Pomeroy Computer Resources, Inc. [*Associated Press*] (SAG)
Pomeroy...... Pomeroy's Reports [*73-128 California*] [*A publication*] (DLA)
POMF...... Polaris Missile Facility
POMFLANT... Polaris Missile Facility, Atlantic (AD)
POMFLANT... Polaris Missile Facility, Atlantic Fleet
POMFPAC .... Polaris Missile Facility, Pacific Fleet
POMGEN...... Program Objective Memorandum Generator [*Military*]
POMH.......... National Association of Post Office Mail Handlers, Watchmen, Messengers, and Group Leaders [*Later, NPOMHWMGL*]
POMI .... Photochromic Microimage (IAA)
POMI .... Preliminary Operating and Maintenance Instructions [*Aerospace*] (AAG)
POMINS...... Portable Mine Neutralization System (MCD)
POMM...... Preliminary Operating and Maintenance Manual [*Military*] (AABC)
Pom Mun Law... Pomeroy on Municipal Law [*A publication*] (DLA)
POMO...... Partially Occupied Molecular Orbitals [*Physical chemistry*]
POMO...... Personnel Objectives Monitoring Operation
POMO.......... Postmodern
POMO.......... Production-Oriented Maintenance Organization (MCD)
POMO.......... Program Operations and Management Office [*Environmental Protection Agency*] (GFGA)
POMOL ...... POMCUS [*Prepositioning of Materiel Configured to Unit Sets*] Objective Levels [*Military*]
pomol.......... Pomologic (AD)
POMOL ...... Pomology
POMOLA...... Poor Man's Optical Landing System
Pomp.......... Epistula ad Pompeium [*of Dionysius Halicarnassensis*] [*Classical studies*] (OCD)
Pomp.......... Pompeius [*of Plutarch*] [*Classical studies*] (OCD)
Pomp.......... Pompey (AD)
POMP .... Pomposo [*Grandly*] [*Music*] (ROG)
POMP .... Pre Coded Originating Mail Processor (PDAA)
POMP .... Prednisone, Oncovin [*Vincristine*], Methotrexate, Purinethol [*Mercaptopurine*] [*Antineoplastic drug regimen*]
POMP .... Principal Outer Membrane Protein
POMP .... Purinethol, Oncovin, Methotrexate, Prednisone [*Medicine*] (MEDA)
POMPAC...... Polaris Missile Facility, Pacific (AD)
POMPr...... Potomac Elec Pwr $2.44 Cv Pfd [*NYSE symbol*] (TTSB)
POMPrA...... Potomac El Pwr$3.89'91 Pfd [*NYSE symbol*] (TTSB)
POMPrH...... Potomac Elec Pwr $3.37cm'87 Pfd [*NYSE symbol*] (TTSB)
POMR...... Problem-Oriented Medical Record
Pom Rem .... Pomeroy on Civil Remedies [*A publication*] (DLA)
Pom Rem & Rem Rights... Pomeroy on Civil Remedies and Remedial Rights [*A publication*] (DLA)
POMR/PST... Partido Obrero Marxista Revolucionario/Partido Socialista de los Trabajadores [*Marxist Revolutionary Workers' Party/Socialist Workers' Party*] [*Peru*] [*Political party*] (PPW)
POMS .... Panel on Operational Meteorological Satellites
POMS .... Persistent Object Management System (NITA)
POMS .... Plain Old Mail Service (CIST)

POMS .... Polar Operational Meteorological Satellite (USDC)
POMS .... Poly-Ortho-methylstyrene [*Organic chemistry*]
POMS .... Process Operating Management System [*Manufacturing*]
POMS .... Production and Operations Management Society (EA)
POMS .... Professional Office Management System (CIST)
POMS .... Profile of Mood States [*A questionnaire*]
POMS .... Program Operations Manual System [*Social Security Administration*]
POMSA ...... Post Office Management Staffs Association [*A union*] [*British*] (DCTA)
POMS-BI...... Profile of Mood States-Bipolar Form
POMSEE ..... Performance, Operating and Maintenance Standards for Electronic Equipment (NG)
pomsee...... Preparation, Operation, Maintenance, Shipboard Electronics Equipment (AD)
POMSIP ...... Post Office Management and Service Improvement Program [*Obsolete*]
Pom Spec Perf... Pomeroy on Specific Performance of Contracts [*A publication*] (DLA)
POMT...... Patriot Organizational Maintenance Trainer [*Army*]
POMT...... Planning and Operations Management Team (MCD)
POMV...... National Federation Post Office Motor Vehicle Employees [*Later, APWU*] (EA)
POMV...... Privately Owned Motor Vehicle (NATG)
PON...... Paraoxonase [*An enzyme*]
PON...... Particulate Organic Nitrogen
PON...... Phosphorotioate Oligonucleotide [*Biochemistry*]
PON...... Ponce [*Puerto Rico*] [*Seismograph station code, US Geological Survey*] (SEIS)
PON...... Ponder Oils Ltd. [*Toronto Stock Exchange symbol*]
Pon...... Pontius [*Authority cited in pre-1607 legal work*] (DSA)
PON...... Pontoon (AAG)
pon...... Pontoon (AD)
PON...... Portuguese Navy [*ICAO designator*] (FAAC)
PON...... Position (IAA)
PON...... Pride of Newark [*Feigenspan beer*]
PON...... Program Opportunity Notice [*Energy Research and Development Administration*]
PON...... Program Opportunity Notification (AD)
pona ...... Paraffin, Olefin, Naphthene, Aromatic (AD)
PONA...... Paraffins, Olefins, Naphthenes, Aromatics
PONA...... Provisions for Ozone Nonattainment Areas [*Environmental science*] (COE)
Pon Ble....... Poncius Blegerii [*Flourished, 14th century*] [*Authority cited in pre-1607 legal work*] (DSA)
PONBRG...... Pontoon Bridge (MUGU)
PonBrg.......... Pontoon Bridge (AD)
Poncebk....... Poncebank [*Associated Press*] (SAG)
Ponce Sch Med... Ponce School of Medicine (GAGS)
PONCHO ..... Patrons of Northwest Civic Cultural and Charitable Organizations
POND...... Parents of Near Drownings [*An association*] (EA)
POND...... Pondere [*By Weight*] [*Latin*]
pond...... Pondere [*By Weigh*] [*Latin*] (AD)
POND...... Ponderosus [*Heavy*] [*Pharmacy*]
Ponder.......... Ponder Industries, Inc. [*Associated Press*] (SAG)
Pondo...... Pondoland (AD)
PONG...... Poet of the New Generation [*Term used to describe poets writing for entertainment value*] (ECON)
PONI...... Postoperative Narcotic Infusion (STED)
ponl--........... New Caledonia [*MARC geographic area code Library of Congress*] (LCCP)
ponn--........... New Hebrides [*MARC geographic area code Library of Congress*] (LCCP)
PONN...... Positive-on-Negative (IAA)
p-on-n........... Positive on Negative (AD)
PONS...... Platt's Oilgram News Service
PONS...... Profile of Nonverbal Sensitivity [*Psychology*]
pons.......... Profile of Nonverbal Sensitivity (AD)
PONSE....... Personnel of the Naval Shore Establishment [*Report*] (NG)
PONSI.......... Program of Noncollegiate Sponsored Instruction (OICC)
Pont........... Epistulae ex Ponto [*of Ovid*] [*Classical studies*] (OCD)
Pont........... Pontevedra (AD)
PONT...... Pontiac [*Automotive engineering*]
PONT...... Pontifex [*Bishop*] [*Latin*] (WGA)
Pont........... Pontoon (WGA)
PONTA...... Popular New Titles from Abroad [*Book acquisition program for libraries*]
pont b.......... Pontoon Bridge (AD)
Ponti........... Pontiac (AD)
Pont Max.... Pontifex Maximus [*Supreme Pontiff*] [*Latin*] (AD)
ponu--........... Nauru [*MARC geographic area code Library of Congress*] (LCCP)
PONUC...... Post Office National Users' Council [*British*]
PONVER...... Project on National Vocational Education Resources (EDAC)
PONYr...... Pennsylvania, Ohio, New York Baseball League (IIA)
PONY...... Pennsylvania-Ontario-New York League [*Old baseball league*]
PONY........ Pride of the Navy Yard (DNAB)
PONY...... Prostitutes of New York
PONY...... Protect Our Nation's Youth [*Baseball league*] [*Name usually written Pony*]
PONY...... Purpose of Neighborhood Youth [*Foundation*]
PONYA...... Port of New York Authority [*Later, PANYNJ*]
POO...... Panel on Oceanography
POO .... Parents Opposed to Opting Out [*An association*] (AIE)
POO .... Payload Operations Office [*NASA*]
POO .... Platform of Opportunity Program [*National Oceanic and Atmospheric Administration*] (MSC)

POO .... Pocos De Caldas [*Brazil*] [*Airport symbol*] (OAG)
Poo .... Poole (AD)
POO .... Poona [*India*] [*Seismograph station code, US Geological Survey*] (SEIS)
POO .... Port Operations Officer (DS)
POO .... Post Office Order
POO .... Priority Operational Objective [*Military*]
POO .... Program Operations Officer [*Social Security Administration*]
POOD .... Permanent Officer of the Day [*or Deck*] [*Navy*]
pood .... Poodle Dog (AD)
POOD .... Provisioning Order Obligating Document
POOEL .... Petty Officer Ordnance Electrician [*British military*] (DMA)
poof .... Peripheral On-Line-Oriented Function [*Computer science*] (AD)
POOFF .... Preservation of Our Femininity and Finances [*Women's group opposing below-the-knee fashions introduced in 1970*]
POOFF .... Professional Oglers of Female Figures [*Men's group opposing below-the-knee fashions introduced in 1970*]
POOH .... Postoperative Open-Heart [*Surgery*] (STED)
POOL .... SCP Pool [*NASDAQ symbol*] (TTSB)
POOL .... SCP Pool Corp. [*NASDAQ symbol*] (SAG)
PoolEn .... Pool Energy Services Co. [*Associated Press*] (SAG)
poop .... Nincompoop (AD)
POOP .... Process Oriented Observation Program [*NORPAX*] (MSC)
POOR .... Poor Clot [*Medicine*] (STED)
POOR .... Prevention of Over-Radiation [*Military*]
Poore Const... Poore's Federal and State Constitution [*A publication*] (DLA)
Poor L & Local Gov't... Poor Law and Local Government Magazine [*A publication*] (DLA)
POOS .... Priority Order Output System [*Japan*] (DIT)
poosslq....... Person of Opposite Sex Sharing Living Quarters (AD)
POOW .... Petty Officer of the Watch [*Navy*] (NVT)
POoW .... Petty Officer on Watch [*Military*] (AD)
POP .... Pacific Ocean Perch
POP .... Package for Online Programming [*Computer science*] (CDE)
POP .... Palletizing Optimization Potential (AD)
POP .... Panoramic Office Planning
POP .... Paperless Ordering Placement [*System*] (DOMA)
POP .... Parallel Output Platform
POP .... Parents of Punkers (EA)
POP .... Paroxypropione [*or Paraoxypropiophenone*] [*Endocrinology*]
POP .... Particle-Oriented Paper (IAA)
POP .... Particulate Organic Phosphorus
POP .... Partido de Orientacion Popular [*Popular Orientation Party*] [*El Salvador*] [*Political party*] (PPW)
POP .... Parti Ouvrier et Paysan du Congo [*Congolese Workers' and Peasants' Party*] [*Zaire*] [*Political party*]
POP .... Parti Ouvrier Progressiste [*Canada*]
POP .... Patrexes of the Panopticon (EA)
POP .... Payload Optimized Program [*NASA*] (KSC)
POP .... Pay One Price
POP .... Peak Overpressure [*Nuclear energy*] (NRCH)
POP .... Perceived Outcome Potential (MHDI)
POP .... Performance-Oriented Packaging [*for hazardous materials*]
POP .... Period of Performance (MCD)
POP .... Perpendicular Ocean Platform [*Oceanography*]
pop .... Perpendicular Ocean Platform (AD)
POP .... Perpendicular-to-Orbit Plane [*Aerospace*] (KSC)
pop .... Persistent Occipito-Posterior (AD)
POP .... Persistent Occipit Posterior [*A fetal position*] [*Obstetrics*]
POP .... Persistent Organic Pollutant [*Environmental science*]
POP .... Pharmacists in Ophthalmic Practice [*Later, PIOP*] (EA)
POP .... Picture-outside-Picture [*Television technology*] (PS)
POP .... Pipeline Outfit, Petroleum (MCD)
POP .... Pituitary Opioid Peptide [*Medicine*] (DMAA)
POP .... Plasma Oncotic Pressure [*Medicine*] (MAE)
POP .... Plasma Osmotic Pressure [*Medicine*]
pop .... Plasma Osmotic Pressure (AD)
pop .... Plaster of Paris (AD)
POP .... Plaster of Paris
POP .... Pneumatic Operated Piston (ECII)
POP .... Point of Presence [*Telecommunications*] (DOM)
PoP .... Point of Presence [*Telecommunications*] (PCM)
PoP .... Point of Purchase [*Advertising*]
POP .... Polar Orbiting Platform (SSD)
POP .... Pollution and Overpopulation
POP .... Polymyositis Ossificans Progressiva [*Medicine*] (DMAA)
POP .... Polyolefin Plastomer [*Organic chemistry*]
POP .... Poly Phenylene Oxide (EDCT)
POP .... Pope & Talbot [*NYSE symbol*] (TTSB)
POP .... Pope & Talbot, Inc. [*NYSE symbol*] (SPSG)
Pop .... Popham's English King's Bench Reports [*1592-1627*] [*A publication*] (DLA)
POP .... Popliteal [*Artery*] [*Anatomy*] (AAMN)
POP .... Popondetta [*Papua New Guinea*] [*Seismograph station code, US Geological Survey Closed*] (SEIS)
Pop .... Poppa (AD)
pop .... Poppet (AD)
POP .... Popping [*Mining engineering*]
POP .... Popular
pop .... Popular (AD)
Pop .... Populare [*Record label*] [*Romania*]
POP .... Population (AAG)
pop .... Population (AD)
Pop .... Population (TBD)
POP .... Population Division [*Bureau of the Census*] (OICC)

POP .... Portuguese Overseas Province (AD)
POP .... Posterior Odds Processing [*Weather forecasting*] [*National Science Foundation*]
POP .... Post Office Plan
POP .... Post Office Preferred (DCTA)
POP .... Post Office Protocol [*Telecommunications*]
POP .... Postoperative [*Medicine*]
p-op .... Post-Operative (AD)
POP .... Power On/Off Protection
POP .... Practical Ordered Program (OA)
POP .... Preburner Oxidizer Pump (MCD)
POP .... Preflight Operations Procedure (MCD)
POP .... Prelaunch Operations Plan [*NASA*] (NASA)
POP .... Premanagement Orientation Program [*LIMRA*]
POP .... Pressurizer Overpressure Protection System [*Nuclear energy*] (IEEE)
POP .... Primary Operation
pop .... Printer of Plates [*MARC relator code*] [*Library of Congress*] (LCCP)
POP .... Printing-Out Paper
POP .... Profit Option Plan [*Retailing*]
POP .... Programmed Operators and Primitives [*Computer science*]
POP .... Program Obligation Plan (KSC)
POP .... Program Operating Plan
POP .... Progressive Overload Program [*Weight training*]
POP .... Project Objective Plan (NG)
POP .... Project Optimization Procedure (IAA)
POP .... Prompt Ordering Plan
POP .... Proof-Of Principle [*Test*]
POP .... Proof of Purchase
POP .... Public Offering Price (AD)
POP .... Puerto Plata [*Dominican Republic*] [*Airport symbol*] (OAG)
POP .... Pump Optimizing Program
POP .... Purchase Outside Production (SAA)
POP3 .... Post Office Protocol 3 [*Computer science*]
POPA .... Patent Office Professional Association (EA)
POPA .... Payload Ordnance Processing Area (NASA)
POPA .... Pet Owners' Protective Association
Popa .... Popayan, Colombia (AD)
POPA .... Prevention of Oil Pollution Act [*1971*]
POPA .... Property Owners' Protection Association
pop advertising... Point-of-Purchase Advertising (AD)
POPAE .... Protons on Protons and Electrons [*Physics*]
POPAI .... Point-of-Purchase Advertising Institute [*Fort Lee, NJ*] (EA)
POPAL .... Pre-Operational Peculiar Age List
POP & B ...... Proposed Operating Program and Budget [*Army*]
pop art........ Popular Art (AD)
popb .... Proposed Operating Plan and Budget (AD)
POPC .... Pamitoyl-Oleoylphosphatidylcholine [*Biochemistry*]
popc-- .... Pitcairn [*MARC geographic area code Library of Congress*] (LCCP)
POP-CON .... Populist Conservative [*Wing of the Republican Party represented by Congressmen Gingrich, Kemp, and Lott*]
POPCRU ..... Police and Prison Civil Rights Union [*Founded in 1989*] [*South Africa*] (ECON)
POPCX .... PIMCO: Opportunity Cl.C [*Mutual fund ticker symbol*] (SG)
POPD .... Power-Operated
POPDA........ Polyoxypropylenediamine [*Organic chemistry*]
POPE .... Parents for Orthodoxy in Parochial Education [*Group opposing sex education in schools*]
POPE .... Product Oriented Procedures Evaluation (AD)
Pope Cust.... Pope on Customs and Excise [*11th ed.*] [*1828*] [*A publication*] (DLA)
POP ED .... Popular Edition [*Publishing*]
Pope Lun.... Pope on Lunacy [*A publication*] (DLA)
PopeRes...... Pope Resources Ltd. [*Associated Press*] (SAG)
PopeTal...... Pope & Talbot, Inc. [*Associated Press*] (SAG)
popex......... Population Explosion (AD)
POPEZ .... Pope Resources L.P. [*NASDAQ symbol*] (TTSB)
POPEZ .... Pope Resources Ltd. [*NASDAQ symbol*] (SPSG)
popf .... Prepared-on-Premises Flavor (AD)
POPGUN ..... Policy and Procedure Governing the Use of Nicknames [*Army*] (AABC)
Poph .... Popham's English King's Bench Reports [*1592-1627*] [*A publication*] (DLA)
Poph (2) ..... Cases at the End of Popham's Reports [*A publication*] (DLA)
Popham....... Popham's English King's Bench Reports [*79 English Reprint*] [*1592-1626*] [*A publication*] (DLA)
Poph Insol ... Popham's Insolvency Act of Canada [*A publication*] (DLA)
POPI .... Post Office Position Indicator [*A form of long-range position indicator*] [*British*]
popi .... Post Office Position Indicator [*British*] (AD)
POPINFORM... Population Information Network [*UNESCO*]
POPINS....... Population Information System [*UNESCO*]
POPLAB ...... International Program of Laboratories for Population Statistics
POPLINE...... Population Information On-Line [*Bibliographic database*] (IID)
POPLINE...... Population Online (NITA)
POPLIT .... Popliteal [*Anatomy*]
poplit .... Popliteal (AD)
POPMIP ...... Portable Ocean Platform Motion Instrumentation Package [*Marine science*] (MSC)
Pop Mo L Tr... Popular Monthly Law Tracts [*1877-78*] [*A publication*] (DLA)
pop music ... Popular Music (AD)
POPMV .... Poplar Mosaic Virus [*Plant pathology*]
Popn .... Population
POPO .... Poured-On, Passed-Over [*Bowdlerized version*]
POPO .... Push-On, Pull-Off [*Computer science*]
POPP .... Prison Officer in a Private Prison (WDAA)
pop psych.... Popular Psychiatry (AD)

popr	Pilot Overhaul Provisioning Review (AD)
POPR	Pilot Overhaul Provisioning Review
POPR	Prototype Organic Power Reactor [*Nuclear energy*]
POPS	Free-Fall Pop-Up Ocean Bottom Seismometer [*Marine science*] (MSC)
POPS	National Beverage Corp. [*NASDAQ symbol*] (SAG)
POPS	Pantograph Optical Projection System (IEEE)
POPS	Parachute Opening Proximity Sensor (MCD)
POPS	Partners of Prisoners & Families Support Group (WDAA)
POPS	People Opposed to Pornography in Schools [*Group opposing sex education in schools*]
POPS	Performance-Oriented Packing Standard
POPS	Platt's Oilgram Price Service
pops--	Polynesia [*MARC geographic area code Library of Congress*] (LCCP)
pops.	Popular Concerts (AD)
POPS	Positioning Orbital Propulsion System (MCD)
POPS	Preserve Our Presidential Sites (EA)
POPS	Pressurizer Overpressure Protection System [*Nuclear energy*] (NRCH)
POPS	Process Operating System [*Toshiba Corp.*] [*Japan*]
POPS	Procurers of Painted-Label Sodas [*Defunct*] (EA)
POPS	Profiles of Problem Solving [*Test*] (TMMY)
POPS	Program for Operator Scheduling [*Bell System computer program*]
POPS	Project Operations [*Navy*] (NVT)
POPS	Protect Our Pelican Society [*Later, PMBS*] (EA)
POPS	Pyrotechnic Optical Plume Simulator (MCD)
Pop Sci	Popular Science [*A publication*] (AD)
POP SCI MO...	Popular Science Monthly [*A publication*] (ROG)
POPSE	Project Office for Physical Security Equipment [*Army*] (RDA)
POPSER	Polaris Operational Performance Surveillance Engineering Report [*Missiles*]
POPSI	Postulate-Based Permuted Subject Indexing (PDAA)
POPSI	Precipitation and Off-Path Scattered Interference [*Report*] [*FCC*]
POPSIPT	Project Operations in Port [*Navy*] (NVT)
POPT	Petty Officer Physical Trainer [*British military*] (DMA)
POPT	Pretesting Orientation on the Purpose of Testing [*US Employment Service*] [*Department of Labor*]
POPU	Push Over Pull Up (NASA)
Populuxe	Popular Luxury [*Coined by Thomas Hine, design critic for the Philadelphia Inquirer, to describe the period from the mid-1950's to the mid-1960's*]
POPUS	Post Office Processing Utility Subsystem [*Telecommunications*] (TEL)
poq	Periodic Order Quantity (AD)
POQ	Period Order Quantity (PDAA)
POQ	Production Offset Quantity [*Military*]
POQ	Provided Otherwise Qualified [*Military*] (AABC)
POQ	Public Opinion Quarterly [*A publication*] (AD)
POQ	Push Off Quickly [*i.e., Be quick about it*] [*British*]
POQL	Probability Outgoing Quality Limit (PDAA)
POQU	Procedure of Questionable Usefulness [*Medicine*] (CPH)
POR	Pacific Ocean Region
POR	Parking Orbit Rendezvous [*NASA*] (MCD)
POR	Partido Obrero Revolucionario [*Revolutionary Workers Party*] [*Peru*] [*Political party*]
POR	Partido Obrero Revolucionario [*Revolutionary Workers Party*] [*Argentina Political party*]
POR	Partido Obrero Revolucionario [*Revolutionary Workers Party*] [*Bolivia*] [*Political party*] (PPW)
POR	Patent Office Reports [*A publication*] (DLA)
POR	Patrol Operations Report
POR	Payable on Receipt [*Business term*]
p-o-r	Pay-on-Receipt
POR	Pay on Return [*Business term*]
POR	Peak Overshoot Ratio (IAA)
POR	Periodic Operation Report
POR	Personnel Occurrence Report [*RAF*] [*British*]
POR	Physician of Record (DAVI)
POR	Pilot Opinion Rating
POR	Plutonium Organic Recycle [*Nuclear energy*] (NRCH)
POR	Point of Resolution (NAKS)
POR	Pola Resources Ltd. [*Vancouver Stock Exchange symbol*]
POR	Pori [*Finland*] [*Airport symbol*] (OAG)
Por	Porifera (AD)
Por	Porogi [*Waterfall*] [*Russian*] (AD)
por	Porosity (AD)
por	Portage (BARN)
POR	Portec, Inc. [*NYSE symbol*] (SPSG)
POR	Portion
POR	Portland [*Maine*] [*Seismograph station code, US Geological Survey Closed*] (SEIS)
Por	Portland (AD)
POR	Port of Refuge [*Shipping*]
POR	Portrait
Por	Portugal (AD)
Por	Portuguese (AD)
por	Portuguese [*MARC language code Library of Congress*] (LCCP)
POR	Portuguese
POR	Position of Responsibility (ADA)
POR	Postocclusive Oscillatory Response (DB)
POR	Post Office Return
POR	Post Office Rifles [*Military British*] (ROG)
POR	Preparation of Overseas Replacement [*Military*] (RDA)
POR	Preparation of Replacements for Oversea Movement [*MTMC*] (TAG)
POR	Press on Regardless [*Automotive marathon*]
POR	Price on Request
POR	Problem-Oriented Records [*Medicine*]
POR	Problem-Oriented Routine (IEEE)
POR	Processing Overseas Replacement Training [*Military*] (VNW)
POR	Process-of-Record (AAEL)
POR	Production Order Records (SAA)
POR	Production Order Request (SAA)
POR	Project Officers Report (MCD)
POR	Psychotherapy Outcome Research
por	Public Opinion Research (AD)
POR	Purchase Order Request
PORA	Police Officers Research Association (AD)
PORAC	Peace Officers Research Association of California
PORACC	Principles of Radiation and Contamination Control [*Nuclear energy*]
PORAG	Presiding Officers' Review and Advisory Group [*Commonwealth Parliament*] [*Australia*]
PORB	Production Operations Review Board [*NASA*] (NASA)
PORC	Partido Obrero Revolucionario-Combate [*Revolutionary Struggle Workers' Party*] [*Bolivia*] [*Political party*] (PPW)
PORC	Peralta Oaks Research Center (AD)
PORC	Plant Operations Review Committee [*Nuclear energy*] (NRCH)
PORC	Plant Overnight Review Committee [*Environmental science*] (COE)
porc	Porcelain (AD)
PORC	Porcelain (AAG)
PORC	Porphyria, Chester Type (DMAA)
PORCN	Production Order Records Change Notice (KSC)
PORCO	Port Control Office
PORD	Performance and Operations Requirements Document [*NASA*] (NASA)
PORDA	Personnel Officers of Research and Development Agencies
PORDIR	Port Director
PORE	Point Reyes National Seashore [*National Park Service designation*]
POREA	Post Office Regional Employees' Association [*Defunct*] (EA)
POREL(A)	Petty Officer Radio Electrician (Air) [*British military*] (DMA)
POREP	Position Report [*Air Force*]
PORES	Purchase Order Receiving System (MCD)
PORF	Pacific Ocean Research Foundation (EA)
Porg	Person of Restricted Growth [*Slang term used to describe a person of limi ted cultural awareness*] [*Lifestyle classification*]
PORGIE	Paperback Original [*Award for best original paperback books of the year*]
PORI	Polaris Operational Readiness Instrumentation [*Missiles*]
PORI	Preoperational Readiness Inspection (MCD)
PORIS	Post Office Radio Interference Service [*British*] (DI)
PORIS	Post Office Radio Interference Station (AD)
PORK	Partnership for Over-Regulated Kar [*Humorous description of government-auto industry technology research program*]
porksan	Pork Sandwich (AD)
porkwich	Pork Sandwich (AD)
PORL	Peninsular/Oriental Steam Nav [*LO Symbol*] (TTSB)
porm	Plus or Minus (AD)
PORM	Plus or Minus
P or M	Plus or Minus (MSA)
PORM-PST	Partido Obrero Revolucionario Marxista-Partido Socialista de los Trabajadores [*Peru*] [*Political party*] (EY)
porn	Pornographic (AD)
PORN	Pornography (DSUE)
PORN	Protect Our Responsibilities Now [*Book title*]
pornette	Pornographic Cassette (AD)
pornfilm	Pornographic Motion Picture Film (AD)
porno	Pornofilm (AD)
porno	Pornographer (AD)
PORNO	Pornography (DSUE)
pornobio	Pornographic Biography (AD)
pornofilm	Pornographic Motion Picture (AD)
porno mag	Pornographic Magazine (AD)
pornovel	Pornographic Novel (AD)
pornovelist	Pornographic Novelist (AD)
Porn Squad	Pornographic Squad (AD)
pornzines	Pornographic Magazines (AD)
PORP	Partial Ossicular Replacement Prosthesis
PORP	Printed on Recycled Paoer (AD)
P or P	Publish or Perish [*Said of scholars, scientists, etc.*]
Porph	Porphyry [*Third century AD*] [*Classical studies*] (OCD)
porph	Porphyry (VRA)
PORR	Preliminary Operations Requirements Review [*NASA*] (NASA)
PORR	Purchase Order Revision Request
PORS	Post Office Research Station (AD)
PORS	Power-On Reset [*Electronics*]
PORS	Product Output Reporting System
PORSE	Post Overhaul Reaction Safeguard Examination [*Navy*] (NVT)
PORT	Bayport Restaurant Group [*NASDAQ symbol*] (TTSB)
PORT	Bayport Restaurant Group, Inc. [*NASDAQ symbol*] (SAG)
PORT	Patient Outcome Research Team (PCM)
PORT	Photo-Optical Recorder Tracker
port	Photo-Optical Recorder Tracker (AD)
PORT	Port [*Commonly used*] (OPSA)
port	Portable (AD)
PORT	Portable (KSC)
PORT	Porter (DSUE)
Port	Porter's Alabama Supreme Court Reports [*1834-39*] [*A publication*] (DLA)
Port	Porter's Indiana Reports [*3-7 Indiana*] [*A publication*] (DLA)
PORT	Portfolio (WGA)
PORT	Portland Railroad

PORT .... Portmanteau (DSUE)
PORT .... Portrait
port............. Portrait (AD)
PORT .... Portugal
Port............. Portugal (VRA)
port............. Portugiesisch [*Portuguese*] [*German*] (AD)
Port............. Portuguese (ODBW)
PORT .... Postoperative Respiratory Therapy (DAVI)
PORT .... Prescriptive Objective Reference Testing [*Vocational guidance*]
PORT .... Presentation Portfolio (VRA)
Port Ade ...... Port Adelaide [*South Australia*] (AD)
Portage........ Portage Industries Corp. [*Associated Press*] (SAG)
PORTAL ...... Process-Oriented Real-Time Algorithmic Language [*1978*] [*Computer science*] (CSR)
Port (Ala).... Porter's Alabama Reports [*A publication*] (DLA)
Port Ala R ... Porter's Alabama Reports [*A publication*] (DLA)
Port Ald ...... Port Alberni [*Vancouver Island, British Columbia*] (AD)
portalet........ Portable Toilet (AD)
Port Alex ..... Port Alexander [*Alaska*] (AD)
Port Ant ...... Port Antonio [*Jamaica*] (AD)
PORTAPAK... Portable, Self-Contained, Instrument Package
Port Art....... Port Arthur (AD)
PORTAS........ Penetration of Radiation Through Aperture Simulation (PDAA)
PortBk........ Portsmouth Bank Shares, Inc. [*Associated Press*] (SAG)
PORT CEM... Portland Cement [*Technical drawings*] (DAC)
Port Chi ...... Port Chicago (AD)
Port Chi ...... Portuguese China (AD)
Port Dal....... Port Dalhousie [*Ontario, Canada*] (AD)
Portec......... Portec, Inc. [*Associated Press*] (SAG)
Porter .... Porter's Alabama Reports [*A publication*] (DLA)
Porter .... Porter's Indiana Reports [*3-7 Indiana*] [*A publication*] (DLA)
Porter (Ala)... Porter's Alabama Reports [*A publication*] (DLA)
Porter R....... Porter's Alabama Reports [*A publication*] (DLA)
Porter's Ala R... Porter's Alabama Reports [*A publication*] (DLA)
Porter's R.... Porter's Alabama Reports [*A publication*] (DLA)
Porter's Repts... Porter's Alabama Reports [*A publication*] (DLA)
PortG35 ...... Portland General Electric Co. [*Associated Press*] (SAG)
PortGC .... Portland General Corp. [*Associated Press*] (SAG)
PortglT........ Portugal Telecom SA [*Associated Press*] (SAG)
PORTIA .... Port Operations, Transport and Integrated Accountancy (MHDB)
Port Ind ...... Portuguese India (AD)
Port Ins....... Porter's Laws of Insurance [*A publication*] (DLA)
Port Jack .... Port Jackson Sydney [*Sydney, New South Wales, Australia*] (AD)
Portland St U... Portland State University (GAGS)
Portland UL Rev... Portland University. Law Review [*A publication*] (DLA)
Port Liz .... Port Elizabeth [*New Jersey*] (AD)
Port Liz....... Port Elizabeth [*South Africa*] (AD)
PORTN........ Portion (ROG)
Port Nick .... Port Nicholson [*Wellington, New Zealand*] (AD)
PORTP .... Partido Obrero Revolucionaria Trotskista Posadista [*Bolivia*] [*Political party*] (PPW)
Port P .... Portuguese Pharmacopoeia [*A publication*]
Port Phil ..... Port Phillip [*Melbourne, Victoria, Australia*] (AD)
PORTREP.... Port [*or Anchorage*] Capacity Report [*Navy*] (NVT)
Port Rich ..... Port Richmond [*Staten Island, New York*] (AD)
PORTS .... Physical Oceanographic Real-Time System [*Marine science*] (OSRA)
PORTS .... Portable Remote Telecommunications System (DOMA)
PORTS .... Port Objective for Real-Time Systems [*Marine science*] (OSRA)
PORTS .... Ports [*Commonly used*] (OPSA)
PORTS .... Portsmouth [*City in England*]
PORTS .... Portsmouth Gaseous Diffusion Plant [*Department of Energy*] [*Portsmouth, OH*] (GAAI)
PortsBk .... Portsmouth Bank Shares [*Associated Press*] (SAG)
PORTSM...... Portsmouth [*County borough in England*]
Ports NSW Jl... Ports of New South Wales Journal [*A publication*]
PORTSREP.. Ports Report File (MCD)
Port Sud ..... Port Sudan (AD)
PORTSUM.... Port [*or Anchorage*] Summary Report [*Navy*] (NVT)
Port Swett ... Port Swettenham [*Malaysia*] (AD)
PortSys....... Porta Systems Corp. [*Associated Press*] (SAG)
Port Talb .... Port Talbot [*Wales*] (AD)
Port Tew...... Port Tewfik [*Egypt*] (AD)
Port Tim ..... Portuguese Timor (AD)
Portug......... Portugais [*Portuguese*] [*French*] (AD)
Portgl........ Portugal Fund [*Associated Press*] (SAG)
Port UL Rev... Portland University. Law Review [*A publication*] (DLA)
Port Wash ... Port Washington [*Long Island, New York*] (AD)
Port Wel ..... Port Wellen [*Ontario, CAN*] (AD)
PORV.......... Pilot-Operated Relief Valve [*Nuclear energy*] (NRCH)
PORV.......... Power-Operated Relief Valve [*Nuclear energy*] (NRCH)
POS .... Aeroposta SA [*Argentina ICAO designator*] (FAAC)
POS .... Catalina Marketing [*NYSE symbol*] (TTSB)
POS .... Catalina Marketing Corp. [*NYSE symbol*] (SPSG)
POS .... Pacific Ocean Ship (NASA)
POS .... Pacific Orchid Society of Hawaii (EA)
POS .... Parent Operating Service (MCD)
POS .... Parosteal Osteosarcoma [*Oncology*] (DAVI)
POS .... Partially Ordered Set (OA)
POS .... Patent Office Society (EA)
POS .... Peacetime Operating Stock [*Military*] (CINC)
POS .... Period of Service [*Military*]
POS .... Permanent Orbital Station [*NASA*] (IAA)
POS .... Photo Optic System
POS .... Pico Resources [*Vancouver Stock Exchange symbol*]
POS .... Piper Owner Society (EA)

POS .... Planar Oxygen Sensor
POS .... Plan of Service (OICC)
POS .... Plant Operating System [*Nuclear energy*] (NRCH)
POS .... Play Observation Scale [*Test*] (TMMY)
pos............. Point of Sale (AD)
PoS............. Point of Sale
POS .... Point of Sale (ODBW)
POS .... Point of Service [*Health plan option*]
POS .... Point of Service Option
POS .... Point-of-Service Plan [*Insurance*] (PAZ)
POS .... Polar Orbiting Satellite [*Marine science*] (OSRA)
POs............. Police Officers (AD)
POS .... Policy Statements [*Australian Broadcasting Tribunal*] [*A publication*]
POS .... Polycystic Ovarian Syndrome [*Also, PCOS*] [*Gynecology*]
POS .... Portable Oxygen System (MCD)
PoS .... Port of Service (AD)
PoS .... Port of Spain (AD)
POS .... Port Of Spain [*Trinidad and Tobago*] [*Airport symbol*] (OAG)
POS .... Port(s) of Support (DOMA)
pos............. Position (WDMC)
POS .... Position (KSC)
POS .... Positive (AFM)
pos............. Positive (AD)
POS .... Possession [*or Possessive*] (WGA)
pos............. Possibility (AD)
Pos .... Possible
POs............. Postal Orders (AD)
POS .... Post Office Scheme [*Regulations*] [*British*]
POS .... Preferred Overseas Shore Duty
POS .... Pressure on Space [*Publishing*] (DGA)
POS .... Pressure-Operated Switch (IAA)
POS .... Primary Operating Stock [*DoD*]
POS .... Primary Operating System (IEEE)
POS .... Primary Oxygen System
POS .... Probability of Success (COE)
POS .... Probability of Survival [*Automotive componant analysis*]
POS .... Problem Oriented System
POS .... Production-Oriented Survey (MCD)
pos............. Product of Sums (AD)
POS .... Products of Sums (IAA)
POS .... Professional Operating System (NITA)
POS .... Professions and Occupations Sourcebook [*A publication*]
POS .... Programmable Option Select [*Computer science*]
PoS .... Programme of Study [*British*] (DET)
POS .... Programming Optimizing System (IAA)
POS .... Program of Study (AEE)
POS .... Program Operations Staff [*Environmental Protection Agency*] (GFGA)
PORTN........ Program Order Sequence
POS .... Protein, Oil, and Starch [*Pilot manufacturing plant established by the Canadian government*]
POS .... Pupil Observation Survey [*Education*]
POS .... Purchase Order Supplement
POSA .... Patriotic Order Sons of America (EA)
POSA .... Payment Outstanding Suspence Accounts (NATG)
posa............ Payment Outstanding Suspense Accounts (AD)
POSA .... Petty Officer Stores Accountant [*British military*] (DMA)
POSA .... Preliminary Operating Safety Analysis [*Nuclear energy*] (NRCH)
POSARS...... Plan of Service Automated Reporting System [*Employment and Training Administration*] [*Department of Labor*]
posb........... Possibly (VRA)
POSB .... Post Office Savings Bank
POSC .... Little Workers of the Sacred Heart (TOCD)
POSC .... Problem-Oriented System of Charting (AAMN)
posc-- .... Santa Cruz Islands [*MARC geographic area code Library of Congress*] (LCCP)
POSCH........ Program of Surgical Control of Hyperlipidemia
POSCO........ Pohang Iron & Steel Co. (ECON)
POSCOR ...... Position Correct (CAAL)
POSCORB ... Planning, Organizing, Staffing, Coordinating, Reporting, and Budgeting [*Management*]
POSD .... Personnel on Station Date [*Army*] (AABC)
POSD .... Post Office Savings Department (AD)
POSD .... Program for Optical System Design
POSD .... Project Operation Support Division [*NASA*]
posdcorb...... Planning-Organization-Staffing-Directing-Coordinating-Reporting-Budgeting g (AD)
POSDCORB... Planning, Organizing, Staffing, Directing, Coordinating, Reporting, and Budgeting [*Principles of management*]
posdsplt....... Port Side Out, Starboard Side Home [*British slang*] (AD)
posdsplt....... Positive Displacement (AD)
POSDSPLT... Positive Displacement
POSE .... Parents Opposed to Sex Education
POSE .... Photogrammetric Ocean Survey Equipment
POSE .... Picture-Oriented Software Engineering [*Computer science*] (CIST)
POSE .... Power Operational Support Equipment
POSE .... Promotion of Social Education [*British*] (DI)
PO SEC ...... Principal Officer's Secretary [*Foreign service*]
POSER .... Process Organization to Simplify Error Recovery (PDAA)
POSET .... Partially Ordered Set (HGAA)
Posey.......... Posey's Unreported Cases [*Texas*] [*A publication*] (ILCA)
Posey UC..... Texas Unreported Cases [*A publication*] (AD)
Posey Unrep Cas... Posey's Unreported Cases [*Texas*] [*A publication*] (DLA)
POSF .... Port of Support File (DOMA)
POSG .... After Glucose Infusion Started [*Biochemistry*] (DAVI)
POSH.......... Permuted on Subject Headings [*Indexing technique*]

posh............	Permuted on Subject Headings (AD)
POSH..........	Personal & Organizational Security Handbook [*A publication*]
POSH..........	Port Outwardbound, Starboard Homewardbound [*Refers to shaded cabins of British naval officers in the Far East*]
POSH..........	Probability of Severe Hail (USDC)
posh............	Samoa Islands [*MARC geographic area code Library of Congress*] (LCCP)
POSI	Personnel On-Site Integration (SAA)
POSI	Positron Corp. [*NASDAQ symbol*] (SAG)
POS INIT......	Position Initialization (GAVI)
POSIP	Portable Ship Instrumentation Package
positor	Positive Resistor (AD)
posit	Position (AD)
POSIT	Position (NVT)
POSIT	Positive
posit	Positive (AD)
POSIT	Positivism (ROG)
posit	Positron (AD)
POSIT	Profile for Open Systems Internetworking Technologies [*Computer science*] (CDE)
POSITIVE	Parents of Surrogate-Borne Infants and Toddlers in Verbal Exchange (EA)
Positr..........	Positron Corp. [*Associated Press*] (SAG)
POSITREPS...	Position Reports
POSITRON ...	Positive Electron
positron	Positive Electron (AD)
Positron	Positron Corp. [*Associated Press*] (SAG)
POSIW........	Positron Corp. Wrrt [*NASDAQ symbol*] (TTSB)
POSIX	Portable Operating System Interface Exchange
POSIX	Portable Operating System Interface for Computer Environments (AAGC)
POSIX	Portable Operating System Interface for Unix [*Computer science*] (PCM)
POSIX	Portable Operating Systems for Computer Environments (AD)
POSIX	Portable Operating System Specification [*IEEE*]
POSK	Polski Osrodek Spoleczno-Kulturalny [*Polish Social and Cultural Association - PSCA*] (EAIO)
POSKP	Polski Osrodek Spoleczno-Kulturalny Posk [*Polish Social and Cultural Association - PSCA*] (EAIO)
POsl............	Papyri Osloenses [*A publication*] (OCD)
POSL	Parti Ouvrier Socialiste Luxembourgeois [*Luxembourg Socialist Workers' Party*] (EAIO)
POSM	National Association of Post Office and General Service Maintenance Employees [*Later, APWU*] [*AFL-CIO*]
posm	Patient-Operated Selected Mechanisms (AD)
POSM	Patient-Operated Selector Mechanism [*Pronounced "possum"*]
POSMA........	Postal Service Manual [*A publication*]
Posmo	Osmotic Permeability [*Biochemistry*] (DAVI)
POSN	Position (AFM)
posn............	Position (AD)
posn--.........	Solomon Islands [*MARC geographic area code Library of Congress*] (LCCP)
POSNA........	Pediatric Orthopaedic Society of North America (EA)
POS/NAV......	Position/Navigation [*System*] [*Military*] (INF)
POSNO	Position Number [*Military*] (ADDR)
POSNY	People of the State of New York (AD)
POSO	Prosoft I-Net Solutions, Inc. [*NASDAQ symbol*] (SAG)
POSP	Pacific Ocean Stations Program (SAA)
pos pr..........	Positive Pressure (MAE)
Pos Press	Positive Pressure (CPH)
pos pron......	Possessive Pronoun (AD)
POSR	Peacetime Operating Stock Requirement [*Military*] (AFIT)
POS R..........	Positive Review [*A publication*] (ROG)
POS REF......	Position Reference (GAVI)
PosResp	Positive Response Television [*Associated Press*] (SAG)
POSRIP........	People Organized to Stop Rape of Imprisoned Persons (EA)
POSS	Palomar Observatory Sky Survey [*NASA*]
POSS	Passive Optical Satellite Surveillance [*System*] (NATG)
POSS	Photo-Optical Surveillance Subsystem
P-O-S S	Point-of-Sale System (AD)
P-O-S S	Point-of-Service System (AD)
POSS	Portable Oceanographic Survey System (MCD)
POSS	Possession [*or Possessive*] (AFM)
poss............	Possession (AD)
poss............	Possessive (WDMC)
poss............	Possible (WDMC)
POSS	Possible
poss............	Possibly (WDMC)
POSS	Possis Medical [*NASDAQ symbol*] (TTSB)
POSS	Possis Medical, Inc. [*NASDAQ symbol*] (NQ)
POSS	Program Operations Support Staff [*Environmental Protection Agency*] (GFGA)
POSS	Prototype Optical Surveillance System
POSS	Proximal Over-Shoulder Strap [*Medicine*]
POSSE	Parents Opposed to Sex and Sensitivity Education [*An association*]
POSSE	Police Operations Systems Support System Elementary
POSSE	Progressive Onslaught to Stamp out Stock Errors [*Navy*] (NG)
POSSED	Possessed (ROG)
posses	Possessive (AD)
POSSF	Post Office Staff Superannuation Fund [*British*] (DI)
Possis..........	Possis Medical, Inc. [*Associated Press*] (SAG)
posslq..........	Person of the Opposite Sex in Same Living Quarters (AD)
POSSLQ.......	Persons of Opposite Sex Sharing Living Quarters [*Bureau of the Census*]
POSSN........	Possession (WGA)

POSSNC	Post Office Senior Staff Negotiating Council [*British*]
POSSON	Possession
POSSUB......	Possible Submarine [*Navy*] (NVT)
POSSUM......	Pictures of Specific Syndromes and Unknown Malformations [*Database*]
POSSUM......	Polar Orbiting Satellite System - University of Michigan [*Designed by engineering students*]
Post	De Posteritate Caini [*of Philo*] (BJA)
POST	Frederick Post Drafting Equipment (AD)
POST	International Post Ltd. [*NASDAQ symbol*] (SAG)
POST	Intl Post Ltd [*NASDAQ symbol*] (TTSB)
POST	Parliamentary Office of Science and Technology [*British*]
POST	Passive Optical Scan Tracker (MCD)
POST	Passive Optical Seeker Technique
POST	Payload Operations Support Team [*NASA*] (MCD)
POST	Peace Officer Standards and Training
POST	Peritoneal Ovum Sperm Transfer [*Medicine*]
POST	Piezoelectric-Oscillator Self-Tuned [*Electric system*]
POST	Point-of-Sale Terminal [*Business term*]
POST	Point-of-Sale Transaction
POST	Polaris Operation Support Task Group [*Missiles*]
POST	Polar Stratospheric Telescope
POST	Police Officer Student Training (AD)
POST	Positive (AAG)
post	Postage (AD)
POST	Postemergence [*Weed control*]
POST	[*The*] Poster [*A publication*] (ROG)
post	Poster (VRA)
post	Posterior
POST	Postmortem (AAMN)
post	Post Mortem (AD)
Post	Post's Reports [*23-26 Michigan*] [*A publication*] (DLA)
Post	Post's Reports [*42-64 Missouri*] [*A publication*] (DLA)
POST	Power-On Self Test [*IBM-PC feature*]
POST	Processes of Science Test (AD)
POST	Production-Oriented Scheduling Techniques (MCD)
POST	Programmer Operating Standards Technique
POST	Program to Operate Simulated Trajectories
POST	Program to Optimize Shuttle [*or Simulated*] Trajectories [*NASA*] (KSC)
POST	Prototype Ocean Surveillance Terminal [*Navy*] (ANA)
Post & Ins ...	Postage and Insurance (ILCA)
Post & Reg...	Postage and Registration (DLA)
post-Aug......	Post-Augustan (AD)
post aur.......	Post Aurem [*Behind the Ear*] [*Latin*] (AD)
POST AUR....	Post Aurem [*Behind the Ear*] [*Pharmacy*]
POSTD	Petty Officer Steward [*British military*] (DMA)
post d	Posterior Diameter (AD)
POSTE	Postage (ROG)
POSTEC	Powder Science and Technology Research Association [*Norway*] (EAIO)
poster	Posterior (AD)
POSTER	Post Strike Emergency Reporting
pos terminal...	Point-of-Sale Terminal (AD)
Poste's Gai...	Poste's Translation of Gaius [*A publication*] (ILCA)
Poste's Gaius Inst...	Poste's Translation of Gaius [*A publication*] (DLA)
POSTFAT	Postfinal Acceptance Trials [*Navy*] (NVT)
POSTFAX	Post Office Facsimile [*British*]
postgangl	Postganglionic [*Medicine*] (MEDA)
PostgradDipAgr...	Postgraduate Diploma in Agriculture
PostGradDipEdStud(IndArts)...	Postgraduate Diploma in Educational Studies (Industrial Arts)
Postgrad Med Inst...	Postgraduate Medical Institute (AD)
Postgraduate D...	Postgraduate Diploma (PGP)
posth	Posthumous (AD)
POSTH	Posthumous
postl	Postlude (AD)
Postl Dict.....	Postlethwaite's Dictionary of Trade and Commerce [*A publication*] (DLA)
post-mort.....	Post Mortem (AD)
POSTNET	Postnumeric Encoding Technique [*US Postal Service*]
post-obit......	Post Obitum [*After Death*] [*Latin*]
post ofc	Post Office (VRA)
POSTOP.......	Postoperative [*Medicine*]
post-op........	Post-Operative (AD)
POSTP	Posterior Probability [*Computations*]
POSTP	Postprocessor [*Computer science*]
post part.....	Post Partum [*Afterbirth*] [*Latin*] (AD)
PostPr..........	Post Properties, Inc. [*Associated Press*] (SAG)
POSTPRO	Postprocessor [*Computer science*]
PostPrp........	Post Properties, Inc. [*Associated Press*] (SAG)
POSTS	Positive Occipital Sharp Transients of Sleep [*On electroencephalogram*] [*Neurology*] (DAVI)
Post Sag D...	Posterior Sagittal Diameter [*Anatomy*] (MAE)
Post Script...	Post Script: Essays in Film and the Humanities [*A publication*] (BRI)
POST SING SED LIQ...	Post Singulas Sedes Liquidas [*After Every Loose Stool*] [*Pharmacy*] (ROG)
post-sync.....	Post-Synchronization (AD)
POSV	Pilot-Operated Solenoid Valve [*Nuclear energy*] (IAA)
POSWG.......	Poseidon Software Working Group [*Missiles*]
pot..............	Dashpot (IDOE)
POT.............	Paint on Tangent (IAA)
POT.............	Parallel Output
POT.............	Pennsylvania-Ontario Transportation Co. [*AAR code*]
POT.............	Periostitis Ossificans Toxica [*Medicine*] (DMAA)

POT	Physical Organization Table (HGAA)
POT	Picture Object Table (MHDI)
POT	Piston Operated Transducer
POT	Pitch-Orthogonal Thrust
POT	Plain Old Telephone [Bell System's basic model]
pot	Point of tangency (AD)
POT	Polet [Former USSR] [FAA designator] (FAAC)
pot	Portable Outdoor Toilet (AD)
POT	Portable Outside Toilet [A unit of mobility equipment] [Military]
POT	Port Antonio [Jamaica] [Airport symbol] (OAG)
POT	Post Office Telecommunications [British]
POT	Post-Operative Treatment [Medicine] (DMAA)
POT	Potable
pot	Potash (AD)
POT	Potash Corp. of Saskatchewan [NYSE symbol] (SPSG)
POT	Potash Corp. Saskatchewan [NYSE symbol] (TTSB)
pot	Potassa [Chemistry] (MAE)
POT	Potassium [Chemical symbol is K]
POT	Potato (ROG)
POT	Potentate
POT	Potential (AFM)
pot	Potential (AD)
POT	Potentiometer [or Potentiometric]
pot	Potentiometer (IDOE)
Pot	Potion
POT	Potsdam [Germany] [Later, NGK] [Seismograph station code, US Geological Survey] (SEIS)
POT	Pottery
POT	Pottle [Unit of measure] (ROG)
POT	Pottsville Free Public Library, Pottsville, PA [OCLC symbol] (OCLC)
POT	Potus [A Drink] [Pharmacy]
POT	Prevailing-Out Torque [Automotive engineering]
POT	Program for Operational Trajectories [Marine science] (OSRA)
POT	Propeller Order Transmitter (OA)
POTAD	Program for Operational Transport and Dispersion (USDC)
PotAGT	Potential Abnormality of Glucose Tolerance [Medicine]
POT & I	Preoverhaul Tests and Inspections [Navy] (NVT)
POTANN	Potomac Annex [Navy]
Potash	Potash Corp. of Saskatchewan, Inc. [Associated Press] (SAG)
potash alum	Potassium Aluminum Sulfate (AD)
potass	Potassium [An element] (DAVI)
POTASWG	Poseidon Test Analysis Software Working Group [Missiles]
potats	Potatoes (AD)
POTBI	Places, Organizations, Things, Biographics, Intangibles
POTC	PERT [Program Evaluation and Review Technique] Orientation and Training Center
POTCP	Partially Oxidized Tetracyanoplatinate Compound [Inorganic, one-dimensional conductor]
POTD	Player of the Decade [Sports]
P o TD	Port of The Dalles (AD)
POTDIF	Potential Difference [Electronics] (IAA)
Pot Dwar	Potter's Edition of Dwarris on Statutes [A publication] (DLA)
PotEd25	Potomac Edison [Associated Press] (SAG)
PotEl	Potomac Electric Power Co. [Associated Press] (OAG)
POTELECTROMET	Potentiometric Electrometer (IAA)
POTEN	Potential (AAMN)
POTF	Polychromatic Optical Thickness Fringe (OA)
POTF	Psychological Operations Task Force [Army] (INF)
Poth Cont	Pothier's Contracts [A publication] (DLA)
Poth Contr Sale	Pothier's Treatise on the Contract of Sale [A publication] (DLA)
Poth Cont Sale	Pothier's Treatise on the Contract of Sale [A publication] (DLA)
Pothier Pand	Pothier's Pandectae Justinianeae, Etc. [A publication] (DLA)
Poth Mar Cont	Pothier's Treatise on Maritime Contracts [A publication] (DLA)
Poth Ob	Pothier on the Law of Obligations [A publication] (DLA)
Poth Obl	Pothier on the Law of Obligations [A publication] (DLA)
Poth Oblig	Pothier on the Law of Obligations [A publication] (DLA)
Poth Oeuv	Oeuvres de Pothier [A publication] (DLA)
Poth Pand	Pothier's Pandects [A publication] (DLA)
Poth Part	Pothier on Partnership [A publication] (DLA)
Poth Proc Civ	Pothier. Procedure Civile [A publication] (DLA)
POTIB	Polaris Technical Information Bulletin [Missiles]
POTIB	Poseidon Technical Information Bulletin [A publication] (AD)
potl--	Tokelau Islands [MARC geographic area code Library of Congress] (LCCP)
Pot LD	Pott's Law Dictionary [3rd ed.] [1815] [A publication] (DLA)
Potltch	Potlatch Corp. [Associated Press] (SAG)
POTMC	Protective Outfit Toxicological Microclimate Controlled (RDA)
PotmEl	Potomac Electric Power Co. [Associated Press] (SAG)
POTMLD	Potential Mixed Layer Depth
poto--	Tonga [MARC geographic area code Library of Congress] (LCCP)
POTOMAC	Patent Office Techniques of Mechanized Access and Classification [Automation project, shut down in 1972]
potosslq	Persons of the Opposite Sex Sharing Living Quarters (AD)
potr	Potrero [Cattle Ranch] [Spanish] (AD)
PotrSvg	Potters Savings & Loan Co. [Associated Press] (SAG)
POTS	Perials of the Sea (MHDB)
POTS	Petty Officer Telegraphist Special (DSUE)
POTS	Photo-Optical Terrain Simulator (MUGU)
POTS	Plain Old Telephone Service [or System] [Humorous term for Long Lines Department of AT & T See also PANS]
pots	Plain Old Telephone Service (AD)
POTS	PORI [Polaris Operational Readiness Instrumentation] Operational Test System [Missiles]
pots	Potentiometers (AD)
POTS	Potentiometers (COE)
POTS	Precision Optical Tracking System (KSC)
POTS	Preoverhaul Tests [Navy] (NVT)
POTS	Purchase of Telephones and Services Program (AAGC)
POTS	Purchase of Telephone Services Contracts
pott	Pottery (AD)
pott--	Trust Territory of the Pacific Islands [MARC geographic area code Library of Congress] (LCCP)
Pott Corp	Potter on Corporations [A publication] (DLA)
Pott Dwarris	Potter's Edition of Dwarris on Statutes [A publication] (DLA)
Potter	Potter's Reports [4-7 Wyoming] [A publication] (DLA)
PottrFinl	Potters Financial Corp. [Associated Press] (SAG)
Potts LD	Potts' Law Dictionary [3rd ed.] [1815] [A publication] (DLA)
POTUS	President of the United States
POTV	Personnel Orbit Transfer Vehicle (MCD)
pot w	Portable Water (AD)
POTW	Potable Water (KSC)
POTW	Publically-Owned Treatment Works (DNAB)
POTW	Publicly Owned Treatment Works (EG)
POU	Paramount Resources Ltd. [Toronto Stock Exchange symbol]
POU	Placenta, Ovary, Uterus [Medicine]
POU	Point of Use
POU	Poughkeepsie [New York] [Airport symbol] (OAG)
POU	Poughkeepsie, NY [Location identifier FAA] (FAAL)
POU	Pouilloux [France] [Seismograph station code, US Geological Survey] (SEIS)
POUCC	Post Office Users Coordination Committee [British]
POUCG	Point-of-Use Chemical Generation (AAEL)
POUF	Projects of Optimum Urgency and Feasibility
PoughSv	[The] Poughkeepsie Savings Bank FSB [Associated Press] (SAG)
POUL	Poultry
poul	Poultry (AD)
POUM	Partido Obrero de Unificacion Marxista [Workers' Party of Marxist Unification] [Former USSR] (LAIN)
POUNC	Post Office Users' National Council [British] (ILCA)
POUP	Post Overhaul Upkeep Period
poup--	United States Miscellaneous Pacific Islands [MARC geographic area code Library of Congress] (LCCP)
POU/POE	Point-of-Use/Point-of-Entry [Water standards] (FFDE)
POUR	President's Organization for Unemployment Relief (AD)
POUS	Partido Operario de Unidade Socialista [Workers' Party for Socialist Unity] [Portugal Political party] (PPW)
POUT	Prison Officer under Training (WDAA)
POV	Peak Operated Valve (MCD)
POV	Peak Operating Voltage
POV	Pend Oreille Valley Railroad (AD)
POV	Persistence of Vision - Ray [Computer program]
POV	Personally Owned Vehicle
POV	Pinch-Off Voltage
POV	Pittsburgh & Ohio Valley Railway Co. [AAR code]
POV	Plane of Vibration
POV	Pneumatically Operated Valve
POV	Point of View
p-o-v	Point-of-View (AD)
POV	Presov [Czechoslovakia] [Airport symbol] (AD)
POV	Pressure-Operated Valve (MCD)
POV	Privately Owned Vehicle (NVT)
pov	Privately Owned Vehicle (AD)
POV	Proximity Operations Vehicle (SSD)
POV	Purchase, Outside Vendors
POV	Putting-On Voltage [Doppler navigation] (DEN)
POVC	Probation Officers and Volunteers in Corrections [Victoria, Australia]
POVEU	Program Operations Vocational Education Unit (OICC)
Pov L Rep	Poverty Law Reporter [Commerce Clearing House] [A publication] (DLA)
POVT	Puerperal Ovarian-Vein Thrombophlebitis [Medicine]
POW	Paying Their Own Way
POW	Pay Order of Withdrawal
POW	Peoples of the World [A publication]
POW	Perception of Ward [Scales] [Psychology]
POW	Petty Officer of the Watch [Navy]
POW	Powassan Encephalitis [Medicine]
POW	Powder [Navy]
POW	Power
pow	Power (AD)
POW	Power Corp. of Canada [Toronto Stock Exchange symbol Vancouver Stock Exchange symbol]
POW	Powhatan [Arkansas] [Seismograph station code, US Geological Survey] (SEIS)
POW	Prince of Wales
P o W	Prince of Wales (AD)
pow	Prisoner of War (AD)
PoW	Prisoner of War (WDAA)
POW	Prisoner of War [Also, PW]
P o W	Prisoner of Watergate (AD)
POW	Prisoner Outreach Work (WDAA)
POW	Progressive Order of the West [Defunct] (EA)
POWACO	Portable Water Coolant Circulator
Pow App Proc	Powell's Law of Appellate Proceedings [A publication] (DLA)
PoWBN	Biblioteka Narodowa [National Library], Warsaw, Poland [Library symbol Library of Congress] (LCLS)
PoWC	Instytut Informacji Naukowej, Technicznej, i Ekonomicznej, Warsaw, Poland [Library symbol Library of Congress] (LCLS)
Pow Car	Powell's Inland Carriers [2nd ed.] [1861] [A publication] (DLA)
Pow Cont	Powell on Contracts [A publication] (DLA)
Pow Conv	Powell. Conveyancing [1810] [A publication] (ILCA)

POW Country... Potash, Oil, and Wheat Country [*Saskatoon, Saskatchewan*] (AD)
powd............ Powder (AD)
POWD......... Powder [*England*]
POWD......... Powdered
Pow Dev...... Powell's Essay upon the Learning of Devises, Etc. [*A publication*] (DLA)
POWDR........ Protect Our Wetlands and Duck Resources [*Department of the Interior*] [*Washington, DC*]
Powell........ Powell Industries, Inc. [*Associated Press*] (SAG)
POWER........ Pension Opportunities for Workers' Expanded Retirement [*Plan proposed in 1991 by the Department of Labor*]
POWER........ People Organized and Working for Economic Rebirth [*Program for black economic development*] [*Later, Nationway Ventures International Ltd.*]
POWER........ Performance Optimization with Enhanced RISC [*Reduced Instruction Set Computer*] (PCM)
POWER........ Planning Operation With Enabling Resources
POWER........ Priority Output Writers Execution Processor [*Computer science*] (IAA)
POWER........ Priority Output Writers, Execution Processors, and Input Readers (MHDI)
POWER........ Priority Output Writes Execution Process [*Computer science*] (IAA)
POWER........ Producing Organized Writing and Effective Reviewing
POWER........ Professionals Organized for Women's Equal Rights [*Feminist group*]
POWER........ PROFS [*Program for Regional Observing and Forecasting Services*] Operational Weather Education and Research [*Marine science*] (OSRA)
POWER........ Programmed Operational Warshot Evaluation and Review
power......... Programmed Operational Warshot Evaluation and Review (AD)
POWER........ Promote Our Wonderful Energy Resources (EA)
Powers....... Powers' Reports, New York Surrogate Court [*A publication*] (DLA)
Power's Sur.. Powers' Reports, New York Surrogate Court [*A publication*] (DLA)
Pow Ev....... Powell on Evidence [*10th ed.*] [*1921*] [*A publication*] (DLA)
powf--........ Wallis and Futuna [*MARC geographic area code Library of Congress*] (LCCP)
POWG......... Procurement Officers Work Group (AAGC)
Pow Inl Car... Powell on the Law of Inland Carriers [*A publication*] (DLA)
POW(J)........ Prisoner of War of Japan
powk--........ Wake Island [*MARC geographic area code Library of Congress*] (LCCP)
POWL......... Powell Indus [*NASDAQ symbol*] (TTSB)
POWL......... Powell Industries, Inc. [*NASDAQ symbol*] (NQ)
POW/MIG..... Place of Work and Migration Sample [*Bureau of the Census*] (GFGA)
Pow Mort..... Powell on Mortgages [*6th ed.*] [*1826*] [*A publication*] (DLA)
Pow Mortg... Powell on Mortgages [*A publication*] (DLA)
POWO......... Prince [*or Princess*] of Wales' Own [*Military unit*] [*British*] (DMA)
PoWP.......... Biblioteka Golowna Politechniki Warszawsjiej (Warsaw Technical University Central Library), Warsaw, Poland [*Library symbol Library of Congress*] (LCLS)
POWP......... Preliminary Overhaul Work Package (DNAB)
POWR......... Environmental Power [*NASDAQ symbol*] (SAG)
Pow R & D... Power, Rodwell, and Drew's English Election Cases [*1847-56*] [*A publication*] (DLA)
PowrCrv...... PowerCerv Corp. [*Associated Press*] (SAG)
POWRENAF.. Petty Officer WREN [*Women's Royal Naval Service*] Air Fitter [*British military*] (DMA)
POWRENCINE.... Petty Officer WREN [*Women's Royal Naval Service*] Cinema Operator [*British military*] (DMA)
POWRENCK... Petty Officer WREN [*Women's Royal Naval Service*] Cook [*British military*] (DMA)
POWRENDHYG... Petty Officer WREN [*Women's Royal Naval Service*] Dental Hygienist [*British military*] (DMA)
POWRENDSA... Petty Officer WREN [*Women's Royal Naval Service*] Dental Surgery Assistant [*British military*] (DMA)
POWRENMET... Petty Officer WREN [*Women's Royal Naval Service*] Meteorological Observer [*British military*] (DMA)
POWRENMT... Petty Officer WREN [*Women's Royal Naval Service*] Motor Transport Driver [*British military*] (DMA)
POWRENPHOT... Petty Officer WREN [*Women's Royal Naval Service*] Photographer [*British military*] (DMA)
POWRENQA... Petty Officer WREN [*Women's Royal Naval Service*] Quarters Assistant [*British military*] (DMA)
POWREN(R)... Petty Officer WREN [*Women's Royal Naval Service*] (RADAR) [*British military*] (DMA)
POWRENREL.. Petty Officer WREN [*Women's Royal Naval Service*] Radio Electrician [*British military*] (DMA)
POWRENRS(M)... Petty Officer WREN [*Women's Royal Naval Service*] Radio Supervisor (Morse) [*British military*] (DMA)
POWRENSA... Petty Officer WREN [*Women's Royal Naval Service*] Stores Accountant [*British military*] (DMA)
POWRENS(C)... Petty Officer WREN [*Women's Royal Naval Service*] Stores Assistant (Clothes) [*British military*] (DMA)
POWRENS(S)... Petty Officer WREN [*Women's Royal Naval Service*] Stores Assistant (Stores) [*British military*] (DMA)
POWRENSTD... Petty Officer WREN [*Women's Royal Naval Service*] Steward [*British military*] (DMA)
POWRENS(V)... Petty Officer WREN [*Women's Royal Naval Service*] Stores Assistant (Victualling) [*British military*] (DMA)
POWRENTEL... Petty Officer WREN [*Women's Royal Naval Service*] Telephonist [*British military*] (DMA)
POWRENTSA... Petty Officer WREN [*Women's Royal Naval Service*] Training Support Assistant [*British military*] (DMA)
POWRENWA... Petty Officer WREN [*Women's Royal Naval Service*] Weapon Analyst [*British military*] (DMA)

POWRENWTR(G)... Petty Officer WREN [*Women's Royal Naval Service*] Writer (General) [*British military*] (DMA)
POWRENWTR(P)... Petty Officer WREN [*Women's Royal Naval Service*] Writer (Pay) [*British military*] (DMA)
POWRENWW... Petty Officer WREN [*Women's Royal Naval Service*] Welfare Worker [*British military*] (DMA)
Powrwv........ Powerwave Technologies, Inc. [*Associated Press*] (SAG)
POWS.......... PROFS [*Program for Regional Observing and Forecasting Services*] Operational Work Station [*Marine science*] (OSRA)
POWS.......... Project Operating Work Statement [*NASA*] (NASA)
POWS.......... Pyrotechnic Outside Warning System (IEEE)
pows--......... Western Samoa [*MARC geographic area code Library of Congress*] (LCCP)
POW-SIG...... Pagan/Occult/Witchcraft Special Interest Group (EA)
Pow Surr...... Powers' Reports, New York Surrogate Court [*A publication*] (DLA)
POWTECH... International Powder and Bulk Solids Technology Exhibition and Conference
POWTR........ Petty Officer Writer [*British military*] (DMA)
POWU.......... Post Office Work Unit [*Computer performance measure*] [*British Telecom*]
PoWU.......... Uniwersytet Warszawski [*University of Warsaw*], Warsaw, Poland [*Library symbol Library of Congress*] (LCLS)
POW:WE...... Peoples of the World: Western Europeans [*A publication*]
POWWER..... Power of World Wide Energy Resources [*In organization name "Natural POWWER"*] (EA)
POX .... Partial Oxidation [*Organic chemistry*]
POX .... Point of Exit
POX .... Port Alexander [*Alaska*] [*Airport symbol*] (AD)
P-OX .... Pressure Oxidation
POX .... Purgeable Organic Halogen [*Chemistry*] (FFDE)
POX-AC....... Pox Battery, Acute [*Biochemistry*] (DAVI)
poxd--.......... Mariana Islands [*MARC geographic area code Library of Congress*] (LCCP)
poxe--.......... Marshall Islands [*MARC geographic area code Library of Congress*] (LCCP)
poxf--.......... Midway Islands [*MARC geographic area code Library of Congress*] (LCCP)
poxh--.......... Niue [*MARC geographic area code Library of Congress*] (LCCP)
POY .... Lovell-Powell [*Wyoming*] [*Airport symbol*] (AD)
POY .... Partially Oriented Yarns
POY .... Polyester Oriented Yarn (DICI)
POY .... Powell, WY [*Location identifier FAA*] (FAAL)
POY .... Prairie Oil Royalties Co. Ltd. [*AMEX symbol Toronto Stock Exchange symbol*] (SPSG)
poy............. Pre-Oriented Yarn (AD)
Poynt M & D... Poynter on Marriage and Divorce [*2nd ed.*] [*1824*] [*A publication*] (DLA)
POYO .... Pollo Tropical [*NASDAQ symbol*] (SAG)
POZ.............. Poznan [*Poland*] [*Airport symbol*] (OAG)
Poz............... Poznan (AD)
PP .... Brazil [*International civil aircraft marking*] (ODBW)
PP .... Eisai Co. Ltd. [*Japan*] [*Research code symbol*]
PP .... Free Library of Philadelphia, Philadelphia, PA [*Library symbol Library of Congress*] (LCLS)
PP .... Head Injury Hotline [*Formerly, Phoenix Project*] (EA)
PP .... Pacific Petroleum (AD)
PP .... Page Printer (NVT)
PP .... Pages
Pp .... Pages (WDMC)
pp .... Pages (WDMC)
PP .... Pages from the Past [*Later, PIR*] [*An association*] (EA)
PP .... Palisades Plant [*Nuclear energy*] (NRCH)
PP .... Palus Putretudinis [*Lunar area*]
PP .... Pancreatic Polypeptide [*Biochemistry*]
PP .... Pandectes Periodiques [*A publication*] (ILCA)
PP .... Panel Point [*Technical drawings*]
pp .... Panel Point (AD)
PP .... Pangu Pati [*Papua New Guinea*] [*Political party*] (PPW)
PP .... Papa [*Pope*]
Pp .... Papa [*Father*] [*Latin*] (AD)
PP .... Paper Profit
pp .... Papua New Guinea [*MARC country of publication code Library of Congress*] (LCCP)
PP .... Paradigm Publishing Ltd. [*British*]
PP .... Paradoxical Pulse [*Medicine*] (DMAA)
PP .... Parallel Processor
PP .... Parcel Post
pp .... Parcel Post (AD)
PP .... Parish Priest
PP .... Paris Publications, Inc.
PP .... Parity Price (MHDW)
PP .... Parliamentary Papers [*A publication British*]
P/P .... Partial Pay [*Air Force*]
PP .... Partial Pressure
pp .... Partial Pressure (NAKS)
PP .... Partial Product (IAA)
PP .... Partial Program
PP .... Partia Popullore [*Popular Party*] [*Albania*] [*Political party*] (PPE)
PP .... Particular [*Named*] Port [*British*] (ROG)
PP .... Partido Panamenista [*Panamanian Party*] [*Political party*] (PPW)
PP .... Partido Popular [*Popular Party*] [*Spain Political party*] (PPE)
PP................ Partido Populista [*Populist Party*] [*Argentina Political party*]
PP................ Parti du Peuple [*People's Party*] [*Burundi*] [*Political party*]
PP .... Partners in Politics (EA)
PP .... Part Paid [*Business and trade*]

PP	Part Paid (AD)
PP	Parts Per
PP	[The] Passionate Pilgrim [Shakespearean work]
PP	Passive Participle
PP	Passive Participle (AD)
PP	Pastor Pastorum [Shepherd of the Shepherds] [Latin] (ROG)
PP	Past Participle
PP	Past Participle (WDMC)
PP	Past Patriarch [Freemasonry] (ROG)
PP	Past President
P/P	Patch Panel (NASA)
PP	Patent Pending (IAA)
PP	Pater Patriae [The Father of His Country] [Latin]
PP	Patres [Fathers] [Latin]
PP	Patriotic Party [British]
PP	Patrol Vessels [Navy symbol] (MUGU)
PP	Peace PAC (EA)
PP	Peak Power (IAA)
PP	Peak Pressure
PP	Peak-to-Peak
PP	Peanut Pals (EA)
PP	Pedal Power
PP	Pedal Pulse
PP	Pellagra Preventive [Factor] [See also PPF] [Biochemistry]
PP	Pellagra Preventive (AD)
P-P	Pellagra-Preventive Factor (AD)
PP	Pension Plan
PP	People's Party [Spain Political party] (ECON)
PP	People's Party [Halkci Partisi] [Turkey Political party] (PPW)
PP	Pep Pill [Slang]
PP	Perceptual Performance (AD)
PP	Perfusion Pressure [Cardiology] (DAVI)
PP	Periodical Publications [British Library shelf designation]
PP	Peripheral Processor [Computer science]
PP	Periportal [Anatomy]
PP	Periproct [Invertebrate anatomy]
PP	Permanent Partial [Dentistry] (MAE)
PP	Permanent Party [Military]
PP	Permanent Party (AD)
PP	Permanent Pasture [Agriculture]
PP	Permanent Press (ADA)
PP	Permanent Professor
PP	Peroxisome Proliferator [Biochemistry]
PP	Per Person (AD)
PP	Per Procurationem [By Proxy, By the Action Of] [Legal term Latin]
PP	Personal Prelatures [Diocesan abbreviation] (TOCD)
PP	Personal Property
P-P	Person to Person [Word processing]
PP	Pet Pride (EA)
PP	Petroleum Point
PP	Petrus Piccoli de Monteforte [Flourished, 14th century] [Authority cited in pre-1607 legal work] (DSA)
PP	Petticoat Peeping [From one girl to another, in reference to dress disarrangement]
PP	Peyer's Patch [Immunology]
PP	Phillips Airlines [ICAO designator] (AD)
PP	Philo-Phobe [Psychological testing]
PP	Phoenix Project [An association] (EA)
PP	Phony Peach Bacteria [Plant pathology]
PP	Photosynthetic Panel [i.e., leaf] [Slang]
PP	Physical Profile
PP	Physical Profile (AD)
PP	Physical Properties (AD)
PP	Physical Properties
PP	Phytophthora Parasitica [A fungus]
PP	Pianissimo [Very Softly] [Music]
PP	Pianissimo [Very Softly] [Italian] [Music] (WDAA)
PP	Picked Ports
PP	Pickpocket
PP	Pickpocket (AD)
PP	Picture Peace [Defunct] (EA)
PP	Piena Pelle [Full Leather] [Italian] (AD)
PP	Piers Plowman [Middle English poem]
P/P	Pier to Pier (ADA)
PP	Piissimus [Most Holy] [Latin]
PP	Pilotless Plane
PP	Pilot Parents (EA)
PP	Pilot Punch
PP	Pine Bark Mixed with Peat
PP	Pink Puffer [Emphysema] (MAE)
PP	Pinpoint [Pupils] [Ophthalmology] (DAVI)
PP	Pinprick [Medicine] (DMAA)
PP	Pipeline Processor (IAA)
PP	Piping
PP	Piscataqua Pioneers (EA)
PP	Piu Piano [More Softly] [Music]
PP	PIXEL-Processing [Computer science]
PP	Placental Protein [Gynecology]
PP	Place of Publisher (NITA)
PP	Plane Parallel
PP	Plane Polarized [Telecommunications] (TEL)
PP	Planetary Programs [NASA]
PP	Planned Parenthood
PP	Planning Package [NASA] (NASA)
PP	Planning Package (NAKS)
PP	Planning Permission (AD)
PP	Planning Purpose
PP	Plan Profile
PP	Plant Protection
PP	Plasmapheresis [Hematology]
PP	Plasma Protein
PP	Plaster of Paris
PP	Plate Power (IAA)
PP	Plate Pulse (IAA)
PP	Play or Pay (ROG)
PP	Please Pay (ROG)
PP	Plenum Pressure (COE)
PP	Plethysmograph Pressure [Measurement] [Medicine] (DAVI)
PP	Pleural Pressure [Medicine]
PP	Plot Points [Computer science]
PP	Pluvius Policy [Insurance against rain]
PP	Pocketpiece [A. C. Nielsen Co.] [Rating report] (NTCM)
PP	Poetry Project (EA)
P/P	Point-to-Point [Air Force]
PP	Polar Pacific [American air mass]
PP	Pole Piece (DEN)
PP	Pole Position [Automobile racing]
PP	Polizei Pistole [Police Pistol] [Walther Waffenfabrik, German arms manufacturer]
PP	Polypeptide [Biochemistry]
PP	Polyphosphate [Inorganic chemistry] (AAMN)
PP	Polypropylene [Organic chemistry]
PP	Polypyrrole [Photovoltaic energy systems]
PP	Polystyrene Agglutination Plate (DB)
PP	Pom-Pom [Gun]
PP	Pontificum [Of the Popes] [Latin]
PP	Popular Party [European political movement] (ECON)
PP	Population Planning (DAVI)
PP	Populist Party of America [Political party] (EA)
PP	Porcelain Pavers (DICI)
PP	Port Pipe (ADA)
PP	Posa Piano [Handle with Care] [Shipping] [Italian]
PP	Position Paper (MCD)
PP	Postage Paid [Shipping]
PP	Postage Paid (AD)
PP	Posted Price (MENA)
PP	Posterior Parietal Cortex [Neuroanatomy]
PP	Posterior Pituitary [Medicine]
PP	Post Pagado [Postage Paid] [Shipping] [Spanish]
PP	Postpaid
PP	Post Partum [After Birth] [Latin] (ADA)
PP	Post Partum [Afterbirth] [Latin] (AD)
PP	Postpass
PP	Postponed
PP	Post Position [Racing]
PP	Postprandial [After Meals] [Pharmacy]
PP	Post Processing
PP	Postprocessor [Computer science] (IAA)
PP	Pounds Pressure
PP	Pour Point [Petroleum characteristic]
PP	Power Package
PP	Power People
PP	Power Plan (IAA)
PP	Power Plant
PP	Power Play [Hockey]
PP	Power Pole (NASA)
PP	Power Pole (NAKS)
PP	Power Supplies [JETDS nomenclature] [Military] (CET)
PP	Praemissis Praemittendis [Omitting Preliminaries, To Whom It May Concern] [Latin]
PP	Praepter Propter [Approximately] [Pharmacy]
Pp	Pratylenchus penetrans [A nematode]
PP	Preferred Provider [Medicine] (DMAA)
PP	Prentiss Properties Trust [NYSE symbol] (SAG)
PP	Prepaid
PP	Preparative Flag [Navy British]
PP	Preparing, Providing [Pharmacy] (ROG)
PP	Preposition [Industrial engineering]
PP	Prepositional Phrase (BYTE)
PP	Prepregnancy [Medicine]
PP	Preprinted
PP	Preprocessor
PP	Preproduction (KSC)
PP	Prescribed Period [Social Security Administration] (OICC)
PP	Present Participle [Grammar]
PP	Present Position [Military]
PP	Present Position (AD)
PP	Present Pupil (AIE)
PP	Press Packed
PP	Press Pressure (SSD)
PP	Pressure Pattern (MCD)
PP	Pressure-Proof [Technical drawings]
PP	Pressure-Proof (AD)
PP	Pretty Poor [Slang Bowdlerized version]
PP	Primarily Primates [An association] (EA)
PP	Primary Pressure [Nuclear energy] (NRCH)
PP	Primary Producers (ADA)
PP	Princess Pat's [Princess Patricia of Connaught's Light Infantry] [Military unit] [Canada]
PP	Principal

PP	Principal Point
pp	Printed Pages [*Publishing*] (WDAA)
PP	Printer Page [*Computer science*]
P/P	Printer/Plotter (NASA)
PP	Print Positions
PP	Print-Punch [*Computer science*] (BUR)
PP	Priority Message Precedence [*Telecommunications*] (ADDR)
PP	Priority Processor
PP	Prior Permission
PP	Private Jet Services AG [*Sweden ICAO designator*] (ICDA)
PP	Privately Printed
pp	Privately Printed (AD)
P/P	Private Passenger
PP	Private Patient [*Medicine*]
PP	Private Practice [*Chiropody*] [*British*]
PP	Private Property [*Military*]
pp	Private Property (AD)
PP	Procurement Package (AAGC)
PP	Procurement Plan (MCD)
PP	Producer Price
PP	Production Processes
PP	Product Publication (IAA)
PP	Professional Paper
pp	Professional Paper (AD)
PP	Professor Publicus [*Public Professor*] [*Latin*] (ROG)
PP	Programming Plan (AFM)
PP	Program Package (MCD)
PP	Program Paper
PP	Program Performance (NASA)
pp	Program Performance (NAKS)
PP	Program Planning (COE)
PP	Program Product [*Computer science*]
PP	Progress Payments [*Military procurement*]
PP	Project Priesthood (AD)
PP	Project Proposal (KSC)
PP	Proletarian Party
PP	Proodeftiki Parataxis [*Progressive Front*] [*Greek Cyprus*] [*Political party*] (PPE)
pp	Pro Parte [*In Part*] [*Latin*]
PP	Propeller Pitch
PP	Proportional Part
PP	Proposals Paper
PP	Proposed Plan (BCP)
PP	Propria Persona [*In His or Her Own Person*] [*Latin*] (WGA)
PP	Propulsion Power (KSC)
PP	Protein Phosphatase [*An enzyme*]
PP	Prothrombin-Proconvertin [*Hematology*]
PP	Proton-Proton [*Nuclear physics*]
PP	Protoporphyria [*Medicine*]
PP	Protoporphyrin [*Biochemistry*]
PP	Provisioning Procedures [*Corps of Engineers*]
PP	Proximal Phalanx [*Anatomy*]
PP	Pseudomyxoma Peritonei [*Medicine*] (DMAA)
PP	Pseudoprogram (IAA)
PP	Psychic Phenomena
PP	Psychological Profile
PP	Psychologists and Psychiatrists [*in service*] [*British*]
P/P	Pterocephaliid-Ptychaspid [*Paleogeologic boundary*]
PP	Public Property
PP	Published Price [*of a book*]
PP	Pulse Pair (IAA)
PP	Pulse Polarography [*Analytical chemistry*]
PP	Pulse Pressure [*Medicine*]
P-P	Pulse to Pulse
PP	Pulvis Patrum [*The Fathers' Powder (or Jesuits' Powder)*] [*Pharmacy*] (ROG)
PP	Pump-Priming (MHDB)
PP	Punctum Proximum [*Near Point*] [*Latin*]
pp	Purchased Part (AD)
PP	Purchased Parts
PP	Purchase Power [*Commercial firm*] (EA)
PP	Purchase Price
PP	Pusher Plane
PP	Push-Pull [*Technical drawings*]
p-p	Push-Pull (AD)
pp	Push-Pull (NAKS)
PP1	Pyrophosphate [*Chemistry*]
PP1	Protein Phosphatase 1 [*An enzyme*]
PPA	Athenaeum of Philadelphia, Philadelphia, PA [*Library symbol Library of Congress*] (LCLS)
PPA	National Plant Protection Association
PPA	Pakistan Press Association (AD)
PPA	Paleopathology Association (EA)
PPA	Palpation, Percussion, and Auscultation [*Medicine*]
ppa	Palpitation, Percussion, Auscultation (AD)
PPA	Pampa, TX [*Location identifier FAA*] (FAAL)
PPA	Panamerican/Panafrican Association (EA)
PPA	Paper Pail Association [*Defunct*] (EA)
PPA	Paper Plate Association [*Later, SSI*] (EA)
PPA	Parallel Port Adapter [*Computer science*] (CIST)
PPA	Parallel Processing Automata (PDAA)
PPA	Parcel Post Association [*Later, PSA*] (EA)
PPA	Parenting Publications of America (NTPA)
PPA	Parents for Private Adoption [*Defunct*] (EA)
PPA	Partido Panamenista Autentico [*Panama*] [*Political party*] (EY)

PPA	Partido Patriotico Arubano [*Aruban Patriotic Party*] [*Netherlands Antilles*] [*Political party*] (PPW)
PPA	Partido Peronista Autentico [*Authentic Peronist Party*] [*Argentina Political party*] (EY)
PPA	Pathology Practice Association (EA)
PPA	Peat Producers Association [*British*] (EAIO)
PPA	Pensioner Party of Australia [*Political party*]
PPA	Pension Portability Act of 1992 (WYGK)
PPA	Pension Protection Act (GFGA)
PPA	People for Prison Alternatives [*An association*] (AD)
PPA	Peppa Resources [*Vancouver Stock Exchange symbol*]
PPA	Perennial Plant Association (EA)
PPA	Periodical Publishers Association [*Later, MCA*] (EA)
PPA	Per Power of Attorney [*Business term*]
ppa	Per Procura [*By Proxy*] [*Latin*]
PPA	Personnel Pool of America [*An association*] (AD)
PPA	Pesticide Producers Association [*Defunct*] (EA)
PPA	Pet Producers of America (EA)
PPA	Phenylpropanolamine [*Organic chemistry*]
ppa	Phenylpropanolamine (AD)
PPA	Phenylpropanolamine(hydrochloride) [*Also, PPH, PPM*] [*Decongestant*]
PPA	Phenylpyruvic Acid [*Organic chemistry*]
PPA	Phiala Prius Agitata [*Having First Shaken the Bottle*] [*Pharmacy*]
ppa	Phiala Prius Agitate [*Bottle Having First Been Shaken*] [*Latin*] (AD)
PPA	Phosphoric Acid Anodized (PDAA)
PPA	Photo Peak Analysis (IEEE)
ppa	Photo-Peak Analysis (AD)
PPA	Physical Page Address [*Computer science*] (CIST)
PPA	Pianoforte Publicity Association [*British*] (BI)
PPA	Pictorial Photographers of America (EAIO)
PPA	Pie De Palo [*Argentina*] [*Seismograph station code, US Geological Survey*] (SEIS)
PPA	Pilot Pulse Amplitude
PPA	Pilots and Passengers Association [*Defunct*] (EA)
PPA	Pitch Precession Amplifier
PPA	Pittsburgh Pneumonia Agent [*Microbiology*]
PPA	Planned Program Accomplishment (GNE)
PPA	Plant Patent Act [*1930*]
PPA	Plasminogen Proactivator [*Hematology*]
PPA	Plutonium Preparation Area [*Nuclear energy*] (GFGA)
PPA	Policyholders Protective Association of America (EA)
PPA	Pollution Prevention Act [*1990*]
PPA	Polycrystalline Products Association (NTPA)
PPA	Polymer Permeation Analyzer
PPA	Poly(phosphoric Acid) [*Inorganic chemistry*]
PPA	Pool Promoters Association [*British*] (BI)
PPA	Popcorn Processors Association [*Later, PI*]
PPA	Popski's Private Army [*Commando force led by Vladimir Peniakoff*] [*World War II*]
PPA	Population Planning Associates (BABM)
PPA	Portland Port Authority [*Australia*]
PPA	Postpartum Amenorrhea [*Medicine*]
PPA	Post-Pill Amenorrhea [*Medicine*] (MEDA)
PPA	Potato Processors' Association [*Australia*]
PPA	Poultry Publishers Association (EA)
PPA	Power Plant Automation
PPA	Powerplant Performance Analysis
PPA	Preferred Provider Arrangement [*Information service or system*] (HCT)
PPA	Preliminary Pile Assembly (IAA)
PPA	Preschool Playgrounds Association [*British*]
PPA	Prescription Pricing Authority (PDAA)
PPA	Presidents' Professional Association [*Later, Presidents Association*] (EA)
PPA	Press and Publications Administration [*China*]
PPA	Princeton Particle Accelerator (IAA)
PPA	Princeton-Pennsylvania Accelerator [*Closed, 1972*] [*AEC*]
PPA	Princeton-Pennsylvania Proton Accelerator [*Closed, 1972*] [*AEC*] (IAA)
PPA	Principal Port Authority [*British*] (ROG)
PPA	Printers' Provident Association (DGA)
PPA	Printing Platemakers Association [*Later, GPA*]
PPA	Priority Problem Areas (MCD)
PPA	Prison Parole Assessment (WDAA)
PPA	Process Plan Association [*British*] (DS)
PPA	Process Plant Association [*British*] (DBA)
PPA	Produce Packaging Association [*Later, PMA*] (EA)
PPA	Professional Paddlesports Association (NTPA)
PPA	Professional Panhellenic Association [*Later, PFA*] (EA)
PPA	Professional Photographers of America (AD)
PPA	Professional Programmers Association (EA)
PPA	Professional Putters Association (EA)
PPA	Program Problem Area
PPA	Progressive Party of America [*Third party in 1948 Presidential race*]
PPA	Progress Presse Agentur GmbH [*Press agency*] [*Germany*]
PPA	Proletarian Party of America [*Political party*] (AD)
PPA	Promotional Products Association International (NTPA)
PPA	Prompt Payment Act (AAGC)
PPA	Propane Phosphonic Acid Anhydride [*Organic chemistry*]
PPA	Propane-Precipitated Asphalt [*Petroleum technology*]
PPA	Property Protection Area
PPA	Propheter Construction Co., Inc. [*ICAO designator*] (FAAC)
PPA	Protected Partition Area [*Telecommunications*] (IAA)
PPA	Protestant Press Agency [*British*]

PPA............. Prudent Purchaser Arrangement [Medical insurance]
PPA............. Pseudopassive Array
PPA............. Public Personnel Association [Later, IPMA] (EA)
PPA............. Publishers' Publicity Association (EA)
PPA............. Pulmonary Artery Pressure [Cardiology]
Ppa .... Pulmonary Artery Pressure [Medicine] (DMAA)
PPA............. Pulsed Power Amplifier
PPA............. Pulse Plasma Accelerator
PPA............. Pure Pulmonary Atresia [Medicine] (DMAA)
PPA............. Purple Plum Association [Defunct] (EA)
PPA............. Push-Pull Amplifier (IAA)
PPAA .... Patres Amplissimi [Cardinals] [Latin]
PPAA .... Personal Protective Armor Association (EA)
PPAAR .... Princeton University, Pennsylvania University, Army Avionics
              Research (PDAA)
PPAB .... Program and Policy Advisory Board [UN Food and Agriculture
              Organization]
PPABP .... American Baptist Publication Society, Philadelphia, PA [Library
              symbol Library of Congress Obsolete] (LCLS)
PP-AC......... Air-Conditioning Power Panel (DAC)
PPAC .... Pesticide Policy Advisory Committee [Environmental Protection
              Agency]
PPAC .... Primary Progress Assessment Chart [Psychology]
PPAC .... Private Planning Association of Canada
PPAC .... Product Performance Agreement Center [Military]
PPAC .... Progressive Political Action Committee [Defunct]
PPAC .... Public Parks Advisory Committee [South Australia]
PPACE .... United States Army, Corps of Engineers, Philadelphia District Library,
              Custom House, Philadelphia, PA [Library symbol Library of
              Congress] (LCLS)
PPAChi .... American Catholic Historical Society, Philadelphia, PA [Library
              symbol Library of Congress] (LCLS)
PPADS......... Parawing Precision Aerial Delivery System (MCD)
PPAEM .... Albert Einstein Medical Center, Northern Division, Philadelphia, PA
              [Library symbol Library of Congress] (LCLS)
PPAFA .... Pennsylvania Academy of the Fine Arts, Philadelphia, PA [Library
              symbol Library of Congress Obsolete] (LCLS)
PPAG .... Personnel Profile - Age by Grade [Army]
PPAG .... Proposed Public Affairs Guidance (COE)
PPAI........... Pinpoint Assignment Instructions [Army] (INF)
PPAK .... Atwater Kent Museum, Philadelphia, PA [Library symbol Library of
              Congress] (LCLS)
PPAL........... Pennsylvania Power & Light Co. (IAA)
PPAL........... Principal (ROG)
PPalZ .... New Jersey Zinc Co. [of Pennsylvania], Technical Library, Palmerton,
              PA [Library symbol Library of Congress] (LCLS)
PPAmP .... American Philosophical Society, Philadelphia, PA [Library symbol
              Library of Congress] (LCLS)
PPAmS .... American Sunday School Union, Philadelphia, PA [Library symbol
              Library of Congress Obsolete] (LCLS)
PPAmSR ...... American Sugar Refining Co., Philadelphia, PA [Library symbol
              Library of Congress Obsolete] (LCLS)
PPAmSwM... American Swedish Historical Foundation, Philadelphia, PA [Library
              symbol Library of Congress] (LCLS)
PPAN .... Academy of Natural Sciences of Philadelphia, Philadelphia, PA
              [Library symbol Library of Congress] (LCLS)
PPAN .... Pyrolyzed Polyacrylonitrile [Organic chemistry]
PP & A .... Palpation, Percussion, and Auscultation [Medicine]
pp & a .... Palpitation, Percussion, and Auscultation (AD)
PP & A .... Percussion, Palpation, and Auscultation [Medicine] (DAVI)
pp&b........... Paper, Printing, and Binding (AD)
PP & B .... Paper, Printing, and Binding [Publishing]
PP & C .... Pickpocket and Confidence [Police term]
PP & C .... Production Planning and Control [Military] (AABC)
PP & C .... Project Planning and Control (NG)
PP & E .... Program Planning and Evaluation (AD)
PP&L .... Pacific Power and Light (AD)
PP&L .... Pennsylvania Power and Light (AD)
PP&L Res... PP & L Resources, Inc. [Associated Press] (SAG)
PP & NA...... Private Plants and Naval Activities
PP & T....... Packaging, Preservation, and Transportation
PPAnR .... Annenberg Research Institute for Judaic and Middle Eastern Studies,
              Philadelphia, PA [Library symbol] [Library of Congress] (LCLS)
PPAp........... Apprentices' Free Library, Philadelphia, PA [Library symbol Library of
              Congress Obsolete] (LCLS)
PPAP .... People's Party of Arunachal Pradesh [India] [Political party] (PPW)
PPAP .... Precedents of Private Acts of Parliament [A publication] (DLA)
PPA pos...... Phenylpyruvic Acid Positive [Biochemistry] (DAVI)
PPAR .... Paging Partners [NASDAQ symbol] (TTSB)
PPAR .... Paging Partners Corp. [NASDAQ symbol] (SAG)
PPAR .... Peroxisome Proliferator-Activated Receptor [Genetics]
PPAR .... Priority Problem Analysis Report [Military] (DNAB)
PPAR .... Project Performance Audit Report
PPARA .... ARA Historical Foundation, ARA Industries, Philadelphia, PA [Closed]
              [Library symbol] [Library of Congress] (LCLS)
PPARC........ Particle Physics and Astronomy Research Council [British]
PPArmA ...... Armstrong Association of Philadelphia, Philadelphia, PA [Library
              symbol Library of Congress Obsolete] (LCLS)
PPARW .... Paging Partners Wrrt [NASDAQ symbol] (TTSB)
PPAS .... Patti Page Appreciation Society (EA)
PPAS .... Peripheral Pulmonary Artery Stenosis [Medicine] (DMAA)
PPAS .... Portable Public Address System (MCD)
PPAS .... Postpolio Atrophy Syndrome [Medicine] (STED)
PPAS .... Potassium Picrate Active Substances [Measure of detergent content
              of water]

PPAS .... Probability Proportional to Aggregate Size [Statistics]
PPAtR .... Atlantic Refining Co., Philadelphia, PA [Library symbol Library of
              Congress] (LCLS)
PPATRA ...... Printing, Packaging, and Allied Trades Research Association (AD)
PPATY .... Preparatory (ROG)
PPAuC .... Automobile Club of Philadelphia, Philadelphia, PA [Library symbol
              Library of Congress Obsolete] (LCLS)
PPAUS .... Peat Producers Association of the United States (EA)
PPAW .... Public Policy Affecting Women Task Force (EA)
PPAWA .... Poultry Producers' Association of Western Australia
Ppb............. Pappaband [Hard Cover] [German] (AD)
PPB............. Parachute Paraglider Building [NASA] (KSC)
PPB............. Parts per Billion
ppb............. Parts per Billion (AD)
ppb............. Parts per Billion 10 (IDOE)
PPB............. Petro-Canada Products, Inc. [Toronto Stock Exchange symbol
              Vancouver Stock Exchange symbol]
PPB............. Philadelphia Bar Association, Philadelphia, PA [Library symbol
              Library of Congress] (LCLS)
P-P-B......... Planning-Programming-Budgeting [System] [Army]
PPB............. Platelet-Poor Blood [Hematology] (MAE)
PPB............. Platoon Patrol Base [Military] (VNW)
PPB............. Political Party Broadcast [Television] [British]
PPB............. Polybrominated-Biphenyl (AD)
PPB............. Poly(para-benzamide) [Organic chemistry]
PPB............. Positive Pressure Breathing [Aerospace]
PPb............. Postparotid Basic Protein (DMAA)
PPB............. Power Plant Bulletin (MCD)
PPB............. Precision Pressure Balance
PPB............. Preprophase Band [Cytology]
PPB............. Presidente Prudente [Brazil] [Airport symbol] (AD)
PPB............. Pres Prudente [Brazil] [Airport symbol] (OAG)
PPB............. Primary Propulsion Branch [Manned Spacecraft Center]
PPB............. Printing, Paper, and Binding [Publishing] (WDMC)
PPB............. Private Posting Box
PPB............. Procurement Policy Board [ABA Public Contract Law Section]
              (AAGC)
PPB............. Production Parts Breakdown (MCD)
PPB............. Program Performance Baseline (NASA)
PPB............. Program Planning Budget (NOAA)
PPB............. Program-Planning-Budgeting
PPB............. PROM [Programmable Read-Only Memory] Programmer Board
PPB............. Provisioning Parts Breakdown
PPB............. Purchasing Power Benefit (ADA)
PPB............. Push-Pull Bearing
PPBANSW.... Pasture Protection Boards' Association of New South Wales
              [Australia]
PPBAS .... Planning-Programming-Budgeting-Accounting System (AD)
PPBB .... Partai Pesaka Bumiputra Bersatu [United Traditional Bumiputra
              Party] [Malaysia] [Political party] (PPW)
PPBB .... PCI-toPCI Bridge Board (ACII)
PPBB .... Prime Power Brass Board (MCD)
PPBC .... Pittsburgh Penguins Booster Club (EA)
PPBC .... Plant Pathogenic Bacteria Committee (EA)
PPBC .... Portland Problem Behavior Checklist (EDAC)
PPBC-R...... Portland Problem Behavior Checklist - Revised [Educational test]
P PBD......... Paper or Paperboard [Freight]
PPBD .... Port of Palm Beach District [AAR code]
PPBE .... Passenger Protective Breathing Equipment [Aviation] (DA)
PPBERS ...... Program Performance and Budget Execution Review System [Army]
PPBES .... Planning, Programming, Budgeting, and Execution System [Army]
              (RDA)
PPBES .... Program Planning and Budget Execution System [Army]
PPBES .... Program Planning-Budgeting-Evaluation System Project (EA)
PPBESP .... Program Planning-Budgeting-Evaluation System Project (EA)
PPBF .... Pan-American Pharmaceutical and Biochemical Federation
PPBFSPS .... Pen and Pocket Blade Forgers' and Smithers' Protective Society [A
              union] [British]
PPBG .... Preliminary Program and Budget Guidance
PPBH .... Pharmaceutical Partners for Better Healthcare (ECON)
PPBI........... Balch Institute, Philadelphia, PA [Library symbol Library of
              Congress] (LCLS)
PPBM.......... Pulse Polarization Binary Modulation (MCD)
PPBMIS .... Planning, Programming, and Budgeting Management Information
              System [Army]
PPBP.......... Pro-Platelet Basic Protein (DMAA)
PPBR .... Program Plan and Budget Request (OICC)
PPBS .... Planning, Programming, and Budgeting System [Army]
PPBS .... Positive Pressure Breathing System [Aerospace]
PPBS .... Postprandial Blood Sugar [Clinical chemistry]
PPBS .... Program Planning and Budgeting Staff [Environmental Protection
              Agency] (GFGA)
PPBS .... Program, Planning, and Budgeting System [Johnson Administration]
              [Executive Office of the President] (GFGA)
PPC............. College of Physicians of Philadelphia, Philadelphia, PA [Library
              symbol Library of Congress OCLC symbol] (LCLS)
PP-C......... Free Library of Philadelphia, Carson Collection, Philadelphia, PA
              [Library symbol Library of Congress] (LCLS)
PPC............. Palm Personal Computer
PPC............. Pan Pacific Centers [Defunct] (EA)
PPC............. Paperboard Packaging Council (EA)
PPC............. Parallel Path Counter [Electronics] (IAA)
PPC............. Partial Pay Card
PPC............. Partido Popular Cristiano [Christian Popular Party] [Peru] [Political
              party] (PPW)

PPC............... Parting Post Calls (MCD)
PPC............... Partitu Populare Corsu [*Corsica*] [*Political party*] (PD)
PPc............... Parts Preference Code [*Military*] (AFIT)
PPC............... Patres Conscripti [*Senators*] [*Latin*] (ROG)
PPC............... Patrick Petroleum Co. (EFIS)
PPC............... Patrol Plane Commander
PPC............... Peak Power Control [*Telecommunications*] (TEL)
PPC............... Permission to Photocopy (MCD)
PPC............... Per Pupil Cost (AFM)
PPC............... Persistent Photoconductivity [*Physics*]
PPC............... Personal Portable Computer
PPC............... Personal Productivity Center
PPC............... Personal Programmable Calculator (MHDI)
PPC............... Personal Protective Clothing (GNE)
PPC............... Pet Population Control (AD)
PPC............... Petroleum Packaging Council (NTPA)
PPC............... Petroleum Planning Committee [*Obsolete NATO*] (NATG)
PPC............... Phased Program Construction (IAA)
PPC............... Phased Provisioning Code (NASA)
PPC............... Philatelic Press Club [*Later, IPPC*]
PPC............... Photographic Processing Cells (AFM)
PPC............... Photo Persistent Conductivity (AAEL)
PpC............... Pick Publishing Corporation, New York, NY [*Library symbol Library of Congress*] (LCLS)
PPC............... Picture Postcard
ppc............... Picture Postcard (AD)
PPC............... Pierce's Perpetual Code [*1943*] [*A publication*] (DLA)
PPC............... Pine Pass [*British Columbia*] [*Seismograph station code, US Geological Survey Closed*] (SEIS)
PPC............... Plain Paper Copier [*Electrophotography*]
PPC............... Plain Plaster Cornice [*Construction*]
PPC............... Planar Postive Column (IAA)
PPC............... Plane Paper Copier (IAA)
ppc............... Plan-Paper Copier (AD)
PPC............... Plant Pest Control Division [*of ARS, Department of Agriculture*]
PPC............... Plant Process Computer
PPC............... Plasma Prothrombin Conversion (DB)
PPc............... Platform Position Computer
PPC............... Platinum-Palladium Colloid (DB)
PPc............... Plug Patch Cord
PPC............... Plutonium Process Cell [*Nuclear energy*] (NRCH)
PPC............... Plutonium Product Cell [*Nuclear energy*] (NRCH)
PPC............... Point of Possible Collision [*Navigation*]
PPC............... Point-to-Point Correlation [*Graphing*]
PPC............... Polarizable Point Charge [*Model for the water molecule*]
PPC............... Policy Planning Council [*U.S. Department of State*] (BARN)
PPC............... Polyphthalate-Polycarbonate
PPC............... Pooled Platelet Concentrate [*Medicine*] (MEDA)
PPC............... Portable Personal Computer (DGA)
PPC............... Positive Peer Control
PPC............... Positive Peer Culture (AD)
PPC............... Posterior Parietal Cortex [*Brain anatomy*]
PPC............... Postpulmonary Complications
PPC............... Potential Points of Collision [*Navigation*]
PPC............... Potentional Performance Capability (IAA)
PPC............... Pour Prendre Conge [*To Take Leave*] [*French*]
p p c............... Pour Prendre Conge [*To Take Leave*] [*French*] (AD)
PPC............... Power Pack Charger
PPC............... Power Plant Change (NVT)
PPC............... PPC Oil & Gas Corp. [*Toronto Stock Exchange symbol*]
PPC............... Precision Photomechanical Corp.
PPC............... Predicted Propagation Correction (PDAA)
PPC............... Preliminary Phase Correction (IAA)
PPC............... Preprocessing Center [*NASA*] (NASA)
PPC............... Pre-Proposal Conference (MCD)
PPC............... President of the Privy Council [*Canada*]
PPC............... Pressure Pulse Contour [*Cardiac computer*] (PDAA)
PPC............... Primary Power Control (MCD)
PPC............... Printers' Pension Corp. (DGA)
PPC............... Print Position Counter
PPC............... Priority Placement Certificate [*Military*] (AFM)
PPC............... Production Planning and Control
PPC............... Product Planning Committee
PPC............... Professional Personal Computer
PPC............... Professional Personnel Consultant (WDAA)
PPC............... Program Planning and Control (AAG)
PPC............... Program Planning Coordination Office [*United Nations*]
PPC............... Progressive Patient Care
ppc............... Progressive Patient Care (AD)
PPC............... Project Parts Coordinator
PPC............... Project Physics Course [*National Science Foundation*]
PPC............... Project Planning and Control (COE)
PPC............... Project Planning Centre for Developing Countries [*Research center British*] (IRC)
PPC............... Proof-of-Passing Certificate (OTD)
PPC............... Pro-Personal Computer (NITA)
PPC............... Prospect Creek, AK [*Location identifier FAA*] (FAAL)
PPC............... Prospective Parliamentary Candidate [*British*]
PPC............... Proximal Palmar Crease [*Anatomy*]
PPC............... Psychorotrophic Plate Count [*Bacteriology*]
PPC............... Publishers Publicity Circle
PPc............... Pulsed Power Circuit (IEEE)
PPc............... Purchase Price Control (AD)
pPc............... Pure Peruvian Cocaine (AD)
ppca............... Plasma Prothrombin Conversion Accelerator (AD)

PPCA .... Plasma [*or Proserum*] Prothrombin Conversion Accelerator [*Factor VII*] [*Also, SPCA Hematology*]
PPCAA .... Parole and Probation Compact Administrators Association (EA)
PPCAP .... People to People Citizen Ambassador Program (EA)
PPCB .... Page Printer Control Block [*Computer science*]
PPCB .... Patrick Petroleum Co. [*NASDAQ symbol*] (SAG)
PPCC .... Carpenters' Co., Philadelphia, PA [*Library symbol Library of Congress*] (LCLS)
PPCC .... Particles per Cubic Centimeter
PPCC .... Parts per Cubic Centimeter (IAA)
PPCC .... Port Phillip Conservation Council [*Australia*]
PPCC .... Postmolded Plastic Chip Carrier [*Computer science*]
PPCCD .... Profiled Peristaltic Charge Coupled-Device [*Computer science*] (IAA)
PPCCH .... Chestnut Hill College, Philadelphia, PA [*Library symbol Library of Congress*] (LCLS)
PPCD .... Plant Pest Control Division (AD)
PPCD .... Polymorphous Posterior Corneal Dystropy [*Medicine*] (DMAA)
PPCE .... Portable Pneumatic Checkout Equipment (KSC)
PPCE .... Post-Proline Cleaving Enzyme [*Biochemistry*]
ppcf .... Plasma Prothrombin Conversion Factor (AD)
PPCF .... Plasmin Prothrombin Conversion Factor [*Factor V*] [*Hematology*]
PPCH .... People-to-People Committee for the Handicapped (EA)
PPCI............ Curtis Institute of Music, Philadelphia, PA [*Library symbol Library of Congress*] (LCLS)
PPCI............ Presentation Protocol Control Information [*Telecommunications*]
PPCiC .... Civic Club of Philadelphia, Philadelphia, PA [*Library symbol Library of Congress Obsolete*] (LCLS)
PPCIG .... Personal Property Consignment Instruction Guide (MCD)
PPCLI.......... Princess Patricia of Connaught's Light Infantry [*Military unit*] [*Canada*]
PPCLI.......... Princess Patricia's Canadian Light Infantry (AD)
PPCM.......... Philadelphia County Medical Society, Philadelphia, PA [*Library symbol Library of Congress Obsolete*] (LCLS)
PPCO .... Philadelphia College of Osteopathic Medicine, Philadelphia, PA [*Library symbol Library of Congress*] (LCLS)
PPCO2 .... Partial Pressure Carbon Dioxide
PPCoC .... Community College of Philadelphia, Philadelphia, PA [*Library symbol Library of Congress*] (LCLS)
PPCOD........ People-to-People Committee on Disability (EA)
PPCoIP .... Colonial Penn Group, Inc., Marketing Research Library, Philadelphia, PA [*Library symbol Library of Congress*] (LCLS)
PPComm....... Commercial Museum, Philadelphia, PA [*Library symbol Library of Congress Obsolete*] (LCLS)
PPCP .... College of Physicians of Philadelphia, Philadelphia, PA [*Library symbol*] [*Library of Congress*] (LCLS)
PPCP .... Propellant Pneumatic Control Panel (KSC)
PPCPC .... Philadelphia City Planning Commission, Philadelphia, PA [*Library symbol Library of Congress*] (LCLS)
PPCPSG........ Polish POW Camps Philatelic Study Group (EA)
PPCR .... Production Planning Change Request (SAA)
PPCS .... National Carl Schurz Memorial Foundation, Philadelphia, PA [*Library symbol Library of Congress Obsolete*] (LCLS)
PPCS .... Page Printer Control System [*Computer science*]
PPCS .... Personnel Protection and Communication Services [*British*] (AD)
PPCS .... Person to Person: Collect and Special Instruction [*Telecommunications*] (TEL)
PPCS .... Precision Pointing Control System [*Engineering*]
PPCS .... Primary Producers' Cooperative Society (AD)
PPCS .... Production Planning and Control System
PPCS .... Project Planning and Control System [*Social Security Administration*]
PPCuP .... Curtis Publishing Co., Research Library, Philadelphia, PA [*Library symbol Library of Congress Obsolete*] (LCLS)
PPD .... A Posteriori Probability Distribution [*Mathematics*]
PPD .... Drexel University, Philadelphia, PA [*Library symbol Library of Congress*] (LCLS)
PPD .... Humacao-Palmas [*Puerto Rico*] [*Airport symbol*] (OAG)
PPD .... Packs per Day [*Cigarettes*] [*Medicine*]
PPD .... Panel Power Distribution (MCD)
PPD .... Papered (ROG)
PPD .... Paranoid Personality Disorder (AD)
PPD .... Para-Phenylenediamine [*Organic chemistry*]
PPD .... Partido Popular Democratico [*Popular Democratic Party*] [*Puerto Rico*] [*Political party*] (PPW)
PPD .... Partido Popular Democratico [*Popular Democratic Party of Puerto Rico*] [*Spanish*] (BARN)
PPD .... Partido por la Democracia [*Democratic Party*] [*Chile*] [*Political party*] (EY)
PPD .... Parti Populaire Djiboutien [*Djibouti People's Party*] [*Political party*] (PPW)
PPD .... Parti Progressiste Dahomeen [*Dahomey Progressive Party*] [*Political party*]
PPD .... Parts Provisioning Document
PPD .... Party for Peace and Democracy [*South Korea*] [*Political party*]
PPD .... Payload Position Data
PPD .... Pay Packets Deficiency [*British*]
PPD .... Pepsin Pancreatin Digest [*Food protein digestibility assay*]
PPD .... Permanent Partial Disability [*Dentistry*] (MAE)
PPD .... Personal Protective Device [*Toxicology*]
PPD .... Personnel Planning Data [*Navy*]
PPD .... Personnel Priority Designator [*Military*] (AFM)
PPD .... Petroleum Production Division
PPD .... Phenyldiphenyloxadiazole [*Organic chemistry*] (MAE)
PPD .... Pitch Phase Detector
PPD .... Plains Petroleum Co. [*Vancouver Stock Exchange symbol*]
PPD .... Plot Plan Drawing (SAA)

PPD .... Point Position Data
PPD .... Politieke Partij Democraten 66 [*Political Party Democrats 66*] [*Netherlands*] (EAIO)
PPD .... Portland Public Docks (AD)
PPD .... Portuguese Popular Democrats
PPD .... Posterior Polymorphous Dystrophy [*Neurology*] (DAVI)
ppd .... Postpaid (WDMC)
PPD .... Postpaid
PPD .... Postpartum Day [*Obstetrics*] (DAVI)
PPD .... Postpartum Depression (PAZ)
PPD .... PostScript Printer Description [*Computer science*] (PCM)
PPD .... Preferred Policyholders' Discount [*British*] (BARN)
ppd .... Prepaid (WDMC)
PPD .... Prepaid
PPD .... Prepaid Dental Plan [*Insurance*] (MCD)
PPD .... Pre-Paid Legal Services, Inc. [*AMEX symbol*] (SPSG)
PPD .... Pre-Paid Legal Svcs [*AMEX symbol*] (TTSB)
ppd .... Prepared (MAE)
PPD .... Preprototype Demonstration
PPD .... Presidential Protective Division [*US Secret Service*]
PPD .... Prime Power Distribution
PPD .... Principal Project Designer [*Engineering project management*]
PPD .... Printer Page Description [*Computer science*]
PPD .... Processed Payment Document (GFGA)
PPD .... Proficiency Pay Designator [*Military*] (AABC)
PPD .... Prognostic Prediction Devices
PPD .... Program Package Document
PPD .... Program Planning Directives [*NASA*] (KSC)
PPD .... Program Planning Document (NG)
PPD .... Progressive Perceptive Deafness [*Medicine*]
PPD .... Projectile Pull and Drain [*Machine*] (MCD)
PPD .... Project Planning Directive (NG)
PPD .... Prompt Payment Discount (AAGC)
PPD .... Propria Pecunia Dedicavit [*With His Own Money He Offered It*] [*Latin*] (ROG)
PPD .... Propulsion and Power Division [*Manned Spacecraft Center*] [*NASA*]
PPD .... Provisioning Procurement Data
PPD .... Pulse-Type Phase Detector
PPD .... Purchasing Power of the Dollar (MHDW)
PPD .... Purified Protein Derivative [*Tuberculin*]
ppd .... Purified Protein Derivative (AD)
PPDA .... Para-Phenylenediamine [*Organic chemistry*]
PPDA .... Phenyl Phosphorodiamidate [*Fertilizer technology*]
PPDA .... Produce Packaging Development Association (AD)
PPDB .... Personnel Planning Data Book [*Navy*]
PPDB .... Point-Positioning Data Base [*Cartography*] (RDA)
PPD-B .... Purified Protein Derivative - Battey [*Tuberculin*] (AAMN)
PPDC .... Dental Cosmos Library, Philadelphia, PA [*Library symbol Library of Congress Obsolete*] (LCLS)
PPDC .... Paraguayan People's Documentation Center [*Mestre, Italy*] (EAIO)
PPDC .... Partido Popular Democratica Cristiana [*Popular Christian Democratic Party*] [*Spain Political party*] (PPE)
PPDC .... Perfusion Program Directors Council [*Cardiology*] (DAVI)
PPDC .... Polymer Products Development Center (AD)
PPDC .... Programming Panels and Decoding Circuits
PPDD .... Pershing Physical Deception Device [*Army*]
PPDD .... Plan Position Data Display
PPDD .... Preliminary Project Design Description (NRCH)
PPDDS .... Private Practice Dental Delivery System
PPDef-M ...... Defense Personnel Support Center, Directorate of Medical Material Library, Philadelphia, PA [*Library symbol*] [*Library of Congress*] (LCLS)
PPDF .... Poisson Probability Distribution Function [*Mathematics*]
PPDG .... Parti Progressiste Democratique Guadeloupeen [*Political party*] (EY)
PPDGF .... Porcine Platelet-Derived Growth Factor [*Biochemistry*]
PPDI .... Paraphenylene Diisocyanate [*Organic chemistry*]
PPDI .... Pharmaceutical Product Development, Inc. [*NASDAQ symbol*] (SAG)
PPDI .... Pharmaceutical Product Devlpmt [*NASDAQ symbol*] (TTSB)
ppdi .... Pilot's Projected-Display Indicator (AD)
PPDI .... Pre-Pre-Delivery Inspection [*Automotive project management*]
PPDIL .... Pre-Power-Dependent Insertion Limit [*Nuclear energy*] (NRCH)
PPDio .... Diocesan Library, Philadelphia, PA [*Library symbol Library of Congress Obsolete*] (LCLS)
PPDL .... Postscript Page Description Language [*Computer science*] (CIST)
PPDM .... E. I. Du Pont de Nemours & Co., Marshall Laboratory, Philadelphia, PA [*Library symbol Library of Congress*] (LCLS)
PPDM .... Pseudo-Pinch Design Method [*Heat exchange design*]
PPDMG .... Popular Priced Dress Manufacturers Group [*Later, AMA*] (EA)
ppdo .... Per Person, Double Occupancy (AD)
PPDO .... Personal Paid Days Off
PPDP .... Preliminary Project Development Plan [*NASA*]
PPDP .... Preprogram Definition Phase
PP-DPH .... Free Library of Philadelphia, Library for the Blind and Physically Handicapped, Philadelphia, PA [*Library symbol Library of Congress*] (LCLS)
PPDR .... Philadelphia Department of Records, Philadelphia, PA [*Library symbol*] [*Library of Congress*] (LCLS)
PPDR .... Pilot Performance Description Record
PP/DR .... Preliminary Performance Design Requirements
PPDR .... Preproliferative Diabetic Retinopathy [*Medicine*] (STED)
PPDR .... Production Packing Depth Range (NG)
PPDrop .... Dropsie University, Philadelphia, PA [*Library symbol Library of Congress*] (LCLS)
PPDS .... Personal Printer Data Stream [*IBM Corp.*] (PCM)
PPDS .... Phonologic Programming Deficit Syndrome (DMAA)

PPDS .... Physical Property Data Service [*Institution of Chemical Engineers*] [*Databank*] [*Information service or system*] (IID)
PPDS .... Planning Production Data Sheet
PPDS .... Preservation and Packaging Data Sheet [*DoD*]
PPDS .... Publishers' Parcels Delivery Service (AD)
PPD-S .... Purified Protein Derivative-Standard [*Tuberculin*]
PPDSE .... International Plate Printers, Die Stampers, and Engravers' Union of North America
PPDSE .... Plate Printers, Die Stampers, and Engravers [*Union*] (AD)
PPDT .... (Phenylpyridyl)diphenyltriazine [*Analytical chemistry*]
PPDT .... Poly(phenyleneterephthalamide) [*Organic chemistry*]
PPDU .... Presentation Protocol Data Unit [*Computer science*] (TNIG)
PPE .... Independent Union of Plant Protection Employees in the Electrical and Machine Industry
PPE .... Partial Plasma Exchange (STED)
PPE .... Parti Populaire Europeen [*European Peoples' Party - EPP*] (EAIO)
PPE .... Permeability Pulmonary Edema (STED)
PPE .... Personal Protective Equipment [*General Motors Corp.*]
ppe .... Philosophy, Politics, and Economics (AD)
PPE .... Philosophy, Politics, Economics [*Oxford University*]
PPE .... Pholbe Phillips Editions [*Publisher*] [*British*]
PPE .... Pipette [*Chemistry*]
PPE .... Platform Position Equipment
PPE .... Polypentene [*Organic chemistry*]
PPE .... Polyphenylene Ether Plastic [*Materials science*]
PPE .... Polyphenylether (IEEE)
PPE .... Polyphosphate Ester [*Inorganic chemistry*]
PPE .... Polyphosphoric Ester (STED)
PPE .... Porcine Pancreatic Elastase [*An enzyme*]
PPE .... Portable Purge Equipment [*NASA*]
PPE .... Potomac Pacific Engineering, Inc.
PPE .... Predicted Period-of-Effect [*Meteorology*]
PPE .... Premodulation Processing Equipment
PPE .... Preproduction Engineering
PPE .... Preproduction Evaluation (NG)
PPE .... Preproduction Proposal Evaluation
PPE .... Preproenkephalin [*Biochemistry*]
PPE .... Print-Punch Editor [*Computer science*] (SAA)
PPE .... Problem Program Efficiency (IEEE)
PPE .... Problem Program Evaluator
PPE .... Programmed Physical Examination (STED)
PPE .... Program Performance Evaluator (NITA)
PPE .... Program Planning and Evaluation
PPE .... Prototype Production Evaluation (NG)
PPE .... Purchasing Power Equivalent
PPE .... Pyridoxal Phosphate Effect [*Medicine*]
PPEA .... Plant Performance Evaluation Activity [*Military*] (DNAB)
PPEB .... Eastern Baptist Theological Seminary, Philadelphia, PA [*Library symbol Library of Congress*] (LCLS)
PPEB .... [*The*] Pottery of Palestine from the Earliest Times to the End of the EarlyBronze Age [*A publication*] (BJA)
PPECP .... Pollution Prevention and Emissions Control Program (COE)
PPEF .... Public Policy Education Fund (EA)
PPEFH .... E. F. Hutton & Co., Philadelphia, PA [*Library symbol Library of Congress Obsolete*] (LCLS)
PPEMA .... Portable Power Equipment Manufacturers Association (EA)
PPEN .... Purchased Parts Equipment Notice (SAA)
PPEng .... Engineers' Club, Philadelphia, PA [*Library symbol Library of Congress Obsolete*] (LCLS)
PPEP .... Eastern Pennsylvania Psychiatric Institute, Philadelphia, PA [*Library symbol Library of Congress*] (LCLS)
PPEP .... Pen Plotter Emulation Program [*Computer science*] (MHDI)
PPEP .... Plasma Physics and Environmental Perturbation (NASA)
P/PEP .... Progress Performance Evaluation Panel [*Job Corps*]
PPER .... Procurement Package Engineering Release (MCD)
PPES .... Physical Performance Evaluation System [*Army*]
PPES .... Pilot Performance Evaluation System [*Air Force*]
PPES .... Planning, Programming, and Execution System [*Army*] (AAGC)
PPeSchw ..... Schwenkfelder Historical Library, Pennsburg, PA [*Library symbol Library of Congress*] (LCLS)
PPETS .... Pretreatment Permitting and Enforcement Tracking System [*Environmental Protection Agency*] (ERG)
PPF .... Franklin Institute, Philadelphia, PA [*Library symbol Library of Congress OCLC Obsolete*] (LCLS)
PPF .... Hancock [*John*] Patriot Preferred Dividend Fund [*NYSE symbol*] (SPSG)
PPF .... John Hancock Patr Pfd Div Fd [*NYSE symbol*] (TTSB)
PPF .... Pacific Peace Fund (EA)
PPF .... Paired-Pulse Facilitation [*Neurophysiology*]
PPF .... Panamanian Public Force (AD)
PPF .... Panels Per Facing [*Outdoor advertising*] (WDMC)
PPF .... Parsons [*Kansas*] [*Airport symbol*] (OAG)
PPF .... Parsons, KS [*Location identifier FAA*] (FAAL)
PPF .... Parti Populaire Francais [*French Popular Party*] [*Political party*] (PPE)
PPF .... Patriotic People's Front [*Hungary Political party*]
PPF .... Payload Processing Facility [*Air Force*] (NASA)
PPF .... Peacetime Planning Factors
PPF .... Peak Power Frequency
PPF .... Pellagra Preventive Factor [*See also PP*] [*Biochemistry*]
PPF .... People's Police Force
PPF .... Personal Property Floater [*Insurance*]
ppf .... Personal Property Floater [*Insurance*] (AD)
PPF .... Phagocytosis Promoting Factor [*Immunology*] (DAVI)
PPF .... Phase Pushing Factor

PPF............ Photophoretic Force [*Pressure exerted by light*]
PPF............ Plasma Protein Fraction [*Hematology*]
PPF............ Plumbers and Pipefitters [*Union*] (AD)
PPF............ Poetarum Philosophorum Graecorum Fragmenta [*A publication*] (OCD)
PPF............ Polarization-Preserving Fiber
PPF............ Poly(phenolformaldehyde) [*Organic chemistry*]
PPF............ Porous Polyurethane Foam [*Also, PUF*] [*Plastics technology*]
PPF............ Power Plant Frame [*Mazda Miata*] [*Connecting engine and transmission to final drive*]
PPF............ Presbyterian Peace Fellowship (EA)
PPF............ Primary Part Failure (DNAB)
PPF............ Principal Profile Forms [*Soil classification*]
PPF............ Privatefoeretagarnas Partioganisation i Finland [*Finnish Private Entrepreneurs' Party*] [*Political party*] (PPE)
PPF............ Production Possibility Frontier [*Economics*]
PPF............ Provision of Production Facilities [*Military*] (AABC)
PPF............ United Association of Journeymen and Apprentices of the Plumbing and Pipe Fitting Industry of the United States and Canada
PPFA.......... Page Printer Formatting Aid [*Computer science*] (CIST)
PPFA.......... Planned Parenthood Federation of America (EA)
PPFA.......... Plastic Pipe and Fittings Association (EA)
PPFA.......... Professional Picture Framers Association (EA)
PPFA.......... United States Army, Frankford Arsenal Library, Philadelphia, PA [*Library symbol Library of Congress*] (LCLS)
p-p factor.... Pellagra-Preventive Factor (AD)
PPFAR .... Federal Archives and Records Center, General Services Administration, Philadelphia, PA [*Library symbol Library of Congress*] (LCLS)
PPFAS .... Past President of the Faculty of Architects and Surveyors [*British*] (DBQ)
PPF-B .... Biochemical Research Foundation, Franklin Institute, Newark, DE [*Closed*] [*Library symbol*] [*Library of Congress*] (LCLS)
PPFC.......... Philadelphia Fellowship Commission, Philadelphia, PA [*Library symbol Library of Congress Obsolete*] (LCLS)
PPFC.......... Priscilla Presley Fan Club [*Defunct*] (EA)
PPFD .... Photosynthetically Active Photon Flux Density [*Botany*]
PPFF .... Poisson Probability Frequency Function [*Mathematics*]
PPF-G .... Germantown Laboratories, Inc., Philadelphia, PA [*Library symbol Library of Congress*] (LCLS)
PPFHi .... Historical Society of Frankford, Philadelphia, PA [*Library symbol Library of Congress Obsolete*] (LCLS)
PPFJC .... Federation of Jewish Charities, Philadelphia, PA [*Library symbol Library of Congress Obsolete*] (LCLS)
PPFML........ Fidelity Mutual Life Insurance Co., Philadelphia, PA [*Library symbol Library of Congress*] (LCLS)
PPFO .... Paris Procurement Field Office
PPFPR .... F. P. Ristine & Co., Philadelphia, PA [*Library symbol Library of Congress Obsolete*] (LCLS)
PPFr.......... Friends' Free Library of Germantown, Philadelphia, PA [*Library symbol Library of Congress*] (LCLS)
PPFR .... Plutonium Product Filter Room [*Nuclear energy*] (NRCH)
PPFRB .... Federal Reserve Bank of Philadelphia, Philadelphia, PA [*Library symbol Library of Congress*] (LCLS)
PPFRT .... Prototype Preliminary Flight Rating Test
PPFS.......... Pergamon Professional and Financial Services [*Commercial firm British*]
PPG .... German Society of Pennsylvania, Philadelphia, PA [*Library symbol Library of Congress*] (LCLS)
PPG .... Pacific Proving Ground [*AEC*]
PPG .... Pago Pago [*Samoa*] [*Airport symbol*] (OAG)
PPG .... Pago Pago, AQ [*Location identifier FAA*] (FAAL)
PPG .... Pediatric Pneumogram [*Radiology*] (DAVI)
PPG .... PEMA Policy and Guidance [*Military*] (AABC)
PPG .... Periodical Press Gallery [*US Senate*]
PPG .... Permanent Planning Group [*Military British*]
PPG .... Personnel Processing Group [*Army*]
PPG .... Photoplethysmography [*Medicine*]
PPG .... Picopicogram [*One trillionth of one trillionth of a gram*]
PPG .... Piezoelectric Power Generation
PPG .... Pipe Plug
PPG .... Pittsburgh Plate Glass [*Commercial firm*]
PPG .... Planned Procurement Guide
PPG .... Planning and Policy Guidance (MCD)
PPG .... Planning and Programming Guidance [*Army*] (AABC)
ppg .... Planning and Programming Guidance (AD)
PPG .... Plasma Power Generator
PPG .... Player Piano Group (EAIO)
PPG .... Points per Game (WGA)
PPG .... Policies and Procedures Guide (SAA)
PPG .... Polymorphonuclear Cells per Glomerulus (STED)
PPG .... Poly(propylene Glycol) [*Organic chemistry*]
PPG .... Polyurethane-Polyvinyl Graphite (STED)
PPG .... Portal Pressure Gradient [*Medicine*] (DMAA)
PPG .... Postprandial Glucose (STED)
ppg .... Pounds per Gallon
PPG .... Power-Play Goal [*Hockey*]
PPG .... PPG Indus [*NYSE symbol*] (TTSB)
PPG .... PPG Industries, Inc. [*Formerly, Pittsburgh Plate Glass Co.*] [*Associated Press*] (SAG)
PPG .... PPG Industries, Inc., Coatings and Resins Division, Allison Park, PA [*OCLC symbol*] (OCLC)
PPG .... Predictive Proportional Guidance
PPG .... Pre-School Playgroup [*British*] (DET)
PPG .... Pretragal Parotid Gland (STED)

PPG .... Primary Pattern Generator [*Bell Laboratories*]
PPG .... Print Pattern Generator (IAA)
PPG .... Program for Population Genetics [*Collaboration of US and China Groups*]
PPG .... Program Planning Guide (OICC)
PPG .... Program Policy Guidelines
PPG .... Program Pulse Generator (IEEE)
PPG .... Propulsion and Power Generation
PPGA .... Pennsylvania Personnel and Guidance Association (AD)
PPGA .... Personal Producing General Agent [*Insurance*]
PPGA .... Plastic Pin Grid Array (PCM)
PPGA .... Post Pill Galactorrhea-Amenorrhea [*Medicine*] -
ppga .... Post-Pill Galactorrheamenorrhea [*Medicine*] (AD)
PPGA .... Potplant Growers Association [*British*] (DBA)
PPGA .... Preschool Play-Group Association [*British*] (DI)
PPGA .... Professional Plant Growers Association (NTPA)
PPGBL .... Personal Property Government Bill of Lading (DNAB)
PPGE .... General Electric Co., Philadelphia, PA [*Library symbol Library of Congress*] (LCLS)
PPGE .... Partido del Progreso de Guinea Ecuatorial [*Progressive Party of Equatorial Guinea*] [*Political party*] (EY)
PPGE-M .... General Electric Co., Missile and Space Vehicle Department, Aerosciences Laboratory, Philadelphia, PA [*Library symbol Library of Congress*] (LCLS)
PPGen .... Genealogical Society of Pennsylvania, Philadelphia, PA [*Library symbol Library of Congress*] (LCLS)
PPGenH .... Philadelphia General Hospital Laboratories, Philadelphia, PA [*Library symbol Library of Congress Obsolete*] (LCLS)
PPGeo .... Geographical Society of Philadelphia, Philadelphia, PA [*Library symbol Library of Congress Obsolete*] (LCLS)
PPGF .... Polypeptide Growth Factor [*Endocrinology*] (DAVI)
PPGH .... Philadelphia General Hospital, Philadelphia, PA [*Library symbol Library of Congress*] (LCLS)
PPGi .... Girard College, Philadelphia, PA [*Library symbol Library of Congress Obsolete*] (LCLS)
PPGJW .... Past Pro-Grand Junior Warden [*Freemasonry*] (ROG)
PPGL .... Polished Plate Glass [*Technical drawings*] (DAC)
PPGM .... Past Provincial Grand Master [*Freemasonry*]
PPGM .... Planning-Programming Guidance Memo [*Navy*]
PPGO .... Past Pro-Grand Organist [*Freemasonry*] (ROG)
PPGO .... Past Pro-Grand Orient [*Freemasonry*] (ROG)
PPGP .... Past Pro-Grand Pursuivant [*Freemasonry*] (ROG)
PPGP .... Prepaid Group Practice [*Insurance*] (DHSM)
PPGraph ...... Graphic Sketch Club, Philadelphia, PA [*Library symbol Library of Congress Obsolete*] (LCLS)
PPGratz....... Gratz College, Philadelphia, PA [*Library symbol Library of Congress Obsolete*] (LCLS)
PPGRC........ Public Policy and Government Relations Council
PPGSB .... Past Pro-Grand Sword Bearer [*Freemasonry*] (ROG)
PPGSN........ Past Provincial Grand Senior [*Freemasonry*] (ROG)
PPGSW........ Past Provincial Grand Senior Warden [*Freemasonry*]
PPGW .... Past Pro-Grand Warden [*Freemasonry*] (ROG)
PPH .... Pages per Hour
PPH .... Paid Personal Holiday
PPH .... Pamphlet
pph .... Pamphlet (AD)
pph .... Papers Per Hour [*News*] (WDMC)
PPH .... Parts per Hundred
PPH .... Peak-to-Peak Heights [*Spectrometry*]
PPH .... Persistent Pulmonary Hypertension [*Medicine*]
PPH .... Petroleum Pipehead
PPH .... Phenylpropanolamine(hydrochloride) [*Also, PPA, PPM*] [*Decongestant*]
PPH .... Phosphopyruvate Hydratase [*An enzyme*]
PPH .... PHP Healthcare [*NYSE symbol*] (TTSB)
PPH .... PHP Healthcare Corp. [*NYSE symbol*] (SPSG)
PPH .... Postpartum Hemorrhage [*Medicine*]
pph .... Post-Partum Hemorrhage [*Medicine*] (AD)
pph .... Pounds Per Hour (AD)
PPH .... Pounds per Hour (NG)
PPH .... Primary Pulmonary Hypertension [*Medicine*]
PPH .... Prophet Resources Ltd. [*Vancouver Stock Exchange symbol*]
PPH .... Protocollagen Proline Hydroxylase [*An enzyme*] (MAE)
PPH .... Pulses per Hour
pph .... Pulses Per Hour (AD)
PPHa .... Hahnemann Medical College and Hospital, Philadelphia, PA [*Library symbol Library of Congress*] (LCLS)
PPHA .... Peak Pulse Height Analysis
PPHA .... Private Proprietary Homes for Adults
PPHBA........ Peruvian Paso Half-Blood Association [*Later, PPPBR*] (EA)
PPHFC........ Holy Family College, Philadelphia, PA [*Library symbol Library of Congress*] (LCLS)
PPH/LB .... Pounds per Hour per Pound (SAA)
PPHM .... Parts per Hundred Million
P-PH-M .... Pulse Phase Modulation (DEN)
PPHN .... Persistent Pulmonary Hypertension of the Newborn [*Medicine*]
PPHOPT....... Pseudo-Pseudohypoparathyroidism [*Also, PPHP*] [*Endocrinology*]
PPHor .... Pennsylvania Horticultural Society, Philadelphia, PA [*Library symbol Library of Congress*] (LCLS)
P Php.......... Port Phillip (AD)
PPHP .... Pseudo-Pseudohypoparathyroidism [*Also, PPHOPT*] [*Endocrinology*]
PPHPI.......... Henry Phipps Institute, Philadelphia, PA [*Library symbol Library of Congress Obsolete*] (LCLS)
pphpm .... Parts Per Hundred Parts of Mix (AD)
pphpm .... Pints Per Hundred Parts of Mix (AD)

pphr............ Parts Per Hundred Parts of Rubber (AD)
PPHRII......... Parents of Premature and High Risk Infants International (EA)
PPHRNA ...... Peruvian Paso Horse Registry of North America (EA)
PPHS .... Partisan Prohibition Historical Society (EA)
PPHSL .... Periodical Publication in Harvard Science Libraries
PPHT .... (Phenylethyl-propylamino)hydroxytetralin [Biochemistry]
PPHx........... Previous Psychiatric History (MEDA)
PPi.............. Carnegie Library of Pittsburgh, Pittsburgh, PA [Library symbol Library of Congress] (LCLS)
PPI.............. Institute for Psychosomatic and Psychiatric Research and Training [Research center] (RCD)
PPI.............. Packing, Postage, and Insurance [Shipping]
PPI.............. Padangpandjang [Sumatra] [Seismograph station code, US Geological Survey] (SEIS)
PPI.............. Pages per Inch [Publishing]
ppi............... Pages Per Inch (AD)
PPI.............. Pakistan Press International
PPI.............. Pan Pacific Institute [Flinders University, Australia]
PPI.............. Parallel Peripheral Interface [Computer science]
PPI.............. Parcel Post, Insured [Shipping]
ppi............... Parcel Post Insured (AD)
PPI.............. Particles per Inch
PPI.............. Partito Popolare Italiano [Italian Popular Party] [Political party] (WDAA)
PPI.............. Patient Package Insert [Pharmacy] (DAVI)
PPI.............. Pensioners for Peace International (EAIO)
PPI.............. Pergamon Press, Inc.
PPI.............. Personality and Personal Illness Questionnaires [Psychology]
PPI.............. Personnel Planning Information
PPI.............. Phoenix Precision Instrument Co.
PPI.............. Pickle Packers International (EA)
ppi............... Picks Per Inch [Weaving] (DICI)
PPI.............. Pico Products [AMEX symbol] (TTSB)
PPI.............. Pico Products, Inc. [AMEX symbol] (SPSG)
PPI.............. Pictorial Position Indicator
PPI.............. Pilgrim Holdings Ltd. [Vancouver Stock Exchange symbol]
PPI.............. PIPA [Pulsed Integrating Pendulous Accelerometer] Pulse Integrator
PPI.............. Piston Position Indicator
PPI.............. PIXEL [Picture Element] per Inch [Computer science] (PCM)
ppi............... Pixels Per Inch [Computer graphics] (WDMC)
PPI.............. Plane Position Indicator [RADAR]
ppi............... Plan Position Indicator (AD)
PPI.............. Plan Position Indicator Mode [Computer science] (ADA)
PPI.............. Plasma Protein Isolate [Food technology]
PPI.............. Plastics Pipe Institute (EA)
PPI.............. Plot Position Indicator
PPI.............. Point per Inch (IAA)
ppi............... Points Per Inch (WDMC)
PPI.............. Policy Proof of Interest
ppi............... Policy Proof of Interest (AD)
PPI.............. Polymeric Polyisocyanate (EDCT)
PPI.............. Polyphosphonositides
PPI.............. Polyphthalimide [Organic chemistry]
PPI.............. POM [Program Objective Memorandum] Preparation Instructions [Military]
ppi............... Pores per Inch
PPI.............. Port Pirie [Australia Airport symbol] (OAG)
PPI.............. Ports [Harbors] Performance Indicator [Australia]
PPI.............. Postage Paid Impression [Freight] (DCTA)
PPI.............. Potash and Phosphate Institute (EA)
PPI.............. Potato Protease Inhibitor (DB)
PPI.............. Pounds per Inch [Lubrication load]
PPI.............. Preceding Preparatory Interval [Psychometrics]
PPI.............. Precise-Pixel Interpolation [Computer science]
PPI.............. Preferred Parts Index
PPI.............. Pre Phase-In
PPI.............. Preplant Inc. [Herbicides] [Agriculture]
PPI.............. Prepleading Investigation [Law]
PPI.............. Pre-production Part Index
PPI.............. Preproinsulin [Medicine] (DB)
PPI.............. Present Pain Intensity
PPI.............. Present Position Indicator [Aviation]
PPI.............. Prices Paid Index [Economics]
PPI.............. Primarily Primates, Inc. [An association] (EA)
PPI.............. Primary Personal Interest [Personnel study]
PPI.............. Prince Patrick Island [Canada]
PPI.............. Producer Price Index [Bureau of Labor Statistics] [Information service or system]
PPI.............. Professional Photographers of Israel (PDAA)
PPI.............. Programmable Peripheral Interface (MCD)
PPI.............. Program Position Indicator
PPI.............. Progressive Policy Institute [Research center] (RCD)
PPI.............. Project Procurement Instructions [Jet Propulsion Laboratory, NASA]
PPI.............. Project Public Information [Department of Education] (AEBS)
PPI.............. Property Protection Insurance
PPI.............. Proportional Plus Integral
PPI.............. Protective Packaging, Inc. (AD)
PPI.............. Public-Private Interface
PPI.............. Pulse Position Indicator (MCD)
PPI.............. Pulses per Inch (CMD)
ppi............... Pulses Per Inch (WDMC)
PPI.............. Pyrophosphate Index [Agronomy]
PPi.............. Pyrophosphate, Inorganic [Chemistry]
PPi-A .... Carnegie Library of Pittsburgh, Allegheny Regional Branch, Monroeville, PA [Library symbol Library of Congress] (LCLS)

PPIA............ Poultry Products Inspection Act (GFGA)
PPIA............ Programme du Pipeline des Iles de l'Arctique [Canada]
PPiAC .... Community College of Allegheny County, Pittsburgh, PA [Library symbol Library of Congress] (LCLS)
PPiAL .... Allegheny County Law Library, Pittsburgh, PA [Library symbol Library of Congress] (LCLS)
PPiAM .... Pittsburgh Academy of Medicine, Pittsburgh, PA [Library symbol Library of Congress] (LCLS)
PPIAS .... Parent-to-Parent Information on Adoption Services [British] (DI)
PPIB............ Programmable Protocol Interface Board
PPiC............ Carnegie-Mellon University, Pittsburgh, PA [Library symbol Library of Congress] (LCLS)
PPIC............ Plumbing and Piping Industry Council (AD)
PPIC............ Pollution Prevention Information Clearinghouse [Environmental Protection Agency]
PPiCa.......... Carlow College, Pittsburgh, PA [Library symbol Library of Congress] (LCLS)
PPiCa-O ...... Carlow College, Our Lady of Mercy Academy, Pittsburgh, PA [Library symbol Library of Congress] (LCLS)
PPiCC .... Chatham College, Pittsburgh, PA [Library symbol Library of Congress] (LCLS)
PPICR .... Institute for Cancer Research, Philadelphia, PA [Library symbol Library of Congress] (LCLS)
PPICS .... Production Planning Inventory Control System (PDAA)
PPiD .... Duquesne University, Pittsburgh, PA [Library symbol Library of Congress] (LCLS)
PPID .... Peak Pain Intensity Difference Score [Medicine] (DMAA)
PPID .... Polaris-Poseidon Intelligence Digest (MCD)
PPID .... Process Program Identification (AAEL)
PPiD-L......... Duquesne University, School of Law, Pittsburgh, PA [Library symbol Library of Congress] (LCLS)
PPiE............ E. D'Appolonia Consulting Engineers, Pittsburgh, PA [Library symbol Library of Congress] (LCLS)
PPIE............ Prolonged Postictal Encephalopathy [Medicine] (DMAA)
PPIE............ Pseudophase Ion Exchange [Chemistry]
PPIF............ Photo Processing Interpretation Facility
ppif............. Photo-Processing Interpretation Facility (AD)
PPIFC.......... Pauline Pinkney International Fan Club (EA)
PPIFIA .... Policy Proof of Interest, Full Interest Admitted (EBF)
PPIGB .... Plant Pathology Internet Guide Book
PPiGulf .... Gulf Research & Development Co., Pittsburgh, PA [Library symbol Library of Congress] (LCLS)
PPiHB .... Carnegie-Mellon University, Hunt Institute for Botanical Documentation, Pittsburgh, PA [Library symbol Library of Congress] (LCLS)
PPiHi........... Historical Society of Western Pennsylvania, Pittsburgh, PA [Library symbol Library of Congress] (LCLS)
PPil............. International Poetry Forum, Pittsburgh, PA [Library symbol Library of Congress] (LCLS)
PPiK............ Ketchum, McLeod & Grove, Inc., Pittsburgh, PA [Library symbol Library of Congress] (LCLS)
PPiL............ LaRoche College, Pittsburgh, PA [Library symbol Library of Congress] (LCLS)
PPIL............ Priced Provisioned Item List (MCD)
p-pille......... Praeventivpille [Dano-Norwegian] [Contraceptive pill] (AD)
PPiM............ Carnegie-Mellon University, Mellon Institute, Pittsburgh, PA [Library symbol Library of Congress] (LCLS)
PPIM........... Programmable Peripheral Interface Microcomputer (IAA)
PPiMS .... Mine Safety Appliances Co., Pittsburgh, PA [Library symbol Library of Congress] (LCLS)
PPIMS .... Past Performance Information Management System [Army]
PPIn............ Independence National Historical Park, Philadelphia, PA [Library symbol Library of Congress] (LCLS)
pp/in .... Pages Per Inch (AD)
PPINA.......... Insurance Co., of North America, Corporate Archives, Philadelphia, PA [Library symbol Library of Congress] (LCLS)
PPINA.......... RADAR Weather Report Not Available [NWS] (FAAC)
PPINE.......... RADAR Weather Report Equipment No Echoes Observed [NWS] (FAAC)
PPINICI........ Pulsed Positive Ion-Negative Ion Chemical Ionization [Instrumentation]
PPINO.......... RADAR Weather Report Equipment Inoperative Due to Breakdown [NWS] (FAAC)
PPInstHE..... Past President of the Institution of Highway Engineers [British] (DI)
PPIOK .... RADAR Weather Report Equipment Operation REsumed [NWS] (FAAC)
PPIOM......... RADAR Weather Report Equipment Inoperative Due to Maintenance [NWS] (FAAC)
PPIP............ Physics Post-Doctoral Information Pool [American Institute of Physics] (PDAA)
PPiPP.......... Point Park College, Pittsburgh, PA [Library symbol Library of Congress] (LCLS)
PPiPPG........ PPG Industries, Inc., Glass Research Center, Information Services Library, Pittsburgh, PA [Library symbol Library of Congress] (LCLS)
PPiPT.......... Pittsburgh Theological Seminary, Pittsburgh, PA [Library symbol Library of Congress] (LCLS)
PPIQ .... Personality and Personal Illness Questionnaire (AD)
PPIR .... Personnel Planning Information Report (MCD)
PPiR .... Rockwell International Corp., Pittsburgh, PA [Library symbol Library of Congress] (LCLS)
PPIRO.......... Planned Position Indicator Readout (NVT)
PPiRP .... Reformed Presbyterian Theological Seminary, Pittsburgh, PA [Library symbol] [Library of Congress] (LCLS)

PPIS............ Pesticide Product Information System [*Environmental Protection Agency*] (GFGA)
PPIS............ Product Profile Information System [*Shell Oil Co.*]
PPIStructE ... Past President of the Institution of Structural Engineers [*British*] (DI)
PPIU .... Policy, Planning and Implementation Unit
PPIU .... Programmable Peripheral Interface Unit
PPiU .... University of Pittsburgh, Pittsburgh, PA [*Library symbol Library of Congress*] (LCLS)
PPiU-A .... University of Pittsburgh, Henry Clay Frick Fine Arts Center, Pittsburgh, PA [*Library symbol Library of Congress*] (LCLS)
PPiU-BL ...... University of Pittsburgh, Blair-Lippincott Library, Eye and Ear Hospital of Pittsburgh, Pittsburgh, PA [*Library symbol Library of Congress*] (LCLS)
PPiU-H......... University of Pittsburgh, Maurice and Laura Falk Library of the Health Professions, Pittsburgh, PA [*Library symbol Library of Congress*] (LCLS)
PPiU-IS .... University of Pittsburgh, Archives of Industrial Society, Pittsburgh, PA [*Library symbol*] [*Library of Congress*] (LCLS)
PPiU-L .... University of Pittsburgh, Law School, Pittsburgh, PA [*Library symbol Library of Congress*] (LCLS)
PPiU-LS ...... University of Pittsburgh, Graduate School of Library and Information Sciences, Pittsburgh, PA [*Library symbol Library of Congress*] (LCLS)
PPiU-NS ...... University of Pittsburgh, Natural Sciences Library, Pittsburgh, PA [*Library symbol Library of Congress*] (LCLS)
PPiU-PH ...... University of Pittsburgh, Graduate School of Public Health, Pittsburgh, PA [*Library symbol Library of Congress*] (LCLS)
PPiU-PIA...... University of Pittsburgh, Graduate School of Public and International Affairs, Pittsburgh, PA [*Library symbol Library of Congress*] (LCLS)
PPiUS .... United States Steel Corp., Pittsburgh, PA [*Library symbol Library of Congress*] (LCLS)
PPiU-SF ...... University of Pittsburgh, Stephen Collins Foster Memorial [*Music*] Library, Pittsburgh, PA [*Library symbol Library of Congress*] (LCLS)
PPiUSM .... United States Department of the Interior, Bureau of Mines, Pittsburgh Research Center, Pittsburgh, PA [*Library symbol Library of Congress*] (LCLS)
PPIV............ Per Person Interview Value [*Marketing*] (WDMC)
PPIV............ Positive Personnel Identity Verification (PDAA)
PPiW .... Westinghouse Electric Corp., Research and Development Center, Pittsburgh, PA [*Library symbol Library of Congress*] (LCLS)
PPiW-N....... Westinghouse Electric Corp., Nuclear Center Library, Pittsburgh, PA [*Library symbol Library of Congress*] (LCLS)
PPiWP .... Western Psychiatric Institute and Clinic, University of Pittsburgh, Pittsburgh, PA [*Library symbol Library of Congress*] (LCLS)
PPJ............. Pressure Plane Joint
PPJ............. Pure Pancreatic Juice
PPJ............. Thomas Jefferson University, Philadelphia, PA [*Library symbol Library of Congress*] (LCLS)
PPJea .... Jeanes Hospital, Philadelphia, PA [*Library symbol Library of Congress Obsolete*] (LCLS)
PPJO........... Pli Premier Jour Officiel [*Official First Day Cover - OFDC*] [*Canada Post Corp.*]
PPJ-S.......... Thomas Jefferson University, Scott Memorial Library, Philadelphia, PA [*Library symbol Library of Congress*] (LCLS)
PPJW.......... Past Pro-Junior Warden [*Freemasonry*] (ROG)
PPK............ Paired Perpendicular Keratotomy [*Procedure to correct astigmatism*]
PPK............ Palmoplantar Keratoderma [*Dermatology*]
PPK............ Palmoplantar Keratosis [*Medicine*] (DMAA)
PPK............ Parametrized Post-Keplerian [*Physics*]
PPK............ Paramp Pump Klystron
PPK............ Parti Progressiste Katangais [*Political party*]
PPK............ Personal Preference Kit [*Small bag in which astronauts are allowed to take personal mementos*]
PPK............ Polizei Pistole Kriminal [*Pistol suitable for undercover police or detective use*] [*Walther Waffenfabrik, German arms manufacturer*]
PPK............ Punt, Pass, and Kick [*Youth competition sponsored by professional football*]
pPk............ Purplish Pink (AD)
PPK............ Ramp 66, Inc. [*ICAO designator*] (FAAC)
PPKB .... Partai Perpaduan Kebang-Saan Brunei [*Brunei National United Party*] [*Political party*] (EY)
PPKCA .... Pen and Pocket Knife Cutters' Association [*A union*] [*British*]
PPKG .... Power Package (MSA)
Ppl............. Intrapleural Pressure [*Medicine*] (DAVI)
PPL............. Library Co. of Philadelphia, Philadelphia, PA [*Library symbol Library of Congress*] (LCLS)
PPL............. Package Programs of London (NITA)
PPL............. Palach Press Ltd. [*British*] (EAIO)
PPL............. Palmer Physical Laboratory [*Princeton University*] (MCD)
PPL............. Pars Planus Lensectomy [*Ophthalmology*] (DAVI)
PPL............. Participle [*Grammar*] (WGA)
PPL............. PCBoard Programming Language [*Clark Development Co.*] (PCM)
PPL............. Pembina Resources Ltd. [*Toronto Stock Exchange symbol*]
PPL............. Penicilloyl Polylysine [*Pharmacology*]
PPL............. Pennsylvania Power & Light Co. [*NYSE symbol*] (SPSG)
PPL............. People
PPL............. Peripheral Blood Leukocyte [*Medicine*] (PDAA)
PPL............. Per Pupil Limitation (AFM)
PPL............. Peter Peregrinus Ltd. [*Publisher*]
PPL............. Phenylpropanolamine [*Organic chemistry*]
PPL............. Philadelphia Public Library (AD)
PPL............. Phoenix Public Library (AD)

PPL............. Phonographic Performance Ltd. [*British*]
PPL............. Photogrammetric Programming Language [*Computer science*] (PDAA)
PPL............. Physical Properties Laboratory [*Oklahoma State University*] [*Research center*] (RCD)
ppl............. Pipeline (AD)
PPL............. Pittsburgh Public Library (AD)
PPL............. Pixel per Line [*Computer science*] (IAA)
PPL............. Planned Parenthood League (AD)
PPL............. Planning Parts List
PPL............. Plan Position Landing (DEN)
PPL............. Plant Physiology Laboratory (SSD)
PPL............. Plasma Physics Laboratory [*Also known as PPPL*]
PPL............. Plasma Propulsion Laboratory (MCD)
PPL............. Plus Programming Language [*Computer science*]
PPL............. Plutonium Product Loadout [*Nuclear energy*] (NRCH)
PPL............. Police Protective League (AD)
PPL............. Polymorphic Programming Language [*1971*] [*Computer science*] (CSR)
PPL............. Populated Place [*Board on Geographic Names*]
PPL............. Population Paper Listing [*US Census Bureau*] [*A publication*]
PPL............. Porcine Pancreatic Lipase [*An enzyme*]
PPL............. Posterior Pole Plasm [*Insect embryology*]
PPL............. Power Plant Laboratory (MUGU)
PPL............. PP&L Resources [*NYSE symbol*] (TTSB)
PPL............. PP & L Resources, Inc. [*NYSE symbol*] (SAG)
PPL............. Precise Participant Location
PPL............. Predictive Period LASER (KSC)
PPL............. Preferential Planning List
PPL............. Preferred Parts List
PPL............. Preliminary Parts List
PPL............. Preliminary Power Laboratory (IAA)
PPL............. Presbyterians Pro-Life [*An association*] (EA)
PPL............. Priced Parts List (NASA)
P/PL........... Primary Payload [*NASA*] (NASA)
PPL............. Princeton Polymer Laboratories
PPL............. Print Positions per Line [*Computer science*] (MHDI)
PPL............. Private Pilot's Licence [*British*]
PPL............. Program Production Library [*Computer science*]
PPL............. Project Priority List [*Environmental Protection Agency*]
PPL............. Protein-Polysaccharide [*Biochemistry*] (DAVI)
PPL............. Protein Preprolactin [*Biochemistry*]
PPL............. Providence Public Library (AD)
PPL............. Provisioning Parts List (AAG)
PPL............. Purchased Parts List
PPL............. Pure Prairie League [*Musical group*]
PPL............. Purple
PPL............. Puu Pili [*Hawaii*] [*Seismograph station code, US Geological Survey*] (SEIS)
PpL .... W. & F. Pascoe Proprietory Ltd., Milsons Point, Australia [*Library symbol Library of Congress*] (LCLS)
PPLA .... Practice Precautionary Landing Approach [*Aviation*]
PPLA .... Professional Photographic Laboratories Association [*British*] (DBA)
P-plane........ Pilotless Airplane (AD)
PPLas .... La Salle College, Philadelphia, PA [*Library symbol Library of Congress*] (LCLS)
PPlase .... Peptidylprolyl Cis-Trans Isomerase [*An enzyme*]
PPLB .... Postprocessor Call Library [*Computer science*] (IAA)
PPLC .... Patients Protection Law Commission (AD)
PPLD .... Pikes Peak Library District [*Internationally recognized computerized library system*]
PPLDF .... Professional Protector and Legal Defense Fund
PPLE .... Partial Preliminary Logistic Evaluation
PPLE .... Participle [*Grammar*]
pple .... Past Participle (AD)
PPLE .... Principle (ROG)
PPL/H .... Private Pilot's Licence/Helicopters [*British*] (AIA)
PPLI .... Precise Participant Location-Identification [*Navigation*]
PPLI .... Precise Position Location Information
PPLI .... Provisioning Parts List Index (MCD)
PPLIF.......... Pulsed Photolysis LASER-Induced Fluorescence [*Environmental science*]
PPLL........... Military Order of the Loyal Legion of the United States, [*Civil*] War Library and Museum, Philadelphia, PA [*Library symbol Library of Congress*] (LCLS)
PPLLT......... Provisional Program Load Library Tape [*Computer science*] (MHDI)
PPLN .... Pipeline
pplo .... Pleuropneumonia-Like Organism (AD)
PPLO .... Pleuropneumonia-Like Organisms [*Bacteriology*]
PPLO .... Pleuropneumonia-Link Oganism [*Medicine*] (WDAA)
PPLP.......... Photopolymers Lithograph Plate
P PLPBD ..... Paper or Pulpboard [*Freight*]
PPLPrA .... Penn Pwr & Lt 4.40% Pfd [*NYSE symbol*] (TTSB)
PPLPrB .... Penn Pwr & Lt 4.50% Pfd [*NYSE symbol*] (TTSB)
ppls .... Peoples [*Internet language*] [*Computer science*]
PPLS .... Peoples Bank Corp. (Indianapolis, IN) [*NASDAQ symbol*] (SAG)
PPLS .... Peoples Bank Indianapolis [*NASDAQ symbol*] (TTSB)
PPLS .... Precision Position Locator System [*Army*]
PPLS .... Preferred Parts List System (MCD)
PPLS .... Propellant and Pressurant Loading System [*NASA*] (KSC)
PPLT .... Lutheran Theological Seminary, Philadelphia, PA [*Library symbol Library of Congress*] (LCLS)
PPLV .... Preliminary Pollutant Limit Value (MCD)
PPLX .... Section of Populated Place [*Board on Geographic Names*]
PPM............ Aberdeen, MD [*Location identifier FAA*] (FAAL)

PPM	Investment Grade Municipal Income Fund [*NYSE symbol*] (SAG)
PPM	Investment Grade Muni Inc. [*NYSE symbol*] (TTSB)
PPM	Mercantile Library, Philadelphia, PA [*Library symbol Library of Congress Obsolete*] (LCLS)
PPM	Page-per-Minute [*Computer science*] (PCM)
PPM	Pages per Minute [*Printer technology*]
ppm	Pages per Minute
ppm	Papermaker [*MARC relator code*] [*Library of Congress*] (LCCP)
PPM	Parallel Processing Machine [*Computer science*] (IAA)
PPM	Particuliere Participatiemaatschappy [*Private Joint Stock Company*] [*Dutch*]
PPM	Partido del Pueblo Mexicano [*Mexican People's Party*] [*Political party*] (PPW)
PPM	Partido Proletario de Mexico [*Proletarian Party of Mexico*] [*Political party*] (AD)
PPM	Parti Pekerja-Pekerja Malaysia [*Workers' Party of Malaysia*] [*Political party*] (PPW)
PPM	Parti Progressiste Martiniquais [*Progressive Party of Martinique*] [*Political party*] (PPW)
PPM	Partitioned-Pipe Mixer [*Engineering*]
PPM	Part Program Manager
PPM	Parts per Million
ppm	Parts Per Million (AD)
PPM	Parts per Minute (MCD)
PPM	Pattani People's Movement [*Thailand*] [*Political party*]
PPM	Peak Power Meter
PPM	Peak Program Meter [*Television*]
ppm	Peak Program Meter (AD)
PPM	Periodic Permanent Magnet
PPM	Periodic Permanent Magnet Focusing (IAA)
PPM	Periodic Pulse Metering [*Telecommunications*] (TEL)
PPM	Permanent Pacemaker [*Cardiology*] (MAE)
PPM	Pershing Project Manager
PPM	Personnel Priority Model (MCD)
PPM	Personnel Program Manager [*Navy*]
PPM	Persutuan Perpustakaan Malaysia [*Library Association of the Federation of Malaysia*] (AD)
PPM	Phenylpropanolamine(hydrochloride) [*Also, PPA, PPH*] [*Decongestant*]
PPM	Phosphopentomutase [*An enzyme*]
PPM	Physician Practice Management
PPM	Pictures per Minute (NTCM)
PPM	Piecewise Parabolic Method [*Mathematical model of fluid flow*]
PPM	Pigmented Pupillary Membrane [*Medicine*] (STED)
PPM	Pilot Production Model [*Military*] (CAAL)
PPM	Pistol Prize Money [*British military*] (DMA)
PPM	Planned Preventive Maintenance (IEEE)
PPM	Popocatepetl [*Mexico*] [*Seismograph station code, US Geological Survey*] (SEIS)
PPM	Portable Pix Map [*Computer science*]
PPM	Position and Pay Management [*Army*] (AABC)
PPM	Position and Proper Motion [*Catalog of star positions*]
PPM	Postage Prepaid in Money
PPM	Posterior Papillary Muscle [*Image on transesophageal echocardiography*] [*Cardiology*] (DAVI)
PPM	Postpass Message
PPM	Post-Program Monitoring
PPM	Pounds per Minute
ppm	Pounds Per Minute (AD)
PPM	Prairie Print Makers [*Defunct*] (EA)
PPM	Prenegotiation Position Memorandum (AAGC)
PPM	Presentation Protocol Machine [*Telecommunications*] (OSI)
PPM	Previous Processor Mode
PPM	Principal Period of Maintenance (AAGC)
PPM	Problem Program Monitor (IAA)
PPM	Production Planning Memorandum
PPM	Program, Project Management [*Army*]
PPM	Project Profile Manual
PPM	Prudential Portfolio Managers Ltd. [*British*]
PPM	Pulse Phase Modulation [*Telecommunications*] (IAA)
PPM	Pulse Position Modulation [*Radio data transmission*]
ppm	Pulse Position Modulation (AD)
PPM	Pulse Power Module (RDA)
PPM	Pulses per Minute
ppm	Pulses per Minute (IDOE)
PPM	Pyrite-Pyrrhotite-Magnetite [*Mineralogy*]
PPMA	Petroleum Marketers Association of America
PPMA	Petrol Pump Manufacturers Association [*British*] (DBA)
PPMA	Plastic Products Manufacturers Association [*Later, Plastic and Metal Products Manufacturers Association*] (EA)
PPMA	Political Products Manufacturers Association (EA)
PPMA	Polypropyl Methacrylate [*Organic chemistry*]
ppma	Post-Polio Muscular Atrophy [*Medicine*] (AD)
PPMA	Post-Poliomyelitis Muscular Atrophy [*Medicine*]
PPMA	Precision Potentiometer Manufacturers Association [*Later, Variable Resistive Components Institute*] (EA)
PPMA	Produce Packaging and Marketing Association [*British*] (DBA)
PPMA	Progressive Postmyelitis Muscular Atrophy [*Medicine*] (DMAA)
PPMA	Pulp and Paper Manufacturers Association [*Later, PPMMA*] (EA)
PPMAP	Power Planning Modeling Application Procedure [*Environmental Protection Agency*] (GFGA)
PPMC	Parts Per Million Carbon [*Automotive engineering*]
PPMC	People to People Music Committee (EA)
PPMCX	PIMCO: Precious Metals Cl.C [*Mutual fund ticker symbol*] (SG)
PPMD	Posterior Polymorphous Dystrophy of the Cornea [*Ophthalmology*] (DAVI)
PPME	Pacific Plate Motion Experiment (NASA)
PPMFA	Pulp and Paper Manufacturers' Federation of Australia
PPMFC	Preprints on Precision Measurement and Fundamental Constants [*National Institute of Standards and Technology*]
PPMG	Professional Publishers Marketing Group (EA)
PPMI	Pilot Plant Meat Irradiator
PPMI	Printed Paper Mat Institute (EA)
PPMIN	Pulses per Minute (MSA)
PPMis	Misericordia Hospital, Philadelphia, PA [*Library symbol Library of Congress Obsolete*] (LCLS)
PPML	Preferred Parts and Materials List [*NASA*]
PPMM	Postpolycythemia Myeloid Metaplasia [*Medicine*] (AAMN)
PPMMA	Pulp and Paper Machinery Manufacturers Association [*Later, APMA*] (EA)
PPMN	Preliminary Program Management Network [*Military*]
PPMNA	Provisions for Particulate Matter Nonattainment Areas [*Environmental science*] (COE)
PPMO	Pershing Project Manager's Office (RDA)
PPMO	Provisional Program Management Office [*Army*]
PPMol	Moore College of Art, Philadelphia, PA [*Library symbol Library of Congress*] (LCLS)
PPMPC	Pilot Parachute Mortar Pyrotechnic Cartridge (SAA)
PPMR	Purchased Parts Material Requirements
PPMRC	Pre-Positioned Materiel Receipt Card
PPMRD	Pre-Positioned Material Receipt Document
PPMS	Performax's Personal Matrix System (DMAA)
PPMS	Physical Properties Measurement System (AAEL)
PPMS	Pitt Press Mathematical Series [*A publication*]
PPMS	Plastic Pipe Manufacturers Society [*British*] (DBA)
PPMS	Poly(para-Methylstyrene) [*Organic chemistry*]
PPMS	Polyphenylmethylsiloxane [*Organic chemistry*]
PPMS	Professional Productivity Management System (HGAA)
PPMS	Programme and Project Management System [*United Nations Development Programme*] (DUND)
PPMS	Program Performance Measurement Systems (IEEE)
PPMS	Psychophysiologic Musculoskeletal [*Reaction*] [*Medicine*] (STED)
PPMS	Purdue Perceptual-Motor Survey [*Kephart Scale*]
PPMV	Parts per Million by Volume
ppmv	Parts per Million by Volume [*Marine science*] (OSRA)
PPMW	Parts per Million by Weight (MCD)
PPMW	Primary Plant Mineralized Water (IAA)
PPN	Numismatic and Antiquarian Society, Philadelphia, PA [*Library symbol Library of Congress Obsolete*] (LCLS)
PPN	Papenoo [*Society Islands*] [*Seismograph station code, US Geological Survey*] (SEIS)
PPN	Parameterized Post-Newtonian [*Gravity*]
PPN	Parametrized Post-Newtonian [*Physics*]
PPN	Partial Parenteral Nutrition [*Medicine*] (DMAA)
PPN	Partido Patriotico Nobo [*New Patriotic Party*] [*Aruba*] [*Political party*] (EY)
PPN	Partido Progreso Nacional [*National Progress Party*] [*Costa Rica*] [*Political party*] (PPW)
PPN	Parti Progressiste Nigerien [*Nigerian Progressive Party*] [*Political party*]
PPN	Patrol Plane Navigator (DNAB)
PPN	Peak-to-Peak Noise [*Instrumentation*]
PPN	Pedunculopontine Nucleus (DMAA)
PPN	Peripheral Parenteral Nutrition [*Medicine*] (DAVI)
PPN	Peroxypropionyl Nitrate [*Organic chemistry*]
PPN	Polyphosphonate [*Organic chemistry*]
PPN	Popayan [*Colombia*] [*Airport symbol*] (OAG)
PPN	Portland Public Library, Portland, ME [*OCLC symbol*] (OCLC)
PPN	Precipitation (WGA)
PPN	Predictive Proportional Navigation
PPN	Procurement Program Number [*Military*]
PPN	Project, Programmer Number
PPN	Proportion (ROG)
ppn	Proportion (AD)
PPN	Protoplanetary Nebulae [*Astrophysics*]
PPN	Public Packet Network [*Computer science*] (ODBW)
PPN	Pyramidopallidonigral (DB)
PPNA	Peak Phrenic Nerve Activity [*Medicine*]
PPNA	Pupil-Perceived Needs Assessment [*Education*] (EDAC)
PPNAD	Primary Pigmented Nodular Adrenocortical Disease [*Medicine*] (STED)
PPNB	Pre-Pottery Neolithic B Period [*Paleontology*]
PPNC	Patrol Plane Navigator/Communicator (DNAB)
PPNC	Pre-Pottery Neolithic C Phase [*Paleontology*]
PPNDG	Petition Pending
PPNF	Price-Pottenger Nutrition Foundation (EA)
PPNG	Penicillinase-Producing Neisseria gonorrhoeae
PPNICI	Pulsed Positive/Negative Ion Chemical Ionization
P/PNL	Pocket Panel [*Automotive engineering*]
PPNMC	United States Navy, Naval Regional Medical Center, Philadelphia, PA [*Library symbol Library of Congress*] (LCLS)
PPNP	Point Pelee National Park [*Ontario, Canada*] (AD)
PPNSC	Preferred Procurement Number Selector Code [*Military*] (AFIT)
PPNSCA	Policy Plans and National Security Council Affairs
PPNS-IE	Preschool and Primary Nowicki-Strickland Internal-External Control Scale (EDAC)
PPNT	Proponent
PPNW	Physicians for the Prevention of Nuclear War (AD)

PPNWA	N. W. Ayer & Son, Philadelphia, PA [*Library symbol Library of Congress Obsolete*] (LCLS)
PPO	Diphenyloxazole [*Chemistry*] (DAVI)
PPO	Parking Patrol Officer
PPO	Patriot Project Office [*Army*]
PPO	Pepsi-Cola Puerto Rico Bott'B' [*NYSE symbol*] (TTSB)
PPO	Pepsi Cola Puerto Rico Bottling [*NYSE symbol*] (SAG)
PPO	Permanent Paranormal Object
PPO	Photographic Program Office [*NASA*] (KSC)
PPO	Platelet Peroxidase [*An enzyme*]
PPO	Pleuropneumonia Organisms [*Bacteriology*]
PPO	Police Petty Officer (DNAB)
PPO	Pollution Prevention Office [*Environmental Protection Agency*]
PPO	Polyphenol Oxidase [*An enzyme*]
PPO	Polyphenylene Oxide [*Organic chemistry*]
ppo	Polyphenylene Oxide (AD)
PPO	Poly(propylene Oxide) [*Organic chemistry*]
PPO	Port Postal Office (AFM)
PPo	Pottsville Free Public Library, Pottsville, PA [*Library symbol*] [*Library of Congress*] (LCLS)
PPO	Power Plant Operating
PPO	Preferred-Provided Organization [*Insurance*] (AD)
PPO	Preferred-Provider Option [*Insurance*]
PPO	Preferred-Provider Organization [*Insurance*]
PPO	Pre Phase-Out
PPO	Pressed Plutonium Oxide
PPO	Primary Party Organization [*Politics*]
PPO	Principal Priority Officer
PPO	Prior Permission Only (AFM)
ppo	Prior Permission Only (AD)
PPO	Procurement Planning Officer
PPO	Program Printout (MCD)
PPO	Projected Program Objective (NG)
PPO	Publications and Printing Office [*Army*]
PPO	Public Pension Offset [*Federal Employees Retirement System*] (GFGA)
PPO	Pure Plutonium Oxide
PPO	Push-Pull Output (DEN)
PPO₂	Partial Pressure of Oxygen (CAAL)
PPoAr	Schuylkill County Archives, Pottsville, PA [*Library symbol*] [*Library of Congress*] (LCLS)
PPOC	Per Pupil Operating Cost (ADA)
PP of A	Professional Photographers of America [*Atlanta, GA*] (WDMC)
PPOG	Polytechnic Personnel Officers Group (AIE)
p-p-ola	Political Plugola (AD)
PPOLL	Parallel Poll (CIST)
ppom	Particulate Polycyclic Organic Matter (AD)
P-POP	Plain Paper Optimized Printing [*Canon*] [*Computer science*]
PPORT	Prostate Patient Outcomes Research Team
PPOS	Present Position (GAVI)
PPOS	Saint George United Methodist Church, Philadelphia, PA [*Library symbol Library of Congress*] (LCLS)
PPOSN	Proposition (ROG)
PPOX	Polypropylene Oxide (EDCT)
PPOX	Polypropylene Oxide Plastic
PPP	Pacific Peacemaker Project [*Defunct*] (EA)
PPP	Pakistan People's Party [*Political party*] (PD)
PPP	Palmoplantar Pustulosis [*Medicine*] (DMAA)
PPP	Pan Pacific Petroleum [*Vancouver Stock Exchange symbol*]
PPP	Paper, Printing, Publishing [*Department of Employment*] [*British*]
PPP	Parallel Pattern Processor
PPP	Parallel Push Pull (IAA)
PPP	Pariser-Parr-Pople [*Physical chemistry*]
PPP	Partai Persatuan Pembangunan [*United Development Party*] [*Indonesia*] [*Political party*] (PPW)
PPP	Partido del Pueblo de Panama [*Panamanian People's Party*] [*Political party*] (PPW)
PPP	Passage, Power, and Passenger [*Evaluation of labor progress*] [*Obstetrics*] (DAVI)
PPP	Payload Patch Panel [*NASA*] (NAKS)
ppp	Peak Pulse Power (NAKS)
PPP	Peak Pulse Power
PPP	Pentose-Phosphate Pathway [*Metabolism*]
PPP	Penultimate Profit [*Investment term*] (DFIT)
PPP	Peoples Party of Pakistan [*Political party*] (AD)
PPP	People's Patriotic Party [*Myanmar*] [*Political party*] (PD)
PPP	People's Political Party [*St. Vincent*] [*Political party*] (PPW)
PPP	People's Progressive Party [*Mauritania*] [*Political party*] (EY)
PPP	People's Progressive Party [*Gambia*] [*Political party*] (PPW)
PPP	People's Progressive Party [*Guyana*] [*Political party*] (PD)
PPP	People's Progressive Party [*Anguilla*] [*Political party*] (PPW)
PPP	People's Progressive Party [*Solomon Islands*] [*Political party*] (PPW)
PPP	People's Progress Party [*Papua New Guinea*] [*Political party*] (PPW)
PPP	Permanent Party Personnel (MCD)
PPP	Perpex Peristaltic Pump
PPP	Personal Property Policy [*Insurance*]
PPP	Personnel Performance Profile
PPP	Petroleum Production Pioneers (AD)
PPP	Phased Project Planning [*NASA*] (KSC)
PPP	Pianississimo [*As Softly As Possible*] [*Music*]
PPP	Pickford Projective Pictures [*Psychology*]
ppp	Piu Pianissimo [*Very Very Softly*] [*Italian*] [*Music*] (AD)
PPP	Planning Purpose Proposal
PPP	Plan Position Presentation
PPP	Platelet-Poor Plasma [*Hematology*]
PPP	Pluripotent Progenitor [*Cytology*]
PPP	Pogo Producing [*NYSE symbol*] (TTSB)
PPP	Pogo Producing Co. [*NYSE symbol*] (SPSG)
PPP	Point-to-Point Protocol [*Computer science*] (PCM)
PPP	Polluter Pays Principle
PPP	Pollution Prevention Plan [*Environmental science*] (COE)
PPP	Poly(para-phenylene) [*Organic chemistry*]
PPP	Polyphoretic Phosphate [*Organic chemistry*] (DAVI)
PPP	Polypropylene-Paper-Polypropylene [*Biochemistry*]
PPP	Popular Power Package (IAA)
PPP	Portable Plotting Package [*Nuclear energy*] (NRCH)
PPP	Positive Pressure Paradox
PPP	Post-Painted Parts
PPP	Postpartum Psychosis [*Obstetrics*] [*Psychiatry*] (DAVI)
PPP	Powerful Permutation Procedure [*Meteorology*]
PPP	Preferred Pharmacy Program
PPP	Prepositional Procurement Package (DOMA)
PPP	Prescriptive Parent Programming [*Education*]
PPP	Prescriptive Program Plan [*Education*]
PPP	Pretty Poor Planning
PPP	Primary Products Promotion [*Australia*]
PPP	Priority Placement Program (DOMA)
PPP	Prior-Participating Preferred [*Stock*] (MHDW)
PPP	Prison Pen Pals (EA)
PPP	Private Patients' Plan [*British*]
PPP	Production Part Pattern (MCD)
PPP	Profit and Performance Planning (DCTA)
PPP	Program Protection Plan [*DoD*] (RDA)
PPP	Progressive People's Party [*Liberia*] [*Political party*] (PPW)
PPP	Progressive People's Party [*Sierra Leone*] [*Political party*] (EY)
PPP	Progressive People's Party [*Sudan*] [*Political party*] (EY)
PPP	Propria Pecunia Posuit [*Erected at His Own Expense*] [*Latin*]
PPP	Proserpine [*Australia Airport symbol*] (OAG)
PPP	Province Pacification Plan (CINC)
PPP	Provisioning Program Plan (MCD)
PPP	Public Policy Program [*Australian National University*]
PPP	Purchasing Power Parity [*Economics*]
PPP	Push-Pull Power (IAA)
PPPA	Poison Prevention Packaging Act
PPPA	Professional Pool Players Association [*Defunct*] (EA)
PPPA	Protein Phosphatase Alpha (DMAA)
PPPA	Pulp and Paper Prepackaging Association [*Later, SSI*]
PPPA	Push-Pull Power Amplifier (IAA)
PPP & M	Preservation, Packaging, Packing, and Marking
PPPBL	Peripheral Pulses Palpable Both Legs [*Medicine*] (DMAA)
PPPBR	Peruvian Paso Part-Blood Registry (EA)
PPPC	Petroleum Pool Pacific Coast
PPPC	Pipe Plug Producers Council (EA)
PPPCA	Philadelphia College of Art Library, Philadelphia, PA [*Library symbol Library of Congress*] (LCLS)
PPPCity	Philadelphia City Institute Branch Free Library, Philadelphia, PA [*Library symbol Library of Congress Obsolete*] (LCLS)
PPPCO	Pennsylvania College of Optometry, Philadelphia, PA [*Library symbol Library of Congress*] (LCLS)
PPPCPh	Philadelphia College of Pharmacy and Science, Philadelphia, PA [*Library symbol Library of Congress*] (LCLS)
PPPE	Pennsylvania Economy League, Inc., Eastern Division, Philadelphia, PA [*Library symbol Library of Congress*] (LCLS)
PPPEA	Pulp, Paper, and Paperboard Export Association of the United States (EA)
PPPEC	Philadelphia Electric Co., Philadelphia, PA [*Library symbol Library of Congress*] (LCLS)
PPPEE	Pulsed Pinch Plasma Electromagnetic Engine (AAG)
PPPF	Positive Pregnancy and Parenting Fitness (EA)
PPPFM	Free and Accepted Masons of Pennsylvania, Grand Lodge Library, Philadelphia, PA [*Library symbol Library of Congress*] (LCLS)
PPPG	People's Progressive Party of Guyana [*Political party*]
PPPG	Postprandial Plasma Glucose [*Endocrinology*] (DAVI)
PPPH	Pennsylvania Hospital, Philadelphia, PA [*Library symbol Library of Congress*] (LCLS)
PPPHA	Philadelphia Housing Association, Philadelphia, PA [*Library symbol Library of Congress Obsolete*] (LCLS)
PPPHC	Philadelphia Tuberculosis and Health Association, Philadelphia, PA [*Library symbol Library of Congress Obsolete*] (LCLS)
PPPH-I	Institute of the Pennsylvania Hospital, Philadelphia, PA [*Library symbol Library of Congress*] (LCLS)
PPPI	Insurance Society of Philadelphia, Philadelphia, PA [*Library symbol Library of Congress Obsolete*] (LCLS)
PPPI	Personnel Performance Problems Inventory [*Test*]
PPPI	Plan Positional Plot Indicator
PPPI	Precision Plan Position Indicator
PPPI	Preliminary Process Potential Index
PPPI	Preplanned Product Improvement [*DoD*] (MCD)
PPPI	Primary Private Practice Income [*Medicine*] (MAE)
PPPI	Primary Private Practice Insurance [*Medicine*] (DMAA)
PPPI	Projection Plan Position Indicator
PPPI	Pulp, Paper, and Paperboard Institute USA [*Later, API*]
PPPL	Philadelphia Board of Public Education, Pedagogical Library, Philadelphia, PA [*Library symbol Library of Congress*] (LCLS)
PPPL	Planetary Physical Processes Laboratory (SSD)
PPPL	Princeton Plasma Physics Laboratory [*Also known as PPL - Plasma Physics Laboratory*] [*Princeton, NJ*] [*Department of Energy*]
PPPL	Printed Planning Parts List
PPPL	Program Preferred Parts List

PPPlanP ...... Planned Parenthood of Southeast Pennsylvania, Philadelphia, PA [Library symbol Library of Congress] (LCLS)

PPPlay........ Plays and Players Club, Philadelphia, PA [Library symbol Library of Congress Obsolete] (LCLS)

PPPLS .... Public Policy for Public Libraries Section [Public Library Association] [American Library Association]

PPPM........... Philadelphia Museum of Art, Philadelphia, PA [Library symbol Library of Congress] (LCLS)

PPPM-I........ Philadelphia Museum of Art, College of Art, Philadelphia, PA [Library symbol Library of Congress Obsolete] (LCLS)

PPPP .... Past Performance and Present Posture (AAG)

PPPP .... People's Peace and Prosperity Party [Defunct] (EA)

pppp........... Piu Piu Piu Pianissimo [Very, Very, Very Softly] [Italian] [Music] (AD)

PPPP .... Porokeratosis Punctata Palmaris et Plantaris [Medicine] (DMAA)

PPPP .... Proposed Partial Package Program (MUGU)

PPPPI .... Photographic Projection Plan Position Indicator (DEN)

PPPPP .... Pain, Pallor, Pulse Loss, Paresthesia, Paralysis [Medicine] (MEDA)

PPPR .... Philadelphia Transportation Co., Philadelphia, PA [Library symbol Library of Congress Obsolete] (LCLS)

PPPRC......... Poor Richard Club, Philadelphia, PA [Library symbol Library of Congress Obsolete] (LCLS)

PPPres......... Presbyterian University of Pennsylvania, Scheie Eye Institute Library, Philadelphia, PA [Library symbol Library of Congress] (LCLS)

PPPRF .... Pan Pacific Public Relations Federation [Thailand] [Defunct]

PPPrHi........ Presbyterian Historical Society, Philadelphia, PA [Library symbol Library of Congress] (LCLS)

PPPrl .... Printing Institute, Philadelphia, PA [Library symbol Library of Congress Obsolete] (LCLS)

PPProM....... Provident Mutual Life Insurance Co., Philadelphia, PA [Library symbol Library of Congress Obsolete] (LCLS)

PPPS .... People's Press Printing Society [British]

PPPSB .... Philadelphia College of the Bible, Philadelphia, PA [Library symbol Library of Congress] (LCLS)

PPPTe......... Philadelphia College of Textiles and Science, Philadelphia, PA [Library symbol Library of Congress] (LCLS)

PPQ .... Abandoned Police Post [Board on Geographic Names]

PPQ .... Parts per Quadrillion

PPQ .... Person Perception Questionnaire [Psychology] (EDAC)

PPQ .... Pittsfield, IL [Location identifier FAA] (FAAL)

PPQ .... Planning Purpose Quote

PPQ .... Plant Protection and Quarantine Programs [Department of Agriculture] (IMH)

PPQ .... Polyphenylquinoxaline [Resin]

ppq .... Polyphenylquinoxaline (AD)

PPQ .... Possible Parliamentary Question [Australia]

PPQA .... Pageable Partition Queue Area [Computer science]

PPQN .... Parts per Quarter Note [Computer science] (PCM)

PPQR .... Priority Parts Quality Review

PPQT .... Preproduction Qualification Test [Army]

PPQT & E .... Pre-Production Qualification Test and Evaluation [Army]

PPR .... Paid Pensioner Recruiter [British military] (DMA)

PPH .... Palomino Pony Registry

PPR .... Paper

PPr............. Paraprosthetic (DB)

PPH .... Partido Panamenista Republicano [Panama] [Political party] (EY)

PPR .... Partido Patriotico Revolucionario [Mexico Political party] (EY)

PPR .... Partido Proletariano Revolucionario [Proletarian Revolutionary Party] [Portugal Political party] (PPW)

PPR .... Payload Preparation Room [VAFB] [NASA] (MCD)

PPR .... Peak Production Rate

PPR .... Periodicals Publishing Record [Alberta Public Affairs Bureau] [Canada Information service or system] (CRD)

PPR .... Periodic Personnel Report

PPR .... Permanent Pay Record [Military]

PPR .... Permanent Personal Registration [Voting] (BARN)

PPR .... Peste des Petits Ruminants [Rinderpest-like disease] [Veterinary medicine]

PPR .... Photographic Press Review [A publication British]

PPR .... Photo-Plastic-Recording

PPR .... Photopolarimeter Radiometer [Instrumentation]

PPR .... Physician Payment Reform

PPR .... Pilgrim America Prime Rate Trust [NYSE symbol] (SAG)

PPR .... Pilgrim America Prime Rt [NYSE symbol] (TTSB)

PPR .... Pilgrim Prime Rate Trust [NYSE symbol] (SPSG)

PPR .... Pilot, Pressure Regulator (MCD)

PPR .... Pinault Printemps-Redoute [A non-food retail group] [France]

PPR .... Pirapora [Brazil] [Airport symbol] (AD)

PPR .... Polish People's Republic

PPR .... Politieke Partij Radikalen [Radical Political Party] [Netherlands Political party] (PPE)

PPR .... Polska Partia Robotnicza [Polish Workers' Party] [Political party]

PPr............. Port Pirie (AD)

PPR .... Portable Propagation Recorder [Bell System]

PPR .... Potential Problem Report [Navy] (CAAL)

PPR .... Present Participle [Grammar]

ppr............. Present Participle (AD)

PPR .... Price. Procedural Regulation [United States] [A publication] (DLA)

PPR .... Price's Precipitation Reaction [Medicine]

PPR .... Principal Private Residence [Income tax] [British]

PPR .... Principal Probate Registry (DLA)

PPR .... Printed Paper Rate [British] (ILCA)

ppr............. Printed Paper Rate (AD)

ppr............. Prior Permission Required (AD)

PPR .... Prior Permission Required (FAAC)

PPR .... Procurement Problem Report (AD)

PPR .... Production Parts Release (KSC)

PPR .... Production Progress Report (MCD)

PPR .... Program Planning Report (IAA)

PPR .... Program Progress Review

PPR .... Program Proposal Request

PPR .... Progress Payment Report (AAGC)

PPR .... Project Progress Report (OICC)

PPR .... Proper [Heraldry]

PPR .... Proprietary Procurement Request (NG)

PPR .... Provisioning Preparedness Review [Navy] (CAAL)

PPR .... Purchase Parts Request (KSC)

PPRA .... Past President of the Royal Academy [British] (EY)

PPRA .... Preliminary Personnel Requirements Analysis [Navy]

PPRA .... Protection of Pupil Rights Amendment

PPRAM .... Parallel Processing Random Access Memory (AAEL)

pprbd.......... Paperboard (AD)

PPRBD........ Paperboard

PPRC.......... Personnel Program Review Committee [Military]

PPRC.......... Physician Payment Review Commission

PPRC.......... Pollution Prevention Research Center [North Carolina State University] [Research center] (RCD)

PPRC.......... Prepositioned Receipt Card (AABC)

PPRCI.......... Rittenhouse Club, Philadelphia, PA [Library symbol Library of Congress Obsolete] (LCLS)

PPRD.......... Pontypool Road [Welsh depot code]

PPRDS........ Products and Process Research and Development Support (DCTA)

PPRE .... Peroxisome Proliferator Response Element [Biochemistry]

PPREC .... Pulp and Paper Research and Education Center [Auburn University] [Research center] (RCD)

PPREF .... Process Program Reference (AAEL)

PPREPT .... Periodic Personnel Report [Military] (AABC)

PPRETS .... Reformed Episcopal Seminary, Philadelphia, PA [Library symbol Library of Congress Obsolete]

PPRF .... Paramedian Pontine Reticular Formation [Neuroanatomy]

PPRF .... Postpartum Renal Failure [Medicine] (DMAA)

PPRF .... Pulse Pair Repetition Frequency (MCD)

PPRF .... Rosenbach Foundation, Philadelphia, PA [Library symbol Library of Congress] (LCLS)

PPRG .... Precambrian Paleobiology Research Group

PPRGF......... Richard Gimbel Foundation for Literary Research, Philadelphia, PA [Library symbol Library of Congress Obsolete] (LCLS)

PPRI .... PACOM [Pacific Command] Priority Number (CINC)

PPRIBA........ Past President of the Royal Institute of British Architects (EY)

PPRibP........ Phosphoribose Diphosphate [Biochemistry]

PPRIC .... Pulp and Paper Research Institute of Canada

PPRICA........ Pulp and Paper Research Institute of Canada (AD)

PPrIT .... Putnam Premier Income Trust [Associated Press] (SAG)

PPRL .... Poisonous Plant Research Laboratory [Agricultural Research Service] [Research center] (RCD)

PPRM .... Population Protection and Resources Management [Military British]

PPRM .... Pure Premium Rating Method [Insurance]

PPRN .... Preliminary Publication Revision Notice

PPRN .... Purchased Parts Requirement Notice (KSC)

PPRNCM...... Professional Performance of the Royal Northern College of Music [British] (DBQ)

PPRNS......... Pulse-Phased Radio Navigation System

PPRO.......... Per Procuration [Business term]

PPROM........ Prolonged Premature Rupture of Membranes [Obstetrics] (DAVI)

PPROP......... Personal Property [Legal shorthand] (LWAP)

PPRP .... Polydenosine Diphosphate-Ribose Polymerase (DMAA)

PPRPF .... Regional Planning Federation, Philadelphia, PA [Library symbol Library of Congress Obsolete] (LCLS)

PPRR .... Performance Planning & Review Record (WDAA)

PPRS .... Perceptions of Parental Role Scales

PPRS .... Pharmaceutical Price Regulation Scheme [British]

PPRS .... Preferred Planning Reporting System (WDAA)

PPRS .... Program Planning and Review Staff [Environmental Protection Agency] (GFGA)

PPRS .... Promotions and Placements Referral System (MCD)

PPRSA......... Past President of the Royal Society of Arts [British] (DI)

PPRV .... Peste des Petits Ruminants Virus [Rinderpest-like disease] [Veterinary medicine]

PPRWP........ Poor Precordial R-Wave Progression [Cardiology]

PPS............. Butte Aviation, Inc. [FAA designator] (FAAC)

PPS............. Pacific Passenger Services (AD)

PPS............. Packets per Second [Computer science] (PCM)

PPS............. Page Printing System [Honeywell, Inc.] [Computer science]

PPS............. Page Processing System (NITA)

PPS............. Paint, Pesticide Chemicals, and Solvents

PPS............. Paper Publications Society [Amsterdam, Netherlands] (EA)

PPS............. Parallel Processing System [Computer science] (MDG)

PPS............. Parameter Processing System (CAAL)

PPS............. Parliamentary Private Secretary [British]

PPS............. Partia e Punes e Shqiperise [Party of Labor of Albania - PLA] [Political party] (PPW)

PPS............. Partial Pressure Sensor

PPS............. Participating Preferred Stock (MHDW)

PPS............. Partido Popular Salvadoreno [Salvadoran Popular Party] [Political party] (PPW)

PPS............. Partido Popular Socialista [Popular Socialist Party] [Argentina Political party] (PPW)

PPS............. Partido Popular Socialista [Popular Socialist Party] [Mexico Political party]

PPS............. Parti du Progres et du Socialisme [Party of Progress and Socialism] [Morocco] [Political party] (PPW)

PPS............ Parti du Progres Social [*Burkina Faso*] [*Political party*] (EY)
PPS............ Parti Populaire Senegalais [*Senegalese People's Party*] [*Political party*] (PPW)
PPS............ Parti Populaire Syrien [*Syrian People's Party*] [*Political party*] (BJA)
PPS............ Parti Progressiste Soudanais [*Sudanese Progressive Party*] [*Political party*]
PPS............ Partito Populare Somalo [*Somali People's Party*]
PPS............ Parts Provisioning System (KSC)
PPS............ Patchboard Programming System
PPS............ Payload Pointing System (SSD)
PPS............ Payload Power Switch
PPS............ Pennsylvania Prison Society (AD)
PPS............ Peoples Oil Ltd. [*Vancouver Stock Exchange symbol*]
PPS............ Pepsin A [*Medicine*] (MAE)
PPS............ Performance Program Statement [*Australia*]
PPS............ Period per Second (IAA)
PPS............ Peripheral Processor System [*Computer science*] (IAA)
PPS............ Personal Plane Service [*Aircraft restoration firm*] [*British*]
PPS............ Personal Portable Shopper [*Computer science*]
PPS............ Personal Preference Scale [*Psychology*]
PPS............ Personal Printer Series [*IBM Corp.*]
PPS............ Personal Printing System [*Computer science*]
PPS............ Personal Process Service (LAIN)
PPS............ Personal Protection Squad [*of the London Metropolitan Police*]
PPS............ Personnel/Payroll System
PPS............ Personnel Processing Squadron
PPS............ Persutuan Perpustakaan Singapura [*Library Association of Singapore*] (AD)
PPS............ Petroleum Press Service
PPS............ Petroleum Production Survey [*Bureau of Mines*]
PPS............ Phantom Phanatics Society (EA)
PPS............ Phlogopite-Peridotite Solidus [*Geology*]
PPS............ Phosphorous Propellant System (KSC)
PPS............ Photophoretic Spectroscopy
PPS............ Photopolarimeter Spectrometer
PPS............ Photovoltaic Power Supply
PPS............ Pictures per Second (WDAA)
pps............. Pictures Per Second (AD)
PPS............ Piece Part Specification (MCD)
PPS............ Pierpont [*South Carolina*] [*Seismograph station code, US Geological Survey*] (SEIS)
PPS............ Pitt Press Series [*A publication*]
PPS............ Plant Parasitic Systems
PPS............ Plant Protection System [*Nuclear energy*] (NRCH)
PPS............ Plasma Power Supply
PPS............ Plutonium Product Storage [*Nuclear energy*] (NRCH)
PPS............ Pneumatic Power Subsystem (NASA)
PPS............ Point-to-Point System (IAA)
PPS............ Policy Processing Sheet [*Insurance*]
PPS............ Polonus Philatelic Society (EA)
PPS............ Polska Partia Socjalistyczna [*Polish Socialist Party*]
PPS............ Poly(para-phenylene Sulfide) [*Organic chemistry*]
PPS............ Polyphenylene Sulfide Plastic
PPS............ Polyvalance Pneumococcal Polysaccharides [*A vaccine for patients with splenectomies*] [*Medicine*] (DAVI)
PPS............ Portable Personal Shopper
PPS............ Ported Pressure Switch [*Automotive engineering*]
PPS............ Postpartum Sterilization [*Gynecology*] (DAVI)
PPS............ Postperfusion Syndrome [*Medicine*]
PPS............ Postpericardiotomy Syndrome [*Medicine*] (DMAA)
PPS............ Post-Polio Sequelae [*Medicine*]
p-ps.......... Post-Polio Syndrome [*Medicine*] (AD)
PPS............ Post-Postscriptum [*Further Postscript*] [*Latin*]
PPS............ Post Production Service (AAG)
PPS............ Post Production Support (MCD)
PPS............ Post Properties [*NYSE symbol*] (TTSB)
PPS............ Post Properties, Inc. [*NYSE symbol*] (SPSG)
PPS............ Postpump Syndrome [*Medicine*] (MAE)
PPS............ Pounds per Second (AAG)
pps............. Pounds Per Second (AD)
PPS............ Precise Positioning Service [*Military*]
PPS............ Precision Positioning Service
PPS............ Precision Power Supply
PPS............ Prepositioned Stock (NG)
PPS............ Prescribed Payments System (ADA)
PPS............ Primary Paraffin Sulfonate [*Organic chemistry*]
PPS............ Primary Power Standard
PPS............ Primary Power System [*Nuclear energy*] (NRCH)
PPS............ Primary Pressure Standard
PPS............ Primary Propulsion System [*Spacecraft*]
PPS............ Primary Protection System [*Computer science*]
PPS............ Principal Private Secretary [*British*]
PPS............ Printer/Plotter System (MCD)
PPS............ Prior Preferred Stock
pps............. Private Parliamentary Secretary [*British*] (AD)
PPS............ Private Practice Section [*American Physical Therapy Association*] (EA)
PPS............ Probability Proportional to Size [*Statistics*]
PPS............ Procurement Planning Schedule [*DoD*]
PPS............ Production Planning System [*TDS Business Systems Ltd.*] [*Software package*] (NCC)
PPS............ Programmable Patch System
PPS............ Programmable Power Supply
PPS............ Programmed Processor System
PPS............ Programming Program Strela [*Computer science*]

PPS............ Program Performance Specification (CAAL)
PPS............ Program Planning Summary (OICC)
PPS............ Program Planning System [*DoD*]
PPS............ Program Policy Staff [*UN Food and Agriculture Organization*]
PPS............ Progressive Pneumonia of Sheep
PPS............ Project for Public Spaces (EA)
PPS............ Propose (FAAC)
PPS............ Propulsion and Propellant Section [*Picatinny Arsenal*] [*Dover, NJ*]
PPS............ Propulsion Pressurization Subsystem
PPS............ Prospective Payment System [*For hospital care*]
PPS............ Prospective Pricing System [*Information service or system*] (HCT)
PPS............ Provisioning Parts Schedule (MCD)
PPS............ Provisioning Performance Schedule (AFM)
PPS............ Provisioning Policy Statement (MCD)
PPS............ Prudential Property Services [*Prudential Group*] [*British*]
PPS............ Public and Private [*Nongovernment*] Schools [*Public-performance tariff class*] [*British*]
PPS............ Puerto Princesa [*Philippines*] [*Airport symbol*] (OAG)
PPS............ Pulses per Second [*Data transmission*]
pps............. Pulses Per Second (AD)
PPSA .... Pan-Pacific Surgical Association (EA)
PPSAS .... Program Planning and Status Assessment System [*Nuclear energy*] (NRCH)
PPSAT .... Peripheral Processor Saturation (MHDI)
PPSAWA ...... Pan Pacific and Southeast Asia Women's Association (AD)
PPSB .... Periodical Publishers' Service Bureau (NADA)
PPSB .... Prothrombin, Proconvertin, Stuart Factor, Antihemophilic B Factor [*Blood coagulation factors*] [*Hematology*]
PPSC .... Physical Profile Serial Code [*Military*]
PPSC .... Privacy Protection Study Commission [*Government commission*]
PPSC .... Processor Program State Control (NITA)
PPSCA .... Partido Popular Social Cristiano Autentico [*Political party*] (EY)
PPSCI .... Seamen's Church Institute, Philadelphia, PA [*Library symbol Library of Congress Obsolete*] (LCLS)
PPSD .... Polska Partia Socialno-Demokratyczna [*Polish Social-Democrat Party*] [*Political party*]
PPSD .... Proposed
PPSE .... Programmer Support Environment [*Computer science*] (LAIN)
PPSE .... Purpose
PPSEAWA .... Pan-Pacific and South-East Asia Women's Association [*Tokyo, Japan*] (EAIO)
PPSEAWA-USA... Pan Pacific and Southeast Asia Women's Association of the USA (EA)
PPSF .... Palestinian Popular Struggle Front [*Political party*] (BJA)
PPSFP .... Parallel-Pattern Single-Fault Propagation [*Computer science*] (CIST)
PPS-FR .... Polska Partia Socjalistyczna - Frakcja Rewolucyjna [*Polish Socialist Party - Revolutionary Faction*] [*Political party*] (PPE)
PPSG .... Piston and Pin Standardization Group [*Later, NEPMA*] (EA)
PPSG .... Spring Garden College, Philadelphia, PA [*Library symbol Library of Congress*] (LCLS)
PPSh .... Partia e Punes e Shqiperise [*Labor Party of Albania*] [*Formerly, PKSh*] [*Political party*] (PPE)
PPSH .... Pseudovaginal Perineoscrotal Hypospadias [*Medicine*]
PPSI .... Pacific Physician Services (SPSG)
PPSI .... Pacific Physician Services, Inc. [*NASDAQ symbol*] (SAG)
PPSI .... Parent Problem-Solving Instrument (EDAC)
PPSIA .... "Personal Property Shipping Information" [*Pamphlet*] Is Applicable [*Military*] (AABC)
PPSIAD .... Past President of the Society of Industrial Artists and Designers [*British*] (DI)
PPSJ .... Pressure Plane Swivel Joint
PPSJ .... Saint Joseph's College, Philadelphia, PA [*Library symbol Library of Congress*] (LCLS)
PPSJ-AF ...... Saint Joseph's College, Academy of Food Marketing, Philadelphia, PA [*Library symbol Library of Congress*] (LCLS)
PPSKED .... Provisioning Performance Schedule (MCD)
PPSKF .... SmithKline Corp., Philadelphia, PA [*Library symbol Library of Congress*] (LCLS)
PPSL .... Program Parts Selection List
PPSL .... Provisioning Parts Selection List (MCD)
PPSMEC ...... Procurement, Precedence of Supplies, Material and Equipment Committee [*Joint Communications Board*]
ppsn........... Present Position (AD)
PPSN .... Present Position [*Aviation*] (FAAC)
PPSN .... Public Packet Switched [*or Switching*] Network [*Telecommunications*]
PPSN .... Purchased Part Shortage Notice
ppso........... Per Person, Single Occupancy (AD)
PPSO .... Personal Property Shipping Office [*Military*]
PPSOPR....... Sun Oil Co., General Office Library, Philadelphia, PA [*Library symbol Library of Congress Obsolete*] (LCLS)
PPSP .... Page Printer Spooling System [*Computer science*]
PPSP .... Ponderosa Pine or Sugar Pine [*Lumber*]
PPSP .... Power Plant Siting Program [*Environmental Protection Agency*] (GFGA)
PPSPS .... Plutonium Product Shipping Preparation Station [*Nuclear energy*] (NRCH)
PPSQ .... Principal Problem Strategy Questionnaire (EDAC)
PPSR .... Periodic Personnel Strength Report [*Army*] (AABC)
PPSS .... Foundation for the President's Private Sector Survey on Cost Control (EA)
PPSS .... Polyphenylene Sulfide Sulfone [*Organic chemistry*]
PPSS .... Public Packet Switching Service (NITA)
PPSSCC ...... Foundation for the President's Private Sector Survey on Cost Control (EA)
P-PST .... Pre-Professional Skill Test (EDAC)

PPStarr........	Starr Center Association, Philadelphia, PA [*Library symbol Library of Congress Obsolete*] (LCLS)
PPStCh........	Saint Charles Borromeo Seminary, Philadelphia, PA [*Library symbol Library of Congress*] (LCLS)
PPSteph.......	William B. Stephens Memorial Library, Philadelphia, PA [*Library symbol Library of Congress Obsolete*] (LCLS)
PPSTH	Population Post-stimulus Time Histogram [*Statistics*]
PPSU	Poly Phenylene Sulfone (EDCT)
PPSU	Polyphenylene Sulfone Plastic
PPSU	Programmable Power Supply Unit (EECA)
PPSV	Plutonium Product Storage Vault [*Nuclear energy*] (NRCH)
PPSV	Printing and Publishing Services, Victoria [*Australia*]
PPSWA	Plant Protection Society of Western Australia [*Australia*]
PPS-WRN	Polska Partia Socjalistyczna - Wolnosc, Rownosc, Niepodleglosc [*Polish Socialist Party - Freedom, Equality, Independence*] [*Political party*] (PPE)
PPT	Palmitoyl-Protein Thioesterase [*An enzyme*]
PPT	Pamatai [*French Polynesia*] [*Geomagnetic observatory code*]
PPT	Papeete [*French Polynesia*] [*Airport symbol*] (OAG)
PPT	Papeete [*French Polynesia*] [*Seismograph station code, US Geological Survey*] (SEIS)
PPT	Papeete, Society Islands [*Airport*] (AD)
PPT	Parietal Pleural Tissue (DB)
PPT	Partial Prothrombin Time [*Hematology*]
PPT	Parti Progressiste Tchadien [*Progressive Party of Chad*] [*Political party*]
PPT	Parts per Thousand (DNAB)
ppt	Parts per Thousand (IDOE)
ppt	Parts per Trillion [*Marine science*] (OSRA)
PPT	Parts per Trillion
p-p-t	Pay-per-Transaction [*Agreement between video cassette rental stores and owners of film rights*]
PPT	Peak-to-Peak Threshold (DB)
PPT	Pedunculopontine Tegmentum [*Neurology*]
PPT	Pericles, Prince of Tyre [*A publication*] (AD)
PPT	Periodic Programs Termination [*Computer science*]
PPT	Period Pulse Train
PPT	Peripheral Performance Test (CAAL)
PPT	Permanent Part-Time (ADA)
PPT	Personal Property Tax (MHDW)
PPT	Phosphinothricin [*Organic chemistry*]
PPT	Pilot's Power Tool
PPT	Pine Point Mines Ltd. [*Toronto Stock Exchange symbol Vancouver Stock Exchange symbol*]
PPT	Pitch Precession Torquer
PPT	Plant Protease Test (MAE)
PPT	Poly Propylene Terephthalate (EDCT)
PPT	Polypurine Tract [*Genetics*]
PPT	Polypyrimidine Tract [*Genetics*]
PPT	Pooh Property Trust [*A.A. Milne estate*] [*British*]
PPT	Poppet [*Engineering*]
PPT	Post Production Test
PPT	PowerPoint [*Computer science*] (PCM)
PPT	Practical Policy Test [*Psychology*]
PPT	Praecipitatus [*Precipitated*] [*Pharmacy*]
PPT	Praeparata [*Prepared*] [*Pharmacy*] (ROG)
PPT	Precipitate (MSA)
ppt	Precipitate (AD)
ppt	Precipitat Prepared [*Laboratory science*] (DAVI)
PPT	Preproduction Test [*Army*]
PPT	Preprotachykinin [*Biochemistry*]
PPT	Preprototype (SAA)
PPT	Private Purchasing Tariff [*British*]
PPT	Probabilistic Potential Theory (PDAA)
PPT	Process Page Table [*Telecommunications*] (TEL)
PPT	Production Prototype
PPT	Product Positioning Time (AFM)
PPT	Programmer Productivity Technique (IAA)
PPT	Project Planning Technique (MCD)
PPT	Prompt (ROG)
PPT	Propyl(thio)uracil [*Biochemistry*]
PPT	Public and Private Transport
PPT	Pulse Plasma Thruster
PPT	Punched Paper Tape [*Computer science*]
PPT	Putnam Premier Income Tr [*NYSE symbol*] (TTSB)
PPT	Putnam Premier Income Trust [*NYSE symbol*] (SPSG)
PPT	Temple University, Philadelphia, PA [*Library symbol Library of Congress*] (LCLS)
PPT	Theosophical Society, Philadelphia, PA [*Library symbol Library of Congress Obsolete*] (LCLS)
PPTA...........	Post-Primary Teachers Association [*New Zealand*] (WDAA)
PPTB	Pin-Pack Test Board
PPTBA	Pattern and Plastic Tool Builders Association [*Defunct*] (EA)
PPTC...........	People-to-People Tennis Committee (EA)
PPTC...........	Purchased Part Tab Card
PPTD	Precipitated
pptd	Precipitated (AD)
PPT-D	Temple University, Dental-Pharmacy School, Philadelphia, PA [*Library symbol Library of Congress*] (LCLS)
PPTE...........	Permanent Part-Time Employment
PPTF...........	Public Policy Task Force [*Defunct*] (EA)
PPTF...........	Public-Private Task Force
ppth	Parts Per Thousand (GNE)
pPTH	Porcine Parathyroid Hormone [*Endocrinology*]
PPTI	Protein Polymer Technologies [*NASDAQ symbol*] (TTSB)
PPTI............	Protein Polymer Technologies, Inc. [*NASDAQ symbol*] (SAG)
PPT-ISA	Picture Personality Test for Indian South Africans
PPTIW	Protein Polymer Technol Wrrt [*NASDAQ symbol*] (TTSB)
PPTJ	Theodore F. Jenkins Memorial Law Library, Philadelphia, PA [*Library symbol Library of Congress*] (LCLS)
PPTL	Postpartum Tubal Ligation [*Medicine*]
PPTL	Pulp and Paper Traffic League [*Defunct*] (EA)
PPT-L..........	Temple University, Law School, Philadelphia, PA [*Library symbol Library of Congress*] (LCLS)
PPT-M	Temple University, Medical School, Philadelphia, PA [*Library symbol Library of Congress*] (LCLS)
PPTMR	Personal Property Traffic Management Regulation
PPTN	Precipitation
pptn	Precipitation (AD)
PPTO	Personal Property Transportation Officer
PPTO	Principal Professional and Technology Officer [*British*]
PPTP...........	Point-to-Point Tunneling Protocol [*Microsoft Corp.*]
PPTP...........	Power-Proportioning Temperature Programmer (IAA)
PPTPP	Promulgators of Public Toilets in Public Parks (AD)
PPTR	Punched Paper Tape Reader [*Computer science*]
PPTri	Tri-Institutional Library, Philadelphia, PA [*Library symbol Library of Congress*] (LCLS)
PPTS	Pianoforte Polishers' Trade Society [*A union*] [*British*]
PPTS	Portable Perishable Tool System (MCD)
PPTS	Pre-Planned Training System (PDAA)
PPTS	Pre-Problem Training Situation (SAA)
PPTS	Pyridinium Para-Toluenesulfonate [*Organic chemistry*]
PPTS	Pyridinium-para-Tosylate [*Organic chemistry*]
PP/TSD	Post Placement and Training Support Program for People with Disabilities [*Australia*]
PPT-T..........	Temple University, School of Theology, Philadelphia, PA [*Library symbol Library of Congress*] (LCLS)
PPTTG	Personal Property Transit Time Guide [*MTMC*] (TAG)
PPTV..........	Parts per Trillion by Volume
PPTV..........	PPT Vision [*NASDAQ symbol*] (TTSB)
PPTV..........	PPT Vision, Inc. [*NASDAQ symbol*] (SAG)
PPT Vis.......	PPT Vision, Inc. [*Associated Press*] (SAG)
PPTW..........	Permanent Part-Time Work
PPTY..........	Property (AFM)
ppty.............	Property (AD)
PPU	Cocoa, FL [*Location identifier FAA*] (FAAL)
PPU	Papun [*Myanmar*] [*Airport symbol*] (OAG)
PPU	Parti Populaire des Ueles [*Ueles People's Party*] [*Political party*]
PPU	Payment for Public Use [*Canada*]
PPU	Peace Pledge Union [*British*]
PPU	Peninsula Petroleum Corp. [*Vancouver Stock Exchange symbol*]
PPU	Peoria & Pekin Union Railway Co. [*AAR code*]
PPU	Peripheral Processing Unit [*Computer science*]
PPU	Picture Processing Unit [*Computer science*]
PPU	Platform Position Unit
ppu	Platform Position Unit (AD)
PPU	Power Processing Unit (MCD)
PPU	Pre-Processor Utility (NITA)
PPU	Preproduction Unit (MCD)
PPU	Primary Producers Union (AD)
PPU	Prime Power Unit
PPU	Professional Psychics United (EA)
PPU	Promontory Point [*Utah*] [*Seismograph station code, US Geological Survey Closed*] (SEIS)
PPUG..........	United Gas Improvement Corp., Philadelphia, PA [*Library symbol Library of Congress Obsolete*] (LCLS)
PPUI	Pitch and Putt Union of Ireland (EAIO)
PPULC	Union Library Catalogue of Pennsylvania, Philadelphia, PA [*Library symbol Library of Congress*] (LCLS)
PPUNA	United States Naval Aircraft Factory, Philadelphia, PA [*Library symbol Library of Congress Obsolete*] (LCLS)
PPUnC	University Club, Philadelphia, PA [*Library symbol Library of Congress Obsolete*] (LCLS)
PPUNH........	United States Naval Home, Philadelphia, PA [*Library symbol Library of Congress Obsolete*] (LCLS)
PPUSDA.......	United States Department of Agriculture, Agricultural Research Service, Eastern Utilization Research and Development Division, Philadelphia, PA [*Library symbol*] [*Library of Congress*] (LCLS)
PPV..............	Paraphenylene Vinylene [*Organic chemistry*]
PPV..............	Pay-per-View [*Pay-television service*]
ppv..............	Pay-Per-View (AD)
ppv..............	People-Powered Vehicle (AD)
PPV..............	People-Powered Vehicle [*Recreational vehicle powered by pedaling*]
PPV..............	Pitch Power Valve (IAA)
PPV..............	Plum Pox Virus [*Plant pathology*]
PPV..............	Polarized Platen Viewer (OA)
PPV..............	Poly (Phenylenevinylene) [*Organic chemistry*]
PPV..............	Porcine Parvovirus [*Veterinary science*] (DMAA)
PPV..............	Positive Predictive Value [*Experimentation*]
PPV..............	Positive Pressure Ventilation [*Medicine*]
PPV..............	Preprogrammed Vehicles (MCD)
PPV..............	Primary Pressure Vessel (MCD)
PPV..............	Progressive Pneumonia Virus [*Medicine*] (DB)
P/PV.............	Public/Private Ventures [*Philadelphia, PA*] [*Research center*] (RCD)
PPV..............	United States Veterans Administration Hospital, Philadelphia, PA [*Library symbol Library of Congress*] (LCLS)
PPVT...........	Peabody Picture Vocabulary Test [*Education*]
PPVT-R	Peabody Picture Vocabulary Test - Revised [*Education*]

PP-W .... Free Library of Philadelphia, H. Josephine Widener Memorial Branch, Philadelphia, PA [*Library symbol Library of Congress Obsolete*] (LCLS)
PPW............. PacifiCorp [*NYSE symbol*] (SPSG)
PPW............. Pacificorp Capital [*NYSE symbol*] (SAG)
PPW............. Papa Westray [*Scotland*] [*Airport symbol*] (OAG)
PPW............. Parts per Weight
PPW............. Petitions for Patent Waiver
PPW............. Plane-Polarized Wave
PPW............. Ponderosa Pine Woodwork Association [*NWWDA*] [*Absorbed by*] (EA)
PPW............. Potato Processing Waste
PPWA........... Ponderosa Pine Woodwork Association [*NWWDA*] [*Absorbed by*]
PPWa........... Wagner Free Institute of Science, Philadelphia, PA [*Library symbol Library of Congress*] (LCLS)
PPWC .... Pulp, Paper, and Woodworkers of Canada
PPWD .... S. S. White Co., Philadelphia, PA [*Library symbol Library of Congress Obsolete*] (LCLS)
PPWe........... Westminster Theological Seminary, Philadelphia, PA [*Library symbol Library of Congress*] (LCLS)
PPWI .... Wistar Institute of Anatomy and Biology, Philadelphia, PA [*Library symbol Library of Congress*] (LCLS)
PPWiH .... Wills Eye Hospital, Philadelphia, PA [*Library symbol Library of Congress*] (LCLS)
PPWL........... Present Practice Waste Load (DICI)
PPWM .... Medical College of Pennsylvania, Philadelphia, PA [*Library symbol Library of Congress*] (LCLS)
PPWP .... Planned Parenthood - World Population [*Later, PPFA*] (EA)
PPWPr......... PacifiCorp 5% Pfd [*AMEX symbol*] (TTSB)
PPWrE .... PacifiCorp $1.98 cm Pfd [*NYSE symbol*] (TTSB)
PPWR .... Prepositioned War Reserves [*Army*]
PPWRS .... Prepositioned War Reserve Stocks [*Army*]
PPX............. Packet Protocol Extension
PPX............. Port Moller, AK [*Location identifier FAA*] (FAAL)
PPX............. Private Packet Exchange
PPY............. Pages per Year [*Facetious criterion for determining insignificance of Supreme Court Justices*] [*Proposed by University of Chicago professor David P. Currie*]
PPY............. Pancreatic Polypeptide [*Medicine*] (DMAA)
PPY............. Prophesy Development [*Vancouver Stock Exchange symbol*]
PPYH .... Young Men's and Young Women's Hebrew Association, Philadelphia, PA [*Library symbol Library of Congress Obsolete*] (LCLS)
PPYU .... Party of Popular Yemenite Unity [*Political party*] (PD)
PPZ............. Proton Polar Zone
PPZ............. Puerto Paez [*Venezuela*] [*Airport symbol*] (AD)
PPZ............. Zoological Society of Philadelphia, PA [*Library symbol Library of Congress Obsolete*] (LCLS)
PQ................. Pack Quickly [*Humorous interpretation for Parti Quebecois*] [*Canada*]
PQ................. Panic in Quebec [*Humorous interpretation for Parti Quebecois*] [*Canada*]
PQ................. Parametric Quantron [*Physics*]
PQ................. Parliamentary Question [*British*]
PQ................. Parti Quebecois [*Quebec separatist political party*]
pq................. Peculiar (AD)
PQ................. Performance Qualification (ACII)
PQ................. Performer Quotient [*TV-performer rating*]
PQ................. Permeability Quotient
pq................. Permeability Quotient (AD)
pq................. Personality Quotient (AD)
PQ................. Personality Quotient [*Psychology*]
p-q................. Phenol-Hydroquinone [*Photography*] (AD)
PQ................. Philological Quarterly [*A publication*] (BRI)
PQ................. Photo Quality (PCM)
PQ................. Physically Qualified
PQ................. Physician's Questionnaire (AAMN)
PQ................. Planetary Quarantine [*NASA*]
PQ................. Plant Quarantine Division [*of ARS, Department of Agriculture*]
PQ................. Plasma Quad [*Instrumentation*]
PQ................. Plastoquinone [*Biochemistry*]
PQ................. Pollution Quotient
PQ................. Polyquinoxaline [*Organic chemistry*]
P-Q................. Porphyrin-Quinone [*Photochemistry*]
PQ................. PQ Corp. [*Formerly, Philadelphia Quartz Co.*]
PQ................. Premium Quality (MUGU)
PQ................. Preparative Quencher [*Spectroscopy*]
PQ................. Presentation Quotient [*Business Term*]
PQ................. Previous Question [*Parliamentary law*]
pq................. Previous Question (AD)
Pq................. Primaquine [*Antimalarial*]
PQ................. Pronator Quadratus [*Muscle*] [*Anatomy*] (DAVI)
pq................. Pro Querente [*For the Plaintiff*] [*Latin Legal term*] (DLA)
PQ................. Province Quebec [*Quebec*] [*Canadian province Postal code*]
PQ................. Psi Quotient [*Parapsychology*]
PQ................. Public Quarters
PQ................. Puerto Rico International Airlines, Inc. [*Prinair*] [*ICAO designator*] (OAG)
pq................. Punishment Quarters (AD)
PQ................. Pyrimethamine-Quinine [*Organic chemistry*] (MAE)
PQ................. Quebec [*Postal code*] (CDAI)
PQ................. South Pacific Airlines of New Zealand (AD)
PQ-W .... United States Patent Quarterly [*A publication*] (DLA)
PQA .... Pacific Coast Airlines [*ICAO designator*] (FAAC)
PQA .... Parts Quality Assurance
PQA .... Petroleum Quality Assurance
PQA .... Plant Quality Assurance

PQA .... Preliminary Quantitative Analysis
PQA .... Procurement Quality Assurance [*Program*] [*DoD*]
pqa .... Procurement Quality Assurance (AD)
PQA .... Production Quality Assurance
PQA .... Project Quality Assurance
PQA .... Protected Queue Area [*Computer science*] (BUR)
PQAA .... Province of Quebec Association of Architects [*1890, OAQ from 1974*] [*Canada*] (NGC)
PQAD .... Plant Quality Assurance Director [*Nuclear energy*] (NRCH)
PQAI .... Procurement Quality Assurance Instruction
PQAM .... Project Quality Assurance Manager [*Nuclear energy*] (NRCH)
PQANSW........ Paraplegic and Quadriplegic Association of New South Wales [*Australia*]
PQAP .... Planned Quality Assurance Program [*Navy*]
PQAP .... Procurement Quality Assurance Program [*DoD*]
PQAQ .... Paraplegic and Quadriplegic Association of Queensland [*Australia*]
PQAR .... Petroleum Quality Assurance Representative
PQASA............ Paraplegic and Quadriplegic Association of South Australia
PQAV .... Paraplegic and Quadriplegic Association of Victoria [*Australia*]
PQAWA .... Paraplegic and Quadriplegic Association of Western Australia
PQB .... Quebecor CI'A' [*AMEX symbol*] (TTSB)
PQB .... Quebecor, Inc. [*AMEX symbol*] (SPSG)
PQC .... Chieftain Airways PLC [*British ICAO designator*] (FAAC)
PQC .... Paul Quinn College [*Texas*]
PQC .... Paul Quinn College, Waco, TX [*OCLC symbol*] (OCLC)
PQC .... Phuquoc [*South Vietnam*] [*Airport symbol*] (AD)
PQC .... Precision Quartz Crystal
PQC .... Procurement Quality Control (IAA)
PQC .... Production Quality Control
PQCS .... Process Quality Control System
PQD .... Partido Quisqueyano Democrata [*Quisqueyan Democratic Party*] [*Dominican Republic*] [*Political party*] (PPW)
PQD .... Percentage Quartile Deviation [*Statistics*]
PQD .... Plant Quarantine Division (AD)
PQD .... Predicted Quarterly Demand
PQD .... Pyroelectric Quad Detector
PQDMB .... Percentage Quartile Deviation Median Bias [*Statistics*]
PQE .... Parents for Quality Education [*Defunct*] (EA)
PQE .... Post-Qualification Education (PDAA)
pqe .... Post-Qualification Education (AD)
PQE .... Principal Quality Engineers [*British*] (RDA)
PQE .... Professional Qualification Examination [*National Security Agency*] (EDAC)
PQE .... Project Quality Engineering
PQEP .... Product Quality Evaluation Plan [*Military*] (AABC)
PQET............ Print Quality Enhancement Technology [*IBM*] (PCM)
PQFP .... Plastic Quad Flat Package [*Computer science*] (PCM)
PQGS .... Propellant Quantity Gauge [*or Gauging*] System [*Apollo*] [*NASA*]
PQI .... Presque Isle [*Maine*] [*Airport symbol*] (OAG)
PQI .... Presque Isle, ME [*Location identifier FAA*] (FAAL)
PQI .... Print Quality Improvement [*Advanced photo system*]
PQI .... Product Quality Improvement [*Program*] [*Chrysler Corp.*]
PQI .... Professional Qualification Index (AFM)
pqi .... Professional Qualification Index (AD)
PQI .... Propellant Quantity Indicator (NASA)
PQIH .... Plant Quarantine Inspection House (AD)
PQL .... Practical Quantitation Level [*Environmental chemistry*] (ERG)
PQL .... Practical Quantitation Limit [*Environmental chemistry*]
PQL .... Prior Quarter Liability [*IRS*]
PQLI .... Physical Quality of Life Index [*Overseas Development Council*]
PQM .... Pilot Qualified in Model (NVT)
PQM .... Post Quartermaster [*Marine Corps*]
PQM .... Print Quality Monitor [*Computer science*] (IAA)
PQM .... Pulse Quaternary Modulation
PQMC .... Philadelphia Quartermaster Center [*Merged with Defense Clothing and Textile Supply Center*] [*Military*]
PQMD .... Philadelphia Quartermaster Depot [*Military*]
PQMD .... Propellant Quantity Measuring Device
PQMDO........ Proposed Quality Material Development Objective (NATG)
PQMF............ Parallel Quadrature Mirror Filter (PDAA)
PQMR .... Preliminary Quantitative Material Requirements (MCD)
PQMS .... Process Quality Measurement System [*Chemical process engineering*]
PQN .... Consolidated Petroquin [*Vancouver Stock Exchange symbol*]
PQN .... Pahaquarry [*New Jersey*] [*Seismograph station code, US Geological Survey*] (SEIS)
PQN .... Pipestone, MN [*Location identifier FAA*] (FAAL)
PQN .... Principal Quantum Number [*Atomic physics*]
PQNCX............ PIMCO: Renaissance CI.C [*Mutual fund ticker symbol*] (SG)
PQNS .... Protein, Quantity Not Sufficient [*Laboratory science*] (DAVI)
PQO .... Phoenix, AZ [*Location identifier FAA*] (FAAL)
PQOL .... Perceived Quality of Life [*Medicine*] (DMAA)
PQOS .... Pre-Qualified Offsets Supplier
PQOSS .... Pre-Qualified Offsets Supplier Status
PQP .... Planetary Quarantine Plan [*NASA*]
PQP .... Prequalification Prototype (KSC)
PQQ .... Port Macquarie [*Australia Airport symbol*] (OAG)
PQQ .... Pyrroloquinoline Quinone [*Biochemistry*]
PQQPRI............ Provisional Qualitative and Quantitative Personnel Requirements Information [*Army*] (AABC)
PQR .... Pantan Resources [*Vancouver Stock Exchange symbol*]
PQR .... Performance Qualification Requirement
PQR .... Personnel Qualification Record [*Military*] (INF)
PQR .... Personnel Qualification Roster [*Military*] (AABC)
PQR .... Procedure Qualification Record [*Nuclear energy*] (NRCH)

PQR	Program Quality Review (AD)
PQRI	Product Quality Research Initiative [Drug evalution]
pqrs	Productivity Increases, Quality Control, Robotization, and Savings [Japanese formula for economic success] (AD)
PQRST	Personal Questionnaire Rapid Scaling Technique [Personality development test] [Psychology]
PQRST	Product-Quality-Routing-Service-Timing [Industrial engineering]
PQS	Percentage Quota System (AD)
PQS	Personnel Qualification Standard (AD)
PQS	Personnel Qualification Standards [Military] (NVT)
PQS	Pilot Station [Alaska] [Airport symbol] (OAG)
PQS	Production Quotation Support
PQS	Progressive Qualification Scheme [British]
PQS	Promotion Qualification Score [Military]
PQSF	Preparative Quencher Stopped Flow [Spectroscopy]
PQT	Parquet Resources, Inc. [Toronto Stock Exchange symbol]
PQT	PC Quote [AMEX symbol] (TTSB)
PQT	PC Quote, Inc. [AMEX symbol] (SAG)
PQT	Performance Qualification Test (MCD)
PQT	Polyquinazolotriazole [Organic chemistry]
PQT	Preliminary Qualification Test (MCD)
PQT	Production Qualification and Testing
PQT	Professional Qualification Test [of the National Security Agency]
PQT	Prototype Qualification Testing (RDA)
PQT & E	Production Qualification Test and Evaluation
PQT-C	Prototype Qualification Test - Contractor (MCD)
PQT-G	Prototype Qualification Test - Government (MCD)
PQT/LOT	Production Qualification Test / Limited Operational Test
PQT-SE	Prototype Qualification Test - Service Evaluation (MCD)
PQU	Salisbury, MD [Location identifier FAA] (FAAL)
PQUE	Petroquest Energy [Formerly, Optima Petroleum] [NASDAQ symbol]
PQUE	Print Queue Processor [Computer science]
PQW	Placita de Quo Warranto, Record Commission [England] [A publication] (DLA)
PQX	Physically Qualified Except
PQZ	Premium Quality Zinc
PR	Abbott Laboratories [Research code symbol]
PR	Aircrew Survival Equipmentman [Navy rating]
PR	Pacific Reporter [A publication] (DLA)
P(R)	Packet (Receive)
PR	Painter (ADA)
PR	Pair (KSC)
pr	Pair (AD)
PR	Pakistan Railways (DCTA)
PR	Panama Red [Variety of marijuana]
Pr	Panama-Red Marijuana (AD)
PR	Panel Receptacle
PR	Pangenesis Related [Protein chemistry]
PR	Panthere Rose [France] [An association Defunct] (EAIO)
pr	Paper (WDAA)
PR	Paper Tape Reader
PR	Parachute Rigger [Navy] (KSC)
PR	Paradise Regained [A publication] (AD)
PR	Parallax and Refraction
Pr	Parana (AD)
pr	Parcel Receipt (AD)
PR	Parcel Receipt [Shipping]
PR	Parental Recommendation [Movie rating] (CDAI)
PR	Parents Rights (EA)
PR	Parish Register
PR	Park Ranger (AD)
PR	Parliamentary Report [British]
PR	Parrott Rifle
PR	Partial Remission [Medicine]
PR	Partial Response [Medicine] (DAVI)
PR	Partido Radical [Radical Party] [Chile] [Political party]
PR	Partido Radical [Radical Party] [Spain Political party] (PPE)
PR	Partido Reformista [Reformist Party] [Dominican Republic] [Political party] (PPW)
PR	Partido Republicano [Republican Party] [Panama] [Political party] (EY)
PR	Partido Republicano [Republican Party] [Ecuador] [Political party] (EY)
PR	Partido Revolucionario [Revolutionary Party] [Guatemala] [Political party] (PPW)
PR	Partido Riojano [Spain Political party] (EY)
PR	Parti Republicain [Republican Party] [France Political party] (PPW)
PR	Parti Republicain [Republican Party] [Reunion] [Political party] (EY)
PR	Parti Republicain [Republican Party] [Martinique] [Political party] (PPW)
PR	Parti Republicain [Republican Party] [New Caledonia] [Political party] (FEA)
PR	Partisan Review [A publication] (BRI)
PR	Partito Radicale [Radical Party] [Founded, 1955] [Italy] [Political party] (PPE)
PR	Party Raayat [Leftist organization in Singapore]
PR	Passengers' Risk (ROG)
PR	Passive Ranging [Military] (LAIN)
PR	Past in Review [Later, PIR] (EA)
PR	Pastor
PR	Pathogenesis Related [Biology]
PR	Patient Relations (DAVI)
PR	Patria Roja [Red Fatherland] [Peru] (PD)
PR	Patrol Vessel, River Gunboat [Navy symbol]
PR	Pattern Recognition (BUR)
PR	Payroll
pr	Payroll (AD)
PR	Peer Review
PR	Peking Review [A publication] (AD)
PR	Pelvic Rock [Orthopedics] (DAVI)
PR	Peng-Robinson [Equation of state]
PR	Penicillium roqueforti [Toxin] [Medicine]
P-R	Pennsylvania-Reading [Seashore Lines] (AD)
PR	Pennsylvania Reports (Penrose and Watts) [A publication] (DLA)
PR	Penny Resistance (EA)
PR	Pen Record (SAA)
PR	Per
PR	Percentage Rates
PR	Percentile Rank
pr	Percentile Rank (AD)
PR	Percent Recovery [Plant pathology]
PR	Performance Rating (OICC)
PR	Performance Ratio (AAG)
PR	Performance Report (AFM)
PR	Performance Requirement
PR	Perfusion Rate [Cardiology] (DAVI)
PR	Periodic Report (IAA)
PR	Periodic Reversal (IAA)
PR	Periodic Review [Social Security Administration] (DHP)
PR	Peripheral Resistance [Medicine]
pr	Peripheral Resistance (AD)
PR	Peripheral rheumatism [Medicine] (DB)
PR	Perirenal [Nephrology]
PR	Permanens Rector [Permanent Rector]
PR	Permeance (IAA)
PR	Permissive Reassignment [Air Force] (AFM)
PR	Per Price [Business term]
PR	Per Rectum [Medicine]
pr	Per Rectum [By the Rectum] [Latin] (AD)
PR	Pershing Rifles [Honorary military organization]
PR	Persistency Rater [LIMRA]
PR	Personality Record [Psychological testing]
PR	Personnel Resources (EA)
PR	Pesikta Rabbati (BJA)
PR	Pesticide Registration [Environmental Protection Agency]
PR	Phenol Red
PR	Philadelphia Reports [Pennsylvania] [A publication] (DLA)
PR	Philanthropic Roundtable (EA)
PR	Philippine Airlines [ICAO designator] (AD)
PR	Philippine Island Reports [A publication] (DLA)
P-R	Philips Roxane [Commercial firm] (DAVI)
PR	Phosphate Rock [Petrology]
PR	Phosphorylase-Rupturing [Biochemistry]
PR	Photographic Reconnaissance [Military] (MCD)
PR	Photographic Recorder
PR	Photoreacting [or Photoreactivation] [Biochemistry]
PR	Photo Reconnaissance [ICAO designator] (FAAC)
PR	Photorecorder
PR	Photorefractive [Optics]
PR	Photoresist
P/R	Photosynthesis/Respiration [Biochemistry]
PR	Physical Record [Computer science]
PR	Physican Reviewer (MEDA)
PR	Picture Ratio (IAA)
PR	Piezo Resistive [Automotive electronics]
PR	Pilot Rating
PR	Pinar del Rio (AD)
PR	Pinch Runner [Baseball]
PR	Pineal Recess [Neuroanatomy]
PR	Pipe Rail (AAG)
PR	Pitch Ratio
P/R	Pitch/Roll (MCD)
PR	Pittsburgh Reports [1853-73] [Pennsylvania] [A publication] (DLA)
PR	Pityriasis [Dermatology]
PR	Pityriasis Rosea [Dermatology] (MAE)
PR	Planetary RADAR [Equipment box]
P/R	Planned Requirements (DNAB)
PR	Planning Reference
PR	Plant Recovery [Nuclear energy] (NRCH)
PR	Plant Report
PR	Please Return
PR	Plotting and RADAR
PR	Ply Rating [Tires] (NATG)
PR	Pneumatic Retinopathy [Ophthalmology]
PR	Polarized Relay (IAA)
PR	Policy Review (MCD)
PR	Polish Register [Polish ship classification society] (DS)
PR	Polskie Radio [Polish Radio] (AD)
PR	Ponceau Red [Biological stain]
PR	Poor Rate [British] (ROG)
PR	Populus Romanus [The Roman People] [Latin]
PR	Position Record (NASA)
PR	Position Register (IAA)
PR	Position Report [Air Force]
PR	Postal Regulations (DLA)
PR	Poste Recommandee [Registered Post]
PR	Posterior Repair [Gynecology] (DAVI)
PR	Posterior Ridge
PR	Posterior Root [Medicine] (DMAA)
PR	Post Request

PR.............. Post-Resuscitation
PR.............. Potency Ratio [Medicine] (DMAA)
PR.............. Pounder [Gun]
PR.............. Pour Remercier [To Express Thanks] [French]
PR.............. Power Range [Nuclear energy] (NRCH)
PR.............. Power Rating
PR.............. Power Ratio
PR.............. Power Return
Pr.............. Praca [Plaza] [Portuguese] (AD)
Pr.............. Practice Reports [Various jurisdictions] [A publication] (DLA)
PR.............. Prairie (MCD)
Pr.............. Prairie (AD)
Pr.............. Prandtl Number [IUPAC]
Pr.............. Praseodymium [Chemical element]
PR.............. Prayer
PR.............. Preacher
Pr.............. Preamble (ILCA)
Pr.............. Precancelled [Philately]
PR.............. Precedence Rating [Military] (AFIT)
PR.............. Preconstruction Requirement [Environmental Protection Agency]
PR.............. Predicted Rate [Medicine] (DAVI)
Pr.............. Prednisone [Also, P, PDN, Pred, Pro] [Endocrinology] [Antineoplastic drug]
PR.............. Preferred [Stock exchange term] (SPSG)
pr.............. Preferred (WDAA)
PR.............. Prefix [Indicating a private radiotelegram] (BUR)
PR.............. Pregnancy Rate [Medicine]
PR.............. Preliminary Report
PR.............. Preliminary Review [Army]
PR.............. Premature Release [Telecommunications] (TEL)
PR.............. Prepare Reply
PR.............. Preposition
PR.............. Pre-Raphaelite
PR.............. Presbyopia [Ophthalmology]
Pr.............. Presbyopia (AD)
Pr.............. Presbyter [Elder] [Latin] (AD)
PR.............. Presbyterian (ROG)
PR.............. Present
Pr.............. Presentation [Gynecology]
PR.............. Presidency (ROG)
Pr.............. Press (AD)
PR.............. Pressoreceptor [Laboratory science] (DAVI)
PR.............. Press Release
PR.............. Press Revise (DGA)
PR.............. Pressure
PR.............. Pressure Ratio
PR.............. Pressure Recorder (NRCH)
PR.............. Pressure Regulator (KSC)
PR.............. Preston [Postcode] (ODBW)
PR.............. Prevention (DAVI)
PR.............. Price [Online database field identifier]
pr.............. Price (ODBW)
PR.............. Price Communications [AMEX symbol] (TTSB)
PR.............. Price Communications Corp. [AMEX symbol] (SAG)
PR.............. Price Received
PR.............. Price Redetermination [Economics]
PR.............. Price Reduced [of a book]
Pr.............. Price's English Exchequer Reports [1814-24] [A publication] (DLA)
PR.............. Priest
Pr.............. Priest (WDAA)
PR.............. Primary (NASA)
PR.............. Primary RADAR (DA)
PR.............. Primary Reference [Automobile fuel] (DICI)
PR.............. Primary Zone [Environmental science] (COE)
PR.............. Primitive
PR.............. Prince
Pr.............. Prince (WDAA)
PR.............. Prince Regent (ROG)
PR.............. Princess Royal's [Military unit] [British]
Pr.............. Principal
PR.............. Principal Register [Computer science]
PR.............. Print [or Printed] (NTCM)
pr.............. Print (VRA)
PR.............. Printed [or Printer]
PR.............. Printer [Computer science] (IAA)
PR.............. Printing Request (MCD)
PR.............. Print Register (IAA)
PR.............. Print Restore [Computer science] (MHDB)
PR.............. Prior
PR.............. Priority Regulation
PR.............. Priority Resolver
PR.............. Priory
PR.............. Prism
pr.............. Prismatic Tank [Liquid gas carriers]
PR.............. Prison Riot (WDAA)
Pr.............. Pristane [Organic chemistry]
pr.............. Private (DLA)
PR.............. Private Road [Maps and charts] [British] (ROG)
PR.............. Prize Ring [Boxing]
PR.............. Probabilistic Risk Assessment [Computer-based technique for accident prediction]
PR.............. Probability
Pr.............. Probable
PR.............. Probate Reports [A publication] (DLA)
Pr.............. Problemata [of Aristotle] [Classical studies] (OCD)

PR.............. Problem Report (MCD)
Pr.............. Procarbazine [Also, P, PC, PCB] [Antineoplastic drug]
Pr.............. Procedural Regulations [Civil Aeronautics Board]
PR.............. Procedures Review [DoD]
PR.............. Proceedings (IAA)
PR.............. Processor [Computer science] (IAA)
PR.............. Process-Reactive [Scale] [Psychometrics]
PR.............. Proctologist
Pr.............. Proctoscopy (AD)
PR.............. Proctosigmoidoscopy [Medicine] (AD)
PR.............. Procurement Regulation [Military]
PR.............. Procurement Request [or Requisition]
PR.............. Producing Region [Agriculture]
PR.............. Production Rate
PR.............. Production Requirements [Military] (AFIT)
PR.............. Production Review [Automotive project management]
P/R.............. Productivity/Respiration [Physiology]
PR.............. Profile (DAVI)
PR.............. Profile Reliability (MCD)
PR.............. Profit Rate (WGA)
P-R.............. Progesterone Receptor [Endocrinology]
PR.............. Programming [Computer science] (IAA)
PR.............. Program Register [Computer science] (BUR)
PR.............. Program Requirements (KSC)
PR.............. Progressive Resistance
PR.............. Progress Report
PR.............. Project Release (EA)
PR.............. Project Report
PR.............. Project Rover (SAA)
PR.............. Prolactin [Also, LTH, PRL] [Endocrinology]
PR.............. Prolonged-Release [Pharmacy]
Pr.............. Promenade (DD)
PR.............. Pronominal [Grammar] (ROG)
PR.............. Pronoun
PR.............. Pronounced
PR.............. Propagating Rift [Geology]
PR.............. Proper
PR.............. Property
PR.............. Proportional Representation [in legislatures, etc.]
PR.............. Proposed Regulation
PR.............. Proposed Request
PR.............. Proposed Rule [Federal government] (GFGA)
PR.............. Propulsion Range
Pr.............. Propyl [Organic chemistry]
PR.............. Pro Rata
pr.............. Prose
PR.............. Prosthetic-Group Removing [Enzyme] [Biochemistry] (DAVI)
PR.............. Prosthion [Medicine] (MAE)
PR.............. Protease [Chemistry]
PR.............. Protective Reaction [Bombing raid] [Vietnam]
PR.............. Protectorate Regiment [British military] (DMA)
PR.............. Protein (MAE)
PR.............. Protestant (ADA)
PR.............. Prototype
PR.............. Proved
PR.............. Provencal [Language, etc.]
Pr.............. Proverbs [Old Testament book] (BJA)
PR.............. Provost (WDAA)
Pr.............. Proximal
PR.............. Pseudorandom
PR.............. Pseudoresidual
PR.............. Psychedelic Review [A publication]
PR.............. Psychiatric Record (AD)
PR.............. Publicity Release (NTCM)
PR.............. Public Relations
pr.............. Public Relations (AD)
PR.............. Public Responsibility
PR.............. Puerto Rican [Derogatory term]
pr.............. Puerto Rico [IYRU nationality code] [MARC country of publication code Library of Congress] (LCCP)
PR.............. Puerto Rico [Postal code]
PR.............. Puerto Rico [ANSI two-letter standard code] (CNC)
PR.............. Puerto Rico Supreme Court Reports [A publication] (DLA)
PR.............. Pulmonic Regurgitation [Cardiology] (DAVI)
PR.............. Pulse Rate
PR.............. Pulse Ratio (IEEE)
PR.............. Pulse Regenerator
PR.............. Punctum Remotum [Far Point] [Latin]
pr.............. Punctum Remotum [Remote Point] [Latin] (AD)
PR.............. Punjab Record [India] [A publication] (DLA)
PR.............. Purchase Request
PR.............. Purple (AAG)
PR.............. Purplish Red
pR.............. Purplish Red (AD)
PR.............. Pyke's Reports [Canada] [A publication] (DLA)
PR.............. Pyramidal Response (DB)
pr.............. Pyrite [CIPW classification] [Geology]
PR.............. Pyrogallol Red [Also, PGR] [An indicator Chemistry]
PR.............. Pyrolytic Release
PR+.............. Reactor Pressure Plus (NRCH)
PR.............. Reading Public Library, Reading, PA [Library symbol Library of Congress] (LCLS)
PR.............. River Gunboat [Navy symbol]
PR.............. Upper Canada Practice Reports [1850-1900] [Ontario] [A publication] (DLA)

PR1	Parachute Rigger, First Class [*Navy*]
PR2	Parachute Rigger, Second Class [*Navy*]
PR3	Parachute Rigger, Third Class [*Navy*]
PRA	Albright College, Reading, PA [*Library symbol Library of Congress*] (LCLS)
PRA	Division of Policy Research and Analysis [*National Science Foundation*]
PRA	Page Replacement Algorithm [*Computer science*] (MHDI)
PRA	Paint Research Association [*British*]
PRA	Paperwork Reduction Act (GFGA)
PRA	Parabolic Reflector Antenna
PRA	Parana [*Argentina*] [*Airport symbol*] (OAG)
PRA	Participant Record Advice
PRA	Partido Revolucionario Autentico [*Authentic Revolutionary Party*] [*Bolivia*] [*Political party*] (PPW)
PRA	Parti du Regroupement Africain [*African Regroupment Party*] [*Banned, 1974 Burkina Faso*] [*Political party*]
PRA	Parti du Regroupement Africain [*African Regroupment Party*] [*Niger*] [*Political party*] (PD)
PRA	Paymaster-Rear-Admiral [*Navy British*]
PRA	Pay Readjustment Act [*1942*]
PRA	Pay Record Access
pra	Payroll Audit (AD)
PRA	Payroll Auditor [*Insurance*]
PRA	Peace Research Abstracts (NITA)
PRA	Peak Recording Accelerograph [*Accelerometer*] (IEEE)
PRA	Pendulous Reference Axis [*Accelerometer*] (IEEE)
PRA	People's Revolutionary Army [*Grenada*]
PRA	Permanent Restricted Area [*Former USSR*] (NATG)
PRA	Personal Rights Association [*British*] (BI)
PRA	Personnel Research Activity [*Later, NPTRL*] [*Navy*]
PRA	Petrol Retailers' Association [*British*]
PRA	Pharmacy Restructuring Authority [*Australia*]
PRA	Phosphoribosylamine
PRA	Pilots Rights Association (EA)
PRA	Pitch and Roll Attitude (IAA)
PRA	Planetary Radio Astronomy
PRA	Planned Regulatory Action [*Federal government*] (GFGA)
PRA	Planned Restricted Availability [*Military*] (NVT)
PRA	Plasma Renin Activity [*Hematology*]
pra	Plasma Renin Activity [*Medicine*] (AD)
PRA	Plutonium Recycle Acid [*Nuclear energy*] (NRCH)
PRA	Polar Regions Award (IAA)
PRA	Policy Research and Analysis
PRA	Popular Rotorcraft Association (EA)
PRA	Postal Reorganization Act (AD)
PRA	Postal Reorganization Act of 1970 (AAGC)
PRA	Praha [*Prague*] [*Czechoslovakia*] [*Seismograph station code, US Geological Survey*] (SEIS)
PRA	Prairiefire Rural Action (EA)
pra	Prakrit [*MARC language code Library of Congress*] (LCCP)
PRA	Precision Axis (KSC)
PRA	Premium Audit
PRA	Prerefund Audit [*IRS*]
PRA	Pre-Retirement Association [*British*] (DI)
PRA	President of the Royal Academy [*British*]
PRA	President's Re-Employment Agreement [*New Deal*]
PRA	Primary Reviewing Authority
PRA	Prime Responsible Authority (IAA)
PRA	Print Alphanumerically [*Computer science*] (MDG)
pra	Print Alphanumerically (AD)
PRA	Probabilistic Risk Assessment [*Computer-based technique for accident prediction*]
PRA	Probation and Rehabilitation of Airmen [*Air Force*] (AFM)
pra	Probation and Rehabilitation of Airmen (AD)
PRA	Production Reader Assembly (KSC)
PRA	Production Readiness Assessment [*Army*]
PRA	Progesterone Receptor Assay [*Clinical chemistry*]
PRA	Program Reader Assembly [*Computer science*]
pra	Progressive Retinal Atrophy [*Medicine*] (AD)
PRA	Projected Requisition Authority [*Army*] (AABC)
PRA	Prompt Radiation Analysis (MCD)
PRA	Propionic Acid [*Organic chemistry*]
PRA	Prospair Ltd. [*British ICAO designator*] (FAAC)
PRA	Proust Research Association (EA)
PRA	Psoriasis Research Association (EA)
PRA	Psychiatric Rehabilitation Association [*British*]
PRA	Psychological Research Associates
PRA	Public Resources Association [*Defunct*] (EA)
PRA	Public Roads Administration
PRA	Puerto Rico Area Office [*AEC*]
PRA	Puerto Rico Association (AD)
PRA	Purchase and Resale Agreement [*Canada*] (BARN)
PRA	US 1869 Pictorial Research Associates (EA)
PRAA	Airman Apprentice, Parachute Rigger, Striker [*Navy rating*]
Prac	Practical (DLA)
PRAC	Practice (AABC)
prac	Practice (AD)
PRAC	Pressure Ratio Acceleration Control [*Gas turbine engine*]
PRAC	Productivity Technologies Corp. [*NASDAQ symbol*] (SAG)
PRAC	Program Resource Advisory Committee [*TRADOC*] (MCD)
PRAC	Public Relations Advisory Committee
PRACA	Problem Reporting and Corrective Action (MCD)
PRACA3	Puerto Rican Association for Community Affairs (EA)
Prac Act	Practice Act [*A publication*] (DLA)
Pra Cas	Prater's Cases on Conflict of Laws [*A publication*] (DLA)
PRaCHS	Archbishop Carroll High School, Radnor, PA [*Library symbol*] [*Library of Congress*] (LCLS)
pracl	Page-Replacement Algorithm and Control Logic (AD)
PRACL	Page-Replacement Algorithm and Control Logic [*Computer science*]
PRACL	Practical
PRACSATS	Practical Satellites
PRACT	Practical (ROG)
pract	Practical (AD)
PRACT	Practice [*Legal shorthand*] (LWAP)
pract	Practitioner (AD)
PRACT	Practitioner
PRACT	Practolol (DB)
Pract Law	Practical Lawyer [*A publication*] (DLA)
PRACTNR	Practitioner
Pract Reg	Practical Register in the Common Pleas [*England*] [*A publication*] (DLA)
PRAD	Pitch Ratio Adjust Device (MCD)
PRAD	Program Research and Development (IAA)
PRADA	Partido Revolucionario Dominicano Autentico [*Dominican Republic*] [*Political party*]
Pr Adm Dig	Pritchard's Admiralty Digest [*3rd ed.*] [*1887*] [*A publication*] (DLA)
PRADOR	PRF [*Pulse Repetition Frequency*] Ranging Doppler RADAR
PRADS	Parachute Retrorocket Airdrop System (MCD)
praef	Praefatio [*Latin*] (OCD)
Praeger	Frederick A. Praeger (AD)
Praegtzr	Praegitzer Industries, Inc. [*Associated Press*] (SAG)
Praem	De Praemiis et Poenis [*of Philo*] (BJA)
praen	Praenomen (AD)
Praep Evang	Praeparatio Evangelica [*of Eusebius*] [*Classical studies*] (OCD)
Praepo	Praepositus [*Deceased, 1509*] [*Authority cited in pre-1607 legal work*] (DSA)
praes	Praesens [*Present Tense*] [*Latin*]
praet	Praeteritum [*Past Tense*] [*Latin*]
PRAF	Passenger-Reserved Air Freight
PRAG	Pensions Research Accountants Group (MHDB)
prag	Pragmatic (AD)
pragma	Processing Routines Aided by Graphics for Manipulation of Arrays (AD)
PRAGMA	Processing Routines Aided by Graphics for Manipulation of Arrays (PDAA)
Pra H & W	Prater on Husband and Wife [*2nd ed.*] [*1836*] [*A publication*] (DLA)
PrA-HPA	Protein A Hemolytic Plaque Assay [*Medicine*] (DMAA)
PRAI	Peer Review Analysis (EFIS)
PRAI	Phosphoribosyl Anthranilate Isomerase
PRAI	Pre-Reading Assessment Inventory [*Education*] (EDAC)
PRAIC	President of the Royal Architectural Institute of Canada (NGC)
PRAICO	Puerto Rican American Insurance Co. (AD)
PRAIRIE	Prairie [*Commonly used*] (OPSA)
Prairie View A&M U	Prairie View Agricultural and Mechanical University (GAGS)
prais	Passive-Hanging Interferometer Sensor (AD)
PRAIS	Passive Ranging Interferometer Sensor
PRAIS	Pesticide Residue Analysis Information Service [*British*]
PRAISE	Pilot Records of Achievement in Schools Evaluation (AIE)
PRAISE	Prospective Randomized Amlodipine Survival Evaluation [*Medicine*] (DMAA)
pral	Principal [*Principal*] [*Spanish*] (AD)
PRAM	Parallel Random Access Machine [*Computer science*]
PRAM	Perambulator [*British*]
pram	Perambulator (AD)
Pram	Poseidon Random-Access Memory (AD)
PRAM	Poseidon Random Access Memory [*Missiles*]
Pram	Prambanam (VRA)
PRAM	Preliminary Repair Level Decision Analysis Model (PDAA)
PRAM	Pre-Recorded Announcement and Boarding Music Reproducer
PRAM	Primary Report of Aircraft Mishap [*Army*] (DOMA)
pram	Productivity, Reliability, Availability, and Maintainability (AD)
PRAM	Productivity, Reliability, Availability, and Maintainability Office [*Air Force*]
PRAM	Product Reliability and Maintainability
PRAM	Programmable Random Access Memory [*Computer science*] (IAA)
PRAM	Program Requirements Analysis Method
PRAM	Propelled Ascent Mine
PRAM	Propelled Rapid Ascent Mine (MCD)
PRAM	Pseudorandom Access Memory [*Computer science*] (IAA)
PRAMPO	Productivity, Reliability, Availability, and Maintenance Program Office [*Air Force*] (DOMA)
PRAMS	Processing Asset Management System (WDAA)
PRAN	Airman, Parachute Rigger, Striker [*Navy*]
PRAN	Production Analyzer (IAA)
PRAND	Prandium [*Dinner*] [*Pharmacy*]
prand	Prandium [*dinner*] [*Latin*] (AD)
PR & D	Personal Rest and Delay [*Air Force*] (AFM)
PR & D	Power, Rodwell, and Drew's English Election Cases [*1847-56*] [*A publication*] (DLA)
PR & D	Public Research and Development
PR & D El Cas	Power, Rodwell, and Drew's English Election Cases [*A publication*] (DLA)
Pr & Div	Law Reports, Probate and Divorce [*England*] [*A publication*] (DLA)
PR & R	Professional Rights and Responsibilities
PRANG	Puerto Rico Air National Guard
PRAP	Patient Resident Assessment Profile [*Geriatrics*]
PRAP	Provincial/Regional Library Association Presidents [*Canada*]
PRAP	Provisions of Following Reference Apply [*Army*] (AABC)
PRAQ	Playground and Recreation Association of Queensland [*Australia*]

PRAR	Partido Revolucionario Autentico Rios [Bolivia] [Political party] (PPW)
PRARE	Precise Range and Range-Rate Experiment
PRARIE	Prairie [Commonly used] (OPSA)
PRARS	Pitch, Roll, Azimuth Reference System (NG)
PRAS	Pacific Regional Advisory Service [South Pacific Bureau for Economic Co-Operation] (EY)
PRAS	Particle Reactor Analysis Services (AAEL)
PRAS	Pension and Retirement Annuity System
PRAS	Prereduced, Anaerobically Sterilized [Microbiology]
PRAS	Pseudo-Renal Artery Syndrome [Medicine] (DMAA)
PRAS	Pulsed Realistic Age-Structured [Model for disease persitence]
PRASD	Personnel Research Activity, San Diego [California] [Navy]
PRAT	Parliamentary Retiring Allowances Trust [Australia]
PRAT	Platelet Radioactive Antiglobulin Test [Hematology] (DAVI)
PRAT	Prattsburgh Railroad (AD)
PRAT	Predicted Range Against Target [Military] (NVT)
PRAT	Pressure-Retaining Amphipod Trap [Deep-sea biology]
PRAT	Production Reliability Acceptance Test
P RAT AET	Pro Ratione Aetatis [According to Age] [Pharmacy] (ROG)
p rat aet	Pro Ratione Aetatis [In Proportion to Age] [Latin] (AD)
P RAT AETAT	Pro Rata Aetatis [According to Age] [Pharmacy]
p rat aetat	Pro Ratione Aetatis [In Proportion to Age] [Latin] (MAE)
PratHtl	Pratt Hotel Corp. [Associated Press] (SAG)
PratLm	Pratt & Lambert United, Inc. [Associated Press] (SAG)
PRATRA	Philippines Relief and Trade Rebilitation Administration (AD)
Pratt	Pratt's Contraband-of-War Cases [A publication] (DLA)
Pratt	Pratt's Supplement to Bott's Poor Laws [1833] [A publication] (DLA)
Pratt BS	Pratt's Law of Benefit Building Societies [A publication] (DLA)
Pratt Cont	Pratt's Contraband-of-War Cases [A publication] (DLA)
Pratt Cts Req	Pratt's Statutes Establishing Courts of Request [A publication] (DLA)
Pratt Fr Soc	Pratt on Friendly Societies [15th ed.] [1931] [A publication] (DLA)
Pratt High	Pratt and Mackenzie on Highways [21st ed.] [1967] [A publication] (DLA)
Pratt Inst	Pratt Institute (GAGS)
Pratt PL	Pratt's Edition of Bott on the Poor Laws [A publication] (DLA)
Pratt Prop T	Pratt on the Property Tax Act [A publication] (DLA)
Pratt Sav B	Pratt on Savings Banks [6th ed.] [1845] [A publication] (DLA)
Pratt SL	Pratt on Sea Lights [2nd ed.] [1858] [A publication] (DLA)
PRAUS	Programme de Recherche sur l'Amiante de l'Universite de Sherbrooke [Asbestos Research Program] [University of Sherbrooke Quebec] [Information service or system] (IID)
PRAV	Planned Restricted Availability [Navy] (ANA)
PRAV	Playground and Recreation Association of Victoria [Australia]
PRAW	Personnel Research Activity, Washington, DC [Obsolete Navy]
PRaW	Wyeth Laboratories, Radnor, PA [Library symbol Library of Congress] (LCLS)
PRAWL	Puerto Rican American Women's League
Prax	Brown's Practice (Praxis) [or Precedents] in Chancery [A publication] (DLA)
Praxair	Praxair, Inc. [Associated Press] (SAG)
Prax Can	Praxis Almae Curiae Cancellariae (Brown) [A publication] (DLA)
PRAY	Paul Revere Associated Yeoman (AD)
PRAZ	Prazosin [A vasodilator]
PRB	Basic Proline-Rich Protein (DMAA)
PRB	Painters' Registration Board [Western Australia]
PRB	Panel Review Board [NASA] (KSC)
PRB	Parabola [Mathematics]
PRB	Parachute Refurbishment Building [NASA] (NASA)
PRB	Partido de la Revolucion Boliviana [Bolivian Revolutionary Party] [Political party] (AD)
PRB	Partido Republicano Brasileiro [Brazil Political party] (EY)
PRB	Paso Robles [California] [Airport symbol] (AD)
PRB	Paso Robles, CA [Location identifier FAA] (FAAL)
PRB	Pension Review Board [Canada]
PRB	People's Republic of Bonin (AD)
PRB	Personal Reaction Blank [Psychology] (DAVI)
PRB	Personnel Reaction Blank [Psychology]
PRB	Personnel Records Branch [Army] (AABC)
PRB	Personnel Requirements Branch (MUGU)
PRB	Personnel Research Branch [Army] (MCD)
PRB	Personnel Review Board (AD)
PRB	Physiotherapists' Registration Board [New South Wales, Australia]
PRB	Planned Requirements - Bureau Directed
PRB	Plant Review Board [Nuclear energy] (NRCH)
PRB	Podiatrists' Registration Board [New South Wales, Australia]
PRB	Polar Research Board [National Academy of Sciences]
PRB	Population Reference Bureau (EA)
PRB	Post-Retirement Benefits (AAGC)
PRB	Pre-Raphaelite Brotherhood (WDAA)
PRB	Press-Radio Bureau (NTCM)
prb	Principal Borehole (AD)
PRB	Private Radio Bureau [FCC] (NTCM)
PRB	Procedure Review Board [Nuclear energy] (NRCH)
PRB	Procurement Review Board (MCD)
PRB	Professional Registration Boards of the Northern Territory [Australia]
PRB	Program Request Block (IAA)
PRB	Program Review Board
PRB	Project Review Board [NASA] (NASA)
PRB	Prosthetics Research Board
PRB	Proteus Air Systeme [France ICAO designator] (FAAC)
PRB	Pseudo-Random Binary (AAEL)
PRB	Psychosurgery Review Board [Victoria, Australia]
PRB	Public Roads Bureau
PRBA	Portable Rechargeable Battery Association (NTPA)
PRBA	Puerto Rican Bar Association (EA)
PRBA(AG)	Personnel Research Board of the Army, Adjutant General
PrBayA	American Junior College of Puerto Rico, Bayamon, PR [Library symbol Library of Congress] (LCLS)
PrBayC	Bayamon Central University (Universidad Central de Bayamon), Bayamon, Puerto Rico [Library symbol Library of Congress] (LCLS)
PRBC	Packed Red Blood Cells [Medicine]
PRBC	Parasitized Red Blood Cell [Medicine]
PRBC	Placental Residual Blood Volume [Medicine] (DMAA)
PRBC	Premier Bancorp, Inc. [NASDAQ symbol] (NQ)
PRBC	Prestige Bancorp, Inc. [NASDAQ symbol] (SAG)
PRBD	Paraboloid
PRBG	Puerto Rican Board of Guardians [Defunct] (EA)
PRBK	Provident Bancorp [NASDAQ symbol] (TTSB)
PRBK	Provident Bancorp, Inc. [NASDAQ symbol] (SAG)
PRBLC	Parabolic
PRBLTY	Probability [NWS] (FAAC)
PRBMECAB	Permanent Regional Bureau of the Middle East Committee for the Affairs of the Blind [Riyadh, Saudi Arabia] (EAIO)
PRBNT	Prebent
PRBO	Position Relief Briefing Observed [Aviation] (FAAC)
PRBS	Pseudorandom Binary Sequence [Computer science]
PRBSG	Pseudorandom Binary Sequence Generator [Computer science] (NRCH)
PRBT	Precision Remote Bathythermograph
PRBV	Placental Residual Blood Volume [Hematology] (MAE)
PRC	Chief Aircrew Survival Equipmentman [Formerly, Chief Parachute Rigger] [Navy rating]
PRC	Pacific Air Charter, Inc. [ICAO designator] (FAAC)
PRC	Packed Red Cell [Hematology] (MAE)
PRC	Pain Rehabilitation Center (AD)
PRC	Palestine Red Crescent (AD)
PRC	Park Ridge Center (EA)
PRC	Partial Response Coding (IEEE)
PRC	Partido Regionalista de Cantabria [Spain Political party] (EY)
PRC	Partido Republicano Calderonista [Calderonista Republican Party] [Costa Rica] [Political party] (PPW)
PRC	Partido Revolucionario Comunista [Brazil Political party] (EY)
PRC	Parti Republicain Caledonien [New Caledonia] [Political party] (FEA)
PRC	Part Requirement Card
PRC	Parts Release Card (KSC)
PRC	Passaic River Coalition (EA)
PRC	Passenger Reservation Center [Army]
PRC	Pay-Raise Commission (AD)
PRC	Penrose Resources Corp. [Vancouver Stock Exchange symbol]
PRC	Pension Research Council (EA)
PRC	Pension Rights Center [Washington, DC] (EA)
PRC	People's Redemption Council [Liberia] (PD)
PRC	People's Republic of China [Mainland China]
PRC	People's Republic of the Congo
PRC	Periodic Reverse Current (IAA)
PRC	Permanent Regular Commissions [Army British]
PRC	Personality Research Center [University of Texas at Austin] [Research center] (RCD)
PRC	Personnel Readiness Center [Air Force]
PRC	Personnel Reception Centre [British military] (DMA)
PRC	Personnel Recovery Center [Military]
PRC	Personnel Reporting Code [Army] (AABC)
PRC	Phase-Response Curve
PRC	Philippine Resource Center [An association] (EA)
PRC	Physical Review Council [DoD]
PRC	Picatinny Research Center [Picatinny Arsenal] (AD)
PRC	Pierce (MSA)
PRC	Pitch Rate Command (MCD)
PRC	Pitch Ratio Controller (MCD)
PRC	Planar Random Composite (MCD)
PRC	Planned Requirements, Conversion (NG)
PRC	Planning Research Corp. [Telecommunications service] (TSSD)
PRC	Planning Research Corporation [Marine science] (OSRA)
PRC	Plant Records Center [of the American Horticultural Society] (IID)
PRC	Plasma Renin Concentration [Hematology]
PRC	Plastic Roller Conveyor
PRC	Plutonium Rework Cell [Nuclear energy] (NRCH)
PRC	Point of Reverse Curve (MSA)
PRC	Point Reyes [California] [Seismograph station code, US Geological Survey Closed] (SEIS)
PRC	Policy Review Committee [Terminated, 1981] [National Security Council] (EGAO)
PRC	Polish Resettlement Corps [British military] (DMA)
PRC	Polysulphide Rubber Compound (PDAA)
prc	Polysulphide Rubber Compound (AD)
PRC	Populace and Resources Control (COE)
PRC	Population Research Center [University of Chicago] [Research center] (RCD)
PRC	Population Resource Center (EA)
PRC	Postal Rate Commission [Federal government]
PRC	Postconsumer Recycled Content [Plastics technology]
PRC	Post Roman Conditam [After the Founding of Rome] [Latin]
PRC	Poultry Research Centre [of the Agricultural Research Council] [British] (ARC)
PRC	Power Reflection Coefficient [of RADAR signals]
PRC(AG)	Prattsburgh Railway Corp. [AAR code]
PRC	Preoral Ciliary [Gland]
PRC	Pre-Ranger Course [Army] (INF)

PRC	Prescott [Arizona] [Airport symbol] (OAG)
PRC	Prescott, AZ [Location identifier FAA] (FAAL)
PRC	Prescription Rate Carryover [Health insurance] (GHCT)
PRC	Pressure Recorder Controller [Nuclear energy] (NRCH)
PRC	Pressure Response Cell [For chemical kinetic studies]
PRC	Prevention Research Center [Pacific Institute for Research and Evaluation] [Research center] (RCD)
PRC	Price
PRC	Price Redetermination Contract (SAA)
PRC	Primary Routing Center [Telecommunications] (TEL)
PRC	Primate Research Center
PRC	Prime Responder Cell (DB)
PRC	Printer Control
PRC	Priory Cell
Pr C	Prize Cases [A publication] (DLA)
PRC	Problem Resolution Coordinator [IRS]
PRC	Procaterol [Pharmacology]
PRC	Procedure Review Committee (AAG)
PRC	Procession Register Clock
PRC	Proconsul
PRC	Procurement Request Code [Military] (AFIT)
PRC	Production Control (IAA)
PRC	Production Readjustments Committee [WPB]
PRC	Product Regional Center [Department of Supply and Service] [Canada] (IMH)
PRC	Professional Reference Center [Los Angeles County Office of Education] [Downey, CA] [Library network]
PRC	Professional Relations Council [American Chemical Society]
PRC	Programmed Rate Control (NITA)
PRC	Program Rest Code (MCD)
PRC	Program Review Committee (AFM)
PRC	Prologic Management Systems, Inc. [AMEX symbol] (SAG)
PRC	Propeller Change (MCD)
PRC	Providence College, Phillips Memorial Library, Providence, RI [OCLC symbol] (OCLC)
PRC	Pseudo-Range Correction
PRC	Public Relations Club (AD)
PRC	Pyrotechnic Rocket Container
PRC a	Revolutionary Socialist Party [Peru] [Political party] (PD)
Pr Ca	Great War Prize Cases, by Evans [England] [A publication] (DLA)
PRCA	Packaging Research [NASDAQ symbol] (TTSB)
PRCA	Packaging Research Corp. [NASDAQ symbol] (SAG)
PRCA	Palomino Rabbit Co-Breeders Association (EA)
PRCA	Parks, Recreation and Cultural Affairs Administration [New York City]
PRCA	People's Republic of China Army (MCD)
PRCA	Pitch and Roll Channel Assembly (MCD)
PRCA	Presbyterian Reformed Church of Australia
PRCA	President of the Royal Canadian Academy
PRCA	President of the Royal Canadian Academy of Arts (NGC)
PRCA	Problem Reporting and Corrective Action (NASA)
PRCA	Professional Rodeo Cowboys Association (EA)
PRCA	Public Relations Consultants Association (FAIO)
PRCA	Puerto Rico Communications Authority
PRCA	Pure Red Cell Agenesis [Hematology] (MAE)
PRCA	Pure Red Cell Aplasia [Hematology]
PrCoC	Colegio Universitario de Cayey, Cayey, PR [Library symbol Library of Congress] (LCLS)
PRC & NW	Pierre, Rapid City & Northwestern Railroad [Nickname: Plenty Rough Country and No Women]
PRCAW	Packaging Research Wrrt [NASDAQ symbol] (TTSB)
PRCB	Program Requirements Change Board [NASA] (NASA)
PRCB	Program Requirements Control Board [NASA]
PRCB	Program Review Control Board [NASA] (NASA)
PRCBD	Program Requirements Control Board Directive [NASA] (NASA)
PRCBD	Program Review Control Board Directive [NASA] (NASA)
PRCC	Partial Rank Correlation Coefficient [Nuclear energy] (NUCP)
PRCC	Peoria Record Club [Record label]
PRCC	Pollution Research and Control Corp. [NASDAQ symbol] (SAG)
PRCC	Pollution Resh & Ctl CA [NASDAQ symbol] (TTSB)
PRCC	Procurement Research Coordinating Counsel (AAGC)
PRCC	Puerto Rico Cancer Center [University of Puerto Rico] [Research center] (RCD)
PRCCh	Principal Roman Catholic Chaplain [Navy British]
PrcCm	Price Communications Corp. [Associated Press] (SAG)
PRCCT	Printed Circuit [Computer science] (IAA)
prcd	Priced (AD)
PRCEC	Pearce Sys Intl [NASDAQ symbol] (TTSB)
PR Cem	Puerto Rican Cement Co., Inc. [Associated Press] (SAG)
PRCESSN	Processing
PRCF	Petroleum Resources Communications Foundation [Canada]
PRCF	Plutonium Recycle Critical Facility [Nuclear energy]
Pr Ch	Parish Church (AD)
PR Ch	Practical Register in Chancery [England] [A publication] (DLA)
Pr Ch	Precedents in Chancery, Edited by Finch [1689-1722] [England] [A publication] (DLA)
PRCH	Precharge
PRCH	Proprietary Chapel [Church of England]
PRCHNG	Purchasing
prchst	Parachutist (AD)
prcht	Parachute (AD)
PRCHT	Parachute (AFM)
Prcht Bad	Parachutist Badge [Military decoration]
PRCI	Parti Republicain de la Cote d'Ivoire [Republicaqn Party of the Ivory Coast] [Political party] (EY)
PRCI	Policy Review Committee Intelligence [Military]
PRCI	Production Reliability Cost Improvement (DWSG)
PRCIX	Price T. Rowe: New Income [Mutual fund ticker symbol] (SG)
Pr CKB	Practice Cases, in the King's Bench [England] [A publication] (DLA)
PRCM	Master Chief Aircrew Survival Equipmentman [Formerly, Master Chief Parachute R igger] [Navy rating]
PRCM	Passive Radiation Countermeasure [Military]
PRCM	Pericom Semiconductor Corp. [NASDAQ symbol] (SAG)
PRCM	Procom Technology Inc. [NASDAQ symbol] (SAG)
PRCMNT	Procurement
PRCMT	Procurement (MSA)
PRCN	Percon, Inc. [NASDAQ symbol] (SAG)
PRCN	Porcine Respiratory Coronavirus (DB)
PRCN	Precision (MSA)
PR-CNTL	Product Control Register
PRCO	Pacific Requisition Control Office [Navy]
Pr Co	Prerogative Court (DLA)
PR/COM	Vessel Delivered in Partially-Completed Status [Navy] (DNAB)
Pr Cont	Pratt's Contraband-of-War Cases [1861] [A publication] (DLA)
PrcOptCp	Precision Optics Corp. [Associated Press] (SAG)
PRCP	Perceptron, Inc. [NASDAQ symbol] (SAG)
PRCP	Personnel Readiness Capability Program [Navy] (DNAB)
PRCP	Power Remote Control Panel (AAG)
PRCP	Practical Register in the Common Pleas [A publication] (DLA)
PRCP	President of the Royal College of Physicians [British]
PRCP	President of the Royal College of Preceptors [British] (ROG)
PRCP	Puerto Rican Communist Party [Political party]
PRCPTN	Precipitin [Test] [Immunology]
PRCR	Protective Cover (AAG)
PrcREI	Price REIT, Inc. [Associated Press] (SAG)
PRCS	Passive and Remote Crosswind Sensor (MCD)
PRCS	Personal Radio Communications System [General Electric Co.]
PRCS	Personal Report of Confidence as a Speaker [Psychology]
PRCS	Polish Red Cross Society
PRCS	President of the Royal College of Surgeons [British]
PRCS	Prevention and Removal of Corrosion and Scale [Engineering]
PRCS	Process (AFM)
prcs	Process (AD)
PRCS	Processing (IAA)
P/RCS	Propulsion and Reaction Control Subsystem [NASA] (KSC)
PRCS	Psychological Response Classification System
PRCS	Purchase Requisition Change Supplement
PRCS	Senior Chief Aircrew Survival Equipmentman [Formerly, Senior Chief Parachute R igger] [Navy rating]
PRCSG	Processing (MSA)
PRCSR	Processor
prcst	Precast (AD)
PRCST	Precast (AAG)
PRCT	Pool Repair Cycle Time (MCD)
PRCT	Procept, Inc. [NASDAQ symbol] (SAG)
PRCTN	Precaution [ICAO designator] (FAAC)
PRCU	Power Regulating and Control Unit (CET)
prcu	Power Regulation and Control Unit (AD)
PRCUA	Polish Roman Catholic Union of America (EA)
PRCY	ProCyte Corp. [NASDAQ symbol] (NQ)
PRD	Partial Roqotion of Degeneration
prd	Partial Reaction of Degeneration (AD)
PRD	Parti Democratique Dahomeen [Dahomey Democratic Party] [Political party]
PRD	Partido de la Revolucion Democratica [Mexico Political party] (EY)
PRD	Partido de Renovacion Democratica [Democratic Renewal Party] [Costa Rica] [Political party] (PPW)
PRD	Partido Reformista Democratico [Democratic Reformist Party] [Spain Political party] (PPW)
PRD	Partido Revolucionario Democratico [Democratic Revolutionary Party] [Panama] [Political party] (PPW)
PRD	Partido Revolucionario Dominicano [Dominican Revolutionary Party] [Dominican Republic] [Political party] (PPW)
PRD	Parti du Renouveau Democratique [Benin] [Political party] (EY)
PRD	Parti Radical-Democratique Suisse [Radical Democratic Party of Switzerland] [Political party] (PPE)
PRD	Part Reference Designator
PRD	Party of the Democratic Revolution [Mexico Political party]
PRD	Payroll Deduction
PRD	Performance-Related Pay [Business term] (ECON)
PRD	Period
PRD	Periodontics and Restorative Dentistry
PRD	Personal Radiation Dosimeter (KSC)
PRD	Personnel Readiness Date [Army] (AABC)
PRD	Personnel Records Division [Army] (AABC)
PRD	Personnel Requirements Data (AAG)
PRD	Personnel Research Division [Navy] (MCD)
PRD	Personnel Resources Data
PRD	Pesticides Regulation Division (AD)
PRD	Physician Relations Department (DMAA)
PRD	Piezoelectric Resonating Device
PRD	Planned Residential Development
PRD	Polaroid Corp. [NYSE symbol] (SPSG)
PRD	Political Resource Directory [A publication]
PRD	Polytechnic Research & Development Co. (AAG)
PRD	Positive Regulatory Domain [Genetics]
PRD	Postal Regulating Detachment [Military]
PRD	Postradiation Dysplasia [Medicine]
PRD	Potentially Reportable Deficiency [Nuclear energy] (NRCH)
PRD	Power Range Detector (IEEE)
PRD	Power Requirement Data

PRD	Precompetitive Research and Development
PRD	Predicted Range of the Day [*Military*] (NVT)
PRD	Preretro Update Display
PRD	Presidential Review Directive (USDC)
PRD	Pressing Direction
PRD	Pride
PRD	Prime RADAR Digitizer (IAA)
PRD	Princeton Reference Design (MCD)
PRD	Printer Driver
PRD	Printer Dump
prd	Printer Dump (AD)
PRD	Process Requirements Drawing (MCD)
PRD	Procurement Regulation Directive [*NASA*] (NASA)
PRD	Procurement Regulation Directive (NAKS)
PRD	Procurement Requirements Document [*NASA*] (NASA)
PRD	Production Responsibilities Document (MCD)
PRD	Productivity Research Division [*Office of Personnel Management*] (GRD)
PRD	Product Research and Development [*Advertising*] (DOAD)
PRD	Proficiency Rating Designator [*Military*]
PRD	Program [*or Project*] Requirement Data [*NASA*] (KSC)
PRD	Program Requirements Document
PRD	Projected Rotation Date (NG)
PRD	Proline-Rich Domain [*Genetics*]
prd	Pro-Rata Distribution (AD)
PRD	Pro Rate Distribution [*Clause*] [*Insurance*]
PRD	Puerto Rico, Decisiones [*A publication*] (DLA)
PRD	Push Rod [*Mechanical engineering*]
PRDA	Pony Riding for the Disabled Association [*Australia*]
PRDA	Program Research and Development Announcement [*Energy Research and Development Administration*]
PRDC	Personnel Research and Development Center [*Office of Personnel Management*] (GRD)
PRDC	Pig Research and Development Corp. [*Australia*]
PRDC	Polar Research and Development Center [*Army*]
PRDCTVTY	Productivity
PRDDO	Partial Retention of Diatomic Differential Overlap [*Physics*]
PRDE	Pride International [*NASDAQ symbol*] [*Formerly, Pride Petroleum*] (SG)
PRDE	Pride Petroleum Services, Inc. [*NASDAQ symbol*] (CTT)
PRDE	Pride Petroleum Svcs [*NASDAQ symbol*] (TTSB)
PrdEn	Producers Entertainment Group Ltd. [*Associated Press*] (SAG)
PrdEnt	Producers Entertainment Group Ltd. [*Associated Press*] (SAG)
PrdePt	Pride Petroleum Services, Inc. [*Associated Press*] (SAG)
PRDF	Page Reference Distribution Function [*Computer science*] (IAA)
PRDF	Political Rights Defense Fund [*Defunct*] (EA)
PRDG	Princess Royal's Dragoon Guards [*Military unit*] [*British*] (ROG)
PRDIAG	Primary Diagnosis [*Medicine*]
PRDL	Personnel Research and Development Laboratory [*Navy*] (MCD)
prdl	Predella (VRA)
PRDM	Paradigm Technology [*NASDAQ symbol*] (TTSB)
PRDM	Paradigm Technology, Inc. [*NASDAQ symbol*] (SAG)
PRDM	Parti pour le Rassemblement Democratique des Mahorais [*Mayotte*] [*Political party*] (EY)
PRDN	Partido de Reconciliacion Democratica Nacional [*Party of National Democratic Reconciliation*] [*Guatemala*] [*Political party*]
PRDNTST	Periodontist
PRDP	Power Reactor Demonstration Program
PRDPEC	Power Reactor Development Programme Evaluation Committee [*Canada*] (HGAA)
PRDR	Preproduction Reliability Design Review [*Navy*] (CAAL)
PRDR	Production Request Design Review
PRDS	Paradise
PRDS	Processed RADAR Display System (PDAA)
PRDV	Peak Reading Digital Voltmeter
PRDX	Prediction Program [*NASA*]
PRE	Bureau for Private Enterprise
PRE	Federation Europeenne des Fabricants de Produits Refractaires [*Zurich, Switzerland*] (EAIO)
PRE	Partido Republicano Evolucionista [*Republican Evolutionist Party*] [*Portugal Political party*] (PPE)
PRE	Partido Roldosista Ecuatoriano [*Ecuador*] [*Political party*] (EY)
PRE	Partner-Resisted Exercise [*Army*] (INF)
PRE	Personal Rescue Enclosure (NASA)
PRE	Personnel Restraint Equipment (SAA)
PRE	Petroleum Refining Engineer
PRE	Photoreactivating
PRE	Physical Reconditioning Exercises [*Orthopedics*] (DAVI)
PRE	Pineridge Capital [*Vancouver Stock Exchange symbol*]
PRE	Planetary Rotation Engine (IAA)
PRE	Portable RADAR Equipment
pre	Pre-Choice [*Advertising*] (WDMC)
PRE	Precinct
PRE	Precision Valley Aviation [*ICAO designator*] (FAAC)
PRE	Predecessor (KSC)
pre	Prefatory (WDMC)
PRE	Prefect
pre	Preferred (WDMC)
pre	Prefix (WDMC)
PRE	Prefix
PRE	Preliminary
PRE	Preliminary Amplifier (IAA)
PRE	Premier Industrial Corp. [*NYSE symbol*] (SPSG)
pre	Preoperative [*Surgery*] (DAVI)
PRE	Prepayment Coin Telephone [*Telecommunications*] (TEL)
PRE	Pre-Retirement Education (AIE)
PRE	Presbyterian Historical Society, Philadelphia, PA [*OCLC symbol*] (OCLC)
PRE	President of the Royal Society of Painter-Etchers and Engravers [*British*]
pre	Pretest [*Advertising*] (WDMC)
PRE	Pretoria [*South Africa*] [*Seismograph station code, US Geological Survey*] (SEIS)
PRE	Problem Reproducer Equipment (SAA)
PRE	Processing Refabrication Experiment [*Nuclear energy*] (NRCH)
PRE	Progesterone [*A hormone*]
PRE	Progesterone Response Element [*Endocrinology*]
PRE	Progressive Resistive Exercise [*Medicine*]
PRE	Progressive Resistive Exercise [*Ophthalmology*] (STED)
PRE	Proportional Reduction of Error
PRE	Protein Relaxation Enhancement (OA)
PRE	Protein Retention Efficiency [*Medicine*] (WDAA)
PRE	Proton Relaxation Enhancement [*Physics*]
PRE	Public Relations Exchange [*Later, PRXI*] (EA)
PRE	Pulse Radiation Effect
PRE	Realencykopaedie fuer Protestantische Theologie und Kirche [*A publication*] (ODCC)
PRE	Spanish Catalonian Battalion (PD)
PREA	Pension Real Estate Association (EA)
P/REA	Probationary Radio Electrical Artificer [*British military*] (DMA)
PREAG	Parks Residents Environmental Action Group [*Australia*]
PREAG	Photographic Reconnaissance Equipment Advisory Group [*Military*]
PREAMP	Preamplifier (AAG)
PREAP	Prison Research Education Action Project (EA)
PRE-ARM	People's Rights Enforced Against Riots and Murder [*Vigilante group in New Jersey*]
PREB	Prebendary
PREB	Pupil Record of Educational Behavior [*Aptitude test*]
Preb Dig	Preble. Digest, Patent Cases [*A publication*] (DLA)
Preb Pat Cas	Preble. Digest, Patent Cases [*A publication*] (DLA)
PREC	Palestine Research and Educational Center (EA)
p rec	Per Rectum [*Through the rectum*] [*Pharmacology*] (DAVI)
PREC	Precambrian [*Period, era, or system*] [*Geology*]
PREC	Precedence (AABC)
PREC	Preceding
PREC	Precentor (ROG)
PREC	Precious (ROG)
prec	Precious (VRA)
PREC	Precision (AABC)
Prec	Precite [*Supra, Cited Before*] [*French*] (ILCA)
PREC	Propulsion Research Environmental Chamber
PREC	Public Revenue Education Council (EA)
PrecCst	Precision Castparts Corp. [*Associated Press*] (SAG)
PRECD	Precede (FAAC)
PrecDr	Precision Drilling Corp. [*Associated Press*] (SAG)
PRECEDE	Predisposing, Reinforcing, and Enabling Causes in Educational Diagnosis and Evaluation [*Occupational therapy*]
Pre Ch	Precedents in Chancery, Edited by Finch [*A publication*] (DLA)
Prec in Ch	Precedents in Chancery, Edited by Finch [*24 English Reprint*] [*1689-1722*] [*A publication*] (DLA)
Prec in Ch (Eng)	Precedents in Chancery, Edited by Finch [*24 English Reprint*] [*A publication*] (DLA)
precip	Precipitate [*Laboratory science*] (DAVI)
PRECIP	Precipitation
PRECIS	Pre-Coordinate Indexing System
PRECIS	Preserved Context Index System [*British Library*] [*London, England*] [*Information service or system*]
PRECO	Preparatory Commission of the United Nations Organization
PRECOM	Precommissioning [*Military*]
PRECOM	Preliminary Communications Search [*Military*] (NVT)
PRECOMDET	Precommissioning Detail [*Navy*] (NVT)
PRECOMG	Precommissioning [*Military*] (NVT)
PRECOMM	Preliminary Communications [*Military*] (NVT)
PRECOMMDET	Precommissioning Detail [*Navy*]
PRECOMMSCOL	Precommissioning School [*Navy*]
precomp	Precomputed Loan
PRECOMP	Prediction of Contingency Maintenance and Parts Requirements (MCD)
PRECOMUNIT	Precommissioning Unit [*Navy*] (DNAB)
precon	Previous Conviction (WDAA)
PrecRes	Precision Response Corp. [*Associated Press*] (SAG)
PRECSN	Precision
PrecStd	Precision Standard, Inc. [*Associated Press*] (SAG)
PrecSy	Precision Systems, Inc. [*Associated Press*] (SAG)
PRED	Predicate
PRED	Predicted
pred	Predicted (STED)
PRED	Prediction (AFM)
Pred	Prednisone [*Also, P, PDN, Pr, Pro*] [*Endocrinology*] [*Antineoplastic drug*]
PRED	Prednisone (DMAA)
PreD₃	Previtamin D3 [*A precursor to vitamin D3*] (DAVI)
PREDA	Puerto Rico Economic Development Administration (NADA)
PREDECE	Predecease (ROG)
PREDICT	Pollution Reduction by Information and Control Technology
PREDICT	Prediction of Radiation Effects by Digital Computer Techniques
Pr Edw I	Prince Edward Island (DLA)
Pr Edw I	Prince Edward Island Reports [*Canada*] [*A publication*] (DLA)
Pr Edw Isl	Prince Edward Island (DLA)
Pr Edw Isl	Prince Edward Island Reports [*Canada*] [*A publication*] (DLA)

PREE............ Partial Reinforcement Extinction Effect (STED)
PREEMIE...... Premature Baby [Medical slang] (WDAA)
PRE-EMPTN... Pre-Emption (ROG)
PREF............ Preface
pref............. Preface (WDAA)
PREF............ Prefecture
PREF............ Preference [or Preferred] (AFM)
PREF............ Preferred (KSC)
PREF............ Prefix (AAG)
PREF............ Prefocused
PREF............ Propulsion Research Environmental Facility
PREFAB...... Prefabricated (KSC)
PREFACE...... Pre-Freshman and Cooperative Education for Minorities in
              Engineering
PREF-AP...... Prefect-Apostolic [Roman Catholic]
PREFAT....... Prepare Final Acceptance Trials [Navy] (NVT)
PREFCE....... Preface (ROG)
PREFD........ Preferred (WDAA)
prefd........... Preferred (STED)
PREFLT....... Preflight (KSC)
PREFLTSCOL.. Preflight School [Military]
PREFMD...... Preformed
PREFRAM..... Prepare Fleet Rehabilitation and Modernization Overhaul [Navy]
              (NVT)
preft........... Prefecture
PREG .... Pregnancy [or Pregnant]
PREG .... Pregnelone (STED)
PREG .... Pregnenolone [Endocrinology]
pregang....... Preganglionic [Anatomy]
PREGN........ Pregnancy [or Pregnant] (AAMN)
prehis.......... Prehistory [or Prehistoric] (BARN)
PREHIST...... Prehistory [or Prehistoric] (WDAA)
PREIA .... Professional Radio and Electronics Institute of Australia
PREINACT.... Prepare Inactivation [Navy] (NVT)
PREINSURV.. Prepare for Board of Inspection and Survey [Navy] (NVT)
PreissM....... Preiss [Byron] Multimedia Co., Inc. [Associated Press] (SAG)
PREJ........... Prejudice (AABC)
PREL........... Pain Relief Level [Medicine]
PREL........... Preliminary
PREL........... Preliminary Evaluation [Orbit identification]
PREL........... Prelude [Music] (ROG)
PREL........... Priority Reconnaissance Exploitation List (CINC)
PREL........... Programmable Rotary Encoded Logic [Computer science] (MHDB)
PRELA .... Prensa Latina, Angencia Informativa Latinoamericana [Press agency]
              [Cuba]
PRELIM....... Preliminary (AFM)
prelim......... Preliminary (STED)
Prelim .... Preliminary (AL)
prelim diag... Preliminary Diagnosis [Medicine] (DAVI)
prelims........ Preliminary Pages [Frontmatter] [Publishing]
PRELIMY ..... Preliminary (ROG)
prelm......... Preliminary (VRA)
PRELOG...... People's Revolutionary League of Ghana [Political party] (PPW)
PRELORT..... Precision Long Range Tracking RADAR
PRELUDE..... Pre-Optimization Linearization of Undulation and Detection of Errors
              (PDAA)
PREM.......... Preliminary Reference Earth Model [Geology]
PREM.......... Premature [Medicine]
prem.......... Prematurity (STED)
PREM.......... Premier (ROG)
prem.......... Premiere (WDMC)
PREM.......... Premier Financial Services, Inc. [Freeport, IL] [NASDAQ symbol]
              (NQ)
PREM.......... Premier Financial Svcs [NASDAQ symbol] (TTSB)
Prem........... Premises (TBD)
Prem........... Premium (EBF)
PREM.......... Premium (AFM)
prem.......... Premium (WDMC)
PREM.......... Probe-Microphone Real Ear Measurement [Audiology]
PREMA .... Pulp Refining Equipment Manufacturers Association (EA)
PremBksh.... Premier Bankshares [Associated Press] (SAG)
Premdr .... Premdor, Inc. [Associated Press] (SAG)
PREMED ...... Premedical Student (WDAA)
PRE-MED..... Previous to Appearance in MEDLINE [Latham, NY] [Bibliographic
              database]
PREMEDU.... Preventive Medicine Unit
Premerk ...... Premark International, Inc. [Associated Press] (SAG)
PREMES ...... Premises (ROG)
PremFin....... Premier Financial Bancorp, Inc. [Associated Press] (SAG)
PremFn....... Premier Financial Services [Associated Press] (SAG)
premie .... Premature [Infant] (DAVI)
Premis........ Premis Corp. [Associated Press] (SAG)
PREMOD..... Premodeling Data Output [Environmental Protection Agency]
PREMOD..... Premodulation (NASA)
PREMODE..... Preliminary Mid-Ocean Dynamics Experiment [Marine science]
              (MSC)
Premrln ...... Premier Industrial Corp. [Associated Press] (SAG)
pre-mRNA.... Precursor-Messenger Ribonucleic Acid
PREMS .... Premises (DSUE)
PREMSS ...... Photographic Reconnaissance and Exploitation Management Support
              System (MCD)
PremT......... Premiere Technologies, Inc. [Associated Press] (SAG)
PREN .... Price Enterprises [NASDAQ symbol] (TTSB)
PREN .... Price Enterprises, Inc. [NASDAQ symbol] (SAG)

Pren Act ...... Prentice's Proceedings in an Action [2nd ed.] [1880] [A publication]
              (DLA)
prenat......... Prenatal
PrEng.......... Professional Engineer
PrentPr .... Prentiss Properties Trust [Associated Press] (SAG)
preocc .... Preoccupied [Biology, taxonomy]
PREOP .... Preoperative [Medicine]
PRE-OPS..... Pre-Operational Support [Military]
PREOS .... Predicted Range for Electrooptical Systems [Military] (CAAL)
PREOVHL.... Prepare for Shipyard Overhaul [Navy] (NVT)
PREP .... Pacific Range Electromagnetic Platform (AAG)
PREP .... Parent Readiness Evaluation of Preschoolers [Child development
              test]
PREP .... Pattern Reversal Evoked Potential
PREP .... Peace Research and Education Project
PREP .... Peacetime Requirements and Procedures [Strategic Air Command]
              (MUGU)
PREP .... Personal Responsibility Education Process
PREP .... Persons Responsive to Educational Problems (EA)
PREP .... Plan, Rehearse, Edit, and Psych [Public speaking preparation
              technique]
PREP .... Plasma Rotating Electrode Process [Metallurgy]
PREP .... Population, Resources, and Environment Program [American
              Association for the Advancement of Science]
PReP .... Power PC [Personal Computer] Reference Platform [Configuration
              standard] (PCM)
PREP .... Predischarge Education Program [DoD]
PREP .... Preparation [or Preparatory]
prep.......... Preparation (WDMC)
Prep.......... Preparations (AL)
Prep.......... Preparatory (AL)
prep.......... Prepare (WDMC)
PREP .... Prepare (AFM)
PREP .... Preposition
prep.......... Preposition (WDMC)
PREP .... Productivity Research and Extension Program [North Carolina State
              University] [Research center] (RCD)
PREP .... Programmed Educational Package
PREP .... Programmed Electronics Pattern (PDAA)
PREP .... Pupil Record of Educational Progress [Education] (AEBS)
PREP .... Purchasing, Receiving, and Payable System
PREP .... Putting Research into Educational Practice [Information service of
              ERIC]
Prepak........ People's Revolutionary Party of Kungleipak [India] [Political party]
              (PD)
PREPARE ..... Premarital Personal and Relationship Evaluation
PREPARE.... Project for Retraining of Employable Persons as Relates to EDP
PREPAS ...... Precise Personnel Assignment System [Marine Corps] (GFGA)
PrepCom..... Preparatory Committee [United Nations Committee on Environment
              and Development]
PREPD .... Prepared
PREPE .... Prepare (ROG)
PREPG .... Preparing
PREPN .... Preparation
PREPnet ..... [The] Pennsylvania Research & Economic Partnership Network
              [Computer science] (TNIG)
Prepo.......... Praepositus [Deceased, 1509] [Authority cited in pre-1607 legal
              work] (DSA)
Prepos........ Praepositus [Deceased, 1509] [Authority cited in pre-1607 legal
              work] (DSA)
PREPOS...... Preposition (AABC)
PREPOSTOR... Prepositioned Storage [Army] (AABC)
PREPP .... Process Experimental Pilot Plant (COE)
PREPPSA..... Prepare Postshakedown Availability [Navy] (NVT)
Preppy .... Preparatory School Alumnus [Lifestyle classification]
PREPREG.... Pre-Impregnated Glass Fibers [Fiberglass production]
PREPRO...... Prepositioning [Ship] [Navy] (DOMA)
PREPRO...... Preprocessor [Computer] [Coast Guard]
PREPROD.... Preproduction Model [Military] (AFIT)
PREPS .... Predischarge Remedial Education Program [For servicemen]
PREPS .... Program of Research and Evaluation in Public Schools [Mississippi
              State University] [Research center] (RCD)
PREPSCOL... Preparatory School
prepub........ Prepublication
PREQUAL..... Prequalified [NASA] (KSC)
Prer .... Prerogative Court (DLA)
PRER .... Putting Research into Educational Research
PRE-RE....... Prerefunded Municipal Note [Investment term] (DFIT)
PRERECPAC... Preplanned Reconnaissance Pacific (CINC)
PREREQ...... Prerequisite (WGA)
PRERLA....... Pupils Round, Equal, React to Light and Accommodation
              [Medicine] (MAE)
Prerog Ct..... Prerogative Court, New Jersey (DLA)
PRES .... Premises (ROG)
PRES .... Pre-Release Employment Scheme (WDAA)
PRES .... Presbyterian
PRES .... Presence
PRES .... Present (AAG)
Pres........... Presentation (EBF)
PRES .... Preserved
PRE-S........ Preshaving (MSA)
PRES .... President (EY)
pres........... President (DD)
Pres........... President (ODBW)
PRES .... President of the Royal Entomological Society [British]

PRES .... Pressure (FAAC)
PRES .... Preston R. R. [AAR code]
PRES .... Presumptive [Grammar]
PRES .... Prime Residential, Inc. [NASDAQ symbol] (SAG)
PRES .... Proton Resonance (IAA)
PRES100...... Presidential's Hundred Tab [Military]
Pres Abs ...... Preston's Abstracts of Title [2nd ed.] [1823-24] [A publication] (DLA)
PRESAC....... Photographic Reconnaissance System Analysis by Computer
PRESAGE..... Program to Realistically Evaluate Strategic Anti-Ballistic Missile Gaming Effectiveness [Military] (PDAA)
PRESAILEDREP... Forecast Sailing Report [Navy] (NVT)
PRESAIR...... Pressurized Air Compressor (DNAB)
PRESB .... Presbyterian
PRESB .... Prescribe (AABC)
PresBnc .... Prestige Bancorp, Inc. [Associated Press] (SAG)
PRESBY .... Presbyterian
PRESBY .... Presbytery
presby .... Presbytery (VRA)
PresCasn ..... President Casinos, Inc. [Associated Press] (SAG)
Pres C of E Ch... Presbyterian Church of England Chaplain [Navy British]
PRESCOM...... Personnel Command [Army] (DOMA)
Pres Conv .... Preston on Conveyancing [5th ed.] [1819-29] [A publication] (DLA)
PRESCORE.. Program for the Rapid Estimation of Construction Requirements
PRESCR....... Prescription (MSA)
Presd .... Presidio Oil Co. [Associated Press] (SAG)
PRESDL....... Presidential (WGA)
presen .... Presentation (VRA)
PRESERV..... Preservation
Pres Est...... Preston on Estates [3rd ed.] [1829] [A publication] (DLA)
PRESET....... Preset Spin Echo Technique
Pres Fal....... Falconer's Decisions, Scotch Court of Session [1744-51] [A publication] (DLA)
Pres Fal....... Gilmour and Falconer's Reports, Scotch Court of Session [A publication] (DLA)
Pres Falc ..... President Falconer's Scotch Session Cases (Gilmour and Falconer) [1681-86] [A publication] (DLA)
PRESFR....... Pressure Falling Rapidly [NWS] (FAAC)
PRESIG....... Pressurizing (KSC)
PRESIGN..... Procedure Sign
PRESINSURV... Inspection and Survey Board [Navy]
Pres Leg...... Preston on Legacies [1824] [A publication] (DLA)
PresLf.......... Presidential Life Corp. [Associated Press] (SAG)
Presly......... Presley Companies [Associated Press] (SAG)
Pres Mer ..... Preston on Merger [A publication] (DLA)
PRESNAVWARCOL... Naval War College
PRES PART... Present Participle [Grammar] (WDAA)
PRESPROC... Presidential Proclamation
Pres Proc.... Presidential Proclamation (AAGC)
PresR......... Presidential Realty Corp. [Associated Press] (SAG)
PRESRR....... Pressure Rising Rapidly [NWS] (FAAC)
PRESS .... Pacific Range Electromagnetic Signature Studies [or System] [Military] (NG)
PRESS .... Parti Republicain Social du Senegal [Social Republican Party of Senegal] [Political party]
PRESS .... Predicted Residual Sum of Squares
PRESS .... Prediction Error Sum of Squares (AAEL)
PRESS .... Prereading Expectancy Screening Scale [Educational test]
PRESS .... Pressurant (NAKS)
PRESS .... Pressure (MCD)
PRESS .... Prolog Equation Solving System (BYTE)
PRESS .... Property Record for Equipment Servicing and Sharing (MCD)
PRESSAR..... Presentation Equipment for Slow Scan RADAR
PRESSDUCTOR... Pressure Inductor (IAA)
PRESSO....... Program for Elective Surgical Second Opinion [Blue Cross/Blue Shield]
Pres SQ...... Presidential Studies Quarterly [A publication] (BRI)
PRESSURS... Pre-Strike Surveillance/Reconnaissance System (MCD)
PREST .... Party on Scientific and Technical Research Policy [European community] (MHDB)
PREST .... Present (ROG)
PRES'T .... President
PRE-ST .... Prestart (AAG)
PREST .... Programme of Policy Research in Engineering Science and Technology [British]
Prest Conv .... Preston on Conveyancing [A publication] (DLA)
Prestek .... Presstek, Inc. [Associated Press] (SAG)
Prest Est...... Preston on Estates [A publication] (DLA)
PrestFn .... Prestige Financial Corp. [Associated Press] (SAG)
Prest Merg... Preston on Merger [A publication] (DLA)
PRESTMO..... Prestissimo [Very Fast] [Music] (ROG)
PRESTO .... Personnel Response and Evaluation System for Target Obscuration [Military] (RDA)
PRESTO ...... Prediction of Radiological Effects Due to Shallow Trench Operations [Environmental Protection Agency] (AEPA)
PRESTO ...... Prestissimo [Very Fast] [Music] (ROG)
PRESTO ...... Program for Rapid Earth-to-Space Trajectory Optimization [NASA]
PRESTO ...... Program Reporting and Evaluation System for Total Operations [AFSC]
PRE-STORM... Preliminary Regional Experiment for STORM [Stormscale Operational and Research Meteorology] [Marine science] (OSRA)
Prest Shep T... Sheppard's Touchstone by Preston [A publication] (DLA)
presv .... Preservation (BARN)
Presv .... Preservation (AL)
Presync....... Presynchronization
PRET.......... Periodic Reliability Evaluation Test (MCD)

PRET.......... Preterit [Past tense] [Grammar] (ROG)
PRET.......... Pretoria [South Africa] (ROG)
PRETCHREP... Preliminary Technical Report (MCD)
PRETECHREP... Preliminary Technical Report [Army] (AABC)
PRETOS....... Proofreading Tests of Spelling [Educational test]
PRETTYBLUEBATCH... Philadelphia Regular Exchange Tea Total Young Belles Lettres Universal Experimental Bibliographical Association To Civilize Humanity [From Edgar Allan Poe essay "How to Write a Blackwood Article"]
PREV .... Medical and Psychological Previews [Database] [BRS Information Technologies] [Information service or system] (IID)
PREV .... Prevention
PREV .... Previous (AFM)
PREV .... Previous Program Selection [In-car entertainment] [Electronics]
PrevAGT ..... Previous Abnormality of Glucose Tolerance
PREVENT .... Pacific Northwest Regional Visibility Experiment using Natural Tracers [Marine science] (OSRA)
PREVENT .... Pacific NW Regional Visibility EXperiment using Natural Tracers (USDC)
PREVENT .... Precertification to Verify Necessary Treatment
PRevere...... Paul Revere Corp. [Associated Press] (SAG)
PREVLV ...... Prevalve
PrevMed...... Preventive Medicine (DAVI)
PREVMEDU... Preventive Medicine Unit
pre-voc .... Prevocational [Education] (DAVI)
PREVT .... Preventative
PREWI........ Press Wireless [A radio service for the transmission of news]
Pr Exch ...... Price's English Exchequer Reports [1814-24] [A publication] (DLA)
PREZ.......... President Casinos [NASDAQ symbol] (TTSB)
PREZ.......... President Riverboat Casinos [NASDAQ symbol] (SAG)
PRF........... Palestine Rejection Front (BJA)
PRF........... Parachute Refurbishment Facility [NASA] (NASA)
PRF........... Partial Reinforcement [Training]
PRF........... Partido Revolucionario Febrerista [Febrerista Revolutionary Party] [Paraguay] [Political party] (PPW)
PRF........... Patient Record Form
PRF........... Patient Report Form (DB)
PRF........... Penetration Room Filtration [Nuclear energy] (NRCH)
prf............ Performer [MARC relator code] [Library of Congress] (LCCP)
PRF........... Permanent Requirements File [Computer science] (CIST)
PRF........... Personality Research Form [Psychology]
PRF........... Personnel Readiness File [Army] (AABC)
PRF........... Petroleum Research Fund
PRF........... Phenol/Resorcinol/Formaldehyde [Plastics technology]
PRF........... Plant Response Fertilization [Agriculture]
PRF........... Plasmacytoma Repressor Factor [Cytology]
PRF........... Plastics Recycling Foundation (EA)
PRF........... Plutonium Reclamation Facility [Nuclear energy]
PRF........... Plymouth Rock Foundation (EA)
PRF........... Plywood Research Foundation (EA)
PRF........... Point Response Function [Of a telescope]
PRF........... Polyclonal Rheumatoid Factor [Medicine] (DMAA)
PRF........... Pontine Reticular Formation [Neurophysiology]
PRF........... Porpoise Rescue Foundation (EA)
PRF........... Potential Requirements File (NITA)
PRF........... Power Radio Frequency [Telecommunications] (IAA)
PRF........... Prefac Enterprises, Inc. [Toronto Stock Exchange symbol]
PRF........... Preformed [Technical drawings]
PRF........... Pride Co. $2.60cm Cv L.P. [NYSE symbol] (TTSB)
PRF........... Pride Companies Ltd. [NYSE symbol] (SPSG)
PRF........... Primary Reference Fuel [Automotive engineering]
PRF........... Processor Request Flag [Telecommunications] (TEL)
PRF........... Progressive Renal Failure [Medicine] (AAMN)
PRF........... Prolactin-Releasing Factor [Endocrinology]
PRF........... Proliferation Regulatory Factor [Biochemistry]
PRF........... Proof (KSC)
prf............ Proof (VRA)
PRF........... Protein Rich Fraction [Food analysis]
PRF........... Psychiatric Research Foundation
PRF........... Psychical Research Foundation (EA)
PRF........... Psychosynthesis Research Foundation (EA)
PRF........... Publications Reference File [Government Printing Office] [Database] [Washington, DC] (MCD)
PRF........... Public Relations Foundation
PRF........... Public Residential Facility
PRF........... Puerto Rico Federal Reports [A publication] (DLA)
PRF........... Pulse Rate Frequency (MUGU)
PRF........... Pulse Recurrence Frequency
PRF........... Pulse Repetition Frequency [Computer science]
prf............ Pulse Repetition Frequency (IDOE)
PRF........... Purchase Rate Factor
PRF........... Purdue Research Foundation [Purdue University] [Research center] (MCD)
PRFA .... Plasma Recognition Factor Activity [Hematology] (AAMN)
Pr Falc........ President Falconer's Scotch Session Cases [1744-51] [A publication] (DLA)
PRFAW .... Personnel Research Field Activity, Washington [Navy] (MUGU)
PrfBcp........ Professional Bancorp [Associated Press] (SAG)
PRFC .... Plymouth Rock Fanciers Club (EA)
PRFC .... Potomac River Fisheries Commission [Maryland and Virginia] (NOAA)
PRFCN .... Purification
PRFCS .... Pattern Recognition Feedback Control System [Computer science] (IAA)
PRFCS .... Prefocus

PRFD .... Pulse Recurrence Frequency Discrimination [*Telecommunications*] (TEL)
PRFDX .... Price T. Rowe: Equity Income [*Mutual fund ticker symbol*] (SG)
PRFE............ Polar Reflection Faraday Effect
PR Fed .... Puerto Rico Federal Reports [*A publication*] (DLA)
PRFG .... Proofing [*Freight*]
PRFI............. Portable Range-Finder/Illuminator
PRFI............. Puerto Rican Family Institute (EA)
PRFIA.......... Phase-Resolved Fluoroimmunoassay
PRFIC.......... Plume RADAR Frequency Interference Code (MCD)
PrflOF......... Preferred Income Opportunity Fund [*Associated Press*] (SAG)
PRFL........... Pressure Fed Liquid (KSC)
PRFM........... Performance (MSA)
PRFM........... Perfumania, Inc. [*NASDAQ symbol*] (SAG)
PRFM........... Premature [*or Prolonged*] Rupture of Fetal Membrane [*Gynecology*] (MAE)
PRFM........... Prolonged Rupture of Fetal Membranes [*Obstetrics*] (DAVI)
PRFM........... Pseudorandom Frequency Modulated [*Computer science*]
PRFN .... Prestige Financial [*NASDAQ symbol*] (TTSB)
PRFN .... Prestige Financial Corp. [*NASDAQ symbol*] (SAG)
PRFR .... Proofer [*Freight*]
PRFRD......... Proofread (MSA)
PRFRT......... Partially Relaxed Fourier Transform (DB)
PRFS .... Phase-Resolved Fluorescence Spectroscopy
PRFS .... Pulse Recurrence Frequency Stagger (OA)
PRFSS......... Peterborough Royal Foxhound Show Society [*British*] (DBA)
PRFT........... Partially Relaxed Fourier Transform [*Mathematics*]
PRFT............ Portable Rod-and-Frame Test (EDAC)
PRFT........... Presser Foot
PRFT........... Press Fit
PRFT........... Proffitt's, Inc. [*NASDAQ symbol*] (NQ)
PRFU .... Processor Ready for Use [*Telecommunications*] (TEL)
PRG .... Empresa Aero-Servicios Parrague Ltd. [*Chile*] [*ICAO designator*] (FAAC)
PRG .... Gilbert Associates, Inc., Reading, PA [*Library symbol Library of Congress*] (LCLS)
PRG .... Parabolic Radius Gage (MCD)
PRG .... Paris, IL [*Location identifier FAA*] (FAAL)
PRG .... Peacekeeper Rail Garrison [*Cancelled 1991*] [*Air Force*] (DOMA)
PRG .... Peerless Carpet Corp. [*Toronto Stock Exchange symbol*]
PRG .... People's Revolutionary Government [*Grenada*] (PD)
PRG .... Perennial Rye Grass [*Immunology*]
PRG .... Performance Related Gift [*Business Management*]
PRG .... Personnel Requirements Generator
PRG .... Personnel Resources Group [*Military*]
PRG .... Perugia [*Italy*] [*Seismograph station code, US Geological Survey*] (SEIS)
PRG .... Phleborrheogram [*Hematology*] (DAVI)
PRG .... Physician Resources Group, Inc. [*NYSE symbol*] (SAG)
PRG .... Physicians Resource Group [*NYSE symbol*] (TTSB)
PRG .... Pick Resources Guide [*ALLM Books*] [*England*] [*Information service or system*] (IID)
PRG .... Plastic Radial Grating
PRG .... Policy Research Group [*Australian Labor Party*]
PRG .... Powerful Radio Galaxy [*Cosmology*]
PRG .... Prague [*Former Czechoslovakia*] [*Airport symbol*] (OAG)
PRG .... Procedure Review Group [*Nuclear energy*] (NRCH)
PRG .... Program Regulation Guide
PRG .... Program Review Group [*Military*]
PRG .... Provisional Revolutionary Government [*Political arm of the Vietcong*] (VNW)
PRG .... Purge (AAG)
PRGC .... Past Royal Grand Cross [*Freemasonry*] (ROG)
PRGFX .... Price T. Rowe: Growth Stock [*Mutual fund ticker symbol*] (SG)
PRG/I........... Pick Resources Guide/International [*ALLM Books*] [*Information service or system*] (IID)
PRGIX .... Price T. Rowe: Growth & Income [*Mutual fund ticker symbol*] (SG)
PRGM .... Program (AFM)
Prgm........... Program (PHSD)
PRGMG .... Programming (MSA)
PRGMNG ..... Programming
PRGMR ..... Programmer (AFM)
Prgmr .... Programmer (AL)
PRGO .... Perrigo Co. [*NASDAQ symbol*] (SPSG)
PRGPrB........ Pub Sv E&G 4.18% Pfd [*NYSE symbol*] (TTSB)
PRGR........... ProGroup, Inc. [*NASDAQ symbol*] (NQ)
PRGRMR ..... Programmer
PRGS .... President of the Royal Geographical Society [*British*]
PRGS .... Prognosis (AABC)
PRGS .... Progress Software [*NASDAQ symbol*] (SPSG)
PrgSoft .... Progress Software Corp. [*Associated Press*] (SAG)
PRGVN......... Provisional Revolutionary Government of South Vietnam (VNW)
PRGX........... Profit Recovery Group International, Inc. (The) [*NASDAQ symbol*] (SAG)
PRGX .... Profit Recovery Grp Intl [*NASDAQ symbol*] (TTSB)
PRH .... Partido Revolucionario Hondureno [*Honduras Revolutionary Party*] [*Political party*] (PPW)
PRH .... Petrol Railhead
PRH .... Phrae [*Thailand*] [*Airport symbol*] (OAG)
PrH .... Prepositus Hypoglossi [*Neuroanatomy*]
PRH .... Program Requirements Handbook (MUGU)
PRH .... Prolactin-Releasing Hormone [*Endocrinology*]
PRH .... Promus Hotel [*NYSE symbol*] (TTSB)
PRH .... Promus Hotel Corp. [*NYSE symbol*] (SAG)
PRH .... Psychiatric Regional Hospital [*Health insurance*] (GHCT)

PRHA........... People Refreshment House Association [*British*] (BI)
PRHA........... President of the Royal Hibernian Academy [*British*]
PRHB........... Pacific Rehabilitation & Sports Medicine, Inc. [*NASDAQ symbol*] (SAG)
PRHB .... Pacific Rehab/Sports Medicine [*NASDAQ symbol*] (TTSB)
PRHBF......... Peak Reactive Hyperemia Blood Flow [*Hematology*] (MAE)
Pr HC Ch ... Practice of the High Court of Chancery [*A publication*] (DLA)
PRHi........... Historical Society of Berks County, Reading, PA [*Library symbol Library of Congress*] (LCLS)
PRHYX........ Price T. Rowe: High Yield [*Mutual fund ticker symbol*] (SG)
PRI.............. Farmington, MO [*Location identifier FAA*] (FAAL)
PRI.............. Institutional Revolutionary Party [*Mexico*] [*Political party*]
PRI.............. Pacific Research Institute for Public Policy (EA)
PRI.............. Pacific Resources, Inc. (EFIS)
PRI.............. Pain Rating Index
PRI.............. Paint Research Institute [*Defunct*] (EA)
PRI.............. Paleontological Research Institution (EA)
PRI.............. Partido Revolucionario Institucional [*Party of the Institutionalized Revolution*] [*Mexico Political party*]
PRI.............. Partito Repubblicano Italiano [*Italian Republican Party*] [*Political party*] (PPW)
PRI.............. Partner Relationship Inventory [*Marital relations test*] [*Psychology*]
PRI.............. Partnership for Rural Improvement [*Washington*] (EDAC)
PRI.............. Peace Research Institute [*Later, Institute for Policy Studies*] (EA)
PRI.............. Performance Registry International
PRI.............. Personal Reaction Index [*Interpersonal skills and attitudes test*]
PRI.............. Personal Resource Inventory (DB)
PRI.............. Personnel Research, Inc. [*Information service or system*] (IID)
PRI.............. Personnel Research Institute Test (AEBS)
PRI.............. Petroleum Recovery Institute [*Research center*] (RCD)
PRI.............. Phosphate Rock Institute [*Defunct*] (EA)
PRI.............. Phosphoribose Isomerase [*An enzyme*] (MAE)
PRI.............. Photographic Reconnaissance and Interpretation (NATG)
PRI.............. Photo RADAR Intelligence
PRI.............. Pineapple Research Institute of Hawaii (EA)
PRI.............. Plan Repeater Indicator (IAA)
PRI.............. Plasticity Retention Index [*Rubber test method*]
PRI.............. Plastics and Rubber Institute [*Institution of the Rubber Industry and Plastics Institute*] [*Formed by a merger of*] (EAIO)
PRI.............. Polymer Research Institute [*Polytechnic Institute of New York*] [*Research center*] (RCD)
PRI.............. Polymer Research Institute [*University of Massachusetts*] [*Research center*] (RCD)
PRI.............. Population Reference Intake (WDAA)
PRI.............. Practice Training Index
PRI.............. Praslin Island [*Seychelles Islands*] [*Airport symbol*] (OAG)
PRI.............. Preliminary Rifle Instruction [*Military*]
PRI.............. Prescriptive Reading Inventory
PRI.............. President of the Royal Institute (of Painters in Water Colours) [*British*] (ROG)
PRI.............. President of the Royal Institution (London) (ROG)
PRI.............. President Regimental Institutes [*British*]
PRI.............. Prevention Routiere Internationale [*International Road Safety Organization*] [*Luxembourg*] (EAIO)
Pri.............. Price's English Exchequer Reports [*1814-24*] [*A publication*] (DLA)
Pri.............. Price's English Mining Commissioners' Cases [*A publication*] (DLA)
PRI.............. Priest [*California*] [*Seismograph station code, US Geological Survey*] (SEIS)
PRI.............. Primary (KSC)
pri.............. Primary (IDOE)
PRI.............. Primary Rate, Inc.
PRI.............. Primary Rate Interface (PCM)
PRI.............. Primary Winding (IAA)
PRI.............. Primate Research Institute [*New Mexico State University*] [*Hollman, NM*]
PRI.............. Prime Computer Inc., Corporation Library, Framingham, MA [*OCLC symbol*] (OCLC)
PRI.............. Primer (IAA)
PRI.............. Princeville Airways, Inc. [*ICAO designator*] (FAAC)
PRI.............. Printer Interface [*Computer science*] (CIST)
PRI.............. Priority (AFM)
PRI.............. Priority Repair Induction [*Code*]
PRI.............. Priority Requirement for Information (AFM)
Pri.............. Priscianus [*Authority cited in pre-1607 legal work*] (DSA)
PRI.............. Prison
PRI.............. Private
PRI.............. Prize [*or Prizeman*] [*British*] (ROG)
PRI.............. Processing Research Institute [*Carnegie Mellon University*]
PRI.............. Production Rate Index (OA)
PRI.............. Production Records, Inc. (EA)
PRI.............. Program Interrupt [*Computer science*] (IAA)
PRI.............. Program Revision Intent
PRI.............. Projection Readout Indicator [*Aviation*] (OA)
PRI.............. Proteus Resources, Inc. [*Vancouver Stock Exchange symbol*]
PRI.............. Prout Research Institute (EA)
PRI.............. Psoriasis Research Institute (EA)
PRI.............. Public Radio International
PRI.............. Public Relations Institute of Ireland (BI)
PRI.............. Puerto Rican Independence [*Later, GPRG*] [*An association*] (EA)
PRI.............. Puerto Rico [*ANSI three-letter standard code*] (CNC)
PRI.............. Pulse Rate Increase [*Medicine*]
PRI.............. Pulse Rate Indicator
PRI.............. Pulse Recurrence [*or Repetition*] Interval (NATG)
PRI.............. Pulse Repetition Internal
PRI.............. Pulse Repetition Interval (CIST)

PRI	Pure Research Institute [*Later, BRINC*] (EA)
PRIA	Peer Review Improvement Act of 1982
PRIA	President of the Royal Irish Academy
PRIA	PRI Automation [*NASDAQ symbol*] (SAG)
PRIA	Public Rangelands Improvement Act of 1978
PRIA	Society for Participatory Research in Asia [*India*] (EAIO)
PRIAM	Precision Range Information Analysis for Missiles (MCD)
PRIAM	Pre-Normative Requirements for Intelligent Actuation & Measurements (ACII)
PRIAS	Packard's Radioimmunoassay System [*Medicine*] (DMAA)
PrIAU-SJ	Inter-American University of Puerto Rico, San Juan Campus, San Juan, PR [*Library symbol Library of Congress*] (LCLS)
PRI Auto	PRI Automation [*Associated Press*] (SAG)
PRIBA	President of the Royal Institute of British Architects
PRIBAG	Priority Baggage (DNAB)
PRI BIL	Primary Billet (DNAB)
PRIC Dec	Puerto Rico Industrial Commission Decisions [*A publication*] (DLA)
PRICE	Physicians for Research in Cost-Effectiveness (EA)
Price	Price's English Exchequer Reports [*A publication*] (DLA)
Price	Price's English Mining Commissioners' Cases [*A publication*] (DLA)
PRICE	Pricing Review to Intensify Competitive Environment [*Computer science*]
PRICE	Programmed Review of Information for Costing and Evaluation (MCD)
PRICE	Protection, Rest, Ice, Compression, Evaluation [*Medicine*]
Price & St	Price and Stewart's Trade Mark Cases [*A publication*] (DLA)
PriceCst	Price Costco, Inc. [*Associated Press*] (SAG)
PriceEnt	Price Enterprises, Inc. [*Associated Press*] (SAG)
Price Gen Pr	Price's General Practice [*A publication*] (DLA)
Price Liens	Price on Maritime Liens [*1940*] [*A publication*] (DLA)
Pricell	Pricellular Corp. [*Associated Press*] (SAG)
Price Min Cas	Price's Mining Cases [*A publication*] (DLA)
Price Notes PC	Price's Notes of Practice Cases in Exchequer [*1830-31*] [*England*] [*A publication*] (DLA)
Price Notes PP	Price's Notes of Points of Practice, English Exchequer Cases [*A publication*] (DLA)
Price PC	Price's English Practice Cases [*1830-31*] [*A publication*] (DLA)
Price Pr Cas	Price's English Practice Cases [*A publication*] (DLA)
Price R Est	Price on Acts Relating to Real Estate [*A publication*] (DLA)
PriceTR	Price [*T. Rowe*] Associates, Inc. [*Associated Press*] (SAG)
Prickett	Prickett's Reports [*1 Idaho*] [*A publication*] (DLA)
PRICOM	Prison Commission [*British*]
PRI-D	Peace Research Institute - Dundas [*Canada*] (IRC)
PRID	Pridie [*The Day Before*] [*Latin*]
PriD	Princeton Datafilm, Inc., Princeton, NJ [*Library symbol Library of Congress*] (LCLS)
Prid & C	Prideaux and Cole's English Reports [*4 New Sessions Cases*] [*1850-51*] [*A publication*] (DLA)
Prid & Co	Prideaux and Cole's English Reports [*4 New Sessions Cases*] [*1850-51*] [*A publication*] (DLA)
Prid Ch W	Prideaux's Directions to Churchwardens [*10th ed.*] [*1835*] [*A publication*] (DLA)
PRIDCO	Puerto Rico Industrial Development Co.
Prid Conv	Prideaux's Forms and Precedents in Conveyancing [*24th ed.*] [*1952*] [*A publication*] (DLA)
PRIDE	National Parents' Resource Institute for Drug Education (EA)
PRIDE	People and Resources Identified for Distributed Environments (TELE)
PRIDE	People for Rehabilitating and Integrating the Disabled through Education [*New York City*]
PRIDE	Perfection Requires Individual Defect Elimination
PRIDE	Personal Responsibility in Daily Effort [*Military Airlift Command's acronym for the Zero Defects Program*]
PRIDE	Preschool and Kindergarten Interest Descriptor [*Educational test*]
Pride	Pride Companies Ltd. [*Associated Press*] (SAG)
PRIDE	Priority Receiving with Inter-Departmental Efficiency [*Computer science*]
PRIDE	Production of Reliable Items Demands Excellence [*Navy*] (NG)
PRIDE	Productive Rehabilitation Institute of Dallas for Ergonomics [*Research center*] (RCD)
PRIDE	Productivity Improvements for the Decade of the Eighties
PRIDE	Professional Results in Daily Effort [*Strategic Air Command's acronym for the Zero Defects Program*]
PRIDE	Profitable Information by Design (MHDI)
PRIDE	Profitable Information by Design through Phased Planning and Control (MHDB)
PRIDE	Programmed Reliability in Design Engineering
PRIDE	Promote Real Independence for the Disabled and Elderly (EA)
PRIDE	Prompt Response Insurance Delivery Express
PRIDE	Protection of Reefs and Islands from Degradation and Exploitation
PRIDE	Provisioning Review Input Data Evaluation (MCD)
PRIDE	Pulse RADAR Intelligent Diagnostic Environment [*US Army Missile Command*] (RDA)
PrideA	Pride Automotive Group, Inc. [*Associated Press*] (SAG)
PrideAto	Pride Automotive Group, Inc. [*Associated Press*] (SAG)
Prid Judg	Prideaux's Judgments and Crown Debts [*4th ed.*] [*1854*] [*A publication*] (DLA)
PRIF	Prior Year Refund Information File [*IRS*]
PRI-FLY	Primary Flight Control [*on an aircraft carrier*] [*Navy*]
PRIH	Prolactin-Release Inhibiting Factor [*Also, PIF*] [*Endocrinology*]
PRIISM	Pacific Research Institute for Information Systems and Management [*University of Hawaii at Manoa*] [*Research center*] (RCD)
PRIL	Penarth Research International Ltd. [*British*]
PRIM	Pac Rim Holding [*NASDAQ symbol*] (SPSG)
PRIM	Plans and Reports Improvement Memorandum [*Military*] (CAAL)
PRIM	Plume Radiation Intensity Measurement (MUGU)

PRIM	Pre-Referral Intervention Manual [*Test*] (TMMY)
PRIM	Primary (AFM)
PRIM	Primase (DMAA)
PRIM	Primate
PRIM	Primitive
PRIM	Program for Information Managers [*Later, AIM*] [*An association*]
PRIM	Programmed Instruction for Management Education (HGAA)
PRIMA	Pollutant Response in Marine Animals [*Marine science*] (MSC)
PRIMA	Public Radio in Mid-America (NTCM)
PRIMA	Public Risk and Insurance Management Association [*Washington, DC*] (EA)
PRIMA	Public Risk Management Association (NTPA)
Primadn	Primadonna Resorts, Inc. [*Associated Press*] (SAG)
PrimaE	Prima Energy Corp. [*Associated Press*] (SAG)
PRIM & R	Public Responsibility in Medicine and Research (EA)
PRIMAR	Program to Improve Management of Army Resources (AABC)
PrimaryB	Primary Bank [*Associated Press*] (SAG)
Primary Ed	Primary Education [*A publication*]
PRIMATE	Personal Retrieval of Information by Microcomputer and Terminal Ensemble
PRIM BIB	Primary Bibliography (DGA)
PRIMCOM	Pacific Rim Interactive Multimedia Computing [*Australia*]
PRIME	Planning through Retrieval of Information for Management Extrapolation
PRIME	Precision Integrator for Meteorological Echoes (IEEE)
PRIME	Precision Range Integrated Maneuver Exercise [*Army*] (RDA)
PRIME	Precision Recovery Including Maneuvering Entry [*Air Force*]
PRIME	Prematriculation Program in Medical Education (DMAA)
PRIME	Preparedness of Resources in Mission Evaluation (SAA)
PRIME	Prescribed Right to Income and Maximum Equity
PRIME	Primary Initiatives in Mathematics Education (AIE)
PRIME	Priority Improved Management Effort (KSC)
PRIME	Priority Improvement Effort [*DoD*]
PRIME	Priority Management Effort [*Army*]
PRIME	Priority Management Evaluation [*Navy*]
PRIME	Procarbazine, Ifosfamide, Methotrexate [*Antineoplastic drug regimen*]
PRIME	Processing, Research, Inspection, and Marine Extension Program [*National Oceanic and Atmospheric Administration*] (MSC)
PRIME	Profession Related Intern-Mentorship Experience
PRIME	Program Independence, Modularity, Economy
PRIME	Programmed Instruction for Management Education [*American Management Association*]
PRIME	Programme for International Managers in Europe [*Business program*]
PRIME	Program Research in Integrated Multiethnic Education [*Defunct*] (EA)
PRIME BEEF	Priority Improvement Management Effort Base Engineering Emergency Force [*Air Force*] (DOMA)
PrimeCp	Prime Capital Corp. [*Associated Press*] (SAG)
PrimeMg	Prime Management Group, Inc. [*Associated Press*] (SAG)
PRIMENET	Prime Network Software Package [*Prime Computer, Inc.*]
PrimEq	Prime Equities International [*Associated Press*] (SAG)
PRIMER	Patient Record Information for Education Requirements [*Computer science*]
PRIME RIBS	Priority Improvement Management Effort Readiness in Base Services [*Air Force*] (DOMA)
PrimeRsd	Prime Residential, Inc. [*Associated Press*] (SAG)
PRIMES	Preflight Integration of Munitions and Electronic Systems (MCD)
PRIMES	Productivity Integrated Measurement System [*Army*]
PrimeSrc	PrimeSource Corp. [*Associated Press*] (SAG)
PRIMEX	Primary Care Extender [*Insurance*] (DMAA)
Primex	Primex Technologies, Inc. [*Associated Press*] (SAG)
PRIMEX	Private Message Switching [*Telecommunications British*]
PRIMIP	Primipara [*Woman bearing first child*] [*Medicine*] (AAMN)
PRIMIR	Product Improvement Management Information Report
PRIM LUC	Prima Luce [*Early in the Morning*] [*Pharmacy*]
PRIM M	Primo Mane [*Early in the Morning*] [*Pharmacy*]
PRIM METH	Primitive Methodist [*A publication*]
PRIMO	Programmable, Realtime, Incoherent, Matrix, Optical Processor [*Computer science*]
PRIMORDIAL	Primary Order Dial (NITA)
PRIMOS	Prime Operating System [*Prime Computer, Inc.*]
PRIMP	Primipara [*Woman bearing first child*] [*Obstetrics*] (DAVI)
Primrk	Primark Corp. [*Associated Press*] (SAG)
PRIMS	Product Requirement Information Management System (MCD)
PRIMSCO	Pilot Run Item Master Schedule Committee (IAA)
PRIMTEC	Pacific Rim Interactive Multi-Media Technology
PRIMTRA	Air Primary Training
PRIMUS	Physician Reservists in Medical Universities and Schools [*Military*]
PRIMUS	Primary Medical Care for the Uniformed Services [*DoD*]
PrimusT	Primus Telecommunications Group, Inc. [*Associated Press*] (SAG)
PRIN	Partido Revolucionario de la Izquierda Nacionalista [*National Leftist Revolutionary Party*] [*Bolivia*] [*Political party*] (PPW)
PRIN	Performance Risk Index Number (NG)
PRIN	Princeton [*New Jersey*] [*Seismograph station code, US Geological Survey*] (SEIS)
PRIN	Principal
Prin	Principal (AL)
PRIN	Principality (ROG)
PRIN	Principally (ROG)
PRIN	Princlpia [*Elements*] [*Latin*] (ROG)
PRIN	Principle (ROG)
prin	Principle (VRA)
PRINAIR	Puerto Rico National Airlines
PrinAm	Princeton American Corp. [*Associated Press*] (SAG)
PRINC	Principal
PRINC	Principle

PRINCE....... Parts Reliability Information Center [*NASA*]
PRINCE....... Programmed International Computer Environment [*International relations simulation game*]
PRINCE....... Programmed Reinforced Instruction Necessary to Continuing Education
PRINCE/APIC... Parts Reliability Information Center/Apollo Parts Information Center [*NASA*]
PrinceM...... Princeton Media Group, Inc. [*Associated Press*] (SAG)
Prince NML... Prince's New Mexico Laws [*A publication*] (DLA)
Princeton U... Princeton University (GAGS)
PRINCIR ...... Printed Circuit (IAA)
PrincNtl ...... Princeton National Bancorp [*Associated Press*] (SAG)
PRIND........ Present Indication [*Aviation*] (IAA)
PRIND........ Prolonged Reversible Ischemic Neurologic Deficit [*Medicine*] (DMAA)
PRINDUS...... Prison Industries [*Industries conducted in English prisons*]
PRINFO....... Printed Information Distribution (SAA)
PRING........ Partido Revolucionario de Izquierda Nacional Gueiler [*Revolutionary Party of the National Left - Gueiler Wing*] [*Bolivia*] [*Political party*] (PPW)
PRIN-L........ Partido Revolucionario de la Izquierda Nacional Laboral [*Political party*] (PPW)
PRINM........ Partido Revolucionario de la Izquierda Nacional Moller [*Bolivia*] [*Political party*] (PPW)
PRINMUS .... Principal Musician [*Marine Corps*]
PRINOBC/NEC... Primary Navy Officer Billet Classification and Navy Enlisted Classification
Prin PL .... Eden's Principles of Penal Law [*A publication*] (DLA)
Prins & Conderlag... Prins and Conderlag's Reports [*Ceylon*] [*A publication*] (ILCA)
PrinsRec...... Prins Recycling Corp. [*Associated Press*] (SAG)
PRINSYS....... Product Information System (IAA)
PRINT .... Preedited Interpreter (IAA)
PRINT .... Pre-Edited Interpretive System [*Computer science*]
print.......... Printing (WDMC)
PRINT .... Public Release of Information and Transcripts [*Student legal action organization*]
PRINTG....... Printing
printout....... Printer Output [*Computer science*] (CDE)
PRINTR....... Printer
PRINUL....... Puerto Rico International Undersea Laboratory
PRIO .... International Peace Research Institution, Oslo [*Norway*]
PRIO .... Priority [*Telecommunications*]
PRION .... Proteinaceous Infectious Particle
PRIOR........ Program for In-Orbital Rendezvous [*Antisatellite system*] [*Air Force*]
PRIP .... Park Restoration and Improvement Program [*National Park Service*]
PRIP .... Parts Reliability Improvement Program
PRIP .... Planned Retirement Income Program [*Institute of Financial Management*]
PRIPACSEVOCAM... Primary Pacific Secure Voice Communications [*Navy*] (CAAL)
PRIPP .... Pacific Research Institute for Public Policy (EA)
PRIRA .... Primary RADAR (FAAC)
PRIS .... Pacific Range Instrumentation Satellite (MUGU)
PRIS .... Pest Management Research Information System [*Agriculture Canada*] [*Information service or system*] (IID)
PRIS .... Prison (ROG)
PRIS .... Prisoner (AFM)
PRIS .... Program Resource Information System [*Department of Agriculture*]
PRIS .... Propeller Revolution Indicator System (MSA)
PRISCO....... Price Stabilization Corp.
PRISE .... Page Reader Input System with Editing (NVT)
PRISE .... Pennsylvania Resources and Information Center for Special Education [*Montgomery County Intermediate Unit*] [*King of Prussia*] [*Information service or system*] (IID)
PRISE .... Pennsylvania's Regional Instruction System for Education [*Network of colleges and universities*]
PRISE .... Program for Integrated Shipboard Electronics
PRISIC........ Photographic Reconnaissance Interpretation Section [*Squadron*] IntelligenceCenter [*JICPOA*]
PRISM .... Parameter Related Internal Standard Method [*Statistical procedure*]
PRISM .... Paraxial-Ray Imaging Spectro Microscope
PRISM .... Partnership for Regulatory Innovation and Sustainable Manufacturing
PRISM .... Pattern Recognition Information Synthesis Modeling [*Market analysis*]
PRISM .... Peace and Reconciliation Inter-Schools Movement (AIE)
PRISM .... Pediatric Risk of Mortality [*Medicine*]
PRISM .... Pediatric Risk of Mortality Score [*Medicine*] (STED)
PRISM .... Personnel Record Information Systems for Management
PRISM .... Personnel Related Information System for Management (NITA)
PRISM .... Personnel Requirements Information System Methodology (NVT)
PRISM .... Photorefractive Information Storage Materials Consortium (CDE)
PRISM .... Pittsburgh Research-Based Instructional Supervising Model (EDAC)
PRISM .... Plant Risk Status Information Management System [*Environmental science*] (COE)
PRISM .... Pliocene Research, Interpretations and Synoptic Mapping [*Climatology*]
PRISM .... Powerful Resource for Information and System Management [*Computer science*] (IAA)
PRISM .... Power Reactor Inherently Safe Module [*Nuclear energy*]
PRISM .... Power Reactor Innovation Small Module [*Nuclear energy*]
PRISM .... Priorities in School Mathematics Project (EDAC)
Prism .... Prism Group [*Associated Press*] (SAG)
PRISM .... Programmable Integrated Scripts for MIRROR [*Management Information Reporting and review of Operational Resources Systems*] [*Computer Language*] (PCM)
PRISM .... Programmed Integrated System Maintenance (NG)
PRISM .... Program Reliability Information System for Management [*Polaris*]
PRISM .... Progressive Refinement of Integrated Supply Management (AFM)

PRISM .... Projection and Integrated Standalone Monitor [*Dolch Computer Systems*] [*Computer science*] (PCM)
PrismEnt...... Prism Entertainment Corp. [*Associated Press*] (SAG)
PRISM Internatl... Professional Records and Information Services Management International (NTPA)
PrismS........ Prism Solutions [*Associated Press*] (SAG)
PRISN......... Prime Stock Number
PRISNET ...... Private Switching Network Service [*Telecommunications*]
Prison L Reptr... Prison Law Reporter [*A publication*] (ILCA)
Prison L Rptr... Prison Law Reporter [*A publication*] (DLA)
Prison Serv J... Prison Service Journal [*A publication*] (DLA)
PRISS .... Post Deployment Software Support Real-Time Interactive Simulation System
PRISSECIMP... Primary Secondary Impedance (IAA)
PrissSys ..... Peerless Systems Corp. [*Associated Press*] (SAG)
PRIST .... Paper Radioimmunosorbent Test [*Analytical biochemistry*]
Pritch Adm Dig... Pritchard's Admiralty Digest [*3rd ed.*] [*1887*] [*A publication*] (DLA)
Pritch M & D... Pritchard's Divorce and Matrimonial Causes [*3rd ed.*] [*1874*] [*A publication*] (DLA)
Pritch Quar Sess... Pritchard's Quarter Sessions [*A publication*] (DLA)
PRITX .... Price T. Rowe: Intl. Stock [*Mutual fund ticker symbol*] (SG)
priv .... Private (STED)
PRIV .... Private
PRIV .... Privative
PRIV .... Privilege
PRIVAUTH ... Travel Authorized via Privately-Owned Vehicle with Understanding No Additional Cost to Government Involved
Priv C App.. Privy Council Appeals [*England*] [*A publication*] (DLA)
Priv CDI..... Indian Privy Council Decisions [*A publication*] (DLA)
Priv Counc App... Privy Council Appeals [*England*] [*A publication*] (DLA)
Priv Counc DI... Privy Council Decisions [*India*] [*A publication*] (DLA)
PRIVE .... Private (ROG)
Priv Hous Fin... Private Housing Finance [*A publication*] (DLA)
Priv Lond... Privilegia Londini [*A publication*] (DLA)
Priv Maintd... Privately Maintained [*Nautical charts*]
PRIV PROP... Private Property [*Military*] (DNAB)
PRIVX .... Private Exchange (IAA)
PRIZE.......... Program for Research in Information Systems Engineering [*University of Michigan*] [*Research center*] (RCD)
Prize CR ...... Prize Court Reports [*South Africa*] [*A publication*] (DLA)
PRIZM .... Potential Rating Index by ZIP [*Zone Improvement Plan*] Market [*Advertising*]
PRJ............. Aero Servicios Pro-Bajio, SA de CV [*Mexico*] [*FAA designator*] (FAAC)
PRJ............. American Junior College of Puerto Rico, Bayamon, PR [*OCLC symbol*] (OCLC)
PRJ............. Capri [*Italy*] [*Airport symbol*] (AD)
PRJ............. Payroll Journal [*Accounting*]
PRJ............. Port Royal [*Jamaica*] [*Seismograph station code, US Geological Survey*] (SEIS)
PRJC.......... Pearl River Junior College [*Poplarville, MS*]
PRJC.......... Puerto Rico Junior College
PRJMP........ Pressure Jump [*NWS*] (FAAC)
PRK .... Democratic People's Republic of Korea [*ANSI three-letter standard code*] (CNC)
PRK .... Paraskevi [*Lesbos*] [*Greece*] [*Seismograph station code, US Geological Survey*] (SEIS)
PRK .... Park
PRK .... Park National Corp. [*AMEX symbol*] (SAG)
PRK .... Parkside Petroleum, Inc. [*Toronto Stock Exchange symbol Vancouver Stock Exchange symbol*]
PRK .... People's Republic of Kampuchea [*From 1979 to 1989*] [*Formerly, Cambodia*] [*Later, SOC*] (PD)
PRK .... Phase Reversal Keying [*Computer science*] (IAA)
PRK .... Photorefractive Keratectomy [*Ophthalmology*]
PRK .... Photorefractive Keratectomy
PRK .... Pridie Kalendas [*The Day before the Calends*] [*Latin*]
PRK .... Primary Rabbit Kidney [*Medicine*] (DMAA)
PRK .... Primary Rat Kidney [*Cells*]
PRKC.......... Protein Kinase C (DMAA)
PRKCA........ Protein Kinase C Alpha (DMAA)
PRKG.......... Parking
PRKO.......... Progesterone Receptor Knockout [*Mouse strain*]
PRKR.......... Parkervision, Inc. [*NASDAQ symbol*] (SAG)
PRL............. Aviaprima [*Russian Federation*] [*ICAO designator*] (FAAC)
PRL............. Pacht, Ross et Al, Los Angeles, CA [*OCLC symbol*] (OCLC)
PRL............. Page Revision Log (NASA)
PRL............. Parallel (MSA)
PRL............. Partido Radical Liberal [*Radical Liberal Party*] [*Ecuador*] [*Political party*]
PRL............. Parti Reformateur Liberal [*Liberal Reform Party*] [*Belgium Political party*] (PPW)
PRL............. Parti Republicain de la Liberte [*Republican Party for Liberty*] [*France Political party*] (PPE)
PRL............. Parti Republicain de la Liberte [*Republican Party for Liberty*] [*Burkina Faso*] [*Political party*]
PRL............. Parts Requirement List (KSC)
PRL............. Paul Revere [*NYSE symbol*] (SPSG)
PRL............. Peace Research Laboratory [*Later, LPRL*] [*An association*] (EA)
prl............. Pearl (VRA)
PRL............. Personnel Research Laboratory [*Lackland Air Force Base, TX*]
PRL............. Pesticide Research Laboratory and Graduate Study Center [*Pennsylvania State University*] [*Research center*] (RCD)

PRL.............. Petroleum Refining Laboratory [*Pennsylvania State University*] (MCD)
PRL.............. Philco Resources [*Vancouver Stock Exchange symbol*]
PRL.............. Philips Research Laboratories (NITA)
PRL.............. Photoreactivating Light
PRL.............. Physical Review Letters [*A publication*]
PRL.............. Physical Review Letters (AAEL)
PRL.............. Physiological Research Laboratories [*University of California at San Diego*] [*Research center*]
PRL.............. Pioneering Research Laboratory [*Massachusetts*] [*Army*]
PRL.............. Planning Requirements List (MCD)
PRL.............. Plastics Research Laboratory [*MIT*] (MCD)
PRL.............. Polar Research Laboratory [*USA*] [*Marine science*] (OSRA)
PRL.............. Political Risk Letter [*Database*] [*Frost & Sullivan, Inc.*] [*Information service or system*] (CRD)
PRLan... Population Research Laboratory [*University of Alberta*] [*Research center*] (RCD)
PRL.............. Postal Reform League (IAA)
PRL.............. Preamble
PRL.............. Precision Reduction Laboratory (AFM)
PRL.............. Predicted Repair Level (MCD)
PRL.............. Pressure Ratio Limiter (MCD)
PRL.............. Priority Rate Limiting (MCD)
PRL.............. Progressive Republican League
PRL.............. Project Research Laboratory
PRL.............. Prolactin [*Also, LTH, PR*] [*Endocrinology*]
Prl.............. Prolactin (STED)
PRL.............. Properties Research Laboratory [*Purdue University*] [*Lafayette, IN*]
PRL.............. Propulsion Research Laboratory
PRL.............. Proton Reference Level [*Chemistry*]
PRL.............. Publications Requirements List (NG)
PRL.............. Pulse-Reflection Logic (IAA)
PRLA .... Prairie Religious Library Association
PRLA .... Pupils React to Light and Accommodation [*Medicine*] (STED)
PrLas... Premier Laser Systems, Inc. [*Associated Press*] (SAG)
PR Laws Ann... Laws of Puerto Rico, Annotated [*A publication*] (DLA)
PRLC .... Pittsburgh Regional Library Center [*Chatham College*] [*Pittsburgh, PA*] [*Library network*]
PRLCA .... Power Research Library of Contemporary Art [*University of Sydney, Australia*]
PRLDEF .... Puerto Rican Legal Defense and Education Fund (EA)
PRLI............ Purchase Request Line Item [*DoD*]
PRLINK....... Public Relations Society of America Online Information Service (IID)
PRLN .... Paracelsian, Inc. [*NASDAQ symbol*] (SAG)
Pr Ln .... Prior Lien [*Business term*] (MHDW)
PRLNW....... Paracelsian Inc. Wrrt [*NASDAQ symbol*] (TTSB)
PRLO .... Prologic Management Systems, Inc. [*NASDAQ symbol*] (SAG)
PRLO .... PROLOGIC Mgmt Sys [*NASDAQ symbol*] (TTSB)
PRLOW....... PROLOGIC Mgmt Sys Wrrt [*NASDAQ symbol*] (TTSB)
PRLP .... Planetary Rocket Launcher Platform (AAG)
PRLP .... Puerto Rico Legal Project [*of the National Lawyers Guild*] (EA)
PRLR .... Parlor
PRLS .... Peerless Systems Corp. [*NASDAQ symbol*] (SAG)
PRLS .... Pima Regional Library Service [*Library network*]
PRLS .... Pulsed Ruby LASER System
PRLST .... Price List
PRLTRL & M... Printer, Lithographer, and Multilith Operator [*Navy*]
PRLW .... Parti des Reformes et de la Liberte de Wallonie [*Belgium Political party*] (PPW)
PRLX .... Parallax (AAG)
PRLX .... Parlex Corp. [*NASDAQ symbol*] (NQ)
PRM.............. Panarim Resources, Inc. [*Vancouver Stock Exchange symbol*]
PRM.............. Parameter (ECII)
PRM.............. Parma Byzantine [*Diocesan abbreviation*] [*Ohio*] (TOCD)
Prm.............. Parmenides [*of Plato*] [*Classical studies*] (OCD)
PRM.............. Parsons Mountain [*South Carolina*] [*Seismograph station code, US Geological Survey*] (SEIS)
PRM.............. Partially Reflecting Mirror
PRM.............. Partially Regulated Module
PRM.............. Partial Response Method
PRM.............. Payload Retention Mechanism [*NASA*] (NASA)
PRM.............. Period of Reduced Melting [*Climatology*]
PRM.............. Personal Radiation Monitor
PRM.............. Petition [*or Proposal*] for Rule Making (NRCH)
PRM.............. Phosphoribomutase [*An enzyme*] (MAE)
PRM.............. Photoreceptor Membrane [*Of the eye*]
PRM.............. Pilots Radio Manual
PRM.............. Pit Rib Meristem [*Botany*]
PRM.............. Posigrade Rocket Motor (NASA)
PRM.............. Power Range Monitor (IEEE)
PRM.............. Precision Runway Monitor [*FAA*] (TAG)
PRM.............. Preformed Road Markings [*Road markings embedded in the pavement rather than painted on street's surface*]
PRM.............. Preliminary Requirements Model [*NASA*]
PRM.............. Prematurely Ruptured Membrane [*Medicine*] (STED)
PRM.............. Premature [*or Prolonged*] Rupture of Membranes [*Gynecology*] (MAE)
PRM.............. Premium
PRM.............. Presbyterian Renewal Ministries (EA)
PRM.............. Presidential Review Memorandum [*Jimmy Carter Administration*]
PRM.............. Pressure Monitoring Module [*Mechanical engineering*]
PRM.............. Pressure Remanent Magnetization
PRM.............. Prevention Reference Manuals [*Environmental science*] (COE)
PRM.............. Preventive Medicine (MAE)
PRM.............. Primary Reference Material [*Medicine*] (MAE)
PRM.............. Primary Reference Material [*Library science*] (DAVI)

PRM.............. Prime (AAG)
PRM.............. Prime Air, Inc. [*ICAO designator*] (FAAC)
PRM.............. PRIMEDIA, Inc. [*NYSE symbol*] [*Formerly, K-III Communications*] (SG)
PRM.............. Primidone [*Antiepileptic drug*]
PRM.............. Process Radiation Monitor [*Nuclear energy*] (NRCH)
PRM.............. Programmer Reference Manual [*Computer science*]
PRM.............. Programming and Resources Management [*NASA*] (MCD)
PRM.............. Promote (AABC)
PRM.............. Publications Requirements Manager [*DoD*]
PRM.............. Puerto Lopez [*Colombia*] [*Airport symbol*] (AD)
PRM.............. Pulse Rate Modulation
PRMA .... Primadonna Resorts [*NASDAQ symbol*] (TTSB)
PRMA .... Primadonna Resorts, Inc. [*NASDAQ symbol*] (SAG)
PrMan.......... Prayer of Manasses [*Apocrypha*] (BJA)
PRMAR .... Primary Mission Area [*Military*] (CAAL)
PrmBcp........ Prime Bancorp, Inc. [*Associated Press*] (SAG)
PrmBn .... Premier Bankshares Corp. [*Associated Press*] (SAG)
PRMC .... Paper and Plastic Representatives Management Council (NTPA)
PRMC .... Periodically Replenished Magma Chambers [*Geology*]
PRMC .... Puerto Rican Migration Consortium (EA)
PRMD .... Private Management Domain [*Telecommunications*] (OSI)
PRME .... Prime Retail [*NASDAQ symbol*] (TTSB)
PRME .... Prime Retail, Inc. [*NASDAQ symbol*] (SAG)
PrmEgy........ Prime Energy [*Associated Press*] (SAG)
PrmeMd....... Prime Medics [*Associated Press*] (SAG)
PRMEP .... Prime Retail 8.5%Ptc Cv'B'Pfd [*NASDAQ symbol*] (TTSB)
PrmFar .... Premier Farnell PLC [*Associated Press*] (SAG)
PRMG .... Piston Ring Manufacturers Group [*Later, NEPMA*] (EA)
PRM GR .... Permanent Grade (DNAB)
PRMGX .... Principal Balanced Fund Cl.A [*Mutual fund ticker symbol*] (SG)
PRMH .... Parti Republicain Modere Haitien [*Political party*] (EY)
PRMH .... Profoundly Retarded Multiply Handicapped (AIE)
PrmHsp........ Prime Hospitality Corp. [*Associated Press*] (SAG)
Prmian......... Permian Basin Royalty Trust [*Associated Press*] (SAG)
Pr Min .... Printed Minutes of Evidence [*A publication*] (DLA)
PR/MIPR....... Purchase Request/Military Interdepartmental Purchase Request (AFIT)
PRMIS .... Printing Resources Management Information System (DNAB)
Prmisy......... Premisys Communications [*Associated Press*] (SAG)
Prmk........... Paramark Enterprises, Inc. [*Associated Press*] (SAG)
PRML.......... Partial Response Maximum Likelihood [*Computer science*]
PrmLasr....... Premier Laser Systems, Inc. [*Associated Press*] (SAG)
PRMLD .... Premolded [*Technical drawings*] (MSA)
PrMLtd........ Prime Motor Inns Ltd. [*Associated Press*] (SAG)
PRMO .... Premenos Technology [*NASDAQ symbol*] (TTSB)
PRMO .... Premenos Technology Corp. [*NASDAQ symbol*] (SAG)
PrmosT........ Premenos Technology Corp. [*Associated Press*] (SAG)
PRMP .... Plutonium Recovery Modification Project [*Department of Energy*]
PRMP .... Production Readiness Master Plan
PrmPks........ Premier Parks, Inc. [*Associated Press*] (SAG)
PRMR .... Pitch Rate/Moment Ratio [*Automotive engineering*]
PRMR .... Primer (MSA)
PrmRad........ Premier Radio Network [*Associated Press*] (SAG)
PrmBc......... Premier Bancorp, Inc. [*Associated Press*] (SAG)
PrmRetl....... Prime Retail, Inc. [*Associated Press*] (SAG)
PrmRtl .... Prime Retail, Inc. [*Associated Press*] (SAG)
PRMS .... Premisys Communications [*NASDAQ symbol*] (SAG)
PRM-SDX ..... Pyrimethamine-Sulfadoxine [*Pharmacology*] (DAVI)
PrmsH .... Promus Hotel Corp. [*Associated Press*] (SAG)
PRMSS .... Patriotic Resistance Movement of South Sudan
PRMSS .... Patriotic Resistance Movement of South Sudan [*Political party*]
PRMTR .... Parameter (AAG)
PRMV .... Peach Rosette Mosaic Virus [*Plant pathology*]
PRMX .... Primex Technologies, Inc. [*NASDAQ symbol*] (SAG)
PRN .... Greenville, AL [*Location identifier FAA*] (FAAL)
PRN .... Packet Radio Network [*Telecommunications*] (OSI)
PRN .... Pahrock Range [*Nevada*] [*Seismograph station code, US Geological Survey*] (SEIS)
PRN .... Park Reverse Neutral [*Automotive engineering*]
PRN .... Partido de la Resistencia Nicaraguense [*Political party*] (EY)
PRN .... Partido de la Revolucion Nacional [*Party of the National Revolution*] [*Bolivia*] [*Political party*] (PPW)
PRN .... Partido de Reconstrucao Nacional [*Brazil Political party*] (EY)
PRN .... Partido Republicano Nacional [*National Republican Party*] [*Costa Rica*] [*Political party*]
PRN .... Parts Requirement Notice (KSC)
PRN .... Peace Research Network [*Later, PSA*] (EA)
PRN .... Peace RES Network (EA)
PRN .... Physicians Radio Network
PRN .... Polyradiculoneuropathy [*Medicine*] (DB)
PRN .... Previous Result Negative (IAA)
PRN .... Pridie Nonas [*The Day before the Nones*] [*Latin*]
PRN .... Princess Air [*British ICAO designator*] (FAAC)
PRN .... Printer [*Computer science*]
PRN .... Print Numerically (DEN)
PRN .... Pristina [*Former Yugoslavia*] [*Airport symbol*] (OAG)
PRN .... PR Newswire [*PR Newswire, Inc.*] [*Information service or system*] (IID)
PRN .... Procurement Reallocation Notice
PRN .... Program Release Notice [*NASA*] (NASA)
PRN .... Prominent Resources Corp. [*Vancouver Stock Exchange symbol*]
PRN .... Pronasale [*Anatomy*]
PRN .... Pro Re Nata [*Whenever Necessary*] [*Pharmacy*]
PRN .... Pseudorandom Noise

PRN	Pseudorandom Number
PRN	Puerto Rican Cement [*NYSE symbol*] (TTSB)
PRN	Puerto Rican Cement Co., Inc. [*NYSE symbol*] (SPSG)
PRN	Pulse Ranging Navigation
PRN	Pulse Ranging Network (KSC)
PRN	Purchase Request Notice [*Banking*]
PRN	Purchase Request Number
pRNA	Ribonucleic Acid, Polysomal [*Biochemistry, genetics*]
PRNC	Potomac River Naval Command [*Washington, DC*]
PRNC	Prince
PRNC	Puerto Rico Nuclear Center
PRNDI	Public Radio News Directors (NTPA)
PRNDL	Park, Reverse, Neutral, Drive, Low [*Automotive term for automatic gearshift indicator in cars; pronounced "prindle"*]
PrnDn	Princeton Dental Management Corp. [*Associated Press*] (SAG)
PrnDnt	Princeton Dental Management Corp. [*Associated Press*] (SAG)
PRNET	Packet Radio Network
PRNEX	Price T. Rowe: New Era [*Mutual fund ticker symbol*] (SG)
PRNG	Paper Negative (VRA)
PRNG	Purging (MSA)
PRNHX	Price T. Rowe: New Horizons [*Mutual fund ticker symbol*] (SG)
PRNI	Premiere Radio Networks [*NASDAQ symbol*] (TTSB)
PRNI	Premier Radio Network [*NASDAQ symbol*] (SAG)
PRNIA	Premiere Radio Networks 'A' [*NASDAQ symbol*] (TTSB)
prnnl	Perennial [*Botany*]
PRNP	Prion Protein (DMAA)
PRNS	Prins Recycling [*NASDAQ symbol*] (TTSB)
PRNS	Prins Recycling Corp. [*NASDAQ symbol*] (SAG)
PRNT	Plaque Reduction Neutralization Test [*Immunochemistry*]
PRNTG	Printing (MSA)
PRNTR	Printer
PRNTV	Preventive
PRNU	Photoresponse Nonuniformity
PRO	Pacific Research Office (CINC)
PRO	Parallel Rod Oscillator
PRO	Parents Reaching Out [*An association*] (EA)
PRO	Parents Rights Organization (EA)
PRO	Particle Reduction Oven
PRO	Parts Release Order
PRO	Patients' Rights Organization (EA)
PRO	Pay and Records Office [*British military*] (DMA)
PRO	Peer Review Organization [*Medicare*]
PRO	Pen Recorder Output (SAA)
PRO	Performing Rights Organization [*Formerly, BMI-Canada Ltd.*] [*Canada*]
PRO	Perry, IA [*Location identifier FAA*] (FAAL)
PRO	Personnel Relations Officer [*for Shore Stations*] [*Navy*]
PR/O	Pilot Repair/Overhaul [*Military*]
PRO	Pitch Response Operator
PRO	Planned Requirements, Outfitting [*Navy*] (NG)
PRO	Planning Rooident Order (KSC)
PRO	Plant Representative Officer (MCD)
PRO	Population Renewal Office
PRO	Procision RISC [*Reduced Instruction Set Computer*] Organization
Pro	Prednisone [*Also, P, PDN, PR, Pred*] [*Antineoplastic drug, Endocrinology*]
PRO	Principal Public Library [*Library network*]
PRO	Print Octal (DEN)
PRO	Probate
PRO	Probation [*or Probationer*]
PRO	Probation Services for Adults (PHSD)
PRO	Problem Resolution Office [*IRS*]
PRO	Procedure (AABC)
PRO	Proceed (NAKS)
Pro	Proculus [*Flourished, 1st century*] [*Authority cited in pre-1607 legal work*] (DSA)
PRO	Procurement Research Office [*Army*]
PRO	Production Repair Order
PRO	Professional
pro	Professional (ODBW)
PRO	Professional Dental Technologies, Inc. [*AMEX symbol*] (SAG)
PRO	Professional Racing Organization of America [*Later, USCF*] (EA)
PRO	Professional Resellers Organization [*Defunct*] (EA)
PRO	Professional Review Organization [*Medicare*]
PRO	Proficiency
PRO	Proflavine [*An antiseptic*]
PRO	Programmable Remote Operation [*Computer Devices, Inc.*]
PRO	Program Representative Office (AAGC)
PRO	Progressive
Pro	Proline [*Also, P*] [*An amino acid*]
pro	Proline [*An amino acid*] (DOG)
Pro	Prolyl [*Biochemistry*]
PRO	Pronation [*Medicine*]
PRO	Pronoun [*Grammar*] (WGA)
PRO	Pronto Explorations Ltd. [*Toronto Stock Exchange symbol*]
PRO	Propagation [*Military*]
PRO	Propagation Prediction Report (SAA)
PRO	Propair, Inc. [*Canada ICAO designator*] (FAAC)
PRO	Propeller Order
PRO	Prophylactic (AABC)
PRO	Prostitute (ADA)
Pro	Protein
Pro	Protest
Pro	Protest (EBF)
Pro	Prothrombin [*Factor II*] [*Hematology*]

PRO	Proved
pro	Provencal [*MARC language code Library of Congress*] (LCCP)
Pro	Proverbs [*Old Testament book*] (BJA)
PRO	Providence [*Diocesan abbreviation*] [*Rhode Island*] (TOCD)
PRO	Province (ROG)
PRO	Provost
PRO	Public Record Office [*British*]
PRO	Public Relations Office [*or Officer*] [*Usually military*]
PRO	Puchase Request Order
PROA	Polymer Research Corp. of America [*NASDAQ symbol*] (NQ)
PROA	Polymer Resh America [*NASDAQ symbol*] (TTSB)
PROA	Puerto Rico Operations Area
ProActiv	ProActive Technologies, Inc. [*Associated Press*] (SAG)
PRO-AM	Professional-Amateur (WDAA)
pro-am	Professionals and Amateurs [*Sports*] (WDMC)
PROAP	Principal Regional Office for Asia and the Pacific [*UNESCO*]
Prob	English Probate and Admiralty Reports for Year Cited [*A publication*] (DLA)
Prob	Law Reports, Probate Division [*England*] [*A publication*] (DLA)
PROB	Probability (KSC)
prob	Probable
PROB	Probably
prob	Probably (VRA)
Prob	Probate [*Legal term*] (DLA)
PROB	Probation [*FBI standardized term*]
PROB	Problem
Prob	Quod Omnis Probus Liber Sit [*of Philo*] (BJA)
PROB40	Probability 40 Percent [*ICAO*] (FAAC)
Prob (1891)	Law Reports, Probate Division [*1891*] [*England*] [*A publication*] (DLA)
Prob & Adm Div	Probate and Admiralty Division Law Reports [*A publication*] (DLA)
Prob & Div	Probate and Divorce, English Law Reports [*A publication*] (DLA)
Prob & Mat	Probate and Matrimonial Cases [*A publication*] (DLA)
Probat	Probation [*Legal term*] (DLA)
Probation & Parole L Rep	Probation and Parole Law Reports [*A publication*] (DLA)
Probation & Parole L Summ	Probation and Parole Law Summaries [*A publication*] (DLA)
Probat J	Probation Journal [*A publication*] (ILCA)
Prob C	Probate Code [*A publication*] (DLA)
PROBCOST	Probabilistic Budgeting and Forward Costing
Prob Ct Rep	Probate Court Reporter [*Ohio*] [*A publication*] (DLA)
PROBDET	Probability of Detection [*Navy*] (NVT)
Prob Div	Probate Division, English Law Reports [*A publication*] (DLA)
PROBE	Performance Review of Base Supply Effectiveness [*Air Force*] (AFM)
PROBE	Pilot Radiation Observation Experiment [*Marine science*] (OSRA)
PROBE	Practical Research into Organizational Behavior and Effectiveness (EDAC)
PROBE	Profile Resolution Obtained by Excitation (PDAA)
PROBE	Program for Research on Objectives-Based Evaluation [*UCLA*]
PROBE	Program Optimization and Budget Evaluation [*Military*]
PROBES	Processes and Resources of the Bering Sea Shelf [*University of Alaska*]
PROBFOR	Probability Forecasting [*Computer program*] [*Bell System*]
PROBIT	Probability Unit [*Statistics*]
Prob J	Probation Journal [*A publication*] (DLA)
Prob LT	Probyn on Land Tenure [*4th ed.*] [*1881*] [*A publication*] (DLA)
PROBO	Product/Ore/Bulk/Oil Carrier [*Shipping*] (DS)
PROBOUT	Proceed On or About (MUGU)
Prob Pr Act	Probate Practice Act [*A publication*] (DLA)
Prob R	Probate Reports [*A publication*] (DLA)
Prob Rep	Probate Reports [*A publication*] (DLA)
Prob Rep Ann	Probate Reports, Annotated [*A publication*] (DLA)
PROBSUB	Probable Submarine (NVT)
PROBUS	Program Budget System [*Military*]
Proby	Probationary [*British military*] (DMA)
PROC	Performing Rights Organization of Canada [*See also SDE*]
PROC	Preliminary Required Operational Capability [*Military*]
PROC	Procedure (AAG)
PROC	Proceedings
proc	Proceedings (WDMC)
proc	Process (VRA)
PROC	Process (AABC)
Proc	Processes (AL)
Proc	Processing (AL)
PROC	Procession (ROG)
PROC	Processor [*or Processing*]
Proc	Proclamation (DLA)
PROC	Proctor
PROC	Procure (AABC)
PROC	Procurement (MSA)
PROC	Programming Computer [*Computer science*]
PROC	Proposed Required Operational Capability [*Military*] (AABC)
PROC	Protein C (DMAA)
PROCAL	Programmable Calculator [*Computer science*] (IAA)
Proc Amer Soc of Internat L	Proceedings. American Society of International Law [*A publication*] (DLA)
Proc Amp	Processing Amplifier (NTCM)
PRO CAPILL	Pro Capillis [*For the Hair*] [*Pharmacy*]
Procarb	Procarbazine [*Antineoplastic drug*] (DAVI)
PROCAS	Process-Oriented Contract Administration Services
Proc B & B	Proctor's Bench and Bar of New York [*A publication*] (DLA)
Proc Ch	Proceedings in Chancery [*A publication*] (DLA)
PROCCIR	Procurement Circular [*Air Force*] (AFIT)

Proc Cir .... Procurement Circular (AAGC)
PROCD.......... Procedure (AFM)
PROCD.......... Proceed (AFM)
PROCDRE ...... Procedure (ROG)
PROCED .... Procedure
Proc Elec Assoc Aust... Proceedings. Electrical Association of Australia [A publication]
Proc Elec Assoc NSW... Proceedings. Electrical Association of New South Wales [Australia A publication]
Proc Eng Assoc NSW... Proceedings. Engineering Association of New South Wales [Australia A publication]
Procept........ Procept, Inc. [Associated Press] (SAG)
PROCIEE...... Proceedings of the Institute of Electrical Engineers [A publication] (IAA)
Proc Inst Criminol Univ Sydney... University of Sydney. Institute of Criminology. Proceedings [A publication]
Proc Instn Radio Eng Aust... Proceedings. Institution of Radio Engineers of Australia [A publication]
PROCLIB...... Procedure Library [Computer science]
Proc Med-Leg Soc Vic... Medico-Legal Society of Victoria. Proceedings [A publication]
Proc Microscopical Soc Vic... Proceedings. Microscopical Society of Victoria [Australia A publication]
ProcmT........ Procom Technology Inc. [Associated Press] (SAG)
Proc Natl Acad Sci USA... Proceedings of the National Academy of Science of the United States of America (MEC)
PROCO......... Procurement Officer [Military]
PROCO......... Programmed Combustion [Ford Motor Co.]
PROCO......... Projects for Continental Operations [World War II]
PROCOL....... Process Control Language (NITA)
PROCOL...... Process Control Oriented Language [Computer science] (IAA)
PROCOM...... Procedures Committee [Institute of Electrical and Electronics Engineers] (IEEE)
PROCOM...... Procurement Committee
PROCOM...... Prognose Compiler [Computer science] (IAA)
PROCOMEXCHI... Mexican-Chicano Cooperative Programs on Mexican-US-Chicano Futures (EA)
PROCOMP ... Process Compiler [Computer science] (IAA)
PROCOMP ... Process Computer [Computer science]
PROCOMP ... Program Compiler [Computer science] (IEEE)
PROCON ..... Protocol Converter (DA)
PROCON ...... Request Diagnosis, Prognosis, Present Condition, Probable Date and Mode of Disposition of Following Patient Reported in Your Hospital [Military]
Procop .... Procopius [Sixth century AD] [Classical studies] (OCD)
PROCOPT ... Processing Option [Computer science] (MHDB)
PROCOTIP ... Promotion Cooperative du Transport Individuel Publique [Public cars for private use to reduce traffic congestion] [Also known as TIP] [France]
Proc Pr .... Proctor's Practice [A publication] (DLA)
Proc Prac..... Proctor's Practice [A publication] (DLA)
Proc Roy Soc Qld... Proceedings. Royal Society of Queensland [Australia A publication]
Proc Roy Soc Vic... Proceedings. Royal Society of Victoria [Australia A publication]
Proc R Soc Edin... Proceedings of the Royal Society of Edinburgh (MEC)
Proc R Soc London... Proceedings of the Royal Society of London (MEC)
PROCS......... Proceedings
Proc Sci Soc Univ Adel... Proceedings. Scientific Society. University of Adelaide [A publication]
PROCSD ...... Processed
PROCSEQ ... Processing Sequence [Computer science] (MHDB)
PROCSIM .... Processor Simulation Language [Computer science] (PDAA)
Proc Soc Chem Indust Vic... Proceedings. Society of Chemical Industry of Victoria [Australia A publication]
PROCT......... Proctology
ProctGm ...... Procter & Gamble Co. [Associated Press] (SAG)
PROCTO....... Proctology [Gastroenterology] (DAVI)
PROCTO....... Proctoscopy [Medicine]
PROCTOR .... Priority Routine Organizer for Computer Transfers and Operations of Registers
PROCTOT..... Priority Routine Organizer for Computer Transfers and Operations and Transfers
PROCU......... Processing Unit
PROCUP ...... Partido Revolucionario Obrerista y Clandestino de Union Popular [Mexico Political party] (EY)
PROCVAL..... Validation Procedures Library [Social Security Administration]
Proc WA Instn Eng... Proceedings. Western Australian Institution of Engineers [A publication]
Procyt.......... ProCyte Corp. [Associated Press] (SAG)
PROD.......... Office of Production [National Security Agency]
PROD.......... Photographic Retrieval from Optical Disk
PROD.......... Produce
prod .... Produce (WDAA)
prod .... Product (WDMC)
PROD.......... Product [or Production] (AABC)
Prod............ Production (AAGC)
prod............ Production (WDMC)
PROD.......... Production (DOMA)
PROD.......... Professional Drivers Council for Safety and Health
PROD.......... Professional Over-the-Road Drivers [Part of Teamsters Union]
PRODAC ..... Production Advisers Consortium (NADA)
PRODAC ...... Programmed Digital Automatic Control [Computer science]
PRODAM...... Production Orientated Draughting and Manufacturing (PDAA)
PRODAN ...... Propionyl(dimethylamino)naphthalene [Organic chemistry]
PRODASE .... Protein Database

Prod Aust..... Productivity Australia [A publication]
PRODC......... Production Command [Army]
PROD/DEPL... Production and Deployment [Phase] (DOMA)
Proden......... Proyecto de Desarrollo Nacional [Project for National Development] [Chile] (PPW)
ProDex........ ProDex, Inc. [Associated Press] (SAG)
PRODISCO.... Producers Distributing Corp.
Prod Liab Int'l... Product Liability International [A publication] (DLA)
Prod Liab Rep... Product Liability Reporter [Commerce Clearing House] [A publication] (DLA)
Prodn.......... Production
PRODN .... Production
PRODNG ...... Producing
ProDnt .... Professional Dental Technologies, Inc. [Associated Press] (SAG)
PRODOC ...... Procedure Documentation [Computer science] (MHDB)
PRODON ..... Production
ProdOp........ Production Operators Corp. [Associated Press] (SAG)
PRO DOS ..... Pro Dose [For a Dose] [Pharmacy]
ProDOS....... Professional Disk Operating System [Computer science]
PRODR .... Producer
Prods .... Products (AAGC)
Prod Safety & Liab Rep... Product Safety and Liability Reporter [A publication] (DLA)
PRODT......... Product
PRODUCE .... Production Distribution Using Component Evaluation (IAA)
Product........ Productivity Technologies Corp. [Associated Press] (SAG)
PRODUCTN... Production
Productv ...... Productivity Technologies Corp. [Associated Press] (SAG)
PRODUTAS... Proceed on Duty Assigned [Military]
PRODVAL ..... Product Validation (MCD)
PROE .... Programme Regional Oceanien de l'Environnement [South Pacific Regional Environmental Programme - SPREP] (EAIO)
PRO.EC........ Professional Dental Tech [ECM, Symbol] (TTSB)
PRO EL .... Protein Electrophoresis [Biochemistry] (DAVI)
Pro Ex.......... Protein Exchange [Dietetics]
PROF .... Peace Research Organization Fund
PROF .... Personal Radio Operators Federation [Defunct] (EA)
PROF .... Prediction and Optimization of Failure Rate (MHDB)
PROF .... Profanity [FBI standardized term]
PROF .... Profession [or Professional]
Prof.............. Professional (AL)
PROF .... Professional Office System
PROF .... Professor (EY)
Prof.............. Professor (ODBW)
PROF .... Profile (GAVI)
prof.............. Profile (VRA)
Prof.............. Profile
PROF .... Pupil Registering and Operational Filing [Computer science]
ProFac .... Pro-Fac Cooperative, Inc. [Associated Press] (SAG)
PROFAC...... Propulsive Fluid Accumulator
PROFACTS.... Production Formulation, Accounting, and Cost System (MHDI)
Prof Admin.... Professional Administrator [A publication]
PROFAGTRANS... Proceed by First Available Government Transportation [Military]
PROFAT .... Projet des Francophones de l'Atlantique [Canada]
pro-fax......... Production Facilities (WDMC)
Pro-Fax........ Production Facility (NTCM)
ProfBTM ...... Professional Business and Technical Management [British] [An association] (DBA)
Prof Burd .... Commemoratio Professorum Burdigalensium [of Ausonius] [Classical studies] (OCD)
Prof Corp ..... Proffatt on Private Corporations in California [A publication] (DLA)
Prof Corp Guide (P-H)... Professional Corporation Guide (Prentice-Hall, Inc.) [A publication] (DLA)
PROFCY...... Proficiency
PROF-E........ Programmed Review of Operator Functions - Elementary (DNAB)
Prof Eng ...... Professional Engineer
Prof Engr ..... Professional Engineer [A publication]
PROFERI...... Programme for Refugee Reintegration and Rehabilitation of Resettlement Areas in Eritrea
PROFESSL.... Professional
PROFFIS ...... Professional Filler System [Military]
Proffitt .... Proffitt's, Inc. [Associated Press] (SAG)
PROFILE ...... Programmed Functional Indices for Laboratory Evaluation [RAND Corp.]
PROFILES .... Personal Reflection on Family Life and Employment Stressors [Psychology]
PROFIS........ Programminformationssystem Sozialwissenschaften [Informationszentrum Sozialwissenschaften] [Germany Defunct Information service or system] (CRD)
PROFIT .... Program for Financed Insurance Techniques
PROFIT .... Programmed Reviewing, Ordering, and Forecasting Inventory Technique
PROFIT .... Propulsion Flight Control Integration Technology (MCD)
Prof Jur .... Proffatt on Trial by Jury [A publication] (DLA)
PROFL .... Professional
PR of MAN ... [The] Prayer of Manasses, King of Judah [Apocrypha]
Prof Not .... Proffatt on Notaries [A publication] (DLA)
Prof Officer... Professional Officer [A publication]
PROFP......... Proficiency Pay [Military]
ProfRec........ Profit Recovery Group International, Inc. (The) [Associated Press] (SAG)
PROFS......... Professional Office System [IBM Corp.]
PROFS......... Program for Regional Observing and Forecasting Services [Boulder, CO] [Department of Commerce] (GRD)

PROFS......... Prototype Regional Observation and Forecasting Service [*National Oceanic and Atmospheric Administration*] (GRD)
Profsnl......... Professional (TBD)
ProfStaff...... Professional Staff [*Associated Press*] (SAG)
Prof Wills.... Proffatt on Wills [*A publication*] (DLA)
PROG........... Peer Review Oversight Group [*National Institutes of Health*]
prog........... Progesterone [*Endocrinology*] (DAVI)
prog........... Prognathism [*Dentistry*] (DAVI)
PROG........... Prognosis [*or Prognostication*] (AAG)
PROG........... Program (KSC)
Prog........... Program (AL)
PROG........... Programmer [*or Programming*]
PROG........... Programmer's Paradise [*NASDAQ symbol*] (TTSB)
PROG........... Programmers Paradise, Inc. [*NASDAQ symbol*] (SAG)
PROG........... Progress (AABC)
Prog........... Progressive [*A publication*] (BRI)
Prog Arch.... Progressive Architecture [*A publication*] (BRI)
PROG BK.... Programmed Book [*Publishing*]
ProgBk........ Progressive Bank, Inc. [*Associated Press*] (SAG)
ProgCp........ Progressive Corp. [*Associated Press*] (SAG)
PROGDEV... Program Device (KSC)
ProgFn........ Progress Financial Corp. [*Associated Press*] (SAG)
PROGLIB...... Production Program Library [*Social Security Administration*]
PRO GM...... Pro Grand Master [*Freemasonry*]
PROGMG..... Programming
PROGN....... Prognosis (AAMN)
PROGNO...... Prognosen-Trends-Entwicklungen [*Forecasts-Trends-Developments*] [*Society for Business Information*] [*Information service or system*] (IID)
PROGOFOP... Program of Operation [*Computer science*]
ProgPar....... Programmers Paradise, Inc. [*Associated Press*] (SAG)
PROGR........ Programmer (ECII)
progr........... Progress (DAVI)
Progrp........ ProGroup, Inc. [*Associated Press*] (SAG)
Progr Polym Sci... Progress in Polymer Science (MEC)
PROGS....... Progressive
PROGS........ Progressive Proofs [*Graphic arts*] (DGA)
PROGVAL...... Validation Program Library [*Social Security Administration*]
PROH......... Prohibit
PROH......... Prohibition [*FBI standardized term*]
Prohib.......... Prohibited
PROI........... CFI ProServices [*NASDAQ symbol*] (TTSB)
PROI........... CFI Proservices, Inc. [*NASDAQ symbol*] (SAG)
PROI........... President of the Royal Institute of Oil Painters [*British*]
PROI........... Project Return on Investment (MHDW)
PRO-IF........ Personal Radio Operators International Federation [*Formerly, ARC*] (EA)
PROIMREP... Proceed Immediately - Report for Purpose Indicated [*Military*]
Pro Indian Soc of Internat L... Proceedings of the Conference. Indian Society of International Law [*New Delhi, India*] [*A publication*] (DLA)
PROJ........... Project
Proj............ Project (TBD)
proj............. Project (VRA)
PROJ........... Projectile (AFM)
PROJ........... Projector [*or Projection*]
PROJACS..... Project Analysis and Control System (MHDI)
PROJECT...... Project Engineering Control
PROJENGR... Project Engineer
PROJID........ Project Identification [*Computer science*]
PROJMGR..... Project Manager [*Military*]
PROJMGRASWS... Project Manager, Antisubmarine Warfare Systems
PROJMGRFBM... Project Manager, Fleet Ballistic Missile [*Navy*]
PROJMGRSMS... Project Manager, Surface Missile Systems [*Navy*]
ProjSft......... Project Software & Development, Inc. [*Associated Press*] (SAG)
projt............ Projector (VRA)
PROJTRNS... Project Transition [*DoD*]
PROL........... Priority Requirement Objective List (AFM)
Prol............ Prologic Management Systems, Inc. [*Associated Press*] (SAG)
PROL........... Prologue
prol............. Prologue (WDAA)
PRO L......... Province Laws (DLA)
PROLAC...... Prolactin [*Biochemistry*] (DAVI)
PROLAMAT... Programming Languages for Machine Tools [*Conference*]
PROLAMAT... Programming Languages for Numerically Controlled Machine Tools [*Conference*] [*Computer science*] (IAA)
PROLAN...... Processed Language [*Computer science*]
PROLE........ Proletarian (WDAA)
Proler.......... Proler International Corp. [*Associated Press*] (SAG)
Prolif........... Proliferative [*or Proliferation*]
PROLLAP.... Professional Library Literature Acquisition Program
PRO LOC et TEM... Pro Loco et Tempore [*For the Place and Time*] [*Latin*] (ROG)
PROLOG...... Production of Onshore Lower 48 Oil and Gas Model [*Department of Energy*] (GFGA)
PROLOG...... Program Logistics (NG)
PROLOG...... Programming in Logic [*Programing language*] [*1970*]
PROLOG...... Project Logic Planning (IAA)
Prolog........ Prologic Management Systems, Inc. [*Associated Press*] (SAG)
Prologc....... Prologic Management Systems, Inc. [*Associated Press*] (SAG)
Prologic....... Prologic Management Systems, Inc. [*Associated Press*] (SAG)
prolong........ Prolongatus [*Prolonged*] [*Latin*] (DAVI)
PROLT........ Procurement Lead Time
PROM......... Passive Range of Motion [*Medicine*]
PROM......... Pockels Readout Optical Modulator
PROM......... Premature [*or Prolonged*] Rupture of Membranes [*Gynecology*]
PROM......... Programmable Read-Only Memory [*Computer science*]

PROM......... Program, Resources, Objectives, Management [*Air Force Systems Command technique*]
PROM......... Progressive Range of Motion [*Medicine*]
PROM......... Prolonged Rupture of Membranes [*Gynecology*] (DAVI)
PROM......... Promenade [*Maps and charts*]
prom......... Promenade (DD)
PROM......... Prominent
PROM......... Promise [*Legal shorthand*] (LWAP)
Prom......... Promissory [*A publication*] (DLA)
PROM......... Promontory
PROM......... Promote [*or Promotion*] (AFM)
PROM......... Promotion
PROM......... Promulgate (AABC)
Pro-MACE.... Prednisone, Methotrexate with Leucovorin, Adriamycin, Cyclophosphamide, Epipodophyllin [*Etoposide, VP-16*] [*Antineoplastic drug regimen*]
PROMACE-MOPP... Procarbazine, Methotrexate, Adriamycin, Cyclophosphamide, Etoposide, Mustargen [*Nitrogen mustard*], Oncovin , Procarbazine, Prednisone [*Vincristine*] [*Antineoplastic drug regimen*]
PROMAG...... Production Management Action Group [*British*]
PROMAP...... Program for the Refinement of the Materiel Acquisition Process [*Army*] (AABC)
PROMAR...... Program on the Promotion of Marine Sciences [*Marine science*] (OSRA)
PROMAST.... Production Master Scheduling System (PDAA)
PROMATS.... Probabilistic Materials System (PDAA)
Prom dk...... Promenade Deck [*of a ship*] (DS)
ProMED...... Program to Monitor Emerging Diseases
PROMEE...... Promisee [*Legal shorthand*] (LWAP)
PROMETHEUS... Program for European Traffic with Highest Efficiency and Unprecedented Safety (ECON)
PROMEX...... Productivity Measurement Experiment [*National Institute of Standards and Technology*]
PROMIM...... Programmable Multiple Ion Monitor
PROMIS...... Problem-Oriented Medical Information System [*Computerized patient-management system*]
PROMIS...... Process Management and Information System [*I. P. Sharp Associates Ltd.*] [*Software package*] (NCC)
PROMIS...... Project Management Integrated System (NITA)
PROMIS...... Project-Oriented Management Information System
PROMIS...... Prosecutor's Management Information System [*Law Enforcement Assistance Administration*]
PROMISE..... Programming Managers Information System (MHDI)
PROMISE..... Prospective Randomized Milrinone Survival Evaluation [*Medicine*]
PROMISS..... Packaging Requirements for Optimum Malfunction Isolation by Systematic Substitution (IAA)
PROML....... Promulgate
PROMO...... Promotion [*Slang*] (DSUE)
Promo........ Promotional Announcement (NTCM)
PROMOR..... Promisor [*Legal shorthand*] (LWAP)
PROMPT..... Production, Reviewing, Organizing, and Monitoring of Performance Techniques (BUR)
PROMPT..... Program Monitoring and Planning Techniques (IEEE)
PROMPT..... Program Reporting, Organization, and Management Planning Technique (IAA)
PROMPT..... Program to Record Official Mail Point-to-Point Times [*Postal Service program*]
PROMPT..... Project Management and Production Team Technique [*Computer science*]
PROMPT..... Project Reporting Organization and Management Planning Technique
PROMS...... Procurement Management System (MCD)
PROMS...... Programmable Read Only Memory System [*Computer science*]
PROMS...... Program Monitoring System (MCD)
PROMS...... Projectile Measurement System [*Computer science Army*]
PROMSS..... Procedures and Relationships for the Operation of Manual Stations and Spaces (DNAB)
PROM STAT... Promotion Status (DNAB)
PROMT....... Precision Optimized Measurement Time [*Spectroscopy*]
PROMT....... Predicasts Overview of Markets and Terminology (NITA)
PROMT....... Predicasts Overviews of Marketing and Technology [*Business database*]
PROMT....... Programmable Miniature Message Terminal (MCD)
PROMUS..... Provincial-Municipal Simulator [*Computer-based urban management system*]
PROMY...... Promissory (ROG)
PRON......... Patriotyczny Ruch Odrodzenia Narodowego [*Patriotic Movement for National Rebirth*] [*Poland*] (EY)
PRON......... Procurement Request Order Number [*Army*] (AABC)
PRON......... Pronation
PRON......... Pronominal (ADA)
PRON......... Pronoun
PRON......... Pronounced
PRON......... Pronunciation (ROG)
pron......... Pronunciation (WDMC)
PRONED...... Promotion of Non-Executive Directors (ODBW)
Pronet........ ProNet, Inc. [*Associated Press*] (SAG)
Pro-Nica...... Professionals - Nicaragua (EA)
PRO-NICA.... Professionals - Nicaragua [*An association*] (EA)
PRONTO...... Program for Numeric Tool Operation [*Computer science*]
PRONTO...... Programmable Network Telecommunications Operating System
prooem........ Prooemium (BJA)
PROOF....... Precision Recording (Optical) of Fingerprints
PROOF....... Projected Return on Open Office Facilities [*Computer program*]
proOLMC.... Pro-Opiolipomelanocortin [*Endocrinology*]

PRO-OP ...... Project Optimization [*Industrial engineering*]
PROP .... Performance Review for Operating Programs (BUR)
PROP .... Pilot Repair Overhaul and Provisioning (MUGU)
PROP .... Planetary Rocket Ocean Platform
PROP .... Prerelease Orientation Program [*Reformatory program*]
PROP .... Preservation of the Rights of Prisoners [*An association British*]
PROP .... Primary Operand Unit (IAA)
PROP .... Prisoners' Right of Privacy [*British*] (DI)
PROP .... Production Operators [*NASDAQ symbol*] (TTSB)
PROP .... Production Operators Corp. [*NASDAQ symbol*] (NQ)
PROP .... Production Planning (IAA)
PROP .... Profit Rating of Projects
PROP .... Proof of Purchase (WDMC)
PROP .... Propaganda (AFM)
Prop .... Propagate [*Botany*]
PROP .... Propellant (KSC)
PROP .... Propeller
PROP .... Proper
PROP .... Propertius [*Roman poet, c. 29BC*] [*Classical studies*] (ROG)
PROP .... Property
Prop .... Property (TBD)
prop .... Property (WDAA)
PROP .... Property Release Option Program [*HUD*]
PROP .... Proportional (KSC)
PROP .... Proportioning (NAKS)
PROP .... Proposal (AAG)
PROP .... Proposed (AFM)
PROP .... Proposition
PROP .... Propranolol (DB)
PROP .... Proprietor
prop .... Proprietor (WDAA)
PROP .... Propulsion (AAG)
PROP .... Propulsion Engineer (NAKS)
PROP .... Propylthiouracil [*Also, PT, PTU*] [*Thyroid inhibitor*]
PROPAC...... Progressive Political Action Committee [*Defunct*] (EA)
PROPAC...... Prospective Payment Assessment Commission [*Washington, DC*] (EGAO)
ProPAC .... Prospective Payment Assessment Commission
PROPAKASIA... International Food Processing and Packaging Technology Exhibition and Conferencefor South East Asia
PROPAL....... Proportional
Prop & Comp... Property and Compensation Reports [*A publication*] (DLA)
Prop & Comp R... Property and Compensation Reports [*A publication*] (DLA)
PRO-PAY ..... Proficiency Pay [*Military*]
PropCT......... Property Capital Trust [*Associated Press*] (SAG)
pro per .... Propria Persona [*In His or Her Own Person*] [*Latin*] (WGA)
PROPER COUNT... Property Accountability (MCD)
PROPH...... Porphyrins [*Chemistry*] (DAVI)
PROPH...... Profile of Phonology (AIE)
PROPH...... Prophylactic
Proph21...... Prophet 21, Inc. [*Associated Press*] (SAG)
PROPHET.... Proactive Rehabilitation of Outside Plant Using Heuristic Expert Techniques [*GTE computer software*]
prophy .... Prophylactic (DAVI)
PROPIN....... Proprietary Information
PROPL......... Proportional
Prop Law..... Property Lawyer [*1826-30*] [*A publication*] (DLA)
Prop Law Bull... Property Law Bulletin [*A publication*] (DLA)
Prop Law NS... Property Lawyer, New Series [*England*] [*A publication*] (DLA)
PROPLING ... Propelling
PROPLOSS... Propagation Loss (NVT)
PROPLT....... Propellant (NASA)
PROPN......... Propane
PROPN......... Proportion (MSA)
proPO .... Prophenoloxidase
PROPON ...... Proportion (ROG)
PROPORICH... Proceed to Port in Which Unit is Located [*Navy*] (DNAB)
PROPR....... Proprietary (ROG)
PROPR......... Proprietor (EY)
propr......... Proprietor (WDAA)
PROPRE....... Property Press (DLA)
PROPRSS ... Proprietress (ROG)
PROPTRY ... Proprietary [*Freight*]
PROPUL...... Propulsion
PROPY .... Proprietary
Pro Quer...... Pro Querente [*For the Plaintiff*] [*Latin*] (ILCA)
PROR......... Predicted Orbit
PRORA........ Programs for Research on Romance Authors
PRORAT...... Projected Rating
PRO RAT AET... Pro Ratione Aetatis [*According to Age*] [*Pharmacy*]
PRO RECT ... Pro Recto [*Rectal*] [*Pharmacy*]
pro rect....... pro recto [*By rectum*] [*Latin*] [*Pharmacy*] (DAVI)
PROREP...... Proceed Ship, Command Station Reporting Duty or Purpose Indicated [*Military*]
PROS .... Preventive Maintenance, Repair, and Operational Services (ODBW)
PROS .... Procurement Squadron
PROS .... Professional Reactor Operator Society (EA)
PROS .... Proscenium [*Theater term*] (DSUE)
PROS .... Prosecution (ROG)
PROS .... Prosody
PROS .... Prospect Group [*NASDAQ symbol*] (TTSB)
PROS .... [*The*] Prospect Group, Inc. [*New York, NY NASDAQ symbol*] (NQ)
pros .... Prostate [*Anatomy*] (DAVI)
PROS .... Prosthetic (AABC)
PROS .... Prostitute (DSUE)

PROS .... Prostrate
PROSA........ Programming System with Symbolic Addresses [*Computer science*] (IAA)
PROSAM...... Programmed Single-Axis Mount [*Military camera*]
PROSAMO .. Planned Release of Selected and Modified Organisms [*British*]
Pros Atty.... Prosecuting Attorney (DLA)
PROSC........ Proscenium [*Theater term*] (WDAA)
PRosC......... Rosemont College, Rosemont, PA [*Library symbol Library of Congress*] (LCLS)
PROSD........ Performance Records for Optimizing System Design (IAA)
PROSE....... Personal Record of School Experiences (EDAC)
PROSE....... Problem Solution Engineering [*Programming language*] [*Computer science*] (CSR)
PROSE....... Program System Example (SAA)
PROSEA...... Plant Resources of South-East Asia [*A publication*]
PROSECON... Prosecution (ROG)
PROSEL....... Process Control and Sequencing Language [*Computer science*] (IAA)
ProsGp........ [*The*] Prospect Group, Inc. [*Associated Press*] (SAG)
PROSI......... Public Relations Office of the Sugar Industry
PROSIG....... Procedure Signal [*Navy*]
PROSIGN..... Procedure Sign [*Military*] (AABC)
PROSIM...... Production System Simulator [*Computer science*]
PROSIN....... Procedure Sign [*Military*] (IAA)
PROSINE...... Procedure Sign [*Military*]
PROSMATEC... Progressive Shift Schedule Management Technology [*Automotive engineering*]
PROSO........ Protamine Sulfate [*Biochemistry*] (DAVI)
ProSoc........ Prometheus Society (EA)
Prosoft........ Prosoft I-Net Solutions, Inc. [*Associated Press*] (SAG)
Prosop Att .. Prosopographia Attica [*A publication*] (OCD)
prosp......... Prospectively (DLA)
PROSPEC..... PRO Specification (NITA)
PROSPECT... Proponent Sponsored Engineer Corps Training [*Army Corps of Engineers*]
PROSPER .... Profit Simulation, Planning and Evaluation of Risk (MHDB)
ProSport ...... Professional Sports Care Management, Inc. [*Associated Press*] (SAG)
PROSPRO ... Process Systems Program
ProsSt........ Prospect Street High Income Portfolio, Inc. [*Associated Press*] (SAG)
PROST........ Pronuclear Oocyte and Sperm Transfer [*Embryology*]
prost......... Prostate (CPH)
PROST........ Prostitute [*or Prostitution*] [*FBI standardized term*]
PROSTAT..... Prostatic (AAMN)
PROSTH...... Prosthesis
PROSY........ People's Republic of South Yemen (BJA)
PROT .... Protect [*or Protection*] (MSA)
Prot........... Protectorate (WDAA)
PROT .... Protein
PROT .... Protest (ROG)
PROT .... Protestant
Prot........... Protestant (WDAA)
PROT .... Proteus [*Bacterium*]
PROT .... Protinus [*Speedily*] [*Pharmacy*]
Prot........... Protocol (DLA)
PROT .... Prototype
PROT .... Protractor (AAG)
PROTA........ Protection Actual [*Probability for avoidance of ship*]
ProTACA ...... Procurement Technical Assistance Cooperative Agreement Program [*DoD*]
PROTAP....... Professional Opportunities through Academic Partnership [*National War College*]
PROTAP....... Protonotary Apostolic [*Roman Catholic*]
Prot CJ ...... Protocol on the Statute of the European Communities Court of Justice [*A publication*] (DLA)
PROTCT...... Protective (AAG)
ProtDg........ Protein Design Labs [*Associated Press*] (SAG)
PROTEC...... Protection
PROTECON... Process and Test Control [*Pendar Technical Association Ltd.*] [*Software package*] (NCC)
PROTECT .... Probabilities Recall Optimizing the Employment of Calibration Time (KSC)
PROTECT .... Protection
ProtectO ...... Protection One, Inc. [*Associated Press*] (SAG)
PRO TEM .... Pro Tempore [*For the Time Being*] [*Latin*]
PRO TEM et LOC... Pro Tempore et Loco [*For the Time and Place*] [*Latin*] (ROG)
Proteon....... Proteon, Inc. [*Associated Press*] (SAG)
PROTEUS..... Profile Telemetry of Upper Ocean Currents [*Marine science*] (OSRA)
PROTEUS..... Project to Research Objects Theories, Extraterrestrials, and Unusual Sightings (EA)
PROTEUS..... Propulsion Research and Open Water Testing of Experimental Underwater Systems (MCD)
PROTHROM... Prothrombin [*Hematology*]
PROTIMEREP... Proceed in Time Report Not Later Than [*Hour and/or date indicated*] [*Military*]
ProtLf......... Protective Life Corp. [*Associated Press*] (SAG)
PROTO........ Protoporphyrin [*Hematology*]
Proto.......... ProtoSource Corp. [*Associated Press*] (SAG)
PROTO........ Prototype (KSC)
ProtoS........ ProtoSource Corp. [*Associated Press*] (SAG)
ProtP .... Protein Polymer Technologies, Inc. [*Associated Press*] (SAG)
Prot PI .... Protocol on Privileges and Immunities of the European Economic Community [*A publication*] (DLA)
ProtPoly...... Protein Polymer Technologies, Inc. [*Associated Press*] (SAG)
PROTR........ Protractor (MSA)

Protr .... Protrepticus [of Clemens Alexandrinus] [Classical studies] (OCD)
ProtSy......... Protocol Systems, Inc. [Associated Press] (SAG)
Proud Dom Pub... Proudhon's Domaine Public [A publication] (DLA)
Proudf Land Dec... United States Land Decisions (Proudfit) [A publication] (DLA)
PROUS.......... Proceed to a Port in Continental United States [Military]
PRO US EXT... Pro Usu Externo [For External Use] [Pharmacy]
Prouty......... Prouty's Reports [61-68 Vermont] [A publication] (DLA)
Prov .... De Providentia [of Seneca the Younger] [Classical studies] (OCD)
prov .... Provenance (VRA)
PROV .... Provencal [Language, etc.]
PROV .... Provence [France] (ROG)
PROV .... Proverb
Prov .... Proverbs [Old Testament book]
PROV .... Provide (KSC)
PROV .... Provident Financial Holdings, Inc. [NASDAQ symbol] (SAG)
PROV .... Province
PROV .... Provincial
Prov .... Provincial (AL)
PROV .... Provinciale [Provincial] [Netherlands] (EY)
PROV .... Proving Ground [Navy]
PROV .... Provision [or Provisional] (AFM)
Prov .... Provisional (TBD)
Prov .... Provisional Light [Navigation signal]
PROV .... Provost
ProvBcp....... Provident Bancorp, Inc. [Associated Press] (SAG)
Prov Can Stat... Statutes of the Province of Canada [A publication] (DLA)
ProvCo........ Provident Companies, Inc. [Associated Press] (SAG)
Prov Cons.... De Provinciis Consularibus [of Cicero] [Classical studies] (OCD)
PROVCORPV.. Provisional Corps, Vietnam
PROVD........ Provided
PROVER....... Procurement for Minimum Total Cost through Value Engineering and Reliability
ProvFinl...... Provident Financial Holdings, Inc. [Associated Press] (SAG)
ProvGM....... Provincial Grand Master [Freemasonry]
PROVGR ...... Proving Grounds
PROVIB........ Propulsion System Decision and Vibration Analysis (DNAB)
Provid......... De Providentia [of Philo] (BJA)
Providence C... Providence College (GAGS)
Providn....... Providian Corp. [Formerly, Capital Holding] [Associated Press] (SAG)
PROVIMI...... Proteins, Vitamins, and Minerals [Pharmacology] (DAVI)
PROVIS........ Provision
PROVMAAG... Provisional Military Assistance Advisory Group (CINC)
PROVMAAG-K.. Provisional Military Assistance Advisory Group, Korea (CINC)
PROVMAIN... Other Provisions Basic Orders Remain in Effect
PROVMAINTCO... Provisional Maintenance Company [Navy] (DNAB)
PROVMUSTCO... Provisional Medical Unit Self-Contained Company [Navy] (DNAB)
PROVNC ...... Province
provns .... Provisions (DLA)
PROVO......... Proviso [Contract clause] (ROG)
PROVO......... Provocateur (DSUE)
PROVONS .... Provisions
PROVORG..... Providing Organization (DOMA)
PROVOST .... Priority Research Objectives for Vietnam Operations Support
PROVSN ...... Provision
Prov St .... Statutes, Laws, of the Province of Massachusetts [A publication] (DLA)
PROWDELREP... Proceed Without Delay Report Duty or Purpose Indicated [Military]
PROWL........ Procedure Work Log System (IAA)
PROWLER.... Programmable Robot Observer with Logical Enemy Response [Developed by Robot Defense Systems of Thornton, CO]
PROWORD... Procedure Word
PRO-X.......... Prothrombin Time [Hematology] (CPH)
prox .... Proximal (CPH)
PROX.......... Proxim, Inc. [NASDAQ symbol] (SAG)
PROX.......... Proximity (AABC)
PROX.......... Proximo [In Next Month] [Latin]
Prox .... Proximo (EBF)
prox .... Proximo [In Next Month] [Latin] (ODBW)
PROX ACC ... Proxime Accessit [Next in Order of Merit] [Latin]
PRO-XAN..... Protein-Xanthophyll [Alfalfa protein concentrate process]
PROXI......... Projection by Reflection Optics of Xerographic Images (IEEE)
Proxim........ Proxim, Inc. [Associated Press] (SAG)
Proxima...... Proxima Corp. [Associated Press] (SAG)
prox luc ...... Proxima Luce [Day Before] [Latin] (MAE)
Proxymd...... ProxyMed, Inc. [Associated Press] (SAG)
PRP .... Panretinal Photocoagulation [Ophthalmology]
PRP .... Parent Rule Point (MCD)
PRP .... Parti de la Revolution Populaire [People's Revolutionary Party] [Zaire] [Political party] (PD)
PRP .... Partido de Renovacion Puertorriqueno [Puerto Rican Renewal Party] [Political party] (EY)
PRP .... Partido de Representacao Popular [Brazil Political party]
PRP .... Partido Renovacion Patriotica [Honduras] [Political party] (EY)
PRP .... Partido Republicano Portugues [Portuguese Republican Party] [Political party] (PPE)
PRP .... Partido Revolucionario Popular [Popular Revolutionary Party] [Portugal Political party] (PPE)
PRP .... Parti Republicain du Progres [Republican Progress Party] [Central Africa] [Political party] (PD)
PRP .... Parti Republicain Progressif [Algeria] [Political party] (EY)
PRP .... Peace Resource Project (EA)
PRP .... Peak Radiated Power (CET)
PRP .... People's Redemption Party [Nigeria] [Political party] (PPW)
PRP .... People's Reform Party [Philippines] [Political party] (EY)

PRP .... People's Revolutionary Party [Benin] [Political party]
PRP .... People's Revolutionary Party [North Vietnam] [Political party]
PRP .... Peptide Recognition Protein [Biochemistry]
PRP .... Performance-Related Pay (ECON)
PRP .... Performance, Requirements, Practices [Military]
PRP .... Personnel Reliability Program [Air Force]
PRP .... Phantom Range Pod (MCD)
PRP .... Phase Review Package (MCD)
PRP .... Physical Readiness Program [Navy] (DNAB)
PRP .... Physiologic Rest Position [Medicine] (DMAA)
PRP .... Pickup-Zone Release Point
PRP .... Pityriasis Rubra Pilaris [Dermatology] (MAE)
PRP .... Placement Route and Patch [Computer science] (IAA)
PRP .... Platelet-Rich Plasma [Hematology]
PRP .... Pneumatically-Released Pilot (DNAB)
PRP .... Polymer of Ribose Phosphate [Organic chemistry] (MAE)
PRP .... Polyribitol Phosphate [Organic chemistry]
PRP .... Position Report Printout
PRP .... Postbuckled Rectangular Plate
PRP .... Potentially Responsible Party [Environmental Protection Agency]
PRP .... Power-Deployed Reserve Parachute (MCD)
PRP .... Premature-Removal Period (MCD)
PRP .... Prepare (FAAC)
PRP .... Prerigor Pressurization [Meat processing]
PR P .... Present Participle (WGA)
PRP .... President's Reorganization Project [Carter Administration] [Executive Office of the President] (GFGA)
PRP .... Pressure Rate Product [In treadmill test]
PRP .... Primary Raynaud's Phenomenon [Medicine]
PRP .... Principal Responsible Party
PRP .... Print Out [Computer science] (IAA)
PrP............. Prion Protein [Biochemistry]
PRP .... Problem Resolution Program [IRS]
PRP .... Procurement Requirements Package (MCD)
PRP .... Production Readiness Plan
PRP .... Production Requirements Plan
PRP .... Production Reserve Policy
PRP .... Profit-Related Pay [Economics]
PRP .... Program Random Process (PDAA)
PRP .... Program Requirements Package [Computer science]
PRP .... Program Review Panel [Army] (AABC)
PRP .... Progressive Rework Plan
PRP .... Progressive Rubella Panencephalitis [Medicine]
PRP .... Proliferative Retinopathy Photocoagulation
PRP .... Proliferin Related Protein [Biochemistry]
PRP .... Proline-Rich Protein [Biochemistry]
PRP .... Proper Return Port [Shipping]
PRP .... Prospective Reimbursement Plan [Medicaid]
PRP .... Protease-Resistant Prion [Medicine]
PrP............. Protease-Resistant Protein [Microbiology]
PrP............. Protein Phosphatase [An enzyme]
PRP .... Pseudorandom Pulse
PRP .... Psychotic Reaction Profile [Psychology]
PRP .... Public Relations Personnel [Navy]
PRP .... Pulse Recurrence [or Repetition] Period (CET)
PRP .... Pulse Repetition Frequency [Medicine] (DAVI)
PRP .... Pulse Repetition Period [Computer science] (IAA)
PRP .... Purchase Request Package [Shipping] (MCD)
PRP .... Purple (MSA)
PRP .... Purpose (MSA)
PRP .... Reformed Presbyterian Theological Seminary, Pittsburgh, PA [OCLC symbol] (OCLC)
PRPA .... Professional Race Pilots Association [Later, USARA] (EA)
PRPB .... Parti de la Revolution Populaire du Benin [Benin People's Revolutionary Party] [Political party] (PD)
PRPC .... Parti Republicain du Peuple Camerounais [Political party] (EY)
PRPC .... Public Relations Policy Committee [NATO] (NATG)
PrPCU-L....... Catholic University of Puerto Rico, Law Library, Ponce, Puerto Rico [Library symbol] [Library of Congress] (LCLS)
PRP-D......... Polyribosylribitol Phosphate-Diptheria Toxoid [Medicine]
PRPDA......... Public Radio Program Directors Association (NTPA)
PrpdLg........ Pre-Paid Legal Services, Inc. [Associated Press] (SAG)
PRPF .... Planar Radial Peaking Factor [Network analysis] (IEEE)
PRPG .... Proportioning
PRPH .... Peripherin (DMAA)
Pr/Ph .... Pristane/Phytane Ratio [Environmental science]
PRPHL .... Peripheral
PRPL .... PACOM [Pacific Command] Reconnaissance Priority List (CINC)
PRPL .... People's Democratic Republic of Laos
PRPL .... Procurement Repair Parts List (AAG)
PRPLN .... Propulsion (MSA)
PRPLNT .... Propellant (KSC)
PRPLT .... Propellant (MSA)
PRPNE .... Propane [Organic chemistry]
PRPOOS ...... Plankton Rate Processes in Oligotrophic Oceans [Cooperative research project]
PRPP .... Phosphoribosylpyrophosphate [Biochemistry]
PRPP .... Phosphorylribose Pyrophosphate [Biochemistry]
PRPP .... Pseudoresidual Plot Program
PRPQ .... Programming Request for Price Quotation [Computer science]
PR PR .... Praeter Propter [About, Nearly] [Latin] (ROG)
PRPRR......... Preparer
PRPS .... Pressure Rise per Stage (MCD)
PRPS .... Program Requirement Process Specification [NASA] (KSC)
PRPS .... Prostatic Secretory Protein (DMAA)

PRPSA.........	Personal Report of Public Speaking Apprehension (EDAC)
PRPSD.........	Proposed (MSA)
PRPSL.........	Proposal (MSA)
PRPT	Parti Revolutionnaire du Peuple Tunisien [*Revolutionary Party of the Tunisian People*] [*Political party*] (PD)
PRP-T	Polyribosylribitol Phosphate Conjugated to Tetanus Toxoid [*Medicine*]
PRPT	Procoriptive Reading Performance Test [*Educational test*]
PRPUC........	Philippine Republic Presidential Unit Citation [*Military decoration*]
PRPUCE.......	Philippine Republic Presidential Unit Citation Emblem [*Military decoration*]
prpylm.........	Propylaeum (VRA)
PRQ	Houston, TX [*Location identifier FAA*] (FAAL)
PRQ	Personal Resources Questionnaire (DMAA)
PRQ	Presidente Roque Saenz Pena [*Argentina*] [*Airport symbol*] (AD)
PRQA..........	Passenger Ride Quality Apparatus [*Public transportation*]
PRR	Partner Airlines [*Former USSR*] [*FAA designator*] (FAAC)
PRR	Parts Replacement Request (KSC)
PRR	Passenger Reservation Request (NVT)
PRR	Passive Ranging RADAR
PRR	Pawling Research Reactor
PRR	Pennsylvania Railroad Co. [*AAR code Obsolete*]
PRR	Performance-Related Remuneration (ADA)
PRR	Perrine, FL [*Location identifier FAA*] (FAAL)
PRR	Perris [*California*] [*Seismograph station code, US Geological Survey Closed*] (SEIS)
PRR	Personnel Requirements Report [*Army*]
PRR	Philippine Research Reactor (SAA)
PRR	Placement Revision Request
PRR	Planning Release Record (AAG)
PRR	Plans and Requirements Review
PRR	Political Risk Review [*A publication*] (EAAP)
PRR	Post-Recall Release (WDAA)
Pr R	Practice Reports [*Ontario*] [*A publication*] (DLA)
Pr R	Practice Reports [*Quebec*] [*A publication*] (DLA)
PRR	Prairie [*Commonly used*] (OPSA)
PRR	Preliminary Requirements Review [*NASA*] (KSC)
PRR	Premature Removal Rate
PRR	Presbyterian and Reformed Renewal Ministries International [*Formerly, PCC*] (EA)
PRR	Pressure Rise Rate [*Nuclear energy*] (NRCH)
PRR	Primary Production Required [*Resource management*]
PRR	Prism Resources Ltd. [*Vancouver Stock Exchange symbol*]
PRR	Problem Reporting and Resolution
PRR	Producer's Reliability Risk
PRR	Production Readiness Review
PRR	Production Research Reports
PRR	Program Requirements Review [*NASA*] (NASA)
PRR	Program Revision Report (KSC)
PRR	Proline-Rich Protein [*Biochemistry*]
PRR	Proton Relaxation Rate
PRR	Pseudoresident Reader (MHDB)
PRR	Publication Revision Request (AAG)
PRR	Puerto Rico Reactor (NRCH)
PRR	Puerto Rico Supreme Court Reports [*A publication*] (DLA)
PRR	Pulse Recurrence [*or Repetition*] Rate (MUGU)
PrRA	Academia Maria Reina, Rio Piedras, PR [*Library symbol Library of Congress*] (LCLS)
PRRA..........	Puerto Rico Reconstruction Administration [*Terminated, 1955*]
PrRadA........	Premiere Radio Networks, Inc. [*Associated Press*] (SAG)
PRR & Regs...	Commonwealth of Puerto Rico Rules and Regulations [*A publication*] (DLA)
PRRB..........	Provider Reimbursement Review Board [*Medicare*]
PRRC..........	New Mexico Petroleum Recovery Research Center [*New Mexico Institute of Mining and Technology*] [*Research center*] (RCD)
PRRC..........	Pitch/Roll Rate Changer Assembly (MCD)
PRRC..........	Precision Response Corp. [*NASDAQ symbol*] (SAG)
PrRe	Evangelical Seminary, Rio Piedras, PR [*Library symbol Library of Congress*] (LCLS)
PRRE	Pupils Round, Regular, and Equal [*Medicine*] (MAE)
Pr Reg BC ...	Practical Register in the Bail Court [*A publication*] (DLA)
Pr Reg Ch....	Practical Register in Chancery [*1 vol.*] [*A publication*] (DLA)
Pr Reg CP ...	Practical Register in the Common Pleas [*1705-42*] [*A publication*] (DLA)
Pr Rep........	Practice Reports [*Ontario*] [*A publication*] (DLA)
Pr Rep........	Practice Reports [*England*] [*A publication*] (DLA)
Pr Rep BC ...	Lowndes, Maxwell, and Pollock's English Bail Court Practice Reports [*1850-51*] [*A publication*] (DLA)
PRRFC........	Planar Randomly Reinforced Fiber Composite
PRRI	Puerto Rico Rum Institute [*Later, PRRPA*]
PRRM.........	Presbyterian and Reformed Renewal Ministries International (EA)
PRRM.........	Program Review and Resources Management [*NASA*]
PRRM.........	Pulse Repetition Rate Modulation [*Data transmission*] [*Computer science*] (TEL)
PRRMI........	Presbyterian and Reformed Renewal Ministries International (EA)
PRRPA........	Puerto Rico Rum Producers Association [*Defunct*] (EA)
PRRR..........	Pioneer Railcorp [*NASDAQ symbol*] (SAG)
PRRS..........	Positioning Reporting Recording System (RDA)
PRRS..........	Problem Reporting and Resolution System [*Military*] (CAAL)
PR-RSV.......	Rous Sarcoma Virus, Prague Strain
PRRWO.......	Puerto Rican Revolutionary Workers Organization (NADA)
PRS	Pacific Railroad Society (EA)
PRS	Pacific Rocket Society (EA)
PRSD	Padre Resources [*Vancouver Stock Exchange symbol*]
PRSL	Paint Research Station [*British*] (BI)
PRS	Pairs
PRS	Paraiso [*California*] [*Seismograph station code, US Geological Survey*] (SEIS)
PRS	Parametric Ruled Surface (MCD)
PRS	Parasi [*Solomon Islands*] [*Airport symbol*] (OAG)
PRS	Parliamentary Research Services [*British*]
PRS	Pars Systems (CRS) [*ICAO designator*] (FAAC)
PRS	Partei fuer Renten-, Steuer-, und Soziale Gerechtigkeit [*Party for Equitable Pensions, Taxation, and Social Services*] [*Germany Political party*] (PPW)
PR's	Partial Responders [*to medication*]
PRS	Partial Response Signalling (NITA)
PRS	Parti de la Revolution Socialiste [*Party of Socialist Revolution*] [*Benin*] [*Political party*]
PRS	Parti de la Revolution Socialiste [*Party of Socialist Revolution*] [*Senegal*] [*Political party*]
PRS	Partido de la Revolucion Socialista [*Party of the Socialist Revolution*] [*Cuba*] [*Political party*]
PRS	Partido para a Renovacao Social [*Party for Social Renovation*] [*Guinea-Bissau*] [*Political party*] (EY)
PRS	Partido Revolucionario Socialista [*Mexico Political party*] (EY)
PRS	Partito Republicano Sammarinese [*Republican Party*] [*San Marino*] [*Political party*] (EY)
PRS	Passive RADAR Surveillance [*Military*] (CAAL)
PRS	Pattern Recognition Society (EA)
PRS	Pattern Recognition System
PRS	Payload Retention Subsystem [*NASA*] (NASA)
PRS	Pennsylvania-Reading Seashore Lines [*Absorbed into Consolidated Rail Corp.*]
PRS	Perceptual Respresentation System [*Memory*]
PRS	Performance Rating System (OICC)
PRS	Performing Right Society [*British*]
PRS	Personality Rating Scale [*Psychology*]
PRS	Personal Recording System
PRS	Personal Relations Survey [*Managerial skills test*]
PRS	Personnel Readiness System [*Air Force*]
PRS	Personnel Rescue Service [*NASA*] (NASA)
PRS	Personnel Rescue System [*NASA*] (MCD)
PRS	Personnel Research Section [*Army*]
PRS	Personnel Research Staff [*Department of Agriculture*]
PRS	Philatelic Research Society
PRS	Philosophical Research Society (EA)
PRS	Photographic Reconnaissance System
PRS	Photo Resist Spinner
PRS	Physically Restricted Status [*Military*]
PRS	Pipe Roll Society (EA)
PRS	Planar Rider System
PRS	Planners Referral Service [*Information service or system*] (IID)
PRS	Planning Record Sheet
PR's	Planning References (AAG)
PRS	Planning Research & Systems Ltd. [*British*]
PRS	Plasma Renin Substrate [*Hematology*]
PRS	Pneumatic Reading System
PRS	Pointing Reference System (KSC)
PRS	Population Research Service [*Information service or system*] (IID)
PRS	Positive Rolandic Spikes [*Neurology*] (DAVI)
PRS	Power Reactant Subsystem [*NASA*] (NASA)
PRS	Power Relay Satellite
PRS	Prayers (ROG)
PRS	Precipitate Reduction Sinter [*Metal*] (DICI)
PRS	Precision Ranging System
PRS	Precision Rotary Stripper
PRS	Present (WGA)
PRS	President of the Royal Society [*British*]
PRS	Presidio Oil Co. [*AMEX symbol*] (SPSG)
PRS	Presidio, TX [*Location identifier FAA*] (FAAL)
PRS	Press (MSA)
PRS	Pressure Reducing Station
PRS	Pressure Response Spectrum [*Nuclear energy*] (NRCH)
PR/S	Prestrike (SAA)
PRS	Price Reporting System (NUMA)
PRS	Primary Recovery Ship [*NASA*]
PRS	Primary Recovery Site [*NASA*] (KSC)
PRS	Primary Representational System (EDAC)
PRS	Primary Rescue Site [*NASA*] (NASA)
PRS	Procedure Review Section [*Social Security Administration*]
PRS	Process Radiation Sampler [*Nuclear energy*] (NRCH)
PRS	Production Recording System
PRS	Production Release System (MCD)
PRS	Product Requirement Schedule (MCD)
PRS	Programmed RADAR Simulator (IAA)
PRS	Program Rating Summary Report [*Television ratings*] (NTCM)
PRS	Program Requirements Summary (MUGU)
PRS	Property Recovery Section
PRS	Propodial Sinus [*Zoology*]
PRS	Prospective Reimbursement System [*Health insurance*] (GHCT)
PRS	Prospectors Air [*Vancouver Stock Exchange symbol*]
PRS	Protestant Reformation Society (EA)
PRS	Provide Repair Service [*Navy*] (NVT)
PRS	Provisioning Requirements Statement
PRS	Pseudorandom Sequence
PRS	Psycholinguistic Rating Scale
PRS	Public Relations Section [*Library Administration and Management Association*]
PRS	Puerto Lempira [*Honduras*] [*Airport symbol*] (AD)
PRS	Pure Random Search [*Optimization method*]

PRSA	Pan-Rhodian Society of America (EA)
PRSA	Permigewasset River Study Act of 1989 (COE)
PRSA	Power Reactant Storage Assembly [NASA] (MCD)
PRSA	President of the Royal Scottish Academy
PRSA	Proportional Representation Society of Australia
PRSA	Public Relations Society of America (EA)
PRSA	Puerto Rico Statehood Commission (EA)
PrSaC	Colegio Universitario del Sagrado Corazon [College of the Sacred Heart], Santurce, PR [Library symbol Library of Congress] (LCLS)
PRSC	Parametric Response Surface Control (AAEL)
PRSC	Plutonium Rework Sample Cell [Nuclear energy] (NRCH)
PRSC	Puerto Rico Solidarity Committee (EA)
Pr Scale	Prejudice Scale [Psychology] (DHP)
PRSCHL	Preschool
PRSCR	Puerto Rico Supreme Court Reports [A publication] (DLA)
PRSD	Portable Rectilinear Scanning Device
PRSD	Power Reactant Storage [or Supply] and Distribution [NASA] (NASA)
PRSD	Pressed (AAG)
PRSDS	Power Reactant Storage and Distribution System (MCD)
PrSE	El Mundo Publishing Co., San Juan, PR [Library symbol Library of Congress] (LCLS)
PRSE	President of the Royal Society of Edinburgh
PRSEC	Payroll Section
Prsfdr	Pressfeeder [Printing]
PRSG	Personal Radio Steering Group [Ann Arbor, MI] [Telecommunications service] (TSSD)
PRSG	Pressing
PRSG	Pulse-Rebalanced Strapdown Gyro (MCD)
PRSH	President of the Royal Society for the Promotion of Health [British]
PRSIS	Prospective Rate Setting Information System [Medicine] (DMAA)
PRSL	Pennsylvania-Reading Seashore Lines [Absorbed into Consolidated Rail Corp.] [AAR code]
PRSM	Prism Group [NASDAQ symbol] (SAG)
PR/SM	Processor Resource/Systems Manager [Computer science] (CDE)
prsmc	Prismacolor (VRA)
PRSMC	Prism Group [NASDAQ symbol] (TTSB)
PRSMN	Pressman (AABC)
PRSN	Provisional Relative Sunspot Number [NASA]
PRSNG	Pressing
PRSNL	Personal
PRSNNL	Personnel
PRSNT	Present [NWS] (FAAC)
PRSP	Penicillin-Resistant S. Pneumoniae [Clinical chemistry]
PRSP	Puerto Rico Socialist Party (NADA)
PRSPL	Planning and Role Setting for Public Libraries [Public Library Association] [A publication]
PRSR	Presser (MSA)
PR/SR	Price Redetermination/Service Reallocation (AAGC)
PRSRV	Preservative (AAG)
PRSRZ	Pressurize (MSA)
PRSS	Pennsylvania-Reading Seashore Lines [Absorbed into Consolidated Rail Corp.]
PRSS	Problem Report Squawk Shoot [NASA] (NASA)
PRSSA	Public Relations Student Society of America (EA)
PRSSA	Puerto Rico Mainland US Statehood Students Association (EA)
PRSSD	Pressed
PRST	Persist (FAAC)
PRST	Presstek, Inc. [NASDAQ symbol] (NQ)
PRST	Priest
PRST	Probability Reliability Sequential Tests (MCD)
Pr Stat	Private Statutes [Legal term] (DLA)
PRSTC	Prosthetic
PRSTG	Prestige
PRSU	Police Requirements Support Unit [Home Office] [British]
PRSV	Papaya Ringspot Virus [Plant pathology]
PRSV	Preserving
PRSVN	Preservation (AABC)
PRSW	President of the Royal Scottish Water Colour Society
PRSW	Pure Software [NASDAQ symbol] (TTSB)
PRSW	Pure Software, Inc. [NASDAQ symbol] (SAG)
PrSW	World University, San Juan, PR [Library symbol Library of Congress] (LCLS)
PrSW-I	World University, International Institute of the Americas, Barbosa Esq. Guayama, San Juan, PR [Library symbol Library of Congress] (LCLS)
PRT	Air Cargo Carriers, Inc. [ICAO designator] (FAAC)
PRT	Parachute Radio Transmitter [Telecommunications] (IAA)
PRT	Pararescue Team (COE)
PRT	Parliamentary Remuneration Tribunal [New South Wales, Australia]
PRT	Parr Terminal Railroad [AAR code]
PRT	Part (AAG)
PRT	Participating Research Teams [Department of Energy]
PRT	Partido Revolucionario de los Trabajadores [Workers' Revolutionary Party] [Argentina Political party] (PD)
PRT	Partido Revolucionario de los Trabajadores [Workers' Revolutionary Party] [Peru] [Political party] (PPW)
PRT	Partido Revolucionario de los Trabajadores [Revolutionary Workers' Party] [Costa Rica] [Political party] (EY)
PRT	Partido Revolucionario de los Trabajadores [Workers' Revolutionary Party] [Uruguay] [Political party] (PD)
PRT	Partido Revolucionario de Trabajadores [Revolutionary Worker's Party] [Colorado Political party] (EY)
PRT	Passage Reading Test [Education] (EDAC)
PRT	Patient Review Tribunal [Queensland, Australia]

PRT	Patten Recognition Technology (NITA)
PRT	Pattern Recognition Technique
PRT	Payroll Tax (ADA)
PRT	Penicillium Roqueforti Toxin (DB)
PRT	Periodic Reevaluation Tests
PRT	Permanent Recording Traffic [Telecommunications] (IAA)
PRT	Personal Rapid Transit [Computer-guided transit system]
PRT	Personnel Research Test [Military]
PRT	Petroleum Revenue Tax [British]
PRT	Pharmaceutical Research and Testing [Public Health Service] (GRD)
PRT	Philadelphia Reading Test [Education]
PRT	Phosphoribosyltransferase [Also, PRTase] [An enzyme]
PRT	Photoradiation Therapy [Oncology]
PRT	Physical Readiness Training [Army] (INF)
PRT	Pictorial Reasoning Test [Job screening test]
PRT	Planar Resistor Technology (AAEL)
PRT	Platinum Resistance Thermometer
PRT	Point Retreat, AK [Location identifier FAA] (FAAL)
PRT	Port
PRT	Portable Radiation Thermometer
PRT	Portable Radio Telephone
PRT	Portable Remote Terminal
PRT	Portable Router Template (MCD)
PRT	Portable Router Tool
PRT	Portland [Diocesan abbreviation] [Maine] (TOCD)
PRT	Portugal [ANSI three-letter standard code] (CNC)
PRT	Power Recovery Turbine
PRT	Prato [Italy] [Seismograph station code, US Geological Survey] (SEIS)
PRT	Precision Radiation Thermometer
PRT	Preliminary Reference Trajectory [NASA] (KSC)
PRT	Pressurized Relief Tank (NRCH)
PRT	Primary Ranging Test (OA)
PRT	Print
PRT	Printer [Computer science] (MDG)
prt	Printer [MARC relator code] [Library of Congress] (LCCP)
PRT	Prison Reform Trust (WDAA)
Prt.	Private [British military] (DMA)
PRT	Problem Resolution Tasking System [Army] (INF)
PRT	Procurement Review Team
PRT	Procurement Round Table (EA)
PRT	Production Reliability Test
PRT	Production Run Tape
PRT	Product Range Testing [Business term]
PRT	Program Reference Table
PRT	Program Review Team [Navy] (DNAB)
PRT	Promotion, Transfer, and Redundancy [Railway union agreement] [British] (ECON)
PRT	Prompt Air, Inc. [FAA designator] (FAAC)
PRT	Prompt Relief Trip [Nuclear energy] (NRCH)
Prt.	Protagoras [of Plato] [Classical studies] (OCD)
PRT	Prova di Restituzione Termica [Italy] [Medicine]
PRT	Provost
PRT	Psychiatric Rehabilitation Team (EA)
PRT	Publications Requirements Tables (AAG)
PRT	Pulsed RADAR Transmitter
prt.	Pulse Frequency (IDOE)
PRT	Pulse Recurrence [or Repetition] Time (CET)
PRTase	Phosphoribosyltransferase [Medicine] (MEDA)
PRTAX	Price T. Rowe: Tax-Free Income [Mutual fund ticker symbol] (SG)
PRTB	Partido Revolucionario de Trabajadores Bolivianos [Bolivian Workers' Revolutionary Party] [Political party] (PD)
PRTBR	Partido Revolucionario de los Trabajadores de Bolivia Romero [Bolivia] [Political party] (PPW)
PRTC	Partido Revolucionario de los Trabajadores Centroamericanos [Revolutionary Party of Central American Workers] [El Salvador] [Political party] (PD)
PRTC	Pediatric Research and Training Center [University of Connecticut] [Research center] (RCD)
PRTC	Ports Canada
PRTC	Professional Rate Training Course (DNAB)
PRTCD	Puerto Rico Tax Court Decisions [A publication] (DLA)
PRTC-H	Partido Revolucionario de los Trabajadores Centroamericanos - Seccion de Hondur as [Revolutionary Party of Central American Workers - Honduras] [Political party]
PRTCTV	Protective
PRTD	Portland Traction Co. [AAR code]
PRTD	Printed (DGA)
prtd	Printed (VRA)
PRTF	Pheromone and Receptor Transcription Factor [Genetics]
PRTF	Psychiatric Review Technique Form [Social Security Administration]
PRTG	Printing (AFM)
PRTH	Pituitary Resistance to Thyroid Hormone [Medicine] (DMAA)
PRTH	Prothrombin Time [Hematology] (DAVI)
PRTH-C	Prothrombin Time Control [Hematology] (DAVI)
PRTHS	Pennsylvania Railroad Technical and Historical Society (EA)
PRTI	Physical and Recreational Training Instructor [British military] (DMA)
PRTKT	Parts Kit
PRTL	Portable (DNAB)
PRTL	Primus Telecommunications Group, Inc. [NASDAQ symbol] (SAG)
PRTLS	Powered Return to Launch Site [NASA] (MCD)
PRTLY	Partially
PRTM	Printing Response-Time Monitor
PrtMcled	Porter McLeod National Retail [Associated Press] (SAG)
PRTN	Partition

PRTN	Proteinase (DMAA)
PRTNR	Partner
PRTNRSHP...	Partnership
PRTO	Preservation Research and Testing Office [*Library of Congress*] (EA)
PRTOT	Prototype Real-Time Optical Tracker [*Computer science*]
PRTP	Prototype (IAA)
PRTQ	Peer Role-Taking Questionnaire [*Psychology*] (EDAC)
PRTR	Plutonium Recycle Test Reactor [*Nuclear energy*]
PRTR	Porter
PRTR	Printer
Prt Rep	Practice Reports [*A publication*] (DLA)
PRTRL	Printer, Lithographer [*Navy*]
PRTRM	Printer, Offset Process [*Navy*]
PRTRNS	Programmable Transformer Converter (MCD)
Prtronx	Printronix, Inc. [*Associated Press*] (SAG)
PRTS	Personal Rapid Transit System [*Computer-guided transit system*]
PRTS	Ports [*Postal Service standard*] (OPSA)
PRTSc	Pretoria Theological Series [*A publication*] (BJA)
PrtSc	Print Screen [*Computer keyboard*]
PRTSTNT	Protestant
PRTV	Positive Response Television [*NASDAQ symbol*] (SAG)
Prtw	Propeller Twist [*Genetics*]
PRTY	Priority
PrtyCty	Party City Corp. [*Associated Press*] (SAG)
PRU	Packet Radio Unit
PRU	Paranagua [*Brazil*] [*Airport symbol*] (AD)
PRU	Pararescue Unit (COE)
PRU	Peripheral Resistance Unit [*Medicine*]
PRU	Photographic Reconnaissance Unit [*Aircraft*] [*Marine Corps*]
PRU	Physical Record Unit (NITA)
PRU	Physical Research Unit (IAA)
PRU	Pneumatic Regulation Unit (AAG)
PRU	Polarity Reversal Unit [*Electrochemistry*]
PRU	Polish-Russian Union (NADA)
PRU	Primary Replacement Unit
PRU	Prisoner's Rights Union (EA)
PRU	Programs Research Unit (KSC)
PRU	Prome [*Myanmar*] [*Airport symbol*] (OAG)
PRU	Provincial Reconnaissance Unit [*Military*]
PRU	Prudential Property & Casualty Insurance Co., Holmdel, NJ [*OCLC symbol*] (OCLC)
PRU	Pruhonice [*Czechoslovakia*] [*Seismograph station code, US Geological Survey*] (SEIS)
PrU	University of Puerto Rico, Rio Piedras, PR [*Library symbol Library of Congress*] (LCLS)
PRUAA	President of the Royal Ulster Academy of Arts
PRUC	Partido Revolucionario de Union Civico [*Revolutionary Party for Civic Union*] [*Costa Rica*] [*Political party*]
PRUC	Practice Reports [*1848-1900*] [*Upper Canada*] [*A publication*] (DLA)
PRUD	Partido Revolucionario de Unification Democratica [*Revolutionary Party of Democratic Unification*] [*El Salvador*]
PrudRe	Prudential Reinsurance Holdings, Inc. [*Associated Press*] (SAG)
PrU-H	University of Puerto Rico, Humacao Regional College, Humacao, PR [*Library symbol Library of Congress*] (LCLS)
PrU-L	University of Puerto Rico, Law Library, San Juan, PR [*Library symbol Library of Congress*] (LCLS)
PrU-M	University of Puerto Rico, School of Medicine, San Juan, PR [*Library symbol Library of Congress*] (LCLS)
PrU-MA	University of Puerto Rico, Mayaguez Campus, Mayaguez, Puerto Rico [*Library symbol Library of Congress*] (LCLS)
PrU-MS	University of Puerto Rico, Department of Marine Sciences, Mayaguez, PR [*Library symbol Library of Congress*] (LCLS)
PRUNIT	Photo Roentgen Unit (IAA)
PrU-NS	University of Puerto Rico, Natural Science Library, Rio Piedras, PR [*Library symbol Library of Congress*] (LCLS)
PRUS	Prussia [*Obsolete*]
Prus	Prussian [*Philately*]
PRUSAF	Puerto Rico, USA Foundation (EA)
PRV	Papaya Ringspot Virus
PRV	Parsley Rhabdovirus [*Plant pathology*]
PRV	Peak Rated Voltage (IAA)
PRV	Peak Reserve Voltage (IAA)
PRV	Peak Reverse Voltage
PRV	Pearl River Valley Railroad Co. [*AAR code*]
PRV	Peugeot Renault Volvo [*Automobile joint project partners*]
PRV	Polycythemia Rubra Vera [*Medicine*]
PRV	Porvoo [*Finland*] [*Seismograph station code, US Geological Survey Closed*] (SEIS)
PRV	Pour Rendre Visite [*To Make a Call*] [*French*]
PRV	Pressure Reducing [*or Regulation or Relief*] Valve
PRV	Pressure Regulator Valve (COE)
PRV	Princess Ventures [*Vancouver Stock Exchange symbol*]
PRV	Prior Record Variable [*Criminal sentencing*]
prv	Private (VRA)
PRV	Propeller Revolution
Prv	Proverbs [*Old Testament book*]
PRV	Provincial
PRV	Provincial Express, Inc. [*Canada ICAO designator*] (FAAC)
PRV	Provisional Reconnaissance Unit
PRV	Pseudorabies Virus
PRV	Pseudorelative Velocity
Prv	Pyruvenol [*Biochemistry*]
PrvAm	Provident American Corp. [*Associated Press*] (SAG)
PrvBksh	Provident Bankshares Corp. [*Associated Press*] (SAG)
prv coll	Private Collection (VRA)

PRVD	Procurement [*or Purchase*] Request for Vendor Data (AAG)
PRVDNC	Providence
Prvena	Provena Foods, Inc. [*Associated Press*] (SAG)
PrvEng	Providence Energy Corp. [*Associated Press*] (SAG)
PRVEP	Pattern Reversal Visual Evoked Potential
PrvLf	Provident Life & Accident Insurance Co. of America [*Associated Press*] (SAG)
PrvLLC	Providian LLC, Inc. [*Associated Press*] (SAG)
PRVNTN	Prevention
PRVNTV	Preventive
PRVS	Penetration Room Ventilation System [*Nuclear energy*] (IEEE)
PRVT	Production Readiness Verification Testing (MCD)
PRVT	Product Reliability Validation Test (MCD)
PRVW	Preview (MSA)
PrvWor	Providence & Worcester Railroad Co. [*Associated Press*] (SAG)
PrvWor	Providence Worcester Railroad Co. [*Associated Press*] (SAG)
PRW	Paired Wire [*Telecommunications*] (TEL)
PRW	Percent Rated Wattage
PRW	Polymerized Ragweed [*Immunology*]
PRW	Press Relations Wire [*Commercial firm*] (EA)
PRW	Promark Software [*Vancouver Stock Exchange symbol*]
PRW	Prosser [*Washington*] [*Seismograph station code, US Geological Survey*] (SEIS)
PRW	Quebecor Printing [*NYSE symbol*] (TTSB)
PRW	Quebecor Printing, Inc. [*NYSE symbol*] (SAG)
PRW	World University, San Juan, PR [*OCLC symbol*] (OCLC)
PRWAD	Professional Rehabilitation Workers with the Adult Deaf [*Later, ADARA*] (EA)
PRWD	Priority Regular World Day
PRWI	Prince William Forest Park [*National Park Service designation*]
PRWO	Puerto Rican Revolutionary Workers Organization
PRWP	Poor R-Wave Progression [*On electrocardiogram*] [*Cardiology*] (DAVI)
PRWRA	Puerto Rican Water Resources Authority
PRWS	President of the Royal Society of Painters in Water Colours [*British*]
PRWV	Peak Reserve Working Voltage
PRX	Paris [*Texas*] [*Airport symbol*] (OAG)
PRX	Paris, TX [*Location identifier FAA*] (FAAL)
PRX	Pharmaceutical Resources [*NYSE symbol*] (SPSG)
PRX	Pressure Regulation Exhaust
PRX	Pseudoexfoliation (DMAA)
PRXI	PRX [*Public Relations Exchange*] International (EA)
PRXL	Parexel International Corp. [*NASDAQ symbol*] (SAG)
PRXL	PAREXEL Intl [*NASDAQ symbol*] (TTSB)
PRXM	Proxima Corp. [*NASDAQ symbol*] (SAG)
PRY	Paraguay [*ANSI three-letter standard code*] (CNC)
PRY	Parys [*South Africa*] [*Seismograph station code, US Geological Survey*] (SEIS)
PRY	Pittway Corp. [*AMEX symbol*] (SPSG)
PRY.A	Pittway Corp.'A' [*AMEX symbol*] (TTSB)
P Ryl	Catalogue of the Greek Papyri in the John Rylands Library at Manchester [*A publication*] (OCD)
PRZ	Portales, NM [*Location identifier FAA*] (FAAL)
PRZ	Potential Repository Zone [*Nuclear waste storage*]
PRZ	Prism Entertainment [*AMEX symbol*] (TTSB)
PRZ	Prism Entertainment Corp. [*AMEX symbol*] (SPSG)
PRZ	Przhevalsk [*Former USSR Seismograph station code, US Geological Survey*] (SEIS)
PRZF	Pyrazofurin [*Antineoplastic drug*]
PRZM	Pesticide Root Zone Model [*Environmental Protection Agency*] (AEPA)
PRZM	Prism Solutions [*NASDAQ symbol*] (SAG)
PS	Abbott Laboratories [*Research code symbol*]
PS	American Political Science Association. Quarterly [*A publication*]
PS	Chloropicrin [*Poison gas*] [*Army symbol*]
PS	Elementary and Early Childhood Education [*Educational Resources Information Center (ERIC) Clearinghouse*] [*University of Illinois*] (PAZ)
PS	Pace Setter (MHDI)
PS	Pacific Southwest Airlines [*ICAO designator*] (OAG)
PS	Pacific Star Communication [*Vancouver Stock Exchange symbol*]
P(S)	Packet (Send)
PS	Packet Switching [*Telecommunications*]
PS	Packet Switch Stream [*British*] [*Computer science*] (TNIG)
PS	Packing Sheet (MCD)
PS	Paddle Steamer (ADA)
PS	Paediatric Surgery
PS	Paget-Schroetter [*Syndrome*] [*Medicine*] (DB)
PS	Painting System
PS	Pakistan Standard (IAA)
PS	Paleontological Society (EA)
PS	Palm Society [*Later, IPS*] (EA)
PS	Paltauf-Sternberg [*Disease*] [*Medicine*] (DB)
PS	Pan Salicornia Zone [*Ecology*]
PS	Parachute Subsystem [*NASA*] (NASA)
PS	Paradoxical Sleep
PS	Parallel Single [*Outdoor advertising*] (NTCM)
PS	Parallel to Serial (NITA)
P/S	Parallel to Serial Converter (MCD)
PS	Paramagnetic Scheromak
PS	Parents of Suicides (EA)
PS	Parents' Section of the Alexander Graham Bell Association for the Deaf (EA)
PS	Parity Switch
PS	Parliamentary Secretary [*British*]

PS	Parlor Snake [Slang for "to escort visitors around post"]
PS	Parochial School
PS	Parrot Society (EA)
ps	PARSEC [Parallax Second] [See PARSEC]
PS	Par Selling (MHDB)
PS	Partially Sighted (AIE)
PS	Partially Smutted [Plant pathology]
PS	Partially Synergistic [Pharmacology]
PS	Partido Socialista [Socialist Party] [Chile] [Political party]
PS	Partido Socialista [Socialist Party] [Uruguay] [Political party]
PS	Partido Socialista Portuguesa [Portuguese Socialist Party] [Political party] (PPE)
PS	Partido Socialista - Uno [Socialist Party - One] [Also, PS-1 Bolivia] [Political party] (PPW)
PS	Parti Socialiste [Socialist Party] [Belgium Political party] (PPW)
PS	Parti Socialiste - Federation de la Reunion [Reunion Federation of the Socialist Party] [Political party] (PPW)
PS	Parts Shipper
PS	Part Surface (IAA)
PS	Passed School of Instruction [of Officers] [British]
PS	Passenger Service
PS	Passenger Steamer
PS	Passing Scuttle
ps	Pastel (VRA)
PS	Pastel Society [British]
PS	Pathological (Surgical) Staging [For Hodgkin's Disease]
PS	Pathologic Stage
PS	Patient's Serum [Medicine]
PS	Patrologia Syriaca (BJA)
PS	Patrol Service [British military] (DMA)
PS	Patrol Ship (CINC)
PS	Patton Society (EA)
P/S	Pause/Still [Video technology]
PS	Payload Shroud (MCD)
PS	Payload Specialist [NASA] (MCD)
PS	Payload Station [NASA] (MCD)
PS	Payload Support [NASA] (NASA)
PS	Paymaster Sergeant
PS	Pedal Sinus
PS	Pediatric Surgery (DAVI)
PS	Pellegrini-Stieda [Disease] [Medicine] (DB)
PS	Pellet Size
PS	Penal Servitude
PS	Penny Stock [Investment term]
PS	Peperomia Society [Later, PEPS] (EA)
PS	Perception Schedule
PS	Perceptual Speed (Test) [Psychology]
PS	Perfect Shuffle (MHDI)
PS	Performance Score
PS	Performance Standard
PS	Performance Status [Rehabilitation] (DAVI)
PS	Performing Scale [Medicine] (MAE)
PS	Perimeter Surveillance (LAIN)
PS	Periodic Syndrome [Medicine]
PS	Peripheral Shock [Psychology]
PS	Permanent Secretary
PS	Permanent Signal [Telecommunications] (TEL)
PS	Per Second (AAMN)
PS	Per Ship
PS	Personal Secretary (DCTA)
PS	Personal Skills
PS	Personal Survival
PS	Personal System [IBM computer introduced in 1987]
PS	Personnel Subsystem [Army]
PS	Per Speculum [Medicine]
PS	Peru Solidarity [An association] (EA)
Ps	Peseta [Monetary unit] [Andorra and Spain] (BARN)
PS	Pet Switchboard [Defunct] (EA)
PS	Petty Sessions (DLA)
PS	Pharmaceutical Society (NADA)
P/S	Phaser/Subarray
PS	Phase Separation
PS	Phase-Shift
PS	Phasing System [Telecommunications] (OA)
PS	Phenix Society (EA)
PS	Phenomenally Speedy Ordinary [Photographic plates] (ROG)
PS	Philalethes Society (EA)
PS	Phillnathean Society (EA)
PS	Philolexian Society (EA)
PS	Philological Society (EAIO)
PS	Philomathean Society (EA)
PS	Phosphate-Saline [A buffer] [Cell culture]
PS	Phosphatidylserine [Biochemistry]
PS	Photochemical System
PS	Photoemission Scintillation (MCD)
PS	Photographic Service
PS	Photographic Squadron
PS	Photometer System (KSC)
PS	Photosystems
PS	Phrase Structure (WGA)
PS	Phylaxis Society (EA)
PS	Physical Sciences
PS	Physical Security
PS	Physical Sequential (HGAA)
PS	Physical Status [Medicine]
PS	Physiological Society (BUAC)
PS	Picket Ships [Navy]
ps	Picosecond [One trillionth of a second]
PS	Pilgrim Power Station (NRCH)
PS	Pilgrim Society (EA)
PS	Pineal Stalk [Neuroanatomy]
PS	Pine Bark Mixed with Clay Loam Soil
PS	Pine Siskin [Ornithology]
PS	Pink Sheet [Investment term]
PS	Pipe Size (BARN)
PS	Pirandello Society (EA)
PS	Pisosecond (IAA)
PS	Pistol Sharpshooter [Army]
PS	Pitot/Static Tube (MCD)
PS	[The] Pittsburg & Shawmut Railroad Co. [AAR code]
PS	Pituitary Stalk [Neuroanatomy]
PS	Planetary Society (EA)
PS	Planetary Surface (IAA)
PS	Planning and Scheduling
PS	Planning Study (AAG)
PS	Plant Stress [Horticulture]
PS	Plastic Surgery [Medicine]
PS	Plate Sunk [Printing] (DGA)
PS	Platform (Sided) (DCTA)
P/S	Platoon/Section [Army]
PS	Plea Side (ROG)
PS	Pleural Sclerite [Entomology]
PS	Plotting System
PS	Plus
PS	Pneumatic Suspension [Automotive engineering]
PS	Pneumatic System
PS	Poetry Society [British]
P/S	Point of Shipment
PS	Point of Switch
PS	Point of Symmetry
PS	Point Source (COE)
PS	Point Sparger [Engineering]
PS	Point Spread [In visual cortex]
PS	Polanyi Society (EA)
PS	Polaris Standard [Missiles]
PS	Polarity Scale [Psychology]
PS	Polarity Selector (IAA)
PS	Police Sergeant [Scotland Yard]
PS	Policy Statement
PS	Polio Society (EA)
PS	Polite Society (BUAC)
Ps	Polyporus sulphureus [A fungus]
PS	Polysaccharide (DB)
PS	Polystyrene [Organic chemistry]
PS	Polysulfone [Also, PSO] [Organic chemistry]
P/S	Polyunsaturated/Saturated [Fatty acid ratio]
PS	Population Sample (MAE)
PS	Porlock Society (EA)
PS	Porous Silicon [Physics]
PS	Porter-Silber Chromogen [Medicine] (MAE)
P/S	Port or Starboard
PS	Port Security
PS	Port Store [Telecommunications] (TEL)
PS	Port Strobe [Telecommunications] (TEL)
PS	Pos-Escrito [Postscript] [Portuguese]
PS	Position-Specific Antigen
PS	Positive Value (DA)
PS	Postal Satsang [An association] (EA)
PS	Postal Service [US]
PS	Poster Society (EA)
PS	PostScript [Adobe printer language]
ps	PostScript [Computer science]
PS	Post Scriptum [Written Afterwards, Postscript] [Latin]
PS	Potassium Sorbate [Food additive]
PS	Potentiometer Synchro
P/S	Power Section (NG)
PS	Power Series (IAA)
PS	Power Source
PS	Power-Specific (MCD)
PS	Power Spectra [Neurophysiology]
PS	Power Station (MCD)
PS	Power Steering [Automobile ads]
PS	Power Supply
PS	Powys Society (EA)
PS	Prairie Schooner [A publication] (BRI)
PS	Prairies Service [Record series prefix] [Canada]
PS	Predictive Saccades [Ophthalmology]
PS	Preduzece Soko [Former Yugoslavia] [ICAO aircraft manufacturer identifier] (ICAO)
PS	Preferred Stock [Investment term]
PS	Prehistoric Society (EA)
PS	Preliminary Study
PS	Preparedness Staff [Environmental Protection Agency] (GFGA)
Ps	Prescription (AAMN)
PS	Presenilin [Biochemistry]
PS	Presentation Services [Computer science] (IBMDP)
PS	Press Secretary (ILCA)
PS	Press to Start (KSC)
PS	Pressure [or Propellant] Seal
P-S	Pressure-Sensitive

PS	Pressure Sensor
PS	Pressure Switch
Ps	Pressure, Systolic [Cardiology]
PS	Price Spreading [Business term]
PS	Primary School (ADA)
PS	Prime Select (MCD)
PS	Prime Sponsor
PS	Principal Sojourner [Freemasonry] (ROG)
PS	Principal Subject [In a sonata or rondo] [Music] (ROG)
PS	Print Scan [Computer science] (IAA)
PS	Prior Service [Military]
PS	Private Screenings [Cable TV programming service]
PS	Private Secretary
PS	Private Security Program [Association of Independent Colleges and Schools specialization code]
PS	Private Siding [Rail] [Shipping] (DS)
PS	Privy Seal [British]
PS	Probability of Survival (MCD)
PS	Problem Specification
PS	Problem Statement [Computer science] (IAA)
PS	Procambial Strand [Botany]
PS	Processor Status
PS²	Process Sheet
PS	Process Solution (MCD)
PS	Process Specification
PS	Process Storage [Computer science] (IAA)
PS	Process Subsystem [Telecommunications] (TEL)
PS	Procurement Specification (MCD)
PS	Product Service (IAA)
PS	Product Software (MCD)
PS	Product Standards (MCD)
PS	Product Support
PS	Profit Sharing [Business term]
PS	Programmable Switch [Computer science] (IAA)
PS	Programmed Symbols (MEDA)
PS	Programming System
PS	Program Section [Computer science] (IAA)
PS	Program Simulation (OICC)
PS	Program Source [Computer science] (IAA)
PS	Program Specification (MCD)
PS	Program Start (KSC)
PS	Program Stateword [Computer science] (IAA)
PS	Program Status [Computer science] (IAA)
PS	Program Store [Computer science] (IEEE)
PS	Program Summary (NG)
PS	Project Slip
PS	Project Start [Milestone chart]
PS	Project Stock [Military] (AABC)
PS	Project Study [British military] (DMA)
PS	Proler International Corp. [NYSE symbol] (SPSG)
PS	Proler Intl [NYSE symbol] (TTSB)
PS	Prolifers for Survival [Defunct] (EA)
PS	Prometheus Society (EA)
PS	Prompt Side [of a stage] [i.e., the right side A stage direction]
PS	Proof Shot [Ammunition]
PS	Proof Stress
PS	Propellant Supply (KSC)
PS	Propellant System
PS	Proportional Spacing [Typography] (WDMC)
PS	Propulsion Section
PS	Prostaglandin Synthetase [An enzyme]
PS	Protection Strategy (COE)
PS	Protective Service
PS	Protective Shelter
PS	Protective Subsystem [Military] (INF)
PS	Protect Status (MHDB)
PS	Protein Society (BUAC)
PS	Protein Synthesis
PS	Proton Synchrotron [Nuclear energy]
PS	Protoplasmic Surface [Freeze etching in microscopy]
PS	Proto-Semitic (BJA)
PS	Provost-Sergeant
PS	Psalm
Ps	Psalms [Old Testament book]
PS	Pseudo [Classical studies] (OCD)
Ps	Pseudomonas [Bacterium] (MAE)
PS	Pseudomonas Stutzeri [Bacterium]
PS	Pseudonym (WGA)
PS	Psychiatric (MAE)
PS	Psychology Society (EA)
PS	Psychometric Society (EA)
PS	Psychonomic Society (EA)
PS	Psychotic
PS	Publication Standard
PS	Public Sale
PS	Public School
PS	Public Service
PS	Public Statutes [Legal term] (DLA)
PS	Public Stenographer
PS	Public Storage (EFIS)
PS	Publishing Services [American Library Association]
PS	Puget Sound [Also, Puget Sound Naval Shipyard] [Washington]
PS	Pull Switch
PS	Pulmonary Sequestration
PS	Pulmonary Stenosis [Medicine]
PS	Pulse per Second (IAA)
PS	Pulse Sensor (KSC)
PS	Pulse Shaper
PS	Pulses per Second [Data transmission] (DEN)
PS	Pulse Stretcher
PS	Pumping Station (NATG)
PS	Purdon's Pennsylvania Statutes [A publication] (DLA)
PS	Purity-Supreme [Supermarkets]
PS	Pyloric Stenosis [Medicine]
PS	Serum From a Pregnant Woman (DAVI)
ps----	South Pacific [MARC geographic area code Library of Congress] (LCCP)
PS	South Pole [Also, SP]
PS	Static Pressure
PS	Swarthmore Public Library, Swarthmore, PA [Library symbol Library of Congress] (LCLS)
PS	Transport [Russian aircraft symbol]
PS	US Postal Service (AAGC)
PS-1	Partido Socialista - Uno [Socialist Party - One] [Also, PS Bolivia] [Political party] (PD)
PS/2	Personal System/2 [IBM Corp.]
PS2	Picture System 2 [Evans & Sutherland Computer Corp.] (MCD)
PS²	Profound Sensitivity Syndrome [Psychology]
PS3	PROBE [Program Optimization and Budget Evaluation] Staff Support System [Military]
PS2000	Public Service 2000 Program [Canada]
PSA	Pacific Island Aviation, Inc. [Mariana Islands] [ICAO designator] (FAAC)
PSA	Pacific Science Association [Hawaii] (BUAC)
PSA	Pacific Seedsmens Association (BUAC)
PSA	Pacific Southwest Airlines
PSA	Pakistan Sociological Association (BUAC)
PSA	Parametric Semiconductor Amplifier
PSA	Parametric Sound Amplifier [Blaupunkt]
PSA	Parcel Shippers Association (EA)
PSA	Particle Size Analyzer
PSA	Partido Socialista Aponte [Bolivia] [Political party] (PPW)
PSA	Partido Socialista Argentino [Socialist Party of Argentina] [Political party]
PSA	Parti Socialiste Autonome [Autonomous Socialist Party] [France Political party] (PPE)
PSA	Parti Solidaire Africain [African Solidarity Party] [Congo] [Political party]
PSA	Partito Socialista Autonomo [Autonomous Socialist Party] [Switzerland Political party] (PPW)
PSA	Part Stress Analysis (MCD)
PSA	Passenger Shipping Association [British] (DBA)
PSA	Pastel Society of America (EA)
PSA	Past Shakedown Availability [Military]
PSA	Path of Steepest Ascent [Statistical design of experiments]
PSA	Path Selection Algorithm [Telecommunications] (TEL)
PSA	Patient Care Associate [Medicine]
PSA	Payload Service Area [NASA] (NASA)
PSA	Payload Support Avionics [NASA] (NASA)
PSA	Peace and Solidarity Alliance (EA)
PSA	Peace Studies Association (EA)
PSA	People's Supreme Assembly [Yemen] [Political party] (PPW)
PSA	Personal Service Agreements (MCD)
PSA	Personal Statement Analyzer (HGAA)
PSA	Personnel and Service Area [Nuclear energy] (NRCH)
PSA	Personnel Support Activity (DOMA)
PSA	Petersburg [Alaska] [Seismograph station code, US Geological Survey] (SEIS)
PSA	Petites Soeurs de l'Assumption [Little Sisters of the Assumption - LSA] [Paris, France] (EAIO)
PSA	Peugot Societe Anonyme [Peugeot Co. Ltd.] [French]
PSA	Philippine Standards Association (IAA)
PSA	Philippine Sugar Association [Later, PSC] (EA)
PSA	Philosophy of Science Association (EA)
PSA	Phlebology Society of America (NTPA)
PSA	Phobia Society of America [Later, ADAA] (EA)
PSA	Photographic Society of America (EA)
PSA	Phycological Society of America (EA)
PSA	Pickles and Sauces Association [British] (DBA)
PSA	Pipe Stress Analysis (PDAA)
PSA	Pirandello Society of America (EA)
PSA	Pisa [Italy] [Airport symbol] (OAG)
PsA	Pisces Austrinus [Constellation]
PSA	Pisces Society of America
PSA	Play Schools Association (EA)
PSA	Pleasant Sunday Afternoons
PSA	Plumeria Society of America (EA)
PSA	Pneumatic Sensor Assembly
PSA	Poe Studies Association (EA)
PSA	Poetry Society of America (EA)
PSA	Police Superintendents' Association [New Zealand] (WDAA)
PSA	Political Studies Association [British]
PSA	Political Studies Association of the United Kingdom (BUAC)
PSA	Polycrystalline Silicon Self-Aligned [Photovoltaic energy systems] (MHDI)
PSA	Polyethylene Sulfonic Acid [Organic chemistry] (MAE)
PSA	Polysialic Acid [Organic chemistry]
PSA	Polysilicic Acid [Organic chemistry]
PSA	Portable Sanitation Association (EA)
PSA	Portable Sound Analyzer

PSA............	Port Storage Area [Telecommunications] (TEL)
PSA............	Port Support Activity (DOMA)
PSA............	Post Shakedown Availability
PSA............	Post-Sleep Activity
PSA............	Potential Surface Analysis (ADA)
PSA............	Potters' Society of Australia
PSA............	Poultry Science Association (EA)
PSA............	Power Saw Association [British] (BI)
PSA............	Power Servo Amplifier (KSC)
PSA............	Power Servo Assembly (MCD)
PSA............	Power Supply Assembly
PSA............	Power Switching Amplifier
PSA............	Power Switching Assembly
PSA............	Precipitation Series Algorithm [Marine science] (OSRA)
PSA............	Prefabricated Surfacing Aluminum
PSA............	Preferred Storage Area (MCD)
PSA............	Prefix Storage Area [Computer science] (OA)
PSA............	Preliminary Safety Analysis [NASA] (SSD)
PSA............	Pre/Post Sleep Activity (NASA)
PSA............	President of the Society of Antiquaries [British]
PSA............	Pressure Sensitive Adhesive [Trademark]
PSA............	Pressure Suit Assembly
PSA............	Pressure-Swing Adsorption [Chemical engineering]
PSA............	Pressure Switch Assembly (NASA)
PSA............	Pressure Switching Alarm [Engineering]
PSA............	Presunrise Authority
PSA............	Presunrise Service Authority (NTCM)
PSA............	Prices Surveillance Authority (BUAC)
PSA............	Principal Supervisory Agent (EBF)
PSA............	Private Schools Association [British]
PSA............	Probabilistic Safety Analysis (NRCH)
PSA............	Problem Statement Analyzer [Computer science] (IAA)
PSA............	Process Service Area (IAA)
PSA............	Procurement Seminar for Auditors [Army]
PSA............	Product Safety Association [Defunct] (EA)
PSA............	Product Support Administration (MCD)
PSA............	Professional Sales Association (NTPA)
PSA............	Professional Salespersons of America [Defunct] (EA)
PSA............	Professional Service Association (EA)
PSA............	Professional Services Agreement (COE)
PSA............	Professional Skaters Association (NTPA)
PSA............	Professional Skills Alliance (EA)
PSA............	Professional Squash Association (NTPA)
PSA............	Professional Stringers Association [Defunct] (EA)
PSA............	Programmed Shutter and Aperture [Photography] (DICI)
PSA............	Program Study Authorization (KSC)
PSA............	Progressive Spinal Ataxia [Medicine] (DMAA)
PSA............	Prolonged Sleep Apnea
PSA............	Promoting Stress & Anxiety (WDAA)
PSA............	Promotional Sourcing Association (BUAC)
PSA............	Property Services Agency [Department of the Environment] [British]
PSA............	Prostate-Specific Antigen [Immunochemistry]
PSA............	Protective Security Attendant [Australia]
PSA............	Province Senior Advisor [Army] (VNW)
PSA............	Provisional Site Acceptance (NATG)
PSA............	Provisions Stowage Assembly (NASA)
PSA............	Psalm
Psa............	Psalms [Old Testament book]
PSA............	Pseudomonic Acid [Biochemistry]
PsA............	Psoriatic Arthritis (DAVI)
PSA............	Psychological Operations Support Activity [Military] (MCD)
PSA............	Psychological Semantic Analysis (NITA)
PSA............	Psychologists for Social Action [Defunct] (EA)
PSA............	Publication Systems Associates, Inc. [Information service or system] (IID)
PSA............	Public Securities Association [Database producer] (EA)
PSA............	Public Service Act
PSA............	Public Service Alliance (BUAC)
PSA............	Public Service Announcement
PSA............	Public Service Association [New Zealand] (WDAA)
PSA............	Public Storage [NYSE symbol] (TTSB)
PSA............	Public Storage, Inc. [NYSE symbol] (SAG)
PSA............	Push Down Stack Automaton [Computer science]
PSA............	Storage Properties, Inc. [AMEX symbol] (SPSG)
PSAA	Pacific Special Activities Area [Military]
PSAA	Pakistan Students' Association of America
PSAA	Plasma Sciences and Applications (IAA)
PSAA	Polish Singers Alliance of America (EA)
PSAA	Polwarth Sheepbreeders' Association of Australia
PSAA	Poststimulatory Auditory Adaptation
PSAAV	Provincial Sewerage Authorities Association of Victoria [Australia]
PSAB	Pathology Services Accreditation Board [Victoria, Australia]
PSAB	Prime Bancorp [NASDAQ symbol] (TTSB)
PSAB	Prime Bancorp, Inc. [NASDAQ symbol] (CTT)
PSAB	Production Systems Acceptance Branch [Social Security Administration]
PSAC	Passive Satellite Attitude Control
PSAC	Pennsylvania State Athletic Conference (PSS)
PSAC	Personnel Service Company [Army] (AABC)
PSAC	Policy Signing and Accounting Centre [Insurance firm] [British]
PSAC	Preferred Stock Advisory Committee [New Deal]
PSAC	President's Science Advisory Committee [Terminated, 1973] [Executive Office of the President]
PSAC	Private Security Advisory Council [Terminated, 1977] [Department of Justice] (EGAO)
PSAC	Production Statistics Advisory Committee (BUAC)
PSAC	Product Safety Advisory Council [Consumer Product Safety Commission]
PSAC	Professional Skating Association of Canada
PSAC	Public Service Alliance of Canada [Labor union of federal government employees]
PSACH	Pseudoachondrodysplasia [Medicine] (DMAA)
PSACN	Process Specification Advance Change Notice (SAA)
PSAcPh........	Prostate-Specific Acid Phosphatase [An enzyme]
PSACPOO	President's Scientific Advisory Committee Panel on Oceanography [Marine science] (MSC)
PSAD	Predicted Site Acquisition Data [NASA]
PSAD	Prediction, Simulation, Adaptation, Decision [Computer science]
PSAD	Procurement and Systems Acquisition Division (AAGC)
PSAE	Philippine Society of Agricultural Engineers (BUAC)
PSAF...........	Private Sector Adjustment Factor [Banking]
PSAG	Pelvic Sonoangiography [Medicine] (DMAA)
PSAGN	Poststreptococcal Acute Glomerulonephritis [Medicine]
PSAI...........	Pediatric Services of Amer [NASDAQ symbol] (TTSB)
PSAI...........	Pediatric Services of America, Inc. [NASDAQ symbol] (SAG)
PSAI...........	Political Studies Association of Ireland (BUAC)
PSAI...........	Portable Sanitation Association International (NTPA)
PSAIR	Priority Specific Air Information Request [Defense Mapping Agency] (MCD)
PSAJ	Peace Studies Association of Japan (BUAC)
PSAL	Permanent Supplementary Artificial Lighting (IAA)
PSAL	Programming System Activity Log [Computer science]
PSAL	Public Schools Athletic League
PSALI..........	Permanent Supplementary Artificial Lighting of Interiors (IEEE)
P Salin	Petrus de Salinis [Flourished, 13th century] [Authority cited in pre-1607 legal work] (DSA)
PSALM	Project Structured Analysis of LOGEX [Logistical Exercise] Methodology (MCD)
PSAM	Partitioned Sequence Access Method
PSAM	Point Source Ambient Monitoring [Environmental Protection Agency] (GFGA)
PSAMS	Plessey Scientific-Atlanta Multistar System (NITA)
PSAN	Phase Stabilized Ammonium Nitrate (MCD)
PSAn..........	Psychoanalysis [or Psychoanalyst] (DAVI)
PS & A	Pharmacy, Supply, and Administration (DOMA)
PS & B	Power Steering and Brakes [Automotive engineering] (IIA)
PS & C	Private Siding and Collected One End
PS&C	Production Scheduling and Control (AAGC)
PS & CC	Packaging, Storage, and Containerization Center [DARCOM] (MCD)
PS & D	Private Siding and Delivered One End
PS & DS	Program Statistics and Data Systems
PS & E........	Plans, Specifications, and Estimates [Construction]
PS & ER	Production Support and Equipment Replacement [Military] (AABC)
PS & L	Power Switching and Logic
PS & M	Personnel Supervision and Management Division of ASTSECNAV's Office [Absorbed into SECP, 1944]
PS & T........	Pay, Subsistence, and Transportation [Military]
PSANDT.......	Pay, Subsistence, and Transportation [Military]
PS & TC	Population Studies and Training Center [Brown University] [Research center] (RCD)
PS & TN	Pay, Subsistence, and Transportation, Navy
PS & W	Pacific, Southern & Western Railroad [Nickname: Play Safe and Walk]
PSANP	Phenol-Soluble Acidic Nuclear Protein [s] [Biochemistry]
PSAO	Pharmacy Services Administrative Organization
PSAO	Primary Staff Action Officer [Military]
PSAP	Phenylsulfonylacetophenone
PSAP	Plane Stress Analysis and Plot [Computer science]
PSAP	Presentation Service Access Point [Telecommunications] (OSI)
PSAP	Primary Public Safety Answering Point (DMAA)
PSAP	Public Safety Answering Point [Telecommunications] (TEL)
PSAP	Public Service Answering Point
PSAP	Pulmonary Surfactant Apoprotein [Biochemistry]
PSAPR	Pathology Society of Asia and Pacific Region (BUAC)
PSAPrA	Public Storage 10% cm'A'Pfd [NYSE symbol] (TTSB)
PSAPrB	Public Storage 9.20% cm'B'Pfd [NYSE symbol] (TTSB)
PSAPrC	Public Storage Adj Rt'C'Pfd [NYSE symbol] (TTSB)
PSAPrD........	Public Storage 9.50%'D'Pfd [NYSE symbol] (TTSB)
PSAPrE	Public Storage 10%'E'Pfd [NYSE symbol] (TTSB)
PSAPrF	Public Storage 9.75% 'F' Pfd [NYSE symbol] (TTSB)
PSAPrG	Public Storage 8.875% Dep Pfd [NYSE symbol] (TTSB)
PSAPrH........	Public Storage 8.45%'H'Dep Pfd [NYSE symbol] (TTSB)
PSAPrX	Public Storage 8.25%Cv Pfd [NYSE symbol] (TTSB)
PSAR	Platform Shock Attenuation and Realignment System (MCD)
PSAR	Pneumatic [or Pressure] System Automatic Regulator (AAG)
PSAR	Preliminary Safety Analysis Report
PSAR	Pressure System Automatic Regulator (IAA)
PSAR	Process Storage Address Register [Computer science] (IAA)
PSAR	Programmable Synchronous/Asynchronous Receiver (IEEE)
PSAR	Propulsion Systems Analysis Report (SAA)
PSarg..........	Pre-Sargonic (BJA)
PSAS	Prespeech Assessment Scale [Occupational therapy]
PSAS	Production Systems Acceptance Section [Social Security Administration]
PSAS	Program Support and Advanced Systems (SAA)
PSASA	Public Service Association of South Australia
PSASS	Perishable Subsistence Automated Supply System [DoD]
PSASV	Phase-Sensitive Anodic Stripping Voltammetry
PSAT...........	Predicted Site Acquisition Table [NASA]
PSAT...........	Preliminary Scholastic Aptitude Test

PSAT........... Programmable Synchronous/Asynchronous Transmitter (IEEE)
PSAT/NMSQT... Preliminary Scholastic Aptitude/National Merit Scholarship Qualifying Test (PAZ)
PSAUK........ Political Studies Association of the United Kingdom
PSAUSA...... Polish Socialist Alliance of the United States of America (EA)
PSAX .... Pacific Southwest Airlines [Air carrier designation symbol]
PSB............. Bellefonte-Clearfield-Philipsburg [Pennsylvania] [Airport symbol] (AD)
PSB............. Pacific Science Board [National Academy of Sciences]
PSB............. Phase Shifting Blank (AAEL)
PSB............. Philatelic Sales Branch [Later, PSD] [US Postal Service]
PSB............. Philipsburg, PA [Location identifier FAA] (FAAL)
PSB............. Phosphorus-Solubilizing Bacteria [Microbiology]
PSB............. Plant Safety Bureau
PSB............. Plant Service Building [Nuclear energy] (NRCH)
PSB............. Plough, Sweeper, and Blower (DA)
PSB............. Police Superannuation Board [Australia]
PSB............. Polytechnic of the South Bank [London, England]
PSB............. Premium Savings Bond [British] (DCTA)
PSB............. Professional and Statutory Board (AIE)
PSB............. Program Specification Block [IBM Corp.]
PSB............. Program Station Basis [Rating system] (WDMC)
PSB............. Protected Specimen Brush [Medicine]
PSB............. Protein S Beta (DMAA)
PSB............. PS Business Parks, Inc. [AMEX symbol] (SPSG)
PSB............. Psychological Services Bureau (AEBS)
PSB............. Psychological Strategy Board [Military] (LAIN)
PSB............. Public Service Board (NADA)
PSBA .... Power-Specific Biological Activity [Engine emissions testing]
PSBA .... Public School Bursars' Association [British] (BI)
PSBBF .... Pearl S. Buck Birthplace Foundation (EA)
PSBBrc .... Peoples Savings Bank of Brockton [Associated Press] (SAG)
PSBCA .... Painted Soda Bottles Collectors Association (EA)
PSBCA .... Postal Service Board of Contract Appeals (AAGC)
PSbetaG ...... Pregnancy-Specific Beta-1-Glycoprotein [Medicine] (DMAA)
PSBF .... Pearl S. Buck Foundation (EA)
PSBG .... Pregnancy-Specific beta-Glycoprotein [Gynecology]
PSBH .... Pad Safety in Blockhouse
PSBH .... Phonon Side-Band Hole [Spectroscopy]
PSBI........... Performance Standardization Branch Instruction (SAA)
PSBK .... Progressive Bank [NASDAQ symbol] (TTSB)
PSBK .... Progressive Bank, Inc. [Pawling, NY] [NASDAQ symbol] (NQ)
PSBL .... Possible (FAAC)
PSBLS .... Permanent Space Based Logistics System
PSBMA .... Professional Services Business Management Association [Later, PSMA] (EA)
PsbMV .... Pea Seed-Borne Mosaic Virus
PSBNAME.... Program Specification Block Name [Computer science] (MHDB)
PSBO .... Partial Small Bowel Obstruction [Medicine] (MEDA)
PSBP .... PS Business Parks, Inc. [Associated Press] (SAG)
PSBPrB .... Pub Sv Colo, 8.40% Pfd [NYSE symbol] (TTSB)
PSBR .... Pennsylvania State University Breazeale Nuclear Reactor [Research center] (RCD)
PSBR .... Public Sector Borrowing Requirement
PSBS .... Phoenix Society for Burn Survivors (EA)
PSBT........... Pilot Self-Briefing Terminal [Aviation] (FAAC)
PSBU .... Propeller Shaft Bearing Unit [Truck engineering]
PSBU .... Public Sector and Broadcasting Union [Australia]
PSBV .... Public Service Board Victoria [Australia]
PSC............. Congolese Socialist Party [Zaire] [Political party] (PD)
PSC............. Isla De Pascua [Easter Island] [Seismograph station code, US Geological Survey Closed] (SEIS)
PSC............. Pacific Salmon Commission (EA)
PSC............. Pacific Science Center
PSC............. Pacific Science Council
PSC............. Pacific South Coast Freight Bureau, San Francisco CA [STAC]
PSC............. Pacific Studies Center (EA)
PSC............. Palaeontological Society of China (BUAC)
PSC............. Palestine Solidarity Campaign (BUAC)
PSC............. Palestine Solidarity Committee [Defunct] (EA)
PSC............. Palmer Skin Conductance
PSC............. Parallel Switch Control (MCD)
PSC............. Parallel to Serial Converter
PSC............. Parents Sharing Custody (EA)
PSC............. Partido Social Conservador Colombiano [Colombian Social Conservative Party] [Political party] (EY)
PSC............. Partido Social Cristiano [Social Christian Party] [Guatemala] [Political party] (PPW)
PSC............. Partido Social Cristiano [Social Christian Party] [Bolivia] [Political party]
PSC............. Partido Social Cristiano [Social Christian Party] [Ecuador] [Political party] (PPW)
PSC............. Partido Socialcristiano Nicaraguense [Nicaraguan Social Christian Party] [Political party] (PPW)
PSC............. Partido Socialista de Catalunya [Catalan Socialist Party] [Spain Political party] (PPE)
PSC............. Parti Socialiste Caledonien [New Caledonia] [Political party] (FEA)
PSC............. Parti Socialiste Camerounais [Cameroon Socialist Party] [Political party]
PSC............. Parti Socialiste Centrafricain [Central African Socialist Party] [Political party] (PD)
PSC............. Pasco [Washington] [Airport symbol] (OAG)
PSC............. Pasco, WA [Location identifier FAA] (FAAL)
PSC............. Passaic Byzantine [Diocesan abbreviation] [New Jersey] (TOCD)
PSC............. Passed Staff College [British]
PSC............. Passenger Services Conference [IATA] (DS)

psc............. Passes Staff College [British] (WA)
PSC............. Patriot Steering Committee
PSC............. Paul Smiths College [New York]
PSC............. Peacetime Subcontract
PSC............. Pembroke State College [North Carolina]
PSC............. Percentage of Successful Collisions [Obstetrics]
PSC............. Permanent Split Capacitor (IAA)
PSC............. Personal Service Corporation (EBF)
PSC............. Personal Services Contractor
PSC............. Personal Supercomputer [Culler Scientific Systems Corp.]
PSC............. Personnel Service Center [or Company] [Military] (INF)
PSC............. Personnel Status Change (KSC)
PSC............. Personnel Subsystem Cost
PSC............. Per Standard Compass [Navigation]
PSC............. Petty Sessional Court [British] (ROG)
PSC............. Phase-Sensitive Converter
PSC............. Philadelphia Service Center [IRS]
PSC............. Philadelphia Suburban Corp. [NYSE symbol] (SPSG)
PSC............. Philander Smith College [Little Rock, AR]
PSC............. Phila Suburban [NYSE symbol] (TTSB)
PSC............. Philippine Sugar Commission (EA)
PSC............. Phonemic Spelling Council [Defunct] (EA)
PSC............. Photographic Sciences Corp. (EFIS)
PSC............. Photosensitive Cell (IEEE)
PSC............. Phylogenetic Species Concept [Biology]
PSC............. Physical Sciences Center
PSC............. Physical Sciences Committee [Terminated, 1977] [NASA] (EGAO)
PSC............. Physical Security/Pilferage Code (MCD)
PSC............. Pipe Smokers' Council (BUAC)
Psc............. Pisces [Constellation]
PSC............. Pittsburgh Supercomputing Center [National Science Foundation Research center] (RCD)
PSC............. Pittsburgh Superconducting Center [Pennsylvania] (GRD)
pSC............. Plasmid Stanley Cohen [Molecular biology]
PSC............. Platform Support Center [NASA] (SSD)
PSC............. Pluripotent Stem Cell [Cytology]
PSC............. Plutonium Stripping Concentrate [Nuclear energy] (NRCH)
PSC............. Point Shipping Co. [Steamship] (MHDW)
PSC............. Polaroid Stereoscopic Chroncyclegraph
PSC............. Polar Science Center [University of Washington] [Research center] (RCD)
PSC............. Polar Stratospheric Cloud [Meteorology]
PSC............. Population Studies Center [University of Michigan] [Research center] (RCD)
PSC............. Porcelain on Steel Council [Defunct] (EA)
PSC............. Porous Silicon Capacitor (AAEL)
PSC............. Porter-Silber Chromogen [Medicine] (MAE)
PSC............. Portland Society for Calligraphy (EA)
PSC............. Postal Service Center (AFM)
PSC............. Posterior Subcapsular Cataracts [Ophthalmology]
PSC............. Post-Storage Checkout [NASA] (KSC)
PSC............. Postsynaptic Current [Neurophysiology]
PSC............. Potentiometer Strip Chart
PSC............. Potomac State College [of West Virginia University]
PSC............. Power Supply Calibrator
PSC............. Power System Communications (IAA)
PSC............. Prairie Swine Centre [University of Saskatchewan] [Canada] (IRC)
PSC............. Prairie Swine Centre, Inc. [Canada] (BUAC)
PSC............. Preferred Semiconductor Circuit [Electronics] (IAA)
PSC............. Pressure Suit Circuit (KSC)
PSC............. Pressure System Control (AAG)
PSC............. Prestressed Cement (EDCT)
PSC............. Prestressed Concrete (ADA)
PSC............. Presumptive Hematopoietic Stem Cell
PSC............. Price Signal Code [Military] (AABC)
PSC............. Primary Sclerosing Cholangitis [Medicine]
PSC............. Principal Subordinate Command (NATG)
PSC............. Private Secretary's Certificate [British] (DI)
PSC............. Private Sector Council (EA)
PSC............. PROBE [Program Optimization and Budget Evaluation] Steering Committee [Military]
PSC............. Processing and Spectral Control
PSC............. Processing Service Centers [Social Security Administration]
PSC............. Procurement Source Code (AFM)
PSC............. Product and Service Code (AAGC)
PSC............. Production Scheduling and Control (IAA)
PSC............. Product Safety Committee [New South Wales, Australia]
PSC............. Product Support Confidential (AAG)
PSC............. Professional Service Corporation [Medicine] (HCT)
PSC............. Professional Services Council [Washington, DC] (EA)
PSC............. Programmable Sample Changer [Spectroscopy]
PSC............. Program Schedule Chart (NASA)
PSC............. Program Sequence Control (NITA)
PSC............. Program Service Center [Social Security Administration] (OICC)
PSC............. Program Standards Checker [Computer science]
PSC............. Program Status Chart [Computer science]
PSC............. Program Structure Code (AFM)
PSC............. Program Support Contract (SSD)
PSC............. Program Switching Center [Computer science] (IAA)
PSC............. Project Systems Control (MCD)
PSC............. Propagating Space Charge (PDAA)
PSC............. Protosolar Cloud [Astronomy]
PSC............. Prototype System Characteristics
PSC............. PSC, Inc. [Associated Press] (SAG)
PSC............. Public Service Careers [Program] [Department of Labor]

PSC............	Public Service Co.
PSC............	Public Service Commission [*Usually, of a specific state*]
PSC............	Public Service Commission [*Canada*] (BUAC)
PSC............	Pulse Shape Control Circuit (IAA)
PSC............	Pulse Synchronized Contraction [*In the vascular system*] [*Medicine*]
PSC............	Sandoz AG [*Switzerland*] [*Research code symbol*]
PSc............	Scranton Public Library, Scranton, PA [*Library symbol Library of Congress*] (LCLS)
PSC............	Swarthmore College, Swarthmore, PA [*Library symbol Library of Congress OCLC symbol*] (LCLS)
PSCA...........	Parliamentary Select Committee on Agriculture [*British*]
PscA...........	Pisces Austrinus [*Constellation*]
PSCA...........	Polish Social and Cultural Association [*British*] (EAIO)
PSCA...........	Pressure Suit Conditioning Assembly (MCD)
PSCA...........	Profit Sharing Council of America (EA)
PSCACM......	Permanent Secretariat of the Central American Common Market
PSCAGNT.....	Podhale Social-Cultural Association of Gypsies in Nowy Targ [*Poland*] (BUAC)
PSCAN........	Purchase Order Scan
PSCAV........	Professional Squash Coaches' Association of Victoria [*Australia*]
PSCB..........	Padded Sample Collection Bag [*NASA*]
PSCB..........	Parliamentary Standing Committee on Broadcasting [*Australia*]
PSCBG........	Paper Shipping-Containers Buyers Group
PSCC..........	Photo Systems Controller Console (KSC)
PSCC..........	Posterior Subcapsular Cataract [*Medicine*] (STED)
PSCC..........	Power System Communications (IAA)
PSCC..........	Projets de Services Communautaires du Canada
PSCD..........	Plutonium Stripping Concentration Distillate [*Nuclear energy*] (NRCH)
PSCD..........	Postcard (VRA)
PSCD..........	Program for the Study of Crime and Delinquency [*Ohio State University*] [*Research center*] (RCD)
PSCE..........	Presurgical Coagulation Evaluation [*Medicine*] (DAVI)
PSCEC........	Planning Status of Committed Engineering Changes (SAA)
PSCF..........	Personal Security Clearance File
PSCF..........	Processor Storage Control Function
PSCFB........	Pacific South Coast Freight Bureau
PSCG..........	Power Supply and Control Gear
PSCG..........	Power Supply Control Group [*Military*] (CAAL)
PSCH..........	Postoperative Suprachoroidal Hemorrhage [*Medicine*]
PsChE........	Pseudocholinesterase (STED)
PSC-Hi.......	Friends Historical Library of Swarthmore College, Swarthmore, PA [*Library symbol Library of Congress*] (LCLS)
PSCI..........	Perez Self-Concept Inventory [*Psychology*] (EDAC)
PSCI..........	Plastic Shipping Container Institute (EA)
Psci...........	Pressure at Slow Component Intercept [*Medicine*] (STED)
PSCI..........	Primary Self-Concept Inventory [*Psychology*] (EDAC)
PSCJ..........	Perseverance Society of Carpenters and Joiners [*A union*] [*British*]
PSCJ..........	Progressive Society of Carpenters and Joiners [*A union*] [*British*]
PSCL..........	Programmed Sequential Control Language
PSCL..........	Propellants System Components Laboratory [*Kennedy Space Center*] [*NASA*]
PSCL..........	Propellant Systems Cleaning Laboratory [*NASA*] (NASA)
PScL..........	Scranton Public Library, Scranton, PA [*Library symbol*] [*Library of Congress*] (LCLS)
PScLL........	Lackawanna Bar Association Law Library, Scranton, PA [*Library symbol Library of Congress*] (LCLS)
PScM.........	Marywood College, Scranton, PA [*Library symbol Library of Congress*] (LCLS)
PSCM.........	Pokeweed Activated Spleen Conditioned Medium [*Medicine*] (STED)
PSCM.........	Process Steering and Control Module [*Telecommunications*] (TEL)
PSCM.........	Professinal Sports Care Management, Inc. [*NASDAQ symbol*] (SAG)
PSCM.........	Professional Sports Care Mgmt [*NASDAQ symbol*] (TTSB)
PSCN.........	Partido Socialcristiano Nicaraguense [*Nicaraguan Social Christian Party*] [*Political party*] (PPW)
PSCN.........	Permanent System Control Number (MCD)
PSCN.........	Preliminary Specification Change Notice [*NASA*] (NASA)
PSCN.........	Program Support Communications Network (SSD)
PSCN.........	Proposed Specification Change Notice
PSCNET......	Pittsburgh Superconducting Center Network
PSCO.........	Pennsylvania State College of Optometry
PSCO.........	Personnel Survey Control Officer [*Military*] (AABC)
PSCO.........	ProtoSource Corp. [*NASDAQ symbol*] (SAG)
PSCol.........	Public Service Co. of Colorado [*Associated Press*] (SAG)
P/score......	Pressure Score [*Medicine*] (STED)
PSCOU.......	ProtoSource Corp. Unit [*NASDAQ symbol*] (TTSB)
PSCOW......	ProtoSource Corp. Wrrt [*NASDAQ symbol*] (TTSB)
PSCP.........	Palestine Symphonic Choir Project (EA)
P/S CP.......	Platoon/Section Command Post
PSCP.........	Polar Continental Shelf Project [*Canada*]
PSCP.........	Posterior Subcapsular Cataractous Plaque [*Ophthalmology*] (DAVI)
PSCP.........	Public Service Careers Program [*Department of Labor*]
PSC-P.......	Swarthmore College Peace Collection, Swarthmore, PA [*Library symbol Library of Congress*] (LCLS)
PSCPD.......	Philadelphia Signal Corps Procurement District [*Army*]
PSC-PSOE....	Partit dels Socialistes de Catalunya [*Party of Socialists of Catalonia*] [*Political party*] (PPW)
PSCPT.......	Preschool Self-Concept Picture Test [*Psychology*]
PSCR.........	Permanent Scratch File [*Computer science*]
PSCR.........	Photo-Selective Copper Reduction [*For circuit board manufacture*]
PSCR.........	Priority System Change Request
PSCR.........	Production Schedule Completion Report [*DoD*]
PSCR.........	Programmable Scanning Receiver (DWSG)
PSCR.........	Public Service Commission Reports [*A publication*] (DLA)
PSCRD.......	Program Support Communications Requirements Document (SSD)
PSCRL.......	Patent Security Category Review List (AAGC)
PSCRT.......	Passive Satellite Communications Research Terminal (SAA)
PSCS.........	Pacific Scatter Communications System [*Air Force*] (CET)
PSCS.........	Packet-Switched Communication System (CIST)
PSCS.........	Program Support Control System
PSCT.........	Peripheral Stem Cell Transplant [*Medicine*] (STED)
PSCT.........	Polite Sentence Completion Test (TES)
PSCU.........	Power Supply Control Unit (CET)
PScU.........	University of Scranton, Scranton, PA [*Library symbol Library of Congress*] (LCLS)
PSCUS.......	Peters' United States Surpeme Court Reports [*26-41 United States*] [*A publication*] (DLA)
PSCX.........	PSC, Inc. [*Formerly, Photographic Sciences Corp.*] [*NASDAQ symbol*] (NQ)
PSD..........	Destour Socialist Party [*Tunisia*] [*Political party*] (PD)
PSD..........	Doctor of Political Science
Ps D.........	Doctor of Psychology
Ps D.........	Doctor of Psychology in Metaphysics
PSD..........	Doctor of Public Service
PSD..........	Packed Switched Data
PSD..........	Particle Size Distribution
PSD..........	Partido Socialdemocracia [*Social Democratic Party*] [*Chile*] [*Political party*] (EY)
PSD..........	Partido Social Democrata [*Social Democratic Party*] [*Mexico Political party*] (PPW)
PSD..........	Partido Social Democrata [*Social Democratic Party*] [*Bolivia*] [*Political party*] (PPW)
PSD..........	Partido Social Democrata [*Social Democratic Party*] [*Spain Political party*] (PPE)
PSD..........	Partido Social Democratico [*Social Democratic Party*] [*Nicaragua*] [*Political party*] (PPW)
PSD..........	Partido Social Democratico [*Social Democratic Party*] [*Brazil Political party*]
PSD..........	Partido Social Democratico [*Social Democratic Party*] [*El Salvador*] [*Political party*]
PSD..........	Partido Socialista Democratico [*Social Democratic Party*] [*Guatemala*] [*Political party*] (PD)
PSD..........	Partido Socialista Democratico [*Social Democratic Party*] [*Argentina Political party*] (PPW)
PSD..........	Parti Social-Democrate [*Social Democratic Party*] [*France Political party*] (PPW)
PSD..........	Parti Social-Democrate [*Algeria*] [*Political party*] (EY)
PSD..........	Parti Social Democrate de Madagascar et des Comores [*Social Democratic Party of Madagascar and Comores*]
PSD..........	Parti Social-Democratie [*Benin*] [*Political party*] (EY)
PSD..........	Parti Socialiste Democratique [*Cameroon*] [*Political party*] (EY)
PSD..........	Passed (ROG)
PSD..........	Passing Scene Display
PSD..........	Past Start Date
PSD..........	Patent Search Documentation (NITA)
PSD..........	Paternal Sister Dam (OA)
PSD..........	Patient Symptom Diary
PSD..........	Pay Supply Depot (WDAA)
PSD..........	Peptone-Starch-Dextrose [*Microbiology*] (MAE)
PSD..........	Permanent Signal Detection [*Telecommunications*] (TEL)
PSD..........	Personal Services Department [*Navy British*]
PSD..........	Personnel Services Division [*Army*]
PSD..........	Personnel Support Detachment (DOMA)
PSD..........	Personnel System [*or Subsystem*] Development (AAG)
PSD..........	Pescadero [*California*] [*Seismograph station code, US Geological Survey*] (SEIS)
PSD..........	Pesticides Safety Directorate (BUAC)
PSD..........	Petroleum Safety Data [*American Petroleum Institute*]
PSD..........	Petty Session Division [*Legal term*] (DLA)
PSD..........	Phase-Sensitive Demodulator [*or Detector*]
PSD..........	Phase Shifter Driver
PSD..........	Philatelic Sales Division [*Formerly, PSB*] [*US Postal Service*]
PSD..........	Photoconductive, Semiconductive Device
PSD..........	Photon Stimulated Desorption [*For analysis of surfaces*]
PSD..........	Pictorialized Scatter Diagram [*Botany*]
PSD..........	Pitch Servo Drive
PSD..........	Planning Systems Division (COE)
PSD..........	Platform Specific Driver [*Computer science*]
PSD..........	Polysilicon Diode (IAA)
PSD..........	Polystyrene, Deuterated [*Organic chemistry*]
PSD..........	Pore Size Distribution
PSD..........	Port Said [*Egypt*] [*Airport symbol*] (AD)
PSD..........	Port Security Detachment [*Military*] (GFGA)
PSD..........	Port Status Display (AAEL)
PSD..........	Position Sensitive Light Detector (IAA)
PSD..........	Postal Security Device [*Computer science*]
PSD..........	Post Sending Delay
PSD..........	Postsynaptic Density [*Neurophysiology*]
PSD..........	Power Spectral [*or Spectrum*] Density
PSD..........	Power Spectrum Distribution [*Electronics*]
PSD..........	Preferred Sea Duty
PSD..........	Pressure-Sensitive Devices (MCD)
PSD..........	Prevention of Significant Deterioration [*Environmental Protection Agency*]
PSD..........	Printed Side Down [*Graphic arts*] (DGA)
PSD..........	Printing Systems Division (NITA)
PSD..........	Private-Sector Development (ECON)
PSD..........	Procedural Support Data
PSD..........	Processing Status Display [*NASA*]
PSD..........	Process Specification Departure (SAA)
PSD..........	Procurement Surveys Division [*NASA*] (MCD)

PSD .... Professional Service Dates [*Formerly, ADBD*]
PSD .... Professional Systems Division [*American Institute of Architects Service Corp.*] [*Information service or system*] (IID)
PSD .... Programmed Slip Differential [*Automotive engineering*]
PSD .... Programme Support and Development [*British*]
PSD .... Program Status Documents [*Computer science*]
PSD .... Program Status Doubleword
PSD .... Program Support Document (MUGU)
PSD .... Program System Description (SAA)
PSD .... Program Systems Division [*Environmental Protection Agency*] (GFGA)
PSD .... Promotion Service Date
PSD .... Propellant Slosh Dynamics
PSD .... Propellant Storage Depot [*NASA*]
PSD .... Proportional Stock Density [*Pisciculture*]
PSD .... Propulsion System Demonstrator [*Marine Corps*] (DOMA)
PSD .... Protective Serum Dilution
PSD .... Protective Structures Division [*Office of Civil Defense*]
PSD .... Pseudosingle Domain [*Behavior of grains in rocks*] [*Geophysics*]
PSD .... Pseudo Stow Document (DNAB)
PSD .... Puget Sound P&L [*NYSE symbol*] (TTSB)
PSD .... Puget Sound Power & Light Co. [*NYSE symbol*] (SPSG)
PSD .... Pulse Shape Discriminator
PSD .... Pure Screw Dislocation
PSDA .... Paper Sack Development Association [*British*] (BI)
PSDA .... Partial Source Data Automation (NVT)
PSDA .... Particle Size Distribution Analysis [*Statistics*]
PSDA .... Patient Self-Determination Act
P/SDA .... Power/Signal Distribution Assembly
PSDB .... Partido da Social Democracia Brasiliera [*Brazilian Social Democratic Party*] [*Political party*] (EY)
PSDB .... Police Scientific Development Branch [*British*] (WDAA)
PSDC .... Pennsylvania State Data Center [*Middletown*] [*Information service or system*] (IID)
PSDC .... Plant Sciences Data Center [*Formerly, Plant Records Center*] [*American Horticultural Society*] [*Mt. Vernon, VA*]
PSDC .... Power Sprayer and Duster Council (EA)
PSDC .... Protective Structures Development Center [*Military*]
PSDD .... Preliminary System Design Description [*Nuclear energy*] (NRCH)
PSDDS .... Pilot [*or Public*] Switched Digital Data Service [*Telecommunications*] (TEL)
PS de G .... Partido dos Socialistas de Galicia [*Spain Political party*] (EY)
Psdepgr .... Pseudepigrapha (BJA)
PSDF .... People's Self-Defense Force [*South Vietnamese militia force*] (VNW)
PSDF .... Popular Self-Defense Force [*Local armed units protecting Vietnamese hamlets*]
PSDF .... Propulsion Systems Development Facility (KSC)
PSDI .... Partido Social Democratico Independente [*Independent Social Democratic Party*] [*Portugal Political party*] (PPE)
PSDI .... Partito Socialista Democratico Italiano [*Italian Social Democratic Party*] [*Political party*]
PSDI .... Project Software & Development, Inc. [*NASDAQ symbol*] (SAG)
PSDI .... Project Software & Dvlp [*NASDAQ symbol*] (TTSB)
PSDIAD .... Photostimulated Desorption Ion Angular Distribution [*Surface analysis*]
PSDIS .... Partito Socialista Democratico Indipendente Sammarinese [*Independent Social Democratic Party of San Marino*] [*Political party*] (PPE)
PSdM .... Mennonite Publishing House, Scottsdale, PA [*Library symbol Library of Congress*] (LCLS)
PSDM .... Presentation Services for Data Management (MHDB)
PSD(MS)...... Photon Stimulated Desorption (Mass Spectroscopy) (MCD)
PSDN .... Packet Switched Data Network [*Telecommunications*]
PSDN .... Packet-Switching Data Network [*Computer science*] (DOM)
PSDN .... Public Switched Data Network (NITA)
PSDP .... Payload Station Distribution Panel [*NASA*] (MCD)
PSDP .... Personnel Subsystem Development Plan
PSDP .... Phrase Structure and Dependency Parser (DIT)
PSDP .... Professional Skills Development Program [*Bureau of the Census*] (GFGA)
PSDP .... Programmable Signal Data Processor (MCD)
PSDPr......... Puget Sound P&L 7.875% Pfd [*NYSE symbol*] (TTSB)
PSDPrB....... Puget Sound P&L Adj Rt'B'Pfd [*NYSE symbol*] (TTSB)
PSDR .... Planning and Scheduling Document Record [*NASA*] (NASA)
PSDR .... Process Storage Data Register (IAA)
PSDR .... Program Status Doubleword Register [*Computer science*] (MHDB)
PSDR .... Public Sector Debt Repayment [*British*] (ECON)
PSDS .... Packet Switch Data System [*Information retrieval*] (IID)
PSDS .... Packet Switched Data Service [*Telecommunications*] (TEL)
PSDS .... Partito Socialista Democratico Sammarinese [*Social Democratic Party of San Marino*] [*Political party*] (PPE)
PSDS .... Passing Scene Display System
PSDS .... Permanently Separated from Duty Station [*Military*]
PSDS .... Postal Source Data System [*U.S. Postal Service*] (CIST)
PSDS .... Prison Service Drug Strategy (WDAA)
PSDS .... Public Switched Data Service [*Telecommunications*]
PSDS .... Public Switched Digital Service [*Computer science*] (TNIG)
PSDSP .... Pious Society of the Daughters of Saint Paul [*See also FSP*] [*Rome, Italy*] (EAIO)
PSDT .... President (ROG)
PSDTC .... Pacific Securities Depository Trust Co.
PSDU .... Polish Social Democratic Union [*Political party*]
PSDU .... Power Switching Distribution Unit
PSDU .... Presentation Service Data Unit [*Telecommunications*] (OSI)
PSDVB .... Poly(styrene-Divinylbenzene) [*Organic chemistry*]

PSE .... Aeroservicio Sipse SA de CV [*Mexico ICAO designator*] (FAAC)
PSE .... Pacific School of English [*Australia*]
PSE .... Pacific Stock Exchange (EA)
PSE .... Packet Switching Exchange [*Telecommunications*]
PSE .... Pale Soft Exudative [*Pork*]
PSE .... Paper Surface Efficiency (DGA)
PSE .... Partido Socialista de Euskadi [*Basque Socialist Party*] [*Spain Political party*] (EY)
PSE .... Partido Socialista Ecuatoriano [*Ecuadorean Socialist Party*] [*Political party*] (PPW)
PSE .... Passage
PSE .... Passive Seismic Experiment [*NASA*]
PSE .... Payload Service Equipment [*NASA*] (MCD)
PSE .... Payload Servicing Equipment [*NASA*] (NAKS)
PSE .... Payload Support Equipment [*NASA*] (MCD)
PSE .... Peculiar Support Equipment [*NASA*] (NASA)
PSE .... Penicillin-Sensitive Enzymes [*Biochemistry*]
PSE .... Personal and Social Education (DET)
PSE .... Personnel Subsystem Elements [*Army*] (AABC)
PSE .... Perth Stock Exchange [*Australia*]
PSE .... Phase-Shifter, Electronic
PSE .... Philadelphia Stock Exchange
PSE .... Photosensitive Epilepsy
PSE .... Physical Security Equipment [*Army*] (RDA)
PSE .... Phytochemical Society of Europe (EA)
PSE .... Pigin Signed English
PSE .... Pitch Steering Error
pse .... Planed and Square-Edge (DAC)
PSE .... Pleasant Saturday Evenings
PSE .... Pleasant Sunday Evenings (ROG)
PSE .... Please (MDG)
PSE .... Point of Subjective Equality [*Psychology*]
PSE .... Polestar Exploration, Inc. [*Vancouver Stock Exchange symbol*]
PSE .... Ponce [*Puerto Rico*] [*Airport symbol*] (OAG)
PSE .... Portal Systemic Encephalopathy [*Medicine*]
PSE .... Post-Separation Employment
PSE .... Postshunt Encephalopathy [*Medicine*]
PSE .... Power Spectrum Equalization [*Electronics*]
PSE .... Power System Engineering (MCD)
PSE .... Present State Examination [*Medicine*] (DMAA)
PSE .... Pressurized Subcritical Experiment [*Nuclear energy*]
PSE .... Pre-Stamped Envelope
PSE .... Prevention of Stripping Equipment (NATG)
PSE .... Principal Staff Element [*Defense Supply Agency*]
PSE .... Priority Standardization Effort [*Army*] (AABC)
PSE .... Prison Service Establishment (AIE)
PSE .... Probability of Successful Engagement [*Military*] (CAAL)
PSE .... Process Systems Engineering
PSE .... Producer Subsidy Equivalent [*OECD model for the study of farm-support policies in the EC, Japan, America, Canada, Australia, and New Zealand*]
PSE .... Product Support Engineering (MCD)
PSE .... Programmed System Evolution (MCD)
PSE .... Program Supplement (COE)
PSE .... Protein Separation Efficiency [*Food technology*]
PSE .... Proximal Sequence Element [*Genetics*]
PSE .... Proximal Stimulating Electrode (DB)
PSE .... Psychological Stress Evaluator [*Lie detector*]
PSE .... Public Sector [*or Service*] Employment
PSE .... Public Service Electric & Gas Co., Newark, NJ [*OCLC symbol*] (OCLC)
PSE .... Public Service Employment (EBF)
PSE .... Pulse Sense
PSE .... Purified Spleen Extract [*Medicine*] (DMAA)
PSEA .... Pacific and Southeast Asia (DNAB)
PSEA .... Physical Security Equipment Agency [*Army*]
PSEA .... Pleaters, Stitchers, and Embroiderers Association (EA)
PSE & C ...... Power Supply Engineering and Construction [*Nuclear energy*] (NRCH)
PSE & G ...... Public Service Electric & Gas Co.
PSEB .... Poisoning Surveillance and Epidemiology Branch [*Defunct*] (EA)
PSEB .... Punjab State Electricity Board [*India*] (BUAC)
PSEBM .... Proceedings of the Society for Experimental Biology and Medicine [*A publication*]
P/SEC.......... Personal Secretary (DCTA)
PSEC.......... Picosecond [*One trillionth of a second*]
psec.......... Picosecond [*Alternative of preferred ps*] (IDOE)
PSED.......... Preliminary Systems Engineering Design
PSEF.......... Pennsylvania Science and Engineering Foundation
PSEF.......... Plastic Surgery Educational Foundation (EA)
PSEG.......... PSE & G Capital Trust [*Associated Press*] (SAG)
PSEG.......... Public Service Electric & Gas Co. [*Associated Press*] (SAG)
PSEG.......... Public Service Enterprise Group, Inc. (EFIS)
PSEK.......... Probability of Single Shot Engagement Kill [*Military*]
PSEK.......... Progressive Symmetrical Erythrokeratoderma [*Medicine*] (DMAA)
PSelS.......... Susquehanna University, Selinsgrove, PA [*Library symbol Library of Congress*] (LCLS)
PSEMA........ Parti Social d'Education des Masses Africaines [*African Party for Social Education of the Masses*] [*Burkina Faso*]
PseOG .... Pease Oil & Gas Co. [*Associated Press*] (SAG)
PSEP.......... Passive Seismic Experiments Package [*NASA*]
PSEP.......... Physical Security Evaluation Procedure [*US Army Construction Engineering Research Laboratory*] (RDA)
PSEQ .... Pupil Services Expectation Questionnaire

PSERC .... Public Sector Economics Research Centre [*University of Leicester*] [*British*] (CB)
PSES............ Pretreatment Standards for Existing Sources [*Environmental Protection Agency*]
PSET............ Pre-Selection English Test [*Australia*]
PSEU .... Production Support Equipment Unit (MCD)
PSEU .... Public Service Executive Union [*Ireland*] (BUAC)
PSEU .... Public Services Employees' Union [*Afghanistan*] (BUAC)
Pseud .... Pseudepigrapha (BJA)
PSEUD .... Pseudonym
Pseudep ...... Pseudepigrapha (BJA)
PSEUDO ...... Pseudonym [*Legal shorthand*] (LWAP)
PSEW .... Project on the Status and Education of Women (EA)
PSewD......... Dixmont State Hospital, Sewickley, PA [*Library symbol Library of Congress*] (LCLS)
PSF............. Pakistan Science Foundation
PSF............. Panama Sea Frontier
PSF............. Panhandle & Santa Fe Railway Co. [*AAR code*]
PSF............. Parents for Safe Food [*An association*] (BUAC)
PSF............. Parti Social Francais [*French Social Party*] [*Political party*] (PPE)
PSF............. Passive Solar Foundation [*Defunct*] (EA)
PSF............. Payload Structure Fuel [*Ratio*]
PSF............. Peptide Supply Factor [*Biochemistry*]
PSF............. Performance Shaping Factor [*Engineering*]
PSF............. Permanent Signal Finder
PSF............. Personal Silicon Foundry (IAA)
PSF............. Per Square Foot (ADA)
PSF............. Philippine Sea Frontier
PSF............. Pittsfield [*Massachusetts*] [*Airport symbol*] (AD)
PSF............. Pittsfield, MA [*Location identifier FAA*] (FAAL)
PSF............. Plutonium Stripper Feed [*Nuclear energy*] (NRCH)
PSF............. Point Spread Function
PSF............. Polysulfone [*Organic chemistry*]
PSF............. Popular Struggle Front [*Palestine*] [*Political party*] (PD)
PSF............. Port Stanley [*Falkland Islands*] [*Seismograph station code, US Geological Survey Closed*] (SEIS)
PSF............. Posterior Spinal Fusion [*Medicine*] (DAVI)
PSF............. Pound-Force per Square Foot (IAA)
PSF............. Pounds per Square Foot
psf............. Pounds per Square Foot (IDOE)
PSF............. Power Separation Filter (IAA)
PSF............. Preservation Services Fund
PSF............. Presidio of San Francisco [*Military*] (AABC)
PSF............. Prime Subframe (MCD)
PSF............. Private Source Funds (DNAB)
PSF............. Probability of Spurious Fire [*Military*] (CAAL)
PSF............. Probability Sample File [*Human Relations Area Files*] [*Information retrieval*]
PSF............. Processing and Staging Facility [*Solid rocket booster*] (NASA)
PSF............. Processing and Storage Facility [*NASA*] (NASA)
PSF............. Process Signal Former (IAA)
PSF............. Program for the Study of the Future (EA)
PSF............. Program Support Facility (USDC)
PSF............. Progressive Space Forum [*Defunct*] (EA)
PSF............. Progres Social Francais [*French Social Progress*] [*Political party*] (PPE)
PSF............. Provisional Sinn Fein [*Northern Ireland*]
PSF............. Provisional System Feature [*Telecommunications*] (TEL)
PSF............. Pseudosarcomatous Fasciitis [*Medicine*]
PSF............. Saint Francis College, Loretto, PA [*OCLC symbol*] (OCLC)
PSFAM........ Parameter Sensitive Frequency Assignment Method (MCD)
PSFC........... Pacific Salmon Fisheries Commission (BUAC)
PS/FC.......... Power Supply / Frequency Converter (DWSG)
PSFC........... Power Supply/Fuel Cell (NAKS)
PSFC........... Process Supercritical Fluid Chromatography
PSFC........... Provisional Special Forces Co. (CINC)
PSFC/HIMH... Pete Shelley Fan Club/Harmony in My Head (EA)
PSFD .... Public Sector Financial Deficit
PSFI............ PS Financial, Inc. [*NASDAQ symbol*] (SAG)
PS Fincl....... PS Financial, Inc. [*Associated Press*] (SAG)
PSFL........... Puget Sound Freight Lines [*AAR code*]
PSFQ .... Pupil Services Fulfillment Questionnaire
PSFT........... Peoplesoft, Inc. [*NASDAQ symbol*] (SAG)
PSG .... Pacific Seabird Group (EA)
PSG .... Palestine Study Group (EA)
PSG .... Parachute Study Group (EA)
PSG .... Parti Socialiste Guyanais [*Guiana Socialist Party*] [*Political party*] (PPW)
PSG .... Passage [*NWS*] (FAAC)
PSG .... Peak Systolic Gradient [*Medicine*] (MAE)
PSG .... Pershing [*Missile*] (GFGA)
PSG .... Personnel Subsystem Group (SAA)
PSG .... Peru Support Group (BUAC)
PSG .... Petersburg [*Alaska*] [*Airport symbol*] (OAG)
PSG .... Petersburg, AK [*Location identifier FAA*] (FAAL)
PSG .... Phenol Sector Group [*European Council of Chemical Manufacturers Federations*] [*Belgium*] (EAIO)
PSG .... Phosphate-Saline-Glucose [*A buffer*] [*Cell culture*]
PSG .... Phosphosilicate Glass [*IEEE*]
PSG .... Phrase-Structure Grammar [*Computer science*]
PSG .... Planning Systems Generator
PSG .... Platoon Sergeant [*Army*] (AABC)
PSG .... Polysomnogram [*Medicine*] (MAE)
PSG .... Post Stall Gyration (MCD)
PSG .... Power Subsystem Group [*NASA*] (MCD)

PSG .... Pregnancy-Specific Glycoprotein [*Biochemistry*]
PSG .... Presystolic Gallop [*Cardiology*]
PSG .... Production Support Group (NITA)
PSG .... Production System Generator
PSG .... Professional Specialty Group
PSG .... Programmable Sequence Generator [*Computer science*] (CIST)
PSG .... Programmable Sound Generator [*Chip*] [*Atari, Inc.*]
PSG .... Programmable Symbol Generator
PSG .... Pseudomonas Syringae PV Glycinea [*Plant pathology*]
PSG .... PS Group Holdings [*NYSE symbol*] [*Formerly, PS Group, Inc.*] (SG)
PSG .... PS Group, Inc. [*NYSE symbol*] (SPSG)
PSG .... Psychogalvanometer
PSG .... Psychological Studies Group [*Military*] (VNW)
PSG .... Public Strategies Group, Inc. [*Consulting firm hired in 1993 to improve Minneapolis school district*] (ECON)
PSG .... Publishing Systems Group [*Later, CPSUG*] (EA)
PSG .... Pulsed Strain Gauge (IAA)
PSG .... Pulse Sequence Generation [*Instrumentation*]
PSG .... Pulse Signal Generator (IAA)
PSGA .... Parkinson Support Groups of America (EA)
PSGA .... Pedal Steel Guitar Association (EA)
PSGA .... Professional Skaters Guild of America (EA)
PSGB .... Pharmaceutical Society of Great Britain
PSGB .... Primate Society of Great Britain (DBA)
PSGCU .... Palm Springs Golf 'Unit' [*NASDAQ symbol*] (TTSB)
PSGD .... Past Senior Grand Deacon [*Freemasonry*]
PSGE .... Partido Socialdemocrata de Guinea Ecuatorial [*Social Democratic Party of Equatorial Guinea*] [*Political party*] (EY)
PSGE .... Passage [*Postal Service standard*] (OPSA)
PSGE .... Photosynthetic Gas Exchanger (SAA)
PSG-EG........ Partido Socialista Galego - Esquerda Galega [*Spain Political party*] (EY)
PSGL .... P-Selectin Glycoprotein Ligand [*Biochemistry*]
PSGM .... Past Supreme Grand Master [*Freemasonry*]
PSGN .... Post-Streptococcal Glomerulonephritis [*Medicine*]
PSGR .... Passenger (AFM)
PS Grp......... PS Group, Inc. [*Associated Press*] (SAG)
PSGT........... Platoon Sergeant [*Military*]
PSGTCAEI..... Permanent Secretariat of the General Treaty on Central American Economic Integration (EAIO)
PSGV .... Pacific Sentinel Gold Corp. [*NASDAQ symbol*] (SAG)
PSGVF .... Pacific Sentinel Gold [*NASDAQ symbol*] (TTSB)
PSGW .... Past Senior Grand Warden [*Freemasonry*]
PSH .... Friends Historical Library of Swarthmore College, Swarthmore, PA [*OCLC symbol*] (OCLC)
PSH .... Parshall, ND [*Location identifier FAA*] (FAAL)
PSH .... Past Social History (CPH)
PSH .... Past Surgical History [*Medicine*] (DMAA)
PSH .... Permanent Shift of Hearing
PSH .... Peshawar [*Pakistan*] [*Seismograph station code, US Geological Survey*] (SEIS)
PSH .... Phase Shift (MSA)
PSH .... Polystyrene, Hydrogenous [*Organic chemistry*]
PSH .... Postspinal Headache (AAMN)
PSH .... Post-Stimulus Histogram [*Psychometrics*]
PSH .... Preselect Heading (NG)
PSH .... Pressure Switch, High [*Nuclear energy*] (NRCH)
PSH .... Productive Standard Hour (PDAA)
PSH .... Program Support Handbook
PSH .... Proximity Sensing Head
PSH .... Publications Statistiques Hongroises [*Hungary*]
PSH .... Public Storage Canadian Properties IIIa Ltd. [*Toronto Stock Exchange symbol*]
P Shaw .... Patrick Shaw's Justiciary Cases [*1819-31*] [*Scotland*] [*A publication*] (DLA)
PSHB .... Persistent Spectral Hole-Burning [*Spectroscopy*]
PSHC.......... Permanent Secretariat of the Hemispheric Congress (EA)
PSHC.......... Public Speaking and Humor Club (EA)
PSHCJ .... Philanthropic Society of House Carpenters and Joiners [*A union*] [*British*]
PSHD .... Phase-Shift Driver (MSA)
PSHD .... Port Security Harbor Defense (DOMA)
PSHF .... Polysulfone Hollow Fiber [*Filtration membrane*]
PSHFA .... Public Servants' Housing and Finance Association [*British*] (BI)
PSHR .... Pusher [*Freight*]
PSHS .... Propulsion Systems Hazards Subcommittee [*Military*]
PShS........... Shippensburg State College, Shippensburg, PA [*Library symbol Library of Congress*] (LCLS)
PSHSGB....... Polar System History Society of Great Britain (BUAC)
PSHT.......... Powys Self-Help Trust [*British*]
PSI............. Pacific Semiconductors, Inc. (MCD)
PSI............. Pacific Stratus Investigation [*Marine science*] (OSRA)
PSI............. Pacific Sulfur Investigation [*Marine science*] (OSRA)
PSI............. Pacific Sulfur/Stratus Investigation (USDC)
PSI............. Page Survival Index (PDAA)
PSI............. Paid Service Indication [*Telecommunications*] (TEL)
PSI............. Pakistan Standards Institution (IAA)
PSI............. Palmar Sweat Index (EDAC)
PSI............. Paper Stock Institute of America (EA)
PSI............. Parapat [*Sumatra*] [*Seismograph station code, US Geological Survey*] (SEIS)
PSI............. Parapsychological Services Institute (EA)
PSI............. Parenting Stress Index [*Psychology*]
PSI............. Partai Socialis Indonesia [*Socialist Party of Indonesia*]

PSI............... Participation Systems, Inc. [*Electronics Communications Co.*] [*Winchester , MA*] [*Telecommunications*] (TSSD)
PSI............... Particle-Sizing Interferometer (MCD)
PSI............... Parti Socialiste Ivoirien [*Ivorian Socialist Party*] [*The Ivory Coast*] [*Political party*] (EY)
PSI............... Partito Socialista Italiano [*Italian Socialist Party*] [*Political party*] (PPE)
PSI............... Pasni [*Pakistan*] [*Airport symbol*] (OAG)
PSI............... Passive Solar Institute [*Defunct*] (EA)
PSI............... Paul Scherrer Institute [*Switzerland*] (BUAC)
PSI............... Percent Similarity Index
PSI............... Performance Systems International, Inc.
PSI............... Peripherally Synapsing Interneuron [*Neurology*]
PSI............... Peripheral Subsystem Interface [*Computer science*] (IAA)
PSI............... Permanent Staff Instructor [*Military British*]
PSI............... Permuterm Subject Index [*Institute for Scientific Information*] [*A publication*] (IID)
PsI............... Perpetual Storage, Inc., Salt Lake City, UT [*Library symbol Library of Congress*] (LCLS)
PSI............... Personalised System of Induction (AIE)
PSI............... Personalized System of Instruction
PSI............... Personal Sequential-Inference Machine [*Computer science*]
PSI............... Personal Service Income
PSI............... Personal Style Indicator [*Test*] (TMMY)
PSI............... Personnel Security Investigation [*Military*]
PSI............... Personnel Selection Inventory [*Test*]
PSI............... Person of Special Importance [*British military*] (DMA)
PSI............... Per Square Inch (ADA)
PSI............... Pet Sitters International (NTPA)
PSI............... Pharmaceutical Society of Ireland (BI)
PSI............... Phenomenological Systems, Inc.
PSI............... Photographic Society International (EA)
PSI............... Photographic Society of Ireland (BI)
PSI............... Photometric Sunspot Index
PSI............... Photo Services Industrial Ltd. [*British*]
PSI............... Physical, Sensitivity, Intellectual [*Biorhythmics*]
PSI............... Planned Start Installation [*Telecommunications*] (TEL)
PSI............... Plan Speed Indicator [*Military*]
PSI............... Plas Speed Indicator (IAA)
PSI............... Platoon Sector Indicator [*Army*]
PSI............... Play Skills Inventory
PSI............... Policy Studies Institute [*Research center British*] (IRC)
PSI............... Pollutant Standards Index [*Environmental Protection Agency*]
p-Si............... Polycrystalline Silicon [*Photovoltaic energy systems*]
PSI............... Population Services International (BUAC)
PSI............... Porta Systems [*AMEX symbol*] (TTSB)
PSI............... Porta Systems Corp. [*AMEX symbol*] (SPSG)
PSI............... Positive Self-Image [*Psychology*]
PSI............... Posterior Sagittal Index [*Anatomy*] (AAMN)
PSI............... Posterior Superior Iliac Spine [*Posterosuperior iliac spine*] [*Anatomy*] (DAVI)
PSI............... Postpartum Support, International (EA)
PSI............... Post-Tensioning Institute (WPI)
PSI............... Pound-Force per Square Inch (IAA)
PSI............... Pounds per Square Inch
psi............... Pounds per Square Inch (IDOE)
PSI............... Pounds per Square Inch Absolute (IAA)
PSI............... Power per Square Inch
PSI............... Power Static Inverter (NASA)
PSI............... Praed Street Irregulars (EA)
PSI............... Preprogrammed Self-Instruction [*Computer science*] (IEEE)
PSI............... Preschool Inventory (EDAC)
PSI............... Pre-Sentence Investigation (OICC)
PSI............... Present Serviceability Index (IEEE)
PSI............... Preservice Inspection [*Nuclear energy*] (NRCH)
PSI............... Preshipment Inspection [*International trade*]
PSI............... Pressure Sensitive Identification
PSI............... Pressurized Sphere Injection (DNAB)
PSI............... Prime System Indicator
PSI............... Probe Systems, Inc.
PSI............... Problem-Solving and Inference Machine (IAA)
PSI............... Problem-Solving Information [*Apparatus*]
PSI............... Problem-Solving Interpreter [*Computer language*]
PSI............... Process System Index
PSI............... Process Systems, Inc.
PSI............... Proctorial System of Instruction (IEEE)
PSI............... Production Stock Item (MCD)
PSI............... Product Support Instructions (AAG)
PSI............... Professional Secretaries International [*Kansas City, MO*] (EA)
PSI............... Professional Services Income (WDAA)
PSI............... Programmed School Input (NVT)
PSI............... Program Status Information [*Computer science*] (MCD)
PSI............... Program Supply Interest (MCD)
PSI............... Project Starlight International (EA)
PSI............... Protosynthetic Indexing (NITA)
PSI............... Protosynthex Index
PSI............... PSI Energy [*Associated Press*] (SAG)
PSI............... Psychological Screening Inventory [*Personality development test*]
PSI............... Psychological Society of Ireland (BUAC)
PSI............... Psychosomatic Inventory [*Psychology*]
PSI............... Publications Standing Instruction (AAG)
PSI............... Public Services International [*See also ISP*] [*Ferney Voltaire, France*] (EAIO)
PSI............... Pulse Sciences, Inc.
PSIA............. Paper Stock Institute of America (EA)

PSIA............. Pounds per Square Inch Absolute
psia.............. Pounds per Square Inch Absolute (IDOE)
PSIA............. President of the Society of Industrial Artists [*British*]
PSIA............. Pressure Absolute [*AGA*] (TAG)
PSIA............. Production System Integration Area
PSIA............. Professional Ski Instructors of America (EA)
PSIA............. Public Security Investigation Agency [*Japan*] (CINC)
PSI-B........... Personnel Selection Inventory for Banking [*Test*] (TES)
PSIC............. Passenger Service Improvement Corp.
PSIC............. Passive Solar Industries Council (EA)
PSIC............. Process Signal Interface Controller
PSIC............. Production Scheduling and Inventory Control
PSICOMP.... Predicted Speech Intelligibility Computer (IAA)
Psicor.......... PSICOR, Inc. [*Associated Press*] (SAG)
PSICP .... Program Support Inventory Control Point
PSID............. Partial Seismic Intrusion Device (MCD)
PSID............. Patrol Seismic Intrusion Detector [*or Device*] [*DoD*]
PSID............. Pounds per Square Inch Differential (MCD)
psid.............. Pounds per Square Inch, Differential [*Marine science*] (OSRA)
PSID............. Preliminary Safety Information Document [*Nuclear energy*] (NRCH)
PSIDC.......... Punjab State Industrial Development Corp. [*India*] (BUAC)
PS/IDS........ Physical Security/Intrusion Detection System (MCD)
PSIEP.......... Project on Scientific Information Exchange in Psychology [*Superseded by Office of Communication*]
PSIF............. Prison Service Industries & Farming (WDAA)
PSIF............. Prison Service Industries and Farms (BUAC)
PSIFT........... Platelet Suspension Immunofluorescence Test [*Medicine*] (DMAA)
PSIG............. Per-Square-Inch Gauge (AAGC)
psig.............. Pounds per Square Inch Gauge (IDOE)
psig.............. Pressure per Square Inch Gauge (COE)
PSIG............. Propulsion Systems Integration Group [*NASA*] (NASA)
PSII............. Plasma Source Ion Implantation (AAEL)
PSII............. Process Safety Incident Investigation [*Engineering*]
PSIL............. Philippine Society of International Law (BUAC)
PSIL............. Potential Selected Item List (MCD)
PSIL............. Preferred Speech Interference Level
PSI-LOGO .... Listing of Oil and Gas Opportunities [*Online Resource Exchange, Inc.*] [*Database*]
PSIM........... Power System Instrumentation and Measurement (MCD)
PSIM........... Problem-Solving Instructional Material [*National Science Foundation project*]
PSINet .... PSINet, Inc. [*Associated Press*] (SAG)
PSIO............ Performance Scales Intelligence Quotient (EDAC)
PSIP........... Private Sector Initiative Program [*Department of Labor*]
PSIS............ Posterior Sacroiliac Spine [*Anatomy*] (DAVI)
PSIS............ Posterior Superior Iliac Spine [*Medicine*] (STED)
psis............. Pounds per Square Inch Sealed (NAKS)
PSIS............ Pounds per Square Inch Sealed (NASA)
PSIS............ Programme for Strategic and International Security Studies [*Switzerland*] (PDAA)
PSISIG........ Psychic Science International Special Interest Group (EA)
PSIT............ Property Security Investment Trust [*British*]
PSIU............ Power/Sequence Interface Unit (MCD)
PSIUP......... Partito Socialista Italiano di Unita Proletaria [*Italian Socialist Party of Proletarian Unity (1945-1947)*] [*Political party*] (PPE)
PSIV............ Passive
PSIX............ Performance Systems International, Inc. [*NASDAQ symbol*] (SAG)
PSIX............ PSINet, Inc. [*NASDAQ symbol*] [*Formerly, Performance Systems International*] (SG)
PSJ............. Parallel Swivel Joint
PSJ............. Petites Soeurs de Jesus [*Little Sisters of Jesus*] [*Italy*] (EAIO)
PSJ............. Pharmaceutical Society of Japan (BUAC)
psj............. Planed and Square-Jointed (DAC)
PSJ............. Plane Swivel Joint
PSJ............. Point Spread Junction (IAA)
PSJ............. Poso [*Indonesia*] [*Airport symbol*] (OAG)
PSJ............. Pressure Switch Joint
PSJ............. Public Service Job (OICC)
PSJS........... Pier and Span Junction Set (MCD)
PSK............ Dublin, VA [*Location identifier FAA*] (FAAL)
PSK............ Phase Shift Keying [*Computer science*]
PSK............ PostSparKasse [*Post Office Savings Bank*] [*Austria*]
PSK............ Power Supply Kit
PSK............ Private Secretary to the King [*British*]
PSK............ Program Selection Key [*Computer science*] (BUR)
PSK............ Protection Survey Kit
PSK............ Protein Serine Kinase (DMAA)
PSK............ Public Storage Properties IX, Inc. [*AMEX symbol*] (SAG)
PSK............ Pulse Shift Keying (CAAL)
PSKM........... Phase Shift Keyed Modulation (NITA)
PSKM........... Phase-Shift Keying MODEM
PSK-PCM..... Phase-Shift Keying - Pulse Code Modulation
PSL............ Palouse Silt Loam [*Agronomy*]
PSL............ Parallel Strand Lumber
PSL............ Parasternal Line [*Anatomy*] (MAE)
PSL............ Parti Social-Liberal [*Algeria*] [*Political party*] (EY)
PSL............ Paymaster-Sub-Lieutenant [*Navy British*]
PSL............ Peabody Short Line R. R. [*Army*]
PSL............ Percent Stroke Length [*Medicine*] (STED)
PSL............ Personnel Skill Levels (AAG)
PSL............ Perth [*Scotland*] [*Airport symbol*] (AD)
PSL............ Petroleum Ether-Soluble Lipid
PSL............ Phase Sequence Logic (IAA)
PSL............ Photographic Science Laboratory [*Navy*]
PSL............ Photostimulated Luminescence [*Physics*]

PSL	Physical Sciences Laboratory [*University of Wisconsin - Madison, New Mexico State University*] [*Research center*]
PSL	Physical Sciences Laboratory [*Bethesda, MD*] [*National Institutes of Health*] (GRD)
PSL	Pipe Sleeve
PSL	Pocket Select Language [*Burroughs Corp.*]
PSL	Polskie Stronnictwo Ludowe [*Polish Peasant Party*] [*Political party*] (PPE)
PSL	Polystyrene Latex (PDAA)
PSL	Portable Standard List Processing [*Computer science*]
PSL	Potassium, Sodium Chloride, Sodium Lactate [*Solution*] (AAMN)
PSL	Potential Source List (MCD)
PSL	Power and Signal List [*Telecommunications*] (TEL)
PSL	Power Source Logic
PSL	Practical Storage Life
PSL	Pressure Seal (NASA)
PSL	Pressure-Sensitive Label
PSL	Primary Standards Laboratory
PSL	Private Sector Liquidity
PSL	Problem-Solving Language
PSL	Problem Specification Language
PSL	Problem Statement Language [*Computer science*] (IAA)
PSL	Process Simulation Language [*Computer science*] (TEL)
PSL	Process Status Longword [*Number*] [*Computer science*] (BYTE)
PSL	Professionnel Air Systems [*France ICAO designator*] (FAAC)
PSL	Programming Script Language (PCM)
PSL	Program Support Library (MCD)
PSL	Project Support Laboratory [*Military*] (CAAL)
PSL	Propellant Seal
PSL	Propulsion Systems Laboratory [*USATACOM*] (RDA)
PSL	Public School League [*Sports*]
PSL	Public Storage Prop'A' X [*AMEX symbol*] (TTSB)
PSL	Public Storage Properties X, Inc. [*AMEX symbol*] (SAG)
PSL	Pycnocline Scattering Layer (DNAB)
PSL	South Hills Library Association, Pittsburgh, PA [*OCLC symbol*] (OCLC)
PSLA	Palaung State Liberation Army [*Myanmar*] [*Political party*] (EY)
PSLA	Polish Sea League of America (EA)
PSLA	Pre-School Learning Alliance (WDAA)
PSLC	Post-Schistosomal Liver Cirrhosis [*Medicine*]
PSLC	Private Security Liaison Council (EA)
PSLI	Packet Switch Level Interface
PSLI	Partito Socialista dei Lavoratori Italiani [*Socialist Party of Italian Workers*] [*Political party*] (PPE)
PSLI	Physalaemin-Like Immunoreactivity [*Medicine*]
P-slip	Process Slip
PSL-Lewica	Polskie Stronnictwo-Lewica [*Polish Peasant Party-Left (1947-1949)*] [*Political party*] (PPE)
PSL-Lewica	Polskie Stronnictwo Ludowe-Lewica [*Polish Peasant Party-Left (1913-1920)*] [*Political party*] (PPE)
PSLLS	Pulsed Solid-State LASER Light Source
PSL-NW	Polskie Stronnictwo Ludowe-Nowe Wyzwolenie [*Polish Peasant Party-New Liberation*] [*Political party*] (PPE)
PSLO	Palaung State Liberation Organization [*Myanmar*] [*Political party*] (EY)
PSL-Piast	Polskie Stronnictwo Ludowe-Piast [*Polish Peasant Party-Piast*] [*Political party*] (PPE)
PSL/PSA	Problem Statement Language/Problem Specification Analyzer [*Computer science*]
PSLR	Product Safety and Liability Reporter [*A publication*]
PSLS	Pan Stock Line Station (MCD)
PSLS	Polystyrene Latex Sphere (AAEL)
PSL sol	Potassium, Sodium Chloride, Sodium Lactate Solution [*Pharmacology*] (DAVI)
PSL SOL	Potassium, Sodium Chloride, Sodium Lactate Solution (BABM)
PSLT	Picture Story Language Test
PSLT	Port Side Light (IAA)
PSLT	Pressurized Sonobuoy Launch Tube [*Navy*] (CAAL)
pslt	Psalter (VRA)
PSLV	Poa Semilatent Virus
PSLV	Polar Satellite Launch Vehicle
PSL-Wyzwolenie	Polskie Stronnictwo Ludowe-Wyzwolenie [*Polish Peasant Party-Liberation*] [*Political party*] (PPE)
PSM	Packet Switched Signaling Message (CIST)
PSM	Panasystolic Murmur [*Cardiology*] (DAVI)
PSM	Parallel Slit Map (OA)
PSM	Parcel Sorting Machine [*Freight*] (DCTA)
PSM	Parc Saint-Maur [*France*] [*Later, CLF*] [*Geomagnetic observatory code*]
PSM	Particle Size Monitor [*Instrumentation*]
PSM	Parti Socialiste Mauricien [*Mauritian Socialist Party*] [*Political party*] (EY)
PSM	Parti Socialiste Monegasque [*Monaco Socialist Party*] [*Political party*] (PPW)
psm	Passed School of Music [*Certificate of the Royal Military School of Music*] (WDAA)
PSM	Passenger Service Manager [*Travel industry*]
PSM	Past Savio Movement [*Defunct*] (EA)
PSM	Peak Selector Memory [*Computer science*]
PSM	People for Self Management [*An association*] (NADA)
PSM	Personal Skills Map [*Career effectiveness test*]
PSM	Personnel Subsystem Management [*Army*] (AABC)
PSM	Personnel Systems Management [*Air Force*] (AFM)
PSM	Petroleum Supply Monthly [*Database*] [*Department of Energy Information service or system*] (CRD)

PSM	Phase-Sensitive Modulator (MCD)
PSM	Phase-Shifter Module
PSM	Phase Shifting Mask (AAEL)
PSM	Physical Society of Moldova (BUAC)
PSM	Physician and Sports Medicine [*A publication*]
PSM	Pia Societas Missionum [*Fathers of the Pious Society of Missions, Pallottini*] [*Roman Catholic religious order*]
PSM	Pioneer Metals Corp. [*Toronto Stock Exchange symbol Vancouver Stock Exchange symbol*]
PSM	Platyschisma Shale Member [*Geology*]
PSM	Please See Me
PSM	Plymouth State College of the University of New Hampshere, Plymouth, NH [*OCLC symbol*] (OCLC)
PSM	Point Source Monitoring [*Environmental Protection Agency*] (GFGA)
PSM	Portsmouth [*New Hampshire*] [*Airport symbol*] (AD)
PSM	Portsmouth, NH [*Location identifier FAA*] (FAAL)
PSM	Postal Service Manual [*A publication*] (AFM)
PSM	Postmitochondrial Supernatant [*Medicine*] (DMAA)
PSM	Postsynaptic Membrane [*Neurology*]
PSM	Power Strapping Machine
PSM	Power Supply Module (MHDI)
PSM	Power System Module
PSM	Preservation Security Manager
PSM	Pressure Switch Manifold [*Automotive transmissions*]
PSM	Presystolic Murmur [*Cardiology*]
PSM	Prism (MSA)
PSM	Process Safety Management [*Chemical engineering*]
PSM	Production Systems Management (IAA)
PSM	Productive Standard Minute (MHDI)
PSM	Product Support Manual (AAG)
PSM	Professional Staff Member [*Congress*] (DOMA)
PSM	Programming Support Monitor [*Texas Instruments, Inc.*]
PSM	Program-Sensitive Malfunction
PSM	Program Support Management [*NASA*] (KSC)
PSM	Progressive Series Modulator (IAA)
PSM	Project Safety Management
PSM	Propellant Storage Module [*NASA*]
PSM	Pro Sanctity Movement (EA)
PSM	Public Service Medal
PSM	Public Storage Prop'A' XI [*AMEX symbol*] (TTSB)
PSM	Public Storage Properties XI, Inc. [*AMEX symbol*] (SAG)
PSM	Pulse Slope Modulation (IAA)
PSM	Pulse-Spacing Modulation (ECII)
PSm	Pyro Substitute Monitor [*NASA*] (NASA)
PSm	Thesaurus Syriacus [*R. Paine Smith*] [*A publication*] (BJA)
PSMA	Power Saw Manufacturers Association [*Later, CSMA*] (EA)
PSMA	Power Sources Manufacturers Association (NTPA)
PSMA	Power Supply Manufacturers Association [*British*] (DBA)
PSMA	President of the Society of Marine Artists [*British*]
PSMA	Pressure Sensitive Manufacturers Association [*British*] (DBA)
PSMA	Professional Services Management Association [*Alexandria, VA*] (EA)
PSMA	Progressive Spinal Muscular Atrophy [*Medicine*]
PSMA	Proximal Spinal Muscular [*Medicine*] (DMAA)
PSMA	Proximal Spinal Muscular Atrophy [*Medicine*] (DMAA)
PSMA	Pyrotechnic Signal Manufacturers Association (EA)
PSMD	Photo Selective Metal Deposition
PSME	Partido Socialista de Melilla [*See also PSOE*] [*Spanish North Africa*] [*Political party*] (MENA)
PSME	Personal Social and Moral Education (AIE)
PSMed	Psychosomatic Medicine (DAVI)
PSME-PSOE	Partido Socialista de Melilla - Partido Socialista Obrero Espanol [*Political party*] (EY)
PSMF	Protein Sparing Modified Fast
PSMFC	Pacific States Marine Fisheries Commission
PSMI	Phase-Shift Modal Interference
PSMI	Precise Ship Motion Instrument
PSMIT	Programming Services for Multimedia Industry Terminals [*IBM Corp.*]
PSML	Processor System Modeling Language [*1976*] [*Computer science*] (CSR)
PSMM	Multimission Patrol Ship [*Symbol*]
PSMMA	Plastic Soft Materials Manufacturers Association (EA)
PSMP	Program on Short- and Medium-Range Weather Prediction Research [*Marine science*] (OSRA)
PSMP	Project Software Management Plan (SSD)
PSMPA	Per Square Meter per Annum
PSMR	Parts Specification Management for Reliability
PSMR	Pneumatic [*or Pressure*] System Manifold Regulator [*or Manual*] (AAG)
PSMRD	Postsurgical Minimum Residual Disease [*Medicine*] (DB)
PSMS	Permanent Section of Microbiological Standardization (MCD)
PSMS	Physical Self Maintenance Scale
PSMSL	Permanent Service for Mean Sea Level [*of the Federation of Astronomical and Geophysical Data Analysis Services*] [*Birkenhead, Merseyside, England*] (EAIO)
PSMT	Paced Sequential Memory Task (PDAA)
PSMT	Pedestal Sight Manipulation Test (IAA)
PSMT	Perishable Sheet Metal Tool (MCD)
PSMT	Psychiatric Services Management Team (STED)
PSMU	Power Supply and Multiplexer Unit [*Telecommunications*] (TSSD)
PSMV	Paspalum Striate Mosaic Virus [*Plant pathology*]
PSMV	Pea Seed-Borne Mosaic Virus [*Plant pathology*]
PSN	Package Sequence Number
PSN	Packet Switched Network
PSN	Packet Switching Node

PSN .... Palestine, TX [*Location identifier FAA*] (FAAL)
PSN .... Parent Support Network [*Australia*]
PSN .... Partial Shipment Number [*DoD*]
PSN .... Parti de la Solidarite Nationale [*Party of National Solidarity*] [*Luxembourg*] [*Political party*] (PPE)
PSN .... Partido Socialista Nicaraguense [*Nicaraguan Socialist Party*] [*Political party*] (PPW)
PSN .... Payment Systems Network, Inc. (TBD)
PSN .... Pentium Serial Number [*Computer science*]
PSN .... Permanent Sort Number [*Computer science*]
PSN .... Polish Surname Network (EA)
PSN .... Poor Sisters of Nazareth (TOCD)
PSN .... Position
PSN .... Potosina del Aire SA de CV [*Mexico ICAO designator*] (FAAC)
PSN .... Private Satellite Network, Inc. [*New York, NY*] [*Telecommunications*] (TSSD)
PSN .... Processing Serial Number (MCD)
PSN .... Professional Speakers Network (NTPA)
PSN .... Program Summary Network (MCD)
PSN .... Progressive Student Network (EA)
PSN .... Provisioning Sequence Number (MCD)
PSN .... Public Storage Prop 'A' XII [*AMEX symbol*] (TTSB)
PSN .... Public Storage Properties XII, Inc. [*AMEX symbol*] (SAG)
PSN .... Public Switched Network (BUR)
PSNA .... Phytochemical Society of North America (EA)
PSNA .... Powys Society of North America (EA)
PSNAL .... Personal (FAAC)
PSNB .... Puget Sound Bancorp (EFIS)
PSNC .... Pacific Steam Navigation Co. (MHDW)
PSNC .... Parti Socialiste de la Nouvelle Caledonie [*Socialist Party of New Caledonia*] [*Political party*] (PPW)
PSNC .... Pharmaceutical Services Negotiating Committee (BUAC)
PSNCF .... Pacific Southern Naval Coastal Frontier
PSNCO .... Personnel Staff Noncommissioned Officer [*Military*]
PSNI .... Pharmaceutical Society of Northern Ireland (BUAC)
PSNL .... Personnel (FAAC)
PSNP .... Pebble Springs Nuclear Plant (NRCH)
PSNR .... Pasifik Satelit Nusantara (PT) [*NASDAQ symbol*] (SAG)
PSNR .... Positioner
PSNR .... Power Signal-to-Noise Ratio
PSNRP .... Position Report [*Aviation*] (FAAC)
PSNS .... Parasympathetic Nervous System (STED)
PSNS .... Physical Science for Nonscience Students
PSNS .... Pretreatment Standards for New Indirect Sources [*Environmental Protection Agency*]
PSNS .... Programmable Sampling Network Switch
PSNS .... Puget Sound Naval Shipyard [*Bremerton, WA*] (MCD)
PSNS-MATLABS... Puget Sound Naval Shipyard Material Laboratories [*Bremerton, WA*]
PSNSR .... Position Sensor (MCD)
PSNSW .... Philatelic Society of New South Wales [*Australia*]
PSNSY .... Puget Sound Naval Shipyard [*Bremerton, WA*]
PSNT .... Present [*Legal term*] (ROG)
PSNZ .... Perinatal Society of New Zealand (BUAC)
PSO .... Pad Safety Officer [*Aerospace*] (MCD)
PSO .... Paint Spray Outfit
PSO .... Paseo
PSO .... Pasto [*Colombia*] [*Airport symbol*] (OAG)
PSO .... Pasto [*Colombia*] [*Seismograph station code, US Geological Survey*] (SEIS)
PSO .... Pauli Spin Operator [*Physics*]
PSO .... Peacetime Stockage Objective [*DoD*] (AFIT)
PSO .... Penobscot Shoe [*AMEX symbol*] (TTSB)
PSO .... Penobscot Shoe Co. [*AMEX symbol*] (SPSG)
PSO .... Personal Staff Officer [*Australia*]
PSO .... Personnel Security Officer [*Military*]
PSO .... Personnel Selection Officer [*British military*] (DMA)
PSO .... Personnel Services Organisation [*Australia*]
PSO .... Piano-Shaped Object
PSO .... Pilot Systems Operator
PSO .... Planet Sensor Output
PSO .... Point Surface Origin
PSO .... Polaris Systems Officer [*British military*] (DMA)
PSO .... Policy Studies Organization (EA)
PSO .... Political Survey Officers [*Navy*]
PSO .... Polysulfone [*Also, PS*] [*Organic chemistry*]
PSO .... Port Services Office [*or Officer*] (DNAB)
PSO .... Primary Standardization Office [*Military*] (AABC)
PSO .... Principal Scientific Officer [*British*]
PSO .... Principal Staff Officer [*British military*] (DMA)
PSO .... Procurement Services Office
PSO .... Product Support Organization
PSO .... Profco Resources Ltd. [*Vancouver Stock Exchange symbol*]
PSO .... Programmable Storage Oscilloscope (CIST)
PSO .... Program Secretarial Officer (COE)
PSO .... Program Senior Official (COE)
PSO .... Program Staff Officer
PSO .... Progressive Supranuclear Ophthalmoplegia (CPH)
PSO .... Prospective Supply Officer (DNAB)
PSO .... Protective Security Officer
PSO .... Provider Sponsored Organization
PSO .... Provisions Supply Office [*Military*]
PSO .... Proximal Subungual Onychomycosis
PSO .... Psychiatric Services Officer [*Australia*]
PSO .... Publications Supply Officer [*Military*]

PSO .... Publicity Security Officer [*Navy*]
PSO .... Public Safety Officer
PSO .... Public Service Obligation [*Australia*]
PSO .... Public Service Organisation [*Government grant*] [*British*]
PSOA .... Postal Supervisory Officers' Association [*Australia*]
PSOA .... Pro Stock Owners Association (EA)
PSOB .... Paper Society for the Overseas Blind [*Defunct*] (EA)
PSOC .... Preliminary System Operational Concept (MCD)
PSOE .... Partido Socialista Obrero Espanol [*Spanish Socialist Workers' Party*] [*See also PSME*] [*Political party*] (PPE)
PSOJ .... Private Sector Organisation of Jamaica (BUAC)
P sol .... Partly Soluble [*Chemistry*] (DAVI)
P Sol .... Partly Soluble (WGA)
PSOLMHT .... Pious Society of Our Lady of the Most Holy Trinity (EA)
PSom .... Mary S. Biesecker Public Library, Somerset, PA [*Library symbol Library of Congress*] (LCLS)
PSomHi .... Somerset County Historical and Genealogical Society, Somerset, PA [*Library symbol Library of Congress*] (LCLS)
PSON .... Paul-Son Gaming [*NASDAQ symbol*] (TTSB)
PSON .... Paul-Son Gaming Corp. [*NASDAQ symbol*] (SAG)
PSON .... Person (ROG)
PSONAL .... Personal (ROG)
PSOP .... Parti Socialiste des Ouvriers et Paysans [*Socialist Party of Workers and Peasants*] [*France Political party*]
PSOP .... Payload Systems Operating Procedures [*NASA*] (NASA)
PSOP .... Power System Optimization Program [*Computer science*]
PSOR .... Preliminary System of Requirements
PSOS .... Probably Secure Operating System (MHDB)
PSP .... Pace-Setting Potential [*Physiology*]
PSP .... Pacifistische Socialistische Partij [*Pacific Socialist Party*] [*Political party Netherlands*]
PSP .... Package Size Proneness [*Marketing*]
PSP .... Packaging Shipping Procedures
PSP .... Packet Switching Processor
PSP .... Pad Safety Plan
PSP .... Palm Springs [*California*] [*Airport symbol*] (OAG)
PSP .... Palm Springs, CA [*Location identifier FAA*] (FAAL)
PSP .... Pancreatic Spasmolytic Peptide [*Biochemistry*]
PSP .... Paralytic Shellfish Poisoning [*Marine biology*]
PSP .... Parathyroid Secretory Protein [*Biochemistry*]
PSP .... Parti de la Solidarite du Peuple [*Cameroon*] [*Political party*] (EY)
PSP .... Partido Socialista del Peru [*Socialist Party of Peru*] [*Political party*] (PPW)
PSP .... Partido Socialista Popular [*Popular Socialist Party*] [*Spain Political party*] (PPE)
PSP .... Partido Socialista Popular [*Popular Socialist Party*] [*Peru*] [*Political party*] (PPW)
PSP .... Partido Socialista Portuguesa [*Portuguese Socialist Party*] [*Political party*] (PPW)
PSP .... Partido Social Progresista [*Social Progressive Party*] [*Brazil Political party*]
PSP .... Parti Socialiste Polynesien [*Polynesian Socialist Party*] [*Political party*] (PPW)
PSP .... Parti Social pour le Progres [*Tunisia*] [*Political party*] (EY)
PSP .... Parti Soudanais Progressiste [*Sudanese Progressive Party*] [*Political party*]
PSP .... Parts Screening Program
PSP .... Patrol Seaplane
PSP .... Payload Signal Processor [*NASA*] (NASA)
PSP .... Payload Specialist Panel [*NASA*] (NASA)
PSP .... Payload Support Plan [*NASA*] (MCD)
PSP .... Payroll Savings Plan (GFGA)
PSP .... Peak Sideband Power (DEN)
PSP .... Perforated Steel Planking (SAA)
PSP .... Perforated Steel Plate (VNW)
PSP .... Perforated Steel Plating (DNAB)
PSP .... Performance Shaping Parameters (IEEE)
P sp .... Performance Share Plan [*Human resources*] (WYGK)
PSP .... Performance Standards Program
PSP .... Periodic Short Pulse (MAE)
PSP .... Permanent Sample Plot [*For ecological studies*]
PSP .... Personal Security Preview [*Psychology*] (DAVI)
PSP .... Personal Success Program
PSP .... Personnel Subsystem Process [*Army*] (AABC)
PSP .... Pharmaceutical Society of Pakistan (BUAC)
PSP .... Pharmacological Sciences Program [*Bethesda, MD*] [*National Institute of General Medical Sciences*] (GRD)
PSP .... Phenolsulfonephthalein [*Chemical indicator*]
PSP .... Pierced Steel Planking [*Military*]
PSP .... Plane Strain Plastometer
PSP .... Planet Scan Platform [*NASA*] (KSC)
PSP .... Planned Standard Programming [*Computer science*]
PSP .... Plasma Spraying [*Welding*]
PSP .... Plasmon Surface Polariton [*Physics*]
PSP .... Platform Sensor Package
PSP .... Pointed Soft Point [*Ammunition*]
PSP .... Pointed Soft Point Bullet
PSP .... Policies, Systems, and Procedures
PSP .... Polyfactorial Study of Personality [*Psychology*]
PSP .... Poly(styrene peroxide) [*Organic chemistry*]
PSP .... Popular Socialist Party [*Political party*] (BUAC)
PSP .... Portable Service Processor (IEEE)
PSP .... Positive Spike Pattern (MAE)
psp .... Posterior Subcapsular Plaque [*Ophthalmology*] (DAVI)
PSP .... Postipankki [*National savings bank*] [*Finland*]

PSP............	Post-Shoring-Polyethylene [*Method of constructing underground homes*]
PSP............	Post-Surgical Pain [*Medicine*]
PSP............	Postsynaptic Potential [*Neurophysiology*]
PSP............	Potential for Successful Performance [*Test*]
PSP............	Power System Planning
PSP............	Praja Socialist Party [*India*] [*Political party*] (PPW)
PSP............	Precision Spot Positioning
PSP............	Predictable System Performance (SAA)
PSP............	Predictive Smooth Pursuit [*Ophthalmology*]
PSP............	Pre-Season Predictor Model [*Television ratings*] (NTCM)
PSP............	Presending Pause (NITA)
PSP............	Presensitized Photoplate
PSP............	Prestart Panel [*Aerospace*] (AAG)
PSP............	Priced Spare Parts [*Military*] (AFIT)
PSP............	Primary Smog Product (PDAA)
PSP............	Primary Sodium Pump [*Nuclear energy*] (NRCH)
PSP............	Primary Supply Point [*Military*] (AFM)
PSP............	Primary Support Point [*Military*] (AFM)
PSP............	Priority Strike Program
PSP............	Problem Solving Process
PSP............	Product Service Publication [*General Motors Corp.*]
PSP............	Product Support Program (NG)
PSP............	Professional and Scholarly Publishing Division [*Association of American Publishers*] (EDAC)
PSP............	Profit Sharing Plan [*Business term*] (MHDW)
PSP............	Programmable Signal Processor (MCD)
PSP............	Program Segment Prefix [*Computer science*]
PSP............	Program Support Plan [*NASA*]
PSP............	Progressive Socialist Party [*Lebanon*] [*Political party*] (BJA)
PSP............	Progressive Supranuclear Palsy [*Neurology*]
PSP............	Project Schedule Plan (NASA)
PSP............	Project Standard Practice (DNAB)
PSP............	Protective Shielding Program
PSP............	Protocol for Specific Purpose
PSP............	Pseudopregnancy [*Gynecology*]
PSP............	Pseudostatic Spontaneous Potential (IAA)
PSP............	Public Storage Canadian Properties [*Limited Partnership Units*] [*Toronto Stock Exchange symbol*]
PSP............	Public Storage Prop'A' XIV [*AMEX symbol*] (TTSB)
PSP............	Public Storage Properties XIV, Inc. [*AMEX symbol*] (SAG)
PSP............	Puerto Rican Socialist Party [*Political party*] (PD)
PSP............	Swarthmore College Peace Collection, Swarthmore, PA [*OCLC symbol*] (OCLC)
PSPA	Pacific Seafood Processors Association (EA)
PSPA	Passive Solar Products Association (EA)
PSPA	Pre-School Play Apparatus (WDAA)
PSPA	Pressure Static Probe Assembly (MCD)
PSPA	Professional School Photographers of America (EA)
PSPA	Professional Sports Photographers Association [*British*] (EAIO)
PSP & E	Product Support Planning and Estimating (AAG)
PSPC	Partido Socialista del Pueblo de Ceuta [*Political party*] (EY)
PSPC	Permanent South Pacific Commission (BUAC)
PSPC	Physical Security / Pilferage Code
PSPC	Polystyrene Packaging Council (EA)
PSPC	Position-Sensitive Proportional Counter [*Instrumentation*]
PSPC	President's Soviet Protocol Committee [*World War II*]
PSPD	Permits and State Programs Division [*Environmental Protection Agency*] (GFGA)
PSPD	Position-Sensitive Proportional Detector [*For X-ray diffraction*]
PSPDN........	Packet Switched Public Data Network [*Computer science*] (TNIG)
PSPEN........	Primary/Secondary Peace Education Network [*Later, PEN*] (EA)
PSPF...........	Potential Single Point Failures [*NASA*] (KSC)
PSPF...........	Prostacyclin Stimulating Plasma Factor [*Endocrinology*]
PSPFLI.......	Pulsed Single Photon Fluorescence Lifetime Instrumentation
PSPG	Phase-Shifting Pulse Gate (WDAA)
PSPGV	Primary Sodium Pump Guard Vesel [*Nuclear energy*] (NRCH)
PSphR	Rohm & Haas Co., Research Library Services, Spring House, PA [*Library symbol Library of Congress*] (LCLS)
PSPI...........	Psychosocial Pain Inventory [*Psychology*]
PSPL..........	Priced Spare Parts List
PSPL..........	Progressive Socialist Party of Lebanon
PSPLR	Priced Spare Parts List Revision
PSPM.........	Procurement Seminar for Project Management [*Army*]
PSPMW	International Brotherhood of Pulp, Sulphite, and Paper Mill Workers [*Later, UPIU*]
PSPP	Preliminary System Package Plan
PSPP	Program System Package Plan
PSPP	Proposed System Package Plan [*Military*]
PSPR	Personnel Subsystem Products [*Army*] (AABC)
PSPR	Programmable Signal Processor RADAR
PSPRT	Partial Sequential Probability Ratio Test (PDAA)
PSPS	Paddle Steamer Preservation Society [*British*] (BI)
PSPS	Pesticides Safety Precautions Scheme [*British*]
PSPS	Planar Silicon Photoswitch (IEEE)
PSPS	Power-Steering Pressure Sensor [*Automotive engineering*]
PSPS	Power Steering Pressure Switch [*Automotive engineering*]
PSPS	Product Support Procurement Summary (MCD)
PSPS	Program Support Plan Summary
PSPSK	Previous Signaling Element Phase Shift Keying [*Computer science*] (IAA)
PSPSV	Pre-School Playgroup Support Visitor (WDAA)
PSPT...........	Parisi Spanish Proficiency Test (EDAC)
PSPT...........	Passport (AABC)
PSPT...........	Planar Silicon Power Transistor

PSptv	PerSeptive Biosystems, Inc. [*Associated Press*] (SAG)
PSPV	Partido Socialista del Pais Valenciano [*Spain Political party*] (EY)
PSQ	Parent Symptom Questionnaire [*Medicine*] (DMAA)
PSQ	Patient Satisfaction Questionnaire [*Medicine*] (DMAA)
PSQ	Personnel Security Questionnaire
PSQ	Personnel Squadron
PSQ	Political Science Quarterly [*A publication*] (BRI)
PSQ	Protein Sequence Query
PSQ	Public Storage Prop'A' XV [*AMEX symbol*] (TTSB)
PSQ	Public Storage Properties XV [*AMEX symbol*] (SPSG)
PSQA	Pageable System Queue Area [*Computer science*] (MCD)
PSQC	Philippine Society for Quality Control (BUAC)
PSQI	Pittsburgh Sleep Quality Index
PSQL	Platinum Software [*NASDAQ symbol*] (TTSB)
PSQL	Platinum Software Corp. [*NASDAQ symbol*] (SAG)
PSR	Pacific Security Region
PSR	Pacific-Sierra Research Corp.
PSR	Packed Snow on Runway [*NWS*] (FAAC)
PSR	Pad Safety Report [*NASA*]
PSR	Page Send-Receive [*Teletypewriter*]
PSR	Pain Sensitivity Range [*Biometrics*]
PSR	Panoramic Stereo Rectification
PSR	Paper Stock Record [*DGA*]
PSR	Parachute Status Report [*Army*] (AABC)
PSR	Partido Socialista Revolucionario [*Revolutionary Socialist Party*] [*Peru*] [*Political party*] (PPW)
PSR	Partido Socialista Revolucionario [*Revolutionary Socialist Party*] [*Mexico Political party*] (PPW)
PSR	Partido Socialista Revolucionario [*Revolutionary Socialist Party*] [*Portugal Political party*] (PPE)
PSR	Parts and Supply Requisition (IAA)
PSR	Party Socialiste Revolutionnaire [*Socialist Revolutionary Party*] [*Lebanon*] [*Political party*] (PPW)
psr	Paternal Sex Ratio Gene [*Genetics*]
PSR	Paul's Scarlet Rose [*Plant cell line*]
PSR	Pennsylvania State Reports [*A publication*] (DLA)
PSR	Pennsylvania State University Reactor (NRCH)
PSR	Perfectly Stirred Reactor
PSR	Performance Summary Report (NG)
PSR	Peripheral Shim Rod [*Nuclear energy*] (NRCH)
PSR	Personnel Status Report [*Military*]
PSR	Pescara [*Italy*] [*Airport symbol*] (OAG)
PSR	Petaluma & Santa Rosa Railroad Co. [*AAR code*]
PSR	Petrostates Resource Corp. [*Vancouver Stock Exchange symbol*]
PSR	Pharmaceutical Sales Representative
PSR	Phase Sensitive Rectifier (NITA)
PSR	Phase Sequence Relay
PSR	Philatelic Societies' Record [*A publication British*]
PSR	Photo Scale Reciprocal (DNAB)
PSR	Physical Sciences Research Program [*North Carolina State University*] [*Research center*] (RCD)
PSR	Physicians for Social Responsibility (EA)
PSR	Plow-Steel Rope
PSR	Point of Safe Return (MCD)
PSR	Point Source Range (IAA)
PSR	Policy Status Report [*Insurance*]
PSR	Political and Social Reform Movement [*British*]
PSR	Political Science Reviewer [*A publication*] (BRI)
PSR	Portable Seismic Recorder
PSR	Positive Support Review, Inc. [*Telecommunications service*] (TSSD)
PSR	Postal Service Representative [*British*] (DCTA)
PSR	Post-Sinusoidal Resistance
PSR	Power System Relaying (MCD)
PSR	Predicted SONAR Range [*Military*] (NVT)
PSR	Pre-Sentence Report (WDAA)
PSR	Present Serviceability Rating [*FHWA*] (TAG)
PSR	Presidential Special Representative (BARN)
PSR	Price-Sales Ratio [*Economics*]
PSR	Primary Surveillance RADAR
PSR	Primary System Relief (COE)
PSR	Problem Status Report (MCD)
PSR	Processor State Register
PSR	Procurement Status Report (IEEE)
PSR	Productivity Savings Reward (AAGC)
PSR	Programming Status Report [*Computer science*]
PSR	Programming Support Representative [*IBM Corp.*]
PSR	Program Status Register
PSR	Program Status Report [*or Review*]
PSR	Program Status Review [*NASA*] (NASA)
PSR	Program Study Request (AAG)
PSR	Program Summary Record [*Military*] (AFIT)
PSR	Program Support Representative (NITA)
PSR	Program Support Requirements (KSC)
PSR	Progress Summary Report
PSR	Project Safe Run (EA)
PSR	Project Scan Record
PSR	Project Summary Report (MCD)
PSR	Proliferative Sickle Retinopathy (DB)
PSR	Propeller Shaft Rate [*Navy*] (CAAL)
PSR	Pro Seniors [*International Bowhunting Organization*] [*Class Equipment*]
PSRtv	Proton Storage Ring [*Nuclear physics*]
PSR	Prototype Systems Review
PSR	Provisioning Support Request [*Military*] (CAAL)
PSR	Public Service Company of Colorado [*AMEX symbol*] (SAG)

PSR .... Public Service Co. of Colorado [*NYSE symbol*] (SPSG)
PSR .... Public Social Responsibility [*Unit of the Anglican Church of Canada General Synod*]
PSR .... Public SvcColorado [*NYSE symbol*] (TTSB)
PSR .... Pulmonary Stretch Receptors [*Medicine*]
PSRA .... Persil Stain Release Agent (WDAA)
PSRA .... Presunrise Service Authorization [*Telecommunications*] (OTD)
PSRA .... Problem Status Report Analysis (SAA)
PSRA .... Professional Soccer Reporter's Association (EA)
PSRAAALAA... President's Special Representative and Adviser on African, Asian, and Latin American Affairs [*Department of State*]
PSRAM .... Physical Security Requirements Assessment Methodology [*Civil Engineering Research Laboratory*] [*Navy*] (RDA)
PSRAM .... Pseudostatic Random Access Memory [*Apple Computer Inc.*]
PSRBOW...... Premature Spontaneous Rupture of Bag of Waters [*Medicine*] (MEDA)
PSRC .... Plastic Surgery Research Council (EA)
PSRC .... Pretrial Services Resource Center (EA)
PSRC .... PrimeSource Corp. [*NASDAQ symbol*] (SAG)
PSRC .... Public Service Research Council (EA)
PSRCA .... Professional Standards Review Council of America (EA)
PSRD .... Personnel Shipment Ready Date [*Army*] (AABC)
PSRD .... Program Support Requirements Document [*NASA*] (KSC)
PSRE .... Partido Socialista Revolucionario Ecuatoriano [*Socialist Revolutionary Party of Ecuador*] [*Political party*] (PPW)
PSRE .... Propulsion System Rocket Engine (MCD)
PSRF .... Product Support Reports and Functions
PSRF .... Profit Sharing Research Foundation (EA)
PSRI .... Particulate Solid Research Institute
PSRI .... Personnel Specialities and Record Inventory (SAA)
PSRI .... Position Subject to Return of Incumbent [*Aviation*] (FAAC)
PSRI .... Psycho-Social Rehabilitation International (EAIO)
PSRL .... Post Strike Reconnaissance List [*Military*] (CINC)
PSRM .... Parti Sosialis Rakyat Malaya [*People's Socialist Party of Malaya*]
PSRM .... Post-Scram Reactivity Monitor [*Nuclear energy*] (NRCH)
PSRM .... Pressurization Systems Regulator Manifold (AAG)
PSRM .... Processor State Register Main [*Computer science*]
PSRMA .... Pacific Southwest Railway Museum Association [*Later, SDRM*] (EA)
PSR-ML/MIR... Partido Socialista Revolucionario (Marxista-Leninista)/Movimiento de Izquierda Revolucionaria [*Revolutionary Socialist Party (Marxist-Leninist)/Mi litant Movement of the Revolutionary Left*] [*Peru*] [*Political party*] (PPW)
PSRMLS ...... Pacific Southwest Regional Medical Library [*Library network*]
PSRMT .... Piecewise-Sinusoidal Reaction Matching Technique [*Antenna*] [*Navy*]
PSRO .... Passenger Standing Route Order [*Army*] (AABC)
PSRO .... Professional Standards Review Organization (NADA)
PSR-P .... Packed Snow on Runway - Patchy [*Aviation*] (DNAB)
PSRP .... Physical Sciences Research Papers [*Air Force*] (MCD)
PSRP .... Production Support Repair Plan (SAA)
PSRPr .... Pub Sv of Colo.,4 1/4% Pfd [*AMEX symbol*] (TTSB)
PSRPrA .... Pub Sv Colo.,7.15% Pfd [*NYSE symbol*] (TTSB)
PSRR .... Parachute Supported Radio Relay
PSRR .... Power Supply Rejection Ratio (IAA)
PSRR .... Product and Support Requirements Request [*Computer science*] (IBMDP)
PSRS .... Pictographic Self-Rating Scale [*Psychology*] (AEBS)
PSRS .... Portable Seismic Recording System
PSRS .... Position Subject to Rotating Shifts [*Aviation*] (FAAC)
PSrS .... Slippery Rock State College, Slippery Rock, PA [*Library symbol Library of Congress*] (LCLS)
PSRT .... Passive Satellite Research Terminal
PS-RTP .... Paper-Substrate Room-Temperature Phosphorescence [*Analytical chemistry*]
PSRU .... Processor State Register Utility [*Computer science*]
PSRU .... Production Support Repair Unit (SAA)
PSS............. Hastings, NE [*Location identifier FAA*] (FAAL)
PSS............. International Production, Service, and Sales Union
PSS............. Packet Switched System (NITA)
PSS............. Packet Switching Service [*Telecommunications Information service or system British*] (IID)
PSS............. Packet SwitchStream [*British Telecommunications Plc*] [*London*] [*Information service or system*] (IID)
PSS............. Pad Safety Supervision [*Aerospace*] (AAG)
PSS............. Pad Safety Supervisor [*NASA*] (NAKS)
PSS............. Palomar Sky Survey [*NASA*]
PSS............. Partially Sighted Society [*British*]
PSS............. Partia Socialiste e Shqiperise [*Socialist Party of Albania*] [*Political party*] (EAIO)
PSS............. Parti de Solidarite Senegalaise [*Senegalese Solidarity Party*] [*Political party*]
PSS............. Parti Socialiste Suisse [*Social Democratic Party of Switzerland*] [*Political party*] (PPE)
PSS............. Partito Socialista Sammarinese [*Socialist Party of San Marino*] [*Political party*] (PPE)
PSS............. Partito Socialista Somalo [*Somali Socialist Party*] [*Political party*]
PSS............. Passenger Service Supervisor [*Travel industry*]
PSS............. Passenger Service Systems [*Airlines*]
PSS............. Patent Search System [*Pergamon*] [*Database*] [*Computer science*] [*British*]
PSS............. Pauli Spin Susceptibility [*Physics*]
PSS............. Payless ShoeSource [*NYSE symbol*] (TTSB)
PSS............. Payless ShoeSource, Inc. [*NYSE symbol*] (SAG)
PSS............. Payload Specialist Station [*NASA*] (NASA)
PSS............. Payload Support System [*NASA*] (MCD)
PSS............. Perceived Stress Scale [*Psychology*] (DHP)
PSS............. Performance Standard Sheet
PSS............. Performance Support System [*Human resources*] (WYGK)
PSS............. Periscope Simulation System [*Navy*]
PSS............. Personal Signaling System
PSS............. Personnel Service Support [*Army*] (DOMA)
PSS............. Personnel Staffing Specialist (GFGA)
PSS............. Personnel Subsystem [*Air Force*] (AFM)
PSS............. Personnel Support System [*Army*] (AABC)
PSS............. Phase-System Switching [*Physical chemistry*]
PSS............. Physical Security Subsystem
PSS............. Physiological Saline Solution [*Physiology*]
PSS............. Planetary Scan System [*or Subsystem*]
PSS............. Planned Systems Schedule (AAG)
PSS............. Planning Summary Sheets (AAG)
PSS............. Plant Science Seminar [*Later, ASP*]
PS/S........... Plumbing Supervisor/Specialist (AAG)
PSS............. Plume Suppression System [*Combustion technology*]
PSS............. Plunger Snap Switch
PSS............. Pneumatic Supply Subsystem (AAG)
PSS............. Polar Subsurface Sounder (SSD)
PSS............. Poly(styrenesulfonate) [*Organic chemistry*]
PSS............. Porcine Stress Syndrome [*Veterinary medicine*]
PSS............. Portable Simulation System (MCD)
PSS............. Port Safety and Security [*USCG*] (TAG)
PSS............. Posadas [*Argentina*] [*Airport symbol*] (OAG)
PSS............. Postal Savings System [*Terminated, 1966*]
PSS............. Postal Separation System (SAA)
PSS............. Postscripta [*Postscripts*] [*Latin*]
PSS............. Power Supply Section
PSS............. Power Supply Subsystem (IAA)
PSS............. Power System Synthesizer
PSS............. Precancel Stamp Society (EA)
PSS............. Premature Separation Switch (SAA)
PSS............. Presbyteri Sancti Sulpicii [*Sulpicians*] [*Roman Catholic men's religious order*]
P/S/S .... Price/Stern/Sloan Publishers, Inc.
PSS............. Primary Sampling System [*Nuclear energy*] (NRCH)
PSS............. Princess (ROG)
PSS............. Printer Storage System [*Computer science*] (MHDI)
PSS............. Probabilistic Safety Study [*Nuclear energy*] (NRCH)
PSS............. Process Sampling System [*Nuclear energy*] (NRCH)
PSS............. Process Standard Specification
PSS............. Process Switching Service (IAA)
PSS............. Professional Services Section (BARN)
PSS............. Professor of Sacred Scripture
PSS............. Programming Support System (SAA)
PSS............. Program Support Staff [*Environmental Protection Agency*] (GFGA)
PSS............. Progressive Science Series [*A publication*]
PSS............. Progressive Systemic Sclerosis [*Medicine*]
PSS............. Propellant Supply System [*or Subsystem*]
PSS............. Proposed Sale of Securities (GFGA)
PSS............. Proprietary Software Systems [*Computer science*] (IEEE)
PSS............. Proprietary Support System [*Computer science*] (IAA)
PSS............. Propulsion Subsystem Structure
PSS............. Propulsion Support System (KSC)
PSS............. Protective Security Service
PSS............. Protective Signature Service (MCD)
PSS............. Psalms [*Old Testament book*]
Pss.............. Pseudomonas Syringae Syringae [*Plant pathology*]
PSS............. Pseudo Spread Spectrum (MCD)
PSS............. Psychiatric Services Section [*of the American Hospital Association*] [*Later, SCSMHPS*] (EA)
PSS............. Psychiatric Status Schedules [*Psychology*]
PSS............. Psychological Saline Solution (BARN)
PSS............. Public Services Satellite
PSS............. Public Storage Canadian Properties II [*Limited Partnership Units*] [*Toronto Stock Exchange symbol*]
PSS............. Push-Button Selection Station
PS(SA)......... Photographic Society of Southern Africa (BUAC)
PSSA .... Pilot Signal Selector Adaptor (SAA)
PSSA .... Pitch Starting Synchro Assembly
PSSA .... Postsunset Service Authorization [*Telecommunications*] (OTD)
PSSA .... Pseudo-Steady-State Approximation [*Chemical engineering*]
PSSAA .... Pacific Stars and Stripes Alumni Association (EA)
PSSAANDPS... Permanent Secretariat of the South American Agreement on Narcotic Drugs and Psychotropic Substances (EAIO)
PSSB .... Palm Springs Savings Bank [*Palm Springs, CA*] [*NASDAQ symbol*] (NQ)
PSSB .... Palm Springs Svgs Bk [*NASDAQ symbol*] (TTSB)
PSSB .... Passing Stopped School Bus [*Traffic offense charge*]
PSSBB .... Public School System Blanket Bond [*Insurance*]
PSSC .... Parachute Subsystem Sequence Controller [*NASA*] (SAA)
PSSC .... Personal Social Services Council [*British*] (DI)
PSSC .... Petroleum Security Subcommittee [*of Foreign Petroleum Supply Committee*] [*Terminated, 1976*] (EGAO)
PSSC .... Physical Science Study Committee [*National Science Foundation*]
PSSC .... Pious Society of Missionaries of St. Charles [*Later, CS*] [*Roman Catholic men's religious order*]
PSSC .... Public Service Satellite Consortium (EA)
PSSCC .... Peter Symonds School Cadet Corps [*British military*] (DMA)
PSSD .... Parallel-Serial Scan Design [*Electronics*]
PSSD .... Personnel Service Support Directorate (DOMA)
PSSDC .... Production Service and Sales District Council (NTPA)
PSSDS .... Portable Surface Supported Diving System (PDAA)
PSSEP .... Preliminary System Safety Engineering Plan

PSSES .... Public Service Senior Executive Service [Australia]
PSSF............ Petites Soeurs de la Sainte-Famille [Little Sisters of the Holy Family] [Sherbrooke, PQ] (EAIO)
PSSG .... Physical Science Study Group
PSSGNR ...... Passenger
PSS-I .... Peace Science Society (International) (EA)
PSSI............ Physician Sales & Service [NASDAQ symbol] (TTSB)
PSSI............ Physician Sales & Service, Inc. [NASDAQ symbol] (SAG)
PSSI............ Plasma Source Ion Implantation
PSSI............ Primary Specialty Skill Identifier [Military] (AABC)
PSSI............ PSS World Medical [NASDAQ symbol] [Formerly, Physician Sales & Service]
PSSIIS .... Partito Socialista: Sezione Italiana del Internazionale Socialista [Socialist Party: Italian Section of International Socialism] [Political party] (PPE)
PSS(Int)...... Peace Science Society (International)
PSSJ........... Poor Sisters of St. Joseph (TOCD)
PSSK .... Probability of Single Shot Kill [Of a guided missile]
PSSL .... Princeton University Solid State and Materials Laboratory [New Jersey]
PSSM.......... Preliminary Science Meeting [NASA]
PSSMA .... Paper Shipping Sack Manufacturers Association (EA)
PSSMLF...... Provincial Society of Spanish and Moroccan Leather Finishers [A union] [British]
PSSO .... Pass Slip Stitch Over [Knitting]
PsSol .... Psalms of Solomon [Pseudepigrapha] (BJA)
PSSP .... Partition with Self Substitution Property (IAA)
PSSP .... Payload Specialist Station Panel [NASA] (MCD)
PSSP .... Personnel Security and Surety Program [Military] (ADDR)
PSSP .... Phone Center Staffing and Sizing Program [Telecommunications] (TEL)
PSSR .... Parallel-Shaft Speed Reducer
PSSR .... Pre-Startup Safety Review [Chemical engineering]
PSSR .... Primary School Staff Relations [Project] (AIE)
PSSR .... Problem Status and Summary Report [NASA] (KSC)
PSSR .... Provisioning Supply Support Requests [DoD]
PSSRA .... Public Service Staff Relations Act [Canada]
PSSRB .... Public Service Staff Relations Board [Canada]
PSSS .... Philosophic Society for the Study of Sport (EA)
PSSS .... Presidential Survivability Support System
PSST........... Periodic Significant Scheduled Tasks [NASA] (NASA)
PSS(T) .... Pregnancy Support Service (Tasmania) [Australia]
PSSTA .... Port Security Station [Coast Guard]
PSSU .... Patch Survey and Switching Unit (MCD)
PST............. Airwork (New Zealand) Ltd. [ICAO designator] (FAAC)
PST............. Pacific Standard Time
PST............. Pacific Summer Time
PST............. Paired Selected Ternary (IAA)
PST............. Pair Selected Ternary [Computer science]
PST............. Pancreastatin [Biochemistry]
PST............. Pancreatic Suppression Test [Medicine] (AAMN)
PST............. Paroxysmal Superaventricular Tachycardia [Medicine] (MEDA)
PST............. Paroxysmal Supraventricular Tachycardia [Cardiology] (DAVI)
PST............. Partido Socialista de los Trabajadores [Socialist Workers' Party] [Mexico Political party] (PPW)
PST............. Partido Socialista de los Trabajadores [Socialist Workers Party] [Panama] [Political party] (EY)
PST............. Partido Socialista de los Trabajadores [Socialist Workers' Party] [Colombia] [Political party] (PPW)
PST............. Partition Specification Table (MHDI)
PST............. Pascal-Suttle Test [Psychology] (DAVI)
PST............. Pass Time [Military]
PST............. Paste
pst............. Paste (VRA)
PST............. Pastry (MSA)
PST............. Pasture Canyon [Utah] [Seismograph station code, US Geological Survey Closed] (SEIS)
PST............. Penicillin, Streptomycin, and Tetracycline [Antibiotics] (MAE)
PSt............. Pennsylvania State University, University Park, PA [Library symbol Library of Congress] (LCLS)
PST............. Performance Specification Tree
PST............. Periodic Self-Test [Computer science]
PST............. Peristimulus Time [Neurophysiology]
PST............. Personnel Subsystem Team [Military] (AFIT)
PST............. Peseta [Monetary unit] [Spain and Latin America]
PST............. Pesticide
PST............. Petrie Stores (EFIS)
PST............. Petrie Stores Corp. [NYSE symbol] (SPSG)
PST............. Phase Space Theory [Physical chemistry]
PST............. Phenol Sulfotransferase [An enzyme]
PST............. Philadelphia Suburban Transportation [AAR code]
PST............. Piston Shock Tunnel
PST............. Planetary Spectroscopy Telescope (SSD)
PST............. Point of Spiral Tangent (KSC)
PST............. Polaris Star Tracker [Missiles]
PST............. Polished Surface Technique (IEEE)
PST............. Pooled Superannuation Trust
PST............. Porcine Somatotropin [Gene-spliced animal hormone] [Monsanto Co.]
PST............. Portuguese Speaking Test [Center for Applied Linguistics] (TES)
PST............. Poststenotic [Medicine] (DMAA)
PST............. Post-Stimulus Time
PST............. Pressure-Sensitive Tape
PST............. Preston [Cuba] [Airport symbol] (AD)
PST............. Primary Surge Tank [Nuclear energy] (NRCH)

PST............. Priority Selection Table [Computer science] (IBMDP)
PST............. Prior Service Training [US Army Reserve] (INF)
PST............. Production Sampling Test (IAA)
PST............. Production Special Tooling (MCD)
PST............. Production Surveillance Test (MCD)
PST............. Product Support Technician
PST............. Professional, Scientific, and Technical
PST............. Profit Sharing Trustee (DLA)
PST............. Program Status Table [Computer science] (IAA)
PST............. Program Synchronization Table (CMD)
PST............. Project ST [Later, NSTA] (EA)
PST............. Propeller STOL [Short Takeoff and Landing] Transport
PST............. Pro Sight Technology
PST............. Shepard's Preparing for Settlement and Trial [A publication]
Pst............. Static Transpulmonary Pressure at a Specific Lung Volume [Medicine] (DAVI)
PSTA .... Monterey Pasta [NASDAQ symbol] (SAG)
PSTA .... Packaging Science and Technology Abstracts [International Food Information Service] [Germany Information service or system]
PSTA .... Partido Socialista Tito Atahuichi [Bolivia] [Political party] (PPW)
PSt-A .... Pennsylvania State University, Agricultural Library, University Park, PA [Library symbol Library of Congress] (LCLS)
PSTA .... Pre-Sea Trial Audit (MCD)
PSTA .... Public Safety and Training Association (NADA)
PSt-All .... Pennsylvania State University, Allentown Campus, Allentown, PA [Library symbol Library of Congress] (LCLS)
PSt-Alt .... Pennsylvania State University, Altoona Campus, Altoona, PA [Library symbol Library of Congress] (LCLS)
PSt-B .... Pennsylvania State University, Berks Campus, Wyomissing, PA [Library symbol Library of Congress] (LCLS)
PSTB .... Perpetual State Bank (North Carolina) [NASDAQ symbol] (SAG)
PSTB .... Picture Story Test Blank [Psychology]
PSTB .... Propulsion System Test Bed [for ABC helicopters] (RDA)
PSTB .... Puget Sound Tug & Barge [AAR code]
pstbd .... Pasteboard (VRA)
PSt-Be .... Pennsylvania State University, Beaver Campus, Monaca, PA [Library symbol Library of Congress] (LCLS)
PSTC .... Pressure Sensitive Tape Council (EA)
PSTC .... Product Support Task Control (AAG)
PSTC .... Public Switched Telephone Circuits [Telecommunications] (TEL)
PStcA.......... American Philatelic Research Library, State College, PA [Library symbol Library of Congress] (LCLS)
PSt-Ca .... Pennsylvania State University, Capitol Campus, Middletown, PA [Library symbol Library of Congress] (LCLS)
PSTCA .... Public Services Temporary Clerks' Association [A union] [British]
PStcH.......... HRB-Singer, Inc., Science Park, State College, PA [Library symbol Library of Congress] (LCLS)
PSTCO .... Per Steering Compass [Navigation] (DNAB)
PSt-D .... Pennsylvania State University, DuBois Campus, DuBois, PA [Library symbol Library of Congress] (LCLS)
PSTD .... Potato Spindle Tuber Disease
PSTD .... Promotable Second-Tier Debt [Economics]
PstdE.......... Eastern College, St. Davids, PA [Library symbol Library of Congress] (LCLS)
PSt-De .... Pennsylvania State University, Delaware Campus, Chester, PA [Library symbol Library of Congress] (LCLS)
PSt-E .... Pennsylvania State University, Behrend Campus, Erie, PA [Library symbol Library of Congress] (LCLS)
PSTE .... Personnel Subsystem Test and Evaluation [Military]
PST-E.......... Priority Selection Table Extension [Computer science] (IBMDP)
PSTE .... Production Special Testing Equipment (MCD)
PSTEP.......... Pre-Service Teacher Education Program [National Science Foundation]
PSTF .... Payload Spin Test Facility (MCD)
PSt-F .... Pennsylvania State University, Fayette Campus, Uniontown, PA [Library symbol Library of Congress] (LCLS)
PSTF .... Pioneer Station Training Facility [NASA]
PSTF .... Pressure Suppression Test Facility [Nuclear energy] (IEEE)
PSTF .... Privately-Owned Sewage Treatment Facility
PSTF .... Professional Staff [NASDAQ symbol] (SAG)
PSTF .... Profit Sharing Trust Fund
PSTF .... Proximity Sensor Test Facility [Nuclear energy] (NRCH)
PSTF............ Pump Seal Test Facility [Nuclear energy] (NRCH)
PSTG .... Postage (WGA)
PSTGC .... Per Steering Compass [Navigation]
PSt-H .... Pennsylvania State University, Hazelton Campus, Hazelton, PA [Library symbol Library of Congress] (LCLS)
PSTH .... Peristimulus Time Histogram
PSTH .... Posthumously
PSTH .... Poststimulus Time Histogram [Medical statistics]
PSTH .... Poststimulus Time Histogram (STED)
PSTH .... Professional Sports Teams Histories [A publication]
PSTI........... Pancreatic Secretory Trypsin Inhibitor [Biochemistry]
PSTIAC .... Pavements and Soil Trafficability Information Analysis Center [Army Corps of Engineers] (IID)
PSt-KP .... Pennsylvania State University, King of Prussia Graduate Center, King of Prussia, PA [Library symbol Library of Congress] (LCLS)
PSTL .... Pastoral
PSTL .... Pistol (MSA)
PSTL .... Postal (AFM)
PSTL .... Pressure Model Static and Transient Launch Configuration (SAA)
PSTM.......... Persistent Standoff Target Marker (MCD)
PSTM.......... Photon Scanning Tunnelling Microscope
PSTMA........ Paper Stationery and Tablet Manufacturers Association [Later, PCA] (EA)

PSt-MA .... Pennsylvania State University, Mont Alto Campus, Mont Alto, PA [*Library symbol Library of Congress*] (LCLS)
PSt-McK ..... Pennsylvania State University, McKeesport Campus, McKeesport, PA [*Library symbol Library of Congress*] (LCLS)
PSTN .... Pesticide Safety Team Network (GNE)
PSTN .... Piston (MSA)
PSTN .... Position
PSTN .... Public Service Telephone Network (WDAA)
PSTN .... Public Switched Telephone Network
PSt-NK .... Pennsylvania State University, New Kensington Campus, New Kensington, PA [*Library symbol Library of Congress*] (LCLS)
PSt-O .... Pennsylvania State University, Ogontz Campus, Abington, PA [*Library symbol Library of Congress*] (LCLS)
PSTO .... Principal Sea Transport Officer
PSTO .... Purdue Student-Teacher Opinionaire [*Test*]
PS to PS ..... Private Siding to Private Siding
PS to S .... Private Siding to Station
PSTP.......... Pentasodium Triphosphate (STED)
PSt-PiN ...... Pennsylvania State University, School of Nursing, Allegheny General Hospital, Pittsburgh, PA [*Library symbol Library of Congress*] (LCLS)
PSTR .... Pastor
PSTR .... Penn State TRIGA [*Training Reactor, Isotopes General Atomic*] Reactor
P/STRG....... Power Steering [*Automotive engineering*]
PSTS.......... Passive SONAR Tracking System
PSt-S .... Pennsylvania State University, Scranton Campus, Scranton, PA [*Library symbol Library of Congress*] (LCLS)
PSTS.......... Primary School Teachers and Science [*Project*] (AIE)
PSt-Sk .... Pennsylvania State University, Schuylkill Campus, Schuylkill Haven, PA [*Library symbol Library of Congress*] (LCLS)
PSt-SV .... Pennsylvania State University, Shenango Valley Campus, Sharon, PA [*Library symbol Library of Congress*] (LCLS)
PSTTX........ Pioneer Short Term Income [*Mutual fund ticker symbol*] (SG)
PSTV.......... Potato Spindle Tuber Viroid (STED)
PSTV.......... Potato Spindle Tuber Virus
PSTV.......... PST Vans [*NASDAQ symbol*] (TTSB)
PSTV.......... PST Vans, Inc. [*NASDAQ symbol*] (SAG)
PSTVd........ Potato Spindle Tuber Viroid [*Plant pathology*]
PST Vn .... PST Vans, Inc. [*Associated Press*] (SAG)
PSt-WB....... Pennsylvania State University, Wilkes-Barre Campus, Wilkes-Barre, PA [*Library symbol Library of Congress*] (LCLS)
PSt-WS....... Pennsylvania State University, Worthington Scranton Campus, Dunmore, PA [*Library symbol Library of Congress*] (LCLS)
PSt-X .... Pennsylvania State University, Off-Campus Libraries [*Library symbol*] [*Library of Congress*] (LCLS)
PSt-Y .... Pennsylvania State University, York Campus, York, PA [*Library symbol Library of Congress*] (LCLS)
pstyl........... Peristyle (VRA)
P'STYL....... Pronestyl [*Procainamide*] [*Bristol-Myers Squibb Co.*] [*Pharmacology*] (DAVI)
PSTZG .... Pasteurizing [*Freight*]
PSU .... Aeropeninsular, SA de CV [*Mexico*] [*FAA designator*] (FAAC)
PSu............ John R. Kaufman, Jr., [*Sunbury*] Public Library, Sunbury, PA [*Library symbol Library of Congress*] (LCLS)
PSU .... Package Size Unspecified
PSU .... Packet Switching Unit
PSU .... Partido Socialista Unificado [*Socialist Unification Party*] [*Argentina Political party*] (PPW)
PSU .... Partido Socialista Uruguayo [*Uruguayan Socialist Party*] [*Political party*] (PD)
PSU .... Partidul Socialist Unitar [*Unitary Socialist Party*] [*Romania*] [*Political party*] (PPE)
PSU .... Parti Socialiste Unifie [*Unified Socialist Party*] [*France Political party*] (PPW)
PSU .... Partito Socialista Unificato [*Unified Socialist Party*] [*Italy Political party*] (PPE)
PSU .... Partito Socialista Unitario [*Socialist Unity Party*] [*Italy Political party*] (PPE)
PSU .... Path Setup [*Telecommunications*] (TEL)
PSU .... Pennsylvania State University
PSU .... Pennsylvania State University, University Park (USDC)
PSU .... Peripheral Switching Unit (CIST)
PSU .... Pet Services, Unlimited [*Commercial firm*] (EA)
PSU .... Philatelic Sales Unit
PSU .... Photosynthetic Unit
PSU .... Plasma Spray Unit
PSU .... Polyphenylene Sulfone [*Organic chemistry*]
PSU .... Portland State University
PSU .... Port Security Unit [*Coast Guard*] (DOMA)
PSU .... Port Sharing Unit (IAA)
PSU .... Port Storage Utility [*Telecommunications*] (TEL)
PSU .... Postsurgical Unit (DAVI)
PSU .... Power Supply Unit (MSA)
PSU .... Power Switching Unit (MCD)
PSU .... Pressure Status Unit (AAG)
PSU .... Primary Sampling Unit [*Statistics*]
PSU .... Printed Side Up [*Graphic arts*] (DGA)
PSU .... Probability Sampling Unit (WDMC)
PSU .... Processor Service Unit (ECII)
PSU .... Processor Speed Up [*Computer memory core*]
PSU .... Processor Storage Unit [*Computer science*] (CIST)
PSU .... Program Storage Unit [*Computer science*] (MDG)
PSU .... Public Services Unit (EERA)
PSU .... Public Storage Prop'A'XVI [*AMEX symbol*] (TTSB)

PSU .... Public Storage Properties XVI [*AMEX symbol*] (SPSG)
PSU .... Tatoo-a-Pet [*Commercial firm*] (EA)
PSUB .... Piston-Supported Upper Bearing
PSUC .... Partit Socialista Unificat de Catalunya [*Unified Socialist Party of Catalonia*] [*Spain Political party*] (PPE)
PSUD .... Psychoactive Substance Use Disorder
PSU/IRL ..... Pennsylvania State University Ionosphere Research Laboratory
PSULI .... Partito Socialista Unitario de Lavoratori Italiani [*Unitary Socialist Party of Italian Workers*] [*Political party*] (PPE)
PSUN .... Pacific Sunwear of Calif [*NASDAQ symbol*] (TTSB)
PSUN .... Pacific Sunwear of California, Inc. [*NASDAQ symbol*] (SAG)
PSUP .... Pennsylvania State University Press (DGA)
PSUR .... Pennsylvania State University Reactor
PSURAO ..... Pennsylvania State University Radio Astronomy Observatory
PSurg......... Plastic Surgery [*Medicine*]
P-SURG...... Presurgery Coagulation Profile [*Hematology and surgery*] (DAVI)
PSUSAM .... Philippine Statehood USA Movement [*An association*] (EA)
PSV .... Pair Shield Video (NITA)
PSV .... Paleosecular Variation [*Geology*]
PSV .... Papillitis Stenosans Vateri (DB)
PSV .... Peanut Stunt Virus
PSV .... Photographic-Spatial Volume (SAA)
PSV .... Pictorial Study of Values [*Psychology*]
PSV .... Planetary Space Vehicle [*NASA*] (NASA)
PSV .... Polished-Stone Value (PDAA)
PSV .... Portable Sensor Verifier (AAG)
PSV .... Positive Start Voltage
PSV .... Preserve (MSA)
PSV .... Pressure Safety Valve
PSV .... Pressure Support Ventilation [*Medicine*] (DAVI)
PSV .... Probability State Variable [*Statistics*]
PSV .... Progressieve Surinaamse Volkspartij [*Progressive Suriname People's Party*] [*Political party*] (PPW)
PSV .... Pseudo-Synthetic Video (DOMA)
PSV .... Psychological, Social, and Vocational [*Adjustment factors*]
PSV .... Public Service Vehicle
PSV .... Public Storage Prop'A'XVII [*AMEX symbol*] (TTSB)
PSV .... Public Storage Properties XVII, Inc. [*AMEX symbol*] (SAG)
PSV .... Saint Vincent College, Latrobe, PA [*OCLC symbol*] (OCLC)
PSvcBad..... Presidential Service Badge [*Military decoration*] (AABC)
PSvCol ...... Public Service Co. of Colorado [*Associated Press*] (SAG)
PSVD .... Polystyrene-Divinylbenzene Copolymer [*Organic chemistry*]
PSVER .... Pattern-Shift Visual Evoked Response [*Medicine*] (MEDA)
PSVM......... Phase-Sensitive Voltmeter
psvm......... Phase-Sensitive Voltmeter (IDOE)
PSvNM ...... Public Service Co. of New Mexico [*Associated Press*] (SAG)
PSVOA....... Purse Seine Vessel Owners Association (EA)
PSVOMA..... Purse Seine Vessel Owners Marketing Association [*Later, PSVOA*] (EA)
PSVP .... Pilot Secure Voice Project [*NATO Integrated Communications System*] (NATG)
PSVT .... Paroxysmal Supraventricular Tachycardia [*Cardiology*]
PSVT .... Passivate [*Metallurgy*]
PSVTN .... Preservation (MSA)
PSVTV .... Preservative (MSA)
PSW.......... Pacific Southwest Forest and Range Experiment Station [*Berkeley, CA*] [*Department of Agriculture*] (GRD)
PSW.......... Past Sleepwalker (STED)
PSW.......... Peripheral Switching Unit (NITA)
PSW.......... Pinetree Software Canada Ltd. [*Vancouver Stock Exchange symbol*]
PSW.......... Plasma Spray Welder
PSW.......... Politically Simulated World [*Computer-assisted political science game*]
PSW.......... Potential Switch
PSW.......... Potentiometer Slidewire
PSW.......... Powerplant Specific Weight
PSW.......... Primary Shield Water (DNAB)
PSW.......... Processor Status Word
PSW.......... Program Status Word [*Computer science*]
PSW.......... Pskov State Aviation Enterprise [*Former USSR*] [*FAA designator*] (FAAC)
PSW.......... Psychiatric Social Worker [*British*]
PSW.......... Public Storage Prop'A'XVIII [*AMEX symbol*] (TTSB)
PSW.......... Public Storage Properties XVIII [*AMEX symbol*] (SPSG)
PSWA .... Partially Smooth Water Area (DS)
PSWAD....... Perspective Study of World Agricultural Development [*FAO*] [*United Nations*] (MSC)
PSWB .... Patented Steel Wire Bureau [*British*] (BI)
PSWB .... Public School Word-Book [*A publication*]
PSWBD....... Power Switchboard
PSWBS ...... Project Summary Work Breakdown Structure
PSWF .... Prolate Spheroidal Wave Function (PDAA)
PSWFRES .... Pacific Southwest Forest and Range Experiment Station [*Berkeley, CA*] (SAA)
PSWG .... Pressure Sine Wave Generator
PSWMOW .... Psychiatric Social Work in Mental Observation Wards [*British*]
PSWO .... Picture and Sound World Organization
PSWO .... Princess of Wales' Own [*Military unit*] [*British*] (ROG)
PSWO .... Product Support Work Order
PSWOPC..... Psychiatric Social Work in Out-Patient Clinics [*British*]
PSWP......... Plant Service Water Pump (IEEE)
PSWR .... Powell Sport Wagon Registry (EA)
PSWR .... Power Standing Wave Ratio
PSWR .... Program Status Word Register [*Computer science*] (MHDB)
PSWS .... Potable and Sanitary Water System [*Nuclear energy*] (NRCH)

PSwS	Smith, Kline & French Co. [*Later, SmithKline Corp.*], Swedeland, PA [*Library symbol Library of Congress*] (LCLS)
PSWT	Polysonic Wind Tunnel (MCD)
PSWT	Psychiatric Social Work Training [*British*]
PSWTUF	Public Service Workers' Trade Union Federation [*Ceylon*]
PSX	Pacific Scientific [*NYSE symbol*] (TTSB)
PSX	Pacific Scientific Co. [*NYSE symbol*] (SPSG)
PSX	Palacios, TX [*Location identifier FAA*] (FAAL)
PSX	Pseudoexfoliation (DMAA)
PSY	Port Stanley [*Falkland Islands*] [*Airport symbol*]
PSY	PSM Technologies, Inc. [*Vancouver Stock Exchange symbol*]
PSY	Psychiatry
PSY	Psychological (CINC)
PSY	Public Storage Prop'A' XIX [*AMEX symbol*] (TTSB)
PSY	Public Storage Properties XIX, Inc. [*AMEX symbol*] (SAG)
PSYC	Psychologist
PSYC	Psychology
PsycCp	Psychemedics Corp. [*Associated Press*] (SAG)
PSYCH	Psychiatrist (DSUE)
PSYCH	Psychiatry
PSYCH	Psychic (ROG)
PSYCH	Psychology (AFM)
Psych	Psychology (DD)
Psych & MLJ	Psychological and Medico-Legal Journal [*A publication*] (DLA)
PSYCHC	Psychiatric
PSYCHEM	Psychiatric Chemistry
PSyCHES	Psychiatric Case History Event System (PDAA)
psychiat	Psychiatry [*or Psychiatric*] (DAVI)
PSYCHL	Psychological (AFM)
PSYCHO	Psychoanalysis (DSUE)
psycho	Psychopath [*Psychiatry*] (DAVI)
psychoan	Psychoanalysis [*Medicine*] (DMAA)
PSYCHOL	Psychology
psychopathol	Psychopathology (DAVI)
psychophys	Psychophysics [*Psychiatry*] (DAVI)
psychophysiol	Psychophysiology [*Psychiatry*] (DAVI)
PsychosMed	Psychosomatic Medicine [*Psychiatry*] (DAVI)
psychother	Psychotherapy [*Psychiatry*] (DAVI)
PSYCHY	Psychiatry
PsycINFO	Psychological Abstracts Information Services [*American Psychological Association*] (IID)
PSYCINFO	Psychological Information (NITA)
PSYCTRC	Psychiatric
PSYCTRY	Psychiatry
PSYCY	Psychology
PsyD	Doctor of Psychology
PsyD, LCP	Doctor of Psychology, Licensed Clinical Psychologist
PsyETA	Psychologists for the Ethical Treatment of Animals (EA)
PSYETA	Psychologists for the Ethical Treatment of Animals [*An association*] (EA)
Psy M	Master of Psychology (PGP)
PSYOP	Psychological Operation [*Military*]
PSYOPS	Psychological Operations [*Military*]
PSY-OPS	Psychological Warfare Operations (DNAB)
psy-path	Psychopath [*Psychiatry*] (DAVI)
PSYS	Precision Systems [*NASDAQ symbol*] (TTSB)
PSYS	Precision Systems, Inc. [*NASDAQ symbol*] (SAG)
Psy S	Specialist in Psychology (PGP)
PSY-SDIV	Psychological Sciences Division [*Office of Naval Research*] (DNAB)
psy-som	Psychosomatic (DAVI)
PsySR	Psychologists for Social Responsibility (EA)
PSYU	Public Sustained Yield Unit [*Forestry*]
PSYWAR	Psychological Warfare
PSYWPN	Psychological Weapon [*Military*] (AFM)
PSZ	Partially-Stabilized Zirconia [*Ceramics*]
PSZ	Piszkesteto [*Hungary*] [*Seismograph station code, US Geological Survey*] (SEIS)
PSZ	Pressure Sealing Zipper
PSZ	Pro Air Service [*ICAO designator*] (FAAC)
PSZ	Public Storage Prop'A' XX [*AMEX symbol*] (TTSB)
PSZ	Public Storage Properties XX [*AMEX symbol*] (SPSG)
PSZ	Puerto Suarez [*Bolivia*] [*Airport symbol*] (OAG)
PSZN	Pubblicazioni. Stazione Zoologica di Napoli [*A publication*]
PT	Advanced Planning and Technology Office [*Kennedy Space Center Directorate*] (NASA)
PT	Brazil [*International civil aircraft marking*] (ODBW)
PT	Duffryn Yard [*Welsh depot code*]
PT	Motor Torpedo Boat [*Navy symbol Obsolete*]
PT	Pacific Time
PT	Packet Terminal (NITA)
PT	Page Table [*Computer science*] (IAA)
pt	Paint (VRA)
PT	Pain Threshold
PT	Pallet Truck (DCTA)
P-T	Palomero Toluqueno [*Race of maize*]
PT	Paper Tape
PT	Paper Title [*Business term*]
PT	Paper Trooper [*One who salvaged paper for war effort*] [*World War II*]
PT	Para-Terphenyl [*Organic chemistry*]
PT	Parathormone (DB)
PT	Parathyroid [*Medicine*]
PT	Parcel Ticket [*Freight*]
PT	Paroxysmal Tachycardia [*Cardiology*]
PT	Part [*Online database field identifier*]

pt	Part (DAVI)
PT	Partially Tested (IAA)
PT	Participative Teams (MCD)
PT	Partido de los Trabajadores [*Paraguay*] [*Political party*] (EY)
PT	Partido Trabajador [*Mexico Political party*] (EY)
PT	Partition Table [*Computer science*] (IAA)
PT	Part Throttle [*Engines*]
P-T	Part-Time [*Employment*]
PT	Part Total [*Earnings less than weekly benefit amount*] [*Unemployment insurance*] (OICC)
PT	Paschale Tempore [*Easter Time*] [*Latin*]
PT	Passenger Traffic [*MTMC*] (TAG)
PT	Passenger Transport
PT	Passing Title [*Real estate*]
PT	Passive Track [*Military*] (CAAL)
PT	Past Tense
PT	Pataca [*Monetary unit*] [*Macau*]
PT	Patellar Tendon [*Anatomy*]
PT	Patentee (NITA)
Pt	Patient (WDAA)
PT	Patient
PT	Patrol Torpedo Boat [*Later, PTF*] [*Navy symbol*]
PT	Paying Teller [*Banking*]
PT	Payment
pt	Payment (WDMC)
PT	Payout Time [*Business term*]
PT	Pay Tone [*Telecommunications*] (TEL)
PT	Pencil Tube
PT	Penetrant Test [*Nuclear energy*] (NRCH)
PT	Penetration Test (NATG)
PT	Peninsula Terminal Co. [*AAR code*]
PT	Pennant [*British naval signaling*]
PT	Pensacola-Tallahassee [*Diocesan abbreviation*] [*Florida*] (TOCD)
PT	Pension Trustee (DLA)
PT	Perfect Title [*Business term*]
PT	Perforated Tape [*Computer science*] (IAA)
PT	Performance Technology [*Human resources*] (WYGK)
PT	Performance Test
PT	Pericardial Tamponade [*Medicine*] (DMAA)
PT	Periodic Test [*Nuclear energy*] (NRCH)
PT	Period Tapering (IAA)
PT	Permeability Transition [*Biochemistry*]
PT	Perpetual Traveller (ECON)
PT	Persepolis Texts (BJA)
PT	Persistent Tease [*Slang Bowdlerized version*]
P/T	Personal Time [*Employment*]
PT	Personal Trade [*Marketing and retail terminology referring to customers*]
PT	Personal Transporter
PT	Perstetur [*Let It Be Continued*] [*Pharmacy*]
PT	Per Truck
PT	Perturbation Theory [*Physical chemistry*]
PT	Pertussis Toxin [*Pharmacology*]
PT	Peseta [*Monetary unit*] [*Spain and Latin America*]
Pt	Peter [*New Testament book*]
PT	Petrol Tractor [*British*]
PT	Petty Theft
PT	Phase Transfer [*Physical chemistry*]
PT	Phase Type (NITA)
PT	Pheasant Trust (EA)
PT	Phenytoin [*Pharmacology*] (DAVI)
PT	Phoenix Theatre [*Defunct*] (EA)
PT	Photoconductive Thermoplastic [*Materials science*]
PT	Photographic Intelligenceman [*Navy rating*]
PT	Phototherapy [*Medicine*]
PT	Phototoxity [*Medicine*]
PT	Phototransistor (NRCH)
PT	Physical Teardown (MCD)
PT	Physical Therapist
PT	Physical Therapy [*or Therapist*]
PT	Physical Training [*Military*]
PT	Physiotherapy [*Medicine*]
PT	Piaster [*Monetary unit*] [*Spain, Republic of Vietnam, and some Middle Eastern countries*] (IMH)
PT	Picture Telegraphy [*Telecommunications*] (IAA)
PT	Pine Tar [*Medicine*]
PT	Pint
pt	Pint (ODBW)
PT	Pipe Tap (MSA)
PT	Pitch Trim (MCD)
PT	Placebo Treated [*Medicine*]
PT	Plain Talk (EA)
PT	Plain Test (MCD)
PT	Planning and Timing [*of Investments*]
PT	Planum Temporale [*Brain anatomy*]
P-T	Plasma Thermocouple Reactor [*Nuclear energy*] (NRCH)
PT	Plasticized Transparent [*Flexography*] (DGA)
PT	Plastics Technology [*A publication*]
PT	Plastic Tube
Pt	Platinum [*Chemical element*]
PT	Platoon Truck [*British*]
PT	Pleno Titulo [*With Full Title*] [*Latin*]
PT	Plenty Tough [*Slang*]
PT	Plenty Trouble [*Slang*]
PT	Plonia Technica

PT .... Plotting Equipment [*JETDS nomenclature*] [*Military*] (CET)
PT .... Plot Titles [*Test*] [*Psychology*]
PT .... Pneumatic Tube [*Technical drawings*]
PT .... Pneumothorax [*Medicine*]
PT .... Poetry Treasury [*An association Defunct*] (EA)
PT .... Point [*Maps and charts*]
pt .... Point (ODBW)
P/T .... Pointer/Tracker (MCD)
PT .... Point of Tangency
PT .... Point of Turn [*Navigation*]
PT .... Pollen Tube [*Botany*]
PT .... Poll-Tax Rolls [*British*]
PT .... Polymeric Triglyceride [*Food science*]
PT .... Polythiophene [*Organic chemistry*]
PT .... Polyvalent Tolerance (BABM)
PT .... Pool Temperature [*Nuclear energy*] (NRCH)
PT .... Pope and Talbot [*Steamship*] (MHDW)
PT .... Popliteal Tendon [*Anatomy*]
PT .... Port
pt .... Port (ODBW)
PT .... Portal Tract [*Anatomy*]
PT .... Port Number [*Telecommunications*] (TEL)
PT .... Port Talbot Railway [*Wales*]
PT .... Portugal [*ANSI two-letter standard code*] (CNC)
PT .... Portugal Telecom ADS [*NYSE symbol*] (TTSB)
PT .... Portugal Telecom SA [*NYSE symbol*] (SAG)
pt .... Portuguese Timor [*io (Indonesia) used in records cataloged after January 1978*] [*MARC country of publication code Library of Congress*] (LCCP)
PT .... Positional Tolerance (AAEL)
PT .... Positional Tolerancing
PT .... Postal Telegraph Co. [*Terminated*]
PT .... Post and Telegraphy [*Telecommunications*] (IAA)
PT .... Poste e Telegrafi [*Post and Telegraph Service*] [*Italy*]
PT .... Posterior Tibial [*Anatomy*]
PT .... Post Town
PT .... Potential Transformer
PT .... Power Transfer (KSC)
PT .... Prachakorn Thai [*Thai Citizens Party*] [*Political party*]
PT .... Precision Teaching
PT .... Precision Time Fuze
PT .... Precision Transform [*Eastman Kodak Co.*] [*Computer science*] (PCM)
PT .... Preferential Treatment (OICC)
PT .... Preoperational Test [*Nuclear energy*] (NRCH)
PT .... Press Test [*Psychology*]
P/T .... Pressure/Temperature (KSC)
PT .... Pressure Test (AAG)
PT .... Pressure Time Fuel System [*Cummins Engine Co., Inc.*]
PT .... Pressure Transducer (KSC)
PT .... Pressure Transmitter (NRCH)
PT .... Pressure Tubing
PT .... Pretectal [*Neuroanatomy*]
pt .... Preterit [*Past tense*] [*Grammar*]
PT .... Previous Operating Time (AFIT)
PT .... Primal Therapy
PT .... Primary Target [*Army*]
PT .... Primary Trainer [*Aircraft*]
PT .... Print (MSA)
PT .... Printed Text
PT .... Printer Terminal
PT .... Priority Telegram
PT .... Prior Treatment [*Medicine*]
PT .... Private Terms
PT .... Procedure Turn [*FAA*] (TAG)
PT .... Processing Tax Division [*United States Internal Revenue Bureau*] (DLA)
PT .... Processing Time
PT .... Production Techniques (MCD)
PT .... Production Test [*Military*]
PT .... Productive Time [*Computer order entry*]
PT .... Product Team (AAGC)
PT .... Product Test (IAA)
PT .... Proficiency Testing
PT .... Profile Template
PT .... Profit Taking [*Investment term*]
PT .... Program (Exercise) on Treadmill
PT .... Programmable Terminal [*Computer science*]
PT .... Programmer and Timer
PT .... Progress in Technology [*Automotive industry*]
PT .... Progressive Tax (MHDW)
PT .... Prohibited Telegrams
PT .... Project Tibet (EA)
PT .... Project Transition [*DoD*] (OICC)
PT .... Project Trust (EAIO)
PT .... Prolong Tablets [*Pharmacy*]
PT .... Pronator Teres [*Musle*] [*Orthopedics*] (DAVI)
PT .... Proof Test (AAG)
PT .... Propanethiol [*Organic chemistry*]
PT .... Propellant Transfer
PT .... Propeller Torpedo [*Boat*]
PT .... Property Tax (MHDW)
PT .... Property Transfer [*Real estate*] (KSC)
PT .... Prophet
PT .... Propylthiouracil [*Also, PROP, PTU*] [*Thyroid inhibitor*]

PT .... Pro Tempore [*For the Time Being*] [*Latin*]
PT .... Prothrombin Time [*Hematology*]
PT .... Prototype (IAA)
PT .... Provascular Tissue [*Botany*]
PT .... Provincetown-Boston Airline [*ICAO designator*] (AD)
PT .... Provisioning Team (AAG)
Pt .... Pseudoword Target [*Psychology*]
PT .... Psychology Today [*A publication*] (BRI)
PT .... Pteropods [*Quality of the bottom*] [*Nautical charts*]
PT .... PTP Resource Corp. [*Formerly, Petrologic Petroleum Ltd.*] [*Vancouver Stock Exchange symbol*]
PT .... Publication Type [*Online database field identifier*]
PT .... Public Transport (DA)
PT .... Public Trustee
PT .... Pull-Through [*Gun cleaning*]
PT .... Pulmonary Tuberculosis [*Medicine*]
PT .... Pulp Testing [*Dentistry*]
PT .... Pulse Timer
PT .... Pulse Train
PT .... Pulse Transformer (IAA)
PT .... Punched Tape [*Computer science*]
PT .... Punch Through [*Computer science*] (IAA)
PT .... Pupil Teacher
PT .... Purchase Tax [*British*]
PT .... Pure Telepathy [*Psychical research*]
PT .... Pyramidal Tract [*Anatomy*]
PT .... Pyramid Texts (BJA)
PT .... [*Serum Glutamic*] Pyruvic Transaminase [*Also, SGPT*] [*An enzyme*] (DAVI)
PT .... Total Pressure
PT1 .... Photographic Intelligenceman, First Class [*Navy rating*]
PT2 .... Photographic Intelligenceman, Second Class [*Navy rating*]
PT3 .... Photographic Intelligenceman, Third Class [*Navy rating*]
PTA .... National Postal Transport Association [*Later, APWU*]
PTA .... Packed Tower Aeration (MEC)
PTA .... Page Table Address [*Computer science*] (IAA)
PTA .... Palatines to America (EA)
PTA .... Pantorama Industries, Inc. [*Toronto Stock Exchange symbol*]
PTA .... Paper and Twine Association (EA)
PTA .... Paper Tape Accessory (MHDI)
PTA .... Paper Towel Association [*British*] (BI)
PTA .... Parallel Tubular Array [*Cytology*]
PTA .... Parathyroid Adenoma [*Medicine*] (STED)
PTA .... Parent-Teacher Association
PTA .... Part Throttle Acceleration [*Engines*] (EG)
PTA .... Passenger Transport Authorities [*British*]
PTA .... People Taking Action
PTA .... Percent Time Active (CAAL)
PTA .... Percutaneous Transluminal Angioplasty [*Medicine*]
PTA .... Periodical Title Abbreviations [*A publication*]
PTA .... Peritonsillar Abscess [*Medicine*]
PTA .... Persistent Truncus Arteriosus [*Medicine*] (MAE)
PTA .... Peseta [*Monetary unit*] [*Spain and Latin America*]
PTA .... Phenyltrimethylammonium [*Also, PTM, PTMA*] [*Organic chemistry*]
PTA .... Phorbol Tetradecanoyl Acetate [*Also, PMA, TPA*] [*Organic chemistry*]
PTA .... Phosphoryl Triamide [*Organic chemistry*]
PTA .... Phosphotransacetylase [*An enzyme*]
PTA .... Phosphotungstic Acid [*Inorganic chemistry*]
PTA .... Photographers' Telegraph Association
PTA .... Phototransistor Amplifier
PTA .... Physical Therapy Assistant
PTA .... Pianoforte Tuners' Association [*British*] (DBA)
PTA .... Picatinny Arsenal [*New Jersey*] [*Later, Armament Development Center*] [*Army*]
PTA .... Pilotless Target Aircraft [*Military*]
PTA .... Pitch Trim Adjustment
PTA .... Pitch Trim Angle
PTA .... Planar Turbulence Amplifier (IEEE)
PTA .... Plasma Thromboplastin Antecedent [*Factor XI*] [*Hematology*]
PTA .... Plasma Transferred Arc [*Metallurgy*]
PTA .... Platelet Thromboplastin Antecendent [*Medicine*] (STED)
PTA .... Platinized Titanium Anode
PTA .... Point of Total Assumption (MCD)
PTA .... Port Alsworth [*Alaska*] [*Airport symbol*] (OAG)
PTA .... Postcard Traders' Association [*British*] (DBA)
PTA .... Posterior Tibial [*Pulse*] [*Medicine*] (DAVI)
PTA .... Post-Test Analysis [*NASA*] (NASA)
PTA .... Post-Traumatic Amnesia [*Medicine*]
PTA .... Potential Toxic Area (NASA)
PTA .... Power Transfer Assembly (IAA)
PTA .... Preferential Trade Arrangements [*ASEAN*] (IMH)
PTA .... Premium Transportation Authorization (AAG)
PTA .... Prepaid Ticket Advice [*Travel industry*]
PTA .... Preparation through Acceptance
PTA .... Pressure Transducer Assembly
PTA .... Pre-Treatment Anxiety [*Medicine*] (DMAA)
PTA .... Prevention of Terrorism Act [*British*] (ECON)
PTA .... Price-Tag Awareness [*See also PTS*]
PTA .... Primary Target Area [*Military*]
PTA .... Primary Tungsten Association [*British*] (EAIO)
PTA .... Printing Trades Alliance [*British*] (DBA)
PTA .... Prior to Admission [*Medicine*]
PTA .... Prior to Arrival [*Medicine*] (MAE)
PTA .... Procrustes Target Analysis [*Marine science*] (OSRA)
PTA .... Programmable Translation Array

PTA............	Program Time Analyzer
PTA............	Proposed Technical Approach
PTA............	Propulsion Test Article [*NASA*] (NASA)
PTA............	Protestant Teachers Association (NADA)
PTA............	Prothrombin Activity [*Hematology*]
PTA............	Proton Target Area
PTA............	Ptarmigan Airways Ltd. [*Canada ICAO designator*] (FAAC)
PTA............	Pulse Torquing Assembly (KSC)
PTA............	Punta Arenas [*Chile*] [*Seismograph station code, US Geological Survey Closed*] (SEIS)
PTA............	Purchase Transaction Analysis
PTA............	Pure Terephthalic Acid (DICI)
PTA............	Pure Tone Acuity (STED)
PTA............	Pure Tone Average [*Otorhinolaryngology*] (DAVI)
PTA............	Purified Terephthalic Acid [*Organic chemistry*]
PTAA............	Airman Apprentice, Photographic Intelligenceman, Striker [*Navy rating*]
PTA-A	Periodical Title Abbreviations: by Abbreviation [*A publication*]
PTAA............	Professional Tattooists Association of Australia
PTAB............	Photographic Technical Advisory Board [*American National Standards Institute*]
PTAB............	Program Status Table [*Computer science*] (IAA)
PTAB............	Project Technical Advisory Board (AAEL)
PTAC............	Penn Treaty American [*NASDAQ symbol*] (TTSB)
PTAC............	Penn Treaty American Corp. [*NASDAQ symbol*] (NQ)
PTAC............	Plant Transportation Advisory Committee
PTAC............	Professional and Technical Advisory Committee [*JCAH*]
P'TACH	Parents for Torah for All Children [*Program for learning disabled children*]
PTACV	Prototype Tracked Air-Cushion Vehicle
PTACX	PIMCO: Target CI.C [*Mutual fund ticker symbol*] (SG)
PTAD	(Phenyl)triazolinedione [*Organic chemistry*]
PTAD	Productivity and Technical Assistance Division [*Mutual Security Agency*] [*Abolished, 1953*]
PT AEQ	Partes Aequales [*Equal Parts*] [*Pharmacy*]
PTAF............	Platelet Activating Factor (DMAA)
PTAF............	Policy Target Adjustment Factor (MEDA)
PTAFR.........	Platelet Activating Factor Receptor (DMAA)
PTAG	Professional Tattoo Artists Guild (EA)
P-TAG	Target-Attaching Globulin Precursor [*Medicine*] (STED)
PTAH	Phosphotungstic Acid-Hematoxylin [*A stain*]
PTAL	Para-Tolualdehyde [*Organic chemistry*]
PTAN	Airman, Photographic Intelligenceman, Striker [*Navy rating*]
PT & E	Physical Teardown and Evaluation (MCD)
PT & E	Progress Tests and Examinations
PT & ER	Physical Teardown and Evaluation Review (MCD)
PT & ME......	Physical Teardown and Maintenance Evaluation [*Army*]
PT & W	Physical Training and Welfare [*British military*] (DMA)
PTANYC	Protestant Teachers Association of New York City (EA)
PTAP...........	Phenyltrimethylammonium Perbromide [*Organic chemistry*]
PTAP...........	Profiler Triangle Analysis Package [*Marine science*] (OSRA)
PTAP...........	Purified Diphtheria Toxoid Precipitated by Aluminum Phosphate (AAMN)
PTAR	Prime Time Access Rule [*Television*]
PTASE.........	Phosphatase [*An enzyme*] (DHSM)
PTA-T..........	Periodical Title Abbreviations: by Title [*A publication*]
PTAT...........	Pesticides, Toxics, and Air Team (COE)
PTAT...........	Proportional to Absolute Temperature (IAA)
PTAT...........	Pure Tone Average Threshold (DMAA)
PTAV	Percutaneous Transluminal Aortic Valvuloplasty [*Cardiology*] (CPH)
PTAVE.........	Parents and Teachers Against Violence in Education (EA)
PTAWT........	Atlantic Wind Test Site, Tignish, Prince Edward Island [*Library symbol National Library of Canada*] (NLC)
PTB............	Page Table Base [*Computer science*] (IAA)
PTB............	Paragon Trade Brands [*NYSE symbol*] (SPSG)
ptB............	Part Bunkers [*Shipping*] (DS)
PTB............	Partido Trabalhista Brasileiro [*Brazilian Labor Party*] [*Political party*] (PPW)
PTB............	Parti du Travail de Belgique [*Belgian Labour Party*] [*Political party*] (EY)
PTB............	Parti du Travail du Burkina [*Burkina Faso*] [*Political party*] (EY)
PTB............	Patellar Tendon Bearing [*Medicine*]
PTB............	Patrol Torpedo Boat (WDAA)
PTB............	Payload Timing Buffer [*NASA*] (NASA)
PTB............	Perishables Tariff Bureau, Atlanta GA [*STAC*]
PTB............	Permian-Triassic Boundary [*Geology*]
PTB............	Personnel Test Battery
PTB............	Petersburg, VA [*Location identifier FAA*] (FAAL)
PTB............	Phenacylthiazolium Bromide [*Organic chemistry*]
PTB............	Phosphotyrosine-Binding [*Biochemistry*]
PTB............	Physical Transaction Block
PTB............	Physikalisch Technische Bundesanstalt (ACII)
PTB............	Point Barrow [*Alaska*] [*Later, BRW*] [*Seismograph station code, US Geological Survey*] [*Closed*] (SEIS)
PTB............	Pounds per Thousand Barrels [*Petroleum technology*]
PTB............	Pressure Test Barrel
PTB............	Prior to Birth [*Medicine*]
PTB............	Process Technical Bulletin (MCD)
PTB............	Production and Test Branch (IAA)
PTB............	Program Time Base [*Military*] (AFIT)
PTB............	PT Boats, Inc. (EA)
PTBA...........	Percutaneous Transluminal Balloon Angioplasty [*Cardiology*] (DMAA)
PTBA...........	Proud to be Australian [*Political party*]
PTBB...........	Para-tertiary-butylbenzaldehyde [*Organic chemistry*]
PTBBA	Para-tertiary-butylbenzoic Acid [*Organic chemistry*]

PTBD	Percutaneous Transhepatic Biliary Drainage [*Medicine*]
PTBD-EF	Percutaneous Transhepatic Biliary Drainage - Enteric Feeding [*Medicine*] (DAVI)
PTBE	Pyretic Tick-Borne Encephalitis [*Medicine*] (DMAA)
PTBF	Portal Tributary Blood Flow [*Physiology*]
PTBI	PT Boats, Inc. (EAIO)
PTBIPK	Poly(t-Butyl Isopropenyl Ketone) [*Organic chemistry*]
PTBK..........	Partbook [*Music*]
PTBL..........	Portable (AABC)
PTBPD	Posttraumatic Borderline Personality Disorder [*Medicine*] (DMAA)
PTBR..........	Processing Tax Board of Review Decisions [*United States Internal Revenue Bureau*] [*A publication*] (DLA)
PTBR..........	Punched Tape Block Reader [*Computer science*]
PtBS..........	Poly(tertiary-butylstyrene) [*Organic chemistry*]
PTBS..........	Posttraumatic Brain Syndrome [*Medicine*] (DMAA)
PTBT..........	Para-tertiary-butyltoluene [*Organic chemistry*]
PTBT..........	Partial Test-Ban Treaty
PTBT..........	Pretransplant Blood Transfusion [*Medicine*]
PTBVK	Poly(t-Butyl Vinyl Ketone) [*Organic chemistry*]
PTC............	Chief Photographic Intelligenceman [*Navy rating*]
PTC............	Motor Boat Subchaser [*Navy symbol Obsolete*]
PTC............	Pacific Telecommunications Council (EA)
PTC............	Pacific Tuna Conference
PTC............	PAR Technology [*NYSE symbol*] (TTSB)
PTC............	PAR Technology Corp. [*NYSE symbol*] (SPSG)
Ptc............	Participating [*Business term*]
PTC............	Parti Travailliste Congolais [*Congolese Labor Party*] [*Political party*]
PTC............	Part Through Crack [*Alloy tension*]
PTC............	Passive Thermal Control
PTC............	Patent, Trademark, and Copyright Institute [*Franklin Pierce College*] (IID)
PTC............	Patrol Vessel, Motor Torpedo Boat, Submarine Chaser [*Navy symbol*]
PTC............	Peace Tax Campaign [*Australia*]
PTC............	Pentagon Telecommunications Center (MCD)
PTC............	Peoples Telephone Co., Inc. (EFIS)
PTC............	Peoria Terminal Co. [*AAR code*]
PTC............	Percutaneous Cholangiography [*Medicine*]
PTC............	Percutaneous Transhepatic Cholangiogram [*Medicine*]
PTC............	Performance Test Chamber (MCD)
PTC............	Performance Test Code
PTC............	Periscope Television Camera [*Telecommunications*] (IAA)
PTC............	Permission to Take Classes [*Education*]
PTC............	Personal Transfer Capsule
PTC............	Personal Typing Centre (NITA)
PTC............	Personnel Transfer Capsule [*Undersea technology*]
PTC............	Personnel Transport Carrier
PTC............	Phase Transfer Catalysis [*Physical chemistry*]
PTC............	Phenylisothiocyanate [*Organic chemistry*]
PTC............	Phenylthiocarbamide [*or Phenylthiocarbamyl*] [*Organic chemistry*]
PTC............	Pheochromocytoma, Thyroid Carcinoma Syndrome [*Oncology*] (MAE)
PTC............	Photographic Training Centre [*British*] (CB)
PTC............	Photographic Type Composition (ADA)
PTC............	Pipe and Tobacco Council of America [*Defunct*] (EA)
PTC............	Pipe Tobacco Council (EA)
PTC............	Pitch Trim Compensator
PTC............	Pitch Trim Controller (MCD)
PTC............	Plan to Clear [*Aviation*] (FAAC)
PTC............	Plasma Thromboplastin Component [*Factor IX*] [*Also, CF Hematology*]
PTC............	Plastic Training Cartridge [*Army*] (INF)
PTC............	Plugged Telescoping Catheter [*Clinical chemistry*]
PTC............	Pneumatic Temperature Control
PTC............	Pneumatic Test Console
PTC............	Points to Consider
PTC............	Police Training Centre [*British*]
PTC............	Portable Tele-Transaction Computer [*Telxon*]
PTC............	Portable Temperature Control (KSC)
PTC............	Portable Temperature Controller [*NASA*] (NAKS)
PTC............	Porto Cannone [*Italy*] [*Seismograph station code, US Geological Survey*] (SEIS)
PTC............	Portuguese Trade Commission (EA)
PTC............	Positive Target Control [*Aviation*] (FAAC)
PTC............	Positive Temperature Coefficient
PTC............	Positive Transmitter Control
PTC............	Postal and Telegraphic Censorship [*Telecommunications*] (IAA)
PTC............	Postal Telegraph Cable
PTC............	Posterior Trabeculae Carneae [*Heart anatomy*]
PTC............	Post-Tensioned Concrete [*Technical drawings*]
PTC............	Post-Turnover Change [*Nuclear energy*] (NRCH)
PTC............	Power Testing Code (MCD)
PTC............	Power Transfer Coefficient
PTC............	Power Transmission Council
PTC............	Pre- and Post-Process Treatment Chambers (AAEL)
PTC............	Premature Tricuspid Closure [*Medicine*] (DMAA)
PTC............	Preoperative Testing Center
PTC............	Pressure and Temperature Control (KSC)
PTC............	Pressure Transducer Calibrator
PTC............	Primary Teaching Certificate [*Australia*]
PTC............	Primary Technical Course [*Military*]
PTC............	Primary Training Centre [*British military*] (DMA)
PTC............	Princeton Resources Corp. [*Vancouver Stock Exchange symbol*]
PTC............	Programmable Temperature Controls
PTC............	Programmable Test Console
PTC............	Programmed Transmission Control (BUR)

PTC............	Programmer Training Center
PTC............	Program of Technical Cooperation [Organization of American States]
PTC............	Promotional Telephone Call [Marketing] (OICC)
PTC............	Proof Test Capsule [NASA]
PTC............	Propellant Tanking Console (AAG)
PTC............	Propensity to Consume (MHDW)
PTC............	Propulsion Test Complex (KSC)
PTC............	Prothrombin Complex [Hematology]
PTC............	Pseudotumor Cerebri [Medicine] (AAMN)
PTC............	Psychophysical Timing Curve
PTC............	Public Services, Tax & Commerce Union (WDAA)
PTC............	Publishing Technology Corp. [Information service or system] (IID)
PTC............	Pulse Time Code
PTCA...........	Patience T'ai Chi Association (EA)
PTCA...........	Percutaneous Transluminal Coronary Angioplasty [Medicine]
PTCA...........	Plains Tribal Council of Assam [India] [Political party] (PPW)
PTCA...........	Postal Telegraph Clerks' Association [A union] [British]
PTCA...........	Pressure Technology Corp. of America
PTCA...........	Private Truck Council of America (EA)
PTCA...........	Professional Tennis Coaches' Association [Australia]
PTCAA.........	Professional Turkey Calling Association of America (EA)
PTCAD.........	Provisional Troop Carrier Airborne Division
PTCC...........	Pacific Division Transport Control Center
PTCC...........	PerSeptive Tech II Corp. [NASDAQ symbol] (SAG)
PT/CC..........	Problem Tracking and Change Control [Computer science]
PTCCS.........	Polaris Target Card Computing System [Missiles]
PtcD...........	Phosphatidylcholine [Biochemistry]
PTCD	Private Training College for the Disabled (AIE)
PTCH..........	Pacer Technology [NASDAQ symbol] (NQ)
PTCHY........	Patchy [Meteorology] (DA)
PTCI...........	Programmable Telecommunications Interface (MCD)
PTCI...........	Programmable Terminal Communications Interface (MCD)
PT CL..........	Part Called [Stock exchange term] (MHDB)
PTCL...........	Peripheral T-Cell Lymphoma [Oncology]
PTCLD.........	Part Called [Stock exchange term] (SPSG)
PTCM..........	Master Chief Photographic Intelligenceman [Navy rating]
Pt Copyright & TM Cas...	Patent, Copyright, and Trade Mark Cases [United States] [A publication] (DLA)
PTCP..........	Parameter Test Control Program [Computer science] (IAA)
PTCP..........	Participate (FAAC)
PTCP..........	Positive Turnaround Control Point (MCD)
PTCR	Pad Terminal Connection Room [NASA]
PTCR	Payload Terminal Connector Room [NASA] (MCD)
PTCR	Percutaneous Transluminal Coronary Recanalization [Cardiology] (DMAA)
PTCR	Positive Temperature Coefficient Resistance [Materials science and technology]
PTCRA	Percutaneous Transluminal Coronary Rotational Ablation [Cardiology] (DMAA)
PTCRM	Partial Thermochemical Remanent Magnetization
PTCS...........	Passive Thermal Control Section [NASA] (NASA)
PTCS...........	Passive Thermal Control System (NASA)
PTCS...........	Pax Tibi cum Sanctis [Peace to Thee with the Saints] [Latin]
PTCS...........	Percutaneous Transhepatic Cholangioscopy [Medicine]
PTCS...........	Phenyltrichlorosilane [Organic chemistry]
PTCS...........	Planning, Training, and Checkout System [NASA] (MCD)
PTCS...........	Powertrain Control Signal [Automotive engineering]
PTCS...........	Pressure Transducer Calibration System
PTCS...........	Propellant Tanking Computer System (KSC)
PTCS...........	Senior Chief Photographic Intelligenceman [Navy rating]
PTCT..........	Protect (MSA)
PT-CT.........	Prothrombin Time Control [Hematology] (DAVI)
PTCV..........	Pilot-Operated Temperature Control Valve
PTCV..........	Plowright Tissue Culture Vaccine [Against rinderpest]
PTD............	Package Travel Directive (WDAA)
ptd............	Painted (VRA)
PTD............	Painted (AAG)
PTD............	Paper Towel Dispenser [Technical drawings]
PTD............	Parallel Transfer Disk [Computer science]
PTD............	Particle Transfer Device
PTD............	Part Throttle Deceleration [Engines] (EG)
PTD............	Patented (IAA)
PTD............	Percutaneous Transluminal Dilatation [Medicine] (DMAA)
PTD............	Period to Discharge [Medicine] (DAVI)
PTD............	Permanent Total Disability [Medicine]
PTD............	Phenyltriazolinedione [Organic chemistry]
Ptd............	Phosphatidyl
PTD............	Photodiode Detector [Instrumentation]
PTD............	Photothermal Deflection
PTD............	Physical Teardown (MCD)
PTD............	Pilot to Dispatcher
PTD............	Plant Test Date [Telecommunications] (TEL)
PTD............	Pointed (WGA)
PTD............	Portland [Oregon] [Seismograph station code, US Geological Survey] (SEIS)
PTD............	Posttuning Drift
PTD............	Potsdam, NY [Location identifier FAA] (FAAL)
PTD............	Potter Distilleries Ltd. [Toronto Stock Exchange symbol Vancouver Stock Exchange symbol]
PTD............	Printed
PTD............	Prior to Discharge [Medicine] (MAE)
PTD............	Programmable Threshold Detector (MCD)
PTD............	Programmed Thermal Desorber
PTD............	Provisioning Technical Documentation
PTD............	Provisioning Transcript Documentation (MCD)

PTDA	Per Task Data Area [Computer science] (BYTE)
PTDA	Power Transmission Distributors Association (EA)
PTDB	Point Target Data Base (SAA)
PTDC	Pacific Trade and Development Conference [OPTAD] (FEA)
PtdCho.........	Phosphatidylcholine (STED)
PTDDSS	Provisioning Technical Documentation Data Selection Sheet [NASA] (NASA)
PtdEtn.........	Phosphatidylethanolamine (STED)
PTDF..........	Pacific Tuna Development Foundation (EA)
PTDF..........	Procurement Technical Data File [DoD]
Pt Dhgtr.......	Patient's Daughter [Also, Pt DTR] (DAVI)
PTDIA.........	Professional Truck Driver Institute of America (EA)
PtdIns.........	Phosphatidylinositol [Also, PI] [Biochemistry]
PTDL..........	Programmable Tapped Delay Line (PDAA)
PTDOS.........	Processor Technology Disk Operating System
PTDP..........	Permanent Transvenous Demand Pacemaker (STED)
PTDP..........	Preliminary Technical Development Plan (AFM)
PTDP..........	Proposed Technical Development Plan
PTDQ..........	Polymerized Trimethyldihydroquinoline [Organic chemistry]
PtdS...........	Phosphatidylserine [Biochemistry]
PTDS..........	Photo Target Detection System
PtdSer.........	Phosphatidylserine (STED)
PTDTL.........	Pumped Tunnel Diode Transistor Logic
PT DTR.......	Patient's Daughter [Also, Pt Dhgtr] (DAVI)
PTDU..........	Pointing and Tracking Demonstration Unit (MCD)
PTe............	Indian Valley Public Library, Telford, PA [Library symbol Library of Congress] (LCLS)
PTE............	International Federation of Professional and Technical Engineers
PTE............	Nouadhibou [Mauritania] [Airport symbol] (AD)
PTE............	Packet Transfer Engine [Newbridge Networks Corp.]
PTE............	Packet Transport Equipment [Computer science] (PCM)
PTE............	Page Table Entry
PTE............	Parathyroid Extract [Medicine]
PTE............	Partido de Trabajadores Espanoles [Spanish Workers' Party] [Political party] (PPE)
PTE............	Part-Time Education (WDAA)
PTE............	Party to Exemption [RSPA] (TAG)
PTE............	Passenger Transport Executive [British]
PTE............	Peace through Education Project [An association]
PTE............	Pectin transeliminase [or Pectate Lyase] [An enzyme]
PTE............	Peculiar Test Equipment
PTE............	Photographic Tasks and Equipment [NASA]
PTE............	Plate (ROG)
PTE............	Portable Test Equipment (AAG)
PTE............	Portage [Alaska] [Seismograph station code, US Geological Survey] (SEIS)
PTE............	Port Stephens [Australia Airport symbol] (OAG)
PTE............	Posttraumatic Endophthalmitis (STED)
PTE............	Potential to Emit (GNE)
PTE............	Power Transport Equipment
PTE............	Pressure Test Equipment (MCD)
PTE............	Pressure-Tolerant Electronics (IEEE)
PTE............	Pretax Earnings [Employment]
PTE............	Pretibial Edema [Medicine] (DAVI)
PTE............	Primrose Technology Corp. [Vancouver Stock Exchange symbol]
PTE............	Private [British]
Pte............	Private (WDAA)
PTE............	Private Trade Entity
PTE............	ProActive Technologies, Inc. [AMEX symbol] (SAG)
PTE............	Problem Trend Evaluation (MCD)
PTE............	Production Test Equipment (MCD)
PTE............	Proximal Tibial Epiphysis [Orthopedics] (DAVI)
PTE............	Proxylem Tracheary Element [Botany]
Pte............	Pteroyl [Biochemistry]
PTE............	Pulmonary Thromboembolism [Medicine]
PTEA..........	Preliminary Training Effectiveness Analysis
PTEAR	Physical Teardown
PTEAR	Physical Teardown and Maintenance Allocation Review (MCD)
PTeb..........	Tebtunis Papyri [A publication] (OCD)
PTEC..........	Phoenix Technologies [NASDAQ symbol] (TTSB)
PTEC..........	Phoenix Technologies Ltd. [NASDAQ symbol] (NQ)
PTEC..........	Plastics Technical Evaluation Center [Military]
pt ed..........	Patient Education (DAVI)
PTED..........	Pulmonary Thromboembolic Disease [Medicine]
PteGlu........	Pteroylmonoglutamic Acid [Folic acid] [Also, FA, PGA] [Biochemistry]
PTEK..........	Premiere Technologies [NASDAQ symbol] (TTSB)
PTEK..........	Premiere Technologies, Inc. [NASDAQ symbol] (SAG)
PTEL..........	Peoples Telephone Co. [NASDAQ symbol] (TTSB)
PTEL..........	People's Telephone Co., Inc. [NASDAQ symbol] (NQ)
PTEN..........	Patterson Energy [NASDAQ symbol] (TTSB)
PTEN..........	Patterson Energy, Inc. [NASDAQ symbol] (SAG)
PTEN..........	Pentaerythritol Tetranitrate [An explosive and a vasodilator] [Cardiology] (DAVI)
PTEN..........	Prime Time Entertainment Network [Television broadcasting]
pter...........	End of Short Arm of Chromosome [Medicine] (STED)
PTER..........	Physical Teardown and Evaluation Review (MCD)
PTES..........	Productivity Trend Evaluation System (MCD)
PTES..........	Purdue Teacher Evaluation Scale
PTET..........	Platinum Entertainment [NASDAQ symbol] (TTSB)
PTETD........	Production Test Engineering Task Description (MCD)
PTETPC.......	Party to Expose the Petrov Conspiracy [Australia Political party]
PTETS........	Pioneer Television and Electronic Technicians Society [Defunct] (EA)
PT EX.........	Part Exchange (WDAA)
PTF............	Malololailai [Fiji] [Airport symbol] (OAG)
PTF............	Paralemniscal Tegmental Field [Neuroanatomy]

PTF	Parathyroid Fever [*Medicine*] (CPH)
PTF	Parts Transfer Form (SAA)
PTF	Patch and Test Facility
PTF	Patient Treatment File [*Medicine*] (DMAA)
PTF	Patrol Torpedo Boat, Fast [*Formerly, PT*] [*Navy symbol*]
PTF	Payload Test Facility [*VAFB*] [*NASA*] (MCD)
PTF	Permit to Fly [*Aviation*] (AIA)
PTF	Petersfield Oil & Minerals [*Vancouver Stock Exchange symbol*]
PTF	Phase Transfer Function (MCD)
PTF	Plaintiff [*Legal term*] (ROG)
PTF	Plasma Thromboplastin Factor [*Factor VIII*] [*Also, AHF, AHG, TPC Hematology*]
PTF	Police Training Foundation
PTF	Polymer Thick Film
PTF	Polytetrafluoroethylene (EDCT)
PTF	Port Task Force
PTF	Power Test Fail
PTF	Production Tabulating Form (AAG)
PTF	Programmable Transversal Filter [*SMP*]
PTF	Program Temporary Fix [*Computer science*]
PTF	Proof Test Facility [*Nuclear energy*]
PTF	Propellant Tank Flow
PTF	Proximal Tubule Fluid [*Laboratory science*] (DAVI)
PTF	Pulse Transfer Function
PTFA	Preliminary Tool and Facility Analysis (MCD)
PTFA	Prothrombin Time Fixing Agent (DMAA)
PTFC	Pretty Things Fan Club (EA)
PTFCE	Polytrifluorochloroethene (BARN)
PTFD	Personnel, Training and Force Development [*Army*]
PTFDA	Professional Travel Film Directors Association [*Later, Professional Travelogue Sponsors - PTS*] (EA)
PTFE	Polytetrafluoroethylene [*Organic chemistry*]
PTFG	Large Guided Missile Motorboat [*Navy symbol*] (DNAB)
PTFHA	Physician Task Force on Hunger in America [*Defunct*] (EA)
PTFHC	Putnam Tax Free Health Care Fund [*Associated Press*] (SAG)
PTFM	Platform (AAG)
PTFMA	Peacetime Force Material Assets [*Navy*] (AFIT)
PTFMA	Public Telecommunications Financial Management Association (EA)
PTFMO	Peacetime Force Materiel Objective [*Army*]
PTFMPO	Peacetime Force Materiel Procurement Objective [*Army*]
PTFMR	Peacetime Force Materiel Requirements [*Army*]
PTFMR-A	Peacetime Force Materiel Requirements - Acquisition [*Army*] (AABC)
PTFMR-R	Peacetime Force Materiel Requirements - Retention [*Army*] (AABC)
PTFP	Public Telecommunications Facilities Program [*Department of Commerce*]
PTFS	Pilot-to-Forecaster Service (NOAA)
PTFS	Posttraumatic Fibromyalgia Syndrome [*Medicine*] (DMAA)
PTFT	Production Temporary Facility Tool (SAA)
PTFUR	President's Task Force on Urban Renewal (EA)
PTFX	Plating Fixture (AAG)
ptg	Painting (VRA)
PTG	Parathyroid Gland [*Medicine*] (DMAA)
PTG	Parent-Teacher Group
PTG	Pennington Gap, VA [*Location identifier FAA*] (FAAL)
PTG	Piano Technicians Guild (EA)
PTG	Pietersburg [*South Africa*] [*Airport symbol*] (OAG)
PTG	Place to Go (IAA)
PTG	Planed, Tongued, and Grooved (DAC)
PTG	Polaris Task Group [*Missiles*]
PTG	Portage Industries Corp. [*AMEX symbol*] (SPSG)
PTG	Portageville [*Missouri*] [*Seismograph station code, US Geological Survey Closed*] (SEIS)
PTG	Portuguese (ROG)
PTG	Precise Tone Generator [*Telecommunications*] (TEL)
PTG	Pressure Test Gauge
PTG	Pressure Transfer Gauge
PTG	Printing
ptg	Printing (WDMC)
PTG	Professional Technical Group
PTG	Prothoracic Gland [*Insect anatomy*]
PTG	Pulse Target Generator
PTG	Small Guided Missile Motorboat [*Navy symbol*] (DNAB)
PTG	Teniposide [*Antineoplastic drug regimen*] (DAVI)
PTGA	Pteroyltriglutamic Acid [*Pharmacology*]
PTGAP	Professional Technical Group on Antennas and Propagation [*of the IEEE*]
PTGBD	Percutaneous Transhepatic Gallbladder Drainage [*Medicine*]
PTGC	Programmed Temperature Gas Chromatography
PTG CYL	Printing Cylinder (DGA)
PTGEC	Professional Technical Group on Electronic Computers [*Later, IEEE Computer Society*]
PT GEO	Posted to Geographics
PTGEWS	Professional Technical Group on Engineering Writing and Speech [*of the IEEE*]
pTGF	Porcine Transforming Growth Factor
PTGL	Pyrolysis to Gases and Liquids [*Chemical processing*]
PTGS	Paper Trade Golfing Society [*British*]
PTGS	Portable Telemetry Ground Station
PTGT	Primary Target [*Military*]
PTH	Hydrofoil Motor Torpedo Boat [*Ship symbol*] (NATG)
PTH	Pacer Technology (EFIS)
PTH	Pallet Torque Hook
PTH	Panther Mines Ltd. [*Vancouver Stock Exchange symbol*]
PTH	Paper Tape Half-Duplex
PTH	Parathormone [*Medicine*] (MAE)

PTH	Parathyroid Hormone [*Endocrinology*]
PTH	Path (GAVI)
PTH	Pathology [*Medical specialty*] (DHSM)
PTH	Peak Tanning Hours [*Supposedly occurring between 10am and 2pm*] [*See also BROTS, SROTS*]
PTH	Phenylthiohydantoin [*Organic chemistry*]
PTH	Plasma Thromboplastin Component [*Medicine*] (DMAA)
PTH	Plated through Hole
Pth	Polythiophene [*Organic chemistry*]
PTH	Port Heiden [*Alaska*] [*Airport symbol*] (OAG)
PTH	Port Heiden, AK [*Location identifier FAA*] (FAAL)
PTH	Post-Transfusion Hepatitis [*Medicine*]
PTH	Project Team Head (MHDI)
PTH	Project Top Hat [*Defunct*] (EA)
PtHA	Pinto Horse Association of America (EA)
P Th B	Bachelor of Practical Theology
PThD	Punch-Through Device (PDAA)
PtHeat	Petroleum Heat & Power Corp. [*Associated Press*] (SAG)
PtHel	Petroleum Helicopter, Inc. [*Associated Press*] (SAG)
PTHF	Polytetrahydrofuran [*Organic chemistry*]
PtHg	Partially Hearing (AIE)
PTHLGST	Pathologist
PTH-LP	Parathyroid Hormone-Like Peptide [*Endocrinology*]
PTHrP	Parathyroid Hormone-Related Protein [*Biochemistry*]
PTHS	Parathyroid Hormone Secretion Rate [*Endocrinology*] (MAE)
PTI	First USA Paymentech [*NYSE symbol*] (TTSB)
PTI	First USA Paymentech, Inc. [*NYSE symbol*] (SAG)
PTI	Package Turn In (MCD)
PTI	Pancreatic Trypsin Inhibitor [*Biochemistry*]
PTI	Parent Training and Information [*Centers*] [*Established under the Individuals with Disabilities Education Act (IDEA)*] (PAZ)
PTI	Parkes-Tidbinbilla Interferometer [*Astronomy*]
PTI	Party Identity [*Telecommunications*] (TEL)
PTI	Pathways to Independence [*An association*] (EA)
PTI	Paymentech, Inc. [*NYSE symbol*] [*Formerly, First USA Paymentech*] (SG)
PTI	Pennsylvania Transportation Institute [*Pennsylvania State University*] [*Research center*] (RCD)
PTI	Penn Telecom, Inc. [*Gibsonia, PA*] (TSSD)
PTI	Persistent Tolerant Infection
PTI	Personnel Tests for Industry
PTI	Personnel Transaction Identifier [*Air Force*] (AFM)
PTI	Philadelphia Textile Institute
PTI	Physical-Technical Institute [*Former USSR*]
PTI	Physical Training Instructor [*British*]
PTI	Pictorial Test of Intelligence [*Education*]
PTI	Pipe Test Insert [*Liquid Metal Engineering Center*] [*Energy Research and Development Administration*] (IEEE)
PTI	Plugging Temperature Indicator [*Nuclear energy*] (NRCH)
PTI	Poetry Therapy Institute (EA)
PTI	Porous Tungsten Ionizer
PTI	Post-Tensioning Institute [*Defunct*] (EA)
PTI	Power Tool Institute (EA)
PTI	Precision Technology, Inc. (AAG)
PTI	Preliminary Test Information (KSC)
PTI	[*The*] Press Trust of India
PTI	Pretrial Intervention (BARN)
PTI	Pre-Trial Investigation (DNAB)
PTI	Pre-Trip Inspection [*Shipping*]
PTI	Previously-Taxed Income
PTI	Prinicipal-Teacher Interaction Study (EDAC)
PTI	Production Training Indicator [*Computer science*]
PTI	Programmed Test Input (MCD)
PTI	Programming Tools and Information [*IBM Corp.*] [*Computer science*]
PTI	Program Transfer Interface
PTI	Promethean Technologies, Inc. [*Vancouver Stock Exchange symbol*]
PTI	Protein Technologies International
PTI	Publicacoes Tecnicas Internacionais Ltda. [*International Technical Publications Ltd.*] [*Information service or system*] (IID)
PTI	Public Technology, Inc. [*Research center*] (RCD)
PTI	Public Tool Interface [*Computer science*] (ODBW)
PTI	Puntilla Lake, AK [*Location identifier FAA*] (FAAL)
PTIA	Pet Trade and Industry Association (EAIO)
PTIB	Program Testing Information Bulletin (IAA)
PTIC	Patent and Trade Mark Institute of Canada
PTIE	Pet Trade and Industry Exhibition [*British*] (ITD)
PTIG	Presentation of Technical Information Group (SAA)
PTIHd	PTI Holding, Inc. [*Associated Press*] (SAG)
PTI Hold	PTI Holding, Inc. [*Associated Press*] (SAG)
PTII	PTI Holding [*NASDAQ symbol*] (TTSB)
PTII	PTI Holding, Inc. [*NASDAQ symbol*] (SAG)
PTIIW	PTI Hldg Wrrt [*NASDAQ symbol*] (TTSB)
PTIL	Parts Test Information List (KSC)
PTI-ODT	Personnel Tests for Industry - Oral Directions Test
PTIP	Physical Therapist in Independent Practice (GFGA)
PTIP	Pluribus Terminal Interface Processor [*Computer science*] (CIST)
PTIRFM	Polarized Total Internal Reflection Fluorescence Microscopy
PTIS	Pacific Triangle Information Services [*Information service or system*] (IID)
PTIS	Photo Thermal Ionization Spectroscopy (AAEL)
PTIS	Plasma Therm [*NASDAQ symbol*] (TTSB)
PTIS	Plasma-Therm, Inc. [*NASDAQ symbol*] (NQ)
PTIS	Powertrain Input Signal [*Automotive engineering*]
PTIS	Programmed Test Input System (MCD)
PTIS	Propulsion Test Instrumentation System (KSC)

PTIWU .... Posts and Telegraphs Industrial Workers' Union [*India*]
PTIX............ Performance Technologies [*NASDAQ symbol*] (TTSB)
PTIX............ Performance Technologies, Inc. [*NASDAQ symbol*] (SAG)
PTJ .... Part-Time Job
PTJ .... Portland [*Australia Airport symbol*] (OAG)
PTJ .... Pulse Train Jitter [*Computer science*] (IAA)
PTK............. Passport to Knowledge [*Program*]
PTK............. Phototherapeutic Keratectomy [*Ophthalmology*]
PTK............. Polishing Tool Kit
PTK............. Pontiac, MI [*Location identifier FAA*] (FAAL)
PTK............. Potentiometer Tapping Kit
PTK............. Probability of Track [*Military*]
PTK............. Protein-Tyrosine Kinase [*An enzyme*]
PTKK............ Truk [*Caroline Islands*] [*ICAO location identifier*] (ICLI)
PTL............. Partial Total Loss [*Insurance*] (DS)
PTL............. Part Time Legislature
PTL............. Patrol [*or Patrolman*] (AABC)
PTL............. Patrol Boat
PTL............. Peacetime Losses [*Military*]
PTL............. Penteli [*Greece*] [*Seismograph station code, US Geological Survey*] (SEIS)
PTL............. [*Sodium*] Pentothal [*An anesthetic*] (DAVI)
PTL............. People That Love [*Of television's "PTL Club"*] [*Facetious translations: "Pass the Loot" and "Pay the Lady"*]
PTL............. Perinatal Telencephalic Leukoencephalopathy [*Medicine*]
PTL............. Peripheral T-Cell Lymphoma [*Oncology*]
PTL............. Petroleum Testing Laboratory
PTL............. Phase Tracking Loop (MCD)
PTL............. Photographic Technology Laboratory (KSC)
PTL............. Pietermaritzburg [*South Africa*] [*Airport symbol*] (AD)
PTL............. Pintle [*Design engineering*]
PTL............. Pittsburgh Testing Laboratory (EFIS)
PTL............. Planning Test List
PTL............. Pocket Testament League (EA)
ptl .... Portal (VRA)
PTL............. Power Transmission Line (OA)
PTL............. Praise the Lord [*Of television's "PTL Club"*] [*Facetious translations: "Pass the Loot" and "Pay the Lady"*]
PTL............. Pressure, Torque, and Load
PTL............. Preterm Labor [*Obstetrics*] (DAVI)
PTL............. Pre-Test Laboratory (DNAB)
PTL............. Pretty Tough Lawyer [*Refers to Melvin Belli, attorney for Tammy and Jim Bakker of the PTL Club*]
PTL .... Primary Target Line [*Military*]
PTL............. Process and Test Language
PTL............. Providence Air Charter [*ICAO designator*] (FAAC)
PTL............. Public Television Library
PTL............. Pulse Transmission Logic (IAA)
PTLA............ Praise the Lord Anyway
PTLA............ Publishers' Trade List Annual
PTLAP......... Petroleum Test Laboratory Accreditation Program
PTLBD......... Particleboard
PTLC........... Piedmont Triad Library Council [*Library network*]
PTLC........... Precipitation Thin-Layer Chromatography [*Medicine*] (DMAA)
PTLC........... Preparative Thin-Layer Chromatography (DB)
PT-LD.......... Physical Teardown - Logistics Demonstration (MCD)
PTLD........... Post-Transfusion Liver Disease [*Medicine*]
PTLD........... Prescribed Tumor Lethal Dose [*Oncology*]
PTLEF......... Peace through Law Education Fund (EA)
PTLEN......... Petal Length [*Botany*]
PTLF........... Pressure, Temperature, Level, and Flow [*Chemical engineering*]
PTLRS .... Publications and Technical Literature Research Section [*Environmental Protection Agency*] (IID)
PTLV........... Primate T-Lymphotropic Viruses
PTLX........... Patlex Corp. [*NASDAQ symbol*] (SAG)
PTLY........... Partly [*NWS*] (FAAC)
PTM............ Palmarito [*Venezuela*] [*Airport symbol*] (OAG)
PTM............ Pancake Torquer Motor (SAA)
PTM............ Parasite Tubing Method (PDAA)
PTM............ Passenger Traffic Manager
PTM............ Pattern Transformation Memory
PTM............ Performance Test Model (OA)
PTM............ Petromac Energy, Inc. [*Vancouver Stock Exchange symbol*]
PTM............ Phase Time Modulation
PTM............ Phenyltrimethylammonium [*Also, PTA, PTMA*] [*Organic chemistry*]
PTM............ Photomultiplier (IAA)
PTM............ Photon Tunneling Microscope
PTM............ Physical Teardown and Maintenance (MCD)
PTM............ Pietermaritzburg [*South Africa*] [*Seismograph station code, US Geological Survey*] (SEIS)
PTM............ Pneumatic Telescope Mast
PTM............ Polaris Tactical Missile
PTM............ Portable Traffic Monitor [*Telecommunications*] (TEL)
PTM............ Portland Terminal Co. [*AAR code*]
PTM............ Posttransfusion Mononucleosis [*Medicine*]
PTM............ Pressure-Transmitting Medium [*Engineering*]
Ptm............ Pressure Transmural [*Pretaining to an airway or blood vessel*] [*Medicine*] (DAVI)
PTM............ Preterm Milk [*Medicine*]
PTM............ Pretuned Module [*Telecommunications*] (IAA)
PTM............ Primary Thickening Meristem [*Botany*]
PTM............ Programmable Terminal Multiplexer [*Texas Instruments, Inc.*]
PTM............ Programmable Timer Module
PTM............ Program Timing and Maintenance [*Electronics*] (IAA)
PTM............ Program Timing and Miscellaneous [*Electronics*]

PTM .... Program Trouble Memorandum [*NASA*] (IAA)
PTM .... Proof Test Model [*NASA*]
PTM .... Pulse Time Modulation [*Radio*]
PTM .... Pulse Time Multiplex
PTM .... Pulse Transmission Mode (MCD)
PTM .... Putnam Managed High Yield Trust [*NYSE symbol*] (SPSG)
PTM .... Putnam Managed Hi Yield Tr [*NYSE symbol*] (TTSB)
PTM .... Southeastern Airways Corp. [*ICAO designator*] (FAAC)
PTMA............ Phenyltrimethylammonium [*Also, PTA, PTM*] [*Organic chemistry*]
PTMA............ Phosphotungstomolybdic Acid [*Inorganic chemistry*]
PTMA............ Prothymosin Alpha (DMAA)
PTMAS......... Professional, Technical, Managerial, and Administrative Staff
PTMC........... Photomechanical (VRA)
PTMC........... Polaris Tender Management Computer [*Missiles*]
PTMC........... Polish Telephones & Microwave Corp. [*NASDAQ symbol*] (SAG)
PTMC........... Polish Tels & Microwave Corp. [*NASDAQ symbol*] (TTSB)
PTMCA......... Pit Tub and Mine Car Manufacturers' Association [*British*] (BI)
PTMCW......... Polish Tels & Microwave Wrrt [*NASDAQ symbol*] (TTSB)
PTMD........... Propellant Toxicity Monitoring Devices (KSC)
PTMDF......... Pupils, Tension, Media, Disc, Fundus [*Medicine*]
PTMEG......... Polytetramethylene Ether Glycol [*Organic chemistry*]
PTML........... PNPN [*Positive-Negative-Positive-Negative*] Transistor Magnetic Logic (IAA)
PTML........... PNP [*Positive-Negative-Positive*] Transistor Magnetic Logic (IEEE)
PTML........... Proxicom Template Markup Language [*Computer science*]
PTM/OS .... Programmable Terminal Monitor/Operating System (NITA)
PTMPY......... Per Thousand Members per Year (DMAA)
PTMS........... Parathymosin (DMAA)
PTMS........... Para-Toluidine-meta-sulfonic Acid [*Also, PTMSA*] [*Organic chemistry*]
PTMS........... Pattern Transformation Memory System
PTMS........... Precision Torque Measuring System (NASA)
PTMS........... Publication Text Management System (MCD)
PTMS........... Public Transportation Facilities and Equipment Management System [*FHWA*] (TAG)
PTMSA......... Para-Toluidine-meta-sulfonic Acid [*Also, PTMS*] [*Organic chemistry*]
PTMSP......... Poly(trimethylsilyl-propyne) [*Organic chemistry*]
PTMT........... Poly(tetramethylene Terephthalate) [*Organic chemistry*]
PTMTLG....... Pitometer-Log [*Engineering*]
PTMU........... Power and Temperature Monitor Unit (KSC)
PTMUX .... Pulse Time Multiplex (MSA)
PTMV........... Percutaneous Transvenous Mitral Valvotomy [*Cardiology*]
PTN............ Morgan City/Patterson [*Louisiana*] [*Airport symbol*] (OAG)
PTN............ Pantanal Linhas Aereas Sul-Matogrossenses SA [*Brazil*] [*ICAO designator*] (FAAC)
PTN............ Particulate Total Nitrogen [*Analytical chemistry*]
PTN............ Partido Trabalhista Nacional [*National Workers' Party*] [*Brazil*]
PTN............ Partition (KSC)
PTN............ Patterson, LA [*Location identifier FAA*] (FAAL)
PTN............ Phenotemperature Normogram [*Phenology*]
PTN............ Phenytoin [*Anticonvulsant*]
PTN............ Plant Test Number [*Telecommunications*] (TEL)
PTN............ Pluton Industries Ltd. [*Vancouver Stock Exchange symbol*]
PTN............ Potsdam [*New York*] [*Seismograph station code, US Geological Survey*] (SEIS)
PTN............ Private Telecommunication Network [*Telecommunications*] (OSI)
PTN............ Procedure Turn [*ICAO*] (FAAC)
Ptn............ Pterin [*Biochemistry*]
PTN............ Public Telephone Network (DA)
PTN............ Pull-Thru Network (EA)
PTNA........... Pituitary Tumor Network Association (EA)
pTNM.......... Postsurgical, Tumor, Nodes, and Metastases [*Classifications for postsurgical resection pathological staging of cancer*] [*Oncology*] (DAVI)
Ptnr........... Partner (TBD)
PTNR .... Partner (ROG)
PTNRSHIP ... Partnership (ROG)
PTNX .... Printronix, Inc. [*NASDAQ symbol*] (NQ)
PTNX .... Private Telecommunication Network Exchange [*Telecommunications*] (OSI)
PTO............. North West Geomatics Ltd. [*Canada ICAO designator*] (FAAC)
PTO............. Pacific Theater of Operations [*World War II*]
PTO............. Packard Truck Organization [*Defunct*] (EA)
PTO............. Paid Time Off (NFD)
PTO............. Participating Test Organization [*Air Force*]
PTO............. Partners Oil & Mining [*Vancouver Stock Exchange symbol*]
PTO............. Part Time Operation (DA)
PTO............. Patent and Trademark Office [*Formerly, PO*] [*Department of Commerce*]
PTO............. Pato Branco [*Brazil*] [*Airport symbol*] (OAG)
PTO............. People, Topics, Opinions [*A publication British*]
PTO............. Percutaneous Transhepatic Obliteration (STED)
PTO............. Perlsucht Tuberculin Original [*Medicine*] (MAE)
PTO............. Permeability-Tuned Oscillator (IAA)
PTO............. Personal Time Off (DAVI)
PTO............. Personal Trust Officer [*Banking*] (TBD)
PTO............. Please Turn Over [*the page*]
pto .... Please Turn Over (WDMC)
PTO............. Porto [*Serro Do Pilar*] [*Portugal*] [*Seismograph station code, US Geological Survey*] (SEIS)
PTO............. Port Transportation Officer
PTO............. Power Takeoff [*Automotive engineering*]
PTO............. Power Test Operations (MCD)
PTO............. Powertrain Operations [*Auto manufacturer corporate structure*]
PTO............. Professional and Technology Officer [*British*]
PTO............. Project Technical Office [*Military*] (DNAB)

PTO	Project Type Organization (AAG)
PTO	Proof Test Orbiter [*NASA*]
PTO	Propellant Transfer Operation (AFM)
PTO	Public Telecommunications Operator (NITA)
PTO	Public Trustee Office (DLA)
PTO	Public Trust Office [*Australia*]
PTO	Purdue Teacher Opinionaire [*Test*]
PTO	Pyridinethiol Oxide [*Pharmacology*]
PTOA	Projective Tests of Attitudes
PTobA	United States Army, Tobyhanna Army Depot Library, Tobyhanna, PA [*Library symbol Library of Congress*] (LCLS)
PTO Board	Patent and Trademark Office Board of Patent Appeals and Interferences (AAGC)
PToG	General Telephone & Electronics, GTE Sylvania, Inc., Towanda, PA [*Library symbol Library of Congress*] (LCLS)
PTOJ	Passive Track-On-Jam
PTOL	Peacetime Operating Level (AFM)
Ptol	Ptolemaeus Mathematicus [*Second century AD*] [*Classical studies*] (OCD)
Ptol	Ptolemaic (BJA)
PTOMAIN	Project to Optimize Many Individual Numbers (SAA)
PTON	Proteon, Inc. [*NASDAQ symbol*] (SPSG)
P to P	Plate to Plate (DEN)
P to P	Port to Port [*Shipping*] (DS)
PTOP	Program Test and Operations Plan
PTOPC	Program to Program Communications (MHDI)
PTOS	Paper Tape Oriented Operating System
PTOS	Patent and Trademark Office Society (EA)
PTOS	Patriot Tactical Operations Simulator [*Army*]
PTOS	Peacetime Operating Stock [*Military*]
PTOUT	Printout (MSA)
PTP	Paper Tape Perforator [*or Punch*]
PTP	Paper Tape Punch (ECII)
PTP	Parameter Test Program (SAA)
PTP	Parent to Parent, Inc. [*Australia*]
PTP	Parti Togolais du Progres [*Party for Togolese Progress*]
PTP	Peak-to-Peak [*Nuclear energy*]
PTP	Pensions for Technical Professionals [*An association*]
PTP	People to People International (EA)
PTP	percutaneous Transhepatic Portography (STED)
PTP	Percutaneous Transhepatic Selective Portography [*Roentgenography*]
PTP	Petrologic Petroleum [*Vancouver Stock Exchange symbol*]
PTP	Phenyltetrahydropyridine [*Biochemistry*]
PTP	Platinum Temperature Probe
PTP	Pointe-A-Pitre [*Guadeloupe*] [*Airport symbol*] (OAG)
PTP	Point Park College, Pittsburgh, PA [*Inactive*] [*OCLC symbol*] (OCLC)
PTP	Point-to-Point [*Robotics*] [*Telecommunications*]
PTP	Point-to-Point Phone (NAKS)
PTP	Pollution Transfer Program [*Marine science*] (MSC)
PTP	Porous Tungsten Plug
PTP	Posterior Tibial Pulse [*Cardiology*] (DAVI)
PTP	Posto Telefonico Pubblico [*Public Telephone*] [*Italy*]
PTP	Post-Tetanic Potentiation [*Neurology*]
PTP	Post-Transfusion Purpura [*Medicine*]
PTP	Potato Tuber Peroxidase [*An enzyme*]
PTP	Preferred Target Point (KSC)
PTP	Preliminary Task Plan (MCD)
PTP	Pretransmission Precautionary Answer to Nature's Call [*Especially before a long program*] [*Television*]
PTP	Pre-Turbo Pressure
PTP	Primary Target Point [*NASA*]
PTP	Print-to-Point [*Telecommunications*] (IAA)
PTP	Prior to Program [*Medicine*] (MAE)
PTP	Production Test Plan (MCD)
PTP	Production Test Procedure (NATG)
PTP	Professional Tax Planner
PTP	Programmable Text Processor [*Programming language*] (CSR)
PTP	Programmable Touch Panel [*Electronics*]
PTP	Programmed Turn Phase
PTP	Program Task Planning (MCD)
PTPJ	Promise to Pay (MHDW)
PTPL	Protect the Planet [*Manual*]
PTP	Protein Tyrosine Phosphatase [*An enzyme*]
PTP	Prothrombin-Proconvertin (STED)
PTP	Prothrombin-Procovertin (STED)
PTP	Proximal Tubular Pressure (STED)
PTP	Proximity Test Plug [*Nuclear energy*] (NRCH)
PTP	Pueblo to People (EA)
Ptp	Transpulmonary Pressure (MAE)
PTPA	Portal-to-Portal Act of 1947 (WYGK)
PT-PAC	Physical Therapy Political Action Committee
PTPase	Protein Tyrosine Phosphatase [*An enzyme*]
PTPC	Permeability Transition Pore Complex [*Biochemistry*]
PTPC	Professional Teaching Practices Commission (OICC)
PTPC	Protein-Tyrosine Phosphatase C (DMAA)
PTPD	Part Paid [*Business term*]
Pt Pd	Part paid (EBF)
PTPE	Powertrain Product Engineering [*Automotive*]
PTP'er	Prime Time Performer [*In book title, "Vitale: Just Your Average Bald, One-Eyed Basketball Wacko Who Beat the Ziggy and Became a PTP'er"*]
PTPF	Payee TIN [*Taxpayer Identification Number*] Perfection File [*IRS*]
PTPG	Protein-Tyrosine Phosphatase Gamma (DMAA)
PTPI	People to People International (EAIO)

PTPI	Posttraumatic Pulmonary Insufficiency [*Medicine*] (STED)
PTPI	Professional and Technical Programs, Inc.
PTPM	Posttraumatic Progressive Myelopathy [*Neurology*] (DAVI)
PTPN	Peripheral [*Vein*] Total Parenteral Nutrition [*Gastroenterology*] (DAVI)
PTPN	Ponape Island [*Caroline Islands*] [*ICAO location identifier*] (ICLI)
PTPN	Protein-Tyrosine Phosphatase, Non-Receptor (DMAA)
PTPR	Production Test Program Report
PTPS	Package Test Power Supply
PTPS	Parallel-Tuned Parallel-Stabilized (IAA)
PTPS	Parker Team Player Survey [*Test*] (TMMY)
PTPS	Propellant Transfer Pressurization System (KSC)
PTPS	Pumped Two-Phase System (SSD)
PTPSC	People-to-People Sports Committee (EA)
PTPSK	Pilot Tone Phase Shift Keying [*Computer science*] (IAA)
PTPT	Platinum Print (VRA)
P-TPT	Portable Tactual Performance Test [*Child development test*] [*Psychology*]
PTPU	Program Tape Preparation Unit
PTQ	Ludlow Aviation, Inc. [*FAA designator*] (FAAC)
PTQ	Parent-Teacher Questionnaire (DMAA)
PTQ	Poly(tolyquinoxaline) [*Organic chemistry*]
PTQ	Pulse-Taking Questionnaire
PTR	Nova Scotia Department of Lands and Forests [*Canada*] [*FAA designator*] (FAAC)
PTR	Pacific Test Range (MUGU)
PTR	Painter
ptr	Painter (VRA)
PTR	Paper Tape Reader
PTR	Paper Towel Receptor [*Technical drawings*]
PTR	Parr Terminal Railroad (MHDW)
PTR	Partido Tercera Republica [*Chile*] [*Political party*] (EY)
PTR	Partner
PTR	Parts Tool Requirements File
PTR	Parts Transfer Record (SAA)
PTR	Part Throttle Reheat [*Aviation*] (OA)
PTR	Patient Termination Record [*Medicine*] (DB)
PTR	Patuxent River [*Navy*] (MCD)
PTR	Perforated Tape Reader
PTR	Peripheral Total Resistance [*Medicine*] (MAE)
PTR	Perlsucht Tuberculin Rest [*Medicine*] (MAE)
P/Tr	Permian/Triassic [*A geological period boundary*]
PTR	Personal Technology Research [*Commercial firm*]
PTR	Peterson [*Alabama*] [*Seismograph station code, US Geological Survey*] (SEIS)
Ptr	Petrine [*Of, or relating to, Peter the Apostle or Peter the Great*] (BJA)
PTR	Photoelectric Tape Reader
PTR	Physikalisch-Technische Reichsanstalt
PTR	Pilot Training Rate [*Navy*]
PTR	Pleasant Harbor [*Alaska*] [*Airport symbol*] (OAG)
PTR	Plug-Type Receptacle
PTR	Pointer [*Computer science*]
PTR	Point in Time Repair [*Computer science*]
PTR	Polar to Rectangular (SAA)
PTR	Pool Test Reactor [*Nuclear energy*]
PTR	Pool Training Reactor [*Nuclear energy*]
PTR	Poor Transmission [*Telecommunications*] (TEL)
PTr	Porcine Trypsin (DB)
PTR	Portable Tape Recorder
PTR	Port Macquarie [*New South Wales*] [*Airport symbol*] (AD)
PTR	Position Track RADAR
PTR	Positive Termination Rate [*Job Training and Partnership Act*] (OICC)
PTR	Post-Trip Review
PTR	Power Transformers (MCD)
PTR	Precision Transmitter Receiver
PTR	Preliminary Technical Report
PTR	Preliminary Test Report [*NASA*] (KSC)
PTR	Pressure Test Record
PTR	Pressure Transmitter Recorder (ECII)
PTR	Pressure-Tube Reactor [*Nuclear energy*]
PTR	Pretransmit Receiving
PTR	Pre-Trial Release (OICC)
PTR	Printer (MSA)
P Tr	Private Trust [*Includes testamentary, investment, life insurance, holding title, etc.*] [*Legal term*] (DLA)
PTR	Processor Tape Read
PTR	Production Test Record
PTR	Production Test Requirements (KSC)
PTR	Professional Tennis Registry, USA (EA)
PTR	Proficiency Testing Research (EA)
PTR	Programmer Trouble Report [*Nuclear energy*] (GFGA)
PTR	Program Technical Review (MCD)
PTR	Program Trouble Report [*NASA*] (KSC)
PTR	Proof Test Reactor [*Nuclear energy*]
PTR	Punched Tape Reader [*Computer science*]
PTR	Pupil-Teacher Ratio
PTR	Security Capital Pacific Trust [*NYSE symbol*] (SAG)
PTR	Security Cap Pacific Tr [*NYSE symbol*] (TTSB)
PTRA	Percutaneous Transluminal Renal Angioplasty [*Medicine*] (DMAA)
PTRA	Port Terminal Railroad Association
PTRA	Power-Motion Technology Representatives Association (NTPA)
PTRA	Power Transmission Representatives Association (EA)
P/TRAC	Positraction [*Automotive engineering*]
PTrB	Betz Laboratories, Inc., Trevose, PA [*Library symbol Library of Congress*] (LCLS)

PTRC	Personnel and Training Research Center [*Air Force*]
PTRD	Part Redeemed [*Stock exchange term*] (SPSG)
PTRE	PartnerRe Ltd. [*NASDAQ symbol*] (SAG)
PTRE	Pressure Tube Reactor Experiment [*Nuclear energy*] (NUCP)
PTREF	PartnerRe Ltd [*NASDAQ symbol*] (TTSB)
PTRF	Peacetime Rate Factor [*Military*] (AABC)
PTRF	Peacetime Replacement Factor [*Military*]
PTRI	Pharmaceutical and Toxicological Research Institute [*Ohio State University*] [*Research center*] (RCD)
PTRIA	Polystyrene-Tube Radioimmunoassay [*Medicine*] (DMAA)
PtrixMd	Pediatrix Medical Group, Inc. [*Associated Press*] (SAG)
PTRJ	Powered Thermocouple Reference Junction
PTRM	Partial Thermoremanent Magnetization [*Geophysics*]
PTRN	Photran Corp. [*NASDAQ symbol*] (TTSB)
PTRNMKR	Patternmaker (WGA)
PTRO	Koror [*Caroline Islands*] [*ICAO location identifier*] (ICLI)
PTRO	Personnel Transaction Register by Originator [*Military*] (AABC)
PTRO	Petrominerals Corp. [*NASDAQ symbol*] (NQ)
PTRO	Preoverhaul Test Requirement Outline
PTRP	Paper Tape Reader Punch [*Computer science*] (IAA)
PTRP	Post-Treatment Resource Program [*Medicine*]
PTRPrA	Security Cap Pac Cv'A'Pfd [*NYSE symbol*] (TTSB)
PTRPrB	Security Cap Pac Tr Sr'B'Pfd [*NYSE symbol*] (TTSB)
PTRR	Port Townsend Railroad, Inc. [*Formerly, PTS*] [*AAR code*]
PTRS	Philosophical Transactions. Royal Society of London [*A publication*]
PTRS	Potters Financial [*NASDAQ symbol*] (TTSB)
PTRS	Potters Financial Corp. [*NASDAQ symbol*] (SAG)
PTRS	Potters Savings & Loan Co. [*NASDAQ symbol*] (SAG)
ptrt	Portrait (VRA)
PTRU	Petro Union, Inc. [*NASDAQ symbol*] (SAG)
PT Rulings	Pay-Roll Tax Rulings [*Australia A publication*]
PTRUQ	Petro Union [*NASDAQ symbol*] (TTSB)
PTRV	Peak Transient Reverse Voltage [*Electronics*] (IAA)
PTRY	Pantry, Inc. [*NASDAQ symbol*]
PTRY	Pottery [*Freight*]
ptry	Pottery (VRA)
PTS	Painful Tonic Seizure (AAMN)
PTS	Pali Text Society (EA)
PTS	Paper Tape Sender
PTS	Paper Tape System [*Computer science*] (IAA)
PTS	Paper Tape-to-Magnetic Tape Conversion System (DIT)
PTS	Papiertechnische Stiftung [*Database producer*]
PTS	Parachute Training School [*British military*] (DMA)
PTS	Parameter Test Setup
PTS	Para-Toluenesulfonic Acid
Pts	Participating (EBF)
PTS	Parts
PTS	Patellar-Tendon Supracondylar [*Anatomy*]
PTS	Payload Test Set [*NASA*] (NASA)
PTS	Payload Transportation System [*NASA*] (MCD)
PTS	People's Translation Service (EA)
PTS	Perforated Tape Subsystem [*Computer science*] (IAA)
PTS	Performance Tracking System
PTS	Permanent Threshold Shift [*Hearing evaluation*]
PTS	Personal Typography System (DGA)
PTS	Petro-Sun International, Inc. [*Toronto Stock Exchange symbol*]
PTS	Philatelic Traders' Society Ltd. [*British*] (BI)
PTS	Phosphotransferase System [*Organic chemistry*]
PTS	Photogrammetric Target System [*Air Force*]
PTS	Photogrammetric Triangulation System [*Air Force*] (IAA)
PTS	Photothermal Spectroscopy
PTS	Phototransmission System [*Telecommunications*] (IAA)
PTS	Phototypesetting (DGA)
PTS	Pilot Training Squadron [*Air Force*]
PTS	Pi Tau Sigma [*Society*]
PTS	Pittsburg, KS [*Location identifier FAA*] (FAAL)
PTS	Plane Transport System (DA)
PTS	Planning Tracking System (MCD)
PTS	Player Trade Society [*A union*] [*British*]
PTS	Pneumatic Test Sequencer (AFM)
PTS	Pneumatic Test Set (KSC)
PTS	Pneumatic Tube System
PTS	Pod Tail Section
PTS	Pointing and Tracking Scope
PTS	Points [*Postal Service standard*] (OPSA)
PTS	Points of Call Airlines Ltd. [*Canada ICAO designator*] (FAAC)
PTS	Polar Track Structure [*Aviation*] (FAAC)
PTS	Port Townsend Railroad, Inc. [*Later, PTRR*] [*AAR code*]
PTS	Post and Telecommunications Service (IAA)
PTS	Post-Traumatic Stress [*Medicine*]
PTS	Power Transfer Switch
PTS	Power Transient Suppressor (IEEE)
PTS	Practical Test Standards [*FAA*] (TAG)
PTS	Precision Timing System
PTS	Predicasts Terminal Systems [*Predicasts, Inc.*] [*Cleveland, OH Database*]
PTS	Predicasts Time Series [*Series of databases*] [*Predicasts, Inc. Cleveland, OH*]
PTS	Preflight Test Set (DNAB)
PTS	Pressure Test Station (DNAB)
PTS	Pressurized Thermal Shock [*Nuclear energy*]
PTS	Price-Tag Shock [*See also PTA*]
PTS	Primary Trait System (EDAC)
PTS	Prime Time Sunday [*TV program*]
PTS	Princeton Theological Seminary, Princeton, NJ [*OCLC symbol*] (OCLC)
PTS	Printing Technical School (DGA)
PTS	Prior to Surgery (DAVI)
PTS	Private Telecommunications Systems [*Radio-Suisse Ltd.*] [*Switzerland Telecommunications*]
PTS	Proactive TMDE Support (RDA)
PTS	Proceed to Select [*Telecommunications*] (TEL)
PTS	Proceed to Send [*Telecommunications*] (TEL)
PTS	Processor Transaction Server [*Computer science*] (CIST)
PTS	Production Test Specification
PTS	Professional Tank Services, Ltd. (EFIS)
PTS	Professional Travelogue Sponsors (EA)
PTS	Programmable Terminal System [*Computer science*] (IAA)
PTS	Programmer Test Station
PTS	Program of Technology and Society [*Later, DTS*] (EA)
PTS	Program Test System [*Computer science*] (IEEE)
PTS	Program Triple Store
PTS	Project Tracking System [*Environmental Protection Agency*] (ERG)
PTS	Propellant Transfer System
PTS	Protestant Truth Society [*British*] (DBA)
PTS	Provisional Technical Secretariat [*United Nations*]
PTS	Public Telephone Service [*or System*] [*Telecommunications*] (TEL)
PTS	Pure Time Sharing [*Computer science*] (IEEE)
PTS	Put to Sleep [*ASPCA terminology*]
PTSA	Kusaie [*Caroline Islands*] [*ICAO location identifier*] (ICLI)
PTSA	Para-Toluenesulfonic Acid [*Organic chemistry*]
PTSA	Parent-Teacher-Student Association [*Nickname: "Pizza"*]
PTSA	Piano Trade Suppliers' Association [*British*] (BI)
PTSA	Professional Trucking Services Association (EA)
PTSC	Paper Tape Selectric Composer (DGA)
PT-S/C	Proof Test Spacecraft [*NASA*]
PTSD	Pesticides and Toxic Substances Division [*Environmental Protection Agency*] (GFGA)
PTSD	Post-Traumatic Stress Disorder [*Psychiatry*]
PTSE	Paper Tape Splicing Equipment
PTSED	Pesticides and Toxic Substances Enforcement Division (COE)
PTSH	Poststimulus Time Histogram [*Medicine*] (DMAA)
PTSI	PAM Transportation Services, Inc. [*NASDAQ symbol*] (NQ)
PTSI	P.A.M. Transportation Svcs [*NASDAQ symbol*] (TTSB)
PTSI	Para-Toluene Sulfonylisocyanate [*Organic chemistry*]
PTSM	Plant, Technology, and Safety Management (HCT)
PTSO	Personnel Transaction Summary by Originator [*Military*] (AABC)
PTSP	Paper Tape Software Package (NITA)
PTSP	Peacetime Support Period [*DoD*]
PT/SP	Pressure Tube to Spool Piece [*Nuclear energy*] (NRCH)
PTS PROMT	Predicasts Overview of Markets and Technology [*Predicasts, Inc.*] [*Cleveland, OH Bibliographic database*]
PTSR	Performance Technical Survey Report
PTSR	Preliminary Technical Survey Report [*Military*] (AFIT)
PTSR	Pressure-Tube Superheat Reactor [*Nuclear energy*]
PTSS	Parallel Tuned Series Stabilized (IAA)
PTSS	Photon Target Scoring System (AAG)
PTSS	Posttraumatic Stress Syndrome [*Medicine*] (DMAA)
PTSS	Post-Traumatic Stress System [*Medicine*]
PTSS	Princeton Time Sharing Services, Inc.
ptst	Paintstick (VRA)
PTST	Personnel Transaction Summary by Type Transaction [*Military*] (AABC)
PTST	Pretransfusion Serologic Testing
PTST	Prime Time School Television [*Defunct*] (EA)
PTT	Partial Thromboplastin Time [*Hematology*]
PTT	Particle Transport Time (MAE)
PTT	Part Task Trainer (MCD)
PTT	Party Test [*Telecommunications*] (TEL)
PTT	Peak Twitch Tension [*Physiology*]
PTT	Perth Theatre Trust [*Australia*]
PTT	Petrotex Resources [*Vancouver Stock Exchange symbol*]
PTT	Physical Therapist Technician
PTT	Platform Transmitter Terminal [*Satellite-based tracking system*]
PTT	Postal, Telegraph, and Telephone Administration (NATG)
PTT	Postes, Telegraphes, et Telediffusion [*Post, Telegraph, and Telephone*] [*General Post Office Facetious translation: Prostitution Telematique et Telephonique*] [*France*]
PTT	Post, Telegraph and Telephone Authority (NITA)
PTT	Post, Telephone, and Telegraph [*Telecommunications*] (IAA)
PTT	Post Telephone & Telegraph Administration (WDAA)
PTT	Post Telephone or Telex (NITA)
PTT	Post, Telephon und Telegraphenbetriebe [*Switzerland Telecommunications*]
PTT	Post Ten Tumblers [*Pseudonym used by William Maginn*]
PTT	Post und Telegraphenverwaltung [*Postal and Telegraph Administration*] [*Austria Telecommunications*]
PTT	Pratt, KS [*Location identifier FAA*] (FAAL)
PTT	Press-to-Talk (IDOE)
PTT	Press to Transmit
PTT	Private Tombs at Thebes [*Oxford*] [*A publication*] (BJA)
PTT	Processing Telecom Technologies (PCM)
PTT	Production Type Test
PTT	Program Technical Training (AFM)
PTT	Program Test Tape [*Computer science*] (IEEE)
PTT	Protein Truncation Test [*Analytical biochemistry*]
PTT	Prothrombin Time [*Hematology*] (AAMN)
PTT	Public Telecommunications Trust [*Proposed replacement for Corporation for Public Broadcasting*]

PTT .... Pulmonary Transit Time [*Physiology*]
PTT .... Pulse Transmission Time [*Medicine*] (DMAA)
PTT .... Push to Talk
PTT/8 .... Paper Tape Code on Eight Levels (NITA)
PTTC .... Pacific Transportation Terminal Command [*Army*]
PTTC .... Paper Tape and Transmission Code
PTTC .... Perforated Tape and Transmission Code [*Telecommunications*] (IAA)
PTTC .... Petroleum Technology Transfer Council (NTPA)
PTT-CT .... Activated Partial Thromboplastin Time, Control [*Hematology*] (DAVI)
PTTDAR ...... Personnel Training and Training Devices Analysis Report (MCD)
PTTH .... Prothoracicotropic Hormone
PTTI .... Postal, Telegraph, and Telephone International [*See also IPTT*] [*Geneva, Switzerland*] (EAIO)
PTTI .... Precise Time and Time Interval (AFM)
PTTK .... Kosrae Island [*Caroline Islands*] [*ICAO location identifier*] (ICLI)
PTTK .... Partial Thromboplastin Time with Kaolin [*Hematology*]
PTTL .... Photo-Transferred Thermoluminescence (PDAA)
PTTL .... Press-to-Test Light
PTTMC .... PACOM [*Pacific Command*] Tactical Target Materials Catalog (CINC)
PTTRN .... Pattern
PTTS .... Pressure Temperature Test Set (DWSG)
PTTS .... Private Telegraph and Telephone Service [*Telecommunications*] (IAA)
PTTY .... Petty
PTU .... Package Transfer Unit
PTU .... Pallet Transporter Unit [*Military*] (CAAL)
PTU .... Parallel Transmission Unit (AAG)
PTU .... Part-Throttle Unlock [*Automotive engineering*]
PTU .... Pathology Transcription Unit
PTU .... Phenylthiourea [*Organic chemistry*]
PTU .... Pilot Test Unit [*Air Force*]
PTU .... Planning Tracking Unit (MCD)
PTU .... Platinum [*Alaska*] [*Airport symbol*] (OAG)
PTU .... Platinum, AK [*Location identifier FAA*] (FAAL)
PTU .... Plumbing Trades Union [*British*]
PTU .... Plumbing Trade Union (NADA)
PTU .... Portable Test Unit
PTU .... Power Transfer Unit
PTU .... Program Track Unit [*Telecommunications*] (LAIN)
PTU .... Propylthiouracil [*Also, PROP, PT*] [*Thyroid inhibitor*]
P-TUBE .... Pneumatic Tube (NAKS)
PTUC .... Pacific Trade Union Community [*Australia*] (EAIO)
PTUV .... Public Tenants' Union of Victoria [*Australia*]
PTV .... Parachute Test Vehicle
PTV .... Paratransit Vehicle
PTV .... Passenger Transfer Vehicle [*Airport transportation*]
PTV .... Passenger Transport Vehicle
PTV .... Pathfinder Test Vehicle [*NASA*] (MCD)
PTV .... Pay Television
PTV .... Peach Tree Valley [*California*] [*Seismograph station code, US Geological Survey*] (SEIS)
PTV .... Peak-to-Valley
PTV .... Penetration Test Vehicle [*Aerospace*]
PTV .... Pietas Tutissima Virtus [*Piety Is the Safest Virtue*] [*Motto of Ernst, Margrave of Brandenburg (1583-1613)*] [*Latin*]
PTV .... Pitch Thrust Vector (KSC)
PTV .... Poly(thienylenevinylene) [*Organic chemistry*]
PTV .... Porous Tungsten Vaporizer
PTV .... Porterville, CA [*Location identifier FAA*] (FAAL)
PTV .... Predetermined Time Value (IEEE)
PTV .... Programmable Temperature Vaporizer
PTV .... Programmed-Temperature Vaporizing [*Analytical chemistry*]
PTV .... Propulsion Technology Validation (MCD)
PTV .... Propulsion Test Vehicle
PTV .... Prototype Test Vehicle (MCD)
PTV .... Public Television
PTV .... Punched Tape Verifier [*Computer science*]
PTV .... Punch through Varactor [*Computer science*] (IAA)
PTV .... Puntavia Air Services [*Djibouti*] [*FAA designator*] (FAAC)
PTVA .... Propulsion Test Vehicle Assembly [*NASA*]
PTVC .... Pitch Thrust Vector Control (KSC)
PTVD .... Portable Toxic Vapor Detector
PTVE .... Propulsion Test Vehicle Engineering [*NASA*] (MCD)
PTVST .... Port Visit [*Navy*] (NVT)
PTVV .... Peak-to-Valley Variation (MCD)
PTW .... Page Table Word [*Computer science*] (IAA)
PTW .... Personal Typesetting Workstation (DGA)
PTW .... Physikalisch-Technische-Werkstatten [*Roentgenology*]
PTW .... Pilot Training Wing [*Air Force*]
PTW .... Playing to Win (EA)
PTW .... Point Target Weapon
PTW .... Pottstown, PA [*Location identifier FAA*] (FAAL)
PTW .... Pressure-Treated Wood
PTW .... Pressure-Type Window
PTWAM .... Page Table Word Associative Memory [*Computer science*] (IAA)
PTWC .... Pacific Tsunami Warning Center [*National Weather Service*] (MSC)
PTWC .... Project on Technology, Work, and Character (EA)
PT-WEX .... Part-Time Work Experience Program [*Texas*] (EDAC)
PTWF .... Pakistan Transport Workers' Federation
PTWG .... Provisioning Technical Working Group
PTWI .... Provisional Tolerable Weekly Intake [*Toxicology*]
PTWM .... Power Transformation Weighting Method [*Mathematics*]
PTWMASA ... Private Treaty Wool Merchants' Association of South Australia
PTWMAV .... Private Treaty Wool Merchants' Association of Victoria [*Australia*]
PTWMAWA... Private Treaty Wool Merchants' Association of Western Australia

P-TWP .... Post-Township
PTWT .... Photo-Type Traveling Wave Tube (NG)
PTX .... Aereo Postal de Mexico SA de CV [*ICAO designator*] (FAAC)
PTX .... Pacific Trans-Ocean Resources Ltd. [*Toronto Stock Exchange symbol*]
PTX .... Palytoxin [*Organic chemistry*]
PTx .... Parathyroidectomy [*Medicine*]
PTX .... Pertussis Toxin [*Pharmacology*]
PTX .... Picrotoxin [*Biochemistry*]
PTX .... Pillowtex Corp. [*NYSE symbol*] (SPSG)
PTX .... Pneumothorax [*Medicine*] (AAMN)
PTX .... Polythermalex (IAA)
PTX .... Polythiazide [*Organic chemistry*]
PTX .... Pressure-Temperature Composition
PTX .... Proprietary Format [*Computer science*]
PTXA .... Parathyroidectomy and Autotransplantation [*Endocrinology*] (DAVI)
PTXB .... Pumiliotoxin B [*Organic chemistry*]
PTY .... Panama City [*Panama*] [*Airport symbol*] (OAG)
PTY .... Parity (IAA)
PTY .... Party (AAG)
PTY .... Proprietary
Pty .... Proprietary (DD)
PTYA .... Yap [*Caroline Islands*] [*ICAO location identifier*] (ICLI)
PTZ .... Pentylenetetrazole [*CNS stimulant*]
PTZ .... Phenothiazine (EDCT)
PTZ .... Pulitzer Publishing [*NYSE symbol*] (TTSB)
PTZ .... Pulitzer Publishing Co. [*NYSE symbol*] (SPSG)
PU .... Pack Unit [*Single title, multiple orders*] [*Publishing*] [*British*]
PU .... Paid Up [*Insurance*] (EY)
pu .... Paid Up [*Insurance*] (ODBW)
PU .... Parents United (EA)
PU .... Participating Unit (NVT)
PU .... Parts Used [*Medicine*]
PU .... Passed Urine [*Medicine*]
PU .... Paste Up (ADA)
PU .... Peptic Ulcer [*Medicine*]
PU .... Perbonate Unit [*Analytical biochemistry*]
PU .... Percent Utilization [*Anesthesiology*]
PU .... Peripheral Unit [*Computers*] (MSA)
PU .... Personnel, Utility [*British military*] (DMA)
PU .... Persons Using [*Television*] (WDMC)
PU .... Peru [*IYRU nationality code*] (IYR)
PU .... Per Unit (EECA)
PU .... Per Urethra [*Medicine*]
PU .... Physical Unit [*Computer science*] (IBMDP)
PU .... Pick Up [*Business term*]
PU .... Plant Unit
PU .... Players' Union [*Football*] [*British*]
PU .... Pluggable Unit (SAA)
PU .... Pluna [*Airline flight code*] (ODBW)
Pu .... Plutonium [*Chemical element*]
PU .... Polyurethane [*Also, PUR*] [*Organic chemistry*]
PU .... Power Equipment [*JETDS nomenclature*] [*Military*] (CET)
PU .... Power Unit
PU .... Pregnancy Urine [*Medicine*]
PU .... Prilled Urea [*A fertilizer*]
PU .... Princeton University
PU .... Prisoner's Union [*Later, PRU*] (EA)
PU .... Processing Unit [*Computer science*]
PU .... Processor Utility [*Telecommunications*] (TEL)
PU .... Production Unit (CAAL)
PU .... Propellant Unit (NASA)
PU .... Propellant Utilization [*Aerospace*]
PU .... Propulsion Unit (KSC)
PU .... Propyleneurea [*Organic chemistry*]
PU .... Prostatic Urethra [*Anatomy*] [*Urology*] (DAVI)
PU .... Proutist Universal (EA)
PU .... Publications (MCD)
PU .... Publisher [*Online database field identifier*]
PU .... Puetzer [*Germany ICAO aircraft manufacturer identifier*] (ICAO)
PU .... Pump Unit (AAG)
Pu .... Punic (BJA)
Pu .... Punjab Regiment [*India*] [*Army*]
PU .... Purdue University
Pu .... Purine [*Biochemistry*]
PU .... Purple (ROG)
PU .... University of Pennsylvania, Philadelphia, PA [*Library symbol Library of Congress*] (LCLS)
PUA .... Partido de Unificacion Anticomunista [*Anti-Communist Unification Party*] [*Guatemala*] [*Political party*] (PPW)
PUA .... Patient Unit Assistant [*Medicine*] (DMAA)
PUA .... Plant-Unique Analysis [*Nuclear energy*] (NRCH)
PUA .... Polish Union of America (EA)
PUA .... Pride Users' Association [*Defunct*] (EA)
PUA .... Primeras Lineas Uruguayas de Navegacion Aerea [*Uruguay*] [*ICAO designator*] (FAAC)
PU-A .... University of Pennsylvania, Morris Arboretum, Philadelphia, PA [*Library symbol Library of Congress*] (LCLS)
PUAA .... Public Utilities Advertising Association [*Later, PUCA*] (EA)
PUAC .... Propellant Utilization Acoustical Checkout (AAG)
PUAC .... Public Athletic Conference (PSS)
PU-AC .... University of Pennsylvania, Annenberg School of Communications, Philadelphia, PA [*Library symbol Library of Congress*] (LCLS)
PUAD .... Pueblo Army Depot [*Colorado*] (AABC)
PUADA .... Pueblo Army Depot Activity (AABC)

PUAID .... Parti d'Unite Arabe Islamique-Democratique [*Algeria*] [*Political party*] (EY)
PU & D .... Pick Up and Delivery [*Business term*]
PUAR .... Pulse Acquisition RADAR [*Military*] (MSA)
PU-Ar .... University of Pennsylvania Archives, Philadelphia, PA [*Library symbol*] [*Library of Congress*] (LCLS)
PUAS .... Postal Union of the Americas and Spain [*See also UPAE*] [*Montevideo, Uruguay*] (EAIO)
PUASP .... Postal Union of the Americas, Spain, and Portugal [*Uruguay*] (EAIO)
PUB .... Partido Union Boliviana [*Bolivian Unity Party*] [*Political party*] (PPW)
PUB .... Percutaneous Umbilical Blood [*Pediatrics*] (CPH)
PUB .... Phycourobilin [*Biochemistry*]
PUB .... Physical Unit Block [*Computer science*]
PUB .... Puale Bay [*Alaska*] [*Seismograph station code, US Geological Survey*] (SEIS)
PUB .... Public
Pub .... Public (TBD)
pub .... Public (WDMC)
pub .... Publication (WDMC)
PUB .... Publication (AFM)
PUB .... Public House [*A drinking establishment*] [*British*]
pub .... Public House (ODBW)
PUB .... Publicity
PUB .... Public Utilities Board (NADA)
PUB .... Published (AABC)
pub .... Published (WDMC)
pub .... Publisher (WDMC)
PUB .... Publisher
PUB .... Pueblo [*Colorado*] [*Airport symbol*] (OAG)
PUB .... Pueblo, CO [*Location identifier FAA*] (FAAL)
PUBAFF .... Public Affairs (DNAB)
PUBAFFRRU... Public Affairs Ready Reserve Unit (DNAB)
Pub Bargaining Cas (CCH)... Public Bargaining Cases (Commerce Clearing House) [*A publication*] (DLA)
PUB BDG .... Publisher's Binding (DGA)
PUBC .... Presbyterians United for Biblical Concerns [*Later, PBC*] (EA)
Pubcaster ... Public Broadcaster [*Radio or TV station affiliated with NPR or PBS*]
PubcoC .... Pubco Corp [*Associated Press*] (SAG)
PUBD .... Published (ROG)
pubd .... Published (WDAA)
PUB DOC .... Public Documents (ROG)
Pub Employee Bargaining Rep (CCH)... Public Employee Bargaining Reports (Commerce Clearing House) [*A publication*] (DLA)
Pub Employee Rel Rep... Public Employee Relations Reports [*A publication*] (DLA)
Pub Ent Advert & Allied Fields LQ... Publishing, Entertainment, Advertising, and Allied Fields Law Quarterly [*A publication*] (DLA)
Pub Gen Laws... Public General Laws [*A publication*] (DLA)
PUB HA....... Public Hall [*Freemasonry*] (ROG)
Pub Health... United States Public Health Service, Court Decisions [*A publication*] (DLA)
Pub Hist ..... [*The*] Public Historian [*A publication*]
PUBINFO...... Office of Public Information [*Formerly, OPR*] [*Navy*]
Pub Int........ Public Interest [*A publication*]
PUBL .... Public (WGA)
PUBL .... Publication [*or Published or Publisher*] (EY)
PUBL .... Publish (FAAC)
Publ .... Publisher (AL)
Publ .... Publishing (AL)
Publ Admin... Public Administration [*A publication*]
Pub Land L Rev... Public Land Law Review [*A publication*] (DLA)
Pub Lands Dec... Department of the Interior, Decisions Relating to Public Lands [*A publication*] (DLA)
Pub Law ...... Public Law (AAGC)
PUBLCTN ... Publication
PUBLD .... Published (ROG)
Pub LF........ Public Law Forum [*A publication*] (DLA)
public .... Publicist
PUBLICA ..... Public Libraries Concerted Action (TELE)
Publick .... Publicker Industries, Inc. [*Associated Press*] (SAG)
PUBLINX...... Public Links [*Amateur golf*]
PUBLR .... Publisher
Publ Serv Rev... Public Service Review [*A publication*]
PUBLSHG .... Publishing (DCTA)
PUBN .... Publication (MSA)
pubn .... Publication (WDAA)
Pubn .... Publication (AL)
PUBNET ...... American Association of Publishers' electronic ordering system
PUBO .... Pubco Corp. [*NASDAQ symbol*] (NQ)
Pub Op Q ... Public Opinion Quarterly [*A publication*] (BRI)
Pub Papers... Public Papers of the President [*A publication*] (DLA)
Pub Rel ...... Public Relations
Pub Rel Bull... Public Relations Bulletin [*American Bar Association A publication*] (DLA)
Pub Rel J .... Public Relations Journal [*A publication*] (BRI)
Pub Res....... Public Resolution (AAGC)
Pub Res C ... Public Resources Code [*California*] [*A publication*] (ILCA)
Pub Res No... Public Resolution Number [*Congress*] (ILCA)
PUB RM....... Publisher's Ream (DGA)
PUBS .... Elephant & Castle Group, Inc. [*NASDAQ symbol*] (SAG)
PUBS .... Percutaneous Umbilical Blood Sampling [*Medicine*]
PUBS .... Percutaneous Umbilical Cord Sampling [*Also, Cordocentesus*] [*Medical test*] (PAZ)
PUBS .... Pop-Up Bottom Seismograph [*Marine science*] (MSC)
PUBS .... Publications (CDAI)
PUBS .... Publication Series

PUBS .... Purple Urine Bag Syndrome [*Medicine*] (DMAA)
PUBSAT ...... Publications Special Assistance Team [*Military*]
Pub Ser Comm... Public Service Commission [*Usually, of a specific state*] (DLA)
PUBSF .... Elephant & Castle Group [*NASDAQ symbol*] (TTSB)
PubSNC ...... Public Service Co. North Carolina [*Associated Press*] (SAG)
Pub St .... Public Statutes [*A publication*] (DLA)
PubSt .... Public Storage, Inc. [*Associated Press*] (SAG)
PubStrg....... Public Storage, Inc. [*Associated Press*] (SAG)
Pub U Rep... Public Utilities Reports [*A publication*] (DLA)
Pub Util C ... Public Utilities Code [*A publication*] (DLA)
Pub Util L Anthol... Public Utilities Law Anthology [*A publication*] (DLA)
Pub Util Rep... Public Utilities Reports [*A publication*] (DLA)
PU-BZ .... University of Pennsylvania, Biology Library, Philadelphia, PA [*Library symbol Library of Congress*] (LCLS)
PUC .... Pacific Unicorn [*Vancouver Stock Exchange symbol*]
PUC .... Pacific Union College [*Angwin, CA*]
PUC .... Papers under Consideration
PUC .... Parti de l'Unite Congolaise [*Congolese Unity Party*] [*Political party*]
PUC .... Pediatric Urine Collector [*Medicine*]
PUC .... Peripheral Unit Controller [*Computer science*] (CIST)
PUC .... Permanent Unit Code (NG)
PUC .... Pick-Up Car
PUC .... Planification d'Urgence Canada [*Emergency Planning Canada - EPC*]
PUC .... Player Unit Component (MCD)
PUC .... Pontificia Universidade Catolica [*Rio de Janeiro*]
PUC .... Popular Unity of Chile [*Political party*]
PUC .... Port Utilization Committee
PUC .... Post Urbem Condita [*After the Building of the City of Rome*] [*Latin*]
PUC .... Presidential Unit Citation [*Military decoration*]
PUC .... Price [*Utah*] [*Airport symbol*] (OAG)
PUC .... Price, UT [*Location identifier FAA*] (FAAL)
PUC .... Processing Unit Cabinet [*Computer science*]
PUC .... Production Urgency Committee [*WPB*]
PUC .... Program Under Control (NITA)
PUC .... Program Unit Code [*Military*] (AFIT)
PUC .... Provided You Concur [*Army*]
PUC .... Public Utilities Commission
PUC .... Public Utility Co.
PUC .... Punctured Uniform Code [*Computer science*] (IAA)
PU-C .... University of Pennsylvania, Chemistry Library, Philadelphia, PA [*Library symbol Library of Congress*] (LCLS)
PUCA .... Partido Unionista Centro Americana [*Nicaragua*] [*Political party*] (EY)
PUCA .... Public Utilities Communicators Association [*Later, UCI*] [*New Castle, PA*] (EA)
PUCC .... Port Utilities [*AAR code*]
PUCK .... Florida Panthers Holdings, Inc. [*NASDAQ symbol*] (SAG)
PUCK .... Propellant Utilization Checkout Kit (KSC)
PUCK .... Pucklechurch [*England*]
PuCl .... Plutonium Chloride
PUCM .... Progressive Union of Cabinet Makers [*British*]
PUCP .... Process Unit Control Panel [*Computer science*] (IAA)
PUCS .... Propellant Utilization Control System (KSC)
PUCU .... Propellant Utilization Control Unit
PUD .... Parallel Undocumented Development (PDAA)
PUD .... Partido Union Democratica [*Guatemala*] [*Political party*]
PUD .... Peptic Ulcer Disease
PUD .... Physical Unit Directory [*Computer science*] (MHDI)
PUD .... Pick Up and Delivery [*Business term*]
PUD .... Planned Unit Development [*Housing*]
PUD .... Planned Urban Development
PUD .... Preretro Update Display
PUD .... Prisoner under Detention (ADA)
PUD .... Public Utility District [*Bonds*]
pud .... Pudding (BARN)
PUD .... Pudendal (DMAA)
PUD .... Puerto Deseado [*Argentina*] [*Airport symbol*] (OAG)
PUD .... Pulmonary Disease [*Medicine*]
PuD .... Pulmonary Disease [*Medicine*] (STED)
PU-D .... University of Pennsylvania, Evans Dental Library, Philadelphia, PA [*Library symbol Library of Congress*] (LCLS)
PUDA .... Pueblo Depot Activity [*Colorado*] [*Army*]
PUDD .... Programmable Universal Direct Drive
PUDG .... Pudgie's Chicken [*NASDAQ symbol*] (TTSB)
PUDG .... Pudgies Chicken, Inc. [*NASDAQ symbol*] (SAG)
Pudgie .... Pudgies Chicken, Inc. [*Associated Press*] (SAG)
Pudgies ...... Pudgies Chicken, Inc. [*Associated Press*] (SAG)
PUDGW....... Pudgies Chicken Wrrt [*NASDAQ symbol*] (TTSB)
PUDL .... Push Down List [*Computer science*] (IAA)
PUDN .... Perpetuation of Unit Documentation Number (MCD)
PUDOC........ Centrum voor Landbouwpublikaties en Landbouwdocumentatie [*Center for Agricultural Publishing and Documentation*] [*Ministry of Agriculture and Fisheries*] [*Information service or system*] (IID)
PU-DPL....... Princeton University Device Physics Laboratory [*New Jersey*]
PUDT .... Propellant Utilization Data Translator (AAG)
PUDVM........ Pulsed Ultrasound Doppler Velocity Meter
PUE .... Phosphorus Utilization Efficiency [*Ecology*]
PUE .... Physiotherapists' Union of Employees [*Australia*]
PUE .... Presidential Unit Emblem [*Military decoration*] (AABC)
PUE .... Pre-Stock Unit Equipment [*Military British*]
PUE .... Propellant Utilization Exerciser
PUE............ Puebla [*Mexico*] [*Seismograph station code, US Geological Survey Closed*] (SEIS)
PUE .... Puerto Obaldia [*Panama*] [*Airport symbol*] (OAG)
PUE .... Pyrexia of Unknown Etiology [*Medicine*]
PUEC .... Portsmouth Uranium Enrichment Complex (COE)

PU-EI .... University of Pennsylvania, Moore School of Electrical Engineering, Philadelphia, PA [Library symbol Library of Congress] (LCLS)
Puerto Rico... Puerto Rico Reports [A publication] (DLA)
Puerto Rico F... Puerto Rico Federal Reports [A publication] (DLA)
Puerto Rico Fed... Puerto Rico Federal Reports [A publication] (DLA)
Puerto Rico Rep... Puerto Rico Supreme Court Reports [A publication] (DLA)
PUF .... Partially Unfolded Form [Biochemistry]
PUF .... Partido Union Federal [Federal Union Party] [Argentina Political party]
PUF .... Pau [France] [Airport symbol] (OAG)
PUF .... People's United Front [Papua New Guinea] [Political party] (PPW)
PUF .... People's United Front [Bangladesh] [Political party]
PUF .... Percent Unaccounted For
PUF .... Polyurethane Film [Plastics technology]
PUF .... Polyurethane Foam
PUF .... Porous Polyurethane Foam [Also, PPF] [Plastics technology]
PUF .... Prime Underwriting Facility [Banking]
Puf .... Puffendorf's Law of Nature and Nations [A publication] (DLA)
PUF .... Pure Ultrafiltration (DMAA)
PU-F .... University of Pennsylvania, H. H. Furness Memorial Library, Philadelphia, PA [Library symbol Library of Congress] (LCLS)
PUFA .... Polyunsaturated Fatty Acid [Nutrition]
PU-FA .... University of Pennsylvania, School of Fine Arts, Philadelphia, PA [Library symbol Library of Congress] (LCLS)
PUFF .... People United to Fight Frustrations (EA)
PUFF .... Picofarad (MDG)
PUFF .... Proposed Uses of Federal Funds [Health Planning and Resource Development Act of 1974]
PUFFIN .... Pedestrian User-Friendly Intelligent Crossing (WDAA)
PUFFS .... Passive Underwater Fire Control Feasibility Study
PUFFS .... Passive Underwater Fire Control Feasibility System
PUFFT .... Purdue University Fast FORTRAN [Formula Translation] Translator [Computer science]
PUFI .... Packed under Federal Inspection
PUFL .... Pump Fed Liquid (KSC)
PUFO .... Pack Up and Fade Out [End of military exercise] [British] (DSUE)
PUFS .... Programmer's Utility Filing System (DIT)
PUFS .... Proposed Underwater Fire Control Feasibility Study (SAA)
PUG .... Partially Underground [Military]
PUG .... PASCAL Users' Group [Defunct] (EA)
PUG .... Penta Users Group (EA)
PUG .... Port Augusta [Australia Airport symbol] (OAG)
PUG .... Prestel Users Group (NITA)
PUG .... PRIME Users Group (EA)
PUG .... Print under Glaze [Ceramics]
PUG .... Propellant Utilization and Gauging [Apollo] [NASA]
PUG .... Pugilist
PUG .... Pugillus [A Handful] [Pharmacy] (ROG)
Pug .... Pugsley's New Brunswick Reports [14-16 New Brunswick] [A publication] (DLA)
PUG .... Pulsed Universal Grid
PUG .... Pure Gold Resources, Inc. [Toronto Stock Exchange symbol]
PugetP .... Puget Sound Power & Light Co. [Associated Press] (SAG)
PUGLIG .... PUG Library Information Group (NITA)
PUGS .... Propellant Utilization and Gaging System (NAKS)
PUGS .... Propellant Utilization and Gauging System [Apollo] [NASA] (KSC)
Pugs .... Pugsley's New Brunswick Reports [14-16 New Brunswick] [A publication] (DLA)
Pugs & Bur... Pugsley and Burbridge's New Brunswick Reports [17-20 New Brunswick] [A publication] (DLA)
Pugs & Burg... Pugsley and Burbridge's New Brunswick Reports [17-20 New Brunswick] [A publication] (DLA)
Pugs & T ..... Pugsley and Trueman's New Brunswick Reports [A publication] (DLA)
Pugs & Tru... Pugsley and Trueman's New Brunswick Reports [1882-83] [A publication] (DLA)
PugtP .... Puget Sound Power & Light Co. [Associated Press] (SAG)
PUH .... Pauahi [Hawaii] [Seismograph station code, US Geological Survey] (SEIS)
PUH .... Pregnancy Urine Hormone [Endocrinology]
PUHCA .... Public Utility Holding Co. Act of 1935
PUI .... Pen User Interface [Computer science]
PUI .... Physical Unit of Information [Computer science] (IAA)
PUI .... Pilot-under-Instruction [Navy]
PUI .... Platelet Uptake Index [Clinical chemistry]
PUIC .... Project Unique Identification Code (AAGC)
PU-Ind .... University of Pennsylvania, Industrial Research Department, Philadelphia, PA [Library symbol Library of Congress Obsolete] (LCLS)
PUIWP .... People for a United India and World Peace (EA)
PUJ .... Punta Cana [Dominican Republic] [Airport symbol] (OAG)
PUJT .... Programmable Unijunction Transistor (IAA)
PUK .... Pack-Up Kit (MCD)
PUK .... Paducah [Kentucky] [Airport symbol] (AD)
PUK .... Parti d'Unite Katangaise [Katanga Unity Party] [Political party]
PUK .... Patriotic Union of Kurdistan [Iraq] [Political party] (PD)
PUK .... Pechiney-Ugine-Kuhlmann [France] [Commercial firm]
PUK .... Prourokinase [Thrombolytic] [An enzyme]
PUK .... Pukarua [French Polynesia] [Airport symbol] (OAG)
PUKO .... Pan-American Union of Karatedo Organizations (EA)
PUKS .... Pivotal Unknowables
PUL .... Percutaneous Ultrasonic Lithotripsy [Medicine]
PUL .... Preconfiguration Unit Load
PUL .... Press Union of Liberia
PUL .... Princeton University, Princeton, NJ [Inactive] [OCLC symbol] (OCLC)

PUL .... Program Update Library
PUL .... Propellant Utilization and Loading
PUL .... Publicker Indus [NYSE symbol] (TTSB)
PUL .... Publicker Industries, Inc. [NYSE symbol] (SPSG)
PUL .... Pubourethral Ligament (STED)
PUL .... Pulkovo [Former USSR Seismograph station code, US Geological Survey] (SEIS)
PUL .... Pulley (AAG)
PUL .... Pulmonary
pul .... Pulmonary (STED)
PUL .... Pul. Przedsiebiorstwo Uslug Lotniczych [Poland ICAO designator] (FAAC)
PUL .... Pulse Resources [Vancouver Stock Exchange symbol]
PU-L .... University of Pennsylvania, Biddle Law Library, Philadelphia, PA [Library symbol Library of Congress] (LCLS)
PULA .... Public Laws
PulaskF .... Pulaski Furniture Corp. [Associated Press] (SAG)
PulaskiB ...... Pulaski Bank, A Savings Bank [Associated Press] (SAG)
PULB .... Pulaski Bank, A Savings Bank [NASDAQ symbol] (SAG)
PULB .... Pulaski Bank A Svgs Bk MO [NASDAQ symbol] (TTSB)
PULHES .... Physical Capacity, Upper Extremities, Lower Extremities, Hearing, Eyes, and Psychiatric System (DNAB)
PULHHEEMS... Physical Capacity, Upper Limbs, Left Hearing, Right Hearing, Left Eye, Right Eye, Mental Capacity, Stability [Military medical assessment] (WDAA)
PULL .... Power for Underwater Logistics and Living
Pull Acc .... Pulling on Mercantile Accounts [1846] [A publication] (DLA)
Pull Accts ..... Pulling's Law of Mercantile Accounts [A publication] (DLA)
Pull Att .... Pulling on Attorneys and Solicitors [3rd ed.] [1862] [A publication] (DLA)
Pull Laws & Cust Lond... Pulling's Treatise on the Laws, Customs, and Regulations of the City and Port o f London [A publication] (DLA)
Pull Port of London... Pulling's Treatise on the Laws, Customs, and Regulations of the City and Port ofLondon [A publication] (DLA)
pulm .... Pulmentum [Gruel Pulmonary] [Latin] (MAE)
PULM .... Pulmonary
PULO .... Pattani United Liberation Organization [Thailand] [Political party] (PD)
PULP .... Premium Unleaded Petrol
pulpbd .... Pulpboard (VRA)
PULPP .... Peripheral Ultra-Low Power Processor (PDAA)
pulpwd .... Pulpwood (VRA)
PULS .... Poseidon Undersea Launching System (NOAA)
PULS .... Propellant Utilization Loading System (AAG)
PULS .... Pulse Bancorp [NASDAQ symbol] (TTSB)
PULS .... Pulse Bancorp, Inc. [NASDAQ symbol] (SAG)
PULSAR ...... Pulsating Star
PULSAR ...... Pulsed Sequential Access Relay [Electronics] (ECII)
PULSAR ...... Pulsed Uniform LASER-Stimulated Artificial Radiation [Proposed acronymic designation for pulsars, in the event they are found to be artificially caused by intelligent life from outer space]
PULSE .... Patented Uniform Lateral Stability Element
PULSE .... Public Urban Locator Service
PulseBcp ..... Pulse Bancorp, Inc. [Associated Press] (SAG)
PULSES .... Physical Condition, Upper Extremity Function, Lower Extremity Function, Sensory and Communication Abilities, Excretory Control, Social Support [A neurological disability profile]
Pulsifer (ME)... Pulsifer's Reports [35-68 Maine] [A publication] (DLA)
PULSTAR ..... Pulse Training Assembled Reactor [Nuclear energy] (NRCH)
Pult .... Pulton. De Pace Regis [A publication] (DLA)
Pulte .... Pulte Corp. [Associated Press] (SAG)
PultzPb .... Pulitzer Publishing Co. [Associated Press] (SAG)
PULV .... Pulverized
PULV .... Pulvis [Powder] [Pharmacy]
PULV CONSPER... Pulvis Conspersus [Dusting Powder] [Pharmacy]
pulv gros ..... Pulvis Grossus [Coarse Powder] [Pharmacy] [Latin] (MAE)
pulv subtil ..... Pulvis Subtilis [Smooth Powder] [Pharmacy] [Latin] (MAE)
pulv tenu ..... Pulvis Tenuis [Very fine powder] [Latin] (DMAA)
PUM .... Partido Unificado Mariateguista [Peru] [Political party] (EY)
PUM .... Peanut Urinary Mucins (DB)
PUM .... Pennsylvania University Museum
PUM .... Per Unit Monthly (DNAB)
PUM .... Pomalaa [Indonesia] [Airport symbol] (OAG)
PUM .... President of the United Mineworkers
PUM .... Processor Utility Monitor [Telecommunications] (TEL)
PUMA .... Powered Ultralight Manufacturers Association [Defunct] (EA)
PUMA .... Processor-Upgradable Microcomputer Architecture [DFI, Inc.] (PCM)
PUMA .... Programmable Universal Manipulator (NITA)
PUMA .... Programmable Universal Manipulator for Assembly [General Motors Corp. assembly robot]
PUMA .... Programmable Universal Micro Accelerator [Computer science] (CDE)
PUMA Acc .... Prostitutes' Union of Massachusetts
PUMA .... Puma Technology, Inc. [NASDAQ symbol] (SAG)
PumaT .... Puma Technology, Inc. [Associated Press] (SAG)
PU-Math ...... University of Pennsylvania, Mathematics-Physics Library, Philadelphia, PA [Library symbol Library of Congress] (LCLS)
PUMCODOXPURSACOMLOPAR... Pulse-Modulated Coherent Doppler-Effect X-Band Pulse-Repetition Synthetic-Array Pulse Compression Side Lobe Planar Array
PU-Med .... University of Pennsylvania, Medical School, Philadelphia, PA [Library symbol Library of Congress] (LCLS)
PU-Med-TS... University of Pennsylvania, Medical School, Hospital Nurses Library, Philadelphia, PA [Library symbol Library of Congress] (LCLS)
PUMF .... Peaceful Uses of Military Forces

PUMGC.........	Pious Union of Our Mother of Good Counsel [*See also SMBC*] [*Genazzano, Italy*] (EAIO)
PUMP	Parts Usage Maintenance Program [*Computer science*] (IAA)
PUMP	Plant Uncoupling Mitochondrial Protein [*Biochemistry*]
PUMP	Production Upgrade Management Program (DNAB)
PUMP	Protesting Unfair Marketing Practices [*Student legal action organization*]
PUMS	Permanently Unfit for Military Service [*British*]
PUMS	Physical Unit Management Services [*Computer science*] (CIST)
PUMS	Public Use Microdata Sample [*Bureau of the Census*] (GFGA)
PUMS	Public Use Microdata Samples
PUMST	Polish Underground Movement (1939-1945) Study Trust (EA)
PU-Mu	University of Pennsylvania, University Museum, Philadelphia, PA [*Library symbol Library of Congress*] (LCLS)
PU-Music.....	University of Pennsylvania, School of Music, Philadelphia, PA [*Library symbol Library of Congress*] (LCLS)
Pun	All India Reporter, Punjab [*A publication*] (DLA)
Pun	Indian Law Reports, Punjab Series [*A publication*] (DLA)
PUN	Parti de l'Unite Nationale [*Party of National Unity*] [*Haiti*] [*Political party*] (PPW)
PUN	Partido Union Nacional [*National Union Party*] [*Costa Rica*] [*Political party*]
PUN	Plasma Urea Nitrogen (AAMN)
PUN	Plutonyl Nitrate [*Inorganic chemistry*]
PUN	Precision Underwater Navigation
PUN	Punch
PUN	Puncheon [*Unit of measurement*]
PUN	Punia [*Zaire*] [*Airport symbol*] (AD)
Pun	Punica [*of Silius Italicus*] [*Classical studies*] (OCD)
PUN	Punishment (DSUE)
PUN	Puno [*Peru*] [*Seismograph station code, US Geological Survey*] (SEIS)
PUN	Punta [*Flamenco dance term*]
PU-N	University of Pennsylvania, Center for the Study of the History of Nursing, Philadelphia, PA [*Library symbol*] [*Library of Congress*] (LCLS)
PUNA	Parti de l'Unite Nationale [*National Unity Party*] [*Congo*]
PUNC	Partido de Unidad Nacional Conservadora [*Nicaragua*] [*Political party*] (EY)
PUNC	Practical, Unpretentious, Nomographic Computer
PUNC	Probable Ultimate Net Cost [*Accounting*]
PUNC	Program Unit Counter
PUNC	Punctuation
PUNC	Puncture (DAVI)
punceq	Punctuated Equilibrium [*Bacteriology*]
PUNCT	Punctuation (ROG)
PUNGA	Parti de l'Unite Nationale Gabonaise [*Party for Gabonese National Unity*] [*Political party*]
Punj Rec.....	Punjab Record [*India*] [*A publication*] (DLA)
PUNL	Percutaneous Ultrasonic Nephrolithotripsy [*Nephrology*] [*Radiology*] (DAVI)
PUNS	Partido de Union Nacional del Sahara [*Western Sahara*] [*Political party*]
PUNS	Permanently Unfit for Naval Service [*British*]
PUNSW	Poets' Union of New South Wales [*Australia*]
PUO	Placed under Observation [*Medicine*]
PUO	Princeton University Observatory [*New Jersey*]
PUO	Prudhoe Bay [*Arkansas*] [*Airport symbol*] (OAG)
PUO	Prudhoe Bay, AK [*Location identifier FAA*] (FAAL)
Puo	[*A*] Purine Nucleoside [*Also, R*]
PUO	Pyrexia [*fever*] of Unknown Origin [*Commonly called Trench Fever*]
PuO2	Plutonium Dioxide
PUOS	Public Understanding of Science Program (EDAC)
PUOW	Proposed Units of Work
PUP	Paid-Up Policy [*Insurance*] (DSUE)
PUP	Parti de l'Unite du Peuple Gabonais [*Political party*] (EY)
PUP	Parti de l'Unite Populaire [*Tunisia*] [*Political party*] (EY)
PUP	Partido Union Patriotica [*Patriotic Union Party*] [*Dominican Republic*] [*Political party*] (PPW)
PUP	Peak Underpressure [*Nuclear energy*] (NRCH)
PUP	People's United Party [*Belize*] [*Political party*] (PPW)
PUP	Performance Units Plan (MHDB)
PUP	Performance Update Program [*Air Force*] (DOMA)
PUP	Peripheral Unit Processor [*Computer science*]
PUP	Peripheral Universal Processor (NITA)
PUP	Pious Union of Prayer (EA)
PUP	Plutonium Utilization Program [*Nuclear Regulatory Commission*] (NRCH)
PUP	Po [*Upper Volta*] [*Airport symbol*] (AD)
PUP	Popular Unity Party [*Bangladesh*] [*Political party*] (PPW)
PUP	Power Upgrade Program
PUP	Power Utility Pak [*Computer software*] [*Jwalk and Associates*] (PCM)
Pup	Pre-Urban Professional [*Acronym coined by TeenAge magazine to describe it s typical reader*] [*Lifestyle classification*]
PUP	Princeton University Press (DGA)
PUP	Product Upgrade Program (MUSM)
PUP	Program Unit Punch (SAA)
PUP	Progressive Unionist Party [*Northern Ireland*] [*Political party*] (PPW)
PUP	Public Utilities Panel [*EECE*]
PUP	Pull Up Point
PUP	Pupakea [*Hawaii*] [*Seismograph station code, US Geological Survey Closed*] (SEIS)
PUP	Pupil (DSUE)
Pup	Puppis [*Constellation*]
PUPA	Polish Union Printers Association [*Chicago*]

PU-Penn	University of Pennsylvania, Penniman Library of Education, Philadelphia, PA [*Library symbol Library of Congress Obsolete*] (LCLS)
PUPG	Production Unit Price Goals (MCD)
PUPID	Pulp and Paper Industry Division [*Instrument Society of America*]
PUPO	Pull Up Push Over (NASA)
PUPP	Pruritic Urticarial Papules and Plaques [*Dermatology*] (BARN)
Pupp	Puppis [*Constellation*]
PUPPI	Pop-Up Pore Pressure Instrument [*Oceanography*]
Puppie	Pregnant Urban Professional [*Terminology used in "The Yuppie Handbook"*] [*Lifestyle classification*]
PUPPP	Pruritic Urticarial Papules and Plaques of Pregnancy [*Medicine*]
PU-PSW......	University of Pennsylvania, Pennsylvania School of Social Work, Philadelphia, PA [*Library symbol Library of Congress*] (LCLS)
PUQ	Punta Arenas [*Chile*] [*Airport symbol*] (OAG)
PUR	Partido de Unificacion Revolucionaria [*Party of Revolutionary Unification*] [*Guatemala*] [*Political party*]
PUR	Partido Union Revolucionaria [*Cuba*]
PUR	Patch Unit Radio [*Bell System*]
PUR	Persons Using Radio [*Radio ratings*] (WDMC)
PUR	Polyurethane [*Also, PU*] [*Organic chemistry*]
PUR	Procurement Request [*Army*] (IAA)
PUR	Program of University Research
PUR	Program Utility Routines [*Computer science*]
PUR	Public Utilities Reports [*A publication Information service or system*] (IID)
PUR	Purari [*Papua New Guinea*] [*Seismograph station code, US Geological Survey*] (SEIS)
PUR	Purchase (AFM)
PUR	Purchasing Receipt [*Business term*]
PUR	Purdue University Reactor
PUR	Purdue University Research (MCD)
PUR	Purgative [*Medicine*] (ROG)
PUR	Purichloro Technology Ltd. [*Vancouver Stock Exchange symbol*]
PUR	Purifier (AAG)
Pur	[*A*] Purine [*Biochemistry*]
PUR	Purity [*of the Drug*] [*Pharmacy*] (ROG)
PUR	Puromycin [*Trypanocide*] [*Antineoplastic drug*]
pur	Purple [*Philately*]
PUR	Purpure [*Purple*] [*Heraldry*]
PUR	Pursuant (AABC)
PUR	Pursuit (AABC)
pur	Purus [*Pure*] [*Latin*]
PUR	Spurwing Airlines (Pty) Ltd. [*South Africa ICAO designator*] (FAAC)
PUR 3d	Public Utilities Reports, Third Series [*A publication*] (DLA)
PURA	PACOM [*Pacific Command*] Utilization and Redistribution Agency
PURA	Public Utilities Review Act [*1934*]
PURAC	Personal Use Radio Advisory Committee [*FCC Defunct*] (TSSD)
PURB	Purbeck [*District in England*]
PURC	Pacific Utilization Research Center [*Marine science*] (MSC)
PURC	Princeton University Research Center [*Marine science*] (MSC)
PURC	Public Utility Research Center [*University of Florida*] [*Research center*] (RCD)
PURC	Purchasing
PURCH	Purchase
Purch	Purchase (TBD)
purch	Purchasing (DD)
PURCHG	Purchasing (ROG)
Purd Dig	Purdon's Digest of Laws [*Pennsylvania*] [*A publication*] (DLA)
Purd Dig Laws...	Purdon's Digest of Laws [*Pennsylvania*] [*A publication*] (DLA)
Purdue U	Purdue University (GAGS)
Purdue U (Calumet)...	Purdue University-Calumet (GAGS)
PURE	Innovative Medical Services [*NASDAQ symbol*] (SAG)
PURE	People United for Rural Education (EA)
PURE	Present University Research Efforts [*Database*] [*Harperson Data Services*]
PURE	Purepac, Inc [*NASDAQ symbol*] (SAG)
Pure Appl Chem...	Pure and Applied Chemistry (MEC)
PureAtria	Pure Atria Corp. [*Associated Press*] (SAG)
Purepac	Purepac, Inc. [*Associated Press*] (SAG)
PUREQ	Purchase Requisition (NOAA)
PureSf	Pure Software, Inc. [*Associated Press*] (SAG)
PureTc	Pure Tech International, Inc. [*Associated Press*] (SAG)
PureWld	Pure World, Inc. [*Associated Press*] (SAG)
PUREX	Plutonium Uranium Extraction [*Nuclear energy*]
purg	Purgativus [*Cathartic, purgative*] [*Latin*] (MAE)
PURGE	Pearson Universal Random Generator
PURIF	Purification
PURL	Persistent Uniform Resource Locator [*Computer science*] (IGQR)
PURL	Persistent Universal Resource Locator [*Computer science*]
PURM	Project for Utilization and Redistribution of Materiel [*Air Force*]
PUR (NS)....	Public Utilities Reports, New Series [*A publication*] (DLA)
PURP	Purpose (AFM)
PURP	Purpure [*Purple*] [*Heraldry*] (ROG)
PURPA	Public Utilities Regulatory Policy Act [*1978*]
Purple's St...	Purple's Statutes, Scates' Compilation [*A publication*] (DLA)
PurR	Purine Repressor [*Biochemistry*]
PURRC	Polyurethane Recycle and Recovery Council [*Plastics recycling research*]
PURS	Partido de la Union Republicana Socialista [*Socialist Republican Union Party*] [*Bolivia*]
PURS	Program Usage Replenishment System
PURS	Pursuit
PURS	Purus, Inc. [*NASDAQ symbol*] (SAG)

PURSC........ Partido Unido de la Revolucion Socialista Cubana [Cuba] [Political party] (EY)
PURSCE....... Pursuance (ROG)
PURST........ Pursuant
PURT.......... PureTec Corp. [NASDAQ symbol] [Formerly, Pure Tech International] (SG)
PURT.......... Pure Tech International, Inc. [NASDAQ symbol] (NQ)
Purus.......... Purus, Inc. [Associated Press] (SAG)
PURV.......... Powered Underwater Research Vehicle [Navy]
Purv Coll ..... Purvis' Collection of the Laws of Virginia [A publication] (DLA)
PURW.......... Pure World, Inc. [NASDAQ symbol] (SAG)
PUS .... Parliamentary Under Secretary [British]
PUS .... Passive Ultrasonic Sensor (PDAA)
PUS .... Permanently Unfit for Service [Military] (ADA)
PUS .... Permanent Under Secretary [British]
PUS .... Personnel Utilization Sheet
PUS .... Pharmacopeia of the United States
PUS .... President of the United States
PUS .... Processor Utility Subsystem [Telecommunications] (TEL)
PUS .... Propellant Utilization System
PUS .... Public Use Samples
PUS .... Pusan [South Korea] [Airport symbol] (OAG)
PUS .... Pusan [South Korea] [Seismograph station code, US Geological Survey Closed] (SEIS)
pus.............. Pushto [MARC language code Library of Congress] (LCCP)
PU-S .... University of Pennsylvania, Edgar Fah Smith Memorial Library, Philadelphia, PA [Library symbol Library of Congress] (LCLS)
PUSAS........ Proposed United States of America Standard
PUSC.......... Partido Unidad Social Cristiana [Costa Rica] [Political party] (EY)
PU-Sc .... University of Pennsylvania, Towne Scientific School, Philadelphia, PA [Library symbol Library of Congress] (LCLS)
PUSCC........ Portugal-United States Chamber of Commerce (NTPA)
PUSD.......... Partido Unido Social Democratico [United Social-Democratic Party] [Guinea-Bissau] [Political party] (EY)
PUSD.......... Polska Unia Socjaldemokratyczna [Polish Social Democratic Union] [Political party]
PUSE .... Propellant Utilization System Exerciser
PUSEC........ Polish-US Economic Council (EA)
PUSGX........ Pioneer Amer. Income Cl.A [Mutual fund ticker symbol] (SG)
PUSH.......... People United to Save Humanity [In organization name "Operation PUSH"]
PUSH.......... Play Units for Severely Handicapped (EDAC)
PUSH.......... Public Use Sample Helper (PDAA)
PUSJD........ Pious Union of St. Joseph for the Dying [Defunct] (EA)
PUSJDS....... Pious Union of St. Joseph for Dying Sinners [Later, PUSJD] (EA)
PUSMM....... Parti d'Union Socialiste des Musulmans Mauritaniens [Party for Socialist Unity of Moslems of Mauritania] [Political party]
PUSO .... Principal Unit Security Officer (AAG)
PU-Sp .... University of Pennsylvania, Van Pelt Library, Special Collections, Philadelphia, PA [Library symbol] [Library of Congress] (LCLS)
PU-SHS....... University of Pennsylvania, South Asia Regional Studies Library, Philadelphia, PA [Library symbol Library of Congress] (LCLS)
PUSS .... Pallet Utility Support Structure [NASA] (MCD)
PUSS .... Pilots Universal Sighting System
PUSSI......... Prostitutes United for Social and Sexual Integration [British] (DI)
PUST .... Panafrican Union of Science and Technology
PUT............ Aeroput [Yugoslavia] [ICAO designator] (FAAC)
PUT/.......... Persons Using Television [Television ratings]
pU/T........... Pilot Under Training [Aviation] (DA)
PUT............ Programmable Unijunction Transistor
PUT............ Program Update Tape
PUT............ Property Unit Trust [Finance British]
PUT............ Provocative Use Test [Medicine] (DMAA)
PUT............ Punta De Talca [Chile] [Seismograph station code, US Geological Survey] (SEIS)
PUT............ Putao [Burma] [Airport symbol] (AD)
PUT............ Putnam, CT [Location identifier FAA] (FAAL)
PUT............ Putrescine [Organic chemistry]
Puter Ch ...... Puterbaugh's Illinois Chancery Pleading [A publication] (DLA)
Puter Pl ...... Puterbaugh's Illinois Common Law Pleading [A publication] (DLA)
Putnam........ Putnam's Proceedings before the Justice of the Peace [A publication] (DLA)
PutnCA........ Putnam California Investment Grade [Associated Press] (SAG)
PutNY .... Putnam New York Investment Grade [Associated Press] (SAG)
PUTR .... Pacific Underwater Test Range (SAA)
PUTT.......... Brassie Golf Corp. [NASDAQ symbol] (SAG)
PUTT.......... Portable Underwater Tracking Transducer
PUTT.......... Propellant Utilization Time Trace
PUTWS .... Put Word in String (SAA)
PUU .... Piute Reservoir [Utah] [Seismograph station code, US Geological Survey] (SEIS)
PUU .... Puerto Asis [Colombia] [Airport symbol] (OAG)
PU-UH .... University of Pennsylvania, University Hospital, Philadelphia, PA [Library symbol Library of Congress] (LCLS)
PU-UH-DeS... University of Pennsylvania, University Hospital, De Schweinitz Collection of Ophthalmology, Philadelphia, PA [Library symbol Library of Congress] (LCLS)
PUUSNA ...... Polish Union of the United States of North America (EA)
PUV .... Posterior Urethral Valve [Medicine] (DMAA)
PUV .... Propellant Utilization Valve [NASA] (NASA)
PUV .... Pulaski [Virginia] [Seismograph station code, US Geological Survey Closed] (SEIS)
PUV .... Puumala Virus
PU-V .... University of Pennsylvania, School of Veterinary Medicine, Philadelphia, PA [Library symbol Library of Congress] (LCLS)

PUVA .... Photochemotherapy with Ultraviolet A [Oncology]
PUVA .... Psoralens and Ultraviolet A [Therapy] [Medicine]
PUVD .... Pulsed Ultrasonic Blood Velocity Detector (AAMN)
PUVEP .... Propellant Utilization Vehicle Electronic Package (MCD)
PUVLV .... Propellant Utilization Valve [NASA] (AAG)
PUW .... Pick-Up Walker (MEDA)
PUW .... Pullman [Washington] [Airport symbol] (OAG)
PUW .... Pullman, WA [Location identifier FAA] (FAAL)
PU-W .... University of Pennsylvania, Wharton School of Finance and Commerce, Philadelphia, PA [Library symbol Library of Congress] (LCLS)
PUWP .... Polish United Workers' Party [See also PZPR] [Political party] (PD)
PUY .... Pula [Former Yugoslavia] [Airport symbol] (OAG)
PUZ .... Puerto Cabezas [Nicaragua] [Airport symbol] (AD)
PV .... Association Quebecoise Plaidoyer-Victimes (AC)
PV .... Eastern Provincial Airways [Labrador] [ICAO designator] (OAG)
P-V .... Panton-Valentine [Leukocidin] [Bacteriology] (DAVI)
PV .... Papillomavirus
PV .... Paravane [Anti-moored-mine device] [Obsolete]
PV .... Paraventricular [Neuroanatomy] (MAE)
PV .... Parole Violator
PV .... Paromomycin-Vancomycin [Blood agar] [Microbiology]
PV .... Par Value [Finance]
pv .... Pathovar [Microbiology]
PV .... Path Verification
PV .... Patrol Vessel
PV .... Paving [Technical drawings]
P/V .... Peak-to-Valley
PV .... Pemphigus Vulgaris [Dermatology]
PV .... [The] People's Voice [Pre-World War II publication of Adam Clayton Powell, Jr., and Charlie Buchanan]
PV .... Peripheral Vascular [Medicine]
PV .... Peripheral Vein [Anatomy]
PV .... Peripheral Vessel [Cardiology] (MAE)
PV .... Peritoneo-Venous (WDAA)
PV .... Peroxide Value [Food analysis]
PV .... Per Vaginam [Medicine]
PV .... Petite Vitesse [Goods train] [French]
PV .... Pfeiffer Vacuum Technology AG [NYSE symbol] (SAG)
PV .... Photographic Vision [Filter]
PV .... Photovoltaic
Pv .... Photovoltaics (COE)
PV .... Physical Vulnerability [Number] (NATG)
pV .... Picovolt (IDOE)
PV .... Pigment Volume
PV .... Pilot Vessel
PV .... Pioneer Venus [Spacecraft]
PV .... Pipe Ventilated
PV .... Piston Valve [Automotive engineering]
PV .... Pisum Virus [Plant pathology]
PV .... Planetary Vehicle [NASA]
PV .... Planuebergang [Grade Crossing] [German military - World War II]
PV .... Plan View (MSA)
PV .... Plasma Volume [Medicine]
PV .... Plastic Viscosity
PV .... Playback Verifier (MCD)
PV .... Plummer-Vinson [Syndrome] [Medicine] (DB)
PV .... Pole Vault
PV .... Polio Vaccine
PV .... Poliovirus
PV .... Polycythemia Vera [Also, PCV] [Hematology]
PV .... Polydor/Deutsche-Grammophon Variable Microgroove [Record label] [Germany]
PV .... Polyoma Virus
PV .... Polyvinyl (WGA)
PV .... Pore Volume [Geology]
PV .... Pornovision [Television]
PV .... Portal Vein [Anatomy]
PV .... Position Vacant (ADA)
PV .... Position Value
PV .... Positively Vet [British] (BARN)
PV .... Positive Volume (IEEE)
PV .... Postvaccination
PV .... Post Village
PV .... Post-Virgil
PV .... Postvoiding [Medicine] (MAE)
PV .... Potential Viewer [Television ratings] (NTCM)
PV .... Potential Vorticity [Meteorology] [Fluid mechanics]
PV .... Present Value [Finance]
PV .... Pressure [or Pressurized] Control Valve (IAA)
P/V .... Pressure/Vacuum
PV .... Pressure Velocity
PV .... Pressure Vessel (MSA)
P-V .... Pressure-Volume
PV .... Pressurization Valve
PV .... Prevailing Visibility
PV .... Prevalve (NASA)
PV .... Prevention of Violence (DICI)
P/V .... Preview
PV .... Preview Monitor [A TV monitor] [Filmmaking] (WDMC)
PV .... Priest Vicar
PV .... Primary Valve
PV .... Prime Vertical
PV .... Princess Victoria's Royal Irish Fusiliers [Military British] (ROG)
PV .... Private Varnish [Privately owned railroad cars]

PV.............. Process Variable (IAA)
PV.............. Production Validation [*Military*] (AABC)
PV.............. Professional Virgin (DSUE)
PV.............. Professional Volunteer
P/V.............. Profit/Volume Ratio
PV.............. Project Verification (COE)
PV.............. Project Volunteer (EA)
PV.............. Prometheus Vinctus [*of Aeschylus*] [*Classical studies*] (OCD)
PV.............. Proteus Vulgaris [*Bacterium*]
PV.............. Public Volunteer
PV.............. Public Voucher
PV.............. Pull and Void (MCD)
PV.............. Pulmonary Valvotomy [*Cardiology*]
PV.............. Pulmonary Vascularity [*Medicine*]
PV.............. Pulmonary Vein [*Medicine*]
PV.............. Pulmonic Valve [*Cardiology*] (DAVI)
PV.............. Pulse Voltammetry [*Analytical chemistry*]
PV.............. Pyrocatechol Violet [*Also, PCV*] [*An indicator Chemistry*]
Pv.............. Ventral Pressure Neurons [*of a leech*]
PV.............. Villanova University, Villanova, PA [*Library symbol Library of Congress*] (LCLS)
PV1.............. Private E-1 [*Army*]
PV-1(M)....... Poliovirus Type 1, Maloney
PV2.............. Private E-2 [*Army*]
PV-2(L)....... Poliovirus Type 2, Lansing
PV 4.............. Pickup Trucks, Vans, and Four-Wheel-Drive Vehicles [*Initialism used as title of a publication*]
PVA.............. Aerotransportes Privados SA de CV [*Mexico ICAO designator*] (FAAC)
PVA.............. Paralyzed Veterans of America (EA)
PVA.............. Passenger Vessel Association (NTPA)
PVA.............. Personal Values Abstract [*Scale*]
PVA.............. Platinova Resources Ltd. [*Toronto Stock Exchange symbol*]
PVA.............. Polyvinyl Acetate [*Organic chemistry*] (IAA)
PVA.............. Poly(vinyl Alcohol) [*Also, PVAL*] [*Organic chemistry*]
PVA.............. Population Viability Analysis [*Biology*]
PVA.............. Portable Vehicle Analyzer [*Auto repair*] [*Electronics*]
PVA.............. Positive Vorticity Advection [*NWS*] (FAAC)
PVA.............. Potato Virus A [*Plant pathology*]
PVA.............. Preburner Valve Actuator [*NASA*] (NASA)
PVA.............. Present Value Analysis (MCD)
PVA.............. Prison Visitors' Association (NADA)
PVA.............. Privacy Act (MCD)
PVA.............. Procedure Value Analysis (PDAA)
PVA.............. Propellant Valve Actuator (MCD)
PVA.............. Providencia [*Colombia*] [*Airport symbol*] (OAG)
PVA.............. Provident Life Accident Insurance Co. of America [*NYSE symbol*] (SPSG)
PVAC.......... Peak Volts Alternating Current (KSC)
PVAC.......... Poly(vinyl Acetate) [*Organic chemistry*]
PVAC.......... Present Value of Annual Charges
PVAE.......... Poly(vinyl Acetate) [*Organic chemistry*]
PVAHI........ Augustinian Historical Institute, Villanova University, Villanova, PA [*Library symbol Library of Congress*] (LCLS)
PVAL.......... Poly(vinyl Alcohol) [*Also, PVA*] [*Organic chemistry*]
PV & D........ Purge, Vent, and Drain (NASA)
PVAR.......... Percentage Variance [*Statistics*]
PVAS.......... Postvasectomy Specimen [*Urology*] (DAVI)
PVAS.......... Primary Voice Alert System [*NORAD*] (MCD)
PVASI........ Pulsating/Steady Visual Approach Slope Indicator [*Aviation*] (FAAC)
PVAT.......... Paravant Computer Systems, Inc. [*NASDAQ symbol*] (SAG)
PVat II........ Il Papiro Vaticano Greco II [*A publication*] (OCD)
PVAX.......... Personal Virtual Address Extension [*Computer science*] (CIST)
PVB.......... Platinol [*Cisplatin*], Vinblastine, Bleomycin [*Antineoplastic drug regimen*]
PVB.......... Platteville, WI [*Location identifier FAA*] (FAAL)
PVB.......... Poly(vinyl Butyral) [*Safety glass laminating material*] [*Organic chemistry*]
PVB.......... Portametric Voltmeter Bridge
PVB.......... Post-Vacation Blues
PVB.......... Potentionmetric Voltmeter Bridge (IAA)
PVB.......... Premature Ventricular Beat [*Cardiology*]
PVB.......... Provident Life & Accident Insurance Co. of America [*NYSE symbol*] (SPSG)
PV-B.......... Villanova University, Business and Finance Library, Villanova, PA [*Library symbol Library of Congress*] (LCLS)
PVBE.......... Polyvinyl Butyl Ether [*Organic chemistry*]
PVBr.......... Polyvinyl Bromide (PDAA)
PVBS.......... Possible Vertebral-Basilar System [*Medicine*] (BABM)
PVC.......... Pacvest Capital, Inc. [*Toronto Stock Exchange symbol*]
PVC.......... Partido de Veteranos Civiles [*Civilian Veterans' Party*] [*Dominican Republic*] [*Political party*] (PPW)
PVC.......... Peripheral Vasoconstriction [*Medicine*]
PVC.......... Periscope Viewer/Controller (MCD)
PVC.......... Permanent Virtual Circuit
PVC.......... Photovoltaic Cell (IAA)
PVC.......... Pigment Volume Concentration
PVC.......... Point of Vertical Curve
PVC.......... Polyvinyl Carbazol (IAA)
PVC.......... Poly(vinyl Chloride) [*Organic chemistry*]
PVC.......... Port Vila [*New Hebrides*] [*Seismograph station code, US Geological Survey*] (SEIS)
PVC.......... Position and Velocity Computer
PVC.......... Postvoiding Cystogram [*Medicine*] (MAE)
PVC.......... Potential Volume Change

PVC.......... Premature Ventricular Contraction [*Cardiology*]
PVC.......... Pressure Vacuum Chamber
PVC.......... Pressure Velocity Correction (AAEL)
PVC.......... Pressure Volume Compensator (KSC)
pvc.......... Price Variation Clause (DS)
PVC.......... Primary Visual Cortex [*Anatomy*]
PVC.......... Private Virtual Circuit [*Telecommunications*]
PVC.......... Prosthetic Valve (Disk) Closing [*Cardiology*]
PVC.......... Provincetown [*Massachusetts*] [*Airport symbol*] (OAG)
PVC.......... Provincetown, MA [*Location identifier FAA*] (FAAL)
PVC.......... Pulmonary Venous Congestion [*Medicine*]
PVC.......... Pulse Voltage Converter (OA)
PVC.......... PVC Container Corp. [*Associated Press*] (SAG)
PVCA.......... Polyvinylchloride Acetate [*Organic chemistry*]
PVCBMA...... PVC [*Polyvinylchloride*] Belting Manufacturers Association [*Defunct*] (EA)
PVCC.......... Permanent Virtual Channel Connection (DDC)
PVCC.......... PVC Container [*NASDAQ symbol*] (TTSB)
PVCC.......... PVC Container Corp. [*Eatontown, NJ*] [*NASDAQ symbol*] (NQ)
PVCCF........ Polyvinyl Chloride-Coated Fabric (PDAA)
PVCF.......... Phase Variable Canonical Form (PDAA)
PVCF.......... Present Value Cash Flow [*Finance*]
PVCI.......... Peripheral Vision Command Indicator
PVCN.......... Poly(vinyl Cinnamate) [*Organic chemistry*]
PVco2.......... Venous Carbon Dioxide Pressure [*Medicine*] (MAE)
PVCS.......... Portable Voice Communications System
PVCV.......... Pelargonium Vein Clearing Virus [*Plant pathology*]
PVD.......... Administradora de Fondos ADS [*NYSE symbol*] (TTSB)
PVD.......... Administradora de Fondos de Pensiones Provida SA [*NYSE symbol*] (SAG)
PVD.......... Pancreatic Ventral Duct [*Anatomy*]
PVD.......... Paravisual Director [*British*]
PVD.......... Parent Very Disturbed [*Pediatrics*] (DAVI)
PVD.......... Percussion, Vibration, and Drainage [*Medicine*] (DAVI)
PVD.......... Peripheral Vascular Disease [*Medicine*]
PVD.......... Persistent Virus Disease [*Medicine*] (WDAA)
PVD.......... Physical Vapor Deposition [*Coating technology*]
PVD.......... Physical Vulnerability Division [*Air Force*]
PVD.......... Planned Variations Demonstration [*HUD*]
PVD.......... Plan Video Display (NITA)
PVD.......... Plan View Display (GAVI)
PVD.......... Plasma Vapor Deposition (IAA)
PVD.......... Polyvinyl Dichloride (EDCT)
PVD.......... Portable Vapor Detector
PVD.......... Posterior Vitreous Detachment [*Ophthalmology*]
PVD.......... Product Verification Demonstration (MCD)
PVD.......... Protective Vehicle Division [*US Secret Service*]
PVD.......... Providence [*Rhode Island*] [*Airport symbol*] (OAG)
PVD.......... Pulmonary Vascular Disease [*Medicine*]
PVD.......... Purge, Vent, Drain System (MCD)
PVD.......... Theodore Francis Green State Airport [*FAA*] (TAG)
PvdA.......... Partij van de Arbeid [*Labor Party*] [*Netherlands Political party*] (PPE)
PvdA/PTA..... Partij van de Arbeid van Belgiee/Parti du Travail de Belgique [*Belgian Labor Party*] [*Political party*] (PPW)
PVDC.......... Polyvinyl Dichloride (EDCT)
PVDC.......... Poly(vinylidene Chloride) [*Organic chemistry*]
PVDF.......... Poly(vinylidene Difluoride) [*Organic chemistry*]
PVDF.......... Poly(vinylidene Fluoride) [*Organic chemistry*]
PVDL.......... Precision Variable Delay Line
PVDS.......... Physical Vulnerability Data Sheets (MCD)
PvdV.......... Partij van de Vrijheid [*Party of Freedom*] [*Netherlands Political party*] (PPE)
PVE.......... Perivenous Encephalomyelitis [*Neurology*] (DAVI)
PVE.......... Pine Valley Explorers [*Vancouver Stock Exchange symbol*]
PVE.......... Polyvinyl Ether [*Organic chemistry*]
PVE.......... Porvenir [*Panama*] [*Airport symbol*] (OAG)
PVE.......... Premature Ventricular Extrasystole [*Cardiology*] (AAMN)
PVE.......... Process Validation Enterprise [*Army*] (RDA)
PVE.......... Prolonged Vacuum Exposure
PVE.......... Prosthetic Valve Echogram [*Cardiology*]
PVE.......... Prosthetic Valve Endocarditis [*Medicine*]
PVE.......... Provisioning Engineer
PVE.......... Pulmonary Vascular Effect [*Physiology*]
PVED.......... Parity Violating Energy Difference [*Physical chemistry*]
PVED.......... Parity Violation Energy Difference [*Physics*]
PVED.......... Periventricular Echo Density (DB)
PVEE.......... Polyvinyl Ethyl Ether [*Organic chemistry*]
PVEN.......... Primate Vaccine Evaluation Network
PVEP.......... Pattern Visual Evoked Potential [*neurology*] (DAVI)
PVEPP........ Preliminary Value Engineering Program Plan (MCD)
PVF.......... Peak Visibility Factor
PVF.......... Pension Valuation Factor
PVF.......... Peripheral Visual Field [*Optics*]
PVF.......... Placerville, CA [*Location identifier FAA*] (FAAL)
PVF.......... Political Victory Fund [*National Rifle Association*]
PVF.......... Poly(vinyl Fluoride) [*Organic chemistry*]
PVF.......... Polyvinyl Formal [*Organic chemistry*]
PVF.......... Portal Venous Flow [*Physiology*]
PVF.......... Posterior Vitreous Face [*Ophthalmology*] (DAVI)
PVF.......... Primary Ventricular Fibrillation (CPH)
PVF2.......... Poly(vinylidene Fluoride) [*Organic chemistry*]
PVFC.......... PVF Capital [*NASDAQ symbol*] (TTSB)
PVFC.......... PVF Capital Corp. [*NASDAQ symbol*] (SAG)
PVFCap........ PVF Capital Corp. [*Associated Press*] (SAG)
PVFD.......... Pipe Ventilated, Forced Draught

PVfHi	Valley Forge Historical Society, Valley Forge, PA [*Library symbol Library of Congress*] (LCLS)
PVFHP	Public Voice for Food and Health Policy (EA)
PVFM	Polyvinyl Formal [*Organic chemistry*]
PVFO	Polyvinyl Formal (EDCT)
PVfP	Philadelphia Quartz Co., Valley Forge, PA [*Library symbol Library of Congress*] (LCLS)
PVFS	Physicians for a Violence-Free Society
PVFS	Pinnacle Virtual File System [*Pinnacle Micro, Inc.*] [*Computer science*] (PCM)
PVFS	Postviral Fatigue Syndrome [*Medicine*] (DMAA)
PVG	Periventricular Gray [*Neurobiology*]
PVG	Portsmouth, VA [*Location identifier FAA*] (FAAL)
PVG	Programmable Variations Generator [*Computer science*]
PVG	Project on the Vietnam Generation [*Later, II*] (EA)
PVG	Pulmonary Valve Gradient [*Medicine*] (DMAA)
PVGA	Processed Vegetable Growers Association [*British*] (DBA)
PVGC	Pioneer Venus Gas Chromatograph [*NASA*]
PVH	Papilloma Virus Hominis (DB)
PVH	Paraventricular Hypothalmic Nucleus [*Neuroanatomy*]
PVH	Periventricular Hemorrhage [*Medicine*]
PVH	Phillips-Van Heusen [*NYSE symbol*] (TTSB)
PVH	Phillips-Van Heusen Corp. [*NYSE symbol*] (SPSG)
PVH	Pope Valley Holding [*Vancouver Stock Exchange symbol*]
PVH	Porto Velho [*Brazil*] [*Airport symbol*] (OAG)
PVH	Pulmonary Venous Hypertension [*Medicine*]
PVHE	Polyvinyl Hexyl Ether [*Organic chemistry*]
PVHO	Pressure Vessel for Human Occupancy [*Deep-sea diving*]
PVHS	Photorefractive Volume Holographic Storage
PVI	Pacific Vocational Institute Library [*UTLAS symbol*]
PVI	Paranavai [*Brazil*] [*Airport symbol*] (AD)
PVI	Peripheral Vascular Insufficiency [*Medicine*]
PVI	Perpendicular Vegetation Index [*Botany*]
PVI	Personal Values Inventory [*Psychology*]
PVI	Picture Vocational Interest Questionnaire for Adults [*Vocational guidance test*]
PVI	Pilot-Vehicle Interface [*Search technology*]
PVI	Point of Vertical Intersection
PVI	Poly(vinyl Isobutyl Ether) [*Organic chemistry*]
PVI	Portal Vein Inflow [*Physiology*]
PVI	Premature Vulcanization Inhibitor (MCD)
PVI	Present Value Index (EBF)
PVI	Prevulcanization Inhibitor
PVI	Primary Vocational Interest [*Personnel study*]
PVI	Product Verification Inspection [*DoD*]
PVI	Programmable Video Interface
PVID	Pipe Ventilated, Induced Draught
PVIF	Present Value Interest Factor [*Finance*]
PVIFA	Present Value Interest Factor of an Annuity [*Real estate*]
PVIIX	Putnam Voyager II Cl.A [*Mutual fund ticker symbol*] (SG)
PVIR	Penn Virginia [*NASDAQ symbol*] (TTSB)
PVIR	Penn Virginia Corp. [*NASDAQ symbol*] (NQ)
PVIZT	Phenyl(vinyl)imidazolidinethione [*Organic chemistry*]
PVJ	Pauls Valley, OK [*Location identifier FAA*] (FAAL)
PVJC	Palo Verde Junior College [*California*]
PVK	Packaged Ventilation Kit [*Civil Defense*]
PVK	Penicillin V Potassium [*Medicine*] (DMAA)
PVK	Polyvinylcarbazol [*Organic chemistry*] (IEEE)
PVK	Preveza/Lefkas [*Greece*] [*Airport symbol*] (OAG)
P-VL	Panton-Valentine Leukocidin
PVL	Pavlikeny [*Bulgaria*] [*Seismograph station code, US Geological Survey*] (SEIS)
PVL	Perivalvular Leakage [*Medicine*] (DMAA)
PVL	Periventricular Leukomalacia [*Medicine*]
PVL	Permanent Vision Loss [*Medicine*] (DMAA)
PVL	Pressure to Vertical Locks
PVL	Prevail (FAAC)
PV-L	Villanova University, Law School, Villanova, PA [*Library symbol Library of Congress*] (LCLS)
PVLR	Publisher/Vendor/Library Relations [*Committee of Association for Library Collections and Technical Services*]
PVLR	Publisher/Vendor-Library Relations Committee [*ALCTS*] (AL)
PVLT	Prevalent (FAAC)
PVM	Parallel Virtual Machine [*Software package*]
PVM	Parasitophorous Vacuole Membrane [*Malaria*]
PVM	Pneumonia Virus of Mice
PVM	Poly(vinyl Methyl Ether) [*Organic chemistry*]
PVM	Posterior Ventral Microtubule [*Anatomy*]
PVM	Potato Virus M [*Plant pathology*]
PVM	Potentiometric Voltmeter
PVM	Power Vacuum Module [*Automotive engineering*]
PVM	Pressure Vessel Material
PVM	Prisons Video Magazine (WDAA)
PVM	Progressive Minerals [*Vancouver Stock Exchange symbol*]
PVM	Projection Video Monitor
PVM	Protein, Vitamins, Minerals [*J. B. Williams Co. brand of liquid protein*]
PVM	Proton Vector Magnetometer (NOAA)
PVMA	Pressure Vessel Manufacturers Association (EA)
PVMB	Potential Variation Mixed Basis [*Photovoltaic energy systems*]
PVME	Poly(vinyl Methyl Ether) [*Organic chemistry*]
PVMed	Preventative Medicine (DAVI)
PVMI	Parish Visitors of Mary Immaculate [*Roman Catholic women's religious order*]
PVMK	Polyvinyl Methyl Ketone [*Organic chemistry*] (DICI)
PVMT	Pavement [*Technical drawings*]
PVMTD	Preservation Method
PVMV	Pepper Veinal Mottle Virus [*Plant pathology*]
PVN	Paraventricular Nucleus [*Brain anatomy*]
PVN	Patient Very Nervous [*Medicine*] (WDAA)
PVN	Peters Valley [*New Jersey*] [*Seismograph station code, US Geological Survey Closed*] (SEIS)
PVN	Poly(vinyl Nitrate) [*Organic chemistry*]
PVN	Proven Resources Ltd. [*Vancouver Stock Exchange symbol*]
PVN	Providian Corp. [*Formerly, Capital Holding*] [*NYSE symbol*] (SAG)
PVN	Providian LLC [*NYSE symbol*] (SAG)
PVNGS	Palo Verde Nuclear Generating Station (NRCH)
PVNO	Polyvinylpyridine-N-Oxide [*Organic chemistry*]
PVNPrM	Providian LLC'MIPS' [*NYSE symbol*] (TTSB)
PVNPS	Post-Vietnam Psychiatric Syndrome
PVNS	Pigmented Villonodular Synovitis [*Also, PVS*] [*Medicine*]
PVNT	Prevent (AAG)
PVNTMED	Preventive Medicine [*Also, PM*]
PVO	Atlantic City, NJ [*Location identifier FAA*] (FAAL)
PVO	Bearing Supplies Ltd. [*British ICAO designator*] (FAAC)
PVO	Peripheral Vascular Occlusion [*Medicine*] (DAVI)
PVO	Phosphorus Vanadium Oxide [*Inorganic chemistry*]
PVO	Pioneer Venus Orbiter [*NASA*]
PVO	Portoviejo [*Ecuador*] [*Airport symbol*] (OAG)
PVO	Principal Veterinary Officer (ROG)
PVO	Principal Visiting Officer [*Australia*]
PVO	Private Voluntary Organization
PVO	Privileged Visiting Order (WDAA)
PVO	Project Vietnam Orphans [*British*] (DI)
PVO	Prosthetic Valve (Disk) Opening [*Cardiology*]
PVO	Protivo-Voxdushnaia Oborona [*Antiaircraft Defense*] [*Former USSR*]
PVO	Pulmonary Venous Obstruction [*Medicine*] (DMAA)
PVO	Pulmonary Venous Occlusion [*Cardiology*] (DAVI)
PvO₂	Partial Pressure of Venous Oxygen [*Hematology*] (CPH)
PVOA	Passenger Vehicle Operation Association Ltd. [*British*] (BI)
PVOA	Public Vehicle Operators' Association [*Later, CBRPT*] [*British*] (DI)
PVOD	Peripheral Vascular Occlusive Disease [*Medicine*]
PVOD	Pulmonary Veno-Occlusive Disease [*Medicine*] (STED)
PVOD	Pulmonary Venous Obstructive Disease [*Cardiology*] (DAVI)
PVOH	Polyvinyl Alcohol (EDCT)
PVOR	Precision VHF [*Very High-Frequency*] Omnidirectional Range (IAA)
PVOR	Precision VHF Omnirange
PVOUVS	Pioneer Venus Orbiter Ultraviolet Spectrometer [*NASA*]
PVOYX	Putnam Voyager Cl.A [*Mutual fund ticker symbol*] (SG)
PV-P	Past Vice-President
PVP	Penicillin V Potassium [*Biochemistry*] (MAE)
PVP	Peripheral Vein Plasma [*Cardiology*] (MAE)
PVP	Peripheral Venous Pressure [*Cardiology*]
PVP	Pipelined Vector Processor (NITA)
PVP	Plant Variety Protection
PVP	Plasma Vaporization Process
PVP	Poly(vinylpyrrolidone) [*Organic chemistry*]
PVP	Portal Venous Pressure [*Physiology*]
PVP	Preferred Vision Provider
PVP	President's Veterans Program [*Employment*]
PVP	Professional Video Productions, Inc. [*Telecommunications service*] (TSSD)
PVP	Pueblo Viejo [*Peru*] [*Seismograph station code, US Geological Survey Closed*] (SEIS)
PVP	Pulmonary Venous Pressure [*Medicine*] (STED)
PVPA	Plant Variety Protection Act [*1970*]
PVPC	Permanent Virtual Path Connection (DDC)
PVPDC	Poly(vinylpyridinium) Dichromate [*Organic chemistry*]
PVP-I	Poly(vinylpyrrolidone) Iodine Complex
PVP-I	Polyvinylpyrrolidone Povidone-Iodine (STED)
PVPMPC	Perpetual Vice-President-Member Pickwick Club [*From "The Pickwick Papers" by Charles Dickens*]
PVPO	Plant Variety Protection Office [*Department of Agriculture*]
PVPS	Plasma Varactor Phase Shifter
PVQ	Deadhorse, AK [*Location identifier FAA*] (FAAL)
PVQ	Personal Value Questionnaire [*Navy*]
PVR	Palos Verdes [*California*] [*Seismograph station code, US Geological Survey Closed*] (SEIS)
PVR	Paraventricular Nuclear Stratum (STED)
PVR	Peripheral Vascular Resistance [*Cardiology*]
PVR	Personnel Vehicle Radar (LAIN)
PVR	Phase Volume Ratio [*Physical chemistry*]
PVR	Photo Voltaic Relay (NITA)
PVR	Pontefract Volunteer Rifles [*British military*] (DMA)
PVR	Portable Vehicular Ramp [*MTMC*] (TAG)
PVR	Postvoiding Residual [*Medicine*]
PVR	Precision Voltage Reference (MDG)
PVR	Premature Voluntary Release [*British military*] (DMA)
PVR	Procedure Validation Report (AAG)
PVR	Process Variable Record
PVR	Profit/Volume Ratio
PVR	Proliferative Vitreoretinopathy [*Ophthalmology*]
PVR	Puerto Vallarta [*Mexico*] [*Airport symbol*] (OAG)
PVR	Pulmonary Vascular Resistance [*Physiology*]
PVR	Pulmonary Venous Redistribution (STED)
PVR	Pulse Volume Rate [*Physiology*]
PVR	Pulse Volume Recording [*Medicine*]
PVR	Pure and Vulcanized Rubber (IAA)
PVRC	Pressure Vessel Research Committee [*National Institute of Standards and Technology*]
PVRD	Purge, Vent, Repressurize, and Drain (NASA)

PVRI .... Pulmonary Vascular Resistance Index [*Medicine*] (DMAA)
PVRO .... Plant Variety Rights Office [*Ministry of Agriculture, Fisheries, and Food*] [*British*]
PVRO .... Pyrotechnics (NAKS)
PVRV .... Purified Vero-Cell Rabies Vaccine [*Medicine*] (DB)
PVS .... Partner Violence Screen [*Health*]
PVS .... [*The*] Pecos Valley Southern Railway Co. [*AAR code*]
PVS .... Percussion, Vibration and Suction [*Medicine*] (DAVI)
PVS .... Performance Verification System
PVS .... Peripheral Vascular Surgery [*Cardiology*] (DAVI)
PVS .... Peritoneovenous Shunt [*Medicine*]
PVS .... Periventricular Nuclear Stratum (DB)
PVS .... Persistent Vegetative State [*Medicine*]
PVS .... Personal Videoconferencing Station [*Widcom, Inc.*] [*Los Gatos, CA*] [*Telecommunications service*] (TSSD)
PVS .... Personal Videoconferencing System (NITA)
PVS .... Photovoltaic System
PVS .... Pigmented Villonodular Synovitis [*Also, PVNS*] [*Medicine*]
PVS .... Plant Vent Stack [*Nuclear energy*] (NRCH)
PVS .... Plan-View Size (PDAA)
PVS .... Plexus Visibility Score [*Medicine*]
PVS .... Polyvinylsulfonate [*Organic chemistry*]
PVS .... Ported Vacuum Switch [*Automotive engineering*]
PVS .... Postal Vehicle Service
PVS .... Post-Vietnam Syndrome
PVS .... Postviral Syndrome [*Medicine*] (WDAA)
PVS .... Potato Virus S [*Plant pathology*]
PVS .... Premature Ventricular Systole [*Cardiology*] (MAE)
PVS .... Present Value Service [*LIMRA*]
PVS .... Pressure Vacuum System
PVS .... Prime Vendor Support [*Army*]
PVS .... Principal Veterinary Surgeon [*British*]
PVS .... Priority Ventures [*Vancouver Stock Exchange symbol*]
PVS .... Private Viewdata System [*Computer science*]
PVS .... Product Verification Specification
PVS .... Professional Video Services Corp. [*Telecommunications service*] (TSSD)
PVS .... Programmed Ventricular Stimulation (DB)
PVS .... Program Validation Services [*Computer science*]
PVS .... Propellant Venting System
PVS .... Pulmonary Valve Stenosis [*Cardiology*]
PVSA .... Parkvale Financial [*NASDAQ symbol*] (TTSB)
PVSA .... Parkvale Financial Corp. [*NASDAQ symbol*] (NQ)
PVSC .... Professional Video Services Corp. [*Telecommunications service*] (TSSD)
PVSG .... Paravertebral Sympathetic Ganglion [*Neuroanatomy*]
PVSG .... Periscope Visual Scene Generation
PVSG .... Polycythemia Vera Study Group (MEDA)
PV Slg .... Polyvalent Surface Immunoglobulin [*Immunology*]
PV/ST .... Premate Verification/System Test [*NASA*] (KSC)
PVT .... Pacific Vending Technology Ltd. [*Vancouver Stock Exchange symbol*]
PVT .... Page View Terminal [*Typography*] [*Videotex terminal*]
PVT .... Parameter Variable Table (CIST)
PVT .... Paroxysmal Ventricular Tachycardia [*Medicine*]
PVT .... Par Voie Telegraphique [*By Telegraph*] [*French*]
PVT .... Performance Validation Test (CIST)
PVT .... Performance Verification Test
PVT .... Personal Verifier Terminal (DA)
PVT .... Persons Viewing Television [*Television ratings*] (NTCM)
PV/T .... Photovoltaic/Thermal
PVT .... Physical Vapor Transport [*Materials processing*]
PVT .... Pivot (MSA)
PVT .... Point of Vertical Tangent
PVT .... Polyvalent Tolerance [*Immunology*]
PVT .... Poly(vinyltoluene) [*Organic chemistry*]
PVT .... Portal Vein Thrombosis [*Physiology*]
PVT .... Position Velocity-Time
PVT .... Potato Virus T [*Plant pathology*]
PVT .... Precision Verification Team
PVT .... Precision Verification Test (MCD)
PVT .... Preflight Verification Test (NASA)
PVT .... Pressure, Volume, Temperature
PVT .... Private
Pvt .... Private (DD)
PVT .... Private Patient [*Medicine*] (DMAA)
PVT .... Probe Velocity Transducer (KSC)
PVT .... Product Verification Test (MCD)
PVT .... Prototype Validation Test (MCD)
PVT .... Provident Companies [*NYSE symbol*] (TTSB)
PVT .... Provident Companies, Inc. [*NYSE symbol*] (SAG)
PVT .... Provisioning Technician
PVT .... Pulse Video Thermography [*Nondestructive testing technique*]
PVTAP .... Pyrotechnic Verification Test [*NASA*] (NASA)
PVTAP .... Photovoltaic Transient Analysis Computer Program
PVTB .... Private Bancorp, Inc. [*NASDAQ symbol*]
PVT-C .... Production Validation Test - Contractor (MCD)
PVT-C .... Product Verification Test - Contractor (MCD)
PVT-C .... Prototype Validation Test - Contractor (MCD)
PVTE .... Private
PVT-G .... Production Validation Test - Government
PVT-G .... Prototype Validation Test - Government
PVTI .... Piping and Valve Test Insert [*Nuclear energy*] (NRCH)
PVTM .... Physical Vulnerability Technical Memorandum (MCD)
PVTOS .... Physical Vapor Transport of Organic Solutions [*Materials processing*]

PVTPr .... Provident Companies Dep Pfd [*NYSE symbol*] (TTSB)
PVTR .... Portable Video Tape Recorder
PVTS .... Pressure Vessel Thermal Shock (PDAA)
PVU .... Perimeter Ventures Ltd. [*Vancouver Stock Exchange symbol*]
PVU .... Precision Velocity Update (MCD)
PVU .... Provo [*Utah*] [*Airport symbol*] (OAG)
PVU .... Provo, UT [*Location identifier FAA*] (FAAL)
PVU .... Villanova University, Villanova, PA [*OCLC symbol*] (OCLC)
PVV .... Fondation Europeenne "Pro Venetia Viva" [*European Foundation "Pro Venetia Viva"*] (EAIO)
PVV .... Partij voor Vrijheid en Vooruitgang [*Freedom and Progress Party*] [*See also PLP*] [*Belgium*] [*Political party*] (PPW)
PVV .... Portal Venous Velocity [*Physiology*]
PVV .... Pressure, Vent, and Vacuum
PVW .... Plainview, TX [*Location identifier FAA*] (FAAL)
PVW .... Posterior Vaginal Wall [*Medicine*] (DMAA)
PVW .... Wilson College, Chambersburg, PA [*OCLC symbol*] (OCLC)
PVWA .... Planned Value of Work Accomplished
PVWA .... Plan Value of Work Accounting (MCD)
PVWS .... Planned Value of Work Scheduled (MCD)
PVX .... Phosphorous-Doped Vapor-Deposited Oxide (IAA)
PVX .... Potato Virus X [*Plant pathology*]
PVY .... Pope Vanoy [*Alaska*] [*Airport symbol*] (OAG)
PVY .... Potato Virus Y
PVY .... Providence Energy [*AMEX symbol*] (TTSB)
PVY .... Providence Energy Corp. [*AMEX symbol*] (SPSG)
PVYV .... Pittosporum Vein Yellowing Virus [*Plant pathology*]
PVZ .... Painesville, OH [*Location identifier FAA*] (FAAL)
PW .... Citizens Library, Washington, PA [*Library symbol Library of Congress*] (LCLS)
PW .... Pacific Western Airlines Ltd. [*Canada ICAO designator*] (OAG)
PW .... Packed Weight
PW .... Paine Webber, Inc. (EFIS)
PW .... Palau [*ANSI two-letter standard code*] (CNC)
PW .... Paper Wrapper (ADA)
PW .... Paraguay Watch (EA)
PW .... Parallel With (IAA)
PW .... Parkes-Weber [*Syndrome*] [*Medicine*] (DB)
PW .... Passing Window (MSA)
PW .... Password [*Computer science*]
PW .... Peere-Williams' English Chancery Reports [*1695-1736*] [*A publication*] (DLA)
PW .... Pension for Wounds [*Navy British*] (ROG)
PW .... Pericardium Wall [*Medicine*]
PW .... Per Week
pw .... Per Week (ODBW)
PW .... Petroleum Week [*A publication*]
PW .... Philadelphia & Western Railroad [*AAR code Terminated*]
pW .... Picowatt
PW .... Pilot Wire (MSA)
PW .... Pine Bark Mixed with Weblite and Peat
PW .... Pitts & W Va RR SBI [*AMEX symbol*] (TTSB)
PW .... Pittsburgh & West Virginia Railroad [*AMEX symbol*] (SPSG)
PW .... Pivoted Window (AAG)
PW .... Plain Washer (MSA)
PW .... Plantar Wart [*Orthopedics*] (DAVI)
PW .... Platoon Weapons [*British military*] (DMA)
PW .... Poets and Writers (EA)
PW .... Policewoman (WDAA)
PW .... Ports and Waterways
PW .... Position Wanted [*Employment*]
PW .... Positive Women [*An association Australia*]
PW .... Postal Wire [*Telecommunications*] (IAA)
PW .... Posterior Wall [*Medicine*]
PW .... Postwar
PW .... Potable Water [*Nuclear energy*] (NRCH)
PW .... Power
PW .... Power Wagon [*Military vehicle*]
PW .... Power Windows [*Automobile ads*]
P-W .... Prader-Willi [*Syndrome*] [*Medicine*] (AAMN)
PW .... PRECIS Word (NITA)
PW .... Presbyterian Women [*An association*] (EA)
PW .... Present Worth [*Economics*]
PW .... Pressurized Water
PW .... Prevailing Wage (MHDW)
PW .... Prime Western [*Zinc*]
PW .... Prince of Wales [*Military unit*] [*British*]
PW .... Printed Wiring (MSA)
PW .... Printing World [*A publication*] (DGA)
PW .... Prisoner of War [*Also, POW*]
PW .... Private Wire (NATG)
PW .... Process Water [*Environmental science*] (COE)
PW .... Progesterone Withdrawal [*Endocrinology*]
PW .... Program Word [*Computer science*] (IAA)
PW .... Projected Window (MSA)
PW .... Projection Welding
PW .... Proven Winners
PW .... Providence & Worcester Co. [*AAR code*]
PW .... Psychological Warfare
PW .... Public Welfare
PW .... Public Works
PWPr .... Publishers Weekly [*A publication*] (BRI)
PW .... Pulmonary Wedge [*Pressure*] (DB)
PW .... Pulpwash [*Byproduct of citrus processing*]
PW .... Pulse Width [*RADAR*]

PW..............	Purlwise [Knitting]
PW..............	Royal Warrant for Pay and Promotion [British military] (DMA)
Pw..............	Transthoracic Pressure [Medicine] (DAVI)
pW0p..........	Picowatts, Psophometrically Weighted at a Point of Zero Reference Level
PW2............	Personal Workstation 2 [Computer hardware] [Unisys Corp.] (PCM)
PWA............	Challeng'Air [France] [FAA designator] (FAAC)
PWA............	Oklahoma City, OK [Location identifier FAA] (FAAL)
PWA............	Pacific Western Airlines Ltd. [Toronto Stock Exchange symbol Vancouver Stock Exchange symbol]
PWA............	Palmer-Houston [Alaska] [Seismograph station code, US Geological Survey] (SEIS)
PWA............	Patient [or Person] with [AIDS] Acquired Immunodeficiency Syndrome [Immunology] (DAVI)
PWA............	People with AIDS Coalition (EA)
PWA............	Performance Warehouse Association (EA)
PWA............	Person with AIDS [Acquired Immune Deficiency Syndrome] [Medicine]
PWA............	Pharmaceutical Wholesalers Association [Later, DWA]
PWA............	Please Wait Awhile [Humorous interpretation for Pacific Western Airlines Corp.]
PWA............	Polish Women's Association [Australia]
PWA............	Portuguese West Africa [Angola]
PWA............	Power and Water Authority [Northern Territory, Australia]
PWA............	Pratt & Whitney Aircraft (MCD)
PWA............	Pray while Aloft [Humorous interpretation for Pacific Western Airlines Corp.]
PWA............	Printed Wire Assembly [Computer science]
PWA............	Prison Wardens Association (NADA)
PWA............	Private Eye Writers of America [An association]
PWA............	Private Write Area [NASA] (NASA)
PWA............	Probably Won't Arrive [Humorous interpretation for Pacific Western Airlines Corp.]
PWA............	Process Waste Assessment [Environmental science] (COE)
PWA............	Product Work Authorization (NASA)
PWA............	Professional Writers of America (NADA)
PWA............	Project Work Authorization
PWA............	Psychic Workers Association (NADA)
PWA............	Public Works Administration [All functions transferred to office of Federal Works Agency, 1943]
PWA............	Publishers' Weekly Announcements [Title changed to Forthcoming Books] [A publication]
PWA............	PWA Corp. [Toronto Stock Exchange symbol Vancouver Stock Exchange symbol]
PWa............	Warren Library Association and County Division, Warren, PA [Library symbol Library of Congress] (LCLS)
PWA............	Waynesburg College, Waynesburg, PA [OCLC symbol] (OCLC)
PWAA	Paint and Wallpaper Association of America [Later, NDPA] (EA)
PWAA	Polish Western Association of America (EA)
PWAA	Polish Women's Alliance of America (EA)
PWAA	Professional Women's Appraisal Association (EA)
PWAC..........	Periodical Writers Association of Canada
PWAC..........	Pratt & Whitney Aircraft (AAG)
PWAC..........	Present Worth of Annual Charges [Pronounced "p-wack"] [Bell System]
PWacD.........	David Library of the American Revolution, Washington Crossing, PA [Library symbol Library of Congress] (LCLS)
PWAF..........	Polish Workers' Aid Fund [Defunct] (EA)
PWAFRR.......	Present Worth of All Future Revenue Requirements [Finance]
PWAK..........	Wake Island Air Force Base [Wake Island] [ICAO location identifier] (ICLI)
PWal...........	Helen Kate Furness Free Library, Wallingford, PA [Library symbol Library of Congress] (LCLS)
PWalPH.......	Pendle Hill Library, Wallingford, PA [Library symbol Library of Congress] (LCLS)
PW & B	Philadelphia, Wilmington & Baltimore Railroad
PWAP	Public Works of Art Projects [New Deal]
PWARC........	Person With AIDS-Related Complex (CPH)
PWarN	United States Naval Air Development Center, Technical Information Library, Warminster, PA [Library symbol] [Library of Congress] (LCLS)
PWASA........	Poliomyelitis Welfare Association of South Australia
PWAV	Powerwave Technologies, Inc. [NASDAQ symbol] (SAG)
PWayC........	Waynesburg College, Waynesburg, PA [Library symbol Library of Congress] (LCLS)
PWB............	Directorate of Post War Building [British] (DAS)
PWb............	Osterhout Free Library, Wilkes-Barre, PA [Library symbol Library of Congress] (LCLS)
PWB............	Partial Weight Bearing [Medicine]
PWB............	Pencil Writing on Back [Deltiology]
PWB............	Permanent Water Ballast [DS]
PWB............	Pilot Weather Briefing [Aviation] (FAAC)
PWB............	Printed Wire Board (NAKS)
PWB............	Printed Wiring Board (DOMA)
PWB............	Private Wine Buyers' Society [British] (BI)
PWB............	Programmer's Workbench [Microsoft, Inc.] (PCM)
PWB............	Psychological Warfare Branch [Allied Forces] [World War II]
PWB............	Pulling Whaleboat
PWBA	Pension and Welfare Benefits Administration [Department of Labor]
PWBA	Plane-Wave Born Approximation
PWBA	Printed Wiring Board Assembly (MCD)
PWBA	Professional Women Bowlers Association [Later, LPBT] (EA)
PWBC	PennFirst Bancorp [NASDAQ symbol] (SAG)
PWBC	Peripheral White Blood Cells [Medicine]
PWbH	Wyoming Historical and Geological Society, Wilkes-Barre, PA [Library symbol Library of Congress]
PWBI	Posterior Wall of Bronchus Intermedius [Anatomy]
PWbK..........	King's College, Wilkes-Barre, PA [Library symbol Library of Congress] (LCLS)
PWBK	Pennwood Savings Bank [NASDAQ symbol] (SAG)
PWB/MM	Programmer's Workbench Memorandum Macros [Computer science] (MHDI)
PWBP	Pension and Welfare Benefit Programs [Labor-Management Services Administration]
PWBRT	Prophylactic Whole Brain Radiation Therapy [Medicine] (DMAA)
PWBS	Program Work Breakdown Structure (NASA)
PWbW	Wilkes College, Wilkes-Barre, PA [Library symbol Library of Congress] (LCLS)
PWC............	Chester County District Library Center, Exton, PA [OCLC symbol] (OCLC)
PWC............	Pacific War Council [World War II]
PWC............	Parents Who Care [An association] (NADA)
PWC............	Paws with a Cause [An association] (EA)
PWC............	Peak Work Capacity
PWC............	Pentecostal World Conference [Emmetten, Switzerland] (EA)
PWC............	Personal Watercraft
PWC............	Pfeifer-Weber-Christian [Syndrome] [Medicine] (DB)
PWC............	Physical Work Capacity
PWC............	Physicians Who Care (EA)
PWC............	Pilgrim Wrestling Conference (PSS)
PWC............	Poland Watch Center [Defunct] (EA)
PWC............	Portable Windows Change [Computer science]
PWC............	Port Workers' Committee [British]
PWC............	Pratt & Whitney Canada, Inc. [ICAO designator] (FAAC)
PWC............	PricewaterhouseCoopers
PWC............	Primary Work Code (SSD)
PWC............	Printed Wiring Cards [Telecommunications]
PWC............	Prisoner of War Cage
PWC............	Prisoner of War Camp
PWC............	Prisoner of War Command
PWC............	Prisoner of War Compound
PWC............	Process Water Cooler (MSA)
PWC............	Professional Women in Construction (EA)
PWC............	Professional Women's Caucus (EA)
PWC............	Provincial Warning Center [NATO] (NATG)
PWC............	Public Works Canada [See also TPC]
PWC............	Public Works Center [Navy]
PWC............	Pulse-Width Coded
PWCA	Pure White Cell Aplasia [Medicine] (DMAA)
PWCACE	Public Works Center Activity Civil Engineer [Navy] (DNAB)
PWcC..........	Chester County District Library Center, West Chester, PA [Library symbol Library of Congress] (LCLS)
PWCC	Political Warfare Coordination Committee [London] [World War II]
PWCCA	Pembroke Welsh Corgi Club of America (EA)
PWCDET	Public Works Center Detachment [Navy] (DNAB)
PWCEN	Public Works Center [Navy]
PWcHi	Chester County Historical Society, West Chester, PA [Library symbol Library of Congress] (LCLS)
PWCI	Price Warehouse Coopers & Lybrand
PW/CI/DET....	Prisoner of War/Civilian Internees/Detainees (MCD)
PWCLANT	Public Works Center, Atlantic [Navy]
PWCMIS	Public Works Center Management Information System [Navy] (DNAB)
PWCMS	Public Works Center Management System [Navy]
PWCOU	Public Workers and Constructional Operatives' Union [British]
PWCPAC	Public Works Center, Pacific [Navy]
PWCR	Prader-Willi Chromosome Region [Medicine] (DMAA)
PWcS...........	West Chester State College, West Chester, PA [Library symbol Library of Congress] (LCLS)
PwCtIT........	Power Control Technologies, Inc. [Associated Press] (SAG)
PWD............	Pan World Ventures, Inc. [Vancouver Stock Exchange symbol]
PWD............	Participative Work Design
PWD............	People with Disabilities
PWD............	Permanent Wants Directory [A publication]
PWD............	Petroleum Warfare Department [Ministry of Fuel and Power] [British World War II]
PWD............	Plentywood, MT [Location identifier FAA] (FAAL)
PWD............	Plywood [Technical drawings]
PWD............	Post-Write Disturb (IAA)
PWD............	Powder (KSC)
PWD............	Power Distributor (KSC)
PWD............	Powered (IAA)
PWD............	Process Word (IAA)
PWD............	Procurement Work Directive [Army] (AABC)
PWD............	Proximity Warning Device (MCD)
PWD............	Psychological Warfare Division [SHAEF] [World War II]
PWD............	Public Works Department (NADA)
PWDC..........	Pulse-Width Detector [or Discriminator] [RADAR]
PWDC..........	Philippine War Damage Commission [Post-World War II]
PWDCA	Portuguese Water Dog Club of America (EA)
PWDEPT	Public Works Department [Navy]
PWDG	Prince of Wales' Dragoon Guards [Military British] (ROG)
PWDI	Program with Developing Institutions (EA)
PWDMS	Public Works Developmental Management System [Navy]
PWDP	Powder Passing
PWDR	Partial Wave Dispersing Relation
pwdr	Powder [Pharmacy] (DAVI)
PWDRD........	Powdered [Freight]
PWDS	Postweaning Diarrhea Syndrome [Medicine] (DMAA)

PWDS .... Protected Wireline Distribution System (CET)
PWDY .... PaineWebber Group [Associated Press] (SAG)
PWDY496 .... PaineWebber Group [Associated Press] (SAG)
PWE .... Pauli-Weisskopf Equation [Physics]
PWE .... Pawnee City, NE [Location identifier FAA] (FAAL)
PWE .... Political Warfare Executive [World War II]
PWE .... Posterior Wall Excursion [Anatomy] (DMAA)
PWE .... Present Worth Expenditures [Telecommunications] (TEL)
PWE .... Pre-Warfare Executive (WDAA)
PWE .... Primary Weapons and Equipment
PWE .... Prisoner of War Enclosure
PWE .... Pulse-Width Encoder
PWEA.......... Printed Wiring and Electronic Assemblies [NASA]
PWEA.......... Public Works Employment Act (AAGC)
PW/ED .... Pratt & Whitney Engineering Division
PWEDA........ Public Works and Economic Development Act
PWEDA........ Public Works and Economic Development Association (EA)
PWEHC........ Public Works Emergency Housing Corp. [New Deal]
PWES.......... Price Waterhouse Energy Solutions
PWesAC ...... Community College of Allegheny County, South Campus, West Mifflin, PA [Library symbol Library of Congress] (LCLS)
PWesD........ Dresser Industries, Inc., Harbison-Walker Refractories Co., West Mifflin, PA [Library symbol Library of Congress] (LCLS)
PWF............ Pacific Whale Foundation (EA)
PWF............ Package Will Follow [Birthday-card notation]
PWF............ Pax World Foundation (EA)
PWF............ Permanent Wood Foundation [Building term]
PWF............ Personnel Working File (DOMA)
PWF............ Photoelectric Work Function
PWF............ Pop Warner Football (EA)
PWF............ Portable Windows Format [Computer science]
PWF............ Power Financial Corp. [Toronto Stock Exchange symbol]
PWF............ Present Worth Factor [Real estate]
PWF............ Private Wagon Federation [British] (DBA)
PWF............ Propellant Weight Fraction (NATG)
PWF............ Pulse Wave Form
PWF............ Pure Water Flux [Engineering]
PWFA.......... Papermakers' Woven Felt Association (DGA)
PWFG.......... Primary Waveform Generator [Telecommunications] (TEL)
PWFN .... Projection Weld Flange Nut
PWFR.......... Plantwide Failure Reporting (MCD)
PWFS.......... Price Waterhouse Financial Solutions
PWG............ Panzerwagen [Tank] [German military - World War II]
PWG .... Pathology Work Group (GNE)
PWG .... Permanent Working Group (NATG)
PWG .... Photoelectric Web Guide
PWG .... Plastic Wire Guide
PWG .... Powergem Resources Corp. [Vancouver Stock Exchange symbol]
PWG .... Powergen PLC [NYSE symbol] (SAG)
PWG .... PowerGen PLC ADS [NYSE symbol] (TTSB)
PWG C........ PWG Capital Trust I [Associated Press] (SAG)
PWGM .... Process Water Gamma Monitor [Environmental science] (COE)
PwgnADS..... Powergan PLC [Associated Press] (SAG)
PwgnIntr...... Powergan PLC [Associated Press] (SAG)
PWG.PP....... PowerGen PLC Interim ADS [NYSE symbol] (TTSB)
PWGSC .... Public Works and Government Services Canada (ACII)
PWH .... Pellet Warhead
PWH .... Poliokeawe [Pali] [Hawaii] [Seismograph station code, US Geological Survey] (SEIS)
PWH .... Precision Welding-Head
PWH .... Proprietor of Copyright on a Work Made for Hire
PWH .... Prototype Wave Height
PWHA.......... Plutonium Waste Handling Area [Nuclear energy] (NRCH)
Pwhe........... Person Who Has Everything [Lifestyle classification]
PWhi........... Whitehall Township Public Library, Whitehall, PA [Library symbol Library of Congress] (LCLS)
PWHK.......... PaineWebber Group, Inc. [Associated Press] (SAG)
PWHQ.......... Peace War Headquarters (NATG)
PWHS.......... Public Works Historical Society (EA)
PWHT.......... Post-Weld Heat Treatment [Nuclear energy] (NRCH)
PWI............. Alas Panamenas SA [Panama] [ICAO designator] (FAAC)
PWI............. PACOM [Pacific Command] Warning Intelligence [Army]
PWI............. Permanent Ware Institute [Defunct] (EA)
PWI............. Permanent Way Institution [Fleet, Hampshire, England] (EAIO)
PWI............. Perry Williams, Inc. (EFIS)
PWI............. Physiological Workload Index [Aviation]
PWI............. Piecewise-Linear (IAA)
PWI............. Pilot Warning Indicator [or Instrument] [Aviation]
PWI............. Plasma Wave Instrument [Physics]
PWI............. Platoon Weapons Instructor [British military] (DMA)
PWI............. Posterior Wall Infarct [Anatomy] (MAE)
PWI............. Potable Water Intake
PWI............. Precedence Work Item
PWI............. Prince of Wales' Island (ROG)
PWI............. Prisoner of War Interrogation
PWI............. Projects with Industry Program [Department of Education]
PWI............. Proximity Warning Indicator [or Instrument] [Aviation]
PWI............. Public Windows Interface [Computer science] (PCM)
PWIA........... Personal Watercraft Industry Association (EA)
PWIB........... Prisoner of War Information Bureau [Post-World War II]
PWIC........... Prisoner of War Information Center (DOMA)
PWIF........... Plantation Workers' International Federation [Later, IFPAAW]
PWIFC......... Porter Wagoner International Fan Club [Defunct] (EA)
PWIN........... Prototype WWMCCS Intercomputer Network (MCD)
PWINO......... Precipitation Identifier Information Not Available [NWS] (FAAC)

PWIR .... Palmar Wireless [NASDAQ symbol] (SAG)
PWIR .... Palmer Wireless 'A' [NASDAQ symbol] (TTSB)
PWIS .... Prisoner of War Information System (DOMA)
PWJ .... Paine Webber Group [NYSE symbol] (TTSB)
PWJ .... PaineWebber Group, Inc. [NYSE symbol] (SPSG)
PWJ .... Pulsating Water-Jet Lavager [Medicine] (RDA)
PWJ .... PWG Capital Trust I [NYSE symbol] (SAG)
PWJC .... Paine, Webber, Jackson & Curtis [Later, Paine Webber, Inc.]
PWK............ Chicago/Wheeling, IL [Location identifier FAA] (FAAL)
PWK............ Prestwick BAE [British ICAO designator] (FAAC)
PWL............ Petroleum and Water Logistics [Army] (RDA)
PWL............ Piecewise-Linear
PWL............ Piecework Linear
PWL............ Port Wells [Alaska] [Seismograph station code, US Geological Survey] (SEIS)
PWL............ Poughkeepsie, NY [Location identifier FAA] (FAAL)
PWL............ Powell Air Ltd. [Canada ICAO designator] (FAAC)
PWL............ Power Level
PWL............ Printed Wiring Laboratory (MCD)
PWLB........... Public Works Loan Board [British]
PWLV........... Posterior Wall of Left Ventricle [Anatomy] (AAMN)
PWM............ Parentship for World Mission (NADA)
PWM............ Planar Wing Module (MCD)
PWM............ Plated Wire Memory
PWM............ Pokeweed Mitogen [Genetics]
PWM............ Portable Welding Machine
PWM............ Portland [Maine] [Airport symbol] (OAG)
PWM............ Portland, ME [Location identifier FAA] (FAAL)
PWM............ Printed Wiring Master
PWM............ Pulse Width Modulation [Electronic instrumentation]
PWM............ Pulse-Width Multiplier (IEEE)
PWMA.......... Portable Wear Metal Analyzer [Air Force]
PWMAF........ Pulse-Width Modulated Audio Frequency (IAA)
PWMD.......... Printed Wiring Master Drawing (NASA)
PWM-FM .... Pulse-Width Modulation - Frequency Modulation [RADAR]
PWmL.......... Lycoming College, Williamsport, PA [Library symbol Library of Congress] (LCLS)
PWML........... Patchy White Matter Lesion [Medicine]
PWMM.......... Polly Woodside Maritime Museum [Australia]
PWmP .... James V. Brown Library of Williamsport and Lycoming County, Williamsport, PA [Library symbol Library of Congress] (LCLS)
PWMR.......... Periventricular White-Matter Radiolucency [Medicine]
P Wms......... Peere-Williams' English Chancery Reports [1695-1736] [A publication] (DLA)
PWMS.......... Public Works Management System [Navy]
PWMSCM .... Pokeweed Mitogen-Stimulated Spleen-Cell-Conditioned Medium [For growing cells]
P Wms (Eng)... Peere-Williams' English Chancery Reports [1695-1736] [A publication] (DLA)
PWN .... Cash America International, Inc. [NYSE symbol] (SPSG)
PWN .... Cash Amer Intl [NYSE symbol] (TTSB)
PWN .... Patna Weekly Notes [India] [A publication] (ILCA)
PWN .... Pinewood Nematode
PWN .... Pulsar Wind Nebula [Astronomy]
PWN .... West Plains, MO [Location identifier FAA] (FAAL)
PWNA .... Power Washers of North America (NTPA)
PWNBKR...... Pawnbroker
PWNDA........ Provincial Wholesale Newspaper Distributors' Association [British] (BI)
PW-NWLZOA... Pioneer Women/Na'amat, the Women's Labor Zionist Organization of America [Later, MWWV] (EA)
PWO .... Parliamentarians for World Order (EA)
PWO .... Performance Work Standard (AAGC)
PWO .... Plane-Wave Orbital [Physics]
PWO .... Prince of Wales' Own [Military unit] [British]
PWO .... Principal Welfare Officer [Navy British]
PWO .... Principle Warfare Officer [British]
PWO .... Production Work Order (MCD)
PWO .... Public Works Officer [Navy]
PWOC.......... Protestant Women of the Chapel
PWOP.......... Pregnant without Permission [Military World War II]
PWOR.......... Prince of Wales' Own Royal [Military unit] [British]
PWP............. Barrio Florida [Puerto Rico] [Seismograph station code, US Geological Survey] (SEIS)
PWP............. PaineWebber Group [NYSE symbol] (SAG)
PWP............. Parents without Partners (EA)
PWP............. Particles per Wafer Pass (AAEL)
PWP............. Past Worthy Patriarch
PWP............. Peasants' and Workers' Party [India] [Political party] (PPW)
PWP............. Personal Word Processor (WDMC)
PWP............. Picowatt Power (CET)
PWP............. Picowatt Psophometric (IAA)
pWp............. Picowatts, Psophometrically Weighted
PWP............. Planning Work Package (MCD)
PWP............. Plasticized White Phosphorus
PWP............. Plastic Waste Processor (DWSG)
PWP............. Polish Workers' Party
PWP............. Portable Word Processor
PWP............. Postwar Planning [World War II]
PWP............. Prelaunch Wind Profile (SAA)
PWP............. Preliminary Working Paper (AAGC)
P-W-P.......... Product-with-Purchase (WDMC)
p-w-p.......... Product-with-Purchase (WDMC)
PWP............. Professional Women Photographers (EA)
PWP............. Public Watering Place (ADA)

PWP............ Public Works Planning (GFGA)
PWP............ Pulmonary Wedge Pressure [Medicine]
PWP............ Purchase-with-Purchase [Sales promotion]
PWPHIT....... PaineWebber Premier High Income Trust [Associated Press] (SAG)
PWPIM .... PaineWebber Premier Insured Municipal Income Fund [Associated Press] (SAG)
PWpM.......... Merck, Sharp & Dohme [Later, Merck & Co., Inc.] Research Laboratories, Library Services, West Point, PA [Library symbol Library of Congress] (LCLS)
PWPP .... Professionwide Pension Plan [American Chemical Society]
PWPS .... Pure Water Preservation Society [British]
PWQ .... Petersburg, WV [Location identifier FAA] (FAAL)
PWQ .... Preferred and Well Qualified [Candidate designation]
PWQM .... Protection Water Quality Management
PWR .... Peak Watt Rating [Electrical engineering]
PWR .... Pilot Wire Regulator
PWR .... Point of Weapon Release [Military]
PWR .... Police War Reserve [British] (DAS)
PWR .... Port Walter, AK [Location identifier FAA] (FAAL)
PWR .... Power (KSC)
pwr .... Power (IDOE)
PWR .... Power Explorations, Inc. [Toronto Stock Exchange symbol]
PWR .... Power On [Modem status information light] [Computer science] (IGQR)
PWR .... Power Wirewound Resistor
PWR .... Pressurized-Water Reactor [Nuclear energy]
PWR .... Prevailing Wage Rate [US Employment Service] [Department of Labor]
PWR .... Prince of Wales' Royal [Military unit] [British]
PWR .... Program Work Request
PWR .... Program Work Requirement (MCD)
PWR .... Project Work Review [Army] (AFIT)
PWR .... Publication Work Request (MCD)
PWR .... Public Worship Regulation Act [1874] [British] (ROG)
PWR .... Punjab Weekly Reporter [India] [A publication] (ILCA)
PWRCB........ President's War Relief Control Board [World War II]
PWRDEVELENGR... Power Development Engineer (IAA)
PWRE .... Prepositioned War Reserve Equipment [Army]
PWREMR ..... Prepositioned War Reserve Material Requirements [Navy] (MCD)
PWREMS ..... Prepositioned War Reserve Material Stocks [Navy] (MCD)
PWR-FLECHT... Pressurized Water Ractor - Full Length Emergency Cooling Heat Transfer [Nuclear energy] (PDAA)
PWRH.......... Powerhouse (MSA)
PwrhsRs ...... Powerhouse Resources, Inc. [Associated Press] (SAG)
PWRIMC ...... Prince of Wales Royal Indian Military College [British military] (DMA)
PWRM .... Prepositioned War Reserve Materiel (MCD)
PWRMON .... Power Monitor (IAA)
PWRMR .... Prepositioned War Reserve Materiel Requirement (NVT)
PWRMRB..... Prepositioned War Reserve Materiel Requirement Balance (AFIT)
PWRMS .... Prepositioned War Reserve Materiel Stock (NVT)
PWRNO........ Power Failure (FAAC)
PWRO .... Pending Work Release Order (MCD)
PWROK........ Power Restored (FAAC)
PWRPLT ...... Power Plant (IAA)
PWRPNL ...... Power Panel (IAA)
PWRR.......... Prepositioned War Reserve Requirements [Army] (NG)
PWRR.......... Providence and Worcester Railroad Co. [NASDAQ symbol] (NQ)
PWRR.......... Providence & Worcester RR [NASDAQ symbol] (TTSB)
PWRR.......... Providence Worcester Railroad Co. [NASDAQ symbol] (SAG)
PWRR-MF.... Prepositioned War Reserve Requirements for Medical Facilities [Army] (AABC)
PWRS .... Prepositioned War Reserve Stocks [Army]
PWRS .... Programmable Weapons Release System (IEEE)
PWRSEMICOND... Power Semiconductor (IAA)
PWRS-MF.... Prepositioned War Reserve Stocks for Medical Facilities [Army] (AABC)
PWRSUP...... Power Supply (IAA)
PWRU.......... Power Unit (IAA)
PWS............ Paddle-Wheel Steamer [Shipping] (ROG)
PWS............ Parallel Working System
PWS............ Pattern Weavers' Society [A union] [British] (DCTA)
PWS............ Pax World Service (EA)
PWS............ Performance Work Standard
PWS............ Performance Work Statement [DoD]
PWS............ Peter Warlock Society (EA)
PWS............ Petrified Wood Society (EA)
PWS............ Petroleum and Water Systems [Army] (RDA)
PWS............ Phoenix Weapons System
PWS............ Plane-Wave Spectrum
PWS............ Plasma Wave Guide Switch (IAA)
PWS............ Plasma Wave Source [Physics]
PWS............ Plasma Wave System [Instrumentation]
PWS............ Port-Wine Stain
PWS............ Potable Water System (KSC)
PWS............ Prader-Willi Syndrome Association (EA)
PWS............ Predicted Wave Signaling
PWS............ Preliminary Work Statement (MCD)
PWS............ Pressure Wave Supercharger [Automotive engineering]
PWS............ Pricing Work Statement (MCD)
PWS............ Prisoners' Wives' Service (WDAA)
PWS............ Private Wire Service
PWS............ Private Wire System (AAG)
PWS............ Programmer Work Station
PWS............ Program Work Statement (MCD)
PWS............ Project Work Schedule [Computer science]

PWS............ Proximity Warning System (IAA)
PWS............ Psychological Warfare Service [Allied Forces] [World War II]
PWS............ Psychological Warfare Society [Birmingham, England] (EA)
PWS............ Public Water Supply (PA)
PWS............ Public Water System
PWS............ Pulau-Weh [Sumatra] [Seismograph station code, US Geological Survey Closed] (SEIS)
PWSA .... Pheasant and Waterfowl Society of Australia
PWSA .... Ports and Waterways Safety Act (GFGA)
PWSA .... Professional Women Singers Association (EA)
PWSC .... Post-War Scientific Collaboration [British]
PWSCC .... Prince William Sound Community College [Alaska]
PWSO .... Pilot Weapons System Officer
PWSPMid .... PaineWebber Group, Inc. [Associated Press] (SAG)
PWSPP .... Payne Whitney Suicide Prevention Program [New York Hospital] (EA)
PWSS .... Port War Signal Station [British military] (DMA)
PWSS .... Public Water Supply System (GFGA)
PWST .... Protected Water Storage Tank [Nuclear energy] (NRCH)
PWSWA ...... Processed Woodchip, Sawdust, and Woodflour Association [British] (BI)
PWT............ Bremerton, WA [Location identifier FAA] (FAAL)
PWT............ Pacific War Time (IAA)
PWT............ Pacific Winter Time (IAA)
PWT............ Penn West Petroleum Ltd. [Toronto Stock Exchange symbol]
PWT............ Pennyweight
PWT............ Picture World Test [Psychology]
PWT............ Professional Walleye Trail
PWT............ Progressive Wave Tube
PWT............ Propulsion Wind Tunnel Facility [Arnold Air Force Base, TN] [Air Force]
PWTC......... Public Works Training Center [Navy]
PWTC......... Public Works Transportation Center (MCD)
PWTCVA ..... Procurement of Weapons and Tracked Combat Vehicles, Army (AABC)
PWTF......... Polish Workers Task Force (EA)
PWTN......... Power Train (AABC)
PWTO......... Principal Wireless Telegraphy Officer (IAA)
PWTP......... Process Waste Treatment Plant [Engineering]
PWTR......... Pewter (MSA)
PWTR......... Philadelphia War Tax Resistance (EA)
PWTVA .... Procurement of Weapons and Tracked Vehicles, Army (AABC)
PWU........... Pacific Western University [Hawaii]
PWU........... Political World Union (EA)
PWUSA....... Project Wolf USA (EA)
PWUSD....... PaineWebber Group, Inc. [Associated Press] (SAG)
PWUSJ .... PaineWebber Group [Associated Press] (SAG)
PWV........... Passionfruit Woodiness Virus [Plant pathology]
PWV........... Pittsburgh & West Virginia Railroad [AAR code]
PWV........... Polistes Wasp Venom [Laboratory science] (DAVI)
PWV........... Precipitable Water Vapor
PWV........... Pressure Wave Velocity [Cardiology]
PWV........... Pretoria-Witwatersrand [South Africa]
PWV........... Prince of Wales' Volunteers [Military unit] [British]
PWV........... Pulse Wave Velocity
PWVA .... Pacific War Veterans of America [Defunct]
PWVS .... Prince of Wales' Volunteer Service [British]
PWW .... Plannar Wing Weapon (MCD)
PWW .... Point Weather Warning
PWW .... Project West Wing (MCD)
PWW .... Washington and Jefferson College, Washington, PA [Library symbol Library of Congress] (LCLS)
PWWC .... Post War World Council [Defunct] (EA)
PW-WLZOA... Pioneer Women, the Women's Labor Zionist Organization of America [Later, PW-MWLZOA] (EA)
PWWR .... Power Wirewound Resistor
PWX........... Permanent Working Staff [NATO] (NATG)
PWX........... Prisoners of War Executive [Branch of SHAEF] [World War II]
PWY........... PaineWebber Group [AMEX symbol] (SAG)
PX............. Air Niugini [Air New Guinea] [ICAO designator] (AD)
PX............. Pancreatectomized [Medicine]
Px............. Past History (DAVI)
PX............. Pedro Ximenez [A blending sherry]
PX............. Peroxidase [Also, PO, POD] [An enzyme]
PX............. Physical Examination
PX............. Piroxicam [Anti-inflammatory]
Px............. Plantwax [A fungicide]
PX............. Please Exchange
PX............. Pneumothorax [Medicine]
PX............. Post Exchange [Military]
PX............. Praxair, Inc. [NYSE symbol] (SPSG)
PX............. Private Examination (WDAA)
PX............. Private Exchange
PX............. Production Executive of the War Cabinet [World War II]
Px............. Prognosis [Medicine] (WGA)
PX............. Pyroxene [Also, PYX] [A mineral]
PXA .... Parana [Brazil] [Airport symbol] (AD)
PXA .... Place Index in Address (SAA)
PXA .... Pulsed Xenon Arc
PXC........... Proximity Computer (MCD)
PXCMD .... Phoenix Contract Management District (SAA)
PXD .... Pioneer Natural Resources [NYSE symbol] [Formerly, Parker & Parsley Petrol] (SG)
PXD .... Place Index in Decrement
PXD .... Post-Exercise Discussion [NATO] (NATG)

PXD .... Price Ex-Dividend [*Stock market*]
PXE .... Pacific Exchange, Inc.
PXE .... Pacific Research & Engineering Corp. [*AMEX symbol*] (SAG)
PXE .... Phenylxylylethane [*Organic chemistry*]
PXE .... Poly(xylenyl ether) [*Organic chemistry*]
PXE .... Provinces X Explorations [*Vancouver Stock Exchange symbol*]
PXE .... Pseudoxanthoma Elasticum [*Medicine*]
PXE.U .... Pacific Res & Engineering Unit [*AMEX symbol*] (TTSB)
PXF .... Primex Forest Industries Ltd. [*Toronto Stock Exchange symbol Vancouver Stock Exchange symbol*]
PXG .... Phoenix Gold Mines Ltd. [*Toronto Stock Exchange symbol*]
PXH .... Pacific Express Holdings Ltd. [*New Zealand*] [*ICAO designator*] (FAAC)
PXI .... Pax Christi International (EA)
PXI .... Pulsed Xenon Illuminator
PxIMP .... Peroxisomal Integral Membrane Protein [*Biochemistry*]
PX In .... Arrival Time [*Aviation*]
PXL .... Poney Explorations Ltd. [*Vancouver Stock Exchange symbol*]
PXL .... Pulsed Xenon LASER
Pxl .... Pyridoxal [*Also, PL*] [*Biochemistry*]
PXLS .... Pulsed Xenon Light Source
PXLSS .... Pulsed Xenon Light Source System
PXM .... Projection X-Ray Microscope
Pxm .... Pyridoxamine [*Also, PM*] [*Biochemistry*]
PX Me .... Report My Arrival or Departure [*Aviation slang*]
PXN .... Panoche, CA [*Location identifier FAA*] (FAAL)
PXN .... Paxson Communications 'A' [*AMEX symbol*] (TTSB)
PXN .... Paxson Communications Corp. [*AMEX symbol*] (SAG)
Pxn .... Pyridoxine [*Also, PN*] [*Biochemistry*]
PXO .... Porto Santo [*Portugal*] [*Airport symbol*] (OAG)
PXO .... Prospective Executive Officer
PX Out .... Takeoff Time [*Aviation*]
PXP .... Packet Exchange Protocol [*Computer science*] (TNIG)
PXP .... Phoenix Investment Partners [*NYSE symbol*] [*Formerly, Phoenix Duff & Phelps*]
PXPPL .... Pull and Push Plate
PXR .... Paxar Corp. [*NYSE symbol*] (SAG)
PXR .... Plus-X-Reversal
PXR .... Praxis Resources Ltd. [*Vancouver Stock Exchange symbol*]
PXRD .... Powder X-Ray Diffraction
PXRE .... Phoenix Re Corp. [*NASDAQ symbol*] (NQ)
PXRE .... PXRE Corp. [*NASDAQ symbol*] (TTSB)
PXRE Cp ...... PXRE Corp. [*Associated Press*] (SAG)
PXS .... Plexus Resources Corp. [*Toronto Stock Exchange symbol*]
PXS .... Pulsed Xenon System
PXSC .... Proximity Sensing Computer (MCD)
PXSS .... Pulsed Xenon Solar Simulator
PXSTR .... Phototransistor (IEEE)
PXT .... Patuxent River, MD [*Location identifier FAA*] (FAAL)
PXT .... Pinxit [*He, or She, Painted It*] [*Latin*]
PXT .... Praxis Technologies Corp. [*Toronto Stock Exchange symbol*]
PXU .... Pleiku [*South Vietnam*] [*Airport symbol*] (AD)
PXU .... Portable X-Ray Unit
PXV .... Evansville, IN [*Location identifier FAA*] (FAAL)
PXV .... Pedro Ximenez Viejo [*A blending sherry*]
PXX .... Aroostook Aviation, Inc. [*FAA designator*] (FAAC)
PXX .... Porto Alfonso [*Brazil*] [*Airport symbol*] (AD)
PXXI .... Prophet 21, Inc. [*NASDAQ symbol*] (SAG)
PXY .... Milwaukee, WI [*Location identifier FAA*] (FAAL)
Pxy .... Pyridoxyl [*Biochemistry*]
PY .... Martin Memorial [*York City and County*] Library, York, PA [*Library symbol Library of Congress*] (LCLS)
PY .... Pack Year [*Cigarettes*] (MEDA)
PY .... Pack Years [*of cigarette consumption*] (DAVI)
PY .... Paraguay [*ANSI two-letter standard code*] (CNC)
py .... Paraguay [*IYRU nationality code*] [*MARC country of publication code Library of Congress*] (LCCP)
PY .... Patrol Vessel, Yacht [*Navy symbol*]
PY .... Pechiney ADS [*NYSE symbol*] (TTSB)
PY .... Pembroke Yeomanry [*British military*] (DMA)
PY .... Person Years [*After radiation exposure*]
p/y .... Per Year (WDAA)
Py .... Phosphopyridoxal [*Medicine*] (DMAA)
PY .... Physical Year
P/Y .... Pitch or Yaw
Py .... Polyoma Virus [*Medicine*] (DMAA)
PY .... Polysar Ltd. [*Toronto Stock Exchange symbol Vancouver Stock Exchange symbol*]
PY .... Prior Year (AABC)
PY .... Program Year (AFM)
py .... Program Year (NAKS)
PY .... Project Yedid [*Defunct*] (EA)
PY .... Proto Yiddish (BJA)
PY .... Publication Year [*Online database field identifier*]
Py .... Pyrene [*Organic chemistry*] (AAMN)
Py .... Pyridine [*Organic chemistry*]
Py .... Pyrimidine (DOG)
Py .... Pyrogen [*Medicine*]
PY .... Pyrometer (IEEE)
PY .... Pyronin Y [*A biological dye*]
PY .... Pythium [*A fungus*]
PY .... Spray [*ICAO*] (FAAC)
PY .... Surinam Airways [*ICAO designator*] (AD)
PYA .... Partners Preferred Yield [*AMEX symbol*] (SAG)
PYA .... Partners Preferred Yld'A' [*AMEX symbol*] (TTSB)

PYA .... Penn Yan, NY [*Location identifier FAA*] (FAAL)
PYA .... Pioneer Youth of America (EA)
PYA .... Pittsburgh, Youngstown & Ashland Railway Co. (IIA)
PYA .... Plan, Year, and Age [*Insurance designations*]
PYA .... Psychoanalysis [*Medicine*]
PYA .... Pyatigorsk [*Former USSR Seismograph station code, US Geological Survey*] (SEIS)
PYA .... Pyroair Tech [*Vancouver Stock Exchange symbol*]
PYAC .... Penn-York Athletic Conference (PSS)
PYAR .... Person-Years-at-Risk [*After radiation exposure*] (FFDE)
PYarE .... Electric Storage Battery Co., Yardley, PA [*Library symbol Library of Congress*] (LCLS)
Py B .... Bachelor of Pedagogy
PYB .... Borg-Warner Corp., York Division, York, PA [*Library symbol Library of Congress*] (LCLS)
PYB .... [*The*] Palestine Year Book [*New York*] [*A publication*] (BJA)
PYB .... Partners Preferred Yield II [*AMEX symbol*] (SAG)
PYB .... Partners Preferred Yld'A' II [*AMEX symbol*] (TTSB)
PYB .... Pittsburgh Youth Ballet
PYBT .... [*The*] Prince's Youth Business Trust [*British*]
PYC .... Aeropycsa SA de CV [*Mexico ICAO designator*] (FAAC)
PYC .... Kuparuk, AK [*Location identifier FAA*] (FAAL)
PYC .... Pale Yellow Candle [*Baltic coffee-house*] [*London*] (DSUE)
PYC .... Partners Preferred Yield III [*AMEX symbol*] (SAG)
PYC .... Partners Preferred Yld'A' III [*AMEX symbol*] (TTSB)
PYC .... Patrol Vessel, Yacht, Coastal [*Navy symbol Obsolete*]
PYC .... Pembroke Yeomanry Cavalry [*British military*] (DMA)
PYC .... Perishability Code [*Military*] (AFIT)
PYC .... Playon Chico [*Panama*] [*Airport symbol*] (OAG)
PYC .... Pope and Young Club (EA)
PYC .... Proteose-Yeast Castione Medium [*Microbiology*] (MAE)
PyC .... Pyogenic Culture [*Medicine*] (MAE)
PYC .... York College of Pennsylvania, York, PA [*Library symbol Library of Congress*] (LCLS)
PYCG .... Pyrochromatogram [*Analytical chemistry*]
PYCR .... Pyrroline-5-Carboxylate Reductase (DMAA)
Pyd .... [*A*] Pyrimidine Nucleoside [*Also, Y*]
PYDV .... Potato Yellow Dwarf Virus [*Plant pathology*]
PYE .... Peptone Yeast Extract [*Medium*] [*Microbiology*] (DAVI)
PYE .... Point Reyes, CA [*Location identifier FAA*] (FAAL)
PYE .... Protect Your Environment [*Groups*]
PYE .... Pryme Energy Resources [*Vancouver Stock Exchange symbol*]
PYF .... French Polynesia [*ANSI three-letter standard code*] (CNC)
PYF .... Pyrenees [*France*] [*Seismograph station code, US Geological Survey*] (SEIS)
Py-FD-MS .... Pyrolysis Field Desorption Mass Spectrometry
PYFV .... Parsnip Yellow Fleck Virus [*Plant pathology*]
PYG .... Peptone-Yeast-Glucose [*Medium*] [*Microbiology*]
PYGC .... Pyrolysis Gas Chromatography
PYGM .... Peptone-Yeast Glucose Maltose Agar [*Microbiology*] (MAE)
PYGN .... Pyrogen Unit [*Biochemistry*]
PYGS .... Church of Jesus Christ of Latter-Day Saints, Genealogical Society Library, Gettysburg Branch, York, PA [*Library symbol Library of Congress*] (LCLS)
PYH .... Puerto Ayacucho [*Venezuela*] [*Airport symbol*] (OAG)
PYH .... York Hospital, York, PA [*Library symbol Library of Congress*] (LCLS)
PYHi .... Historical Society of York County, York, PA [*Library symbol Library of Congress*] (LCLS)
Py-HRMS .... Pyrolysis High-Resolution Mass Spectrometry
PYI .... Presidential Young Investigator Program [*National Science Foundation*]
PYJ .... Louisville, KY [*Location identifier FAA*] (FAAL)
Pyke .... Pyke's Lower Canada King's Bench Reports [*1809-10*] [*A publication*] (ILCA)
Pyke LC ...... Pyke's Lower Canada King's Bench Reports [*1809-10*] [*A publication*] (ILCA)
Pyke's R ..... Pyke's Lower Canada King's Bench Reports [*1809-10*] [*A publication*] (ILCA)
PYL .... Perry Island, AK [*Location identifier FAA*] (FAAL)
PYLL .... Potential Years of Life Lost [*Medicine*] (DMAA)
PYLR .... Peach Yellow Leaf Roll [*Plant pathology*]
PYM .... Martin Memorial [*York City and County*] Library, York, PA [*OCLC symbol*] (OCLC)
PYM .... Pan-African Youth Movement (EA)
PYM .... Plymouth, MA [*Location identifier FAA*] (FAAL)
PYM .... Psychosomatic [*Medicine*] (DMAA)
PYM .... Psychosomatic Medicine
PYM .... Putnam High Yield Municipal [*NYSE symbol*] (SPSG)
PYM .... Putnam Hi Yield Muni [*NYSE symbol*] (TTSB)
Py-MS .... Pyrolysis Mass Spectrometry
Pymt .... Payment
PYMT .... Payment
PYMV .... Peanut Yellow Mottle Virus [*Plant pathology*]
PYN .... Chicago, IL [*Location identifier FAA*] (FAAL)
PYN .... Poneloya [*Nicaragua*] [*Seismograph station code, US Geological Survey*] (SEIS)
PYNC .... Prior Year Notice [*IRS*]
PYO .... Person-Years of Observation [*Medicine*]
PYO .... Pick Your Own [*Fruits and vegetables*] (DSUE)
PYO .... Prior Year Overhead (AAGC)
PYO .... Pyongyang [*Heizo*] [*North Korea*] [*Seismograph station code, US Geological Survey*] [*Closed*] (SEIS)
PYOL .... Pyramid Oil (EFIS)
PYoW .... Westmoreland County Community College, Youngwood, PA [*Library symbol Library of Congress*] (LCLS)

PYP..............	Photoactive Yellow Protein [*Biochemistry*]
PYP..............	Pyrophosphate [*Scintiscanning*]
PYPER........	Promote Yard Performance Efficiency and Reliability (DNAB)
PYPH..........	Polyphase
P-Y-R..........	Pitch-Yaw-Roll (AAG)
PYR	Player Resources, Inc. [*Vancouver Stock Exchange symbol*]
PYR	Prior Year Report
PYR	Prior Year's Return [*IRS*]
Py R.............	Pyke's Lower Canada King's Bench Reports [*1809-10*] [*A publication*] (ILCA)
Pyr...............	Pyralidae [*Entomology*]
PYR	Pyramid [*California*] [*Seismograph station code, US Geological Survey*] (SEIS)
PYR	Pyramid Air Lines [*Egypt*] [*ICAO designator*] (FAAC)
Pyr...............	Pyramidal Tract [*Neuroanatomy*]
PYR	Pyrgos [*Greece*] [*Airport symbol*] (AD)
PYR	Pyridine [*Organic chemistry*]
Pyr...............	[*A*] Pyrimidine [*Biochemistry*]
Pyr...............	Pyrocap International Corp. [*Associated Press*] (SAG)
PYR	Pyrocap International Corp. [*AMEX symbol*] (SAG)
PYR	Pyrometer (AAG)
PYR.EC........	Pyruvate [*Biochemistry*]
PYR.EC........	Pyrocap International [*ECM Symbol*] (TTSB)
PYRETH.......	Pyrethrum [*Pellitory*] [*Pharmacology*] (ROG)
PYRKIN.......	Pyruvate Kinase [*An enzyme*] (DAVI)
pyrm	Pyramid (VRA)
PYRMD.......	Pyramid [*Freight*]
PYRO	Pyrogallic Acid (ROG)
PYRO	Pyromaniac (WDAA)
PYRO	Pyrotechnic
Pyrocp	Pyrocap International Corp. [*Associated Press*] (SAG)
PYROM	Pyrometer [*Engineering*]
PYROTECH..	Pyrotechnical (ROG)
pyrox	Pyroxiline (VRA)
PYROX GN..	Pyroxene Gneisses [*Agronomy*]
PyrP............	Pyridoxamine Phosphate [*or Pyridoxyl Phosphate*] [*Organic chemistry*] (DAVI)
PyrP............	Pyridoxyl (Pyridoxamine) Phosphate (BABM)
PYRR	Pyrrolidine [*Organic chemistry*]
PYRREC.......	Pyrrolidinoethyl Chloride [*Organic chemistry*]
Pyrrh...........	Pyrrhus [*of Plutarch*] [*Classical studies*] (OCD)
PYRS	Pyramids [*Board on Geographic Names*]
PYRUV.........	Pyruvate [*Organic chemistry*] (DAVI)
PYS	Parietal Yolk Sac [*Cells*] (DB)
PYS	Partial Yield Spectroscopy (MCD)
PYS	Photoelectron Yield Spectroscopy
PYS	Photo Yield Spectroscopy (AAEL)
PYS	Primitive Yolk Sac [*Embryology*]
PYSZ...........	Partially Yttria-Stabilized Zirconia [*Industrial ceramics*]
PYT	Payment (DCTA)
PYT	Playitas [*Nicaragua*] [*Seismograph station code, US Geological Survey*] (SEIS)
PYT	Prentiss, MS [*Location identifier FAA*] (FAAL)
PYT	Pretty Young Thing [*In song title from the Michael Jackson album "Thriller"*]
PYT	Pyng Tech [*Vancouver Stock Exchange symbol*]
Pyth............	Pythian [*of Pindar*] [*Classical studies*] (OCD)
Py-TRMS	Pyrolysis Time-Resolved Mass Spectrometry
PYTV...........	TV Filme, Inc. [*NASDAQ symbol*] (SAG)
PYV	Payton Ventures [*Vancouver Stock Exchange symbol*]
PyV	Polyoma Virus
PYV	Yaviza [*Panama*] [*Airport symbol*] (OAG)
PYX	Perryton, TX [*Location identifier FAA*] (FAAL)
PYX	Playtex Products [*NYSE symbol*] (SPSG)
PYX	Pyroxene [*Also, PX*] [*A mineral*]
Pyx..............	Pyxis [*Constellation*]
Pyxi.............	Pyxis [*Constellation*]
Pyxis...........	Pyxis Corp. [*Associated Press*] (SAG)
PYXS	Pyxis Corp. [*NASDAQ symbol*] (SAG)
PZ................	Canal Zone [*ANSI two-letter standard code Obsolete*] (CNC)
PZ................	Pancreozymin [*Also, CCK*] [*Endocrinology*]
PZ................	Panzerbrechend [*Armor-Piercing*] [*German military - World War II*]
PZ................	Pastural Zone [*Agriculture*]
PZ................	Past Z
PZ................	Paterson Zochonis [*Commercial firm*] [*British*]
PZ................	Peak-to-Zero (IAA)
PZ................	Penzance [*British depot code*]
PZ................	Peripheral Zone [*Botany*] [*Anatomy*]
PZ................	Phase Zero
Pz................	Phenylazobenzyloxycarbonyl [*Biochemistry*]
PZ................	Pick Up Zone [*Shipping*]
PZ................	Pickup Zone [*Military*] (INF)
pz................	Pieze [*Unit of pressure*]

PZ................	Pie Zeses [*May You Live Piously*] [*Italian*]
PZ................	Pizza
PZ................	Poland [*IYRU nationality code*] (IYR)
PZ................	Potez [*Etablissements Henri Potez*] [*France ICAO aircraft manufacturer identifier*] (ICAO)
PZ................	Prazosin [*A vasodilator*]
PZ................	Pregnancy Zone Protein (AAMN)
PZ................	Primary Zone [*Military*]
PZ................	Prisoner of Zion (BJA)
PZ................	Protective Zone
PZ................	Prozone Phenomenon [*Immunology*]
PZ................	Psychic Zodiac
PZ................	Pyrazine [*Organic chemistry*]
PZ................	Surinam [*Aircraft nationality and registration mark*] (FAAC)
PZA.............	Patrol Zone Area (MCD)
PZA.............	Paz De Ariporo [*Colombia*] [*Airport symbol*] (OAG)
PZA.............	Pizzeria
PZA.............	Provena Foods [*AMEX symbol*] (TTSB)
PZA.............	Provena Foods, Inc. [*AMEX symbol*] (SPSG)
PZA.............	Pyrazinamide [*Antibacterial compound*]
PZAA...........	Polarized Zeeman Atomic Absorption
PZB.............	Pietermaritzburg [*South Africa*] [*Airport symbol*] (OAG)
PZB.............	Pittston Brinks Group [*NYSE symbol*] [*Formerly, Pittston Services Group*] (SG)
PZB.............	Pittston Brinks Grp [*NYSE symbol*] (TTSB)
PZC.............	Pezamerica Resources Corp. [*Vancouver Stock Exchange symbol*]
PZC.............	Point of Zero Charge [*Electrochemistry*]
PZC.............	Progressive Zionist Caucus (EA)
PZ-CCK	Pancreozymin-Cholecystokinin [*Endocrinology*] (MAE)
PZCO...........	Pickup-Zone Control Officer [*Military*] (INF)
PZD.............	Partial Zona Dissection [*In-vitro fertilization*] (PAZ)
PZD.............	Partial Zonal Drilling [*In vitro fertilization*] [*Medicine*] (BARN)
PZD.............	Phase Zero Defense
PZDV...........	Panzer-Division [*Armored Division*] [*German military*]
PZE.............	Penzance [*England*] [*Airport symbol*] (OAG)
PZE.............	Piezoelectric
PZFC...........	Pia Zadora Fan Club (EA)
PZH.............	Zhob [*Pakistan*] [*Airport symbol*] (OAG)
PZI..............	Indiana University of Pennsylvania, Indiana, PA [*OCLC symbol*] (OCLC)
PZI..............	Protamine Zinc Insulin
PZKPFW......	Panzerkampfwagen [*German tank*] [*World War II*]
PZKW..........	Panzerkampfwagen [*German tank*] [*World War II*]
PZL.............	Panstwowe Zaklady Lotnicze [*Poland ICAO designator*] (FAAC)
PZL.............	Pennzoil Co. [*NYSE symbol Toronto Stock Exchange symbol*] (SPSG)
PZL.............	Progressive Zionist League-Hashomer Hatzair (EA)
PZM............	Piezoelectric Mount (IAA)
PZM............	Pittston Minerals Group [*NYSE symbol*] (SPSG)
PZM............	Pressurized Zone Microphone
PZO.............	Peebles, OH [*Location identifier FAA*] (FAAL)
PZO.............	Puerto Ordaz [*Venezuela*] [*Airport symbol*] (OAG)
PZP.............	Phase Zero Program
P7P.............	Porcine Zona Pellucida [*Experimental animal contraceptive*]
PZP.............	Pregnancy Zone Protein
PZPR	Polska Zjednoczona Partia Robotnicza [*Polish United Workers' Party - PUWP*] [*Political party*] (PPW)
PZQ.............	Rogers City, MI [*Location identifier FAA*] (FAAL)
PZ(R)...........	Penetration Zone (Radius) (MCD)
PZR.............	Pressurizer (NRCH)
PZR LCS	Pressurizer Level Control System [*Nuclear energy*] (GFGA)
PZR PCS.....	Pressurizer Pressure Control System [*Nuclear energy*] (GFGA)
PZS.............	Pittston Services Group [*Formerly, The Pittston Co.*] [*NYSE symbol*] (SPSG)
PZS.............	President of the Zoological Society [*British*]
PZSV...........	Pelargonium Zonate Spot Virus [*Plant pathology*]
PZT.............	Lead [*Plumbum*] Zirconate-Titanate [*Piezoelectric transducer*]
PZT.............	Photographic Zenith Tube
PZT.............	Piezoelectric Transducer [*or Translator*]
PZT.............	Piezoelectric Zirconate Titanate
PZT.............	Polycrystalline Lead Zirconate Titanate [*Piezoelectricity*]
PZU.............	Port Sudan [*Sudan*] [*Airport symbol*] (OAG)
PZV.............	New York, NY [*Location identifier FAA*] (FAAL)
PZX.............	Paragould, AR [*Location identifier FAA*] (FAAL)
PZX.............	Pittston BAX Group [*NYSE symbol*] [*Formerly, Pittston Burlington Group*]
PZX.............	Pittston Burlington Group [*NYSE symbol*] (TTSB)
PZY.............	Performance Executive Airlines Ltd. [*British ICAO designator*] (FAAC)
PZY.............	Piestany [*Former Czechoslovakia*] [*Airport symbol*] (OAG)
PZZ.............	Pizza Patio Ltd. [*Vancouver Stock Exchange symbol*]
PZZA...........	Papa Johns International, Inc. [*NASDAQ symbol*] (SAG)
PZZA...........	Papa John's Intl [*NASDAQ symbol*] (TTSB)
PZZI............	Pizza Inn [*NASDAQ symbol*] (TTSB)
PZZI............	Pizza Inn, Inc. [*NASDAQ symbol*] (SAG)

Q

By Acronym

Q	Atomic Shell of 98 Electrons per Shell (BARN)
Q	Blood Volume (DAVI)
Q	Cardiac Output (DAVI)
Q	Chicago, Burlington & Quincy Railroad [*Also known as Burlington Route*] [*Slang*]
Q	Clerical Perception [*On General Aptitude Test Battery*] (DAVI)
Q	Codex Marchalianus (BJA)
Q	Coefficient of Association [*Statistics*]
Q	Coenzyme Q [*Ubiquinone*] [*Also, CoQ, U, UQ*] [*Biochemistry*]
Q	Combination of Purpose [*JETDS nomenclature*]
Q	Coulomb [*Unit of quality*] [*Electronics*] (WDAA)
Q	Drone [*Designation for all US military aircraft*]
Q	Dynamic Pressure [*NASA*]
Q	Electrical Charge (WDAA)
q	Electrical Quantity (IDOE)
Q	Electrocardiographic Wave (STED)
q	Frequency of the Rarer Allele of a Pair [*Genetics*] (DAVI)
Q	Glutamine [*One-letter symbol; see Gln*]
Q	Heat [*or q*] [*Symbol IUPAC*]
Q	Kuwait [*IYRU nationality code*] (IYR)
Q	Merit of a Coil or Capacitor [*Electronics*]
Q	Moment of Area (BARN)
Q	One Billion [*British thermal units*] (GNE)
Q	Output [*Business term*]
q	Partition Function, Particle [*Symbol*] [*IUPAC*]
Q	Partition Function, System [*Symbol*] [*IUPAC*]
Q	Perfusion [*Cardiology*] (DAVI)
Q	Perihelion Distance [*Astronomy*] (BARN)
Q	Pitch Rate [*Angular Rate*] (NAKS)
Q	Polaris Correction [*Missiles*]
Q	Promotional Fare [*Also, K, L, V*] [*Airline fare code*]
Q	Proportion Not in a Specific Class
Q	Qarar (BARN)
Q	Q Band (IDOE)
Q	Qere (BJA)
Q	Q-Factor (DEN)
Q	Q Output (IDOE)
Q	Quaalude [*or Methaqualone*] [*A trademark*] [*Pharmacology*] (DAVI)
Q	Quad (IAA)
Q	Quadragesms [*Year Books of Edward III*] [*A publication*] (ILCA)
Q	Quadrans [*A Farthing*] [*Monetary unit*] [*British*]
Q	Quadriceps [*Anatomy*]
Q	Quadrillion (AD)
Q	Quadrillion BTU's [*Also known as "quads"*]
Q	Quadruple
Q	Quadruple Expansion Engine
Q	Quaere [*Inquire*] [*Latin*]
Q	Quai [*Embankment*] [*French*] (AD)
Q	Quaker Line
Q	Qualifier [*Linguistics*]
Q	Quality (IAA)
Q	Quality Factor
q	Quality Factor (AD)
q	Quality of Output [*Economics*]
Q	Quantity
Q	Quantity of Electric Charge (IAA)
Q	Quantity of Electricity [*Symbol*] [*IUPAC*]
Q	Quantity of Heat (STED)
q	[*Value of*] Quantum (IDOE)
q	Quaque [*Each*] [*Latin*] (AD)
q	Quaque [*Each or Every*] [*Latin*]
Q	Quarantine (AD)
Q	Quark [*Physics*]
Q	Quart
q	Quart (AD)
Q	Quarter
q	Quarter (WDMC)
Q	Quarterback [*Football*]
Q	Quartering [*Military British*]
Q	Quarterly
q	Quarterly (ODBW)
Q	Quartermaster [*Military*]
Q	Quarternary [*Geology*]
Q	Quarters [*Officer's rating*] [*British Royal Navy*]
Q	Quarter Word Designator [*Computer science*]
Q	Quartile

q	Quartile (AD)
Q	Quartile Variation [*Symbol*] (AD)
q	Quarto (AD)
Q	Quarto [*Book from 25 to 30 centimeters in height*]
Q	Quarto Edition [*Shakespearean work*]
Q	Quartoquadrillion (WDAA)
Q	Quartz [*CIPW classification*] [*Geology*]
Q	Quasi [*Almost, As It Were*] [*Latin*]
Q	Quatrefage's Angle [*Parietal Angle*] (DAVI)
Q	Quebec [*Phonetic alphabet*] [*International*] (DSUE)
Q	Queen [*Chess*]
Q	Queen [*Phonetic alphabet*] [*Pre-World War II*] [*World War II*] (DSUE)
Q	Queenie [*Phonetic alphabet*] [*Royal Navy World War I*] (DSUE)
Q	Queensland [*Fever*] [*Medicine*] (BABM)
Q	Queensland Fever [*Medicine*] (DAVI)
Q	Queensway [*Furniture store chain*] [*British*]
q	Queer (AD)
q	Quench (AD)
Q	Quench (IAA)
Q	Quercetin [*Botany*]
Q	Querwellen [*of transverse seismic waves*] (BARN)
q	Query (ODBW)
Q	Query
Q	Query Fever [*Medicine*] (DAVI)
Q	Query Language [*1975*] (CSR)
Q	Question
q	Question (AD)
q	Questioned [*Soundness of decision or reasoning in cited case questioned*] [*Used in Shepard's Citations*] [*Legal term*] (DLA)
Q	Questionnaire
Q	Quetzal [*Monetary unit*] [*Guatemala*]
Q	Queue
Q	Quick
q	Quick (AD)
Q	Quick [*Flashing*] Light [*Navigation signal*]
Q	Quiescent [*Cytology*]
Q	Quiescit [*He Rests*] [*Latin*]
Q	Quiller-Couch [*Sir Arthur, 1863-1944, English man of letters*] [*Letter used as pen name*]
Q	Quiller Press [*Publisher*] [*British*]
Q	Quilting
Q	Quinacrine [*Fluorescent method*] [*Chromosome stain*]
Q	Quinidine [*Pharmacology*] (DAVI)
Q	Quinone [*An oxidizing agent*] [*Chemistry*] (DAVI)
Q	Quint [*Energy unit*] (FFDE)
Q	Quintal [*Unit of weight*]
q	Quintal (AD)
Q	Quintar [*Monetary unit*] [*Albania*]
Q	Quintus [*Fifth*] [*Latin*]
Q	Quire [*Measure of paper*]
q	Quire (AD)
Q	Quisque [*Each, Every*] [*Pharmacy*]
Q	Qumran (BJA)
Q	Quorum (DLA)
Q	Quotient (ADA)
Q	Radiant Energy [*Symbol*] [*IUPAC*]
Q	Reaction Energy (STED)
Q	Reactive Power (STED)
Q	Receivership [*or Bankruptcy*] [*Designation used with NYSE symbols*] (SPSG)
Q	Respiratory Quotient [*Also, RQ*] [*Physiology*]
Q	San Quentin [*Prison*]
Q	San Quentin Prison (AD)
Q	Semi-Interquartile Range or Quartile Deviation [*Statistics*]
Q	Sonar [*JETDS nomenclature*]
Q	Special Purpose [*JETDS nomenclature*]
Q	Squalls [*Meteorology*] (BARN)
Q	Stagnation Pressure (WDAA)
Q	Thermoelectric Power [*Physics*] (BARN)
Q	Volume Rate [*Heat transmission symbol*]
Q1	First Quarto [*The earliest publication of the plays of William Shakespeare*] (WDMC)
Q1	Quintal [*Hundred-weight*] [*Spanish*] (AD)
Q2H	Quaque Secunda Hora [*Every Second Hour*] [*Pharmacy*]
Q3H	Quaque Tertia Hora [*Every Third Hour*] [*Pharmacy*]
Q4H	Quaque Quartus Hora [*Every Fourth Hour*] [*Pharmacy*]

Q4V	Quicker for Victory [*World War II*]
Q8	Quadraphonic Eight [*Tape cartridge format*] (NTCM)
Q₉	Ubichromanol-9 (DAVI)
Q₉	Ubichromenol-9 (DAVI)
Q₁₀	Coefficient of Temperature (DAVI)
Q1⁰	Every Hour around the Clock [*Q2⁰ is evey 2 hours, etc.*] [*Pharmacy*] (DAVI)
QA	Air Caribe [*ICAO designator*] (AD)
QA	Bibliotheque Municipale, Alma, Quebec [*Library symbol National Library of Canada*] (NLC)
QA	National Restaurant Association Quality Assurance Study Group (EA)
QA	QANTAS Airways Ltd. [*Australia*] (DS)
qa	Qatar [*MARC country of publication code Library of Congress*] (LCCP)
QA	Qatar [*IYRU nationality code*] [*ANSI two-letter standard code*] (CNC)
QA	Quadrans [*A Farthing*] [*Monetary unit*] [*British*] (ROG)
QA	Quadripartite Agreement
QA	Qualification Approval (WDAA)
QA	Quality Acceptance (AD)
QA	Quality Analysis (IAA)
QA	Quality Appraisal [*Social Security Administration*] (DHP)
QA	Quality Assessment (HCT)
QA	Quality Assurance
qa	Quality Assurance (AD)
QA	Quantum Access, Inc. [*Database producer*] (IID)
QA	Quarternary Ammonium [*Chemistry*]
QA	Quarters Allowance
QA	Quarters Armourer [*British military*] (DMA)
QA	Quarters Assistant [*British military*] (DMA)
QA	Quasi Algorithm (OA)
QA	Queen Alexandra's Imperial Military Nursing Service [*British*] (BARN)
QA	Query Analyzer (IEEE)
QA	Query Author [*Proofreader's notation*]
QA	Quick-Acting
qa	Quick-Acting (AD)
qa	Quick Assembly (AD)
QA	Quick Assembly [*Furniture*]
QA	Quick Asset [*Finance*]
QA	Quiescent Aerial [*or Antenna*]
qa	Quiescent Aerial (AD)
QA	Quinic Acid [*Organic chemistry*]
Q-A	Quint-A (AD)
QA	Quisqualic Acid [*Biochemistry*]
QAA	ALCAN International Ltee. [*ALCAN International Ltd.*] Jonquiere, Quebec [*Library symbol National Library of Canada*] (NLC)
QAA	Qualified Administrative Assistant [*Canada*] (ASC)
QAA	Quality Ash Association (BUAC)
QAA	Quality Assurance Acceptance (COE)
QAA	Quality Assurance Assistant [*DoD*]
QAA	Quality Assurance Audit (MCD)
QAA	Question and Answer (IAA)
QAA	Quinoline Amino Alcohol [*Organic chemistry*]
QA & O	Quality Assurance and Operations [*Nuclear Regulatory Commission*] (GFGA)
QA & P	Quanah, Acme & Pacific Railroad (AD)
QA & R	Quality Assurance and Reliability
QAAO	Quality Assurance and Operations (IAA)
QAAS	Quality Assurance Acceptance Standard (IAA)
QAAS	Quality Assurance Ammunition Specialist [*or Speciality*] (MCD)
QAB	Quality Assurance Board (AD)
QAB	Quality Assurance Bulletin (AD)
QAB	Queen Anne's Bounty
QAB	Queensland Agricultural Bank [*Australia*]
QAB	Quick Action Button [*Military*] (CAAL)
QABA	Bibliotheque et Audiovisuel, Alma, Quebec [*Library symbol National Library of Canada*] (NLC)
QAC	Qatar Air Cargo [*FAA designator*] (FAAC)
QAC	Quadrant Aimable Charge Warhead (MCD)
QAC	Quadripartite Agreements Committee [*Military*]
QAC	Quality Assessment Coordinator (MEDA)
QAC	Quality Assurance Chart (MCD)
QAC	Quality Assurance Check (AD)
QAC	Quality Assurance Checklist (NRCH)
QAC	Quality Assurance Code
QAC	Quality Assurance Coding (AD)
QAC	Quality Assurance Coordinator [*Environmental Protection Agency*] (GFGA)
QAC	Quality Assurance Criterion [*Nuclear energy*] (NRCH)
QAC	Quarternary Ammonium Compound [*Chemistry*]
qac	Quaternary Ammonium Compound (AD)
QAC	Quaternary Ammonium Compound [*Chemistry*] (DAVI)
QAC	Quebec Appeal Cases [*Maritime Law Book Co. Ltd.*] [*Canada Information service or system*] (CRD)
QAC	Queensland Arts Council [*Australia*]
QACAD	Quick-Acting Choke [*Automotive engineering*]
QACAD	Quality Assurance Corrective Action Document (NASA)
QACC	Quality Assurance Coordination Committee (DMAA)
QACHL	Centre de Documentation, Centre Hospitalier des Laurentides et Centre d'Accueil et de Readaptation des Hautes-Vallees, L'Annonciation, Quebec [*Library symbol National Library of Canada*] (BIB)
QACUE	Quebec Association of Computer Users in Education [*Canada*] (EDAC)
Qad	Qadmoniot [*Jerusalem*] (BJA)
QAD	Quadriceps Active Displacement [*Sports medicine*]
QAD	Quality Assessment Director (MEDA)
QAD	Quality Assessment Division [*Higher Education Funding Council*] (AIE)
QAD	Quality Assurance Data
QAD	Quality Assurance Department (AD)
QAD	Quality Assurance Directive
QAD	Quality Assurance Directorate [*Materials*] [*British*]
QAD	Quality Assurance Division [*Picatinny Arsenal*] [*Dover, NJ*]
QAD	Quarter Amplitude Damped (ACII)
QAD	Quick Attach-Detach [*Engine*]
qad	Quick-Attach-Detach (AD)
QADC	Queen's Aide-de-Camp [*Military British*]
QADI	Quality Assurance Department Instruction (AD)
qadk	Quick Attach-Detach-Kit (AD)
QADK	Quick Attach-Detach Kit
QAD(MATS)	Quality Assurance Directorate (Materials) [*British*]
QADS	Quality Assurance Data Summary (AD)
QADS	Quality Assurance Data System
QAE	Quality Assurance Engineering
QAE	Quality Assurance Evaluator [*Military*]
QAE	Queen's Awards for Export [*British*]
QAES	Quality Assurance and Expert Systems [*Computer science*]
QAET	Quality Assurance Environment Testing [*Military*] (CAAL)
QAET	Quality Assurance Evaluation Test (NG)
QAF	Qatar Amiri Flight [*ICAO designator*] (FAAC)
QAF	Quality Achievement Factor (RDA)
QAF	Quality Adjustment Factor (DMAA)
qaf	Quality-Assurance Firing (AD)
QAF	Quality Assurance Function
QAFA	Quality Assurance Field Activity
QAFCO	Qatar Fertiliser Co. (BUAC)
QAFCO	Quatar Fertilizer Co. (AD)
QAFL	Queensland Australian Football League (AD)
QAFM	Quality Assurance Forms Guide Manual (SAA)
qafo	Quality-Assurance Field Operation (AD)
QAFO	Quality Assurance Field Operations
QAG	Quaker Action Group (AD)
QAG	Quality Assurance Group
QAG	Queensland Art Gallery [*Australia*]
QAGA	Queensland Amateur Gymnastic Association [*Australia*] (AD)
qagc	Quiet Automatic Gain Control (AD)
QAGC	Quiet Automatic Gain Control (IAA)
QAGTC	Queensland Association for Gifted and Talented Children [*Australia*]
QAH	Quick Airways Holland BV [*Netherlands ICAO designator*] (FAAC)
QAHA	Queensland Allergy and Hyperactivity Association [*Australia*]
QAHD	Centre de Documentation, Hotel-Dieu d'Arthabaska, Quebec [*Library symbol National Library of Canada*] (BIB)
Qahira	El Qahira [*Cairo*] [*Egyptian Arabic*] (AD)
QAI	Quality Assurance Index (MCD)
QAI	Quality Assurance Inspection
QAI	Quality Assurance Instruction (NRCH)
QAI	Quality Assurance International
QAI	Queen's Award to Industry [*British*] (AD)
QAIA	Queen Alia International Airport [*Jordan*]
QAICG	Quality Assurance Interface Coordination Group (AD)
QAID	Queensland Association of Industries for the Disabled [*Australia*]
QAIL	Quality Assurance Information Letter (MCD)
QAILS	Queensland Association of Independent Legal Services [*Australia*]
QAIMNS	Queen Alexandra's Imperial Military Nursing Service [*British*]
QAIMNSR	Queen Alexandra's Imperial Military Nursing Service Reserve [*British military*] (DMA)
QAIP	Quality Assurance Inspection Procedure
QAIRG	Quality Assurance Installation Review Group [*Nuclear energy*] (NRCH)
QA + IS	Quality Association and Inspection Service [*British*]
QAK	Quick Attach Kit
qak	Quick-Attach Kit (AD)
QAL	Q Allowance List [*Aviation*] (DNAB)
QAL	Quality Assurance Laboratory
QAL	Quarterly Acceptance List (AFIT)
QAL	Quarterly Accession List
QAL	Quartz Aircraft Lamp
qal	Quartz Aircraft Lamp (AD)
qal	Quaternary Alluvium (AD)
QAL	Quebec Airways Ltd. (MCD)
QAL	Queensland Alumina Ltd. [*Australia*] (AD)
qal	Quintal [*Hundred-weight*] [*French*] (AD)
QALAS	Qualified Associate of the Land Agents' Society [*British*]
QALC	College d'Alma, Lac St.-Jean, Quebec [*Library symbol National Library of Canada*] (NLC)
QALD	Quality-Assurance Liaison Division (AD)
QALE	Quality-Adjusted Life Expectancy [*Medicine*] (DMAA)
QALI	Quality Assurance Letter of Instructions
QALL	Quartz Aircraft Landing Lamp
qall	Quartz Aircraft Landing Lamp (AD)
QALPACS	Quality Patient Care Scale [*Medicine*] (DMAA)
QALTR	Quality Assurance Laboratory Test Request (MCD)
QALY	Quality-Adjusted Life Year (DMAA)
QALY's	Quality Adjusted Life Years
QAM	Quadrature Amplified Modulation (NITA)
QAM	Quadrature Amplitude Modulation
qam	Quadrature Amplitude Modulation (AD)
QAM	Quality Assurance Manager
QAM	Quality Assurance Manual
QAM	Quality Assurance Monitor (HCT)

QAM............ Quality Assurance Monitoring (DMAA)
QAM............ Quaque Aente Meridiem [Every Morning] [Pharmacy]
QAM............ Queensland Arts Movement [Australia]
QAM............ Queued Access Method [Computer science]
qam............ Queued Access Method
QAMDO...... Quadripartite Agreed Materiel Development Objective [Military]
QAMFNS...... Queen Alexandra's Military Family Nursing Service [British military] (DMA)
QAMIS .... Quality Assurance Management and Information System [Environmental Protection Agency] (GFGA)
QAMIS .... Quality Assurance Monitoring Information System (AD)
QAML........... Centre de Documentation, Musee Laurier, Arthabaska, Quebec [Library symbol National Library of Canada] (NLC)
QAMM .... Quality Assurance Management Meeting [DoD]
QAMR........... Quadripartite Agreed Materiel Requirement [Military]
QAMR........... Quality Assurance Management Review [DoD]
QAMS .... Quad-Phase Amplitude Modulation System (AD)
QAMS .... Quality Assurance Management Staff [Environmental Protection Agency] (GFGA)
QAMS .... Queensland Air Museum Society [Australia]
QAN .... Queensland Air Navigation Co. Ltd. [Australia] (ADA)
Q & A .... Question and Answer (MSA)
Q and A ...... Question and Answer (WDMC)
Q & D .... Quick and Dirty [Computer science]
q & d .... Quick and Dirty (AD)
Q & O .... Quebec and Ontario [Canada] (AD)
Q & R .... Quality and Reliability
Q & RA .... Quality and Reliability Assurance
Q & SL .... Qualifications and Standards Laboratory (WDAA)
q & t .... Quenched and Tempered (AD)
QANTAS...... Queensland & Northern Territory Aerial Service [Later, QANTAS Airways Ltd.] [Australia]
QAO .... Quality Assurance Office [Navy]
QAO .... Quality Assurance Officer [Environmental Protection Agency] (GFGA)
QAO .... Quality Assurance Operation
qao .... Quality Assurance Operation (AD)
QAO .... Quality Assurance Outline
QAO .... Queen's Awards Office [British]
QAOC........... Quality Assurance Overview Contractor (AD)
QAOGR .... Queen Alexandra's Own Gurkha Rifles [British military] (DMA)
QAOP .... Quality Assurance Operating Plan
QAOP .... Quality Assurance Operating Procedure (AD)
QAP .... Quadratic Assignment Problem [Mathematics]
QAP .... Qualifications Appraisal Panel (OICC)
QAP .... Quality Assurance Package
QAP .... Quality Assurance Plan
QAP .... Quality Assurance Planning (AD)
QAP .... Quality Assurance Procedure
QAP .... Quality Assurance Professional (HCT)
QAP .... Quality Assurance Program [Nuclear energy]
QAP .... Quality Assurance Provision
QAP .... Quanah, Acme & Pacific Railway Co. [AAR code]
QAP .... Quinine, Atabrine, Plasmoquine [Treatment for malaria]
qap .... Quinine, Atebrin, Plasmoquine [Medicine] (AD)
QAPBS........ Queensland Association of Permanent Building Societies [Australia]
QAPCO........ Qatar Petrochemical Co. (BUAC)
QAPED........ Quadripartite Agreed Plans of Engineering Design [Military]
QAPET........ Quadripartite Agreed Plans of Engineering Tests [Military]
QAPI .... Quality Assurance Program Index [Nuclear energy] (NRCH)
QAPL .... Queensland Airlines Party Ltd.
QAPL .... Queensland Airlines Proprietary Ltd. [Australia] (AD)
QAPP .... Quality Assurance Program Plan [Nuclear energy] (NRCH)
QAPS .... Queensland Association of Personnel Services [Australia] (AD)
QAPST .... Quadripartite Agreed Plans of Service Tests [Military]
QA/QC .... Quality Assurance/Quality Control (BCP)
QAR .... Quality and Reliability (IAA)
QAR .... Quality Assurance Reagent [Cardiology] (DAVI)
QAR .... Quality Assurance Record
QAR .... Quality Assurance Report [A publication] (AD)
QAR .... Quality Assurance Representative
QAR .... Quality Assurance Requirements (NRCH)
QAR .... Quality Assurance Responsible/Witness (MCD)
QAR .... Quantitative Autoradiography [Medicine]
QAR .... Quasi-Adiabatic Representation
QAR .... Questionable Activity Report [Employment and Training Administration] [Department of Labor]
QAR .... Quick Access Recording
qar .... Quick-Access Recording (AD)
QARAFNS ... Queen Alexandra's Royal Air Force Nursing Service [British] (AD)
QARANC ..... Queen Alexandra's Royal Army Nursing Corps [British]
QARANC ..... Queen Alexandra's Royal Army Nursing Service [British] (AD)
QARC.......... Quality Assurance Record Center (MCD)
QARC.......... Quality Assurance Review Center [National Cancer Institute]
QARI .... Quality Assurance Receipt Inspection [Military] (DNAB)
QARM .... Bibliotheque Municipale, Arthabaska, Quebec [Library symbol National Library of Canada] (NLC)
QA/RM .... Quality Assurance/Risk Management (MEDA)
QARNNS ..... Queen Alexandra's Royal Navy Nursing Service [British]
QARNNSR ... Queen Alexandra's Royal Naval Nursing Service Reserve [British military] (DMA)
QAR-R .... Quality Assurance Record - Receiving (MCD)
QAR-T .... Quality Assurance Record - Tooling (MCD)
QART .... Quality Assurance Review Technique (MHDB)
QAS .... Quality Answering System (AD)
QAS .... Quality Assurance Service [Medicine]

QAS .... Quality Assurance Specialist [DoD]
QAS .... Quality Assurance Standards [Business] (DAVI)
QAS .... Quality Assurance System (AD)
QAS .... Queensland Academy of Sport [Australia]
QAS .... Question-Answering System
qas .... Quick-Acting Scuttle (AD)
QAS .... Quick Action Shuttle
QAS .... Quisqueya Airlines SA [Haiti] [ICAO designator] (FAAC)
QASA .... Queensland Amateur Swimming Association [Australia] (AD)
QASAC .... Quality Assurance Spacecraft Acceptance Center (MCD)
QASAG........ Experimental Farm, Agriculture Canada [Ferme Experimentale, Agriculture Canada] L'Assomption, Quebec [Library symbol National Library of Canada] (NLC)
QASAR........ Quality Assurance Systems Analysis Review (AD)
QASAS .... Quality Assurance Specialist, Ammunition Surveillance (MCD)
QASB .... Bibliotheque Municipale, Asbestos, Quebec [Library symbol National Library of Canada] (NLC)
QASB .... Queensland Ambulance Service Board [Australia]
QASC .... Quadripartite Armaments Standardization Committee [Military] (AABC)
QASCO........ Qatar Steel Co. (BUAC)
QASDM........ Quality Assurance, Sample, and Data Management
QASK .... Quadrature Amplitude Shift Keying
QASL .... Quality Assurance Systems List (IEEE)
QASP .... Quality Assurance Standard Practice (MCD)
QASP .... Quality Assurance Surveillance Plan (NITA)
QASPR........ QUALCOMM, Inc. Automatic Satellite Position Reporting
QASS .... Queensland Academy of Space Sciences [Australia]
QAST .... Quality Assurance Service [or Serviceability] Test [Nuclear energy] (NG)
QAT .... Aero Taxi [Canada ICAO designator] (FAAC)
Qat .... Qatabanian (BJA)
QAT .... Qatar [ANSI three-letter standard code] (CNC)
Qat .... Qatar (AD)
QAT .... Quaker Oats Co. [Toronto Stock Exchange symbol]
QAT .... Qualification Approval Test (NATG)
QAT .... Quality Action Team [Industrial engineering]
QAT .... Quality Assurance Team (MCD)
QAT .... Quality Assurance Technical [Material] (DAVI)
QAT .... Quantitative Assessment and Training Center (AD)
QATA .... Queensland Art Teachers' Association [Australia]
QATARGAS... Qatar Liquified Gas Co. (BUAC)
QATB .... Queensland Ambulance Transport Brigade [Australia] (AD)
QATIP .... Quality Assurance Test and Inspection Procedures (MCD)
QATP .... Quality Assurance Technical Publications (AAG)
QATP .... Quality Assurance Test Procedure (AD)
QATS .... Quality Assurance and Test Service (IAA)
QATS .... Quarterly Advanced Training Schedule [Navy] (DNAB)
QATT .... Qualification for Acceptance Thermal Testing [NASA] (NASA)
QAU .... Quality Assurance Unit
QAUR.......... Quality Assurance and Utilization Review [Medicine] (DMAA)
QAVC .... Quiet Automatic Voltage Control [Electronics] (ECII)
QAVC .... Quiet Automatic Volume Control
qavc .... Quiet Automatic Volume Control (AD)
QAVP .... Quality Assurance Verification Procedures [Military] (DNAB)
QAVT .... Qualification Acceptance Vibration Test [NASA] (NASA)
QAVT .... Qualification for Acceptance Vibration Testing (NAKS)
QAW .... Quality at Work [Quality Decision Management] [Computer science] (PCM)
QAWA .... Queensland Amateur Wrestling Association [Australia] (AD)
QAWT .... Quick-Acting Water-Tight (DNAB)
QAY .... Bibliotheque Municipale, Aylmer, Quebec [Library symbol National Library of Canada] (NLC)
QB............... Bibliotheque Municipale, Brossard, Quebec [Library symbol National Library of Canada] (BIB)
qb .... Qualified Bidders (AD)
QB............... Qualified Buyer
QB............... Quantitative (Electrophysiological) Battery [Cardiology] (DAVI)
qb .... Quarterback (AD)
QB............... Quarterback [Football]
QB............... Quasi-Biennial
QB............... Quebecair, Inc. [Airlines] [ICAO designator] (OAG)
QB............... Queen's Bays [Later, QDG] [Military unit] [British]
QB............... Queen's Bench [Legal] [British]
QB............... Queen's Bench Reports, by Adolphus and Ellis, New Series [A publication] (DLA)
QB............... Queen's Bishop [Chess]
QB............... Queensboro Bridge [New York City] (AD)
QB............... Queensland Ballet [Australia]
QB............... Query Buffer [Computer science] (IAA)
QB............... Quick Batch (MHDI)
QB............... Quick Break (MSA)
qb .... Quick Break
QB............... Quickbrew [Brand of tea] [British]
QB............... Quiet Birdmen [An association] (EA)
Qb............... Total Body Clearance (MAE)
QB............... Whole Blood [Hematology] (DAVI)
QBA .... Quality Bakers of America Cooperative (EA)
QBA .... Quality Brands Associates of America [Defunct] (EA)
QBA .... Quantitative Budget Analysis (MCD)
QBA .... Quebecair (AD)
QBA .... Quebecair, Inc. [Airlines]
QBA .... Queensland Band Association [Australia]
QBA .... Queensland Beekeepers' Association [Australia]
QBA .... Queensland Bowling Association [Australia] (AD)

QBA .... Queensland Bridge Association [*Australia*]
QBAA .... Quality Brands Associates of America (AD)
QBAC .... Quality Bakers of America Cooperative (EA)
QBAL .... Jillians Entertainment [*NASDAQ symbol*] (TTSB)
QBAL .... Jillians Entertainment Corp. [*NASDAQ symbol*] (SAG)
QBAN .... Qui Bixit Annos [*Who Lived ____ Years*] [*Latin*]
QBB .... Queen's Bad Bargain [*Undesirable serviceman*] [*Slang British*] (DSUE)
QBB .... Queensland Barristers' Board [*Australia*]
QBB .... Queensland Butter Board [*Australia*] (AD)
QBC .... Bella Coola [*Canada*] [*Airport symbol*] (OAG)
QBC .... Quality British Celery Association (BUAC)
QBC .... Quality Buffy Coat [*Hematology*] (DAVI)
QBC .... Quantitative Buffy Coat [*Hematology*] (DAVI)
Qbc .... Quebec (AD)
QBC .... Quebec [*Canada*] (WDAA)
QBCA .... Quantitative Buffy-Coat Analysis (MEDA)
QBCCL .... Centre de Documentation, CLSC de l'Aquilon, Baie-Comeau, Quebec [*Library symbol National Library of Canada*] (BIB)
QBCH .... Centre de Documentation, Pavillon St.-Joseph, Centre Hospitalier Regional de Beauceville, Quebec [*Library symbol National Library of Canada*] (BIB)
QBCHS .... Queensland Bush Children's Health Scheme [*Australia*]
QBD .... Quasi-Bidirectional (MHDI)
QBD .... Quasi Birth and Death [*Statistics*]
QBD .... Queen's Bench Division [*Military unit*] [*British*]
QBD .... Queen's Bench Division, Law Reports [*A publication*]
QBD .... Queensland Book Depot [*Australia*] (AD)
QBDA .... Quebrada
QB Div .... English Law Reports, Queen's Bench Division [*1865-75*] [*A publication*] (DLA)
QBE .... Beaconsfield Public Library, Quebec [*Library symbol National Library of Canada*] (NLC)
QBE .... Query by Example [*Data processing search method*]
QBEAU .... Bibliotheque Municipale, Beauport, Quebec [*Library symbol National Library of Canada*] (BIB)
QBEC .... Bibliotheque Municipale, Becancour, Quebec [*Library symbol National Library of Canada*] (NLC)
QBEC .... Quebec Building Envelope Council (AC)
QBEHBI .... H. Bergstrom International Ltd., Beaconsfield, Quebec [*Library symbol National Library of Canada*] (NLC)
QBES .... Queensland Bureau of Emergency Services [*Australia*]
QBF .... Query-by-Forms [*Data processing search method*]
QBFJOTF .... [*The*] Quick Brown Fox Jumped over the Fence [*Typing exercise*]
QBFJOTLD ..... [*The*] Quick Brown Fox Jumped over the Lazy Dogs [*Typing exercise*]
QBFP .... Queensland Boating and Fisheries Patrol [*Australia*]
QBG .... Qualified Binary Grouping [*Computer science*] (IAA)
QBG .... Queensland Bookbinders' Guild [*Australia*]
QBI .... Queen's Bureau of Investigation [*British*] (AD)
qbi .... Quite Bloody Impossible [*Slang*] (AD)
QBI .... Quite Bloody Impossible [*British slang, applied particularly to flying conditions*]
QBIC .... Query by Image Content [*Computer science*]
QBID .... Queensland Business and Industry Directory [*Australia A publication*]
QBIR .... Quarterly Printing Industry Business Indicator Report [*A publication*] (EAAP)
QBJ .... Juniorat des Freres du Sacre-Coeur, Bramptonville, Quebec [*Library symbol National Library of Canada*] (NLC)
QBL .... Qualified Bidders List
QBL .... Queensland Baseball League [*Australia*]
QBLC .... Queen's Bench Reports, Lower Canada [*A publication*] (DLA)
QBMS .... Mitel Semiconductor, Bromont, Quebec [*Library symbol National Library of Canada*] (NLC)
QBNA .... Queensland Bush Nursing Association [*Australia*]
QBO .... Bibliotheque Municipale, Boucherville, Quebec [*Library symbol National Library of Canada*] (NLC)
QBO .... Mail Advertising Service Association International. Quarterly Business Outlook [*A publication*]
QBO .... Quarterly Business Outlook [*A publication*] (EAAP)
QBO .... Quasi-Biennial Oscillation [*Earth science*]
QBOA .... Quebec Bus Owners Association (AC)
qbop .... Quality Basic-Oxygen Process (AD)
Q-BOP .... Quick Basic Oxygen Process [*Steelmaking*]
QBP .... Queen's Bishop's Pawn [*Chess*] (IIA)
QBPL .... Queens Borough Public Library [*New York, NY*]
QBR .... Quebecor, Inc. [*Toronto Stock Exchange symbol*]
QBR .... Queen's Bench Reports [*Legal*] [*British*]
QBR .... Queen's Bench Reports, by Adolphus and Ellis, New Series [*A publication*] (DLA)
QBRA .... ACS Biblio-information, Inc., Brossard, Quebec [*Library symbol National Library of Canada*] (BIB)
QBRG .... Centre Hospitalier Robert Giffard, Beauport, Quebec [*Library symbol National Library of Canada*] (NLC)
QBRs .... Queen's Bench Reports [*A publication*] (AD)
QBS .... Qatar Broadcasting Service (BUAC)
QBS .... Qualifications-Based Selection [*Metallurgy*]
QBS .... Quebec Bureau of Standards [*Canada*] (BUAC)
QBSA .... Centre Hospitalier St.-Augustin, Beauport, Quebec [*Library symbol National Library of Canada*] (BIB)
QBSA .... Queensland Blinded Soldiers' Association [*Australia*]
QBSM .... Que Besa su Mano [*Who Kisses Your Hand*] [*Spanish*] (AD)
QBSM .... Que Besa Sus Manos [*Kissing Your Hands*] [*Spanish*]
QBSP .... Que Besa sus Pies [*Who Kisses Your Feet*] [*Spanish*] (AD)

QBSPH .... Centre Hospitalier de Charlevoix, Baie St.-Paul, Quebec [*Library symbol National Library of Canada*] (BIB)
QBT .... Quad Bus Transceiver (NITA)
qBtu .... Quadrillion British Thermal Units (GNE)
QBU .... Bibliotheque Municipale, Buckingham, Quebec [*Library symbol National Library of Canada*] (NLC)
QBUC .... Queen's Bench Reports, Upper Canada [*A publication*] (DLA)
Q Bull Natn Counc Women Aust... National Council of Women of Australia. Quarterly Bulletin [*A publication*]
QBV .... Whole Blood Volume [*Hematology*] (DAVI)
QBWA .... Queensland Braille Writing Association [*Australia*]
QBWUE .... Queensland Blind Workers Union of Employees [*Australia*]
QBX .... Quick-BASIC [*Beginner's All-Purpose Symbolic Instruction Code*] Extended [*Computer science*] (PCM)
QC .... Air Zaire SA [*Zaire*] [*ICAO designator*] (ICDA)
QC .... Bibliotheque Municipale, Cowansville, Quebec [*Library symbol National Library of Canada*] (BIB)
Qc .... Capillary Blood Volume (DAVI)
QC .... Impact Pressure [*Symbol*] (WDAA)
Qc .... Pulmonary Capillary Blood Flow [*Medicine*] (DAVI)
QC .... QC Explorations [*Vancouver Stock Exchange symbol*]
QC .... Quad Center [*Typography*]
qc .... Quad Column [*Typesetting*] (WDMC)
QC .... Quad Crown [*Paper*] (DGA)
QC .... Quadrantal Correction (AD)
qc .... Qualcosa [*Something*] [*Italian*] (AD)
qc .... Qualification Course (AD)
QC .... Qualification Course
QC .... Qualifying Certificate
QC .... Quality Certificate
QC .... Quality Circle [*Labor-management team organized to increase industrial productivity*]
QC .... Quality Control [*or Controller*]
qc .... Quality Control (AD)
QC .... Quantek Corp. [*Trademark*]
QC .... Quantitative Chemiluminescence
qc .... Quantitative Command (AD)
QC .... Quantitative Command
QC .... Quantum Cascade [*LASER*] (ECON)
QC .... Quantum Computer [*Physics*]
QC .... Quantum Coprocessors [*Computer science*]
qc .... Quantum Counter (AD)
QC .... Quantum Counter
QC .... Quarterly Credit
QC .... Quartermaster Corps [*Army*] (WGA)
QC .... Quarter of Coverage [*Social Security Administration*] (OICC)
QC .... Quarters of Coverage [*Social Security Administration*] (GFGA)
QC .... Quartz Crystal
qc .... Quartz Crystal (AD)
QC .... Quasi-Contract [*Business term*]
QC .... Quaternary Carrier [*Biochemistry*]
QC .... Quebec Central Railway Co. [*AAR code*]
QC .... Quebec City (AD)
QC .... Queen Consort [*British*] (ROG)
QC .... Queen's College [*Oxford and Cambridge Universities*] (ROG)
QC .... Queen's Counsel [*British*]
QC .... Quench Correction
QC .... Queue Control (NITA)
QC .... Quezon City (AD)
QC .... Quick Catheter [*Medicine*] (STED)
q/c .... Quick Change (AD)
QC .... Quick Change (IAA)
QC .... Quick Charge [*Airplane*] (IIA)
QC .... Quick Cleaning (MSA)
QC .... Quick Code (NITA)
QC .... Quick Connect
qc .... Quick Connect (AD)
QC .... Quick Curl [*Refers to Barbie doll hair*] [*Doll collecting*]
QC .... Quiesce-Completed [*Computer science*] (IBMDP)
QC .... Quiescent Center [*Plant root growth*]
QC .... Quincy College (AD)
QC .... Quinine-Colchicine [*Medicine*] (MAE)
QC .... Quinnipiac College (AD)
qc .... Quit Claim (AD)
QC .... Quit Claim (WDAA)
QC .... Quixote Center (EA)
QCA .... Bibliotheque Municipale, Candiac, Quebec [*Library symbol National Library of Canada*] (BIB)
QCA .... Quaker Concern for Animals [*An association*] (BUAC)
QCA .... Quality Control Analysis
QCA .... Quantitative Coronary Angiography [*Cardiology*] (DAVI)
QCA .... Quantum-Dot Cellular Automata [*Microelectronics*]
QCA .... Quarterly Compilation of Abstracts [*A publication*]
QCA .... Queen Charlotte Airlines Ltd.
QCA .... Queensland Coal Associates [*Australia*] (AD)
QCA .... Queensland Coal Association [*Australia*]
QCA .... Queensland Colonial Association [*Australia*]
QCA .... Queensland Colostomy Association [*Australia*]
QCA .... Queensland Cricket Association [*Australia*] (AD)
QCA .... Queensland Croquet Association (AD)
QCA .... Quiet Communities Act (GFGA)
Q-cab .... Quiet Cab (AD)
QCAG .... Ministere de l'Agriculture, des Pecheries et de l'Alimentation, Chateauguay, Quebec [*Library symbol National Library of Canada*] (NLC)

QCAI	Quality Conformance Acceptance Inspection (MCD)
QCAL	Centre de Documentation, Centre Hospitalier Anna-Laberge, Chateauguay, Quebec [*Library symbol National Library of Canada*] (BIB)
QC & R	Quality Control and Reliability (AD)
QC & T	Quality Control and Techniques (SAA)
QC & T	Quality Control and Test (AD)
Q CAP	Quad Foolscap [*Paper*] (DGA)
QCAR	Queensland Criminal Reports [*A publication*]
Q-card	Qualification Card (AD)
QCAS	Queensland Chamber of Agricultural Societies [*Australia*]
QCAT	Quality Control and Techniques (IAA)
QCB	Bibliotheque Municipale, Coaticook, Quebec [*Library symbol National Library of Canada*] (NLC)
QCB	Quality Control Board (MCD)
QCB	Quality Control Branch
QCB	Quality Control Bulletin (AD)
QCB	Queensland Coal Board [*Australia*]
QCB	Queue Control Block [*Computer science*]
qcb	Queue Control Block [*Data processing*] (AD)
QCBC	Quaker City Bancorp [*NASDAQ symbol*] (SAG)
QCBC	Queen's Commendation for Brave Conduct [*British*] (AD)
QCBC	Quick Change Boost Control [*Automotive engineering*]
qcbm	Quick-Connects Bulkhead Mounting (AD)
QCC	Bibliotheque Gaspesienne, Cap-Chat, Quebec [*Library symbol National Library of Canada*] (NLC)
QCC	Qualification Correlation Certification
qcc	Qualification Correlation Certification (AD)
QCC	Quality Communications Circle (MCD)
QCC	Quality Control Centre (NITA)
QCC	Quality Control Chain (IAA)
QCC	Quality Control Committee (MCD)
QCC	Queen Charlotte [*British Columbia*] [*Seismograph station code, US Geological Survey*] (SEIS)
QCC	Queensland Conservation Council [*Australia*] (AD)
QCC	Queensland Cotton Corp. [*Australia*]
QCC	Quenched Carbonaceous Composite [*Plasma technology*]
QCC	Quick Connect Coupling
qcc	Quick-Connect Coupling (AD)
QCC	Quinsigamond Community College [*Worcester, MA*]
QCC	Qwest Commuter Corp. [*ICAO designator*] (FAAC)
QCCA	Quality Control Council of America [*Defunct*] (EA)
QCCA	Queensland Cleaning Contractors Association [*Australia*] (AD)
QCCARS	Quality Control Collection Analysis and Reporting System
QCCB	Queen's College Cadet Battalion [*Taunton*] [*British military*] (DMA)
QCCL	CLSC Albert Samson, Coaticook, Quebec [*Library symbol National Library of Canada*] (NLC)
QCCR	Quality Control Change Request (SAA)
QCCRS	Conseil Regional de la Sante et des Services Sociaux, Chicoutimi, Quebec [*Library symbol National Library of Canada*] (NLC)
QCCS	Cree School Board, Chisasibi, James Bay, Quebec [*Library symbol National Library of Canada*] (BIB)
QCCT	Queensland Cultural Centre Trust [*Australia*]
QCD	Quality Control Data
qcd	Quality-Control Data (AD)
QCD	Quality Control Directive (MCD)
QCD	Quantum Chromodynamics [*Nuclear physics*]
qcd	Quantum Chromodynamics (AD)
QCD	Query Complexity Degree (MHDB)
QCD	Quick Claim Deed (MHDB)
QCD	Quick Control Dial [*Photography*]
qcd	Quit-Claim Deed (AD)
QCDI	Quality Control Departmental Instruction (AD)
QCDP	Quality Color Dithering Process [*Computer science*] (PCM)
QCDPA	Quality Chekd Dairy Products Association (EA)
QCDR	Quality Control Deficiency Report (AFM)
QCDSU	Quality Control Directive Supplement (SAA)
QCE	Quality Control and Evaluation (MCD)
QCE	Quality Control Engineering (AD)
QCE	Quality Control Engineers
QCEA	Quaker Council for European Affairs (EA)
QCENGR	Quality Control Engineer (IAA)
QCEU	Queensland Colliery Employees Union [*Australia*] (AD)
QCF	Quality Control [*Tabulating*] Form (AAG)
QCF	Quarterly Control Contract Factor (MCD)
QCF	Quartz Crystal Filter
qcf	Quartz-Crystal Filter (AD)
QCF	Queensland Cancer Fund [*Australia*]
QCF	Quench Compensation Factor
QCFB	QCF Bancorp [*NASDAQ symbol*] (TTSB)
QCFB	QCF Bancorp, Inc. [*NASDAQ symbol*] (SAG)
QCF Bc	QCF Bancorp, Inc. [*Associated Press*] (SAG)
QCFCLB	Queensland Council of Finance Counsellors and Lease Brokers [*Australia*]
QCFO	Quartz Crystal Frequency Oscillator
qcfo	Quartz-Crystal Frequency Oscillator (AD)
QCG	Quartz Creek Gold Mines (BC), Inc. [*Vancouver Stock Exchange symbol*]
QCGA	Queensland Cane Growers' Association [*Australia*]
QCGAT	Quiet, Clean, General Aviation Turbofan [*NASA*]
QCGC	Queensland Cane-Growers Council [*Australia*] (AD)
QCH	Hopital de Chicoutimi, Inc., Quebec [*Library symbol National Library of Canada*] (NLC)
QCH	Quick Connect Handle
qch	Quick-Connect Handle (AD)
QCHI	Quad City Hldgs [*NASDAQ symbol*] (TTSB)
QCHI	Quad City Holdings [*NASDAQ symbol*] (SAG)
QCHJC	Health Sciences Information Centre, Jewish Rehabilitation Hospital [*Centre d'Information sur les Sciences de la Sante, Hopital Juif de Readaptation*] Chomedey, Quebec [*Library symbol National Library of Canada*] (NLC)
QCHM	Quaker Chemical [*NASDAQ symbol*] (TTSB)
QCHM	Quaker Chemical Corp. [*NASDAQ symbol*] (NQ)
QCHR	Quality Control History Record
QCI	Quality Conformance Inspection (MSA)
QCI	Quality Control Index [*Environmental Protection Agency*] (GFGA)
QCI	Quality Control Information (AABC)
qci	Quality-Control Information (AD)
QCI	Quality Control Inspection
QCI	Quarto Castello [*Italy*] [*Seismograph station code, US Geological Survey Closed*] (SEIS)
QCI	Queen's College, Ireland (ROG)
QCI	Queensland Confederation of Industry [*Australia*] (AD)
QCI	Quota Club International [*Later, QI*]
Q Cic	Quintus Tullius Cicero (AD)
QCID	Quality Control and Inspection Department [*Navy*] (DNAB)
QCIE	Quality Control Inspection Element (AFIT)
QCIF	Quarter Common Intermediate Format (TELE)
QCIM	Quarterly Cumulative Index Medicus [*A publication*]
QCIP	Quality Control Inspection Procedure [*Nuclear energy*] (NRCH)
QCIR	Queen's Centre for International Relations [*Canada*] (BUAC)
QCIR	Queen's University at Kingston Centre for International Relations [*Canada Research center*] (RCD)
QCI's	Queen Charlotte Islands
QC Isl	Queen Charlotte Islands (AD)
Q City	Quezon City [*Philippines*] (AD)
QCJC	Queensland Criminal Justice Commission [*Australia*]
QCJJ	Quaker Committee on Jails and Justice [*Canada*]
QCK	Quick
QCK	Quick Connect Kit
qck	Quick-Connect Kit (AD)
QCL	Logilab, Inc., Charlebois, Quebec [*Library symbol National Library of Canada*] (NLC)
QCL	Quality Characteristics List (MSA)
QCL	Quality Checklist
QCL	Quality Control Level
qcl	Quality-Control Level (AD)
QCLPC	National Historic Park, Parks Canada [*Parc Historique National, Parcs Canada*] Coteau-du-Lac, Quebec [*Library symbol National Library of Canada*] (NLC)
QCM	Bibliotheque Municipale, Chateauguay, Quebec [*Library symbol National Library of Canada*] (BIB)
QCM	Quality Construction Master
QCM	Quality Control Manager
QCM	Quality Control Manual
QCM	Quality Courts Motels [*Later, QM*]
QCM	Quality of Care Measurement [*Insurance*] (WYGK)
QCM	Quantitative Computer Management (IEEE)
QCM	Quantum Conformal Fluctuation [*Theoretical physics*]
QCM	Quartz Crystal Microbalance
QCM	Quartz Crystal Monitor
QCM	Queensland Chamber of Mines [*Australia*]
QCM	Queensland Coal Mining [*Australia*] (AD)
QCM	Quick-Connects for Bulkhead Mounting (PDAA)
QCMA	Queensland Cooperative Milling Association [*Australia*] (AD)
QCMB	Centre de Documentation, Musee Beaulne, Coaticook, Quebec [*Library symbol National Library of Canada*] (NLC)
QCMC	Queensland Chicken Meat Council [*Australia*]
QCMM	Bibliotheque Municipale, Cap-De-La-Madeleine, Quebec [*Library symbol National Library of Canada*] (NLC)
QCMP	Queens' Council Member of Parliament [*British*] (AD)
QCMPE	Quantum Chemistry Microcomputer Program Exchange
QCNIC	Quad-Cities Nuclear Information Center (AD)
QCO	Quality Completion Order (AD)
QCO	Quality Control Officer (AAG)
QCO	Quality Control Organization
QCO	Quantity at Captain's Option [*Shipping*] (DS)
QCO	Quartz Crystal Oscillator
qco	Quartz-Crystal Oscillator (AD)
Q Co	Queens County (AD)
QCO	Quick Changeover [*Manufacturing*]
QCO_2	Microliters of Carbon Dioxide Given Off per Milligram of Tissue per Hour [*Medicine*] (DAVI)
QCOI	Queensland Chamber of Industry [*Australia*]
QCOM	Qualcomm, Inc. [*NASDAQ symbol*] (SPSG)
Q Conv R	Queensland Conveyancing Cases [*Australia A publication*]
QCOP	Quality Control Operating Procedure
QC Opt	QC Optics [*Associated Press*] (SAG)
QCOTA	Queensland Council on the Ageing [*Australia*]
QCP	Quality Check Program [*DoD*]
QCP	Quality Continuation Plan [*BMW manufacturer's warranty*]
QCP	Quality Control Procedure
QCP	Quantum Critical Point [*Physics*]
QCP	Queens College Press [*Australia*] (AD)
QCP	Quezon City [*Philippines*] [*Seismograph station code, US Geological Survey*] (SEIS)
QCP	Quiet Community Program [*Environmental Protection Agency*] (GFGA)
QCPA	Queensland Country Press Association [*Australia*]
QCPC	Quality Control Property Clearance (SAA)

QC-PCR....... Quantitative Competitive Polymerase Chain Reaction [*Analytical biochemistry*]
QC-PCR....... Quantitative Competive Polymerase Chain Reaction [*Genetics*]
QCPE .... Quantum Chemistry Program Exchange
QCPI .... Queen's College of Physicians, Ireland (ROG)
QCPLL .... Quadrature Channel Phase-Locked Loop (IAA)
QCPM .... Quality Control Procedures Manual (SAA)
QCPMS .... Quality Control and Performance Monitoring System (MCD)
QCPP .... Quality Control Planning Procedure (IAA)
QC/PS .... Impact/Static Pressure Ratio (WDAA)
QCPSA .... Quaker Center for Prisoner Support Activities (EA)
QCPSK .... Quaternary Coherent Phase-Shift Keying
QCQ .... Quebec [*Quebec*] [*Seismograph station code, US Geological Survey*] (SEIS)
QCR .... Qualitative Construction Requirement [*Army*]
QCR .... Quality Control/Reliability
qcr .... Quality Control/Reliability (AD)
QCR .... Quality Control Report
QCR .... Quality Control Representative [*Military*] (AABC)
QCR .... Quality Control Review
QCR .... Quality Control Room
QCR .... Quick Change Response [*System*]
qcr .... Quick-Change Response (AD)
QCR .... Quick Connect Relay
QCRC .... Quebec Central Railway Co. [*Canada*] (AD)
QCRCN....... Campus Notre-Dame-De-Foy, Cap-Rouge, Quebec [*Library symbol National Library of Canada*] (NLC)
QC Rep ...... Quality-Control Representative (AD)
QC Rept ..... Quality-Control Report (AD)
QCRF .... Queensland Children's Research Foundation [*Australia*]
QCRI .... Quality Control Reliability Investigator (AD)
QCRM .... Bibliotheque Municipale, Cap-Rouge, Quebec [*Library symbol National Library of Canada*] (BIB)
QCRS .... Quality Control Reference [*Analytical chemistry*]
QCRS .... Seminaire St-Augustin, Cap-Rouge, Quebec [*Library symbol National Library of Canada*] (NLC)
QCRT .... Quick Change Real-Time (MHDI)
qcrt .... Quick-Change Real Time (AD)
QC Ry .... Quebec Central Railway [*Canada*] (AD)
QCS .... Quad-Cities Station [*Nuclear energy*] (NRCH)
QCS .... Quality Control Standard (AAG)
QCS .... Quality Control Survey (SAA)
QCS .... Quality Control System
QCS .... Quality Cost System
QCS .... Query Control Station (MCD)
QCS .... Service de la Bibliotheque de Ville de Laval, Chomedey, Quebec [*Library symbol National Library of Canada*] (BIB)
QCSB .... Queens County Bancorp [*NASDAQ symbol*] (SAG)
QCSC .... Quadripartite Chemical, Biological, Radiological Standardization Committee [*Military*] (AABC)
QCSE .... Quantum-Confined Stark Effect [*Physics*]
QCSEE .... Quiet, Clean, Short-Haul Experimental Engine [*NASA*]
QCSEL .... Quality Control Select Vendor (MCD)
QCSH .... Societe Historique du Saguenay, Chicoutimi, Quebec [*Library symbol National Library of Canada*] (NLC)
QCSHEE ..... Quiet, Clean, Short-Haul Experimental Engine (DICI)
QCSM .... Quiescent Command/Service Module (MCD)
QCSO .... Quality Control Stop Order (AD)
QCSR .... Quaker Committee on Social Rehabilitation (NADA)
QCSR .... Quality Control Service Request (SAA)
QCSSO .... Queensland Council of State School Organisations [*Australia*]
QCSSP .... Quality Control Single Source Procurement (MCD)
QC Stand .... Quality-Control Standard (AD)
QCSTL .... Cote St. Luc Public Library, Quebec [*Library symbol National Library of Canada*] (NLC)
QCT............ Quality Control Technology (WDAA)
QCT............ Quantitative Computed Tomography [*Medicine*] (STED)
QCT............ Quantitative Computerized Tomography [*Biomedical engineering*]
QCT............ Quasiclassical Trajectory [*Chemical physics*]
QCT............ Quasi Classical Trajetory [*Physical chemistry*]
qct .... Questionable Corrective Task (AD)
QCT............ Questionable Corrective Task
QCT............ Quiescent Carrier Telephony (WDAA)
qct .... Quiescent Carrier Telephony (AD)
QCTE .... Quality Control Test Engineering (SAA)
QCTR .... Quality Control Test Report
QCTT.......... Quality Control Test Team [*Military*]
QCU .... Quality Courts United [*Later, QM*] (EA)
QCU .... Quartz Crystal Unit
qcu............. Quartz Crystal Unit (AD)
qcu............. Quick-Change Unit (AD)
QCU .... Quick Change Unit (MCD)
QCU .... Universite du Quebec, Chicoutimi, Quebec [*Library symbol National Library of Canada*] (NLC)
QCUG .... Departement de Geographie, Universite du Quebec, Chicoutimi, Quebec [*Library symbol National Library of Canada*] (NLC)
QCUGC....... Cartotheque, Universite du Quebec, Chicoutimi, Quebec [*Library symbol National Library of Canada*] (NLC)
QCUS .... Quartz Crystal Unit Set
qcus........... Quartz Crystal Unit Set (AD)
qcvc........... Quick-Connect Valve Coupler (AD)
QCVC .... Quick Connect Valve Coupler
QCVTI .... Quality Control Verification Test Inspection (SAA)
QCW .... Q-Phase CW Signal [*Television*] (IDOE)
QCW .... Quadrant Continuous Wave

qcw............ Quadrant Continuous Wave (AD)
QCW .... Quality Criteria for Water (EG)
QCWA .... Quarter Century Wireless Association (EA)
QCWA .... Queensland Country Women's Association [*Australia*] (AD)
Qcy .... Quincy (AD)
QCYC .... Queensland Cruising Yacht Club [*Australia*]
QD .... Bibliotheque Municipale, Dorval, Quebec [*Library symbol National Library of Canada*] (BIB)
QD .... QData Systems, Inc. [*Vancouver Stock Exchange symbol*]
QD .... Quad Demy [*Paper*] (DGA)
QD .... Quaestiones Disputatae (BJA)
QD .... Quantity Distance [*Explosives*]
QD .... Quantum Design, Inc.
QD .... Quantum Dot [*Solid state physics*]
QD .... Quaque Die [*Every Day*] [*Pharmacy*]
QD .... Quarterdeck
qd .... Quarterdeck (AD)
QD .... Quarter Distribution [*Parapsychology*]
QD .... Quartile Deviation [*Statistics*]
qd .... Quartile Deviation (AD)
QD .... Quasi Dicat [*As If One Should Say, or As Though One Should Say*] [*Latin*]
QD .... Quasi Dictum [*As If Said, or As Though It Had Been Said*] [*Latin*]
QD .... Quasi Dixisset [*As If One Had Said*] [*Latin*]
QD .... Quater in Die [*Four Times a Day*] [*Pharmacy*]
qd .... Quater in Die [*Four Times a Day*] [*Latin*] (AD)
qd .... Questioned Document [*Army*]
QD .... Questioned Document [*Criminology*]
QD .... Quick Delivery (WDAA)
qd .... Quick Delivery (AD)
qd .... Quick Detachable [*Weapon*] (AD)
QD .... Quick Detachable
q-d .... Quick-Disconnect (AD)
QD .... Quick Disconnect
QD .... Quicksilver Data [*Information service or system*] (IID)
QD .... Transbrasil SA Linhas Aereas [*Brazil ICAO designator*] (ICDA)
QDA .... Quadratic Discriminant Analysis [*Mathematics*]
QDA .... Qualifying Dividend Account
QDA .... Quantitative Descriptive Analysis
QDA .... Quantity Discount Agreement
qda .... Quantity Discount Agreement (AD)
Q-DBS........ Quasi-Direct Broadcast Satellite
QDC .... Quantum Development Corp.
QDC .... Quick Dependable Communications
qdc .... Quick Detachable Communication (AD)
QDC .... Quick Die Change [*Automotive engineering*]
QDC .... Quick Disconnect Cap
qdc............ Quick-Disconnect Cap (AD)
QDC .... Quick Disconnect Connector
QDC & E...... Quartz Devices Conference and Exhibition
qdcc........... Quick-Disconnect Circular Connection (AD)
QDCC......... Quick Disconnect Circular Connector
QDCE .... College Bourgchemin (CEGEP), Drummondville, Quebec [*Library symbol National Library of Canada*] (NLC)
qdd .... Qualified for Deep Diving (AD)
QDD .... Qualified for Deep Diving Duties [*Navy British*]
QDD .... Quantized Decision Detection
qdd .... Quantized Decision Detection (AD)
QDE .... Etablessement Donnacona, Quebec [*Library symbol National Library of Canada*] (BIB)
QDE .... Qualified Designated Entities [*Independent counseling groups and churches involved with aiding aliens*] [*Immigration and Naturalization Service term*]
QDE .... Quality Data Evaluation (MCD)
QDEAS .... Quality Deficiency Evaluation and Action System (MCD)
QDEBUG ..... Quick Diagnostic Debugging Program [*Computer science*] (MHDI)
QDEC .... Queensland Development Education Centre [*Australia*]
QDEC .... Queensland Distance Education College [*Australia*]
QDEK .... Quarterdeck Corp. [*NASDAQ symbol*] (SAG)
QDEK .... Quarterdeck Office Systems [*NASDAQ symbol*] (SPSG)
QDEL .... Quidel Corp. [*NASDAQ symbol*] (SPSG)
QDELW .... Quidel Corp. Wrrt [*NASDAQ symbol*] (TTSB)
QDF .... Quantum Distribution Function
QDF .... Queensland Department of Forestry [*Australia*]
QDG .... Queen's Dragoon Guards [*Formerly, KDG, QB*] [*Military unit*] [*British*]
QD/GD .... Quincy Division/General Dynamics (AD)
Qd Govt Mining J... Queensland Government Mining Journal [*A publication*]
Qd Graingrower... Queensland Graingrower [*A publication*]
QDGS.......... Quick-Draw Graphics System (PDAA)
QDH .... Quick Disconnect Handle
qdh .... Quick-Disconnect Handle (AD)
QDHSC........ Hopital Sainte-Croix, Drummondville, Quebec [*Library symbol National Library of Canada*] (NLC)
QDIN .... Quality Dining [*NASDAQ symbol*] (TTSB)
QDIN .... Quality Dining, Inc. [*NASDAQ symbol*] (SAG)
Qd Ind .... Queensland Industry [*A publication*]
QDISC......... Quick Disconnect
QDK .... Quick Disconnect Kit
qdk............. Quick-Disconnect Kit (AD)
Qd L .... Queensland Lawyer [*Australia A publication*]
QDL .... Quick Disconnect, Large
Qd Law Soc J.... Queensland Law Society. Journal [*A publication*]
QDM .... Centre d'Information Documentaire Come-Saint-Germain, Drummondville, Quebec [*Library symbol National Library of Canada*] (NLC)

QDM .... Quad Driver Module [*Electronics*]
QDM .... Quick Disconnect, Miniature
QDMA .... Quality Deer Management Association
QDMBPT ...... Quasi-Degenerate Many-Body Perturbation Theory [*Physics*]
QDMC .... Quadratic Dynamic Matrix Control
QDMC .... Quadratic Matrix Control [*Chemical engineering*] [*Computer science*]
QDN .... Quick Disconnect Nipple
qdn .... Quick-Disconnect Nipple (AD)
qdo .... Quadripartite Development Objective (AD)
QDO .... Quadripartite Development Objective [*Military*] (AABC)
Qd'O .... Quai d'Orsay (AD)
QDO .... Quantitative Design Objective
QDO .... Queensland Dairyfarmers' Organisation [*Australia*]
QDO .... Queensland Dairymens Organisation [*Australia*] (AD)
QDO .... Quick Delivery Order
QDOF .... Queensland Department of Forests [*Australia*]
QDOPH .... Office des Personnes Handicapees du Quebec, Drummondville, Quebec [*Library symbol National Library of Canada*] (NLC)
QDOS .... Quick and Dirty Operating System [*Microsoft Corp.*] (ECON)
QDP .... Quick Disconnect Pivot
qdp .... Quick-Disconnect Pivot (AD)
Qd Police J... Queensland Police Journal [*A publication*]
QDPR .... Quinoid Dehydropteridine Reductase [*An enzyme*] (DAVI)
QDPSK .... Quaternary Differential Phase Keying [*Telecommunications*] (CIST)
QDPSK .... Quaternary Differential Phase-Shift Keying (TEL)
QDR .... Dubai Riyal [*Monetary unit*]
QDR .... Quadrennial Defence Review [*Defense policy*]
QDR .... Quadrennial Defense Review [*Army*]
QDR .... Qualification Design Review [*NASA*] (MCD)
QDR .... Quality Data and Reporting (MCD)
QDR .... Quality Deficiency Record [*DoD*]
QDR .... Quality Deficiency Report [*DoD*]
QDR .... Quick Disk Reformatter [*Vernon Buerg*] [*Computer utility tool*] (PCM)
QDR .... Quick Dump Rinse (AAEL)
Qdrax .... Quadrax Corp. [*Associated Press*] (SAG)
QDRI .... Qualitative Development Requirement Information
QDRL .... Questionnaire Design Research Laboratory [*Department of Health and Human Services*] (GFGA)
QDRM .... Banca Quadrum SA [*NASDAQ symbol*] (SAG)
QDRMY .... Banca QuadruADS [*NASDAQ symbol*] (TTSB)
qdrnt .... Quadrant (AD)
QDRNT .... Quadrant (MSA)
QDRO .... Qualified Domestic Relations Order [*Court authorization for retirement distribution*]
QDRT .... Quadrant
QDRTR .... Quadrature
QDRX .... Quadrax Corp. [*NASDAQ symbol*] (NQ)
QDRXZ .... Quadrax Corp. Wrrt 'C' [*NASDAQ symbol*] (TTSB)
QDS .... Quality Data System (NASA)
QDS .... Quantitative Decision System (AD)
QDS .... Quarantine Document System [*Information retrieval*] [*NASA*]
QDS .... Quarter Die Sumendum [*To be taken four times a day*] [*Latin*] [*Pharmacy*] (DAVI)
qds .... Quick-Disconnect Series (AD)
QDS .... Quick Disconnect Series
QDS .... Quick Disconnect, Small
QDS .... Quick Disconnect Swivel
qds .... Quick-Disconnect Swivel (AD)
QDSB .... Quadrature Double Sideband (MCD)
QDSPA .... Queensland Dance Studio Proprietors' Association [*Australia*]
QDT .... Qualified Domestic Trust
QDT .... Quintessence of Dental Technology
QDTA .... Quantitative Differential Thermal Analysis
qdta .... Quantitative Differential Thermal Analysis (AD)
QDTAA .... Queensland Dive Tourism Association of Australia
Qd Teach J... Queensland Teachers' Journal [*A publication*]
QDU .... Dusseldorf-Main RR [*Germany Airport symbol*] (OAG)
QDV .... Quick Disconnect Valve
qdv .... Quick Disconnect Valve (AD)
QDX .... Quick Decision Exercise [*Training simulation*] [*Army*]
QDXR .... Quadriplexer
QE .... Bibliotheque Municipale, St.-Eustache, Quebec [*Library symbol National Library of Canada*] (BIB)
QE .... Journal of Quantum Electronics [*A publication*] (MCD)
QE .... Quadrant Elevation
qe .... Quadrant Elevation (AD)
QE .... Quadruple Expansion (DS)
QE .... Quaestiones et Salutationes in Exodum [*Philo*] (BJA)
QE .... Quality Engineer [*or Engineering*]
QE .... Quality Evaluation (NG)
QE .... Quality Excellence [*Chrysler Corp.*]
QE .... Quantum Efficiency
QE .... Quebec (AD)
QE .... Queen's Evidence [*British*] [*Legal term*] (BARN)
QE .... Queue Empty (MHDI)
QE .... Queue Entry
qe .... Quick Estimate (AD)
qe .... Quod Est [*Which Is*] [*Latin*] (AD)
QE .... Quod Est [*Which Is*] [*Latin*]
QE .... Quotation Estimate (MCD)
QE .... Quoted Exhibit (SAA)
QE 2 .... Queen Elizabeth 2 [*Luxury liner*]
QEA .... QANTAS Empire Airways Ltd. [*Later, QANTAS Airways Ltd.*]
QEA .... Quantum Electronics and Applications (IAA)
QEA .... Queensland Exporters' Association [*Australia*]

QEA .... Queue Element Area [*Computer science*] (IAA)
QEA .... Quick Electrolyte Analyzer [*Laboratory science*] (DAVI)
QEAD .... Quality Engineering and Assurance Division [*Navy*] (DNAB)
QEAE .... Quarternary Ethylaminoethyl [*Organic chemistry*]
QEAM .... Quick Erecting Antenna Mast [*Army*] (RDA)
QEAS .... Quantum Electronics and Applications Society (MCD)
QEAV .... Quick Exhaust Air Valve
qeav .... Quick-Exhaust Air Valve (AD)
QEB .... Quality Engineering Bulletin [*NASA*]
QEC .... Quantum Electronics Council
QEC .... Quantum Energy [*Vancouver Stock Exchange symbol*]
QEC .... Queen Elizabeth College [*British*]
QEC .... Quick Engine Change
qec .... Quick Engine Change (AD)
QEC .... Quiesce-at-End-of-Chain [*Computer science*] (IBMDP)
QECA .... Quick Engine Change Assembly (NG)
QECC .... Queen Elizabeth Chemical Center [*British*] (AD)
QECCH .... Compton County Historical and Museum Society [*Societe d'Histoire et du Musee du Comte de Compton*] Eaton Corner, Quebec [*Library symbol National Library of Canada*] (NLC)
QECK .... Quick Engine Change Kit (NG)
QECS .... Quick Engine Change Stand (NG)
QECU .... Quick Engine Change Unit
qecu .... Quick Engine-Change Unit (AD)
QED .... Quality Education Data [*Information service or system*] (IID)
QED .... Quality, Efficiency, Dependability (AD)
qed .... Quantitative Evaluative Device (AD)
QED .... Quantitative Evaluative Device (AEBS)
QED .... Quantum Electrodynamics [*Theory*]
qed .... Quantum Electrodynamics (AD)
QED .... Quantum Emission Domain [*Spectral physics*]
QED .... Quentin E. Deverill [*Protagonist in TV series; initialism also used as title of the series*]
QED .... Quick Editor [*Computer science*] (ECII)
QED .... Quick Erection Dome
qed .... Quick-Reaction Dome (AD)
QED .... Quick Text Editor
QED .... Quod Erat Demonstrandum [*Which Was the Thing to Be Proved*] [*Latin*]
qed .... Quod Erat Demonstrandum [*That Which Was to Be Proved*] [*Latin*] (AD)
QEDL .... Quality Engineering Diagnostic Laboratory (MCD)
QEE .... Quadriceps Extension Exercise [*Orthopedics*] (DAVI)
qee .... Quadruple Expansion Engine (AD)
QEEL .... Quality Evaluation and Engineering Laboratory [*Navy*]
QEEL/CO ..... Quality Evaluation and Engineering Laboratory, Concord [*California*] [*Navy*]
qeev .... Quantum Electrodynamics Electron Volts (AD)
QEF .... Quail Embryo Fibroblast [*Medicine*] (DMAA)
QEF .... Queensland Employers' Federation [*Australia*] (AD)
qef .... Quod Erat Faciendum [*That Which Was to Be Done*] [*Latin*] (AD)
QEF .... Quod Erat Faciendum [*Which Was to Be Made, or Done*] [*Latin*]
QEFFD .... Queen Elizabeth's Foundation for the Disabled [*British*] (AD)
QEH .... Queen Elizabeth Hall [*London, England*]
QEH .... Queen Elizabeth's Hospital School [*England*]
QEI .... Quod Erat Inveniendum [*Which Was to Be Found Out*] [*Latin*]
qei .... Quod Erat Inveniendum [*That Which Was to Be Discovered*] [*Latin*] (AD)
QEIC .... Queensland Education Information Centre [*Australia*]
QEIC .... Queensland Egg Industry Council [*Australia*]
QEIM .... Qinhuangdao Engineering & Research Institute for Ferrous Metallurgical Mines [*China*] (BUAC)
QE/K .... Quality Evaluation and Engineering Laboratory, Keyport [*Washington*] [*Naval Torpedo Station*]
QEKG .... Q-Med, Inc. [*Clark, NJ*] [*NASDAQ symbol*] (NQ)
QEL .... Quality Evaluation Laboratory
QEL .... Queue Element [*Computer science*]
QEL .... Quiet Extended Life
qel .... Quiet Extended Life (AD)
QElecSC ...... Quadripartite Electronic Standardization Committee [*Military*] (AABC)
QELS .... Quantitative Evaluation of Library Searching [*Spectra matching technique*]
QELS .... Quasi-Elastic Light Scattering [*Also, QLS, QUELS*] [*Physics*]
QEM .... Quadrant Electrometer
qem .... Quadrant Electrometer (AD)
QEM .... Qualified Export Manager [*American Society of International Executives*] [*Designation awarded by*]
QEM .... Quality Education for Minorities (AD)
QEM .... Quality Education for Minorities Project (EA)
QEMH .... Queen Elizabeth Military Hospital [*Ministry of Defense*] [*British*] (PDAA)
QEMM .... Quarterdeck Expanded Memory Manager [*Computer science*]
QEN .... Quare Executionem Non [*Wherefore Execution Should Not Be Issued*] [*Latin Legal term*] (DLA)
QEngrSC ..... Quadripartite Engineer Standardization Committee [*Military*] (AABC)
QENP .... Queen Elizabeth National Park [*Uganda*] (AD)
QENS .... Quasi-Elastic Neutron Scattering [*Physics*]
QEO .... Quality Engineering Operations
qeo .... Quality Engineering Operations (AD)
QEO .... Queen Elizabeth's Own [*British military*] (DMA)
QEONS .... Queen Elizabeth's Overseas Nursing Service [*British*] (DAVI)
QEOP .... Quartermaster Emergency Operation Plan [*Army*]
QEP .... Quality Evaluation Program [*College of American Pathologists*]
QEP .... Quality Examination Program (AFM)
QEP .... Queen Elizabeth Park (AD)

QEP	Queen Elizabeth Planetarium (AD)
QEP	Queensland Environmental Program [Australia] (AD)
QEPC	QEP Co., Inc. [NASDAQ symbol] (SAG)
QEP Co	QEP Co., Inc. [Associated Press] (SAG)
QEPL	Quality Engineering Planning List (MCD)
QER	Qualitative Equipment Requirements [Army] (AABC)
qer	Qualitative Equipment Requirements (AD)
QER	Quarterly Economic Review [A publication] (AD)
QER	Queen's Edinburgh Rifles [British military] (DMA)
QERI	Qingdao Electronics Research Institute [China] (BUAC)
QES	Quadrant Eleventh-Gram Second
QES	Quaker Esperanto Society (EA)
QESCP	Quality Engineering Significant Control Points (MCD)
qescp	Quality Engineering Significant Control Points (AD)
QESISB	Queensland Electricity Supply Industry Superannuation Board [Australia]
QESP	Queen Emma Summer Palace (AD)
QEST	Quality Evaluation System Tests (NG)
QEST	Query, Update Entry, Search, Time-Sharing System (NVT)
QESTS	Query, Update Entry, Search, Time Sharing [Computer science] (AD)
QET	Quality Expo TIME-International (ITD)
QET	Quality in Education [Project] (AIE)
QET	Quasi-Equilibrium Theory [Physical chemistry]
QET	Queen Elizabeth Theatre [Vancouver] (AD)
QETE	Quality Engineering Test Establishment [Department of National Defence] [Canada] (IRC)
QEV	Quick Exhaust Valve
qev	Quick Exhaust Valve (AD)
QEW	Queen Elizabeth Way [Canada]
QEW	Quick Early Warning Test [Medicine] (MAE)
QF	Qabel Foundation (EA)
QF	QANTAS Airways Ltd. [Australia ICAO designator]
QF	Qualifying Facility [Electric power]
QF	Quality Factor [Nuclear energy]
qf	Quality Factor (AD)
QF	Quality Form [Nuclear energy] (NRCH)
QF	Quarterfinals (WGA)
QF	Quench Frequency (DEN)
qf	Quench Frequency (AD)
QF	Queue Full
QF	Quick-Firing [Gun]
QF	Quick Fix (MCD)
QF	Quick Freeze
qf	Quick Freeze (AD)
QFA	Qantas Airways Ltd. [Australia ICAO designator] (FAAC)
QFA	Qualification Firings Alignment (DNAB)
qfa	Quality per Final Article (AD)
QFA	Quantitative Fibrinogen Assay [Clinical chemistry]
QFAB	Quaker Fabric [NASDAQ symbol] (TTSB)
QFAB	Quaker Fabric Corp. [NASDAQ symbol] (SAG)
QFB	Quiet Fast Boat [Navy symbol]
QF-BH	Quick Fix - Black Hawk
QFC	Quantitative Flight Characteristics
qfc	Quantitative Flight Characteristics (AD)
QFCC	Qantas Flight Catering Centre [Australia]
QFCC	Quantitative Flight Characteristics Criteria
qfcc	Quantitative Flight Characteristics Criteria (AD)
QFCI	Quality Food Centers [NASDAQ symbol] (TTSB)
QFCI	Quality Food Centers, Inc. [NASDAQ symbol] (NQ)
QFCI	Quartermaster Food and Container Institute for the Armed Forces
QFD	Quality Function Deployment [Automotive engineering]
QFD	Quality Function Development [Failure analysis]
QFD	Quantum Flavor Dynamics
QFD	Quarterly Forecast Demand
QFDA	Queensland Funeral Directors' Association [Australia]
QFDO	Queensland Film Development Office [Australia]
QFE	Columbus [Georgia] Fort Benning [Airport symbol] (OAG)
QFE	Quartz Fiber Electrometer (WDAA)
qfe	Quartz Fiber Electrometer (AD)
QFE	Query Formulation and Encoding
Q-fellows	Quartermaster Fellows (AD)
Q-fellows	Queer Fellows (AD)
QFET	Quantum Field-Effect Transistor (CIST)
Q-fever	Queensland Fever [Medicine] (DB)
Q fever	Query Fever (AD)
QFF	Atmospheric Pressure Converted to Mean Sea Level Elevation [Aviation code] (AIA)
qff	Quadruple Flip-Flop (AD)
QFF	Quadrupole Flip-Flop [Computer science]
QFF	Queensland Farmers' Federation [Australia]
QFGA	Queensland Farmers and Graziers' Association [Australia]
QFGA	Queensland Flower Growers' Association [Australia]
QFHS	Quebec Federation of Historical Societies [Canada] (EAIO)
QFI	Qualified Flight Instructor
QFI	Qualified Flying Instructor
QFIA	Quantitative Fluorescence Image Analysis [Medicine]
QFIRC	Quick Fix Interference Reduction Capability (AFM)
qfirc	Quick-Fix Interference-Reduction Capability (AD)
QFITC	Queensland Fishing Industry Training Committee [Australia]
QFITC	Queensland Food Industry Training Council [Australia]
QFITC	Queensland Furniture Industry Training Committee [Australia]
QFL	Quasi-Fermi Level
qfl	Quasi-Fermi Level (AD)
QFLGE	Queensland Foundation for Local Government Engineering [Australia]

QFM	Quantized Frequency Modulation
qfm	Quantized Frequency Modulation (AD)
QFM	Quartz-Fayalite-Magnetite [Geology]
QFMA	Quarters Furniture Manufacturers Association (NTPA)
QFMA	Quebec Fertilizer Manufacturers Association (AC)
QFMA	Queensland Flour Millers' Association [Australia]
QFMR	Quantized Frequency Modulation Repeater
QFN	Quicken Financial Network (PCM)
QFO	Quartz Frequency Oscillator
qfo	Quartz Frequency Oscillator (AD)
QFOBI	Qualified Family-Owned Business Interests
QFP	Quad Flat Pack (NITA)
qfp	Quartz Fiber Product (AD)
QFP	Quartz Fiber Product
QFP	Quick Fix Program
QFPL	Qualified Film Producers List (AAGC)
QFr	Epistulae ad Quintum Fratrem [of Cicero] [Classical studies] (OCD)
QFR	Quarterly Force Revision [Military] (NVT)
Q fract	Quick Fraction [Reference to membrane potentials] (DAVI)
QFRI	Queensland Fisheries Research Institute [Australia] (AD)
QFS	Queensland Fire Service [Australia]
QFS	Queensland Fisheries Service [Australia] (AD)
QFS	Queensland Forest Service [Australia]
QFS	Quick-Fit Sea (DNAB)
QFSM	Queen's Fire Service Medal for Distinguished Service [British]
QFSM	Queen's Fire Services Medal [British] (AD)
QFSR	Quartus Foundation for Spiritual Research (EA)
QFT	Quantized Field Theory
qft	Quantized Field Theory (AD)
QFT	Quantum Field Theory (AAEL)
QG	Bibliotheque Municipale, Gatineau, Quebec [Library symbol National Library of Canada] (NLC)
QG	Quadrature Grid
qg	Quadrature Grid (AD)
QG	Quaestiones et Salutationes in Genesin [Philo] (BJA)
QG	Qualified in Gunnery [British military] (DMA)
QG	Quartermaster General [Military]
QG	Quartier General [Headquarters] [French] (AD)
QG	Quartier Generale [Headquarters] [Italian] (AD)
QG	Queensland Grains [Australia Commercial firm]
QGA	Queensland Graingrowers' Association [Australia]
QGA	Queensland Gymnastic Association [Australia]
QGAH	Hotel-Dieu de Gaspe, Quebec [Library symbol National Library of Canada] (NLC)
QGAP	Centre de Documentation, Peches Maritimes, Ministere de l'Agriculture, des Pe cheries, et de l'Alimentation du Quebec, Gaspe, Quebec [Library symbol National Library of Canada] (NLC)
QGBES	Queensland Government Bureau of Emergency Services [Australia]
QGBF	Quasi-Grain Boundary Free [Photovoltaic energy systems]
QGC	College de la Gaspesie, Gaspe, Quebec [Library symbol National Library of Canada] (NLC)
QGCH	Centre Hospitalier de Gatineau, Quebec [Library symbol National Library of Canada] (NLC)
QGE	Queen's Gurkha Engineers [British military] (DMA)
QGEN	QIAGEN [NASDAQ symbol] (SAG)
QGFM	Queensland Guild of Furniture Manufacturers [Australia]
QGGA	Queensland Grain Growers Association [Australia] (AD)
QGI	Grosse Ile Library, Magdalen Islands, Quebec [Library symbol National Library of Canada] (NLC)
QGL	Granby Leader Mail Office, Quebec [Library symbol National Library of Canada] (NLC)
QGM	Bibliotheque Municipale, Granby, Quebec [Library symbol National Library of Canada] (NLC)
qgm	Quarter-Girth Measure (AD)
QGM	Queen's Gallantry Medal [British]
QGMG	Musee de la Gaspesie, Gaspe, Quebec [Library symbol National Library of Canada] (BIB)
QGMM	Bibliotheque Municipale, Grand'Mere, Quebec [Library symbol National Library of Canada] (NLC)
QGNG	Ecole Secondaire Nicolas-Gatineau, Gatineau, Quebec [Library symbol National Library of Canada] (BIB)
QGO	Queen's Gurkha Officer [Military British]
QGPC	Qatar General Petroleum Corp.
QGPO	Qatar General Petroleum Organization (AD)
QGS	Quantity Gauging System (NASA)
QGSH	Societe Historique du Comte de Shefford, Granby, Quebec [Library symbol National Library of Canada] (NLC)
QGTB	Queensland Government Tourist Bureau [Australia] (AD)
QGU	Queensland Golf Union [Australia]
Q Guild	Quality Guild (BUAC)
qgv	Quantized Gate Video (AD)
QGV	Quantized Gate Video [RADAR]
QH	Bibliotheque Municipale, Hull, Quebec [Library symbol National Library of Canada] (NLC)
QH	Quadrature Hybrid (IAA)
QH	Quaque Hora [Every Hour] [Pharmacy]
qh	Quaque Hora [Every Hour] [Latin] (AD)
q-h	Quartz-Halogen (AD)
QH	Quartz Halogen
QH	Quartz Helix
qh	Quartz Helix (AD)
QH	Queen's Hall (AD)
QH	Quorn Hounds
QH	West African Airways [ICAO designator] (AD)

Q-H₂ .... Ubihydroquinone [*Ubiquinol*] [*Laboratory science*] (DAVI)
QHAC .... CEGEP [*College d'Enseignement General et Professionnel*] de Hauterive, BaieComeau, Quebec [*Library symbol National Library of Canada*] (NLC)
QHACR .... Conseil Regional de la Sante et des Services Sociaux de la Region Cote-Nord, Hauterive, Quebec [*Library symbol National Library of Canada*] (NLC)
QHB .... Economics Information Centre, Bell Canada, Hull, Quebec [*Library symbol National Library of Canada*] (NLC)
QHB .... Queen's Hard Bargain [*Undesirable serviceman*] [*Slang British*] (DSUE)
QHBC .... Bibliotheque Centrale de Pret d'Outaouais, Hull, Quebec [*Library symbol National Library of Canada*] (BIB)
QHBEER .... Headquarters Engineering Economics Reference Centre, Bell Canada, Hull, Quebec [*Library symbol National Library of Canada*] (NLC)
QHBRM .... Bell Canada Headquarters, Regulatory Matters-Regulatory Information Bank, Hull, Quebec [*Library symbol National Library of Canada*] (NLC)
QHC .... CEGEP [*College d'Enseignement General et Professionnel*] de l'Outaouais, Hull, Quebec [*Library symbol National Library of Canada*] (NLC)
QHC .... Quarter Half Circle (IAA)
QHC .... Queen's Honorary Chaplain [*British*]
QHC .... Queensland Housing Commission [*Australia*]
QHCH .... Heritage Campus, CEGEP de l'Outaouais, Hull, Quebec [*Library symbol National Library of Canada*] (NLC)
QHCL .... Centre de Documentation, CLSC de Hull, Quebec [*Library symbol National Library of Canada*] (NLC)
QHCRS .... Conseil Regional de la Sante et des Services Sociaux de la Region Outaouais-Hull, Hull, Quebec [*Library symbol National Library of Canada*] (NLC)
QHDS .... Queen's Honorary Dental Surgeon [*British*]
QHE .... E. B. Eddy Co., Hull, Quebec [*Library symbol National Library of Canada*] (NLC)
QHE .... Quantum Hall Effect [*Physics*]
QHE .... Quantum Hall Experiment (AAEL)
QHEA .... Queensland Horticultural Export Association [*Australia*]
Q Her .... Queensland Heritage [*A publication*]
QHESJ .... Ecole Secondaire St.-Joseph, Hull, Quebec [*Library symbol National Library of Canada*] (BIB)
QHGI .... Quorum Health Group [*NASDAQ symbol*] (TTSB)
QHGI .... Quorum Health Group, Inc. [*NASDAQ symbol*] (SAG)
QHI .... Qualified Helicopter Instructor
Q Hist Soc J ... Queensland Historical Society. Journal [*A publication*]
QHM .... Quartz Horizontal Magnetometer (NOAA)
QHM .... Queen's Harbour Master [*British*]
QHMML .... Micromedia Ltee., Hull, Quebec [*Library symbol National Library of Canada*] (BIB)
QHNS .... Queen's Honorary Nursing Sister [*British*]
QHO .... Queen's Hall Orchestra
QHP .... Quasi-Hydrostatic Pressure [*Physics*]
QHP .... Queen's Honorary Physician [*British*]
QHP .... Quiet Helicopter Program (RDA)
QHPJ .... Centre Hospitalier Pierre Janet, Hull, Quebec [*Library symbol National Library of Canada*] (NLC)
QHQAR .... Centre Regional de l'Outaouais, Archives Nationales du Quebec, Hull, Quebec [*Library symbol National Library of Canada*] (BIB)
QHR .... Quality History Record [*Nuclear energy*] (NRCH)
q hr .... Quaque Hora [*Every Hour*] [*Latin Pharmacy*] (WGA)
QHRI .... Quantum Health Resources [*NASDAQ symbol*] (SPSG)
QHRI .... Quantum Hlth Resources [*NASDAQ symbol*] (TTSB)
QHS .... Qinghaosu [*Antimalarial drug*]
qhs .... Quaque Hora Somni [*Every Hour of Sleep*] [*Pharmacy*] [*Latin*] (MAE)
QHS .... Queen's Honorary Surgeon [*British*]
QHS .... Queensland Historical Society [*Australia*]
QHS .... Quick Hot-Swap [*Computer disk drive*]
QHSA .... Societe d'Amenagement de l'Outaouais, Hull, Quebec [*Library symbol National Library of Canada*] (NLC)
QHSC .... Centre Hospitalier Regional de l'Outaouais, Hull, Quebec [*Library symbol National Library of Canada*] (NLC)
QHSIA .... Queensland Hide and Skin Industries Association [*Australia*]
QHSS .... Queensland Healthy Soil Society [*Australia*]
QHU .... Universite du Quebec, Hull, Quebec [*Library symbol National Library of Canada*] (NLC)
QHV .... Queen's Honorary Veterinarian [*British*] (AD)
QHV .... Quiet Heavy Vehicle [*Automotive engineering*]
QHY .... Quantized High Y [*Picture resolution*] (NTCM)
QI .... Cimber Air [*ICAO designator*] (AD)
QI .... Quad Imperial [*Paper*] (DGA)
QI .... Qualified Indorsement (MHDB)
QI .... Qualified Instructor [*British military*] (DMA)
QI .... Quality Improvement (HCT)
qi .... Quality Improvement (AD)
QI .... Quality Increase (AABC)
QI .... Quality Index
QI .... Quality Indices (WDAA)
qi .... Quality Indices (AD)
QI .... Quantity Indicator (KSC)
QI .... Quarterly Index [*A publication*] (AD)
QI .... Quart Imperial (DNAB)
QI .... Quartz Iodine
QI .... Quasi-Inertial
QI .... Queensland Insurance [*Australia*] (AD)
QI .... Quiet Ionosphere (IAA)

QI .... Quota International (EA)
QIA .... Quantitative Infrared Analysis
QIA .... Queensland Institute of Architects [*Australia*] (AD)
QIA .... Queensland Irish Association [*Australia*]
QIA .... Quick Informal Assessment [*Test*] (TMMY)
QIAC .... Quantimet Image Analyzing Computer (PDAA)
QIAET .... Quartzsite Integrated Acoustic and Engine Test Site
QIAGEN .... QIAGEN [*Associated Press*] (SAG)
QIAM .... Queued Indexed Access Memory [*Computer science*] (IAA)
qiam .... Queued Indexed Access Memory [*Computer science*] (AD)
QIB .... Qatar Islamic Bank (BUAC)
QIB .... Quarterly Information Bulletin [*Navy*] (DNAB)
QIB .... Queensland Imperial Bushmen [*British military*] (DMA)
QIB .... Quick Is Beautiful [*NASA project philosophy*]
QIC .... Aero Quick [*Mexico ICAO designator*] (FAAC)
QIC .... Quaker International Centre (BUAC)
QIC .... Quality Information Center
QIC .... Quality Inspection Control [*Environmental science*] (COE)
qic .... Quality Inspection Criteria (AD)
QIC .... Quality Inspection Criteria
QIC .... Quality Insurance Chain (IAA)
QIC .... Quarter Inch Cartridge [*Computer science*]
QIC .... Quarter-Inch Cartridge Drive Standards, Inc. (DDC)
QIC .... Quarter-Inch Compatibility [*Format*]
QIC .... Quartz Iodine Crystal
qic .... Quartz-Iodine Crystal (AD)
QICA .... Queensland Immigration Control Association [*Australia*]
QIC-Wide ..... Quarter Inch Cartridge-Wide
qid .... Quater in Die [*Four Times a Day*] [*Latin*] (AD)
QID .... Quater in Die [*Four Times a Day*] [*Pharmacy*]
QIDN .... Queen's Institute of District Nursing [*British*]
QIE .... Qualified International Executive (AD)
QIE .... Quantitative Immunoelectrophoresis Methods [*Analytical biochemistry*]
qie .... Qunatitative Immuno-Electrophoresis (AD)
QIE-AF .... Qualified International Executive - Air Forwarding [*American Society of International Executives, Inc.*] [*Designation awarded by*]
QIE-EM .... Qualified International Executive - Export Management [*American Society of International Executives, Inc.*] [*Designation awarded by*]
QIE-F .... Qualified International Executive - Forwarding [*American Society of International Executives, Inc.*] [*Designation awarded by*]
QIER .... Queensland Institute for Educational Research [*Australia*] (AD)
QIE-TM .... Qualified International Executive - Traffic Management [*American Society of International Executives, Inc.*] [*Designation awarded by*]
QIF .... Quantitative Immunofluorescence
QIF .... Quartz-Iron-Fayalite [*Geology*]
QIF .... Quicken Interchange File [*Computer science*] (PCM)
QIFMA .... Archives des Freres Maristes, Iberville, Quebec [*Library symbol National Library of Canada*] (NLC)
QIG .... Quantitative Immunoglobulin [*Immunology*] (DAVI)
QIG .... Queensland Industrial Gazette [*A publication*]
QIH .... Quality International Hotels (AD)
QIK .... Quick (MSA)
QIL .... Quad In-Line
QIL .... Quartz Incandescent Lamp
qil .... Quartz Incandescent Lamp (AD)
qil .... Quartz Iodine Lamp (AD)
QIL .... Quartz Iodine Lamp
QILS .... Quantification of Integrated Logistics Support
QIMA .... Queensland Institute of Municipal Administration (BUAC)
QIMR .... Queensland Institute of Medical Research [*Australia*] (AD)
QIN .... Quality Improvement Network (DMAA)
QIO .... Queue Input/Output
QIP .... PALINET [*Pennsylvania Area Library Network*] Central, Philadelphia, PA [*OCLC symbol*] (OCLC)
QIP .... Quad-in-Line Package [*Computer science*] (IAA)
QIP .... Quality Improvement Process [*Quality control*]
QIP .... Quality Improvement Program (ACII)
QIP .... Quality Improvement Project (HCT)
QIP .... Quality Inspection Point (KSC)
QIP .... Quarterly Intercession Paper [*A publication*] (ROG)
QIP .... Quarters Improvement Program (MCD)
QIP .... Quartz Insulation Part
qip .... Quartz Insulation Part (AD)
QIP .... Query Interpretation Program (SAA)
QIP .... Quiescat in Pace [*May He, or She, Rest in Peace*] [*Latin*]
QIPA .... Queensland Institute of Public Affairs [*Australia*] (AD)
QIPS .... Qualitative Incentive Procurement Service (AD)
QIPS .... Quality Improvement Projects (WDAA)
QIR .... Quechan Indian Reservation (AD)
QIRC .... Queensland Industrial Relations Commission [*Australia*]
QIS .... Quality Information System (IAA)
QIS .... Quality Insurance System (IAA)
QISAM .... Queued Indexed Sequential Access Method [*IBM Corp.*] [*Computer science*]
qisam .... Queued-Indexed Sequential-Access Method [*Computer science*] (AD)
qit .... Qualification Information and Test (AD)
QIT .... Quality Information and Test [*System*]
QIT .... Queensland Institute of Technology [*Australia*] (AD)
QITLJ .... Queensland Institute of Technology. Law Journal [*A publication*]
QITS .... Quality Information and Test System (WDAA)
QIXX .... Quest International Resources Corp. [*NASDAQ symbol*] (SAG)

QIXXF .... Quest International Res. [*NASDAQ symbol*] [*Formerly, Consolidated Ramrod Gold*] (SG)

QIXXF .... Quest Intl Res [*NASDAQ symbol*] (TTSB)

QJ .... Bibliotheque Municipale, Jonquiere, Quebec [*Library symbol National Library of Canada*] (BIB)

QJ .... Quadriceps Jerk [*Neurology*] (DAVI)

QJ .... Quick Junction [*Electronics*]

Q Japan Com'l Arb Ass'n...   Quarterly. Japan Commercial Arbitration Association [*A publication*] (DLA)

QJC .... College de Joliette, Quebec [*Library symbol National Library of Canada*] (NLC)

QJC .... Quincy Junior College (AD)

QJCCI .... Queensland Japan Chamber of Commerce and Industry [*Australia*]

QJCH .... Centre de Documentation, Departement de Sante Communautaire de Lanaudiere, Joliette, Quebec [*Library symbol National Library of Canada*] (BIB)

QJCSVA ...... Archives Provinciales des Clercs de Saint-Viateur, Joliette, Quebec [*Library symbol National Library of Canada*] (NLC)

Q/JET .... Quadrajet Carburetor [*Automotive engineering*]

QJH .... Centre Hospitalier Regional de Lanaudiere, Joliette, Quebec [*Library symbol National Library of Canada*] (NLC)

QJJ .... Seminaire de Joliette, Quebec [*Library symbol National Library of Canada*] (NLC)

QJL .... Querner, J. L., San Antonio TX [*STAC*]

QJMA .... Musee d'Art de Joliette, Quebec [*Library symbol National Library of Canada*] (NLC)

QJMP .... Queue Jump Command

QJOC .... College de Jonquiere, Quebec [*Library symbol National Library of Canada*] (NLC)

QJS .... Quarterly Journal of Speech [*A publication*] (BRI)

QJSA .... Quarterly Journal of Studies in Alcohol [*A publication*] (AD)

qjump .... Queue Jump (AD)

QK .... Kirkland Municipal Library [*Bibliotheque Municipale de Kirkland*] Quebec [*Library symbol National Library of Canada*] (NLC)

QK .... Quasi Contract [*Legal shorthand*] (LWAP)

QK .... Queen's Knight [*Chess*]

qk .... Quick (AD)

QK .... Quick Kinescope [*Film replay*] (NTCM)

QKB .... Brome County Historical Society, Knowlton, Quebec [*Library symbol National Library of Canada*] (NLC)

QKBW .... Burroughs Wellcome & Co., Kirkland, Quebec [*Library symbol National Library of Canada*] (NLC)

QKC .... Aero Taxi Aviation, Inc. [*ICAO designator*] (FAAC)

QKD .... Quantum Key Distribution [*For encrypting communication*]

QKFA .... Queensland Keep Fit Association [*Australia*]

Qk Fl .... Quick Flashing (AD)

QKFL .... Quick Flashing Light [*Navigation signal*]

QKITA .... Institut de Technologie Agricole, Kamouraska, Quebec [*Library symbol National Library of Canada*] (NLC)

QKL .... Aeromaritime (CAAA) [*France ICAO designator*] (FAAC)

QKL .... Cologne/Bonn-Main RR [*Germany Airport symbol*] (OAG)

QKLN .... Laboratoires Nordic, Inc., Kirkland, Quebec [*Library symbol National Library of Canada*] (BIB)

qkly .... Quickly (AD)

qkm .... Quadratkilometer [*Square Kilometer*] [*German*] (AD)

QKOA .... Quarantine Kennel Owners' Association (BUAC)

QKPC .... Medical Library, Pfizer Canada, Inc., Kirkland, Quebec [*Library symbol National Library of Canada*] (NLC)

QkReily ...... Quick & Reilly Group, Inc. [*Associated Press*] (SAG)

QKT .... Queen's Knight [*Chess*]

QKTN .... Quickturn Design Sys [*NASDAQ symbol*] (TTSB)

QKTN .... Quickturn Design System [*NASDAQ symbol*] (SAG)

QKTP .... Queen's Knight's Pawn [*Chess*] (IIA)

QL .... Ethyl 2-(Diisopropylamino)ethylmethylphosphonite [*See EDMP*] [*Army symbol*]

QL .... Lesotho Airways [*ICAO designator*] (AD)

QL .... Quad Left [*Typography*]

QL .... Quality of Living

QL .... Quantum League [*An association*] (EA)

QL .... Quantum Leap (WDAA)

QL .... Quantum Libet [*As Much as Is Desired*] [*Pharmacy*]

ql .... Quantum Libet [*As Much as You Like*] [*Latin*] (AD)

Q/L .... Quarantine Launch (AD)

ql .... Quarrel (AD)

QL .... Quarrel (ROG)

QL .... Quartz-Locked

QL .... Quebec Law [*A publication*] (DLA)

QL .... Queen's Lancers [*Military unit*] [*British*]

QL .... Queensland [*Airline code*] (AD)

ql .... Query Language (AD)

QL .... Query Language [*Computer science*] (DIT)

QL .... Queue Length [*Telecommunications*] (TEL)

ql .... Quick Look (AD)

QL .... Quick Look (NAKS)

ql .... Quilate [*Carat*] [*Portuguese*] (AD)

ql .... Quintal (AD)

QL .... Quintal [*Unit of weight*]

QL .... Qumran Literature (BJA)

QL .... Quoc-Lo [*Main national highway in South Vietnam*] (VNW)

QL/1 .... Query Language/One [*Computer science*] (MHDI)

QLA .... Aviation Quebec Labrador Ltd. [*Canada ICAO designator*] (FAAC)

QLA .... Bibliotheque Municipale, Laval, Quebec [*Library symbol National Library of Canada*] (NLC)

QLA .... Lasham [*England*] [*Airport symbol*]

QLA .... Quebec Library Association (AC)

QLA/ABQ ...... Quebec Library Association/Association des Bibliothecaires du Quebec [*Canada*]

QLAB .... Quick Like a Bunny

QLAC .... CEGEP [*College d'Enseignement General et Professionnel*] Montmorency, Laval, Quebec [*Library symbol National Library of Canada*] (NLC)

QLACS .... Cite de la Sante de Laval, Quebec [*Library symbol National Library of Canada*] (NLC)

QLACW .... Canadian Workplace Automation Research Centre [*Centre Canadien de Recherche sur l'Informatisation du Travail*] Laval, Quebec [*Library symbol National Library of Canada*] (NLC)

QLAG .... Research Station, Agriculture Canada [*Station de Recherches, Agriculture Canada*] Lennoxville, Quebec [*Library symbol National Library of Canada*] (NLC)

QLAH .... Lennoxville-Ascot Historical Society Museum, Lennoxville, Quebec [*Library symbol National Library of Canada*] (NLC)

QLAID .... Ateliers d'Ingenierie Dominion, Lachine, Quebec [*Library symbol National Library of Canada*] (NLC)

QLAP .... Quick Look Analysis Program

QLAR .... Canadian Arsenals Ltd. [*Arsenaux Canada Ltee.*], Le Gardeur, Quebec [*Library symbol National Library of Canada*] (BIB)

QLASC .... College de l'Assomption, Quebec [*Library symbol National Library of Canada*] (NLC)

QLASGPT .... Federal Training Centre, Penitentiary, Ministry of the Solicitor General [*Centre Federal de Formation, Penitencier, Ministere du Solliciteur General*] Laval, Quebec [*Library symbol National Library of Canada*] (NLC)

QLAVD .... Centre de Documentation, Assurance-Vie Desjardins, Levis, Quebec [*Library symbol National Library of Canada*] (NLC)

QLB .... Bishop's University, Lennoxville, Quebec [*Library symbol National Library of Canada*] (NLC)

QLBG .... Department of Geography, Bishop's University, Lennoxville, Quebec [*Library symbol National Library of Canada*] (NLC)

QLC .... College de Levis, Quebec [*Library symbol National Library of Canada*] (NLC)

QLC .... Quasi-Liquid Crystal [*Organic chemistry*]

QLCCP .... Service de Documentation et de Reference, Confederation des Caisses Populaires et d'Economie Desjardins du Quebec, Levis, Quebec [*Library symbol National Library of Canada*] (NLC)

QLCLL .... CEGEP [*College d'Enseignement General et Professionnel*] de Levis-Lauzon, Lauzon, Quebec [*Library symbol National Library of Canada*] (BIB)

QLCRS .... Conseil Regional de la Sante et des Services Sociaux, Longueuil, Quebec [*Library symbol National Library of Canada*] (NLC)

QLCS .... Quick Look and Checkout System

Qld .... Queensland (AD)

QLD .... Queen's Light Dragoons [*British military*] (DMA)

QLD .... Quillo Resources, Inc. [*Vancouver Stock Exchange symbol*]

QLDC .... Delmar Chemicals, La Salle, Quebec [*Library symbol National Library of Canada*] (NLC)

Qld Ind ...... Queensland Industry [*A publication*]

Qld Law ...... Queensland Lawyer [*A publication*]

QLDR .... Quick Look Data Reference (NASA)

QLDS .... Quick Look Data Station [*NASA*] (KSC)

QLE .... Bibliotheque Municipale, Levis, Quebec [*Library symbol National Library of Canada*] (NLC)

QLFCP .... Federation des Caisses Populaires Desjardins, Levis, Quebec [*Library symbol National Library of Canada*] (NLC)

QLFD .... Qualified (KSC)

QLFECA .... Archives des Freres des Ecoles Chretiennes, Ville de Laval, Quebec [*Library symbol National Library of Canada*] (NLC)

QlFood .... Quality Food Centers, Inc. [*Associated Press*] (SAG)

qlfy .... Qualify (AD)

qlfyg .... Qualifying (AD)

qlfyn .... Qualification (AD)

QLG .... Quick-Look Guide

QLGA .... Queensland Local Government Association [*Australia*] (AD)

QLGC .... Qlogic Corp. [*NASDAQ symbol*] (SAG)

QLGU .... Queensland Ladies Golf Union [*Australia*]

QLHD .... Hotel-Dieu de Levis, Quebec [*Library symbol National Library of Canada*] (NLC)

QLI .... Quality of Life Index

qli .... Quality of Life Index (AD)

Q Lib .... Quantum Libet [*As Much as You Please*] [*Pharmacy*]

qlii .... Quais-LASER-Intensity Interferometer (AD)

Q-Link .... QuantumLink [*Quantum Computer Services, Inc.*] [*Vienna, VA*] [*Information service or system*] (IID)

QLIT .... Quick Look Intermediate Tape

qlit .... Quick-Look Intermediate Tape (AD)

qll .... Quartz Landing Lamp (AD)

QLL .... Quartz Landing Lamp [*Aviation*]

QLLC .... Qualified Logical Link Control [*Telecommunications*]

QLM .... Bibliotheque Municipale de Lachine, Quebec [*Library symbol National Library of Canada*] (NLC)

QLM .... Quasi-Lagrangian Model [*Marine science*] (OSRA)

qlm .... Quasi-LASER Machine (AD)

QLM .... Quasi-Linear Machine

QLNLB .... Institut Nazareth et Louis-Braille, Longueuil, Quebec [*Library symbol National Library of Canada*] (NLC)

QLO .... Bibliotheque Municipale, Longueuil, Quebec [*Library symbol National Library of Canada*] (NLC)

QLOC .... Queensland Light Opera Co. [*Australia*] (AD)

QLOCE .... College Edouard-Montpetit, Longueuil, Quebec [*Library symbol National Library of Canada*] (NLC)

QLOCSS .... Centre de Services Sociaux Richelieu, Longueuil, Quebec [*Library symbol National Library of Canada*] (NLC)
Qlogic .... Qlogic Corp. [*Associated Press*] (SAG)
QLOPB .... Centre de Documentation, Centre Hospitalier Pierre Boucher, Longueuil, Quebec [*Library symbol National Library of Canada*] (NLC)
QLOU .... Pratt & Whitney Aircraft Ltd., Longueuil, Quebec [*Library symbol National Library of Canada*] (NLC)
QLP .... Quality Low-Priced [*Art series*]
QLP .... Query Language Processor [*Computer science*]
QLP .... Quinoxaline Ladder Polymer [*Organic chemistry*]
QLPC .... Queensland Library Promotion Council [*Australia*] (AD)
QLPED .... Pylon Electronic Development Co. Ltd., Lachine, Quebec [*Library symbol National Library of Canada*] (NLC)
QLPS .... Petro-Sun International, Inc., Longueuil, Quebec [*Library symbol National Library of Canada*] (NLC)
QLR .... Quebec Law Reports
QLR .... Queen's Lancashire Regiment [*Military unit*] [*British*]
QL(R) .... Quick Look (Report)
QLRA .... Queensland Litter Research Association [*Australia*]
QL Rev .... Quarterly Law Review [*A publication*] (DLA)
QLS .... Bibliotheque Municipale, La Salle, Quebec [*Library symbol National Library of Canada*] (NLC)
QLS .... Quantum Leap Society (BUAC)
QLS .... Quasi-Elastic Light Scattering [*Also, QELS, QUELS*] [*Physics*]
QLS .... Quebec Land Surveyor [*Canada*] (ASC)
QLS .... Queensland Law Society [*Australia*] (AD)
QLS .... Queensland Littoral Society [*Australia*] (AD)
QLS .... Quick Law Systems (AD)
QLS .... Quick Loading System (AD)
QLS .... Quick Look Station [*NASA*] (MCD)
QLSA .... Queue Line Sharing Adapter [*Computer science*]
QLSAA .... Archives des Soeurs de Sainte-Anne, Lachine, Quebec [*Library symbol National Library of Canada*] (NLC)
QLSD .... Societe de Developpement International Desjardins, Levis, Quebec [*Library symbol National Library of Canada*] (BIB)
QLSE .... ESSO Building Products of Canada Ltd., La Salle, Quebec [*Library symbol National Library of Canada*] (NLC)
QLSEA .... Queensland Livestock Exporters' Association [*Australia*]
QLSHG .... Bibliotheque Medicale, Hopital General La Salle, Quebec [*Library symbol National Library of Canada*] (NLC)
QLSI .... Quantum Learning Sys [*NASDAQ symbol*] (TTSB)
QLSI .... Quantum Learning Systems, Inc. [*NASDAQ symbol*] (SAG)
qlsm .... Quasi-LASER Sequential Machine (AD)
QLSM .... Quasi-Linear Sequential Machine
QLSO .... L'Octogone, Centre de la Culture, La Salle, Quebec [*Library symbol National Library of Canada*] (NLC)
QL Soc J ...... Queensland Law Society. Journal [*A publication*]
QLSS .... Research Department, J. E. Seagram & Sons Ltd., La Salle, Quebec [*Library symbol National Library of Canada*] (NLC)
QLT .... Bibliotheque Municipale, La Tuque, Quebec [*Library symbol National Library of Canada*] (NLC)
QLT .... Quadra Logic Technologies [*Associated Press*] (SAG)
QLT .... Quadra Logic Technologies, Inc. [*Vancouver Stock Exchange symbol Toronto Stock Exchange symbol*]
QLT .... Quantitative Leak Test
qlt .... Quantitative Leak Test (AD)
QLT .... Quasi-Linear Theory
QLTA .... Queensland Lawn Tennis Association [*Australia*] (AD)
QLTI .... Quadra Logic Technologies, Inc. [*NASDAQ symbol*] (NQ)
QLTIF .... QLT Phototherapeutics [*NASDAQ symbol*] (TTSB)
qlty .... Quality (AD)
QLTY .... Quality (AFM)
QLTYCONO... Quality Control Officer [*Military*]
QltyDin .... Quality Dino Entertainment [*Commercial firm Associated Press*] (SAG)
qly .... Quarterly (ODBW)
Qly Land R... Fitzgibbon's Irish Land Reports [*A publication*] (DLA)
QM .... Air Malawi [*ICAO designator*] (AD)
QM .... Bulgaria [*License plate code assigned to foreign diplomats in the US*]
QM .... Quad Medium [*Paper*] (DGA)
qm .... Quadratmeter [*Square Meter*] [*German*] (AD)
Q-M .... Quadrature Modulation
QM .... Qualification Motor (MCD)
QM .... Quality Management (HCT)
QM .... Quality Manual [*A publication*] (MCD)
QM .... Quality Memorandum
QM .... Quality Motels (EA)
QM .... Quality of Merit
QM .... Quantitative Methods
QM .... Quantum Mechanics
qm .... Quantum Mechanics (AD)
qm .... Quaque Mane [*Every Morning*] [*Latin*] (AD)
QM .... Quaque Matin [*Every Morning*] [*Pharmacy*]
QM .... Quarterly Meetings [*Quakers*]
QM .... Quarterly Memorandum
QM .... Quartermaster [*Military*] (VNW)
Qm .... Quartermaster (WDAA)
QM .... Quartermaster Corps (AAGC)
QM .... Quartz Manometer (ACII)
QM .... Quasi-Monoclonal [*Mouse strain*]
QM .... Queen Mother [*British*]
QM .... Queen's Messenger [*British*]
QM .... Queens Museum (AD)
Q-M .... Quenu-Muret Sign [*Cardiology*] (DAVI)

qm .... Query Message (AD)
QM .... Query Message (WDAA)
QM .... Query Module (MCD)
QM .... Queue Manager [*Computer science*] (CMD)
QM .... Quick-Make [*Contact*] (IAA)
QM .... Quinacrine Mustard [*Chromosome stain*]
QM .... Quinonemethide [*Organic chemistry*]
qm .... Quintal Metrico [*Metric Quintal*] [*Spain*] (AD)
QM .... Qumran Manuscripts (BJA)
QM .... Quo Modo [*In What Manner*] [*Latin*]
qm .... Quo Modo [*In What Manner*] [*Latin*] (AD)
QM1 .... Quartermaster, First Class [*Navy rating*]
QM2 .... Quartermaster, Second Class [*Navy rating*]
QM3 .... Quartermaster, Third Class [*Navy rating*]
QMA .... Group Information Centre, Alcan Aluminum Ltd. [*Centre d'Information du Groupe, Alcan Aluminium Ltee*] Montreal, Quebec [*Library symbol National Library of Canada*] (NLC)
QMA .... Qatar Monetary Agency (AD)
qma .... Qualified Military Available (AD)
QMA .... Qualified Military Available
QMA .... Qualitative Materiel Approach [*Army*] (AABC)
QMA .... Quality Management Approach [*Business term*]
qma .... Quality Material Approach (AD)
QMA .... Quarry Masters' Association [*Australia*]
QMA .... Quarterly Moving Average
QMA .... Quartermasters Association [*Later, ALA*]
QMA .... Quebec Medical Association (AC)
QMAA .... Archives de la Chancellerie, L'Archeveche de Montreal, Quebec [*Library symbol National Library of Canada*] (NLC)
QMAAC .... Queen Mary's Army Auxiliary Corps [*The WAAC*] [*British*]
QMAB .... Montreal Association for the Blind, Quebec [*Library symbol National Library of Canada*] (NLC)
QMABB .... TECSULT, Montreal, Quebec [*Library symbol National Library of Canada*] (NLC)
QMAC .... Macdonald College Library, Ste-Anne-De-Bellevue, Quebec [*Library symbol National Library of Canada*] (NLC)
QMAC .... Quadripartite Materiel and Agreements Committee [*Military*] (AABC)
QMAC .... Quarter-Orbit Magnetic Attitude Control (PDAA)
QMACL .... Quebec Association for Children with Learning Disabilities [*Association Quebecoise pour les Enfants Souffrant de Troubles d'Apprentissage*] Montreal, Quebec [*Library symbol National Library of Canada*] (NLC)
QMACM .... Centre des Dossiers et de Documentation, Direction de Montreal, Ministere des Affaires Culturelles du Quebec [*Library symbol National Library of Canada*] (BIB)
QMACN .... Archives de la Congregation de Notre-Dame, Montreal, Quebec [*Library symbol National Library of Canada*] (NLC)
QMADMA ..... Archives, Diocese of Montreal, Anglican Church of Canada, Quebec [*Library symbol National Library of Canada*] (NLC)
QMAE .... Aviation Electric Ltd., Montreal, Quebec [*Library symbol National Library of Canada*] (NLC)
QMAEC .... Atomic Energy of Canada [*L'Energie Atomique du Canada*] Montreal, Quebec [*Library symbol National Library of Canada*] (NLC)
QMAGB .... Bibliotheque Municipale, Magog, Quebec [*Library symbol National Library of Canada*] (NLC)
Q(Maint) ...... Quartermaster Maintenance [*World War II*]
QMAL .... Air Liquide Canada Ltee., Montreal, Quebec [*Library symbol National Library of Canada*] (NLC)
QMALL .... Abbott Laboratories Ltd., Montreal, Quebec [*Library symbol National Library of Canada*] (NLC)
QMAM .... Allan Memorial Institute, Montreal, Quebec [*Library symbol National Library of Canada*] (NLC)
QMAMA .... Lavalin Environnement, Montreal, Quebec [*Library symbol National Library of Canada*] (NLC)
QMAMI .... Minerais LAC Ltee., Malartic, Quebec [*Library symbol National Library of Canada*] (NLC)
QMANSW ..... Quarry Masters' Association of New South Wales [*Australia*]
QMAO .... Qualified for Mobilization Ashore Only [*Navy*]
qmao .... Qualified for Mobilization Ashore Only (AD)
QMAPO .... Centre de Documentation, APO Quebec, Montreal, Quebec [*Library symbol National Library of Canada*] (NLC)
QMAPS .... Quebec Aid for the Partially-Sighted [*Aide aux Insuffisants Visuels du Quebec*] Montreal, Quebec [*Library symbol National Library of Canada*] (NLC)
QMARC .... Archives Provinciales des Capucins, Montreal, Quebec [*Library symbol National Library of Canada*] (NLC)
QMAS .... Archives du Seminaire de Saint-Sulpice, Montreal, Quebec [*Library symbol National Library of Canada*] (NLC)
QMASBB .... ASEA [*Allmaenna Svenska Elektriska Aktiebolaget*] Brown Boveri, Inc., Montreal, Quebec [*Library symbol National Library of Canada*] (BIB)
QMASC .... Bibliotheque Municipale, Mascouche, Quebec [*Library symbol National Library of Canada*] (BIB)
QMASRC ...... Space Research Corp., Mansonville, Quebec [*Library symbol National Library of Canada*] (NLC)
QMASSAS .... Centre de Documentation, Secteur Affaires Sociales, Association pour la Sante etla Securite du Travail, Montreal, Quebec [*Library symbol National Library of Canada*] (NLC)
QMATC .... College de Matane, Quebec [*Library symbol National Library of Canada*] (NLC)
QMAV .... Bibliotheque des Avocats, Barreau de Montreal, Quebec [*Library symbol National Library of Canada*] (NLC)
Q-max .... Quarantine Maximum (AD)
QMAY .... Ayerst, McKenna & Harrison, Inc. Montreal, Quebec [*Library symbol National Library of Canada*] (NLC)

QMB............ Information Resource Centre, Bell Canada [*Centre d'Information Specialisee, Bell Canada*], Montreal, Quebec [*Library symbol National Library of Canada*] (NLC)

QMB............ Qualified Medicare Beneficiary

QMB............ Qualified Mortgage Bond

QMB............ Quality Management Board (DOMA)

QMB............ Quarterly Management Bulletin [*A publication*] (DNAB)

QMB............ Queensbury [*England*] [*Seismograph station code, US Geological Survey*] (SEIS)

QMB............ Queensland Milk Board [*Australia*]

QMB............ Quick Make-and-Break [*Contact*] (DEN)

qmb............ Quick Make-and-Break (AD)

QMBA.......... Ecole des Beaux-Arts, Montreal, Quebec [*Library symbol National Library of Canada*] (NLC)

QMBA.......... Queensland Master Builders Association [*Australia*] (AD)

QMBAE........ Bristol Aero Engines Ltd., Montreal, Quebec [*Library symbol National Library of Canada*] (NLC)

QMBAN........ Centre de Documentation, Banque Nationale du Canada, Montreal, Quebec [*Library symbol National Library of Canada*] (NLC)

QMBB.......... College Bois-De-Boulogne, Montreal, Quebec [*Library symbol National Library of Canada*] (NLC)

QMBBL........ Beauchemin, Beaton, Lapointe, Inc., Montreal, Quebec [*Library symbol National Library of Canada*] (NLC)

QMBC.......... Byers, Casgrain, Montreal, Quebec [*Library symbol National Library of Canada*] (BIB)

QMBD.......... Translation Bureau, Canada Department of the Secretary of State [*Bureau des Traductions, Secretariat d'Etat*] Montreal, Quebec [*Library symbol National Library of Canada*] (NLC)

QMBE............ Centre de Documentation, Bureau des Economies d'Energie du Quebec, Mont real, Quebec [*Library symbol National Library of Canada*] (NLC)

QMBGC........ Bibliotheque d'Ingenierie, BG Checo International Ltee., Montreal, Quebec [*Library symbol National Library of Canada*] (NLC)

QMBIM........ Bio-Mega, Inc., Montreal, Quebec [*Library symbol National Library of Canada*] (NLC)

QMBL.......... Law Library, Bell Canada, Montreal, Quebec [*Library symbol National Library of Canada*] (NLC)

QMBM.......... Bibliotheque de la Ville de Montreal, Quebec [*Library symbol National Library of Canada*] (NLC)

QMBMO....... Bank of Montreal [*Banque de Montreal*], Quebec [*Library symbol National Library of Canada*] (NLC)

QMBMS....... Management Sciences Library, Bell Canada, Montreal, Quebec [*Library symbol Obsolete National Library of Canada*] (NLC)

QMBN.......... Bibliotheque Nationale du Quebec, Montreal, Quebec [*Library symbol National Library of Canada*] (NLC)

QMBNR........ Bell Northern Research, Montreal, Quebec [*Library symbol National Library of Canada*] (NLC)

QMBP.......... Building Products Ltd., Montreal, Quebec [*Library symbol National Library of Canada*] (NLC)

QMBR.......... Bio-Research Laboratories Ltd., Pointe-Claire, Quebec [*Library symbol National Library of Canada*] (NLC)

QMBT........... Montreal Board of Trade [*Chambre de Commerce du District de Montreal*] Quebec [*Library symbol National Library of Canada*] (NLC)

QMC............ Chief Quartermaster [*Navy rating*]

QMC............ College de Montreal, Quebec [*Library symbol National Library of Canada*] (NLC)

QMC............ James Carson Breckinridge Library, Quantico, VA [*OCLC symbol*] (OCLC)

QMC............ Quadripartite Materiel Committee [*Military*]

QMC............ Quartermaster Clerk [*Marine Corps*]

QMC............ Quartermaster Corps [*Army*]

QMC............ Queen Mary College [*England*] (WDAA)

QMC............ Queensland Mining Council [*Australia*]

QMC............ Quekett Microscopical Club [*British*] (BI)

QMC............ Quick Modification Concept (MCD)

QMCA.......... Engineering Library, Canadair Ltd., Montreal, Quebec [*Library symbol National Library of Canada*] (NLC)

QMCAD........ Centre d'Animation, de Developpement, et de Recherche en Education, Montreal, Quebec [*Library symbol National Library of Canada*] (NLC)

QMCADM..... Centre d'Accueil Domremy-Montreal, Ste.-Genevieve, Quebec [*Library symbol National Library of Canada*] (NLC)

QMCADQ..... Conservatoire d'Art Dramatique de Montreal, Quebec [*Library symbol National Library of Canada*] (NLC)

QMCAE........ CAE Electronics Ltd., Montreal, Quebec [*Library symbol National Library of Canada*] (NLC)

QMCAG....... College Andre Grasset, Montreal, Quebec [*Library symbol National Library of Canada*] (NLC)

QMCAI......... Canadian Asbestos Information Centre [*Centre Canadien d'Information sur l'Amiante*] Montreal, Quebec [*Library symbol National Library of Canada*] (NLC)

QMC&S....... Quartermaster Center and School [*Army*] (RDA)

QMC & SO... Quartermaster Cataloging and Standardization Office [*Army*]

QMCAR........ Carmel de Montreal, Quebec [*Library symbol National Library of Canada*] (NLC)

QMCAT........ Commission de la Sante et de la Securite du Travail du Quebec, Montreal [*Library symbol National Library of Canada*] (NLC)

QMCAV........ Direction Generale du Cinema et de l'Audio-Visuel, Ministere des Communications du Quebec, Montreal, Quebec [*Library symbol National Library of Canada*] (NLC)

QMCB.......... Canadian Broadcasting Corp. [*Societe Radio-Canada*] Montreal, Quebec [*Library symbol National Library of Canada*] (NLC)

QMCBE........ Engineering Headquarters, Canadian Broadcasting Corp. [*Service de l'Ingenierie, Societe Radio-Canada*] Montreal, Quebec [*Library symbol National Library of Canada*] (NLC)

QMCBH........ Catherine Booth Hospital, Montreal, Quebec [*Library symbol National Library of Canada*] (NLC)

QMCBM....... Music Library, Canadian Broadcasting Corp. [*Musicotheque et Discotheque, Societe Radio-Canada*], Montreal, Quebec [*Library symbol National Library of Canada*] (BIB)

QMCC.......... Canada Cement Co., Montreal, Quebec [*Library symbol National Library of Canada*] (NLC)

QMCCA........ Centre Canadien d'Architecture [*Canadian Centre for Architecture*] Montreal, Quebec [*Library symbol National Library of Canada*] (NLC)

QMCCL........ Currie, Coopers & Lybrand Ltd., Montreal, Quebec [*Library symbol National Library of Canada*] (NLC)

QMCCR........ Canadian Council of Resource Ministers [*Conseil Canadien des Ministres des Ressources*] Montreal, Quebec [*Library symbol National Library of Canada*] (NLC)

QMCCS........ Centraide, Montreal, Quebec [*Library symbol National Library of Canada*] (NLC)

QMCD......... Centre Documentaire, Centrale des Bibliotheques, Montreal, Quebec [*Library symbol National Library of Canada*] (NLC)

QMCDM....... College de Maisonneuve, Montreal, Quebec [*Library symbol National Library of Canada*] (NLC)

QMCDP........ Caisse de Depot et Placement du Quebec, Montreal, Quebec [*Library symbol National Library of Canada*] (NLC)

QMCE.......... Celanese Canada Ltd., Montreal, Quebec [*Library symbol National Library of Canada*] (NLC)

QMCEA........ Canadian Export Association [*Association Canadienne d'Exportation*] Montreal, Quebec [*Library symbol National Library of Canada*] (NLC)

QMCEC........ Catholic School Commission [*Commission des Ecoles Catholiques*] Montreal, Quebec [*Library symbol National Library of Canada*] (NLC)

QMCECI....... Centre Canadien d'Etudes et de Cooperation Internationale, Montreal, Quebec [*Library symbol National Library of Canada*] (NLC)

QMCED........ Centre de Documentation, Ministere du Commerce Exterieur et du Developpement Technologique du Quebec, Montreal, Quebec [*Library symbol National Library of Canada*] (BIB)

QMCF.......... Merck Frosst Laboratories [*Laboratoires Merck Frosst*] Montreal, Quebec [*Library symbol National Library of Canada*] (NLC)

QMCFH........ Centre de Documentation, Charette, Fortier, Hawey, Touche, Ross, Montreal, Quebec [*Library symbol National Library of Canada*] (NLC)

QMCGW....... Clarkson, Gordon, Woods, Gordon, Montreal, Quebec [*Library symbol National Library of Canada*] (NLC)

QMCHA........ Queensland Mechanical Cane Harvesters' Association [*Australia*]

QMCHC........ Montreal Chest Hospital Centre [*Centre Hospitalier Thoracique de Montreal*]Quebec [*Library symbol National Library of Canada*] (NLC)

QMCHF........ Centre de Documentation, Centre Hospitalier Fleury, Montreal, Quebec [*Library symbol National Library of Canada*] (NLC)

QMCHL........ Centre Hospitalier de Lachine, Montreal, Quebec [*Library symbol National Library of Canada*] (NLC)

QMCICM....... Centre Interculturel Monchanin, Montreal, Quebec [*Library symbol National Library of Canada*] (NLC)

QMCIH......... Bibliotheque de Documentation des Archives, Ville de Montreal, Quebec [*Library symbol National Library of Canada*] (NLC)

QMCIM........ Canadian Institute of Mining and Metallurgy [*Institut Canadien des Mines et de la Metallurgie*] Montreal, Quebec [*Library symbol National Library of Canada*] (NLC)

QMC-IRL...... Queen Mary College Industrial Research Ltd. [*Research center British*] (IRUK)

QMCJ.......... Canadian Jewish Congress [*Congres Juif Canadien*] Montreal, Quebec [*Library symbol National Library of Canada*] (NLC)

QMCL.......... CanAtom Ltd., Montreal, Quebec [*Library symbol National Library of Canada*] (NLC)

QMCLG........ College Lionel Groulx, Ste-Therese, Quebec [*Library symbol National Library of Canada*] (NLC)

QMCLK........ Quartermaster Clerk [*Navy rating*]

QMCM.......... Canadian Marconi Co., Montreal, Quebec [*Library symbol National Library of Canada*] (NLC)

QMCM.......... Master Chief Quartermaster [*Navy rating*]

QMCM.......... Quartermaster Corporal-Major [*British military*] (DMA)

QMCN.......... Canadian National Railways [*Chemins de fer Nationaux du Canada*] Montreal, Quebec [*Library symbol National Library of Canada*] (NLC)

QMCNC........ Chemical Library, Canadian National Railways [*Bibliotheque Chimique, Chemins de fer Nationaux du Canada*] Montreal, Quebec [*Library symbol Obsolete National Library of Canada*] (NLC)

QMCOM....... Conservatoire de Musique de Montreal, Quebec [*Library symbol National Library of Canada*] (NLC)

QMCP.......... Canadian Pacific Ltd. [*Le Canadien Pacifique*] Montreal, Quebec [*Library symbol National Library of Canada*] (NLC)

QMCQ.......... Cinematheque Quebecoise, Montreal, Quebec [*Library symbol National Library of Canada*] (BIB)

QMCR.......... Canadian Copper Refiners Ltd., Montreal, Quebec [*Library symbol National Library of Canada*] (NLC)

QMCR.......... Quartermaster Corps Regulations [*Army*]

QMCRI......... Centre de Recherche Industrielle du Quebec, Montreal, Quebec [*Library symbol National Library of Canada*] (NLC)

QMCRIM...... Centre de Documentation, Centre de Recherche Informatique de Montreal, Quebec [*Library symbol National Library of Canada*] (BIB)

QMCRP........ Conference des Recteurs et des Principaux des Universites du Quebec, Montreal, Quebec [*Library symbol National Library of Canada*]

QMCS .... Christian Science Reading Room, Montreal, Quebec [*Library symbol National Library of Canada*]

QMCS .... Quality Monitoring Control System [*Military*] (CAAL)

QMCS .... Senior Chief Quartermaster [*Navy rating*]

QMCSCA...... Archives de la Congregation de Sainte-Croix, Montreal, Quebec [*Library symbol National Library of Canada*] (NLC)

QMCSSMM... CSSMM [*Centre de Services Sociaux du Montreal Metropolitain*], Montreal, Quebec [*Library symbol National Library of Canada*] (NLC)

QMCSSS...... Service de Reference, Conseil de la Sante et des Services Sociaux de la Region de Montreal Metropolitain, Montreal, Quebec [*Library symbol National Library of Canada*] (NLC)

QMCSVA...... Archives des Clercs de Saint-Viateur, Province de Montreal, Outremont, Quebec [*Library symbol National Library of Canada*] (NLC)

QMCT.......... Commission de Transport de la Communaute Urbaine de Montreal, Quebec [*Library symbol National Library of Canada*] (NLC)

QMCTC .... Quartermaster Corps Technical Committee [*Army*]

QMCTM........ Canadian Tobacco Manufacturers' Council [*Conseil Canadien des Fabricants des Produits du Tabac*] Montreal, Quebec [*Library symbol National Library of Canada*] (NLC)

QMCVDDH ... Que Me - Comite Vietnam pour la Defense des Droits de l'Homme [*Que Me - Vietnam Committee on Human Rights*] (EAIO)

QMCVM .... Commission des Valeurs Mobilieres du Quebec, Montreal, Quebec [*Library symbol National Library of Canada*] (NLC)

QMCW .... Canada Wire & Cable Co. Ltd., Montreal, Quebec [*Library symbol National Library of Canada*] (NLC)

QMD .... Institut Genealogique Drouin, Montreal, Quebec [*Library symbol National Library of Canada*] (NLC)

QMDA .... Daniel Arbour & Associes, Montreal, Quebec [*Library symbol National Library of Canada*] (NLC)

QMDB .... College Jean-De-Brebeuf, Montreal, Quebec [*Library symbol National Library of Canada*] (NLC)

QMDC .... Dawson College, Montreal, Quebec [*Library symbol National Library of Canada*] (NLC)

QMDE .... Dominion Engineering Works Ltd., Montreal, Quebec [*Library symbol National Library of Canada*] (NLC)

QMDEP .... Quartermaster Depot [*Army*]

QMDH .... Douglas Hospital Centre [*Centre Hospitalier Douglas*] Montreal, Quebec [*Library symbol National Library of Canada*] (NLC)

QMDK .... Quick Mechanical Disconnect Kit

qmdk .... Quick Mechanical Disconnect Kit (AD)

QMDL .... Domtar Ltd., Montreal, Quebec [*Library symbol National Library of Canada*] (NLC)

QMDM .... Montreal Association for the Mentally Retarded [*Association de Montreal pour les Deficients Mentaux*] Quebec [*Library symbol National Library of Canada*] (NLC)

QMDMR....... Groupe DMR, Inc., Montreal, Quebec [*Library symbol National Library of Canada*] (BIB)

QMDO.......... Qualitative Materiel Development Objective [*Army*]

QMDOM....... Dominion Bridge Co. Ltd., Montreal, Quebec [*Library symbol National Library of Canada*] (NLC)

QMDPC........ Quartermaster Data Processing Center [*Army*]

QMDT .... Dominion Textile, Montreal, Quebec [*Library symbol National Library of Canada*] (NLC)

QME .... Quantock Marine Enterprises (AD)

qme .... Queueing Matrix Evaluation (AD)

QME .... Queueing Matrix Evaluation (PDAA)

QMEA.......... Atmospheric Environment Service, Environment Canada [*Service de l'Environnement Atmospherique, Environnement Canada*] Dorval, Quebec [*Library symbol National Library of Canada*] (NLC)

QMEA.......... Queensland Meat Exporters' Association [*Australia*]

QMEC.......... Monenco Consultants Ltd., Montreal, Quebec [*Library symbol National Library of Canada*] (NLC)

QMECB .... Centrale des Bibliotheques, Services Documentaires Multimedia, Inc., Montreal, Quebec [*Library symbol National Library of Canada*] (NLC)

QMECS .... Experts-Conseils Shawinigan, Montreal, Quebec [*Library symbol National Library of Canada*] (NLC)

Q Med .... Q-Med, Inc. [*Associated Press*] (SAG)

QMED .... Quest Medical [*NASDAQ symbol*] (TTSB)

QMED .... Quest Medical, Inc. [*NASDAQ symbol*] (NQ)

QMEE........... Environmental Protection Service, Environment Canada [*Service de la Protection de l'Environnement, Environnement Canada*] Montreal, Quebec [*Library symbol National Library of Canada*] (NLC)

QMEM.......... Bibliotheque Municipale de la Ville de Montreal-Est, Quebec [*Library symbol National Library of Canada*] (BIB)

QMEN .... Ministere de l'Environnement, Montreal, Quebec [*Library symbol National Library of Canada*] (NLC)

QMENT .... National Theatre School [*Ecole Nationale de Theatre*] Montreal, Quebec [*Library symbol National Library of Canada*] (NLC)

QMEP........... Ecole Polytechnique, Montreal, Quebec [*Library symbol National Library of Canada*] (NLC)

QMEPCC...... Quartermaster Equipment and Parts Commodity Center [*Army*]

QMERS .... E. R. Squibb & Sons Ltd., Montreal, Quebec [*Library symbol National Library of Canada*] (NLC)

QMES........... Ecole Secondaire Saint-Stanislas, Montreal, Quebec [*Library symbol National Library of Canada*] (NLC)

QMF............. Fraser-Hickson Institute, Montreal, Quebec [*Library symbol National Library of Canada*] (NLC)

QMF............. Query Management Facility [*Database*] (BYTE)

QMFA........... Montreal Museum of Fine Arts [*Musee des Beaux-Arts de Montreal*] Quebec [*Library symbol National Library of Canada*] (NLC)

QMFAC........ Farinon Canada, Dorval, Quebec [*Library symbol National Library of Canada*] (NLC)

QMFBD .... Federal Business Development Bank [*Banque Federale de Developpement*] Montreal, Quebec [*Library symbol National Library of Canada*] (NLC)

QMFC........... First Church of Christ, Scientist, Montreal, Quebec [*Library symbol National Library of Canada*] (NLC)

QMFCI .... Quartermaster Food and Container Institute (AD)

QMFCIAF ..... Quartermaster Food and Container Institute for the Armed Forces

QMFCJ......... Bibliotheque de Theologie, les Facultes de la Compagnie de Jesus, Montreal, Quebec [*Library symbol National Library of Canada*] (NLC)

QMFER .... Forest Engineering Research Institute of Canada [*Institut Canadien de Recherches en Genie Forestier*] Pointe-Claire, Quebec [*Library symbol National Library of Canada*] (NLC)

QMFH .... Frank W. Horner Ltd., Montreal, Quebec [*Library symbol National Library of Canada*] (NLC)

QMFMO .... Federation des Medecins Omnipraticiens du Quebec, Montreal, Quebec [*Library symbol National Library of Canada*] (NLC)

QMFMS........ Federation des Medecins Specialistes du Quebec, Montreal, Quebec [*Library symbol National Library of Canada*] (NLC)

QMFR .... Arctic Biological Station, Fisheries and Oceans Canada [*Station Biologique del'Arctique, Peches et Oceans Canada*] Ste-Anne-De-Bellevue, Quebec [*Library symbol National Library of Canada*] (NLC)

QMFRA .... Archives des Franciscains, Montreal, Quebec [*Library symbol National Library of Canada*] (NLC)

QMFRAN...... Studium Franciscain de Theologie, Montreal, Quebec [*Library symbol National Library of Canada*] (NLC)

QMFSGA...... Archives des Freres de Saint-Gabriel, Montreal, Quebec [*Library symbol National Library of Canada*] (NLC)

QMG .... QMG Holdings, Inc. [*Toronto Stock Exchange symbol*]

QMG .... Quartermaster General [*Army*]

QMG .... Quench Melt Growth [*Physics*]

QMG .... Sir George Williams Campus, Concordia University, Montreal, Quebec [*Library symbol National Library of Canada*] (NLC)

QMGA .... Montreal Gazette, Quebec [*Library symbol National Library of Canada*] (NLC)

QMGB .... Grands Ballets Canadiens, Montreal, Quebec [*Library symbol National Library of Canada*] (NLC)

QMGDH....... Grace Dart Hospital Center, Montreal, Quebec [*Library symbol National Library of Canada*] (NLC)

QM Gen ...... Quartermaster General [*Military*] (GFGA)

QMGF .... Quartermaster-General to the Forces [*Military British*]

QMGG......... Department of Geography, Sir George Williams Campus, Concordia University, Montreal, Quebec [*Library symbol National Library of Canada*], (NLC)

QMGGM....... University Map Collection, Department of Geography, Sir George Williams Campus, Concordia University, Montreal, Quebec [*Library symbol National Library of Canada*] (NLC)

QMGH.......... Montreal General Hospital [*Hopital General de Montreal*] Quebec [*Library symbol National Library of Canada*] (NLC)

QMGHC........ Community Health Department, Montreal General Hospital [*Departement de Sante Communautaire, Hopital General de Montreal*], Quebec [*Library symbol National Library of Canada*] (NLC)

QMGHN........ Nurses' Library, Montreal General Hospital [*Bibliotheque des Infirmieres, Hopital General de Montreal*], Quebec [*Library symbol National Library of Canada*] (NLC)

QMGL .... Genstar Ltd., Montreal, Quebec [*Library symbol National Library of Canada*] (NLC)

QMGLS .... Library Studies Program, Concordia University, Montreal, Quebec [*Library symbol National Library of Canada*] (NLC)

QMGM .... Gaz Metropolitain, Montreal, Quebec [*Library symbol National Library of Canada*] (BIB)

QMGMC....... Quartermaster-General of the Marine Corps

QMGO......... Quartermaster-General's Office [*Military British*] (ROG)

QMGP .... Gerard Parizeau Ltee, Montreal, Quebec [*Library symbol National Library of Canada*] (NLC)

QMGS .... Grand Seminaire, Montreal, Quebec [*Library symbol National Library of Canada*] (NLC)

QMH .... Hydro-Quebec, Montreal, Quebec [*Library symbol National Library of Canada*] (NLC)

QMH .... Queens Moat Houses [*Hotelier*] [*British*]

QMHC.......... Medical Library, Hoechst Canada, Inc., Montreal, Quebec [*Library symbol National Library of Canada*] (BIB)

QMHC.......... Quinhon Missionary Sisters of the Holy Cross (TOCD)

QMHCL .... Bibliotheque Medicale, Hopital Charles Lemoyne, Greenfield Park, Quebec [*Library symbol National Library of Canada*] (NLC)

QMHCLC....... Departement de Sante Communautaire, Hopital Charles Lemoyne, Greenfield Park, Quebec [*Library symbol National Library of Canada*] (NLC)

QMHD.......... Hotel-Dieu de Montreal, Quebec [*Library symbol National Library of Canada*] (NLC)

QMHDE........ Centre de Documentation, Direction de l'Environnement, Hydro-Quebec, Montreal, Quebec [*Library symbol National Library of Canada*] (NLC)

QMHE.......... Ecole des Hautes Etudes Commerciales, Montreal, Quebec [*Library symbol National Library of Canada*] (NLC)

QMHGC........ Centre Hospitalier de Verdun, Quebec [*Library symbol National Library of Canada*] (NLC)

QMHGF........ Hopital General Fleury, Montreal, Quebec [*Library symbol National Library of Canada*] (NLC)

QMHI.......... Centre de Documentation, Hydro-Quebec International, Montreal, Quebec [*Library symbol National Library of Canada*] (BIB)

QMHJR........ Centre de Documentation du Personnel, Hopital de Convalescents Julius Richardson[*Staff Library, Julius Richardson Convalescent Hospital, Inc.*], Montreal, Quebec [*Library symbol National Library of Canada*] (NLC)

QMHJT........ Hopital Jean Talon, Montreal, Quebec [*Library symbol National Library of Canada*] (NLC)

QMHM........ Centre Hospitalier Jacques Viger, Montreal, Quebec [*Library symbol National Library of Canada*] (NLC)

QMHME....... Hopital Marie-Enfant, Montreal, Quebec [*Library symbol National Library of Canada*] (NLC)

QMHMR....... Hopital Maisonneuve-Rosemont, Montreal, Quebec [*Library symbol National Library of Canada*] (NLC)

QMHND....... Hopital Notre-Dame, Montreal, Quebec [*Library symbol National Library of Canada*] (NLC)

QMHNDI...... Bibliotheque des Services Infirmiers, Hopital Notre-Dame, Montreal, Quebec [*Library symbol National Library of Canada*] (NLC)

QMHP......... Qualified Mental Health Professional

QMHRP....... Hopital Riviere-Des-Prairies, Montreal, Quebec [*Library symbol National Library of Canada*] (NLC)

QMHRT........ Centre de Documentation, Redaction et Terminologie, Hydro-Quebec, Montreal, Quebec [*Library symbol National Library of Canada*] (BIB)

QMHSC....... Hopital du Sacre-Coeur, Montreal, Quebec [*Library symbol National Library of Canada*] (NLC)

QMHSCA..... Hopital Santa Cabrini, Montreal, Quebec [*Library symbol National Library of Canada*] (NLC)

QMHSJ....... Hopital Louis H. LaFonataine, Montreal, Quebec [*Library symbol National Library of Canada*] (NLC)

QMHSJA..... Hopital Ste-Jeanne-D'Arc, Montreal, Quebec [*Library symbol National Library of Canada*] (NLC)

QMHSL....... Hopital Saint-Luc, Montreal, Quebec [*Library symbol National Library of Canada*] (NLC)

QMHSLC..... Departement de Sante Communautaire, Hopital Saint-Luc, Montreal, Quebec [*Library symbol National Library of Canada*] (NLC)

QMHVG....... Centre de Documentation, Verification Generale, Hydro-Quebec, Montreal, Quebec [*Library symbol National Library of Canada*] (BIB)

QMI............ Insurance Institute of the Province of Quebec [*Insitut d'Assurance du Quebec*] Montreal, Quebec [*Library symbol National Library of Canada*] (NLC)

QMI............ Qualification Maintainability Inspection

QMIA .... International Air Transport Association [*Association du Transport Aerien International*] Montreal, Quebec [*Library symbol National Library of Canada*] (NLC)

QMIA .... Quartermaster Intelligence Agency [*Merged with Defense Intelligence Agency*]

QMIA .... Queensland Motor Industry Association [*Australia*] (AD)

QMIAA .... Institut des Arts Appliques, Montreal, Quebec [*Library symbol National Library of Canada*] (NLC)

QMIAG .... Institut des Arts Graphiques, Montreal, Quebec [*Library symbol National Library of Canada*] (NLC)

QMIAP .... Pavillon Albert Prevost, Montreal, Quebec [*Library symbol National Library of Canada*] (NLC)

QMIC .... International Civil Aviation Organization [*Organisation de l'Aviation Civile Internationale*] Montreal, Quebec [*Library symbol National Library of Canada*] (NLC)

QMICA .... Institute of Chartered Accountants of Quebec [*Institut Canadien des Comptables Agrees du Quebec*] Montreal, Quebec [*Library symbol National Library of Canada*] (NLC)

QMICAV ...... Institut Culturel Avataq, Montreal, Quebec [*Library symbol National Library of Canada*] (BIB)

QMICE .... Canadian Institute of Adult Education [*Institut Canadien d'Education des Adultes*] Montreal, Quebec [*Library symbol National Library of Canada*] (NLC)

QMICM .... Institut de Cardiologie de Montreal, Quebec [*Library symbol National Library of Canada*] (NLC)

QMIF........... Imasco Foods Ltd., Montreal, Quebec [*Library symbol National Library of Canada*] (NLC)

QMIFQ .... Informatech France-Quebec, Montreal, Quebec [*Library symbol National Library of Canada*] (NLC)

QMIG .... Industrial Grain Products Ltd., Montreal, Quebec [*Library symbol National Library of Canada*] (NLC)

QMII........... Istituto Italiano di Cultura, Montreal, Quebec [*Library symbol National Library of Canada*] (NLC)

QMIIS .... Islamic Studies Library, McGill University, Montreal, Quebec [*Library symbol National Library of Canada*] (NLC)

QMIIST .... International Institute of Stress [*Institut International du Stress*] Montreal, Quebec [*Library symbol Obsolete National Library of Canada*] (BIB)

QMIKES ...... Quadrupole Mass Analyzed Ion Kinetic Energy Spectroscopy

QMILO .... International Labour Office [*Bureau International du Travail*] Montreal, Quebec [*Library symbol National Library of Canada*] (NLC)

QMIM......... Institut Armand-Frappier, Universite du Quebc, Laval, Quebec [*Library symbol National Library of Canada*] (NLC)

QMIMM....... Ministere des Communautes Culturelles et de l'Immigration, Montreal, Quebec [*Library symbol National Library of Canada*] (NLC)

QMIMSO..... Quartermaster Industrial Mobilization Services Offices [*Army*]

QMINC........ Institut du Cancer de Montreal, Quebec [*Library symbol National Library of Canada*] (NLC)

QMINCA....... Institut National Canadien pour les Aveugles, Montreal, Quebec [*Library symbol National Library of Canada*] (NLC)

QMINP .... Institut National de Productivite, Montreal, Quebec [*Library symbol National Library of Canada*] (NLC)

QMIP .... Institute of Parasitoloy, Macdonald College, Ste-Anne-De-Bellevue, Quebec [*Library symbol National Library of Canada*] (NLC)

QMIPP .... Institut Philippe Pinel de Montreal, Quebec [*Library symbol National Library of Canada*] (NLC)

QMIRC .... Institut de Recherches Cliniques, Montreal, Quebec [*Library symbol National Library of Canada*] (NLC)

QMIRP .... Institute for Research on Public Policy [*Institut de Recherches Politiques*] Montreal, Quebec [*Library symbol National Library of Canada*] (NLC)

QMIRS .... Informatheque IRSST [*Institut de Recherche en Sante et Securite au Travail*] Montreal, Quebec [*Library symbol National Library of Canada*] (NLC)

QMIS .... Quality Review Management Information System [*IRS*]

QMISM .... Centre de Documentation, Institut Raymond-Dewar, Montreal, Quebec [*Library symbol National Library of Canada*] (NLC)

QMIST .... Centre d'Information, IST [*Industriel Services Techniques*], Montreal, Quebec [*Library symbol National Library of Canada*] (BIB)

QMIT........... Imperial Tobacco Co. of Canada Ltd., Montreal, Quebec [*Library symbol National Library of Canada*] (NLC)

QMITR .... Research Library, Imperial Tobacco Co. of Canada Ltd., Montreal, Quebec [*Library symbol National Library of Canada*] (NLC)

QMJ........... Jewish Public Library [*Bibliotheque Juive Publique, Montreal*] Quebec [*Library symbol National Library of Canada*] (NLC)

QMJB .... Jardin Botanique, Montreal, Quebec [*Library symbol National Library of Canada*] (NLC)

QMJES........ Technical Services, Joseph E. Seagram & Sons Ltd., La Salle, Quebec [*Library symbol National Library of Canada*] (NLC)

QMJG......... Jewish General Hospital, Montreal, Quebec [*Library symbol National Library of Canada*] (NLC)

QMJGI .... Institute of Community and Family Psychiatry, Jewish General Hospital, Montreal,Quebec [*Library symbol National Library of Canada*] (NLC)

QMJGL........ Lady Davis Institute for Medical Research, Jewish General Hospital, Montreal, Quebec [*Library symbol National Library of Canada*] (NLC)

QMJH.......... Hopital de Mont-Joli, Inc., Quebec [*Library symbol National Library of Canada*] (NLC)

QMJHW .... Johnson & Higgins, Willis, Faber Ltd., Montreal, Quebec [*Library symbol National Library of Canada*] (NLC)

QMJJ .... Johnson & Johnson Ltd., Montreal, Quebec [*Library symbol National Library of Canada*] (NLC)

QMJL.......... John Lovell & Son City Directories Ltd., Montreal, Quebec [*Library symbol National Library of Canada*] (NLC)

QMJLP........ Laboratoire de Police Scientifique, Montreal, Quebec [*Library symbol National Library of Canada*] (NLC)

QMJM......... Canada Department of Justice [*Ministere de la Justice*] Montreal, Quebec [*Library symbol National Library of Canada*] (NLC)

QMJRH .... James R. Hay & Associates, Pointe Claire, Quebec [*Library symbol National Library of Canada*] (BIB)

QMJSJ........ Commission des Services Juridiques du Quebec, Montreal, Quebec [*Library symbol National Library of Canada*] (NLC)

QML............ Loyola Campus, Concordia University, Montreal, Quebec [*Library symbol National Library of Canada*] (NLC)

QML............ Qayyum Moslem League [*Pakistan*] (PD)

QML............ Qualified Manufacturers List [*DoD*]

QMLA.......... Laboratoires Abbott Ltee, Montreal, Quebec [*Library symbol National Library of Canada*] (NLC)

QMLAV .... Lavalin, Inc., Montreal, Quebec [*Library symbol National Library of Canada*] (BIB)

QMLAVE ...... Lavalin Environment, Inc., Montreal, Quebec [*Library symbol National Library of Canada*] (BIB)

QMLBD .... Lafleur, Brown & De Granpre, Montreal, Quebec [*Library symbol National Library of Canada*] (BIB)

QMLCA .... Lower Canada Arms Collectors Association, Montreal, Quebec [*Library symbol National Library of Canada*] (NLC)

QMLCC .... Lower Canada College Montreal, Quebec [*Library symbol National Library of Canada*] (NLC)

QMLCPF ..... Bibliotheque de la Faune, Ministere du Loisir, de la Chasse et de la Peche, Montreal, Quebec [*Library symbol National Library of Canada*] (NLC)

QMLF.......... Librairies Flammarion, Montreal, Quebec [*Library symbol National Library of Canada*] (NLC)

QMLG .... Lakeshore General Hospital [*Hopital General du Lakeshore*] Pointe-Claire, Quebec [*Library symbol National Library of Canada*] (NLC)

QMLGC .... Community Health Department, Lakeshore General Hospital [*Departement de SanteCommunautaire, Hopital General du Lakeshore*], Pointe-Claire, Quebec [*Library symbol National Library of Canada*] (NLC)

QMLM.......... Bibliotheque Municipale, Mont-Laurier, Quebec [*Library symbol National Library of Canada*] (BIB)

QMLP.......... Centre de Documentation, La Presse Ltee., Montreal, Quebec [*Library symbol National Library of Canada*] (NLC)

QMLPT........ Librairie Pointe-Aux-Trembles, Quebec [*Library symbol National Library of Canada*] (NLC)

QMLQ......... Centre de Documentation, Loto-Quebec, Montreal, Quebec [*Library symbol National Library of Canada*] (NLC)

QMLR.......... Constance-Lethbridge Rehabilitation Centre [*Centre de Readaptation Constance-Lethbridge*] Montreal, Quebec [*Library symbol National Library of Canada*] (NLC)

QMM........... Marina di Massa [*Italy*] [*Airport symbol*] (AD)

QMM............ McLennan Library, McGill University, Montreal, Quebec [*Library symbol National Library of Canada*] (NLC)

QMM............ Queensland Maritime Museum [*Australia*]

QMMAC .... Musee d'Art Contemporain, Montreal, Quebec [*Library symbol National Library of Canada*] (NLC)

QMMAQ .... La Magnetotheque, Montreal, Quebec [*Library symbol National Library of Canada*] (NLC)

QMMAR .... Marianapolis College, Montreal, Quebec [*Library symbol National Library of Canada*] (NLC)

QMMB .... Blackader/Lauterman Library of Architecture and Art, McGill University, Montreal, Quebec [*Library symbol National Library of Canada*] (NLC)

QMMBC .... Molson Breweries of Canada Ltd., Montreal, Quebec [*Library symbol Obsolete National Library of Canada*] (NLC)

QMMBG .... Botany-Genetics Library, McGill University, Montreal, Quebec [*Library symbol National Library of Canada*] (BIB)

QMMBZ........ Blacker-Wood Library of Zoology and Ornithology, McGill University, Montreal, Quebec [*Library symbol National Library of Canada*] (NLC)

QMMC .... Miron Co. Ltd., Montreal, Quebec [*Library symbol National Library of Canada*] (NLC)

QMMCH .... Montreal Children's Hospital, Quebec [*Library symbol National Library of Canada*] (NLC)

QMMCR .... Musee du Chatau de Ramezay, Montreal, Quebec [*Library symbol National Library of Canada*] (NLC)

QMMD .... Religious Studies Library, McGill University, Montreal, Quebec [*Library symbol National Library of Canada*] (NLC)

QMME.......... Physical Sciences and Engineering Library, McGill University, Montreal, Quebec [*Library symbol National Library of Canada*] (NLC)

QMMG .... Map and Air Photo Library, McGill University, Montreal, Quebec [*Library symbol National Library of Canada*] (NLC)

QMMGS .... Department of Geological Sciences, McGill University, Montreal, Quebec [*Library symbol National Library of Canada*] (NLC)

QMMH .... Mental Hygiene Istitute [*Institut de l'Hygiene Mentale*] Montreal, Quebec [*Library symbol National Library of Canada*] (NLC)

QMMHH .... Maimonides Hospital Geriatric Center [*Centre Hospitalier Geriatrique Maimonides*], Montreal, Quebec [*Library symbol National Library of Canada*] (NLC)

QMMI........... Atwater Library [*Formerly, Mechanics Institute Library*] Montreal, Quebec [*Library symbol National Library of Canada*] (NLC)

QMMIQ .... Quebec Regional Office, Employment and Immigration Canada [*Bureau Regional duQuebec, Emploi et Immigration Canada*] Montreal, Quebec [*Library symbol National Library of Canada*] (NLC)

QMML.......... Law Library, McGill University, Montreal, Quebec [*Library symbol National Library of Canada*] (NLC)

QMMLS........ Library Science Library, McGill University, Montreal, Quebec [*Library symbol National Library of Canada*] (NLC)

QMMM.......... Medical Library, McGill University, Montreal, Quebec [*Library symbol National Library of Canada*] (NLC)

QMMMCM ... McCord Museum, McGill University, Montreal, Quebec [*Library symbol National Library of Canada*] (NLC)

QMMMDM ... Marvin Duchow Music Library, McGill University, Montreal, Quebec [*Library symbol National Library of Canada*] (NLC)

QMMMM ...... Montreal Military and Maritime Museum, Quebec [*Library symbol National Library of Canada*] (NLC)

QMMN .... Nursing/Social Work Library, McGill University, Montreal, Quebec [*Library symbol National Library of Canada*] (NLC)

QMMO .... Osler Library, McGill University, Montreal, Quebec [*Library symbol National Library of Canada*] (NLC)

QMMOC .... Monsanto Canada Ltd., Montreal, Quebec [*Library symbol National Library of Canada*] (NLC)

QMMOS .... Montreal Star, Quebec [*Library symbol National Library of Canada*] (NLC)

QMMPB .... MPB Technologies, Dorval, Quebec [*Library symbol National Library of Canada*] (NLC)

QMMRB .... Department of Rare Books and Special Collections, McGill University, Montreal, Quebec [*Library symbol National Library of Canada*] (NLC)

QMMRS .... Mendelsohn Rosentzveig Shacter, Montreal, Quebec [*Library symbol National Library of Canada*] (BIB)

QMMSC .... Howard Ross Library of Management, McGill University, Montreal, Quebec [*Library symbol National Library of Canada*] (NLC)

QMMSR .... Centre de Documentation, Ministere de la Main-d'Oeuvre et de la Securite du Revenu du Quebec, Montreal, Quebec [*Library symbol National Library of Canada*] (NLC)

QMN .... Centres Biblio-Culturels de Montreal-Nord, Quebec [*Library symbol National Library of Canada*] (NLC)

QMNA .... Canadian Pulp and Paper Asssociation [*Association Canadienne des Producteurs dePates et Papiers*] Montreal, Quebec [*Library symbol National Library of Canada*] (NLC)

QMNB .... Biotechnology Branch, CISTI , Montreal, Quebec [*Canada Institute for Scienctific and Technical Information*] [*Annexe de Biotechnologie, ICIST*] [*Library symbol*] [*National Library of Canada*] (BIB)

QMNDE......... Hopital Notre-Dame-De-L'Esperance-De-St-Laurent, Montreal, Quebec [*Library symbol National Library of Canada*] (NLC)

QMNE .... Northern Electric Co. Ltd., Montreal, Quebec [*Library symbol National Library of Canada*] (NLC)

QMNF .... National Film Board, Montreal Quebec [*Formerly, Ottawa*] [*Office National du Film, Montreal (Anciennement Ottawa)*] [*Library symbol*] [*National Library of Canada*] (NLC)

QMNFNI....... National Information/Distribution System, National Film Board [*Systeme d'Information et de Distribution pour les Produits Audio-Visuels Canadiens, Office National du film*] Montreal, Quebec [*Library symbol National Library of Canada*] (NLC)

QMNHH........ Health Protection Branch, Canada Department of National Health and Welfare [*Direction Generale de la Protection de la Sante, Ministere de la Sante Nationale et du Bien-Etre Social*] Montreal, Quebec [*Library symbol National Library of Canada*] (NLC)

QMNIH.......... Montreal Neurological Institute and Hospital [*Institut et Hopital Neurologiques de Montreal*] Quebec [*Library symbol National Library of Canada*] (NLC)

QMNOT .... Northern Telecom Canada Ltd., Montreal, Quebec [*Library symbol National Library of Canada*] (NLC)

QMNR .... Noranda Research Centre, Pointe-Claire, Quebec [*Library symbol National Library of Canada*] (NLC)

QMNT .... Nesbitt, Thomson & Co. Ltd., Montreal, Quebec [*Library symbol National Library of Canada*] (NLC)

QMO .... Oratoire Saint-Joseph, Montreal, Quebec [*Library symbol National Library of Canada*] (NLC)

qmo .... Qualitative Material Objective (AD)

QMO .... Qualitative Materiel Objective [*Army*] (AABC)

QMO .... Quartz Mountain State Park [*Oklahoma*] [*Seismograph station code, US Geological Survey*] (SEIS)

QMO .... Queen Mary's Own [*British military*] (DMA)

QMO & O ..... Quebec, Montreal, Ottawa & Occidental [*Railway*]

QMOB .... Office de Biologie, Ministere du Loisir, de la Chasse et de la Peche, Montreal, Quebec [*Library symbol Obsolete National Library of Canada*] (NLC)

QMobSC ...... Quadripartite Mobility Standardization Committee [*Military*] (AABC)

QMOCP........ Canadian Livestock Feed Board [*Office Canadien des Provendes*] Montreal, Quebec [*Library symbol National Library of Canada*] (NLC)

QMOCQ........ Office de la Construction du Quebec, Montreal, Quebec [*Library symbol National Library of Canada*] (NLC)

QMOD .... Queue Modification Process

QMOF .... Ogilvie Flour Mills Co. Ltd., Montreal, Quebec [*Library symbol National Library of Canada*] (NLC)

QMOFJ......... Office Franco-Quebecois pour la Jeunesse, Montreal, Quebec [*Library symbol National Library of Canada*] (NLC)

QMOI .... Ordre des Infirmieres et Infirmiers du Quebec, Montreal, Quebec [*Library symbol National Library of Canada*] (NLC)

QMOLF .... Office de la Langue Francaise, Montreal, PQ, Canada [*Library symbol National Library of Canada*] (NLC)

QMOP .... Centre de Documentation, Office de Planification et de Developpement du Quebec, Montreal, Quebec [*Library symbol National Library of Canada*] (BIB)

QMOR .... Ogilvy, Renaud Law Library, Montreal, Quebec [*Library symbol National Library of Canada*] (BIB)

QMORC .... Quartermaster Officers' Reserve Corps [*Military*]

Q(Mov) .... Quartermaster Movements [*World War II*]

QMOW .... Quartermaster of the Watch [*Navy*] (DNAB)

QMP............. Qualitative Management Program [*Army*] (INF)

QMP............. Quality Milk Producers (BUAC)

QMP............. Quezon Memorial Park [*Philippines*] (AD)

QMPA .... Centre de Documentation, Projet Archipel de Montreal, Quebec [*Library symbol National Library of Canada*] (NLC)

QMPA .... Quartermaster Purchasing Agency [*Army*]

QMPA .... Queensland Master Painters Association [*Australia*] (AD)

QMPAE .... Paramax Electronics, Montreal, Quebec [*Library symbol National Library of Canada*] (BIB)

QMPC .... Presbyterian College, Montreal, Quebec [*Library symbol National Library of Canada*] (NLC)

QMPC .... Quartermaster Petroleum Center [*Army*] (MUGU)

QMPCA .... Agriculture Canada, Montreal, Quebec [*Library symbol National Library of Canada*] (NLC)

QMPCG .... Documentation Centre, George Etienne Cartier House, Parks Canada [*Centre de Documentation, Maison George-Etienne Cartier, Parcs Canada*], Montreal, Quebec [*Library symbol National Library of Canada*] (NLC)

QMPCUSA.... Quartermaster Petroleum Center, United States Army

QMPE........... Pezaris Electronics Co., Montreal, Quebec [*Library symbol National Library of Canada*] (NLC)

QMPI .... Polish Institute of Arts and Sciences in Canada [*Institut Polonais des Arts et des Sciences au Canada*] Montreal, Quebec [*Library symbol National Library of Canada*] (NLC)

QMPM .... Peat, Marwick, Mitchell et Cie., Montreal, Quebec [*Library symbol National Library of Canada*] (NLC)

QMPM .... Quantitative Methods for Public Management [*Course*]

QMPP .... Pulp and Paper Research Institute of Canada [*Institut Canadien de Recherches sur les Pates et Papiers*] Pointe-Claire, Quebec [*Library symbol National Library of Canada*] (NLC)

QMPPM .... Montreal Branch, Pulp and Paper Research Institute of Canada [*Succursale de Montreal, Centre Canadien de Recherche sur les Pates et Papiers*], Quebec [*Library symbol National Library of Canada*] (BIB)

QMPRA .... Archives Providence, Montreal, Quebec [*Library symbol National Library of Canada*] (NLC)

QMPSB .... Protestant School Board of Greater Montreal, Quebec [*Library symbol National Library of Canada*] (NLC)

QMPSR .... P. S. Ross & Partners, Montreal, Quebec (NLC)

QMPTI .... Potton Technical Industries, Mansonville, Quebec [*Library symbol National Library of Canada*] (NLC)

QMPWQ....... Quebec Region Library, Public Works Canada [*Bibliotheque de la Region du Quebec, Travaux Publics Canada*] Montreal, Quebec [*Library symbol National Library of Canada*] (NLC)

QMQ .... Queen Mary Veterans Hospital [*Hopital Reine-Marie (Anciens combattants)*] Montreal, Quebec [*Library symbol National Library of Canada*] (NLC)

QMQAR .... Centre Regional de Montreal, Archives Nationales du Quebec, Quebec [*Library symbol National Library of Canada*] (NLC)

QMQAR .... Quebec Archives, Montreal, Quebec [*Library symbol National Library of Canada*] (NLC)

QMQB .... Quick-Make, Quick-Break

qmqb .... Quick-Make Quick-Break (AD)

QMQDP .... Commission des Droits de la Personne du Quebec, Montreal, Quebec [*Library symbol National Library of Canada*] (NLC)

QMQE .... Queen Elizabeth Hospital, Montreal, Quebec [*Library symbol National Library of Canada*] (NLC)

QMR .... Qualitative Material Report

qmr .... Qualitative Material Requirement (AD)

QMR .... Qualitative Material Requirement [*Army*]

QMR .... Qualitative Military Requirements [*NATO*] (NATG)

QMR .... Quartermaster

Qmr .... Quartermaster [*Military*] (AD)

QMR .... Queen Mary's Regiment [*British military*] (DMA)

QMR .... Quick Medical Reference [*Computer system*]

QMR .... Royal Bank of Canada [*Banque Royale du Canada*] Montreal, Quebec [*Library symbol National Library of Canada*] (NLC)

QMRA .... Railway Association of Canada, Montreal, Quebec [*Library symbol National Library of Canada*] (NLC)

QMRAD .... Centre de Documentation, Institut de Recherche Appliquee sur le Travail, Montreal, Quebec [*Library symbol National Library of Canada*] (NLC)

QMR & E ..... Quartermaster Research and Engineering [*Military*] (AD)

QMRAQ .... Recherches Amerindiennes au Quebec, Montreal, Quebec [*Library symbol National Library of Canada*] (NLC)

QMRC .... Quartermaster Reserve Corps [*Military*]

QMRC .... Royal Canadian Air Force [*Corps d'Aviation Royale du Canada*] Montreal, Quebec [*Library symbol National Library of Canada*] (NLC)

QMRCH .... Richmond County Historical Society [*Societe d'Histoire du Comte de Richmond*] Melbourne, Quebec (NLC)

QMRCM .... Raymond, Chabot, Martin, Pare, Montreal, Quebec [*Library symbol National Library of Canada*] (NLC)

QMRD .... Reader's Digest of Canada Ltd., Montreal, Quebec [*Library symbol National Library of Canada*] (NLC)

QMRE .... Revenue Canada [*Revenu Canada*] Montreal, Quebec [*Library symbol National Library of Canada*] (NLC)

QMREC .... Quartermaster Research and Engineering Command [*Army*]

QMREFEA .... Quartermaster Research and Engineering Field Evaluation Agency [*Merged with Troop Evaluation Test*]

QMREG .... Regie de l'Electricite et du Gaz, Montreal, Quebec [*Library symbol National Library of Canada*] (NLC)

QMREX .... Canada Department of Regional Industrial Expansion [*Ministere de l'Expansion Industrielle Regionale*] Montreal, Quebec [*Library symbol National Library of Canada*] (NLC)

QMRH .... Centre de Recherches en Relations Humaines, Montreal, Quebec [*Library symbol National Library of Canada*] (NLC)

QMRI .... Rehabilitation Institute of Montreal [*Institut de Rehabilitation de Montreal*] Quebec [*Library symbol National Library of Canada*] (NLC)

QMRK .... QualMark Corp. [*NASDAQ symbol*] (TTSB)

QMRL .... Quartermaster Radiation Laboratory [*Army*]

QMRL .... Regie du Logement, Montreal, Quebec [*Library symbol National Library of Canada*] (NLC)

QMRM .... Reddy Memorial Hospital, Montreal, Quebec [*Library symbol National Library of Canada*] (NLC)

QMROS .... Robinson-Sheppard, Montreal, Quebec [*Library symbol National Library of Canada*] (BIB)

QMRP .... Qualified Mental Retardation Professional

QMRP .... Rhone-Poulenc Pharma, Inc., Montreal, Quebec [*Library symbol National Library of Canada*] (NLC)

QMRPA .... Quartermaster Radiation Planning Agency [*Army*]

QMRQ .... Societe de Radio-Television du Quebec, Montreal, Quebec [*Library symbol National Library of Canada*] (NLC)

QMRR .... Rolls-Royce of Canada Ltd., Montreal, Quebec [*Library symbol National Library of Canada*] (NLC)

QMRRD .... Reginald P. Dawson Library, Town of Mount Royal, Quebec [*Library symbol National Library of Canada*] (NLC)

QMRS .... Information Centre, Canadian Security Intelligence Service [*Centre d'Information, Service Canadien du Renseignement de Securite*], Montreal, Quebec [*Library symbol National Library of Canada*] (BIB)

QMRSJA ...... Archives des Religieuses Hospitalieres de Saint-Joseph, Montreal, Quebec [*Library symbol National Library of Canada*] (NLC)

QMRV .... Royal Victoria Hospital, Montreal, Quebec [*Library symbol National Library of Canada*] (NLC)

QMRVW .... Women's Pavilion, Royal Victoria Hospital, Montreal, Quebec [*Library symbol National Library of Canada*] (NLC)

QMS .... QMS, Inc. [*Associated Press*] (SAG)

QMS .... Quadrupole Mass Spectrometer

QMS .... Quality Management System

QMS .... Quality Micro Systems [*Trademark*]

QMS .... Quality Monitoring System (MCD)

QMS .... Quarterly Meteorological Summary [*Navy*] (DNAB)

QMS .... Quartermaster School [*Army*]

QMS .... Quartermaster Sergeant [*Military*]

QMS .... Quartermaster Stores [*Military*]

QMS .... Quicksilver Messenger Service [*Pop music group*]

QMS .... Sun Life of Canada [*Sun Life du Canada*] Montreal, Quebec [*Library symbol National Library of Canada*] (NLC)

QMSA .... Seaman Apprentice, Quartermaster, Striker [*Navy rating*]

QMSA .... Service de la Documentation, Ministere de la Sante et des Services Sociaux du Quebec, Montreal, Quebec [*Library symbol National Library of Canada*] (NLC)

QMSAC .... Sandoz Canada, Inc., Dorval, Quebec [*Library symbol National Library of Canada*] (NLC)

QMSAP .... Societe des Artistes Professionnels du Quebec, Montreal, Quebec [*Library symbol National Library of Canada*] (NLC)

QMSC .... Queensland Mathematical Sciences Council [*Australia*]

QMSC .... Southern Canada Power Co., Montreal, Quebec [*Library symbol National Library of Canada*] (NLC)

QMSCA .... Statistics Canada [*Statistique Canada*] Montreal, Quebec [*Library symbol National Library of Canada*] (NLC)

QMSCC .... Queen Mary's School Cadet Corps [*British military*] (DMA)

QMSCM .... Canadian Microfilming Co. Ltd. [*Societe Canadienne du Microfilm, Inc.*] Montreal, Quebec [*Library symbol National Library of Canada*] (NLC)

QMSD .... Information Resource Centre, Systems Development [*Centre d'Information Specialise, Systemes-Applications Pratiques*], Montreal, Quebec [*Library symbol National Library of Canada*] (BIB)

QMSDB .... Societe de Developpement de la Baie James, Montreal, Quebec [*Library symbol National Library of Canada*] (NLC)

QMSDI .... Centre de Documentation, SOGIC [*Societe Generale des Industries Culturelles du Quebec*], Montreal, Quebec [*Library symbol National Library of Canada*] (BIB)

QMSDL .... Sidbec-Dosco Ltd./Ltee., Montreal, Quebec [*Library symbol National Library of Canada*] (NLC)

QM Segt ...... Quartermaster-Sergeant [*British military*] (DMA)

QMSG .... Queue Message [*Computer science*] (PCM)

QMSGA .... Archives Generales des Soeurs Grises, Montreal, Quebec [*Library symbol National Library of Canada*] (NLC)

QMSGE .... Office des Services de Garde a l'Enfance, Montreal, Quebec [*Library symbol National Library of Canada*] (NLC)

QMSGME ..... Service General des Moyens d'Enseignement, Ministere de l'Education du Quebec, Montreal, Quebec [*Library symbol National Library of Canada*] (NLC)

QMSGT .... Quartermaster Sergeant [*Marine Corps*]

Qm Sgt .... Quartermaster Sergeant [*Military*] (AD)

QMSH .... Societe Historique de Montreal, Quebec [*Library symbol National Library of Canada*] (NLC)

QMSHE .... Stadler Hurter, Montreal, Quebec [*Library symbol National Library of Canada*] (NLC)

QMSHQ .... Centre de Documentation, Societe d'Habitation du Quebec, Montreal, Quebec [*Library symbol National Library of Canada*] (BIB)

QMSI .... Quartermaster-Sergeant Instructor [*British military*] (DMA)

QMSI .... Scolasticat de l'Immaculee-Conception, Montreal, Quebec [*Library symbol National Library of Canada*] (NLC)

QMSIL .... Silicart, Inc., Montreal, Quebec [*Library symbol National Library of Canada*] (NLC)

QMSJ .... St. Joseph's Teachers' College, Montreal, Quebec [*Library symbol National Library of Canada*] (NLC)

QMSMA .... St. Mary's Hospital, Montreal, Quebec [*Library symbol National Library of Canada*] (NLC)

QMSN .... Seaman, Quartermaster, Striker [*Navy rating*]

QMSNC .... SNC, Inc., Montreal, Quebec [*Library symbol National Library of Canada*] (NLC)

QMSO .... Quartermaster Supply Officer [*Army*]

QMSO .... Shell Oil Co. of Canada, Montreal, Quebec [*Library symbol National Library of Canada*] (NLC)

QMSOB .... Le Groupe SOBECO, Montreal, Quebec [*Library symbol National Library of Canada*] (NLC)

QMSQC .... Squibb Canada, Inc., Montreal, Quebec [*Library symbol National Library of Canada*] (NLC)

QMSSA .... Queensland Merino Stud Sheepbreeders' Association [*Australia*]

QMST .... Legal Department, Steinberg, Inc., Montreal, Quebec [*Library symbol National Library of Canada*] (NLC)

QMSTJ .... Centre d'Information sur la Sante de l'Enfant, Hopital Sainte-Justine, Montreal,Quebec [*Library symbol National Library of Canada*] (NLC)

QMSTJS .... Departement de Sante Communautaire, Hopital Sainte-Justine, Montreal, Quebec [*Library symbol National Library of Canada*] (NLC)

QMSU .... Surete du Quebec, Montreal, Quebec [*Library symbol National Library of Canada*] (NLC)

QMSVM .... Centre de Service Social Ville-Marie [*Ville-Marie Social Service Centre*] Montreal, Quebec [*Library symbol National Library of Canada*] (NLC)

QMSW .... Quartz Metal Sealed Window

qmsw .... Quartz Metal Sealed Window (AD)

QMSW .... Sherwin-Williams Co. of Canada Ltd., Montreal, Quebec [*Library symbol National Library of Canada*] (NLC)

QMSWP .... Shawinigan Engineering Ltd. Co., Montreal, Quebec [*Library symbol National Library of Canada*] (NLC)

QMT .... Montreal Trust Co., Quebec [*Library symbol National Library of Canada*] (NLC)

QMT .... Quantitative Muscle Testing [*Medicine*] (MAE)

QM-T .... Quartermaster-Trainee [*Navy*] (DNAB)

QMT .... Queens-Midtown Tunnel (AD)

QMTA .... Tomenson Alexander Ltd., Montreal, Quebec [*Library symbol National Library of Canada*] (NLC)

QMTC .... Air Canada, Montreal, Quebec [*Library symbol National Library of Canada*] (NLC)

QMTD .... Transportation Development Centre, Transport Canada [*Centre de Developpement des Transports, Transports Canada*] Montreal, Quebec [*Library symbol National Library of Canada*] (NLC)

QMTGC .... Teleglobe Canada, Montreal, Quebec [*Library symbol National Library of Canada*] (NLC)

QMTH .... Institut de Tourisme et d'Hotellerie du Quebec, Montreal, Quebec [*Library symbol National Library of Canada*] (NLC)

QMTMO .... Centre de Documentation, Ministere du Travail du Quebec, Montreal, Quebec [*Library symbol National Library of Canada*] (NLC)

QMTOE .... Quartermaster Table of Organization and Equipment [*Units*] [*Military*]

QMTQ .... Direction des Communications, Tourisme Quebec, Montreal, Quebec [*Library symbol National Library of Canada*] (BIB)

QMTQM .... Trans Quebec & Maritimes, Montreal, Quebec [*Library symbol National Library of Canada*] (NLC)

QMTR .... Waterways Development, Transport Canada [*Developpement des vois Navigables, Transports Canada*] Montreal, Quebec [*Library symbol National Library of Canada*] (NLC)

QMTRA .... Centre de Documentation, Ministere des Transports du Quebec, Montreal, Quebec [*Library symbol National Library of Canada*] (NLC)

QMU .... Universite de Montreal, Quebec [*Library symbol National Library of Canada*] (NLC)

QMUA .... Service des Archives de l'Universite de Montreal, Quebec [*Library symbol National Library of Canada*] (NLC)

QMUC .... Union Carbide Canada Ltd., Pointe-Aux-Trembles, Quebec [*Library symbol National Library of Canada*] (NLC)

QMUDD .... Departement de Demographie, Universite de Montreal, Quebec [*Library symbol National Library of Canada*] (NLC)

QMUE .... Bibliotheque de l'Institut d'Etudes Medievales, Universite de Montreal, Quebec [*Library symbol National Library of Canada*] (NLC)

QMUEB .... Ecole de Biblioteconomie, Universite de Montreal, Quebec [*Library symbol National Library of Canada*] (NLC)

QMUEC .... L'Ecole de Criminologie, Universite de Montreal, Quebec [*Library symbol National Library of Canada*] (NLC)

QMUGC .... Cartotheque, Departement de Geographie, Universite de Montreal, Quebec [*Library symbol National Library of Canada*] (NLC)

QMUGL .... Cartotheque, Institut de Geologie, Universite de Montreal, Quebec [*Library symbol National Library of Canada*] (NLC)

QMUQ .... Universite de Quebec, Montreal, Quebec [*Library symbol National Library of Canada*] (NLC)

QMUQA .... Service des Archives de l'Universite du Quebec a Montreal [*Library symbol National Library of Canada*] (BIB)

QMUQC .... Cartotheque, Universite du Quebec, Montreal, Quebec [*Library symbol National Library of Canada*] (NLC)

QMUQEN ...... Ecole Nationale d'Administration Publique, Universite du Quebec, Montreal, Quebec [*Library symbol National Library of Canada*] (NLC)

QMUQET ...... Ecole de Technologie Superieure, Universite de Quebec, Montreal, Quebec [*Library symbol National Library of Canada*] (NLC)

QMUQIC .... Cartotheque, INRS-Urbanisation, Montreal, Quebec [*Library symbol National Library of Canada*] (NLC)

QMUQIS .... Centre de Documentation, INRS [*Institut National de la Recherche Scientifique*]-Sante, Montreal, Quebec [*Library symbol National Library of Canada*] (NLC)

QMUQIU ...... Centre de Documentation INRS [*Institut National de la Recherche Scientifique*]-Urbanisation, Montreal, Quebec [*Library symbol National Library of Canada*] (NLC)

QMUQPA ...... Pavillon des Arts, Universite du Quebec, Montreal, Quebec [*Library symbol National Library of Canada*] (NLC)

QMUQS .... Bibliotheque des Sciences, Universite du Quebec, Montreal [*Library symbol National Library of Canada*] (BIB)

QMUQTM ..... Tele-Universite, Universite du Quebec, Montreal, Quebec [*Library symbol National Library of Canada*] (NLC)

QMV .... Qualified Majority Voting [*Napoleonic Code*]

QMV .... Quality Majority Vote (WDAA)

QMV .... RCA Victor Co. Ltd., Montreal, Quebec [*Library symbol National Library of Canada*] (NLC)

QMVC .... Media Resource Centre, Vanier College, Montreal, Quebec [*Library symbol National Library of Canada*] (NLC)

QMVR .... Resource Centre, VIA Rail Canada, Inc. [*Centre de Documentation, VIA Rai l Canada, Inc.*] Montreal, Quebec [*Library symbol National Library of Canada*] (NLC)

QMVRM .... Centre de Maintenance, VIA Rail, Montreal, Quebec [*Library symbol National Library of Canada*] (BIB)

QMW .... Quartz Metal Window

qmw .... Quartz Metal Window (AD)

QMW .... Queen Mary and Westfield College, University of London [*England*] (BUAC)

QMW .... Warnock Hersey Co. Ltd., Montreal, Quebec [*Library symbol National Library of Canada*] (NLC)

QMWM .... William M. Mercer, Montreal, Quebec [*Library symbol National Library of Canada*] (NLC)

QMWS .... Quasi-Morphine Withdrawal Syndrome [*Medicine*] (DMAA)

QMY .... Queen Mary's Yeomanry [*British military*] (DMA)

QMY .... YWCA, Montreal, Quebec [*Library symbol National Library of Canada*] (NLC)

QMYH .... YM - YWHA, Montreal, Quebec [*Library symbol National Library of Canada*] (NLC)

QN .... Bush Pilots Airways [*ICAO designator*] (AD)

QN .... Quantifier Negation [*Principle of logic*]

QN .... Quantum Number

QN .... Quaque Nocte [*Every Night*] [*Pharmacy*]

qn .... Quaque Nocte [*Every Night*] [*Latin*] (AD)

QN .... Quarterly Newsletter. American Bar Association [*A publication*] (DLA)

QN .... Quarterly Notes (ILCA)

QN .... Quarternote [*A publication*] (EAAP)

QN .... Queen (ADA)

Qn .... Queen (AD)

QN .... Queen's Knight [*Chess*] (IIA)

QN .... Query Normalization

qn .... Question (AD)

QN .... Question (FAAC)

QN .... Quetzalcoatlus Northropi [*Pterosaur, a model constructed for the Smithsonian Institution and referred to by these initials*]

QN .... Quintuple Screw (DS)

QN .... Quotation [*Investment term*]

qn .... Quotation (AD)

QNA .... Qatar News Agency (BUAC)

qna .... Quality per Next Assembly (AD)

QNA .... Quarterly National Accounts (NITA)

QNA .... Queensland Netball Association [*Australia*]

QNA .... Quinuclidinol Atrolactate [*Organic chemistry*]

QNaN .... Quiet Not a Number [*Computer programming*] (BYTE)

QNat .... Quaestiones Naturales [*of Seneca the Younger*] [*Classical studies*] (OCD)

QNB .... Qatar National Bank (BUAC)

QNB .... Quinuclidinyl Benzilate [*Also, BZ*] [*Hallucinogen*]

QNC .... New Castle Free Public Library, New Castle, PA [*OCLC symbol*] (OCLC)

QNC .... Qatar National Cement Co. (BUAC)

QNC .... Queensland Naturalists Club [*Australia*] (BUAC)

QNCH .... Quenched (MSA)

QNCHRN ..... Centre Hospitalier Rouyn-Noranda, Noranda, Quebec [*Library symbol National Library of Canada*] (NLC)

QNCR .... Quarterly Noncompliance Report [*Environmental Protection Agency*] (GFGA)

QNCRS .... Conseil Regional de la Sante et des Services Sociaux Rouyn-Noranda, Noranda, Quebec [*Library symbol National Library of Canada*] (NLC)

QND .... Quantum Nondemolition [*Method of measurement*]

QNDE .... Quantitative Non-Destructive Evaluation (CIST)

Qndk .... Quensk [*Language of the Quains*] (AD)

QNE .... Height Altimeter Set to 1013.2 Millibars Will Read on Landing [*Aviation code*] (AIA)

QNEC .... Qualified Non-Elective Contribution

Q Newl-Spec Comm Env L... Quarterly Newsletter. Special Committee on Environmental Law [*A publication*] (DLA)

QNF .... Queensland Newsagents' Federation [*Australia*]

QNH .... Quantity (GAVI)

QNH .... Qui Nhon [*Vietnam*] (VNW)

QNI .... Queen's Nursing Institute [*British*]

QNIA .... Queensland Nursery Industry Association [*Australia*]

QNICA .... Soeurs de L'Assomption, Nicolet, Quebec [*Library symbol National Library of Canada*] (NLC)

QNICS .... Seminaire de Nicolet, Quebec [*Library symbol National Library of Canada*] (NLC)

QNIP .... Institut de Police du Quebec, Nicolet, Quebec [*Library symbol National Library of Canada*] (NLC)

QNK .... Kabo Air Travels [*Nigeria*] [*ICAO designator*] (FAAC)

QN MAQ .... Quilter's Newsletter Magazine [*A publication*]

QNMC .... Quadripartite Nonmateriel Committee [*Military*] (AABC)

QNNTC .... Qatar National Navigation and Transport Co. (BUAC)

QNO .... Quinidine-N-oxide [*Organic chemistry*]

QNOAG .... Experimental Farm, Agriculture Canada [*Ferme Experimentale, Agriculture Canada*] Normandin, Quebec [*Library symbol National Library of Canada*] (NLC)

QNP .... Queen's Knight's Pawn [*Chess*] (IIA)

QNP .... Quezon National Park [*Philippines*] (AD)

qns. .... Quantity Not Sufficient (AD)

QNS .... Quantity Not Sufficient [*Pharmacy*]

Qns .... Queens (AD)

QNS .... Queen's Nursing Sister [*British*] (DAVI)

QNS & L ...... Quebec North Shore and Labrador Railway [*Canada*] (AD)

QNSC .... Qui Nhon Support Command [*Vietnam*]

Qns Coll ...... Queen's College (AD)

Qnsd .... Queensland (AD)

Qnsld .... Queensland [*Australia*] (BARN)

Qns Pk .... Queens Park (AD)

QNST .... Quick Neurological Screening Test

qnt .... Quantisizer (AD)

QNT .... Quantizer (MDG)

QNT .... Quintet [*Music*]

qnt .... Quintet (WDAA)

QNTJB .... Queensland and Northern Territory Judgements Bulletin [*Australia A publication*]

QNTM .... Quantum Corp. [*NASDAQ symbol*] (NQ)

QNTY .... Quantity (AFM)

qnty .... Quantity (AD)

QNUE .... Queensland Nurses' Union of Employees [*Australia*]

QNWR .... Quivira National Wildlife Refuge [*Kansas*] (AD)

QNX .... Quinnex, Inc. [*FAA designator*] (FAAC)

QO .... Bar Harbor Airlines [*ICAO designator*] (AD)

QO .... Oxygen Consumption [*Biochemistry*] (DAVI)

QO .... Quaker Oats [*Trade name*]

QO .... Qualified in Ordnance [*Obsolete Navy*]

QO .... Qualified Optician [*British*]

QO .... Quartermaster Operation [*Military*]

QO .... Quarters Officer [*British military*] (DMA)

QO .... Queen's Own [*Military unit*] [*British*]

QO .... Quick Opening [*Nuclear energy*] (NRCH)

qo	Quick Opening (AD)
QO	Quick Outlet (WDAA)
QO	Quinoline Oxide [*Biochemistry*] (OA)
QO₂	Oxygen Quotient (AAMN)
QOA	Quasi-Official Agencies (AD)
QOBV	Quick-Opening Blowdown Valve [*Nuclear energy*] (NRCH)
QOC	Quality of Conformance
QOC	Quality of Contact (DAVI)
QOC	Quasi-Optical Circuit
QOC	Queensland Opera Company [*Australia*]
QOCG	Queen's Own Corps of Guides [*British military*] (DMA)
QOCH	Queen's Own Cameron Highlanders [*Military unit*] [*British*]
QOD	Quality of Design
QOD	Quantitative Oceanographic Data
QOD	Quaque Otra Die [*Every Other Day*] [*Pharmacy*]
QOD	Quebec Order of Dentists [*Canada*] (AD)
qod	Quick-Opening Device (AD)
QOD	Quick-Opening Device
QOD & WSY	Queen's Own Dorset and West Somerset Yeomanry [*British military*] (DMA)
QODY	Queen's Own Dorsetshire Yeomanry [*British military*] (DMA)
QOF	Quaker Oats Foundation (AD)
Q of C	Quality of Care [*Medicine*] (DAVI)
QOH	Quantity on Hand
QOH	Quaque Otra Hora [*Every Other Hour*] [*Pharmacy*]
QOH	Queen's Own Hussars [*Military unit*] [*British*]
QOI	Quality Operating Instruction
QOIB	Queensland Office of International Business [*Australia*]
QOIC	Quarantine Officer in Charge [*Military*] (AD)
QOL	Quality of Life [*Program*] [*Army*]
QOLCPF	Bibliotheque de la Faune, Ministere du Loisir, de la Chasse, et de la Peche, Orsainville, Quebec [*Library symbol National Library of Canada*] (NLC)
QOLI	Quality of Life Index [*Medicine*] (DMAA)
QOLP	Queensland Open Learning Project [*Australia*]
QOLY	Queen's Own Lowland Yeomanry [*Military unit*] [*British*] (DMA)
QOMAC	Quarter Orbit Magnetic Attitude Control
QOMY	Queen's Own Mercian Yeomanry [*Military unit*] [*British*]
QON	Quaque Otra Nocte [*Every Other Night*] [*Pharmacy*]
QON	Quarter Ocean Net
qon	Quarter Ocean Net (AD)
QONR	Queen's Own Nigeria Regiment [*British military*] (DMA)
QOOH	Queen's Own Oxfordshire Hussars [*British military*] (DMA)
qopri	Qualitative Operational Requirements (AD)
Q(Ops)	Quartermaster Operations [*World War II*]
QOR	Qualitative Operational Requirement [*Military*]
qor	Qualitative Operational Requirement (AD)
QOR	Quarterly Operating Report
QOR	Quebec Official Reports [*A publication*] (DLA)
QOR	Queen's Own Rifles [*Military unit*] [*British*]
QOR	Queen's Own Royal [*Military unit*] [*British*]
QORC	Queen's Own Rifles, Canada [*Military*] (ROG)
QORGIY	Queen's Own Royal Glasgow Imperial Yeomanry [*British military*] (DMA)
QORGS	Quasi-Optimal Rendezvous Guidance System
QORGY	Queen's Own Royal Glasgow Yeomanry [*British military*] (DMA)
QORR	Queen's Own Royal Regiment [*British military*] (DMA)
QORWKR	Queen's Own Royal West Kent Regiment [*Military unit*] [*British*]
QOS	Quality of Service [*Telecommunications*] (TEL)
QoS	Quality of Service [*Telecommunications*]
QOS	Quality Operating System
QOS	Quick on System (AD)
QOSMC	Quingdao Ocean Shipping Mariners' College [*China*] (BUAC)
QOT	Quasi-Optical Technique
qot	Quote (AD)
QOT & E	Qualification, Operational Test, and Evaluation
qotn	Quotation (AD)
QOWH	Queen's Own Worcestershire Hussars [*British military*] (DMA)
QOWVR	Queen's Own Westminster Volunteer Rifles [*Military British*] (ROG)
QOY	Queen's Own Yeomanry [*British military*] (DMA)
QP	Perceptual Quotient [*Education*] (AEE)
Qp	Pulmonary Blood Flow [*Medicine*] (DAVI)
Qp	Quadrant Pain [*Gastroenterology*] (DAVI)
QP	Quadrant Pain (STED)
QP	Quadratic Programming [*Computer science*] (BUR)
QP	Quadruple Play (DEN)
QP	Qualification Proposal
QP	Qualified Psychiatrist (MAE)
QP	Quality People
QP	Quality Product (IAA)
QP	Quanti-Pirquet [*Reaction or test for tuberculin*] (AAMN)
QP	Quantum Placet [*As Much as You Please*] [*Pharmacy*]
qp	Quantum Placet [*At Discretion*] [*Latin*] (AD)
QP	Quartered Partition
Q/P	Quartz/Phenolic
QP	Quasiparticle [*Physics*]
QP	Quasi-Peak
QP	Queen Post
qp	Queen Post (AD)
QP	Queen's Pawn [*Chess*] (ADA)
QP	Queen's Pleasure [*British*]
QP	Queen's Printer [*British*] (AD)
QP	Query Processing (MCD)
QP	Quest for Peace (EA)
qp	Quick Process (AD)

QP	Quick Processing [*Chemicals*]
QP	Quoted Price [*Investment term*]
QP	Sunbird [*ICAO designator*] (AD)
QPA	Bibliotheque Municipale, Port-Alfred, Quebec [*Library symbol National Library of Canada*] (NLC)
QPA	Qualitative Point Average (WDAA)
qpa	Qualitative Point Average (AD)
QPA	Quality Product Assurance
Q/PA	Quality/Productivity Assessment (MCD)
QPA	Quantity per Application (MCD)
qpa	Quantity per Article (AD)
qpa	Quantity per Assembly (AD)
QPA	Quantity per Assembly (MCD)
QPA	Queensland Photolab Association [*Australia*]
QPA	Queensland Police Academy [*Australia*] (AD)
QPA	Queensland Polynesian Association [*Australia*] (AD)
QPAA	Quality Planning and Administration (MCD)
QPAC	Qualified Productivity Aid for Computing (IAA)
QPAG	Experimental Farm, Agriculture Canada [*Ferme Experimentale, Agriculture Canada*] La Pocatiere, Quebec [*Library symbol National Library of Canada*] (NLC)
QPAM	Quadrature Phase and Amplitude Modulation (NITA)
QPAM	Quantized Pulsed Amplitude Modulation
Q P & S	Quaker Peace and Service (AD)
QPAT	Quad Pulse Output Module (ACII)
QPB	Quality Paperback Book Club [*Trademark of Book-of-the-Month Club, Inc.*]
QPBC	Quality Paperback Book Club [*Trademark of Book-of-the-Month Club, Inc.*] (CDAI)
QPC	College de Ste.-Anne, La Pocatiere, Quebec [*Library symbol National Library of Canada*] (NLC)
Qpc	Pulmonary Capillary Blood Flow [*Cardiology*] (DAVI)
QPC	Qatar Petroleum Co. (AD)
QPC	Quadrigeminal Plate Cistern [*Neurology*] (DAVI)
QPC	Quality of Patient Care [*Hospital administration*] (DAVI)
QPC	Quality Performance Chart (SAA)
QPC	Quantity per Equipment/Component
QPC	Quantum Point Contact [*Physics*]
QPC	Quasi-Propulsive Coefficient (DS)
QPC	Quasi-Public Company
QPC	Queensland Philatelic Council [*Australia*]
QPC	Queensland Police Club [*Australia*]
QPCAI Report	Queensland Parliamentary Commissioner for Administration. Investigations Report [*Australia A publication*]
QPCB	Quench Particle Collection Bomb (MCD)
QPCE	CEGEP [*College d'Enseignement General et Professionnel*] de La Pocatiere, Quebec [*Library symbol National Library of Canada*] (NLC)
QPCM	Bibliotheque Municipale, Port-Cartier, Quebec [*Library symbol National Library of Canada*] (BIB)
QPD	Bibliotheque Intermunicipale de Pierrefonds et Dollard-Des-Ormeaux, Pierrefonds, Quebec [*Library symbol National Library of Canada*] (NLC)
QPD	Quadrature Phase Detection [*Physics*]
QPD	Quality Paperbacks Direct (WDAA)
QPDM	Quadpixel Data-Flow Manager [*Computer science*]
QPDOLL	Quarterly Payment Demand on Legal Loan
QPE	Quantum Paraelectric [*Physics*]
QPEEG	Quantitative Pharmaco-Electro-Encephalography [*Medicine*] (DMAA)
qpei	Quality per End Item (AD)
QPEI	Quantity per End Item (MCD)
QPES	Centre de Documentation, Institut de Technologie Agro-Alimentaire de La Pocatiere, Quebec [*Library symbol National Library of Canada*] (NLC)
QPF	Quantitative Precipitation Forecast (NOAA)
qpf	Quantitative Precipitation Forecast (AD)
QPF	Quebec Police Force [*Canada*] (AD)
QPF	Queensland Producers' Federation [*Australia*]
QPFC	Queen's Park Football Club (AD)
QPFL	Queensland Professional Fishermens League [*Australia*] (AD)
QPH	Queen's Park Harriers [*British*] (ROG)
QPI	Quadratic Performance Index
qpi	Quadratic Performance Index (AD)
Q/PI	Quality and Productivity Improvement (AAGC)
QPI	Quality Productivity Improvement (MCD)
QPIMC	Quadratic Programming Internal Model Control [*Chemical engineering*] [*Computer science*]
QPIR	EBRI [*Employee Benefit Research Institute*] Quarterly Pension Investment Report [*A publication*]
QPIS	Quality Performance Instruction Sheet (AD)
QPIS	Quality Planning Instruction Sheet (MCD)
QPIT	Quantitative Pilocarpine Ionophoresis Test
QPL	Qualified Parts List (AAG)
QPL	Qualified Producers List (IAA)
QPL	Qualified Products List [*Military*]
Q PL	Quantum Placet [*As Much as You Please*] [*Pharmacy*]
QPL	Queensland Press Ltd. [*Australia*]
QPL	Queens Public Library (AD)
QPL & S	Qualified Products Lists and Sources
QPLM	Bibliotheque Municipale, Plessisville, Quebec [*Library symbol National Library of Canada*] (NLC)
QPLT	Quiet Propulsion Lift Technology [*NASA*]
qplt	Quiet Propulsion Lift Technology (AD)
QPM	Quality Practice Manual [*A publication*]
QPM	Quality Program Manager [*Nuclear energy*] (NRCH)

QPM	Quality-Protein Maize
QPM	Quantized Pulse Modulation
QPM	Quaque Post Meridiem [*Every night*] [*Latin*] [*Pharmacy*] (DAVI)
QPM	Quasi-Phase-Matching [*Physics*]
QPM	Queen's Polar Medal [*British*] (AD)
QPM	Queen's Police Medal [*British*]
QPM	Queen's [*Victoria*] Prime Ministers [*A publication*]
QPM	Questions of Procedure for Ministers
QPM	Quick Printing Management [*A publication*] (DGA)
QPMV	Quail Pea Mosaic Virus [*Plant pathology*]
Q/PNL	Quarter Panel [*Automotive engineering*]
QPO	Quasi-Periodic Oscillation [*Astronomy*]
QPOC	Pointe-Claire Public Library [*Bibliotheque Publique de Pointe-Claire*] Quebec [*Library symbol National Library of Canada*] (NLC)
QPOCQ	Quebec Family History Society, Pointe Claire, Quebec [*Library symbol National Library of Canada*] (BIB)
QPP	Quality Program Plan (MCD)
QPP	Quality Program Provision
QPP	Quantized Pulse Position
QPP	Quebec Pension Plan [*Canada*]
QPP	Quebec Provincial Police [*Canada*] (AD)
QPP	Queensland People's Party [*Australia Political party*]
QPP	Quetico Provincial Park [*Ontario, Canada*] (AD)
QPP	Quiescent Push-Pull [*Electronics*] (DEN)
QPPC	Quarterly Production Progress Conference [*Navy*] (NG)
QPPM	Quantized Pulse Position Modulation [*Telecommunications*] (IAA)
QPPO	Queensland Pork Producers' Organisation [*Australia*]
QPPR	Quantitative Property-Property Relationship
QPQ	QPQ Corp. [*Associated Press*] (SAG)
QPQ	Quench Polish Quench (PDAA)
QPQ	Quid Pro Quid
QPQ Cp	QPQ Corp. [*Associated Press*] (SAG)
QPQQ	QPQ Corp. [*NASDAQ symbol*] (SAG)
QPQQW	QPQ Corp. Wrrt [*NASDAQ symbol*] (TTSB)
QPR	Pittsburgh Regional Library Center - Union List, Pittsburgh, PA [*OCLC symbol*] (OCLC)
QPR	Quadrature Partial Response (NITA)
QPR	Qualitative Personnel Requirements [*NASA*] (KSC)
QPR	Quality Progress Review (MCD)
QPR	Quantity Progress Report (AD)
QPR	Quarterly Process Review
QPR	Quarterly Progress Report
QPR	Quebec Practice Reports [*A publication*] (DLA)
QPR	Queen's Park Ranger [*British*] (DI)
QPR	Question, Persuade, and Refer [*A suicide prevention effort*]
QPRD	Quality Planning Requirements Document [*NASA*] (NASA)
QPRF	Quantitative Precipitation Ratio Forecasts [*National Weather Service*]
QPRI	Qualitative Personnel Requirements Information [*NASA*] (MCD)
QPRI	Qualitative Personnel Requirements Inventory (MCD)
QPRM	Bibliotheque Municipale, Princeville, Quebec [*Library symbol National Library of Canada*] (NLC)
QPRS	Quadrature Partial-Response System [*Telecommunications*] (TEL)
QPRS	Quarterly Project Reliability Summary [*Navy*] (NG)
QPRT	Qualified Personal Residence Trust [*Investment term*]
QPS	Quaker Peace and Service [*An association*] (EAIU)
QPS	Qualified Processing Source
QPS	Qualified Process Supplies (MCD)
QPS	Quality Planning Specification [*NASA*] (NASA)
QPS	Quantitative Physical Science
qps	Quantitative Physical Science (AD)
QPS	Quantity Planning Specification (NASA)
QPS	Queensland Purchasing and Sales [*Australia*]
QPS	Query Property Similarity (MHDI)
QPS	Quick Program Search (WDAA)
QPS	Quiescent Power Supply
QPSC	Quiescent Power Supply Current
QPSII	Qualified Possession Source Investment Income [*IRS*]
qpsk	Quad-Phase Shift Key [*Computer science*] (AD)
QPSK	Quadrature Phase Shift Key [*or Keying*] [*Telecommunications*]
QPSK	Quaternary Phase Shift Keying (NITA)
QPSL	Qualified Parts and Suppliers List (MCD)
QPSX	Queued Packet Synchronous Exchange [*Telecommunications*] (OSI)
QPT	Quadrant Power Tilt (IEEE)
QPT	Quarterly Provisional Tax
QPT	Quartz Pressure Transducer [*Telecommunications*] (IAA)
QPT	Quick Prothrombin Time [*Hematology*] (DAVI)
QPTC	Quarry Products Training Council (AIE)
QPU	Queensland Police Union [*Australia*]
QPVT	Quick Picture Vocabulary Test [*Speech and language therapy*] (DAVI)
QPW	Quattro Pro for Windows [*Borland International*] [*Computer science*] (PCM)
QPX	QPX Minerals, Inc. [*Vancouver Stock Exchange symbol*]
QQ	Aerovias Quisqueyana [*Airlines*] [*Dominican Republic*] [*ICAO designator*] (OAG)
QQ	Bibliotheque de Quebec, Quebec [*Library symbol National Library of Canada*] (NLC)
QQ	Michigan Airways [*ICAO designator*] (AD)
QQ	Potential Hijacker [*Airline notation*]
QQ	Qara Qash [*Sinkiang province of China*] (AD)
QQ	Qara Qum [*Sinkiang province of China*] (AD)
QQ	Qualitate Qua [*In the Capacity Of*] [*Latin*]
Q-Q	Quantile-Quantile [*Computer science*]
QQ	Quaque [*Each or Every*] [*Pharmacy*]
qq	Quaque [*Each*] [*Latin*] (AD)

qq	Quartos (AD)
QQ	Quartos (WDAA)
QQ	Quasi-Quadrennial
qq	Quelques [*Some*] [*French*] (AD)
QQ	Que Que [*Rhodesia*] (AD)
qq	Questionable Questionnaire (AD)
QQ	Questionable Questionnaires
QQ	Questions
qq	Questions (WDMC)
qq	Quintales [*Quintals*] [*Spanish*] (AD)
QQ	Quisque [*Each, Every*] [*Pharmacy*]
QQ	Quoque [*Also*] [*Pharmacy*]
qq	Quoque [*Every*] [*Latin*] (AD)
QQA	Archives Nationales du Quebec, Quebec [*Library symbol National Library of Canada*] (NLC)
QQA	Quarterly Quality Assurance [*Environmental Protection Agency*]
QQAA	Archives de l'Archeveche de Quebec, Quebec [*Library symbol National Library of Canada*] (NLC)
QQAC	Ministere des Affaires Culturelles du Quebec, Quebec, Quebec [*Library symbol National Library of Canada*] (NLC)
QQACJ	Archives de la Compagnie de Jesus, Province du Canada - Francais, Saint-Jerome, Quebec, Quebec [*Library symbol National Library of Canada*] (NLC)
QQAG	Centre de Documentation du 200, Ministere de l'Agriculture, des Pecheries, et del'Alimentation, Quebec, Quebec [*Library symbol National Library of Canada*] (NLC)
QQAI	Bibliotheque Administrative, Ministere des Affaires Inter-Gouvernementales du Quebec, Quebec, Quebec [*Library symbol Obsolete National Library of Canada*] (NLC)
QQAM	Centre de Documentation, Ministere des Affaires Municipales du Quebec, Quebec, Quebec [*Library symbol National Library of Canada*] (NLC)
QQAND	Archives du Monastere Notre-Dame-Des-Anges, Quebec, Quebec [*Library symbol National Library of Canada*] (NLC)
QQAPC	Cerebral Palsy Association of Quebec, Inc. [*L'Association de Paralysie Cerebrale du Quebec, Inc.*] Quebec, Quebec [*Library symbol National Library of Canada*] (NLC)
QQAQ	Bibliotheque des Services Diocesains, Archeveche de Quebec, Quebec [*Library symbol National Library of Canada*] (BIB)
QQAQS	Synod Office, Diocese of Quebec, Anglican Church of Canada, Quebec, Quebec [*Library symbol National Library of Canada*] (NLC)
QQAS	Archives du Seminaire de Quebec, Quebec, Quebec [*Library symbol National Library of Canada*] (NLC)
QQASF	Conseil des Affaires Sociales et de la Famille, Quebec, Quebec [*Library symbol National Library of Canada*] (NLC)
QQBJNQ	Bureau de la Baie James et du Nord Quebecois, Ste.-Foy, Quebec [*Library symbol National Library of Canada*] (NLC)
QQBL	Bibliotheque des Freres des Ecoles Chretiennes, Quebec [*Library symbol National Library of Canada*] (NLC)
QQBMC	Bibliotheque Municipale, Charlesbourg, Quebec [*Library symbol National Library of Canada*] (BIB)
QQBS	Bureau de la Statistique du Quebec, Quebec, Quebec [*Library symbol National Library of Canada*] (NLC)
QQBST	Centre de Documentation, Ministere de l'Enseignement Superieur et de la Science du Quebec, Ste.-Foy, Quebec [*Library symbol National Library of Canada*] (NLC)
QQC	Defence Research Establishment Valcartier, Canada Department of National Defence[*Centre de Recherches pour la Defense Valcartier, Ministere de la Defense Na tionale*] Courcelette, Quebec [*Library symbol National Library of Canada*] (NLC)
QQC	Quantitative Quality Characteristics
QQC	Queensland Quality Centre [*Australia*]
QQCAD	Conservatoire d'Art Dramatique du Quebec, Quebec [*Library symbol National Library of Canada*] (NLC)
QQCAI	Centre de Documentation, Commission d'Acces a l'Information, Quebec, Quebec [*Library symbol National Library of Canada*] (NLC)
QQCAT	Commission de la Sante et de la Securite du Travail du Quebec, Quebec, Quebec [*Library symbol National Library of Canada*] (NLC)
QQCC	Centre de Documentation, Conseil des Colleges du Quebec, Quebec, Quebec [*Library symbol National Library of Canada*] (BIB)
QQCDP	Commission des Droits de la Personne du Quebec, Quebec, Quebec [*Library symbol National Library of Canada*] (NLC)
QQCDT	Centre de Documentation, Commission des Normes du Travail, Quebec [*Library symbol National Library of Canada*] (NLC)
QQCE	CEGEP [*College d'Enseignement General et Professionnel*] de Limoilou, Quebec, Quebec [*Library symbol National Library of Canada*] (NLC)
QQCF	Centre Francois Charron, Quebec, Quebec [*Library symbol National Library of Canada*] (BIB)
QQCFP	Centre de Documentation, Commission de la Fonction Publique du Quebec, Quebec, Quebec [*Library symbol National Library of Canada*] (BIB)
QQCFX	CEGEP [*College d'Enseignement General et Professionnel*] F. X. Garneau, Sillery, Quebec [*Library symbol National Library of Canada*] (NLC)
QQCGI	Centre de Documentation, CGI [*Conseillers en Gestion et Informatique*], I nc., Quebec [*Library symbol National Library of Canada*] (NLC)
QQCH	Departement des Archives et Statistiques de la Ville de Quebec, Quebec, Quebec [*Library symbol National Library of Canada*] (NLC)

QQCHJH...... Centre Hospitalier Jeffery Hale, Quebec, Quebec [*Library symbol National Library of Canada*] (BIB)

QQCLF......... Conseil de la Langue Francaise, Quebec, Quebec [*Library symbol National Library of Canada*] (NLC)

QQCM.......... College Merici, Quebec, Quebec [*Library symbol National Library of Canada*] (NLC)

QQCMQ........ Service de la Documentation et de l'Audiovisuel, Conservatoire de Musique de Quebec, Quebec [*Library symbol National Library of Canada*] (NLC)

QQCOC........ Centre de Documentation - DGTI [*Direction Generale des Technologies de l'Information*], Ministere des Communications du Quebec, Ste.-Foy, Quebec [*Library symbol National Library of Canada*] (BIB)

QQCOM........ Centre de Documentation, Direction Generale des Medias, Ministere des Communications du Quebec, Quebec, Quebec [*Library symbol National Library of Canada*] (BIB)

QQCPQ......... Parks Service, Environment Canada [*Service des Parcs, Environnement Canada*], Quebec [*Library symbol National Library of Canada*] (BIB)

QQCPS......... Centre de Documentation, Conseil de la Science et de la Technologie du Quebec, Ste.-Foy, Quebec [*Library symbol National Library of Canada*] (NLC)

QQCR........... Centre Hospitalier Christ-Roi, Quebec, Quebec [*Library symbol National Library of Canada*] (BIB)

QQCRS......... Conseil Regional de la Sante et des Services Sociaux, Quebec, Quebec [*Library symbol National Library of Canada*] (NLC)

QQCS........... Service de Documentation et de Bibliotheque, Complexe Scientifique, Ste.-Foy, Quebec [*Library symbol National Library of Canada*] (NLC)

QQCSF......... Conseil du Statut de la Femme, Quebec, Quebec [*Library symbol National Library of Canada*] (NLC)

QQCSS......... Centre de Documentation, Centre de Services Sociaux de Quebec, Quebec [*Library symbol National Library of Canada*] (BIB)

QQCT........... Commission de Toponymie du Quebec, Quebec, Quebec [*Library symbol National Library of Canada*] (NLC)

QQCU........... Conseil des Universites du Quebec, Ste.-Foy, Quebec [*Library symbol National Library of Canada*] (NLC)

QQCUQ......... Communaute Urbaine de Quebec [*Library symbol National Library of Canada*] (BIB)

qqd.............. Quantum Quatra Die [*Every Fourth Day*] [*Latin*] (AD)

QQE............. Wildlife and Inland Waters Library, Environment Canada [*Bibliotheque de la Faune et des Eaux Interieures, Environement Canada*] Ste-Foy, Quebec [*Library symbol National Library of Canada*] (NLC)

QQED........... Centre de Documentation, Ministere de l'Education du Quebec, Quebec, Quebec [*Library symbol National Library of Canada*] (BIB)

QQEDOP...... Centre de Documentation, Office des Professions du Quebec, Quebec [*Library symbol National Library of Canada*] (NLC)

QQEN........... Ministere de l'Environnement, Ste-Foy, Quebec [*Library symbol National Library of Canada*] (NLC)

QQERE......... Centre de Documentation-Energie, Ministere de l'Energie et des Ressources du Quebec, Quebec, Quebec [*Library symbol National Library of Canada*] (NLC)

QQERM........ Centre de Documentation-Mines, Ministere de l'Energie et des Ressources du Quebec, Quebec, Quebec [*Library symbol National Library of Canada*] (NLC)

QQERT......... Centre de Documentation-Terres et Forets, Ministere de l'Energie et des Ressources du Quebec, Quebec, Quebec [*Library symbol National Library of Canada*] (NLC)

QQESE......... Centre de Documentation, Direction Generale de l'Enseignement et de la RechercheUniversitaires, Ministere de l'Enseignement Superieur et de la Science du Quebe c, Quebec, Quebec [*Library symbol National Library of Canada*] (BIB)

QQF............. Bibliotheque Franclscalne, Quebec, Quebec [*Llbrary symbol National Library of Canada*] (NLC)

qqf.............. Quelquefois [*Sometimes*] [*French*] (AD)

QQFPCE....... Direction de la Classification et de l'Evaluation des Emplois, Ministere de la Fonction Publique, Quebec, Quebec [*Library symbol National Library of Canada*] (NLC)

QQFTI.......... Service du Traitement de l'Information, Ministere des Finances, Duberger, Quebec [*Library symbol National Library of Canada*] (NLC)

QQGR........... Bibliotheque Gabrielle-Roy, Quebec, Quebec [*Library symbol National Library of Canada*] (BIB)

qqh.............. Quantum Quatra Hora [*Every Four Hours*] [*Latin*] (AD)

QQH............. Quaque Hora [*Every Hour*] [*Pharmacy*]

QQH............. Quaque Quarta Hora [*Every Fourth Hour*] [*Pharmacy*]

QQHA........... Queensland Quarter Horse Association [*Australia*]

QQHD........... Hotel-Dieu de Quebec, Quebec [*Library symbol National Library of Canada*] (NLC)

QQHDM........ Musee des Augustines de l'Hotel-Dieu de Quebec, Quebec [*Library symbol National Library of Canada*] (NLC)

QQHDS........ Hotel-Dieu du Sacre-Coeur, Quebec, Quebec [*Library symbol National Library of Canada*] (NLC)

QQHEJ......... Hopital de l'Enfant-Jesus, Quebec, Quebec [*Library symbol National Library of Canada*] (NLC)

QQHFA......... Hopital St-Francois d'Assise, Quebec, Quebec [*Library symbol National Library of Canada*] (NLC)

QQ HOR....... Quaque Hora [*Every Hour*] [*Pharmacy*]

qq hor.......... Quaque Hora [*Every Hour*] [*Latin*] (AD)

QQHSS......... Hopital du Saint-Sacrement, Quebec, Quebec [*Library symbol National Library of Canada*] (NLC)

QQHSSC...... Centre de Documentation, Departement de Sante Communautaire, Hopital du Saint-Sacrement, Quebec, Quebec [*Library symbol National Library of Canada*] (BIB)

QQIAS.......... Service de la Documentation, Ministere de la Sante et des Services Sociaux du Q uebec, Quebec, Quebec [*Library symbol National Library of Canada*] (NLC)

QQIC............ Ministere de l'Industrie, du Commerce et du Tourisme, Quebec, Quebec [*Library symbol National Library of Canada*] (NLC)

QQIF............ Inspecteur General des Institutions Financieres, Quebec, Quebec [*Library symbol National Library of Canada*] (NLC)

QQIN............ Indian and Northern Affairs Canada [*Affaires Indiennes et du Nord Canada*],Quebec [*Library symbol National Library of Canada*] (BIB)

QQIQRC....... Institut Quebecois de Recherche sur la Culture, Quebec, Quebec [*Library symbol National Library of Canada*] (NLC)

QQJ............. Ministere de la Justice du Quebec, Ste-Foy, Quebec [*Library symbol National Library of Canada*] (NLC)

QQL............. Bibliotheque de l'Assemblee Nationale, Quebec, Quebec [*Library symbol National Library of Canada*] (NLC)

QQLA........... Universite Laval, Quebec, Quebec [*Library symbol National Library of Canada*] (NLC)

QQLAAA...... Secteur Art et Architecture, Universite Laval, Quebec, Quebec [*Library symbol National Library of Canada*] (NLC)

QQLAAV...... Ecole des Arts Visuels, Universite Laval, Quebec, Quebec [*Library symbol National Library of Canada*] (NLC)

QQLACA...... Cartotheque, Universite Laval, Quebec, Quebec [*Library symbol National Library of Canada*] (NLC)

QQLACH...... Centre Hospitalier de l'Universite Laval, Quebec, Quebec [*Library symbol National Library of Canada*] (NLC)

QQLACHC.... Centre de Documentation, Departement de Sante Communautaire, Centre Hospitalier,Universite Laval, Quebec, Quebec [*Library symbol National Library of Canada*] (NLC)

QQLACHR.... Centre de Recherche, Centre Hospitalier, Universite Laval, Quebec, Quebec [*Library symbol National Library of Canada*] (BIB)

QQLACHT.... Centre de Toxicologie, Centre Hospitalier, Universite Laval, Quebec, Quebec [*Library symbol National Library of Canada*] (BIB)

QQLACI........ Centre International de Recherches sur le Bilinguisme, Universite Laval, Quebec,Quebec [*Library symbol National Library of Canada*] (NLC)

QQLAD......... Faculte de Droit, Universite Laval, Quebec, Quebec [*Library symbol National Library of Canada*] (NLC)

QQLAG......... Institut de Geographie, Universite Laval, Quebec, Quebec [*Library symbol National Library of Canada*] (NLC)

QQLAGM...... Departement de Geologie et de Mineralogie, Universite Laval, Quebec, Quebec [*Library symbol National Library of Canada*] (NLC)

QQLAI.......... Societa Dante Alighieri, Universite Laval, Quebec, Quebec [*Library symbol National Library of Canada*] (NLC)

QQLAS......... Bibliotheque Scientifique, Universite Laval, Quebec, Quebec [*Library symbol National Library of Canada*] (NLC)

QQLCP......... Ministere du Loisir, de la Chasse et de la Peche, Quebec, Quebec [*Library symbol National Library of Canada*] (NLC)

QQLH........... Literary and Historical Society of Quebec [*Societe Litteraire et Historique de Quebec*] Quebec [*Library symbol National Library of Canada*] (NLC)

QQLM.......... Centre de Documentation, Laurentienne Mutuelle d'Assurance, Quebec, Quebec [*Library symbol National Library of Canada*] (BIB)

qqma........... Quality Qualified Military Availability (AD)

QQMAA........ Archives du Monastere des Augustines, Quebec, Quebec [*Library symbol National Library of Canada*] (NLC)

QQMAB........ Bibliotheque du Monastere des Augustines, Quebec, Quebec [*Library symbol National Library of Canada*] (NLC)

QQMAGA...... Archives des Augustines du Monastere de l'Hopital General de Quebec, Quebec [*Library symbol National Library of Canada*] (NLC)

QQM & R.... Quantitative, Qualitative, Maintainability, and Reliability

QQMC.......... Forestry Canada [*Forets Canada*], Ste.-Foy, Quebec [*Library symbol National Library of Canada*] (NLC)

QQMCH....... Bibliotheque Administrative, (Edifice H), Ministere des Communications du Quebec, Quebec [*Library symbol National Library of Canada*] (NLC)

QQMF.......... Laurentian Forestry Centre, Canadian Forestry Service [*Centre de Foresterie des Laurentides, Service Canadien des Forets*] Ste.-Foy, Quebec [*Library symbol National Library of Canada*] (NLC)

QQMQ.......... Musee du Quebec, Quebec [*Library symbol National Library of Canada*] (NLC)

QQMR.......... Le Mussee du Royal 22e Regiment et la Regie du Royal 22e Regiment, Quebec, Quebec [*Library symbol National Library of Canada*] (NLC)

QQMSRD..... Centre de Documentation, Direction Generale des Ressources Informationnelles, Ministere de la Main d'Oeuvre et de la Securite du Revenu du Quebec, Quebec, Quebec [*Library symbol National Library of Canada*] (NLC)

QQMSRP...... Centre de Documentation, Direction Generale de la Planification, Ministere de laMain-d'Oeuvre et de la Securite du Revenu du Quebec, Quebec, Quebec [*Library symbol National Library of Canada*] (BIB)

QQMUC....... Centre de Documentation, Musee de la Civilisation, Quebec [*Library symbol National Library of Canada*] (BIB)

QQO............. Quasiquadrennial Oscillation [*Astronomy*]

QQOLF......... Office de la Langue Francaise, Quebec, Quebec [*Library symbol National Library of Canada*] (NLC)

QQOPC........ Office de la Protection du Consommateur, Quebec, Quebec [*Library symbol National Library of Canada*] (NLC)

QQOPD .... Direction de la Documentation, Office des Promotions du Quebec, Quebec, Quebec [*Library symbol National Library of Canada*] (NLC)

QQP .... Quick Query Program

QQPCQ .... Canadian Park Service, Environment Canada [*Service Canadien des Parcs, Environnement Canada*], Quebec, Quebec [*Library symbol National Library of Canada*] (NLC)

QQPEA .... Archives des Peres Eudistes, Charlesbourg, Quebec [*Library symbol National Library of Canada*] (NLC)

QQPR .... Quantitative and Qualitative Personnel Requirements

qqpr .... Quantitative and Qualitative Personnel Requirements (AD)

QQPRI .... Quantitative and Qualitative Personnel Requirements Information [*Military*]

QQPSM .... Maurice Lamontagne Institute, Fisheries and Oceans Canada [*Institut Maurice Lamontagne, Peches et Oceans Canada*], Mont-Joli, Quebec [*Library symbol National Library of Canada*] (NLC)

QQQE .... Centre Quebecois des Sciences de l'Eau, Universite du Quebec, Quebec, Quebec [*Library symbol National Library of Canada*] (NLC)

QQR .... Technical Information Centre, Reed Ltd., Quebec, Quebec [*Library symbol National Library of Canada*] (NLC)

QQRA .... Roche Associes Ltee., Group-Conseil, Ste.-Foy, Quebec [*Library symbol National Library of Canada*] (NLC)

QQRAA .... Regie de l'Assurance Automobile du Quebec, Sillery, Quebec [*Library symbol National Library of Canada*] (NLC)

QQRAMQ ..... Regie de l'Assurance-Maladie du Quebec, Sillery, Quebec [*Library symbol National Library of Canada*] (NLC)

QQRE .... Ministere du Revenu, Ste.-Foy, Quebec [*Library symbol National Library of Canada*] (NLC)

QQRRQ .... Regie des Rentes du Quebec, Ste.-Foy, Quebec [*Library symbol National Library of Canada*] (NLC)

QQRSP .... Regie des Services Publics, Ste.-Foy, Quebec [*Library symbol National Library of Canada*] (NLC)

QQS .... Quality Quest System [*Vancouver Stock Exchange symbol*]

QQS .... Seminaire de Quebec, Quebec [*Library symbol National Library of Canada*] (NLC)

QQSAA .... Centre de Documentation, Secretariat aux Affaires Autochtones, Quebec [*Library symbol National Library of Canada*] (BIB)

QQSAJ .... Secretariat a la Jeunesse, Conseil Executif, Quebec, Quebec [*Library symbol National Library of Canada*] (NLC)

QQSC .... Quadripartite Quartermaster Standardization Committee [*Military*] (AABC)

QQSCA .... Archives des Soeurs de la Charite de Quebec, Quebec, Quebec [*Library symbol National Library of Canada*] (NLC)

QQSCF .... Centre de Documentation, Secretariat a la Condition Feminine du Quebec, Quebec, Quebec [*Library symbol National Library of Canada*] (BIB)

QQSHQ .... Centre de Documentation, Societe d'Habitation du Quebec, Quebec [*Library symbol National Library of Canada*] (BIB)

QQSIP .... Societe Quebecoise d'Initiatives Petrolieres, Ste.-Foy, Quebec [*Library symbol National Library of Canada*] (NLC)

QQSP .... Centre de Documentation, Syndicat de Professionnels et de Professionnelles du Gouvernement du Quebec, Quebec [*Library symbol National Library of Canada*] (BIB)

QQSS .... Quebec Library, Translation Bureau, Secretary of State Canada [*Bibliotheque de Quebec, Bureau des Traductions, Secretariat d'Etat*], Ste.-Foy, Quebec [*Library symbol National Library of Canada*] (NLC)

QQST .... Centre de Documentation, Conseil de la Science et de la Technologie, Quebec [*Library symbol National Library of Canada*] (NLC)

QQTCG .... Canadian Coast Guard [*Garde Cotiere Canadienne*] Quebec, Quebec [*Library symbol National Library of Canada*] (NLC)

QQTE .... Tecrad, Inc., Ancienne-Lorette, Quebec [*Library symbol National Library of Canada*] (NLC)

QQTO .... Ministere du Tourisme du Quebec, Quebec [*Library symbol National Library of Canada*] (NLC)

QQTQ .... Centre de Documentation, Ministere du Travail du Quebec, Quebec [*Library symbol National Library of Canada*] (BIB)

QQTR .... Ministere des Transports, Quebec, Quebec [*Library symbol National Library of Canada*] (NLC)

QQTRD .... Centre de Documentation, Ministere des Transports - Rue Dorchester, Quebec [*Library symbol National Library of Canada*] (NLC)

QQU .... Couvent des Ursulines, Quebec, Quebec [*Library symbol National Library of Canada*] (NLC)

QQUA .... Archives du Monastere des Ursulines de Merici, Quebec, Quebec [*Library symbol National Library of Canada*] (NLC)

QQUIE .... Centre de Documentation, INRS [*Institut National de la Recherche Scientifique*]-Eau, Quebec, Quebec [*Library symbol National Library of Canada*] (NLC)

QQUQ .... Universite du Quebec, Quebec, Quebec [*Library symbol National Library of Canada*] (NLC)

QQUQEN ...... Ecole Nationale d'Administration Publique, Universite du Quebec, Quebec, Quebec [*Library symbol National Library of Canada*] (NLC)

QQUQT .... Tele-Universite, Universite du Quebec, Quebec, Quebec [*Library symbol National Library of Canada*] (NLC)

QQV .... Centre de Documentation, le Verificateur General du Quebec, Quebec, Quebec [*Library symbol National Library of Canada*] (BIB)

QQ V .... Quae Vide [*Which See*] [*Plural form*] [*Latin*]

qqv .... Quae Vide [*Which See*] [*Latin*] (AD)

QQV .... Quantum Vis [*As Much as You Wish*] [*Pharmacy*] (ADA)

qqv .... Quod Vide [*Which see*] [*Latin*] (WDMC)

Q-QY .... Question or Query (AAG)

q/qy .... Question/Query (AD)

QQZ .... Jardin Zoologique de Quebec, Charlesbourg, Quebec [*Library symbol National Library of Canada*] (NLC)

QR .... Air Satellite [*ICAO designator*] (AD)

QR .... Qatar Riyal [*Monetary unit*] (BJA)

Qr .... Qere (BJA)

QR .... Quadrans [*A Farthing*] [*Monetary unit*] [*British*] (ROG)

QR .... Quadratic Residues (MHDB)

QR .... Quad Right [*Typography*]

QR .... Quadriradial [*Genetics*] (DAVI)

QR .... Quad Royal [*Paper*] (DGA)

QR .... Quadrupole Resonance

QR .... Qualifications Record (AEBS)

qr .... Qualifications Record (AD)

QR .... Quality Requirement (IAA)

QR .... Quality Review

QR .... Quantitative Restrictions [*International trade*]

QR .... Quantity Requested

QR .... Quantity Required

QR .... Quantum Rectum [*The Quantity Is Correct*] [*Pharmacy*]

qr .... Quantum Rectus [*Quantity is Correct*] [*Latin*] (AD)

QR .... Quantum Resources [*Vancouver Stock Exchange symbol*]

QR .... Quarantine Report [*HEW*]

QR .... Quart

QR .... Quarter

qr .... Quarter (AD)

QR .... Quarterly (ROG)

qr .... Quarterly [*A periodical published four times a year*] (WDMC)

QR .... Quarterly Replenishment

QR .... Quarterly Report (OICC)

QR .... Quarter-Round [*Technical drawings*] (DAC)

QR .... Quarters Rating [*British military*] (DMA)

QR .... Quebec Official Reports [*A publication*] (DLA)

QR .... Queensland Railways [*Australia*] (AD)

QR .... Queen's Rangers [*British military*]

QR .... Queen's Regulation [*Military British*]

QR .... Queen's Rook [*Chess*] (ADA)

QR .... Queen's Royal [*Military unit*] [*British*]

Q/R .... Query/Response (MCD)

QR .... Quick Reaction

qr .... Quick Reaction (AD)

qr .... Quick Receipt (AD)

QR .... Quick Recovery (DAVI)

QR .... Quick Recovery Defibrillator [*Cardiology*] (DAVI)

QR .... Quick Response

QR .... Quieting Reflex [*In book title "Q-R: The Quieting Reflex" by Charles F. Stroebel*]

QR .... Quieting Response [*Medicine*] (DMAA)

QR .... Quinaldine Red [*Medicine*] (DMAA)

QR .... Quintana Roo (AD)

QR .... Quire [*Measure of paper*]

qr .... Quire [*Paper*] (WDMC)

QR .... Quota Restriction

QR .... Quotation Request

QR .... Sources Public Library [*Bibliotheque Municipale des Sources*] Roxboro, Quebec [*Library symbol National Library of Canada*] (NLC)

QRA .... Archeveche de Rimouski, Quebec [*Library symbol National Library of Canada*] (NLC)

QRA .... Quality and Reliability Assurance (NG)

QRA .... Quality Recording Alarm [*Engineering*]

qra .... Quality Reliability Assurance (AD)

QRA .... Quantified Risk Analysis

QRA .... Quarterly Review and Analysis

QRA .... Queensland Rifle Association [*Australia*] (AD)

QRA .... Quick Reaction Acquisition (MCD)

QRA .... Quick Reaction Aircraft (MCD)

QRA .... Quick Reaction Alert [*Military*] (AFM)

qra .... Quick Reaction Alert (AD)

QRA .... Quick Reaction Area (MCD)

QRA .... Quick Replaceable Assembly

QRAAT .... Centre de l'Abitibi-Temiscamingue, Archives Nationales du Quebec, Rouyn-Noranda, Quebec [*Library symbol National Library of Canada*] (BIB)

QRAC .... Quality and Reliability Assessment Council

QRAC .... Quality and Reliability Assurance Committee (AAGC)

QR Air .... Queen's Regulations and Orders for the Royal Canadian Air Force

QRAL .... Quality and Reliability Assurance Laboratory [*NASA*] (KSC)

QRAN .... Archives Nationales du Quebec, Rimouski, Quebec [*Library symbol National Library of Canada*] (BIB)

QR & AI ...... Queen's Regulations and Admiralty Instructions [*Obsolete Navy British*]

QR & O (Can)... Queen's Regulations and Orders for the Canadian Army

QRB .... Quality Review Bulletin [*A publication*] (DMAA)

QRB .... Quarterly Review of Biology [*A publication*] (BRI)

QRBC .... Bibliotheque Centrale de Pret d'Abitibi-Temiscamingue, Rouyn-Noranda, Quebec [*Library symbol National Library of Canada*] (NLC)

QRBM .... Quasi-Random Band Model

qrbm .... Quasi-Random Band Model (AD)

QRC .... Quaker Resources Canada Ltd. [*Vancouver Stock Exchange symbol*]

QRC .... Queensland Rubber Co. [*Australia*] (AD)

QRC .... Quick RAM [*Random Access Memory*] Change [*Computer science*] (IAA)

QRC .... Quick Reaction Capability [*Military*]
qrc .... Quick Reaction Capability (AD)
QRC .... Quick Reaction Change (MCD)
QRC .... Quick Reaction Communications (MHDI)
QRC .... Quick Response Capability [*Military*]
QRC .... Quick Response Controller (NITA)
QRCA .... Qualitative Research Consultants Association (EA)
QRCB .... College Bourget, Rigaud, Quebec [*Library symbol National Library of Canada*] (NLC)
QRCC .... Quadripartite Research Coordination Committee [*Military*] (AABC)
QRCC .... Query Response Communications Console
QRCC .... Quick Reaction Combat Capability (DOMA)
QRCG .... Quasi-Random Code Generator (CET)
qrcg .... Quasi-Random Code Generator (AD)
QRCH .... Centre de Documentation, Centre Hospitalier Regional de Rimouski, Quebec [*Library symbol National Library of Canada*] (NLC)
QRCN .... College de l'Abitibi-Temiscamingue, Rouyn, Quebec [*Library symbol National Library of Canada*] (NLC)
QRCN .... Queen's Regulations and Orders for the Royal Canadian Navy
QRCR .... Quality Reliability Consumption Reports
QRCRS .... Conseil Regional de la Sante et des Services Sociaux, Rimouski, Quebec [*Library symbol National Library of Canada*] (NLC)
QRCUP .... Quebec Region Canadian University Press (AD)
QRD .... Quality Reliability Deployment [*Automotive engineering*]
QRD .... Quarterly Review of Doublespeak [*A publication*]
QRD .... Quick Reaction Development
QRDC .... Quartermaster Research and Development Center [*or Command*] [*Natick, MA*]
QRDEA .... Quartermaster Research and Development Evaluation Agency [*Army*]
QRDN .... Quality Requirement Discrepancy Notice (SAA)
QRDS .... Quarterly Review of Drilling Statistics [*American Petroleum Institute*]
QRE .... Bibliotheque Municipale, Repentigny, Quebec [*Library symbol National Library of Canada*] (NLC)
QRE .... Quick Reaction Element (COE)
QRE .... Quick Reaction [*or Response*] Estimate
QREC .... Quartermaster Research and Engineering Center [*or Command*] [*Natick, MA*]
QRECS .... Centre Regional de Documentation Pedagogique, Commission Scolaire de Le Gardeur,Repentigny, Quebec [*Library symbol National Library of Canada*] (BIB)
Q Rev Juris... Quarterly Review of Jurisprudence [*1887-88*] [*A publication*] (DLA)
Q Rev Rural Econ... Quarterly Review of the Rural Economy [*A publication*]
QRF .... Quadrature Rejection Frequency
QRF .... Quality Review File [*IRS*]
QRF .... Quick Reaction Force [*Military*] (CINC)
QRG .... Quadrupole Residual Gas
QRG .... Quick Reaction Grooming
QRG .... Quick Response Graphic
qrg .... Quick Response Graphic (AD)
qrga .... Quadrupole Residual Gas Analyzer (AD)
QRGA .... Quadrupole Residual Gas Analyzer
QRGAS .... Quadrupole Residual Gas Analyzer System
QRGS .... Grand Seminaire de Rimouski, Quebec [*Library symbol National Library of Canada*] (NLC)
QRH .... Rosemere High School, Quebec [*Library symbol National Library of Canada*] (BIB)
QRHD .... Bibliotheque Medicale, Hotel-Dieu de Roberval, Quebec [*Library symbol National Library of Canada*] (NLC)
QRI .... Qualitative Requirements Information [*Army*]
qri .... Qualitative Requirements Information (AD)
QRI .... Quick Reaction Integration (NASA)
QRIA .... Quick Reaction Integration Activity (NASA)
QRIB .... Haskell Free Library, Rock Island, Quebec [*Library symbol National Library of Canada*] (NLC)
QRIC .... CEGEP [*College d'Enseignement General et Professionnel*] de Rimouski, Quebec [*Library symbol National Library of Canada*] (NLC)
QRIC .... Quick Reaction Installation Capability (CET)
qric .... Quick Reaction Installation Capability (AD)
QRICC .... Quick Reaction Inventory Control Center [*Army*] (MCD)
QRIH .... Queen's Royal Irish Hussars [*Military unit*] [*British*]
QRIM .... Institut Maritime, CEGEP de Rimouski, Quebec [*Library symbol National Library of Canada*] (NLC)
QRISTHRA ... Qiqihar Research Institute of Science and Technology, Harbin Railway Administration [*China*] (BUAC)
QRKB .... Quebec King's Bench Reports [*A publication*] (DLA)
QRKB .... Rapports Judiciaires de Quebec, Cour du Banc du Roi [*Quebec Law Reports, King's Bench*] [*A publication*] (DLA)
QRL .... Bibliotheque Municipale, Riviere-Du-Loup, Quebec [*Library symbol National Library of Canada*] (BIB)
QRL .... Q-Switch Ruby LASER
QRL .... Quadripartite Research List [*Military*] (AABC)
QRL .... Quaternary Research Laboratory [*University of Michigan*] [*Research center*] (RCD)
QRL .... Queensland Research League [*Australia*] (AD)
QRL .... Quick Reference List
QRL .... Quick Relocate and Link
QRLC .... CEGEP [*College d'Enseignement General et Professionnel*] de Riviere-Du-Loup, Quebec [*Library symbol National Library of Canada*] (BIB)
QRLH .... Centre de Documentation DSC, Hotel-Dieu de Riviere-Du-Loup, Quebec [*Library symbol National Library of Canada*] (BIB)
QRLP .... Centre de Recherche, Tourbieres Premier Ltee., Riviere-Du-Loup, Quebec [*Library symbol National Library of Canada*] (BIB)
QRLY .... Quarterly

QRM .... Artificial Interference to Transmission or Reception [*Broadcasting*]
QRM .... Bibliotheque Municipale, Rimouski, Quebec [*Library symbol National Library of Canada*] (NLC)
QRM .... Quality and Resource Management (HCT)
QRM .... Quorum Resource Corp. [*Vancouver Stock Exchange symbol*]
QRMC .... Quadrennial Review of Military Compensation [*DoD*]
QRMC .... Quick Response Multicolor Copier (MCD)
QRMF .... Quick Reacting, Mobile Force [*Military NATO*] (NATG)
QRMP .... Quick-Response Multicolor Printer (RDA)
Qr Mr .... Quartermaster [*British military*] (DMA)
Qrmr .... Quartermaster (AD)
QRN .... Soeurs de Notre-Dame du Saint-Rosaire, Rimouski, Quebec [*Library symbol National Library of Canada*] (NLC)
QRO .... Quality Review Organization (AD)
Qro .... Queretaro (AD)
qro .... Quick Reaction Operation (AD)
QRO .... Quick Reaction Operation (WDAA)
QRO .... Quick Reaction Organization (WDAA)
QROA .... Quarter Racing Owners of America (EA)
Q Roo .... Quintana Roo (AD)
QRosc .... Pro Roscio Comoedo [*of Cicero*] [*Classical studies*] (OCD)
QRP .... Queen's Rook's Pawn [*Chess*] (IIA)
QRP .... Query and Reporting Processor
QRP .... Quick Reaction Program [*Army*]
QRP .... Quick Response Proposal [*Navy*]
QRPA .... Quartermaster Radiation Planning Agency (AD)
QRPAO .... Qualified Radium Plaque Adaptometer Operator [*Navy*]
QRPG .... Quebec Rubber and Plastics Group [*Canada*] (BUAC)
QRPS .... Quick Reaction Procurement System [*Army*] (AABC)
QRQB .... Quebec Queen's Bench Reports [*Canada*] [*A publication*] (DLA)
QRR .... Quadrature Rejection Ratio
QRR .... Quadrupole Resonance Response
QRR .... Qualitative Research Requirement for Nuclear Weapons Effects Information (AABC)
QRR .... Quality Readiness Review (MCD)
QRR .... Quarterly Research Review
QRR .... Queen's Royal Regiment [*Military unit*] [*British*]
QRR .... Queen's Royal Rifles [*British military*] (DMA)
QRR .... Quincy Railroad Co. [*AAR code*]
QRRB .... Qualified Railroad Retirement Beneficiary
QRRF .... Master Quality Review Report File [*IRS*]
QRRI .... Qualitative Research Requirements Information [*Army*]
QRRK .... Quantum Rice-Ramsperger-Kassel [*Chemical kinetics methodology*]
QRRS .... Quality Response Rating Scales (EDAC)
QRS .... Natural Interference to Transmission or Reception [*Broadcasting*]
QRS .... Qualification Review Sheet (KSC)
QRS .... Qualified Repair Source (AFIT)
QRS .... Quantum Readout System [*Method of measurement*]
QRS .... Quarters
qrs .... Quarters (AD)
QRS .... Queensland Rose Society [*Australia*]
QRS .... Queen's Row Spare
QRS .... Quick Reaction Sortie (NASA)
QRSC .... Quebec Superior Court Reports [*A publication*] (DLA)
QRSC .... Rapports Judiciaires de Quebec, Cour Superieure [*Quebec Law Reports, Superior Court*] [*A publication*] (DLA)
QRSI .... QRS Corp. [*NASDAQ symbol*] [*Formerly, Quick Response Services*]
QRSI .... Queensland Raw Sugar Industry [*Australia*]
QRSI .... Quick Response Services [*NASDAQ symbol*] (SAG)
QRSL .... Qualified Repair Source List (AFIT)
QRSL .... Quick Reaction Space Laboratory [*NASA*] (NASA)
qrt .... Quarter (AD)
QRT .... Queue Run-Time [*Computer science*]
QRT .... Quick Reaction Task (MCD)
QRT .... Quick Reaction Team [*Military*]
QRT .... Quiet Radio Transmission (DNAB)
QRTA .... Queensland Road Transport Association [*Australia*]
qrtg .... Quartering (AD)
QRTL .... Queensland Right to Life [*An association Australia*]
QRTLY .... Quarterly (ROG)
qrtly .... Quarterly (AD)
qrtmstr .... Quartermaster (AD)
QRTP .... Quick Response Targeting Program [*Lunar*]
QRTR .... Quarter (IAA)
QRTR .... Quarter-Plate (VRA)
QRTSA .... Queensland Retail Traders and Shopkeepers' Association [*Australia*]
QRU .... Queen's Row Unit
QRU .... Universite du Quebec, Rimouski, Quebec [*Library symbol National Library of Canada*] (NLC)
QRUC .... Cartotheque, Universite du Quebec, Rimouski, Quebec [*Library symbol National Library of Canada*] (NLC)
QRUQR .... Universite du Quebec en Abitibi-Temiscamingue, Rouyn, Quebec [*Library symbol National Library of Canada*] (NLC)
QRUS .... Queen's Row Unit Spare
QRV .... Qualified Real-Estate Valuer
QRV .... Queenstown Rifle Volunteers [*British military*] (DMA)
QRV .... Quick Release Valve
qrv .... Quick-Release Valve (AD)
QRV .... Quinn River Valley [*Nevada*] [*Seismograph station code, US Geological Survey Closed*] (SEIS)
QRVB .... Queen's Rifle Volunteer Brigade [*British military*] (DMA)
QRW .... Quail Ridge Winery [*Vancouver Stock Exchange symbol*]
QRX .... Queensland Railfast Express [*Australia*] (AD)
qry .... Quality and Reliability Year (AD)
QRY .... Quality and Reliability Year

QRY	Quarry (KSC)
QRZ	Quaddel Reaktion Zeit [*Wheal Reaction Time*] [*German*]
QRZ	Who is Calling [*Amateur Radio*] (BARN)
QS	Cal Sierra [*ICAO designator*] (AD)
QS	Every Shift [*Nursing*] (DAVI)
QS	Les Quatre Saisons [*Record label*] [*France*]
QS	Quadratic Sieve [*Computer science*] (BARN)
qs	Quadrophonic Stereo (AD)
QS	Quadrophonic Stereo (WDAA)
QS	Quadruple Screw (IAA)
QS	Quadrupole Splitting (OA)
QS	Quality Standard
QS	Quality Stock
QS	Quality Surveillance [*Navy*] (DNAB)
QS	Quantity Share [*Economics*]
QS	Quantity Surveying
qs	Quantum Satis [*Sufficient Quantity*] [*Latin*]
QS	Quantum Sufficit [*A Sufficient Quantity*] [*Pharmacy*] (ADA)
qs	Quantum Sufficit [*As Much as Suffices*] [*Latin*] (AD)
QS	Quarantine Station
QS	Quartermaster Sergeant [*Military*]
QS	Quarternote Society (AD)
qs	Quarter Section (AD)
QS	Quarter Section
QS-	Quarter Sessions
Q-S	Queckenstedt-Stookey Test [*Neurology*] (DAVI)
QS	Quecksilbersaeule [*Mercury Column*] [*German*] (AD)
QS	Queensland Society [*Australia*] (AD)
QS	Queen's Scarf (ADA)
QS	Queen's Scholar [*British*]
QS	Queen's Serjeant [*Military British*] (ROG)
Q-S	Queneau-Schuhmann [*Lead process*]
QS	Query Similarity [*Computer science*] (MHDI)
QS	Query System [*Computer science*]
QS	Question Standard (NATG)
QS	Queueing System (AD)
QS	Queue Select [*Computer science*]
QS	Quickie Strike (MHDB)
QS	Quick Service
QS	Quick Sweep [*Construction*]
QS	Quiet Sleep [*Physiology*]
QS	Quota Source (AABC)
Qs2	systemic Blood Flow [*Medicine*] (STED)
QS2	Total Electromechanical Systole [*Cardiology*] (DAVI)
QS$_2$I	Shortened Electrochemical Systole [*Cardiology*] (DAVI)
QSA	Quad Synchronous Adapter [*Perkin-Elmer*]
QSA	Qualification Site Approval [*NASA*] (NASA)
QSA	Qualified in Small Arms [*British military*] (DMA)
QSA	Queensland Shopkeepers Association [*Australia*] (AD)
QSA	Queensland Swimming Association [*Australia*]
QSA	Quick Service Assistant (MCD)
QSABS	Laboratoire de Sante Publique du Quebec, Ste-Anne-De-Bellevue, Quebec [*Library symbol National Library of Canada*] (NLC)
QS AD	Quantum Sufficiat Ad [*To a Sufficient Quantity*] [*Pharmacy*]
QSAL	Quadripartito Standardication Agrooment Liot [*Auotralia*]
QSAL	Quadripartite Standardization Agreements List [*Military*]
QSAM	Quadrature Sideband Amplitude Modulation [*Telecommunications*]
QSAM	Queued Sequential Access Method [*IBM Corp.*] [*Computer science*]
qsam	Queued Sequential Access Method (AD)
Qsan	Anatomic Shunt Flow [*Medicine*] (DAVI)
QS & L	Quarters, Subsistence, and Laundry [*Military*]
qs & l	Quarters, Subsistence, and Laundry (AD)
QSAR	Quantitative Structure-Activity Relationship (STED)
QSAR	Quantitative Structure Activity Relationships (AEPA)
QSAT	Quality Systems Acquisition Technology [*Army*] (RDA)
QSAT	Queensland Scholastic Aptitude Test [*Australia*]
Q-SAT	Quick-Score Achievement Test (TES)
QSATS	Quiet Short-Haul Air Transportation System
QSBC	Qualified Small Business Corp.
QSBC	Queensland Small Business Council [*Australia*]
QSBE	Quicken Small Business Expert [*Financial software*]
qsbg	Quasi-Stellar Blue Galaxies (AD)
qsbo	Quasi-Stellar Blue Objects (AD)
QSBR	Bio-Research Laboratory, Senneville, Quebec [*Library symbol National Library of Canada*] (NLC)
QSC	African Safari Airways Ltd. [*Kenya*] [*ICAO designator*] (FAAC)
QSC	Al-Ahli Bank of Qatar (MENA)
QSC	College de Shawinigan, Quebec [*Library symbol National Library of Canada*] (NLC)
QSC	Quality, Service, Cleanliness [*McDonald's Hamburger stands motto*]
QSC	Quasi-Sensory Communication [*Parapsychology*]
QSC	Quasistatic Compliance [*Measurement*] (DAVI)
QSC	Quebec Securities Commission [*Canada*] (AD)
QSC	Queensland Sugar Corp. [*Australia*]
QSC	Queen Street Camera, Inc. [*Toronto Stock Exchange symbol*]
QSC	Questionnaire Service Co. [*Information service or system*] (IID)
QSCA	Quick Set Compound
QSCA	Queensland Specialist Contractors' Association [*Australia*]
QSCC	Queensland Society for Crippled Children [*Australia*]
QSCV	Quality, Service, Cleanliness, and Value [*Formula for successful fast-food restaurants as taught by McDonald's Corp. at its Hamburger University*]
QSD	Quality Surveillance Division [*Navy*]
QSDC	Quantitative Structural Design Criteria [*NASA*]
QSDMA	Queensland Soft Drink Manufacturers' Association [*Australia*]

QSE	Qualified Scientists and Engineers
qse	Qualified Scientists and Engineers (AD)
QSE	Quantum Size Effect (PDAA)
QSED	Research Centre, Domtar Ltd., Senneville, Quebec [*Library symbol National Library of Canada*] (NLC)
QSEE	Quiet STOL [*Short Takeoff and Landing*] Experimental Engine [*Aviation*] (OA)
QSEMH	Missisquoi Historical Society [*Societe d'Histoire de Missisquoi*] Stanbridge-East, Quebec [*Library symbol National Library of Canada*] (NLC)
QSF	Bibliotheque Municipale, Ste-Foy, Quebec [*Library symbol National Library of Canada*] (NLC)
QSF	Quasi-Static Field
qsf	Quasi-Static Field (AD)
QSF	Quasi-Stationary Front
QSF	Queensland Soccer Federation [*Australia*] (AD)
QSFAG	Research Station, Agriculture Canada [*Station de Recherches, Agriculture Canada*] Ste-Foy, Quebec [*Library symbol National Library of Canada*] (NLC)
QSFB	Biorex, Ste.-Foy, Quebec [*Library symbol National Library of Canada*] (BIB)
QSFBP	Maison Generalice des Soeurs du Bon Pasteur, Ste-Foy, Quebec [*Library symbol National Library of Canada*] (NLC)
QSFC	Centre des Medias, CEGEP [*College d'Enseignement General et Professionnel*]de Ste.-Foy, Quebec [*Library symbol National Library of Canada*] (NLC)
QSFC	College d'Enseignement, Ste.-Foy, Quebec [*Library symbol National Library of Canada*] (NLC)
QSFCAE	Clinique d'Aide a l'Enfance, Ste.-Foy, Quebec [*Library symbol National Library of Canada*] (NLC)
QSFCD	Societe de Cooperation pour le Developpement International, Ste.-Foy, Quebec [*Library symbol National Library of Canada*] (BIB)
QSFCM	College Marguerite d'Youville, Ste.-Foy, Quebec [*Library symbol National Library of Canada*] (NLC)
QSFCP	Commission de Police du Quebec, Ste.-Foy, Quebec [*Library symbol National Library of Canada*] (NLC)
QSFCR	Centre de Recherche Industrielle du Quebec, Ste.-Foy, Quebec [*Library symbol National Library of Canada*] (NLC)
QSFCRO	Centre de Documentation, Commission Rochon, Ste.-Foy, Quebec [*Library symbol National Library of Canada*] (BIB)
QSFCSE	Centre de Documentation, Conseil Superieur de l'Education du Quebec, Ste.-Foy, Quebec [*Library symbol National Library of Canada*] (BIB)
QSFE	Centre de Documentation, Directeur General des Elections du Quebec, Ste.-Foy, Quebec [*Library symbol National Library of Canada*] (BIB)
QSFHL	Hopital Laval, Ste.-Foy, Quebec [*Library symbol National Library of Canada*] (NLC)
QSFIG	Centre de Documentation, INRS [*Institut National de la Recherche Scientifique*]-Georessources, Ste.-Foy, Quebec [*Library symbol National Library of Canada*] (NLC)
QSFIO	Institut National d'Optique, Ste.-Foy, Quebec [*Library symbol National Library of Canada*] (BIB)
QSFPC	Centre de Documentation, Bureau de la Protection Civile du Quebec, Ste.-Foy, Quebec [*Library symbol National Library of Canada*] (BIB)
QSFS	SOQUEM [*Societe Quebecoise d'Exploration Miniere*] Documentation, Ste.-Foy,Quebec [*Library symbol National Library of Canada*] (NLC)
QSG	Quasi-Steady Glide [*NASA*]
QSG	Quasi-Stellar Galaxy
qsg	Quasi-Stellar Galaxy (AD)
QSGVT	Quarter Scale Ground Vibration Test (MCD)
QSH	Stanstead Historical Society, Quebec [*Library symbol National Library of Canada*] (NLC)
QSHAG	Saint Hyacinthe Food Research Centre, Agriculture Canada [*Centre de Recherches Alimentaires de Saint-Hyacinthe, Agriculture Canada*] Quebec [*Library symbol National Library of Canada*] (NLC)
QSHC	CEGEP [*College d'Enseignement General et Professionnel*] de Shawinigan, Quebec [*Library symbol National Library of Canada*] (NLC)
QSHCH	Centre Hospitalier Regional de La Mauricie, Shawinigan, Quebec [*Library symbol National Library of Canada*] (NLC)
QSHCHS	Departement de Sante Communautaire, Centre Hospitalier Regional de la Mauricie, Shawinigan, Quebec [*Library symbol National Library of Canada*] (BIB)
QSHCP	Hopital Communautaire du Pontiac [*Pontiac Community Hospital*], Shawville, Quebec [*Library symbol National Library of Canada*] (NLC)
QSHERAN	Centre Regional de l'Estrie, Archives Nationales du Quebec, Sherbooke, Quebec [*Library symbol National Library of Canada*] (NLC)
QSHERB	Bibliotheque Centrale de Pret de l'Estrie, Sherbrooke, Quebec [*Library symbol National Library of Canada*] (BIB)
QSHERC	Bibliotheque des Sciences de la Sante, Universite de Sherbrooke, Quebec [*Library symbol National Library of Canada*] (NLC)
QSHERCR	Conseil Regional de la Sante et des Services Sociaux des Cantons de l'Est, Sherbrooke, Quebec [*Library symbol National Library of Canada*] (NLC)
QSHERD	Sherbrooke Daily Record, Quebec [*Library symbol National Library of Canada*] (NLC)
QSHERE	College de Sherbrooke (CEGEP) [*College d'Enseignement General et Professionnel*], Quebec [*Library symbol National Library of Canada*] (NLC)

QSHERG ...... Bibliotheque du Grand Seminaire, Sherbrooke, Quebec [*Library symbol National Library of Canada*] (NLC)

QSHERH ...... Huntingdon Gleaner, Quebec [*Library symbol National Library of Canada*] (NLC)

QSHERHD .... Centre Hospitalier Hotel-Dieu, Sherbrooke, Quebec [*Library symbol National Library of Canada*] (NLC)

QSHERM ...... Monastere des Peres Redemptoristes, Sherbrooke, Quebec [*Library symbol Obsolete National Library of Canada*] (NLC)

QSHERN ...... Bibliotheque Municipale, Sherbrooke, Quebec [*Library symbol National Library of Canada*] (NLC)

QSHERS ...... Seminaire de Sherbrooke, Quebec [*Library symbol National Library of Canada*] (NLC)

QSHERSB .... Les Conseillers Samson Belair, Inc., Sherbrooke, Quebec [*Library symbol National Library of Canada*] (NLC)

QSHERSC .... College du Sacre-Coeur, Sherbrooke, Quebec [*Library symbol National Library of Canada*] (NLC)

QSHERSF .... Ecole Secondaire St.-Francois, Sherbrooke, Quebec [*Library symbol National Library of Canada*] (NLC)

QSHERSG .... Societe de Genealogie des Cantons de l'Est, Sherbrooke, Quebec [*Library symbol National Library of Canada*] (NLC)

QSHERSH .... La Societe d'Histoire des Cantons de l'Est, Sherbrooke, Quebec [*Library symbol National Library of Canada*] (NLC)

QSHERSV .... Centre Hospitalier St.-Vincent-De-Paul, Sherbrooke, Quebec [*Library symbol National Library of Canada*] (NLC)

QSHERU ...... Bibliotheque Generale, Universite de Sherbrooke, Quebec [*Library symbol National Library of Canada*] (NLC)

QSHERUA ... Galerie d'Art et Centre Culturel, Universite de Sherbrooke, Quebec [*Library symbol National Library of Canada*] (NLC)

QSHERUD ... Bibliotheque de Droit, Universite de Sherbrooke, Quebec [*Library symbol National Library of Canada*] (NLC)

QSHERUG ... Departement de Geographie, Universite de Sherbrooke, Quebec [*Library symbol National Library of Canada*] (NLC)

QSHERUGC... Cartotheque, Departement de Geographie, Universite de Sherbrooke, Quebec [*Library symbol National Library of Canada*] (NLC)

QSHERURA... Centre de Documentation, Programme de Recherche sur l'Amiante, Universite de Sherbrooke, Quebec [*Library symbol National Library of Canada*] (NLC)

QSHERUS .... Bibliotheque des Sciences, Universite de Sherbrooke, Quebec [*Library symbol National Library of Canada*] (NLC)

QSHERY ...... Centre de Documentation et d'Audio-Visuel, Hopital d'Youville de Sherbrooke, Quebec [*Library symbol National Library of Canada*] (NLC)

Q-ship .... Query-Ship [*Military*] (WDAA)

QSHM .... Municipal Library [*Bibliotheque Municipale*] Shawinigan, Quebec [*Library symbol National Library of Canada*] (NLC)

QSHS .... Seminaire Ste-Marie, Shawinigan, Quebec [*Library symbol National Library of Canada*] (NLC)

QSI .... Bibliotheque Municipale, Sept-Iles, Quebec [*Library symbol National Library of Canada*] (NLC)

QSI .... Quality Salary Increase (AFM)

qsi .... Quality Salary Increase (AD)

QSI .... Quality Service Indicator

QSI .... Quality Step Increase (GFGA)

QSI .... Quantum Scalar Irradiance [*Instrumentation*]

QSI .... Quantum Systems, Inc.

QSI .... Quarterly Survey of Intentions [*Became Consumer Buying Expectations Survey*] [*Bureau of the Census*]

QSIA .... Centre Regional de la Cote-Nord, Archives Nationales du Quebec, Sept-Iles, Quebec [*Library symbol National Library of Canada*] (BIB)

QSIBCP .... Bibliotheque Centrale de Pret de la Cote-Nord, Sept-Iles, Quebec [*Library symbol National Library of Canada*] (NLC)

QSIC .... CEGEP [*College d'Enseignement General et Professionnel*] de Sept-Iles, Quebec [*Library symbol National Library of Canada*] (BIB)

QSIC .... Quality Standard Inspection Criteria

qsic............ Quality Standard Inspection Criteria (AD)

QSIH .... Hopital des Sept-Iles, Quebec [*Library symbol National Library of Canada*] (NLC)

QSII .... Quality Systems [*NASDAQ symbol*] (TTSB)

QSII .... Quality Systems, Inc. [*NASDAQ symbol*] (NQ)

QSIIOM .... Mineralogy Laboratory, Iron Ore Co., Sept-Iles, Quebec [*Library symbol National Library of Canada*] (NLC)

QSILC .... College Jesus-Marie de Sillery, Quebec [*Library symbol National Library of Canada*] (NLC)

QSIM .... Qualitative Simulation Algorithm [*Mathematics*]

QSJ .... Stanstead Journal, Quebec [*Library symbol National Library of Canada*] (NLC)

QSJHD .... Hotel-Dieu de Saint-Jerome, Quebec [*Library symbol National Library of Canada*] (NLC)

QSJM .... Queen's Silver Jubilee Medal [*British*] (AD)

QSK .... Quadriphase Shift Keying (MCD)

QSL............ Q-Switch LASER

QSL............ Qualification Status List (KSC)

QSL............ Qualified Source List [*NASA*] (NASA)

QSL............ Quality of School Life Scale [*Educational test*]

QSL............ Quarterly Stock List

QSL............ Queensland State Library [*Australia*] (AD)

QSL............ Queue Search Limit [*Computer science*]

QSLCR .... Campus 1, Champlain Regional College, St.-Lambert, Quebec [*Library symbol National Library of Canada*] (NLC)

QSLE.......... Bibliotheque Municipale, Saint-Leonard, Quebec [*Library symbol National Library of Canada*] (NLC)

qsm .... Quadruple-Screw Motorship (AD)

QSM........... Quality Systems Management [*DoD*]

QSM........... Quarter Scale Model (MCD)

QSM........... Quarter Square Multiplier

qsm........... Quarter-Square Multipliers (AD)

QSM........... Quasi-Linear Sequential Machine

qsm........... Queen's Service Medal [*British*] (AD)

QSM........... Queen's Service Medal [*New Zealand*] (WDAA)

QSM........... South Molle Islands [*Queensland*] [*Airport symbol*] (AD)

QSMO .... Quaker State Motor Oils (AD)

QSMVMAC... Queen Street Mall and Valley Mall Advisory Committee [*Brisbane, Australia*]

QSMVT .... Quarter Scale Model Vibration Testing (NASA)

QSND.......... Qsound Labs, Inc. [*NASDAQ symbol*] (SAG)

QSNDF........ QSound Labs [*NASDAQ symbol*] (TTSB)

QSNT.......... (Quinolinesulfonyl)nitrotriazole [*Organic chemistry*]

QSO .... Bibliotheque Municipale, Sorel, Quebec [*Library symbol National Library of Canada*] (NLC)

QSO .... Contact [*Amateur Radio*] (BARN)

QSO .... QUASAR [*Quasi-Stellar*] [*Astronomy*] (IAA)

QSO .... Quasi-Biennial Stratospheric Oscillation

qso............ Quasibiennial Stratospheric Oscillation (AD)

qso............ Quasistellar Object (AD)

QSO .... Quasi-Stellar [*or QUASAR*] Object

QSO .... Quebec Symphony Orchestra [*Canada*] (AD)

QSO .... Queensland Symphony Orchestra [*Australia*] (AD)

QSO .... Queen's Service Order [*British*] (AD)

QSOCS .... C. Stroemgren, Sorel, Quebec [*Library symbol National Library of Canada*] (NLC)

QSOCS........ QIT - Fer et Titane, Inc., Sorel, Quebec [*Library symbol National Library of Canada*] (NLC)

QSOP .... Quadripartite Standing Operating Procedures [*Military*]

QSOP .... Quad Small-Outline Package [*Electronics*] (MED)

QSOP .... Quarter Size Outline Package (AAEL)

Qsound ...... Qsound Labs, Inc. [*Associated Press*] (SAG)

QSP .... Air ACG [*France*] [*FAA designator*] (FAAC)

Qsp .... Physiologic Shunt Flow [*Total venous admixture*] [*Medicine*] (DAVI)

qsp............ Quality Search Procedure (AD)

QSP .... Quench Spray Pump (IEEE)

QSP .... Quick Search Procedure

QSPA .... Queensland Secondary Principals' Association [*Australia*]

QSPP .... Quebec Society for the Protection of Plants [*Canada*] (AD)

QSPR .... Quantitative Structure [*Pharmacokinetic relationship*] (DB)

QSPR .... Quantitative Structure-Property Relationship

QSPS .... Qualification Standards for Postal Field Service

QSPV .... Quasistatic Pressure Volume [*Measurement*] (DAVI)

Qs/Qt .... Intropulmonary Shunt Ratio [*Medicine*] (DAVI)

Qs/Qt .... Right-to-Left Shunt Ratio [*Medicine*] (DAVI)

QSR .... Quality Statistics Report [*Nuclear energy*] (NUCP)

QSR .... Quality Status Review (MCD)

QSR .... Quality Strike Reconnaissance

QSR .... Quality System Review

QSR .... Quantum State Reconstruction [*Physics*]

QSR .... Quarterly Statistical Report (NRCH)

QSR .... Quarterly Status Report

QSR .... Quarterly Summary Report

QSR .... Quartier de Securite Renforcee [*Maximum Security Prison*] [*French*] (AD)

QSR .... Quasar [*Galaxy*]

QSR .... Quasi-Stellar Radio Source

QSR .... Quebec Sturgeon River Mines Ltd. [*Toronto Stock Exchange symbol*]

QSR .... Quick Service Restaurant

QSR .... Quick-Start Recording [*Video technology*]

QSR .... Quick Strike Reconnaissance (MCD)

qsr............ Quick-Strike Reconnaissance (AD)

QSR .... Quien Sabe Ranch [*California*] [*Seismograph station code, US Geological Survey*] (SEIS)

QSR .... Quinoline Still Residue [*Coal tar technology*]

QSRA .... Queensland Smallbore Rifle Association [*Australia*]

QSRA .... Quiet Short-Haul Research Aircraft [*NASA*]

qsra .... Quiet Short-Haul Research Aircraft (AD)

Qsrel......... Relative Shunt Flow [*Medicine*] (DAVI)

QSRFC........ Queensland Sport and Recreational Fishing Council [*Australia*]

QSRIG........ Quantity Surveyors Research and Information Group (AD)

QSRMC....... Quality Scheme for Ready Mixed Concrete (EAIO)

QSRS .... Quasi-Stellar Blue Galaxies (SAA)

QSRS .... Quasi-Stellar Radio Source

qsrs .... Quasi-Stellar Radio Sources (AD)

QSRT .... QSR Ltd. [*NASDAQ symbol*] (SAG)

QSRTCG....... Queensland Sales Representatives and Commercial Travellers' Guild [*Australia*]

QSRTF .... QSR Ltd [*NASDAQ symbol*] (TTSB)

QSS .... Quadratic Score Statistic [*Test*]

QSS .... Quadruple-Screw Ship (AD)

QSS .... Quadrupole Screw Ship

QSS .... Quantitative Sacroiliac Scintigraphy [*Orthopedics*] [*Radiology*] (DAVI)

QSS .... Quasi-Steady State

QSS .... Quasi-Stellar Source

qss............ Quasi-Stellar Source (AD)

QSS .... Quench Spray Subsystem (IEEE)

QSS .... Quick Service Supervisor (MCD)

QSS .... Quick Supply Store [*Military*] (AABC)

QSS .... Quill and Scroll Society (EA)

QSS .... Quindar Scanning System (NASA)

QSS .... Quota Sample Survey (WDAA)

QSSA .... Quasi-Stationary State Approximation

qssa........... Quasi-Stationary-State Approximation (AD)

QSSCT .... Queensland Society of Sugar Cane Technologists [Australia] (AD)
QSSI .... Quarterly Surprise Security Inspection [Navy] (DNAB)
Q's Signs .... Quant's Sign (STED)
QSSP .... Quasi-Solid State Panel
qssp .... Quasi-Solid-State Panel (AD)
QSSR .... Quarterly Stock Status Report
QST .... General Call Preceding a Message [Amateur Radio] (BARN)
QST .... QSA Tech, Inc. [Vancouver Stock Exchange symbol]
QST .... Quality Scottish Trout [An association] (BUAC)
QST .... Quantitative Sensory Test [Medicine] (DMAA)
QST .... Quebec Standard Test [Canada] (AD)
QST .... Questmont Mines [Vancouver Stock Exchange symbol]
QSTAG .... Quadripartite Standardization Agreement [Military]
QSTAG .... Quality Standardization Agreements (MCD)
QSTAH .... Ste-Anne's Hospital, Ste.-Anne-De-Bellevue, Quebec [Library symbol National Library of Canada] (NLC)
QSTAJ .... John Abbott College, Ste-Anne-De-Bellevue, Quebec [Library symbol National Library of Canada] (NLC)
QSTAMP ...... Quality Stamp
QSTAR .... Quantitative Structure-Time-Activity Relationship [Chemistry]
QSTAS .... Spar Technology Ltd., Ste-Anne-De-Bellevue, Quebec [Library symbol National Library of Canada] (NLC)
QSTB .... Bibliotheque Municipale, Saint-Bruno-De-Montarville, Quebec [Library symbol National Library of Canada] (BIB)
QSTBL .... Abbaye de Saint-Benoit-Du-Lac, Comte De Brome, Quebec [Library symbol National Library of Canada] (NLC)
QSTC .... Tioxide Canada, Inc., Sorel, Quebec [Library symbol National Library of Canada] (NLC)
QstDiag .... Quest Diagnostics, Inc. [Associated Press] (SAG)
Q-S test ...... Queckenstedt-Stookey Test (STED)
QSTFAG ...... Centre de Documentation, Ministere de l'Agriculture, des Pecheries, et de l'Alimentation, Ste.-Foy, Quebec [Library symbol National Library of Canada] (NLC)
QSTFCE .... Centre de Documentation, Centrale de l'Enseignement du Quebec, Ste.-Foy, Quebec [Library symbol National Library of Canada] (NLC)
QSTFCR .... Resource Centre, St. Lawrence Campus, Champlain Regional College, Ste.-Foy, Quebec [Library symbol National Library of Canada] (NLC)
QSTFP .... Protecteur du Citoyen du Quebec, Ste.-Foy [Library symbol National Library of Canada] (BIB)
QSTFR .... Rexfor, Ste.-Foy, Quebec [Library symbol National Library of Canada] (NLC)
QSTFRA ...... Centre de Documentation, Roche Associes Ltee., Ste.-Foy, Quebec [Library symbol National Library of Canada] (NLC)
QSTHHR ...... Societe d'Histoire Regionale de St-Hyacinthe, Quebec [Library symbol National Library of Canada] (NLC)
QSTHS .... Seminaire de St-Hyacinthe, Quebec [Library symbol National Library of Canada] (NLC)
QSTHTA ...... Institut de Technologie Agricole et Alimentaire de St.-Hyacinthe, Quebec [Library symbol National Library of Canada] (NLC)
QSTHUM ..... Headquarters Mobile Command, Canada Department of National Defence [Quartier-General du Commandement de la Defense Nationale] St-Hubert, Quebec [Library symbol National Library of Canada] (NLC)
QSTHV .... Faulte de Medecine Veterinaire de l'Universite de Montreal, Saint-Hyacinthe, Quebec [Library symbol National Library of Canada] (NLC)
QSTING .... Quasi-Spectral Time Integration on Nested Grids
QSTJ .... College Militaire Royal de Saint-Jean, Quebec [Library symbol National Library of Canada] (NLC)
QSTJA .... Bibliotheque Adelard-Berger, St.-Jean-Sur-Richelieu, Quebec [Library symbol National Library of Canada] (BIB)
QSTJAG .... Research Station, Agriculture Canada [Station de Recherches, Agriculture Canada] Saint-Jean, Quebec [Library symbol National Library of Canada] (NLC)
QSTJB .... Bibliotheque Municipale, Saint-Jean, Quebec [Library symbol National Library of Canada] (NLC)
QSTJC .... College Saint-Jean-Sur-Richelieu, Saint-Jean, Quebec [Library symbol National Library of Canada] (NLC)
QSTJCF .... Canadian Forces Base St. Jean [Base des Forces Canadiennes St.-Jean], Quebec [Library symbol National Library of Canada] (NLC)
QSTJE .... Bibliotheque Municipale, Saint-Jerome, Quebec [Library symbol National Library of Canada] (NLC)
QSTJEC .... CEGEP [College d'Enseignement General et Professionnel] de St.-Jerome, Quebec [Library symbol National Library of Canada] (BIB)
QSTJECR ..... Conseil Regional de la Sante et des Services Sociaux Laurentides-Lanaudiere, Saint-Jerome, Quebec [Library symbol National Library of Canada] (NLC)
QSTJEJ .... Jesuites/Bibliotheque, Saint-Jerome, Quebec [Library symbol National Library of Canada] (NLC)
QSTJH .... Bibliotheque Medicale, Hopital du Haut-Richelieu, St.-Jean-Sur-Richelieu, Quebec [Library symbol National Library of Canada] (BIB)
QSTJSC .... Centre de Documentation, Departement de Sante Communautaire du Haut-Richelieu, St.-Jean, Quebec [Library symbol National Library of Canada] (NLC)
QSTK .... Q Steaks, Inc. [NASDAQ symbol] (SAG)
QSTL .... Bibliotheque Municipale, Saint-Laurent, Quebec [Library symbol National Library of Canada] (NLC)
QSTLD .... Dominion Yarn Co., St. Laurent, Quebec [Library symbol National Library of Canada] (BIB)
QSTN .... Question (WDAA)

qstn .... Question (AD)
qstnr .... Questionnaire (AD)
qstol .... Quiet-and-Short Takeoff and Landing (AD)
QSTOL .... Quiet-Short-Takeoff-and-Landing [Airplane] [Japan]
QSTR .... Bibliotheque Municipale de Saint-Raphael-De-L'Ile-Bizard, Quebec [Library symbol National Library of Canada] (NLC)
qsts .... Quadruple-Screw Turbine Steamship (AD)
QSTTB .... Engineering Library, Bell Helicopter Textron, Ste. Therese, Quebec [Library symbol National Library of Canada] (NLC)
QSTTH .... Les Industries Harnois, St-Thomas-De-Joliette, Quebec [Library symbol National Library of Canada] (NLC)
QstVC......... Quest for Value Fund [Associated Press] (SAG)
QstVI.......... Quest for Value Fund [Associated Press] (SAG)
qsuff .... Quantum Sufficit [As Much As Will Suffice] [Latin] (MAE)
Q-switch ..... Quantum Switch (AD)
QSWL .... Queensland Spastic Welfare League [Australia]
QSY .... Quiet Sun Year
qsy .... Quiet Sun Year (AD)
QSYS .... Quad Systems Corp. [NASDAQ symbol] (SAG)
Q-SYSTEM ... Inventory Control System With Varying Reorders (MHDB)
QT .... Bibliotheque Municipale, Trois-Rivieres, Quebec [Library symbol National Library of Canada] (NLC)
QT .... Blood Volume Quantity per Unit of Time [Cardiology] (DAVI)
QT .... Cardiac Output [Cardiology] (DAVI)
QT .... Quadruple Thermoplastic (SAA)
QT .... Qualification Test
QT .... Qualifier Type (NITA)
QT .... Quality Test (AD)
qt .... Quality Test (AD)
qt .... Quantitative (DAVI)
QT .... Quantity
qt .... Quantity (AD)
qt .... Quarry Tile (AD)
QT .... Quarry Tile [Technical drawings]
QT .... Quart (AFM)
qt .... Quart (ODBW)
qt .... Quarter (AD)
QT .... Quarters
QT .... Quartet [Music]
qt .... Quartet (WDAA)
QT .... Quasi-Triennial
QT .... Quebec-Telephone [Toronto Stock Exchange symbol]
QT .... Queckenstedt's Test [Neurology] (DAVI)
QT .... Quenched and Tempered (MCD)
QT .... Questioned Trade [on a stock exchange]
QT .... Queuing Theory [Telecommunications]
QT .... Queuing Time [Telecommunications] (TEL)
QT .... Quick's Test [For pregnancy or prothrombin] [Laboratory science] (DAVI)
QT .... Quick Tan [Trademark of Plough, Inc.]
QT .... Quick Test
qt .... Quick Test (AD)
qt .... Quiet (AD)
QT .... Quiet [or sub rosa, as, "On the QT"]
QT .... Qui Tam [Who as Well] [Latin] (ILCA)
QT .... Quotation Ticker [Business term]
QT .... Quotient
QT .... Vaengir [ICAO designator] (AD)
QTA............ Archives Nationales du Quebec, Trois-Rivieres, Quebec [Library symbol National Library of Canada] (NLC)
QTA............ Quadrant Transformer Assembly
qta............. Quadrant Transformer Assembly (AD)
QTA............ Quick Turn Around (AAEL)
QTAC .... Queensland Tertiary Admissions Centre [Australia] (AD)
QTAM......... Quadrature Amplitude Modulation (MCD)
qtam.......... Queued Telecommunication Access Method (AD)
QTAM......... Queued Telecommunications Access Method [IBM Corp.] [Computer science]
QTAM......... Queued Terminal Access Method [Computer science]
QT & E........ Qualification Test and Evaluation [Military]
QTAT.......... Quick Turn Around Time (NITA)
qtaux .... Quintaux [Quintals] [French] (AD)
QTB............ Le Boreal Express, Montreal, Quebec [Library symbol National Library of Canada] (NLC)
QTB............ Quarry-Tile Base [Technical drawings]
qtb .... Quarry-Tile Base (AD)
QTB............ Quarterly Training Briefing [Army] (INF)
QTB............ Queensland Timber Board [Australia] (AD)
QTB............ Queensland Trotting Board [Australia] (AD)
QTBC .... Bibliotheque Centrale de Pret de la Mauricie, Trois-Rivieres, Quebec [Library symbol National Library of Canada] (NLC)
QTBUE .... Queensland Timber Board Union of Employees [Australia]
QTC............ Quantitative Trait Loci [Genetics]
QTC............ Quebec Teaching Congress [Canada] (AD)
QTC............ Queensland Turf Club [Australia] (AD)
QTC............ Quick Transmission Change (MCD)
QTC............ Quick Turnaround Cell [Engineering] (RDA)
QTCE.......... CEGEP [College d'Enseignement General et Professionnel], Trois-Rivieres, Quebec [Library symbol National Library of Canada] (NLC)
QTCHC........ Centre Hospitalier Cooke, Trois-Rivieres, Quebec [Library symbol National Library of Canada] (NLC)
QTCL.......... College Lafleche, Trois-Rivieres, Quebec [Library symbol National Library of Canada] (NLC)

QTCO .... Communication-Quebec, Trois-Rivieres, Quebec [*Library symbol National Library of Canada*] (NLC)

QTCPB .... Corporation Pierre Boucher, Trois-Rivieres, Quebec [*Library symbol National Library of Canada*] (NLC)

QTCRD .... Conseil Regional de Developpement, Trois-Rivieres, Quebec [*Library symbol National Library of Canada*] (NLC)

QTCRS .... Conseil Regional de la Sante et des Services Sociaux, Trois-Rivieres, Quebec [*Library symbol National Library of Canada*] (NLC)

QTCSRV ...... Commission Scolaire Regionale des Vieilles-Forges, Trois-Rivieres, Quebec [*Library symbol National Library of Canada*] (NLC)

QTCSS .... Centre de Services Sociaux, Trois-Rivieres, Quebec [*Library symbol National Library of Canada*] (NLC)

QTD .... Quadruple Terminal Digits (AABC)

QTD .... Quartered

qtd .... Quartered (AD)

Qtd .... Quarter-Sawed [*Forest industry*] (WPI)

QTD .... Quasi-Two-Dimensional

QTDG .... Quaker Theological Discussion Group (EA)

QT DX .... Quantitas Duplex [*Double Quantity*] [*Pharmacy*]

QTE .... Ecole Normale M. L. Duplessis, Trois-Rivieres, Quebec [*Library symbol National Library of Canada*] (NLC)

QTE .... Qualite [*Quality*] [*French*] (ROG)

QTE .... Quote

qte .... Quote (AD)

QTEC........... QuesTech, Inc. [*NASDAQ symbol*] (NQ)

Q-TECH .... Quality-Technology

QTED .... Quick Text Editor (WDAA)

qted .... Quick Text Editor (AD)

qted .... Quoted (AD)

QTED .... Quoted (WDAA)

QTEF........... Queensland Tertiary Education Foundation [*Australia*]

QTEL........... Quintel Communications [*Formerly, Quintel Entertainment, Inc.*] [*NASDAQ symbol*]

QTEL........... Quintel Entertainment [*NASDAQ symbol*] (TTSB)

QTEL........... Quintel Entertainment, Inc. [*NASDAQ symbol*] (SAG)

QTER .... Bibliotheque Municipale, Terrebonne, Quebec [*Library symbol National Library of Canada*] (NLC)

Qtest........... Quantitative Test (NITA)

QTEV........... Quadruple Turbo-Electric Vessel (DS)

QTF .... Quarry-Tile Floor [*Technical drawings*]

qtf .... Quarry-Tile Floor (AD)

QTF .... Quebec Teachers' Federation [*Canada*] (AD)

qtfl .... Quatrefoil (VRA)

qtg .... Quoting (AD)

QTH .... Queued Transaction Handling [*Computer science*]

QTHSJ .... Hopital Saint-Joseph, Trois-Rivieres, Quebec [*Library symbol National Library of Canada*] (NLC)

QTHSM .... Hopital Sainte-Marie, Trois-Rivieres, Quebec [*Library symbol National Library of Canada*] (NLC)

QTI............. Institut Albert Tessier, Trois-Rivieres, Quebec [*Library symbol National Library of Canada*] (NLC)

QTIA........... Queensland Tourism Industry Authority [*Australia*]

QTIB........... Quebec Tourist Information Bureau [*Canada*] (AD)

QTIEA......... Queensland Timber Importers and Exporters' Association [*Australia*]

Q-TIP .... Qualified Terminable Interest Property [*Plan*] [*Tax law*]

QTIP .... Qualified Terminable Interest Property Trust [*Investment term*] (DFIT)

QTITC......... Queensland Timber Industry Training Council [*Australia*]

QTL .... Qualified Thrift Lender

QTL .... Quantitative Trait Loci [*Genetics*]

QTL .... Quantum Theory of LASERS

QTL .... Quarterly Title List

QTL .... Quintel Industries Ltd. [*Vancouver Stock Exchange symbol*]

QTLC .... Queensland Trades and Labor Council [*Australia*] (AD)

QTLMB........ Queensland Tobacco Leaf Marketing Board [*Australia*]

Qtly............. Quarterly

qtly .... Quarterly (ODBW)

QTM........... Qualification Test Model

QTM........... Quechon Tribal Museum [*Yuma, Arizona*] (AD)

QTMC.......... College de la Region de l'Amiante (CEGEP), Thetford-Mines, Quebec [*Library symbol National Library of Canada*] (NLC)

QTME.......... Ministere de l'Energie et des Ressources du Quebec, Trois-Rivieres, Quebec [*Library symbol National Library of Canada*] (BIB)

QTMH .... Hopital General de la Regie de l'Amiante, Inc., Thetford Mines, Quebec [*Library symbol National Library of Canada*] (BIB)

QTN .... Quasithermal Noise [*Plasma physics*]

qtn .... Quotation (AD)

QTN .... Quotation (WDAA)

QTO .... Qualified Testing Officer [*British military*] (DMA)

QTO .... Quarto [*Book from 25 to 30 centimeters in height*]

qto .... Quarto (WDAA)

QTOL .... Quiet Takeoff and Landing [*Aviation*]

qtol .... Quiet Takeoff and Landing (AD)

QTOPDQ ...... Centre de Documentation, Office de Planification et de Developpement du Quebe c, Trois-Rivieres, Quebec [*Library symbol National Library of Canada*] (NLC)

QTP .... Qualification Test Plan [*NASA*] (NASA)

QTP .... Qualification Test Procedure

QTP .... Qualification Test Program

QTP .... Quality Test Plan [*Nuclear energy*] (NRCH)

QTP .... Quantum Theory of Paramagnetism

qtp .... Quantum Theory of Paramagnetism (AD)

QTP .... Quantum Theory Project [*University of Florida*] [*Research center*] (RCD)

QTPC .... Quadripartite Technical Procedures Committee [*Military*] (AABC)

QTPR .... Quarterly Technical Progress Report

QTPT .... Qualification Test and Proof (IAA)

QTR .... Qatar Airways [*FAA designator*] (FAAC)

QTR .... Qualification Test Report

QTR .... Qualified Tuition Reduction [*IRS*]

QTR .... Quality Technical Report (AD)

QTR .... Quality Technical Requirement (AD)

qtr .... Quarry-Tile Roof (AD)

QTR .... Quarry-Tile Roof [*Technical drawings*]

QTR .... Quarter (AFM)

Qtr .... Quarter (EBF)

qtr .... Quarter (ODBW)

QTR .... Quarterly (AFM)

QTR .... Quarterly Technical Report

QTR .... Quarterly Technical Review [*Jet Propulsion Laboratory publication*]

QTR .... Queenstake Resources [*TS Symbol*] (TTSB)

QTR .... Queenstake Resources Ltd. [*Toronto Stock Exchange symbol*]

QTRLY .... Quarterly

QTRN .... Quintiles Transnational [*NASDAQ symbol*] (TTSB)

QTRN .... Quintiles Transnational Corp. [*NASDAQ symbol*] (SAG)

QTRRSS....... Centre de Documentation, Regie de la Securite dans les Sports du Quebec, Trois-Rivieres, Quebec [*Library symbol National Library of Canada*] (NLC)

QTRS .... Quarters

QTS .... Qualification Test Specification

QTS .... Qualified Teacher Status [*British*] (DET)

QTS .... Quantizer Threshold Spacing [*Telecommunications*] (MHDB)

qts .... Quarts (AD)

QTS .... Quartz Thermometer Sensor

qts .... Quick Turn Stock (AD)

QTS .... Seminaire de Trois-Rivieres, Quebec [*Library symbol National Library of Canada*] (NLC)

QTSC .... Queensland Transmission and Supply Corp. [*Australia*]

QTT .... Quartet [*Music*]

QTT .... Trois-Rivieres High School, Quebec [*Library symbol National Library of Canada*] (NLC)

QTTA .... Queensland Table Tennis Association [*Australia*]

QTTC .... Queensland Tourist and Travel Corp. [*Australia*] (AD)

qtte .... Quartette (AD)

QTTE .... Quartette [*Music*]

QTTF........... Temifibre, Inc., Temiscaming, Quebec [*Library symbol National Library of Canada*] (NLC)

QTTP........... Q-Tags Test of Personality [*Psychology*]

QTU .... Qualification Test Unit

QTU .... Queensland Teachers Union [*Australia*] (AD)

QTU .... Universite du Quebec, Trois-Rivieres, Quebec [*Library symbol National Library of Canada*] (NLC)

QTUAH........ Archives Historiques, Universite du Quebec, Trois-Rivieres, Quebec [*Library symbol National Library of Canada*] (NLC)

QTUGC........ Cartotheque, Departement de Geographie, Universite du Quebec, Trois-Rivieres, Quebec [*Library symbol National Library of Canada*] (NLC)

QTUIH......... Imprimes Historiques, Universite du Quebec, Trois-Rivieres, Quebec [*Library symbol National Library of Canada*] (NLC)

QTURA........ Archives des Ursulines, Trois-Rivieres, Quebec [*Library symbol National Library of Canada*] (NLC)

QTUTH .... Centre de Documentation en Theatre Quebecois, Trois-Rivieres, Quebec [*Library symbol National Library of Canada*] (NLC)

QTV .... Qualification Test Vehicle

Q-TWIST...... Quality-Adjusted Time without Symptoms and Toxicity [*Medicine*] (CDI)

QTX............. Beaufort Leasing Ltd. [*Canada*] [*FAA designator*] (FAAC)

Qty............. Quality (DS)

QTY .... Quantity (KSC)

qty .... Quantity (AD)

QTYDESREQ... Quantity Desired as Requested [*Military*]

qtydesreq...... Quantity Desired or Requested (AD)

qtz............... Quartz (AD)

QTZ .... Quartz (AAG)

QTZ............. Quartzite [*Lithology*]

qtze .... Quartzose (AD)

qtzic............ Quartzitic (AD)

QTZN .... Quantization [*Telecommunications*] (IAA)

QTZR .... Quantizer [*Telecommunications*] (IAA)

qtzt.............. Quartzite (AD)

QU .... Nicaragua [*License plate code assigned to foreign diplomats in the US*]

QU .... Quadrantectomy [*Medicine*]

QU .... Quaere [*Query*] [*Latin*]

QU .... Quail Unlimited (EA)

QU .... Quart (WGA)

qu .... Quart (AD)

qu .... Quarter (AD)

QU .... Quarter (ADA)

qu .... Quarterly (AD)

QU .... Quartermaster (ROG)

QU .... Quartern (ROG)

QU .... Quasi [*Almost, As It Were*] [*Latin*]

qu .... Quasi [*As It Were*] [*Latin*] (AD)

QU .... Quay (ROG)

QU .... Queen

Qu .... Queen (AD)

QU .... Queen's College [*Cambridge, Oxford*] (AD)

QU .... Queen's University [*Canada*]

qu .... Query (AD)

qu	Question (AD)
QU	Question
QU	Questionnaire
QU	Quina [Quinine] [Pharmacy] (ROG)
QU	Quinto Mining [Vancouver Stock Exchange symbol]
QU	Quotation (ROG)
QU	Uganda Airlines [ICAO designator] (AD)
QUA	Quabbin [Massachusetts] [Seismograph station code, US Geological Survey] (SEIS)
qua	Quadrate (AD)
QUA	Quassar de Mexico SA de CV [ICAO designator] (FAAC)
QUA	Quinterra Resources, Inc. [Toronto Stock Exchange symbol Vancouver Stock Exchange symbol]
quaal	Quaalude (AD)
QUABX	Alliance Quasar Fund Cl.B [Mutual fund ticker symbol] (SG)
QUAC	Quadriatic Arc Computer
quack	Quacksalver
quacks	Quacksalvers (AD)
quackupunc...	Quackupuncture (AD)
quad	Quaalude (AD)
QUAD..........	Quadrajet Carburetor [Automotive engineering]
QUAD..........	Quadrangle (AAG)
quad	Quadrangle (ODBW)
quad	Quadrant (AD)
Quad	Quadrant [A publication]
QUAD..........	Quadraphonic
quad	Quadrat (AD)
QUAD..........	Quadrature (NASA)
quad	Quadriceps [Muscle] [Anatomy] (DAVI)
QUAD..........	Quadrilateral (WGA)
QUAD..........	Quadrillion
Quad	Quadriplegic
quad	Quadriplegic [Medicine] (DMAA)
QUAD..........	Quadrophonic (NITA)
QUAD..........	Quadruple
quad	Quadruplet (ODBW)
QUAD..........	Quadruplex [Videotape recording] (NTCM)
Qu-AD	Quality-Assurance Department (AD)
Qu-AD	Quality-Assurance Division (AD)
quad c	Quadripod Cane (AD)
QUAD CAP...	Quad Foolscap [Paper] (DGA)
QuadCty.......	Quad City Holdings [Associated Press] (SAG)
quad ex	Quadriceps Exercise [Orthopedics] (DAVI)
QUADPAN	Quadrilateral Element Panel Method [Aerospace propulsion]
quadplex	Quadriplex (AD)
Quadr..........	Quadragesms [Yearbooks of Edward III] [A publication] (DLA)
Quadr..........	Quadrant [A publication]
QUADR	Quadruple
QUADRADAR...	Four-Way RADAR Surveillance
quadrap	Quadraphonic (AD)
Quadrax......	Quadrax Corp. [Associated Press] (SAG)
quadrip	Quadriplegia (AD)
quadro........	Quadroon (AD)
quadrup	Quadruped (AD)
quadrupl......	Quadruplicato [Four Times as Much] [Latin] (AD)
Quadrupl......	Quadruplicato [Four Times as Much] [Pharmacy]
QUADS........	Quality Achievement Data System (NASA)
QuadSy.......	Quad Systems Corp. [Associated Press] (SAG)
Quaest Conv...	Quaestiones Convivales [of Plutarch] [Classical studies] (OCD)
Quaest Graec...	Quaestiones Graecae [of Plutarch] [Classical studies] (OCD)
Quaest Plat...	Quaestiones Platonicae [of Plutarch] [Classical studies] (OCD)
Quaest Rom...	Quaestiones Romanae [of Plutarch] [Classical studies] (OCD)
quag	Quagmire (AD)
QUAILLS	Quick Update and Access Interlibrary Loans System
QuakCh.......	Quaker Chemical Corp. [Associated Press] (SAG)
QuakCty.......	Quaker City Bancorp [Associated Press] (SAG)
Quaker.......	Quaker Oats (AD)
Quaker.......	Quaker Press (AD)
QuakFab	Quaker Fabric Corp. [Associated Press] (SAG)
QuakrOat	Quaker Oats Co. [Associated Press] (SAG)
QuakSC.......	Quaker State Corp. [Associated Press] (SAG)
QUAL	Qualification (NG)
qual	Qualification (AD)
QUAL	Qualified (NAKS)
qual	Qualify (AD)
QUAL	Qualitative
Qual..........	Qualiton & MHV [Record label] [Hungary]
QUAL	Quality (KSC)
qual	Quality (AD)
QUAL	Quality Semiconductor [NASDAQ symbol] (TTSB)
QUAL	Quality Semiconductor, Inc. [NASDAQ symbol] (SAG)
QUAL ANAL...	Qualitative Analysis (WDAA)
qual anal	Qualitative Analysis (AD)
QualCert	Qualifying Certificate [Australia]
Qualcom......	Qualcomm, Inc. [Associated Press] (SAG)
QualDin	Quality Dining, Inc. [Associated Press] (SAG)
QUALENGR...	Quality Engineer (IAA)
QUALGO	Quasi-Autonomous Local Government Organisation [British] (DI)
QUALN	Qualification (ROG)
QUALOD	Quaalude [Methaqualone] [A trademark] [Pharmacology] (DAVI)
quals	Qualifying Examinations (AD)
quals	Qualifying Tests (AD)
QualSemi	Quality Semiconductor, Inc. [Associated Press] (SAG)
QualSy........	Quality Systems, Inc. [Associated Press] (SAG)
QUALT	Queensland University Aphasia and Language Test

QUALTA	Quad Asynchronous Local Terminal Adapter [Computer science] (MHDB)
QUALTIS	Quality Technical Information Service (NITA)
QUALTIS	Quality Technology Information Service [Atomic Energy Authority] [British] (IID)
QUAM	Quadrature Amplitude Modulation (IEEE)
quam	Quadrature-Amplitude Modulation (AD)
QUAM	Quantized Amplitude Modulation (NITA)
QUAN	Quantity (KSC)
QUANA........	Authorized Newsagents Association of Queensland [Australia] (BUAC)
Quandary	Quandary Peak [Colorado] (AD)
Quanex	Quanex Corp. [Associated Press] (SAG)
QUANGO	Quasi-Autonomous Non-Governmental [or National Governmental] Organisation [British]
quango	Quasi-Autonomous Non-Governmental Organization [British] (WA)
QuanRst	Quantum Restaurant Group [Associated Press] (SAG)
QUANSY	Question Answering System (MHDB)
QUANT........	Quantitative [or Quantity]
quant	Quantity (AD)
quant	Quantum (AD)
quant anal ...	Quantitative Analysis [Laboratory science] (DAVI)
QuantHlt	Quantum Health Resources, Inc. [Associated Press] (SAG)
QuantLrn......	Quantum Learning Systems, Inc. [Associated Press] (SAG)
QUANTRAS...	Question Analysis Transformation and Search [Computer science]
quantras	Question Analysis Transformation and Search [Data processing] (AD)
QUANT SUFF...	Quantum Sufficiat [A Sufficient Quantity] [Pharmacy]
Quant Suff ...	Quantum Sufficit [A Sufficient Quantity] [Pharmacy]
quant suff ...	Quantum Suffict [Sufficient Quantity] [Latin] (AD)
Quantum......	Quantum Corp. [Associated Press] (SAG)
QUAOPS	Quarantine Operations [Military] (NVT)
quaops........	Quarantine Operations (AD)
QUAP	Quality Assurance Procedures
QUAP	Questionnaire Analysis Program (IAA)
QUAPP........	Qu'Appelle [Canadian river] (ROG)
QUAPS........	Quality Assurance Publications [Navy]
Quaq..........	Quaquero [Quaker] [Spanish] (AD)
quar	Quarantine (AD)
QUAR	Quarantine (AABC)
QUAR	Quarry
QUAR	Quarter [Business term]
Quar..........	Quarter (EBF)
QUAR	Quarterly
QUARAM.......	Quality and Reliability Management [DoD]
QUARC........	Quarterdeck Anti-Virus Research Center
Quar Crim Dig...	Quarles' Tennessee Criminal Digest [A publication] (DLA)
QUARG	Quality of Urban Air Review Group [British] (ECON)
QUARK........	Quantizer, Analyzer, and Record Keeper [Telecommunications] (TEL)
Quar Law Journal...	Quarterly Law Journal [Virginia] [A publication] (DLA)
Quar L Rev...	Quarterly Law Review [Virginia] [A publication] (DLA)
QUARLY.......	Quarterly (ROG)
quar pars	Quarta Pars [One-Fourth Part] [Latin] (AD)
quarpel	Quartermaster Water-Repellent [Military] (AD)
QUARPEL.....	Quartermaster Water-Repellent Clothing [Military]
quarr..........	Quarry (AD)
QUART........	Quadrantectomy, Axillary Dissection, Radiotherapy [Oncology]
QUART........	Quality Assurance and Reliability Team
quart..........	Quarter Gallon (AD)
Quart..........	Quarterly (AD)
quart..........	Quarterly (AD)
QUART........	Quarterly
quart..........	Quartet (AD)
QUART........	Quartetto [Quartet] [Music] (ROG)
QUART........	Quartus [Fourth] [Pharmacy]
Quart Bull Instn Eng Aust...	Quarterly Bulletin. Institution of Engineers of Australia [A publication]
Quart Ital	Quartetto Italiano [Italian Quartet] [Italian] (AD)
Quart J Roy Met Soc...	Quarterly Journal of the Royal Meteorological Society (MEC)
Quart LJ (VA)...	Quarterly Law Journal [Virginia] [A publication] (DLA)
Quart L Rev (VA)...	Quarterly Law Review [Virginia] [A publication] (DLA)
QUARTM.......	Quartermaster (ROG)
Quartrdk	Quarterdeck Corp. [Associated Press] (SAG)
QUARTZ GR...	Quartzite Granite [Agronomy]
quartzite	Granular Quartz Rock (AD)
QUASAR	Quasi-Stellar [Astronomy]
quasar	Quasi-Stellar Radio (AD)
QUASAT	Quasar Satellite [Proposed observatory in space]
QUASER......	Quantum Amplification by Stimulated Emission of Radiation
quaser	Quantum Amplification by Stimulated-Emission of Radiation (AD)
Quash........	Quashey (AD)
QUASS	Quassia [Pharmacology] (ROG)
QUAST........	Quality Assurance Service Test (PDAA)
QUAT	Quater [Four Times] [Pharmacy]
QUAT	Quaternary [Period, era, or system] [Geology]
Quat..........	Quaternary (AD)
quat	Quaternary (AD)
QUAT	Quaternary Ammonium Compound [Class of antimicrobial agents]
QUAT	Quaternion (NASA)
QUAT	Quatrefoil [Numismatics]
QUAT	Quattuor [Four] [Latin] (DAVI)
quat	Quattuor [Four] [Latin]
QUATIP.......	Quality Assurance Test and Inspection Plan [Military] (CAAL)
QUATS........	Quaternary Ammonium Compound [Biochemistry] (DB)

QUB .... Queen's University, Belfast [Ireland]
QUBMIS ...... Quantitatively Based Management Information System
quc .... Quebec [MARC country of publication code Library of Congress] (LCCP)
QUD .... Queen's University of Dublin (AD)
QUE .... Albuquerque Public Library, Albuquerque, NM [OCLC symbol] (OCLC)
QUE .... Gouvernement du Quebec, Service Aerien Gouvernemental [Canada] [FAA designator] (FAAC)
Que .... Quebec [Canada] (DD)
QUE .... Quebec [Canadian province]
QUE .... Quebecair (AD)
Que .... Quebecois (AD)
Que .... Quechua (AD)
que .... Quechua [MARC language code Library of Congress] (LCCP)
QUE .... Queenston Gold Mines Ltd. [Toronto Stock Exchange symbol]
Que .... Quenia [Kenya] [Portuguese] (AD)
QUE .... Quetta [Pakistan] [Seismograph station code, US Geological Survey] (SEIS)
Quebcor .... Quebecor, Inc. [Associated Press] (SAG)
Quebec L (Can)... Quebec Law Reports [Canada] [A publication] (DLA)
Quebec Pr (Can)... Quebec Practice [Canada] [A publication] (DLA)
Queb KB ...... Quebec Official Reports, King's Bench [Canada] [A publication] (DLA)
QuebPr .... Quebecor Printing, Inc. [Associated Press] (SAG)
Queb Pr .... Quebec Practice Reports [1897-1943] [A publication] (DLA)
Que BR .... Quebec Rapports Judiciaires Officiels (Banc de la Reine, Cour Superieure) [A publication] (DLA)
Que C A .... Quebec Official Reports, Court of Appeals [A publication]
Que CA .... Rapports Judiciaires Officiels, Cour d'Appel [1892-date] [Official Law Reports, Court of Appeal Quebec] [A publication] (DLA)
Que CBR ...... Rapports Judiciaires Officiels, Cour du Banc du Roi [ou de la Reine] [Official Law Reports, Court of King's, or Queen's, Bench Quebec] [A publication] (DLA)
Que CS .... Rapports Judiciaires Officiels, Cour Superieure [Official Law Reports, Superior Court] [Quebec] [A publication] (DLA)
QueenCB ...... Queens County Bancorp [Associated Press] (SAG)
QueenCtB .... Queens County Bancorp [Associated Press] (SAG)
Queens .... Queensland [Australia]
Queens .... Queensway Studios [Record label] [Great Britain]
Queens B Bull... Queens Bar Bulletin [United States] [A publication] (DLA)
Queens CBA Bull... Queens County Bar Association. Bulletin [United States] [A publication] (DLA)
Queens C (CUNY)... Queens College of The City University of New York (GAGS)
Queens Intra LJ... Queen's Intramural Law Journal [1968-70] [Canada] [A publication] (DLA)
Queen's Intramural LJ... Queen's Intramural Law Journal [A publication] (DLA)
Queens JP & Loc Auth Jo... Queensland Justice of the Peace and Local Authorities' Journal [A publication] (DLA)
Queensl .... Queensland (AD)
Queensl Acts... Queensland Public Acts [A publication] (DLA)
Queens Law... Queensland Lawyer [Australia] [A publication] (DLA)
Queensl Cr Lands LR... Queensland Crown Lands Law Reports [A publication] (DLA)
Queensl JPR... Queensland Justice of the Peace. Reports [A publication] (DLA)
Queensl JP Rep... Queensland Justice of the Peace. Reports [A publication] (DLA)
Queensl L.... Queensland Law [A publication] (DLA)
Queensl LSJ... Queensland Law Society. Journal [A publication A publication] (DLA)
Queensl Pub Acts... Queensland Public Acts [A publication] (DLA)
Queensl R .. Queensland State Reports [A publication] (DLA)
Queensl SCR... Queensland. Supreme Court. Reports [A publication] (DLA)
Queens L Soc'y J... Queensland Law Society. Journal [A publication] (DLA)
Queensl St R... Queensland State Reports [Australia] [A publication] (DLA)
Queensl St Rep... Queensland State Reports [Australia] [A publication] (DLA)
Queens Q..... Queen's Quarterly [A publication] (BRI)
Queens St R... Queensland State Reports [A publication] (DLA)
Que KB .... Quebec Official Reports, King's Bench [A publication] (DLA)
Que L........... Quebec Law [A publication] (DLA)
QUEL .... Query Language [Computer science] (MHDI)
Que LR .... Quebec Law Reports [Canada] [A publication] (DLA)
QUELS .... Quasi-Elastic Light Scattering [Also, QELS, QLS] [Physics]
Quen .... Quentin (AD)
Quent .... San Quentin [California State Prison] (AD)
Que Pr .... Quebec Practice [A publication] (DLA)
Que PR .... Quebec Practice Reports [A publication] (DLA)
Que Prac .... Quebec Practice Reports [A publication] (DLA)
Que QB .... Quebec Official Reports, Queen's Bench [A publication] (DLA)
Quer .... Queretaro (AD)
quer .... Querulous (DAVI)
QUERC .... Quercus [Oak] [Pharmacology] (ROG)
Que Rev Jud... Quebec Revised Judicial [A publication] (DLA)
Que Rev Stat... Quebec Revised Statutes [Canada] [A publication] (DLA)
QUES .... Questa Oil & Gas [NASDAQ symbol] (TTSB)
QUES .... Questa Oil & Gas Co. [NASDAQ symbol] (SAG)
QUES .... Question (AAG)
ques............ Question (AD)
QUES .... Question Mark (AABC)
Que SC .... Quebec Official Reports, Superior Court [A publication] (DLA)
QUEST .... Qualitative Experimental Stress Tomography
QuEST......... Quality Educational Standards in Teaching
QUEST .... Quality Electrical Systems Test [Interpreter]
quest .... Quality Electrical System Test (AD)
QUEST .... Quality Utilization Effectiveness Statistically Qualified
QUEST .... Quantification of Uncertainty in Estimating Support Tradeoffs (PDAA)

QUEST .... Quantitative Environmental Science and Technology [ULDECO Ltd.] [British] (IRUK)
QUEST .... Quantitative Understanding of Explosive Stimulus Transfer
QUEST .... Quantitative Utility Estimates for Science and Technology [RAND Corp.]
QUEST .... Queens Educational and Social Team (AD)
QUEST .... Query Evaluation and Search Technique
QUEST .... Question
quest .... Question (STED)
quest .... Questionable (DAVI)
quest .... Questioned (AD)
Questa .... Questa Oil & Gas Co. [Associated Press] (SAG)
QUESTA .... Questionnaire for Students, Teachers, and Administrators (EDAC)
questal .... Quiet, Experimental, Short-Takeoff-and-Landing [NASA] (AD)
questar .... Quantitative Utility Evaluation Suggesting Targets for the Allocations of Resources (AD)
Questar........ Questar Corp. [Associated Press] (SAG)
Que Stat ..... Quebec Statutes [Canada] [A publication] (DLA)
Questch .... QuesTech, Inc. [Associated Press] (SAG)
QUESTER ..... Quick and Effective System to Enhance Retrieval [Computer science]
quester .... Quick and Efficient System to Enhance Retrieval (AD)
QuestInt....... Quest International Resources Corp. [Associated Press] (SAG)
QuestM........ Quest Medical, Inc. [Associated Press] (SAG)
QUESTN ...... Question
Questn .... Questionnaire (ADA)
questn .... Questionnaire (AD)
QUESTOL ..... Quiet Experimental Short Takeoff and Landing [Program] [NASA]
Questron ..... Questron Technology [Associated Press] (SAG)
Que Super ... Quebec Official Reports, Superior Court [A publication] (DLA)
Que Tax Rep (CCH)... Quebec Tax Reporter (Commerce Clearing House) [A publication] (DLA)
QuF............. Australian Queensland Fever (DAVI)
qufyd .... Qualified (AD)
QUGA .... Queensland United Graziers' Association [Australia]
QUH .... Queen's University Highland Battalion [British military] (DMA)
QUI .... Aero Quimmco SA de CV [Mexico ICAO designator] (FAAC)
QUI .... Queen's University, Ireland
QUI .... Quincy Railroad Co. [Later, QRR] [AAR code]
QUI .... Quirindi [New South Wales] [Airport symbol] (AD)
QUI .... Quito [Ecuador] [Seismograph station code, US Geological Survey Closed] (SEIS)
QUI .... Quito, Ecuador, Tracking Station [NASA] (NASA)
QUI .... Thomas Crane Public Library, Quincy, MA [OCLC symbol] (OCLC)
QUIC .... Quality Data Information and Control (NASA)
QUIC .... Quantum Information and Computing [Consortium sponsored by DARPA]
QUIC .... Question and Information Connection [St. Louis Public Library] (AD)
Quich .... Quichua (AD)
quicha .... Quantitative Inhalation Challenge Apparatus [Medicine] (AD)
QUICHA .... Quantitative Inhalation Challenge Apparatus [Medicine] (MAE)
QUICK.......... Quality, Understanding, Integrity, Creativity, Knowledge [Business philosophy of Flag Communications Ltd.] (WDAA)
QUICK.......... Queens University Interpretative Code (AD)
QUICK.......... Quotation Information Center KK [Nihon Keizai Shimbun, Inc.] [Information service or system] (IID)
QuickRsp ..... Quick Response Services [Commercial firm Associated Press] (SAG)
Quicktr........ Quickturn Design System [Commercial firm Associated Press] (SAG)
QUICKTRAN... Quick FORTRAN [Programming language] [1979]
QUICO.......... Quality Improvement through Cost Optimization (MHDB)
quico .... Quality Improvement through Cost Optimization (AD)
QUID .... Quantified Intrapersonal Decision-Making [In book title]
Quidel.......... Quidel Corp. [Associated Press] (SAG)
QUIDS.......... Quick Interactive Documentation System (WDAA)
QUIES .... Quiescent (AD)
QUIK .... Quiksilver, Inc. [Costa Mesa, CA] [NASDAQ symbol] (NQ)
Quikslv .... Quiksilver, Inc. [Associated Press] (SAG)
quiktran ...... Quick Fortran [Computer science] (AD)
QUIL .... Quad in Line [Electronics Telecommunications] (TEL)
QUILL .... Queen's University Interrogation of Legal Language (NITA)
QUILL .... Queen's University Interrogation of Legal Literature [Queen's University of Belfast] [Northern Ireland] [Information service or system] (IID)
Quill & Q..... Quill & Quire [A publication] (BRI)
Quilmas....... San Quilmas (AD)
QUILS .... Quarterly Index of Lubricant Sales [Industry report]
QUILT .... Quantitative Intelligence Analysis Technique (PDAA)
quilwk.......... Quillwork (VRA)
quim .... Quimica [Chemistry] [Spanish] (AD)
Quimigal...... Quimica de Portugal (AD)
QUIN .... Quina [Quinine] [Pharmacy] (ROG)
Quin............ Quincy (AD)
Quin............ Quincy's Massachusetts Reports [A publication] (DLA)
Quin .... Quinten (AD)
quin .... Quintet (AD)
Quin............ Quintilianus (AD)
Quin............ Quintilius (AD)
Quin............ Quintillian (AD)
Quin............ Quintino (AD)
Quin............ Quintius (AD)
QUIN .... Quintuple
quin .... Quintuplet (AD)
Quin Bank... Quin on Banking [1833] [A publication] (DLA)
Quinct.......... Pro Quinctio [of Cicero] [Classical studies] (OCD)
Quincy .... Quincy's Massachusetts Reports [A publication] (DLA)
QUINID .... Quinidine [Pharmacology] (DAVI)

QUININ .... Quinine [*Pharmacology*] (DAVI)
quinq .... Quinque [*Five*] [*Latin*] (MAE)
quins .... Quintuplets (AD)
QUINT .... Quintetto [*Quintet*] [*Music*] (ROG)
Quint........... Quintilian [*First century AD*] [*Classical studies*] (OCD)
QUINT.......... Quintuple
quint........... Quintuplet [*Neonatology*] (DAVI)
quint .... Quintuplicate (AD)
quint .... Quintus [*Fifth*] [*Latin*] (AD)
QUINT.......... Quintus [*Fifth*] [*Latin*] (WGA)
Quintel........ Quintel Entertainment, Inc. [*Associated Press*] (SAG)
Quintiles...... Quintiles Transnational Corp. [*Associated Press*] (SAG)
Quinti Quinto... Year Book 5 Henry V [*England*] [*A publication*] (DLA)
Quint Smyrn... Quintus Smyrnaeus [*Classical studies*] (OCD)
quintupl .... Quintuplicate (AD)
QUIP .... Quad In-Line Package
QUIP .... Quantum-Well Infrared Photodetector [*Physics*]
QUIP .... Query Interactive Processor (IEEE)
QUIP .... Questionnaire Interpreter Program (IAA)
QUIP .... Quick-Inline Package (NITA)
QUIP .... Quipp, Inc. [*NASDAQ symbol*] (NQ)
QUIP .... QUOTA [*Query Online Terminal Assistance*] Input Processor [*Computer science*]
Quipp.......... Quipp, Inc. [*Associated Press*] (SAG)
QUIS .... Queen's University Information Systems (NITA)
quis .... Quisling [*World War II*] (AD)
Quit............ National Society of Non Smokers [*An association*] (BUAC)
QUIV .... Quiver (ROG)
quix .... Quixote (AD)
QUIX .... Quixote Corp. [*NASDAQ symbol*] (NQ)
Quixte .... Quixote Corp. [*Associated Press*] (SAG)
QUIZ .... Quizno's Corp. [*NASDAQ symbol*] (TTSB)
QUIZ .... Quizno's Franchise Corp. [*NASDAQ symbol*] (SAG)
Quiznos....... Quizno's Franchise Corp. [*Associated Press*] (SAG)
Qu Jour Int-Amer Rel... Quarterly Journal of Inter-American Relations [*A publication*] (DLA)
QUK .... Quaker Resources, Inc. [*Vancouver Stock Exchange symbol*]
QUL .... Queen's University Library (AD)
QUL .... Quillagua [*Chile*] [*Seismograph station code, US Geological Survey*] (SEIS)
Qu LJ .... Quarterly Law Journal [*A publication*] (DLA)
QULOC........ Queensland University Libraries Office of Cooperation [*Australia*]
Qu L Rev .... Quarterly Law Review [*A publication*] (DLA)
QUM .... Queen's University, Medical Library [*UTLAS symbol*]
QUM .... Quillmana [*Peru*] [*Seismograph station code, US Geological Survey Closed*] (SEIS)
QUMDO....... Qualitative Materiel Development Objective [*Army*] (AFIT)
QUMR.......... Quality Unsatisfactory Material Report (MCD)
QUN .... Qutdligssat [*Greenland*] [*Airport symbol*] (AD)
QUNG.......... Quaker United Nations Group (BUAC)
UUNU .... Quaker United Nations Office (EAIO)
QUO .... Quadex Users' Organization (EA)
QUO .... Quote Resources, Inc. [*Vancouver Stock Exchange symbol*]
QUOBIRD..... Queen's University Online Bibliographic Information Retrieval and Dissemination (NITA)
QuoBO .... Query on Business Objects [*Computer science*] (PCM)
quod .... Quodlibet [*As You Please*] [*Latin*] (AD)
Quoddy .... Passamaquoddy Bay (AD)
quok.......... Quokka (AD)
Quomodo Adul... Quomodo Adulescens Poetas Audire Debeat [*of Plutarch*] [*Classical studies*] (OCD)
QUON.......... Question (ROG)
Quon Attach... Quoniam Attachiamenta [*A publication*] (DLA)
QUONBLE .... Questionable (ROG)
Quon Pt .... Quonset Point [*Rhode Island*] (AD)
quor........... Quorom [*Of Which*] [*Latin*] (AD)
quor........... Quorum (AD)
QUOR.......... Quorum [*Of Which*] [*Pharmacy*]
QuorumH ..... Quorum Health Group, Inc. [*Associated Press*] (SAG)
QUOT .... Quotation
quot .... Quotation (AD)
quot .... Quoted In [*or Quoting*] [*Legal term*] (DLA)
quot .... Quotidie [*Daily*] [*Latin*] (AD)
QUOT .... Quotient (MSA)
quot .... Quotient (STED)
quot .... Quoties [*As often as necessary*] [*Latin*] [*Pharmacology*] (DAVI)
QUOT .... Quoties [*As Often as Needed*] [*Pharmacy*]
QUOTA........ Query Online Terminal Assistance [*Computer science*]
QUOTID....... Quotidie [*Daily*] [*Pharmacy*]
quotid .... Quotidie [*Every Day*] [*Latin*] (AD)
QUOT OP SIT... Quoties Opus Sit [*As Often as Necessary*] [*Pharmacy*]
quot os .... Quoties Opus Sit [*As often as necessary*] [*Latin*] [*Pharmacy*] (DAVI)
QUP .... Quality Unit Pack
qup .... Quantity per Unit Pack (AD)
QUP .... Quantity Unit Pack
QUP .... Quincemil [*Peru*] [*Airport symbol*] (AD)
QUP .... Quonset Point [*Navy*]
QUR .... Quinstar Resources [*Vancouver Stock Exchange symbol*]
Qur........... Quran [*Koran*] [*Malay*] (AD)
QuSAR........ Quantitative Structure Activity Relationships [*National Institute on Drug Abuse*]
QUST .... Questron Technology [*NASDAQ symbol*] (TTSB)
QUTLJ......... Queensland University of Technology. Law Journal [*A publication*]
QUX .... Quinella Exploration Ltd. [*Vancouver Stock Exchange symbol*]
QUY .... Quest Energy Corp. [*Vancouver Stock Exchange symbol*]

QV............. Bibliotheque Municipale, Victoriaville, Quebec [*Library symbol National Library of Canada*] (NLC)
QV............. Lao Aviation [*Laos*] [*ICAO designator*] (ICDA)
QV............. Qualification and Validation Board [*Army*] (RDA)
QV............. Quality Verification [*Nuclear energy*] (NRCH)
qv............. Quality Verification (AD)
QV............. Quantum Vis [*or Voleris*] [*As Much as You Wish*] [*Pharmacy*]
QV............. Quattrovalvole [*Four valves per cylinder*] [*Italian*]
QV............. Queen Victoria [*British*]
QV............. Qui Vixit [*Who Lived*] [*Latin*]
QV............. Quod Vide [*or Videte*] [*Which See*] [*Latin*]
qv............. Quod Vide [*Which see*] [*Latin*] (WDMC)
q-v........... Q-Value (AD)
QVAH .... Institut de Recherche d'Hydro-Quebec, Varennes, Quebec [*Library symbol National Library of Canada*] (NLC)
QVAI .... Centre de Documentation, INRS [*Institut National de la Recherche Scientifique*]-Energie, Varennes, Quebec [*Library symbol National Library of Canada*] (NLC)
Q Van Weyt... Q. Van Weytson on Average [*A publication*] (DLA)
QVBFL .... Bibliotheque Felix-Leclerc, Val-Belair, Quebec [*Library symbol National Library of Canada*] (NLC)
QVC .... College de Victoriaville, Quebec [*Library symbol National Library of Canada*] (NLC)
QVC .... Qualification, Validation, and Certification Board [*Army*] (RDA)
QVC .... Quality Value Convenience Network, Inc. [*Television*]
QVCEMBO.... Ecole Quebecoise du Meuble et du Bois Ouvre, College de Victoriaville, Quebec [*Library symbol National Library of Canada*] (NLC)
QVCSF .... Queen Victoria's Clergy Sustentation Fund [*British*]
QVE........... Bibliotheque Municipale, Verdun, Quebec [*Library symbol National Library of Canada*] (BIB)
QVEC .... Cultural Centre [*Centre Culturel*] Verdun, Quebec [*Library symbol National Library of Canada*] (NLC)
QVEC .... Qualified Voluntary Employee Contribution
QVGCCQ...... Cree Regional Authority, Grand Council of the Crees (of Quebec) [*Administration Regionale Crie, Grand Conseil des Cris (du Quebec)*] Val D'Or, Quebec [*Library symbol National Library of Canada*] (NLC)
QVI............ Quality Verification Inspection
Q Vic .... Statutes of Quebec in the Reign of Victoria [*A publication*] (DLA)
QVL........... Qualified Vendors List
QVLBI .... Quasi-Very-Long-Baseline Interferometry
QVM .... Qualified Vehicle Modifier
QVM .... Queen Victoria Museum [*Launceston, Tasmania*] (AD)
QVM .... Que Viva Mexico [*Long Live Mexico*] [*Spanish*] (AD)
QVO .... Queen Victoria's Own [*British military*] (DMA)
QVP .... Quality Verification Plan
QVP .... Quick View Plus (PCM)
QVPL .... Qualified Verification Procedures List
QVR .... Quality Verification Report
UVR .... Queen Victoria's Rifles [*Military unit*] [*British*]
QVRF .... Queensland Victoria Research Foundation [*Australia*]
QVS .... Quality Verification Surveillance (AD)
QVS .... Queen Victoria's School [*British military*] (DMA)
QVSLEA ...... Atmospheric Environment Service, Environment Canada [*Service de l'Environnement Atmospherique, Environnement Canada*] Ville St-Laurent, Quebec [*Library symbol National Library of Canada*] (NLC)
QVT .... Qualified Verification Testing [*NASA*]
qvt .... Quality Verification Test (AD)
QVT........... Qume Video Terminal (NITA)
QVVT .... Qualified Verification Vibration Testing [*NASA*] (NASA)
QW........... Air Turks and Caicos [*ICAO designator*] (AD)
QW........... Poland [*License plate code assigned to foreign diplomats in the US*]
QW........... Quality of Working Life (DAVI)
QW........... Quantum Well [*Physics*]
QW........... Quarter Wave
qw........... Quarter Wave (AD)
QW........... Waterloo Public Library, Quebec [*Library symbol National Library of Canada*] (NLC)
QWA .... Quarter-Wave Antenna
qwa........... Quarter-Wave Antenna (AD)
QWA .... Qwestair [*Australia ICAO designator*] (FAAC)
QWAM .... Qualified for Warrant Air Mechanic [*British military*] (DMA)
Q WAR....... Quo Warranto [*Latin Legal term*] (DLA)
QWASP........ Quebec White Anglo-Saxon Protestant
QWB .... Quality of Well-Being [*Medicine*] (DMAA)
QWBI .... Quality of Well Being Index
QWBP .... Qualification Standards for Wage Board Positions
QWC .... Queensland Writers' Centre [*Australia*]
QWC .... West Chester State College, West Chester, PA [*OCLC symbol*] (OCLC)
QWD .... Quarterly World Day
qwd........... Quarterly World Day (AD)
Q/WDO........ Quarter Window [*Automotive engineering*]
QWE........... Qualified for Warrant Engineer [*British military*] (DMA)
q-wedge ..... Quartz Wedge (AD)
QWERTY...... [*The*] Standard English Language Typewriter Keyboard (BARN)
QWG .... Quadripartite Working Group [*Military*]
QWGCD....... Quadripartite Working Group for Combat Development [*American, Australian, British, and Canadian armies*]
QWG/CD .... Quadripartite Working Group on Combat Developments (MCD)
QWG/ENG .... Quadripartite Working Group on Engineering (MCD)
QWG/EW...... Quadripartite Working Group on Electronic Warfare (MCD)
QWG/LOG.... Quadripartite Working Group on Logistics [*Military*] (RDA)

QWG/PIQA ... Quadripartite Working Group on Proofing Inspection Quality Assurance (MCD)
QWG/STANO ... Quadripartite Working Group on Surveillance and Target Acquisition/Night Observation (MCD)
QWHS .... Queensland Women's Historical Society [*Australia*]
QWIKTRAN ... Quick FORTRAN [*Programming language*] [*1979*] (CSR)
QWIP .... Quantum Well Infra-red Photodetectors
QWIR .... Quantum Well, Infra-Red [*Detector*] (AAEL)
qwk .... Once a Week [*Every Week*] [*Pharmacy*] (DAVI)
QWL .... Quality of Working Life [*Labour Canada program*]
qwl .... Quality of Working Life (AD)
QWL .... Quality of Work Life [*Anti-recession program of Ford Motor Co.*]
QWL .... Quick Weight Loss
qwl .... Quick Weight Loss (AD)
QWLD .... Quality of Worklife Database [*Management Directions*] [*Information service or system*] (IID)
QWM .... Qualified for Warrant Mechanician [*British military*] (DMA)
QWMP .... Quadruped Walking Machine Program [*Army*]
QWOT .... Quarter-Wave Optical Thickness (WDAA)
qwot .... Quarter-Wave Optical Thickness (AD)
qwp .... Quarter-Wave Plate (AD)
QWP .... Quarter-Wave Plate
QWR .... Quantum Wire (AAEL)
QWR .... Quarterly Weight Report (DNAB)
QWR .... Queen's Westminster Rifles [*British military*] (DMA)
QWR .... Que West Resources Ltd. [*Toronto Stock Exchange symbol*]
QWRC .... Queensland Water Resources Commission [*Australia*]
QWRV .... Queen's Westminster Rifle Volunteers [*British military*] (DMA)
QWSH .... Congregation Shaar Hashomayim Library-Museum, Westmount, Quebec [*Library symbol National Library of Canada*] (NLC)
QWSMM ...... Westmount Public Library, Quebec [*Library symbol National Library of Canada*] (NLC)
QWSSUA .... Quasi-Wide-Sense-Stationary Uncorrelated Scattering (PDAA)
QWSSUS ..... Quasi-Wide Sense Stationary Uncorrelated Scattering (IAA)
QWT .... Quick Word Test [*Education*] (EDAC)

QX .... Century Airlines [*ICAO designator*] (AD)
QX .... Horizon Air [*ICAO designator*] (AD)
QX .... Qatar Amiri Flight [*Qatar*] [*ICAO designator*] (ICDA)
qx .... Quintaux [*Hundred-Weights*] [*French*] (AD)
QXE .... Horizon Airlines, Inc. [*ICAO designator*] (FAAC)
QXI .... Queue Executive Interface [*Computer science*] (MHDB)
QY .... Aero Virgin Islands [*ICAO designator*] (AD)
qy .... Quantum Yield (AD)
QY .... Quantum Yield
QY .... Quay (ROG)
Qy .... Quay (AD)
qy .... Query (AD)
QY .... Query
QY .... Quota Year [*Pisciculture*]
QYC .... Quincy Yacht Club (AD)
QYD .... Qi and Yin Deficiency (DMAA)
QYM .... SOLINET [*Southeastern Library Network*] Center, Atlanta, GA [*OCLC symbol*] (OCLC)
QYO .... Queensland Youth Orchestra [*Australia*] (AD)
Qz .... Quartz (AD)
qz .... Quartz (AD)
QZ .... Quartz [*Quality of the bottom*] [*Nautical charts*]
QZ .... Stockholm University Computing Center [*Sweden*] (TSSD)
QZ .... Zambia Airways [*Airline flight code*] (ODBW)
QZ .... Zambia Airways [*ICAO designator*] (AD)
Q-Zar .... Q-Zar, Inc. [*Associated Press*] (SAG)
QZAR .... Q-Zar, Inc. [*NASDAQ symbol*] (SAG)
QZARF .... Q-Zar Inc. [*NASDAQ symbol*] (TTSB)
QZE .... Quadratic Zeeman Effect [*Physics*]
QZM .... Quartz Mountain Gold Corp. [*Vancouver Stock Exchange symbol Toronto Stock Exchange symbol*]
QZMGF .... Quartz Mountain Gold Corp. (MHDW)
QZN .... Quan Zhou [*Republic of China*] [*Seismograph station code, US Geological Survey*] (SEIS)
QZS .... Quebec Zoological Society [*Canada*] (AD)

R
By Acronym

R................. Abstracted Reappraisement Decisions [*A publication*] (DLA)
R................. Acknowledgment of Receipt [*Message handling*]
    [*Telecommunications*]
R................. All India Reporter, Rajasthan [*A publication*] (DLA)
r................. Angular Yaw Velocity (AAG)
R................. Antenna with Reflector
r----- .... Arctic Ocean and Region [*MARC geographic area code Library of Congress*] (LCCP)
R................. Arginine [*One-letter symbol; see Arg*]
R................. Behnken's Unit [*Of Roentgen-Ray Exposure*] [*Radiology*] (DAVI)
R................. Carbon Stars [*Astronomy*] (BARN)
R................. [*A*] Chemical Radical (DOG)
R................. Cilag-Chemie AG [*Switzerland*] [*Research code symbol*]
r................. Correlation Coefficient (DAVI)
R................. Correlation Coefficient [*Statistics*] (BARN)
R................. Declared or Paid in the Preceding 12 Months Plus Stock Dividend [*Investment term*] (DFIT)
R................. Denver Laboratories [*Great Britain*] [*Research code symbol*]
R................. Drug-Resistant Plasmid (STED)
R................. Electric Resistance [*Symbol*]
R................. Gas Constant (STED)
R................. Janssen [*Belgium*] [*Research code symbol*]
R................. Jeudi [*French*] (ASC)
R................. Kentucky Law Reporter [*A publication*] (DLA)
R................. Metabolic Respiratory Quotient (STED)
R................. Molar Gas Constant [*Symbol*] [*IUPAC*] (NASA)
R................. Nicolaus Rufulus [*Flourished, 13th century*] [*Authority cited in pre-1607 legal work*] (DSA)
R................. Option Not Traded [*Investment term*] (DFIT)
R................. Parti Republicain Radical et Radical-Socialiste [*France*] [*Political party*] (ECED)
R................. Product Moment Coefficient of Correlation [*Statistics*]
R................. [*A*] Purine Nucleoside [*One-letter symbol; see Puo*]
R................. Rabba (BJA)
R................. Rabbanite (BJA)
R................. Rabbi
r................. Racemic [*Also, dl, rac*] [*Chemistry*]
R................. RACON [*RADAR Beacon*]
R................. Radfahrabteilung [*Bicycle Battalion*] [*German military - World War II*]
R................. Radial [*Followed by three digits; for use on instrument approach charts*] [*Aviation*]
R................. Radian
R................. Radiancy
R................. Radiation
R................. Radical
R................. Radio
R................. Radioactive Mineral (MAE)
R................. Radiographer [*British military*] (DMA)
R................. Radiolocation (IAA)
R................. Radiology [*or Radiologist*] (ADA)
R................. Radiotelegram
R................. Radium [*Chemical symbol is Ra*] (KSC)
r................. Radius [*Symbol*] [*IUPAC*]
R................. Radius (NAKS)
r................. Radius of Gyration (AAG)
R................. Rail (MSA)
R................. Railroad [*or Railway*]
R................. Rain [*Meteorology*]
R................. Raleigh [*Diocesan abbreviation*] [*North Carolina*] (TOCD)
R................. Ram
R................. Rand [*Monetary unit*] [*Botswana, Lesotho, South Africa, and Swaziland*]
R................. Random Number
R................. Range
R................. Range Rate (NAKS)
R................. Rank
R................. Rankine [*Temperature scale*]
R................. Raphe Nucleus [*Neuroanatomy*]
R................. Rare [*When applied to species*] [*Biology*]
R................. Rare [*Numismatics*]
r................. Rarus [*Rate*] [*Latin*] (EES)
R................. Rate
R................. Ratio
R................. Rational Number (MDG)
R................. Rationing [*British*]
R................. Raw (STED)

R................. Rawle's Pennsylvania Reports [*1828-35*] [*A publication*] (DLA)
R................. Rayleigh Wave [*Seismology*]
R................. Raymundus de Pennafort [*Deceased, 1275*] [*Authority cited in pre-1607 legal work*] (DSA)
R................. Raymundus de Sabanacho [*Authority cited in pre-1607 legal work*] (DSA)
R................. Rays
R................. Reaction (AAG)
R................. Read (AAG)
R................. Readability (IAA)
R................. Reader (NTCM)
R................. Readiness Count
R................. Real
R................. Ream (ADA)
R................. Rear
R................. Reasoning Factor [*or Ability*] [*Psychology*]
R................. Reaumur [*Temperature scale*] [*German*]
R................. Rebounds [*Basketball, hockey*]
R................. Receipt (ROG)
R................. Receive (NAKS)
r................. Received (ODBW)
R................. Received Solid [*Amateur radio*]
R................. Receiver
R................. Receiving (IAA)
R................. Reception (IAA)
R................. Receptor [*Biochemistry*]
R................. Recessed [*Electrical outlet symbol*]
R................. Recht [*Law*] [*German*]
R................. Recipe [*Take*] [*Pharmacy*]
R................. Reciprocating
R................. Recite [*Swell Organ*] [*Music*]
R................. Recluse
R................. Recognition [*Experimentation*]
R................. Recommendation (MHDB)
R................. Reconditioned (DCTA)
R................. Reconnaissance [*Designation for all US military aircraft*]
R................. Reconstruction Committee [*British World War II*]
R................. Record
R................. Recorder (ECII)
R................. Recovery (IAA)
R................. Recreations
R................. Recruit (ROG)
R................. Rectal [*or Rectum*] [*Medicine*]
r................. Rectangular Tank [*Liquid gas carriers*]
R................. Rectifier (IAA)
R................. Rectilinear Polarization [*Physics*] (ECON)
R................. Recto [*Also, RO*] [*Right-hand page*]
R................. Rector [*or Rectory*]
(R)............. Rectus [*Clockwise configuration*] [*See RS*] [*Biochemistry*]
R................. Rectus [*Muscle*] [*Anatomy*] (DAVI)
R................. Recurrence [*Medicine*]
R................. Red
R................. Redemption Fee [*Finance*]
R................. Redetermination
R................. Red Primary (IAA)
R................. Reducer [*Photographic processing*] (DGA)
R................. Reductase Test [*Biochemistry*] (DAVI)
R................. Redundancy [*Used in correcting manuscripts, etc.*]
R................. Redundant (NAKS)
R................. Reel (DGA)
R................. Referee [*Football*]
R................. Referred (OICC)
R................. Refill [*of bract liquid*] [*Botany*]
R................. Reflectance
R................. Reflection [*Angle of*]
R................. Reflector Lamp
R................. Reflexive
R................. Reform [*Judaism*]
R................. Refraction
R................. Refrigerated [*Shipping*] (DS)
R................. Refrigerated Tank [*Liquid gas carriers*]
R................. Refrigerator
R................. Refused
R................. Refuse Disposal [*British Waterways Board sign*]
R................. Regenerated [*Biology*]
R................. Regiment

R..................	Regina [Queen] [Latin]
R..................	Register [Computer science]
R..................	Registered
R..................	Registered Trademark (DAVI)
R..................	Registrar (ROG)
R..................	Regna [Queen] [Latin] (DLA)
R..................	Regression Coefficient (AAMN)
R..................	Regular (ADA)
R..................	Regular Priority [Wire service symbol] (NTCM)
R..................	Regulate (NAKS)
R..................	Regulating
R..................	Regulatory [Gene] [Genetics] (DAVI)
R..................	Rehydratable (NAKS)
R..................	Reigned
R..................	Reiz [Stimulus] [German Psychology]
R..................	Relapse [Medicine] (DMAA)
R..................	Relation [Computer science]
R..................	Relative Humidity
R..................	Relative Signal Strength (IAA)
R..................	Relaxed
R..................	Relay (DNAB)
R..................	Relevant [Computer science] [Telecommunications]
R..................	Reliability (MCD)
R..................	Religious (DNAB)
R..................	Religious Program (NTCM)
R..................	Reluctance
R..................	Remote [Telecommunications] (TEL)
R..................	Remotum [Far Respiration] [Latin] (MAE)
R..................	Render (IAA)
R..................	Renewed License [FCC] (NTCM)
R..................	Repair (DNAB)
R..................	Repeal [Legal term] (DLA)
R..................	Repeat (WDMC)
R..................	Repeater (IAA)
R..................	Repetitive [Electronics]
R..................	Replace (NAKS)
R..................	Replaceability (AAG)
R..................	Replaced [Dentistry]
R..................	Reply (ADA)
R..................	Reports
R..................	[The] Reports, Coke's English King's Bench [A publication] (DLA)
R..................	Repressor [Psychology] (MAE)
R..................	Reprint
R..................	Reproducible (DNAB)
r..................	Reproductive Potential [Genetics] (DOG)
R..................	Republic
R..................	Republican
R..................	Request
R..................	Requiescat [He, or She Rests] [Latin]
R..................	Rerun [of a television show]
R..................	Resazurin [A pH indicator] (DAVI)
R..................	Rescinded [Legal term] (DLA)
R..................	Research
R..................	Resentment [Psychology]
R..................	Reserve
R..................	Reset (MDG)
R..................	Reside [or Resident]
R..................	Resistance [Symbol] [IUPAC]
R..................	Resistor
R..................	Resolution
R..................	Resolved [Legal term] (DLA)
R..................	Respectfully [Letter closing]
R..................	Respiration
R..................	Respond [or Response]
R..................	Responder [Strain of mice]
R..................	Response (WDAA)
R..................	Responsorium [Responsory]
R..................	Respublica [Commonwealth] [Latin]
R..................	Rest [in cell cycles] [Cytology] (DAVI)
R..................	Restricted [Immunology]
R..................	Restricted [Persons under eighteen (sixteen in some localities) not admitted unless accompanied by parent or adult guardian] [Movie rating]
R..................	Restricted [Military document classification]
R..................	Restricted Area [Followed by identification]
R..................	Retarder [Slow] [On clock-regulators] [French]
R..................	Reticular [Nucleus of thalamus] [Neuroanatomy]
R..................	Retired [or Retiree]
R..................	Rettie's Scotch Court of Session Reports, Fourth Series [A publication] (DLA)
R..................	Returning
R..................	Reverse [Giemsa method] [Chromosome stain]
R..................	Review (AAMN)
R..................	Revised (MCD)
R..................	Revision [Legal term] (DLA)
R..................	Revoked [Legal term] (DLA)
R..................	Revolute Joint (IAA)
R..................	Reward
R..................	Rewind
R..................	Rewritten [FAR clauses] (AAGC)
R..................	Rex [King] [Latin]
R..................	Reynolds Number [Viscosity]
R..................	Rhinitis [Medicine]
R..................	Rhizoctonia [A fungus]
R..................	Rho (NUCP)

R..................	Rhode Island State Library, Providence, RI [Library symbol Library of Congress] (LCLS)
R..................	Rhodesia [Later, Zimbabwe] (ROG)
R..................	Rhodium [Symbol is Rh] [Chemical element] (ROG)
R..................	Rhodopsin [Visual purple]
R..................	Rhythm
R..................	Rial [Monetary unit] [Iran, Saudi Arabia, etc.]
r..................	Ribose [One-letter symbol; see Rib]
R..................	Ricardus Anglicus [Deceased, 1242] [Authority cited in pre-1607 legal work] (DSA)
R..................	Richard (King of England) (DLA)
R..................	Richtkreis [Aiming Circle] [Gunnery term] [German military - World War II]
R..................	Rickettsia
R..................	Riffle
R..................	Rifle
R..................	Rigger [British military] (DMA)
R..................	Right [Politics]
R..................	Right [Direction]
R..................	Right Edge [Skating]
R..................	Right Eye [Ophthalmology] (DAVI)
R..................	Right-Hand [Music] (DAS)
R..................	Riker Laboratories, Inc. [Research code symbol]
R..................	Rimus (BJA)
R..................	Ring [Technical drawings]
r..................	Ring Chromosome [Medicine] (MAE)
R..................	Ring Lead [Telecommunications] (TEL)
R..................	Ring Road [Traffic sign] [British]
R..................	Rinne [Test] [Hearing Test] (DAVI)
-R..................	Rinne's Test Negative [Hearing test]
+R..................	Rinne's Test Positive [Hearing test]
R..................	Rio [River] [Spanish] (ROG)
R..................	Rise [Electronics]
R..................	Riser [Technical drawings]
R..................	Rises
R..................	Risk
R..................	River [Maps and charts]
R..................	Riveted (DS)
R..................	Road
R..................	Road-Holding [In automobile name Rolls-Royce Bentley Turbo R]
R..................	Roan (Leather) [Bookbinding] (ROG)
R..................	Robert [Phonetic alphabet] [Royal Navy World War I Pre-World War II] (DSUE)
R..................	Robertus [Authority cited in pre-1607 legal work] (DSA)
R..................	Robin Avions [Pierre Robin] [France ICAO aircraft manufacturer identifier] (ICAO)
R..................	Robotics
R..................	Rock [Maps and charts]
R..................	Rocket [Missile vehicle type symbol]
R..................	Rod [Measurement]
r..................	Roentgen [Also, RU] [Unit measuring X and gamma radiations]
R..................	Roentgen (NAKS)
R..................	Roger [All right or OK] [Communications slang]
R..................	Roger [Phonetic alphabet] [World War II] (DSUE)
R..................	Roll
R..................	Roller-Skating Rinks [Public-performance tariff class] [British]
R..................	Rollout (KSC)
R..................	Roman
R..................	Roman Catholic School [British]
R..................	Romania
R..................	Romans [New Testament book] (BJA)
R..................	Romeo [Phonetic alphabet] [International] (DSUE)
R..................	Rontgen [Measurement] (EECA)
R..................	Rood [Unit of measurement]
R..................	Rook [Chess]
R..................	Room (NFPA)
R..................	Rorschach [Test] [Psychology] (DAVI)
R..................	Rosary
R..................	Roscoe's Cape Of Good Hope [A publication] (DLA)
R..................	Rosin, [Standard material for soldering]
R..................	Rostral [Anatomy]
R..................	Rotary Wing [Aircraft designation]
R..................	Rotor
R..................	Rough [Appearance of bacterial colony]
R..................	Rough Sea [Navigation]
R..................	Roussel [France] [Research code symbol]
R..................	Route
R..................	Routine (KSC)
R..................	Royal
R..................	Royalty Monthly [A publication]
R..................	R-Register [Computer science]
R..................	Rub [Medicine] (MAE)
R..................	Rubber
R..................	Rubidomycin [See also D, Daunorubicin] [Antineoplastic drug]
R..................	Ruble [Monetary unit] [Former USSR]
R..................	Rue [Street] [French]
R..................	Rule
R..................	Ruled [Followed by the dates of a monarch's reign]
r..................	Ruler
R..................	Rum (ROG)
R..................	Run [Distance sailed from noon to noon] [Navy British] (ROG)
R..................	Runic
R..................	Runs [scored] [Baseball or cricket]
R..................	Runway [Aviation] (DA)
R..................	Rupee [Monetary unit] [Ceylon, India, and Pakistan]

R................	Rural (MCD)
R................	Rydberg Constant [Spectroscopy] [Symbol] (DEN)
R................	Ryder System [NYSE symbol] (TTSB)
R................	Ryder System, Inc. [NYSE symbol] (SPSG)
R................	Ryman [Office equipment and furniture store chain] [British]
R................	Ryom [Catalog of music of Vivaldi] (BARN)
R................	Ship [Missile launch environment symbol]
R................	Stauffer Chemical Co. [Research code symbol]
R................	Transfer Payments [Economics]
R................	Transport [Naval aircraft designation]
R................	Yaw Control Axis [Symbol]
R(00)...........	Rydberg Constant (IDOE)
R1	Stage Right [Theater] (WDMC)
R1 Cro	Croke's English King's Bench Reports Tempore Elizabeth [1582-1603] [A publication] (DLA)
R 1 DIY.......	Royal 1st Devon Imperial Yeomanry [British military] (DMA)
R2..............	Reporting Responsibility [DoD]
R2..............	Richard II [Shakespearean work]
R2 Cro	Croke's English King's Bench Reports Tempore James [Jacobus] I [A publication] (DLA)
R2CSE.........	Relaxed Two-Color Stimulated Echo [Spectroscopy]
R2DC3	Rapid Reaction, Deployable Command, Control, and Communications
R2E............	Realisations et Etudes Electronique [Computer manufacturer] [France]
R2P2...........	Rapid Retargeting and Precision Pointing [Strategic Defense Initiative]
R2R	Run-to-Run (AAEL)
R3..............	Rearm, Resupply, Refuel [Army]
R³	Relay, Reporter, Responder [Military] (CAAL)
R³	Requirements Resources Review [Board] [DoD] (DOMA)
R3..............	Richard III [Shakespearean work]
R3 Cro	Croke's English King's Bench Reports Tempore Charles I [1625-41] [A publication] (DLA)
R-5-P	Ribose-5-Phosphate [Biochemistry] (MAE)
R-19/CA	Rhodes 19 Class Association (EA)
Ra..............	Airway Resistance [Medicine] (MAE)
RA..............	Antonine Sisters (TOCD)
RA..............	Coast RADAR Station [Maps and charts]
RA..............	High-Powered Radio Range (Adcock)
RA..............	Rabbinical Assembly (EA)
RA..............	Racecourse Association (BUAC)
Ra..............	RADAR
RA..............	RADAR Altimeter [Aviation] (KSC)
Ra..............	RADAR Station
RA..............	Radiation Oncology Services (MEDA)
RA..............	Radio (WDAA)
RA..............	Radioactive
RA..............	Radio Altimeter
RA..............	Radio Antenna
RA..............	Radio Authority [Government regulatory agency] [British]
RA..............	Radiocommunications Agency (BUAC)
RA..............	Radiology (DAVI)
RA..............	Radionic Association (EA)
Ra..............	Radium [Chemical element]
RA..............	Radius of Action (AAG)
RA..............	Ragocyte [Medicine] (DMAA)
RA..............	Ragweed Antigen [Immunology]
RA..............	Rain [ICAO] (FAAC)
Ra..............	Rainerius [Authority cited in pre-1607 legal work] (DSA)
RA..............	Rainforest Alliance (EA)
RA..............	Raise (AAG)
RA..............	Raker Act of 1913 (COE)
RA..............	Ramblers' Association [British] (DBA)
RA..............	Ramp Actuator
RA..............	Random Access [Computer science] (AAG)
RA..............	Range [Aviation]
RA..............	Range Area (NASA)
RA..............	Range Assessor [British military] (DMA)
RA..............	Rape [Division in the county of Sussex] [British]
RA..............	Rapid Access [Film] (DGA)
RA..............	Rapid-American Corp.
RA..............	Rapid Anastigmatic (Lens) [Photography] (ROG)
RA..............	Raritan Arsenal (AAG)
Ra..............	Rastell's Entries [A publication] (DSA)
RA..............	Rate Action (AAG)
RA..............	Rate of Application
RA..............	Rate of Approach (IIA)
RA..............	Ratepayers' Association [British] (ILCA)
RA..............	Ratio Actuator (MCD)
RA..............	Ration
RA..............	Ration Allowance [British military] (DMA)
Ra..............	Rayleigh Number [IUPAC]
Ra..............	Raymundus de Pennafort [Deceased, 1275] [Authority cited in pre-1607 legal work] (DSA)
RA..............	Raynaud's Phenomenon [Medicine]
RA..............	Rayon (AAG)
RA..............	Read Amplifier
RA..............	Reading Age (WDAA)
RA..............	Ready-Access [Telecommunications] (TEL)
RA..............	Ready Alert [Navy] (NVT)
RA..............	Rear Admiral [Also, RADM, RADML]
RA..............	Rear Artillery
R/A.............	Rear Axle [Automotive engineering]
RA..............	Reasonable Alternative (GNE)
RA..............	Rebuild America (EA)
RA..............	Receiver Attenuation
RA..............	Receiver Auxiliary (IAA)
RA..............	Recipient Agency [Federal government] (GFGA)
RA..............	Recipient Rights Adviser
RA..............	Reciprocal Asymmetrical [Medicine] (DMAA)
RA..............	Reckson Associates Realty [NYSE symbol] (TTSB)
RA..............	Reckson Associates Realty Corp. [NYSE symbol] (SAG)
RA..............	Reclamation Act of 1902 (COE)
RA..............	Reclamation Association (BUAC)
RA..............	Reconnaissance Aircraft (DNAB)
RA..............	Record Address (IAA)
R/A.............	Recorded Announcement [Telecommunications] (TEL)
RA..............	Recording Annunciator (IAA)
RA..............	Records Administration (MCD)
RA..............	Recreation Aide [Red Cross]
RA..............	Recrystallization-Anneal (PDAA)
RA..............	Rectifier (IAA)
RA..............	Redevelopment Act (OICC)
RA..............	Redstone Arsenal [Huntsville, AL] [Army]
RA..............	Reduced Aperture (MCD)
RA..............	Reduction of Area
RA..............	Referees' Association [British] (DBA)
RA..............	Refer to Accepter [Banking]
R/A.............	Refer to Acceptor (EBF)
RA..............	Refractories Association of Great Britain (BUAC)
RA..............	Refractory Anemia [Medicine]
RA..............	Refractory Ascites [Medicine] (DMAA)
RA..............	Refugee Action [An association] (BUAC)
RA..............	Refugee Agency [NATO] (NATG)
RA..............	Regia Anglorum [British] [An association] (DBA)
RA..............	Regional Administrator
RA..............	Regional Associations [Marine science] (MSC)
RA..............	Register Allocator (IAA)
RA..............	Registered Architect (IIA)
RA..............	Registration Act
RA..............	Registration Appeals [A publication] (DLA)
RA..............	Regular Army
RA..............	Regulation Appeals [A publication] (DLA)
RA..............	Regulatory Alternative [Federal government] (GFGA)
RA..............	Regulatory Analysis [Federal government] (GFGA)
RA..............	Rehabilitation Act (OICC)
RA..............	Reimbursement Authorization (AFM)
RA..............	Reims Aviation [France ICAO aircraft manufacturer identifier] (ICAO)
RA..............	Reinforced Alert (NATG)
RA..............	Relative Abundance [Chemistry]
RA..............	Relative Activity [Physiology]
RA..............	Relative Address
RA..............	Release Authorization
RA..............	Released-Action [Pharmacy]
RA..............	Reliability Analysis (AAG)
RA..............	Reliability Assessment (KSC)
RA..............	Reliability Assurance (MCD)
RA..............	Religious of the Apostolate of the Sacred Heart [Roman Catholic women's religious order]
RA..............	Religious of the Assumption [Roman Catholic women's religious order]
RA..............	Relocation Address
RA..............	Relocation Assistance [HUD]
RA..............	Remedial Action [Navy]
RA..............	Remittance Advice (MCD)
RA..............	Remote Access [Telecommunications] (IAA)
RA..............	Remote Area
RA..............	Renal Artery [Anatomy]
RA..............	Renin Activity (AAMN)
RA..............	Renin-Angiotensin [Medicine] (DMAA)
RA..............	Rental Agreement
RA..............	Repair Assignment (AAG)
RA..............	Repeat Action [Medicine]
R/A.............	Repeat Attempt [Telecommunications] (TEL)
RA..............	Repeated Attacks [Medicine]
RA..............	Replacement Algorithm
RA..............	Reporting Activity (MCD)
RA..............	Representative Assembly
RA..............	Republicans Abroad (EA)
RA..............	Requesting Agency (MUGU)
RA..............	Requirements Analysis
RA..............	Rescue Ambulance [Emergency medicine] (DAVI)
RA..............	Reserve Affairs (DOMA)
RA..............	Resident Agent (AFM)
RA..............	Resident Alien
RA..............	Resident Assistant
RA..............	Resident Auditor
RA..............	Residual Air
RA..............	Resistor Assembly
RA..............	Resource Allocation (MCD)
RA..............	Resource Application (ERG)
RA..............	Resource Assistant (GNE)
RA..............	Respiratory Allergy [Immunology]
RA..............	Respiratory Arrest [Medicine]
R-A.............	Response Errors [Statistics]
RA..............	Restricted Account [Banking]
RA..............	Resume-Accelerate [Automotive engineering]
RA..............	Retinal Anlage [Ophthalmology]
RA..............	Retinoic Acid [Biochemistry]

RA	Retrograde Amnesia [*Medicine*]
RA	Return Address
RA	Return Air [*Technical drawings*]
R/A	Return to Author [*Bookselling*]
RA	Revenue Act [*1962, 1964, 1971, 1976, 1978*]
RA	Revenue Agent [*IRS*]
RA	Reverendus Admodum [*Very Reverend*] [*Latin*]
RA	Reviewing Activity (MCD)
RA	Reviewing Authority
RA	Reviews in Anthropology [*A publication*] (BRI)
RA	Revue Administrative [*A publication*] (ILCA)
RA	Rheumatoid Agglutinins [*Clinical chemistry*]
RA	Rheumatoid Arthritis [*Medicine*]
rA	Riboadenylate (STED)
RA	Rice Association [*British*] (DBA)
RA	Riders Association [*Defunct*] (EA)
RA	Right Accumulator (IAA)
RA	Right Aft (MCD)
RA	Right Angle (DEN)
RA	Right Aortic [*Medicine*] (DB)
RA	Right Arch [*Freemasonry*]
RA	Right Arm [*Medicine*]
RA	Right Ascension [*Navigation*]
RA	Right Atrium [*Cardiology*]
RA	Right Auricle [*Anatomy*]
RA	Right Axilla (KSC)
RA	Ripple Adder
RA	Risk Analysis (MCD)
RA	Risk Assessment (GFGA)
RA	Road America [*Automotive raceway*]
RA	Robbery Armed
RA	Robustrus Archistriatalis [*Bird brain anatomy*]
RA	Rocket Assist (RDA)
RA	Rokitansky-Aschoff [*Sinus*] [*Gastroenterology*]
RA	Room Air (MEDA)
RA	Root Apex [*Botany*]
RA	Roquefort Association (EA)
RA	Rosin Acid [*Organic chemistry*]
RA	Rosin Activated [*Standard material for soldering*].
RA	Rotary Assembly
RA	Rotation Angiography [*Medicine*] (DMAA)
RA	Rotogravure Association
RA	Routing Arbiter [*Telecommunications*]
RA	Royal Academician [*or Academy*] [*British*]
RA	Royal Academy [*British*] (WDAA)
RA	Royal Academy of Arts (BUAC)
RA	Royal Academy of Arts in London [*British*]
RA	Royal Arch [*Freemasonry*]
RA	Royal Armouries [*Tower of London*]
RA	Royal Art
RA	Royal Artillery [*British*]
RA	Royal Artist
RA	Royal Nepal Airlines [*ICAO designator*] (AD)
RA	Royal Regiment of Artillery [*Military British*]
RA	Rueckwaertiges Armeegebiet [*Rear area of an army*] [*German military*]
RA	Rules on Appeal [*A publication*] (DLA)
RA	Rural Action [*An association*] (BUAC)
RA	Russian Air [*To distinguish call-signs and frequencies*] [*World War II British*]
RA	Russian American
RA	Thermal Resistance of Unit Area [*Heat transmission symbol*]
RAA	Blackrock CA Inv Qual Muni [*AMEX symbol*] (TTSB)
RAA	Blackrock California Investment Quality Municipal [*AMEX symbol*] (SPSG)
RAA	Rabbinical Alliance of America (EA)
RAA	RADAR Aircraft Altitude (IAA)
RAA	Random Access Array (NITA)
RAA	Reagan Alumni Association (EA)
RA(A)	Rear-Admiral of Aircraft Carriers [*Obsolete British*]
RAA	Reeve Aleutian Airways, Inc. [*Air carrier designation symbol*]
RAA	Regenerative Agriculture Association [*Later, RI*] (EA)
RAA	Regional Administrative Assistant (ADA)
RAA	Regional Airline Association (EA)
RAA	Regional Arts Association [*British*]
RAA	Regression-Associated Antigen (DB)
RAA	Reinsurance Association of America [*Washington, DC*] (EA)
RAA	Relational Algebra Accelerator [*Computer board*]
RAA	Remote Access Audio (NITA)
RAA	Remote Access Audio Device [*Computer science*] (MHDB)
RAA	Renewal Assistance Administration [*HUD*]
RAA	Renin-Angiotensin-Aldosterone [*Clinical nephrology*]
RAA	Research and Analysis (IAA)
RAA	Research Animal Alliance (EA)
RAA	Respiratory Aid Apparatus
RAA	Ricegrowers' Association of Australia
RAA	Right Angle Adapter
RAA	Right Ascension Angle
RAA	Right Atrial Abnormality [*Medicine*] (STED)
RAA	Right Atrial Appendage [*Medicine*]
RAA	Rockette Alumnae Association (EA)
RAA	Royal Academy Association [*British*] (NADA)
RAA	Royal Academy of Arts [*British*] (ROG)
RAA	Royal Australian Artillery (BUAC)
RAA	Rural Assistance Authority [*New South Wales, Australia*]

RAA	Rynes Aviation, Inc. [*ICAO designator*] (FAAC)
RAAA	Red Angus Association of America (EA)
RAAA	Relocation Assistance Association of America [*Defunct*] (EA)
RAAAS	Remote Antiarmor Assault System (MCD)
RAAB	Remote Amplifier Acquisition and Advisory Box [*NASA*] (NAKS)
RAAB	Remote Amplifier and Adaption Box (NASA)
RAAB	Remote Amplifier and Adoption Box [*NASA*] (NAKS)
RAAB	Remote Application and Advisory Box (MCD)
RAABF	Royal Artillery Association Benevolent Fund [*British military*] (DMA)
RAAC	Reference Areas Advisory Committee [*Victoria, Australia*]
RAAC	Rhodesian Air Askari Corps [*British military*] (DMA)
RAAC	Rome Allied Area Command [*World War II*]
RAACC	Robotics and Automation Applications Consulting Center [*Ford Motor Co.*]
RAACEF	Rear-Admiral of Aircraft Carriers, Eastern Fleet [*British*]
RAACT	Radioactive
RAAD	Radford Army Ammunition Depot [*Virginia*] (MCD)
RAAD	Restructured Air Assault Division (MCD)
RAADC	Regional Accounting and Disbursing Center (DNAB)
RAADES	Relative Antiair Defense Effectiveness Simulation [*Military*] (CAAL)
RA(A)EF	Rear-Admiral (Administration) Eastern Fleet [*British*]
RAAF	Redstone Army Airfield [*Huntsville, AL*]
RAAF	Royal Australian Air Force [*ICAO designator*] (FAAC)
RAAFA	Royal Australian Air Force Association
RAAG	Regional Aviation Assistance Group [*FAA*]
RAAG	Research Association of Applied Geometry [*Japan*] (BUAC)
RAAGG	Rheumatoid Arthritis Agglutinin [*Medicine*] (STED)
RAAM	Race Across America [*Annual cycling event*]
RAAM	Reagent Array Analysis Method [*Analytical biochemistry*]
RAAM	Remote Antiarmor Mine (RDA)
RAAM	Residual-Area-Analysis Method [*Spectrometry*]
RAAMC	Royal Australian Army Medical Corps (DAVI)
RAAMS	Remote Antiarmor Mine System [*Military*] (AABC)
RAAN	Repair Activity Accounting Number [*Navy*]
RAAP	Radford Army Ammunition Plant (AABC)
RAAP	Residue Arithmetic Associative Processor [*Computer science*] (OA)
RAAR	RAM Address Register
RAAS	Racial Adjustment Action Society (BUAC)
RAAS	Remedial Action Assessment System [*Environmental science*] (COE)
RAAS	Renin-Angiotensin-Aldosterone System [*Medicine*] (DMAA)
RAAS	Royal Amateur Art Society [*British*]
RAAT	Recombinant Alpha 1-Antitrypsin [*Biochemistry*]
RAATS	RCRA [*Resource Conservation and Recovery Act*] Administrative Action Tracking System (ERG)
RAAW	Rural, Agricultural, and Allied Workers (BUAC)
RAAWS	RADAR Altimeter and Altitude Warning System [*Military*] (CAAL)
RAAWS	Ranger Antiarmor, Antipersonnel Weapon System [*Army*] (INF)
RAB	Rabaul [*New Britain Island*] [*Airport symbol*] (OAG)
RAB	Rabaul [*New Britain Island*] [*Seismograph station code, US Geological Survey*] (SEIS)
RAB	Rabbet (MSA)
RAB	Rabbinical
Rab	Rabbit (STED)
RAB	Rabbit Oil & Gas [*Vancouver Stock Exchange symbol*]
RAB	Rabelais [*French author, 1494-1553*] (ROG)
RAB	Radio Advertising Bureau [*New York, NY*] (EA)
RAB	Reactor Auxiliary Building [*Nuclear energy*] (NRCH)
RAB	Regional Advisory Board [*American Hospital Association*]
RAB	Remote Afterload Brachytherapy [*Radiology*] (DAVI)
RAB	Renewal-at-Birth [*A periodical subscription*] (WDMC)
RAB	Rent Advisory Board [*Cost of Living Council*]
RAB	Research Advisory Board (DAVI)
RAB	Restoration Advisory Board
RAB	Rice, Applesauce, and Banana [*Diet*] (DAVI)
RAB	Richard Austen Butler [*1902-1982*] [*In book title "RAB: The Life of R. A. Butler"*]
RAB	Rotating Arm Basin
RABA	Rabbit Antibladder Antibody (STED)
RABA	Radioantigen-Binding Assay [*Medicine*]
RABA	Re-Chargeable Air-Breathing Apparatus (PDAA)
RABAC	Real Americans Buy American Cars [*An association Defunct*]
RABAL	Radiosonde Balloon
RABAL	Radiosonde Balloon Wind Data [*Meteorology*] (FAAC)
RABAR	Raytheon Advanced Battery Acquisition RADAR
RABATS	Rapid Analytical Block Aerial Triangulation System (PDAA)
Rabb	Rabbinic [*Hebrew*] [*Language*] (BARN)
RABB	Rabbinical
RABBI	Rapid Access Blood Bank Information (MAE)
RABCa	Rabbit Antibladder Cancer (STED)
RABDF	Royal Association of British Dairy Farmers [*British*] (BI)
RABET	RADAR Beacon Transponder
RABFAC	RADAR Beacon, Forward Air Controller
RABFAC-TDC	RADAR Beacon Forward Air Controller - Target Data Communicator (MCD)
RABG	Room Air Blood Gas (STED)
RABG	Room Air Blood Gases [*Medicine*] (DAVI)
RABH	Reported Altitude Block Height (SAA)
RABI	Royal Agricultural Benevolent Institution [*Church of England*]
RABIN	Netherlands Advisory Council for Libraries and Information Services (BUAC)
RABiTS	Rolling-Assisted Biaxially Textured Substrate [*Physics*]
RABNVS	Reactor Auxiliary Building Normal Ventilation System [*Nuclear energy*] (NRCH)
RABP	Renal Artery Bypass [*Medicine*]
RABP	Retinoic Acid-Binding Protein [*Biochemistry*] (DAVI)

Rab Post......	Pro Rabirio Postumo [of Cicero] [Classical studies] (OCD)
RABR...........	Rainbow Bridge National Monument
RABR...........	Right Angle Bulkhead Receptacle
RABS	Rear-Wheel Antilock Brake System [Automotive engineering]
RABS	Remote Air Battle Station
RABV	Reflood Assist Bypass Valve [Nuclear energy] (NRCH)
RABVAL......	RADAR Bomb Evaluation (MCD)
R_{ac}...............	AC Resistance (IDOE)
RAC	IEEE Robotics and Automation Council (EA)
rac	Racemate (DB)
rac	Racemic [Also, dl, r] [Chemistry]
RAC	Racer Resources Ltd. [Vancouver Stock Exchange symbol]
RAC	Raciborz [Poland] [Seismograph station code, US Geological Survey] (SEIS)
RAC	Racine, WI [Location identifier FAA] (FAAL)
RAC	RADAR Address Counter
RAC	RADAR Area Correlator
RAC	RADAR Azimuth Converter
RAC	Radiation Advisory Committee (GNE)
RAC	Radio Adaptive Communications
RAC	Radio Advisory Committee [Corporation for Public Broadcasting] (NTCM)
RAC	Radiological Assessment Coordinator [Nuclear energy] (NRCH)
RAC	Radiometric Area Correlator (MCD)
RAC	Radio Service Code (IAA)
RAC	Raisin Administrative Committee (EA)
RAC	Ram Air Cushion [Aerospace] (AAG)
RAC	Ramsay's Appeal Cases [Canada] [A publication] (DLA)
RAC	Random Access Capability [Microscopy]
RAC	Random Access Computer (IIA)
RAC	Random Access Controller [Computer science] (IAA)
RAC	Rangefinder with Automatic Compensator [Firearms]
RAC	Rapid Action Change [DoD]
RAC	Ration Accessory Convenience [World War II]
RAC	Rational Activity Coefficient
RAC	Raw Agricultural Commodity
RAC	Reactor Accident Calculation
RAC	Read Address Counter
RAC	Reallexikon fuer Antike und Christentum [A publication] (OCD)
RAC	Rear-Admiral Commanding [British]
RAC	Rebuild America Coalition (EA)
RAC	Receptor-Affinity Chromatography
RAC	Recessed Annular Connector
RAC	Recombinant DNA Advisory Committee [National Institutes of Health]
RAC	Reconnaissance Airplane Company [Army] (VNW)
RAC	Recreation Advisory Council [Bureau of Outdoor Recreation]
rac	Rectified Alternating Current (IDOE)
RAC	Rectified Alternating Current [Electronics] (ECII)
RAC	Recycling Advisory Council (GNE)
RAC	Reflect Array Pulse Compressor (RDA)
RAC	Refrigerant-Air Condition (DNAB)
RAC	Refueling Area Commander [Navy] (ANA)
RAC	Regional Advisory Council (ACII)
RAC	Regional Asbestos Coordinator (GNE)
RAC	Regional Assistance Committee [Environmental science] (COE)
RAC	Registrar of Aboriginal Corporations [Australia]
RAC	Release and Approval Center (MCD)
RAC	Reliability Action Center [NASA] (NASA)
RAC	Reliability Analysis Center [Griffiss Air Force Base, NY] [DoD] (GRD)
RAC	Reliability Assessment of Components (KSC)
RAC	Remote Access [Telecommunications] (IAA)
RAC	Remote Access and Control (AAEL)
RAC	Remote Access Computing System (IAA)
RAC	Renal Arterial Constriction [Medicine]
RAC	Repair, Alignment, and Calibration (NVT)
RAC	Reparable Assets Control (AFM)
RAC	Representation des Artistes Canadiens
RAC	Request for Authority to Complete (DOMA)
RAC	Request for Authority to Contract [Military]
RAC	Requisition Advice Care [Military]
RAC	Research Advisory Committee
RAC	Research Advisory Council
RAC	Research Analysis Corp. [Nonprofit contract agency] [Army]
RAC	Resource Assessment Commission (BUAC)
RAC	Response Action Contractor [Metallurgy]
RAC	Response Action Contracts [Environmental science] (COE)
RAC	Response Action Coordinator [Environmental Protection Agency] (ERG)
RAC	Responsibility Analysis Chart (DNAB)
RAC	Retail Advertising Conference (EA)
RAC	Rework After Completion (SAA)
RAC	Rhomboidal Air Controller (PDAA)
RAC	Right Atrial Catheter [Medicine] (MEDA)
RAC	Risk Assessment Code (MCD)
RAC	River Assault Craft [Navy] (ANA)
RAC	Roadside Assistance Center [Automotive Customer Service]
RAC	Rotorua Aero Club [New Zealand] [ICAO designator] (FAAC)
RAC	Royal Academician (of Canada) (ROG)
RAC	Royal Aero Club [British]
RAC	Royal Agricultural College [British]
RAC	Royal Arch Chapter [Freemasonry]
RAC	Royal Armoured Corps [British]
RAC	Royal Artillery Committee [British military] (DMA)
RAC	Royal Automobile Club [Controlling body of motor racing in Britain]
RAC	Rubber Allocation Committee
RAC	Rubber Association of Canada (BUAC)
RAC	Rules of the Air and Air Traffic Control [ICAO Air Navigation Commission]
Ra Ca	English Railway and Canal Cases [A publication] (DLA)
RACA	Recovered Alcoholic Clergy Association (EA)
RACA	Regroupement d'Artistes des Centres Alternatifs [Association of National Non-Profit Artists' Centres ANNPAC] [Canada]
RACA	Requiring Activity Contract Administrator [DoD]
RACA	Resource Accounting and Cost Allocation (MHDI)
RACA	Rural Arts and Crafts Association [Defunct] (EA)
RACAS	Radiation Automatic Casualty Assessment System [Military]
RACC	Radiation and Contamination Control
RACC	Regional Agricultural Credit Corp.
RACC	Regional ASW [Antisubmarine Warfare] Command Center [Navy] (DOMA)
RACC	Remote ARIA [Apollo Range Instrumentation Aircraft] Control Center [NASA]
RACC	Remotely Activated Command and Control [Military] (CAAL)
RACC	Reporting Activity Control Card [Army] (AABC)
RACC	Research Aviation Coordinating Committee
RACC	Rituels Accadiens [A publication] (BJA)
RACC	Romanian-American Chamber of Commerce (NTPA)
RACC	Royal Armoured Corps Centre [British] (MCD)
RACC	Royal Automobile Club of Canada
RACCA	Refrigeration and Air Conditioning Contractors Association - National [Later, National Environmental Systems Contractors Association] (EA)
RACD	Royal Army Chaplains' Department [British]
RACD	Royal Army Clothing Department [British]
RACE	Data Race [NASDAQ symbol] (TTSB)
RACE	Date Race, Inc. [NASDAQ symbol] (SAG)
RACNE	Racial Attitudes and Consciousness Exam [Two-part television program broadcast in 1989]
RACE	Radiation Adaptive Compression Equipment
RACE	Random Access Card Equipment [Computer science] (CDE)
RACE	Random Access Computer Equipment
RACE	Random Access Control Equipment (IEEE)
RACE	Rapid Amplification of CDNA [Complementary Deoxyribonucleic Acid] Ends [Genetics]
RACE	Rapid Amplification of Cloned Ends [Analytical biochemistry]
RACE	Rapid Automatic Checkout Equipment
RACE	Regional Automatic Circuit Exchange (IAA)
RACE	Request Altitude Changes En Route [Aviation]
RACE	Research and Development in Advanced Communications for Europe [European Community] (MHDB)
RACE	Research and Development in Advanced Communication Technologies for Europe (NITA)
RACE	Research in Advanced Communications in Europe [European Commission]
RACE	Research on Automatic Computation Electronics
RACE	Resource Assessment and Conservation Engineering [Environmental protection]
RACE	Response Analysis for Call Evaluation (IAA)
RACE	Restoration of Aircraft to Combat Effectivity [Army]
RACE	Results Analysis, Computation, and Evaluation (MHDI)
RACE	Routing and Cost Estimate (IAA)
RACEL	Record of Access/Eligibility [DoD]
RACEP	Random Access and Correlation for Extended Performance [Telecommunications]
RACER	Rankine-Cycle Energy Recovery [System] [Navy] (DOMA)
RACER	Redbook Assumption Cost Estimating Request
RACER	Runner Administration and Computerized Entry Routine [Computer science] (MHDI)
Race Rel L Rep...	Race Relations Law Reporter [A publication] (DLA)
RACES	Radio Amateur Civil Emergency Service [Civil defense]
RACES	Remote Arming Common Element System
RACF	RAC Financial Group, Inc. [NASDAQ symbol] (SAG)
RACF	RAC Fin'l Grp [NASDAQ symbol] (TTSB)
RACF	Resource Access Control Facility [IBM Corp.]
RACFI	Radio and Communication Facilities Inoperative
RAC Fin	RAC Financial Group, Inc. [Associated Press] (SAG)
RACFO	Radio and Communications Facilities Operative (IAA)
RACFOE......	Research Analysis Corporation Field Office, Europe [Army] (AABC)
RACG	Racing
RACG	Radiometric Area Correlation Guidance
RACGP........	Royal Australian College of General Practitioners (BUAC)
RACGPFMP...	Royal Australian College of General Practitioners Family Medicine Program
RAChD	Royal Army Chaplains' Department [British]
RACI	Reported Altitude Change Indicator (IAA)
RACI	Royal Australian Chemical Institute
RACIC	Remote Area Conflict Information Center [Battelle Memorial Institute]
RACIS	RADAR Computer Interaction Simulator
RACM	Reasonable Available Control Measures [Environmental Protection Agency] (GFGA)
RACMD.......	Radio Countermeasures and Detection (IAA)
RAC MSA	Royal Automobile Club Motor Sports Association (BUAC)
RACMSC	Royal Automobile Club Motor Sports Council [British] (DI)
RACNE	Regional Advisory Committee on Nuclear Energy
RACNSC	Religious Activities Committee, National Safety Council (EA)
RACO	Racotek, Inc. [NASDAQ symbol] (SAG)
RACO	RADAR-Absorbing Coating [Military] (RDA)
RACO	Rear Area Combat Operations (INF)
RACOB(WA)...	Rear-Admiral Commanding Combined Operational Bases (Western Approaches) [British]

RACOG.........	Royal Australian College of Obstetricians and Gynaecologists (BUAC)
RACOM.........	Random Communication (IAA)
RACOMS.......	Rapid Combat Mapping Service [*or System*] [*Military*]
RACON........	RADAR Beacon (IAA)
Racon..........	Radar Beacon (IDOE)
RACON........	RADAR Responder Beacon
RACON........	Radiobeacon [*Telecommunications*] (OTD)
Ra (Conspic)...	RADAR Conspicuous Object
RACOON.......	Radiation Controlled Balloon [*Meteorology*]
Racotek.......	Racotek, Inc. [*Associated Press*] (SAG)
RACP	Royal Australasian College of Physicians
RACPAS.....	RADAR Coverage Penetration Analysis
RACQ.........	Radiological Advisory Council of Queensland [*Australia*]
RACR..........	Resources Allocation Change Request
Rac Rel L Survey...	Race Relations Law Survey [*A publication*] (DLA)
RAC/RJ........	Religious Action Center of Reform Judaism (EA)
RACS	Random Access Communications System
RACS	Reactor Auxiliary Cooling System [*Nuclear energy*] (NUCP)
RACS	Recruit Allocation Control System [*Navy*] (NVT)
RACS	Redundant Attitude Control System (MCD)
RACS	Regenerable Affinity Chromatography Support
RACS	Remote Access Computing System [*Computer science*]
RACS	Remote Automatic Calibration System (NASA)
RACS	Remote Automatic Control System (KSC)
RACS	Request for Approval of Contractual Support ·
RACS	Road/Automobile Communication System [*Automotive engineering*]
RACS	Rotation Axis Coordinate System (MCD)
RACS	Royal Australasian College of Surgeons
RACT	Reasonable Available Control Technology [*Environmental Protection Agency*]
RACT	Remote Access Computer Technique [*Computer science*] (IEEE)
RACT	Reverse-Acting
RACU..........	Remote Acquisiton and Command Unit [*NASA*] (NASA)
RACU..........	Remote Acquistion and Command Unit (NAKS)
RACUAHC	Religious Action Center of the Union of American Hebrew Congregations [*Later, RAC/RJ*] (EA)
RACV	Royal Automobile Club of Victoria
RAD	Parti Radical [*Radical Party*] [*France*] [*Political party*] (EAIO)
RAD	RADAR
RAD	RADAR Approach Aid [*Aviation*] (DA)
RAD	RADAR Augmentation Device
RAD	Radford Army Ammunition Plant [*Virginia*]
RAD	Radford Arsenal [*Army*] (AAG)
rad.............	Radiac (IDOE)
RAD	RADIAC [*Radiation Detection, Indication, and Computation*] Equipment (NATG)
RAD	Radial
rad..............	Radian [*Symbol*] [*SI unit of plane angle*]
RAD	Radian (NAKS)
RAD	Radiation (KSC)
RAD	Radiation Absorbed Dose [*Unit of measurement of radiation energy*]
rad..............	Radiation Absorbed Dose (DOG)
RAD	Radiation Dosage (NAKS)
RAD	Radiator (AAG)
RAD	Radical
rad..............	Radical (IDOE)
rad..............	Radio (IDOE)
RAD	Radio (AAG)
RaD	Radioactive Lead [*or Pb²¹⁰*] [*Radiology*] (DAVI)
RAD	Radioactivity Detection
RAD	Radiogram
RAD	Radiographer (HCT)
Rad.............	Radiola [*Record label*] [*Australia*]
RAD	Radiologist
RAD	Radiology [*or Radiologist*] (ADA)
Rad.............	Radiotherapist (MAE)
RAD	Radium [*Chemical symbol is Ra*]
RAD	Radius (AAG)
rad.............	Radius (IDOE)
rad.............	Radix (IDOE)
RAD	Radix [*Root*] [*Latin*]
RAD	Radnorshire [*County in Wales*] (ROG)
RAD	Raised Afterdeck [*of a ship*] (DS)
RAD	Random Access Data (BUR)
RAD	Random Access Device
RAD	Random Access Disc (MCD)
RAD	Rapid Access Data [*Xerox Corp.*]
RAD	Rapid Access Data Drum (NITA)
RAD	Rapid Access Device
RAD	Rapid Access Disk
RAD	Rapid Access Drive (BUR)
RAD	Rapid Access Drum (IAA)
RAD	Rapid Application Development [*Computer science*]
RAD	Rapid Automatic Drill
RAD	Ratio Adjust Device (MCD)
RAD	Ratio Analysis Diagram [*Metallurgy*]
RAD	Reactive Airway Disease [*Medicine*] (MAE)
RA(D)..........	Rear-Admiral (Destroyers) [*Obsolete Navy British*]
RAD	Receptor Affinity Distribution [*Biochemistry*]
RAD	Recommendation Approval Document (MCD)
RAD	Records Arrival Date [*Bell System*] (TEL)
RAD(BPF)......	Recruiting Aids Department [*Navy*]
RADC	Reference Attitude Display
RAD	Reflex Anal Dilatation [*Medicine*]
RAD	Regional Accountable Depot [*Military*]

RAD	Regional Administrative Directors
RAD	Relative Air Density (OA)
RAD	Released from Active Duty [*Navy*]
RAD	Repair at Depot (MCD)
RAD	Reported for Active Duty [*Navy*]
RAD	Request for Apollo Documents [*NASA*] (KSC)
RAD	Required Availability Date [*Military*]
RAD	Requirements Action Directive (AFM)
RAD	Research and Advanced Development (MCD)
RAD	Research and Development (IAA)
RAD	Reservists on Active Duty [*Navy*]
RAD	Resource Allocation Display [*Navy*]
RAD	Resource Availability Determination (MCD)
RAD	Respect voor Arbeid en Democratie [*Belgium Political party*] (EY)
RAD	Restricted Activity Day [*Environmental medicine*]
RAD	Restricted Activity Days [*Veterans Administration*] (GFGA)
RAD	Restricted Shipyard Availability Requiring Drydocking [*Navy*] (NVT)
RAD	Return to Active Duty [*Military*]
RAD	Review and Approval Document (MCD)
RAD	Right Angle Drive (PDAA)
RAD	Right Anterior Descending [*Medicine*] (DAVI)
RAD	Right Anterior Digestive [*Gland*]
RAD	Right Axis Deviation [*Medicine*]
RAD	Rite Aid [*NYSE symbol*] (TTSB)
RAD	Rite Aid Corp. [*NYSE symbol*] (SPSG)
RAD	River Assault Division [*Navy*] (VNW)
RAD	Roentgen Absorbed Dosage (NAKS)
RAD	Roentgen Administered Dose
RAD	Royal Academy of Dancing [*British*] (EAIO)
RAD	Royal Academy of Dancing, United States Branch (EA)
RAD	Royal Albert Dock [*British*]
RAD	Royal Association in Aid of Deaf People (BUAC)
RAD	Rural Areas Development
RAD	Sisters of the Love of God (TOCD)
RAD	Warroad, MN [*Location identifier FAA*] (FAAL)
RADA	Radica Games Ltd. [*NASDAQ symbol*] (SAG)
RadA	Radical Alliance [*British*]
RADA	Radioactive
RADA	Random Access Discrete Address [*Army division-level battlefield radio communications system*]
RADA	Realignment of Airdrop Activities (MCD)
RADA	Right Acromio-Dorsoanterior [*A fetal position*] [*Obstetrics*]
RADA	Rosin Amine-D-Acetate [*Medicine*] (DMAA)
RADA	Royal Academy of Dramatic Art [*British*]
RADAC	RADAR Analog Digital Data and Control (KSC)
RADAC	Rapid Digital Automatic Computing
RADAC	Raytheon Automatic Drafting Artwork Compiler
RADACS.......	Random Access Discrete Address Communications System [*Army*]
RadaElc	Rada Electronics Industries Ltd. [*Associated Press*] (SAG)
RADAF	Radica Games [*NASDAQ symbol*] (TTSB)
RADAG........	RADAR Area Correlation Guidance System (PDAA)
RaDaK	Rabbi David Kimhi [*Biblical scholar, 1160-1235*] (BJA)
RADAL	Radio Detection and Location
RADALT	RADAR Altimeter [*Aviation*] (SSD)
RADAM........	Remote Area Denial Artillery Munition [*Military*]
RADAN........	RADAR Analysis System (MCD)
RADAN........	RADAR Doppler Automatic Navigator
RADAN........	RADAR Navigation
RADANT.......	RADOME [*RADAR Dome*] Antenna (NVT)
Radar.	Radar's Reports [*138-163 Missouri*] [*A publication*] (DLA)
RADAR........	Radio Association Defending Airwave Rights (EA)
RADAR........	Radio Detection and Ranging
RADAR........	Radio's All-Dimension Audience Research (NTCM)
RADAR........	Random Access Dump and Reload (IAA)
RADAR........	Rassemblement des Democrates pour l'Avenir de la Reunion [*Rally of Democrats for the Future of Reunion*] [*Political party*] (PPW)
RADAR........	Receivable Accounts Data Entry and Retrieval [*Computer science*] (MHDI)
RADAR........	Reseau d'Approvisionnement et de Debouches d'Affaires [*Business Opportunities Sourcing System - BOSS*] [*Canada*]
RAD-AR	Risk/Benefit Assessment of Drugs - Analysis and Response [*Post-marketing surveillance*]
RADAR........	Royal Association for Disability and Rehabilitation [*British*]
RADARC	Radially Distributed Annular Rocket Chamber
RADAREVALSq...	RADAR Evaluation Squadron [*Air Force*]
RADARSAT...	RADAR Satellite [*Canada*]
RADAS	Random Access Discrete Address System
RADAT	RADAR Alignment Designation Accuracy Test (MCD)
RADAT	RADAR Data Transmission
RADAT	Radio Direction and Track
RADAT	Radiosonde Observation Data
RADATA	RADAR Automatic Data Transmission Assembly (IAA)
RADATA	RADAR Data Transmission and Assembly (IEEE)
RADATAC....	Radiation Data Acquisition Chart
RADATS.......	RADAR Data-Transmission System (WDAA)
RADAUS.......	Radio-Austria AG
RADAY........	Radio Day (CET)
RADB	Radiometric Age Data Bank [*Geological Survey*] [*Information service or system Defunct*] (IID)
RADBIOL.....	Radiobiology
RADBN........	Radio Battalion [*Marine Corps*]
RAD(BPF)......	Rear-Admiral Commanding Destroyers (British Pacific Fleet)
RADC	RADAR Countermeasures and Deception [*Military*] (MCD)
RADC	Regiment Air Defense Center (NATG)
RADC	Review, Approve or Disapprove, and Comment (MCD)

RADC........... Rome Air Development Center [*Griffiss Air Force Base, NY*] [*Air Force*]
RADC.......... Royal Army Dental Corps [*British*]
RADCAP....... Research and Development Contributions to Aviation Progress [*Air Force*]
RADCAS....... Radiation Casualty [*Criteria for battlefield targets*] (MCD)
RADCAT....... RADAR Calibration Target (MCD)
RADCC........ Radiation Control Center
RADCC........ Radiological Control Center [*Army*] (KSC)
RADCC........ Rear Area Damage Control Center (AABC)
RADC/ETR.... Rome Air Development Center Deputy for Electronic Technology [*ESD*]
RADCHM...... Radiochemistry
RADCM........ RADAR Countermeasures and Deception [*Military*]
RADCOL........ RADC [*Rome Air Development Center*] Automatic Document Classification On-Line [*Air Force Information service or system*] (IID)
RADCOM...... Radio Communications (MCD)
RADCOM...... Radiometric Contrast Matching (MCD)
RADCOM...... Research and Development Command (MCD)
RADCON...... RADAR Control
RADCON...... RADAR Data Converter (AFM)
RADCON...... Radiological Control [*Military*] (AABC)
RADCOT....... Radial Optical Tracking Theodolite (MUGU)
RADCS........ RADAR Control Squadron
RADD.......... Royal Association in Aid of the Deaf and Dumb [*British*] (BI)
RADDEF....... Radiological Defense [*To minimize the effect of nuclear radiation on people and resources*]
RADDOL ...... Raddolcendo [*Gradually Softer*] [*Music*]
RADDS........ RADAR Display Distribution System (DWSG)
RADDS........ Raytheon Automated Digital Design System (PDAA)
RADE .... Research and Development Division [*National Security Agency*] [*Obsolete*]
RADEC........ Radiation Detection Capability (MCD)
RADEF........ Radiological Defense [*To minimize the effect of nuclear radiation on people and resources*]
Ra de Hacur... Raoul d'Harcourt [*Deceased, 1307*] [*Authority cited in pre-1607 legal work*] (DSA)
RADELECTENG... Radio and Electronic Engineer (IAA)
RADEM........ Random Access Delta Modulation
RADEP......... RADAR Departure [*Aviation*] (FAAC)
RADER......... Rassemblement Democratique du Ruanda [*Democratic Rally of Rwanda*]
RADES......... RADAR Evaluation Squadron [*Air Force*]
RADES......... Realistic Air Defense Engagement System [*Army*] (RDA)
RADEX........ RADAR Data Extractor (PDAA)
RADEX........ RADAR Exercise (NVT)
RADEX........ Radiation Exclusion Plot [*Chart of actual or predicted fallout*]
RADFAC....... Radiating Facility
RADFAL....... Radiological Prediction Fallout Plot
RADFET....... Radiation-Sensing Field Effect Transistor [*Instrumentation*]
RADFO........ Radiological Fallout [*Army*]
Radford U.... Radford University (GAGS)
RADHAZ...... Radiation Hazards
RADHAZ...... Radio Frequency Hazard (IAA)
RADI .... Rada Electronic Industries Ltd. [*New York, NY NASDAQ symbol*] (NQ)
RADI .... Radio Area of Dominant Influence [*Advertising*] (DOAD)
RADI .... Radiographic Inspection [*NASA*] (AAG)
Radi........... Radium [*Record label*] [*France*]
RADI .... Register of Approved Driving Instructors (WDAA)
RADI .... Retail Alarm for Display and Intruder (PDAA)
RADIAC....... Radiation Detection, Indication, and Computation [*Radiological measuring instruments*]
RADIAC....... Radioactive Detection and Measurement
RADIAC....... Radio Activity Detection, Identification and Computation (IAA)
RADIAL....... Radial [*Commonly used*] (OPSA)
RADIALS...... Research and Development in Information and Library Science (NITA)
RADIAT....... Radiation
RADIC......... Radical (ROG)
RADIC......... Radio Interior Communications
RADIC......... Redifon Analog-Digital Computer [*British*]
RADIC......... Research and Development Information Center (AFM)
RadicaG...... Radica Games Ltd. [*Associated Press*] (SAG)
Radical Ed... Radical Education [*A publication*]
Radical Ed Dossier... Radical Education Dossier [*A publication*]
RADIC-LIB ... Radical Liberal
RADICS....... Research and Development in Computer System (IAA)
RADIEL....... Radial [*Commonly used*] (OPSA)
RADIF......... Rada Electronics Industries [*NASDAQ symbol*] (TTSB)
RADIL......... Research Animal Diagnostic and Investigative Laboratory [*University of Missouri-Columbia*] [*Research center*] (RCD)
RADINJCLRDS... Radiation Injury Claims Record (DNAB)
RADINT........ RADAR Intelligence
RADINT........ Radio Intelligence [*Military*] (IAA)
RADIO......... Radiotherapy
RADIOBIOL.... Radiobiology
RADIOCHEM... Radiochemistry
RADIOG ...... Radiography (IAA)
Radio Hobbies Aust... Radio and Hobbies Australia [*A publication*]
radio-IEP..... Radioimmunoelectrophoresis [*Biochemistry*] (DAVI)
Radiol......... Radiology
Radio Rev Aust... Radio Review of Australia [*A publication*]
RADIQUAD... Radio Quadrangle [*Military*]

RADIR.......... Random Access Document Indexing and Retrieval
RADISH........ Rheumatoid Arthritis Diffuse Idiopathic Skeletal Hyperostosis (DAVI)
RAD ISO VENO BILAT... Radioactive Isotopic Venogram, Bilateral [*Nuclear Medicine*] (DAVI)
RADIST......... RADAR Distance Indicator
RadiSys........ RadiSys Corp. [*Associated Press*] (SAG)
RADIT......... Radio Teletype (IEEE)
Radius......... Radius, Inc. [*Associated Press*] (SAG)
RADIUS........ Religious Drama Society of Great Britain (BUAC)
RADIUS........ Remote Access Dial-In User Service [*Computer science*] (IGQR)
RADIUS........ Remote Authentication Dial-In User Service [*Computer science*] (PCM)
RADIUS........ Research and Development Institute of the United States [*Research center*] (RCD)
RADIUS........ Research and Development in the United States [*Database*]
RADL .... Radial
RADL .... Radiological [*or Radiology*] (AAG)
RADLAB....... Radiation Laboratory (AAG)
RADLAC....... Radial Pulse Line Accelerators (MCD)
RADLCEN..... Radiological Center
RADLDEF...... Radiological Defense [*To minimize the effect of nuclear radiation on people and resources*]
RADLDEFLAB... Radiological Defense Laboratory [*NASA*]
RADLFO....... Radiological Fallout [*Army*] (AABC)
RADLGC....... Radiologic
RADLGCL...... Radiological
RADLGY....... Radiology
RADLMON ... Radiological Monitor [*or Monitoring*] [*Military*]
RADLO .... Radiological Officer
RADLOPS..... Radiological Operations [*Military*] (AABC)
RADLSAFE... Radiological Safety [*Military*]
RADLSO...... Radiological Survey Officer [*Military*]
RADLSV...... Radiological Survey [*Military*]
RadLV........ Radiation Leukemia Virus [*Medicine*] (DMAA)
RADLWAR ... Radiological Warfare
RADM .... RADARman (GFGA)
RADM .... Random Walk Advection and Dispersion Model [*Environmental Protection Agency*] (GFGA)
RADM .... Rear Admiral [*Also, RA, RADML*] (AAG)
Radm.......... Rear Admiral
RADM .... Regional Acid Deposition Model [*for acid rain*] [*Environmental Protection Agency*]
RADMAP...... Radiological Monitoring Assessment Prediction System (PDAA)
RADMIS....... Research Activities Designators Management Information System
RADMON .... Radiological Monitoring (AFM)
RADN......... Radiation (AAG)
RADN......... Radnorshire [*County in Wales*]
RADNAV ..... Radio Navigation [*USCG*] (TAG)
RADNO........ Report Missing Account Radio Failure [*Meteorology*] (FAAC)
RADNORS.... Radnorshire [*County in Wales*] (ROG)
RADNOS ...... No Radio [*Military*]
RADNOTE .... Radio Note [*Military*]
RADOC........ Regional Air Defense Operations Center (NATO)
RADOC........ Remote Automatic Detection Contingencies
RADOD .... Research and Development Objectives Document (MCD)
RADOME...... RADAR Dome [*NASA*]
RADON .... RADAR Beacon
RADON .... Research and Development Operational Needs (MCD)
RADOP........ RADAR Doppler [*Missile-tracking system*] (AAG)
RADOP........ RADAR Operator (CET)
RADOP........ RADAR/Optical Weapons [*Military*]
RADOP........ Radio Operator [*Navy*]
RADOPR....... Radio Operator (AAG)
RADOPWEAP... RADAR Optical Weapons (IEEE)
RADOSE...... Radiation Dosimeter Satellite [*NASA*]
RADOT........ Real-Time [*or Recording*] Automatic Digital Optical Tracker
RADP......... Right Acromio-Dorsoposterior [*A fetal position*] [*Obstetrics*]
RADPLANBD... Radio Planning Board [*Navy*]
RADPROPCAST... Radio Propagation Forecast
RADREF....... RADAR Refraction (MCD)
RADREL....... Radio Relay [*Military*]
RADRELRON... Radio Relay Squadron [*Military*] (IAA)
RADREPMN... Radio Repairman (IAA)
RADRON ...... RADAR Squadron [*Air Force*]
RADRONMOB... Radio Squadron, Mobile [*Military*] (IAA)
RADRU........ Rapid Access Data Retrieval Unit [*Computer science*] (PDAA)
RADS.......... RADAR Alphanumeric Display Sub-System (PDAA)
RADS.......... Radar and Algorithm Display Model (USDC)
RADS.......... RADAR Squadron [*Air Force*]
RAD/S......... Radians per Second
RADS.......... Radiation and Dosimetry Services (NRCH)
RADS.......... Radiation Systems, Inc. (EFIS)
RADS.......... Radius (AAG)
RADS.......... Rapid Area Distribution Support [*Air Force*]
RADS.......... Raw Data System
RADS.......... Reactive Airway Disease Sydrome [*Medicine*] (STED)
RADS.......... Reactive Airways Dysfunction Syndrome [*Medicine*] (DMAA)
RADS.......... Real-Time Analysis and Display System [*Marine science*] (OSRA)
RADS.......... Retiree Activity Days [*DoD*]
RADS.......... Retrospective Assessment of Drug Safety [*Medicine*] (DB)
RADS.......... Reynolds Adolescent Depression Scale [*Test*] (TES)
RADS.......... Ryukyu Air Defense System
RAD/S²........ Radians per Second Squared
RADSAFE..... Radiological Safety [*Military*]
RADSCAT..... Radiometer/Scatterometer [*Sensor*] [*Meteorology*]

RADSEC	Radio Section (IAA)
RADSIM	Random Access Discrete Address System Simulator [*Army*] (IAA)
RADSL	Rate Adaptive Digital Subscriber Line (PCM)
RADSO	Radiological Survey Officer (IEEE)
RADSOC	Request for Authority to Develop a System or Change [*Military*] (AFIT)
RADSTA	Radio Station
RadT	Radiola-Telefunken [*Record label*] [*Australia*]
R/ADT	Registration/Admission, Disposition and Transfer [*Tri-Service Medical Information System*] (DNAB)
Rad Ther	Radiation Therapy (DAVI)
Rad Ther	Radiotherapy (STED)
RADTR	Radiator
RADTS	Rabbit Antidog Thymus Serum [*Immunology*] (MAE)
RADTT	Radiation Therapy Technologist (HCT)
RADTT	Radio Teletypewriter (CET)
RADU	RADAR Analysis and Detection Unit (WDAA)
RADU	RADAR Analysis and Development Unit [*National Severe Storms Forecast Center*] (NOAA)
RADU	Ram Air-Driven Unit
RAD-UDRT	Respect voor Arbeid en Democratie/Union Democratique pour le Respect du Travail [*Respect for Labor and Democracy/Democratic Union for the Respect of Labor*] [*Belgium Political party*] (PPE)
Rad UI	Radius-Ulna [*Medicine*] (MAE)
RADVS	RADAR Altimeter and Doppler Velocity Sensor
RADWAR	Radiological Warfare
RADWASTE	Radioactive Waste
RADY	Radiology
RAE	Arar [*Saudi Arabia*] [*Airport symbol*] (OAG)
RA(E)	Engineer Rear-Admiral [*Navy British*] (DMA)
RAE	Farnborough Rae [*British*] [*FAA designator*] (FAAC)
RaE	Rabbit Erythrocyte (STED)
RAE	RADAR Altimeter Equipment
RAE	Radio Astronomy Explorer [*Satellite*]
RAE	Radiodifusion Argentina al Exterior [*Broadcasting organization*] [*Argentina*]
RAE	Range, Azimuth, and Elevation (MCD)
RAE	Report After Execution (AAGC)
RAE	Research and Engineering (IAA)
RAE	Research Assessment Exercise [*Higher Education Funding Council*] (AIE)
RAE	Residue After Evaporation (AAEL)
RAE	Review of Applied Entomology [*Database*] [*Commonwealth Institute of Entomology*] [*Information service or system*] (CRD)
RAE	Right Arithmetic Element
RAE	Right Ascension Encoder
RAE	Right Atrial Enlargement [*Cardiology*]
RAE	Royal Aeronautical Establishment [*British*] (IAA)
RAE	Royal Aerospace Establishment [*British*] (WA)
RAE	Royal Aircraft Establishment [*British Ministry of Defense*] [*Research center*]
RAE	Royal Army Establishment [*British*]
RAE	Russian Antarctic Expedition
RAEA	Regroupement des Auteurs-Editeurs Autonomes [*Canada*]
RAEB	Refractory Anemia, Erythroblastic [*Hematology*] (DAVI)
RAEB	Refractory Anemia with Excess of Blasts [*Hematology*]
RAEB-T	Refractory Anemia with Excess of Blasts in Transformation [*Hematology*]
RAEC	Rabbit Aortic Endothelial Cells
R Ae C	Royal Aero Club [*British*] (BARN)
RAEC	Royal Army Educational Corps [*British*]
RAECO	Rare-Earth Cobalt
RAEDOT	Range, Azimuth, and Elevation Detection of Optical Targets
RA EM	Radium Emanation (WDAA)
RAEM	Refractory Anemia with Excess Myeloblast [*Hematology*] (MAE)
RAEN	Radio Amateur Emergency Network (IEEE)
RAEN	Russian Academy of the Natural Sciences (BUAC)
RaeRG	Reallexikon der Aegyptischen Religionsgeschichte [*Berlin*] [*A publication*] (BJA)
RAES	Radio Astronomy Experiment Selection Panel
RAES	Rapid Access with Extensive Search [*Algorithm*]
RAES	Ratios for Automotive Executives [*Computer software*]
RAES	Remote Access Editing System [*Computer science*] (IEEE)
RAES	Retail Automated Execution System (NUMA)
RAeS	Royal Aeronautical Society [*British*] (EAIO)
RAET	Range, Azimuth, Elevation, and Time
RAETDS	Reciprocating Aircraft Engine Type Designation System
RAETU	Reserve Airborne Electronics Training Unit (DNAB)
RAF	Farnas Aviation Services [*Sudan*] [*FAA designator*] (FAAC)
RAF	Racial Awareness Facilitator [*School*] [*Navy*] (NVT)
Ra F	Raphael Fulgosius [*Deceased, 1427*] [*Authority cited in pre-1607 legal work*] (DSA)
RAF	Regional Arab Federation of Associations for Voluntary Fertility Control (BUAC)
RAF	Regular Air Force
RAF	Repetitive Atrial Firing [*Medicine*] (DMAA)
RAF	Requirements Allocation Form
RAF	Requirements Analysis From [*NASA*] (NASA)
RAF	Research Aviation Facility [*National Center for Atmospheric Research*]
RAF	Reserved Air Freight
RAF	Resource Allocation Formula
RAF	Reynolds Analogy Factor [*Physics*]
RAF	Rheumatoid Arthritis Factor [*Medicine*] (MAE)

RAF	River Assault Flotilla [*Navy*] (VNW)
RAF	Rote Armee Faktion [*Red Army Faction (Baader-Meinhof Group)*] [*Terrorist group*] [*Germany*]
RAF	Royal Aircraft Factory [*World War I*] [*British*]
RAF	Royal Air Force [*British*]
RAF	Sacramento, CA [*Location identifier FAA*] (FAAL)
RAFA	Rank Annihilation Factor Analysis [*Computer science*]
RAFA	Royal Air Forces Association (EAIO)
Ra Fab	Raymundus Fabri [*Flourished, 14th century*] [*Authority cited in pre-1607 legal work*] (DSA)
RAFAC	Radio Aids and Facilities (IAA)
Rafair	Royal Air Force [*Airline call sign*] [*British*]
RAFAR	Radio Automated Facsimile and Reproduction
RAFAX	RADAR Facsimile
RAFB	Randolph Air Force Base [*Texas*]
RAFB	Rickenbacker Air Force Base [*Formerly, Lockbourne Air Force Base*] [*Ohio*]
RAFB	Royal Air Force Base [*British*]
RAFBF	Royal Air Force Benevolent Fund [*British military*] (DMA)
RAFC	Regional Area Forecast Center [*ICAO designator*] (FAAC)
RAFC	Richmond Area Film Cooperative [*Library network*]
RAFC	Royal Air Force Club [*British*]
RAFC	Royal Air Force College [*British*]
RAFC	Royal Artillery Flying Club [*British military*] (DMA)
RAFCC	Royal Air Force Cinema Corp. [*British military*] (DMA)
RAFCC	Royal Air Force Coastal Command [*British*]
RAFCWA	Rural Adjustment and Finance Corp. of Western Australia [*Computer science*]
RAFD	Rome Air Force Depot
RAFES	Royal Air Force Educational Service [*British military*] (DMA)
RAFFC	Royal Air Force Fighter Command [*British*]
Raff Pens Man	Raff's Pension Manual [*A publication*] (DLA)
RAFG	Royal Air Force, Germany [*British military*] (DMA)
RAFGSA	Royal Air Force Gliding and Soaring Association (BUAC)
RAFH	Royal Air Force Historical Society (BUAC)
RAFHS	Royal Air Force Historical Society [*British*] (DBA)
RAFI	Radiosonde Observation Not Filed [*NWS*] (FAAC)
RAFI	Rural Advancement Foundation International
RAFI	Rural Advancement Fund International [*Later, RAFI-USA*] (EA)
RAFIAM	Royal Air Force Institute of Aviation Medicine [*British*] (IAA)
RAFLO	Radio Frequency Liaison Office [*Navy*] (DNAB)
RAFM	Repair-at-Failure Maintenance (PDAA)
RAFME	Royal Air Force, Middle East [*British military*] (DMA)
RAFMS	Royal Air Force Medical Service [*British*]
RAFNS	Royal Air Force Nursing Service [*British military*] (DMA)
RAFO	Reserve Air Force Officers [*Later, RAFRO*] [*British*]
RAFO	Resident Air Force Officer [*Australia*]
RAFOS	Royal Air Force Ornithological Society (BUAC)
RAFR	Royal Air Force Regiment [*British*]
RAFRC	Revolutionary Armed Forces of the Republic of Cuba
RAFRO	Royal Air Force Reserve of Officers [*Formerly, RAFO*] [*British*]
RAFRZ	Radiosonde Observation Freezing Levels [*NWS*] (FAAC)
RAFS	R. Austin Freeman Society (EA)
RAFS	Regional Analysis and Forecast System [*National Meteorological Center*]
RAFS	Remote Area Families Service [*Uniting Church*] [*Australia*]
RAFS	Royal Air Force Station [*British*] (MCD)
RAFSA	Royal Air Force Sailing Association [*British*] (BI)
RAFSAA	Royal Air Force Small Arms Association [*British military*] (DMA)
RAFSC	Royal Air Force Staff College [*British*]
RAFSC	Royal Air Force Strike Command (BUAC)
RAFSC	Royal Air Force Support Command [*British*]
RAFSP	Royal Air Force Service Police [*British military*] (DMA)
RAFSTN	Royal Air Force Air Station
RAFT	Racial Awareness Facilitator Training [*Navy program*]
RAFT	Radially Adjustable Facility Tube (IEEE)
RAFT	Rear-Admiral Fleet Train [*British Pacific Fleet*]
RAFT	Receiving Ambient Function Test (PDAA)
RAFT	Recomp Algebraic Formula Translator [*Computer science*]
RAFT	Reentry Advanced Fusing Test (IAA)
RAFT	Regional Accounting and Finance Test [*Military*] (AFM)
RAFT	Resource Allocation for Transportation (DNAB)
RAFT	Retail Association for the Furnishing Trade [*British*] (BI)
RAFT	Reunion des Amateurs de Fox Terriers [*An association*] (EAIO)
RAFT	Revolving Acceptance Facility by Tender [*Finance*]
RAFT	Rotate and Flip Test [*Taylor and Ebertsohn*] (TES)
RAFTC	Royal Air Forces Transport Command [*British*]
Ra Fulgo	Raphael Fulgosius [*Deceased, 1427*] [*Authority cited in pre-1607 legal work*] (DSA)
RAFVR	Royal Air Force Volunteer Reserve [*British*]
RAFW	Right Atrial Free Wall [*Medicine*] (DMAA)
RAG	Radical Anthropology Group (BUAC)
Rag	Ragland's California Superior Court Decisions [*A publication*] (DLA)
RAG	Ragweed [*Medicine*] (DMAA)
RAG	Ragweed Pollen Antigen (DB)
RAG	Rainforest Action Group [*Australia*]
RAG	Readiness Analysis Group
RAG	Recombination-Activating Gene
RAG	Regimental Artillery Group [*OPFOR*] (GFGA)
RAG	Regional Advisory Group [*Generic term*] (DHSM)
RAg	Related Antigen [*Immunology*]
RAG	Religious Arts Guild [*Defunct*] (EA)
RAG	Replacement Air Group
RAG	Requirements Advisory Group [*Air Force*] (MCD)
RAG	Resource Appraisal Group [*US Geological Survey*]

RAG .... Retail Associates Group, Inc. [*Homesewing industry trade group*]
RAG .... Returned Ammunition Group (NATG)
RAG .... Reusable Agena [*NASA*] (NASA)
RAG .... Ring Airfoil Grenade [*Army*]
RAG .... River Assault Group [*Military*]
RAG .... ROM [*Read-Only Memory*] Address Gate [*Computer science*]
RAG .... Runway Arresting Gear [*Aviation*]
RAG-1 .... Rosenberg, Avraham, and Gutnick [*Strain of bacteria named for its researchers: Eugene Rosenberg, Avraham Reisfield, and David Gutnick*]
Ragan .... Ragan [*Brad*], Inc. [*Associated Press*] (SAG)
RAGB .... Refractories Association of Great Britain (BI)
RAGB .... Restaurateurs Association (BUAC)
RAGBRAI .... Register's Annual Great Bicycle Ride Across Iowa
RAGC .... Rainbows for All God's Children [*Later, RFAGC*] (EA)
RAGC .... Relief General Communications Vessel
RAGC .... Royal and Ancient Golf Club [*Scotland*]
RAGE .... Radio Amplification of Gamma Emissions [*Antiguerrilla weapon*]
RAGE .... Radiotherapy Action Group Exposure [*An association*] (BUAC)
RAGE .... Rapid Gradient Echo (DMAA)
RAGE .... Receptor for Advanced Glycation End-Product [*Biochemistry*]
RAGEMS ...... Radioactive Gaseous Effluent Monitoring System
RAGES .... Rail Armed Guard Escort Service [*Military Traffic Management Command*]
RAGF .... Remote Air-Ground Facility [*Aviation*]
Ragg .... Rheumatoid Agglutinator [*Immunology*]
RAGS .... Rag Shops [*NASDAQ symbol*] (TTSB)
RAGS .... Rag Shops, Inc. [*NASDAQ symbol*] (SAG)
RAGS .... Recycling Advisory Group Scotland (BUAC)
RAGS .... Repulsive Axon Guidance Signal [*Biochemistry*]
RAGS .... Risk Assessment Guidance for Superfund [*Environmental science*]
RAGS .... Risk Assessments Guidance for Superfund [*Environmental Protection Agency*]
RagShp .... Rag Shops, Inc. [*Associated Press*] (SAG)
Rag Super Ct Dec (Calif)... Ragland's California Superior Court Decisions [*A publication*] (DLA)
RAH .... Rabbit Anti-Human [*Immunology*]
RAH .... Radiation-Anneal Hardening [*Alloy*]
RAH .... Rafha [*Saudi Arabia*] [*Airport symbol*] (OAG)
RAH .... Ralcorp Holdings [*NYSE symbol*] (SAG)
RAH .... Receipt, Excess, Adjustment, Due-In History File [*Army*]
RAH .... Receiving Array Hydrophone
RAH .... Reconnaissance Attack Helicopter
RAH .... Regent Air [*Canada ICAO designator*] (FAAC)
RAH .... Regressing Atypical Histiocytosis [*Medicine*]
RAH .... Reviews in American History [*A publication*] (BRI)
RAH .... Right Anterior Hemiblock [*Medicine*] (AAMN)
RAH .... Right Atrial Hypertrophy [*Cardiology*]
RAH .... Royal Albert Hall [*London, England*]
RAHCAR ...... Refugee Ad Hoc Campaign for Asylum Rights (BUAC)
RAHF .... Research Animal Holding Facility [*NASA*] (NASA)
RaHGBM ...... Rabbit Anti-Human Glomerular Basement Membrane [*Immunology*]
RAHLO .... Regional Aboriginal Health Liaison Officer [*Australia*]
RAHO .... Rabbit Antibody to Human Ovary [*Medicine*] (DMAA)
RAHO .... Rabbits Against Human Ovary [*Immunology*]
RAHO .... Royal Albert Hall Orchestra
RAHS .... Royal Australian Historical Society (BUAC)
RAHTG .... Rabbit Anti-Human Thymocyte Globulin [*Immunology*] (AAMN)
RAHTS .... Rabbit Anti-Human Thymocyte Serum [*Immunology*] (OA)
RAI .... Praia [*Cape Verde Islands*] [*Airport symbol*] (OAG)
RAI .... Racquetball Association of Ireland (EAIO)
RAI .... RADAR Altimeter Indicator (MCD)
RAI .... Radiational Aridity Index (EES)
RAI .... Radiation Applications, Inc.
RAI .... Radioactive Interference [*NASA*]
RAI .... Radioactive Iodine [*Medicine*]
RAI .... Radioactive Isotope [*Roentgenology*]
Rai .... Rainerius [*Authority cited in pre-1607 legal work*] (DSA)
RAI .... Random Access and Inquiry [*Computer science*]
RAI .... Range Azimuth Indicator
RAI .... Rapid Attentional Integration (DB)
RAI .... Raspberry Island [*Alaska*] [*Seismograph station code, US Geological Survey*] (SEIS)
RAI .... Rassemblement Arabique-Islamique [*Algeria*] [*Political party*] (EY)
RAI .... Reading Association of Ireland (BUAC)
RAI .... Receiving and Inspection (IAA)
RAI .... Reliability Assurance Instructions (KSC)
RAI .... Removal and Installation (IAA)
RAI .... Repair at Intermediate (MCD)
RAI .... Request for Additional Information (NRCH)
RAI .... Research Advisory Institute, Inc.
RAI .... Resource Analysts, Inc.
RAI .... Restaurants Association of Ireland (BUAC)
RAI .... Roll Attitude Indicator [*NASA*]
RAI .... Rounders Association of Ireland (EAIO)
RAI .... Royal Air Inter-Compagnie d'Exploitation de Lignes Aer Interieures [*Morocco*] [*ICAO designator*] (FAAC)
RAI .... Royal Albert Institution [*British*] (DAS)
RAI .... Royal Anthropological Institute [*British*]
RAI .... Royal Archaeological Institute [*British*]
RAI .... Royal Artillery Institution [*British military*] (DMA)
RAI .... Runway Alignment Indicator [*Aviation*]
RAI .... Rural America, Inc. (EA)
RAIA .... Royal Australian Institute of Architects (BUAC)

RAIAD .... Reverse Acronyms, Initialisms, and Abbreviations Dictionary [*Formerly, RAID*] [*A publication*]
RAIAM .... Random Access Indestructive Advanced Memory [*Computer science*] (MSA)
RAIC .... Radiological Accident and Incident Control
RAIC .... Red Andina de Informacion Comercial [*Andean Trade Information Network*] (EAIO)
RAIC .... Redstone Arsenal Information Center [*Army*]
RAIC .... Royal Architectural Institute of Canada
RAICG .... Radiosonde Observation Icing At [*NWS*] (FAAC)
RAID .... RADAR Identification and Direction System (NG)
RAID .... Radioimmunodetection [*Medicine*] (DB)
RAID .... Ram Air-Inflated Drogue [*Military*] (CAAL)
RAID .... Ram-Air Inflation Decelerator [*Munitions*] (RDA)
RAID .... Random Access Image Device [*Computer science*] (IAA)
RAID .... Random Access Interactive Debugger (IAA)
RAID .... Rapid Alerting and Identification Display (PDAA)
RAID .... Real-Time Applications Interactive Debugger (MCD)
RAID .... Recallable Airborne Infrared Display
RAID .... Reconnaissance and Interdiction Detachment [*Army*] (DOMA)
RAID .... Reduced Array of Inexpensive Drives [*Computer science*]
RAID .... Redundant Array of Independent Disks [*Computer science*] (CDE)
RAID .... Redundant Arrays of Inexpensive Disks [*Computer science*]
RAID .... Remote Access Interactive Debugger [*Computer science*] (IEEE)
RAID .... Reverse Acronyms and Initialisms Dictionary [*Later, RAIAD*] [*A publication*]
RAID .... River Assault Interdiction Division [*Navy*] (NVT)
RAIDERS ..... Remote Automated Issue, Document Entry, and Register System [*Army*]
RAIDEX .... Antisurface Raiders Exercise [*NATO*] (NATG)
RAIDS .... Rapid Acquisition and Identification System
RAIDS .... Rapid Availability of Information and Data for Safety [*NASA*] (KSC)
RAIDS .... Recently Acquired Income Deficiency Syndrome
RAIDS .... Reduced Annual Income Deficiency Syndrome [*British*]
RAIF .... Reseau d'Action et d'Information pour les Femmes [*Canada*]
RAIL .... RailAmerica, Inc. [*NASDAQ symbol*] (SAG)
RAIL .... Railroad Advancement through Information and Law Foundation
RAIL .... Railway (ROG)
RAIL .... Runway Alignment Indicator Light [*or Lighting*] [*Aviation*]
RailAm .... RailAmerica, Inc. [*Associated Press*] (SAG)
Rail & Can Cas... English Railway and Canal Cases [*A publication*] (DLA)
Rail & Can Cas... Railway and Canal Traffic Cases [*A publication*] (DLA)
Rail Ca .... Railway and Canal Cases [*1835-54*] [*A publication*] (DLA)
Rail Cas ...... Railway Cases [*A publication*] (DLA)
RailFn .... Railroad Financial Corp. [*Associated Press*] (SAG)
RAILS .... Remote Area Instrument Landing Sensor [*Army*]
RAILS .... Remote Area Instrument Landing System [*Army*]
RAILS .... Report of Assets in Long Supply
RAILS .... Runway Alignment Indicator Light [*or Lighting*] System [*Aviation*] (MCD)
Railtex .... Railtex, Inc. [*Associated Press*] (SAG)
Railway & Corp Law J... Railway and Corporation Law Journal [*A publication*] (DLA)
Railw Cas .... Railway Cases [*A publication*] (DLA)
RAILZ .... RailAmerica Inc. Wrrt 'B' [*NASDAQ symbol*] (TTSB)
RAIM .... Receiver Autonomous Integrity Monitoring [*Computer software*]
RAIMAZ .... Records, Archives, and Information Management Association of Zimbabwe (BUAC)
RAIN .... Rainforest Cafe [*NASDAQ symbol*] (TTSB)
RAIN .... Rainforest Cafe, Inc. [*NASDAQ symbol*] (SAG)
RAIN .... Relational Algebraic Interpreter
RAIN .... Relief for Africans in Need (EA)
RAIN .... Reporting Advocacy and Information Network [*National Court Reporters Association*]
RAIN .... Reversing Acidification in Norway
RAIN .... Royal Anthropological Institute News [*Later, Anthropology Today*] [*A publication*]
RAINBO .... Research and Instrumentation for National Bio-Science Operations (MUGU)
RaInCfe .... Rainforest Cafe, Inc. [*Associated Press*] (SAG)
RAINDX .... Random Access Index Edit [*Computer science*] (IAA)
RAINIT .... Random Access Initializer [*Computer science*] (IAA)
RAINN .... Rape, Abuse, and Incest National Network
RAINPAL ...... Recursive Aided Inertial Navigation for Precision Approach and Landing [*NASA*]
RAINS .... Regional Acidification Information and Simulation [*International Institute for Applied Systems Analysis*]
RainTc .... Rainbow Technologies, Inc. [*Associated Press*] (SAG)
RAI/OP .... Repetitive Activity Input/Output Plan (PDAA)
RAIP .... Recruiting Advertising Improvement Program [*Navy*] (DNAB)
RAIP .... Requester's Approval in Principle (NRCH)
RAIPA .... Royal Australian Institute of Public Administration (BUAC)
RAIPR .... Royal Australian Institute of Parks and Recreation (BUAC)
RAIR .... Ram-Augmented Interstellar Rocket (WDAA)
RAIR .... Random Access Information Retrieval [*Computer science*] (IEEE)
RAIR .... Rapid Advancement in Reading [*Education*]
RAIR .... Recordak Automated Information Retrieval [*System*]
RAIR .... Reflection Absorption Infrared Spectroscopy [*Also, IRAS, IRRAS, RAIRS, RAIS*]
RAIR .... Remote-Access Immediate Response [*Computer science*] (MHDB)
RAIRE .... Recognition Awards for the Integration of Research and Education [*National Science Foundation*]
RAIRS .... Railroad Accident/Incident Reporting System [*Department of Transportation*]

RAIRS......... Reflection Absorption Infrared Spectroscopy [*Also, IRAS, IRRAS, RAIR, RAIS*]
RAIS .... Rabbit Antiserum to Rat Lymphocytes (DB)
RAIS .... Rail Air International Service (PDAA)
RAIS .... Range Automated Information System (KSC)
RAIS .... Reflection Absorption Infrared Spectroscopy [*Also, IRAS, IRRAS, RAIR, RAIRS*]
RAISE .... Reliability Accelerated In-Service Echelon (MCD)
RAISE .... Rigorous Approach to Industrial Software Engineering [*British*]
RAIST .... Reseau Africain d'Institutions Scientifiques et Technologiques [*African Network of Scientific and Technological Institutions*] (EAIO)
RAIT............. Radioimmunotherapy [*Medicine*]
RAIT............. Reading Attitude Imagination Technique (EDAC)
Raith St ...... Raithby's English Statutes at Large [*A publication*] (DLA)
Raith St ...... Raithby's Study of the Law [*A publication*] (DLA)
RAI-TV .... Radio Audizioni Italiana-Televisione [*Italian Radio Broadcasting and Television Company*]
RAIU .... Radioiodide Uptake [*Endocrinology*]
RAIX .... Rosenbalm Aviation [*Air carrier designation symbol*]
Raj................ All India Reporter, Rajasthan [*A publication*] (DLA)
Raj................ Rajaratam Revised Reports [*Ceylon*] [*A publication*] (DLA)
raj................. Rajasthani [*MARC language code Library of Congress*] (LCCP)
RAJ.............. Raji Airlines [*Pakistan*] [*ICAO designator*] (FAAC)
RAJ.............. Rajkot [*India*] [*Airport symbol*] (OAG)
Rajasthan .... Indian Law Reports, Rajasthan Series [*A publication*] (DLA)
RAJFC.......... Rex Allen, Jr. Fan Club (EA)
RAJPO .... Range Applications Joint Program Office
RAK .... Marrakech [*Morocco*] [*Airport symbol*] (OAG)
RAK .... Rakhov [*Former USSR Seismograph station code, US Geological Survey Closed*] (SEIS)
RAK .... Read Access Key
RAK .... Remote Access Key
RAK .... Riga Airclub (Latvian Professional Air Sport Center) [*FAA designator*] (FAAC)
RAKE .... Rocket Assisted Kinetic Energy [*Army*] (DOMA)
RAKKASANS... 187th Airborne Regimental Combat Team Association (EA)
RAKO .... Rawson-Koenig [*NASDAQ symbol*] (TTSB)
RAKO .... Rawson-Koenig, Inc. [*NASDAQ symbol*] (NQ)
RAKTP .... Royal Arch Knight Templar Priest [*Freemasonry*]
RAL .... Rabalanakaia [*New Britain*] [*Seismograph station code, US Geological Survey*] (SEIS)
RAL.............. Radio Annoyance Level (OA)
RAL.............. Radio Astronomy Laboratory [*Research center*] (RCD)
RAL.............. Ralston-Purina Group [*NYSE symbol*] (SPSG)
RAL.............. Rapid Access Loop
RAL.............. Rear-Admiral, Alexandria [*British*]
RAL.............. Reenlistment Allowance [*Military*]
RAL.............. Regional Adjunct Language [*Computer science*] (PDAA)
RAL.............. Register of Additional Locations [*Library of Congress*]
RAL.............. Remote Area Landing (NG)
RAL.............. Reports and Analysis Letter (OICC)
RAL.............. Required Average Life (MCD)
RAL.............. Resorcylic Acid Lactone [*Veterinary pharmacology*]
RAL.............. Responsibility Assignment List [*NASA*] (NASA)
RAL.............. Reynold's Aluminum Co. of Canada Ltd. [*Toronto Stock Exchange symbol*]
RAL.............. Riverband Acoustical Laboratory (KSC)
RAL.............. Riverside [*California*] [*Airport symbol*] (OAG)
RAL.............. Riverside, CA [*Location identifier FAA*] (FAAL)
RAL.............. Robotics & Automation Research Laboratory [*University of Toronto*] [*Research center*] (RCD)
RAL.............. Roswell Airlines, Inc. [*ICAO designator*] (FAAC)
RAL.............. Rubber-Air-Lead [*Tile*]
RAL.............. Rutherford and Appleton Laboratory [*Observatory*] [*British*]
RALA .... Registered Automatic Line Adapter [*Computer science*] (CIST)
RALAC .... RADAR Altimeter Low-Altitude Control [*Military*] (CAAL)
RALAC .... Refuse and Litter Advisory Committee [*Australia*]
RALAC .... Rehabilitation Artificial Limb, and Appliance Centre [*Australia*]
RALACS .... RADAR Altimeter Low-Altitude Control System [*Military*] (NG)
RALA-EHF.... Roycrofters-at-Large Association/Elbert Hubbard Foundation (EA)
Ralcorp........ Ralcorp Holdings [*Associated Press*] (SAG)
RALD........... Richmond Area Library Directors [*Library network*]
RALF........... Rapid Access to Literature Via Fragmentation Codes (NITA)
RALF........... Relocatable Assembly Language Floating Point
RALF........... Robotic Assistant Labor Facilitator [*In the movie "Flight of the Navigator" (1986)*]
RALFH .... Random Access Logical File Handler (MCD)
RALI............ Regimento de Artilharia Ligeira [*Light Artillery Regiment*] [*Portuguese*]
RALI............ Remarried Association of Long Island (EA)
RALI............ Resource and Land Investigation [*Program*] [*Department of the Interior*] (GRD)
RALL........... Rallentando [*Gradually Slower*] [*Music*]
rall.............. Rallentando [*Slackening the Pace*] [*Italian*] [*Music*] (WDAA)
RALLA .... Regional Allied Long-Lines Agency [*Formerly, RELLA*] (NATG)
RALLEN ...... Rallentando [*Gradually Slower*] [*Music*] (ROG)
RALLO .... Rallentando [*Gradually Slower*] [*Music*] (ROG)
RALLOC ...... Random Access Allocation [*Computer science*] (IAA)
Rallys......... Rally's, Inc. [*Associated Press*] (SAG)
RALMC .... Remote Aboriginal Language Management Committee [*Australia*]
RALPH .... Rapidly Adapting Lateral Position Handler
RALPH .... Reduction and Acquisition of Lunar Pulse Heights [*NASA*] (NASA)
RALPH .... Royal Association for the Longevity and Preservation of the Honeymooners (EA)
RALS .... Remote Augmented Lift System (MCD)

RALS .... Right Add, Left Subtract [*Army field artillery technique*] (INF)
RALS .... Robotic Ammunition Landing System
RALSA .... Restraint and Life Support Assembly (MCD)
RalsRP .... Ralston Ralston Purina Group [*Associated Press*] (SAG)
RALT............ RADAR Altimeter [*Aviation*] (NASA)
RALT............ Radio Altitude (IAA)
RALT............ Range Light (AAG)
RALT............ Ranging Airborne LASER Tracker (MCD)
RALT............ Reported Altitude (IAA)
RALT............ Routine Admission Laboratory Tests [*Medicine*]
RALU............ Register and Arithmetic/Logic Unit [*Computer science*]
RALU............ Rotary Analog Logic Unit (MCD)
RALV............ Random Access Light Valve
RaLV............ Rasheed (Rat) Leukemia Virus
RALW........... Radioactive Liquid Waste (IEEE)
Ralw & Corp LJ... Railway and Corporation Law Journal [*A publication*] (DLA)
RAM............. Rabbit Alveolar Macrophage [*Clinical chemistry*]
RAM............. Rabbit Antimouse [*Hematology*]
RAM............. RADAR-Absorbent Material [*Aviation*]
RAM............. RADAR-Absorbing Material
RAM............. Radar Absorption Material (NAKS)
RAM............. Radiation Attenuation Measurement (CET)
RAM............. Radioactive Material
RAM............. Radio Attenuation Measurement [*Spacecraft for testing communications*]
RAM............. Radio Audience Measurement (NTCM)
RAM............. Radon Assessment and Mitigation [*Environmental science*] (COE)
RAM............. RAID Assessment Mode (MCD)
RAM............. Raman [*Turkey*] [*Seismograph station code, US Geological Survey*] (SEIS)
Ram............. Ramanathan's Reports [*Ceylon*] [*A publication*] (DLA)
Ram............. Ramcor Resources, Inc. [*Vancouver Stock Exchange symbol*]
RAM............. Ramenskoye [*US prefix for Soviet-Russian developmental aircraft flown at the Ramenskoye test facility*] (DOMA)
RAM............. Ramingining [*Australia Airport symbol*] (OAG)
Ram............. Ramsey's Quebec Appeal Cases [*A publication*] (DLA)
RAM............. Random Access Measurement [*System*] [*Computer science*]
RAM............. Random Access Memory [*Computer science*]
RAM............. Random Access Method [*Computer science*] (WDAA)
RAM............. Random Angle Modulation
RAM............. Range-Altitude Monitor
RAM............. Range Assessment Mode (MCD)
RAM............. Rapid Alternating Movement
RAM............. Rapid Amortization Mortgage
RAM............. Rapid Area Maintenance [*Air Force*]
RAM............. Raytheon Airborne Microwave (MCD)
RAM............. Readiness and Money (DNAB)
RAM............. Recent Advances in Manufacturing [*Information service or system*] (IID)
RAM............. Reconnaissance Air Meet (DOMA)
RAM............. Recovery Aids Material (MUGU)
RAM............. Red Artillery Model [*Military*]
RAM............. Redeye Air Missile [*System*] (RDA)
RAM............. Reentry Antimissile
RAM............. Reentry Attenuation Measurement [*NASA*]
RAM............. Reflection Anisotropy Microscopy
RAM............. Reform the Armed Forces Movement [*Philippines*]
RAM............. Regional Audit Manager
RAM............. Registered Apartment Manager [*National Association of Home Builders*] [*Designation awarded by*]
RAM............. Regular Army and Militia [*British*]
RAM............. Relaxing Avalanche Mode (IAA)
RAM............. Releasable Asset Program [*Military*] (AFIT)
RAM............. Reliability and Maintainability (IAA)
RAM............. Reliability Assessment for Management
RAM............. Reliability, Availability, and Maintainability [*Army*]
RAM............. Religions, Ancient and Modern [*A publication*]
RAM............. Remote Access Monitor (MCD)
RAM............. Remote Area Monitoring (KSC)
RAM............. Repair and Maintenance (IAA)
RAM............. Repeater Amplitude Modulation (MCD)
RAM............. Repeating Antipersonnel Mine
RAM............. Research and Applications Module [*NASA*]
RAM............. Research Aviation Medicine [*Navy program of research into aerospace medical techniques*]
RAM............. Reserve Adjustment Magnitude
RAM............. Resident Access Methods (MCD)
RAM............. Resident Aerospace Medicine [*Physician in specialty training*] [*Military*]
RAM............. Resources Analysis and Management
RAM............. Responsibility Assignment Matrix [*NASA*] (NASA)
RAM............. Restricted Access Memory [*Computer science*] (MCD)
RAM............. Reverse Annuity Mortgage
RAM............. Revolutionary Action Movement
RAM............. Right Ascension of the Meridian [*Navigation*]
RAM............. Rocket and Missile System [*Army*]
RAM............. Rocket Assisted Motor (WDAA)
RAM............. Rolling Airframe Missile
RAM............. Rothschild Asset Management (WDAA)
RAM............. Royal Academy of Music [*British*]
RAM............. Royal Air Maroc [*Morocco*]
RAM............. Royal Air Maroc - Compagnie Nationale de Transports Aeriens [*Morocco*] [*ICAO designator*] (FAAC)
RAM............. Royal Appliance Manufacturing [*NYSE symbol*] (SPSG)
RAMRP......... Royal Appliance Mfg [*NYSE symbol*] (TTSB)

RAM.............	Royal Arch Mason [*Freemasonry*]
RAM.............	Royal Ark Mariners
RAMA	Railway Automotive Management Association [*Defunct*] (EA)
RAMA	Reactor Accident Mitigation Project [*Nuclear energy*] (NUCP)
RAMA	Recap and Movement Authorization [*NASA*] (NASA)
RAMA	Region of Assured Mission Abort [*Military*] (CAAL)
RAMA	Retail Advertising and Marketing Association International (NTPA)
RAMA	Rome Air Materiel Area [*Deactivated*] [*Air Force*]
RAMAB	Ready Afloat Marine Amphibious Brigade (CINC)
RAMAC	Radio Marine Associated Companies (BUAC)
RAMAC	Random Access Memory Accounting Computer [*Computer science*] (IAA)
RAMAC	Random Access Method of Accounting and Control [*Computer science*]
Ramachandrier A...	Ramachandrier's Cases on Adoption [*1892*] [*India*] [*A publication*] (DLA)
Ramachandrier DG...	Ramachandrier's Cases on Dancing Girls [*1892*] [*India*] [*A publication*] (DLA)
Ramachandrier HML...	Ramachandrier's Cases on Hindu Marriage Law [*1891*] [*India*] [*A publication*] (DLA)
RAMADCS....	Reliability, Availability, and Maintainability Automated Data Collection System [*Army*]
RAMAIDB.....	RAM [*Radioactive Materials*] Accident/Incident Database [*Nuclear energy*]
RAMAN	Regional Atmosphere Measurement and Analysis Network [*Marine science*] (OSRA)
RAMAN	Regional Atmospheric Measurement and Analysis Network (USDC)
Ram & Mor...	Ramsey and Morin's Montreal Law Reporter [*A publication*] (DLA)
RAMARK	RADAR Marker [*Military*]
Ram Ass......	Ram on Assets, Debts, and Incumbrances [*2nd ed.*] [*1837*] [*A publication*] (DLA)
RAMAZ	Rabbi Moses Zacuto (BJA)
RAMB	Rabbit Anti-Mouse Brain (PDAA)
RAMB	Random Access Memory Buffer [*Computer science*]
RaM-BaM ...	Rabbi Moses ben Maimon [*Maimonides*] [*Jewish philosopher, 1135-1204*]
RAMBAN......	Rabbi Moses ben Nahman [*Spanish Talmudist, 1195-1270*] (BJA)
RAMBO........	Real-Time Acquisitions Management and Bibliographic Order System [*Suggested name for the Library of Congress computer system*]
RAMBO........	Remove Aquino from Malacanang before October [*Operation proposed by rebel military leader "Gringo" Honasan*] [*1987 Philippines*]
RAMBO........	Restore a More Benevolent Order Coalition [*Later, NCAN*] (EA)
RAMC	Resource Allocation and Mine Costing Model [*Department of Energy*] (GFGA)
RAMC	Risk Assessment and Management Commission [*Environmental science*] (COE)
RAMC	Royal Army Medical College [*British*] (MCD)
RAMC	Royal Army Medical Corps [*Initialism also facetiously translated during World War I as "Rats after Moldy Cheese," "Rob All My Comrades," or "Run Away, Matron's Coming"*] [*British*]
Ram Cas P & E...	Ram's Cases of Pleading and Evidence [*A publication*] (DLA)
RAMCEASE...	Reliability, Availability, Maintainability, Cost Effectiveness and Systems Effectiveness (MHDB)
RamcoG.......	Ramco Gershenson Properties Trust [*Associated Press*] (SAG)
RAMCT	Royal Army Medical Corps, Territorials [*British*] (ROG)
RAMD	Random Access Memory Device [*Computer science*]
RAMD	Receiving Agency Materiel Division [*Military*]
RAMD	Reliability, Availability, and Maintainability Demonstration
RAM-D........	Reliability, Availability, Maintainability, and Durability [*Army*] (AABC)
RAMDAC......	Random Access Memory Digital to Analog Converter [*Computer science*] (CDE)
RAMEC	Rapid Action Maintenance Engineering Change [*Navy*] (MCD)
RAMEC	Rapid Action Minor Engineering Change
RAMECES ...	Reliability, Availability, Maintainability, Enhancement of Communications-Electronic Systems (AAGC)
Ram F	Ram on Facts [*A publication*] (DLA)
RAMFAS.......	Reliability Analysis of Microcircuit Failure in Avionic Systems (MCD)
RamFin........	Ramapo Financial Corp. [*Associated Press*] (SAG)
RAMHR	Risk-Adjusted Multiple Hurdle Rates (ADA)
RAMI	Royal Academy of Medicine in Ireland (BUAC)
RAMIG........	Rabbit Antimouse Immunoglobulin G [*Immunology*]
RAMIO	RAM Plus Input/Output (NITA)
RAMIS	Rapid Access Management Information System [*Computer science*]
RAMIS	Rapid Automatic Malfunction Isolation System
RAMIS	Receive, Assemble, Maintain, Inspect, and Store (IAA)
RAMIS	Receiving, Assembly Maintenance, Inspection, Storage [*Military*]
RAMIS	Repair, Assemble, Maintain, Issue, and Supply (MUGU)
RAMIT	Rate-Aided Manually Implemented Tracking (NATG)
Ram Leg J...	Ram's Science of Legal Judgment [*2nd ed.*] [*1834*] [*A publication*] (DLA)
Ram Leg Judgm (Towns Ed)...	Ram's Science of Legal Judgment, Notes by Townshend [*A publication*] (DLA)
RAM/LOG....	Reliability, Availability, Maintainability, and Logistics (MCD)
RAMM	Random Access Memory Module [*Computer science*]
RAMM	Random Access Metal-Oxide-Semiconductor Memory [*Computer science*] (IAA)
RAMM	Recording Ammeter (MSA)
RAMM	Regional and Mesoscale Meteorology [*Branch*] [*National Environmental Satellite, Data, and Information Service*] (USDC)
RAMMIT	Reliability and Maintainability Management Improvement Techniques [*Army*]
RAMMIT	Reliability, Availability, and Maintenance Management Improvements Technique
RAMMS	Responsive Automated Materiel Management System [*Army*] (AABC)
RAMNAC......	Radio Aids to Marine Navigation Application Committee (BUAC)
RAMNAC......	Radio Aids to Marine Navigation Committee [*British*]
RAMOGE......	Regional Pollution Studies in the Ligurian Sea [*Marine science*] (MSC)
RAMONT......	Radiological Monitoring
RAMOS........	Reading and Mathematics Observation System (EDAC)
RAMOS........	Remote Automatic Meteorological Observing Station
RAMP	RADAR Mapping of Panama
RAMP	RADAR Masking Parameter (IAA)
RAMP	RADAR Modification Program (NG)
RAMP	Radiation Airborne Measurement Program
RAMP	Radio Attenuation Measurement Project
RAMP	Raising Achievements in Mathematics Project (AIE)
RAMP	Ramp [*Postal Service standard*] (OPSA)
RAMP	Random Access Mechanization of Phosphorus
RAMP	Rapid Absorbent Matrix Pad (DB)
RAMP	Rapid Acquisition of Manufactured Parts [*Military*]
RAMP	Rate and Acceleration Measuring Pendulum (PDAA)
RAMP	Raytheon Airborne Microwave Platform [*Sky station*]
RAMP	Receptor-Activity-Modifying Protein [*Endocrinology*]
RAMP	Records and Archives Management Programme [*UNESCO*]
RAMP	Recovered Allied Military Personnel
RAMP	Regional Administrative Management Plan [*Department of Labor*]
RAMP	Reliability Analysis and Modeling Program (AAEL)
RAMP	Reliability and Maintainability Program
RAMP	Reliability, Availability, Maintainability Program [*Army*] (IAA)
RAMP	Remedial Action Master Plan [*Environmental science*] (COE)
RAMP	Remote Access Maintenance Protocol [*Telecommunications*]
RAMP	Research Association of Minority Professors (EA)
RAMP	Reserve Associate Manning Program [*Military*]
RAMP	Resource Allocation and Management Program (EDAC)
RAMP	Review of Army Mobilization Planning (MCD)
R/AMP	Rifampin [*Also, RF, RIF, RMP*] [*Bactericide*]
RAMP	Ring Airfoil Munition Projectile [*Army*]
RAMP	Rural Abandoned Mine Program [*Department of Agriculture*]
RAMPAC......	Radioactive Materials Packaging [*Nuclear energy*]
RAMPART....	RADAR Advanced Measurements Program for Analysis of Reentry Techniques [*ARPA - Raytheon*]
RAMPART....	Route to Airlift Mobility through Partnership (MCD)
RAMPI	Raw Material Price Index (NITA)
RAMPLAN....	Rock Mechanics Applied to Mine Planning (PDAA)
RAMPS	Rapid Message Preparation System (NATG)
RaMPS	Rapid Multiple Peptide System [*Biotechnology*]
RAMPS	Repatriated American Military Personnel [*World War II*]
RAMPS	Resources Allocation and Multiproject Scheduling
Ram Rep	Ramanathan's Supreme Court Reports [*Ceylon*] [*A publication*] (ILCA)
RAMS	RADAR Target Scattering Advanced Measurement System
RAMS	Radiation Measuring System
RAMS	Radio Amateur Megacycle Society (IAA)
RAMS	Random Access Measurement System [*Computer science*]
RAMS	Random Access Memorix Storage [*Computer science*] (IAA)
RAMS	Random Access Memory Store [*Computer science*] (TEL)
RAMS	Rapid Munitions Assembly System (DWSG)
RAMS	Rascal Avionics Management System (MCD)
RAMS	Record Archival Management System (HGAA)
RAMS	Recovery and Modification Services (MCD)
RAMS	Recruiting Advertising Management System [*Navy*] (DNAB)
RAMS	Reduced-Size Antenna Monopulse System
RAMS	Regional Air Monitoring Station [*or System*] [*Environmental Protection Agency*]
RAMS	Regional Atmospheric Modeling System [*Marine science*] (OSRA)
RAMS	Registered Australian Mortgage Securities Trust
RAMS	Regulatory Activities Manpower System [*Nuclear energy*] (NRCH)
RAMS	Reliability and Maintainability Studies [*Army*] (RDA)
RAM-S	Reliability, Availability, Maintainability - Supportability (MCD)
RAMS	Remote Area Mobility Study (MCD)
RAMS	Remote Automatic Multipurpose Station
RAMS	Remotely Accessible Management Systems [*Computer science*]
RAMS	Repairables Asset Management System [*Military*] (CAAL)
RAMS	Repair, Assembly, and Maintenance Shop (IAA)
RAMS	Requirements Analysis Material Sheet [*or Study*] (MCD)
RAMS	Right Ascension Mean Sun [*Navigation*]
RAMS	Rocket and Missile System [*Army*]
RAMSA	Radio Aeronautica Mexicana, Sociedad Anonima
Rams App....	Ramsey's Quebec Appeal Cases [*1873-86*] [*A publication*] (DLA)
Ramsay	Ramsey Health Care, Inc. [*Associated Press*] (SAG)
Ramsay App Cas...	Ramsay's Appeal Cases [*Canada*] [*A publication*] (DLA)
Ramsay App Cas (Can)...	Ramsay's Appeal Cases [*Canada*] [*A publication*] (DLA)
Ram SC	Ramanathan's Supreme Court Reports [*Ceylon*] [*A publication*] (DLA)
RAMSES	Reprogrammable Advanced Multimode Shipborne ECM System [*Canadian Navy*]
RAMSH........	Reliability, Availability, Maintainability, Safety, and Human Factors [*Telecommunications*] (TEL)
RAMSIM	Reliability, Availability, Maintenance, Simulation [*Navy*] (DNAB)
RAMSS	Royal Alfred Merchant Seamen's Society [*British*]
RAMT	Rabbit Antimouse Thymocyte [*Immunology*]
RAMT	Rudder Angle Master Transmitter
RAMTAC	Reentry Analysis and Modeling of Target Characteristics
RAMTIP	Reliability and Maintainability Technology Insertion Program [*DoD*]
RAMTRA	Reserve Air Maintenance Training (DNAB)
Ramtrn	Ramtron International Corp. [*Associated Press*] (SAG)
Ramtron	Ramtron International Corp. [*Associated Press*] (SAG)
RAMUS........	Remote Access Multi-User System (DNAB)

RAMV	Radish Mosaic Virus [*Plant pathology*]
RAMVAN	Reconnaissance Aircraft Maintenance Van
Ram W	Ram on Exposition of Wills of Landed Property [*1827*] [*A publication*] (DLA)
RAN	Defence Products Ltd. [*British ICAO designator*] (FAAC)
RAN	RADAR Navigation (DNAB)
RAN	Railway Abidjan-Niger
RAN	Rainforest Action Network (EA)
Ran	Ranae [*Frogs*] [*of Aristophanes*] [*Classical studies*] (OCD)
RAN	Random (DNAB)
RAN	Rangoon [*Burma*] [*Seismograph station code, US Geological Survey Closed*] (SEIS)
RAN	Ranitidine [*An antiulcer drug*]
RAN	Read around Number
RAN	Reconnaissance/Attack Navigator
RAN	Regional Air Navigation [*ICAO*]
RAN	Remote Area Nurse
RAN	Renan Ltd. [*Moldova*] [*FAA designator*] (FAAC)
RAN	Repair Activity Accounting Number [*Navy*]
RAN	Reporting Accounting Number (NG)
RAN	Request for Authority to Negotiate
RAN	Requirement Action Number
RAN	Requisition Account Number
RAN	Resident's Admission Notes [*Medical records*] (DAVI)
RAN	Resource-Adjacent Nation [*Ocean fishery management*]
RAN	Revenue Anticipation Note
RAN	Royal Australian Navy (VNW)
RANA	Rheumatoid Arthritis Nuclear Antigen [*Immunology*]
RANA	Rhodesia & Nyasaland Airways
RANAS	Rear-Admiral, Naval Air Stations [*British military*] (DMA)
RANC	RADAR Absorption Noise and Clutter (NASA)
RANCA	Retired Army Nurse Corps Association (EA)
RANCH	Ranch [*Commonly used*] (OPSA)
RANCHES	Ranch [*Commonly used*] (OPSA)
RANCID	Real and Not Corrected Input Data [*Computer science*]
RANCIN	Retrieval and Analysis of Navy Classified Information (DNAB)
RANCOM	Random Communication Satellite
Rand	Randall's Reports [*62-71 Ohio State*] [*A publication*] (DLA)
RAND	Rand Cap [*NASDAQ symbol*] (TTSB)
RAND	Rand Capital Corp. [*NASDAQ symbol*] (NQ)
Rand	Randolph's Reports [*22-27 Virginia*] [*1821-28*] [*A publication*] (DLA)
Rand	Randolph's Reports [*7-11 Louisiana*] [*A publication*] (DLA)
Rand	Randolph's Reports [*21-56 Kansas*] [*A publication*] (DLA)
RAND	Random [*Sample or Specimen*] (DAVI)
RAND	Research and Development (IAA)
RAND	Research and No Development [*Origin of name of RAND Corporation, a nonprofit national defense research organization*]
R & A	Rates and Allotments [*Eight-Sheet Outdoor Advertising Association*] [*A publication*]
R & A	Reliability and Availability
R & A	Reports and Analysis
R & A	Rescue and Assistance
R & A	Research and Analysis
R & A	Responsibility and Action
R & A	Review and Analysis
R & A	Review and Approval
R & A	Royal and Ancient Golf Club of St. Andrews [*Recognized as the game's legislative authority in all countries except the US*] [*British*]
R & A	Rules and Administration Committee [*US Senate*]
R & AC	RADAR and Air Communications
R & AD	Research and Advanced Development
RANDAM	Random Access Nondestructive Advanced Memory [*Computer science*]
RANDANAL...	Randomization Analyser (IAA)
Rand & Fur Poi...	Rand and Furness on Poisons [*A publication*] (DLA)
Rand Ann.....	Randolph Annual [*A publication*] (DLA)
R & AT	Research and Advanced Technology
R & B	Red and Blue (KSC)
R&B	Regional Arts Bureau (BUAC)
R & B	Remington and Ballinger's Code [*1910*] [*A publication*] (DLA)
R & B	Rhythm and Blues [*Music*]
R & B	Right and Below (MEDA)
R & B	Room and Board
R & B Inc	R & B, Inc. [*Associated Press*] (SAG)
R & B Supp...	Remington and Ballinger's Code, Supplement [*1913*] [*A publication*] (DLA)
R & C	Rail and Canal
R & C	Reasonable and Customary [*Refers to medical charges*] [*Insurance*]
R&C	Reckitt & Colman (WDAA)
R & C	Records and Control
R & C	Reed and Carnrick [*Commercial firm*] (DAVI)
R&C	Request & Complaint (WDAA)
R & C	Requirements and Configuration
R & C	Rest and Convalescence (ADA)
R & C	Review and Comment [*Aerospace*]
R & C	Rod and Custom [*A publication*]
R & C	Russell and Chesley's Nova Scotia Equity Reports [*A publication*] (DLA)
R & C	Russell and Chesley's Nova Scotia Reports [*A publication*] (DLA)
RandCa........	Rand Capital Corp. [*Associated Press*] (SAG)
R & Can Cas...	Railway and Canal Cases [*England*] [*A publication*] (DLA)
R & Can Tr...	Railway and Canal Traffic Cases [*England*] [*A publication*] (DLA)
R & Can Tr Cas...	Railway and Canal Traffic Cases [*England*] [*A publication*] (DLA)
R & CC	Railway and Canal Cases [*1835-54*] [*A publication*] (DLA)
R & CC	Recorder and Communications Control (NASA)
R & CC	Riot and Civil Commotion
R & C Ca	Railway and Canal Cases [*England*] [*A publication*] (DLA)
R & C Cas ...	Railway and Canal Cases [*England*] [*A publication*] (DLA)
R & C N Sc...	Russell and Chesley's Nova Scotia Reports [*A publication*] (DLA)
Rand Com Paper...	Randolph on Commercial Paper [*A publication*] (DLA)
R & CS	Radiological and Chemical Support [*Nuclear energy*] (NRCH)
R & C Tr Cas...	Railway and Canal Traffic Cases (Neville) [*England*] [*A publication*] (DLA)
R & D	Read and Destroy
R & D	Requirements and Distribution (AFM)
R & D	Research and Demonstration [*Labor training*]
R&D	Research and Development (IDOE)
R & DA	Research and Development Associates for Military Food and Packaging Systems (EA)
R & DCTE ...	Research and Development Center for Teacher Education [*Department of Education*] (GRD)
R & DELSEC...	Research and Development Electronic Security [*Military*] (AABC)
R & DNET ...	Research and Development Network [*Formerly, ARPANET*]
R & DO	Research and Development Operations [*Marshall Space Flight Center*] [*NASA*] (NASA)
R & DPP	Research and Development Program Planning [*Database*] [*DTIC*]
R & DSoc	Research and Development Society [*British*] (DBA)
R & E	Research and Education (MAE)
R&E	Research and Education Community
R & E	Research and Engineering
R&E	Rest and Exercise (STED)
R & E	Restructuring and Efficiency
R&E	Round and Equal [*Medicine*] (STED)
R & EA	Readiness and Emergency Action [*Red Cross Disaster Services*]
R&EC	Research and Engineering Council (NADA)
R&E Council...	Research and Engineering Council of the Graphic Arts Industry (NTPA)
Rand Em Dom...	Randolph on Eminent Domain [*A publication*] (DLA)
Rander........	Randers Group, Inc. [*Associated Press*] (SAG)
R & EW	Rest and Exercise (DAVI)
R & F	Rank and File
R & F	Reach and Frequency [*Advertising*] (WDMC)
R & G	Russell and Geldert's Nova Scotia Reports [*A publication*] (DLA)
R & G N Sc...	Russell and Geldert's Nova Scotia Reports [*A publication*] (DLA)
R & H Bank...	Roche and Hazlitt's Bankruptcy Practice [*2nd ed.*] [*1873*] [*A publication*] (DLA)
R & H Dig ...	Robinson and Harrison's Digest [*Ontario*] [*A publication*] (DLA)
R & I	Radical and Intense [*Extremely great*] [*Slang*]
R & I	Receiving and Inspection (KSC)
R & I	Removal and Installation (NRCH)
R & IBWA	Rural and Industries Bank of Western Australia
RANDID	Rapid Alphanumeric Digital Indicating Device
RANDIS	Random Disc File [*Computer science*] (IAA)
R & IT	Rating and Income Tax Reports [*England*] [*A publication*] (DLA)
R & J	Rabkin and Johnson's Federal, Income, Gift, and Estate Taxation [*A publication*] (DLA)
R & J	Rafique and Jackson's Privy Council Decisions [*India*] [*A publication*] (DLA)
R & J	Romeo and Juliet [*Shakespearean work*]
R & J Dig ...	Robinson and Joseph's Digest [*Ontario*] [*A publication*] (DLA)
R & L	Bureau for Reference and Loan Services [*Library network*]
R & L	Rail and Lake
R & LH	Right and Left Hands [*Work-factor system*]
R & LL & T...	Redman and Lyon on Landlord and Tenant [*8th ed.*] [*1924*] [*A publication*] (DLA)
R & LO	Reliability and Launch Operations (MCD)
R & M	Law Reporter, Montreal [*Canada*] [*A publication*] (DLA)
R & M	Redistribution and Marketing (AFM)
R & M	Refurbishment and Modification
R & M	Release and Material (MCD)
R & M	Reliability and Maintainability [*Navy*]
R & M	Reliability and Marketing (WDAA)
R & M	Repairs and Maintenance
R & M	Reports and Memorandum (MCD)
R & M	Routine and Microscopic (DAVI)
R & M	Russell and Mylne's English Chancery Reports [*A publication*] (DLA)
R & M	Ryan and Moody's English Nisi Prius Reports [*A publication*] (DLA)
R & M/2	Averaged [*Motor Octane Number*] [*Antiknock index Fuel technology*]
R & MCC	Ryan and Moody's English Crown Cases Reserved [*A publication*] (DLA)
R & MNP	Ryan and Moody's English Nisi Prius Reports [*A publication*] (DLA)
R & My	Russell and Mylne's English Chancery Reports [*A publication*] (DLA)
R & N	Rhodesia and Nyasaland Law Reports [*1956*] [*A publication*] (DLA)
R & NLR	Rhodesia and Nyasaland Law Reports [*1956-64*] [*A publication*] (DLA)
RANDO	Radiotherapy Analog Dosimetry
R & O	Rail and Ocean
R & O	Requirements and Objectives
RANDOLS	Random Domain Library Screening [*Genetic laboratory technique*]
R & P	Recruitment and Placement (MCD)
R & P	Reserve and Process (NASA)
R & P	Ring and Pinion [*Automotive engineering*]
R & P	Rules and Procedures (MSA)
Rand Peak...	Randall's Edition of Peake on Evidence [*A publication*] (DLA)
Rand Perp...	Randall on Perpetuities [*A publication*] (DLA)
R & PI	Rubber and Plastics Industry (MCD)
R&PM	Research and Program Management (NAKS)
R & PM	Resources and Program Management [*NASA*]

R & PP	Recreation and Public Purposes Act
R & P SEC	Radio and Panel Section [*Navy*]
R & PT	Rifle and Pistol Team [*Navy*]
R & QA	Reliability and Quality Assurance
R&R	Rape & Robbery [*Legal term*] (WDAA)
R & R	Rate and Rhythm [*of pulse*]
R & R	Records and Reports
R & R	Refueling and Rearming [*Air Force*]
R & R	Regurgitate and Reingest [*Animal behavior*]
R & R	Reinstatement and Replacement (ADA)
R&R	Reliability and Response (CIST)
R & R	Remove and Replace (KSC)
R & R	Rendezvous and Recovery (NASA)
R & R	Repair and Return
R & R	Reporting and Requisitioning [*Air Force*]
R & R	Research and Reporting Committee [*Interstate Conference of Employment Security Agencies*] (OICC)
R & R	Rest and Recreation
R & R	Rest and Recuperation [*Military*]
R & R	Rest and Rehabilitation [*Marine Corps*]
R & R	Rich & Rare Canadian Whisky [*Gooderham's*]
R & R	Rock and Roll [*Music*]
R & R	Rock and Rye
R & R	Routing and Record Sheet [*Air Force*]
R & R	Russell and Ryan's English Crown Cases [*A publication*] (DLA)
R & RA	Retraining and Reemployment Administration [*Terminated, 1947*]
R&R Bk N	Reference & Research Book News [*A publication*] (BRI)
R & RC	Reactors and Reactor Control (MCD)
R & RCC	Russell and Ryan's English Crown Cases Reserved [*A publication*] (DLA)
R & RE	Radiation and Repair Engineering [*Nuclear energy*] (NRCH)
R & ROTC	Reserve and Reserve Officers' Training Corps [*Army*]
R & Ry CC	Russell and Ryan's English Crown Cases [*A publication*] (DLA)
R & S	Raben & Sjogren [*Publisher*] [*Sweden*]
R & S	Range and Safety (AAG)
R & S	Reconnaissance and Security [*Military*] (INF)
R & S	Reconnaissance and Surveillance (MCD)
R & S	Reenlistment and Separation [*Military*] (AFM)
R&S	Reliability and Serviceability (CIST)
R & S	Ren and Stimpy [*Cartoon characters*]
R & S	Renovation and Storage [*Military*] (AFIT)
R & S	Reports and Statistics Branch [*US Military Government, Germany*]
R & S	Research and Statistics (IEEE)
R & S	Research and Study
R & S	Restraints and Seclusion [*Psychiatry*] (DAVI)
R&S	Ritonavir & Saquinavir [*Medicine*] (WDAA)
R & SC	Replacement and School Command [*Military*]
R & S SQ	Repair and Salvage Squadron [*Military*]
R & T	Research and Technology
R & T	Rough and Tumble Engineers' Historical Association (EA)
R & T	Rush & Tomkins [*Commercial firm British*]
R & T WUIS	Research and Technology Work Unit Information System [*Database*] [*Defense Technical Information Center*] (CRD)
R & TWUS	Research and Technology Work Unit Summary
R & U	Repairs and Upkeep [*Military*]
R & U	Repairs and Utilities [*Military*]
R&VA	Rating and Valuation Association (BUAC)
R & VR	Rating and Valuation Reporter [*A publication*]
R & W	Rail and Water [*Shipping*]
R & W	Routing and Work [*Military*]
R&X	Register and Indexed [*Computer science*] (CIST)
R & Z	Range and Zero [*NASA*] (KSC)
Rane	Rainerius de Forlivio [*Deceased, 1358*] [*Authority cited in pre-1607 legal work*] (DSA)
Raney	Raney's Reports [*16-20 Florida*] [*A publication*] (DLA)
RANG	Rangaire Corp. (MHDW)
RANG	Range Group [*Military*]
RANG	Rangoon [*City in Burma*] (ROG)
Rang Cr LJ	Rangoon Criminal Law Journal [*A publication*] (DLA)
Rang Dec	Sparks' Rangoon Decisions [*British Burma*] [*A publication*] (DLA)
RANGECO	Range Company (DNAB)
RangKoM	[*The*] Rangkaian Komputer Malaysia [*Computer science*] (TNIG)
Rang LR	Rangoon Law Reports [*India*] [*A publication*] (DLA)
RangrO	Ranger Oil Ltd. [*Associated Press*] (SAG)
RANK	Rank Group PLC (The) [*NASDAQ symbol*] (SAG)
RANK	[*The*] Rank Organisation Ltd. [*NASDAQ symbol*] (NQ)
RANK	Replacement Alpha Numeric Keyboard [*Computer science*] (DA)
Rank & S Comp L	Ranking and Spicer's Company Law [*11th ed.*] [*1970*] [*A publication*] (DLA)
RankGrp	Rank Group PLC (The) [*Associated Press*] (SAG)
RankinA	Rankin Automotive Group, Inc. [*Associated Press*] (SAG)
RankOrg	[*The*] Rank Organisation PLC [*Associated Press*] (SAG)
Rank P	Rankin on Patents [*1824*] [*A publication*] (DLA)
Rank S & P Exec	Ranking, Spicer, and Pegler on Executorship [*21st ed.*] [*1971*] [*A publication*] (DLA)
RANKY	Rank Organisation ADR [*NASDAQ symbol*] (TTSB)
RANMOG	Reactivity-Adjusted Non-Methane Organic Gas [*Automotive emissions*]
RANN	Research Applied to National Needs [*Formerly, IRRPOS*] [*National Science Foundation Obsolete*]
RANOSP	Radiological North Sea Project [*British*]
rANP	Rat Atrial Natriuretic Peptide [*Biochemistry*]
RANS	Range Squadron
RANS	Revenue Anticipation Notes
RANSA	Royal Australian Naval Sailing Association (BUAC)

RANSA	Rutas Aereas Nacionales Sociedad Anonima [*Cargo airline*] [*Venezuela*]
RANSAD	Random Access Noiselike Signal Address [*Telecommunications*] (IAA)
RANSW	Ratepayers' Association of New South Wales [*Australia*]
RANSW	Rationalist Association of New South Wales [*Australia*]
RANT	Reentry Antenna Test
RANT	Right Anterior (STED)
RANTE	Royal Australian Navy Training Establishment
RANTES	Regulated-upon-Activation, Normal T Expressed and Secreted [*Immunology*]
RANXPE	Resident Army Nike-X Project Engineer (AABC)
RANZCP	Royal Australian and New Zealand College of Psychiatrists (BUAC)
RAO	National Radio Astronomy Observatory, Charlottesville, VA [*OCLC symbol*] (OCLC)
RAO	RADAR Operator
RAO	Radio Astronomy Observatory [*University of Michigan*] [*Research center*]
RAO	Rado Reef Resources [*Vancouver Stock Exchange symbol*]
RAO	Raoul [*Raoul Island*] [*Seismograph station code, US Geological Survey*] (SEIS)
RAO	Regimental Amalgamation Officer [*British military*] (DMA)
RAO	Regional Accounting Office [*Telecommunications*] (TEL)
RAO	Regional Administrative Office
RAO	Regional Agricultural Officer [*Ministry of Agriculture, Fisheries, and Food*] [*British*]
RAO	Response Amplitude Operator (PDAA)
RAO	Retired Affairs Officers (EA)
RAO	Ribeirao Preto [*Brazil*] [*Airport symbol*] (OAG)
RAO	Right Anterior Oblique [*Medicine*]
RAO	Right Anterior Occipital [*Neurology*] (DAVI)
RAO	Rudder Angle Order (MSA)
RAOA	Railway Accounting Officers Association [*Later, AAR*]
RAOB	Radiosonde Observation
RAOB	Rawindsonde Observation [*Marine science*] (OSRA)
RAOB	Royal Antediluvian Order of Buffaloes
RAOBS	Radiometeorograph Observation (IAA)
RAOC	Rear Area Operations Center (MCD)
RAOC	Regional Air Operations Center (NATG)
RAOC	Royal Army Ordnance Corps [*Formerly, AOC*] [*British*]
RAOC(E)	Royal Army Ordnance Corps (Engineering) [*British military*] (DMA)
Rao DHL	Rao's Decisions on Hindu Law [*1893*] [*India*] [*A publication*] (DLA)
RAOMP	Report of Accrued Obligations, Military Pay (AFM)
RaONC	Radiation Oncology [*Medicine*] (DMAA)
RAOP	Regional Air Operations Plan (NATG)
RAOT	Rocker Arm Oiling Time (PDAA)
RAOTA	Radio Amateur Old Timers' Association [*British*] (BI)
RAOU	Royal Australasian Ornithologists Union (BUAC)
RAP	I Will Call You Again [*International telex abbreviation*] (WDMC)
RAP	RADAR-Absorbing Paint [*Military*] (RDA)
RAP	RADAR Aim Point
RAP	Radical Alternatives to Prison [*British*]
RAP	Radio Access Point (MCD)
RAP	Radio Air Play
RAP	Radiological Assistance Plan [*AEC*]
RAP	Radon Action Program (GNE)
RAP	Random Access Program [*Computer science*]
RAP	Random Access Projector
RAP	Ranger Assessment Phase [*Army*] (INF)
RAP	Rapid (AAG)
RAP	Rapid Air [*France ICAO designator*] (FAAC)
RAP	Rapid Assessment Program [*Environmental evaluation strategy*]
RAP	Rapid City [*South Dakota*] [*Airport symbol*] (OAG)
RAP	Rapid City, SD [*Location identifier FAA*] (FAAL)
RAP	Rapindik [*New Britain*] [*Seismograph station code, US Geological Survey Closed*] (SEIS)
RAP	Reactive Atmosphere Process
RAP	Readiness Action Proposal (MCD)
RAP	Readiness Assessment Program [*Navy*]
RAP	Rear Area Protection [*Military*] (AABC)
RAP	Receptor-Associated Protein [*Biochemistry*]
RAP	Recognize All Potential (DNAB)
RAP	Recommended Area for Protection [*Australia*]
RAP	Recruiter Assistance [*or Assistant*] Program [*Navy*] (DNAB)
RAP	Recurrent Abdominal Pain [*Medicine*] (STED)
RAP	Reduced Acreage Program [*Agriculture*]
RAP	Redundancy Adjustment of Probability (IEEE)
RAP	Refugee Arrival Project [*An association*] (BUAC)
RAP	Regimental Aid Post [*British*]
RAP	Regional Acceleratory Phenomenon [*Physiology*]
RAP	Regional Analysis and Prediction [*Branch*] [*Marine science*] (OSRA)
RAP	Regression Analysis Program [*Military*]
RAP	Regression-Associated Protein [*Biochemistry*]
RAP	Regulatory Accounting Practices [*or Principles*] [*Business term*]
RAP	Regulatory Account Procedures (EBF)
RAP	Regulatory Analysis Program [*Federal government*]
RAP	Relational Associative Processor (IEEE)
RAP	Relationship Anecdotes Paradigm Method [*Psychology*]
RAP	Relative Accident Probability
RAP	Releasable Assets Program
RAP	Reliability Assessment Prediction
RAP	Reliability Assessment Program
RAP	Reliability Assurance Program (IAA)
RAP	Reliable Acoustic Path
RAP	Remedial Accomplishment Plan [*Environmental science*] (COE)

RAP	Remedial Action Program [*or Project, Plan*] (MCD)
RAP	Remote Access Point [*Telecommunications*]
RAP ....:	Renal Artery Pressure [*Medicine*]
RAP	Rental Assistance Payment Program [*HUD*]
RAP	Rent Assessment Panel [*Northern Ireland*] (BUAC)
RAP	Requirements Analysis Package [*Computer science*]
RAP	Reset After Punch [*Computer science*] (IAA)
RAP	Resident Assembler Program
RAP	Resident Assessment Protocol [*Occupational therapy*]
RAP	Resident Associate Program [*Smithsonian Institution*]
RAP	Residual Analysis Program [*Space Flight Operations Facility, NASA*]
RAP	Resource Access Projects [*Administration for Children, Youth and Families*] (EDAC)
RAP	Resource Allocation Process (AAGC)
RAP	Resource Allocation Processor (CMD)
RAP	Response Action Plan (GNE)
RAP	Response Analysis Program [*Computer science*] (IBMDP)
RAP	Responsible Apparel Production
RAP	Restricted Access Processor (SSD)
RAP	Results Analysis Plan (MCD)
RAP	Retained Accessory Power [*Automotive engineering*]
RAP	Review and Analysis Process
RAP	Revised Accounting Procedures
RAP	Rheumatoid Arthritis Precipitin [*Medicine*] (STED)
RAP	Right Angle Plug
RAP	Right Atrial Pressure [*Cardiology*]
RAP	Ring-Around Programming (CAAL)
RAP	Rocket-Assisted Projectile (RDA)
RAP	"Round Up" Administration Planning Staff [*for the invasion of France*] [*World War II*]
RAP	Rubidium Acid Phthalate [*Organic chemistry*]
RAP	Rules for Admission to Practice [*A publication*] (DLA)
RA-P	Rumex Acetosa Polysaccharide [*Antineoplastic drug*]
RAP	Rupees, Annas, Pies [*Monetary units*] [*India*]
RAP	Smithsonian Resident Associate Program (EA)
RAPAC	Research Applications Policy Advisory Committee [*National Science Foundation*] (EGAO)
RAPAD	Research Association for Petroleum Alternative Development
Rapal & L....	Rapalje and Lawrence's American and English Cases [*A publication*] (DLA)
Rapalje & L...	Rapalje and Lawrence's Law Dictionary [*A publication*] (DLA)
RAPAM	Red de Accion sobre Plaguicidas y Alternativas en Mexico [*Member of the Pesticide Action Network*] (CROSS)
Rap & L.......	Rapalje and Lawrence's American and English Cases [*A publication*] (DLA)
Rap & Law...	Rapalje and Lawrence's American and English Cases [*A publication*] (DLA)
Rap & L Law Dict...	Rapalje and Lawrence's Law Dictionary [*A publication*] (DLA)
RAPBPPI......	Research Association for the Paper and Board, Printing, and Packaging Industries [*Research center British*] (IRC)
RAPC	Radio Administration Plenipotentiary Conference
RAPC	Right Angle Pressure Cartridge
RAPC	Royal Army Pay Corps [*Formerly, APC*] [*British*]
RAPCAP.......	RADAR Picket Combat Air Patrol (NVT)
RAPCC........	RADAR Approach Control Center (MCD)
RAPCO........	Regional Air Priorities Control Office [*Army*] (AABC)
RAPCOE......	Random Access Programming and Checkout Equipment
RAPCON	RADAR Approach Control [*Air Force*]
Rap Contempt...	Rapalje on Contempt [*A publication*] (DLA)
RAPD	Random Amplified Polymorphic DNA [*Deoxyribonucleic Acid*] [*Genetics*]
RAPD	Reach Avalanche Photodiode (IAA)
RAPD	Relatively Afferent Pupillary Defect [*Ophthalmology*]
RAPD	Response Amplitude Probability Data
RAPE	RADAR Arithmetic Processing Element [*Navy*]
RAPE	Right Atrial Pressure Elevation [*Medicine*] (STED)
RAPEC	Rocket-Assisted Personnel Ejection Catapult
RAPECA......	Rassemblement du Peuple Camerounais [*Camerounese People's Rally*]
RAP-EX........	Rear Area Protection Operations Extended (MCD)
Rap Fed Ref Dig...	Rapalje's Federal Reference Digest [*A publication*] (DLA)
Raph.............	Raphael Fulgosius [*Deceased, 1427*] [*Authority cited in pre-1607 legal work*] (DSA)
Raph Cum ...	Raphael Cumanus [*Deceased, 1427*] [*Authority cited in pre-1607 legal work*] (DSA)
RAPI	Radiosonde Report Already Sent in PIBAL [*Pilot Balloon Observation*] Collection [*Aviation*] (FAAC)
RAPI	Royal Australian Planning Institute (BUAC)
RAPIC	Remedial Action Program Information Center [*Department of Energy*] [*Also, an information service or system*] (IID)
RAPID..........	Rail Gun Armature Plasma Investigation Device (PDAA)
RAPID..........	Random Access Personnel Information Dissemination
RAPID..........	Random Access Personnel Information Disseminatora (NITA)
RAPID..........	Rapid [*Commonly used*] (OPSA)
RAPID..........	Rapid Access for Phoenix Intermodal Development
RAPID..........	Rapid Accurate Polynomial Interpolation Device (IAA)
RAPID..........	Reactor and Plant Integrated Dynamics [*Computer science*] (KSC)
RAPID..........	Reader-to-Advertiser Phone Inquiry Delivery System [*Chilton Corp.*]
RAPID..........	Readily Accessible Parts Information Directory [*Information service or system*] (IID)
RAPID..........	Real-Time Acquisition and Processing of Inflight Data
RAPID..........	Real-Time Application Program Interface to DISOSS (NITA)
RAPID..........	Relative Address Programming Implementation Device [*Computer science*]
RAPID..........	Reliability Assessment Program with In-Plant Data

RAPID..........	Remote Access Planning for Institutional Development [*Computer science*]
RAPID..........	Remote Access Procedure for Interactive Design [*General Motors Corp.*]
RAPID..........	Remote Automatic Parts Input for Dealers (IAA)
RAPID..........	Research in Automatic Photocomposition and Information Dissemination
RAPID..........	Retrieval and Processing Information for Display
RAPID..........	Retrieval and Production for Integrated Data [*Computer science*] (MHDB)
RAPID..........	Retrieval through Automated Publication and Information Digest [*Computer science*] (DIT)
RAPID..........	Retrorocket-Assisted Parachute in Flight Delivery
RAPID..........	Rocketdyne Automatic Processing of Integrated Data [*Computer science*]
RAPID..........	Ryan Automatic Plot Indicator Device
RAPIDS.........	Random Access Personnel Information Dissemination System [*Army*] (AABC)
RAPIDS........	Rapid Automated Problem Identification System [*DoD*]
RAPIDS........	Rapids Commonly used (OPSA)
RAPIDS........	Real-Time Automated Personnel Identification System [*DoD*]
RAPIER........	Rapid Analysis of Products by Integrated Engineering Routines [*Computer-assisted design*]
RAPIER........	Rapid Emergency Reconstitution Team [*Military*]
RAPIT	Record and Process Input Tables (IAA)
Rap Jud QBR...	Rapports Judiciaires de Quebec, Cour du Banc de la Reine [*Quebec Law Reports, Queen's Bench*] [*A publication*] (DLA)
Rap Jud QCS...	Rapports Judiciaires de Quebec. Cour Superieure [*Quebec Law Reports, Superior Court*] [*A publication*] (DLA)
Rap Jud Quebec CS (Can)...	Rapports Judiciaires de Quebec [*Quebec Law Reports*] [*Canada*] [*A publication*] (DLA)
Rap Jud Quebec KB (Can)...	Rapports Judiciaires de Quebec [*Quebec Law Reports*] [*Canada*] [*A publication*] (DLA)
Rap Jud Quebec QB (Can)...	Rapports Judiciaires de Quebec [*Quebec Law Reports*] [*Canada*] [*A publication*] (DLA)
Rap Lar	Rapalje on Larceny [*A publication*] (DLA)
RAPLOC........	Rapid Passive Localization (MCD)
RAPLOC-LSI...	Rapid Passive Localization - Low-Ship Impact [*Navy*] (CAAL)
RAPLOC-WAA...	Rapid Passive Localization - Wide Aperture Array [*Military*] (CAAL)
RAPM	Refractory Anemia With Partial Myeloblastosis [*Medicine*] (STED)
RAPM	Reliability Assessment Prediction Model
RAPM	Risk-Adjusted Profitability Measure [*Banking*] (ECON)
Rap NY Dig...	Rapalje's New York Digest [*A publication*] (DLA)
RAPO	Rabbit Antibodies to Pig Ovary [*Immunology*]
RAPO	Resident Apollo Project Office [*NASA*] (KSC)
RAPP	Racial Awareness Pilot Project [*University of Cincinnati*]
RAPP	Reconciliation and Purification Program [*Air Force*]
RAPP	Registered Air Parcel Post
RAPP	Remedial Action Projects Program (COE)
Rapp Bount...	Rapp on the Bounty Laws [*A publication*] (DLA)
RAPPI	Random Access Plan-Position Indicator [*Air Force*]
RAPPORT	Rapid Alert Programmed, Power Management of RADAR Targets [*Military*] (PDAA)
Rapport........	Rapport: The Modern Guide to Books, Music & More [*A publication*] (BRI)
RAPP's	Radiologists, Anesthesiologists, Pathologists, and Physiatrists
RAPR	RADAR Processor (CET)
RAPR	Right Angle Panel Receptacle
RAPR	Russian Association of Public Relations (BUAC)
RAPRA........	RAPRA Technology [*Formerly, Rubber and Plastics Research Association*] (EA)
RAPRA........	Rubber and Plastics Research Association (NITA)
RAPRA........	Rubber and Plastics Research Association of Great Britain (BUAC)
RAPRENOx...	Rapid Reduction of Nitrogen Oxides [*Automotive engineering*]
RAPS	RADAR-Absorbing Primary Structure (MCD)
RAPS	RADAR Prediction System (MCD)
RAPS	RADAR Proficiency Simulator
RAPS	Radioactive Argon Processing System (NRCH)
RAPS	Radiologist, Anesthesiologist, and Pathologist (HCT)
RAPS	Rate and Position Sensor (IAA)
RAPS	Recovery Access Presentation System (GAVI)
RAPS	Regional Air Pollution Study [*Environmental Protection Agency*]
RAPS	Regulated Air Pressure System (MCD)
RAPS	Regulatory Affairs Professionals Society (EA)
RAPS	Reliable Acoustic Path SONAR (MCD)
RAPS	Remote Access Power Support (NITA)
RAPS	Remote Applications Protocol Suite (ACII)
RAPS	Remote Area Power Supply
RAPS	Resource Analysis and Planning System [*DoD*] (DOMA)
RAPS	Retired Annuitant Pay Statement [*DoD*]
RAPS	Retired Army Personnel System
RAPS	Retiree Annuitant Pay System
RAPS	Retrieval Analysis and Presentation System [*Computer science*]
RAPS	Right Aft Propulsion System [*Aerospace*] (GFGA)
RAPS	Risk Appraisal of Programs System
RAPS	Role Activity Performance Scale [*Mental health*]
RAPSAG.......	Rapid Sealift Acquisition Group [*Navy*]
RAPSAT	Ranging and Processing Satellite (DA)
RAPSG.........	Rapsgate [*England*]
RAPT	Raptor Systems [*NASDAQ symbol*] (TTSB)
RAPT	Raptor Systems, Inc. [*NASDAQ symbol*] (SAG)
RAPT	Reception Automatic Picture Transmission (PDAA)
RAPT	Rehabilitation of Addicted Prisoners Trust [*British*] [*An association*]
RAPT	Reusable Aerospace Passenger Transport (MCD)
RAPTAP.......	Random Access Parallel Tape

RAPTAP ...... Rapid Access Parallel Tape [*Computer science*] (IAA)
RAP-TAP ..... Releasable Assets Program - Transferable Assets Program [*Navy*] (NG)
RAPTN .... RAPRA Trade Names [*RAPRA Technology Ltd.*] [*Information service or system*] (IID)
RaptorS ...... Raptor Systems, Inc. [*Associated Press*] (SAG)
RAPTS .... Resource Accounting Project Tracking System (DNAB)
RAPTUS .... Rapid Thorium-Uranium System [*Nuclear energy*]
RAPUD .... Revenue Analysis from Parametric Usage Descriptions [*Telecommunications*] (TEL)
RAPWI .... Organization for the Recovery of Allied Prisoners of War and Internees [*Initially in Headquarters of Allied Land Forces, Southeast Asia*] [*World War II*]
Rap Wit ...... Rapalje's Treatise on Witnesses [*A publication*] (DLA)
RAPYHT .... Retrieval and Acceleration of Promising Young Handicapped and Talented Program (EDAC)
RAQ .... Raha [*Indonesia*] [*Airport symbol*] (OAG)
RAQ .... Regional Air Quality
RAQ .... Right Anterior Quadrant [*Medicine*] (STED)
RAR .... Aviaross [*Russian Federation*] [*ICAO designator*] (FAAC)
RAR .... RADAR Arrival Route [*Aviation*] (DA)
RAR .... RADAR Augmentation Reliability (MCD)
RAR .... Radio Acoustic Ranging
RAR .... Random Age Replacement
RAR .... Rapid Access Recording (IEEE)
Rar .... Rare Records [*Record label*]
RAR .... Rarotonga [*Cook Islands*] [*Seismograph station code, US Geological Survey*] (SEIS)
RAR .... Rarotonga [*Cook Islands*] [*Airport symbol*] (OAG)
RAR .... Rat Insulin Receptor (STED)
RAR .... Read around Ratio
RAR .... Real Aperture RADAR
RAR .... Reallexikon der Aegyptischen Religionsgeschichte [*Berlin*] [*A publication*] (BJA)
RAR .... Reasonable Assumed [*or Assured*] Resources [*Minerals*]
RAR .... Record and Report
RAR .... Redevelopment Area Resident
RAR .... Reduced Aspect Ratio
RAR .... Regular Army Reserve
RAR .... Relative Accumulation Rate [*Ecology*]
RAR .... Relative Adherence Ratio (DB)
RAR .... Reliability Action Report [*or Request*]
RAR .... Remote Arm Reset (MCD)
RAR .... Remove and Replace (IAA)
RAR .... Remove Audible Ring
RAR .... Repair and Retrofix (IAA)
RAR .... Repair as Required (AAG)
RAR .... Report Authorization Record [*or Request*] (AAG)
RAR .... Reserve Asset Ratio [*Banking*] (ADA)
RAR .... Residential Appraisal Report [*Real estate*] (EMRF)
RAR .... Resource Allocation Recommendations [*Military*]
RAR .... Restricted Articles Regulation (DS)
RAR .... Retinoic Acid Receptor [*Biochemistry*]
RAR .... Return Address Register
RAR .... Revenue Agent's Report [*IRS*]
RAR .... Revenue and Retrieval (IAA)
RAR .... Revise as Required (MCD)
R-Ar .... Rhode Island State Archives, Providence, RI [*Library symbol Library of Congress*] (LCLS)
RAR .... Rhodesian African Rifles [*Military unit*]
RAR .... Right Arm Reclining (STED)
RAR .... Right Arm Recumbent [*Medicine*] (AAMN)
RAR .... ROM [*Read-Only Memory*] Address Register
RAR .... Routing and Recording (IAA)
RAR .... Royal Army Reserve [*British*]
RAR .... Royal Australian Regiment (VNW)
RAR .... Rules and Regulations (IAA)
RAR .... Rural Area Redevelopment
RARA .... Random Access-to-Random Access [*Computer science*] (IAA)
RARA .... Retinoic Acid Receptor (HGEN)
RARA .... Retinoic Acid Receptor Alpha (DMAA)
RARA .... Rural and Remote Area
RARAD .... RADAR Advisory [*Aviation*] (FAAC)
RARAF .... Radiological Research Accelorator Facility [*Department of Energy*]
RARB .... Raritan Bancorp [*NASDAQ symbol*] (TTSB)
RARB .... Raritan Bancorp, Inc. [*NASDAQ symbol*] (NQ)
R Arb .... Recht der Arbeit [*Right to Work*] [*German*] (DLA)
RARB .... Retinoic Acid Receptor Beta (DMAA)
RARC .... Reactors and Reactor Control (IAA)
RARC .... Regional Administrative Radio Conference (NITA)
RARC .... Revoked Appointment and Returned to Civilian Status [*Navy*]
RARC .... Ruakura Agricultural Research Centre [*New Zealand*] (BUAC)
RARDE .... Royal Armament Research and Development Establishment [*British*]
RARDEN ..... Royal Armament Research and Development Establishment, Enfield [*British military*] (DMA)
RARE .... Associated Networks for European Research [*EC*] (ECED)
RARE .... Bugaboo Creek Steak House [*NASDAQ symbol*] (SAG)
RARE .... Radiation and Repair Engineering [*Nuclear energy*] (IAA)
RARE .... Rail Archaeological Research Effort [*An association*]
RARE .... Ram Air Rocket Engine
RARE .... Rare Animal Relief Effort
RARE .... Rare Antigen/Antibody Resource Exchange Program [*American Association of Blood Banks*]
RARE .... Rare Hospitality Intl., Inc. [*NASDAQ symbol*] (SAG)
RARE .... Rehabilitation of Addicts by Relatives and Employers

RARE .... Reinforcement and Resupply of Europe (MCD)
RARE .... Reseaux Associes pour la Recherche Europeene [*Associated Networks for European Research*]
RARE .... Retinoic Acid Responsive Element [*Biochemistry*]
RARE .... Roadless Area Resource Evaluation
RARE .... Ronne Antarctic Research Expedition [*1947-48*]
Ra Ref .... RADAR Reflector
RAREF .... Radiation and Repair Engineering Facility [*Nuclear energy*] (NRCH)
RareHosp. .... Rare Hospitality Intl., Inc. [*Associated Press*] (SAG)
RAREP .... RADAR Report [*FAA*]
RAREP .... RADAR Weather Report (IAA)
RARES .... Rotating Associative Relational Store (MHDI)
RARF .... RADOME [*RADAR Dome*], Antenna, and Radio Frequency [*Array*] [*Electronics*]
RARG .... Regulatory Analysis Review Group [*Comprising several federal agencies*]
RARI .... Reporting and Routing Instructions [*Navy*]
RarintnBc ... Raritan Bancorp [*Associated Press*] (SAG)
rariss .... Rarissimum [*Extremely Rare*] [*Latin*]
RaritnBc .... Raritan Bancorp [*Associated Press*] (SAG)
RARLS .... Rabbit Antirat Lymphocyte Serum [*Immunology*] (MAE)
RARO .... Regular Army Reserve of Officers [*British*]
RAROC .... Risk-Adjusted Return on Capital [*Economics*]
RAR OCC ..... Raro Occurrit [*Rarely Occurs*] [*Latin*] (ROG)
RAROM .... RAM and ROM (NITA)
RARP .... Radio Affiliate Replacement Plan [*Canadian Broadcasting Corporation*]
RARP .... Reverse Address Resolution Protocol [*Computer science*] (PCM)
RARR .... Range and Range Rate (IAA)
RARR .... Reinstallation and Removal Record (KSC)
RARS .... Refractory Anemia with Ringed Sideroblasts [*Hematology*]
RArt .... Royal Artillery [*British*]
RARTS .... Rabbit Anti-Rat Thymocyte Serum [*Immunology*] (DMAA)
RARU .... Rackham Arthritis Research Unit [*University of Michigan*] [*Research center*] (RCD)
RARU .... Radio Range Station Reported Unreliable [*Message abbreviation*]
RAS .... Jim Ratliff Air Service, Inc. [*FAA designator*] (FAAC)
RAS .... Rabbonim Aid Society
RAS .... RADAR-Absorbing Structures
RAS .... RADAR Advisory Service
RAS .... RADAR Assembly Spares (NG)
RAS .... RADAR Augmentation System (MCD)
RAS .... Radio Astronomy Satellite (IAA)
RAS .... RADOME [*RADAR Dome*] Antenna Structure
RAS .... Radula Sinus
RAS .... Random Access Storage [*Computer science*] (IAA)
RAS .... Rapid Access Storage (NITA)
RAS .... Rasht [*Iran*] [*Airport symbol*] (OAG)
ras .... Rasurae [*Scrapings or Filings*] [*Latin*] (MAE)
RAS .... Rathus Assertiveness Scale [*Psychology*] (EDAC)
RAS .... Reaction Augmentation System
RAS .... Reactor Alarm System (IEEE)
RAS .... Reactor Analysis and Safety [*Nuclear energy*] (NRCH)
RAS .... Readers Admission System [*Online Public Access Catalog*]
RAS .... Reading Association Sydney [*Australia*]
RAS .... Realistic Age-Structured [*Model for disease persitence*]
RAS .... Rear Area Security [*Army*] (AABC)
RAS .... Recirculation Actuation Signal [*Nuclear energy*] (NRCH)
RAS .... Record Assigned System (MCD)
RAS .... Records and Analysis Subsystem (TEL)
RAS .... Recruiting Analysis Service [*LIMRA*]
RAS .... Recruitment and Assessment Services [*British Civil Service*] (ECON)
RAS .... Rectified Air Speed [*Navigation*]
RAS .... Recurrent Aphthous Stomatitis [*Medicine*]
RAS .... Reference Address for Small Core Memory (IAA)
RAS .... Reflector Antenna System
RAS .... Refractory Anemia with Ringed Sideroblasts [*Hematology*]
RAS .... Regimental Aviation Squadron [*Army*] (ADDR)
RAS .... Regional Automated Systems
RAS .... Relative Aerobic Strain (PDAA)
RAS .... Relay Antenna Subsystem [*NASA*]
RAS .... Reliability, Availability, and Serviceability [*IBM Corp. slogan*] (MCD)
RAS .... Reliability, Availability, Security (IAA)
RAS .... Remote Access Server [*Computer science*] (PCM)
RAS .... Remote Access Service [*Telecommunications*]
RAS .... Remote Access Services [*Microsoft Corp.*] [*Computer networking*] (PCM)
RAS .... Remote Acquisition Station [*Nuclear energy*] (NRCH)
RAS .... Remote Active Spectrometer
RAS .... Remote Area Support (MCD)
RAS .... Remote Arm Set (MCD)
RAS .... Renal Artery Stenosis [*Medicine*] (MAE)
RAS .... Renin-Angiotensin System [*Endocrinology*]
RAS .... Replenishment at Sea [*Navy*]
RAS .... Report Audit Summary (AAG)
RAS .... Reproduction Assembly Sheet (MCD)
RAS .... Requirements Allocation Sheet
RAS .... Requirements Analysis Sheet [*NASA*] (KSC)
RAS .... Requirements Audit System
RAS .... Reserve Advisory Squadron
RAS .... Reset and Start (IAA)
RAS .... Resource Analysis System (HGAA)
RAS .... Reticular Activating System [*Diffuse network of neurons in the brain*]
RAS .... Retiree Account Statement [*DoD*]
RAS .... Return Address Stack (ECII)

RAS	Return of Activated Sludge (DICI)
RAS	Reutter Anderson Schoor (EFIS)
RAS	Rheumatoid Arthritis Serum [Factor] [Medicine]
RAS	River Assault Squadron [Navy] (NVT)
RAS	Rocket-Assisted Artillery Shell [Military] (MUSM)
RAS	Rockhampton Aerial Services [Australia]
RAS	Route Accounting Subsystem [Telecommunications] (TEL)
RAS	Row Address Select (IAA)
RAS	Row-Address Strobe (IEEE)
RAS	Royal Accounting System [United States Geological Survey]
RAS	Royal Adelaide Show [Australia]
RAS	Royal Aeronautical Society [British]
RAS	Royal African Society (EAIO)
RAS	Royal Agricultural Society [British] (DAS)
RAS	Royal Asiatic Society [British]
RAS	Royal Asiatic Society of Great Britain and Ireland (BUAC)
RAS	Royal Astronomical Society [British]
RAS	Royal International Agricultural Show [British] (ITD)
RAS	Russian Academy Of Sciences
RAS	Sun Raster [Image format] (AAEL)
RASA	Radionuclide Aerosol Sampler/Analyzer [Chemistry]
RASA	Railway and Airline Supervisors Association [AFL-CIO]
RASA	Realignment of Supply Activities (MCD)
RASA	Redstone Arsenal Support Activity (MCD)
RASA	Regional Aeronautical Support Activity (AFIT)
RASAC	Rural Assistance Scheme Advisory Committee (BUAC)
RASAU	Reserve Antisubmarine Warfare Systems Analysis Mobilization Unit (DNAB)
RASB	Rapid Access to Sequential Block [Computer science] (PDAA)
RASB	Royal Asiatic Society of Bengal (BUAC)
RASC	Radiological Affairs Safety Committee (DNAB)
RASC	Rear Area Security Controller [Military]
RASC	Religious Altered State of Consciousness [Psychology]
RASC	Rome Air Service Command [Air Force]
RASC	Royal Agricultural Society of the Commonwealth (EAIO)
RASC	Royal Army Service Corps [Formerly, ASC; later, RCT] [British]
RASC	Royal Astronomical Society of Canada
RASCAL	Random Access Secure Communications Antijam Link
RASCAL	Rotorcraft-Aircrew Systems Concepts Airborne Laboratory (RDA)
RASCAL	Royal Aircraft Establishment Sequence Calculator [British] (DEN)
RASCAL	Rudimentary Adaptive System for Computer-Aided Learning (PDAA)
RASCAP	Replenishment at Sea Corrective Action Program (MCD)
RASCC	Rear Area Security Control Center [Military]
RASC/DC	Rear Area Security and Area Damage Control [Military]
RASCOM	Regional African Satellite Communications System (ECON)
RASCOM	Regional African Satellite Communication System for the Development of Africa [ITU] [United Nations] (DUND)
RASCORE	RADAR Scorer (MCD)
RASC/RCT	Royal Army Service Corps/Royal Corps of Transport [British]
RASD	Reference and Adult Services Division [American Library Association] (EA)
RASD	Requirements and Specification Documentation [Computer science]
RASD BRASS	RASD [Reference and Adult Services Division] Business Reference Services Section
RASD CODES	RASD [Reference and Adult Services Division] Collection Development and Evaluation Section
RASD HS	RASD [Reference and Adult Services Division] History Section
RASD ILC	RASD [Reference and Adult Services Division] Interlibrary Loan Committee [American Library Association]
RASD MARS	RASD [Reference and Adult Services Division] Machine-Assisted Reference Section
RASDS	Regional Advisory Service in Demographic Statistics [United Nations] (EY)
RASE	Rapid Acquisition by Sequential Estimation (IAA)
RASE	Rapid Automatic Sweep Equipment [Air Force]
RASE	Royal Agricultural Society of England
RASER	Radio Amplification by Stimulated Emission of Radiation
RASER	Random-to-Serial Converter
RASER	Range and Sensitivity Extending Resonator [Electronics]
RASGN	Reassignment
RASH	Rain Showers [Meteorology]
RASHI	Rabbi Shlomo Yitzhaqi [Medieval Jewish commentator]
RaSHI	Rabbi Solomon Bar Isaac (BJA)
RASI	Reliability, Availability, Serviceability and Improvability (NITA)
RASI	Reliability, Availability, Service, Improvement (MHDI)
RASI	Resident Assistant Stress Inventory [Psychology] (DHP)
RASIDS	Range Safety Impact Display System
RASILA	Rannikko- ja Sisaevesiliikenteen Tvoenantajaliitto [Employers' Federation of Coastal and Inland Waterways Transportation] [Finland] (EY)
RASIS	Reliability, Availability, Serviceability, Integrity and Security (NITA)
RASK	Royal Agricultural Society of Kenya (BUAC)
RASL	Reserve Active Status List (DOMA)
RASM	Remote Analog Submultiplexer (MCD)
rASMC	Rat Aortic Smooth Muscle Cells
RASN	Rain and Snow [Sleet] [Meteorology]
RASNSW	Royal Art Society of New South Wales [Australia]
RASNZ	Royal Astronomical Society of New Zealand (BUAC)
RASO	Radio Allocations Study Organization (NTCM)
RASO	Radiological Affairs Support Office [Obsolete Navy]
RASO	Rear Airfield Supply Organization [Military]
RASO	Regional Aviation Supply Officer [Navy] (AFIT)
RASONDE	Radiosonde Observation
RASP	Rapid Acquisition of Spare Parts (DOMA)
RASP	Receiver Active Signal Processor [Military] (CAAL)

RASP	Refined Aeronautical Support Program (NG)
RASP	Reliability and Aging Surveillance Program [Air Force]
RASP	Remote Access Switching and Patching
RASP	Resource Allocation and Stress in Plants [Research initiative] [bbsrc-Biotechnology and Biological Sciences Research Council] [British]
RASP	Retrieval and Sort Processor [Computer science]
RASP	Retrieval and Statistics Processing (NITA)
RASP	Rheumatoid Arthritis Specific Protein [Medicine] (DB)
RASPE	Resident Army SENSCOM [Sentinel Systems Command] Project Engineer (AABC)
RASPO	Resident Apollo Spacecraft Program Office [NASA] (KSC)
RASR	Regular Army Special Reserve (ADA)
RASR	Rodders Against Street Racing
RASS	RADAR Acoustic Sounding System [National Oceanic and Atmospheric Administration]
RASS	RADAR Attitude Sensing System (MCD)
RASS	Radio Acoustic Sounding System
RASS	Rapid Area Supply Support [Military] (AFM)
RASS	Register, Address, Skip and Special Chip (IAA)
RASS	Relief Association for Southern Sudan
RASS	Remote Activated Stores System (MCD)
RASS	Remote Area Services Subsidy Scheme [Australia]
RASS	Rheumatoid Arthritis and Sjoegren Syndrome [Medicine] (DMAA)
RASS	Rock Analysis Storage System [United States Geological Survey] [Information service or system] (IID)
RASS	ROSAT [Roentgen Satellite] All Sky Survey
RASS	Rotating Acoustic Stereo-Scanner [Telecommunications] (OA)
RASS	Ruggedized Airborne Seeker Simulator (MCD)
RASSAN	RADAR Sea State Analyzer [Marine science] (MSC)
RASSAS	Radio Astronomical Space System of Aperture Synthesis (MCD)
RASSH	Radiosondes Shipped From (NOAA)
RASSR	Reliable Advanced Solid-State RADAR
RAS-STADES	Records Association System - Standard Data Elements System (MCD)
RASSW	Radical Alliance of Social Service Workers (EA)
RAST	Radioallergosorbent Test [Immunochemistry]
Rast	Rastell's Entries and Statutes [England] [A publication] (DLA)
RAST	Recovery Assistance, Securing, and Traversing [Environmental science] (COE)
RAST	Recovery, Assist, Secure, and Traverse System [Navy]
RAST	Reliability and System Test
RASTA	Radiant Augmented Special Test Apparatus (MCD)
RASTA	Radiation Special Test Apparatus (IAA)
RASTA	Radio Station [Coast Guard]
Rast Abr	Rastell's Abridgment of the Statutes [A publication] (DLA)
RASTAC	Random Access Storage and Control [Computer science]
RASTAD	Random Access Storage and Display [Computer science]
RASTAS	Radiating Site Target Acquisition System (MCD)
RASTBC	Research Association for Scientific and Technical Bulletins of China (BUAC)
Rast Ent	Rastell's Entries and Statutes [A publication] (DLA)
RasterG	Raster Graphics, Inc. [Associated Press] (SAG)
RASTI	Rapid Speech Transition Index [Acoustics]
RASTIC	Rail, Automatic Straightening, Intrinsically Controlled [Railroad maintenance device] [British]
RASTR	Recorded Acoustic Signal Target Repeater
RASU	Rangoon Arts and Science University (BUAC)
RASUI	Reliability, Availability, Serviceability, Useability, Installability (IAA)
RaSV	Rasheed (Rat) Sarcoma Virus
RASV	Reusable Aerodynamic Space Vehicle
RASVY	Royal Australian Survey Corps (BUAC)
RAT	Radiatively-Active Trace [Analytical chemistry]
RAT	Radiological Assessment Team [Nuclear energy] (NRCH)
RAT	Ram Air Temperature
RAT	Ram Air Turbine (MCD)
RAT	Ranges, Ammunition, and Targets (MCD)
RAT	Rated
RAT	Rating (AABC)
RAT	Ratio (AAG)
RAT	Ratioflug Luftfahrtunternehmen GmbH [Germany ICAO designator] (FAAC)
RAT	Ration (IAA)
RAT	Rations [Military] (AABC)
RAT	Rat Island [Alaska] [Seismograph station code, US Geological Survey Closed] (SEIS)
RAT	Rat Resources [Vancouver Stock Exchange symbol]
RAT	Raynaud's Association Trust (EA)
RAT	Receipt Account Title File [Office of Management and Budget] (GFGA)
RAT	Register Alias Table [Computer science]
RAT	Regular Associated Troupers (EA)
RAT	Relative Accuracy Test (GFGA)
RAT	Reliability Assurance Test
RAT	Remote Area Terminal
RAT	Remote Associates Test [Psychology]
RAT	Repeat Action Tablet [Pharmacology]
RAT	Reseau des Amis de la Terre [Network of Friends of the Earth] [France Political party] (PPE)
RAT	Reserve Auxiliary Transformer (IEEE)
RAT	Resistance Armee Tunisienne [Tunisian Armed Resistance] (PD)
RAT	Restricted Articles Tariff
RAT	Right Anterior Thigh [Anatomy]
RAT	Rocket-Assisted Torpedo [Antisubmarine warfare]
RAT	Rocket Launched Antisubmarine Torpedo (IAA)

RAT..............	Rotational Autonomic Tester
RAT..............	Routing Automation Technique (PDAA)
RATA.........	Rankine Cycle Air Turboaccelerator
RA/TA.........	Restricted Availability/Technical Availability (NVT)
RATAC........	RADAR Analog Target Acquisition Computer
RATAC........	RADAR Coverage via Tactical Air Navigation (IAA)
RATAC........	RADAR Target Acquisition (IAA)
RATAC........	Raytheon Acoustic Telemetry and Control
RATAC........	Remote Airborne Television Display of Ground RADAR Coverage via TACAN (CET)
RATAN........	RADAR and Television Aid to Navigation
RATAN........	Radio and Television Aids to Navigation
RATAV........	RADAR Terrain Avoidance
RATBP.........	Revised Appendix to Be Published (MCD)
RATC..........	RADAR-Aided Tracking Computer (WDAA)
RATC..........	Rate-Aided Tracking Computer
RATC..........	Rhodesian Air Training Centre [British military] (DMA)
RATCC........	RADAR Air Traffic Control Center [Later, RATCF] [Navy]
RATCC........	Regional Air Traffic Control Center (NATG)
RATCF........	Radar Air Traffic Control Facilities [FAA] (TAG)
RATCHET....	Regional Atmospheric Transport Code for Hanford Emission Tracking (USDC)
RATCON......	RADAR Terminal Control
RATD..........	RADAR Automatic Target Detection [Military] (CAAL)
RATD..........	Register of Apparel and Textile Designers [British] (DBA)
RATD..........	Russian Aviation Trade [House] [Russia; established in 1991] (DOMA)
RATDA........	Regional African Telecommunication Database [International Telecommunication Union] (DUND)
RATE..........	Rate Analysis and Transportation Evaluation [Student legal action organization]
RATE..........	Record and Tape Exchange [Defunct] (EA)
RATE..........	Remote Area Teacher Education [Australia]
RATE..........	Remote Automatic Telemetry Equipment
RATE..........	Retention and Transfer Enhancement [Military]
RATEL.........	Radiotelephone
RATEL.........	Raytheon Automatic Test Equipment Language [Computer science] (CSR)
RATELO......	Radiotelephone Operator (AABC)
RATEP........	Remote Area Teacher Education Program [Australia]
RATER........	Response Analysis Tester [NASA]
RATES........	Rapid Access Tariff Expediting Service [Journal of Commerce, Inc.] [Database]
RATEX........	Rational Expectations [Economics]
RATF..........	Radio Aids Training Flight [British military] (DMA)
RATFNSC....	Religious Activities Task Force National Safety Council (EA)
RATFOR......	Rational FORTRAN [Computer science]
RA-TFR......	RADAR Altimeter - Terrain Following RADAR (MCD)
RATG..........	Rabbit Antithymocyte Globulin [Immunochemistry]
RATG..........	Radiotelegram [or Radiotelegraph]
RATG..........	Radio Telegraphy
RATG..........	Rhodesian Air Training Group [British military] (DMA)
RATHAS......	Rat Thymus Antiserum [Biochemistry] (MAE)
RATIG........	Robert A. Taft Institute of Government [Later, TTI] (EA)
RATIO........	Radio Telescope in Orbit (IEEE)
RATL..........	Rational Software [NASDAQ symbol] (SAG)
RATLER......	Robotic All-Terrain Lunar Exploration Rover [NASA]
RatnSft.......	Rational Software [Associated Press] (SAG)
RATNY........	Ratners Group PLC (MHDW)
RATO..........	Rocket-Assisted Takeoff [Aerospace]
RATOG.......	Rocket-Assisted Takeoff Gear [Aviation] (IEEE)
RATPAC......	RADAR Acquisition Tracking Probe for Active Calibration (DNAB)
RATR..........	Reliability Abstracts and Technical Reviews [NASA]
RATRAN......	RADAR Triangle Navigation (IAA)
RATS..........	RADAR Acquisition and Tracking System (MCD)
RATS..........	RADAR Altimeter Target Simulator (MCD)
RATS..........	Radio Amateur Telecommunications Society (EA)
RATS..........	Ram Air Turbine System
RATS..........	Rapid Area Transportation Support [Air Force] (MCD)
RATS..........	Rate and Track Subsystem
RATS..........	Rear Area Types [Military slang for rear support troops] (VNW)
RATS..........	Reconnaissance and Tactical Security [Teams] [Military]
RATS..........	Reform of the Australian Taxation System [1985] [A publication]
RATS..........	Remote Alarm Transmission System
RATS..........	Remote Area Tactical [Location and Landing] System
RATS..........	Remote Area Terminal System
RATS..........	Resolver Alignment Test Set
RATS..........	Restricted Articles Terminal System [IATA] (DS)
RATSC........	Rome Air Technical Service Command [Air Force]
RATSCAT.....	RADAR Target Scatter [RADAR program]
RATSEC......	Robert A. Taft Sanitary Engineering Center (AABC)
Rat Sel Cas...	Rattigan's Select Hindu Law Cases [A publication] (DLA)
RATT..........	Radio Airborne Teletype (MCD)
RATT..........	Radio Telephone/Teleprinter (INF)
RATT..........	Radioteletype
RATT..........	Radio Teletypewriter (IAA)
RATTC........	Radio and Teletype Control Center
Rattigan......	Rattigan's Select Hindu Law Cases [India] [A publication] (DLA)
Ratt LC......	Rattigan's Leading Cases on Hindu Law [A publication] (DLA)
RATTLE.......	Road Accident Tabulation Language (PDAA)
Rattlsnk......	[The] Rattlesnake Holding Co., Inc. [Associated Press] (SAG)
Rat Unrep Cr...	Ratanlal's Unreported Criminal Cases [India] [A publication] (DLA)
RATWUS......	Research and Technology Work Unit Summary
RATx..........	Radiation Therapy [Medicine] (MAE)
RAU...........	Radioactive Uptake [Medicine] (DMAA)

RAU	Radion Access Unit [Army]
RAU	Rangpur [Bangladesh] [Airport symbol] (AD)
RAU	Recurrent Aphthous Ulceration [Medicine]
RAU	Regional Acquisition Unit [NASA] (NASA)
RAU	Remote Acquisition Unit [NASA] (NASA)
RAU	Repairs and Utilities [Military] (IAA)
RAU	River Assault Unit [Navy]
Rauch	Rauch Industries, Inc. [Associated Press] (SAG)
RA-UDAA	Robbery Armed - Unlawful Driving Away of an Automobile [Police code]
RAUIC........	Repair Activity Unit Identification Code (MCD)
RAUIS.........	Remote Acquisition Unit Interconnecting Station [NASA] (NASA)
RAUK	Rear-Admiral of the United Kingdom [Navy British] (ROG)
Rauma	Rauma Oy [Associated Press] (SAG)
RaumaOy....	Rauma Oy [Associated Press] (SAG)
RAUS	Retired Association for the Uniformed Services (NADA)
R Aust Plan Inst J...	Royal Australian Planning Institute. Journal [A publication]
RAUT	Republic Automotive [NASDAQ symbol] (TTSB)
RAUT	Republic Automotive Parts, Inc. [NASDAQ symbol] (NQ)
R Aux AF ...	Royal Auxiliary Air Force [Formerly, AAF] [British]
RAV	Cravo Norte [Colombia] [Airport symbol] (OAG)
RAV	Ramm Venture [Vancouver Stock Exchange symbol]
RAV	Random Access Viewer
RAV	Ravensburg [Federal Republic of Germany] [Seismograph station code, US Geological Survey] (SEIS)
RAV	Ravine, PA [Location identifier FAA] (FAAL)
RAV	Receipt Authority Voucher
RAV	Recreation-Active Vehicle
RAV	Recreational Active Vehicle
RAV	Reduced Availability (MCD)
RAV	Remotely Augmented Vehicle [Aircraft]
RAV	Repackaged Asset Vehicle
RAV	Restricted Availability (NG)
RAV	Rogers Aviation Ltd. [British ICAO designator] (FAAC)
RAV	Rous-Associated Virus (MAE)
RAV4	Recreation-Active Vehicle 4-Wheel Drive
RAVC	Royal Army Veterinary Corps [Formerly, AVC] [British]
RAVE	RADAR Acquisition Visual-Tracking Equipment
RAVE	Random Access Video Editing [Computerized film editing]
RAVE	Random Access Viewing Equipment
RAVE	Rankin Automotive Group, Inc. [NASDAQ symbol] (SAG)
RAVE	Readjustment Assistance Act 74 for Vietnam Era Veterans (OICC)
RAV-E	Recreational Active Vehicle-Electric
RAVE	Research Aircraft for the Visual Environment [Helicopters] [Army]
RAVEC	RADAR Vector
RAVEN	Ranging and Velocity Navigation
Raven	Raven Industries, Inc. [Associated Press] (SAG)
RAVES	Rapid Aerospace Vehicle Evaluation System [Grumman Corp.]
RAVIR	RADAR Video Recorder (NVT)
RAVN	Raven Indus [NASDAQ symbol] (TTSB)
RAVN	Raven Industries, Inc. [NASDAQ symbol] (SAG)
RAVPRO	Resource Allocation and Validation Program
R-AVR........	Ruggedized Airborne Video Recorder
RAVU	Radiosonde Analysis and Verification Unit
RAW	Airway Resistance [Medicine]
RAW	Arawa [Papua New Guinea] [Airport symbol] (OAG)
RAW	Rapid American Withdrawal [Antiwar march sponsored by Vietnam Veterans Against the War] (EA)
Raw	Rawle's Pennsylvania Reports [5 vols.] [A publication] (DLA)
RAW	Read after Write
RAW	Read Alter Wire
RAW	Ready and Waiting [or Willing] [Slang]
RAW	Rear Axle Weight [Automotive engineering]
RAW	Reconnaissance Attack Wing [Navy] (NVT)
RAW	Redmond, OR [Location identifier FAA] (FAAL)
RAW	Regional Air (Pty) Ltd. [South Africa ICAO designator] (FAAC)
RAW	Reliability Assurance Warranty (MCD)
RAW	Rent-a-Wreck Industries Corp. [Vancouver Stock Exchange symbol]
RAW	Request for Additional Work [Navy] (DNAB)
RAW	Research and Analysis Wing [India] (BUAC)
RAW	Return America to Work [Also translated as "Reaganomics Ain't Working"] [UAW bumper sticker slogan]
RAW	Revenue Anticipation Warrant
RAW	Rifleman's Assault Weapon (MCD)
RAW	Right Atrial Wall [Medicine] (DMAA)
RAW	Right Attack Wing [Women's lacrosse position]
RAW	Rural American Women (EA)
RAWA	Rail-Water [Shipping]
RAWA	Renaissance Artists and Writers Association (EA)
RAWA	Rent-A-Wreck Amer Inc. [NASDAQ symbol] (TTSB)
RAWA	Rent-a-Wreck of America, Inc. [Los Angeles, CA] [NASDAQ symbol] (NQ)
RAWA	Revolutionary Association of the Women of Afghanistan
RAWARA......	Rail-Water-Rail [Shipping]
RAWARC.....	RADAR and Warning Coordination [Teletypewriter circuit]
RAWB	Railroad and Airline Wage Board [Terminated, 1953]
RAWC	Radioactive Waste Co-Ordinating Committee (BUAC)
Raw Const ...	Rawle on the Constitution of the United States [A publication] (DLA)
Raw Cov......	Rawle on Covenants for Title [A publication] (DLA)
RAWEB	Refractory Anemia without Excess of Blasts [Hematology]
Raw Eq	Rawle's Equity in Pennsylvania [A publication] (DLA)
RAWIE	Radio Weather Intercept Element
RAWIN	RADAR Wind [Upper air observation]
RAWIN	Radar Wind Sounding [Determination of winds by radar observation of a balloon] [Marine science] (OSRA)

RAWIND	RADAR Wind [*Upper air observation*]
RAWINDS	RADAR Wind Sounding [*Upper air observation*] (MSA)
RAWINS	RADAR Winds [*Upper air observation*]
RAWINS	Radio-Winds (USDC)
RAWINSONDE...	RADAR Wind Sounding and Radiosonde [*Upper air observation*]
RAWINSONES...	Radiosonde and RAWIN [*Radar Wind Sounding*] [*Combined method*] [*Marine science*] (OSRA)
RAWINSONES...	Radio-Winds and Radiosondes (USDC)
RAWIT	RNA [*Ribonucleic Acid*] Amplification with In/Vitro Translation [*Genetics*]
RAWL	Rawlings Sporting Goods [*NASDAQ symbol*] (TTSB)
RAWL	Rawlings Sporting Goods Company, Inc. [*NASDAQ symbol*] (SAG)
Rawle	Rawle's Pennsylvania Supreme Court Reports [*1828-35*] [*A publication*] (DLA)
Rawle Const US...	Rawle on the Constitution of the United States [*A publication*] (DLA)
Rawle Cov...	Rawle on Covenants for Title [*A publication*] (DLA)
Rawle Pen & W...	Rawle, Penrose, and Watts' Pennsylvania Reports [*1828-40*] [*A publication*] (DLA)
Rawlings	Rawlings Sporting Goods Co., Inc. [*Associated Press*] (SAG)
Rawl Mun Corp...	Rawlinson's Municipal Corporations [*10th ed.*] [*1910*] [*A publication*] (DLA)
RAWO	Reliability Assurance Work Order (MCD)
RAWOOP-SNAP...	Ramo-Wooldridge One-Pass Assembly Program (SAA)
RAWP	Resource Allocation Working Party [*British*]
RAWS	RADAR Altimeter Warning Set (MCD)
RAWS	RADAR Automatic Weather System
RAWS	Remote Area Weather Station (MCD)
RAWS	Remote Automatic Weather Station
RAWSII	Role Adaptable Weapons System [*Military*]
RAWSII	Raw Statement of Intelligence Interest (MCD)
RawsnKo	Rawson-Koenig, Inc. [*Associated Press*] (SAG)
RAWTS	RNA [*Ribonucleic Acid*] Amplification with Transcript Sequencing [*Genetics*]
RAX	Random Access [*Computer science*] (MHDI)
RAX	Remote Access [*Computer science Telecommunications*]
RAX	Remote Access Terminal (NAKS)
RAX	Rio Alto Exploration Ltd. [*Toronto Stock Exchange symbol*]
RAX	Rural Automatic Exchange (DEN)
RAXR	Rax Restaurants (EFIS)
Ray	Raymundus de Pennafort [*Deceased, 1275*] [*Authority cited in pre-1607 legal work*] (DSA)
Ray	Raynerius de Forlivio [*Deceased, 1358*] [*Authority cited in pre-1607 legal work*] (DSA)
RAY	Rayrock Yellowknife Resources, Inc. [*Toronto Stock Exchange symbol*]
RAY	Raytech Corp. [*NYSE symbol*] (SPSG)
RAY	Rothesay [*Scotland*] [*Airport symbol*] (OAG)
Ray B Ex ...	Raymond's Bill of Exceptions [*A publication*] (DLA)
RAYCI	Raytheon Controlled Inventory [*Computer science*]
Raycm	Raychem Corp. [*Associated Press*] (SAG)
RAY-COM	Raytheon Communications Equipment [*Citizens band radio*]
RAYDAC	Raytheon Digital Automatic Computer (MUGU)
Ray de For...	Raynerius de Forlivio [*Deceased, 1358*] [*Authority cited in pre-1607 legal work*] (DSA)
Rayden	Rayden on Divorce [*A publication*] (DLA)
Ray de Saba...	Raymundus de Sabanacho [*Authority cited in pre-1607 legal work*] (DSA)
RAYDIST......	Ray-Path Distance (MUGU)
Ray Ins	Ray's Medical Jurisprudence of Insanity [*A publication*] (DLA)
RAYM	[*The*] Raymond Corp. [*NASDAQ symbol*] (NQ)
Raym B Ex...	Raymond's Bill of Exceptions [*A publication*] (DLA)
Raym Ch Dig...	Raymond's Digested Chancery Cases [*A publication*] (DLA)
Raymd	Raymond Corp. [*Associated Press*] (SAG)
Ray Med Jur...	Ray's Medical Jurisprudence of Insanity [*A publication*] (DLA)
Ray Men Path...	Ray's Mental Pathology [*A publication*] (DLA)
Raym Ld	Lord Raymond's English King's Bench Reports [*3 vols.*] [*A publication*] (DLA)
Raymond	Raymond's Reports [*81-89 Iowa*] [*A publication*] (DLA)
Rayn	Rayner's English Tithe Cases [*3 vols.*] [*A publication*] (DLA)
RAYNET	Radio Amateurs Emergency Network (EECA)
RAYNET	Raytheon Data Communications Network (NITA)
RaynrInc	Rayonier, Inc. [*Associated Press*] (SAG)
Rayn Ti Cas...	Rayner's English Tithe Cases [*1575-1782*] [*A publication*] (DLA)
RAY/RD	Raytheon Co./Research Division
RAYS	Risk and Youth Smoking [*Project*] (AIE)
RAYS	Sunglass Hut International, Inc. [*NASDAQ symbol*] (SAG)
RAYS	Sunglass Hut Intl [*NASDAQ symbol*] (TTSB)
RAYSISTOR...	Raytheon Resistor [*Electro-optical control device*]
RAYSPAN ...	Raytheon Spectrum Analyzer
Raytc	Raytech Corp. [*Associated Press*] (SAG)
Raytel	Raytel Medical Corp. [*Associated Press*] (SAG)
RAY-TEL	Raytheon Telephone [*Citizens band radio*]
Raythn	Raytheon Co. [*Associated Press*] (SAG)
Ray Ti Cas...	Rayner's English Tithe Cases [*1575-1782*] [*A publication*] (DLA)
RayTLP	Rayonier Timberlands Ltd. [*Associated Press*] (SAG)
RAZ	Razoxane [*Medicine*] (DMAA)
RAZ	Rijnmond Air Services BV [*Netherlands ICAO designator*] (FAAC)
RAZ	Rolled Alloyed Zinc
RAZEL	Range, Azimuth, and Elevation
RAZON........	Range and Azimuth Only
RAZPE	Resident ARGMA [*Army Rocket and Guided Missile Agency*] Zeus Project Engineer (AAG)
RAZR	American Safety Razor Co. [*NASDAQ symbol*] (SAG)
RAZR	Amer Safety Razor [*NASDAQ symbol*] (TTSB)

RAZS	Rolled Alloyed Zinc Sheet
R/B	ASE [*National Institute for Automotive Service Excellence*] Test Registration Booklet [*A publication*] (EAAP)
R_B	Base Resistance (IDOE)
RB	Botswana [*IYRU nationality code*] (IYR)
RB	RADAR Beacon
R/B	Radio Beacon
RB	Radio Bearing (DEN)
RB	Radio Brenner [*Radio network*] [*Germany*]
RB	Railroad Bond [*Business term*] (MHDW)
RB	Rate Beacon (AAG)
RB	Rated Boost
RB	Rating Board [*Medicine*] (MAE)
RB	Ration Book
RB	Reactor Building [*Nuclear energy*] (NRCH)
RB	Read Backward
RB	Read Buffer
RB	Reading & Bates [*NYSE symbol*] (TTSB)
RB	Reading & Bates Corp. [*NYSE symbol*] (SPSG)
RB	Reasons to Believe [*An association*] (EA)
rb	Rebreathing [*Medicine*] (DAVI)
RB	Recirculating Ball [*Automotive engineering*]
RB	Reconnaissance Bomber
RB	Recovery Beacon
RB	Red Book [*Full name is "Drug Topics Red Book," a pharmacist's guide*] [*A publication*]
RB	Red Border (COE)
RB	Red Brigades [*Revolutionary group*] [*Italy*]
RB	Redeemable Bond [*Investment term*]
RB	Reentry Body
RB	Reference Burst (LAIN)
RB	Regular Budget [*United Nations*]
RB	Relationship Banking (EBF)
RB	Relative Bearing [*Navigation*]
RB	Relay Block (MSA)
RB	Remote Batch [*Computer science*] (IAA)
RB	Renaut's Bodies [*Neurology*]
RB	Renegotiation Board [*Terminated, 1979*] [*Federal government*]
RB	Renegotiation Bulletins [*A publication*] (DLA)
RB	Report Bibliography
RB	Request Block
RB	Research Bulletin
RB	Reserve Bank (ADA)
RB	Reserve Blocked (IAA)
RB	Resistance Brazing
RB	Respiratory Bronchiole [*Medicine*] (MAE)
RB	Restiform Body [*Neuroanatomy*]
RB	Restricted Bulletin
Rb	Retinoblastoma [*Oncology*]
RB	Retractable Boom
RB	Retraining Benefits [*Employment*] (OICC)
RB	Retrobulbar [*Ophthalmology*] (DAVI)
RB	Return to Bias
RB	Revenue Bond [*Investment term*]
RB	Reverse Blocked
RB	Revision Block (MSA)
RB	Rich Bitch [*Slang*]
RB	Rifle Brigade
RB	Right Base [*Aviation*] (FAAC)
RB	Right Border [*Genetics*]
RB	Right Bronchus [*Anatomy*] (DAVI)
RB	Right Bundle [*Medicine*] (DB)
RB	Right Buttock [*Anatomy*]
RB	Right Fullback [*Soccer*]
RB	Rigid Boat
RB	Rigid Body
RB	Ring Back [*Computer science*] (IAA)
RB	Ripple Banking [*Electronics*] (ECII)
RB	Ritzaus Bureau [*Press agency*] [*Denmark*]
RB	Road Bend
RB	Road Buffer (SAA)
RB	Roast Beef [*Restaurant slang*]
Rb	Rock Bass [*Ichthyology*]
RB	Rocket Branch (AAG)
R_B	Rockwell Hardness B-Scale (WDAA)
RB	Rohon-Beard (Cells) [*Neurology*]
RB	Rollback [*Telecommunications*] (TEL)
RB	Rollback Disability Claims [*Social Security Administration*] (OICC)
RB	Roller Bearing
RB	Roman-British
RB	Rose Bengal [*A dye*]
RB	Roth-Bernhardt [*Syndrome*] [*Medicine*] (DB)
RB	Round Bobbin [*A publication*] (EAAP)
RB	Royal Burgh
RB	Rubber Band (ADA)
RB	Rubber Base [*Technical drawings*]
RB	Rubber Bearing (DS)
RB	Rubber Block (DNAB)
RB	Rubidium [*Chemical element*]
RB	Ruble [*Monetary unit*] [*Former USSR*]
RB	Run Back [*Typography*]
RB	Running Back [*Football*]
RB	Rural Bank (ADA)
RB	Russell Bodies [*Medicine*]
RB	Russet-Burbank Potato

RBa	Barrington Public Library, Barrington, RI [Library symbol Library of Congress] (LCLS)
RBA	Rabat [Morocco] [Airport symbol] (OAG)
RBA	Rabat [Morocco] [Seismograph station code, US Geological Survey] (SEIS)
RBA	RADAR Beacon Antenna
RBA	Radial Blanket Assembly [Nuclear energy] (NRCH)
RBA	Radio Beacon Array
RBA	Radiobinding Assay [Analytical chemistry]
RBA	Raisin Bargaining Association (EA)
RBA	Ranger Battalions Association (EA)
RBA	Rare Bird Alert [Linnaean Society] (BARN)
RBA	Recovery Beacon Antenna [NASA] (KSC)
RBA	Reentry Body Assembly
RBA	Refined Bitumen Association [British] (DBA)
RBA	Rehoboth Baster Association [Namibia] (PPW)
RBA	Reinsurance Brokers Association (BUAC)
RBA	Relative Binding Affinity [Chemistry]
RBA	Relative Byte Address [Computer science] (MCD)
RBA	Religious Booksellers Association (EA)
RBA	Rescue Breathing Apparatus
RBA	Reserve Bank of Australia
RBA	Retail Bakers of America (EA)
RBA	Retail, Book, Stationery, and Allied Trades Employees' Association [A union] [British]
RBA	Retailer's Bakery Association (NTPA)
RBA	Right Brachial Artery [Anatomy] (DAVI)
RBA	Risk-Based Audit
RBA	Road Bitumen Association [British] (BI)
RBA	Roadside Business Association (EA)
RBA	Romanian Banking Association (BUAC)
RBA	Rose Bengal Antigen (MAE)
RBA	Rotary Beam Antenna
RBA	Rotor Blade Antenna
RBA	Royal Bhutanese Army (BUAC)
RBA	Royal Brunei Airlines [ICAO designator] (FAAC)
RBA	Royal Society of British Architects
RBA	Royal Society of British Artists
RBAAP	Riverbank Army Ammunition Plant (AABC)
RBaB	Barrington College, Barrington, RI [Library symbol Library of Congress] (LCLS)
RBAF	Royal Belgian Air Force
RBAF	Royal Brunei Armed Forces
RBAL	Reprocessing Building Analytical Laboratory [Nuclear energy] (NRCH)
RBAM	Remote Batch Access Method (IAA)
RBAN	Regular Best Asymptotically Normal (PDAA)
RBAP	Repetitive Bursts of Action Potential [Electrophysiology]
RBAS	Rostral Basilar Artery Syndrome [Medicine] (DMAA)
RBAUSC	Romanian Baptist Association of United States and Canada [Defunct] (EA)
RBA WWII	Ranger Battalions Association World War II (EA)
RBB	Rabbi
RBB	Rabbit-Air AG, Zurich [Switzerland ICAO designator] (FAAC)
RBB	Reference Books Bulletin (AL)
RBB	Remazolium Brilliant Blue [Reactive dye composition]
RBB	Rental Bond Board [New South Wales, Australia]
RBB	Reuters Business Briefing [A publication]
RBB	Right Breast Biopsy [Gynecology] (DAVI)
RBB	Right Bundle Branch [Cardiology] (AAMN)
RBBB	Right Bundle-Branch Block [Cardiology]
RBBP	Retinoblastoma Binding Protein (DMAA)
RBBR	R-B Rubber Products [NASDAQ symbol] (TTSB)
RBBR	R-B Rubber Products, Inc. [NASDAQ symbol] (SAG)
RBBS	Remote Bulletin Board System [For IBM computers] [Telecommunications]
RBBSB	Right Bundle-Branch System Block [Cardiology]
RBBT	Rebabbit
RBBX	Right Breast Biopsy Examination [Medicine] (AAMN)
RBC	Radio Beam Communications
RBC	Radio Bureau of Canada
RBC	Rail-Borne Crane [British]
RBC	Reactive Bias Circuit (MCD)
RBC	Reactor Building Cooling [Environmental science] (COE)
RBC	Real Estate Brokerage Council (EA)
RBC	Red Badge of Courage (EA)
RBC	Red Blood Cell [or Corpuscle] [Medicine]
RBC	Red Blood Count [Medicine]
RBC	Redundant Battery Charger (KSC)
RBC	Regal Beloit [AMEX symbol] (TTSB)
RBC	Regal-Beloit Corp. [AMEX symbol] (SPSG)
RBC	Regional Blood Center [Red Cross]
RBC	Regulations of British Columbia [Attorney General's Ministry] [No longer available online] [Information service or system] (CRD)
RBC	Remote Balance Control
RBC	Remote Black Concentrator [Telecommunications] (LAIN)
RBC	Retortable Barrier Container [For food]
RBC	Return Beam Camera
RBC	Rhodesia Broadcasting Corp.
rbc	Ribulose Bisphosphate Carboxylase/Oxygenase (DOG)
RBC	Rio Blanco [Colorado] [Seismograph station code, US Geological Survey Closed] (SEIS)
RBC	Roller Bearing Corp. (MCD)
RBC	Ropec Industries, Inc. [Vancouver Stock Exchange symbol]
RBC	Rotating Beam Ceilometer [Aviation]
RBC	Rotating Biological Contractors [Processing equipment]
RBC	Royal Bank of Canada [UTLAS symbol]
RBC	Royal British Colonial Society of Artists
RBC	Royal British-Colonial Society of Artists, London [1886] (NGC)
RBCA	Rhodes Bantam Class Association (EA)
RBC-ADA	Red Blood Cell Adenosine Deaminase [An enzyme] (AAMN)
RBCC	Red Blood Cell Cast [Hematology] (DAVI)
RBCC	Reentry Body Coordination Committee
RBCCW	Reactor Building Closed Cooling Water [Nuclear energy] (NRCH)
RBCD	Right Border Cardiac Dullness [Medicine] (DMAA)
RBC FO	Red Blood Cell Fallout [Hematology] (DAVI)
RBC frag	Red Blood Cell Fragility (STED)
RBCH	Rod Bank Coil Unit [Nuclear energy] (IAA)
RBC/hpf	Red Blood Cells per High Power Field [Hematology] (MAE)
RBCLCW	Reactor Building Closed Loop Cooling Water [Environmental science] (COE)
RBCM	Red Blood Cell Mass [in circulation]
RBCM	Reference Book of Corporate Managements [Dun's Marketing Services] [Information service or system] (CRD)
RBCO	Ryan Beck & Co. [NASDAQ symbol] (TTSB)
RBCO	Ryan, Beck & Co., Inc. [West Orange, NJ] [NASDAQ symbol] (NQ)
RBC/P	Red Blood Cell to Plasma [Ratio] (STED)
RBCR	Reprocessing Building Control Room [Nuclear energy] (NRCH)
RBCS	Radio Beam Communications Set
RBCS	Reactor Building Cooling System [Nuclear energy] (NRCH)
RBC s/f	Red Blood Cells Spun Filtration (STED)
RBCTK	Red Blood Cell Transketolase [Medicine] (PDAA)
RBCU	Reactor Building Cooling Unit [Nuclear energy] (NRCH)
RBCV	Red Blood Cell Volume [Hematology]
RBCWS	Reactor Building Cooling Water System (IEEE)
RBD	Dallas, TX [Location identifier FAA] (FAAL)
RBD	Rapid Beam Deflector (WDAA)
RBD	Recurrent Brief Depression [Psychology] (ECON)
RBD	Refined, Bleached, and Deodorized [Vegetable oil technology]
RBD	Reliability Block Diagram (NITA)
RBD	Reliable Block Diagram (MCD)
RBD	REM [Rapid Eye Movement] Behavior Disorder [Medicine]
RBD	Rice Blast Disease [Fungal disease of crop plants]
RBD	Right Border of Dullness [Cardiology]
RBD	RNA [Ribonucleic Acid] Binding Domain [Biochemistry]
RBD	Rubber Block Drive [Mechanical power transmission]
RBD	Rubbermaid, Inc. [NYSE symbol] (SPSG)
RBD	Trans World Express, Inc. [ICAO designator] (FAAC)
RBDE	RADAR Bright Display Equipment [FAA]
RBDF	Royal Bahamian Defence Force (BUAC)
RBDM	Registrar of Births Deaths and Marriages [Australia]
RBDNRQ	Received but Did Not Return Questionnaire (AABC)
RBDP	Rehoboth Bevryde Demokratiese Party [Rehoboth Free Democratic Party or Liberation Front] [Namibia] [Political party] (EY)
RBDP	Rocket Booster Development Program [Λοгоораоо] (ΛΛQ)
RBDS	RADAR Bomb Directing Systems
RBDS	Radio Broadcast Data Service (WDMC)
RBDS	Radio Broadcast Data System
RBDS	Radio Broadcasting Data System
RBDS	Roberds, Inc. [NASDAQ symbol] (SAG)
RBDT	Reverse Blocking Diode Thyristor (IAA)
RBDV	Raspberry Bushy Dwarf Virus [Plant pathology]
RBE	Arbet International Ltd. [Hungary ICAO designator] (FAAC)
RBE	Bassett, NE [Location identifier FAA] (FAAL)
RBE	Radiation Biological Effectiveness (IAA)
RBE	Radiation Biological Equivalent
RBE	Red Ball Express [Military]
RBE	Relative Biological Effectiveness [or Efficiency] [of stated types of radiation]
rbe	Relative Biological Effectiveness (WDAA)
RBE	Remain Behind Equipment [Navy] (ANA)
RBE	Remote Batch Entry (CMD)
RBE	Renabie Mines (1981) Ltd. [Toronto Stock Exchange symbol]
RBE	Replacement Battery Equipment
RBEB	Ribbon Bridge Erection Boat (MCD)
RBEC	Roller Bearing Engineers Committee (EA)
RBEDT	Reactor Building Equipment Drain Tank [Nuclear energy] (NRCH)
RB/ER	Reduced Blast/Enhanced Radiation
RBES	Rule-Based Expert System (LAIN)
RBESI	Reactor Building Exhaust System Isolation [Nuclear energy] (NRCH)
RBF	Raba Raba [New Guinea] [Airport symbol] (AD)
RBF	Radial Basis Function [Mathematics]
RBF	Read Bit Feedback [Computer science] (WDAA)
RBF	Reconnaissance by Fire [Military] (VNW)
RBF	Red Lake Buffalo Resources Ltd. [Toronto Stock Exchange symbol]
RBF	Regional Blood Flow [Physiology]
RBF	Remote Batch Facility
RBF	Renal Blood Flow [Medicine]
RBF	Retarded Bomb Fuze
RBF	Rice Bran Factor (DB)
RBF	Roberson, Fred, Louisville KY [STAC]
RBFB	Retirement Benefits Fund Board [Australia]
RBFC	Razzy Bailey Fan Club (EA)
RBFC	Reactor Building Fan Coolers [Environmental science] (COE)
RBFC	Retract Before Firing Contractor (NG)
RBFC	Royal Business Funds Corp. (EFIS)
RBFIT	Retirement Benefits Fund Investment Trust [Australia]
RBFPP	Rocket Booster Fuel Pod Pickup (MUGU)
RBFT	Romanian Bank of Foreign Trade (IMH)
RBG	British Guiana Reports of Opinions [A publication] (DLA)

RBG	Right Buccal Ganglion [*Dentistry*]
RBG	Roseburg [*Oregon*] [*Airport symbol*] (AD)
RBG	Roseburg, OR [*Location identifier FAA*] (FAAL)
RBG	Royal Botanic Garden [*British*] (WA)
RBG	Royal Botanic Gardens, Kew (BUAC)
RBGDT	Royal Botanic Gardens and Domain Trust [*Australia*]
RBGF	Resin-Bonded Glass-Fiber (PDAA)
RBGH	Recombinant Bovine Growth Hormone
RBGM	Real Beam Ground Map (MCD)
RBGNH	Royal Botanic Gardens and National Herbarium [*Australia*]
RBGS	Radio Beacon Guidance System (AAG)
RBGS	Royal Botanic Gardens Sydney [*Australia*]
RBH	Regal Bahamas International Airways Ltd. [*ICAO designator*] (FAAC)
RBH	Regimental Beachhead [*Army*]
RBH	Rollins Burdick Hunter Co. (EFIS)
RBH	Royal Blind Homes [*Australia*]
RBH	Royal Bucks Hussars [*British military*] (DMA)
RBH	Rutherford Birchard Hayes [*US president, 1822-1893*]
RBHA	Rotor Blade Homing Antenna
RBHB	Red and Black Horizontal Bands [*Navigation markers*]
RBHC	Regional Bell Holding Co. (BYTE)
RBHPC	Rutherford B. Hayes Presidential Center (EA)
RBHPF	Reactor Building Hydrogen Purge Fan (IEEE)
RBHS	Reactor Building Heating System [*Nuclear energy*] (NRCH)
RBI	Rabi [*Fiji*] [*Airport symbol*] (OAG)
RBI	RADAR Blip Identification Message
RBI	Radio Berlin International
RBI	Radiographic Baseline [*Medicine*] (DMAA)
RBI	Railway Benevolent Institution [*British*]
RBI	Range Bearing Indicator (MCD)
RBI	Recombinant Bio-Catalysis, Inc. [*Commercial firm*]
RBI	Relative Bearing Indicator [*Aviation*] (DA)
RBI	Remote Bus Isolator (SSD)
RBI	Reply by Indorsement
RBI	Reserve Bank of India (ECON)
RBI	Resource-Based Industry (ODBW)
RBI	Ripple-Blanking Input (IEEE)
RBI	Rocketborne Instrumentation (IAA)
RBI	Root Beer Institute [*Defunct*]
RBI	Runs Batted In [*Baseball*]
RBiCalz	Revista Biblica. Rafael Calzada [*Argentina*] [*A publication*] (BJA)
RBID	Reference Burst Identification (LAIN)
RBIF	Red Basic Intelligence File (MCD)
Rb Imp	Rubber Base Impression [*Medicine*] (DMAA)
RBIN	R & B, Inc. [*NASDAQ symbol*] (SPSG)
RBJ	Aeroservicios del Bajio, SA de CV [*Mexico*] [*FAA designator*] (FAAC)
RBJ	Rebun [*Japan*] [*Airport symbol Obsolete*] (OAG)
RBJ	Tucson, AZ [*Location identifier FAA*] (FAAL)
RBK	RBK NT Corp. [*Toronto Stock Exchange symbol*]
RBK	Reebok International Ltd. [*NYSE symbol*] (SPSG)
RBK	Reebok Intl [*NYSE symbol*] (TTSB)
RBK	Right Bank
RBK & C	Royal Borough of Kensington and Chelsea [*England*]
RBKV	Resource Bank [*NASDAQ symbol*] (TTSB)
RBL	Radiation Biology Laboratory [*Smithsonian Institution*]
RBL	Raised Black Letters [*Automobile tires*]
RBL	Range and Bearing Launch [*Navy*] (CAAL)
RBL	Rat Basophilic Leukemia [*Cell line*]
RBL	Reasonable Benefit Limit [*Superannuation*]
RBL	Rebroadcast Link [*Aerial*]
RBL	Recommended Buy List
RBL	Red Bluff [*California*] [*Airport symbol*] (AD)
RBL	Red Bluff, CA [*Location identifier FAA*] (FAAL)
RBL	Reid's Base Line [*Neuroanatomy*]
RBL	Resource Based Learning (ADA)
RBL	Rheological Boundary Layer [*Physics*]
RBL	Rifled Breech-Loading [*Gun*]
RBL	Right Buttock Line (MCD)
RBL	Rio Blanco Resources Ltd. [*Vancouver Stock Exchange symbol*]
RBL	Royal British Legion [*British military*] (DMA)
RBL	Rubblestone [*Technical drawings*]
RBL	Ruble [*Monetary unit*] [*Former USSR*]
RBL	Ruch Biblijny i Liturgiczny (BJA)
RBLAC	Regional Bureau for Latin America and the Caribbean [*United Nations*] (ECON)
RBLC	Renaissance Business and Law Center, Inc. [*Detroit, MI*] (TSSD)
RBLDR	Rebuilder
RBLR	Red-Banded Leaf Roller [*Entomology*]
RBLS	River Bend Library System [*Library network*]
RBLS	Royal British Legion of Scotland [*British*] (DBA)
rblt	Rebuilt (VRA)
RBM	Range Betting Method
RBM	Readiness Based Maintenance [*Army*] (DOMA)
RBM	Real-Time Batch Monitor [*Xerox Corp.*]
RBM	Reasonable Benefit Multiple
RBM	Regional Battle Manager [*DoD*]
RBM	Regional Bone Mass
R-B-M	Reinforced Brick Masonry
RBM	Relative Batch Monitor [*Computer science*] (MHDB)
RBM	Remote Batch Module
RBM	Resistance to Bending Moment [*Automotive engineering*]
RBM	Retractor Bulb Motoneuron [*Neurology*]
RBM	Rifleman's Breaching Munition Program [*Military*] (INF)
RBM	Rod-Block Monitor [*Nuclear energy*] (NRCH)
RBMA	Radiologists Business Managers Association (EA)

RBMA	Radiology Business Management Association [*Formerly, Radiologists Business Managers Association*] (EA)
RBME	, Egon [*Keil*] [*Haydee Madsen In ballet title, "Initials RBME." Refers to the four starring dancers.*]
RBMECAB	Regional Bureau of the Middle East Committee for the Affairs of the Blind [*An association*] (EAIO)
RBML	Rare Books & Manuscript Librarianship [*American Library Association*]
RBMR	Rotating Bubble Membrane Radiator [*Battelle Pacific Northwest Laboratories*]
RBMS	Rare Books and Manuscripts Section [*Association of College and Research Libraries*]
RBMS	Remote Bridge Management Software (HGAA)
RBMT	Retrospective Bibliographies on Magnetic Tape (NASA)
RBMU	Regions Beyond Missionary Union [*Later, Regions Beyond Missionary Union International*] (EA)
RBMX	Robomatix Technologies [*NASDAQ symbol*] (SAG)
RBN	Brown University, Providence, RI [*OCLC symbol*] (OCLC)
RBN	PTS [*Predicasts*] Regional Business News [*Cleveland, OH*] [*Database*] [*Information service or system*] (IID)
RBN	Radiobeacon [*Maps and charts*]
RBN	Random Block Number [*Computer science*]
RBN	Red Baron Aviation, Inc. [*ICAO designator*] (FAAC)
R Bn	Red Beacon [*Nautical charts*]
RBN	Retrobulbar Neuritis [*Medicine*]
RBN	Ribbon (MSA)
RBN	Rybnik [*Poland*] [*Seismograph station code, US Geological Survey*] (SEIS)
RBNA	Royal British Nurses' Association [*British*] (BI)
RBNC	Republic Bancorp [*NASDAQ symbol*] (TTSB)
RBNC	Republic Bancorp, Inc. [*NASDAQ symbol*] (NQ)
RBNK	Regent Bancshares Corp. [*NASDAQ symbol*] (NQ)
RBNKE	Regent Bancshares [*NASDAQ symbol*] (TTSB)
RBNKP	Ragent Bancshrs 10% Cv'A'Pfd [*NASDAQ symbol*] (TTSB)
RBNWE	Regent Bancshares Wrrt [*NASDAQ symbol*] (TTSB)
RBNZ	Reserve Bank of New Zealand
RBO	Rainbow Bridge Organization (EA)
RBO	Rainbow Cargo Express [*Ghana*] [*ICAO designator*] (FAAC)
RBO	Relationship by Objective [*Management technique*]
RBO	Ripple-Blanking Output (IEEE)
RBO	Robore [*Bolivia*] [*Airport symbol*] (AD)
RBO	Russian Brotherhood Organization (NADA)
RBO	Russian Brotherhood Organization of the United States of America
RBOA	Residential Boat Owners Association (BUAC)
RBOA	Richardson Boat Owners Association (EA)
RBOB	Reformulated Gasoline Blendstock for Downstream Oxygenated Blending
RBOB	Renewable-Base Oxygenated Blend [*Automotive fuel*]
RBOC	Rapid Bloom Offboard Chaff [*Navy ship system*]
RBOC	Regional Bell Operating Co.
RBOC	Report Back on Course [*Aviation*] (FAAC)
RBOD	Required Beneficial Occupancy Data (SAA)
RBOF	Receiving Basin for Off-Site Fuel [*Nuclear energy*]
RBOF	Regulated Business Operations Fund (AAGC)
RBOF	Report Back on Frequency [*Aviation*] (FAAC)
RBOK	Rinderpest Bovine Old Kabete [*A virus*]
RBOT	Robotics Information [*EIC/Intelligence, Inc.*] [*Information service or system*] (IID)
R-BOT	Rotating Bomb Oxidation Test [*Lubricant testing*] [*Automotive engineering*]
RBOUSA	Russian Brotherhood Organization of the USA (EA)
RBOW	Rupture of the Bag of Waters [*Medicine*] (DMAA)
RBP	Raba Raba [*Papua New Guinea*] [*Airport symbol*] (OAG)
RBP	Ratio Balance Panel
RBP	Ration Breakdown Point [*Military*] (AABC)
RBP	Reactor Building Protection [*Nuclear energy*] (NRCH)
RBP	Registered Business Programmer [*Offered earlier by Data Processing Management Association, now discontinued*] (IEEE)
RBP	Remote Batch Processing [*Computer science*] (IAA)
RBP	Resting Blood Pressure [*Cardiology*] (DAVI)
RBP	Retinol-Binding Protein [*Biochemistry*]
RBP	Retractable Bow Propeller
RBP	Return Battery Pack (KSC)
RBP	Riboflavin-Binding Protein [*Biochemistry*]
RBP	Ribose Binding Protein [*Biochemistry*]
RBP	Rocket Branch Panel (AAG)
RBP	RUBISCO [*Ribulosebisphosphate Carboxylase/Oxygenase*] Binding Protein [*Biochemistry*]
RBPA	Royal Bancshares of Pennsylvania [*NASDAQ symbol*] (SAG)
RBPA	Royal Bank of Pennsylvania [*NASDAQ symbol*] (NQ)
RBPAA	Royal Bancshares(PA)'A' [*NASDAQ symbol*] (TTSB)
RBPB	Raffles and Bingo Permits Board [*Victoria, Australia*]
RBPC	Revised Behavior Problem Checklist [*Test*]
RBPCA	Rare Breeds Poultry Club of America (EA)
RBPCase	Ribulosebisphosphate Carboxylase [*Also, RUBISCO*] [*An enzyme*]
RBPD	Religious Book Publishing Division [*of Association of American Publishers*] [*RPG*] [*Superseded by*]
RBPF	Royal Bahamas Police Force (BUAC)
RBPP	Rotor Burst Protection Program [*NASA*]
RBPr	Reading & Bates $1.625 Cv Pfd [*NYSE symbol*] (TTSB)
RBPT	Rose Bengal Plate Test [*Agriculture*] (OA)
RBQ	Request Block Queue [*Computer science*] (IAA)
RBQ	Rurrenabaque [*Bolivia*] [*Airport symbol*] (OAG)
RBR	RADAR Boresight Range (KSC)
RBR	Rambler Exploration [*Vancouver Stock Exchange symbol*]

RBR .... Refracted Bottom-Reflected Ray
RBR .... Renegotiation Board Regulation [or Ruling]
RBR .... Research Branch [Naval Technical Training Command] [Millington, TN]
RBR .... Rio Branco [Brazil] [Airport symbol] (OAG)
RBr .... Rogers Free Library, Bristol, RI [Library symbol Library of Congress] (LCLS)
RBR .... Rotor Blade RADAR
RBR .... Rubber
rbr .... Rubber (VRA)
rbr .... Rubricator [MARC relator code] [Library of Congress] (LCCP)
RBrHi .... Bristol Historical and Preservation Society, Bristol, RI [Library symbol Library of Congress] (LCLS)
RBRIZED ...... Rubberized
RBRRS .... Rhythm and Blues Rock and Roll Society [Later, RBRRSI] (EA)
RBRRSI .... Rhythm and Blues Rock and Roll Society, Inc. (EA)
RBrRW .... Roger Williams College, Bristol, RI [Library symbol Library of Congress] (LCLS)
R-B Rub ...... R-B Rubber Products, Inc. [Associated Press] (SAG)
RBRV .... Resource-Based Relative Value [Health insurance]
RBRVS .... Resource-Based Relative Value Scale [Medicare]
RBS .... RADAR Beacon Sequencer
RBS .... RADAR Beacon Station (IAA)
RBS .... RADAR Beacon System
RBS .... RADAR Beam Sharpening
RBS .... RADAR Bombardment System (NATG)
RBS .... RADAR Bomb Scoring
RBS .... RADAR Bombsight
RBS .... Radio Beacon Station (IAA)
RBS .... Raise-Bottom-Slightly [Definition of a gentleman] [Slang British] (DI)
RBS .... Random Barrage System [Military]
RBS .... Random Blood Smear [Hematology] (DAVI)
RBS .... Random Blood Sugar [Medicine] (MAE)
RBS .... Rare Books Section [Association of College and Research Libraries]
RBS .... Rare Breeds Society (BUAC)
RBS .... Rated Breaking Strength (IAA)
RBS .... Raydex Bonded Shield (NITA)
RBS .... Reactor Building Spray [Nuclear energy] (NRCH)
RBS .... Reactor Building Sump [Nuclear energy] (IAA)
RBS .... Recoverable Booster System
RBS .... Recreational Boating Safety [USCG] (TAG)
RBS .... Reformer's Book Shelf [A publication]
RBS .... Regional Briefing Station
RBS .... Remote Batch System
RBS .... Remote Battle System
RBS .... Research for Better Schools, Inc. [Philadelphia, PA] [Department of Education]
RBS .... Resonant Bond Scattering (AAEL)
RBS .... Resources Breakdown Structure [Computer science] (PCM)
RBS .... Ribosome Binding Site [Biochemistry]
RBS .... River Bend Station [Nuclear energy] (NRCH)
RBS .... Roberts, IL [Location identifier FAA] (FAAL)
RBS .... Royal Ballet School [British] (DI)
RBS .... Royal Bank of Scotland [NYSE symbol] (SPSG)
RBS .... Royal Blind Society of New South Wales (BUAC)
RBS .... Royal Botanical Society (BUAC)
RBS .... Royal Society of British Sculptors
RBS .... Rutherford Backscattering Spectroscopy
RbSA .... Rabbit Serum Albumin (DB)
RBSC .... RADAR Bomb Scoring Central (NG)
RBSc .... Royal Bank of Scotland Group Ltd. [Associated Press] (SAG)
RBSc .... Royal Bank of Scotland Group PLC [Associated Press] (SAG)
RBSc .... Royal Society of British Sculptors
RBSCD .... Rare Book and Special Collections Division [Library of Congress]
RBSct .... Royal Bank of Scotland Group Ltd. [Associated Press] (SAG)
RBSDS .... Revised Bogardus Social Distance Scale (EDAC)
RBSDV .... Rice Black-Streaked Dwarf Virus [Plant pathology]
RBSE .... RADAR Beam Sharpening Element
RBSE .... Repository-Based Software Engineering
rBSF .... Recombinant B-Cell Stimulatory Factor [Biochemistry]
RBSF .... Retail Branch Stores Forum (EA)
RBSI .... Reactor Building Spray Injection [Environmental science] (COE)
RBSN .... Reaction Bonded Silicon Nitride [Materials science and technology]
RBSNSW ..... Royal Blind Society of New South Wales [Australia]
RBSOA .... Reverse Bias Safe Operating Area (AAEL)
RBSPr .... Royal Bk Scotland Pfd ADS [NYSE symbol] (TTSB)
RBSPrB .... Royal Bk Scotland Pfd'B'ADS [NYSE symbol] (TTSB)
RBSPrC .... Royal Bk Scotland Pfd'C'ADS [NYSE symbol] (TTSB)
RBSPrD .... Royal Bk Scotland Pfd'D' ADS [NYSE symbol] (TTSB)
RBSPrX .... Royal Bk Scotland Ex Cap Sec [NYSE symbol] (TTSB)
RBSR .... Reprocessing Building (Cable) Spreading Room [Nuclear energy] (NRCH)
RBSRA .... Red Berkshire Swine Record Association (EA)
RBSS .... Recoverable Booster Space System (IAA)
RBSS .... Recoverable Booster Support System
RBST .... Rare Breeds Survival Trust [British]
RBST .... Remedial and Basic Skills Training (OICC)
RBSVS .... Reactor Building Standby Ventilation System [Environmental science] (COE)
RBT .... Rabbet [Technical drawings]
RBT .... Radial Beam Tube [Electronics]
RBT .... Rainbow Trout
RBT .... Random Breath Testing (ADA)
RBT .... Rational Behavior Therapy
RBT .... Rebate [Technical drawings]

RBT .... Rebuilt (DS)
RBT .... Remote Batch Terminal
RBT .... Resistance Bulb Thermometer
RBT .... Ribbon Bridge Transporter (MCD)
RBT .... Rich Best Torque [Automotive engineering]
RBT .... Ringback Tone [Telecommunications] (TEL)
RBT .... Robinton Aereo CA [Dominican Republic] [ICAO designator] (FAAC)
RBT .... Rough Blanking Template (MCD)
RBT .... Rubber Tile [Technical drawings]
RBT .... Rutland Biotech Ltd. [Vancouver Stock Exchange symbol]
RBTA .... Road Builders Training Association (EA)
RBTC .... Rational Behavior Therapy Center [Psychology] (DAVI)
RBTC .... Round-Bottom Tissue Culture (DB)
RbtCeco ...... Robertson-Ceco Corp. [Associated Press] (SAG)
RBTE .... Religious Booksellers Trade Exhibit
RBTE .... Replacement Battery Terminal Equipment
RbtHalf .... Robert Half International [Associated Press] (SAG)
RBTIP .... Residential Building Technology Innovation Program (DICI)
RBTL .... RADAR Beacon Tracking Level [FAA]
RbtPhr .... Roberts Pharmaceutical Corp. [Associated Press] (SAG)
RBTS .... Rider Block Tagline System [Military] (CAAL)
RBTWT .... Radial Beam Traveling Wave Tube [Electronics]
RBU .... Red Butte Canyon [Utah] [Seismograph station code, US Geological Survey] (SEIS)
RBU .... Regional Business Unit
RBU .... Remote Buffer Unit (IAA)
Rbu .... Ribulose [Biochemistry]
RBUPC .... Research in British Universities, Polytechnics, and Colleges [Formerly, SRBUC] [British Library]
RBV .... Air Roberval [Canada ICAO designator] (FAAC)
RBV .... Reactor Building Vent (IEEE)
RBV .... Relative Biological Value [Food science]
RBV .... Return Beam Vidicon [Satellite camera]
RBV .... Right Brachial Vein [Anatomy] (DAVI)
RBV .... Robbinsville, NJ [Location identifier FAA] (FAAL)
RBVC .... Return Beam Vidicon Camera
RBVI .... Reactor Building Ventilation Isolation [Nuclear energy] (NRCH)
RBVPRM ..... Reactor Building Vent Process Radiation Monitor [Nuclear energy] (NRCH)
RBW .... Rainbow Group [European political movement] (ECON)
RBW .... Walterboro, SC [Location identifier FAA] (FAAL)
RBWO .... Resonant Backward Wave Oscillator (IAA)
RBX .... Manteo, NC [Location identifier FAA] (FAAL)
Rby .... Ribitol [or Ribityl] [Biochemistry]
RBY .... Royal Bucks Yeomanry [British military] (DMA)
RBY .... Ruby [Alaska] [Airport symbol] (OAG)
rby .... Ruby (VRA)
RBY .... Ruby Resources Ltd. [Vancouver Stock Exchange symbol]
RBYC .... Royal Berkshire Yeomanry Cavalry [British] (ROG)
RRZ .... Rabat Zaers [Morocco] [Seismograph station code, US Geological Survey] (SEIS)
RBZ .... Rubidazone [An antibiotic]
RC .... Circular Radio Beacon
RC .... Congregation de Notre Dame de la Retraite au Cenacle [Congregation of Our Lady of the Retreat in the Cenacle] (EAIO)
RC .... Congregation of Our Lady of the Retreat in the Cenacle [Roman Catholic women's religious order Italy]
RC .... Cuba [IYRU nationality code] (IYR)
RC .... Grupo Radio Centro [NYSE symbol] (SPSG)
RC .... Grupo Radio Centro ADS [NYSE symbol] (TTSB)
RC .... Missouri Revised Statutes [1855] [A publication] (DLA)
RC .... Nicholl, Hare, and Carrow's Railway Cases [1835-55] [A publication] (DLA)
RC .... Nondirectional Radio Beacon [ITU designation] (CET)
RC .... RADAR Computer (MCD)
RC .... RADAR Control (DEN)
RC .... Radio Car [British]
RC .... Radio Code (WDAA)
RC .... Radio Code Aptitude Area [Military]
R/C .... Radio Command [or Control] (KSC)
RC .... Radio Compass
RC .... Radio Components (IAA)
R/C .... Radio Control [British military] (DMA)
RC .... Radio Controlled
RC .... Radix Complement [Mathematics]
RC .... Railway Cases [A publication] (DLA)
RC .... Rainbow Coalition [Named for the 1984 political campaign of Rev. Jesse Jackson] [Later, NRCI] (EA)
RC .... Rainform Compressed (MCD)
R/C .... Range Clearance [NASA] (KSC)
RC .... Range Command [NASA] (NASA)
RC .... Range Contractor [NASA] (KSC)
RC .... Range Control [NASA] (KSC)
RC .... Range Correction
RC .... Rapid Change (MCD)
RC .... Rapid City [Diocesan abbreviation] [South Dakota] (TOCD)
RC .... Rapid Curing [Asphalt grade]
RC .... Rate Center [Telecommunications] (TEL)
RC .... Rate Command
RC .... Rate of Change
R/C .... Rate of Climb [Aviation]
R/C .... Ratio Command (MCD)
RC .... Ray Control
RC .... Ray Control Electrode (IAA)
RC .... Raymond-Cestan [Syndrome] [Medicine] (DB)

RC	Rayon and Cotton [*Freight*]
RC	Reaction Center
RC	Reaction Chamber
RC	Reaction Control
RC	Reaction Coupling (IAA)
RC	Reactor (IAA)
RC	Reactor Cavity [*Nuclear energy*] (NRCH)
RC	Reactor Compartment (MSA)
RC	Reactor Coolant [*Nuclear energy*] (NRCH)
RC	Read and Compute
RC	Read Clock (IAA)
RC	Reader Code
RC	Ready Calendar
RC	Real Circuit
RC	Rear Commodore [*Navy*] (NVT)
RC	Rear Connection (MSA)
RC	Rearwin Club (EA)
RC	Receipt
RC	Receiver (IAA)
RC	Receiver Card
RC	Reception Center [*Army*]
Rc	Receptor (STED)
RC	Receptor-Chemoeffector [*Biochemistry*]
RC	Recipient City (NITA)
RC	Recirculating Cooler
RC	Recirculatory Air (AAG)
R/C	Reclining Chair (DAVI)
RC	Recognition Context [*Computer science*] (PCM)
RC	Reconnaissance Car [*British*]
R/C	Reconsign
RC	Reconstructed Communism Party [*Italy*]
RC	Reconstruction Committee [*British World War II*]
RC	Record Carrier (IAA)
RC	Record Change [*or Changer*] (AAG)
RC	Record Code (IAA)
RC	Record Commissioners [*British*] (DLA)
RC	Record Count [*Computer science*]
RC	Recording Completing [*Trunk*] [*Telecommunications*] (TEL)
RC	Recording Controller [*Nuclear energy*] (NRCH)
RC	Records Check (AFM)
RC	Records Communication Program [*Army*]
R/C	Recovered
RC	Recovery Code
RC	Recovery Controller [*NASA*] (MCD)
R/C	Recredited
RC	Recruiting Center
RC	Recurring Cost (NASA)
RC	Red Cell [*or Corpuscle*] [*Hematology*]
RC	Red Cell Cast [*Hematology*] (MAE)
RC	Red China
RC	Red Cross
RC	Reduced Capability (MCD)
RC	Reduced Cuing
RC	Redundancy Check (IAA)
RC	Reels [*JETDS nomenclature*] [*Military*] (CET)
RC	Reference Cavity
RC	Reference Clock [*Telecommunications*] (TEL)
RC	Reference Configuration (SSD)
RC	Referred Care [*Medicine*]
RC	Reformed Church
RC	Refrigerated Centrifuge
RC	Regiment of Cavalry [*British military*] (DMA)
RC	Regional Center
RC	Regional Commandant [*Air Force British*]
RC	Regional Commissioner [*Social Security Administration*]
RC	Regional Council
RC	Register Containing (SAA)
RC	Registered Check
RC	Registered Criminologist
RC	Register of Copyrights [*US*]
RC	Registration Cases [*A publication*] (DLA)
RC	Regnecentralen Computer (NITA)
RC	Regulatory-Catalytic Unit [*Physiology*]
RC	Regulatory Council [*FAA*] (MCD)
RC	Rehabilitation Center
RC	Rehabilitation Counselor
RC	Reinforced Cement (EDCT)
RC	Reinforced Concrete [*Technical drawings*]
RC	Reinstate Card (IAA)
RC	Relative [*Force*] Cost (MCD)
RC	Relative Covariance [*Statistics*]
RC	Relay Computer (BUR)
RC	Release Card
RC	Release Clause [*Real estate*]
RC	Relief Claim
RC	Remand Center (WDAA)
RC	Remington's Code [*A publication*] (DLA)
RC	Remote Channel (NITA)
RC	Remote Component
RC	Remote Computer
RC	Remote Concentrator
RC	Remote Control
RC	Remote Control Authority [*FCC*] (NTCM)
RC	Rent Charge
RC	Rent Control (MHDB)
RC	Reopened Claim [*Unemployment insurance*] (OICC)
RC	Reorder Cycle
RC	Repair Costs [*Technical drawings*]
RC	Replacement Cost [*Insurance*]
RC	Replication Controller [*Computer science*]
RC	Reply Coupon [*Advertising*]
RC	Report of Contact [*Social Security Administration*] (OICC)
RC	Reprint with Corrections (DGA)
RC	Republic of China (CDAI)
R/C	Request for Checkage [*Navy*]
RC	Requirements Contract
RC	Rescriptum [*Counterpart*] [*Latin*]
RC	Research Center (IEEE)
RC	Reserve Components [*Military*]
RC	Reserve Corps
RC	Reserve Currency
RC	Resin Coated (MCD)
RC	Resistance-Capacitance
RC	Resistance Coupled
R-C	Resistor-Capacitor
RC	Resistor-Capacitor Circuit (IAA)
RC	Resolver Control
RC	Resource Capital International Ltd. [*Toronto Stock Exchange symbol*]
RC	Resources Council (EA)
RC	Respiration Ceased [*Medicine*]
RC	Respiratory Care [*Medicine*]
RC	Respiratory Center [*Medicine*]
Rc	Response, Conditioned [*Psychology*] (DAVI)
RC	Responsibility Center [*Air Force*] (AFM)
RC	Rest Camp
RC	Rest Cure
RC	Restrained Cursor (NITA)
RC	Restrictive Cardiomyopathy [*Cardiology*]
RC	Restrictive Covenant (MHDB)
RC	Retail Consortium [*British*]
RC	Retention Catheter [*Medicine*]
RC	Retrograde Cystogram [*Medicine*] (MAE)
r/c	Return Cargo [*Shipping*] (DS)
RC	Revenue Canada
RC	Revenue Cutter [*Coast Guard*]
RC	Reverse Course [*Aviation*]
RC	Reverse Current
RC	Reversing Gear Clutch (DS)
RC	Review Classification (NITA)
RC	Review Cycle [*Military*] (AFIT)
RC	Revised Code
RC	Revue Critique de Legislation et de Jurisprudence de Canada [*A publication*] (DLA)
RC	Ribbon-Frame Camera (MUGU)
RC	Rib Cage [*Anatomy*]
RC	Richard of Cashel [*Pseudonym used by Richard Laurence*]
RC	Rider Club [*Commercial firm*] (EA)
RC	Right Center [*A stage direction*]
RC	Right Center [*Position in soccer, hockey*]
RC	Right Chest [*Medicine*]
RC	Ring Counter
RC	Ringing Circuit [*Telecommunications*] (IAA)
RC	Risk Capital [*Finance*]
RC	Road Reconnaissance [*FAA*] (TAG)
RC	Roads Corp. [*Victoria, Australia*] [*Commercial firm*]
RC	Robert & Carriere [*France*] [*Research code symbol*]
RC	Robot Controller (IAA)
Rc	Rockwell Hardness C-Scale (WDAA)
RC	Roll Center [*Automotive engineering*]
RC	Roll Channel
RC	Roller Chock [*Shipfitting*]
RC	Roller Coating
RC	Rolling Chassis [*Automotive engineering*]
RC	Rolls Court [*Legal*] [*British*]
RC	Roman Catholic
RC	Romanian Cradle (BUAC)
RC	ROM [*Rough Order of Magnitude*] Control
RC	Root Canal [*Dentistry*]
rc	Root Cast [*Archaeology*]
RC	Rosin Core [*Foundry technology*]
R-C	Rosslyn Connecting Railroad Co. [*AAR code*]
RC	Rotary Combustion [*Automobile*]
RC	Rotary Compression (IAA)
RC	Rotary Converter (IAA)
RC	Rotation Control (NASA)
RC	Rough Cast (ADA)
RC	Rough Cutting [*Construction*]
RC	Round Corners [*Bookselling*]
RC	Rounding Control [*Computer programming*] (BYTE)
RC	Roussy-Cornil [*Syndrome*] [*Medicine*] (DB)
R/C	Routing and Clipping (MCD)
RC	Royal Commission [*British*]
RC	Royal Crest [*British*]
RC	Royal Crown [*Soft drink brand*]
R/C	Rubber-Capped
RC	Rubber Covered (IAA)
RC	Rubber Cushioned (WDAA)
RC	Rudder Club (EA)
RC	Rules Committee [*House of Representatives*] (OICC)
RC	Ruling Cases [*A publication*] (DLA)

RC.............. Rural Coalition (EA)
RC.............. Rural Construction
RC.............. Rural Education and Small Schools [*Educational Resources Information Center (ERIC) Clearinghouse*] [*Appalachia University*] (PAZ)
RC.............. Rushlight Club (EA)
RC.............. Taiwan [*International vehicle registration*] (ODBW)
RCA............ Rabbinical Council of America (EA)
RCA............ Racecourse Association [*British*] (DBA)
RCA............ RADAR Controlled Approach (NVT)
RCA............ Radiative-Convective-Atmospheric [*Meteorology*]
RCA............ Radio Club of America (EA)
RCA............ Radio Collectors of America (EA)
RCA............ Radio Corporation of America (NASA)
RCA............ Radio Correspondents Association (IAA)
RCA............ Radio Council of America (NADA)
RCA............ Radiological Control Area (MCD)
RCA............ Radionuclide Cerebral Angiogram [*Cardiology*] (DAVI)
RCA............ Raji Cell Assay (STED)
RCA............ Rapid City, SD [*Location identifier FAA*] (FAAL)
RCA............ Rate Change Authorization (NVT)
RCA............ Ration Cash Allowance [*British military*] (DMA)
RCA............ Reaction Control Assembly
RCA............ Red Cell Adherence (STED)
RCA............ Red Cell Agglutination [*Hematology*] (DAVI)
RCA............ Red Cell Aggregate [*or Aggregation*] [*Hematology*]
RCA............ Red Cross Act
RCA............ Reformed Church in America (ROG)
RCA............ Refractory Contractors' Association (BUAC)
RCA............ Refugee Cash Assistance [*Office of Refugee Resettlement*] [*Department of Health and Human Services*] (GFGA)
RCA............ Regulator of Complement Activation [*Biochemistry*]
RCA............ Reinforced Concrete Association (BUAC)
RCA............ Relative Chemotactic Activity (STED)
RCA............ Remote Control Amplifier (MCD)
RCA............ Renal Cell Carcinoma [*Medicine*] (DB)
RCA............ Renault Club of America [*Defunct*] (EA)
RCA............ REO [*Rawson E. Olds*] Club of America (EA)
RCA............ Replacement Cost Accounting (ADA)
RCA............ Republican Communications Association (EA)
RCA............ Request for Corrective Action (AAG)
RCA............ Research Council of Alberta [*Canada*] (BUAC)
RCA............ Resident Care Aide
RCA............ Residential Care Alternatives
RCA............ Residential Care Association [*British*]
RCA............ Resource Conservation Act (COE)
RCA............ Retail Confectioners Association (BUAC)
RCA............ Retailers' Council of Australia
RCA............ Retirement Care Assoc [*NYSE symbol*] (TTSB)
RCA............ Retirement Care Associates [*NYSE symbol*] (SAG)
RCA............ Review and Concurrence Authority
RCA............ Revival Centres of Australia
RCA............ Richland Aviation [*ICAO designator*] (FAAC)
RCA............ Ricinus communis Agglutinin [*Immunology*]
RCA............ Right Coronary Artery [*Anatomy*]
RCA............ Riot Control Agent (NVT)
RCA............ Rocket Cruising Association (EA)
RCA............ Rodeo Cowboys Association [*Later, PRCA*] (EA)
RCA............ Root Canal Anterior [*Dentistry*]
RCA............ Root Cause Analysis (MCD)
RCA............ Rostrum Clubs of Australia
RCA............ Royal Cambrian Academy [*British*]
RCA............ Royal Cambrian Academy of Art [*British*]
RCA............ Royal Canadian Academy
RCA............ Royal Canadian Academy of Arts
RCA............ Royal Canadian Army (MCD)
RCA............ Royal Canadian Artillery
RCA............ Royal Choral Association [*British*] (BI)
RCA............ Royal Choral Society (BUAC)
RCA............ Royal College of Art [*British*]
RCA............ Royal Co. of Archers [*British*] (DI)
RCA............ Ruger Collectors Association (EA)
RCA............ Rural Crafts Association [*British*] (DBA)
RCA............ Soil and Water Resources Conservation Act [*1977*]
RCAA.......... Rocket City Astronomical Association [*Later, VBAS*] (EA)
RCAA.......... Royal Canadian Academy of Arts (BUAC)
RCAA.......... Royal Cornwall Agricultural Association [*British*] (DBA)
RCAB.......... Review and Concurrence Advisory Board
RCABV........ Replacement-Cost-Adjusted Book Value (DICI)
RCAC.......... Radio Corp. of America Communications (MCD)
RCAC.......... Remote Computer Access Communications Service
RCAC.......... Reserve Component Assistance Coordinator (MCD)
RCAC.......... Royal Canadian Armoured Corps
RCACS........ USREDCOM [*United States Readiness Command*] Command and Control System (AABC)
RCADV........ Reverse Course and Advise [*Aviation*] (FAAC)
RCADXC...... Radio Club Amsterdam Dx Certificate (IAA)
RCAE.......... Royal Correspondence of the Assyrian Empire [*A publication*] (BJA)
RCAF.......... Rail Cost Adjustment Factor [*Interstate Commerce Commission*]
RCAF.......... Returned Customer Assignment Form (IAA)
RCAF.......... Royal Canadian Air Force
RCAFA........ Royal Canadian Air Force Association
RCAF(WD)... Royal Canadian Air Force, Women's Division
RCAG.......... Remote Center Air-Ground [*NASA*] (NAKS)
RCAG.......... Remote Center Air/Ground Facility [*NASA*]

RCAG.......... Remote Communications Air/Ground Facility [*FAA*] (TAG)
RCAG.......... Remote Control Air-Ground [*NASA*] (NAKS)
RCAG.......... Remote-Controlled Air-Ground Communication Site (MCD)
RCAG.......... Replacement Carrier Air Group [*Military*] (AFIT)
RCAHMS..... Royal Commission on the Ancient and Historical Monuments of Scotland (BUAC)
RCAI.......... Railroadiana Collectors Association Inc. (EA)
R/CAL......... Resistance Calibration (MCD)
RCAMC....... Royal Canadian Army Medical Corps
RCAN.......... Recorded Announcement [*Telecommunications*] (TEL)
RC & CR...... Revenue, Civil, and Criminal Reporter [*Calcutta*] [*A publication*] (DLA)
RC & D........ Resource Conservation and Development [*Department of Agriculture*]
RC & L........ Rail, Canal, and Lake [*Transportation*]
RCANSW...... Registered Clubs Association of New South Wales [*Australia*]
RCANSW...... Restaurant and Caterers' Association of New South Wales [*Australia*]
RCAP.......... Re Capital Corp. [*NASDAQ symbol*] (SAG)
RCAP.......... Rural Community Assistance Program (EA)
RCAPC........ Royal Canadian Army Pay Corps
RCAPDR...... Revolutionary Council of the Algerian People's Democratic Republic
RCAPS........ Roosevelt Center for American Policy Studies [*Defunct*] (EA)
RCAQ.......... Restaurant and Caterers' Association of Queensland [*Australia*]
RCAR.......... Religious Coalition for Abortion Rights (EA)
RCAR.......... Religious Coalition for Reproductive Choice (EA)
RCAS.......... Requirements for Close Air Support [*Army*] (MCD)
RCAS.......... Research Center for Advanced Study [*University of Texas at Arlington*] [*Research center*] (RCD)
RCAS.......... Reserve Component Automation System [*DoD*]
RCAS.......... Riverside Curriculum Assessment System [*Test*] (TMMY)
RCASC........ Royal Central Asian Society [*British*]
RCASC........ Royal Canadian Army Service Corps
RCASNSW ... Radio Controlled Aircraft Society of New South Wales [*Australia*]
RCAT.......... Radio Code Aptitude Test
RCAT.......... Radio-Controlled Aerial Target [*Military*]
RCAT.......... Remote-Controlled Aerial Target (NATG)
RCAT.......... Ridgetown College of Agricultural Technology [*Canada*] (ARC)
RCAV.......... Restaurant and Caterers' Association of Victoria [*Australia*]
RCAVIC....... Radio Corp. of America Victor (IAA)
RCAY.......... Gangshan [*China*] [*ICAO location identifier*] (ICLI)
RCB .... Radiation Control Board (AAG)
RCB .... Radio-Controlled Boat (IAA)
RCB .... Randomized Complete Block [*Statistical design*]
RCB .... Reactor Containment Building [*Nuclear energy*] (NRCH)
RCB .... Ready Crew Building (NATG)
RCB .... Reflection Coefficient Bridge
RCB .... Region Control Block [*Computer science*] (BUR)
RCB .... Regular Commissions Board [*British military*] (DMA)
RCB .... Regulations of the Civil Aeronautics Board
RCB .... Releases Control Branch [*Edison, NJ*] [*Environmental Protection Agency*] (GRD)
RCB .... Remote Circuit Breaker (MCD)
RCB .... Remote Control Bandwidth
RCB .... Representative Church Body [*Ireland*] [*Church of England*]
RCB .... Requirements Control Board (MCD)
RCB .... Resource Control Block [*Computer science*] (IBMDP)
RCB .... Retail Credit Bureau (NADA)
RCB .... Retrieval Containment Building [*Environmental science*] (COE)
RCB .... Revolutionary Communist Party (NADA)
RCB .... Richards Bay [*South Africa*] [*Airport symbol*] (OAG)
RCB .... Right Cornerback [*Football*]
RCB .... Romanian Commercial Bank (BUAC)
RCB .... Root Canal Bicuspid [*Dentistry*]
RCB .... Rubber Control Board
RCB .... Rubber-Covered Braided (IAA)
RCBA .... Ratio Changers and Boosters Assembly (MCD)
RCBA .... Relative Basal Area of Conifer Species [*Ecology*]
RCBA .... Royal Crown Bottlers Association (EA)
RC BASIC .... Regnecentralen BASIC (NITA)
RCBC .... Rapid Cycling Bubble Chamber (IAA)
RCBC .... Red Cross Blood Center
rCBF........... Regional Cerebral Blood Flow [*Medicine*]
RCBHT........ Reactor Coolant Bleed Holdup Tank [*Nuclear energy*] (NRCH)
RCBR.......... Retrospective Cost-Based Reimbursement [*Health insurance*] (GHCT)
RCBR.......... Rotating Catalytic Basket Reactor [*Chemical engineering*]
RCBS.......... Jinmen [*China*] [*ICAO location identifier*] (ICLI)
RCBT.......... Reactor Coolant Bleed Tank [*Nuclear energy*] (NRCH)
RCBV.......... Regional Cerebral Blood Volume [*Medicine*] (MAE)
RCBW.......... Radiological-Chemical-Biological Warfare
RCBWP....... Rubber-Covered, Braided, and Weatherproof (IAA)
RCC .... Belleville, IL [*Location identifier FAA*] (FAAL)
RCC .... International Society of Reply Coupon Collectors (EA)
RCC .... Rachel Carson Council (EA)
RCC .... Rack Clearance Center [*Association of American Publishers*]
RCC .... RADAR Control Clouds
RCC .... RADAR Control Computer (MCD)
RCC .... RADAR Control Console [*Military*] (CAAL)
RCC .... Radiation Coordinating Council [*Environmental Protection Agency*] (GFGA)
RCC .... Radio Chemical Center [*British*] (BARN)
RCC .... Radiochemical Centre [*United Kingdom*] (NRCH)
RCC .... Radio Common Carrier
RCC .... Radio Common Channels
RCC .... Radio Communications Center
RCC .... Radiographic Coronary Calcification [*Medicine*] (STED)

RCC .... Radiological Control Center [*Army*]
RCC .... Rag Chewers' Club [*Amateur radio*]
RCC .... Range Commanders Council [*White Sands Missile Range*] (KSC)
RCC .... Range Communications Component (MCD)
RCC .... Range Control Center [*NASA*]
RCC .... Rape Crisis Center (EA)
RCC .... Ratio of Charges to Costs
RCC .... RCA Corp. Communications
RCC .... Reaction Control Center (KSC)
RCC .... Reactor Closed Cooling [*Nuclear energy*] (NRCH)
RCC .... Read Channel Continue
RCC .... Reader Common Contact
RCC .... Real-Time Computer Complex
RCC .... Recco Corp. [*Vancouver Stock Exchange symbol*]
RCC .... Receptor-Chemoeffector Complex [*Biochemistry*]
RCC .... Record Collectors' Club (EA)
RCC .... Recovery Control Center
RCC .... Rectangular Concrete Columns [*Jacys Computing Services*]
                    [*Software package*] (NCC)
RCC .... Red Carpet Clubs [*United Airlines' club for frequent flyers*] (EA)
RCC .... Red Cell Cast (STED)
RCC .... Red Cell Concentrate (STED)
RCC .... Red Cell Count [*Hematology*] (MAE)
RCC .... Red Cross of Constantine (EA)
RCC .... Reduced Crude Conversion [*Petroleum refining*]
RCC .... Regional Census Center [*Bureau of the Census*] (GFGA)
RCC .... Regional Climate Center [*Marine science*] (OSRA)
RCC .... Regional Control Center [*Air Force*] (DOMA)
RCC .... Regional Coordination Committee [*Department of Health and Human
                    Services*]
RCC .... Regulated Common Carrier [*Computer science*] (TNIG)
RCC .... Regulation Communication Center [*RSPA*] (TAG)
RCC .... Regulator of Chromosome Condensation [*Genetics*]
RCC .... Reinforced Carbon-Carbon (MCD)
RCC .... Relative Casein Content [*Food analysis*]
RCC .... Relative Crowding Coefficient (EES)
RCC .... Remote Center Compliance [*Computer science*]
RCC .... Remote Combat Center (SAA)
RCC .... Remote Communications Central
RCC .... Remote Communications Complex
RCC .... Remote Communications Concentrator
RCC .... Remote Communications Console
RCC .... Remote Computer Center (MCD)
RCC .... Remote Control Complex (SAA)
RCC .... Renal Cell Carcinoma [*Medicine*]
RCC .... Representative Church Council [*Episcopalian*]
RCC .... Request for Contract Clearance (AAGC)
RCC .... Rescue Control Center
RCC .... Rescue Coordination Center [*Coast Guard*]
RCC .... Rescue Crew Commander (AFM)
RCC .... Research Computing Center [*University of New Hampshire*]
                    [*Research center*] (RCD)
RCC .... Reset Control Circuit
RCC .... Residential Colleges Committee (AIE)
RCC .... Resistance-Capacitance Coupling (DNAB)
RCC .... Resistor Color Code (DEN)
RCC .... Resource Category Code [*Military*] (CAAL)
RCC .... Resource Control Center [*Military*] (AFIT)
RCC .... Resources for Community Change [*Defunct*] (EA)
RCC .... Retail Council of Canada (BUAC)
RCC .... Reusable Carbon-Carbon (MCD)
RCC .... Revolutionary Command Council [*Iraq*] (BUAC)
RCC .... Revolutionary Command Council [*Sudan*] (BUAC)
RCC .... Revolutionary Command Council [*Sudan*] [*Political party*]
RCC .... Revolutionary Conservative Caucus (BUAC)
RCC .... Right Common Carotid (STED)
RCC .... Right Coronary Cusp [*Medicine*] (STED)
RCC .... Right to Choose Coalition [*Australia*]
RCC .... Ring-Closed Circuit [*Computer science*] (IAA)
RCC .... Rio Carpintero [*Cuba*] [*Seismograph station code, US Geological
                    Survey*] (SEIS)
RCC .... Riverside City College [*California*]
RCC .... Robotic Command Center [*Army*]
RCC .... Rochester Community College, Rochester, MN [*OCLC symbol*]
                    (OCLC)
RCC .... Rockefeller Center Cable
RCC .... Rocket Combustion Chamber (SAA)
RCC .... Rod Cluster Control [*Nuclear energy*] (NRCH)
RCC .... Roller-Compacted Concrete
RCC .... Roman Catholic Church
RCC .... Roman Catholic Church Curate (ROG)
RCC .... Rough Combustion Cutoff [*NASA*]
RCC .... Routine Coronary Care [*Orders*] [*Cardiology*] (DAVI)
RCC .... Routing Control Center (IAA)
RCC .... Rubber Covered Cable (MSA)
RCC .... Rural Construction Cadre [*Military*]
RCC .... Russian Corps Combatants (EA)
RCCA .... Race Car Club of America [*An association*]
RCCA .... Record Carrier Competition Act [*1981*]
RCCA .... Recovery Control Center, Atlantic (DNAB)
RCCA .... Regional Centre for Cultural Action (BUAC)
RCCA .... Remote Control Rod Cluster Assembly (IAA)
RCCA .... Rickenbacker Car Club of America (EA)
RCCA .... Rod Cluster Control Assembly [*Nuclear energy*] (NRCH)
RCCA .... Rough Combustion Cutoff Assembly [*NASA*] (KSC)

RCCA .... Route Capacity Control Airline (DS)
RCCAM .... Remote Computer Communications Access Method [*Computer
                    science*] (MHDB)
RCC & S .... Riots, Civil Commotions, and Strikes [*Insurance*]
RCCB .... Remote Control Circuit Breaker (NASA)
RCCB .... Residual Current Circuit Breaker [*Electronics*] (EECA)
RCCC .... Range Communications Control Center [*Military*] (MCD)
RCCC .... Regular Common Carrier Conference (EA)
RCCC .... Reserve Component Career Counselor [*Military*] (AABC)
RCCC .... Reserve Component Coordination Council (MCD)
RC/CC .... Responsibility Center/Cost Center [*Military*] (AFIT)
RCCC .... Return Critical Control Circuit
RCCC .... Royal Caledonia Curling Club
RCCC .... Royal Commission on Corporate Concentration [*Canada*]
RCCC .... Royal Curling Club of Canada
RCCC .... Rural Cellular 'A' [*NASDAQ symbol*] (TTSB)
RCCC .... Rural Cellular Corp. [*NASDAQ symbol*] (SAG)
RC/CCI .... Resource Code/Cost Category Input (SAA)
RCCDF .... Remote Control Center Development Facility (SSD)
RCCE .... Regional Congress of Construction Employers (EA)
RC-CE .... Revenue Canada, Customs and Excise
RCCE .... Rotating Cylinder-Collector Electrode [*Electrochemistry*]
RCCES .... Research Centre for Canadian Ethnic Studies [*University of Calgary*]
                    [*Research center*] (RCD)
RCCF .... Reserve Components Contingency Force [*Military*]
RCCh .... Roman Catholic Chaplain [*Navy British*]
RCCH .... Roman Catholic Church
RCCL .... Royal Caribbean Cruise Line
RCCLS .... Resource Center for Consumers of Legal Services [*Later,
                    NRCCLS*] (EA)
RCCM .... Regional Committee for Community Medicine (DMAA)
RCCM .... Regional Contingency Construction Management (DOMA)
RCCM .... Research Council for Complementary Medicine [*British*] (IRUK)
RCC/MG .... Range Commanders Council Meteorological Group [*White Sands
                    Missile Range*]
RCCO .... RADAR Control Console Operator [*Military*] (CAAL)
RCCO .... Royal Canadian College of Organists (BUAC)
RCCOL .... Reinforced Concrete Column [*Camutek*] [*Software package*] (NCC)
RC COMAL .... Regnecentralen COMAL (NITA)
RCCOW .... Return Channel Control Orderwire [*Military*] (CAAL)
RCCP .... Recorder and Communications Control Panel (NASA)
RCCP .... Recovery Control Center, Pacific (DNAB)
RCCP .... Reinforced Concrete Culvert Pipe [*Technical drawings*]
RCCP .... Renal Cell Carcinoma, Papillary [*Medicine*] (DMAA)
RCCP .... Rough Cut Capacity Planning [*Manufacturing management*]
RCCPDS .... Reserve Component Common Personnel Data System [*Marine
                    Corps*] (GFGA)
RCCPLD .... Resistance-Capacitance Coupled
RCCRA .... Rough Combustion Cutoff Replaceable Assembly [*NASA*] (KSC)
RCCS .... Rate Command Control System (AAG)
RCCS .... Reactor Cavity Cooling System [*Nuclear energy*]
RCCS .... Remote Communicatios Central Set (SAA)
RCCS .... Royal Canadian Corps of Signals
RCCT .... Randomized Controlled Clinical Trial [*Medicine*] (DMAA)
RCCT .... Reseau Canadien des Centres de Toxicologie (AC)
RCC/TG .... Range Commanders Council Telemetry Group [*White Sands Missile
                    Range, NM*]
RCCTL .... Resistor Capacitor-Coupled Transistor Logic (IAA)
RCCUS .... Republican Citizens Committee of the United States (EA)
RCCV .... Red Clover Cryptic Virus [*Plant pathology*]
RCD .... Rabbit Calicivirus Disease
RCD .... RADAR Cloud Detection Report [*NWS*] (FAAC)
RCD .... Rapid City [*South Dakota*] [*Seismograph station code, US Geological
                    Survey*] (SEIS)
RCD .... Rassemblement Constitutionnel Democratique [*Tunisia*] [*Political
                    party*] (ECON)
RCD .... Rassemblement pour la Culture et la Democratie [*Algeria*] [*Political
                    party*] (EY)
RCD .... Received
Rcd .... Received (EBF)
rcd .... Received (ODBW)
RCD .... Receiver-Carrier Detector
RCD .... Reconnaissance Cockpit Display
RCD .... Recontact Date [*Automotive retailing*]
RCD .... Record
RCD .... Recordable Compact Disc [*Computer science*]
RCD .... Redox Chemiluminescence Detector [*Instrumentation*] [*Sievers*]
RCD .... Reduced Crude Desulfurization [*Petroleum refining*]
RCD .... Reference Configuration Description (SSD)
RCD .... Regent's Canal Dock [*British*]
RCD .... Registered Connective Device (MHDB)
RCD .... Reinforcement Control Depot [*Air Force*]
RCD .... Relative Cardiac Dullness [*Medicine*]
RCD .... Research and Acquisition Communications Division [*Military*]
RCD .... Research Centers Directory [*A publication*]
RCD .... Residual Current Device [*Electrical circuits*]
RCD .... Resource Conservation and Development (COE)
RCD .... Retrofit Configuration Drawing (MCD)
RCD .... Reverse Circulation Drilling [*Mining technology*]
RCD .... Reverse Current Device [*Electronics*] (MSA)
RCD .... Ringer/Citrate/Dextrose (DB)
RCD .... Rock Coring Device
RCD .... Rocket Cushioning Device (NG)
RCD .... Route Control Digit [*Telecommunications*] (TEL)
RCD .... Royal Canadian Dragoons [*Military*]

RCD .... Rural Civil Defense
RCD .... Sisters of Our Lady of Christian Doctrine [*Roman Catholic religious order*]
RCDA......... Recurrent Chronic Dissecting Aneurysm [*Medicine*] (DMAA)
RCDA......... Religion in Communist Dominated Areas [*A publication*]
RCDA......... Research Career Development Awards [*Department of Health and Human Services*]
RCDA......... Research Center for Religion and Human Rights in Closed Societies (EA)
RCDB......... Rubber-Covered Double-Braided (IAA)
RCDC......... Pingdong (South) [*China*] [*ICAO location identifier*] (ICLI)
RCDC......... RADAR Course-Directing Central [*Military*]
RCDC......... RADAR Course-Directing Control (MUGU)
RCDC......... Radiation Chemistry Data Center [*Notre Dame, IN*] [*Department of Commerce*]
RCDC......... Ross Cosmetics Distribution (EFIS)
RCDC......... Royal Canadian Dental Corps
RCDCB....... Regional Civil Defense Coordination Boards [*DoD*] (AABC)
RCDD......... Registered Communications Distribution Designer [*Building Industry Consulting Service International*] [*Designation awarded by*] (TSSD)
RC de l'E..... Rapports de la Cour de l'Echiquier [*Exchequer Court Reports*] [*Canada*] [*A publication*] (DLA)
RCDEP...... Rural Civil Defense Education Program
RCDG........ Recording (MSA)
RCDHS....... Rehabilitation and Chronic Disease Hospital Section [*American Hospital Association*] (EA)
RCDI.......... Longtan [*China*] [*ICAO location identifier*] (ICLI)
RCDIW....... Royal Commission on the Distribution of Income and Wealth [*British*]
RCDLR....... Remote Control Door Lock Receiver
RCDM......... Regional Centre for Drama and Music [*University of New England, Australia*]
RCDM......... Russian Christian Democratic Movement [*Political party*] (BUAC)
RCDMB...... Regional Civil and Defense Mobilization Boards
RCDMS...... Reliability Central Data Management System [*Air Force*] (DIT)
RCDNA...... RADAR Cloud Detection Report Not Available [*NWS*] (FAAC)
RCDNE...... RADAR Cloud Detection Report No Echoes Observed [*NWS*] (FAAC)
RCDNO ..... RADAR Cloud Detector Inoperative Due to Breakdown Until [*NWS*] (FAAC)
RCDO.......... Regional Case Development Officer [*Environmental Protection Agency*] (GFGA)
RCDOM...... RADAR Cloud Detector Inoperative Due to Maintenance Until [*NWS*] (FAAC)
RCDP .... Record Parallel (MCD)
RCDP .... Romani Christian Democratic Party [*Bulgaria*] [*Political party*] (BUAC)
RCDPB....... Resource Conservation and Development Policy Board (COE)
RCDR......... Recorder (KSC)
RCDR......... Relative Corrected Death Rate [*Medicine*] (DMAA)
RCDS .... Records
RCDS .... Reinforced Concrete Detailing System (PDAA)
RCDS .... Royal College of Defence Studies [*British*]
RCDS .... Rural Community Development Service [*Abolished, 1970*] [*Department of Agriculture*]
RCDT .... Reactor Coolant Drain Tank [*Nuclear energy*] (NRCH)
RCE............. Aerocer SA [*Mexico ICAO designator*] (FAAC)
RCE............. Radio Communications Equipment
RCE............. Radio Control Equipment [*FAA*] (TAG)
RCE............. Railway Construction Engineer [*British military*] (DMA)
RCE............. Rapid Changing Environment (AAG)
RCE............. Rapid Circuit Etch
RCE............. Ray Control Electrode (IAA)
RCE............. Reaction Control Engine
RCE............. Reactor Compatibility Experiment [*Nuclear energy*] (NRCH)
RCE............. Reasonable Compensation Equivalent [*Medicine*] (DMAA)
rce .... Recording Engineer [*MARC relator code*] [*Library of Congress*] (LCCP)
RCE............. Reentry Control Electronics
RCE............. Reliability Control Engineering (AAG)
RCE............. Religious of Christian Education [*Roman Catholic women's religious order*]
RCE............. Remote Control Equipment (DIT)
RCE............. Repetitive Counterelectrophoresis (PDAA)
RCE............. Restricted Coulomb Energy
RCE............. Rice University, Fondren Library, Houston, TX [*OCLC symbol*] (OCLC)
RCE............. Right Center Entrance (WDAA)
RCE............. Roche Harbor [*Washington*] [*Airport symbol*] (OAG)
RCE............. Ross Consumer Electronics [*British*]
RCE............. Rotary Combustion Engine (PDAA)
RCE............. Royal Canadian Engineers
RCE............. Union Restaurants Collectifs Europeens [*European Catering Association*] (EAIO)
RCEA .... Recreational Coach and Equipment Association [*Later, MHI*]
RCEA .... Research Council Employees' Association [*Canada*]
RCEAC....... Regional Civil Emergency Advisory Committee [*Formerly, JRCC*] [*Civil defense*]
RCEDD....... Resources, Community and Economic Development Division (AAGC)
RCEEA ...... Radio Communication and Electronic Engineering Association (BUAC)
RCEEA ...... Radio Communications and Electronic Engineers Association
RCEHMT .... Regional Centre for Energy, Heat, and Mass Transfer for Asia and Pacific [*India*] (BUAC)
RCEI.......... Range Communications Electronics Instructions [*NASA*] (KSC)
RCEID .... Radio-Controlled Improvised Explosive Device [*Criminology*] (LAIN)
RCEME........ Royal Canadian Electrical and Mechanical Engineers

RCEP .... Royal Commission on Environmental Pollution [*British*]
RCEP .... Rural Concentrated Employment Program [*Department of Labor*]
RCERA .... Religious Committee for the ERA [*Equal Rights Amendment*] (EA)
RCERIP....... Reserve Component Equipment Readiness Improvement Program [*Military*] (AABC)
RCEUSA...... Romanian Catholic Exarchy in the United States of America (EA)
RCEVH .... Research Centre for the Education of the Visually Handicapped [*University of Birmingham*] [*British*] (CB)
RCF............. Radcliffe Resources Ltd. [*Vancouver Stock Exchange symbol*]
RCF............. Radiocommunication Failure Message [*Aviation*]
RCF............. Ratio Correction Factor
RCF............. Reader's Comment Form (IBMDP)
RCF............. Recall Finder
RCF............. Red Cell Folate [*Hematology*] (AAMN)
RCF............. Redundant Churches Fund [*British*] (EAIO)
RCF............. Refractory Ceramic Fiber [*Materials science*]
RCF............. Regenerated Cellulose Film [*Organic chemistry*]
RCF............. Relative Centrifugal Force
RCF............. Relative Cumulative Frequency
RCF............. Remote Call Forwarding [*Bell System*]
RCF............. Remote Cluster Facility (IAA)
RCF............. Remote Communication Facility [*FAA*] (TAG)
RCF............. Remote Console Facility [*Computer science*] (CIST)
RCF............. Repair Cost Factor [*Navy*]
RCF............. Repair Cycle Float [*Military*] (AABC)
RCF............. Retail Computer Facilities
RCF............. Review of Contemporary Fiction [*A publication*] (BRI)
RCF............. Ristocetin Cofactor (DB)
RCF............. River Conservation Fund [*Later, ARCC*] (EA)
RCF............. Rock Characterization Facility [*Nuclear waste storage*]
RCF............. Rosicrucian Fellowship (EA)
RCF............. Rotating Cylinder Flap
RCF............. Royal Carmarthen Fusiliers [*British military*] (DMA)
RCFA .... Religious Communities for the Arts [*Defunct*] (EA)
RCFA .... Royal Canadian Field Artillery [*Military*]
RCFC .... Ray Coble Fan Club [*Defunct*] (EA)
RCFC .... Reactor Containment Fan Cooler [*Nuclear energy*] (NRCH)
RCFC .... Refractory Ceramic Fiber Coalition (NTPA)
RCFC .... Ron Craddock Fan Club (EA)
RCFC .... Rosanne Cash Fan Club (EA)
RCFC .... Roy Clark Fan Club (EA)
RCFC .... Roy Clayborne Fan Club (EA)
RCFC(U)..... Reactor Core Fan Cooling (Unit) (IEEE)
RCFF.......... Repair Cycle Float Factor (MCD)
RCFM......... Radiocommunication Failure Message [*Aviation*] (WDAA)
RCFN......... Taidong/Fengnian [*China*] [*ICAO location identifier*] (ICLI)
RCFP.......... Reporters Committee for Freedom of the Press (EA)
RCFR......... Red Cross Field Representative
RCFR......... Royal Canadian Fleet Reserve
RCFS.......... Jiadong [*China*] [*ICAO location identifier*] (IOLI)
RCFSAP ...... Regional Commission on Food Security for Asia and the Pacific (BUAC)
RCFT.......... Randomized Controlled Field Trial [*Statistics*]
RCFT.......... Remove Cloud From Title (MHDB)
RCFTU .... Russian Confederation of Free Trade Unions (BUAC)
RCFU.......... Reactive Crime Fighting Unit [*British*] (WDAA)
RCFU.......... Rotary Carton Feed Unit
RCFZ.......... Fengshan [*China*] [*ICAO location identifier*] (ICLI)
RCG .... Radiation Concentration Guide [*Formerly, MPC*]
RCG .... Radioactivity Concentration Guide (KSC)
RCG .... Radio Command Guidance (AAG)
RCG .... Radioelectrocardiograph (IAA)
rCG .... Rat Chorionic Gonadotropin
RCG .... Reaction Cured Glass [*Ceramic technology*]
RCG .... Receiving (AAG)
RCG .... Recommended Concentration Guide [*Nuclear energy*] (NRCH)
RCG .... Recovery Control Group (IAA)
RCG .... Reference Concept Group (SSD)
RCG .... Restricted Categorical Grammar
RCG .... Resurgens Communications (EFIS)
RCG .... Retail Credit Group [*British*]
RCG .... Reverberation Control of Gain
RCG .... Revolutionary Communist Group [*Political party*] (BUAC)
RCG .... Right Cerebral Ganglion [*Anatomy*]
RCGA .... Royal Canadian Garrison Artillery [*Military*]
RCGC......... Royal Canberra Golf Club [*Australia*]
RCGD......... Research Center for Group Dynamics [*University of Michigan*] [*Research center*] (RCD)
RCGI .... Ludao [*China*] [*ICAO location identifier*] (ICLI)
RCGI .... Renal Care Group [*NASDAQ symbol*] (TTSB)
RCGM......... Reactor Cover Gas Monitor [*Nuclear energy*] (NRCH)
RCGM......... Taoyuan [*China*] [*ICAO location identifier*] (ICLI)
RCGP......... Royal College of General Practitioners [*British*]
rCGRP......... Rat Calcitonin Gene-Related Peptide [*Biochemistry*]
RCGS.......... RADAR Correlation Guidance Study
RCGS.......... Radio Command Guidance System (IAA)
RCGS.......... Recent College Graduates Survey [*Department of Education*] (GFGA)
RCGS.......... Royal Canadian Geographical Society (BUAC)
RCGS.......... Royal Canadian Geological Society (BUAC)
RCGUGA...... Resistance-Capacitance Grounded Unity Gain Amplifier (IAA)
RCH .... Chile [*International vehicle registration*] (ODBW)
RCH .... Helicopter Air Service, Inc. [*ICAO designator*] (FAAC)
RCH .... Rancho
RCH .... Rauch Industries, Inc. [*AMEX symbol*] (SPSG)
RCH .... Rectocolic Hemorrhage [*Medicine*] (DMAA)

RCH .... Residential Children's Home   (AIE)
RCH .... Rich Resources Ltd. [*Vancouver Stock Exchange symbol*]
RCH .... Riohacha [*Colombia*] [*Airport symbol*]   (OAG)
RCH .... Rotary Clothes Hoist   (ADA)
RCH .... Rural Cooperative Housing
RCHA .... Rachel Carson Homestead Association   (EA)
RCHA .... Reference Library of Hispanic America [*A publication*]
RCHA .... Royal Canadian Horse Artillery
RCHB .... Reserve Cargo-Handling Battalion [*Navy*]   (DOMA)
RCHCS .... Regenerable Carbon Dioxide and Humidity Control System   (NASA)
RCHF .... Richfood Hldgs [*NASDAQ symbol*]   (TTSB)
RCHF .... Richfood Holdings, Inc. [*NASDAQ symbol*]   (NQ)
RCHF .... Right Congestive Heart Failure [*Medicine*]   (DMAA)
RCHG .... Reduced Charge   (AAG)
RCHI .... Risk Capital Holdings [*NASDAQ symbol*]   (TTSB)
RCHI .... Risk Capital Holdings, Inc. [*NASDAQ symbol*]   (SAG)
RCHM .... Remote Computer-Controlled Hardware Monitor   (MHDI)
RCHM .... Royal Commission on Historical Monuments [*British*]
RCHME .... Royal Commission on the Historical Monuments of England   (BUAC)
RCHPE .... Regional Clearing House for Population Education   (BUAC)
RCHRA .... Regional Council on Human Rights in Asia   (EAIO)
RCHS .... Railway and Canal Historical Society [*British*]   (BI)
RCHS .... Royal Caledonian Horticultural Society [*British*]   (BI)
RCHT .... Ratchet [*Design engineering*]
RCHTA .... Radio Control Hobby Trade Association   (NTPA)
RCH/TCH ..... Receive Channel/Transmit Channel [*Telecommunications*]   (MCD)
RCHY .... Richey Electronics [*NASDAQ symbol*]   (SAG)
RCI .... RADAR Coverage Indication [*or Indicator*]
RCI .... RADAR Coverage Indicator   (IAA)
RCI .... Radio Canada International
RCI .... Radiochemical Inspectorate [*British*]   (NUCP)
RCI .... Radio Communications Instruction   (MUGU)
RCI .... Range Communications Instruction   (IAA)
RCI .... Range Communications Instructions [*NASA*]   (KSC)
RCI .... Read Channel Initialize
RCI .... Reading Comprehension Interview   (EDAC)
RCI .... Reading Comprehension Inventory [*G. Giordano*]   (TES)
RCI .... Recommended Course Indicator
RCI .... Reggio Calabria [*Italy*] [*Seismograph station code, US Geological Survey*]   (SEIS)
RCI .... Religious of Christian Instruction [*Roman Catholic religious order*]
RCI .... Remote Control Indicator   (CAAL)
RCI .... Remote Control Interface
RCI .... Republique de la Cote d'Ivoire [*Republic of the Ivory Coast*]   (BARN)
RC/I .... Request for Change and/or Information   (SAA)
RCI .... Request for Contract Investigation   (MCD)
RCI .... Research and Control Instruments Ltd.   (BUAC)
RCI .... Resident Classification Index
RCI .... Resident Cost Inspector
RCI .... Resort Condominiums International   (EA)
RCI .... Resource Consultants, Inc.   (EFIS)
RCI .... Respiratory Control Index [*Biochemistry*]
RCI .... Retail Confectioners International   (EA)
RCI .... Roadway Congestion Index [*BTS*]   (TAG)
RCI .... ROC Communities [*NYSE symbol*]   (SPSG)
RCI .... Rochester Commercial and Industrial [*Database*]
RCI .... Rogers Communications, Inc. [*Toronto Stock Exchange symbol Vancouver Stock Exchange symbol*]
RCI .... Roof Consultants Institute   (EA)
RCI .... Routing Control Indicator [*Telecommunications*]   (TEL)
RCI .... Royal Canadian Institute   (BARN)
RCI .... Royal Channel Islands Yacht Club   (BI)
RCI .... Royal Colonial Institute [*British*]
RCIA .... Red Cell Immune Adherence [*Medicine*]   (DMAA)
RCIA .... Remote Control Interface Adapter   (IAA)
RCIA .... Retail Clerks International Association [*Later, UFCWIU*]   (EA)
RCIA .... Retail Credit Institute of America [*Later, NFCC*]
RCIA .... Rite of Christian Intiation [*An association*]   (EA)
RCI.A .... Rogers Commun CI 'A' [*TS, Symbol*]   (TTSB)
RCIADIC ...... Royal Commission into Aboriginal Deaths in Custody [*Australia*]
RCIC .... Reactor Core Isolation Cooling [*Nuclear energy*]   (NRCH)
RCIC .... Red Cross International Committee
RCIC .... Regional Coastal Information Center [*National Marine Advisory Service*]   (MSC)
RCIC .... Reserve Component Issues Conference [*Military*]   (MCD)
RCIC .... Royal Canadian Infantry Corps
RCICS .... Reactor Core Isolation Cooling System [*Nuclear energy*]   (NRCH)
RCID .... Recruiter Code Identification [*Army*]   (AABC)
RCIE .... Regional Council for International Education [*University of Pittsburgh*]
RCII .... Renters Choice [*NASDAQ symbol*]   (TTSB)
RCII .... Renters Choice, Inc. [*NASDAQ symbol*]   (SAG)
RCIL .... Reliability Critical Item List   (AAG)
RCIP .... Reseau Canadien d'Information sur le Patrimoine   (AC)
RCIRF .... Radiologic Contrast-Induced Renal Failure [*Medicine*]   (DMAA)
RCIRR .... Reserve Components, Individual Ready Reserve [*Military*]
RCIS .... Remote Computer Interface Subsystem   (MHDB)
RCIS .... Research Conference on Instrumentation Science
RCITR .... Red Cell Iron Turnover Rate [*Hematology*]   (MAE)
RCIU .... Remote Computer Interface Unit
RCIVS .... Regional Conference on International Voluntary Service [*Commercial firm*]   (EAIO)
RCJ .... RCJ Resources Ltd. [*Vancouver Stock Exchange symbol*]
RCJ .... Reaction Control Jet
RCJ .... Reinforced Composite Joint

RCJ .... Reports of Certain Judgments of the Supreme Court, Vice-Admiralty Court, and Full Court of Appeal, Lagos [*1884-92*] [*Nigeria*] [*A publication*]   (DLA)
RC(J) .... Rettie, Crawford, and Melville's Session Cases, Fourth Series [*1873-98*] [*Scotland*] [*A publication*]   (DLA)
rcj .... Rogationist Fathers   (TOCD)
RCJ .... Rogationist Fathers   (TOCD)
RCJ .... Royal Courts of Justice [*British*]
RCJS .... Ramsey Corporation Job Skills-Reading Electrical Drawings & Schematics [*Test*]   (TMMY)
RCK .... Rockdale, TX [*Location identifier FAA*]   (FAAL)
RCK .... Rockford [*Diocesan abbreviation*] [*Illinois*]   (TOCD)
RCKH .... Gaoxiong [*China*] [*ICAO location identifier*]   (ICLI)
RCKU .... Jiayi [*China*] [*ICAO location identifier*]   (ICLI)
RCKW .... Hengchun [*China*] [*ICAO location identifier*]   (ICLI)
RCKY .... Rockies   (FAAC)
RCKY .... Rocky
RCKY .... Rocky Shoes & Boots [*NASDAQ symbol*]   (TTSB)
RCKY .... Rocky Shoes & Boots, Inc. [*NASDAQ symbol*]   (SAG)
RCL .... Radial Collateral Ligament [*Anatomy*]
RCL .... Radiation Counter Laboratories, Inc.
RCL .... Radio Command Linkage   (AAG)
RCL .... Radio Communications Link [*FAA*]   (TAG)
RCL .... Railway Conversion League   (BUAC)
RCL .... Ramp Craft Logistic [*Navy British*]
RCL .... Ramped Cargo Lighter
RCL .... Ramsey County Public Library, St. Paul, MN [*OCLC symbol*]   (OCLC)
RCL .... Rationalist Concept of Logic
RCL .... Reactor Coolant Loop [*Nuclear energy*]   (NRCH)
RCL .... Read Clock   (IAA)
RCL .... Recall   (MSA)
RCL .... Receive Clock   (IAA)
RCL .... Recoil   (MSA)
RCL .... Recoiless Rifle   (MUSM)
RCL .... Recoilless Launcher
RCL .... Redcliff [*Vanuatu*] [*Airport symbol*]   (OAG)
RCL .... Reichhold Ltd. [*Toronto Stock Exchange symbol*]
RCL .... Reliability Component List   (MCD)
RCL .... Reliability Control Level   (KSC)
RCL .... Remote Control Location
RCL .... Repair Cycle Level
RCL .... Required Cleanliness Level [*Automobile maintenance*]
RCL .... Research Computation Laboratory [*University of Houston*] [*Research center*]   (RCD)
RCL .... Reserved Commodity List [*World War II*]
RCL .... Resistance, Capacitance & Inductive   (NITA)
RCL .... Ricegrowers' Cooperative Ltd. [*Australia*]
RCL .... Royal Canadian Legion
RCL .... Royal Caribbean Cruise Line [*NYSE symbol*]   (SPSG)
RCL .... Royal Caribbean Cruises [*NYSE symbol*]   (TTSB)
RCL .... Rubber Continuous Liner   (DS)
RCL .... Ruby Crystal LASER
RCL .... Ruling Case Law
RCL .... Runway Centerline [*Aviation*]
RCLA .... Regis College Lay Apostolate [*Defunct*]   (EA)
RCLB .... Revolutionary Communist League of Britain [*Political party*]   (PPW)
RCLC .... Reactor Coolant Leakage Calculation   (IEEE)
RCLC .... Reactor Coolant Letdown Cooler [*Nuclear energy*]   (NRCH)
RCLC .... Republican Congressional Leadership Council   (EA)
RCLC .... Xiao Liu Qiu [*China*] [*ICAO location identifier*]   (ICLI)
RCLD .... Reclined   (MSA)
RC-LDAP ..... Reserve Component Leader Development Action Plan [*Army*]   (INF)
RCLED .... Resonantcavity Light-Emitting Diode [*Electronics*]
RCLG .... Recoilless Gun   (AABC)
RCLG .... Taizhong [*China*] [*ICAO location identifier*]   (ICLI)
RCLGGL .... Royal Commission on Local Government in Greater London [*British*]
RCLJ .... Revue Critique de Legislation et de Jurisprudence [*A publication*]   (DLA)
RCLL .... Runway Center Line Lights [*ICAO designator*]   (FAAC)
RCLM .... Reclaim   (AABC)
RCLM .... Runway Centerline Marking [*Aviation*]
RCLMG .... Reclaiming
RCLO .... Reports Control Liaison Officer [*Army*]   (AABC)
RCLR .... Recoilless Rifle   (AABC)
RCLS .... Lishan [*China*] [*ICAO location identifier*]   (ICLI)
RCLS .... Ramapo Catskill Library System [*Library network*]
RCLS .... Recoilless
RCLS .... Runway Centerline Light System [*FAA*]   (TAG)
RCLU .... Jilong [*China*] [*ICAO location identifier*]   (ICLI)
RCLWUNE ..... Regional Commission on Land and Water Use in the Near East   (EA)
RCLY .... Lanyu [*China*] [*ICAO location identifier*]   (ICLI)
RCM .... Aircam Aviation Ltd. [*British ICAO designator*]   (FAAC)
RCM .... ARCO Chemical [*NYSE symbol*]   (TTSB)
RCM .... ARCO Chemical Co. [*NYSE symbol*]   (SPSG)
RCM .... Aviation Radio and RADAR Countermeasures Technician [*Navy*]
RCM .... La Republique des Citoyens du Monde [*Commonwealth of World Citizens*]
RCM .... RADAR [*or Radio*] Countermeasures [*Military*]   (AAG)
RCM .... Radial Compression Model [*Chromatography*]
RCM .... Radiative-Convective Model [*Meteorology*]
RCM .... Radiocontrast Media [*Clinical chemistry*]
RCM .... Radio-Controlled Mine [*Military*]
RCM .... Radio Counter-Measures [*British military*]   (DMA)
RCM .... Radiographic Contrast Media [*Chemistry*]   (DAVI)
RCM .... Random Coefficient Model [*Mathematics*]

RCM............	Random Coincidence Monitor [*Beckman Instruments, Inc.*] [*Instrumentation*]
RCM............	Range Change Method [*Aircraft*]
RCM............	Rassemblement Chretien de Madagascar [*Christian Rally of Madagascar*]
RCM............	RCM Technologies, Inc. [*Associated Press*] (SAG)
RCM............	Reaction Control Motor (IAA)
RCM............	Reactor Materials [*A publication*]
RCM............	Read Clutch Magnet (IAA)
RCM............	Receipt of Classified Material (AAG)
RCM............	Recent Crustal Movements [*Geology*] (NOAA)
RCM............	Red Cell Mass [*Hematology*]
RCM............	Reduced Casualties and Mishaps
RCM............	Refurbished Command Module [*NASA*] (KSC)
RCM............	Regimental Corporal-Major [*British*]
RCM............	Regimental Court-Martial
RCM............	Reinforced Clostridial Medium [*Microbiology*]
RCM............	Reliability-Centered Maintenance [*DoD*]
RCM............	Reliability Corporate Memory (IEEE)
RCM............	Religious Conceptionist Missionaries [*Roman Catholic women's religious order*]
RCM............	Repair Cycle Monitor
RCM............	Replacement Culture Medium [*Microbiology*]
RCM............	Requirements Correlation Matrix [*Air Force*] (DOMA)
RCM............	Resource Cost Model (EDAC)
RCM............	Responsibility Center Monthly (COE)
RCM............	Revised Code of Montana [*A publication*]
RCM............	Revolutionary Communist Maoists [*Political party*] (BUAC)
RCM............	Rhode Island College, Providence, RI [*OCLC symbol*] (OCLC)
RCM............	Richmond [*Australia Airport symbol*] (OAG)
RCM............	Right Costal Margin [*Medicine*]
RCM............	Rod Cell Memory (IAA)
RCM............	Root Canal Molar [*Dentistry*]
RCM............	Rosmac Resources Ltd. [*Vancouver Stock Exchange symbol*]
RCM............	Rotor Current Meter
RCM............	Rous Conditioned Medium
RCM............	Royal Canadian Mint
RCM............	Royal College of Midwives [*British*]
RCM............	Royal College of Mines (BUAC)
RCM............	Royal College of Music [*British*]
RCM............	Royal Conservatory of Music [*Leipzig*]
RCM............	Rule for Court-Martial [*Military*] (INF)
RCM............	Sisters of the Immaculate Conception (TOCD)
RCMA	Radio Communications Monitoring Association (EA)
RCMA	Railroad Construction and Maintenance Association [*Later, NRC/MAI*] (EA)
RCMA	Religious Conference Management Association (EA)
RCMA	Research Council of Makeup Artists (NTCM)
RCMA	Reservist Clothing Maintenance Allowance [*Military*]
RCMA	Roof Coatings Manufacturers Association (EA)
RCM and E...	Radio Control Models and Electronics [*A publication*]
RCMAS........	Revised Children's Manifest Anxiety Scale [*Psychology*] (DHP)
RCMASA......	Russian Consolidated Mutual Aid Society of America (EA)
RCMAT	Radio-Controlled Miniature Aerial Target [*Military*] (MCD)
RCMD.........	Rice Council for Market Development (EA)
RCME.........	Russian Commodity and Raw Materials Exchange [*Russian Federation*] (EY)
RCMF.........	Radio Component Manufacturers' Federation (IAA)
RCMF.........	Royal Commonwealth Military Forces (ADA)
RCMG	Reseau Canadien sur les Maladies Genetiques (AC)
RCMI	Research Centers in Minority Institutions Program [*Bethesda, MD*] [*National Institutes of Health*] (GRD)
RCMIF	Rogers Cantel Mobile Communications [*NASDAQ symbol*] (SAG)
RCMIS........	Reserve Components Management Information System [*Army*]
RCMJ.........	Donggang [*China*] [*ICAO location identifier*] (ICLI)
RCMM	Registered Competitive Market Maker [*Stock exchange term*] (SPSG)
R + CMO.....	[*The*] Rose + Croix Martinist Order (EA)
RCMP	Recompute Last Fix [*Navy Navigation Satellite System*] (DNAB)
RCMP	Royal Canadian Mounted Police [*Formerly, RNWMP*]
RCMPRS......	Recompression
RCMQ.........	Qingquangang [*China*] [*ICAO location identifier*] (ICLI)
rCMR.........	Regional Cerebral Metabolic Rate [*Brain research*]
RCMS	Ilan [*China*] [*ICAO location identifier*] (ICLI)
RCMS	Reliability Centered Maintenance Strategy (MCD)
RCMS	Research Careers for Minority Scholars [*National Science Foundation*]
RCMS	Resonator-Controlled Microwave Source (PDAA)
RCM Str.......	RCM Strategic Global Government Fund [*Associated Press*] (SAG)
RCMT.........	RCM Technologies [*NASDAQ symbol*] (TTSB)
RCMT.........	RCM Technologies, Inc. [*NASDAQ symbol*] (NQ)
RCMTZ........	RCM Technologies Wrrt'C' [*NASDAQ symbol*] (TTSB)
RCMV.........	Red Clover Mottle Virus [*Plant pathology*]
RCN	Receipt of Change Notice
RCN	Reconnaissance
RCN	Record Control Number [*Military*] (AFM)
RCN	Record Number [*Online database field identifier*]
RCN	Recovery Communications Network
RCN	Recreation (MSA)
RCN	Relay-Contact Network (PDAA)
RCN	Report Change Notice (MCD)
RCN	Report Control Number (MCD)
RCN	Requirements Change Notice [*NASA*] (NASA)
RCN	Residential Communications Network [*Telecommunications service*]
RCN	Resource Center for Nonviolence (EA)
RCN	Reticulum-Cell Neoplasia [*Oncology*]

RCN	Right Caudate Nucleus [*Medicine*] (DMAA)
RCN	Rimacan Resources Ltd. [*Vancouver Stock Exchange symbol*]
RCN	Rogers Cantel MobComm'B' [*NYSE symbol*] (TTSB)
RCN	Rogers Cantel Mobile Communications [*NYSE symbol*] (SAG)
RCN	Royal Canadian Navy [*Obsolete*]
RCN	Royal College of Nursing [*British*]
RCNA........	Royal College of Nursing, Australia
RCNAS........	Royal Canadian Naval Air Station
RCNC.........	Royal Canadian Naval College [*1943-1948*]
RCNC.........	Royal Corps of Naval Constructors [*British*]
RCNCOES	Reserve Components Noncommissioned Officer Education System [*Army*]
RCNDT........	Recondition
RCNLR........	Reconnaissance Long Range [*Army*]
RCNMV.......	Red Clover Necrotic Mosaic Virus [*Plant pathology*]
RCNN........	Tainan [*China*] [*ICAO location identifier*] (ICLI)
RCNO.........	Dongshi [*China*] [*ICAO location identifier*] (ICLI)
RCNR.........	Royal Canadian Naval Reserve
RCNSC........	Reserve Component National Security Course [*National Defense University*] (INF)
RCNSS........	Reserve Component National Security Seminar (MCD)
RCNTR........	Ring Counter (MSA)
RCNV.........	Resource Center for Nonviolence (EA)
RCNVR.......	Royal Canadian Naval Volunteer Reserve [*1923-1945*]
RCO	Aero Renta de Coahuila SA de CV [*Mexico ICAO designator*] (FAAC)
RCO	Aliphatic Acyl Radical [*Biochemistry*] (DAVI)
RCO	RADAR Control Officer
RCO	Radio Control Operator
RCO	Range Control Office [*or Officer*] [*NASA*] (KSC)
RCO	Range Cutoff (MCD)
RCO	Reactor Core (IEEE)
RCO	Receiver Cuts Out [*Telecommunications*] (TEL)
RCO	Reclamation Control Officer [*Military*] (AFIT)
RCO	Recuperative Catalytic Oxidation [*Chemical engineering*]
RCO	Regional Catering Officer [*British*] (DCTA)
RCO	Remedy Coordination Official (AAGC)
RCO	Remote Communication Outlet [*ATCS*]
RCO	Remote Control Office
RCO	Remote Control Operator
RCO	Remote Control Oscillator
RCO	Rendezvous Compatible Orbit [*Aerospace*]
RCO	Reports Control Officer [*Army*] (AABC)
RCO	Representative Calculating Operation
RCO	Requisition Control Office
RCO	Research Contracting Officer
RCO	Resistance-Controlled Oscillator
RCo	Ristocetin Cofactor
RCO	Rococco Resources Ltd. [*Vancouver Stock Exchange symbol*]
RCO	Royal College of Organists [*British*]
RCOA	Radio Club of America
RCOA	Record Club of America [*Defunct*]
RCOA	Refugee Council of Australia
RC-OAC	Reserve Component Infantry Officer Advance Course [*Military*] (INF)
RCOC.........	Regional Communications Operations Center [*Military*] (MCD)
RC/OC........	Reverse Current/Overcurrent (KSC)
RCOC.........	Royal Canadian Ordnance Corps
RC-OES.......	Reserve Component Officer Education System [*Army*] (INF)
RCoF.........	Ristocetin Cofactor (STED)
RCOG.........	Royal College of Obstetricians and Gynaecologists [*British*]
RCOM........	Enroute Communications [*Aviation*] (FAAC)
RCOM........	Remote Communication Message (IAA)
RCON.........	Reconfiguration [*Aviation*] (FAAC)
RCON.........	Regional Consular Affairs Officer [*Foreign service*]
R/CONT.......	Remote Control [*Automotive engineering*]
RCONT.......	Rod Control
RCOR.........	Quality Dino Entertainment [*NASDAQ symbol*] (SAG)
RCOR.........	Remote Computer Output Room (MCD)
RCORF.......	Quality Dino Entmt [*NASDAQ symbol*] (TTSB)
RCOT.........	Recoton Corp. [*NASDAQ symbol*] (NQ)
RCOT.........	Rolling Contour Optimization Theory [*Bridgestone Corp.*]
R (Count)....	Readiness Count (MCD)
RCP	Racal Communications Processor [*Racal Datacom, Inc.*]
RCP	RADAR Chart Protector (DNAB)
RCP	RADAR Control Panel (MCD)
RCP	RADAR Conversion Program
RCP	Radiation Constraints Panel [*NASA*] (MCD)
RCP	Radiative-Convective-Photochemical [*Meteorology*]
RCP	Radical Caucus in Psychiatry (EA)
RCP	Radio Control Panel [*Aviation*]
RCP	Radiological Control Program [*Nuclear energy*] (NRCH)
RCP	Random Chemistry Profile (DAVI)
RCP	Random Close-Packed [*Granular physics*]
RCP	Rapid City Public Library, Rapid City, SD [*OCLC symbol*] (OCLC)
RCP	Reactor Characterization Program [*Nuclear energy*] (NRCH)
RCP	Reactor Coolant Pump [*Nuclear energy*] (NRCH)
RCP	Receive Clock Pulse
rcp	Recipient [*MARC relator code*] [*Library of Congress*] (LCCP)
rcp	Reciprocal [*Translocation*] (STED)
RCP	Reciprocity (DB)
RCP	Recognition and Control Processor [*Computer science*] (IBMDP)
RCP	Reconciling Congregation Program (EA)
RCP	Recording Control Panel
RCP	Recovery Command Post
RCP	Recruiting Command Post
RCP	Rectangular Coordinate Plotter

RCP	Reenlistment Control Point (DOMA)
RCP	Reflector-cum-Periscope [British military] (DMA)
RCP	Regimental Command Post
RCP	Regional Conservation Program
RCP	Register Clock Pulse
RCP	Registry of Comparative Pathology (EA)
RCP	Reinforced Concrete Pavement
RCP	Reinforced Concrete Pipe [Technical drawings]
RCP	Relative Competitive Preference [Marketing]
RCP	Relative Corrector Program (IAA)
RCP	Reliability Critical Problem (AAG)
RCP	Remote Communication Processor (IAA)
RCP	Remote Control Panel
RCP	Request for Contractual Procurement
RCP	Requirements Change Proposal
RCP	Restartable Cryogenic Propellant
RCP	Restoration Control Point [Telecommunications] (TEL)
RCP	Retention Control Point [Military] (INF)
RCP	Retrocorneal Pigmentation [Medicine] (DMAA)
RCP	Returns Compliance Program [Internal Revenue Service]
RCP	Revolutionary Communist Party [Political party] (BUAC)
RCP	Revolutionary Communist Party of India [Political party] (PPW)
RCP	Riboflavin Carrier Protein [Immunology]
RCP	Right Circular Polarization
RCP	Right-Hand Circular Polarization [NASA] (IAA)
RCP	Rockefeller Center Properties, Inc. [NYSE symbol] (SPSG)
RCP	Rockefeller Ctr Prop [NYSE symbol] (TTSB)
RCP	Roll Centering Pickoff (SAA)
RCP	Roman Catholic Priest (ROG)
RCP	Romanian Communist Party [Political party]
RCP	Rotation Combat Personnel
RCP	Royal College of Pathologists [British]
RCP	Royal College of Physicians of London [British]
RCP	Royal College of Preceptors [British] (ROG)
RCP	Royal College of Psychiatrists [British] (DAVI)
RCP	Royal Commission on the Press [British]
RCP	Rural Counselling Program [Australia]
RCPA	Regional Colleges Principals' Association of Victoria [Australia]
RCPA	Reserve Components Program of the Army (AABC)
RCPA	Rice and Corn Production Administration [Philippines] (BUAC)
RCPA	Rural Cooperative Power Association
RCPAC	Reserve Components Personnel and Administration Center [Army] (AABC)
RCPAC	Reserve Personnel and Administrative Center [Army] (DOMA)
RCPath	Royal College of Pathologists [British]
RCPB	Reactor Coolant Pressure Boundary [Nuclear energy] (NRCH)
RCP(B)	Romanian Communist Party (Bolshevik) [Political party]
RCP(b)	Russian Communist Party (Bolsheviks) [Political party]
RCPB(M-L)	Revolutionary Communist Party of Britain [Marxist-Leninist] [Political party] (BUAC)
RCPC	Regional Check Processing Centers
RCPC	Royal Canadian Postal Corps [Formerly, CPC]
RCPCC	Rice and Corn Production Coordinating Council [Philippines] (BUAC)
RCPCR	Recombinant Circle Polymerase Chain Reaction [Genetics]
RCPD	Reserve Components Personnel Directorate [Office of Personnel Operations] [Army]
RCPE	Radiological Control Practices Evaluation (MCD)
RCPE	Royal College of Physicians, Edinburgh
RCPEd	Royal College of Physicians, Edinburgh
RCPG	Regional Cooperative Physics Group [Educational institutions in Ohio, Michigan, Illinois and Pennsylvania] (PDAA)
RCPGlas	Royal College of Physicians and Surgeons of Glasgow
RCPH	Red Cell Peroxide Hemolysis (STED)
RCPI	Revolutionary Communist Party of India [Political party] (PPW)
RCPI	Royal College of Physicians, Ireland
RCPL	Requirements Contract Price List (AAGC)
RCPL	Right Circularly Polarized Light
RCPL	Royal College of Physicians, London (ROG)
RCPM	Raven Colored Progressive Matrix (STED)
RCPM	Raven Coloured Progressive Matrices [Psychiatry] (DAVI)
RCPO	Regional Contract Property Officer
RCPO	Xinzhu [China] [ICAO location identifier] (ICLI)
RCPP	Refrigeration, Compressor and Electrical Power, Airborne Pod Enclosure (DNAB)
RCPP	Reinforced Concrete Pressure Pipe
RCPR	Response-Contingent Positive Reinforcement [Psychology] (DHP)
RCPS	Royal College of Physicians and Surgeons of Glasgow
RCPS	Royal College of Physicians and Surgeons (of United States of America) (EA)
RCPSA	Retired Civil and Public Servants' Asssociation [Ireland] (BUAC)
RCPSC	Royal College of Physicians and Surgeons of Canada (BUAC)
RCPS(C)	Royal College of Physicians and Surgeons of Canada
RCPSGlas	Royal College of Physicians and Surgeons of Glasgow [Scotland] (BUAC)
RCPS(Glasg)	Royal College of Physicians and Surgeons of Glasgow (DBQ)
RCPsych	Royal College of Psychiatrists [British] (DAVI)
rcpt	Receipt (WDAA)
Rcpt	Receipt (EBF)
RCPT	Receipt (AFM)
RCPT	Receptacle (MSA)
RCPT	Reception (AABC)
RCPT	Refrigeration, Compressor and Electrical Power, Trailer-Mounted (DNAB)
RCPT	Registered Cardiopulmonary Technologist [Medicine] (WGA)
RCPTN	Reception (MSA)

RCPV	Riot Control Patrol Vehicle
RCQ	Reconquista [Argentina] [Airport symbol] (OAG)
RCQ	Rich Capital Corp. [Vancouver Stock Exchange symbol]
RCQ	Role Category Questionnaire [Psychology] (EDAC)
RCQC	Magong [China] [ICAO location identifier] (ICLI)
RCQG	Right Caudal Quarter Ganglion [Medicine] (STED)
RCQS	Taidong/Zhihang [China] [ICAO location identifier] (ICLI)
RCR	RADAR Control Room
RCR	Ramsbottom Carbon Residue [Analysis of petroleum products]
RCR	Randle Cliff RADAR (PDAA)
RCR	Rated Capacity Report [Army]
RCR	Reactor Control Room
RCR	Reader Control Relay
RCR	Receiver [Telecommunications] (ECII)
RCR	Reciprocating Cryogenic Refrigerator
RCR	Recrystallization Controlled Rolling (PDAA)
RCR	Regenerative Cyclic Reactor [Chemical engineering]
RCR	Registered Commodity Representative [Investment term] (NUMA)
RCR	Relative Citation Rate [Bibliography]
RCR	Relative Consumption Rate [Entomology]
RCR	Required Carrier Return Character [Computer science]
RCR	Respiratory Control Ratio [Medicine]
RCR	Restitution of Conjugal Rights [Legal] [British] (ROG)
RCR	Retrofit Configuration Record [NASA] (NASA)
RCR	Reverse Contactor (IAA)
RCR	Reverse Current Relay (IAA)
RCR	Rochester, IN [Location identifier FAA] (FAAL)
RCR	Room Cavity Ratio [Lighting]
RCR	Route Contingency Reserve [Aviation] (DA)
RCR	Royal Canadian Regiment [Military]
RCR	Royal Canadian Rifles [Military unit]
RCR	Royal College of Radiologists [British]
RCR	Runway Condition Reading [FAA] (TAG)
RCRA	Radiologically-Controlled Radiation Area (DNAB)
RCRA	Refrigeration Compressor Rebuilders Association (EA)
RCRA	Resort and Commercial Recreation Association (EA)
RCRA	Resource Conservation and Recovery Act [Pronounced "rickra"] [1976]
RCRA	Rural Cooperative and Recovery Act (OICC)
RCRA	Zouying [China] [ICAO location identifier] (ICLI)
R-CRAS	Rogers Criminal Responsibility Assessment Scales [Personality development test] [Psychology]
RCRB	Reseau Canadian de Recherce sur les Bacterioses (AC)
RCRBSJ	Research Council on Riveted and Bolted Structural Joints [Later, RCSC] (EA)
RCRC	Rabbinic Center for Research and Counseling (EA)
RCRC	Reinforced Concrete Research Council (EA)
RCRC	Revoked Commission, Returned to Civilian Status [Navy]
RCRD	Record (AFM)
RCRDC	Radio Components Research and Development Committee (BUAC)
RCRE	Retirement Care Associates, Inc. [NASDAQ symbol] (SAG)
RCRHRCS	Research Center for Religion and Human Rights in Closed Societies (EA)
RCRIS	Resource Conservation and Recovery Information System (ERG)
RCRL	Reliability Critical Ranking List (AAG)
RCRP	Regional Centers for Radiological Physics [National Cancer Institute]
RCRR	Roster Chaplain - Ready Reserve [Army]
RCRS	Regenerative Carbon-Dioxide Removal System (MCD)
RCRS	Rehabilitation Client Rating Scale (STED)
R-CRS	Report on Course [Aviation] (DA)
RCRS	Reserve Combat Replacement Squadron (DNAB)
RCRTN	Recreation
RCRTNL	Recreational
RCRTR	Recruiter
RCS	Rabbit Aorta Contracting Substance [TA_2 - see TA, Thromboxane] [Biochemistry]
RCS	RADAR Calibration Sphere
RCS	RADAR Collimator System
RCS	RADAR Control Ship
RCS	RADAR Cross Section
RCS	Radio Command System
RCS	Radio Communications Set
RCS	Radio Communications System [Military] (CAAL)
RCS	Radio Control System
RCS	Range Calibration Satellite (SAA)
RCS	Range Control Station [or System] [Army]
RCS	Rapports de la Cour Supreme du Canada [Database] [Federal Department of Justice] [Information service or system] (CRD)
RCS	Rate Command System (AAG)
RCS	RCM Strategic Global Government Fund [NYSE symbol] (SAG)
RCS	RCM Strategic Global Gvt Fund [NYSE symbol] (TTSB)
RCS	Reaction Control System [or Subsystem] [Steering system in spacecraft] [NASA]
RCS	Reactive Current Sensing (MCD)
RCS	Reactor Coolant System [Nuclear energy] (NRCH)
RCS	Rearward Communications System (MDG)
RCS	Recurrent Change of Station (SAA)
RCS	Recurrent Change of Status (SAA)
RCS	Red Cell Suspension (STED)
RCS	Reentry Control System [Aerospace] (AFM)
RCS	Reference Color Space [Computer science]
RCS	Refurbishment Cost Study (KSC)
RCS	Regional Control Station [Military] (MCD)
RCS	Registrar of Cooperative Societies [New South Wales, Australia]
RCS	Rehost Computer System [Aviation] (FAAC)

RCS	Reliability Control, Specification
RCS	Reliable Corrective Action Summary (AAG)
RCS	Reloadable Control Storage [Computer science]
RCS	Remington's Compiled Statutes [1922] [A publication] (DLA)
RCS	Remote Characterization System [Remote controlled vehicle] [Hazardous materials control]
RCS	Remote Computing Service
RCS	Remote Control Set
RCS	Remote Control Station (NITA)
RC(S)	Remote Control (System) (DEN)
RCS	Rent Control System
R/CS	Repeat Cesarean Section [Obstetrics] (MAE)
RCS	Reports Control Symbol [Military]
RCS	Reports Creation System
RCS	Representative Conflict Situations [Army]
RCS	Request for Consultation Service (MCD)
RCS	Requirement Clearance Symbol [Military] (AFM)
RCS	Requirements Control Symbol [Military] (MCD)
RCS	Requirements Control System
RCS	Residential Conservation Service [Offered by major electric and gas utilities]
Rcs	Resources [Army]
RCS	Reticulum Cell Sarcoma [Medicine]
RCS	Retrofit Configuration System (MCD)
RCS	Revenue Cutter Service [Coast Guard]
RCS	Revision Control System [Computer science]
RCS	Rich Coast Sulphur Ltd. [Vancouver Stock Exchange symbol]
RCS	Ride-Control Segment [or System] [Aviation]
RCS	Right Coronary Sinus [Cardiology] (AAMN)
RCS	Rip-Out Control Sheet (DNAB)
RCS	Rizzoli Corriere della Sera [Publisher]
RCS	Rochester [England] [Airport symbol] (AD)
RCS	Royal Choral Society [British] (EAIO)
RCS	Royal College of Science [British]
RCS	Royal College of Surgeons [British]
RCS	Royal Commonwealth Society [British]
RCS	Royal Corps of Signals [British]
RCSB	RCSB Financial [NASDAQ symbol] (TTSB)
RCSB	RCSB Financial, Inc. [Associated Press] (SAG)
RCSB	[The] Rochester Community Savings Bank [NASDAQ symbol] (NQ)
RCSB	Royal Commonwealth Society for the Blind [British] (DBA)
RCSBDE	Round Corners Silver Bevelled Deckle Edges [Bookbinding] (DGA)
RCSBE	Round Corners Silver Bevelled Edges [Bookbinding] (DGA)
RCSB Fn	RCSB Financial, Inc. [Associated Press] (SAG)
RCSBP	RCSB Finl 7% Perp Cv 'B' Pfd [NASDAQ symbol] (TTSB)
RCSBP	Reserve Components Survivor Benefits Plan [Military]
RCSC	Huwei [China] [ICAO location identifier] (ICLI)
RCSC	Radio Component Standardization Committee [British]
RCSC	Reaction Control System [or Subsystem] Controller [Apollo] [NASA] (NASA)
RCSC	Research Council on Structural Connections (EA)
RCSC	Royal Canadian Sea Cadets
RCSCC	Royal Canadian Sea Cadets Corps
RCSCJ	Sisters of the Cross of the Sacred Heart of Jesus (Mexico) (TOCD)
RCSDE	Reactor Coolant System Dose Equivalent (IEEE)
RCSDF	Reconfigurable Computer System Design Facility (MHDB)
RCSDP	League of Red Cross Societies Development Program
RCSE	Remote Control and Status Equipment (MCD)
RCSE	Round Corners Silver Edges [Bookbinding] (DGA)
RCSE	Royal College of Surgeons, Edinburgh
RCSEd	Royal College of Surgeons, Edinburgh
RCSEL	Recommended Common Support Equipment List (MCD)
RCSEng	Royal College of Surgeons, England
RCSG	Restarting Computer and Symbol Generator (IAA)
RCSHSB	Red Cedar Shingle and Handsplit Shake Bureau [Later, CSSB] (EA)
RCSI	Reactor Coolant System Integrity [Environmental science] (COE)
RCSI	Receipt for [or of] Classified Security Information
RCSI	Rede CONSISDATA de Servicos Integrados [CONSISDATA Integrated Services Network] [Consultoria, Sistemas, e Processamento de Dados Ltda.] [Brazil] [Information service or system] (CRD)
RCSI	Royal College of Surgeons, Ireland
RCSIS	Radio/Cable Switching Integration System (MCD)
RCSM	Ri Yue Tan [China] [ICAO location identifier] (ICLI)
RCSO	Research Contract Support Office
RCSP	Royal Commission on Social Policy [Australia]
RCSQ	Pingdong (North) [China] [ICAO location identifier] (ICLI)
RCSQ	Royal Commonwealth Society of Queensland [Australia]
RCS-RF	Rabbit Aorta Contracting Substance-Releasing Factor [Medicine] (PDAA)
RCSS	Radial Compression Separation System [Chromatography]
RCSS	Random Communication Satellite System
RCSS	Recruiting Command Support System [Navy] (DNAB)
RCSS	Reduced Chi-Square Statistic
RCSS	Taibei/Songshan [China] [ICAO location identifier] (ICLI)
RCSSA	Regional Centre for Seismology for South America (EAIO)
RCSSMRS	Regional Centre for Services in Surveying, Mapping, and Remote Sensing [West Africa]
RCS Supp	Remington's Compiled Statutes, Supplement [A publication] (DLA)
RCSTN	Radio Compass Station (IAA)
RCSU	Repair Cycle Support Unit
RCSX	North American Car Corp. [AAR code]
RCT	RADAR Control Trailer [Military] (AABC)
RCT	Radiation/Chemical Technician (IEEE)
RCT	Radiobeacon Calibration Transmitter

RCT	Radiological Control Technician [Environmental science] (COE)
RCT	Randomized Clinical Trial [Medicine]
RCT	Randomized Control Trial [Statistics]
RCT	Raw Cycle Time (AAGC)
RCT	Real Estate Investment Trust [NYSE symbol] (SAG)
RCT	Receipt (IAA)
rct	Receipt (EBF)
RCT	Receipts [Stock exchange term] (SPSG)
RCT	Received Copy of Temporary Pay Record
RCT	Recruit
rct	Recruit (WDAA)
RCT	Reed City, MI [Location identifier FAA] (FAAL)
RCT	Reference Clock Trigger [Telecommunications] (IAA)
RCT	Reference Cluster Tool (AAEL)
RCT	Regimental Combat Team
RCT	Regional Control Task [Computer science] (CIST)
RCT	Region Control Task [Computer science] (BUR)
RCT	Registered Care Technician [Proposed by American Medical Association to alleviate nursing shortage]
RCT	Regular Care Technologist
RCT	Rehabilitation and Research Center for Torture Victims (EAIO)
RCT	Remote Control [Systems] (MCD)
RCT	Remote Control Terminal (MCD)
RCT	Renal Cortical Tumor [Oncology]
RCT	Repair Cycle Time (MCD)
RCT	Repeat Cycle Timer
RCT	Resistor-Capacitor Transistor (IAA)
RCT	Resolver Control Transformer
RCT	Resource Consulting Teacher
RCT	Response Coordination Team [Nuclear energy] (NRCH)
RCT	Retention Control Training [Medicine]
RCT	Retrograde Conduction Time [Medicine] (DMAA)
RC-T	Revenue Canada, Taxation
RCT	Reverseconducting Thyristor (IAA)
RCT	Reversible Counter
RCT	Rework/Completion Tag [Nuclear energy] (NRCH)
RCT	Ridgecrest Resources [Vancouver Stock Exchange symbol]
RCT	Roll Call Training
RCT	Root Canal Therapy [Dentistry]
RCT	Root Canal Treatment [Dentistry] (DAVI)
RCT	Rorschach Content Test [Psychology]
RCT	Royal Clinical Teacher [British]
RCT	Royal Corps of Transport [Army British]
RCT	Royal Cosmic Theology [British]
RCT	Running Call Telephone (WDAA)
RCT	Ryan Air Service, Inc. [FAA designator] (FAAC)
RCTA	Retail Confectionery and Tobacconists' Association [British] (DI)
RCTB	Reserve Components Troop Basis [Army] (AABC)
RCTC	Regeneratively-Cooled Thrust Chamber
RCTC	Reserve Components Training Center [Military]
RCTC	Union of Rail Canada Traffic Controllers [See also CCFC]
RCTDAP	Reserve Components Training Development Action Plan [Army] (DOMA)
RCTDPOVALCAN	Request Concurrent Travel of Dependents by Privately Owned Vehicle [ALCAN Highway or Via Route Required] [Army] (AABC)
RCTG	Recruiting (AABC)
RCTI	Rajawali Citra Televisi Indonesia (EY)
RCTL	Resistance-Coupled Transistor Logic
RCTL	Resistor-Capacitor Transistor Logic
RCTM	Radio Technical Committee for Maritime services
RCTM	Regional Center for Tropical Meteorology [National Hurricane Center]
RCTM	Remote Control Tunnelling Machine
RCTN	Reaction (MSA)
R (Ct of Sess)	Rettie, Crawford, and Melville's Session Cases, Fourth Series [1873-98] [Scotland] [A publication] (DLA)
RCTP	Reserve Components Troop Program [Army]
RCTP	Taibei City/Taibei International Airport [China] [ICAO location identifier] (ICLI)
RCTPS	Revue Canadienne de Theorie Politique et Sociale [A publication]
RCTRANSMOD	Reserve Components Transition to Modernization
RCTS	Railway Correspondence and Travel Society [British]
RCTS	Reactor Coolant Treatment System [Nuclear energy] (NRCH)
RCTSR	Radio Code Test, Speed of Response [Military]
RCTSS	Regional Computerized Traffic Signal System
RCTV	Radio Caracas Television [Venezuela] (EY)
RCTV	RCA Cable and Rockefeller Center Cable Pay-TV Program Service
RCTV	Remote Controlled Target Vehicle [Military] (INF)
RCU	Atlantic, SL [Spain] [FAA designator] (FAAC)
RCU	Rack Controller Unit [Computer science] (PCM)
RCU	RADAR Calibration Unit
RCU	RADAR Control Unit [Military] (CAAL)
RCU	Rate Changes Unit (COE)
RCU	Rate Construction Unit [Hypothetical basic currency unit] (DCTA)
RCU	Receiver Control Unit (IAA)
RCU	Reference Control Unit (MCD)
RCU	Regional Coordinating Unit [Advisory Committee on Pollution of the Sea]
RCU	Relay Control Unit (AAG)
RCU	Remote Control Unit
RCU	Requisition Control Unit
R/CU	Research and Curriculum Unit [Mississippi State University] [Research center] (RCD)
RCU	Research Coordinating Unit [Oklahoma State Department of Vocational and Technical Education] [Stillwater, OK]
RCU	Research into Chronic Unemployment [British]

RCU .... Reserve Component Unit [Army]   (AABC)
RCU .... Resistor-Capacitor Unit   (IAA)
RCU .... Respiratory Care Unit [Medicine]
RCU .... Revolution Control Unit [Automotive engineering]
RCU .... Rio Cuarto [Argentina] [Airport symbol]   (OAG)
RCU .... Road Construction Unit   (PDAA)
RCU .... Rocket Countermeasure Unit
RCUA .... Remote Checkout Umbilical Array
RCUC .... Redundant Churches' Users' Committee [British]   (WDAA)
RCUEP .... Research Center for Urban and Environmental Planning [Princeton University]
RCUK .... Bakuai [China] [ICAO location identifier]   (ICLI)
RCUL .... Reference Control Unit Launch   (MCD)
RCUR .... Recurrent   (MSA)
RCUT .... Rapid Carbohydrate Utilization Test   (PDAA)
RCV .... RADAR Control Van   (NATG)
RCV .... Radiation Control Valve [Nuclear energy]   (NRCH)
RCV .... Reaction-Control Valve
RCV .... Receive   (AFM)
rcv .... Receive   (IDOE)
RCV .... Receiver
RCV .... Receiver/Exciter Subsystem [Deep Space Instrumentation Facility, NASA]
RCV .... Red Cell Volume [Hematology]
RCV .... Relative Conductor Volume
RCV .... Remote-Controlled Vehicle   (MCD)
RCV .... Replacement Cost Valuation [Insurance]
RCV .... Restartable Cryogenic Vehicle
RCV .... Reversed Circular Vection [Optics]
RCV .... Revised Claim Valuation [Insurance]
RCV .... Rich Cut Virginia [Tobacco]   (ROG)
RCV .... Riot Control Vehicle
RCV .... Robotic Combat Vehicle [Army]   (RDA)
RCV .... Routine Coefficient of Variation [Statistics]
RCV .... Ryegrass Cryptic Virus [Plant pathology]
RCVBL .... Receivable
RCV-COMMZ... Rear Combat Vehicle/Communications Zone   (MCD)
RCVD .... Reactive Chemical Vapor Deposition [Coating technology]
RCVD .... Received   (MSA)
RCVG .... Receiving   (MSA)
RCVG .... Replacement Carrier Fighter Group [V is Navy code for Fighter]
RCVGX .... Oppenheimer Bond Fund for Growth [Mutual fund ticker symbol]   (SG)
RCVMV .... Red Clover Vein Mosaic Virus
RCVNG .... Receiving
RCVNO .... Receiving Capability Out [Aviation]   (FAAC)
RCVR .... Receiver   (AAG)
rcvr .... Receiver   (IDOE)
RCVS .... Remote Control Video Switch   (MCD)
RCVS .... Royal College of Veterinary Surgeons [British]
RCVSG .... Readiness Antisubmarine Warfare Carrier Air Wing [Navy]   (NVT)
RCVT .... Registered Cardiovascular Technologist [Medicine]   (WGA)
RCVTP .... Reserve Component Virtual Training Program [Army]   (RDA)
RCVV .... Rear Compressor Variable Vane
RCVW .... Readiness Attack Carrier Air Wing [Navy]   (NVT)
RCVY .... Recovery   (MSA)
RCW .... Raw Cooling Water [Nuclear energy]   (NRCH)
RCW .... Reactor Cooling Water [Nuclear energy]   (NRCH)
RCW .... Read, Compute, Write   (IAA)
RCW .... Recirculated Cooling Water [Environmental science]   (COE)
RCW .... Record Control Word [Computer science]
RCW .... Red-Cockaded Woodpecker
RCW .... Redwood Cultural Work/Redwood Records   (EA)
RCW .... Reformed Church Women [An association]   (EA)
RCW .... Register Containing Word
RCW .... Research Center on Women   (EA)
RCW .... Resident Careworker
RCW .... Return Control Word
RCWA .... Revised Code of Washington Annotated [A publication]   (DLA)
RCWAT .... Retarded Citizens' Welfare Association of Tasmania [Australia]
RCWI .... Right Ventricular Cardiac Work Index [Cardiology]
RCWK .... Xinshe [China] [ICAO location identifier]   (ICLI)
RCWP .... Rubber Covered, Weatherproof   (IAA)
RCWP .... Rural Clean Water Program [Department of Agriculture]
RCWS .... Remote Control Water Sampler
RCWS .... Research Centre for Women's Studies [University of Adelaide, Australia]
RCWS .... Russian Children's Welfare Society - Outside of Russia   (EA)
RCWV .... Rated Continuous Working Voltage   (IAA)
RCX .... Ladysmith, WI [Location identifier FAA]   (FAAL)
RCX .... Remote Cluster Executive   (IAA)
RCXY .... Guiren [China] [ICAO location identifier]   (ICLI)
RCY .... Recovery   (NASA)
RCY .... Red Cross and Red Crescent Youth [Geneva, Switzerland]
RCY .... Remaining Cycles   (MCD)
RCY .... Rotating Coil Yoke
RCY .... Royal Crystal [Vancouver Stock Exchange symbol]
RCYRA .... Rooster Class Yacht Racing Association [Defunct]   (EA)
RCYU .... Hualian [China] [ICAO location identifier]   (ICLI)
RCZ .... Radiation Control Zone
RCZ .... Rear Combat Zone   (NATG)
RCZ .... Rockingham, NC [Location identifier FAA]   (FAAL)
RD .... Airlift International, Inc. [ICAO designator]
Rd .... Albert Rolland [France] [Research code symbol]
RD .... Aviona [ICAO designator]   (AD)

RD .... Boots Pure Drug Co. [Great Britain] [Research code symbol]
RD .... Directional Radio Beacon [ITU designation]   (CET)
R_D .... Drain Resistance   (IDOE)
RD .... Indian Revenue Decisions [A publication]   (DLA)
rd .... Rad [Non-SI unit; preferred unit is Gy, Gray]
RD .... RADAR   (DEN)
RD .... RADAR Data
RD .... RADAR Display
RD .... RADARman [Also, RDM] [Navy rating]
RD .... Radiation Absorbed Dose [Unit of measurement of radiation energy]   (IAA)
RD .... Radiation Damage [Nucleonics]   (OA)
RD .... Radiation Detection
RD .... Radio Detector
Rd .... Radiolaria [Quality of the bottom] [Nautical charts]
RD .... Radiological Defense [To minimize the effect of nuclear radiation on people and resources]
Rd .... Rainbow Darter [Ichthyology]
RD .... Random Drift
RD .... Random Driver [Nuclear energy]   (NRCH)
RD .... Range Development   (MUGU)
RD .... Rated   (IAA)
RD .... Rated Duty   (IAA)
RD .... Rate Difference [Toxicology]
R/D .... Rate of Descent [Aviation]   (MCD)
RD .... Ratio Detector   (IAA)
RD .... Raynaud's Disease [Medicine]
RD .... Reaction of Degeneration [Physiology]
RD .... Read   (AAG)
RD .... Read Data
RD .... Read Delay   (IAA)
RD .... Read Direct
RD .... Reader's Digest [A publication]
RD .... Readiness Data
RD .... Readiness Date
RD .... Reading Disability
RD .... Reappraisement Decisions [A publication]   (DLA)
RD .... Rear Door
RD .... Receipt Day   (NRCH)
RD .... Received Data   (IEEE)
RD .... Receiving Data [Modem status information light] [Computer science]   (IGQR)
RD .... Recemment Degorgee [Recently Disgorged] [Refers to aging of wine] [French]
RD .... Recognition Differential
RD .... Record Description [Computer science]
RD .... Recorder   (IAA)
RD .... Recorders-Reproducers [JETDS nomenclature] [Military]   (CET)
RD .... Recording Demand   (DEN)
RD .... Rectifier Diode   (IAA)
RD .... Red
RD .... Redirect [Computer science]   (TNIG)
RD .... Red Pennant [Navy British]
Rd .... Reduce [Army]
RD .... Reference Designator   (NASA)
RD .... Reference Document
RD .... Reference Drawing   (NATG)
RD .... Refer to Drawer [Banking]
RD .... Regio Decreto [Royal Decree] [Latin]   (DLA)
RD .... Regional Director
RD .... Register Drive   (MSA)
RD .... Registered   (ROG)
RD .... Registered Dietitian
RD .... Registration Division [Environmental Protection Agency]   (EPA)
RD .... Reinforcement Designee [Air Force]   (AFM)
RD .... Reiter's Disease [Medicine]   (DMAA)
RD .... Relative Density
RD .... Relaxation Delay
RD .... Relay Drawer
RD .... Relay Driver
RD .... Relocatable Directory [Computer science]   (IAA)
RD .... Remedial Design   (EPA)
RD .... Remove Directory [Computer science]
RD .... Renal Disease [Medicine]
RD .... Rendered   (ROG)
rd .... Rendered   (WDAA)
RD .... Renon-Delille [Syndrome] [Medicine]   (DB)
RD .... Replacement Detachment [Army]
RD .... Replenishable Demand
RD .... Reply Delay   (MUGU)
RD .... Report Departing [Aviation]   (DA)
RD .... Request Disconnect [Telecommunications]   (OSI)
RD .... Required Date
RD .... Requirements Document [NASA]   (KSC)
RD .... Research and Development [Army]
RD .... Reserve Decoration [Navy British]
RD .... Resistance Determinant [Medicine]   (MAE)
RD .... Resistor Diode   (IAA)
RD .... Resolver Differential   (IAA)
RD .... Resource Development
RD .... Respiratory Disease
RD .... Respiratory Distress [Medicine]   (DAVI)
RD .... Restricted Data [Security classification]
RD .... Retention and Disposal
RD .... Retinal Detachment [Ophthalmology]

RD .... Revision Directive [*Drawings*]
RD .... Revolutionary Development [*South Vietnam*]
RD .... Reye's Disease [*Medicine*]
RD .... Right Defense
RD .... Right Deltoid [*Medicine*]
RD .... Right Door [*Theater*]
RD .... Right Dorso Anterior [*Medicine*] (MAE)
RD .... Rights in Data (OICC)
RD .... Riley-Day [*Syndrome*] [*Medicine*] (DB)
RD .... Ringdown [*Telecommunications*] (TEL)
RD .... Rive Droite [*Right Bank*] [*French*]
RD .... Rix-Dollar
RD .... Road [*Maps and charts*] (AAG)
Rd .... Road (ASC)
RD .... Rod
RD .... Romanovsky Dye [*Biological stain*]
RD .... Rood [*Unit of measurement*]
RD .... Roof Diameter (IAA)
RD .... Roof Drain (AAG)
RD .... Root Diameter (MSA)
R/D .... Rotary to Digital (MCD)
RD .... Rotodrome
RD .... Round (AAG)
RD .... Routing Domain [*Computer science*] (TNIG)
RD .... Royal Dragoons [*British*]
RD .... Royal Dutch Petrol [*NYSE symbol*] (TTSB)
RD .... Royal Dutch Petroleum Co. [*NYSE symbol*] (SPSG)
RD .... Royal Naval Reserve Decoration [*British*]
RD .... Rubber Dam [*Medicine*] (DMAA)
RD .... Ruling Date [*IRS*]
RD .... Run Down [*Typography*]
RD .... Running Days
rd .... Running Days (ODBW)
RD .... Rupture Disk (KSC)
RD .... Rural Deacon [*or Deaconry*] [*Church of England*]
RD .... Rural Dean [*Church of England*]
RD .... Rural Delivery
RD .... Rural Development
RD .... Rural District
rd .... Rutherford [*Unit of strength of a radioactive source*]
RD1 .... RADARman, First Class [*Navy rating*]
RD2 .... RADARman, Second Class [*Navy rating*]
rd² .... Square Rod (CDAI)
RD3 .... RADARman, Third Class [*Navy rating*]
RDA .... Radioactive Dentin Abrasion [*Dentistry*]
RDA .... Railway Development Association [*British*]
RDA .... Ranging Demodulator Assembly [*Deep Space Instrumentation Facility, NASA*]
RDA .... Rassemblement Democratique Africain [*Niger*] [*Political party*] (PD)
RDA .... Rassemblement Democratique Africain [*Ivory Coast*] [*Political party*] (PPW)
RDA .... Read Data Available
RDA .... Reader's Digest Assn'A' [*NYSE symbol*] (TTSB)
RDA .... Reader's Digest Association [*NYSE symbol*] (SPSG)
RdA .... Reading Age [*Education*] (DAVI)
RDA .... Real-Time Debugging Aid
RDA .... Receive Data and Acknowledge [*Telecommunications*] (OSI)
RDA .... Recirculation Duct Assembly
RDA .... Recommended Daily Allowance [*Dietary*]
RDA .... Recommended Dietary Allowance (DAVI)
RDA .... Recommended Duty Assignment (AFM)
RDA .... Redevelopment Authority (PA)
RDA .... Regional Dance America [*Defunct*] (EA)
RDA .... Regional Dance Association
RDA .... Regional Data Associates [*Information service or system*] (IID)
RDA .... Regional Dental Activity (AABC)
RDA .... Regional Development Authority [*Victoria, Australia*]
RDA .... Register Display Assembly
RDA .... Registered Dental Assistant (DMAA)
RDA .... Regularize Discriminant Analysis [*Mathematics*]
RDA .... Reliability Design Analysis (MCD)
RDA .... Remote Data [*or Database*] Access (NASA)
RDA .... Representational Difference Analysis [*Genetic technique*]
RDA .... Request for Deviation Approval (MCD)
RDA1 .... Research and Development Abstracts [*A publication*]
RDA .... Research and Development, Army
RDA .... Research, Development, and Acquisition (AAGC)
RDA .... Resent, Demand, Appreciate [*In Sidney Simon, Leland Howe, and Howard Kirschenbaum's book "Values Clarification"*]
RDA .... Resident Data Area (NASA)
RDA .... Retail Display Agreement (WDMC)
RDA .... Retail Distributors Association, Inc. [*British*] (BI)
RDA .... Reverse Diels-Alder [*Organic chemistry*]
RDA .... Riding for the Disabled Association (EAIO)
RDA .... Right Dorso Anterior [*Medicine*] (ROG)
RDA .... Rod Drop Accident (IEEE)
RDA .... Rome Daily American [*An English-language newspaper in Italy*] [*A publication*]
RDA .... Royal Danish Army (NATG)
RDA .... Royal Defence Academy [*British*]
RDA .... Royal Docks Association [*British*] (BI)
RDA .... Rules for the Discipline of Attorneys [*A publication*] (DLA)
RDA .... Run-Time Debugging Aid (MHDB)
RDA .... Run-Time Debugging Unit (NITA)

RDA .... Rural Development Abstracts [*Database*] [*Commonwealth Bureau of Agricultural Economics*] [*Information service or system*] (CRD)
RDA .... Rural Development Act [*1972*] (OICC)
RDA .... Rural Development Administration [*AEC*]
RDA .... TK Travel Ltd. [*Gambia*] [*ICAO designator*] (FAAC)
RDAA .... Range Doppler Angle Angle (IAA)
RDAA .... Riding for the Disabled Association of Australia
RDAA .... Rural Doctors' Association of Australia
RDAAC .... Research into Drug Abuse Advisory Committee [*Australia*]
RdAc .... Radioactinium [*Nuclear physics*] (WGA)
RDAC .... Recruiting District Assistance Council [*Navy*] (DNAB)
RDAC .... Research and Development Acquisition Committee [*Military*]
RDAF .... Revue de Droit Administratif et de Droit Fiscal [*Lausanne, Switzerland*] [*A publication*] (DLA)
RDAF .... Royal Danish Air Force
RDAFCI .... Research and Development Associates, Food and Container Institute (EA)
RDAISA .... Research Development and Acquisition Information Systems Activity [*Army*] (AAGC)
RDAISA .... Research, Development, and Acquisition Information Systems Agency [*Army*] (AABC)
RDAL .... Representation Dependent Accessing Language
RD & A .... Research, Development, and Acquisition [*DoD*]
RD & D .... Research, Development, and Demonstration
RD & E .... Research, Development, and Engineering
RD & ES ..... Requirements Determination and Exercise System [*Military*] (MCD)
RD & P .... Research, Development, and Production [*NATO*] (NATG)
RD & S .... Research, Development, and Studies [*Marine Corps*]
RD & T .... Research, Development, and Testing
RDAR .... Reliability Design Analysis Report (AAG)
RDARA .... Regional and Domestic Air Route Area
RDAS .... Reflectivity Data Acquisition System
RDAT .... Registered Designs Appeal Tribunal (DLA)
RDAT .... Remote Data Acquisition Terminal (NRCH)
RDAT .... Research and Development Acceptance Test
RDAT .... Research, Development, and Test
RDAT .... Rotary [*or Rotating*] Digital Audio Tape
RDAU .... Remote Data Acquisition Unit
RDAV .... Reset Data Available [*Computer science*] (MHDI)
RDAVS .... Recovered Doppler Airborne Vector Scorer
R (Day) .... Redeployment Day [*Military*]
RDB .... Racecourses Development Board [*South Australia*]
RDB .... RADAR Decoy Balloon [*Air Force*]
RDB .... Ramped Dump Barge
RDB .... Random Double-Blind Trial [*Medicine*] (DMAA)
RDB .... Rapidly Deployable Barge [*Military*] (MCD)
RDB .... Rare Disease Database [*National Organization for Rare Disorders*] [*Information service or system*] (IID)
RDB .... Reader's Digest Assn'B' [*NYSE symbol*] (TTSB)
RDB .... Readers Digest Association [*NYSE symbol*] (SAG)
RDB .... Red Data Book (EES)
RDB .... Red Data Books (GNE)
RDB .... Reference Data and Bias (SAA)
RDB .... Relational Data Base (PDAA)
RDB .... Requirements and Design Branch (SAA)
RDB .... Requirements Data Bank [*Air Force*] (GFGA)
RDB .... Research and Development Board [*Abolished, 1953, functions transferred to Department of Defense*]
RDB .... Resistance Decade Box
RDB .... Round Die Bushing
RDB .... Royal Danish Ballet
RDB .... Rural Development Board [*British*]
RDBA .... Roll Drive and Brake Assembly
RDBL .... Readable
RDBMS .... Relational Database Management System [*Computer science*] (BYTE)
RdBrick .... Red Brick Systems, Inc. [*Associated Press*] (SAG)
RDC .... Chief RADARman [*Navy rating*]
R_dc .... DC Resistance (IDOE)
RDC .... Racecourse Development Committee [*New South Wales*]
RDC .... RADAR Data Converter (MCD)
RDC .... RADAR Design Corp.
RDC .... RADAR Display Console
RDC .... Radiac [*Nucleonics*]
RDC .... Radiation Density Constant
RDC .... Radioactivity Decay Constant
RDC .... Rail Diesel Car
RDC .... Rand Development Corp. (IAA)
RDC .... Rapaport Diamond Corp. [*Information service or system*] (IID)
RDC .... Rapid Development Capability [*Military*] (NG)
RDC .... Rassemblement Democratique Caledonien [*Caledonian Democratic Rally*] [*Political party*] (PPW)
RDC .... Rassemblement Democratique Centrafricain [*Central African Republic*] [*Political party*]
RDC .... Rate Damping Control
RDC .... Read Data Check (CMD)
RDC .... Reading Development Continuum (AIE)
RDC .... Real Decisions Corp. [*Information service or system*] (IID)
RDC .... Recording Doppler Comparator [*Astronomy*] (OA)
RDC .... Reduce (MSA)
RDC .... Reference Designator Code (NASA)
RDC .... Reflex Digital Control
RDC .... Refugee Documentation Centre [*Information service or system*] (IID)
RDC .... Regional Data Center [*Marine science*] (MSC)
RDC .... Regional Dissemination Center [*NASA*]

RDC	Regional Dissemination Centers [NASA] (PDAA)
RDC	Regional Distribution Center [TRW Automotive Aftermarket Group]
RDC	Reliability Data Center (KSC)
RDC	Reliability Data Control (IAA)
RDC	Remote Data Collection (MCD)
RDC	Remote Data Concentrator
RDC	Reply Delay Compensation (MUGU)
RDC	Request for Document Change (NASA)
RDC	Research and Development Command [Military]
RDC	Research Diagnostic Criteria [Medicine, psychiatry]
RDC	Revolutionary Development Cadre [South Vietnam]
RDC	Rotary Dispersion Colorimeter
RDC	Rotating Diffusion Cell [Chemistry]
RDC	Rotating Disk Contractor [Chemical engineering]
RDC	Rowan Companies, Inc. [NYSE symbol] (SPSG)
RDC	Rowan Cos. [NYSE symbol] (TTSB)
RDC	Royal Defence Corps [British]
RDC	Rubber Development Corp. [Expired, 1947]
RDC	Running-Down Clause [Business term]
RDC	Rural Development and Conservation [Department of Agriculture]
RDC	Rural Development Centre [University of New England, Australia]
RDC	Rural District Council [British]
RDC	Sisters of Divine Compassion [Roman Catholic religious order]
RDCA	Rural District Councils Association [British]
RDCAA	Registered Dairy Cattle Association of Australia
RDCC	Regional and Distribution Carriers Conference (NTPA)
RDCC	Regional Distributors and Carriers Conference (EA)
RD-CCSA	Reciprocal Derivative Constant-Current Stripping Analysis [Analytical electrochemistry]
RDCE	Radio Distribution and Control Equipment [Aviation] (DA)
RDCEHCY	Research and Demonstration Center for the Education of Handicapped Children and Youth [Defunct] (EA)
RDCEO	Rural District Council Executive Officer [British]
RDCF	Restricted Data Cover Folder (AAG)
RDCHE	Rene Dubos Center for Human Environments (EA)
RDCHK	Read Check [Computer science] (IAA)
RDCLP	Response Document Capability List Positive (IAA)
RDCM	Master Chief RADARman [Navy rating]
RDCM	Reduced Delta Code Modulation [Digital memory]
RDCN	Reduction (MSA)
RDCO	Reliability Data Control Office (AAG)
RDCP	Remote Display Control Panel (MCD)
RDCR	Reducer (MSA)
RDCRIT	Read Criteria (SAA)
RDCS	Reconfiguration Data Collection System [or Subsystem] (MCD)
RDCS	Senior Chief RADARman [Navy rating]
RDCTN	Reduction
RDCU	Receipt Delivery Control Unit [Social Security Administration]
RDD	Random Digit Dialing [Telecommunications]
RDD	Rapid Demolition Device
RDD	Rassemblement Democratique Dahomeen [Dahomean Democratic Rally]
RDD	Reactor Development Division [of AEC]
RDD	Read Disconnect Delay [Computer science] (IAA)
RDD	Redding [California] [Airport symbol] (OAG)
RDD	Reference Design Document (KSC)
RDD	Required Delivery Date (AABC)
rdd	Required Delivery Date (ODBW)
RDD	Requirements Definition Document [NASA] (NASA)
RDD	Requisition Due Date (TEL)
RDD	Research and Development Directorate [Army]
RDD	Return Due Date [IRS]
RDD	Routine Dynamic Display (MCD)
RDDA	Recommended Daily Dietary Allowance
RDD & E	Research, Development, Diffusion [or Dissemination], and Evaluation
RDDCS	Range Drone Data Control System [Military] (CAAL)
RDDM	Reactor Deck Development Mock-Up [Nuclear energy] (NRCH)
RDDMI	Radio Digital Distance Magnetic Indicator (MCD)
RDDP	Polymerase [Deoxyribonucleic Acid] [Formerly, RIDP] [An enzyme]
RDDP	Response Document Discard Positive [Computer science] (IAA)
RDDR	Rod Drive
RDDS	RADAR Data Distribution Switchboard [Military] (CAAL)
RDDS	Range Data Distributive System [Military]
RDDS	Research and Development Descriptive Summaries [DoD]
RDDS	Retail Dental Delivery System [Dentistry]
RDDSEM	Real Data System Element Model [Computer science] (MHDB)
RDDT&E	Research, Development, Demonstration, Testing, and Evaluation [Environmental science] (COE)
RDE	RADAR Display Equipment
RDE	Radial Defect Examination (IEEE)
RDE	Receive Data Enable [Computer science] (CIST)
RDE	Receptor-Destroying Enzyme [A neuraminidase] [Immunochemistry]
RDE	Recommended Distribution of Effort [Civil defense]
RDE	Relational Database Engine (PCM)
RDE	Reliability Data Extractor (MCD)
RDE	Remote Data Entry (NITA)
RDE	Research and Development Establishment [British]
RDE	Research, Development, and Engineering (RDA)
RDE	Research Development Exchange (OICC)
RDE	Roating Disk Electrode
RDE	Rotating Disc Electrode
RDE & A	Research, Development, Engineering, and Acquisition (RDA)
RDEB	Recessive Dystrophic Epidermolysis Bullosa [Also, EBDR] [Dermatology]

RDEC	Rabbit Diarrheal Escherichia Coli
RDEC	Research, Development, and Engineering Center (RDA)
R de D McGill	Revue de Droit de McGill [A publication] (DLA)
R de J	Revue de Jurisprudence [Quebec] [A publication] (DLA)
R de Jur	Revue de Jurisprudence [Quebec] [A publication] (DLA)
R de L	Revue de Legislation et de Jurisprudence [Canada] [A publication] (DLA)
R de L et de J	Revue de Legislation et de Jurisprudence [A publication] (DLA)
RDEP	Recruit Depot [Navy]
RDEP	Response Document End Positive [Computer science] (IAA)
RDES	Remote Data Entry System (DMAA)
RDES	Requirement and Determination Execution System
R de S	Ricardus Petronius de Senis [Deceased, 1314] [Authority cited in pre-1607 legal work] (DSA)
RDF	RADAR Direction Finder [or Finding] (CET)
RDF	Radial Distribution Function [X-ray diffraction]
RDF	Radio Direction Finder [or Finding] (AABC)
RDF	Rapid Deployment Force [Military]
RDF	Recirculating Document Feeder (NITA)
RDF	Record Definition Field [Computer science] (BUR)
RDF	Recursive Digital Filter [Computer science] (IAA)
RDF	Redford Resources, Inc. [Vancouver Stock Exchange symbol]
RDF	Reflection Direction Finding
RDF	Refuse-Derived Fuel (ERG)
RDF	Repeater Distribution Frame (NATG)
RDF	Research, Development, and Facilities (NOAA)
RDF	Reserve Defense Fleet [Navy]
RDF	Resource Data File (MCD)
RDF	Resource Description Framework [Computer science]
RDF	Robotech Defense Force [Defunct] (EA)
RDF	Roger Wyburn-Mason and Jack M. Blount Foundation for the Eradication of Rheumatoid Disease (EA)
RDF	Royal Dublin Fusiliers [British]
RDF-A	Rapid Deployment Force - Army
RDFC	Recurring Digital Fibroma of Childhood [Medicine] (DMAA)
RDFI	Receiving Depository Financial Institution
RDFL	Reflection Direction Finding, Low Angle (MCD)
RDF/LT	Rapid Deployment Force/Light Tank [Military] (MCD)
RDFQ	Recueil de Droit Fiscal Quebecois [A publication] (DLA)
RDFS	Ratio of Decayed and Filled Surfaces [Dentistry] (MEDA)
RDFSTA	Radio Direction Finder Station
RDFT	Ratio of Decayed and Filled Teeth [Dentistry] (MEDA)
RDFU	Research and Development Field Unit [Military]
RDFU-V	Research and Development Field Unit - Vietnam [Military] (MCD)
RDFWA	Regular Defence Force Welfare Association [Australia]
RDG	Radio Directors' Guild [Defunct] (IAA)
RDG	Reading [Pennsylvania] [Airport symbol] (OAG)
RDG	Reading [British depot code]
Rdg	Reducing (WGA)
RDG	Reference Drawing Group [NATO] (NATG)
RDG	Regional Development Grant [British] (DCTA)
RDG	Registrar Data Group [Information service or system] (IID)
RDG	Relative Disturbance Gain [Control engineering]
RDG	Research Discussion Group (EA)
RDG	Resolver Differential Generator
RDG	Resource Development Group Ltd. [British]
RDG	Ridge (MSA)
RDG	Right Digestive Gland
RDG	Rounding
RDG	Rover P4 Drivers Guild [An association] (EAIO)
RdgBate	Reading & Bates Corp. [Associated Press] (SAG)
RdgBt	Reading & Bates Corp. [Associated Press] (SAG)
RDGC	Reading Co. [NASDAQ symbol] (NQ)
RDGCA	Reading Co. Cl'A' [NASDAQ symbol] (TTSB)
RDGE	Reading Entertainment, Inc. [NASDAQ symbol] (SAG)
RDGE	Resorcinol Diglycidyl Ether [Organic chemistry]
RDGE	Ridge [Commonly used] (OPSA)
RDGF	Retina-Derived Growth Factor [Biochemistry]
RDGL	Radiological (IAA)
RDGR	Response Document General Reject (IAA)
RDGS	Ridges [Postal Service standard] (OPSA)
RDGT	Reliability Development Growth Testing (RDA)
RDGY	Radiology (IAA)
RDH	Radioactive Drain Header [Nuclear energy] (NRCH)
RDH	Rapid Displacement Heating [Pulp and paper technology]
RDH	Red Hill Marketing Group Ltd. [Vancouver Stock Exchange symbol]
RDH	Reference Datum Height [Aviation] (DA)
RDH	Registered Dental Hygienist
RDH	Remote Device Handler (IAA)
RDH	Resource Dispersion Hypothesis [Animal ecology]
RDH	Round Head
RDH	Royal Deccan Horse [British military] (DMA)
RDHBF	Regional Distribution of Hepatic Blood Flow [Medicine] (DB)
RDHD	Round Head (IAA)
RDHER	Revolutionary Development Hamlet Evaluation Report [South Vietnam]
RDHM	Royal Dental Hospital, Melbourne [Australia]
RDHS	Logan's Roadhouse [NASDAQ symbol] (TTSB)
RdhseGr	Roadhouse Grill, Inc. [Associated Press] (SAG)
RDI	Radio Doppler Inertial
RDI	Rassemblement Democratique pour l'Independance [Quebec]
RDI	Rassemblement des Democrates Liberaux pour la Reconstruction Nationale [Benin] [Political party] (EY)
RDI	Readicare, Inc. [AMEX symbol] (SAG)
RDI	Recommended Daily Intake [Dietary]

RDI .... Reference Daily Intake [FDA]
RDI .... Reference Designation Index (MCD)
RDI .... Regulated Deficit Irrigation
RDI .... Rejection and Disposition Item
RDI .... Relative Drought Index (EES)
RDI .... Released Data Index
RDI .... Reliability Design Index (DNAB)
RDI .... Relief and Development Institute [Formerly, International Disaster Institute] [Defunct] (EA)
RDI .... Remote Data Input
RDI .... Research and Development Institute, Inc. [Montana State University] [Research center] (RCD)
RDI .... Research and Development of Instrumentation [Program] [Army]
RDI .... Riley's Datashare International Ltd. [Toronto Stock Exchange symbol]
RDI .... Route Digit Indicator [Telecommunications] (TEL)
RDI .... Routing Domain Identifier (TNIG)
RDI .... Royal Designer for Industry [British]
RDI .... Rupture Delivery Interval [Obstetrics]
RDIA .... Regional Development Incentives Act
RDIC .... ReadiCare, Inc. [NASDAQ symbol] (TTSB)
RDIF .... Rural Development Insurance Fund [Farmers Home Administration] [Department of Agriculture] (GFGA) *
RDIM .... Revolving Door Identification Model (EDAC)
RDIO .... Multi-Market Radio, Inc. [NASDAQ symbol] (SAG)
RDIOA .... Multi-Mkt Radio 'A' [NASDAQ symbol] (TTSB)
RDIOW .... Multi-Mkt Radio Wrrt 'A' [NASDAQ symbol] (TTSB)
RDIOZ .... Multi-Mkt Radio Wrrt 'B' [NASDAQ symbol] (TTSB)
RDIPP .... Rivista di Diritto Internazionale Privato e Processuale [A publication] (DLA)
RDIS .... Replenishment Demand Inventory System
RDIS .... Research and Development Information System [Later, EPD/RDIS] [Electric Power Research Institute] [Information service or system] (IID)
RDISSS .... Royal Dockyard Iron and Steel Shipbuilders' Society [A union] [British]
RDIT .... Rapid Deployment Imagery Terminal (DOMA)
RDIT .... Replication, Distribution, Installation, and Training [Army] (RDA)
RDIU .... Remote Device Interface Unit
RDIXS .... Research and Development Information Exchange System [Navy] (DOMA)
RDJ .... Readjustment
Rdj .... Readjustment (EBF)
RDJ .... Rio De Janeiro [Brazil] [Later, VSS] [Seismograph station code, US Geological Survey] (SEIS)
RDJCT .... Register, Department of Justice and the Courts of the United States [A publication]
RDJTF .... Rapid Deployment Joint Task Force [Military] (RDA)
RDK .... Irish Air Tours [ICAO designator] (FAAC)
R dk .... Raised Deck [of a ship] (DS)
RDK .... Random-Dot Kinematogram [For motion detection]
RDK .... Red Oak, IA [Location identifier FAA] (FAAL)
RDK .... Research and Development Kit
RDK .... Ruddick Corp. [NYSE symbol] (SPSG)
RDL .... Radial (MSA)
RDL .... Radioactive Decay Law
RDL .... Radiological Defense Laboratory [NASA] (KSC)
RDL .... Rail Dynamics Laboratory
RDL .... Random Dynamic Load
RDL .... Rapid Draft Letter (DNAB)
RDL .... [The] Reactor Development Laboratory [UKAEA] [British]
RDL .... Rear Defence Locality [British military] (DMA)
RDL .... Reciprocal Detection Latency
RDL .... Recurring Document Listing (MCD)
RDL .... Redlaw Industries [AMEX symbol] (TTSB)
RDL .... Redlaw Industries, Inc. [AMEX symbol Toronto Stock Exchange symbol] (SPSG)
RDL .... Regional Development Laboratory [Philadelphia, PA]
RDL .... Reliable Detection Limit [Analytical chemistry]
RDL .... Remote Display Link
RDL .... Replaceable Display Light
RDL .... Report Definition Language [Computer science] (MHDB)
RDL .... Resistance Diode Logic (IAA)
RDL .... Resistor Diode Logic
RDL .... Rim of Dorsal Lip
RDL .... Roadair Lines IC [Canada ICAO designator] (FAAC)
RDL .... Rocket Development Laboratory [Air Force]
RDLBBB .... Rate-Dependent Left Bundle Branch Block [Medicine] (DMAA)
RDLGE .... Reunion Democratica para la Liberacion de Guinea Ecuatorial [Democratic Movement for the Liberation of Equatorial Guinea] [Political party] (PD)
RDLI .... Royal Durban Light Infantry [British military] (DMA)
RD-LMXB ..... Radiation-Driven Low-Mass X-Ray Binary [Cosmology]
RDLN .... Retrodorsolateral Nucleus [Neuroanatomy]
RDLP .... Research and Development Limited Partnership [Tax-shelter investment]
Rdlw .... Redlaw Industries [Associated Press] (SAG)
RDLWS .... Redlaw Ind 2001 Wrrts [AMEX symbol] (TTSB)
RDLX .... Airlift International, Inc. [Air carrier designation symbol]
RdM .... Die Religionen der Menschheit [A publication] (BJA)
RDM .... RADARman [Also, RD]
RDM .... Radial Distribution Method
RDM .... Random (WGA)
RDM .... Random Dimer Model [Physics]
RDM .... Real-Time Data Manager (MCD)
RDM .... Recording Demand Meter

RDM .... Redmond [Oregon] [Airport symbol] (OAG)
RDM .... Relay Driver Module
RDM .... Remote Data Management
RDM .... Remote Digital Multiplexer (MCD)
RDM .... Respirable Dust Monitor (PDAA)
RDM .... Roadmaster Industries [NYSE symbol] (SAG)
RDM .... Rod Disk Membrane (DB)
RDMC .... Regional Director of Motor Carriers [FHWA] (TAG)
RDMC .... Research and Development Management Course [Army]
RDME .... Range and Distance Measuring Equipment
RDMF .... Rapidly Deployable Medical Facilities
RDMGA ...... Railway Dock and Marine Grades Association [A union] [British]
RDMI .... Roof Drainage Manufacturers Institute [Defunct] (EA)
RDMN .... Redman Industries [NASDAQ symbol] (SAG)
RDMS .... Range Data Measurement Subsystem (MCD)
RDMS .... Registered Diagnostic Medical Sonologist
RDMS .... Relational Data Management System (MHDI)
RDMS .... Retail Development Management Services [British]
RDMS .... Retrospective Data Management System
RDMSR ...... Read Machine-Specific Register [Computer science]
RDMSS ...... Rapidly Deployable Mobile SIGINT [Signal Intelligence] System (MCD)
RDMTR ...... Radiometer (NASA)
RDMU .... Range-Drift Measuring Unit
RDN .... Dinar SA [Argentina ICAO designator] (FAAC)
RDN .... Real de Minas Mine [Vancouver Stock Exchange symbol]
RDN .... Redundancy (IAA)
RDN .... Rejection Disposition Notice
RDN .... Relative Distinguished Name [Telecommunications] (OSI)
RDN .... Resource Decision Network (PDAA)
RDN .... Royal Danish Navy (NATG)
RDN .... Rural Deanery [Church of England]
rDNA .... Deoxyribonucleic Acid, Recombinant [Biochemistry, genetics]
rDNA .... Deoxyribonucleic Acid, Ribosomal [Biochemistry, genetics]
RDNA .... Recombinant DNA [Deoxyribonucleic Acid]
rDNA .... Ribosomal DNA [Deoxyribonucleic Acid] [Marine science] (OSRA)
Rdng .... Reading (AL)
RDNG .... Reading (MSA)
RDNP .... Rassemblement Democratique Nationaliste et Progressiste [Progressive Nationalist and Democratic Assembly] [Haiti] (PD)
RDNS .... Readiness (MSA)
RDNSSA ..... Royal District Nursing Society of South Australia
RDNU .... Rally for Democracy and National Unity [Mauritania] [Political party] (EY)
RDO .... Radio (AABC)
RDO .... Radiological Defense Officer [Civil defense]
RDO .... Radio Readout
RDO .... Range Development Officer (MUGU)
RDO .... Readout [Computer science] (IAA)
RDO .... Recoonnaiooanoo Duty Officer
RDO .... Redistribution Order [Military] (AFM)
RDO .... Regional Defense Organization (DNAB)
RDO .... Regional Disbursing Office
RDO .... Remote Data Objects [Computer science]
RDO .... Research and Development Objectives [Military] (AFM)
RDO .... Research, Development, and Operation [Military appropriation]
RDO .... River District Office [National Weather Service]
RDO .... Rodeo Resources Ltd. [Vancouver Stock Exchange symbol]
RDO .... Runway Duty Officer [Aviation] (MCD)
RDOC .... Integrated Surgical Systems, Inc. [NASDAQ symbol] (SAG)
RDOC .... Reference Designation Overflow Code (NASA)
RDOC .... Residential Distillate Oil Combustion [Industrial medicine]
RDOD .... Retinal Detachment, Oculus Dexter [Right Eye] [Ophthalmology] (DAVI)
RDOINT ...... Radio Intelligence [Military] (IAA)
RDOM .... Restructured Division Operations Manual (MCD)
RDON .... Road Octane Number [Fuel technology]
RDOS .... R Disc Operating System (NITA)
RDOS .... Real-Time Disk-Operating System [Computer science]
RDOS .... Residual Density of States [Solid state physics]
RDOS .... Retinal Detachment, Oculus Sinister [Left Eye] [Ophthalmology] (DAVI)
RDOSEC ..... Radio Section (IAA)
RDOSTN ..... Radio Service (IAA)
RDOTRANS... Radio Transmitter (IAA)
RDOUT .... Readout
RDP .... RADAR Data Processing
RDP .... RADAR Digital Probe
RDP .... Radiation Degradation Product
RDP .... Radiodifusao Portuguesa [State Broadcasting Service]
RDP .... Radio Distribution Point (IAA)
RDP .... Radiosonde Data Processor (IAA)
RDP .... Range Data Processor (MCD)
RDP .... Range Deflection Protractor [Weaponry] (INF)
RDP .... Rassemblement pour la Democratie et le Progres [Mali] [Political party] (EY)
RDP .... Ration Distributing Point [Military]
RDP .... Reactor Development Program [Nuclear Regulatory Commission] (NRCH)
RDP .... Receiver and Data Processor (MCD)
RDP .... Reconstruction and Development Program [South Africa]
RDP .... Recreational Dive Planner
RDP .... Rectifying-Demodulating Phonopneumograph [Medicine]
RDP .... Redeployment Point [Military] (INF)
RDP .... Regional Development Program [Australia]

RDP .... Remote Data Processor
RDP .... Renal Dipeptidase [*An enzyme*]
RDP .... Requirements Data Plan (NASA)
RDP .... Requirements Development Plan [*NASA*] (NASA)
RDP .... Research and Development Plan
RDP .... Research Data Publication [*Center*]
RDP .... Reunification Democracy Party [*Political party South Korea*]
RDP .... Revolutionary Development Program [*South Vietnam*]
RDP .... Ribulosediphosphate [*Also, RuBP*] [*Biochemistry*]
RDP .... Right Dorso Posterior [*Medicine*] (ROG)
RDP .... Rocca Di Papa [*Italy*] [*Seismograph station code, US Geological Survey*] (SEIS)
RDPB .... RADAR Data Plotting Board
RDPB .... Research and Development Planning and Budgeting (AFIT)
RD/PBM .... Research and Development/Programming Budget Memorandum (MCD)
RDPBN .... Response Document Page Boundary Negative [*Computer science*] (IAA)
RDPBP .... Response Document Page Boundary Positive [*Computer science*] (IAA)
RDPC .... RADAR Data Processing Center [*Military*]
RDPE .... RADAR Data Processing Equipment (AABC)
RDPE .... Reticular Degeneration of the Pigment Epithelium [*Biochemistry*] (DAVI)
RDPG .... Revolutionary Development Peoples Group [*South Vietnam*] [*Military*] (VNW)
RDPJ .... Rail Discharge Point Jet (NATG)
RDPL .... Laos [*International civil aircraft marking*] (ODBW)
RDPM .... Rail Discharge Point Mogas (NATG)
RDPM .... Revised Draft Presidential Memorandum
RDPM .... Rotary Drive Piston Motor
RDPR .... Refer to Drawer Please Represent [*Business term*] (DCTA)
RDPS .... RADAR Data Processing System
RDPS .... Remote Docking Procedures Simulator (MCD)
RDPS .... Research and Development Planning Summary
RdQ .... Reading Quotient
RDR .... Grand Forks, ND [*Location identifier FAA*] (FAAL)
RDR .... RADAR (AAG)
RDR .... RADAR Departure Route [*Aviation*] (DA)
RDR .... RADAR Diagnostic Report (IAA)
RDR .... RADAR Display Room (IAA)
RDR .... Raider
RDR .... Rapid Canadian Resource Corp. [*Vancouver Stock Exchange symbol*]
RDR .... Raw Data Recorder (NASA)
RDR .... Read Drum (IAA)
RDR .... Reader (MSA)
Rdr .... Reader (AL)
R/DR .... Rear Door [*Automotive engineering*]
RDR .... Receive Data Register [*Computer science*] (MDG)
RDR .... Registered Diplomate Reporter
RDR .... Rejection Disposition Report [*NASA*] (KSC)
RDR .... Relative Digestion Rate [*Nutrition*]
RDR .... Reliability Design Review
RDR .... Reliability Diagnostic Report (AAG)
RDR .... Remote Digital Readout
RDR .... Repeat Discrepancy Report (MCD)
RDR .... Request Data and Respond [*Telecommunications*] (OSI)
RDR .... Research and Development Report
RDR .... Research Division Report
RDR .... Restart Delay Relay (IAA)
RDR .... Ribonucleoside Diphosphate Reductase [*An enzyme*]
RDR .... Risk Data Report [*Insurance*]
RDR .... Risk-Driven Remediation
RDR .... Rotating Disk Reactor (AAEL)
RDR .... Rudder (NASA)
RD/RA .... Remedial Design/Remedial Action [*Environmental Protection Agency*] (ERG)
RDRAM .... Rambus Dynamic Random Access Memory (AAEL)
RDRBCN ...... RADAR Beacon (KSC)
RDRC .... Road Design and Road Costs [*British*]
RDRD .... Remote Digital Readout
RdrDB .... Readers Digest Association [*Associated Press*] (SAG)
RdrDg .... Reader's Digest Association [*Associated Press*] (SAG)
RDR/EO .... RADAR/Electro-Optical (MCD)
RDRINT .... RADAR Intermittent (IEEE)
RDRM .... Return Data Relay Measurement (SSD)
RDRP .... Response Document Resynchronization Positive [*Computer science*] (IAA)
RDRSMTR ... RADAR Transmitter (AAG)
RDRT .... Read-Rite Corp. [*NASDAQ symbol*] (SPSG)
RDRV .... Rhesus Diploid-Cell-Strain Rabies Vaccine
RDR XMTR... RADAR Transmitter
RDS .... RADAR Distribution Switchboard
RDS .... RADAUS [*Radio-Austria AG*] Data-Service [*Telecommunications*]
RDS .... Radio Data System [*Telecommunications*]
RDS .... Radio Digital System [*Telecommunications*] (TEL)
RDS .... Radio Display Service
RDS .... Railway Development Society [*British*] (DBA)
RDS .... Random Digit Sample (NTCM)
RDS .... Random Dot Stereogram
RDS .... Range Destruct System
RDS .... Rate-Determining Step [*Chemical kinetics*]
rds .... Rate-Determining Step [*Chemistry*] (MEC)
RDS .... Rate of Dispersal Success [*Ecology*]

RDS .... Raytheon Data Systems Co.
RDS .... Read Select (SAA)
RDS .... Read Strobe
RDS .... Reeds [*Music*]
RDS .... Relational Database Systems Inc. (NITA)
RDS .... Relative Detector Sensitivity [*Robotics technology*]
RDS .... Religious Drama Society of Great Britain (BI)
RDS .... Remote Data Service [*Computer science*]
RDS .... Rendezvous Docking Simulator [*Aerospace*]
RDS .... Reperimento Documentazione Siderurgica [*Iron and Steel Documentation Service*] [*Information service or system*] (IID)
RDS .... Request for Data Services
RDS .... Required Number of Days of Stock
RDS .... Requisition Distribution System
RDS .... Research and Development Service [*Army-Ordnance*]
RDS .... Research and Development Survey
RDS .... Research Defence Society [*British*]
RDS .... Research, Development, and Standardization [*Groups*] [*Army*] (RDA)
RDS .... Research Documentation Section [*Public Health Service*] [*Information service or system*] (IID)
RDS .... Research Documents Search [*Information service or system*] (IID)
RDS .... Residuum Desulfurization [*Petroleum technology*]
Rds .... Resistance of the Airways on the Oral Side of the Point in the Airways Where Intraluminal Pressure Equals Intrapleural Pressure [*Medicine*] (DAVI)
RDS .... Resistive Divider Standard
RDS .... Resolver Differential Transmitter (IAA)
RDS .... Resource Development Services (EA)
RDS .... Respiratory Distress Syndrome [*Formerly, HMD*] [*Medicine*]
RDS .... Responsive Database Services, Inc
RDS .... Retail Distribution Station [*Military*] (AFM)
RDS .... Reticuloendothelial Depressing Substance [*Medicine*] (AAMN)
RDS .... Retinal Degeneration Slow [*Genetics*]
RDS .... Revolutionary Development Support [*South Vietnam*]
RDS .... Revolving Discussion Sequence
RDS .... Rhoades Aviation, Inc. [*ICAO designator*] (FAAC)
RDS .... Rhode Island Department of State Library Services, Providence, RI [*OCLC symbol*] (OCLC)
RDS .... Richard D. Siegrest [*Alaska*] [*Seismograph station code, US Geological Survey*] (SEIS)
RDS .... Rio Grande do Sul [*Brazil*] [*Airport symbol*] (AD)
RDS .... Roads [*Postal Service standard*] (OPSA)
RDS .... Robotic Deriveter System
RDS .... Robust Detection Scheme [*Navigation*] (OA)
RDS .... Rocket Development Section [*Picatinny Arsenal*] [*Dover, NJ*]
RDS .... Rocketdyne Digital Simulator [*NASA*] (NASA)
RDS .... Rokeach Dogmatism Scale
RDS .... Rounds [*of ammunition*] [*Military*]
RDS .... Royal Drawing Society [*British*]
RDS .... Royal Dublin Society
RDS .... Rural Development Service [*Department of Agriculture*]
RDS .... Rural Development Society (NADA)
RDSA .... Seaman Apprentice, RADARman Striker [*Navy rating*]
RD/SB .... Rudder Speed Brake [*Aviation*] (MCD)
RDSD .... Reliability Design Support Document [*Nuclear energy*] (NRCH)
RDSD .... Revolutionary Development Support Division [*South Vietnam*]
RDSIM .... Runway Delay Simulation Model [*FAA*] (TAG)
RDSM .... Remote Digital Submultiplexer (KSC)
RDSM .... Research Development Safety Management [*Air Force*]
RDS/M .... Rounds per Minute [*Military*]
RDSN .... RADARman, Seaman [*Navy rating*]
RDSN .... Seaman, RADARman, Striker [*Navy rating*]
RDSO .... Research, Design, and Standardization Organization [*Indian Railways*] [*India*] (PDAA)
RDSP .... Revolutionary Development Support Plan [*or Program*] [*South Vietnam*]
RDSPA .... Redispatch Accepted (FAAC)
RDSS .... RADAR Determination Satellite System [*Aviation*] (DA)
RDSS .... Radio Determination Satellite Service [*Geostar Corp.*]
RDSS .... Rapid Deployable Surveillance Systems [*Military*] (NVT)
RDSS .... Remote Determination Satellite Service
RDS-TMC ..... Radio Data System - Traffic Management Channel
RDS-TMS ..... Radio Data System - Traffic Message Channel [*Traffic and highway management*] (ECON)
RD Sup .... Revenue Decisions, Supplement [*India*] [*A publication*] (DLA)
RDT .... Radio Digital Terminal [*Bell System*]
RDT .... Rapid Decompression Test
RDT .... Reactor Development and Technology [*Nuclear energy*] (MCD)
RDT .... Reactor Drain Tank [*Nuclear energy*] (NRCH)
RDT .... Redoubt [*Alaska*] [*Seismograph station code, US Geological Survey*] (SEIS)
RDT .... Regular Dialysis Treatment [*Medicine*]
RDT .... Reliability Demonstration Test
RDT .... Reliability Design Test
RDT .... Reliability Development Testing (CAAL)
RDT .... Remote Data Transmitter
RDT .... Renal Dialysis Treatment [*Nephrology*]
RDT .... Repertory Dance Theatre [*Salt Lake City, UT*]
RDT .... Reserve Duty Training [*Military*]
RDT .... Resistor Diode Transistor Technique (IAA)
RDT .... Resource Definition Table [*Computer science*] (IBMDP)
RDT .... Retinal Damage Threshold [*Ophthalmology*]
RDT .... Revue de Droit du Travail [*A publication*] (DLA)
RDT .... Richard-Toll [*Senegal*] [*Airport symbol*] (OAG)
RDT .... Rotational Direction Transmission

RDT	Routine Dialysis Therapy [*Medicine*] (DMAA)
RDT & E	Research, Development, Test, and Engineering (SSD)
RDT&E	Research, Development, Test, and Evaluation (AAGC)
RDT&E	Research, Development, Testing, and Evaluation (BCP)
RDT & EN	Research, Development, Test, and Evaluation, Navy
RDTC	Remote Distributed Terminal Controller (NITA)
RDTE	Research, Development, Test, and Evaluation [*DoD*]
RDTEA	Research, Development, Test, and Evaluation, Army
RDTE & E	Research, Development, Test, Evaluation, and Engineering Program [*DoD*] (RDA)
RDTF	Revolutionary Development Task Force [*South Vietnam*]
RdTh	Radiothorium [*Nuclear physics*] (WGA)
RDTI	Research, Development and Technology Investigation
RDTL	Resistor Diode Transistor Logic (IEEE)
RDTLC	Rotating Disc Thin-Layer Chromatography
RDTM	Rated Distribution and Training Management
RDTR	Radiator (MSA)
RDTR	Research Division Technical Report
RDTSC	Read Time Stamp Counter [*Computer science*]
RDTSR	Rapid Data Transmission System for Requisitioning [*Navy*]
RDU	RADAR Display Unit
RDU	Raleigh/Durham [*North Carolina*] [*Airport symbol*]
RDU	Receipt and Despatch Unit [*Aircraft*]
RDU	Recreational Drug User
RDU	Refrigerated Detector Unit (SAA)
RDU	Regional Decision Unit (COE)
RDU	Regional Development Unit [*Manpower Services Commission*] (AIE)
RDU	Remote Data Uplink [*SmartOffice*] [*Computer science*]
RDU	Remote Display Unit [*American Solenoid Co.*] [*Somerset, NJ*]
RDU	Rideau Resources Corp. [*Vancouver Stock Exchange symbol*]
R du B Can	Revue. Barreau Canadien [*A publication*] (DLA)
RDUC	Receiver Data from Unit Control (MCD)
R du D	Revue du Droit [*A publication*] (DLA)
RDUS	Radius, Inc. [*NASDAQ symbol*] (SAG)
RDV	Recoverable Drop Vehicle (MCD)
RDV	Red Devil [*Alaska*] [*Airport symbol*] (OAG)
RDV	Rice Dwarf Virus [*Plant pathology*]
RDV	Rotary Disk Valve [*Automotive engineering*]
RDV	Rotating Dome Valve [*Military*] (RDA)
RDVM	Remote Digital Voice Multiplexer [*AT&T*] (CIST)
RDVT	Recurrent Deep Vein Thrombosis [*Medicine*] (DAVI)
RDVT	Reliability Design Verification Test
RDVU	Rendezvous (AABC)
RDW	Red Blood Cell Distribution Width Index [*Medicine*] (DMAA)
RDW	Red Cell Size Distribution Width [*Hematology*]
RDW	Redwood Resources, Inc. [*Vancouver Stock Exchange symbol*]
RDW	Response Data Word (MCD)
RDW	Return Data Word (MCD)
RDW	Right Defense Wing [*Women's lacrosse position*]
RDWA	Returned Development Workers Association (EAIO)
RDWCA	Royal Dockyard Wood Caulkers' Association [*A union*] [*British*]
rdwd	Redwood (VRA)
RDWND	RADAR Dome Wind [*NWS*] (FAAC)
RDWS	Radiological Defense Warning System
RDWW	United Slate Tile and Composition Roofers, Damp and Waterproof Workers Association [*Later, UURWAW*]
RDWY	Roadway
RDX	Cocoa, FL [*Location identifier FAA*] (FAAL)
RDX	Radixin (DMAA)
RDX	Ready [*Broadcasting*] (WDMC)
RDX	Research Department Explosive [*Cyclonite*]
RDY	Aspen, CO [*Location identifier FAA*] (FAAL)
RDY	Ready (AAG)
RDY	Roadway
RDY	Royal Devon Yeomanry [*British military*] (DMA)
RDY	Royal Dockyard [*British*]
RDYA	Royal Devon Yeomanry Artillery [*British military*] (DMA)
rdymd	Readymade (VRA)
RdysRst	Rudys Restaurant Group [*Associated Press*] (SAG)
RDZ	Radiation Danger Zone (IAA)
RDZ	Ringier Dokumentationszentrum [*Ringier Documentation Center*] [*Switzerland Information service or system*] (IID)
RDZ	Rodez [*France*] [*Airport symbol*] (OAG)
RE	Aer Arann Teo [*ICAO designator*] (AD)
Re	Earth or Geocentric Radius (AAG)
R$_E$	Emitter Resistance (IDOE)
RE	Everest Reinsurance Hldgs [*NYSE symbol*] (TTSB)
RE	Everest Reinsurance Holdings [*NYSE symbol*] [*Formerly, Prudential Reinsurance Holdings*] (SG)
RE	Everest Reinsurance Holdings, Inc. [*NYSE symbol*] (SAG)
RE	Fellow of the Royal Society of Painter-Etchers and Engravers [*British*]
Re	Ohio Decisions Reprint [*A publication*] (DLA)
Re	Prudential Reinsurance Holdings, Inc. [*NYSE symbol*] (SAG)
RE	Radiated Emission (IEEE)
RE	Radiation Effects (AAG)
RE	Radiation Equipment (NRCH)
RE	Radio-Eireann [*Eire*] [*Record label*]
RE	Radio Electrician
RE	Radio Equipment (IAA)
RE	Radio Exposure (AAG)
RE	Radium Emanation
RE	Railway Executive [*British*]
Re	Rainerius [*Authority cited in pre-1607 legal work*] (DSA)
RE	Rainform Expanded (MCD)
RE	Ram Effect [*Mechanical engineering*] (OA)
RE	Rare Earth
RE	Rate Effect (IEEE)
RE	Rate of Exchange
RE	Rational Expectations [*Economics*] (ECON)
RE	Rattus Exulans [*The Polynesian rat*]
RE	Raw End (OA)
RE	Reactive Evaporation [*Coating technology*]
RE	Read Emitter [*Computer science*] (IAA)
RE	Read Error [*Computer science*] (IAA)
RE	Reading-Ease [*Score*] [*Advertising*]
Re	Real [*Mathematics*]
RE	Real Estate
RE	Real Estate Program [*Association of Independent Colleges and Schools specialization code*]
RE	Real Number (DEN)
RE	Reasonable Effort (GNE)
RE	Receiver/Exciter
RE	Recent [*Used to qualify weather phenomena*]
RE	Reconnaissance Experimental [*British military*] (DMA)
RE	Recording Electrode (DB)
RE	Recovery Equipment (IAA)
RE	Rectal Examination [*Medicine*]
RE	Recursively Enumerable (IAA)
RE	Red Edges
RE	Reel (MSA)
R/E	Reentry [*Aerospace*] (KSC)
RE	Reference [*Online database field identifier*]
RE	Reference Equivalent [*Telecommunications*] (TEL)
RE	Reflux
RE	Reformed Episcopal [*Church*]
RE	Refrigeration Effect
RE	Regarding
re	Regarding (STED)
RE	Regional Enteritis [*Medicine*]
RE	Regular Expression (IAA)
RE	Rehearsal Engineer (MCD)
RE	Reinforced [*Technical drawings*]
RE	Relative Effectiveness [*or Efficiency*] (MCD)
RE	Relay Assemblies [*JETDS nomenclature*] [*Military*] (CET)
RE	Relay Engineer (IAA)
RE	Release
RE	Religious Education [*Secondary school course*] [*British*]
RE	Religious of the Eucharist [*Roman Catholic women's religious order*]
RE	Remote Pickup [*FCC*] (NTCM)
RE	Renewal Registration [*US Copyright Office class*]
RE	Renovacion Espanola [*Spanish Renovation*] (PPE)
RE	Repair Equipment [*Navy*]
RE	Repair Equipment for F-15 and Subsequent Programs [*Military*] (MCD)
RE	Repayable to Either
RE	Repetitive Extrasystole [*Cardiology*]
RE	Reportable Event (EPA)
RE	Republication [*NASA*]
RE	Request for Estimate
RE	Research and Engineering
RE	Research and Experiments Department [*Ministry of Home Security*] [*British World War II*]
RE	Reset (MDG)
RE	Resolution Enhancement [*Computer graphics*]
Re	Respiratory Exchange Ratio [*Medicine*] (MAE)
RE	Responsible Engineer (NASA)
RE	Rest [*or Resting*] Energy [*Medicine*]
RE	Restriction Endonuclease [*An enzyme*]
RE	Restriction of Extension (IAA)
RE	Retained Earnings (EBF)
RE	Reticuloendothelial [*or Reticuloendothelium*] [*Medicine*]
RE	Retinal Equivalent [*For Vitamin A*]
RE	Retinyl Ester [*Organic chemistry*]
re	Reunion [*MARC country of publication code Library of Congress*] (LCCP)
RE	Reunion [*ANSI two-letter standard code*] (CNC)
RE	Reversal of Prior Entry [*Banking*]
RE	Revised Edition [*Publishing*]
Re	Reynolds Number [*Viscosity*] [*IUPAC*]
Re	Rhenium [*Chemical element*]
RE	Rifle Expert
RE	Right Ear (DB)
RE	Right Eminent [*Freemasonry*]
RE	Right End
RE	Right Excellent
RE	Right Eye
RE	Risk Evaluation [*Insurance*]
RE	Risk Exercise
RE	Riviera Explorations Ltd. [*Vancouver Stock Exchange symbol*]
RE	Rotary Engine [*Automotive engineering*]
RE	Royal Engineers [*Military British*]
RE	Royal Exchange [*British*]
RE	Royal Society of Painter-Etchers and Engravers [*British*]
RE	Royal Society of Painter-Etchers and Engravers, London [*1880*] (NGC)
RE	Rupee [*Monetary unit*] [*Ceylon, India, and Pakistan*]
RE	Rural Electrification
REA	Aer Arann Teoranta [*Ireland*] [*ICAO designator*] (FAAC)
REA	American Real Estate Investment Corp. [*AMEX symbol*] (SAG)

REA.............. Amer Real Estate Investment [*AMEX symbol*] (TTSB)
REA.............. RADAR Echoing Area
REA.............. Radiation Emergency Area
REA.............. Radiative Energy Attenuation [*Analytical chemistry*]
REA.............. Radio Electrical Artificer [*British military*] (DMA)
REA.............. Radioenzymatic Assay [*Analytical biochemistry*]
REA.............. Railroad Evangelistic Association (EA)
REA.............. Railway Express Agency [*Later, REA Express*] [*Defunct*]
REA.............. Range Error Average (MUGU)
REA.............. Rare-Earth Alloy
REA.............. Realcap Holdings Ltd. [*Toronto Stock Exchange symbol*]
REA.............. Reao [*French Polynesia*] [*Airport symbol*] (OAG)
REA.............. Recycle Acid [*Nuclear energy*] (NRCH)
REA.............. Reentry Angle
REA.............. Regional Economic Area
REA.............. Regional Executive Agent (BCP)
REA.............. Registered Environmental Assessor
REA.............. Religious Education Association (EA)
REA.............. Renaissance Educational Associates [*Defunct*] (EA)
REA.............. Renaissance Education Association (EA)
REA.............. Renal Anastomosis [*Medicine*]
REA.............. Request for Engineering Action (IAA)
REA.............. Request for Engineering Authorization
REA.............. Request for Equitable Adjustment [*Navy*]
REA.............. Research and Education Association
REA.............. Research Engineering Authorization (AAG)
REA.............. Research in Accrediting Efforts Project [*Illinois*] (EDAC)
REA.............. Reserve Enlisted Association [*Defunct*] (EA)
REA.............. Responsible Engineering Activity
REA.............. Retirement Equity Act of 1984 (WYGK)
REA.............. Rice Export Association
REA.............. Ridihalgh, Eggers & Associates, Columbus, OH [*OCLC symbol*] (OCLC)
REA.............. Right Ear Advantage [*Medicine*] (DMAA)
REA.............. Rocket Engine Assembly
REA.............. Rubber Export Association [*Defunct*] (EA)
REA.............. Rural Education Association [*Later, NREA*] (EA)
REA.............. Rural Electric Association (IAA)
REA.............. Rural Electrification Administration [*Department of Agriculture*]
REA Bull...... Rural Electrification Administration. Bulletin [*A publication*] (DLA)
REAC.......... Radiation Equipment and Accessories Corporation (SAA)
REAC.......... Radiological Emergency Assessment Center [*National Science Foundation*] (NUCP)
REAC.......... Reactant (NAKS)
REAC.......... Reaction (AAG)
REAC.......... Reactive
REAC.......... Reactor (AAG)
REAC.......... Real Estate Aviation Chapter (EA)
REAC.......... Reeves Electronic Analog Computer
REAC.......... Regional Educational Advisory Council [*British*]
ReAC.......... Reinsurance Australia Corp. [*Commercial firm*]
REACCS...... Reaction Access System [*Computer program*]
REACDU...... Recalled to Active Duty
REACH........ Rape Emergency Aid and Counseling for Her [*An association*] (NADA)
REACH........ Reassurance to Each [*To help families of the mentally ill*]
REACH........ Recognizing Exceptional Achievement in Community Help Award [*Association of Personal Computer User Groups*] (PCM)
REACH........ Research, Education, and Assistance for Canadians with Herpes
REACH........ Research on the Early Abilities of Children with Handicaps Project (EDAC)
REACH........ Responsible Educated Adolescents Can Help (EA)
REACH........ Retired Executives Action Clearing House [*British*] (DI)
REACH........ Review and Analysis of Companies in Holland [*Database*] (IID)
REACH........ Rural Employment Action and Counseling Help [*Project*]
REACK........ Receipt Acknowledged
REACOT...... Remove Errors and Complete on Time (DNAB)
REACQ........ Reacquire
REACT........ RADAR Electrooptical Area Correlation Tracker [*Military*] (CAAL)
REACT........ Radio Emergency Associated Citizens Teams [*Acronym alone is now used as official association name*] (EA)
RE ACT........ Rapid Execution and Combat Targeting [*Air Force*]
REACT........ Reaction Time Measure of Visual Field (TES)
RE ACT........ Reconnaissance/Reaction (MCD)
REACT........ Record Evaluate and Control Time System (IAA)
REACT........ Register Enforced Automated Control Technique [*Cash register-computing system*]
REACT........ Reliability Evaluation and Control Technique
REACT........ Requirements Evaluated against Cargo Transportation (PDAA)
REACT........ Rese Engineering Automatic Core Tester
REACT........ Resource Allocation and Control Technique [*Management*]
REAC/TS...... Radiation Emergency Assistance Center/Training Site [*Department of Energy*]
REAC/TS...... Radiological Emergency Assistance Center/Training Site [*Environmental science*] (COE)
REACTS...... Reader Action Service [*ZIP code computer*]
REACTS...... Regional Educators Annual Chemistry Teaching Symposium
REACTVT...... Reactivate
READ.......... RADAR Echo Augmentation Device
READ.......... Readability Ease Assessment Device (MCD)
READ.......... Reading [*County borough in England*]
READ.......... Reading Efficiency and Delinquency [*Program*]
READ.......... Real-Time Electronic Access and Display [*System*] [*Computer science*]
READ.......... Regulatory and Economics Analysis Division (COE)

READ .... Relative Element Address Designate (NITA)
READ.......... Remedial Education for Adults
READ.......... Remote Electronic Alphanumeric Display [*Computer science*] (IEEE)
READ.......... Research and Economic Analysis Division [*Office of Transportation*] (GRD)
READ.......... Reserve on Extended Active Duty [*Military*]
Read Dec.... Read's Declarations and Pleadings [*A publication*] (DLA)
READE........ Reduce Errors and Decrease Expense (DNAB)
READEF...... Reason for Deficiency (SAA)
Readex........ Readex Microprint Corp., New York, NY [*Library symbol Library of Congress*] (LCLS)
Readg........ Reading Co. [*Associated Press*] (SAG)
ReadgE........ Reading Entertainment, Inc. [*Associated Press*] (SAG)
READI........ Rocket Engine Analyzer and Decision Instrumentation
READIEX...... Readiness Exercise [*Navy*] (DOMA)
READIMP...... Readiness Improvement (MCD)
Readings...... Readings: A Journal of Reviews and Commentary in Mental Health [*A publication*] (BRI)
READJ........ Readjusted
READJP........ Readjustment Pay [*Military*]
READL........ Railway Employers' Association Defence League [*British*]
readm.......... Readmission [*Hospital administration*] (DAVI)
Read PL...... Read's Declarations and Pleadings [*A publication*] (DLA)
READR........ Remain in Effect after Discharge and Reenlistment [*Refers to orders*] [*Army*]
ReadRt........ Read-Rite Corp. [*Associated Press*] (SAG)
READS........ Reader Enrollment and Delivery System [*Library of Congress Washington, DC Information service or system*] (IID)
READS........ Reentry Air Data System (ADA)
READS........ Reno Air Defense Sector [*ADC*]
READSUPPGRUDET... Readiness Support Group Detachment (DNAB)
READTRAFAC... Readiness Training Facility (DNAB)
READU........ Ready Duty (NVT)
READU........ Ready Unit (NVT)
READYREP.. Ready-to-Sail Report [*Navy*] (NVT)
REA et A...... Rite Ecossais Ancien et Accepte [*Ancient and Accepted Scottish Rite*] [*Freemasonry*] [*French*]
REAF.......... Reorganization of Engineer Active Forces (MCD)
REAF.......... Resources Exchange Association Foundation [*Also known as REA Foundation*] (EA)
REAF.......... Revised Engineer Active Force (MCD)
REAG.......... Reproductive Effects Assessment Group [*Environmental Protection Agency*] (EPA)
ReaGld........ Rea Gold Corp. [*Associated Press*] (SAG)
ReaGold...... Rea Gold Corp. [*Associated Press*] (SAG)
REAGX........ Rea-Graham Fund [*Mutual fund ticker symbol*] (SG)
R/EAL.......... Reading/Everyday Activities in Life [*Educational test*]
REAL.......... Realistic, Equal, Active, for Life Women of Canada [*An association*]
REAL.......... Reliability, Inc. [*NASDAQ symbol*] (NQ)
REAL.......... Research-Extension Analytical Laboratory [*Ohio State University*] [*Research center*] (RCD)
REAL.......... Road Emulsion Association [*British*] (DBA)
REAL.......... Routine Economic Air Lift [*Army*]
Realco........ Realco, Inc. [*Associated Press*] (SAG)
REALCOM.... Real-Time Communications [*RCA*]
Real Est L Rep... Real Estate Law Report [*A publication*] (DLA)
Real Est Rec... Real Estate Record [*New York*] [*A publication*] (DLA)
REAL FAMMIS... Real-Time Finance and Manpower Management Information System [*Marine Corps*] (MCD)
RealGd........ Real Goods Trading Corp. [*Associated Press*] (SAG)
Reality........ Reality Interactive, Inc. [*Associated Press*] (SAG)
REALIZN...... Realization (ROG)
REALM........ Remote Access Line Monitor [*Cornet, Inc.*]
Real Pr Cas.. Real Property Cases [*England*] [*A publication*] (DLA)
Real Prop Acts... Real Property Actions and Proceedings [*A publication*] (DLA)
Real Prop Cas... Real Property Cases [*1843-47*] [*A publication*] (DLA)
Real Prop Prob & Trust J... Real Property, Probate, and Trust Journal [*A publication*] (DLA)
REAM.......... Rapid Excavation and Mining [*Project*] [*Bureau of Mines*]
REAMS........ Resources Evaluation and Management System [*Army*]
REAN.......... Royal East African Navy [*British military*] (DMA)
RE & D........ Research, Engineering, and Development
RE & T........ Research Engineering and Test (NASA)
RE&T.......... Research Engineering and Test [*NASA*] (NAKS)
REANSW...... Real Estate Association of New South Wales [*Australia*]
REAP.......... Read, Encode, Annotate, Ponder [*Reading improvement method*]
REAP.......... Regional Enforcement Activities Plan [*Environmental Protection Agency*] (ERG)
REAP.......... Reliability Engineering Analysis and Planning (PDAA)
REAP.......... Remote Entry Acquisition Package
REAP.......... Research and Engineering Apprenticeship Program [*Army*] (RDA)
REAP.......... Resource Center for Efficient Agricultural Production [*Macdonald College*] [*Research center*] (RCD)
REAP.......... Resource Engineering & Planning Co.
REAP.......... Reutilization Expedite Assets Program [*DoD*]
REAP.......... Rural Environmental Assistance Program [*Department of Agriculture*]
Reap Dec.... United States Customs Court Reports, Reappraisement Decision [*A publication*] (DLA)
REAPOR...... Real Estate Accounts Payable and Operating Reports
Reapp Dec... United States Customs Court Reports, Reappraisement Decision [*A publication*] (DLA)
REAPS........ Rotary Engine Air Pollution System [*Automotive engineering*]
REAPS........ Rotary Engine Antipollution System
REAPT........ Reappoint (AFM)
REAPTD...... Reappointed (WGA)

REAR	Reliability Engineering Analysis Report (IEEE)
REARF	Rearm and Refuel [*Military*] (VNW)
REARM	Renovation of Armament Manufacturing Program [*Army*] (MCD)
REARM	Underway Rearming [*Navy*] (NVT)
REART	Restricted Articles [*IATA*] (DS)
REAS	Real Estate Appraisal School [*Federal Home Loan Bank Board*]
REAS	Reasonable (ROG)
REAS	Reasonably Expected as Safe [*Medicine*] (DMAA)
REAS	Register of Environment Assessments and Statements (MCD)
REAS	Resources, Entities Accounting Subsystem (MCD)
REASM	Reassemble (AAG)
REASN	Reason (ROG)
REASSCE	Reassurance (ROG)
REASSEM	Reassemble (MSA)
REASSN	Reassign (ROG)
REASSND	Reassigned (ROG)
REASST	Reassignment (ROG)
REASSY	Reassembly (MSA)
REASTAN	Renton Electrical Analog for Solution of Thermal Analogous Networks
REAT	Radiological Emergency Assistance Team [*AEC*]
REAUM	Reaumur (ROG)
REAV	Renewable Energy Authority of Victoria [*Australia*]
reax	Reaction Shot [*TV news*] (WDMC)
REB	RADAR Evaluation Branch [*ADC*]
REB	Rare Earth Boride (PDAA)
REB	Real Estate Business [*Realtors National Marketing Institute*] [*A publication*]
REB	Reba Resources Ltd. [*Vancouver Stock Exchange symbol*]
REB	Rebecca/Eureka [*Navigation*] (AIA)
REB	Rebecca Eureka Beacon [*Navigation*] (IAA)
REB	Rebel
REB	R. E. Blake [*Record label*]
REB	Rebounds [*Basketball, hockey*]
REB	Rebuilt
REB	Redwood Empire Bancorp [*AMEX symbol*] (SPSG)
REB	Reentry Body
REB	Reentry Body Building (IAA)
REB	Regional Education Board of the Christian Brothers (EA)
REB	Regional Examining Bodies [*British*] (DI)
REB	Relativistic Electron Beam (MCD)
REB	Research Earth Borer
REB	Research Ethics Board [*Canada*]
REB	Reviewed Event Bulletin [*A publication*]
REB	Revised English Bible [*1989*] [*A publication*] (ODCC)
REB	Rocket Engine Band
REB	Rod End Bearing [*Army helicopter*]
REB	Roentgen-Equivalent-Biological [*Irradiation unit*]
REB	Royal Exhibition Buildings [*Melbourne, Australia*]
REBA	Relativistic Electron Beam Accelerator
REBAC	Real Estate Buyers Agent Council (NTPA)
REBAR	Reinforcing Bar (AAG)
REBASB	Real Estate and Business Agents' Supervisory Board [*Western Australia*]
REBAT	Reference Breakdown Air Traffic Control Services Report (FAAC)
REBAT	Restricted Bandwidth Techniques (NG)
REBC	Real Estate Brokerage Council (EA)
R-EBD-HS	Recessive Epidermolysis Bullosa Dystrophia-Hallopeaun Siemens [*Dermatology*]
REBE	Recovery Beacon Evaluation
REBECCA	RADAR Responder Beacon [*System*] (MUGU)
REBECCA	Remote Electrical Block Energization Clock Control Arrangement (IAA)
REBEEL	Realistic Battlefield Environment-Electronic [*Military*] (PDAA)
REBIA	Regional Educational Building Institute for Africa
REBK	Repertoire des Banques de Donnees en Conversationnel [*Association Nationale de la Recherche Technique*] [*Information service or system*]
REBLT	Rebuilt [*Automotive advertising*]
REBPr	Redwood Empire Bcp 7.80% Cv Pfd [*AMEX symbol*] (TTSB)
REBS	Royal Engineers Balloon School [*British military*] (DMA)
REBUD	Rehabilitation Budgeting Program [*Telecommunications*] (TEL)
REBUS	Reseau des Bibliotheques Utilisant SIBIL [*Library Network of SIBIL Users*] [*University of Lausanne Switzerland*] [*Information service or system*] (IID)
REBUS	Routine for Executing Biological Unit Simulations [*Computer program*]
REC	Clarion State College, Clarion, PA [*OCLC symbol*] (OCLC)
REC	Radiant Energy Conversion
REC	Radioelectrocomplexing [*Clinical chemistry*] (AAMN)
REC	Radio Electronic Combat [*Communications*]
REC	Radio Executives Club (NTCM)
REC	Railway Enthusiasts' Club [*British*] (BI)
REC	Railway Executive Committee [*British*]
REC	Rain Erosion Coating
REC	Rare-Earth Catalyst [*Automotive engineering*]
REC	Reactive [*Laboratory science*] (DAVI)
REC	Reactor Engineer Console
REC	Real Estate Council
REC	Receipt
Rec	Receipt (EBF)
Rec	Receivable [*Banking*] (TBD)
REC	Receive (NAKS)
REC	Received (DS)
REC	Receiver (AAG)
REC	Recens [*Fresh*] [*Pharmacy*]

REC	Recent (ROG)
REC	Receptacle (WGA)
REC	Reception
RECs	Recess (MSA)
REC	Recherches sur l'Origine de l'Ecriture Cuneiforme [*A publication*] (BJA)
REC	Recife [*Brazil*] [*Airport symbol*] (OAG)
REC	Recipe
REC	Reclamation (WGA)
REC	Recognition Equipment, Inc. (EFIS)
rec	Recombinant (DB)
REC	Recommendation (AFM)
REC	Reconnaissance and Radioelectronic Combat [*Military*] (INF)
rec	Record (WDMC)
Rec	Record (AL)
REC	Record (AAG)
Rec	Recordati [*Italy*] [*Research code symbol*]
REC	Recorded Program (NTCM)
REC	Recorder
rec	Recorder (WDAA)
Rec	Recording (AL)
rec	Recording (WDMC)
REC	Recording (ECII)
REC	Recover [*or Recovery*]
REC	Recreation
REC	Recreo [*Guatemala*] [*Seismograph station code, US Geological Survey*] (SEIS)
Rec	Recruiter [*British military*] (DMA)
REC	Rectifier (IEEE)
Rec	Recueil (BJA)
rec	Recurrence [*or Recurrent*] [*Medicine*] (MAE)
REC	Recurring (MCD)
REC	Regiment Etranger de Cavalerie [*Foreign Cavalry Regiment*] [*French*]
REC	Regional Electricity Co. [*British*] (ECON)
REC	Regional Electronics Centers [*British*]
REC	Regional Evaluation Center (NVT)
REC	Regional Express Co. [*ICAO designator*] (FAAC)
REC	Rehabilitation Engineering Center for the Hearing Impaired [*Gallaudet College*] [*Research center*] (RCD)
REC	Rehabilitation Engineering Centers [*Department of Health and Human Services*]
REC	Religious Education Centre (AIE)
REC	REM [*Roentgen-Equivalent-Man*] Equivalent Chemical [*Irradiation unit*]
REC	Request for Engineering Change (MCD)
REC	Research Ethics Committee
REC	Reserve Equalization Committee [*Military*]
REC	Residual Evaluation Center (MCD)
REC	Revloc, PA [*Location identifier FAA*] (FAAL)
REC	Ripling Electrochemical
REC	Rudge Enthusiasts Club (EA)
RECA	Repetitive Element Column Analysis (PDAA)
RECA	Residual Capabilities Assessment (MCD)
RECA	Revenue and Expenditure Control Act of 1968
RECA	Right External Carotid Artery [*Medicine*] (MEDA)
RECALC	Recalculated
RECAP	Real Estate Cost Analysis Program
Recap	Recapitalization (EBF)
Recap	Recapitulation (EBF)
RECAP	Recapitulation (AABC)
RECAP	Reformatter Electronic Circuit Analysis Program (CIST)
RECAP	Reliability Engineering and Corrective Action Program
RECAP	Reliability Evaluation Continuous Analysis Program
RECAP	Research and Education Center for Architectural Preservation [*University of Florida*] [*Research center*] (RCD)
RECAP	Resource and Capabilities Model (KSC)
RECAP	Review and Command Assessment of Project [*Military*]
RECAP	Rural Enterprises Community Action Program
RECAPS	Read Encode/Capture/Proof/Sort [*Computer science*] (MHDB)
RECAPS	Regionalized Civilian Automated Pay System [*Air Force*]
Rec Asst	Recreation Assistant (MEDA)
RECAT	Ad Hoc Committee on the Cumulative Regulatory Effects on the Cost of Automotive Transportation [*Terminated, 1972*] (EGAO)
RECAT	Reduced Energy Consumption for Commercial Air Transportation (DICI)
RECAU	Receipt Acknowledged and Understood
RECBAD	United States Army Recruiter Badge [*Military decoration*] (GFGA)
RECBKS	Receiving Barracks
RECC	Rhine Evacuation and Control Command [*NATO*] (NATG)
RECCB	Regional Education Committee of the Christian Brothers [*Later, REB*] (EA)
RECCE	Reconnaissance (CINC)
RECCEN	Reception Center [*Army*] (IAA)
RECCEXREP	Reconnaisance Exploitation Report (MCD)
RECCFO	Received in Connection with Fitting Out (DNAB)
RECCO	Reconnaissance (NVT)
REC COM	Record Commissioner [*British*] (DLA)
RECD	Received (AAG)
recd	Received (ODBW)
RECD	Recorded (WDAA)
RECDC	Regional Early Childhood Direction Centers (EDAC)
Rec Dec	Vaux's Recorder's Decisions [*1841-45*] [*Philadelphia, PA*] [*A publication*] (DLA)
RecdSys	Reconditioned Systems, Inc. [*Associated Press*] (SAG)

RECDUINS ... Received for Duty under Instruction
RECDUT .... Received for Duty
RECE............ Cuban Representation of Exiles [*Also known as Representacion Cubana del Exilio*] (EA)
RECE............ Relativistic Electron Coil Experiment (MCD)
RE CEL .... Reticulum Cell [*On Differential*] [*Hematology*] (DAVI)
RECENT ...... Recentis [*Fresh*] [*Pharmacy*] (ROG)
RECEP .... Reception (ADA)
RECERT ...... Recertification (NASA)
RECETED .... Receipted (ROG)
RecFIN........ Recreational Fisheries Information Network [*Database*] [*National Marine Fisheries Service*]
RECFM........ Record Format [*Computer science*]
RECG .... Radioelectrocardiograph
RECG .... Reciting
RECGA........ Research and Engineering Council of the Graphic Arts Industry
RECGAI ...... Research and Engineering Council of the Graphic Arts Industry (EA)
RECGP........ Recovery Group [*Air Force*]
RECH.......... Reformed Episcopal Church
RECHAR...... Recombiner Charcoal Adsorber [*Nuclear energy*] (NRCH)
RECHG .... Recharge (NASA)
RECHRG ..... Recharger
RECID .... Recidivism [*or Recidivist*] (WDAA)
RECIP .... Recipient
RECIP .... Reciprocate (AAG)
RECIP .... Reciprocating Gas-Fueled Engine
RECIPE .... Recomp Computer Interpretive Program Expediter [*Computer science*]
RECIR .... Recirculating [*Automotive engineering*]
RECIRC .... Recirculate (AAG)
RECIT......... Recitation
RECIT......... Recitative [*Music*]
recit............ Recitative (WDAA)
Reckson...... Reckson Associates Realty Corp. [*Associated Press*] (SAG)
REC L .... Recent Law (DLA)
RECL........... Recital (ROG)
RECL........... Reclamation
RECL........... Reclose
Reclaim....... Reclaim, Inc. [*Associated Press*] (SAG)
RECLAIM .... Regional Clean Air Incentive Market [*Environmental program*] (ECON)
Rec Laws.... Recent Laws in Canada [*A publication*] (DLA)
RECLR .... Recleared [*Aviation*] (FAAC)
RECM.......... Recommend (KSC)
REC MAN.... Recreation Management Exhibition [*British*] (ITD)
RECMD .... Recommend (AAG)
Recmd........ Recommissioned (DS)
RECMECH ... Recoil Mechanism (AAG)
RECMF........ Radio and Electronic Component Manufacturers' Federation
RECMFA ...... Radio and Electronic Component Manufacturers Association (IAA)
RECMN .... Recommendation
RECMOP...... Received [*Payment under Provisions of the*] Mustering Out Payment Act [*Military*] (DNAB)
RECMPT ...... Recomputation
RECMS .... Record Maintenance Statistics (MHDB)
RECN .... Reconnaissance
RECNCLN.... Reconciliation (AABC)
RECNO........ This Office Has No Record Of [*Army*] (AABC)
RECNSTRCTV... Reconstructive
RECNUM...... Record Number [*Online database field identifier*]
RECO .... Remote Command and Control (MCD)
RECO .... Remote Control [*Of mines*] (DOMA)
RECOC........ Reading and Comprehension in Chemistry
RECODEX..... Report Collection Index [*Studsvik Energiteknik AB*] [*Database Nykoping, Sweden*]
RECOG........ Recognition [*or Recognize*] (AAG)
RECOGE ...... Recognisance (ROG)
RECOGN ...... Recognizance
RECOGS...... Recognisances (ROG)
RECOGSIG ... Recognition Signal [*Navy*]
RECOL .... Retrieval Command Language [*Computer search language*]
RECOM .... Recommend (WDAA)
RECOMB...... Conference on Computational Molecular Biology (HGEN)
Recomm...... Recommendation (DAVI)
RECOMMTRANSO... Upon Receipt of These Orders Communicate with Transportation Officer for Priority Designator via Government Air If Available to ____
RECOMP...... Recommended Completion
RECOMP...... Recomplement
RECOMP...... Redstone Computer
RECOMP...... Repairs Completed [*Military*] (NVT)
RECOMP...... Retrieval and Composition (DIT)
RECON........ Readiness Condition [*Military*]
RECON........ Reconcentration (WDAA)
RECON........ Reconciliation
RECON........ Recondition (WDAA)
RECON........ Reconnaissance (NATG)
RECON........ Reconnoitre (WDAA)
RECON........ Reconsignment (WDAA)
recon .... Reconstruction (VRA)
RECON........ Reliability and Configuration Accountability System
RECON........ Remote Console [*NASA computer*]
RECON........ Remote Control (KSC)
RECON......... Resources Conservation (MCD)
RECON......... Retrospective Conversion (NITA)

RECON.......... Retrospective Conversion of Bibliographic Records [*Library of Congress*]
RECONATKRON... Reconnaissance Attack Squadron [*Navy*] (DNAB)
RECONATKWING... Reconnaissance Attack Wing [*Navy*] (DNAB)
RECONBN....... Reconnaissance Battalion [*Navy*] (DNAB)
RECONCE....... Reconveyance (ROG)
RECONCO....... Reconnaissance Co. [*Military*]
RECOND .... Recondition (AABC)
RECONDO....... Reconnaissance Commando Doughboy [*Military*] (AABC)
RECONEX....... Raid/Reconnaissance Exercise [*Military*] (NVT)
RECONFIG ..... Reconfiguration (NASA)
RECONN .... Reconnaissance (AAG)
R Econ S ...... Royal Economic Society [*British*]
recons denied... Reconsideration Denied (AAGC)
RECONST....... Reconstruct (AABC)
reconstr .... Reconstruction (CPH)
RECONVCE...... Reconveyance (ROG)
Recoton .... Recoton Corp. [*Associated Press*] (SAG)
RECOV........... Recovery (KSC)
RECOVER..... Remote Continual Verification [*Telephonic monitoring system*]
RECOVER..... Remote Control Verification [*Nuclear safeguards*]
RECOVY .... Recovery
RECP .... International College of Real Estate Consulting Professionals (EAIO)
RECP .... Real Estate Consulting Professional [*International College of Real Estate Consulting Professionals*] [*Designation awarded by*]
RECP .... Receptacle
RECP .... Reception (WGA)
RECP .... Reciprocal (AAG)
RECP .... Release Engineering Change Proposal (MCD)
RECP .... Request for Engineering Change Proposal [*NASA*]
RECP .... Rural Environmental Conservation Program
Recp Cen ..... Reception Center [*Army*]
RECPOM....... Resource Constrained Procurement Objectives for Munitions Model [*Army*]
RECPST........ Receptionist (WGA)
RECPT .... Receipt
RECPT .... Receptacle (AAG)
RECPT .... Reception (AAG)
RECR .... Receiver
RECR .... Recreation (AABC)
RECRA......... Real Estate Capital Resources Association (NTPA)
RECRAS....... Retrieval System for Current Research in Agricultural Sciences [*Japan*]
RECRC .... Recirculate (NASA)
RECRE .... Recreation
Rec Rm .... Recovery Room (BARN)
recrm.......... Recreation Room (REAL)
RECRN........ Recreation
RECRSHIP ... Receivership (LWAP)
RECRT......... Recruit (AFM)
RECRUIT...... Recruiting
RECRYST...... Recrystallized
RECS .... Radiological Emergency Communications System [*Nuclear energy*] (NRCH)
RECS .... Rear Echelon COMINT [*Communications Intelligence*] System [*Military*] (MCD)
RecS........... Reconditioned Systems, Inc. [*Associated Press*] (SAG)
RECS .... Reconfigurable EC System (MCD)
RECS .... Reconstitutable Emergency Communications System
RECS .... Representative Shuttle Environmental Control System [*NASA*] (MCD)
RECS .... Residential Energy Consumption Survey [*Department of Energy*] (GFGA)
RECSAM ...... Southeast Asian Regional Center for Education in Science and Mathematics [*Malaysia*]
RECSAT .... Reconnaissance Satellite (NVT)
RECSATSUM... Reconnaissance Satellite Summary (DNAB)
rec sec .... Recording Secretary (WGA)
RECSG .... Renewable Energy Congressional Staff Group [*Defunct*] (EA)
RECSHIP...... Receiving Ship
Rec Spec ..... Recreation Specialist (MEDA)
RECSQUAD... Reconnaissance Squadron [*Military*]
RECSTA .... Receiving Station [*Military*]
RECSYS .... Recreation Systems Analysis [*Computer science*]
RECT........... Receipt
rect............. Receipt (WDAA)
RECT........... Reception (IAA)
RECT........... Rectangle (AAG)
RECT........... Rectification [*or Rectifier*] (IAA)
rect............. Rectification (IDOE)
RECT Rm ...... Rectificatus [*Rectified*] [*Pharmacy*]
rect............. Rectified (IDOE)
rect............. Rectifier (IDOE)
RECT........... Rectifier (NAKS)
RECT........... Rectify (AAG)
RECT........... Rector
Rect............ Rectory (WDAA)
rect............. Rectum [*Medicine*] (MAE)
RECT........... Rectus [*Muscle*] [*Anatomy*]
RECTAD........ Received for Temporary Additional Duty
RECTADINS... Received for Temporary Additional Duty under Instruction
RECTAS .... Regional Centre for Training in Aerial Surveys (EAIO)
RECTD .... Received for Temporary Duty
RECTD .... Recited (ROG)
Rec Tech ...... Recreation Technician (MEDA)
RECTEMDUINS... Received for Temporary Duty under Instruction

RECTENNA... Rectifying Antenna [*Microwave power transmission*]
RECTG .... Reciting (ROG)
RECTIFON.... Rectification (ROG)
RECTIL........ Rectilineal [*Geometry*] (ROG)
RECTON....... Reduction (ROG)
RECTR........ Recommend Transfer Of (NOAA)
RECTR........ Rectifier
RECTREAT ... Received for Treatment
RECUR......... Recurrence [*or Recurrent*] [*Medicine*]
RECV .... Receive (NASA)
rec v .... Recreational Vehicle (BARN)
RECVD .... Received
recvee .... Recreational Vehicle (BARN)
RecvEng ...... Recovery Engineering, Inc. [*Associated Press*] (SAG)
RECVG .... Receiving
RECVR .... Receiver (NASA)
RECVY .... Recovery
RECY .... Recovery (AAG)
RECY .... Recycling Industries [*NASDAQ symbol*] (TTSB)
RECY .... Recycling Industries, Inc. [*NASDAQ symbol*] (SAG)
RECYCLE ..... Recycling
Recycling..... Recycling Industries, Inc. [*Associated Press*] (SAG)
RED .... Comite International de La Croix-Rouge [*Switzerland ICAO designator*] (FAAC)
ReD .... Doctor of Recreation (GAGS)
RED .... New South Wales Reserved Equity Decisions [*A publication*] (DLA)
RED .... Radian Energy Distribution
RED .... Radiation Experience Data [*Food and Drug Administration*] [*Database*]
RED .... Radio Equipment Department [*British military*] (DMA)
RED .... Railroad Employees' Department [*of AFL-CIO*]
RED .... Range Error Detector
RED .... Rapid Erythrocyte Degeneration [*Medicine*] (DMAA)
RED .... Rapid Excess Disposal [*Military*] (AABC)
RED .... Rare-Earth Device
RED .... RCRA [*Resource Conservation and Recovery Act*] Enforcement Division [*Environmental Protection Agency*] (GFGA)
RED .... Redactor (WGA)
red............. Redeemable [*Finance*] (ODBW)
RED .... Redeemed
Red.......... Redfield's New York Surrogate Reports [*A publication*] (DLA)
Red............ Redington's Reports [*31-35 Maine*] [*A publication*] (DLA)
RED .... Red Lion Inns L.P. [*AMEX symbol*] (TTSB)
RED .... Red Lion Inns Ltd. [*AMEX symbol*] (SPSG)
RED .... Red Lodge, MT [*Location identifier FAA*] (FAAL)
RED .... Redoubt Volcano [*Alaska*] [*Seismograph station code, US Geological Survey*] (SEIS)
RED .... Reduce [*or Reduction*] (AAG)
red.............. Reduced (WDMC)
red.............. Reduction (WDMC)
RFD .... Reduction (NAKS)
RED .... Redundant (KSC)
Red............ Rodwar's Comments on Ordinances of the Gold Coast Colony [*1889-1909*] [*Ghana*] [*A publication*] (DLA)
Re-D .... Re-Evaluation Deadline [*Rehabilitation*] (DAVI)
RED .... Reflection Electron Diffraction [*For surface structure analysis*]
RED .... Refunding Escrow Deposit [*Finance*] (DFIT)
RED .... Registered Expected Death
RED .... Repairable Equipment Depot [*British military*] (DMA)
RED .... Repeat Expansion Detection [*Genetics*]
RED .... Reregistration Eligibility Decision [*Environmental Protection Agency*] (AEPA)
RED .... Restructured Expanded Data (MCD)
RED .... Resume Entry Device
RED .... Review, Evaluation, Disposition Board (AAG)
RED .... Ritchie's Equity Decisions (Russell) [*Canada*] [*A publication*] (DLA)
REDA .... Rural Educational and Development Association [*Canada*]
REDAC......... Racal Electronic Design and Analysis by Computer (IAA)
REDAC......... Real-Time Data Acquisition
REDAC......... Remote Detection and Control [*Environmental science*] (COE)
Red Am R Cas... Redfield's American Railway Cases [*A publication*] (DLA)
Red Am RR Cas... Redfield's Leading American Railway Cases [*A publication*] (DLA)
Red & Big Cas B & N... Redfield and Bigelow's Leading Cases on Bills and Notes [*A publication*] (DLA)
REDAP......... Reentrant Data Processing
REDAS......... Reduced to Apprentice Seaman [*Navy*]
REDB .... Redbourne [*England*]
REDB .... Red Brick Systems [*NASDAQ symbol*] (TTSB)
REDB .... Red Brick Systems, Inc. [*NASDAQ symbol*] (SAG)
Red Bail ...... Redfield on Carriers and Bailments [*A publication*] (DLA)
REDBR......... Redbridge [*England*]
REDC .... Regional Economic Development Center [*Memphis State University*] [*Research center*] (RCD)
REDC .... Reinsertion of Direct Current (IAA)
REDCAP....... Real-Time Electromagnetic Digitally Controlled Analyser and Processor
REDCAPE..... Readiness Capability [*Military*]
Red Car....... Redfield on Carriers and Bailments [*A publication*] (DLA)
Red Cas RR... Redfield's Leading American Railway Cases [*A publication*] (DLA)
Red Cas Wills... Redfield's Leading Cases on Wills [*A publication*] (DLA)
REDCAT....... Racial and Ethnic Category [*Army*] (INF)
REDCAT....... Range-Extended Directionally-Controlled Antitank Missile (MCD)
REDCAT....... Readiness Category [*Military*]
REDCN......... Reducing (ROG)

REDCOM...... Readiness Command [*Army*]
REDCON...... Readiness Condition [*Military*]
REDD .... Reduced (ROG)
ReddiBrk...... Reddi Brake Supply Corp. [*Associated Press*] (SAG)
REDE .... Regents External Degree Examinations [*New York*] (EDAC)
Re de J........ Revue de Jurisprudence [*Montreal*] [*A publication*] (DLA)
Re de L .... Revue de Jurisprudence et Legislation [*Montreal*] [*A publication*] (DLA)
Redem......... Redemption (DLA)
RedEm........ Redwood Empire Bancorp [*Associated Press*] (SAG)
RedEmp....... Redwood Empire Bancorp [*Associated Press*] (SAG)
Redes Pl...... Redesdale's Treatise upon Equity Pleading [*A publication*] (DLA)
REDF .... Redfed Bancorp [*NASDAQ symbol*] (SAG)
Redf........... Redfield's New York Surrogate Reports [*A publication*] (DLA)
Redf Am Railw Cas... Redfield's American Railway Cases [*A publication*] (DLA)
Redf & B ..... Redfield and Bigelow's Leading Cases [*England*] [*A publication*] (DLA)
Redf Carr..... Redfield on Carriers and Bailments [*A publication*] (DLA)
RedfedBc..... Redfed Bancorp [*Associated Press*] (SAG)
RED FG....... Red Flint Glazed [*Paper*] (DGA)
Redf (NY)..... Redfield's New York Surrogate Reports [*A publication*] (DLA)
Redf Railways... Redfield on Railways [*A publication*] (DLA)
Redf R Cas... Redfield's Railway Cases [*England*] [*A publication*] (DLA)
Redf Sur (NY)... Redfield's New York Surrogate Court Reports [*A publication*] (DLA)
Redf Surr..... Redfield's New York Surrogate Reports [*A publication*] (DLA)
Redf Surr (NY)... Redfield's New York Surrogate Court Reports [*5 vols.*] [*A publication*] (DLA)
Redf Wills ... Redfield's Leading Cases on Wills [*A publication*] (DLA)
REDGF........ Rea Gold Corp. [*NASDAQ symbol*] (SAG)
RedhkA........ Redhook Ale Brewery, Inc. [*Associated Press*] (SAG)
RED HORSE... Rapid Engineer Development, Heavy Operational Repair Squadron, Engineering [*Air Force*] (AFM)
RED HORSE... Rapid Engineering Deployable, Heavy Operational Repair Squadron, Engineer [*Air Force*] (AFM)
RedHot .... Red Hot Concepts, Inc. [*Associated Press*] (SAG)
RedHt .... Red Hot Concepts, Inc. [*Associated Press*] (SAG)
REDI .... Rapid Earthquake Data Integration
REDI .... Real Estate Data, Inc. [*Information service or system*] (IID)
REDI .... Reddi Brake Supply [*NASDAQ symbol*] (TTSB)
REDI .... Reddi Brake Supply Corp. [*NASDAQ symbol*] (SAG)
REDI .... Remote Electronic Delivery of Information [*Library science*] (DOMA)
REDICORT ... Readiness Improvement through Correspondence Training (MCD)
RediCr .... ReadiCare, Inc. [*Associated Press*] (SAG)
REDIG IN PULV... Redigatur In Pulverent [*Let It Be Reduced to Powder*] [*Pharmacy*] (ROG)
Redington.... Redington's Reports [*31-35 Maine*] [*A publication*] (DLA)
RED in PULV... Redactus in Pulverem [*Reduce to a Powder*] [*Pharmacy*]
Red Int L ..... Reddie's Inquiries in International Law [*2nd ed.*] [*1851*] [*A publication*] (DLA)
Re Dir......... Director of Recreation (PGP)
REDIS .... Reference Dispatch (NOAA)
REDISC........ Rediscount [*Banking*]
Redisc........ Rediscount (EBF)
REDIST .... Redistilled
REDISTR...... Redistribution (AFM)
REDL .... Redlane [*England*]
REDL .... Runway Edge Light [*ICAO designator*] (FAAC)
Redlaw........ Redlaw Industries, Inc. [*Associated Press*] (SAG)
REDLOG....... Logistic Readiness Report [*Navy*] (CINC)
Redlw......... Redlaw Industries, Inc. [*Associated Press*] (SAG)
Redman....... Redman Industries [*Associated Press*] (SAG)
Redman....... Redman on Landlord and Tenant [*A publication*] (DLA)
Redm Arb .... Redman on Arbitration [*A publication*] (DLA)
Red Mar Com... Reddie's Law of Maritime Commerce [*1841*] [*A publication*] (DLA)
Red Mar Int L... Reddie's Researches in Maritime International Law [*1844-45*] [*A publication*] (DLA)
REDN.......... Reduction
REDNON...... Operational Readiness Report (Nonatomic) (CINC)
REDNT......... Redundant (AAG)
REDO .... RADAR Engineering Design Objectives (NG)
REDO .... Red Documental [*Ministerio de Educacion Publica*] [*Chile*] [*Information service or system*] (CRD)
REDOPS....... Ready for Operations [*Reporting system*] [*DoD*]
REDOX........ Reduction and Oxidation
REDP.......... Redondo Peak [*New Mexico*] [*Seismograph station code, US Geological Survey*] (SEIS)
Red Pop ...... Post Reditum ad Populum [*of Cicero*] [*Classical studies*] (OCD)
Red Pr .... Redfield's New York Practice Reports [*A publication*] (DLA)
REDR.......... Redruth [*England*]
REDRAT....... Readiness Rating
REDREP....... Redeployment Report [*Military*]
Red RL .... Reddie's Roman Law [*A publication*] (DLA)
RedRoof ...... Red Roof Inns, Inc. [*Associated Press*] (SAG)
Red RR........ Redfield on the Law of Railroads [*A publication*] (DLA)
Red RR Cas... Redfield's Leading American Railway Cases [*A publication*] (DLA)
REDS .... Reactor Electric Distribution System (COE)
REDS .... Retrovirus Epidemiology Donor Study [*Medicine*]
REDS .... Revised Engine-Delivery Schedule
REDS .... Royal Engineers Diving School [*British military*] (DMA)
Red Sc L ..... Reddie's Science of Law [*2nd ed.*] [*A publication*] (DLA)
Red Sen ...... Post Reditum in Senatu [*of Cicero*] [*Classical studies*] (OCD)
REDSG........ Redesignate (AFM)
redsh.......... Reddish [*Philately*]
REDSO........ Regional Economic Development Services Office [*USAID*]

REDSOD	Repetitive Explosive Device for Soil Displacement
REDSO/ESA...	Regional Economic Development Services Office for East and Southern Africa
RED-T	Remote Electric Drive Turret
REDTOP	Reactor Design from Thermal-Hydraulic Operating Parameters [*NASA*]
REDTRAIN ...	Readiness Training (MCD)
REDUC	Red Latinoamericana de Documentacion en Educacion [*Latin American Education Documentation Network*] (PDAA)
REDUC	Reduction (KSC)
REDUCE	Reduction of Electrical Demand Using Computer Equipment [*Energy management system designed by John Helwig of Jance Associates, Inc.*]
REDUN	Redundancy (NASA)
REDUPL	Reduplication
REDW	Redwood National Park
Redwar	Redwar's Comments on Ordinances of the Gold Coast Colony [*1889-1909*] [*Ghana*] [*A publication*] (DLA)
Redwd	Redwood Trust, Inc. [*Associated Press*] (SAG)
Red Wills	Redfield on the Law of Wills [*A publication*] (DLA)
REDWN	Redrawn
REDX	Red Eagle Resources (EFIS)
REDY	Ready (DAVI)
REDY	Recirculating Dialyzate [*Artificial kidney dialysis system*]
REDYP	Reentry Dynamics Program
REDZ	Recent Drizzle [*Meteorology*] (DA)
REE	Lubbock, TX [*Location identifier FAA*] (FAAL)
REE	Radio Exterior Espana (EY)
REE	Rapid Extinction Effect [*Electrophysiology*]
REE	Rare-Earth Element [*Chemistry*]
REE	Rational Expectations Equilibrium [*Economics*]
REE	Red Earth Energy Ltd. [*Vancouver Stock Exchange symbol*]
REE	Registered Export Establishment
REE	Respiratory Energy Expenditure [*Physiology*]
REE	Resting Energy Expenditure
REEA	Radio and Electronics Engineering Association (IAA)
REEA	Real Estate Educators Association (NTPA)
Reebok	Reebok International Ltd. [*Associated Press*] (SAG)
REEC	Regional Export Expansion Council [*Department of Commerce*]
REECO	Reynolds Electrical & Engineering Co.
Reed	Reed on Bills of Sale [*A publication*] (DLA)
REED	Reeds Jewelers [*NASDAQ symbol*] (TTSB)
REED	Reeds Jewelers, Inc. [*Wilmington, NC*] [*NASDAQ symbol*] (NQ)
re-ed	Re-Education (DAVI)
REED	Resources on Educational Equity for the Disabled
REED	Restricted Edge Emitting Diode [*Electronics*] (EECA)
Reed Am LS...	Reed's American Law Studies [*A publication*] (DLA)
Reed BS	Reed on Bills of Sale [*A publication*] (DLA)
Reed C	Reed College (GAGS)
Reed Car	Reed on Railways as Carriers [*A publication*] (DLA)
Reed Fraud...	Reed's Leading Cases on Statute of Frauds [*A publication*] (DLA)
ReedIntl	Reed International Ltd. [*Associated Press*] (SAG)
ReedJwl	Reeds Jewelers, Inc. [*Associated Press*] (SAG)
Reed PA Black...	Reed's Pennsylvania Blackstone [*A publication*] (DLA)
Reed Pr Sug...	Reed's Practical Suggestions for the Management of Lawsuits [*A publication*] (DLA)
REEDS	Retention of Tears, Ectrodactyly, Ectodermal Dysplasia, and Strange Hair, Skin and Teeth Syndrome [*Medicine*] (DMAA)
REEEVAC	Renewable Energy and Energy Efficiency Joint Ventures Advisory Committee [*Department of Energy*] (EGAO)
REEF	Rocket Exhaust Effects Facility (MCD)
REEFER	Refrigerator, Refrigerated, or Cold Storage [*Airplane, railway car, truck*]
REEFNSW	Real Estate Employers Federation of New South Wales [*Australia*]
REEG	Radioelectroencephalograph
R-EEG	Resting Electroencephalogram [*Medicine*] (STED)
REEGT	Registered Electroencephalographic Technician [*Medicine*] (AAMN)
REEI	Russian and East European Institute [*Indiana University*] [*Research center*] (RCD)
REEL	Radiation Exposure Evaluation Laboratory (DNAB)
REEL	Recessive-Expressive Emergent Language Scores [*For the hearing-impaired*]
REELS	Receptive-Expressive Emergent Language Scale (STED)
REELS	Reflected Electron Energy Loss Spectra
REEM	Reserves Embarked [*Navy*] (NVT)
REEN	Regional Energy Education Network [*National Science Teachers Association*]
ReEND	Reproductive Endocrinology (STED)
REENL	Reenlist [*Military*] (AFM)
REENLA	Reenlistment Allowance [*Military*]
REENL ALLOW...	Reenlistment Allowance [*Military*] (DNAB)
REENLB	Reenlistment Bonus [*Military*]
Reenlmt	Re-Enlistment [*Army*]
REEP	Range Estimating and Evaluation Procedure [*Computer science*]
REEP	Reasonable Extra Efforts Program [*Environmental science*] (COE)
REEP	Regression Estimation of Event Probabilities (IEEE)
REEP	Review of Environmental Effects of Pollutants [*Environmental Protection Agency*] (GFGA)
REEP	Right End-Expiratory Pressure [*Medicine*] (DMAA)
REEP	Role Exchange/Education-Practice (MEDA)
REES	Center for Russian and East European Studies [*University of Pittsburgh*] [*Research center*] (RCD)
REES	Reactive Electronic Equipment Simulator (RDA)
REES	Regular Educator Expectancy Scale (EDAC)

REES...........	Russian and East European Studies Area Program [*University of Pittsburgh*] [*Research center*] (RCD)
Reese	Reporter of Vols. 5 and 11, Heiskell's Tennessee Reports [*A publication*] (DLA)
REETA.........	Rural Extension, Education and Training Abstracts [*Database*] [*Commonwealth Bureau of Agricultural Economics*] [*Information service or system*] (CRD)
REETS.........	Radiological Effluent and Environmental Technical Specifications [*Nuclear Regulatory Commission*] (NRCH)
Reeve Des...	Reeve on Descents [*A publication*] (DLA)
Reeve Dom Rel...	Reeve on Domestic Relations [*A publication*] (DLA)
Reeve Eng L...	Reeve's History of the English Law [*A publication*] (DLA)
Reeve Eng Law...	Reeve's History of the English Law [*A publication*] (DLA)
Reeve Hist Eng Law...	Reeve's History of the English Law [*A publication*] (DLA)
Reeve Sh....	Reeve on the Law of Shipping [*A publication*] (DLA)
Reeves HEL...	Reeve's History of the English Law [*A publication*] (DLA)
Reeves Hist Eng Law...	Reeve's History of the English Law [*A publication*] (DLA)
REF...........	Ejection Fraction at Rest (STED)
REF...........	Range Error Function [*Aerospace*] (AAG)
REF...........	Rat Embryo Fibroblast [*Cells*]
REF...........	Recovery Educational Foundation (EA)
REF...........	REFAC Technology Develop [*AMEX symbol*] (TTSB)
REF...........	Refac Technology Development Corp. [*AMEX symbol*] (SAG)
REF...........	Refectory (DSUE)
REF...........	Refer (EY)
REF...........	Referee
Ref...........	Referee (EBF)
ref...........	Referee (WDAA)
Ref...........	Reference (AL)
REF...........	Reference
ref...........	Reference (IDOE)
REF...........	Referendum
REF...........	Refinery [*or Refining*]
REF...........	Reflection Resources [*Vancouver Stock Exchange symbol*]
REF...........	Reflector
ref...........	Reflex (STED)
REF...........	Reformation
REF...........	Reformed
REF...........	Refrain (WGA)
REF...........	Refresher (AABC)
REF...........	Refrigerant [*Cooling*] [*Medicine British*] (ROG)
REF...........	Refrigerator (WGA)
REF...........	Refugee Coordinator [*Department of State*] (GFGA)
REF...........	Refund [*or Refunding*]
Ref...........	Refunding (EBF)
REF...........	Refurbish (NAKS)
REF...........	Refurbishment (NASA)
REF...........	Refused (ADA)
REF...........	Release of Excess Funds
REF...........	Renal Erythropoietic Factor [*Medicine*]
REF...........	Restriction Endonuclease Fingerprinting [*Analytical biochemistry*]
REF...........	Risk Evaluation Force (DOMA)
REF...........	Unclear Pronoun Reference [*Used in correcting manuscripts, etc.*]
REFA..........	Real Estate Fund of America
Refac	Refac Technology Development Corp. [*Associated Press*] (SAG)
Re fa lo	Recordari Facias Loquelam [*Have the Record Before the Court*] [*Latin*] [*Legal term*] (BARN)
Ref Aust	Reference Australia [*A publication*]
Ref Bk R	Reference Book Review [*A publication*] (BRI)
REFC..........	Reference (ROG)
REFC..........	Reflections of Elvis Fan Club (EA)
REFC..........	Richard Eden Fan Club (EA)
REFCD	Research and Education Foundation for Chest Disease [*Defunct*] (EA)
REFCO	Resolution Funding Corp. [*Established by the Financial Institutions Reform, Recovery, and Enforcement Act of 1989*]
REFCON	Reference Configuration (SSD)
RefCorp	Resolution Funding Corp. [*Established by the Financial Institutions Reform, Recovery, and Enforcement Act of 1989*]
REFCORP.....	Resolution Funding Corporation (USGC)
REFD	Referred
REFD	Refined
REFD	Reformed (WGA)
REFD	Refund (AFM)
REFD CON ...	Reinforced Concrete [*Freight*]
Ref Dec	Referee's Decision [*Legal term*] (DLA)
REF/DES	Reference Designator Number (MCD)
REFD MTL ...	Reinforced Metal [*Freight*]
ref doc.......	Referring Doctor [*Medicine*] (AAMN)
REFD PLYWD...	Reinforced Plywood [*Freight*]
REFEC........	Refectory (DSUE)
R$_{eff}$........	Effective Resistance (IDOE)
REFF..........	References (WGA)
REFFREQ	Reference Frequency [*Telecommunications*] (IAA)
REFG	Refrigerating [*or Refrigeration*]
Ref Girl	Refractory Girl [*A publication*]
REFGR........	Refrigerator
REFI..........	Regional Ejection Fraction Image [*Medicine*] (DMAA)
REFIC........	Research Fire Control (SAA)
REFIL........	Recharged from Inversion Layer (PDAA)
REFL..........	Reference Line (AAG)
REFL..........	Reflectance [*or Reflector*] (AAG)
REFL..........	Reflection [*or Reflector*] (IAA)
REFL..........	Reflex
REFL..........	Reflexive

REFL............	Specimen Lost by Reference Laboratory (DAVI)
Reflctn.........	Reflectone, Inc. [*Associated Press*] (SAG)
REFLD	Reflected
REFLEC........	Reflection (IAA)
REFLECS.....	Retrieval from the Literature on Electronics and Computer Sciences (PDAA)
Reflectn.......	Reflectone, Inc. [*Associated Press*] (SAG)
REFLES........	Reference Librarian Enhancement System [*University of California*] [*Online microcomputer system*]
REFLEX........	Reserve Flexibility [*Military*] (MCD)
REFM............	Resource Ecology and Fisheries Management [*Marine science*] (OSRA)
REFMCHY	Refrigerating Machinery
REFMS.........	Recreation and Education for Multiple Sclerosis
REFMT.........	Reinforcement
REFNO.........	Reference Number (CINC)
Ref NRE......	Refused, Not Reversible Error [*Legal term*] (DLA)
REFONE	Reference Our Telephone Conversation (FAAC)
REFORGER...	Return of Forces to Germany [*Military*]
REFORM.......	Reformatory (ROG)
REFORMA....	National Association to Promote Library Services to the Spanish-Speaking
REFORS.......	Replacement Forecasting System (IAA)
REFP............	Reference Papers [*Army*] (AABC)
ref phys	Referring Physician (DAVI)
REFR	Refractory
REFR	Refrigerate (KSC)
REFR	Research Frontiers [*NASDAQ symbol*] (TTSB)
REFR	Research Frontiers, Inc. [*NASDAQ symbol*] (SAG)
REFRA	Recent Freezing Rain [*Meteorology*] (DA)
REFRACDUTRA...	Release from Active Duty for Training [*Army*] (AABC)
REFRAD......	Release from Active Duty [*Army*]
REFRADT......	Release from Active Duty for Training [*Army*] (AABC)
REFRANACDUTRA...	Release from Annual Active Duty for Training [*Army*] (AABC)
REFRAT.......	Release from Annual Training [*Army*] (AABC)
REFRD.........	Refrigerated (AAG)
Refr G.........	Refractory Girl [*A publication*]
REFRG.........	Refrigerate (AAG)
REFRIG.......	Refrigerate (NAKS)
REFRIG.......	Refrigerated Service [*Shipping*] [*British*]
REFRIG.......	Refrigeration
REFRIG.......	Refrigerator [*Classified advertising*]
REFRIGN......	Refrigeration
REFS..........	Remote Entry Flexible Security [*Computer science*] (MHDB)
REFSEARCH...	Reference Materials Searching System (NITA)
REFSMMAT...	Reference Stable Member Matrix (KSC)
Ref Sp	Reformed Spelling (BARN)
REFSRV	[*The*] Reference Service [*Mead Data Central, Inc.*] [*Information service or system*] (IID)
REFT............	Release for Experimental Flight Test (NG)
REFTEL........	Reference Telegram (NATG)
Reftel.........	Reference Telegram
REFTEMP.....	Reference Temperature (IAA)
REFTO	Reference Travel Order (NOAA)
REFTRA	Refresher Training (NVT)
REFTS.........	Resonant Frequency Tracking System
refty...........	Refectory (VRA)
REFUL	Refueling
REFURB	Refurbished
REFURDIS ...	Reference Your Dispatch
REFURLTR...	Reference Your Letter
RefWID.......	Refugee Women in Development (EA)
Ref WM	Refused, Want of Merit [*Legal term*] (DLA)
REFY...........	Refinery
REG	Aircraft Nationality and Registration Marks
Reg.............	Daily Register [*New York City*] [*A publication*] (DLA)
REG	Radiation Exposure Guide
REG	Radioencephalogram
REG	Radioisotope Electrogenerator (IAA)
REG	Random Event Generator [*Psychology*]
REG	Range Extender with Gain [*Bell System*]
REG	Reeves Entertainment Group [*Television*]
Reg.............	Regal, Branch of EMI [*Record label*] [*Spain*]
REG	Regarding
REG	Regency Realty [*NYSE symbol*] (SPSG)
REG	Regency Resources [*Vancouver Stock Exchange symbol*]
REG	Regeneration (IAA)
REG	Regent
REG	Reggio Calabria [*Italy*] [*Airport symbol*] (OAG)
REG	Regiment
reg..............	Regiment (WDAA)
REG	Regina [*Queen*] [*Latin*]
REG	Region (AAG)
Reg.............	Region (TBD)
reg..............	Region (DD)
REG	Regis College, Weston, MA [*OCLC symbol*] (OCLC)
REG	Register (AAG)
REG	Registered [*Stock exchange term*] (SPSG)
reg..............	Registered (WDAA)
Reg.............	Registered (EBF)
Reg.............	Registrar (EBF)
REG	Registrar (ROG)
reg..............	Registrar (WDAA)
reg..............	Registration (ODBW)
REG	Registration [*ICAO designator*] (FAAC)

Reg.............	Registration Cases [*A publication*] (DLA)
Reg.............	Registrum Omnium Brevium [*Register of Writs*] [*Latin A publication*] (DSA)
REG	Registry
REG	Regourd Aviation [*France ICAO designator*] (FAAC)
REG	Regression Analysis [*Military*] (IAA)
REG	Regular (AAG)
Reg.............	Regular (EBF)
REG	Regulate· (AAG)
REG	Regulating [*Duties*] [*Navy British*]
REG	Regulation
REG	Regulator (DEN)
REG	Repair-Evacuator Group [*Former USSR*]
REG	Rheoencephalography [*Medicine*]
REG	Rock Eagle [*Georgia*] [*Seismograph station code, US Geological Survey*] (SEIS)
REGA	Regional Acceptance [*NASDAQ symbol*] (TTSB)
REGA	Regional Acceptance Corp. [*NASDAQ symbol*] (SAG)
RegAcp........	Regional Acceptance Corp. [*Associated Press*] (SAG)
REGAD........	Regenerate Address [*Computer science*] (MHDB)
REGAF	Regular Air Force
REGAL	Remote Generalized Application Language [*Computer science*] (PDAA)
REGAL	Remotely Guided Autonomous Lightweight Torpedo (MCD)
RegalBel......	Regal-Beloit Corp. [*Associated Press*] (SAG)
Reg App	Registration Appeals [*England*] [*A publication*] (DLA)
Reg Arch	Registered Architect
REGARD......	Ruby, Emerald, Garnet, Amethyst, Ruby, Diamond [*Jewelry*]
RegBn..........	Regent Bancshares Corp. [*Associated Press*] (SAG)
RegBnc........	Regent Bancshares Corp. [*Associated Press*] (SAG)
Reg Brev	Registrum Omnium Brevium [*Register of Writs*] [*Latin A publication*] (DLA)
REGC	Right Eminent Grand Commander [*Freemasonry*]
REG/CAN.....	Registry Number/Chemical Abstracts Number [*American Chemical Society information file*]
Reg Cas......	Registration Cases [*England*] [*A publication*] (DLA)
RegCin.........	Regal Cinemas, Inc. [*Associated Press*] (SAG)
REGD..........	Registered
Reg'd..........	Registered (EBF)
Reg Deb	Gales and Seaton's Register of Debates in Congress [*1824-37*] [*A publication*] (DLA)
Reg Deb (Gales)...	Register of Debates in Congress (Gales) [*1789-91*] [*A publication*] (DLA)
Reg Deb (G & S)...	Gales and Seaton's Register of Debates in Congress [*1824-37*] [*A publication*] (DLA)
REGE	Regular Eight [*Motion picture*] (VRA)
REGEM	Release of Genetically Engineered Microorganisms [*A conference*]
REGEN........	Regenerate (NAKS)
regen..........	Regenerate [*Computer science*] (WDMC)
REGEN........	Regeneration (AAG)
REGEN........	Regenerative Generator [*Electronics*] (ECII)
regen..........	Regeration [*Computer science*] (WDMC)
Regenrn.......	Regeneron Pharmaceuticals, Inc. [*Associated Press*] (SAG)
REGENT......	Reduce Geography in No Time (SAA)
REGEXP......	Regular Expression [*Computer science*] (NHD)
Reg Gen	Regulae Generales [*A publication*] (DLA)
RegHlt.........	Regency Health Services, Inc. [*Associated Press*] (SAG)
REGI...........	Registry, Inc. (The) [*NASDAQ symbol*] (SAG)
ReGI...........	Renninger & Graves, Inc., Philadelphia, PA [*Closed*] [*Library symbol*] [*Library of Congress*] (LCLS)
REGIM........	Regimental (ROG)
REGING.......	Registering (ROG)
Regional Rail Reorg Ct...	Special Court Regional Railroad Reorganization Act [*A publication*] (DLA)
Regis..........	Regis Corp. [*Associated Press*] (SAG)
REGIS........	Register (AABC)
Regis..........	Registration (AL)
REGIS........	Relational General Information System
ReGIS.........	Remote Graphics Instruction Set (HGAA)
Registry......	Registry, Inc. (The) [*Associated Press*] (SAG)
Reg J Social Issues...	Regional Journal of Social Issues [*A publication*]
REGL	Regal Cinemas [*NASDAQ symbol*] (TTSB)
REGL	Regal Cinemas, Inc. [*NASDAQ symbol*] (SAG)
REGL	Regimental
REGL	Regional
regl.............	Regional (DD)
Regl............	Regional (PHSD)
Regl............	Reglement [*Administrative Ordinance or Rule of Procedure*] [*French*] (ILCA)
ReglCin........	Regal Cinemas, Inc. [*Associated Press*] (SAG)
Reg Lib........	Register Book [*A publication*] (DLA)
Reg Lib........	Registrar's Book, Chancery [*A publication*] (DLA)
REGLN........	Regulation (AAG)
REGLON.......	Regulation (ROG)
REGLOS.......	Reserve and Guard Logistic Operations-Streamline [*Army*] (AABC)
REGM.........	Register Module
Reg Maj	Books of Regiam Majestatem [*Scotland*] [*A publication*] (DLA)
REGN.........	Regeneron Pharmaceuticals [*NASDAQ symbol*] (SPSG)
REGN.........	Regional
REGN.........	Registry Number
REG-NEG	Regulatory Negotiation
RegnFn........	Regions Financial Corp. [*Associated Press*] (SAG)
reg nsy	Regular Nursery [*Neonatology*] (DAVI)
Regnt..........	Regent Bancshares Corp. [*Associated Press*] (SAG)
RegntBc.......	Regent Bancshares Corp. [*Associated Press*] (SAG)

ReGo .... Reinventing Government [*Nickname for National Performance Review*]
Reg Om Brev... Registrum Omnium Brevium [*Register of Writs*] [*Latin A publication*] (DLA)
Reg Orig...... Registrum Originale [*Latin A publication*] (DLA)
Reg Pl .... Regula Placitandi [*Rule of Pleading*] [*Latin*] [*Legal term*] (BARN)
REGPOWREN... Regulating Petty Officer WREN [*Women's Royal Naval Service*] [*British military*] (DMA)
RegProf .... Regius Professor [*The King's Professor*] [*British*]
REGR .... Recent Hail [*Meteorology*] (DA)
REGR .... Register (ROG)
REGR .... Registrar
REGR .... Regulator (AAG)
REGRA .... Regression Analysis [*Military*] (IAA)
Regs .... Registered Tonnage (EBF)
REGS .... Regulations
Regs Conn State Agencies... Regulations of Connecticut State Agencies (AAGC)
REGSTD....... Registered
REGSTR....... Registrar
REGSTRTN... Registration
REGT .... Regent
REGT .... Regiment (AABC)
REGT .... Regulator
RegtAsst..... Regent Assisted Living, Inc. [*Associated Press*] (SAG)
REGTL .... Regimental
Reg TM...... Registered Trademark (BARN)
REGUL .... Regular (ROG)
REGULAT.... Regulation
Reg Umb ..... Regio Umbilici [*Region of the Umbilicus*] [*Pharmacy*]
regurg........ Regurgitation [*Medicine*] (DAVI)
Reg US Pat Off... Registered at the United States Patent Office (BARN)
Reg Writ..... Register of Writs [*A publication*] (DLA)
REGY .... Registry (ROG)
REH .... Random Evolutionary Hits
REH .... Rational Expectations Hypothesis [*Economics*]
REH .... Rehoboth Beach [*Delaware*] [*Airport symbol*] (AD)
REH .... Rehoboth Beach, DE [*Location identifier FAA*] (FAAL)
REH .... Renin Essential Hypertension [*Medicine*] (DMAA)
REHAB .... Rehabilitate [*or Rehabilitation*] (AFM)
REHAB .... Rehabilitation
Rehab Aust... Rehabilitation in Australia [*A publication*]
Rehabcre..... Rehabilicare, Inc. [*Associated Press*] (SAG)
RehabG....... RehabCare Group, Inc. [*Associated Press*] (SAG)
RehabGp...... RehabCare Group, Inc. [*Associated Press*] (SAG)
REHABIL...... Rehabilitation
REHABIT ...... Reitan Evaluation of Hemispheric Abilities and Brain Improvement Training [*Neuropsychology test*]
Reh Allowed... Rehearing Allowed [*Used in Shepard's Citations*] [*Legal term*] (DLA)
REHB .... Rehabilicare, Inc. [*NASDAQ symbol*] (SAG)
REHC .... Random Evolutionary Hits per Codon
Reh Den ...... Rehearing Denied [*Used in Shepard's Citations*] [*Legal term*] (DLA)
Reh Dis .... Rehearing Dismissed [*Used in Shepard's Citations*] [*Legal term*] (DLA)
Reh'g .... Rehearing [*Legal term*] (DLA)
REHIS .... Royal Environmental Health Institute of Scotland [*British*]
REHNRAP ... Recreational, Entertainment, and Health Naturally Radioactive Products (NRCH)
REHR .... Reactor Heat Removal (COE)
REHT .... Reheat (KSC)
REHVA .... Representatives of European Heating and Ventilating Associations
REI .... Range from Entry Interface (NASA)
REI........... Rat der Europaeischen Industrieverbaende [*Council of European Industrial Federations*]
REI.......... Real Estate Investment Trust of America (MHDW)
REI............ Real Estate Issues [*American Society of Real Estate Counselors*] [*A publication*]
REI............ Recognition and Engraving Institute (NTPA)
REI............ Recognition Equipment, Inc. (IAA)
REI............ Recreational Equipment Inc. [*Commercial firm*]
REI............ Regiment Etranger d'Infanterie [*Foreign Infantry Regiment*] [*French*]
REI............ Reidovoe [*Former USSR Seismograph station code, US Geological Survey*] (SEIS)
REI............ Religion and Ethics Institute (EA)
REI............ Request for Engineering Information (NG)
REI............ Request for Engineering Investigation [*Nuclear energy*] (NRCH)
REI............ Research-Engineering Interaction (IEEE)
REI............ Reusable External Insulation [*of space shuttle*] [*NASA*]
REI............ Runway-End Identification [*Aviation*] (NASA)
REI............ Rural Economics Institute (OICC)
REIB........... Report Established in Block [*Aviation*] (FAAC)
REIC........... Radiation Effects Information Center [*Battelle Memorial Institute*] [*Defunct*]
REIC........... Rare Earth Information Center (NITA)
REIC........... Renewable Energy Info Center (EA)
REIC........... Research Industries Corp. [*NASDAQ symbol*] (NQ)
Reid PL Dig... Reid's Digest of Scotch Poor Law Cases [*A publication*] (DLA)
REIG........... Rare-Earth Iron Garnet (IAA)
REIL........... Real Estate Investing Letter [*Harcourt Brace Jovanovich, Inc.*] [*No longer available online*] [*Information service or system*] (CRD)
REIL........... Runway-End Identification Lights [*Aviation*]
Reilly.......... Reilly's English Arbitration Cases [*A publication*] (DLA)
Reilly EA ..... Reilly's European Arbitration. Lord Westbury's Decisions [*A publication*] (DLA)

REI(M)......... Regiment Etranger d'Infanterie (de Marche) [*Foreign Marching Infantry Regiment*] [*French*]
REIM........... Reimburse (AABC)
REIMB .... Reimburse (MSA)
REIMBJTR ... Reimbursement [*in Accordance with*] Joint Travel Regulations [*Military*] (DNAB)
REIN .... Real Estate Information Network [*Database*]
REIN .... Recovery Engineering [*NASDAQ symbol*] (TTSB)
REIN .... Recovery Engineering, Inc. [*NASDAQ symbol*] (SAG)
REIN .... Reinforce
Rein .... Reinstated [*Regulation or order reinstated*] [*Used in Shepard's Citations*] [*Legal term*] (DLA)
REINCH........ Reinsch Test [*For urine mercury and arsenic*] (DAVI)
REINET .... Real Estate Information Network [*National Association of Realtors*] [*Information service or system*] (IID)
REINF .... Refund Information File [*IRS*]
REINF .... Reinforce (AAG)
REINFD .... Reinforced (AAG)
REINFG .... Reinforcing (AAG)
REINFM .... Reinforcement (AAG)
REINIT .... Reinitialize (MCD)
REINS .... RADAR-Equipped Inertial Navigation System
REINS .... Requirements Electronic Input System [*NASA*] (KSC)
ReinsGp....... Reinsurance Group of America [*Associated Press*] (SAG)
REINSR........ Reinsurance
REINV .... REfernce Invoice (FAAC)
REIPA .... Real Estate Information Providers Association (NTPA)
REIQ .... Refrigeration Installation Equipment (SAA)
REIS........... Readiness Information System [*Army*]
REIS........... Reconstitutable and Enduring Intelligence System
REIS........... Regional Economic Information System [*Department of Commerce*] [*Information service or system*] (IID)
REIS........... Regional Energy Information System [*Minnesota State Department of Energy and Economic Development*] [*St. Paul*] [*Information service or system*] (IID)
REIS........... Research and Engineering Information Services [*Exxon Research & Engineering Co.*] (IID)
REIS........... Reseau Europeen Integre d'Image et de Services [*European Integrated Network of Image and Services*] (EAIO)
REIT........... Real Estate Investment Trust [*Associated Press*] (SAG)
REIT........... Reiteration [*Printing*] (ROG)
REITS .... Racial Equality in Training Schemes (AIE)
REIV........... Rocket Engine Injector Valve
REJ............ Imperial Airlines [*British*] [*FAA designator*] (FAAC)
REJ............ Redig, SD [*Location identifier FAA*] (FAAL)
REJ............ Reject (MSA)
rej............ Reject (IDOE)
rej............ Rejection (IDOE)
REJ............ Religious Education Journal of Australia [*A publication*] (APTA)
REJASE........ Reusing Junk as Something Else [*Conversion of junk into reusable items*]
Rejasing...... Reusing Junk as Something Else (BARN)
REJD........... Rejoined (WGA)
REJEN.......... Remote Job Entry [*Computer science*] (MHDI)
REJIS.......... Regional Justice Information Service [*St. Louis, MO*]
REJN........... Rejoin (AABC)
REJO........... Rod Easterling and Jim Osburn [*Automobile named for designers*]
REJU........... Reject Unit [*IRS*]
REK............ Reykjavik [*Iceland*] [*Airport symbol*] (OAG)
REKR........... Royal East Kent Rgiment [*British*] (WDAA)
REKY .... Royal East Kent Yeomanry [*Military unit*] [*British*]
REL............ Radiation Evaluation Loop [*Nuclear energy*] (NRCH)
REL............ Radio Electrician [*Navy British*]
REL............ Radio Engineering Laboratories
REL............ Rapidly Extensible Language System [*Computer science*] (CSR)
REL............ Rare-Earth LASER
REL............ Rassemblement Europeen de la Liberte [*European Liberty Rally*] [*France Political party*] (PPE)
REL............ Rate of Energy Loss
REL............ Reactor Equipment Ltd. [*Nuclear energy*] (NRCH)
REL............ Recommended Exposure Limit
REL............ Regional Education Laboratory
REL............ Related
REL............ Relation
rel............ Relation (DD)
REL............ Relations
Rel............ Relations (TBD)
REL............ Relative
rel............ Relative (IDOE)
REL............ Relativity
Rel............ Relatore [*Reporter*] [*Italian*] (ILCA)
REL............ Relay (AAG)
REL............ Release (AAG)
rel............ Released (WDAA)
REL............ Reliability
REL............ Reliance Group Hldgs [*NYSE symbol*] (TTSB)
REL............ Reliance Group Holdings, Inc. [*Formerly, Leasco Corp.*] [*NYSE symbol*] (SPSG)
REL............ Relic
REL............ Relie [*Bound*] [*Publishing*] [*French*]
REL............ Relief (AAG)
rel............ Relief (VRA)
REL............ Religion
REL............ Reliquary and Illustrated Archaeologist [*A publication*] (ROG)
REL............ Reliquiae [*Remains*] [*Latin*]

Rel	Reliquiae [of Suetonius] [Classical studies] (OCD)
REL	Relizane [Algeria] [Seismograph station code, US Geological Survey Closed] (SEIS)
REL	Relocatable [Computer science]
REL	Reluctance (DEN)
REL	Rescue Equipment Locker (AAG)
REL	Resting Expiratory Level [Medicine] (DMAA)
REL	Restricted Energy Loss
REL	Trelew [Argentina] [Airport symbol] (OAG)
RELA	Real Estate Leaders of America [Montgomery, AL] (EA)
RELACDU	Released from Active Duty [Navy] (DNAB)
RELACS	RADAR Emission Location Attack Control System
Rel & Pub Order...	Religion and the Public Order [A publication] (DLA)
RELARN	Russian Electronic Academic and Research Network (DDC)
RELAT	Related
RELATN	Relation (ROG)
RELAY	Relayed Correlation Spectroscopy (DMAA)
RELB	Reading Efficiency Level Battery [R. Carver] (TES)
RelBcp	Reliance Bancorp [Associated Press] (SAG)
RELBL	Reliability
RelbLfe	[The] Reliable Life Insurance Co. [Associated Press] (SAG)
RELBY	When Relieved By [Army]
RELC	Regional Language Centre [SEAMEO] [Singapore] [Research center] (IRC)
RELC	Reliability Committee [NASA]
RELCODE	Relative Code (NITA)
RELCT	Relocate (FAAC)
RELCTD	Relocated
RELCV	Regional Educational Laboratory for the Carolinas and Virginia
RELD	Rare-Earth LASER Device
RELD	Relieved (WGA)
RELDET	When Relieved Detached [Duty Indicated]
Rel d Griech...	Die Religion der Griechen [A publication] (OCD)
RELDIRDET...	When Relieved and When Directed Detached [Duty Indicated]
RELE	Ariely Advertising Ltd. [NASDAQ symbol] (SAG)
RELE	Radio Electrician
RELE	Release (ROG)
RELE	Resistive Exercise of Lower Extremities [Medicine] (DMAA)
Rel Ed	Religious Education [A publication] (BRI)
RELEF	Ariely Advertising Ltd [NASDAQ symbol] (TTSB)
RELET	Refernce Letter (FAAC)
RelGrp	Reliance Group Holdings, Inc. [Formerly, Leasco Corp.] [Associated Press] (SAG)
REL HUM	Relative Humidity (WDAA)
RELI	Real Estate Law Institute (EA)
RELI	Reliance Bancshares [NASDAQ symbol] (TTSB)
RELI	Reliance Bancshares, Inc. [NASDAQ symbol] (SAG)
RELI	Religion Index [American Theological Library Association] [Information service or system]
RELIA	Regional European Long Lines Agency (IAA)
Reliab	Reliability, Inc. [Associated Press] (SAG)
ReliaS	ReliaStar Financial Co. [Associated Press] (SAG)
ReliaStar	ReliaStar Financial Co. [Associated Press] (SAG)
ReliBsh	Reliance Bancshares, Inc. [Associated Press] (SAG)
relig	Religion (VRA)
RELIG	Religion [or Religious]
RELIP	Radially Extended Linear Impeller Propulsion [Submarine technology]
RELIPOSIS...	Research Liaison Panel on Scientific Information Services (NITA)
reliq	Reliquary (VRA)
RELIQ	Reliquiae [Remains] [Latin]
RELIQ	Reliquum [The Remainder] [Pharmacy]
Reliv	Reliv International, Inc. [Associated Press] (SAG)
RELKIN	Relativistic Kinematics (PDAA)
RELL	Reinforced Education Learning Laboratory (EA)
RELL	Richardson Electr [NASDAQ symbol] (TTSB)
RELL	Richardson Electronics Ltd. [NASDAQ symbol] (NQ)
RELLA	Regional European Long-Lines Agency [Later, RALLA] (NATG)
RELLI	Reliable
RELMA	Robert E. Lee Memorial Association (EA)
RELMAP	Regional Lagrangian Model of Air Pollution [Marine science] (OSRA)
RELMAT	Relative Matrix (MCD)
RELOC	Relocate (AAG)
RELP	Real Estate Limited Partnership
RELPAS	Restricted Express Lists/Physiological Activity Section [National Science Foundation]
REL PRON	Relative Pronoun [Grammar] (WDAA)
RELQ	Release-Quiesce [Computer science]
REL-R	Reliability Report (AAG)
RELR	Revised and Expurgated Law Reports [India] [A publication] (DLA)
RELS	Real Estate Listing Service [Database] [MDR Telecom] [Information service or system] (CRD)
RELS	Redeye Launch Simulator (MCD)
RELS	Relations
Rel St	Religious Studies [A publication] (BRI)
RelStlAl	Reliance Steel & Aluminum Co. [Associated Press] (SAG)
Rel St Rev...	Religious Studies Review [A publication] (BRI)
RELT	Rauding Efficiency Level Test [R. Carver] (TES)
RELTD	Related
RELV	Reliv International, Inc. [NASDAQ symbol] (SAG)
RELY	Relational Technology, Inc. (MHDW)
RELY	Reliance Bancorp [NASDAQ symbol] (SAG)
REM	Rack Entry Module (PDAA)
REM	Radiation Equivalent Man (IAA)
REM	Radiation Exposure Module [Environmental science] (COE)

REM	Radioactivity Environmental Monitoring [Information service or system] (IID)
REM	Radio Electrical Mechanic [British military] (DMA)
REM	Random Entry Memory (ADA)
REM	Range Evaluation Missile
REM	Rapid Eye Movement
REM	Rare Earth Metal [Inorganic chemistry]
REM	Raumbildentfernungsmesser [Stereoscopic range-finder] [German military - World War II]
REM	Reaction Engine Module [NASA] (KSC)
REM	Recognition Memory [Semionics Associates] [Computer science]
REM	Recovery Exercise Module (MCD)
REM	Reentry Module
REM	Reflection Electron Microscopy
REM	Registered Environmental Manager
REMN	Registered Equipment Management [Air Force] (AFM)
REM	Release-Engage [or Engagement] Mechanism (NASA)
REM	Release Engine Mechanism (NASA)
REM	Release Engine Module (MCD)
REM	Release Escape Mechanism (MCD)
REM	Reliability Engineering Model (KSC)
REM	Remainder (MSA)
REM	Remark
Rem	Remigius [Flourished, 841-908] [Authority cited in pre-1607 legal work] (DSA)
Rem	Remington [Record label] [USA, Europe, etc.]
REM	Remit (AABC)
Rem	Remit (EBF)
Rem	Remittance (DLA)
REM	Remote [Alaska] [Seismograph station code, US Geological Survey] (SEIS)
REM	Remote Event Module [Computer science]
REM	Remove [or Removal] (AAG)
REM	Reserves Embarked [Navy] (NVT)
REM	Reticular Erythematous Mucinosis [Medicine] (DMAA)
REM	Return Electrode Monitor (DB)
REM	Riecam, SA [Honduras] [FAA designator] (FAAC)
REM	Rocket Engine Module (MCD)
rem	Roentgen Equivalent in Man (NAKS)
REM	Roentgen-Equivalent-Mammal [Irradiation unit]
REM	Roentgen-Equivalent-Man [Later, Sv] [Irradiation unit]
rem	Roentgen Equivalent Man (COE)
REMA	Refrigeration Equipment Manufacturers Association [Later, ARI] (MCD)
REMA	Repetitive Excess Mixed Anhydride [Medicine] (DMAA)
REMA	Rotating Electrical Machines Association [British] (DBA)
REMAB	Radiation Equivalent Manikin Absorption
REMAB	Remote Marshalling Base (MCD)
REMAC	Remote Data Acquistion Subsystem [Computer science] (MHDB)
REMAD	Remote Magnetic Anomaly Detection
Rem Am	Remedia Amoris [of Ovid] [Classical studies] (OCD)
REMAP	Record Extraction, Manipulation, and Print
REMAP	Regional Environment Management Allocation Process (PDAA)
REMAP	Rehabilitation Engineering Movement Advisory Panel (ACII)
REMARC	Retrospective Machine Readable Catalog [Carrollton Press, Inc.] [Arlington, VA Bibliographic database Online version of the US Library of Congress Shelflist]
REMAS	Radiation Effects Machine Analysis System (AAG)
REMAS	Remote Energy Monitor Alarm System [Computer science] (MHDI)
REMAT	Research Centre for Management of New Technology [Wilfrid Laurier University] [Canada Research center] (RCD)
REMBASS	Remotely Monitored Battlefield Area Sensor System (MCD)
REMBI	Real Estate Management Brokers Institute (NTPA)
REMBJTR	Reimbursement in Accordance with Joint Travel Regulations
REMC	Radio and Electronics Measurements Committee [London, England] (DEN)
REMC	REMEC Inc. [NASDAQ symbol] (TTSB)
REMC	Resin-Encapsulated Mica Capacitor
REMCA	Reliability, Maintainability, Cost Analysis (MCD)
REMCAL	Radiation Equivalent Manikin Calibration
REMCALC	Relative Motion Collision Avoidance Calculator (PDAA)
REMCE	Remittance (ROG)
REMCO	Committee on Reference Materials [ISO] (DS)
REMCO	Rear Echelon Maintenance Combined Operation [Military]
Rem Cr Tr	Remarkable Criminal Trials [A publication] (DLA)
REMD	Rapid Eye Movement Deprivation
Rem'd	Remanded [Legal term] (DLA)
REMDOS	Remote Disc Operating System (NITA)
Remdy	Remedy Corp. [Associated Press] (SAG)
REME	Royal Electrical and Mechanical Engineers [Military British]
REMED	Remedium [Remedy] [Pharmacy] (ROG)
Remedy	Remedy Corp. [Associated Press] (SAG)
REMES	Reference Message (FAAC)
REMG	Radioelectromyograph
Rem'g	Remanding [Legal term] (DLA)
REMI	Reliability Engineering and Management Institute (EA)
REMI	Resource Bancshares Mortgage Group [NASDAQ symbol] (SAG)
REMI	Resource Bancshares Mtg Gp [NASDAQ symbol] (TTSB)
REMIC	Real Estate Mortgage Investment Conduit [Federal National Mortgage Association]
REMICS	Real-Time Manufacturing Information Control System [Computer science] (MHDI)
REMIDS	Remote Minefield Identification and Deployment [or Display] System (MCD)

Remigi........	Remigius de Gonni [Deceased, 1554] [Authority cited in pre-1607 legal work] (DSA)
REMILOC	Required Inservice Manyears in Lieu of Controls [Military]
REMIS	Real Estate Management Information System (BUR)
REMIS	Reliability and Maintainability Information System [Air Force] (GFGA)
REMIT........	Remittance (DSUE)
REMIT........	Research Effort Management Information Tabulation
Remitt	Remittance (DLA)
REML..........	Radiation Effects Mobile Laboratory
REML..........	Removal (ROG)
REML..........	Restricted Maximum Likelihood [Statistics]
REML..........	Risley Engineering and Materials Laboratory (PDAA)
REM-M	Rapid Eye Movement-Movement Period
Remma	Reese, "Musik in the Middle Ages" [A publication]
REMMAN	Remainderman [Legal shorthand] (LWAP)
REMMPS	Reserve Manpower Management and Pay System [Marine Corps]
REMN	Radio Electrical Mechanician [British military] (DMA)
REMN	Remain (ROG)
REMOBE	Readiness for Mobilization Evaluation (MCD)
REMOD	Remodeling
REMON	Real-Time Event Monitor [Computer science] (IAA)
REMOS	Real-Time Event Monitor [Computer science] (IEEE)
REMOS	Resources Management Online System (HGAA)
REMOSS	Reliability Monitoring of Subcontractors/Suppliers (MCD)
REMOTE	Reflective Mossbauer Technique (PDAA)
REMP..........	Radiological Environmental Monitoring Program [Nuclear energy] (NRCH)
REMP..........	Rapid Eye Movement Period (PDAA)
REMP..........	Research and Evaluation Methods Program [University of Massachusetts] [Research center] (RCD)
REMP..........	Research, Engineering, Mathematics, and Physics Division [National Security Agency] [Obsolete]
REMP..........	Research Group for European Migration Problems
REMP..........	Roentgen-Equivalent-Man Period [Irradiation Unit] (MAE)
REMPAC	Reflectivity Measurements Pacific
REMPAN	Radiation Emergency Medical Preparedness and Assistance Network [World health organization]
REMPC	Remedial Planning Contractor (COE)
REMPI	Resonance Enhanced Multiple Photon Ionisation [Physics]
REMPI	Resonant Enhanced Multiphoton Ionization [Spectroscopy]
REMPI	Resonant Multiphoton Ionization [Physics]
REM-Q	Rapid Eye Movement - Quiescent Period
REMR	Remainder
REMR	Repair, Evaluation, Maintenance, Rehabilitation
REM-RAND...	Remington Rand Corp. [Later, a division of Sperry-Rand]
REMRO	Remote RADAR Operator (MCD)
REMS..........	Rapid Excavation and Maintenance System [for gas piping repair]
REMS..........	Rapid Eye Movement Sleep [Neurology] (DAVI)
REMS..........	Rapid Eye Movement State
REMS..........	Reduced Exposure Mining System
REMS..........	Reentry Measurement System
REMS..........	Refinery Evaluation Modeling System [Department of Energy] (GFGA)
REMS..........	Registered Equipment Management System [Air Force]
REMS..........	Remotely Employed Sensor [Military] (GFGA)
REMS..........	Robust Expert Maintenance System [US Army Tank-Automotive Command] (RDA)
REMS..........	Rohm Electronic Message System (CIST)
REMSA	Railway Electrical and Mechanical Supply Association (IAA)
REMSA	Railway Engineering Maintenance Suppliers Association (EA)
REM sleep...	Rapid Eye Movement Sleep (WDAA)
REMSTA	Remote Electronic Microfilm Storage Transmission and Retrieval
REMSTAR	Remote Electronic Microfilm in Storage Transmission and Retrieval [Computer science] (EECA)
REMSTAR	Remote Electronic Microfilm Storage Transmission and Retrieval (NITA)
REMT..........	Radiological Emergency Medical Team [Military] (AABC)
REMT..........	Relief Electronic Maintenance Technician
REMT..........	Remote
REMTDS	Rocket Engine and Motor Type Designation System
RemTp........	Remedy Temp, Inc. [Associated Press] (SAG)
Rem Tr	Cummins and Dunphy's Remarkable Trials [A publication] (DLA)
Rem Tr No Ch...	Benson's Remarkable Trials and Notorious Characters [A publication] (DLA)
REMUS	Routine for Executive Multi-Unit Simulation (PDAA)
REMX..........	RemedyTemp, Inc. [NASDAQ symbol] (SAG)
Remy..........	Remy's Reports [145-162 Indiana] [15-33 Indiana Appellate] [A publication] (DLA)
REN	Aero-Rent SA de CV [Mexico ICAO designator] (FAAC)
REN	Religion and Ethics Network (EA)
REN	Remote Enable (IEEE)
Ren.............	Renaissance [Record label]
REN	Renaissance
ren..............	Renal [Medicine] (MAE)
REN	Rename File [Computer science]
REN	Rencon Mining Co. [Vancouver Stock Exchange symbol]
REN	Renewable
REN	Renewal
REN	Renin [An enzyme]
Ren.............	Renner's Gold Coast Colony Reports [A publication] (DLA)
REN	Reno [Nevada] [Seismograph station code, US Geological Survey Closed] (SEIS)
ren..............	Renovetur [Renew] [Pharmacy] [Latin] (MAE)
REN	Ringer Equivalence Number [Telephones]
REN	Rollins Environmental Services, Inc. [NYSE symbol] (SPSG)
REN	Rollins Environ Sv [NYSE symbol] (TTSB)
RenaCap......	Renaissance Capital Growth & Income Fund III [Associated Press] (SAG)
Renais.........	Renaissance (VRA)
RenaissRe ..	RenaissanceRe Holdings Ltd. [Associated Press] (SAG)
RenalT........	Renal Treatment Centers, Inc. [Associated Press] (SAG)
RenalTrt......	Renal Treatment Centers, Inc. [Associated Press] (SAG)
RENAMO	Resistencia Nacional Mocambicana [Mozambique]
Ren & Ref...	Renaissance and Reformation [A publication] (BRI)
RENAT	Revolutsiya, Nauka, Trud [Revolution, Science, Labor] [Given name popular in Russia after the Bolshevik Revolution]
RenCm........	Renaissance Communications Corp. [Associated Press] (SAG)
REND	Rendered (ADA)
REND	Rendezvous (NAKS)
RENDD	Rendered (ROG)
RendeR.......	Reversible Non-Linear Dimension Reduction
RENDOCK	Rendezvous and Docking [Aerospace] (MCD)
RENDZ	Rendezvous (KSC)
RenE	Renaissance Entertainment Corp. [Associated Press] (SAG)
RENE	Rocket Engine/Nozzle Ejector
Reneg..........	Renegotiation (AAGC)
RenEnt........	Renaissance Entertainment Corp. [Associated Press] (SAG)
RENEW	Republican Network to Elect Women
RENEW	Resourcing Enabling, Network for Evangelical Women
RENFE	Red Nacional de los Ferrocariles Espanoles [Spanish National Railways] (EY)
RENG	Radio Electronic News Gathering (NTCM)
RENG	Research Engineers, Inc. [NASDAQ symbol] (SAG)
R ENG..........	Royal Engineers [Military British] (ROG)
RenHtl	Renaissance Hotel Group NV [Associated Press] (SAG)
RENL	Runway End Light [Aviation] (FAAC)
RENM	Ready for Next Message (IAA)
RENM	Request for Next Message
RENMR	Reconnaissance Medium Range [Army]
RENN	Renaissance Cap Growth & Inc Fd [NASDAQ symbol] (TTSB)
RENN	Renaissance Capital Growth & Income Fund III [NASDAQ symbol] (SAG)
Renn..........	Renner's Reports, Notes of Cases, Gold Coast Colony and Colony of Nigeria [1861-1914] [A publication] (DLA)
RENO	Reno Air [NASDAQ symbol] (TTSB)
RENO	Reno Air, Inc. [NASDAQ symbol] (SAG)
RenoAir	Reno Air, Inc. [Associated Press] (SAG)
RENOT	Regional Notice [FAA]
RENOT	Regional Office Notice [Aviation] (FAAC)
RENOVAND...	Renovandus [To Be Renewed] [Pharmacy] (ROG)
RENPE	Rare and Endangered Native Plant Exchange (EA)
Ren Q	Renaissance Quarterly [A publication] (BRI)
RENRAD	Rendezvous RADAR [NASA] (NASA)
RenRe	RenaissanceRe Holdings Ltd. [Associated Press] (SAG)
RENS	Radiation Effects on Network Systems
RENS	Reconnaissance, Electronic Warfare, and Naval Intelligence System
RENS	Renaissance Solutions [NASDAQ symbol] (TTSB)
RENS	Renaissance Solutions, Inc. [NASDAQ symbol] (SAG)
REN SEM	Renovetur Semel [Renew Once] [Pharmacy]
RenSolu.......	RenaissanceRe Solutions, Inc. [Associated Press] (SAG)
RENSONIP ...	Reconnaissance Electronic Warfare, Special Operations, and Naval Intelligence Processing (MCD)
RENT	Reentry Nose Tip [Air Force]
RENT	Rental
RENT	Rentrak Corp. [NASDAQ symbol] (NQ)
Rentch	Rentech, Inc. [Associated Press] (SAG)
Renters........	Renters Choice, Inc. [Associated Press] (SAG)
RentlSrv	Rental Service Corp. [Associated Press] (SAG)
RENU	Reconstruction Education for National Understanding [An association] (EA)
RENUNCN	Renunciation (ROG)
RENV	Renovate (AABC)
REO	Ransom Eli Olds [Acronym used as name of automobile manufactured by Ransom E. Olds Co.]
REO	Rare-Earth Oxide
REO	Rea Gold [AMEX symbol] (TTSB)
REO	Rea Gold Corp. [Toronto Stock Exchange symbol Vancouver Stock Exchange symbol]
REO	Real Estate Owned [Banking]
REO	Receptive-Expressive Observation [Sensorimotor skills test]
REO	Regenerated Electrical Output
REO	Regional Environmental Offices [Air Force] (DOMA)
REO	Regional Executive Officer [British]
REO	Reinforcements (DSUE)
REO	Respiratory and Enteric Orphan [Virus] (MAE)
REO	Responsible Engineering Office [Military] (AFIT)
REO	Rio Airways, Inc. [ICAO designator] (FAAC)
REO	Rome, OR [Location identifier FAA] (FAAL)
REOC	Report When Established on Course [Aviation] (FAAC)
REOC	Royal Enfield Owners Club (EA)
REON	Rocket Engine Operations - Nuclear (IEEE)
REOP	Reopening [Investment term]
ReOpt	Remedial Option [Computer science]
REOPT	Reorder Point [Army]
REORG........	Reorganize (EY)
REOS	Racal Electronic Optical System [Software package] [Racal Imaging Systems]
REOS	Rare-Earth Oxysulfide
REOS	Reflective Electron Optical System
REOT	Right-End-of-Tape

REOU .... Radio and Electronic Officers' Union [*British*] (DCTA)
Rep .... Coke's English King's Bench Reports [*1572-1616*] [*A publication*] (DLA)
Rep .... De Republica [*of Cicero*] [*Classical studies*] (OCD)
REP .... Die Republikaner [*Republican Party*] [*Germany Political party*] (PPW)
Rep .... General system Design [*Computer science*]
Rep .... Knapp's Privy Council Reports [*England*] [*A publication*] (DLA)
REP .... RADAR Effects Processor (MCD)
REP .... RADAR Evaluation Pod [*Spacecraft*]
REP .... Radical Education Project [*Students for a Democratic Society*]
REP .... Radioelektronnoye Podavleniye [*Radio Electronic Suppression*] [*Soviet counterintelligence*] (LAIN)
REP .... Radiological Emergency Plan [*Nuclear energy*] (NRCH)
REP .... Railway Equipment and Publication Co., The, New York NY [*STAC*]
REP .... Range Error Probable [*Military*]
REP .... Range Estimation Program (MCD)
REP .... Rapid Electrophoresis
REP .... Reaction Energy Profile
REP .... Reasonable Efforts Program [*Environmental Protection Agency*] (EPA)
REP .... Recovery and Evacuation Program [*Marine Corps*]
REP .... Reentrant Processor [*Telecommunications*]
REP .... Reentry Physics Program
REP .... Regional Employment Premium [*British*]
REP .... Registered Environmental Professional
REP .... Rehabilitation Engineering Program [*Research center*] (RCD)
REP .... Relativistic Electron Precipitation [*Meteorology*]
REP .... Reliability Evaluation Program (IAA)
REP .... Rendezvous Evaluation Pad [*NASA*] (KSC)
REP .... Rendezvous Exercise Pod (SAA)
REP .... Repair (AAG)
REP .... Repeal (ROG)
REP .... Repeat (AAG)
rep .... Repeat (WDMC)
Rep .... Repertoire (DLA)
REP .... Repertory (ADA)
rep .... Repertory (ODBW)
REP .... Repertory Theater (DSUE)
rep .... Repertory Theatre (ODBW)
REP .... Repetatur [*Let It Be Repeated*] [*Pharmacy*]
REP .... Repetition (DSUE)
rep .... Repetition (WDMC)
REP .... Repetitive Extragenic Palindrome [*or Palindromic*] [*Genetics*]
REP .... Replace (NVT)
REP .... Replication [*Telecommunications*] (TEL)
REP .... Report (AAG)
rep .... Report (WDMC)
rep .... Reporter (WDMC)
REP .... Reporter
REP .... Report Evaluation Program (SAA)
REP .... Reporting Point [*Aviation*]
REP .... Representative (AAG)
rep .... Representative (ODBW)
Rep .... Representative (WDAA)
Rep .... Representing (DLA)
REPI .... Reprimand (DSUE)
Rep .... Reprint (DLA)
rep .... Reprint (WDMC)
REP .... Reproducing Programs [*Computer science*]
REP .... Reproductive Endocrinology Program [*University of Michigan*] [*Research center*] (RCD)
REP .... Repsol SA ADS [*NYSE symbol*] (SPSG)
REP .... Republic (EY)
Rep .... Republic (WDAA)
Rep .... Republican
Rep .... Republican (WA)
REP .... Repulsion
REP .... Reputation (DSUE)
rep .... Reputation (WDAA)
REP .... Request for Proposal (MUGU)
REP .... Research and Economic Programs [*Department of the Treasury*] (GRD)
REP .... Research Expenditure Proposal
REP .... Reserve Enlisted Program [*Military*]
REP .... Resonance Escape Probability [*Nuclear energy*] (NRCH)
REP .... Retrograde Pyelogram [*Medicine*]
REP .... Rework Excellence Program [*Navy*] (DNAB)
REP .... Richardson Emergency Psychodiagnostic Summary [*Psychology*]
REP .... Road Environment Pollutant [*Automotive corrosion testing*]
REP .... Rocket Engine Processor
REP .... Roentgen-Equivalent-Physical [*Irradiation unit*]
rep .... Roentgen Equivalent Physical (DOG)
REP .... Siem Reap [*Cambodia*] [*Airport symbol*] (AD)
REP .... Unnecessary Repetition [*Used in correcting manuscripts, etc.*]
Rep .... Wallace's "The Reporters" [*A publication*] (DLA)
REP 63 .... Reserve Enlistment Program 1963 (MCD)
REPA .... Registered Environmental Property Assessor
REPA .... Rural Environment Planning Association [*Australia*]
REPACCS .... Remote Cable-Pair Cross-Connect System [*Telecommunications*] (ITD)
REPAIR .... Reperfusion in Acute Infarction, Rotterdam [*Cardiology study*]
REPAIRS ..... Readiness Evaluation Program for Avionics Intermediate Repair Simulation (MCD)
Rep & Ops Atty Gen Ind... Indiana Attorney General Reports [*A publication*] (DLA)
Repap .... Repap Enterprises Corp., Inc. [*Associated Press*] (SAG)

REPAS .... Research, Evaluation, and Planning Assistance Staff [*AID*]
Rep Ass Y ... Clayton's English Reports, York Assizes [*A publication*] (DLA)
REPAT .... Repatriate (AABC)
REPB .... Republic (MSA)
REPB .... Republic Bancshares [*NASDAQ symbol*] (TTSB)
REPB .... Republic Bancshares, Inc. [*NASDAQ symbol*] (SAG)
REPB .... Republic Bank [*NASDAQ symbol*] (NQ)
RepBcp .... Republic Bancorp, Inc. [*Associated Press*] (SAG)
REPBX .... Reference Private Branch Exchange Message (SAA)
REPC .... Regional Economic Planning Council [*British*]
REPC .... Representation Commissioner [*Canada*]
REPC .... Research and Educational Planning Center [*University of Nevada - Reno*] [*Research center*] (RCD)
REPC .... Research and Engineering Policy Council [*DoD*]
Rep Cas Eq... Gilbert's English Chancery Reports [*1705-27*] [*A publication*] (DLA)
Rep Cas Inc Tax... Reports of Cases Relating to Income Tax [*1875*] [*A publication*] (DLA)
Rep Cas Madr... Reports of Cases, Diwani Adalat, Madras [*A publication*] (DLA)
Rep Cas Pr... Cooke's Practice Cases [*1706-47*] [*England*] [*A publication*] (DLA)
REPCAT .... Report Corrective Action Taken [*Military*]
Rep Ch .... Reports in Chancery [*1615-1710*] [*England*] [*A publication*] (DLA)
Rep Ch Pr.... Reports on Chancery Practice [*England*] [*A publication*] (DLA)
REPCO .... Replacement Parts Co.
Rep Com Cas... Commercial Cases, Small Cause Court [*1851-60*] [*Bengal, India*] [*A publication*] (DLA)
Rep Com Cas... Report of Commercial Cases [*1895-1941*] [*A publication*] (DLA)
REPCOMDESPAC... Representative of Commander Destroyers, Pacific Fleet
REPCON .... Rain Repellant and Surface Conditioner (PDAA)
Rep Const Ct... South Carolina Constitutional Court Reports [*A publication*] (DLA)
Rep Cr L Com... Reports of Criminal Law Commissioners [*England*] [*A publication*] (DLA)
REPCY .... Repair Cycle
Rep de Jur Com... Repertoire de Jurisprudence Commerciale [*Paris*] [*A publication*] (DLA)
Rep de Not... Repertoire de Notariae [*Paris*] [*A publication*] (DLA)
REPDN .... Reproduction (AFM)
REPDU .... Report for Duty [*Military*]
REPEA .... Research and Engineers Professional Employees Association
REPEET .... Reusabler Engines, Partially External Expendable Tankage (PDAA)
REPEM- CEAAL... Red de Educacion Popular Entre Mujeres Afiliada al Consejo de Educacion de A dultos de America Latino [*Women's Network of the Council for Adult Education in Latin American*] [*Ecuador*] (EAIO)
RepEnv .... Republic Environmental Systems, Inc. [*Associated Press*] (SAG)
Rep Eq........ Gilbert's Reports in Equity [*England*] [*A publication*] (DLA)
REPERF .... Reperforator [*Telecommunications*] (TEL)
REPERMSG... Report in Person or by Message to Command or Person Indicated
RepEStl .... Republic Engineered Steels, Inc. [*Associated Press*] (SAG)
REPET.......... Repetatur [*Let It Be Repeated*] [*Pharmacy*]
REPET .... Repetition (IAA)
REPFORMAINT... Representative of Maintenance Force
RepGrp .... Republic Group [*Associated Press*] (SAG)
REPH .... Republic Health Corp. (EFI3)
Rep Hawaii Att'y Gen... Hawaii Attorney General Report [*A publication*] (DLA)
REPHO .... Reference Telephone Conversation (NOAA)
REPI .... Ross Educational Philosophical Inventory (EDAC)
REPIDISCA... Red Panamericana de Informacion y Documentacion en Ingenieria Sanitaria y Ciencias del Ambiente [*Pan American Network for Information and Documentation in Sanitary Engineering and Environmental Sciences*] [*WHO*] [*United Nations*] (DUND)
REPIN .... Reply If Negative [*Military*]
Rep in CA.... Court of Appeal Reports [*New Zealand*] [*A publication*] (DLA)
Rep in Can... Reports in Chancery [*21 English Reprint*] [*A publication*] (DLA)
Rep in Ch.... Reports in Chancery [*21 English Reprint*] [*A publication*] (DLA)
Rep in Cha... Bittleston's Chamber Cases [*1883-84*] [*A publication*] (DLA)
Rep in Ch (Eng)... Reports in Chancery [*21 English Reprint*] [*A publication*] (DLA)
Rep in C of A... Reports in Courts of Appeal [*New Zealand*] [*A publication*] (DLA)
RepInd........ Republic Industries, Inc. [*Associated Press*] (SAG)
REPISIC....... Report Immediate Superior in Command [*Navy*]
Rep Jur........ Repertorium Juridicum [*Latin A publication*] (DLA)
REPL........... Replace (AAG)
repl .... Replacement (DLA)
REPL........... Replacement (ECII)
repl .... Replica (VRA)
REPLAB .... Responsive Environment Programmed Laboratory (IEEE)
Replgn .... Repligen Corp. [*Associated Press*] (SAG)
REPLN .... Replenish (AABC)
REPLTR .... Report by Letter (NVT)
REPM.......... Rare Earth Permanent Magnet
REPM.......... Repairman (NATG)
REPM.......... Representatives of Electronic Products Manufacturers [*Later, ERA*]
RePMA........ Release Paper Manufacturers Association [*British*] (DBA)
Rep Mass Att'y Gen... Report of the Attorney General of the State of Massachusetts [*A publication*] (DLA)
Rep MC .... Reports of Municipal Corporations [*A publication*] (DLA)
REPMC .... Representative to the Military Committee [*NATO*]
REPMES ...... Reply by Message (FAAC)
REPMIS ...... Reserve Personnel Management Information System [*Military*]
REPML .... Reply by Mail (FAAC)
REPMSG...... Report by Message (DNAB)
REPNAVRESCEN... Report to Naval Reserve Center (DNAB)
Rep NC Att'y Gen... North Carolina Attorney General Reports [*A publication*] (DLA)
Rep Neb Att'y Gen... Report of the Attorney General of the State of Nebraska [*A publication*] (DLA)
RepNY .... Republic New York Corp. [*Associated Press*] (SAG)

REPO .... Remote Emergency Power Off (CIST)
REPO .... Reporting Officer [*Navy*]
REPO .... Repossess
REPO .... Repurchase Agreement [*Also, RP*] [*Investment term*]
Repo .... Repurchase Agreement [*Finance*] (DFIT)
repol .... Repolarization [*Cardiology*] (DAVI)
REPOL .... Reporting Emergency Petroleum, Oils, and Lubricants [*Environmental science*] (COE)
REP-OP ...... Repetitive Operation [*Computer science*] (MDG)
Reports .... Coke's English King's Bench Reports [*1572-1616*] [*A publication*] (DLA)
REPOS .... Dealers Repurchase Agreement (TDOB)
REPOS .... Repurchase Agreement (EBF)
REPPAC ...... Repetitively Pulsed Plasma Accelerator
Rep Pat Cas... Reports of Patent, Design, and Trade Mark Cases [*England*] [*A publication*] (DLA)
Rep Pat Des & Tr Cas... Reports of Patent, Design, and Trade Mark Cases [*A publication*] (DLA)
Rep QA .... Reports Tempore Queen Anne [*11 Modern*] [*A publication*] (DLA)
REPR .... Real Estate Planning Report [*Military*] (AABC)
REPR .... Repair (ROG)
repr .... Represent (WDAA)
REPR .... Representative
REPR .... Repressurization (MCD)
repr .... Reprint [*Publishing*] (WDAA)
REPR .... Reprinted
reprd .... Reproduction (VRA)
repres .... Representation (VRA)
Reprint .... English Reports, Full Reprint [*A publication*] (DLA)
REPRO .... Reproduce (KSC)
REPRO .... Reproduction (NAKS)
repro .... Reproduction (ODBW)
REPROC ...... Reprocess (MCD)
REPROD ...... Receiver Protective Device (DEN)
REPROD ...... Reproduction
REPROM ...... Reprogrammable Programmable Read-Only Memory [*Computer science*] (TEL)
REPROM ...... Reprogrammable Read-Only Memory (NITA)
REPRON ...... Representation (ROG)
REPROTOX... Reproductive Toxicology Center [*Database*] [*Washington, DC*]
REPRO TYP... Reproduction Typing (DGA)
Repr Stat NZ... Reprint of the Statutes of New Zealand [*A publication*] (DLA)
REPS .... Regional Economic Projections Series [*NPA Data Services, Inc.*] [*Information service or system*] (CRD)
REPS .... Regional Emissions Projection System [*Environmental Protection Agency*]
REPS .... Repetitive Electromagnetic Pulse Simulator [*Army*] (RDA)
REPS .... Representative
REPS .... Republic Engineered Steels [*NASDAQ symbol*] (TTSB)
REPS .... Republic Engineered Steels, Inc. [*NASDAQ symbol*] (SAG)
REPS .... Royal Engineers Postal Section [*British military*] (DMA)
RepSc .... Republic Security Financial [*Associated Press*] (SAG)
RepSec .... Republic Security Financial [*Associated Press*] (SAG)
REPSHIPS.... Reports of Shipments [*Military*]
REPSNO...... Report through Senior Naval Officer
Repsol .... Repsol SA [*Associated Press*] (SAG)
REPT .... Receipt
rept .... Receipt (WDAA)
REPT .... Repeat (ADA)
REPT .... Repetatur [*Let It Be Repeated*] [*Pharmacy*]
REPT .... Report
REPT .... Represent (ROG)
rept .... Reprint (BJA)
REPT .... Reptron Electronics [*NASDAQ symbol*] (TTSB)
REPT .... Reptron Electronics, Inc. [*NASDAQ symbol*] (SAG)
Rep T F ...... Reports, Court of Chancery Tempore Finch [*1673-81*] [*A publication*] (DLA)
Rep T Finch... Reports, Court of Chancery Tempore Finch [*1673-81*] [*A publication*] (DLA)
Rep T Finch (Eng)... Reports, Court of Chancery Tempore Finch [*1673-81*] [*England*] [*A publication*] (DLA)
Rep T Hard... Lee's English King's Bench Reports Tempore Hardwicke [*1733-38*] [*A publication*] (DLA)
Rep T Hardw... Lee's English King's Bench Reports Tempore Hardwicke [*1733-38*] [*A publication*] (DLA)
Rep T Holt... Reports Tempore Holt, English Cases of Settlement [*A publication*] (DLA)
Rept Mtg AAAS... Report. Meeting of the Australasian Association for the Advancement of Science [*A publication*]
Rept Mtg ANZAAS... Report. Meeting of the Australian and New Zealand Association for the Advancement of Science [*A publication*]
REPTO .... Rear Engine Power-Take-Off [*Automotive engineering*]
REPTO .... Reparto
Rep T O Br... Carter's English Common Pleas Reports Tempore Orlando Bridgman [*A publication*] (DLA)
REPTOF ...... Reporting Officer (NATG)
Rep T QA..... Reports Tempore Queen Anne [*11 Modern*] [*A publication*] (DLA)
Reptr .... [*The*] Reporter [*Boston, Los Angeles, New York, Washington*] [*A publication*] (DLA)
REPTR ...... Reporter
REPTRANS... Report for Transportation
Rept Res .... Reporting Research [*Queensland, Department of Education, Research Branch*] [*A publication*]
Reptrn .... Reptron Electronics, Inc. [*Associated Press*] (SAG)
Rep T Talb... Reports Tempore Talbot, English Chancery [*A publication*] (DLA)

Rept T Finch... Cases Tempore Finch, English Chancery [*1673-81*] [*23 English Reprint*] [*A publication*] (DLA)
Rept T Holt... Cases Tempore Holt, English King's Bench [*A publication*] (DLA)
Rep T Wood... Manitoba Reports Tempore Wood [*Canada A publication*] (DLA)
repu .... Repousse (VRA)
REPUB .... Republican
RepubBk .... Republic Bank [*Associated Press*] (SAG)
RepubBsh .... Republic Bancshares, Inc. [*Associated Press*] (SAG)
REPUD .... Repudiate
REPULSE ...... Russian Efforts to Publish Unsavory Love Secrets of Edgar
repunit .... Repeating Unit [*Mathematics*] (BARN)
REPVE .... Representative (ROG)
RepWst .... Republic Waste Industries, Inc. [*Associated Press*] (SAG)
Rep York Ass... Clayton's English Reports, York Assizes [*A publication*] (DLA)
REQ .... Request (AAG)
REQ .... Require (AAG)
REQ .... Requisition
req .... Requisition (WDAA)
REQAFA .... Request Advise as to Further Action [*Army*] (AABC)
REQANA .... Requirements Analysis (MCD)
REQANS...... Request Answer By [*Date*] [*Military*]
REQAURQN... Request Authority to Requisition [*Army*] (AFIT)
REQCAPS ...... Requirements and Capabilities Automated Planning System (MCD)
REQD .... Required (AAG)
REQDI .... Request Disposition Instructions [*Army*] (AABC)
REQED .... Required Execution Date (MCD)
REQF .... Wrong Test Requested - Floor Error [*Medicine*] (DAVI)
REQFOLINFO... Request Following Information Be Forwarded This Office [*Army*] (AABC)
REQIBO...... Request Item Be Placed on Back Order [*Army*]
REQID .... Request if Desired (FAAC)
REQINT .... Request Interim Reply By [*Date*] [*Military*] (AABC)
REQL .... Wrong Test Requested - Laboratory Error [*Medicine*] (DAVI)
REQMNT .... Requirement (NVT)
REQMT ...... Requirement
REQN .... Requisition (AAG)
REQNOM...... Request Nomination
REQOON ...... Request Consideration (SAA)
REQP .... Recursive Equality Quadratic Program (PDAA)
REQPER...... Request Permission [*Navy*] (NVT)
REQRCM...... Request Your Recommendation (FAAC)
REQRE .... Require (ROG)
REQREC ...... Request Recommendation (NVT)
REQS .... Requires
REQSI .... Request Shipping Instructions [*Military*]
REQSSD .... Request Supply Status and Expected Delivery Date [*Army*] (AABC)
REQSTD .... Requested (FAAC)
REQSUPSTAFOL... Request Supply Status of Following [*Army*] (AABC)
REQT .... Request (ROG)
REQT .... Requirement (AAG)
REQTRAC .... Request Tracer Be Initiated [*Military*]
REQU .... Require (IAA)
REQUAL...... Requalify
REQUCHRD... Request Unit of Issue Be Changed to Read [*Army*] (AABC)
REQUEST.... Restricted English Question-Answering (HGAA)
REQUONS.... Requisitions
REQVER ...... Requirements Verification (IEEE)
RER .... Potrerillos [*Chile*] [*Airport symbol*] (AD)
RER .... RADAR Effects Reactor
RER .... Radiation Effects Reactor [*Nuclear energy*]
RER .... Radioelektronnaya Razvedka [*Reconnaissance and Intelligence*] [*Soviet counterintelligence*] (LAIN)
RER .... Radio Expenditure Report [*A publication*] (DOAD)
RER .... Railway Equipment Register
RER .... Receiver/Exciter Ranging [*NASA*]
RER .... Redundant Element Removal (IAA)
ReR .... Remington Rand Corp., Blue Bell, PA [*Library symbol Library of Congress*] (LCLS)
RER .... Renal Excretion Rate [*Medicine*] (MAE)
RER .... Representatives for Experiment Review [*Nuclear energy*] (NRCH)
RER .... Rerun (AAG)
RER .... Residual Error Rate
RER .... Resource Evaluation Report (MCD)
RER .... Respiratory Exchange Rate
RER .... Respiratory Exchange Ratio [*Medicine*] (DAVI)
RER .... Retlaw Resources, Inc. [*Vancouver Stock Exchange symbol*]
RER .... Reusable-Expendable-Reusable
RER .... Rough [*Surfaced*] Endoplasmic Reticulum [*Cytology*]
RER .... Rubberized Equipment Repair
RERA .... Recent Rain [*Meteorology*] (DA)
RERAD .... Reference Radio
RERAD .... Reradiation
RER & D...... Rehabilitative Engineering Research and Development Service [*Veterans Administration*] (GRD)
RERC .... Radiological Emergency Response Coordination [*Nuclear energy*] (NRCH)
RERC .... Rare Earth Research Conference (EA)
RERC .... Real Estate Research Corp.
Re/Re .... Reinforcement/Resupply [*To Europe*] (DOMA)
REREPS ...... Repair and Rehabilitation of Paved Surfaces (MCD)
REREQ ...... Reference Requisition (NOAA)
REREX .... Remote Readout Experiment
RERF .... Radiation Effects Research Foundation [*Formerly, ABCC*]
RERI .... Radiation Effect Research Institute

RERIC .... Regional Energy Resources Information Center [*Asian Institute of Technology*] [*British Information service or system*] (IID)
RERL .... Residual Equivalent Return Loss
Rer Nat Scr Graec Min... Rerum Naturalium Scriptores Graeci Minores [*A publication*] (OCD)
RERO .... Radiological Emergency Response Operation [*Nuclear energy*] (NRCH)
RERO .... Royal Engineers Reserve of Officers [*British*]
RERP .... Radiological Emergency Response Planning (NRCH)
RERTE .... Reroute [*Aviation*] (FAAC)
RERTR .... Reduced Enrichment in Research and Test Reactions [*Department of Energy*]
RERTR .... Research Enrichment in Research and Test Reactors Program [*Department of Energy*]
RES .... Eastman School of Music, Rochester, NY [*OCLC symbol*] (OCLC)
RES .... Office of Nuclear Regulatory Research [*Nuclear Regulatory Commission*]
RES .... Office of Research [*Bureau of Intelligence and Research*] [*Department of State*] [*Washington, DC*] (GRD)
RES .... On Reserved List [*Army British*] (ROG)
RES .... RADAR Environment Simulation (NATG)
RES .... RADAR Evaluation Squadron [*Military*]
RES .... Radiation Exposure State (NATG)
RES .... Radio-Echo Sounding [*Geophysics*]
RES .... Rapid Evaluation System (IAA)
RES .... Raytheon Electronic Systems
RES .... Readiness Estimation System (MCD)
RES .... Record Element Specification [*Computer science*]
RES .... Record Evaluation System
RES .... Reentry System (ADA)
RES .... Regional Environmental Study [*Australia*]
RES .... Rehabilitation Evolution System [*Medicine*]
RES .... Relative Electric Strength (MCD)
RES .... Relief Electronics Specialist
RES .... Remote Access Editing System [*Computer science*] (IAA)
RES .... Remote Entry Services (MCD)
RES .... Remote Entry Subsystem (IAA)
RES .... Remote Job Entry System (NITA)
RES .... Renaissance Energy Ltd. [*Toronto Stock Exchange symbol*]
RES .... Reprint Expediting Service
RES .... Resawed (WGA)
RES .... Rescue (WDAA)
RES .... Research (AAG)
res .... Research (IDOE)
Res .... Research (AL)
RES .... Reserve (CY)
res .... Reserve (WDAA)
Res .... Reserve (TBD)
Res .... Reserved (EBF)
RES .... Reservoir (AAG)
RES .... Reset
RES .... Residence
RES .... Residencial
RES .... Resident
RE3 .... Residual (KSC)
RES .... Residue
RES .... Resigned
RES .... Resilient [*Technical drawings*]
res .... Resin (VRA)
res .... Resistance (IDOE)
RES .... Resistance [*or Resistor*] (AAG)
RES .... Resistencia [*Argentina*] [*Airport symbol*] (OAG)
RES .... Resistor
res .... Resistor (IDOE)
Res .... Resolu [*Resolved, Decided*] [*French*] (ILCA)
RES .... Resolute [*Northwest Territories*] [*Seismograph station code, US Geological Survey*] (SEIS)
RES .... Resolute Bay [*Northwest Territories*] [*Geomagnetic observatory code*]
RES .... Resolution
res .... Resolution (IDOE)
Res .... Resolved [*Legal term*] (DLA)
RES .... Resolver (IAA)
RES .... Resonator [*Automotive engineering*]
RES .... Resources
Res .... Resources (TBD)
RES .... Respiratory Emergency Syndrome [*Medicine*] (DB)
RES .... Restauraciones Aeronauticas SA de CV [*Mexico ICAO designator*] (FAAC)
RES .... Restaurant (DSUE)
RES .... Restore
Res .... Resurrection (BJA)
RES .... Reticuloendothelial Society (EA)
RES .... Reticuloendothelial [*Medicine*]
RES .... Review of English Studies [*A publication*] (BRI)
RES .... Romance of Empire Series [*A publication*]
RES .... Royal Easter Show [*Australia*]
RES .... Royal Economic Society [*British*]
RES .... Royal Empire Society [*British*]
RES .... Royal Entomological Society [*British*]
RES .... RPC Energy Services, Inc. [*NYSE symbol*] (SPSG)
RES .... RPC, Inc. [*NYSE symbol*] [*Formerly, RPC Energy Services*] (SG)
ResA .... R & E Research Associates, Palo Alto, CA [*Library symbol Library of Congress*] (LCLS)
RESA .... Real Estate Settlement Act (COE)

RESA .... Regional Education Service Agency
RESA .... Research, Evaluation, and System Analysis [*Navy*]
RESA .... Research Society of America (IAA)
RESA .... Ring-Infected Erythrocyte Surface Antigen [*Immunochemistry*]
RESA .... Runway End Safety Area [*Aviation*] (DA)
RESA .... Scientific Research Society of America (EA)
RESAF .... Reserve of the Air Force
RESALIFT ... Reserve Airlift (NVT)
Res & Exp ... Research and Exploration [*A publication*] (BRI)
RESANTISUBCARIARGRU... Reserve Antisubmarine Warfare Carrier Air Group [*Navy*] (DNAB)
RESAR .... Reference Safety Analysis Report [*Nuclear energy*] (NRCH)
RESASWCARAIREGRU... Reserve Antisubmarine Warfare Carrier Air Group [*Navy*] (DNAB)
RESASWTRACEN... Reserve Antisubmarine Warfare Training Center [*Navy*] (DNAB)
RESAV .... Real Estate Salespersons' Association of Victoria [*Australia*]
RESAWA ...... Real Estate Salespersons' Association of Western Australia
RESC .... Reactor Subcriticality [*Environmental science*] (COE)
RESC .... Regional Educational Service Center
RESC .... Rescind (AAG)
RESC .... Rescue (AFM)
RESC .... Resource
RESC .... Resuscitation [*Medicine*] (DAVI)
RESC .... Roanoke Electric Steel [*NASDAQ symbol*] (TTSB)
RESC .... Roanoke Electric Steel Corp. [*NASDAQ symbol*] (NQ)
RESC .... Royal Engineers and Signal Corps [*Military British*] (IAA)
RescAm .... Resource America [*Commercial firm Associated Press*] (SAG)
RESCAN ...... Reflecting Satellite Communication Antenna
RESCAP ...... Rescue Combat Air Patrol [*Army*]
RESCAP ...... Resistor-Capacitor (IAA)
ResCare .... Res Care, Inc. [*Associated Press*] (SAG)
Res Cas .... Reserved Cases [*Ireland*] [*A publication*] (DLA)
RESCD .... Rescind [*Legal shorthand*] (LWAP)
RESCEN ...... Reserve Center [*Navy*] (DNAB)
RescM .... Resource Mortgage Capital, Inc. [*Associated Press*] (SAG)
resco .... Resin-Coated (VRA)
RESCOMMIS... Reserve Command Management Information System (DNAB)
RESCRU ...... Reserve Cruise [*Navy*] (NVT)
RESCU .... Radio Emergency Search Communications Unit
RESCU .... Remote Emergency Satellite Cellular Unit [*Ford Motor Co.*]
RESCU .... Rocket-Ejection Seat Catapult Upward [*Aviation*]
RESCUE ...... Recovery Employing Storage Chute Used in Emergencies [*Inflatable aircraft wing*]
RESCUE ...... Referring Emergency Service for Consumers' Ultimate Enjoyment [*Service plan of Recreational Vehicle Dealers of America*] (EA)
RESCUE ...... Remote Emergency Salvage and Clean Up Equipment
RESCUER ... Rocket Escape System with Cruise Using Electric Rotor (MCD)
RESD .... Reentry Environmental Systems Division [*General Electric Co.*] (MCD)
RESD .... Resigned
RESD .... Resolved (ROG)
RESDAT ...... Restricted Data [*Atomic Energy Act of 1954*]
RESDESDIV... Reserve Destroyer Division (DNAB)
RESDESRON... Reserve Destroyer Squadron (DNAB)
RESDICT ...... Reserve District
Research L & Econ... Research in Law and Economics [*A publication*] (DLA)
ResEdit .... Resource Editor [*Computer science*] (DOM)
ResEngn ...... Research Engineers, Inc. [*Associated Press*] (SAG)
RESEP .... Reentry System Environmental Protection
RESER .... Reentry Systems Evaluation RADAR [*Aerospace*]
reserva .... Reservation
Reserv Cas... Reserved Cases [*1860-64*] [*A publication*] (DLA)
RESERVE ..... Reserve Training [*USCG*] (TAG)
RESERVON... Reservation (ROG)
RESET .... Regression Specification Error Test [*Statistics*]
RESEX .... Resource Executive (IAA)
RESF .... Research and Engineering Support Facility (MCD)
RESFAC ...... Reserve Facility (DNAB)
RESFLD ...... Residual Field (AAG)
RESFLY ...... Respectfully (ROG)
RESFOR ...... AUTODIN CRT for Secure Reserve Force (MCD)
RESFORON... Reserve Force Squadron (DNAB)
RESG .... Research Engineering Standing Group [*DoD*]
Res Gamma Eta Gamma... Rescript of Gamma Eta Gamma [*A publication*] (DLA)
RESGD .... Resigned
RESGND ...... Resigned
RESH .... Recent Shower [*Meteorology*] (DA)
RESHAPE ..... Resource Self-Help/Affordability Planning Effort [*Program*] [*Federal government*] (RDA)
ReshInc .... Research, Inc. [*Associated Press*] (SAG)
ReshInd ...... Research Industries Corp. [*Associated Press*] (SAG)
ReshMed ...... Research Medical, Inc. [*Associated Press*] (SAG)
RESHUS ...... Reseau Documentaire en Sciences Humaines de la Sante [*Network for Documentation in the Human Sciences of Health*] [*Institut de l'Information Scientifique et Technique*] [*Information service or system*] (IID)
RESI .... Republic Environmental Systems [*NASDAQ symbol*] (TTSB)
RESI .... Republic Environmental Systems, Inc. [*NASDAQ symbol*] (SAG)
RES I .... Research EMP [*Electromagnetic Pulse*] Simulator I [*Air Force*]
RESIC .... Redstone Scientific Information Center [*Army*]
RES/IC .... Reserve - In Commission [*Vessel status*]
resid .... Residency
RESID .... Residual (AAG)
RESIG .... Resignation (AFM)
RESIL .... Resilient

RESIN .... Resina [*Resin*] [*Pharmacy*] (ROG)
Res Ipsa ...... Res Ipsa Loquitur [*The Thing Speaks for Itself*] [*Latin*] (DLA)
RES/IS .... Reserve - In Service [*Vessel status*]
RESIS .... Resistance
RESIS .... Resistor (IAA)
RESIST .... Replace Essential Supplies in Sufficient Time [*Navy*] (NVT)
RESIST .... Resistant
RESIST .... Resistor (WDAA)
RESIST .... Retirees to Eliminate State Income Source Tax [*An association*]
RESIST ex ..... Reusable Surface Insulation Stresses [*NASA computer program*]
resist ex ...... Resistive Exercises [*orhtopedics*] (DAVI)
RESIV .... Real Estate and Stock Institute of Victoria [*Australia*]
Res Judic .... Res Judicatae [*A publication*] (DLA)
RESL .... Radiological and Environmental Sciences Laboratory [*Nuclear energy*] (NRCH)
RESLAB .... Research Laboratory
RESLOAD ..... Resident Loader (MHDI)
RESLV .... Resolve (KSC)
RESM .... ResMed, Inc. [*NASDAQ symbol*] (SAG)
RESMA .... Railway Electric Supply Manufacturers Association [*Later, RSA*]
ResMed .... ResMed, Inc. [*Associated Press*] (SAG)
RESMILCON... Reserve Military Construction (DNAB)
RESN .... Recent Snow [*Meteorology*] (DA)
RESN .... Resonant
RESNA .... Rehabilitation Engineering and Assistive Technology Society of North America (NTPA)
RESNA .... RESNA [*Rehabilitation Engineering Society of North America*]: Association for the Advancement of Rehabilitation Technology [*Association retains acronym from former name*] (EA)
RESO .... Regional Environmental Support Office (DNAB)
RESO .... Resoluta [*Music*] (ROG)
RESOC .... Research Sonobuoy Configuration (NG)
RES/OC .... Reserve - Out of Commission [*Vessel status*]
RESOJET ...... Resonant Pulse Jet
RESOLN .... Resolution (MSA)
RESORS .... Remote Scanning Online Retrieval System (NITA)
RESORS .... Remote Sensing On-Line Retrieval System [*Canada Centre for Remote Sensing*] [*Department of Energy, Mines, and Resources Database*] [*Information service or system*] (IID)
RES/OS .... Reserve - Out of Service [*Vessel status*]
Resound ...... Resound Corp. [*Associated Press*] (SAG)
Resp .... De Respiratione [*of Aristotle*] [*Classical studies*] (OCD)
RESP .... Registered Education Savings Plan [*Canada*]
RESP .... Regulated Electrical Supply Package
ResP .... Research Publications, Inc., New Haven, CT [*Library symbol Library of Congress*] (LCLS)
RESP .... Respectively
RESP .... Respiration (KSC)
RESP .... Respirator
Resp .... Respiratory (CPH)
RESP .... Respironics, Inc. [*NASDAQ symbol*] (NQ)
RESP .... Respondent
resp .... Respondent (WDAA)
RESP .... Response (AAG)
Resp .... Response USA, Inc. [*Associated Press*] (SAG)
RESP .... Responsibility (NAKS)
RESP .... Responsible (AFM)
Resp .... Republica [*of Plato*] [*Classical studies*] (OCD)
RESPA .... Real Estate Settlement Procedures Act of 1974
RESP-A .... Respiratory Battery, Acute [*Medicine*] (DAVI)
RES PHYS ... Resident Physician (WDAA)
respir .... Respirations [*Medicine*] (DAVI)
Respirn .... Respironics, Inc. [*Associated Press*] (SAG)
RESPLY .... Respectively
RESPO .... Responsible Property Officer [*Army*] (AABC)
RespOnc ...... Response Oncology, Inc. [*Associated Press*] (SAG)
RESPOND .... Respondere [*To Answer*] [*Pharmacy*] (ROG)
Respons ...... Response USA, Inc. [*Associated Press*] (SAG)
RESPONSA... Retrieval of Special Portions from Nuclear Science Abstracts (DIT)
RESPT .... Respondent
Res Pub....... Res Publica [*A publication*] (ILCA)
RESPY .... Respectfully (ROG)
RESQ .... Research Queueing (MHDB)
RESR .... Research, Inc. [*NASDAQ symbol*] (NQ)
RESR .... Resources (AABC)
RESRC .... Resource
RESRC .... Resources
RESREP .... Resident Representative (MUGU)
RESRT .... Resort
RESRT .... Restart [*Computer science*]
RESRV .... Reserve
RESS .... RADAR Echo Simulation Study [*or Subsystem*]
RESS .... Rapid Expansion of Supercritical Solution [*Chemical engineering*]
RESS .... Recruiting Enlisted Selection System [*Military*] (DNAB)
RESSFOX ..... Recessed Sealed Sidewall Field Oxidation (AAEL)
RESSI .... Real Estate Securities and Syndication Institute (EA)
REST .... RADAR Electronic Scan Technique
REST .... RADAR Electronic Scan Test (IAA)
REST .... Rain Erosion Seed Test
REST .... Range Endurance Speed and Time [*Computer*]
REST .... Raynaud's Phenomenon, Esophageal Motor Dysfuntion, Sclerodactyly, and Telangiectasis Syndrome [*Medicine*] (DMAA)
REST Ip........ Reentry Environment and Systems Technology
REST/ .... Reentry System Test Program
REST .... Reporting System for Training [*Navy*] (NG)

REST .... Residence in Science and Technology
REST .... Respiratory Therapist (HCT)
REST .... Rest [*Commonly used*] (OPSA)
REST .... Restaurant (ROG)
REST .... Restitution [*Legal shorthand*] (LWAP)
rest .... Restorative [*Pharmacology*] (DAVI)
REST .... Restored
rest .... Restored (VRA)
REST .... Restor Industries [*NASDAQ symbol*] (TTSB)
REST .... Restor Industries, Inc. [*NASDAQ symbol*] (SAG)
REST .... Restrict (AAG)
REST .... Restricted Environmental Stimulation Technique
REST .... Restricted RADAR Electronic Scan Technique (IAA)
REST .... Routine Execution Selection Table [*Computer science*] (WDAA)
RESTA .... Reconnaissance, Surveillance, and Target Acquisition [*Military*] (AABC)
RESTAS ...... Reception Station System [*Army*]
RESTAT....... Reserve Components Status Reporting [*Army*] (AABC)
RESTD .... Restricted [*Security classification*] [*Military*]
RESTO .... Restaurant
RESTOR....... Restoration
Restor.......... Restor Industries, Inc. [*Associated Press*] (SAG)
RESTR .... Restaurant (WGA)
RESTR .... Restorer
RESTR .... Restrict (AABC)
RESTRACEN... Reserve Training Center
RESTRAFAC... Reserve Training Facility
Restric Prac... Reports of Restrictive Practices Cases [*A publication*] (DLA)
RESTS .... Restoration Survey
RESTT .... Respiratory Therapy Technician (HCT)
RESUB .... Resublimed
RESUP........ Resupply (AABC)
RESUPSHIP... Resident Supervisor of Shipbuilding Conversion and Repair (DNAB)
ResurP .... Resurgence Properties [*Associated Press*] (SAG)
RESURR ...... Resurrection
RESUS .... Resuscitation
RESV .... Reserve Fleet [*Navy*]
RESVD .... Reserved (ROG)
RESVON....... Reservation (ROG)
RESVR .... Réservoir (AAG)
RESY .... Reconditioned Sys [*NASDAQ symbol*] (TTSB)
RESY .... Residuary (ROG)
RESYNCING... Resynchronizing (GAVI)
RESYZ .... Reconditioned Sys Wrrt'B' [*NASDAQ symbol*] (TTSB)
RET............ Price REIT [*NYSE symbol*] (TTSB)
RET............ Price REIT, Inc. [*NYSE symbol*] (SAG)
RET............ RADAR Equipment Trailer (MCD)
RET............ Rad-Equivalent Therapy [*Radiology*]
R-ET............ Rational-Emotive Psychotherapy [*Also known as R-EP, RT*]
RET............ Rational-Emotive Therapy [*Medicine*] (WDAA)
RET............ Readiness Enhancement Technology [*Military*]
RET............ Regional Entry Test
RET............ Registered Engineering Technologist (DD)
RET............ Reiteration [*Printers' term*] (DSUE)
RET............ Reitman's (Canada) Ltd. [*Toronto Stock Exchange symbol*]
RET............ Relay Extractor Tool
RET............ Reliability Evaluation Test
RET............ Repetitive Extrasystole Threshold [*Cardiology*]
RET............ Resolution Enhancement Technology [*Printer feature*] [*Hewlett-Packard Co.*] [*Computer science*] (PCM)
RET............ Resonance Energy Transfer [*Physical chemistry*]
RET............ Retailer
RET............ Retain (AAG)
Ret............ Retained (WDAA)
RET............ Retard (AAG)
RET............ Reticulocyte [*Hematology*] (DAVI)
Ret............ Reticulum [*Constellation*]
RET............ Retired (AFM)
ret............ Retired (DD)
RET............ Retired after Finishing [*Yacht racing*] (IYR)
RET............ Retract
RET............ Return [*or Returnable*] (AAG)
RET............ Right Esotropia [*Ophthalmology*]
RET............ Ring Emitter Transistor
RET............ Road Equivalent Tariff [*To finance ferries*] [*British*] (DI)
RET............ Rost [*Norway*] [*Airport symbol*] (OAG)
RET............ Roster of Employees Transferred [*Army*]
RET............ Rotational Energy Transfer [*Chemical physics*]
RETA.......... Reactor Environmental Test Apparatus (MCD)
RETA.......... Refrigerating Engineers and Technicians Association (EA)
RETA.......... Retrieval of Enriched Textual Abstracts [*Information retrieval program*]\
RET-ABSTEE... Returned Absentee (DNAB)
RETAC .... Regional Educational Television Advisory Council
RETACT........ Real-Time Advanced Core and Thermohydraulic
RETAI.......... Real Estate Trainers Association, International (EA)
RETAIN .... Remote Technical Assistance and Information Network [*Computer science*]
RETAP .... Regular Education Teachers and Principals Project (EDAC)
RET BREV ... Retorna Brevium [*The Return of Writs*] [*Latin Legal term*] (DLA)
RETC.......... Railroad Equipment Trust Certificate
RETC.......... Rat Embryo Tissue Culture
RETC.......... Regional Emergency Transportation Center [*Military*]
RETC.......... Retention Curve [*U.S. EPA*]

RETC............ Retention Curve Computer Code [*Environmental Protection Agency*] (AEPA)
Ret Cath ...... Retention Catheter [*Medicine*] (CPH)
RETCO.......... Regional Emergency Transportation Coordinator [*Military*]
RETCON........ Retroactive Continuity [*Computer science*] (NHD)
RETD .... Retained
RETD .... Retired (EY)
RETD .... Returned
RETEN .... Retention [*Insurance*] (MCD)
RETEST........ Reinforcement Testing for System Training (SAA)
RETF............ Retired Document File [*IRS*]
RETG .... Retaining
RETI............ Communaute de Travail des Regions Europeennes de Tradition Industrielle [*Association of Traditional Industrial Regions of Europe*] [*Lille, France*] (EAIO)
R et I .... Regina et Imperatrix [*Queen and Empress*] [*Latin*]
Reti............ Reticulum [*Constellation*]
R et I .... Rex et Imperator [*King and Emperor*] [*Latin*]
RETIC.......... Reticulocyte [*Hematology*]
Retic Ct ...... Reticulocyte Count [*Hematology*] (CPH)
RETIMP........ Raleigh-Edwards Tensile Impact Machine Pendulum
RETIREX...... Retirement Exhibition [*British*] (ITD)
Retix............ Retix, Inc. [*Associated Press*] (SAG)
RETL............ Retail
RETL............ Rocket Engine Test Laboratory [*Air Force*]
RETM............ Rare Earth Transition Metal [*Computer science*]
RETMA........ Radio-Electronics-Television Manufacturers Association [*Later, Electronic Industries Association*]
RETMOB ...... Requirements for Total Mobilization Study
RETN............ Return (ROG)
RETNDU...... Return to Duty [*Military*] (DNAB)
RETNG........ Retraining
RETNN.......... Retention [*Insurance*]
RETNR.......... Retainer (ADA)
RETO .... Retouched (VRA)
RETO .... Review of Education and Training for Officers [*Military*] (RDA)
RETORC........ Research Torpedo Configuration (NG)
RETP............ Reliability Evaluation Test Procedure
RETP............ Reserve Entry Training Plan [*Canada*]
RETP............ Retape
RETR .... Retainer (ROG)
RETR .... Retention Register [*Computer science*]
RETR .... Retraced
RETR .... Retract (AAG)
RETR .... Retrieve (KSC)
RETRA........ Radio, Electrical, and Television Retailers' Association [*British*]
Retract........ Retractationes [*of Augustine*] [*Classical studies*] (OCD)
RETRAN...... Refined Trajectory Analysis
RETRANS.... Retransmit
RetiCre........ Retirement Care Associates, Inc. [*Associated Press*] (SAG)
RETRD.......... Retarded
RETREAD.... Retiree Training for Extended Active Duty [*Military*] (MCD)
RETREP...... Regional Emergency Transportation Representative
RETRF .... Rural Electrification and Telephone Revolving Fund [*Department of Agriculture*]
RETRG........ Retracting (WGA)
RETRNG...... Retraining
RETRO .... Regional Environmental Training and Research Organization [*Retraining program for unemployed space-industry workers*]
RETRO .... Retroactive (AAG)
RETRO .... Retro Controller [*NASA*] (NAKS)
RETRO .... Retrofire (KSC)
RETRO .... Retrofire Officer
RETRO .... Retrofit
RETRO .... Retrograde
RETRO .... Retro-Rocket (AAG)
Retro .... Retrospective Rate Derivation
RETROCON.. Retroactive Conversion (WDMC)
RETROEUR... Retrograde Europe [*Army*]
RETROF........ Retrofire (SAA)
RETRO FA.... Retroactive Family Allowance [*Military*] (DNAB)
RETROG...... Retrogressive
Retro pyelo... Retrograde Pyelogram [*Nephrology*] (DAVI)
Retrosp........ Retrospectively (DLA)
RETROSPEC... Retrospective Search System (NITA)
RETRV .... Retrieve (MCD)
RETS............ Radio Electronics Television School (IAA)
RETS............ Radiological Environmental Technical Specifications [*Nuclear energy*] (NRCH)
RETS............ Real-Time Sonobuoy (MCD)
RETS............ Recent Thunderstorm (DA)
RETS............ Reconfigurable Electrical Test Stand (NASA)
RETS............ Remoted Targets System (MCD)
RETS............ Renaissance English Text Society (EA)
RETSCP ...... Rocket Engine Thermal Strains with Cyclic Plasticity [*Propellant*]
RETSER ...... Retained in Service [*Military*] (DNAB)
RETSIE........ Renewable Energy Technologies Symposium and International Exposition [*Renewable Energy Institute*] (TSPED)
RETSPL........ Reference Equivalent Threshold Sound Pain [*or Pressure*] Level
RETT............ Relatively Easy to Test [*Audiology*]
Rett............ Rettie's Scotch Court of Session Cases, Fourth Series [*A publication*] (DLA)
Rettie.......... Rettie's Scotch Court of Session Cases, Fourth Series [*A publication*] (DLA)
RETUL .... Reticulum Cells [*On differential*] [*Hematology*] (DAVI)

RETULSIGN... Retain on Board until Ultimate Assignment Received
RETX .... Retix [*NASDAQ symbol*] (SPSG)
REU .... Air Austral [*France*] [*FAA designator*] (FAAC)
REU .... Air Reunion [*France ICAO designator*] (FAAC)
REU .... Radio Engineering Unit (IAA)
REU .... Rated Exposure Unit [*Advertising*] (NTCM)
REU .... Ready Extension Unit (MHDB)
REU .... Rectifier Enclosure Unit [*Power supply*] [*Telecommunications*] (TEL)
REU .... Requesting Expeditor Unit (DNAB)
REU .... Research Experiences for Undergraduates [*NSF grant program*]
REU .... Reunion [*ANSI three-letter standard code*] (CNC)
REU .... Reunion Island [*Seismograph station code, US Geological Survey*] (SEIS)
REU .... Reus [*Spain*] [*Airport symbol*] (OAG)
ReunInd........ Reunion Resources [*Associated Press*] (SAG)
REUNIR........ Reseau des Universites et de la Recherche [*Network of Universities and Research*] [*French*] [*Computer science*] (TNIG)
ReunRsc...... Reunion Resources [*Commercial firm Associated Press*] (SAG)
REUR............ Reference Your
REURAD ...... Reference Your Radio
REURTWX.... Reference Your TWX [*Teletypewriter communications*] (AAG)
REUSE .... Revitalize Effective Utilization of Supply Excess [*Navy*] (NG)
ReutrHd........ Reuters Holdings Ltd. [*Associated Press*] (SAG)
REV............ Range Extender Vehicle [*Gasoline-electric hybrid*]
REV/............ Ratio of Earth-to-Vehicle Radii
REV............ Reentry Vehicle [*Aerospace*]
REV............ Regulator of Virion-Protein Expression [*Genetics*]
REV............ Representative Elementary Volume [*Sampling for analysis*]
REV............ Reticuloendotheliosis Virus
Rev............ Revelation [*New Testament book*]
REV............ Revelstoke Companies Ltd. [*Toronto Stock Exchange symbol*]
REV............ Reventador [*Race of maize*]
REV............ Revenue
rev .... Revenue (WDAA)
REV............ Reverend
Rev............ Reverend (ASC)
REV............ Reversal Film [*Cinematography*] (NTCM)
REV............ Reverse (AAG)
rev .... Reverse (VRA)
rev .... Reversed (WDMC)
rev .... Review (WDMC)
REV............ Review (AFM)
rev .... Reviewed (WDMC)
rev .... Revise (WDMC)
REV............ Revise [*or Revision*] (AAG)
Rev............ Reviser (AL)
rev .... Revision (WDMC)
REV............ Revision (NAKS)
REV............ Revision Message [*Aviation*] (DA)
REV............ Revlon Inc'A' [*NYSE symbol*] (TTSB)
Rev............ Revocable (EBF)
REV............ Revocable [*Business term*]
REV............ Revolution (AAG)
rev .... Revolution (WDMC)
REV............ Revolve (WDAA)
REV............ Rotor Entry Vehicle [*Aerospace*]
REVA .... Recommended Vehicle Adjustment [*Military*] (AABC)
REVAB .... Relief Valve Augmented Bypass [*Nuclear energy*] (NRCH)
REV A/C ...... Revenue Account (WDAA)
Rev & TC .... Revenue and Taxation Code [*A publication*] (DLA)
REVAR........ Authorized Revisit Above-Mentioned Places and Vary Itinerary as Necessary
Rev C Abo PR... Revista de Derecho. Colegio de Abogados de Puerto Rico [*A publication*] (DLA)
Rev Can...... Revue Canadienne [*Quebec*] [*A publication*] (DLA)
Rev C & C Rep... Revenue, Civil, and Criminal Reporter [*Calcutta*] [*A publication*] (DLA)
Rev Can D Fam... Revue Canadienne de Droit Familial [*A publication*] (DLA)
Rev Can Dr Com... Revue Canadienne de Droit Communautaire [*A publication*] (DLA)
Rev Cas...... Revenue Cases [*A publication*] (DLA)
Rev Cas (Ind)... Revised Cases [*India*] [*A publication*] (DLA)
Rev Civ Code... Revised Civil Code [*A publication*] (DLA)
Rev Civ St ... Revised Civil Statutes [*A publication*] (DLA)
Revco .... Revco DS, Inc. [*Associated Press*] (SAG)
Rev Code Civ Proc... Revised Code of Civil Procedure [*A publication*] (DLA)
Rev Code Cr Proc... Revised Code of Criminal Procedure [*A publication*] (DLA)
REVCOM...... Revolutionary Committee [*China*]
REVCON...... Review Conference
Rev Contemp L... Review of Contemporary Law [*A publication*] (DLA)
REV CPY .... Review Copy (DGA)
Rev Cr Code... Revised Criminal Code [*A publication*] (DLA)
Rev Crit ...... Revue Critique de Legislation et de Jurisprudence de Canada [*A publication*] (DLA)
Rev Crit de Leg... Revue Critique de Legislation [*Paris*] [*A publication*] (DLA)
Rev Crit de Legis et Jur... Revue Critique de Legislation et de Jurisprudence [*Montreal*] [*A publication*] (DLA)
Rev Cubana de Derecho... Revista Cubana de Derecho [*Havana, Cuba*] [*A publication*] (DLA)
REVCUR...... Reverse Current (AAG)
REVD............ Reverend (ROG)
Rev'd .... Reversed [*Legal term*] (DLA)
Rev da Fac de Direito (Lisbon)... Revista. Faculdade de Direito. Universidade de Lisboa (Lisbon) [*A publication*] (DLA)

Rev de Derecho Esp y Amer... Revista de Derecho Espanol y Americano [*Madrid, Spain*] [*A publication*] (DLA)

Rev de Derecho Jurispr y Cienc Soc... Revista de Derecho, Jurisprudencia, y Ciencias Sociales y Gaceta de los Tribunales [*A publication*] (DLA)

Rev de Droit Contemp... Revue de Droit Contemporain [*Brussels, Belgium*] [*A publication*] (DLA)

Rev de Droit Hong... Revue de Droit Hongrois [*A publication*] (DLA)

Rev de Droit Penal Mil et de Droit de la Guerre... Revue de Droit Penal Militaire et de Droit de la Guerre [*A publication*] (DLA)

Rev de Droit Unif... Revue de Droit Uniforme [*A publication*] (DLA)

Rev de Droit Uniforme... Revue de Droit Uniforme [*A publication*] (DLA)

Rev de Fac de Direito (Sao Paulo)... Revista. Faculdade de Direito. Universidade de Sao Paulo [*Sao Paulo, Brazil*] [*A publication*] (DLA)

Rev de Jur... Revue de Jurisprudence [*Quebec*] [*A publication*] (DLA)

Rev de la Fac de Derecho (Caraboba)... Revista. Facultad de Derecho. Universidad de Caraboba [*Valencia, Venezuela*] [*A publication*] (DLA)

Rev de la Fac de Derecho (Caracas)... Revista. Facultad de Derecho. Universidad Catolica Andres Bello (Caracas) [*A publication*] (DLA)

Rev de la Fac de Derecho y Cienc Soc... Revista. Facultad de Derecho y Ciencias Sociales [*Montevideo, Uruguay*] [*A publication*] (DLA)

Rev de Leg... Revue de Legislation et de Jurisprudence [*Montreal*] [*A publication*] (DLA)

Rev de Legis... Revue de Legislation [*Canada*] [*A publication*] (DLA)

Rev del Inst de Derecho Comparado... Revista. Instituto de Derecho Comparado [*Barcelona, Spain*] [*A publication*] (DLA)

Rev de Sci Criminelle et de Droit Penal Compare... Revue de Science Criminelle et de Droit Penal Compare [*Paris, France*] [*A publication*] (DLA)

REV DEV...... Revolutionary Development [*South Vietnam*]

Rev Droit Int'l Moyen-Orient... Revue de Droit International pour le Moyen-Orient [*A publication*] (DLA)

Rev Droit Penal Militaire et Dr de la Guerre... Revue de Droit Penal Militaire et de Droit de la Guerre [*A publication*] (DLA)

Rev du Dr.... Revue du Droit [*Quebec*] [*A publication*] (DLA)

Rev D US..... Revue de Droit. Universite de Sherbrooke [*A publication*] (DLA)

REV ED...... Revised Edition (WDAA)

REVEL.......... Reverberation Elimination

REVERB....... Reverberation (NTCM)

reverb.......... Reverberation [*Sound*] (WDMC)

REVERB....... Reverberator [*Automotive engineering*]

REVERSY.... Reversionary (ROG)

Rev Et Anc.. Revue des Etudes Anciennes [*A publication*] (OCD)

Rev Et Grec.. Revue des Etudes Grecques [*A publication*] (OCD)

Rev Et Lat ... Revue des Etudes Latines [*A publication*] (OCD)

rev'g.......... Reversing [*Legal term*] (DLA)

Rev Gen ...... Revue Generale de Droit [*A publication*] (DLA)

Rev Gen D... Revue Generale de Droit [*A publication*] (DLA)

Rev Gen de Legis y Jurispr... Revista General de Legislacion y Jurisprudencia [*Madrid, Spain*] [*A publication*] (DLA)

Rev Gen Reg... Revised General Regulation, General Accounting Office [*United States*] [*A publication*] (DLA)

Rev Ghana L... Review of Ghana Law [*A publication*] (DLA)

Rev Hist Rel... Revue de l'Histoire des Religions [*A publication*] (OCD)

REVIEW....... Recording and Video Playback of Electronic Warfare Information

Rev Internac y Diplom... Revista Internacional y Diplomatica. Publicacion Mensual [*Mexico*] [*A publication*] (DLA)

Rev Internat Franc du Droit des Gens... Revue Internationale Francaise du Droit des Gens [*A publication*] (DLA)

Rev Int'l Comm Jur... Review. International Commission of Jurists [*A publication*] (DLA)

Rev Int'l des Droits de l'Antiquite... Revue Internationale des Droits de l'Antiquite [*A publication*] (DLA)

Rev Int'l Dr Auteur... Revue Internationale du Droit d'Auteur [*A publication*] (DLA)

Rev Int'l Droit Comp... Revue Internationale de Droit Compare [*A publication*] (DLA)

Rev Int'l Dr Penal... Revue Internationale de Droit Penal [*A publication*] (DLA)

Revised Rep... Revised Reports [*England*] [*A publication*] (DLA)

Rev Ivoirienne de Droit... Revue Ivoirienne de Droit [*A publication*] (DLA)

Rev J & PJ... Revenue, Judicial, and Police Journal [*Bengal*] [*A publication*] (DLA)

Rev Jud & Police J... Revenue, Judicial, and Police Journal [*A publication*] (DLA)

Rev Jur d'Alsace et de Lorraine... Revue Juridique d'Alsace et de Lorraine [*A publication*] (DLA)

Rev Jur de Buenos Aires... Revista Juridica de Buenos Aires [*A publication*] (DLA)

Rev Jur du Congo... Revue Juridique du Congo [*A publication*] (DLA)

REVL............ [*To Be*] Reviewed by Pathologist [*Laboratory science*] (DAVI)

Rev L & Soc... Review of Law and Social Change [*A publication*] (DLA)

Rev Leg....... Revue de Legislation et de Jurisprudence [*Quebec*] [*A publication*] (DLA)

Rev Leg....... Revue Legale [*Canada*] [*A publication*] (DLA)

Rev Legale.... Revue Legale [*A publication*] (DLA)

Rev Leg NS... Revue Legale. New Series [*Canada*] [*A publication*] (DLA)

Rev Leg (OS)... Revue Legale (Old Series) [*A publication*] (DLA)

RevMex......... Revolutionary Mexican Historical Society (EA)

REV/MIN...... Revolutions per Minute [*e.g., in reference to phonograph records*]

Rev Mod Phys... Reviews of Modern Physics (MEC)

REVN .... Reversion (ROG)

REVNRY....... Revolutionary

REVO .... Revoke (AABC)

REVO .... Revolution (DSUE)

REVOCN...... Revocation (ROG)

REVOCON .... Remote Volume Control

REVOCON .... Revocation

Rev of Polish Law and Econ... Review of Polish Law and Economics [*Warsaw, Poland*] [*A publication*] (DLA)

Rev of Sym... Review of Symptoms [*Medical Records*] (DAVI)

Rev of Sys... Review of Systems [*Medical records*] (DAVI)

REVOL......... Revolution (WGA)

REVON....... Reversion

REVOP....... Random Evolutionary Operation

Rev Ord....... Revised Ordinances [*A publication*] (DLA)

Rev Ord NWT... Revised Ordinances, Northwest Territories [*1888*] [*Canada*] [*A publication*] (DLA)

Rev Pen Code... Revised Penal Code [*A publication*] (DLA)

Rev Pol Code... Revised Political Code [*A publication*] (DLA)

Rev Pol L.... Review of Polish Law [*A publication*] (DLA)

REV PROC... Revenue Procedure [*Internal Revenue Service*]

REVR .... Receiver (AAG)

REVR .... Reversioner (ROG)

REVR .... Reviewer (AFM)

Rev R .... Revised Reports [*1759-1866*] [*England*] [*A publication*] (DLA)

Rev Reh ..... Reversed [*or Reversing*] on Rehearing [*Used in Shepard's Citations*] [*Legal term*] (DLA)

Rev Rep ..... Revised Reports [*England*] [*A publication*] (DLA)

Rev Rev (A)... Review of Reviews. Australian Edition [*A publication*]

REV RUL...... Revenue Ruling [*Internal Revenue Service*]

REVS .... Reconnaissance Electro-Optical Viewing System

REVS .... Requirements Engineering and Validation System

REVS .... Reverse Shot [*Photography*] (WDMC)

RevS .... Reverse Shot [*Filmmaking*] (WDMC)

REV/S........ Revolutions per Second

REVS .... Rotor Entry Vehicle System [*Aerospace*]

Rev Sel Code Leg... Review of Selected Code Legislation [*A publication*] (DLA)

Revs Geophys Space Phys... Reviews of Geophysics and Space Physics (MEC)

Rev St .... Revised Statutes [*A publication*] (DLA)

Rev Stat ..... Revised Statutes [*Various jurisdictions*] [*A publication*] (DLA)

Rev Suisse Dr Int'l Concurrence... Revue Suisse du Droit International de la Concurrence [*Swiss Review of International Antitrust Law*]

Rev Sw Dig... Revision of Swift's Digest of Connecticut Laws [*A publication*] (DLA)

RevTar........ Revenue Tariff [*Australia Political party*]

Rev Tax'n Indiv... Review of Taxation of Individuals [*A publication*] (DLA)

Rev Trimestr de Jurispr... Revista Trimestral de Jurisprudencia [*Rio De Janeiro, Brazil*] [*A publication*] (DLA)

Rev Tunisienne de Droit... Revue Tunisienne de Droit [*Tunis, Tunisia*] [*A publication*] (DLA)

REV VER...... Revised Version (WDAA)

REVW .... Review (NVT)

REVWR .... Reviewer (DGA)

REVY .... Reversionary (ROG)

REW.......... Incised Wound [*On Autopsy*] [*Pathology*] (DAVI)

REW.......... Read, Execute, Write [*Computer science*] (IAA)

REW.......... Recycle Water [*Nuclear energy*] (NRCH)

REW.......... Redwood Valley, CA [*Location identifier FAA*] (FAAL)

REW.......... Reward (AFM)

REW.......... Rewind (MDG)

REWARD..... Reading, Writing and Arithmetic Development System (EDAC)

REWDAC..... Retrieval by Title Words, Descriptors, and Classification (DIT)

REWK........ Rework (MSA)

REWRC....... Report When Established Well to Right of Course [*Aviation*] (FAAC)

REWS........ Radio Electronic Warfare Service (MCD)

REWSON..... Reconnaissance, Electronic Warfare, Special Operations, and Naval Intelligence Processing Systems

REWSONIP... Reconnaissance Electronic Warfare Special Operation and Naval Intelligence Processing (IAA)

REWTEL...... Radio and Electronics World Telecommunications (NITA)

REX.......... Radio Exploration Satellite (PDAA)

REX.......... Ram Air Freight, Inc. [*ICAO designator*] (FAAC)

REX.......... Rapid Text Search [*Computer science*] (IT)

REX.......... Rare-Earth Exchanged [*Faujasite, a zeolite*]

REX.......... Reactor Experimental [*Former USSR*] (DEN)

REX.......... Real-Time Executive Routine [*Computer science*]

REX.......... Real-Time Executive System [*Computer science*] (MHDI)

REX.......... Rechtswissenschaftliche Experten und Gutachter [*NOMOS Datapool*] [*Database*]

REX.......... Reduced Exoatmospheric Cross Section

REX.......... Reentry Experiment

REX.......... Reflector Erosion Experiment [*NASA*]

REX.......... Regression Expert [*Computer science*]

REX.......... Related Experience (SAA)

REX.......... Requisition Exception Code [*Air Force*] (AFIT)

REX.......... Research, Evaluation, and Experimental Program [*Bureau of the Census*] (GFGA)

REX.......... Resonance-Enhanced X-Ray [*Physics*]

REX.......... Rexburg [*Idaho*] [*Seismograph station code, US Geological Survey*] (SEIS)

REX.......... Rex Silver Mines [*Vancouver Stock Exchange symbol*]

REX.......... Reynosa [*Mexico*] [*Airport symbol*] (OAG)

REX.......... Robot Excavation [*Carnegie-Mellon Robotics Institute*]

REX.......... Rolodex Electronic Express

REX.......... Run Executive [*Computer science*]

REXA......... Radioisotope-Excited X-Ray Analyzer (PDAA)

Rexam........ Rexam PLC [*Associated Press*] (SAG)

Rexel......... Rexel, Inc. [*Associated Press*] (SAG)

Rexene .... Rexene Corp. [*Associated Press*] (SAG)

Rexhall....... Rexhall Industries [*Associated Press*] (SAG)

REXI.......... Resource America [*NASDAQ symbol*] (SAG)

REXI.......... Resource America'A' [*NASDAQ symbol*] (TTSB)

REXL.......... Rexhall Indus [*NASDAQ symbol*] (TTSB)

REXL.......... Rexhall Industries, Inc. [*NASDAQ symbol*] (NQ)

RexlSun.......	Rexall Sundown, Inc. [*Associated Press*] (SAG)
REXMIT.......	Retransmitted (AABC)
REXMY	Rexam PLC [*NASDAQ symbol*] (SAG)
REXMY	Rexam Plc ADR [*NASDAQ symbol*] (TTSB)
REXN	Rexon, Inc. [*NASDAQ symbol*] (NQ)
REXS	Radio Exploration Satellite [*Japan*]
RexStore......	Rex Stores Corp. [*Associated Press*] (SAG)
REXW	Rexworks, Inc. [*NASDAQ symbol*] (NQ)
Rexwks	Rexworks, Inc. [*Associated Press*] (SAG)
REXX	Restructured Extended Executor [*IBM command language*] (PCM)
REY..............	Aero-Rey SA de CV [*Mexico ICAO designator*] (FAAC)
REY..............	Reentry
REY..............	Reyes [*Bolivia*] [*Airport symbol*] (OAG)
REY..............	Reykjavik [*Iceland*] [*Seismograph station code, US Geological Survey*] (SEIS)
REY..............	Reynolds & Reynolds'A' [*NYSE symbol*] (TTSB)
REY..............	Reynolds & Reynolds Co. [*NYSE symbol*] (SPSG)
REY..............	Rush Ventures, Inc. [*Vancouver Stock Exchange symbol*]
ReyMt........	Reynolds Metals Co. [*Associated Press*] (SAG)
ReyMtl........	Reynolds Metals Co. [*Associated Press*] (SAG)
Reyn	Reynolds, Reports [*40-42 Mississippi*] [*A publication*] (DLA)
Reyn L Ins...	Reynold's Life Insurance [*A publication*] (DLA)
Reynolds	Reynolds, Reports [*40-42 Mississippi*] [*A publication*] (DLA)
Reynolds' Land Laws...	Reynolds' Spanish and Mexican Land Laws [*A publication*] (DLA)
ReyPrp........	Revenue Properties Co. Ltd. [*Associated Press*] (SAG)
ReyRey........	Reynolds & Reynolds Co. [*Associated Press*] (SAG)
REYRTWX....	Reference Your Telegraph Wire Exchange [*Telecommunications*] (IAA)
REZ..............	Airplanes, Inc. [*ICAO designator*] (FAAC)
REZ..............	Mary Esther, FL [*Location identifier FAA*] (FAAL)
REZ..............	Radioelektronnaya Zashchita [*Radioelectronic Defense*] [*Soviet counterintelligence*] (LAIN)
RF..............	Fournier [*France ICAO aircraft manufacturer identifier*] (ICAO)
RF..............	Franc [*Monetary unit*] [*Rwanda*]
RF..............	RADAR Frequency (IAA)
RF..............	Radial Fibers [*Ear anatomy*]
RF..............	Radial Flow (AAG)
RF..............	Radical Force (EA)
RF..............	Radio Facility
RF..............	Radio France (IAA)
RF..............	Radio Frequency [*Transmission*]
rf..............	Radio Frequency (GAVI)
RF..............	Railroad Financial (EFIS)
RF..............	Rainer Foundation [*British*] (BI)
RF..............	Rainfed [*Agriculture*]
RF..............	Rainform (MCD)
RF..............	Raised Face (MSA)
RF..............	Range-Finder [*Gunnery*]
RF..............	Rapeseed Flour [*Food technology*]
RF..............	Rapid-Fire
Rf..............	Rate of Flow [*Medicine*] (MAE)
RF..............	Rating Factor (IFFF)
RF..............	Reactive Factor (IAA)
RF..............	Head Forward
RF..............	Reason Foundation (EA)
RF..............	Reception Fair [*Radio logs*]
RF..............	Receptive Field [*of visual cortex*]
RF..............	Receptor Floor (DB)
RF..............	Recombination Frequency [*Genetics*] (DOG)
RF..............	Reconnaissance Fighter (MUGU)
RF..............	Reconnaissance Force
RF..............	Recovery Forces
RF..............	Recovery Forecast
RF..............	Recruitment for the Armed Forces [*British*]
RF..............	Rectus Femoris [*A muscle*] [*Anatomy*]
RF..............	Red Fumes (NATG)
RF..............	Reducing Flame
RF..............	Reef
RF..............	Reference [*Online database field identifier*]
RF..............	Reference Fuel
RF..............	Reflecting Platelet (DB)
RF..............	Reflight
RF..............	Refunding
RF..............	Regional Forces [*ARVN*]
RF..............	Registered Forester (WPI)
RF..............	Register File
RF..............	Register Finder
RF..............	Reitland-Franklin Unit (AAMN)
RF..............	Relative Flow [*Rate*]
RF..............	Relative Fluorescence [*Analytical chemistry*] (MAE)
Rf..............	Relative to the Solvent Front [*Paper chromatography*] [*Analytical chemistry*]
RF..............	Release Factor (NRCH)
RF..............	Releasing Factor [*Also, RH*] [*Endocrinology*]
RF..............	Reliability Factor
RF..............	Renal Failure [*Medicine*]
RF..............	Rent Free
RF..............	Replacement Factor [*Military*]
RF..............	Replicative Factor [*or Form*] [*Genetics*]
RF..............	Reply Finding [*Nuclear energy*] (NRCH)
RF..............	Reported Frequency (NTCM)
RF..............	Reporting File
RF..............	Representative Fraction
RF..............	Republique Francaise [*French Republic*]

RF..............	Reserve Flight [*British military*] (DMA)
RF..............	Reserve Force
RF..............	Resistance Factor
RF..............	Resonance Frequency (AAEL)
RF..............	Resorcinol-Formaldehyde [*Organic chemistry*]
RF..............	Respectable Frere [*Worshipful Brother*] [*Freemasonry*] [*French*] (ROG)
RF..............	Respiratory Failure [*Medicine*]
RF..............	Response Factor
RF..............	Retardation Factor
Rf..............	Retardation Factor [*Chromatography*] (DB)
RF..............	Retention File [*IRS*]
RF..............	Reticular Formation [*Sleep*]
RF..............	Retroperitoneal Fibromatosis [*Oncology*]
RF..............	Reverse Free
RF..............	Revolving Fund [*Finance*]
RF..............	Rex Francorum [*King of the Franks*] [*Latin*]
RF..............	Rheumatic Fever [*Medicine*]
RF..............	Rheumatoid Factor [*Also known as IgM*] [*Immunology*]
RF..............	Rhinal Fissure [*Anatomy*]
RF..............	Rhodesian Front [*Later, Republican Front*]
RF..............	Riboflavin [*Biochemistry*]
RF..............	Rice Flour (OA)
RF..............	Richmond Fellowship (EAIO)
RF..............	Rifampin [*Also, R/AMP, RIF, RMP*] [*Bactericide*]
RF..............	Riffle Frequency
RF..............	Riga-Fede [*Syndrome*] [*Medicine*] (DB)
RF..............	Rigging Fixtures (MCD)
RF..............	Right Field [*or Fielder*] [*Baseball*]
RF..............	Right Foot
RF..............	Right Forward [*Football*]
RF..............	Right Front
RF..............	Right Fullback [*Soccer*]
RF..............	Rigid Frame [*Revolver*] (DICI)
RF..............	Rinforzando [*With Special Emphasis*] [*Music*]
rf..............	Rinforzando [*Enforcing*] [*Italian*] (WDAA)
RF..............	Ring Frame
RF..............	Ripple Factor
rf..............	Rise of Floor (DS)
RF..............	Rockefeller Foundation
RF..............	Rodeo Foundation (EA)
RF..............	Roll Film [*Photography*]
RF..............	Roof (WGA)
rf..............	Roof (VRA)
RF..............	Roof Fan (OA)
RF..............	Root Canal, Filing of [*Dentistry*] (DAVI)
RF..............	Rosette Formation (DB)
RF..............	Rosicrucian Fellowship (EA)
RF..............	Rosicrucian Fraternity (EA)
RF..............	Rossair [*ICAO designator*] (AD)
RF..............	Rough Finish
RF..............	Routes Forestieres [*Forested Routes*] [*French*] (BARN)
RF..............	Royal Fusiliers [*Military unit*] [*British*]
RF..............	Royal Windsor Foresters [*British military*] (DMA)
RF..............	Ruled Feint [*Paper*] (DGA)
RF..............	Rundles-Falls [*Syndrome*] [*Medicine*] (DB)
RF..............	Running Forward
Rf..............	Rutherfordium [*Proposed name for chemical element 104*] [*See also Ku*]
RF..............	Sisters of St. Philip Neri Missionary Teachers [*Roman Catholic religious order*]
RF..............	Travelair Goteborg [*ICAO designator*] (AD)
RF1...........	Federal Reserve Bank of Boston, Boston, MA [*OCLC symbol*] (OCLC)
RFA...........	Blackrock FL Inv Qual Muni [*AMEX symbol*] (TTSB)
RFA...........	Blackrock Florida Investment Quality Municipal [*AMEX symbol*] (SPSG)
RFA...........	RADAR Filter Assembly
RFA...........	Radiation Field Analyzer
RFA...........	Radio Frequency Allocation (MCD)
RFA...........	Radio Frequency Amplifier
RFA...........	Radio Frequency Attenuator (MCD)
RFA...........	Radio Frequency Authorizations [*Air Force*]
RFA...........	Rainforest Foundation Australia
RFA...........	Raleigh Flying Service, Inc. [*ICAO designator*] (FAAC)
RFA...........	Rapid Flow Analysis
RFA...........	RCRA [*Resource Conservation and Recovery Act*] Facility Assessment
RFA...........	Recommendation for Acceptance (AAG)
RFA...........	Record File Address [*Computer science*] (CIST)
RFA...........	Recurrent Fault Analysis [*Telecommunications*] (TEL)
RFA...........	Refrigerated Foods Association (NTPA)
RFA...........	Regional Financial Associates Inc.
RFA...........	Registered Fitness Appraiser [*Canadian Association of Sports Sciences*]
RFA...........	Register Field Address (IAA)
RFA...........	Regulatory Flexibility Act
RFA...........	Regulatory Flexibility Analysis (AAGC)
RFA...........	Relieved from Assigned [*Military*]
RFA...........	Remote File Access
RFA...........	Remote Function Activator
RFA...........	Renewable Fuels Association (EA)
RFA...........	Request for Action (KSC)
RFA...........	Request for Alteration (AAG)
RFA...........	Request for Analysis

RFA .... Request for Application
RFA .... Request for Assistance (GFGA)
RFA .... Request for Grant Applications
RFA .... Reserve Forces Act
RFA .... Resident Functional Atlas (DMAA)
RFA .... Restrictive Fire Area [*Military*] (AABC)
RFA .... Retarding Field Analyzer [*Surface analysis*]
RFA .... Reynolds Family Association (EA)
RFA .... Rich Family Association (EA)
RFA .... Rickey Family Association (EA)
RFA .... Right Femoral Artery [*Anatomy*]
RFA .... Right Forearm [*Medicine*] (MEDA)
RFA .... Right Frontoanterior [*A fetal position*] [*Obstetrics*]
RFA .... Rimfire Adapter (MCD)
RFA .... Risley Family Association (EA)
RFA .... Rocky Flats Area Office (SAA)
RFA .... Roll Follow-Up Amplifier
RF-A .... Rotation Free-Aquatred [*Automobile tire system*]
RFA .... Royal Field Artillery [*Military British*]
RFA .... Royal Fleet Auxiliary [*British*]
RFA .... Rugby Fives Association [*British*] (BI)
RFA .... Rural Forestry Assistance [*Program*] [*Forest Service*]
RFAA .... Relieved from Attached and Assigned [*Army*]
RFAC .... Royal Fine Art Commission [*British*]
R-factor .... Release Factor (DB)
R factor .... Resistance Factor (DOG)
RFAD .... Released from Active Duty Not Result of Demobilization [*Navy*]
RFAD .... Request for Accelerated Delivery (MCD)
RFAED .... Readiness Forecast Authorization Equipment Data [*Air Force*] (AFM)
RFAF .... Request for Additional Fire (MCD)
RF/AFG .... Radio Frequency/Acoustic Firing Group [*Military*] (CAAL)
RFAGC .... Rainbows for All God's Children (EA)
RFALROU .... Request Follow-Up Action on Listed Requisitions Indicated Still Outstanding in Unit [*Army*] (AABC)
RF & OOA .... Railway Fuel and Operating Officers Association [*Later, IAROO*] (EA)
RFAO .... Rocky Flats Area Office [*Energy Research and Development Administration*]
RFAS .... Radio Frequency Attitude Sensor
RFASIX .... Reserve Forces Act of 1955, Six Months Trainee
RFASS .... Rapid Fire Artillery Support System (MCD)
RFAT .... Relieved from Attached [*Army*] (AABC)
RFATE .... Radio Frequency Automatic Test Equipment (MCD)
RFATHREE ... Reserve Forces Act of 1955, Three Months Trainee
RFB .... Air-Cushion Vehicle built by Rhein Flugzeugbau [*Usually used in combinati on with numerals*] [*Germany*]
RFB .... Ready for Baseline (NASA)
RFB .... Reason for Backlog [*Telecommunications*] (TEL)
RFB .... Recording for the Blind (EA)
RFB .... Recording for the Blind, Bethesda, MD [*OCLC symbol*] (OCLC)
RFB .... Registrar of Finance Brokers [*Victoria, Australia*]
RFB .... Reliability Functional Block
RFB .... Request for Bid (AFM)
RFB .... Retained Foreign Body [*Medicine*]
RFB .... Right Fullback [*Soccer*]
RFBA .... Reserve Forces Benefit Association [*Later, REA*] (EA)
RFB&D........ Recording for the Blind and Dyslexic
RFBC .... River Forest Bancorp [*NASDAQ symbol*] (NQ)
RFBD .... Recording for the Blind and Dyslexic [*An association*] (PAZ)
RFBK .... RS Financial Corp. [*Formerly, Raleigh Federal Savings Bank*] [*NASDAQ symbol*] (NQ)
RFBPA .... Raw Fat and Bone Processors Association [*British*] (BI)
RFBR .... Russian Foundation for Basic Research
RFC .... Radio Facility Charts (MCD)
RFC .... Radio Frequency Chart (AAG)
RFC .... Radio Frequency Choke (AAG)
RFC .... Radio Frequency Coil (IAA)
RFC .... Radio Frequency Communications
RFC .... Radio Frequency Compatibility
RFC .... Radio Frequency Controller [*Telecommunications*] (ECII)
RFC .... Radio Frequency Crystal
RFC .... Railroad Freight Classification
RFC .... Ranger Fan Club (EA)
RFC .... Rare Fruit Council [*Later, RFCI*] (EA)
RFC .... Ravan Fan Club [*Defunct*] (EA)
RFC .... Reason for Change (MCD)
RFC .... Recirculation Flow Control [*Nuclear energy*] (NRCH)
RFC .... Reconstruction Finance Corp. [*Abolished, 1957*]
RFC .... Reduced Function Computer [*Computer science*]
RFC .... Reference Concentration [*Toxicology*]
RfC .... Reference Concentration
RFC .... Regenerative Fuel Cell
RFC .... Registered Floor Clerk [*Investment term*] (NUMA)
RFC .... Relative Force Capability (NATG)
RFC .... Religious Formation Conference (EA)
RFC .... Remote Food Carriers [*Army*] (INF)
RFC .... Republicans for Choice (EA)
RFC .... Request for Change (KSC)
RFC .... Request for Change Revolution (NAKS)
RFC .... Request for Comment [*Telecommunications*] (PCM)
RFC .... Request for Confirmation (MCD)
RFC .... Request for Connection [*Telecommunications*] (OSI)
RFC .... Request for Contract (GFGA)
RFC .... Required Functional Capability [*Navy*]

RFC .... Research Facilities Center [*National Oceanic and Atmospheric Administration*] (GRD)
RFC .... Residual Functional Capacity [*Social Security Administration*] (OICC)
RFC .... Residuum Fluid Cracking [*Petroleum refining*]
RFC .... Resolution Funding Corp. [*Established by the Financial Institutions Reform, Recovery, and Enforcement Act of 1989*]
RFC .... Resources for Communication [*Information service or system*] (IID)
RFC .... Retirement-for-Cause [*Program*] [*Air Force*]
RFC .... Retrograde Femoral Catheter [*Medicine*] (DMAA)
RFC .... RFC Resource Finance Corp. [*Toronto Stock Exchange symbol*]
RFC .... RFC Resources Corp. [*Vancouver Stock Exchange symbol*]
RFC .... River Forecast Center [*National Weather Service*] (NOAA)
RFC .... Rosette-Forming Cell [*Immunochemistry*]
RFC .... Royal Flying Corps [*Later, RAF*] [*British*]
RFC .... Royal Flying Cross [*British*] (IIA)
RFC .... Rugby Football Club
RFCA .... Racing Fans Club of America (EA)
RFCA .... Rare Fruit Council of Australia
RFCA .... Reconstruction Finance Corporation Act [*Obsolete*]
RFCA .... Residual Functional Capacity Assessment [*Social Security Administration*] (GFGA)
RFCC .... Regional Freight Consolidation Center (AAGC)
RFCC .... Resid Fluid Catalytic Cracking [*Petroleum refining*]
RFCEA .... Revival Fires (Christian Evangelizers Association) (EA)
RFCG .... Radio Frequency Command Generator (MCD)
RFCI .... Rare Fruit Council International (EA)
RFCI .... Resilient Floor Covering Institute (EA)
RFCM .... Radio Frequency Control Monitor [*Formerly, RFU*] (MCD)
RFCMC .... Reconstruction Finance Corporation Mortgage Co.
RFCO .... Radio Facility Control Officer [*Military*] (IAA)
RFCO .... Radio Frequency Checkout (AAG)
RFCO .... Range Facility Control Officer [*Military*] (IAA)
RFCP .... Radio Frequency Compatibility Program
RFCP .... Request for Computer Program (NASA)
RFCP .... Requests for Contractual Procurement (MUGU)
RFCR .... Refacer
RFCS .... Radio Frequency Carrier Shift (NVT)
RFCS .... Recirculation Flow Control System [*Nuclear energy*] (NRCH)
RFCS .... Regenerative Fuel Cell Subsystem
RFCSEUSG.. Retirement Federation of Civil Service Employees of the United States Government [*Defunct*] (EA)
RFCT .... Report of Federal Cash Transactions (OICC)
RFCV .... Rural Finance Council of Victoria [*Australia*]
RFD .... Radiation Flux Density
RFD .... Radio Frequency Demodulator
RFD .... Radio Frequency Display (MCD)
RFD .... Raised Face Diameter (MSA)
RFD .... Raised Foredeck [*of a ship*] (DS)
RFD .... Reactor Flight Demonstration
RFD .... Read for Data (IAA)
RFD .... Ready for Data (IEEE)
RFD .... Ready for Delivery (MUGU)
RFD .... Ready for Duty
RFD .... Reentry Flight Demonstration
RfD .... Reference Dose [*Environmental science*]
RFD .... Reference Dose [*Toxicology*] (LDT)
RFD .... Reference Dose Values [*Environmental science*] (COE)
RFD .... Refund (WDAA)
RFD .... Refurbish for Delivery (MCD)
RFD .... Released for Delivery (NG)
RFD .... Remote Frequency Display (MCD)
RFD .... Reporting for Duty [*Air Force*]
RFD .... Request for Delivery
RFD .... Request for Deviation
RFD .... Request for Discussion [*Electronic newsgroups*]
RFD .... Request for Parts Disposition (MCD)
RFD .... Requirements Formulation Document [*NASA*] (NASA)
RFD .... Reserve Forces Duty [*Military*] (MCD)
RFD .... Residual Flux Density
RFD .... Reverse-Flow Diverter [*Engineering*]
RFD .... Rockford [*Illinois*] [*Airport symbol*] (OAG)
RFD .... Rockford Minerals, Inc. [*Toronto Stock Exchange symbol*]
RFD .... Rural Free Delivery [*of mail*]
RFDA .... Request for Deviation Approval
RFDB .... Red Flag Database [*Air Force*] (GFGA)
RFDC .... Radio Frequency Data Collection [*Electronic commerce*]
RFDL .... Radio Frequency Data Link (MCD)
RFDT .... Reliability Failure Diagnostic Team (AAG)
RFDU .... Reconfiguration and Fault Detection Unit
RFE .... Aero Fe SA [*Mexico ICAO designator*] (FAAC)
RFE .... Radio Free Europe
RFE .... Relative Fluorescence Efficiency (DB)
RFE .... Request for Effectivity (MCD)
RFE .... Request for Enhancement [*Computer science*] (NHD)
RFE .... Request for Estimate (KSC)
RFE .... Request for Expenditure
RFE .... Rotating Field Electrophoresis [*Analytical biochemistry*]
RFE .... Rutherfordton, NC [*Location identifier FAA*] (FAAL)
RFEA .... Radio Frequency Equipment Analyzer
RFEA .... Regional Further Education Adviser (AIE)
RFEA .... Regular Forces Employment Association [*British military*] (DMA)
RFECM .... Revised for Engineering Change Memorandum (SAA)
RFED .... Radio Frequency Expandable Decoy (DWSG)
RFED .... Research Facilities and Equipment Division [*NASA*] (MCD)
RFED .... Roosevelt Financial Group, Inc. [*NASDAQ symbol*] (NQ)

RFED	Roosevelt Finl [*NASDAQ symbol*] (TTSB)
RFEDP	Roosevelt Finl 6.5% Cv 'B' Pfd [*NASDAQ symbol*] (TTSB)
RFEHB	Retired Federal Employees Health Benefits Program (MCD)
RFEI............	Request for Engineering Information (KSC)
RF/EMI........	Radio Frequency and Electromagnetic-Interference [*Telecommunications*]
RFEP...........	Reserve Female Enlistment Program [*Military*] (DNAB)
RFER	Reefer [*Military*] (DNAB)
RFE/RL	Radio Free Europe/Radio Liberty (EA)
RFETS	Rocky Flats Environmental Technology Site [*Golden, CO*] (GAAI)
RFF	Radio Frequency Filter
RFF	Radio Frequency Finder (NVT)
RFF	Radio Frequency Fuze
RFF	Random Force Field
RFF	Ready for Ferry [*Navy*] (NVT)
RFF	Recirculative Fluid Flow
RFF	REFF, Inc. [*Toronto Stock Exchange symbol*]
RFF	Refuge from Flood (ADA)
RFF	Regular Federal Funds [*Medicaid*] (GFGA)
RFF	Relative Failure Frequency
RFF	Relative Fluorescence Efficiency (DMAA)
RFF	Relief from Face to Face [*Education*]
RFF	Remote Fiber Fluorometer [*Instrumentation*]
RFF	Request for Fire [*Military*]
RFF	Request for Form
RFF	Research Flight Facility [*Air Force*]
RFF	Resources for the Future
RFF	Rift-Fracture-Fracture [*Geology*]
RFF	Royal Filling Factory [*British military*] (DMA)
RFFC	Randy Floyd Fan Club (EA)
RFFD	Radio Frequency Fault Detection
RFFIT	Rapid Fluorescent Focus Inhibition Test [*Medicine*] (MEDA)
RFFO	Request for Factory Order (MCD)
RFFO	Rocky Flats Field Office (COE)
RFFS	River and Flood Forecasting Service (NADA)
RFFSA	Rede Ferroviaria Federal Sociedade Anonima [*Federal Railway Corporation*] [*Brazil*] (EY)
RFFT	Right Front Fluid Temperature [*Automotive engineering*]
RFG	RADAR Field Gradient (IEEE)
RFG	Radio Frequency Generator
RFG	Ramp Function Generator (IAA)
RFG	Rapid-Fire Gun
RFG	Rate and Free Gyro
RFG	Receive Format Generator
RFG	Reformulated Gasoline
RFG	Refugio, TX [*Location identifier FAA*] (FAAL)
RFG	Refunding [*Business term*]
Rfg.............	Refunding (EBF)
RFG	Register Finder Grid (IAA)
RFG	Reise und Industrieflug [*Airline*] [*Germany*]
RFG	Report Format Generator
RFG	Rhodesian Financial Gazette [*A publication*]
RFG	Rifle Fine Grain [*British military*] (DMA)
RFG	Roofing (AAG)
RFG	Royscot Finance Group [*Royal Bank of Scotland*]
RFGC	Royal Fremantle Golf Club [*Australia*]
RFGD	Radio-Frequency Glow Discharge [*Materials science*]
RFGN	Refrigeration [*Charges*]
RFGT	Refrigerant (MSA)
RFH	Radio Frequency Head (IAA)
RFH	Radio Frequency Heating
RFH	Raised Face Height (MSA)
RFH	Reichsfinanzhof [*Reich Finance Court*] [*German*] (ILCA)
RFH	Right Femoral Hernia [*Medicine*] (DMAA)
RFH	Rio Mayo [*Argentina*] [*Airport symbol*] (AD)
RFH	Roof Hatch [*Technical drawings*]
RFH	Royal Festival Hall [*London*]
RFH	Royal Free Hospital (ROG)
RFHCO	Rocket Fuel Handler Clothing Outfit [*Protective suit*]
RFHI	Real Fire Heating International Exhibition [*British*] (ITD)
RFHT	Radio Frequency Horn Technique
RFI.............	Cohen & Steers Total Return Rt. Realty Fund [*NYSE symbol*] (SPSG)
RFI.............	Cohen & Steers Total Rt Rty Fd [*NYSE symbol*] (TTSB)
RFI.............	RADAR Frequency Interferometer (MCD)
RFI.............	Radio France Internationale
RFI.............	Radio Frequency Indicator
RFI.............	Radio Frequency Induction [*Of plasmas*]
RFI.............	Radio Frequency Interchange (MDG)
RFI.............	Radio Frequency Interface (MCD)
RFI.............	Radio Frequency Interference
RFI.............	Rajneesh Foundation International (EA)
RFI.............	RCRA [*Resource Conservation and Recovery Act*] Facility Investigation
RFI.............	Ready for Installation (MCD)
RFI.............	Ready for Issue [*Military*]
RFI.............	Relative Fluorescent Intensity [*Analytical chemistry*]
RFI.............	Release for Issue (MCD)
RFI.............	Remedial Facility Investigation [*Environmental science*] (COE)
RFI.............	Remedial Field Investigation (GNE)
RFI.............	Remote Facility Inquiry [*NASA*] (KSC)
RFI.............	Remote File Inquiry [*NASA*] (NASA)
RFI.............	Report/File Language (HGAA)
RFI.............	Representative of a Foreign Interest
RFI.............	Requested for Information

RFI.............	Request for Information
RFI.............	Request for Inspection (IAA)
RFI.............	Request for Investigation
RFI.............	Request for Issue
RFI.............	Retail Floorcovering Institute [*Later, AFA*] (EA)
RFI.............	Richmond Fellowship International [*British*] (EAIO)
RFIC...........	Radio Frequency Integrated Circuit
RFICP	Radio Frequency Inductively-Coupled Plasma (AAEL)
RFID	Radio Frequency Identification
RFID	Request for Implementation Date
RFIF...........	Refund Information File [*IRS*]
RFIFO	Receive, First-In, First-Out [*Communications engineering*]
RFIM..........	Radio Frequency Interference Meter
RFIP...........	Radio Frequency Impedance Probe
RF/IR	RADAR Frequency/Infrared Frequency (IEEE)
RFIT...........	Radio Frequency Interference Tests (KSC)
RFJ............	Radio Frequency Joint
RFJI...........	Research Foundation for Jewish Immigration (EA)
RFK............	Anguilla, MS [*Location identifier FAA*] (FAAL)
RFK............	Radio Free Kabul [*British Defunct*] (EAIO)
RFK............	Robert Francis Kennedy [*American politician, 1925-68*]
RFKM..........	Robert F. Kennedy Memorial (EA)
RFL............	Radio Frequency Laboratories
RFL............	Radio Frequency Lens
RFL............	Radio-Frequency LINAC (SDI)
RFL............	Reduced Focal Length
RFL............	Reflect (NASA)
RFL............	Reflector [*or Reflected*]
RFL............	Refuel (AAG)
RFL............	Reiter-Fiessinger-Leroy (DB)
RFL............	Religion and Family Life Section of the National Council on Family Relations (EA)
RFL............	Requested Flight Level
RFL............	Reset Flux Level
RFL............	Resorcinol-Formaldehyde-Latex
RFL............	Restrictive Fire Line [*Military*] (AABC)
Rfl.............	Rifle (DOMA)
RFL............	Right Frontolateral [*Anatomy*] (AAMN)
RFL............	Rotating Field Logic (IAA)
RFL............	Rough Field Landing
RFL............	Rugby Football League [*British*] (DBA)
RFLA	Rheumatoid Factor-Like Activity [*Immunology*] (MAE)
RFLD	Radio Frequency Leakage Detector
RFLG	Refuelling (DA)
RFLMN	Rifleman (AABC)
RFLP	Restriction Fragment Length Polymorphism [*Genetics*]
R/FLR	Rear Floor [*Automotive engineering*]
RFLS	Rheumatoid Factor-Like Substance [*Immunology*] (MAE)
RFLT	Right Front Lining Temperature [*Automotive engineering*]
RFLX	Reflex (MSA)
RFM...........	Radio Frequency Management (NOAA)
RFM...........	Radio Frequency Monitoring [*Military*] (CAAL)
RFM...........	Reactive Factor Meter
RFM...........	Red Fox Minerals [*Vancouver Stock Exchange symbol*]
RFM...........	Refueling Mission [*Air Force*]
RFM...........	Release for Manufacture (DNAB)
RFM...........	Reliability Figure of Merit (IAA)
RFM...........	Reliable Flow Manager [*Computer science*]
RFM...........	Reserve Forces Modernization (MCD)
RF M	RF Management Corp. [*Associated Press*] (SAG)
Rfm...........	Rifampicin (DB)
RFM...........	Rifampin (STED)
Rfm...........	Rifampin (STED)
RFM...........	Roll Follow-Up Motor
RFM...........	Roll Forming Machine
RFM...........	Runway Friction Measurement [*Aviation*]
RFM...........	Rural Financial Market
RFMA	Reliability Figure of Merit Analysis
RFMC..........	Regional Fishery Management Council [*National Oceanic and Atmospheric Administration*] (MSC)
RFMC..........	RF Management [*NASDAQ symbol*] (TTSB)
RFMC..........	RF Management Corp. [*NASDAQ symbol*] (SAG)
RFMCW	R.F. Management Wrrt'A' [*NASDAQ symbol*] (TTSB)
RFMCZ........	R.F. Management Wrrt'B' [*NASDAQ symbol*] (TTSB)
RF Mgt	RF Management Corp. [*Associated Press*] (SAG)
RFMI..........	RF Monolithics [*NASDAQ symbol*] (TTSB)
RFMI..........	RF Monolithics, Inc. [*NASDAQ symbol*] (SAG)
RFMO	Radio Frequency Management Office (MCD)
RF Mono	RF Monolithics, Inc. [*Associated Press*] (SAG)
RFMP..........	Restriction-Fragment Melting Polymorphism [*Genetics*]
RFMS..........	Remote File Management System
RFMT..........	Runway Friction Measurement Test [*Aviation*]
RFMVR	Recency-Frequency-Monetary Value Ratio (NTCM)
RFN...........	Radio Frequency Noise
RFN...........	Raufarhofn [*Iceland*] [*Airport symbol*] (OAG)
RFN...........	Registered Fever Nurse
RFN...........	Remote Filter Niche [*Nuclear energy*] (NRCH)
RFN	Rifleman
RFNA	Radio Frequency Noise Analyzer (DNAB)
RFNA	Red Fuming Nitric Acid
RFNCC.........	Regional Nuclear Fuel Cycle Centers
RFND	Refined (MSA)
RFNG	Refining
RFNG	Roofing
RFNM	Ready for Next Message

RFNRE.........	Revolving Fund for Natural Resources Exploration [*United Nations*] (EY)
RFNRY........	Refinery
RFO	Air Royal [*France ICAO designator*] (FAAC)
RFO	Radio Frequency Oscillator
RFO	Ready for Occupancy (MCD)
RFO	Reconciling with Accounting and Finance Officer (AAGC)
RFO	Regional Field Officer [*Civil Defense*]
RFO	Request for Factory Order (MCD)
RFO	Request for Orders [*Military*]
RFO	Research Fiscal Office (SAA)
RFO	Restricted Flow Orifice (AAEL)
RFO	Retrofire Officer [*NASA*] (KSC)
RFO	Roll Follow-Up Operation
RFOA	Reasonable Factors Other than Age [*Equal Employment Opportunity Commission*]
RFOB	Rear Face of Block [*Automotive engineering*]
RFOFM	Records for Our Fighting Men [*Collected phonograph records during World War II*]
RFOG	Resonant Fiber Optic Gyroscope
RFOL	Results to Follow (DAVI)
RFOP	Regional Financial Operating Plan
RFP	Radio Finger Printing [*Identification of wireless radio operators by individual keying characteristics*]
RFP	Radio Free People [*An association Defunct*]
RFP	Radio Frequency Plasma
RFP	Radio Frequency Pulse (MCD)
RFP	Raiatea [*French Polynesia*] [*Airport symbol*] (OAG)
RFP	Rapid Filling Period [*Cardiology*]
RFP	Reactor Feed Pump [*Nuclear energy*] (NRCH)
RFP	Reasonable Further Progress (COE)
RFP	Registered Financial Planner [*International Association of Registered Financial Planners*] [*Designation awarded by*]
RFP	Relative Frass Production [*Ecology*]
RFP	Remaining Force Potential (MCD)
RFP	Replication Fork Pause [*Genetics*]
RFP	Reproductive Freedom Project [*ACLU*] [*Attempts to enforce the Supreme Court decisions guaranteeing a woman's right to choose abortion*] (EA)
RFP	Republicans for Progress [*Defunct*]
RFP	Request for Price Quotation
RFP	Request for Programming [*Computer science*]
RFP	Request for Proposal
RFP	Request for Purchase
RFP	Requirements and Formulation Phase (MCD)
RFP	Requirements for Production [*Army*] (RDA)
RFP	Requisition for Procurement [*DoD*]
RFP	Retired on Full Pay [*Military British*]
RFP	Reversed Field Pinch [*Plasma physics*] (NRCH)
RFP	RF Power Products [*AMEX symbol*] (SAG)
RFP	Richmond, Fredericksburg & Potomac Railroad Co. [*AAR code*]
RFP	Right Frontoposterior [*A fetal position*] [*Obstetrics*]
RFPA	Request for Part Approval (MCD)
RFPA	Request for Proposal Authorization [*NASA*] (NASA)
RFPA	Right to Financial Privacy Act
RFPB	Reserve Forces Policy Board [*DoD*]
RFPC	Reserve Flag Officer Policy Council [*Navy*]
RF/PF	Regional Forces - Popular Forces [*Republic of Vietnam*] [*Army*]
RFPI	Rapid Force Projection Initiative
RFPI	Registered Financial Planners Institute (EA)
RFPI	Request for Proposal Information [*Competitive bidding*]
RFPI/EFOGM...	Rapid Force Projection Initiative / Enhanced Fiber Optic Guided Missile [*Army*] (INF)
RF Pow	RF Power Products [*Associated Press*] (SAG)
RFPP	Radio Frequency Propagation Program (NG)
RFPR	Radiant Flash Pyrolysis Reactor [*Chemical engineering*]
RFPR	Reversed-Field Pinch Reactor [*Plasma physics*] (PDAA)
RFPRS	Retail Food Price-Reporting System
RFPS	Request for Proposal Supplement (DNAB)
RFPS	Royal Faculty of Physicians and Surgeons of Glasgow
RFPT	Reactor Feed Pump Turbine [*Nuclear energy*] (NRCH)
RFQ	Radio-Frequency Quadrupole [*Accelerator for subatomic physics study*]
RFQ	Rapid Freeze Quench
RFQ	Request for Qualifications (OICC)
RFQ	Request for Quotation
RFQ	Request for Quote (AAEL)
RFR	Radial Flow Reactor [*Chemical engineering*]
RFR	Radio Frequency Receiver
RFR	Radio Frequency Relay
RFR	Rapid Filling Rate (STED)
RFR	Rear Engine, Front and Rear Drive [*Automotive design*]
RFR	Redfern Resources [*Vancouver Stock Exchange symbol*]
RFR	Reduced Frequency Response [*Telecommunications*] (OA)
RFR	Refraction (AAMN)
RFR	Reject Failure Rate
RFR	Required Freight Rate (DS)
RFR	Rio Frio [*Costa Rica*] [*Airport symbol*] (OAG)
RFR	Roofer (WGA)
RFR	Royal Air Force [*British ICAO designator*] (FAAC)
RFR	Royal Fleet Reserve [*British*]
RFR	Sisters of Our Lady of Refuge (TOCD)
RFRA	Religious Freedom Restoration Act
RFRC	Refractory (MSA)
rfrd..............	Referred (BARN)

RFRG	Refrigerator
RFRJ	Radio Frequency Rotary Joint
Rfrs.............	Roofers (WPI)
RFRSH........	Refresh [*Computer graphics*]
RFS.............	Radio Frequency Seal
RFS.............	Radio-Frequency Shift (IEEE)
RFS.............	Radio Frequency Subsystem [*NASA*]
RFS.............	Raman Forward-Scattering [*Physics*]
RFS.............	Random Filing System
RFS.............	Range Frequency Synthesizer
RFS.............	Rapid Frozen Section [*Pathology and surgery*] (DAVI)
RFS.............	Ready for Sea [*Navy*]
RFS.............	Ready for Sending [*Computer science*] (IAA)
RFS.............	Ready for Service
RFS.............	Reduced Friction Strut [*Suspension system*] [*Automotive engineering*]
RFS.............	Regardless of Feature Size [*Manufacturing term*]
RFS.............	Regional Field Specialist [*Civil Defense*]
RFS.............	Regional Frequency Supplies [*Telecommunications*] (TEL)
RFS.............	Registry of Friendly Societies [*British*] (ILCA)
RFS.............	Relapse-Free Survival [*Oncology*]
RFS.............	Religion and Family Life Section (EA)
RFS.............	Remote Fiber Spectroscopy
RFS.............	Remote File Service [*or System*] [*Computer science*] (PCM)
RFS.............	Remote File Sharing [*Computer science*]
RFS.............	Renal Function Studies [*Medicine*]
RFS.............	Render, Float, and Set [*Construction*]
RFS.............	Request for Services [*Social Security Administration*]
RFS.............	Request for Shipment (MCD)
RFS.............	Resources Forecasting System
RFS.............	Response Feedback System [*NASA*]
RFS.............	R. F. Scientific, Inc. [*Telecommunications service*] (TSSD)
RFS.............	RFS Hotel Investors, Inc. [*NYSE symbol*] (SAG)
RFS.............	Roll Follow-Up System
RFS.............	Rossair Pty Ltd. [*Australia ICAO designator*] (FAAC)
RFS.............	Rossendorfer Forschungs-Reaktor [*Rossendorf Research Reactor*] [*German*]
RFS.............	Rotational Flight Simulator [*Air Force*]
RFS.............	Rover Flight Safety
RFS.............	Royal Forestry Society of England [*British*]
RFS.............	Rural Fire Service [*Australia*]
RFSAT	Radio Frequency Saturation (IAA)
RFSB	Regional Forward Scatter Branch [*Supreme Allied Commander, Europe*] (NATG)
RFSE..........	Radio Frequency Shielded Enclosure
RFS/ECM	Radio Frequency Surveillance/Electronic Countermeasures (MCD)
RF-SET	Radio-Frequency Single-Electron Transistor
RFSH..........	Recombinant Follicle-Stimulating Hormone [*Endocrinology*]
RFSH..........	Refresh [*Computer graphics*]
RFS Htl	RFS Hotel Investors, Inc. [*Associated Press*] (SAG)
RFSI...........	RFS Hotel Investors [*NASDAQ symbol*] (TTSB)
RFSI...........	RFS Hotel Investors, Inc. [*NASDAQ symbol*] (SAG)
RFS/ISE	Ready for Sea/Individual Ship Exercise (MCD)
RFSM	Radio Frequency Spectrum Management (LAIN)
RFSMS	Radio Frequency Signal Management System [*Aviation*] (GFGA)
RFSP	Radioactive Fallout Study Program [*Canada*]
RFSP	Replacement Flight Strip Printer [*Aviation*] (DA)
RFSP	Request for System Proposal (MHDI)
RFSP	Rigid Frame Selection Program
RFSS	Radio Frequency Simulation System (MCD)
RFSS	Radio Frequency Surveillance Subsystem
RFSS	Reliability Failure Summary Support (SAA)
RFST...........	Rapid Frequency Settling Time (IAA)
RFST...........	Research Foundation for the Study of Terrorism [*British*]
RFSTF........	Radio Frequency Systems Test Facility (KSC)
RFSU	Rugby Football Schools Union [*British*]
RFT.............	Radio Frequency Transformer (IAA)
RFT.............	Rapid Fermentation Technique
RFT.............	Ready for Training [*Military*]
RFT.............	Ready for Typesetter [*Publishing*]
RFT.............	Real Fourier Transform
RFT.............	Recursive Function Theory (IAA)
RFT.............	Reflectance, Fluorescence, Transmittance [*Densitometer*] [*Instrumentation*]
RFT.............	Refresher Training [*Navy*] (NVT)
RFT.............	Regge Field Theory [*Particle Physics*]
RFT.............	Regional Film Theatre [*British*]
RFT.............	Registered Floor Trader [*Investment term*] (NUMA)
RFT.............	Reinforcement
RFT.............	Repeat Formation Tester [*Well drilling*]
RFT.............	Request for Technology (DOM)
RFT.............	Request for Tender (ADA)
RFT.............	Resistive Force Theory (AAEL)
RFT.............	Respirator Fit Test [*Environmental science*] (FFDE)
RFT.............	Revisable Form Text [*Computer science*] (PCM)
RFT.............	Right Fibrous Trigone (STED)
RFT.............	Right Frontotransverse [*A fetal position*] [*Obstetrics*]
RFT.............	Rod-and-Frame Test (MAE)
RFT.............	Rotary Feed-Through
RFT.............	Routine Fever Therapy [*Medicine*] (STED)
RFTA..........	Regional Fuel Tax Agreement [*FHWA*] (TAG)
RFTC..........	Radio Frequency Test Console
RFTD	Radial Flow Torr Deposition System (IEEE)
RFT:DCA......	Revisable Form Text: Document Content Architecture [*IBM Corp.*] [*Computer science*]

RFTDS	RADAR Frequency Target Discrimination System (MCD)
RFTF	Radio Frequency Test Facility [Oak Ridge National Laboratory]
RFTF	Retail Fruit Trade Federation [British] (DBA)
RF-TK	Radio Frequency Tracking [Military] (MCD)
RFTL	Radio Frequency Transmission Line
RFTM	Radiator Fan Timer Module [Cooling systems] [Automotive engineering]
RFTN	Reflectone, Inc. [NASDAQ symbol] (NQ)
RFTO	Ready for Takeoff [Aviation]
RFTOI	Request for Test or Inspection (MCD)
RFTP	Request for Technical Proposal
RFTS	Radio Frequency Test Set (AABC)
RFTS	Request for Technical Samples (AAGC)
RFTS	Return Free Tax System [Internal Revenue Service] (GFGA)
RFTW	Ready for the World [Rhythm and Blues recording group]
RFTY	Reformatory (AABC)
RFU	Radio Frequency Unit [Later, RFCM] (MCD)
RFU	Ready-for-Use (NG)
RFU	Reference Frequency Unit [Telecommunications] (OA)
RFU	Reliability Field Unit
RFU	Remote Firing Unit (MCD)
RFU	Returns File Unit [IRS]
RFU	Rugby Football Union [British]
RFUA	Roll Follow-Up Amplifier
RFUDL	Radio Frequency Update Link
RFUM	Roll Follow-Up Motor
RFUO	Roll Follow-Up Operation
RFUS	Reversible Follow-Up System
RFUS	Roll Follow-Up System
RFV	RADAR Film Viewer
RFV	Radial Force Variation [Automotive tire testing]
RFV	Ragado Fino Virus
RFV	Regressing Friend Virus
RFV	Resonant Frequency Vibration
RFV	Right Femoral Vein [Anatomy] (DAVI)
RFVC	Radial Four-Valve Combustion [Automotive engineering]
RFVC	Reason for Visit Classification [Medicine] (DHSM)
R-FVII	Reading Free Vocational Interest Inventory [Vocational guidance test]
R-FVII REVISED...	Reading Free Vocational Interest Inventory Revised [Test] [Ralph Leonard Becker] (TES)
RFVM	Radio Frequency Voltmeter
RFW	Radio Free Women [Defunct] (EA)
RFW	Radio Frequency Wave
RFW	Rapid Filling Wave [Cardiology]
RFW	Reactor Feedwater [Nuclear energy] (NRCH)
RFW	Refrigerated Fresh Water Medium [Microbiology]
RFW	Request for Waiver (MCD)
RFW	Reserve Feed Water [Technical drawings]
RFW	Reversible Full Wave
RFW	Robinhood [Queensland] [Airport symbol] (AD)
RFWAC	Reversible Full Wave Alternating Current
RFWAR	Requirements for Work and Resources (MUGU)
RFWCHS	Royal Far West Children's Homes Scheme [Australia]
RFWDC	Reversible Full-Wave Direct Current
RFWF	Radio Frequency Wave Form
RFX	East Hartford, CT [Location identifier FAA] (FAAL)
RFX	J.P. Hunt, Inc. [FAA designator] (FAAC)
RFX	Reversed Field Experiment [Nuclear energy] (NRCH)
RFX	Roxborough [Queensland] [Airport symbol] (AD)
RFYC	Royal Forth Yacht Club [British] (DBA)
RFZ	Restrictive Fire Zone [Military]
RFZ	Rinforzando [With Special Emphasis] [Music]
Rg	Gate Resistance (IDOE)
Rg	Grid Resistance (IDOE)
RG	RADAR Guidance (IAA)
RG	Radial Glial Guide [Neurology]
R/G	Radiation Guidance (MUGU)
RG	Radio Direction Finding Station [ITU designation] (CET)
RG	Radio Frequency Cables; Bulk [JETDS nomenclature] [Military] (CET)
RG	Radiogram (DEN)
RG	Radio Guidance (AAG)
RG	Radio Guide (IAA)
R-G	Radiologist-General
RG	Range (AAG)
RG	Ranging Gun [British military] (DMA)
RG	Rate [Loop] Gain
RG	Rate Grown
RG	Rate Gyro (NAKS)
RG	Rate Gyroscope (KSC)
RG	Readiness Group [Military] (AABC)
RG	Reading [Postcode] (ODBW)
RG	Reagent Grade
RG	Real Gas
R/G	Rear Gunner [British military] (DMA)
RG	Rebuilding Grade [Automotive engineering] [Polymer Steel Corp.]
RG	Reception Good [Radio logs]
RG	Rechtsgeschichte [German] (ILCA)
RG	Recording (IAA)
RG	Recruiting Group [Military] (MUSM)
RG	Rectangular Guide (DEN)
R/G	Red and Gold (Edges) [Bookbinding] (ROG)
RG	Red-Green
RG	Reduction Gear [or Gearbox] (NG)
RG	Register (CET)

RG	Regula Generalis [General Rule or Order of Court] [Latin A publication] (DLA)
RG	Regulated Gallery [Nuclear energy] (NRCH)
RG	Regulatory Guide [Nuclear energy] (NRCH)
RG	Regummed [Philately]
RG	Reichsgericht [Reich Supreme Court] [German] (ILCA)
RG	Release Guard [Telecommunications] (TEL)
RG	Remak's Ganglion [Neurology]
RG	Remedial Gymnast [British]
RG	Renabie Gold Trust [Formerly, Barrick-Cullation Gold Trust] [Toronto Stock Exchange symbol]
RG	Report Generator (CMD)
RG	Report Guide
RG	Report Program Generator [Programming language] [1962] (IAA)
RG	Reserve Grade [Military]
RG	Reset Gate
RG	Resettlement Grants [British World War II]
RG	Resolving Gel [Biochemistry]
RG	Reticle Generator
RG	Reticulated Grating (AAG)
RG	Retrograde (DAVI)
RG	Reverse Gate
RG	Revolutionary Government [Vietnam]
RG	Right Gluteus [Anatomy]
RG	Right Guard [Football]
RG	Right Gun
RG	Ringing Generator [Telecommunications] (TEL)
RG	Rio Group
RG	Robert Graham [Designer's mark on US 1984 $1 Olympic commemorative coin]
Rg	Rodgers Antibodies [Medicine] (BABM)
RG	Rogers CommunCl'B' [NYSE symbol] (TTSB)
RG	Rogers Communications, Inc. [NYSE symbol] (SAG)
RG	Rogers Group (EA)
RG	Rogue's Gallery [Defunct] (EA)
RG	Rolled Gold
RG	Rueckgang [Return] [Music]
RG	Varig Brazilian [Airline flight code] (ODBW)
RG	VEB Fahlberg-List [East Germany] [Research code symbol]
RGA	Range-Gemini to Agena (SAA)
RGA	Rate Gyro Assembly
RGA	Reduction Gearbox Assembly (DNAB)
RGA	Regal Petroleum Ltd. [Vancouver Stock Exchange symbol]
RGA	Region Air [Seychelles] [ICAO designator] (FAAC)
RGA	Reinsurance Group of Amer [NYSE symbol] (TTSB)
RGA	Reinsurance Group of America, Inc. [NYSE symbol] (SPSG)
RGA	Relative Gain Array [Control engineering]
RGA	Remote Gain Amplifier (IAA)
RGA	Republican Governors Association (EA)
RGA	Request for Graphic Arts Service
RGA	Residual Gas Analysis (AAEL)
RGA	Residual Gas Analyzer
RGA	Ring Guild of America [Defunct] (FA)
RGA	Rio Grande [Argentina] [Airport symbol] (OAG)
RGA	Routing Accumulator (IAA)
RGA	Royal Garrison Artillery [British]
RGA	Royal Guernsey Artillery [British military] (DMA)
RGA	Rubber Growers' Association [Later, TGA] (EAIO)
RGAA	Radiochemical Gamma Activation Analysis
RGAL	Rate Gyro Assembly - Left Solid Rocket Booster (MCD)
RGAL	Reference Guide to American Literature [A publication]
RGAO	Rate Gyro Assembly - Orbiter (MCD)
RGAP	Rate Gyro Accelerometer Package (MCD)
RGAR	Rate Gyro Assembly - Right Solid Rocket Booster (MCD)
RGAS	Retained Gastric Antrum Syndrome [Medicine] (DAVI)
RGB	Barry (R.G.) [NYSE symbol] (TTSB)
RGB	Barry (R.G.) Corp. [NYSE symbol] (SAG)
RGB	Red-Giant Branch [Stellar physics]
RGB	Red Green Blue [Video monitor]
RGB	Refractory Grade Bauxite [Geology]
RGB	River Gunboat
RGB Cpt	RGB Computer & Video [Commercial firm Associated Press] (SAG)
RGBI	Red Green Blue Intensity [Video monitor]
RGBK	Regions Financial [NASDAQ symbol] (TTSB)
RGBK	Regions Financial Corp. [NASDAQ symbol] (SAG)
RGB-MB	Resistencia da Guine-Bissau Movimento Bafata [Political party] (EY)
RGB monitor...	Red-Green-Blue Monitor (DDC)
RGB monitor...	Red, Green, Blue Monitor
RGBY	Red, Green, Blue, Yellow [Video monitor] (IAA)
RGC	Radio-Gas Chromatography
RGC	Rangely [Colorado] [Seismograph station code, US Geological Survey] (SEIS)
RGC	Reaction Gas Chromatography (DB)
RGC	Reconstructed Gas Chromatogram
RGC	Reference Gas Cell [Instrumentation]
RGC	Reigate Resources (Canada) Ltd. [Toronto Stock Exchange symbol]
RGC	Repair Group Category [Military] (AFIT)
RGC	Repository for Germinal Choice [A sperm bank]
RGC	Republic Group [NYSE symbol] (TTSB)
RGC	Republic Gypsum Co. [NYSE symbol] (SPSG)
RGC	Retinal Ganglion Cell [Neurochemistry]
RGC	Ribosomal Gene Cluster [Genetics]
RGC	Right Giant Cell (DB)
RGC	Rio Grande College [Ohio]
RGC	Rio Grande College, Rio Grande, OH [OCLC symbol] (OCLC)

RGC .... Royal Greenwich Conservatory [British]
RGC .... Rural Governments Coalition [Defunct] (EA)
RGCAS .... Remote Global Computer Access Service (MHDB)
RGCO .... Roanoke Gas [NASDAQ symbol] (TTSB)
RGCO .... Roanoke Gas Co. [NASDAQ symbol] (SAG)
RGCR .... Renner's Gold Coast Colony Reports [1868-1914] [Ghana] [A publication] (DLA)
RGCSP .... Review of General Concepts of Separation Panel [FAA] (TAG)
Rgcy .... Regency (VRA)
RgcyRlt .... Regency Realty Corp. [Associated Press] (SAG)
RGD .... Radiation Gasdynamics (PDAA)
RGD .... Ragged [NWS] (FAAC)
RGD .... Range Gate Deception [Military] (LAIN)
RGD .... Rarefied Gas Dynamics
RGD .... Reduction Gas Detector [Instrumentation]
RGD .... Regis Development Corp. [Vancouver Stock Exchange symbol]
RGD .... Regular Geophysical Day
RGD .... Report and Graph Designer Module [Solomon Software] [Computer science] (PCM)
RGD .... Revue de Geomorphologie Dynamique [A publication]
RGD .... Rigid (MSA)
RGda .... Radio Grenada
RGDAA .... Royal Guide Dogs Association of Australia
RGDAT .... Royal Guide Dogs Association of Tasmania [Australia]
RGDATA .... Retail Grocery, Dairy, and Allied Trades Association [British] (BI)
RGDT .... Reliability Growth/Development Test
RGDV .... Rice Gall Dwarf Virus [Plant pathology]
RGE .... Porgera [Papua New Guinea] [Airport symbol] (OAG)
RGE .... Range [Maps and charts] (MDG)
RGE .... Rat der Gemeinden Europas [Council of European Municipalities]
RGE .... Reduced Gravity Environment
RGE .... Red under Gold Edges [Books]
RGE .... Regroupement des Guineens a l'Exterieur [Rally of Guineans Abroad] (PD)
RGE .... Relative Gas Expansion (AAMN)
RGE .... Rotating Gel Electrophoresis
RGEA .... Rate Gyro Electronics Assembly (MCD)
RGEN .... Repligen Corp. [Cambridge, MA] [NASDAQ symbol] (NQ)
RGenBelge... Revue General Belge [A publication] (BJA)
RGEPS .... Rucker-Gable Educational Programming Scale [Psychology]
RGF .... Range Gated Filter
RGF .... Rarefied Gas Field [or Flow]
RGF .... Royal Gun Factory [British military] (DMA)
RGFC .... R & G Financial Corp. [NASDAQ symbol] (SAG)
RGFC .... Ray Griff Fan Club (EA)
RGFC .... Remote Gas Filter Correlation (KSC)
RGFC .... Robin George Fan Club (EA)
RG Fincl ...... R & G Financial Corp. [Associated Press] (SAG)
RGFX .... Raster Graphics, Inc. [NASDAQ symbol] (SAG)
RGG .... Die Religion in Geschichte und Gegenwart [A publication] (ODCC)
RGG .... Rotating Gravity Gradiometer
RGG .... Royal Grenadier Guards [British]
RGH .... Rare Gas Halogen [Inorganic chemistry]
RGH .... Rat Growth Hormone [Endocrinology]
RGH .... Rough (AAG)
RghtMg .... Right Management Consultants, Inc. [Associated Press] (SAG)
RGI .... Randers Group, Inc. [AMEX symbol] (SAG)
RGI .... Rand Graduate Institute (AAGC)
RGI .... Rangiroa [French Polynesia] [Airport symbol] (OAG)
RGI .... Regional Airlines [France ICAO designator] (FAAC)
RGI .... Royal Glasgow Institute of Fine Arts [Scotland]
RGICC .... Region Internal Computer Code [Computer science]
RGI.EC .... Randers Group [ECM Symbol] (TTSB)
RGIFA .... Royal Glasgow Institute of Fine Arts [Scotland]
RGIS .... Regis Corp. [NASDAQ symbol] (NQ)
RGIS .... Remote Graphics Instruction Set [Computer science] (CIST)
RGIS .... Route Guidance and Information System
RGIT .... Representative for German Industry and Trade [An association] (EA)
RGIT .... Robert Gordon Institute of Technology [Scotland]
RGJ .... Richmond, VA [Location identifier FAA] (FAAL)
RGJ .... Royal Green Jackets [Military unit] [British]
RGJLond ...... Royal Green Jackets, London [Military unit] [British]
RGJTAVR ..... Royal Green Jackets Territorial and Army Volunteer Reserve [Military unit] [British]
RGK .... Red Wing, MN [Location identifier FAA] (FAAL)
RGK .... Reserv Glavnogo Komandovaniia [Reserve of the High Command] [Former USSR]
RGL .... RADAR Gunlaying (IAA)
RGL .... Rate Gyroscope Limit
RGL .... Reading Grade Level
RGL .... Regionair Ltd. [British ICAO designator] (FAAC)
RGL .... Regional Resources Ltd. [Toronto Stock Exchange symbol Vancouver Stock Exchange symbol]
RGL .... Regulate (MSA)
RGL .... Report Generator Language [Computer science] (IEEE)
RGL .... Rio Gallegos [Argentina] [Airport symbol] (OAG)
RGL .... Runway Guard Light [Aviation] (DA)
RGL .... Wrangell, AK [Location identifier FAA] (FAAL)
RGLC .... Racing, Gaming, and Liquor Commission [Northern Territory, Australia]
RGLD .... Royal Gold, Inc. [NASDAQ symbol] (NQ)
RGLR .... Regular (MSA)
RGLT .... Regulating (MSA)
RGLTD .... Regulated (MSA)
RGLTR .... Regulator (MSA)

RGLTRY .... Regulatory
RGM .... Radiogas Monitor [Nuclear energy] (NRCH)
RGM .... Rangemile Ltd. [British ICAO designator] (FAAC)
RGM .... Recorder Group Monitor
RGM .... Redundant Gyro Monitor (NASA)
RGM .... Reliability Growth Management (MCD)
RGM .... Remote Geophysical Monitor (MCD)
RGM .... Reversible Gelatin Matrix
RGM .... Rietti-Greppi-Micheli [Syndrome] [Medicine] (DB)
RGM .... Right Gluteus Maziums [Muscle] [Anatomy] (DAVI)
RGM .... Rounds per Gun per Minute
RGM .... Royex Gold Mining Corp. [Toronto Stock Exchange symbol Vancouver Stock Exchange symbol]
RGMI .... Regulations Governing the Meat Inspection [of the USDA]
RGMS .... Reversible Gelatin Matrix System
RGMV .... Ryegrass Mosaic Virus [Plant pathology]
RGN .... Ranging (IAA)
RGN .... Rangoon [Myanmar] [Airport symbol] (OAG)
RGN .... Rangoon [Burma] [Airport symbol] (AD)
Rgn .... Region (AL)
RGN .... Region (AFM)
RGN .... Registered General Nurse
RG(N) .... Register (N) Stages (MCD)
RGN .... Riggins Resources [Vancouver Stock Exchange symbol]
RGNG .... Rigging (MSA)
RGNl .... Regional
Rgnl .... Regional (AL)
RGNT .... Regent Assisted Living [NASDAQ symbol] (TTSB)
RGNT .... Regent Assisted Living, Inc. [NASDAQ symbol] (SAG)
RGO .... Akron, OH [Location identifier FAA] (FAAL)
RGO .... Argo SA [Dominican Republic] [ICAO designator] (FAAC)
RGO .... Radio Guidance Operation (DNAB)
RGO .... Ranger Oil Ltd. [NYSE symbol Toronto Stock Exchange symbol] (SPSG)
RGO .... Rosella Plains [Queensland] [Airport symbol] (AD)
RGO .... Royal Greenwich Observatory [British]
RGP .... RADAR Glider Positioning (IAA)
RGP .... Rate Gyro Package
RGP .... Regina Public Library [UTLAS symbol]
RGP .... Reliability Growth Program (PDAA)
RGP .... Remote Graphics Processor
RGP .... Retired Greyhounds as Pets (EA)
RGP .... Retrograde Pyelogram [Nephrology] (DAVI)
RGP .... Rhodesian Government Party
RGP .... Rice Genome Research Program [Japan]
RGP .... Rigid Gas Permeable [Contact lens]
RGP .... Rocketdyne Gun Propellant (MCD)
RGP .... Rolled Gold Plate [Metallurgy]
RGPF .... Royal Gunpowder Factory [British]
RG PH .... Registered Pharmacist
RGPO .... Range Gate Pull Off (NVT)
RGPS .... Razor Grinders' Protection Society [A union] [British]
RGR .... Oklahoma City, OK [Location identifier FAA] (FAAL)
RGR .... Range Gated Receiver
RGR .... Ranger
RGR .... Rare-Gas Recovery [Nuclear energy] (NRCH)
RGR .... Rassemblement des Gauches Republicaines [Assembly of the Republican Left] [France Political party]
RGR .... Receipt of Goods Received
RGR .... Region Air, Inc. [Canada ICAO designator] (FAAC)
RGR .... Regional Rail [TRB] (TAG)
RGR .... Regulus Resources, Inc. [Vancouver Stock Exchange symbol]
RGR .... Relative Growth Rate [Entomology]
RGR .... Ringer (WGA)
RGR .... Rio Grande [Brazil] [Airport symbol] (AD)
RGR .... Routing Register (IAA)
RGR .... Royal Garrison Regiment [Military British] (ROG)
RGR .... Royal Gurkha Regiment [British military] (DMA)
RGR .... Sturm Ruger [NYSE symbol] (TTSB)
RGR .... Sturm Ruger & Co. [NYSE symbol] (SPSG)
RGRDE .... Rotating Gold Ring-Disc Electrode (PDAA)
RGRMA .... Rate Gyro Redundancy Management Algorithm (NASA)
RgrT .... Ranger Tab [Military decoration]
RGS .... RADAR Ground Stabilization
RGS .... Radio Guidance System
RGS .... Rate Gyro System
RGS .... Reference Guides Series (ACII)
RGS .... Refined Gigabit System [High purity hydrogen peroxide]
RGS .... Regulator of G Protein Signaling [Biochemistry]
RGS .... Regulators of G-Protein Signalling [Biochemistry]
RGS .... Release Guard Signal [Telecommunications] (EECA)
RGS .... Remote Ground Switching
RGS .... Rene Guyon Society (EA)
RGS .... Renown Aviation, Inc. [ICAO designator] (FAAC)
RGS .... Research Grants Staff [Environmental Protection Agency] (GFGA)
RGS .... Restructured General Support [Military]
RGS .... Rieger Syndrome [Medicine] (DMAA)
RGS .... Rifleman's Gun Shield [Military] (INF)
RGS .... Rio Grande Southern Railroad (IIA)
RGS .... River Gauging Station
RGS .... Rochester Gas & El [NYSE symbol] (TTSB)
RGS .... Rochester Gas & Electric Corp. [NYSE symbol] (SPSG)
RGS .... Rocket Guidance System (KSC)
RGS .... Royal Geographical Society [British]
RGS .... Royal Gold Enterprises, Inc. [Toronto Stock Exchange symbol]

RGS	Ruffed Grouse Society (EA)
RGS	Sisters of Our Lady of Charity of the Good Shepherd [Roman Catholic religious order]
RGS	[The] Sisters of the Good Shepherd (TOCD)
RGSAT	Radio Guidance Surveillance and Automatic Tracking (AAG)
RGSC	Ramp Generator and Signal Converter (IEEE)
RGSDLR	Rigsdaler [Numismatics]
RGSF	Reference Guide to Short Fiction [A publication]
RGSSA	Royal Geographical Society of Australasia, South Australian Branch
RGSTV	Rice Grassy Stunt Virus [Plant pathology]
RGSTY	Registry
RGSU	Restructured General Support Unit (MCD)
RGT	Airbourne School of Flying [British] [FAA designator] (FAAC)
Rgt	Regent [Record label]
RGT	Regent College Library [UTLAS symbol]
RGT	Regiment
RGT	Rengat [Sumatra, Indonesia] [Airport symbol] (AD)
RGT	Resonant Gate Transistor [Computer science]
RGT	Reverse Garbage Truck (ADA)
RGT	Rigging Template (MCD)
RGT	Right
RGTF	Royal General Theatrical Fund [British] (DI)
RGTM	Regional Government Technical Monitor [Department of Housing and Urban Development] (GFGA)
RGTP	Reseau Gouvernemental de Transmission par Paquets [Government Packet Network - GPN] [Canada]
RGTP	Rough Template (AAG)
RGTR	Register
RgtStrt	Right Start, Inc. [Associated Press] (SAG)
RGU	Rate Gyroscope Unit
RGU	Regional Glucose Utilization [Medicine] (DMAA)
RGV	Relative Gas Vacuolation [In algae]
RGV	Rio Grande Ventures Ltd. [Vancouver Stock Exchange symbol].
R-GVB	Resonating-Generalized Valence Bond [Physical chemistry]
RGW	Ramp Gross Weight [Aviation]
RGW	Reagent Grade Water
RGWO	Range Gate Walk Off [Military] (LAIN)
RGWS	RADAR Guided Weapon System (MCD)
RGX	Reverse Geometry X-Ray (PS)
RGY	Regency Airlines Ltd. [ICAO designator] (FAAC)
RGZ	Recommended Ground Zero [Military] (AABC)
RH	Air Zimbabwe [Zimbabwe] [ICAO designator] (ICDA)
RH	Rabbinic Hebrew (BJA)
RH	Radiant Heat
RH	Radiation Homing (AAG)
RH	Radiation Hybrid (HGEN)
RH	Radiation Hybrid Mapping [Biochemistry]
RH	Radio Hargeisa
RH	Radiological Health (KSC)
r/h	RADs [Radiation Absorbed Doses] per Hour (DEN)
RH	Railhead [British military] (DMA)
RH	Rankine-Hugoniot [Physics]
RH	Reactive Hyperemia [Medicine]
RH	Receive Hub [Telegraph] [Telecommunications] (TEI)
RH	Receiver Hopping Mode (IAA)
RH	Red Heat (IAA)
RH	Red Herring [Investment term]
RH	Redhill [International vehicle registration] (ODBW)
RH	Reduced Haloperidol [An antidepressant] (DAVI)
RH	Regal Bahamas International Airlines [ICAO designator] (AD)
RH	Regional Headquarters (NOAA)
RH	Relative Humidity
RH	Releasing Hormone [Also, RF] [Endocrinology]
RH	Remote Handled (COE)
RH	Remotely Handled
r/h	REMs [Roentgen Equivalents, Man] per Hour (DEN)
RH	Report Heading (BUR)
RH	Requesta Regni Hierosolymitani [A publication] (BJA)
RH	Request-Response Header [Computer science] (BUR)
RH	Research Highlights [A publication] (DIT)
RH	Reserve Shutdown Hours (IAA)
RH	Residential Hotels [Public-performance tariff class] [British]
RH	Response Header (IAA)
RH	Retinal Hemorrhage [Medicine] (DMAA)
RH	Revisionist History [Taby, Sweden] (EAIO)
R/H	Revolutions per Hour (DEN)
RH	Rheostat (IEEE)
Rh	Rhesus [Blood factor]
Rh	Rhetorica [of Aristotle] [Classical studies] (OCD)
rh	Rheumatic [Medicine] (MAE)
Rh	Rheumatism [Medicine]
RH	Rheumatology (DAVI)
RH	Rhinitis [Medicine]
RH	Rhinoceros (ROG)
Rh	Rhipicephalus [A genus of cattle tick] (DAVI)
rh	Rhodesia [Southern Rhodesia] [MARC country of publication code Library of Congress] (LCCP)
Rh	Rhodium [Chemical element]
Rh	Rhodopsin [Visual Purple]
rh	Rhonchi [Rales] [Latin] (MAE)
RH	Richner-Hanhart [Syndrome] [Medicine] (DB)
RH	Right Halfback [Soccer]
RH	Right Hand
RH	Right Hemisphere [Medicine] (DB)
RH	Right Hyperphoria [Medicine]
RH	Road Haulage
RH	Rockwell Hardness
r/h	Roentgens per Hour (DEN)
RH	Roger Houghton Ltd. [Publisher] [British]
RH	Room Humidifier (DMAA)
RH	Rosh Hashanah [New Year] (BJA)
RH	Rotuli Hundredorum [Latin A publication] (DLA)
RH	Round Head
RH	Round Hole [Looseleaf binding] (DGA)
RH	Round House [Maps and charts]
RH	Royal Highlanders [Military unit] [British]
RH	Royal Highness
RH	Royal Hospital [Chelsea] [British military] (DMA)
RH	Royal Hussars [Military unit] [British]
RH	Rueckwaertiges Heeresgebiet [Rear area of a group of armies] [German military]
RH	Runaway Hotline (EA)
RH	Running Head [Printing] (WDMC)
RH	Ryan's Hope [Television program]
RH	Southern Rhodesia [ANSI two-letter standard code Obsolete] (CNC)
RHA	Ranching Heritage Association (EA)
RHA	Records Holding Area [Military]
RHA	Regional Health Authority [British]
RHA	Reichold [Alabama] [Seismograph station code, US Geological Survey] (SEIS)
RHA	Reindeer Herders Association (EA)
RHA	Religious Heritage of America (EA)
RHA	Renewal and Housing Assistance Report [HUD]
RHA	Respiratory Health Association (EA)
RHA	Reykholar [Iceland] [Airport symbol Obsolete] (OAG)
RHA	Rice Husk Ash (PDAA)
RHA	Right Hepatic Artery [Medicine] (DMAA)
RHA	Road Haulage Association [British]
RHA	Rohm & Haas Co., Spring House, PA [OCLC symbol] (OCLC)
RHA	Rolled Homogeneous Armor [Weaponry] (INF)
RHA	Roman High Avoidance [Behavior trait]
RHA	Rose Hybridizers Association (EA)
RHA	Royal Hellenic Army (NATG)
RHA	Royal Hibernian Academy
RHA	Royal Horse Artillery [British]
RHA	Rural Housing Alliance [Later, RAI] (EA)
RHA	Rural Housing Authority [Western Australia]
RHAA	Rivers and Harbors Appropriation Act of 1899 (COE)
RHAAP	Rural Housing Assistance for Aborigines Program [Australia]
RHAB	Random House AudioBooks [Publisher]
RHAF	Royal Hellenic Air Force
RHAG	Rotary Hydraulic Arresting Gear (PDAA)
RH Agglut	Rheumatoid Agglutinins [Clinical chemistry] (CPH)
Rh Al	Rhetorica ad Alexandrum [of Aristotle] [Classical studies] (OCD)
RHAM	Rhammus [Pharmacology] (ROG)
RHAP	Rhapsody (WGA)
RHAPP	Rental Housing Assistance for Pensioners Program [Australia]
RHASS	Royal Highland and Agricultural Society of Scotland [British]
RHA(T)	Regional Health Authority (Teaching) [British]
RHAV	Rat Hepatoma-Associated Virus
RHAW	RADAR Homing and Warning (MCD)
RHAWR	RADAR Homing and Warning Receiver (MCD)
RHAWS	RADAR Homing and Warning System
RHB	RADAR Homing Beacon [Maps and charts] (IAA)
RHB	RADAR Homing Bomb [Air Force]
RHB	Raise Head of the Bed [Medicine] (DAVI)
rHb	Recombinant Haemoglobin [Possible blood substitute]
RHB	Regional Hospital Boards [British]
RHB	RehabCare Group [NYSE symbol]
RHB	Right Halfback [Soccer]
RHB	Right Heart Bypass [Medicine] (MAE)
RHB	Round Head Brass [Screw Head] (ECII)
RHB	Round Hole Broach
RHBA	Racking Horse Breeders Association of America (EA)
RHBA	Racking Horse Breeders Association of America (NTPA)
RHBC	RehabCare Corp. [NASDAQ symbol] (SPSG)
RHBC	RehabCare Group [NASDAQ symbol] (TTSB)
RHBF	Reactive Hyperemia Blood Flow [Medicine] (MAE)
RHBV	Rice Hoja Blanca Virus [Plant pathology]
RHBV	Right-Heart Blood Volume [Medicine] (STED)
RHC	Range-Height Converter (IAA)
RHC	Reactive Hydrocarbon [Environmental science]
RHC	Reactor Head Cooling [Nuclear energy] (NRCH)
RHC	Regional Bell Holding Co. [Computer science] (TNIG)
RHC	Regional Holding Co.
RHC	Resetting Half-Cycle
RHC	Resin Hemoperfusion Column
RHC	Respiration Has Ceased [Medicine] (STED)
RHC	Respirations Have Ceased [Medicine]
RHC	Right-Hand Circular [NASA] (KSC)
RHC	Right-Hand Component (IAA)
RHC	Right-Hand Console
RHC	Right Heart Catheterization [Medicine]
RHC	Right Hypochondrium [Medicine]
RHC	Rio Hotel & Casino [NYSE symbol] (TTSB)
RHC	Riverside Methodist Hospital Library, Columbus, OH [OCLC symbol] (OCLC)
RHC	Road Haulage Cases [1950-55] [England] [A publication] (DLA)
RHC	Rosary Hill College [New York]
RHC	Rotational Hand Controller [NASA]

RHC	Royal Highlanders of Canada [*Military unit*] [*World War I*]
RHC	Royal Holloway College [*British*] (DI)
RHC	Rubber Hydrocarbon
RHC	Rural Health Clinic [*Department of Health and Human Services*] (GFGA)
RHCA	Red Hills Conservation Association (EA)
Rh CA	Rhodesian Court of Appeal Law Reports [*1939-46*] [*A publication*] (DLA)
RHCA	Roller Hockey Coaches Association (EA)
RHCC	Reproductive Health Care Center
RHCC/PP	Reproductive Health Care Center/Planned Parenthood
RHCF	Residential Health Care Facility [*Medicine*] (DHSM)
RHCG	Research for Health Charities Group [*British*]
RHCI	Radiant Heating and Cooling Institute
RHCI	Ramsay Health Care [*NASDAQ symbol*] (TTSB)
RHCI	Ramsay Health Care, Inc. [*NASDAQ symbol*] (NQ)
RHCM	Relative Humidity Control/Monitor (NASA)
RHCP	Right-Hand Circularly Polarized [*LASER waves*]
RHCS	Red Hot Concepts, Inc. [*NASDAQ symbol*] (SAG)
RHCSA	Regional Hospitals Consultants' and Specialists' Association
RHCSU	Red Hot Concepts Unit [*NASDAQ symbol*] (TTSB)
RHCTL	Right-Hand Control (IAA)
RHD	Archangelos [*Greece*] [*Seismograph station code, US Geological Survey*] (SEIS)
RhD	Doctor of Rehabilitation (GAGS)
RHD	RADAR Horizon Distance (IAA)
RHD	Radial Head Dislocation (STED)
RHD	Radiological Health Data
RHD	Railhead
RHD	Random House Dictionary [*A publication*]
RHD	Regional Health Director [*HEW*]
RHD	Relative Hepatic Dullness [*Medicine*]
RHD	Renal Hypertensive Disease [*Medicine*]
RHD	Required Hangar Depth (MCD)
RHD	Return Head
RHD	R.H. Donnelley [*NYSE symbol*] [*Formerly, Dun & Bradstreet*]
RhD	Rhesus Hemolytic Disease (STED)
RHD	Rheumatic Heart Disease [*Medicine*]
RHD	Rhodes, Inc. [*NYSE symbol*] (SPSG)
RHD	Right Hand Drive [*Automotive engineering*]
RHD	Rio Hondo [*Argentina*] [*Airport symbol*] (AD)
RHD	Rural Housing Disaster
RHD & R	Radiological Health Data and Reports [*A publication*]
RHDEL-II	[*The*] Random House Dictionary of the English Language: Second Edition - Unabridged [*A publication*]
RHD-II	[*The*] Random House Dictionary of the English Language: Second Edition - Unabridged [*A publication*]
RHDV	Rabbit Hemorrhagic Disease Virus
RHE	Radiation Hazard Effects (KSC)
RHE	Random House Encyclopedia [*A publication*]
RHE	Record Handling Electronics
RHE	Reims [*France*] [*Airport symbol*] (OAG)
RHE	Reliability Human Engineering (AAG)
RHE	Remote Hellfire Electronics [*Army*]
RHE	Research in Higher Education [*A publication*] (DHP)
RHE	Respiratory Heat Exchange (STED)
RHE	Retinohepatoendocrinologic [*Syndrome*] [*Medicine*] (DMAA)
RHE	Reversible Hydrogen Electrode
RHE	Revue d'Histoire Ecclasiastique [*A publication*] (ODCC)
RHE	Rheims [*France*] [*Airport symbol*] (AD)
RHEA	Reentry Heating Energies Analyzer [*Air Force*]
RHEB	Right-Hand Equipment Bay [*Apollo*] [*NASA*]
RHEED	Reflectance High Energy Electron Diffraction (CIST)
RHEED	Reflected High-Energy Electron Diffraction [*Spectroscopy*]
RHEED	Reflection High-Energy Electron Diffraction (DMAA)
RHEED	Reflective High-Energy Electron Diffraction
RHEINHYP	Rheinische Hypothekenbank AG [*Germany*] (EY)
RHEL	Rutherford High Energy Laboratory (MCD)
RHEM	Rheometrics, Inc. [*Piscataway, NJ*] [*NASDAQ symbol*] (NQ)
RHEM	Rheometrics Scientific [*NASDAQ symbol*] (TTSB)
rheo	Rheostat (STED)
RHEO	Rheostat (AAG)
Rheomt	Rheometrics, Inc. [*Associated Press*] (SAG)
Rhes	Rhesus [*of Euripides*] [*Classical studies*] (OCD)
Rhet	Ars Rhetorica [*of Dionysius Halicarnassensis*] [*Classical studies*] (OCD)
Rhet	De Rhetoribus [*of Suetonius*] [*Classical studies*] (OCD)
RHET	Resonant Hot-Tunnelling Electron Transistor [*Electronics*] (AAEL)
Rhet	Rhetores Graeci [*A publication*] (OCD)
RHET	Rhetoric
Rhet Her	Rhetorica ad Herennium [*First century BC*] [*Classical studies*] (OCD)
Rhet Lat Min	Rhetores Latini Minores [*A publication*] (OCD)
RHEU	Rheumatology (DAVI)
rheu fev	Rheumatic Fever (DAVI)
rheu ht dis	Rheumatic Heart Disease (DAVI)
RHEUM	Rheumatism [*Medicine*]
R_{HF}	High-Frequency Resistance (IDOE)
RHF	Rarefied Hypersonic Flow
RHF	Remembrance of the Holocaust Foundation (EA)
RHF	Restricted Hartree-Fock [*Quantum mechanics*]
RHF	Retired History File [*Army*]
RHF	Right Heart Failure [*Medicine*]
RHF	Roller Hockey Federation (EA)
RHF	Royal Highland Fusiliers [*Military unit*] [*British*]
RHFC	Richard Hatch Fan Club (EA)

RHFC	Robyn Hitchcock Fan Club (EA)
RHFEB	Right-Hand Forward Equipment Bay [*NASA*] (KSC)
RHFF	Richard Hatch Fan Fellowship [*Defunct*] (EAIO)
RHFS	Receiving Hospital Field Station
RHFS	Round Hill Field Station [*MIT*] (MCD)
RHG	Renaissance Hotel Group NV [*NYSE symbol*] (SAG)
RHG	Right Hand Grip (DMAA)
RHG	Royal Horse Guards [*British*]
RHG1D	Royal Horse Guards and 1st Dragoons [*British military*] (DMA)
RHG-CSF	Recombinant Human Granulocyte, Colony Stimulating Factor [*Hematology*]
RHGH	Recombinant Human Growth Hormone [*Biochemistry*]
RHGP	Russian Human Genome Project
rhGRF	Rat Hypothalamus Growth Hormone-Releasing Factor [*Endocrinology*]
RHGSA	Russian Historical and Genealogical Society in America [*Later, RNAA*] (EA)
RHH	Right-Hand Head
RHH	Right Homonymous Hemianopia [*Medicine*] (MEDA)
RHH	Robertson-Ceco Corp. [*NYSE symbol*] (SPSG)
RHI	RADAR Height Indicator (CET)
RHI	Range-Height Indicator [*RADAR*]
RHI	Real Hazard Index
RHI	Relative Humidity Indicator (AAG)
RHI	Responsible Hospitality Institute (EA)
RHI	Rhinelander [*Wisconsin*] [*Airport symbol*] (OAG)
RHI	Rhinology [*Medicine*] (DHSM)
RHI	Rhode Island
RHI	Rhode Island Historical Society Library, Providence, RI [*OCLC symbol*] (OCLC)
RHi	Rhode Island Historical Society, Providence, RI [*Library symbol Library of Congress*] (LCLS)
Rh I	Rhode Island Reports [*A publication*] (DLA)
Rh I	Rhode Island Supreme Court Reports [*A publication*] (DLA)
RHI	Rigid-Hull Inflatable [*US Coast Guard vessel*]
RHI	Robert Half International, Inc. [*NYSE symbol*] (SPSG)
RHI	Robert Half Intl [*NYSE symbol*] (TTSB)
RHI	Round Hill Installation (SAA)
RHI	Rural Health Initiative [*Medicine*] (DMAA)
RHIA	Radiation-Hardened Interfacing Amplifier
RHIB	Rain and Hail Insurance Bureau [*Defunct*] (EA)
RHIB	Rigid-Hull Inflatable Boat (DOMA)
RHIC	Relativistic Heavy Ion Collider [*Nuclear physics*]
RHIDEC	[*The*] Restaurant/Hotel Interior Design Exposition (ITD)
RHIE	RAND Health Insurance Experiment [*Managed care study*]
RHIF	Rural Housing Insurance Fund [*Department of Agriculture*] (GFGA)
RHIFC	Ray Heatherton Irish Friends Club [*Defunct*] (EA)
RHIG	RH [*or Rhesus*] Immune Globulin [*Immunology*]
RHIMO	Agency for Navigation on the Rhine and the Moselle (NATG)
Rhin	Rhinology [*Medicine*]
RHINO	RADAR Range Height Indicator Not Operating on Scan [*Meteorology*] (FAAC)
Rhino	Really Here in Name Only [*Education*] [*British*]
RHINO	Repeating Handheld Improved Non-Rifled Ordnance (PDAA)
RHINO	Rhinoceros (DSUE)
RHINOL	Rhinology [*Medicine*]
RHIO	Rank Has Its Obligations [*Military slang*]
RHIP	Radiation Health Information Project [*Defunct*] (EA)
RHIP	Rank Has Its Privileges [*Military slang*]
RHIR	Rank Has Its Responsibilities [*Military slang*]
RHi-Sh	Rhode Island Historical Society, George L. Shepley Collection, Providence, RI [*Library symbol Library of Congress*] (LCLS)
RHistS	Royal Historical Society [*British*]
RhITC	Rhodamine Isothiocyanate [*Biochemistry*]
RHittAs	Revue Hittite et Asianique [*Paris*] [*A publication*] (BJA)
Rhiz	Rhizobium [*A bacterium*] (DAVI)
RHJ	Rubber Hose Jacket (MSA)
RHJSC	Regional Hospital Junior Staff Committee [*British*] (DAVI)
RHK	Radio Hong Kong
RHK	Reefing Hook
RHL	Radiological Health Laboratory
RHL	Rat Hepatic Lectin [*Biochemistry*]
RHL	Rectangular Hysteresis Loop (PDAA)
RHL	Recurrent Herpes Labialis [*Medicine*] (DMAA)
RHL	Residual Hazards List [*NASA*] (NASA)
RHL	Rettie's Scotch Court of Session Cases, Fourth Series [*House of Lords' Part*] [*A publication*] (DLA)
RHL	Reverse Half-Line [*Feed*]
RHL	Richland Mine, Inc. [*Vancouver Stock Exchange symbol*]
RHL	Right Hemisphere Lesion [*Cardiology*] (DAVI)
RHL	Right Hepatic Lobe [*Anatomy*]
RHL	Roy Hill [*Western Australia*] [*Airport symbol*] (AD)
RHLG	Radiometric Homing Level Gauge
RHLI	Royal Hamilton Light Infantry [*British military*] (DMA)
Rh LJ	Rhodesian Law Journal [*A publication*] (DLA)
RHLN	Right Hilar Lymph Node [*Anatomy*] (MAE)
RHM	Ranks Hovis McDougall [*Commercial firm British*] (ECON)
RHM	Refractory Heavy Minerals [*In sands used for glass making*]
RHM	Relative Humidity Monitor (GFGA)
RHM	Renewal and Housing Management [*HUD*]
RHM	Rhabdomyosarcoma [*Also, RMS*] [*Oncology*]
RHM	Right-Hand Polarized Mode (IAA)
RHM	Rio Hardy [*Mexico*] [*Seismograph station code, US Geological Survey*] (SEIS)
RHM	Roentgen per Hour at One Meter

RHMII........	Right Hand Man II [Computer package] [Futurus, Inc.] (PCM)
RhMk........	Rhesus Monkey [Medicine] (DMAA)
RhMK........	Rhesus Monkey Kidney [Medicine] (DMAA)
RhMkK........	Rhesus Monkey Kidney [Medicine] (DMAA)
RHMS........	Royal Hibernian Military School [Dublin]
Rh Mus.......	Rheinisches Museum fuer Philologie [A publication] (OCD)
RHN........	Rhonavia [France ICAO designator] (FAAC)
RHN........	Royal Hellenic Navy [Obsolete] (NATG)
Rh Neg.......	Rhesus Factor Negative [Hematology] (MAE)
RhnPl........	Rhone-Poulenc, Inc. [Associated Press] (SAG)
Rh null........	Rhesus Factor Null [Indicates all Rhesus factors are missing] [Hematology] (DAVI)
RHO........	Railhead Officer [Military Obsolete]
RHO........	Remanufactured High Output
RHO........	Rhodes [Greece] [Seismograph station code, US Geological Survey Closed] (SEIS)
RHO........	Rhodesia [Later, Zimbabwe]
RHO........	Rhodes Island [Greece] [Airport symbol] (OAG)
RHO........	Rhodopsin [Optics] [Genetics] (DOG)
RHO........	Rhombic [Antenna]
RHO........	Southern Rhodesia [ANSI three-letter standard code Obsolete] (CNC)
RHOB........	Rayburn House Office Building [Washington, DC] (DLA)
Rhod........	Rhodesia
RHOD........	Rhodium [Chemistry]
Rhode Island C...	Rhode Island College (GAGS)
Rhode Island Rep...	Rhode Island Reports [A publication] (DLA)
Rhode Island Sch Design...	Rhode Island School of Design (GAGS)
Rhodes........	Rhodes, Inc. [Associated Press] (SAG)
Rhodesian LJ...	Rhodesian Law Journal [A publication] (DLA)
RHOGI........	RADAR Homing Guidance Investigation (MCD)
RHOJ........	RADAR Home on Jam
Rho L........	Rhodian Law [A publication] (DLA)
rhom........	Rhomboid [Muscle] [Anatomy] (DAVI)
RHOM........	Rottlund Co. [NASDAQ symbol] (SAG)
RHOMB........	Rhomboid [Mathematics]
RHOSP........	Registered Home Ownership Savings Plan
RHOV........	Du Variant [Laboratory science] (DAVI)
RHP........	Radiant Heat Pump
RHP........	Rated Horsepower
RHP........	Reduced Hard Pressure (MSA)
RHP........	Resource Holding Potential
RHP........	Resource Holding Power [Fighting ability - animal defense]
RHP........	Rhodospirillum Heme Protein (DB)
RHP........	Right-Handed Pitcher [Baseball]
RHP........	Right-Hand Page (WDMC)
rhp........	Right-Hand Page [Also, called Recto] (WDMC)
RHP........	Right Hand Panel (MCD)
RHP........	Rural Health Program [Military] (CINC)
RHPA........	Reverse Hemolytic Plaque Assay [Clinical chemistry]
RHPC........	Rapid-Hardening Portland Cement
rhPF........	Recombinant Human Platelet Factor [Biochemistry]
RH PL........	Rhodium Plate (MSA)
RHPLC........	Radio-High-Performance Liquid Chromatography
Rh Poз........	Rhesus Factor Positive [Hematology] (MAE)
RhPOv........	Rhone Poulenc Overseas Ltd. [Associated Press] (SAG)
RhPOv........	Rhone-Poulenc Overseas Ltd. [Associated Press] (SAG)
RHPOY........	Rhone-Poulenc SA (MHDW)
RHPR........	Revue d'Histoire et de Philosophie Religeuses [A publication] (ODCC)
RHPS........	Phillips [R.H.], Inc. [NASDAQ symbol] (SAG)
RHPS........	Radiation-Hardened Power Supply
RHPS........	Rapid Housing Payment System [Department of Housing and Urban Development] (GFGA)
RHPSW........	Phillips(R.H.)Inc. Wrrt [NASDAQ symbol] (TTSB)
RHQ........	Regimental Headquarters
RHQ........	Regional Headquarters (NITA)
RHR........	Rear Headrest
RHR........	Receiver Holding Register
RHR........	Reheater (AAG)
RHR........	Rejectable Hazard Rate (IEEE)
RHR........	Renal Hypertensive Rat [Medicine] (DMAA)
RHR........	Residual Heat Removal [Nuclear energy] (NRCH)
RHR........	Resting Heart Rate [Cardiology]
r/hr........	Roentgens per Hour (AABC)
RHR........	Rohr, Inc. [NYSE symbol] (SPSG)
RHR........	Roughness Height Rating (MSA)
RHR........	Royal Highland Regiment [Military unit] [British]
RHRP........	Residual Heat Removal Pump [Nuclear energy] (NRCH)
RHRS........	Residual Heat Removal System [Nuclear energy] (NRCH)
RHRSD........	Revised Hamilton Rating Scale for Depression [Test] (TMMY)
RHRSW........	Residual Heat Removal Service Water [Nuclear energy] (NRCH)
RHS........	Rectangular Hollow Section [Metal industry]
RHS........	Regency Health Services [NYSE symbol] (TTSB)
RHS........	Regency Health Services, Inc. [NYSE symbol] (SAG)
RHS........	Retirement History Survey
RHS........	Right-Hand Side
RHS........	Robin Hood Society [British] (DBA)
RHS........	Rocketdyne Hybrid Simulator [NASA] (NASA)
RHS........	Rodeo Historical Society (EA)
RHS........	Rolled Hollow Section
RHS........	Rough Hard Sphere [Model of liquids]
rhs........	Roundheaded Screw (BARN)
RHS........	Royal Historical Society [British]
RHS........	Royal Horticultural Society [British] (ARC)
RHS........	Royal Humane Society [British]
RHSA........	Radio Historical Society of America (NTCM)
RHSC........	Richmond Hill School Company [British military] (DMA)
RHSC........	Right-Hand-Side by Centroid
RHSC........	Right-Hand Side Console [NASA] (KSC)
RHSCH........	Rhodes Scholar
RhSh........	Rosh Hashanah [New Year] (BJA)
RHSI........	Royal Horticultural Society of Ireland (PDAA)
RHSI........	Rubber Heel and Sole Institute [Defunct] (EA)
RHSJ........	Religious Hospitallers of St. Joseph [Roman Catholic women's religious order]
RhSNA........	National Archives of Rhodesia, Salisbury, Rhodesia [Library symbol Library of Congress] (LCLS)
RHSNSW........	Royal Humane Society of New South Wales
RHSP........	Registered Hazardous Substances Professional [Environmental science]
RHSSA........	Royal Humane Society of South Australia [Australia]
RHSV........	Royal Horticultural Society of Victoria [Australia]
RHT........	Radiant Heat Temperature (NASA)
RHT........	Register Holding Time (NITA)
RHT........	Renal Homotransplantation [Medicine] (DMAA)
RHT........	Reynolds Hydrodynamic Theory [Physics]
RHT........	Richton International Corp. [AMEX symbol] (SPSG)
RHT........	Richton Intl [AMEX symbol] (TTSB)
RHT........	Right Hypertropia [Ophthalmology]
RHTM........	Regional Highway Traffic Model [Database] [Obsolete]
rhTPO........	Recombinant Human Thrombopoietin [Hematology]
RHTPS........	Razor Hafters' Trade Protection Society [A union] [British]
RHTS........	Reactor Heat Transport System (NRCH)
RHU........	Radioisotope Heater Unit (NASA)
RHU........	Registered Health Underwriter [NAHU]
RHU........	Requisition Held Up (DNAB)
RHU........	Reserved for Hardware Use [Computer science] (IAA)
RHU........	Residuum Hydrocracking Unit [Petroleum refining]
RHU........	Rheumatology [Medical specialty] (DHSM)
RHUDO........	Regional Housing and Urban Development Office
rHuEPO........	Recombinant Human Erythropoietin [Biochemistry]
RHV........	Registered Health Visitor [British]
RHV........	Remnant Hepatic Volume [Hematology]
RHV........	RHYS Industries Ltd. [Vancouver Stock Exchange symbol]
RHV........	Road Haulage Vehicle (DCTA)
RHV........	San Jose, CA [Location identifier FAA] (FAAL)
RHW........	Radiant Heat Warmer (STED)
RHW........	Required Hangar Width (MCD)
RHW........	Reversible Half-Wave
RHW........	Right Half Word
RHW........	Router Header Word (NASA)
RHWAC........	Reversible Half-Wave Alternating Current
RHWACDC........	Reversible Half-Wave Alternating Current - Direct Current
RHWB........	[The] Reverend Henry Ward Beecher [American clergyman, 1813-1887]
RHWDC........	Reversible Half-Wave Direct Current
RHWR........	RADAR Homing and Warning Receiver (MCD)
RHX........	Atlanta, GA [Location identifier FAA] (FAAL)
RHX........	Regenerative Heat Exchanger [Nuclear energy] (NRCH)
RHY........	Rhyolite Resources [Vancouver Stock Exchange symbol]
RHYTHM........	Remember How You Treat Hazardous Materials [E. I. Du Pont De Nemours & Co. program]
Rhythm........	Rhythmica [of Aristoxenus] [Classical studies] (OCD)
RI........	Chicago, Rock Island & Pacific Railroad Co. (MHDB)
RI........	Eastern Airlines [ICAO designator] (AD)
RI........	Indonesia [IYRU nationality code] (IYR)
Ri........	Input Resistance (IDOE)
RI........	Input Resistor (STED)
RI........	Member of the Royal Institute of Painters in Water Colours [British]
RI........	Morrison Restaurants, Inc. [NYSE symbol] (SPSG)
RI........	RADAR Input
RI........	RADAR Intercept (IAA)
RI........	RADAR Interference (LAIN)
RI........	Radiation Indicator [Nuclear energy] (NRCH)
RI........	Radiation Intensity (AABC)
RI........	Radicalist International [Defunct] (EA)
RI........	Radioimmunology (DB)
RI........	Radio Industry [Telecommunications] (IAA)
RI........	Radio Inertial (MCD)
RI........	Radio Influence
RI........	Radio Inspector
RI........	Radio Interference (MCD)
RI........	Radioisotope
RI........	Radix Institute (EA)
RI........	Rampart Institute (EA)
RI........	Random Interlace [Television]
RI........	Random Interval (AEBS)
RI........	Range Instrumentation (MCD)
RI........	Ranger Instructor [Army] (INF)
R/I........	Rate of Interest [Economics]
RI........	REACT International (EA)
RI........	Reactor Island [Nuclear energy] (NRCH)
RI........	Readers International [Subscription book club] [British]
RI........	Read-In (DEN)
RI........	Reallocation Inventory (AFIT)
RI........	Receiver Interface
RI........	Receiving Inspection (AAG)
RI........	Recession Index (STED)
RI........	Recipe Index [A publication]

RI	Recombinant Inbred [*Genetics*]
RI	Reconnaissance Inspection [*Military*] (GFGA)
RI	Recovery, Inc.
RI	Recruit Induction [*Military*]
RI	Recruit Instruction [*Navy*]
RI	Recurrent Intussusception
RI	Redheads International · (EA)
RI	Referential Integrity [*Computer science*] (PCM)
RI	Reflective Insulation [*Technical drawings*]
RI	Refractive Index
RI	Refugees International (EA)
RI	Regenerative Index (STED)
RI	Regimental Institute [*British military*] (DMA)
RI	Regina Imperatrix [*Queen Empress*] [*Latin*]
RI	Regional Ileitis [*Medicine*]
RI	Registro Italiano [*Italian ship classification society*] (DS)
RI	Regular Insulin [*Pharmacology*] (DAVI)
RI	Rehabilitation International (EA)
RI	Reimplantation [*Dentistry*]
RI	Reinitiate (SAA)
RI	Reinsurance (ADA)
RI	Reissue [*of a book or periodical*] [*Publishing*]
RI	Relative Intensity
RI	Relaxation Instruction [*Psychology*]
RI	Release-Inhibiting Factor [*Endocrinology*] (MAE)
RI	Release Inhibition (STED)
RI	Reliability Index
RI	Religious Instruction (ADA)
RI	Remedial Investigation [*Environmental Protection Agency*] (DOMA)
RI	Remission Induction [*Oncology*]
RI	Renal Insufficiency [*Medicine*] (STED)
RI	Repeat Indication [*Telecommunications*] (TEL)
RI	Replaceable Item
RI	Replicative Intermediate [*Medicine*] (MAE)
RI	Report of Investigation
RI	Repulsion Induction [*Motor*]
RI	Request for Information (MCD)
RI	Require Identification
RI	Rescue, Inc. (EA)
RI	Research Institute [*Fort Belvoir, VA*] [*United States Army Engineer Topographic Laboratories*] (GRD)
RI	Residual Income
RI	Resistance Index
RI	Resistance Inductance (IEEE)
RI	Resistance International (EA)
RI	Resolve, Inc. (EA)
RI	Resonance Integral [*Nuclear energy*] (NRCH)
RI	Respiratory Illness [*Medicine*]
RI	Respiratory Index (STED)
RI	Retention Index
RI	Reticulocyte Index (STED)
RI	Retirement Income
RI	Retreats International (EA)
RI	Retroactive Inhibition [*Psychology*]
RI	Retroactive Interference (STED)
RI	Reunite, Inc. (EA)
RI	Reverberation Index
RI	RHEMA [*Restoring Hope through Educational and Medical Aid*] International (EA)
RI	Rhode Island [*Postal code*]
RI	Rhode Island Supreme Court Reports [*A publication*] (ILCA)
RI	Ribonuclease Inhibitor
RI	Ribosomal [*Protein*] [*Cytology*]
Ri	Ricardus Anglicus [*Deceased, 1242*] [*Authority cited in pre-1607 legal work*] (DSA)
RI	Richardson Number [*Physics*]
RI	Right Iliac [*Crest*] [*Anatomy*] (DAVI)
RI	Rigorous Imprisonment [*British military*] (DMA)
RI	Ring Index [*of chemical compounds*] [*A publication*]
RI	Ring Indicator [*MODEM*] (PCM)
RI	Ringing [*Modem status information light*] [*Computer science*] (IGQR)
RI	Rio-Sul, Servicos Aereos Regionais SA [*Brazil ICAO designator*] (ICDA)
RI	Robotics International Association of the Society of Manufacturing Engineers (BTTJ)
RI	Rock Island Lines [*Railroad*]
RI	Rockwell International Corp. (MCD)
RI	Rodale Intstitute (EA)
R-I	Rodeway Inns of America (EFIS)
RI	Rolf Institute (EA)
RI	Room Index (PDAA)
RI	Roses, Inc. (NTPA)
RI	Rosette Inhibition (STED)
RI	Rotary International (EA)
RI	Routing Identifier [*or Indicator*] (AFM)
RI	Royal Institute of Painters in Watercolours [*British*] (WA)
RI	Royal Institute of Painters in Water-Colours, London [*1831*] (NGC)
RI	Royal Institution [*British*]
RI	Royal Irish [*Military unit*] [*British*]
RI	Rubber Insulation [*Technical drawings*]
RI	Ruby Tuesday [*NYSE symbol*] [*Formerly, Morrison Restaurants*] (SG)
RI	Ruby Tuesday, Inc. [*NYSE symbol*] (SAG)
R/I	Rule In (DAVI)
RI	Rule Interpretation

RI	Rulers of India [*A publication*]
RI	Runaway Inflation (MHDB)
RI	Rutherford Institute (EA)
RIA	Radioimmunoassay [*Clinical chemistry*]
RIA	Railroad Insurance Association
RIA	Railway Industry Association [*British*] (EAIO)
RIA	Rain in Area (ADA)
RIA	Randomized Intervention Analysis [*Experimental design*]
RIA	Reactivity Initiated Accident [*Nuclear energy*] (NRCH)
RIA	Registered Industrial and Cost Accountant
RIA	Registered Investment Adviser [*Securities*]
RIA	Regulatory Impact Analysis [*or Assessment*]
RIA	Regulatory Impact Assessment [*Environmental science*] (COE)
RIA	Religious Instruction Association [*Later, PERSC*]
RIA	Remote Intelligence Acquisition
RIA	Removable Instrument Assembly [*Nuclear energy*] (NRCH)
RIA	Research Institute of America [*New York, NY*] [*Information service or system*] (IID)
RIA	Research into Aging (WDAA)
RIA	Reset Indicators from Accumulator [*Computer science*] (IAA)
RIA	Retroactive Liability Insurance
RIA	Reversible Ischemic Attack [*Medicine*] (DMAA)
RIA	Rich International Airways, Inc. [*ICAO designator*] (FAAC)
RIA	Robotic Industries Association
RIA	Robot Institute of America (NADA)
RIA	Rock Island Arsenal [*Illinois*] [*Army*]
RIA	Royal Irish Academy
RIA	Santa Maria [*Brazil*] [*Airport symbol*] (OAG)
RIAA	Recording Industry Association of America (EA)
RIAADA	Research Institute of African and African Diaspora Arts (EA)
RIAC	Regional Industry Advisory Committee [*Civil Defense*]
RIAC	Royal Irish Automobile Club (EAIO)
RIACS	Research Institute for Advanced Computer Science [*University Space Research Association*] [*Research center*] (RCD)
RIAD	Rencontres Internationales des Assureurs Defense [*Genoa, Italy*] (EA)
RIA-DA	Radioimmunoassay Double Antibody [*Test*] [*Clinical chemistry*]
RIAEC	Rhode Island Atomic Energy Commission
RIAES	Rhode Island Agricultural Experiment Station [*University of Rhode Island*] [*Research center*] (RCD)
RIAF	Royal Indian Air Force
RIAF	Royal Iraqi Air Force
RIAI	Royal Institute of the Architects of Ireland
RIAIAD	Reverse International Acronyms, Initialisms, and Abbreviations Dictionary [*A publication*]
RIAL	Religion in American Life (EA)
RIAL	Revised Individual Allowance List [*Navy*] (NVT)
RIAL	Rock Island Arsenal Laboratories [*Illinois*] (MCD)
RIAL	Runway Identifiers and Approach Lighting [*Aviation*] (IAA)
RIAM	Royal Irish Academy of Music
RIAP	Research Institute for Asia and the Pacific [*Australia*]
RIAQRA	Radon Gas and Indoor Air Quality Research Act of 1986 (COE)
RIAR	Requirements Inventory Analysis Report (AFM)
RIA-R	Rock Island Arsenal General Thomas J. Rodman Laboratory [*Army*]
RIAS	Radio in American Sector [*of Berlin*] (SAA)
RIAS	Readiness Information Access System (MCD)
RIAS	Research Initiation and Support [*National Science Foundation program*]
RIAS	Research Institute for Advanced Studies [*Martin Marietta Corp.*]
RIAS	Roter Interactional Analysis System [*Medicine*] (DMAA)
RIAS	Royal Incorporation of Architects in Scotland
RIAS	Rundfunk im Amerikanischen Sektor Berlins [*Radio in American Sector*] [*Germany*]
RIASC	Royal Indian Army Service Corps [*British*]
RIA/SE	Rock Island Arsenal/Science and Engineering Directorate [*Illinois*]
RIAST	Reitan Indiana Aphasic Screening Test [*Speech and Language Therapy*] (DAVI)
RIA Tax	Research Institute of America Tax Coordinator [*A publication*] (DLA)
RIAX	Rich International Airways, Inc. [*Air carrier designation symbol*]
RIB	Racing Information Bureau [*British*] (CB)
RIB	Radioactive Ion Beam (COE)
RIB	Railway Information Bureau
RIB	Receiver Interface Board [*Navy Navigation Satellite System*] (DNAB)
RIB	Recoverable Item Breakdown
RIB	Recyclable, Incineratable, Biodegradable [*Food packaging*]
RIB	Ribbed (AAG)
RIB	Riberalta [*Bolivia*] [*Airport symbol*] (OAG)
Rib	Ribose [*Also, r*] [*A sugar*]
RIB	Right Inboard (MCD)
RIB	Right Intermediate Bronchus [*Anatomy*]
RIB	Rigid Inflatable Boat (MUSM)
RIB	River Ice Breaker (PDAA)
RIB	[*The*] Roman Inscriptions of Britain [*A publication*] (OCD)
RIB	Rubberized Inflatable Boat (DOMA)
RIB	Rural and Industries Bank of Western Australia [*Commercial firm*]
RIB	Rural Industries Bureau
RIBA	Recombinant Immunoblot Assay [*Medicine*]
RIBA	Royal Institute of British Architects (IID)
RIBA	Royal Institute of British Architects, London [*1834*] (NGC)
RIBC	Rigid Intermediate Bulk Container
RI Bd RC	Rhode Island Board of Railroad Commission Reports [*A publication*] (DLA)
RIBE	Reactive Ion Beam Etching
RIBEA	Rhode Island Business Educators Association (EDAC)
RIBI	Ribi ImmunoChem Res [*NASDAQ symbol*] (TTSB)

RIBI	Ribi Immunochem Research, Inc. [*NASDAQ symbol*] (NQ)
RibiIm	Ribi Immunochem Research, Inc. [*Associated Press*] (SAG)
RIBIT	Read in Bed - It's Terrific
RIBLIM	Reduction in Benefit Limitation
RIBMESC	Resources Information Bank on Multicultural Education (AIE)
ribnwk	Ribbonwork (VRA)
Ribozym	Ribozyme Pharmaceuticals, Inc. [*Associated Press*] (SAG)
RIBS	Readiness in Base Service [*Air Force*] (DOMA)
RIBS	Restructured Infantry Battalion System (AABC)
RIBS	Royal Institute of British Sculptors
RIBSS	Rutherford Ion Backscattering [*Medicine*] (DMAA)
RIBSS	Research Institute for the Behavioral and Social Sciences [*Army*]
rib vlt	Ribbed Vault (VRA)
RIC	RADAR Indicating Console [*FAA*]
RIC	RADAR Input Control
RIC	RADAR Intercept Calculator
RIC	RADAR Intercept Control
RIC	Radioimmunoconjugate
RIC	Radio Industry Council [*British*]
RIC	Radon Information Council (COE)
RIC	Rafter Input Converter
RIC	Rainforest Information Centre [*Australia*] (EAIO)
RIC	Range Instrumentation Conference (MUGU)
RIC	Range Instrumentation Coordination (KSC)
RIC	Raptor Information Center (EA)
RIC	Rare-Earth Information Center (EA)
RIC	Read-In Counter
RIC	Receiver Impulse Characteristic (IAA)
RIC	Reciprocal Impedance Converter (PDAA)
RIC	Reconstituted Ion Current [*Chromatography*]
RIC	Reconstructed Ion Chromatogram
RIC	Record Identification Code [*Navy*]
RIC	Recruiter Identification Code [*Military*]
RIC	Regolamento Internazionale Carrozze [*International Carriage and Van Union*]
RIC	Regulated Investment Company [*Business term*]
RIC	Relocation Instruction Counter [*Computer science*] (OA)
RIC	Remand in Custody (WDAA)
RIC	Remote Information Center
RIC	Remote Interactive Communications [*Xerox Corp.*]
RIC	Renomedullary Interstitial Cell (DB)
RIC	Repairable Identification Code
RIC	Repairable Item Code
RIC	Repair Induction Code [*Module Maintenance Facility*]
RIC	Repertoire Bibliographique des Institutions Chretiennes [*Bibliographical Repertory of Christian Institutions*] [*Centre de Recherche et de Documentation des Institutions Chretiennes*] [*France*] [*Information service or system*] (CRD)
RIC	Replaceable Item Code
RIC	Replacement Ion Chromatography [*Spectrometry*]
RIC	Request for Instrumentation Clarification [*NASA*] (KSC)
RIC	Resident Inspector-in-Charge
RIC	Resistance, Inductance, and Capacitance (NASA)
RIC	Resource Conservation and Recovery Act Docket and Information Center [*Environmental Protection Agency*] (AEPA)
RIC	Resource Identification Code [*Navy*]
RIC	Resource Information Center System [*Search system*]
RIC	Retirement Income Credit
Ric	Ricardus Malumbra [*Deceased, 1334*] [*Authority cited in pre-1607 legal work*] (DSA)
Ric	Richard (King of England) (DLA)
RIC	Richardson's Airway, Inc. [*ICAO designator*] (FAAC)
RIC	Richmond [*Virginia*] [*Airport symbol*]
RIC	Richmond [*Florida*] [*Seismograph station code, US Geological Survey Closed*] (SEIS)
RIC	Richmond [*Diocesan abbreviation*] [*Virginia*] (TOCD)
RIC	Ricks College, David O. McKay Learning Resources Center, Rexburg, ID [*OCLC symbol*] (OCLC)
RIC	Right Iliac Crest [*Anatomy*] (DAVI)
RIC	Right Internal Capsule [*Medicine*] (MEDA)
RIC	Right Internal Carotid [*Artery*] [*Anatomy*] (DAVI)
RIC	Right Internal Cartoid [*Medicine*] (MEDA)
RIC	Road Information Center [*Arab Contractors Co.*] (IID)
RIC	Rockwell International Corp. (NASA)
RIC	Rodeo Information Commission (EA)
RIC	Roman Imperial Coinage [*A publication*] (OCD)
RIC	Routing Identification Code (NATG)
RIC	Royal Institute of Chemistry [*Later, RSC*] [*British*]
RIC	Royal Irish Constabulary
RIC	Rural Information Center [*Department of Agriculture Information service or system*] (IID)
RIC	Rural Innovation Centre [*Western Australia*]
RICA	Costa Rica International, Inc. [*NASDAQ symbol*] (SAG)
RICA	Railway Industry Clearance Association (EA)
RICA	Research Institute for Consumer Affairs [*British*]
RICA	Right Internal Cartoid Artery (MEDA)
RICA	Rural Industry Council of Australia
RICAL	Research Information Center and Library [*Foster Wheeler Corp.*] [*Information service or system*] (IID)
Ric & S.	Rickards and Saunders' English Locus Standi Reports [*1890-94*] [*A publication*] (DLA)
Ricar	Ricardus [*Authority cited in pre-1607 legal work*] (DSA)
RICASIP	Research Information Center and Advisory Service on Information Processing [*National Bureau of Standards - National Science Foundation*]

RICB	Research into Child Blindness [*British*] (DI)
RICC	Regional Interagency Coordinating Committee [*Department of Labor*]
RICC	Remote Intercomputer Communications Interface (MCD)
RICC	Reportable Item Control Code [*Army*] (AABC)
RICC	Rice Industry Coordination Committee [*New South Wales, Australia*]
RICE	American Rice, Inc. [*NASDAQ symbol*] (SAG)
RICE	Amer Rice [*NASDAQ symbol*] (TTSB)
RICE	Recreational Industries Council on Exporting (EA)
RICE	Regional Information and Communications Exchange [*Rice University Library*] [*Houston, TX*]
RICE	Relative Index of Combat Effectiveness [*Military British*]
RICE	Research and Information Centre on Eritrea (EA)
RICE	Research Institute on Care for the Elderly [*British*] (DBA)
RICE	Resources in Computer Education [*Northwest Regional Educational Laboratory Microcomputer Software and Information for Teachers*] [*No longer available online*] [*Information service or system*]
RICE	Rest, Ice, Compression, Elevation [*Medicine*]
Rice	Rice's South Carolina Law Reports [*1838-39*] [*A publication*] (DLA)
RICE	Right to a Comprehensive Education (EAIO)
Rice Ch	Rice's South Carolina Equity Reports [*A publication*] (DLA)
RICE-DIETS	Rest, Ice, Compression, and Elevation, - Drugs, Incision, Exercise Therapy, and Surgery [*Treatment for knee injuries*]
Rice Dig	Rice's Digest of Patent Office Decisions [*A publication*] (DLA)
Rice Eq	Rice's South Carolina Equity Reports [*1838-39*] [*A publication*] (DLA)
Rice Ev	Rice's Law of Evidence [*A publication*] (DLA)
Rice L (SC)	Rice's South Carolina Law Reports [*A publication*] (DLA)
Rice's Code	Rice's Code of Practice [*Colorado*] [*A publication*] (DLA)
Rice U	Rice University (GAGS)
RICH	Radiation-Induced Color Halo [*Physics*]
Rich	Richard (King of England) (DLA)
Rich	Richardson's Reports [*2-5 New Hampshire*] [*A publication*] (DLA)
RICH	Richland, WA [*Commercial waste site*] (GAAI)
RICH	Richmond National Battlefield Park
Rich & H	Richardson and Hook's Street Railway Decisions [*A publication*] (DLA)
Rich & S	Richardson and Sayles' Select Cases of Procedure without Writ [*Selden Society Publication 60*] [*A publication*] (DLA)
Rich & W	Richardson and Woodbury's Reports [*2 New Hampshire*] [*A publication*] (DLA)
Richardson Law Practice	Richardson's Establishing a Law Practice [*A publication*] (DLA)
Rich Ch Pr	Richardson's Chancery Practice [*1838*] [*A publication*] (DLA)
Rich CP	Richardson's Practice Common Pleas [*England*] [*A publication*] (DLA)
RichCst	Rich Coast Resources [*Associated Press*] (SAG)
Rich Ct Cl	Richardson's Court of Claims Reports [*A publication*] (DLA)
Rich Dict	Richardson's New Dictionary of the English Language [*A publication*] (DLA)
RICHE	Reseaud'Information et de Communication Hospitalier (OSI)
RichEl	Richardson Electronics Ltd. [*Associated Press*] (SAG)
RICHEL	Richmond - Cape Henry Environmental Laboratory [*NASA/USGS*]
Richfood	Richfood Holdings, Inc. [*Associated Press*] (SAG)
Rich Land A	Richey's Irish Land Act [*A publication*] (DLA)
Rich NH	Richardson's Reports [*3-5 New Hampshire*] [*A publication*] (DLA)
Rich PRCP	Richardson's Practical Register of English Common Pleas [*A publication*] (DLA)
Rich Pr KB	Richardson's Attorney's Practice in the Court of King's Bench [*8th ed.*] [*1792*] [*A publication*] (DLA)
Rich Pr Reg	Richardson's Practical Register of English Common Pleas [*A publication*] (DLA)
Richton	Richton International Corp. [*Associated Press*] (SAG)
Rich Wills	Richardson's Law of Testaments and Last Wills [*A publication*] (DLA)
RichyEl	Richey Electronics [*Associated Press*] (SAG)
RICI	Remanufacturing Industries Council International (NTPA)
RICK	Ricks Cabaret International, Inc. [*NASDAQ symbol*] (SAG)
RICK	Rick's Cabaret Intl [*NASDAQ symbol*] (TTSB)
RICK-A	Rickettsial Battery [*Bacteriology*] (DAVI)
Rick & M	Rickards and Michael's English Locus Standi Reports [*A publication*] (DLA)
Rick & S	Rickards and Saunders' English Locus Standi Reports [*A publication*] (DLA)
RickCab	Ricks Cabaret International, Inc. [*Associated Press*] (SAG)
Rick Eng St	Rickard's English Statutes [*A publication*] (DLA)
Ricks	Ricks Cabaret International, Inc. [*Associated Press*] (SAG)
RICKW	Rick's Cabaret Intl Wrrt [*NASDAQ symbol*] (TTSB)
RICL	Receipt Inspection Checklist (DNAB)
RICM	Reflection Interference Contrast Microscopy
RICM	Registre International des Citoyens du Monde [*International Registry of World Citizens*]
RICM	Right Intercostal Margin [*Medicine*]
RICMD	Richmond Contract Management District (SAA)
RICMO	RADAR Input Countermeasures Officer [*Air Force*]
RICMT	RADAR Input Countermeasures Technician [*Air Force*]
RICO	Racketeer Influenced and Corrupt Organization Act (DFIT)
RICO	Racketeer-Influenced and Corrupt Organizations [*Nickname of a 1970 law used by federal prosecutors to indict organized crime leaders*]
RICO	Racketeering in Interstate Commerce (DICI)
RI Comp of Rules of St Agencies	Rhode Island Compilation of Rules of State Agencies [*A publication*] (DLA)
RI Const	Rhode Island Constitution [*A publication*] (DLA)
RICP	Recurrent Intrahepatic Cholestasis of Pregnancy [*Obstetrics*] (DMAA)
RICRS	Rockford Institute Center on Religion and Society (EA)
Ric Ruf	Ricardus Rufulus [*Authority cited in pre-1607 legal work*] (DSA)

RICS .... Range Instrumentation Control System
RICS .... Remote Image Confirming Sensor (MCD)
RICS .... Reports Index Control (MCD)
RICS .... Respiratory Intensive Care System [*Medicine*]
RICS .... Right Intercostal Space [*Anatomy*] (DAVI)
RICS .... Royal Institution of Chartered Surveyors [*British*]
RICS .... Rubber-Impregnated Chopped Strand (PDAA)
RI Ct Rec.... Rhode Island Court Records [*A publication*] (DLA)
RICU .... Respiratory Intensive Care Unit [*Medicine*]
RID .... RADAR Input Drum
RID .... Radial Immunodiffusion [*Analytical biochemistry*]
RID .... Radio Intelligence Division [*of the Federal Communications Commission*]
RID .... Radioisotope Detection
RID .... Range Instruments Development (MCD)
RID .... Rapidate Interactive Debugger [*Computer science*] (MHDI)
RID .... Real-Fluid Isentropic Decompression [*Engineering*]
RID .... Recepter Interacting Domain [*Biochemistry*]
RID .... Record Identity [*Military*] (AFIT)
RID .... Records Issue Date [*Bell System*] (TEL)
RID .... Reduced Ignition Relay (MCD)
RID .... Refractive Index Detector [*Instrumentation*]
RID .... Regimented Inmate Discipline [*Mississippi State Penitentiary*]
RID .... Registry of Interpreters for the Deaf (EA)
RID .... Reglement International Concernant le Transport des Marchandises Dangereuses [*International Regulation Governing the Carriage of Dangerous Goods*]
RID .... Regulatory Integration Division [*Environmental Protection Agency*] (GFGA)
RID .... Released to Inactive Duty
RID .... Reliability Index Determination (MCD)
RID .... Remission-Inducing Drug [*Medicine*]
RID .... Remove Intoxicated Drivers [*An association*]
RID .... Research Institutes and Divisions [*of National Institutes of Health*]
RID .... Reset Inhibit Drive
RID .... Reset Inhibit Drum
RID .... Retrofit Installation Data (MCD)
RID .... Reversible Intravas Device
RID .... Review Item Discrepancy (MCD)
RID .... Review Item Disposition [*NASA*] (NASA)
RID .... Richmond, IN [*Location identifier FAA*] (FAAL)
RID .... Rider College Library, Lawrenceville, NJ [*OCLC symbol*] (OCLC)
RID .... Royal Irish Dragoons [*British military*] (DMA)
RIDA .... Raster Image Device Accelerator [*Printer technology*]
RIDA .... Reverse Isotope Dilution Assay [*Chemical analysis*]
RIDA .... Rural and Industrial Development Authority (NADA)
RIDAC .... Range Interference Detecting and Control
RIDAURA ..... Remission Inducing Drug, Au [*Chemical symbol for gold*], Rheumatoid Arthritis [*Gold-based drug manufactured by SmithKline Beckman Corp.*]
RIDB .... Readiness Intergrated Database
RIDC .... Ryerson International Development Centre [*Ryerson Polytechnical Institute*] [*Canada Research center*] (RCD)
RIDCSF .... Radial Immunodiffusion Cerebrospinal Fluid [*or Colloidal Gold*] [*Immunology*] (DAVI)
RIDD .... Range Instrumentation Development Division (SAA)
Riddell........... Riddell Sports, Inc. [*Associated Press*] (SAG)
RIDDLE........ Rapid Information Display and Dissemination in Library Environments (TELE)
Riddle's Lex... Riddle's Lexicon [*A publication*] (DLA)
RIDDOR .... Reporting of Injuries, Diseases, and Dangerous Occurrences Regulations [*British*]
RIDE .... Research Institute for Diagnostic Engineering
RIDE .... Ride Inc. [*NASDAQ symbol*] (TTSB)
RIDE .... Ride Snowboard Co. [*NASDAQ symbol*] (SAG)
RI Dec .... Rhode Island Decisions [*A publication*] (DLA)
RideInc......... Ride, Inc. [*Associated Press*] (SAG)
Rider C .... Rider College (GAGS)
RIDES .... Rockford Infant Developmental Scales [*Child development test*]
RIDEX .... Ridexchange (EA)
RIDF .... Random Input Describing Function [*Computer science*]
RIDG .... Ridgeview, Inc. [*NASDAQ symbol*] (SAG)
Ridg............. Ridgeway's Reports Tempore Hardwicke, Chancery and English King's Bench [*A publication*] (DLA)
RIDG............ Royal Inniskilling Dragoon Guards [*Military unit*] [*British*]
RIDG............ Royal Irish Dragoon Guards [*British military*] (DMA)
Ridg & Hard... Ridgeway's Reports Tempore Hardwicke, Chancery and English King's Bench [*A publication*] (DLA)
Ridg Ap .... Ridgeway's Irish Appeal (or Parliamentary) Cases [*A publication*] (DLA)
Ridg App ...... Ridgeway's Irish Appeal (or Parliamentary) Cases [*A publication*] (DLA)
Ridg Cas...... Ridgeway's Reports Tempore Hardwicke, Chancery and English King's Bench [*A publication*] (DLA)
RIDGE.......... Ridge [*Commonly used*] (OPSA)
RIDGE.......... Ridge InterDisciplinary Global Experiments [*Program*] [*Marine science*] (OSRA)
RIDGES........ Ridges [*Commonly used*] (OPSA)
Ridgevw .... Ridgeview, Inc. [*Associated Press*] (SAG)
Ridgew .... Ridgeway's Reports Tempore Hardwicke, Chancery and English King's Bench [*A publication*] (DLA)
Ridgew Ir PC... Ridgeway's Irish Parliamentary Reports [*1784-96*] [*A publication*] (DLA)
Ridgew L & S (Ir)... Ridgeway, Lapp, and Schoales' Irish Term Reports [*A publication*] (DLA)

Ridgew L & S (Ire)... Ridgeway, Lapp, and Schoales' Irish Term Reports [*A publication*] (ILCA)
Ridgew T Hardw... Ridgeway's Reports Tempore Hardwicke, Chancery [*27 English Reprint*] [*1744-46*] [*A publication*] (DLA)
Ridgew T Hardw (Eng)... Ridgeway Tempore Hardwicke [*27 English Reprint*] [*A publication*] (DLA)
Ridg L & S... Ridgeway, Lapp, and Schoales' Irish Term Reports [*A publication*] (DLA)
Ridg Parl Rep... Ridgeway's Irish Parliamentary Reports [*1784-96*] [*A publication*] (DLA)
Ridg PC ...... Ridgeway's Irish Appeal (or Parliamentary) Cases [*A publication*] (DLA)
Ridg Pr Rep... Ridgeway's Irish Appeal (or Parliamentary) Cases [*A publication*] (DLA)
Ridg Rep .... Ridgeway's Reports of State Trials in Ireland [*A publication*] (DLA)
Ridg St Tr... Ridgeway's (Individual) Reports of State Trials in Ireland [*A publication*] (DLA)
Ridg Temp H... Ridgeway's Reports Tempore Hardwicke, Chancery [*27 English Reprint*] [*1744-46*] [*A publication*] (DLA)
Ridg T H...... Ridgeway's Reports Tempore Hardwicke, Chancery [*27 English Reprint*] [*1744-46*] [*A publication*] (DLA)
Ridg T Hard... Ridgeway's Reports Tempore Hardwicke, Chancery and English King's Bench [*27 English Reprint*] [*A publication*] (DLA)
Ridg T Hardw... Ridgeway's Reports Tempore Hardwicke, Chancery and English King's Bench [*27 English Reprint*] [*A publication*] (DLA)
Ridgw Ir PC... Ridgeway's Irish Parliamentary Cases [*A publication*] (DLA)
RIDI .... Receiving Inspection Detail Instruction [*NASA*] (NASA)
RIDIC .... Radiopharmaceutical Internal Dose Information Center [*Oak Ridge, TN*] [*Department of Energy*] (GRD)
RIDIR.......... Resonant Ion-Dip Infrared [*Spectroscopy*]
RIDIT .... Relative to an Identified Distribution Transformation [*Pharmacology*]
RIDL .... Radiation Instrument Development Laboratory
RIDL .... Riddell Sports [*NASDAQ symbol*] (TTSB)
RIDL .... Riddell Sports, Inc. [*NASDAQ symbol*] (SPSG)
RIDL .... Ridge Instrument Development Laboratory [*Navy*]
Ridley Civil & Ecc Law... Ridley's Civil and Ecclesiastical Law [*A publication*] (DLA)
RIDP .... Polymerase [*Deoxyribonucleic Acid*] [*Later, RDDP*] [*An enzyme*]
RIDP .... RADAR-IFF Data Processor (MCD)
RIDS .... Radio Information Distribution System (MCD)
RIDS .... Range Information Display System (MCD)
RIDS .... Receiving Inspection Data Status [*Report*] [*Nuclear energy*] (NRCH)
RIDS .... Regional Operations Control Centre Information Display System [*NORAD*]
RIDS .... Regulatory Information Distribution System [*Nuclear energy*] (NRCH)
Rid Sup Proc... Riddle's Supplementary Proceedings [*New York*] [*A publication*] (DLA)
RIE .... RADAR Intercept Event
RIE .... Range of Incentive Effectiveness
RIE .... Reactive Ion Etching [*Semiconductor technology*]
RIE .... Recognised Investment Exchange [*British*]
RIE .... Refrigeration Installation Equipment (SAA)
RIE .... Research in Education [*Monthly publication of ERIC*]
RIE .... Resources in Education [*Formerly, Research in Education*] [*National Institute of Education Database*]
RIE .... Retirement Income Endowment [*Insurance*]
RIE .... Rice Lake [*Wisconsin*] [*Airport symbol*] (OAG)
RIE .... Riedel Environmental Technology (EFIS)
RIE .... Right Inboard Elevon [*Aviation*] (MCD)
RIE .... Royal Institute of Engineers [*British*]
RIEC .... Royal Indian Engineering College [*British*]
Ried............ Riedell's Reports [*68, 69 New Hampshire*] [*A publication*] (DLA)
RIEDA .... Reseau d'Innovations Educatives pour le Developpement en Afrique [*Network of Educational Innovation for Development in Africa*] (EAIO)
RIEDAC........ Research in International Economics of Disarmament and Arms Control [*A program of Columbia University School of International Affairs*]
RIEF............ Recycling Isoelectric Focusing [*Preparative electrophoresis*]
RIEI............ Roofing Industry Educational Institute (EA)
RIEM............ Research Institute for Environmental Medicine [*Army*] (MCD)
RIEP............ Rocket Immunoelectrophoresis (DB)
RIES............ Research Institute for Engineering Sciences [*Wayne State University*] [*Research center*] (RCD)
RIES............ Resonance Ionization Emission Spectroscopy
RIETCOM...... Regional Interagency Emergency Transportation Committee
RIF............ Cohen & Steers Realty Income Fund [*Formerly, Real Estate Securities Income Fund, Inc.*] [*AMEX symbol*] (CTT)
RIF............ Cohen & Steers Rlty Inc. Fd [*AMEX symbol*] (TTSB)
RIF............ Radio-Influence Field (IEEE)
RIF............ Radio Interference Filter
RIF............ Rapid Infrared Forming Technique [*Materials science*]
RIF............ Rate Increase Factor (DDC)
RIF............ Rate Input Form (NVT)
RIF............ Readiness Index Factor
RIF............ Reading Is Fundamental (EA)
RIF............ Receipt Inspection Form [*Military*] (DNAB)
RIF............ Reclearance in Flight [*Aviation*] (FAAC)
RIF............ Reconnaissance in Force [*Military*] (VNW)
RIF............ Reduced Injury Factor Baseball
RIF............ Reduction in Force [*Military*]
RIF............ Refund Information File [*IRS*]
RIF............ Relative Importance Factor (NASA)
RIF............ Release-Inhibiting Factor [*Endocrinology*]
RIF............ Reliability Improvement Factor

RIF	Reportable Item File [*Military*] (AFIT)
RIF	Resistance Inducing Factor (ADA)
RIF	Richfield [*Utah*] [*Airport symbol*] (OAG)
RIF	Richfield, UT [*Location identifier FAA*] (FAAL)
RIF	Rifampicin [*An antibacterial, antibiotic, and antituberculin*] (DAVI)
RIF	Rifampin [*Also, R/AMP, RF, RMP*] [*Bactericide*]
RIF	Rifle
RIF	Right Iliac Fossa [*Medicine*]
RIF	Right Internal Fixation [*Orthopedics*] (DAVI)
RIF	Rodeo Information Foundation [*Later, Rodeo News Bureau*]
RIF	Royal Inniskilling Fusiliers [*Military unit*] [*British*]
RIF	Royal Irish Fusiliers [*Military unit*] [*British*]
RIFA	Radioiodinated Fatty Acid [*Medicine*] (MAE)
RIFC	Radioactive Illuminated Fire Control (MCD)
RIFC	Radio In-Flight Correction
RIFC	Rat Intrinsic Factor Concentrate
RIFCM	Roll Integrated Flight Control Module (MCD)
RIFF	Raster Image File Format [*Computer science*] (BTTJ)
RIFF	Resource Interchange File Format [*Computer science*] (CDE)
RIFFED	Forced Out by a Reduction in Force
RIFFI	Riksforbundet Internationella Foereningen foer Invandrarkvinnor [*Sweden*]
RIFI	Radio Interference Field Intensity [*Meter*] (NG)
RIFI	Radio-Interference-Free Instrument
RIFIM	Radio Interference Field Intensity Meter
RIFL	Random Item File Locater
RIFLIP	Restriction Fragment-Length Polymorphism (BARN)
RIFM	Research Institute for Fragrance Materials (EA)
RIFMA	Roentgen-Isotope-Fluorescent Method of Analysis
RIFN	Recombinant Interferon [*Biochemistry*]
RIFS	Radioisotope Field Support
RIFS	Reflectometric Interference Spectroscopy [*Sensor for optical thickness*]
RI/FS	Remedial Investigation and Feasibility Study [*Environmental Protection Agency*]
RIFT	Reactor-in-Flight Test [*NASA*]
RIFT	Resin Infusion Under Flexible Tooling
RIFT/S	Reactor-in-Flight Test/System [*NASA*] (AAG)
RIG	Rabies Immune Globulin [*Immunology*]
RIG	Radio Inertial Guidance (AAG)
RIG	Radio Interference Guard
RIG	Rate Integrating Gyro
RIG	Refractive Index Gradient [*Analytical chemistry*]
RIG	Ridgeling [*Horse racing*]
RIG	Riga Airlines [*Latvia*] [*ICAO designator*] (FAAC)
RIG	Rigging (ROG)
RIG	Rio Grande [*Brazil*] [*Airport symbol*] (OAG)
RIG	Roll-Imitation Gold
RIG	Royal Institue of Geology [*British*] (NUCP)
RIG	Sonat Offshore Drilling [*NYSE symbol*] (TTSB)
RIG	Sonat Offshore Drilling, Inc. [*NYSE symbol*] (SPSG)
RIG	Transocean Offshore, Inc. [*NYSE symbol*] (SAG)
RIGB	Royal Institution of Great Britain
Rigel	Rigel Energy [*Associated Press*] (SAG)
RI Gen Laws	General Laws of Rhode Island [*A publication*] (DLA)
RIGES	Renewable Intensive Global Energy Scenario
RIGFET	Resistive Insulated-Gate Field Effect Transistor
Rigg	Select Pleas, Starrs, and Other Records from the Rolls of the Exchequer of the Jews, Edited by J. M. Riggs [*Selden Society Publications, Vol. 15*] [*A publication*] (DLA)
RIGGS	Ross Ice Shelf Geophysical and Glaciological Survey [*Ross Ice Shelf Project*]
RIGH	Rabies Immune Globulin, Human [*Immunology*] (MAE)
Rightch	Rightchoice Managed Care Co. [*Associated Press*] (SAG)
RIGHTS	Reforming Institutions to Guarantee Humane Treatment Standards [*Student legal action organization*]
RIGI	Receiving Inspection General Instruction [*NASA*] (NASA)
rIGIF	Recombinant Interferon Gamma-Inducing Factor [*Biochemistry*]
RIGR	Rhode Island Government Register [*A publication*] (AAGC)
RIGS	Radioimmunoguided Surgery [*Medicine*]
RIGS	Radio Inertial Guidance System
RIGS	Resonant Infrasonic Gauging System
RIGS	Riggs National Corp. [*NASDAQ symbol*] (NQ)
RIGS	Riggs Natl Corp. [*NASDAQ symbol*] (TTSB)
RIGS	Runway Identifiers with Glide Slope [*Aviation*]
RigsNt	Riggs National Corp. [*Associated Press*] (SAG)
RIH	Rhode Island Hospital, Providence, RI [*OCLC symbol*] (OCLC)
RIH	Right Inguinal Hernia [*Medicine*]
RIHANS	River and Harbor Aid to Navigation System [*Coast Guard*]
RIHED	Regional Institute of Higher Education and Development
RIHL	Richton International Corp. (MHDW)
RiHM	Riemann, "Handbuch der Musikgeschichte" [*A publication*]
RIHS	Royal International Horse Show [*British*]
RIHSA	Radioactive Iodinate Human Serum Albumin [*Clinical chemistry*] (AAMN)
RIHSC	Research Involving Human Subjects Committee [*U.S. Food and Drug Administration*]
RII	RADAR Intelligence Information
RII	Receiving Inspection Instruction [*Nuclear energy*] (NRCH)
RII	Request for Intelligence Acornmation [*Military*] (INF)
RII	Resort Income Investors, Inc. [*AMEX symbol*] (CTT)
RIIA	Royal Institute of International Affairs [*British*]
RIIC	Research Institute on International Change [*Columbia University*]
RIIES	Research Institute on Immigration and Ethnic Studies [*Smithsonian Institution*]

RIIS	Route Integration Instrumentation System (LAIN)
RIISE	Research Institute for Information Science and Engineering, Inc. [*Information service or system*] (IID)
RIISOM	Research Institute for Iron, Steel, and Other Metals (MHDB)
RIIXS	Remote Interrogation Information Exchange System (DNAB)
RIJ	International Romani Union - U.S. Branch
RIJ	Right Internal Jugular [*Vein*] [*Anatomy*]
RIJ	Rioja [*Peru*] [*Airport symbol*] (OAG)
RIJ	Romano Internacionalno Jekhethanibe [*International Romani Union*] (EA)
RIJC	Rhode Island Junior College [*Later, CCRI*]
RIK	Eurojet Compagnie [*British ICAO designator*] (FAAC)
RIK	Replacement in Kind (NG)
RIKE	Raman-Induced Kerr Effect (PDAA)
RIKES	Raman-Induced Kerr Effect Scattering [*Spectroscopy*]
RIL	Radio Influence Level
RIL	Radio Interference Level
RIL	Radiolocation (IAA)
RIL	Recombinant Interleukin [*Immunotherapy*]
RIL	Recoverable Item List
RIL	Red Indicator Light
RIL	Reduction in Leadtime (MCD)
RIL	Reliability Intensity Level (CAAL)
RIL	Repairable Item List (CAAL)
RIL	Representation Independent Language (NITA)
RIL	Reset Indicators of the Left Half (IAA)
RIL	Res Ipsa Loquitur [*Speaks for Itself*] [*Latin*] (LWAP)
RIL	Rifle, CO [*Location identifier FAA*] (FAAL)
RIl	Riley's South Carolina Chancery Reports [*1836-37*] [*A publication*] (DLA)
RIl	Riley's South Carolina Equity Reports [*A publication*] (DLA)
RIL	University of Rhode Island, Graduate Library School, Kingston, RI [*OCLC symbol*] (OCLC)
RILAMAC	Research in Laboratory Animal Medicine and Care
RILEM	Reunion Internationale des Laboratoires d'Essais et de Recherches sur les Materiaux et les Constructions [*International Union of Testing and Research Laboratories for Materials and Structures*] (EAIO)
Riley	Riley's Reports [*37-42 West Virginia*] [*A publication*] (DLA)
Riley	Riley's South Carolina Chancery Reports [*A publication*] (DLA)
Riley	Riley's South Carolina Law Reports [*A publication*] (DLA)
Riley Ch	Riley's South Carolina Equity Reports [*A publication*] (DLA)
Riley Eq	Riley's South Carolina Equity Reports [*A publication*] (DLA)
Riley Eq (SC)	Riley's South Carolina Equity Reports [*A publication*] (DLA)
Riley L (SC)	Riley's South Carolina Law Reports [*A publication*] (DLA)
RILFC	Rhode Island Library Film Cooperative [*Library network*]
Ril Harp	Riley's Edition of Harper's South Carolina Reports [*A publication*] (DLA)
RILKO	Research into Lost Knowledge Organisation Trust (EAIO)
RILOP	Reclamation in Lieu of Procurement [*Navy*] (NG)
RILPG	Regenerative Injection Liquid Propellant Gun (MCD)
RILS	Ranging Integration Location System
RILS	Rapid Integrated Logistic Support System [*Military*] (AABC)
RILSA	Resident Integrated Logistics Support Activity [*Military*] (AFIT)
RILSD	Resident Integrated Logistics Support Detachment [*Military*] (MCD)
RILST	Remote Integrated Logistics Support Team [*Military*] (MCD)
RILT	Rabbit Ileal Loop Test [*for enterotoxins*]
RILWAS	Regionalized Integrated Lake-Watershed Acidification Study [*Adirondack mountains*]
RIM	Mauritania [*International vehicle registration*] (ODBW)
RIM	Merrill Lynch & Co. [*AMEX symbol*] (SAG)
RIM	RADAR Input Mapper
RIM	RADAR Input Monitor (CET)
RIM	RADAR Intelligence Map
RIM	Radial Inlet Manifold
RIM	Radiant Intensity Measurements (MUGU)
RIM	Radio Imaging Method (CIST)
RIM	Radioisotope Medicine
RIM	Radioisotope Method [*Analytical chemistry*]
RIM	Railroad Interdiction Mine [*DoD*]
RIM	Rate Improvement Mortgage [*Banking*]
RIM	Reaction Injection Molding [*Plastics technology*]
RIM	Readiness Indicator Model (MCD)
RIM	Read-In Mode
RIM	Read Interrupt Mask [*Computer science*]
RIM	Receipt, Inspection, and Maintenance [*Military*]
RIM	Receiver Intermodulation [*Telecommunications*] (TEL)
RIM	Recreation Information Management System [*Department of Agriculture Washington, DC Information service or system*] (IID)
RIM	Recurrent Induced Malaria [*Medicine*] (DMAA)
RIM	Refractive Index Matching [*Coal technology*]
RIM	Regulation Interpretation Memorandum [*Environmental Protection Agency*]
RIM	Regulatory Information Memorandum [*Environmental science*] (COE)
RIM	Rehabilitation Institute of Michigan
RIM	Relational Information Management [*Acronym is title of a book by Wayne Erickson*] (PCM)
RIM	Relative Importance Measure [*Environmental science*] (COE)
RIM	Relative-Intensity Measure [*Medicine*] (DMAA)
RIM	Relative Intensity Measures [*of nursing care*]
RIM	Request Initialization Mode (IAA)
RIM	Research in Motion [*Wireless Message Device*]
RIM	Research Instrument Module (IAA)
RIM	Resident Industrial Manager
RIM	Resource Interface Module [*Datapoint*]

RIM............ Rim [*Hawaii*] [*Seismograph station code, US Geological Survey*] (SEIS)
RIM............ Rimrock Airlines, Inc. [*ICAO designator*] (FAAC)
RIM............ Rockridge Mining [*Vancouver Stock Exchange symbol*]
RIM............ Rotors in Motion [*Aviation*] (AIA)
RIM............ Royal Indian Marine
RIM............ RSU [*Remote Subscriber Unit*] Interface Module [*Telecommunications*]
RIM............ Rubber Insulation Material
RIMA .... Right Internal Mammary Anastomosis [*Cardiology*] (DAVI)
RIMA .... Right Internal Mammary Artery [*Anatomy*] (AAMN)
RIMAD .... Refractive Index Matched Anomalous Diffraction [*Light measurement*]
Rimage .... Rimage Corp. [*Associated Press*] (SAG)
RIMAS .... Russian Independent Mutual Aid Society (EA)
RIMAT .... Must Ride Company Material (FAAC)
RiMB .... Riemann, "Musikgeschichte in Beispielen" [*A publication*]
RIMB .... Roche Institute of Molecular Biology
RIMC .... Reparable Item Movement Control [*Military*] (AFIT)
RIMC .... Reportable Items of Major Combinations [*Army*] (AABC)
RIMCS .... Reparable Item Movement Control System [*Military*] (AFIT)
RIMD .... Regulation and Information Management Division [*Environmental Protection Agency*] (EPA)
RIMD .... Resources and Institutional Management Division [*NASA*]
RIME.......... Radio Inertial Missile Equipment
RIME.......... Radio Inertial Monitoring Equipment (KSC)
RIME.......... Ranking Index for Maintenance Expenditures (PDAA)
RIME.......... Relaynet International Message Exchange [*Information network*] [*Computer science*] (PCM)
RIME.......... Research Institute for Management Executives [*Washington, DC*]
RIMF.......... Reportable Item Master File [*Military*] (AFIT)
RIMG.......... Rimage Corp. [*NASDAQ symbol*] (SAG)
RIMI........... Research Improvement in Minority Institutions [*Program*] [*National Science Foundation*]
RiML .... Riemann, "Musik Lexikon" [*A publication*]
RIMLF .... Rostral Interstitial Nucleus of Medial Longitudinal Fasciculus [*Neuroanatomy*]
RIMM......... Report on Improved Manpower Management
RIMMS .... RVNAF [*Republic of Vietnam Air Force*] Improvement and Modernization Management System
RIMOB .... Reserve Indication of Mobilization [*Army*] (AABC)
RIMP .... Minimum Range to Avoid Plumb Impingement (MCD)
RIMP .... Remote Input Message Processor
RIMP .... Risk Management Program (MCD)
RIMPAC ..... Rim of the Pacific [*Naval exercise; name refers to the four participating countries: Australia, Canada, New Zealand, and the United States*]
RIMPTF....... Recording Industries Music Performance Trust Funds [*Later, MPTF*] (EA)
RIMR .... Rockefeller Institute for Medical Research
RIMRASP.... Reserve Intelligence Mobilization Readiness and Support Projects (MCD)
RIMS .... RADAR In-Flight Monitoring System
RIMS .... Radiant Intensity Measuring System
RIMS .... Radio Interference Measuring System
RIMS .... Record Information Movement Study (KSC)
RIMS .... Redrawn Inviscid Melt Spinning (EDCT)
RIMS .... Regional Information Management System [*FHWA*] (TAG)
RIMS .... Remote Information Management System
RIMS .... Replacement Inertial Measurement System
RIMS .... Requirements Inventory Management System (MCD)
RIMS .... Resonance Ionization Mass Spectrometry
RIMS .... Retarding Ion Mass Spectrometer [*Instrumentation*]
RIMS .... Revised Interheater Mobility Study (DOMA)
RIMS .... Risk and Insurance Management Society [*Database producer*] (EA)
RIMSE .... Relative Integrated Mean Square Error [*Statistics*]
RIMS II .... Regional Input-Output Modeling System
RIMSTOP.... Retail Inventory Management/Stockage Policy [*DoD*]
RIMTech ..... Research Institute for the Management of Technology [*Southern California Technology Executives Network*] [*Research center*] (RCD)
R$_{in}$............ Input Resistance (IDOE)
RIN .... Radio Inertial (MSA)
RIN .... Rassemblement pour l'Independance Nationale [*Quebec separatist party, 1960-1968*] [*Canada*]
RIN .... Rat Insulinoma [*A cell line*]
RIN .... Record Identification Number
RIN .... Redpath Industries Ltd. [*Toronto Stock Exchange symbol*]
RIN .... Reference Indication Number
RIN .... Register in Instruction [*Computer science*] (IAA)
RIN .... Regular Inertial Navigator (MCD)
RIN .... Regulatory Identifier Number [*Environmental Protection Agency*]
RIN .... Relative Intensity Noise (CIST)
RIN .... Report Identification Number [*Military*] (AABC)
Rin............. Riner's Reports [*2 Wyoming*] [*A publication*] (DLA)
RIN .... Ringi Cove [*Solomon Islands*] [*Airport symbol*] (OAG)
RIN .... Rotor Impulsive Noise [*Helicopters*]
RIN .... Royal Indian Navy
RIN .... Royal Institute of Navigation (DS)
RIN .... Springfield, MO [*Location identifier FAA*] (FAAL)
RINA.......... Resident Inspector of Naval Aircraft
RINA.......... Royal Institution of Naval Architects [*British*]
RINAL........ RADAR Inertial Altimeter
RINC.......... Recruiter-in-Charge (DNAB)
RIND.......... Research Institute of National Defense (NADA)
RIND.......... Reversible Ischemic Neurological Deficit [*or Disability*] [*Medicine*]

Riner .... Riner's Reports [*2 Wyoming*] [*A publication*] (DLA)
RINEX .... Receiver-Independent Exchange [*Navigation systems*] [*Data communications*]
RINF........... Rinforzando [*With Special Emphasis*] [*Music*]
rinf............. Rinforzando [*Enforcing*] [*Italian*] (WDAA)
RINFZ......... Rinforzando [*With Special Emphasis*] [*Music*]
RING.......... Ringer
RING.......... Ringer Corp. [*NASDAQ symbol*] (SAG)
Ring Bank.... Ringwood's Principles of Bankruptcy [*18th ed.*] [*1947*] [*A publication*] (DLA)
RINGDOC..... Pharmaceutical Literature Documentation [*Derwent Publications Ltd.*] [*British Information service or system*] (IID)
RINGDOC..... Ring Documentation (NITA)
Ringer .... Ringer Corp. [*Associated Press*] (SAG)
RINM.......... Resident Inspector of Naval Material
RINN.......... Recommended International Nonproprietary Name [*Drug research*]
RINR.......... Royal Indian Naval Reserve [*British military*] (DMA)
RINS.......... Research Institute for the Natural Sciences
RINS.......... Resident Inspector
RINS.......... Rotorace Inertial Navigation System (MCD)
RINSMAT..... Resident Inspector of Naval Material (MUGU)
RINSORD..... Resident Naval Inspector of Ordnance
RINSPOW.... Resident Naval Inspector of Powder
RINSUL....... Rubber Insulation
RINT........... RADAR Intermittent (MSA)
RINT........... Radiation Intelligence
RINT........... Reality Interactive [*NASDAQ symbol*] (TTSB)
RINT........... Reality Interactive, Inc. [*NASDAQ symbol*] (SAG)
R Int'l Arb Awards... United Nations Reports of International Arbitral Awards [*A publication*] (DLA)
RINTU......... Reality Interactive Unit [*NASDAQ symbol*] (TTSB)
RINTW........ Reality Interactive Wrrt [*NASDAQ symbol*] (TTSB)
RINVR........ Royal Indian Naval Volunteer Reserve [*British military*] (DMA)
RIO .... RADAR Intercept Officer [*Navy*]
RIO .... RADAR-Intercept Operator
RIO .... Radio Information Office [*National Audience Board*] (NTCM)
RIO .... Radio Intercept Officer (MCD)
RIO .... Ramus Infraorbitalis [*Anatomy*]
RIO .... Registry of Italian Oddities (EA)
RIO .... Relocatable Input/Output
RIO .... Remain Intact Organization (EA)
RIO .... Remote Input/Output (NITA)
RIO .... Reporting In and Out [*Military*]
RIO .... Research Industry Office (MCD)
RIO .... Reshaping the International Order [*Title of Club of Rome report*]
RIO .... Resident Inspector Office [*Coast Guard*]
RIO .... Resident Inspector of Ordnance (AAG)
RIO .... Resin-in-Pulp [*Process for uranium ore treatment*] (IIA)
RIO .... Retail Issue Outlets (NG)
RIO .... Ride-It-Out
RIO .... Right Inferior Oblique [*Projection*] [*Radiology*] (DAVI)
RIO .... Rio De Janeiro [*Brazil*] [*Airport symbol*] (OAG)
RIO .... Rio Grant [*Caja Del Rio*] [*New Mexico*] [*Seismograph station code, US Geological Survey*] [*Closed*] (SEIS)
RIO .... Rio Sierra Silver [*Vancouver Stock Exchange symbol*]
RIO .... Roll in Only (NITA)
RIO .... Royal Italian Opera
RioAl .... Rio Algom Ltd. [*Associated Press*] (SAG)
RIOC .... Remote Input/Output Controller [*Computer science*] (MHDB)
RIOGD .... Rio Grande (FAAC)
RIOH .... Rio Hotel & Casino [*Formerly, MarCor Resorts, Inc.*] [*NASDAQ symbol*] (SPSG)
RioHtl .... Rio Hotel & Casino [*Associated Press*] (SAG)
RIOJ........... Recurrent Intrahepatic Obstructive Jaundice [*Medicine*] (MAE)
RIOMETER... Relative Ionospheric Opacity Meter
RIOPR......... Rhode Island Open Pool Reactor
RIO-RIT-RIM... Religion Index Database - Religion Index One; Religion Index Two; Research in Ministry [*American Theological Library Association*] [*Information service or system*] (CRD)
RIOS .... Joint Working Group on River Inputs to Ocean Systems [*Marine science*] (MSC)
RIOS .... Receiving Inspection Operating Sheet (MCD)
RIOS .... Remote Input-Output System [*Computer science*] (IAA)
RIOS .... ROM [*Read-Only Memory*] BIOS [*Pronounced "rye-ose"*] [*Computer science*]
RIOS .... Rotating Image Optical Scanner
RIOT .... RAM Input/Output Timer
RIOT .... Real-Time Input-Output Transducer [*or Translator*] [*Computer science*]
RIOT .... Remote Independently-Operated Transceiver
RIOT .... Remote Input/Output Terminal [*Computer science*]
RIOT .... Resolution of Initial Operational Techniques
RIOT .... Retrieval of Information by On-Line Terminal [*Atomic Energy Authority*] [*Computer science British*]
RIOTEX .... Riot Exercise (DNAB)
RIP............. RADAR Identification Point (AFM)
RIP............. RADAR Improvement Plan (NATG)
RIP............. RADAR Improvement Program
RIP............. Radioimmunoprecipitation [*Clinical chemistry*]
RIP............. Radioisotopic Pathology [*Medical specialty*] (DHSM)
RIP............. Radiological Information Plot (NATG)
RIP............. Random Input Sampling [*Computer science*]
RIP............. Rapid Ignition Propagation (MCD)
RIP............. Rapid Infusion Pump [*Chemotherapy*] (DAVI)
RIP............. Rapid Installation Plan

RIP............ Raster Image Processor [*Printer technology*]
RIP............ Rate-Invariant Path [*Economic theory*]
RIP............ Rays Initiating from a Point (MCD)
RIP............ RCRA [*Resource Conservation and Recovery Act*] Implementation Plan [*Environmental Protection Agency*] (GFGA)
RIP............ Reactive Ion Plating [*Coating technology*]
RIP............ Reactor Instrument Penetration Valve (IEEE)
RIP............ Readiness Improvement Program [*Military*] (CAAL)
RIP............ Rearrangement Induced Premeiotically [*Genetics*]
RIP............ Receiving Inspection Plan [*Nuclear energy*] (NRCH)
RIP............ Recoverable Item Program [*Marine Corps*]
RIP............ Reduction Implementation Panel [*DoD*]
RIP............ Reduction in Paperwork (SAA)
RIP............ Reenlistment Incentive Program (DNAB)
RIP............ Refractive Index Profile
RIP............ Register Indicator Panel
RIP............ Register of Intelligence Publications (MCD)
RIP............ Relationship Improvement Program (SAA)
RIP............ Reliability Improvement Program
RIP............ Remain in Place (MCD)
RIP............ Remote Image Protocol [*Computer science*]
RIP............ Remote Indicator Panel (CAAL)
RIP............ Remote Instrument Package (PDAA)
RIP............ Renin Inhibitory Peptide [*Biochemistry*]
RIP............ Repeat-Induced Point Mutation [*Genetic engineering technique*]
RIP............ Replication Initiation Point [*Mapping for deoxyribonucleic acid synthesis*]
RIP............ Report on Individual Personnel (MCD)
RIP............ Requiescat [*or Requiescant*] in Pace [*May He (She, or They) Rest in Peace*] [*Latin*] (GPO)
RIP............ Research in Parapsychology [*A publication*]
RIP............ Research in Progress (MCD)
RIP............ Reset In Proportion [*A printing instruction*] (WDMC)
RIP............ Resin-in-Pulp [*Ore processing*]
RIP............ Respiratory Inversion Point [*Physiology*]
RIP............ Rest in Peace (TAG)
RIP............ Rest in Proportion [*Printing*] (WDMC)
RIP............ Retired in Place [*Telecommunications*] (TEL)
RIP............ Retirement Improvement Program [*Air Force*] (AFM)
RIP............ Retirement Income Plan [*Insurance*] (MCD)
RIP............ Ribosome Inactivating [*or Inhibiting*] Protein [*Biochemistry*]
RIP............ Ring Index Pointer [*Computer science*] (OA)
RIP............ Ripieno [*Additional*] [*Music*]
rip............ Ripped [*Lumber*] (BARN)
RIP............ Ripple Resources Ltd. [*Vancouver Stock Exchange symbol*]
RIP............ Rolling Injection Planter (GNE)
RIP............ Routing Information Process [*or Protocol*] [*Telecommunications*] (TEL)
RIP............ Rural Industrialization Program [*Department of Agriculture*]
RIPA............ Radioimmunoprecipitation Assay [*Clinical chemistry*]
RIPA............ Royal Institute of Public Administration [*British*]
RIPAA............ Royal Institute of Public Administration Australia [*Australia*]
RIPC............ Regroupement des Independants et Paysans Camerounais [*Regrouping of Independents and Farmers of the Cameroons*]
RIPCO............ Receiving Inspection and Preparation for Checkout (SAA)
RIPD............ RLG [*Research Libraries Group, Inc.*] Research-in-Progress Database [*Information service or system*] (CRD)
RIPE............ Range Instrumentation Performance Evaluation (MUGU)
RIPE............ Robot-Independent Programming Environment (CIST)
RIPEM............ Riordan's Internet Privacy Enhanced Mail [*Computer science*]
RIPFCOMTF... Rapid Item Processor to Facilitate Complex Operations on Magnetic Tape Files [*Computer science*]
RIPH & H..... Royal Institute of Public Health and Hygiene [*British*]
RIPILS............ Recently Immigrated Professional Irish Legals [*Lifestyle classification*]
RIPIS............ Rhode Island Pupil Identification Scale [*Psychology*]
RIPL............ Remote Initial Program Load [*Computer science*]
RIPL............ Representation-Independent Programming Language
RIPN............ Russian Institute for Public Networks (DDC)
RIPOM............ Report [*command indicated*] If Present, Otherwise by Message [*Navy*]
RIPOSTE...... Restitution Incentive Program Operationalized as a Strategy Toward an Effective Learning Environment [*HEW*]
RIPP............ RADAR Intelligence Photo Producer
RIPP............ Regulatory Information on Pesticide Products [*Database*] (IT)
RIPP............ Resistive-Intermittent Positive Pressure [*Medicine*] (DMAA)
RIPP............ Russian-American Institute for President Programs [*For technology transfer*]
RIPPLE............ Radioactive Isotope-Powered Pulse Light Equipment (IEEE)
RIPPLE............ Radioisotope-Powered Prolonged Life Equipment (IEEE)
RIPPLE............ Radioisotope Power Packages for Electricity [*Nuclear energy*] (NUCP)
RIPPLE............ Ripplesmere [*England*]
RIPR............ Recommended Immediate Procurement Records (MCD)
RIPRS............ Recovery Improvement Program Reporting System
RIPS............ RADAR Impact Prediction System (CET)
RIPS............ Radio-Isotope Power Supply [*or System*] [*Nuclear energy*] (NG)
RIPS............ Range Instrumentation Planning Study [*AFSC*]
RIPS............ Raster Image Processor System (PCM)
RIPS............ Remote Image Processing System
RIPS............ Research Institute of Pharmaceutical Sciences [*University of Mississippi*] (PDAA)
RI Pub Laws... Public Laws of Rhode Island [*A publication*] (DLA)
RIPV............ Reactor Isolation Pressure Valve (IEEE)
RIPWC............ Royal Institute of Painters in Water-Colours [*British*]
RIQAP............ Reduced Inspection Quality Assurance Program
RIQS............ Remote Information Query System [*Information retrieval service*] [*Computer science*]
RIR............ RADAR Interface Recorder (MCD)
RIR............ Range Illumination RADAR
RIR............ Read-Only Memory Instruction Register [*Computer science*] (IAA)
RIR............ Receiving Inspection Report
RIR............ Redgrave Information Resources Corp. [*Publisher*]
RiR............ Redgrave Information Resources Corp., Westport, CT [*Library symbol Library of Congress*] (LCLS)
RIR............ Reduction in Requirement [*Air Force*] (AFM)
RIR............ Regimental Inquiry Regulations [*British military*] (DMA)
RIR............ Rehabilitation Information Round Table (EA)
RIR............ Relative Index Register (NITA)
RIR............ Reliability Investigation Requests (KSC)
RIR............ Reportable Item Report [*NASA*] (NASA)
RIR............ Reporting Interface Record [*Computer science*] (IAA)
RIR............ Request Immediate Reply [*Business term*] (MHDB)
RIR............ Reset Indicators of the Right Half (IAA)
RIR............ Resonant Internal Reflection
RIR............ Rhode Island Red [*Poultry*]
RIR............ Ribbon-to-Ribbon (IAA)
RIR............ Richmond International Raceway [*Auto racing*]
RIR............ Right Iliac Region [*Medicine*] (MAE)
RIR............ Right Inferior Rectus [*Muscle*] [*Anatomy*] (DAVI)
RIR............ Riverside/Rubidoux, CA [*Location identifier FAA*] (FAAL)
RIR............ ROM [*Read-Only Memory*] Instruction Register
RIR............ Royal Irish Regiment [*British*] (WA)
RIR............ Royal Irish Rifles [*British military*] (DMA)
RIRA............ Reports and Information Retrieval Activity (NITA)
RIRAA............ Russian Immigrants' Representative Association In America
RIRAP............ Recombinant Interleukin Receptor Antagonist Protein [*Biochemistry*]
RIRB............ Radioiodinated Rose Bengal [*Medicine*] (MAE)
RIRB............ Railway Insurance Rating Bureau [*Defunct*] (EA)
RIRCA............ Rhode Island Red Club of America (EA)
RI/RD............ Rockwell International/Rocketdyne Division
RI Rep............ Rhode Island Reports [*A publication*] (DLA)
RIrF............ Royal Irish Fusiliers [*Military unit*] [*British*] (DMA)
RIRIG............ Reduced-Excitation Inertial Reference Integrating Gyro
RIRJ............ Research Institute of Religious Jewry (EA)
RIRMA............ Revisers, Ink and Roller Makers' Auxiliaries [*A union*] [*British*] (DI)
RIRMS............ Remote Information Retrieval and Management System [*Computer science*] (BUR)
RIRO............ Roll-In/Roll-Out [*Storage allocation*] [*Computer science*]
RIRS............ Railroad Inspection Reporting System [*BTS*] (TAG)
RIRS............ Reliability Information Retrieval System (MCD)
RIRT............ Rehabilitation Information Round Table (EA)
RIRT............ Rhodium-Iron Resistance Thermometer
RIRTI............ Recording Infrared Tracking Instrument
RIS............ Air Services Ltd. [*Czechoslovakia*] [*ICAO designator*] (FAAC)
RIS............ Kansas City, MO [*Location identifier FAA*] (FAAL)
RIS............ RADAR Information Service [*Aviation*] (DA)
RIS............ RADIAC [*Radiation Detection, Indication, and Computation*] Instrument System
RIS............ Radio Information Service (WDAA)
RIS............ Radio Interference Service [*Department of Trade*] [*British*]
RIS............ Radiology Information System [*Computer science*]
RIS............ Railway Invigoration Society [*British*] (BI)
RIS............ Ramjet Inlet System
RIS............ Range Information System [*For aircraft*] (MCD)
RIS............ Range Instrumentation Ship
RIS............ Range Instrumentation Station
RIS............ Raster Input Scanner (NITA)
RIS............ Reblooming Iris Society (EA)
RIS............ Receipt Inspection Segment (OA)
RIS............ Receiving Inspection Segment
RIS............ RECON Information System (MCD)
RIS............ Recorded Information Service [*Telecommunications*] (TEL)
RIS............ Record Input Subroutine
RIS............ Redwood Inspection Service (EA)
RIS............ Regional Information Service [*Library science*] (TELE)
RIS............ Regulatory Impact Statement
RIS............ Regulatory Information Service [*Congressional Information Service, Inc.*] [*Information service or system Defunct*]
RIS............ Relative Impact Strength [*Mechanical engineering*]
RIS............ Relevent Industry Sales (PDAA)
RIS............ Reliability Information System
RIS............ Remote Information System
RIS............ Reporting Identification Symbol (IAA)
RIS............ Reports Identification Symbol
RIS............ Requirements Planning and Inventory Control System [*Computer science*] (IAA)
RIS............ Research Information Service [*John Crerar Library*] [*Information service or system*] (IID)
RIS............ Research Information Services [*Georgia Institute of Technology*] [*Atlanta*] [*Information service or system*] (IID)
RIS............ Research Information System [*Rehabilitation Services Administration*] (IID)
RIS............ Reset Indicators Form Storage [*Computer science*] (IAA)
RIS............ Resistor Insulator Semiconductor (IAA)
RIS............ Resonance Ionization Spectroscopy
RIS............ Retail Information System (BUR)
RIS............ Retarded Infants Services [*Later, CFS*] (EA)
RIS............ Retransmission Identity Signal [*Telecommunications*] (TEL)
RIS............ Retroreflector in Space [*Instrumentation*]
RIS............ Revolution Indicating System (MSA)

RIS.............. Rise Resources, Inc. [*Vancouver Stock Exchange symbol*]
RIS.............. Rishiri [*Japan*] [*Airport symbol Obsolete*] (OAG)
RIS.............. Rock Island Southern Railroad (IIA)
RIS.............. Ross Incineration Services, Inc. (EFIS)
RIS.............. Rotatable Initial Susceptibility
RIS.............. Rotating Image Scanner
RIS.............. Routine Interest Shipping (MCD)
RIS.............. Russian Intelligence Service
RISA .... Radioactive Iodinated Serum Albumin [*Scan or Study*] [*Medicine*] (DAVI)
RISA .... Radioimmunosorbent Assay [*Clinical chemistry*]
RISA .... Radioiodinated Serum Albumin [*Medicine*]
RISA .... Railway and Industrial Spring Association [*Later, RISRI*]
RISA .... Romani Imperii Semper Auctor [*Continual Increaser of the Roman Empire*] [*Latin*]
RIS-ALEX..... Research Information Services - Alexander Library
RISB .... Rotter Incomplete Sentences Blank [*Psychology*]
RISC .... Reduced Instruction Set Chip (NITA)
RISC .... Reduced Instruction Set Computer
RISC .... Reduced Instruction-Set Computing (PCM)
RISC .... Refractive Index Sounding Central
RISC .... Regulatory Information Service Center [*Office of Management and Budget*] (GFGA)
RISC .... Remote Information Systems Center
RISC .... Research Institute of Scripps Clinic [*Research center*] (RCD)
RISC .... RISCORP Inc. 'A' [*NASDAQ symbol*] (TTSB)
RISC .... Rockwell International Science Center
RISC .... Rust Inventory of Schizotypal Cognitions [*Test*] (TMMY)
RISCT .... Research Institute of the Study of Conflict and Terrorism [*British*] (DBA)
RISD .... Requisition and Invoice Shipping Document
RISD .... Rhode Island School of Design
RISD .... Rural Institutions and Services Division [*FAO*]
RISE.......... National Institute for Resources in Science and Engineering (EA)
RISE.......... Radiation-Induced Surface Effect
RISE.......... RAM [*Reliability, Availability, and Maintainability*] Improvement of Selected Equipment [*Military*] (MCD)
RISE.......... Readiness Improvement Status Evaluation (MCD)
RISE.......... Readiness Improvement Summary Evaluation (MCD)
RISE.......... Reform of Intermediate and Secondary Education (OICC)
RISE.......... Regional Initiative in Science Education
RISE.......... Regional Initiatives in Science Education [*National Academy of Sciences*]
RISE.......... Register for International Service in Education [*Institute of International Education*] (IID)
RISE.......... Relative Integral Square Error [*Statistics*] (IAA)
RISE.......... Reliability Improvement Selected Equipment (AABC)
RISEL.......... Research and Information Services for Education [*Montgomery County Intermediate Unit*] [*King of Prussia, PA*]
RISE.......... Research and Information State Education Trust (AIE)
RISE.......... Research in Science Education [*National Science Foundation*] (GRD)
RISE.......... Research Institute for Small and Emerging Business
RISE.......... Research Institute for Studies in Education [*Iowa State University*] [*Research center*] (RCD)
RISE.......... Research in Supersonic Environment
RISE.......... Responsible Industry for a Sound Environment (EA)
RISE.......... Reusable Inflatable Salvage Equipment
RISE.......... Rulings Information System, Excise [*Revenue Canada - Customs and Excise*] [*Information service or system*] (CRD)
RISEAP .... Regional Islamic Da'Wah Council of Southeast Asia and the Pacific (EAIO)
Riser............ Riser Foods, Inc. [*Associated Press*] (SAG)
RISH .... Research Initiative into Silicon Hybrids [*British*]
RISHE .... Research Institute for Supersensonic Healing Energies
RISI .... Resource Information Systems, Inc. (IID)
RISIC .... Rubber-Insert Sound Isolation Coupling (DNAB)
RISK .... Rating Inventory for Screening Kindergartners [*Coleman and Dover*] (TES)
RISK .... Rock Is Stoning Kids [*Defunct*] (EA)
RISKAC........ Risk Acceptance (NASA)
RiskCap........ Risk Capital Holdings, Inc. [*Associated Press*] (SAG)
RISL.......... Rand Information Systems Ltd. (NITA)
RISL.......... Residual Item Selection List
RISLU .... Reduced Instruction Set Logical Unit (CIST)
RISM .... International Inventory of Musical Scores (WDAA)
RISM .... Reference Interaction Site Model [*Chemical physics*]
RISM .... Research Institute for the Study of Man [*Army*] (MCD)
RI/SME .... Robotics International of SME [*Society of Manufacturing Engineers*] (EA)
RISO .... Range Instrumentation Systems Office [*White Sands Missile Range*]
RISO .... Rocket Impacts on Stratospheric Ozone [*Air Force*]
RISOL .... Risoluto [*Resolutely*] [*Music*] (ROG)
RISOP.......... Red Integrated Strategic Offensive Plan [*Army*] (AABC)
RISP .... Recoverable Interplanetary Space Probe (IAA)
RISP .... Regional Information Services Plan (NITA)
RISP .... Robotics and Intelligent Systems Program [*Oak Ridge National Laboratory*]
RISP .... Ross Ice Shelf Project [*International cooperative research project*]
RISQ .... [*The*] Reseau Interordinateur Scientifique Quebecois [*Canada*] [*Computer science*] (TNIG)
RI-SR.......... Removal Item - Ship's Record (MCD)
RISRI .... Railway and Industrial Spring Research Institute [*Defunct*] (EA)
RISS .... Range Instrumentation and Support Systems
RISS .... Recommended Initial System Stockage
RISS .... Refractive Index Sounding System

RISS .... Regional Information Sharing System [*Department of Justice*]
RISS .... Rockwell International Suspension Systems Co.
RISSB .... Research Institute on the Sino-Soviet Bloc (EA)
RIST.......... RADAR Installed System Tester (KSC)
RIST.......... Radioimmunosorbent Technique [*or Test*] [*Clinical chemistry*]
RIST.......... Radioisotopic Sand Tracer [*Marine science*] (MSC)
RIST.......... Rule Induction and Statistical Testing (AAEL)
RISVD.......... Risvegliato [*Reanimated*] [*Music*] (ROG)
RISW .... Registered Industrial Social Worker [*Designation awarded by the American Association of Industrial Social Workers*]
RISW .... Royal Institution of South Wales [*British*]
RISWR .... Regional Institute of Social Welfare Research (EA)
RIT.......... RADAR Inputs Test
RIT.......... Radio Information Test
RIT.......... Radioiodinated Triolein [*Medicine*] (MAE)
RIT.......... Radio Network for Inter-American Telecommunications
RIT.......... Railway Inclusive Tour (DCTA)
RIT.......... Rate of Information Throughput [*Computer science*] (BUR)
RIT.......... Readiness Initiative Team [*Military*]
RIT.......... Receiver Incremental Tuning
RIT.......... Receiving and Inspection Test (IAA)
RIT.......... Reclamation Insurance Type [*Military*] (AFIT)
RIT.......... Red Interamericana de Telecomunicaciones [*Inter-American Telecommunication Network*] (NTCM)
RIT.......... Refining in Transit
RIT.......... Relative Ignition Temperature
RIT.......... Remote Imagery Transceiver (DOMA)
RIT.......... Request for Interface Tool [*NASA*] (NASA)
RIT.......... Retrieval Injury Threshold
RIT.......... Reverse Income Tax (MHDW)
RIT.......... RightCHOICE Managed Care'A' [*NYSE symbol*] (TTSB)
RIT.......... Rightchoice Managed Care Co. [*NYSE symbol*] (SAG)
RIT.......... Rio Tigre [*Panama*] [*Airport symbol*] (OAG)
RIT.......... Ritardando [*Gradually Slower*] [*Music*]
rit.......... Ritardando [*Gradually Slower*] [*Music*] (ODBW)
RIT.......... Ritenuto [*Immediately Slower*] [*Music*]
rit.......... Ritenuto [*Held Back*] [*Italian*] [*Music*] (WDAA)
rit.......... Ritual (BJA)
RIT.......... Rochester Institute of Technology [*New York*]
RIT.......... Rochester Institute of Technology Library [*UTLAS symbol*]
RIT.......... Rocket Interferometer Tracking
RIT.......... Rod-in-Tube
RIT.......... Rorschach Inkblot Test [*Psychiatry*] (DAVI)
RIT.......... Rosette Inhibition Titer [*Medicine*] (DMAA)
RIT.......... Rotary Indexing Table
RIT.......... Rothschild Investment Trust
RITA.......... Rand Intelligent Terminal Agent
RITA.......... Real-Time Integrated Ticket Administration (NITA)
RITA.......... Recognition for Information Technology Achievement [*An award*] (PDAA)
RITA.......... Recoverable Interplanetary Transport Approach
RITA.......... Refundable Income Tax Account
RITA.......... Reservation, Information, Tourist Accommodation [*Computerized system for booking hotel rooms*] [*British*]
RITA.......... Resist Inside the Army [*Peace-movement slang*]
RITA.......... Resistor-in-the Army [*Peace movement slang during Vietnam War*] (VNW)
RITA.......... Retirement Industry Trust Association (NTPA)
RITA.......... Reusable Interplanetary Transport Approach Vehicle
RITA.......... Rivera and Tamayo Fault Exploration [*Marine science*] (MSC)
RITA.......... Romance Is Treasured Always [*Annual award bestowed by Romance Writers of America. Acronym selected to honor cofounder, Rita Clay Estrada*]
RITA.......... Rural Industrial Technical Assistance [*Latin American building program*]
RITA.......... Russian Information Telegraph Agency [*Formerly, TASS*]
RITA .... Retail Industry Trade Action Coalition [*Washington, DC*] (EA)
RitAcc.......... Rituels Accadiens [*A publication*] (BJA)
RITAD .... Radiation-Induced Thermally Activated Depolarization [*Radiation dosimetry technique*]
RITAL.......... Red Internacional de American Latina [*International Telecommunication Network for Latin America*] (NTCM)
RITAR .... Ritardando [*Gradually Slower*] [*Music*]
RITARD.......... Ritardando [*Gradually Slower*] [*Music*]
ritard .... Ritardando [*Holding Back*] [*Italian*] [*Music*] (WDAA)
RITARO .... Ritardando [*Gradually Slower*] [*Music*] (ROG)
RITB.......... Road Transport Industry Training Board [*British*]
RITC.......... Regional Information Technology Coordinators (NITA)
RITC.......... Request in Trail Climb [*Aviation*] (FAAC)
RITC.......... Rhodamine Isothiocyanate [*Biochemistry*]
Ritch.......... Ritchie's Cases Decided by Francis Bacon [*1617-21*] [*A publication*] (DLA)
Ritch.......... Ritchie's Equity Reports [*1872-82*] [*Nova Scotia*] [*A publication*] (DLA)
Ritch Eq Dec... Ritchie's Equity Decisions [*Nova Scotia*] [*A publication*] (DLA)
Ritch Eq Rep... Ritchie's Equity Reports [*Nova Scotia*] [*A publication*] (DLA)
Ritchie.......... Ritchie's Equity [*Canada*] [*A publication*] (DLA)
RITD.......... Request in Trail Descent [*Aviation*] (FAAC)
RITE.......... Rapidata Interactive Text Editor (IEEE)
RITE.......... Rapid Information Technique for Evaluation
RITE.......... Regenerative Intercooled Turbine Engine (MCD)
RITE.......... Research Institute for Innovative Technolgies for the Earth
RITE.......... Research Institute for Telecommunications and Economics (NITA)
RITE.......... Right [*Direction of Turn*] [*ICAO designator*] (FAAC)
RiteA .... Rite Aid Corp. [*Associated Press*] (SAG)

RITEA........... Rock Island Railroad Transportation and Employee Assistance Act [1980]
RiteAid........ Rite Aid Corp. [Associated Press] (SAG)
RITEN......... Ritenuto [Immediately Slower] [Music]
RITENA........ Reunion Internacional de Tecnicos de la Nutricion Animal [International Meeting of Animal Nutrition Experts] (EAIO)
RITENO........ Ritenuto [Immediately Slower] [Music] (ROG)
RITG........... Radiatively Important Trace Gas
RITI............ Resident Inspection Test Instruction
RITL........... Royal Institute of Technology Library (NITA)
RITLS.......... Rhode Island Test of Language Structure
RITOP......... Red Integrated Tactical Operational Plan (CINC)
RITQ........... Revised Infant Temperament Questionnaire
RITR.......... Rework Inspection Team Report
RITRC......... RIT Research Corp.
RITREAD...... Rapid Iterative Reanalysis for Automated Design [Computer program]
RITS........... Radiatively Important Trace Species [Program] (USDC)
RITS........... Radiatively Important Trace Substances
RITS........... Rapid Information Transmission System
RITS........... Reconnaissance Intelligence Technical Squadron
RITS........... Remote Input Terminal System [Computer science] (IAA)
Rits Cts Leet... Ritson's Jurisdiction of Courts-Leet [A publication] (DLA)
Rits Int....... Ritso's Introduction to the Science [A publication] (DLA)
RITSL.......... Reconfigured Integrated Two-Stage Liquefaction [Chemical engineering]
RITSq.......... Reconnaissance Intelligence Technical Squadron [Air Force]
RITU........... Research Institute of Temple University (KSC)
RITZ........... Regulatory and Investigative Treatment Zone Model [Environmental Protection Agency] (AEPA)
RIU............ Andalusia, AL [Location identifier FAA] (FAAL)
RIU............ RADAR Interface Unit [Military] (CAAL)
RIU............ Radioactive Iodine Uptake [Medicine]
RIU............ Railroad Insurance Underwriters [Later, RTI] (EA)
RIU............ Refractive Index Unit
RIU............ Remote Interface Unit [NASA] (NASA)
riu............ Rhode Island [MARC country of publication code Library of Congress] (LCCP)
RIU............ Ring Interface Unit [Telecommunications] (OSI)
RIU............ University of Rhode Island, Kingston, RI [OCLC symbol] (OCLC)
RIUSA......... Rehabilitation International USA
RIV............ Radio Influence Voltage
RIV............ Ramus Interventricularis [First-order branch of coronary artery] [Medicine]
RIV............ Rapid Intervention Vehicle (DA)
RIV............ Rapid Isolation Valve [Analytical chemistry]
RIV............ Recirculation Isolation Valve (NASA)
RIV............ Regolamento Internazionale Veicoli [Italian generic term meaning "International Regulation of Vehicles"] [Initialism also refers to International Wagon Union]
RIV............ Right Innominate Vein [Anatomy] (DAVI)
RIV............ River
RIV............ Riverside, CA [Location identifier FAA] (FAAL)
RIV............ Riverview [Australia Seismograph station code, US Geological Survey] (SEIS)
RIV............ Rivet (AAG)
Riv............ Riviera [Record label] [France]
RIV............ Riviera Holding Corp. [AMEX symbol] (SAG)
RIV............ Riviera Holdings [AMEX symbol] (TTSB)
Riv............ Rivista [Review] [Italian] (BJA)
RIVA.......... Recreational Industry Vehicle Association (IAA)
RIVAL......... Rapid Insurance Valuation Language (IAA)
Rival.......... Rival Co. [Associated Press] (SAG)
Riv Ann Reg... Rivington's Annual Register [A publication] (DLA)
RIVC.......... Radionuclide Imaging of the Inferior Vena Cava [Medicine] (DMAA)
Riv d Arch Crist... Rivista di Archeologia Cristiana [A publication] (OCD)
Riv di Diritto Internaz e Comparato del Lavoro... Rivista di Diritto Internazionale e Comparato del Lavoro [Padua, Italy] [A publication] (DLA)
Riv Dir Int e Comp del Lavoro... Rivista di Diritto Internazionale e Comparato del Lavoro [Bologna, Italy] [A publication] (DLA)
Riv Dir Int'le Priv & Proc... Rivista di Diritto Internazionale Privato e Processuale [Padova, Italy] [A publication] (DLA)
RIVDIV........ River Assault Division [Military]
RIVE.......... Resources in Vocational Education [Database] [National Center for Research in Vocational Education] [Information service or system] (CRD)
RIVER........ River [Commonly used] (OPSA)
RIVFLOT...... River Flotilla [Military]
RIVFLOTONE... River Flotilla One [Military]
RivFor........ River Forest Bancorp [Associated Press] (SAG)
Rivian........ Riviana Foods, Inc. [Associated Press] (SAG)
RivianaF...... Riviana Foods, Inc. [Associated Press] (SAG)
Riviera........ Riviera Holding Corp. [Associated Press] (SAG)
Rivier C....... Rivier College (GAGS)
Riv Ital per le Sc Giur... Rivista Italiana per le Scienze Giuridiche [A publication] (OCD)
RIVL.......... Rival Co. [NASDAQ symbol] (TTSB)
RIVL.......... Rival Manufacturing [NASDAQ symbol] (NQ)
RIVPACS...... River Invertebrate Prediction and Classification System
RIVPATFLOT... River Patrol Flotilla [Navy] (DNAB)
RIVPATFOR... River Patrol Force [Navy] (DNAB)
RIVR.......... River [Commonly used] (OPSA)
RIVR.......... River Valley Bancorp [NASDAQ symbol] (SAG)
RivrNtl........ Riverside National Bank [Associated Press] (SAG)
RIVRON...... River Assault Squadron [Navy] (DNAB)
RivrVlly....... River Valley Bancorp [Associated Press] (SAG)

RIVS .... Ruptured Interventricular Septum [Medicine] (AAMN)
RIVSEC .... River Section (DNAB)
RIVSUPPRON... River Support Squadron [Navy] (DNAB)
RivSvgs .... Riverview Savings Bank [Associated Press] (SAG)
RIVT.......... Rivulet (ADA)
RivwdInt ...... Riverwood International Corp. [Associated Press] (SAG)
RIW .... Reliability Improvement Warranty [Navy]
RIW .... Repaired in Works [British military] (DMA)
RIW .... Riverton [Wyoming] [Airport symbol] (OAG)
RIWC .... Royal Institute of Painters in Water-Colours [British] (ROG)
Riwt .... Rich International White Trash [Lifestyle classification]
RIX .... Riga [Former USSR Airport symbol] (OAG)
RIX .... University of Rhode Island, Extension Division Library, Providence, RI [OCLC symbol] (OCLC)
RIXOS......... Rosat International X-Ray Optical Survey [Cosmology]
RIXT.......... Remote Information Exchange Terminal (MCD)
RIY.......... Renaissance of Italian Youth (EA)
RIY.......... Riyan Mukalla [South Arabia (Yemen)] [Airport symbol] (AD)
RIZ.......... Radio Industry Zagreb [Former Yugoslavia]
RIZ.......... Rio Alzucar [Panama] [Airport symbol] (OAG)
RJ.......... A'Beckett's Reserved Judgements [Port Phillip] [A publication] (ILCA)
R(J).......... Justiciary Cases [Scotland] [A publication] (DLA)
RJ.......... La Reveil Juif. Sfax [A publication] (BJA)
RJ.......... RADAR/Jimsphere
RJ.......... Radial Jerk [Reflex] [Neurology] (DAVI)
RJ.......... Ramjet
RJ.......... Reform Judaism (BJA)
RJ.......... Regional Jet [British Aerospace/Taiwan Aerospace Corp. joint venture] (ECON)
RJ.......... Registered Jack (DDC)
RJ.......... Reject
RJ.......... Revue de Jurisprudence [A publication] (DLA)
RJ.......... Revue Judiciaire, by Bruzard [1843-44] [Mauritius] [A publication] (DLA)
RJ.......... Rights and Justice [An association British] (EAIO)
RJ.......... [The] River Jordan [A publication] (BJA)
RJ.......... Rivet Joint [RC-135 reconnaissance aircraft] [Air Force] (DOMA)
RJ.......... Road Junction [Maps and charts]
RJ.......... Robert Jones [Dressing] [Surgery] (DAVI)
RJ.......... Rotary Joint
RJ 500........ Rolls-Japan 500 [Type of Rolls-Royce engine]
RJA.......... Ramjet Addition (AAG)
RJA.......... Reform Jewish Appeal (EA)
RJA.......... Retail Jewelers of America [Later, JA] (EA)
RJA.......... Rotary Joint Assembly
RJA.......... Royal Jersey Artillery [Military unit] [British]
RJA.......... Royal Jordanian [ICAO designator] (FAAC)
RJA.......... Russko-Jewrejsky Archiw [A publication] (BJA)
RJAA.......... Tokyo/New Tokyo International [Japan ICAO location identifier] (ICLI)
RJAF.......... Matsumoto [Japan ICAO location identifier] (IOLI)
HJAF.......... Royal Jordanian Air Force
RJAH.......... Hyakuri [Japan ICAO location identifier] (ICLI)
RJAI.......... Ichigaya [Japan ICAO location identifier] (ICLI)
RJAK.......... Kasumigaura [Japan ICAO location identifier] (ICLI)
RJAM.......... Miharnitorishima [Japan ICAO location identifier] (ICLI)
RJamFn........ Raymond James Financial, Inc. [Associated Press] (SAG)
RJ & PJ....... Revenue, Judicial, and Police Journal [Calcutta] [A publication] (DLA)
RJAO.......... Chichijima [Japan ICAO location identifier] (ICLI)
RJAT.......... Takigahara [Japan ICAO location identifier] (ICLI)
RJAW.......... Iwo Jima [Japan ICAO location identifier] (ICLI)
RJB.......... Rajbiraj [Nepal] [Airport symbol Obsolete] (OAG)
RJB.......... Relay Junction Box (KSC)
RJB.......... Ruby Jewel Bearing
RJBD.......... Nanki-Shirahama [Japan ICAO location identifier] (ICLI)
RJBE.......... Relative Jostle Biological Effectiveness
RJC.......... Ranger Junior College [Texas]
RJC.......... Reaction Jet Control [NASA] (NASA)
RJC.......... Robinson Jeffers Committee (EA)
RJC.......... Rochester Junior College [Minnesota] [Later, Rochester Community College]
RJCA.......... Asahikawa [Japan ICAO location identifier] (ICLI)
RJCB.......... Obihiro [Japan ICAO location identifier] (ICLI)
RJCC.......... Sapporo/Chitose [Japan ICAO location identifier] (ICLI)
RJCG.......... Sapporo [Japan ICAO location identifier] (ICLI)
RJCH.......... Hakodate [Japan ICAO location identifier] (ICLI)
RJCK.......... Kushiro [Japan ICAO location identifier] (ICLI)
RJCM.......... New Memanbetsu [Japan ICAO location identifier] (ICLI)
RJCN.......... Nakashibetsu [Japan ICAO location identifier] (ICLI)
RJCO.......... Sapporo/Okadama [Japan ICAO location identifier] (ICLI)
RJCR.......... Rebun [Japan ICAO location identifier] (ICLI)
RJCS.......... Kushiro/Kenebetsu [Japan ICAO location identifier] (ICLI)
RJCT.......... Tokachi [Japan ICAO location identifier] (ICLI)
RJCW.......... Wakkanai [Japan ICAO location identifier] (ICLI)
RJCY.......... Muroran/Yakumo [Japan ICAO location identifier] (ICLI)
RJD.......... Reaction Jet Device [NASA] (NASA)
RJD.......... Reaction Jet Driver [NASA] (NASA)
RJDA.......... Rassemblement des Jeunesses Democratiques Africaines [Rally of African Democratic Youth]
RJDA.......... Reaction Jet Driver - Aft [NASA] (NASA)
RJDB.......... Iki [Japan ICAO location identifier] (ICLI)
RJDC.......... Yamaguchi-Ube, Honshu Island [Japan ICAO location identifier] (ICLI)
RJDF.......... Reaction Jet Driver - Forward [NASA] (NASA)
RJDG.......... Fukuoka [Japan ICAO location identifier] (ICLI)

RJDK .... Kamigoto [Japan ICAO location identifier] (ICLI)
RJDM .... Metabaru [Japan ICAO location identifier] (ICLI)
RJDO .... Ojika [Japan ICAO location identifier] (ICLI)
RJDT .... Tsushima [Japan ICAO location identifier] (ICLI)
RJE .... Ramjet Engine
RJE .... Rayleigh-Jeans Equation [Physics]
RJE .... Remote Job Entry [Computer science]
RJEB .... Monbetsu [Japan ICAO location identifier] (ICLI)
RJEC .... Asahikawa [Japan ICAO location identifier] (ICLI)
RJ/EC .... Reaction Jet/Engine Control [NASA] (NASA)
RJEO .... Okushiri [Japan ICAO location identifier] (ICLI)
RJEP .... Remote Job Entry Protocol [Telecommunications] (OSI)
RJER .... Rishiri Island [Japan ICAO location identifier] (ICLI)
RJETS .... Remote Job Entry Terminal System [Computer science] (MCD)
RJF .... Les Rejaudoux [France] [Seismograph station code, US Geological Survey] (SEIS)
RJF .... Raymond James Financial, Inc. [NYSE symbol] (SPSG)
RJF .... Raymond James Finl [NYSE symbol] (TTSB)
RJFA .... Ashiya [Japan ICAO location identifier] (ICLI)
RJFA .... Roumanian Jewish Federation of America [Defunct] (EA)
RJFB .... Gannosu/Brady [Japan ICAO location identifier] (ICLI)
RJFC .... Yakushima [Japan ICAO location identifier] (ICLI)
RJFE .... Fukue [Japan ICAO location identifier] (ICLI)
RJFF .... Fukuoka [Japan ICAO location identifier] (ICLI)
RJFG .... Tanegashima [Japan ICAO location identifier] (ICLI)
RJFK .... Kagoshima [Japan ICAO location identifier] (ICLI)
RJFM .... Miyazaki [Japan ICAO location identifier] (ICLI)
RJFN .... Nyutabaru [Japan ICAO location identifier] (ICLI)
RJFO .... Oita [Japan ICAO location identifier] (ICLI)
RJFR .... Kitakyushu [Japan ICAO location identifier] (ICLI)
RJFT .... Kumamoto [Japan ICAO location identifier] (ICLI)
RJFU .... Nagasaki [Japan ICAO location identifier] (ICLI)
RJFY .... Kanoya [Japan ICAO location identifier] (ICLI)
RJFZ .... Tsuiki [Japan ICAO location identifier] (ICLI)
RJH .... Rajshahi [Bangladesh] [Airport symbol] (AD)
RJIS .... Regional Justice Information System
RJK .... Rijeka [Former Yugoslavia] [Airport symbol] (OAG)
RJKA .... Amami [Japan ICAO location identifier] (ICLI)
RJKB .... Okierabu [Japan ICAO location identifier] (ICLI)
RJKI .... Kikai/Kikaigashima Island [Japan ICAO location identifier] (ICLI)
RJKN .... Tokunoshima Island [Japan ICAO location identifier] (ICLI)
RJL .... Rigel Energy [Formerly, Total Canada Oil & Gas Ltd.] [AMEX symbol] (SPSG)
RJLI .... Royal Jersey Light Infantry [Military unit] [British]
RJM .... Reed, John M., San Antonio TX [STAC]
RJM .... Religious of Jesus-Mary [Roman Catholic women's religious order]
RJM .... Royal Jersey Militia [Military unit] [British]
RJM .... Warner Robins, GA [Location identifier FAA] (FAAL)
RJNF .... Fukui [Japan ICAO location identifier] (ICLI)
RJNG .... Gifu [Japan ICAO location identifier] (ICLI)
RJNH .... Hamamatsu [Japan ICAO location identifier] (ICLI)
RJNK .... Kanazawa/Komatsu [Japan ICAO location identifier] (ICLI)
RJNN .... Nagoya [Japan ICAO location identifier] (ICLI)
RJNO .... Oki [Japan ICAO location identifier] (ICLI)
RJNT .... Toyama [Japan ICAO location identifier] (ICLI)
RJNY .... Yaizu/Shizuhama [Japan ICAO location identifier] (ICLI)
RJO .... Rapports Judiciaires Officiels de Quebec [Quebec Official Law Reports] [A publication] (ILCA)
RJO .... Remote Job Output [Computer science]
RJO .... Revolutionary Justice Organization [Lebanese terrorist group]
RJOA .... Hiroshima [Japan ICAO location identifier] (ICLI)
RJOB .... Okayama [Japan ICAO location identifier] (ICLI)
RJOC .... Izumo [Japan ICAO location identifier] (ICLI)
RJOD .... Reaction Jet OMS [Orbital Maneuvering Subsystem] Driver [NASA] (NASA)
RJOE .... Akeno [Japan ICAO location identifier] (ICLI)
RJOF .... Hofu [Japan ICAO location identifier] (ICLI)
RJOH .... Miho [Japan ICAO location identifier] (ICLI)
RJOI .... Iwakuni [Japan ICAO location identifier] (ICLI)
RJOK .... Kochi [Japan ICAO location identifier] (ICLI)
RJOM .... Matsuyama [Japan ICAO location identifier] (ICLI)
RJOO .... Osaka/International [Japan ICAO location identifier] (ICLI)
RJOP .... Komatsujima [Japan ICAO location identifier] (ICLI)
RJOQ (BR).. Rapports Judiciaires Officiels de Quebec, Cour du Banc du Roi [Quebec Official Law Reports, King's Bench] [A publication] (ILCA)
RJOQ (CS).. Rapports Judiciaires Officiels de Quebec, Cour Superieure [Quebec Official Law Reports, Superior Court] [A publication] (ILCA)
RJOR .... Tottori [Japan ICAO location identifier] (ICLI)
RJOS .... Ruth Jackson Orthopaedic Society (NTPA)
RJOS .... Tokushima [Japan ICAO location identifier] (ICLI)
RJOT .... Takamatsu [Japan ICAO location identifier] (ICLI)
RJOY .... Osaka/Yao [Japan ICAO location identifier] (ICLI)
RJOZ .... Ozuki [Japan ICAO location identifier] (ICLI)
RJP .... Reaction Jet Pipe
RJP .... Realistic Job Preview
RJP .... Remote Job Processing [Computer science]
RJP .... Remote Job Processor [NITA]
RJP .... RJP Electronics [Vancouver Stock Exchange symbol]
RJP .... Rocket Jet Plume
RJPA .... Ramjet Performance Analysis (MCD)
RJQ .... Rapports Judiciaires [Quebec Law Reports] [A publication] (DLA)
RJQ BR........ Rapports Judiciaires de Quebec, Cour du Banc du Roi [Quebec Law Reports, King's Bench] [A publication] (DLA)

RJQ CS .... Rapports Judiciaires de Quebec, Cour Superieure [Quebec Law Reports, Superior Court] [A publication] (DLA)
RJR .... Mathieu's Quebec Revised Reports [A publication] (DLA)
RJR .... R. J. Reynolds Tobacco Co.
RJR .... RJR Nabisco Holding Corp. [Associated Press] (SAG)
RJR .... Rotary Joint Reed
RJRA .... Rotary Joint Reed Assembly
RJR Nab .... RJR Nabisco Holding Corp. [Associated Press] (SAG)
RJRQ .... Mathieu's Quebec Revised Reports [A publication] (DLA)
RJS .... Reaction Jet System (KSC)
RJS .... Remote Job System [Computer science] (MCD)
RJS .... Richard Jeffries Society (EAIO)
RJS .... Roberta Jo Society (EA)
RJS .... Rocket and JATO [Jet-Assisted Takeoff] Section [Picatinny Arsenal] [Dover, NJ]
RJS .... Ruth Jackson Society (EA)
RJSA .... Aomori [Japan ICAO location identifier] (ICLI)
RJSC .... Yamagata [Japan ICAO location identifier] (ICLI)
RJSD .... Sado [Japan ICAO location identifier] (ICLI)
RJSFC .... R. J. Sutton Fan Club (EA)
RJSH .... Hachinohe [Japan ICAO location identifier] (ICLI)
RJSI .... Hanamaki [Japan ICAO location identifier] (ICLI)
RJSK .... Akita [Japan ICAO location identifier] (ICLI)
RJSM .... Misawa [Japan ICAO location identifier] (ICLI)
RJSN .... Niigata [Japan ICAO location identifier] (ICLI)
RJSO .... Ominato [Japan ICAO location identifier] (ICLI)
RJSS .... Sendai [Japan ICAO location identifier] (ICLI)
RJST .... Matsushima [Japan ICAO location identifier] (ICLI)
RJSU .... Kasuminome [Japan ICAO location identifier] (ICLI)
RJT .... Rassemblement des Jeunes Togolais [Togolese Youth Rally]
RJT .... Reference Jet Transport
RJT .... Royal Jubilee Trust [Provides financial aid to start new businesses] [British]
RJTA .... Atsugi [Japan ICAO location identifier] (ICLI)
RJTC .... Tachikawa [Japan ICAO location identifier] (ICLI)
RJTD .... Tokyo [Japan ICAO location identifier] (ICLI)
RJTE .... Tateyama [Japan ICAO location identifier] (ICLI)
RJTF .... Chofu [Japan ICAO location identifier] (ICLI)
RJTG .... Tokyo [Japan ICAO location identifier] (ICLI)
RJTH .... Hachijojima [Japan ICAO location identifier] (ICLI)
RJTI .... Tokyo [Japan ICAO location identifier] (ICLI)
RJTJ .... Iruma [Japan ICAO location identifier] (ICLI)
RJTK .... Kisarazu [Japan ICAO location identifier] (ICLI)
RJTL .... Shimofusa [Japan ICAO location identifier] (ICLI)
RJTO .... Oshima [Japan ICAO location identifier] (ICLI)
RJTQ .... Miyakejima [Japan ICAO location identifier] (ICLI)
RJTR .... Zama/Rankin [Japan ICAO location identifier] (ICLI)
RJTT .... Tokyo/International [Japan ICAO location identifier] (ICLI)
RJTU .... Utsunomiya [Japan ICAO location identifier] (ICLI)
RJTV .... Ramjet Test Vehicle
RJTW .... Zama [Japan ICAO location identifier] (ICLI)
RJTY .... Yokota [Japan ICAO location identifier] (ICLI)
RJTZ .... Fuchu [Japan ICAO location identifier] (ICLI)
RJZ .... Royal Jordanian Air Force [ICAO designator] (FAAC)
RK .... Air Afrique [Ivory Coast] [ICAO designator] (ICDA)
R_K .... Cathode Resistance (IDOE)
RK .... Rabbit Kidney
RK .... Rack
RK .... Radial Keratoplasty [Ophthalmology] (DAVI)
RK .... Radial Keratotomy [Ophthalmology]
RK .... Rassemblement Katangais [Katanga Rally]
RK .... Rat Kidney
RK .... Realkatalog der Aegyptologie [A publication] (BJA)
R-K .... Redlich-Kwong [Physics]
RK .... Republic of Korea [IYRU nationality code] (IYR)
RK .... Rhodopsin Kinase [An enzyme]
RK .... Right Kidney
RK .... Right to Know (EA)
RK .... Rock [Maps and charts] (MCD)
RK .... Royal Knight [British]
RK .... Rubbing Keel [of a ship] (DS)
RK .... Run of Kiln
RKA .... Air Afrique [Ivory Coast] [ICAO designator] (FAAC)
RKA .... Reaction Kinetic Analysis (PDAA)
RKA .... Rockdale, NY [Location identifier FAA] (FAAL)
RKAF .... Royal Khmer Air Force [Cambodia]
RKB .... Red Kidney Bean
RKBCAC .... Rose Kushner Breast Cancer Advisory Center (EA)
RKCC .... Right to Know Committee of Correspondence [Defunct] (EA)
RKD .... Rockland [Maine] [Airport symbol] (OAG)
RKE .... Roskilde [Denmark] [Airport symbol] (OAG)
RKFC .... Ray Kirkland Fan Club (EA)
RKG .... Radiocardiogram
RKG .... Rockingham R. R. [AAR code]
RKG .... Royal Khmer Government [Cambodia]
RKH .... Rock Hill [South Carolina] [Airport symbol] (OAG)
RKH .... Rockingham Resources, Inc. [Vancouver Stock Exchange symbol]
RKH .... Rokitansky-Kuster-Hauser [Syndrome] [Gynecology] (DAVI)
RKHS .... Reducing Kernel Hilbert Space [Electronics] (OA)
RKID .... Right Kidney [Urine Sample] (DAVI)
RK II .... Runge-Kutta Second Order [Mathematics]
RKInt .... Rockwell International Corp. [Associated Press] (SAG)
RKJ .... Ramsey, Kenneth J., Pittsburgh PA [STAC]
RKJJ .... Kwangju [South Korea ICAO location identifier] (ICLI)
RKJK .... Kunsan [South Korea ICAO location identifier] (ICLI)

RKJM..........	Mokpo [*South Korea ICAO location identifier*] (ICLI)
RKJO..........	Hongjungri [*South Korea ICAO location identifier*] (ICLI)
RKJU..........	Jhunju [*South Korea ICAO location identifier*] (ICLI)
RKJY..........	Yeosu [*South Korea ICAO location identifier*] (ICLI)
RKKA..........	Raboche-Krest'ianskaia Krasnaia Armiia [*Workers' and Peasants' Red Army*] [*Redesignated Soviety Army*] [*Former USSR*]
RKKY..........	Ruderman-Kittel-Kasuya-Yoshida (AAEL)
RKL	Right Knee Left [*Guitar playing*]
RKL	Ruskin Developments Ltd. [*Vancouver Stock Exchange symbol*]
RKM	RADAR Keyboard Multiplexer [*Computer science*] (MHDI)
RKM	Runge-Kutta Method [*Mathematics*]
RkMCh	Rocky Mountain Chocolate Factory [*Associated Press*] (SAG)
RkMCn	Rocky Mountain Chocolate Factory [*Associated Press*] (SAG)
RkMInet.......	Rocky Mountain Internet, Inc. [*Associated Press*] (SAG)
RkMInt.......	Rocky Mountain Internet, Inc. [*Associated Press*] (SAG)
RKN	Root Knot Nematode [*Plant pathology*]
RKN	Runge-Kutta-Nystroem [*Formula*] [*Mathematics*]
RKNC..........	Chunchon [*South Korea ICAO location identifier*] (ICLI)
RKND..........	Sokcho [*South Korea ICAO location identifier*] (ICLI)
RKNFSYS....	Rock Information System [*Carnegie Institution*] [*Databank*] [*National Science Foundation*] (IID)
RKNH..........	Heongsung [*South Korea ICAO location identifier*] (ICLI)
RKNI..........	Injae [*South Korea ICAO location identifier*] (ICLI)
RKNK..........	Kwandaeri [*South Korea ICAO location identifier*] (ICLI)
RKNN..........	Kangnung [*South Korea ICAO location identifier*] (ICLI)
RKNW..........	Wonju [*South Korea ICAO location identifier*] (ICLI)
RKNY..........	Yangku [*South Korea ICAO location identifier*] (ICLI)
RKO..........	Radio-Keith-Orpheum [*Motion picture production and exhibition firm, also active in broadcasting*]
RKO..........	Range Keeper Operator [*Navy*]
RKP..........	Rockport, TX [*Location identifier FAA*] (FAAL)
RKP..........	Routledge & Kegan Paul [*British publisher*]
RKPC..........	Cheju/International [*South Korea ICAO location identifier*] (ICLI)
RKPD..........	Chedong [*South Korea ICAO location identifier*] (ICLI)
RKPE..........	Chinhae [*South Korea ICAO location identifier*] (ICLI)
RKPK..........	Kimhae/International [*South Korea ICAO location identifier*] (ICLI)
RKPM..........	Cheju/Mosulpo [*South Korea ICAO location identifier*] (ICLI)
RKPN..........	Rooms Katholieke Partij Nederland [*Roman Catholic Party of the Netherlands*] [*Political party*] (PPE)
RKPP	Busan [*South Korea ICAO location identifier*] (ICLI)
RKPS..........	Sachon [*South Korea ICAO location identifier*] (ICLI)
RKPU	Ulsan [*South Korea ICAO location identifier*] (ICLI)
RKR..........	Poteau, OK [*Location identifier FAA*] (FAAL)
RKR..........	Rack Register (MHDB)
RKR..........	Rocker (AAG)
RKR..........	Rockspan Resources [*Vancouver Stock Exchange symbol*]
RKRA..........	Rocker Arm [*Mechanical engineering*]
RKS..........	Reko [*Solomon Islands*] [*Seismograph station code, US Geological Survey*] (SEIS)
RKS..........	Rock Springs [*Wyoming*] [*Airport symbol*] (OAG)
RKSA..........	Ascom City [*South Korea ICAO location identifier*] (ICLI)
RKSB..........	Uijeongbu [*South Korea ICAO location identifier*] (ICLI)
RKSC..........	Cheongokri [*South Korea ICAO location identifier*] (ICLI)
RKSD..........	Kanamni [*South Korea ICAO location identifier*] (ICLI)
RKSE..........	Paekryoungdo Beach [*South Korea ICAO location identifier*] (ICLI)
RKSF..........	Republic of Korea Air Force Headquarters [*South Korea ICAO location identifier*] (ICLI)
RKSG..........	Pyongtaek [*South Korea ICAO location identifier*] (ICLI)
RKSH..........	Kwanak [*South Korea ICAO location identifier*] (ICLI)
RKSI..........	Chajangni [*South Korea ICAO location identifier*] (ICLI)
RKSK..........	Susaek [*South Korea ICAO location identifier*] (ICLI)
RKSL..........	Seoul City [*South Korea ICAO location identifier*] (ICLI)
RKSM..........	Seoul East [*Sinchonri*] [*South Korea ICAO location identifier*] (ICLI)
RKSO..........	Osan [*South Korea ICAO location identifier*] (ICLI)
RKSP..........	Paekryoungdo Site [*South Korea ICAO location identifier*] (ICLI)
RKSP	Rooms Katholieke Staatspartij [*Roman Catholic State Party*] [*Netherlands Political party*] (PPE)
RKSR..........	Yeongdongri [*South Korea ICAO location identifier*] (ICLI)
RKSS..........	Seoul/Kimpo International [*South Korea ICAO location identifier*] (ICLI)
RKST..........	Tongoucheon [*South Korea ICAO location identifier*] (ICLI)
RKSU..........	Yeoju [*South Korea ICAO location identifier*] (ICLI)
RKSW..........	Suwon [*South Korea ICAO location identifier*] (ICLI)
RKSX..........	Song San-Ri [*South Korea ICAO location identifier*] (ICLI)
RKSY..........	Seoul/Yungsan [*South Korea ICAO location identifier*] (ICLI)
RKT..........	Air 21, Inc. [*FAA designator*] (FAAC)
RKT..........	Ras-al-Khaima [*Trucial Oman*] [*Airport symbol*] (AD)
RKT..........	Ras Al Khaymah [*United Arab Emirates*] [*Airport symbol*] (OAG)
RKT..........	Rikitea [*Tuamotu Archipelago*] [*Seismograph station code, US Geological Survey*] (SEIS)
RKT..........	Rocket (AAG)
RKT..........	Rock Tenn Co. [*NYSE symbol*] (SAG)
RKTA..........	Andong [*South Korea ICAO location identifier*] (ICLI)
RKTC..........	Chungju [*South Korea ICAO location identifier*] (ICLI)
RKTD..........	Taejon [*South Korea ICAO location identifier*] (ICLI)
RKTH..........	Pohang [*South Korea ICAO location identifier*] (ICLI)
RKTJ..........	Kyungju [*South Korea ICAO location identifier*] (ICLI)
RKTM..........	Seosan [*South Korea ICAO location identifier*] (ICLI)
RKTM..........	Rock-Tenn 'A' [*NASDAQ symbol*] (TTSB)
RKTN..........	Rock Tenn Co. [*NASDAQ symbol*] (SAG)
RKTN..........	Taegu [*South Korea ICAO location identifier*] (ICLI)
RKTO..........	Nonsan [*South Korea ICAO location identifier*] (ICLI)
RKTR..........	Rocketeer
RKTS	Sangju [*South Korea ICAO location identifier*] (ICLI)
RKTSTA	Rocket Station

RKTT..........	Taegu [*South Korea ICAO location identifier*] (ICLI)
RKTY..........	Yechon [*South Korea ICAO location identifier*] (ICLI)
RKU..........	Yule Island [*Papua New Guinea*] [*Airport symbol*] (OAG)
RKV	Rabbit Kidney Vacuolating Virus
RKV	Rose Knot Victor [*Gemini tracking ship*]
RKVA	Reactive Kilovolt-Ampere
RKVAM	Recording Kilovolt-Ampere Meter (MSA)
RKVP	Rooms Katholieke Volkspartij [*Roman Catholic People's Party*] [*Netherlands Political party*] (PPE)
RKW	Renal Potassium Wasting (MAE)
RKW	Rockwood, TN [*Location identifier FAA*] (FAAL)
RKX	Maxton, NC [*Location identifier FAA*] (FAAL)
Rky	Rocky [*Quality of the bottom*] [*Nautical charts*]
RKY	Roentgen Kymography
RKY	Rokeby [*Australia Airport symbol Obsolete*] (OAG)
RL	Aerolineas Nicaraguenses [*ICAO designator*] (AD)
RL	Coarse Rales [*On chest ausculation*] [*Medicine*] (DAVI)
RL	Crown International Airlines [*ICAO designator*] (AD)
R_L	Load Resistance (IDOE)
RL	Master Cross-Reference List
RL	Radiation Laboratory
RL	Radiation Level [*Nuclear energy*]
RL	Radio Liberty [*Board for International Broadcasting*]
RL	Radio Link (OA)
RL	Radiolocation
RL	Radioluminescent
RL	Radionavigation land station using two separate loop antennas, and a single transmitter, and operating at a power of 150 watts or more [*ITU designation*] (CET)
RL	Ragged Left [*Printing*] (WDMC)
rl	Ragged Left [*Typesetting*] (WDMC)
RL	Rahmana Litslan (BJA)
RL	Rail (AAG)
RL	Ralph Lauren [*Fashion designer, 1939-*]
RL	Raman LASER
RL	Random Lengths [*Lumber*]
rl	Random Lengths [*Wood industry*] (WPI)
RL	Random Logic
RL	Rated Load
R/L	Rate/Limited (MCD)
RL	Reactive Loss (IAA)
RL	Reactor Licensing [*Nuclear energy*] (NRCH)
RL	Reader's Library [*A publication*]
RL	Reading List
RL	Real Life (NHD)
Rl	Receive Leg [*Telecommunications*] (TEL)
R/L	Receive Location (DOMA)
RL	Receptor-Ligand Complex
RL	Record Length
RL	Record Librarian [*Medial records*] (DAVI)
RL	Red Lamp (IAA)
R/L	Redline (KSC)
RL	Red Lion Hotels [*NYSE symbol*] (TTSB)
RL	Red Lion Hotels, Inc. [*NYSE symbol*] (SAG)
RL	Reduced [*or Reduction*] Level
RL	Reel
RL	Reeling Machines [*JETDS nomenclature*] [*Military*] (CET)
RL	Reference Library
RL	Reference Line (IAA)
RL	Reference List
RL	Reflection Loss [*Telecommunications*] (TEL)
RL	Regent's Line [*Steamship*] (MHDW)
RL	Reiz-Limen [*Stimulus threshold*] [*Psychology*]
RL	Relay Logic
RL	Release Load
RL	Religious [*A radio station format*] (WDMC)
RL	Relocation (IAA)
RL	Relocation Library (HGAA)
R/L	Remote/Local (NASA)
RL	Remote Location (IAA)
RL	Report Immediately Upon Leaving [*Aviation*] (FAAC)
RL	Report Leaving [*ICAO*] (FAAC)
RL	Research Laboratory
RL	Reserve List (ADA)
RL	Residential Lease [*Real estate*] (ADA)
RL	Resistance-Inductance (IDOE)
RL	Resistor Logic (IEEE)
RL	Respectable Loge [*Worshipful Lodge*] [*Freemasonry*] [*French*] (ROG)
R_L	Respiratory Resistance [*Medicine*] (DAVI)
RL	Restaurant Liquor [*License*]
RL	Restricted Line Officer
RL	Retarded Learner [*Education*]
RL	Reticular Lamina [*Ear anatomy*]
RL	Retired List
RL	Retirement Loss
R/L	Return Link (MCD)
RL	Return Loss
RL	Revised Laws [*A publication*] (DLA)
RL	Revue Legale [*Canada*] [*A publication*] (DLA)
RL	Rhumb Line
RL	Rial [*Monetary unit*] [*Iran, Saudi Arabia, etc.*]
RL	Richland Operations Office [*Energy Research and Development Administration*]
RL	Richtlinien [*Instructions, Directions*] [*German*] (ILCA)
R/L	Right and Left

RL	Right Lateral (DAVI)
RL	Right Leg
RL	Right Line
RL	Right Lower [*Medicine*]
RL	Right Lung
RL	Right to Left
RL	Ringer Lactated [*Medicine*]
RL	Ring Level (BUR)
RL	Rive'on Le-Khalkalah [*Tel Aviv*] (BJA)
RL	River Lines, Inc. [*AAR code*]
RL	Road Load [*Automotive engineering*]
RL	Road Locomotive [*British*]
RL	Rocket Launcher
RL	Roll
RL	Rolland, Inc. [*Toronto Stock Exchange symbol*]
RL	Roll Lift [*NASA*] (KSC)
RL	Roman Law (DLA)
RL	Romeo Series L [*Alfa-Romeo*] [*Automotive model designation*]
RL	Roof Leader (MSA)
RL	Round Lot [*Unit of trading*]
RL	Roussy-Levy [*Syndrome*] [*Medicine*] (DB)
RL	Royal (ROG)
RL	Royal Lancers [*British military*] (DMA)
RL	Royal Licence [*British*]
RL	Rugby League [*British*] (DI)
RL	Run Length [*Computer science*]
RL	Running Losses [*Automotive engineering*]
RL	Runway Light [*Aviation*] (DA)
R_L	Total Pulmonary Resistance [*Medicine*] (DAVI)
RLA	Aeronautical Marker Beacon [*ITU designation*] (CET)
RLA	Lar-Liniile Aeriene Romance [*Romania*] [*ICAO designator*] (FAAC)
RLA	Radiographic Lung Area [*Medicine*] (STED)
RLA	Reallexikon der Assyriologie [*Berlin*] [*A publication*] (BJA)
RLA	Rebuild Los Angeles [*Commission established after 1992 riots*] (ECON)
RLA	Receptive Language Age [*of the hearing-impaired*]
RLA	Redevelopment Land Agency [*Washington, DC*]
RLA	Regional Land Agent [*Ministry of Agriculture, Fisheries, and Food*] [*British*]
RLA	Regional Letter of Acceptance [*Department of Housing and Urban Development*] (GFGA)
RLA	Relay To [*ICAO*] (FAAC)
RLA	Religious Leaders of America [*A publication*]
RLA	Religious Liberty Association (NADA)
RLA	Remote Line Adapter
RLA	Remote Loop Adapter [*Telecommunications*]
RLA	Repair Level Analysis [*Military*] (AFIT)
RLA	Repair Line Agreement (NASA)
RLA	Research Laboratory for Archeology [*British*]
RLA	Responsible Local Agencies (OICC)
RLA	Restricted Landing Area [*Aviation*]
RLA	Roll Lock Actuator (MCD)
RLA	Royal Lao [*or Laotian*] Army [*Laos*]
RLA	Rui Lopes Associates, Inc. [*Sunnyvale, CA*] [*Telecommunications*] (TSSD)
RLA	Run Length/Amplitude [*Computer science*]
RLA	Rural Land Alliance (EA)
RLAB	Royce Laboratories [*NASDAQ symbol*] (TTSB)
RLAB	Royce Laboratories, Inc. [*Miami, FL*] [*NASDAQ symbol*] (NQ)
RLAC	Recycling Legislation Action Coalition [*Defunct*] (EA)
RLADD	RADAR Low-Angle Drogue Delivery (AFM)
RLAF	Royal Laotian Air Force
RL & R	Rail, Lake, and Rail
RL & S	Ridgeway, Lapp, and Schoales' Irish King's Bench Reports [*1793-95*] [*A publication*] (DLA)
RL & W	Roberts, Leaming, and Wallis' County Court Reports [*1849-51*] [*A publication*] (DLA)
RLANO	Relay Equipment out of Operation (FAAC)
RLAOK	Relay Equipment Resumed Operation (FAAC)
RLAS	Rocket Lunar Attitude System
RLAss	Reallexikon der Assyriologie [*Berlin*] [*A publication*] (BJA)
R LAT	Right Lateral [*Medicine*] (MEDA)
R Lat	Right Lateral [*Medicine*] (STED)
RLB	Air Alba Ltd. [*British ICAO designator*] (FAAC)
RLB	Racecourses Licences Board [*Victoria, Australia*]
RLB	RACON Station [*ITU designation*] (CET)
RLB	Reliability [*or Reliable*] (AAG)
RLB	Remontant-Leucocytes Beljansky (DB)
RLB	Rickettsia-Like Bodies (CPH)
RLB	Right Linebacker (WGA)
RLB	United States Railroad Labor Board Decisions [*A publication*] (DLA)
RLBCD	Right Lower Border of Cardiac Dullness [*Cardiology*]
RLB Dec	Railroad Labor Board Decisions [*A publication*] (DLA)
RLBG	Relative Bearing [*Aviation*] (FAAC)
RLBI	Right Left Bearing Indicator [*Navigation*] (IAA)
RLBL	Regional Laser and Biotechnology Laboratories [*University of Pennsylvania*] [*Research center*] (RCD)
RLBM	Rearward Launched Ballistic Missile
RLC	Avial (Russian Co. Ltd.) [*Former USSR ICAO designator*] (FAAC)
RLC	Radio Launch Control System (IEEE)
RLC	Radio Liberty Committee [*Later, RFE/RL*] (EA)
RLC	Reaction Liquid Chromatography (DB)
RLC	Real-time Lens Error Correction [*Computer science*] (NTCM)
RLC	Receive Logic Chassis
RLC	Rectus and Longus Capitus (STED)
RLC	Refund Litigation Coordinator [*IRS*]
RLC	Regulatory Light Chain [*Physiology*]
RLC	Remote Line Concentrator
RLC	Remote Load Controller [*NASA*] (MCD)
RLC	Remote Lock Control [*Automotive engineering*]
RLC	Report Landing Completed [*Aviation*] (FAAC)
RLC	Republican Liberty Caucus (EA)
RLC	Residual Lung Capacity [*Medicine*]
RLC	Resistance Inductance Capacitance (MSA)
RLC	Revival Life Centre [*Australia*]
RLC	Rhodopsin-Lipid Complex (STED)
RLC	Ribosome-Lamella Complex [*Physiology*]
RLC	Right Line Contactor (MCD)
RLC	Right Line Contractor
RLC	Robinson Little & Co. Ltd. [*Toronto Stock Exchange symbol*]
RLC	Rollins Truck Leasing [*NYSE symbol*] (SPSG)
RLC	ROM [*Read-Only Memory*] Location Counter
RLC	Rotating Litter Chair [*NASA*] (KSC)
RLC	Run Length Coding
RLCA	National Rural Letter Carriers' Association
RLCA	Reaction-Limited Cluster Aggregation
RLCA	Rear Lower Control Arm
RLCA	Religion and Labor Council of America [*Defunct*] (EA)
RLCA	Rural Letter Carriers' Association (NADA)
RLCD	Relocated
RLCE	Request Level Change Enroute [*Aviation*] (DA)
RLCM	Rat Lung-Conditioned Medium [*Culture media*]
RLCO	Realco, Inc. [*NASDAQ symbol*] (SAG)
RLCOW	Realco Inc. Wrrt [*NASDAQ symbol*] (TTSB)
RLCR	Railcar (MSA)
RLCS	Radio Launch Control System
RLCTN	Relocation
RLCU	Reference Link Control Unit [*Telecommunications*] (TEL)
RLD	RADAR Laydown Delivery (AFM)
RLD	Ready-to-Load Date [*At origin*] (DOMA)
RLD	Related Living Donor [*Medicine*]
RLD	Relocation Dictionary
RLD	Relocation Directory (NITA)
RLD	Relocation List Directory
RLD	Remote Launch Demonstration [*Army*] (DOMA)
RLD	Repetitive LASER Desorption
RLD	Resistive Load Detection (STED)
RLD	Retail Liquor Dealer
RLD	Rheinland Air Service [*Germany ICAO designator*] (FAAC)
RLD	Richland [*Washington*] [*Airport symbol Obsolete*] (OAG)
RLD	Right Lateral Decubitus [*Position*] (STED)
RLD	Rolled (AAG)
RLD	Round Vesicles, Large Profile and Dark Mitochondria [*Synaptic terminals*] (DB)
RLD	Run Length Discriminator (MCD)
RLD	Ruptured Lumbar Disc [*Medicine*]
RLDB	Reference Library Data Base
RLDS	Reorganized Church of Jesus Christ of Latter-Day Saints
RLDU	Resources for Learning Development Unit (AIE)
RLE	Raleigh Energy [*Vancouver Stock Exchange symbol*]
RLE	Rate of Loss of Energy (IAA)
RLE	Recent Life Events (STED)
RLE	Relative Luminous Efficiency (NATG)
RLE	Request Loading Entry [*Computer science*]
RLE	Research Laboratory of Electronics [*MIT*] [*Research center*]
RLE	Resorts Leisure Exchange [*Commercial firm British*]
RLE	Right Lower Extremity [*Medicine*]
RLE	Run-Length Encoding [*Computer science*]
RLEA	Railway Labor Executives' Association (EA)
RLED	Resettlement Licence Eligibility Date (WDAA)
RLEO	Request Liaison Engineering Order [*NASA*] (NASA)
RLETFL	Report Leaving Each Thousand Foot Level [*Aviation*] (FAAC)
RLEW	Research Library for Edward Woodward (EA)
R_{LF}	Low-Frequency Resistance (IDOE)
RLF	Reactive Load Factor (IAA)
RLF	Reduced Layer Formation (BARN)
RLF	Relevant Labor Force (DNAB)
RLF	Relief (AAG)
RLF	Religion and Labor Foundation
RLF	Religious Liberty Foundation [*Defunct*] (EA)
RLF	Remote Lift Fan [*Aviation*]
RLF	Replication Licensing Factor [*Genetics*]
RLF	Retained Lund Fluid (DAVI)
RLF	Retrograde Lipid Flow [*Hypothesis for biological cell movement*]
RLF	Retrolental Fibroplasia [*Eye disease in premature babies*]
RLF	Reverse Line Feed [*Telecommunications*] (OSI)
RLF	Rhizoctonia-Like Fungus
RLF	Right Lateral Femoral [*Site of injection*] [*Medicine*]
RLF	Royal Laotian Forces
RLF	Royal Literary Fund [*British*]
RLFC	Rebel Lee Fan Club (EA)
RLG	Glidepath [*Slope*] Station [*ITU designation*] (CET)
RLG	Kremmling, CO [*Location identifier FAA*] (FAAL)
RLG	Railing (AAG)
RLG	Regimental Landing Group
RLG	Regional Liaison Group (CINC)
RLG	Release Guard [*Telecommunications*] (TEL)
RLG	Relief Landing Ground [*British military*] (DMA)
RLG	Research Libraries Group [*An association Also, an information service or system*] (EA)

RLG .... Rifle Large Grain [*British military*] (DMA)
RLG .... Ring LASER Gyro [*Navy*]
RLG .... Royal Laotian Government
RLG .... Royal Lepage Ltd. [*Toronto Stock Exchange symbol Vancouver Stock Exchange symbol*]
RLGD .... Realigned
RLGM .... Remote Look Group Multiplexer (MCD)
RLGM-CD .... Remote Look Group Multiplexer Cable Drive (MCD)
RLGN .... Ring LASER Gyro Navigation (MCD)
RLGS .... Restriction Landmark Genomic Scanning (HGEN)
RLH .... Run Like Hell [*Slang*]
RLHIT .... Royal Life High Income Trust [*British*]
RLHP .... Road Load Horsepower [*Automotive engineering*]
RLHS .... Railway and Locomotive Historical Society (EA)
RLHTE .... Research Laboratory of Heat Transfer in Electronics [*MIT*] (MCD)
RLI .... Anniston, AL [*Location identifier FAA*] (FAAL)
RLI .... Radiation Level Indicator
RLI .... Rand Light Infantry [*British military*] (DMA)
RLI .... Realtors Land Institute (EA)
RLI .... Red Line Instrumentation (IAA)
RLI .... Resist Lithography (AAEL)
RLI .... Retirement Life Item
RLI .... Rhodesian Light Infantry [*Military unit*]
RLI .... Right/Left Indicator (NVT)
RLI .... RLI Corp. [*NYSE symbol*] (SPSG)
RLI .... Rostral Length Index
RLIB........... Relocatable Library [*Computer science*]
RLI Cp .... RLI Corp. [*Associated Press*] (SAG)
RLIEVDP ...... Request Line Items Be Expedited for Vehicles [*or Equipment*] Deadlined for Parts [*Army*] (AABC)
RLIF........... [*The*] Reliable Life Insurance Co. [*NASDAQ symbol*] (NQ)
RLIFA.......... Reliable Life Ins [*NASDAQ symbol*] (TTSB)
R Lim E ...... Roll-Limiting Engine
RLIN .... Research Libraries Information Network [*Pronounced "arlen"*] [*Formerly, BALLOTS Research Libraries Group, Inc. Stanford, CA*] [*Library network*] [*Information service or system*]
RLIN .... Royale Investments, Inc. [*NASDAQ symbol*] (SAG)
RLIN .... Royale Invts Inc. [*NASDAQ symbol*] (TTSB)
RLionH .... Red Lion Hotels, Inc. [*Associated Press*] (SAG)
RLionInn...... Red Lion Inns Ltd. [*Associated Press*] (SAG)
RLJ .... Rhodesian Law Journal [*A publication*] (DLA)
RLK........... Air Nelson Ltd. [*New Zealand*] [*ICAO designator*] (FAAC)
RLL........... Localizer Station [*ITU designation*] (CET)
RLL........... Rapid and Large Leakage (GNE)
RLL........... Relay Ladder Logic (ACII)
RLL........... Religion in Literature and Life [*A publication*]
RLL........... Relocating Linking Loader
RLL........... Representation-Language Language [*Computer science*]
RLL........... Right Lower Limb [*Medicine*]
RLL........... Right Lower Lobe [*Lungs*]
RLL........... Rim of Lateral Lip
RLL........... Rocket Launcher Locator
RLL........... Rolla, ND [*Location identifier FAA*] (FAAL)
RLL........... Run-Length-Limited [*Computer science*]
RLLB........... Right Long Leg Brace [*Medicine*]
RLLB........... Right Lower Leg Brace [*Medicine*]
RLLD .... Registered Laundry and Linen Director [*National Association of Institutional Linen Management*] [*Designation awarded by*]
RLLS........... Runway Lead-In Lighting System [*Aviation*] (FAAC)
RLLSC .... Right to Life League of Southern California (EA)
RLLY........... Rally's Hamburgers [*NASDAQ symbol*] (TTSB)
RLLY........... Rally's, Inc. [*NASDAQ symbol*] (NQ)
RLM........... Marine Radio Beacon Station [*ITU designation*] (CET)
RLM........... Rat Liver Mitochondria (DB)
RLM........... Rearward Launched Missile
RLM........... Reflector and Lighting Equipment Manufacturers (IAA)
RLM........... Reflector Lamps Manufacturer (IAA)
RLM........... Regional Library of Medicine [*Pan American Health Organization*]
RLM........... Reichsleftfahrt Ministerium [*German Air Ministry*] [*World War II*]
RLM........... Remote Line Module [*Telecommunications*]
RLM........... Research and Laboratory Management [*Army*]
RLM........... Return to Land and Management [*Agriculture*]
RLM........... Reynolds Metals [*NYSE symbol*] (TTSB)
RLM........... Reynolds Metals Co. [*NYSE symbol*] (SPSG)
RLM........... Right Lower Medial [*Medicine*] (DMAA)
RLM........... Royal American Airways, Inc. [*ICAO designator*] (FAAC)
RLM........... Royal Lancashire Militia [*British military*] (DMA)
RLM........... Royal London Militia
RLM........... Roy-L Merchant Group, Inc. [*Toronto Stock Exchange symbol*]
RLMA.......... Roll Label Manufacturers Association (EA)
RLMD .... Rat Liver Mitochondria (MAE)
RLME .... Rapid Liquid Metal Embrittlement (MCD)
RLMM.......... Research Laboratory for Mechanics of Materials (MCD)
RLMPrD........ Reynolds Metals 7%'PRIDES' [*NYSE symbol*] (TTSB)
RLMS.......... RADAR Land Mass Simulation
RLMS.......... Reproduction of Library Materials Section [*Resources and Technical Services Division of ALA*]
RLN .... LORAN Station [*ITU designation*] (CET)
RLN .... Recurrent Laryngeal Nerve [*Medicine*] (MAE)
RLN .... Regional Lymph Node [*Medicine*] (CPH)
RLN .... Remote LAN [*Linked Access Network*] Node [*DCA, Inc.*] (PCM)
RLN .... Romeo Series L Normale [*Alfa-Romeo*] [*Automotive model designation*]
RLNA .... Request Level Not Available [*Aviation*] (FAAC)
RLNC .... Regional Lymph Node Cell [*Medicine*] (DMAA)

RLND .... Regional Lymph Node Dissection [*Medicine*]
RLNS .... Revue Legale. New Series [*Canada*] [*A publication*] (DLA)
RLO .... Omnidirectional Range Station [*ITU designation*] (CET)
RLO .... RADAR Lock-On
RLO .... Records Liaison Officers [*Environmental Protection Agency*] (AEPA)
RLO .... Regional Liaison Office [*Military*] (AFM)
RLO .... Repairs Liaison Officer [*Landing craft and barges*] [*Navy*]
RLO .... Residual Lymphatic Output [*Medicine*] (DMAA)
R/LO .... Response/Lockout (MCD)
RLO .... Restricted Line Officer (DNAB)
RLO .... Returned Letter Office
RLO .... Richland Operations Office [*Energy Research and Development Administration*]
RLO .... Rose Lookout Tower [*Oklahoma*] [*Seismograph station code, US Geological Survey*] (SEIS)
RLO .... Round Lot Orders [*Unit of trading*] (MHDW)
RLO .... Rudder Lock-Out (MCD)
RLOCK........ Record Lock
rlogin.......... Remote Login [*Computer science*] (IGQR)
RLOP .... Reactor Licensing Operating Procedure [*Nuclear energy*] (NRCH)
RLOS .... Retention Level of Supply [*Navy*] (NG)
RLOS .... Revue Legale (Old Series) [*Canada*] [*A publication*] (DLA)
RLP .... Radiation-Leukemia-Protection (MAE)
RLP .... Rail Loading Point (NATG)
RLP .... Random Loose-Packed [*Granular physics*]
RLP .... Remote Line Printer (MCD)
RLP .... Ribosome-Like Particle [*Cytology*]
RLP .... Roads and Landscape Planning [*British*]
RLP .... Rosella Plains [*Australia Airport symbol Obsolete*] (OAG)
RLP .... Rotatable Log Periodic Antenna (MCD)
RLP .... Rotating Linear Polarization
RLP .... Ruby LASER Pulse
RLPA .... Religious Liberty Protection Act
RLPA .... Retail Loss Prevention Association [*New York, NY*] (EA)
RLPA .... Rotating Log Periodic Antenna
RLPB .... Rural Land Protection Board [*Australia*]
RLPG .... Regenerative Liquid Propellant Gun (MCD)
RLPH .... Reflected Light Photohead
RLPL .... Railway Labor's Political League
RLPNLP .... Retired League Postmasters of the National League of Postmasters (EA)
RLPS .... Royal Liverpool Philharmonic Society [*British*] (DBA)
RLQ .... Right Lower Quadrant [*of abdomen*] [*Medicine*]
RLQB .... Revue Legale Reports, Queen's Bench [*Canada*] [*A publication*] (DLA)
RLR .... Radioactive Lighting Rod [*Nuclear energy*] (NRCH)
RLR .... Radio Range Station [*ITU designation*] (CET)
RLR .... Record Length Register
RLR .... Red Light Running [*NHTSA*] (TAG)
RLR .... ReliaStar Financial [*NYSE symbol*] (TTOD)
RLR .... ReliaStar Financial Co. [*NYSE symbol*] (SAG)
RLR .... Reserves to Loans Ratio
RLR .... Retired Lives Reserve [*Insurance*]
RLR .... Reverse Locking Relay (IAA)
RLR .... Right Larval Retractor
RLR .... Right Lateral Rectus [*Eye anatomy*]
RLR .... Right Lateral Rotation [*Medicine*]
RLR .... Roller (MSA)
RLRD .... Register Load and Read
RLRIU .... Radio Logic Routing Interface Unit (MCD)
RLRPr......... ReliaStar Finl 10% Dep Pfd [*NYSE symbol*] (TTSB)
RLRPrA........ ReliaStar Fin I 8.20%'TOPrS' [*NYSE symbol*] (TTSB)
RLRS .... Regional Learning Resources Services [*Veterans Administration*] (GFGA)
RLS............ RADAR Line of Sight
RLS............ Radius of Landing Site [*NASA*] (KSC)
RLS............ Raman LASER Source
RLS............ Ranfurly Library Service [*An association*] (EAIO)
RLS............ Rate-Lock Standby [*FNMA*] (EMRF)
RLS............ Recursive Least Squares [*Mathematics*]
RLS............ Regularized Least-Squares [*Mathematics*]
RLS............ Remote Line Switch [*Telecommunications*] (TEL)
RLS............ Research in the Life Sciences Committee [*National Academy of Sciences*]
RLS............ Reservoir Level Sensor (MCD)
RLS............ Resonance Light Scattering [*Physics*]
RLS............ Restless Legs Syndrome [*Medicine*]
RLS............ Restricted Least Squares [*Statistics*]
RLS............ Reusable Launch System [*Aerospace*] (IAA)
RLS............ Rim Latch Set
RLS............ Ringer's Lactate Solution [*Physiology*]
RLS............ Riolos of Patras [*Greece*] [*Seismograph station code, US Geological Survey*] (SEIS)
RLS............ Robert Louis Stevenson [*Nineteenth-century Scottish author*]
RLS............ Rocket Launching System
RLS............ Roll Limit Switch
RLS............ Romeo Series L Sport [*Alfa-Romeo*] [*Automotive model designation*]
RLS............ Rotary Limit Switch
RLS............ Rotating Lighthouse System (IAA)
RLS............ Ruby LASER System
RLS............ Surveillance RADAR Station [*ITU designation*] (CET)
RLS............ Westerly, RI [*Location identifier FAA*] (FAAL)
RLSA.......... Republican Law Students Association of New York (EA)
RLSA NY ..... Republican Law Students Association of New York (EA)
RLSB.......... Right Lower Scapular Border [*Medicine*] (DMAA)

RLSC .... Revue Legale Reports, Supreme Court [*Canada*] [*A publication*] (DLA)
RLSD .... Received Line Signal Detector
RLSD .... Research and Laboratory Services Division [*Health and Safety Executive*] [*British*] (IRUK)
RLSE .... Release (MSA)
RLSL .... Recursive Least Square Lattice (DMAA)
RLSO .... Regional Logistical Support Offices (DOMA)
RLSO .... Unit Released by Blood Bank (DAVI)
RLSP .... Ruby LASER Single Pulse
RLSS .... Regenerative Life Support System [*NASA*] (NASA)
RLSS .... Romeo Series L Super Sport [*Alfa-Romeo*] [*Automotive model designation*]
RLSS .... Royal Life Saving Society [*Studley, Warwickshire, England*] (EAIO)
RLST .... Read Least Significant Time [*Military*]
RLST .... Release Timer [*Telecommunications*] (TEL)
RLT .... Arlit [*Niger*] [*Airport symbol*] (OAG)
RLT .... Radionavigation Land Test (PDAA)
RLT .... Rate Level Test [*R. Carver*] (TES)
RLT .... Redeemable Listed Trust
RLT .... Regimental Landing Team [*Military*]
RLT .... Registered Laboratory Technician [*Medicine*] (WGA)
RLT .... Relating To (AABC)
RLT .... Reliability Life Test
RLT .... Reliant Airlines, Inc [*ICAO designator*] (FAAC)
RLT .... Remote Line Tester (PDAA)
RLT .... Reorder Lead Time [*Navy*] (NG)
RLT .... Repair Lead Time
RLT .... Research & Laser Technology, Inc.
RLT .... Return Line Tether [*NASA*] (MCD)
RLT .... Right Lateral Thigh [*Medicine*]
RLT .... Ring LASER Technique
RLT .... Rolling Liquid Transporter [*Army*]
RLT .... Romeo Series L Turismo [*Alfa-Romeo*] [*Automotive model designation*]
RLTA .... Reenlistment Leave Travel Allowance [*Military*]
RLTA .... Rhodesian Lawn Tennis Association
RLTD .... Related
RLTF .... Romeo Series L Targa Florio [*Alfa-Romeo*] [*Automotive model designation*]
RLTK .... Rhumbline Track [*Aviation*] (FAAC)
RLTM .... Research Laboratories Technical Memorandum
RLTN .... Relation (MSA)
RLTO .... Regional Lime Technical Officer [*Ministry of Agriculture, Fisheries, and Food*] [*British*]
Rltr .... Realtor (WGA)
RLTR .... Realtor
RltRef .... Realty Refund Trust [*Associated Press*] (SAG)
RLTS .... Radio Linked Telemetry System
RLTV .... Relative (AFM)
RLTY .... Realty [*Classified advertising*]
RltyInco .... Realty Income Corp. [*Associated Press*] (SAG)
RLU .... RADAR Logic Unit (MCD)
RLU .... Relative Light Units [*Analysis of light intensity*]
RLU .... Relay Logic Unit (IAA)
RLU .... Remote Line Unit [*Telecommunications*]
RLU .... Reserve Liaison Unit (DNAB)
RLU .... Waterville, ME [*Location identifier FAA*] (FAAL)
RLUD .... Routing Logic [*Radio Interface*] Unit Diagnostic Program [*Telecommunications*]
RLUF .... Refundable Life Use Fee [*Housing*] (DICI)
RLV .... Range Location Velocity
RLV .... Rauscher [*Murine*] Leukemia Virus
RLV .... Real Aviation Ltd. [*Ghana*] [*ICAO designator*] (FAAC)
RLV .... Reallexikon der Vorgeschichte [*Berlin*] [*A publication*] (BJA)
RLV .... Recordable LASER Videodisc [*Optical Disc Corp.*] (DOM)
RLV .... Relieve (AFM)
RLV .... Reliv' International [*AMEX symbol*] (TTSB)
RLV .... Reliv' International, Inc. [*AMEX symbol*] (SPSG)
RLV .... Reusable Launch Vehicle [*NASA*]
RLV .... Roving Lunar Vehicle (AAG)
RLVD .... Relieved
RLVDT .... Rotary Linear Variable Differential Transformer
RLVL .... Report Level [*Aviation*] (FAAC)
RLVS .... Recoverable Launch Vehicle Structure (KSC)
RLW .... Rajasthan Law Weekly [*India*] [*A publication*] (DLA)
RLW-30 .... Ration Lightweight-30 Day [*Military*] (RDA)
RLWL .... Reactor Low-Water Level (IEEE)
RLWY .... Railway (AAG)
RLX .... Relaxin [*Biochemistry*]
RLXN .... Relaxation (MSA)
RLY .... Aerolineas Yasi, SA de CV [*Mexico*] [*FAA designator*] (FAAC)
RLY .... Railway
RLY .... Relay (AAG)
RLY .... Worland, WY [*Location identifier FAA*] (FAAL)
RM .... Lab. Roland-Marie [*France*] [*Research code symbol*]
RM .... Marianitas (TOCD)
RM .... Maritime Radionavigation Mobile Station [*ITU designation*] (OET)
R$_m$ .... Meter Resistance (IDOE)
RM .... Office of Resource Management [*Nuclear energy*] (NRCH)
RM .... Rack Mounted (IAA)
RM .... RADAR Mapper
RM .... RADAR Missile (MUGU)
RM .... Radiation Measurement
R/M .... Radiation/Meteoroid [*NASA satellite*]

RM .... Radiation Monitor (NRCH)
RM .... Radical Mastectomy [*Medicine*]
RM .... Radioman [*Navy rating*]
RM .... Radio Marker (IAA)
RM .... Radio Marti [*Cuba*]
RM .... Radio Material Officer (MCD)
RM .... Radio Message (IAA)
RM .... Radio Monitor
RM .... Range Marks
RM .... Range of Movement [*Medicine*]
RM .... Raven's Matrices [*Intelligence test*]
RM .... Raw Material
RM .... Raybestos-Manhattan, Inc. (EFIS)
RM .... Reactance Meter (IAA)
RM .... Reaction Mass
RM .... Reactor Manufacturer [*Nuclear energy*] (NRCH)
RM .... Readiness Manager [*DARCOM*] [*Army*]
R/M .... Read/Mostly [*Computer science*] (TEL)
RM .... Read Out Material [*Computer science*] (IAA)
RM .... Readout Matrix
RM .... Ready Money (ROG)
RM .... Ream
rm .... Ream (WDMC)
RM .... Reasonable Man [*Legal shorthand*] (LWAP)
RM .... Reasoning Module [*Computer science*]
RM .... Receiver, Mobile
RM .... Receiving Memo
RM .... Recordimeter (NTCM)
RM .... Record Mark (BUR)
RM .... Recovery Manager [*Environmental science*] (COE)
RM .... Rectangular Module (IAA)
RM .... Red Marrow [*Hematology*]
RM .... Redundancy Management (MCD)
RM .... Reference Manual (IAA)
RM .... Reference Mark (IAA)
RM .... Reference Material
RM .... Reference Memory [*Psychology*]
RM .... Reference Method
RM .... Reference Mission [*NASA*] (NASA)
RM .... Reflection Modulation (IAA)
RM .... Refresh Memory (MCD)
RM .... Regeneration Medium [*Biology*]
RM .... Regional Manager
RM .... Regional Meetings [*Quakers*]
RM .... Regional Myocardial [*Medicine*] (DB)
RM .... Registered Magistrate (WDAA)
RM .... Registered Mail (WDAA)
RM .... Registered Midwife [*British*] (DBQ)
RM .... Register Memory
RM .... Reichsmark [*Later, DM*] [*Monetary unit*] [*German*]
RM .... Relais Musique [*Phonorecord series*] [*Canada*]
RM .... Relative Mobility [*of ions*] [*Chemistry*]
RM .... Remark [*Aviation*] (FAAC)
RM .... Remedial Maintenance (AFM)
Rm .... Remission [*Medicine*]
RM .... Remote (IAA)
RM .... Remote Manipulator [*NASA*] (NASA)
RM .... Remote Manual (NRCH)
RM .... Remote Multiplexer [*Computer science*] (CAAL)
rm .... Remove [*Computer science*] [*Telecommunications*]
RM .... Rendezvous Maneuver (MCD)
RM .... Repair Manual
RM .... Repetition Maximum [*Medicine*]
RM .... Replaceable Module
RM .... Rescue Module [*NASA*] (NASA)
RM .... Research Machines (NITA)
RM .... Research Materials [*National Institute of Standards and Technology*]
RM .... Research Memorandum
RM .... Residential Member [*American Institute of Real Estate Appraisers of the National Association of Realtors*] [*Designation awarded by*]
RM .... Resident Magistrate
RM .... Residue Manipulator (IAA)
RM .... Resolution Multiplier (IAA)
RM .... Resource Management (DDC)
RM .... Resource Manager
RM .... Resource Module (SSD)
RM .... Respiratory Movement
RM .... Response Memoranda [*Jimmy Carter administration*]
RM .... Retail Manager
RM .... Retrospective Method [*Insurance*]
RM .... Return Material [*Navy*] (NG)
RM .... Review of Metaphysics [*A publication*] (BRI)
R/M .... Revolutions per Minute
RM .... Rhesus Monkey
RM .... Richmark Resources Ltd. [*Vancouver Stock Exchange symbol*]
RM .... Riding Master [*British*]
RM .... Right Mid
RM .... Ring Micrometer
RM .... Rocket Management (MCD)
RM .... Rocket Motor
RM .... Rocky Mountains
RM .... Rod Memory (IAA)
RM .... Rogosa SL Medium [*Microbiology*] (DAVI)
RM .... Rollback Module [*Telecommunications*] (TEL)
RM .... Rolling Moment [*Physics*]

rm...............	Romania [MARC country of publication code Library of Congress] (LCCP)
RM...............	Roman Martyrology
RM...............	Romans [New Testament book]
RM...............	Romford [Postcode] (ODBW)
rm...............	Room (ODBW)
RM...............	Room
Rm...............	Room (DD)
RM...............	Rosenthal-Melkersson [Syndrome] [Medicine] (DB)
RM...............	Rotating Machinery (IAA)
RM...............	Rothmann-Makai [Disease] [Medicine] (DB)
RM...............	Roumania [IYRU nationality code] (IYR)
RM...............	Routine Maintenance (AAG)
RM...............	Routing Manager
RM...............	Routing Matrix (IAA)
RM...............	Rowley Mile [Horseracing] [British]
RM...............	Royal Mail [British]
RM...............	Royal Marines [British]
RM...............	Royal Mint [British] (DAS)
RM...............	Rubber Mold (MCD)
RM...............	Rule Making [Nuclear energy] (NRCH)
RM...............	Ruptured Membrane [Medicine]
RM...............	Rural Municipality (DLA)
RM...............	Russian Military [World War II]
RM...............	RYMAC Mortgage Investment Corp. [AMEX symbol] (CTT)
RM...............	RYMAC Mtge Invest [AMEX symbol] (TTSB)
RM...............	Wings West [ICAO designator] (AD)
RM-1............	Madison Chromosome [Genetics] (DAVI)
RM1.............	Radioman, First Class [Navy rating]
RM2.............	Radioman, Second Class [Navy rating]
RM3.............	Radioman, Third Class [Navy rating]
RM³.............	Remote Multimedia Mode [Army]
RMA.............	Racquetball Manufacturers Association [Defunct] (EA)
RMA.............	Radio-Labeled Monoclonal Antiglobulin [Clinical chemistry]
RMA.............	Radio Manufacturers Association [Later, Electronic Industries Association]
RMA.............	Radiometric Microbiological Assay
RMA.............	Rail Makers' Association [British] (BI)
RMA.............	Random Multiple Access
RMA.............	Rauma Oy [NYSE symbol] (SAG)
RMA.............	Rauma Oy ADS [NYSE symbol] (TTSB)
RMA.............	Reactive Modulation Amplifier
RMA.............	Readiness Management Assembly [Military] (INF)
RMA.............	Rear Maintenance Area [Military British]
RMA.............	Receiver Measurement Adapter (MCD)
RMA.............	Reclaim Managers Association [Defunct] (EA)
RMA.............	Records Management Officer (COE)
RMA.............	Recreation Managers' Association [British] (DBA)
RMA.............	Regiment de Marche d'Afrique [African Marching Regiment] [French]
RMA.............	Regional Manpower Administration
RMA.............	Registered Medical Assistants [Later, ARMA] (EA)
RMA.............	Relative Medullary Area [Medicine] (DMAA)
RMA.............	Relaxation Map Analysis [Coatings]
RMA.............	Relevant Market Area [Automotive dealership territory]
RMA.............	Reliability and Maintenance Analysis (CAAL)
RMA.............	Reliability, Maintainability, and Availability [Standards]
RMA.............	Remote Manipulator Arm [NASA] (NAKS)
RMA.............	Research and Marketing Act [1946]
RMA.............	Reserve Military Aviator
RMA.............	Retail Merchants' Association of Canada
RMA.............	Retread Manufacturers Association [British] (DBA)
RMA.............	Revolution in Military Affairs [Defense policy]
RMA.............	Rhythmic Motor Activity [Physiology]
RMA.............	Rice Millers' Association (EA)
RMA.............	Right Mentoanterior [A fetal position] [Obstetrics]
RMA.............	Riparian Management Area (WPI)
RMA.............	Robert Morris Associates [National Association of Bank Loan and Credit Officers] [Philadelphia, PA] (EA)
RMA.............	Rockefeller Mountains [Antarctica] [Seismograph station code, US Geological Survey Closed] (SEIS)
RMA.............	Rocky Mountain Airways, Inc. [ICAO designator] (FAAC)
RMA.............	Rocky Mountain Arsenal [Army] (AABC)
RMA.............	Rodeo Media Association [Defunct] (EA)
RMA.............	Roma [Australia Airport symbol] (OAG)
RMA.............	Rosin Mildly Activated [Standard material for soldering]
RMA.............	Royal Malta Artillery [Military unit] [British]
RMA.............	Royal Marine Academy [British]
RMA.............	Royal Marine Artillery [Obsolete British]
RMA.............	Royal Marines Association [British military] (DMA)
RMA.............	Royal Military Academy [For cadets of Royal Engineers and Royal Artillery; frequently referred to as Woolwich] [British]
RMA.............	Royal Military Asylum [British]
RMA.............	Royal Musical Association [British]
RMA.............	Rubber Manufacturers Association (EA)
RMA.............	Rusk Manufacturers Association [British] (DBA)
RMAA.........	Rubber Manufacturers' Association of Australia
RMAAMT.....	Registered Medical Assistants of American Medical Technologists (EA)
RMAAS........	Reactivity Monitoring and Alarm System [Nuclear energy] (NRCH)
RMAB	Royal Marines Auxiliary Brigade [British military] (DMA)
RMAC	Reactor Monitoring and Control [Nuclear energy] (IAA)
RMAC	Remote Master Aircraft (MCD)
RMAC	Rocky Mountain Athletic Conference (PSS)
RMACHA......	Rocky Mountain Automated Clearing House Association
R-MAD........	Reactor Maintenance, Assembly, and Disassembly
RMAF..........	Royal Moroccan Air Force
RMAG	Recursive Macroactuated Generator (MHDI)
RMAG	Rocky Mountain Association of Geologists (IAA)
RMAI	Retail Management Assessment Inventory [London House, Inc.] (TES)
RMAL..........	Revised Master Allowance List [Military] (AFIT)
RMALAN......	Royal Malaysian Navy
RMALC	Red Mexicana de Accion Frente al Libre Comercio [Mexican Action Network on Free Trade] (CROSS)
RMAN.........	Recovered Materials Advisory Notice [EPA] (AAGC)
RM & C	Reactor Monitoring and Control [Nuclear energy] (NRCH)
RM & PP	Raw Material and Purchase Parts (MCD)
RM&S..........	Reliability, Maintainability, and Sustainability [Military]
RMANOVA ..	Repeated Measures Analysis of Variance [Statistics]
RMAO..........	Resources Management and Administration Office [Environmental Protection Agency] (GFGA)
RMAS	Royal Military Academy Sandhurst [British]
RMA/SPRI....	Rubber Manufacturers Association/Single Ply Roofing Institute
R MAST	Radio Mast
RMAT..........	Royal Marine Advisory Team [British military] (DMA)
RMATS	Remote Maintenance and Testing Service [AT&T] (CIST)
RMATS-1	Remote Maintenance, Administration, and Traffic System-1 [Telecommunications] (TEL)
RMAX	Range, Maximum
RMB...........	Radio Marker Beacon
RMB...........	Radio Marketing Bureau [British] (CB)
RMB...........	Rambler Oil Co. [Toronto Stock Exchange symbol]
RMB...........	Rand Merchant Bank [South Africa]
RMB...........	Raw Materials Board [of the Reconstruction Finance Corp.]
RMB...........	Renminbi [Monetary unit] [China]
RMB...........	Right Mainstem Bronchus [Medicine] (DMAA)
RMB...........	Roadside Mailbox (ADA)
RMB...........	Rocky Mountain Motor Tariff Bureau, Inc., Denver CO [STAC]
RMB...........	Rombauer [Missouri] [Seismograph station code, US Geological Survey] (SEIS)
RMB...........	ROM Memory Band (NITA)
RMB...........	Royal Marine Bands [British military] (DMA)
RMB...........	Royal Marines Badge [British]
RMBA.........	Residual Mantle Bouguer Anomaly [Geology]
RMBAA.......	Rocky Mountain Business Aircraft Association (IAA)
RMBC	Regional Marine Biological Centre [UNESCO] (MSC)
RMBF..........	Regional Myocardial Blood Flow [Cardiology] (DAVI)
RMBF..........	Required Myocardial Blood Flow [Cardiology]
RMBNSW.....	Rice Marketing Board of New South Wales [Australia]
R-MBP-A......	Rat-Mannose-Binding Protein A
R-MBP-C......	Rat-Mannose-Binding Protein C
RMBPD.......	Royal Marine Boom Patrol Detachment [World War II]
RMBQ	Rice Marketing Board of Queensland [Australia]
RMBS	Rambus [Stock market symbol]
RMBS	Responsive Multicultural Basic Skills Approach (EDAC)
RMC...........	American Restaurant Partners Ltd. [AMEX symbol] (SPSG)
RMC...........	Amer Restaurant Ptnrs'A' [AMEX symbol] (TTSB)
RMC...........	Captain of Royal Marines [Military British]
RMC...........	Chief Radioman [Navy rating]
RMC...........	Radiation Management Corp. (NRCH)
RMC...........	Radiation Material Corp.
RMC...........	Radioactive Materials Committee [National Science Foundation] (NUCP)
RMC...........	Radio Management Control (MCD)
RMC...........	Radio Materials Co. (IAA)
RMC...........	Radio Monte Carlo [Monaco] (EY)
RMC...........	Randolph-Macon College [Virginia]
RMC...........	Rating Method Code [Insurance]
RMC...........	Rat Mast Cell
RMC...........	Raytheon Manufacturing Co. (MCD)
RMC...........	Ready Mixed Cement [Commercial firm British]
RMC...........	Ready Mixed Concrete (ADA)
RMC...........	Recursive Monte Carlo Method
RMC...........	Reduced Material Condition (NVT)
RMC...........	Redundancy Management Control (MCD)
RMC...........	Regional Management Centre (AIE)
RMC...........	Regional Media Center
RMC...........	Regular Military Compensation (AABC)
RMC...........	Regulated Motor Carriers
RMC...........	Relative-Motion Control [Microcopy]
RMC...........	Relay Mode Control (IAA)
RMC...........	Remote Control (IAA)
RMC...........	Remote Manual Control (NRCH)
RMC...........	Remote Message Concentrator (IAA)
RMC...........	Remote Multiplexer Combiner (MCD)
RMC...........	Rendezvous Mercury Capsule [NASA] (AAG)
RMC...........	Repair Manufacturer Codes
RMC...........	Representative in Medical Council [Royal College of Physicians] [British] (ROG)
RMC...........	Republican Mainstream Committee (EA)
RMC...........	Republican Majority Coalition [Republican party faction]
RMC...........	Residential Manpower Center [Job Corps]
RMC...........	Resident Management Corp. [Public housing]
RMC...........	Resource Management Consultants [Salem, NH] [Telecommunications] (TSSD)
RMC...........	Resource Management Corp.
RMC...........	[Series] Resources in Measurement & Control (ACII)
RMC...........	Return to Military Control (AABC)
RMC...........	Revolutionary Military Council [Grenada]

RMC............	Revue du Marche Commun [*Review of the Common Market*] [*French*]
RMC............	Revue Musicale [*A publication*]
RMC............	Right Middle Cerebral [*Artery*] [*Medicine*] (DB)
RMC............	Rocket Motor Case
RMC............	Rocky Mountain College [*Billings, MT*]
RMC............	Rod Memory Computer [*NCR Corp.*]
RMC............	Rosemont College, Rosemont, PA [*OCLC symbol*] (OCLC)
RMC............	Rotary Mirror Camera
RMC............	Rotating Modulation Collimator
RMC............	Royal Marine Commandos [*British*]
RMC............	Royal Military College [*For army cadets; often referred to as Sandhurst*] [*British*]
RMC............	Rural Manpower Center [*Michigan State University*]
RMCA	Right Main Coronary Artery [*Medicine*] (STED)
RMCA	Right Man Coronary Artery [*Anatomy*] (DAVI)
RMCA	Right Middle Cerebral Artery [*Anatomy*]
RMCAT	Ralph Mayer Center for Artists' Techniques [*University of Delaware*] [*Newark*] [*Information service or system*] (IID)
RMCAT	Right Middle Cerebral Artery Thrombosis [*Cardiology*] (DAVI)
RMCB	Registered Mail Central Bureau [*Later, RMIA*] (EA)
RMCB	Reserve Mobile Construction Battalion
RMCB	Royal Marine Commando Brigade [*British*]
RMCC	RADAR Monitor and Control Console [*Military*] (CAAL)
RMCC	Regional Ministers Conference on Cooperatives [*Australia*]
RMCC	Rotating Map, Cursor Centered [*Automotive engineering*]
RMCC	Royal Military College of Canada [*British military*] (DMA)
RMCC	Ryan and Moody's English Crown Cases [*A publication*] (DLA)
RMCCR	Ryan and Moody's English Crown Cases [*A publication*] (DLA)
RMCCSC	Raw Materials Committee of the Commonwealth Supply Council [*British World War II*]
RMCDC	Rocky Mountain Child Development Center [*University of Colorado*] [*Research center*] (RCD)
RMCDE	RADAR Message Conversion and Distribution (DA)
RM-CEAAL ...	Red de Mujeres del Consejo de Educacion de Adultos de Americana Latina [*Women's Network of the Council for Adult Education in Latin America - WN-CAELA*] [*Quito, Ecuador*] (EAIO)
RMCF...........	Rocky Mountain Chocolate Factory, Inc. [*Durango, CO*] [*NASDAQ symbol*] (NQ)
RMCF...........	Rocky Mtn Choc Factory [*NASDAQ symbol*] (TTSB)
RMCG	Reactor Materials Control Group [*Environmental science*] (COE)
RMCI	Right Management Consultants, Inc. [*Philadelphia, PA*] [*NASDAQ symbol*] (NQ)
RMCI	Right Mgmt Consultants [*NASDAQ symbol*] (TTSB)
RMCL..........	Recommended Maximum Contaminant Level [*Environmental Protection Agency*]
RMCL..........	Right Midclavicular Line [*Anatomy*] (DAVI)
RMCM	Master Chief Radioman [*Navy rating*]
RMCM	Reduced Material Condition Maintenance (MCD)
RMCM	Return Material Credit Memo
RMCM	Rotating Map, Cursor Moving [*Automotive engineering*]
RMCM	Royal Manchester College of Music [*British*]
RMCMI	Rocky Mountain Coal Mining Institute (EA)
RMCO	Raymond Manufacturing Co.
RMCOEH......	Rocky Mountain Center for Occupational and Environmental Health [*University of Utah*] [*Research center*] (RCD)
RMCP	Rat Mast Cell Protease [*An enzyme*]
RMCPA	Rocky Mountain College Placement Association (AEBS)
RMCS	Range Monitoring and Control Subsystem (MCD)
RMCS	Reactor Manual Control System [*Nuclear energy*] (NRCH)
RMCS	Remote Monitoring and Control System [*Telecommunications*]
RMCS	Royal Medical and Chirurgical Society [*British*] (ROG)
RMCS	Royal Military College of Science [*British*]
RMCS	Russian Mendeleev Chemical Society
RMCS	Senior Chief Radioman [*Navy rating*]
RMCSF	Recombinant Macrophage Colony-Stimulating Factor [*Biochemistry*]
RMCT..........	Rat Mast Cell Technique [*Allergy*] (DAVI)
RMCU	Royal Martyr Church Union [*British*] (DBA)
RMCUSA	Riley Motor Club USA (EA)
RMD	Rapid Movement Disorder [*Neurology*] (DAVI)
RMD	Ratio of Midsagittal Diameters (STED)
RMD	Raw Materials Department [*Ministry of Supply*] [*British*]
RMD	Reaction Motors Division (SAA)
RMD	Reading Matter Depth (DGA)
RMD	Ready Money Down [*Immediate payment*]
RMD	Repair and Modification Directive (AAG)
RMD	Required Markup Declaration [*Computer science*]
RMD	Retromanubrial Dullness [*Medicine*]
RMD	Right Manubrial Dullness [*Anatomy*] (MAE)
RMDA	Request for Manufacturing Development Authorization (AAG)
RMDHS........	Regional Model Data Handling System [*Environmental Protection Agency*] (GFGA)
RMDI	Radio Magnetic Deviation Indicator (AAG)
RM Dig........	Rapalje and Mack's Digest of Railway Law [*A publication*] (DLA)
RMDIR.........	Remove Directory [*Computer science*]
RMDL	Remedial
RMDP	Radon Mitigation Demonstration Program [*Environmental science*] (COE)
RMDP	Resource Mothers Development Project
RMDP	Rural Manpower Development Program
Rmdr	Remainder (DLA)
RMDU	Remote Multiplexer/Demultiplexer Unit (SSD)
RMDY	Remedy Corp. [*NASDAQ symbol*] (SAG)
RME.............	Armenian International Airlines [*ICAO designator*] (FAAC)
RME.............	Rack-Mount Extender (MHDI)
RME.............	Radiation Monitoring Equipment
RME.............	Rape Methyl Ester [*Fuel technology*]
RME.............	Raw Materials (MCD)
RME.............	Reasonable Maximum Exposure [*Toxicology*]
RME.............	Receptor Mediated Endocytosis [*Biochemistry*]
RME.............	Reflex Milk Ejection (OA)
RME.............	Relay Mirror Experiment
RME.............	Request Monitor Entry [*Computer science*]
RME.............	Resident Maintenance Engineer (NATG)
RME.............	Right Mediolateral Episiotomy [*Obstetrics*] (DAVI)
RME.............	Rocket Mission Evaluator (MCD)
RME.............	Rocky Mountain Energy [*Vancouver Stock Exchange symbol*]
RME.............	Rome, NY [*Location identifier FAA*] (FAAL)
RME.............	Royal Marine Engineers [*British*]
RMEC	Refractory Metals Electrofinishing Corp.
RMEC	Regional Medical Education Center [*Veterans Administration*] (GFGA)
RMED	Recruit, Retrain, Reemploy Medics [*Program*]
RMED	Research Medical [*NASDAQ symbol*] (TTSB)
RMED	Research Medical, Inc. [*NASDAQ symbol*] (SAG)
RMedSoc......	Royal Medical Society, Edinburgh
RMEE	Right Middle Ear Exploration [*otorhinolaryngology*] (DAVI)
RMEF	Rocky Mountain Elk Foundation (EA)
RMEL	Rocky Mountain Educational Laboratory [*Closed*]
R Melb Hosp Q...	Royal Melbourne Hospital. Quarterly [*A publication*]
RMER	Resource Management Expense Reporting System (MCD)
R Met S.......	Royal Meteorological Society [*British*]
RMEX	Reynolds Metals Co. (EFIS)
RMF.............	Raw Materials Finance Department [*Ministry of Supply*] [*British*]
RMF.............	RCS [*Reaction Control System*] Module Forward [*NASA*] (NASA)
RMF.............	Reactivity Measurement Facility [*Nuclear energy*]
RMF.............	Reamfixture (MCD)
RMF.............	Reduced Magnetic Field [*Computer science*] (PCM)
RMF.............	Reflectivity Measuring Facility
RMF.............	Residual Master File [*Computer science*]
RMF.............	Resource Measurement Facility [*Computer science*]
RMF.............	Reymann Memorial Farms [*West Virginia University*] [*Research center*] (RCD)
RMF.............	Right Middle Finger (DMAA)
RMF.............	Rotating Magnetic Field [*Spectrometry*]
RMF.............	Royal Malaysian Air Force [*ICAO designator*] (FAAC)
RMF.............	Royal Munster Fusiliers [*Military unit*] [*British*]
RMFA...........	Royal Malta Fencible Artillery [*British military*] (DMA)
RMFC...........	Rachel Minke Fan Club (EA)
RMFC...........	Ronnie McDowell Fan Club (EA)
RMFC...........	Ronnie Milsap Fan Club (EA)
RMFVR	Royal Marine Forces Volunteer Reserve [*Obsolete British*]
RMG	RADAR Mapper Gapfiller
RMG	RAL Marketing Group, Inc. [*Vancouver Stock Exchange symbol*]
RMG	Ranging Machine Gun [*British military*] (DMA)
RMG	Recommended for Medal and Gratuity [*British*]
RMG	Relative-Motion Gauge
RMG	Resource Management Group [*Military*]
RMG	Right Main Gear (MCD)
RMG	Rome [*Georgia*] [*Airport symbol Obsolete*] (OAG)
RMG	Rome [*Georgia*] [*Seismograph station code, US Geological Survey*] (SEIS)
RMG	Ronald Martin Groome [*Commercial firm British*]
RMG	Royal Marine Gunner [*British*]
RMGF	RADAR Mapper, Gap Filler (MSA)
RMGIC	Resin-Modified Glass-Ionomer Cement [*Dental material*]
RMGO	Regional Military Government Officer [*World War II*]
RMH	Rabbit-Mouse Hybridomas [*Immunochemistry*]
RMH	Refrigerator Mechanical Household (MSA)
RMH	Riemann's Metrical Hypothesis [*Mathematics*]
RMHA	Rocky Mountain Horse Association (EA)
RMHCSDI	Robert Maynard Hutchins Center for the Study of Democratic Institutions (EA)
RMHDDHG...	Regiere Mich Herr durch Deinen Heiligen Geist [*Rule Me, Lord, Through Thy Holy Spirit*] [*Motto of Ann, Margravine of Brandenburg (1575-1612)*] [*German*]
RMHF	Rat, Mouse, and Hamster Fanciers (EA)
RMHI	Religious and Mental Health Inventory
RMHT	RMH Teleservices, Inc. [*NASDAQ symbol*] (SAG)
RMH Tel......	RMH Teleservices, Inc. [*Associated Press*] (SAG)
RMI.............	Claretian Missionary Sisters (TOCD)
RMI.............	Merrell-National Laboratories [*Research code symbol*]
RMI.............	Rack Manufacturers Institute (EA)
RMI.............	Radiological Monitoring for Instructors [*Civil Defense*]
RMI.............	Radio Magnetic Indicator
RMi.............	Radio Magnetic Indicator [*NASA*] (NAKS)
RMI.............	Reactive Metals, Inc. Titanium Co. Extrusion Plant [*Department of Energy*] [*Ashtabula, OH*] (GAAI)
RMI.............	Reich Ministry of Interior
RMI.............	Release of Material for Issue
RMI.............	Reliability Maturity Index [*Polaris*]
RMI.............	Reliability Monitoring Index
RMI.............	Religious of Mary Immaculate [*Roman Catholic women's religious order*]
RMI.............	Remote Magnetic Indication
RMI.............	Remote Method Invocation [*Computer science*] (DOM)
RMI.............	Renewable Materials Institute [*College of Environmental Science and Forestry at Syracuse*] [*Research center*] (RCD)
RMI.............	Repair and Maintenance Instruction [*Military*]
RMI.............	Repairs, Maintenance, and Improvements
RMI.............	Repetitive Motion Injury

RMI..............	Republic of the Marshall Islands
RMI..............	Resource Management, Inc. (EFIS)
RMI..............	Richardson-Merrell, Inc. [*Later, Richardson-Vicks, Inc.*]
RMI..............	Rimini [*Italy*] [*Airport symbol*] (AD)
RMI..............	Rocket Motor Igniter
RMI..............	Rocky Mountain Institute (GNE)
RMI..............	Roll Manufacturers Institute (EA)
RMI..............	Rotonics Manufacturing [*Formerly, Koala Technologies*] [*AMEX symbol*] (SPSG)
RMI..............	Route Monitoring Information [*Telecommunications*] (TEL)
RMI..............	Rural Ministry Institute (EA)
RMIA	Rattan Manufacturers and Importers Association
RMIA	Registered Mail Insurance Association (EA)
RMIB	Rothwell Miller Interest Blank [*Test*] (TMMY)
RMIC	Research Materials Information Center [*ORNL*]
RMICBM	Road Mobile Intercontinental Ballistic Missile
rMIF	Recombinant Migration Inhibitory Factor [*Biochemistry*]
RMIFC	Reba McEntire International Fan Club (EA)
RMIG	Royal Masonic Institution for Girls [*British*] (BI)
RMIGA	Rocky Mountain Intercollegiate Golf Association (PSS)
RMII..........	Reference Method Item Identification [*DoD*]
RMII..........	Rocky Mountain Internet, Inc. [*NASDAQ symbol*] (SAG)
RMILL	Rocky Mountain Intercollegiate Lacrosse League (PSS)
RMIM	Repeater Media Interface Module [*Telecommunications*]
RMI/MO	Routine Manual In / Manual Out [*Military*] (DNAB)
R/MIN	Revolutions per Minute
RMIN	Roentgen per Minute (IAA)
RMIP	Reentry Measurements Instrumentation Package
RMIS	Readiness Management Information System [*Military*] (AABC)
RMIS	Resource Management Information System [*Environmental Protection Agency*]
RMISC	Rocky Mountain Intercollegiate Skiing Conference (PSS)
RMISL	Rocky Mountain Intercollegiate Soccer League (PSS)
RMIT	Rolland Maintenance Institutional Trainer [*Army*]
RMI Ti	RMI Titanium Co. [*Associated Press*] (SAG)
RMJ..............	Ramjet (MSA)
RMJ..............	Rumoi [*Japan*] [*Seismograph station code, US Geological Survey*] (SEIS)
RMJM	Recluse Missionaries of Jesus and Mary [*Roman Catholic women's religious order*]
RMK..............	Remark (AFM)
RMK..............	Renmark [*Australia Airport symbol*] (OAG)
RMK..............	Retrofit Modification Kit
RMK..............	Rhesus Monkey Kidney [*Medicine*]
RMK..............	Roxmark Mines Ltd. [*Toronto Stock Exchange symbol*]
RML..............	Lieutenant, Royal Marines [*Navy British*] (ROG)
RML..............	RADAR Mapper, Long Range
RML..............	RADAR Microwave Link (IEEE)
RML..............	Radiation Myeloid Leukemia [*Medicine*] (DB)
RML..............	Range Measurements Laboratory [*Air Force*]
RML..............	Read Major Line [*Computer science*] (IAA)
RML..............	Refresher Maintenance Lab
RML..............	Regional Medical Library
RML..............	Relational Machine Language
RML..............	Remote Maintenance Line [*Bell Laboratories*]
RML..............	Remote Measurements Laboratory
RML..............	Rescue Motor Launch [*Air/sea rescue*] [*Navy*]
RML..............	Research Machines Ltd. (NITA)
RML..............	Restricted Maximum Likelihood [*Statistics*]
RML..............	Revolution in Military Logistics [*Army*]
RML..............	Rhizomucor Meihei Lipase [*An enzyme*]
RML..............	Rifled Muzzle-Loading [*Gun*]
RML..............	Right Mediolateral [*Episiotomy*] [*Obstetrics*]
RML..............	Right Mentolateral [*Episiotomy*] [*Obstetrics*]
RML..............	Right Middle Lobe [*Lungs*]
RML..............	Rock Mechanics Laboratory [*Pennsylvania State University*] [*Research center*] (RCD)
RML..............	Rocky Mountain Laboratories [*National Institutes of Health*]
RML..............	Rotating Mirror LASER
RML..............	Russell Corp. [*NYSE symbol*] (SPSG)
RMLA	Rocky Mountain Lama Association (EA)
RMLC	Royal Marine Labour Corps [*British military*] (DMA)
RMLE..........	Regiment de Marche de la Legion Etrangere [*Foreign Legion Marching Regiment*] [*French*]
RMLI..........	Royal Marine Light Infantry [*Obsolete British*]
RML IV	Mid-Atlantic Regional Medical Library Program [*Library network*]
RMLO	Reports Management Liaison Officer [*Defense Supply Agency*]
RMLP..........	Regional Medical Library Program [*Department of Health and Human Services*]
RMLR	RADAR Mapper, Long Range (MSA)
RMLR	RADAR Microwave Link Repeater (FAAC)
RMLS	Right Middle Lobe Syndrome [*Medicine*] (MEDA)
RMLT..........	RADAR Microwave Link Terminal (FAAC)
RMLV..........	Rauscher Murine Leukemia Virus [*Medicine*] (DMAA)
RMM..........	Mercedarian Sisters (TOCD)
RMM..........	RADAR Map Matching
RMM..........	Rapid Micromedia Method [*Analytical biochemistry*]
RMM..........	Read-Mostly Memory [*Computer science*]
RMM..........	Read-Mostly Mode [*Computer science*]
RMM..........	Remote Maintenance Monitor [*Computer science*] (MCD)
RMM..........	Rifle Marksman
RMM..........	Ripple Mark Meter
RMM..........	Rosedale Mennonite Missions (EA)
RMMC	Regiment Materiel Management Latent Center [*Military*] (AABC)
RMMC	Rocky Mountain Mapping Center [*Colorado*]

RMMCA	Road Markings Manufacturers and Contractors Association [*British*] (DBA)
RMMDBO.......	Royal Marine Mobile Defended Base Organisation [*British military*] (DMA)
RMMEA.......	Rolling Mill Machinery and Equipment Association [*Defunct*] (EA)
RMMLA.......	Rocky Mountain Modern Language Association (EDAC)
RMMLF	Rocky Mountain Mineral Law Foundation (EA)
RMMLR	Rocky Mountain Mineral Law Review [*A publication*] (DLA)
RMMP	Riceland Mosquito Management Plan [*Department of Agriculture*]
RMMRA	Rocky Mountain Midget Racing Association [*Automobile competition organizer*]
RMMS	Remote Maintenance Monitoring System [*FAA*] (TAG)
RM/MS & C...	Redundancy Management/Moding, Sequencing, and Control (MCD)
RMMTB.......	Rocky Mountain Motor Tariff Bureau, Inc.
RMMU	Removable Media Memory Units
RMN	Registered Mental Nurse
RMN	Remain (FAAC)
RMN	Reserve Material [*Account*] Navy
RMN	Reuters Money Network [*Reality Technologies*] (PCM)
RMN	Richard Milhous Nixon [*US president, 1913-*]
RMN	RN Aviation Ltd. [*British ICAO designator*] (FAAC)
RMN	Roman Corp. Ltd. [*Toronto Stock Exchange symbol*]
RMNS	Royal Malayan Navy Ship [*British military*] (DMA)
RMNSW.......	Railway Museum of New South Wales [*Australia*]
RMO	RADAR Master Oscillator
RMO	RADAR Material Office [*Navy*] (MCD)
RMO	Radio Material Office [*or Officer*] [*Navy*] (IEEE)
RMO	Radio Mogadishu
RMO	Records Management Office [*or Officer*] [*Military*] (AFM)
RMO	Recruitment and Manning Organization [*WSA*]
RMO	Refined Menhaden Oil [*Food science*]
RMO	Regimental Medical Officer (NATG)
RMO	Regimental Munitions Officer [*Army*]
RMO	Regional Management Officer [*Social Security Administration*]
RMO	Regional Medical Officer [*British*]
RMO	Reports Management Officer [*DoD*]
RMO	Resident Medical Officer [*British*]
RMO	Resource Management Office [*Army*]
RMO	Resources Management Office [*NASA*] (KSC)
RMO	Rochester-Mercier [*New York*] [*Seismograph station code, US Geological Survey Closed*] (SEIS)
RMO	Rocket Management Office [*Army*] (RDA)
RMO	Royal Marine Office [*British*]
RM Obs	Royal Marine Observer [*British military*] (DMA)
RMOC	Recommended Maintenance Operation Chart [*Army*] (AABC)
RMOGA	Rocky Mountain Oil and Gas Association
RMOKHS.....	Religious and Military Order of Knights of the Holy Sepulchre (EA)
RMON..........	Remote Monitor (CIST)
RMON..........	Remote Monitoring [*Computer science*] (IGQR)
RMON..........	Resident Monitor
RMON MIB...	Remote Network Monitoring Management Information Base [*Telecommunications*]
R MON RE(M)...	Royal Monmouthshire Royal Engineers (Militia) [*British military*] (DMA)
RMOS	Real Memory Operating System [*Computer science*] (IAA)
RMOS	Refractory Metal-Oxide Semiconductor (IEEE)
RMP..........	Radio Management Panel (GAVI)
RMP..........	Radio Motor Patrol [*New York police cars*]
RMP..........	Rainform Message Processing (MCD)
RMP..........	Raman Microprobe [*Spectrometer*]
RMP..........	Rampart [*Alaska*] [*Airport symbol*] (OAG)
RMP..........	Rampart Resources Ltd. [*Vancouver Stock Exchange symbol*]
RMP..........	Range Maintenance Plan (MCD)
RMP..........	Rapidly Miscible Pool [*Medicine*] (MAE)
RMP..........	Rated Maximum Pressure (SAA)
RMP..........	Rate Measuring Package (MCD)
RMP..........	Raw Materials Processing
RMP..........	Receptor-Mediated Permeabilizer [*Medicine*]
RMP..........	Reduction of the Membrane Potential
RMP..........	Reentry Measurement Program [*Military*]
RMP..........	Refiner Mechanical Pulp [*Papermaking*]
RMP..........	Regional Medical Program
RMP..........	Registered Medical Practitioner [*British*] (ROG)
RMP..........	Reprogrammable Microprocessor
RMP..........	Research and Microfilm Publications
RMP..........	Research Management Plan
RMP..........	Resident Manufacturing Plan (SAA)
RMP..........	Resistance Management Plans [*To prevent insect adaptation to toxins*]
RMP..........	Resource Management Plan (GNE)
RMP..........	Resting Membrane Potential [*Neuroelectrochemistry*]
RMP..........	Revised Management Procedure
RMP..........	Rifampicin [*An antibacterial, Antibiotic, and antituberculin*] (DAVI)
RMP..........	Rifampin [*Also, R/AMP, RF, RIF*] [*Bactericide*]
RMP..........	Right Mentoposterior [*A fetal position*] [*Obstetrics*]
RMP..........	Risk Management Plan [*Environmental Protection Agency*]
RMP..........	Risk Management Program [*Environmental Protection Agency*]
RMP..........	RMP: Rural Marketing and Policy [*A publication*]
RMP..........	Rocketdyne Mortar Propellant (MCD)
RMP..........	Rocket Motor Plume
RMP..........	Rocket Motor Propellant (MUGU)
RMPCA.......	Rome [*Monte Porzio Catone*] [*Italy*] [*Seismograph station code, US Geological Survey*] (SEIS)
RMP..........	Rotorcraft Master Plan [*FAA*] (TAG)
RMP..........	Round Maximum Pressure (NATG)

RMP............	Royal Marine Police [British military] (DMA)
RMP............	Royal Military Police [British]
RMPA.........	Rocky Mountain Psychological Association (MCD)
RMPA.........	Royal Medico-Psychological Association [British]
RMPCK.......	Ramp Check [Aviation] (FAAC)
RMPE.........	Root Mean Percentage Error [Statistics]
RMPF.........	Rocky Mountain Poison Foundation
RMPI	Remote Memory Port Interface
RMPM	Rich Man, Poor Man [Book title]
RMPM	Royal Mail Parcels Marketing [British Post Office]
RMPO	Ramapo Financial [NASDAQ symbol] (TTSB)
RMPO	Ramapo Financial Corp. [NASDAQ symbol] (NQ)
RMPP	Risk Management and the Prevention Plan [Hazardous materials]
RMPR	Rassemblement Mahorais pour la Republique [Mayotte Rally for the Republic] [Political party] (PPW)
RMPR	Rated Mobilization and Professional Resource (MUGU)
RMPR	Revised Maximum Price Regulation [World War II]
RMPS	Regional Medical Programs Service [Health Services and Mental Health Administration, HEW]
RMPS	Royal Melbourne Philharmonic Society [Australia]
RMPTC	Royal Military Police Training Centre [British]
RMQ	Air Armorique [France] [FAA designator] (FAAC)
RMQM	Quarter-Master, Royal Marines [Navy British] (ROG)
RMR	Air Co. Ltd. [Romania] [FAA designator] (FAAC)
RMR	Malraux Society (EAIO)
RMR	Rapid Memory Reload (MCD)
RMR	Reamer [Design engineering]
RMR	Reference Mixture Radio (KSC)
RMR	Reflector Moderated Reactor (AAG)
RMR	Regional Maintenance Representative [Military]
RMR	Registered Merit Reporter
RMR	Remote Map Reader
RMR	Remote Meter Reading
RMR	Reserve Minority Report [Army]
RMR	Resource Management Review [Military]
RMR	Resource Mortgage Capital [Formerly, RAC Mortgage Investment] [NYSE symbol] (SPSG)
RMR	Resting Metabolic Rate [Physiology]
RMR	Right Medial Rectus [Eye anatomy]
RMR	Rock-Mass Rating [Mining technology]
RMR	Rocky Mountain Review of Language & Literature [A publication] (BRI)
RMR	Rotational Magnetic-Dipole Radiation [Astronomy]
RMR	Rotation Magnitude Ratio
RMR	Royal Malayan Regiment [British military] (DMA)
RMR	Royal Marines Reserve [British]
RMR	Royal Montreal Regiment [Military unit]
RMRA	Royal Marines Rifle Association [British military] (DMA)
RMREL	Rocky Mountain Regional Education Laboratory (AEBS)
RMRK	Remark (FAAC)
RMRM	Radioactive Materials Reference Manual (NRCH)
RMRO	Royal Marine Routine Orders [British military] (DMA)
RMROCK......	Rocket Motors Records Office Center [Navy]
RMRPO	Resource Mortgage Capital, Inc. [NASDAQ symbol] (SAG)
RMRPO	Resource Mtg Cap cm Cv'B'Pfd [NASDAQ symbol] (TTSB)
RMRPP	Resource Mtg Cap 9.75% Cv 'A' Pfd [NASDAQ symbol] (TTSB)
RMRS	Remote Meter Resetting System [Postage meter]
RMRS	Repeatable Maintenance and Recall System (NASA)
RMS............	RADAR Maintenance Spares (NG)
RMS............	RADAR Manual System (DNAB)
RMS............	RADAR Mapping Set [or System]
RMS............	Radian Means per Second (NASA)
RMS............	Radiation and Meteoroid Satellite [NASA]
RMS............	Radiation Monitoring Satellite (IAA)
RMS............	Radiation Monitoring System [Nuclear energy] (NUCP)
RMS............	Radio and Microwave Systems [British]
RMS............	Radiological Monitoring System
RMS............	Radiology Management System
RMS............	Radio Marker Station
RMS............	Radio Merchandise Sales (IAA)
RMS............	Radiometric Sextant Subsystem
RMS............	Rail Mail Steamer
RMS............	Railway Mail Service
RMS............	Random Mass Storage [Computer science]
RMS............	Random Motion Simulator [NASA] (NASA)
RMS............	Range Measuring System [Air Force]
RMS............	Range Modification System
RMS............	Rapid Multistream
RMS............	Rathkamp Matchcover Society (EA)
RMS............	Reactor Monitor System (IEEE)
RMS............	Real Market Share [Business term] (MHDB)
RMS............	Recipe Management Standard (AAEL)
RMS............	Reconnaissance Management System
RMS............	Record Management System
RMS............	Records Management Society [British] (DBA)
RMS............	Recovery Management Support [Computer science]
RMS............	Recruiting Main Station [Military]
RMS............	Rectal Morphine Sulfate Suppository [Medicine] (DMAA)
RMS............	Redundancy Management System [NASA] (MCD)
RMS............	Reentry Measurement System
RMS............	Reflective Memory System (NITA)
RMS............	Regulator of Mitotic Spindle Assembly [Cytology]
RMS............	Regulatory Manpower System [Nuclear energy] (NRCH)
RMS............	Regulatory Monitoring System (NRCH)
RMS............	Rehabilitation Medicine Service [Veterans Administration]

RMS............	Reliability and Maintainability Simulator
RMS............	Reliability, Maintainability, Supportability [Automotive engineering]
RMS............	Remote Maintenance System
RMS............	Remote Manipulator Subsystem [NASA] (NASA)
RMS............	Remote Manipulator System [NASA] (NAKS)
RMS............	Remote Manual Switch [Nuclear energy] (NRCH)
RMS............	Remote Master Station (MCD)
RMS............	Remote Missile Select
RMS............	Remote Monitor System
RMS............	Remote Multiplexer System [Computer science] (IAA)
RMS............	Reports Management System [Office of Management and Budget] [Database]
RMS............	Resource Management Squadron [Military]
RMS............	Resource Management Support (NITA)
RMS............	Resource Management System (IAA)
RMS............	Resources Management Staff [Environmental Protection Agency] (GFGA)
RMS............	Resources Management System [Army]
RMS............	Respiratory Muscle Strength [Physiology]
RMS............	Retromotor Simulator
RMS............	Reusable Multipurpose Spacecraft [Aerospace] (IIA)
RMS............	Revenue Management System (ECON)
RMS............	Revised Magnetic Standard
RMS............	Revised Management Scheme [International Whaling Commission]
RMS............	Rhabdomyosarcoma [Also, RHM] [Oncology]
RMS............	Rheometrics Mechanical Spectrometer
RMS............	Rheumatic Mitral Stenosis [Medicine] (DB)
RmS............	RL Microfilm Systems, Feasterville, PA [Library symbol] [Library of Congress] (LCLS)
RMS............	Rocket Management System (MCD)
RMS............	Roll Microwave Sensor
RMS............	Romanian Missionary Society (EA)
RMS............	Root Mean Square [Physics, statistics]
rms	Root Mean Square (COE)
rms	Root Mean Squared (DOM)
RMS............	Rostral Migratory Stream [Brain anatomy]
RMS............	Royal Mail Service [British]
RMS............	Royal Mail Steamship [British]
RMS............	Royal Marine Signaller [British military] (DMA)
RMS............	Royal Medical Society [British] (DBA)
RMS............	Royal Meteorological Society [British]
RMS............	Royal Microscopical Society [British]
RMS............	Royal Museum of Scotland
RMS............	Royal Society of Miniature Painters, Sculptors, and Gravers [British]
RMS............	Rural Manpower Services (OICC)
RMS............	TAS Aviation, Inc. [ICAO designator] (FAAC)
RMSA	Regulator of Mitotic Spindle Assembly (DMAA)
RMSA	Rhabdomyosarcoma, Alveolar [Medicine] (DMAA)
RMSA	Rural Marketing and Supply Association [Australia]
RMSA	Rural Music Schools Association [British]
RMSA	Seaman Apprentice, Radioman, Striker [Navy rating]
RM/SAD	Remote Motor/Safe and Arming Device
RMSchMus...	Royal Marines School of Music [British]
RMSCR	Rhabdomyosarcoma Chromosomal Region (DMAA)
RMSD	Root Mean Square Deviation [Statistics]
RMSD	Royal Mail Special Delivery [British Post Office facility] (DCTA)
RMSDS	Reserve Merchant Ship Defense System [Navy] (MCD)
RMSE..........	Relative Mean Square Error [Statistics]
RMSE..........	Root Mean Square Error
RMSEP	Root Mean Square Error of Prediction (AAEL)
RMSF..........	Rocky Mountain Spotted Fever
RMSG..........	Resource Management Study Group [Military]
RMSI	Royal Marine Signalling Instructor [British military] (DMA)
RMSM	Royal Military School of Music [British]
RMSN	Seaman, Radioman, Striker [Navy rating]
RMSP..........	Refractory Metal Sheet Program [Navy] (NG)
RMSP..........	Resource and Mission Sponsor Plan [Navy]
RMSP..........	Royal Mail Steam Packet Co.
RMSP..........	Rubber Modified Silica Phenolic
Rmsq..........	Romanesque (VRA)
RMSR..........	Recovery Management Support Recorder (MHDI)
RMSS	Range Meteorological Sounding System (MCD)
RMSS	Religious Mercedarians of the Blessed Sacrament [Roman Catholic women's religious order]
RMSS	Ruvalcaba-Myhre-Smith Syndrome [Medicine] (DMAA)
RMSU	Remote Monitoring Sensor Unit (MCD)
RMSU	Rocket Motor Switching Unit (MCD)
RMSV	Root Mean Square Value [Statistics] (IAA)
RMSVP	Remote Manipulation Subsystem Verification Plan [NASA] (MCD)
RMSVp	Remote Manipulator Subsystem Verification Plan [NASA] (NAKS)
RMT............	Radioman Telegrapher [Telecommunications] (IAA)
RMT............	Radiometric Moon Tracer
RMT............	Rail, Maritime, and Transport Union [British] (ECON)
RMT............	Rapidly Moving Telescope [Astronomy]
RMT............	Rapid Mass Transfer [Physics]
RMT............	Recognition Memory Test (DHP)
RMT............	Rectangular Midwater Trawl (ADA)
RMT............	Registered Massage Therapist
RMT............	Registered Music Teacher
RMT............	Registered Music Therapist
RMT............	Registry of Medical Technologists
RMT............	Relative Medullary Thickness [Of kidney] [Medicine] (BABM)
RMT............	Remote [Telecommunications] (MSA)
RMT............	Remount (WGA)
RMT............	Renal Mesenchymal Tumor [Oncology]

RMT............	Required Monthly Test [Telecommunications] (OTD)
RMT............	Research Methods and Techniques
RMT............	Reserve Mechanical Transport [British military] (DMA)
RMT............	Resource Management Team (MCD)
RMT............	Retromolar Trigone [Dentistry] (MAE)
RMT............	Rework Monitoring Test
RMT............	Right Mentotransverse [A fetal position] [Obstetrics]
RMT............	River Management Tool
RMT............	Rocky Mount [North Carolina] [Airport symbol] (AD)
RMTB..........	Reconfiguration Maximum Theoretical Bandwidth
RMTC..........	RADAR Maintenance and Test Control (MCD)
RMTC..........	Regional Medical Training Center
RMTC..........	Rider Motorcycle Touring Club [Later, RC] [Commercial firm] (EA)
RMTE..........	Remote (AAG)
RMTF..........	Ready Missile Test Facility [Military] (CAAL)
RMTF..........	Recipe Management Task Force (AAEL)
RMTF..........	Rigoberta Menchu Tum Foundation (EA)
RMTH	Regular Member of the Third House [Pseudonym used by Dr. Francis Bacon]
RMTH	River Mouth [Board on Geographic Names]
RMTO..........	Regional Motor Transport Officer [British] (DCTA)
RMTR..........	Ramtron International Corp. [NASDAQ symbol] (SAG)
RMTR..........	Ramtron Int'l [NASDAQ symbol] (TTSB)
RMTR..........	Redesigned Missile Tracking RADAR [Army] (AABC)
RMTR..........	Repair and Maintenance Time Rate [Automobile service]
RMTS..........	Remote Mode Transfer Switch (CIST)
RMTS..........	Research Member of the Technical Staff (ROG)
RMU	Radio Maintenance Unit (DEN)
RMU	Rainbow Monument [Utah] [Seismograph station code, US Geological Survey] (SEIS)
RMU	Reference Measuring Unit (MCD)
RMU	Remote Maneuvering Unit [NASA]
RMU	Remote Monitoring Unit [Telecommunications]
RMU	Remote Multiplexer Unit [Computer science] (KSC)
RMU	Romeo Series M Unificto [Alfa-Romeo] [Automotive model designation]
RMUC	Reference Measuring Unit Computer
RMUC	Rocky Mountain Undergarment (EFIS)
RMUI	Relief Medication Unit Index [Medicine] (DMAA)
RMuLV........	Rauscher Murine Leukemia Virus [Medicine] (DB)
RMUNX.......	Rochester Fund Municipals [Mutual fund ticker symbol] (SG)
RMV	Reentry Measurement Vehicle [Military]
RMV	Remotely Manned Vehicle
RMV	Remove (AAG)
RMV	Respiratory Minute Volume [Physiology]
RMV	Ribgrass Mosaic Virus [Plant pathology]
RMV	Romavia [Romania] [ICAO designator] (FAAC)
RMVBL........	Removable (AAG)
RMVD.........	Removed (AAG)
RMVE..........	Regiment de Marche de Volontiers Etrangers [Foreign Volunteers Marching Regiment] [French]
RMVG	Removing (AAG)
RMVL.........	Removal (AAG)
RMVM	Review of Medical and Veterinary Mycology [Database] [Commonwealth Mycological Institute] [Information service or system] (CRD)
RMVT..........	Repetitive Monomorphic Ventricular Tachycardia [Cardiology]
RMW	Rattlesnake Mountain [Washington] [Seismograph station code, US Geological Survey] (SEIS)
RMW	Reactor Makeup Water [Nuclear energy] (NRCH)
RMW	Read Modify Write (NITA)
RMW	Resource Management Wing [Military]
RMWAA	Roadmasters and Maintenance of Way Association of America (EA)
RMWC	Randolph-Macon Woman's College [Virginia]
RMWO	Warrant Officer, Royal Marines [Navy British] (ROG)
RMWR	Religious, Morale, Welfare, and Recreation [Military] (AFM)
RMWS	Reactor Makeup Water Storage [Nuclear energy] (NRCH)
RMWS	Reactor Make-Up Water System [Nuclear energy] (IAA)
RMWT	Reactor Makeup Water Tank [Nuclear energy] (NRCH)
RMX............	Remote Multiplexer (NITA)
RMX............	Resource Management Executive (MCD)
RMYC	Royal Motor Yacht Club [British] (BI)
RMZ............	Right Midzone [Medicine] (DMAA)
Rn...............	Negative Resistance (IDOE)
RN	Neptune Radii [Astronomy]
RN	Newport Public Library, Newport, RI [Library symbol Library of Congress] (LCLS)
RN	Radio National [Australian Broadcasting Corp.]
RN	Radio Navigation
RN	Radio Noise (IAA)
RN	Radionuclide [Radiology]
Rn...............	Radon (AAEL)
RN	Random Number (IEEE)
RN	Rassemblement National [Canada Political party] (PPW)
RN	Rattus Norvegicus [The Norway or brown rat]
rn...............	Read News [Computer science] (CDE)
RN	Real Name [British Library indexing for pseudonymous author]
RN	Reception Nil [Radio logs]
RN	Reception Node
RN	Recipient Name (NITA)
RN	Record Number [Online database field identifier]
RN	Red Nucleus [Brain anatomy]
RN	Reference Noise [Telecommunications]
RN	Reference Number
RN	Reflex Nephropathy [Medicine] (STED)
RN	Registered Nurse
RN	Registry Number
RN	Rejection Notice (AAG)
RN	Release Note [Shipping] (DS)
RN	Removable Needle [Medicine]
RN	Renastera Noastra [Rumania] [A publication] (BJA)
RN	Renovacion Nacional [National Renovation] [Chile] [Political party] (EY)
Rn...............	Renumbered [Existing article renumbered] [Used in Shepard's Citations] [Legal term] (DLA)
RN	Report Number (NITA)
RN	Research Note
RN	Reticular Nucleus (STED)
RN	Reuters News Agency (WDMC)
RN	Revision Notice (KSC)
RN	Revolucion Nacional [Spain Political party] (EY)
RN	Reynolds Number [Viscosity]
RN	Richard Nixon [In book title "RN - The Memoirs of Richard Nixon"]
RN	River Name (BJA)
RN	RJR Nabisco Holdings [NYSE symbol] (SPSG)
RN	Roan (Leather) [Bookbinding] (ROG)
RN	Root Tip Necrosis [Plant pathology]
RN	Royal Air International [ICAO designator] (AD)
RN	Royal Name (BJA)
RN	Royal Navy [British]
RN	Rubber Non-Continuous Liner (DS)
RN	Ruin (ROG)
RN	Ruritan National (EA)
RNA	Radio Naval Association [British]
RNA	Radio Navigational Aids (NATG)
RNA	Radionuclide Angiography [Medicine]
RNA	Rassemblement National Arabe [Arab National Rally] [Tunisia] (PD)
RNA	Rations Not Available [Military] (AABC)
RNA	Recurring Nuisances Act [British]
RNA	Regina Resources [Vancouver Stock Exchange symbol]
RNA	Registered Nurse Anesthetist
RNA	Registered Nursing Assistant
RNA	Religion Newswriters Association (EA)
RNA	Republic of New Africa (EA)
RNA	Research Natural Area [National Science Foundation]
RNA	Research Natural Areas (WPI)
RNA	Ribonucleic Acid [Biochemistry, genetics]
RNA	Ribonucleic Acid [A publication]
RNA	Robbery Not Armed
RNA	Romantic Novelists' Association [British]
RNA	Rotatable Nozzle Assembly
RNA	Rough, Noncapsulated, Avirulent [With reference to bacteria]
RNA	Royal Naval Association [British military] (DMA)
RNA	Royal Neighbors of America (EA)
RNA	Royal Nepal Airlines Corp. [ICAO designator] (FAAC)
RNA	Royal Netherlands Army
RNA	Royal Norwegian Army (MCD)
RNAA	Radiochemical Neutron Activation Analysis
RNAA	Radiometric Neutron Activation Analysis
R/NAA.........	Rocketdyne - North American Aviation [Later, Rockwell International Corp.] (AAG)
RNAA	Russian Nobility Association in America (EA)
RNAAC........	Reference Number Action Activity Code (MCD)
RNAAF........	Royal Norwegian Army and Air Force
RNAC	Remote Network Access Controller
RNAC	Royal Nepal Airlines Corp.
RNAD	Royal Naval Armament Depot [British]
RNAEC	Rhodesia and Nyasaland Army Educational Corps [British military] (DMA)
RNAF	Royal Naval Air Force [British]
RNAF	Royal Netherlands Air Force
RNAF	Royal Norwegian Air Force
RNAH	Royal Naval Auxiliary Hospital [British military] (DMA)
RNAIA	Royal National Agricultural and Industrial Association [Australia]
RNAL	Radionuclear Applications Laboratory [Pennsylvania State University] [Research center] (RCD)
RNAM	Regional Network for Agricultural Machinery [Institute of Agricultural Engineering and Technology] [Philippines]
RNAMY	Royal Naval Aircraft Maintenance Yard [British]
RN & CR......	Ryde, Newport & Cowes Railway [British]
RNaNP........	National Sea Grant Depository Library, Pell Marine Science Library, Narragansett, RI [Library symbol] [Library of Congress] (LCLS)
RNAP	Ribonucleic Acid Polymerase [An enzyme]
RNAPII........	Ribonucleic Acid Polymerase II [An enzyme]
RNAS	Royal Naval Air Service [Precursor of Fleet Air Arm] [Initialism also facetiously translated during World War I as "Really Not a Sailor"] [British]
RNAS	Royal Naval Air Station [British]
RNAS	Royal Northern Agricultural Society [British] (DBA)
RNASBR	Royal Naval Auxiliary Sick Berth Reserve [British military] (DMA)
RNAse	Ribonuclease [An enzyme]
RNaseP.......	Ribonuclease-P [An enzyme]
RNasin........	Ribonuclease Inhibitor [Biochemistry]
RNASS	Royal North Australian Show Society
RNATE	Royal Naval Air Training Establishment [British]
RNAV	Area Navigation
R/NAV.........	Radio Navigation [Military] (EECA)
R-NAV.........	Random Navigation
RNAV	Remote Area Navigation [FAA] (TAG)
RNAV	Royal Naval Artillery Volunteers [British]

RNAW.......... Royal Naval Aircraft Workshop [British]
RNAY........... Royal Naval Aircraft Yard [British]
RNB............. Millville, NJ [Location identifier FAA] (FAAL)
RNB............. Received, Not Billed (AFM)
RNB............. Renegotiation Board [Terminated, 1979] [Federal government]
RNB............. Republic New York [NYSE symbol] (TTSB)
RNB............. Republic New York Corp. [NYSE symbol] (SPSG)
RNB............. Resonant Nuclear Battery
r'n'b............ Rhythm and Blues [Music] (BARN)
RNB............. RibonuCleoprotein Particle [Biochemistry]
RNB............. Ronneby [Sweden] [Airport symbol] (OAG)
RNB............. Royal Naval Barracks [British]
RNBC........... Royal Naval Beach Commando [British]
RNBD........... Royal North British Dragoons [British military] (DMA)
RNBF........... Royal North British Fusiliers [British military] (DMA)
RNBM.......... Radio Noise Burst Monitor (MCD)
RNBM.......... Royal Navy Ballistic Missile [British]
RNBO........... Rainbow Technologies [NASDAQ symbol] (TTSB)
RNBO........... Rainbow Technologies, Inc. [NASDAQ symbol] (NQ)
RNBPrC........ Republic NY $1.9375 cm Pfd [NYSE symbol] (TTSB)
RNBPrD........ Republic NY Adj Rt Dep Pfd [NYSE symbol] (TTSB)
RNBPrE........ Republic NY $1.8125 cm Pfd [NYSE symbol] (TTSB)
RNBT........... Royal Naval Benevolent Trust [British]
RNBW.......... Rainbow
RNBWS......... Royal Naval Bird Watching Society [British]
RNC............. Little Raleigh [North Carolina] [Seismograph station code, US Geological Survey] (SEIS)
RNC............. McMinnville, TN [Location identifier FAA] (FAAL)
RNC............. Radio Noncontingent
RNC............. Rainbow Network Communications [Floral Park, NY] [Telecommunications] (TSSD)
RNC............. Registered Nurse, Certified (MEDA)
RNC............. Republican National Committee (EA)
RNC............. Request Next Character
RNC............. Ribosome-Nascent Chain [Biochemistry]
RNC............. Rockwood Nat'l [PC Symbol] (TTSB)
RNC............. Romanian National Council (EA)
RNC............. Royal Naval College [For future officers; often spoken of as Dartmouth] [British]
RNC............. Rumanian National Committee [Later, Romanian National Tourist Office] (EA)
RNCA........... Rhodesia and Nyasaland Court of Appeal Law Reports [A publication] (DLA)
RNCBC......... Reserve Naval Construction Battalion Center (DNAB)
RNCBCDET.... Reserve Naval Construction Battalion Center Detachment (DNAB)
RNCBMU....... Reserve Naval Construction Battalion Maintenance Unit (DNAB)
RNCC........... Reference Number Category Code (MCD)
RNCC........... Royal Naval College of Canada [1911-1922]
RNCF........... Read Natural Childbirth Foundation (EA)
RNCF........... Reserve Naval Construction Force [Navy] (PDAA)
RNCH........... Ranch (MCD)
RNCHS......... Ranch [Commonly used] (OPSA)
RNCM.......... Royal Northern College of Music [British]
RN CNAA..... Registered Nurse, Certified in Nursing Administration, Advanced (MEDA)
RNCO........... Alrenco, Inc. [NASDAQ symbol] (SAG)
RNColl......... Royal Naval College, Greenwich [British]
RNCR........... Reserve Naval Construction Regiment (DNAB)
RN CS.......... Registered Nurse, Certified Specialist (MEDA)
RNCSIR........ Royal Norwegian Council for Scientific and Industrial Research (EAIO)
RNCV.......... Radio Nacional de Cabo Verde [National Radio of Cape Verde] (EY)
RNCV.......... Royal Navy Coast Volunteers [British military] (DMA)
RNCVR......... Royal Naval Canadian Volunteer Reserve [World War I]
RNCYC......... Royal Northern and Clyde Yacht Club [British] (DBA)
RND............. Radical Neck Dissection [Medicine]
RND............. Railroads for National Defense [MTMC] (TAG)
RND............. Random
RND............. Rassemblement National Democratique [National Democratic Rally] [Senegal] [Political party] (PPW)
RND............. Rassemblement National pour la Democratie [Benin] [Political party] (EY)
RND............. Reactive Neurotic Depression [Medicine] (STED)
RND............. Real-Fluid Nonisentropic Decompression [Engineering]
RND............. Resistance-Nodulation-Division [Biochemistry]
RND............. Round
RND............. Royal Naval Division [British]
RND............. San Antonio, TX [Location identifier FAA] (FAAL)
RNDH........... Royal North Devon Hussars [British military] (DMA)
RNDM.......... Random (MSA)
RNDQ........... Royal Naval Detention Quarter [British] (DI)
RNDr........... Doctor of Natural Sciences
rndr............ Rendering (VRA)
RNDZ........... Rendezvous (KSC)
RNE............. Aspen, CO [Location identifier FAA] (FAAL)
RNE............. Morgan Stanley Russia & New Europe Fund, Inc. [NYSE symbol] (SAG)
RNE............. Risley Nuclear Establishment [British] (NUCP)
RNE............. Roanne [France] [Airport symbol] (OAG)
RNEC........... Royal Naval Engineering College [British]
RNEColl....... Royal Naval Engineering College [British]
RNEE........... Royal Navy Equipment Exhibition [British]
RNEF........... Resting (Radio-)Nuclide Ejection Fraction [Cardiology] (DAVI)
RNEIA.......... Royal Netherlands East Indies Army
RNEIAF........ Royal Netherlands East Indies Air Force

RNEIN.......... Royal Netherlands East Indies Navy
RNERL......... Radiochemistry and Nuclear Engineering Research Laboratory [National Environmental Research Center]
RNES........... Royal Naval Engineering Service [British]
RNET........... Remote Network (MHDB)
RNETA......... Royal Naval Endurance Triathlon Association [British]
RNEW.......... Religious Network for Equality for Women (EA)
RNF............. Radial Nerve Factor [of sea urchin]
RNF............. Radio Noise Figure (CET)
RNF............. Receiver Noise Figure
RNF............. Refounded National Party [South Africa Political party] (EAIO)
RNF............. Refracted Near Field [Optics]
RNF............. Royal Naval Fund [British] (DAS)
RNF............. Royal Northumberland Fusiliers [Military unit] [British]
RNF............. Rudolf Nureyev Foundation
RNFC........... Reference Number Format Code (MCD)
RNFC........... Royal Naval Film Corp. [British military] (DMA)
RNFCC......... Regional Nuclear Fuel Cycle Center [National Science Foundation] (NUCP)
rnfd............ Reinforced (VRA)
RNFL........... Rainfall [NWS] (FAAC)
RNFL........... Retinal Nerve Fiber Layer [Anatomy]
RNFP........... RADAR Not Functioning Properly [Military] (AFIT)
RNG............. Radionuclide Angiography (STED)
RNG............. Radio Range
RNG............. Random Number Generator [Parapsychology]
RNG............. Range [or Ranging] (AAG)
RNG............. Ranging Noise Generator
RNG............. Reference Noise Generator
RNG............. Regulations under the Natural Gas Act
RNG............. Ringing [Modem status information light] [Computer science] (IGQR)
RNG............. Running
RNGCOMP..... Range Computer (IAA)
RNGG........... Ringing (MSA)
RNGHQ......... Royal Navy General Headquarters [British]
RNGLND........ Rangeland
RNGM.......... Royal North Gloucestershire Militia [British military] (DMA)
RNG RT........ Range Rate (MCD)
RNGT........... Renegotiate
RNH............. New Richmond, WI [Location identifier FAA] (FAAL)
RNH............. Royal Naval Hospital [British]
RNHA........... Registered Nursing Home Association [British] (DBA)
RNHA........... Republican National Hispanic Assembly of the United States (EA)
RNHi........... Newport Historical Society, Newport, RI [Library symbol Library of Congress] (LCLS)
RN-HSG....... Radionuclide Hysterosalpingogram [Medicine]
RNHU........... Royal National Homing Union [British] (BI)
RNI............. Kansas City, MO [Location identifier FAA] (FAAL)
RNI............. Reference Nutrient Intake [Medicine] (WDAA)
RNI............. Resident Navy Inspector
RNIB........... Royal National Institute for the Blind [British]
RNIC........... Robinson Nugent [NASDAQ symbol] (TTSB)
RNIC........... Robinson Nugent, Inc. [NASDAQ symbol] (NQ)
RNICU......... Regional Neonatal Intensive-Care Unit (MEDA)
RNID........... Routine Network-In-Dial (DNAB)
RNID........... Royal National Institute for the Deaf [British]
RNID/NOD..... Routine Network-In-Dial / Network-Out-Dial (DNAB)
RNIE........... Royal Netherlands Institute of Engineers
RNIM........... Rotors Not in Motion [Aviation] (AIA)
RNIO........... Resident Naval Inspector of Ordnance
RNIP........... Registered Nurse, Interim Permit (MEDA)
RNIR........... Reduction to Next Inferior Rank
RNIT........... Radio Noise Interference Test
RNJ............. Blackrock New Jersey Investment Quality Municipal [AMEX symbol] (SPSG)
RNJ............. Blackrock NJ Inv Qual Muni [AMEX symbol] (TTSB)
RNJ............. Ramapo College of New Jersey, Mahwah, NJ [OCLC symbol] (OCLC)
RNJ............. Rektorskommitten for de Nordiska Journalist Hogskolorna [Committee for Nordic Universities of Journalism - CNUJ] [Defunct] (EAIO)
RNJ............. Yoron-Jima [Japan] [Airport symbol] (OAG)
RNk............. North Kingstown Free Library, North Kingstown, RI [Library symbol Library of Congress] (LCLS)
RNL............. Rainelle, WV [Location identifier FAA] (FAAL)
RNL............. Renal Laboratory Profile [Medicine] (STED)
RNL............. Renewal (MSA)
RNL............. Rennell Island [Solomon Islands] [Airport symbol] (OAG)
RNL............. Risley Nuclear Laboratories [British] (NUCP)
RNLA........... Royal Netherlands Army
RNLAF......... Royal Netherlands Air Force
RNLBI.......... Royal National Life-Boat Institution [British]
RNLC........... Rosary Novena for Life Committee (EA)
RNLI........... Royal National Life-Boat Institution [British]
RNLJ........... Rhodesia and Nyasaland Law Journal [A publication] (DLA)
RNLN........... Royal Netherlands Navy (DOMA)
RNLO........... Royal Naval Liaison Officer [British]
RNLS........... Resume Normal Speed [Aviation] (FAAC)
RNLT........... Running Light
RNM............. Radio-Navigation Mobile
RNM............. Radionuclide Migration
RNm............. Red Nucleus, Magnocellular [Division] [Hematology] (DAVI)
RNM............. Resistencia Nacional Mocambicana [Mozambican National Resistance] (PD)
RNM............. University of Rochester, Miner Medical Library, Rochester, NY [OCLC symbol] (OCLC)

RNMBR........ Royal Naval Motor Boat Reserve [British military] (DMA)
RNMC......... Regional Network Measurement Center (MHDI)
RNMC......... Regional Nursing Midwifery Committee [National Health Service] [British] (DI)
RNMC......... Royal Netherlands Marine Corps
RNMCB....... Reserve Naval Mobile Construction Battalion (DNAB)
RNMCBDET... Reserve Naval Mobile Construction Battalion Detachment (DNAB)
RNMCC....... Reference Number Mandatory Category Code [DoD]
RNMD......... Registered Nurse for Mental Defectives
RNMDSF...... Royal National Mission to Deep Sea Fishermen [British]
RNMH......... Registered Nurse for the Mentally Handicapped [British] (DBQ)
RNMI.......... Realtors National Marketing Institute [Chicago, IL] (EA)
RNMP......... Remote Network Monitoring Probe [Computer science] (DDC)
RNMS......... Registered Nurse for the Mentally Subnormal [British]
RNMS......... Royal Naval Minewatching Service [British military] (DMA)
RNMT......... Registered Nuclear Medicine Technologist (DAVI)
RNMV......... Rice Necrosis Mosaic Virus [Plant pathology]
RNMWS...... Royal Naval Minewatching Service [British] (BI)
RNN.......... Naval War College, Newport, RI [Library symbol Library of Congress] (LCLS)
RNN.......... Recurrent Neural Network (AAEL)
RNN.......... Regional NOCN [National Ocean Communications Network] Node [Marine science] (OSRA)
RNN.......... Ronne [Denmark] [Airport symbol] (OAG)
RNN.......... Royal Netherlands Navy
RNN.......... Royal Norwegian Navy
RNNAS....... Royal Netherlands Naval Air Service
RNNU........ United States Navy, Naval Underwater Systems Center, Technical Library, Newport, RI [Library symbol Library of Congress] (LCLS)
RNO.......... Air Normandie [France ICAO designator] (FAAC)
RNO.......... Regional Nuclear Option (MCD)
RNO.......... Regional Nursing Officer [British]
RNO.......... Reno [Nevada] [Airport symbol] (OAG)
RNO.......... Resident Naval Officer [Followed by place name] (NATG)
RNO.......... Results Not Observed (DNAB)
RNO.......... Rhino Resources [Vancouver Stock Exchange symbol]
RNOA......... Royal Norwegian Army (NATG)
RNOAF....... Royal Norwegian Air Force
RNOC......... Resistencia Nicaraguense de Organizacion Civica [Political party] (EY)
RNOC......... Royal Naval Officers Club [Defunct] (EA)
RNODC ...... Responsible National Oceanographic Data Center [Marine science] (MSC)
RNON......... Royal Norwegian Navy (NATG)
RNORA...... Royal Norwegian Army
RNORN...... Royal Norwegian Navy
RNP.......... Radio Navigation Point [Military] (MCD)
RNP.......... Rassemblement National Populaire [National People's Rally] [France]
RNP.......... Registered Nurse Practitioner (AAMN)
RNP.......... Remote Network Processor
RNP.......... Required Navigation Performance [Aviation] (FAAC)
RNP.......... Ribonucleoprotein [Biochemistry]
RNP.......... RNA [Ribonucleic Acid] Nuclear Protein
RNP.......... Rongelap [Marshall Islands] [Airport symbol] (OAG)
RNP.......... Roscoe's Nisi Prius Evidence [20th ed.] [1934] [A publication] (DLA)
RNP.......... Royal Naval Personnel Research Committee [British]
RNPA......... Regional Nuclear Power Authority
RNPC......... Regional Nuclear Power Co.
RNPC......... Required Navigation Performance Capability
RNPDL....... Risley Nuclear Power Development Laboratories [British] (NUCP)
RNPL........ Royal Naval Physiological Laboratory [Later, AMTE (PL)] [British]
RNPR......... Relative Net Protein Ratio [Nutrition]
RNPrB........ RJR Nabisco Sr'B'Dep Pfd [NYSE symbol] (TTSB)
RNPrC........ RJR Nabisco SrC'PERCS [NYSE symbol] (TTSB)
RNPRC....... Royal Naval Personnel Research Committee [British] (MCD)
RNPrT........ RJR Nabisco 10% 'TOPrS' [NYSE symbol] (TTSB)
RNPS......... Royal Naval Patrol Service [Obsolete British]
RNPS......... Royal Navy Polaris School [British]
RNQ.......... Waycross, GA [Location identifier FAA] (FAAL)
RNR.......... Air Cargo Masters, Inc. [FAA designator] (FAAC)
RNR.......... Rate Not Reported (DS)
RNR.......... Receive Not Ready [Computer science] (IEEE)
RNR.......... Redwood Library and Athenaeum, Newport, RI [Library symbol Library of Congress] (LCLS)
RNR.......... RenaissanceRe Holdings Ltd. [NYSE symbol] (SAG)
RNR.......... Renewable Natural Resources (DI)
RNR.......... Renewal Not Required (AIA)
RNR.......... Resonant Nuclear Reaction [Physics]
RNR.......... Ribonucleotide Reductase [An enzyme]
RNR.......... Ring Number Read [Telecommunications] (IAA)
RNR.......... Robinson River [Papua New Guinea] [Airport symbol] (OAG)
r'n'r .... Rock and Roll [Music] (BARN)
RNR.......... Royal Naval Reserve [British]
RNR.......... Runner (MSA)
RNRA........ Resonant Nuclear Reaction Analysis [Physics]
RNRA........ Royal Naval Rifle Association [British military] (DMA)
RNRB........ Relative Navigational Reference Beacon [Military] (CAAL)
RNRC........ Riverside National Bank [NASDAQ symbol] (NQ)
RNRE........ Refused, Not Reversible Error [Legal term] (ILCA)
RNREF....... RenaissanceRe Holdings [NASDAQ symbol] (TTSB)
RNREF....... RenaissanceRe Holdings Ltd. [NASDAQ symbol] (SAG)
RNRF........ Renewable Natural Resources Foundation (EA)
RnRHoF&M... Rock and Roll Hall of Fame and Museum
RNRS........ Royal National Rose Society [British] (EAIO)
RNR(T) .... Royal Naval Reserve (Trawlers) [British military] (DMA)

RNS .... Race, National Origin, and Sex (DNAB)
RNS .... RADAR Netting Station [Military] (AABC)
RNS .... Ransom Resources Ltd. [Vancouver Stock Exchange symbol]
RNS .... Reference Normal Serum [Clincial chemistry] (AAMN)
RNS .... Religious News Service (EA)
RNS .... Rennes [France] [Airport symbol] (OAG)
RNS .... Respiratory Nursing Society (EA)
RNS .... Reusable Nuclear Shuttle [NASA]
RNS .... Reusable Nuclear Stage [Aerospace]
RNS .... Ribonuclease S [An enzyme]
RNS .... Royal Naval School [British]
RNS .... Royal Numismatic Society [British]
RNS .... Russian Numismatic Society (EA)
RNS .... Services Aeronautiques Roannais [France ICAO designator] (FAAC)
RNSA .... Royal Naval Sailing Association [British]
RNSAC .... Range Surveillance Aircraft (MCD)
RNSC......... Radionuclide Superior Cavography [Medicine] (DMAA)
RNSC......... Reference Number Status Code (MCD)
RNSC......... Rocket/Nimbus Sounder Comparison [NASA]
RNSC......... Royal Naval Staff College [British]
RNSD......... Royal Naval Stores Depot [British]
RNSG......... Reserve Naval Security Group (DNAB)
RNSGC....... Reserve Naval Security Group Course (DNAB)
RNSH......... Royal National Scottish Hospital
RNSI......... Rational National Standards Initiative
RNS of M.... Royal Naval School of Music [British military] (DMA)
RNSP......... Round-Nose Soft-Point Bullet
RNSQ......... Royal Naval Sick Quarters [British]
RNSR......... Royal Naval Special Reserve [British military] (DMA)
RNSR......... Royal Nova Scotia Regiment [Military unit]
RNSS......... Royal Naval Scientific Service [British] (DEN)
RNSS......... Royal Norwegian Society of Sciences
RNSTS........ Royal Naval Supply and Transport Service [British]
RNSYS........ Royal Nova Scotia Yacht Squadron
RNT .... Regensburger Neues Testament [A publication] (BJA)
RNT .... Registered Nurse Tutor [British]
RNT .... Rentavion CA [Venezuela] [ICAO designator] (FAAC)
RNT .... Renton, WA [Location identifier FAA] (FAAL)
Rnt........... Roentgenology [Radiology] (DAVI)
RNTE......... Royal Naval Training Establishment [British military] (DMA)
RNTK......... Rentech, Inc. [NASDAQ symbol] (SAG)
rNTP......... Ribonucleoside Triphosphate [Biochemistry]
Rntrak........ Rentrak Corp. [Associated Press] (SAG)
RNTU........ Royal Naval Training Unit [British military] (DMA)
RntWay...... Rent Way, Inc. [Associated Press] (SAG)
RntWck...... Rent-a-Wreck of America, Inc. [Associated Press] (SAG)
RNTWPA..... Radio-Newsreel-Television Working Press Association (EA)
RNU .... RADAR Netting Unit [Military] (AABC)
RNU .... Radio National Unity
RNU .... Ranau [Malaysia] [Airport symbol] (OAG)
RNV .... Cleveland, MS [Location identifier FAA] (FAAL)
RNV .... Radio Noise Voltage
RNV .... Radionuclide Venography [Clinical chemistry] (AAMN)
RNV .... Radionuclide Ventriculography [Medicine]
RNV .... Random Noise Voltmeter
RNV .... Relative Nutritive Value [Nutrition]
RNV .... Replacement Naval Vessels
RNV .... Resistive Null Voltage
RNV .... Reusable Nuclear Vehicle [Aerospace] (KSC)
RNV .... Royal Naval Volunteer (Reserve) [British] (ROG)
RNVC......... Reference Number Variation Code (MCD)
RNVG......... Radionuclide Ventriculography [Medicine] (DMAA)
RNVPR....... Royal Naval Volunteer Postal Reserve [British military] (IAA)
RN(V)R....... Royal Naval (Volunteer) Reserve [Obsolete World War II British]
RNVR(A)...... Royal Naval Volunteer Reserve (Air) [British military] (DMA)
RNVSR........ Royal Naval Volunteer Supplementary Reserve [Obsolete World War II British]
RNV(W)R...... Royal Naval Volunteer (Wireless) Reserve [British military] (DMA)
RNW .... Radio Navigational Warning (WDAA)
RNW .... Ring Number Write [Telecommunications] (IAA)
RNWAR....... Royal Naval Wireless Auxiliary Reserve [British military] (DMA)
RNWBL....... Renewable (MSA)
RNWMP..... Royal North West Mounted Police [Later, RCMP] [Canada]
RNWY........ Runway (AABC)
RNX .... Renox Creek Resources [Vancouver Stock Exchange symbol]
RNXS......... Royal Naval Auxiliary Service [British]
RNY .... Blackrock New York Investment Quality Municipal [AMEX symbol] (SPSG)
RNY .... Blackrock NY Inv Qual Muni [AMEX symbol] (TTSB)
RNY .... Rainier Energy Resources [Vancouver Stock Exchange symbol]
RNY .... Republic New York Corp. [Associated Press] (SAG)
RNY .... Required Net Yield [Business term] (EMRF)
RNY .... Runway Lights [Aviation] (AIA)
RNYPO........ Regional Navy Youth Programs Officer (DNAB)
RNZ .... Radio New Zealand
RNZ .... Royal New Zealand
RNZA......... Royal New Zealand Army (VNW)
RNZAF....... Royal New Zealand Air Force
RNZE......... Royal New Zealand Engineers
RNZIR........ Royal New Zealand Infantry Regiment (VNW)
RNZN......... Royal New Zealand Navy
RNZN(V)R.... Royal New Zealand Naval (Volunteer) Reserve
Ro............ Hoffmann-La Roche, Inc. [Switzerland, USA] [Research code symbol]
RO .... Observer (Radio) [British military] (DMA)

RO	Omani Rial [*Monetary unit*] (IMH)
R₀	Output Resistance (IDOE)
RO	RADAR Observer
RO	RADAR Operator
RO	Radiation Office [*Environmental Protection Agency*]
RO	Radionavigation Mobile Station [*ITU designation*] (CET)
RO	Radioopaque
RO	Radio Operator
RO	Radio Orchestra
RO	Radio Orient (IAA)
RO	Railway Office [*British*] (ROG)
RO	Range Only (CAAL)
RO	Range Operation (AAG)
RO	Rank Organisation Ltd. [*Toronto Stock Exchange symbol*]
RO	Reactor Operator [*Nuclear energy*] (NRCH)
RO	Read Only [*Computer science*] (IBMDP)
RO	Readout (KSC)
RO	Reality Orientation
RO	Receive Only
RO	Receiving Office [*or Officer*]
RO	Receiving Order [*Business term*] (DCTA)
RO	Reconnaissance Officer
RO	Recorders [*JETDS nomenclature*] [*Military*] (CET)
RO	Records Office [*or Officer*] [*Air Force*] (AFM)
RO	Recovery Operations [*NASA*]
RO	Recruiting Officer [*Military*]
RO	Recto [*Also, R*]
Ro	Recto [*On the right hand page*] (WA)
RO	Reddish Orange
RO	Redistribution Order [*Military*] (DNAB)
RO	Reference Oscillator [*Telecommunications*] (OA)
RO	Referral Order [*Military*] (DNAB)
RO	Regimental Orders [*Army*]
RO	Regional Office [*or Officer*]
RO	Registered Office (WDAA)
RO	Register Output
R/O	Regular Order
RO	Regulated Output (FAAC)
RO	Relieving Officer (ROG)
RO	Relocatable Output [*Computer science*]
RO	Remains Open [*Environmental science*] (COE)
RO	Remote Operations [*Telecommunications*] (OSI)
RO	Rent Officer [*British*] (ILCA)
R/O	Repair and Overhaul (MCD)
RO	Repair Order
RO	Repolarization Opening [*Biochemistry*]
RO	Reportable Occurrence [*Nuclear energy*] (NRCH)
RO	Reporting Officer [*Army*] (AABC)
RO	Report Over (DA)
RO	Reproducible Ozalid (DNAB)
RO	Requirements Objective
RO	Requisitioning Objective [*Military*] (AABC)
R/O	Requisitions/Objectives (CINC)
RO	Research Objective (MCD)
RO	Research Officer [*British*]
RO	Reserve of Officers [*British*]
RO	Reserve Order
RO	Responding Officer [*Police term*]
RO	Responsible Office (AAGC)
RO	Restriction Orifice [*Nuclear energy*] (NRCH)
RO	Retired Officer [*Military British*]
RO	Retrofit Order [*Navy*] (NG)
RO	Returning Officer (ROG)
RO	Revenue Officer [*IRS*]
RO	Reverse-Osmosis [*Physical chemistry*]
RO	Rework Order (MCD)
R/O	Rewritable/Optical
Ro	Rhodium [*Correct symbol is Rh*] [*Chemical element*]
RO	Right Opening (WDAA)
RO	Right Orifice (WDAA)
RO	Right Outboard (MCD)
RO	Rimoil Corp. [*Toronto Stock Exchange symbol*]
RO	Rip Out (DNAB)
RO	Ritter-Oleson Technique [*Medicine*] (MAE)
RO	Road (WGA)
RO	Roan [*Thoroughbred racing*]
RO	Rock [*Germany ICAO aircraft manufacturer identifier*] (ICAO)
Ro	Rodoicus [*Authority cited in pre-1607 legal work*] (DSA)
Ro	Roffredus Beneventanus [*Flourished, 1215-43*] [*Authority cited in pre-1607 legal work*] (DSA)
Ro	Rolandus Bandinelli [*Deceased, 1181*] [*Authority cited in pre-1607 legal work*] (DSA)
RO	Roll
Ro	Rolle's Abridgment [*A publication*] (DLA)
Ro	Roll-On [*Trailer ship*] (DICI)
R/O	Rollout (MCD)
R/O	Rollover
RO	Romania [*ANSI two-letter standard code*] (CNC)
RO	Romans [*Old Testament book*]
Ro	Rome Stock Exchange [*Italy*]
RO	Rood [*Unit of measurement*]
RO	Room Only
RO	Roper Organization (EA)
RO	Rose (ROG)
RO	Rough

RO	Rough Opening [*Technical drawings*]
RO	Round Off (IAA)
RO	Route Order [*Military*]
RO	Routine Order
RO	Routing Office [*or Officer*] [*Navy*]
RO	Rowed Over [*Rowing*] [*British*] (ROG)
RO	Royal Observatory [*British*]
RO	Royal Octavo
RO	Royal Ordnance Factory [*British*]
R/O	Rule Out [*Medicine*]
RO	Runoff Election
R-O	Run-On [*Used in correcting manuscripts, etc.*]
RO	Runout (MSA)
RO	Runover [*Publishing*]
RO	Russian Obuckhoff Rifle
RO	Rust and Oxidation (DNAB)
RO1(G)	Radio Operator (General) 1st Class [*British military*] (DMA)
RO1(W)	Radio Operator (Warfare) 1st Class [*British military*] (DMA)
RO2(G)	Radio Operator (General) 2nd Class [*British military*] (DMA)
RO2(W)	Radio Operator (Warfare) 2nd Class [*British military*] (DMA)
RO 7 R	Rey Osterreigh and Recall [*Test*] [*Psychiatry*] (DAVI)
ROA	Altimeter Station [*ITU designation*] (CET)
ROA	Racehorse Owners Association [*British*] (DBA)
ROA	Radiation Oncology Administrators [*Later, SROA*] (EA)
ROA	Radio Operator's Aptitude Test [*Military*]
ROA	Radius of Action (CAAL)
ROA	Raman Optical Activity [*Spectrometry*]
ROA	Recorder Announcement (DNAB)
ROA	Record of Acquisition (WDAA)
ROA	Reference Optical Alignment
ROA	Rehabilitation of Offenders Act [*1974*] [*British*] (DCTA)
ROA	Reinsurance Offices Association [*British*] (AIA)
ROA	Reno Air, Inc. [*ICAO designator*] (FAAC)
ROA	Research Opportunity Announcement (AAGC)
ROA	Reserve Officers Association (NADA)
ROA	Reserve Officers Association of the United States (EA)
ROA	Restricted Operations Area [*Environmental science*] (COE)
ROA	Retired Officers Association [*Military*]
ROA	Return on Assets [*Business term*]
ROA	Right Occipitoantorior [*A fetal position*] [*Obstetrics*]
ROA	Roanoke [*Virginia*] [*Airport symbol*]
ROA	Robert Owen Association (EA)
ROA	Roller Owners' Association [*British*] (BI)
roa	Romance [*MARC language code Library of Congress*] (LCCP)
ROA	Rules of the Air (AFM)
ROA	Russian Orchestra of the Americas
Ro Abr	Rolle's Abridgment [*A publication*] (ILCA)
ROAC	Rock of Ages [*Stock exchange term*]
ROAD	Inroads [*Database*] [*Australia*]
ROAD	Reorganization Objectives, Army Division [*Military*]
ROAD	Retires on Active Duty [*Military*] (MCD)
ROAD	Reversible Obstructive Airway Disease (DAVI)
ROAD	Road [*Commonly used*] (OPSA)
ROAD	Roadway Express [*NASDAQ symbol*] (TTSB)
ROAD	Roadway Express, Inc. [*NASDAQ symbol*] (SAG)
ROAD	Roadway Services, Inc. [*NASDAQ symbol*] (NQ)
ROAD	Ruch Obywatelski-Akcja Demokratyczna [*Civil Movement for Democratic Action*] [*P oland*] [*Political party*]
Roadmst	Roadmaster Industries [*Associated Press*] (SAG)
ROADS	Real-Time Optical Alignment and Diagnostic System [*Module*]
ROADS	Resource Organization and Discovery in Subject-Based Services [*British*] (TELE)
ROADS	Roads [*Commonly used*] (OPSA)
ROADS	Roadway Analysis and Design System [*Computer science*]
RoadSv	Roadway Services, Inc. [*Associated Press*] (SAG)
RoadwyEx	Roadway Express, Inc. [*Associated Press*] (SAG)
ROAH	Naha [*Ryukyu Islands*] [*ICAO location identifier*] (ICLI)
ROAM	Return on Assets Managed [*Finance*]
ROAMA	Rome Air Materiel Area [*Deactivated*] [*Air Force*]
ROANA	Rover Owners' Association of North America [*Defunct*] (EA)
Roan El	Roanoke Electric Steel Corp. [*Associated Press*] (SAG)
RoanGas	Roanoke Gas Co. [*Associated Press*] (SAG)
ROAP	, ara-C , Prednisone [*Vincristine*] [*Cytarabine*] [*Antineoplastic drug regimen*]
ROAR	Radio Operated Auto Racing
ROAR	Recovery and Overpayment Accounting and Reporting System [*Social Security Administration*] (GFGA)
ROAR	Regional Organization for Airways Restudy
ROAR	Restore Our Alienated Rights [*Boston antibusing group*]
ROAR	Return of Army Repairables (AABC)
ROAR	Royal Optimizing Assembly Routine [*Computer science*] (IAA)
ROAR	Royal Optimizing Assembly Routing [*Royal McBee Corp.*] [*Computer science*]
ROARE	Reduction of Attitudes and Repressed Emotions [*Treatment given to sex offenders*] [*Psychology*]
ROARS	Rutgers Online Automated Retrieval Service [*Rutgers University*] (OLDSS)
ROAST	Ring Out and Stress Tester (PDAA)
ROAT	Radio Operator's Aptitude Test [*Military*]
ROATS	Rabbit Ovarian Antitumor Serum [*Medicine*] (DMAA)
ROB	African International Airways (West Africa) Ltd. [*Nigeria*] [*FAA designator*] (FAAC)
ROB	Monrovia [*Liberia*] Roberts International Airport [*Airport symbol*] (OAG)
ROB	RADAR Order of Battle

ROB	RADAR Out of Battle (CET)
ROB Eq.........	Recovery Operations Branch [NASA] (KSC)
ROB	Regional Office Building
ROB	Relieve of Booty [Crime term]
ROB	Remaining on Board
ROB	Reorder Buffer [Computer science]
ROB	Report on Board [Navy]
ROB	Report on Business (IT)
ROB	Reserveoffizier-Bewerber [Reserve officer applicant] [German military - World War II]
ROB	Reserve on Board
ROB	Right of Baseline (MCD)
ROB	Right Outboard (MCD)
Rob	Robards' Reports [12, 13 Missouri] [A publication] (DLA)
Rob	Robards' Texas Conscript Cases [A publication] (DLA)
ROB	Robert Morris College, Coraopolis, PA [OCLC symbol] (OCLC)
ROB	Robertsfield [Liberia] [Airport symbol]
Rob	Robertson's English Ecclesiastical Reports [A publication] (DLA)
Rob	Robertson's Reports [24-30 New York Superior Court] [1863-68] [A publication] (DLA)
Rob	Robertson's Reports [1 Hawaii] [A publication] (DLA)
Rob	Robertson's Scotch Appeal Cases [1707-27] [A publication] (DLA)
Rob	Roberts' Reports [29-31 Louisiana Annual] [A publication] (DLA)
ROB	Robin International, Inc. [Toronto Stock Exchange symbol]
Rob	Robinson's English Admiralty Reports [1799-1809, 1838-1852] [A publication] (DLA)
Rob	Robinson's English Ecclesiastical Reports [1844-53] [A publication] (DLA)
Rob	Robinson's Louisiana Reports [1-4 Louisiana Annual] [1841-46] [A publication] (DLA)
Rob	Robinson's Reports [2-9, 17-23 Colorado Appeals] [A publication] (DLA)
Rob	Robinson's Reports [38 California] [A publication] (DLA)
Rob	Robinson's Reports [40, 41 Virginia] [A publication] (DLA)
Rob	Robinson's Reports [1 Nevada] [A publication] (DLA)
Rob	Robinson's Reports [1-8 Ontario] [A publication] (DLA)
Rob	Robinson's Scotch Appeal Cases [1840-41] [A publication] (DLA)
Rob	Robinson's Upper Canada Reports [A publication] (DLA)
ROB	Roborough [England]
ROB	Robotic Operating Buddy [Nintendo video game system accessory]
ROB	Roburent [Italy] [Seismograph station code, US Geological Survey] (SEIS)
ROB	Round of Beam (DS)
ROB	Run of Book [Advertising] (WDMC)
ROB	Run on Bank (MHDB)
ROB	Waco, TX [Location identifier FAA] (FAAL)
RoBA	Academia R.S. Romania [Academy of Romania], Bucharest, Romania [Library symbol Library of Congress] (LCLS)
Rob Adm & Pr...	Roberts on Admiralty and Prize [A publication] (DLA)
ROBAMP	Rotational Base for Aviation Maintenance Personnel
Rob & J	Robards and Jackson's Reports [26, 27 Texas] [A publication] (DLA)
Rob App	Robinson's Scotch Appeal Cases [1840-41] [A publication] (DLA)
ROBAR	Read Only Back-Up Address Register [Computer science] (MHDB)
Robards	Robards' Reports [12, 13 Missouri] [A publication] (DLA)
Robards	Robards' Texas Conscript Cases [1862-65] [A publication] (DLA)
Robards & Jackson...	Robards and Jackson's Reports [26-27 Texas] [A publication] (DLA)
ROBAT	Robotic Obstacle-Breaching Assault Tank
Robb	Robbins' New Jersey Equity Reports [67-70 New Jersey] [A publication] (DLA)
Robb	Robb's United States Patent Cases [A publication] (DLA)
Rob Bank	Robertson's Handbook of Bankers' Law [A publication] (DLA)
Rob Bank	Robson on Law and Practice in Bankruptcy [7th ed.] [1894] [A publication] (DLA)
RoBBC	Biblioteca Centrala de Stat a R.S. Romania [Central State Library of Romania], Bucharest, Romania [Library symbol Library of Congress] (LCLS)
Robb (NJ)	Robbins' New Jersey Equity Reports [A publication] (DLA)
Robb Pat Cas...	Robb's United States Patent Cases [A publication] (DLA)
Rob Cal	Robinson's Reports [38 California] [A publication] (DLA)
Rob Car V....	Robertson's History of the Reign of the Emperor Charles V [A publication] (DLA)
Rob Cas	Robinson's Scotch Appeal Cases [1840-41] [A publication] (DLA)
Rob Chr	Robinson's Reports [2-9, 17-23 Colorado Appeals] [A publication] (DLA)
ROBCO	Readiness Objective Code [Military] (AABC)
ROBCO	Requirement Objective Code
Rob Colo	Robinson's Reports [2-9, 17-23 Colorado Appeals] [A publication] (ILCA)
Rob Cons Cas (Tex)...	Robards' Texas Conscript Cases [A publication] (DLA)
Rob Consc Cas...	Robards' Texas Conscript Cases [A publication] (DLA)
Rob Dig	Robert's Digest [Lower Canada] [A publication] (DLA)
Rob Dig	Robert's Digest of Vermont Reports [A publication] (DLA)
Rob E	Robertson's English Ecclesiastical Reports [2 vols.] [1844-53] [A publication] (DLA)
Rob Ecc	Robertson's English Ecclesiastical Reports [2 vols.] [1844-53] [A publication] (DLA)
Rob Eccl	Robertson's English Ecclesiastical Reports [2 vols.] [1844-53] [A publication] (DLA)
Rob El Law...	Robinson's Elementary Law [A publication] (DLA)
Rob Ent........	Robinson's Book of Entries [A publication] (DLA)
ROBEPS	RADAR Operating Below Prescribed Standard [NWS] (FAAC)
Rob Eq........	Roberts' Principles of Equity [A publication] (DLA)
Rober........	Robertus [Authority cited in pre-1607 legal work] (DSA)
Roberds.......	Roberds, Inc. [Associated Press] (SAG)
Rober Maran...	Robertus Maranta [Flourished, 16th century] [Authority cited in pre-1607 legal work] (DSA)
Robert	Robertson's Scotch Appeal Cases [1707-27] [A publication] (DLA)
Robert App...	Robertson's Scotch House of Lords Appeals [A publication] (DLA)
Robert App Cas...	Robertson's Scotch House of Lords Appeals [A publication] (DLA)
Roberts........	Roberts' Reports [29-31 Louisiana Annual] [A publication] (DLA)
Roberts Emp Liab...	Roberts on Federal Liabilities of Carriers [A publication] (DLA)
Robertson......	Robertson's English Ecclesiastical Reports [A publication] (DLA)
Robertson....	Robertson's Reports [24-30 New York Superior Court] [A publication] (DLA)
Robertson....	Robertson's Reports [New York Marine Court] [A publication] (DLA)
Robertson....	Robertson's Reports [1 Hawaii] [A publication] (DLA)
Robertson....	Robertson's Scotch Appeal Cases [1707-27] [A publication] (DLA)
Robertson's Rep...	Robertson's Reports [24-30 New York Superior Court] [A publication] (DLA)
Rob Forms...	Robinson's Virginia Forms [A publication] (DLA)
Rob Fr	Roberts on Frauds [1805] [A publication] (DLA)
Rob Fr Conv...	Roberts on Fraudulent Conveyances [A publication] (DLA)
Rob Gav	Robinson's Common Law of Kent, or Custom on Gavelkind [5th ed.] [1897] [A publication] (DLA)
Rob Hawaii...	Robinson's Reports [1 Hawaii] [A publication] (DLA)
ROBIN.........	Register of Business Opportunities in New South Wales [Australia]
ROBIN.........	Remote On-Line Business Information Network [Computer science] (IEEE)
ROBIN.........	Rocket Balloon Instrument [Air Force]
Robin App ...	Robinson's Scotch House of Lords Appeals [A publication] (DLA)
ROBINS........	Roberts Information Services, Inc. [Information service or system] (IID)
Robin Sc App...	Robinson's Scotch Appeal Cases [1840-41] [A publication] (DLA)
Robinson	Robinson's English Ecclesiastical Reports [1844-53] [A publication] (DLA)
Robinson	Robinson's Louisiana Reports [1-12 Louisiana] [A publication] (DLA)
Robinson	Robinson's Ontario Reports [A publication] (DLA)
Robinson	Robinson's Reports [1 Nevada] [A publication] (DLA)
Robinson	Robinson's Reports [38 California] [A publication] (DLA)
Robinson	Robinson's Reports [40-41 Virginia] [A publication] (DLA)
Robinson	Robinson's Reports [17-23 Colorado] [A publication] (DLA)
Robinson	Robinson's Scotch House of Lords Appeals [A publication] (DLA)
Robinson Sc App Cas...	Robinson's Scotch Appeal Cases [1840-41] [A publication] (DLA)
Rob Jun	William Robinson's English Admiralty Reports [1838-52] [A publication] (DLA)
Rob Jus	Robinson's Justice of the Peace [1836] [A publication] (DLA)
Rob LA	Robinson's Louisiana Reports [1-4 Louisiana Annual] [1841-46] [A publication] (DLA)
Rob (LA Ann)...	Robinson's Louisiana Reports [1-4 Louisiana Annual]
Rob L & W...	Roberts, Leaming, and Wallis' County Court Reports [1849-51] [A publication] (DLA)
Rob Leg.......	Robertson's Legitimation by Subsequent Marriage [1829] [A publication] (DLA)
Rob Louis....	Robinson's Louisiana Reports [1-12 Louisiana] [A publication] (DLA)
Rob Mar (NY)...	Robertson and Jacob's New York Marine Court Reports [A publication] (DLA)
Rob MO	Robards' Reports [12, 13 Missouri] [A publication] (DLA)
ROBMV.......	Robinia Mosaic Virus [Plant pathology]
RobMyr.......	Robbins & Myers [Associated Press] (SAG)
ROBN.........	Robbins & Myers [NASDAQ symbol] (TTSB)
ROBN.........	Robbins & Myers, Inc. [NASDAQ symbol] (NQ)
Rob Nev	Robinson's Reports [1 Nevada] [A publication] (DLA)
RobNug.......	Robinson Nugent, Inc. [Associated Press] (SAG)
Rob (NY)	Robertson's Reports [24-30 New York Superior Court] [A publication] (DLA)
ROBO..........	Eshed Robotec Ltd. [NASDAQ symbol] (SAG)
ROBO..........	Rocket Orbital Bomber
ROBOF........	Eshed Robotec 1982 Ltd [NASDAQ symbol] (TTSB)
ROBOMB.......	Robot Bomb [Air Force]
Rob Ont	Robinson's Reports [1-8 Ontario] [A publication] (DLA)
ROBOT........	Record Organization Based on Transposition (PDAA)
RobotVs.......	Robotic Vision Systems, Inc. [Associated Press] (SAG)
Rob Pat	Robinson on Patents [A publication] (DLA)
Rob Per Suc...	Robertson's Law of Personal Succession [1836] [A publication] (DLA)
Rob Pr.........	Robinson's Practice [A publication] (DLA)
Rob Prior......	Robertson's Law of Priority of Incumbrances [A publication] (DLA)
Robs Bank...	Robson on Law and Practice in Bankruptcy [7th ed.] [1894] [A publication] (DLA)
Robs Bankr...	Robertson's Handbook of Bankers' Law [A publication] (DLA)
Rob Sc App...	Robinson's Scotch Appeal Cases [A publication] (DLA)
Rob SI	Robertson's Sandwich Island Reports [1 Hawaii] [A publication] (DLA)
Robson	Robson on Law and Practice in Bankruptcy [7 eds.] [1870-94] [A publication] (DLA)
Rob Sr Ct...	Robertson's New York Superior Court Reports [24-30] [A publication] (DLA)
Rob Succ	Roberts on the Law of Personal Succession [A publication] (DLA)
Rob Super Ct...	Robertson's Reports [24-30 New York Superior Court] [A publication] (DLA)
Robt Eccl	Robertson's English Ecclesiastical Reports [163 English Reprint] [1844-53] [A publication] (DLA)
Robt Eccl (Eng)...	Robertson's English Ecclesiastical Reports [163 English Reprint] [A publication] (DLA)
RobtHalf	Robert Half International [Associated Press] (SAG)

Robt (NY) .... Robertson's Reports [*24-30 New York Superior Court*] [*A publication*] (DLA)

Robt Sc App Cas... Robertson's Scotch Appeal Cases [*A publication*] (DLA)

Rob UC .... Robinson's Upper Canada Reports [*A publication*] (DLA)

ROBV .... Robotic Vision Sys [*NASDAQ symbol*] (TTSB)

ROBV .... Robotic Vision Systems, Inc. [*NASDAQ symbol*] (NQ)

Rob VA .... Robinson's Reports [*40, 41 Virginia*] [*A publication*] (DLA)

Rob W .... Roberts. Wills and Codicils [*1826*] [*A publication*] (ILCA)

Roc .... New Hampshire Reports [*A publication*] (DLA)

ROC .... Radius of Curvature

ROC .... Rail Operations Center [*MTMC*] (TAG)

ROC .... Railton Owners Club (EA)

ROC .... Range Operations Center [*Western Test Range*] (MCD)

ROC .... Range Operations Conference [*NASA*] (KSC)

ROC .... Rapid Omnidirectional Compaction [*Materials technology*] [*Dow Chemical Co.*]

ROC .... Rate of Climb [*Aviation*]

ROC .... Rate of Convergence (IEEE)

ROC .... Ratio of Charges [*Health insurance*] (GHCT)

ROC .... Readily-Oxidizable Carbon (PDAA)

ROC .... Receiver Operating Characteristic Curve

ROC .... Receiver [*or Relative*] Operating Characteristics [*Signal detection*] [*Graph for assessing diagnostic tests*]

ROC .... Receptor-Operated Channel (DB)

ROC .... Recommended Operating Condition [*Computer science*]

ROC .... Reconnaissance and Operations Center (NATG)

ROC .... Reconnaissance Optique de Caracteres [*Optical Character Recognition*] [*French*]

ROC .... Record of Changes (DNAB)

ROC .... Record of Comments (NASA)

ROC .... Record of Communication (COE)

ROC .... Recovery Operations Center (CIST)

ROC .... Redeem Our Country (EA)

ROC .... Reduced Operational Capability Program [*Navy*] (NVT)

ROC .... Reduced Oxygen Concentration (MCD)

ROC .... Reduce Operating Costs [*Air Force project*]

ROC .... Reevaluation of Capital [*Business term*] (MHDB)

ROC .... Regional Operating Center [*NATO Integrated Communications System*] (NATG)

ROC .... Region One Cooperative Library Service Unit [*Library network*]

ROC .... Regroupement des Officiers Communistes [*Burkina Faso*] [*Political party*] (EY)

ROC .... Relative Operating Characteristics (MCD)

ROC .... Reliability Operating Characteristic

ROC .... Remote Object Communications (AAEL)

ROC .... Remote Operator's Console

ROC .... Republican Organizing Committee [*Political organization in opposition to the NPL of North Dakota*]

ROC .... Republic of China

ROC .... Request of Change (NASA)

ROC .... Required Operational Capability [*Military*] (RDA)

ROC .... Requirements Document [*Army*] (RDA)

ROC .... Research into Ovarian Cancer (WDAA)

ROC .... Reserve Officer Candidate

ROC .... Residual Organic Carbon [*Organic chemistry*] (DAVI)

ROC .... Rest of Canada [*English-speaking portion of Canada*] (ECON)

ROC .... Return on Capital [*Finance*]

ROC .... Reusable Orbital Carrier [*Aerospace*] (MCD)

ROC .... Rochester [*New York*] [*Airport symbol*] (OAG)

ROC .... Rochester-Odenbach [*New York*] [*Seismograph station code, US Geological Survey*] (SEIS)

ROC .... Rochester Public Library, Rochester, MN [*OCLC symbol*] (OCLC)

Roc .... Rochus Curtius [*Flourished, 1470-1515*] [*Authority cited in pre-1607 legal work*] (DSA)

ROC .... Rocky Mountain [*Canada ICAO designator*] (FAAC)

Roc .... Rococo Records [*Record label*] [*Canada, USA*]

ROC .... ROC Taiwan Fund SBI [*NYSE symbol*] (SPSG)

ROC .... Rotatable Optical Cube

ROC .... Rothmans Inc. [*Formerly, Rothmans of Pall Mall Canada*] [*Toronto Stock Exchange symbol Vancouver Stock Exchange symbol*]

ROC .... Royal Observer Corps [*British civilian aircraft observers*] [*World War II*]

ROC .... Royal Ordnance Corps [*British*]

ROCAF .... Republic of China Air Force

ROCALDIS ... Routine Calls May Be Dispensed With

ROCAP .... Regional Office for Central America and Panama

ROCAP .... Regional Office [*or Officer*] for Central American Programs [*Department of State*]

ROCAPPI ...... Research on Computer Applications for the Printing and Publishing Industries

ROCAT .... Rocket Catapult

ROCC .... Range Operations Conference Circuit (MUGU)

ROCC .... Range Operations Control Center (MCD)

ROCC .... Receptor-Operated Calcium Channel [*Physiology*]

ROCC .... Regional Oil Combating Center [*United Nations Environment Programme*] (MSC)

ROCC .... Regional Operations Control Center [*AT & T*]

ROCC .... Region Operations Control Center [*NORAD*] [*ICAO designator*] (FAAC)

ROCC .... Remote Operational Control Center

Rocc .... Roccus. De Navibus et Naulo [*Maritime law*] [*A publication*] (DLA)

ROCC .... Russell's Owl Collectors Club (EA)

Rocc De Nav et Nau... Roccus. De Navibus et Naulo [*Maritime law*] [*A publication*] (DLA)

ROC Cm....... ROC Communities [*Associated Press*] (SAG)

Roccus Ins... Roccus on Insurance [*A publication*] (DLA)

ROCE .... Return on Capital Employed [*Accounting term*]

ROCF .... Rockford Industries [*NASDAQ symbol*] (TTSB)

ROCF .... Rockford Industries, Inc. [*NASDAQ symbol*] (SAG)

ROC Fd .... ROC Taiwan Fund [*Associated Press*] (SAG)

ROCH .... Rochester [*Municipal borough in England*] (ROG)

Roch .... Rochus Curtius [*Flourished, 1470-1515*] [*Authority cited in pre-1607 legal work*] (DSA)

ROCH .... Ruch Oporu Chlopskiego [*Movement of Peasant Resistance*] [*Poland Political party*] (PPE)

Roch Curt .... Rochus Curtius [*Flourished, 1470-1515*] [*Authority cited in pre-1607 legal work*] (DSA)

Roche & H Bank... Roche and Hazlitt's Bankruptcy Practice [*2nd ed.*] [*1873*] [*A publication*] (DLA)

Roche D & K... Roche, Dillon, and Kehoe's Irish Land Reports [*1881-82*] [*A publication*] (DLA)

RochG......... Rochester Gas & Electric Corp. [*Associated Press*] (SAG)

RochMed...... Rochester Medical Corp. [*Associated Press*] (SAG)

ROCI .... Rahim Organizational Conflict Inventories [*Interpersonal skills and attitudes test*]

ROCI .... Rauschenberg Overseas Cultural Interchange [*Retrospective exhibit of artist Robert Rauschenberg's work*]

ROCI .... Rickman Owners Club International (EA)

ROCID .... Reorganization of Combat Infantry Division [*Army*] (AABC)

Roc Ins .... Roccus on Insurance [*A publication*] (DLA)

ROCK .... Gibraltar Steel [*NASDAQ symbol*] (TTSB)

ROCK .... Gibraltar Steel Corp. [*NASDAQ symbol*] (SAG)

Rock .... New Hampshire Reports [*A publication*] (DLA)

ROCK .... Rocket (MCD)

Rock .... Smith's New Hampshire Reports [*A publication*] (DLA)

RockBott...... Rock Bottom Restaurants, Inc. [*Associated Press*] (SAG)

RockCtr........ Rockefeller Center Properties [*Associated Press*] (SAG)

Rockefeller U... [*The*] Rockefeller University (GAGS)

ROCKET ...... Rand's Omnibus Calculator of the Kinetics of Earth Trajectories

ROCKEX ...... Rocket Exercise [*Military*] (NVT)

ROCKF .... Rockford [*England*]

Rockford C.... Rockford College (GAGS)

Rockfrd........ Rockford Industries, Inc. [*Associated Press*] (SAG)

Rockingham... Smith's New Hampshire Reports [*A publication*] (DLA)

Rock Min ..... Rockwell on Mines [*A publication*] (DLA)

ROCKOON.... Rocket Balloon [*Navy*]

RocksMiner... Rocks & Minerals [*A publication*] (BRI)

Rock Sp Law... Rockwell's Spanish and Mexican Law Relating to Mines [*A publication*] (DLA)

ROCKSTORE... Rock Storage [*Storage in excavated rock caverns*]

RockTen....... Rock Tenn Co. [*Associated Press*] (SAG)

Rockwl......... Rockwell International Corp. [*Associated Press*] (SAG)

Rocky Mt Miner L Rev... Rocky Mountain Mineral Law Review [*A publication*] (DLA)

RockySh....... Rocky Shoes & Boots, Inc. [*Associated Press*] (SAG)

ROCM .... Rochester Medical [*NASDAQ symbol*] (TTSB)

ROCM .... Rochester Medical Corp. [*NASDAQ symbol*] (SAG)

ROCMAGV .. Republic of China, Military Assistance Group, Vietnam

ROCMAS...... Russian Orthodox Catholic Mutual Aid Society of USA (EA)

ROCMC........ Republic of China Marine Corps

ROCMM........ Regional Office of Civilian Manpower Management

ROCN.......... Reclamation Order Control Number

ROCN.......... Republic of China Navy

ROCNA........ Retraining Objective Control Number [*Air Force*] (AFM)

ROCOA........ Renault Owners Club of America (EA)

ROCOB........ Rocketsonde Observation (NOAA)

ROCOCO...... Rocailles, Coquilles, et Cordeau [*Rocks, Shells, and String*] [*French*]

ROCOMP...... Radio or Computer Operated Mobile Platform [*Army*]

ROCOZ........ Rocket-Borne Ozonesonde (SAA)

ROCP .... RADAR Out of Commission for Parts [*ADC*]

ROCP .... Regional Occupation Center Program (OICC)

ROCP .... Remote Operator Control Panel [*Electronics*] (IAA)

ROCPEX....... Republic of China Philatelic Exhibition

ROCR.......... Recovery Operations Control Room [*NASA*] (KSC)

ROCR.......... Remote Optical Character Recognition [*Computer science*]

ROCS.......... Railroad Operations Control System (PDAA)

ROCS.......... Range Operations Control System (SAA)

ROCS.......... Resource-Oriented Computer System (CIST)

ROCSIM....... Railroad Operations Computer Simulation [*FTA*] (TAG)

ROCU.......... Remote Operational Control Unit [*Military*] (CAAL)

ROCWMAS... Russian Orthodox Catholic Women's Mutual Aid Society (EA)

ROD .... Aerodan, SA de CV [*Mexico*] [*FAA designator*] (FAAC)

ROD .... Railway Operating Department [*British military*] (DMA)

ROD .... Range of the Day [*Military*] (CAAL)

ROD .... Range Operations Directorate [*White Sands Missile Range*]

ROD .... Rate of Descent (KSC)

ROD .... Recorder on Demand

ROD .... Record of Decision [*Environmental Protection Agency*]

ROD .... Record of Discussion (MCD)

ROD .... Release Order Directive [*Later, ERO*] (NRCH)

ROD .... Remote Operated Door (MCD)

ROD .... Renal Osteodystrophy [*Medicine*] (DB)

ROD .... Repair and Overhaul Directive (AAG)

ROD .... Repair on Demand (DA)

ROD .... Report of Discrepancies

ROD .... Required on Dock (KSC)

ROD .... Required Operational Date

ROD .... Reverse-Osmosis Desalination

ROD .... Rewritable Optical Disk [*Computer science*] (BARN)

R-O-D .... Rise-Off-Disconnect (AAG)

ROD	Roddy Resources, Inc. [*Toronto Stock Exchange symbol*]
Rod	Rodericus Suarez [*Flourished, 15th century*] [*Authority cited in pre-1607 legal work*] (DSA)
ROD	Rosewood, OH [*Location identifier FAA*] (FAAL)
ROD	Route Opening Detachment (MCD)
RODA	Regardless of Destination Airport (FAAC)
RODA	Sisters Oblates to Divine Love [*Roman Catholic religious order*]
RODAC	Reorganization Objectives, Army Division, Army and Corps [*Military*] (AABC)
ROD/AC	Rotary Dual Input for Analog Computation (SAA)
RODATA	Registered Organization Data Bank
RODC	Regional Oceanographic Data Center [*Marine science*] (MSC)
RODC	Registered Organization Development Consultant [*Organization Development Institute*] [*Designation awarded by*]
RODE	Iejima United States Air Force Base [*Ryukyu Islands*] [*ICAO location identifier*] (ICLI)
RO-DI	Reverse Osmosis - Deionization System [*Water purification*]
RODIAC	Rotary Dual Input for Analog Computation
R-O Dis	Reality-Oriented Discussion
Rodm	Rodman's Reports [*78-82 Kentucky*] [*A publication*] (DLA)
Rodman	Rodman's Reports [*78-82 Kentucky*] [*A publication*] (DLA)
RODN	Kadena Air Base [*Ryukyu Islands*] [*ICAO location identifier*] (ICLI)
RODO	Range Operations Duty Officer (MUGU)
Rodo	Rodoicus [*Authority cited in pre-1607 legal work*] (DSA)
RodRen	Rodman & Renshaw Capital Group [*Associated Press*] (SAG)
RODS	Real-Time Operations, Dispatching, and Scheduling [*System*] [*TRW, Inc.*]
RODS	Records of Decision System [*Environmental Protection Agency*] (AEPA)
ROE	Birmingham, AL [*Location identifier FAA*] (FAAL)
ROE	Rate of Exchange [*Finance*]
ROE	Reflector Orbital Equipment
ROE	Reflector Orbital Experiment (MCD)
ROE	Return on Equity [*Finance*]
ROE	Roster of Exception [*Military*] (AABC)
ROE	Round Off Error
ROE	Royal Observatory, Edinburgh [*Scotland*]
ROE	Rules of Engagement [*Military*] (AABC)
ROEAP	Regional Office for Education, Asia and Pacific [*UNESCO*] (AIE)
ROEFEX	Rotterdam Energy Futures Exchange [*Netherlands*] (EY)
Roelk Man	Roelker's Manual for Notaries and Bankers [*A publication*] (DLA)
ROEM	Removable, Optical, Erasable Media [*Computer science*] (BTTJ)
Roent	Roentgenology [*Radiology*]
Roent M	Master of Roentgenology
ROESY	Rotating-Frame Overhauser Enchancement Spectroscopy [*Organic chemistry*]
Roe US Com	Roe's Manual for United States Commissioners [*A publication*] (DLA)
ROEX	Rules of Engagement Exercise (DOMA)
ROF	Aerofrance [*France ICAO designator*] (FAAC)
ROF	Rate of Fire [*In rounds per minute*] [*Military*]
ROF	Reformed Ogboni Fraternity [*Nigeria*]
ROF	Remote Operator Facility [*Honeywell, Inc.*]
ROF	Reporting Organizational File [*Military*] (AFM)
Rof	Roffredus Beneventanus [*Flourished, 1215-43*] [*Authority cited in pre-1607 legal work*] (DSA)
ROF	Rose Hall [*Guyana*] [*Airport symbol*] (AD)
ROF	Royal Oak Foundation (EA)
ROFA	Royal Ordnance Factory [*British*] (NATG)
ROFA	Radio of Free Asia (NTCM)
ROF-B	Royal Ordnance Factory, Bishopton [*Scotland*]
Rof Bn	Roffredus Beneventanus [*Flourished, 1215-43*] [*Authority cited in pre-1607 legal work*] (DSA)
R of D	Reporter of Debate [*US Senate*]
R of E	Rate of Exchange
ROFF	Retail Office Furniture Forum (EA)
Roffe Be	Roffredus Beneventanus [*Flourished, 1215-43*] [*Authority cited in pre-1607 legal work*] (DSA)
ROFFEN	Roffensis [*Signature of Bishop of Rochester*] [*Latin*] (ROG)
ROFL	Rolling on the Floor Laughing [*Internet language*] (PCM)
ROFL	Rolls on Floor Laughing [*Internet language*] [*Computer science*]
ROFL	Russian Orthodox Fraternity Lubov (EA)
RO/FLO	Roll-On/Float-Off (DOMA)
RofnSinr	Rofin-Sinar Technologies, Inc. [*Associated Press*] (SAG)
R of O	Reserve of Officers [*British*]
ROFOR	Route Forcast [*Aviation*] (FAAC)
ROFR	Repair of Repairables (MCD)
ROFT	RADAR Off Target
ROFT	Rapid Optics Fabrication Technology (MCD)
R of W	Right of Way
ROG	Reactive Organic Gas [*Environmental chemistry*]
ROG	Receipt of Goods
ROG	Recruiting Operations Group [*Military*]
ROG	Residency Operations Group
R-O-G	Rise-Off-Ground [*Model airplane*] (AAG)
ROG	Rodale's Organic Gardening [*A publication*]
ROG	Rogel [*C.C. Sergio Gonzales*], Ing. [*Mexico ICAO designator*] (FAAC)
Rog	Rogerius Beneventanus [*Flourished, 12th century*] [*Authority cited in pre-1607 legal work*] (DSA)
ROG	Rogers, AR [*Location identifier FAA*] (FAAL)
ROG	Rogers Corp. [*AMEX symbol*] (SPSG)
ROG	Roggianite [*A zeolite*]
ROG	Rothchild Gold [*Vancouver Stock Exchange symbol*]
ROGAR	Review of Guard and Reserve Task Force (MCD)
RogCantl	Rogers Cantel Mobile Communications [*Associated Press*] (SAG)

Rog CHR	Rogers' City Hall Recorder [*1816-22*] [*New York*] [*A publication*] (DLA)
RogCm	Rogers Communications, Inc. [*Associated Press*] (SAG)
Rog Ecc L	Rogers' Ecclesiastical Law [*5th ed.*] [*1857*] [*A publication*] (DLA)
Rog Ecc Law	Rogers' Ecclesiastical Law [*A publication*] (DLA)
Rog Elec	Rogers on Elections and Registration [*A publication*] (DLA)
Rogers	Rogers Corp. [*Associated Press*] (SAG)
Rogers	Rogers on Elections [*A publication*] (DLA)
Rogers	Rogers' Reports [*47-51 Louisiana Annual*] [*A publication*] (DLA)
Rog Hov	Roger De Hoveden's Chronica [*A publication*] (DLA)
Rog Jud Acts	Rogers on the Judicature Acts [*A publication*] (DLA)
Rog Min	Rogers. Mines, Minerals, and Quarries [*A publication*] (ILCA)
Rog Min	Rogers on Mines and Minerals [*A publication*] (DLA)
ROGOPAG	Rossellini, Jr.; Godard, Pasolini, Gregoretti [*Title of episodic motion picture formed from surnames of its directors*]
Rog Rec	Rogers' New City Hall Recorder [*A publication*] (DLA)
Rog Trav	Rogers' Wrongs and Rights of a Traveller [*A publication*] (DLA)
RogWve	Rogue Wave Software, Inc. [*Associated Press*] (SAG)
ROH	Rat Ovarian Hyperemia [*Test*] (MAE)
ROH	Ray of Hope [*An association*] (EA)
ROH	Rear Overhead [*TII*] (TAG)
R-O-H	Receiver Off the Hook
ROH	Regular Overhaul [*Navy*] (NG)
ROH	Returned on Hire
roh	Rhaeto-Romance [*MARC language code Library of Congress*] (LCCP)
ROH	Robinhood [*Australia Airport symbol Obsolete*] (OAG)
ROH	Rohm & Haas [*NYSE symbol*] (TTSB)
ROH	Rohm & Haas Co. [*NYSE symbol*] (SPSG)
ROH	Rohtak [*India*] [*Seismograph station code, US Geological Survey Closed*] (SEIS)
ROH	Royal Opera House [*Covent Garden, London*]
RoHaas	Rohm & Haas Co. [*Associated Press*] (SAG)
ROHCG	Royal Opera House, Covent Garden [*British*] (WDAA)
ROHN	ROHN Industries [*NASDAQ symbol*] [*Formerly, UNR Industries*] (SG)
Rohr	Rohr Industries, Inc. [*Associated Press*] (SAG)
ROI	Member of the Royal Institute of Oil Painters [*British*]
ROI	Radiological Operating Instructions [*Environmental science*] (COE)
ROI	Radio, Optical, Inertial
ROI	Range Operations Instruction [*NASA*] (KSC)
ROI	Reactive Oxygen Intermediate [*Biochemistry*]
ROI	Region of Influence
ROI	Region of Interest [*Nuclear energy*] (NRCH)
ROI	Registration of Interest
ROI	Relevant, Original, Impact [*Advertising*] (WDMC)
ROI	Reliability Organization Instruction (AAG)
ROI	Religious Observance Index (BJA)
ROI	Remnant of Israel (EA)
ROI	Rendezvous Orbit Insertion [*Aerospace*]
ROI	Report of Investigation [*Military*] (AFM)
ROI	Research Online International, Inc. [*Information service or system*] (IID)
ROI	Resource Objectives, Inc. [*Ridgewood, NJ*] (TSSD)
ROI	Return on Investment [*Finance*]
roi	Return on Investment (WDMC)
ROI	Rotating Optical Interferometer
ROI	Royal Institute of Oil Painters [*British*]
ROI	Royal Institute of Oil Painters, London [*1883*] (NGC)
ROIC	Regional Officer in Charge [*CIA*] (VNW)
ROIC	Resident Officer-in-Charge [*Military*]
ROICC	Resident Officer-in-Charge of Construction [*Military*]
ROICM	Resident Officer-in-Charge of Material [*Navy*] (DNAB)
ROID	Report of Item Discrepancy [*Army*] (AABC)
ROIG	Ishigaki Jima [*Ryukyu Islands*] [*ICAO location identifier*] (ICLI)
ROIH	Right Oblique Inguinal Hernia [*Medicine*] (DMAA)
ROIN	Reorganization of the Interconnection Network (MHDI)
RO in C	Resident Officer-in-Charge [*Navy*]
ROINST	Range Operations Instruction [*NASA*] (MUGU)
ROIP	Remaining Oil in Place [*Petroleum industry*]
ROIS	Radio Operational Intercom System (KSC)
ROITL	Reports of Interest to Lawyers [*Merton Allen Associates*] [*Information service or system*] (CRD)
ROIX	Response Oncology [*NASDAQ symbol*] (TTSB)
ROIXD	Response Oncology, Inc. [*NASDAQ symbol*] (SAG)
ROJ	Range of Jamming
ROJ	Royal Order of Jagie Ilo [*Later, SHOSJ*] (EA)
ROJM	Range of Joint Motion [*Medicine*] (DMAA)
ROK	Republic of Korea
ROK	Rockhampton [*Australia Airport symbol*] (OAG)
ROK	Rockwell International Corp. [*NYSE symbol Toronto Stock Exchange symbol*] (SPSG)
ROK	Rockwell Intl [*NYSE symbol*] (TTSB)
ROKA	Republic of Korea Army
ROKAF	Republic of Korea Air Force
ROKAP	Republic of Korea Civic Action Program
ROKDTF	Republic of Korea Division Task Force
ROKF	Republic of Korea Forces
ROKFV	Republic of Korea Forces in Vietnam
ROKG	Republic of Korea Government
ROKG	Rocking
ROKIT	Republic of Korea Indigenous Tank Program (MCD)
ROKJ	Kume Jima [*Ryukyu Islands*] [*ICAO location identifier*] (ICLI)
ROKMC	Republic of Korea Marine Corps
ROKN	Republic of Korea Navy
ROKPr	Rockwell Intl $4.75 Cv Pfd [*NYSE symbol*] (TTSB)

ROKPrB....... Rockwell Intl $1.35 Cv PFd [*NYSE symbol*] (TTSB)
ROKPTN...... Rockhampton (ROG)
ROKPUC ..... Republic of Korea Presidential Unit Citation Badge [*Military decoration*]
ROKPUCE .... Republic of Korea Presidential Unit Citation [*Military decoration*]
ROKUSCFC... Republic of Korea and US Combined Forces Command (MCD)
ROKW......... Yomitan [*Ryukyu Islands*] [*ICAO location identifier*] (ICLI)
ROL .... Aeroel Airways Ltd. [*Israel*] [*FAA designator*] (FAAC)
ROL .... RADAR Observer License
ROL .... Record of Oral Language (ADA)
ROL .... Reduction-Option Loan [*Banking*]
RoL .... Register of Lists [*Environmental Protection Agency*] (AEPA)
ROL .... Remote Operating Location (MCD)
ROL .... Reordering Level
ROL .... Rest of Life
ROL .... Right Occipitolateral [*Obstetrics*]
ROL .... Rolla [*Missouri*] [*Seismograph station code, US Geological Survey*] (SEIS)
Rol .... Rolle's Abridgment [*A publication*] (DLA)
Rol .... Rolle's English King's Bench Reports [*2 vols.*] [*A publication*] (DLA)
ROL .... Rollins, Inc. [*NYSE symbol*] (SPSG)
ROL .... Rotate Left [*Computer science*]
ROL .... Royal Oak Resources Ltd. [*Toronto Stock Exchange symbol*]
ROL .... Royal Overseas League [*British*] (EAIO)
Rol Ab .... Rolle's Abridgment [*A publication*] (DLA)
ROLAC .... Regional Office for Latin America and the Caribbean [*United Nations Environment Programme*] (EAIO)
ROLAC .... Regional Organization of Liaison for Allocation of Circuit (NATG)
ROLAC .... Registry of Life Assurance Commission [*British*]
ROLADES .... Roland Air Defense System (MCD)
ROLC .... Our Lady of Charity of Refuge (TOCD)
ROLE .... Receive Only Link Eleven [*Naval datalink system*] [*British*]
ROLET .... Reference Our Letter (NOAA)
ROLF .... Remotely Operated Longwall Face (IEEE)
ROLFE .... Review of Law in Further Education (AIE)
ROLL .... Roll Angle (NAKS)
Roll .... Rolle's Abridgment [*A publication*] (DLA)
Roll .... Rolle's English King's Bench Reports [*2 vols.*] [*A publication*] (DLA)
Roll Abr ...... Rolle's Abridgment [*A publication*] (DLA)
Rolle .... Rolle's Abridgment [*A publication*] (DLA)
Rolle .... Rolle's English King's Bench Reports [*2 vols.*] [*1614-25*] [*A publication*] (DLA)
Rolle Abr .... Rolle's Abridgment of the Common Law [*A publication*] (DLA)
Rolle R .... Rolle's English King's Bench Reports [*2 vols.*] [*1614-25*] [*A publication*] (DLA)
RollinE........ Rollins Environmental Services, Inc. [*Associated Press*] (SAG)
Rollins........ Rollins, Inc. [*Associated Press*] (SAG)
Rollins C ..... Rollins College (GAGS)
RollLeas...... Rollins Truck Leasing [*Associated Press*] (SAG)
Roll Rep ..... Rolle's English King's Bench Reports [*2 vols.*] [*1614-25*] [*A publication*] (DLA)
Rolls Ct Rep... Rolls' Court Reports [*A publication*] (DLA)
Ro/Lo .... Roll-On, Roll-Off/Lift-On, Lift-Off [*Shipping*] (DS)
ROLR .... Receiving Objective Loudness Rating [*Telephones*] (IEEE)
ROLS .... Rainbow Optical Landing System (PDAA)
ROLS .... Recoverable Orbital Launch System
ROLS .... Remote On-Line Subsystem [*Computer science*] (MHDI)
ROLS .... Remote Online System (NITA)
ROLSIM .... Roland Simulation (MCD)
ROLTP .... Remote On-Line Transaction Processing [*Computer science*] (TELE)
ROM .... Empresa Aeromar [*Dominican Republic*] [*ICAO designator*] (FAAC)
ROM .... Priest, CA [*Location identifier FAA*] (FAAL)
ROM .... RADAR Operator Mechanic (WDAA)
ROM .... Radiopaque Contrast Material (WGA)
ROM .... Range of Motion [*or Movement*]
ROM .... Reactive Oxygen Metabolites [*Biochemistry*]
ROM .... Read-Only Memory [*Computer memory*] [*Computer science*]
ROM .... Read-Only Men [*On Board car window sign's version of the computer term, Read-Only Memory*]
ROM .... Readout Memory (IEEE)
ROM .... Reciprocal Ohmmeter [*Electronics*] (IAA)
rom .... Reciprocal Ohm Meter (STED)
ROM .... Recruiter of the Month [*Navy*] (DNAB)
ROM .... Refuel-On-The-Move [*Army*] (DOMA)
ROM .... Regional Oxidant Model [*Environmental Protection Agency*] (GFGA)
ROM .... Register of Merit (WGA)
ROM .... Return on Market Value [*Finance*]
ROM .... Right Otitis Media [*Medicine*] (STED)
ROM .... Rio Algom Ltd. [*AMEX symbol Toronto Stock Exchange symbol*] (SPSG)
Rom............ Roemisch [*Roman*] [*German*]
ROM .... Roman [*Type*] [*Publishing*]
rom .... Roman [*Type*] [*Publishing*] (ODBW)
ROM .... Romance
Rom............ Romance [*Literary genre*] (WDAA)
Rom............ Romania [*ANSI three-letter standard code*] (CNC)
Rom............ Romania (VRA)
Rom............ Romans [*New Testament book*]
rom .... Romany [*MARC language code Library of Congress*] (LCCP)
Rom............ Romany Records [*Record label*]
ROM .... Romberg [*Medicine*]
Rom............ Romberg [*Sign*] (STED)
ROM .... Rome [*Italy*] [*Seismograph station code, US Geological Survey Closed*] (SEIS)
ROM .... Rome [*Italy*] [*Airport symbol*] (OAG)

Rom............ Romeo and Juliet [*Shakespearean work*]
Rom............ Romilly's Notes of English Chancery Cases [*1767-87*] [*A publication*] (DLA)
Rom............ Romulus [*of Plutarch*] [*Classical studies*] (OCD)
ROM .... Rotating Piston Machine (IAA)
ROM .... Rough Order of Magnitude [*Army*] (AABC)
ROM .... Royal Ontario Museum [*Toronto, ON*] [*Research center*]
ROM .... Run of Mine
ROM .... Rupture of Membranes [*Medicine*]
ROMA .... Return on Managed Assets [*Business term*]
ROMAC......... Range Operations Monitor Analysis Center (MCD)
ROMAC......... Range Operations Monitoring and Control
ROMAC......... Robotic Muscle Activator
Romac .... Romac Industries, Inc. [*Associated Press*] (SAG)
ROMACC....... Range Operational Monitoring and Control Center
ROMAD........ Radio Operator/Maintenance Driver
ROMAD........ Read Only Memory Automatic Design [*Computer science*] (MHDB)
Rom Adelsparteien... Roemische Adelsparteien und Adelsfamilien [*A publication*] (OCD)
ROMAN........ Remotely-Operated Mobile Manipulator (PDAA)
Rom & Jul.... Romeo and Juliet [*Shakespearean work*] (BARN)
ROMANS..... Range-Only Multiple Aircraft Navigation System [*Air Force*]
ROMANS..... Remote Manipulation Systems [*NASA*]
RO(M)B .... Reduction of (Military) Budgets
Romb.......... Romberg [*Sign*] (STED)
ROMBI .... Results of Marine Biological Investigations [*Marine science*] (MSC)
ROM BIOS ... Read Only Memory Basic Input Output System [*Computer science*] (IGQR)
ROMBUS..... Reusable Orbital Module Booster and Utility Shuttle [*Aerospace*]
ROMC .... Romac Industries, Inc. [*NASDAQ symbol*] (SAG)
ROMC .... Romac Intl [*NASDAQ symbol*] (TTSB)
Rom Cas..... Romilly's Notes of English Chancery Cases [*1767-87*] [*A publication*] (DLA)
Rom Cath .... Roman Catholic (WDAA)
ROMCOE..... Rocky Mountain Center on Environment (EPA)
Rom Cr Law... Romilly's Observations on the Criminal Law [*3rd ed.*] [*1813*] [*A publication*] (DLA)
ROMD .... Minami Daito Jima [*Ryukyu Islands*] [*ICAO location identifier*] (ICLI)
ROMD .... Remote Operations and Maintenance Demonstration [*Nuclear energy*]
ROME .... Resource Organizations and Meetings for Educators [*National Center for Research in Vocational Education*] [*Information service or system Defunct*] (CRD)
ROMEMO..... Reference Our Memorandum (FAAC)
ROMES .... Reference Message from Our Office (FAAC)
Rom Forsch... Roemische Forschungen [*A publication*] (OCD)
Rom Gesch... Grundriss der Romischen Geschichte [*A publication*] (OCD)
Rom Gesch... Romische Geschichte bis zum Beginn der Punischen Kriege [*A publication*] (OCD)
ROMI .... Rule Out Myocardial Infarction [*Medicine*]
Romilly NC (Eng)... Romilly's Notes of English Chancery Cases [*A publication*] (DLA)
ROMIO........ ROM Plus Input/Output (NITA)
Rom Law..... Mackeldey's Handbook of the Roman Law [*A publication*] (DLA)
ROMM .... Read-Only Memory Module [*Computer science*]
ROMN .... Film Roman, Inc. [*NASDAQ symbol*] (SAG)
ROMO .... Rocky Mountain National Park
ROMON....... Receiving-Only Monitor
ROMOSS...... Revised Officer Military Occupational Speciality System (MCD)
ROMOTAR ... Range-Only Measurement of Trajectory and Recording
ROMP .... Radiotelephone Operator Maintenance Proficiency (DNAB)
ROMP .... Recovery of Male Potency (EA)
ROMP .... Report of Obligation Military Pay (AFM)
ROMP .... Review of Management Practices [*or Processes*]
ROMP .... Ring Opening Metathesis Polymerization [*Organic chemistry*]
Rom Pol ...... Roman Politics 220-150BC [*A publication*] (OCD)
ROMPS........ Regional Office Monthly Personnel Status [*Department of Labor*]
ROMR......... Read-Only Memory Register [*Computer science*] (IAA)
Rom Rev ..... [*The*] Roman Revolution [*1939*] [*A publication*] (OCD)
Rom Rule Asia Min... Roman Rule in Asia Minor [*A publication*] (OCD)
ROMS .... Read-Only Memory Storage [*Computer science*] (IAA)
ROMS .... Remote Ocean Surface Measuring System [*Navy*] (CAAL)
ROMSA........ Right Otitis Media Suppurative, Acute [*Medicine*] (STED)
ROMSC........ Right Otitis Media Suppurative, Chronic [*Medicine*] (STED)
Rom Staatsr... Roemisches Staatsrecht [*A publication*] (OCD)
Rom Strafr... Roemisches Strafrecht [*A publication*] (OCD)
Rom Stud ... Roemische Studien [*A publication*] (OCD)
ROMT .... Rom Tech [*NASDAQ symbol*] (TTSB)
ROMT .... Rom Tech, Inc. [*NASDAQ symbol*] (SAG)
RomTch ...... Rom Tech, Inc. [*Associated Press*] (SAG)
ROMV .... Return on Market Value [*Finance*] (WDAA)
ROM WNL ... Range of Motion Within Normal Limits [*Medicine*] (STED)
ROMY .... Miyako [*Ryukyu Islands*] [*ICAO location identifier*] (ICLI)
RON .... Air Nauru [*ICAO designator*] (FAAC)
RON .... Cooper Cameron [*NYSE symbol*] (TTSB)
RON .... Cooper Cameron Corp. [*NYSE symbol*] (SAG)
RON .... Reality or Nothing (WDAA)
RON .... Remaining [*or Rest*] Overnight [*Aviation*]
RON .... Remain Overnight Position [*Military*] (VNW)
RON .... Remote [*Alaska*] [*Seismograph station code, US Geological Survey Closed*] (SEIS)
RON .... Report of NAC/ENTAC (MCD)
RON .... Research-Octane-Number [*Fuel technology*]

RON .... Rest Overnight [*or Rest-of-Night*] [*Pronounced "ron" Chance for a candidate to catch some sleep during a traveling political campaign*]
RON .... Rondon [*Colombia*] [*Airport symbol Obsolete*] (OAG)
RON .... Run Occurrence Number (IAA)
RON .... Squadron (MUGU)
RONA .... Naha United States Naval Base [*Ryukyu Islands*] [*ICAO location identifier*] (ICLI)
RONA .... Return on Net Assets
RONAG .... Reserve Officers Naval Architecture Group
RONB .... Research-Octane-Number-Barrels [*Fuel technology*]
RONC .... Ronson Corp. [*NASDAQ symbol*] (SAG)
RONCO .... Rock-Oldies-News-Commercials Operation [*Formula radio*]
RONCOM .... Ronald Como, Inc. [*Perry Como's production firm; Ronald is his son*]
RONCP .... Ronson Corp. 12% Cv Pfd [*NASDAQ symbol*] (TTSB)
ROND .... Remote Ordnance Neutralization Device (DWSG)
RONEO .... Rotary and Neostyle [*Duplicating machine*] [*Acronym is trademark*]
Roneo .... Rotary Neostyle (WDAA)
RONLY .... Receiver Only [*Radio*]
RONS .... Read-Only Name Store (NITA)
RONS .... Read Only Nano Store (MHDB)
RONS .... Reserve Officers of the Naval Service [*Later, ROA*]
Ronson .... Ronson Corp. [*Associated Press*] (SAG)
RONWT .... Revised Ordinances, Northwest Territories [*Canada*] [*A publication*] (DLA)
ROO .... Radio Optical Observatory
ROO .... Railhead Ordnance Officer
ROO .... Range Operations Officer
ROO .... Reserve of Officers [*British*]
ROO .... Resident Obstetric Officer [*British*]
ROO .... Richland Operations Office [*Energy Research and Development Administration*]
ROO .... Rondonopolis [*Brazil*] [*Airport symbol*] (OAG)
ROOF .... Reclaim, Inc. [*NASDAQ symbol*] (SAG)
ROOF .... Roofing
ROOI .... Return on Original Investment [*Business term*] (MHDW)
ROOM .... Hospitality Worldwide Services, Inc. [*NASDAQ symbol*] (SAG)
RoomP .... Room Plus, Inc. [*Associated Press*] (SAG)
RoomPl .... Room Plus, Inc. [*Associated Press*] (SAG)
ROOPH .... Readily Operative Overhead Protection by Hippos [*Facetious proposal for protection against nuclear attack*]
ROOSCH ...... Royal Order of Sputnik Chasers
Roosevelt U... Roosevelt University (GAGS)
ROOST .... Rapid Optical Ocean Surveillance Testbed [*Navy*] (EECA)
ROOST .... Reusable One-Stage Orbital Space Truck [*Aerospace*]
ROOT .... Relaxation Oscillator Optically Tuned
Root .... Root's Connecticut Reports [*1774-89*] [*A publication*] (DLA)
Root .... Root's Connecticut Supreme Court Reports [*1789-98*] [*A publication*] (DLA)
Root Bt Laws... Root's Digest of Law and Practice in Bankruptcy [*1818*] [*A publication*] (DLA)
Root R .... Root's Connecticut Reports [*A publication*] (DLA)
Roots .... Root's Connecticut Reports [*A publication*] (DLA)
Root's Rep .... Root's Connecticut Reports [*A publication*] (DLA)
ROP .... Raster Operation
ROP .... Rate of Pay [*British military*] (DMA)
ROP .... Rate of Penetration [*Drilling technology*]
ROP .... Receive-Only Printer [*Computer science*]
ROP .... Receiving Operations Package [*DoD*]
ROP .... Record of Performance
ROP .... Record of Production
ROP .... Record of Purchase (NRCH)
ROP .... Recovery Operating Plan [*NASA*] (IAA)
ROP .... Refined Oil Products
ROP .... Regional Operating Plan [*Department of Labor*]
ROP .... Regional Oversight Policy [*Environmental Protection Agency*] (GFGA)
ROP .... Registered Options Principal
ROP .... Reorder Point [*Navy*] (NG)
ROP .... Reorder Price
ROP .... Repeat Offenders Project
ROP .... Republic of Panama
ROP .... Republic of the Philippines
ROP .... Requirements Objectives Period
ROP .... Retinopathy of Prematurity [*Medicine*]
ROP .... Right Occipitoposterior [*A fetal position*] [*Obstetrics*]
ROP .... Right Outside Position [*Dancing*]
ROP .... Rites of Passage
ROP .... Robson Petroleum Ltd. [*Toronto Stock Exchange symbol*]
ROP .... Roll-Over Protection Equipment (MCD)
ROP .... Rookie Orientation Program [*Automobile racing*]
Rop .... Roper on Legacies [*4 eds.*] [*1799-1847*] [*A publication*] (DLA)
ROP .... Rota [*Mariana Islands*] [*Airport symbol*] (OAG)
ROP .... Rotating Observation Platform (IAA)
ROP .... Royal Oman Police [*ICAO designator*] (FAAC)
ROP .... Royal Order of Piast (EA)
ROP .... Run of Paper [*Business term*]
ROP .... Run of Press [*i.e., on an unspecified page or plate in web press set-up*] [*Printing*]
ROP .... Run of Publication (NTCM)
ROP₃ .... Revision of Procurement Policy and Procedures
ROPA .... Record of Procurement Action (COE)
ROPA .... Regional Organ Procurement Agency [*Medicine*] (DAVI)
ROPA .... Reserve Officer Personnel Act of 1954
ROPAR .... Regional Operators Program for Aircraft Reliability
ROPB .... Reserve Officers Promotion Board [*Air Force*]

ROPBX .... Reference Our Private Branch Exchange Message (SAA)
ROPE .... Remotely Operated Platform Electronic [*Submarine technology*]
ROPE .... Respiratory-Ordered Phase Encoding [*Medicine*] (DMAA)
ROPE .... Reunion of Professional Entertainers (EA)
ROPER .... Regional Operators Program for Engine Reliability
Roper .... Roper Industries, Inc. [*Associated Press*] (SAG)
ROPES .... Regional Occupation Planning and Evaluation System (EDAC)
ROPES .... Remote Online Print Executive System
ROPEVAL .... Readiness/Operational Evaluation (NVT)
ROPEVAL .... Rim of the Pacific Evaluation (MCD)
ROPF .... Research into One-Parent Families [*British*]
Rop H & W ... Roper's Law of Property between Husband and Wife [*2nd ed.*] [*1826*] [*A publication*] (DLA)
ROPHO .... Reference Our Telephone Call (NOAA)
Rop Husb & Wife... Roper's Law of Property between Husband and Wife [*A publication*] (DLA)
ROPIS .... Response of Plants to Interacting Stress Program [*Electric Power Research Institute*]
Rop Leg .... Roper on Legacies [*A publication*] (DLA)
ROPM .... Remote Operations Protocol Machine [*Telecommunications*] (OSI)
ROPMA .... Reserve Officers Personnel Management Act [*Proposed*]
ROPME .... Regional Organization for the Protection of the Marine Environment [*Safat, Kuwait*] (EAIO)
ROPOS .... Remotely Operated Platform for Ocean Science [*Marine science*] (OSRA)
ROPP .... Receive-Only Page Printer
ROPP .... Review of Plant Pathology [*Database*] [*Commonwealth Mycological Institute*] [*Information service or system*] (CRD)
Rop Prop ..... Roper's Law of Property between Husband and Wife [*2nd ed.*] [*1826*] [*A publication*] (DLA)
ROPR .... Roper Industries [*NASDAQ symbol*] (TTSB)
ROPR .... Roper Industries, Inc. [*NASDAQ symbol*] (SAG)
ROPRA .... Reserve Officer Performance Recording Activity
Rop Rev ..... Roper on Revocation of Wills [*A publication*] (DLA)
ROPS .... Range Operation Performance Summary
ROPS .... RasterOps (EFIS)
R(OPS) .... Ring Off-Premises Station [*Telecommunications*] (OTD)
ROPS .... Roll-Over Protection Standards (WPI)
ROPS .... Roll-Over Protection System [*for tractors*]
ROPS .... Roll Over Protective Structures [*NASA*] (KSC)
ROPT .... Remaining Number of Operations
ROPU .... RADAR Overheat Protection Unit (MCD)
ROQ .... Houghton Lake, MI [*Location identifier FAA*] (FAAL)
ROQ .... Recruiter of the Quarter [*Navy*] (DNAB)
ROQ .... Reordering Quality
ROR .... Koror [*Palau Islands*] [*Airport symbol*] (OAG)
ROR .... Range-Only RADAR [*Military*] (AABC)
ROR .... Rapid-Onset-Rate [*Air Force*] (DOMA)
ROR .... Rate of Read
ROR .... Rate of Return (MCD)
ROR .... Released on Own Recognizance [*Law*]
ROR .... Repair of Repairables (MCD)
ROR .... Repair, Overhaul, Restoration (MCD)
ROR .... Residual Oil Remover [*Lens cleaner*] [*V-Vax Products*]
ROR .... Return of Repairables
ROR .... Return on Revenue
ROR .... Right of Rescission [*Business term*]
ROR .... Rochester Minerals [*Vancouver Stock Exchange symbol*]
ROR .... Rocket on Rotor
ROR .... Rockton & Rion Railway [*AAR code*]
ROR .... Roraima Airways [*Guyana*] [*FAA designator*] (FAAC)
Ror .... Rorschach [*Inkblot test*] (STED)
ROR .... Rorschach [*Test*]
ROR .... Rotate Right [*Computer science*]
ROR .... Rubery Owen-Rockwell [*Automotive industry supplier*]
ror .... Run of Reel [*Broadcasting*] (WDMC)
RORA .... Aguni [*Ryukyu Islands*] [*ICAO location identifier*] (ICLI)
RORA .... Reliable Operate RADAR Altimeter
RORA .... Reserve Officer Recording Activity
RORC .... Royal Ocean Racing Club [*British*]
RORCE .... Rate of Return on Capital Employed (DS)
RORD .... Return on Receipt of Document [*Business term*]
RORE .... Iejima [*Ryukyu Islands*] [*ICAO location identifier*] (ICLI)
Ro Rep .... Robards' Texas Conscript Cases [*1862-65*] [*A publication*] (DLA)
Ro Rep .... Rolle's English King's Bench Reports [*A publication*] (DLA)
ROREQ .... Reference Our Requisition (NOAA)
Rorer Jud Sales... Rorer on Void Judicial Sales [*A publication*] (DLA)
Rorer RR ..... Rorer on Railways [*A publication*] (DLA)
RORET .... Authorized Rotational Retention [*Navy*]
RORG .... Naha [*Ryukyu Islands*] [*ICAO location identifier*] (ICLI)
RORH .... Hateruma [*Ryukyu Islands*] [*ICAO location identifier*] (ICLI)
RO/RI .... Redistribution Out/Redistribution In (CINC)
Ror Int St L... Rorer on Inter-State Law [*A publication*] (DLA)
RORIS .... Remote Operated Radiographic Inspection System
Ror Jud Sal... Rorer on Void Judicial Sales [*A publication*] (DLA)
RORK .... Kitadaito [*Ryukyu Islands*] [*ICAO location identifier*] (ICLI)
RO/RO .... Roll-On/Roll-Off [*Shipping*] (AFM)
RO-RO .... Rolls Royce [*Automobile*] [*Slang*] (DSUE)
RORQN .... Reference Requisition from Our Office (FAAC)
RORS .... Realignment of Resources and Services (MCD)
RORS .... Shimojishima [*Ryukyu Islands*] [*ICAO location identifier*] (ICLI)
RORSAT .... RADAR Ocean Reconnaissance Satellite (MCD)
RORT .... Report on Reimbursable Transactions [*DoD*]
RORT .... Tarama [*Ryukyu Islands*] [*ICAO location identifier*] (ICLI)
RORU .... Rest of Route Unchanged [*Aviation*] (FAAC)

RoRx............	Radiation Therapy (DAVI)
RORY............	Yoron [Ryukyu Islands] [ICAO location identifier] (ICLI)
ROS...............	ATS-Servicii de Transport Aerian [Italy ICAO designator] (FAAC)
ROS...............	RADAR Order Switch
ROS...............	Radius of Suspension
ROS...............	Range of Spares (MCD)
ROS...............	Range Operations Supervisor (MUGU)
ROS...............	Range Operation Station
ROS...............	Rate of Speed (MCD)
ROS...............	Rat Osteosarcoma [Cell line]
ROS...............	Reactive Oxygen Species
ROS...............	Read-Only Storage [Computer science]
ROS...............	Ready Operating Status (DNAB)
ROS...............	Record-on-Silicon (AAEL)
ROS...............	Reduced Operational Status [Military]
ROS...............	Reed Organ Society (EA)
ROS...............	Registration Offering Statistics System [Securities and Exchange Commission] (GFGA)
ROS...............	Regulated Oxygen Supply (MCD)
ROS...............	Regulated Oxygen System (NASA)
ROS...............	Remote Operating System (IAA)
ROS...............	Remote Operations Service [Telecommunications] (OSI)
ROS...............	Remote Optical Sight [Military] (CAAL)
ROS...............	Remote Optical System
ROS...............	Removable Overhead Structure (MCD)
ROS...............	Reporter on Scene (NTCM)
ROS...............	Report Originator System [Military] (CAAL)
ROS...............	Representative Observation Site [Weather observing facility] [Air Force]
ROS...............	Requisition on Stores [Nuclear energy] (NRCH)
ROS...............	Research Optical Sensor (MCD)
ROS...............	Resident Operating System
ROS...............	Residual Oil Saturation [Petroleum technology]
ROS...............	Restored Oil Shales
ROS...............	Return from Overseas [Military]
ROS...............	Return on Sales
ROS...............	Review of Systems [Medicine]
ROS...............	Revised Occupant Simulation
ROS...............	Rights of Stockholders [Investment term] (MHDW)
ROS...............	Robotics Operating System
ROS...............	Rod Outer Segments [of the retina]
ROS...............	Rosa [Rose] [Pharmacology] (ROG)
ROS...............	Rosario [Argentina] [Airport symbol] (OAG)
ROS...............	Rosary
Ros...............	Roscommon [County in Ireland] (WGA)
ROS...............	Roseneath [New Zealand] [Seismograph station code, US Geological Survey Closed] (SEIS)
ROS...............	Rose Resources Corp. [Vancouver Stock Exchange symbol]
RoS...............	Rostral Sulcus (DB)
ROS...............	Roswell Public Library, Roswell, NM [OCLC symbol] (OCLC)
ROS...............	Rotary on Stamps Fellowship (EA)
ROS...............	Rotating Optical Scanner
ROS...............	Royal Order of Scotland (EA)
ROS...............	Run of Schedule [Commercial announcement to be broadcast throughout the program schedule] [Advertising]
ROS...............	Run-of-Station [Broadcasting] (WDMC)
ROS...............	Rush Order Service
ROSA............	Recording Optical Spectrum Analyzer (MCD)
ROSA............	Record One Stop Association [Defunct] (EA)
ROSA............	Remotely-Operated Service Arm [Nuclear energy] (NUCP)
ROSA............	Report of Student Answers [Scoring sheet for the Scholastic Aptitude Test (SAT)] (PAZ)
ROSA............	Report of Supply Activity (MCD)
ROSAR........	Read-Only Storage Address Register
Rosary C......	Rosary College (GAGS)
ROSAT........	RADAR Ocean Surveillance Satellite (NVT)
ROSAT........	Roentgen Satellite [Space research]
ROSC...........	Reserve Officers Sanitary Corps
ROSC...........	Restoration of Spontaneous Circulation
ROSC...........	Road Operators Safety Council [British]
Rosc............	Roscoe's Reports of the Supreme Court [1861-78] [South Africa] [A publication] (DLA)
ROSC...........	Roscommon [County in Ireland] (ROG)
Rosc Act.....	Roscoe on Actions [1825] [A publication] (DLA)
Rosc Adm....	Roscoe's Admiralty Jurisdiction and Practice [A publication] (DLA)
Rosc Am......	Pro Sexto Roscio Amerino [of Cicero] [Classical studies] (OCD)
Rosc Bdg Cas...	Roscoe's Digest of Building Cases [4th ed.] [1900] [A publication] (DLA)
Rosc Bills....	Roscoe's Bills of Exchange [2nd ed.] [1843] [A publication] (DLA)
Rosc Civ Pr...	Roscoe's Outlines of Civil Procedure [2nd ed.] [1880] [A publication] (DLA)
Rosc Cr.......	Roscoe's Law of Evidence in Criminal Cases [16 eds.] [1835-1952] [A publication] (DLA)
Rosc Crim Ev...	Roscoe's Law of Evidence in Criminal Cases [16 eds.] [1835-1952] [A publication] (DLA)
Rosc Ev......	Roscoe's Nisi Prius Evidence [20th ed.] [1934] [A publication] (DLA)
Rosc Jur......	Roscoe's Jurist [England] [A publication] (DLA)
Rosc Light...	Roscoe's Law of Light [4th ed.] [1904] [A publication] (DLA)
Rosc NP	Roscoe's Law of Evidence at Nisi Prius [20 eds.] [1827-1934] [A publication] (DLA)
ROSCO.......	Rotating Stratified Combustion [Automotive engineering]
ROSCOE......	RADAR and Optical Systems Code
ROSCOE.......	Remote Operating System Conventional Operating Environment [Computer science] (IAA)
Roscoe	Roscoe's Reports of the Supreme Court of Cape Of Good Hope [South Africa] [A publication] (DLA)
Roscoe Bldg Cas...	Roscoe's Digest of Building Cases [England] [A publication] (DLA)
Roscoe Cr Ev...	Roscoe's Law of Evidence in Criminal Cases [16 eds.] [1835-1952] [A publication] (DLA)
Roscoe's BC..	Roscoe's Digest of Building Cases [England] [A publication] (DLA)
ROSCOM......	Roscommon [County in Ireland]
ROSCOP	Report of Observations/Samples Collected by Oceanographic Programs [Intergovernmental Oceanographic Commission] (MSC)
ROSCOP	Report on Oceanographic Cruises and Data Stations (GNE)
Rosc PC	Roscoe's English Prize Cases [1745-1859] [A publication] (DLA)
Rosc Pl	Roscoe's Pleading [1845] [A publication] (DLA)
ROSDAL.......	Representation of Structure Diagrams Arranged Linearly [Structure notation shorthand] [Chemistry]
ROSDR	Read-Only Storage Data Register
ROSE	Reconstruction by Optimized Series Expansion [Of large molecules]
ROSE	Remotely Operated Special Equipment [Nuclear energy]
ROSE	Remote Operations Service Element [Computer science] (TNIG)
ROSE	Remote Optical Sensing of Emissions [Instrumentation]
ROSE	Research Open Systems in Europe [Computer science] (BARN)
ROSE	Resident Operational Support Equipment
ROSE	Residuum Oil Supercritical Extraction [Petroleum refining]
ROSE	Retrieval by Online Search [Computer science]
ROSE	Rising Observational Sounding Equipment
ROSE	Rivera Ocean Seismic Experiment
Rose	Rose's English Bankruptcy Reports [A publication] (DLA)
ROSE	Rosette [Cytology] (DAVI)
ROSE	Rural Oxidants in the Southern Environment [Marine science] (OSRA)
ROSE	T R Financial [NASDAQ symbol] (TTSB)
ROSE	TR Financial Corp. [NASDAQ symbol] (SAG)
Rose Bankr...	Rose's English Bankruptcy Reports [1810-16] [A publication] (DLA)
Rose Bankr (Eng)...	Rose's English Bankruptcy Reports [A publication] (DLA)
Rose BC	Rose's English Bankruptcy Reports [A publication] (DLA)
ROSEBUD	Rare Object Searches with Bolometers Underground [Astrophysics]
Rose Dig	Rose's Digest of Arkansas Reports [A publication] (DLA)
Rose-Hulman Inst Tech...	Rose-Hulman Institute of Technology (GAGS)
Rosenberger...	Street Railway Law [United States] [A publication] (DLA)
Rosenberger Pock LJ...	Rosenberger's Pocket Law Journal [A publication] (DLA)
Rose Notes...	Rose's Notes on United States Reports [A publication] (DLA)
Rose RA	Roscoe on Real Actions [A publication] (DLA)
Rose St D....	Roscoe on Stamp Duties [A publication] (DLA)
RoseStr........	Rose's Stores [Associated Press] (SAG)
ROSET	Register of Solicitors Employing Trainees (ILCA)
Rose WC	Rose. Will Case [New York] [A publication] (DLA)
ROSIE	Reconnaissance by Orbiting Ship-Identification Equipment
ROSIE	Rooters Organized to Stimulate Interest and Enthusiasm [Women baseball fans, Cincinnati]
ROSIE	Rule Oriented System for Implementing Expertise (MCD)
ROSL	Royal Overseas League [British] (DI)
ROSLA	Raising of the School-Leaving Age (WDAA)
ROSMAR......	Rosmarinus [Rosemary] [Pharmacology] (ROG)
ROSO...........	Relay-Operated Sampling Oscilloscope
ROSP	Report on Syndicated Programs [A.C. Nielsen Co.] [A publication] (DOAD)
RoSPA	Royal Society for the Prevention of Accidents [British]
ROSPA........	Royal Society for the Prevention of Accidents [British] (AIE)
ROSR...........	Radio On-Scene Report (WDMC)
ROSR...........	Real-Time On-Scene Report (NTCM)
ROSS	Review of Subjective Symptoms [Medicine] (DMAA)
ROSS	Ross Systems [NASDAQ symbol] (TTSB)
ROSS	Ross Systems, Inc. [NASDAQ symbol] (SPSG)
Ross Cont ...	Ross on Contracts [A publication] (DLA)
Ross Conv...	Ross' Lectures on Conveyancing, Etc. [Sc.] [A publication] (DLA)
Ross LC......	Ross's Leading Cases in the Law of Scotland (Land Rights) [1638-1840] [A publication] (DLA)
Ross LC......	Ross's Leading Cases on Commercial Law [England] [A publication] (DLA)
Ross Ldg Cas...	Ross's Leading Cases in the Law of Scotland (Land Rights) [A publication] (DLA)
Ross Ldg Cas...	Ross's Leading Cases on Commercial Law [A publication] (DLA)
Ross Lead Cas...	Ross' Leading Cases [England] [A publication] (DLA)
Ross Lead Cas...	Ross's Leading Cases in the Law of Scotland (Land Rights) [1638-1840] [A publication] (DLA)
RossStr........	Ross Stores, Inc. [Associated Press] (SAG)
RossSy........	Ross Systems, Inc. [Associated Press] (SAG)
RossTch.......	Ross Technology, Inc. [Associated Press] (SAG)
ROSS TEST...	Ross Test of Higher Congnitive Processes (TES)
Ross V & P...	Ross on Vendors and Purchasers [2nd ed.] [1826] [A publication] (DLA)
ROST	Regional Office of Science and Technology [UNESCO] (MSC)
ROST	Ross Stores [NASDAQ symbol] (TTSB)
ROST	Ross Stores, Inc. [Newark, CA] [NASDAQ symbol] (NQ)
ROSTA	Regional Office for Science and Technology in Africa [UNESCO] [See also BRUSTA] [Nairobi, Kenya] (EAIO)
ROSTE	Regional Office for Science and Technology for Europe [UNESCO] [Italy] (EAIO)
ROSTSCA.....	Regional Office of Science and Technology for South and Central Asia [UNESCO] (IRC)
ROSTSEA.....	Regional Office of Science and Technology for Southeast Asia [UNESCO] (IRC)
roswd..........	Rosewood (VRA)
ROT	RADAR on Target

ROT	Range on Target
ROT	Rate of Turn
ROT	Read-Only Tag
ROT	Red Oak Tannins [*in leaves*]
ROT	Reference Our Telex (DS)
ROT	Registered Occupational Therapist (DAVI)
ROT	Registered Options Trader [*Investment term*] (NUMA)
ROT	Remaining Operating Time (NASA)
ROT	Remedial Occupation Therapy
ROT	Reserve Oil Tank (MSA)
ROT	Reusable Orbital Transport [*Aerospace*]
ROT	Right Occipitotransverse [*A fetal position*] [*Obstetrics*]
ROT	Right Outer Thigh [*Injection site*]
ROT	Rotary (AAG)
ROT	Rotate (AAG)
ROT	Rotating Light [*Navigation signal*]
ROT	Rotation (NAKS)
ROT	Rotator [*A type of muscle*] (DAVI)
ROT	Rotor (ADA)
ROT	Rotorua [*New Zealand*] [*Seismograph station code, US Geological Survey Closed*] (SEIS)
ROT	Rotorua [*New Zealand*] [*Airport symbol*] (OAG)
ROT	Rule of Thumb
ROT	Running Object Table [*Computer science*]
ROT	Runway Occupancy Time [*FAA*] (TAG)
ROT	Tarom, Romanian Air Transport [*ICAO designator*] (FAAC)
ROTAB	Rotable Table
ROT ABCCC	Rotational Airborne Command and Control Center (CINC)
ROTAC	Rotary Oscillating Torque Actuators
ROTAD	Required Overseas Terminal Arrival Date (DNAB)
RotaryPw	Rotary Power International, Inc. [*Associated Press*] (SAG)
ROTAS	Rotate and Slide (DNAB)
Rotavapor	Rotary Evaporator
ROT AWS	Rotational Air Weather Squadron (CINC)
ROT BS	Rotational Bomb Squadron (CINC)
ROTC	Reserve Officers' Training Corps [*Separate units for Army, Navy, Air Force*]
ROTC	Rotech Medical [*NASDAQ symbol*] (TTSB)
ROTC	RoTech Medical Corp. [*Orlando, FL*] [*NASDAQ symbol*] (NQ)
ROTCC	Receiver-Off-Hook Tone Connecting Circuit
Rot Chart	Rotulus Chartarum [*Charter Roll*] [*Latin A publication*] (DLA)
Rot Claus	Rotuli Clause [*Close Roll*] [*Latin A publication*] (DLA)
ROTCM	Reserve Officers' Training Corps Manual (AABC)
ROTCR	Reserve Officers' Training Corps Region (AABC)
Rot Cur Reg	Rotuli Curiae Regis [*1194-99*] [*Latin A publication*] (DLA)
ROTE	Range Optical Tracking Equipment (AAG)
ROTE	Role of Occupational Therapy with the Elderly [*Project*]
ROTE AREFS	Rotating Air Refueling Squadron (CINC)
Rotech	Rotech Medical Corp. [*Associated Press*] (SAG)
ROTEL	Rolling Hotel [*European bus-tour system*]
ROTFI	Rotational Tolometry
RO terminal	Receive Only Terminal [*Computer science*]
ROTERO	Roterodamum [*Rotterdam*] (ROG)
ROTF	Rolling on the Floor
ROTF	Russian Orthodox Theological Fund (EA)
ROT FIS	Rotating Fighter Interceptor Squadron (CINC)
ROT FIS DET	Rotating Fighter Interceptor Squadron Detachment (CINC)
ROTFL	Rolling on the Floor Laughing [*Computer hacker terminology*] (NHD)
Rot Flor	Rotae Florentine [*Reports of the Supreme Court of Florence*] [*Latin A publication*] (DLA)
ROTH	Read-Only Tape Handler
R-OTH	Relocatable Over-The-Horizon [*Radar*] (DOMA)
ROTHR	Relocatable Over-the-Horizon RADAR
ROTI	CluckCorp International, Inc. [*NASDAQ symbol*] (SAG)
ROTI	Range Optical Tracking Instrument
ROTI	Recording Optical Tracking Instrument [*Missiles*]
ROTI	Reinforced Oxide Throat Insert
ROTL	Remote Office Test Line [*Bell Laboratories*]
ROTLT/BCN	Rotating Light or Beacon
ROTM	Futema [*Ryukyu Islands*] [*ICAO location identifier*] (ICLI)
ROTMH	Raised Oil-Tight Manhole [*Shipfitting*]
ROTN	Rotation (ROG)
ROTO	Rotogravure [*Printing process*] (NTCM)
ROTO	Roto-Rooter, Inc. [*Cincinnati, OH*] [*NASDAQ symbol*] (NQ)
ROTOMT	Rotometer
Rotonic	Rotonics Manufacturing [*Associated Press*] (SAG)
ROTOR	Rotorcraft Helicopter [*Pilot rating*] (AIA)
RotoRtr	Roto Rooter, Inc. [*Associated Press*] (SAG)
ROTP	Regular Officer Training Plan [*Canada*]
Rot Parl	Rotulae Parliamentariae [*Latin A publication*] (DLA)
Rot Pat	Rotuli Patenes [*Latin A publication*] (DLA)
Rot Plac	Rotuli Placitorum [*Latin A publication*] (DLA)
ROT PROJ	Rotation Project (DNAB)
ROTR	Read-Only Typing Reperforator (NITA)
ROTR	Receive-Only Tape Reperforator [*Computer science*] (IAA)
ROTR	Receive-Only Typing Reperforator
ROTR	Rotator [*Electromagnetics*]
ROT RCS	Rotational RADAR Calibration Squadron (CINC)
ROTR-S/P	Receive-Only Typing Reperforator - Series to Parallel
ROTS	RADAR Observer Testing System
ROTS	Range on Target Signal
ROTS	Remote Operator Task Station [*Air Force*]
ROTS	Reusable Orbital Transport System [*Aerospace*] (IAA)
ROTS	Rotary Out Trunk Switch [*Telecommunications*] (TEL)
ROTSAL	Rotate and Scale [*Computer science*]
ROTT	Rate of Turntable
ROTT	Reorder Tone Trunks [*Telecommunications*] (TEL)
ROT TAS	Rotational Tactical Assault Squadron (CINC)
ROT TBS	Rotational Tactical Bomber Squadron (CINC)
ROT TCS	Rotational Troop Carrier Squadron (CINC)
ROTTER	Rotterdam (ROG)
Rottlund	Rottlund Co. [*Associated Press*] (SAG)
ROT TX	Rotating Transformer
Rotuli Curiae Reg	Rotuli Curiae Regis [*1194-99*] [*Latin A publication*] (DLA)
ROTV	Reusable Orbital Transport Vehicle [*Aerospace*]
ROU	Radio Officers Union [*British*]
ROU	Recurrent Oral Ulcer [*Medicine*] (DMAA)
ROU	Rouge Industries [*NYSE symbol*] [*Formerly, Rouge Steel*] (SG)
ROU	Rouge Steel 'A' [*NYSE symbol*] (TTSB)
ROU	Rouge Steel Co. [*NYSE symbol*] (SAG)
ROU	Rougiers [*France*] [*Seismograph station code, US Geological Survey Closed*] (SEIS)
ROU	Rouyn Ressources Minieres, Inc. [*Toronto Stock Exchange symbol*]
ROU	Russe [*Bulgaria*] [*Airport symbol*] (OAG)
ROU	Uruguay [*International vehicle registration*] (ODBW)
RougeStl	Rouge Steel Co. [*Associated Press*] (SAG)
ROUL	Rouleaux [*Formation Differential*] [*Cytology*] (DAVI)
ROUL	Rouletted (ROG)
Roum P	Roumanian Pharmacopoeia [*A publication*]
Round Dom	Round's Law of Domicil [*1861*] [*A publication*] (DLA)
Round L & A	Round's Right of Light and Air [*1868*] [*A publication*] (DLA)
Round Lien	Round's Law of Lien [*1863*] [*A publication*] (DLA)
Roundup M	Roundup Magazine [*A publication*] (BRI)
Rouse	Rouse Co. [*Associated Press*] (SAG)
Rouse Conv	Rouse's Practical Conveyancer [*3rd ed.*] [*1867*] [*A publication*] (DLA)
Rouse Cop	Rouse's Copyhold Enfranchisement Manual [*3rd ed.*] [*1866*] [*A publication*] (DLA)
Rouse Pr Mort	Rouse's Precedents and Conveyances of Mortgaged Property [*A publication*] (DLA)
R$_{OUT}$	Output Resistance (IDOE)
ROUT	Rollout (NAKS)
ROUT	Routine (AABC)
ROUTE	Route [*Commonly used*] (OPSA)
ROV	Refined Oil of Vitriol
ROV	Remotely Operated Vehicle [*Underwater robot*]
ROV	Remote Operated Valve (KSC)
ROV	Remote Optical Viewing
ROV	Repairs to Other Vessels
ROV	Report of Visit [*LIMRA*]
ROV	Restricted Overhaul (MCD)
ROV	Risk, Originality, and Virtuousity [*Scoring considerations in gymnastics competition*]
ROV	Rostov [*Former USSR Airport symbol*] (OAG)
ROV	Rover Airways International, Inc. [*ICAO designator*] (FAAC)
ROVAC	Rotary Vane Air Cycle (MCD)
ROVD	Relay-Operated Voltage Divider
ROVNITE	Remaining Overnight
ROVS	Remote Optical Viewing System
ROVS	Russkly Obshche-Voyenskiy Soyuz [*Russian Armed Forces Union*] (LAIN)
ROW	Randstrom Manufacturing Corp. [*Vancouver Stock Exchange symbol*]
ROW	Relocate Out of Washington [*Navy*] (NG)
ROW	Rendu-Osler-Weber Syndrome [*Medicine*] (DMAA)
ROW	Requisition on Warehouse [*Nuclear energy*] (NRCH)
ROW	Rest of World [*Newly industrialized countries of Asia*]
ROW	Right of Way
ROW	Rights of Women [*British*] [*An association*] (DBA)
ROW	Risk of War
ROW	Roll Welding
ROW	Roswell [*New Mexico*] [*Airport symbol*] (OAG)
ROW	Row [*Postal Service standard*] (OPSA)
ROW	Rowe Furniture [*NYSE symbol*] (TTSB)
ROW	Rowe Furniture Corp. [*NYSE symbol*] (SPSG)
ROW	Rowesville [*South Carolina*] [*Seismograph station code, US Geological Survey*] (SEIS)
ROWA	Read Once, Write All [*Computer science*]
Rowan	Rowan Companies, Inc. [*Associated Press*] (SAG)
ROW & PF	Rake Out, Wedge, and Point Flashings [*Construction*]
ROWB	Rowberrow [*England*]
Rowe	Rowe's Interesting Cases [*England and Ireland*] [*1798-1823*] [*A publication*] (DLA)
Rowe	Rowe's Interesting Parliamentary and Military Cases [*A publication*] (DLA)
RoweFrn	Rowe Furniture Corp. [*Associated Press*] (SAG)
Rowell	Rowell's Reports [*45-52 Vermont*] [*A publication*] (DLA)
Rowell El Cas	Rowell's Contested Election Cases [*A publication*] (DLA)
Row Eng Const	Rowland's Manual of the English Constitution [*1859*] [*A publication*] (DLA)
Rowe Rep	Rowe's Irish Reports [*A publication*] (DLA)
Rowe Sci Jur	Rowe's Scintilla Juris [*A publication*] (DLA)
ROW/FEPA	Riders of the Wind, the Field Events Player's Association (EA)
ROWP	Reference Overhaul Work Package (DNAB)
ROWPE	Reverse Osmosis Water Purification Equipment (MCD)
ROWPS	Reverse Osmosis Water Purification System (MCD)
ROWPU	Reverse Osmosis Water Purification Unit [*Army*] (RDA)
ROWPVT	Receptive One-Word Picture Vocabulary Test [*Educational test*]
ROWPVT-UE	Receptive One-Word Picture Vocabulary Test-Upper Extension (TES)
ROWS	RADAR Ocean Wave Spectrometer

ROWS......... Register of Weather Stations [*Meteorological Office*] (PDAA)
ROX........... Roseau, MN [*Location identifier FAA*] (FAAL)
ROX........... Roxburgh [*New Zealand*] [*Seismograph station code, US Geological Survey*] (SEIS)
ROX........... Run of Experiments (AAEL)
ROXB......... Roxburghe [*Style of bookbinding*] (ROG)
ROXB......... Roxburghshire [*County in Scotland*]
ROXL......... Rotate through X Left [*Computer science*]
ROXR......... Rotate through X Right [*Computer science*]
ROY........... Conifair Aviation, Inc. [*Canada ICAO designator*] (FAAC)
ROY........... Moultonboro, NH [*Location identifier FAA*] (FAAL)
ROY........... Rest of You (IIA)
ROY........... Rio Mayo [*Argentina*] [*Airport symbol*] (OAG)
ROY........... Rookie of the Year
ROY........... Royal
Roy........... Royale & Allegro-Royale [*Record label*]
Royal Aust Hist Soc J Proc... Royal Australian Historical Society. Journal and Proceedings [*A publication*]
RoyaleE...... Royale Energy Corp. [*Associated Press*] (SAG)
RoyalO....... Royal Oak Mines [*Associated Press*] (SAG)
RoyBk........ Royal Bank of Canada, Inc. [*Associated Press*] (SAG)
Royce......... Royce Value Trust, Inc. [*Associated Press*] (SAG)
RoyceMC.... Royce OTC Micro Capital Fund [*Associated Press*] (SAG)
RoycLab..... Royce Laboratories, Inc. [*Associated Press*] (SAG)
Roy Dig...... Royall's Digest Virginia Reports [*A publication*] (DLA)
ROYGBIV.... Red, Orange, Yellow, Green, Blue, Indigo, Violet [*Primary Colors*] [*Mnemonic aid*]
RoyGld....... Royal Gold Corp. [*Associated Press*] (SAG)
ROYL......... Royale Energy [*NASDAQ symbol*] (TTSB)
ROYL......... Royale Energy Corp. [*NASDAQ symbol*] (SAG)
RoylApl...... Royal Appliance Manufacturing [*Associated Press*] (SAG)
RoylD......... Royal Dutch Petroleum Co. [*Associated Press*] (SAG)
Royle Stock Sh... Royle on the Law of Stock Shares, Etc. [*A publication*] (DLA)
RoylGrip..... Royal Grip, Inc. [*Associated Press*] (SAG)
RoylInv...... Royale Investments, Inc. [*Associated Press*] (SAG)
ROYN......... Yonagunijima [*Ryukyu Islands*] [*ICAO location identifier*] (ICLI)
RoyPlm....... Royal Palm Beach Ltd. [*Associated Press*] (SAG)
RoyPls........ Royal Plastics Group Ltd. [*Associated Press*] (SAG)
Roy Soc Med... Royal Society of Medicine Journal (MEC)
ROZ........... Restricted Operations Zone [*Environmental science*] (COE)
RP............ Bristol-Myers Co. [*Research code symbol*]
R_p........... Parallel Resistance (IDOE)
R_p........... Plate Resistance (IDOE)
RP............ Precision Airlines [*ICAO designator*] (AD)
R_p........... Primary Resistance (IDOE)
RP............ Problems of Reconstruction [*British World War II*]
RP............ Providence Public Library, Providence, RI [*Library symbol Library of Congress*] (LCLS)
R_p........... Pulmonary Resistance [*Cardiology*] (MAE)
RP............ RADAR Plot (DEN)
RP............ Radial Artery Pressure [*Medicine*]
RP............ Radial Pulse [*Medicine*]
RP............ Radiation Pressure
RP............ Radiation Protection
RP............ Radical Proverbs [*A publication*]
R-P............ Radiologist-Pediatric
RP............ Radio Phone (DS)
RP............ Raid Plotter
RP............ Rally Point [*Air Force*]
RP............ Ranchers for Peace (EA)
RP............ Range Pulse
RP............ Raphe Pallidus [*Anatomy*]
RP............ Rapid Processing [*Film*] (MAE)
RP............ Rappen [*Monetary unit*] [*Switzerland*]
RP............ Rated Pressure (NATG)
RP............ Rate Package (AAG)
RP............ Rating Pending
RP............ Raynaud's Phenomenon [*Medicine*]
RP............ Reactive Protein [*Clinical chemistry*] (MAE)
RP............ Reactor Pressure [*Nuclear energy*] (NRCH)
RP............ Reactor Project [*Nuclear energy*] (NRCH)
RP............ Reader Printer
RP............ Reader Punch
RP............ Readiness Potential
RP............ Read Printer (NITA)
RP............ Real Part [*of complex number*] (DEN)
RP............ Real Property
RP............ Rear Projection [*Television*]
RP............ Receipt Pass (AAG)
RP............ Received Pronunciation [*of the English language*]
RP............ Receive Processor
RP............ Reception Poor [*Radio logs*]
RP............ Receptor Potential
RP............ Recommended Practice
RP............ Recorded Program (IAA)
RP............ Recorder Point (MCD)
RP............ Record Position (AAGC)
RP............ Record Processor [*Computer science*] (OA)
RP............ Records of the Past [*A publication*] (BJA)
RP............ Recovery Phase (IEEE)
RP............ Reddish Purple
RP............ Red Phosphorus [*Military*] (RDA)
RP............ Reduced Pressure (COE)
RP............ Reference Paper
RP............ Reference Pattern (NATG)

RP............ Reference Point
RP............ Reference Publication (MCD)
RP............ Reference Pulse
RP............ Refilling Point
RP............ Reformed Presbyterian
RP............ Refractory Period [*Medicine*]
RP............ Regeneration Project [*Later, CR*] (EA)
RP............ Re-Geniusing Project [*Defunct*] (EA)
RP............ Regimental Paymaster [*British military*] (DMA)
RP............ Regimental Police [*British*]
RP............ Registered Pharmacist (DAVI)
RP............ Registered Plumbers [*British*]
RP............ Regius Professor [*The King's Professor*] [*British*]
RP............ Regulatory Protein (DB)
R-P............ Reid-Provident [*Commercial firm*] (DAVI)
RP............ Reinforced Plastic [*Packaging*]
RP............ Relative Potency (DAVI)
RP............ Relative Pressure (KSC)
RP............ Relay Panel
RP............ Release Point [*Ground traffic*] [*Military*]
RP............ Reliability Program (IAA)
RP............ Relief Pitcher [*Baseball*]
R/P............ Relief Printing (DGA)
RP............ Religious Program Specialist [*Navy*] (DNAB)
RP............ Remote Pickup
RP............ Remote Printer (BUR)
RP............ Remote Processor (NITA)
RP............ Rent Regulation (Office of Price Stabilization) [*Economic Stabilization Agency*] [*A publication*] (DLA)
RP............ Reorder Point [*Army*]
RP............ Repair Period (NASA)
RP............ Repeater
RP............ Repetitively Pulsed (MCD)
RP............ Replaceable Pad (MCD)
RP............ Replacement Pilot [*Navy*]
RP............ Replenishment Park [*British*]
RP............ Reply Paid
RP............ Reply Prepaid (IAA)
RP............ Reporting Post [*RADAR*]
RP............ Reprint
RP............ Reproducers [*JETDS nomenclature*] [*Military*] (CET)
RP............ Reproducing Punch [*Computer science*] (IAA)
RP............ Republican Party [*Iraq*] [*Political party*] (BJA)
RP............ Republic of Panama
RP............ Republic of Portugal (BARN)
RP............ Republic of the Philippines
RP............ Republikeinse Party van Suidwesafrika [*Republican Party of South West Africa*] [*Namibia*] [*Political party*] (PPW)
RP............ Repurchase Agreement [*Also, REPO*] [*Investment term*]
RP............ Research Paper
RP............ Research Publications
RP............ Reserve Personnel [*Air Force*] (AFM)
RP............ Reserve Purchase
RP............ Resistance Plate (AAG)
RP............ Resist Pressure [*Industrial engineering*]
RP............ Resolving Power [*of a lens*]
RP............ Resource Processor [*Telecommunications*] (TSSD)
RP............ Respirable Particulate [*Environmental science*] (GFGA)
RP............ Respiratory Rate:Pulse Rate [*Index*] [*Medicine*]
RP............ Responsible Party (GNE)
RP............ Resting Potential [*Medicine*] (DB)
RP............ Resting Pressure [*Physiology*] (MAE)
RP............ Resting Pulse [*Physiology*]
RP............ Restoration Priority (CET)
RP............ Rest Pain [*Medicine*] (MAE)
RP............ Restriction of Privileges [*British military*] (DMA)
RP............ Resupply Provisions [*NASA*] (KSC)
RP............ Retained Personnel [*Military*]
RP............ Retinitis Pigmentosa [*Eye disease*] [*Ophthalmology*]
RP............ Retinitis Proliferans [*Ophthalmology*] (DAVI)
RP............ Retinyl Palmitate [*Organic chemistry*]
RP............ Retractor Penis [*Medicine*] (DB)
RP............ Retrograde Pyelography [*Medicine*]
RP............ Retroperitoneal [*Medicine*]
RP............ Return of Post
RP............ Return Premium
R/P............ Return to Port [*for Orders*] (DS)
RP............ Revealed Preference Analysis [*Economics*]
RP............ Reverend Pere [*Reverend Father*] [*French*]
RP............ Reverendus Pater [*Reverend Father*] [*Latin*]
R-P............ Reversed Phase [*Chromatography*]
RP............ Reverse Processing [*Chemical engineering*]
RP............ Revertive Pulsing
RP............ Review of Politics [*A publication*] (BRI)
RP............ Revision Proposal (NG)
Rp............ Revoked or Rescinded in Part [*Existing regulation or order abrogated in part*] [*Used in Shepard's Citations*] [*Legal term*] (DLA)
R/P............ Reward/Penalty
RP............ Rheumatoid Polyarthritis [*Medicine*] (DB)
RP............ Rhone-Poulenc [*France*] [*Research code symbol*]
RP............ Rhone-Poulenc ADR [*NYSE symbol*] (TTSB)
RP............ Rhone-Poulenc Co. [*NYSE symbol*] (SAG)
RP............ Ribosomal Protein [*Biochemistry*]
RP............ Ribos Phosphate [*Laboratory science*] (DAVI)
R/P............ Rise/Passive (MCD)

RP...............	Ristocetin-Polymyxin [*Antibacterial mixture*]
RP...............	Rocket Projectile
RP...............	Rocket Propellant
RP...............	Rockland and Pollin [*Scale*] [*Psychology*]
RP...............	Rodent Potency Dose
RP...............	Rollback Process [*Telecommunications*] (TEL)
RP...............	Roll Pad (MCD)
RP...............	Ron Pair
RP...............	Room and Pillar [*Coal mining*]
RP...............	Root Primordia [*Botany*]
RP...............	Rotary Pursuit [*Test for motor skill*]
RP...............	Rotatable Pool Quantity
RP...............	Rotuli Parliamentorum [*1278-1533*] [*Latin A publication*] (DLA)
RP...............	Round Punch
RP...............	Route Package (CINC)
RP...............	Royal Panopticon (ROG)
RP...............	Royal Provincials [*British military*] (DMA)
RP...............	Royal Society of Portrait Painters [*British*] (WA)
RP...............	Rules of Procedure
RP...............	Rupiah [*Monetary unit*] [*Indonesia*]
RP...............	Rust Preventive
RP...............	Specia [*France*] [*Research code symbol*]
RPA.............	Provence Aero Service [*France ICAO designator*] (FAAC)
RPA.............	Providence Athenaeum, Providence, RI [*Library symbol Library of Congress*] (LCLS)
RPA.............	RADAR Performance Analyzer
RPA.............	Radial Photon Absorptiometry [*Chemistry*] (DAVI)
RPA.............	Radio Paging Association [*British*] (DBA)
RPA.............	Radium Plaque Adaptometer [*Navy*]
RPA.............	Random Phase Approximation
RPA.............	Rationalist Press Association [*British*] (EAIO)
RPA.............	Real Property Administrator [*Building Owners and Managers Institute*] [*Designation awarded by*]
RPA.............	Record and Playback Assembly (MCD)
RPA.............	Record of Procurement Action (MCD)
RPA.............	Redundancy Payments Act [*1965*] [*British*] (DCTA)
RPA.............	Reentrant Process Allocator [*Telecommunications*] (TEL)
RPA.............	Regional Plan Association (EA)
RPA.............	Regional Planning Agency (PA)
RPA.............	Regional Planning Association (NADA)
RPA.............	Regional Ports Authority [*British*]
RPA.............	Regional Publishers Association (NTPA)
RPA.............	Registered Public Accountant
RPA.............	Register of Private Agents [*Victoria, Australia*]
RPA.............	Relative Peak Area [*Medicine*]
RPA.............	Renal Physicians Association (EA)
RPA.............	Renewal Projects Administration [*HUD*]
RPA.............	Replacement Price Accounting (ADA)
RPA.............	Replication Protein A [*Genetics*]
RPA.............	Republican Party of Australia [*Political party*]
RPA.............	Request for Procurement Action [*Authorization*] [*NASA*] (NASA)
RPA.............	Request Present Altitude [*Aviation*] (FAAC)
RPA.............	Reserve Personnel Appropriation
RPA.............	Reserve Personnel, Army
RPA.............	Resident Programmer Analyst [*Computer science*]
RPA.............	Resource Planning Associates, Cambridge, MA [*OCLC symbol*] (OCLC)
RPA.............	Response Profile Analysis [*National Demographics & Lifestyles, Inc.*]
RPA.............	Resultant Physiological Acceleration
RPA.............	Retarding Potential Analyzer [*NASA*]
RPA.............	Retinoylphorbolacetate [*Biochemistry*]
RPA.............	Retired Philosphers Association (EA)
RPA.............	Reverse Passive Anaphylazis [*Medicine*] (DMAA)
RPA.............	Ribonuclease Protection Assay [*Analytical biochemistry*]
RPA.............	Right Pulmonary Artery [*Medicine*]
RPA.............	Rolpa [*Nepal*] [*Airport symbol*] (OAG)
RPA.............	Rotorcraft Pilot's Associate [*Army*] (RDA)
RPA.............	Royal Pakistan Artillery [*British military*] (DMA)
RPA.............	Rubber Peptizing Agent
RPA.............	Rubber Proofers' Association [*British*] (BI)
RPA.............	Rural Pharmacists Association [*British*] (DBA)
RPA.............	Rural Preservation Association [*British*]
RPA.............	Rust Prevention Association [*Later, Crop Quality Council*]
RPAA...........	Rotating Phase Array Antenna
RPAB...........	Brown University, Annmary Brown Memorial Library, Providence, RI [*Library symbol Library of Congress*] (LCLS)
RPAC...........	Regional Paramedic Advisory Committee [*Emergency medicine*] (DAVI)
RPAE...........	Retarding Potential Analyzer Experiment [*NASA*]
RPAG...........	Retired Professionals Action Group [*Later, Gray Panthers*]
RPAM..........	American Mathematical Society, Providence, RI [*Library symbol Library of Congress*] (LCLS)
RPAM..........	Regional Public Affairs Manager [*Nuclear energy*] (NRCH)
RPAM..........	Research in Public Administration and Management [*British*]
RP & W.......	Rawle, Penrose, and Watts' Pennsylvania Reports [*1828-40*] [*A publication*] (DLA)
RPAO..........	Radium Plaque Adaptometer Operator [*Navy*]
RPAODS	Remotely Piloted Aerial Observation Detection System (MCD)
RPAP...........	Repap Enterprises Corp., Inc. [*NASDAQ symbol*] (NQ)
RPAPC........	Religious Press Associations Postal Coalition (EA)
RPAPF........	Repap Enterprises [*NASDAQ symbol*] (TTSB)
RPAPL........	Real Property Actions and Proceedings Law [*New York, NY A publication*]
RPAR...........	Rebuttable Presumption Against Regulation [*of pesticides*] [*Environmental Protection Agency*]

RPAS	Audubon Society of Rhode Island, Providence, RI [*Library symbol Library of Congress*] (LCLS)
RPAS	Reactor Protection Actuating Signal [*Nuclear energy*] (NRCH)
RPASC........	Royal Pakistan Army Service Corps [*British military*] (DMA)
RPASMC.....	Rubber and Plastic Adhesive and Sealant Manufacturers Council [*Later, Adhesive and Sealant Council*] (EA)
R Pat Cas....	Reports of Patent, Design, and Trade Mark Cases [*A publication*] (DLA)
RP-ATLF	Roscoe Pound - American Trial Lawyers Foundation (EA)
RpAuto........	Republic Automotive Parts, Inc. [*Associated Press*] (SAG)
RPaw	Pawtucket Public Library, Pawtucket, RI [*Library symbol Library of Congress*] (LCLS)
RPB	Aerorepublica [*Columbia*] [*FAA designator*] (FAAC)
RPB	Belleville, KS [*Location identifier FAA*] (FAAL)
RPB	Brown University, Providence, RI [*Library symbol Library of Congress*] (LCLS)
RPB	RADAR Plotting Board
RPB	Recognised Professional Body [*Marketing of Investments Board Organising Committee, London Stock Exchange*] [*Finance*]
RPB	Regional Preparedness Board [*Military*] (AABC)
RPB	Research to Prevent Blindness (EA)
RPB	Resources Protection Board
RPB	River Purification Board [*British*] (DCTA)
RPB	Royal Palm Beach Ltd. [*AMEX symbol*] (SPSG)
RPB	Royal Protection Branch [*of the London Metropolitan Police*]
Rpba	Periosteal Bone Apposition Rate [*Laboratory science*] (DAVI)
RPBG..........	Revised Program and Budget Guidance [*Military*]
RPBH..........	Butler Health Center, Providence, RI [*Library symbol Library of Congress*] (LCLS)
RPBio	Registered Professional Biologist [*Canada*] (ASC)
RPB-JH	Brown University, John Hay Library of Rare Books annd Special Collections, Providence, RI [*Library symbol Library of Congress*] (LCLS)
RPB-S	Brown University, Sciences Library, Providence, RI [*Library symbol Library of Congress*] (LCLS)
RPBSC	Rules Peculiar to the Business of the Supreme Court [*A publication*] (DLA)
RPC	Baltimore Regional Planning Commission [*Library network*]
RPC	RADAR Planning Chart
RPC	RADAR Processing Center
RPC	Radiation Protection Committee [*South Australia*]
RPC	Radiological Physics Center [*National Cancer Institute*]
RPC	Rapeseed Protein Concentrate [*Food technology*]
RPC	Readers per Copy [*Newspapers and magazines*]
RPC	Real Property Cases [*1843-48*] [*England*] [*A publication*] (DLA)
RPC	Real Property Commissioner's Report [*1832*] [*England*] [*A publication*] (DLA)
RPC	Records Processing Center [*Veterans Administration*]
RPC	Recreational Pilot Certificate [*Aviation*] (DA)
RPC	Recruiting Publicity Center [*Military*]
RPC	Reefed Parachute Canopy
RPC	Refugee Processing Center (MCD)
RPC	Regional Planning Center
RPC	Regional Planning Commission
RPC	Regional Preparedness Committee [*Civil Defense*]
RPC	Registered Protective Circuit
RPC	Registered Publication Clerk [*or Custodian*] [*Navy*]
RPC	Reliability Policy Committee (AAG)
RPC	Remotely Piloted Craft [*Navy*]
RPC	Remote Parameter Control [*Automotive engineering*]
RPC	Remote Position Control
RPC	Remote Power Controller
RPC	Remote Procedure Call [*Computer science*]
RPC	Remote Process Cell [*Nuclear energy*] (NRCH)
RPC	Remote Processor Controller (NITA)
RPC	Remount Purchasing Commission [*British military*] (DMA)
RPC	Renopericardial Canal [*Medicine*]
RPC	Repairable Provisioning Center (MCD)
RPC	Repair Parts Catalog
RPC	Repair Parts Cost (MCD)
RPC	Reparable Processing Center (AFM)
RPC	Reply Postcard
RPC	Reported Post Coastal (NATG)
RPC	Reports of English Patent Cases [*A publication*] (DLA)
RPC	Reports of Patent Cases [*Legal*] [*British*]
RPC	Reports of Patent, Design, and Trade Mark Cases [*A publication*] (DLA)
RPC	Report to Commander [*Military*]
RPC	Republican Policy Committee
RPC	Request the Pleasure of Your Company [*On invitations*] (DSUE)
RPC	Requisition Processing Cycle (MCD)
RPC	Research and Productivity Council [*Canada*] (IRC)
RPC	Research Planning Conference [*LIMRA*]
RPC	Resource Policy Center [*Dartmouth College*] [*Research center*] (RCD)
RPC	Ressources Phytogenetiques du Canada [*Plant Gene Resources of Canada - PGRC*]
RPC	Restrictive Practices Court [*Legal*] [*British*]
RPC	Restructured Pork Chop [*Food industry*]
RPC	Reticularis Pontis Caudalis [*Brain anatomy*]
RPC	Reverse-Phase Chromatography
RPC	Reverse-Phase Column
RPC	Rice Polishing Concentrate (OA)
RPC	River Patrol Craft [*Military*] (CINC)
RPC	Romanian Philatelic Club [*Defunct*] (EA)

RPC	Rotation Planar Chromatography
RPC	Row Parity Check (IEEE)
RPC	Royal Parks Constabulary [*British*]
RPC	Royal Pioneer Corps [*British*]
RPC	RPC Energy Services, Inc. [*Associated Press*] (SAG)
RPC	Rules of Practice in Patent Cases [*A publication*]
RPC	Rural Political Cadre [*Vietnam*]
RPC	Russian People's Center (EA)
RPC	Russian Privatization Center (ECON)
RPCA	Remotely Programmable Conference Arranger [*Telecommunications*] (TSSD)
RPCA	Reverse Passive Anaphylaxis [*Immunology*]
RPCAS	Requisition Priority Code Analysis System [*Army*]
RPCC	Reactor Physics Constants Center [*Argonne National Laboratory*]
RPCC	Remote Process Crane Cave [*Nuclear energy*] (NRCH)
RPCCA	Red Poll Cattle Club of America [*Later, ARPA*] (EA)
RPCF	Reiter Protein Complement Fixation [*Obsolete test for syphilis*]
RPCGN	Rapidly Progressive Crescenting Glomerulonephritis [*Medicine*] (DMAA)
RPCH	Reformed Presbyterian Church
RPCH	Rural Primary Care Hospital
RPCI	Regroupement des Partis de la Cote-D'Ivoire [*Regroupment of the Parties of the Ivory Coast*]
RP/CI	Reinforced Plastics/Composites Institute [*Later, SPICI*] (EA)
RPCK	Renopericardial Canal, Kidney [*Medicine*]
RP/CL	Reporting Post, Coastal Low [*RADAR*]
RPCLF	Revenue Properties Co. Ltd. [*NASDAQ symbol*] (SAG)
RPCLF	Revenue Properties Ltd [*NASDAQ symbol*] (TTSB)
RPCM	Rassemblement Populaire Caledonien et Metropolitain [*Caledonian and Metropolitan Popular Rally*] [*Political party*] (PPW)
RP/CM	Reporting Post, Coastal Medium [*RADAR*]
RPCO	Reclamation Program Control Officer [*Military*] (AFIT)
RPCP	Radioisotope-Powered Cardiac Pacemaker (MCD)
RPCP	Renopericardial Canal, Pericardium [*Medicine*]
RPCQ	Rural Press Club [*Queensland, Australia*]
RPCR	Rassemblement pour la Caledonie dans la Republique [*Popular Caledonian Rally for the Republic*] [*Political party*] (PPW)
RPCRAAIO ...	Receive and Process Complaints and Requests for Assistance, Advice, or Information Only [*Army*] (AABC)
RPC Rep......	Real Property Commissioner's Report [*1832*] [*England*] [*A publication*] (DLA)
RPCRS	Reactor Protection Control Rod System (IEEE)
RPCS	Reactor Plant Control System [*Nuclear energy*] (NRCH)
RPCS	Reject Processing and Control System (MHDB)
RPCU	Retropubic Cystourethropexy [*Urology*] (DAVI)
RPCV	Returned Peace Corps Volunteer
RPCV	Rural Press Club of Victoria [*Australia*]
RPCVCCA.....	Returned Peace Corps Volunteers Committee on Central America [*Defunct*] (EA)
RPCVD	Remote Plasma Chemical Vapor Deposition [*Coating technology*] [*Semiconductor technology*]
RPCWA	Rural Press Club of Western Australia
RPCX	Roberts Pharmaceutical [*NASDAQ symbol*] (TTSB)
RPCX	Roberts Pharmaceutical Corp. [*NASDAQ symbol*] (SAG)
RPD	RADAR Planning Device
RPD	RADAR Prediction Device
RPD	Radioisotope Power Device
RPD	Rapid (AAG)
RPD	Reactive Plasma Deposition
RPD	Reactor Plant Designer [*Nuclear energy*] (NRCH)
RPD	Reductive Photo Dehalogenation
RPD	Reflex Plasma Discharge
RPD	Regius Professor of Divinity (ROG)
RPD	Regulatory Policy Division [*Environmental Protection Agency*] (EPA)
RPD	Relative Power Density
RPD	Removable Partial Denture (DAVI)
RPD	Renewal Parts Data (MSA)
RPD	Repadre Resources Ltd. [*Vancouver Stock Exchange symbol*]
RPD	Repatriation Pension Decisions [*Australia A publication*]
RPD	Rerum Politicarum Doctor [*Doctor of Political Science*]
RPD	Research Planning Diagram (PDAA)
RPD	Reserves Available to Support Private, Noninterbank Deposits [*Federal Reserve System*]
RPD	Resistance Pressure Detector
RPD	Respiratory Protective Device [*Medicine*]
RPD	Retarding Potential Difference (IEEE)
RPD	Retired Pay Defense (NVT)
RPD	Rhode Island School of Design, Providence, RI [*Library symbol Library of Congress*] (LCLS)
RPD	Rocket Propulsion Department [*Royal Aircraft Establishment*] [*British*]
RPD & TM Cas...	Reports of Patent Design and Trade Mark Cases [*United Kingdom*] [*A publication*] (DLA)
RPDB	Repertoire Pratique de Droit Belge [*A publication*] (ILCA)
RPDES	Research Program Development and Evaluation Staff [*Department of Agriculture*]
RPDF	Radiation Protection Design Features (NRCH)
RPDH..........	Reserve Shutdown Planned Derated Hours [*Electronics*] (IEEE)
RPDL	Radioisotope Process Development Laboratory [*ORNL*]
RPDL	Rensselaer Polytechnic Institute Plasma Dynamics Laboratory [*Research center*] (RCD)
RPDL	Repair Parts Decision List [*Military*] (CAAL)
RPD LMG.....	Ruchnoy Pulemyot Degtyaryov Light Machine Gun [*Soviet-made weaponry*] [*Also, RPDM, RPDM LMG*]
RPDM	Ruchnoy Pulemyot Degtyaryov Light Machine Gun [*Soviet-made weaponry*] [*Also, RPD LMG, RPDM LMG*] [*Military*] (VNW)
RPDM LMG...	Ruchnoy Pulemyot Degtyaryov Light Machine Gun [*Soviet-made weaponry*] [*Also, RPD LMG, RPDM*] [*Military*] (VNW)
RPDMRC......	Reference or Partial Description Method Reason Code (MCD)
RPDO	Repair Parts Directive Order
RPDP	Recoverable Plasma Diagnostics Package (SSD)
R-PDQ	Revised Prescreening Developmental Questionnaire (TES)
RPDR	Reproducer (MSA)
RPDR	Rotating Packed Disk Reactor [*Chemical engineering*]
RPDS	Rapids (MCD)
RPDS	Retired Personnel Data System [*Air Force*]
RPDT	RADAR Prediction Data Table (PDAA)
RPDt	Registered Professional Dietitian
RPDTMC......	Reports of Patent, Design, and Trade Mark Cases [*Australia A publication*]
RPDWR........	Revised Primary Drinking Water Regulations
RPE	Elmwood Public Library, Providence, RI [*Library symbol Library of Congress*] (LCLS)
RPE	Radial Probable Error (IEEE)
RPE	Radio Production Executive (IAA)
RPE	Range Planning Estimate (MUGU)
RPE	Range Probable Error [*Formerly, Range Error Probable*] [*Air Force*] (NATG)
RPE	Rating of Perceived Exertion
RPE	Record of Personal Experience (AIE)
RPE	Reformed Protestant Episcopal
RPE	Registered Professional Engineer (IEEE)
RPE	Related Payroll Expense
RPE	Related Production Equipment (SAA)
RPE	Relative Price Effect
RPE	Reliability Project Engineer (NASA)
RPE	Remote Peripheral Equipment (IEEE)
RPE	Repair Parts Estimate (MCD)
RPE	Report of Patients Evacuated [*Aeromedical evacuation*]
RPE	Required Page-End Character [*Computer science*]
RPE	Resource Planning and Evaluation [*Nuclear energy*] (NRCH)
RPE	Retinal Pigment Epithelium
RPE	Rocket Propulsion Establishment [*British*] (KSC)
RPE	Ron Pair Enterprises [*Division of Wilson, Inc.*]
RPE	Rotating Platinum Electrode [*Electrochemistry*]
RPE	Royal Pakistan Engineers [*British military*] (DMA)
RPEA	Regional Planning and Evaluation Agency [*California State Board of Education*]
RP/ED	Rapid Prototyping/Evolutionary Design (MCD)
RPEN	Retry Pending (SSD)
RPEng.........	Providence Engineering Society, Providence, RI [*Library symbol Library of Congress*] (LCLS)
RPEP	Rabies Post-Exposure Prophylaxis [*Medicine*] (DMAA)
RPEP	Register of Planned Emergency Procedures [*Military*]
RPEV	Roadway Powered Electric Vehicle
RPF.............	RADAR Performance Figure (IAA)
RPF.............	Radiometer Performance Factor
RPF.............	Radio Position Finding [*A term for RADAR before early 1942*]
RPF.............	Radio Proximity Fuze
RPF.............	Rally for the Republic [*French Political party*] (ECON)
RPF.............	Real Property Facilities [*Army*] (AABC)
RPF.............	Reduced Physical Fidelity (MCD)
RPF.............	Reference Point Foundation (EA)
RPF.............	Reformatorische Politieke Federatie [*Reformist Political Federation*] [*Netherlands Political party*] (PPE)
RPF.............	Region Peaking Factor [*Nuclear energy*] (NRCH)
RPF.............	Registered Professional Forester
RPF.............	Reiter Protein Complement Fixation [*Obsolete test for syphilis*] (CPH)
RPF.............	Relaxed Pelvic Floor [*Medicine*]
RPF.............	Remote Personnel Facility
RPF.............	Remote Processing Facility (MCD)
RPF.............	Renal Plasma Flow [*Medicine*]
RPF.............	Repair Parts Facility (MCD)
rpf..............	Reperforated [*Philately*]
RPF.............	Retroperitoneal Fibrosis [*Medicine*] (DB)
RPF.............	Retroperitonel Fibrosis [*Medicine*] (WDAA)
RPF.............	Right Panel Front [*Nuclear energy*] (NRCH)
RPF.............	Rigid Plastic Foam
RPF.............	Roscoe Programming Facility (NITA)
RPF.............	Rotable Pool Factor (MCD)
RPF.............	Royal Pacific Sea Farms Ltd. [*Toronto Stock Exchange symbol Vancouver Stock Exchange symbol*]
RPF.............	Rwandan Patriotic Front [*Political party*]
RPFC	Ray Price Fan Club (EA)
RPFC	Recurrent Peak Forward Current
RPFCX	Davis Convertible Fund Cl.A [*Mutual fund ticker symbol*] (SG)
RPFFB	Foundation Fighting Blindness [*Formerly, RP Foundation Fighting Blindness*] (EA)
RPFFB	RP [*Retinitis Pigmentosa*] Foundation Fighting Blindness (EA)
RPFGX	Davis Financial Fund Cl.A [*Mutual fund ticker symbol*] (SG)
RPFMA	Rubber and Plastic Footwear Manufacturers' Association [*British*] (BI)
RPFOD	Reported for Duty (FAAC)
RPFRX	Davis Real Estate Fund Cl.A [*Mutual fund ticker symbol*] (SG)
RPFS	Radio Position Fixing System [*Aviation*] (DA)
RPFS	Rudder Pedal Force Sensor (MCD)
RPFT...........	Rudder Pedal Force Transducer (MCD)
RPG	Radar Product General [*Marine science*] (OSRA)
RPG	Radiation Protection Guide [*AEC*]
RPG	Radioisotopic Power Generator [*Navy*]
RPG	Rampage Resources Ltd. [*Vancouver Stock Exchange symbol*]

RPG	Random Pulse Generator [Telecommunications] (OA)
RPG	Rebounds per Game [Basketball, hockey]
RPG	Reflection Phase Grating [Acoustics]
RPG	Refugee Policy Group (EA)
RPG	Regional Planning Group (NATG)
RPG	Register Program Generator (HGAA)
RPG	Religion Publishing Group [Defunct] (EA)
RPG	Report Processor Generator (MCD)
RPG	Report Program Generator [Programming language] [1962]
RPG	Research Planning Guide (MCD)
RPG	Retrograde Pyelogram [Medicine]
RPG	Right Pedal Ganglion
RPG	River Patrol Group [Military] (VNW)
RPG	Rocket-Propelled Grenade
RPG	Role-Playing Game [Video game]
RPG	Rotary Pulse Generator
RPG	Rounds per Gun
RPGAN	Role-Playing Game Association Network (EA)
RPGC	Royal Perth Golf Club [Australia]
RPGG	Retroplacental Gamma Globulin [Immunology] (DAVI)
RPGMEC	Regional Postgraduate Medical Education Committee [Medicine] (DMAA)
RPGN	Rapidly Progressive Glomerular Nephritis [Medicine]
RPGN	Rapidly Progressive Glomerulonephritis [Nephrology] (DAVI)
RPGN	Right Pedal Giant Neuron (DB)
RPGPM	Rounds per Gun per Minute
RPH	Raypath Resources Ltd. [Vancouver Stock Exchange symbol]
RPH	Registered Pharmacist
RPH	Relative Pulse Height (OA)
RPH	Remember Pearl Harbor [Group] [World War II]
RPH	Remotely Piloted Helicopter
RP/H	Repairs, Heavy
RPH	Retroperitoneal Hemorrhage [Medicine] (DAVI)
RPH	Reverse Passive Hemagglutination (DB)
RPH	Revolutions per Hour
RPH	Rhode Island Hospital, Peters House Medical Library, Providence, RI [Library symbol Library of Congress] (LCLS)
RPH	Rideout Pyrohydrolysis
RPHA	Reverse Passive Hemagglutination [Clinical chemistry]
RPHAMFCA...	Reversed Passive Hemagglutination by Miniature Centrifugal Fast Analysis [Medicine] (DMAA)
RPhilS	Royal Philharmonic Society [British] (DI)
RPhO	Regional Pharmaceutical Officer [National Health Service] [British] (DI)
RPHPLC	Reversed-Phase High-Performance Liquid Chromatography (DB)
RPHST	Research Participation for High School Teachers [National Science Foundation]
RPI..............	Paradise Air (Pvt) Ltd. [Sri Lanka] [FAA designator] (FAAC)
RPI..............	RADAR Precipitation Integrator [National Weather Service]
RPI..............	Railway Progress Institute (EA)
RPI..............	Random Procedure Information (WDAA)
RPI..............	Rapeseed Protein Isolate [Food technology]
RPI..............	Rassemblement Populaire pour l'Independance [People's Rally for Independance] [Djibouti] [Political party] (PPW)
RPI..............	Rated Position Identifier (AFM)
RPI..............	Reaction Product Imaging [Chemistry]
RPI..............	Read, Punch, and Interpret
RPI..............	Real Property Inventory [Military]
RPI..............	Recover Processor Improvement (DWSG)
RPI..............	Registro de la Propiedad Industrial [Spanish Patent Office] [Information service or system] (IID)
RPI..............	Relative Position Indication (NRCH)
RPI..............	Relay Position Indicator
RPI..............	Remarried Parents, Inc. [Defunct] (EA)
RPI..............	Rensselaer Polytechnic Institute [Troy, NY] (MCD)
RPI..............	Republican Party of India [Political party] (PPW)
RPI..............	Research Price Index
RPI..............	Research Publications International [Database producer] (IID)
RPI..............	Resource Policy Institute (EA)
RPI..............	Responsive Production Inventory
RPI..............	Retail Prices Index [British]
RPI..............	Reticulocyte Production Index [Hematology]
RPI..............	Reversals per Inch (IAA)
RPI..............	Revolutions per Inch (IAA)
RPI..............	Rework Print Image (IAA)
RPI..............	Richmond Professional Institute [Virginia]
RPI..............	Rimpac Industries [Vancouver Stock Exchange symbol]
RPI..............	Rod Position Indicator [Nuclear energy] (NRCH)
RPI..............	Roller Path Inclination [Navy] (DOMA)
RPI..............	Roll Position Indicator (MCD)
RPI..............	Rose Polytechnic Institute [Indiana]
RPI..............	Rows per Inch (CIST)
RPI..............	Royal Polytechnic Institute (ROG)
RPIA	Resurgence Properties [NASDAQ symbol] (SAG)
RPIA	Rocket Propellant Information Agency (MCD)
RPIA	Roll Position Indicator Assembly
RPIAC	Retail Prices Index Advisory Committee [Department of Employment] [British]
RPIC	Reagan Political Items Collectors (EA)
RPIC	Republic Pictures (EFIS)
RPIC	Rock Properties Information Center [Purdue University] [National Science Foundation] (IID)
RPIC	Rubber and Plastics Industry Conference of the United Steelworkers of America (NTPA)

RPICCE	Round Pupil Intracapsular Cataract Extraction [Ophthalmology] (DAVI)
RPI/CIE	Rensselaer Polytechnic Institute/Center for Integrated Electronics [Troy, NY]
RPIE	Real Property Installed Equipment [Air Force] (MCD)
RPIE	Replacement of Photography Imagery Equipment (RDA)
RPIF	Real Property Industrial Fund
RPIFC	Robert Plant International Fan Club (EA)
RPIFC	Ronnie Prophet International Fan Club (EA)
RPII	Rotary Power Internationsl, Inc. [NASDAQ symbol] (SAG)
RPII	Rotary Power Intl [NASDAQ symbol] (TTSB)
RPI/MA	Rensselaer Polytechnic Institute/Microwave Acoustics Laboratory [Troy, NY]
RPIO	Registered Publication Issuing Office [Military]
RPIO	Responsible Planning and Implementation Officer (COE)
RPIPP	Reversed-Phase Ion-Pair Partition (DB)
RPIPP	Reverse Phase Ion-Pair Partition (DMAA)
RPIS	Real Property Inventory System (COE)
RPIS	Regional Plant Introduction Station (GNE)
RPIS	Rod Position Indication System [Nuclear energy] (NRCH)
RPIS	Rod Position Information System [Nuclear energy] (NRCH)
RPISU	Radon Progeny Integrating Sampling Unit (GNE)
RPIT	Related-Party International Transaction
RPJ	[The] Rise of Provincial Jewry [A publication] (BJA)
RPJ	Rotary Pressure Joint
RPJCB	John Carter Brown Library, Providence, RI [Library symbol Library of Congress] (LCLS)
RPK	Revenue Passenger Kilometer (AIA)
RPK	Ribophosphate Pyrophosphokinase [An enzyme]
RPK	Ribosephosphate Kinase (DMAA)
RPK	Roosevelt [Washington] [Seismograph station code, US Geological Survey] (SEIS)
RPL..............	Adrien Arpel [AMEX symbol] [Formerly, Alfin, Inc.]
RPL..............	RADAR Processing Language [Computer science] (IEEE)
RPL..............	Radiation Physics Laboratory [National Institute of Standards and Technology] (MCD)
RPL..............	Radio-Photo Luminescent [Dosimetry]
RPL..............	Radio Physics Laboratory (IAA)
RPL..............	Ramped Powered Lighter [British military] (DMA)
RPL..............	Ram Petroleums Ltd. [Toronto Stock Exchange symbol]
RPL..............	Ramseur Pilot Light Teaching System
RPL..............	Rapid Pole Line [A type of pole line construction]
RPL..............	Rated Power Level (NASA)
RPL..............	Reactor Primary Loop
RPL..............	Reading Public Library, Reading, PA [OCLC symbol] (OCLC)
RPL..............	Receive Replenishment From [Navy] (NVT)
RPL..............	Recommended Provisioning List
RPL..............	Reemployment Priority List [DoD]
RPL..............	Remote Program Load
RPL..............	Renewal Parts Leaflet (MSA)
RPL..............	Repair Parts List [Army] (AABC)
RP/L...........	Repairs, Light
RPL..............	Repeal [Legal shorthand] (LWAP)
RPL..............	Repetitive Flight Plan [ICAO] (FAAC)
RPL..............	Replacement (IAA)
RPL..............	Replenish (NVT)
RPL..............	Requested Privilege Level [Computer science]
RPL..............	Request Parameter List [Computer science] (BUR)
RPL..............	Resident Programming Language [Computer science]
RPL..............	Resident Pulmonary Lymphocyte [Immunology]
RPL..............	Reverse Polish Logic (NITA)
RPL..............	Rhode Island State Law Library, Providence, RI [Library symbol Library of Congress] (LCLS)
RPL..............	Richmond Public Library [UTLAS symbol]
RPL..............	Ripe Pulp Liquid [A banana substrate]
RPL..............	Ripple
RPL..............	Robot Programming Language [Computer science]
RPL..............	Rocket Propulsion Laboratory [Air Force]
RPL..............	Rodent and Primate Laboratory (SSD)
RPL..............	Rotary Pellet Launcher [Military] (PDAA)
RPL..............	Running Program Language [Computer science]
RPLAD	Retroperitoneal Lymphoadenectomy [Medicine] (BABM)
RPLC	Replace (FAAC)
RPLC	Reversed-Phase Liquid Chromatography
RPLIND	Retroperitoneal Lymph Node Dissection [Medicine] (CDI)
RPLN	Retroperitoneal Lymph Nodes [Medicine]
RPLND........	Retroperitoneal Lymphadenectomy [Oncology] (DAVI)
RPLND........	Retroperitoneal Lymph Node Dissection [Medicine] (MEDA)
RPLNG	Replenishing
RPLR	Repeller (MSA)
RPLS	Radionuclide Perfusion Lung Scan
RPLS	Random Primary Library Screening [Chemistry]
RPLS	Reactor Protection Logic System (IEEE)
RPLSN	Repulsion (MSA)
RPLT...........	Repellent (MSA)
RPLV	Reentry Payload Launch Vehicle
rplx	Rhoplex (VRA)
RPM	Ngukurr [Airport symbol]
RPM	RADAR Performance Monitor
RPM	Radial-Burning Pulse Motor (MCD)
RPM	Radial Power Monitor [Environmental science] (COE)
RPM	Radiation Polarization Measurement
RPM	Raised Pavement Marker [Highway design]
RPM	Random Phase Model (OA)
RPM	Rapid Processing Mode [Medicine] (MAE)

RPM............	Rate per Minute
RPM............	Raven's Proressive Matrices [*Psychiatry*] (DAVI)
RPM............	Reactive Plume Model [*Environmental Protection Agency*] (GFGA)
RPM............	Read Program Memory [*Computer science*] (MDG)
RPM............	Real Property Maintenance (DOMA)
RPM............	Real Property Management
RPM............	Reasonable Prudent Man [*Legal shorthand*] (LWAP)
RPM............	Reclamation Program Manager [*Military*] (AFIT)
RPM............	Refractory Platinum Metal
RPM............	Regional Particulate Model (USDC)
RPM............	Registered Publications Manual [*Navy*]
RPM............	Registered Publications Memorandum
RPM............	Register of Preservation Microfilms (TELE)
RPM............	Registrants Processing Manual [*Selective Service System*]
RPM............	Regulated Power Module
RPM............	Relative Plate Motion [*Geophysics*]
RPM............	Relaxation Potential Model [*Physics*]
RPM............	Reliability Performance Measure [*QCR*]
RPM............	Reliability Planning and Management (MCD)
RPM............	Remedial Project Manager [*Navy*]
RPM............	Remotely Piloted Munitions [*Army*]
RPM............	Remote Performance Monitoring (CET)
RPM............	Remote Program Management
RPM............	Reprogram Mode
RPM............	Resale Price Maintenance
RPM............	Research and Program Management [*NASA*]
RPM............	Resident Process Manager [*Computer science*] (PCM)
RPM............	Resistant Plant Material [*Soil science*]
RPM............	Response-per-Thousand [*Marketing*]
RPM............	Resupply Provisions Module [*NASA*] (KSC)
RPM............	Retail Price Maintenance (DCTA)
RPM............	Returns Program Manager [*IRS*]
RPM............	Revenue Passenger Mile
RPM............	Revenue per Mile
RPM............	Revolutions per Mile [*Automobile tires*]
RPM............	Revolutions per Minute [*e.g., in reference to phonograph records*]
rpm............	Revolutions per Minute (IDOE)
RPM............	Rhode Island Medical Society, Providence, RI [*Library symbol Library of Congress*] (LCLS)
RPM............	Rifle Prize Money [*British military*] (DMA)
RPM............	Rocket-Propelled Mines (NATG)
RPM............	Roll Position Mechanism (MCD)
RPM............	Rotations per Minute
RPM............	Rounds per Minute [*Military*] (INF)
RPM............	Royalty Payment Mechanism
RPM............	RPM, Inc. [*Associated Press*] (SAG)
RPM............	Runs per Minute (IAA)
RPMa..........	Masonic Temple Library, Providence, RI [*Library symbol Library of Congress*] (LCLS)
RPMA	Real Property Maintenance Activities [*or Administration*] [*Army*] (AABC)
RPMA	Retail Packaging Manufacturers Association (NTPA)
RPMB	Cubi Naval Air Station, Bataan [*Philippines*] [*ICAO location identifier*] (ICLI)
RPMB	Remotely-Piloted Mini-Blimp (PDAA)
RPMC	Cebu/Lahug, Cebu [*Philippines*] [*ICAO location identifier*] (ICLI)
RPMC	Remote Performance Monitoring and Control
RPMC	Reserve Personnel, Marine Corps (MCD)
RPMD	Resources Planning and Mobilization Division [*of OEP*]
RPMD	Rheumatic Pain Modulation Disorder [*Medicine*] (DMAA)
RPMDA	Retail Print Music Dealers Association (NTPA)
RPMF..........	Reserve Personnel Master File [*Military*]
RPMI	Radiant Power Measuring Instrument [*Geophysics*]
RPMI	Revolutions-per-Minute Indicator
RPMI	Roswell Park Memorial Institute [*State University of New York at Buffalo*] [*Research center*] (RCD)
RPMIO	Registered Publication Mobile Issuing Office [*Military*]
RPMK	Clark Air Base, Pampanga [*Philippines*] [*ICAO location identifier*] (ICLI)
RPML..........	Laoag/International, Ilocos Norte [*Philippines*] [*ICAO location identifier*] (ICLI)
RPMM	Manila/International [*Philippines*] [*ICAO location identifier*] (ICLI)
RPMN	Repairman (AABC)
RPMO	Radio Projects Management Office
RPMOR.......	Rounds per Mortar
RPMORPM...	Rounds per Mortar per Minute
RPMP	Legazpi, Albay [*Philippines*] [*ICAO location identifier*] (ICLI)
RPMP	Register of Plan Mobilization Producers
RPMR	Romblon, Tablas Island [*Philippines*] [*ICAO location identifier*] (ICLI)
RPMS	Real Property Management System (MCD)
RPM/S	Revolutions per Minute/Second (DEN)
RPMS	Royal Postgraduate Medical School [*British*]
RPMS	Sangley Point Naval Station, Cavite [*Philippines*] [*ICAO location identifier*] (ICLI)
RPMT..........	Lapu-Lapu/Mactan International [*Philippines*] [*ICAO location identifier*] (ICLI)
RPMZ..........	Zamboanga/International [*Philippines*] [*ICAO location identifier*] (ICLI)
RPN............	Registered Professional Nurse
RPN............	Renal Papillary Necrosis [*Nephrology*] (DAVI)
RPN............	Reserve Personnel, Navy [*An appropriation*]
RPN............	Reverse Polish Notation [*Arithmetic evaluation*] [*Computer science*] (IEEE)
RPN............	Rosh-Pina [*Israel*] [*Airport symbol*] (OAG)
RPN............	Royal Pakistan Navy [*British military*] (DMA)
RPND...........	Reprinting, No Date [*Publishing*]
RPNSM........	Replenishment
RPNVR.........	Royal Pakistan Naval Volunteer Reserve [*British military*] (DMA)
RPO............	Aeroposta, SA [*Argentina*] [*FAA designator*] (FAAC)
RPO............	Radiation Protection Officer [*NASA*] (NASA)
RPO............	Radiophare Omnidirectionnel [*Omnidirectional Radio Beacon*] (NATG)
RPO............	Railway Post Office
RPO............	Range Planning Office (MUGU)
RPO............	Rapids [*Real Time Automated Personnel Identification System*] Program Office
RPO............	Readiness Project Officer
RPO............	Regional Personnel Officer [*Social Security Administration*]
RPO............	Regional Pests Officer [*Ministry of Agriculture, Fisheries, and Food*] [*British*]
RPO............	Regional Planning Officer (COE)
RPO............	Regional Program [*or Project*] Officer (OICC)
RPO............	Regional Purchasing Office [*Defense Supply Agency*]
RPO............	Registered Publications Officer [*Navy*] (DNAB)
RPO............	Regular Production Option [*Automotive engineering*]
RPO............	Regulating Petty Officer [*British*]
RPO............	Rejection Purchase Order (MCD)
RPO............	Repair Parts Order [*Navy*]
RPO............	Replacement Purchase Order
RPO............	Responsible Property Officer [*Military*] (AFIT)
RPO............	Retail Postal Outlet (ASC)
RPO............	Retired Pay Operations [*Army*]
RPO............	Returned by the Post Office (WDMC)
RPO............	Revolution per Orbit
RPO............	Rhone-Poulenc Overseas [*NYSE symbol*] (SPSG)
RPO............	Right Posterior Oblique [*View*] [*Radiology*] (DAVI)
RPO............	Rotor Power Output
RPO............	Royal Philharmonic Orchestra [*British*] (WDAA)
RPOA..........	Recognized Private Operating Agencies (NATG)
RPOADS......	Remotely-Piloted Observation Aircraft Designator System (PDAA)
RPOC..........	Remote Payload Operations Center [*NASA*] (MCD)
RPOC..........	Report Proceeding on Course [*Aviation*] (FAAC)
RPOC..........	Residual Particulate Organic Carbon [*Environmental science*]
RPOCC........	Remote Payload Operations Control Center [*NASA*] (SSD)
RPOCN........	Request for Purchase Order Change Notice (AAG)
RPOOK........	Receive Pulse On/Off Keyed (MCD)
RPOP..........	Rover Preflight Operations Procedures [*NASA*] (KSC)
RPoPrA.......	Rhone-Poul Overseas 8.125% Pref [*NYSE symbol*] (TTSB)
RPorP	Portsmouth Priory, Portsmouth, RI [*Library symbol Library of Congress*] (LCLS)
RPOW.........	RPM, Inc. [*NASDAQ symbol*] (SAG)
RPP.............	RADAR Power Programmer
RPP.............	Radiation Protection Plan [*Nuclear energy*] (NRCH)
RPP.............	Radiochemical Processing Plant [*Oak Ridge National Laboratory*]
RPP.............	Rassemblement Populaire pour le Progres [*Popular Rally for Progress*] [*Djibouti*] [*Political party*] (PPW)
RPP.............	Rate Pressure Product [*Cardiology*]
RPP.............	Reactor Plant Planning (DNAB)
RPP.............	Rechargeable Power Pack
RPP.............	Recovered Polypropylene [*Organic chemistry*]
RPP.............	Recovery Pilot Plant (ACII)
RPP.............	Reductive Pentose Phosphate [*Photosynthesis cycle*]
RPP.............	Regional Priority Program [*Army*] (AABC)
RPP.............	Registered Postal Packet
RPP.............	Reinforced Pyrolytic Plastic (NASA)
RPP.............	Reliability Program Plan (MCD)
RPP.............	Removable Patch Panel
RPP.............	Rendezvous Point Position [*Aerospace*]
RPP.............	Repair Parts Provisioning
RPP.............	Repap Enterprises Corp., Inc. [*Toronto Stock Exchange symbol Vancouver Stock Exchange symbol*]
RPP.............	Reply Paid Postcard
RPP.............	Republican People's Party [*Cumhuriyet Halk Partisi - CHP*] [*Turkey Political party*] (PPW)
RPP.............	Request for Proposal Preparation (SAA)
RPP.............	Requisition Processing Point [*Military*]
RPP.............	Retrograde Processing Point (MCD)
RPP.............	Retropubic Prostatectomy [*Medicine*]
RPP.............	Reverse Pulse Polarography [*Analytical chemistry*]
RPP.............	Rivers Pollution Prevention (ROG)
RPP.............	Roll-Pitch Pickoff
RPP.............	Rules of Practices and Procedure
RPP.............	Rural Practice Project [*An association Defunct*] (EA)
RPPA..........	Repetitively-Pulsed Plasma Accelerator (IAA)
RPPA..........	Republican Postwar Policy Association [*Encouraged Republican Party to drop its isolationist viewpoint and take a stand for an American share in international collaboration after the war*] [*World War II*]
RPPC..........	Providence College, Providence, RI [*Library symbol Library of Congress*] (LCLS)
RPPDL........	Random Peptide Phage Display Library [*Biochemistry*]
RPPE..........	Research, Program, Planning, and Evaluation
RPPI...........	Remote Plan Position Indicator (MCD)
RPPI...........	Repeater Plan Position Indicator (NVT)
RPPI...........	Role Perception Picture Inventory
RPPL..........	Repair Parts Price List
RPPL..........	Repair Parts Provisioning List
RPPM.........	Park Museum Reference Library, Providence, RI [*Library symbol Library of Congress*] (LCLS)
RPPMP	Repair Parts Program Management Plans
RPPO..........	Regional Printing Procurement Office [*Army*]

RPPP	Repair Parts Program Plan [*Army*]
RPPP	Rules of Pleading, Practice, and Procedure [*A publication*] (DLA)
RPPR	Red Cell Precursor Production Rate [*Hematology*] (DAVI)
RPPS	Reactive Perfluoroalkyl Polymeric Surfactant [*Organic chemistry*]
RPPS	Retired Pay / Personnel System [*Military*] (DNAB)
RPPS	Robotnicza Partia Polskich Socjalistow [*Workers Party of Polish Socialists*] [*Political party*] (PPE)
RPPS-Lewica	Robotnicza Partia Polskich Socjalistow - Lewica [*Workers Party of Polish Socialists - Left*] [*Political party*] (PPE)
RPPTF	Rotatable Porous-Prism Test Fixture
RPPY	Reactor Plant Planning Year (DNAB)
RPQ	Rapports de Pratique de Quebec [*Quebec Practice Reports*] [*Canada*] [*A publication*] (DLA)
RPQ	Request for Price Quotation
RPQ	Rutter Parent Questionnaire
RPQC	Right to Peace & Quiet Campaign (WDAA)
RPR	Federation Guadeloupeenne du Rassemblement pour la Republique [*Guadeloupe Federation of the Rally for the Republic*] [*Political party*] (PPW)
RPR	Radio Physics Research
RPR	Railway Pioneer Regiment [*British military*] (DMA)
RPR	Raipur [*India*] [*Airport symbol*] (OAG)
RPR	Rally for the Republic [*France*] [*Political party*]
RPR	Rapid Plasma Reagin [*Card test for venereal disease*]
RPR	Rapid Power Reduction (IEEE)
RPR	Rassemblement pour la Republique [*Rally for the Republic*] [*France Political party*] (ECON)
RPR	Rassemblement pour la Republique [*Rally for the Republic*] [*Wallis and Futuna Islands*] [*Political party*] (PD)
RPR	Rassemblement pour la Republique [*Rally for the Republic*] [*Martinique*] [*Political party*] (PPW)
RPR	Rassemblement pour la Republique [*Rally for the Republic*] [*French Guiana*] [*Political party*] (PPW)
RPR	Rassemblement pour la Republique [*Rally for the Republic*] [*Mayotte*] [*Political party*] (EY)
RPR	Rassemblement pour la Republique [*Rally for the Republic*] [*French Polynesia*] [*Political party*] (PPW)
RPR	Rassemblement pour la Republique [*Rally for the Republic*] [*Reunion*] [*Political party*] (PPW)
RPR	Rated Pressure Ratio (EG)
RPR	Read Printer
RPR	Rear Projection Readout
RPR	Rectangular Parallelepiped Resonant Method [*Crystal elasticity*]
RPR	Red Blood Cell Precursor Production Rate [*Hematology*]
RPR	Registered Professional Reporter
RPR	Reiter Protein Reagin [*Biochemistry*] (DAVI)
RPR	Rent Procedural Regulation (Office of Rent Stabilization) [*Economic Stabilization Agency*] [*A publication*] (DLA)
RPR	Repair (MSA)
RPR	Repair Parts Requisition
RPR	Research Project Report [*A publication*] (EAAP)
RPR	Reverse Phase Relay (IAA)
RPR	Reverse Power Relay (IAA)
RPR	Reverse Price Risk [*Finance*] (EMRF)
RPR	Rhone-Poulenc Rorer [*NYSE symbol*] (SPSG)
RPR	Rings Present (NITA)
RPR	Rockport Resources Ltd. [*Vancouver Stock Exchange symbol*]
RPR	Roger Williams College, Providence Campus, Providence, RI [*Library symbol Library of Congress*] (LCLS)
RPR	Roll-Pitch Resolver
RPR	Rotatable Pool Rate (MCD)
RPRA	Racing Public Relations Association
RPRA	Railroad Public Relations Association (EA)
RPRA	Royal Pigeon Racing Association [*British*] (DBA)
R Prac Patent Cases	Rules of Practice in Patent Cases [*A publication*] (DLA)
RPRC	Regional Primate Research Centers
RPRC	Religious Public Relations Council (EA)
RPRC	Retired and Pioneer Rural Carriers of United States (EA)
RPRC	Rhode Island College, Providence, RI [*Library symbol Library of Congress*] (LCLS)
RPRCF	Rapid Plasma Reagin Complement Fixation (STED)
RPR-CT	Rapid Plasma Reagin Card Test [*Clinical chemistry*]
RPRD	Research Policy and Review Division [*of OEP*]
R$_{pri}$	Primary Resistance (IDOE)
RPRI	Radiata Pine Research Institute [*Australia*]
rPRL	Rat Prolactin [*Biochemistry*]
RPRL	Regional Parasite Research Laboratory [*US Department of Agriculture*] [*Research center*] (RCD)
RPRL	Regional Poultry Research Laboratory [*East Lansing, MI*] [*Department of Agriculture*] (GRD)
RPRMN	Repairman
RPROM	Reprogrammable Read-Only Memory [*Computer science*] (HGAA)
RPROP	Real Property [*Legal shorthand*] (LWAP)
RPROP	Receiving Proficiency Pay [*Military*]
RPRRB	Real Property Resource Review Board (AFM)
RPRS	Random-Pulse RADAR System (AAG)
RPRS	Roll-Pitch Resolver System
RPRT	Report (AFM)
RPRT	Right Place at the Right Time [*A criterion for success*]
RPRV	Remotely Piloted Research Vehicle [*NASA*]
RPRWP	Reactor Plant River Water Pump (IEEE)
RPS	Racial Preservation Society [*British*]
RPS	RADAR Plotting Sheet (OA)
RPS	RADAR Position Symbol [*ICAO*] (FAAC)
RPS	Radiation Protection Standards (SAA)

RPS	Radical Philosophy Society [*British*]
RPS	Radioisotope Power System (COE)
RPS	Radiological Protection Service (DEN)
RPS	Radio Program Standard [*Australian Broadcasting Tribunal*]
RPS	Randomized Pattern Search (PDAA)
RPS	Range Pad Service
RPS	Range Positioning System
RPS-Lewica	Rapid Patent Service [*Research Publications, Inc.*] [*Information service or system*] (IID)
RPS	Rapid Photo Screening
RPS	Rare Poultry Society [*British*]
RPS	Reactor Protection System [*Nuclear energy*] (NRCH)
RPS	Real-Time Processing System (NITA)
RPS	Real-Time Programming System [*Computer science*] (IEEE)
RPS	Record and Playback Subsystem (NASA)
RPS	Records per Sector [*Computer science*]
RPS	Regional Pressure Setting (DA)
RPS	Registered Publications System
RPS	Regulated Power Supply
RPS	Regulatory Performance Summary [*Report*] [*Nuclear energy*] (NRCH)
RPS	Reinforced Porcelain System [*Dentistry*]
RPS	Relative Performance Score [*Telecommunications*] (TEL)
RPS	Relay Power Supply (MCD)
RPS	Remittance Processing Systems [*IRS*]
RPS	Remote Printing System
RPS	Remote Processing Service (BUR)
RPS	Remote Processing System (IAA)
RPS	Remote Programming System (MCD)
RPS	Renal Pressor Substance [*Medicine*]
RPS	Request for Procurement Services
RPS	Requirements Planning System [*Computer science*]
RPS	Response-Produced Stimulation
RPS	Retired Persons Services (EA)
RPS	Return Pressure Sensing (MCD)
RPS	Reversed-Phase Series (PDAA)
RPS	Revolutions per Second (AFM)
rps	Revolutions per Second (IDOE)
rps	Rhodopseudomonas Virldes [*A bacterium*]
RPS	Rhone-Poulenc Systems (NITA)
RPS	Right Pedal Sinus
RPS	Rigid Proctosigmoidoscopy [*Proctoscopy*]
RPS	Ripe Pulp Solid [*A banana substrate*]
RPS	RMS [*Remote Manipulator System*] Planning System (SSD)
RPS	Rochester Public Schools, Library Processing Center, Rochester, MN [*OCLC symbol*] (OCLC)
RPS	Role Performance Scale [*Occupational therapy*]
RPS	Rotary Precision Switch
RPS	Rotating Passing Scuttle
RPS	Rotational Position Sensing [*Computer science*]
RPS	Royal Philharmonic Society (EAIO)
RPS	Royal Photographic Society [*British*] (WDAA)
RPS	Royal Photographic Society of Great Britain (DEN)
RPS	RPS Realty Trust [*NYSE symbol*] (SPSG)
RPS	Rutile-Paper-Slurry [*Grade of titanium dioxide*]
RPSA	Religious Program Specialist Seaman Apprentice [*Navy rating*] (DNAB)
RPSA	Rudder Pedal Sensor Assembly (MCD)
RPSC	Royal Philatelic Society of Canada
RPSCTDY	Return to Proper Station Upon Completion of Temporary Duty [*Military*]
RPS-DL	Registered Publications Section - District Library [*Navy*]
RPSEL	Recommended Peculiar Support Equipment List (MCD)
RPSF	Rotation, Processing, and Surge Facility [*NASA*] (NAKS)
RPSG	Report Passing [*Aviation*] (FAAC)
RPSGB	Royal Pharmaceutical Society of Great Britain (EAIO)
RPSGB	Royal Photographic Society of Great Britain (EAIO)
RP (Ships)	Registered Ships' Plumbers [*British*]
RPSI	Railway Preservation Society of Ireland (BI)
RPSI	Roche Psychiatric Service Institute
RPSIO	Registered Publications Subissuing Office [*Military*] (NVT)
RPSL	Repair Parts Selective List
RPSL	Rhode Island Department of State Library Services, Providence, RI [*Library symbol Library of Congress*] (LCLS)
RPSM	Registered Publication Shipment Memorandum
RPSM	Residency Program in Social Medicine (DMAA)
RPSM	Resources Planning and Scheduling Method
RPSMG	Reactor Protective System Motor Generator (IEEE)
RPSML	Repair Parts Support Material List
RPSN	Religious Program Specialist Seaman [*Navy rating*] (DNAB)
RPSO	Regional Procurement and Support Office [*Foreign service*]
RPSP	RADAR Programmable Signal Processor
RPSP	Reference Preparation for Serum Proteins (DMAA)
RPS-PL	Registered Publications Section - Personnel Library [*Navy*]
RPSS	Ryukyu Philatelic Specialist Society (EA)
RPST	Reaction Products Separator Tank [*Nuclear energy*] (NRCH)
RPST	Recombinant Porcine Somatotropin
RPSTL	Repair Parts and Special Tools List [*Army*] (AABC)
RPT	Congregation Sons of Israel and David, Temple Beth-El, Providence, RI [*Library symbol Library of Congress*] (LCLS)
RPT	Raluana Point [*New Britain*] [*Seismograph station code, US Geological Survey*] (SEIS)
RPT	Ramco Gershenson Properties Trust [*NYSE symbol*] (SAG)
RPT	Ramco-Gershenson Property Trust [*NYSE symbol*] [*Formerly, RPS Realty Trust*] (SG)
RPT	Ramco-Gershenson Prop Tr [*NYSE symbol*] (TTSB)

RPT............... Rapid Pull Through [*Gastroenterology*]
RPT............... Rassemblement du Peuple Togolais [*Rally of the Togolese People*] [*Political party*] (PPW)
RPT............... Reactor for Physical and Technical Investigations [*Former USSR Nuclear energy*]
RPT............... Reactor Plant Test (DNAB)
RPT............... Recirculation Pump Trip [*Nuclear energy*] (NRCH)
RPT............... Recruit Performance Test (OA)
RPT............... Reference Point Tracking
RPT............... Refractory Period of Transmission (STED)
RPT............... Registered Physical Therapist
RPT............... Regular Public Transport (ADA)
RPT............... Relative Prime Transform
RPT............... Repair Parts Transporter (MCD)
rpt............... Repeat [*International telex abbreviation and wire-service jargon*] (WDMC)
RPT............... Repeat [*International telex abbreviation and wire-service jargon*] (WDMC)
RPT............... Reply Paid Telegram
RPT............... Report
RPT............... Reporting Time [*Filmmaking*] (WDMC)
RPT............... Reprint
RPT............... Request Programs Termination [*Computer science*]
RPT............... Resident Provisioning Team [*NASA*]
RPT............... Rocket-Powered Target
RPT............... Rocket Propulsion Technician [*Air Force*]
RPT............... Rotary Power Transformer
RPT............... Rudder Pedal Transducer (NASA)
RPTA .... Recycled Paperboard Technical Association (NTPA)
RPTA .... Renal Percutaneous Transluminal Angioplasty [*Medicine*] (STED)
RPTA .... Rudder Pedal Transducer Assembly (NASA)
RPTC .... Relative Priority Test Circuit (MHDI)
RPTC .... Repeating Coil (MSA)
RPTD .... Repeated
RPTD .... Reported
RPTD .... Reprinted (WGA)
RPTD .... Ruptured
Rptd............ Ruptured [*Medicine*] (STED)
RPTF............ Republican Presidential Task Force (EA)
RPTF............ Rotatable Porro-Mirror Test Fixture
RPTIA .... Recreational Park Trailer Industry Association (NTPA)
RPTL............ Real Property Tax Law [*New York, NY A publication*]
RPTLC .... Reverse Phase Thin-Layer Chromatography
RPTN .... Repetition (AAG)
RPTOR.......... Reporting Organization (COE)
RPTP .... Receptor Protein Tyrosine Phosphatase [*Biochemistry*]
RPTR .... Repeater (MSA)
RPTS .... Reactor Plant Test Section (DNAB)
RPTS .... Regional Priority Tracking System (COE)
RPTS .... Roadway-Powered Transporter System [*Experimental vehicle*]
RPTSO .... Reactor Plant Test Support Organization (DNAB)
RPU .... RADAR Prediction Uncertainty
RPU .... Radio Phone Unit [*Navy*]
RPU .... Radio Propagation Unit [*Army*] (MCD)
RPU .... Railway Patrolmen's International Union [*Later, BRAC*] (EA)
RPU .... Receiver Processor Unit [*Electronics*]
RPU .... Rectifier Power Unit
RPU .... Regional Planning Unit (OICC)
RPU .... Regional Processing Unit
RPU .... Registered Publication Unit
RPU .... Release Program Unit (DWSG)
RPU .... Remote Pickup Unit
RPU .... Remote Processing Unit (KSC)
RPU .... Retention Pending Use [*Air Force*]
RPU .... Retropubic Urethropexy [*Gynecology*] (DAVI)
RPU .... Rotatable Pool Unit (DNAB)
RPUA .... Aparri, Cagayan [*Philippines*] [*ICAO location identifier*] (ICLI)
RPUB .... Baguio, Benguet [*Philippines*] [*ICAO location identifier*] (ICLI)
RPUC .... Cabanatuan, Nueva Ecija [*Philippines*] [*ICAO location identifier*] (ICLI)
RPUC .... Reprint under Consideration [*Publishing*]
RPUD .... Daet, Camarines Norte [*Philippines*] [*ICAO location identifier*] (ICLI)
RPUE .... Lucena, Quezon [*Philippines*] [*ICAO location identifier*] (ICLI)
RPUF .... Floridablanca Air Base, Pampanga [*Philippines*] [*ICAO location identifier*] (ICLI)
RPUG .... Lingayen, Pangasinan [*Philippines*] [*ICAO location identifier*] (ICLI)
RPUH .... San Jose, Occidental Mindoro [*Philippines*] [*ICAO location identifier*] (ICLI)
RPUI .... Iba, Zambales [*Philippines*] [*ICAO location identifier*] (ICLI)
RPUJ .... Castillejos, Zambales [*Philippines*] [*ICAO location identifier*] (ICLI)
RPUK .... Calapan, Oriental Mindoro [*Philippines*] [*ICAO location identifier*] (ICLI)
RPUL .... Lipa/Fernando Air Base, Batangas [*Philippines*] [*ICAO location identifier*] (ICLI)
RPUM .... Mamburao, Occidental Mindoro [*Philippines*] [*ICAO location identifier*] (ICLI)
RPUN .... Naga, Camarines Sur [*Philippines*] [*ICAO location identifier*] (ICLI)
RPUO .... Basco, Batanes Island [*Philippines*] [*ICAO location identifier*] (ICLI)
RPUP .... Jose Panganiban/PIM, Camarines Norte [*Philippines*] [*ICAO location identifier*] (ICLI)
RPUQ .... Vigan, Ilocos Sur [*Philippines*] [*ICAO location identifier*] (ICLI)
RPUR .... Baler, Aurora Sub-Province [*Philippines*] [*ICAO location identifier*] (ICLI)
RPUS .... San Fernando, La Union [*Philippines*] [*ICAO location identifier*] (ICLI)
RPUT .... Tuguegarao, Cagayan [*Philippines*] [*ICAO location identifier*] (ICLI)

RPUU .... Bulan, Sorsogon [*Philippines*] [*ICAO location identifier*] (ICLI)
RPUV .... Virac, Catanduanes [*Philippines*] [*ICAO location identifier*] (ICLI)
RPUW .... Marinduque/Gasan, Marinduque [*Philippines*] [*ICAO location identifier*] (ICLI)
RPUX .... Plaridel, Bulacan [*Philippines*] [*ICAO location identifier*] (ICLI)
RPUY .... Cauayan, Isabela [*Philippines*] [*ICAO location identifier*] (ICLI)
RPUZ .... Bagabag, Neuva Viscaya [*Philippines*] [*ICAO location identifier*] (ICLI)
RPV .... Reactor Pressure Vessel [*Nuclear energy*] (NRCH)
RPV .... Real Program Value (CAAL)
RPV .... Recorder Processor Viewer
RPV .... Reduced Product Verification [*DoD*]
RPV .... Relatvie Protein Value [*Medicine*] (WDAA)
RPV .... Remotely Piloted Vehicle [*Aircraft*]
RPV .... Remotely Piloted Vehicles
RPV .... Remote Positioning Valve
RPV .... Reserve Personnel Navy (DOMA)
RPV .... Residual Pressure Valve [*Automotive engineering*]
RPV .... Rhopalosiphum padi Virus
RPV .... Right Portal Vein [*Medicine*] (STED)
RPV .... Right Portal Vein [*Medicine*] (DB)
RPV .... Right Pulmonary Vein [*Medicine*]
RPV .... Rinderpest Virus
RPV .... Roadway Powered Vehicle [*Automotive engineering*]
RPV .... United States Veterans Administration Hospital, Davis Park, Providence, RI [*Library symbol Library of Congress*] (LCLS)
RPVA .... Tacloban/Daniel Z. Romualdez, Leyte [*Philippines*] [*ICAO location identifier*] (ICLI)
RPVB .... Bacolod, Negros Occidental [*Philippines*] [*ICAO location identifier*] (ICLI)
RPVC .... Calbayog, Western Samar [*Philippines*] [*ICAO location identifier*] (ICLI)
RPVD .... Dumaguete/Sibulan Negros Oriental [*Philippines*] [*ICAO location identifier*] (ICLI)
RPVE .... Caticlan, Aklan [*Philippines*] [*ICAO location identifier*] (ICLI)
RPVF .... Catarman, Northern Samar [*Philippines*] [*ICAO location identifier*] (ICLI)
RPVG .... Guiuan, Eastern Samar [*Philippines*] [*ICAO location identifier*] (ICLI)
RPVH .... Hilongos, Leyte Del Norte [*Philippines*] [*ICAO location identifier*] (ICLI)
RPVI .... Iloilo, Iloilo [*Philippines*] [*ICAO location identifier*] (ICLI)
RPVI-AIAF.... Remotely Piloted Vehicle Investigation - Adjustment of Indirect Artillery Fire
RPVI-ES........ Remotely Piloted Vehicle Investigation - Emerging Sensors (MCD)
RPVIO........ Registered Publication Van Issuing Office [*Military*] (NVT)
RPV-IT........ Remotely Piloted Vehicle - Institutional Trainer [*Military*]
RPVK........ Kalibo, Aklan [*Philippines*] [*ICAO location identifier*] (ICLI)
RPVL........ Roxas/Del Pilar, Palawan [*Philippines*] [*ICAO location identifier*] (ICLI)
RPVM........ Masbate [*Philippines*] [*ICAO location identifier*] (ICLI)
RPVN........ Medellin, Cebu [*Philippines*] [*ICAO location identifier*] (ICLI)
RPVNTV...... Rust Preventative
RPVO........ Ormoc, Leyte [*Philippines*] [*ICAO location identifier*] (ICLI)
RPVP........ Puerto Princesa, Palawan [*Philippines*] [*ICAO location identifier*] (ICLI)
RPVP........ Right Posterior Ventricular Preexcitation [*Medicine*] (DMAA)
RPVR........ Roxas, Capiz [*Philippines*] [*ICAO location identifier*] (ICLI)
RPVS........ San Jose De Buenavista/Antique [*Philippines*] [*ICAO location identifier*] (ICLI)
RPVT........ Relative Position Velocity Technique
RPVT........ Tagbilaran, Bohol [*Philippines*] [*ICAO location identifier*] (ICLI)
RPVX........ Remote-Piloted Vehicle Experiment
RPW .... Rawle, Penrose, and Watts' Pennsylvania Reports [*1828-40*] [*A publication*] (DLA)
RPW .... Resistance Projection Welding [*Manufacturing term*]
RPW .... Running Process Word (IAA)
RPWA........ Surallah/Allah Valley, Cotabato (South) [*Philippines*] [*ICAO location identifier*] (ICLI)
RPWB........ Buayan/General Santos, Cotabato (South) [*Philippines*] [*ICAO location identifier*] (ICLI)
RPWC........ Cotabato, North Cotabato [*Philippines*] [*ICAO location identifier*] (ICLI)
RPWD........ Davao/Francisco Bangoy International [*Philippines*] [*ICAO location identifier*] (ICLI)
RPWDA....... Retail Paint and Wallpaper Distributors of America [*Later, NDPA*]
RPWE........ Butuan, Agusan [*Philippines*] [*ICAO location identifier*] (ICLI)
RPW Foundation... Alberta Recreation, Parks & Wildlife Foundation (AC)
RPWG........ Dipolog, Zamboanga Del Norte [*Philippines*] [*ICAO location identifier*] (ICLI)
RPWI........ Ozamis, Misamis Oriental [*Philippines*] [*ICAO location identifier*] (ICLI)
RPWJ........ Jolo, Sulu [*Philippines*] [*ICAO location identifier*] (ICLI)
RPWK........ Tacurong/Kenram, Cotabato [*Philippines*] [*ICAO location identifier*] (ICLI)
RPWL........ Cagayan De Oro, Misamis Oriental [*Philippines*] [*ICAO location identifier*] (ICLI)
RPWM........ Malabang, Lanao Del Sur [*Philippines*] [*ICAO location identifier*] (ICLI)
RPWN........ Bongao/Sanga-Sanga, Sulu [*Philippines*] [*ICAO location identifier*] (ICLI)
RPWP........ Pagadian, Zamboanga Del Sur [*Philippines*] [*ICAO location identifier*] (ICLI)
RPWS........ Surigao, Surigao Del Norte [*Philippines*] [*ICAO location identifier*] (ICLI)
RPWT........ Del Monte, Bukidnon [*Philippines*] [*ICAO location identifier*] (ICLI)

RPWV	Buenavista, Agusan [*Philippines*] [*ICAO location identifier*] (ICLI)
RPWW	Tandag, Surigao Del Sur [*Philippines*] [*ICAO location identifier*] (ICLI)
RPWX	Iligan, Lanao Del Norte [*Philippines*] [*ICAO location identifier*] (ICLI)
RPWY	Malaybalay, Bukidnon [*Philippines*] [*ICAO location identifier*] (ICLI)
RPWZ	Bislig, Surigao Del Sur [*Philippines*] [*ICAO location identifier*] (ICLI)
RPX	BAC Aircraft Ltd. [*British ICAO designator*] (FAAC)
RPX	Roundup, MT [*Location identifier FAA*] (FAAL)
RPXC	Tarlac (Crow Valley) [*Philippines*] [*ICAO location identifier*] (ICLI)
RPXG	Lubang, Occidental Mindoro [*Philippines*] [*ICAO location identifier*] (ICLI)
RPXI	Itbayat, Batanes [*Philippines*] [*ICAO location identifier*] (ICLI)
RPXJ	Jomalig, Quezon [*Philippines*] [*ICAO location identifier*] (ICLI)
RPXM	Fort Magsaysay, Nueva Ecija [*Philippines*] [*ICAO location identifier*] (ICLI)
RPXP	Poro Point, La Union [*Philippines*] [*ICAO location identifier*] (ICLI)
RPXR	Corregidor, Cavite [*Philippines*] [*ICAO location identifier*] (ICLI)
RPXT	Alabat, Quezon [*Philippines*] [*ICAO location identifier*] (ICLI)
RPXU	Sorsogon, Sorsogon [*Philippines*] [*ICAO location identifier*] (ICLI)
RPY	Blythe, CA [*Location identifier FAA*] (FAAL)
RPY	Roll, Pitch, and Yaw
RPZ	Runway Protection Zone [*FAA*] (TAG)
RQ	Maldives International Airlines [*ICAO designator*] (AD)
RQ	RASD Quarterly [*American Library Association A publication*]
RQ	Recovery Quotient [*Medicine*] (DMAA)
RQ	Reportable Quantity [*Hazardous substance emergency response*]
R/Q	Request for Quotation (AAG)
R/Q	Resolver/Quantizer (IEEE)
RQ	Respiratory Quotient [*Also, Q*] [*Physiology*]
RQA	Recursive Queue Analyzer (IEEE)
RQAO	Reliability and Quality Assurance Office [*NASA*]
RQBCHS	Royal Queensland Bush Children's Health Scheme [*Australia*]
RQBE	Relational Query-by-Example [*Computer interface*] [*FoxPro*] (PCM)
RQC	RADAR Quality Control
RQC	Receiving Quality Control (IAA)
RQC	Reliability and Quality Control (MCD)
RQCL	Request Clearance [*Aviation*] (FAAC)
RQD	Raised Quarter Deck [*of a ship*] (DS)
RQD	Rock Quality Designation [*Mining technology*] [*Nuclear energy*] (NRCH)
RQDP	Request, Quandary and Deferment Plan
RQE	Relative Quantum Efficiency (OA)
RQE	Responsive Quantum Efficiency
RQG	Reduced Quantity Generator (ERG)
RQGC	Royal Queensland Golf Club [*Australia*]
RQH	Revue des Questions Historiques [*A publication*] (ODCC)
RQI	Rayleigh Quotient Iteration
RQIAC	Requires Immediate Action (NOAA)
RQL	Reference Quality Level (IEEE)
RQL	Rejectable Quality Level
RQLTA	Royal Queensland Lawn Tennis Association [*Australia*]
RQM	Real-Time Quality Measurement (CIST)
RQM	Ride Quality Meter [*Automotive testing*]
RQMC	Regimental Quartermaster-Corporal [*British*]
RQMD	Richmond Quartermaster Depot [*Virginia*] [*Merged with Defense General Supply Center*]
RQMNTS	Requirements (FAAC)
RQMS	Regimental Quartermaster-Sergeant [*British*]
RQMT	Requirement (AFM)
RQMTS	Requirements (NAKS)
RQN	Radial Quantum Number
RQN	Requisition (AFM)
RQO	River Quality Objective [*British*] (DCTA)
RQOF	Request on File (FAAC)
RQP	Request Flight Plan [*Aviation*] (DA)
RQP	Resistor Qualification Program
RQPP	Request Present Position [*Aviation*] (FAAC)
RQQPRI	Recommended Qualitative and Quantitative Personnel Requirements Information [*Military*] (MCD)
RQR	Require (AAG)
RQR	Requirement (IAA)
RQRD	Required
RQRMNT	Requirement
RQS	Rate Quoting System
RQS	Ready Qualified for Standby [*Military*]
RQS	Request Supplementary Flight Plan Message [*Aviation code*]
RQS	River Quality Standard [*British*] (DCTA)
RQT	Reenlistment Qualification Test [*Military*] (MCD)
RQT	Reliability Qualification Test (CAAL)
RQT	Resistor Qualification Test
RQTAO	Request Time and Altitude Over [*Aviation*] (FAAC)
RQTO	Request Travel Order (NOAA)
RQTP	Resistor Qualification Test Program
R/QTR	Rear Quarter [*Automotive engineering*]
RQTS	Requirements (KSC)
RQTV	Requirements Volatility
RQUS	Remote Query Update System [*Computer science*]
RQX	Air Engiadina [*Switzerland ICAO designator*] (FAAC)
RQY	Elkins, WV [*Location identifier FAA*] (FAAL)
RQY	Relative Quantum Yield
RQZ	Huntsville, AL [*Location identifier FAA*] (FAAL)
RR	Pike and Fischer's Radio Regulations [*A publication*] (DLA)
RR	Radiation Reaction [*Cells*] [*Medicine*]
RR	Radiation-Resistant
RR	Radiation Response
RR	Radiation Retinopathy [*Ophthalmology*]
R/R	Radio and RADAR
RR	Radio Range
RR	Radio Receptor (IAA)
RR	Radio Recognition
RR	Radio Regulations
RR	Radio Regulations, Geneva (OTD)
RR	Radio Relay (CINC)
RR	Radio Research
rr	Ragged Right [*Typography*] (BARN)
RR	Railroad
RR	Raised Ranch [*Architecture*] (BARN)
RR	Rand Rifles [*British military*] (DMA)
RR	Range Rate (NASA)
RR	Range Recorder [*NASA*] (IAA)
RR	Rapid Rectilinear
RR	Rarely Reversed [*Decisions in law*]
rr	Rarissime [*Very Rarely*] [*Latin*] (GPO)
RR	Raritan River Rail Road Co. [*AAR code*]
RR	Rated Radius [*Automotive engineering*]
RR	Rate Ratio
RR	Rate Rebate [*British*]
RR	Rattus Rattus [*The ship or black rat*]
RR	Readiness Region [*Military*]
RR	Readiness Review (KSC)
RR	Readout and Relay
RR	Ready Reckoner (DGA)
RR	Ready Reference
RR	Rear (AABC)
RR	Rear Engine, Rear Drive [*Automotive engineering*]
RR	Receive Ready [*Computer science*] (IEEE)
RR	Receiver Room [*Navy*] (CAAL)
RR	Receiving Report (AAG)
RR	Recipient Rights
RR	Recoilless Rifle
RR	Recommended for Re-Engagement [*British*]
RR	Record Rarities [*Record label*]
R/R	Record/Retirement
R/R	Record/Retransmit (IEEE)
RR	Recovery Reliability (MCD)
RR	Recovery Room
RR	Recruit Roll [*Navy*]
RR	Recurrence Rate
RR	Rediscount Rate
RR	Red Reflex [*Ophthalmology*] (DAVI)
RR	Redstone Resources, Inc. [*Toronto Stock Exchange symbol*]
RR	Reduced Range
RR	Redundancy Reduction (AAG)
RR	Reentry Range
RR	Reference Receiver
RR	Reference Register [*Computer science*]
RR	Reflectors [*JETDS nomenclature*] [*Military*] (CET)
RR	Regional Railroad
RR	Registered Representative [*Wall Street stock salesman*]
RR	Register to Register (MCD)
RR	Register-to-Register Instruction (IAA)
RR	Register-to-Register Operation (IAA)
RR	Regular Respirations [*Medicine*] (MEDA)
RR	Regular Rhythm [*Cardiology*] (DAVI)
RR	Rehabilitation Record
RR	Relative Rank
RR	Relative Response
RR	Relative Risk [*Medicine*]
RR	Relay Rack [*Telecommunications*] (TEL)
RR	Relief Radii (MSA)
RR	Religious Roundtable (EA)
RR	Remington Rand [*Commercial firm*] (NADA)
RR	Removal Rate (AAEL)
RR	Removal-Replacement
RR	Rendezvous RADAR [*NASA*]
RR	Renegotiation Regulations
RR	Renewable Resources
RR	Renin Release [*Endocrinology*] (MAE)
RR	Rent Regulation (Office of Rent Stabilization) [*Economic Stabilization Agency*] [*A publication*] (DLA)
R/R	Repair or Replacement
R/R	Repair/Rebuild (MCD)
RR	Repeatedly Reactive
RR	Repetition Rate
RR	Report Reaching [*ICAO*] (FAAC)
RR	Republic at Romania (BARN)
RR	Required Reserves
RR	Requirements Review [*NASA*] (NASA)
RR	Requisition Restriction Code (DNAB)
RR	Reroute [*Telecommunications*] (TEL)
RR	Research Reactor [*Nuclear energy*] (IAA)
RR	Research Report
RR	Reservatis Reservandis [*With All Reserve*] [*Latin*]
RR	Reserve Regiment [*British military*] (DMA)
RR	Residue Register (IAA)
RR	Resonance Raman
RR	Resource Report
RR	Respiratory Rate [*Medicine*]
RR	Response Rate (DAVI)
RR	Response Regulator [*Biochemistry*]
RR	Responsible Receiver

RR	Retired Reserve [*Military*]
RR	Retro-Rocket [*Army*] (AABC)
RR	Return Rate (IEEE)
RR	Return Register
RR	Revenue Release [*A publication*] (DLA)
RR	Reverse Recovery [*Electronics*]
RR	Reverse Reduction (DS)
RR	Review for Religious [*A publication*] (BRI)
RR	Revised Reports [*Legal*] [*British*]
RR	Revision Record (MSA)
RR	Rheumatoid Rosette [*Medicine*] (DB)
RR	Rhodesia Regiment [*British military*] (DMA)
RR	Rhymney Railway [*Wales*]
RR	Ridge Regression [*Statistics*]
RR	Rifle Range
RR	Right Rear
RR	Right Reverend [*Of an abbot, bishop, or monsignor*]
RR	Rights Reserved
RR	Rigid-Rotor [*Calculations*]
RR	Risk Ratio
RR	Risk Reduction [*Branch*] [*Forecast Systems Laboratory*] (USDC)
RR	Riva-Rocci Sphygmomanometer [*Medicine*] (DMAA)
RR	Rodman&Renshaw Cap [*NYSE symbol*] (TTSB)
RR	Rodman & Renshaw Capital Group [*NYSE symbol*] (SPSG)
RR	Roemische Religions-Geschichte [*A publication*] (OCD)
RR	Rolling Resistance [*Automotive engineering*]
RR	Roll Radius (MCD)
RR	Roll Roofing (AAG)
RR	Rolls-Royce [*Automobile*]
RR	Ronald Reagan [*US president, 1911-*]
RR	Root Rot [*Plant pathology*]
RR	Rough Riders [*The City of London Yeomanry*] [*Military unit*] [*British*]
RR	Round Robin (IEEE)
RR	Routine Message Precedence [*Telecommunications*] (ADDR)
RR	Routine Relay (KSC)
RR	Royal Air Force [*ICAO designator*] (AD)
RR	Running Reverse
R/R	Run Round [*Typography*] (DGA)
RR	Rural Resident (OICC)
RR	Rural Route
RR	Rush and Run (WDAA)
RR	Rush Release
RR	Ruthenium Red [*Inorganic chemistry*] (OA)
RR	Very Rare [*Numismatics*]
RRA	Dallas-Fort Worth, TX [*Location identifier FAA*] (FAAL)
RRA	Race Relations Act [*1976*] [*British*] (DCTA)
RRA	RADAR Recording and Analysis Equipment (DA)
RRA	Radiation Research Associates, Inc. (NRCH)
RRA	Radioreceptor Assay [*Clinical chemistry*]
RRA	Radio Relay Aircraft (CET)
RRA	Railroad Retirement Act (GFGA)
RRA	RAM [*Reliability, Availability, and Maintainablity*] Rationale Annex [*Army*]
RRA	Ranger Regimental Association (EA)
RRA	Ready Reserve Agreement [*Navy*] (DOMA)
RRA	Reclamation Reform Act [*1982*]
RRA	Record Retention Agreement [*IRS*]
RRA	Redmond, R. A., Los Angeles CA [*STAC*]
RRA	Regional Railroads of America (NTPA)
RRA	Registered Record Administrator [*American Medical Record Association*] [*Medicine*]
RRA	Religious Research Association (EA)
RRA	Remote Record Address
RRA	Renal Renin Activity [*Nephrology*] (DAVI)
RRA	Reserve Recognition Accounting [*Securities and Exchange Commission*]
RRA	Resident Research Associate
RRA	Revenue Reconciliation Act of 1990 (WYGK)
RRA	Rubber Reclaimers Association [*Later, NARI*] (EA)
RRA	Rubber Recyclers Association (EA)
RRAC	Race Relations Advisory Committee [*Trades Union Congress*] [*British*] (DCTA)
RRAC	Reactor Review and Audit Committee [*Oak Ridge National Laboratory*]
RRAC	Regional Resources Advisory Committee [*Army*] (AABC)
RRAD	Red River Army Depot [*Texas*] (AABC)
RRAD	Roll Ratio Adjust Device (MCD)
RRAF	Ready Reserve of the Armed Forces
RRAF	Royal Rhodesian Air Force
RRAM	Repetitive and Rapid Alternating Movements [*Neurology*] (DAVI)
RR & C	Records, Reports, and Control (AFM)
RR & Can Cas	Railway and Canal Cases [*England*] [*A publication*] (DLA)
RR & Cn Cas	Railway and Canal Cases [*1835-54*] [*A publication*] (DLA)
RR & D	Rehabilitation Research and Development Program [*Veterans Administration*] (GFGA)
RR & D	Reparations, Removal, and Demolition [*Section*] [*Industry Branch, US Military Government, Germany*]
RR & E	Round, Regular, and Equal [*With reference to pupils of eyes*]
RRAP	Residential Rehabilitation Assistance Program [*Canada*]
RRAR	ROM Return Address Register
RRAS	Radiofrequency Resonance Absorption (MCD)
RRAS	Routing and Remote Access Service [*Microsoft Corp.*]
RRB	Race Relations Board [*Military*] (VNW)
RRB	RADAR Reflective Balloon
RRB	Radiographers Registration Board [*Tasmania, Australia*]
RRB	Radio Range Beacon (IAA)
RRB	Radio Research Board (DEN)
RRB	Railroad Retirement Board
RRB	Rapid Response Bibliography Service [*Information retrieval*] (AEBS)
RRB	Regular Reenlistment Bonus [*Military*]
RRB	Requirements Review Board (SSD)
RRB	R. R. Bowker Co. [*Publisher*]
RRB	Rubber Reserve Board [*of the Reconstruction Finance Corp.*]
RR-BB	Rayon-Rayon Bias-Belted (PDAA)
RRBC	Rat Red Blood Cell
RRBFC	Red River Boys Fan Club [*Inactive*] (EA)
RRBLB	United States Railroad Retirement Board. Law Bulletin [*A publication*] (DLA)
RRBN	Round Robin [*Aviation*] (FAAC)
RRB Rept	Radio Research Board. Report. [*Australia*] [*A publication*]
RRC	RADAR Return Code
RRC	Radiation Recorder Controller (NRCH)
RRC	Radiation Resistance Cable
RRC	Radio Receptor Co.
RRC	Radio Relay Center (NATG)
RRC	Radio Research Co.
RRC	Railroad Record Club [*Commercial firm*] (EA)
RRC	Rainy River Community College, International Falls, MN [*OCLC symbol*] (OCLC)
RRC	Ravenroc Resources Ltd. [*Vancouver Stock Exchange symbol*]
RRC	Reactor Recirculation Cooling [*Nuclear energy*] (NRCH)
RRC	Readiness Reportable Code (DNAB)
RRC	Receiving Report Change (AAG)
RRC	Recognized Rescue Center [*Navy*] (DNAB)
RRC	Reconstructionist Rabbinical College [*Pennsylvania*]
RRC	Recreation Resources Center [*University of Wisconsin*] [*Research center*] (RCD)
RRC	Recruit Reception Center
RRC	Red River Community College [*UTLAS symbol*]
RRC	Reentry Rate Command [*NASA*]
RRC	Refractories Research Center [*Ohio State University*] [*Research center*] (RCD)
RRC	Refugee Resource Center [*Defunct*] (EA)
RRC	Regional Reporting Centers [*Navy*] (DOMA)
RRC	Regional Resource Center
RRC	Regional Response Center [*Environmental Protection Agency*] (EG)
RRC	Regional Review Consultants [*American Occupational Therapy Association*]
RRC	Regular Route Carrier
R/RC	Removal/Recertification
RRC	Reporting Requirements Code (DNAB)
RRC	Report Review Committee [*National Academy of Sciences*]
RRC	Reports of Rating Cases [*Legal*] [*British*]
RRC	Requirements Review Committee [*Navy*]
RRC	Research Resources Center [*University of Illinois at Chicago*] [*Research center*] (RCD)
RRC	Residency Review Committee [*Medicine*]
RRC	Resuscitation Research Center [*University of Pittsburgh*] [*Research center*] (RCD)
RRC	Retrograde River Crossing (MCD)
RRC	Retrovirus Research Center [*Veterans Administration Medical Center*] [*Baltimore, MD*]
RRC	Rheology Research Center [*University of Wisconsin - Madison*] [*Research center*] (RCD)
RRC	Rigid Raiding Craft [*British military*] (DMA)
RRC	Road Runners Club of America
RRC	Rocket Research Corp. (MCD)
RRC	Rodale Research Center [*Horticulture*]
RRC	Rollin' Rock Club (EA)
RRC	Roll Ratio Controller (MCD)
RRC	Roof Research Center [*Oak Ridge, TN*] [*Oak Ridge National Laboratory*] [*Department of Energy*] (GRD)
RRC	Routine Respiratory Care [*Medicine*]
RRC	Royal Red Cross [*British*]
RRC	Rubber Reserve Co. [*Dissolved, 1935, functions transferred to Reconstruction Finance Corporation*]
RRC	Rubber Reserve Committee [*Navy*]
RRC	Rural Referral Center [*Health care*]
RRC	Russell Research Center [*Department of Agriculture*]
RRC	Russian Research Center [*Harvard University*] [*Research center*] (RCD)
RRC	Ryde's Rating Cases [*A publication*] (DLA)
RRCA	Rhinelander Rabbit Club of America (EA)
RRCA	Road Runners Club of America (EA)
RRCAH	Roll Rate Command/Attitude Hold (MCD)
RRCC	Reduced Rate Contribution Clause [*Insurance*]
RRCCC	Regional Recreation and Conservation Consultative Committee [*Thames Water Authority*] [*British*]
RRCEF	Redwood Records Cultural and Educational Fund (EA)
RRCEM	Residency Review Committee for Emergency Medicine (EA)
RRCM	Roberts Radio Current Meter (NOAA)
RRCN	Receiving Report Change Notice (AAG)
RRCO	Radio Research Coordination Officer [*Air Force*]
RRCOTAAOSOCOTWAOS	Rollin' Rock Club of Texas and Any Other State or Country of the World and OuterSpace
RR Cr R	Revised Reports, Criminal Rulings [*1862-75*] [*India*] [*A publication*] (DLA)
RRCS	Railroad Communication System
RRCS	Reentry RADAR Cross Section
RRCS	Revenue Receipts Control Sheets [*IRS*]

RRCU .... Remote Range Control Unit (MCD)
RRCUS .... Rhodesian Ridgeback Club of the US (EA)
RRD .... Reactor Radiation Division [*National Institute of Standards and Technology*]
RRD .... Reactor Research and Development
RRD .... Receive, Record, Display
RRD .... Reliability Requirements Directive
RRD .... Replacement Regulating Detachment [*Army*]
RRD .... Requisition Received Date [*Bell System*] (TEL)
RRD .... Resonant Reed Decoder
RRD .... Retendering Receipt Day (NRCH)
RRD .... Roosevelt Roads [*Puerto Rico*] [*Seismograph station code, US Geological Survey*] (SEIS)
RRD .... Route/Route Destination [*Telecommunications*] (TEL)
RRDA .... Rendezvous Retrieval, Docking, and Assembly [*of space vehicle or orbital station*] [*NASA*] (AAG)
RRDA .... Repetitive Report Distribution Audit (AAG)
RRDB .... Research Results Data Base [*Department of Agriculture*] [*Information service or system*] (IID)
RRDC .... Railroad Data Center [*Association of American Railroad*] (PDAA)
RRDC .... Road Racing Drivers Club
RRDE .... RADAR Research and Development Establishment (IAA)
RRDE .... Radio Research and Development Establishment (MCD)
RRDE .... Rotating Ring Disk Electrode
RRDECA .... Roy Rogers - Dale Evans Collectors Association (EA)
RRDF .... RO/RO [*Roll-On/Roll-Off*] Discharge Facility [*Army*] (RDA)
RRDFCS .... Redundant Reconfigurable Digital Flight Control System (MCD)
RRDO .... Register of Rivers Discharging into the Oceans [*United Nations Environment Programme*] (MSC)
RRDR .... Raw RADAR Data Recorder
RRDS .... Relative Record Data Set
RRDTRL ...... Resistor-Resistor Diode Transistor Logic (IAA)
RRDU .... Recreation Research Demonstration Unit (RDA)
RRE .... Marree [*Australia Airport symbol Obsolete*] (OAG)
RRE .... Race-Relations Education Program [*Military*] (DNAB)
RRE .... RADAR Research Establishment [*British*]
RRE .... Radiation Related Eosinophilia [*Medicine*] (AAMN)
RRE .... Railroad Enthusiasts (EA)
RRE .... Raloxifene Response Element [*Biochemistry*]
RRE .... Range Rate Error
RRE .... Ras Responsive Element [*Genetics*]
RRE .... Receive Reference Equivalent [*Telecommunications*] (TEL)
RRE .... Reg Resources Corp. [*Vancouver Stock Exchange symbol*]
RRE .... Rolls-Royce Enthusiasts (EA)
RRE .... Roster of Required Events
RRE .... Royal RADAR Establishment [*British Research center*]
RREA .... Rendezvous RADAR Electronics Assembly [*NASA*] (MCD)
RREA .... Renewable Resources Extension Act (COE)
R/REA .... Rural/Regional Education Association (AEE)
RREAC .... Royal RADAR Establishment Automatic Computer (IAA)
RREAS .... Race Relations Employment Advisory Service [*British*]
RREB .... Race Relations Education Board [*Military*] (DNAB)
RREC .... Reading Research and Education Center [*Champaign, IL*] [*Department of Education*] (GRD)
RREC .... Rehabilitation Record
RREC .... Rice Research and Extension Center [*University of Arkansas*] [*Research center*] (RCD)
RREF .... Resting Radionuclide Ejection Fraction [*Medicine*] (DAVI)
RREL .... Risk Reduction Engineering Laboratory
RR/EO .... Race Relations/Equal Opportunity [*Military*] (AABC)
RRep .... Records Repository [*Air Force*] (AFM)
RREP .... Reed Reference Electronic Publishing
Rreq .... Required Resistance (IDOE)
RRESA .... Registered Real Estate Salespersons' Association [*Australia*]
RR et AC .... Rosea Rubeae et Aureae Crucis [*The Order of the Rose of Ruby and the Cross of Gold*]
RREU .... Rendezvous RADAR Electronics Unit [*NASA*] (MCD)
RRev .... Records Review [*Air Force*] (AFM)
RRF .... Racing Research Fund [*Defunct*] (EA)
RRF .... Ragged Red Fibers [*Muscle pathology*]
RRF .... Rapid Reaction Forces [*Army*] (AABC)
RRF .... Raptor Research Foundation (EA)
RRF .... Reading Reform Foundation (EA)
RRF .... Ready Reserve Fleet
RRF .... Ready Reserve Force [*Military*]
RRF .... Realty Refund SBI [*NYSE symbol*] (TTSB)
RRF .... Realty Refund Trust SBI [*NYSE symbol*] (SPSG)
RRF .... Reconnaissance Reporting Facility
RRF .... Red Resistance Front [*Netherlands Political party*]
RRF .... Reed Reactor Facility [*Reed College*] [*Research center*] (RCD)
RRF .... Regional Relay Facility (DNAB)
RRF .... Rehabilitation Research Foundation (EA)
RRF .... Residual Renal Function [*Medicine*] (DMAA)
RRF .... Resin Regeneration Facility [*Department of Energy*]
RRF .... Resonant Reed Filter
RRF .... Resonant Ring Filter [*Computer science*] (IAA)
RRF .... Retirement Register File [*Computer science*]
RRF .... Revised Recommended Findings
RRF .... Rift-Rift-Fracture [*Geology*]
RRF .... Riot Relief Fund (EA)
RRF .... Royal Regiment of Fusiliers [*Military unit*] [*British*]
RRFC .... Robert Redford Fan Club (EA)
RRFC .... Robin Right Fan Club (EA)
RRfd .... Risk Reference Dose (GNE)
RRFO .... Rhine River Field Organization [*Post-World War II*]

RRFS .... Range Rate Frequency Synthesizer
RRFT .... Right Rear Fluid Temperature [*Automotive engineering*]
RRFWG .... Ready Reserve Force Working Group (DOMA)
RRG .... Point Mugu, CA [*Location identifier FAA*] (FAAL)
RRG .... RADAR Range Gate
RRG .... Rental Rehabilitation Grant [*Department of Housing and Urban Development*] (GFGA)
RRG .... Requirements Review Group [*Air Staff*] [*Air Force*] (MCD)
RRG .... Research Review Group (NRCH)
RRG .... Resource Request Generator
RRG .... Restabilization Reset Generator (SAA)
RRG .... Rodrigues Island [*Mauritius*] [*Airport symbol*] (OAG)
RRG .... Roll Reference Gyro (AAG)
RRH .... Rural Rental Housing [*Loans*] [*Farmers Home Administration*]
RRHFF .... Rock and Roll Hall of Fame Foundation (EA)
RRHICMD ..... Remote Reading High Intensity Constant Monitoring Device (IAA)
RRHPF .... Ronald Reagan Home Preservation Foundation (EA)
RR-HPO ...... Rapid Recompression-High Pressure Oxygen [*Medicine*] (MAE)
RRHR .... Regional Radiological Health Representative [*U.S. Food and Drug Administration*]
RRI .... Barora [*Solomon Islands*] [*Airport symbol*] (OAG)
RRI .... Radio Republic Indonesia (IAA)
RRI .... Radio Republik Indonesia [*Radio network*]
RRI .... Range Rate Indicator
RRI .... Red Roof Inns [*NYSE symbol*] (TTSB)
RRI .... Red Roof Inns, Inc. [*NYSE symbol*] (SAG)
RRI .... Reference Roughness Index [*FHWA*] (TAG)
RRI .... Refugee Relief International (EA)
RRI .... Reimbursement Refund Indicator [*Military*] (AFIT)
RRI .... Rendezvous RADAR Indicator [*NASA*] (NASA)
RRI .... Reroute Inhibit [*Telecommunications*] (TEL)
RRI .... Resident Reactor Inspector [*Nuclear energy*] (NRCH)
RRI .... Revised Ring Index [*A publication*]
RRI .... Riverside Research Institute (MCD)
RRI .... Rocket Research Institute
RRI .... Romex Resources, Inc. [*Vancouver Stock Exchange symbol*]
RRI .... Rowett Research Institute [*British*] (BI)
RRI .... Rubber Research Institute (NADA)
RRI & StL ... Rockford, Rock Island & St. Louis Railroad
RRIC .... Race Relations Information Center [*Defunct*]
RRIC .... RADAR Repeater Indicator Console
RRID .... Reverse Radial Immunodiffusion (PDAA)
RRIF .... Registered Retirement Investment Fund [*Canada*]
RRIHS .... Regional Research Institute for Human Services [*Portland State University*] [*Research center*] (RCD)
RR-IM .... Office of Research and Reports, Intelligence Memoranda [*CIA*]
RRIM .... Reinforced Reaction Injection Molding [*Plastics technology*]
RRIN .... Readiness Risk Index Number (NG)
RRIPM .... Rapid Response Interference Prediction Model (MCD)
RRIS .... Radiological Release Information System (MCD)
RRIS .... Railroad Research Information Service [*National Academy of Sciences*] [*Defunct*]
RRIS .... Remote RADAR Integration Station [*Military*]
RRJE .... Range Remote Job Entry [*Telecommunications*] (OSI)
RRK .... Redaurum Red Lake Mines Ltd. [*Toronto Stock Exchange symbol*]
RRK .... Retaining Ring Kit
RRK .... Rourkela [*India*] [*Airport symbol*] (AD)
RRKM .... Rice, Ramsperger, Kassel, Marcus [*Developers of a theorem in chemical kinetics, designated by the initial letters of their last names*]
RRL .... Merrill, WI [*Location identifier FAA*] (FAAL)
RRL .... Rabbit Reticulocyte Lysate [*Biochemistry*]
RRL .... Radio Relay Link (NATG)
RRL .... Radio Research Laboratory
RRL AC .... Ralston Purina Co., Corporate Library, St. Louis, MO [*OCLC symbol*] (OCLC)
RRL .... Ranchmen's Resources Ltd. [*Toronto Stock Exchange symbol*]
RRL .... Rayleigh Radiation Law [*Physics*]
RRL .... Reference Repository Location
RRL .... Regimental Reserve Line
RRL .... Registered Record Librarian [*Medicine*]
RRL .... Reserve Retired List [*Military*]
RRL .... Road Research Laboratory [*British*]
RRL .... Rocket Research Laboratories (KSC)
RRL .... Rolls Royce Ltd. [*British ICAO designator*] (FAAC)
RRL .... Ruby Rod LASER
RRL .... Rudder Reference Line [*NASA*] (NASA)
RRL .... Runway Remaining Lights [*Aviation*]
RRL .... Ruthenium Red Staining Layer [*Biology*]
RRLC .... Radiation-Resistant Linear Circuit
RRLC .... Redwood Region Logging Conference (EA)
RRLC .... Rochester Regional Library Council [*Information service or system*] (IID)
RRLG .... Rocket, Radio, Longitudinal, Generator Powered (IAA)
RRLL .... Relative Rumble Loudness Level (DICI)
RRLO .... Race Relations Liaison Officer (WDAA)
RRLR .... Road Race Lincoln Register (EA)
RRLT .... Right Rear Lining Temperature [*Automotive engineering*]
RRLTU .... Recruit Remedial Literacy Training Unit (DNAB)
RRM .... Acvila Air-Romanian Carrier [*FAA designator*] (FAAC)
RRM .... Rate of Return Method [*Insurance*]
RRM .... Rayleigh-Ritz Method [*Physics*]
RRM .... Red Resource Monitoring (MCD)
RRM .... Reliant Resources Ltd. [*Vancouver Stock Exchange symbol*]
RRM .... Renegotiated-Rate Mortgage

RRM	Reports, Reviews, Meetings
RRM	RNA [*Ribonucleic Acid*] Recognition Motif [*Genetics*]
RRM	Rotation Remanent Magnetization (PDAA)
RRM	Runaway Rotating Machine
RRMC	Royal Roads Military College [*Royal Roads, BC*]
RRMF	RADAR Reflectivity Measuring Facility
RRMG	Reactor Recirculation Motor Generator (IEEE)
RRMRP	Ready Reserve Mobilization Reinforcement Pool [*Army*]
RRMRS	Ready Reserve Mobilization Reinforcement System [*Army*]
RRMS	Reserve Readiness and Mobility Squadron
RRMS	Revenue Requirements Modeling System [*Department of Energy*] (GFGA)
RRMSEP	Relative Root Mean Square Error of Prediction (AAEL)
RRMT	Race Relations Management Team (WDAA)
RRMT	Reactor and Reactor Material Technology [*Environmental science*] (COE)
RRN	Rapid Reinforcement of NATO (MCD)
RRN	Relative Record Number [*Computer science*]
RRN	Serra Norte [*Brazil*] [*Airport symbol*] (OAG)
rRNA	Ribonucleic Acid, Ribosomal [*Biochemistry, genetics*]
RRNC	Ranger Rick's Nature Club (EA)
RRND	Right Radical Neck Dissection [*Surgery*] (DAVI)
RRNN	Reproductive Rights National Network [*Defunct*] (EA)
RRNS	Redundant Residue Number System (IEEE)
RRNS	Related Returns Notification System [*IRS*]
RRO	Recipient Rights Officer
RRO	Regimental Reserve Officer (ADA)
RRO	Renegotiation Regional Office
RRO	Reproduction Rights Organisation (TELE)
RRO	Responsible Reporting Office [*Telecommunications*] (TEL)
RRO	Richport Resources Ltd. [*Vancouver Stock Exchange symbol*]
RROA	Railroadians of America (EA)
RROC	Rolls-Royce Owners' Club (EA)
RROCA	Rolls Royce Owners' Club of Australia
RROM	Resistive Range of Motion (STED)
RROS	Resistive Read-Only Storage
RROSP	Race Relations and Overseas Students Panel (AIE)
RROU	Remote Readout Unit
RRP	Radio Relay Pod
RRP	Radio Ripple Proximity (IAA)
RRP	Range Ring Profile (MCD)
RRP	Rapid Reinforcement Plan [*Military*] (MUSM)
RRP	Reactor Refueling Plug (NRCH)
RRP	Reader and Reader-Printer (PDAA)
RRP	Ready Replacement Pilot
RRP	Recommended Retail Price
RRP	Recoverable Repair Parts
RRP	Refugee Resettlement Program (MEDA)
RRP	Regional Project Research Program (EA)
RRP	Regular Retail Price
RRP	Relative Refractory Period [*Medicine*]
RRP	Relay Rack Panel
RRP	Religious Requirements and Practices [*A publication*]
RRP	Rental Rehabilitation Program [*Department of Housing and Urban Development*] (GFGA)
RRP	Republican Reliance Party [*Cumhuriyetci Guven Partisi - CGP*] [*Turkey Political party*] (PPW)
RRP	Resource Referral Program (WYGK)
RRP	Reverse Repurchase Agreement [*Investment term*]
RRP	Rock Hill, SC [*Location identifier FAA*] (FAAL)
RRP	Roosevelt Roads [*Puerto Rico*] [*Seismograph station code, US Geological Survey Closed*] (SEIS)
RRP	Rotterdam-Rhine Pipeline [*Oil*]
RRP	Rough River Petroleum Corp. [*Vancouver Stock Exchange symbol*]
RRP	Rudder Reference Plane [*NASA*] (NASA)
RRPA	Relativistic Random-Phase Approximation [*Electrodynamics*]
RRPA	Ruhr Regional Planning Authority [*Post-World War II*]
RRPB	Retraining and Reemployment Policy Board
RRPC	Reserve Reinforcement Processing Center [*Army*] (AABC)
RRPD	Runway Reference Point Downwind [*Aviation*] (FAAC)
RRPE	Union for Radical Review of Radical Political Economics [*A publication*] (EAAP)
RRPG	Regular Right Part Grammar (IAA)
RRPI	Relative Rod Position Indication [*Nuclear energy*] (NRCH)
RRPI	Rotary Relative Position Indicator [*Nuclear energy*] (NRCH)
RRPL	Recommend Repair Parts List
RRPM	Reflective Raised Pavement Marker [*Highway design*]
RRPM	Representatives of Radio Parts Manufacturers (IAA)
RRPP	Reverends Peres [*Reverend Fathers*] [*French*]
RRPR	Reduced Range Practice Rocket [*Army*]
RRPS	Ready Reinforcement Personnel Section [*Air Force*] (AFM)
RRPS	Ronald Reagan Philatelic Society (EA)
RRPU	Runway Reference Point Upwind [*Aviation*] (FAAC)
RRQ	Rock Rapids, IA [*Location identifier FAA*] (FAAL)
RRQG	Right Rostal Quarter Ganglion [*Medicine*] (STED)
RRR	Exceedingly Rare [*Numismatics*]
RRR	RADAR Radiation Receiver
RRR	RAF-HQSTC (Air Transport) [*British ICAO designator*] (FAAC)
RRR	Railroad Reports [*United States*] [*A publication*] (DLA)
RRR	Raleigh Research Reactor
RRR	RAM [*Reliability, Availability, and Maintainability*] Rationale Report [*Army*]
RRR	Range and Range Rate
RRR	Range Rover Register [*An association*] (EAIO)
RRR	Rapid Runway Repair

RRR	Reader Railroad [*AAR code*]
RRR	Readiness Removal Rate (DNAB)
RRR	Readin', Ritin', and Rithmetic [*Also, 3R's*]
RRR	Records, Racing, and Rallying [*Sporting aviation*]
RRR	Red Red Rose [*An association Defunct*] (EA)
RRR	Reduced Residual Radiation
RRR	Regular Rate and Rhythm [*Cardiology*] (AAMN)
RRR	Relay, Reporter, Responder (DWSG)
RRR	Relief, Recovery, Reform [*Elements of the New Deal*]
RRR	Renaissance Commun [*NYSE symbol*] (TTSB)
RRR	Renaissance Communications Corp. [*NYSE symbol*] (SAG)
RRR	Renin-Release Rate [*Endocrinology*] (MAE)
RRR	Renin-Release Ratio (STED)
RRR	Repairable Return Rate (DNAB)
RRR	Required Rate of Return [*Finance*]
RRR	Residual Resistance Ratio [*Metal purity*]
RRR	Resistor-Reactor Rectifier
RRR	Resource Rent Royalty
RRR	Resource Requirements Request [*Military*] (MCD)
RRR	Resurfacing, Restoration, and Rehabilitation [*US Federal Highway Administration*]
RRR	Rework Removal Rate
RRR	Ridge-Ridge-Ridge [*Triple junction of lithospheric plates*]
RRR	Risk Rescue Rating (STED)
RRR	Riverton Resources Corp. [*Vancouver Stock Exchange symbol*]
RRR	Royal Rhodesia Regiment [*British military*] (DMA)
RRR	Rum, Romanism, and Rebellion [*Phrase coined during the Presidential campaign of 1884 to describe the Democratic party*]
RRR	Run-Time Reduction Ratio (MHDB)
RRR	University of Rochester, Rochester, NY [*OCLC symbol*] (OCLC)
RRRC	Regulatory Requirements Review Committee [*Nuclear energy*] (NRCH)
RRRE	RADAR Range-Rate Error
RR Rep	Railroad Reports [*A publication*] (DLA)
RRRLC	Rochester Regional Research Library Council [*Rochester, NY*] [*Library network*]
RRRN	Round, Regular, and React Normally [*Referring to the pupils of the eyes*] (DAVI)
RRRPD	Reseau de Radio Rurale des Pays en Developpement [*Developing Countries Farm Radio Network*] (EAIO)
RRRR	Railroad Revitalization and Regulatory Reform Act [*1976*]
RRRR	Rare Medium Group [*Stock market symbol*]
RRRRR	Receipt [*British naval signaling*]
RRRRRR	Remedial Readin', Remedial Ritin', and Remedial Rithmetic [*Also, 6R's*] [*Humorous interpretation of the three R's*]
RRRS	Route Relief Requirements System [*Telecommunications*] (TEL)
RRRV	Rate of Rise of Restriking Voltage (IEEE)
RRS	Bedford Rae [*British ICAO designator*] (FAAC)
RRS	Dothan, AL [*Location identifier FAA*] (FAAL)
RRS	RADAR Ranging System
RRS	Radiation Research Society (EA)
RRS	Radiological Research Society (COE)
RRS	Radio Receiver Set
RRS	Radio Recording Spectrophotometer
RRS	Radio Relay Squadron
RRS	Radio Relay Station
RRS	Radio Relay System
RRS	Radio Remote Set (CAAL)
RRS	Radio Research Station [*British*]
RRS	Range Rate Search (MCD)
RRS	Rational Recovery Systems (EA)
RRS	Reaction Research Society (EA)
RRS	Reactor Recirculating System (NRCH)
RRS	Reactor Refueling System (NRCH)
RRS	Reactor Regulating System (NRCH)
RRS	Readiness Reportable Status (NVT)
RRS	Ready Reportable Status (MCD)
RRS	Reconnaissance Reporting System
RRS	Red River Settlement [*Canada*]
RRS	Reed Relay Scanner
RRS	Regulatory Reform Staff [*Environmental Protection Agency*] (EPA)
RRS	Relay Radio Subsystem [*NASA*]
RRS	Remaining Radiation Service (NATG)
RRS	Reminder of Route Same (SAA)
RRS	Remington's Revised Statutes [*A publication*] (DLA)
RRS	Rendezvous RADAR System [*NASA*] (MCD)
RRS	Required Response Spectrum (IEEE)
RRS	Research Referral Service [*International Federation for Documentation*] [*Information service or system*] (IID)
RRS	Resin Regeneration Subsystem [*Nuclear energy*] (NRCH)
RRS	Resonance Raman Scattering [*Spectroscopy*]
RRS	Resonance Raman Spectroscopy
RRS	Resources and Referral Services (OICC)
RRS	Restraint Release System (KSC)
RRS	Retired Reserve Section
RRS	Retransmission Request Signal [*Telecommunications*] (TEL)
RRS	Retrograde Rocket System
RRS	Retrorectal Space (STED)
RRS	Revised Statutes of Nebraska, Reissue
RRS	Ribs of Reinforced Shotcrete [*Engineering*]
RRS	Richards-Rundle Syndrome (STED)
RRS	Riva-Rocci Sphygmomanometer (STED)
RRS	River and Rainfall Station [*National Weather Service*] (NOAA)
RRS	Roll Rate Sensor
RRS	Roo Rat Society (EA)

RRS	Roros [Norway] [Airport symbol] (OAG)
RRS	Royal Research Ship [British]
RRSA	Radio Republic South Africa (IAA)
RRSCS	Rate Stabilization and Control System (MCD)
RRSM	Rough Riding Sergeant-Major [British military] (DMA)
RRSP	Registered Retirement Savings Plan [Canada]
RRSQ	Radio Relay Squadron [Military] (IAA)
RRSSM	Rough Riding Staff Sergeant-Major [British military] (DMA)
RR sta	Railroad Station (VRA)
RRSTRAF	Ready Reserve Strategic Army Forces
RRSV	Red Ringspot Virus [of blueberry]
RRSV	Rice Ragged Stunt Virus [Plant pathology]
RRSW	Rosin-Rammler-Sperling-Weibull [Equation for microcapsules] (DB)
RRT	Radio Relay Terminal
RRT	Rail Rapid Transit [TXDOT] (TAG)
RRT	Railroad Retirement Tax [IRS]
RRT	Railroad Transport (NATG)
RRT	Randomized Response Technique [Statistics]
RRT	Ready Round Transporter (NATG)
RRT	Reentry Reference Time [NASA]
RRT	Reflected-Reflected-Transmitted [Wave mechanics]
RRT	Regional Response Team [Environmental Protection Agency] (EG)
RRT	Registered Recreation Therapist
RRT	Registered Respiratory Therapist
RRT	Relative Rate Test (DB)
RRT	Relative Retention Time
RRT	Rendezvous RADAR Transducer [NASA] (NASA)
RR/T	Rendezvous RADAR/Transponder [NASA] (KSC)
RRT	Request for Review of Tooling
RRT	Requirements Review Team
RRT	Requisite Remedial Technology (EPA)
RRT	Resazurin Reduction Time [Medicine] (MAE)
RRT	Ring-Ring Trip [Telecommunications] (TEL)
RRT	Robert Mines Ltd. [Vancouver Stock Exchange symbol]
RRTA	Railroad Retirement Tax [IRS]
RRTD	Rural Rehabilitation Technologies Database [University of North Dakota] [Information service or system] (IID)
RRTIS	Renewable Resources Technical Information System [Forest Service]
RRTS	Radiometer Recording Titration System [Experimentation]
RRTS	Range-Rate Tracking System
RRTS	Remote RADAR Tracking System (MHDI)
RRTTL	Resistor-Resistor Transistor-Transistor Logic [Computer science] (IAA)
RRU	Cedar Rapids, IA [Location identifier FAA] (FAAL)
RRU	Radiobiological Research Unit (IEEE)
RRU	Radio Research Unit [Army] (AABC)
RRU	Remington-Rand UNIVAC
RRU	Remote Readout Unit
RRU	Remote Request Unit (CAAL)
RRU	Resource Recycling Unit
RRU	Respiratory Resistance Unit [Medicine] (DMAA)
RRU	Retro-Rocket UNIVAC (MUGU)
R RUL	Renegotiation Rulings (DLA)
RRV	Denver, CO [Location identifier FAA] (FAAL)
RRV	Raspberry Ringspot Virus [Plant pathology]
RRV	Rate of Rise of Voltage [Electronics] (IAA)
RRV	Remote Reconnaissance Vehicle (NITA)
RRV	Rhesus Rotavirus [Medicine]
RRV	Right Renal Vein [Medicine] (STED)
RRV	Rotor Reentry Vehicle
RRV & W	Red River Valley & Western Railroad [North Dakota]
RRVSGA	Red River Valley Sugarbeet Growers Association (EA)
RRW	Jacksonville, FL [Location identifier FAA] (FAAL)
RRW	Radiation-Resistant Wire
RRW	Royal Regiment of Wales [Military unit] [British]
RRWU	Rhodesia Railway Workers' Union
RRX	Railroad Crossing [Telecommunications] (TEL)
RRX	Ronrico Explorations Ltd. [Vancouver Stock Exchange symbol]
RRZ	RADAR Regulation Zone (DA)
RS	Aeropesca [ICAO designator] (AD)
RS	IEEE Reliability Society (EA)
RS	Rabbinical School (BJA)
RS	Rabbinical Seminary (BJA)
RS	Rabbinic Supervisor (BJA)
RS	Rachmaninoff Society [Record label]
RS	RADAR Scanner
RS	RADAR Scattering
RS	RADAR Selector (MCD)
RS	RADAR Set
RS	RADAR Simulator (CET)
RS	RADAR Start (CET)
RS	Radial Sedan [Class of racing cars]
RS	Radiated Susceptibility (IEEE)
RS	Radiation Sensitive [Physiology]
RS	Radiation Source (NRCH)
RS	Radio Communication Supervisor (IAA)
RS	Radio Duties - Special
RS	Radio School (IAA)
RS	Radio Set (IAA)
RS	Radio Simulator
RS	Radiospare (IAA)
RS	Radio Station [Maps and charts]
RS	Radio Supervisor [British]
RS	Radio Switchboard (CAAL)
RS	Radiotelegram Service (IAA)

RS	Radius of Safety (MCD)
RS	Radular Sac
RS	Ragtime Society (EA)
RS	Railway Station (ROG)
RS	Rain and Snow [Sleet] [Meteorology]
RS	Raman Scattering [Spectroscopy]
RS	Raman Spectroscopy
RS	Random Saccades [Ophthalmology]
RS	Random Splice [Telecommunications] (TEL)
RS	Range Safety [NASA] (KSC)
RS	Range Selector
RS	Range Setter (IAA)
R/S	Range Surveillance
RS	Rapid Setting [Asphalt grade]
RS	Ras Shamra (BJA)
RS	Raster Suppression [of color images]
RS	Rating Schedule [Medicine] (MAE)
RS	Rating Sheet [Psychometrics]
RS	Rauwolfia Serpentina [A plant, the root extract of which is used medicinally]
RS	RAWINSONDE [Radiosonde and RADAR Wind Sounding] [Upper air observation] (NASA)
RS	Raw Stock
RS	Ray Society (EA)
RS	Reactor Safeguards (NRCH)
RS	Reader Stop [Computer science] (BUR)
RS	Readiness Squadron (DNAB)
RS	Reading of Standard
RS	Ready Service (AAG)
RS	Real Storage
RS	Rearranging Sequence [Genetics]
RS	Rebuild Standard [Marine Corps]
RS	Receiver Station
RS	Receiving Ship [or Station]
RS	Reception Station
RS	Recipient's Serum [In blood matching]
RS	Recipient State (NITA)
RS	Reciprocating Steam (MCD)
RS	Reclaimed Wheat Grass/Shrub Cover [Agriculture]
RS	Recognition Structure [Immunochemistry]
RS	Recommended Standard [Telecommunications] (TEL)
RS	Reconfiguration System (MCD)
RS	Reconnaissance Satellite
RS	Reconnaissance Squadron [Military]
RS	Reconnaissance-Strike [Military]
RS	Reconnaissance Strip [Military] (AFM)
RS	Reconstitution Site (NVT)
RS	Recording Secretary
RS	Record Separator [Control character] [Computer science]
RS	Recreation Supervisor [Red Cross]
RS	Recruiting Service
RS	Recruiting Station
RS	Recruitment Surveys [Army British]
RS	Rectal Sinus
RS	Rectal Suppository [Medicine]
RS	Rectified Spirits (ROG)
RS	Rectus-Sinister [Nomenclature system] [Biochemistry]
RS	Redeemable Stock
RS	Reduced Smoke (MCD)
RS	Reduced Strength (MCD)
RS	Reducing Substance [Laboratory science] (DAVI)
RS	Reducing Sugar
RS	Redundancy Status [NASA] (MCD)
RS	Redundant Set [NASA] (MCD)
RS	Reed-Sternberg Cell [Medicine] (MAE)
RS	Reel Sequence [Computer science]
RS	Reentry System (AFM)
RS	Reference Serum [Clinical chemistry]
R/S	Reference Standard
RS	Reformed Spelling
RS	Refrigeration System (MCD)
RS	Refurbishment Spare (NASA)
RS	Regional Authorities (Scotland)
RS	Register and Storage (MCD)
RS	Registered Sanitarian
RS	Register of Shipping of the USSR [Ship classification society] (DS)
RS	Register Select
RS	Register to Storage (NITA)
RS	Registration Services
RS	Regularly Scheduled [Red Cross Volunteer]
RS	Regular Savings
RS	Regular Station [Military]
RS	Regulated Substance [Environmental Protection Agency]
RS	Regulating Station [Military]
RS	Regulation Station [Air Force]
RS	Reinforcing Stimulus
RS	Reiter's Syndrome [Medicine]
R/S	Rejection Slip (ADA)
RS	Relative Sweetness
RS	Relay Selector (IAA)
R/S	Relay Set [Telecommunications] (TEL)
RS	Reliability Standard
RS	Reliability Summary (KSC)
RS	Reliance Steel & Aluminum [NYSE symbol] (TTSB)
RS	Reliance Steel & Aluminum Co. [NYSE symbol] (SAG)

RS..............	Relief Stamped (DGA)
RS..............	Religious Studies [Secondary school course] [British]
RS..............	Relocation Site (NVT)
RS..............	Reminder Shock
RS..............	Remotely Settable Fuze (MCD)
RS..............	Remote Sentry [Army]
R/S..............	Remote Site [NASA] (KSC)
RS..............	Remote Station
RS..............	Renal Specialist [Medicine]
RS..............	Render and Set [Construction] (IAA)
RS..............	Renin Substrate [Biochemistry]
RS..............	Rephael Society (EA)
RS..............	Report of Survey [Military]
RS..............	Reproductive Success [Genetics]
RS..............	Republicains Sociaux [Social Republicans] [France Political party] (PPE)
RS..............	Request for Services [Social Security Administration]
RS..............	Request for Support (MCD)
RS..............	Request to Send
RS..............	Requirement Submission [Environmental science] (COE)
RS..............	Research Scientist (ADA)
RS..............	Research Summary
RS..............	Research Systems (MCD)
RS..............	Reserve Section [Military]
RS..............	Reserve Stock (SAA)
RS..............	Reset
RS..............	Reset-Set [Computer science]
RS..............	Reset Steering
RS..............	Resident School (MUGU)
RS..............	Resistance Soldering
RS..............	Resistant Sporangia [Botany]
RS..............	Resistor (IAA)
RS..............	Re-Solv, the Society for the Prevention of Solvent and Volatile Substance Abuse [British] (EAIO)
RS..............	Resonator [Electronics] (IAA)
RS..............	Resorcinol-Sulfur [Organic chemistry] (MAE)
RS..............	Resources Section [Resources and Technical Services Division] [American Library Association]
RS..............	Respiratory Syncytial [Virus]
RS..............	Respiratory System [Medicine]
RS..............	Response-Stimulus
RS..............	Response to Stimulus [Ratio] [Neurology] (DAVI)
RS..............	Responsus [To Answer] [Latin]
RS..............	Resume Sheet
RS..............	Resynchronizing State (IAA)
RS..............	Retail Shops and Stores [Public-performance tariff class] [British]
R-S..............	Reticulated Siderocyte [Cytology] (AAMN)
RS..............	Return to Saturation
RS..............	Return to Situation (SAA)
RS..............	Revenue Sharing
RS..............	Reverberation Strength
RS..............	Reversal Shift [Psychometrics]
RS..............	Reverse Shot [Cinematography] (NTCM)
RS..............	Reverse Signal (IAA)
RS..............	Review of Symptoms [Medicine]
RS..............	Review of Systems [Medical records] (DAVI)
RS..............	Revised Statutes
R/S..............	Revolutions per Second
RS..............	Reye's Syndrome [Medicine]
RS..............	Rheinflugzeugbau [Germany ICAO aircraft manufacturer identifier] (ICAO)
RS..............	Rheumatoid Spondylitis [Medicine] (DAVI)
RS..............	Rhinal Sulcus (DB)
RS..............	Rhythm Strip [Electrocardiogram] (CPH)
RS..............	Right Sacrum [Medicine] (KSC)
RS..............	Right Safety [Sports]
RS..............	Right Septum [Medicine] (DB)
RS..............	Right Side
RS..............	Right Stellate [Ganglion] [Medicine] (DB)
RS..............	Riley-Schwachmann (DB)
RS..............	Ringer's Solution [Physiology]
RS..............	Ripon Society (EA)
R/S..............	Road Service
RS..............	Road Space [Military]
RS..............	Roberts Syndrome [Medicine] (DMAA)
RS..............	[The] Roberval & Saguenay Railway Co. [AAR code]
RS..............	Rochelle Salt [Potassium Sodium Tartrate] [Organic chemistry]
RS..............	Rocket Station (IAA)
RS..............	Rocket System (MCD)
RS..............	Roller Shutter
RS..............	Rolls Series [A publication] (DLA)
RS..............	Roll Stabilization
RS..............	Root Mean Square Average [Statistics] (IAA)
RS..............	Root Stock [Botany]
RS..............	Rotary Selector (IAA)
RS..............	Rotary Switch (IAA)
RS..............	Rotary System (IAA)
R-S..............	Rough-Smooth Variation [Bacteriology] (DAVI)
RS..............	Route Selector
RS..............	Route Signal (IAA)
RS..............	Route Switching [Telecommunications] (TEL)
RS..............	Routing Slip [Military]
RS..............	Royal Scots [Military unit]
RS..............	Royal Society [British]
RS..............	Rubble Stone (AAG)

RS..............	Rudder Station (MCD)
RS..............	Runaway Shop (MHDB)
R_s..............	Screen Resistance (IDOE)
R_s..............	Secondary Resistance (IDOE)
R_s..............	Series Resistance (IDOE)
rs..............	Sleet [Meteorology] (BARN)
R_s..............	Source Resistance (IDOE)
Rs..............	Sri Lanka Rupee [Monetary unit] (IMH)
RS..............	Syntex Laboratories, Inc. [Research code symbol]
RS-232	Recommended Standard-232 [Computer science] (IGQR)
RSA..............	Air Service Affaires [France ICAO designator] (FAAC)
RSA..............	American Railway and Airline Supervisors Association (EA)
RSA..............	Rabbit Serum Albumin [Immunology]
RSA..............	Rack Service Association (EA)
RSA..............	RADAR Service Area
RSA..............	RADAR Signature Analysis [Air Force]
RSA..............	Radiation Safety Advisor [British] (NUCP)
RSA..............	Railway Security Agency [South Vietnam government security] (VNW)
RSA..............	Railway Supervisors Association (NADA)
RSA..............	Railway Supply Association (EA)
RSA..............	Random Sequential Automaton (IAA)
RSA..............	Range Safety Approval (MUGU)
RSA..............	Rated Sail Area [IOR] [Yacht racing]
RSA..............	Rate Sensitive Assets (EBF)
RSA..............	Rate Sensor Assembly (MCD)
RSA..............	Rate Subsystem Analyst (MUGU)
RSA..............	Rationalist Society of Australia
RSA..............	Rational Self-Analysis [Psychology] (DHSM)
RSA..............	Rat Serum Albumin [Immunology]
RSA..............	Receptive Services Association (NTPA)
RSA..............	Redstone Arsenal [Huntsville, AL] [Army]
RSA..............	Reference Satellite A (NASA)
RSA..............	Refined Sugar Association [British] (DBA)
RSA..............	Regional Office Systems [Computer science]
RSA..............	Regional Science Association (EA)
RSA..............	Regional Studies Association [British] (EAIO)
RSA..............	Regular Spiking Activity [Electrophysiology]
RSA..............	Rehabilitation Services Administration [Office of Special Education and Rehabilitive Services, Department of Education]
RSA..............	Relative Specific Activity
RSA..............	Relative Standard Accuracy [Testing methodology]
RSA..............	Relay Services Association of Great Britain (BI)
RSA..............	Remote Session Access [Telecommunications] (OSI)
RSA..............	Remote Station Alarm
RSA..............	Remote Storage Activities
RSA..............	Renaissance Society of America (EA)
RSA..............	Rental Service Association (EA)
RSA..............	Repair Sevice Attendant [Telecommunications] (TEL)
RSA..............	Republiek van Suid-Afrika [Republic of South Africa] [Afrikaans]
RSA..............	Requirements Statement Analyzer
RSA..............	Research Security Administrators
RSA..............	Research Society on Alcoholism (EA)
RSA..............	Resource Sharing Alliance [Library consortium] (IT)
RSA..............	Respiratory Sinus Arrhythmia [Medicine]
RSA..............	Responsibility for Student Achievement Scale (EDAC)
RSA..............	Reticulum Cell Sarcoma [Pathology] (DAVI)
RSA..............	Retire to Staging Area [Military]
RSA..............	Returned Services Association (BARN)
RSA..............	Revest-Shamir-Adelman [Encryption Algorithm] [Theoretical mathematics] (PCM)
RSA..............	Revised Shapley Ames [Catalogue of Bright Galaxies]
RSA..............	Revised Statutes Annotated [A publication] (DLA)
RSA..............	Revised Statutes of Alberta [Canada] [A publication] (DLA)
RSA..............	Rheometrics Sound Analyzer
RSA..............	Rhetoric Society of America (EA)
RSA..............	Rhythmic Slow Activity [Electroencephalography]
RSA..............	Ridden Standardbred Association (EA)
RSA..............	Right Sacroanterior [A fetal position] [Obstetrics]
RSA..............	Right Subclavian Artery [Anatomy] (DAVI)
RSA..............	Rivest-Shamir-Adelman [Cryptography]
RSA..............	Rivest Shamir Adleman
RSA..............	Roller Skating Association (NTPA)
RSA..............	Rotary Servo Actuator
RSA..............	Rotary Switch Art (IAA)
RSA..............	Royal & Sun Alliance [Insurance] [British]
RSA..............	Royal Scottish Academician
RSA..............	[The] Royal Scottish Academy
RSA..............	Royal Scottish Academy, Edinburgh [1826] (NGC)
RSA..............	Royal Society for the Encouragement of Arts, Manufactures, and Commerce [British] (EAIO)
RSA..............	Royal Society of Antiquaries
RSA..............	Royal Society of Australia (BARN)
RSA..............	Royal Society of the Arts [British]
RSA..............	Royal Sun Alliance (WDAA)
RSA..............	Rubber Shippers Association [Defunct]
RSA..............	Runway Safety Area [FAA] (TAG)
RSA..............	Rural Sanitary Authority [British]
RSA..............	Rural Service Area (CIST)
RSA..............	Russian Space Agency
RSA..............	Santa Rosa [Argentina] [Airport symbol] (OAG)
RSAA..........	Romanian Studies Association of America (EA)
RSAA..........	Royal Society for Asian Affairs [British] (DI)
RSAAF........	Royal South African Air Force
RSABA........	Royal South Australian Bowling Association

RSAC	RADAR Significance Analysis Code
RSAC	Radiological Safety Analysis Computer (MCD)
RSAC	Reactor Safety Advisory Committee [Canada] (BARN)
RSAC	Recreational Software Advisory Council
RSAC	Region, State, Area, County [Code] [DoD]
RSAC	Reliability Surveillance and Control (IAA)
RSAC	Remote Slave Aircraft (MCD)
RSAC	Royal Scottish Automobile Club (DBA)
RSACi	Recreational Software Advisory Council on the Internet [Computer science]
RSACI	Recreational Software Advisory Council on the Internet
RSAD	Remote Safe-and-Arm Device
RSAF	Republic of Singapore Air Force (PDAA)
RSAF	Royal Saudi Air Force
RSAF	Royal Small Arms Factory [British]
RSAF	Royal Swedish Air Force
RSAG	Reserve Storage Activity, Germersheim, West Germany [Military]
RSAI	Regional Science Association, International (NTPA)
RSAI	Royal Society of Antiquaries of Ireland
RSAI	Rules, Standards and Instruction (IAA)
RSAI	Rutgers Social Attribute Inventory [Psychology]
RSAK	Reserve Storage Activity, Kaiserslautern, West Germany [Military]
RSAL	Reserve Storage Activity, Luxembourg [Military]
RSALT	Running, Signal, and Anchor Lights
RSAM	Real-Time Seismic Amplitude Measurement
RSAM	Royal Scottish Academy of Music and Drama (AIE)
RSAMC	Royal Society of Arts, Manufacturing and Commerce [London]
RSAND	Reserve Systems Analysis Division [Military] (DNAB)
RS & C	Reliability, Surveillance, and Control (SAA)
RS & D	Receipt, Storage, and Delivery [Business term]
RS&H	Reynolds, Smith, & Hills, Inc. (NAKS)
RS & I	Rules, Standards, and Instructions
RS & M	Royal Sappers and Miners [British military] (DMA)
RS & MD	Riots, Strikes, and Malicious Damage [Insurance] (ADA)
RS & R	Retail, Service, and Repair
RS & S	Receiving, Shipping, and Storage (NASA)
R San I	Royal Sanitary Institute [Later, RSH] [British]
RSAP	Response Session Abort Positive (IAA)
RSAP	Revolutionaire Socialistische Arbeiders Partij [Revolutionary Socialist Workers' Party] [Netherlands Political party] (PPE)
RSARR	Republic of South Africa Research Reactor
RSAS	Revenue Sharing Advisory Service (EA)
RSAS	Royal Sanitary Association of Scotland
RSAS	Royal Surgical Aid Society [British] (BI)
RSAT	Raynaud's and Scleroderma Association Trust [British] (EAIO)
RSB	Radiation Safety Booklet (DNAB)
RSB	Range Safety Beacon [NASA] (AAG)
RSB	Ravensbos [Netherlands] [Seismograph station code, US Geological Survey] (SEIS)
RSB	Reactor Service Building (NRCH)
RSB	Reconnaissance Strike Bomber
RSB	Recycling Sourcebook [A publication]
RSB	Reduced-Size Blueprint (NG)
RSB	Reference Standards Book [Military]
RSB	Regimental Stretcher-Bearer
RSB	Regional Shipping Boards [NATO] (NATG)
RSB	Registered Schools Board [Victoria, Australia]
RSB	Remote System Base (MHDI)
RSB	Repair Service Bureau [Telecommunications] (TEL)
RSB	Retail Sales Battery [Employment test]
RSB	Reticulocyte Standard Buffer [Medicine] (DMAA)
RSB	Rhondda & Swansea Bay Railway [Wales]
RSB	Right Sternal Border [Medicine]
RSB	Rochester Subway Co. [AAR code]
RSB	Roller Skating Business Magazine [A publication] (EAAP)
RSB	Roseberth [Australia Airport symbol Obsolete] (OAG)
RSB	Royal Swedish Ballet
RSB	Rudder Speed Brake (MCD)
RSB	Samaero SA [Romania] [ICAO designator] (FAAC)
RSBA	Rail Steel Bar Association [Later, SMA] (EA)
RSBC	Revised Statutes of British Columbia [A publication] (ILCA)
RSBDC	Regional Small Business Development Center [Rutgers University] [Research center] (RCD)
RSB(E)	Regional Shipping Board (East) [NATO]
RSBEI	Registered Student of the Institution of Body Engineers [British] (DBQ)
RSBO	Refined Soybean Oil
RSBRC	Reference and Subscription Books Review Committee [American Library Association]
RSBS	RADAR Safety Beacon System (MCD)
RSBT	Recovery Storage Unit Boot Test [Military]
RSB(W)	Regional Shipping Board (West) [NATO]
RSC	Racing Service Center [Motorcycle racing]
RSC	RADAR Scan Converter [Military] (CAAL)
RSC	RADAR Sea Clutter
RSC	RADAR Set Control
RSC	RADAR System Console [Military] (CAAL)
RSC	RADAR System Controller [Military] (CAAL)
RSC	Radiation Shielding Computer Codes [Database] [Oak Ridge National Laboratory] [Department of Energy] [Information service or system] (CRD)
RSC	Range Safety Command [or Control] [NASA]
RSC	Rational Self-Counseling [Psychology] (DHSM)
RSC	Rat Skin Collagen
RSC	Rat Spleen Cell [Medicine] (DMAA)

RSC	Raytheon Service Co.
RSC	Reactor Safety Commission [Germany]
RSC	Reactor Safety Coordinator [Nuclear energy] (NRCH)
RSC	Reactor Steam Cycle
RSC	Reader Service Card
RSC	Record Status Code [Military] (AABC)
RSC	Referee Stops Contest [Amateur boxing]
RSC	Regional Safety Coordinator [Australia]
RSC	Regional Service Center [Military] (CINC)
RSC	Regular, Slotted, Corrugated [Container]
RSC	Reinforcement Support Category [DoD]
RSC	Relative System Capability
RSC	Relaxation-Sensitive Cell (PDAA)
RSC	Release Schedule Code (SAA)
RSC	Religious Sisters of Charity [Roman Catholic religious order]
RSC	Remote Sensing Center [Texas A & M University] [Research center] (RCD)
RSC	Remote Store Controller
RSC	Replacement and School Command [Military]
RSC	Rescue Sub-Center [ICAO] (FAAC)
RSC	Reserve Service Control [Navy]
RSC	Residential Sales Council (EA)
RSC	Residential Support Center (OICC)
RSC	Resident Shop Control (SAA)
RSC	Respiratory Symptoms Complex [Medicine]
RSC	Restart Capability (AAG)
RSC	Rested-State Contraction [Obstetrics] (MAE)
RSC	Reversible Sickled Cell [Hematology]
RSC	Revised Statutes of Canada [Canada Department of Justice] [Information service or system] (CRD)
RSC	Rework Support Conference [Military] (DNAB)
RSC	Rex Stores [NYSE symbol] (TTSB)
RSC	Rex Stores Corp. [Formerly, Audio/Video Affiliates, Inc.] [NYSE symbol] (SPSG)
RSC	Riga Skulte Airport [Former USSR Airport symbol Obsolete] (OAG)
RSC	Right-Sided Colon Cancer [Medicine]
RSC	Right Stage Center [A stage direction]
RSC	Right Subclavian [Medicine] (DMAA)
RSC	RISC Single Chip [IBM] [Computer science]
RSC	Road Safety Committee [British police]
RSC	Road Safety Council [Australia]
RSC	Royal Shakespeare Company [British]
RSC	Royal Society of Canada
RSC	Royal Society of Chemistry [Chemical Society and Royal Institute of Chemistry] [Formed by a merger of] (EAIO)
RSC	Rules of the Supreme Court [A publication] (DLA)
RSC	Runway Surface Condition [Aviation] (MCD)
RSC	Rural Service Center [Agency for International Development]
RSC	Russell Sage College [New York]
RSC	Saint Charles Borromeo Seminary, Overbrook, PA [OCLC symbol] (OCLC)
RSCA	Religious Speech Communication Association (EA)
RScA	Right Scapulo-Anterior [A fetal position] [Obstetrics]
RSCAA	Radio Shack Computer Alumni Association (EA)
RSCAAL	Remote Sensing Chemical Agent Alarm [Army] (INF)
RSCACT	Road Safety Council of the Australian Capital Territory
RscBnc	Resource Bancshares Mortgage Group [Associated Press] (SAG)
RSCC	Regional Sample Control Center (GNE)
RSCC	Remote-Site Command Computer [NASA]
RSCC	Remote-Site Computer Complex [NASA]
RSCC	Republican Senatorial Campaign Committee
RSCCP	Response Session Change Control Positive (IAA)
RSCD	Report Series Codes Dictionary [A publication]
RSCD	Request to Start Contract Definition
RSCD	Runway Surface Condition [Aviation] (FAAC)
RSCDS	Royal Scottish Country Dance Society (EAIO)
RSCDSA	Religion and Socialism Commission of the Democratic Socialists of America (EA)
RSCF	Rotating Spherical Convection Facility (SSD)
RSCG	Radio Set Control Group
RSCG	Roux Seguela Cayzac & Goudard [Advertising agency] (ECON)
RSCH	Range Scheduling (MUGU)
RSCH	Ready Spares Chassis
RSCH	Research (AFM)
Rsch	Research (TBD)
RschFrnt	Research Frontiers [Associated Press] (SAG)
RschFrt	Research Frontiers, Inc. [Associated Press] (SAG)
RSCHM	Royal School of Church Music [British]
RSCHOPSDET	Research Operations Detachment (DNAB)
RSCIE	Remote Station Communication Interface Equipment
RSCJ	Society of the Sacred Heart [Roman Catholic women's religious order]
RSCL	Radioactive Sodium Chemistry Loop
RSCM	Recoiling Structural Contour Map [Surface analysis]
RscM	Resource Mortgage Capital, Inc. [Associated Press] (SAG)
RSCM	Royal School of Church Music [British]
RscMtg	Resource Mortgage Capital, Inc. [Associated Press] (SAG)
RscMtge	Resource Mortgage Capital, Inc. [Associated Press] (SAG)
RSCN	Registered Sick Children's Nurse [British]
RSCNT	Road Safety Council of the Northern Territory [Australia]
RSCO	Rules of the Supreme Court, Order [Number] (ILCA)
RS Comp	Statutes of Connecticut, Compilation of 1854 [A publication] (DLA)
RScP	Right Scapuloposterior [A fetal position] [Obstetrics]
RSCR	Range Safety Command Receiver [NASA] (KSC)
RSCR	Res Care, Inc. [NASDAQ symbol] (SAG)

RSCR .... Reserve Special Commendation Ribbon
RSCS .... Range Safety Command System [NASA] (AAG)
RSCS .... Rate Stabilization and Control System
RSCS .... Remote Spooling Communications Subsystem [IBM Corp.] [Computer science] (IBMDP)
RSCS .... Remote Spooling Control System [Computer science] (TNIG)
RSCS .... Rod Sequence Control System [Nuclear energy] (NRCH)
RSCSA .... Railway Signal and Communications Suppliers Association [Later, RSS] (EA)
RSCSS .... Range Safety Command Shutdown System (IAA)
RSCT .... Rach Sentence Completion Test [Speech and language therapy] (DAVI)
RSCT .... Rohde Sentence Completions Test [Psychology]
RSCT .... Rotter Sentence Completion Test [Speech and language therapy] (DAVI)
RSCW .... Research Reactor, State College of Washington (NRCH)
RSD .... RADAR System Development (IAA)
RSD .... Radiance Spectral Distribution
RSD .... Raised (MSA)
RSD .... Raised Shelter Deck (DS)
RSD .... Range Support Directive (SAA)
RSD .... Rassemblement des Socialistes et des Democrates [Rally of Socialists and Democrats] [Reunion] [Political party] (PPW)
RSD .... Ratoon Stunting Disease [of sugarcane]
RSD .... Reentry Systems Department
RSD .... Reference Services Division [of ALA] [Later, RASD] (EA)
RSD .... Reflex Sympathetic Dystrophy [Medicine]
RSD .... Refueling Shutdown (IEEE)
RSD .... Relative Standard Deviation [Statistics]
RSD .... Relative Stock Density [Pisciculture]
RSD .... Reliability Status Document (IAA)
RSD .... Remote Sensing Device
RSD .... Reporting Systems Division [National Shorthand Reporters Association]
RSD .... Requirements and Specifications Document [NASA] (NASA)
RSD .... Research Services Department [United Way of Greater Indianapolis] [Indiana] [Information service or system] (IID)
RSD .... Research Services Directory [A publication]
RSD .... Resigned
RSD .... Responsible System Designer (NRCH)
RSD .... Ring System Descriptor (NITA)
RSD .... Risk-Specific Dose [Environmental science] (FFDE)
RSD .... Roadside Delivery (ADA)
RSD .... Rock Sound [Bahamas] [Airport symbol] (OAG)
RSD .... Rolling Steel Door [Technical drawings]
RSD .... Rosehaugh Stanhope Developments [Commercial firm British]
RSD .... Round Vesicles, Small Profile and Dark Mitochondria [Synaptic terminals] (DB)
RSD .... Royal Society, Dublin
RSD .... Runcible System Duplexer [Telecommunications] (IAA)
RSDA .... Reflex Sympathetic Dystrophy Association (EA)
RSDA .... Road Surface Dressing Association [British] (DBA)
RSDB .... SCB [Statistika Centralbyran] Regional Statistical Data Base [Sweden Information service or system] (CRD)
RSDC .... Radiation Subprogramme Data Center [Marine science] (MSC)
RSDC .... Range Safety Data Coordinator (SAA)
RSDC .... Remote Secure Data Change (DNAB)
RSDG .... Raster Scan Display Generator (MCD)
RSDG .... Royal Scots Dragoon Guards [British military] (DMA)
RSDI .... Retirement, Survivors, or Disability Insurance [Social Security Administration] (GFGA)
RSDLP .... Russian Social-Democratic Labor Party [Political party]
RSDLP(B) .... Russian Social-Democratic Labor Party (Bolsheviks) [Political party]
RSDNC .... Residence
RSDNT .... Resident
Rsdnt .... Resident (TBD)
RSDP .... Remote Shutdown Panel (IEEE)
RSDP .... Remote-Site Data Processor [NASA]
RSDP .... Rural School Development Program [Australia]
RSDr .... Doctor Rerum Socialium [Doctor of Social Sciences] [Latin]
RSDRP .... Rossiiskaia Sotsial-Demokraticheskaia Rabochaya Partiia [Russian Social Democratic Workers' Party] [Political party] (PPE)
RSDS .... RADAR Systems Design Section
RSDS .... Range Safety Destruct System
RSDS .... Reflex Sympathetic Dystrophy Syndrome [Medicine] (DMAA)
RSDSA .... Reflex Sympathetic Dystrophy Association (EA)
RSDT .... Regulations of Office of the Secretary, Department of Transportation
RSDT .... Remote Station Data Terminal
RSDU .... RADAR Storm Detection Unit
RSDW .... Ross Sea Deep Water [Marine science] (MSC)
RSDWP .... Russian Social-Democratic Workers Party
RSE .... RADAR Search Equipment
RSE .... Raid Size Estimate
RSE .... Rat Synaptic Ending (DB)
RSE .... Reactive Sputter Etch (AAEL)
RSE .... Receiving Site Equipment [NASA]
RSE .... Record Selection Expression (MHDI)
RSE .... Reference Sensing Element (DNAB)
RSE .... Reference Standards Equipment [Deep Space Instrumentation Facility, NASA]
RSE .... Relative Standard Error [DOE] (TAG)
RSE .... Remote Sensing of Environment [A publication] (DNAB)
RSE .... Removal Site Evaluations [Environmental science] (COE)
RSE .... Request for Self Enhancement (IAA)
RSE .... Request Select Entry [Computer science]

RSE .... Resistance Soldering Equipment
RSE .... Reverse Sutured Eye [Ophthalmology] (DAVI)
RSE .... Richmond Stock Exchange (IIA)
RSE .... Right Sternal Edge [On Examination] [Cardiology] (DAVI)
RSE .... Rouse Co. [NYSE symbol] (SAG)
RSE .... Royal Society of Edinburgh
RSE .... Sydney-Rose Bay [Australia Airport symbol] (OAG)
RSEA .... Reference Sensing Element Amplifier
RSEC .... Regional Science.Experience Center
RSEC .... Regional Solar Energy Center
RSEC .... Representative Shuttle Environmental Control [System] [NASA]
R_sec .... Secondary Resistance (IDOE)
RSECS .... Representative Shuttle Environmental Control System [NASA] (MCD)
RSED .... Refund Statute Expiration Date [IRS]
RSEP .... Response Session End Positive (IAA)
RSEP .... Restraint System Evaluation Program [Department of Transportation]
RSEPrA .... Rouse Co. Sr'A'Cv Pfd [NYSE symbol] (TTSB)
RSEPrZ .... Rouse Capital 9.25%'QUIPS' [NYSE symbol] (TTSB)
RSER .... Remote Sensing of Earth Resources
RSER .... Rotary Stylus Electronics Recorder
RSERV .... Relocatable Library Service Function [Computer science] (IAA)
RSES .... Refrigeration Service Engineers Society (EA)
RSES .... Rosenberg Self-Esteem Scale
RSET .... Receiver Signal Element Timing (IAA)
RSET .... Register Set [Computer science] (CIST)
RSEU .... Remote Scanner-Encoder Unit [Bell Laboratories]
RSEW .... Resistance Seam Welding
RSEW-HF ...... Resistance Seam Welding - High Frequency
RSEW-I .... Resistance Seam Welding - Induction
RSEXEC .... Resource Sharing Executive (MHDI)
RSF .... Radial Stress-Field [Hypothesis describing forces in a sand-pile]
RSF .... Radial Structure Function [of solid catalysts]
RSF .... Receiving-Safing Facility [NASA] (MCD)
RSF .... Reciprocal Cross Sterile Females [Genetics]
RSF .... Refurbish and Subassemblies Facilities [NASA] (NASA)
RSF .... Refurbishment and Subassembly Facility [Kennedy Space Center] (NAKS)
RSF .... Reject Suspense File [Army]
RSF .... Relative Sensitivity Factor [Analytical chemistry]
RSF .... Relative Substitution Frequency [of amino acids in proteins]
RSF .... Remote Service Facility (IAA)
RSF .... Remote Support Facility
RSF .... Requisition Status File (DNAB)
RSF .... Research Systems Facility
RSF .... Residual Support Force [After main force redeployment] [Military]
RSF .... Retail Stores Forum (EA)
RSF .... Rhododendron Species Foundation (EA)
RSF .... Risk Studies Foundation (EA)
RSF .... Roll Sheet Feeder
RSF .... Rough Sunk Face [Construction]
RSF .... Royal Scots Fusiliers [Military unit]
RSF .... Russian Student Fund [Defunct] (EA)
RSFA .... Roller Skating Federation of America [Defunct] (EA)
RSFC .... Republic Security Financial Corp. [NASDAQ symbol] (NQ)
RSFC .... Republic Security Finl [NASDAQ symbol] (TTSB)
RSFC .... Ricky Skaggs International Fan Club (EA)
RSFC .... Rolling Stones Fan Club (EA)
RSFC .... Ronnie Smith Fan Club (EA)
RSFCO .... Republic Sec Finl Cv'C'Pfd [NASDAQ symbol] (TTSB)
RSFCP .... Republic Sec Finl 7.5% Cv 'A' Pfd [NASDAQ symbol] (TTSB)
RS Fnl .... RS Financial Group [Formerly, Raleigh Federal Savings Bank] [Associated Press] (SAG)
RSFPP .... Retired Servicemen's Family Protection Plan [Military]
RSFQ .... Rapid Single-Flux Quantum Circuit [Physics]
RSFS .... Real Scene Focus Sensor (PDAA)
RSFS .... Royal Scottish Forestry Society (EAIO)
RSFSR .... Russian Soviet Federated Socialist Republic
RSG .... Rabbi Saadia Gaon [Jewish scholar, 882-942] (BJA)
RSG .... RADAR Set Group [HAWK missile] (MCD)
RSG .... RADAR Signal Generator (MCD)
RSG .... RADAR Systems Group [of General Motors Corp.]
RSG .... Range Safety Group [Range Commanders Council] [White Sands Missile Range, NM]
RSG .... Rate Signal Generator (AAG)
RSG .... Rate Support Grant [British]
RSG .... Rate Switching Gyro (MCD)
RSG .... Reassign (AABC)
RSG .... Receiving Stolen Goods
RSG .... Red Supergiant [Astronomy]
RSG .... Reenlistment Steering Group [Military] (MCD)
RSG .... Reference Signal Generator
RSG .... Regional Seat of Government
RSG .... Reitan Strength of Grip [Medicine] (DAVI)
RSG .... Relay Switch Group
RSG .... Research Study Group (NATG)
RSG .... Resident Study Group [Army] (MCD)
RSG .... Resource Service Group Ltd. [Toronto Stock Exchange symbol]
RSG .... Revenue Support Grant (AIE)
RSG .... Rocksprings, TX [Location identifier FAA] (FAAL)
RSG .... Royal Scots Greys [Military unit]
RSGB .... Radio Society of Great Britain [Potters Bar, Hertfordshire, England] (EAIO)
RSGB .... Research Surveys of Great Britain Ltd.
RSGC .... Royal Sydney Golf Club [Australia]
RSGI .... Riverside Group, Inc. [Jacksonville, FL] [NASDAQ symbol] (NQ)

RSGMT	Reassignment
RSGN	Reassign
RSGS	Ranges and Space Ground Support (AAG)
RSGS	Royal Scottish Geographical Society
RSH	RADAR Status History
rsh	Remote Shell [Computer science] (CDE)
RSH	Resin Sluice Header (NRCH)
RSH	Ring Systems Handbook [American Chemical Society] [A publication]
RSH	Royal Society of Health [Formerly, R San I] [British]
RSH	Russian Mission [Alaska] [Airport symbol] (OAG)
RSHA	Reichssicherheitshauptampt [Central Security Office of the Reich] [NAZI Germany]
RSHF	Room Sensible Heat Factor
RSHI	Rough Service, High Impact (DNAB)
RSHM	Religious of the Sacred Heart of Mary [Roman Catholic women's religious order]
RSHMI	Russian Hydrometeorological Institute [Marine science] (OSRA)
RSHS	Railroad Station Historical Society (EA)
RSHX	Recirculation Spray Heat Exchanger [Nuclear energy] (NRCH)
RSI	Air Sunshine, Inc. [ICAO designator] (FAAC)
RSI	East-West Resource Systems Institute [Research center] (RCD)
rsi	Race Specific Incompatibility
RSI	RADAR Scope Interpretation (AAG)
RSI	Radiation Shielding Information Data Base [Oak Ridge National Laboratory] [Department of Energy Information service or system] (CRD)
RSI	Radiation Systems, Inc. (EFIS)
RSI	Rationalization, Standardization, and Integration [or Interoperability] [Program] [Army] (INF)
RSI	Reactor Siting Index (NRCH)
RSI	Receipt, Storage, and Issue [Army] (AABC)
R(SI)	Reconstruction, Social Insurance [British World War II]
RSI	Record Status Indicator [Military] (AABC)
RSI	Reflected Signal Indication [Air Force]
RSI	Refractory Reusable Surface Insulation (PDAA)
RSI	Regional Safety Inspector [Ministry of Agriculture, Fisheries, and Food] [British]
RSI	Register Sender Inward [Telecommunications] (TEL)
RSI	Relative Strength Indicator (NUMA)
RSI	Religious Science International (EA)
RSI	Relocation Services Institute [British] (DBA)
RSI	Remote Sensing Institute [South Dakota State University] [Research center] (RCD)
RSI	Repetitive Strain Injury (PCM)
RSI	Replacement Stream Input [Military]
RSI	Repressor-Sensitizer Index [Psychology]
RSI	Repubblica Sociale Italiana [Italian Socialist Republic] [Founded by Mussolini 1943-1945]
RSI	Research Studies Institute
R-SI	Restricted-Security Information (DNAB)
RSI	Reusable Surface Insulation [NASA]
RSI	Ring State Indicator [Telecommunications] (IAA)
RSI	Rio Sidra [Panama] [Airport symbol] (OAG)
RSI	Roll Stability Indicator [NASA] (KSC)
RSI	Rotary Shaft Indicator
RSI	Rough Sleepers' Initiative [British] (WDAA)
RSI	Royal Sanitary Institute (ROG)
RSI	Royal Signals Institution [British] (DEN)
RSIC	Radiation Shielding Information Center [Department of Energy] [Oak Ridge, TN]
RSIC	Redstone Scientific Information Center [Army]
RSIC	Responding Superior in Command (MCD)
R-SICU	Respiratory-Surgical Intensive Care Unit [of a hospital] (AAMN)
RSID	Resource Identification Table [Computer science]
RSIGG	Rocket Signal, Green (IAA)
RSIGR	Rocket Signal, Red (IAA)
R SIGS	Royal Corps of Signals [British] (DMA)
RSIHM	Reparation Society of the Immaculate Heart of Mary (EA)
RSIM	RADAR Simulator (MSA)
RSIM	Retrospective Single Ion Monitoring [Analytical chemistry]
RSIN	Rural Stress Information Network (WDAA)
RSIP	RADAR Systems Improvement Program (DWSG)
RSIP	Reusable Software Implementation Program (SSD)
RSIPR	Reactor System with Interstage Product Removal [Chemical engineering]
RSIS	Radical Science Information Service [News service attempting to interrelate radical politics and scientific issues]
RSIS	Reed Stenhouse Investment Services [British]
RSIS	Rotorcraft Systems Integration Simulator [Joint Army-NASA program] (RDA)
RSIS	RSI Systems [NASDAQ symbol] (TTSB)
RSIS	RSI Systems, Inc. [NASDAQ symbol] (SAG)
RSI Sys	RSI Systems, Inc. [Associated Press] (SAG)
RSITA	Reglement du Service International des Telecommunications de l'Aeronautique
R/SITU	Respiratory/Surgical Intensive Therapy Unit [of a hospital]
RSIUFL	Release Suspension for Issue and Use of Following Lots [Military]
RSIVP	Rapid Sequence Intravenous Pyelogram [Medicine]
RSJ	Religious of St. Joseph of Australia (TOCD)
RSJ	Resistively-Shunted Junction [Physics]
RSJ	Rolled-Steel Joist
RSJ	Rolling-Stock Jigsaws [British]
RSK	Ransiki [West Irian, Indonesia] [Airport symbol] (AD)
RSKERL	Robert S. Kerr Environmental Research Laboratory [Ada, OK] [Environmental Protection Agency] (GRD)

RSKU	Reza Shah Kibur University [Iran]
RSL	Radio Standards Laboratory [National Institute of Standards and Technology]
RSL	Rate-Sensitive Liabilities (TDOB)
RSL	Reading on Statute Law [A publication] (DLA)
RSL	Received Signal Level [Telecommunications] (TEL)
RSL	Received Signal Power Level [Telecommunications] (OTD)
RSL	Reconnaissance and Security Line
RSL	Red Suspender League (EA)
RSL	Reference Standards Laboratory [Deep Space Instrumentation Facility, NASA]
RSL	Relative Sea Level
RSL	Remote Sensing Laboratory [University of Kansas, University of Minnesota] [Research center] (MCD)
RSL	Remote Sprint Launching [Military]
RSL	Requirements Statement Language
RSL	Research Services Ltd. [Database producer] [Wembley, Middlesex, England]
RSL	Resource Support List [NASA] (MCD)
RSL	Returned Servicemen's League [British military] (DMA)
RSL	Returned Services League [Australia] (WDAA)
RSL	Revolutionary Socialist League (EA)
RSL	Right Sacrolateral [Position] [Obstetrics] (DAVI)
RSL	Rio-Sul, Servicos Aereos Regionais SA [Brazil] [ICAO designator] (FAAC)
RSL	Ripe Skin Liquid [A banana substrate]
RSL	Road Service Licence [British] (DCTA)
RSL	Roselend [France] [Seismograph station code, US Geological Survey] (SEIS)
RSL	Royal Society, London [British]
RSL	Royal Society of Literature [British]
RSL	RSI Retail Solutions, Inc. [Vancouver Stock Exchange symbol]
RSL	Rumsford Sandy Loam [Type of soil]
RSL	Russell, KS [Location identifier FAA] (FAAL)
RSLA	Range Safety Launch Approval (AFM)
RSLB	Right Short Leg Brace [Medicine]
RSLPI	Recombinant Secretory Leukoprotease Inhibitor [Biochemistry]
RSLS	Receiver Side Lobe Suppression (MCD)
RSLS	Redundant Set Launch Sequencer (MCD)
RSLS	Reply Path Side Lobe Suppression (IAA)
RSLS	Runway Status Light System [FAA] (TAG)
RSLSI	Renzulli/Smith Learning Style Inventory (EDAC)
RSLT	Result (IAA)
RSLTS	Results
RSLV	Resolve (NASA)
RSLVR	Resolver (MSA)
RSM	Diocesan Sisters of Mercy (TOCD)
RSM	Radiation Signature Measurement
RSM	Radiation Survey Meter [NASA]
RSM	Radio Squadron Mobile (MUQU)
RSM	Rapeseed Meal
RSM	Rapidly Solidified Materials
RSM	Readability, Strength, Modulation (IAA)
RSM	Ready Service Magazine [Military] (DNAR)
RSM	Real Storage Management [Computer science] (IBMDP)
RSM	Reconnaissance Strategic Missile
RSM	Reed Switching Matrix
RSM	Regimental Sergeant Major [Army]
RSM	Religious Sisters of Mercy of Alma, Michigan (TOCD)
RSM	Remote Monitoring Services Manager [Telecommunications]
RSM	Research into Site Management (MHDB)
RSM	Resident Sector Management [Computer science] (IAA)
RSM	Resident System Monitor
RSM	Resource Management System (IAA)
RSM	Resource Status Monitor [Systems Center, Inc.]
RSM	Response Surface Methodology
RSM	Resume (NASA)
RSM	Revised Statutes of Manitoba [Canada] [A publication] (DLA)
RSM	Rivet Setting Machine
RSM	Robert Strange McNamara [US Secretary of Defense, 1961-68]
RSM	Rotterdam School of Management [Netherlands] (ECON)
RSM	Royal School of Mines [British]
RSM	Royal School of Musketry [Hythe] [Military British] (ROG)
RSM	Royal Society of Medicine [British]
RSM	Royal Society of Musicians of Great Britain
RSM	Royal Surrey Militia [British military] (DMA)
RSM	San Marino [International vehicle registration] (ODBW)
RSM	Sisters of Mercy [Roman Catholic religious order]
RSM	Sisters of Mercy (Ballyahannon, Ireland) (TOCD)
RSM	Sisters of Mercy (Mayo, Ireland) (TOCD)
RSM	Sisters of Mercy of Ardagh & Clonmacnois (TOCD)
RSM	Sisters of Mercy of Portland (TOCD)
RSM	Sisters of Mercy of the Americas (TOCD)
RSM	Sisters of Mercy (Sligo) (TOCD)
RSMA	Radiological Systems Microfilm Associates (EA)
RSMA	Railway Supply Manufacturers Association [Defunct] (EA)
RSMA	Railway Systems and Management Association [Defunct] (EA)
RSMA	Royal Society of Marine Artists [Formerly, SMA] [British]
RSMAS	Rosenstiel School of Marine and Atmospheric Science [University of Miami] [Research center] (RCD)
RSmB	Bryant College, Smithfield, RI [Library symbol Library of Congress] (LCLS)
RSMC	Regional Specialized Meteorological Center [Marine science] (OSRA)
RSMD	Resource Systems Management Division [Environmental Protection Agency] (GFGA)

RSME	Royal School of Military Engineering [*British military*] (DMA)
RSMF	Royal Society of Medicine Foundation (EA)
RSMG	Rotorcraft Simulator Motion Generator [*Army*] (RDA)
RSMGB	Royal Society of Musicians of Great Britain (EAIO)
RSMIS	Real Estate and Space Management Information System [*Marine science*] (OSRA)
RSMLC	Red de Salud de las Mujeres Latinoamericanas y del Caribe [*Latin American and Caribbean Women's Health Network*] (EAIO)
RSMM	Redundant System Monitor Model [*NASA*] (MCD)
RSMR	Raw Stock Material Requirements
RSMR	Rayleigh Scattering of Moessbauer Resonance [*Physics*]
RSMR	Relative Standard Mortality Rate (DMAA)
RSMS	Radio Spectrum Measurement System [*National Telecommunications and Information Administration*]
RSMT	Ras Shamra Mythological Texts (BJA)
RSMT	Red Sea Mission Team (EA)
RSMT	Reliability Safety Margin Test
RSN	Radiation Surveillance Network [*Public Health Service*]
RSN	Radio Supernovae [*Astrophysics*]
RSN	Random Sequence Number (DNAB)
RSN	Rassemblement pour le Salut National [*Rally for National Salvation*] [*Senegal*] (PD)
RSN	Ready, Soon, Now (Approach) [*Marketing*]
RSN	Real Soon Now [*Internet language*] [*Computer science*]
RSN	Reason (AFM)
RSN	Record Sequence Number [*Computer science*] (IAA)
RSN	Reference Sequence Number [*Online bibliographies*]
RSN	Reject Sequence Number [*Computer science*]
RSN	Report Serial Number [*Army*]
RSN	Research Surveillance Network
RSN	Resonate (KSC)
RSN	Revised Statutes of Newfoundland [*Canada*] [*A publication*] (DLA)
RSN	Right Substantia Nigra [*Medicine*] (DMAA)
RSN	Royal School of Needlework [*British*]
RSN	Royal Swazi National Airways Corp. [*Swaziland*] [*ICAO designator*] (FAAC)
RSN	Ruston, LA [*Location identifier FAA*] (FAAL)
RSNA	Radiological Society of North America (EA)
RSNA	Royal Society of Northern Antiquaries (ROG)
RSNB	Revised Statutes of New Brunswick [*Canada*] [*A publication*] (DLA)
RSNC	Royal Society for Nature Conservation Wildlife Trusts Partnership (EAIO)
RSND	Resound Corp. [*NASDAQ symbol*] (SAG)
RSNF	Royal Saudi Arabian Navy Forces (MCD)
RSNGS	Rancho Seco Nuclear Generating Station (NRCH)
RSNO	Referral Service Network Office
RSNP	Registered Student Nurse Program [*Military*] (AABC)
RSNS	Revised Statutes of Nova Scotia [*Canada*] [*A publication*] (DLA)
RSNT	Research Society for Natural Therapeutics [*British*] (DBA)
RSNT	Revised Single Negotiating Text [*UN Law of the Sea Conference*]
RSNZ	Royal Society of New Zealand (WDAA)
RSO	Aero Asia [*Pakistan*] [*ICAO designator*] (FAAC)
RSO	Radiation Safety Officer [*Nuclear energy*] (NRCH)
RSO	Radiation Service Organization (EFIS)
RSO	Radiological Safety Office [*or Officer*] (NASA)
RSO	Radiosonde Observation (MUGU)
RSO	Radio Symphony Orchestra
RSO	Railway Sorting Office
RSO	Railway Suboffice
RSO	Ramus Supraorbitalis [*Anatomy*]
RSO	Range Safety Officer [*Military*]
RSO	Range Support Operation
RSO	Reactor Standards Office [*Oak Ridge National Laboratory*]
RSO	Reactor System Outline [*Nuclear energy*] (NRCH)
RSO	Reconnaissance and Survey Officer [*Military*] (AABC)
RSO	Reconnaissance System Officer (MCD)
RSO	Rectified Skew Orthomorphic (PDAA)
RSO	Regimental Supply Officer [*Army*]
RSO	Regional Safety Officer [*British*] (DCTA)
RSO	Regional Security Officer [*Foreign Service*]
RSO	Register Sender Outward [*Telecommunications*] (TEL)
RSO	Relativistic and Spin-Orbit (PDAA)
RSO	Remanso [*Brazil*] [*Airport symbol*] (AD)
RSO	Reported Significant Observations [*Environmental science*] (COE)
RSO	Reproduction Service Order (SAA)
RSO	Research Ship of Opportunity
RSO	Resident Surgical Officer [*British*]
RSO	Retirement Service Officer [*DoD*]
RSO	Revenue Sharing Office [*Treasury*] (OICC)
RSO	Revised Statutes of Ontario [*Canada*] [*A publication*] (DLA)
RSO	Revolutionaere Sozialisten (Oesterreichs) [*Revolutionary Socialists (Austria)*] [*Political party*] (PPE)
RSO	Right Salpingo-Oophorectomy [*Medicine*]
RSO	Robert Stigwood Orginazation [*Record label*]
RSO	Runway Supervisory Officer [*Aviation*] (MCD)
RSO	Rural Suboffice [*British*]
RSOB	Russell Senate Office Building [*Also, OSOB*] [*Washington, DC*] (DLA)
RSOC	Remote Sensing Oceanography [*Navy*]
RSOG	Reserve Special Operations Group [*Army*]
RSOI	Reception, Staging, Onward Movement and Integration [*Military*] (INF)
RSO/MFSO	Range Safety Officer / Missile Flight Safety Officer [*Military*] (SAA)
RSOP	Range Safety Operational Plan (MUGU)
RSOP	Readiness Standing Operating Procedures [*Military*] (INF)

RSOP	Reconnaissance, Selection, and Occupation of Position [*Military*]
RSOPN	Resumed Operation [*Aviation*] (FAAC)
RSOR	Range Safety Operations Requirement
RS or L	Rated Same or Lower
RSOS	Resident Supervisor of Shipping [*Navy*] (DNAB)
RSP	RADAR Signal Processor
RSP	Radii of Standard Parallels
RSP	Radio Switch Panel
RSP	Random Smooth Pursuit [*Ophthalmology*]
RSP	Range Solar Panel
RSP	Range Sorting Program
RSP	Range Support Plan (MUGU)
RSP	Rapid Site Preparation
RSP	Rapid Solidification Process (MCD)
RSP	Rassemblement Socialiste Progressiste [*Tunisia*] [*Political party*] (EY)
RSP	Rate Sensing Package (AAG)
RSP	Reactive Soil Pool [*Agriculture*]
RSP	Reactivity-Selectivity Principle (MEC)
RSP	Reactivity Surveillance Procedures [*Nuclear energy*] (NRCH)
RSP	Reader/Sorter Processor
RSP	Real-Time Signal Processor (MCD)
RSP	Rear-Screen Projection (WDAA)
RSP	Receiving Stolen Property
RSP	Recirculating Single Pass [*Medicine*] (BARN)
RSP	Reconnaissance and Security Positions [*Military*]
RSP	Record Select Program [*Computer science*]
RSP	Recoverable Sparoair Probe (MUGU)
RSP	Red Switch Project [*Military*] (MUSM)
RSP	Reinforced Structural Plastic
RSP	Relative Stopping Power [*Nuclear energy*] (NUCP)
RSP	Remote Sensor Platoon
RSP	Remote Shutdown Panel [*Nuclear energy*] (NRCH)
RSP	Remote Switching Partition (HGAA)
RSP	Render Safe Procedure [*Military*]
RSP	Rendezvous Station Panel [*NASA*] (MCD)
RSP	Replenishment Spare Part
RSP	Replication Synchronization Process [*Telecommunications*] (TEL)
RSP	Required Space Character [*Computer science*]
RSP	Reserve Stock Point
RSP	Resource Sharing Protocol (IAA)
RSP	Resource Specialist Program
RSP	Respirable Suspended Particulates
RSP	Responder Beacon
RSP	Response Byte [*Computer science*]
RSP	Restoration Priority [*Telecommunications*] (TEL)
RSP	Retail Stockage Policy
RSP	Revolutionaire Socialistische Partij [*Revolutionary Socialist Party*] [*Netherlands Political party*] (PPE)
RSP	Revolutionary Socialist Party [*India*] [*Political party*] (PPW)
RSP	Rhinoseptoplasty [*Otorhinolaryngology*] (DAVI)
RSP	Right Sacroposterior [*A fetal position*] [*Obstetrics*]
RSP	Robotic Sample Processor [*Automation*]
RSP	Rocky Slope Pipeline
RSP	Roll Stabilization Platform
RSP	Roscoe, Snyder & Pacific Railway Co. [*AAR code*]
RSP	Rotating Shield Plug [*Nuclear energy*] (NRCH)
RSP	Rotation in a Selected Plane
RSPr	Route Selection Program (SAA)
RSP	Rural Satellite Program [*US Agency for International Development*] [*Washington, DC*] [*Telecommunications*] (TSSD)
RSP	Southern Pacific Rail [*NYSE symbol*] (TTSB)
RSP	Southern Pacific Railroad Co. [*NYSE symbol*] (SPSG)
RSPA	Railway Systems and Procedures Association [*Later, RSMA*]
RSPA	Research and Special Programs Administration [*Department of Transportation*] [*Washington, DC*] (GRD)
RSPA	Royal Society for the Prevention of Accidents [*British*]
RSPAS	[*The*] Research School of Pacific and Asian Studies [*Australian National University*] (ECON)
RSPB	Retail Stockage Policy, Bulk Supplies (MCD)
RSPB	Royal Society for the Protection of Birds [*British*]
RSPBA	Royal Scottish Pipe Band Association [*British*] (DBA)
RSPCA	Royal Society for the Prevention of Cruelty to Animals [*British*]
RSPD	Rapid Solidification Plasma Deposition [*Metallurgy*]
RSPD	Research and Special Project Division [*Bureau of National Affairs*] [*Information service or system*] (IID)
RSPD	Respond (MSA)
RSPE	RADAR Signalling Processing Equipment
RSPE	Retail Stockage Policy, Evaluation (MCD)
RSPEI	Revised Statutes of Prince Edward Island [*Canada*]
RSPH	Royal Society for the Promotion of Health [*British*] (DAVI)
RSPI	Residential Space Planners International (EA)
RSPI	Resident-Shared Page Index [*Computer science*] (OA)
RSPK	Recurrent Spontaneous Psychokinesis [*Poltergeist*] [*Parapsychology*]
RSPL	RADAR Significant Power Line
RSPL	Recommended Spare Parts List [*NASA*]
RSPM	Random Spatial Phase Modulator
RS/PM	Rapid Solidification/Powder Metallurgy
RSPMP	Ready Store Positive Maintenance Program (MCD)
RSPO	Rail Services Planning Office [*Interstate Commerce Commission*]
RSPO	Railway Station Police Officer [*British*]
RSPP	Radio Simulation Patch Panel (CET)
RSPP	Royal Society of Portrait Painters [*British*]
Rspr	Rechtspraak [*Case Law, Judicial Decisions*] [*Netherlands*] (ILCA)
Rspr	Rechtsprechung [*Court Practice*] [*German*] (ILCA)

Rspr Arb ...... Rechtsprechung in Arbeitssachen [*Labor Court Reports*] [*German*] (ILCA)
RSPRT .... Robust Sequential Probability Ratio Test [*Navy*]
RSPS .... Range Solar Panel Substrate
RSPS .... Response (MSA)
RSPS .... Royal Scottish Pipers' Society [*British*] (DBA)
RSPT .... Rayleigh-Schrodinger Perturbation Theory [*Physical chemistry*]
RSPT .... Real Storage Page Table [*Computer science*] (BUR)
RSPT .... Report Starting Procedure Turn [*Aviation*] (DA)
RSPT .... Revue des Sciences Philosophiques et Theologiques [*A publication*] (ODCC)
RSPTR .... Respirator (MSA)
RSPV .... Respective (AABC)
RSPWC .... Royal Society of Painters in Water-Colours [*British*]
RSQ .... Rescue (AAG)
RSQ .... Revised Statutes of Quebec [*Canada*] [*A publication*] (DLA)
RSQBT .... Rescue Boat
RSQC .... Reliability, Safety, and Quality Control
RSR .... Congregation of Our Lady of the Holy Rosary [*Roman Catholic women's religious order*]
RSR .... En Route Surveillance RADAR
RSR .... Radiological Safety Review [*Nuclear energy*] (NRCH)
RSR .... Raiding Support Regiment [*British Royal Marines*] [*World War II*]
RSR .... Range Safety Report [*NASA*] (AAG)
RSR .... Rapid Solidification Rate (IEEE)
RSR .... Rate Stabilization Reserve [*Health insurance*] (GHCT)
RSR .... Reactor Safety Research [*Nuclear energy*]
RSR .... Ready Service Ring (NG)
RSR .... Red Sulfhydryl Reagent
RSR .... Reference Services Review [*A publication*] (BRI)
RSR .... Refracted Surface-Reflected Ray
RSR .... Regular Sinus Rhythm [*Physiology*]
RSR .... Relative Survival Rate [*Statistics*] (DAVI)
RSR .... Relay Set Receiver [*Telecommunications*] (IAA)
RSR .... Remote Start Relay (IAA)
RSR .... Republica Socialista Romania [*Socialist Republic of Romania*] (EY)
RSR .... Republic of Sudan Radio
RSR .... Request for Scientific Research (AAG)
RSR .... Required Supply Rate [*Military*] (AABC)
RSR .... Research Study Requests
RSR .... Residue Solvent Refining [*Lummus Crest, Inc. process*]
RSR .... Resorufin [*Organic chemistry*]
RSR .... Resources Status Report
RSR .... Restore [*Computer science*] (ECII)
RSR .... Reverse Switching Rectifier (IAA)
RSR .... Revised Supplementary Regulation
RSR .... Right Element Shift Right (SAA)
RSR .... Riser Foods Cl'A' [*AMEX symbol*] (TTSB)
RSR .... Riser Foods, Inc. [*AMEX symbol*] (SPSG)
RSR .... Rocket Scoring Reliability (MCD)
RSR .... Rocket Stabilized Rod
RSR .... Rod Select Relay (IEEE)
RSR .... Rotary Seal Ring
RSR .... Rotating Shadowband Radiometer (USDC)
RSR .... Route Surveillance RADAR
RSR .... Rover Sports Register [*An association*] (EAIO)
RSR .... Royal Sussex Regiment [*Military unit*] [*British*]
RSR .... Worcester, MA [*Location identifier FAA*] (FAAL)
RSRA .... Rotor Systems Research Aircraft [*Army/NASA*]
RSRB .... Redesigned Solid Rocket Booster
RSRCH .... Research
RSRE .... Royal Signals and RADAR Establishment [*Computer chip designer*] [*England*]
RSRE .... Royal Signals Research Establishment [*British*]
RSRM .... Raiding Squadron Royal Marines [*British military*] (DMA)
RSRM .... Redesigned Solid Rocket Motor
RSRM .... Reduced Smoke Rocket Motor (MCD)
RSRM .... Reusable Solid Rocket Motor
RSROA .... Roller Skating Rink Operators Association (EA)
RSROAA ...... Roller Skating Rink Operators Association (NADA)
RSROM .... Row Select Read-Only Memory [*Computer science*] (IAA)
RSRP .... Remote Sensing Research Program [*University of California*]
RSRP .... Rossica Society of Russian Philately (EA)
RSRS .... Radio and Space Research Station [*Later, Appleton Laboratory*] [*British*] (MCD)
RSRS .... Range Safety Receiving Station
Rsrt .... Resort
RsrtIn .... Resort Income Investors, Inc. [*Associated Press*] (SAG)
RSRV .... Rotor Systems Research Vehicle
RSRW .... Remote Short Range Wind Sensor (MCD)
RSS .... RADAR Seeker Simulator [*Military*] (CAAL)
RSS .... RADAR Sensing System [*Military*] (CAAL)
RSS .... RADAR Signal Simulator
RSS .... Radiated Simulation System (MCD)
RSS .... Radio Security Service [*British*]
RSS .... Radio Subsystem
RS(S) .... Radio Supervisor (Special) [*British military*] (DMA)
RSS .... Rail Security Service [*MTMC*] (TAG)
RSS .... Rail Surveillance Service [*Military Traffic Management Command*]
RSS .... Railway Systems Suppliers (EA)
RSS .... Range Safety Switch [*NASA*] (MCD)
RSS .... Range Safety System [*NASA*]
RSS .... Range Slaving System
RSS .... Rapid Scanning of Spectra [*Instrumentation*]

RSS .... Rashtriya Swayamsevak Sangh [*National Union of Selfless Servers*] [*Militant Hindu organization India*]
RSS .... Rat Stomach Strip [*Medicine*] (DMAA)
RSS .... Reactant Service System
RSS .... Reactants Supply System [*NASA*] (KSC)
RSS .... Reactive Stream Separation (MCD)
RSS .... Reactive System Sensitivity (IAA)
RSS .... Reactor Safety Study [*Nuclear energy*]
RSS .... Reactor Shutdown System [*Nuclear energy*] (NRCH)
RSS .... Ready Service Spares
RSS .... Real-Time Switching System
RSS .... Recombination Signal Sequence [*Immunology*]
RSS .... Reed Stenhouse Companies Ltd. [*Toronto Stock Exchange symbol*]
RSS .... Reference Sound Source
RSS .... Refrigeration System [*or Subsystem*] [*Skylab*] [*NASA*]
RSS .... Refrigeration System Shield (MCD)
RSS .... Regiae Societatis Sodalis [*Fellow of the Royal Society*] [*Latin*]
RSS .... Registered Shoeing Smith [*Blacksmith*] [*Scotland*]
RSS .... Regression Sum of Squares
RSS .... Rehabilitation Service Series
RSS .... Rehabilitation Support Schedule (AFM)
RSS .... Relational Storage System [*Computer science*] (CIST)
RSS .... Relative System Sensitivity
RSS .... Relaxed Static Stability [*Aviation*]
RSS .... Remote Safing Switch
RSS .... Remote Sensing Society [*Nottingham, England*] (EAIO)
RSS .... Remote Shutdown System (IEEE)
RSS .... Remote Slave Station (MCD)
RSS .... Remote Switching System [*Telecommunications*]
RSS .... Repair and Storage Shelter (SAA)
RSS .... Repeat Squawk Sheet (MCD)
RSS .... Requirements Status System [*NASA*]
RSS .... Residual Sum of Squares [*Statistics*]
RSS .... Resource Survey Satellite
RSS .... Restricted Stepsize [*Statistics*]
RSS .... Retention Spermatemia Syndrome [*Medicine*]
RSS .... Retentive Substrate Shield [*i.e., saucer*] [*Slang*]
RSS .... Revised Statutes of Saskatchewan [*Canada A publication*] (DLA)
RSS .... Reye's Syndrome Society [*Later, NRSF*] (EA)
RSS .... Ribbed Smoke Sheet [*Natural rubber*]
RSS .... Rib Structure Station [*NASA*] (MCD)
RSS .... Ride Smoothing System [*Aviation*]
RSS .... Rifle Sharpshooter
RSS .... Rigid Space Structure
RSS .... Ripe Skin Solid [*A banana substrate*]
RSS .... River Support Squadron [*Navy*] (VNW)
RSS .... Road Sensing Suspension [*Automotive engineering*]
RSS .... Rockdale, Sandow & Southern Railroad Co. [*AAR code*]
RSS .... Roger Sessions Society (EA)
RSS .... Roland International Corp. Sound Space [*Electronic music*]
RSS .... Romance of Science Series [*A publication*]
RSS .... Romanche Sedimentary Sequence [*Geology*]
RSS .... Rome and the Study of Scripture [*A publication*] (BJA)
RSS .... Root Sum Square (DA)
RSS .... Roseires [*Sudan*] [*Airport symbol*] (OAG)
RSS .... Rosette Scan Seeker [*Army*] (DOMA)
RSS .... Rotary Shaft Seal
RSS .... Rotary Stepping Switch
RSS .... Rotary Symbol Switch (MCD)
RSS .... Rotating Service Structure [*Kennedy Space Center*] (MCD)
RSS .... Route Switching Subsystem (NITA)
RSS .... Routing and Switching System
RSS .... Royal Shakespeare Society [*British*] (DI)
RSS .... Royal Statistical Society [*British*] (DI)
RSS .... Rural Sociological Society (EA)
RSS .... Russian Spring-Summer Encephalitis [*Medicine*] (MAH)
RSSA .... Resource Services Support Agreement (GNE)
RSSA .... Resources Support Services Agreement
RSSAILA ...... Returned Sailors', Soldiers', Airmen's Imperial League of Australia [*British military*] (DMA)
RSSC .... Remote-Site Simulator Console [*NASA*]
RSSE .... Russian Spring-Summer Encephalitis [*Medicine*]
RSSEL .... Recommended Special Support Equipment List
RSSF .... Retrievable Surface Storage Facility [*Nuclear energy*]
RSSF .... Roller Speed Skating Federation (EA)
RSSI .... Railway Systems Suppliers (EA)
RSSK .... Rigid Seat Survival Kit (NG)
RSSMAP ...... Reactor Safety Study Methodology Application Program [*Nuclear energy*] (NRCH)
RSSN .... Reaction-Sintered Silicon Nitride
RSSN .... Research Space Surveillance Network
RSSP .... Range Single Shot Probability [*Military*]
RSSPCC .... Royal Scottish Society for Prevention of Cruelty to Children
RSSPL .... Recommended Spares and Spare Parts List
RSSPO .... Resident Space Shuttle Project Office [*NASA*] (NASA)
RSSR .... Reactor Building Spray Recirculation [*Environmental science*] (COE)
RSSRT .... Russell Sage Social Relations Test [*Psychology*]
RSSS .... Rashtriya Swayamseyak Sangh [*National Union of Selfless Servers*] [*Militant Hindu organization India*] (PD)
RSSS .... Reusable Space Shuttle System [*Aerospace*] (KSC)
RSSS .... Robotic Substrate Servicing System [*Space Automation and Robotics Center*] [*NASA*]
RSST .... Reserve Station Service Transformer [*Nuclear energy*] (NRCH)
RSSU .... Remote-Site Simulation Unit [*Navy*] (NVT)
RSSU .... Remote System Support Utility [*Telematics International, Inc.*]

RS Supp ...... Supplement to the Revised Statutes [*A publication*] (DLA)
RSSW .... Ross Sea Shelf Water [*Ross Ice Shelf Project*]
RSSZ .... Rung Sat Special Zone [*Vietnam*]
RST .... RADAR Start (MSA)
RST .... RADAR Systems Technician (MCD)
RST .... Radiometric Sun Tracer
RST .... Radiosensitivity Test (AAMN)
RST .... Range Search and Track (MCD)
RST .... Rapid Solidification Technology [*Metallurgy*]
RST .... Rapid Surfactant Test [*Medicine*] (MEDA)
RST .... Readability, Signal Strength & Tone [*Amateur radio shorthand*] (WDAA)
RST .... Readability, Strength, Tone
RST .... Read Symbol Table
RST .... Reagin Screen Test [*Medicine*] (MEDA)
RST .... Recessed Selectromatic Terminal (NASA)
RST .... Recognition Suppression Technique
RST .... Recovery Sequence Tester
RST .... Reentry System Technology [*Aerospace*]
RST .... Reflector Support Truss
RST .... Register and Self-Test
RST .... Regularly-Scheduled Training [*Military*] (ADDR)
RST .... Reinforcing Steel [*Technical drawings*]
RST .... Reliability Shakedown Test (PDAA)
RST .... Religious of St. Andrew [*Roman Catholic religious order*]
RST .... Remote Sensing Technology [*Automotive exhaust emissions*]
RST .... Remote Station [*Computer science*]
RST .... Requirements for Scheduled Test (MUGU)
RST .... Research Study Team
RST .... Reset [*Telecommunications*] (TEL)
RST .... Reset-Set Trigger
RST .... Residential Subsurface Transformer (IAA)
RST .... Resin Skived Tape
RST .... Resistance (AABC)
RST .... Resort Airline, Inc. [*ICAO designator*] (FAAC)
RST .... Rest
RST .... Restore (MSA)
RST .... Rework/Scrap Tag (MCD)
RST .... Reynolds Stress (AAEL)
RST .... Right Sacrotransverse [*A fetal position*] [*Obstetrics*]
RST .... Right Store (SAA)
RST .... Rochester [*Minnesota*] [*Airport symbol*] (OAG)
RST .... Rodney Smith Tube [*Medicine*] (DAVI)
RST .... Rolling Stock (CINC)
RST .... Rough Saw Template (MCD)
RST .... Routine Sequence Table
RST .... Royal Scot Resources [*Vancouver Stock Exchange symbol*]
RST .... Royal Society of Tasmania [*Australia*]
RST .... Royal Society of Teachers [*British*]
R Sta .... Radio Telegraph Station
RSTA .... Reconnaissance, Surveillance, and Target Acquisition Center [*Fort Monmout h, NJ*] [*Army*] (MCD)
RSta .... Regulating Station [*Army*]
RSTA .... Sunresorts Ltd. NV [*NASDAQ symbol*] (SAG)
RSTAA .... Reconnaissance, Surveillance, and Target Acquisition Aircraft (MCD)
RSTA & E .... Reconnaissance, Surveillance, Target Acquisition, and Engagement (MCD)
RSTA/BMC3.. Reconnaissance, Surveillance, and Target Acquisition/Battle Management Command, Control, and Communications (MCD)
RSTAF .... Sunresorts Ltd NV 'A' [*NASDAQ symbol*] (TTSB)
RSTC .... RADAR Ship Target Classification [*Military*] (CAAL)
RSTC .... Recreational Scuba Training Council (EA)
RSTC .... Remote-Site Telemetry Computer [*NASA*]
RSTCP .... Remote Synchronous Terminal Control Program (MHDI)
RSTD .... Restricted
RSTG .... Roasting (MSA)
RSTI .... Radiological Service Training Institute (DMAA)
RSTI .... Rofin-Sinar Technologies, Inc. [*NASDAQ symbol*] (SAG)
RSTK .... Relay Servicing Tool Kit
RSTL .... Red Status Timeline
RSTL .... Relaxed Skin Tension Line [*Dermatology*]
RSTMH .... Royal Society of Tropical Medicine and Hygiene [*British*] (EAIO)
RSTN .... Radio Solar Telescope Network (MCD)
RSTN .... Regional Seismic Test Network [*Nuclear explosion detection*]
RSTN .... Relay Station (IAA)
RSTO .... Rose's Stores [*NASDAQ symbol*] (SAG)
R/STOL .... Reduced/Short Takeoff and Landing [*Aircraft*]
RStorLettRel... Rivista di Storia e Letteratura Religiosa [*Florence*] [*A publication*] (BJA)
RSTOW .... Rose's Stores Wrrt [*NASDAQ symbol*] (TTSB)
RSTP .... Real-Time Statistical and Terminal Profile [*IRS*]
RSTP .... Remote-Site Telemetry Processor [*NASA*] (KSC)
RSTPF .... Rustproof (MSA)
RSTR .... Resistor
RSTR .... Restrict (MSA)
rstrau .... Restaurant (VRA)
RSTRD .... Restricted
RSTRNT ...... Restaurant
RSTRT .... Restart (NASA)
RSTS .... RADAR System Test Station (MCD)
RSTS .... Recovery Systems Track Site (IAA)
RSTS .... Resource Sharing Time Sharing (NITA)
RSTS .... Resource-Sharing Time-Sharing System
RSTS .... Retirement Systems Testing Section [*Social Security Administration*]
RSTS .... Retropharyngeal Soft Tissue Space [*Medicine*] (DMAA)

RSTS/E .... Resource System Time Sharing/Extended [*Computer science*] (BTTJ)
RST-V .... Reconnaissance, Surveillance, and Targeting Vehicle [*Military*]
RSTV .... Rice Stripe Virus [*Plant pathology*]
RSU .... Radiological Sciences Unit [*Medicine*] (DMAA)
RSU .... Railway Services Unit [*MTMC*] (TAG)
RSU .... Rating Scale Unit [*Acoustics*]
RSU .... Recorder Switch Unit
RSU .... Recovery Storage Unit [*Military*]
RSU .... Register Storage Unit
RSU .... Relay Storage Unit
RSU .... Remote Service Unit (NASA)
RSU .... Remote Subscriber Unit [*Telecommunications*]
RSU .... Remote Switching Unit [*Telecommunications*]
RSU .... Repair and Salvage Unit [*British military*] (DMA)
RSU .... Rescue Support Umbilical (MCD)
RSU .... Reserved for Software Use (IAA)
RSU .... Rio Sucio [*Colombia*] [*Airport symbol*] (AD)
RSU .... Runway Supervisory [*MTMC*] (TAG)
RSU .... Runway Supervisory Unit [*Aviation*] (FAAC)
RSUA .... Royal Society of Ulster Architects [*British*] (BI)
RSUP .... REGIS [*Relational General Information System*] System Users' Group (EA)
RSUT .... Remote Start Unit Trainer (DWSG)
RSV .... Armored Reconnaissance Scout Vehicle [*Army*] (RDA)
RSV .... Diesel Run Control Solenoid Valve (IEEE)
RSV .... Random Sine Vibration
RSV .... Rat Sarcoma Virus
RSV .... Rat Seminal Vesicle
RSV .... Recently Separated Veteran
RSV .... Reconnaissance Scout Vehicle (MCD)
RSV .... Red Lake & Sun Valley [*Vancouver Stock Exchange symbol*]
RSV .... Remove Shutoff Valve (KSC)
RSV .... Research Safety Vehicle [*Department of Transportation*]
RSV .... Reserve (MSA)
RSV .... Reservoir [*Board on Geographic Names*]
RSV .... Respiratory Syncytial Virus [*Medicine*]
RSV .... Resupply Vehicle [*Military*]
RSV .... Revised Standard Version [*of the Bible, 1952*]
RSV .... Right Subclavian Vein [*Anatomy*]
RSV .... Robinson, IL [*Location identifier FAA*] (FAAL)
RSV .... Rous Sarcoma Virus [*Same as ASV*]
RSVA .... Randolph-Sheppard Vendors of America (EA)
RSV-Br......... Rous Sarcoma Virus, Bryan [*Strain*]
RSVC .... Rental Service Corp. [*NASDAQ symbol*] (SAG)
RSVC .... Resident Supervisor Call (BUR)
RSVC .... Right Superior Vena Cava [*Medicine*] (DMAA)
RSVCEF .... Rous Sarcoma Virus-Transformed Chick Embryo Fibroblast (DB)
RSVE .... Reconstituted Sendai Virus Envelope [*Immunology*]
RsvltF .... Roosevelt Financial Group, Inc. [*Associated Press*] (SAG)
RsvltFn .... Roosevelt Financial Group, Inc. [*Associated Press*] (SAG)
RSVM .... Ram Seminal Vesicle Microsomal (DB)
RSVP .... Please Call Back [*International telex abbreviation*] (WDMC)
RSVP .... Radiation Spectral Visual Data Distribution (IAA)
RSVP .... Radiation Spectral Visual Photometer
RSVP .... Random Signal Vibration Protector (PDAA)
RSVP .... Rapid Sampling Vertical Profiler [*Oceanography*]
RSVP .... Rapid Serial Visual Presentation [*Computer science*]
RSVP .... Relational Structure Vertex Processor (PDAA)
RSVP .... Remote System Verification Program
RSVP .... Repondez, s'll Vous Plait [*The Favor of an Answer is Requested*] [*French*]
RSVP .... Research Selected Vote Profile [*Election poll*]
RSVP .... Research Society for Victorian Periodicals (EA)
RSVP .... Reservation Protocol [*Computer science*] (IGQR)
RSVP .... Resource Reservation Protocol [*Computer science*]
RSVP .... Response Segmentation and Validation Program [*Donnelley Marketing InformationServices*] [*Information service or system*] (IID)
RSVP .... Response System with Variable Prescriptions (EDAC)
RSVP .... Restartable Solid Variable Pulse [*Motor*] (MCD)
RSVP .... Retired Senior Volunteer Program (EA)
RSVP .... Ride Shared Vehicle Paratransit [*Transportation system*]
RSVP .... Rotating Surveillance Vehicle Platform [*Military*] (MCD)
RSVP .... Rural Southern Voice for Peace [*An association*] (EA)
RSVP .... Rural Student Vocational Program [*Washington*] (EDAC)
RSVPI .... Retired Senior Volunteer Program International (EA)
RSVR .... Reservoir (AAG)
RSVR .... Resolver (AAG)
RSV(RV) ...... Revised Standard Version of the Bible [*A publication*] (BJA)
RSV-SR........ Rous Sarcoma Virus, Schmidt-Ruppin [*Strain*]
RSVT .... Stetson Reading-Spelling Vocabulary Test [*Educational test*]
RSVTN .... Reservation
RSW .... Fort Myers [*Florida*] [*Airport symbol*] (OAG)
RSW .... Fort Myers, FL [*Location identifier FAA*] (FAAL)
RS(W).......... Radio Supervisor (Warfare) [*British military*] (DMA)
RSW .... Rattlesnake Hills [*Washington*] [*Seismograph station code, US Geological Survey*] (SEIS)
RSW .... Raw Service Water [*Nuclear energy*] (NRCH)
RSW .... Refrigerated Seawater
RSW .... Registered Specification Writer [*Canada*] (ASC)
RSW .... Repeating Slide Wire
RSW .... Residential Social Worker (AIE)
RSW-V .... Resistance Spot Welding
RSW .... Retarded Surface Wave
RSW .... Right-Sided Weakness [*Neurology*] (DAVI)

RSW	Royal Scottish Society of Painters in Water Colours
RSW	Southwest Florida International Airport [FAA] (TAG)
RSWB	Raumordnung, Stadtebau, Wohnungswesen, Bauwesen [Fraunhofer Society] [Germany] (IID)
RSWC	Right Side Up with Care
RSWC	Royal Society of Painters in Water-Colours [British] (ROG)
RSWD	Regiment South Western District [British military] (DMA)
RSWF	Radioactive Scrap and Waste Facility
RSWPS	Repetitive Square Wave Potential Signal [Electrochemistry]
RSWS	Royal Scottish Water-Colour Society (ROG)
RSWW	Ross Sea Winter Water [Marine science] (MSC)
RSX	Realtime Resource Sharing Executive [Computer science] (CIST)
RSX	Resource-Sharing Executive (NITA)
RSX	Resource Sharing Extention [Computer science] (CDE)
RSY	Lumberton, NC [Location identifier FAA] (FAAL)
RSY	Rigelyn Security [Vancouver Stock Exchange symbol]
RSYCS	Rosy Cross [Freemasonry]
RSYN	Reactor Synthesis
RSYS	RadiSys Corp. [NASDAQ symbol] (SAG)
RSYS	Responsible System (NASA)
RSZ	Air Service State Co. [Hungary ICAO designator] (FAAC)
RSZ	Phoenix, AZ [Location identifier FAA] (FAAL)
RT	Air Tungaru (Gilbert Islands) [British ICAO designator] (ICDA)
RT	Electric Current Relay
RT	Norving [ICAO designator] (AD)
RT	Rachidian Tooth
RT	RADAR Tracking Radiotelegraphy (IAA)
RT	RADAR Transparency (MCD)
R/T	RADAR Trigger (CET)
RT	Radiation Therapy [Medicine]
RT	Radiographic Test [Nuclear energy] (NRCH)
RT	Radiologic Technologist
RT	Radio Technician
RT	Radiotelegraphy
RT	Radiotelephone
RT	Radio Telephony (NTCM)
RT	Radio/Television Repair Program [Association of Independent Colleges and Schools specialization code]
RT	Radiotherapy (AAMN)
RT	Radio Times (WDAA)
RT	Radio Tower (IAA)
RT	Radio Tracking (KSC)
RT	Radio Transmitter
RT	Radium Therapy [Clinical chemistry] (MAE)
RT	Radular Teeth
RT	Rail Tractor [British]
RT	Rail Transit [BTS] (TAG)
RT	Rail Transport
RT	Raintight (MSA)
RT	Raise Top (OA)
RT	Randomized Trial [Statistics]
RT	Ranger Tab [Military decoration]
RT	Rangetaker [British military] (DMA)
RT	Range Timing (AAG)
RT	Range-to-Target (NASA)
RT	Range Tracking
RT	Rapid Transit (IAA)
RT	Rate (AAG)
RT	Rated Time (IEEE)
RT	Rate Transmitter
RT	Rational Therapy [Short form for rational-emotive therapy]
RT	Ratio Transfer (IAA)
RT	Ratio Transformer [Unit]
RT	Reaction Time
RT	Reactor Trip [Nuclear energy] (NRCH)
RT	Reader Tape [Contact] (MCD)
RT	Reading Teacher [A publication] (BRI)
RT	Reading Test
RT	Readout Technique
RT	Read Tape [Computer science]
RT	Real Time [Computer] [Computer science]
RT	Received Text (ROG)
R/T	Receiver/Transmitter [Radio] (KSC)
RT	Receive-Transmit [Radio]
RT	Receiving Terminal (IAA)
RT	Receiving Test (DNAB)
RT	Receiving Tube
RT	Recipient Type (NITA)
RT	Reconnaissance Team [Military] (VNW)
R/T	Record of Trial [Army] (AABC)
RT	Record Transfer
RT	Recovery Time [Military] (AFIT)
RT	Recreational Therapist [or Therapy]
R/T	Rectal Temperature (DAVI)
RT	Recueillis Temporaires [Temporarily Taken In] [Of unadoptable children] [French]
RT	Red Tetrazolium [Also, TPTZ, TTC] [Chemical indicator]
RT	Reduced Tillage System [Agriculture]
RT	Reduction Tables
RT	Reference Trajectory [NASA] (KSC)
RT	Refrigerated Trap [Biotechnology]
RT	Regional Total (COE)
RT	Regional Treasurer [British]
RT	Registered Technician [American Registry of X-ray Technicians]
RT	Registered Technologist [Radiology] (DAVI)
RT	Registered Trademark (CDAI)
RT	Registered Transmitter (IAA)
RT	Register Ton
RT	Register Traffic [Telecommunications] (TEL)
RT	Register Transfer [Computer science]
R/T	Register Translator [Telecommunications] (TEL)
RT	Registration Type (NITA)
RT	Regression Testing [Computer science] (IEEE)
RT	Regressive Tax (MHDW)
RT	Rehabilitation Therapist [or Therapy]
RT	Rejection Tag (AAG)
RT	Related Term [Indexing]
R/T	Related To (DAVI)
RT	Relaxation Time
RT	Relaxation Training [Psychology]
RT	Relay Tester
RT	Relay Transmitter
RT	Released Time
RT	Release Transmittal (MCD)
RT	Reliable Transfer [Telecommunications] (OSI)
RT	Relocatable Term [Computer science] (IAA)
RT	Relocation Time
RT	Remote Terminal [Computer science]
RT	Renal Transplant [Nephrology]
RT	Repair Time
R/T	Reperforator/Transmitter [Teletypewriter] [Computer science]
RT	Request Translator (SAA)
RT	Research and Technology
RT	Reserve Training
RT	Reset Trigger
RT	Residence Time [Chemistry]
R-T	Resistance Test (NASA)
RT	Resistance Thermometer [Electronics] (IAA)
RT	Resistance Transfer [Laboratory science] (DAVI)
RT	Resistor Tolerance
RT	Resistor Transistor
RT	Resolver Transformer [Computer science] (IAA)
RT	Resonant Transfer (IAA)
RT	Respiratory Therapy [Medicine]
RT	Respiratory Tract [Medicine] (DB)
RT	Response Time [Computer science]
RT	Resting Tension [Biology]
RT	Restraint of Trade (MHDW)
RT	Rest Tremor [Medicine] (DB)
RT	Resuscitation Team
RT	Resuscitation Therapy
RT	Resynchronization Timer [Telecommunications] (OSI)
RT	Retention Time [Computer science]
R/T	Retouch [Graphic arts] (DGA)
RT	Retraining (OICC)
RT	Retransformation [Medicine] (DMAA)
RT	Retro Table [NASA]
RT	Retroviral Transcript [Genetics]
RT	Return Ticket
RT	Reverberation Time (NTCM)
RT	Reverse Transcriptase [An enzyme]
RT	Revolving Radio Beacon [ITU designation] (CET)
RT	Revolving Transmitter [Telecommunications] (IAA)
R/T	Rho/Theta
rT	Ribothymidine (DB)
RT	Rigging Tool (MCD)
RT	Right (EY)
rt	Right (VRA)
RT	Right Tackle [Football]
RT	Right Thigh [Medicine] (MAE)
RT	Right Time of Departure/Arrival (DS)
RT	Ringing Tone [Telecommunications] (TEL)
RT	Ring Time [Telecommunications] (IAA)
RT	Ring Trip [Telecommunications] (TEL)
RT	RISC [Reduced-Instruction Set Computer] Technology [IBM Corp.]
RT	Rise Time (DEN)
RT	[The] River Terminal Railway Co. [AAR code]
RT	Road Traffic
RT	Road Transport (NATG)
RT	Road Truck [Shipping] (DCTA)
RT	Robotic Telepresence
RT	Rocket Target
RT	Romain de Tirtoff [Also known as ERTE] [Couturier]
RT	Room Temperature
RT	Root [Mathematics] (ROG)
RT	Rotary Transformer (IAA)
RT	Rotation Discrete Rate
rt	Rotten [Quality of the bottom] [Nautical charts]
Rt	Rotundus Nucleus (DAVI)
RT	Rough Terrain [Military] (AABC)
RT	Roundtable [Bulletin board system] [Computer science] (PCM)
RT	Round Trip
RT	Route (AABC)
RT	Router Template
RT	Route Treatment [Telecommunications] (TEL)
RT	Routine Tag (SAA)
RT	Routine Test (IAA)
Rt	Routing (TBD)
RT	Royalty Trust
RT	Rubber-Tired (SAA)

RT...............	Rubinstein-Taybi [*Syndrome*] [*Medicine*] (DB)
RT...............	Rufous-Sided Towhee [*Ornithology*]
RT...............	Running Time [*Movies*] (CDAI)
RT...............	Running Title
RT...............	Running Total (DAVI)
RT...............	Runnymede Trust [*An association*] (EAIO)
RT...............	Runup and Taxi [*Air Force*]
RT...............	Ruth [*Old Testament book*]
RT...............	Ryerson Tull [*NYSE symbol*] (SAG)
RT...............	Rye Terms
Rt...............	Tetrachoric Correlation [*Psychology*]
RT...............	Theatine Sisters of the Immaculate Conception (TOCD)
R_T...............	Thermal Resistance (IDOE)
R_T...............	Total Pulmonary Resistance [*Medicine*] (DAVI)
R_T...............	Total Reserves
R_t...............	Total Resistance (IDOE)
rT_3	Reverse Triiodothyronine [*Endocrinology*]
RT_3	Serum Resin Triiodothyronine [*Uptake*] [*Endocrinology*] (DAVI)
RT_3U	Resin T_3 Uptake [*Endocrinology*]
RT_4U	Resin T_4 Uptake [*Endocrinology*]
RTA...............	Racehorse Transporters Association [*British*] (DBA)
RTA...............	RADAR Terrain Analysis
RTA...............	Radically Tapered Antenna
RTA...............	Radiology Telephone Access (DAVI)
RTA...............	Radix Teachers Association (EA)
RTA...............	Rail Travel Authorization [*Military*]
RTA...............	Railway Tie Association (EA)
RTA...............	Rapid Thermal Annealing [*Physics*]
RTA...............	Rattler Resources [*Vancouver Stock Exchange symbol*]
RTA...............	Reactivity Test Assembly [*Nuclear energy*]
RTA...............	Ready-to-Assemble
RTA...............	Real-Time Accumulator
RTA...............	Real-Time Analyzer [*Electronics*]
RTA...............	Reciprocal Trade Agreement
RTA...............	Refrigeration Trade Association (NADA)
RTA...............	Refrigeration Trade Association of America
RTA...............	Regional Transportation Authority (EFIS)
RTA...............	Reliability Test Assembly
RTA...............	Reliable Test Analyzer [*Computer science*]
RTA...............	Remote Technical Assistance (NITA)
RTA...............	Remote Test Access [*Telecommunications*] (TEL)
RTA...............	Remote Trunk Arrangement [*Telecommunications*] (TEL)
RTA...............	Renal Tubule Acidosis [*Medicine*]
RTA...............	Request for Technical Action (MCD)
RTA...............	Required Time of Arrival (DA)
RTA...............	Resident Transient Area [*Computer science*] (IAA)
RTA...............	Retired Teachers Association (BARN)
RTA...............	Riberalta [*Bolivia*] [*Seismograph station code, US Geological Survey Closed*] (SEIS)
RTA...............	Rise-Time Analyzer
RTA...............	Road Traffic Accident [*British*]
RTA...............	Road Traffic Act [*1962*] [*British A publication*] (DLA)
RTA...............	Rose Trade Association [*British*] (DBA)
RTA...............	Rotor Test Apparatus (MCD)
RTA...............	Rotuma [*Fiji*] [*Airport symbol*] (OAG)
RTA...............	Royal Thai Army
RTA...............	Rubber Trade Association [*British*] (DBA)
RTA...............	Rubber Trade Association of New York (EA)
RTAB............	Royal Thai Air Force Base [*Also, RTAFB*] (VNW)
RTAC............	Real-Time Adaptive Control
RTAC............	Real-Time Atmospheric Compensation [*Astronomy*]
RTAC............	Regional Technical Aid Center [*Agency for International Development*]
RTAC............	Research and Technology Advisory Council [*Terminated, 1977*] [*NASA*] (EGAO)
RTAC............	Roads and Transportation Association of Canada [*Ottawa, ON*] [*Formerly, Canadian Good Roads Association*] [*Research center*]
RTACF.........	Real-Time Auxiliary Computing Facility [*Apollo*] [*NASA*]
RTACS.........	Real-Time Adaptive Control System [*Military*] (CAAL)
RTAD...........	Renal Tubular Acidification Defect [*Medicine*] (DMAA)
RTAD...........	Router Adapter
RTAF...........	Report to Armed Forces
RTAF...........	Robot Testing and Assessment Facility
RTAF...........	Royal Thai Air Force
RTAFB.........	Royal Thai Air Force Base [*Also, RTAB*] (VNW)
RTAFCONV..	Royal Thai Air Force Contingent, Vietnam
RTAG...........	Range Technical Advisory Group
RTAM...........	Recherches de Theologie Ancienne et Medievale [*A publication*] (ODCC)
RTAM...........	Remote Telecommunications Access Method [*Computer science*]
RTAM...........	Remote Terminal Access Method [*Computer science*] (BUR)
RTAM...........	Resident Terminal Access Method [*Computer science*]
RTAMA........	Railway Tyre and Axle Manufacturers Association [*British*] (BI)
RTAN...........	Rubber-Toughened Amorphous Nylon [*Organic chemistry*]
RT & EPS....	Rapid Transit and Electrical Power Systems
RTANG........	Right Angle
RTAP...........	Rural Technical Assistance Program [*Department of Transportation*]
RTAPS.........	Real-Time Terminal Application Program System [*Computer science*]
RTAQ..........	Remedial Teachers' Association of Queensland [*Australia*]
RTARF.........	Royal Thai Armed Forces (CINC)
RTARP........	Royal Thai Army Rebuild Plant (MCD)
RT(ARRT)....	Registered Technologist Certified by American Registry of Radiologic Technolgists (STED)
RTAS	Rapid Telephone Access System (IAA)

RTASS	Remote Tactical Airborne SIGINT [*Signals Intelligence*] System [*Air Force*] (DOMA)
RTAVF	Royal Thai Army Volunteer Force (VNW)
RTAWA	Retail Traders' Association of Western Australia
RTB.............	Radial Time Base
RTB.............	Radiodiffusion-Television Belge [*Belgian Radio Broadcasting and Television System*]
RTB.............	Range and True Bearing (IAA)
RTB.............	Ranger Training Brigade [*Fort Benning, GA*] [*Army*] (INF)
RTB.............	Read Tape Binary [*Computer science*] (IEEE)
RTB.............	Real-Time Backplane (AAEL)
RTB.............	Reasons to Believe [*An association*] (EA)
RTB.............	Reason to Believe (ECON)
RTB.............	Regional Training Brigade [*Army*] (INF)
RTB.............	Resistance Temperature Bridge (SAA)
RTB.............	Resistance Temperature Bulb [*NASA*]
RTB.............	Resolver Tracking Bridge
RTB.............	Response/Throughput Bias [*Computer science*] (BUR)
RTB.............	Return to Base [*Military*]
RTB.............	Return to Bias (IAA)
RTB.............	Richard Thomas & Bladwins Ltd. (WDAA)
RTB.............	Roatan [*Honduras*] [*Airport symbol*] (OAG)
RTB.............	Rocket Test Base
RTB.............	Rural Telephone Bank [*Department of Agriculture*]
RTBA............	Rate to Be Agreed [*Business term*] (DCTA)
RTBF............	Radio-Television Belge de la Communaute Culturelle Francaise [*Broadcasting organization*] [*Belgium*] (EY)
RTBISC	Radiodiffusion-Television Belge - Institut des Services Comuns [*Belgian Radio Broadcasting and Television - Common Services Institute*]
RTBM...........	Real-Time BIT [*Binary Digit*] Mapping
RTBM...........	Recoverable Test Bed Missile
RTBT............	Resonant Tunneling Bipolar Transistor [*Electronics*]
RTBV	Rice Tungro Bacilliform Virus [*Plant pathology*]
RTC.............	RADAR Tracking Center [*or Control*]
RTC.............	Radiodiffusion-Television Congolaise [*Congolese Radio and Television*] (AF)
RTC.............	Radio Technical Committee for Aeronautics (NTCM)
RTC.............	Radio Tecnica Colombiana
RTC.............	Radiotelegraph Communication (IAA)
RTC.............	Radiotelephone Communication (IAA)
RTC.............	Radio Transmission Control (NATG)
RTC.............	Radio Tuned Circuit (DEN)
RTC.............	Rails-to-Trails Conservancy (EA)
RTC.............	Randomized Trial Controlled (STED)
RTC.............	Range Telemetry Central [*Aerospace*]
RTC.............	Ratchet (AAG)
RTC.............	Reader Tape Contact
RTC.............	Real-Time Captioning [*for the deaf*]
RTC.............	Real-Time Clock [*Computer science*] (MCD)
RTC.............	Real-Time Command [*Computer science*]
RTC.............	Real-Time Computation [*Computer science*] (IAA)
RTC.............	Real-Time Computer
RTC.............	Real-Time Conference [*GEnie*] [*Telecommunications*]
RTC.............	Real-Time Control [*Computer science*] (MCD)
RTC.............	Real-Time Counter [*Computer science*]
RTC.............	Reconstruction of Town and Country [*British World War II*]
RTC.............	Recruit Training Center
RTC.............	Reference Test Chart
RTC.............	Reference Transfer Calibrator (OA)
RTC.............	Regional Technical College (ACII)
RTC.............	Regional Term Contract
RTC.............	Regional Transfusion Center (WDAA)
RTC.............	Regional Transport Commissioner
RTC.............	Rehabilitation Research and Training Centers [*Department of Health and Human Services*]
RTC.............	Relative Time Clock [*Computer science*] (MDG)
RTC.............	Religious Technology Center (TELE)
RTC.............	Remote Terminal Controller
RTC.............	Removable Top Closure [*Nuclear energy*] (NRCH)
RTC.............	Renal Tubular Cell (STED)
RTC.............	Replacement Training Center [*Military*]
RTC.............	Reproductive Toxicology Center [*Database*] (IID)
RTC.............	Required Technical Characteristic [*Military*] (CAAL)
RTC.............	Requirements Type Contract [*Military*] (AABC)
RTC.............	Reserve Training Center [*Army*] (DOMA)
RTC.............	Reserve Training Corps
RTC.............	Residential Training College [*for disabled people*] [*British*]
RTC.............	Residential Treatment Center [*Department of Health and Human Services*] (GFGA)
RTC.............	Resolution Trust Corp. [*Federal government instrumentality, established in 1989*]
RTC.............	Resort Timesharing Council (EA)
RTC.............	Responsible Training Center [*Air Training Command*] (MCD)
RTC.............	Return to Clinic [*Nursing*]
RTC.............	Return to Control
RTC.............	Reverse Transfer Capacitance
RTC.............	Ridiculous Theatrical Company
RTC.............	Road Transport Commission [*Australia*]
RTC.............	Rocket Technique Committee
RTC.............	Room Temperature Cure (NASA)
RTC.............	Round Table Conference (WDAA)
RTC.............	Round the Clock (DAVI)
RTC.............	Royal Tank Corps [*Military unit*] [*British*]

RTC-30 .... Rehabilitation Research and Training Center in Blindness and Low Vision [*Mississippi State University*] [*Research center*] (RCD)
RTCA .... Race Track Chaplaincy of America (EA)
RTCA .... Radio Technical Commission for Aeronautics (EA)
RTCA .... Radio-Television Correspondents Association (EA)
RTCA .... Real-Time Casualty Assessment (MCD)
RTCA .... Real-Time Control Area (NTCM)
RTCA .... Ribofuranosyltriazolecarboxamide [*Ribavirin*] [*Antiviral compound*]
RTCA .... Rural Training Council of Australia
RTCAC .... Regional Transport Coordination Advisory Committee [*New South Wales, Australia*]
RTCAD .... Register Transfer Computer-Aided Design (MHDI)
RTCANI .... Rav Tov Committee to Aid New Immigrants [*Later, RTIJRO*] (EA)
RTCB .... ROTI [*Recording Optical Tracking Instrument*] Tracker - Cocoa Beach [*NASA*] (KSC)
RTCB .... Run to Cladding Breach [*Nuclear energy*] (NRCH)
RTCC .... Real-Time Command Controller [*Computer science*] (NASA)
RTCC .... Real-Time Communications Control (NITA)
RTCC .... Real-Time Computer Center [*NASA*] (NASA)
RTCC .... Real-Time Computer Command [*NASA*] (NASA)
RTCC .... Real-Time Computer Complex [*NASA*]
RTCC .... Rolling Thunder Coordinating Committee [*Joint US Navy and Air Force group operating in Vietnam*] (VNW)
RTCDS .... Real-Time Cinetheodolite Data System
RtCE .... Right to a Comprehensive Education [*British*]
RTCE .... Rotation/Translation Control Electronics (NASA)
RTCF .... Real-Time Combined File [*IRS*]
RTCF .... Real-Time Computer Facility
RTCH .... Rough Terrain Container Handler (MCD)
RTCIL .... Research and Training Center on Independent Living (EA)
RTCIP .... Real-Time Cell-Identification Processor (PDAA)
RTCL .... Reticle [*Optics*]
RTCM .... Radio Technical Commission for Maritime [*or Marine*] Services (TSSD)
RTCM .... Reasonable Transportation Control Measure (GNE)
RTCMS .... Radio Technical Commission for Marine Services (IAA)
RTCO .... Record Time Compliance Order
RTCOD .... [*The*] Research and Technology Coordinating Document [*Army*] (RDA)
RTCOMN ...... Radiotelephone Communication (IAA)
RTCP .... Radio Transmission Control Panel (NATG)
RTCP .... Real-Time Communications Processor (NASA)
RTCP .... Real-Time Control Program [*Computer science*] (IAA)
RTCP .... Resident Training and Counseling Programs (OICC)
RTCS .... Real-Time Calling Standards [*Chromatography*]
RTCS .... Real-Time Communication System
RTCS .... Real-Time Composition System (NITA)
RTCS .... Real-Time Computation System [*Computer science*] (IAA)
RTCS .... Real-Time Computer System
RTCS .... Roske-De Toni-Caffey-Smith [*Disease*] [*Medicine*] (DB)
RTCTO .... Record Time Compliance Technical Order (AAG)
RTCU .... Real-Time Control Unit
RTCU .... Router Cutter [*Tool*] (AAG)
RTCV .... Rural Training Council of Victoria [*Australia*]
RTCVD .... Rapid Thermal Chemical Vapor Deposition [*Coating technology*] [*Semiconductor technology*]
RTC(W) .... Recruit Training Command (Women) (DNAB)
RTCWA .... Rural Training Council of Western Australia
RTD .... Radiodiffusion-Television de Djibouti
RTD .... Range Time Decoder
RTD .... Rapid Transit District (COE)
RTD .... Rate Damping (NASA)
RTD .... Rate Dumping (MCD)
RTD .... Reactor Technology Department (COE)
RTD .... Read Tape Decimal
RTD .... Ready-to-Drink [*Bottled and canned beverages*]
RTD .... Real-Time Decoder
RTD .... Real Time Developments [*Commercial firm British*]
RTD .... Real-Time Display
RTD .... Reliability Technical Directive (AAG)
RTD .... Remote Temperature Detector
RTD .... Renal Tubular Defect [*Medicine*] (DMAA)
RTD .... Replacement Task Distribution
RTD .... Replacement Training Detachment (MCD)
RTD .... Research and Technology Division [*Air Force*]
RTD .... Research Thrust Division [*Washington, DC DoD*] (GRD)
RTD .... Residence Time Distribution [*Chemical engineering*]
RTD .... Resident Training Detachment [*Army*] (INF)
RTD .... Resistance Temperature Detector [*Nuclear energy*]
RTD .... Resistance Temperature Device [*Nuclear energy*] (NRCH)
RTD .... Resistance Thermometer Device (ACII)
RTD .... Resonant-Tunnelling Diode [*Solid state physics*]
RTD .... Resubmission Turnaround Documents (MEDA)
RTD .... Retard (MSA)
rtd .... Retarded (MAE)
RTD .... Retired
RTD .... Returned [*Medicine*] (DHSM)
RTD .... Return to Duty [*Military*]
RTD .... Rights in Technical Data (AAGC)
RTD .... Road Traffic Division [*British police*]
RTD .... Routine Test Dilution [*Analysis*]
RTD .... Run-Time Debugger [*Computer science*] (PCM)
RTDA .... Radio and Television Dealers' Association
RTDA .... Retail Tobacco Dealers of America (EA)
RTDA .... Returned Absentees

RTD & E ...... Research, Test, Development, and Evaluation (SSD)
RTDAP .... RADAR Target Data Analog Processor (MCD)
RTDB .... Research Training and Development Branch [*Bethesda, MD*] [*National Heart, Lung, and Blood Institute*] (GRD)
RTDBUG ...... Real-Time Debug [*Computer science*] (MHDI)
RTDC .... Real-Time Data Channel (IEEE)
RTDC .... Retardation Coil (MSA)
RTDC .... Rocket-Thrown Depth Charge (NG)
RTDD .... Real-Time Data Distribution
RTDD .... Remote Timing and Data Distribution
RTDDAS....... Real-Time Digital Data Acquisition System (PDAA)
RTDDC........ Real-Time Digital Data Correction (MUGU)
RTDE .... Range Time Data Editor [*NASA*] (KSC)
RTDF .... Real-Time Data File (NOAA)
RTDG .... Radio and Television Directors Guild [*Later, DGA*]
RTDHS .... Real-Time Data Handling System
RTDM .... Rough Terrain Diffusion Model [*Environmental science*] (COE)
RTDox .... Read the Documentations [*Computer hacker terminology*]
RTDP .... RADAR Target Data Processor (MCD)
RTDP .... Robotics Technology Development Program
RTDR .... Reliability Test Data Report
RTDS .... Rapid Thermal Decomposition in Solution [*Powder processing*]
RTDS .... Real-Time Data System
RTDT .... Real-Time Data Translator
RTDTL .... Resistor Tunnel Diode Transistor Logic (IAA)
RTDVHPEP... Rural Texas Domestic Violence Health Professionals Education Program (EDAC)
RTE........... Aeronorte - Transportes Aereos Lda. [*Portugal ICAO designator*] (FAAC)
RTE........... Radiative Transfer Equation
RTE........... Radio Telefis Eireann [*Radio and television network*] [*Ireland*]
RTE........... Radio Trans-Europe
RTE........... Radio Trunk Extension (NATG)
RTE........... RADOME [*RADAR Dome*] Test Equipment
RTE........... Railway Transport Establishment [*British military*] (DMA)
RTE........... Ready to Eat [*Cereals*]
RTE........... Real-Time Engine (MCD)
RTE........... Real-Time Event [*Computer science*] (IAA)
RTE........... Real-Time Executive [*Computer science*]
RTE........... Receiver Test Equipment
RTE........... Reciprocal Thermal Efficiency (PDAA)
RTE........... Recovery Techniques Evaluation [*NASA*] (KSC)
RTE........... Regenerative Turboprop Engines
RTE........... Reliability Test Evaluation (AAG)
RTE........... Remote Terminal Emulator [*For teleprocessing validation*]
RTE........... Repairs-to-Extend (USDC)
RTE........... Repair Test Equipment [*Aviation*]
RTE........... Request to Expedite
RTE........... Research Training and Evaluation (OICC)
RTE........... Resident Training Equipment (MOD)
RTE........... Residual Total Elongation [*Nuclear energy*] (NRCH)
RTE........... Responsible Test Engineer [*NASA*] (NASA)
RTE........... Return from Exception [*Computer science*]
RTE........... Return to Earth [*NASA*]
RTE........... Robotic Tele-Excavation [*University of Southern California*]
RTE........... Route (AFM)
Rte........... Route (TBD)
rte........... Route (DD)
RTE........... Royal Trust Energy Income Fund Trust Units [*Toronto Stock Exchange symbol*]
RTE........... Run-Time Evaluator [*Computer science*] (CIST)
RTEB.......... Radio Trades Examination Board [*British*] (BI)
RTE-B .... Real-Time Basic [*Computer science*] (MDG)
RTEC.......... Residential Transportation Energy Consumption [*DOE*] (TAG)
RTEC.......... Ross Technology [*NASDAQ symbol*] (TTSB)
RTEC.......... Ross Technology, Inc. [*NASDAQ symbol*] (SAG)
RTech .... Radiology Technician [*or Technologist*] (AAMN)
RTECS .... Registry of Toxic Effects of Chemical Substances [*Department of Health and Human Services Information service or system A publication*]
RTECS .... Residential Transportation Energy Consumption Survey [*Department of Energy*] (GFGA)
RTED .... Return-to-Earth Digital [*NASA*]
RTEG .... River Transport Escort Group (CINC)
RTel .... Radio Telemetry
RTEL.......... Radio Telephony (MSA)
RTEL.......... Raytel Medical [*NASDAQ symbol*] (TTSB)
RTEL.......... Raytel Medical Corp. [*NASDAQ symbol*] (SAG)
RTEM.......... RADAR Tracking Error Measurement
RTES.......... Radio and Television Executives' Society [*Later, IRTS*]
RTES.......... Real-Time Engine Simulation (MCD)
RTES.......... Real-Time Executive System [*SEMIS*]
RTES.......... Research Training Environment Scale (DHP)
RTEX.......... Railtex, Inc. [*NASDAQ symbol*] (SAG)
RTEX.......... Real-Time Executive [*Computer science*] (IAA)
RTEX.......... Real-Time Telecommunications Executive (IAA)
RTF........... Radiodiffusion-Television Francaise [*French Radio Broadcasting and Television System*]
RTF........... Radiotelephone
RTF........... Radio Transmission Facility
RTF........... Razor Trade Federation [*A union*] [*British*]
RTF & E ...... Readiness Task Force
RTF........... Ready to Fire (MCD)
RTF........... Real-Time FORTRAN [*Computer science*]
RTF........... Reconnaissance Task Force (AFM)

RTF..............	Reconnaissance Technical Flight [*Air Force*]
RTF..............	Refilled, Tapped, and Fractionated [*Rock formation*] [*Geology*]
RTF..............	Refrigerated Transportation Foundation (EA)
RTF..............	Reliability Task Force (MCD)
RTF..............	Religious Task Force [*Defunct*] (EA)
RTF..............	Replication and Transfer [*Medicine*] (MAE)
RTF..............	Reports Tempore Finch, English Chancery [*A publication*] (DLA)
RTF..............	Resistance Task Force [*Defunct*] (EA)
RTF..............	Resistance Transfer Factor [*of microorganisms to drugs*]
RTF..............	Respiratory Tract Fluid [*Medicine*]
RTF..............	Rich Text Format [*Computer science*] (BYTE)
rtf...............	Rich Text Format [*Computer science*]
RTF..............	Rocket Test Facility
RTF..............	Room Temperature Fluorescence [*Physics*]
RTF..............	Rotational Test Facility [*NASA*]
RTF..............	Rubber-Tile Floor [*Technical drawings*]
RTF..............	Rutherford [*New Jersey*] [*Airport symbol*] (AD)
RTFAQ.........	Read the Frequently Asked Questions [*Computer hacker terminology*] (NHD)
RTFC...........	Randy Travis Fan Club (EA)
RTFC...........	Retired Teamsters Fellowship Club (EA)
RTFCA	Religious Task Force on Central America (EA)
RTFES.........	Religious Task Force on El Salvador (EA)
RTFFRJ.......	Research Task Force for the Future of Reform Judaism [*Defunct*] (EA)
RTFL...........	Rough Terrain Fork Lift
RTFL...........	Rough Terrain Front Loader (MCD)
RTFLFT.......	Rough Terrain Forklift [*Military*]
RTFLT.........	Rough Terrain Forklift Truck (MCD)
RTFM..........	Read the Fabulous Manual [*Internet language*] [*Computer science*]
RTFM..........	Read the Fascinating Manual [*You can substitute a common profane verbal adjective for the third word*] [*Internet*]
RTFM..........	Read the Fine Manual [*Computer science*] (DOM)
RTFM..........	Read the Flaming Manual [*Bowdlerized version*] (CDE)
RTFM..........	Router Form
RTFMS........	Radio Transmission Frequency Measuring System
RTFO	Rolling Thin Film Oven [*For testing asphaltic binders*]
RTFR..........	Reliability Trouble and Failure Report
RTFS..........	Razor Trade Forgers' Society [*A union*] [*British*]
RTFT...........	Rough Terrain Forklift Truck
RTFV..........	RADAR Target Folder Viewer
RTG	Radioactive Thermoelectric Generator [*Nuclear energy*] (NRCH)
RTG	Radiodiffusion-Television Gabonaise [*Gabonese radio and television network*]
RTG	Radiodiffusion-Television Guineenne [*Guinean radio and television network*]
RTG	Radioisotope Thermal Generation (NAKS)
RTG	Radioisotope Thermoelectric Generator
RTG	Radiotelegraph
RTG	Range to Go
RTG	Range to Ground (MCD)
RTG	Rare Tube Gas
RTG	Rating (MUGU)
RTG	Real Time Geometry
RTG	Reconnaissance Technical Group [*Air Force*]
RTG	Reglement Telegraphique [*Telegraph Regulations*] [*French*]
RTG	Requirements Tape Generator [*NASA*]
RTG	Reusable Training Grenade
RTG	River Transport Group [*South Vietnamese Navy*] (VNW)
RTG	Routing
RTG	Royal Thai Government
RTG	Ruteng [*Indonesia*] [*Airport symbol*] (OAG)
RTGB	Reactor Turbine Generator Board [*Nuclear energy*] (NRCH)
RTGD	Real-Time Graphic Display
RTGD	Room Temperature Gamma Detector
RTG DOM	Routing Domain [*Computer science*] (TNIG)
RTGF	Rat Transforming Growth Factor [*Biochemistry*]
RTGp	Reconnaissance Technical Group [*Air Force*] (AFM)
RTGp	Reconnaissance Training Group [*Air Force*] (AFM)
RTGp	Retraining Group [*Air Force*] (AFM)
RTGS	Real-Time Gross Settlement [*Banking*] (ECON)
RTGS	Return to Government Stores (SAA)
RTGU..........	Router Guide
RTGV	Real-Time Generation of Video
RTH	New York, NY [*Location identifier FAA*] (FAAL)
RTh	Radio-Telephone (High Frequency) [*Telecommunications*] (DS)
RTH	Radio Thailand (FEA)
RTH	Regional Telecommunications Hub [*Telecommunications*] (TEL)
RTH	Relay Transformer Header
RTH	Reports of Cases Concerning Settlements Tempore Holt [*England*] [*A publication*] (DLA)
RTH	Reports Tempore Hardwicke [*England*] [*A publication*] (DLA)
RTH	Ridgeway's Reports Tempore Hardwicke, Chancery and English King's Bench [*A publication*] (DLA)
RtH	Right-Handed (DAVI)
R T Hardw...	Reports Tempore Hardwicke, English King's Bench [*A publication*] (DLA)
RTHC..........	Rotation Translation Hand Controller (NASA)
RTHK..........	Radio Television Hong Kong
RTHL..........	Runway Threshold Light [*Aviation*] (FAAC)
RTHM.........	Rythms Net Connections [*NASDAQ symbol*]
R T Holt......	Reports Tempore Holt, English King's Bench [*A publication*] (DLA)
RtHon	Right Honourable (EY)
RThQr	Revue de Theologie et des Questions Religieuses [*A publication*] (BJA)

RTHS...........	Real-Time Hybrid System (NASA)
RTI...............	RADAR Target Identification
RTI...............	Radiation Transfer Index
RTI...............	Radiodiffusion-Television Ivoirienne [*Ivory Coast Radio and Television*] (AF)
RTI...............	Railroad Transportation Insurers [*Defunct*] (EA)
RTI...............	Real-Time Interface [*Computer science*]
RTI...............	Real-Time Interference [*Computer science*] (IAA)
RTI...............	Referred-to-Input
RTI...............	Related Technical Instruction [*Bureau of Apprenticeship and Training*] [*Department of Labor*]
RTI...............	Relational Technology Inc. (NITA)
RTI...............	Relaxation Time Index [*Cardiology*]
RTI...............	Remnant Tumor Index [*Surgery*]
RTI...............	Remote Telephone Interface
RTI...............	Renault Truck Industries [*British subsidiary of Renault Vehicles Industriels*]
RTI...............	Renewable Term Insurance (MHDB)
RTI.:.............	Request for Technical Information [*Military*]
RTI...............	Research Triangle Institutes [*Duke University, University of North Carolina at Chapel Hill, and North Carolina State University at Raleigh*] [*Research center*]
RTI...............	Resilient Tile Institute [*Later, RFCI*] (EA)
RTI...............	Respiratory Tract Infection [*Medicine*]
RTI...............	Return from Interrupt [*Computer science*] (NHD)
RTI...............	Reverse Transcriptase Inhibitor [*Medicine*]
RTI...............	Ridge Transform Intersection [*Geology*]
RTI...............	Right Turn, International (EA)
RTI...............	Rise-Time Indicator
RTI...............	RMI Titanium [*NYSE symbol*] (SPSG)
RTI...............	Role Taking Inventory
RTI...............	Room, Tax, and Incidentals
RTI...............	Root Tolerance Index [*Botany*]
RTI...............	Roti [*Indonesia*] [*Airport symbol*] (OAG)
RTI...............	Round Table International (EA)
RTI...............	RTI, Inc. [*Associated Press*] (SAG)
Rti..............	Tissue Resistance [*Laboratory science*] (DAVI)
RTIC............	Rotor Temperature Indicator and Control [*Instrumentation*]
RTIC............	RT Inds Inc. [*NASDAQ symbol*] (TTSB)
RTIC............	RT Industries, Inc. [*NASDAQ symbol*] (SAG)
RTIF............	Real-Time Interface [*Computer science*] (NASA)
RTII.............	RTI, Inc. [*NASDAQ symbol*] (NQ)
RTIJRO	Rav Tov International Jewish Rescue Organization (EA)
RT Ind	RT Industries, Inc. [*Associated Press*] (SAG)
RTIO............	Real-Time Input/Output (NITA)
RTIO............	Real-Time Input/Output Interface Subsystem [*Space Flight Operations Facility, NASA*]
RTIO/OC.....	Remote Terminal Input/Output
RTI/OC........	Real-Time Input/Output Controller [*Computer science*] (IEEE)
RTIP............	RADAR Target Identification Point (AFM)
RTIP............	Real-Time Interactive Processor (MCD)
RTIP............	Remote Terminal Interactive Processor (MCD)
RTIP............	Remote Terminal Interface Package
RTIR............	Real-Time Infrared [*Spectroscopy*]
RTIR............	Reliability and Trend Indicator Reports (AAG)
RTIRS.........	Real-Time Information Retrieval System
RTIS...........	Real-Time Information Retrieval System [*Computer science*] (HGAA)
RTIS...........	Rockwell Technical Information System [*Rockwell International Corp.*] [*Information service or system*] (IID)
RTISC.........	River Torrens Improvement Standing Committee [*Australia*]
RTITB.........	Road Transport Industry Training Board [*British*] (DCTA)
RTIV...........	Rice Tungro Isometric Virus [*Plant pathology*]
RTJ.............	Return Jump [*Computer science*] (MHDI)
RTK............	Range Tracker (KSC)
RTK............	Receptor Tyrosine Kinase [*Biochemistry*]
RTK............	Record Test Kit
RTK............	Right to Know [*Laws*]
RTK............	Roanoke Rapids, NC [*Location identifier FAA*] (FAAL)
RTKP	Radiothermokeratoplasty [*Ophthalmology*] (DAVI)
RTL.............	RADAR Threshold Lobe Limit (CET)
RTL.............	Radial Transmission Line
RTL.............	Radioisotope Transport Loop [*Nuclear energy*] (NRCH)
RTL.............	Radiomaritime Telex Letter
RTL.............	Radio Television Luxembourgeoise [*Radio Television Luxembourg*] [*French*]
RTL.............	Reactive to Light [*Referring to the pupils of the eyes*] [*Ophthalmology*] (DAVI)
RTL.............	Real-Time Language [*Computer science*] (IEEE)
RTL.............	Real-Time Link [*Computer science*] (MHDI)
rtl...............	Rectal (DAVI)
RTL.............	Refrigerated Transmission Line
RTL.............	Regeneration Thermoluminescence
RTL.............	Regimental Training Line [*Army*]
RTL.............	Register Transfer Language [*Computer science*] (CSR)
RTL.............	Register Transfer Level
RTL.............	Register-Transistor Logic [*Computer science*]
RTL.............	Reinforced Tile Lintel [*Technical drawings*]
RTL.............	Relative Transcription Level [*Genetics*]
RTL.............	Research and Technology Laboratories [*Army*] (RDA)
RTL.............	Resin-Treated Liner
RTL.............	Resistor-Transistor Logic [*Computer science*] (BUR)
RTLS...........	Resource Tie Line [*An association*]
RTL.............	Responsible Task Leader (SSD)
Rtl..............	Retail (TBD)
RTL.............	Retail

RTL	Rheintalflug-Rolf Seewald [*Austria ICAO designator*] (FAAC)
RTL	Right-to-Life (WDAA)
RTL	Run-Time Library [*Interdata*]
RTLA	Reach-Through License Agreement [*Business term*]
RT LAT	Right Lateral (DAVI)
rt lat	Right Lateral [*Medicine*] (MAE)
Rt Law Rep	Rent Law Reports [*India*] [*A publication*] (DLA)
RTLC	Reaction Thin-Layer Chromatography (DB)
RTLF	Association of Railway Trainmen and Locomotive Firemen
RTLG	Radio Telegraph (MSA)
RTLO	Regional Training Liaison Officer [*Ministry of Agriculture, Fisheries, and Food*] [*British*]
RTLOC	Root Locus (IAA)
RTLP	Reference Transmission Level Point [*Telecommunications*]
RTLS	Return to Launch Site [*NASA*]
RTLT	Round-Trip Light Time
RTM	RADAR Target Materiel (AFM)
RTM	Radiation Test Model
RTm	Radio-Telephone (Medium Frequency) [*Telecommunications*] (DS)
RTM	Radio Television Malaysia
RTM	Radio-Television Malgache [*Malagasy Radio and Television*] (AF)
RTM	Radio-Television Marocaine [*Moroccan Radio and Television*] (AF)
RTM	Radio Thrust Misalignment
RTM	[*The*] Railway Transfer Co. of the City of Minneapolis [*AAR code*]
RTM	Rapid Thermal Multiprocessing (AAEL)
RTM	Rapid Tuning Magnetron
RTM	Rassemblement des Travaillistes Mauriciens [*Mauritius*] [*Political party*] (EY)
RTM	Read the Manual
RTM	Real-Time Management (MHDB)
RTM	Real-Time Metric
RTM	Real-Time Module (NITA)
RTM	Real-Time Monitor [*Systems Engineering Labs*]
RTM	Receiver-Transmitter-Modulator
RTM	Reconnaissance Tactical Missile
RTM	Recording Tachometer (IEEE)
RTM	Recovery Termination Management [*Computer science*]
RTM	Refrigerant Transport Module [*Air-conditioning*] (PS)
RTM	Regional Transport Model [*Environmental Protection Agency*] (GFGA)
RTM	Registered Trademark (DEN)
RTM	Register Transfer Module [*Computer science*] (MDG)
RTM	Regulatory Technical Memorandum [*Nuclear energy*] (NRCH)
RTM	Release to Manufacturing [*Business term*]
RTM	Representative Town Meeting
RTM	Requirements Traceability Matrix
RTM	Research Technical Memorandum
RTM	Resin Transfer Molding [*Plastics technology*]
RTM	Response Time Module
RTM	Revenue Ton-Miles
RTM	Room-Temperature Metallizing (SAA)
RTM	Rotterdam [*Netherlands*] [*Airport symbol*] (OAG)
RTM	Routine Medical Care (DAVI)
RTM	Royal Trust Co. Mortgage Corp. [*Toronto Stock Exchange symbol*]
RTM	Running Time Meter (AAG)
RTM	Runtime Manager [*Computer science*] (ROM)
RTM	Trans Am Compania Ltda. [*Ecuador*] [*ICAO designator*] (FAAC)
RTMA	Radio and Television Manufacturers Association [*Later, EIA*]
RTMAGV	Royal Thai Military Assistance Group, Vietnam
RTMBEP	Real-Time Minimal Byte Error Probability [*Computer science*] (MHDI)
RTMC	Royal Thai Marine Corps (CINC)
RTMD	Real-Time Multiplexer Display
R$_{tmf}$	Total Matrix Formation Rate (DAVI)
RTMLA	Round Table for the Management of Library Associations
RTMON	Real-Time Executive Monitor [*Computer science*] (IAA)
RTMOS	Real-Time Multiprogramming Operating System [*Computer science*] (IEEE)
RTMP	Rapid Thermal Melt Processed [*Inorganic chemistry*]
RTMP	Routing Maintenance Protocol (BYTE)
RTMP	Routing Table Maintenance Protocol [*Computer science*]
RTMS	RADAR Target Measuring System (MCD)
RTMS	Real-Time Memory System
RTMS	Real-Time Multiprogramming System
RTMS	Rocket Thrust Measuring System
RTMSW	Real-Time DSN [*Deep Space Network*] Monitor Software Assembly [*NASA*]
RTMTR	Remote Transmitter (FAAC)
RTN	North Country Library System, Watertown, NY [*OCLC symbol*] (OCLC)
RTN	Radial, Tangential, Normal
RTN	Radio Telescope Network
RTN	Raton, NM [*Location identifier FAA*] (FAAL)
RTN	Raytheon Co. [*NYSE symbol*] (SPSG)
RTN	Recompression Thermonuclear
RTN	Recursive Transition Network [*Language analysis*] (BYTE)
RTN	Registered Technologist, Nuclear Medicine (MEDA)
RTN	Registered Trade Name
RTN	Relative Threat Number [*Military*] (CAAL)
RTN	Remote Terminal Network
RTN	Remote Tracking Network
RTN	Renal Tubule Necrosis [*Medicine*]
RTN	Report Test Number [*NASA*]
RTN	Resistor Terminating Network
RTN	Retain (KSC)
RTN	Return (AAG)
rtn	Return (ODBW)
RTN	Return to Neuter
RTN	Rota [*Nicaragua*] [*Seismograph station code, US Geological Survey*] (SEIS)
RTN	Routine
RTN	Routing Transit Number [*Telecommunications*]
RTN	Royal Thai Navy (CINC)
RTN	Russian Television Network
RTNA	Radio and Television (NADA)
RTNA	Regional Television News Australia
RTN(ARRT)	Registered Technologist in Nuclear Medicine Technology (American Registry of Radiologic Technologists) (MAE)
RTNB	Radio-Television Nationale du Burundi (EY)
RTNC	Radio-Television Nationale Congolaise
RTND	Returned
RTNDA	Radio-Television News Directors Association (EA)
RTNE	Radio Technical New Entrant [*Telecommunications*] (OA)
RTNEE	Returnee [*Military*]
R/T Net	Radio/Telephone Network [*Nuclear energy*] (GFGA)
RTNF	Recombinant Tumor Necrosis Factor [*Biochemistry*]
RTNG	Retaining (MSA)
RT(NM)	Radiology Technologist (Nuclear Medicine) (DAVI)
RTNM	Retreatment [*Staging of Cancer*] [*Medicine*] (STED)
rTNM	Retreatment Tumor, Nodes and Metastasis [*Staging of cancer*] (DAVI)
RTNOBE	Round Table of National Organizations for Better Education [*Defunct*] (EA)
RTNP	Red Tag News Publications [*Later, RTNPA*] (EA)
RTNPA	Red Tag News Publications Association (EA)
RTNR	Retainer (MSA)
RTNR	Ringing Tone No Reply (NITA)
RTNR	Ringtone No Reply [*Telecommunications*] (TEL)
RTNS	Rotating Target Neutron Source [*Nuclear physics*]
RTO	Radiotelephone Operator
RTO	Rail Transportation Officer [*Military*]
RTO	Railway Traffic Officer [*Military*]
RTO	Range Training Officer (MCD)
RTO	Rapid Thermal Oxidation (AAEL)
RTO	Reactor Trip Override [*Nuclear energy*] (NRCH)
RTO	Real-Time Operation
rto	Recto (BJA)
RTO	Referred-to-Output
RTO	Regenerative Thermal Oxidation [*Metallurgy*]
RTO	Regional Team of Officers [*British*]
RTO	Regional Telecommunications Office [*DoD*]
RTO	Regional Training Officer (OICC)
RTO	Rejected Takeoff [*Aviation*] (MCD)
RTO	Reliability Test Outline (AAG)
RTO	Report Time Over (FAAC)
RTO	Request to Off-Load [*Shipping*] (DS)
RTO	Responsible Test Organization [*NASA*] (MCD)
RTO	Return to Office (DAVI)
RTO	Right Toe Off [*Medicine*] (STED)
RTO	Road Traffic Officer [*British police*]
RTOAA	Rejected Takeoff Area Available [*Aviation*] (DA)
RTOG	Radiation Therapy Oncology Group (EA)
RTOK	Retest OK (MCD)
RTOL	Reduced Takeoff and Landing [*Aviation*]
RTOL	Rotary Takeoff and Landing [*Aviation*] (AIA)
RTOP	Real-Time Optional Processing (NITA)
RTOP	Research and Technology Objectives and Plans [*NASA*] (NASA)
RTOP	Research and Technology Operating [*or Operations*] Plan [*NASA*]
RTOP	Research and Technology Operations and Plans [*NASA*] (AAGC)
RTOPS	Research and Technology Objectives and Plans Summary [*NASA Information service or system*] (CRD)
R to R	Reach to Recovery (DAVI)
RTOR	Right Turn on Red [*i.e., on red traffic signal*]
RTOS	Real Time Operating System [*Computer science*]
RTOS	Real-Time Optical System (MCD)
RTOT	Range Track on Target [*Air Force*]
RTOW	Regulated [*or Restricted*] Takeoff Weight (MCD)
RTP	Radio Televisao Portuguesa [*Portuguese Radio-Television System*]
RTP	Rapid Thermal Processing [*Semiconductor technology*]
RTP	Rapid Transport Protocol [*Computer science*] (IGQR)
RTP	Reactor Thermal Power (IEEE)
RTP	Real-Time Peripheral (IEEE)
RTP	Real-Time Position (AAG)
RTP	Real-Time Processing [*Computer science*] (IAA)
RTP	Real-Time Profiler [*Instrumentation*]
RTP	Real-Time Program [*Computer science*] (IAA)
RTP	Real Time Protocol [*Telecommunications*] (OSI)
RTP	Real-Time Transport Protocol [*Computer science*] (IGQR)
RTP	Recruitment and Training Program
RTP	Reebok Tennis Professional [*Shoes*]
RTP	Reference Telephonic Power (DEN)
RTP	Reinforced Theatre Plan [*Military British*]
RTP	Reinforced Thermoplastic
RTP	Reinforced Thermoplastics
RTP	Relative Threat Priority [*Military*] (CAAL)
RTP	Reliability Test Plan (MCD)
RTP	Remote Transfer Point
RTP	Renal Transplant Patient (STED)
RTP	Replication-Terminator Protein [*Genetics*]
RTP	Republican Turkish Party [*Cyprus*] [*Political party*]
RTP	Request for Technical Proposal [*Military*]
RTP	Request to Purchase

RTP	Requirement and Test Procedures
RTP	Research Triangle Park [North Carolina]
RTP	Resistor Test Program
RTP	Resource Teaching Program (OICC)
RTP	Restrictive Trade Practice
RTP	Returned to Produce [Scrapping of automotive prototypes]
RTP	Reverse Tie Point (KSC)
RTP	Rio Tinto Plc ADS [NYSE symbol] [Formerly, RTZ Corp. Plc ADS] (SG)
RTP	Room-Temperature Phosphorimetry [Spectrometry]
RTP	Rotex Turret Punch
RTP	Routing Update Protocol [Telecommunications] (PCM)
RTP	Rutland Plains [Australia Airport symbol Obsolete] (OAG)
RTPA	Rail Travel Promotion Agency [Defunct] (EA)
rtPA	Recombinant Tissue Plasminogen Activator [Biochemistry]
RTPA	Recombinant Tissue-Type Plasminogen Activator [Genetics] (DAVI)
RTPA	Regional Transportation Planning Agency (PA)
RTPC	Real-Time Process Control
RTPC	Restrictive Trade Practices Commission
RT-PCR	Reverse Transcription-Polymerase Chain Reaction
RTPCVD	Rapid Thermal Processing Chemical Vapor Deposition [Coating technology] [Semiconductor technology]
RTPF	Round Tube-Plate Fin [Heat exchanger]
RTPG	Rubinstein-Taybi Parent Group (EA)
RTPH	Round Trips per Hour (MSA)
RTPI	Royal Town Planning Institute [British]
RTPL	Real-Time Procodural Language [Computer science] (MDG)
RTPLRS	Real-Time Position Location Reporting System (MCD)
RTPM	Real-Time Program Management
RTPMMA	Rubber-Toughened Polymethyl Methacrylate [Organic chemistry]
RTPR	Reference Theta Pinch Reactor
RTPR	Ribonucleoside Triphosphate Reductase [An enzyme]
RTPS	Radiation Therapy Planning System [Medicine] (DB)
RTPS	Real-Time Telemetry Processing System (PDAA)
RTPU	Reinforced Thermoplastic Polyurethane [Plastics]
RTPU	Rigid Thermoplastic Polyurethane [Organic chemistry]
RTQ	Real-Time Quotes [Information retrieval]
RTQ	Rutter Teacher Questionnaire
RTQA	Reports Tempore Queen Anne [11 Modern] [England] [A publication] (DLA)
RTQC	Real-Time Quality Control
RTR	Le Regiment de Trois-Rivieres [British military] (DMA)
R TR	Radio Tower
RTR	Real Time Radiography (COE)
RTR	Real-Time Readout
RTR	Real-Time Record (NTCM)
RTR	Real-Time Reliability (NITA)
RTR	Real-Time Reporting (AAEL)
RTR	Recovery Temperature Ratio
RTR	Recreational Therapist Registered
RTR	Recruit Training Regiment [Marine Corps] (DOMA)
RTR	Red Blood Cell Turnover Rate [Hematology]
RTR	Registered Technologist, Radiography (MEDA)
RT(R)	Registered Technologist (Radiology) (DAVI)
RTR	Reliability Test Requirements (AAG)
RTR	Reliable Transaction Router [Digital Equipment Corp.]
RTR	Remote Transmitter
RTR	Repair Time Ratio
RTR	Repeater Test Rack (DEN)
RTR	Resonance Test Reactor
RTR	Response Time Reporting
RTR	Retention Time Ratio (STED)
RTR	Return and Restore Status Register [Computer science]
RTR	Returning to Ramp [Aviation] (FAAC)
RTR	Return to Room (STED)
RTR	Ribbon-to-Ribbon Regrowth [of silicon for photovoltaic cells]
RTR	Road Traffic Reports [A publication] (DLA)
RTR	Roof-Top Ratio (COE)
RTR	Rotor (MSA)
RTR	Royal Tank Regiment [Military unit] [British]
Rtr	Ruth Rabbah (BJA)
RTR	Ryder Truck Rental
RTR	Sociedade Brazileira de Turismo (ROTATUR) [Brazil] [ICAO designator] (FAAC)
RTRA	Radio and Television Retailers' Association (NADA)
RTRA	Road Traffic Regulation Act [Town planning] [British]
RTR(ARRT)	Registered Technologist in Radiography (American Registry of Radiologic Technologists) (MAE)
RT(R)(ARRT)	Registered Technologist in Radiography Certified by American Registry of Radiologic Technologists (STED)
RTRC	Radio and Television Research Council (EA)
RTRC	Radiotelemetry and Remote Control (MCD)
RTRC	Regional Teacher Resource Center [NASA]
RTRC	Regional Technical Report Centers [Department of Commerce]
RTRCDS	Real-Time Reconnaissance Cockpit Display System [or Subsystem]
RTRD	Retard [Aviation] (FAAC)
RTRD	Retired
RTRDTN	Retardation
R Tren	Right Trendelenburg [Position] [Surgery] (DAVI)
RTREV	Right Reverend [Of an abbot, bishop, or monsignor]
RTRI	Real-Time Record Interpreter (NTCM)
RTRMNT	Retirement
RTRN	Return (FAAC)
RTRO	Real-Time Readout
RTRP	Remote Terminal Routine Package [Computer science] (IAA)

RTRR	Return to Recovery Room [Medicine] (DAVI)
RTRRM	Response Type Road Roughness Meter [FHWA] (TAG)
RTRS	Real-Time Rescheduling Subsystem
RTRS	Reuters Holdings Ltd. [New York, NY NASDAQ symbol] (NQ)
RTRSOC	Real-Time Reporting System on Oceanic Conditions (SSD)
RTRSW	Rotary Switch (MSA)
RTRSY	Reuters Hldgs ADS [NASDAQ symbol] (TTSB)
RTRV	Retrieve (MSA)
RT RV	Right Reverend [Of an abbot, bishop, or monsignor]
RTRY	Rotary
RTRYD	Reuters Group ADS [NASDAQ symbol] [Formerly, Reuters Holdings ADS] (SG)
RTS	RADAR Target Simulator
RTS	RADAR Test Set
RTS	RADAR Test Station (MCD)
RTS	RADAR Test System
RTS	RADAR Tracking Station [Military]
RTS	RADAR Tracking System
RTS	Radial Tuned Suspension (ADA)
RTS	Radioactive Waste Treatment System [Nuclear energy] (NUCP)
RTS	Radiodiffusion-Television du Senegal [Radio and television network] [Senegal]
RTS	Radiotelemetry Subsystem
RTS	Radioteletypewriter Set
RTS	Radio-Television Scolaire [French]
RTS	Radio Television Seychelles
RTS	Radio-Television Singapore
RTS	Radio Wire Broadcasting Network
RTS	Rail Transfer System (KSC)
RTS	Random Telegraph Signal (AAEL)
RTS	Range Time Signal
RTS	Range Timing System
RTS	Rapid Transit System (DCTA)
RTS	Rapid Transmission and Storage [Goldmark Corp.] [TV system]
RTS	Ratio Test Set
RTS	Reactive Terminal Service [International Telephone & Telegraph computer]
RTS	Reactor Trip System [Nuclear energy] (NRCH)
RTS	Readiness Training Squadron [Military] (NVT)
RTS	Ready to Send [Computer command] (PCM)
RTS	Real Time Scan [Medicine] (DMAA)
RTS	Real-Time Simulation
RTS	Real-Time Subroutines
RTS	Real-Time Supply [NASA] (MCD)
RTS	Real-Time System
RTS	Reconnaissance Technical Squadron [Air Force] (CINC)
RTS	Recorded Time Signal
RT/S	Refrigeration Technician/Specialist (AAG)
RTS	Refueling Water Transfer and Storage [Nuclear energy] (NRCH)
RTS	Regional Technical Support [Military]
RTS	Relay Telemetry Subsystem [NASA]
RTS	Relay Test System
RTS	Reliable Transfer Server [Telecommunications] (OSI)
RTS	Relief Transport Services Ltd. [British ICAO designator] (FAAC)
RTS	Religious Tract Society [British]
RTS	Remember That Song (EA)
RTS	Remote Targeting System
RTS	Remote Terminal Scanning System [Computer science] (IAA)
RTS	Remote Terminal Site [MTMC] (TAG)
RTS	Remote Terminal Supervisor (CMD)
RTS	Remote Terminal System [Computer science] (IAA)
RTS	Remote Testing System (NITA)
RTS	Remote Test System [Bell System]
RTS	Remote Tracking Site [Military]
RTS	Remote Tracking Station [NASA]
RTS	Repaired This Station (AFM)
RTS	Reparatur-Technische Station [Repair and Technical Station] [German]
RTS	Request to Send
RTS	Research and Technical Services [Military]
RTS	Research Test Site (AAG)
RTS	Resolute Resources [Vancouver Stock Exchange symbol]
RTS	Resolve through Sharing (EA)
RTS	Return from Subroutine [Computer science]
RTS	Return to Search
RTS	Return to Sender
RTS	Return to Service [Aviation]
RTS	Return to Stores
RTS	Return to Supplier (MCD)
RTS	Rights [Stock market term]
Rts	Rights (EBF)
RTS	River Thames Society [British]
RTS	Rosner Television Systems, Inc. [New York, NY] [Telecommunications] (TSSD)
RTS	Rotary Thumbwheel Switch
RTS	Rottnest Island [Australia Airport symbol] (OAG)
RTS	Royal Television Society [British]
RTS	Royal Toxophilite Society [British]
RTS	Rubber Traders Society (NADA)
RTS	Rubinstein-Taybi Syndrome [Medicine]
RTS	Run-Time Smartener [Military]
RTRS	Rural Telephone System [Telecommunications] (OA)
RTS	Russ Togs (EFIS)
RTSA	RADAR Target Signature Analysis
RTSA	Radio Tracking System Analyst (MUGU)

RTSA	Remote Telephone Subscribers' Association [*Australia*]
RTSA	Retail Trading Standards Association (WDAA)
RTSC	Recommended Test Sequence Chart
RTSC	Replacement and Training School Command [*Military*]
RTSD	Resources and Technical Services Division [*Later, ALCTS*] [*American Library Association*] (EA)
RTSD	Royal Thai Survey Department (CINC)
RTSD CCS	RTSD [*Resources and Technical Services Division*] Cataloging and Classification Section
RTSD PLMS	RTSD [*Resources and Technical Services Division*] Preservation of Library Materials Section
RTSD RLMS	RTSD [*Resources and Technical Services Division*] Reproduction of Library Materials Section
RTSD RS	RTSD [*Resources and Technical Services Division*] Resources Section
RTSDS	Real-Time Scheduling Display System
RTSD SS	RTSD [*Resources and Technical Services Division*] Serials Section
RTSE	Reliable Transfer Service Element [*Telecommunications*] (OSI)
RTSF	Real-Time Simulation Facility [*NASA*] (MCD)
RTSM	Return to Stock Memo
RTSP	Real-Time Signal Processor (NVT)
RTSP	Real Time Streaming Protocol (PCM)
RTSPC	Real-Time Statistical Process Control (AAEL)
RTSPG	Rubinstein-Taybi Parent Group (EA)
RTSq	Reconnaissance Technical Squadron [*Air Force*] (AFM)
RTSRS	Real-Time Simulation Research System (WDAA)
RTSS	Real-Time Scientific System
RTSS	Returning to School Syndrome
RTST	Radio Technician Selection Test [*Military*]
RTST	Right Start [*NASDAQ symbol*] (TTSB)
RTST	Right Start, Inc. [*NASDAQ symbol*] (SPSG)
RTSV	Real-Time Synthetic Video (DOMA)
RTSW	Real-Time Software [*Computer science*] (MHDI)
RTT	Radet for Teknisk Terminologi [*Norwegian Council for Technical Terminology*] [*Oslo*] [*Information service or system*] (IID)
RTT	Radiation Therapy Technician
RTT	Radiation Tracking Transducer
RTT	Radiotelemetric Theodolite
RTT	Radioteleprinter (DA)
RTT	Radioteletype (IAA)
RTT	Radioteletypewriter
RTT	Radio Television Tunisien [*Tunisian Radio and Television*] (AF)
RTT	Rate of Turntable
RTT	Real-Time Telemetry (IAA)
RTT	Receiver Threshold Test (CET)
RTT	Rectangular Tongue Terminal
RTT	Regie des Telegraphes et des Telephones [*Belgium Telecommunications service*] (TSSD)
RTT	Regional Training Teams [*Army*]
RT(T)	Registered Technologist (Therapy) (DAVI)
RTT	Remote Tuning Technique
RTT	Request to Talk [*Computer science*] (CIST)
RTT	Requirements Traceability Tool [*Computer science*]
RTT	Resonant Tunnelling Transistor [*Electronics*]
RTT	Return Trip Time
RTT	Revised Token Test (EDAC)
RTT	Ring Tongue Terminal
RTT	Rocket-Thrown Torpedo
RTT	Role-Taking Task
RTT	Round-Trip Time [*Computer science*] (IGQR)
RTTA	Range Tower Transfer Assembly (KSC)
RTTA	Ranging Tone Transfer Assembly
RTTAA	Railway Telegraph and Telephone Appliance Association
RTT(ARRT)	Registered Technologist in Radiation Therapy Technology (American Registry of Radiologic Technologists) (MAE)
RTTC	Redstone Technical Test Center [*Army*] (RDA)
RTTC	Road Time Trials Council [*Bicycle racing competition*] [*British*]
RTTD	Real-Time Telemetry Data (MCD)
RTTDS	Real-Time Telemetry Data System
RTTI	Runtime Type Information [*Computer science*] (PCM)
RTTL	Rattail [*Metallurgy*]
RTTL	Rattlesnake Hldg Co. [*NASDAQ symbol*] (TTSB)
RTTL	[*The*] Rattlesnake Holding Co., Inc. [*NASDAQ symbol*] (SAG)
RTTL	Real-Time Temporal Logic [*Computer science*]
RTTL	Running Telltale Light (MSA)
RTTM	Real-Time Transient Model [*Computer science*]
RTTOS	Real-Time Tactical Operating System (MCD)
RTTP	Radiation Therapy Treatment Planning [*Medicine*] (DMAA)
RTTP	Router Template (AAG)
RT-TRACS	Real-Time Traffic Adaptive Signal Control [*FHWA*] (TAG)
RT-TRACS	Real-Time Traffic Control System
RTTS	RADAR Telephone Transmission System
RTTS	Reaction Torque Temperature Sensitivity
RTTS	Real-Time Telemetry System
RTTS	Rover Tester Test Set
RTTV	Real-Time Television
RTTV	Research Target and Test Vehicle
RTTW	Radioteletypewriter (IAA)
RTTY	Radioteletype (IAA)
RTTY	Radioteletypewriter
RTU	RADAR Timing Unit
RTU	Railroad Telegraphers Union
RTU	Range Transfer Unit (MCD)
RTU	Rate of a Transfer Unit (IAA)
RTU	Ready to Use

RTU	Real-Time Ultrasound [*Medicine*] (DMAA)
RTU	Receiver/Transmitter Unit
RTU	Recovery Task Unit
RTU	Reinforcement Training Unit [*Army*] (AABC)
RTU	Remote Telemetry Unit
RTU	Remote Terminal Unit
RTU	Remote Transmission Unit (CIST)
RTU	Renal Transplant Unit [*National Health Service*] [*British*] (DI)
RTU	Replacement Training Unit [*Military*]
RTU	Reserve Training Unit (MCD)
RTU	Response Test Unit
RTU	Return to Unit [*Military British*]
RTU	Right to Use [*Telecommunications*] (TEL)
rTU	rRNA[*Ribonucleic Acid*] Transcription Unit [*Genetics*] (DOG)
RTUA	Recognition Technologies Users Association (EA)
RTUM	Revolutionary Trade Union Movement [*Czechoslovakia*]
RTV	Radio and Television Research Council (NTPA)
RTV	Radiodiffusion-Television (Upper Volta) [*Radio and television network*]
RTv	Radio-Telephone (Very-High Frequency) [*Telecommunications*] (DS)
RTV	Real-Time Video
RTV	Recovery Test Vehicle
RTV	Reentry Test Vehicle [*Air Force*]
RTV	Research Test Vehicle
RTV	Retrieve Resources Ltd. [*Vancouver Stock Exchange symbol*]
RTV	Returned to Vendor (AAG)
RTV	Rhodesian Television (AF)
RTV	Rice Tungro Virus
RTV	Ritonavir [*An antiviral drug*]
RTV	Rocket Test Vehicle (MCD)
RTV	Room-Temperature Vulcanized (NAKS)
RTV	Room Temperature Vulcanizing (MCD)
RTV	Rough Terrain Vehicle
RTVA	Radio Television de Andalucia [*Spain*] (EY)
RTVB	Rumbo Tools for Visual Bask [*Computer science*]
RTVD	Radiotelevision Dominicana [*Dominican Radio and Television*] [*Dominican Republic*]
RTVE	Radiotelevision Espanola [*Spanish*]
RTVM	Radio Television Madrid [*Spain*] (EY)
RTVM	Real-Time Virtual Memeory [*Computer science*] (IAA)
RTVMU	Radiotelevision Murciana [*Spain*] (EY)
RTVOS	Real-Time Virtual Operating System (NITA)
RTVP	Real-Time Video Processing
RTVS	Radio/Television Services [*Washington State University*] [*Pullman*] [*Telecommunications service*] (TSSD)
RTVS	Real Time Velocimeter System [*Army*] (RDA)
RTVS	Relay Test and Verification System (MCD)
RTVS	Run Time Variable Stack (CIST)
RTVV	Radiotelevision Valencia [*Spain*] (EY)
RTW	Manitoba Reports Tempore Wood [*Canada A publication*] (DLA)
RTW	Railway Tank Wagon [*British military*] (DMA)
RTW	Ready-to-Wear [*Clothing*]
RTW	Roturn to Work (DAVI)
RTW	Right to Work
RTW	Right Worshipful
RTW	Road Tank Wagon (WDAA)
RTW	Round the World
RTW	RTW, Inc. [*Associated Press*] (SAG)
RTWB	Richardson's Theological Word Book [*A publication*] (BJA)
RTWI	RTW, Inc. [*NASDAQ symbol*] (SAG)
RTWS	Raw Type Write Submodule
RTWUS	Research and Technology Work Unit Summary
RTx	Radiation Therapy (DAVI)
RTX	Rapid Transit Experimental [*Gas-turbine bus*]
RTX	Real-Time Executive
RTX	Resiniferatoxin [*Organic chemistry*]
RTX	Revenue Canada Taxation Library [*UTLAS symbol*]
RTXE	Real-Time Executive Extended (PDAA)
RTY	Merty [*Australia Airport symbol Obsolete*] (OAG)
RTY	Muscatine, IA [*Location identifier FAA*] (FAAL)
RTY	Rarity (WGA)
RTY	Retry Limit (AAEL)
RTY	Ross Air Training [*British ICAO designator*] (FAAC)
RTYC	Royal Thames Yachting Club [*British*]
RTYV	Rice Transitory Yellowing Virus [*Plant pathology*]
RTZ	Radio Tanzania Zanzibar
RTZ	Retail Trading Zone (WDMC)
RTZ	Return-to-Zero [*Recording scheme*]
RTZ	Ritz Resources Ltd. [*Vancouver Stock Exchange symbol*]
RTZ	RTZ Corp. [*NYSE symbol*] (SPSG)
RTZ	RTZ Corp. ADR [*Associated Press*] (SAG)
RTZL	RTZ Corp. plc ADS [*NYSE symbol*] (TTSB)
RTZL	Runway Touchdown Zone Light [*Aviation*] (FAAC)
RU	Are You [*Communication*]
RU	Britt Airways [*ICAO designator*] (AD)
Ru	Gosudarstvennaia Biblioteka SSR Imeni V. I. Lenina [*Lenin State Library of the USSR*], Moscow, Soviet Union [*Library symbol Library of Congress*] (LCLS)
RU	RADAR Unit (MCD)
RU	Radioactive Uptake [*Radiology*] (DAVI)
RU	Railway Underwriter
RU	Rain Umbrella [*An association*] (EA)
RU	Range Unit
RU	Range User
RU	Rat Unit

RU .... Readers Union Rugby Union (NADA)
RU .... Reading of Unknown
RU .... Ready Use [British]
R/U .... Record/Update
RU .... Rectourethral (DAVI)
RU .... Refrigeration Unit (KSC)
RU .... Regular Unleaded [Shell Oil Co.]
RU .... Reinforcement Unit [British military] (DMA)
RU .... Relative Unit [Typography]
RU .... Release Unit [Army] (AABC)
RU .... Remote Unit (NASA)
RU .... Renaissance Universal (EA)
RU .... Repeat Unit [Genetics]
RU .... Replaceable Unit
RU .... Replacement Unit
RU .... Reproducing Unit
RU .... Request/Response Unit [Computer science]
RU .... Rescue Unit (COE)
RU .... Reserve Unit [Equal to one US dollar] [International finance] [Former USSR]
RU .... Resin Uptake [Endocrinology]
RU .... Resistance Unit (MAE)
RU .... Respiratory Unit [Medicine]
RU .... Rotransmission Unit [RADA] [Army] (RDA)
RU .... Retrograde Urogram [Medicine] (MAE)
RU .... Right Upper [Medicine]
RU .... Right Upstage [Theater] (WDMC)
RU .... Roentgen Unit [Also, r] [Measuring X and gamma radiations]
RU .... Roussel [France] [Research code symbol]
Ru .... Rufinus [Flourished, 1150-86] [Authority cited in pre-1607 legal work] (DSA)
RU .... Rugby Union [Controlling body of British rugby football]
Ru .... Ruins
RU .... Runic [Language, etc.] (ROG)
Ru .... Run Unit (NITA)
Ru .... Rural
RU .... Russian Federation [Internet country code]
RU .... Rutgers-[The] State University [New Brunswick, NJ] (PDAA)
Ru .... Ruth [Old Testament book]
Ru .... Ruthenium [Chemical element]
ru .... Rutile [CIPW classification] [Geology]
RU .... Rutin [Organic chemistry]
RU .... Unborrowed Reserves
RU .... University of Rhode Island, Kingston, RI [Library symbol Library of Congress] (LCLS)
RU .... Ursuline Nuns of the Congregation of Tildonk, Belgium [Roman Catholic religious order]
RU-486 .... Roussel Uclaf "Once-a-Month" Pill [Contraceptive]
RUA .... Arua [Uganda] [Airport symbol] (OAG)
RUA .... Reduced Under Anesthesia [Medicine] (DMAA)
RUA .... Retailer's Uniform Agency
RUA .... Right Upper Arm [Medicine]
RUA .... Routine Urinalysis (DAVI)
RUA .... Royal Ulster Academy of Painting, Sculpture, and Architecture [Ireland]
RUAC .... Remote User Access System [Telecommunications]
RUAT .... Report upon Arrival Threat [Army] (AABC)
RUB .... Rich Urban Biker [Lifestyle classification]
RUB .... Rubber (AAG)
rub .... Rubbing (VRA)
RUB .... Rubefacient [Producing Heat and Redness of the Skin] [Medicine] (ROG)
RUB .... Ruber [Red] [Pharmacy]
RUB .... Ruble [Monetary unit] [Former USSR]
RUB .... Rubric (DLA)
RUB .... Ruby Mountain Mines [Vancouver Stock Exchange symbol]
RUBAC .... Relative Universal Business Automation Code
RUBB .... Great Amer BackRub [NASDAQ symbol]
RUBB .... Great American Backrub Store, Inc. [NASDAQ symbol] (SAG)
Rub Conv .... Rubinstein on Conveyancing [5th ed.] [1884] [A publication] (DLA)
RUBD .... Rubberized (AAG)
RuBeMiA ..... Akademiia Nauk Belorusskaia SSR, Fundamemtlanaia Biblioteka Imeni Ia. Kolasa [Academy of Sciences of the Belorussian SSR, J. Kolasa Fundamental Library], Minsk, Belorussian SSR, Soviet Union [Library symbol Library of Congress] (LCLS)
RUBIDIC ...... Rubidazone [Zorubicin]/DIC [Dacarbazine] [Antineoplastic drug regimen]
RUBISCO .... Ribulosebisphosphate Carboxylase/Oxygenase [An enzyme]
RUBN .... Russian, Ukrainian, and Belorussian Newspapers [A bibliographic publication]
RuBP .... Ribulosebisphosphate [Also, RDP] [Biochemistry]
RuBPCase... Ribulosebisphosphate Carboxylase [An enzyme]
RuBPC/O...... Ribulosebisphosphate Carboxylase/Oxygenase [Also, RUBISCO] [An enzyme]
Rubrmd........ Rubbermaid, Inc. [Associated Press] (SAG)
RUBSG .... Recovery Unit and Base Support Group [Air Force]
RUBSH......... Rubbish
RUBSSO ...... Rossendale Union of Boot, Shoe, and Slipper Operatives [British] (DCTA)
RubyTu .... Ruby Tuesday, Inc. [Associated Press] (SAG)
RUC .... Rapid Update Cycle [Marine science] (OSRA)
RUC .... Reporting Unit Code [Computer science]
RUC .... Riverine Utility Craft [Vehicle for transporting through shallow water and snow] [Navy symbol]
RUC .... Royal Ulster Constabulary [British]

RUC .... Rutas Aereas, CA [Venezuela] [FAA designator] (FAAC)
RUCA .... Rear Upper Control Arm
RUCA .... Russell Cave National Monument
RUCAG........ Residential Utility Consumer Action Group
RUCAPS....... Really Universal Computer-Aided Production System (PDAA)
RUCATSE..... Runway Capacity to Serve the South East [Airport planning group] [British] (ECON)
Rucker......... Rucker's Reports [43-46 West Virginia] [A publication] (DLA)
RUCS .... Racial Unconscious [Psychiatry]
Rucus .... Run Cutting and Scheduling (DICI)
RUD .... Rational Use of Drugs (DB)
RUD .... Recently Used Directory [Computer science] (MHDI)
RUD .... Recurrent Ulcer of the Duodenal Bulb [Medicine] (DMAA)
RUD .... Rudder (AAG)
RUDAEE ...... Report of Unsatisfactory or Defective Airborne Electronic Equipment [Navy]
RUDAOE ...... Report of Unsatisfactory or Defective Aviation Ordnance Equipment [Navy]
R/UDAT .... Regional/Urban Development Assistance Team (DICI)
RUDD........... Remote Underwater Detection Device [Navy]
Ruddick ...... Ruddick Corp. [Associated Press] (SAG)
RUDH.......... Reserve Shutdown Unplanned Derated Hours [Electronics] (IEEE)
RUDI .... Regional Urban Defense Intercept
RUDI .... Report of Unsatisfactory or Defective Instrumentation [Navy]
RUDI .... Resource for Urban Design Information [British] (TELE)
RUDI .... Restricted Use Digital Instrument (OA)
RUDIM......... Rudimentary (ROG)
RUDIS .... Reference Your Dispatch (NOAA)
RUDM.......... Report of Unsatisfactory or Defective Material [Aircraft] [Navy]
RUDMIN ...... Report of Unsatisfactory or Defective Mine [Navy] (NG)
RUDMINDE... Report of Unsatisfactory or Defective Mine, Depth Charge, or Associated Equipment [Navy] (NG)
RUDS........... Reflectance Units of Dirt Shade (PDAA)
RUDTORPE... Report of Unsatisfactory or Defective Torpedo Equipment [Navy] (NG)
RUDY........... Rudys Restaurant Group [NASDAQ symbol] (SAG)
RUE .... Right Upper Entrance [A stage direction]
RUE .... Right Upper Extremity [Medicine]
RUE .... Rue [Postal Service standard] (OPSA)
RUE .... Russellville, AR [Location identifier FAA] (FAAL)
Ruegg Emp L... Ruegg on Employer's Liability [9th ed.] [1922] [A publication] (DLA)
RUER .... SSRC [Social Science Research Council] Research Unit on Ethnic Relations [Research center British] (IRC)
RUF .... Minocqua-Woodruff, WI [Location identifier FAA] (FAAL)
RUF .... Radiation Usage Factor (MCD)
RUF .... Refractory Users Federation [British] (BI)
RUF .... Resource Utilization Factor
RUF .... Revolutionary United Front [Sierra Leone] [Political party] (EY)
RUF .... Revolving Underwriting Facility [Finance]
RUF .... Rigid Urethane Foam
Ruf .... Rufinus [Flourished, 1150-86] [Authority cited in pre-1607 legal work] (DSA)
RUFAS .... Remote Underwater Fisheries Assessment System [National Oceanic and Atmospheric Administration]
RUFC .... Rugby Union Football Club [British] (DAS)
RUFE .... Zeitschrift fuer Rundfunk und Fernsehen [Journal for Radio and Television] [NOMOS Datapool] [Information service or system]
Ruff............. Ruffhead's Edition of the Statutes, by Serjeant Runnington [1235-1785] [A publication] (DLA)
Ruff............. Ruffin and Hawks' Reports [8 North Carolina] [A publication] (DLA)
Ruff............. Statutes at Large, Ruffhead's Edition [England] [A publication] (DLA)
Ruff & H...... Ruffin and Hawks' Reports [8 North Carolina] [A publication] (DLA)
Ruffh St ...... Ruffhead's English Statutes [A publication] (DLA)
RUFF-PAC... Ruff Political Action Committee (EA)
Ruff St .... Ruffhead's English Statutes [A publication] (DLA)
RUFP .... Regulations under the Federal Power Act
RUG .... Coronet Carpets, Inc. [Toronto Stock Exchange symbol]
RUG .... Recomp Users Group [Computer science]
RUG .... Regional User Group [Computer science]
RUG .... Report and Update Program Generator (IAA)
RUG .... Resource Utilization Group (DHSM)
RUG .... Restricted Users Group [Computer science] (ODBW)
RUG .... Retrograde Ureterogram [Medicine]
RUG .... ROSCOE User Group [Princeton, NJ] (CSR)
RUG .... Rugby, NJ [Location identifier FAA] (FAAL)
RUG .... Rutgers-[The] State University, Graduate School of Library and InformationScience, New Brunswick, NJ [OCLC symbol] (OCLC)
RUH .... Range Users Handbook
RUH .... Riyadh [Saudi Arabia] [Airport symbol] (OAG)
RUHBC........ Research Unit in Health and Behavioral Change [University of Edinburgh] [Scotland] (IRC)
RUHP........... Rescue Unit Home Port [Navy] (NVT)
RUI .... Research in Undergraduate Institutions [A National Science Foundation program]
RUI .... Royal University of Ireland
RUI .... Ruidoso [New Mexico] [Airport symbol] (OAG)
RUI .... Ruidoso, NM [Location identifier FAA] (FAAL)
RUIA .... Railroad Unemployment Insurance Act (GFGA)
RUIN .... Regional and Urban Information Network [Washington, DC]
RUK .... Reed International Ltd. [NYSE symbol]
RUK .... Reed Intl P.L.C. ADS [NYSE symbol] (TTSB)
RUKBA........ Royal United Kingdom Benevolent Institution

RuKiFrA .... Akademiia Nauk Kirgizskoi SSR, Tsentralnaia Nauchaia Biblioteka [*Academy of Sciences of the Kirghiz SSR, Central Scientific Library*], Frunze, Kirghiz SSR, Soviet Union [*Library symbol Library of Congress*] (LCLS)

RuL .... Gosudarstvennaia Publichnaia Biblioteka Imeni Saltykova-Shchedrina [*State Saltikov-Shchedrin Public Library*], Leningrad, Soviet Union [*Library symbol Library of Congress*] (LCLS)

RUL .... Refractoriness under Load (IAA)

RUL .... Representative of the Senate of the University of London (ROG)

RUL .... Right Upper Eyelid [*Medicine*]

RUL .... Right Upper Limb [*Medicine*]

RUL .... Right Upper Lobe [*of lung*] [*Medicine*]

RUL .... Right Upper Lung [*Medicine*] (MAE)

RUL .... Rikkyo University Library [*UTLAS symbol*]

RUL .... Ruled

RUL .... Rule Resources Ltd. [*Vancouver Stock Exchange symbol*]

RuLA .... Akademiia Nauk SSSR [*Academy of Sciences of the USSR*], Leningrad, Soviet Union [*Library symbol Library of Congress*] (LCLS)

Rul Cas .... Campbell's Ruling Cases [*England*] [*A publication*] (DLA)

RULE .... Restructuring the Undergraduate Learning Environment [*National Science Foundation*]

RULE .... Rule Industries, Inc. [*NASDAQ symbol*] (NQ)

RULEG .... Rule Then Example [*Computer science*] (BARN)

RuleInd .... Rule Industries, Inc. [*Associated Press*] (SAG)

RULER .... Remaining Useful Life Evaluation Rig [*Lubricant testing*]

Rules Sup Ct ... Rules of the Supreme Court [*A publication*] (DLA)

RULET .... Reference Your Letter (NOAA)

RULPA .... Revised Uniform Limited Partnership Act (AAGC)

RuLU-N .... Leningradskii Universitet, Nauchnaia Biblioteka Imeni Gor'kogo [*Leningrad State University, Gor'kii Scientific Library*], Leningrad, Soviet Union [*Library symbol Library of Congress*] (LCLS)

RUM .... Railwaymen's Union of Malaya

RUM .... Ranger Uranium Mines [*Commercial firm Australia*]

RUM .... Remote Underwater Manipulator [*Oceanography*]

RUM .... Remote Unit Monitor (MCD)

RUM .... Resource and Unit Monitoring (DOMA)

RUM .... Resource Unit Management

RUM .... Resource Utilization Monitor

rum .... Romanian [*MARC language code Library of Congress*] (LCCP)

RUM .... Rotary Ultrasonic Machining [*Manufacturing term*]

RUM .... Rumangabo [*Zaire*] [*Seismograph station code, US Geological Survey*] (SEIS)

RUM .... Rumania

Rum .... Rumania (VRA)

RUM .... Rumjartar [*Nepal*] [*Airport symbol Obsolete*] (OAG)

RUM .... San Marcos, TX [*Location identifier FAA*] (FAAL)

RUMAC .... Rubber-Modified Asphalt Concrete

RUMAS .... Reserve Unit Manpower Authorization System (MCD)

RUMEM .... Reference Your Memorandum (NOAA)

RUMEMO ...... Reference Your Memorandum (FAAC)

RUMES .... Reference Message from Your Office (FAAC)

RuMG .... Gosudarstvennaia Publichnaia Nauchno Tokhnicheskaia Biblioteka SSSR [*State Public Scientific and Technical Library*], Moscow, Soviet Union [*Library symbol Library of Congress*] (LCLS)

RuMHi .... State Public Historical Library, Moscow, Soviet Union [*Library symbol Library of Congress*] (LCLS)

RUMIC .... Remote Underwater Mine Countermeasure (PDAA)

RuMIN .... Institut Nauchnoi Informatsii po Obshchestvennym Naukam, Akademiia Nauk SSSR [*Institute of Scientific Information on Social Sciences, Academy of Sciences of the USSR*], Moscow, Soviet Union [*Library symbol Library of Congress*] (LCLS)

RUMIN .... Ruminant

RUMINT .... Rumor Intelligence

RuMLit .... Vsesoiuznaia Gosudarstvennaia Biblioteka Inostrannoi Literatury [*All-Union State Library of Foreign Literature*], Moscow, Soviet Union [*Library symbol Library of Congress*] (LCLS)

RUMOD .... Regional Underground Monolith Disposal [*Hazardous wastes*]

RuMoKisA .... Akademiia Nauk Moldavskoi SSR, Tsentralnaia Nauchnaia Biblioteka [*Academy of Sciences of the Moldavian SSR, Central Scientific Library*], Kishivev, Moldavian SSR, Soviet Union [*Library symbol Library of Congress*] (LCLS)

RUMP .... Radio-Controlled Ultraviolet Measurement Program (MUGU)

RUMP .... Remote Underwater Marine Probe (SAA)

RUMPS .... Raw Umber and Maize Preservation Society [*An association*]

RUMR .... Routine Unsatisfactory Material Report (MCD)

RuMVKP .... Vsesoiuznaia Knizhnaia Palata [*All-Union Book Chamber*], Ulitsa Oktiab r Skaia, Moscow, Soviet Union [*Library symbol*] [*Library of Congress*] (LCLS)

RUN .... Rassemblement pout l'Unite Nationale [*Cameroon*] [*Political party*] (EY)

RUN .... Reduction Unlimited

RUN .... Reunion Island [*Airport symbol*] (OAG)

RUN .... Rewind and Unload

RUN .... Rockmaster Resources [*Vancouver Stock Exchange symbol*]

RUN .... Run [*Postal Service standard*] (OPSA)

run .... Rundi [*MARC language code Library of Congress*] (LCCP)

RUN .... Runstream [*Computer science*]

RUN .... Ruthven [*California*] [*Seismograph station code, US Geological Survey*] (SEIS)

RUn .... University of Rhode Island, Kingston, RI [*Library symbol*] [*Library of Congress*] (LCLS)

RUNCIBLE .... Revised Unified New Compiler with Its Basic Language Extended [*Computer science*]

RUNDH .... Reserve Shutdown Unit Derated Hours [*Electronics*] (IEEE)

RUNEL .... Runway-End Lighting [*Aviation*]

RUNI .... Reunion Industries [*NASDAQ symbol*] (TTSB)

RUNI .... Reunion Resources [*NASDAQ symbol*] (SAG)

RUNID .... Run Identification [*Computer science*]

Runn .... Runnell's Reports [*38-56 Iowa*] [*A publication*] (DLA)

Runn .... Statutes at Large, Runnington's Edition [*England*] [*A publication*] (DLA)

Runn Eject .... Runnington on Ejectment [*2nd ed.*] [*1820*] [*A publication*] (DLA)

Runnell .... Runnell's Reports [*38-56 Iowa*] [*A publication*] (DLA)

Runn Stat .... Runnington on Statutes [*A publication*] (DLA)

RUNR .... Reunion Resources [*NASDAQ symbol*] (SAG)

RUNT .... Russian Underground Nuclear Test (MCD)

RUO .... Right Upper Outer [*Quadrant*] [*Anatomy*] (DAVI)

RUO .... Right Ureteral Orifice [*Medicine*]

RUOK .... Are You OK? [*Internet language*] [*Computer science*]

RUOK .... Response USA [*NASDAQ symbol*] (TTSB)

RUOK .... Response USA, Inc. [*NASDAQ symbol*] (SAG)

RUOKW .... Response USA Wrrt'A' [*NASDAQ symbol*] (TTSB)

RUOKZ .... Response USA Wrrt'B' [*NASDAQ symbol*] (TTSB)

RUOQ .... Right Upper Outer Quadrant [*Site of injection*] [*Medicine*]

RUP .... Rat Urine Protein [*Biochemistry*] (DAVI)

RUP .... Raza Unida Party (EA)

RUP .... Restricted Use Pesticide [*Environmental Protection Agency*] (GFGA)

RUP .... Right Upper Pole [*Medicine*] (DMAA)

RUP .... Rockefeller University Press (DGA)

RUP .... Rupertsland Resources Co. Ltd. [*Toronto Stock Exchange symbol*]

RUP .... Rupsi [*India*] [*Airport symbol*] (AD)

RUPBX .... Reference Your Public Branch Exchange Message (SAA)

Rupert J .... Rupert Journal [*A publication*]

Rupert Newsl ... Rupert Newsletter [*A publication*]

RUPHO .... Reference Your Telephone Call (NOAA)

RUPPERT ...... Reserve Unit Personnel Performance Report

Ruppie .... Republican Urban Professional [*Lifestyle classification*]

RUPT .... Interrupt (NASA)

RUPT .... Rupture (NASA)

rupt .... Ruptured [*Medicine*] (STED)

RUQ .... Rifle Unqualified [*Military*]

RUQ .... Right Upper Quadrant [*of abdomen*] [*Medicine*]

RUQ .... Salisbury, NC [*Location identifier FAA*] (FAAL)

RUR .... Reference Update Review (SSD)

RUR .... Resin Uptake Ratio [*Endocrinology*]

RUR .... Rossum's Universal Robots [*Acronym is title of play by Karel Capek*]

RUR .... Royal Ulster Rifles [*Military unit*] [*British*]

RUR .... Rural

RUR .... Rurutu Island [*French Polynesia*] [*Airport symbol*] (OAG)

rur .... Russian SFSR [*MARC country of publication code Library of Congress*] (LCCP)

RuralCel .... Rural Cellular Corp. [*Associated Press*] (SAG)

RuralMet .... Rural Metro Corp. [*Associated Press*] (SAG)

RURALC .... Range Utilization Resources and Allocation Listings (SAA)

RURAX .... Rural Automatic Exchange [*Telecommunications*] (TEL)

RUREQ .... Reference Your Requisition (NOAA)

RURESA .... Revised Uniform Reciprocal Enforcement of Support Act (PAZ)

RURL .... Rural Metro Corp. [*NASDAQ symbol*] (SAG)

RURLAM ...... Replacement Unit Repair Level Analysis Model

RURP .... Realised Ultimate Reality Piton [*Mountain climbing*]

RURPOP .... Rural Population File (MCD)

RURTI .... Recurrent Upper Respiratory Tract Infection [*Medicine*] (ADA)

RUS .... Air Russia Airlines [*Russian Federation*] [*ICAO designator*] (FAAC)

RUS .... Marau [*Solomon Islands*] [*Airport symbol*] (OAG)

RUS .... Radioulnar Synostosis [*Medicine*] (DMAA)

RUS .... Rapid City, SD [*Location identifier FAA*] (FAAL)

RUS .... Recurrent Ulcerative Stomatitis [*Medicine*] (STED)

Rus .... Resistance of the Airways on the Alveolar Side of the Point in the Airways whereIntraluminal Pressure Equals intrapleural Pressure [*Medicine*] (DAVI)

RUS .... Rest of the United States [*Government's official term for its system of determining federal salaries*]

RUS .... Rural Uplook Service [*Ithaca, NY*]

RUS .... Russ Berrie & Co. [*NYSE symbol*] (SPSG)

Rus .... Russell's Election Cases [*1874*] [*Nova Scotia*] [*A publication*] (DLA)

Rus .... Russell's English Chancery Reports [*A publication*] (DLA)

RUS .... Russia

Rus .... Russia (VRA)

rus .... Russian [*MARC language code Library of Congress*] (LCCP)

RUS .... Rust College, Holly Springs, MS [*OCLC symbol*] (OCLC)

RUSA .... Reference and User Services Association [*Formerly, RASD*]

RUSAF .... Russell Metals Cv'A' [*NASDAQ symbol*] (TTSB)

RUSAF .... Russell Metals, Inc. [*NASDAQ symbol*] (SAG)

Rus & C Eq Cas ... Russell and Chesley's Nova Scotia Equity Cases [*A publication*] (DLA)

RUSB .... Right Upper Sternal Border [*Anatomy*] (DMAA)

RUSDIC .... Russian Dictionary [*A publication*]

RUSEC .... Romanian-US Economic Council (EA)

Rus EC .... Russell's Contested Election Cases [*Massachusetts*] [*A publication*]

Rus EC .... Russell's Irish Election Reports [*A publication*] (DLA)

RUSEF .... Rational Use of the Sea Floor Program [*National Oceanic and Atmospheric Administration*] (MSC)

Rus Elec Rep ... Russell's Election Cases [*1874*] [*Nova Scotia*] [*A publication*] (DLA)

Rus Eq Rep ... Russell's Nova Scotia Equity Decisions [*A publication*] (DLA)

Rus ER .... Russell's Election Cases [*1874*] [*Nova Scotia*] [*A publication*] (DLA)

RUSH .... Remote User Shared Hardware [*Computer science*]

RUSH .... Rudder Shaped Hull (PDAA)

RUSH	Rush Enterprises, Inc. [NASDAQ symbol] (SAG)
RushEnt	Rush Enterprises, Inc. [Associated Press] (SAG)
Rush Med C	Rush Medicine College (GAGS)
Rushw	Rushworth's Historical Collections [A publication] (DLA)
RUSI	Royal United Services Institute for Defence Studies [British] (DBA)
RUSM	Royal United Service Museum [British military] (DMA)
RUSNO	Resident United States Naval Officer
Rus P	Russian Pharmacopoeia [A publication]
RUSPAND	Russian-Spanish Dictionary [A publication] (SAA)
RUSS	Recurrent Ulcerative Scarifying Stomatitis [Medicine] (STED)
RUSS	Remote User Service Station (MCD)
Russ	Russell's Contested Election Cases [Massachusetts] [A publication] (DLA)
Russ	Russell's Election Cases [1874] [Nova Scotia] [A publication] (DLA)
Russ	Russell's English Chancery Reports [A publication] (DLA)
RUSS	Russet
RUSS	Russia
Russ & C	Russell and Chesley's Nova Scotia Reports [10-12 Nova Scotia Reports] [1875-79] [A publication] (DLA)
Russ & C Eq Cas	Russell and Chesley's Nova Scotia Equity Cases [A publication] (DLA)
Russ & Ches	Russell and Chesley's Nova Scotia Reports [A publication] (DLA)
Russ & Ches Eq	Russell and Chesley's Nova Scotia Equity Reports [A publication] (DI A)
Russ & Eq	Russell and Chesley's Nova Scotia Equity Reports [A publication] (DLA)
Russ & G	Russell and Geldert's Nova Scotia Reports [13-27 Nova Scotia Reports] [1879-95] [Canada] [A publication] (DLA)
Russ & Geld	Russell and Geldert's Nova Scotia Reports [A publication] (DLA)
Russ & Jap PC	Russian and Japanese Prize Cases [London] [A publication] (DLA)
Russ & M	Russell and Mylne's English Chancery Reports [1829-33] [A publication] (DLA)
Russ & My	Russell and Mylne's English Chancery Reports [1829-33] [A publication] (DLA)
Russ & R	Russell and Ryan's English Crown Cases Reserved [1799-1823] [A publication] (DLA)
Russ & RCC	Russell and Ryan's English Crown Cases Reserved [168 English Reprint] [1799-1823] [A publication] (DLA)
Russ & RCC (Eng)	Russell and Ryan's English Crown Cases Reserved [1799-1823] [A publication] (DLA)
Russ & R Cr Cas	Russell and Ryan's English Crown Cases Reserved [A publication] (DLA)
Russ & Ry	Russell and Ryan's English Crown Cases Reserved [A publication] (DLA)
Russ Arb	Russell on Arbitrators [A publication] (DLA)
RussBer	Russ Berrie & Co., Inc. [Associated Press] (SAG)
Russ Ch	Russell's English Chancery Reports [A publication] (DLA)
Russ Con El (Mass)	Russell's Contested Election Cases [Massachusetts] [A publication] (DLA)
Russ Cr	Russell on Crimes and Misdemeanors [A publication] (DLA)
Russ Crim	Russell on Crime [12th ed.] [1964] [A publication] (DLA)
Russ Crimes	Russell on Crimes and Misdemeanors [A publication] (DLA)
Russ El Cas	Russell's Election Cases [1874] [Nova Scotia] [A publication] (DLA)
Russ Elect Cas	Russell's Contested Election Cases [Massachusetts] [A publication] (DLA)
Russ Elect Cas	Russell's Election Cases [Nova Scotia] [A publication] (DLA)
Russell	Russell Corp. [Associated Press] (SAG)
Russell	Russell's Nova Scotia Equity Decisions [A publication] (DLA)
Russell NS	Russell's Nova Scotia Equity Decisions [A publication] (DLA)
Russ Eq	Russell's Nova Scotia Equity Cases [A publication] (DLA)
Russ Eq Cas	Russell's Nova Scotia Equity Cases [A publication] (DLA)
Russ Eq Rep	Russell's Nova Scotia Equity Decisions [A publication] (DLA)
Russ Fact	Russell on Factors and Brokers [A publication] (DLA)
RUSSICA	Russian Information and Communications Agency (IID)
Russ Merc Ag	Russell on Mercantile Agency [A publication] (DLA)
RussMtl	Russell Metals, Inc. [Associated Press] (SAG)
Russ N Sc	Russell's Nova Scotia Equity Cases [A publication] (DLA)
Russ Rev	Russian Review [A publication] (BRI)
Russ T Eld	Russell's English Chancery Reports Tempore Elden [A publication] (DLA)
RUSSWO	Revised Uniform Summary of Surveyed Weather Observations (MCD)
Rust	De Re Rustica [of Varro] [Classical studies] (OCD)
RUSTAN	Russian Text Analyzer
rustc	Rustication (VRA)
RUSTIC	Regional and Urban Studies Information Center [Department of Energy] (IID)
RUT	Remote User Terminal [Computer science] (CAAL)
RUT	Resource Utilization Time (NASA)
RUT	Rooms Using Television [Television ratings]
RUT	Room Usage Time
RUT	Routair Aviation Services [Nigeria] [FAA designator] (FAAC)
RUT	Ruta [Rue] [Pharmacy] (ROG)
RUT	Ruth [Nevada] [Seismograph station code, US Geological Survey Closed] (SEIS)
RUT	Rutland [Vermont] [Airport symbol] (OAG)
RUT	Rutland Railway Corp. [AAR code Terminated]
RUTD	Rutlandshire [County in England] (ROG)
RUTEL	Reference Telegram from Your Office (FAAC)
Rutg Cas	Rutger-Waddington Case [1784] [New York City] [A publication] (DLA)
Rutgers U	Rutgers University (GAGS)
Rutgers UL Rev	Rutgers University. Law Review [A publication] (DLA)
Ruth Inst	Rutherford's Institutes of Natural Law [A publication] (DLA)

RuthR	Ruth Rabbah (BJA)
RUTLDS	Rutlandshire [County in England]
RUTOP	Rutowski Optimization [Computer program]
RuTuAsA	Akademiia Nauk Turkmenskoi SSR, Tsentralnaia Nauchnaia Biblioteka [Academy ofSciences of Turkmen SSR, Central Scientific Library], Ashkhabad, Turkmen, SS R, Soviet Union [Library symbol Library of Congress] (LCLS)
RuUk	Gosudartsvennaia Publichnaia Biblioteka Ukrainskoi SSR [State Public Library of the Ukrainian SSR], Kiev, Soviet Union [Library symbol Library of Congress] (LCLS)
RUUR	Regrade Unclassified Upon Receipt [Air Force]
RUUWS	Research Underwater-Unmanned Weapons Sensor (DNAB)
RUV	Bellefontaine, OH [Location identifier FAA] (FAAL)
RUV	Rauvai [Tuamotu Archipelago] [Seismograph station code, US Geological Survey] (SEIS)
RUV	Residual Urine Volume [Medicine] (STED)
RUWS	Remote Unmanned Work System [Navy]
RUX	Baltimore, MD [Location identifier FAA] (FAAL)
RUX	Right Upper Extremity (STED)
RUY	Ruinas de Copan [Honduras] [Airport symbol] (AD)
RV	Israel Aircraft Industries Ltd. [ICAO aircraft manufacturer identifier] (ICAO)
RV	Rabies Virus
RV	RADAR Vector (SAA)
RV	Radikale Venstre [Radical Liberals] [Denmark Political party] (PPE)
RV	Radio Vatican [Vatican State] (PDAA)
RV	Radio Vehicle (DEN)
RV	Rahway Valley R. R. [AAR code]
RV	Random Variable [Statistics]
R/V	Range to Velocity [Ratio of the RADAR platform]
RV	Raphanus Virus [Plant pathology]
RV	Rateable Value [Property value] [British]
RV	Rated Voltage
RV	Rat Virus [Immunology] (MAE)
RV	Rauscher Virus [Medicine] (DB)
RV	Reaction Voltage
RV	Reactor Vessel [Nuclear energy]
RV	Reading and Vocabulary Test [Also, RVT] [Military]
RV	Realizable Value (ADA)
RV	Rear View [Technical drawings]
RV	Recipient Value (GFGA)
RV	Recirculation Valve (MCD)
RV	Recovery Vehicle [NASA] (NASA)
RV	Recovery Vessel [NASA] (NASA)
RV	Recreational Vehicle
RV	Rectovaginal [Gynecology] (DAVI)
RV	Recycling Valve
RV	Reduced Voltage (IAA)
RV	Reed Valve [Automotive engineering]
RV	Reentry Vehicle [Aerospace]
RV	Reeve Aleutian Airways, Inc. [ICAO designator] (OAG)
RV	Reeves MacDonald Mines [Vancouver Stock Exchange symbol]
RV	Reference Voltage
RV	Refugee Voices, a Ministry with Uprooted Peoples (EA)
RV	Reinforcement Value [Psychology]
RV	Relative Viscosity (DB)
RV	Relaxation Volume (MAE)
RV	Released Value [Freight]
RV	Release Valve [Nuclear energy] (NRCH)
RV	Relief Valve
RV	Remaining Velocity [Ballistics]
RV	Renal Vessel [Medicine]
RV	Rendezvous
RV	Rendezvous Vehicle [NASA] (KSC)
RV	Rescue Vessel
RV	Research Vehicle
RV	Research Vessel
RV	Residual Variance
RUUWS	Residual Volume [Physiology]
RV	Respiratory Volume [Medicine] (MAE)
RV	Retrieval Vessel (NASA)
RV	Retroversion
RV	Retrovirus
RV	Return Visit (DAVI)
Rv	Revelation [New Testament book]
RV	Reverberation Time
Rv	Revised [Regulation or order revised] [Used in Shepard's Citations] [Legal term] (DLA)
RV	Revised Version [of the Bible, 1881]
RV	Rhinovirus (DB)
RV	Rifle Volunteers
RV	Right Ventricle [of heart] [Cardiology]
RV	Riser Valve [NFPA pre-fire planning symbol] (NFPA)
RV	Robotic Vehicle (RDA)
RV	Rod Valgallianse [Red Electoral Alliance] [Norway] (PPE)
R/V	Routine Verification (SSD)
RV	Roving Vehicle [NASA]
RV	Rubella Vaccine (DAVI)
RV	Rubella Virus
RV	Runway Visibility [Aviation] (AFM)
RV	Russell Viper [Time] (MAE)
RV	Ryom-Vivaldi [Catalog of music of Vivaldi] (BARN)
RVA	Farafangana [Madagascar] [Airport symbol] (OAG)
RVA	RADAR Vectoring Area [Aviation] (DA)
RVA	Rating and Valuation Association [British] (DBA)

RVA .... Raven Air, Inc. [*ICAO designator*] (FAAC)
RVA .... Reactive Volt-Ampere Meter
RVA .... Recorded Voice Announcement [*Telecommunications*] (IBMDP)
RVA .... Regular Veterans Association (NADA)
RVA .... Regular Veterans Association of the United States (EA)
RVA .... Relative Virtual Address [*Computer science*] (PCM)
RVA .... Relative Volt-Ampere
RVA .... Reliability Variation Analysis
RVA .... Remote Voltage Adjustment
RVA .... Returned Volunteer Action [*British*] [*An association*] (DBA)
RVA .... Rib-Vertebra Angle [*Anatomy*]
RVA .... Right Ventricular Assistance [*Cardiology*]
RVA .... Right Visual Acuity [*Medicine*]
RVA .... Roberts Wesleyan College, K. B. Keating Library, Rochester, NY [*OCLC symbol*] (OCLC)
RVAAP .... Ravenna Army Ammunition Plant (AABC)
RVACS .... Reactor Vessel Auxiliary Cooling System
RVAD .... Rib-Vertebra Angle Difference [*Anatomy*]
RVAH .... Reconnaissance Attack Squadron [*Navy*] (NVT)
RVANCS .... Remote View Airborne Night Classification System
RVANSW ...... Retirement Village Association of New South Wales [*Australia*]
RVARM .... Recording Varmeter (MSA)
RVAT .... Retinal Visual Acuity Tester [*Ophthalmology*]
RVAV .... Regulating Valve Actuating Valve (KSC)
RVAW .... Readiness Patrol Squadron [*Navy*] (NVT)
RVB .... RADAR Video Buffer
RVB .... Rear Vacuum Break [*Automotive engineering*]
RVB .... Red Venous Blood [*Hematology*] (MAE)
RVB .... Resonating Valence Bond [*Physical chemistry*]
RVB .... Rochester Gas & Electric Corp., TIC Library, Rochester, NY [*OCLC symbol*] (OCLC)
RVB .... Royal Veteran Battalion [*British military*] (DMA)
RVBR .... Riveting Bar [*Tool*] (AAG)
RVC .... RADAR Video Controller [*Military*] (CAAL)
RVC .... Ramakrishna - Vivekananda Center (EA)
RVC .... Random Vibration Control
RVC .... Reactor Volume Control [*Environmental science*] (COE)
RVC .... Rectovaginal Constriction [*Gynecology*] (DMAA)
RVC .... Relative Velocity Computer
RVC .... Remote-Voice Control
RVC .... Reticulated Vitreous Carbon
RVC .... Retired Volunteer Coordinator
RVC .... Richards Aviation, Inc. [*ICAO designator*] (FAAC)
RVC .... Rifle Volunteer Corps [*Military unit*] [*British*]
RVC .... River Cess [*Liberia*] [*Airport symbol*] (AD)
RVC .... RNA [*Ribonucleic Acid*] Virus Capsid
RVC .... Rochester General Hospital Library, Rochester, NY [*OCLC symbol*] (OCLC)
RVC .... Rockville Centre [*Diocesan abbreviation*] [*New York*] (TOCD)
RVC .... Rotary Voice Coil [*Computer technology*]
RVC .... Royal Veterinary College [*British*]
RVC .... Royal Victorian Chain
RVCDA .... Recreational Vehicle Club Directors of America (EA)
RVCF .... Remote Vehicle Checkout Facility [*NASA*] (NASA)
RVCI .... Royal Veterinary College of Ireland
RVCM .... Recent Vertical Crustal Movement [*Geology*]
RVCM .... Republic of Vietnam Campaign Medal [*Military decoration*]
RVCV .... Raspberry Vein Chlorosis Virus [*Plant pathology*]
RVD .... Dutchess County Mental Health Center, Poughkeepsie, NY [*Inactive*] [*OCLC symbol*] (OCLC)
RVD .... RADAR Video Digitizer
RVD .... Regulatory Volume Decrease [*Cytology*]
RVD .... Relative Vertebral Density
RVD .... Remote Virtual Disk [*Computer science*]
RVD .... Residual Vapor Detector (NATG)
RVD .... Right Ventricular Dimension [*Cardiology*]
RVD .... Right Ventricular Dysfunction [*Medicine*]
RVD .... Royal Victoria Dock [*British*] (ROG)
RVDA .... Recreation Vehicle Dealers Association of North America (EA)
RVDANA ...... Recreational Vehicle Dealers Association of North America
RVDO .... Right Ventricular Diastolic Overload [*Cardiology*] (AAMN)
RVDP .... RADAR Video Data Processor
RVDP .... Relief Valve Discharge Piping [*Nuclear energy*] (NRCH)
RVDT .... Rotary Variable Differential Transducer [*or Transformer*]
RVDT .... Rotational Voltage Displacement Transmitter
RVDV .... Right Ventricular Diastolic Volume [*Cardiology*] (DAVI)
RVE .... Airventure, BVBD [*Belgium*] [*FAA designator*] (FAAC)
RVE .... RADAR Video Extractor
RVE .... Representative Volume Element
RVE .... Right Ventricular Enlargement [*Cardiology*]
RVE .... Rochester Institute of Technology, Wallace Memorial Library, Rochester, NY [*OCLC symbol*] (OCLC)
RVE .... Royce Ventures Ltd. [*Vancouver Stock Exchange symbol*]
RVE .... Saravena [*Colombia*] [*Airport symbol*] (OAG)
RVECP .... Right Ventricular Endocardial [*Cardiology*] (DMAA)
RVED-CMP... Right Ventricular End-Diastolic Compliance [*Cardiology*]
RVEDD .... Right Ventricular End-Diastolic Diameter [*Medicine*] (DMAA)
RVEDP .... Right Ventricular End-Diastolic Pressure [*Cardiology*]
RVEDPI .... Right Ventricular End-Diastolic Pressure Index [*Cardiology*]
RVEDV .... Right Ventricle End-Diastolic Volume [*Cardiology*]
RVEE .... Holiday RV Superstores [*NASDAQ symbol*] (TTSB)
RVEE .... Holiday RV Superstores, Inc. [*NASDAQ symbol*] (NQ)
RVEF .... Right Ventricular Ejection Fraction [*Cardiology*] (DAVI)
RVER .... Regional Veterans Employment Representative [*Department of Labor*]

RVESP .... Right Ventricular End-Systolic Pressure [*Cardiology*] (DAVI)
RVESV .... Right Ventricular End-Systolic Volume [*Cardiology*]
RVET .... Right Ventricular Ejection Time [*Medicine*] (MEDA)
RVF .... Rate Variance Formula [*Air Force*]
RVF .... Rift Valley Fever
RVF .... Right Ventricular Failure [*Medicine*] (DB)
RVF .... Right Visual Field [*Psychometrics*]
RVF .... Rochester Psychiatric Center Library, Rochester, NY [*OCLC symbol*] (OCLC)
RVFD .... Riviana Foods [*NASDAQ symbol*] (TTSB)
RVFD .... Riviana Foods, Inc. [*NASDAQ symbol*] (SAG)
RVFN .... Report of Visit of Foreign Nationals (AAG)
RVFP .... Right Ventricular Filling Pressure [*Medicine*] (MEDA)
RVFV .... Rift Valley Fever Virus [*Medicine*]
RVFX .... Rivet Fixture (AAG)
RVG .... Chicago, IL [*Location identifier FAA*] (FAAL)
RVG .... Radionuclide Ventriculography [*Cardiology*] (CPH)
RVG .... Reference-Voltage Generator
RVG .... Right Ventral Gluteal [*Injection site*]
RVG .... Right Visceral Ganglion [*Medicine*]
RVG .... Rotating Vertical Gradiometer
RVG .... Rumrill-Hoyt Corp., Library, Rochester, NY [*OCLC symbol*] (OCLC)
RV/GC .... Reentry Vehicle and Ground Control [*NASA*] (KSC)
RVGG .... Rotating Vertical Gravity Gradiometer
RVH .... Renovascular Hypertension [*Medicine*]
RVH .... Reserve Veterinary Hospital [*British military*] (DMA)
RVH .... Right Ventricular Hypertrophy [*Cardiology*]
RVH .... St. Bernard's Seminary and College Library, Rochester, NY [*OCLC symbol*] (OCLC)
RVHD .... Rheumatic Valvular Heart Disease [*Medicine*] (DMAA)
RVI .... Recorded Video Imaging (MCD)
RVI .... Recreational Vehicle Institute
RVI .... Regulatory Volume Increase [*Cytology*]
RVI .... Relative Value Index [*Medicine*] (MAE)
RVI .... Renault Vehicules Industriels [*Renault Industrial Vehicles*] [*Finland*]
RVI .... Reverse Interrupt [*Telecommunications*] (IAA)
RVI .... Reverse Interrupt Character [*Keyboard*]
RVI .... RV-Aviation [*Finland ICAO designator*] (FAAC)
RVI .... Saint Mary's Hospital, Medical Library, Rochester, NY [*OCLC symbol*] (OCLC)
RVIA .... Recreation Vehicle Industry Association (EA)
RVIAJ .... Royal Victorian Institute of Architects. Journal [*A publication*]
RVID .... Right Ventricular Internal Dimension [*Medicine*] (MEDA)
RVIDd .... Right Ventricle Internal Dimension Diastole [*Medicine*] (STED)
RVIDP .... Right Ventricular Initial Diastolic Pressure [*Medicine*] (MEDA)
RVIMI .... Rubella Virus-Induced Mitotic Inhibitor
RVIS .... Reactor and Vessel Instrumentation System [*Nuclear energy*] (NRCH)
RVIT .... Right Ventricular Inflow Tract (STED)
RVIT .... Rotary Variable Inductive Transducer [*Electronics*]
RVJ .... Reidsville, GA [*Location identifier FAA*] (FAAL)
RVJ .... Sear-Brown Associates Information Center Library, Rochester, NY [*OCLC symbol*] (OCLC)
RVJS .... Reentry Vehicle Jamming Simulator [*Army*]
RVK .... Rorvik [*Norway*] [*Airport symbol*] (AD)
RVK .... Sybron Corp., Medical Products Division Library, Rochester, NY [*OCLC symbol*] (OCLC)
RVL .... Airvallee SpA-Services Aeriens de Val d'Aoste [*Italy ICAO designator*] (FAAC)
RVL .... Reedsville, PA [*Location identifier FAA*] (FAAL)
RVL .... Revere Resources [*Vancouver Stock Exchange symbol*]
rvl .... Revival (VRA)
RVL .... Right Vastus Lateralis [*Muscle*] [*Anatomy*] (DAVI)
RVL .... Rolling Vertical Landing (MCD)
RVL .... Royal Viking Line [*Kloster Cruises of Norway*]
RVL .... Sybron Corp., Pfaudler Division Technical Library, Henrietta, NY [*OCLC symbol*] (OCLC)
RVLA .... Roanoke Valley Library Association [*Library network*]
RVLG .... Revolving
RVLG .... Right Ventrolateral Gluteal [*Site of injection*] [*Medicine*]
RVLIS .... Reactor Vessel Water Level Indication System (IEEE)
RVLR .... Revolver [*Military*] (AABC)
RVLR .... Road Vehicles Lighting Regulation (IAA)
RVLV .... Revolve (MSA)
RVM .... Reactive Voltmeter
RVM .... Reentry Vehicle Module [*NASA*] (KSC)
RVM .... Religious of the Blessed Virgin Mary (TOCD)
RVM .... Repertoire de Vedettes-Matiere [*Laval Subject Authority Records*] [*UTLAS symbol*]
RVM .... Residual Volatile Matter [*Chemistry*]
RVm .... Revised Version [*of the Bible*], Margin
RVM .... Right Ventricular Mean [*Medicine*] (DMAA)
RVM .... Rio Vista Mine [*California*] [*Seismograph station code, US Geological Survey*] (SEIS)
RVM .... Rostral Ventromedial Medulla [*Brain anatomy*]
RVM .... Royal Victorian Medal [*British*] (WA)
RVM .... Sybron Corp., Taylor Division Research Library, Rochester, NY [*OCLC symbol*] (OCLC)
RVMCA .... Recreational Vehicle Manufacturer's Clubs Association (NTPA)
RVMR .... Routine Unsatisfactory Material Report
RVMYC .... Royal Victorian Motor Yacht Club [*Australia*]
RVN .... Republic of Vietnam
RVN .... Requirements Verification Network [*NASA*] (NASA)
RVN .... Retrolabyrinthine Vestibular Neurectomy [*Medicine*]
RVN .... Rogersville, TN [*Location identifier FAA*] (FAAL)

RVN .... Rovaniemi [Finland] [Airport symbol] (OAG)
RVN .... Women's Career Center Library, Rochester, NY [OCLC symbol]
            (OCLC)
RVNAF .... Republic of Vietnam Air Force
RVNAF .... Republic of Vietnam Armed Forces
RVNAFHMFC... Republic of Vietnam Armed Forces Honor Medal, First Class
            [Military decoration]
RVNAFHMSC... Republic of Vietnam Armed Forces Honor Medal, Second Class
            [Military decoration]
RVNCAMFC... Republic of Vietnam Civil Actions Medal, First Class [Military
            decoration]
RVNCAMSC... Republic of Vietnam Civil Actions Medal, Second Class [Military
            decoration]
RVNCAMUC... Republic of Vietnam Civil Actions Medal, Unit Citation [Military
            decoration] (GFGA)
RVNCM .... Republic of Vietnam Campaign Medal [Military decoration]
RVNF .... Republic of Vietnam Forces
RVNGCUC... Republic of Vietnam Gallantry Cross, Unit Citation [Military
            decoration] (GFGA)
RVNGCUCW/P... Republic of Vietnam Gallantry Cross Unit Citation with Palm
            [Military decoration]
RVNMC .... Republic of Vietnam Marine Corps
RVNN .... Republic of Vietnam Navy
RVNT .... Reentry Vehicle Nosetip [Aerospace] (MCD)
RVO .... Aquinas Institute Library, Rochester, NY [OCLC symbol] (OCLC)
RVO .... Lubbock, TX [Location identifier FAA] (FAAL)
RVO .... Rabaul Volcano Observatory [Papua New Guinea]
RVO .... Regional Veterinary Officer [British]
RVO .... Relaxed Vaginal Outlet [Medicine]
RVO .... Retinal Vein Occlusion [Ophthalmology] (DAVI)
RVO .... Right Ventricular Outflow [Medicine] (MEDA)
RVO .... Right Ventricular Overactivity [Medicine] (MEDA)
RVO .... Royal Victorian Order
RVOA .... Right Ventricular Overactivity [Cardiology] (DAVI)
RVOC .... Research Vessel Operators Council [Defunct] (USDC)
RVOG .... Radio Voice of the Gospel (DICI)
RVOT .... Right Ventricular Outflow Tract [Cardiology]
RVP .... Avon Junior/Senior High School Library, Avon, NY [OCLC symbol]
            (OCLC)
RVP .... RADAR Video Processor [Military] (CAAL)
RVP .... Raster-to-Vector Processor [Computer graphics technology]
RVP .... Rat Ventral Prostate (DB)
RVP .... RCA Video Productions
RVP .... Red Veterinary Petrolatum (MAE)
RVP .... Reid Vapor Pressure
RVP .... Renal Venous Plasma [Biochemistry] (DAVI)
RVP .... Renal Venous Pressure (OA)
RVP .... Resting Venous Pressure [Medicine] (DMAA)
RVP .... Reutilization Value Percentage [DoD]
RVP .... Right Ventricular Pressure [Medicine] (DMAA)
RVP .... Rinderpest Virus (DB)
RVP .... Roll Vertical Pendulum (SAA)
RVP .... Rotary Vacuum Pump
RVPA .... Rivet Pattern (AAG)
RVPAFS .... Register of Veterinary Preparations and Animal Feeding Stuffs
            [Australia]
RVPER .... Right Ventricular Peak Filling Rate [Medicine] (DMAA)
RVPFR .... Right Ventricular Peak Filling Rate [Medicine] (DMAA)
RVPRA .... Renal Vein Plasma Renin Activity [Medicine] (DMAA)
RVQ .... Benjamin Franklin High School Library, Rochester, NY [OCLC
            symbol] (OCLC)
RVQ .... Recursive Vector Quantization [Software compression program]
            (PCM)
RVQ .... Review of Vocational Qualifications (AIE)
RVR .... Bishop Kearney High School Library, Rochester, NY [OCLC
            symbol] (OCLC)
RVR .... Cruise America [AMEX symbol] (TTSB)
RVR .... Cruise America, Inc. [AMEX symbol] (SPSG)
RVR .... RADAR Video Recorder
RVR .... Rapid Ventricular Response [Cardiology] (DAVI)
RVR .... Rapid Virtual Reality (PCM)
RVR .... Raven Air Ltd. [British ICAO designator] (FAAC)
RVR .... Reactor Visual Range (HGAA)
RVR .... Renal Vascular Resistance [Medicine]
RVR .... Repetitive Ventricular Response [Medicine] (DB)
RVR .... Resistance to Venous Return [Medicine] (MAE)
RVR .... Response Vacuum Reducer [Mechanical engineering]
RVR .... Reverse Velocity Rotor
RVR .... Rim Vent Release [Safety device for aerosol containers]
RVR .... River [Commonly used] (OPSA)
RVR .... Riverside [California] [Seismograph station code, US Geological
            Survey] (SEIS)
RVR .... Runway Visual Range [Aviation]
RVRA .... Recreation Vehicle Rental Association (EA)
RV/RA .... Renal Vein/Renal Activity [Ratio] [Medicine]
RVRA .... Renal Venous Renin Assay [Medicine] (MAE)
RVRC .... Renal Vein Renin Concentration [Medicine]
RVRC .... Runway Visual Range Center [Aviation] (DA)
RVRM .... Runway Visual Range Midpoint [Aviation]
RVRME .... Rift Valley Research Mission in Ethiopia [Anthropology]
RvrOaks .... River Oaks Furniture, Inc. [Associated Press] (SAG)
RVRR .... Runway Visual Range Rollout [Aviation] (FAAC)
RVRRNO ...... Runway Visual Range Rollout Not Available [Aviation] (FAAC)
RVRS .... Runway Vision Range System [Aviation] (DWSG)
RvrsGp .... Riverside Group, Inc. [Associated Press] (SAG)

RVRT .... Runway Visual Range Touchdown [Aviation] (FAAC)
RVRTNQ .... Runway Visual Range Touchdown Not Available [Aviation] (FAAC)
RVRU .... RADAR Video Recorder Unit
RVS .... Brighton High School Library, Rochester, NY [OCLC symbol] (OCLC)
RVS .... Rabies Vector Species
RVS .... Radius Vector Subroutine
RVS .... Reentry Vehicle Separation [Aerospace] (MUGU)
RVS .... Reentry Vehicle Simulator [Aerospace] (AAG)
RVS .... Relative Value Scale [or Schedule or Study] [Medicine]
RVS .... Remote Viewing System
RVS .... Reported Visual Sensation [Medicine] (MAE)
RVS .... Requirements Validation Study (MCD)
RVS .... Research Vessel Service [British] (IRUK)
RVS .... Reverse (MSA)
RVS .... Riverside Mountains [California] [Seismograph station code, US
            Geological Survey] (SEIS)
RVS .... Rocketborne Vacuum System
RVS .... Tulsa, OK [Location identifier FAA] (FAAL)
RVSB .... Riverview Savings Bank [NASDAQ symbol] (SAG)
RVSB .... Riverview Svgs Bk FSB Camas [NASDAQ symbol] (TTSB)
RVSBL .... Reversible (MSA)
RVSE .... Reverse (AABC)
RVSFC .... Ricky and Vince Smith Fan Club (EA)
RVSN .... Revision [Legal shorthand] (LWAP)
RVSNY .... Reversionary [Legal shorthand] (LWAP)
RVSS .... Reactor Vessel Support System (IEEE)
RVSSC .... Reverse Self Check (AAG)
RVST .... Russel Viper Serum Time [Clinical chemistry]
RVSVP .... Repondez Vite, s'il Vous Plait [Please Reply at Once] [French]
RVSW .... Right Ventricular Stroke Work [Cardiology]
RVSWI .... Right Ventricular Stroke Work Index [Cardiology]
RVSZ .... Riveting Squeezer [Tool] (AAG)
RVT .... Brockport High School Library, Brockport, NY [OCLC symbol]
            (OCLC)
RVT .... Reading and Vocabulary Test [Also, RV] [Military]
RVT .... Registered Vascular Technologist (DAVI)
RVT .... Reliability Verification Tests
RVT .... Renal Vein Thrombosis [Medicine]
RVT .... Resource Vector Table [Computer science] (IBMDP)
RVT .... Rivet (MSA)
RVT .... Royce Value Trust [NYSE symbol] (TTSB)
RVT .... Royce Value Trust, Inc. [NYSE symbol] (SPSG)
RVTC .... Rochester Volunteer Training Corps [British military] (DMA)
RVTD .... Riveted (MSA)
RVTE .... Recurring Venous Thromboembolism [Medicine] (DMAA)
RV/TLC .... Residual Volume per Total Lung Compliance [Pulmonary function
            test] (CPH)
RV/TLC .... Residual Volume/Total Lung Capacity Ratio [Physiology] (MAE)
RVTO .... Reentry Vehicle Test and Observables [Air Force]
RVTOL .... Rolling Vertical Takeoff and Landing [Aviation] (MCD)
RVTV .... Rear Vision Television [Driver safety systems] [Automotive
            engineering]
RVU .... Caledonia-Mumford Junior/Senior High School Library, Caledonia, NY
            [OCLC symbol] (OCLC)
RVU .... Relative Value Unit
RVU .... Relief Valve Unit
RVV .... Cardinal Mooney High School Library, Rochester, NY [OCLC
            symbol] (OCLC)
rVV .... Recombinant Vaccinia Virus
RVV .... Reeve Aleutian Airways, Inc. [ICAO designator] (FAAC)
RVV .... Regional Vascular Volume [Hematology]
RVV .... Rubella Vaccine-Like Virus (AAMN)
RVV .... Rubella Virus Vaccine [Immunology] (DAVI)
RVV .... Runway Visibility Values [Aviation]
RVV .... Russell Viper Venom [Medicine] (DMAA)
RVVNO .... Runway Visual Range Not Available [Aviation] (FAAC)
RVVO .... Right Ventricular Volume Overload [Medicine] (DMAA)
RVVT .... Russell Viper Venom Time [Medicine] (DMAA)
RVW .... Charles H. Roth High School Library, Henrietta, NY [OCLC symbol]
            (OCLC)
RVW .... Ralph Vaughan Williams [British composer, 1872-1958]
Rvw .... Review (TBD)
RVW .... Right Ventricular Weight [Cardiology]
RVW .... Riverwood International Corp. [NYSE symbol] (SPSG)
RVWT .... Right Ventricle Wall Thickness [Medicine] (DMAA)
RVX .... Charlotte Junior/Senior High School Library, Rochester, NY [OCLC
            symbol] (OCLC)
RVX .... Reentry Vehicle, Experimental [Aerospace]
RVX .... Robot Vehicle Expressway
RVY .... Churchville-Chili Senior High School Library, Rochester, NY [OCLC
            symbol] (OCLC)
RVY .... Rivera [Uruguay] [Airport symbol] (OAG)
RVYC .... Royal Victorian Yacht Club [Australia]
RVZ .... Dansville Senior High School Library, Dansville, NY [OCLC symbol]
            (OCLC)
RW .... Hughes Air Corp. [ICAO designator] (ICDA)
RW .... Race Weight [of a horse]
RW .... Radiation Weapon (AAG)
RW .... Radical Women (EA)
RW .... Radiological Warfare
RW .... Radiological Warhead
RW .... Radiological Weapons
RW .... Ragweed [Immunology]
RW .... Rail and Water [Shipping]
RW .... Railway

RW	Ramo Wooldridge [*Later, TRW, Inc.*]
R/W	Ramo-Wooldridge-Thompson Corp. [*Later, TRW, Inc.*] (AAG)
RW	Random Walk
RW	Random Widths [*Lumber*]
rw	Random Widths [*Wood industry*] (WPI)
RW	RAWINSONDE [*Radiosonde and RADAR Wind Sounding*] [*Upper air observation*]
RW	Raw Water [*Nuclear energy*]
R-W	Read-Write [*Computer science*] (MSA)
R/W	Read/Write (NAKS)
RW	Real Wages [*Economics*]
RW	Ream Wrapped (WDMC)
RW	Rechtswissenschaft [*Jurisprudence*] [*German*] (ILCA)
RW	Reclaimed Wheat Grass Cover [*Agriculture*]
RW	Reconnaissance Wing [*Military*]
R(W)	Reconstruction, Workmen's Compensation [*British World War II*]
RW	Recreation and Welfare [*Navy*]
RW	Recruiting Warrant
RW	Red-Bellied Woodpecker [*Ornithology*]
RW	Reduced Weight (DCTA)
RW	Reel and Wheel [*Freight*]
RW	Regions of the World [*A publication*]
RW	Region Wide [*Forestry*]
RW	Relative Worth (MCD)
R/W	Report Writer [*Computer science*]
RW	Republic [*ICAO designator*] (AD)
RW	Resistance Welding (IEEE)
RW	Response Word (NASA)
RW	Restaurant Wine [*License*]
RW	Retail World [*A publication*]
R/W	Returned to Work
RW	Reverse Work (WGA)
RW	Reverse Wound (MCD)
RW	Review
RW	Rewind
RW	Richardsons Westgarth [*Commercial firm British*]
RW	Rideal-Walter Coefficient [*Pharmacy*]
RW	Right Ear, Warm Stimulus [*Medicine*] (MEDA)
RW	Right of Way
RW	Right Wing
RW	Right Worshipful
RW	Right Worthy
RW	River Water [*Nuclear energy*] (NRCH)
RW	Riveted and Welded [*Shipping*] (DS)
RW	Romano-Ward [*Syndrome*] [*Medicine*] (DB)
RW	Rotary Wing [*Aircraft designation*]
RW	Rothmund-Werner [*Disease*] [*Medicine*] (DB)
RW	Rowa-Wagner KG [*Germany*] [*Research code symbol*]
RW	Royal Warrant [*British*] (ADA)
RW	Royal Warwickshire Regiment [*Military unit*] [*British*]
RW	Runway [*Aviation*]
rw	Rwanda [*MARC country of publication code Library of Congress*] (LCCP)
RW	Rwanda [*ANSI two-letter standard code*] (CNC)
RW	R. Warren [*Pseudonym used by Charles Ashton*]
RWA	Aligiulia SpA [*Italy ICAO designator*] (FAAC)
RWA	E. J. Wilson High School Library, Spencerport, NY [*OCLC symbol*] (OCLC)
RWa	George Hail Free Library, Warren, RI [*Library symbol Library of Congress*] (LCLS)
RWA	Race Walking Association [*British*] (DBA)
RWA	RADWASTE [*Radioactive Waste*] Area [*Nuclear energy*] (NRCH)
RWA	Railway Wheel Association [*Defunct*] (EA)
RWA	Raoul Wallenberg Association [*See also RWF*] (EA)
RWA	Reaction Wheel Assembly (MCD)
RWA	Ready, Willing and Able [*Legal shorthand*] (LWAP)
RWA	Rectangular Wave-Guide Assembly
RWA	Regional Water Authority [*British*]
RWA	Rippled Wall Amplifier
RWA	Romance Writers of America (EA)
RWA	Rotary Wing Aircraft
RWA	Royal West of England Academy
RWA	Rwanda [*ANSI three-letter standard code*] (CNC)
RWAAC	Rural Workers Accommodation Advisory Committee [*New South Wales, Australia*]
RWABA	Royal Western Australian Bowling Association
RWAFF	Royal West African Frontier Force [*Military unit*] [*British*]
RWAGE	Ragweed Antigen E [*Immunology*]
RWAH	Rotor Wing Agricultural Hours [*Aviation*] (AIA)
RWAIB	Royal Western Australian Institute for the Blind [*Australia*]
R/W & L	Random Width and Length (DAC)
RWar	Warwick Public Library, Warwick, RI [*Library symbol Library of Congress*] (LCLS)
RWARF	Royal Warwickshire Fusiliers [*British military*] (DMA)
RWarR	Rhode Island Junior College, Knight Campus, Warwick, RI [*Library symbol Library of Congress*] (LCLS)
R War R	Royal Warwickshire Regiment [*Military unit*] [*British*] (DMA)
RWAS	Royal Welsh Agricultural Society (BI)
RWASG	Radiation Weapons Analysis Systems Group (SAA)
RWAV	Rogue Wave Software, Inc. [*NASDAQ symbol*] (SAG)
RWAW	United Union of Roofers, Waterproofers, and Allied Workers
RWAY	Rent-Way [*NASDAQ symbol*] (TTSB)
RWAY	Rent Way, Inc. [*NASDAQ symbol*] (SAG)
RWB	RADWASTE [*Radioactive Waste*] Building [*Nuclear energy*] (NUCP)
RWB	Rear Wheel Brake

RWB	Rod Withdrawal Block [*Nuclear energy*] (NRCH)
RWB	Roger Williams College, Bristol, RI [*OCLC symbol*] (OCLC)
RWB	Royal Winnipeg Ballet
RWBH	Records Will Be Handcarried [*Army*] (AABC)
RWBN	Red and White Beacon [*Nautical charts*]
RWC	East Junior/Senior High School Library, Rochester, NY [*OCLC symbol*] (OCLC)
RWC	Radioactive Waste Campaign (EA)
RWC	Rainwater Conductor (AAG)
RWC	Raw Water Cooling
RWC	Reactor Water Cleanup [*Nuclear energy*] (NRCH)
RWC	Read, Write and Compare (ECII)
RWC	Read, Write, and Compute
RWC	Read-Write-Continue [*Computer science*]
RWC	Receiving Water Concentration (LDT)
RWC	Relative Water Content
RWC	Remote Workcenter
RWC	Residential Wood Combustion
RWC	Roberts Wesleyan College [*Rochester, NY*]
RWCH	Republican Women of Capitol Hill (EA)
RWCP	Real World Computing Partnership [*Japan*] [*Agreement for conducting cooperative global research*]
RWCS	Reactor Water Cleanup System [*Nuclear energy*] (NRCH)
RWCS	Red Wing Collectors Society (EA)
RWCS	Report Writer Control System [*COBOL*] [*Computer science*]
RWCTF	Radioactive Waste Consultation Task Force [*National Science Foundation*] (NUCP)
RWCU	Reactor Water Cleanup [*Nuclear energy*] (NRCH)
RWCU	Reactor Water Cleanup Unit [*Nuclear energy*] (IAA)
RWCUS	Raoul Wallenberg Committee of the United States (EA)
RWD	Air Rwanda [*ICAO designator*] (FAAC)
RWD	Eastridge High School Library, Rochester, NY [*OCLC symbol*] (OCLC)
RWD	Reaction with Distillation [*Koch Engineering Co.*] [*Chemical engineering*]
RWD	Rear Wheel Drive
RWD	Regional WIN [*Work Incentive*] Director [*Department of Health and Human Services*] (GFGA)
RWD	Regular Way Delivery
RWD	Regular World Day
RWD	Rewind
RWD	Right Wing Down [*Aviation*]
RWDCA	Red and White Dairy Cattle Association (EA)
RWDGM	Right Worshipful Deputy Grand Master [*Freemasonry*]
R/WDO	Rear Window [*Automotive engineering*]
RWDS	RADWASTE [*Radioactive Waste*] Disposal System [*Nuclear energy*] (NRCH)
RWDSU	Retail, Wholesale, and Department Store Union (EA)
RWE	Aero West Airlines, Inc. [*ICAO designator*] (FAAC)
RWE	Edison Technical and Occupational Educational Center Library, Rochester, NY [*OCLC symbol*] (OCLC)
RWE	RADAR Warfare Establishment [*British*] (WDAA)
RWE	Radio Warfare Establishment [*British military*] (DMA)
RWF	Ralph Waldo Emerson [*Initials used as pseudonym*]
RWE	Reactor Works Engineering (COE)
RWE	Rheinisch-Westfaelisches Electrizitaetswerk AG [*Rheine-Westphalian Electricity Co.*] [*Germany*]
RWe	Westerly Public Library, Westerly, RI [*Library symbol Library of Congress*] (LCLS)
RWEA	Royal West of England Academy
RWED	Read/Write Extend Delete
RWEMA	Ralph Waldo Emerson Memorial Association (EA)
RWES	Ralph Waldo Emerson Society (EA)
RWF	Fairport High School Library, Fairport, NY [*OCLC symbol*] (OCLC)
RWF	Radio Wholesalers Federation [*British*] (BI)
RWF	Raoul Wallenberg Foreningen [*Raoul Wallenberg Association - RWA*] (EAIO)
RWF	Redwood Falls, MN [*Location identifier FAA*] (FAAL)
RWF	Roundtable for Women in Foodservice [*Later, RWFBH*] (EA)
RWF	Roush, W. F., Miami FL [*STAC*]
RWF	Royal Welch [*or Welsh*] Fusiliers [*Military unit*] [*British*]
RwF	Rwandan Franc [*Monetary unit*] (IMH)
RWFBH	Roundtable for Women Food-Beverage-Hospitality (EA)
RWFC	Randy Wade Fan Club (EA)
RWFC	Red Wings For'Em Club (EA)
RWG	Gates-Chili Senior High School Library, Rochester, NY [*OCLC symbol*] (OCLC)
RWG	Radio Writers' Guild [*Later, WGA*]
RWG	Redwing Airways, Inc. [*ICAO designator*] (FAAC)
RWG	Redwing Resources, Inc. [*Vancouver Stock Exchange symbol*]
RWG	Reliability Working Group (AAG)
RWG	Rigid Waveguide
RWG	Roebling Wire Gauge
RWGM	Right Worshipful Grand Master [*Freemasonry*]
RWGR	Right Worthy Grand Representative [*Freemasonry*]
RWGS	Right Worthy Grand Secretary [*Freemasonry*] (ADA)
RWGT	Right Worthy Grand Templar [*Freemasonry*]
RWGT	Right Worthy Grand Treasurer [*Freemasonry*]
RWGW	Right Worthy Grand Warden [*Freemasonry*]
RWGW	Right Worthy Grand Worshipful [*Freemasonry*] (ROG)
RWH	Geneseo Junior/Senior High School Library, Geneseo, NY [*OCLC symbol*] (OCLC)
RWH	RADAR Warning and Homing
RWH	Rainwater Head
RWH	Rotor Wing Hours [*Aviation*] (AIA)

RWHA .... Royal Warrant Holders' Association [*British*] (WDAA)
RWHD .... Rawhide (MSA)
rwhi .... Rawhide (VRA)
RWI .... Greece-Arcadia Junior/Senior High School Library, Rochester, NY [*OCLC symbol*] (OCLC)
RWI .... RADAR Warning Installation (NATG)
RWI .... Radio Wire Integration [*Military*]
RWI .... Read-Write-Initialize [*Computer science*]
RWI .... Real World Interval (WDAA)
RWI .... Regular World Interval
RWI .... Remote Weight Indicator
RWI .... Rocky Mount [*North Carolina*] [*Airport symbol*] (OAG)
RWIB .... Rioja Wine Information Bureau (EA)
RWIN .... Republic Industries [*NASDAQ symbol*] [*Formerly, Republic Waste Industries*] (SG)
RWIN .... Republic Industries, Inc. [*NASDAQ symbol*] (SAG)
RWIN .... Republic Waste Industries, Inc. [*NASDAQ symbol*] (SAG)
RWIS .... Raw Water Intake Structure [*Environmental science*] (COE)
RWIS .... Restraint and Water Immersion Stress [*Medicine*] (DMAA)
RWIY .... Royal Wiltshire Imperial Yeomanry [*British military*] (DMA)
RWJ .... Greece-Athena Junior/Senior High School Library, Rochester, NY [*OCLC symbol*] (OCLC)
RWJ .... Robert Wood Johnson Medical School [*New Jersey*]
RWJF .... Robert Wood Johnson Foundation
RWJGW ...... Right Worthy Junior Grand Warden [*Freemasonry*]
RWK .... Greece-Olympia High School Library, Rochester, NY [*OCLC symbol*] (OCLC)
RWK .... Queen's Own Royal West Kent Regiment [*Military unit*] [*British*]
RWK .... Remaining Work
RWK .... Renwick Explorations Ltd. [*Vancouver Stock Exchange symbol*]
RWK .... Rework (AAG)
RWkEPA ...... United States Environmental Protection Agency, National Marine Water Quality Laboratory, West Kingston, RI [*Library symbol Library of Congress*] (LCLS)
RWL .... H. W. Schroeder Junior/Senior High School Library, Webster, NY [*OCLC symbol*] (OCLC)
RWL .... Raised White Letters [*Tire design*] [*Automotive engineering*]
RWL .... Rawlins [*Wyoming*] [*Airport symbol*] (AD)
RWL .... Rawlins, WY [*Location identifier FAA*] (FAAL)
RWL .... Reactor Water Level [*Environmental science*] (COE)
RWL .... Recommended Weight Limit [*Ergonmetrics*]
RWL .... Relative Water Level
RWL .... Revolutionary Workers League [*Canada*]
RWL .... Richwell Resources Ltd. [*Vancouver Stock Exchange symbol*]
RWLB .... Regional War Labor Board
RWLR .... Relative Water-Level Recorder
RWM .... Hilton High School Library, Hilton, NY [*OCLC symbol*] (OCLC)
RWM .... Radioactive Waste Management
RWM .... Read-Write Memory [*Computer science*] (MCD)
RWM .... Rectangular Wave Modulation (IEEE)
RWM .... Regional Wall Motion [*Medicine*] (DMAA)
RWM .... Resistance Welding Machine
RWM .... Right Worshipful Master [*Freemasonry*] (ROG)
RWM .... Rod Worth Minimizer [*Nuclear energy*] (NRCH)
RWM .... Roll Wrapping Machine
RWMA .... Resistance Welder Manufacturers Association (EA)
RWMAC ...... Radioactive Waste Management Advisory Committee
RWMC .... Radioactive Waste Management Center
RWMS .... Radioactive Waste Management Site
RWN .... Holly Junior/Senior High School Library, Holly, NY [*OCLC symbol*] (OCLC)
RWN .... Rawdon Resources Ltd. [*Vancouver Stock Exchange symbol*]
RWN .... Winamac, IN [*Location identifier FAA*] (FAAL)
RWNBH .... Records Will Not Be Handcarried [*Army*] (AABC)
RWND .... Rewind (MSA)
RWNF .... Ryan White National Fund (EA)
RWNTEP ..... Ryan White National Teen Education Program (EA)
RWO .... Honeoye Falls-Lima Senior High School Library, Honeoye Falls, NY [*OCLC symbol*] (OCLC)
RWO .... Kodiak, AK [*Location identifier FAA*] (FAAL)
RWO .... Reconnaissance Watch Officer (MCD)
RWO .... Regional Works Officer [*British*]
RWO .... Reimbursable Work Order [*Navy*] (NG)
RWO .... Riddare af Wasa Order [*Knight of the Order of Vasa*] [*Sweden*]
RWO .... Right Wrong Omit (IAA)
RWO .... Routine Work Order (KSC)
RWoH .... Harris Institute, Woonsocket, RI [*Library symbol Library of Congress*] (LCLS)
RwoH .... Reliability without Hermeticity (AAEL)
RWoU .... Union Saint-Jean-Baptiste d'Amerique, Woonsocket, RI [*Library symbol Library of Congress*] (LCLS)
RWP .... James Madison High School Library, Rochester, NY [*OCLC symbol*] (OCLC)
RWP .... Radiation Work Permit [*Nuclear energy*] (NRCH)
RWP .... Radio Wave Propagation
RWP .... Radio Working Party
RWP .... RADWASTE [*Radioactive Waste*] Work Permit [*Nuclear energy*] (NRCH)
RWP .... Rainwater Pipe [*Construction*]
RWP .... Rawalpindi/Islamabad [*Pakistan*] [*Airport symbol Obsolete*] (OAG)
RWP .... Reactor Work Permit (IEEE)
RWP .... Regiment Western Province [*British military*] (DMA)
RWP .... Rifle and Weapons Platoon [*Army Obsolete*] (AABC)
RWP .... Romanian Workers' Party [*Political party*]
RWP .... R-Wave Progression [*On Electrocardiograms*] [*Cardiology*] (DAVI)

RWPC .... RADWASTE [*Radioactive Waste*] Process Cell [*Nuclear energy*] (NRCH)
RWPG .... Real World Problem Generation
RWPH .... River Water Pumphouse [*Nuclear energy*] (NRCH)
RWQ .... James Monroe High School Library, Rochester, NY [*OCLC symbol*] (OCLC)
RWQCB .... Regional Water Quality Control Board (COE)
RWR .... James Sperry High School Library, Henrietta, NY [*OCLC symbol*] (OCLC)
RWR .... RADAR Warning Receiver (MCD)
RWR .... Radioactive Waste Reduction [*Nuclear energy*] (NRCH)
R-W-R .... Rail-Water-Rail [*Shipping*]
RWR .... Read/Write Register
RWR .... Relative Weight Response
RWR .... Reward Resources Ltd. [*Vancouver Stock Exchange symbol*]
RWR .... Romance Writers Report [*A publication*] (EAAP)
RWR .... Ronald Wilson Reagan [*US president, 1911-*]
RWRAT .... Replacement Weather Reconnaissance Aircraft (DNAB)
RWRC .... Remain Well to Right of Course [*Aviation*] (FAAC)
RWRSq .... Rescue and Weather Reconnaissance Squadron [*Air Force*]
RWRT .... Real World Reading Test (EDAC)
RWRW .... Rescue and Weather Reconnaissance Wing [*Air Force*]
RWS .... Air Whitsunday [*Australia ICAO designator*] (FAAC)
RWS .... Camp Springs, MD [*Location identifier FAA*] (FAAL)
RWS .... John Marshall High School Library, Rochester, NY [*OCLC symbol*] (OCLC)
RWS .... RADAR Warning System (MCD)
RWS .... Radioactive Waste System [*Nuclear energy*] (NRCH)
RWS .... Range While Search
RWS .... Reaction Wheel Scanner
RWS .... Reaction Wheel Systems (AAG)
RWS .... Receiver Waveform Simulation [*Telecommunications*] (OA)
RWS .... Regional Warning System
RWS .... Regional Weather Service (NOAA)
RWS .... Release with Service (OICC)
RWS .... Royal Society of Painters in Water-Colours [*British*]
RWS .... Royal Society of Painters in Water-Colours, London [*1804*] (NGC)
RWS .... Royal Watercolour Society [*British*] (EAIO)
RWS .... Royal West Surrey [*Regiment*] [*Military unit*] [*British*]
RWS .... Royal West Sussex [*Regiment*] [*Military unit*] [*British*]
RWSF .... RADWASTE [*Radioactive Waste*] Solidification Facility [*Nuclear energy*] (NRCH)
RWSF .... Revolutionary War Studies Forum (EA)
RWSF .... Roosevelt Warm Springs Foundation (EA)
RWSGW ...... Right Worshipful Senior Grand Warden [*Freemasonry*]
RWSS .... RADWASTE [*Radioactive Waste*] Sample Station [*Nuclear energy*] (NRCH)
RWSS .... River Water Supply System (IEEE)
RWST .... Refueling Water Storage Tank [*Nuclear energy*] (NRCH)
RWT .... Kendall High School Library, Kendall, NY [*OCLC symbol*] (OCLC)
RWT .... RADAR Warning Trainer (MCD)
RWT .... Read-Write Tape [*Computer science*]
RWT .... Refueling Water Tank [*Nuclear energy*] (NRCH)
RWT .... Required Weekly Test [*Telecommunications*] (OTD)
RWT .... Right When Tested (NITA)
RWT .... R-Wave Threshold (DB)
RWTA .... River Water Treatment Area [*Nuclear energy*] (NRCH)
RWTF .... RAAF [*Royal Australian Air Force*] Welfare Trust Fund [*Australia*]
RWTH .... Rotary Wing Turbine Hours [*Aviation*] (AIA)
RWTI .... Redwood Trust [*NASDAQ symbol*] (TTSB)
RWTI .... Redwood Trust, Inc. [*NASDAQ symbol*] (SAG)
RWTIW .... Redwood Trust Wrrt [*NASDAQ symbol*] (TTSB)
RWTS .... Regenerant Waste Treatment Subsystem [*Nuclear energy*] (NRCH)
RWU .... Keshequa Junior/Senior High School Library, Nunda, NY [*OCLC symbol*] (OCLC)
RWV .... L. C. Obourn High School Library, East Rochester, NY [*OCLC symbol*] (OCLC)
RWV .... Radial Wall Variation [*Tire design*] [*Automotive engineering*]
RWV .... Radioactive Waste Vent [*Nuclear energy*] (NRCH)
RWV .... Read-Write-Verify [*Computer science*]
RWV .... Robbery with Violence [*Legal term*] (WDAA)
RWV .... Rubbery Wood Virus
RWV .... Rustad/Wickhem/Video, Inc. [*Madison, WI*] (TSSD)
RWVD .... Real World Visual Display
RWVR .... Real World Vehicular Rate
RWVRC .... Read-Write Vertical Redundancy Check [*Computer science*] (IAA)
RWW .... Lester B. Forman Central Library, Fairport, NY [*OCLC symbol*] (OCLC)
RWW .... Read while Write [*Computer science*] (IAA)
RWW .... Rear Window Wiper [*Automotive engineering*]
RWX .... Letchworth Junior/Senior High School Library, Gainesville, NY [*OCLC symbol*] (OCLC)
RWX .... Read Write Execute [*Computer science*] (CIST)
RWY .... Livonia High School Library, Livonia, NY [*OCLC symbol*] (OCLC)
RWY .... Railway
RWY .... Royal Wiltshire Yeomanry [*Military unit*] [*British*]
RWY .... Runway (AAG)
RWZ .... McQuaid Jesuit High School Library, Rochester, NY [*OCLC symbol*] (OCLC)
RX .... British Independent Airways [*ICAO designator*] (AD)
RX .... Capitol Air Service [*ICAO designator*] (AD)
RX .... Excess Reserves
RX .... Rank Xerox
rx .... Reaction [*Laboratory science*] (DAVI)
RX .... Receive (NITA)

RX .... Receiver [or Reception] [Radio] (NATG)
Rx .... Recipe [Used as a symbol for medical prescriptions]
RX .... Reconnaissance-Experimental Aircraft
RX .... Register and Indexed Storage (MCD)
RX .... Remote Exchange [Telecommunications] (TEL)
RX .... Repairable Exchange
RX .... Resolver-Transmitter
RX .... Rix-Dollar [British] (ROG)
RX .... Rupees [Monetary unit] [Ceylon, India, and Pakistan] (ROG)
RX .... Rush [on teletype messages]
Rx .... Therapy (DAVI)
R$_x$ .... Unknown Resistance (IDOE)
RXA .... Arax Airlines Ltd. [Nigeria] [ICAO designator] (FAAC)
RXA .... Mount Morris Junior/Senior High School Library, Mount Morris, NY [OCLC symbol] (OCLC)
RXA .... Raudha [South Arabia] [Airport symbol] (AD)
RXA .... Repairable Exchange Activity [Army]
RXA .... Roxana Resources Ltd. [Vancouver Stock Exchange symbol]
RXB .... Nazareth Academy Library, Rochester, NY [OCLC symbol] (OCLC)
RXC .... Our Lady of Mercy High School Library, Rochester, NY [OCLC symbol] (OCLC)
RXD .... Penfield High School Library, Penfield, NY [OCLC symbol] (OCLC)
RXD .... Receiving Data [Modem status information light] [Computer science] (IGQR)
RXD .... Research or Exploratory Development (PDAA)
RXE .... Perry Junior/Senior High School Library, Perry, NY [OCLC symbol] (OCLC)
RXF .... Pittsford-Medon High School Library, Pittsford, NY [OCLC symbol] (OCLC)
RXF .... Rexford [Montana] [Seismograph station code, US Geological Survey] (SEIS)
RXG .... Pittsford-Sutherland High School Library, Pittsford, NY [OCLC symbol] (OCLC)
RXH .... R. L. Thomas High School Library, Webster, NY [OCLC symbol] (OCLC)
RXI .... Rexplore Resources International Ltd. [Vancouver Stock Exchange symbol]
RXI .... St. Agnes High School Library, Rochester, NY [OCLC symbol] (OCLC)
RXJ .... Thomas Jefferson Junior/Senior High School Library, Rochester, NY [OCLC symbol] (OCLC)
RXK .... Newark, OH [Location identifier FAA] (FAAL)
RXK .... Warsaw High School Library, Warsaw, NY [OCLC symbol] (OCLC)
RXK .... Air Exel [France ICAO designator] (FAAC)
RXL .... Rank Xerox Ltd. [Xerox subsidiary]
RXL .... Rexel, Inc. [NYSE symbol] (SAG)
RXL .... Wayland Senior High School Library, Wayland, NY [OCLC symbol] (OCLC)
RXLI .... Recessive X-Linked Ichthyosis [Medicine]
RXM .... Road/Write Expandable Memory [Computer science] (CIST)
RXM .... Rexford Minerals Ltd. [Vancouver Stock Exchange symbol]
RXM .... RX Medical Services [AMEX symbol] (SPSG)
RXM .... West Irondequoit High School Library, Rochester, NY [OCLC symbol] (OCLC)
RX Med ...... RX Medical Services Corp. [Associated Press] (SAG)
RXN .... Islip, NY [Location identifier FAA] (FAAL)
RXN .... Reaction [Medicine]
RXN .... Rexene Corp. [NYSE symbol] (SPSG)
RXN .... Wheatland-Chili Junior/Senior High School Library, Scottsville, NY [OCLC symbol] (OCLC)
RX(NP) .... Return-to-Zero Recording (Non-Polarized) [Computer science] (MHDB)
RXO .... York High School Library, Retsof, NY [OCLC symbol] (OCLC)
RXOS .... Rank Xerox Operating System [Computer science] (IAA)
RXP .... American Baptist Historical Society Library, Rochester, NY [OCLC symbol] (OCLC)
RXP .... Radix Point
RXQ .... Lincoln First Bank of Rochester Library Service, Rochester, NY [OCLC symbol] (OCLC)
RXQ .... Washington, DC [Location identifier FAA] (FAAL)
RXR .... Rainex Industries [Formerly, Rainex Resources Ltd.] [Vancouver Stock Exchange symbol]
RXR .... Revco D.S. [NYSE symbol] (TTSB)
RXR .... Revco DS, Inc. [NYSE symbol] (SPSG)
RXS .... RADAR Cross Section
RXS .... Real-Time Executive System [SEMIS] (IAA)
RXS .... Roxas City [Philippines] [Airport symbol] (OAG)
RXSD .... Rexall Sundown [NASDAQ symbol] (TTSB)
RXSD .... Rexall Sundown, Inc. [NASDAQ symbol] (SAG)
RXT .... Renal Treatment Centers, Inc. [NYSE symbol] (SAG)
RXT .... Renal Treatment Ctrs [NYSE symbol] (TTSB)
RXT .... Right Exotropia [Ophthalmology]
RXTC .... Renal Treatment Center, Inc. [NASDAQ symbol] (SAG)
RXTE .... Rossi X-ray Timing Explorer [A satellite]
RxTV .... Prescription Television
RXW .... Roxwell Gold Mines [Vancouver Stock Exchange symbol]
RXW .... Watermeet, MI [Location identifier FAA] (FAAL)
RXX .... Reako Exploration [Vancouver Stock Exchange symbol]
RXY .... Roxy Petroleum Ltd. [Toronto Stock Exchange symbol]
RXZ .... Chicago, IL [Location identifier FAA] (FAAL)
RY .... Air Rwanda [ICAO designator] (AD)
RY .... Perkiomen Airways [ICAO designator] (AD)
Ry .... Railway (AFIT)
Ry .... Railway (EBF)
RY .... Redcoat Air Cargo Ltd. [British ICAO designator] (ICDA)

RY .... Relative Yield [Agriculture]
RY .... Relay (DEN)
RY .... Residual Yield [Agriculture] (OA)
RY .... Riley Aeronautics Corp. [ICAO aircraft manufacturer identifier] (ICAO)
RY .... Roll Yoke
RY .... Royal (ROG)
RY .... Royal Bank Canada [MS Symbol] (TTSB)
RY .... Royal Bank of Canada [Toronto Stock Exchange symbol Vancouver Stock Exchange symbol]
RY .... Royal Bank of Canada, Inc. [NYSE symbol] (SAG)
RY .... Royal Yeomanry [Military unit] [British]
ry .... Rydberg [Unit of energy] [Atomic physics Symbol]
ry .... Ryukyu Islands, Southern [ja (Japan) used in records cataloged after January 1978] [MARC country of publication code Library of Congress] (LCCP)
RYA .... Railroad Yardmasters of America (EA)
RYA .... Royal Yachting Association [British] (BI)
RYA .... Ryan Air Services, Inc. [ICAO designator] (FAAC)
RYALM .... Relay Alarm (AAG)
RYAN .... Ryan's Family Steak Houses, Inc. [NASDAQ symbol] (NQ)
RYAN .... Ryan's Family Stk Hse [NASDAQ symbol] (TTSB)
Ryan & M ... Ryan and Moody's English Nisi Prius Reports [171 English Reprint] [A publication] (DLA)
Ryan & M (Eng)... Ryan and Moody's English Nisi Prius Reports [171 English Reprint] [A publication] (DLA)
RyanBck ..... Ryan Beck Co., Inc. [Associated Press] (SAG)
Ry & Can ..... Reports of Railway and Canal Traffic Cases [1855-1950] [A publication]
Ry & Can Cas ..... Railway and Canal Cases [England] [A publication] (DLA)
Ry & Can Traf Ca ... Railway and Canal Traffic Cases [A publication] (DLA)
Ry & Can Traf Cas... Reports of Railway and Canal Traffic Cases [1855-1950] [A publication] (ILCA)
Ry & Can Traffic Cas... Railway and Canal Traffic Cases [England] [A publication] (DLA)
Ry & Can Tr Cas... Reports of Railway and Canal Traffic Cases [1855-1950] [A publication] (DLA)
Ry & C Cas (Eng)... Railway and Canal Cases [England] [A publication] (DLA)
Ry & Corp Law J... Railway and Corporation Law Journal [A publication] (DLA)
Ry & Corp Law Jour... Railway and Corporation Law Journal [A publication] (DLA)
Ry & C Traffic Cas (Eng)... Railway and Canal Traffic Cases [England] [A publication] (DLA)
Ry & M .... Ryan and Moody's English Nisi Prius Reports [A publication] (DLA)
Ry & MCC ... Ryan and Moody's English Crown Cases Reserved [A publication] (DLA)
Ry & MNP ... Ryan and Moody's English Nisi Prius Reports [A publication] (DLA)
Ry & Moo ... Ryan and Moody [1823-26] [A publication] (DLA)
RyanF .... Ryans Family Steak Houses, Inc. [Associated Press] (SAG)
RYB .... Raymond, MS [Location identifier FAA] (FAAL)
RYB .... Royal Yacht, Britannia (WDAA)
RYB .... Rybachye [Former USSR Seismograph station code, US Geological Survey] (SEIS)
RyBPA .... Royal Bancshares of Pennsylvania [Associated Press] (SAG)
RYC .... Raychem Corp. [NYSE symbol] (SPSG)
RYC .... Raymac Oil Corp. [Vancouver Stock Exchange symbol]
RYC .... Rural Youth Corps [Defunct] (EA)
Ry Cas........ Reports of English Railway Cases [A publication] (DLA)
Ry Cas........ Reports of Railway and Canal Traffic Cases [1855-1950] [A publication]
Ry Corp Law Jour... Railway and Corporation Law Journal [A publication] (DLA)
RYD .... Real Year Dollars (NASA)
Ryde .... Ryde's Rating Appeals [1871-1904] [A publication] (DLA)
Ryde & K..... Ryde and Konstam's Reports of Rating Appeals [1894-1904] [A publication] (DLA)
Ryde & K Rat App... Ryde and Konstam's Reports of Rating Appeals [1894-1904] [A publication] (DLA)
Ryder........... Ryder Systems, Inc. [Associated Press] (SAG)
Ryde Rat App... Ryde's Rating Appeals [1871-1904] [A publication] (DLA)
Rydges Mgmt Serv... Rydge's Management Service [A publication]
RYDMAR...... Reaction-Yield-Detected Magnetic Resonance [Also, RYDMR] [Spectroscopy]
RYDMR........ Reaction-Yield-Detected Magnetic Resonance [Also, RYDMAR] [Spectroscopy]
RYE............ Retirement Year Ending [Army] (AABC)
RYE............ Royalon Petroleum [Vancouver Stock Exchange symbol]
RyerTull....... Ryerson Tull [Associated Press] (SAG)
RYEV .... Radish Yellow Edge Virus [Plant pathology]
Ry F .... Rymer's Foedera [20 vols.] [1704-35] [A publication] (DLA)
RYFL.......... Family Steak Houses Fla [NASDAQ symbol] (TTSB)
RYFL.......... Family Steak Houses of Florida, Inc. [Neptune Beach, FL] [NASDAQ symbol] (NQ)
RYFO .... Ryan Foundation International [India] (EAIO)
RYG .... Royal Plastics Group [NYSE symbol] (TTSB)
RYG .... Royal Plastics Group Ltd. [NYSE symbol] (SAG)
RYK .... Rahimyar Kahn [Pakistan] [Airport symbol] (AD)
RYK .... Relay Creek Resources Ltd. [Vancouver Stock Exchange symbol]
RYK .... Romulus, NY [Location identifier FAA] (FAAL)
RYK .... Rykoff-Sexton, Inc. [NYSE symbol] (SPSG)
RYK .... Rykoff-Sexton, Inc. [Associated Press] (SAG)
ryl .... Royal [Philately]
RYL............ Royal
RYL............ Royal Trustco Ltd. [Toronto Stock Exchange symbol Vancouver Stock Exchange symbol]
RYL............ Ryland Group [NYSE symbol] (TTSB)
RYL............ Ryland Group, Inc. [NYSE symbol] (SPSG)
Ryland .... Ryland Group, Inc. [Associated Press] (SAG)

RylCarb........ Royal Caribbean Cruises [*Associated Press*] (SAG)
Ryl Plac Parl... Ryley's Placita Parliamentaria [*1290-1307*] [*England*] [*A publication*] (DLA)
RYM............. Reference Your Message [*Military*] (AABC)
RYM............. Report of the Friends of York Minster [*British*] (WDAA)
RYM............. Revolutionary Youth Movement [*Factions of Students for a Democratic Society. See RYM-I and RYM-II*]
Rymac .... Rymac Mortgage Investment Corp. [*Associated Press*] (SAG)
Ry MCC .... Ryan and Moody's English Crown Cases [*A publication*] (DLA)
Ry Med Jur... Ryan's Medical Jurisprudence [*A publication*] (DLA)
Rymer.......... Rymer Foods, Inc. [*Associated Press*] (SAG)
Rym F......... Rymer's Foedera [*20 vols.*] [*1704-35*] [*A publication*] (DLA)
RYM-I.......... Revolutionary Youth Movement I [*Also known as "Weatherman"*] [*A faction of Students for a Democratic Society*]
RYM-II......... Revolutionary Youth Movement II [*A faction of Students for a Democratic Society*]
RYMSA .... Rural Youth Movement of South Australia
RYMV .... Rice Yellow Mottle Virus [*Plant pathology*]
RYN .... Rayon
RYN .... Rayonier, Inc. [*NYSE symbol*] (SAG)
RYN .... Ryan Aviation Corp. [*ICAO designator*] (FAAC)
RYN .... Tucson, AZ [*Location identifier FAA*] (FAAL)
RYNA .... Railroad Yardmasters of North America [*Absorbed by RYA*] (EA)
RYNV .... Rubust Yellow Net Virus [*Plant pathology*]
RYO .... Rio Turbio [*Argentina*] [*Airport symbol*] (OAG)
RYO .... Royal Oak Mines [*AMEX symbol*] (SPSG)
RYONSW ..... Rural Youth Organisation of New South Wales [*Australia*]
RYOQ.......... Rural Youth Organisation of Queensland [*Australia*]
RYOT .... Rural Youth Organisation of Tasmania [*Australia*]
RYP .... Cumberland, MD [*Location identifier FAA*] (FAAL)
R-Y-P.......... Roll, Yaw, Pitch (MCD)
RYQ .... Royalstar Resources [*Vancouver Stock Exchange symbol*]
RYR .... Radyr Junction [*Cardiff*] [*Welsh depot code*]
RYR .... Royal Yeomanry Regiment [*British military*] (DMA)
RYR .... Ryanair [*Ireland*] [*ICAO designator*] (FAAC)
RYR .... Ryanodine Receptor [*Genetics*]
RYR .... Rymer Foods [*NYSE symbol*] (TTSB)
RYR .... Rymer Foods, Inc. [*NYSE symbol*] (SPSG)
RyRC .... Ryanodine Receptor Channel [*Biochemistry*]
RYRQD .... Reply Requested (NOAA)
RYS .... Railway Stations [*Public-performance tariff class*] [*British*]
RYS .... Royal Yacht Squadron [*British*]
RYS .... Ryan Resources Ltd. [*Vancouver Stock Exchange symbol*]
RYT............. Ray-Net Communications Systems, Inc. [*Vancouver Stock Exchange symbol*]
RYT............. Reference Your Telegram (WDAA)
RYT............. Reference Your Telex (WDAA)
RYT............. Relative Yield Total [*Agriculture*]
Ryt............. Rytmi [*Record label*] [*Finland*]

RYU .... Rosanky, TX [*Location identifier FAA*] (FAAL)
RYU .... Ryukoku University [*UTLAS symbol*]
RYV .... Watertown, WI [*Location identifier FAA*] (FAAL)
RYY .... Marietta, GA [*Location identifier FAA*] (FAAL)
RZ................ Arabia [*ICAO designator*] (AD)
RZ................ Radiation Zone [*Environmental science*] (COE)
RZ................ Reaction Zone
RZ................ Reconnaissance Zone
RZ................ Recovery Zone (MCD)
RZ................ Regal-Zonophone [*Record label*] [*Great Britain*]
RZ................ Regiment de Zouaves
RZ................ Reset to Zero [*Computer science*] (CIST)
RZ................ Resistance Zone
RZ................ Return to Zero (IDOE)
RZ................ Return-to-Zero Recording [*Computer science*]
Rz................ Retzius [*Neuron*]
RZ................ Revolutionary Cells [*Revolutionary group*] [*West Germany*]
Rz................ Rhizome [*Botany*]
RZ................ Rueckenfallschirm mit Zwangsausloesung [*Static-line, backpack parachute*] [*German military - World War II*]
RZA .... Religious Zionists of America (EA)
RZA .... Santa Cruz [*Argentina*] [*Airport symbol*] (OAG)
RZB .... Raiffeisen Zentralbank [*Austria*]
RZB .... Roseberth [*Queensland*] [*Airport symbol*] (AD)
RZC .... Fayetteville, AR [*Location identifier FAA*] (FAAL)
RZ code...... Return-to-Zero Code (MED)
RZE .... Rzeszow [*Poland*] [*Airport symbol*] (OAG)
RZF .... Riemann Zeta Function [*Mathematics*]
RZI .... Aero Zambia Ltd. [*FAA designator*] (FAAC)
RZL .... Rensselaer, IN [*Location identifier FAA*] (FAAL)
RZL .... Return-to-Zero Level
RZM............ Return-to-Zero Mark
RZMA.......... Rolled Zinc Manufacturers Association [*Defunct*] (EA)
RZ(NP)......... Nonpolarized Return-to-Zero Recording [*Computer science*] (IBMDP)
RZ(NP)......... Return to Zero (Non-Polarized) (NITA)
RZO .... Demopolis, AL [*Location identifier FAA*] (FAAL)
RZ(P)........... Polarized Return-to-Zero Recording [*Computer science*] (IBMDP)
RZP .... Provincetown, MA [*Location identifier FAA*] (FAAL)
RZ(P)........... Return to Zero (Polarized) (NITA)
RZR .... Ramsar [*Iran*] [*Airport symbol*] (AD)
RZR .... Zephyr Aviation Services, Inc. [*ICAO designator*] (FAAC)
RZS .... Rolled Zinc Sheet
RZS............. Royal Zoological Society [*British*]
RZSI............ [*The*] Royal Zoological Society of Ireland (DI)
RZSS .... Royal Zoological Society of Scotland (EAIO)
RZT............. Chillicothe, OH [*Location identifier FAA*] (FAAL)
RZY............. Rezayeh [*Iran*] [*Airport symbol*] (AD)
RZYM.......... Ribozyme Pharmaceuticals [*NASDAQ symbol*] (TTSB)
RZYM.......... Ribozyme Pharmaceuticals, Inc. [*NASDAQ symbol*] (SAG)
RZZ............. Roanoke Rapids, NC [*Location identifier FAA*] (FAAL)

S
By Acronym

S .... Aerospatiale [*Societe Nationale Industrielle Aerospatiale*] (Sud Aviation) [*France ICAO aircraft manufacturer identifier*] (ICAO)
S .... Antisubmarine [*Designation for all US military aircraft*]
S .... Apparent Power [*Symbol*] (DEN)
S .... Boltzmann Constant [*Statistical mechanics*]
S .... Codex Sinaiticus (BJA)
S .... Condensation [*Physics*] (BARN)
S .... Deflection Sensitivity (IDOE)
S .... Detecting [*JETDS nomenclature*]
S .... Displacement [*Physics*] (BARN)
S .... Distance (DAVI)
S .... Elastance [*Electricity*] (BARN)
S .... Entropy [*Symbol*] [*IUPAC*]
S .... Esophoria [*Ophthalmology*] (DAVI)
S .... Esses [*Phonetic alphabet*] [*Pre-World War II*] (DSUE)
S .... Expenditure Saved [*Economics*]
S .... Fun Fairs [*Public-performance tariff class*] [*British*]
S .... Isis-Chemie KG [*Germany*] [*Research code symbol*]
S .... Magnetic Solar Daily Variation
S .... Mean Dose Per Unit Cumulated Activity (DAVI)
S .... New York Supplement [*A publication*] (DLA)
S .... No Option Offered [*Investment term*] (DFIT)
S .... Path, Length of Arc [*Symbol*] [*IUPAC*]
(S) .... Paymaster [*Navy British*]
S .... Permissible Working Stress
S .... Pitman-Moore Co. [*Research code symbol*]
S .... Pounds per Square Inch (AAG)
S .... Poynting Vector [*Symbol*] [*Electromagnetism*] (DEN)
S .... Range Bearing [*JETDS nomenclature*]
S .... Reluctance [*Symbol*] (DEN)
S .... Sabbath
S .... Sabin [*Unit of acoustic measurement*] (DEN)
S .... Sable [*Heraldry*]
S .... Sacral
S .... Sacred
S .... Sacrifice [*Baseball*]
S .... Sacrum
S .... Sadism [*or Sadist*] (CDAI)
S .... Saduccus [*Flourished, 13th century*] [*Authority cited in pre-1607 legal work*] (DSA)
S .... Saeculum
(S) .... Safe [*Task classification*] [*NASA*] (NASA)
S .... Safety [*Football*]
S .... Sailing Ship
S .... Saint
S .... Saline [*Pharmacology*] (DAVI)
S .... Salmonella [*Bacteriology*] (MAE)
S .... Salvageable (AAG)
S .... Same Case [*Same case as case cited*] [*Used in Shepard's Citations*] [*Legal term*] (DLA)
S .... Samedi [*French*] (ASC)
S .... Sample
S .... Samuel [*Old Testament book*] (BJA)
S .... San (VRA)
S .... Sand [*Quality of the bottom*] [*Nautical charts*]
S .... Sandra [*Genotype of Phlox paniculata*]
S .... San Francisco [*California*] [*Mint mark, when appearing on US coins*]
S .... Sankt (VRA)
S .... Santa (VRA)
S .... Santo (VRA)
S .... Sapwood [*Forestry*]
S .... Satang [*Monetary unit in Thailand*]
S .... Satellite (IAA)
S .... Satellite [*Chromosomal*] [*Medicine*] (MAE)
S .... Saturation (MAE)
S .... Saturation in the Blood Phase [*Medicine*] (DAVI)
S .... Saturday
S .... Saturn
S .... Savanna Zone Soil [*Agriculture*]
S .... Save [*Computer science*] [*Telecommunications*]
S .... Savings [*Economics*]
S .... Saxon
S .... Saybolt Second (IAA)
S .... Scalar [*Mathematics*] (ROG)
S .... Scanning
S .... Scarce [*Numismatics*]

S .... Scattering Coefficient [*Photometry*]
S .... Schedule
S .... Schilling [*Monetary unit*] [*Austria*]
S .... Schistosoma [*A parasitic fluke*] (MAE)
S .... School
S .... Science (WGA)
S .... Scilicet [*Namely*] [*Latin*] (DLA)
S .... Scot
S .... Scott's Standard Postage Stamp Catalogue [*A publication*]
S .... Scouting [*Naval aircraft designation*]
S .... Screen (IAA)
S .... Screen (IDOE)
S .... Scribe
S .... Scruple [*Medicine*] (DMAA)
S .... Scuttle
S .... Scythian [*Geology*]
S .... Sea (ADA)
S .... Sea-Air Temperature Difference Correction
S .... Seaman [*Navy*]
S .... Seamless (DAC)
S .... Seaplane [*Navy*]
S .... Search
S .... Searle's Cape Of Good Hope Reports [*South Africa*] [*A publication*] (DLA)
S .... Searle's Cases in the Supreme Court [*1850-67*] [*South Africa*] [*A publication*] (DLA)
S .... Sears,Roebuck [*NYSE symbol*] (TTSB)
S .... Sears, Roebuck & Co. [*NYSE symbol*] (SPSG)
S .... Seasonal [*Business term*] (OICC)
S .... Seat (WGA)
S .... Second [*Symbol*] [*SI unit of time*]
S .... Second [*or Secondary*]
s .... Secondary [*Preferred form is soo*] [*Chemistry*]
S .... Secondary Modern School [*British*]
S .... Secondary [*or Shake*] Wave [*Earthquakes*]
S .... Secondary Winding (IAA)
S .... Secret [*Security classification*]
S .... Secretary
S .... Secretin [*Endocrinology*]
S .... Secretory Substance [*Botany*]
S .... Section
S .... Section (WDMC)
S .... Sector (IAA)
S .... Security (IAA)
S .... Sedentary [*Biology*]
S .... Seder of Triennial Cycle (BJA)
s .... Sedimentation Coefficient [*Physical chemistry*]
S .... See
S .... Seelenlaenge [*Barrel length*] [*German military - World War II*]
S .... Seguente [*And Following*] [*Italian*] (ILCA)
S .... Seite [*Page*] [*German*]
s .... Selection Coefficient (DOG)
S .... Self-Pollinated [*Botany*]
S .... Selvi [*Italy*] [*Research code symbol*]
S .... Semi
S .... Semiannually
S .... Semilente [*Insulin*] [*Pharmacology*] (DAVI)
S .... Semi-Registered Tank [*Liquid gas carriers*]
S .... Semis [*One-Half*] [*Pharmacy*]
S .... Sen [*Monetary unit in Japan*]
S .... Senate
S .... Senate Bill [*with number*] (GPO)
S .... Senor [*Mister*] [*Spanish*]
S .... Sensation [*Psychology*]
S .... Sensitivity (DEN)
S .... Sentence [*Linguistics*]
S .... Senza [*Without*] [*Music*]
S .... Separation
S .... September
S .... Septum [*Anatomy*] (DAVI)
S .... Sepulchrum [*Sepulchre*] [*Latin*]
S .... Sepultus [*Buried*] [*Latin*]
S .... Serial
S .... Series
S .... Serine [*One-letter symbol; see Ser*]
S .... Sermon

S	Serum
S	Servant [*Legal shorthand*] (LWAP)
S	Service [*Military document classification*] (INF)
S	Servicing
S	Servier [*France*] [*Research code symbol*]
S	Sesquiplane [*Navy*]
S	Set
S	Set Meals [*School meals*] [*British*]
S	Seven (ROG)
S	Seventy (ROG)
S	Severity
S	Sewage Disposal [*British Waterways Board sign*]
S	SGOT [*Surface Serum Glutamic-Oxaloacetic*] (DAVI)
S	Shaft Horsepower
S	Shaft Main Engine
S	Shape Descriptor [*S-curve, for example. The shape resembles the letter for which it is named*]
S	Shape Factor of a Structure [*Heat transmission symbol*]
S	Sharing Time (NTCM)
S	Sharp
s	Sharpshooter [*Army*]
S	Shaw, Dunlop, and Bell's Scotch Court of Session Reports, First Series [*A publication*] (DLA)
S	Shaw's Scotch Appeal Cases, House of Lords [*A publication*] (DLA)
S	Shaw's Scotch Court of Session Cases [*A publication*] (DLA)
S	Shear [*Type of seismic wave*]
S	Sheep (ROG)
S	Sheet [*Genetics*]
S	Shell
S	Shelter [*Bureau of the Census*]
S	Sheltered [*Takeoff area for seaplanes*] [*For chart use only*]
S	Shelters [*JETDS nomenclature*] [*Military*] (CET)
S	Shilling [*Monetary unit in Britain*] [*Obsolete*]
S	Ship
S	Shire (ADA)
S	Short Circuit
S	Shrub [*Botany*]
S	Shunt Ahead [*Railroad signal arm*] [*British*]
S	Sick
S	Side
s	Side (NAKS)
S	Siderocyte [*Hematology*] (AAMN)
S	Side Signal (IAA)
S	Sidrah (BJA)
S	Siecle [*Century*] [*French*]
S	Siemens [*Symbol*] [*SI unit of electric conductance*]
S	Sierra [*Phonetic alphabet*] [*International*] (DSUE)
S	Sigma (NUCP)
S	Sigma Mines (Quebec) Ltd. [*Toronto Stock Exchange symbol*]
S	Sign [*or Signed*]
S	Signa [*Write*] [*Pharmacy*]
S	Signal [*Telecommunications*] (TEL)
S	Signaller [*British military*] (DMA)
S	Signal Strength [*Broadcasting*]
S	Signature
s	Signature (WDMC)
S	Signed (DFIT)
/S/	Signed [*Before signature on typed copy of a document, original of which was signed*]
S	Signetur [*Let It Be Entitled*] [*Pharmacy*] (ROG)
S	Signor [*Mister*] [*Italian*]
S	Silent [*Dance terminology*]
S	Silicate
S	Silk (AAG)
S	Silurian [*Geology*] (DOG)
S	Silver
S	Silversmith
S	Simes [*Italy*] [*Research code symbol*]
S	Similarity Index
S	Simon de Bisignano [*Flourished, 1174-79*] [*Authority cited in pre-1607 legal work*] (DSA)
S	Simon de Paris [*Deceased, 1273*] [*Authority cited in pre-1607 legal work*] (DSA)
S	Simplex
S	Simultaneous Transmission of Range Signals and Voice
S	Sine [*Without*] [*Latin*]
S	Single
S	Single Silk [*Wire insulation*]
S	Singular
S	Sinister [*Left*] [*Latin*]
S	Sinistra [*Left Hand*] [*Music*]
S	Sink
S	Sire
S	Sister
S	Site [*Archaeology*]
S	Situs [*Placed*] [*Latin*]
S	Sixteenmo [*Book from 15 to 17-1/2 centimeters in height*]
S	Sixth Word Designator [*Computer science*]
S	Sized (NTCM)
S	Skid (AAG)
S	Slate (KSC)
S	Slave [*LORAN stations*]
S	Sleeping [*Medicine*]
S	Slewed [*Antenna*]
s	Slides (WDMC)
S	Slip
S	Slipped Up [*Horse racing*]
S	Slope [*Technical drawings*]
S	Slow
S	Slow Muscle [*Skeletal muscle pharmacology*]
S	Small [*Size designation for clothing, etc.*]
S	Small (WDMC)
S	Smoke (NFPA)
S	Smooth [*Appearance of bacterial colony*]
S	Smooth Sea [*Navigation*]
S	Snack (CDAI)
S	Sniper [*British military*] (DMA)
S	Snow [*Meteorology*]
S	Socialist
S	Socialist Group [*EC*] (ECED)
S	Societas [*Society*] [*Latin*]
S	Socius [*or Sodalis*] [*Fellow*]
S	Soft
S	Software [*Computer science*]
S	Soiled [*Deltiology*]
S	Sol [*Monetary unit in Peru*]
S	Solar (ADA)
S	Solco Basel AG [*Switzerland*] [*Research code symbol*]
S	Soldering
S	Solicitor's Opinion [*A publication*] (DLA)
S	Solid
S	Solidus [*Shilling*] [*Latin*]
S	Solitary [*Biology*]
S	Solo [*Music*]
S	Solubility
S	Solute (DAVI)
S	Somaliland Scouts [*Military unit*] [*British*]
S	Son
S	SONAR [*Sonic Azimuth and Ranging*] [*British military*] (DMA)
S	Song (ROG)
S	Soprano [*Music*] (WDAA)
S	Sou [*Monetary unit in France*]
S	Sough (AAG)
S	Sound [*Audiology*]
S	Sound Tape [*Films, television, etc.*]
S	Source
S	South [*or Southern*]
s-----	South America [*MARC geographic area code Library of Congress*] (LCCP)
S	Southern (VRA)
S	Southern Reporter [*A publication*] (DLA)
S	Space (IAA)
S	Spacer
S	Spade (ADA)
S	Spar [*Buoy*]
S	Spares
S	Spatial Ability [*Psychology*]
S	Speak
S	Special
s	Special Abilities of an Individual [*Symbol*] [*Psychology*]
S	Specialist [*Ecology*]
S	Special Preparations Necessary for Test [*Laboratory science*] (DAVI)
S	Special Types [*JETDS nomenclature*]
S	Species
S	Specification
S	Specific Factor
S	Specific Surface
S	Speculum [*A publication*] (WDAA)
S	Speech
S	Speed
S	Sphere [*or Spherical*]
S	Spherical Joint (IAA)
S	Spherical Lens [*Ophthalmology*] (DAVI)
S	Spin Quantum Number [*Atomic physics*] (DEN)
S	Spinster
S	Spirillum [*Bacteriology*] (MAE)
S	Split [*In stock listings of newspapers*]
S	Spoilers in Nozzle
S	Sponsored
S	Spontaneous
S	Spool
S	Sport [*In automobile model name "Honda Civic S"*]
S	Sports Program (NTCM)
S	Spring-Burned [*Ecology*]
S	Spurs [*Horse racing*]
S	Squadron
S	Stack
S	Stackable Container (DCTA)
S	Staff [*License plate code assigned to foreign diplomats in the US*]
S	Stand
S	Standard
s	Standard Deviation [*Also, SD*] [*Statistics*]
S	Staphylococcus [*Medicine*] (MAE)
S	Star (NASA)
S	Starboard
S	Start (KSC)
S	Stat [*Unit of radioactive disintegration rate*]
S	State [*Telecommunications*]
S	Static
S	Station

S	Stationary
S	Statue (ADA)
S	Status Required [*Civil Service*]
S	Statute
S	Steamer
S	Steamship (DS)
S	Steel
s	Stefan-Boltzmann Constant
S	Stem
S	Stephanus Provincialis [*Flourished, 1290-97*] [*Authority cited in pre-1607 legal work*] (DSA)
S	Stere [*Metric measure of volume*]
S	Stereo (CDAI)
S	Stereo Broadcast [*British*]
S	Stimulus
S	Stock
S	Stockbroker
S-1	Stoke (IAA)
S	Stolen Base [*Baseball*]
S	Stopping Power
S	Storage
S	Store (IAA)
S	Stores [*British military*] (DMA)
S	Straight
s	Strange [*Quark*] [*Atomic physics*]
S	Stratum (BJA)
S	Stratus [*Meteorology*]
S	Street [*Bureau of the Census*]
S	Strength (DS)
S	Streptococcus [*Medicine*] (MAE)
S	Streptomycin [*An antibiotic*]
S	Streptozocin [*Antineoplastic drug*]
S	Stroke of Piston in Inches [*Railroad term*]
S	Stung [*by bees*] [*Medicine*]
S	Subcompact [*Car size*]
S	Subcutaneous [*Pharmacology*] (DAVI)
S	Subito [*Immediately; Suddenly*] [*Music*]
S	Subject [*Psychology*]
S	Subject [*of a proposition in logic*]
S	Subjective [*findings*] (DAVI)
S	Subluxation [*Chiropractic*]
S	Submarine
s	Submerged Pump [*Liquid gas carriers*]
S	Substantive
S	Substrate (IAA)
S	Substrate, Free [*Enzyme kinetics*]
S	Succeeded
S	Successor
S	Suckling [*Medicine*] (DMAA)
C	Sucre [*Monetary unit*] [*Ecuador*]
S	Sud [*South*] [*French*] (ROG)
S	Sugar [*Phonetic alphabet*] [*Royal Navy World War I Pre-World War II*] [*World War II*] (DEUF)
S	Suit
S	Suitability (CAAL)
S	Sulfamethoxazole [*Also, SMX, SMZ*] [*Antibacterial compound*]
S	Sulfate
S	Sulfur [*Chemical element*]
S	Sum (MAE)
S	Sumendus [*To Be Taken*] [*Pharmacy*]
S	Summary
S	Summer [*Vessel load line mark*]
S	Summit Books [*Publisher's imprint*]
S	Sun
S	Sunday
S	Sunny [*Meteorology*] (ADA)
S	Super
S	Superb
S	Superficial
S	Superior
S	Supernatant [*Protein*] [*Cytology*]
S	Superseded [*New regulation or order substituted for an existing one*] [*Used in Shepard's Citations*] [*Legal term*] (DLA)
S	Supervisor (IAA)
S	Supplementary Frequency (DA)
S	Supply [*Department aboard a carrier*] [*Navy*]
S	Supply [*Economics*]
S	Supravergence (AAMN)
S	Supreme Court Reporter [*A publication*] (DLA)
S	Sur [*On*] [*French*]
S	Surface Area
S	Surfaced
S	Surgeon [*Navy British*] (ROG)
S	Surgery [*Medical Officer designation*] [*British*]
S/A	Surpine (DAVI)
S	Surplus
S	Surrogate
S	Survey
S	Survival
S	Susceptible
S	Suus [*His*] [*Latin*]
S	Svedberg Unit [*Physical chemistry*]
S	Sweden [*IYRU nationality code*]
S	Swiss Mouse [*Medicine*] (DMAA)
S	Switch

S	Switchboard [*Telecommunications*] (TEL)
s	Symmetrical [*Also, sym*] [*Chemistry*]
S	Symmetrically Substituted (IAA)
s	Symmetry Number [*Symbol*] [*IUPAC*]
S	Sync (IDOE)
S	Synchronized Sleep
S	Synchronous
S	Synoptic [*Meteorology*]
S	Synthesis [*Phase in mitosis*] [*Cytology*]
S	Syria (BARN)
S	System
s	Systolic [*Cardiology*] (DAVI)
s	Thio [*or Mercapto*] [*As substituent on nucleoside*] [*Biochemistry*]
s	Thiouridine [*One-letter symbol; see Srd*]
S	Water Surface Craft [*JETDS nomenclature*]
S	Wyeth Laboratories [*Research code symbol*]
S-1	Personnel Section [*Military*]
S1	Sacral Nerve, First [*S2 is second sacral nerve, etc., through S5*] [*Anatomy*] [*Medicine*] (DAVI)
S1	Sacral Vertebra, First [*S2 is second sacral vertabra, etc., through S5*] [*Anatomy*] (DAVI)
S1	Systolic, First Heart Sound [*S2 is second heart sound, etc., through S4*] [*Cardiology*] (DAVI)
S1C	Seaman, First Class [*Navy*]
S1E	Surfaced One Edge [*Technical drawings*]
S1S	Surfaced or Dressed One Side [*Technical drawings*]
S1S1E	Surfaced or Dressed One Side and One Edge [*Technical drawings*]
S1S2E	Surfaced One Side and Two Edges [*Lumber*] (DAC)
S1W	Security of the First World [*Rap music group*]
S2	Bangladesh [*Aircraft nationality and registration mark*] (FAAC)
S-2	Intelligence Section [*in Army brigades or smaller units, and in Marine Corps units smaller than a brigade; also, the officer in charge of this section*]
S 2d	New York Supplement, Second Series [*A publication*] (DLA)
S2d	Southern Reporter, Second Series [*West*] [*A publication*] (AAGC)
S2E	Surfaced Two Edges [*Lumber*] (DAC)
S2 Glf	STwo Golf, Inc. [*Associated Press*] (SAG)
S2H2	Short, Straight Hollow Hosel [*Golf clubs*]
S2S	Surfaced or Dressed Two Sides [*Technical drawings*]
S2S1E	Surfaced Two Sides and One Edge [*Lumber*] (DAC)
S2S & CM	Surfaced Two Sides and Center Matched [*Lumber*] (DAC)
S2S & SL	Surfaced Two Sides and Shiplapped [*Technical drawings*] (DAC)
S-3	Operations and Training Section [*in Army brigades or smaller units, and in Marine Corps units smaller than a brigade; also, the officer in charge of this section*]
S3	Signal Selection Switchboard (CAAL)
S3	Simulation in the Service of Society
S³	Small Scientific Satellite [*NASA*]
S3	Synergistic Strike System
S3	Systems and Software Simulator
S3E	Safety Emissions Energy Economics [*Automotive research*]
S3 Inc	S3, Inc. [*Associated Press*] (SAG)
S3T	Sesquantially Sampling Sediment Trap [*Marine science*] (SSRA)
S-4	Logistics Section [*in Army brigades or smaller units, and in Marine Corps units smaller than a brigade; also, the officer in charge of this section*]
S4	Stanford School Scheduling System
S4	Supply Officer [*Army*]
S4S	Surfaced or Dressed Four Sides [*Technical drawings*]
S4S & CS	Surfaced Four Sides and Caulking Seam [*Lumber*] (DAC)
S4SCS	Surfaced Four Sides with Chalking Seam on Each Edge [*Wood industry*] (WPI)
S5	Civil Affairs Officer [*Army*] (AABC)
S6C	Super Six Conference (PSS)
S7	Seler's Delivery in Seven Days [*NY Stock Exchange*] (EBF)
S7	Seller's Delivery in Seven Days [*Stock exchange term*]
S7	Seychelles [*Aircraft nationality and registration mark*] (FAAC)
S9	Sao Tome and Principe [*Aircraft nationality and registration mark*] (FAAC)
SA	Air-Cushion Vehicle built by Societe National Industrielle Aerospatiale [*France*] [*Usually used in combination with numerals*]
sa----	Amazon River and Basin [*MARC geographic area code Library of Congress*] (LCCP)
SA	Arsine [*Medicine*] (ADDR)
SA	Franciscan Friars of the Atonement (TOCD)
sa	Franciscan Friars of the Atonement (TOCD)
SA	Franciscan Sisters of the Atonement (TOCD)
SA	Le Syllabaire Accadien [*A publication*] (BJA)
SA	Missionary Sisters of Our Lady of Africa [*White Sisters*] [*Roman Catholic religious order*]
SA	Sable [*Heraldry*]
SA	Sacrum Anterior [*A fetal position*] [*Obstetrics*] (DAVI)
S/A	Safe and Arm (NAKS)
S/A	Safe Arm
S/A	Safe Arrival
sa	Safe Arrival (ODBW)
SA	Safety Altitude [*Aviation*] (DA)
SA	Safety Analysis [*Nuclear energy*] (NRCH)
SA	Safety Assessment
SA	Safing Area [*NASA*] (NASA)
SA	Sail Area
SA	Sales Aid (IAA)
SA	Salicylamide (STED)
SA	Salicylic Acid [*Organic chemistry*]
SA	Saline (STED)

SA	Salt Acid
SA	Salt Added
SA	Salvation Army (EA)
Sa	Samarium [*Obsolete form; see Sm*] [*Chemical element*]
SA	Sample Array
SA	Sample Assembly (MCD)
SA	Sandstorm
Sa	Sanguinarine [*Biochemistry*]
SA	Sanitary Authority [*British*] (ROG)
SA	Sarcastics Anonymous (EA)
SA	Sarcoma [*Medicine*]
SA	Saturday
SA	Saturn Apollo [*NASA*] (KSC)
SA	Saudi Arabia [*ANSI two-letter standard code*] (CNC)
SA	Saunders Aircraft Corp. Ltd. [*Canada ICAO aircraft manufacturer identifier*] (ICAO)
SA	Sausage Aerial [*Radio*]
SA	Savannah & Atlanta Railway Co. [*AAR code*]
SA	Savings Account
SA	Sawmakers' Association [*A union*] [*British*]
SA	Say [*Amateur radio shorthand*] (WDAA)
SA	Scaling Amplifier
SA	Scenic America (EA)
S/A	Scheduled/Actual (NASA)
SA	Schizophrenics Anonymous (EA)
SA	Scholarship Amount (NITA)
SA	Science Advisors [*Army*] (RDA)
SA	Scientific American [*A publication*] (BRI)
SA	Scientific Assistant [*Ministry of Agriculture, Fisheries, and Food*] [*British*]
SA	Scleroderma Association (EA)
SA	Scoliosis Association (EA)
SA	Scout Association (EAIO)
SA	Seaman Apprentice [*Navy rating*]
SA	Seasonally Adjusted (WGA)
SA	Second Antibody (STED)
SA	Secondary Amenorrhea [*Medicine*] (MAE)
SA	Secondary Anemia [*Medicine*] (MAE)
SA	Secondary Arrest (STED)
SA	Second Attack [*Men's lacrosse position*]
SA	Secretary of the Army
SA	Secundum Artem [*According to the Art*] [*Latin*]
SA	Security Alarm Technician Program [*Association of Independent Colleges and Schools specialization code*]
SA	Security Assistance (MCD)
SA	See Also [*Indexing code*]
SA	Seiners Association [*Later, PSVOA*]
SA	Select Address
SA	Selected Ammunition (RDA)
SA	Selective Availability
SA	Self-Administered [*Drugs*]
SA	Self-Agglutinating (STED)
SA	Self-Analysis [*Psychology*] (DAVI)
SA	Semen Analysis
SA	Semiannual
SA	Semiautomatic
SA	Senior Advisor [*Military*]
SA	Sensation [*Unit*] (DAVI)
SA	Sense Amplifier
SA	Sensible Atmosphere (SAA)
SA	Sensitized Activated
SA	Sensitizing Antibody (STED)
S/A	Sensor/Actuator (AAEL)
SA	Separat-Abdruck (BJA)
SA	Separated Atom [*Atomic physics*]
SA	Sequential Access (IAA)
SA	Sequential Automated
SA	Serendipity Association (EA)
SA	Serra
SA	Serum Albumin [*Serology*]
SA	Serum Aldolase (STED)
SA	Servant Allowance [*British military*] (DMA)
S/A	Service Action (AAG)
SA	Service Adviser [*or Attache*] [*British*]
SA	Service Agreement (MCD)
SA	Service Aid (IAA)
SA	Service Air [*Nuclear energy*] (NRCH)
S/A	Service Application [*Military*] (AFIT)
SA	Service Area (IAA)
SA	Service Arm (KSC)
SA	Service Assistant [*Telecommunications*] (TEL)
SA	Serviced Apartment
SA	Services to Adults [*Public human service program*] (PHSD)
SA	Servo Amplifier
SA	Seventh Avenue [*New York City*]
SA	Sexaholics Anonymous (EA)
SA	Sex Appeal [*Slang*]
SA	Sexual Abuse
SA	Shaft Angle [*Technical drawings*]
SA	Shell Analysis
SA	Shift Advance Driver
SA	Ship Abstracts [*Helsinki University of Technology*] [*Bibliographic database*]
S/A	Ship Alteration (MCD)
S/A	Shipped Assembled
SA	Shipping Annual Data [*Department of Commerce*] (GFGA)
SA	Shipping Authority
SA	Ship to Aircraft (DEN)
SA	Shipyard Agreement [*MARAD*] (TAG)
SA	Shirley Association (EA)
SA	Shock Attenuation (AAG)
SA	Shop Accessory [*Drawing*] (NG)
SA	Shoplifters Anonymous [*An association*] (EA)
SA	Shops Act [*1950*] [*British*] (ILCA)
SA	Short Acting (STED)
SA	Shortening Allowance [*Carpentry*]
SA	Sialic Acid (STED)
SA	Sialoadenectomy (STED)
SA	Sicanna Industries Ltd. [*Vancouver Stock Exchange symbol*]
SA	Sideroblastic Anemia [*Hematology*]
SA	Siegfried AG [*Switzerland*] [*Research code symbol*]
SA	Sierra
SA	Signal Access
SA	Signal Analysis
SA	Signal Analyzer
SA	Signal Attenuation (AAG)
SA	Signature Analysis
SA	Simian Adenovirus (STED)
SA	Simple-Adjoint [*Method*] (USDC)
SA	Simple Alert (NATG)
SA	Simulated Annealing [*Physics*]
sa	Sin Ano [*Without Year*] [*Publishing*] [*Spanish*]
SA	Sine Anno [*Without Date of Publication*] [*Latin*]
SA	Single Access (MCD)
SA	Single Action [*Firearm*]
SA	Single Amplitude (IAA)
SA	Single Armor [*Telecommunications*] (TEL)
SA	Sinoatrial [*Medicine*]
SA	Sinoauricular [*Medicine*]
SA	Sinus Aestuum [*Bay of Billows*] [*Lunar area*]
SA	Sinus Arrest (STED)
SA	Sinus Arrhythmia [*Cardiology*] (MAE)
SA	Sister of Arts
SA	Site Activation [*NASA*] (MCD)
SA	Situational Awareness [*Navy*] (DOMA)
SA	Situation Audit (MCD)
SA	Skeletal Age (STED)
SA	Sleep Apnea [*Medicine*] (DMAA)
SA	Slide Agglutination (PDAA)
SA	Slightly Active (MAE)
SA	Slovenian Association [*Australia*]
SA	Slow-Acting [*Pharmacy*]
SA	Slow-Acting Relay (IAA)
SA	Slugging Average [*Baseball*]
SA	Small Arms [*All firearms other than cannon*]
SA	Smithsonian Associates [*Later, Smithsonian Resident Associate Program*]
SA	Snap Action
SA	Socialist Action [*An association*] (EA)
S/A	Societa Anonima [*Stock company*] [*Italian*]
SA	Societas Adunationis [*Franciscan Friars or Sisters of the Atonement*] [*Roman Catholic religious order*]
SA	Societe Anonyme [*French*] (WDMC)
SA	Society of Actuaries
SA	Society of Alexandria [*Defunct*] (EA)
SA	Society of Antiquaries [*British*]
SA	Society of Archivists [*British*]
SA	Society of Arts [*British*]
SA	Society of Authors (DGA)
SA	Sociological Abstracts [*Database*]
SA	Software Applications
SA	Soil Association [*Bristol, England*] (EAIO)
SA	Solar Array (KSC)
SA	Soluble in Alkaline Solution
SA	Solution Annealed (MCD)
SA	Son Altesse [*His or Her Highness*] [*French*]
SA	Sonderabdruck (BJA)
SA	Soprano, Alto
SA	Soul Asylum [*Rock-music group*]
SA	Source Address
sa	South Africa [*MARC country of publication code Library of Congress*] (LCCP)
SA	South Africa [*IYRU nationality code*]
SA	South African Airways [*ICAO designator*]
SA	South America
SA	South Arabian (BJA)
SA	South Atlantic
SA	South Australia [*State in Australia*] (BARN)
SA	Southbank Aviation [*Australia*]
SA	Southern Association [*Baseball league*]
SA	Space Aeronautics [*A publication*]
S/A	Space Available (ADA)
SA	Spacecraft Adapter [*NASA*]
SA	Spaced Antenna [*Marine science*] (OSRA)
SA	Spanish-American (DAVI)
SA	Speaker Amplifier
SA	Special Access
SA	Special Action [*Military*] (AFM)
S/A	Special Activities [*Air Force*]
SA	Special Agent (AFM)

SA	Special Application [*Lift truck*]
SA	Special Area [*RADAR*]
SA	Special Artificer [*Navy*]
SA	Special Assignment [*Navy*]
SA	Special Assistant (GFGA)
SA	Specialty Advertising Business [*A publication*] (EAAP)
SA	Species-Area [*Ecology*]
SA	Specific Activity
SA	Specific Antigen [*Immunology*]
SA	Spectrograph Assembly (KSC)
SA	Spectrum Analysis
SA	Speech Amplifier (IAA)
SA	Sperm Aster [*Cytology*]
SA	Speronara [*Ship's rigging*] (ROG)
SA	Spiking Activity [*Medicine*] (DMAA)
SA	Spin Axis (AAG)
SA	Spiritualist Association of Great Britain (BI)
SA	Splice Acceptor [*Genetics*]
SA	Splitting Amplifier (AFM)
SA	Sponsored [*or Sponsoring*] Agency (MCD)
SA	Sports Ambassadors (EA)
SA	Spouse's Allowance [*Canada*]
SA	Springfield Armory [*Army*]
SA	Squash Australia
SA	Stack Access (MHDI)
SA	Stage II Apparel [*AMEX symbol*] (TTSB)
SA	Stage II Apparel Corp. [*AMEX symbol*] (SPSG)
SA	Standard Accuracy [*Analytical chemistry*]
SA	Standard Addition
SA	Standard Agena [*NASA*] (KSC)
SA	Standards Australia
SA	Staphylococcus Aureus [*Microbiology*]
sA	Statampere [*Also, statA*] [*Unit of electric current*]
SA	State Agency [*Formerly, the Disability Determination Services*] [*Social Security Administration*] (OICC)
S/A	State Agent [*Insurance*]
SA	State Archives [*Australia*]
SA	State's Attorney
SA	Station Address [*Computer science*] (BUR)
SA	Stationary Afterglow [*Chemical kinetic*]
SA	Statocyst Anlage
S/A	Status and Alert (AAG)
SA	Statutes of Alberta [*Canada Information service or system*] (IID)
SA	Sternal Angie [*Anatomy*] (DAVI)
SA	Stokes-Adams [*Syndrome*] [*Medicine*]
SA	Stone Arch [*Bridges*]
SA	Storage Activity
SA	Storage Allocator [*Telecommunications*] (TEL)
S/A	Storage Area (KSC)
SA	Store Address
3A	Store Automation
SA	Stores Accountant [*British military*] (DMA)
SA	Stores Assistant [*British military*] (DMA)
SA	Stress Annual (ICSO)
SA	Stretch-Activated Ion Channel
SA	String Analysis (IAA)
SA	Structured Analysis [*Programming language*] [*1977*] (CSR)
SA	Students for America (EA)
SA	Studio Address (WDMC)
SA	Sturmabteilung [*German Political party*] (PPE)
SA	Styrene-Acrylonitrile [*Also, SAN*] [*Organic chemistry*]
SA	Subaccount (NASA)
SA	Sub Anno [*Under the Year*] [*Latin*]
SA	Subarachnoid [*Medicine*]
SA	Subassembly
SA	Subcontract Agreement (MCD)
SA	Subject to Approval
SA	Submerged Arc (OA)
SA	Subresolution Assist (AAEL)
SA	Subsequent Access (BYTE)
SA	Subsistence Allowance
SA	Substitution Authorization (AAG)
SA	Successive Approximation (IEEE)
SA	Succinylacetone [*Organic chemistry*]
S/A	Such As
SA	Sugar Association
SA	Sulfonamide
Sa	Summa [*or Summe*] [*Sum or Total*] [*Latin*]
SA	Summing Amplifier
SA	Sunshine Act (GNE)
SA	Super America [*Automobile model, Ferrari Motors*]
SA	Supervisory Authority
SA	Superwomen Anonymous [*Later, Overachievers Anonymous*] (EA)
SA	Supplemental Agreement (NG)
SA	Supply Accountant [*Navy British*]
SA	Supply Activity
SA	Supply Assistant (WDAA)
SA	Support Activity (MCD)
SA	Support Agency [*NASA*] (KSC)
SA	Support Area [*NASA*] (MCD)
SA	Supporting Arms [*Navy A publication*]
SA	Surface/Air (NATG)
SA	Surface Antigen [*Immunology*] (DAVI)
SA	Surface Area
SA	Surgeon's Assistant [*Medicine*]
SA	Surgical Anastomosis [*Medicine*]
SA	Surgical and Anesthesia Service (HCT)
SA	Surveillance Approach (FAAC)
S/A	Survivorship Agreement [*Legal term*] (DLA)
SA	Sustained Action [*Pharmacy*]
SA	Sweep, Acoustic [*British military*] (DMA)
SA	Sweet Adelines (EA)
SA	Swept Area [*Automotive engineering*]
SA	Swing Arm (KSC)
SA	Switching Assembly (IAA)
SA	Switching Devices [*JETDS nomenclature*] [*Military*] (CET)
SA	Symbolic Assembler (IEEE)
SA	Sympathetic Activity [*Physiology*]
SA	Synchro Amplifier
SA	System Administrator [*Computer science*]
SA	System Assessment
SA	Systemic Antibiotic [*Medicine*]
SA	Systemic Arterial [*Medicine*] (DB)
SA	Systemic Aspergillosis [*Medicine*] (DMAA)
SA	Systems Address
SA	Systems Analysis
SA	Systems Analyst
SA	Systems Architecture [*British*]
SA	VEB Farbenfabrik Wolfen [*East Germany*] [*Research code symbol*]
SAA	Safety Assurance Analysis (NASA)
SAA	Sakai [*Japan*] [*Seismograph station code, US Geological Survey Closed*] (SEIS)
SAA	Sales Automation Association (EA)
SAA	Santiago Capital [*Vancouver Stock Exchange symbol*]
SAA	Saratoga, WY [*Location identifier FAA*] (FAAL)
SAA	Satellite Active Archive [*Marine science*] (OSRA)
SAA	Satellite Attitude Acquisition
SAA	Saturn Apollo Applications [*NASA*] (KSC)
SAA	Saudia Arabia Airlines
SAA	S-Band Acquisition Antenna [*Deep Space Instrumentation Facility, NASA*]
SAA	Science and Applications [*NASA*] (SSD)
SAA	Scottish Aeromodellers Association (DBA)
SAA	Scottish Archery Association (DBA)
SAA	Scottish Assessors' Association (DBA)
SAA	Scout Association of Australia
SAA	Screen Advertising Association Ltd. [*British*] (BI)
SAA	Secretaries' Association of Australia
SAA	Senior Army Advisor
SAA	Serum Amyloid A [*Clinical chemistry*]
SAA	Service Action Analysis (AAG)
SAA	Servo-Actuated Assembly
SAA	Severe Aplastic Anemia [*Hematology*]
SAA	Sex Addicts Anonymous (EA)
SAA	Sexual Abuse Anonymous (EA)
SAA	Shakespeare Association of America (EA)
SAA	Shelter Advertising Association [*Minneapolis, MN*] (EA)
SAA	Sherman Anti-Trust Act (MHDR)
SAA	Signal Appliance Association [*Later, RSS*]
SAA	Simulated Accelerometer Assembly
SAA	Single Article Announcement [*American Chemical Society publication*]
SAA	Sisters Auxiliaries of the Apostolate (TOCD)
SAA	Slot Array Antenna
SAA	Small Arms Ammunition
SAA	Social Administration Association [*British*]
SAA	Society for Academic Achievement (EA)
SAA	Society for American Archaeology (EA)
SAA	Society for Applied Anthropology (AEBS)
SAA	Society for Asian Art (EA)
SAA	Society of American Archivists (EA)
SAA	Society of Animal Artists (EA)
SAA	Society of Archer-Antiquaries (EA)
SAA	Society of Architectural Administrators (EA)
SAA	Society of Automotive Analysts (EA)
SAA	Some American Artists [*An association*] (EA)
SAA	South African Airways [*ICAO designator*] (FAAC)
SAA	South African Alliance (PPW)
SAA	South Atlantic Anomaly [*NASA*] (KSC)
SAA	South Australian Artillery [*British military*] (DMA)
SAA	Southern Africa Association [*British*] (EAIO)
SAA	Southern Arts Association [*British*] (DBA)
SAA	Southern Ash Association [*Defunct*] (EA)
SAA	Special Arbitrage Account
SAA	Special Assignment Airlift [*Air Force*] (AFM)
SAA	Specialty Advertising Association [*Later, SAAI*]
SAA	Speech Association of America [*Later, SCA*] (EA)
SAA	Spondylitis Association of America (EA)
SAA	Sportswear Apparel Association (NTPA)
SAA	Sri Aurobindo Association (EA)
SAA	Staff Administrative Assistant [*Army*] (AABC)
SAA	Standards Association of Australia (BARN)
SAA	State Aboriginal Affairs [*South Australia*]
SAA	State Administrative Agency (GFGA)
SAA	State Applicant Agency (GFGA)
SAA	State Approving Agency [*Bureau of Apprenticeship and Training*] [*Department of Labor*]
SAA	Static Allegation Analyzer [*Computer science*]
SAA	Static Automated Analysis (AAEL)
SAA	Step Adjustable Antenna

SAA............. Stepfamily Association of America (EA)
SAA............. Stokes-Adams Attack [Medicine] (MAE)
SAA............. Sub-Aqua Association [British] (DBA)
SAA............. Summary Activity Account [Army] (AABC)
SAA............. Sunflower Association of America [Later, NSA] (EA)
SAA............. Sunglass Association of America (EA)
SAA............. Supima Association of America (EA)
SAA............. Supplemental Alert Adapter [AT&T] (ITD)
SAA............. Surety Association of America [Iselin, NJ] (EA)
SAA............. Surface Active Agents (ADA)
SAA............. Survival Air-to-Air (MCD)
SAA............. Suzuki Association of the Americas (EA)
SAA............. Swedish-American Association (NADA)
SAA............. Syrian Arab Airlines
SAA............. System Application Architecture [IBM Corp.]
SAAA........... Salvation Army Association of America (NADA)
SAAA........... San Antonio De Areco [Argentina ICAO location identifier] (ICLI)
SAAA........... Scottish Amateur Athletic Association
SAAABB...... Subcommittee on Accreditation of the American Association of Blood Banks (DAVI)
SAAARNG .... Senior Army Advisor, Army National Guard (AABC)
SAAB........... Selected and Amplified Binding [Sequence or site] [Genetics]
SAAB........... South African Archaeological Bulletin [A publication]
SAAB........... Svenska Aeroplan Aktiebolaget [Swedish automobile manufacturer; acronym used as name of its cars]
SAAC........... Concordia/Commodoro Pierrest Egui [Argentina ICAO location identifier] (ICLI)
SAAC........... Schedule Allocation and Control (NASA)
SA/AC......... Scientific Adviser to the Army Council [World War II]
SAAC........... Security Assistance Accounting Center [Military] (AFIT)
SAAC........... Seismic Array Analysis Center [IBM Corp.]
SAAC........... Shelby American Automobile Club (EA)
SAAC........... Simulator for Air-to-Air Combat [Air Force]
SAAC........... Society for the Advancement of Ambulatory Care [Defunct] (EA)
SAAC........... South American Athletic Confederation (EAIO)
SAAC........... Space Applications Advisory Committee
SAAC........... Special Assistant for Arms Control [Military]
SAAC........... Swiss-American Aircraft Corp. (IAA)
SAACCA...... South Australian Aboriginal Child Care Agency
SAACI......... Salesmen's Association of the American Chemical Industry [Later, SACI] (EA)
SAACONS .... Standard Army Automated Contracting System (RDA)
SAACT........ Surveillance and Accountability Control Team (MCD)
SAA/CUA...... Systems Application Architecture / Common User Access [Computer science]
SAAD .... Sacramento Army Depot [California] (AABC)
SAAD .... San Antonio Air Depot [Air Force]
SAAD .... Small Arms Ammunition Depot
SAAD .... Societe des Amis d'Alexandre Dumas (EA)
SAAD .... Society for the Advancement of Anaesthesia in Dentistry (EAIO)
SAAD .... Sperry Air Arm Division
SAAEB .... South African Atomic Energy Board
SAAF........... Saudi Arabian Air Force
SAAF........... Sherman Army Airfield [Fort Leavenworth, KS]
SAAF........... Sino-American Amity Fund (EA)
SAAF........... Small Arms Alignment Fixture [Weaponry] (INF)
SAAF........... Small Austere Air Field (MCD)
SAAF........... South African Air Force
SAAG .... Gualeguaychu [Argentina ICAO location identifier] (ICLI)
SAAG .... Science and Applications Advocacy Group
SAAG .... Steroid Action Aid Group [British] (DBA)
SAAGS........ Semi-Automated Artwork Generator System (PDAA)
SAAGTC ...... South Australian Association for Gifted and Talented Children
SAAHS .... Stability Augmentation Attitude Hold System [Aviation]
SAAI........... Punta Indio [Argentina ICAO location identifier] (ICLI)
SAAI........... Specialty Advertising Association International [Irving, TX] (EA)
SAAJ........... Junin [Argentina ICAO location identifier] (ICLI)
SAAL........... Single Address Assembly Machine Language [Computer science] (MCD)
SAAL........... Single-Axis Acoustic Levitator
SAAL........... South Australian Athletic League
SA-ALC .... San Antonio Air Logistics Center [Formerly, SAAMA] [Air Force] (NASA)
SAALCK ...... State Assisted Academic Library Council of Kentucky [Library network]
SAALC/MM... San Antonio Air Logistics Center, Directorate of Materiel Management [Kelly Air Force Base, TX]
SAAM.......... Mazaruca [Argentina ICAO location identifier] (ICLI)
SAAM.......... Selective Alpha Air Monitor [Environmental science] (COE)
SAAM.......... Simulation Analysis and Modeling
SAAM.......... Small-Animal Anesthesia Machine [Instrumentation]
SAAM.......... Special Air Force Airlift Mission (NASA)
SAAM.......... Special Assignment Airlift & Mission [MTMC] (TAG)
SAAM.......... Special Assignment Airlift Movement [Army] (AABC)
SAAM.......... Special Assignment Air Mission [Navy] (NVT)
SAAMA .... San Antonio Air Materiel Area [Later, SA-ALC] [Air Force]
SAAMI .... Sporting Arms and Ammunition Manufacturers Institute (EA)
SAAMS .... Special Airlift Assignment Missions [Military]
SAAMS .... Special Application Alarm Monitoring System
SAAN .... Pergamino [Argentina ICAO location identifier] (ICLI)
SAAN .... South African Associated Newspapers
SA&D.......... Structured Analysis and Design (CIST)
SA & F........ Southern Airlines and Freighters [Australia]
SA & MGS ... Small Arms and Machine Gun School [British military] (DMA)
SAAO .... South African Astronomical Observatory

SAAOC......... System of Analysis and Assignment of Operations according to Capacities (MHDI)
SAAP .... Parana/Gral Urquiza [Argentina ICAO location identifier] (ICLI)
SAAP .... Saranton Army Ammunition Plant (AABC)
SAAP .... Saturn Apollo Applications Program [NASA]
SAAP .... Selective Aortic Arch Perfusion [Medicine] (DMAA)
SAAP .... Society for the Advancement of American Philosophy (EA)
SAAP .... South Atlantic Anomaly Probe [NASA-CNAE]
SAAP .... South Australian Adoption Panel
SAAPBS ...... South Australian Association of Permanent Building Societies
SAAPCC...... South African Administrative Pay and Clerical Corps [British military] (DMA)
SAAPE .... Scottish Association of Advisers in Physical Education (DBA)
SAAPSA ...... South Australian Apple and Pear Shippers' Association
SAAR .... Rosario [Argentina ICAO location identifier] (ICLI)
SAAR .... Saw Arbor [Tool]
SAAR .... Seasonally Adjusted Annual Retail [Automotive sales]
SAAR .... Solar Aureole Almucantar Radiance (PDAA)
SAARC .... South Asian Association for Regional Cooperation
SAARD .... Slow-Acting Antirheumatic Drug [Pharmacy]
SAARD's ..... Slow-Acting Antirheumatic Drugs [Medicine]
SAARF .... Special Allied Airborne Reconnaissance Force [Teams parachuted into POW areas to take supplies to prisoners or to help them get out] [World War II]
SAAS .... School of Applied Aerospace Sciences [Air Force]
SAAS .... Science Achievement Awards for Students
SAAS .... Scottish Agricultural Statistics Service [University of Edinburgh] (IRC)
SAAS .... Shuttle Aerosurface Actuator Simulation [NASA] (NAKS)
SAAS .... Shuttle Aerosurface Actuator Simulator [NASA] (MCD)
SAAS .... Society for the Advancement of Agricultural Studies [British]
SAAS .... Society of African and Afro-American Students
SAAS .... Soldier as a System [Symposium] (RDA)
SAAS .... Something about the Author Autobiography Series [A publication]
SAAS .... Southern Association of Agricultural Scientists (EA)
SAAS .... Special Ammunition and Analysis Section [Picatinny Arsenal] [Dover, NJ]
SAAS .... Standard Army Ammunition System (AABC)
SAAS .... Stress Analysis of Axisymmetric Solids (MCD)
SAASC .... San Antonio Air Service Command [Air Force]
SAASRA...... South Australian Aboriginal Sports and Recreation Association
SAAST .... Self-Administered Alcoholism Screening Test
SAASW .... Sub-Antarctic Surface Water [Marine science] (MSC)
SAAT........... Satellite Attitude Acquisition Technique
SAAT........... Society of Architects and Associated Technicians [British] (BI)
SAAT........... Systems Analyst Aptitude Test
SAATE......... South Australian Association for the Teaching of English
SAATMS ...... Satellite-Based Advanced Air Traffic Management System [Department of Transportation]
SAATSC ...... San Antonio Air Technical Service Command [Air Force]
SAAU .... Selfreliance Association of American Ukrainians (EA)
SAAU .... Swiss Association of Autonomous Unions
SAAU .... Villaguay [Argentina ICAO location identifier] (ICLI)
SAAUSAR .... Senior Army Advisor, United States Army Reserve (AABC)
SAAV .... Santa Fe/Sauce Viejo [Argentina ICAO location identifier] (ICLI)
SAAVQ........ Societe des Artistes en Arts Visuels du Quebec [1980, founded 1966 as SAPQ, CPQ from 1978, CAPQ from 1982] [Canada] (NGC)
SAAVS .... Submarine Acceleration and Velocity System
SAAWC .... Sector Antiair Warfare Coordinator [Center] (NVT)
SAAWPA...... South Australian Amateur Water Polo Association
SAAX .... Saturn Airways, Inc. [Air carrier designation symbol]
SAB............. Saba [Netherlands Antilles] [Airport symbol] (OAG)
SAB............. Saba Petroleum [AMEX symbol] (TTSB)
SAB............. Saba Petroleum Co. [AMEX symbol] (SAG)
SAB............. Sabbath
SAB............. SABENA [Societe Anonyme Belge d'Exploitation de la Nav Aerienne] [Belgium ICAO designator] (FAAC)
SAB............. Sabhawala [India] [Geomagnetic observatory code]
Sab............. Sabinus [Flourished, 5th or 6th century] [Authority cited in pre-1607 legal work] (DSA)
SAB............. Sabotage [FBI standardized term]
SAB............. Sabouraud Dextrose Agar [Microbiology]
SAB............. Safety Advisory Board [National Science Foundation] (NUCP)
SAB............. Same as Above
SAB............. Same as Basic (KSC)
SAB............. Satellite Assembly Building (MCD)
SAB............. School of American Ballet [New York]
SAB............. Science Advisory Board [Environmental Protection Agency]
SAB............. Scientific Advisory Board [Air Force]
SAB............. Sealed Argon Bubbling [Steelmaking]
SAB............. Sensor/Actuator Bus (AAEL)
SAB............. Service Area Boundary [Telecommunications] (OTD)
SAB............. Shuttle Avionics Breadboard [NASA] (NASA)
SAB............. Signal Aviation Branch
SAB............. Significant Asymptomatic Bacteriuria [Medicine] (MAE)
SAB............. Silk Association of Great Britain (EAIO)
SAB............. Sisters of St. Anne Bangalore (TOCD)
SAB............. Site Activation Board [NASA] (KSC)
SAB............. Snap Action Bimetal [Automotive engineering]
SAB............. Societe Anonyme Belge d'Exploitation de la Navigation Aerienne [Sabena Belgian World Airlines]
SAB............. Society for Applied Bacteriology (EA)
SAB............. Society of American Bacteriologists [Later, ASM]
SAB............. Solar Alignment Bay (OA)
SAB............. Solar Array Batteries
SAB............. Solid Assembly Building

SAB.............	Soprano, Alto, Bass
SAB.............	South African Breweries [*Commercial firm*]
SAB.............	South Atlantic Bight [*A region off the southeastern coast of the United States*] [*Geography*]
SAB.............	Space Applications Board [*National Academy of Engineering*]
SAB.............	Spacecraft Assembly Building [*NASA*] (MCD)
SAB.............	Special Antarctic Blend [*Fuel*]
SAB.............	Special Assessment Bond
SAB.............	Specific Adaptive Strategy (EDAC)
SAB.............	Speech Adaptor Box (NITA)
SAb.............	Spontaneous Abortion [*Medicine*] (DMAA)
SAB.............	Spontaneous Abortion (DAVI)
SAB.............	Stack Access Block
SAB.............	Staff Accounting Bulletins [*Securities and Exchange Commission*] (EBF)
SAB.............	Statistics and Analysis Branch [*Public Health Service*] [*Information service or system*] (IID)
SAB.............	Storage and Assembly Building [*NASA*] (NASA)
SAB.............	Strategic Assessment Branch [*Office of Oceanography and Marine Assessment*] [*National Oceanic and Atmospheric Administration*]
SAB.............	Structural Adhesive Bond
SAB.............	Subarachnoid Bleed [*Neurology*] (DAVI)
SAB.............	Subarachnoid Block [*Medicine*] (MAE)
SAB.............	Subject as Above [*Military*] (AABC)
SAB.............	Support Activities Building [*National Security Agency*]
SAB.............	Supporting Assistance Bureau [*Agency for International Development*]
SAB.............	Sync Address Bus (IAA)
SAB.............	System Advisory Board
SAB.............	Systems Analysis Branch (IAA)
SABA	Buenos Aires [*Argentina ICAO location identifier*] (ICLI)
SABA	Scottish Amateur Boxing Association [*British*] (DBA)
SABA	Serbian-American Bar Association (EA)
SABA	Small, Able Battlefield Aircraft [*Military British*]
SABA	Small Agile Battlefield Aircraft [*British Aerospace Ltd.*]
SABA	Society for the Advancement of Behavior Analysis (EA)
SABA	South African Black Alliance [*Political party*] (PPW)
SABA	South Australian Badminton Association
SABA	South Australian Bowling Association
SABA	Swimmer's Air Breathing Apparatus [*Deep-sea diving*]
SabaPet........	Saba Petroleum [*Associated Press*] (SAG)
SABAR	Satellites, Balloons, and Rockets [*Air Force program*]
SABB	Santa Barbara Bancorp [*NASDAQ symbol*] (TTSB)
SABBA	System Analysis - Building Block Approach [*Ge Cae International and Gen-Red Ltd.*] [*Software package*] (NCC)
SABC	Buenos Aires (Edificio Condor) [*Argentina ICAO location identifier*] (ICLI)
SABC	South African Broadcasting Corp.
SABC	South Alabama Bancorp [*NASDAQ symbol*] (SAG)
SABC	South Australia Brewing Co. [*Commercial firm*]
SABCO	Society for the Area of Biological and Chemical Overlap
SABDR.........	South Australian Birth Defects Registry
SABE............	Buenos Aires/Aeroparque, Jorge Newbery [*Argentina ICAO location identifier*] (ICLI)
SABE............	Society for Automating Better Education (IAA)
SABE............	Society for Automation in Business Education [*Later, SDE*] (EA)
SABE............	Spanish Assessment of Basic Education [*Test*] (TMMY)
SABENA	Societe Anonyme Belge d'Exploitation de la Navigation Aerienne [*Belgian World Airlines*] [*Facetious translation: Such a Bad Experience, Never Again*]
SABER	SECNAV [*Secretary of the Navy*] Advisory Board on Educational Requirements (NG)
SABER	Simplified Acquisition of Base Engineering Requirements [*Air Force*]
SABER	Surface-to-Air Beam Rider (MCD)
SABER	Swing-Arm Beam Erector (MCD)
SABET.........	SECNAV [*Secretary of the Navy*] Advisory Board on Education and Training [*Pensacola, FL*] (EGAO)
SABEU	Scottish Adult Basic Education Unit (AIE)
SABEW	Society of American Business Editors and Writers [*Columbia, MO*] (EA)
SABF...........	Subarray Beam Former [*Computer science*] (MHDI)
SABFV	Secondary Air Anti-Backfire Valve [*Automotive engineering*]
SABH...........	South Australian Brewing Holdings [*Commercial firm*]
SABHI.........	Sabouraud Dextrose Agar and Brain-Heart Infusion [*Microbiology*]
SaBi............	La Sacra Bibbia [*Turin*] [*A publication*] (BJA)
SABI............	Swiss Army Brands [*NASDAQ symbol*] [*Formerly, Forschner Group*] (SG)
SABINE	Systeme d'Acces a la Banque Informatique des Nomenclatures Europeennes [*Database*] [*EC*] (ECED)
SABINET......	South African Bibliographical and Information Network (NITA)
SABIR	Semiautomatic Bibliographic Information Retrieval
SABIRS........	Semiautomatic Bibliographic Information Retrieval System (DIT)
SABL...........	Serialized Assembly Breakdown List (SAA)
SABL...........	South Australian Bookmakers' League
SABLE.........	Semiautomatic BOMARC Local Environment (MCD)
SABM...........	Buenos Aires (Servicio Meteorologico Nacional) [*Argentina ICAO location identifier*] (ICLI)
SABM...........	Set Asynchronous Balanced Mode
SA/BM	Systems Analysis and Battle Management [*Military*] (RDA)
SABMAR	Service-Craft and Boats Machine Accounting Report [*Navy*] (NG)
SABME.........	Set Asynchronous Balanced Mode Extended [*Telecommunications*] (OSI)
SABMIS.......	Sea-Based Antiballistic Missile (IAA)
SABMIS.......	Seaborne [*or Ship-Launched*] Antiballistic Missile Intercept System [*Navy*]
SABMS	Safeguard Antiballistic Missile System [*Military*] (WDAA)
SabnR..........	Sabine Royalty Trust [*Associated Press*] (SAG)
SABO	Sense Amplifier Blocking Oscillator
SABOC	SAGE [*Semiautomatic Ground Environment*] BOMARC [*Boeing-Michigan Aeronautical Research Center*] (IAA)
SABOD........	Same as Basic Operations Directive (KSC)
SABOR........	Same as Basic Or (MUGU)
SABOSE......	SECNAV [*Secretary of the Navy*] Advisory Board on Scientific Education (DNAB)
SABP	Salicylic Acid Binding Protein [*Biochemistry*]
SABP	Skeletal Axis of Basal Piece
SABP	Spontaneous Acute Bacterial Peritonitis [*Medicine*]
SABR	Society for American Baseball Research (EA)
SABR	Symbolic Assembler for Binary Relocatable Programs
SABRA	Surface Activation Beneath Reaction Adhesives (EDCT)
SABRAC	Sabra Computer (DNAB)
Sabratek......	Sabratek Corp. [*Associated Press*] (SAG)
SABRE	SAGE [*Semiautomatic Ground Environment*] Battery Routing Equipment
SABRE	Sales and Business Reservations Done Electronically
SABRE	Secure Airborne RADAR Bombing Equipment (IAA)
SABRE	Secure Airborne RADAR Equipment
SABRE	Self-Aligning Boost and Reentry [*Air Force*]
SABRE	Semiautomated Business Research Environment [*Computerized reservation network*] [*American Airlines*]
SABRE	Single Army Battlefield Requirements Evaluator [*Army*]
SABRE	South Atlantic Bight Recruitment Experiment [*Marine science*] (OSRA)
SABRE	Steerable Adaptive Broadcast Reception Equipment (PDAA)
SABRE	Store Access Bus Recording Equipment [*Telecommunications*] (TEL)
SABRE	Sweden and Britain RADAR Auroral Experiment [*Ionospheric physics*]
SABRE	System for Autonomous Bodies Reporting and Evaluation [*Joint project of the Government of Bangladesh and United Nations Department of Technical Co-operation for Development*] [*Information service or system*]
SabreGr.......	Sabre Group Holdings, Inc. (The) [*Associated Press*] (SAG)
SABRES	Share Adjusted Broker Remarketed Equity Securities (EBF)
SABRF........	Skeletal Axis of Branchial Filament
SABRI.........	Serikat Buruh Rokok Indonesia [*Cigarette Workers' Union of Indonesia*]
SABRITA......	South Africa - Britain Trade Association (DBA)
SABRS	Social Adjustment Behavior Rating Scale [*Psychology*] (DB)
SABRS	Standard Accounting, Budgeting, and Reporting System [*Military*] (GFGA)
SABS	Congregation of the Sisters of the Adoration of the Blessed Sacrament [*Kerala, India*] (EAIO)
S/ABS	Shock Absorber [*Automotive engineering*]
SABS	South African Bureau of Standards [*National standards organization*]
SABS	Stabilizing Automatic Bomb Sight
SABS	Stanford Automated Bibliographic Systems (NITA)
SABSA	South Australian Brake Specialist Association
SABU	SAGE [*Semiautomatic Ground Environment*] Back-Up (IAA)
SABU	Self-Adjusting Ball-Up [*A state of confusion which may, or may not, clear up of itself*] [*Military slang*]
SABU	Semi-Automatic Back-Up [*Military*] (IAA)
SABV	Secondary Air Bypass Valve [*Automotive engineering*]
SABW	Society of American Business Writers [*Later, SABEW*]
Sac	De Sacrificiis Abelis et Caini [*Philo*] (BJA)
SAC............	Pallotine Missionary Sisters Queen of Apostles Prov (TOCD)
SAC............	Saccharin [*Sweetening agent*]
SAC............	Sacramento [*California*] [*Airport symbol*] (AD)
SAC............	Sacramento, CA [*Location identifier FAA*] (FAAL)
SAC............	Sacrifice [*Baseball*]
SAC............	Sacrifice [*Classified advertising*]
SAC............	Sacristan
SAC............	Safety Advisory Committee (MCD)
SAC............	Sahali Resources, Inc. [*Vancouver Stock Exchange symbol*]
SAC............	Saint Ambrose College [*Davenport, IA*]
SAC............	Saint Anselm's College [*Manchester, NH*]
SAC............	Saint Anselm's College, Manchester, NH [*OCLC symbol*] (OCLC)
SAC............	Saint Augustine's College [*Raleigh, NC*]
SAC............	Salute America Committee (EA)
SAC............	San Andreas Lake [*California*] [*Seismograph station code, US Geological Survey*] (SEIS)
SAC............	San Antonio College [*Texas*]
SAC............	Santa Ana College [*California*]
SAC............	Scene-of-Action Commander [*Navy*] (NVT)
SAC............	School of Army Co-Operation [*Air Force British*]
SAC............	Scientific Advisory Committee [*Presidential*] [*Terminated*]
SAC............	Scientific Advisory Council [*Ministry of Supply*] [*British World War II*]
SAC............	Scottish Arts Council (EAIO)
SAC............	Scottish Automobile Club (DI)
SAC............	Scriptomatic Addressing Computer (HGAA)
SAC............	Secondary Accountability Center (AAG)
SAC............	Secondary Address Code
SAC............	Sectional Aeronautical Chart (NOAA)
SAC............	Security Access Control [*Computer science*]
SAC............	Self-Adjusting Clutch
SAC............	Semiautomatic Coding
SAC............	Semiautomatic Controller (CAAL)
SAC............	Senate Appropriations Committee (NVT)
SAC............	Senior Aircraftman [*British military*] (DMA)
SAC............	Service Application Code [*Navy*]
SAC............	Service Area Computer (IAA)

SAC	Serving Area Concept [*Bell System*]
SAC	Servo Adapter Coupler
SAC	Shipbuilding Advisory Council [*British*]
SAC	Ships Air Coordinator (MCD)
SAC	Short-Arm Cast [*Orthopedics*] (DAVI)
SAC	Side-Arm Controller [*Aviation*]
SAC	Signal Analysis Course [*Navy*] (DNAB)
SAC	Signature Authorization Card [*or Chart*] (AAG)
SAC	Single Acting Cylinder
SAC	Single Address Code (AAG)
SAC	Sisters of the Holy Guardian Angels [*Roman Catholic religious order*]
SAC	Soaring Association of Canada
SAC	Social and Athletic Club
SAC	Sociedad Anglo-Chilena [*Anglo-Chilean Society*] (EAIO)
SAC	Societe Africaine de Culture [*Society of African Culture*]
SAC	Society for American Cuisine [*Later, SCA*] (EA)
SAC	Society for Analytical Chemistry [*British*]
SAC	Society for Analytical Cytology (EA)
SAC	Society of African Culture [*France*] (EAIO)
SAC	Society of the Catholic Apostolate [*Pallottines*] [*Roman Catholic men's religious order*]
sac	Society of the Catholic Apostolate, Pallottine Fathers (TOCD)
SAC	South-African Constabulary [*Military British Defunct*] (ROG)
SAC	South Atlantic Coast
SAC	South Atlantic Conference (PSS)
SAC	South Australian Club
SAC	South Carolina Electric & Gas Co. [*NYSE symbol*] (SPSG)
SAC	Southern Africa Committee (EA)
SAC	Southwest Athletic Conference (EA)
SAC	Special Accounting Class [*Navy*] (DNAB)
SAC	Special Advisory Committee [*Navy*] (DNAB)
SAC	Special Agent in Charge [*FBI*]
SAC	Special Analysis Center [*Marine science*] (OSRA)
SAC	Special Area Code [*Bell System*]
SAC	Specialty Aromatic Compound [*Organic chemistry*]
SAC	Specific Acoustic Capacitance
SAC	Spectrum Analyzer Component (MCD)
SAC	Spiritual Advisory Council (EA)
SAC	Sport for All Clearinghouse [*Belgium*] (EAIO)
SAC	Sprayed Acoustical Ceiling [*Technical drawings*]
S/AC	Stabilization/Attitude Control [*NASA*] (NASA)
SAC	Standard Agena Clamshell [*NASA*] (KSC)
SAC	Standard Aircraft Characteristics
SAC	Standing Armaments Committee [*NATO*] (NATG)
SAC	Staphylococcus Aureus Cervan [*Microbiology*]
SAC	Starptautiskas Apmainas Centrs [*International Exchange Center*] [*Latvia*] (EAIO)
SAC	Starting Air Compressor (CAAL)
SAC	State Advisory Committee [*Department of Education*]
SAC	State Apprenticeship Council [*Bureau of Apprenticeship and Training*] [*Department of Labor*]
SAC	Statistical Advisory Committee [*UN Food and Agriculture Organization*]
SAC	Statistical Analysis Center (OICC)
SAC	Storage Access Channel (CMD)
SAC	Storage Access Control [*Computer science*]
SAC	Storage Access Counter (IAA)
SAC	Storage Address Counter (IAA)
SAC	Store Access Controller (NITA)
SAC	Store and Clear
SAC	Store and Clear Accumulator [*Computer science*]
SAC	Storeman's Action Copy (DNAB)
SAC	Strategic Air Command [*Air Force*]
SAC	Strategic Alert Cadre (NVT)
SAC	Student Access Centre [*Australia*]
SAC	Subarea Advisory Council [*Generic term*] (DHSM)
SAC	Submitting Activity Code
SAC	Substance Abuse Coordinator [*Navy*] (DNAB)
SAC	Sudanese Aeronautical Services Co. Ltd. [*Sudan*] [*ICAO designator*] (FAAC)
SAC	Sudanese African Congress [*Political party*] (MENA)
SAC	Sudania Aviation Co. [*Sudan*] [*ICAO designator*] (FAAC)
SAC	Sugar Association of the Caribbean [*Port Of Spain, Trinidad*] (EAIO)
SAC	Sulfuric Acid Concentrate (MCD)
SAC	Sunbeam Alpine Club (EA)
SAC	Suore Missionarie dell'Apostolato Cattolico [*Missionary Sisters of the Catholic Apostolate*] [*Rome, Italy*] (EAIO)
SAC	Supplemental Air Carrier (MCD)
SAC	Supply Administration Center [*DoD*] (MCD)
SAC	Supply Availability Card (MCD)
SAC	Support Action Center [*NASA*] (MCD)
SAC	Support Assessment Capability
SAC	Supporting Arms Coordinator [*Air Force*] (NVT)
SAC	Supreme Allied Command [*or Commander*] [*Headquarters in London*] [*World War II*]
SAC	Surface-Area-Center [*Mechanical engineering*]
SAC	Surveillance Airplane Company [*Army*] (VNW)
SAC	Surveyors Appointments Consultancy [*Royal Institute of Chartered Surveyors*] [*British*]
SAC	Suspended and Canceled Pesticides [*Environmental Protection Agency*] (GFGA)
SAC	Sustained Abdominal Compression [*Gastroenterology*]
SAC	Sveriges Arbetares Centralorganisation [*Central Organization of Swedish Workers*]
SAC	Synchro Azimuth Converter
SAC	Synchronous Astro Compass (SAA)
SAC	System Assessment Capability
SAC	System Automation Corp. [*Information service or system*] (IID)
SAC	Systems Acquisition Career
SAC	Systems Auditability and Control [*Computer science*]
SACA	Cordoba/Area de Material [*Argentina ICAO location identifier*] (ICLI)
SACA	Service Action Change Analysis (AAG)
SACA	South Australian Council on the Ageing
SACA	Special Assistant for Consumer Affairs [*White House*] [*Obsolete*]
SACA	Steam Automobile Club of America (EA)
SACA	Studebaker Automobile Club of America (EA)
SACA	Student Action Corps for Animals (EA)
SACA	Study Advisory Committee on Aeronautics [*National Academy of Engineering*]
SACA(A)	Subversive Activities Control Act of 1950
SAC(A)	Supporting Arms Coordinator (Airborne) [*Marine Corps*] (DOMA)
SACACCS	Strategic Air Command Automated Command Control System (AFM)
SACAD	Stress Analysis and Computer-Aided Design [*Computer science*] (WDAA)
SACAM	Ship Acquisition Contract Administration Manual (MCD)
SACAM	South Australian Committee on Access and Mobility
SACAY	SECNAV [*Secretary of the Navy*] Advisory Commission on Youth (NG)
SACB	Somalia Aid Coordination Body
SACB	Subversive Activities Control Board [*Later, Federal Internal Security Board*]
SACBA	South Australian Cat Breeders' Association
SACBC	South Australian Children's Ballet Company
SACBC	Southern African Catholic Bishops' Conference (EAIO)
SACBC-JPC	Southern African Catholic Bishops' Conference - Justice and Peace Commission (EAIO)
sacc	Cogwheel [*Respiration*] [*Medicine*] (DAVI)
SACC	La Cumbre [*Argentina ICAO location identifier*] (ICLI)
SACC	San Antonio Contracting Center [*Air Force*]
SACC	School Age Child Care
S/ACC	Scientific/Academic Computing Center [*State University of New York Health Science Center at Brooklyn*] [*Research center*] (RCD)
SACC	Shore ASW [*Antisubmarine Warfare*] Command Center (DOMA)
SACC	Slovak-American Cultural Center (EA)
SACC	Society for Anthropology in Community Colleges (EA)
SACC	Society of All Cargo Correspondents [*British*] [*An association*] (DBA)
SACC	State Auditors Coordinating Committee (EA)
SACC	Supplemental Air Carrier Conference [*Defunct*] (EA)
SACC	Supporting Arms Coordination Center [*Air Force*]
SACC	Systems Acquisition Contracting Course (AAGC)
SACCAR	Southern African Centre for Co-Operation in Agricultural Research (EY)
SACCEI	Strategic Air Command Communications-Electronics Instruction
SACCH	Saccharatae [*Sugar-Coated*] [*Pharmacy*]
SACCHS	Scottish Advisory Committee on Computers in the Health Service
SACCI	Swiss-Australian Chamber of Commerce and Industry [*Australia*]
SACCM	Slow Access Charge-Coupled Memory [*Computer science*] (PDAA)
SACCOM	Strategic Air Command Communications (MCD)
SACCOMNET	Strategic Air Command Communications Network
SACCON	Strategic Air Command Command Control Network
SACCP	Strategic Air Command Command Post
SACCS	Schedule and Cost-Control System (MHDB)
SACCS	Shipping and Air Cargo Commodity Statistics [*Australia*]
SACCS	Strategic Air Command Communications [*or Control*] System [*Military*]
SACCS	Strategic Army Command and Control Software [*Computer science Army*] (RDA)
SACCS-DPS	SAC [*Strategic Air Command*] Automated Command Control System - Data Processing System (MCD)
SACC-USA	Swedish-American Chamber of Commerce in the United States of America (NTPA)
SACD	Coronel Olmedo [*Argentina ICAO location identifier*] (ICLI)
SACD	Societe des Auteurs et Compositeurs Dramatiques [*Society of Dramatic Authors and Composers*] [*Paris, France*] (EAIO)
SACD	Society of Americans of Colonial Descent [*Defunct*] (EA)
SACD	Subacute Combined Degeneration [*of spinal cord*] [*Medicine*] (AAMN)
SACDA	Surplus Agricultural Commodities Disposal Act of 1982
SACDEF	Strategic Avionics Crewstation Design Evaluation Facility
SACDIN	Strategic Air Command Digital Information Network (MCD)
SACDM	Study and Action Course in District Management [*LIMRA*]
SACDNU	Sudan African Closed Districts National Union
SAC(DP)	Scientific Advisory Committee, Defence Services Panel [*British World War II*]
SACDRS	Standard Air Carrier Delay Reporting System
SACDU	Switch and Cable Distribution Unit (IAA)
SACE	Cordoba [*Argentina ICAO location identifier*] (ICLI)
SACE	Semiautomatic Checkout Equipment [*DoD*]
SACE	Serum Angiotensin Converting Enzyme [*Activity*] [*Serology*]
SACE	Shore-Based Acceptance Checkout Equipment
SACEA	Sino-American Cultural and Economic Association
SACEM	Society for the Advancement of Continuing Education for Ministry (EA)
SACEM	Society of Authors, Composers, and Editors of Music (NADA)
SACEP	South Asian Cooperative Environment Programme (GNE)
SACEUR	Supreme Allied Commander, Europe [*NATO*]
SACEUR	Supreme Allied Command, Europe [*World War II*] (NADA)
SACEUREP	Supreme Allied Commander, Europe Representative [*NATO*] (NATG)
SACEX	Supporting Arms Coordination Exercise (DOMA)
SACF	Cordoba [*Argentina ICAO location identifier*] (ICLI)

SACF............ Single Association Control Function [*Telecommunications*] (OSI)
SACF .... South Australian Cycling Federation
SACFA .... South Australian Canning Fruitgrowers' Association
SACFI.......... Scholars and Citizens for Freedom of Information (EA)
SACFS .... South Australian Country Fire Service
SACFVI .... South Australian Chamber of Fruit and Vegetable Industries
SACG .... Cordoba [*Argentina ICAO location identifier*] (ICLI)
SACG .... Senior Arms Control Group [*National Security Council*]
SACH .... Small Animal Care Hospital [*Medicine*] (DMAA)
SACH .... Solid Ankle Cushion Heel [*Foot prosthesis*]
SACHC .... Soviet-American Committee on Health Cooperation
SACHD .... South Australian Centre for Human Development
SACHQ........ Strategic Air Command Headquarters (AAG)
Sachse NM... Sachse's Minutes, Norwich Mayoralty Court [*A publication*] (DLA)
SACHT .... Serum Antichromotrypsin (STED)
SACI............ Pilar [*Argentina ICAO location identifier*] (ICLI)
SACI............ Sales Association of the Chemical Industry (EA)
SACI............ Secondary Address Code Indicator
SACI............ South Atlantic Cooperative Investigations [*Military*]
SACI............ Special Assistant for Contracting Integrity (AAGC)
sac-il .... Sacroiliac (STED)
SACIM .... Society in Aid of Children Inoperable in their Motherland [*Australia*]
SACIM .... Southern African Center for Ivory Marketing
SACK .... Scientific Advisory Committee on Kangaroos [*Australia*]
SACK .... Selection Acknowledge [*Computer science*] (MHDB)
SACL........... Laguna Larga [*Argentina ICAO location identifier*] (ICLI)
SACL........... South African Confederation of Labour
SACL........... Space and Component Log
SACL........... Standards and Calibration Laboratory (KSC)
SACL........... Stress and Arousal Adjective Checklist (PDAA)
SACLAMP .... Strategic Air Command Low-Altitude Missile Program [*Air Force*]
SACLANT .... Supreme Allied Commander, Atlantic [*NATO*]
SACLANTCEN... Supreme Allied Atlantic Command Anti-Submarine Warfare Research Centre [*NATO*] [*Italy*]
SACLANTCEN... Supreme Allied Commander, Atlantic, Antisubmarine Warfare Research Center [*NATO*]
SACLANTREPEUR... Supreme Allied Commander, Atlantic, Representative in Europe [*NATO*]
SACLAU .... SACLANT [*Supreme Allied Commander, Atlantic*] Authentification System [*NATO*] (NATG)
SACLEX........ SACLANT [*Supreme Allied Commander, Atlantic*] Standing Exercise Orders [*NATO*] (NATG)
Sac Lit D .... Doctor of Sacred Literature
SACLO .... Strategic Air Command Liaison Officer
SACLOS ...... Semiautomatic Command to Line of Sight [*Military*]
SACM........... School of Acquisition Management [*Army*]
SACM........... Simulated Aerial Combat Maneuver
SACM........... South Australian Centre for Manufacturing
SACM........... Statistical Adiabatic Channel Model [*Physical chemistry*]
SACM........... Strategic Air Command Manual (IAA)
SACM........... Strategic Air Command Missile (IAA)
SACM........... Superfund Accelerated Cleanup Model [*Environmental science*] (BCP)
SACM........... Villa Gral, Mitre [*Argentina ICAO location identifier*] (ICLI)
SACMA .... Suppliers of Advanced Composite Materials
SACMA .... Suppliers of Advanced Composite Materials Association [*Arlington, VA*] (EA)
SACMAP ..... Selective Automatic Computational Matching and Positioning (MCD)
SACMAPS.... Selective Automatic Computational Matching and Positioning System
SACMC .... South Australian Chicken Meat Council
SACMDR ..... Site Activation Commander [*Army*] (AABC)
SACME........ South Australian Chamber of Mines and Energy
SACMED ..... Supreme Allied Commander, Mediterranean [*World War II*]
SAC/MEP .... Strategic Air Command/Minuteman Education Program (AFM)
SACMFCS .... Small Arms Common Module Fire Control System [*Army*]
SACMP .... South African Corps of Military Police [*British military*] (DMA)
SACMPC ..... Systems Acquisition Career Management Personnel Center [*DoD*]
SACMPC ...... Systems Acquisition Career Management Program for Civilians (AAGC)
SACN .... Ascochinga [*Argentina ICAO location identifier*] (ICLI)
SACNA .... South Africa Club of North America [*Defunct*] (EA)
SACNAS....... Society for Advancement of Chicanos and Native Americans in Science (EA)
SACNET ...... Secure Automatic Communications Network
SACNSW...... Society for Arts and Crafts New South Wales [*Australia*]
SACO .... Cordoba [*Argentina ICAO location identifier*] (ICLI)
SACO .... Select Address and Contract Operate
SACO .... Service Administratif Canadien aux Organismes (AC)
SACO .... Service Administratif Canadien Outre-Mer [*Canadian Executive Service Overseas - CESO*]
SACO .... Sino American Cooperative Organization (EA)
SACO .... Subject Authority Cooperative Program [*American Library Association*]
SACO .... Supporting Administrative Contracting Officer (AFIT)
SACO .... Sveriges Akademikers Centralorganisation [*Swedish Confederation of Professional Associations*]
SACOA........ Southern Appalachian Coal Operators Association (EA)
SAC-OA....... Strategic Air Command Office of Operations Analysis
SACOD .... South African Congress of Democrats
SACOM .... SECNAV [*Secretary of the Navy*] Advisory Commission on Manpower (NG)
SACOM .... Senior Aircraft Communicator (IAA)
SACOM .... Ship's Advanced Communications (IAA)
SACOM .... Southern Area Command [*Military*] (AABC)
SACON......... Shock-Absorbing Concretes (RDA)

SACON .... Shock Attenuating Cellular Concrete [*Army*]
SACON......... Structural Analysis Consultant (MCD)
SACOPD....... Smoking-Attributable Chronic Obstructive Pulmonary Disease
SACOPS....... Strategic Air Command Operational Planning System (MCD)
SACP .... Chepes [*Argentina ICAO location identifier*] (ICLI)
SACP .... Sacrificial Anode Cathodic Protection (MCD)
SACP .... Scottish Association of Children's Panels (DBA)
SACP .... Selected Area Channelling Pattern (MCD)
SACP .... Society for Ambulatory Care Professionals (NTPA)
SACP .... Society for Asian and Comparative Philosophy (EA)
SACP .... South African Communist Party
SACP .... Special Assistant for Civilian Personnel [*Navy*] (DNAB)
SACP .... Strategic Air Command Project Office (AAG)
SACPAN ...... Stemming and Closure Panel [*Terminated, 1975*] [*DoD*] (EGAO)
SACP/EEO ... Special Assistant for Civilian Personnel / Equal Employment Opportunity [*Navy*] (DNAB)
SACPG .... Senior Arms Control Planning Group [*Pronounced "sack pig"*] [*DoD*]
SACPMC ..... Systems Acquisition Career Management Program for Civilians [*Air Force*] (DOMA)
SACPO .... Saigon Area Civilian Personnel Office [*Vietnam*]
SACPO .... South African Colored People's Organization
SACPPL .... Standing Advisory Committee on Private Pilot Licensing [*British*] (AIA)
SACPr .... So.Carolina E&G 5% cmPfd [*NYSE symbol*] (TTSB)
SACPX .... Salomon Bros. Capital Fund [*Mutual fund ticker symbol*] (SG)
SACQ .... Monte Quemado [*Argentina ICAO location identifier*] (ICLI)
SACQ .... Student Adaptation to College Questionaire [*Test*] [*Baker and Siryk*] (TES)
SACR .... Sacrament (ROG)
SACR .... Sacred (ROG)
SACR .... Sacrifice (ROG)
SACR .... Sacrist
SACR .... Semiautomatic Coordinate Reader (DNAB)
SACR .... Strategic Air Command Regulations (AAG)
SACRA .... Student Alliance for Christian Renewal in America
SACRE .... Standing Advisory Council for Religious Education (AIE)
SACRE .... Standing Advisory Council on Religious Education [*British*] (DET)
SACRO .... Scottish Association of Care and Resettlement Offenders (DBA)
SACROC....... Scurry Area Canyon Reef Operators Committee
SACS .... Satellite Attitude-Control Simulator [*NASA*]
SACS .... Satellite Control Squadron
SACS .... Scheduling Activity Control System [*PA Computers & Telecommunications Ltd.*] [*Software package*] (NCC)
SACS .... Secondary Anticoagulation System [*Medicine*] (DMAA)
SACS .... Selective High-Frequency Antenna Coupler System [*Military*] (CAAL)
SACS .... Sensor Accuracy Check Site (MCD)
SACS .... Services After-Care Scheme [*British*]
SACS .... Ship Alteration Completion System
SACS .... Shipyard Accuracy Checksite (MCD)
SACS .... Sino-American Cultural Society (EA)
SACS .... Software Avionics Command Support (NASA)
SACS .... Solar Altitude Control System
SACS .... SONAR Accuracy Check Site (NVT)
SACS .... Southern Association of Colleges and Schools (EA)
SACS .... Structure and Composition System [*Military*] (AABC)
SACS .... Synchronous Altitude Communications Satellite
SACS .... Systems Software Avionics Command Support (MCD)
SACS .... Villa De Soto [*Argentina ICAO location identifier*] (ICLI)
SACSA .... Special Assistant for Counterinsurgency and Special Activities [*Military*] (AFM)
SACSA .... Standing Advisory Committee for Scientific Advice [*Oslo Commission*] (DCTA)
SACSDAC..... South Australian Conference of the Seventh-Day Adventist Church
SACSEA ...... Supreme Allied Commander [*or Commander*], Southeast Asia
SACSF .... Subarachnoid Cerebrospinal Fluid (STED)
SACSIR .... South African Council for Scientific and Industrial Research
SACSS .... South Australian Council of Social Service
SACSS .... Staff Association of Catholic Secondary Schools [*Australia*]
SAC/SSW .... Special Assistant to the Chief of Staff for Special Warfare [*Army*]
SACT........... Gobernador Gordillo [*Argentina ICAO location identifier*] (ICLI)
SACT........... Sinoatrial Conduction Time [*Cardiology*]
SACT........... Special Advisory Committee on Telecommunications (NTCM)
SACT........... System Availability Calculation Tool [*Science Applications International Corp.*] (MCD)
SACTO .... Sacramento Test Operations (MCD)
SACTTYNET... Strategic Air Command Teletype Network
SACTU .... South African Congress of Trade Unions
SACTW .... South African Council of Transport Workers
SACU .... Cordoba [*Argentina ICAO location identifier*] (ICLI)
SACU .... Scottish Auto-Cycle Union (DBA)
SACU .... Service for Admission to College and University [*Canada*] (AEBS)
SACU .... Society for Anglo-Chinese Understanding [*British*] (EAIO)
SACU .... South African Customs Union
SACU .... Southern African Customs Union
SACU .... Stand-Alone Digital Communications Unit (MCD)
SACUBO....... Southern Association of College and University Business Officers (AEBS)
SACUS .... Southern Association on Children under Six (EA)
SACV .... Villa Maria Del Rio Seco [*Argentina ICAO location identifier*] (ICLI)
SACVAR ...... Ship Alteration Cost Variance Account Report
SACVE .... State Advisory Councils for Vocational Education (EDAC)
SACW .... Senior Aircraftwoman [*British military*] (DMA)
SAD .... Saddle (AAG)
SAD .... Saddleback Community College District, Mission Viejo Campus, Mission Viejo, CA [*OCLC symbol*] (OCLC)

SAD	Saddlery
Sad	Sadler's Pennsylvania Cases [*A publication*] (DLA)
SAD	Safe-and-Arm Device
SAD	Safety Analysis [*or Assurance*] Diagram [*Nuclear energy*] (NRCH)
SAD	Safety and Arming Device [*Military*] (AABC)
SAD	Safety, Arming, and Destruct (MCD)
SAD	Safford [*Arizona*] [*Airport symbol*] (AD)
SAD	Safford, AZ [*Location identifier FAA*] (FAAL)
SA/D	Sail-Area/Displacement [*Boating*]
sad.	Sandawe [*MARC language code Library of Congress*] (LCCP)
SAD	Scottish Association for the Deaf (DBA)
SAD	Sealed and Delivery (MHDI)
SAD	Search and Destroy (MCD)
SAD	Seasonal Affective Disorder [*Type of depression caused by long nights, short days*]
SAD	Selected Area [*Electron*] Diffraction [*Also, SAED*] [*Analysis of solids*]
SAD	Self-Assessment Depression Scale (AAMN)
SAD	Semiconductor Anticoincidence Detector
SAD	Sentence Appraiser and Diagrammer
SAD	Separation Anxiety Disorder (STED)
SAD	Serial Analysis Delay [*Computer science*] (ECII)
SAD	Service Action Drawing (AAG)
SAD	Servicios Aereos de La Capital [*Colombia*] [*ICAO designator*] (FAAC)
SAD	Ship Acoustics Department [*David W. Taylor Naval Ship Research and Development Center*]
SAD	Shuttle Authorized Document [*NASA*] (NASA)
SAD	Silicon Alloy Diffused (IAA)
SAD	Silverado Mines Ltd. [*Vancouver Stock Exchange symbol*]
SAD	Simple, Average, or Difficult (AAG)
SAD	Single Administrative Document [*European trade contract*] [*1986*] (DCTA)
SAD	Sinoaortic Deafferentation [*Medicine*]
SAD	Sinoaortic Denervation [*Physiology*]
SAD	Situation Attention Display
S-A-D	Sleep Disturbance with Anxiety and Depression [*Combat behavior disorder*] [*Military*] (INF)
S/AD	Small Advertisement (DGA)
SAD	Small Airway Disease [*Medicine*] (DAVI)
SAD	Small Airway Dysfunction (STED)
SAD	Social Avoidance Distress [*Scale*]
SAD	Society of the Ark and the Dove (EA)
SAD	Source-to-Axis Distance (MAE)
SAD	South American Datum
SAD	South Atlantic Division [*Army Corps of Engineers*]
SAD	Soviet Air Defense
SAD	Soviet Air Demonstration
SAD	Space Antennae Diversity [*Telecommunications*] (TEL)
SAD	Spacecraft Attitude Display (MCD)
SAD	Special Adapter Device (IAA)
SAD	Special Artificer, Special Synthetic Training Devices [*Navy*]
SAD	Special Assessment District (PA)
SAD	Standard American Diet (DAVI)
SAD	Station Address Directory [*Army*]
SAD	Status Advisory Display (MCD)
SAD	Store Access Director (NITA)
SAD	Store Address Director
SAD	Subacute Dialysis [*Medicine*] (STED)
SAD	Submarine Anomaly Detection [*Navy*] (NVT)
SAD	Sugar, Acetone, Diacetic Acid [*Test*] [*Medicine*]
SAD	Sugar and Acetone Determination [*Endocrinology*] (DAVI)
SAD	Supervisory Aptitude Development [*In George Lee Walker novel "The Chronicles of Doodah"*]
SAD	Support Acronym Definition [*Computer science*]
SAD	Support Air Direction [*Navy*]
SAD	Supporting Arms Department [*Navy*] (DNAB)
SAD	Suppressor-Activating Determinant (STED)
SAD	Surface Area Decay [*Plant pathology*]
SAD	Survival Assistance Director [*Federal disaster planning*]
SAD	Sympathetic Aerial Detonation [*Air Force*]
SAD	System Allocation Document [*NASA*] (NASA)
SAD	System Amendment Detail(s) (NITA)
SAD	System Analysis Drawing
SAD	Systems Analysis and Design (NITA)
SAD	Systems Analysis Document (MCD)
SAD	Systems Automation Division [*Navy*] (DNAB)
SADA	Seismic Array Data Analyzer (IEEE)
SADA	South Australian Darts Association
SADA	South Australian Debating Association
SADA	Southern Appalachian Dulcimer Association (EA)
SADA	Standard Advanced Dewar Assembly [*Army*]
SADAP	Simplified Automatic Data Plotter
SADAP	State Alcoholism and Drug Abuse Profile [*Public Health Service*] [*Information service or system*] (IID)
SADAR	Satellite Data Reduction [*Processor system*]
SADARM	Search and Destroy Armor Munition (MCD)
SADARM	Selected Armor Defeating Artillery Munitions (MCD)
SADARM	Sense and Destroy Armor [*Army*] (RDA)
SADARM	Sense [*or Search*] and Destroy Armor Munition
SADAS	Sperry Airborne Data Acquistion System (IAA)
SADBA	South Australian Deer Breeders' Association
SADBE	Squaric Acid Dibutylester [*Medicine*] (MEDA)
SAD Beng	Select Cases, Sadr Diwani [*Bengal*] [*A publication*] (DLA)
SAD Bom	Sadr Diwani Adalat Reports [*Bombay, India*] [*A publication*] (DLA)
SADBU	Small and Disadvantaged Business Utilization [*Department of Commerce*]
SADBUO	Small and Disadvantaged Business Utilization Office [*Army*] (RDA)
SADBUS	Small and Disadvantaged Business Utilization Specialist [*Federal government*] (GFGA)
SADC	Sector Aid Defense Commander (NATG)
SADC	Sequential Analog-Digital Computer (DIT)
SADC	Sneak Attack Defense Coordinator [*Military*] (CAAL)
SADC	Southern African Development Community (ECON)
SADCC	South African Development Coordination Committee [*Australia*]
SADCC	South African Development Co-Ordination Conference (WDAA)
SADD	Buenos Aires/Don Torcuato [*Argentina ICAO location identifier*] (ICLI)
SADD	Semiautomatic Detection Device
SADD	Short-Alcohol Dependence Data [*Medicine*] (DMAA)
SADD	Standardized Assessment of Depressive Disorders [*Medicine*] (DMAA)
SADD	Students Against Driving Drunk (EA)
SaDDC	Durban City Council, Durban, South Africa [*Library symbol Library of Congress*] (LCLS)
SADE	Sensitive Acoustic Detection Equipment (PDAA)
SADE	Solar Array Drive Electronics (LAIN)
SADE	Specialized Armoured Development Establishment [*British military*] (DMA)
SADE	Structural Assembly Demonstration Experiment (MCD)
SADE	Superheat Advanced Demonstration Experiment [*Nuclear energy*]
SADE	Symbolic Application Debugging Environment
SADEC	Spin Axis Declination [*Aerospace*] (MCD)
SADELCA	Sociedad Aerea del Caqueta [*Airline*] [*Colorado*]
SADEMS	Salt Dome Experimental Monitoring System (GFGA)
SADEYA	Sociedad Astronomica de Espana y America [*Hispano-American Astronomical Society*] (EAIO)
SADF	San Fernando [*Argentina ICAO location identifier*] (ICLI)
SADF	Semi-Automatic Document Feed (NITA)
SADF	Semi-Automatic Document Feeder (HGAA)
SADF	South African Defence Forces
SADF	Statistical Analysis of Documentation Files (PDAA)
SADG	Monte Grande [*Argentina ICAO location identifier*] (ICLI)
SADGE	SAGE [*Semiautomatic Ground Environment*] Data Generator (IAA)
SADH	Succinic Acid - Dimethylhydrazide [*Plant growth retardant*]
SADI	Secretarial Automated Data Index
SADI	Selling-Areas Distribution Index (WDMC)
SADIC	Solid-State Analog-to-Digital Computer
SADIE	Scanning Analog-to-Digital Input Equipment [*National Institute of Standards and Technology*]
SADIE	Secure Automatic Data Information Exchange [*System*]
SADIE	Semiautomatic Decentralized Intercept Environment [*Air Force*]
SADIE	Sterling and Decimal Invoicing Electronically (IEEE)
SADIS	Shipboard Automated Decoy Integration System [*Navy*]
SADJ	Jose C. Paz/Dr. Mariano More [*Argentina ICAO location identifier*] (ICLI)
SADL	La Plata [*Argentina ICAO location identifier*] (ICLI)
SADL	Sadlier [*William H.*], Inc. [*NASDAQ symbol*] (NQ)
SADL	Sadlier (William H.) [*NASDAQ symbol*] (TTSB)
SADL	Ships Authorized Data List
SADL	Significant Activities of Daily Living (WYGK)
SADL	Significant Activity of Daily Living [*Insurance*]
SADL	Simulated Activities of Daily Living (DMAA)
SADL	Spares Application Data List
SADL	Special Automated Distribution List (AFIT)
SADL	Sterilization Assembly Development Laboratory [*NASA*]
SADL	Synchronous Automatic Dial Language
Sadler	Sadler's Pennsylvania Cases [*A publication*] (DLA)
Sadler (PA)	Sadler's Pennsylvania Cases [*A publication*] (DLA)
Sadlier	Sadlier [*William H.*], Inc. [*Associated Press*] (SAG)
SADM	Moron [*Argentina ICAO location identifier*] (ICLI)
SADM	Secretary of the Army Decision Memorandum [*Army*] (RDA)
SADM	Solar Array Drive Motor
SADM	Special Atomic Demolition Munitions [*Military*] (AABC)
SADM	System Acquisition Decision Memorandum (MCD)
SADMG	Special Artificer, Special Devices, Machine Gun Trainer [*Navy*]
SADNWF	Sadr Diwani Adalat Cases, Northwest Frontier [*Pakistan*] [*A publication*] (DLA)
SADOPS	Ships Angle Tracking and Doppler System (IAA)
SADOT	Structures Assembly Deployment and Operations Technology (SSD)
SADP	El Palomar [*Argentina ICAO location identifier*] (ICLI)
SADP	Scales of Attitudes toward Disabled Persons [*Occupational therapy*]
SADP	Scandinavian Association of Directory Publishers (EAIO)
SADP	Selected Area Electron Diffraction Pattern [*Analysis of solids*]
SADP	Small Area Direct Path [*Military*] (CAAL)
SADP	Structured Analysis, Design, and Programming [*Computer science*]
SADP	Synthetic Array Data Processor
SADP	System Architecture Design Package
Sad PA Cas	Sadler's Pennsylvania Cases [*1885-88*] [*A publication*] (DLA)
Sad PA Cs	Sadler's Pennsylvania Cases [*1885-88*] [*A publication*] (DLA)
SADPMA	South Australian Dairy Products Manufacturers' Association
SADPO	Senior ADP Policy Officer (AAGC)
SADPO	Systems Analysis and Data Processing Office
SADQ	Quilmes [*Argentina ICAO location identifier*] (ICLI)
SADQ	Severity of Alcohol Dependence Questionnaire
SADR	Merlo [*Argentina ICAO location identifier*] (ICLI)
SADR	Saharan Arab Democratic Republic [*Morocco*] (PD)
SADR	Secure Acoustic Data Relay (NVT)
SADR	Severity Adjusted Death Rate [*Medicine*] (DHSM)
SADR	Six Hundred Megacycle Air Defense RADAR
SADRA	South Australian Drag Racers' Association
SADRAM	Seek and Destroy RADAR-Assisted Mission (MCD)
SADRCB	South Australian Dog Racing Control Board

SADRI.......... Social and Demographic Research Institute [*University of Massachusetts*] [*Research center*] (RCD)
SADRT........ Secure Acoustic Data Relay Terminal (MCD)
SADS .... San Justo/Aeroclub Argentino [*Argentina ICAO location identifier*] (ICLI)
SADS .... Schedule for Affective Disorders and Schizophrenia [*Psychological interview*]
SADS .... Seasonal Affective Disorder Syndrome [*Psychiatry*] (DAVI)
SADS .... Semiautomatic Defense System (NG)
SADS .... Semiconductor Anticoincidence Detection System
SADS .... Senate Appropriations Defense Subcommittee
SADS .... Simulated Air Defense System [*RADAR*]
SADS .... Single Application Data Sheet
SADS .... Social Avoidance and Distress Scale [*Psychology*]
SADS .... Solar Array Drive System
SADS .... Submarine Active Detection System
SADS .... Swiss Air Defense System
SADS .... System Architecture Development Study [*NATO Integrated Communications System*] (NATG)
SADSAC...... Sampled Data Simulator and Computer
SADSAC...... Seiler ALGOL Digitally Simulated Analog Computer
SADSAC...... Small Acoustic Device Simulating Aircraft Carrier (NVT)
SADSACT.... Self-Assigned Descriptors from Self and Cited Titles [*Automatic indexing*]
SADSC......... San Antonio Data Services Center [*Military*]
SADS-C........ Schedule for Affective Disorders and Schizophrenia - Change Version [*Personality development test*] [*Psychology*]
SADS-L........ Schedule for Affective Disorders and Schizophrenia - Lifetime Version [*Personality development test*] [*Psychology*]
SADSSC...... South Australian Deaf Sports and Social Club
SADS-TG...... Submarine Active Detection System - Transmit Group [*Navy*]
SADT .... Same Direction Traffic (FAAC)
SADT .... Self-Accelerating Decomposition Temperature
SADT .... Special Active Duty for Training [*Military*] (AABC)
SADT .... Structured Analysis and Design Technique [*Programming language*] [*1978*]
SADT .... Surface Alloy Diffused-Base Transistor
SADTAC...... Selective Automatic Decade Turnover, Absolute Control (IAA)
SADTC........ SHAPE [*Supreme Headquarters Allied Powers Europe*] Air Defense Technology Center [*Later, STC*] [*NATO*]
SADTS......... Safety and Arming Detection Test Set (DWSG)
SADTU........ South African Democratic Teachers' Union
SADU .... Sea Search Attack Development Unit
SADV .... Semiannual Density Variation [*Geophysics*]
SADZ .... Matanza/Aeroclub Universita Rio [*Argentina ICAO location identifier*] (ICLI)
SAE.............. Ogallala, NE [*Location identifier FAA*] (FAAL)
SAE.............. Sable Resources Ltd. [*Vancouver Stock Exchange symbol*]
SaE.............. Sanguinarine Extract [*Biochemistry*]
SAE.............. Self-Addressed Envelope
SAE.............. Self-Aligned Emitter (IAA)
SAE.............. Semi-Actuator Ejector (MCD)
SAE.............. Senior Assistant Editor [*Publishing*]
SAE.............. Service Acquisition Executive [*DoD*]
SAE.............. Shaft Angle Encoder (KSC)
SAE.............. Simple Arithmetic Expression
SAE.............. Site Acceptance Evaluation [*Army*] (AABC)
SAE.............. Site Area Emergency [*Environmental science*] (COE)
SAE.............. Skyways Africa Ltd. [*Kenya*] [*ICAO designator*] (FAAC)
SAE.............. Society for Aerospace Engineers (AAGC)
SAE.............. Society for the Advancement of Education (EA)
SAE.............. Society for the Anthropology of Europe (EA)
SAE.............. Society of American Etchers (NADA)
SAE.............. Society of Association Executives [*British*] (EAIO)
SAE.............. Society of Automotive Engineers [*Acronym is now organization's official name*] (EA)
SAE.............. Society of Automotive Engineers, Inc. (AAGC)
SAE.............. Solar Array Experiment (SSD)
SAE.............. Son Altesse Electorale [*His Highness the Elector*] [*French*] (ROG)
SAE.............. Soviet Antarctic Expedition
SAE.............. Specialized Armoured Establishment [*British military*] (DMA)
SAE.............. Spiral Aftereffect [*Aerospace*]
SAE.............. Stamped Addressed Envelope
sae.............. Stamped Addressed Envelope (ODBW)
SAE.............. Stand Alone Executive (MHDI)
SAE.............. Standard Australian English
SAE.............. Standard Average European
SAE.............. Standard of Automotive Engineers (IAA)
SAE.............. Steering Angle Error
SAE.............. Stop at Expiration [*Magazine subscriptions*]
SAE.............. Student Action for Education [*Defunct*] (EA)
SAE.............. Subcortical Arteriosclerotic Encephalopathy [*Medicine*]
SAE.............. Suntanning Association for Education (NTPA)
SAE.............. Supersonic Aircraft Engine
SAEA.......... South Australian Exporters Association
SAEA.......... Southeastern Adult Education Association (AEBS)
SAEA.......... Southwest Atomic Energy Associates
SAE abstracts... Society of Automotive Engineers abstracts (NITA)
SAEB.......... Self-Adjusting Electric Brake
SAEB.......... Special Army Evaluation Board (AABC)
SAEC.......... Saeculum [*Age, Century, Generation, Lifetime*] [*Latin*] (ROG)
SAEC.......... South American Explorers Club (EA)
SAEC.......... South Australian Equestrian Centre
SAEC.......... Southern Agricultural Energy Center
SAEC.......... State Administration of Exchange Control [*China*]

SAEC........... Sumitomo Atomic Energy Commission [*Japan*]
SAECG .... Signal Averaged Eectrocardiography [*Medicine*]
SAED .... Selected Area Electron Diffraction [*Also, SAD*] [*Surface analysis*]
SAED .... Societe des Amis d'Eugene Delacroix (EAIO)
SAED .... Systems Analysis and Engineering Development [*Naval Air Development Center*] (MCD)
SAEDA .... Subversion and Espionage Directed Against US Army and Deliberate Security Violations (AABC)
SAEDE .... Sensory Aids Evaluation and Development Center [*MIT*]
SAEDFR ...... Scholars Against the Escalating Danger of the Far Right (EA)
SAEF .... Ezeiza [*Argentina ICAO location identifier*] (ICLI)
SAEF .... SEAQ Automated Execution Facility [*Software package*]
SAEF............ Small-Order Automatic Execution Facility [*London Stock Exchange*] [*British*]
SAEF .... Spacecraft Assembly and Encapsulation Facility [*NASA*] (NASA)
SAEF .... State Administrative Expense Funds
SAEF .... Stock Exchange Automatic Execution Facility
SAEH .... Society for Automation in English and the Humanities [*Later, SDE*]
SAEI .... Sumitomo Atomic Energy Industries Ltd. [*Japan*]
SAEM .... Society for Academic Emergency Medicine (NTPA)
SAEMA........ Scottish Association for Educational Management and Administration (AIE)
SAEMA........ Suspended Access Equipment Manufacturers Association [*British*] (DBA)
SAEMR .... Small Arms Expert Marksmanship Ribbon [*Military decoration*] (AFM)
SAEP .... Salmonella Abortus Equi Pyrogen (DB)
SAEP .... South African Education Program [*New York, NY*]
SAES .... SAES Getters SPA [*NASDAQ symbol*] (SAG)
SAES .... Scanning Auger Electron Spectroscopy
SAES .... Special Assistant for Environmental Services [*Military*]
SAES .... Sputter Auger Electron Spectroscopy (IAA)
SAES .... Stand-Alone Engine Simulator (NASA)
SAES .... State Agricultural Experiment Station
SAESA........ Compania de Servicios Aereos SA [*Spain ICAO designator*] (FAAC)
SAESGet...... SAES Getters SPA [*Associated Press*] (SAG)
SAESIP ...... Saturn Apollo Electrical Systems Integration Panel (IAA)
SAESY .... SAES Getters S.p.A ADS [*NASDAQ symbol*] (TTSB)
SAET .... Society for the Advancement of Economic Theory (EA)
SAET .... Society of Automotive-Electrical Technicians [*British*] (DBA)
SAET .... South Australian Electricity Trust
SAET .... Spiral Aftereffect Test [*Psychology*] (AEBS)
SAETA........ SA Ecuatoriana de Transportes Aereos [*Airline*] [*Ecuador*]
SAEV .... Ezeiza [*Argentina ICAO location identifier*] (ICLI)
SAEW.......... Ship's Advanced Electronic Warfare (MCD)
SAEWG ...... Standing Air Emissions Work Group [*Environmental Protection Agency*] (GFGA)
SAEWS ...... Ship's Advanced Electronic Warfare System (NVT)
SAEZ .... Buenos Aires [*Argentina*]/Ezeiza [*Argentina ICAO location identifier*] (ICLI)
SAF.............. Republic of Singapore Air Force [*ICAO designator*] (FAAC)
SAF.............. Safe, Arm, and Fuze
SAF.............. Safed [*Israel*] [*Seismograph station code, US Geological Survey Closed*] (SEIS)
SAF.............. Safety (KSC)
SAF.............. SAF [*Society of American Florists*]- The Center for Commercial Floriculture (EA)
SAF.............. Sample Air Filter
SAF.............. San Andreas Fault
SAF.............. Santa Fe [*New Mexico*] [*Airport symbol*] (OAG)
SAF.............. Save America's Forests [*An association*] (EA)
SAF.............. Scandinavian American Fraternity (EA)
SAF.............. School of Aerial Fighting [*British military*] (DMA)
SAF.............. Scrapie-Associated Fibrils [*Neuroanatomy*]
SAF.............. Scudder New Asia Fd [*NYSE symbol*] (TTSB)
SAF.............. Scudder New Asia Fund [*NYSE symbol*] (SPSG)
SAF.............. Second Amendment Foundation (EA)
SAF.............. Secretary of the Air Force
SAF.............. Secure Automated Fabrication [*Line*] [*Nuclear energy*]
SAF.............. Segment Address Field
SAF.............. Self-Articulating Femoral [*Medicine*]
SAF.............. Service to the Armed Forces
SAF.............. Shark Attack File (DNAB)
SAF.............. Shielding Analysis Form [*Civil Defense*]
SAF.............. Short Address Form (NITA)
SAF.............. Side and Face Milling [*Cutter*] (IAA)
SAF.............. Single Action [*Maintenance*] Form (NVT)
SAF.............. Small Arms Fire [*Military*] (VNW)
SAF.............. Societe des Artistes Francais, Paris [*1880*] [*French*] (NGC)
SAF.............. Society of American Florists (EA)
SAF.............. Society of American Foresters (EA)
SAF.............. Sound and Flash (IAA)
SAF.............. Source Acquisitions File (MCD)
SAF.............. South Africa (EY)
SAF.............. South Africa Foundation (EA)
SAF.............. Southern Attack Force [*Navy*]
SAF.............. Soviet Air Forces (DOMA)
SAF.............. Spacecraft Assembly Facility [*NASA*]
SAF.............. Spanish Air Force
SAF.............. Special Action Force [*Military*]
SAF.............. Specification Approval Form (MCD)
SAF.............. Spin Armed Fuze
SAF.............. Star Action Foundation (EA)
SAF.............. Stem Cell Activating Factor [*Biochemistry*]
SAF.............. Sterilization Assembly Facility
SAF.............. Strategic Air Force

SAF.............. Structural Adjustment Facility [Finance]
SAF.............. Students Against Fires [International student engineering project for 1972-73 sponsored by Student Competitions on Relevant Engineering - SCORE]
SAF.............. Subject Authority File, Washington, DC [UTLAS symbol]
SAF.............. Subject to the Availability of Funds (MCD)
SAF.............. Sultan's Armed Forces
SAF.............. Super Abrasion Furnace [Carbon black manufacture]
SAF.............. Support Action Form (MCD)
SAF.............. Suppressor Activating Factor [Immunology]
SAF.............. Svenska Arbetsgivareforeningen [An employers' confederation] [Sweden]
SAF.............. Swedish Air Force
SAF.............. Switchable Acoustic Filter
SAF.............. Symmetry-Adapted Function
SAF.............. Symposium on Applications of Ferroelectrics [IEEE]
SAF.............. Syrian Air Force (BJA)
SAF.............. System Administration Facility (CIST)
SAFA........... School Assistance in Federally Affected Areas
SAFA........... Service d'Aide aux Forces Alliees [World War II]
SAFA........... Society for Automation in the Fine Arts [Later, SDE]
SAFA........... Society of Air Force Anesthesiologists [Later, DMEF] (EA)
SAFA........... Socttish Amateur Football Association (DBA)
SAFA........... Solar Array Failure Analysis
SAFA........... Soluble Antigen Fluorescent-Antibody [Immunology]
SAFA........... South Australian Football Association
SAFAA......... Secretary of the Air Force, Administrative Assistant
SAFAD......... Small Arms for Air Defense (MCD)
SAFAD......... Swedish Agency for Administrative Development (NITA)
SAFAH........ Supplemental Assistance for Facilities to Assist the Homeless [Department of Housing and Urban Development] (GFGA)
SAF/AL........ Assistant Secretary of the Air Force (Research, Development, and Logistics)
SAF/AQ....... Assistant Secretary of the Air Force for Acquisition (AAGC)
SAFARI........ Semiautomatic Failure Anticipation Recording Instrumentation
SAFARI........ South African Fundamental Atomic Reactor Installation
SAFARI........ Spiro Agnew Fans and Rooters, Inc.
SAFB........... Scott Air Force Base [Illinois]
SAFB........... Shaw Air Force Base [South Carolina]
SAFB........... Sheppard Air Force Base [Texas] (AAG)
SAFBITC...... South Australian Food and Beverage Industry Training Council
SAFblack...... Super Abrasion Furnace Black (EDCT)
SAFC........... SAFECO Corp. [NASDAQ symbol] (NQ)
SAFC........... Swiss Association for Friendship with China (EAIO)
SAFCA........ Safeguard Communications Agency [Army]
SAFCB........ Secretary of the Air Force Correction Board
SAFCMD...... Safeguard Command [Army] (AABC)
SAFCO........ Standing Advisory Committee on Fisheries of the Caribbean Organization
SAFCOM...... Safeguard System Command [Obsolete Army]
SAFCOS...... Scottish Association of Family Conciliation Services (DBA)
SAFCPM...... Safeguard Communications Program Manager [Army] (AABC)
SAFCPMO.... Safeguard Communications Program Management Office [Army] (AABC)
SAFCS........ Society of Air Force Clinical Surgeons (NTPA)
SAFCS........ Steam and Feedwater Rupture Control System (IAA)
SAFCTF....... Safeguard Central Training Facility [Army] (AABC)
SAFD........... Society of American Fight Directors (EA)
SAFDL......... Specified Acceptable Fuel Design Limit [Nuclear energy] (NRCH)
SAFE........... Invivo Corp. [NASDAQ symbol] [Formerly, SafetyTek Corp.] (SG)
SAFE........... Safe Access to Files of Estate [Howrex Corp.] [Information service or system] (IID)
SAFE........... Safe Areas for Evasion (DOMA)
SAFE........... Safeguards Analysis for Effluents
SAFE........... Safeguards Automated Facility Evaluation [Nuclear energy] (NRCH)
SAFE........... Safety and Functional Evaluation [Occupational therapy]
SAFE........... SafetyTek Corp. [NASDAQ symbol] (SPSG)
SAFE........... San Andreas Fault Experiment
SAFE........... Santa Fe [Argentina ICAO location identifier] (ICLI)
SAFE........... Satellite Alert Force Employment
SAFE........... Save America's Fossils for Everyone
SAFE........... Save Animals from Extinction [Later, WPTI] [An association]
SAFE........... Security and Freedom through Encryption [Proposed legislative bill]
SAFE........... Security, Aptitude, Fitness Evaluation [Test]
SAFE........... Security Audit and Field Evaluation (IAA)
S/AFE.......... Seismic/Acoustic Feature Extraction (MCD)
SAFE........... Selected Areas for Evasion [Military] (MCD)
SAFE........... Self-Acceptance, Faulty Information, Effectiveness Counselling or Training [Sex therapy]
SAFE........... Sequential Analysis for Force Development (MCD)
SAFE........... Settlement and Accelerated Funds Exchange [Chicago, IL]
SAFE........... Shelter Available for Emergency
SAFE........... Simulation-Aided Fault Evaluation (MCD)
SAFE........... Simulation Analysis of Financial Exposure (NUMA)
SAFE........... Society for the Advancement of Fission Energy [Defunct] (EA)
SAFE........... Society for the Application of Free Energy (EA)
SAFE........... Society of Associated Financial Executives
SAFE........... Society to Advance Foreclosure Education [Defunct] (EA)
SAFE........... Software Abstracts for Engineers [CITIS Ltd.] [Ireland] [Information service or system] (CRD)
SAFE........... Solar Array Flight Experiment (MCD)
SAFE........... Solvent Abuse Foundation for Education (EA)
SAFE........... Source and Application Inspection Equipment
SAFE........... South America and Far East

SAFE........... Spectronix Automatic Fire Extinguishing [System] [For armored vehicles]
SAFE........... Stationary Attachment and Flexible Endoskeleton
SAFE........... Stock Assessment and Fishery Investigations [National Marine Fisheries Service] (NOAA)
SAFE........... Store and Forward Element [Telecommunications] (TEL)
SAFE........... Straits Air Freight Express [Australia]
SAFE........... Strategy and Force Evaluation (MCD)
SAFE........... Student Assistance and Family Education
SAFE........... Students Against Famine Everywhere [Defunct] (EA)
SAFE........... Suntanning Association for Education (EA)
SAFE........... Support for the Analysts' File Environment (MCD)
SAFE........... Survival [formerly, Space] and Flight Equipment Association [Later, SAFE Association]
SAFE........... Synthetic Agreement for Forward Exchange (NUMA)
SAFE........... System, Area, Function, Equipment
SAFE........... System for Automated Flight Efficiency (PDAA)
SAFEA......... Space and Flight Equipment Assoication (IAA)
SAFEA......... Survival and Flight Equipment Association [Later, SAFE Association] (EA)
SAFE-BAR.... Safeland Barrier (DNAB)
SAFECEN..... Safety Center (DNAB)
Safeco........ Safeco Corp. [Associated Press] (SAG)
SAFEPLAN... Submarine Air Frequency Plan (DNAB)
SAFER......... Safety and Fitness Electronic Records System [FHWA] (TAG)
SAFE-R........ Security, Aptitude, Fitness Evaluation-Resistance [Test] [John Taccarino] (TES)
SAFER......... Sequential Action Flow Routine [Military British]
SAFER......... Simplified Aid for EVA Rescue [NASA]
SAFER......... Special Application of Finite Element Representation [Marine science] (OSRA)
SAFER......... Special Aviation Fire and Explosion Reduction (EGAO)
SAFER......... Spectral Application of Finite Element Representation (USDC)
SAFER......... Split Access Flexible Egress Routing [AT&T] (CIST)
SAFER......... Structural Analysis, Frailty Evaluation and Redesign (MHDB)
SAFER......... Systematic Aid to Flow on Existing Roads [Traffic-control system]
SAFER......... System for Aircrew Flight Extension and Return (PDAA)
Safeskin...... Safeskin Corp. [Associated Press] (SAG)
SAFE TRIP... Students Against Faulty Tires Ripping in Pieces [Student legal action organization]
SAFETY....... Safety Always Follows Everything You Do [Sign]
Safeway...... Safeway, Inc. [Associated Press] (SAG)
SAFF.......... Safing, Arming, Fusing, and Firing [Military] (MCD)
SAFF.......... Store and Forward Facsimile
SAFFE........ Society of Americans for Firearms Elimination (EA)
SAFFI......... Special Assembly for Fast Installations [Telecommunications] (TEL)
SAFFM........ Secretary of the Air Force, Financial Management
SAFFUC...... Sudan African Freedom Fighters' Union of Conservatives
SAFFWALD... Saffron Walden [Municipal borough in England]
SAFGA........ South Australian Flower Growers' Association
SAFGAR...... Semi-Arid Grain Research and Development (GNE)
SAFGC........ Secretary of the Air Force General Counsel
SafHlt......... Safeguard Health Enterprises, Inc. [Associated Press] (SAG)
SAFI.......... Semiautomatic Flight Inspection [FAA]
SAFI.......... Semiautomatic Flight Inspection Aircraft (FAAC)
SAFI.......... Senior Air Force Instructor
SAFI.......... Sholem Aleichem Folk Institute (EA)
SAFI.......... Stock Assessment and Fishery Investigations Program [National Oceanic and Atmospheric Administration] (GFGA)
SAFIAC....... South Australian Film Investment Advisory Committee
SAFIC........ South Australian Fishing Industry Council
SAFIE........ Secretary of the Air Force, Special Assistant for Installations
SAFIL......... Secretary of the Air Force (Installations and Logistics)
SAFIM........ Separated Associated Fluid Interaction Model [Chemical engineering]
SAFIMDA.... School Aid to Federally Impacted and Major Disaster Areas (OICC)
SAFIN........ Secretary of the Air Force, Special Assistant for Intelligence
SAFIRE....... Systems Analysis for Integrated Relief Variation [Engineering]
SAFIS......... Secretary of the Air Force, Office of Information Services
SAFIS......... Substance Abuse Facility Information System [Department of Health and Human Services] (GFGA)
SAFISY....... Space Agency Forum on International Space Year
SAFITC....... South Australian Fishing Industry Training Council
SAFITP....... Safeguard Integrated Training Plan [Army] (AABC)
SAFLL........ Secretary of the Air Force, Office of Legislative Liaison
SAFLOG...... Safeguard Logistics Command [Army] (AABC)
SAFM......... Sanderson Farms [NASDAQ symbol] (TTSB)
SAFM......... Sanderson Farms, Inc. [NASDAQ symbol] (NQ)
SAFMP....... Assistant Secretary of the Air Force (Manpower and Personnel)
SAFMR....... Secretary of the Air Force, Manpower and Reserve Affairs
SAFMS....... Secretary of the Air Force, Missile and Satellite Systems (SAA)
SAFMSC..... Safeguard Materiel Support Command [Army] (AABC)
SAFNGS...... Small Arms Flash, Noise Gunfire Simulator [Army]
SAFO......... Safe Altitude Fuzing Option (SAA)
SAFO......... Secretary of the Air Force Order (AFM)
SAFO......... Self-Adhesive Foreign Object (PDAA)
SAFO......... Senior Acting Field Officer [Military British] (ROG)
SAFO......... Senior Air Force Officer [Present] (AFM)
SAFOC........ Semiautomatic Flight Operations Center
SAFOC........ Syndicat Autonome des Fonctionnaires d'Oubangi-Chari [Autonomous Union of the Workers of Ubangi-Shari]
SAFOH....... Society of American Florists and Ornamental Horticulturists [Later, SAF]
SAFOI........ Secretary of the Air Force, Office of Information
SAFOR........ Semi-Automated Forces [Army] (RDA)
SAFP.......... Society of Air Force Physicians (EA)

SAFPACC	Safeguard Public Affairs Coordinating Committee [*Army*] (AABC)
SAFPC	Secretary of the Air Force Personnel Council
SAFPLAN	Submarine Area Frequency Plan [*Navy*]
SAFPO	Safeguard Project Office (MCD)
SAFR	Senior Air Force Representative (AFM)
SAFR	Social Assessment of Fisheries Resources
SAFR	Sodium Advanced Fast Reactor
SAFR	Source Application of Funds Report (MCD)
S Afr	South Africa
SAFR	Supplementary Application Forms Required [*Civil Service*]
SAFRAS	Self-Adaptive Flexible Format Retrieval and Storage System [*Computer science*] (IID)
S Afr Bankers J	South African Bankers' Journal [*Cape Town, South Africa*] [*A publication*] (DLA)
SAFRD	Assistant Secretary of the Air Force (Research and Development)
SAFRD	Secretary of the Air Force for Research and Development (IAA)
S Afr LR App	South African Law Reports, Appellate [*A publication*] (DLA)
S Afr L Rev	South African Law Review [*A publication*] (DLA)
S Afr LT	South African Law Times [*A publication*] (DLA)
SAFRR	Secretary of the Air Force, Requirements Review
S Afr Tax	South African Tax Cases [*A publication*] (DLA)
S Afr Tax Cas	South African Tax Cases [*A publication*] (DLA)
SAFS	Safing, Arming, and Fusing System [*Military*] (MCD)
SAFS	Secondary Air Force Specialty
SAFS	Society for Academic Freedom and Scholarship [*Canada*]
SAFSC-D	Safeguard System Command-RDT & E [*Research, Development, Test, and Evaluation*] Directorate [*Obsolete Army*] (MCD)
SAFSCOM	Safeguard System Command [*Obsolete Army*] (AABC)
SAFSEA	Safeguard System Evaluation Agency [*Army*] (AABC)
SAFSIM	Safeguard System Simulation [*Missile system evaluation*] [*Army*] (RDA)
SAFSL	Secretary of the Air Force Space Liaison (MCD)
SAFSM	Safeguard System Manager [*Army*]
SAFSO	Safeguard System Office [*Army*] (AABC)
SAFSP	Secretary of the Air Force, Special Projects
SAFSR	Society for the Advancement of Food Service Research (EA)
SAFT	Safety
SAFT	Safety 1st, Inc. [*NASDAQ symbol*] (SAG)
SAFT	Society for the Advancement of the Field Theory (EA)
SAFT	Spark Analysis for Traces [*Spectrometry*]
SAFT	Synthetic Aperture Focusing Technique [*Computer imaging*]
SAFTAC	Semiautomatic Facility for Terminal Area Control
SAFTCP	Safeguard Tactical Communications Plan [*Army*] (AABC)
SAFTCS	Safeguard Tactical Communications System [*Army*] (AABC)
SAF-TE	SCSI Accessed Fault-Tolerant Enclosures [*Computer science*]
SaftKl	Safety-Kleen Corp. [*Associated Press*] (SAG)
SAFTO	South African Foreign Trade Organisation
SAFTRANS	Safeguard Transportation System [*Army*] (AABC)
SAFTU	South African Federation of Trade Unions
Saftytk	Safetytek Corp. [*Associated Press*] (SAG)
SAFUS	Under Secretary of the Air Force
SAFV	Separator Assembly Fuel-Vacuum [*Automotive engineering*]
SAFWA	Southeastern Association of Fish and Wildlife Agencies (EA)
Safwy	Safeway, Inc. [*Associated Press*] (SAG)
SAFX	Saw Fixture [*Tool*] (AAG)
SAFZ	San Andreas Fault Zone [*Geology*]
s-ag--	Argentina [*MARC geographic area code Library of Congress*] (LCCP)
SAG	Saga [*Japan*] [*Seismograph station code, US Geological Survey*] (SEIS)
SAG	Saginaw [*Diocesan abbreviation*] [*Michigan*] (TOCD)
SAG	Sagitta [*Mathematics*]
sag	Sagittal [*Anatomy*] (DAVI)
SAG	Sagittarius [*Constellation*]
SAG	Sagwon, AK [*Location identifier FAA*] (FAAL)
SAG	Saint Anthony's Guild
SAG	Salicyl Acyl Glucuronide [*Organic chemistry*]
sag	Sango [*MARC language code Library of Congress*] (LCCP)
SAG	Schweizerische Afrika-Gesellschaft [*Swiss Society of African Studies*] (EAIO)
SAG	Screen Actors Guild (EA)
SAG	Secretaria de Agricultura y Ganaderia [*Mexico*]
SAG	Seismic Air Gun
SAG	Self-Agglomerator (PDAA)
SAG	Self-Aligned Gate (IAA)
SAG	Semiactive Guidance [*Military*] (IIA)
SAG	Semiautogenous Grinding System [*Ore-crushing process*]
SAG	Senescence-Associated Gene [*Biochemistry*]
SAG	Senior Advisory Group [*Policymakers who advised President Johnson, especially regarding Vietnam*] (VNW)
SAG	Senior Advisory Group [*Nuclear Regulatory Commission*] (GFGA)
SAG	Service Advisory Group (NATG)
SAG	Signal Actuated Gate
SAG	Significant Air Gap
SAG	Society of Arthritic Gardeners
SAg	Soluble Antigen [*Immunochemistry*]
SAG	Sonoangiography [*Medicine*] (DMAA)
SAG	South Australian Gas Co. [*Commercial firm*]
SAG	Sowjetische Aktiengesellschaften [*Soviet Corporations*] [*Germany*]
SAG	Special Activities Group [*Air Force*]
SAG	Standard Address Generator (IEEE)
SAG	St. Apollonia Guild (EA)
SAG	Strategic Communications Ltd. [*Vancouver Stock Exchange symbol*]
SAG	Study Advisory Group [*Army*]
SAG	Submarine Analysis Group [*Navy*] (CAAL)
SAG	Superantigen [*Immunology*]
S/Ag	Supervised Agency (DLA)
SAG	Surface Action Group [*Military*] (NVT)
SAG	Surface Attack Group [*Navy*] (CAAL)
SAG	Swedish Air Ambulance [*ICAO designator*] (FAAC)
SAG	Swiss Agammaglobulinemia [*Medicine*] (MAE)
SAG	Syntax Analyzer Generator (PDAA)
SAG	System Application Group (SAA)
SAG	Systems Analysis Group
SAGA	Saint-Gaudens National Historic Site
SAGA	Sand and Gravel Association of Great Britain
SAGA	Scottish Amateur Gymnastics Association (DBA)
SAGA	Short-Arc Geodetic Adjustment [*Geophysics*]
SAGA	Smocking Arts Guild of America (EA)
SAGA	Society of American Graphic Artists (EA)
SAGA	South Australian Gymnastic Association
SAGA	Soviet-American Gas and Aerosol [*Experiment*] (USDC)
SAGA	Stage and Arena Guild of America
SAGA	Studies, Analysis, and Gaming Agency [*Military*]
SAGA	System for Automatic Generation and Analysis
SAGA-3	Third Soviet-American Gas and Aerosol [*Experiment*] [*Marine science*] (OSRA)
SagaCm	Saga Communications, Inc. [*Associated Press*] (SAG)
SAGAGB	Sand and Gravel Association of Great Britain (BI)
SAGAN	Scientific Apprehension of God's Awesome Nature
SagaP	Saga Petroleum AS [*Associated Press*] (SAG)
SAGB	Schizophrenia Association of Great Britain
SAGB	Senior Advisory Group on Biotechnology [*British*]
SAGB	Skibob Association of Great Britain (DBA)
SAGB	Spiritualist Association of Great Britain
SAGC	Saint Andrews Golf Corp. [*NASDAQ symbol*] (SAG)
SAGCI	Semiautomatic Ground Control of Interceptors [*Military*] (IAA)
SAGCW	Saint Andrews Golf Wrrt [*NASDAQ symbol*] (TTSB)
Sag D	Sagittal Diameter [*Radiology*] (DAVI)
SagDEG	Sagittarius Dwarf Elliptical Galaxy [*Astrophysics*]
SAGE	Sagebrush Inc. [*NASDAQ symbol*] (TTSB)
SAGE	Science and Geography Education [*Database*]
SAGE	Scientific Advisory Group on Effects [*DoD Washington, DC*] (EGAO)
SAGE	Semiautomatic Ground Environment [*Military*]
SAGE	Senior Action in a Gay Environment (EA)
SAGE	Serial Analysis of Gene Expression [*Genetics*]
SAGE	Skylab Advisory Group for Experiments [*NASA*]
SAGE	Society for the Advancement of Good English [*Defunct*] (EA)
SAGE	Society for the Advancement of the George Economy [*Defunct*] (EA)
SAGE	Solar-Assisted Gas Energy [*Water heating*] [*NASA*]
SAGE	South African General Electric Co.
SAGE	South Australian Group of Chief Executives of Tertiary Institutions
SAGE	Soviet-American Gallium Experiment [*Particle physics*]
SAGE	Special Assistant for Growing Enterprises [*Division of National American Wholesale Grocer's Association*]
SAGE	Spoiler Assisted Ground Effect (MCD)
SAGE	Statistical Analysis Group in Education (EDAC)
SAGE	Sterilization Aerospace Ground Equipment (KSC)
SAGE	Strategic Analysis Guidance and Estimate (MCD)
SAGE	Stratospheric Aerosol Gas Experiment
SAGE	Styrene/Allyl Glycidyl Ether [*Organic chemistry*]
SAGE	System for Assessment and Group Evaluation [*Schaeber & Associates, Creative Development, Inc.*] (TES)
Sage C	Sage Colleges (GAGS)
SAGEE	Surface-Air-Generated Electronic Environment (SAA)
SageLb	Sage Laboratories, Inc. [*Associated Press*] (SAG)
SAGEM	Societe d'Applications Generals d'Electricite et de Mecanique [*France*]
SAGES	Screening Assessment for Gifted Elementary Student [*Johnsen and Corn*] (TES)
SAGES	Society American Gastrointestinal Endoscopic Surgeons (EA)
SAGES	Society of American Gastrointestinal Endoscopic Surgery (CMD)
SAGFC	Southeastern Association of Game and Fish Commissioners [*Later, SAFWA*] (EA)
SAGG	South Australian Government Gazette [*A publication*]
SAGGA	Scout and Guide Graduate Association [*British*] (BI)
SAGGA	South Australian Grape Growers' Association
SAGGBS	Salvation Army Guides and Guards, Brownies, and Sunbeams (EAIO)
SAGGE	Synchronous Altitude Gravity Gradient Experiment
SAGI	South-African Garrisons Institutes [*Military British*] (ROG)
SAGI	Specialty Advertising Guild International [*Later, SAA*] (EA)
SAGJ	South African Geographical Journal [*A publication*]
SAGM	Separate Absorption, Grading, and Multiplication Layers [*Semiconductor technology*]
SAGMI	Surface Attack Guided Missile (MCD)
SAGMOS	Self-Aligning Gate Metal Oxide Semiconductor (IEEE)
SAGO	Latin America Center [*Acronym is based on foreign phrase Belgium*]
SA-GOR	Security Assistance - General Operational Requirement [*Military*] (AFIT)
SAGP	Saturable Absorber Giant Pulsing (IAA)
SAGP	Society for Ancient Greek Philosophy (EA)
SAGP	Streptococcal Acidic Glycoprotein [*Antineoplastic drug*]
SAGPGG	Sheep Anti-Guinea Pig Gamma Globulin (OA)
SAGRCB	South African Greyhound Racing Control Board
SAGS	Scandinavian-American Genealogical Society (EA)
SAGS	Semiactive Gravity-Gradient System [*NASA*]
SAGSET	Society for Academic Gaming and Simulation in Education and Training
SAGSET	Society for the Advancement of Games and Simulation in Education and Training [*British*] (DBA)

SAGT	Scottish Association of Geography Teachers [British]
SAGT	Solarized Advanced Gas Turbine (MCD)
SAGT	Systematic Approach to Group Technology (PDAA)
SAGTA	School and Group Travel Association (EAIO)
SAGU	Saguaro National Monument
Sag Val St C	Saginaw Valley State College (GAGS)
SAGW	Surface-to-Air Guided Weapon [British]
SaH	Saat auf Hoffnung (BJA)
SAH	Sachem Exploration [Vancouver Stock Exchange symbol]
SAH	S-Adenosylhomocysteine [Biochemistry]
Sah	Sahara
SAH	Sample and Hold (IAA)
SAH	Sanaa [Yemen Arab Republic] [Airport symbol] (OAG)
SaH	Sandoz Pharmaceuticals [Research code symbol]
SAH	Sayakhat [Kazakhstan] [ICAO designator] (FAAC)
SAH	School of Applied Health [University of Texas]
SAH	Security Archives Holdings [Data storage company] [British]
SAH	Semiactive Homer [Missiles]
SAH	Society of Aeronautical Historians [Netherlands] (EAIO)
SAH	Society of American Historians [Defunct] (EA)
SAH	Society of Architectural Historians (EA)
SAH	Society of Automotive Historians (EA)
SAH	Standard Allowed Hours
SAH	Standard Average Hour (HGAA)
SAH	Subarachnoid Hemorrhage [Medicine]
SAH	Supreme Allied Headquarters [World War II]
SAH	Systemic Arterial Hypertension [Cardiology] (DAVI)
SAHA	Society of American Historical Artists (EA)
SahaG	Sahara Gaming [Associated Press] (SAG)
SAHAND	Society Against Have a Nice Day (NADA)
SAHARA	Synthetic Aperture High Altitude RADAR (AAG)
SAHC	Chosmadal [Argentina ICAO location identifier] (ICLI)
SAHC	S-Adenosylhomocysteine [Biochemistry]
SAHC	Scottish Australian Heritage Council
SAHC	Scottish Australian Horse Council
SAHC	Self-Aligning Hydraulic Cylinder
SAHC	Sleep Analyzing Hybrid Computer (PDAA)
SAHCTL	South Australian Hard Court Tennis League
SAHDA	South Australian Huntingtons Disease Association
SAHF	Semiautomatic Height Finder
SahGam	Sahara Gaming [Associated Press] (SAG)
SAH(GB)	Society of Architectural Historians (of Great Britain)
SAHH	Society for Austrian and Habsburg History (EA)
SAHI	Sagamore Hill National Historic Site
SAHL	Salvation Army Home League [See also LF] (EAIO)
SaHMI	Sachs, "History of Musical Instruments" [A publication]
SAHP	Solar-Assisted Heat Pump (PDAA)
SAHPS	Solar Energy Assisted Heat Pump System
SAHR	Fuerte Gral Roca [Argentina ICAO location identifier] (ICLI)
SAHR	Semi-Active Homing RADAR [Military] (RDA)
SAHR	Society of Army Historical Research [British] (BI)
SAHR	Spring Apply, Hydraulic Release [Truck brakes]
SAHRA	South Australian Herd Recorders' Association
SAHRC	South Australian Harness Racing Club
SAHRS	Standard Attitude Heading Reference System (MCD)
SAHS	Sleep Apnea-Hypersomnolence Syndrome [Medicine] (DMAA)
SAHS	Swedish-American Historical Society (EA)
SAHS	Swiss-American Historical Society (EA)
SAHSA	Servicio Aereo de Honduras Sociedad Anonima
SAHSPA	South Australian High School Principals' Association
SAHT	South Australian Housing Trust
SAHYB	Simulation of Analog and Hybrid Computers
SAI	Saigo [Japan] [Seismograph station code, US Geological Survey] (SEIS)
SAI	Sales Activity Index [Business] (MHDB)
SAI	Schizophrenics Anonymous International [Later, Canadian Schizophrenia Foundation] (EA)
SAI	Science Applications, Inc. (NRCH)
SAI	Science Associates/International [Publisher] (EA)
SAI	Scientific Aid to Indochina [Task force established 1973 by Scientists' Institute for Public Information]
SAI	Scientific Associates, Inc. (AAG)
SAI	Scottish Agricultural Industries [Commercial firm]
SAI	Scriptwriters' Association International [Defunct] (EA)
SAI	Secondary Air Injection [Automotive engineering]
SAI	Self-Actualization Inventory [Test]
SAI	Self-Analysis Inventory [Psychology]
SAI	Senior Advocates International [Defunct] (EA)
SAI	Senior Army Instructor
SAI	Shaheen Air International [Pakistan] [ICAO designator] (FAAC)
SAI	Shoplifters Anonymous International (EA)
SAI	Sigma Alpha Iota [International professional music fraternity for women] (EA)
SAI	Social Adequacy Index
SAI	Societa Anonima Italiana [Stock company] [Italian]
SAI	Society of American Inventors (EA)
SAI	Software Access International, Inc. [Information service or system] (IID)
SAI	Sold as Is [Philately]
SAI	Son Altesse Imperiale [His or Her Imperial Highness] [French]
sai	South American Indian [MARC language code Library of Congress] (LCCP)
SAI	Southern Alberta Institute of Technology [UTLAS symbol]
SAI	Special Accident Insurance (MCD)
SAI	Specific Acoustic Impedance

SAI	Spherical Attitude Indicator (MCD)
SAI	Standby Airspeed [or Attitude] Indicator (MCD)
SAI	State Agency Issuance [Employment and Training Administration] (OICC)
SAI	Statement of Additional Information [Finances] (BARN)
SAI	Steering Axis Inclination [Automotive engineering]
SAI	Stern Activities Index [Psychology]
SAI	Storage and Inspection (IAA)
SAI	Student Aid Index [Department of Education] (GFGA)
SAI	Subarchitectural Interface
SAI	Suburban Action Institute [Later, MAI] (EA)
SAI	Sudden Auroral Intensity
SAI	Sugar Association, Inc. (EA)
SAI	Sunamerica Capital Trust [NYSE symbol] (SAG)
SAI	Sunamerica Capital Trust II [NYSE symbol] (SAG)
SAI	Sunamerica Capital Trust III [NYSE symbol] (SAG)
SAI	SunAmerica, Inc. [Formerly, Broad, Inc.] [NYSE symbol] (SPSG)
SAI	Surveillance Aided Intercept (NVT)
SAI	Surveillance and Inspection (IAA)
SAI	System Analysis Indicator (MCD)
SAIA	Survival of American Indians Association (EA)
SAIAN	Survey of American Indians and Alaska Natives [Department of Health and Human Services] (GFGA)
SAIAS	Ship Aircraft Inertial Alignment System (NG)
SAIB	Safe Area Intelligence Brief (MCD)
SAIB	Sucrose Acetate Isobutyrate [Organic chemistry]
SAIC	School of the Art Institute of Chicago
SAIC	Science Applications International Corp.
SAIC	Science Applications International Corporation [Marine science] (OSRA)
SAIC	Ship Acquisition and Improvement Council [Navy] (ANA)
SAIC	Small Arms Interpost Competition [Military]
SAIC	South African Indian Congress (PD)
SAIC	Special Agent in Charge [Department of the Treasury]
SAIC	State Actuary and Insurance Commissioner [Queensland, Australia]
SAIC	Switch Action Interrupt Count
SAICAR	Succinoaminoimidazolecarboxamide Ribonucleotide [Biochemistry]
SAICETT	South African Institute of Civil Engineering Technicians and Technologists (EAIO)
SAICIC	South Australian Industrial Court and Industrial Commission
SAIC-WG	Ship Acquisition and Improvement Council-Working Group [Navy] (ANA)
SAID	Safe Area Intelligence Description (MCD)
SAID	Safety Analysis Input Data [Nuclear energy] (NRCH)
SAID	Semiautomatic Integrated Documentation
SAID	Shuttle Avionics Integration Division [NASA] (SSD)
SAID	Society for American Indian Dentists (NTPA)
SAID	Specific Adaptation to Improved Demands [Sports medicine]
SAID	Speech Auto-Instructional Device
SAID	Supplementary Aviation Information Display
SAIDA	Spaced Antenna Imaging Doppler Interferometer [Marine science] (OSRA)
SAIDET	Single-Axis Inertial Drift Erection Test
SAIDI	Spaced Antenna Imaging Doppler Interferometer (USDC)
SAIDS	Simian Acquired Immunodeficiency Syndrome [Animal pathology]
SAIDS	Space Analyst Intervention Display System (MCD)
SAIE	Source and Application Inspection Equipment
SAIE	Special Acceptance Inspection Equipment
SAIER	South Australian Institute of Educational Research
SAIF	Savings Association Insurance Fund [Functions transferred from FSLIC, 1989] [Pronounced "safe"]
SAIF	Southern Africa Institute of Fundraising (NFD)
SAIF	Standard Avionics Integrated Fuzing [Air Force]
SAIFER	Safe Arm Initiation from Electromagnetic Radiation
SAIFX	Salomon Bros. Investors Cl.O [Mutual fund ticker symbol] (SG)
SAIH	Studentenes og Akademikernes Internasjonale Hjelpefond [Norway]
SAII	Sage Analytical International (EFIS)
SAIIC	South and Central American Indian Information Center (EA)
SAIL	Charter Bancshares [NASDAQ symbol] (SPSG)
SAIL	Sea-Air Interaction Laboratory [Oceanography]
SAIL	Serial ASCII Instrument Loop [Computer science] (OSI)
SAIL	Ship Active Item Listing (DNAB)
SAIL	Ship's Armament Inventory List [Navy]
SAIL	Shuttle Avionics Integration Laboratory [NASA]
SAIL	Simple Artificial Interactive Language [Computer science]
SAIL	Staged Assessment in Learning (AIE)
SAIL	Stanford Artificial Intelligence Laboratory [Stanford University]
SAIL	Stanford Artificial Intelligence Language (NITA)
SAIL	Steel Authority of India Ltd. [Commercial firm]
SAILA	Sail Assist International Liaison Associates (EA)
SAILA	Sault Area International Library Association [Library network]
SAILA	Simplified Aircraft Instrument Landing System (PDAA)
SAILEDREP	Sailing Report [Navy] (NVT)
SAILER	Staffing of African Institutions for Legal Education and Research [Later, I nternational Legal Center] [An association]
SAILORD	Sailing Order [Navy] (NVT)
SAILREP	Sailing Report [Navy]
SAILS	Seagoing Assembly-Integration-Launch System
SAILS	Simplified Aircraft Instrument Landing System
SAILS	Standard Army Intermediate Level Supply System [or Subsystem]
SAILS	Swets Automated Independant Library System (NITA)
SAIM	Scottish Amicable Investment Managers [Finance]
SAIM	Semiautomatic Inserting Machine (SAA)
SAIM	South America Indian Mission [Later, SAM] (EA)
SAIM	System Analysis and Integration Model (IAA)

SAIM	Systems Analysis and Integration Model (MCD)
SAIMA	Selected Acquisitions Information and Management System (PDAA)
SAIMI	Societe des Amis de l'Institut Metapsychique International [*Society of Friends of the International Metaphysical Institute*] (EAIO)
SAIMR	South African Institute for Medical Research
SAIMS	Selected Acquisitions, Information, and Management System
SAIMS	Supersonic Airborne Infrared Measurement System (MCD)
SAIN	Society for Advancement in Nursing (EA)
Sainan-G-D	Sainan-Gakuin-Daigaku (BJA)
SAINET	Science Applications, Inc. Global Computer Network (MCD)
Saint	Saint's Digest of Registration Cases [*England*] [*A publication*] (DLA)
SAINT	Salzburg Assembly: Impact of the New Technology
SAINT	Satellite Array for International and National Telecommunications (MCD)
SAINT	Satellite Inspection Technique (MCD)
SAINT	Satellite Inspector and Satellite Interceptor [*Air Force spacecraft program*]
SAINT	Satellite Interceptor (KSC)
SAINT	Self-Aligning Implantation of N-Layer Technology (MCD)
SAINT	Strategic Artificially Intelligent Nuclear Transport [*Robot series designation in 1986 movie "Short Circuit"*]
SAINT	Symbolic Automatic Integrator
SAINT	Systems Analysis of an Integrated Network of Tasks [*Air Force*]
SAINTS	Single Attack Integrated System
SAIORG	Supreme Assembly, International Order of Rainbow for Girls [*Freemasonry*] (EA)
SAIP	Service Aircraft Instrumentation Package (MCD)
SAIP	Ship Acquisition and Improvement Panel [*Navy*] (CAAL)
SAIP	Societe d'Applications Industrielle de la Physique
SAIP	Spares Acquisition Integrated with Production
SAIP	Submarine Antenna Improvement Program [*Military*]
SAIP	Systems Acquisition and Implementation Program [*Environmental Protection Agency*] (GFGA)
SAIPL	Spares Acquisition Incorporated with Production List (MCD)
SAIPMS	Science Applications Incorporated Plan Monitoring System
SAIPrB	SunAmerica 9 1/4% cm'B'Pfd [*NYSE symbol*] (TTSB)
SAIPrE	SunAmerica Dep'E'Pfd [*NYSE symbol*] (TTSB)
SAIPrT	SunAmer Cap 9.95% 'TOPrS' [*NYSE symbol*] (TTSB)
SAIPrV	SunAmer Cap II 8.35%'TOPrS' [*NYSE symbol*] (TTSB)
SAIR	Saugus Ironworks National Historic Site
SAIR	Semiannual Inventory Report [*Military*] (AFM)
SAIR	Southern Association for Institutional Research (EDAC)
SAIRI	Supreme Assembly for the Islamic Revolution in Iraq [*Political party*] (ECON)
SAIRR	South African Institute of Racial Relations
SAIRS	Standardized Advanced Infrared System [*Army*]
SAIS	School of Advanced International Studies [*Johns Hopkins University*]
SAIS	Science and Applications Information System (SSD)
SAIS	Societa Agricola Italo-Somala [*Italo-Somali Agricultural Society*]
SAIS	Society for American Indian Studies (EA)
SAIS	Southwestern American Indian Society [*Later, SAISR*] (FA)
SAISA	South Atlantic Intercollegiate Sailing Association
SAISAC	Ship's Aircraft Inertial System Alignment Console
SAISB	South African Individual Scale for the Blind [*Intelligence test*]
SAISB	South Australian Independent Schools' Board
SAI-SDDL	Science Applications, Inc. - Software Design and Documentation Language (MCD)
SAISR	Society for American Indian Studies and Research [*Formerly, SAIS*] (EA)
SAIT	Southern Alberta Institute of Technology [*Calgary, AB*]
SAITR	Special Artificer, Instruments, Typewriter, and Office Equipment Repairman [*Navy*]
SAIW	Sun Artificial Intelligence Workstation
SAIWR	Special Artificer, Instruments, Watch Repairman [*Navy*]
SAJ	Golden Eagle Air Services Ltd. [*Canada ICAO designator*] (FAAC)
SAJ	Saint Joseph Light & Power [*NYSE symbol*] (SAG)
SAJ	Saints Alive in Jesus (EA)
SAJ	Salon Resources Corp. [*Vancouver Stock Exchange symbol*]
SAJ	Sirajganj [*Bangladesh*] [*Airport symbol*] (AD)
SAJ	Society for the Advancement of Judaism (EA)
SAJ	St. Joseph Light & Power Co. [*NYSE symbol*] (SPSG)
SAJ	St. Joseph Lt & Pwr [*NYSE symbol*] (TTSB)
SAJA	Special Approaches to Juvenile Assistance [*Defunct*] (EA)
SAJAA	South African Journal of African Affairs [*A publication*]
SAJC	Southern Association of Junior Colleges (AEBS)
SAJH	San Juan Island National Historic Park
SAJI	Saw Jig [*Tool*]
SAJIB	Societe d'Animation du Jardin et de l'Institut Botaniques [*Canada*]
SAJMMC	San Antonio Joint Military Medical Command
SAJS	School for Advanced Jewish Studies (BJA)
SAJS	South African Journal of Science [*A publication*]
SAK	Die Sumerischen und Akkadischen Koeningsinschriften [*A publication*] (BJA)
SAK	Kalispell, MT [*Location identifier FAA*] (FAAL)
SAK	Red Arrows Display Squadron [*British ICAO designator*] (FAAC)
SAK	Sakata [*Japan*] [*Seismograph station code, US Geological Survey*] (SEIS)
SAK	Saudarkrokur [*Iceland*] [*Airport symbol*] (OAG)
SAK	Stall Lake Mines [*Vancouver Stock Exchange symbol*]
SAK	Stop Acknowledge (CMD)
SAK	Sveriges Arbetarepartiet Kommunisterna [*Swedish Workers' Communist Party*] [*Political party*] (PPW)
SAK	University of Saskatchewan Libraries [*UTLAS symbol*]
SAKB	Suider Afrikaanse Katolieke Biskopsraad [*Southern African Catholic Bishops' Conference - SACBC*] (EAIO)
SAKI	Saudi Arabia - Kuwait - Iraq
SAKI	Solatron Automatic Keyboard Instructor
SAL	Anderson County Library, Anderson, SC [*OCLC symbol*] (OCLC)
SAL	Caspair Ltd. [*Kenya*] [*ICAO designator*] (FAAC)
SAL	Sacramento Air Logistics Center [*California*] (NAKS)
SAL	Saharan Air Layer [*Meteorology*]
SAL	Salad (WGA)
SAL	Salary (ADA)
SAL	Sale and Leaseback (MHDW)
sal	Salicylate [*Medicine*]
Sal	Salicylate (DB)
SAL	Salina [*Diocesan abbreviation*] [*Kansas*] (TOCD)
SAL	Saline
Sal	Salinger's Reports [*88-117 Iowa*] [*A publication*] (DLA)
SAL	Salinometer (KSC)
sal	Salishan [*MARC language code Library of Congress*] (LCCP)
sal	Saliva (MAE)
SAL	Salivation [*Treatment for syphilis*] [*Slang British*] (DSUE)
sal	Salmon [*Philately*]
Sal	Salmonella [*Bacteriology*]
SAL	Salo [*Italy*] [*Seismograph station code, US Geological Survey*] (SEIS)
sal	Salt (MAE)
SAL	Saluting (MSA)
SAL	Salvation Army Shelter (DSUE)
SAL	Salvex Resources Ltd. [*Vancouver Stock Exchange symbol*]
SAL	Sandhills Agriculture Laboratory [*University of Nebraska - Lincoln*] [*Research center*] (RCD)
SAL	San Salvador [*El Salvador*] [*Airport symbol*] (OAG)
SAL	Saperstein & Associates Ltd. [*Vancouver, BC*] [*Telecommunications*] (TSSD)
SAL	Saskatchewan Accelerator Laboratory [*University of Saskatchewan*] [*Canada*] (IRC)
SAL	Savings and Loan (IAA)
SAL	Scientific Airlock (IAA)
SAL	Sea-Animal Locomotion (SAA)
SAL	Seaboard Air Line Railroad [*Later, SCL*] [*AAR code*]
SAL	Secundum Artis Leges [*According to the Rules of the Art*] [*Latin*] (ADA)
SAL	Selected Altitude Layer [*Decoder*]
SAL	Semiactive LASER [*Military*] (CAAL)
SAL	Senior High Income Portfolio II [*NYSE symbol*] (SPSG)
SAL	Sensorineural Acuity Level [*Medicine*]
SAL	Sequential Analysis of Chemistry Constituents (DAVI)
SAL	Service Action Log (AAG)
SAL	Ship Authorized Leave (NG)
SAL	Ship Authorized Level (MCD)
SAL	Shipboard Allowance List (MSA)
SAL	Short Approach Light [*Aviation*]
SAL	Shuttle Avionics Laboratory [*NASA*] (NASA)
SAL	Small Arms Locker (COE)
SAL	Society of Asian Languages (WDAA)
SAL	Solar Arc Lamp
SAL	Solar Array Leaf
SAL	Sons of the American Legion (EA)
SAL	South American Program Library (IAA)
SAL	South Atlantic League [*Nickname: Sally*] [*Baseball*]
SAL	Southern Airlines [*Australia*]
SAL	Space Astronomy Laboratory [*University of Florida*] [*Research center*] (RCD)
SAL	Special Ammunition Load [*Army*] (AABC)
SAL	SQL [*Structured Query Language*] Windows Application Language [*Computer science*]
SAL	Standard Acceptance Limits
SAL	Station Allowance Unit (NATG)
SAL	Strategic Arms Limitation
SAL	Strong Acid Leach (PDAA)
SAL	Structural Adjustment Loan [*World Bank*]
SAL	Structured Assembly Language
SAL	Subject Authority List [*NASA*]
SAL	Submarine Alerting and Loading System
SAL	Submarine Alerting and Locating [*Navy*]
SAL	Suid-Afrikaanse Lugmag [*South African Air Force*] [*See also SALM, SAAF*]
SAL	Supersonic Aerophysics Laboratory (MCD)
SAL	Supply and Logistics (IAA)
SAL	Surface Mail Air Lifted (ADA)
SAL	Symbolic Assembly Language [*Computer science*] (DIT)
SAL	System Access Layer [*Computer science*]
SAL	Systems and Logistics (IAA)
SAL	Systems Assembly Language [*Computer science*] (IEEE)
SALA	Scientific Assistant Land Agent [*Ministry of Agriculture, Fisheries, and Food*] [*British*]
SALA	Secret Army for the Liberation of Armenia
SALA	Servicios Aeronauticos Latina America
SALA	Solar Arc Lamp Assembly
SALA	Southwest Alliance for Latin America [*Defunct*] (EA)
SALALM	Seminar on the Acquisition of Latin American Library Materials (EA)
SalAMGN	Salomon, Inc. [*Associated Press*] (SAG)
Salant	Salant Corp. [*Associated Press*] (SAG)
SA Law Reports CP	South African Law Reports, Cape Provincial Division [*1910-46*] [*A publication*] (DLA)
SA Law Reports CPD	South African Law Reports, Cape Provincial Division [*1910-46*] [*A publication*] (DLA)
SA Law Reports NPD	South African Law Reports, Natal Province Division [*1910-46*] [*A publication*] (DLA)

SA Law Reports SWA... Reports of the High Court of South-West Africa [*A publication*] (DLA)
SALC........... Sacramento Air Logistics Center (NASA)
SALC........... Secret Army for the Liberation of Corsica
SALC........... Special Associated Logistics Course (MCD)
Sal Comp Cr... Salaman's Liquidation and Composition with Creditors [*2nd ed.*] [*1882*] [*A publication*] (DLA)
SALCV........... Solanum Apical Leaf-Curling Virus
SALD .... Fresh Choice [*NASDAQ symbol*] (TTSB)
SALD .... Fresh Choice, Inc. [*NASDAQ symbol*] (SAG)
SalDEC........... Salomon, Inc. [*Associated Press*] (SAG)
SALDRI........... Semiautomatic Low-Data-Rate Input (SAA)
SALDV........... Salvage Dive [*Military*] (MUGU)
SALE........... Safeguards Analytical Laboratory Evaluation [*Nuclear energy*]
SALE........... Silicon Avalanche Light Emitter
SALE........... Simple Algebraic Language for Engineers [*Computer science*]
SALE........... Simulated Air Launch Environment (MCD)
SALE........... Society for Airline Meteorologists (IAA)
SALE........... Special Ammunition Logistical Element
SALEA........... South Australian Livestock Exporters' Association
Salem........... Salem Corp. [*Associated Press*] (SAG)
Salem St C.. Salem State College (GAGS)
SALES........... Ship Aircraft Locating Equipment
SALF........... Society of American Legion Founders [*Defunct*] (EA)
SALF........... Somali Abo Liberation Front [*Ethiopia*] [*Political party*] (PD)
SALF........... Sudan African Liberation Front
SALFAS........... Stand-Alone Low-Frequency Active Sonar (DOMA)
SALG .... South American Liaison Group (CINC)
SALGEP .... Scottish Association of Local Government to Educational Psychologists [*British*]
SALGGC .... South Australian Local Government Grants Commission
SAL-GP .... Semiactive LASER-Guided Projectile (MCD)
SALH .... South Alberta Light Horse (DMA)
SalHWP .... Salomon, Inc. [*Associated Press*] (SAG)
SALI........... Selected Abstracts: Library, Information [*Australia A publication*]
SALI........... Surface Analysis by LASER Ionization
SALIC........... Salicional [*Music*]
Salick........... Salick Health Care, Inc. [*Associated Press*] (SAG)
salicyl........... Salicylate [*Pharmacology*] (DAVI)
SALINET ...... Satellite Library Information Network
SAL/IR........... Semiactive LASER/Infrared (DWSG)
SALIS........... Salisbury [*England*]
SALIS........... Substance Abuse Librarians and Information Specialists (EA)
Salisbury St U... Salisbury State University (GAGS)
Saliva .... Saliva Diagnostic Systems [*Commercial firm Associated Press*] (SAG)
Salk .... Salkeld's English King's Bench Reports [*91 English Reprint*] [*A publication*] (DLA)
Salk (Eng) ... Salkeld's English King's Bench Reports [*91 English Reprint*] [*A publication*] (DLA)
SALL........... Sallust [*Roman historian, 86-34BC*] [*Classical studies*] (ROG)
SALL........... Shore Activity Load List
SALLB........... South Australian Law Librarians Bulletin [*A publication*]
SallieM........ Student Loan Marketing [*Associated Press*] (SAG)
SALLIE MAE... Student Loan Marketing Association [*See also SLMA*]
SallM........... Student Loan Marketing Association [*Sallie Mae*] [*Associated Press*] (SAG)
Sally Mae.... Student Loan Marketing Association (EBF)
Salm........... Salmagundi [*A publication*] (BRI)
Salm........... Salmanassar (BJA)
SALM........... Salvation Army League of Mercy [*British*] (EAIO)
SALM........... Single Anchor Leg Mooring [*Oil platform*]
SALM........... Society of Air Line Meteorologists
SALMA........... South American Land Mammal Age [*Geological epoch*]
Salm Abr .... Salmon's Abridgment of State Trials [*A publication*] (DLA)
Salmant........ Salmanticensis [*Salamanca, Spain*] [*A publication*] (BJA)
SalmHIF........ Salomon Brothers High Income Fund [*Associated Press*] (SAG)
Salmn........... Salomon, Inc. [*Associated Press*] (SAG)
SalmSBF...... Salomon Brothers Fund [*Associated Press*] (SAG)
SalMSFT...... Salomon, Inc. [*Associated Press*] (SAG)
Salm St R.... Salmon's Edition of the State Trials [*A publication*] (DLA)
Salnt........... Salant Corp. [*Associated Press*] (SAG)
SALO .... State Aviation Liaison Official (NOAA)
SALO .... Stop Authorization and Lift Order (AAG)
SalO8Ww.... Salomon Brothers 2008 Worldwide Dollar Government Term Trust [*Associated Press*] (SAG)
SALOA .... Special Arc Light Operation Area (DNAB)
Salomn........ Salomon, Inc. [*Associated Press*] (SAG)
SALON........... Satellite Balloon (IAA)
SALOON........ Satellite Launched from a Balloon (IAA)
SALOP .... Shrewsbury [*British depot code*]
SALOP .... Shropshire [*County in England*]
SalORCL...... Salomon, Inc. [*Associated Press*] (SAG)
SALORS...... Structural Analysis of Layered Orthotropic Ring-Stiffened Shells [*Computer program*] (NASA)
SALP........... Sodium Aluminum Phosphate [*Inorganic chemistry*]
SALP........... South African Labour Party
SALP........... Systematic Assessment of Licensee Performance [*Nuclear energy*] (NRCH)
SALPA .... Special Adult Learning Programmes Association (AIE)
SalPage........ Salomon Page Group Ltd. [*Associated Press*] (SAG)
SalPge........ Salomon Page Group Ltd. [*Associated Press*] (SAG)
SalPge........ Solomon Page Group Ltd. [*Associated Press*] (SAG)
SalPhib........ Salomon Phibro Oil Trust [*Associated Press*] (SAG)
SalPRI........ Salomon, Inc. [*Associated Press*] (SAG)

SALR .... Saturation Adiabatic Lapse Rate [*Meteorology*] (ADA)
SALR .... Synthetic Aperture LASER RADAR
SALRC .... Society for the Assistance of Ladies in Reduced Circumstances [*British*] (DI)
SALRCP .... South African Law Reports, Cape Provincial Division [*1910-46*] [*A publication*] (DLA)
SAL Reports OPD... South African Law Reports, Orange Free State Provincial Division [*1910-46*] [*A publication*] (DLA)
SALR SWA... South African Law Reports, South West African Reports [*A publication*] (DLA)
SALS........... Separate Access Landing System [*Aviation*] (DA)
SALS........... Short Approach Light System [*Aviation*]
SALS........... Simple Approach Lighting System [*Aviation*] (FAAC)
SALS........... Single Anchor Leg Storage (PDAA)
SALS........... Small-Angle Light Scattering
SALS........... Solid-State Acoustoelectric Light Scanner
SALS........... Southern Adirondack Library System [*Library network*]
SALS........... Southern African Literature Society [*Botswana*] (EAIO)
SALS........... Standard Army Logistics System
SALSC .... Scottish Association of Local Sports Councils (DBA)
SALSF .... Short Approach Light System with Sequenced Flashers [*Aviation*]
SALS-K .... Single Ammunition Logistics System - Korea (MCD)
SalSNPL...... Salomon, Inc. [*Associated Press*] (SAG)
SALSU........... Singapore Admiralty Local Staff Union
SaLSUA ...... Sierra Leone Students Union of the Americas (EA)
Salt........... De Saltatione [*of Lucian*] [*Classical studies*] (OCD)
SALT........... Saltash [*England*]
SALT........... Salton/Maxim Housewares [*NASDAQ symbol*] (SPSG)
SALT........... Salvation and Laughter Together [*Defunct*] (EA)
SALT........... Self-Contained All-Weather Landing and Taxiing (MCD)
SALT........... Serum Alanine Aminotransferase [*An enzyme*]
SALT........... Signal and Homing Light (IAA)
SALT........... Sisters All Learning Together [*Feminist group*]
SALT........... Size, Activity, Location, Type Report [*Military*] (INF)
SALT........... Skin-Associated Lymphoid Tissue [*Dermatology*]
SALT........... Society for Applied Learning Technology (EA)
SALT........... Society of American Law Teachers (EA)
SALT........... South African Large Telescope
SALT........... South African Law Times [*A publication*] (DLA)
SALT........... Speech and Language Technology [*British*]
SALT........... Stand Alone Terminal (IAA)
SALT........... State Agency Libraries of Texas [*Library network*]
SALT........... Strategic Arms Limitation Talks (EBF)
SALT........... Strategic Arms Limitation Treaty (MCD)
SALT........... Subscribers' Apparatus Line Tester [*Telecommunications*] (TEL)
SALT........... Suggestive-Accelerative Learning and Teaching (EDAC)
SALT........... Supporting Arms Liaison Team [*Army*] (INF)
SALT........... Swedish Aspirin Low-Dose Trial
SALT........... Symbolic Algebraic Language Translator [*Computer science*]
SALTE........... Semiautomatic Line Test Equipment (NG)
SalTerz........ Sal Terrae. Revista Hispanoamericana de Cultura Ecclesiastica [*Santander, Spain*] [*A publication*] (BJA)
SALTHQ........ Strike Command Alternate Headquarters [*Military*] (AABC)
SALTI........... Summary Accounting for Low-Dollar Turnover Items [*Army*]
SALTIRE ..... Scottish Academic Live Television Interconnect and Research Environment (AIE)
SaltMax........ Salton Maxim Housewares, Inc. [*Associated Press*] (SAG)
SALT-P .... Slosson Articulation, Language Test with Phonology [*Child development test*]
SALTS........... Streamlined Alternative Logistics Transmission System (DOMA)
SALTS........... Streamlined Automated Logistics Transmission System
SALTS........... Systems Alterations Status
SALUT........... Sea, Air, Land, and Underwater Targets [*Navy*]
SALUTE........ Size, Activity, Location, Unit, Time, Equipment (MCD)
SALV........... Duty Salvage Ship [*Navy*] (NVT)
SALV........... Saliva Diagnostic Systems [*NASDAQ symbol*] (SAG)
SALV........... Salvador [*Brazil*] (OAG)
SALV........... Salvage [*Military*] (AFM)
SALVDIVB.... Salvage Diver Badge [*Military decoration*] (GFGA)
Salv Div Bad... Salvage Diver Badge [*Military decoration*]
SALVDV .... Salvage Dives [*Army*]
SALVEX........ Salvage Exercise (MCD)
SALVOPS.... Salvage Operations [*Navy*] (NVT)
SALVTNG.... Salvage Training [*Navy*] (NVT)
SALVW........ Saliva Diagnostic Sys Wrrt [*NASDAQ symbol*] (TTSB)
SALWIS ...... Shipboard Air-Launched Weapons Installation System (NG)
SalWw........... Salomon Brothers Worldwide Income Fund [*Associated Press*] (SAG)
SALX........... Shamrock Airlines [*Air carrier designation symbol*]
SALX........... Synergistic Holding Corp. [*NASDAQ symbol*] (SAG)
SALY........... Salary (ROG)
SAM........... Boston Beer 'A' [*NYSE symbol*] (TTSB)
SAM........... Boston Beer Co. [*NYSE symbol*] (SAG)
SAM........... Eparchy of St. Maron of Brooklyn [*Diocesan abbreviation*] [*United States of America*] (TOCD)
SAM........... Saba [*Netherlands Antilles*] [*Airport symbol*] (AD)
SAM........... S-Adenosylmethionine [*Also, AdoMet, SAMe*] [*Biochemistry*]
SAM........... Safety Activation Monitor (IEEE)
SAM........... Salamo [*Papua New Guinea*] [*Airport symbol*] (OAG)
SAM........... Salicylamide [*Analgesic compound*]
Sam........... Samaria (BJA)
Sam........... Samaritan (BJA)
sam........... Samaritan Aramaic [*MARC language code Library of Congress*] (LCCP)
SAM........... Samarkand [*Former USSR Seismograph station code, US Geological Survey*] (SEIS)

Sam	Samoa (BARN)
SAM	Sample and Analysis Management System [*Computer science*]
SAM	Sampling and Analytical Method
Sam	Samson (BJA)
SAM	Samsville, IL [*Location identifier FAA*] (FAAL)
Sam	Samuel [*Old Testament book*]
SAM	Scanning Acoustic Microscope
SAM	Scanning Auger Microprobe (IAA)
SAM	Scanning Auger Microscopy
SAM	School-Aged Maternity (EDAC)
SAM	School Apperception Method [*Psychology*]
SAM	School Attitude Measure [*Test*] [*Canadian Comprehensive Assessment Program*]
SAM	School in Agency Management [*LIMRA*]
SAM	School of Aerospace Medicine [*Formerly, School of Aviation Medicine*]
SAM	School of Assets Management [*Later, School of Materiel Readiness*] [*Army*]
SAM	Scottish Association of Metals (DBA)
SAM	Screen Activated Machine [*Parimutuel wagering*]
SAM	Script Applier Mechanism [*Programming language*] [*1975*] (CSR)
SAM	Sea Air Mariner
SAM	Security Accounts Manager
SAM	Selective Automatic Monitoring
SAM	Selective Automonitoring Tracing Routine (IAA)
SAM	Self Addressing Memory (IAA)
SAM	Self-Administered Medication [*Medicine*] (MEDA)
SAM	Self-Assembled Monolayer [*Physical chemistry*]
SAM	Self-Propelled Anthropomorphic Manipulator [*Moon machine*]
SAM	Semantic Analyzing Machine
SAM	Semiautomatic Active Memory (SAA)
SAM	Semiautomatic Film Mounter (SAA)
SAM	Semiautomatic Mathematics (IEEE)
SAM	Semiautomatic Mounter [*3M Co.*]
SAM	Semiautonomous Acoustic/Magnetic [*Vehicle*] (DOMA)
SAM	Semiconductor Active Memory [*Computer science*] (IAA)
SAM	Semiconductor Advanced Memory [*Computer science*] (IAA)
SAM	Send-a-Message (MCD)
SAM	Sensing with Active Microwave
SAM	Sequence and Monitor (IAA)
SAM	Sequential Access Memory [*Computer science*] (IEEE)
SAM	Sequential Access Method [*IBM Corp.*] [*Computer science*]
SAM	Serial Access Memory [*Computer science*]
SAM	Service Aggregated Module
SAM	Service Attitude Measurement [*Bell System*]
SAM	Sex Arousal Mechanism [*Medicine*]
SAM	Shared Appreciation Mortgage [*Banking*]
SAM	Shoot Apical Meristem [*Botany*]
SAM	Shuttle Attachment Manipulator [*NASA*] (NAKS)
SAM	Signal Analyzing Monitor (KSC)
SAM	Signal [*System*] for Assessment and Modification [*of behavior*] [*Patented*]
SAM	Simple Architecture Microprocessor
SAM	Simulated Assignment Model
SAM	Simulation of Analog Methods [*Computer science*]
SAM	Single Application Method [*College admissions*]
SAM	Sinusoidal Amplitude Modulation [*Physics*]
SA/M	Site Assessment and Mitigation
SAM	Site Availability Mode [*Environmental science*] (COE)
SAM	Six-Axis Manipulator (PDAA)
SAM	Skills Assessment Module [*Michelle Rosinek*] (TES)
SAM	Social Accounting Matrix (WDAA)
SAM	Sociedad Aeronautica de Medellin [*Colombia*] [*ICAO designator*] (FAAC)
SAM	Sociedad Aeronautica de Medellin Consolidada [*Colorado*]
SAM	Societe des Americanistes
SAM	Society for Adolescent Medicine (EA)
SAM	Society for Advancement of Management [*Cincinnati, OH*] (EA)
SAM	Society for Asian Music (EA)
SAM	Society of Aerospace Medicine (NADA)
SAM	Society of Americanists [*Paris, France*] (EA)
SAM	Society of American Magicians (EA)
SAM	Society of Antique Modelers (EA)
SAM	Software Acquisition Manager (AAGC)
SAM	Soldier, Sailor, Airman, Marine [*A publication*]
SAM	Soluble Adhesion Molecule [*Biochemistry*]
SAM	Something About Myself Inventory (EDAC)
SAM	Sort and Merge
SAM	Sound Absorption Material [*Aviation*]
SAM	Sound-Activated Mobile (PDAA)
SAM	Sourcebook in Applied Mathematics [*National Science Foundation project*]
S Am	South America (VRA)
SAM	South America Mission (EA)
SAM	South American
SAM	South American Region [*USTTA*] (TAG)
SAM	Southern Appalachian Migrant [*Cincinnati slang*]
SAM	Space Age Microcircuits (IAA)
SAM	Space Assemble and Maintenance (SSD)
SAM	Space Available Mail [*Military*] (AABC)
SAM	Special Advisory Message
SAM	Special Air Mission [*Aircraft*] [*Military*]
SAM	Spills, Accidents, and Mixtures [*of Exxon Corp.'s "Stop SAM" safety program*]
SAM	Spinal Analysis Machine

SAM	Squarewave Amplitude Modulation
SAM	Stabilized Assay Meter (NRCH)
SAM	Stage Assembly and Maintenance [*Building*]
SAM	Standard Addition Method [*Mathematics*]
SAM	Standard Analysis Method
SAM	Standard Assembly Module [*Eastman Kodak Co.*]
SAM	Standard Avionics Module (MCD)
SAM	Station Acquisition Marketing Plan [*PBS*] (NTCM)
SAM	Stationing Analysis Model [*Military*] (GFGA)
SAM	Stimuli and Measurements (KSC)
SAM	Strachey and McIlroy [*in SAM/76, a programming language named after its authors and developed in 1976*] (CSR)
SAM	Stratospheric Aerosol Measurement [*or Monitor*] [*Meteorology*]
SAM	Strela Antiaircraft Missiles
SAM	Streptozocin, Adriamycin, Methyl-CCNU [*or Semustine*] [*Antineoplastic drug regimen*] (DAVI)
SAM	Stroboscopic Analyzing Monitor [*Instrumentation*]
SAM	Strong Absorption Model [*Nuclear physics*] (OA)
SAM	Structural Acoustic Monitor
SAM	Structural Assembly Model [*NASA*]
SAM	Student Achievement Monitoring [*Vocational guidance*]
SAM	Study of American Markets [*US News and World Report*]
SAM	Subject Activity Monitor [*Device used in biological research*]
SAM	Subsequent Address Message [*Telecommunications*] (TEL)
SAM	Substitute Alloy Material [*Nuclear energy*]
SAM	Substrate Adhesion Molecule [*Cytology*]
SAM	Substrate-Attached Material [*Cytology*]
SAM	Subsynoptic Advection Model
SAM	Subsystem Action Message [*Military*]
SAM	Subtraction, Addition, Multiplication
SAM	Sulfated Acid Mucopolysaccharide [*Medicine*] (MAE)
SAM	Sulfur-Asphalt Module [*Road-paving technology*]
SAM	Surface-Active Material
SAM	Surface-to-Air Missile
SAM	Symantec Antivirus for Macintosh [*Computer science*] (CDE)
SAM	Symbolic and Algebraic Manipulation (IEEE)
SAM	Sympathetic Adreno Medullary Axis
SAM	Synchronous Amplitude Modulation
SAM	System Accuracy Model
SAM	System Activation and Monitoring [*NASA*] (NAKS)
SAM	System Activity Monitor [*Computer science*]
SAM	System Administration Manager [*Hewlett-Packard Co.*] (PCM)
SAM	System Administration Menu [*Hewlett-Packard Co.*]
SAM	System Analysis Machine (IAA)
SAM	System for Automatic Message Switching [*Telecommunications*] (TSSD)
SAM	Systems Acquisition Management (AAGC)
SAM	Systems Adapter Module
SAM	Systems Adaptor Module (NITA)
SAM	Systems Analysis Module (IFFF)
SAM	Systolic Anterior Motion [*Cardiology*]
SAMA	Gral Alvear [*Argentina ICAO location identifier*] (ICLI)
SAMA	Sacramento Air Materiel Area
SAMA	Salem Maritime National Historic Site
SAMA	Saudi Arabian Monetary Agency [*Riyadh*]
SAMA	Scientific Apparatus Makers Association [*Later, SAMAGA*] (EA)
SAMA	Scottish Amateur Music Association (DBA)
SAMA	Serum Agar Measuring Aid
SAMA	Site Approval and Market Analysis [*FHA*]
SAMA	Sociedad de Amistad Mexico Albania [*Mexico-Albania Friendship Society*] (EAIO)
SAMA	Specialty Automotive Manufacturers Association [*Newport Beach, CA*] (EA)
SAMA	Student American Medical Association [*Later, AMSA*] (EA)
SAMA	Survey of Adults and Markets of Affluence [*Monroe Mendelsohn Research, Inc.*] [*Information service or system*] (CRD)
SAMAA	Special Assistant for Military Assistance Affairs [*Army*] (AABC)
SAMAC	Scientific and Management Advisory Committee [*Terminated, 1973*] [*Army Computer Systems Command*]
SAMAC	Swedish American Museum Association of Chicago (EA)
SAMADB	State and Metropolitan Area Data Book [*Bureau of the Census*] (GFGA)
SAMAE	Southern Air Materiel Area, Europe
SAMAGA	SAMA [*Scientific Apparatus Makers Association*] Group of Associations (EA)
SAM & R	Ship Activation, Maintenance, and Repair
SAMANTHA	System for the Automated Management of Text from a Hierarchical Arrangement
SAMAP	Southern Air Materiel Area, Pacific [*Army*] (AFIT)
SAM-APD	Separate Absorption and Multiplication Region Avalanche Photodiode
SAMAR	Ship Activation, Maintenance, and Repair
SAMAR	Surface-to-Air Missile Availability Report (NG)
SAMAS	Security Assistance Manpower Accounting System (MCD)
SAMAS	Service-Craft and Boats Machine Accounting System [*Navy*] (DNAB)
SA Mast Build	South Australian Master Builder [*A publication*]
SAM-B	School of Aviation [*later, Aerospace*] Medicine - Brooks
SAMB	[*UK Liaison Committee for*] Sciences Allied to Medicine and Biology (ACII)
SAMB	Scottish Association of Master Bakers (DBA)
SAMB	Secondary Aircraft Maintenance Base
SAMBA	Saudi American Bank
SAMBA	Special Agents Mutual Benefit Association [*FBI standardized term*]
SAMBA	Systems Approach to Managing BUSHIPS [*Bureau of Ships; later, NESC or ESC*] Acquisition [*Navy*] (MCD)
SAMBO	Strategic Antimissile Barrage Objects

SAMBUD...... System for Automation of Materiel Plan for Army Materiel/Budget (AABC)
SAMC........... Cristo Redentor [*Argentina ICAO location identifier*] (ICLI)
SAMC........... Samsonite Corp. [*NASDAQ symbol*] (SAG)
SAMC........... South African Medical Corps
SAMC........... Southern Africa Media Center (EA)
SAMC........... Surface Ammunition Malfunction Control (DNAB)
SAMCAP....... Surface-to-Air Missile Capability (PDAA)
SAM-CD........ Scientific American Medicine - Compact Disc [*Electronic publication*]
SAMCEP ...... Self-Protected Air-to-Air Missile Concept Evaluation Program [*Army*]
SamChron.... Samaritan Chronology (BJA)
SAMCO........ Sales Associates Management Corp. [*Palm Springs, CA*] (EA)
SAMCOS....... Senior Army Materiel Command Orientation Seminar
SAMCTT....... School of Aerospace Medicine Color Threshold Test
SAMCU........ Special Airborne Medical Care Unit (MCD)
SAMD .... S-Adenosyl-L-Methionine Decarboxylase (DB)
SAMD .... Surface-to-Air Missile Development
SAMDA .... Standard Asset Management and Disposition Agreement [*Resolution Trust Corp.*]
SAM-DC....... S-Adenosylmethionine Decarboxylase [*An enzyme*]
SAM-D/CDP... Surface-to-Air Missile-Development, Contract Definition (SAA)
SAMe........... Mendoza/El Plumerillo [*Argentina ICAO location identifier*] (ICLI)
SAMe........... S-Adenosylmethionine [*Also, AdoMet, SAM*] [*Biochemistry*]
SAMe........... S-Adenosyl-Methionine [*Dietary supplement*]
SAME........... Sensory-Afferent/Motor-Efferent [*Neurology*]
SAME........... Society of American Military Engineers (EA)
SAME........... Spanish Association for Medical Education [*British*] (EAIO)
SAME........... Students Against Misleading Enterprises [*Student legal action organization*]
SAMEA........ South Australian Meat Exporters' Association
SAMEAC ..... South Australian Multicultural and Ethnic Affairs Commission
SAMECS ...... Structural Analysis Method for Evaluation of Complex Structures (PDAA)
SAMED .... South African Medical Literature [*South African Research Council*] [*Information service or system*] (CRD)
SAMEM........ Sustained-Attrition Minefield Evaluation Model (DNAB)
S Amer........ South America
SAMEX........ Shuttle Active-Microwave Experiments (MCD)
SAMEX........ Surface-to-Air Missile Exercise (NVT)
SAMF........... Mendoza [*Argentina ICAO location identifier*] (ICLI)
SAMF........... Salvation Army Medical Fellowship (EAIO)
SAMF........... Seaborne Army Maintenance Facilities
SAMF........... Ship's Air Maintenance Facility [*Navy*] (NVT)
SAMF........... Switchable Acoustic Matched Filter
Samford U ... Samford University (GAGS)
SAMFS .... South Australian Metropolitan Fire Service
SAMFU .... Self-Adjusting Military Foul-Up [*Slang*]
SAMH .... Scottish Association for Mental Health [*British*]
SAMH .... Valle Hermoso [*Argentina ICAO location identifier*] (ICLI)
SAMHO .... Society of Administrative Mental Health Offices [*British*] (BI)
Sam Houston St U... Sam Houston State University (GAGS)
SAMHSA ...... Substance Abuse and Mental Health Services Administration [*Formerly, ADAMHA*] [*Department of Health and Human Services*]
SAMHSJ ...... South Australian Methodist Historical Society. Journal [*A publication*] (ADA)
SAMI........... Sales and Marketing Information Ltd. [*Database producer*] (IID)
SAMI........... Sales Areas Marketing, Inc. (DOAD)
SAMI........... San Martin [*Argentina ICAO location identifier*] (ICLI)
SAMI........... Selling Areas-Marketing, Inc. [*Originator and database*] [*New York, NY Information service or system*] (IID)
SAMI........... Sequential Assessment of Mathematics Inventory
SAMI........... Single Action Maintenance Instruction (NG)
SAMI........... Socially Acceptable Monitoring Instrument (BABM)
SAMI........... Socially Acceptable Monitoring Instruments [*Medicine*]
SAMI........... Speed of Approach Measurement Indicator (PDAA)
SAMI........... Systems Acquisition Management Inspection
SAMICS .... Solar Array Manufacturing Industry Costing Standards
SAMICS ...... Systems Applications of Millimeter Wave Contact Seeker (MCD)
SAMID .... Ship Antimissile Integrated Defense [*Program*] [*Navy*]
SAMID .... Surface-to-Air Missile Intercept Development
SAMIDS .... Ships Anti-Missile Integrated Defense System (PDAA)
SAMIP .... Surface-to-Air Missile Improvement Program (MCD)
SAMIPAC ..... Societe Auxiliare et Miniere du Pacifique [*France*] (PDAA)
SAMIS .... Safety Management Information Statistics [*FTA*] (TAG)
SAMIS .... Security Assistance Management Information System (MCD)
SAMIS .... Ship Alteration Management Information System [*Discontinued*] [*Navy*]
SAMIS .... Solar Array Manufacturing Industry Simulation
SAMIS .... Standard Army Management Information System (MCD)
SAMIS .... Structural Analysis and Matrix Interpretive System (IAA)
SAMIS .... Structural Analysis and Matrix Inversion System [*Nuclear energy*] (NRCH)
SAMJ........... Jachal [*Argentina ICAO location identifier*] (ICLI)
SAML........... Nationella Samlingspartiet [*National Coalition Party*] [*Finland Political party*] (PPE)
SAML........... Sam & Libby, Inc. [*NASDAQ symbol*] (SPSG)
Saml........... Samuel [*Old Testament Book*] (WGA)
SAML........... Sinus Histiocytes with Massive Lymphadenopathy [*Clinical chemistry*]
SAML........... Standard Army Management Language (AABC)
SAMLA........ Southern Atlantic Modern Language Association
SamLby .... Sam & Libby, Inc. [*Associated Press*] (SAG)
SAMM........... Malargue [*Argentina ICAO location identifier*] (ICLI)
SAMM........... Security Assistance Management Manual [*A publication*] (AAGC)
SAMM........... South Australian Maritime Museum

SAMM.......... Standard Automated Material Management System [*DoD*]
SAMM.......... Support after Murder & Manslaughter (WDAA)
SAMM.......... Systematic Activity Modeling Method (MHDB)
SAMMA....... Stores Account Material Management Afloat (NG)
SAMMA/SAL... Stores Account Material Management Afloat / Ship Authorization Level (DNAB)
SAMMI........ Signature Analysis Methods for Mission Identification
SAMMIE....... Scheduling Analysis Model for Mission Integrated Experiments [*NASA*] (KSC)
SAMMIE....... System for Aiding Man-Machine Interaction [*Prime Computer (UK) Ltd. and Prime Computers CAD/CAM Ltd.*] [*Software package*] (NCC)
SAMMS........ Ship Alteration Material Management System
SAMMS........ Standard Automated Materiel Management System [*DoD*]
SAMNAM...... Samradet for Nordisk Amatormusik [*Arhus, Denmark*] (EAIO)
SAM-NIS...... Screen for Aeronautical Material - Not in Stock (DNAB)
SAMO .... Senior Administrative Medical Officer (DMAA)
SAMO .... Simulated Ab Initio Molecular Orbitals [*Atomic physics*]
SAMO .... Somali African Muki Organisation
SAMOA .... Systematic Approach to Multidimensional Occupational Analysis (MCD)
Samoan PLJ... Samoan Pacific Law Journal [*A publication*] (DLA)
SAMOD .... Secretary of the Army's Mobility, Opportunity, and Development Program (MCD)
SAMOS .... Satellite-Missile Observation Satellite [*or System*]
SAMOS .... Silicon and Aluminum Metal-Oxide Semiconductor (ADA)
SAMOS .... Spot Accumulation and Melting of Snow (PDAA)
SAMOS .... Stacked-Gate Avalanche Injection Type Metal-Oxide Semiconductor (IAA)
SAMOS .... Surveillance and Missile Observation System [*Military*] (IAA)
SAMP .... La Paz [*Argentina ICAO location identifier*] (ICLI)
SAMP .... Salary Administration and Manpower Planning (PDAA)
SAMP .... Sample (AAG)
SAMP .... Sense Amplifier (NITA)
SAMP .... Shuttle Automated Mass Properties [*NASA*] (MCD)
SAMP .... Small Arms Master Plan [*Military document*] (INF)
SAMP .... Stuntmen's Association of Motion Pictures (EA)
SAMP .... Stuntwomen's Association of Motion Pictures (EA)
SAMPAC ..... Society of Advertising Musicians, Producers, Arrangers, and Composers
SAMPAM ..... System for Automation of Materiel Plans for Army Material (MCD)
SAMPAP ..... Security Assistance Master Planning and Phasing
SAMPD .... Science Analysis and Mission Planning Directorate [*NASA*]
SAMPE .... Society for the Advancement of Material and Process Engineering (EA)
SAMPE........ Society of Aerospace Material and Process Engineers (AEBS)
SAMPEX ...... Solar Anomalous and Magnetospheric Particle Explorer
SAM-PEX .... Solar, Anomalous, and Magnetospheric Particle Explorer Satellite
SAMPF .... Sampford [*England*]
SAMPLE....... Single Assignment Mathematical Programming Language [*1971*] [*Computer science*] (CSR)
SAMPM........ Scottish Association of Milk Product Manufacturers (DBA)
SAMPS .... Shore Activity Manpower Planning System (DNAB)
SAMPS .... Subdivision and Map Plotting System (MHDB)
SAMPSP ...... Security Assistance Master Planning and Phasing (MCD)
SAMQ .... Mendoza Aeroparque [*Argentina ICAO location identifier*] (ICLI)
SAMR .... San Rafael [*Argentina ICAO location identifier*] (ICLI)
SAMR .... Special Assistant for Material Readiness [*Army*]
SAMRA .... Sino-American Medical Rehabilitation Association
SAMRAF ...... South African Military Refugee Aid Fund [*Defunct*] (EA)
SAMRT .... Shared Aperture Medium-Range Tracker (MCD)
SAMS .... Sample Method Survey [*for family housing requirements*] [*Military*] (AABC)
SAMS .... Sampling Analog Memory System
SAMS .... San Carlos [*Argentina ICAO location identifier*] (ICLI)
SAMS .... Sandia Air Force Material Study (MCD)
SAMS .... Satellite Automatic Monitoring System [*Programming language*]
SAMS .... Satellite Auto-Monitor System (NITA)
SAMS .... School for Advanced Military Studies [*Army*]
SAMS .... Scottish Association for Marine Science
SAMS .... Security Assistance Management Squadron
SAMS .... Semiautomatic Meteorological Station (SAA)
SAMS .... Ship Alteration Material Survey (DNAB)
SAMS .... Ship's Alteration Management System [*Navy*]
SAMS .... Shore Activity Management Support [*Navy*] (NVT)
SAMS .... Shuttle Attachment Manipulator System [*NASA*]
SAMS .... Shuttle Automated Management System (SSD)
SAMS .... Six Axis Motion System (PDAA)
SAMS .... Society for Advanced Medical Systems [*Later, AMIA*]
SAMS .... Society of Accredited Marine Surveyors (NTPA)
SAMS .... Society of Advanced Motorists Sydney [*Australia*]
SAMS .... South African Medical Services (WDAA)
SAMS .... Space Assembly, Maintenance, and Servicing (SSD)
SAMS .... Stand-Alone Mudmixing System
SAMS .... Standard Army Maintenance System (AABC)
SAMS .... Stratospheric and Mesospheric Sounder
SAMS .... Study Attitudes and Methods Survey [*Study skills test*]
SAMS .... Surface-to-Air Missile System [*Military*]
SAMSA .... Silica and Moulding Sands Association [*British*] (BI)
SAMSA .... Standard Army Management System - Supply Support Arrangement
SAM-SAC.... Specialized Aircraft Maintenance - Strategic Air Command (AAG)
SAM/SAR .... South America/South Atlantic Region [*DoD*]
SAMSARS ... Satellite-Based Maritime Search and Rescue System [*Telecommunications*] (TEL)
SAMSAT ...... Solar Activity Monitoring Satellite (MCD)

SAM/SAT	South America/South Atlantic Region [Aviation]
SAMSAT	Surface-to-Air Missile Servicing, Assembly, and Test
SAMSEM	Ship Antimissile System Engagement Model [Navy] (CAAL)
SAMSI	Spacecraft Array for Michelson Spectral Inferometry
SAMSIM	Surface-to-Air Missile Simulation Model (MCD)
SAMS/MAMS	Special Airspace Management System/Military Airspace Management System [FAA] (TAG)
Samsnte	Samsonite Corp. [Associated Press] (SAG)
SAMSO	Space and Missile Systems Office [Air Force]
SAMSO	Space and Missile Systems Organization [Merger of Ballistic Systems Division and Space Systems Division] [Air Force]
SAMSO	Systems Analysis of Manned Space Operations (MCD)
SAMSOM	Support Availability Multisystem Operational Model
SAMSON	Sources of Ambient MicroSeismic Oceanic Noise Experiment [Office of Naval Research]
SAMSON	Strategic Automatic Message-Switching Operational Network [Canada] (MCD)
SAMSON	System Analysis of Manned Space Operations (MCD)
SAMSOR	Space and Missile Systems Organization Regulation [Later, SDR] [Air Force] (NASA)
SAMSOT	SAMID [Ship Antimissile Integrated Defense] System Operational Test [Navy] (NVT)
SAMSq	Special Air Mission Squadron [Vietnam Air Force] (AFM)
SAMS-USA	South American Missionary Society of the Episcopal Church (EA)
SAMT	Semiautomated Mechanical Transmission [Automotive engineering]
SAMT	Simulated Aircraft Maintenance Trainer (MCD)
SAMT	State-of-the-Art Medium Terminal
SAMTEC	Space and Missile Test and Evaluation Center [Air Force] (DOMA)
SAMTEC	Space and Missile Test Center [Air Force]
SAMTEC/DET 1	Space and Missile Test Center Detachment 1 [Patrick Air Force Base, FL]
SAMTECM	Space and Missile Test Center Manual [Air Force] (MCD)
SAMTO	Space and Missile Test Organization [Vandenberg Air Force Base, CA] [Air Force]
SAMTS	Simulated A/C Maintenance Training System (MCD)
SAMU	Uspallata [Argentina ICAO location identifier] (ICLI)
SAMUX	Serial Addressable Multiplexer (IAA)
SAMV	Mendoza [Argentina ICAO location identifier] (ICLI)
SAMW	Subantarctic Mode Water [Marine science] (OSRA)
SAMWG	Standing Air Monitoring Work Group [Environmental Protection Agency] (GFGA)
S-AMY	Serum Amylase [Medicine] (DMAA)
SAN	Banco De Santiago [NYSE symbol] (SAG)
SAN	Banco Santiago ADS [NYSE symbol] [Formerly, Banco de Santiago ADS] (SG)
SAN	Gato, CA [Location identifier FAA] (FAAL)
SAN	San Angelo [Diocesan abbreviation] [Texas] (TOCD)
SAN	Sanatorium
SAN	San Carlos Milling [AMEX symbol] (TTSB)
SAN	San Carlos Milling Co., Inc. [AMEX symbol] (SPSG)
SAN	Sandersville Railroad Co. [AAR code]
SAN	San Diego [California] [Airport symbol] (OAG)
SAN	Sandwich (MSA)
San	Sanford's Reports [59 Alabama] [A publication] (DLA)
SAN	San Francisco Helicopter Airlines [Air carrier designation symbol]
SAN	San Francisco Operations Office [Energy Research and Development Administration]
SAN	Sanitary (AAG)
SAN	Sanitation (WGA)
San	Sanitorium (CMD)
san	Sanskrit [MARC language code Library of Congress] (LCCP)
SAN	Santiago [Chile] [Seismograph station code, US Geological Survey] (SEIS)
SAN	Satellite Access Nodes
SAN	School of Air Navigation [British]
SAN	Servicios Aereos Nacionales [Ecuador] [ICAO designator] (FAAC)
SAN	Severe Acoustic Noise
SAN	Ship Account Number [Navy]
SAN	Shipping Accumulation Numbers (AAG)
SAN	Sinoatrial Node [Medicine]
SAN	Sinoauricular Node [Medicine] (DMAA)
SAN	Slept All Night [Medicine] (DMAA)
SAN	Society for Ancient Numismatics (EA)
SAN	Solitary Autonomous Nodule [Medicine] (DMAA)
SAN	Sonic Arts Network [An association British] (EAIO)
SAN	Space Age News (AAG)
SAN	Srpska Akademija Nauka i Umetnosti [Belgrade, Yugoslavia]
SAN	Standard Address Number [Publishing]
SAN	Storage Area Network
SAN	Strong Acid Number (IAA)
SAN	Styrene-Acrylonitrile [Also, SA] [Organic chemistry]
SAN	Styrene-Acrylonitrile Copolymer (EDCT)
SAN	Subsidiary Account Number
SAN	System Advisory Notice
SANA	Scientists Against Nuclear Arms [British] [An association] (DBA)
SANA	Scottish Anglers National Association (DBA)
SANA	Slavic American National Association (EA)
SANA	Societa Anonima Navigazione Aerea [Italy]
SANA	Soycrafters Association of North America (EA)
SANA	Soyfoods Association of North America (EA)
SANA	Specialty Advertising National Association [Later, SAA] (EA)
SANA	State, Army, Navy, Air (AABC)
SANA	Syrian Arab News Agency
SANAA	Servicio Autonomo Nacional de Acueductos y Alcantarillados [Honduras]
SANACC	State-Army-Navy-Air Force Coordinating Committee [Terminated, 1949] (EGAO)
SANAE	South African National Antarctic Expedition
SANAFREQ	Safety/NATOPS Frequency (MCD)
SANAT	Sanatorium
Sanb	Sanborn, Inc. [Associated Press] (SAG)
SANB	South African National Bibliography
Sanb & B Ann St	Sanborn and Berryman's Annotated Statutes [Wisconsin] [A publication] (DLA)
SANBAR	Sanders Barotropic
SANC	Catamarca [Argentina ICAO location identifier] (ICLI)
SANC	Sanctuary [Naval cadet's hiding place for smoking] [Slang British] (DSUE)
SANC	Short-Arm Navicular Cast [Orthopedics] (DAVI)
SANC	Slovak-American National Council (EA)
SANCAD	Scottish Association for National Certificates and Diplomas
SanCarlo	San Carlos Milling Co., Inc. [Associated Press] (SAG)
San Ch	Sandford's New York Chancery Reports [A publication] (DLA)
SANCIP	SACLANT [Supreme Allied Commander, Atlantic] Approved NATO Common Infrastructure Program (NATG)
sanct	Sanctuary (VRA)
SancWod	Sanctuary Wood Multimedia [Commercial firm Associated Press] (SAG)
San D	Doctor of Sanitation
SAND	Sampling Aerospace Nuclear Debris
SAND	Sandata, Inc. [NASDAQ symbol] (NQ)
Sand	Sandford's New York Superior Court Reports [3-7 New York] [A publication] (DLA)
SAND	Shelter Analysis for New Designs (DNAB)
SAND	Site Activation Need Date [NASA] (NASA)
SAND	Sorting and Assembly of New Data
S & A	Bureau of Supplies and Accounts [Later, NSUPSC] [Navy]
S & A	Safe-and-Arm (KSC)
S & A	Safety and Arming Device
S&A	Sampling and Analysis [Environmental science] (COE)
S & A	Saunders and Austin's Locus Standi Reports [1895-1904] [A publication] (DLA)
S & A	Science and Application (NASA)
S & A	Sickness and Accident [Insurance]
S&A	Steak and Ale Restaurant Corp. (EFIS)
S & A	Study and Analysis Center (AAGC)
S & A	Sugar and Acetone [Medicine]
S & A	Supplies and Accounts
SANDA	Supplies and Accounts
S & A	Surveillance and Accountability (NRCH)
S & A	Surveillance and Analysis [Environmental Protection Agency] (GFGA)
SANDAC	Sandia Airborne Computer
S & AD	Science and Applications Directorate [NASA]
Sand & H Dig	Sandels and Hill's Digest of Statutes [Arkansas] [A publication] (DLA)
Sandars Just Inst	Sandars' Edition of Justinian's Institutes [A publication] (DLA)
SANDASO	Bureau of Supplies and Accounts Shipment Order [Obsolete Navy]
Sandata	Sandata, Inc. [Associated Press] (SAG)
S & B	Saunders and Bidder's Locus Standi Reports [1905-19] [A publication] (DLA)
S & B	Smith and Batty's Irish King's Bench Reports [1824-25] [A publication] (DLA)
S & B	Sterilization and Bath
S & C	Saunders and Cole's English Bail Court Reports [A publication] (DLA)
S & C	Search and Clear [Military]
S & C	Shipper and Carrier [Business term]
S & C	Signal and Conditioning (KSC)
S & C	Singh & Choudry [Publisher] [British]
S & C	Sized and Calendered [Paper]
S & C	Stabilization and Control [Aerospace] (KSC)
S & C	Standards and Control
S & C	Star and Crescent [Steamship] (MHDW)
S & C	Strategic and Critical Raw Material [Military]
S & C	Swan and Critchfield's Revised Statutes [Ohio] [A publication] (DLA)
S & CDU	Switch and Cable Distribution Unit (AAG)
Sand Ch	Sandford's New York Chancery Reports [A publication] (DLA)
Sand Ch R	Sandford's New York Chancery Reports [A publication] (DLA)
Sand Chy	Sandford's New York Chancery Reports [A publication] (DLA)
S & CM	Strategic and Critical Materials [Military]
S&CM	Surfaced and Center Matched [Wood industry] (WPI)
S and COH	Son and Coheir [Genealogy]
SandCop	Sandwich Cooperative Bank [Associated Press] (SAG)
S & CP Dec	Ohio Decisions [A publication] (DLA)
S & C Rev St	Swan and Critchfield's Revised Statutes [Ohio] [A publication] (DLA)
S & D	Search and Destroy [Army] (AABC)
S & D	Shaw, Dunlop, and Bell's Scotch Court of Session Reports, First Series [1821-38] [A publication] (DLA)
s&d	Signed and Dated (VRA)
S & D	Single and Double [Reduction gears]
S & D	Song and Dance Act [Slang]
S & D	Stomach and Duodenum (CPH)
S & D	Storage and Distribution
S & DJR	Somerset & Dorset Joint Railway [British]
S&DP	Systems and Data Processing (CIST)
S & DR	Somerset & Dorset Joint Railway [British] (ROG)
S&E	Safety and Efficacy (DB)
S&E	Safety and Efficiency (STED)
S & E	Salaries and Expenses

S&E .... Science and Engineering (NAKS)
S & E .... Scientific and Engineering
S & E .... Scientists and Engineers (RDA)
S & E .... Sensor and Effector (SSD)
S & E .... Services and Equipment
S & E .... Supplies and Equipage [*Military*] (CINC)
S & E .... Surfaced One Side and Edge [*Lumber*] (DAC)
S & E .... Surveillance and Entry
S & EC .... Science & Engineering Consultants [*Reston, VA*] (TSSD)
S & EPS ...... Safety & Environmental Protection Subcommittee [*Joint Army, Navy, NASA, Air Force*]
Sand Essays... Sanders' Essays on Uses and Trusts [*5th ed.*] [*1844*] [*A publication*] (DLA)
S & EV .... Saratoga & Encampment Valley Railroad (IIA)
Sandf .... Sandford's New York Superior Court Reports [*3-7 New York*] [*A publication*] (DLA)
S & F .... Security and Facilities [*DoD*]
S & F .... Staff and Faculty
S & F .... Stock and Fixtures
S&F .... Store and Forward (CIST)
S & FA .... Shipping and Forwarding Agent
Sandf Ch...... Sandford's New York Chancery Reports [*A publication*] (DLA)
Sandf Ch (NY)... Sandford's New York Superior Court Reports [*3-7 New York*] [*A publication*] (DLA)
Sandf Ch Rep... Sandford's New York Chancery Reports [*A publication*] (DLA)
SandFm....... Sanderson Farms, Inc. [*Associated Press*] (SAG)
Sandf (NY).... Sandford's New York Superior Court Reports [*3-7 New York*] [*A publication*] (ILCA)
Sandf (NY) R... Sandford's New York Superior Court Reports [*A publication*] (DLA)
S & FO .... Supply and Fiscal Officer
Sandford...... Sandford's New York Superior Court Reports [*A publication*] (DLA)
Sandford's SCR... Sandford's New York Superior Court Reports [*A publication*] (DLA)
Sandford's Sup Ct R... Sandford's New York Superior Court Reports [*A publication*] (DLA)
Sandf R .... Sandford's New York Superior Court Reports [*A publication*] (DLA)
S & FR .... Stability and Frequency Response
S and FRAN... San Francisco [*California*] [*Navy*]
Sandf SC ..... Sandford's New York Superior Court Reports [*A publication*] (DLA)
Sandf SCR.... Sandford's New York Superior Court Reports [*A publication*] (DLA)
S & FSD ...... Sea and Foreign Service Duty [*A Navy pay status*]
S & FSD(A)... Sea and Foreign Service Duty (Aviation) [*A Navy pay status*]
S & FSD(S)... Sea and Foreign Service Duty (Submarine) [*A Navy pay status*]
SANDFSO .... Sea and Foreign Service Office (DNAB)
Sandf Suc..... Sandford's Heritable Succession in Scotland [*A publication*] (DLA)
Sandf Sup CR... Sandford's New York Superior Court Reports [*A publication*] (DLA)
Sandf Sup Ct... Sandford's New York Superior Court Reports [*A publication*] (DLA)
Sandf Superior Court R... Sandford's New York Superior Court Reports [*A publication*] (DLA)
S & G .... Smale and Giffard's English Vice-Chancery Reports [*A publication*] (DLA)
S & G .... Stone and Graham's Court of Referees Reports [*England*] [*A publication*] (DLA)
S & G .... Stone and Graham's Private Bills Reports [*England*] [*A publication*] (DLA)
S & G .... Stud and Girt (DAC)
S&H .... Sample and Hold (CIST)
S & H .... Sherratt & Hughes [*Commercial firm British*]
S and H .... Shipping and Handling (WDMC)
S and H .... Son and Heir [*Genealogy*]
S & H .... Speech and Hearing [*Medicine*]
S & H .... Sperry & Hutchinson Co.
S & H .... Steering and Hydroplane [*British*]
S & H .... Sundays and Holidays
S & H .... Survivability and Hardening (MCD)
S & H/exct... Sundays and Holidays Excepted in Lay Days (DS)
S & I .... Stocked and Issued (AFM)
S & I .... Suction and Irrigation [*Surgery*] (DAVI)
S & I .... Surveillance and Inspection (AAG)
S & I .... Surveys and Investigation
S&I .... Surveys and Investigations of the House Appropriations Committee (AAGC)
S & ID .... Surveillance and Identification
Sand Inst Just Introd... Sandars' Edition of Justinian's Institutes [*A publication*] (DLA)
Sand I Rep... Sandwich Islands Reports [*Hawaii*] [*A publication*] (DLA)
S & IS .... Survey and Investigation Staff [*Navy*] (NVT)
SanDisk....... SanDisk Corp. [*Associated Press*] (SAG)
Sand Isls ..... Sandwich Islands
S & K .... Skills and Knowledges
S&L .... Sale and Leaseback (DFIT)
S&L .... Savings and Loan (DFIT)
S & L .... Savings and Loan [*Association*]
S & L .... Schoales and Lefroy's Irish Chancery Reports [*1802-06*] [*A publication*] (DLA)
S & L .... Signed and Limited Edition [*Publishing*]
S & L .... Standards and Limits
S & L .... Supply and Logistics
S & L .... System and Logistics
S&L Assn..... Savings and Loan Association (EBF)
S & LB .... Sale and Lease-Back [*Business term*] (MHDB)
Sandl St Pap... Sandler's State Papers [*A publication*] (DLA)
S & M.......... Sadism and Masochism
S&M .... Sales & Marketing (WDAA)

S & M.......... Sappers and Miners [*British military*] (DMA)
S&M .... Semiannual Payments of Interest or Dividends in September and March (EBF)
S & M.......... September and March [*Denotes semiannual payments of interest or dividends in these months*] [*Business term*]
S & M.......... Sequencer and Monitor (KSC)
S & M.......... Sexton and Malone [*Comic book*] [*CBC TV series*]
S & M.......... Shaw and Maclean's House of Lords Cases [*A publication*] (DLA)
S & M.......... Smedes and Marshall's Mississippi Chancery Reports [*A publication*] (DLA)
S & M.......... Smedes and Marshall's Mississippi Reports [*9-22 Mississippi*] [*1843-50*] [*A publication*] (DLA)
S & M.......... Stock and Machinery
S & M.......... Structures and Materials (MCD)
S & M.......... Supply and Maintenance [*Army*] (AABC)
S & M.......... Surfaced and Matched [*Lumber*]
S&M .... Surveillance and Maintenance [*Environmental science*] (COE)
S & M.......... SYNCH [*Synchronize*] and MUX [*Multiplex*] (MCD)
S & MA........ Supply and Maintenance Agency [*System*] [*Army*]
S & Mar ...... Smedes and Marshall's Mississippi Reports [*9-22 Mississippi*] [*A publication*] (DLA)
S & Mar Ch... Smedes and Marshall's Mississippi Chancery Reports [*A publication*] (DLA)
S & M Ch ..... Smedes and Marshall's Mississippi Chancery Reports [*A publication*] (DLA)
S & M Ch R... Smedes and Marshall's Mississippi Chancery Reports [*A publication*] (DLA)
S & M Ch Rep... Smedes and Marshall's Mississippi Chancery Reports [*A publication*] (DLA)
S & M Chy... Smedes and Marshall's Mississippi Chancery Reports [*A publication*] (DLA)
S & MMIS ... Supply and Maintenance Management Information System [*Army*]
S & N .... Scottish & Newcastle Breweries [*Commercial firm British*]
S & OC .... Signed and On Chart [*Hospital administration*] (DAVI)
SANDOCC .... San Diego Oceanic Coordinating Committee
S & P .... Salt and Pepper
S & P .... Save & Prosper [*Financial services group*] [*British*]
S & P .... Stake and Platform [*Technical drawings*]
S&P .... Standard & Poor's (EBF)
S & P .... Standard & Poor's Corp.
S&P .... Standards & Practices Division (ACII)
S & P .... Strategy and Policy Group [*War Department*] [*World War II*]
S&P .... Systems and Procedures (CIST)
S & P (Ala) Rep... Stewart and Porter's Alabama Reports [*A publication*] (DLA)
S & PCS ...... Silver and Pewter Collectors Society [*Defunct*] (EA)
S & P RES DIS... Severn and Potomac Reserve District [*Marine Corps*]
S & PTS ...... Standard & Poor's Trading Systems [*Standard & Poor's Corp.*] [*Information service or system*] (IID)
Sand R .... Sandford's New York Superior Court Reports [*A publication*] (DLA)
S & R .... Sergeant and Rawle's Pennsylvania Reports [*1824-28*] [*A publication*] (DLA)
S & R .... Storage and Retrieval [*Computer science*]
S & R .... Stowage and Repair
SANDRA ...... Structure and Reference Analyzer [*IBM Corp.*] [*Chemistry*]
SandReg...... Sands Regent [*Associated Press*] (SAG)
S & R Neg... Shearman and Redfield on the Law of Negligence [*A publication*] (DLA)
S & R on Neg... Shearman and Redfield on the Law of Negligence [*A publication*] (DLA)
S & RP .... Spares and Repair Parts [*Navy*]
S&S .... Safeguards and Security [*Environmental science*] (COE)
S & S........... Saratoga & Schuylerville Railroad (IIA)
S & S........... Sausse and Scully's Irish Rolls Court Reports [*1837-40*] [*A publication*] (DLA)
S & S........... Schleicher & Schuell [*Filter-paper company*]
S&S .... Science & Society [*A publication*] (BRI)
S & S........... Searle and Smith's English Probate and Divorce Reports [*1859-60*] [*A publication*] (DLA)
S & S........... Sense and Sensibility [*Novel by Jane Austen*]
S & S........... Sex and Shopping [*Themes of Judith Krantz's novels*]
S & S........... Shipping and Storage
S & S........... Signs and Symptoms [*Medicine*]
S & S........... Simon & Schuster [*Publisher*]
S & S........... Simons and Stuart's English Vice-Chancellors' Reports [*1822-26*] [*A publication*] (DLA)
S & S........... Spigot and Socket
SANDS........ Stillbirth and Neonatal Death Society [*British*] (EAIO)
SANDS........ Structural Analysis Numerical Design System
S & S........... Supply and Service [*Army*] (AABC)
S & S........... Support and Stimulation [*Medicine*] (DAVI)
S & S........... Swan and Sayler's Revised Statutes of Ohio [*A publication*] (DLA)
S & S........... Sword and Sorcery
Sand SC ...... Sandford's New York Superior Court Reports [*A publication*] (DLA)
S & Sc........ Sausse and Scully's Irish Rolls Court Reports [*A publication*] (DLA)
S & SC .... Sized and Supercalendered [*Paper*]
Sands Ch...... Sandford's New York Chancery Reports [*A publication*] (DLA)
Sand SCR .... Sandford's New York Superior Court Reports [*A publication*] (DLA)
S & SD .... Sewerage and Sewage Disposal (DCTA)
S & Sm....... Searle and Smith's English Probate and Divorce Reports [*A publication*] (DLA)
Sandst .... Sandstone [*Lithology*]
sandst.......... Sandstone (VRA)
Sand Sup Ct Rep... Sandford's New York Superior Court Reports [*A publication*] (DLA)

Sand Supr Ct R... Sandford's New York Superior Court Reports [*A publication*] (DLA)

S & Sx Yeo... Surrey and Sussex Yeomanry [*British military*] (DMA)

S&T .... Science and Technology (EERA)

S&T .... Scientific and Technical (CIST)

S & T .... Selection and Training [*Military*] (LAIN)

S & T .... Simulation and Training

S&T .... Sky & Telescope [*A publication*] (BRI)

S & T .... Stenographer and Typist [*Examination*] [*Civil Service Commission*]

S & T .... Storm and Tempest (ADA)

S & T .... Supply and Transport [*Military*]

S & T .... Supply and Transport Corps [*British*] (DMA)

S & T .... Swabey and Tristram's Probate and Divorce Reports [*1858-65*] [*A publication*] (DLA)

S & TA........ Salmon and Trout Association (DBA)

S & T Bc..... S & T Bancorp [*Associated Press*] (SAG)

S & T Bcp.... S & T Bancorp [*Associated Press*] (SAG)

SandTc .... Sand Technology Systems International, Inc. [*Associated Press*] (SAG)

S & TI......... Scientific and Technical Intelligence [*Military*] (RDA)

S & U .... Supine and Upright (MEDA)

Sand Uses and Trusts... Sanders' Essays on Uses and Trusts [*A publication*] (DLA)

S & V .... Shock and Vibration

SANDW....... Sandwiched (IAA)

S & W .... Smith and Wesson (MCD)

S & W .... Soap and Water [*Enema*] [*Medicine*]

Sandy .... Sandy Corp. [*Associated Press*] (SAG)

SANE .... National Committee for a Sane Nuclear Policy [*"SANE" alone now used as organization name*] (EA)

San E .... Sanitary Engineer [*Academic degree*]

SANE .... Santiago Del Estero [*Argentina ICAO location identifier*] (ICLI)

SANE .... Schizophrenia: a National Emergency [*An association British*]

SANE .... Scientific Applications of Nuclear Explosions (SAA)

SANE .... Severe Acoustic Noise Environment

SANE .... Standard Apple Numerics Environment [*Software*] [*Apple Computers, Inc.*]

SANE .... Sulfur and Nitrogen Emissions (GNE)

SANF .... Salvation Army Nurses' Fellowship (EAIO)

SANF .... Sanford Recreation Area

Sanf............ Sanford's Reports [*59 Alabama*] [*A publication*] (DLA)

SANF .... South African Naval Forces

SanFeFn ...... Santa Fe Financial Corp. [*Associated Press*] (SAG)

Sanfilp........ Sanfilippo [*John*] & Son, Inc. [*Associated Press*] (SAG)

San FLJ...... San Francisco Law Journal [*A publication*] (DLA)

SANFM .... Source Range Neutron Flux Monitor (IAA)

Sanf (NY)..... Sandford's New York Superior Court Reports [*3-7 New York*] [*A publication*] (DLA)

Sanford's Ch R... Sandford's New York Chancery Reports [*A publication*] (DLA)

San Fran...... San Francisco [*California*] (DANN)

San Fran Art Inst... San Francisco Art Institute (GAGS)

San Fran Conserv Music... San Francisco Conservatory of Music (GAGS)

San Fran Law Bull San Francisco Law Bulletin [*A publication*] (DLA)

San Fran LB.. San Francisco Law Bulletin [*A publication*] (ILCA)

San Fran LJ... San Francisco Law Journal [*A publication*] (DLA)

San Fran St U... San Francisco State University (GAGS)

San Fr LB.... San Francisco Law Bulletin [*A publication*] (DLA)

San Fr LJ..... San Francisco Law Journal [*A publication*] (DLA)

SANG.......... SangStat Medical [*NASDAQ symbol*] (TTSB)

SANG.......... SangStat Medical Corp. [*NASDAQ symbol*] (SAG)

sang........... Sanguineous [*Hematology*] (DAVI)

SANG.......... Saudi Arabian National Guard (RDA)

SANG.......... Standardized Aeronautical Navigation/Guidance [*Program*] [*Air Force*]

SANGB........ Selfridge Army/Air National Guard Base (MCD)

SANGFPT..... Spherical Angles from Points (MCD)

Sangstat ...... SangStat Medical Corp. [*Associated Press*] (SAG)

sangu......... Sanguine (VRA)

SANH.......... Rio Hondo/Las Termas [*Argentina ICAO location identifier*] (ICLI)

Sanh .... Sanhedrin (BJA)

Sanh .... Sanherib (BJA)

SANI .... Sanitary

SANI .... Tinogasta [*Argentina ICAO location identifier*] (ICLI)

Sanifil......... Sanifill, Inc. [*Associated Press*] (SAG)

SANINSP...... Sanitation Inspector [*Military*] (AABC)

Sanit.......... Sanitarium

Sanit.......... Sanitary

sanit.......... Sanitation (DAVI)

SANITN....... Sanitation

SAnitRt .... Santa Anita Realty Enterprises, Inc. [*Associated Press*] (SAG)

San Just ...... Sandars' Edition of Justinian's Institutes [*A publication*] (DLA)

SANKA .... Sans Caffeine [*Acronym used as brand name*]

SANL .... La Rioja/Cap. V. Almandos Almonacid [*Argentina ICAO location identifier*] (ICLI)

SANLF .... Saudi Arabian National Liberation Front [*Political party*] (BJA)

SANM .... Sanmina Corp. [*NASDAQ symbol*] (SAG)

SANM .... Synthetic Algal Nutrient Medium

SAN MIG...... San Miguel Beer (DSUE)

Sanmina ...... Sanmina Corp. [*Associated Press*] (SAG)

SANO .... Chilecito [*Argentina ICAO location identifier*] (ICLI)

SANO .... Sano Corp. [*NASDAQ symbol*] (SAG)

SANO .... South African Astronomical Observatory

SanoCo .... Sano Corp. [*Associated Press*] (SAG)

SANOVA...... Simultaneous Analysis of Variance

SANP .... Secondary Auxiliary Nuclear Power

SANPRM...... Supplemental Advance Notice of Proposed Rulemaking [*RSPA*] (TAG)

SANR .... Subject to Approval No Risk

SANROC ...... South African Non-Racial Olympic Committee (EAIO)

SANS .... Scale for the Assessment of Negative Symptoms [*Medicine*] (DMAA)

SANS .... Schedule for the Assessment of Negative Symptoms [*Psychometrics*]

SANS .... Simplified Account - Numbering System

SANS .... Small-Angle Neutron Scattering

SANS .... South African Naval Service

SANS .... Students Against Nuclear Suicide [*Defunct*] (EA)

SANS .... Swimmer and Navigation System [*Navy*] (CAAL)

SANSAN....... San Francisco, San Diego [*Proposed name for possible "super-city" formed by growth and mergers of other cities*]

SANSC........ Sanscrit

SANSET ...... Seaman Apprentice, Nuclear Submarine Engineering Technician [*Navy rating*] (DNAB)

SANSK .... Sanskrit [*Language, etc.*]

SANSS......... Structure and Nomenclature Search System [*Formerly, SSS*] [*Chemical Information Systems, Inc.*] [*Information service or system*]

SANSW....... Shires Association of New South Wales [*Australia*]

SANT .... Tucuman/Teniente Benjamim Matienzo [*Argentina ICAO location identifier*] (ICLI)

SANTA .... Souvenir and Novelty Trade Association (EA)

Santa Clara LR... Santa Clara Law Review [*A publication*] (ILCA)

SantCrz .... Santa Cruz Operation, Inc. [*Associated Press*] (SAG)

SantF .... Santander Finance Ltd. [*Associated Press*] (SAG)

Santos .... Santos Ltd. [*Associated Press*] (SAG)

SANU .... San Juan [*Argentina ICAO location identifier*] (ICLI)

SANU .... Sudan African National Union [*Political party*]

SANUM .... South Africa National Union for Mineworkers

SANW .... Ceres [*Argentina ICAO location identifier*] (ICLI)

SANWFZ ..... South Asia Nuclear Weapons-Free Zone

SANWS .... Sinoatrial Node Weakness Syndrome [*Medicine*] (DMAA)

SANY .... Sanyo Electric Co. Ltd. [*NASDAQ symbol*] (NQ)

Sanyal .... Sanyal's Criminal Cases between Natives and Europeans [*1796-1895*] [*India*] [*A publication*] (DLA)

Sanyo .... Sanyo Electric Co. Ltd. [*Associated Press*] (SAG)

SANYY .... SANYO Electric Ltd ADS [*NASDAQ symbol*] (TTSB)

SAO .... Saharan Air Outbreak [*Meteorology*]

SAO .... Sahel Aviation Service [*Mali*] [*ICAO designator*] (FAAC)

SAO .... San Andreas Geological Observatory [*California*] [*Seismograph station code, US Geological Survey*] (SEIS)

SAO .... Sandia Area Office [*Energy Research and Development Administration*]

SAO .... Sao Paulo [*Brazil*] [*Airport symbol*] (OAG)

SAO .... Scottish Association of Opticians (DAS)

SAO .... Secret Army Organization [*English initialism for OAS, terrorist group in Algeria and metropolitan France*]

SAO .... Secretin-Stimulated Acid Output [*Clinical chemistry*]

SAO .... Security Assistance Office

SAO .... Security Assistance Organizations (DOMA)

SAO .... Select Address and Operate

SAO .... Selected Attack Option (MCD)

SAO .... Semiannual Oscillation [*Astronomy*]

SAO .... Senior Administrative Officer [*British military*] (DMA)

SAO .... Senior Arboricultural Officer [*British*] (WDAA)

SAO .... Serious Arrestable Offence [*Legal term*] (WDAA)

SAO .... Single Airlift Organization (CINC)

SAO .... Single Association Object [*Telecommunications*] (OSI)

SAO .... Single Attack Option

SAO .... Small Airway Obstruction [*Medicine*] (DMAA)

SAO .... Smithsonian Astrophysical Observatory [*Cambridge, MA*]

SAO .... Smooth Approach Orifice [*Mechanical engineering*]

SAO .... Social Actions Office [*or Officer*] [*Air Force*] (AFM)

SAO .... Sonobuoy Acoustic Operator [*Navy*] (CAAL)

SAO .... Special Access Only (MCD)

SAO .... Special Action Office [*Phased out, 1975*] [*Department of Justice*]

SAO .... Special Activities Office [*Air Force*] (AFM)

SAO .... Special Air Operations

SAO .... Special Analysis Office

SAO .... Special Artificer, Optical [*Navy*]

SAO .... Special Astrophysics Observatory

SAO .... Splanchnic Artery Occlusion [*Medicine*]

SAO .... Squadron Accountant Officer [*Navy British*]

SAO .... Staff Administrative Officer [*Military*]

SAO .... Subsidiary/Affiliate Order (MCD)

SAO .... Subvalvular Aortic Obstruction [*Medicine*] (DMAA)

SAO .... Support Air Observation [*Navy*]

SAO .... Survey of Agency Opinion [*LIMRA*]

SAO .... Survival Assistance Officer [*Army*] (AABC)

SAO .... Systems Acquisition Officer [*Military*] (AFIT)

SAO .... Systems Analysis Office

SaO$_2$ .... Saturation Arterial Oxygen [*Medicine*] (DAVI)

SAOA .... Semi-Ascending Order Arrangement (PDAA)

SAOAS .... Secretary of the Army, Office of the Assistant Secretary

SAOAS .... Staff Association of the Organization of American States (EA)

SAOC .... Rio Cuarto/Area de Material [*Argentina ICAO location identifier*] (ICLI)

SAOC .... Scottish Association of Operative Coachmakers [*A union*]

SAOC .... South Australian Olympic Council

SAOC .... Space and Astronautics Orientation Course (NG)

SAOCS .... Submarine Air Optical Communications System (MCD)

SAOD .... Villa Dolores [*Argentina ICAO location identifier*] (ICLI)

SAODAP...... Special Action Office for Drug Abuse Prevention [*Terminated, 1975*] [*FDA*]
SAOE .... Embalse Rio Tercero [*Argentina ICAO location identifier*] (ICLI)
SAOG .... Satellite Operations Group [*Military*]
SAOHSC...... South Australian Occupational Health and Safety Commission
SAOL .... Laboulaye [*Argentina ICAO location identifier*] (ICLI)
SAOM .... Marcos Juarez [*Argentina ICAO location identifier*] (ICLI)
SAO/MEX..... Special Action Office for Mexico [*Drug Enforcement Administration*]
SAOR .... Villa Reynolds [*Argentina ICAO location identifier*] (ICLI)
SAOS .... Scottish Agricultural Organisation Society (DBA)
SAOS .... Select Address [*and Provide*] Output Signal
SAOT .... Semiactive on Target
SAOTA .... Shrimp Association of the Americas (EA)
SAOU .... San Luis [*Argentina ICAO location identifier*] (ICLI)
SAOUG....... South African Online User Group (NITA)
SAP........... Sampling and Analysis Plan
SAP........... San Antonio Public Library, San Antonio, TX [*OCLC symbol*] (OCLC)
SAP........... San Pedro Sula [*Honduras*] [*Airport symbol*] (OAG)
sap........... Saponification [*or Saponify*] [*Analytical chemistry*] (AAMN)
SAP........... Sapporo [*Japan*] [*Seismograph station code, US Geological Survey*] (SEIS)
sap........... Sapwood [*Lumber*] (BARN)
SAP........... Scampton FTU [*British ICAO designator*] (FAAC)
SAP........... Scientific Advisory Panel [*Arlington, VA*] [*Environmental Protection Agency*] (EGAO)
SAP........... Scorched Aluminum Powder
SAP........... Scouting and Amphibian Plane [*Coast Guard*]
SAP........... Scruple Apothecaries
SAP........... Seaborne Aircraft Platform (ADA)
SAP........... Secondary Audio Program
SAP........... Second Audio Program
SAP........... Security Assistance Program (MCD)
SAP........... Semi-Armor-Piercing [*Projectile*] [*Nickname: Sex-Appeal Pete*] [*Military*]
SAP........... Seminal Acid Phosphatase [*An enzyme*]
SAP........... Separate Audio Program [*Television broadcasting*]
SAP........... Serum Acid Phosphatase (DB)
SAP........... Serum Alkaline Phosphatase [*Clinical chemistry*]
SAP........... Serum Amyloid P [*Clinical chemistry*]
SAP........... Service Access Point
SAP........... Service Advertising Protocol [*Computer science*] (PCM)
SAP........... Seychelles Agence de Presse [*News agency*] (EY)
SAP........... Share Assembly Program [*Computer science*]
SAP........... Ship Acquisition Plan [*Navy*]
SAP........... Ship Alteration Package [*Navy*] (DNAB)
SAP........... Shipboard Acoustic Processor [*Navy*] (CAAL)
SAP........... Shipboard Antenna Pedestal
SAP........... Simple Assembly Plan
SAP........... Simplified Acquisition Procedure (AAGC)
SAP........... Single-Axis Platform
SAP........... Sintered Aluminium Product [*Nuclear energy*] (NUCP)
SAP........... Sintered Aluminum Powder
SAP........... Site Activation Phase
SAP........... Situs Ambiguus with Polysplenia [*Medicine*] (DMAA)
SAP........... Skeletal Axis of Pinnule
SAP........... Social Action Party [*Thailand*] [*Political party*] (FEA)
SAP........... Socialistische Arbeiderspartij [*Socialist Workers' Party*] [*Netherlands Political party*] (PPW)
SAP........... Societe des Arts Plastiques de la Province de Quebec, Quebec City [*1955*] [*Canada*] (NGC)
SAP........... Society for Adolescent Psychiatry (EA)
SAP........... Society for American Philosophy [*Defunct*] (EA)
SAP........... Society for Applied Spectroscopy
SAP........... Society of Analytical Psychology (AIE)
SAP........... Sodium Acid Pyrophosphate [*Also, SAPP*] [*Leavening agent, meat additive*]
SAP........... Soon as Possible
SAP........... South African Party [*Political party*] (PPW)
SAP........... South African Police (ECON)
SAP........... Soysal Adelet Partisi [*Social Justice Party*] [*Turkish Cyprus*] [*Political party*] (PPE)
SAP........... Special Access Program (DOMA)
SAP........... Special and Administrative Provisions [*of the Tariff Act of 1930*]
SAP........... Special Attention Personnel [*US VIP troops*] (VNW)
SAP........... Sphingolipid Activator Protein [*Biochemistry*]
SAP........... Spot Authorization Plan [*WPB*] [*Obsolete*]
SAP........... Spy Against Pollution [*An association*]
SAP........... Squadron Aid Post (ADA)
SAP........... Staphylococcus aureus Protease [*An enzyme*]
SAP........... Start of Active Profile (PDAA)
SAP........... State Association President [*American Occupational Therapy Association*]
SAP........... Statement on Auditing Procedure
SAP........... Steroidogenesis Activator Polypeptide
SAP........... Strain Arrestor Plate [*NASA*] (NASA)
SAP........... Strategic Advantages Profile
SAP........... Strategic Audit Plan
SAP........... Strong Anthropic Principle [*Term coined by authors John Barrow and Frank Tipler in their book, "The Anthropic Cosmological Principle"*]
SAP........... Structural Adjustment Package [*Australia*]
SAP........... Structural Analysis Program (MCD)
SAP........... Student Aid Project
SAP........... Subassembly Precision (MCD)
SAP........... Subject Access Project

SAP............ Substituted Accounting Period
SAP............ Sumerian Animal Proverbs (BJA)
SAP............ Superabsorbent Polymer [*Organic chemistry*]
SAP............ Supervisory Airplane Pilot
SAP............ Supplier-Allied-Price [*Automobile content legislation*]
SAP............ Supportability Assurance Program
SAP............ Surface Aligned Photochemistry [*Physics*]
SAP............ Sveriges Socialdemokratiska Arbetareparti [*Swedish Social Democratic Labor Party*] [*Political party*] (PPW)
SAP............ Symbolic Address Program
SAP............ Symbolic Assembly Program [*Computer science*]
SAP............ System Alignment Procedure (NATG)
SAP............ Systemic Arterial Pressure [*Medicine*]
SAP............ Systems Assurance Program [*IBM Corp.*]
SAPA .... Sciences - A Process Approach [*National Science Foundation*]
SAPA .... Sino-American Pharmaceutical Association
SapA .... Societa in Accomandita per Azioni [*Limited Partnership with Shares*] [*Italian*] (IMH)
SAPA .... South African Press Association
SAPAA .... Substance Abuse Program Administrators Association (NTPA)
SAPAI .... Salesmen's Association of Paper and Allied Industries (EA)
SAPAS .... Semiautomatic Population Analysis System (MCD)
SAPAT .... South African Picture Analysis Test [*Psychology*]
SAPB .... South Australian Psychological Board
SAPC .... Shipowners Association of the Pacific Coast [*Defunct*] (EA)
SAPC .... Small Arms Post Competition
SAPC .... South Australian Philatelic Council
SAPC .... South Australian Planning Commission
SAPC .... Substance Abuse Problem Checklist
SAPC .... Supported Aqueous-Phase Catalysis [*Chemistry*]
SAPC .... Suspended Acoustical-Plaster Ceiling [*Technical drawings*]
SAPCH........ Semiautomatic Program Checkout (IAA)
SAPCHE...... Semiautomatic Program Checkout Equipment (AAG)
SAPCO .... Security Assistance Policy Coordinating Office [*Military*]
SAPCO .... Single-Asset Property Company [*British*]
SAPCO .... Sudanese African People's Congress [*Political party*] (EY)
SAPD .... Self-Administration of Psychotropic Drugs (AAMN)
SAPD .... South Australia. Parliamentary Debates [*A publication*]
SAPDF .... Social Activist Professors Defense Foundation [*Defunct*] (EA)
SAPDO .... Special Accounts Property Disposal Officer [*Military*]
SAPE .... Sapient Corp. [*NASDAQ symbol*] (SAG)
SAPE .... Society for Automation in Professional Education [*Later, SDE*]
SAPE .... Solenoid Array Pattern Evaluator
SAPEC .... Savings Associations Political Education Committee
SAPENF ...... Societe Americaine pour l'Etude de la Numismatique Francaise (EA)
SAPF .... Suider-Afrika Padfederasie [*Southern Africa Road Federation - SARF*] (EAIO)
SAPFE .... Seaman Apprentice, Polaris Field Electronics [*Navy rating*] (DNAB)
SAPFL .... Seaman Apprentice, Polaris Field Launcher [*Navy rating*] (DNAB)
SAPFT........ Special Adviser to the President on Foreign Trade [*New Deal*]
SAPFU .... Surpassing All Previous Foul Ups [*Military slang*] [*Bowdlerized version*]
SAPH .... Saphenous (STED)
saph........... Sapphire [*Philately*]
SAPhA .... Student American Pharmaceutical Association [*Later, APhA-ASP*] (EA)
SAPHE .... Semi-Armor-Piercing High Explosive [*Projectile*] (MCD)
SAPHYDATA... Panel on the Acquisition, Transmission, and Processing of Hydrological Data [*Marine science*] (MSC)
SAPI............ Sales Association of the Paper Industry [*New York, NY*] (EA)
SAPI............ Semi-Armor-Piercing Incendiary [*Projectile*] (NATG)
SAPI............ Service Access Point Identifier [*Telecommunications*] (OSI)
SAPI............ Speech Application Programming Interface [*Microsoft Corp.*]
Sapiens ...... Sapiens International Corp. [*Associated Press*] (SAG)
SAPIENS ...... Spreading Activation Processor for Information Encoded in Network Structure [*Department of Education*]
Sapient .... Sapient Corp. [*Associated Press*] (SAG)
SAPIR .... System of Automatic Processing and Indexing of Reports
SAPIS .... State Alcoholism Profile Information System [*Public Health Service*] (IID)
SAPK .... Stress-Activated Protein Kinase [*An enzyme*]
SAPK .... Stress-Activated Protein Kinases [*An enzyme*]
sapl .... Sailed as Per List (ODBW)
SAPL.......... Seacoast Anti-Pollution League (EA)
SAPL.......... Service Action Parts List (AAG)
SAPL.......... Society for Animal Protective Legislation (EA)
SAPL.......... Spartan-Approved Parts List [*Missiles*] (MCD)
SAPLA .... Standing Advisory Panel on Library Automation (NITA)
SAPLIC .... Small Arms Projected Line Charge [*Military*] (INF)
SAPM.......... Scottish Association of Plane Makers [*A union*]
SAPM.......... Society for thr Aid of Psychological Minorities (NADA)
SAPMS........ Short Arm Posterior Molded Splint [*Medicine*] (MEDA)
SAPNA........ Succinyl-Alanyl-para-Nitroanilide [*Biochemistry*]
SaPNFB ...... National Film Board, Pretoria, South Africa [*Library symbol Library of Congress*] (LCLS)
SAPO.......... Sarawak People's Organization [*Malaysia*] [*Political party*] (PPW)
SAPO.......... Silicoaluminophosphate [*Inorganic chemistry*]
SAPO.......... Special Aircraft Project Office (AAG)
SAPO.......... Subarea Petroleum Office [*Military*]
SAPOAD...... Systems Applications Project Operation Action Detail (IAA)
SAPON........ Saponaria [*Soapwort*] [*Pharmacology*] (ROG)
SAPON........ Saponification [*Analytical chemistry*]
sapon......... Saponification (STED)
SAPOS .... Satellite Positioning Service
SAPOV .... Subarea Petroleum Office, Vietnam [*Military*]

SAPP	Security, Accuracy, Propriety, and Policy
S App	Shaw's Scotch Appeal Cases, House of Lords [1821-24] [A publication] (DLA)
SAPP	Skeletal Axis of Palp
SAPP	Sodium Acid Pyrophosphate [Also, SAP] [Leavening agent, meat additive]
SAPP	Soul Assurance Prayer Plan (EA)
SAPP	South Australian Parliamentary Papers [A publication]
SAPP	Special Airfield Pavement Program (NATG)
SAPPHIRE	Synthetic Aperture Precision Processor High Reliability (MCD)
SAPPMA	San Antonio Procurement and Production Materiel Area [Air Force]
SAPPRAD	Southeast Asian Program for Potato Research and Development (GNE)
SAPQ	Societe des Artistes Professionnels du Quebec [1966, CPQ from 1978, SAAVQ from 1980, CAPQ from 1982] [Canada] (NGC)
SAPR	Semiannual Progress Report
SAPR	Summary Area Problem Report (AAG)
SAPRC	Security Assistance Program Review Commission
SAPRITC	South Australian Plastics and Rubber Industry Training Committee
SAPS	Scandinavian Association of Paediatric Surgeons (EAIO)
SAPS	Scandinavian Association of Plastic Surgeons [See also NPF] (EAIO)
SAPS	Secondary Audio Program Services [Television] (BARN)
SAPS	Selected Alternate Processing Separation (MCD)
SAPS	Servico de Alimentacao da Providencia Social [Brazil]
SAPS	Shippingport Atomic Power Station (NRCH)
SAPS	Short-Arm Plaster Splint (STED)
SAPS	Signal Algorithmic Processing System [Navy]
SAPS	Simplified Acute Physiology Score [Medicine]
SAPS	Small Area Plotting Sheet
SaPS	South African Council for Scientific and Industrial Research, Pretoria, South Africa [Library symbol Library of Congress] (LCLS)
SAPS	Standalone Prediction System
SAPS	Surety Agents Promotional Society [Defunct] (EA)
SAPSFA	South Australian Professional Shark Fishermen's Association
SaPSL	State Library, Pretoria, South Africa [Library symbol Library of Congress] (LCLS)
SA/PSP	Site Activation/Phased Support Plan [Military] (MCD)
SAPST	Special Assistant to the President for Science and Technology
SAPT	Scottish Association of Public Transport (DBA)
SAPT	South Africa Department of Posts and Telecommunications (TSSD)
SAPT	Special Assistant to the President for Telecommunications [Johnson Administration]
SAPT	Symmetry-Adapted Perturbation Theory [Physical chemistry]
SAPU	South African Police Union (ECON)
SAPUC	Sintered Aluminum Powder-Clad Uranium Carbide
SAPV	Secondary Air Pulse Valve [Automotive engineering]
SAPW	United Stone and Allied Products Workers of America [Later, USWA]
SAPX	Salivary Peroxidase [Medicine] (DMAA)
SAQ	Pittsburgh, PA [Location identifier FAA] (FAAL)
SAQ	San Andros [Bahamas] [Airport symbol] (OAG)
SAQ	Short-Arc Quadriceps [test] (STED)
SAQ	Short Arc Quads [Medicine]
SAQ	South Atlantic Quarterly [A publication] (BRI)
SAQAD	Springbank Aviation Ltd. [Canada ICAO designator] (FAAC)
SAQAD	Submarine Antenna Quality Assurance Directory [Navy] (DNAB)
SAQAF	Submarine Antenna Quality Assurance Facility [Navy] (DNAB)
SAQC	Statistical Analysis and Quality Control
SAQM	Standardized Air Quality Monitoring [Environmental Protection Agency]
SAQR	Substance Abuse Quarterly Report [Navy] (DNAB)
SAQT	Sociedad Panamericana de Quimioterapia de la Tuberculosis [Pan American Society for Chemotherapy of Tuberculosis - PASCT] (EA)
SAR	National Society, Sons of the American Revolution (EA)
SAR	Safety Analysis Report [Nuclear energy]
SAR	Safety Assessment Report (MCD)
SAR	Sales Authorization Request
SAR	Sample Acceptance Rate [Statistics]
SAR	Santa Anita Realty Enterprises, Inc. [NYSE symbol] (SPSG)
SAR	Santa Anita Rlty(UNIT) [NYSE symbol] (TTSB)
SAR	Santa Rosa Junior College, Santa Rosa, CA [OCLC symbol] (OCLC)
SAR	Sarajevo [Yugoslavia] [Seismograph station code, US Geological Survey] (SEIS)
SAR	Sarcoidosis [Medicine]
Sar	Sarcosine [Biochemistry]
Sar	Sarcosyl [Biochemistry]
SAR	Sardinia [Italy] (ROG)
Sar	Sarswati's Privy Council Judgments [India] [A publication] (DLA)
SAR	Saturation Alleviation Rules
SAR	Saudi Arabian Riyal [Monetary unit] (DS)
SAR	Save Address Register (IAA)
SAR	Scaffold Attachment Region [Genetics]
SAR	Schedule Allocation Requirements (AAG)
SAR	Schedule and Request (MCD)
SAR	School Achievement Record [Australia]
SAR	School of American Research [Research center] (RCD)
SAR	Sea-Air Rescue
SAR	Search and Release (AAG)
SAR	Search and Rescue (FAAC)
SAR	Search and Rescue Program [Military]
SAR	Seasonal Allergic Rhinitis (STED)
SAR	Segment Address Register [Telecommunications]
SAR	Selected Acquisition Report [Military]
SAR	Semiactive RADAR (MCD)
SAR	Semiannual Report
SAR	Semiautomatic Rifle [Army]
SAR	Senior Army Representative
SAR	Service Analysis Report [Telecommunications] (TEL)
SAR	Service Analysis Request [Telecommunications] (TEL)
SAR	Service Aptitude Rating [Military] (NVT)
SAR	Service Assigned Requests (MCD)
SAR	Servicios Aereos de Pilotos Ejecutivos [Colombia] [ICAO designator] (FAAC)
SAR	Sexual Attitude Reassessment [Medicine]
SAR	Sexual Attitude Restructuring (STED)
SAR	Siemens Agronaut Reactor [Germany]
SAR	Significant Action Report [Military] (MCD)
SAR	Silver Acorn Developments [Vancouver Stock Exchange symbol]
SAR	Simulated Acid Rain
SAR	Single-Axis Reference
SAR	Single-BIT [Binary Digit] Alternation Recording
SAR	Site Acceptance Review [Military]
SAR	Society for Animal Rights [Later, ISAR] (EA)
SAR	Society for Application Research [British] (DBA)
SAR	Society of Authors' Representatives (EA)
SAR	Sodium-Adsorption-Ratio
SAR	Software Acceptance Review
SAR	Son Altesse Royale [His or Her Royal Highness] [French]
SAR	SONAR Acoustique Remorque [Acoustic imaging system] [French]
SAR	Sons of the American Revolution
SAR	Source Address Register [Telecommunications]
SAR	South African Railways
SAR	South African Republic
SAR	South African Republic High Court Reports [A publication] (DLA)
SAR	South Australian Government Railways
SAR	Spacecraft Acceptance Review (MCD)
SAR	Sparta, IL [Location identifier FAA] (FAAL)
SAR	Special Access Required
SAR	Special Administrative Region [Hong Kong]
SAR	Special Aeronautical Requirement [Navy] (NG)
SAR	Special Appaaratus Rack (IAA)
SAR	Specific Absorption Rate
SAR	Specific Acoustic Resistance
SAR	Specific Activity Report
SAR	Specific Air Range [Military] (LAIN)
SAR	Specifically Authorized Representative [Air Force]
SAR	Specification Approval Record (MCD)
SAR	Stable Auroral Red [Arc] [Geophysics]
SAR	Stack Address Register (IAA)
SAR	Staff Appraisal Report (WDAA)
SAR	Standardized Abnormality Ratio (WDAA)
SAR	Standardized Admissions Ratios [Hospital activity analysis]
SAR	Standing Authority Release [For perishables] [Business term]
SAR	Start Action Request [Environmental Protection Agency]
SAR	Starting Address Register (ECII)
SAR	Starting Air Receiver (AAG)
SAR	Stock Appreciation Relief [British]
SAR	Stock Appreciation Right (EBF)
SAR	Stock Appreciation Rights [Method of compensation for top executives]
SAR	Storage Address Register [Telecommunications]
SAR	Street Address Record [Telecommunications] (TEL)
SAR	Structure Activity Relationship
SAR	Student Aid Report [Department of Education]
SAR	Students at Risk [Australia]
SAR	Study and Review [Reports] (RDA)
SAR	Subauroral Red [Arc] [Geophysics]
SAR	Submarine Advanced Reactor
SAR	Subsequent Application Review
SAR	Substance Abuse Report [Navy] (DNAB)
SAR	Substitution Approval Request (MCD)
SAR	Successive Accelerated Replacement
SAR	Successive Approximation Register [Computer science]
Sar	Sulfarsphenamine [or Sulpharsphenamine] [Chemistry] (DAVI)
SAR	Sulfuric Acid Regenerator (MCD)
SAR	Summary Analysis Report (NASA)
SAR	Summary Annual Report
SAR	Sum of Absolute Residuals [Mathematics]
SAR	Super-Abrasion-Resistant [Lucite glazing material]
SAR	Support Air Request [Net] [Navy communications]
SAR	Symbol Acquisition Routine
SAR	Synthetic Aperture RADAR [Computer imaging]
SAR	Syrian Arab Republic
SAR	System Acquisition Report
SAR	System Analysis Report
SAR	System Array RADAR (KSC)
SAR	System Availability Report
SAR	Systemic Acquired Resistance [Biology]
SAR	Systemic Arterial Resistance [Medicine]
SAR	Systemic Availability Ratio [Physiology]
SAR	Systems Assessment Review [NASA] (KSC)
SARA	Saralasin [Antihypertensive]
SARA	Saratoga National Historical Park
SARA	Saratoga Trunk (DSUE)
SARA	Satellite Angular Radiometer (NOAA)
SARA	Saturates, Aromatics, Resins, and Asphaltenes [Crude oil analysis]
SARA	Scottish Amateur Rowing Association (DBA)
SARA	Search and Replace Automatically [Computer science] (DGA)
SARA	Search and Rescue Aid

SARA .... Seminar Announcement, Registration, and Attendance [*National Shorthand Reporters Association*]
SARA .... Sequential Automatic Recorder and Annunciator
SARA .... Sexual Assault Research Association (EA)
SARA .... Sexually-Acquired Reactive Arthritis [*Medicine*] (PDAA)
SARA .... Ship Angle and Range (SAA)
SARA .... Sleep Apnoeia Research Association [*Australia*]
SARA .... Small Antique Restoration Association (NTPA)
SARA .... Society for the Advancement of Research into Anorexia [*British*] (DBA)
SARA .... Society of American Registered Architects (EA)
SARA .... South Australian Restaurant Association
SARA .... South Australian Rowing Association
SARA .... Southeastern Association for Research in Astronomy [*University of Georgia*] [*Research center*] (RCD)
SARA .... Still Another Response Averager
SARA .... Student Admission Records Administratioh (IAA)
SARA .... Substance Abuse Relapse Assessment [*Test*] (TMMY)
SARA .... Superfund Amendment and Reauthorization Act [*1986*]
SARA .... Symantec AntiVirus Research Automation
SARA .... System Availability and Reliability Analysis (MHDB)
SARA .... System for Anesthetic and Respiratory Administration (STED)
SARA .... System for Anesthetic and Respiratory Analysis
SARA .... Systems Analysis and Resource Accounting [*Data processing system*]
S Arab .... Saudi Arabia (VRA)
SARAC .... South Australian Rural Advisory Council
SARAC .... Steerable Array for RADAR and Communications (CET)
SARAD .... South African Rates and Data [*A publication*] (IMH)
SARAH .... Search and Range Homing
SARAH .... Search and Rescue and Homing
SARAH .... Semiactive RADAR Alternate Head
SARAH .... Semiautomatic Range Azimuth and Height [*Subsystem*]
Sarah Lawrence C... Sarah Lawrence College (GAGS)
SaraLee ...... Sara Lee Corp. [*Associated Press*] (SAG)
SARARC....... Subauroral Red Arc [*Geophysics*]
Sarat Ch Sent... Saratoga Chancery Sentinel [*1841-47*] [*New York*] [*A publication*] (DLA)
SaratgB........ Saratoga Brands, Inc. [*Associated Press*] (SAG)
SaratgBrd .... Saratoga Brands, Inc. [*Associated Press*] (SAG)
SaratgBv...... Saratoga Beverage Group [*Associated Press*] (SAG)
SARAW .... Sarawak [*Malaysia*] (ROG)
SARB .... State Air Resources Board
Sarbah........ Sarbah's Fanti Law Reports [*Gold Coast*] [*A publication*] (DLA)
Sarbah FC .. Sarbah's Fanti Customary Laws [*Ghana*] [*A publication*] (DLA)
SARBE .... Search and Rescue-Beacon Equipment (MCD)
SARBICA...... Southeast Asian Regional Branch of the International Council on Archives (EAIO)
SARC .... Corrientes [*Argentina ICAO location identifier*] (ICLI)
SARC .... Sarcasm (DSUE)
sarc .... Sarcoma [*Medicine*] (MAE)
sarc .... Sarcophagi (VRA)
sarc .... Sarcophagus (VRA)
SARC .... Search and Rescue Center (CINC)
SARC .... Secure Airborne RADAR Control
SARC .... Split Armature Receiver Capsule (PDAA)
SARC .... Sutton Avian Research Center
SARC .... Symantec AntiVirus Research Center
SAR-C .... Synthetic Aperture RADAR - C-Band (SSD)
SARC .... System Acquisition Review Council [*Army*]
SARC .... Systems Analysis and Research Corp.
SARCA .... Senior Army Reserve Commanders Association
SARCALM ... Synthetic Array RADAR Command Air-Launched Missile
SARCAP....... Search and Rescue - Civil Air Patrol (MCD)
SARCAP....... Search and Rescue Combat Air Patrol (IAA)
SARCAR....... Smithsonian Archaeometric Research Collection and Records [*Facility*]
SARCC .... Search and Rescue Coordination Center [*Air Force*]
SARCCUS ... South African Regional Committee for Conservation and Utilization of Soil
SARCEN ...... Search and Rescue Central [*Navy*]
Sar Ch Sen... Saratoga Chancery Sentinel [*New York*] [*A publication*] (DLA)
SARCOM...... Search and Rescue Communicator [*Navy*]
SARCUP....... Search and Rescue Capability Upgrade Project [*Canadian Navy*]
SARD .... Resistencia (Ciudad) [*Argentina ICAO location identifier*] (ICLI)
SARD .... Sardinia
Sard .... Sardinia (VRA)
SARD .... Simulated Aircraft RADAR Data
SARD .... Solar Array Release and Deployment (MCD)
SARD .... Special Airlift Requirement Directive [*Air Force*] (AFM)
SARD .... Special Airlift Requirement Document [*Army*]
SARD .... Statistical Analysis and Reports Division [*Administrative Office of the U S Courts*] [*Washington, DC*] (GRD)
SARD .... Support and Range Development (MUGU)
SARD .... Synchronized Accumulating Radioisotope Detection
SARDA........ Society for Aid and Rehabilitation of Drug Addicts [*Hong Kong*]
SARDA........ State and Regional Defense Airlift Plan [*FAA, Civil Defense*]
SARDA........ State and Regional Disaster Airlift Planning [*Telecommunications*] (OTD)
SARDC .... Small Arms Research and Development Center [*Army*]
SARDEC ...... Societe des Auteurs, Recherchistes, Documentalistes, et Compositeurs [*Canada*]
SARDET ...... Search and Rescue Detachment [*Navy*] (NG)
SARDIP........ Stricken Aircraft Reclamation and Disposal Program [*Navy*] (NG)

SARDPO ...... San Antonio Research and Development Procurement Office [*Air Force*]
SARDS........ Special Air Route Designators (CINC)
SARDX........ Sardonyx [*Gemstone*] (ROG)
SARE .... Resistencia [*Argentina ICAO location identifier*] (ICLI)
SARE .... Safety Review [*A publication*]
SAREA .... Sinus Area of Leaf [*Botany*]
SARED .... Supporting Applied Research and Exploratory Development [*National Weather Service*]
SAREF .... Safety Research Experiment Facility [*Nuclear energy*]
SAREP .... Speech and Reading Enrichment Program
SAREX .... Search and Rescue Exercise [*Navy*] (DOMA)
SAREX .... Shuttle Amateur Radio Experiment [*NASA*]
SARF .... Formosa [*Argentina ICAO location identifier*] (ICLI)
SARF .... Semiautomated Reconstruction Facility [*Military*] (CAAL)
SARF .... Southeast Asia Rescue Foundation (EA)
SARF .... Southern Africa Road Federation [*See also SAPF*] (EAIO)
Sar FCL ...... Sarbah's Fanti Customary Laws [*Ghana*] [*A publication*] (DLA)
Sar FLR ...... Sarbah's Fanti Law Cases [*1845-1903*] [*Ghana*] [*A publication*] (DLA)
Sar FNC ..... Sarbah's Fanti National Constitution [*Ghana*] [*A publication*] (DLA)
SARFS .... Subordinate Army Field Services
Sarg .... Sargonic (BJA)
SARG .... Self-Adapting Report Generator [*Computer science*] (MHDI)
SARG .... Synthetic Aperture RADAR Guidance (MCD)
SARG .... Synthetic Aperture Retransmission Guidance (MCD)
SARGE .... Surveillance and Reconnaissance Ground Equipment
SARGUN ..... Synthetic Aperture RADAR Gun [*NASA*]
SARH .... Semi-Active RADAR Homing [*Military*] (MUSM)
SARI .... Iguazu/Cataratas Del Iguazu [*Argentina ICAO location identifier*] (ICLI)
SARI .... Share-a-Ride International (EA)
SARI .... Silicon Architectures Research Initiative [*British*]
SARI .... Small Airport Runway Indicator (IAA)
SARI .... South Australian Recreation Institute
SARI .... Standby Altitude Reference Indicator (MCD)
SARIE .... Semiautomatic RADAR Identification Equipment (MCD)
SARIHHWP... Serendipity Association for Research and Implementation of Holistic Health and World Peace (EA)
SARIMS ...... Swept Angle Retarding Ion Mass Spectrometer (PDAA)
SARIPADI .... Serikat Pamong Desa Indonesia [*Village Officials' Union of Indonesia*]
SARIS .... South African Retrospective Information System (NITA)
SARIS .... Synthetic Aperture RADAR Interpretation System [*NASA*] (MCD)
SARISA .... Surface Analysis by Resonance Ionization of Sputtered Atoms
SARITC .... South Australian Retail Industry Training Council
SARK .... Saville Advanced Remote Keying (MCD)
SARL .... Paso De Los Libres [*Argentina ICAO location identifier*] (ICLI)
SARL .... Societe a Responsabilite Limitee [*Private Limited Company*] [*French*]
SARL .... Subtropical Agricultural Research Laboratory [*Weslaco, TX*] [*Department of Agriculture*] (GRD)
SARLA......... South African Rock Lobster Association [*Defunct*]
SARLANT.... Search and Rescue, Atlantic [*Coast Guard*]
SARM .... Monte Caseros [*Argentina ICAO location identifier*] (ICLI)
SARM .... Set Asynchronous Response Mode
SARM .... Standard Analytical Reference Material (MCD)
SARM .... Standard Antiradiation Missile (MCD)
SARM .... System Acquisition Review Memorandum [*Army*]
SARMC .... Search and Rescue Mission Coordinator [*Australia*]
SARME .... Set Asychronous Response Mode Extended [*Telecommunications*] (OSI)
SARMIS .... Search and Rescue Management Information System (COE)
SARMIT .... Sport and Recreation Association of RMIT [*Royal Melbourne Institute of Techn ology*] Union
SARNI .... Serikat Nelajan Indonesia [*Sailors' Union of Indonesia*]
SARO .... Ituzaingo [*Argentina ICAO location identifier*] (ICLI)
SARO .... Special Applications Routine (IAA)
SAROA........ Salvation Army Retired Officers Association
SAROAD ..... Storage and Retrieval of Aerometric Data [*Database*] [*Sigma Data Services Corp.*] [*Information service or system*] (CRD)
SARP .... Posadas [*Argentina ICAO location identifier*] (ICLI)
SARP .... Safety Analysis Report for Packaging [*NASA*] (NASA)
SARP .... Sardine-Anchovy Recruitment Project [*Marine science*] (OSRA)
SARP .... Schedule, Analysis, and Review Procedure [*NASA*] (KSC)
SARP .... Schedule and Resources Procedure [*NASA*] (KSC)
SARP .... Scheduling and Reporting [*or Review*] Procedure [*NASA*] (KSC)
SARP .... Scramble and Recovery Procedure (SAA)
SARP .... Severe Accident Research Plan [*Nuclear energy*] (NRCH)
SARP .... Ship Alteration and Repair Package [*Navy*] (CAAL)
SARP .... Shuttle Astronaut Recruitment Program [*NASA*] (MCD)
SARP .... Signal Automatic RADAR Processing
SARP .... Small Autonomous Research Package
SARP .... Sophisticated Automatic RADAR Processing (PDAA)
SARP .... Space Allocation and Reservation Program (MCD)
SARP .... Space Allocation Requirement Procedures (MCD)
SARP .... Standards and Recommended Practices
SARP .... Storage and Retrieval Processor (MCD)
SARP .... Summary Analysis Report (NAKS)
SARPAC....... Search and Rescue, Pacific [*Coast Guard*] (DNAB)
SARPE .... Single-Atom Resonant Photoemission [*Physics*]
SARPF .... Strategic Air Relocatable Photographic Facility (CINC)
SARPMA ..... San Antonio Real Property Maintenance Agency [*Military*]
SARPS .... Standards and Recommended Practices [*International Civil Aviation Organization*]
SARR .... Resistencia [*Argentina ICAO location identifier*] (ICLI)

SARRA........	Short-Arc Reduction of RADAR Altimetry
SARRP........	Severe Accident Risk Reduction Program [*Nuclear energy*] (NRCH)
SARS..........	Presidencia R. Saenz Pena [*Argentina ICAO location identifier*] (ICLI)
SaRS..........	Safety and Reliability Society [*British*]
SARS..........	School Archival Records Search [*Test*] (TMMY)
SARS..........	Scots Ancestry Research Society [*British*] (DBA)
SARS..........	Secretary of the Army Research and Study [*Fellowship*]
SARS..........	Semi-Active RADAR Simulator [*Military*]
SARS..........	Semiautomated Reconstruction System [*Military*] (CAAL)
SARS..........	Sensor Analog Relay System
SARS..........	Ship Attitude Record System
SARS..........	Simulated Airborne RADAR System (MCD)
SARS..........	Single Allocation and Reservation Study (MCD)
SARS..........	Single-Axis Reference System
SARS..........	Solar Array Reorientation System
SARS..........	Spares Accounting Replenishment System [*NASA*] (KSC)
SARS..........	Standardized Army Refueling System (DOMA)
SARS..........	Static Automatic Reporting System (MCD)
SARS..........	Stellar Attitude Reference System
SARS..........	Student Association for the Rights of Students [*Australia*]
SARS..........	Synthetic Array RADAR System
SARSAT.......	Social Affairs Recreation and Sports Association
SARSAT.......	Search and Rescue Satellite [*Navy*]
SARSAT.......	Search and Rescue Satellite-Aided Tracking [*NASA*]
SARSAT.......	Synthetic Aperture RADAR Satellite [*NASA*] (SSD)
SARSEP.......	Salary Reduction Simplified Employee Pension
SARSEX.......	Synthetic Aperture RADAR Signature Experiment [*Oceanography*]
SARSIM.......	Search and Rescue Simulation [*Coast Guard*]
SARSN........	Southern Appalachian Regional Seismic Network [*Geology*]
SARSS........	Search and Rescue Satellite System [*Navy*] (MCD)
SARSS........	Standard Army Retail Supply System
SARSS/OSC...	Standard Army Retail Supply System/Objective Supply Capability (RDA)
SART..........	Seattle Army Terminal
SART..........	Shuttle Astronaut Recruitment [*NASA*] (NAKS)
SART..........	Society for Assisted Reproductive Technology (EA)
SART..........	Special Army Review Team (MCD)
SART..........	St. Alban's Repertory Theater [*Washington, DC*]
SART..........	Standard Acid Reflux Test [*Clinical chemistry*]
SART..........	Stimuli Analog Refresh Table [*NASA*] (MCD)
SART..........	Stop All Racist Tours [*An association British*]
SART..........	Strategic Aircraft Reconstitution Team [*Air Force*] (DOMA)
SARTACK.....	Search AntiRADAR Tactical Aircraft, K-Band
SARTAF.......	Search and Rescue Task Force [*Military*] (VNW)
SARTEL.......	Search and Rescue, Telephone [*Coast Guard*]
SARTOC......	Southern Africa Regional Tourism Council (EAIO)
SARTS........	Satisfaction of Army Requirements through Space (MCD)
SARTS........	Small Arms Readiness Training Section [*National Guard*]
SARTS........	Small Arms Remote Target System (MCD)
SARTS........	Switched Access Remote Test System [*Bell System*]
SARU..........	Resistencia [*Argentina ICAO location identifier*] (ICLI)
SARU..........	South Australian Rugby Union
SARU..........	System Analysis Research Unit
SARUM.......	Bishop of Salisbury [*British*]
SARUS........	Search and Rescue Using Satellites [*Air Force*]
SARV..........	Satellite Aeromedical Research Vehicle
SARVIP.......	Survival Army Recovery Vest, Insert, and Pockets
SAS...........	Lithuanian Catholic Students' Association "Ateitis" (EA)
SAS...........	Salicylazosulfapyridine [*Antibacterial*]
SaS...........	Salton City, CA [*Location identifier FAA*] (FAAL)
SAS...........	Sample Array System (KSC)
SAS...........	Sand-Asphalt-Sulfur [*Road paving material*]
SAS...........	Saskatoon [*Saskatchewan*] [*Seismograph station code, US Geological Survey Closed*] (SEIS)
SAS...........	Satellite Attack Sensor
SAS...........	Scandinavian Airlines System [*Sweden ICAO designator*] (FAAC)
SAS...........	Schiapparelli [*Italy*] [*Research code symbol*]
SAS...........	School Administrator and Supervisor (GAGS)
SAS...........	SEAL [*Subsea Equipment Associates Ltd.*] Atmospheric System
SAS...........	Sealed Authentication System [*Military*]
SAS...........	Seasonal Agricultural Service
SAS...........	Secondary Alarm Station [*Nuclear energy*] (NRCH)
SAS...........	Secondary Alerting System (IAA)
SAS...........	Secondary Alkane Sulfonate [*Surfactant*] [*Organic chemistry*]
SAS...........	Secondary Assistance Scheme [*Australia*]
SAS...........	Sections Administratives Specialisees [*French Army*]
SAS...........	Secure Authentication System (IIA)
SAS...........	Security Agency Study [*Nuclear energy*] (NRCH)
SAS...........	Security Assistance and Sales [*DoD*]
SAS...........	Segment Arrival Storage Area (KSC)
SAS...........	Seismic Alert System
SAS...........	Selected Applicant Service (NITA)
SAS...........	Self-Adaptive System
SAS...........	Self-Assessment Survey [*Clarke Reading*] (TES)
SAS...........	Self-Rating Anxiety Scale [*Psychology*] (DB)
SAS...........	Semi-Airspace (NITA)
SAS...........	Semiannual Soils [*Environmental science*] (COE)
SAS...........	Senior Assistant Secretary
SAS...........	Sensor and Source
SAS...........	Service Activity System
SAS...........	Service Air System (NRCH)
SAS...........	Service Annual Survey [*Bureau of the Census*] (GFGA)
SAS...........	Sex Attitudes Survey [*Psychology*]
SAS...........	Shakespearean Authorship Society [*Later, SAT*] (EA)
SAS...........	Sherwood Anderson Society (EA)

SAS...........	Shift Accumulator Left, Including Sign (IAA)
SAS...........	Ship Alteration Suite [*Navy*] (CAAL)
SAS...........	Short-Arm Splint [*Orthopedics*] (DAVI)
SAS...........	Side-Angle-Side (Rule) [*Geometry*]
SAS...........	Signal Airways Service
SAS...........	Signal Analysis System [*Electronics*]
SAS...........	Silicon Avalanche Suppressor [*Telecommunications*]
SAS...........	Single Angle Scattering
SAS...........	Single Anomalous Scattering [*Crystallography*]
SAS...........	Single Attached Stations [*Computer science*] (TNIG)
SAS...........	Single Audio System (CAAL)
SAS...........	Single-Award Schedule (AAGC)
SAS...........	Sklar Aphasia Scale [*Psychology*]
SAS...........	Sleep Apnea Syndrome [*Medicine*]
SAS...........	Small-Angle Scattering (OA)
SAS...........	Small Applications Satellite (KSC)
SAS...........	Small Arms School [*British military*] (DMA)
SAS...........	Small Astronomy Satellite
SAS...........	Small-Probe Atmospheric Structure [*NASA*]
SAS...........	Smart Armor System [*Army*]
SAS...........	Snake Approach Scale [*Psychology*]
SAS...........	Snap Action Switch
SAS...........	Social Adjustment Scale [*Psychology*] (DB)
SAS...........	Societatis Antiquariorum Socius [*Fellow of the Society of Antiquaries*] [*British*]
SAS...........	Society for Applied Sociology (EA)
SAS...........	Society for Applied Spectroscopy (EA)
SAS...........	Society for Armenian Studies (EA)
SAS...........	Society of American Silversmiths (EA)
SAS...........	Society of Antiquaries of Scotland (EAIO)
SAS...........	Society of Australasian Specialists [*Later, SASO*]
SAS...........	Sodium Alkane Sulfonate [*Detergent intermediate*]
SAS...........	Sodium Aluminum Sulfate [*Organic chemistry*]
SAS...........	Solar Array Structure
SAS...........	Solar Array System (MCD)
SAS...........	Solar Aspect Sensor
SAS...........	Solomons Ano Sagufenua [*Solomon Islands*] [*Political party*] (FEA)
SAS...........	Son Altesse Serenissime [*His or Her Serene Highness*] [*French*]
SAS...........	Sound Amplification System
SAS...........	South American Series [*A publication*]
SAS...........	South Asian Seas
SAS...........	Southern Anthropological Society
SAS...........	Southern Appalachian Studies [*Defunct*] (EA)
SAS...........	Soviet Academy of Sciences
SAS...........	Space Activity Suit
SAS...........	Space Adaptation Syndrome [*NASA*]
SAS...........	Spacecraft Antenna System
SAS...........	Special Access Space (CAAL)
SAS...........	Special Activities Squadron [*Air Force*]
SAS...........	Special Administrative Section
SAS...........	Special Airlift Summary [*MTMC*] (TAG)
SAS...........	Special Air Service [*British commando unit*]
SAS...........	Special Air Services [*Australia*] (VNW)
SAS...........	Special Ammunition Section [*Picatinny Arsenal*] [*Army*]
SARS..........	Special Ammunition Site [*Army*]
SAS...........	Special Ammunition Stockage [*Army*] (AABC)
SAS...........	Special Ammunition Storage (RDA)
SAS...........	Special Army Squadron [*British*] (DI)
SAS...........	Speed, Aggression, and Surprise [*Military*] (WDAA)
SAS...........	Stability Augmentation System [*or Subsystem*] [*FAA*]
SAS...........	Staff Activity System (IAA)
SAS...........	Staff Administrative Specialist [*Military*]
SAS...........	Standard Age Score (DHP)
SAS...........	St. Andrew Goldfields Ltd. [*Toronto Stock Exchange symbol*]
SAS...........	St. Andrew Society [*Edinburgh, Scotland*] (EAIO)
SAS...........	Statement of Auditing Standards
SAS...........	Station Air System [*Nuclear energy*] (NRCH)
SAS...........	Statistical Analysis System [*Programming language*] [*1966*]
SAS...........	Sterile Aqueous Suspension
SAS...........	Storage Address Switch (IAA)
SAS...........	Storage Aids Systems [*Air Force*] (DOMA)
SAS...........	Strategic Aerospace Summary
SAS...........	Strategic Area Study (MCD)
SAS...........	Subaortic Stenosis [*Medicine*] (DMAA)
SAS...........	Sulfasalazine [*Pharmacology*] (DAVI)
SAS...........	Sum of Adjacent Spans
SAS...........	Super Accuracy Simplex (IAA)
SAS...........	Supercritical Antisolvent [*Chemical engineering*]
SAS...........	Superior Atrial Septum [*Anatomy*]
SAS...........	Supersonic Attack Seaplane
SAS...........	Support Amplifier Station [*Telecommunications*] (OA)
SAS...........	Supravalvular Aortic Stenosis [*Cardiology*]
SAS...........	Surface Active Substances (IEEE)
SAS...........	Survival Avionics System [*Military*] (CAAL)
SAS...........	Survive at School (WDAA)
SAS...........	Suspended Aluminosilicate
SAS...........	Suspended Array System [*To detect submarines*]
SAS...........	SverigeAmerika Stiftelsen [*Sweden-American Foundation*] (EAIO)
SAS...........	Switched Access System [*Telecommunications*] (TEL)
SAS...........	Synthetic Amorphous Silicas [*Inorganic Chemistry*]
SAS...........	System Acquisition School (MCD)
SAS...........	System Analysis Study
SAS...........	System Application Software [*Computer science*] (BUR)
SASA..........	Salta [*Argentina ICAO location identifier*] (ICLI)
SASA..........	Scottish Amateur Swimming Association (DBA)

SASA .... Severe Accident Sequence Analysis [*Nuclear energy*] (NRCH)
SASA .... Ski Area Suppliers Association (EA)
SASA .... Small Arms Systems Agency [*Army*] (RDA)
SASA .... Soil Association of South Australia
SASA .... South Asian Studies Association of Australia and New Zealand
SASA .... South Australian Sawmillers' Association
SASA .... Special Ammunition Supply Activity (MCD)
SASAR .... Segmented Aperture-Synthetic Aperture RADAR
SASAS .... Southern Africa Society of Aquatic Scientists (EAIO)
SASAT .... Shipboard Antisubmarine Attack Teacher [*Navy*]
SASB .... South Australian Superannuation Board
SASB .... Structural Analysis of Social Behavior
SASBFIT .... South Australian Superannuation Board Fund Investment Trust
SASBO .... Southeastern Association of School Business Officials (AEBS)
SASC .... Salta [*Argentina ICAO location identifier*] (ICLI)
SASC .... Semiautomatic Stock Control
SASC .... Senate Armed Services Committee
SASC .... Senior Appointments Selection Committee [*British*]
SASC .... Small Arms School Corps [*Military British*]
SASC .... Subject Analysis Systems Collection [*University of Toronto*] [*Information service or system*] (IID)
SASC .... Sydney Anglican Schools Corp. [*Commercial firm*]
SASCL .... St. Ansgar's Scandinavian Catholic League (EA)
SASCO .... Sudanese Aeronautical Services Co. Ltd. [*Sudan*] [*ICAO designator*] (FAAC)
SASCOM .... Southern Atlantic Satellite Communication
SASCOM .... Special Ammunition Support Command [*Army*] (AABC)
SASCON .... Southern African Solidarity Congress [*Zimbabwe*] [*Political party*] (PPW)
SAS/CSS .... Stability Augmentation System with Control Stick Steering (PDAA)
SASD .... Static Adjustable Speed Drive
SASD .... Strategies and Air Standards Division [*Environmental Protection Agency*] (GFGA)
SA/SD .... Structured Analysis/Structured Design (MCD)
SASDRA .... Sample Acquisition System for Dissolution Rate Analysis (DB)
SASDT .... Ships and Aircraft Supplemental Data Tables [*Navy*]
SASE .... Sample Sequencing (HGEN)
SASE .... Self-Addressed Stamped Envelope
sase .... Self-Addressed Stamped Envelope (ODBW)
SASE .... Small Arms Suppression Evaluation (MCD)
SASE .... Society for the Advancement of Socio-Economics (NTPA)
SASE .... Space Adaptation Syndrome Experiment [*Pronounced "Sassy"*] [*Space shuttle experiment developed in Canada*]
SASE .... Specific Application Service Element [*Telecommunications*] (OSI)
SASE .... Statistical Analysis of a Series of Events (PDAA)
SASES .... South Australian State Emergency Services
SASF .... SIDPERS [*Standard Installation/Division Personnel System*] Authorized Strength File [*Military*] (AABC)
SASFA .... South Australian Shark Fishermen's Association
SASG .... Security Assistance Steering Group [*Military*]
SASG .... Smoke/Aerosol Steering Group [*DARCOM*] (RDA)
SASH .... Symmetry-Adapted Spherical-Harmonic [*Mathematics*]
SASHEP .... Study of Accreditation of Selected Health Educational Programs
SASI .... Ships and Air Systems Integration [*Navy*]
SASI .... Shugart Associates Standard Interface [*Computer science*] (DDC)
SASI .... Shugart Associates Systems Interface
SASI .... Society of Air Safety Investigators [*Later, ISASI*]
SASI .... Southern Association of Science and Industry (EA)
SASI .... Surface Air System Integration
SASI .... System Automation Software, Inc.
SASI .... System on Automotive Safety Information [*General Motors Corp.*] [*Information service or system*]
SASIDS .... Stochastic Adaptive Sequential Information Dissemination System
SASIS .... Semi-Automatic Speaker Identification System (PDAA)
SASITS .... Submarine Advanced Signal Training System (DNAB)
SASJ .... Jujuy [*Argentina ICAO location identifier*] (ICLI)
SASJ .... Self-Aligning Swivel Joint
SASK .... Saskatchewan [*Canadian province*]
Sask .... Saskatchewan [*Canada*] (DD)
Sask .... Saskatchewan Law Reports [*Canada*] [*A publication*] (DLA)
Sask L .... Saskatchewan Law [*A publication*] (DLA)
Sask LR .... Saskatchewan Law Reports [*Canada*] [*A publication*] (DLA)
Sask R .... Saskatchewan Law Reports [*A publication*] (DLA)
Sask Rev Stat ... Saskatchewan Revised Statutes [*Canada*] [*A publication*] (DLA)
Sask Stat .... Saskatchewan Statutes [*Canada*] [*A publication*] (DLA)
SaskTel .... Saskatchewan Telecommunications [*Regina*] [*Information service or system*] (IID)
SASL .... Service Approved Status List [*Navy*] (DNAB)
SASLA .... South Australian Salaried Lawyers' Association
SASLIC .... Surrey and Sussex Libraries in Cooperation (NITA)
SASM .... Smithsonian Air and Space Museum
SASM .... Society for Automation in the Sciences and Mathematics
SASM .... Special Assistant for Strategic Mobility [*Military*] (AFM)
SASM .... Supersonic Antiship Missile (MCD)
SASMB .... South Australian Stock Medicines Board
SASMC .... South Australian Sports Medicine Centre
SASMS .... Special Assistant for Surface Missile System
SASMSA .... South Australian Stud Merino Sheepbreeders' Association
SASN .... Special Assistant to the Secretary of the Navy
SASO .... Oran [*Algeria*] [*ICAO location identifier*] (ICLI)
SASO .... Sasol Ltd. [*NASDAQ symbol*] (NQ)
SASO .... Senior Air Staff Officer [*British*]
SASO .... Society of Australasian Specialists/Oceania (EA)
SASO .... South African Students' Organization (PD)
SASO .... Superintending Armament Supply Officer [*British military*] (DMA)
SASOC .... School Administrators and Supervisors Organizing Committee [*Later, AFSA*] (EA)
Sasol .... Sasol Ltd. [*Associated Press*] (SAG)
SASOY .... Sasol Ltd ADR [*NASDAQ symbol*] (TTSB)
SASP .... Salicylazosulfapyridine (DMAA)
SASP .... Science and Application Space Platform (MCD)
SASP .... Shortest Activity from Shortest Project
SASP .... Single Advanced Signal Processor [*Military*] (CAAL)
SASP .... Site Activation and Support Plan (MCD)
SASP .... Society for the Advancement of Social Psychology (EA)
SASP .... Society of Sales Professionals [*Automotive sales certification program*]
SASP .... Special Ammunition Supply Point [*Army*]
SASP .... Specialized Acid-Soluble Spore Protein [*Bacteriology*]
SASP .... Stand Alone Support Program
SASP .... State Agency for Surplus Property
SASP .... State Airport System Plan [*Department of Transportation*]
SASP .... Submarine Analytic Search Program [*Navy*] (CAAL)
SA-SPM .... Socialist Alliance - Socialist Party of Macedonia [*Political party*] (EY)
SASPS .... SAMMS [*Standard Automated Materiel Management System*] Automated Small Purchase System
SASQ .... La Quiaca [*Argentina ICAO location identifier*] (ICLI)
SASq .... Strategic Aerospace Squadron [*Air Force*]
SASQUA .... Southern African Society for Quaternary Research (EAIO)
SASR .... Rivadavia [*Argentina ICAO location identifier*] (ICLI)
SASR .... Sandy Spring Bancorp [*NASDAQ symbol*] (TTSB)
SASR .... Sandy Spring Bancorp, Inc. [*NASDAQ symbol*] (SAG)
SASR .... Semi-Annual Status Report (MHDI)
SASR .... Subaqueous Sound Ranging (IAA)
SASRDI .... Subaqueous Sound Ranging Development Installation (IAA)
SASRS .... Satellite-Aided Search and Rescue System [*Telecommunications*]
SASS .... Safety Assurance System Summary [*Environmental science*] (COE)
SASS .... SAGE [*Semiautomatic Ground Environment*] Atabe Simulation System (IAA)
SASS .... Saturn Automatic Software System [*NASA*]
SASS .... Schedules and Status Summary [*NASA*] (KSC)
SASS .... School and Staffing Survey [*Department of Education*] (GFGA)
SASS .... SEASAT [*Sea Satellite*]- A Scatterometer System [*NASA*]
SASS .... Sir Arthur Sullivan Society [*British*] (DBA)
SASS .... Small Aerostat Surveillance System [*Army*] (DOMA)
SASS .... Small Airbreathing System Synthesis (MCD)
SASS .... Society for Automation in the Social Sciences [*Later, SDE*]
SASS .... Society for the Advancement of Scandinavian Study (EA)
SASS .... Source Assessment Sampling System [*Environmental Protection Agency*]
SASS .... Spark Chamber Automatic Scanning System (DNAB)
SASS .... Special Aircraft Service Shop (NG)
SASS .... Special Army Signal Service (IAA)
SASS .... SPEEDEX [*Systemwide Project for Electronic Equipment at Depots Extended*] Automatic Scheduling System [*Military*]
SASS .... Spreadsheet Anthropometric Scaling System [*Army*] (RDA)
SASS .... Standard Analysis Software System [*Astronomy*]
SASS .... Standard Army Supply System
SASS .... Strategic Airborne Surveillance System [*Military*]
SASS .... Strategic Alerting Sound System (AAG)
SASS .... Supplement Aviation Spares Report (MCD)
SASS .... Suspended Array Surveillance System [*To detect submarines*]
SASS .... Swath-Sounding Sonar (BARN)
SASS .... Systems and Services Section [*Library Administration and Management Association*]
SASSA .... South Australian Stock Salesmen's Association
SASSC .... Senate Aeronautical and Space Sciences Committee (AAG)
SASSE .... Synchronous Altitude Spin-Stabilized Experiment
SASSI .... Synthetic Amorphous Silica and Silicates Industry Association (EA)
SASSIA .... Synthetic Amorphous Silica and Silicates Industry Association (EA)
SASSIF .... Self-Adjusting System of Scientific Information Flow
SASS LITE ... Small Airship Surveillance System, Low Intensity Target Exploitation [*Army*]
SASSM .... Surface-to-Air, Surface-to-Surface Missile (MCD)
SASSTIXS .... Satellite Air, Surface, Subsurface Tactical Information Exchange System [*Navy*] (CAAL)
SASSY .... Small Angle Separator System [*Superheavy element research*]
SASSY .... Supported Activities Supply System [*Marine Corps*]
SAST .... Safety Standards
SAST .... Selective Arterial Secretin Injection Test [*Medicine*] (DMAA)
SAST .... Self-Administered Alcoholism Screening Test [*Medicine*] (DMAA)
SAST .... Serum Aspartate Aminotransferase [*An enzyme*]
SAST .... Service Announcements in Science and Technology [*National Technical Information Service*] (EA)
SAST .... Single Asphalt Surface Treatment
SAST .... Society for the Advancement of Space Travel [*Defunct*] (MCD)
SAST .... Substance Abuse Screening Test (TMMY)
SAST .... Tartagal/Gral Mosconi [*Argentina ICAO location identifier*] (ICLI)
SASTA JI ..... SASTA [*South Australian Science Teachers Association*] Journal [*A publication*]
SASTAR .... Support Activities Staffing Review (MCD)
SASTE .... Semiautomatic Shop Test Equipment (NG)
SASTP .... Stand-Alone Self-Test Program [*NASA*] (MCD)
SASTRO .... SAGE [*Semiautomatic Ground Environment*] Strobe Training Operator (IAA)
SASTU .... Signal Amplitude Sampler and Totalizing Unit (IEEE)
SASU .... Saturn Apollo Systems Utilization [*NASA*]
SASU .... Suicide Awareness Support Unit (WDAA)
SASUTA .... Southern African Society of University Teachers of Accounting (EAIO)

SASV	Secondary Air Switching Valve [*Automotive engineering*]
SASV	Sisters of the Assumption (TOCD)
SASV	Sisters of the Assumption of the Blessed Virgin [*Roman Catholic religious order*]
SASV	Snap Action Spool Valve
SASVRC	Sir Albert Sakzewski Virus Research Centre
SASW	Situational Attitude Scale-Women (EDAC)
SASWREC	SACLANT [*Supreme Allied Commander, Atlantic*] Antisubmarine Warfare Research Center (NATG)
SAT	Asia Satellite Telecommunications Holdings Ltd. [*NYSE symbol*] (SAG)
SAT	Canadian Satellite Communications, Inc. [*Toronto Stock Exchange symbol*]
SAT	Safe Arming Time
SAT	Salamaua Aerial Transport [*Australia*]
SAT	Salaries and Allowances Tribunal [*Australia*]
SAT	Salt Aggregation Test [*Clinical chemistry*]
SAT	Sampler Address Translator
SAT	San Antonio [*Texas*] [*Airport symbol*]
SAT	Sang-Tuda [*Former USSR Seismograph station code, US Geological Survey Closed*] (SEIS)
SAT	Satellite
sat	Satin (VRA)
Sat	Satirae [*or Sermones*] [*of Horace*] [*Classical studies*] (OCD)
SAT	Satisfactory (AABC)
Sat	Satura [*of Petronius*] [*Classical studies*] (OCD)
SAT	Saturate (AAG)
sat	Saturate (IDOE)
sat	Saturation (IDOE)
SAT	Saturatus [*Saturated*] [*Pharmacy*]
SAT	Saturday (EY)
Sat	Saturday (ODBW)
Sat	Saturn [*Record label*] [*France*]
SAT	Saturn
Sat	Saturnalia [*of Macrobius*] [*Classical studies*] (OCD)
SAT	Scholastic Aptitude Test [*Trademark of the College Entrance Examination Board*]
SAT	Scholastic Assessment Test [*Formerly, Scholastic Aptitude Test*]
SAT	School Ability Test [*Psychology*]
SAT	School of Applied Tactics [*AAFSAT*]
SAT	Scientific Advisory Team [*Navy*] (MCD)
SAT	Scientific and Technical (MCD)
SAT	Sea Acceptance Trial
SAT	Security Alert Team [*Military*] (AFM)
SAT	Security Appeals Tribunal [*Australia*]
SAT	Security Assistance Team [*Military*] (AABC)
SAT	SEMA [*Specialty Equipment Manufacturers Association*] Action Team
SAT	Semiarid Tropics [*Geography*]
SAT	Semiautomatic Test Equipment [*NASA*]
SAT	Semi-Automatic Trim (COE)
SAT	Senior Apperception Technique [*Personality development test*] [*Psychology*]
SAT	Senior Aptitude Tests [*Educational test*]
SAT	Sennacica Asocio Tutmonda [*Nationless Worldwide Association*] (EAIO)
SAT	Serial Accountability Transmittal
SAT	Serum Agglutination Test (OA)
SAT	Serum Antitrypsin (DB)
SAT	Service Acceptance Trials (NVT)
SAT	Servico Acoriana de Transportes Aereos [*Portugal ICAO designator*] (FAAC)
SAT	Shakespearean Authorship Trust [*England*] (EAIO)
SAT	Ship Acceptance Test [*Navy*] (CAAL)
SAT	Ship's Apparent Time [*Navigation*]
SAT	Silicon Annular Transistor
SAT	Simplified Acquisition Threshold (AAGC)
SAT	Sine Acido Thymonuleico [*Without Thymonucleic Acid*]
SAT	Site Acceptance Test [*Military*] (AABC)
SAT	Site Alteration Tests
SAT	Site Assignment Time
SAT	Sitting Atop [*Molecular configuration*]
SAT	Small Angle Tagger (MCD)
SAT	Small Arms Transmitter [*Army*] (INF)
SAT	Snap Action Thermostat
SAT	Social Assessment of Technology (PDAA)
SAT	Socially-Appropriate Technology (PDAA)
SAT	Societa Anonima Transadriatica [*Italy*]
SAT	Society of Acoustic Technology (IAA)
SAT	Software Acceptance Test
SAT	Solar Atmospheric Tide (IAA)
SAT	Sound-Apperception Test [*Psychology*]
SAT	South Atlantic
SAT	Southern African Territories
SAT	Southern Air Transport, Inc.
SAT	Space Available Travel
SAT	Speaker Authentication Technique
SAT	Special Assistance Team [*Navy*] (NG)
SAT	Specific Aptitude Test
SAT	Specified Actions Table [*Military*]
SAT	Speeck Awareness Threshold [*Otorhinolaryngology*] (DAVI)
SAT	Spiral Aftereffect Test [*Psychology*]
SAT	Spray Acid Tool (AAEL)
SAT	Stabilization Assurance Test (IEEE)
SAT	Standard Area of Tinplate [*100,000 square inches*]
SAT	Standard Assessment Task (DET)
SAT	Stanford Achievement Test [*Education*]
SAT	Staphylococcus Adherence Test [*Clinical chemistry*]
SAT	Static Air Temperature
SAT	Stepped Atomic Time [*National Institute of Standards and Technology*]
SAT	Strategic American Traveler
SAT	Structural Analysis Technologies, Inc.
SAT	Study of Appeal Tribunals [*British*]
SAT	Subacute Thyroiditis [*Medicine*]
SAT	Subassembly Template (MCD)
SAT	Subscriber Access Terminal
SAT	Substance Abuse Treatment [*Health insurance*] (GHCT)
SAT	Subsumed Abilities Test [*Student attitudes test*]
SAT	Successive Approximation Technique (NOAA)
SAT	Sufuric Acid Terrahydrate [*Inorganic chemistry*]
SAT	Support Analysis Test
SAT	Surface Aerospace Technology
SAT	Surface Air Temperature [*Climatology*]
SAT	Surface Alloy Transistor (IAA)
SAT	Surface Antenna Terminal (MCD)
SAT	Surveillance, Acquisition, and Tracking [*Military*] (RDA)
SAT	Sustained Airborne Training [*Army*] (INF)
SAT	Symptomless Autoimmune Thyroiditis [*Medicine*] (DMAA)
SAT	System Access Technique [*Sperry UNIVAC*]
SAT	System Access Terminal AT&T (NITA)
SAT	System Alignment Test (NVT)
SAT	System Analysis Table (IAA)
SAT	Systematic Assertiveness Training
SAT	Systematized Assertive Therapy [*Psychology*] (DAVI)
SAT	Systems Acceptance Tests (KSC)
SAT	Systems Approach to Training [*NASA*] (MCD)
SATA	Alliance of Canadian Travel Associations - Saskatchewan (AC)
SATA	Safety and Arming Test Aid (MCD)
SATA	Satellite Automatic Tracking Antenna (MCD)
SATA	Scholastic Abilities Test for Adults (TES)
SATA	Servicios Auxiliares de Transportes [*ICAO designator*] (FAAC)
SATA	Sherman Anti-Trust Act (MHDB)
SATA	Sociedade Acoriana de Transportes Aereos Ltda. [*Airline*] [*Portugal*]
SATA	Something about the Author [*A publication*]
SATA	South Australian Tennis Association
SATA	Southern Aerosol Technical Association
SATA	Spatial Average, Temporal Average [*Medicine*] (DMAA)
SATA	Student Air Travel Association
SATA	Subsonic Aerodynamic Testing Association (MCD)
SATA	Supervisory, Administrative, and Technical Association [*Union of Ship Distribution and Allied Workers*] [*British*] (DCTA)
SATAB	South Australian Totalisator Board
SATAF	Shuttle Activation Task Force [*NASA*] (NASA)
SATAF	Site Activation Task Force [*Military*]
SATAF	Site Activity [*or Alternation*] Task Force [*NASA*] (KSC)
SATAM	Syndicat Autonome des Travailleurs de la Alimentation de Madagascar [*Autonomous Union of Food Workers of Madagascar*]
SATAN	Satellite Active Nullifier [*Antisatellite weapon*]
SATAN	Satellite Automatic Tracking Antenna
Sat An	Satellite Receiving Antenna (NITA)
SATAN	Security Administrator Tool for Analyzing Networks
SATAN	Security Analysis Tool for Auditing Networks [*Computer science*] (CDE)
SATAN	Self-Contained Automatic Tactical Air Navigation (IAA)
SATAN	Sensor for Airborne Terrain Analysis
SATAN	Speed and Throttle Automatic Network (PDAA)
SATAN	Storage Array Tester and Analyzer (PDAA)
SATAN	Strobes Against Troops at Night (MCD)
SATAN	System Administrator Tool for Analyzing Networks
SATANAS	Semiautomatic Analog Setting (IEEE)
SATANS	Static and Transient Analysis, Nonlinear, Shells [*Computer program*] [*Navy*]
SATANT	Satellite Antenna (DWSG)
SATAR	Satellite for Aerospace Research [*NASA*]
SA Tax Cas	South African Tax Cases [*A publication*] (DLA)
SATB	Simulated Air Training Bundle (MCD)
SATB	Soprano, Alto, Tenor, Bass
SATB	South African Tourism Board
SATB	Specific Aptitude Test Battery
SATBC	South Australian Trailer Boat Club
SATC	Clorinda [*Argentina ICAO location identifier*] (ICLI)
SATC	SatCon Technology [*NASDAQ symbol*] (TTSB)
SATC	Satcon Technology Corp. [*NASDAQ symbol*] (SAG)
SATC	Ship Automatic Torpedo Countermeasures (MCD)
SATC	Situation Assessment and Tactical Control [*Military*] (WDAA)
SATC	South African Tax Cases [*A publication*] (DLA)
SATC	South Australian Timber Corp. [*Commercial firm*]
SATC	Students Army Training Corps
SATC	Suspended Acoustical-Tile Ceiling [*Technical drawings*]
SATCA	Sino-American Technical Cooperation Association
SATCAMS	Semiautomatic Tactical Control and Airspace Management System (MCD)
SATCC	Southern Air Traffic Control Centre [*British*]
SATCH	Salicylaldehyde Thiocarbohydrazone [*Organic chemistry*]
SATCHMO	Satchel Mouth [*Nickname of late trumpeter Louis Armstrong*]
SATCO	Semiautomatic Air Traffic Control (IAA)
SATCO	Senior Air Traffic Control Officer (NATG)
SATCO	Signal Automatic Air Traffic Control System
SATCO	Supervisory Air Traffic Control Organization [*FAA*]

SATCOM	Satellite Command
SATCOM	Satellite Communication (NTCM)
SATCOM	Satellite Communication Agency [Army] (IAA)
SATCOM	Satellite Communications [Military]
SATCOM	Scientific and Technical Communication
SATCOMA	Satellite Communications Agency [AEC/DCA]
SATCOM AGEN	Satellite Communications Agency [Army]
Satcon	Satcon Technology Corp. [Associated Press] (SAG)
SATCON	Satellite Condition [Military] (AABC)
sat cond	Satisfactory Condition (STED)
SATCRIS	Semi-Arid Tropical Crops Information Service (IID)
SATCS	Scandinavian Association for Thoracic and Cardiovascular Surgery (EA)
SATD	El Dorado [Argentina ICAO location identifier] (ICLI)
SATD	Saturated
sat'd	Saturated (STED)
satd	Saturated (IDOE)
SATD	Seattle Army Terminal Detachment (AABC)
SATD	Simulation and Training Device [Army]
SATD	Strike Aircraft Test Directorate [Military] (CAAL)
SATDAT	Satellite Data (MCD)
SATDPI	Salesmen's Association of the Textile Dyeing and Printing Industry (EA)
SATE	Semiautomatic Test Equipment [NASA]
SATE	Special Acceptance Test Equipment (MCD)
SATE	Study of Army Test and Evaluation (MCD)
SATEC	Semiautomatic Technical Control
SATEC	Societe d'Aide Technique et de Cooperation [An independent French company]
SATEFL	Scottish Association for the Teaching of English as a Foreign Language (AIE)
SATEL	Satellite (IAA)
SA Telcm	SA Telecommunications, Inc. [Associated Press] (SAG)
SATELCO	Satellite Telecommunications Co. [Japanese-American firm]
SATELDATA	Satellite Databank [European Space Agency] [Database]
SATELLAB	Satellite Laboratory (IAA)
SATELLITE	Scientific and Technological Library Literature [Conference]
SATELLORB	Satellite Simulation Observation and Research Balloon [Military] (DNAB)
SATEMM	Sectorial Association Transportation Equipment & Machinery Manufacturing (AC)
SATENA	Servicio de Aeronavegacion a Territorios Nacionales [Colombian airline]
SATEX	Semiautomatic Telegraph Exchange (WDAA)
SATF	Shiyan Automotive Transmission Factory [China]
SATF	Shortest Access Time First
SATF	Site Activation Task Force (BARN)
SATF	Strategic Area Task Force (SAA)
SATF	Strike and Terrain Following RADAR [Military] (PDAA)
SATF	Substituted Anilines Task Force (EA)
SATFAL	Satellite Data for Fallout (MCD)
SATFN	Satisfaction [Legal shorthand] (LWAP)
SATFOR	Special Air Task Force [Navy]
SAT for TEE	System Approach to Training for Transfer Effectiveness Evaluation (DNAB)
SATFY	Satisfactory (AFM)
SATG	Goya [Argentina ICAO location identifier] (ICLI)
SATG	Saturating (WGA)
SATGA	Societe Aerienne de Transport Guyane Antilles [French Guiana Air Transport]
SAT GCI	Satellite Ground Controlled Interception (NATG)
SATH	Shop at Home [NASDAQ symbol] (TTSB)
SATH	Shop at Home, Inc. [NASDAQ symbol] (SAG)
SATH	Society for the Advancement of Travel for the Handicapped (EA)
SATH	St. Thomas National Historic Site
SAT-HI	Stanford Achievement Test, Special Edition for Hearing Impaired Students (EDAC)
SATI	Bernardo De Irigoyen [Argentina ICAO location identifier] (ICLI)
SATI	Selective Access to Tactical Information (PDAA)
SATI	Society for the Advancement of the Tourism Industry
SATIATER	Statistical Approach to Investment Appraisal to Evaluate Risk (MHDW)
SATIF	Scientific and Technical Information Facility [NASA]
SATIN	SAC [Strategic Air Command] Automated Total Information Network (MCD)
SATIN	SAGE [Semiautomatic Ground Environment] Air Traffic Integration
SATIN	Satellite Inspection (IAA)
SATIN	Satellite Inspector System (AAG)
SATIPS	Society of Assistants Training in Preparatory Schools [British]
SATIR	System for Evaluation of Tactical Information on Missile Destroyers
SATIRE	Scientific and Technical Information Reviewed and Exploited [A publication] (RDA)
SATIRE	Semiautomatic Technical Information Retrieval
SATIS	Satisfactory (AAG)
SATIS	Science and Technology in Society (AIE)
SATIS	Scientific and Technical Information Service (NITA)
SATIS	Southern Africa - The Imprisoned Society [An association British]
SATISFN	Satisfaction (ROG)
SATISFY	Satisfactory (ROG)
SATITC	South Australian Timber Industry Training Council
SATIVA	Society for Agricultural Training through Integrated Voluntary Activities (EA)
SATK	Las Lomitas [Argentina ICAO location identifier] (ICLI)
SATK	Strike Attack [Military]

SATKA	Surveillance, Acquisition, Tracking, and Kill Assessment [Section of SDI - Strategic Defense Initiative]
SATL	Satellite (AABC)
SATL	Science and Advanced Technology Laboratory [Army] (RDA)
SATL	South Atlantic
SATL	Surgical Achilles Tendon Lengthening [Medicine]
SATLAB	Simulation and Training Laboratory (SSD)
SATLCONO	Satellite Control Officer [Air Force]
SATM	Mercedes [Argentina ICAO location identifier] (ICLI)
SAT-M	Scholastic Aptitude Test - Mathematics [College Entrance Examination Board]
SATM	Sodium Aurothiomalate [Organometallic chemistry]
SATM	Supply and Training Mission [Military] (CINC)
Sat Men	Saturae Menippeae [of Varro] [Classical studies] (OCD)
SATMO	Security Assistance Training Management Office [Army]
SATN	Saturation
satn	Saturation (STED)
SATNAV	Satellite Navigation (AABC)
SATNET	Satellite Data Broadcast Networks, Inc. [New York, NY] [Telecommunications] (TSSD)
SATO	Obera [Argentina ICAO location identifier] (ICLI)
SATO	Scheduled Airlines Ticket Office
SATO	Scheduled Airlines Traffic Office [Military]
SATO	Self-Aligning Thick Oxide [Process]
SATO	Shuttle Attached Teleoperator [NASA] (NASA)
SATO	South American Travel Organization
SATO	Southern African Treaty Organization (NADA)
SATO	Station Airline Ticket Office (MCD)
SATO	Supply and Transportation Operations [NASA] (NASA)
SATO	Synthetic Aircraft Turbine Oil
SATOBS	Satellite Observation (IAA)
SATOBS	Satellite Observations (SAA)
SATODP	Satellite Tracking Orbit Determination Program
SATON	Satisfaction (ROG)
SATO-OS	Schedule Airlines Tour Office - Overseas
SATOUR	South African Tourism Board (EA)
SATP	Security Assistance Training Program [Military]
SATP	Single Aircraft Tracking Program (IAA)
SATP	Small Arms Target Practice [Navy]
SATP	Software Acceptance Test Procedures
SATP	Spatial Average Temporal Peak [Medicine] (DMAA)
SATP	Stabilization, Acquisition, Tracking, and Pointing
SATP	Supplier Assurance Test Procedures
SATPATT	Satellite Paper Tape Transfer
SATR	Reconquista [Argentina ICAO location identifier] (ICLI)
SATR	Scheduled Air Transport Rating
SATRA	Science and Technology Research Abstracts [A publication]
SATRA	Shoe and Allied Trades Research Association [Later, Footwear Technology Centre] [British] (EA)
SATRA	Soviet-American Trade Association
SATRAC	Satellite Automatic Terminal Rendezvous and Coupling (MCD)
SATRACK	Satellite Tracking (MCD)
SATRAM	Systeme d'Atterrissage a Trajectoires Multiples [Aviation]
SATRAN	Satellite Reconnaissance Advance Notice (MCD)
SATROS	Science and Technology Regional Organizations [British]
SATS	S. Allan Taylor Society (EA)
SATS	Satellite Antenna Test System [NASA]
SATS	Selected Abstract Test Suite [Telecommunications] (OSI)
SATS	Short Airfield for Tactical Support [Marine Corps]
SATS	Shuttle Avionics Test System [NASA] (NASA)
SATS	Simulated Airborne Transpondent System (MCD)
SATS	Single Array Test System (MCD)
SATS	Small Applications Technology Satellite (MCD)
SATS	Small Arms Target System [British military] (DMA)
SATS	Social and Technical Sciences
SATS	Station Accommodation Test Set (SSD)
SATS	Surrogate Acquilla Training System [Army]
SATS	Synthetic Armed Aircraft Training System (SAA)
SATSA	Signal Aviation Test and Support Activity
SATSERV	Services by Satellite, Inc. [Defunct]
SATSIM	Satellite Simulation [Military] (CAAL)
SATSIM	Saturation Countermeasures Simulator
SATSLAM	Satellite-Tracked Submarine-Launched Antimissile (MCD)
sat sol	Saturated Solution [Pharmacy] (WGA)
SATSTREAM	Satellite Switchstream (NITA)
SATT	Science, Applications, Technology Transfer, and Training [System] [National Institutes of Health]
SATT	Semiautomatic Transistor Tester [NASA]
SATT	Shear Area Transition Temperature (PDAA)
SATT	Society of Architects and Allied Technicians (NADA)
SATT	Strowger Automatic Toll Ticketing [Telecommunications]
SATTA	South Australian Table Tennis Association
SatTech	Satellite Technology Management, Inc. [Associated Press] (SAG)
SATTR	Satisfactory to Transfer (NOAA)
SATU	Curuzu Cuatia [Argentina ICAO location identifier] (ICLI)
SATU	Singapore Association of Trade Unions
SATU	South African Typographical Union
SATUCC	Southern African Trade Union Coordination Council [Gaborone, Botswana] (EAIO)
SatUK	Satellite United Kingdom
SATUR	Saturate (AAG)
SATURN	Simulation and Assignment of Traffic to Urban Road Networks [Kins Developments Ltd.] [Software package] (NCC)
SAT-V	Scholastic Aptitude Test - Verbal [College Entrance Examination Board]

SATW	Society of American Travel Writers (EA)
satwd	Satinwood (VRA)
SATX	Satellite Express [Telecommunications]
Sau	All India Reporter, Saurashtra [1950-57] [A publication] (DLA)
SAU	Saltair [Utah] [Seismograph station code, US Geological Survey] (SEIS)
SAU	Samarkano Resources [Vancouver Stock Exchange symbol]
SAU	Saudi Arabia [ANSI three-letter standard code] (CNC)
SAU	Saugeen Ontario Library Service [UTLAS symbol]
SAU	Sausalito, CA [Location identifier FAA] (FAAL)
SAU	Sawu [Indonesia] [Airport symbol] (OAG)
SAU	Scandinavian Association of Urology (EA)
SAU	Scientific Arithmetic Unit
SAU	Search Attack Unit
SAU	Secure Access Unit (HGAA)
SAU	Separate Administrative Unit [Work Incentive Program]
SAU	Signal Acquisition Unit (NASA)
SAU	Smallest Addressable Unit
SAU	Social Affairs Unit [British]
SAU	Spectrum Analysis Unit
SAU	Squadron Augmentation Unit [Navy] (DOMA)
SAU	Standard Advertising Unit [System introduced to make national newspaper advertising pages uniform in size and format]
SAU	Statistical Analysis Unit
SAU	Strap-Around Unit [NASA] (NASA)
SAU	Substance Abuse Technology, Inc. [AMEX symbol] (SAG)
SAU	Surface Attack Unit
SAU	System [or Subsystem] Availability Unit
SAU	United Aviation Services SA [Spain ICAO designator] (FAAC)
SAUAC	South Australian Uranium Advisory Committee
SAU & G	San Antonio, Uvalde & Gulf Railroad Co.
Sau & Sc	Sausse and Scully's Irish Rolls Court Reports [1837-40] [A publication] (DLA)
SAUCERS	Space and Unexplained Celestial Events Research Society [Defunct] (EA)
SAUFI	Sindacato Autonomo Unificato Ferrovieri Italiani [Autonomous Union of Italian Railroad Workers]
SAUK	Scoliosis Association of the United Kingdom (EAIO)
SaulCntr	Saul Centers [Associated Press] (SAG)
Sau LR	Saurastra Law Reports [India] [A publication] (DLA)
Sauls	Reports Tempore Saulsbury [5-6 Delaware] [A publication] (DLA)
SAULT	South Australian Urban Land Trust
Saund	Saunders' King's Bench Reports [1666-73] [A publication] (DLA)
Saund & A	Saunders and Austin's Locus Standi Reports [1895-1904] [A publication] (DLA)
Saund & Aust	Saunders and Austin's Locus Standi Reports [A publication] (DLA)
Saund & B	Saunders and Bidder's Locus Standi Reports [England] [A publication] (DLA)
Saund & BC	Saunders and Cole's English Bail Court Reports [1846-48] [A publication] (DLA)
Saund & C	Saunders and Cole's English Bail Court Reports [1846-48] [A publication] (DLA)
Saund & M	Saunders and Macrae's English County Courts and Insolvency Cases [County Courts Cases and Appeals, II-III] [A publication] (DLA)
Saund & Mac	Saunders and Macrae's English County Court Cases [A publication] (DLA)
Saund Ass	Saunders on Assault and Battery [1842] [A publication] (DLA)
Saund Bast	Saunders on Affiliation and Bastardy [11th ed.] [1915] [A publication] (DLA)
Saund BC	Saunders and Cole's English Bail Court Reports [82 RR] [1846-48] [A publication] (DLA)
Saund Mag Pr	Saunders' Magistrates' Courts Practice [6th ed.] [1902] [A publication] (DLA)
Saund Mil L	Saunders' Militia Law [4th ed.] [1855] [A publication] (DLA)
Saund Mun Reg	Saunders' Municipal Registration [2nd ed.] [1873] [A publication] (DLA)
Saund Neg	Saunders on Negligence [2nd ed.] [1878] [A publication] (DLA)
Saund Pl & Ev	Saunders' Pleading and Evidence [A publication] (DLA)
Saund Prec	Saunders' Precedents of Indictments [3rd ed.] [1904] [A publication] (DLA)
Saund War	Saunders on Warranties and Representations [1874] [A publication] (DLA)
SAUOS	St. Andrews Ukrainian Orthodox Society (EA)
SAUR	Small Auxin Up RNA [Ribonucleic Acid] [Botany]
SAUS	Sausage (DSUE)
SAUS	Soccer Association of the United States (EA)
S AUS	South Australia (BARN)
Sausse & Sc	Sausse and Scully's Irish Rolls Court Reports [1837-40] [A publication] (DLA)
S Aust	South Australia
S Aust Indus R	South Australia Industrial Reports [A publication] (DLA)
S Austl Acts	South Australia Acts [1866-1936] [A publication] (DLA)
S Austl Stat	South Australian Statutes [1837-1975] [A publication] (DLA)
S Austrl LR	South Australian Law Reports [A publication] (ILCA)
S Aust Teach J	South Australian Teachers' Journal [A publication]
S Aust Wheatgr	South Australian Wheatgrower [A publication]
SAUT	Scottish Association of University Teachers [A union]
SAUV	Semiautonomous Underwater Vehicle (DOMA)
SaV	Saguaro Cactus Virus
SAV	Sale at Valuation (WDAA)
SAV	Sanair [Ukraine] [FAA designator] (FAAC)
SAV	Savannah [Tasmania] [Seismograph station code, US Geological Survey] (SEIS)
SAV	Savannah [Georgia] [Airport symbol] (OAG)

SAV	Savannah Electric & Power Co. [NYSE symbol] (SPSG)
SAV	Saveloy (DSUE)
Sav	Savile's English Common Pleas Reports [A publication] (DLA)
Sav	Savings (DLA)
SAV	Savior
SAV	Semiannual Vegetation (COE)
SAV	Sequential Atrioventricular [Pacing] [Medicine] (DMAA)
SAV	Service Availability [AT & T]
SAV	Small Affluent Variable [Moko disease of banana] [Plant pathology]
SAV	Society Against Vivisection (EA)
SAV	Society of American Ventriloquists [Defunct] (EA)
SAV	Space Air Vehicle (IAA)
SAV	Spectra Ventures Ltd. [Vancouver Stock Exchange symbol]
SAV	Standard Acceptance Value
SAV	Statens Avtalsverk [Sweden]
SAV	State-of-the-Atmosphere Variables (USDC)
SAV	Stock at Valuation
sav	Stock at Valuation (ODBW)
SAV	Streptavidin (STED)
SAV	Strike Attack Vector [Navy] (ANA)
SAV	Strollad ar Vro [Country Party] [France Political party] (PPW)
SAV	Student Alternatives to Violence [Defunct] (EA)
SAV	Submerged Aquatic Vegetation
SAV	Sudania Aviation Co. [Sudan] [ICAO designator] (FAAC)
SAV	Supra-Anular Valve (STED)
SAV	System Assistance Visit [Army]
SAVA	Piedra Del Aguila [Argentina ICAO location identifier] (ICLI)
SAVA	Servicios do Aerotaxisa e Abastecimento do Vale Amazonica [Airline] [Brazil]
SAVA	Sexual Abuse Victims Anonymous [Canada]
SAVA	Standard Army Vetronics Architecture (RDA)
SAVAC	Simulates, Analyzes, Visualizes, Activated Circuitry (DNAB)
SAVAK	Sazemane Attalat Va Anmiyate Keshvar [Iranian security and intelligence organization]
SAVAS	Six-Factor Automated Vocational Assessment System [Vocational guidance test]
SAVASI	Simple [or Simplified] Abbreviated Visual Approach Slope Indicator [FAA]
SAVB	El Bolson [Argentina ICAO location identifier] (ICLI)
SAVB	Savannah Bancorp [NASDAQ symbol] (TTSB)
SAVB	Savannah Bancorp, Inc. [NASDAQ symbol] (SAG)
SavBcp	Savannah Bancorp, Inc. [Associated Press] (SAG)
SAVBOND	War Savings Bond [Allotment for purchase] [Navy]
SAVC	Air-Cushion Vehicle built by Sealand Air Cushion Vehicles [US] [Usually used in combination with numerals]
SAVC	Comodoro Rivadavia/Gral Mosconi [Argentina ICAO location identifier] (ICLI)
SAVC	Society for the Anthropology of Visual Communication (EA)
Sav Conf Law	Savigny's Conflict of Laws [2nd ed.] [1880] [A publication] (DLA)
SAVD	El Maiten [Argentina ICAO location identifier] (ICLI)
SAVD	Spontaneous Assisted Vaginal Delivery [Medicine] (DMAA)
SAVDAT	Save Data (IAA)
SAVDEP	Savings Depot [Military] (DNAD)
SAV-DEP-SYS	Savings Deposit System [Military] (DNAB)
SAVE	Esquel [Argentina ICAO location identifier] (ICLI)
SAVE	Self-Learning Audio Visual Education [National Foundation for the Prevention of Oral Disease]
SAVE	Sensitive Activity Vulnerability Estimate
SAVE	Service Activities of Voluntary Engineers
SAVE	Shoppers Association for Value Economy (EA)
SAVE	Shortages and Valuable Excesses [Navy] (NG)
SAVE	Situation Analysis and Vulnerability Estimate (MCD)
SAVE	Society of Americans for Vashchenko Emigration (EA)
SAVE	Society of American Value Engineers (EA)
SAVE	Society of American Vintage-Radio Enthusiasts
SAVE	South Atlantic Ventilation Experiment [Marine science] (OSRA)
SAVE	Spray Aeration Vacuum Extraction System [Navy]
SAVE	Stop Addiction through Voluntary Effort
SAVE	Student Action Voters for Ecology
SAVE	Students Against Volvo Exaggerations [Student legal action organization]
SAVE	Survival and Ventricular Enlargement [Medicine]
SAVE	System Analysis of Vulnerability and Effectiveness (IAA)
SAVE	Systematic Alien Verification for Entitlements [Immigration and Naturalization Service]
SAVE	System Availability Estimator
SAVE	System Avionics Value Estimation
SAVE	System for Automatic Value Exchange [Computer science]
SAVED	State-of-the-Art Vehicle Engineering Documentation (MCD)
SAVER	Shuttle Avionics Verification and Evaluation [NASA] (NASA)
SAVER	Stowable Aircrew Vehicle Escape Rotoseat (MCD)
SAVER	Study to Assess and Validate Essential Reports [Military] (AABC)
SAVES	Sizing Aerospace Vehicle Structures [NASA]
SAVES	States Audiovisual Education Study
SAVF	Comodoro Rivadavia [Argentina ICAO location identifier] (ICLI)
SAVH	Las Heras [Argentina ICAO location identifier] (ICLI)
SAVI	Science Activities for the Visually Impaired (AIE)
SAVI	Students Audio Visual Interface (PDAA)
SAVIAC	Shock and Vibration Information Analysis Center [Navy]
SAVICOM	Society for the Anthropology of Visual Communication
Savigny Hist Rom Law	Savigny's History of the Roman Law [A publication] (DLA)
Savile	Savile's English Common Pleas Reports [123 English Reprint] [1580-94] [A publication] (DLA)
Saville	Saville Systems [Associated Press] (SAG)

SAVIM .... Survivability and Vulnerability Improvement Modification [Army] (RDA)
SAVING........ Students Against Violence, Injustice, and Guns
SAVITAR ...... Sanders Associates Video Input/Output Terminal Access Resource [Computer science] (IEEE)
SAVLY .... Saville Systems [NASDAQ symbol] (SAG)
SAVLY .... Saville Systems ADS [NASDAQ symbol] (TTSB)
SAVM .... Lago Musters [Argentina ICAO location identifier] (ICLI)
SAVMO .... Service Audiovisual Management Office [Army]
SavnEl .... Savannah Electric & Power Co. [Associated Press] (SAG)
SavnFd .... Savannah Foods & Industries, Inc. [Associated Press] (SAG)
SAVO .... San Antonio Oeste [Argentina ICAO location identifier] (ICLI)
SAVO .... Schultz Sav-O Stores [NASDAQ symbol] (TTSB)
SAVO .... Schultz Sav-O Stores, Inc. [NASDAQ symbol] (CTT)
SAVOR .... Single-Actuated Voice Recorder
Savoy .... Savoy Pictures Entertainment, Inc. [Associated Press] (SAG)
SAVP .... Paso De Indios [Argentina ICAO location identifier] (ICLI)
Sav Pos ...... Savigny on Possessions [6th ed.] [1848] [A publication] (DLA)
SAVPrB .... Savannah El & Pwr 6.64% Pfd [NYSE symbol] (TTSB)
Sav Priv...... Trial of the Savannah Privateers [A publication] (DLA)
SAVQ .... Maquinchao [Argentina ICAO location identifier] (ICLI)
SAVR .... Alto Rio Senguerr [Argentina ICAO location identifier] (ICLI)
SAVS .... Safeguards Area Ventilation System [Nuclear energy] (NRCH)
SAVS .... Scottish Anti-Vivisection Society (DI)
SAVS .... Sierra Grande [Argentina ICAO location identifier] (ICLI)
SAVS .... Status and Verification System [NASA] (KSC)
SAVT .... Save Area Table [Computer science] (IBMDP)
SAVT .... Secondary Address Vector Table [Computer science] (IBMDP)
SAVT .... Trelew/Almirante Zar [Argentina ICAO location identifier] (ICLI)
SAVU .... Comodoro Rivadavia [Argentina ICAO location identifier] (ICLI)
SAVV .... Viedma/Gobernador Castello [Argentina ICAO location identifier] (ICLI)
SAVY .... Puerto Madryn [Argentina ICAO location identifier] (ICLI)
Sav Zeitschr... Zeitschrift der Savigny-Stiftung fuer Rechtsgeschichte. Romanistische Abteilung [A publication] (OCD)
SAW........... Gwinn, MI [Location identifier FAA] (FAAL)
SAW........... Sample Assignment Word
SAW........... Satellite Attack Warning
Saw .... Sawyer's United States Circuit Court Reports [A publication] (DLA)
SAW........... Scottish Association of Writers [British]
SAW........... Search-a-Word [Neuropsychology test]
SAW........... Seasonal Agricultural Worker
SAW........... Seeking, Asking, and Written [Questionnaire] (PDAA)
SAW........... Selectively Aimable Warhead (MCD)
SAW........... Semiautomatic Weapons
SAW........... Signal Aircraft Warning
SAW........... Signal Air Warning (IAA)
SAW........... Simulate Antiaircraft Weapons (SAA)
SAW........... Small Arms Weapon
SAW........... Society of American Wars (EA)
SAW........... Software Analysis Workstation [Computer science] (CIST)
SAW........... Solar Array Wing (MCD)
SAW........... South Albuquerque Works [AEC]
SAW........... Southern Army Worm [Agronomy]
SAW........... Special Agricultural Worker
SAW........... Special Air Warfare (AFM)
SAW........... Squad Assault Weapon [Marine Corps] (DOMA)
SAW........... Squad Automatic Weapon [Army]
SAW........... St. Andrews [Washington] [Seismograph station code, US Geological Survey] (SEIS)
SAW........... Statistical Abstract of the World [A publication]
SAW........... Sterling Airways Ltd. [Denmark ICAO designator] (FAAC)
SAW........... Stone & Webster, Inc. (EFIS)
SAW........... Strategic Aerospace Wing [Air Force]
SAW........... Strike Anywhere [Match]
SAW........... Subantarctic Water
SAW........... Submerged Arc Weld
SAW........... Surface Acoustic Wave [Engineering]
SAWA .... Lago Argentino [Argentina ICAO location identifier] (ICLI)
SAWA .... Scottish Amateur Wrestling Association (DBA)
SAWA .... Screen Advertising World Association [British] (EAIO)
SAWA .... Society of Anaesthetists of West Africa [Nigeria] (EAIO)
SAWA .... Soil and Water Management Association (NADA)
SawakoC...... Sawako Corp. [Associated Press] (SAG)
SAWANS...... South African Women's Auxiliary Naval Service [British military] (DMA)
SAWAS .... South African Women's Auxiliary Services
SAWB .... Base Marambio [Argentina ICAO location identifier] (ICLI)
SAWBET ..... Supply Action Will Be Taken
SAWC .... South Australian Writers' Centre
SAWC .... Special Air Warfare Center
SAWD .... Puerto Deseado [Argentina ICAO location identifier] (ICLI)
SAWD .... Solid Amine Water Desorbed (NASA)
SAWD .... Surface Acoustic Wave Device (PDAA)
SAWDLO...... Surface Acoustic Wave Delay Line Oscillator (PDAA)
sawdu......... Sawdust (VRA)
SAWE .... Rio Grande [Argentina ICAO location identifier] (ICLI)
SAWE .... Simulated Area Weapons Effects
SAWE .... Society of Aeronautical Weight Engineers (IAA)
SAWE .... Society of Allied Weight Engineers (EA)
SAWE-IF ..... Simulated Area Weapons Effects - Indirect Fire
SAWE-NBC-CAS... Simulated Area Weapons Effects - Nuclear, Biological, Chemical - Casualty Assesment System [Army]
SAWE-RF ..... Simulated Area Weapons Effects-Radio Frequency [Army]
SAWES .... Small Arms Weapons Effects Simulator [Military] (PDAA)

SAWF .... Special Air Warfare Forces (AFM)
SAWFD .... South Australian Woods and Forests Department
SAWG .... Rio Gallegos [Argentina ICAO location identifier] (ICLI)
SAWG .... Schedule and Allocations Working Group [NASA] (KSC)
SAWG .... Special Advisory Working Group (NATG)
SAWg .... Strategic Aerospace Wing [Air Force] (AFM)
SAWGUS...... Standoff/Attack Weapons Guidance Utility Study (MCD)
SAWH .... Ushuaia [Argentina ICAO location identifier] (ICLI)
SAWI .... Society for Animal Welfare in Israel (EAIO)
SAWIC .... South African Water Information Centre [Information service or system] (IID)
SAWID .... Shipboard Acoustic Warfare Integrated Defense (NVT)
SAWJ .... San Julian/Cap. D. J. D. Vasquez [Argentina ICAO location identifier] (ICLI)
SAWLT........ South African Written Language Test [Educational test]
SAWM .... Rio Mayo [Argentina ICAO location identifier] (ICLI)
SAWMA ...... Soil and Water Management Association [British]
SAWMA ...... Southern African Wildlife Management Association [See also NVSA]
SAWMARCS... Standard Aircraft Weapon Monitor and Release Control System (NG)
SAWMC .... South Australian Waste Management Commission
SAWO .... Surface Acoustic Wave Oscillator [Telecommunications] (TEL)
SAWP .... Perito Moreno [Argentina ICAO location identifier] (ICLI)
SAWP .... Socialist Alliance of the Working People [Serbia] [Political party]
SAWP .... Society of American Wood Preservers [Defunct] (EA)
SAWPY .... Socialist Alliance of the Working People of Yugoslavia [Political party] (EY)
SAWR .... Gobernador Gregores [Argentina ICAO location identifier] (ICLI)
SAWRC .... South Australian Water Resources Council
SAWRS .... Supplementary Aviation Weather Reporting Station (FAAC)
SAWS .... Jose De San Martin [Argentina ICAO location identifier] (ICLI)
SAWS .... Satellite Attack Warning System
SAWS .... Sawtek Inc. [NASDAQ symbol] (TTSB)
SAWS .... Seventh-Day Adventist World Service [ADRA] [Superseded by] (EA)
SAWS .... Silent Attack Warning System (MCD)
SAWS .... Small Arms Weapons System (NATG)
SAWS .... Small Arms Weapon Study [Army]
SAWS .... Solar Array Wing Simulator (MCD)
SAWS .... Special Airborne Weapon Subsystem (MCD)
SAWS .... Squad Automatic Weapon System [Army]
SAWS .... Subacoustic Warfare System
SAWS .... Submarine Acoustic Warfare System [Navy] (MCD)
SAWT .... Rio Turbio [Argentina ICAO location identifier] (ICLI)
SAWTOC ...... Special Asian Warfare Training and Orientation Center [Located on the Hawaiian island of Oahu] (VNW)
SAWU .... Santa Cruz [Argentina ICAO location identifier] (ICLI)
Sawy.......... Sawyer's United States Circuit Court Reports [A publication] (DLA)
Sawyer Circt... Sawyer's United States Circuit Court Reports [A publication] (DLA)
Sawyer US Ct Rep... Sawyer's United States Circuit Court Reports [A publication] (DLA)
SAX............ Sabah Air [Malaysia] [ICAO designator] (FAAC)
SAX............ Sambu [Panama] [Airport symbol] (OAG)
SAX............ Saxon
Sax .... Saxony
SAX............ Saxophone [Music]
sax............ Saxophone (ODBW)
Sax .... Saxton's New Jersey Chancery Reports [A publication] (DLA)
SAX............ Short Axis [Medicine] (DMAA)
SAX............ Small-Angle X-ray [Instrumentation]
SAX............ Small Automatic Exchange [Telecommunications] (TEL)
SAX............ Sparta, NJ [Location identifier FAA] (FAAL)
SAX............ States Exploration Ltd. [Toronto Stock Exchange symbol]
SAX............ Strong Anion Exchanger [Chemistry]
SAX............ Surface Antigen [Medicine] (DMAA)
SAXA .... Slotted Array X-Band Antenna
SAXAS .... Scanning Automated X-Ray Analysis Spectrometer (DICI)
SAXD .... Small-Angle X-Ray Diffraction
SAXL.......... Short-Arc Xenon Lamp
SAXLE........ Single Cantilevered Axle
SAXS .... Small-Angle X-Ray Scattering
Saxt .... Saxton's New Jersey Chancery Reports [A publication] (DLA)
Saxt Ch ...... Saxton's New Jersey Chancery Reports [A publication] (DLA)
SAY........... Salisbury [Zimbabwe] [Airport symbol Obsolete] (OAG)
Say .... Sayer's English King's Bench Reports [96 English Reprint] [A publication] (DLA)
SAY........... Severe Aster Yellows [Plant pathology]
SAY........... Soccer Association for Youth (EA)
SAY........... Speaking to American Youth (AEBS)
SAY........... Stanley Resources [Vancouver Stock Exchange symbol]
SAY........... Suckling Airways [British ICAO designator] (FAAC)
SAYE.......... Save as You Earn [National Savings Plan] [British]
Sayer .... Sayer's English King's Bench Reports [96 English Reprint] [1751-56] [A publication] (DLA)
Sayer (Eng)... Sayer's English King's Bench Reports [96 English Reprint] [A publication] (DLA)
Sayett .... Sayett Group, Inc. [Associated Press] (SAG)
SAYFC........ Scottish Association of Young Farmers' Clubs (EAIO)
Sayles' Ann Civ St... Sayles' Annotated Civil Statutes [Texas] [A publication] (DLA)
Sayles' Civ St... Sayles' Revised Civil Statutes [Texas] [A publication] (DLA)
Sayles' Rev Civ St... Sayles' Revised Civil Statutes [Texas] [A publication] (DLA)
Sayles' St... Sayles' Revised Civil Statutes [Texas] [A publication] (DLA)
Sayles' Supp... Supplement to Sayles' Annotated Civil Statutes [Texas] [A publication] (DLA)
SAYOS......... Salvation Army Youth Outreach Service [Australia]

Sayre Adm Cas...	Sayre's Cases on Admiralty [*A publication*] (DLA)
SAYT	Sayett Group [*NASDAQ symbol*] (SAG)
SAYTA	Say Time Able [*Aviation*] (FAAC)
SAZ	Sasstown [*Liberia*] [*Airport symbol*] (OAG)
SAZ	Staples, MN [*Location identifier FAA*] (FAAL)
SAZ	Sulfasalazine (STED)
SAZ	Swiss Air-Ambulance Ltd. [*ICAO designator*] (FAAC)
SAZA	Azul [*Argentina ICAO location identifier*] (ICLI)
SAZB	Bahia Blanca/Comdte. Espora [*Argentina ICAO location identifier*] (ICLI)
SAZC	Cnel. Suarez [*Argentina ICAO location identifier*] (ICLI)
SAZD	Dolores [*Argentina ICAO location identifier*] (ICLI)
SAZE	Pigue [*Argentina ICAO location identifier*] (ICLI)
SAZF	Olavarria [*Argentina ICAO location identifier*] (ICLI)
SAZG	General Pico [*Argentina ICAO location identifier*] (ICLI)
SAZH	Tres Arroyos [*Argentina ICAO location identifier*] (ICLI)
SAZI	Bolivar [*Argentina ICAO location identifier*] (ICLI)
SAZJ	Benito Juarez [*Argentina ICAO location identifier*] (ICLI)
SAZK	Cerro Catedral [*Argentina ICAO location identifier*] (ICLI)
SAZL	Santa Teresita [*Argentina ICAO location identifier*] (ICLI)
SAZM	Mar Del Plata [*Argentina ICAO location identifier*] (ICLI)
SAZN	Neuquen [*Argentina ICAO location identifier*] (ICLI)
SAZO	Necochea [*Argentina ICAO location identifier*] (ICLI)
SAZO	Seeker Azimuth Orientation [*Air Force*]
SAZP	Pehuajo/Comodoro P. Zanni [*Argentina ICAO location identifier*] (ICLI)
SAZQ	Rio Colorado [*Argentina ICAO location identifier*] (ICLI)
SAZR	Santa Rosa [*Argentina ICAO location identifier*] (ICLI)
SAZS	San Carlos De Bariloche [*Argentina ICAO location identifier*] (ICLI)
SAZT	Tandil [*Argentina ICAO location identifier*] (ICLI)
SAZU	Puelches [*Argentina ICAO location identifier*] (ICLI)
SAZV	Villa Gesell [*Argentina ICAO location identifier*] (ICLI)
SAZW	Cutral-Co [*Argentina ICAO location identifier*] (ICLI)
SAZX	Nueve De Julio [*Argentina ICAO location identifier*] (ICLI)
SAZY	San Martin De Los Andes/Chapelco [*Argentina ICAO location identifier*] (ICLI)
SB	Air Caledonie International [*ICAO designator*] (AD)
Sb	Antimony [*Chemical element*] (DOG)
SB	Automotive Engine Rebuilders Association. Service Bulletin [*A publication*] (EAAP)
SB	Bachelor of Science
SB	Beauval Public Library, Saskatchewan [*Library symbol National Library of Canada*] (NLC)
SB	International Standard Book Number [*Online database field identifier*]
SB	La Sacra Bibbia [*Turin*] [*A publication*] (BJA)
SB	La Sainte Bible [*A publication*] (BJA)
SB	SAAB-Scania AB [*Sweden ICAO aircraft manufacturer identifier*] (ICAO)
SB	Safety Belt (STED)
SB	Safety Bulletin
SB	Salary Band [*British*] (DCTA)
SB	Sales Book
SB	Salomon, Inc. [*NYSE symbol*] (SPSG)
SB	San Bernadino [*Diocesan abbreviation*] [*California*] (TOCD)
SB	Sandbag (STED)
SB	Santa Barbara [*Television program*]
SB	Sarah Bernhardt [*French actress, 1844-1923*]
SB	Savannah Bank of Nigeria
SB	Save a Baby [*Later, LGM*] (EA)
SB	Savings Bank
SB	Savings Bond [*Treasury Department security*]
SB	S-Band (KSC)
SB	Schistosoma Bovis [*Parasitic fluke*]
SB	Schwartz-Bartter [*Syndrome*] [*Medicine*] (DB)
SB	Science Books & Films [*A publication*] (BRI)
SB	Scissors Bridge (DWSG)
SB	Scleral Buckle (STED)
SB	Scleral Buckling [*Ophthalmalogy*] (CPH)
SB	Scoring Booklet (MCD)
SB	Scouting-Bombing Plane [*When prefixed to Navy aircraft designation*]
SB	Scrieve Board
SB	Sea Base (MCD)
SB	Seaboard World Airlines, Inc. [*ICAO designator*]
SB	Secondary Battery [*Military*]
SB	Secondary Buffer [*Chemistry*]
SB	Section Base [*Military*]
SB	Securing Bands
SB	Sediment Basin [*Environmental science*] (COE)
SB	Selection Board [*Military*]
SB	Selective Bibliography (MCD)
SB	Semi-Balance [*Model*] (USDC)
SB	Senate Bill [*in state legislatures*]
SB	Sengstaken-Blakemore [*Tube*] [*Gastroenterology*] (DAVI)
SB	Senior Beadle [*Ancient Order of Foresters*]
SB	Senior Bond (MHDW)
SB	Sense Byte [*Computer science*] (IAA)
SB	Separately Binned
SB	Serial Binary (CET)
SB	Serial Block (MSA)
SB	Serum Bilirubin [*Clinical chemistry*]
SB	Service Bulletin
SB	Service Bureau (IAA)
SB	Serving Brother [*Church of England*]
SB	Shanti Bahini [*Peace Force*] [*Bangladesh*] [*Political party*]
SB	Shaper Block (MCD)
SB	Shipbuilding [*Navy*]
SB	Shipping Board
SB	Shoot Bud [*Botany*]
SB	Short Bill
S/b	Short Bill (EBF)
SB	Shortness of Breath [*Cardiology*]
S/B	Should Be
SB	Shrunk Back-to-Back [*Packaging of volumes*] [*Publishing*]
SB	Sick Bay
SB	Sideband [*Radio frequency*] (AAG)
SB	Sideroblast [*Hematology*] (AAMN)
SB	Signal Band
SB	Signal Battalion [*Army*]
SB	Signal Boatswain
SB	Signal to Background
SB	Signature Book (ROG)
SB	Silver Braze (MSA)
SB	Silvestroni-Bianco [*Syndrome*] [*Medicine*] (DB)
SB	Simultaneous Broadcast
SB	Single Bayonet [*Lamp base*] (NTCM)
SB	Single Blind [*Experimental condition*]
SB	Single Braid (CET)
SB	Single-Breasted
SB	Single Breath
SB	Single-Ended Boiler (DS)
SB	Sink Beater (ADA)
SB	Sinus Bradycardia [*Cardiology*]
SB	Sitzungsbericht [*Transaction*] [*German*]
SB	Sleeve Bearing (KSC)
SB	Slow Blowing (IAA)
SB	Slow Burning
SB	Small Block [*Automotive engineering*]
SB	Small Bonds
SB	Small Bore (ADA)
SB	Small Bowel
SB	Small Business
Sb	Small-Mouth Bass [*Ichthyology*]
SB	Smooth Bore [*Ballistics*]
SB	Snow Biz [*An association*] (EA)
SB	Social Biology Films [*National Science Foundation project*]
SB	Society for Biomaterials (EA)
SB	Sociologists in Business (EA)
SB	Sodium Balance (DB)
SB	Sodium Bicarbonate [*Inorganic chemistry*]
SB	Sodium Bisulfite [*Inorganic chemistry*]
SB	Sodium Borate [*Inorganic chemistry*]
SB	Solicitors' Board [*Queensland, Australia*]
SB	Solid Base Bullet
SB	Solid Body [*Technical drawings*]
SB	Solomon Islands [*ANSI two-letter standard code*] (CNC)
SB	Sonobuoy (NVT)
SB	Soot Blower (AAG)
SB	Sound Blaster [*Computer science*] (DOM)
SB	Southbound
SB	South Britain [*England and Wales*]
SB	South Buffalo Railway Co. [*AAR code*]
SB	Soybean [*Medicine*] (DMAA)
SB	Space Base [*NASA*] (KSC)
SB	Space Booster (SAA)
SB	Space Branch (IAA)
SB	Special Bibliography
SB	Special Billing [*Telecommunications*] (TEL)
SB	Special Branch [*British police*]
SB	Special Bulletin. New York Department of Labor [*A publication*] (DLA)
SB	Speed Brake (MCD)
SB	Spina Bifida [*Medicine*]
SB	Spin Block (MSA)
Sb	Spiral Having Nuclear Regions Less Conspicuous than Sa Class and Greater than Sc with Arms Wider Open than Sa Class [*Astronomy*] (BARN)
SB	Splash Block
SB	Spontaneous Blastogenesis [*Medicine*] (DMAA)
SB	Sports Bribery [*FBI standardized term*]
SB	Spring Back (ADA)
SB	Stabilized Breakdown
SB	Standard Babylonian (BJA)
SB	Standard Bead
SB	Standby
SB	Standby Base [*Air Force*] (AFM)
SB	Stanford-Binet [*Intelligence test*] [*Education*]
SB	Statement of Billing
SB	Statistical Bulletin
SB	Status Board [*Automated*] (MCD)
SB	Statute Book (ADA)
SB	Steamboat
SB	Stereotyped Behavior [*Medicine*] (DMAA)
SB	Sternal Border [*Anatomy*]
Sb	Stibium [*Antimony*] [*Chemical element*]
sb	Stilb [*Unit of luminance*]
SB	Stillborn [*Medicine*]
SB	Stockbroker
SB	Stolen Base [*Baseball*]
SB	Stop Bath [*Photography*] (DGA)
SB	Stove Bolt
Sb	Strabismus [*Medicine*]

SB	Straight Binary
SB	Straw Boss (MHDB)
SB	Stretcher-Bearer
SB	Strike Benefits (MHDB)
SB	Strong Base [Ion Exchange] (AAEL)
SB	Stuffing Box
SB	Styrene-Butadience Copolymer (EDCT)
SB	Styrene Butadiene [Organic chemistry]
SB	Subbituminous
SB	Sub Branch [Banking]
SB	Submarine Base [Navy]
SB	Submarine Boat [British] (ROG)
SB	Submarine Fog Bell [Mechanical] [Maps and charts]
SB	Substantive
SB	Substitute Blank (IAA)
SBAN	Superbananas
SB	Supplementary Benefits
SB	Supply Bulletin [Military]
SB	Support Box
SB	Supreme Bench [Legal term] (DLA)
SB	Surety Bond (MHDB)
S/B	Surface Based (WDAA)
SB	Surface Binding [Immunochemistry]
SB	Surplus Budget
SB	Sustained Breakdown (IAA)
sb	Svalbard and Jan Mayen [MARC country of publication code Library of Congress] (LCCP)
SB	Switchboard
SB	Switchboard Operator [Navy]
SB	Symbiotic Bacteria [Ecology]
SB	Synchronization Base [NASA] (NASA)
SB	Synchronization Bit (MSA)
SBA	Saabruecker Beitraege zur Altertumskunde [Bonn] [A publication] (BJA)
SBA	Santa Barbara [California] [Airport symbol] (OAG)
SBA	Satellite Broadcasters Association (EA)
SBA	Sbarro, Inc. [NYSE symbol] (SAG)
SBA	Scene Balance Algorithm [Color-correction look-up tables for Photo CDs] (PCM)
SBA	School Band of America (AEBS)
SBA	School Bookshop Association [British] (DI)
SBA	Scott Base [Antarctica] [Seismograph station code, US Geological Survey] (SEIS)
SBA	Scottish Basketball Association (DBA)
SBA	Seat Back Assembly [Aerospace] (MCD)
SBA	Secondary Butyl Alcohol [Organic chemistry]
SBA	Second Bombardment Association (EA)
SBA	Sequential Boolean Analyzer (PDAA)
SBA	Serum Bile Acid [Medicine] (DMAA)
SBA	Service Brake Activator [Automotive engineering]
SBA	Setback Axle [Truck engineering]
SBA	Shaped Beam Antenna
SBA	Shared Batch Area [Computer science] (IBMDP)
SBA	Show Business Association [New York, NY] (EA)
SBA	Siamese Breeders of America [Later, GSCC] (EA)
SBA	Sick Bay Attendant [Navy]
SBAAM	Sideband Address (PCM)
SBA	Simulation-Based Acquisition
SBA	Singapore Badminton Association (EAIO)
SBA	Singapore Broadcast Authority
SBA	Small Business Act (COE)
SBA	Small Business Administration
SBA	Small Business Assessment [Test] (TMMY)
SBA	Small Businesses' Association [British] (DCTA)
SBA	Social Behavior Assessment [Social skills test]
SBA	Society of Batik Artists [Defunct] (EA)
SBQ	Sovereign Base Area (DNAB)
SBA	Soybean Agglutinin [Immunology]
SBA	Spina Bifida and Anencephaly [Medicine]
SBA	Spina Bifida Aperta [Medicine] (DMAA)
SBA	Spirit and Breath Association (EA)
SBA	STA-Mali [ICAO designator] (FAAC)
SBA	Standard Beam Approach [British aircraft landing method]
SBA	Stand-By Assistance [Medicine] (MEDA)
SBA	Standing British Army
SBA	Steamboat Association [British] (DBA)
SBA	Steroid-Binding Assay [Clinical chemistry]
SBA	Structural Board Association (EA)
SBA	Structure Borne Acoustics (KSC)
SBA	Summary Basis for Approval (DB)
SBA	Support Base Activation (AAG)
SBA	Susan B. Anthony Dollar
SBA	Sustaining Base Automation [Army] (RDA)
SBA	Sweet Bugger All [An exclamation] [Slang British] (DSUE)
SBA	System for Business Automation (IAA)
SBA	Systems Builders Association (EA)
SBA	Welsh Bowling Association (DBA)
SBAA	Conceicao Do Araguaia [Brazil ICAO location identifier] (ICLI)
SBAA	Ships-in-Bottles Association of America (EA)
SBAA	Small Business Association of Australia
SBAAM	Spina Bifida Association of America (EA)
SBAAM	Small Business Association of Apparel Manufacturers (EA)
SBABX	SunAmerica Balanced Assets Cl.B [Mutual fund ticker symbol] (SG)
SBAC	SBA Communications 'A' [NASDAQ symbol]
SBAC	Small Business Assistance Center [Worcester, MA] (EA)
SBAC	Society of British Aerospace Companies (MCD)
SBAC	Society of British Aircraft Constructors
SBAC	Susan B. Anthony Conference (PSS)
SBAE	Stabilized Bombing Approach Equipment [Navy]
SBAEDS	Satellite-Based Atomic Energy Detection System (IAA)
SBAF	Rio De Janeiro/Afonsos [Brazil ICAO location identifier] (ICLI)
SBAFWP	Standby Auxiliary Feed Water Pump (IEEE)
SBAH	Sodium Bis(methoxyethoxy)aluminum Hydride [Organic chemistry]
S-Bahn	Schnellbahn [High-Speed Railway] [German]
SBAkWissWien	Sitzungsberichte der Oesterreichischen Akademie der Wissenschaften in Wien [A publication] (BJA)
SBAM	Amapa [Brazil ICAO location identifier] (ICLI)
SBAM	Space-Based Antimissile
SBAMA	San Bernardino Air Materiel Area
SBAMP	Sea-Based Air Master Plan (MCD)
SBAN	Anapolis (Base Aerea) [Brazil ICAO location identifier] (ICLI)
SB & CR	Stock Balance and Consumption Report (AFM)
SBANE	Smaller Business Association of New England [Waltham, MA] (EA)
SBAP	Simple Bin Assignment Problem
SBAP	Small Business Assistance Program
SBAP	Society of Business Advisory Professions (EA)
SBAR	Aracaju/Santa Maria [Brazil ICAO location identifier] (ICLI)
SBarbBc	Santa Barbara Bancorp [Associated Press] (SAG)
S Bar J	State Bar Journal of California [A publication] (DLA)
Sbarro	Sbarro, Inc. [Associated Press] (SAG)
SBAS	S-Band Antenna Switch (MCD)
SBAS	Starbase Corp. [NASDAQ symbol] (SAG)
SBASA	Spina Bifida Association of South Australia
SBASI	Single Bridgewire Apollo Standard Initiator [Explosive]
SBAT	Spina Bifida Association of Tasmania [Australia]
SBAU	Aracatuba [Brazil ICAO location identifier] (ICLI)
SBAV	Spina Bifida Association of Victoria [Australia]
SBAV	Teodoro Sampaio/Usina Porto Primavera [Brazil ICAO location identifier] (ICLI)
SBAWA	Spina Bifida Association of Western Australia
SBAWSEF	Susan B. Anthony Women's Spirituality Education Forum (EA)
SBB	Sabina Resources Ltd. [Vancouver Stock Exchange symbol]
SBB	Saddle Back Butte [California] [Seismograph station code, US Geological Survey] (SEIS)
SBB	Santa Barbara-Barinas [Venezuela] [Airport symbol] (AD)
SBB	Satellite Busy Box (SSD)
SBB	Saudi-British Bank
SBB	Schweizerische Bundesbahnen [Swiss Federal Railways]
SBB	Self-Balancing Bridge
SBB	Serikat Buruh Batik [Batik Workers' Union] [Indonesia]
SBB	Silicon Borne Bond (IAA)
SBB	Silicon-Borne Bonds (SAA)
SBB	Single-Band Beaconry [RADAR]
SBB	Soncino Books of the Bible [London] [A publication] (BJA)
SBB	Specialist Blood Banking (DAVI)
SBB	Specialist in Blood Bank Technical (DAVI)
SBB	Steinman Aviation, Inc. [FAA designator] (FAAC)
SBB	Stimulation-Bound Behavior [Medicine] (DMAA)
SBB	Subtract with Borrow [Computer science] (PCM)
SBB	System Building Block [Computer science]
SBBA	Boca Do Acre [Brazil ICAO location identifier] (ICLI)
SBBA	Spanish-Barb Breeders Association (EA)
SBBE	Belem/Val-De-Caes [Brazil ICAO location identifier] (ICLI)
SBBF	Silicone-Based Brake Fluid [Automotive engineering]
SBBG	Baje/Cmt. Gustavo Kraemer [Brazil ICAO location identifier] (ICLI)
SBBH	Belo Horizonte/Pampulha [Brazil ICAO location identifier] (ICLI)
SBBI	Curitiba/Bacacheri [Brazil ICAO location identifier] (ICLI)
SBBI	Stocks, Bonds, Bills, and Inflation [Investment term]
SBBL	Belem [Brazil ICAO location identifier] (ICLI)
SBBN	Standard Big Bang Nucleosynthesis [Cosmology]
SBBO	Strontium Beryllium Boron Oxide [Inorganic chemistry]
SBBQ	Barbacena [Brazil ICAO location identifier] (ICLI)
SBBR	Brasilia/Internacional [Brazil ICAO location identifier] (ICLI)
SBBS	Brasilia [Brazil ICAO location identifier] (ICLI)
SBBT	Barretos [Brazil ICAO location identifier] (ICLI)
SBBT	Short Basic Battery Test (NVT)
SBBT	Specialist in Blood Bank Technology (HCT)
SBBU	Bauru [Brazil ICAO location identifier] (ICLI)
SBBV	Boa Vista/Internacional [Brazil ICAO location identifier] (ICLI)
SBBW	Barra Do Garcas [Brazil ICAO location identifier] (ICLI)
SBC	Baptist College at Charleston, Charleston, SC [OCLC symbol] (OCLC)
SBC	Ferrocarril Sonora Baja California SA de CV [AAR code]
SBC	Saint Basil's College [Stamford, CT]
SBC	Saint Benedict College [Indiana]
SBC	Saint Bernard College [Alabama]
SBC	Sam Browne's Cavalry [British military] (DMA)
SBC	Santa Barbara [California] [Seismograph station code, US Geological Survey] (SEIS)
SBC	Save the Battlefield Coalition (EA)
SBC	SBC Communications [NYSE symbol] (TTSB)
SBC	SBC Communications, Inc. [NYSE symbol] (SAG)
SBC	Schmidt-Baker Camera (IIA)
SBC	Senate Budget Committee
SBC	Service Bureau Corp.
SBC	Sibasa [South Africa] [Airport symbol] (OAG)
SBC	Signal Board Computer (HGAA)
SBC	Simpson Bible College [Later, Simpson College] [California]
SBC	Single Board Computer
SBC	Single Burst Correcting

SBC	Small Bayonet Cap
SBC	Small Business Centre [British]
SBC	Small Business Computer (BUR)
SBC	Small Business Council (NADA)
SBC	Societe Bibliographique du Canada (AC)
SBC	Society for Bioethics Consultation (NTPA)
SBC	Soleil-Babinet Compensator [Optics]
SBC	Solid Bowl Centrifuge
SBC	SONAR Breakout Cable
SBC	Southeastern Bible College [Lakeland, FL]
SBC	Southern Baptist College [Walnut Ridge, AR]
SBC	Southern Baptist Convention
SBC	Southwestern Bell Corp. (EFIS)
SBC	Spaceborne Computer
SBC	Special Back Care [Medicine]
SBC	Speed Brake Command (NASA)
SBC	Standard Bicarbonate [Pharmacology] (DAVI)
SBC	Standard Boundary Condition
SBC	Standard Buried Collector [Circuit]
SBC	Standing Balance: Eyes Closed [Test] [Occupational therapy]
SBC	Start Breguet Cruise [SST]
SBC	Statutes of British Columbia [British Columbia Attorney General's Ministry] [Information service or system A publication] (CRD)
SBC	Strict Bed Confinement [Medicine]
SBC	Styrene Block Copolymer [Plastics technology]
SBC	Subtract Contents (NITA)
SBC	Sue Bennett College [London, KY]
SBC	Summary Billing Card (AFM)
SBC	Sun Belt Conference (PSS)
SBC	Supplementary Benefits Commission [Department of Employment] [British]
SBC	Surrogates by Choice (EA)
SBC	Survey of Basic Competencies [Achievement test]
SBC	Sweet Briar College [Virginia]
SBC	Swiss Bank Corp.
SBC	Swiss Broadcasting Corp.
SBC	Sydney Basketball Council [Australia]
SBC	System Bus Controller (NITA)
SBCA	Cascavel [Brazil ICAO location identifier] (ICLI)
SBCA	Saint Bernard Club of America (EA)
SBCA	Satellite Broadcasting and Communications Association (EA)
SBCA	SBC [Swiss Bank Corp.] Australia
SBCA	Scottish Building Contractors Association (DBA)
SBCA	Seat Belt Control Apparatus
SBCA	Sensor-Based Control Adapter
SBCA	Small Business Combined Association [Australia]
SBCA	Small Business Council of America (EA)
SBCA	Soybean Council of America [Defunct]
SBCAO	State Business and Corporate Affairs Office [South Australia]
SBCC	Cachimbo [Brazil ICAO location identifier] (ICLI)
SBCC	Senate Bonding and Currency Committee (OICC)
SBCC	Separate Bias, Common Control
SBCC	Southern Building Code Congress, International
SBCC	St. Brendan Cup Committee in America [Defunct] (EA)
SBCCA	Still Bank Collectors Club of America (EA)
SBCCI	Southern Building Code Congress, International (EA)
SBC Com	SBC Communications, Inc. [Associated Press] (SAG)
SBCCS	Single Byte Command Code Set Mapping [Computer science]
SBCD	Campo Grande [Brazil ICAO location identifier] (ICLI)
SBCD	School-Based Curriculum Development (ADA)
SB/CD	Short Bed/Continuous Development [Chamber for thin-layer chromatography] [Analytical biochemistry]
SBCD	Special Business and Contract Directories [A publication]
SBCD	Subtract BCD [Binary Coded Decimal] Number [Computer science]
SBCDP	Small Business Competitiveness Demonstration Program (AAGC)
SBCE	Bachelor of Science in Civil Engineering
SBCE	Concordia [Brazil ICAO location identifier] (ICLI)
SBCF	Belo Horizonte/Confins [Brazil ICAO location identifier] (ICLI)
SBCF	Seacoast Banking Corp. of Florida [Stuart, FL] [NASDAQ symbol] (NQ)
SBCF	Southern Baptist Convention Flyers [Defunct] (EA)
SBCFA	Seacoast Banking FL'A' [NASDAQ symbol] (TTSB)
SBCG	Campo Grande/Internacional [Brazil ICAO location identifier] (ICLI)
SBCH	Chapeco [Brazil ICAO location identifier] (ICLI)
SBCI	Carolina [Brazil ICAO location identifier] (ICLI)
SBCI	Solar Box Cookers International [An association] (EA)
SBCI	Swiss Bank Corp. International
SBCIC	Standard Buried Collector Integrated Circuit (IAA)
SBCIX	Smith Barney Equity Income Cl.A [Mutual fund ticker symbol] (SG)
SBCJ	Maraba/Carajas [Brazil ICAO location identifier] (ICLI)
SBCJ	Store Block Control Journal [Military] (AABC)
SBCL	Cruz Alta/Carlos Ruhl [Brazil ICAO location identifier] (ICLI)
SBCL	SmithKline Beecham Clinical Laboratories
SBCLS	Special Buyer Credit Limit (MHDW)
SBCLS	South Bay Cooperative Library System [Library network]
SBCM	Criciuma [Brazil ICAO location identifier] (ICLI)
SBCM	Security Bank Corp. [NASDAQ symbol] (SAG)
SBCN	Suburban Bancorp [NASDAQ symbol] (SAG)
SBCN	Suburban Bancorp Inc. [NASDAQ symbol] (TTSB)
SBCO	Porto Alegre/Canoas [Brazil ICAO location identifier] (ICLI)
SBCO	Shipbuilding Company
SBCO	Southside Bancshares [NASDAQ symbol] (SAG)
SBC/OC	Swiss Bank Corp./O'Connor & Associates Services (ECON)
SBCORP	Shipbuilding Corp.
SBCP	Campos/Bartolomeu Lisandro [Brazil ICAO location identifier] (ICLI)

SBCP	Spanish Base Construction Program
SBCPO	Sick Bay Chief Petty Officer [British military] (DMA)
SBCR	Corumba/Internacional [Brazil ICAO location identifier] (ICLI)
SBCR	Stock Balance and Consumption Report (NASA)
SBCS	Satellite-Based Communication System
SBCS	Series Book Collectors' Society (EA)
SBCS	Shore-Based Correlation Subsystem [Navy] (CAAL)
SBCS	Steam Bypass Control System [Nuclear energy] (NRCH)
SBCSA	Small Business Corp. of South Australia [Commercial firm]
SBCT	Curitiba/Afonso Pena [Brazil ICAO location identifier] (ICLI)
SBCT	Schilling Body Coordination Test (EDAC)
SBCT	Schottky Barrier Collector Transistor (IAA)
SBCU	Sensor-Based Control Unit [Computer science]
SBCU	Sensor Board Control Unit (NITA)
SBCUK	School Broadcasting Council for the United Kingdom (BI)
SBCV	Caravelas [Brazil ICAO location identifier] (ICLI)
SBCW	Curitiba [Brazil ICAO location identifier] (ICLI)
SBCY	Cuiaba/Marechal Rondon [Brazil ICAO location identifier] (ICLI)
SBCZ	Cruzeiro Do Sul/Internacional [Brazil ICAO location identifier] (ICLI)
SBD	San Bernardino, CA [Location identifier FAA] (FAAL)
SBD	San Bernardino Public Library, San Bernardino, CA [OCLC symbol] (OCLC)
SBD	Savings Bond Division [Navy]
S-BD	S-Band (NASA)
SBD	Schematic Block Diagram [NASA] (NASA)
SBD	Schottky Barrier Diode [Electronics]
S-BD	Seizure-Brain Damage [Medicine] (DMAA)
SBD	Senile Brain Disease [Medicine] (DMAA)
SBD	Shipboard Decoy (DWSG)
SBD	Smart Battery Data
SBD	Southeast Aviation Group, Inc. [ICAO designator] (FAAC)
SBD	Special Business Directories [A publication]
SBD	Standard Bibliographic Description
SBD	Steel Beam Design [Modray Ltd.] [Software package] (NCC)
SBD	Straight Bag Drainage [Medicine] (MAE)
SBD	Strawboard [Shipping]
SBD	Structured Block Diagram [Computer science] (MHDB)
SBD	Subcontractor Bid Document (MCD)
SBD	Surface Barrier Detector
SBDA	Structural Biology and Design Applications [bbscrc-Biotechnology and Biological Sciences Research Council] [British]
SBDAD	Surveillance and Battle Damage Assessment Device [Military]
SbdBcp	Seaboard Bancorp [Associated Press] (SAG)
SBDC	Shipbuilding and Drydock Company
SBDC	Small Business Development Center [Lehigh University, University of Alabama in Birmingham] [Research center]
SBDC	Small Business Development Corp.
SbdCp	Seaboard Corp. [Associated Press] (SAG)
SBDD	Structure-Based Drug Design [Organic chemistry]
SBDE	Silver Bevelled Deckle Edges [Bookbinding] (DGA)
SBDET	Switchboard Detachment (IAA)
SBDFX	Security Inc. Corp. Bond [Mutual fund ticker symbol] (SG)
SBDH	Sociedade Brasileira de Discos Historicos J. Leon [Record label] [Brazil]
SBDK	Sound Bytes Developer's Kit [Computer science]
SBDL	Solid Blank Delay Line
SBDM	School-Based Decision Making (ADA)
SBDN	Presidente Prudente [Brazil ICAO location identifier] (ICLI)
SBDO	Space Business Development Operation (AAG)
SBDP	Serikat Buruh Djawatan Perindustrian [Department of Industry Workers' Union] [Indonesia]
SBDPU	Serikat Buruh Djawatan Pekerdjaan Umun [Public Works' Union] [Indonesia]
SBDQ	Supervisory Behavior Description Questionnaire (EDAC)
SBDT	Schottky Barrier Diode Transistor (IAA)
SBDT	Surface Barrier Diffused Transistor
SBDTTL	Schottky Barrier Diode Transistor-Transistor Logic (IAA)
SBE	Sabre Airways Ltd. [British] [FAA designator] (FAAC)
SBE	Sacred Books of the East [A publication] (BJA)
SBE	S-Band Exciter [System] [Also, SBES]
SBE	SBE, Inc. [Associated Press] (SAG)
SBE	Screen-Based Equipment
SBE	Selebi-Pikwe [Botswana] [Later, PKW] [Airport symbol] (OAG)
SBE	Self Breast Examination [for cancer]
SBE	Shortness of Breath on Exertion [Cardiology]
SBE	Silver Bevelled Edges [Bookbinding] (DGA)
SBE	Simple Boolean Expression [Mathematics]
SBE	Small Business Edition [Microsoft Corp.] [Computer software] (PCM)
SBE	Smithkline Beecham Ltd. [NYSE symbol] (SAG)
SBE	Societe de Biologie Experimentale [Society for Experimental Biology] (EAIO)
SBE	Society for Business Ethics [Santa Clara, CA] (EA)
SBE	Society of Broadcast Engineers (EA)
SBE	Society of Business Economists (EAIO)
SBE	Solar Beam Experiment
SbE	South by East
SBE	Sporadic Bovine Encephalomyelitis [Veterinary medicine]
SBE	State Board of Education (OICC)
SBE	Strategic Bomber Enhancement (MCD)
SBE	Subacute Bacterial Endocarditis [Medicine]
SBE	Sub BIT [Binary Digit] Encoder (MCD)
SBE	Supertwisted Birefringence Effect (NITA)
SBE	System Buffer Element (NITA)
SBEA	Small Business Exporters Association (EA)
SBEC	Single-Board Engine Controller [Automotive engineering]

SBED .... Serial BIT [Binary Digit] Error Detector
SBEE .... Bachelor of Science in Electrical Engineering
SBEED .... Storage Battery Electric Energy Demonstration
SBEG .... Manaus/Eduardo Gomes [Brazil ICAO location identifier] (ICLI)
SBEI .... SBE, Inc. [NASDAQ symbol] (NQ)
SBEI .... Starch-Branching Enzyme I [Plant genetics]
SBEK .... Jacare-Acanga [Brazil ICAO location identifier] (ICLI)
S Bell .... Bell's House of Lords Scotch Appeal Cases [1842-50] [A publication] (DLA)
SBEN .... Campos/Plataforma SS-17 [Brazil ICAO location identifier] (ICLI)
SBEP .... Somatosensory Brain Stem Evoked Potential [Neurology] (DAVI)
SBER .... Eirunepe [Brazil ICAO location identifier] (ICLI)
SBER .... Self-Balancing Electronics Recorder
Sber .... Sitzungsbericht [Transaction] [German] (BJA)
SBER .... Subbit Error Rate
SBES .... Sao Pedro Da Aldeia [Brazil ICAO location identifier] (ICLI)
SBES .... S-Band Exciter System [Also, SBE]
SBET .... Pedregulho/Estreito [Brazil ICAO location identifier] (ICLI)
SBET .... Screen-Based Electronic Typewriter (WDMC)
SBET .... Society for Biomedical Engineering Technicians (DMAA)
SBET .... Society of Biomedical Equipment Technicians (EA)
SBETC .... Small Business Export Trade Corp.
SBEU .... Singapore Bank Employees' Union
SBEUA .... Small Business and Economic Utilization Advisor [Army] (AABC)
SBF .... Salomon Bros Fund [NYSE symbol] (TTSB)
SBF .... Salomon Brothers Fund [NYSE symbol] (SPSG)
SBF .... Scientific Balloon Facility
SBF .... Serologic Blocking Factor [Cardiology]
SBF .... Serum-Blocking Factor (DB)
SBF .... Seven Bar Flying Service, Inc. [ICAO designator] (FAAC)
SBF .... Short Backfire [Antenna]
SBF .... Silicone Brake Fluid (MCD)
SBF .... Single Barrier Failure (SSD)
SBF .... Single Black Female [Classified advertising] (CDAI)
SBF .... Small Business Funding
SBF .... Societe Burundaise de Financement [Development bank] (EY)
SBF .... Society of Business Folk [Defunct] (EA)
SBF .... Southern Baptist Foundation (EA)
SBF .... Soy Base Formula [Nutrition]
SBF .... Splanchnic Blood Flow [Physiology]
SBF .... Standby Flying [British military] (DMA)
SBF .... Stonebridge, Inc. [Toronto Stock Exchange symbol]
SBF .... Subic Bay Freeport
SBF .... Sun Banks of Florida, Inc. (EFIS)
SBF .... Support by Fire [Military] (INF)
SBF .... Surface Burst Fuze
SBFA .... Set Back Front Axle [Automotive engineering]
SBFA .... Small Business Foundation of America [Boston, MA] (EA)
SBFC .... Franca [Brazil ICAO location identifier] (ICLI)
SBFC .... Sawyer Brown Fan Club (EA)
SBFD .... Society of British Fight Directors (DBA)
SBFET .... Schottky Barrier Gate Field Effect Transistor (IAA)
SBFI .... Foz Do Iguacu/Cataratas [Brazil ICAO location identifier] (ICLI)
SBFI .... Specialised Banking Furniture International [Manufacturer] [British]
SB FingL ..... Savings Bank of the Finger Lakes FSB [Associated Press] (SAG)
SBFL .... Florianopolis/Hercilioluz [Brazil ICAO location identifier] (ICLI)
SBFL .... Savings Bank of the Finger Lakes FSB [NASDAQ symbol] (SAG)
SBFL .... Savings Bk of Finger Lakes [NASDAQ symbol] (TTSB)
SBFL .... Super Buffer FET Logic [NITA)
SBFLA .... Studii Biblici Franciscani. Liber Annuus [A publication] (BJA)
SBFM .... Silver-Band Frequency Modulation (IEEE)
SBFM .... Small Business Financial Manager [Microsoft] [Computer science]
SBFN .... Fernando De Noronha [Brazil ICAO location identifier] (ICLI)
SBFT .... Fronteira [Brazil ICAO location identifier] (ICLI)
SBFT .... Small Bowel Follow-Through [Medicine] (MAE)
SBFU .... Alpinopolis/Furnas [Brazil ICAO location identifier] (ICLI)
SBFU .... Standby Filter Unit (IEEE)
SBFZ .... Fortaleza/Pinto Martins [Brazil ICAO location identifier] (ICLI)
SBG .... Salomon Bros 2008 WW Dlr Gvt [NYSE symbol] (TTSB)
SBG .... Salomon Brothers 2008 World-Wide Direct Government Fund [NYSE symbol] (SPSG)
SBG .... Scottish Bus Group Ltd. (DCTA)
SBG .... Selenite Brilliant Green (MAE)
SBG .... Southern Business Group [Commercial firm] [British]
SBG .... Staatsbibliothek Preuss. Kulturbesitz - Gesamtkat. U. Dok., Berlin, Federal Republic of Germany [OCLC symbol] (OCLC)
SBG .... Standard Battery Grade
SBG .... Starburst Galaxy [Astronomy]
SBG .... Steinberg, Inc. [Toronto Stock Exchange symbol]
SBG .... Strategic Bomber Group
SBG .... Submarine Basaltic Glasses [Geology]
SBG .... Universite de Sherbrooke, Publications Officielles [UTLAS symbol]
SBGA .... Brasilia/Gama [Brazil ICAO location identifier] (ICLI)
SBGA .... Serum Beta-Glucuronidase Activity [Serology]
SBGA .... Summit Bank Corp. [NASDAQ symbol] (SAG)
SBGA .... Super Blue Green Algae
SBG GEDD ... Schottky-Barrier Gate Gunn-Effect Digital Device [Electronics] (PDAA)
SBGI .... Serikat Buruh Gelas Indonesia [Glass Workers' Union of Indonesia]
SBGI .... Sinclair Broadcast Group 'A' [NASDAQ symbol] (TTSB)
SBGI .... Sinclair Broadcast Group, Inc. [NASDAQ symbol] (SAG)
SBGI .... Society of British Gas Industries (BI)
SBGL .... Rio De Janeiro/Internacional Galeao [Brazil ICAO location identifier] (ICLI)
SBGM .... Guajara-Mirim [Brazil ICAO location identifier] (ICLI)

SBGM .... Self Blood-Glucose Monitoring [Medicine] (STED)
SBGM .... Self Blood Glucose Monitoring [Endocrinology] (DAVI)
SBGMS .... Shipbuilders', Boiler, and Gasometer Makers' Society [A union] [British]
SBGO .... Goiania/Santa Genoveva [Brazil ICAO location identifier] (ICLI)
SBGP .... Campos/Plataforma PNA-1 [Brazil ICAO location identifier] (ICLI)
SBGP .... Serikat Buruh Gula Proklamasi [Sugar Workers' Union] [Indonesia]
SBGP .... Strategic Bomber Group
SBGR .... Sao Paulo/Internacional Guarulhos [Brazil ICAO location identifier] (ICLI)
SBGS .... Ponta Grossa [Brazil ICAO location identifier] (ICLI)
SBGSN .... Serikat Buruh Garam dan Soda Negeri [Salt Workers' Association] [Indonesia]
SBGT .... Standby Gas Treatment [Nuclear energy] (GFGA)
SBGTS .... Standby Gas Treatment System [Nuclear energy] (NRCH)
SBGW .... Guaratingueta [Brazil ICAO location identifier] (ICLI)
SBH .... Sea-Blue Histiocyte (STED)
SBH .... Sea Blue Histiocytosis [Medicine]
SBH .... Sequencing by Hybridization [Genetics]
SBH .... SmithKline Beecham ADS [NYSE symbol] (TTSB)
SBH .... SmithKline Beecham Ltd. ADS [NYSE symbol] (SPSG)
SBH .... Sodium Borohydride [Inorganic chemistry]
SBH .... Southern Blot Hybridization [Biochemistry]
SBH .... State Board of Health (MAE)
SBH .... State University of New York, Health Sciences Library, Buffalo, NY [OCLC symbol] (OCLC)
SBH .... St. Barthelemy [Leeward Islands] [Airport symbol] (OAG)
SBH .... Strip-Buried Heterostructure [Telecommunications] (TEL)
SBH .... Sumerisch-Babylonische Hymnen [A publication] (BJA)
SBH .... Supermassive Black Hole [Cosmology]
SBH .... Switch Busy Hour [Telecommunications] (IEEE)
SBHC .... Security Bank Holding Co. [NASDAQ symbol] (SAG)
SBHC .... Society of the Bible in the Hands of Its Creators [Defunct] (EA)
SBHC .... Speed Brake Hand Control (NASA)
SBHC .... Speed Brake Hand Controller [NASA] (NAKS)
SBHEU .... Singapore Business Houses Employees' Union
SBHRG .... Space-Based Hypervelocity Rail Gun [Military] (SDI)
SBHRT .... Serikat Buruh Hotel, Rumah-Makan dan Toko [Hotel, Restaurant and Shops' Workers' Union] [Indonesia]
SBHS .... Strict Baptist Historical Society [British] (DBA)
SBHT .... Altamira [Brazil ICAO location identifier] (ICLI)
SBI .... Columbia Bible College, Columbia, SC [OCLC symbol] (OCLC)
SBI .... Sabine Pass, TX [Location identifier FAA] (FAAL)
SBI .... Santa Barbara Island (MUGU)
SBI .... Satellite-Borne Instrumentation (SAA)
SBI .... Scientific Bureau of Investigation [In radio series "Armstrong of the SBI"]
SBI .... Serikat Buruh Industri [Industrial Workers' Union] [Indonesia]
SB-I .... Service de Bibliographie sur l'Informatique [Paris Gestion Informatique] [France Information service or system] (CRD)
SBI .... Shared Bibliographic Input
SBI .... Shares of Beneficial Interest [Stock exchange term]
SBI .... Shriners Burn Institute
SBI .... Signal Band Indication
SBI .... Significant Business Issue (MCD)
SBI .... Single Byte Interleaved
SBI .... Small Business Institute [Small Business Administration]
SBI .... Smith Barney Intermediate Quality Municipal Fund [AMEX symbol] (SAG)
SBI .... Smith Barney Inter Muni Fd [AMEX symbol] (TTSB)
SBI .... Soil Brightness Index
SBI .... Somerville Belkin Industries Ltd. [Toronto Stock Exchange symbol]
SBI .... Sound Blaster Instrument [PC sound format]
SBI .... Soviet Bureau of Information
SBI .... Soybean (Trypsin) Inhibitor [Biochemistry]
SBI .... Space-Based Interceptor [Military] (SDI)
SBI .... Special Background Investigation (NVT)
SBI .... State Bank of India (PDAA)
SBI .... Steel Boiler Institute [Defunct]
SBI .... Sterol Biosynthesis Inhibitors [Chemotherapentic agent]
SBI .... Study Behavior Inventory (EDAC)
SBI .... Sun Belt Institute (EA)
SBI .... Sustainable Biosphere Initiative (GNE)
SBI .... Synchronous Bus Interface [Computer science] (HGAA)
SBI .... Synfuels Bibliography and Index [A publication]
SBI .... Systemic Bacterial Infection (DAVI)
SBIA .... Small Business Innovation Development Act [1982]
SBIB .... Sterling Bancshares [NASDAQ symbol] (TTSB)
SBIB .... Sterling Bancshares, Inc. [NASDAQ symbol] (SAG)
SBIBD .... Symmetrical Balanced Incomplete Block Designs (MCD)
SBIC .... Small Business Investment Company [Generic term]
SBIC .... Small Business Investment Corp. (DFIT)
SBIC .... Small Business Investment Corporation (EBF)
SBICo .... Small Business Investment Company [Generic term]
SBIE .... Shared Bibliographic Input Experiment [Special Libraries Association]
SBIG .... [The] Seibels Bruce Group, Inc. [NASDAQ symbol] (NQ)
SBIGE .... Seibels Bruce Group [NASDAQ symbol] (TTSB)
SBIL .... Ilheus [Brazil ICAO location identifier] (ICLI)
SBILS .... Scanning Beam Instrument Landing System (KSC)
SBIN .... Fort Battleford National Historic Park, Parks Canada [Parc Historique National Fort Battleford, Parcs Canada] Battleford, Saskatchewan [Library symbol National Library of Canada] (NLC)
SBIO .... Synbiotics Corp. [NASDAQ symbol] (NQ)
SBIP .... Ipatinga/Usiminas [Brazil ICAO location identifier] (ICLI)
SBIR .... Small Business Innovation Research (AAGC)

SBIR .... Small Business Innovation Research Program [*Small Business Administration*]
SBIR .... Small Business Innovative Research [*Program*]
SBIR .... Storage Bus in Register
SBIRS .... Space-Based Infrared System [*Military*]
SBIR/STTR ... Small Business Innovation Research/Small Business Technology Transfer [*Army*] (RDA)
SBIS .... Satellite-Based Interceptor System (IAA)
SBIS .... Stanford-Binet Intelligence Scale [*Psychology*] (DAVI)
SBIS .... Sustaining Base Information Service [*or System*] [*Army*] (RDA)
SBIT .... Itumbiara/Hidroelectrica [*Brazil ICAO location identifier*] (ICLI)
SBIT .... Summit Bancshares [*NASDAQ symbol*] (TTSB)
SBIT .... Summit Bancshares Texas [*NASDAQ symbol*] (SAG)
SBIZ .... Imperatriz [*Brazil ICAO location identifier*] (ICLI)
SBJ .... Journal. State Bar of California [*A publication*] (DLA)
SBJ .... Schottky Barrier Junction [*Electronics*]
SBJ .... Simla [*India*] [*Airport symbol*] (AD)
SBJ .... Skin, Bones, Joints (STED)
SBJ .... Solberg, NJ [*Location identifier FAA*] (FAAL)
SBJ .... Subjunctive [*Grammar*] (WGA)
SBJC .... Belem/Julio Cesar [*Brazil ICAO location identifier*] (ICLI)
SBJF .... Juiz De Fora/Francisco De Assis [*Brazil ICAO location identifier*] (ICLI)
SBJP .... Joao Pessoa/Presidente Castro Pinto [*Brazil ICAO location identifier*] (ICLI)
SBJR .... Rio De Janeiro/Jacarepagua [*Brazil ICAO location identifier*] (ICLI)
SBJV .... Joinville [*Brazil ICAO location identifier*] (ICLI)
SBK .... Signet Banking [*NYSE symbol*] (TTSB)
SBK .... Signet Banking Corp. [*NYSE symbol*] (SPSG)
SBK .... Single-Beam Klystron (MSA)
SBK .... Society for Behavioral Kinesiology
SBK .... Softwood Bleached Kraft [*Pulp and paper technology*]
SBK .... South Brooklyn Railway Co. [*AAR code*]
SBK .... St. Brieuc [*France*] [*Airport symbol*] (OAG)
sbk .... Subangular Blocky Soil [*Agriculture*]
SBK .... System Builder Kit [*Digital Research, Inc.*] [*Computer science*] (PCM)
SBK .... Universite de Sherbrooke, Bibliotheque [*UTLAS symbol*]
SBKEW .... Space-Based Kinetic Energy Weapon [*Military*] (MCD)
SBKG .... Campina Grande/Joao Suassuna [*Brazil ICAO location identifier*] (ICLI)
SBKKV .... Space-Based Kinetic Kill Vehicle [*Military*]
SBKP .... Sao Paulo (Campinas)/Viracopos [*Brazil ICAO location identifier*] (ICLI)
SBKU .... Cucui [*Brazil ICAO location identifier*] (ICLI)
s-bl-- .... Brazil [*MARC geographic area code Library of Congress*] (LCCP)
SBL .... Santa Ana [*Bolivia*] [*Airport symbol Obsolete*] (OAG)
SBL .... Scanned Beam Laminography (AAEL)
SBL .... Sealed Beam Lamp
SBL .... Serrated Black Letters [*Tire design*] [*Automotive engineering*]
SBL .... Serum Bactericidal Level [*Medicine*] (STED)
SBL .... Short Brothers PLC [*British ICAO designator*] (FAAC)
SBL .... Society of Biblical Literature (EA)
SBL .... Soybean Lecithin [*Biochemistry*]
SBL .... Space Based LASER
SBL .... Sporadic Burkitt's Lymphoma [*Medicine*]
SBL .... Staphylococcal Bacteriophage Lysate
SBL .... State University of New York at Buffalo, Law Library, Buffalo, NY [*OCLC symbol*] (OCLC)
SBL .... Strong Black Liquor [*Pulp and paper technology*]
SBL .... Structure Building Language (PDAA)
SBL .... Styrene-Butadiene Latexes [*Organic chemistry*]
SBL .... Surface Boundary Layer (MCD)
SBL .... Symbol Technologies [*NYSE symbol*] (TTSB)
SBL .... Symbol Technologies, Inc. [*NYSE symbol*] (SPSG)
SBLA .... Shore-Based Landing Aids (MCD)
SBLA .... Small Business Loans Act [*Canada*]
SBLB .... Labrea [*Brazil ICAO location identifier*] (ICLI)
SBLC .... SB Latex Council (NTPA)
SBLC .... Shallow Bed Liquid Chromatography
SBLC .... Small Business Legislative Council [*Washington, DC*] (EA)
SBLC .... Standby Liquid Control [*Nuclear energy*] (NRCH)
SBLE .... Society of Biblical Literature and Exegesis [*Later, SBL*] (EA)
SBLI .... Savings Bank Life Insurance
SBLI .... Staff Builders 'A' [*NASDAQ symbol*] (TTSB)
SBLI .... Staff Builders, Inc. [*NASDAQ symbol*] (NQ)
SBLJ .... Lajes [*Brazil ICAO location identifier*] (ICLI)
SBLMC .... Styrene Butadiene Latex Manufacturers Council (EA)
SBLN .... Lins [*Brazil ICAO location identifier*] (ICLI)
SBLO .... Londrina [*Brazil ICAO location identifier*] (ICLI)
SBLO .... Strong Black Liquor Oxidation [*Pulp and paper technology*]
SBLOCA .... Small-Break Loss of Coolant Accident [*Nuclear energy*] (NRCH)
SBLP .... Bom Jesus Da Lapa [*Brazil ICAO location identifier*] (ICLI)
SBLP .... Simplified Bank Loan Participation Plan [*Small Business Administration*]
SBLS .... Lagoa Santa [*Brazil ICAO location identifier*] (ICLI)
SBLS .... Spaceborne LASER Ranging
SBLSA .... Small Business and Labor Surplus Advisor (AABC)
SBLT .... Sunbelt Companies [*NASDAQ symbol*] (SAG)
SBM .... College of Charleston, Charleston, SC [*OCLC symbol*] (OCLC)
SBM .... SBM Industries [*Formerly, Speed-O-Print Business Machines Corp.*] [*AMEX symbol*] (SPSG)
SBM .... School in Basic Management [*LIMRA*]
SBM .... Science-by-Mail (EA)
SBM .... Send a Block Message [*Computer science*] (ECII)
SBM .... Sheboygan [*Wisconsin*] [*Airport symbol*] (OAG)

SBM .... Sheboygan, WI [*Location identifier FAA*] (FAAL)
SBM .... Single Black Male [*Classified advertising*]
SBM .... Single-Buoy Mooring [*Oil tanker*]
SBM .... Single-Point Mooring Buoy [*Navy*]
SBM .... Societe des Bains de Mer [*Monte Carlo*]
SBM .... Society of Behavioral Medicine (EA)
SBM .... Solomon-Bloembergen-Morgan Equation [*Medicine*] (DMAA)
SBM .... Space Block Map (CIST)
SBM .... Speed-O-Print Business Machines (EFIS)
SBM .... St. Louis, Brownsville & Mexico [*AAR code*]
SBM .... Submerge [*or Submersible*] (KSC)
SBM .... Submit (AABC)
SBM .... Subtract Magnitude (IAA)
SBM .... Super Bit Mapping [*Compact-disc technology*] (PS)
SBM .... System Balance Measure (BUR)
SBMA .... Maraba [*Brazil ICAO location identifier*] (ICLI)
SBMA .... Sand and Ballast Merchants' Alliance [*British*] (BI)
SBMA .... Service Business Marketing Association (EA)
SBMA .... SINS [*Ship Inertial Navigational System*] Bedplate Mirror Assembly
SBMA .... Snowboard Manufacturers Association (NTPA)
SBMA .... Spinal and Bulbar Muscular Atrophy [*Medicine*]
SBMA .... Spino-Bulbar Muscular Atrophy [*Medicine*]
SBMA .... Steel Bar Mills Association [*Later, SMA*] (EA)
SBMA .... Stock Brick Manufacturers Association [*British*] (BI)
SBMA .... Subic Bay Metropolitan Authority [*Philippines*]
SBMD .... Stochastic Boundary Molecular Dynamics [*Force energy simulation method*]
SBMDL .... Submodel
SBME .... Macae [*Brazil ICAO location identifier*] (ICLI)
SBME .... Society of Business Magazine Editors [*Later, ASBPE*]
SBME .... State Board of Medical Examiners (NADA)
SBMG .... Maringa [*Brazil ICAO location identifier*] (ICLI)
SBMG .... Scottish Book Marketing Group
SBMI .... School Bus Manufacturers Institute (EA)
SBM Ind ...... SBM Industries [*Associated Press*] (SAG)
SBMK .... Montes Claros [*Brazil ICAO location identifier*] (ICLI)
SBML .... Marilia [*Brazil ICAO location identifier*] (ICLI)
SBML .... Signal Band Mainlobe
SBML .... Smooth Bore Muzzle Loading [*British military*] (DMA)
SBMLCNT .... Signal Band (Energy) in Mainlobe Count [*Military*]
SBMN .... Manaus/Ponta Pelada [*Brazil ICAO location identifier*] (ICLI)
SBMO .... Maceio/Palmares [*Brazil ICAO location identifier*] (ICLI)
SBMP .... Safety Base Motion Picture (VRA)
SBMPL .... Simultaneous Binaural Midplace Localization (STED)
SBMPL .... Simultaneous Binaural Midplane Localization [*Audiometry*]
SBMQ .... Macapa/Internacional [*Brazil ICAO location identifier*] (ICLI)
SBMR .... Manoel Ribas [*Brazil ICAO location identifier*] (ICLI)
SBMS .... Mocoro/Dix-Sept Rosado [*Brazil ICAO location identifier*] (ICLI)
SBMSI .... Serikat Buruh Minjak Shell Indonesia [*Union of Oil Workers for Shell of Indonesia*]
SBMSS .... Shore-Based Message Service System (DNAB)
SBMSTE ...... Space and Ballistic Missile System Training Equipment (SAA)
SBMT .... Sao Paulo/Marte [*Brazil ICAO location identifier*] (ICLI)
SBMU .... Manaus [*Brazil ICAO location identifier*] (ICLI)
SBMV .... Southern Bean Mosaic Virus
SBMV-B ...... Southern Bean Mosaic Virus - Strain B
SBMV-C ...... Southern Bean Mosaic Virus - Cowpea Strain
SBMW .... Serikat Buruh Maclaine, Watson [*Maclaine Watson Co. Workers' Union*] [*Indones ia*]
SBMY .... Manicore [*Brazil ICAO location identifier*] (ICLI)
SBMZ .... Porto De Moz [*Brazil ICAO location identifier*] (ICLI)
SBN .... Buffalo Narrows Public Library, Saskatchewan [*Library symbol National Library of Canada*] (NLC)
SBN .... Sheridan Broadcasting Network
SBN .... Single-Breath Nitrogen [*Test*] (DAVI)
SBN .... Sino Business Machine [*Vancouver Stock Exchange symbol*]
SBN .... Small Business Network [*Baltimore, MD*] (EA)
SBN .... South Bend [*Indiana*] [*Airport symbol*] (OAG)
SBN .... Spaceborne (KSC)
SBN .... Standard Book Number
SBN .... Strong Base Number (IAA)
SBN .... Strontium-Barium-Niobidium [*Inorganic chemistry*]
SBN .... Subic Bay News [*A publication*] (DNAB)
SBN .... Sunbelt Nursery Group [*AMEX symbol*] (TTSB)
SBN .... Sunbelt Nursery Group, Inc. [*AMEX symbol*] (SPSG)
SBN₂ .... Single Breath Nitrogen [*Test*] [*Medicine*]
SBNF .... Navegantes [*Brazil ICAO location identifier*] (ICLI)
SBNH .... Society for the Bibliography of Natural History (EA)
SBNK .... Suburban Bancsharees, Inc. [*NASDAQ symbol*] (SAG)
SBNK .... Suburban Bancshares [*NASDAQ symbol*] (TTSB)
SBNL .... Submarine Base, New London [*Connecticut*] [*Navy*]
SBNM .... Santo Angelo [*Brazil ICAO location identifier*] (ICLI)
SBNO .... Senior British Naval Officer
SBNOWA..... Senior British Naval Officer, Western Atlantic
SBNPB .... Space-Based Neutral Particle Beam [*Military*] (SDI)
SBNS .... Society of British Neurological Surgeons
SBNSW .... State Bank of New South Wales [*Australia*]
SBNT .... Natal/Augusto Severo [*Brazil ICAO location identifier*] (ICLI)
SBNT .... Single-Breath Nitrogen Test [*Physiology*]
SBNW .... Single-Breath Nitrogen Washout (STED)
s-bo-- .... Bolivia [*MARC geographic area code Library of Congress*] (LCCP)
SBO .... Classification of Galactic Nebulae Between Elliptical and Spiral Types Having a Bright Nucleus and Dark Bands of Matter But No Distinguishable Arms [*Astronomy*] (BARN)
SBO .... Salina [*Utah*] [*Airport symbol*] (OAG)

SBO .... Secure Base of Operation (WDAA)
SBO .... Showboat, Inc. [NYSE symbol] (SPSG)
SBO .... Sidebands Only (IAA)
SBO .... Silver Box Resources [Vancouver Stock Exchange symbol]
SBO .... Small Bowel Obstruction [Medicine] (MAE)
SBO .... Small Business Office
SBO .... Small Business Ombudsman (COE)
SBO .... Soybean Oil
SBO .... Specific Behavioral Objectives [Aviation]
SBO .... Specified Bovine Offal [Animal feed regulation]
SBO .... Spina Bifida Occulta [Medicine] (STED)
SBO .... Stabo Air Ltd. [Zambia] [FAA designator] (FAAC)
SBO .... Standing Balance: Eyes Open [Test] [Occupational therapy]
SBO .... Studia Biblica et Orientalia [Rome] [A publication] (BJA)
SBO .... Swainsboro, GA [Location identifier FAA] (FAAL)
SBOA .... Specialty Bakery Owners of America (EA)
SB of A .... Smaller Business of America [Defunct] (EA)
SBOI .... Oiapoque [Brazil ICAO location identifier] (ICLI)
SBOLS .... Shadow Box Optical Landing System
SBOM .... Soybean Oil Meal
SBOOM .... Sonic Boom [Computer program] [NASA]
SBOPERDET... Switchboard Operation Detachment (IAA)
SBOR .... Successive Block Overrelaxation (IAA)
SBOS .... Boston Bancorp [Formerly, South Boston Savings Bank] [NASDAQ symbol] (NQ)
SBOS .... Silicon-Borne Oxygen System (SAA)
SBOSI .... Serikat Buruh Obat Seluruh Indonesia [All Indonesian Medicinal Factory Workers' Union]
SBOST .... Slavonic Benevolent Order of the State of Texas [Temple, TX] (EA)
SBOT .... Sacred Books of the Old Testament [The "Rainbow Bible"] [A publication] (BJA)
SBOU .... Ourinhos [Brazil ICAO location identifier] (ICLI)
S/BOY .... Secondary Boycott [Legal shorthand] (LWAP)
SBP .... San Luis Obispo [California] [Airport symbol] (OAG)
SBP .... Scleral Buckling Procedure [Medicine] (MAE)
SBP .... Sec-Butyl Percarbonate [Organic chemistry]
SBP .... Serikat Buruh Pegadaian [Pawnshop Workers' Union] [Indonesia]
SBP .... Serikat Buruh Penerbangan [Airways' Unions] [Indonesia]
SBP .... Service Benefit Plan [Military] (AABC)
SBP .... Shop Procedure Bulletin [A publication] (EAAP)
SBP .... Shore-Based Prototype [Nuclear energy] (OA)
SBP .... Simulated BOMARC [Boeing-Michigan Aeronautical Research Center] Program (IAA)
SBP .... Societe Beneluxienne de Phlebologie [Benelux Phlebology Society - BPS] (EA)
SBP .... Society for Behaviorial Pediatrics (EA)
SBP .... Society of Biological Psychiatry (EA)
SBP .... Sonic Boom Panel [Aerospace] (MCD)
SBP .... Sosyalist Birlik Partisi [Socialist Unity Party] [Turkey Political party] (EY)
SBP .... Soziale Buergerpartei [Social Citizen's Party] [Germany Political party] (PPW)
SBP .... Spaceborne Programmer
SBP .... Special Block Purchase
SBP .... Special Boiling Point (IAA)
SBP .... Special Businessowners Policy [Insurance]
SBP .... Spontaneous Bacterial Peritonitis [Medicine]
SBP .... Squalene-Binding Protein [Biochemistry]
SBP .... Standard Brands Paint Co. [NYSE symbol] (SPSG)
SBP .... Standard Businessowners Policy [Insurance]
SBP .... State Bank of Pakistan
SBP .... Steroid-Binding Plasma Protein
SBP .... Subacute Bacterial Peritonitis (DAVI)
SBP .... Subic Bay [Philippines] [Seismograph station code, US Geological Survey Closed] (SEIS)
SBP .... Sugar Beet Pulp (PDAA)
SBP .... Sulfate-Binding Protein [Biochemistry]
SBP .... Sulphobromophthalein (DB)
SBP .... Sumerian and Babylonian Psalms [A publication] (BJA)
SBP .... Survivor Benefit Plan [For survivors of retired military personnel]
SBP .... Systemic Blood Pressure [Medicine] (MAE)
SBP .... Systolic Blood Pressure [Medicine]
SBPA .... Porto Alegre/Salgado Filho [Brazil ICAO location identifier] (ICLI)
SBPA .... Southern Baptist Press Association (EA)
SBPB .... Parnaiba [Brazil ICAO location identifier] (ICLI)
SBPB .... Space-Based Particle Beam [Military] (SDI)
SBPC .... Pocos De Caldas [Brazil ICAO location identifier] (ICLI)
SBPD .... Society of Business Publication Designers [Later, SPD] (EA)
SBPE .... Standard Battle Plan Emplacement [Military]
SBPF .... Passo Fundo/Lauro Kurtz [Brazil ICAO location identifier] (ICLI)
SBPG .... Paranagua [Brazil ICAO location identifier] (ICLI)
SBPG .... Serikat Buruh Perusahaan Gula [Sugar Workers' Union] [Indonesia]
SBPH .... Porto Velho [Brazil ICAO location identifier] (ICLI)
SBPH .... Single Burst Probability of Hit [Military] (AABC)
SBPH .... Submarine Base, Pearl Harbor [Navy] (DNAB)
SBPI .... Petropolis/Pico do Couto [Brazil ICAO location identifier] (ICLI)
SBPI .... Serikat Buruh Pelabuhan Indonesia [Dockworkers' Union of Indonesia]
SBPI .... Serikat Buruh Pendjahit Indonesia [Tailors' Union of Indonesia]
SBPIM .... Society of British Printing Ink Manufacturers (BI)
SBPK .... Pelotas [Brazil ICAO location identifier] (ICLI)
SBPKB .... Serikat Buruh Persuahaan Kaju and Bangunan [Building, Road and Irrigation Workers' Union] [Indonesia]
SBPL .... Petrolina [Brazil ICAO location identifier] (ICLI)
SBPN .... Porto Nacional [Brazil ICAO location identifier] (ICLI)

SBPP .... Ponta Pora/Internacional [ICAO location identifier] (ICLI)
SBPP .... Serikat Buruh Pelabuhan dan Pelajaran [Dockworkers' Union] [Indonesia]
SBPPK .... Serikat Buruh Pendidikan, Pengadjaran dan Kebudjaan [Department of Education Workers' Union] [Indonesia]
SBPR .... Piracaba [Brazil ICAO location identifier] (ICLI)
SBPR .... Society for Back Pain Research [British]
SBPrC .... Salomon Inc. 9.50% Dep Pfd [NYSE symbol] (TTSB)
SBPrD .... Salomon Inc. 8.08% Dep Pfd [NYSE symbol] (TTSB)
SBPrE .... Salomon Inc. 8.40% Dep Pfd [NYSE symbol] (TTSB)
SBPT .... Serikat Buruh Perhubungan dan Transport [Communications and Transportation Workers' Union] [Indonesia]
SBPT .... Serikat Buruh Pertambangan Timah [Tin Mine Labor Union] [Indonesia]
SBPT .... Societe Beninoise pour la Promotion du Tourisme (EY)
SBPU .... Serikat Buruh Pekerdjaan Umum [Public Workers' Ministry Union] [Indonesia]
SBPV .... Porto Velho [Brazil ICAO location identifier] (ICLI)
SBPW .... Pindamonhangaba/Visaba [Brazil ICAO location identifier] (ICLI)
SBPW .... Special Board for Public Works [New Deal]
SBQ .... Grenada, MS [Location identifier FAA] (FAAL)
SBQ .... Sao Borja [Brazil] [Airport symbol] (AD)
SBQ .... Serikat Buruh Qantas [Qantas Labor Union] [Indonesia]
SBQ .... Smithkline Beacham Clincal Labs [ICAO designator] (FAAC)
SBQ .... Surveyors' Board of Queensland [Australia]
SBQV .... Vitoria Da Conquista [Brazil ICAO location identifier] (ICLI)
SBR .... Saber Aviation, Inc. [ICAO designator] (FAAC)
SBR .... Sabine Royalty Tr UBI [NYSE symbol] (TTSB)
SBR .... Sabine Royalty Trust [NYSE symbol] (SPSG)
SBR .... Sale by Reference
SBR .... Santa Barbara [Monagas, Venezuela] [Airport symbol] (AD)
SBR .... Scripps-Booth Register [An association] (EA)
SBR .... Seat Bucket Read (NG)
SBR .... Segment Base Register (BUR)
SBR .... Sequencing Batch Reactor [Chemical engineering]
SBR .... Service Billing Record
SBR .... Signal to Background Ratio [Instrumentation]
SBR .... Small Box-Respirator [British military] (DMA)
SBR .... Society for Biological Rhythm
SBR .... Society of Bead Researchers (EA)
SBR .... Soviet Breeder Reactor
SBR .... Space-Based RADAR (MCD)
SBR .... Standard Busy Rate (NATG)
SBR .... Starburst Energy [Vancouver Stock Exchange symbol]
SBR .... Stimulus-Bound Repetition [Medicine]
SBR .... Storage Buffer Register
SBR .... Strand Burning Rate (MCD)
SBR .... Strict Bed Rest [Medicine]
SBR .... Styrene-Butadiene Rubber [Also, GR-S] [Synthetic rubber]
SBR .... Supplemental Budget Request
SBRB .... Rio Branco/Presidente Medici [Brazil ICAO location identifier] (ICLI)
SBRC .... Santa Barbara Research Center [Hughes Aircraft Co.]
SBRC .... Single-Braided Rubber-Covered (IAA)
SBRC .... Southwest Border Regional Commission [Department of Commerce]
SBRD .... Seaboard Oil [NASDAQ symbol] (TTSB)
SBRD .... Seaboard Oil Co. [NASDAQ symbol] (SAG)
SBRE .... Recife [Brazil ICAO location identifier] (ICLI)
SBRF .... Recife/Guararapes [Brazil ICAO location identifier] (ICLI)
SBRI .... Serikat Buruh Rokok Indonesia [Cigarette Workers' Union of Indonesia]
SBRI .... Southwest Biomedical Research Institute [Arizona State University] [Research center] (RCD)
SBRI .... Space Biomedical Research Institute [Houston, TX] [NASA]
SBRIMCD.... Sun Bay Recovery - International Missing Children's Division (EA)
SBRJ .... Rio De Janeiro/Santos Dumont [Brazil ICAO location identifier] (ICLI)
SB-RK .... Bomber [Russian aircraft symbol]
SBRP .... Ribeirao Preto/Leite Lopes [Brazil ICAO location identifier] (ICLI)
SBRP .... Sonic Boom Research Program
SBRP .... Special Bridge Replacement Program 1970 [MTMC] (TAG)
SBRP .... Submarine Reportback Processor Unit (DWSG)
SBRQ .... Sao Roque [Brazil ICAO location identifier] (ICLI)
SBRRI .... Serikat Buruh Radio Republik Indonesia [Broadcasting Workers' Association of Indonesia]
SBRS .... Resende [Brazil ICAO location identifier] (ICLI)
SBRS .... Side and Back Rack System (PDAA)
SBRS .... Social Behavior Rating Scale
SBrSPO1 ..... Smith Barney Holdings [Associated Press] (SAG)
SBRV .... Small Ballistic Reentry Vehicle
SBRZ .... Sanborn, Inc. [NASDAQ symbol] (SAG)
SBS .... Salem Corp. [AMEX symbol] (SPSG)
SBS .... Samuel Butler Society [Defunct] (EA)
SBS .... Satellite Business Systems [McLean, VA] [Telecommunications] (MCD)
SBS .... Save British Science [An association] (AIE)
SBS .... Save British Science Society (DBA)
SBS .... Scandinavian Broadcast System
SBS .... Scarborough Board of Education [UTLAS symbol]
SBS .... Scientific Business Systems (NITA)
SBS .... See Before Setting [Typography] (DGA)
SBS .... Semiconductor Bilateral Switch (MSA)
SBS .... Sensor Based System (BUR)
SBS .... Serially Balanced Sequence [Statistics]
SBS .... Servicios Aereos Barsa SA de CV [Mexico ICAO designator] (FAAC)
SBS .... Shaken Baby Syndrome (CPH)
SBS .... Shipboard Simulators [Navy] (DOMA)

SBS............. Short Baseline SONAR (PDAA)
SBS............. Short Beam Shear
SBS............. Sick Building Syndrome [Medicine]
SBS............. Side-by-side [Structure] (DB)
SBS............. Sidi-Bou-Said [Tunisia] [Seismograph station code, US Geological Survey] (SEIS)
SBS............. Silicon Bidirectional Switch (IAA)
SBS............. Silicon Bilateral Switch
SBS............. Simultaneous Buying and Selling Arrangement
SBS............. Single-Business Service
SBS............. Sisters of the Blessed Sacrament [Roman Catholic religious order]
SBS............. [The] Sisters of the Blessed Sacrament for Indians and Colored People (TOCD)
SBS............. Small-Bowel Syndrome (DAVI)
SBS............. Small Business Server [Microsoft Corp.]
SBS............. Small Business Sourcebook [A publication]
SBS............. Small Business Specialist [DoD]
SBS............. Small Business System (ADA)
SBS............. Smart Business Supersite [Internet resource] [Computer science]
SBS............. Social Behavior Standards
SBS............. Social-Breakdown Syndrome (MAE)
SBS............. Society for Biomolecular Screening
SBS............. Soeurs de Bon Sauveur [France] (EAIO)
SBS............. Solid Bleached Sulphate [Fiber for paperboard packaging]
SBS............. Southern Base Section [England]
SBS............. Spaniel Breeders Society (EA)
SBS............. Spanish Benevolent Society "La Nacional" (EA)
SBS............. Spanish Broadcasting System
SBS............. Special Block Sale
SBS............. Special Boat Section [British military] (DMA)
SBS............. Special Boat Service [Military] (WDAA)
SBS............. Special Boat Squadron [British commando unit]
SBS............. Staff Burn-Out Scale [Medicine] (MEDA)
SBS............. Standby Status (AAG)
SBS............. Steamboat Springs [Colorado] [Airport symbol] (OAG)
SBS............. Steel Building System
SBS............. Stimulated Brillouin Scattering
SBS............. Straight Binary Second
SBS............. Strategic Balkan Services [World War II]
SBS............. Strategic Bombing Survey
SBS............. Strategic Business Segment
SBS............. Stuttgarter Bibelstudien. Katholisches Bibelwerk [Stuttgart] [A publication] (BJA)
SBS............. Styrene-Butadiene-Styrene [Copolymer]
SBS............. Subscript Character [Computer science]
SBS............. Superburn Systems Ltd. [Vancouver Stock Exchange symbol]
SBS............. Surveyed Before Shipment [Business term] (MHDB)
SBS............. Survey of Basic Skills [Achievement test]
SBS............. Swedish Behavioural Sciences [Database] [National Library for Psychology and Education] [Information service or system] (CRD)
SBS............. Sweep Back Station (MCD)
SBS............. Swiss Benevolent Society of New York (EA)
SBS............. System Breakdown Structure [Military] (AFIT)
SBSA .... Sao Carlos/Francisco Pereira Lopez [Brazil ICAO location identifier] (ICLI)
SBSA .... Show and Breed Secretaries' Association [British] (BI)
SBSA .... Society of Basque Studies in America (EA)
SBSA .... Standard Business Software Award (NITA)
SBSA .... State Bank of South Australia
SBSanE....... Bachelor of Science in Sanitary Engineering
SBSB .... Small Business Service Bureau [Worcester, MA] (EA)
SBSB .... Society of British Snuff Blenders (EAIO)
SBSBA .... Scottish Blackface Sheep Breeders Association (EA)
SBSBS .... Smith Benevolent Sick and Burial Society [British]
SBSC .... Rio De Janeiro/Santa Cruz [Brazil ICAO location identifier] (ICLI)
SBSC .... Saint Bernardine of Siena College [New York]
SBSC .... Saint Bernard's Seminary and College [New York]
SBSC .... Schottky Barrier Solar Cell [Electronics] (PDAA)
SBSC .... Separate Bias, Single Control
SBSCA .... Small Business Support Center Association [Houston, TX] (EA)
SB/SDB .... Small Business / Small Disadvantaged Business (SSD)
SBSE........... SBS Engineering, Inc. [NASDAQ symbol] (SAG)
SBSE........... SBS Technologies [NASDAQ symbol] (TTSB)
SBSE........... SBS Technologies, Inc. [NASDAQ symbol] (SAG)
SBSG .... Small Business Systems Group [Westford, MA] [Telecommunications] (TSSD)
SBSI........... Seabrook Sea Island Cotton
SBSI........... Serikat Buruh Seluruh Indonesia [All Indonesian Laborers' Union]
SBSI........... Small Business Start-Up Index [A publication]
SBSJ .... Sao Jose Dos Campos [Brazil ICAO location identifier] (ICLI)
SBSK .... Samodzielna Brygada Strzelcow Karpackich [Poland]
SBSKK .... Serikat Buruh Sepatu Keradjinan Kulit Karet [Shoe Workers' Union] [Indonesia]
SBSL .... Sao Luis/Marechal Cunha Machado [Brazil ICAO location identifier] (ICLI)
SBSL........... Single-Bubble Sonoluminescence [Physics]
SBSM .... Santa Maria [Brazil ICAO location identifier] (ICLI)
SBSM .... Sisterhood of Black Single Mothers (EA)
SBSN .... Santarem/Internacional [Brazil ICAO location identifier] (ICLI)
SBSP .... Sao Paulo/Congonhas [Brazil ICAO location identifier] (ICLI)
SBSP .... Single Base Solid Propellant (MSA)
SB Sqn .... Special Boat Squadron [British commando unit] (DMA)
SBSR .... Sao Jose Do Rio Preto [Brazil ICAO location identifier] (ICLI)

SBSRT .... Spreen-Benton Sentence Repetition Test [Speech and language therapy] (DAVI)
SBSS .... Science-Based Stockpile Stewardship [For nuclear weapons]
SBSS .... Seligmann's Buffered Salt Solution [Medicine] (DMAA)
SBSS .... Space-Based Space Surveillance (MCD)
SBSS .... Spare Band Surveillance System (MCD)
SBSS .... Standard Base Supply System [Military] (AFIT)
SBST .... Santos [Brazil ICAO location identifier] (ICLI)
SBSTA .... Sound Bearing Station (IAA)
SBS Tech..... SBS Technologies, Inc. [Associated Press] (SAG)
SBStJ.......... Serving Brother, Order of St. John of Jerusalem [British]
SBStJ.......... Serving Brother, Venerable Order of St. John of Jerusalem [Decoration] (CMD)
SBSTNC ...... Substance
SBSTR .... Substrate [Electronics]
SBSUSA....... Sport Balloon Society of the United States of America (EA)
SBSV .... Salvador/Dois de Julho [Brazil ICAO location identifier] (ICLI)
SBSY .... Cristalandia/Santa Isabel do Morro [Brazil ICAO location identifier] (ICLI)
SBT............. Safe Break Terminator (IAA)
SBT............. Salina Board of Trade (EA)
SBT............. San Benito [California] [Seismograph station code, US Geological Survey] (SEIS)
SBT............. San Bernardino [California] [Airport symbol] (AD)
SBT............. San Bernardino, CA [Location identifier FAA] (FAAL)
SBT............. Schools Board of Tasmania [Australia]
SBT............. Screening Breath Tester [Drunken driving]
SBT............. Seabright Resources, Inc. [Toronto Stock Exchange symbol]
SBT............. Segregated Ballast Tank [Shipping construction]
SBT............. Serikat Buruh Tambang [Mine Workers' Union] [Indonesia]
SBT............. Serikat Buruh Teknik [Technicians' Union] [Indonesia]
SBT............. Serikat Buruh Textil [Textile Workers' Union] [Indonesia]
SBT............. Serum Bactericidal Titer [Clinical chemistry]
SBT............. Shakespeare Birthplace Trust (EA)
SBT............. Shanghai Book Traders
SBT............. Sheet, Bar, Tubing (IAA)
SBT............. Shipboard Test [Navy] (DNAB)
SBT............. Side Buoyancy Tank
SBT............. Simultaneous Baseband Transmission [of information]
SBT............. Single-Breath Test (MAE)
SBT............. Six BIT [Binary Digit] Transcode (CMD)
SBT............. Slender Body Theory (AAEL)
SBT............. Small Boat
SBT............. Smith Barney Municipal Fund [AMEX symbol] (SPSG)
SBT............. Smith Barney Muni Fund [AMEX symbol] (TTSB)
SBT............. Sodium Bitartrate [Inorganic chemistry]
SBT............. Southern Bluefin Tuna [Fish]
SBT............. Space-Based Tug [NASA]
SBT............. Submarine Bathythermograph
SBT............. Submarine Bubble Target [British military] (DMA)
SBT............. Sulbactam (DMAA)
SBT............. Surface Barrier Transistor
SBT............. System Burning Time
SBTA .... Small Business Technical Adviser (AAGC)
SBTC.......... Sino-British Trade Council (DS)
SBTC.......... Speedbrake Thrust Control [Aerospace] (MCD)
SBTC.......... Tapuruquara [Brazil ICAO location identifier] (ICLI)
SBTD.......... Society of British Theatre Designers (DBA)
SBTE.......... Teresina [Brazil ICAO location identifier] (ICLI)
SBTF.......... Tefe [Brazil ICAO location identifier] (ICLI)
SBTG .... Sabotage (AABC)
SBTI........... Soybean Trypsin Inhibitor
SBTK.......... Sabratek Corp. [NASDAQ symbol] (SAG)
SBTK.......... Tarauaca [Brazil ICAO location identifier] (ICLI)
SBTM.......... S-Band Telemetry Modification Kit (SAA)
SBTOW .... Standby Towship [Navy] (NVT)
SBTP.......... Serikat Buruh Teknik dan Pelabuhan [Technical and Harbour Workers' Union] [Indonesia]
SBTPE......... State Boards Test Pool Examination [Medicine] (DMAA)
SBTS.......... Shore-Based Tracking System
SBTS.......... Strategic Bombardment Training Squadron
SBTS.......... Stretch Block Template Set (MCD)
SBTT.......... Serikat Buruh Tambang Timah [Tin Mine Laborers' Union] [Indonesia]
SBTT.......... Small Bowel Transit Time [Medicine] (DMAA)
SBTT.......... Small Business Technology Transfer (AAGC)
SBTT.......... Southern Bell Telephone & Telegraph Co. (KSC)
SBTT.......... Tabatinga/Internacional [Brazil ICAO location identifier] (ICLI)
SBTTL.......... Schottky Barrier Transistor-Transistor Logic (IAA)
SBTU.......... Serikat Buruh Teknik Umum [Indonesia]
SBTU.......... Tucurui [Brazil ICAO location identifier] (ICLI)
SBTV.......... Scandinavian Broadcasting [NASDAQ symbol] (SAG)
SBTVF......... Scandinavian Broadcstg Sys [NASDAQ symbol] (TTSB)
SBU............ Blue Earth, MN [Location identifier FAA] (FAAL)
SBU............ Saint Bonaventure University [New York]
SBU............ Scottish Badminton Union (EAIO)
SBU............ Secondary Building Unit [Physical chemistry]
SBU............ Sequential Build-Up (AAEL)
SBU............ Silver Brazing Union (MSA)
SBU............ Skirt Buildup (SAA)
SBU .... Small Base Unit [Telecommunications]
SBU .... Small Battle Unit [Navy] (NVT)
SBU .... Small Boat Unit (DOMA)
SBU .... Small Business United [Later, NSBU] (EA)
SBU .... Sociedades Biblicas Unidas [United Bible Societies] [British] (EAIO)

SBU .... Software Block Update [Army]
SBU .... Special Business Unit
SBU .... Springbok [South Africa] [Airport symbol] (OAG)
SBU .... Stansbury Island [Utah] [Seismograph station code, US Geological Survey Closed] (SEIS)
SBU .... Starwelt Airways [Burundi] [ICAO designator] (FAAC)
SBU .... Station Buffer Unit [Computer science]
SBU .... Strategic Business Unit
SBU .... Svensk Biblisk Uppslagverk [A publication] (BJA)
SBU .... System Billing Unit (NITA)
SBUA .... Sao Gabriel Da Cachoeira [Brazil ICAO location identifier] (ICLI)
SBUE .... Switch-Backup Entry [NASA] (KSC)
SBUF .... Paulo Afonso [Brazil ICAO location identifier] (ICLI)
SBUF .... Staceys Buffet [NASDAQ symbol] (SAG)
SBUFW .... Staceys Buffet Wrrt [NASDAQ symbol] (TTSB)
SBUG .... Uruguaiana/Rubem Berta [Brazil ICAO location identifier] (ICLI)
SBUI .... Carauari [Brazil ICAO location identifier] (ICLI)
SBUL .... Uberlandia [Brazil ICAO location identifier] (ICLI)
SBUP .... Castilho/Urubupunga [Brazil ICAO location identifier] (ICLI)
SBUR .... Uberaba [Brazil ICAO location identifier] (ICLI)
SBURCS .... Six-BIT [Binary Digit] Universal Random Character Set [Computer science]
SBUV .... Solar and Backscatter Ultraviolet Spectrometer (MCD)
SBUV .... Solar Backscatter Ultraviolet [Ozone measurement]
SBUV .... Solar Backscatter Ultraviolet Experiment (IAA)
SBUV/TOMS... Solar and Backscattered Ultraviolet and Total Ozone Mapping System
SBUX .... Starbucks Corp. [NASDAQ symbol] (SAG)
SBV .... Sabah [Papua New Guinea] [Airport symbol] (OAG)
SBV .... Semiautomatic Bleeder Valve
SBV .... Shield Building Vent [Nuclear energy] (IAA)
SBV .... Single Binocular Vision
SBV .... South Boston, VA [Location identifier FAA] (FAAL)
SBV .... Space Biospheres Venture [Commercial firm] (ECON)
SBV .... State Bank of Victoria [Australia]
SBVC .... San Bernardino Valley College [California]
SBVE .... State Board of Vocational Education [State Board of Education] (OICC)
SBVG .... Varginha/Jam Brigadeiro Trompowsky [Brazil ICAO location identifier] (ICLI)
SBVH .... Vilhena [Brazil ICAO location identifier] (ICLI)
SBVM .... Societe de la Bourse de Valeurs Mobilieres de Bruxelles [Stock exchange] [Belgium] (EY)
SBVS .... Shield Building Ventilation System [Nuclear energy] (NRCH)
SBVT .... Vitoria/Goiabeira [Brazil ICAO location identifier] (ICLI)
SBW .... Salomon Bros W W Income Fd [NYSE symbol] (TTSB)
SBW .... Salomon Brothers Worldwide Income Fund [NYSE symbol] (SPSG)
SBW .... Shebandowan Resources [Vancouver Stock Exchange symbol]
SBW .... Sibu [Malaysia] [Airport symbol] (OAG)
SbW .... South by West
SBW .... Space Bandwidth Product (IAA)
SBW .... Spectral Bandwidth
SBW .... Spruce Budworm
SBW .... Steel Basement Window
SBW .... Submarine Warfare (MCD)
SBW .... Surety Bond Waiver [SBA program] (AAGC)
SBWA .... 2nd Bomb Wing Association (EA)
SBWAS .... Space-Based Wide-Area Surveillance [Air Force] (DOMA)
SBWC .... Stepped-Bore Wheel Cylinder [Automotive brake systems]
SBWG .... Strategic Bomb Wing [Military]
SBWM/F ...... Southern Baptist Women in Ministry/Folio (EA)
SBWMV .... Soilborne Wheat Mosaic Virus
SBWR .... Simplified Boiling Water Reactor [Developed by General Electric Co.] [Nuclear energy]
SBWU .... Singapore Bus Workers' Union
SBWX .... Seaboard World Airlines, Inc. [Air carrier designation symbol]
SBWY .... Subway
SBX .... S-Band Transponder
SBX .... Seabright Explorations, Inc. [Toronto Stock Exchange symbol]
SBX .... Shelby, MT [Location identifier FAA] (FAAL)
SBX .... Student Book Exchange
SBX .... Subsea Beacon/Transponder
SBXG .... Barra Do Garcas/Xingu [Brazil ICAO location identifier] (ICLI)
SBXV .... Xavantina [Brazil ICAO location identifier] (ICLI)
SBY .... BFS [Berliner Spezial Flug], Luftahrtunternehmen GmbH [Germany ICAO designator] (FAAC)
SBY .... Salisbury [Maryland] [Airport symbol] (OAG)
SBY .... Salisbury, MD [Location identifier FAA] (FAAL)
SBY .... Sand Bay [Alaska] [Seismograph station code, US Geological Survey Closed] (SEIS)
SBY .... Shapiro, Barney, Newark NJ [STAC]
SBY .... Standby [Airlines]
SBYA .... Iauarete [Brazil ICAO location identifier] (ICLI)
SBYen .... Salomon, Inc. [Associated Press] (SAG)
SBYS .... Piracununga/Campo Fontenelle [Brazil ICAO location identifier] (ICLI)
SBYT .... Spectrum HoloByte [NASDAQ symbol] (TTSB)
SBYT .... Spectrum HoloByte, Inc. [NASDAQ symbol] (SAG)
SBZ .... Scibe Airlift [Zaire] [ICAO designator] (FAAC)
SBZ .... Sibiu [Romania] [Airport symbol] (OAG)
SBZ .... Sowjetische Besatzungszone [Soviet Occupation Zone] [East Germany]
SBZ .... Sulfabromomethazine [Antibacterial] [Veterinary medicine]
SC .... All India Reporter, Supreme Court Reports [A publication] (DLA)
SC .... Brothers of the Sacred Heart (TOCD)
sc .... Brothers of the Sacred Heart (TOCD)

SC .... Cape Of Good Hope Reports [South Africa] [A publication] (DLA)
SC .... Catalan Solidarity [Political party] (PPW)
SC .... Christian Scientist
SC .... Closure of Semilunar Valves [Gastroenterology] (DAVI)
SC .... Congregation of the Servants of Christ [Anglican religious community]
SC .... Court of Session Cases [Scotland] [A publication] (DLA)
SC .... Cruiser Submarine [Navy symbol Obsolete]
SC .... Cruzeiro do Sul [ICAO designator] (AD)
SC .... Juta's Supreme Court Reports [1880-1910] [Cape Of Good Hope, South Africa] [A publication] (DLA)
SC .... Manetti Roberts [Italy] [Research code symbol]
SC .... Quebec Official Reports, Superior Court [A publication] (DLA)
SC .... Sabra Connection [An association] (EA)
SC .... Saccharomyces Cerevisiae [Bacterium]
SC .... Sacra Congregatio [Sacred Congregation] [Latin]
SC .... Sacrococcygeal [Anatomy]
SC .... Sacrosanctam Concilium [Constitution on the Sacred Liturgy] [Vatican II document]
SC .... Sad Case [An unpopular person] [Teen slang]
SC .... Safe Custody [Banking]
SC .... Safety Computer (COE)
SC .... Saffery Champness International [British accounting firm]
S/C .... Sales Code
S/C .... Sales Costs
SC .... Salesianorum Congregatio [Congregation of St. Francis of Sales] [Salesian Fathers] [Roman Catholic religious order]
SC .... Salmagundi Club (EA)
SC .... Salvage Charges
sc .... Salvage Charges (ODBW)
SC .... Same Case [Law]
SC .... Same Coupling [Music]
SC .... Sandia Corp.
SC .... Sanetis-Cacchione [Syndrome] [Medicine] (DB)
SC .... Sanitary Corps
SC .... Sanitation Center [Food Service] [Army]
sc .... Sans Correction [Without correction or without spectacles] [Ophthalmology] (DAVI)
SC .... Satellite Carrier (IAA)
SC .... Satellite Communications [Military]
SC .... Satellite Computer
SC .... Saturable Core (MSA)
SC .... Saturn Coupe [An automobile] (ECON)
Sc .... Scaccaria [Exchequer] [Latin] (DLA)
SC .... Scale
sc .... Scale (IDOE)
Sc .... Scammon's Reports [2-5 Illinois] [A publication] (DLA)
SC .... Scandinavian
Sc .... Scandium [Chemical element]
SC .... Scanner (IAA)
SC .... Scapula
SC .... Scarce [Bookselling] (ROG)
SC .... Scavenge (AAG)
SC .... Scene
sc .... Scene [Script notation] (WDMC)
SC .... Scented Cape [Tea trade] (ROG)
SC .... Schilling [Monetary unit] (ROG)
S/C .... Schmidt-Cassegrain [Telescope]
Sc .... Schmidt Number [IUPAC]
SC .... School Certificate
SC .... School Construction (OICC)
SC .... Schools Council [British]
SC .... Schooner (ROG)
SC .... Schueller-Christian [Disease] [Medicine] (DB)
SC .... Schwann Cell [Biology]
SC .... Sclatic [Nerve] [Anatomy] (DAVI)
SC .... Science
sc .... Science (IDOE)
sc .... Scilicet [Scire Licet] [It is permitted to know] [Latin] (WDMC)
SC .... Scilicet [Namely] [Legal term Latin]
SC .... Scintillation Counter [Instrumentation]
SC .... Scleral Cautery [Ophthalmology] (CPH)
SC .... Sclerocorneall [Ophthalmology] (DAVI)
SC .... Scope Change (MCD)
SC .... Score (AABC)
Sc .... Scoriae [Quality of the bottom] [Nautical charts]
SC .... Scoring Criteria (MCD)
SC .... Scots
SC .... Scottish Aviation Ltd. [ICAO aircraft manufacturer identifier] (ICAO)
SC .... Scottish Constitution (ADA)
Sc .... Scott's English Common Pleas Reports [A publication] (DLA)
SC .... Scrap Carriage [British military] (DMA)
SC .... Screen Coordinator [Military] (CAAL)
SC .... Screen Flag [Navy British]
SC .... Screw
S/C .... Screwed and Coupled
SC .... Script [Films, television, etc.]
SC .... Scruple
SC .... Scrupulus [Scruple] [Latin] [Pharmacy] (DAVI)
SC .... Sculpsit [He, or She, Engraved It] [Latin]
SC .... Sculptor
SC .... Sculpture Center (EA)
Sc .... Scutum [of Hesiod] [Classical studies] (OCD)
SC .... [The] Seal Cylinders of Western Asia [A publication] (BJA)
SC .... Seamen's Center [Later, Seamen and International House] (EA)

SC	Search Control (IEEE)
SC	Searchlight Carrier [British]
SC	Searle [G. D.] & Co. [Research code symbol]
SC	Seat Cabs
SC	Seco-Cemp Ltd. [Toronto Stock Exchange symbol]
SC	Secondary Code
SC	Secondary Confinement [or Containment] [Nuclear energy] (IEEE)
S-C	Secret and Confidential Files [Navy]
SC	Secretory Coil [Medicine] (MEDA)
SC	Secretory Component [Supersedes SP, TP] [Immunology]
SC	Sectional Center (EECA)
SC	Section Code (NITA)
SC	Secular College
SC	Security Call [Economics]
SC	Security Council (NADA)
SC	Security Council of the United Nations
SC	See Comments [Routing slip]
SC	See Copy
SC	Seed Coat [Botany]
SC	Segment Control (SSD)
SC	Select Cases [Oudh, India] [A publication] (DLA)
SC	Select Committee
SC	Selector Channel
SC	Self-Care [Medicine]
SC	Self-Check (AAG)
SC	Self-Closing
SC	Self Compatible
S/C	Self-Contained [Housing] [British]
SC	Selling Commission [Real estate] (REAL)
sc	Selling Commission [Real estate] (REAL)
SC	Semicactus [Horticulture]
SC	Semicircular (MAE)
SC	Semiclosed [Anatomy]
SC	Semi-Conducting [Electronics] (AAEL)
SC	Semiconductor
SC	Senatus Consulto [By the Decree of the Senate] [Latin]
SC	Senatus Consultum [Classical studies] (OCD)
SC	Send Common [Computer science] (MHDI)
SC	Sending Complete [Telecommunications] (TEL)
SC	Senior Cameraman
SC	Senior Counsel [Ireland]
S/C	Sensor Controller (MCD)
SC	Separate Cover
SC	Sequence Charts (AAG)
SC	Sequence Controller
SC	Sequence Counter
SC	Serum Complement [Medicine] (DMAA)
SC	Servants of Charity [Roman Catholic men's religious order]
sc	Servants of Charity (TOCD)
S/C	Service Ceiling
SC	Service Center [IRS]
SC	Service Certificate [Military British]
SC	Service Change
SC	Service Charge [Banking]
SC	Service Club [Military enlisted men's club]
SC	Service Code [Telecommunications] (TEL)
SC	Service Command [Marine Corps]
SC	Service Connected [Medicine]
SC	Service Corporation [Medicine] (HCT)
SC	Session Cases [Legal term British]
SC	Session Control [Computer science] (IBMDP)
SC	Set/Clear [Flip-flop] [Computer science]
SC	Set Clock
S/C	Set Course [Navigation]
SC	Severest Critic [Initialism used by E. B. White to describe his wife]
SC	Sex Change [Biology]
SC	Sex Chromatin (MAE)
SC	Seychelles [ANSI two-letter standard code] (CNC)
SC	Sezary Cell [Medicine] (DMAA)
SC	Shaft Center (MSA)
SC	Shakespearean Criticism [A publication]
SC	Shallow Compartment (DB)
SC	Shaped Charge [of explosive]
SC	Shaping Circuit [Electronics] (OA)
SC	Sharp Cash [Prompt payment]
SC	Shell Transport & Trading Co. Ltd. [NYSE symbol] (SPSG)
SC	Shell Transp/Trad ADR [NYSE symbol] (TTSB)
SC	Shift Control [Computer science] (IAA)
SC	Shift Control Counter [Computer science] (MDG)
SC	Ship Casualty Library [Maritime Data Network, Inc.] [Information service or system] (CRD)
SC	Shipping Container
SC	Shipping Contract (MCD)
SC	Ship's Cook [Navy]
SC	Shop Call (MCD)
SC	Shop Carpenter
SC	Shopping Center (MHDW)
SC	Shopping Concourses [Public-performance tariff class] [British]
SC	Short Circuit
SC	Short Course [of instruction]
SC	Should Cost (MCD)
S/C	Show Cause [Legal shorthand] (LWAP)
SC	Shunt Capacitor (IAA)
SC	Sick Call [Medicine] (DMAA)
SC	Sickle Cell [Medicine]
S-C	Sickle-Cell Hemoglobin C [Disease] (DAVI)
SC	Side Cabin
Sc	Side Car [Army]
SC	Side Contact [Valves] (DEN)
SC	Sierra Club (EA)
SC	Sieving Coefficient [Laboratory science] (DAVI)
SC	Signal Comparator
SC	Signal Conditioner
SC	Signal Corps [Later, Communications and Electronics Command] [Army]
S/C	Signal-to-Clutter
SC	Significant Characteristics (MCD)
SC	Silicone Coated
SC	Silk Covered (IAA)
SC	Silver Certificate
SC	Silver Crown [Class of racing cars]
SC	Silvered Copper [Wire] (IEEE)
SC	Simulation Coordinator
SC	Simulation Council (IAA)
SC	Simulator Control (MCD)
SC	Sine Correction [Without lenses] [Ophthalmology]
SC	Sine-Cosine
sc	Sine-Cosine (IDOE)
SC	Single Carburetor [Automotive engineering]
SC	Single Case
SC	Single Cell
SC	Single Chemical (MAE)
SC	Single Circuit [Electricity]
SC	Single Column
SC	Single Comb
SC	Single Contact [Switch]
SC	Single Counter
SC	Single Crochet
SC	Single Crystal
sc	Single Crystal (IDOE)
SC	Single Current (IAA)
SC	Sinusoidal Collagen [Anatomy]
SC	Sioux City [Diocesan abbreviation] [Iowa] (TOCD)
SC	Sisters of Charity [Anglican religious community]
SC	Sisters of Charity of Cincinnati, Ohio (TOCD)
SC	Sisters of Charity of Saint Vincent de Paul (EA)
SC	Sisters of Charity of Seton Hill, Greensburg, PA (TOCD)
SC	Sisters of St. Elizabeth, Convent Station (TOCD)
SC	Site Contingency [Nuclear energy] (NRCH)
SC	Situation Console (IAA)
SC	Sized and Calendered [Paper]
SC	Skill Component
SC	Skin Conductance
SC	Slave Clock (IAA)
SC	Slip Coupling (DS)
SC	Slow Call (WDAA)
SC	Slow Component
SC	Slow Curing [Asphalt grade]
SC	Small Cap (WDAA)
SC	Small Capitals [Typography]
sc	Small Capitals [Publishing] (WDAA)
SC	Small Compact [Car size]
SC	Small Craft
SC	Smooth Contour [Technical drawings]
SC	Snellen Chart [Ophthalmology]
SC	Snow Cover [Meteorology]
SC	So-Called
SC	Social Credit Party [British]
SC	Societas Fratrum Sacris Cordis [Brothers of the Sacred Heart] [Roman Catholic religious order]
SC	Society for Cryobiology (EA)
SC	Society of the Cincinnati (EA)
S/C	Software Contractor [NASA] (NASA)
SC	Soil Characteristics
SC	Solar Cell
SC	Solar Coil (IAA)
SC	Solar Constant (IAA)
SC	Soldier Capabilities
SC	Sole Charge [Ecclesiastical] [British] (ROG)
SC	Solid Core [Technical drawings]
SC	Solid-State Circuit (MCD)
SC	SONAR Channel [Navy] (CAAL)
SC	Soncino Chumash [A publication] (BJA)
S/C	Son Compte [His, or Her, Account] [French]
SC	Songwriters Club [Later, SLC] (EA)
SC	Sons of Charity [France] (EAIO)
SC	Sound Channel [Navy] (CAAL)
SC	Source Code
SC	Sources Chretiennes [A publication] (ODCC)
SC	South Carolina [Postal code]
SC	South Carolina Reports [A publication] (DLA)
Sc	South Carolina State Library, Columbia, SC [Library symbol Library of Congress] (LCLS)
SC	Southern California
SC	Southern Classification
SC	Southern Command [British military] (DMA)
SC	Southern Conference (EA)
SC	Southwark College [London, England]
SC	Space Capsule (IAA)

SC	Space Council [*National Aeronautics and Space Administration*] (USDC)
SC	Spacecraft (MCD)
S/C	Spacecraft/Capsule
SC	Spacecraft Communicator (IAA)
SC	Spark Control [*Automotive engineering*]
SC	Special Access, Compartmented (MCD)
SC	Special Care [*Medicine*]
SC	Special Circuit
SC	Special Circular
S/C	Special Conditions (MCD)
SC	Special Constable
SC	Specialty Code
SC	Specification Change
SC	Specification Control (IAA)
SC	Specific Cueing
SC	Speech Communication (IAA)
SC	Speed Controller [*Nuclear energy*] (NRCH)
SC	Spermatocyte
Sc	Spiral Having the Least Conspicuous Nuclear Regions and with Arms Very Loosely Coiled [*Astronomy*] (BARN)
SC	Spiroplasmavirus citri [*Bacteriology*]
SC	Splat Cooled (OA)
SC	Splenic Collateral [*Gastroenterology*] (DAVI)
S/C	Splitter/Combiner (NASA)
SC	Sponsor Code (NITA)
SC	Sports Council [*British*] (EAIO)
SC	Sporulation Capacity [*of fungi*]
SC	Spot Check (AAG)
SC	Spray Calciner [*Nuclear energy*] (NUCP)
SC	Spread Correlation
SC	Spreading Coefficient
SC	Spring Conditions [*Skiing*]
SC	Squamous Cell Carcinoma [*Also, SCC*] [*Medicine*]
SC	Square Corners [*Bookbinding*] (DGA)
SC	Squirrel Cage (IAA)
S/C	Stabilization and Control [*Aerospace*] (GFGA)
SC	Stack (Pipe) Cut [*Sanitation*] [*British*] (ROG)
SC	Staff Captain [*Military British*]
SC	Staff Car [*British*]
SC	Staff College [*Military*]
SC	Staff Corps
SC	Stage Center [*A stage direction*]
SC	Standard Candle [*Power*]
SC	Standard Channel (IAA)
SC	Standard Conditions
SC	Standing Committee (ADA)
SC	Standing Crop
SC	Stanley Consultants, Inc. (EFIS)
SC	Starfleet Command [*An association*] (EA)
SC	Star of Courage [*Award*] [*British*]
SC	Start Computer
SC	Start Conversion [*Computer science*]
SC	Starting Charge [*Bookbinding*] (DGA)
sC	Statcoulomb [*Also, Fr, statC*] [*Unit of electric charge*]
SC	Statement of Capability [*NASA*]
S/C	Statement of Charges [*Army*]
SC	Statement of Compatibility [*NASA*] (MCD)
SC	Statistical Control
SC	Statistics Canada
SC	Status Statement [*Online database field identifier*]
SC	Statutes of Canada
SC	Steel Casting
SC	Steel Cored [*Conductors*]
SC	Steering Committee (NATG)
Sc	Stellacyanin
SC	Stellar Camera
SC	Stepchild [*or Children*] (DNAB)
S/C	Step Climb (GAVI)
SC	Step Counter (IAA)
SC	Stepped Care [*Medicine*]
SC	Sternoclavicular [*Joint*] [*Anatomy*]
SC	Stimulus, Conditioned (AAMN)
SC	Stock Certificate [*Investment term*]
Sc	Stonecat [*Ichthyology*]
SC	Stopcock
SC	Stop-Continue (DEN)
SC	Storage Capacity (AAG)
SC	Storage Circuit (IAA)
SC	Storage Council (NTPA)
SC	Stored Command
S/C	Stowage Container
SC	Stratified Charge [*Automotive engineering*]
SC	Stratocumulus [*Cloud*] [*Meteorology*]
SC	Stratum Corneum [*Skin membrane*]
SC	Streptococcus [*Medicine*] (DB)
SC	Stress Cracking [*Metallurgy*]
SC	Strike Command [*Military*]
S/C	Strip Chart [*Recorder*] [*NASA*] (NASA)
SC	Stronnictwo Chlopskie [*Peasants' Party*] [*Poland Political party*] (PPE)
S/C	Subcable (KSC)
S/C	Subcarrier (AAG)
SC	Subchannel (IAA)
SC	Subclavian [*Anatomy*]

SC	Subcommittee
S/C	Subcontract
SC	Subcontractor (NATG)
SC	Subcorneal [*Ophthalmology*] (AAMN)
SC	Subcours
SC	Subcutaneous [*Beneath the Skin*] [*Medicine*]
SC	Subject Classification [*Library science*]
SC	Subject Code (NITA)
SC	Submarine Chaser [*110 foot*]
S/C	Submarine Coxswain [*British military*] (DMA)
SC	Subscriber Computer (MHDI)
SC	Subsidiary Company (MHDB)
SC	Succinylcholine [*Biochemistry*] (MAE)
SC	Su Cuenta [*Your Account*] [*Business term Spanish*]
SC	Sudden Commencement
SC	Suffolk and Cambridgeshire Regiment [*British military*] (DMA)
SC	Sugar-Coated [*Pharmacy*]
SC	Sulfur Colloid [*Chemistry*] (DAVI)
SC	Summary Court [*Navy*]
SC	Sumter & Choctaw Railway Co. [*AAR code*]
SC	Sunburn Cell [*For measuring phototoxicity*]
SC	Supercalendered [*Paper*]
SC	Super Caster [*Monotype*] (DGA)
SC	Supercharger [*Automotive engineering*]
SC	Super Computer (IAA)
S/C	Superconducting Magnetic (MCD)
SC	Super Coupe [*Model of automobile*]
SC	Supercritical Chromatography
SC	Super Current (IAA)
SC	Superimposed Coding [*Computer science*] (DIT)
SC	Superimposed Current
SC	Superintending Cartographer [*Navy British*]
SC	Superior Colliculus [*Brain anatomy*]
SC	Superior Court (DLA)
SC	Supervisor Call (IAA)
SC	Supervisor's Console
SC	Supervisory Control
SC	Supplemental Contract (AAG)
SC	Supplementary Information [*Telecommunications*] (TEL)
SC	Supply Catalog [*Military*] (AABC)
SC	Supply Control [*Military*]
SC	Supply Corps
SC	Supply Cost (AAGC)
SC	Support Center
SC	Support Chief
SC	Support Command [*Army*]
SC	Support Concept Manual [*Marine Corps*]
SC	Support Contractor (MCD)
SC	Support Controller [*NASA*] (KSC)
SC	Support Coordinator (AAG)
SC	Supporting Cells [*Zoology*]
SC	Suppressed Carrier (IEEE)
SC	Supreme Council [*Freemasonry*] (ROG)
SC	Supreme Court
SC	Supreme Court Reporter [*National Reporter System*] [*A publication*] (DLA)
SC	Surface Combustion [*Reducing gas process*]
SC	Surface Command [*NASA*] (MCD)
SC	Surgeon-Captain [*British military*]
SC	Surgeon-Commander [*British military*]
SC	Surgical Capsule [*of prostate gland*]
SC	Surrogates by Choice [*Defunct*] (EA)
SC	Surveillance Compliance [*Nuclear energy*] (NRCH)
SC	Sweetheart Contract [*Business term*] (MHDB)
SC	Swimmer-Canoeist [*British military*] (DMA)
SC	Swimming Club
SC	Switched Capacitor [*Electronics*] (IAA)
SC	Switching Cell (IEEE)
SC	Sylvania Central Railroad (IIA)
SC	Symbolic Code (AAG)
SC	Synanon Church (EA)
SC	Synaptonemal Complex [*Botanical cytology*]
SC	Synchro-Cyclotron
SC	Synchronization Coefficient
SC	Synclinal [*Geology*]
SC	System Capability
SC	System Category Code (NITA)
SC	System Controller [*Military*] (CAAL)
SC	Systemic Candidiasis (DB)
SC	Systems Command [*Air Force*]
SC	Systolic Click [*Cardiology*]
SC1	Standard Clean 1 (AAEL)
SC2	Standard Clean 2 (AAEL)
SCA	Air Weather Service, Technical Library, Scott AFB, IL [*OCLC symbol*] (OCLC)
SCA	Archibald Library, Caronport, Saskatchewan [*Library symbol National Library of Canada*] (NLC)
SCA	La Societe Canadienne d'Aerophilatelie (AC)
SCA	SAAB Club of North America [*SAAB Clubs of America*] [*Acronym is based on former name,*] (EA)
SCA	Sag-Control Agent [*Automotive painting and finishing*]
SCA	Sako Collectors Association (EA)
SCA	Saluki Club of America (EA)
SCA	Samoyed Club of America (EA)
SCA	Santa Catalina [*Colombia*] [*Airport symbol*] (AD)

SCA.............. Santa Cruz [Argentina] [Seismograph station code, US Geological Survey Closed] (SEIS)
SCA.............. Satellite Committee Agency [Army] (MCD)
SCA.............. Satellite Communications Agency [Army]
SCA.............. Save the Children Alliance [Gentofte, Denmark] (EAIO)
Sca .... Scala [Record label]
SCA.............. Scarborough Public Library [UTLAS symbol]
SCA.............. Schedule Change Authorization [NASA] (NASA)
SCA.............. Schipperke Club of America (EA)
SCA.............. School and College Ability [Test] [of ETS]
SCA.............. Science Clubs of America (EA)
SCA.............. Scientific Computing and Automation
SCA.............. Scottish Canoe Association (DBA)
SCA.............. Scottish Cashmere Association (DBA)
SCA.............. Scottish Chess Association (DBA)
SCA.............. Scottish Courts Administration (ILCA)
SCA.............. Scottish Croquet Association (DBA)
SCA.............. Screen Composers Association (NADA)
SCA.............. Screen Composers of America (EA)
SCA.............. Sea Cadet Association (EAIO)
SCA.............. Sebright Club of America (EA)
SCA.............. Secondary Communications Authorization (IEEE)
SCA.............. Secondary Control Assembly [Nuclear energy] (NRCH)
SCA.............. Sectional Chamber Association [British] (DBA)
SCA.............. Security Capital Atlantic, Inc. [NYSE symbol] (SAG)
SCA.............. Selective Coronary Angiogram (DAVI)
SCA.............. Selectivity Clear Accumulator
SCA.............. Self-Controlled Analgesia [Medicine] (CDI)
SCA.............. Senior Citizens of America [Defunct] (EA)
SCA.............. Sequence Chart Analyzer (IAA)
SCA.............. Sequence Control Area [NASA] (KSC)
SCA.............. Sequencer Control Assembly
S_{ca}.............. Serum Calcium [Biochemistry] (DAVI)
SCA.............. Service and Compliance Administration [US wage/price controls agency]
SCA.............. Service Cinematographique des Armees [France]
SCA.............. Service Contract Act [1965]
SCA.............. Service Corp. of America (EFIS)
SCA.............. Service Cryptologic Agencies [Military]
SCA.............. Sex Chromosome Abnormality
SCA.............. Shadow Communications Agency [British Labour Party]
SCA.............. Shareholder Credit Accounting
SCA.............. Sheepmeat Council of Australia
SCA.............. Shelby Can-Am [Racing car]
SCA.............. Shepherd's Center of America
SCA.............. Shields Class Association (EA)
SCA.............. Shipbuilders Council of America (EA)
SCA.............. Ship Constructive Association [A union] [British]
SCA.............. Ship Cost Adjustment [Navy]
SCA.............. Shipping Control Authority (NVT)
SCA.............. Shooters Club of America [Defunct]
SCA.............. Short Circuit Ampere (IAA)
SCA.............. Short Code Address (NITA)
SCA.............. Should Cost Analysis (MCD)
SCA.............. Shuttle Carrier Aircraft [NASA] (NASA)
SCA.............. Sickle Cell Anemia [Medicine]
SCA.............. Signal Conditioning Assembly [NASA] (KSC)
SCA.............. Simulated Core Assembly [Nuclear energy] (NRCH)
SCA.............. Simulation Control Area [NASA] (MCD)
SCA.............. Simulation Conversion Assembly [Deep Space Instrumentation Facility, NASA]
SCA.............. Single Camshaft Type A [Cosworth racing engines] [Automotive engineering]
SCA.............. Single Channel Analyzer
SCA.............. Ski Council of America [Defunct] (EA)
SCA.............. Small-Caliber Ammunition (MSA)
SCA.............. Smoke Control Association [Defunct] (EA)
SCA.............. Sneak Circuit Analysis [NASA] (NASA)
SCA.............. Social Care Association [British] (DBA)
SCA.............. Societe Canadienne d'Astronomie
SCA.............. Societe Canadienne des Anesthesistes [Canadian Anaesthetists' Society] (EAIO)
SCA.............. Society for Commercial Archeology (EA)
SCA.............. Society for Coptic Archaeology (EA)
SCA.............. Society for Creative Anachronism (EA)
SCA.............. Society for Cultural Anthropology (EA)
SCA.............. Society of Canadian Artists [Formerly, Society of Co-Operative Artists]
SCA.............. Society of Canadian Artists, Montreal [1868-72] (NGC)
SCA.............. Society of Cardiovascular Anesthesiologists (EA)
SCA.............. Society of Consumer Affairs (NADA)
SCA.............. Software Control Authorization [NASA] (KSC)
SCA.............. Soldiers Christian Association [British military] (DMA)
SCA.............. Sonar Class Association (EA)
S Ca.............. South Carolina Reports [A publication] (DLA)
SCA.............. South Central Air, Inc. [ICAO designator] (FAAC)
SCA.............. Southern Communications Area [Military]
SCA.............. Southern Cotton Association (EA)
SCA.............. Soybean Council of America [Defunct] (EA)
SCA.............. Spacecraft Adapter [NASA] (KSC)
SCA.............. SPALTRA [Special Projects Alterations, Training] Control Activity
SCA.............. Special Competition Advocate (AAGC)
SCA.............. Specialist Cheesemakers Association (WDAA)
SCA.............. Specification Compliance Agreement (MCD)
SCA.............. Specific Collection Area [Environmental science] (FFDE)

SCA.............. Specific Combining Ability
SCA.............. Speech Communication Association (EA)
SCA.............. Speed Coaches Association (EA)
SCA.............. Sperm-Coating Antigen
SCA.............. Spinach Carbonic Anhydrase [An enzyme]
SCA.............. Spinocerebellar Ataxia [Genetics]
SCA.............. Sprayed Concrete Association [British] (EAIO)
SCA.............. Stamp Collectors' Association [British] (BI)
SCA.............. Standard Consolidated Area [Bureau of Census]
SCA.............. Stealth Club of America (EA)
SCA.............. Steel Castings Association [British] (BI)
SCA.............. Steel-Cored-Aluminium
SCA.............. Sterba Curtain Antenna
SCA.............. Stevengraph Collectors' Association (EA)
SCA.............. Stock Company Association [Defunct] (EA)
SCA.............. Stock Control Activity (AFIT)
SCA.............. Storecast Carrier Authorization [Broadcasting] (WDMC)
SCA.............. Student Conservation Association (EA)
SCA.............. Subcarrier Authorization (MSA)
SCA.............. Subcarrier Channel [Telecommunications]
SCA.............. Subchannel Adapter
SCA.............. Subclavian Artery [Medicine] (DMAA)
SCA.............. Subcontract Authorization (AAG)
SCA.............. Subcritical Assembly (DEN)
SCA.............. Subcutaneous Abdominal [Block] [Anesthesiology] (DAVI)
SCA.............. Subsequent Coupons Attached
SCA.............. Subsidiary Channel Authorization (IAA)
SCA.............. Subsidiary Communications Allocation (IAA)
SCA.............. Subsidiary Communications Authorization [Facilities used to transmit background music to subscribing customers]
SCA.............. Subsurface Charge Accumulation [Solid state physics]
SCA.............. Sudden Cardiac Arrest [Medicine]
SCA.............. Sulfur-Containing Additive [Chemistry]
SCA.............. Summary Cost Account [Military] (AABC)
SCA.............. Superior Cerebellar Artery [Anatomy]
SCA.............. Supersonic Cruise Aircraft (PDAA)
SCA.............. Supervising Customs Agent [U.S. Customs Service] (BARN)
SCA.............. Support Centers of America [An association] (EA)
SCA.............. Suppressor Cell Activity [Medicine] (DMAA)
SCA.............. Supreme and Exchequer Courts Act [Canada] (ILCA)
SCA.............. Supreme Court Appeals [India] [A publication] (ILCA)
SCA.............. Surface Charge Analysis (AAEL)
SCA.............. Surface Coatings Abstracts [Paint Research Association of Great Britain] [Bibliographic database]
SCA.............. Surgical Care Affiliates, Inc. [NYSE symbol] (SPSG)
SCA.............. Suspended Ceilings Association [British] (DBA)
SCA.............. Swedish Council of America (EA)
SCA.............. Switch Control Assembly
SCA.............. Switzerland Cheese Association [Defunct] (EA)
SCA.............. Synagogue Council of America (EA)
SCA.............. Synchronous Communications Adapter
SCA.............. System Communication Area (ECII)
SCA.............. System Comparison Analysis [Bell System]
SCA.............. System Control Adapter (IAA)
SCA.............. System Control Area
SCA-1 .... Type-1 Spinocerebellar Ataxia [Medicine] (ECON)
SCAA .... School Curriculum and Assessment Authority [British] (DET)
SCAA .... Schools Curriculum & Assessment Authority (WDAA)
SCAA .... Skin Care Association of America (EA)
SCAA .... Specialty Coffee Association of America (EA)
SCAA .... Spill Control Association of America (EA)
SCAA .... Sporadic Cerebral Amyloid Angiopathy [Medicine] (DMAA)
SCAA .... Superconductor Applications Association (EA)
SCAA .... Sussex Cattle Association of America (EA)
SCAAN .... System for Computerized Application Analysis [Automotive engineering]
SCA & I ...... Society for Cardiac Angiography and Interventions (EA)
SCAAP .... Special Commonwealth African Assistance Plan
SCAAP .... Super Computer Automotive Applications Partnership
SCAARF....... Scottish Combined Action Against Racism & Fascism [An association] (BUAC)
SCAAS .... Strategic Communication and Alerting System
SCAB .... Single Chain Antibody Fragment [Botany] (ECON)
SCAB .... South Coast Air Basin (COE)
SCAB .... Streptozocin, CCNU [Lomustine], Adriamycin, Bleomycin [Antineoplastic drug regimen]
SCABA .... Scottish Chartered Accountants Benevolent Association (BUAC)
SCABG .... Single Coronary Artery Bypass [Cardiology] (DMAA)
SCABG .... Single Coronary Artery Bypass Graft [Cardiology]
SCABT .... South Carolina Association of Biology Teachers (EDAC)
SCAC .... Ancud/Pupelde [Chile] [ICAO location identifier] (ICLI)
Scac............ Scaccaria Curia [Court of Exchequer] [Latin] (DLA)
SCAC .... School and College Advisory Center [Later, EGASCAC] (EA)
SCAC .... Scottish Countryside Activities Council (DBA)
SCAC .... Self-Cleaning Air Cleaner
SCAC .... Soil Conservation Advisory Committee (BUAC)
SCAC .... Southern Collegiate Athletic Conference (PSS)
SCAC .... Standard Carriers Alpha Code (MCD)
SCAC .... Support Careers Advisory Committee [Environmental Protection Agency] (EPA)
SCAC .... Syntax-Controlled Acoustic Classifier [Computer science] (MHDI)
SCACT .... Supreme Court of the Australian Capital Territory
SC Acts........ Acts and Joint Resolutions of the State of South Carolina [A publication] (DLA)
SCAD .... Savannah College of Art and Design [Georgia]

SCAD	Scan Converter and Display [Systems]
SCAD	Schedule, Capability, Availability, Dependability (CIST)
SCAD	Schenectady Army Depot (AABC)
SCAD	Short Chain Acyl-Coenzyme A Dehydrogenase (DMAA)
SCAD	Small Current Amplifying Device
SCAD	Societe Canadienne pour l'Analyse de Documents [Indexing and Abstracting Society of Canada]
SCAD	State Commission Against Discrimination
SCAD	Strategic Bomber Penetration Decoy [Air Force]
SCAD	Subprogram Change Affect Diagram (MHDB)
SCAD	Subsonic Cruise Armed Decoy [Air Force]
SCAD	Systeme Communautaire d'Acces a la Documentation [Database] [EC] (ECED)
SCADA	Student Coalition Against Drug Abuse
SCADA	Supervisory Control and Data (IAA)
SCADA	Supervisory Control And Data Acquisition [Industrial engineering] [Computer science]
SCADAR......	Scatter Detection and Ranging
SCADC	Standard Central Air Data Computer
SCADE	Signal Conditioning and Detection Electronics (MCD)
SCADEU	Scottish Adult Basic Education Unit
SCADS	SAS Census Access and Display System [Information service or system] (IID)
SCADS	Scanning Celestial Attitude Determination System
SCADS	Shipborne Containerized Air Defense System
SCADS	Simulation of Combined Analog Digital Systems [Computer science] (IEEE)
SCADS	Sioux City Air Defense Sector [ADC]
SCADS	Speech Command Auditory Display System (MCD)
SCADU	Student Community Action Development Unit (BUAC)
SCAE	Scottish Center for Agricultural Engineering
SCAE	Scottish Centre of Agricultural Engineering [British] (IRUK)
SCAE	Society for Computer-Aided Engineering (EA)
SCAEC	Submarine Contact Analysis and Evaluation Center (NVT)
SCAEF	Supreme Commander, Allied Expeditionary Force [World War II]
Scaen Rom Frag...	Scaenicorum Romanorum Fragmenta [A publication] (OCD)
SCAEPA	Society for Computer Applications in Engineering, Planning, and Architecture [Later, CEPA] (EA)
SCAF.........	Self-Centered-Altruism Fad
SCAF.........	Supersonic Cruise Attack Fighter (MCD)
SCAF.........	Suppressor Cell Activating Factor [Biochemistry]
SCAF..........	Supreme Commander of Allied Forces (ADA)
SCAFA	Scottish Child and Family Alliance (DBA)
SCAFB	Schilling Air Force Base (AAG)
SCAFEDS	Space Construction Automated Fabrication Experiment Definition Study (MCD)
SCAG	Sandoz Clinical Assessment of Geriatrics [Psychometrics]
SCAG	Southern California Association of Governments
SCAG	Special COMSEC Advisory Group [US Army Communications Command] (MCD)
SCAGES	Standing Conference of Associations for Guidance in Education Settings (AIE)
SCAGMSO....	Social-Cultural Association of the German Minority in Silesian Opole [Poland] (BUAC)
SC/AH	System Coordinator / Anomaly Handler (SSD)
SCAHR.........	School of Community and Allied Health Resources
SCAHT	Scottish Churches Architectural Heritage Trust (BUAC)
ScAi	Aiken-Bamberg-Barnwell-Edgefield Regional Library, Aiken, SC [Library symbol Library of Congress] (LCLS)
SCAI.........	Societe des Comptables en Administration Industrielle du Canada
SCAI.........	Switch-to-Computer Applications Interface (CDE)
ScAiD..........	E. I. Du Pont de Nemours & Co., Aiken, SC [Library symbol Library of Congress] (LCLS)
SCAIF.........	Sertoli-Cell Androgenic Inhibitory Factor [Endocrinology]
ScAiTC........	Aiken Technical College, Aiken, SC [Library symbol] [Library of Congress] (LCLS)
SCAJAP.......	Shipping Control Administrator Japan
SCAJAP.......	Shipping Control Authority, Japan (DNAB)
ScAl...........	Allendale-Hampton-Jasper Regional Library, Allendale, SC [Library symbol] [Library of Congress] (LCLS)
SCAL...........	Health o meter Products [NASDAQ symbol] (TTSB)
SCAL...........	Health O Meter Products, Inc. [NASDAQ symbol] (SAG)
SCAL...........	Silver City Airways Ltd.
SCAL...........	Skin Diver Contact Air Lenses
SCAL...........	STAR [Self Testing and Reporting] Computer Assembly Language
SCAL...........	Steel-Cored Aluminum (IAA)
SCALA	Society of Chief Architects of Local Authorities [British]
SCALC.........	Steel-Cored Aluminum Conductor (IAA)
SCALD.........	Structural Computer-Aided Logic Design
SCALE.........	Scalable Architecture for Large Enterprises [Computer software] [Symantec Corp.] (PCM)
SCALE.........	Scales of Creativity and Learning Environment [Educational test]
SCALE.........	Space Checkout and Launch Equipment
SCALE.........	Symmetrically Configured AC [Alternating Current] Light-Emitting [Device]
SCALER	Statistical Calculation and Analysis of Engine Removal [Navy]
SCALO	Scanning Local Oscillator (NG)
SCALOP.......	Standing Committee on Antarctic Logistics and Operations (BUAC)
SCALP........	Small Card Automated Layout Program (IAA)
SCALP........	Students Concerned about Legal Prices [Student legal action organization]
SCALP........	Suit, Contamination Avoidance, and Liquid Protection [Army]
SCALPEL......	Scattering With Aperture Limited Projection Electron Lithography [AT&T development]
SCALRA	Scottish Adult Literacy Resource Agency

SCalWat	Southern California Water Co. [Associated Press] (SAG)
Scam	Scammon's Reports [2-5 Illinois] [A publication] (DLA)
SCAM.........	SCSI [Small Computer System Interface] Configuration Auto Magically [Computer science] (PCM)
SCAM.........	Selection Classification Age Maturity Program [Medical screening procedure for athletes]
SCAM.........	Soil Classification and Mapping Branch [Department of Agriculture] (IID)
SCAM.........	Source-Coder's Cost Analysis Model (PDAA)
SCAM.........	Soviet Cost Analysis Model [CIA]
SCAM.........	Spectrum Characteristics Analysis and Measurement [FAA]
SCAM.........	Standing Conference for Amateur Music [British]
SCAM.........	Station Control and Monitoring
SCAM.........	Strike Camera (MCD)
SCAM.........	Study Course in Agency Management [LIMRA]
SCAM.........	Subcarrier Amplitude Modulation (IAA)
SCAM.........	Subsonic Cruise Armed Missile/Decoy [Air Force] (MCD)
SCAM.........	Synchronous Communications Access Method
SCAMA	Service Central des Approvisionements et Materiels Americains [Central Office of American Supplies and Equipment] [World War II]
SCAMA	Skewed Circular Arc Method of Analysis
SCAMA	Station Conferencing and Monitoring Arrangement [NASA]
SCAMA	Switching, Conferencing, and Monitoring Arrangement [NASA]
SCAMAP	South and Central Asian Medicinal and Aromatic Plants Network (BUAC)
SCAMC	Symposium on Computer Applications in Medical Care [Baltimore, MD]
SCAM/D	Subsonic Cruise Armed Missile/Decoy [Air Force]
SCAMIN	Self-Concept and Motivation Inventory (DMAA)
SCAMM........	Specimen Coordinate Automated Measuring Machine [Defunct]
SCAMP	Scholarships for Children of American Military Personnel (DNAB)
SCAMP	Schools Computers Administration and Management Project (AIE)
SCAMP	Scottish Association of Magazine Publishers (BUAC)
SCAMP	Sectionalized Carrier and Multipurpose Vehicle [Military]
SCAMP	Self-Contained Airborne Multipurpose Pod (MCD)
SCAMP	Self-Contained Ancillary Modular Platform [Woods Hole Oceanographic Institution]
SCAMP	Self-Propelled Crane for Aircraft Maintenance and Positioning (MCD)
SCAMP	Sensor Control and Management Platoon [Marine Corps]
SCAMP	Signal Conditioning Amplifier
SCAMP	Single Channel Amplitude Monopulse Processing
SCAMP	Small-Caliber Ammunition Modernization Program [Army] (RDA)
SCAMP	Space-Controlled Army Measurements Probe
SCAMP	Sperry Computer-Aided Message Processor [British]
SCAMP	Standard Configuration and Modification Program [Military]
SCAMP	Succinyl CAMP [Biochemistry]
SCAMP	Summer Campus, Advanced Mathematics Program [Institute for Defense Analysis]
SCAMP	System/Command Accounting/Monitoring of Projects (DNAB)
SCAMPERS...	Standard Corps-Army-MACOM [Major Army Command] Personnel System (AABC)
SCAMPS	Small Computer Analytical and Mathematical Programming System (IEEE)
SCAMPTME...	Succinyl CAMP Tyrosine Methyl Ester [Biochemistry]
SCAMS	Scanning Microwave Spectrometer
SCAN	Alliance Imaging [NASDAQ symbol] (TTSB)
SCAN	Alliance Imaging, Inc. [NASDAQ symbol] (SPSG)
ScAn...........	Anderson County Library, Anderson, SC [Library symbol Library of Congress] (LCLS)
SCAN	Satellite Cable Audio Networks [Cable-television service]
SCAN	Savings Comparative Analysis [Federal Home Loan Bank Board] [Database]
SCAN	Scandinavian
SCAN	Scanfile [Database] [Australia]
SCAN	Scanner Association of North America (EA)
SCAN	Scanning (IAA)
SCAN	Schedule for Classroom Activity Norms (EDAC)
SCAN	Scintiscan [Medicine]
SCAN	Screening Test for Identifying Central Auditory Disorders
SCAN	Seismic Computerized Alert Network [For warning of an earthquake]
SCAN	Selected Current Aerospace Notices [NASA]
SCAN	Self-Containing Automatic Navigation (IAA)
SCAN	Self-Correcting Automatic Navigator
SCAN	Seniors Cooperative Alert Network [An association] (EA)
SCAN	Sensor Controller Alert Network
SCAN	Sequence Comparison Analysis Program (HGEN)
SCAN	Service Center Advantage Network [Federal-Mogul Corp.]
SCAN	Service Center for Aging Information [Department of Health and Human Services] [Information service or system] (IID)
SCAN	Shipboard Communication Area Network (DWSG)
SCAN	Short Current Abstracts and Notes (DIT)
SCAN	Signal Corps Administrative Network [Obsolete Army]
SCAN	Silent Communication Alarm Network [NASA]
SCAN	Silica-Coated Aluminum Nitride [Materials science]
SCAN	Simplified Colorimetric Analysis (MCD)
SCAN	Small Computers in the Arts Network [Defunct] (EA)
SCAN	Southern California Answering Network [Los Angeles Public Library] [Information service or system]
SCAN	Spares Change Advance Notice (MCD)
SCAN	State of California Answering Network [Information service or system] (IID)
SCAN	Stock Control and Analysis (BUR)
SCAN	Stock Market Computer Answering Network [British]
SCAN	Student Career Automated Network (IEEE)

SCAN	Supermarket Computer Answering Service (OA)
SCAN	Surface Condition Analyzer (MCD)
SCAN	Suspected Child Abuse and Neglect [*Medicine*] (DMAA)
SCAN	Switched Circuit Automatic Network [*Army*]
SCAN	System for Collection and Analysis of Near-Collision Reports (AAG)
SCAN	Visual Scanning [*Test*] (TES)
SCAN-A	SCAN-A: A Test for Auditory Processing Disorders in Adolescents and Adults (TMMY)
SCANA	SCANA Corp. [*Associated Press*] (SAG)
SCANA	Self-Contained Adverse-Weather Night Attack
SCANA	South Carolina Electric & Gas Co. (EFIS)
Scan-Austral	Scandinavian Australia Carriers Ltd. [*Norway*] (BUAC)
ScAnC	Anderson College, Anderson, SC [*Library symbol*] [*Library of Congress*] (LCLS)
SCANCAP	System for Comparative Analysis of Community Action Programs [*Information service or system*] (AEBS)
SCAND	Scandinavia
SCAND	Single Crystal Automatic Neutron Diffractometer
SCANDAL	Select Committee to Arrange a New Deal to Avoid Litigation [*Toledo, OH, group formed in 1973 to humorously protest results of the Michigan-Toledo "War of 18 35"*]
ScandC	Scandinavia Fund [*Associated Press*] (SAG)
SC & D	Stock Control and Distribution (AFM)
Sc & Div	Law Reports, Scotch and Divorce Appeals [*A publication*] (DLA)
Sc & Div App	Scotch and Divorce Appeals [*English Law Reports*] [*A publication*] (DLA)
SCANDEFA	Scandinavian Dental Fair [*Danish Dental Association*]
SC & FE	Sierra Club and Friends of the Earth [*Marine science*] (MSC)
SCANDI	Surveillance Control and Driver Information [*Traffic system*]
SC & J	Signal Collection and Jamming
SCANDLAS	Scandinavian Federation for Laboratory Animal Science (BUAC)
SCANDOC	Scandinavian Documentation Center [*Washington, DC*]
SC & RA	Specialized Carriers and Rigging Association (EA)
SC & S	Strapped, Corded, and Sealed [*As, of a package or bale*]
Scand Stud Criminol	Scandinavian Studies in Criminology [*A publication*] (DLA)
SC & T	Science and Technology (WDAA)
SCANF	Senate Committee on Agriculture, Nutrition, and Family (COE)
Scanfrm	Scanforms, Inc. [*Associated Press*] (SAG)
SCANG	South Carolina Air National Guard (MUSM)
ScanGr	Scan-Graphics, Inc. [*Associated Press*] (SAG)
ScaniaA	Scania AB [*Associated Press*] (SAG)
ScaniaB	Scania AB [*Associated Press*] (SAG)
SCANIIR	Surface Composition by Analysis of Neutral and Ion Impact Radiation [*Qualitative analysis*]
SCAN MAG	Scandalum Magnatum [*Defamation of Dignity*] [*Latin*] (ROG)
SCANN	South Coast against Nuclear Navies [*An association*] (BUAC)
SCANNET	Scandinavian Network (NITA)
SCANO	Automatic Scanning Unit Out of Service (FAAC)
ScanOp	Scan-Optics, Inc. [*Associated Press*] (SAG)
SCANP	Scandinavian Periodicals Index in Economics and Business [*Helsinki School of Economics Library*] [*Information service or system*]
SCANPED	System for Comparative Analysis of Programs For Educational Development [*Information service or system*] (AEBS)
SCANS	Scheduling and Control by Automated Network System
SCANS	Secretary's Commission on Achieving Necessary Skills [*Department of Labor*]
SCANS	Spectra Calculation from Activated Nuclide Sets (PDAA)
SCANS	System Checkout Automatic Network Simulator
SCANSAR	Scanning Synthetic Aperture RADAR
ScanSrce	ScanSource, Inc. [*Associated Press*] (SAG)
SCAN-Test	Scandinavian Pulp, Paper and Board Testing Committee [*Sweden*] (EAIO)
SCANTIE	Submersible Craft Acoustic Navigation and Track Indication Equipment (PDAA)
SCANVAC	Scandinavian Federation of Heating, Air Conditioning, and Sanitary Engineering Associations (BUAC)
ScanVec	ScanVec Co. Ltd. [*Associated Press*] (SAG)
SCAO	Senior Civil Affairs Officer
SCAO	Standing Committee on Army Organization [*British*]
SCAO	Standing Conference of Atlantic Organisations [*British*] (EAIO)
SCAOK	Automatic Scanning Unit Returned to Service (FAAC)
SCAO(P)	Senior Civil Affairs Office, Police [*British*]
SCAP	Alto Palena/Alto Palena [*Chile*] [*ICAO location identifier*] (ICLI)
SCAP	Scapula (DMAA)
SCAP	Service Center Audit Program [*IRS*]
SCAP	Silent Compact Auxiliary Power
SCAP	Silicon Capacitance Absolute Pressure Sensor
SCAP	Slow Component Axonal Particulate [*Neurology*]
SCAP	Small Communications Augmentation Package (MCD)
SCAP	Space Charge Atomizing Precipitaters (KSC)
SCAP	States Cooperative Assistance Program (BUAC)
SCAP	Superfund Comprehensive Accomplishment Plan [*Environmental Protection Agency*] (GFGA)
SCAP	Supreme Commander, Allied Powers [*World War II*] (MUGU)
SCAP	Systems Concepts and Procedures
Scapa	Scottish Campaign for Public Angling (BUAC)
SCAPA	Society for Checking the Abuses of Public Advertising [*British*]
SCAPE	Self-Contained Atmospheric Personnel [*or Protective*] Ensemble [*Suit*] [*Aerospace*]
SCAPE	System Compatibility and Performance Evaluation [*Military*] (CAAL)
ScAPS	Scandinavian Association of Paediatric Surgeons (BUAC)
SCAPS	Site Characterization and Analysis Penetrometer System [*Army*] (RDA)
s caps	Small Capital Letters (WDMC)
SCAPS	Small Capitals [*Typography*]

SCAR	Arica/Internacional Chacalluta [*Chile*] [*ICAO location identifier*] (ICLI)
SCAR	Satellite Capture and Retrieval (AFM)
SCAR	Scandinavian Council for Applied Research
scar	Scarlet [*Philately*]
SCAR	Schools' Campaign Against Racism [*British*] (DI)
SCAR	Scientific Committee on Antarctic Research [*ICSU*] [*Cambridge, England*] (EAIO)
SCAR	Signal Conditioner Assembly Request (MCD)
SCAR	Signal Conditioner Assembly Review (MCD)
SCAR	Society for Computer Applications in Radiology (BUAC)
S Car	South Carolina Reports [*A publication*] (DLA)
SCAR	Spacecraft Assessment Report [*NASA*] (KSC)
SCAR	Special Committee on Atlantic Research
SCAR	Special Committee on Atomic Research [*Pugwash Conference*]
SCAR	Special International Committee on Antarctic Research
SCAR	Standing Committee on Agricultural Research (BUAC)
SCAR	Status Control Alert and Reporting (MCD)
SCAR	Strike Control and Reconnaissance [*Aircraft*]
SCAR	Structure-Carcinogenic Activity Relationship [*Biochemistry*]
SCAR	Student Campaign for Animal Rights (BUAC)
SCAR	Subcaliber Aircraft Rocket
SCAR	Subcell Address Register [*Computer science*] (MHDB)
SCAR	Submarine Celestial Altitude Recorder [*Navy*]
SCAR	Submerged Celestial Altitude Recorder (IAA)
SCAR	Subsequent Contrast Application Review (MCD)
SCAR	Supersonic Cruise Aircraft [*or Airplane*] Research [*NASA*]
SCAR	Supplier Corrective Action Request
SCARA	Selective Compliance Assembly Robot Arm [*IBM Corp.*]
SCARAB	Submersible Craft Assisting Repair and Burial [*Autonomous underwater vehicle*]
SCAR-B	Smoke, Cloud, and Radiation in Brazil
SCARDE	Study Committee on Analysis of Research, Development, and Engineering
SCARE	Sensor Control Anti-Anti-Radiation Missile RADAR Evaluation (PDAA)
SCARE	Structural Ceramic Analysis and Reliability Evaluation [*NASA*]
SCAReU	Stanford Community Against Reagan University [*Group opposed to proposed Ronald Reagan presidential library at Stanford University*]
SCARF	Santa Cruz Acoustic Range Facility [*Navy*]
SCARF	Self-Contained Automated Robotic Factory
SCARF	Sickle Cell Anaemia Research Foundation (BUAC)
SCARF	Side-Looking Coherent All-Range Focused
SCARF	Special Committee on the Adequacy of Range Facilities (MUGU)
SCARF	Standing Committee of the Australian Forestry Council (BUAC)
SCARF	Strategic Cislunar Advanced Retaliatory Force (IAA)
SCARF	Supporters Campaign against Racism in Football [*An association*] (BUAC)
SCARF	Survey of Change and Residential Finance [*Census Bureau*]
SCARF	System Control Audit Review File [*Computer science*]
SCARM	Standing Committee on Agriculture and Resource Management (BUAC)
SCARMD	Severe Childhood Autosomal Recessive Muscular Dystrophy [*Medicine*]
SCARP	Society for Comic Art Research and Preservation
S Car R	South Carolina Law Reports [*A publication*] (DLA)
SCARS	SACEUR [*Supreme Allied Commander, Europe*] Command Alerting Reporting System [*Army*]
SCARS	Serialized Control and Record [*or Reporting*] System (NASA)
SCARS	Sneak Circuit Analysis Report Summary [*NASA*] (GFGA)
SCARS	Software Configuration Accounting and Reporting System
SCARS	Southern's Computer-Assisted Retrieval Service [*University of Southern Mississippi*] (OLDSS)
SCARS	Status Control Alert Reporting System (NATG)
SCARS	System Control and Receiving Station [*Air Force*]
SCART	Sperry Continuity and Resistance Tester
SCARWAF	Special Category Army with Air Force
SCAS	Semicontinuous Activated Sludge [*Test*] [*Environmental Protection Agency*] (FFDE)
SCAS	Signal Corps Aviation School [*Obsolete Army*]
SCAS	Society for Companion Animal Studies (EAIO)
SCAS	South Carolina Academy of Science (BUAC)
SCAS	Southwest Center for Advanced Studies [*Later, University of Texas at Dallas*]
SCAS	Spacecraft Adapter Simulator (IAA)
SCAS	Stability Control Augmentation System (NVT)
SCAS	State Cost Accounting System (OICC)
SCAS	Subsystem Computer Application Software (MCD)
SCASA	Straight Chiropractic Academic Standards Association (EA)
SCASG	SONAR Calibration and Alignment Steering Group
SCASH	Scottish Committee Action on Smoking and Health (EAIO)
SCASP	Sequence of Coverage and Speed (SAA)
SCASS	Signal Corps Aircraft Signal Service [*Obsolete Army*]
SCASS	Standing Conference of Arts and Social Sciences [*British*] (DBA)
SCAT	Scatterometer
SCAT	Scatula [*Package*] [*Pharmacy*]
SCAT	School and College Ability Test [*of ETS*]
SCAT	Schottky Cell Array Technology
SCAT	Science College Ability Test (EDAC)
SCAT	Scout/Antitank Mission [*Army*] (INF)
SCAT	Scout-Attack [*Helicopter*] (MCD)
SCAT	Security Control of Air Traffic [*FAA*]
SCAT	Selected Calibration and Alignment Test (MCD)
SCAT	Self-Contained Automatic Transmitter (MCD)
SCAT	Sequential Component Automatic Testing (MSA)
SCAT	Service Code Automatic Tester [*Automotive engineering*]

SCAT............	Service Command Air Transportation
SCAT............	Severe Combined Anaemia and Thrombocytopenia (ECON)
SCAT............	Share Compiler-Assembler, Translator
SCAT............	Sheep Cell Agglutination Test
SCAT............	Sickle Cell Anemia Test [Medicine] (AAMN)
SCAT............	Silicon Controlled Avalanche Transistor [Electronics] (BARN)
SCAT............	Simulated Catalyst Activity Test [Analytical chemistry]
SCAT............	Small Car Automatic Transit [System]
SCAT............	Societa Ceirano Automobili Torino [Early Italian auto manufacturer]
SCAT............	Solid Catalysts (KSC)
SCAT............	Solution to Customer Aircraft Troubles (MCD)
SCAT............	South Pacific Combat Air Transport [World War II]
SCAT............	Space Communications and Tracking
SCAT............	Special Advisory Committee on Telecommunications
SCAT............	Speed Command Attitude/Target [FAA]
SCAT............	Speed Command of Attitude/Thrust (IAA)
SCAT............	Speed Control Approach/Takeoff
SCAT............	Sperry Canada Automatic Tester
SCAT............	State Change Algorithm Translator
SCAT............	Storage, Checkout, and Transportation [Rack] [Aerospace]
SCAT............	Submarine Classification and Tracking
SCAT............	Supersonic Commercial Air Transport [NASA]
SCAT............	Surface-Controlled Avalanche Transistor
SCAT............	System Commonality Analysis Tool (SSD)
SCAT............	System Configuration Acceptance Test (IAA)
SCAT............	System for Computer Automated Typesetting (PDAA)
SCAT............	Systems Consolidation of Accessions and Trainees [Military] (AABC)
SCATA............	Survival Sited Casualty Treatment Assemblage (AFM)
SCATANA........	Security Control of Air Traffic and Air Navigation Aids [FAA]
SCATBI........	Scales of Cognitive Ability for Traumatic Brain Injury [Test] (TMMY)
SCATE..........	Self-Checking Automatic Testing Equipment
SCATE..........	Space Chamber Analyzer - Thermal Environment [NASA]
SCATE..........	Stromberg-Carlson Automatic Test Equipment
SCATER........	Security Control of Air Traffic and Electromagnetic Radiations [During an air defense emergency] [FAA]
Scates' Comp St...	Treat, Scates, and Blackwell's Compiled Illinois Statutes [A publication] (DLA)
SCATHA......	Satellite Charging at High Altitude (MCD)
SCATHA......	Spacecraft Charging at High Altitudes [Satellite]
SCAT III......	School and College Ability Tests, Series III [Educational Testing Service] (TES)
SCATMINWARIN...	Scatterable Minefield Warning [Army] (ADDR)
SCAT ORIG...	Scatula Originalis [Original Package] [Pharmacy]
SCATS	Scheduling and Tracking System (MCD)
SCATS	Self-Contained Automatic Test System
SCATS	Sequential Controlled Automatic Transistor Start (NITA)
SCATS	Sequentially Controlled Automatic Transmitter Start
SCATS	Simulation, Checkout, and Training System
SCATS	Simulation Control and Training System (NASA)
SCATS	Standing Conference for the Advancement of Training and Supervision [British] (DBA)
SCATS	Storage, Checkout, and Transport [NASA] (NAKS)
SCATS	Surface Combatant Airborne Tactical System (MCD)
SCATS	Sydney Coordinated Adaptive Traffic System [FHWA] (TAG)
SCATSD.......	Signal Corps Aviation Test and Support Detachment [Military] (IAA)
SCATT........	Scatterometer (USDC)
SCATT..........	Scientific Communication and Technology Transfer [System] [University of Pennsylvania]
SCATT..........	Shared Catalog Accessed Through Terminals [Data processing system]
SCATTOR......	Small Craft Assets, Training, and Turnover of Resources (DNAB)
SCAUL........	Standing Conference of African University Libraries [Lagos, Nigeria]
SCAULWA....	Standing Conference of African University Libraries (EAIO)
SCA(UN)......	Department of Security Council Affairs of the United Nations
Scaur	Pro Scauro [of Cicero] [Classical studies] (OCD)
SCAV	Scavenge (AAG)
SCAV	Soil Conservation Association of Victoria (BUAC)
SCAW	Scientists' Center for Animal Welfare (EA)
SCAW	Supreme Camp of the American Woodmen (EA)
SCAWD........	Scottish Churches Action for World Development (EAIO)
SCAWD........	Service Contract Act Wage Determination (AAGC)
SCAWH-SAWRH...	Signal Company Aircraft Warning Hawaii - Signal Aircraft Warning Regiment HawaiiAssociation (EA)
SCAWNA......	Self-Contained Adverse-Weather Night Attack (MCD)
SCAWU........	Singapore Clerical and Administrative Workers' Union
SCAZ..........	South Atlantic Convergence Zone [Marine science] (OSRA)
Sc B.............	Bachelor of Science
ScB.............	Beaufort County Library, Beaufort, SC [Library symbol Library of Congress] (LCLS)
SCB.............	Sample Collection Bag [NASA]
SCB.............	Santa Cruz Basin [California] (GAAI)
SCB.............	Scarborough [Ontario] [Seismograph station code, US Geological Survey Closed] (SEIS)
SCB.............	Schedule Change Board [NASA] (NASA)
SCB.............	Scholarly Book Center [ACCORD] [UTLAS symbol]
SCB.............	School of Classical Ballet [American Ballet Theater Foundation]
Sc B.............	Scientiae Baccalaureus [Bachelor of Science] [Latin]
SCB.............	Scorpion Resources [Vancouver Stock Exchange symbol]
SCB.............	Scribner, NE [Location identifier FAA] (FAAL)
SCB.............	Secondary Carpet Backing
SCB.............	Segment Control BIT [Binary Digit]
SCB.............	Selection Control Board [NASA] (NASA)
SCB.............	Selector Control Box [Aerospace] (MCD)
SCB.............	Selenite Cystine Broth (OA)
SCB.............	Semiconductor Bridge

SCB.............	Session Control Block [Computer science] (BUR)
SCB.............	Shallow Cathode Barrier (IAA)
SCB.............	Ship Characteristics Board
SCB.............	Shipowners Claims Bureau [New York, NY] (EA)
SCB.............	Ships Characteristics Board
SCB.............	Ship's Cook, Butcher [Navy]
SCB.............	Silicon Cell Bridge
SCB.............	Silicon Circuit Board
SCB.............	Silver Cadmium Battery
SCB.............	Single-Cell Biosensor [Analytical biochemistry]
SCB.............	Site Control Block [Computer science] (OA)
SCB.............	Society for Conservation Biology (EA)
SCB.............	Society for the Conservation of Biology (BUAC)
SCB.............	Society of Craftsmen Bakers [British] (BI)
SCB.............	Soeurs de la Charite de Besancon [Sisters of Charity] [France] (EAIO)
SCB.............	Software Control Board [Apollo] [NASA]
SCB.............	Solicitors Compaints Bureau (BUAC)
SCB.............	Specification Control Board [NASA] (NASA)
SCB.............	Speedway Control Board (BUAC)
SCB.............	Stack Control Block
SCB.............	State Capacity Building (EDAC)
SCB.............	Station Control Block [Computer science] (IBMDP)
SCB.............	Stream Control Block [Computer science] (CIST)
SCB.............	Strictly Confined to Bed [Medicine]
SCB.............	Student Contact Book [A publication]
SCB.............	Supervisory Circuit Breaker (IAA)
SCBA...........	Balmaceda/Balmaceda [Chile] [ICAO location identifier] (ICLI)
ScBa...........	Lexington County Circulating Library, Batesburg, SC [Library symbol Library of Congress] (LCLS)
SCBA...........	Savings and Community Bankers of America (TBD)
SCBA...........	Self-Contained Breathing Apparatus (AAEL)
SCBA...........	Supreme Circle Brotherhood of America (EA)
SCBAL.........	Standard Chartered Bank Australia Ltd. (ADA)
Sc BAM.......	Bachelor of Science in Applied Mathematics
Sc BC.........	Bachelor of Science in Chemistry
SCBC	Small-Cell Bronchogenic Carcinoma [Oncology] (DAVI)
SCBCA	Small Claims Board of Contract Appeals
SCBCL-C......	Societe Commerciale de Banque Credit Lyonnais-Cameroun (EY)
SCBCmp	SCB Computer Technology, Inc. [Associated Press] (SAG)
SC Bcp	SC Bancorp [Associated Press] (SAG)
SCBD	Scan Conversion and Bright Display
SCBD	Seller's Approved Configuration Baseline Document [NASA] (NASA)
SCBD	Signal Corps Base Depot [Military] (IAA)
Sc BE	Bachelor of Science in Engineering
SCBE..........	Societe Canadienne des Brevets et d'Exploitation
ScBen........	Marlboro County Public Library, Bennettsville, SC [Library symbol] [Library of Congress] (LCLS)
SCBF..........	Sacred Cat of Burma Fanciers (EA)
SCBF..........	Spinal Cord Blood Flow
SCBG.........	Symmetrical Calcification of Basal Cerebral Ganglia (STED)
SCBH.........	Systemic Cutaneous Basophil Hypersensitivity (STED)
ScBi..........	Lee County Public Library, Bishopville, SC [Library symbol] [Library of Congress] (LCLS)
SCBI..........	SCB Computer Technology [NASDAQ symbol] (TTSB)
SCBI..........	SCB Computer Technology, Inc. [NASDAQ symbol] (SAG)
SCBL..........	Quilpue/Mil el Belloto [Chile] [ICAO location identifier] (ICLI)
SCBL..........	Scotts Bluff and Agate Fossil Beds National Monuments
SCBL..........	Single-Cavitation Bubble Luminescence [Physics]
SCBNP........	Society for the Collection of Brand-Name Pencils [Inactive] (EA)
Sc BP	Bachelor of Science in Physics
SCBP.........	Stratum Corneum Basic Protein (DB)
SCBQ.........	Santiago/Mil el Bosque [Chile] [ICAO location identifier] (ICLI)
SCBQ.........	Science Classroom Behavior Q-Sort (EDAC)
SCBR.........	Serum Cholesterol-Binding Reserve [Medicine]
SCBR.........	Stationary Catalytic Basket Reactor [Chemical engineering]
SCBR.........	Steam-Cooled Breeder Reactor [Nuclear energy]
SCBRO........	Society of Chief Building Regulation Officers (BUAC)
SCBS.........	Saint Charles Borromeo Seminary [Pennsylvania]
SCBS.........	Society for the Conservation of Bighorn Sheep (EA)
SCBS.........	Southern Community Bancshares, Inc. [NASDAQ symbol] (SAG)
SC/BSE	Scientific Co-Operation Bureau for the European and North American Region [United Nations] (EA)
SCBT..........	Society of Computed Body Tomography (EA)
ScBTC........	Beaufort Technical College, Beaufort, SC [Library symbol] [Library of Congress] (LCLS)
SCBT/MR	Society of Computed Body Tomography and Magnetic Resonance (NTPA)
ScBU.........	Screening Bacteriuria (STED)
SCBU.........	Special Care Baby Unit [Medicine]
SCBW.........	Society of Children's Book Writers (EA)
SCBWI........	Society of Children's Book Writers and Illustrators (NTPA)
SCC............	Cameron's Supreme Court Cases [Canada] [A publication] (DLA)
ScC	Charleston Library Society, Charleston, SC [Library symbol Library of Congress] (LCLS)
SCC............	Deadhorse [Alaska] [Airport symbol] (OAG)
SCC............	Deadhorse, AK [Location identifier FAA] (FAAL)
SCC............	Sacra Congregatio Concilii [Sacred Congregation of the Council] [Latin]
SCC............	Safety Control Center (NASA)
SCC............	SAGE [Semiautomatic Ground Environment] Control Center
SCC............	Salivary Caffeine Clearance [Physiology]
SCC............	Santa Cruz [California] [Seismograph station code, US Geological Survey Closed] (SEIS)
SCC............	Sarawak Chamber of Commerce [Malaysia] (BUAC)

SCC	Satellite Communication Concentrator
SCC	Satellite Communications Controller
SCC	Satellite Control Center
SCC	Satellite-Controlled Clock
SCC	Scandinavian Clothing Council (BUAC)
SCC	Scandinavian Collectors Club (EA)
SCC	Scarborough Campus, University of Toronto [UTLAS symbol]
SCC	Schools Councils Classics Committee [British]
SCC	Science Council of Canada
SCC	Scottish Churches Council (BUAC)
SCC	Scottish Consumer Council (BUAC)
SCC	Sea Cadet Corps [Navy British]
SCC	Sears Canada [TS Symbol] (TTSB)
SCC	Sears Canada, Inc. [Toronto Stock Exchange symbol]
SCC	Secondary Category Code (NITA)
SCC	Secondary Combustion Chamber [Furnace technology]
SCC	Secondary Containment Cooling (IEEE)
SCC	Sectional Classification Code (NITA)
SCC	Secure Computing Corp.
SCC	Security Commodity Code (AAG)
SCC	Security Control Center [NASA] (KSC)
SCC	Security Coordination Committee (NATG)
SCC	Seed Certification Committee [Queensland, Australia]
SCC	Select Cases in Chancery [Legal] [British]
SCC	Select Cases in Chancery Tempore King, Edited by Macnaghten [England] [A publication] (DLA)
SCC	Self-Contained Canister (MCD)
SCC	Senate Children's Caucus (EA)
SCC	Senate Copper Caucus (EA)
SCC	Senior Command Course [British military] (DMA)
SCC	Sequence Control Chart
SCC	Sequence Controlled Calculator (IAA)
SCC	Sequential Combination Chemotherapy (STED)
SCC	Sequential Control Counter [Computer science] (BUR)
scc	Serbo-Croatian (Cyrillic) [MARC language code Library of Congress] (LCCP)
SCC	Serial Communications Controller
SCC	Service Change Committee [Military]
SCC	Services for Crippled Children
SCC	Servo Control Cabinet [Military] (CAAL)
SCC	Set Conditionally [Computer science]
SCC	Sexual Concerns Checklist [Premarital and marital relations test]
SCC	Ship Control Center
SCC	Short-Circuit Current
SCC	Short-Course Chemotherapy [Medicine]
SCC	Sickle-Cell Crisis [Hematology] (DAVI)
SCC	Signaling Conversion Circuit [Telecommunications] (TEL)
SCC	Silhouette Collectors' Club (BUAC)
SCC	Simplified Computer Code
SCC	Simulation Control Center [NASA] (KSC)
SCC	Single Conductor Cable (MSA)
SCC	Single Copy Complexity [Genetics]
SCC	Single Cotton-Covered [Wire insulation]
scc	Single Cotton Covered (IDOE)
SCC	Sisters of Christian Charity (TOCD)
SCC	Slice Control Central (SAA)
SCC	Slidell Computer Complex [Slidell, LA] [NASA]
SCC	Small Cell Cancer [Oncology]
SCC	Small-Cell Carcinoma [Medicine] (STED)
SCC	Small Center Contact
SCC	Small Claims Court [Northern Territory, Australia]
SCC	Small Cleaved Cell [Medicine] (DMAA)
SCC	Small College Conference (PSS)
SCC	Small Compressor Colorimeter (MCD)
SCC	Societe Canadienne de Cardiologie [Canadian Cardiovascular Society] (EAIO)
SCC	Societe Canadienne de Criminologie
SCC	Societe Chimique des Charbonnages [France]
SCC	Society for Children with Craniosynostosis (EA)
SCC	Society for the Christian Commonwealth
SCC	Society of Cheese Connoisseurs [British] (DBA)
SCC	Society of Cosmetic Chemists (EA)
SCC	Society of Cost Consultants (BUAC)
SCC	Soeurs de la Croix de Chavanod [Sisters of the Cross of Chavanod] [France] (EAIO)
SCC	Software Checkout Console [Army]
SCC	Soil Conservation Council [South Australia]
SCC	Somatic Cell Concentration (OA)
SCC	Source Classification Code [Environmental Protection Agency]
SCC	Southern Connecticut State College, Division of Library Science, New Haven, CT [OCLC symbol] (OCLC)
SCC	Space Chamber Complex (MCD)
SCC	Space Control Station
SCCam	Spacecraft Control Center [NASA] (KSC)
SCC	Spark Control Computer [Automotive engineering]
SCC	Special Coordinating Committee [National Security Council] [Terminated, 1981]
SCC	Specialist Computer Centres (NITA)
SCC	Specialized Common Carrier [Telecommunications] (NRCH)
SCC	Species Survival Commission (BUAC)
SCC	Specification for Contract Change (DNAB)
SCC	Specific Clauses and Conditions (NATG)
SCC	Speed Control Circuit (DNAB)
SCC	Splenium of the Corpus Callosum [Anatomy]
SCC	Squadron Control Center (AAG)
SCC	Squamous Carcinoma of Cervix [Medicine] (STED)
SCC	Squamous Cell Carcinoma [Also, SC] [Medicine]
SCC	Stabilized Core Composite [Materials science]
SCC	Stamford [Connecticut] [Airport symbol] (AD)
SCC	Standard Commodity Classification [Military]
SCC	Standard Commodity Codes (MCD)
SCC	Standard Consultative Commission [for resolving compliance disputes arising from SALT 1 accord]
SCC	Standard Cubic Centimeter (KSC)
SCC	Standardized Cost Categories
SCC	Standards Council of Canada [See also CCNO]
SCC	Standing Conference of Consultatives [Angling and fisheries] (BUAC)
SCC	Standing Consultative Commission [SALT agreements] [US/USSR]
SCC	Standing Interdepartmental Committee on Censorship [War Cabinet] [British]
SCC	Starcraft Campers Club (EA)
SCC	State Coordination Committee [Responsible for administering the Work Incentive Program at the state level]
SCC	State Corporation Commission
SCC	State/Territories Consultative Committee [Australia]
SCC	Status Change Character (IAA)
SCC	Steel Carriers Conference [Later, RDCC] [An association] (EA)
SCC	Steering Control Console (DNAB)
SCC	Stock Clearing Corp. [NYSE]
SCC	Stock Control Center [Army]
SCC	Storage Connecting Circuit [Teletype]
SCC	Strapped, Corded and Sealed (MHDB)
SCC	Strategic Cell Controller (AAEL)
SCC	Strategic Communications Command [Army] (MCD)
SCC	Stress Control Cracking (EDCT)
SCC	Stress Corrosion Cracking [Metals]
SCC	Structural Concrete Consortium [British] (DBA)
SCC	Student of Codrington College [Barbados]
SCC	Studio Collector's Club (EA)
SCC	Sub-Carrier Channels (NITA)
SC(C)	Submarine Chaser (Control) [110 foot] [Obsolete]
SCC	Submission Control Code (MCD)
SCC	Sudan Council of Churches
SCC	Sunbeam Car Club [Defunct] (EA)
SCC	Suore della Carita Cristiana [Sisters of Christian Charity] [Italy] (EAIO)
SCC	Super-Critical Cryogenics (SAA)
SCC	Super Sonic Car
SCC	Supervisor Control Console
SCC	Supervisory Control Conference (KSC)
SCC	Supply Control Center [Military]
SCC	Supreme Court Cases [India] [A publication] (DLA)
SCC	Supreme Court Circular [Ceylon] [A publication] (ILCA)
SCC	Supreme Court of Canada
SCC	Surface Combat Condition (DNAB)
SCC	Surveillance Coordination Center (NATG)
SCC	Swedish Cooperative Centre (BUAC)
SCC	Switching Control Center [Bell System]
SCC	Sylvac Collectors' Club (BUAC)
SCC	Synchronous Communications Controller
SCC	Syndicat des Communications Canada
SCC	System Communication Controller
SCC	System Control Code (MCD)
SCC	System Control Console (MCD)
SCC	System Coordinate Center [Military] (CAAL)
SCC	Systems Control Center
SCCA	Saab Car Club of Australia
SCCA	Scottish Consumer Credit Association (BUAC)
SCCA	Semiclosed Circle Absorber (DAVI)
SCCA	Semiclosed Circle Absorber System (STED)
SCCA	Single Cell Cytotoxicity Assay [Clinical chemistry]
SCCA	Society of Canadian Cine Amateurs
SCCA	Society of Company and Commercial Accountants [Edgbaston, Birmingham, England] (EAIO)
SCCA	Somali Cat Club of America
SCCA	Sound & Communications Contractors' Association (BUAC)
SCCA	Southeastern Cottonseed Crushers Association (EA)
SCCA	Specification Compliance Concept Agreements (MCD)
SCCA	Sports Car Club of America (EA)
SCCa	Squamous-Cell Carcinoma [Oncology] (DAVI)
SCCA	Squamous Cell Carcinoma [Medicine] (STED)
SCCA	Subcontract Change Authorization (AAG)
SCCAC	Society for Conceptual and Content Analysis by Computer (EA)
SCC-ACO	Strategic Communications Command Advanced Concepts Office [Army]
SCCAIC	Societe Canadienne pour la Couleur dans les Arts, l'Industrie et la Science (EAIO)
ScCam	Kershaw County Library, Camden, SC [Library symbol] [Library of Congress] (LCLS)
SCCAM	Standing Committee of Consumer Affairs Ministers
ScCap	Security Capital Industrial Trust [Associated Press] (SAG)
SCCAPE	Scottish Council for Commercial, Administrative, and Professional Education (BUAC)
SC Cas	Supreme Court Cases [A publication] (DLA)
ScCB	Baptist College at Charleston, Charleston, SC [Library symbol Library of Congress] (LCLS)
SCCB	Safety Change Control Board (MCD)
SCCB	Site Configuration Control Board [NASA] (NASA)
SCCB	Small-Cell Carcinoma of the Bronchus [Medicine] (DMAA)
SCCB	Software Configuration Control Board (KSC)

SCCB .... South Carolina Cmnty Banc [*NASDAQ symbol*] (TTSB)
SCCB .... South Carolina Community Bancshare [*NASDAQ symbol*] (SAG)
SCCB .... State Contracts Control Board [*New South Wales, Australia*]
SCCBcsh...... South Carolina Community Bancshares, Inc. [*Associated Press*] (SAG)
SCCC .... Chile Chico/Chile Chico [*Chile*] [*ICAO location identifier*] (ICLI)
ScCC .... College of Charleston, Charleston, SC [*Library symbol Library of Congress*] (LCLS)
SCCC .... Satellite Communications Control Centre [*British*]
SCCC .... Scottish Consultative Committee on the Curriculum (BUAC)
SCCC .... Security Communications Control Center (COE)
SCCC .... Shared Contingency Computer Center (MHDI)
SCCC .... Single Channel Communications Controller (NITA)
SCCC .... Skyway Community College Conference (PSS)
SCCC .... Squamous Cell Cervical Carcinoma [*Medicine*] (DMAA)
SCCC .... System Casualty Control Console [*Military*] (CAAL)
SCCCE .... Society of Certified Consumer Credit Executives (EA)
ScCCit......... Citadel, Charleston, SC [*Library symbol Library of Congress*] (LCLS)
SCCD .... Iquique/Los Condores [*Chile*] [*ICAO location identifier*] (ICLI)
SCCDEST .... Steering Committee on Crossborder Data Exchange in Science and Technology (NITA)
ScCDHHi...... Dalcho Historical Society of the Episcopal Diocese of South Carolina, Charleston, SC [*Library symbol Library of Congress*] (LCLS)
ScCDHi .... Dalcho Historical Society of the Episcopal Diocese of South Carolina, Charleston, SC [*Library symbol*] [*Library of Congress*] (LCLS)
SCCE .... Satellite Configuration Control Element (MCD)
SCCE .... School and College Conference on English
SCCE .... Scottish Council for Community Education
SCCE .... Society of Certified Credit Executives [*St. Louis, MO*] (EA)
SCCE .... Staged Combustion Compound Engine [*Automotive engineering*]
SCCEA .... Strategic Communications Command Equipment Applications Directorate [*Army*]
ScCenW....... Central Wesleyan College, Central, SC [*Library symbol*] [*Library of Congress*] (LCLS)
SCCF .... Calama/El Loa [*Chile*] [*ICAO location identifier*] (ICLI)
ScCF .... Charleston County Library, Charleston, SC [*Library symbol Library of Congress*] (LCLS)
SCCF .... Satellite Communication Control Facility
SCCF .... Scottish Conservative Christian Forum (BUAC)
SCCF .... Security Clearance Case Files [*Military*] (AABC)
SCCF .... Service Center Control File [*IRS*]
SCCFF .... Second Check Character Flip-Flop [*Computer science*] (MHDB)
SCCG .... Station Communications Control Group [*Ground Communications Facility, NASA*]
ScCh .... Chester County Library, Chester, SC [*Library symbol*] [*Library of Congress*] (LCLS)
SCCH .... Chillan/Gral, Bernardo O'Higgins [*Chile*] [*ICAO location identifier*] (ICLI)
SCCH .... Society of Cinema Collectors and Historians (EA)
SCCH .... Standard Cubic Centimeters per Hour (MCD)
SCCH .... Sternocostoclavicular Hyperostosis [*Medicine*] (DMAA)
ScChf.......... Chesterfield County Library, Chesterfield, SC [*Library symbol*] [*Library of Congress*] (LCLS)
SCCHO........ Sternocostoclavicular Hyperostosis [*Medicine*] (DMAA)
ScChwC ...... Chesterfield-Marlboro Technical College, Cheraw, SC [*Library symbol Library of Congress*] (LCLS)
SCCI........... Punta Arenas/Internacional Carlos Ibanez Del Campo [*Chile*] [*ICAO location identifier*] (ICLI)
SCCI........... Smurf Collectors' Club International (EA)
SCC(I).......... Special Coordination Committee (Intelligence) (MCD)
SCCI........... Supreme Court of Christmas Island [*Australia*]
SCCJ .... Supreme Court of Canada Judgements [*Canada Department of Justice*] [*Information service or system*] (CRD)
SCC(K)I........ Supreme Court of Cocos (Keeling) Islands [*Australia*]
SCCL.......... Safety Compliance Certification Label [*Automotive engineering*]
SCCL.......... Scottish Council for Civil Liberties (DI)
SCCL.......... Scottish Council of Civil Liberties (DBA)
SCCL.......... Small Cell (Anaplastic) Carcinoma of the Lung [*Oncology*]
SCCL.......... Supply Catalog Components List [*Military*]
ScCleU........ Clemson University, Clemson, SC [*Library symbol Library of Congress*] (LCLS)
ScCliJ .... Jacobs Library, Clinton, SC [*Library symbol Library of Congress Obsolete*] (LCLS)
ScCIP.......... Presbyterian College, Clinton, SC [*Library symbol Library of Congress*] (LCLS)
ScCITO........ Thornwell Orphanage, Clinton, SC [*Library symbol Library of Congress*] (LCLS)
ScCM .... Medical University of South Carolina, Charleston, SC [*Library symbol Library of Congress*] (LCLS)
SCCM.......... Sertoli-Cell Culture Medium [*Clinical chemistry*]
SCCM.......... Short Circuit Conductance Matrix (PDAA)
SCCM.......... Single Chamber Controllable Motor (MCD)
SCCM.......... Society of Critical Care Medicine (EA)
SCCM.......... Standard Cubic Centimeters per Minute (NASA)
sccm.......... Standard Cubic Centimeters per Minute (NAKS)
SCCM.......... Standing Committee on Church Music (EA)
SCCML........ Scottish Central Committee on Modern Languages (AIE)
ScCMP........ Middleton Place, Charleston, SC [*Library symbol Library of Congress*] (LCLS)
ScCMu .... Charleston Museum Library, Charleston, SC [*Library symbol Library of Congress*] (LCLS)
SCCN .... Subcontract [*or Subcontractor*] Change Notice (KSC)
SCCNC .... Society of Critical Care Nurses of Canada
SCC NR........ Special Cryptologic Control Number (DNAB)
SCC(NSW) ... State Chamber of Commerce [*New South Wales*] [*Australia*]

SCCO .... Security Classification Control Officer [*Military*]
SCCO .... Steel-Cored Copper (IAA)
ScCoA......... Allen University, Columbia, SC [*Library symbol*] [*Library of Congress*] (LCLS)
ScCoAH........ South Carolina Department of Archives and History, Columbia, SC [*Library symbol Library of Congress*] (LCLS)
ScCoB......... Benedict College, Columbia, SC [*Library symbol Library of Congress*] (LCLS)
ScCoB......... Columbia Bible College, Columbia, SC [*Library symbol Library of Congress*] (LCLS)
ScCoBC........ Columbia Bible College, Columbia, SC [*Library symbol*] [*Library of Congress*] (LCLS)
ScCoC......... Columbia College, Columbia, SC [*Library symbol Library of Congress*] (LCLS)
SCCOC......... Steel-Cored Copper Conductor (IAA)
SC Code ...... Code of Laws of South Carolina [*A publication*] (DLA)
SC Code Ann... Code of Laws of South Carolina, Annotated [*A publication*] (DLA)
ScCoGS........ Church of Jesus Christ of Latter-Day Saints, Genealogical Society Library, Columbia Branch, Columbia, SC [*Library symbol Library of Congress*] (LCLS)
ScCoHE........ South Carolina Department of Health and Environmental Control, Columbia, SC [*Library symbol*] [*Library of Congress*] (LCLS)
ScCoM......... Midlands Technical College, Columbia, SC [*Library symbol*] [*Library of Congress*] (LCLS)
ScCoM-A...... Midland Technical College, Airport Campus, Library and Information Center, Columbia, SC [*Library symbol*] [*Library of Congress*] (LCLS)
ScCoM-B...... Midlands Technical College, Beltline Campus, Columbia, SC [*Library symbol*] [*Library of Congress*] (LCLS)
ScCon .... Horry County Memorial Library, Conway, SC [*Library symbol Library of Congress*] (LCLS)
ScConH........ Horry-Georgetown Technical College, Conway, SC [*Library symbol*] [*Library of Congress*] (LCLS)
ScCoR......... Richland County Library, Columbia, SC [*Library symbol Library of Congress*] (LCLS)
Sc Costs ..... Scott's ABC Guide to Costs [*2nd ed.*] [*1910*] [*A publication*] (DLA)
ScCoT......... Lutheran Theological Southern Seminary, Columbia, SC [*Library symbol Library of Congress*] (LCLS)
ScCoV......... United States Veterans Administration Hospital, Columbia, SC [*Library symbol Library of Congress*] (LCLS)
SCCP .... Sabah Chinese Consolidated Party [*Malaysia*] [*Political party*] (FEA)
SCCP .... Signaling Connection Control Part [*Telecommunications*]
SCCP .... Systems Change Control Procedure [*Social Security Administration*]
SCCPG .... Satellite Communications Contingency Planning Group (NATG)
ScCPT......... Security Capital Pacific Trust [*Associated Press*] (SAG)
SCC(Q)........ State Chamber of Commerce [*Queensland*] [*Australia*]
SCCR .... Society for Cross-Cultural Research (EA)
SCCR .... Stanford Center for Chicano Research [*Stanford University*] [*Research center*] (RCD)
SCCR .... Subcontractor Change Request (MCD)
ScCRC......... Charleston Diocesan Archives, Roman Catholic Church, Charleston, SC [*Library symbol Library of Congress*] (LCLS)
SCCRI .... Swedish Cement and Concrete Research Institute (MCD)
SCCS .... Satellite Communications Control System (MCD)
SCCS .... Secondary Chemical Control System [*Nuclear energy*] (NRCH)
SCCS .... Sodium Chemistry Control System [*Westinghouse Corp.*] (IEEE)
SCCS .... Software Controlled Communication Services (MCD)
SCCS .... Source Code Control System [*Computer science*]
SCCS .... Souvenir Card Collectors Society (EA)
SCCS .... Souvenir China Collectors Society (EA)
SCCS .... Special Consultative Committee on Security [*OAS*]
SCCS .... Standard Commodity Classification System (NG)
SCCS .... Standard Cross-Cultural Sample [*Human Relations Area Files*] [*Information retrieval*]
SCCS .... Standard Cubic Centimeters per Second (NASA)
SCCS .... Standby Core Cooling System [*Nuclear energy*] (NRCH)
SCCS .... Standing Committee of Caribbean Statisticians (BUAC)
SCCS .... Straight Cut Control System (IAA)
SCCS .... STRICOM [*Strike Command*] Command and Control System [*Army*] (AABC)
SCCS .... Switching Control Center System [*Telecommunications*] (TEL)
SCCSA .... Sports Car Collectors Society of America [*Defunct*] (EA)
SCCSIAMRNASNPWPPPPPP... Select Committee to Conduct a Study and Investigation of All Matters Relating to the Need for Adequate Supplies of Newsprint, Printing and Wrapping Paper, Paper Products, Paper, Pulp and Plywood [*US Congress*] [*World War II*]
ScCSM......... Old Slave Mart Museum, Charleston, SC [*Library symbol Library of Congress*] (LCLS)
SCCT .... Specialist in Community College Teaching (GAGS)
ScCT .... Trident Technical College, Palmer Campus, Charleston, SC [*Library symbol Library of Congress*] (LCLS)
SCC-TED ..... Strategic Communications Command - Test and Evaluation Directorate [*Army*]
SCCTR .... Standing Committee for Controlled Thermonuclear Research [*Terminated, 1973*] [*AEC*] (EGAO)
SCCTSD .... Society of Catholic College Teachers of Sacred Doctrine [*Later, CTS*] (EA)
SCCU .... Scottish Cross Country Union (DBA)
SCCU .... Single Channel Control Unit
SCCU .... Spacecraft Command Control Unit (KSC)
SCCU .... Specialist Claims Control Unit [*British*]
SCCUK .... Swedish Chamber of Commerce for the United Kingdom (DS)
SCCUS .... Swedish Chamber of Commerce of the United States [*Later, Swedish-American Chamber of Commerce*]

ScCV.......... United States Veterans Administration Hospital, Charleston, SC [*Library symbol Library of Congress*] (LCLS)

SCCVO........ Scottish Council for Community and Voluntary Organisations (BUAC)

SCCW......... Scarritt College for Christian Workers [*Tennessee*]

SCCWRP..... Southern California Coastal Water Research Project (NOAA)

SCCY......... Coyhaique/Teniente Vidal [*Chile*] [*ICAO location identifier*] (ICLI)

SCCZ......... Punta Arenas [*Chile*] [*ICAO location identifier*] (ICLI)

SCD........... Darlington County Library, Darlington, SC [*OCLC symbol*] (OCLC)

ScD........... Doctorat es Sciences [*Doctor of Science*] [*French*] (ASC)

SCD........... Doctor of Commercial Science

ScD........... Doctor of Science (GAGS)

SCD........... Satellite Control Department

SCD........... S-Band Cassegrain Diplexer

SCD........... Schedule (AABC)

SCD........... Schneider Corp. [*Toronto Stock Exchange symbol*]

SCD........... Science Communication Division [*George Washington University Medical Center*] [*Information service or system*] (IID)

Sc D......... Scientiae Doctor [*Doctor of Science*] [*Latin*]

SCD........... Scientific Computer Division [*Army Tank-Automotive Command*]

ScD........... Scintillation Detector (IEEE)

SCD........... Scottish Council of Dance (DBA)

SCD........... Scottish Council on Disability (BUAC)

SCD........... Screen Door

SCD........... Screwed (MDG)

SCD........... Secondary Current Distribution [*Electroplating*]

SCD........... Security Coding Device (NATG)

SCD........... Self-Control Desensitization [*Psychology*] (DHP)

SCD........... Semiconductor Device (IAA)

SCD........... Senile Cognitive Decline [*Medicine*]

SCD........... Senior Citizen Discount

SCD........... Serial Cryptographic Device (MHDB)

SCD........... Service Computation Date [*Military*] (AFM)

SCD........... Service Connected Disability [*Medicine*] (AAMN)

SCD........... Service Control Drawing

SCD........... Servo Chart Drive

SCD........... Ship's Center Display [*Navy*] (NVT)

SCD........... Sickle Cell Disease [*Medicine*]

SCD........... Signal Canceling Device

SCD........... Significant Construction Deficiency [*Nuclear energy*] (NRCH)

SCD........... Simulated Communications Deception [*Army*] (INF)

SCD........... Slovenian Christian Democrats [*Political party*]

SCD........... Society of Craft Designers (EA)

SCD........... Software Conceptual Design [*Computer science*]

SCD........... Soil Conservation District [*Agriculture*]

SCD........... Source Control Document (NASA)

SCD........... Source Control Drawing

SCD........... Space Control Document [*NASA*] (KSC)

SCD........... Specification Control Document [*or Drawing*] [*NASA*] (NASA)

SCD........... Spinal Cord Disease [*Neurology*] (DAVI)

SCD........... Spreading Cortical Depression

SCD........... State Civil Defense

SCD........... Static Column Decode [*Computer science*]

SCD........... Sterile Connection Device [*Medicine*]

SCD........... Stored-Charge Diode (IAA)

SCD........... Strategic Communications Division [*Military*]

SCD........... Streaming Current Detector

SCD........... Structure-Chart Diagramer [*Computer science*]

SCD........... Subacute Combined Degeneration [*of spinal cord*] [*Medicine*]

SCD........... Subcarrier Discriminator

SCD........... Subcontract Deviation

SCD........... Sudden Cardiac Death [*Medicine*]

SCD........... Sudden Coronary Death (MAE)

SCD........... Sulaco [*Honduras*] [*Airport symbol*] (AD)

SCD........... Sulfur Chemiluminescence Detector

SCD........... Supply, Commissary, and Disbursing [*Navy*]

SCD........... Surrey Commercial Dock [*British*]

SCD........... Surveillance Criticality Designator [*DoD*]

SCD........... Sylacauga, AL [*Location identifier FAA*] (FAAL)

SCD........... System Contents Directory [*Computer science*] (MHDB)

SCD........... System Coordination Document

SCD........... Systems, Components, and Displays

ScDa.......... Darlington County Library, Darlington, SC [*Library symbol Library of Congress*] (LCLS)

SCDA.......... Iquique/Gral Diego Aracena [*Chile*] [*ICAO location identifier*] (ICLI)

SCDA.......... Safing, Cool Down, and Decontamination Area [*NASA*] (NASA)

ScDA.......... Scapulodextra Anterior [*A fetal position*] (AAMN)

SCDA.......... Scottish Community Drama Association (BUAC)

SCDA.......... SEATO [*Southeast Asia Treaty Organization*] Central Distribution Agency (NATG)

SCDA.......... Situational Control of Daily Activities

SCDA.......... Small Card Design Automation (IAA)

SCDA.......... Societe Canadienne des Directeurs d'Association [*Formerly, Institute of Canadian Trade Association Executives*] (AC)

SCDA.......... Sound & Communications Distributors Association (BUAC)

SCDA.......... Standing Conference on Drugs Abuse (WDAA)

SCDA.......... Sullivans Cove Development Authority [*Tasmania, Australia*]

SCDAA........ Sickle Cell Disease Association of America [*Formerly the National Association for Sickle Cell Disease (NASCD)*] (PAZ)

SCDAA........ Soil Conservation and Domestic Allotment Act (COE)

SCDAP........ Severe Core Damage Analysis Package [*Nuclear energy*] (NRCH)

SCDAuto...... Sub Carrier Demodulation, Automatic (PDAA)

SCDC.......... Schools Computer Development Centre (AIE)

SCDC.......... Scottish Cooperative Development Committee

SCDC.......... Service Coding and Data Collection (AAG)

SCDC.......... Single Commutation Direct Current (IAA)

SCDC.......... Societe Canadienne de Droit Canonique (AC)

SCDC.......... Societe des Comptables de Direction au Canada [*Society of Management Accountants of Canada - SMAC*]

SCDC.......... Source Coding and Data Collection

SCDC.......... Strategic Concepts Development Center [*National Defense University*]

SCDC.......... Supreme Court Reports, District of Columbia [*A publication*] (DLA)

SCDC.......... System Control Distribution Computer (MHDB)

SCDCNS....... Supreme Court Reports, District of Columbia, New Series [*A publication*] (DLA)

SCDCU........ Section Chief, Display Control Unit [*Army*]

SC/DDS........ Sensor Control/Data Display Set (MCD)

SCDE.......... School, College, Department of Education (AEE)

ScDeTC....... Denmark Technical College, Denmark, SC [*Library symbol*] [*Library of Congress*] (LCLS)

ScDeV......... Voorhees College, Denmark, SC [*Library symbol Library of Congress*] (LCLS)

SCDF.......... Skin Condition Data Form [*Medicine*] (DMAA)

SCDFGNY .... Sickle Cell Disease Foundation of Greater New York (EA)

Sc D Govt... Doctor of Science in Government

SCDGX........ Scudder Fds: Growth & Inc. [*Mutual fund ticker symbol*] (SG)

SCDH.......... Supreme Council for the Defence of the Homeland [*Afghanistan*] (BUAC)

SCDHEC....... South Carolina Department of Health and Environmental Control (DOGT)

SCDI.......... Scottish Council of Development and Industry (DI)

SCDI.......... Serious Chemical Distribution Incident

SCDI.......... Short Children's Depression Inventory [*Psychology*]

SC Dig....... Cassel's Supreme Court Digest [*Canada*] [*A publication*] (DLA)

Sc D in Ed... Doctor of Science in Education

Sc D in Hyg... Doctor of Science in Hygiene

SC Div Bad... Second Class Diver Badge [*Military decoration*]

SCDL.......... Saturated Current Demand Logic

SCDL.......... Ship Configuration Detail List [*Navy*]

SCDL.......... Stabilized Carbon Dioxide LASER

SCDL.......... Surveillance and Control Data Link [*Military*]

SCDM.......... Solar Corona Diagnostic Mission [*NASA*] (SSD)

Sc D (Med)... Doctor of Medical Science

SCDMR........ Steam-Cooled Deuteriated Water-Moderated Reactor [*Nuclear energy*]

ScdNE......... Scudder New Europe Fund [*Associated Press*] (SAG)

SCD OC of SA... Staff Communications Division, Office, Chief of Staff, Army (AABC)

SCD OCSA ... Staff Communications Division, Office, Chief of Staff, Army (AABC)

Sc DP......... Right Scapuloposterior Position [*of the fetus*] [*Obstetrics*]

ScDP.......... Scapulodextra Posterior [*A fetal position*] (AAMN)

SCDP.......... Sedimentary Chlorophyll Degradation Product [*Paleontology*]

SCDP.......... Simulation Control Data Package [*NASA*] (NASA)

SCDP.......... Slovak Christian Democratic Party [*Political party*] (BUAC)

SCDP.......... Society of Certified Data Processors [*AICCP*] [*Superseded by*] (EA)

SCDP.......... Southern Cooperative Development Program [*Sponsored by Southern Consumers Education Foundation*]

SCDP.......... Steel Cadmium Plated

SCDR.......... Screwdriver (MSA)

SCDR.......... Seller Critical Design Review [*NASA*] (NASA)

SCDR.......... Shuttle Critical Design Review [*NASA*] (NASA)

SCDR.......... Software Critical Design Review [*NASA*] (NASA)

SCDR.......... Subcontractor Critical Design Review [*NASA*]

SCDR.......... Subsystem Controller Definition Record [*Computer science*] (IBMDP)

SCDRL......... Subcontractor Data Requirements List (DNAB)

SCDS.......... Scan Converter Display System (MCD)

SCDS.......... Sensor Communication and Display System (MCD)

SCDS.......... Shipboard Chaff Decoy System [*Navy*]

SCDS.......... Signal Circuits Design Section

SCDS.......... Staff of Chief of Defence Staff [*British*]

SCDSB......... Suppressed Carrier Double Sideband [*Transmission*] (IAA)

SCDSD........ Scientific Clearinghouse and Documentation Services Division [*National Science and Technology Authority*] [*Information service or system*] (IID)

SCD (St V)... Supreme Court Decisions (St. Vincent) [*1928-36*] [*A publication*] (DLA)

SCDU.......... Signal Conditioning and Display Unit [*NASA*] (NASA)

ScDunG........ W.R. Grace & Co., Cryovac Division Technical Library, Duncan, SC [*Library symbol*] [*Library of Congress*] (LCLS)

SCDUX........ Scudder Fds: Large Co. Value [*Mutual fund ticker symbol*] (SG)

SCDW.......... Surface Charge Density Wave [*Physics*]

ScDwE......... Erskine College, Due West, SC [*Library symbol Library of Congress*] (LCLS)

ScDwE-T..... Erskine College, Erskine Theological Seminary, Due West, SC [*Library symbol Library of Congress*] (LCLS)

SCDWG....... System Concept Development Working Group

ScE........... Edgefield County Library, Edgefield, SC [*Library symbol Library of Congress*] (LCLS)

SCE........... Saturated Calomel Electrode [*Electrochemistry*]

SCE........... Scan Conversion Equipment [*Television*]

SCE........... SCEcorp [*NYSE symbol*] (SAG)

SCE........... Schedule Compliance-Evaluation [*Polaris*]

SCE........... Schellex Gold [*Vancouver Stock Exchange symbol*]

SCE........... Schlegeis [*Austria*] [*Seismograph station code, US Geological Survey*] (SEIS)

SCE........... School of Continuing Education (HGEN)

SCE........... Scottish Certificate of Education

SCE........... Scribe Ezra [*Freemasonry*]

SCE........... Secondary Chemical Equilibria [*Chromatography*]

SCE........... Secretory Carcinoma of Endometrium

SCE............ Select Cases Relating to Evidence (Strange) [*A publication*] (DLA)
SCE............ Selection Control Element
SCE............ Sentence Combining Exercise [*Education*] (EDAC)
SCE............ Separated Career Employee
SCE............ Service Checkout Equipment (IAA)
SCE............ Service Cryptologic Elements [*Army*]
SCE............ Short Channel Effect (IAA)
SCE............ Siberia Commodity Exchange [*Russian Federation*] (EY)
SCE............ Signal Conditioning Equipment
SCE............ Signal Conversion Equipment [*Telecommunications*]
SCE............ Signal Conversion Equivalent (NITA)
SCE............ Significant Combat Equipment [*Army*]
SCE............ Single-Charge Exchange [*Physics*] (OA)
SCE............ Single Cotton-Covered Enameled [*Wire insulation*] (DEN)
sce............ Single Cotton Enameled (IDOE)
SCE............ Single Cycle Execute
SCE............ Sister Chromatic Exchange Analysis (DAVI)
SCE............ Sister Chromatid Exchange [*Cytology*]
SCE............ Situationally Caused Error
SCE............ Sky Care Ltd. [*New Zealand*] [*ICAO designator*] (FAAC)
SCE............ Slope-Clearing Events [*Geology*]
SCE............ Small Current Element
SCE............ Societe Canadienne d'Esthetique [*Canadian Society for Aesthetics - CSAC*]
SCE............ Society for Clinical Ecology [*Later, AAEM*] (EA)
SCE............ Society for Creative Ethics [*Later, SPC*] (EA)
SCE............ Society of Carbide Engineers [*Later, SCTE*] (EA)
SCE............ Society of Chemical Engineers [*Japan*] (BUAC)
SCE............ Society of Christian Engineers (EA)
SCE............ Society of Christian Ethics (EA)
SCE............ Society of Computational Economics (BUAC)
SCE............ Software Capability Evaluation (RDA)
SCE............ Solar Corona Explorer [*Project*] [*NASA*]
SCE............ Solder Circuit Etch
SCE............ Source (MSA)
SCE............ Southern California Edison Co. [*AMEX symbol*] (SAG)
SCE............ Space Cabin Environment [*Skylab*] [*NASA*]
SCE............ Spacecraft Command Encoder (MCD)
SCE............ Special Conditioning Equipment
SCE............ Spectrum Communications & Electronics Corp. [*Telecommunications service*] (TSSD)
SCE............ Stabilization Control Electronics
SCE............ Staff Civil Engineer [*Military*] (DNAB)
SCE............ Stage Calibration Equipment (SAA)
SCE............ Standard Calomel Electrode
SCE............ Standard Card Enclosure [*Business term*] (MHDI)
SCE............ Standard Communication Environment (DOMA)
SCE............ State College [*Pennsylvania*] [*Airport symbol*] (OAG)
SCE............ State College, PA [*Location identifier FAA*] (FAAL)
SCE............ Station Cable Equalizer (IAA)
SCE............ Stored Controlled Energy
SCE............ St. Petersburg Commodity Exchange [*Russian Federation*] (EY)
SCE............ Stratified-Charge Engine [*Auto engine*]
SCE............ Supercritical Extract [*Separation technology*]
SCE............ Superintending Civil Engineer [*British*]
SCE............ United States Air Force, Armament Laboratory, Technical Library, Eglin AFB, FL [*OCLC symbol*] (OCLC)
ScEA............ John R. Abney Collection, Edgefield County Library, Edgefield, SC [*Library symbol Library of Congress*] (LCLS)
ScEa............ Pickens County Library, Easley, SC [*Library symbol Library of Congress*] (LCLS)
SCEA............ Scottish Civic Entertainment Association (BUAC)
SCEA............ Service Children's Education Authority [*Ministry of Defence*] [*British*]
SCEA............ Side Cutting Edge Angle (IAA)
SCEA............ Signal Conditioning Electronics Assembly [*NASA*] (NAKS)
SCEA............ Societe Canadienne d'Education par l'Art (AC)
SCEA............ Society of Communications Engineers and Analysts
SCEA............ Society of Cost Estimating and Analysis (EA)
SCE&G........ South Carolina Electric & Gas Co. (EFIS)
SCE & PWD... Staff Civil Engineer and Public Works Department (DNAB)
SCEAR........ Scientific Committee on the Effects of Atomic Radiation
SCEB............ SHAPE [*Supreme Headquarters Allied Powers Europe*] Communications Electronics Board [*NATO*] (NATG)
SCEB............ Societe Canadienne des Etudes Bibliques [*Canadian Society of Biblical Studies - CSBS*]
SCEB............ Syndicat Canadien des Employes de Bureau [*Canadian Office Employees Union - COEU*]
SCEC............ Scottish Community Education Council (EAIO)
SCEC............ Societe Canadienne des Eleveurs de Chevres
SCEC............ Societe Canadienne des Etudes Classiques [*Classical Association of Canada - CAC*]
SCEC............ Southern California Earthquake Center
SCEC............ Spaceborne Computer Engineering Conference (MCD)
SCEC............ Student Council for Exceptional Children (AEBS)
SCEC............ Sunshine Coast Environment Council (BUAC)
SCECC............ Societe Canadienne pour l'Etude Comparee des Civilisations [*Canadian Society for the Comparative Study of Civilisations - CSCSC*]
SCECI............ Societe Canadienne d'Education Comparee et Internationale
SCEcp............ SCEcorp [*Formerly, Southern California Edison Co.*] [*Associated Press*] (SAG)
SCECSAL..... Standing Conference of Eastern, Central, and Southern African Librarians (BUAC)
SCED............ Schedule (IAA)
SCEd............ Southern California Edison Co. [*Associated Press*] (SAG)

SCED........... Standing Conference on Education Development (AIE)
SCEd44........ Southern California Edison Co. [*Associated Press*] (SAG)
Sc Ed D....... Doctor of Science in Education
SCEDS......... Societe Canadienne d'Etude du Dix-Huitieme Siecle (AC)
SCEE........... Societe Canadienne d'Etudes Ethniques (AC)
SCEE........... Societe Canadienne pour l'Etude de l'Education [*Canadian Society for the Study of Education - CSSE*]
SCEE........... Southern Coalition for Educational Equity (EA)
SCEE........... Student Committee for Economic Education (EA)
SCEEB......... Scottish Certificate of Education Examination Board
SCEEE......... Southeastern Center for Electrical Engineering Education [*Air Force*]
SCEERR....... Sacra Congregatio Episcoporum et Regularium [*Sacred Congregation of Bishops and Regulars*] [*Latin*]
SCEES......... Service Central des Enquetes et Etudes Statistiques [*Central Service for Statistical Inquiries and Studies*] [*Ministry of Agriculture Paris, France*]
SCEES......... Societe Canadienne pour l'Etude de l'Enseignement Superieur [*Canadian Society for the Study of Higher Education - CSSHE*]
SCEET......... Support Concept Economic Evaluation Technique (MCD)
SCEF........... Isla Rey Jorge/Centro Meteorologico Antartico Presidente Frei [*Chile*] [*ICAO location identifier*] (ICLI)
SCEF........... Southern Conference Educational Fund (EA)
SC/EFC....... Spoiler Control/Elevator Feel Computer (MCD)
SC/EFC CP... SC/EFC [*Spoiler Control/Elevator Feel Computer*] Control Panel (MCD)
SCEFS......... Spoiler Control Elevator Feel System (MCD)
SCEH.......... Society for Clinical and Experimental Hypnosis (EA)
ScEHi.......... Edgefield County Genealogical and Historical Society, Edgefield, SC [*Library symbol*] [*Library of Congress*] (LCLS)
SCEI........... Safe Car Educational Institute
SCEI........... Serial Carry Enable Input (IAA)
SCEI........... Societe Canadienne pour les Etudes Italiennes [*Canadian Society for Italian Studies - CSIS*]
SCEI........... Special Committee on Environmental Information [*Special Libraries Association*]
SCEIBF....... Standing Conference for Europe of the International Basketball Federation (EAIO)
SCEIL......... Service Ceiling
SCEIO......... Societe Canadienne pour Etudes d'Intelligence par Ordinateur
SCEIU......... Standing Conference on Education for International Understanding [*British*] (DBA)
SCEKS........ Spectrum Clear Except Known Signals (MUGU)
SCEL.......... Santiago/Internacional Arturo Merino Benitez [*Chile*] [*ICAO location identifier*] (ICLI)
scel........... Scellino [*Shilling*] [*Monetary unit*] [*Italian*]
SCEL.......... Signal Corps Engineering Laboratories [*Obsolete Army*]
SCEL.......... Small Components Evaluation Loop [*Nuclear energy*] (NRCH)
SCEL.......... Standing Committee on Education in Librarianship
SCELBAL..... Scientific Elementary Basic Language [*1963*] [*Computer science*] (CSR)
SCELO........ State Committee for the Establishment of Law and Order [*Burma*] (BUAC)
SCEM.......... Santiago/Arturo Merino Benitez (Edificio Direccion Meteorologica) [*Chile*] [*ICAO location identifier*] (ICLI)
SCEME........ Scottish Companies Exporting to the Middle East [*An association*] (BUAC)
SCEMSC...... Standing Conference of Ethnic Minority Senior Citizens (BUAC)
SCEN.......... Santiago/Edificio Navegacion Aerea Arturo Merino Benitez [*Chile*] [*ICAO location identifier*] (ICLI)
SCEN.......... Societe Canadienne pour l'Etude des Noms [*Canadian Society for the Study of Names - CSSN*]
SCEN.......... South Central
SCENE........ Studies of Coastal and Estuarine Environments [*National Oceanic and Atmospheric Administration*] (MSC)
SCENIC....... Scientific Engineering Information Center (KSC)
SCENRUS.... Senate Committee on Energy and Natural Resources of the United States (COE)
SCEO.......... Satellite Control Engineering Office (IAA)
SCEO.......... Scottish Centre for Education Overseas (AIE)
SCEO.......... Senior Chief Executive Officer [*Civil Service*] [*British*]
SCEO.......... Station Construction Engineering Officer
SCEP.......... Sandwich Counterelectrophoresis [*Medicine*] (DMAA)
SCEP.......... Secure Communications Equipment Program [*Air Force*] (CET)
SCEP.......... Significant Criminal Enforcement Project [*Bureau of Alcohol, Tobacco, and Firearms*]
SCEP.......... Societe Canadienne d'Enseignement Postscolaire
SCEP.......... Special Committee on Antarctic Research [*International Council of Scientific Unions*] (USDC)
SCEP.......... Spinal Cord Evoked Potential [*Medicine*] (DMAA)
SCEP.......... Study of Critical Environmental Problems [*MIT*]
SCEP.......... Syndicat Canadien des Communications, de l'Energie et du Papier (AC)
SCEPC........ Senior Civil Emergency Planning Committee [*NATO*] (NATG)
SCEPrB....... South'n Cal Ed 4.08% Pfd [*AMEX symbol*] (TTSB)
SCEPrC....... South'n Cal Ed 4.24% Pfd [*AMEX symbol*] (TTSB)
SCEPrD....... So'n Cal Ed 4.32% cm Pfd [*AMEX symbol*] (TTSB)
SCEPrE....... South'n Cal Ed 4.78% Pfd [*AMEX symbol*] (TTSB)
SCEPrG....... South'n Cal Ed 5.80% Pfd [*AMEX symbol*] (TTSB)
SCEPrP....... South'n Cal Ed 7.36% Pfd [*AMEX symbol*] (TTSB)
SCEPS........ Solar Cell Electric Power System (RDA)
SCEPS........ Stored Chemical Energy Propulsion System
SCEPS........ Strategic and Corporate Europlanners Society [*Belgium*] (BUAC)
SCEPT........ Syndicat Canadien des Employes Professionnels et Techniques (AC)
SCEPTR....... Suitcase Emergency Procedures Trainer (MCD)
Sceptre....... Sceptre Resources Ltd. [*Associated Press*] (SAG)

SCEPTRE ..... Software-Controlled Electronic-Processing Traffic-Recording Equipment (PDAA)
SCEPTRE ..... System Computerized for Economical Performance, Tracking, Recording and Evaluation [*North Central Airlines*]
SCEPTRE ..... System for Circuit Evaluation and Prediction of Transient Radiation Effect (MCD)
SCEPTRE ..... System for Constant Elevation Precipitation Transmission and Recording
SCEPTRON... Spectral Comparative Pattern Recognizer
SCEPW .... Senate Committee on Environment and Public Works (COE)
SCE.Q .... So Cal Edison 8.375%'QUIDS' [*AMEX symbol*] (TTSB)
SC Eq .... South Carolina Equity Reports [*A publication*] (DLA)
SCER .... Quintero [*Chile*] [*ICAO location identifier*] (ICLI)
SCER .... Sheffield Centre for Environmental Research [*British*] (CB)
SCER .... Societe Canadienne d'Etudes de la Renaissance [*Canadian Society for Renaissance Studies - CSRS*]
SCER .... Societe Canadienne pour l'Etude de la Religion [*Canadian Society for the Study of Religion - CSSR*]
SCER .... Standing Commission on Ecumenical Relations of the Episcopal Church (EA)
SCERA .... Senate Committee on Environment, Recreation, and the Arts (BUAC)
SCERGA ...... Societe Canadienne d'Economie Rurale et Gestion Agricole [*Canadian Agricultural Economics and Farm Management Society - CAEFMS*]
SCERP .... Stratospheric Cruise Emissions Reduction Program (DICI)
SCERT .... System and Computer Evaluation Revision Technique
SCERT .... Systems and Computers Evaluation and Review Technique [*Computer science*]
SCES .... State Cooperative Extension Service
SCES .... Successories, Inc. [*NASDAQ symbol*] (SAG)
SCESB .... State Casual Employees Superannuation Board [*Victoria, Australia*]
SCESOM ...... Service Canadien pour les Etudiants et les Stagiaires d'Outre-Mer
SCESWUN.... Standing Committee on the Economic and Social Work of the United Nations
SCET .... Scottish Council for Educational Technology (IID)
SCET .... Society of Civil Engineering Technicians [*British*] (DBA)
SCET .... Spacecraft Event Time
SCET .... Standing Committee on Education and Training (ACII)
SCETA .... Societe de Controle et d'Exploitation de Transports Auxiliaires [*France*]
SCETT .... Standing Committee for the Education and Training of Teachers in the Public Sector (BUAC)
SCETV .... South Carolina Educational Television [*Columbia*] [*Telecommunications*] (TSSD)
SCEU .... Science and Culture Employees' Union [*Afghanistan*] (BUAC)
SCEU .... Selector Channel Emulation Unit
SCEU .... Selector Channel Emulator Unit (NITA)
SCEWA .... Society for Citizen Education in World Affairs [*Later, CEA*]
SCEZ .... Santiago [*Chile*] [*ICAO location identifier*] (ICLI)
SCF .... Florence County Library, Florence, SC [*OCLC symbol*] (OOLO)
SCF .... Phoenix [*Arizona*] Scottsdale [*Airport symbol*] (OAG)
SCF .... Samoth Capital Corp. [*Toronto Stock Exchange symbol*]
SCF .... Sampled Channel Filter
SCF .... Satellite Control Facility [*Sunnyvale, CA*] [*NASA*]
SCF .... Save the Children Federation (EA)
SCF .... Save the Children Fund [*British*] (EAIO)
SCF .... S-Band Composite Feed
SCF .... Scandinavia Co. [*Formerly, Scandinavia Fund, Inc.*] [*AMEX symbol*] (SPSG)
SCF .... Schedule Control File
SCF .... Schematic Concept Formation
SCF .... Scientific Committee for Food [*European union*]
SCF .... Scientific Computing Facility
SCF .... Scientific Computing Feature (NITA)
SCF .... Secondary Checkpoint File
SCF .... Sectional Center Facility [*First three digits of the ZIP code*] [*US Postal Service*]
SCF .... Sectional Center Facility [*Air Force*] (AFM)
SCF .... Self-Consistent Field [*Quantum mechanics*]
SCF .... Senior Chaplain to the Forces [*British*]
SCF .... Sequential Compatibility Firing [*Aerospace*]
SCF .... Signature Characterization Facility (MCD)
SCF .... Single Catastrophic Failure (AAG)
SCF .... Single Cost Factor
SCF .... Single Crystal Filament
SCF .... Skin Cancer Foundation (EA)
SCF .... Skywings AB [*Sweden ICAO designator*] (FAAC)
SCF .... Slovak Catholic Federation (EA)
SCF .... Small Company Fund [*Phillips and Drew Fund Management*] [*British*]
SCF .... SNAP [*Systems for Nuclear Auxiliary Power*] Critical Facility (NRCH)
SCF .... Sociedad Centroamericana de Farmacologia [*Central American Society of Pharmacology - CASP*] (EAIO)
SCF .... Society of the Compassionate Friends [*Later, TCF*] (EA)
SCF .... Sodium Cleaning Facility [*Nuclear energy*] (NRCH)
SCF .... Solution Crystal Facility (SSD)
SCF .... Spacecraft Checkout Facility
SCF .... Spacecraft Control Facility [*NASA*] (MCD)
SCF .... Spanish Cycling Federation (BUAC)
SCF .... Spherical Cavity Flow
SCF .... Spinning Continuous Filament
SCF .... Spinning Crucible Furnace
SCF .... Standard Cascade Form (IAA)
SCF .... Standard Charge Factor (NASA)
SCF .... Standard Cubic Foot
SCF .... Standing Committee on Fishing (BUAC)

SCF .... Standing Committee on Forestry (BUAC)
SCF .... Station Code File
SCF .... Statistical Collection File (NASA)
SCF .... Steinbeck Center Foundation (EA)
SCF .... Stem Cell Factor [*Genetics*]
SCF .... Stress Concentration Factor (MCD)
SCF .... Subchorionic Fibrin [*Obstetrics*]
SCF .... Sunnyvale Control Facility [*California*] [*NASA*] (NASA)
SCF .... Supercritical Fluid
SCF .... Supercritical Fluid Chromatography (EDCT)
SCF .... Support Carrier Force
SCF .... Switched Capacitor Filter (CIST)
SCF .... System Change Failure (SAA)
SCFA .... Antofagasta/Internacional Cerro Moreno [*Chile*] [*ICAO location identifier*] (ICLI)
SCFA .... Save the Children Fund Australia [*An association*] (BUAC)
SCFA .... Segmented Continuous Flow Analysis [*Analytical chemistry*]
SCFA .... Short-Chain Fatty Acids [*Biochemistry*]
SCFA .... Skin and Cancer Foundation of Australia
SCFA .... Slovak Catholic Federation of America [*Later, SCF*] (EA)
SCFA .... South Carolina Forestry Association (WPI)
SCFB .... Swirling Circulating Fluidized Bed
SCFBAC ...... Scottish Central Fire Brigade's Advisory Council (WDAA)
SCFBC .... Staged-Cascade Fluidized Bed Combustion
SCFBR .... Steam-Cooled Fast Breeder Reactor [*Nuclear energy*]
SCFC .... Southern California Film Circuit [*Library network*]
SCFC .... Steve Cochran Fan Club (EA)
SCFCS .... Standing Committee on the Free Circulation of Scientists [*International Council of Scientific Unions*]
SCFD .... Standard Cubic Feet per Day
S/CFDR .... Survivability/Crash Flight Data Recorder (MCD)
SCFE .... Slipped Capital Femoral Epiphysis [*Orthopedics*] (DAVI)
SCFE .... Supercritical Fluid Extraction [*Also, SFE*] [*Chemical engineering*]
SCFEL .... Standard COMSEC [*Communications Security*] Facility Equipment List
SCFF .... Scotopic Critical Flicker Frequency [*Magnetic environment*]
SCFG .... Stochastic Context-Free Grammar (PDAA)
SCFGVPT .... Southern California Figure-Ground Visual Perception Test
SCFH .... Standard Cubic Feet per Hour (AAG)
SCFI .... Streptococcal Chemotactic Factor Inhibitor [*Immunochemistry*]
SCFIX .... Seligman Capital Cl.A [*Mutual fund ticker symbol*] (SG)
ScFl .... Florence County Library, Florence, SC [*Library symbol Library of Congress*] (LCLS)
SCFL .... Source Coupled FET Logic (NITA)
ScFIM .... Francis Marion College, Florence, SC [*Library symbol Library of Congress*] (LCLS)
ScFIT .... Florence-Darlington Technical College Library, Florence, SC [*Library symbol Library of Congress*] (LCLS)
SCFM .... Porvenir/Capitan Fuentes Martinez [*Chile*] [*ICAO location identifier*] (ICLI)
SCFM .... Scanforms, Inc. [*NASDAQ symbol*] (NQ)
SCFM .... Standard Cubic Feet per Minute
SCFM .... Subcarrier Frequency Modulation [*Telecommunications*] (TEL)
SCFMA .... Summer and Casual Furniture Manufacturers Association (EA)
scf/min .... Standard Cubic Feet per Minute (DAVI)
SCFMO .... Self-Consistent Field Molecular Orbital (OA)
SCFP .... Science Career Facilitation Project [*National Science Foundation*]
SCFP .... Syndicat Canadien de la Fonction Publique [*Canadian Union of Public Employees - CUPE*]
SCFPA .... Structural Cement-Fiber Products Association [*Defunct*] (EA)
SCFRS .... Surface Combatant Force Requirements Study [*Navy*] (DOMA)
SCFS .... S-Band Composite Feed System
SCFS .... Slip-Cast-Fused Silica (RDA)
SCFS .... Standard Cubic Feet per Second (AAG)
SCFS .... Subcarrier Frequency Shift (IAA)
SCFSEC .... Standing Committee of French-Speaking Ethnical Communities (EA)
SCFT .... Futaleufu/Futaleufu [*Chile*] [*ICAO location identifier*] (ICLI)
SCFTS .... Small Card Final Test System (SAA)
SCFZ .... Antofagasta [*Chile*] [*ICAO location identifier*] (ICLI)
SCG .... Air Force Geophysics Laboratory Research Library, Hanscom AFB, MA [*OCLC symbol*] (OCLC)
ScG .... Greenville County Library, Greenville, SC [*Library symbol Library of Congress*] (LCLS)
SCG .... SCANA Corp. [*NYSE symbol*] (SPSG)
SCG .... Scientific Computing Group [*University of Toronto*] [*Research center*] (RCD)
SCG .... Scoring (ADA)
SCG .... Screen Cartoonists Guild [*Defunct*] (EA)
SCG .... Search for Common Ground (EA)
SCG .... Security Classification Guide (AFM)
SCG .... Seismocardiography [*Medicine*]
SCG .... Self Changing Gear (DCTA)
SCG .... SEMMS [*Solar Electric Multiple-Mission Spacecraft*] Coordinating Group [*NASA*]
SCG .... Sequential Control Guidance (KSC)
SCG .... Serum Chemistry Graft (MAE)
SCG .... Shipcraft Guild (EA)
SCG .... Sight Current Generator
SCG .... Sigma Science [*Vancouver Stock Exchange symbol*]
SCG .... Sitra Cargo Systems [*Peru*] [*ICAO designator*] (FAAC)
SCG .... Sliding-Coil Gauge (RDA)
SCG .... Social Credit Group [*British*] (DAS)
SCG .... Socialist Campaign Group (BUAC)
SCG .... Societe Canadienne de Geotechnique [*Canadian Geotechnical Society*] (EAIO)

SCG .... Society of the Classic Guitar (EA)
SCG .... Sodium Cromoglycate [*Pharmacology*]
SCG .... Solution Crystal Growth
SCG .... Space and Communications Group [*of General Motors Corp.*]
SCG .... Space Charge Grid
SCG .... Special Consultative Group [*NATO*]
SCG .... Specialist Certificate in Gerontology (GAGS)
SCG .... Specification Control Group (IAA)
SCG .... Standby Diesel Generator (COE)
SCG .... St. Claude [*Guadeloupe*] [*Seismograph station code, US Geological Survey*] (SEIS)
SCG .... Steel Carriers Group [*Later, RDCC*] [*Defunct*] (EA)
SCG .... Stored Cold Gas
SCG .... Supercritical Gas Extraction
SCG .... Superior Cervical Ganglion [*Anatomy*]
ScGa .... Cherokee County Public Library, Gaffney, SC [*Library symbol Library of Congress*] (LCLS)
SCGA .... Sodium-Cooled Graphite Assembly [*Nuclear energy*]
SCGA .... Southern Cotton Ginners Association (EA)
SCGA .... Sugar Cane Growers Association [*Australia*] (BUAC)
Sc Gael........ Scotch Gaelic [*Language*] (BARN)
ScGaL .... Limestone College, Gaffney, SC [*Library symbol Library of Congress*] (LCLS)
SCGB .... Ski Club of Great Britain (DI)
ScGBJ .... Bob Jones University, Greenville, SC [*Library symbol Library of Congress*] (LCLS)
SCGC .... Societe Canadienne de Genie Civil
SCGC .... Society of Carnival Glass Collectors
SCGCh .... Societe Canadienne du Genie Chimique
SCGD .... Specification Control Group Directive (KSC)
SCGDL......... Signal Corps General Development Laboratory [*Obsolete Army*]
SCGE .... Sioux City Grain Exchange (EA)
SCGE .... Societe Canadienne de Genie Electrique
SCGEI .... Societe Canadienne de Genie Electrique et Informatique [*Canadian Society for Electrical and Computer Engineering*] [*Canada*] (EAIO)
ScGeo.......... Georgetown County Memorial Library, Georgetown SC [*Library symbol Library of Congress*] (LCLS)
ScGF........... Furman University, Greenville, SC [*Library symbol Library of Congress*] (LCLS)
SCGGA........ Sonoma County Grape Growers Association (EA)
SCGI .... Small College Goals Inventory [*Test*]
SCGM .... Senior Cook General Mess [*British military*] (DMA)
SCGM .... Societe Canadienne de Genie Mecanique
SCGMB........ Societe Canadienne de Genie Medical et Biologique
SCGN .... SciGenetics, Inc. [*NASDAQ symbol*] (SAG)
SCGO........... Strontium Chromium Gallium Oxide [*Inorganic chemistry*]
SCGP .... Scrabble Crossword Game Players [*Later, NSA*] (EA)
SCGP .... Self-Contained Guidance Package (AAG)
SCGR.......... Societe Canadienne du Genie Rural
SCGRL......... Signal Corps General Research Laboratory [*Military*] (IAA)
ScGrw.......... Abbeville-Greenwood Regional Library, Greenwood, SC [*Library symbol Library of Congress*] (LCLS)
ScGrwL........ Lander College, Greenwood, SC [*Library symbol Library of Congress*] (LCLS)
ScGrwP........ Piedmont Technical College, Greenwood, SC [*Library symbol Library of Congress*] (LCLS)
SCGSA......... Signal Corps Ground Signal Agency [*Military*] (IAA)
SCGSN......... Socialist Campaign Group Supporters Network (BUAC)
SCGSS......... Signal Corps Ground Signal Service [*Obsolete Army*]
SCGSS........ Super-Critical Gas Storage System [*NASA*] (KSC)
SCGT .... Stanford's Compendium of Geography and Travel [*A publication*]
ScGTC.......... Greenville Technical College, Greenville, SC [*Library symbol*] [*Library of Congress*] (LCLS)
SCGZ .... Puerto Williams/Guardia-Marina Zanartu [*Chile*] [*ICAO location identifier*] (ICLI)
SCH .... AFSC Technical Information Center, Washington, DC [*OCLC symbol*] (OCLC)
SCH .... Saudi Consulting House [*Saudi Arabia*] (BUAC)
SCH .... Schedule (AAG)
Sch .... Schedule (ODBW)
SCH .... Schefferville [*Quebec*] [*Seismograph station code, US Geological Survey*] (SEIS)
SCH .... Scheme (ADA)
SCH .... Schenectady, NY [*Location identifier FAA*] (FAAL)
SCH .... Schering [*Italy*] [*Research code symbol*]
SCH .... Schering-Plough Corp. [*Research code symbol*]
SCH .... Schiller [*German poet, 1759-1805*] (ROG)
SCH .... Schilling [*Monetary unit*] [*Austria*]
Sch .... Schist [*Quality of the bottom*] [*Nautical charts*]
SCH .... Schoenaur Rifle
SCH .... Scholar
SCH .... Scholarship
SCH .... Scholium [*Note*] [*Latin*]
SCH .... School (AFM)
sch. .... School (WDAA)
Sch .... School (AL)
SCH .... Schooner
SCH .... Schreiber Resources Ltd. [*Vancouver Stock Exchange symbol*]
SCH .... Schreiner Airways BV [*Netherlands ICAO designator*] (FAAC)
Sch .... Schultz Number
SCH .... Schwab [*Charles*] Corp. [*NYSE symbol*] (SPSG)
SCH .... Search (MCD)
SCH .... Sector Command Headquarters (SAA)
SCH .... Seizures per Circuit per Hour [*Telecommunications*] (TEL)

SCH .... Sequencer Chassis
SCH .... Shelter Complex Headquarters [*Civil Defense*]
SCH .... Sisters of Charity of St. Vincent de Paul, Halifax [*Roman Catholic religious order*]
SCH .... Societe Canadienne d'Hermeneutique [*Canadian Society for Hermeneutics - CSH*]
SCH .... Society for Calligraphy and Handwriting (EA)
SCH .... Society for Colonial History [*Defunct*] (EA)
SCh .... Society of Christ [*Roman Catholic men's religious order*]
sch. .... Society of Christ (TOCD)
SCH .... Society of Classical Homeopathy [*Australia*]
SCH .... Socket Head (AAG)
SCH .... Sole Community Hospital
SCH .... Square Cartridge Heater
SCH .... Store Channel (SAA)
SCH .... Student Contact Hours (EDAC)
SCH .... Student Credit Hours
SCH .... Studia ad Corpus Hellenisticum Novi Testamenti (BJA)
SCh .... Succinylcholine [*Biochemistry*]
SCH .... Supporting Checkout
SCH .... Suprachiasmatic [*Nucleus*] (DB)
SCHA .... Copiapo/Chamonate [*Chile*] [*ICAO location identifier*] (ICLI)
SCHA .... Scottish Catholic Historical Association (BUAC)
SCHA .... St. Croix Hotel and Tourism Association [*Virgin Islands*] (EAIO)
ScHaC .... Coker College, Hartsville, SC [*Library symbol Library of Congress*] (LCLS)
Schalk .... Schalk's Jamaica Reports [*A publication*] (DLA)
Sch & Lef .... Schoales and Lefroy's Irish Chancery Reports [*A publication*] (DLA)
Sch Aq R .... Schultes' Aquatic Rights [*1811*] [*A publication*] (DLA)
Sch Arts...... School Arts [*A publication*] (BRI)
SCHASE....... Steeplechase
SCHAVMED... School of Aviation Medicine [*Later, School of Aerospace Medicine*] (MCD)
Schawk .... Schawk, Inc. [*Formerly, Filtertek Inc.*] [*Associated Press*] (SAG)
SChB........... Small Chemical Businesses [*American Chemical Society*]
Sch Bailm.... Schouler on Bailments [*A publication*] (DLA)
SC-HC........ Scattered-to-Heavy Clouds [*Meteorology*] (DNAB)
SCHC .... Society of the Companions of the Holy Cross (EA)
SCHC .... Southern Christian Conference (PSS)
SCHCR....... Stanford Center for Health Care Research [*Closed, 1978*]
SCHD .... Scheduling
SCHDL .... Schedule (ECII)
Sch Dom Rel... Schouler on Domestic Relations [*A publication*] (DLA)
SCHE .... Scheme (ROG)
SChE .... Serum Cholinesterase [*An enzyme*]
SCHE .... Societe Canadienne de l'Histoire de l'Eglise [*Canadian Society of Church History - CSCH*]
SCHEC .... Societe Canadienne de l'Histoire de l'Eglise Catholique [*Canadian Catholic History Association - CCHA*]
SCHED .... Schedule (KSC)
sched........... Schedule (STED)
SCHED .... Scheduled (NAKS)
SCHEDE....... Schedule (ROG)
Scheib .... Scheib [*Earl*], Inc. [*Associated Press*] (SAG)
Scheif Pr ..... Scheiffer's Practice [*A publication*] (DLA)
SCHEM .... Schematic
Scher........... Scherer's New York Miscellaneous Reports [*22-47*] [*A publication*] (DLA)
Scherer........ Scherer [*R.P.*] Corp. [*Associated Press*] (SAG)
SCHERZ ...... Scherzando [*Playful*] [*Music*]
SchfEx .... Scheffield Explorations [*Associated Press*] (SAG)
SchG.......... Schiedsgericht [*Arbitration Court*] [*German*] (ILCA)
SCHG .... Supercharge
Sch H & W... Schouler on Husband and Wife [*A publication*] (DLA)
ScHI .... South Carolina Historical Society, Charleston, SC [*Library symbol Library of Congress*] (LCLS)
SCHI .... Southern California Horticultural Institute (BUAC)
SCHIS .... Schistocytes [*Hematology*] (DAVI)
SCHISTO...... Schizocyte (STED)
SCHIZ .... Schizocyte (STED)
schiz .... Schizophrenia (STED)
SCHIZ .... Schizophrenia [*Medicine*]
schizo......... Schizophrenia [*Psychology*]
SCHJ........... Societe Canadienne de l'Histoire Juive [*Canadian Jewish Historical Association - CJHS*]
SCHL .... Court of Session Cases, House of Lords [*Scotland*] [*A publication*] (DLA)
SCHL .... Scholastic Corp. [*NASDAQ symbol*] (SAG)
SCHL .... School (WGA)
SC(HL)........ Sessions Cases (House of Lords) [*Legal*] [*British*]
SCHL .... Societe Canadienne d'Hypotheques et de Logement [*Central Mortgage and Housing Corp. - CMHC*]
SCHL .... Subcapsular Hematoma of Liver [*Medicine*] (STED)
SCHLA .... School for Latin America [*Military*] (AFM)
Sch Leg Rec... Schuylkill's Pennsylvania Legal Record [*A publication*] (DLA)
Sch Lib .... School Librarian [*A publication*] (BRI)
Schlmb .... Schlumberger Ltd. [*Associated Press*] (SAG)
SCHLP .... Supracricoid Hemilaryngopharyngectomy (STED)
Sch LR........ Schuylkill's Pennsylvania Legal Record [*A publication*] (DLA)
SCHLS .... Schluszsatz [*Finale*] [*Music*]
SCHLSHIP... Schoolship [*Navy*] (NVT)
SCHLSHP.... Scholarship
SCHLT .... Searchlight (MSA)
Schltzk........ Schlotzskys, Inc. [*Associated Press*] (SAG)

SCHM	International Commission for a History of the Scientific and Cultural Developments of Mankind (BUAC)
SCHM	Schematic (AAG)
schm	Schematic (VRA)
Schm	Schoolmaster [Navy British]
SCHM	Societe Canadienne d'Histoire de la Medecine [Canadian Society for the History of Medicine - CSHM]
SchMau	Schweitzer Mauduit International Inc. [Associated Press] (SAG)
SCHMC	Society of Catering and Hotel Management Consultants [British] (DBA)
Schm Civil Law...	Schmidt's Civil Law of Spain and Mexico [A publication] (DLA)
Schm Exp	Schmitthoff. Export Trade [A publication] (ILCA)
Schmidt Civ Law...	Schmidt's Civil Law of Spain and Mexico [A publication] (DLA)
SCHMILSCIO...	School of Military Sciences Officer [Air Force]
Schmitt	Schmitt Industries, Inc. [Associated Press] (SAG)
Schm LJ	Schmidt's Law Journal [New Orleans] [A publication] (DLA)
SCHMOO.....	Space Cargo Handler and Manipulator for Orbital Operations
SCHMR	Schoolmaster (ROG)
Sch Mus B...	Bachelor of School Music
SCHN	Schnitzer Steel Ind'A' [NASDAQ symbol] (TTSB)
SCHN	Schnitzer Steel Industries, Inc. [NASDAQ symbol] (SAG)
Schnitzr	Schnitzer Steel Industries, Inc. [Associated Press] (SAG)
SCHO	Scholar [or Scholarship] (ROG)
SCHO	Societe Canadienne d'Histoire Orale [Canadian Oral History Association - COHA]
SCHO	Standard Controlled Heteroydne Oscillator
Schoales & L...	Schoales and Lefroy's Irish Chancery Reports [A publication] (DLA)
Schol	Scholar
SCHOL	Scholarship
Schol	Scholia [Classical studies] (OCD)
Schol	Scholiast [Classical studies] (OCD)
SCHOL	Scholium [Note] [Latin] (ROG)
SCHOLAR	Schering-Oriented Literature Analysis and Retrieval System [Schering-Plough Corp.] [Information service or system] (IID)
Schol Bern...	Scholia Bernensia ad Vergilii Bucolica et Georgica [A publication] (OCD)
Schol Bob....	Scholia Bobiensia [Classical studies] (OCD)
ScholCp	Scholastic Corp. [Associated Press] (SAG)
Schol Cruq...	Scholia Cruquiana [Classical studies] (OCD)
Schol Flor Callim...	Scholia Florentina in Callimachum [Classical studies] (OCD)
Schomberg Mar Laws Rhodes...	Schomberg's Treatise on the Maritime Laws of Rhodes [A publication] (DLA)
School Libs Aust...	School Libraries in Australia [A publication]
School L Rep (Nat'l Org on Legal Probs in Educ)...	School Law Reporter. National Organization on Legal Problems in Education [A publication] (DLA)
School of Advanced Studies Rev...	School of Advanced International Studies. Review [A publication] (DLA)
School of LR...	School of Law. Review, Toronto University [Canada] [A publication] (DLA)
Schouler Bailm...	Schouler on Bailments [A publication] (DLA)
Schouler Dom Rel...	Schouler on Domestic Relations [A publication] (DLA)
Schouler Pers Prop...	Schouler on the Law of Personal Property [A publication] (DLA)
Schouler US Hist...	Schouler's History of the United States under the Constitution [A publication] (DLA)
SchP	Ordo Clericorum Regularium Pauperum Matris Dei Scholarum Piarum [Roman Catholic men's religious order]
schp	Piarist Fathers (TOCD)
SchP	Piarist Fathers (TOCD)
SchP	Sisters of the Pious Schools (TOCD)
Sch Per Prop...	Schouler on the Law of Personal Property [A publication] (DLA)
SCHPM	Societe Canadienne d'Histoire et de Philosophie des Mathematiques [Canadian Society for the History and Philosophy of Mathematics - CSHPM]
SCHPS	Societe Canadienne d'Histoire et de Philosophie des Sciences [Canadian Society for the History and Philosophy of Science - CSHPS]
SCHR	Cochrane/Cochrane [Chile] [ICAO location identifier] (ICLI)
SCHR	Scherer Healthcare [NASDAQ symbol] (TTSB)
SCHR	Scherer Healthcare, Inc. [NASDAQ symbol] (CTT)
SCHR	Schooner
SCHR	Societe Canadienne d'Histoire de la Rhetorique [See also CSHR] [Canada]
SCHR	Supervisory Change Relations Test
Sch Reg	Schuylkill's Pennsylvania Register [A publication] (DLA)
SchrHl	Scherer Healthcare, Inc. [Associated Press] (SAG)
SchroAsn	Schroder Asian Growth [Associated Press] (SAG)
SchrPl	Schering-Plough Corp. [Associated Press] (SAG)
SCHRUB	Schmidt Rubin Rifle
SCHS	Salford Centre for Housing Studies (BUAC)
SCHS	School Squadron [Air Force]
SCHS	Scottish Church History Society (EAIO)
SCHS	Small Component Handling System [Nuclear energy] (NRCH)
SCHS	Supreme Court Historical Society (EA)
SCHSIS	South Carolina Handicapped Services Information System (EDAC)
schst	Schist (VRA)
Schuler	Schuler Homes, Inc. [Associated Press] (SAG)
Schuller	Schuller Corp. [Associated Press] (SAG)
Schullr	Schuller Corp. [Associated Press] (SAG)
Schulmn	Schulman [A.], Inc. [Associated Press] (SAG)
Schult	Schult Homes Corp. [Associated Press] (SAG)
Schultz	Schultz Sav-O-Stores, Inc. [Associated Press] (SAG)
Schupo	Schutzpolizist [Policeman] [German]

Schuy Leg Rec (PA)...	Schuylkill's Pennsylvania Legal Record [A publication] (DLA)
Schuyl Legal Rec...	Schuylkill's Pennsylvania Legal Record [A publication] (DLA)
Schuyl Leg Rec...	Schuylkill's Pennsylvania Legal Record [A publication] (DLA)
Schuyl Leg Reg...	Schuylkill's Legal Register [Pennsylvania] [A publication] (ILCA)
Schuy Reg (PA)...	Schuylkill's Pennsylvania Register [A publication] (DLA)
SCHVPT	Southern Counties Historic Vehicle Preservation Trust (BUAC)
Schwab	Schwab [Charles] Corp. [Associated Press] (SAG)
Schwarz Int L...	Schwarzenberger's Manual of International Law [A publication] (DLA)
Schwarz Man Int L...	Schwarzenberger's Manual of International Law [A publication] (ILCA)
Schweiz Jb f Internat Recht...	Schweizerisches Jahrbuch fuer Internationales Recht/Annuaire Suisse de Droit In ternational [Zurich, Switzerland] [A publication] (DLA)
Schweiz Z f Strafrecht...	Schweizerische Zeitschrift fuer Strafrecht/Revue Penale Suisse [Berne, Switzerland] [A publication] (DLA)
SCHWR	Steam-Cooled Heavy-Water Reactor
Schwtz	Schwitzer, Inc. [Associated Press] (SAG)
SCI	Council for the Securities Industry [Levy] [British]
SCI	Sacra Congregatio Indicis [Sacred Congregation of the Index] [Latin]
SCI	Safari Club International (EA)
SCI	San Clemente Island [California] [Seismograph station code, US Geological Survey] (SEIS)
SCI	Sand Collectors International (EAIO)
SCI	Santa Cruz Island (MUGU)
SCI	Savio Club International [Defunct] (EA)
SCI	Scale (ECII)
SCI	Scaleable Coherent Interface [Computer science]
SCI	Schedule-Cost Index (MCD)
SCI	Science (AFM)
Sci	Science [A publication] (BRI)
SCI	Science Citation Index (STED)
SCI	Science Curriculum Improvement [Study] [Education]
SCI	Science of Creative Intelligence [Transcendental meditation]
Sci	Scientific (AL)
SCI	Scientific Attache [Foreign service]
SCI	Scientific Computers, Inc. (MCD)
SCI	SCI Satellite Conferencing International Corp. [Formerly, Valclair Resources, Ltd.] [Vancouver Stock Exchange symbol]
SCI	Seabee Club International (EA)
SCI	Sea Containers Inc. [Steamship] (MHDW)
SCI	Sealable Coherent Interface [Computer science]
SCI	Seamen's Church Institute of New York/New Jersey (EA)
SCI	Secret Compartmented Information (WPI)
SCI	Security Container Institute [Defunct] (EA)
SCI	Selected Configured Item (MCD)
SCI	Seminar Clearinghouse International, Inc. [Information service or system] (IID)
SCI	Sensitive Compartmented Information [Military]
SCI	Sequential Comparison Index [Measures effect of chemical pollution in lakes and streams]
SCI	Serial Communication Interface [Computer science]
SCI	Service Change Information (MCD)
SCI	Service Civil International [International Voluntary Service] [India]
SCI	Service Civil International [Australia]
SCI	SES [Shuttle Engineering System] Cockpit Interface [NASA] (SSD)
SCI	Sexual Communications Inventory [Marital relations test] [Psychology]
SCI	Shapiro Control Inventory [Test] (TMMY)
SCI	Ship Controlled Intercept [RADAR] [Navy]
SCI	Shipping Container Institute
SCI	Shipping Corp. of India (BUAC)
SCI	Shipping Corp. of India Ltd.
SCI	Ship's Capability Impaired [Navy]
SCI	Short Circuit
SCI	Short Crus of Incus (STED)
SCI	Signal Corps Item [Obsolete Army] (NATG)
SCI	Simulation Councils, Inc.
SCI	Single-Channel Interface [Computer science]
SCI	Single Column Inch (ADA)
SCI	Sister Cities International (EA)
SCI	Slot Cell Inserter
SCI	Small Craft Instructor [Red Cross]
SCI	Smoke Curtain Installation [British military] (DMA)
SCI	Societe de Chimie Industrielle (EA)
SCI	Society of Chemical Industries (NADA)
SCI	Society of Chemical Industry (EA)
SCI	Society of Chiropodists in Ireland (BUAC)
SCI	Society of Composers (EA)
SCI	Society of Composers, Inc. (BUAC)
SCI	Society of Computer Intelligence (IAA)
SCI	Society of the Chemical Industry (NADA)
SCI	Soft Cast Iron
SCI	Software Configuration Item [Computer science]
SCI	Source Code Indicator (MCD)
SCI	Southern Cross International [England] (BUAC)
SCI	Special Cargo Airlines [Russian Federation] [ICAO designator] (FAAC)
SCI	Special Compartmented Intelligence [DoD] (MCD)
SCI	Special Control Item [Code]
SCI	Special Customs Invoice
SCI	Specific Case Inventory [Test] [London House, Inc.] (TES)
SCI	Spinal Cord Injury [Medicine]
SCI	Spinal Cord-Insured (MCD)

SCI............ Sponge and Chamois Institute (EA)
SCI............ Staging Connections, Inc. [*Telecommunications service*] (TSSD)
SCI............ Stampe Club International (EA)
SCI............ Steel Construction Institute [*British*] (IRUK)
SCI............ Stein Collectors International (EA)
SCI............ Stem Cell Inhibitor [*Cytology*]
SCI............ Stratospheric Circulation Index [*Geophysics*]
SCI............ Stroke Club International (EA)
SCI............ Structured Clinical Interview
SCI............ Supervisor Call Instruction (IAA)
SCI............ Supervisory Cost Inspector [*Navy*]
SCI............ Surface Charge Imaging (AAEL)
SCI............ Swaythling Club International (BUAC)
SCI............ Swedish Ceramic Institute (BUAC)
sci............ Switch Closure In (NAKS)
SCI............ Switch Closure In (MCD)
SCI............ Switched Collector Impedance [*Electronics*] (OA)
SCI............ System Control Interface
SCIA.......... Signal Corps Intelligence Agency [*Obsolete Army*]
SCIA.......... Simultaneous Converging Instrument Approaches [*FAA*] (TAG)
SCIA.......... Smart Card Industry Association (EA)
SCIA.......... Social Competence Inventory for Adults [*Psychology*]
SCIA.......... Society of Chief Inspectors and Advisers [*British*] (AIE)
SCIA.......... Systems Change Impact Analysis [*Social Security Administration*]
SCIAC........ Southern California Intercollegiate Athletic Conference (PSS)
SCIAF........ Scottish Catholic International Aid Fund (BUAC)
Sci Amer .... Scientific American (MEC)
SCIAPS...... Senate Comprehensive Integrated Automated Printing System
SCIAS........ Society of Chemical Industry, American Section (EA)
SCIAS........ Supreme Council of the Independent Associated Spiritualists [*Defunct*] (EA)
SciAtl......... Scientific-Atlanta, Inc. [*Associated Press*] (SAG)
SCIATS ...... Small Craft Instruction and Training School [*Navy*]
SCIB.......... Ship Characteristics Improvement Board [*Navy*] (DOMA)
SCIB.......... Significant Counterintelligence Briefs (AFM)
SCIBP........ Special Committee for the International Biological Program [*National Research Council*]
SCIBTA ...... Stem Cell Indicated by Transplantation Assay (STED)
SCIC.......... Curico/General Freire [*Chile*] [*ICAO location identifier*] (ICLI)
SCIC.......... Saskatchewan Council for International Cooperation [*Canada*] (BUAC)
SCIC.......... Secretariat des Conferences Intergouvernementales Canadiennes
SCIC.......... Semiconductor Integrated Circuit
SCIC.......... Single-Column Ion Chromatography
SCIC.......... Sisters of Charity of the Immaculate Conception of Ivrea (TOCD)
SCIC.......... Society of Certified Insurance Counselors (NTPA)
SCIC.......... Special Control Item Code
SCICC........ Service Center Internal Computer Code [*Computer science*]
SCICF........ Safari Club International Conservation Fund (EA)
SCICFNDT... Standing Committee for International Cooperation within the Field of Non-Destructive Testing (EA)
SciClone...... SciClone Pharmaceuticals, Inc. [*Associated Press*] (SAG)
SCICLOPS.... Systems Control, Incorporated Computerized Library Operations [*Information service or system*] (IID)
SCICS .... Spinal Cord Injury Care System [*University of Alabama in Birmingham*] [*Research center*] (RCD)
Sci D .... Doctor of Science
SCID .... Scotland's Campaign Against Irresponsible Drivers [*An association*] (BUAC)
SCID .... Severe Combined Immune Deficiency [*Immunology*]
SCID .... Severe Combined Immunodeficiency Disease [*Medicine*] (STED)
SCID .... Small Column Insulated Delays (MCD)
SCID .... Structured Clinical Interview for DSM-III
SCID .... Subcommutator Identification [*NASA*]
SciDCom...... Doctor of Science in Commerce (NADA)
SCIDE .... Servicio Cooperativo Interamericano de Educacion
SciDMet....... Doctor of Science in Metallurgy (NADA)
SCIDNT ...... System Control Incorporated Identification Program [*Navy*]
SCIDS .... Small Container Intermodal Distribution System (PDAA)
SCIDT .... Scottish Country Industries Development Trust (BUAC)
SciDyn........ Science Dynamics Corp. [*Associated Press*] (SAG)
SCIE .... Concepcion/Carriel Sur [*Chile*] [*ICAO location identifier*] (ICLI)
SCIE .... Stolen Children Information Exchange (EA)
SCIEC........ Southern California Industry-Education Council (SAA)
SCIEH .... Scottish Centre for Infection & Environmental Health (WDAA)
SCIENCE ..... Stimulation des Cooperations Internationaux et des Echanges Necessaires aux Chercheurs Europeennes [*Stimulation of International Cooperation and the Necessary Exchanges of European Scientists*] [*EEC*]
SCIENT ...... Scientific
SCIES.......... South China Institute for Environmental Sciences (BUAC)
SCIF........... Congregation of Bethlehemite Religious Women, Daughters of the Sacred Heart (BUAC)
SCIF........... Daughters of the Sacred Heart of Jesus [*Bethlehemite Sisters*] [*Roman Catholic religious order*]
SciF........... Science Foods, Inc. [*Associated Press*] (SAG)
SCIF........... Sound and Communications Industries Federation [*British*] (DBA)
SCIF........... Special Compartmented Intelligence Facility [*DoD*]
SCIF........... Static Column Isoelectric Focusing [*Materials processing*]
SCIF........... Systems Certification and Integration Facility
SCI FA .... Scire Facias [*Make Him Know*] [*Latin*] (LWAP)
Sci Fa ad Dis Deb... Scire Facias ad Disprobandum Debitum [*Latin*] (DLA)
SCIFC.......... Sandy Croft International Fan Club [*Defunct*] (EA)
SCIFC.......... Southern California Intercollegiate Fencing Conference (PSS)
SCI-FI .... Science Fiction [*Also, SF*]

Sci-Fi.......... Science Fiction [*Literary genre*] (WDAA)
SCI Fn .... SCI Finance LLC, Inc. [*Associated Press*] (SAG)
Sci Freedom... Science and Freedom [*A publication*]
SciGen......... SciGenetics, Inc. [*Associated Press*] (SAG)
SciGm......... Scientific Games Holding Corp. [*Associated Press*] (SAG)
SCIGY .... Special Committee for the International Geophysical Year
SCIH .... Societe Canadienne de l'Heritage Industriel (AC)
SCIH .... Societe Canadienne d'Ingenierie Hospitaliere
SCII .... Strong-Campbell Interest Inventory [*Vocational guidance*]
SCIIA .... Sudden Changes in the Integrated Intensity of Atmospherics (PDAA)
SCI-IVS .... SCI-International Voluntary Service (EA)
SCIJ .... Ski-Club International Journalists (BUAC)
SCIL .... Scilicet [*Namely*] [*Legal term Latin*]
SCIL .... Selected Configuration Item List (MCD)
SCIL .... Ship's Construction Item List (MCD)
SCIL .... Soft Consumable Item List
SCIL .... Support Center International Logistics [*Army*]
SCILL .... Southern California Interlibrary Loan Project [*Library network*]
SCILS .... School of Communication, Information, and Library Studies [*Rutgers University*]
SCILT .... Scottish Centre for Information Language Teaching (BUAC)
SCIM .... Congregation des Soeurs Servantes du Coeur Immaculae de Marie [*Servants of the Immaculate Heart of Mary*] [*Good Shepherd Sisters*] [*Roman Catholic religious order*]
SCIM .... Savage's Cognitive Impairment Model
SCIM .... Selected Categories in Microfiche [*National Technical Information Service*]
SCIM .... Silicon Coating by Inverted Meniscus (PDAA)
SCIM .... Speech Communications Index Meter
SCIM .... Standard Cubic Inches per Minute (AAG)
SCiM .... Standard Cubic Inches per Minute (NAKS)
SCIM .... Subject Codes for Intelligence Management (MCD)
SCIMITAR .... System for Countering Interdiction Missiles and Targets RADARs (MCD)
SCIMP .... Selective Cooperative Indexing of Management Periodicals [*Database*] [*European Business School Librarians Group*] [*Information service or system*] (CRD)
SCIMP .... Self-Contained Imaging Micro-Profiler [*Instrumentation*]
SCIMPEX ..... Syndicat des Commercants Importateurs et Exportateurs de l'Ouest African [*Union of Commercial Importers and Exporters of West Africa*]
SCIN .... Self-Canceling Installment Note
SC in Banco... Supreme Court in Banco [*Canada*] [*A publication*] (DLA)
SCINS .... Self-Contained Inertial Navigation System (DOMA)
SCINSET ...... Scottish Colleges In-Service Education of Teachers (AIE)
SCINT .... Scintillator [*Nucleonics*]
SCINX .... Scudder Fds: International [*Mutual fund ticker symbol*] (SG)
SCIO .... Scios, Inc. [*NASDAQ symbol*] (SAG)
SCIO .... Scios Nova, Inc. [*NASDAQ symbol*] (SPSG)
SCIO .... Staff Counterintelligence Officer [*Military*] (NVT)
SCIOP .... Social Competence Inventory for Older Persons [*Psychology*]
Scios .... Scios, Inc. [*Associated Press*] (SAG)
Scios .... Scios Nova, Inc. [*Associated Press*] (SAG)
SciosNov ..... Scios Nova, Inc. [*Associated Press*] (SAG)
SCIOZ .... Scios Inc. Wrrt'D' [*NASDAQ symbol*] (TTSB)
SCIP........... Isla De Pascua/Mataveri [*Easter Island*] [*Chile*] [*ICAO location identifier*] (ICLI)
SCIP........... Sampling Close to the Injector
SCIP........... Scanning for Information Parameters
SCIP........... School Curriculum Industry Partnership [*British*] (ECON)
SCIP........... Schools Council Industry Project [*British*] (DET)
SCIP........... Sea Counterinfiltration Patrol (CINC)
SCIP........... Self-Contained Instrument Package (KSC)
SCIP........... Ship's Capability Impaired for Lack of Parts [*Navy*]
SciP........... Society for Computers in Psychology (BUAC)
SCIP........... Society of Competitor Intelligence Professionals (EA)
SCIP........... Solid Cast Iron Propeller (DS)
SCIP........... Special Crisis Intervention Program (OICC)
SCIP........... Stanford Center for Information Processing [*Stanford University*] [*Later, CIT*]
SCIP........... Stanford Computer Industry Project
SCIP........... System Control Interface Package [*Computer science*] (MHDI)
SCIPHE .... Sparkman Centre for International Public Health Education (AIE)
SCIPIO .... Sales Catalog Index Project Input On-Line [*Cleveland Museum of Art*] [*Information service or system*] (IID)
SCIPMIS ...... Standard Civilian Personnel Management Information System [*Army*]
SCIPP .... Sacrococcygeal to Inferior Pubic Point [*Anatomy*] (MAE)
SCIPP .... Santa Cruz Institute for Particle Physics [*University of California, Santa Cruz*] [*Research center*] (RCD)
SCIPP .... Silicon-Computing Instrument Patch-Programmed (SAA)
SCIPP .... Silicon Computing Instrument, Patch Programmed (IAA)
SCIPPY .... Social Competence Intervention Package for Preschool Youngsters (EDAC)
SCIR .... Society of Cardiovascular and Interventional Radiology (EA)
SCIR .... Subsystem Capability Impact Reporting [*Military*] (NVT)
SCIRA .... Snipe Class International Racing Association (EA)
SCIRA .... Stable Carbon Isotope Ratio Analysis [*For determining material source*]
SCIRA .... State Central Information Reception Agency
SCIRC .... Spinal Cord Injury Research Center [*Ohio State University*] [*Research center*] (RCD)
SCIRI .... Supreme Council of the Islamic Revolution in Iraq (BUAC)
SCIRP .... Semiconductor Infrared Photography (PDAA)
SCIRT .... Supplier Capability Information Retrieval Technique (PDAA)
SCIS........... Safety Containment Isolation System (IEEE)

SCIS	Science Curriculum Improvement Study [Education]
SCIS	SCI Systems [NASDAQ symbol] (TTSB)
SCIS	SCI Systems, Inc. [NASDAQ symbol] (NQ)
SCIS	Scottish Council of Independent Schools (BUAC)
SC Is	Selected Judgments of the Supreme Court of Israel [A publication] (DLA)
SCIS	Spacecraft Interface Specification (MCD)
SCIS	Spinal Cord Injury Service [Medicine]
SCIS	Standard Cubic Inches per Second (NASA)
scis	Standard Cubic Inches per Second (NAKS)
SCIS	Survivable Communications Integration System
SCISCM	Single Carrier Initiated Single Carrier Multiplication (MCD)
SCISD	Signal Corps Intermediate Supply Depot [Army] (IAA)
SCISEARCH	Science Citation Index Search [Institute for Scientific Information] [Philadelphia, PA Bibliographic database]
SCISO	Supreme Court, Individual Slip Opinions
SCISOR	System for Conceptual Information Summarization, Organization, and Retrieval [Software package] (IT)
SCI/SR	Shakaichosa-Kenkyusho Consumer Index Summary Report [Marketing Intelligence Corp.] [Japan Information service or system] (CRD)
SCISR	Societe Canadienne des Infirmieres en Sante Respiratoire (AC)
SCISRS	Sigma Center Information Storage and Retrieval System
SCI Sys	SCI Systems, Inc. [Associated Press] (SAG)
SCIT	Small Craft Instructor Trainer [Red Cross]
SCIT	Smaller Companies International Trust [British]
SCIT	Special Commissions of Income Tax [British]
SCIT	Standard Change Integration and Tracking (NASA)
SCIT	Standardization Control of Industry Quality Tools [Military] (INF)
SCIT	Storm Cell Identification and Tracking [Algorithm] (USDC)
SCIT	Subcommittee on Interzonal Trade [Allied German Occupation Forces]
SCI/TAP	Sister Cities International Municipal and Technical Cooperation Program (BUAC)
SciTch	Scientific Technology, Inc. [Associated Press] (SAG)
SCITEC	[The] Association of the Scientific, Engineering, and Technological Community of Canada
SciTech	SciTech Book News [A publication] (BRI)
SCITEC-PAC	Science and Technology Political Action Committee (EA)
SCITEF	Software and Interoperability Test Facility [Fort Huachuca, AZ] [United States Army Electronic Proving Ground] (GRD)
Scitex	Scitex Corp. Ltd. [Associated Press] (SAG)
SCITT	School-Centred Initial Teacher Training [British] (DET)
SCIU	SDPC [Shuttle Data Processing Complex] Configuration/Isolation Unit [NASA]
SCIU	Selector Control Interface Unit (MCD)
SCiU	Selector Control Interface Unit (NAKS)
SCiU	Spacecraft Interface Unit [NASA] (NAKS)
SCIU	Spacecraft Interface Unit (NASA)
SCI-USA	Service Civil International - United States of America (FA)
CCIV	Society of Chemical Industry of Victoria [Australia] (BUAC)
SCIV	Subclavian Intravenous Injection [Medicine]
SCIV	Subcutaneous Intravenous [Medicine] (DMAA)
SCIVU	Scientific Council of the International Vegetarian Union (BUAC)
SCIWF	Synthesis Contor of the Institute for Wholistic Education (EA)
SCIX	Scitex Corp. Ltd. [NASDAQ symbol] (NQ)
SCIX	Signal Conditioning Index (ECII)
SCIXF	Scitex Corp. Ord [NASDAQ symbol] (TTSB)
SCIZ	Isla De Pascua [Easter Island] [Chile] [ICAO location identifier] (ICLI)
scj	Congregation of the Priests of the Sacred Heart of Jesus (TOCD)
SCJ	Congregatio Sacerdotum a Corde Jesu [Congregation of the Priests of the Sacred Heart of Jesus] [Roman Catholic religious order]
SC J	Nebraska Supreme Court Journal [A publication] (DLA)
SCJ	Scanjet AB [Sweden ICAO designator] (FAAC)
SCJ	Science Council of Japan (MCD)
SCJ	Sclerocorneal Junction [Ophthalmology] (DAVI)
SCJ	Section of Criminal Justice [American Bar Association] (EA)
SC(J)	Sessions Cases (Judiciary Reports) [Legal] [British]
SCJ	Shaped Charge Jet (MCD)
SCJ	Sisters of the Child Jesus [Roman Catholic religious order]
SCJ	Society for Collegiate Journalists (EA)
SCJ	Spertus College of Judaica [Chicago, IL] (BJA)
SCJ	Squamocolumnar Junction [Medicine] (MAE)
SCJ	Sternoclavicular Joints [Anatomy] (DAVI)
SCJ	Stretch Chuck Jaws (MCD)
SCJ	Super Cobra Jet [Automotive engineering]
SC J	Supreme Court Journal [India] [A publication] (DLA)
SCJ	Supreme Court of Justice [British] (ROG)
SCJA	Senior Conformation Judges Association (EA)
SCJAEF	Senior Conformation Judges Association Education Fund (EA)
SCJB	Jamaica Supreme Court Judgment Books [A publication] (DLA)
SCJC	Saint Catharine Junior College [Kentucky]
SCJM	Sisters of Charity of Jesus and Mary [See also ZLJM] [Belgium] (EAIO)
SCJO	Osborno/Canal Bajo [Chile] [ICAO location identifier] (ICLI)
SCJS	Seminary College of Jewish Studies (BJA)
Sc Jur	Scottish Jurist [A publication] (DLA)
SCK	Air Force Weapons Laboratory, Kirtland AFB, NM [OCLC symbol] (OCLC)
SCK	Air Sinclair Ltd. [British ICAO designator] (FAAC)
s-ck--	Colombia [MARC geographic area code Library of Congress] (LCCP)
SCK	SC Bancorp [AMEX symbol] (SPSG)
SCK	Serum Creatine Kinase [An enzyme]
SCK	Set Clock (IAA)
SCK	Sisters of Christ the King [Roman Catholic religious order]

SCK	Stockton [California] [Airport symbol] (OAG)
SCK	Stockton, CA [Location identifier FAA] (FAAL)
SCK	Studiecentrum voor Kernenergie [Also, CEEN, NERC] [Center for Nuclear Energy Studies] [Belgium] (NRCH)
ScK	Williamsburg County Library, Kingstree, SC [Library symbol] [Library of Congress] (LCLS)
SCKBD	Society of Certified Kitchen and Bathroom Designers (NTPA)
SCKD	Society of Certified Kitchen Designers (EA)
SCKLS	South Central Kansas Library System [Library network]
SCKSJ	Supreme Commandery Knights of St. John (EA)
SCKT	Socket Communications [NASDAQ symbol] (TTSB)
SCKT	Socket Communications, Inc. [NASDAQ symbol] (SAG)
SCKTPT	Southern California Kinesthesia and Tactile Perception Tests
SCKTW	Socket Communications Wrrt [NASDAQ symbol] (TTSB)
ScKW	Williamsburg Technical College, Kingstree, SC [Library symbol Library of Congress] (LCLS)
s-cl--	Chile [MARC geographic area code Library of Congress] (LCCP)
SCL	Great Falls, MT [Location identifier FAA] (FAAL)
ScL	Licence es Sciences [Licentiate of Science] [French] (ASC)
SCL	Santa Clara - Ricard [California] [Seismograph station code, US Geological Survey Closed] (SEIS)
SCL	Santiago [Chile] [Airport symbol] (OAG)
SCL	Save a Cat League (EA)
SCL	Scale
SCL	Scarlet (ROG)
SCL	Scleroderma [Medicine] (DAVI)
SCL	Scottish Central Library (PDAA)
SCL	Scrap Classification List [DoD]
scl	Scroll (VRA)
Scl	Sculptor [Constellation]
SCL	Seaboard Coast Line Railroad Co. [Subsidiary of Seaboard Coast Line Industries] [Later, CSX Corp.] [AAR code]
SCL	Secondary Coolant Line [or Loop] [NASA] (NASA)
SCL	Select Cases in Chancery Tempore King [25 English Reprint] [1724-33] [A publication] (DLA)
SCL	Selectively Cross Linked
SCL	Semiconductor Complex, Ltd. [Commercial firm] [India]
SCL	Senior Citizens League [Defunct] (EA)
SCL	Sequential Control Logic
SCL	Serum Cholesterol Level [Clinical chemistry] (OA)
SCL	Serum Copper Level [Clinical chemistry] (AAMN)
SCL	Service Control Layer [Computer science]
SCL	Shaped Charge Liner
SCL	Shaw Cablesystems Ltd. [Toronto Stock Exchange symbol]
SCL	Ship Configuration List [Navy] (CAAL)
SCL	Signal Corps Laboratory [Obsolete Army]
SCL	Signal Corps Letter (MCD)
SCL	Simmons College, Boston, MA [OCLC symbol] (OCLC)
SCL	Single Channel Monitoring (NITA)
SCL	Single Composition Lathe-Cut [Dental alloy]
SCL	Sinus Cycle Length [Cardiology]
SCL	Sisters of Charity (of Leavenworth) [Roman Catholic religious order]
SCL	Site Concurrence Letter (AFM)
SCL	Skin Conductance Level [Physiology]
SCL	Social
SCL	Society for Caribbean Linguistics [St. Augustine, Trinidad] (EAIO)
SCL	Society for Computers and Law [Abingdon, Oxfordshire, England] (EAIO)
SCL	Society of Construction Law [British] (DBA)
SCL	Society of County Librarians [British]
SCL	Sofati Container Line [Shipping line]
SCL	Soft Contact Lens
SCL	Software Career Link [Database producer] [Burlington, MA]
SCL	Sola International, Inc. [NYSE symbol] (SAG)
SCL	South Carolina Law Reports [Pre-1868] [A publication] (DLA)
SCL	South Central Regional Library System [UTLAS symbol]
SCL	Southeastern Composers' League (EA)
SCL	Southern Copper Ltd. [Commercial firm Australia]
SCL	Space-Charge Layer [Electronics] (MED)
SCL	Space Charge Limited
SCL	Space Component Lifetime (SSD)
SCL	Specification Change Log [NASA] (NASA)
SCL	Spinocervicolemniscal (DB)
SCL	Spontaneous Cycle Length
SCL	Standard Chartered Leasing (NITA)
SCL	Standard Classification List [Military]
SCL	Standard Conventional Load
SCL	Static Complementary Logic (ECII)
SCL	St. Cloud [Diocesan abbreviation] [Minnesota] (TOCD)
SCL	Stem Cell Leukaemia [Hematology]
SCL	Stepan Chemical Co. [AMEX symbol] (SPSG)
SCL	Stepan Co. [NYSE symbol] (TTSB)
SCL	Stock Corporation Law [A publication] (DLA)
SCL	String Control Language [Computer science]
SCL	Student of the Civil Law
SCL	Super Chevys Limited [Defunct] (EA)
SCL	Supervisory Control Language [Computer science] (MHDI)
SCL	Swiftair Cargo Ltd. [Canada ICAO designator] (FAAC)
SCL	Switch-to-Computer Link (CDE)
SCL	Symbolic Correction Loader
SCL	Symmetric Clipper
SCL	Symphony Command Language [Computer science]
SCL	Symptom Checklist [Medicine] (DMAA)
SCL	Synthetic Combinatorial Library [Biochemistry]
SCL	System Command Language [Computer science]

SCL............ Systems Component List (KSC)
SCL............ Systems Control Language [*Computer science*]
Sc LA......... Left Scapuloanterior Position [*of the fetus*] [*Obstetrics*]
SCLA......... Section Carry Look Ahead (MHDB)
ScLan......... Lancaster County Library, Lancaster, SC [*Library symbol*] [*Library of Congress*] (LCLS)
ScLangU...... United Merchants Research Center, Langley, SC [*Library symbol Library of Congress*] (LCLS)
Sc La R....... Scottish Land Court Reports [*Supplement to Scottish Law Review*] [*A publication*] (DLA)
Sc La Rep ... Report by the Scottish Land Court [*A publication*] (DLA)
Sc La Rep Ap... Appendices to the Report of the Scottish Land Court [*A publication*] (DLA)
Sc La Rep App... Appendices to the Report of the Scottish Land Court [*A publication*] (DLA)
ScLat.......... Dillon County Library, Latta, SC [*Library symbol*] [*Library of Congress*] (LCLS)
SCLAT......... Service Central de la Lutte Anti-terroriste [*Central Anti-Terrorist Service*] [*France*] (ECON)
ScLau .... Laurens County Library, Laurens, SC [*Library symbol Library of Congress*] (LCLS)
SCLAV .... Sclavonic [*Language, etc.*] (ROG)
SCLB.......... Southern Corn Leaf Blight (OA)
SCLC.......... Scottish Child Law Centre (BUAC)
SCLC.......... Small-Cell Lung Cancer [*Oncology*]
SCLC.......... Southern Christian Leadership Conference (EA)
SCLC.......... Space-Charge-Limited Current
SCLCP........ Side-Chain Liquid Crystalline Polymer [*Organic chemistry*]
SCLCS........ Ship Command-Launch Control Subsystem [*Navy*] (CAAL)
SCLD.......... Sickle-Cell Chronic Lung Disease [*Medicine*] (DMAA)
SCLD.......... Space Charge Limited Diode (IAA)
SCLDF........ Sierra Club Legal Defense Fund (EA)
SCLE.......... Santiago/Los Leones [*Chile*] [*ICAO location identifier*] (ICLI)
SCLE.......... Subacute Cutaneous Lupus Erythematosus [*Medicine*]
SCLE.......... Subcutaneous Lupus Erythematosus [*Medicine*] (DAVI)
SCLEC........ Signal Corps Logistics Evaluation Committee [*Obsolete Army*] (KSC)
SCLER........ Scleroscope
SCLER........ Sclerosis [*Medicine*]
SCLERA ...... Santa Catalina Laboratory for Experimental Relativity by Astrometry [*University of Arizona*] [*Research center*] (RCD)
SCLERO....... Scleroderma [*Medicine*]
SCLF.......... Single Crystal LASER Fusion [*For dating of geological material*]
SCLFM........ Society of Chain Link Fencing Manufacturers [*British*] (DBA)
SCLI.......... Somerset and Cornwall Light Infantry [*British military*] (DMA)
SCLIGFET ... Space-Charge-Limited Insulated-Gate Field Effect Transistor (PDAA)
SCLIR......... Secondary Calibration Laboratories for Ionizing Radiation
Sc LJ......... Scottish Law Journal and Sheriff Court Record [*A publication*] (DLA)
SCLJ.......... South Carolina Law Journal [*A publication*] (DLA)
SCLK.......... Ship's Clerk
SCLL.......... Sandia Corporation, Livermore Laboratory
SCLL.......... Supreme Committee for the Liberation of Lithuania [*Defunct*] (EA)
SCLL.......... Vallenar/Vallenar [*Chile*] [*ICAO location identifier*] (ICLI)
SC LM .... Scottish Law Magazine and Sheriff Court Reporter [*A publication*] (DLA)
SCLM.......... Stability, Control, and Load Maneuvers [*Aerospace*] (MCD)
SCLM.......... Sub-Continental Lithospheric Mantle
SCLN.......... SciClone Pharmaceuticals [*NASDAQ symbol*] (TTSB)
SCLN.......... SciClone Pharmaceuticals, Inc. [*NASDAQ symbol*] (SAG)
SCLO .... Self-Consistent Local Orbital [*Method*] [*Mathematics*]
SCLO .... Statistical Clearance Liaison Officer [*Army*] (AABC)
SCLOG........ Security Log [*Telecommunications*] (TEL)
Sc LP......... Left Scapuloposterior Position [*of the fetus*] [*Obstetrics*]
SCLP.......... Santiago/Lo Prado [*Chile*] [*ICAO location identifier*] (ICLI)
SCLP.......... Scientists Committee on Loyalty Problems (BUAC)
SCLPr......... Stepan Co. 5.50% Cv Pfd [*NYSE symbol*] (TTSB)
SCLR .... Santa Clara Law Review [*A publication*] (ILCA)
Sc LR......... Scottish Law Reporter [*A publication*] (DLA)
Sc LR......... Scottish Law Review and Sheriff Court Reports [*A publication*] (DLA)
Sc L Rep ..... Scottish Law Reporter [*Edinburgh*] [*A publication*] (DLA)
SCLS.......... Serra Cooperative Library System [*Library network*]
SCLS.......... Shipboard Command and Launch Subsystem (MCD)
SCLS.......... South Central Library System [*Library network*]
SCLS.......... Study of Children's Learning Styles (EDAC)
SCLS.......... Systemic Capillary Leak Syndrome [*Medicine*] (DMAA)
Sc LT......... Scots Law Times [*A publication*] (DLA)
SCLT.......... Scottish Civil Liberties Trust (BUAC)
SCLTFT....... Space Charge Limited Thin Film Triode (DICI)
SCLV.......... Socialist Campaign for a Labour Victory (BUAC)
SCLV.......... Subclavian Vein [*Anatomy*]
SCLWR........ Scientific Computing Laboratory Work Request (IAA)
SCLY.......... Scullery (MSA)
SCM........... Aero Servicio de Carga Mexicana SA de CV [*Mexico ICAO designator*] (FAAC)
Sc M .... Master of Science
SCM........... Sacra Caesarea Majestas [*Sacred Imperial Majesty*] [*Latin*]
SCM........... Samarium Cobalt Magnet
SCM........... Sanctae Memoriae [*Of Holy Memory*] [*Latin*]
SCM........... S-Band Cassegrain Monopulse
SCM........... Scammon Bay [*Alaska*] [*Airport symbol*] (OAG)
SCM........... Scammon Bay, AK [*Location identifier FAA*] (FAAL)
SCM........... Scanning Capacitance Microscopy (AAEL)
SCM........... Scientific Calculator Machine (NITA)
SCM........... Scratch Pad Memory (IAA)
SCM........... ScreenCam Movie [*Computer software*] (CDE)
SCM........... Segment Control Module (IAA)

SCM........... Selective Complement Accumulator
SCM........... Self-Contained Munitions
SCM........... Sender's Composition Message [*Cable*]
SCM........... Service Command Module [*Aerospace*] (MCD)
SCM........... Service Control Manager [*Computer science*]
SCM........... Shaft Cutting Machine [*Mining technology*]
SCM........... Sheep Creek Mountain [*Alaska*] [*Seismograph station code, US Geological Survey*] (SEIS)
SCM........... Shorthaul Customer Modem (NITA)
SCM........... Signal Conditioning Module
SCM........... Simulated Command Module (IAA)
SCM........... Simulated Core Mock-Up [*or Model*] [*Nuclear energy*] (NRCH)
SCM........... Sine Cosine Multiplier (IAA)
SCM........... Single-Channel MODEM [*Telecommunications*] (TEL)
SCM........... Single Chip Module [*Electronics*] (CDE)
SCM........... Single Column Model (USDC)
SCM........... Single Crystal Meteorite
SCM........... Siscoe Callahan [*Vancouver Stock Exchange symbol*]
SCM........... Site Configuration Message [*NASA*]
SCM........... Skill Centre Manager (AIE)
SCM........... Small Capacity Memory [*Computer science*] (IAA)
SCM........... Small-Core Memory [*Computer science*]
SCM........... Smaller Companies Market [*Business term*]
SCM........... Social Change Media [*Australia*]
SCM........... Societe Canadienne des Microbiologistes [*Canadian Society of Microbiologists*] (EAIO)
SCM........... Society for Computer Medicine [*Later, AMIA*] (EA)
SCM........... Society of Clinical Masseurs [*Australia*]
SCM........... Society of Coal Merchants (BUAC)
SCM........... Society of Community Medicine [*Later, SPH*] (EAIO)
SCM........... Software Configuration Management (IEEE)
SCM........... Solar Cell Module
SCM........... Soluble Cytotoxic Mediator [*Immunology*]
SCM........... Spacecraft Material [*NASA*] (SSD)
SCM........... Spares Calculation Model
SCM........... Special Court-Martial
SCM........... Specification Change Memorandum
SCM........... Spleen Cell-Conditioned Medium (DB)
SCM........... Spleen Concanavalin A Medium [*Immunoassay*]
SCM........... Spondylitic Caudal Myelopathy [*Medicine*] (DMAA)
SCM........... Squadron Corporal-Major [*British military*] (DMA)
SCM........... Stamp Cancelling Machine (DCTA)
SCM........... Standard Cubic Meter
SCM........... STARAN [*Stellar Attitude Reference and Navigation*] Control Module (OA)
SCM........... State-Certified Midwife [*British*]
SCM........... Steam Condensing Mode [*Nuclear energy*] (NRCH)
SCM........... Sternocleidomastoid [*Anatomy*]
SCM........... Stillman College, Tuscaloosa, AL [*OCLC symbol*] (OCLC)
SCM........... Strategic Cruise Missile (MCD)
SCM........... Streamline Curvature Method [*Computer program*]
SCM........... Streptococcal Cell Membrane [*Microbiology*]
SCM........... Strouds Creek & Muddlety Railroad [*AAR code*]
SCM........... Student Christian Movement [*British*]
SCM........... Student Christian Movement of Great Britain and Ireland (BUAC)
SCM........... Subscribers' Concentration Module [*Telecommunications*] (TEL)
SCM........... Subsystem Configuration Management [*or Monitoring*] [*NASA*] (NASA)
SCM........... Summary Court-Martial [*Army*]
SCM........... Superconducting Magnet (IEEE)
SCM........... Supervision Control Module [*Telecommunications*] (TEL)
SCM........... Supply Categories of Material (MCD)
SCM........... Suppressed-Carrier Modulation
SCM........... Surface Contamination Module (DWSG)
SCM........... Sustained Competitive Motivation
SCM........... Sydney Conservatorium of Music [*Australia*]
SCM........... Symmetrically Cyclically Magnetized (IAA)
SCM........... System Control and Monitor [*Telecommunications*] (TSSD)
SCM........... System Control Module [*NASA*] (GFGA)
SCM........... Systems Control Microprocessor
SCMA......... Scottish Carpet Manufacturers Association (DBA)
SCMA......... Scottish Cement Merchants Association (DBA)
SCMA......... Silk Commission Manufacturers Association [*Defunct*] (EA)
SCMA......... Society of Cinema Managers of Great Britain and Ireland, Amalgamated (BUAC)
SCMA......... Sound & Communications Manufacturers' Association (BUAC)
SCMA......... Southern Cypress Manufacturers Association (EA)
SCMA......... Sports Card Manufacturers Association (NTPA)
SCMA......... Sterilised Cat Gut Manufacturers' Association [*British*] (BI)
SCMA......... Stilton Cheese Makers Association [*British*] (DBA)
SCMA......... Systems Communications Management Association (IAA)
SCMAC....... Scottish Catholic Marriage Advisory Council (BUAC)
SCMAI .... Staff Committee on Mediation, Arbitration, and Inquiry [*American Library Association*]
ScMan........ Clarendon County Public Library, Manning, SC [*Library symbol*] [*Library of Congress*] (LCLS)
ScMar......... Marion County Library, Marion, SC [*Library symbol*] [*Library of Congress*] (LCLS)
SCMAT....... Southern California Motor Accuracy Test
ScMb .... Chapin Memorial Library, Myrtle Beach, SC [*Library symbol*] [*Library of Congress*] (LCLS)
SCMB......... Standard Chartered Merchant Bank [*Singapore*]
SCMB......... Subsystem Configuration Management Board [*NASA*] (GFGA)
SCMB......... System Configuration Management Board (SSD)

SCMBCR...... Simulated Countercurrent Moving-Bed Chromatographic Reactor [*Chemical engineering*]
SCMBX .... Scudder Fds: Man. Mun. Bds. [*Mutual fund ticker symbol*] (SG)
ScMc .... McCormick County Library, McCormick, SC [*Library symbol*] [*Library of Congress*] (LCLS)
SCMC.......... S-Carboxymethylcysteine [*An amino acid*]
SCMC.......... Sisters of Charity of Our Lady, Mother of the Church [*Roman Catholic religious order*]
SCMC.......... Societe de Construction des Musees du Canada
SCMC.......... Sodium(carboxymethyl)cellulose [*Organic chemistry*]
SCMC.......... Spontaneous Cell-Mediated Cytotoxicity [*Medicine*] (DMAA)
SCMC.......... Strategic Cruise Missile Carrier
SCMC.......... Supply Category of Material Code
SCMCR .... Simulated Countercurrent Moving-Bed Chromatographic Reactor [*Chemical engineering*]
SCMD .... Santiago/Ministerio de Defensa Nacional [*Chile*] [*ICAO location identifier*] (ICLI)
SCMD .... Selectively Conductive Molding Device
SCMDBMC... Standing Committee of the Murray-Darling Basin Ministerial Council [*Australia*]
SCMDI .... Shenyang Coal Mine Design Institute (BUAC)
SCME.......... American Federation of State, County, and Municipal Employees
SCME.......... Service Center Math Error [*IRS*]
SCME.......... Society of Clinical and Medical Electrologists (EA)
SCME.......... Surgut Commodity and Raw Materials Exchange [*Russian Federation*] (EY)
SCMESS ...... Society of Consulting Marine Engineers and Ship Surveyors (BUAC)
SCMF.......... Single Contact Midge Flange
SCMF.......... Societe Canadienne de Musique Folklorique
SCM file ..... ScreenCam Movie File [*Lotus ScreenCam recorder program*] (IGQR)
SCMG .... Sierra Carriers and Mountaineering Group (EA)
SCMI........... Society to Conquer Mental Illness [*Defunct*] (EA)
Sc M in Hyg... Master of Science in Hygiene
SCMM.......... Medical Mission Sisters (TOCD)
SCMM.......... Sisters of Charity of Our Lady, Mother of Mercy [*Roman Catholic religious order*]
SCMM.......... Society of Catholic Medical Missionaries, Inc. [*Medical Mission Sisters*] [*Roman Catholic religious order*]
SCMO .... Senior Clerical Medical Officer (DMAA)
SCMO .... Senior Clinical Medical Officer [*British*]
SCMO .... Societe Canadienne de Meteorologie et d'Oceanographie [*Canadian Meteorological and Oceanographic Society - CMOS*]
SCMO .... Societe pour une Confederation au Moyen-Orient [*Society for Middle East Confederation - SMEC*] [*Israel*] (EAIO)
SCMO .... Studie- en Informatiecentrum TNO voor Milieu-Onderzoek [*TNO Study and Information Center on Environmental Research*] [*Information service or system*] (IID)
SCMO .... Subsidiary Communications Multiplex Operation [*FM radio frequency unused portion*]
SCMO .... Summary Court-Martial Order [*Army*]
ScMoc .... Berkeley County Library, Moncks Corner, SC [*Library symbol*] [*Library of Congress*] (LCLS)
SCMOD........ Scale Model
SCMOV .... Subterranean Clover Mottle Virus [*Plant pathology*]
SCMP.......... Scottish Computers in Schools Project (AIE)
SCMP.......... Second-Class Mail Publications [*Later, ASCMP*] (EA)
SCMP.......... Service Craft Modernization Program [*Navy*] (CAAL)
SCMP.......... Simple Cost-Effective Microprocessor (MHDI)
SCMP.......... Society of Company Meeting Planners (EA)
SCMP.......... Society of Corporate Meeting Professionals (NTPA)
SCMP.......... Software Configuration Management Plan [*Computer science*]
SCMP.......... Sulfonated Chemimechanical Pulp [*Pulp and paper technology*]
SCMP.......... Support Center Management Plan (AAG)
SCMP.......... System Contractor Management Plan [*NASA*] (NASA)
SCMPT........ Sperm Cervical Mucus Penetration Test [*Clinical chemistry*]
SCMR .... Secretary's Committee on Mental Retardation [*Department of Health and Human Services*]
SCMR .... Society for Cardiovascular Magnetic Resonance (NTPA)
SCMR .... South Canterbury Mounted Rifles [*British military*] (DMA)
SCMR .... Special Committee on Migration and Resettlement [*Department of State*] [*World War II*]
SCMR .... Surface Composition Mapping Radiometer [*NASA*]
SCMRTC ...... Sino-Canadian Mariculture Research and Training Centre (BUAC)
SCMS .... Serial Copy Management System [*for digital audio tape recording machines*]
SCMS .... Serial Copy Master System (DOM)
SCMS .... Signal Command Management System [*Military*] (AABC)
SCMS .... Sodium Colistin Methanesulphonate (DB)
SCMS .... Somali Current Monitoring System [*Marine science*] (MSC)
SCMS .... Standard Configuration Management Systems [*Military*] (AFIT)
SCMT .... Single-Cause Mortality Tape [*National Center for Health Statistics databank*]
SCMT .... Standing Committee of Ministers Responsible for Transportation (BUAC)
SCMT .... Subcontract Management Team [*NASA*] (SSD)
SCMTVS ...... Signal Corps Mobile Television System [*Military*] (IAA)
SCMU .... Scottish Commercial Motormen's Union (BUAC)
SCMU .... Species Conservation Monitoring Unit (GNE)
Sc Mun App Rep... Scotch Munitions Appeals Reports [*Edinburgh and Glasgow*] [*A publication*] (DLA)
SCMV .... Santa Cruz Mountain Vintners (EA)
SCMV.......... Sugar Cane Mosaic Virus
SCN .... Citadel, Daniel Library, Charleston, SC [*OCLC symbol*] (OCLC)
ScN .... Newberry-Saluda Regional Library, Newberry, SC [*Library symbol*] [*Library of Congress*] (LCLS)

SCN .... Potassium Thiocyanate [*or KSCN*] [*Organic chemistry*] (DAVI)
SCN .... Saarbrucken [*Germany Airport symbol*] (OAG)
SCN .... Satellite Communications Network, Inc. [*Edison, NJ*] [*Telecommunications*] (TSSD)
SCN .... Satellite Control Network
SCN .... Scan (IAA)
SCN .... Scanner [*Computer science*]
SCN .... Schematic Change Notice
SCN .... Screen [*Technical drawings*]
SCN .... Scribe Nehemiah [*Freemasonry*]
SCN .... Search Control Number (MCD)
SCN .... Secretary's Commission on Nursing [*Department of Health and Human Services*]
SCN .... Securities Communications Network, Inc. [*Englewood, CO*] (TSSD)
SCN .... Security Capital Ind Tr [*NYSE symbol*] (TTSB)
SCN .... Security Capital Industrial Trust Co. [*NYSE symbol*] (SAG)
SCN .... Self-Checking Number
SCN .... Self-Compensating Network [*Telecommunications*] (TEL)
SCN .... Self-Contained Navigation [*NASA*]
SCN .... Sensitive Command Network
SCN .... Shipbuilding and Conversion, Navy
SCN .... Ships Construction, Navy [*Funding*]
SCN .... Shop Control Number (DNAB)
SCN .... Shortest Connected Network
SCN .... Show Cause Notice
SCN .... Silent Canyon Resources Ltd. [*Vancouver Stock Exchange symbol*]
SCN .... Single Crystal Needle
SCN .... Sisters of Charity (of Nazareth) [*Roman Catholic religious order*]
SCN .... Software Change Notice (DOMA)
SCN .... Sonoco Products Corp. [*NYSE symbol*] (SAG)
SCN .... Sorting Code Number (DCTA)
SCN .... South American Airlines [*Peru*] [*ICAO designator*] (FAAC)
SCN .... Southern Command Network [*Military*] (GFGA)
SCN .... Soybean Cyst Nematode [*Botany*]
SCN .... Special Care Nursery
SCN .... Special Change Notice (KSC)
SCN .... Specification Change Notice [*NASA*]
SCN .... Specific Control Number
SCN .... Stock Control Number
SCN .... Strategic Communications Network [*Military*] (LAIN)
SCN .... Summary and Charge Number
SCN .... Sunset Crater National Monument [*Arizona*] [*Seismograph station code, US Geological Survey*] (SEIS)
SCN .... Supply Corps, Navy
SCN .... Suprachiasmatic Nucleus [*or Nuclei*] [*of the hypothalamus Anatomy*]
SCN .... Sylvania-Corning Nuclear Corp.
SCN .... System Change Notice
SCN .... System Control Number
SCNA .... Self-Contained Night Attack (MCD)
SC$_{Na}$....... Sieving Coefficient for Sodium [*Organic chemistry*] (DAVI)
SCNA .... Sikh Council of North America [*Defunct*] (EA)
SCNA .... Sudden Cosmic-Noise Absorption
SCNAWAF.... Special Category Navy with Air Force
SCNB .... Societe Nationale des Chemins de Fer Belges [*Belgian National Railways*]
ScNC.......... Newberry College, Newberry, SC [*Library symbol Library of Congress*] (LCLS)
SCNCM .... Standing Committee of Nature Conservation Ministers [*Australia*]
SCND .... Scottish Campaign for Nuclear Disarmament (BUAC)
SCND .... Thiocyanate [*Organic chemistry*] (DAVI)
ScndBdc ..... Scandinavian Broadcasting [*Commercial firm Associated Press*] (SAG)
scnDNA....... Deoxyribonucleic Acid, Single Copy Nuclear [*Biochemistry, genetics*]
SCNDVA....... Standing Committee on National Defence and Veterans Affairs [*Canada*]
SCNEA .... Sealing Commission for the Northeast Atlantic (BUAC)
SCNG.......... Scan Graphics [*NASDAQ symbol*] (TTSB)
SCNG.......... Scan-Graphics, Inc. [*NASDAQ symbol*] (NQ)
SCNG.......... Scanning (MSA)
SCNI .... Select Committee on Nationalised Industries [*British*]
SCNI .... Sports Council for Northern Ireland (BUAC)
SCNI .... Supreme Court of Norfolk Island [*Australia*]
SC (Nig)...... Judgments of the Supreme Court of Nigeria [*A publication*] (DLA)
SCNMV........ Sweet Clover Necrotic Mosaic Virus [*Plant pathology*]
SCNO .... Savio Club National Office (EA)
SCNO .... Senior Canadian Naval Officer [*British military*] (DMA)
ScNoaSH .... North Augusta Senior High School, North Augusta, SC [*Library symbol Library of Congress*] (LCLS)
SCNP .... Scottish Council for National Parks (BUAC)
SCNPrA....... Security Cap Ind Tr 9.40% Pfd [*NYSE symbol*] (TTSB)
SCNPrB....... Security Cap Ind Tr 7% Cv Pfd [*NYSE symbol*] (TTSB)
SCNPWC...... Standing Committee for Nobel Prize Winners' Congresses (EA)
SCNR .... Scanner (MSA)
SCNR .... Scientific Committee of National Representatives [*NATO*]
Sc NR .... Scott's New English Common Pleas Reports [*A publication*] (DLA)
SCNR .... Sequence Control Number Register [*Computer science*]
SCNR .... Solid-Core Nuclear Rocket [*NASA*]
SCNR .... Supreme Council for National Reconstruction [*South Korea*]
SCNS .... Self-Contained Navigation System [*NASA*]
SCNS .... Statewide Course Numbering System [*Florida*] (EDAC)
SCNS .... Subcutaneous Nerve Stimulation [*For treatment of pain*]
SCN/SIN...... Sensitive Command Network/Sensitive Information Network (CET)
SCNSW........ Spastic Centre of New South Wales [*Australia*]
SCNSW........ Supreme Court of New South Wales [*Australia*]
SCNT .... Supreme Court of the Northern Territory [*Australia*]

SCNTFC .... Scientific
SCNTN ...... Self-Contained
SCNTST ...... Scientist
SCNUL .... Standing Conference on National and University Libraries [British]
SCNVYO .... Standing Conference of National Voluntary Youth Organisations (BUAC)
SCNWA .... Sealing Commission for the Northwest Atlantic (BUAC)
SCNYA .... Saucony, Inc. "A" [NASDAQ symbol] [Formerly, Hyde Athletic Industry "A"]
SCNYB .... Saucony, Inc. "B" [NASDAQ symbol] [Formerly, Hyde Athletic Industry "B"]
SCO .... Converse College, Spartanburg, SC [OCLC symbol] (OCLC)
SCO .... Euro Air Helicopter Service AB [Sweden ICAO designator] (FAAC)
SCO .... Manetti Roberts [Italy] [Research code symbol]
SCO .... Sales Contracting Officer [Army]
SCO .... Santa Cruz Operation [Computer manufacturer] (PCM)
SCO .... Sarawak Communist Organization [Malaya]
ScO .... Scientific Officer [Also, SO] [Ministry of Agriculture, Fisheries, and Food] [British]
SCO .... Scobey, MT [Location identifier FAA] (FAAL)
SCO .... Score Resources [Vancouver Stock Exchange symbol]
SCO .... Scoresbysund [Greenland] [Seismograph station code, US Geological Survey Closed] (SEIS)
Sco .... Scorpius [Constellation]
SCO .... Scottish (ROG)
SCO .... Scottish Committee of Optometrists (BUAC)
Sco .... Scott's English Common Pleas Reports [A publication] (DLA)
SCO .... Scout [or Scouting] (DNAB)
SCO .... Selective Conscientious Objection
SCO .... Senior Chief Officer [British military] (DMA)
SCO .... Senior Commercial Office [Foreign service]
SCO .... Service Cryptologic Organizations (MCD)
SCO .... Show Cause Order [Legal shorthand] (LWAP)
SCO .... Signal Company [Military] (IAA)
SCO .... Single Crystal Orthoferrites
SCO .... Sisters of Charity of Ottawa [Grey Nuns of the Cross] [Roman Catholic religious order]
SCO .... Sisters of Charity of Quebec (Grey Nuns) (TOCD)
SCO .... Smith Corona Corp. [NYSE symbol] (SPSG)
SCO .... Societe Canadienne d'Onomastique (AC)
SCO .... Society of Commissioned Officers (EA)
SCO .... Software Change Order (MCD)
SCO .... Somatic Crossing-Over [Medicine] (DMAA)
SCO .... Southern College of Optometry [Tennessee]
S/CO .... Spacecraft Observer (KSC)
SCO .... Spacecraft Operations [NASA] (KSC)
SCO .... Squadron Command Officer (AAG)
SCO .... Squadron Constructor Officer [Navy British]
SCO .... Staff Communications Office [Army]
SCO .... Start Checkout [NASA] (NASA)
sco .... Start Checkout (NAKS)
SCO .... State Coordinating Officer [Federal disaster planning]
SCO .... State Coroners' Office [Australia]
SCO .... Statistical Control Office [or Officer] [Military]
SCO .... Subcarrier Oscillator
sco .... Subcarrier Oscillator (IDOE)
SCO .... Subcommissural Organ [Neuroanatomy]
SCO .... Subcontract Consignment Order
SCO .... Successor Contracting Officer (MCD)
SCO .... Supercritical Oxygen (MCD)
SCO .... Switch Closure Out (MCD)
sco .... Switch Closure Out (NAKS)
SCO .... Synthetic Crude Oil [Fuel technology]
SCO .... System Check-Out Computer (PDAA)
SCO .... System Counterpart Officer [Military] (AFIT)
SCOA .... Saluki Club of America (EA)
SCOA .... Sample Cave Operating Area [Nuclear energy] (NRCH)
SCOA .... Supreme Council Order of the Amaranth (EA)
SCOA .... Sydney College of the Arts [Australia]
SCOAL .... Short-Term Coal Analysis System [Department of Energy] (GFGA)
Sco & J Tel... Scott and Jarnigan on the Law of Telegraphs [A publication] (DLA)
SCOAP .... Scandia Controllability and Observability Analysis Program (NITA)
SCOB .... Scattered Clouds or Better (SAA)
SCOB .... Scheduled-Controlled Operant Behavior [Environmental Protection Agency]
SCOBA .... Standing Conference of the Canonical Orthodox Bishops in the Americas (EA)
SCOBBS .... School of Combined Operations, Beach and Boat Section [Military British]
SCOBO .... Satellite Collection Buoy Observations
SCOBOL .... Structured Common Business-Oriented Language
SCOC .... Santa Cruz Operation [NASDAQ symbol] (TTSB)
SCOC .... Santa Cruz Operation, Inc. [NASDAQ symbol] (SAG)
SCOC .... Sediment Community Oxygen Consumption [Marine biology]
SCOC .... Senior Commanders Orientation Course (MCD)
SCOC .... Short-Circuit Output Current
SCOC .... Societe Canadienne d'Orientation et de Consultation
SCOC .... Spanish Chamber of Commerce [Taiwan] (EAIO)
SCOC .... Support Command Operations Center [Military]
SCOC .... Systems Control and Operations Concept (COE)
SCOCE .... Special Committee on Compromising Emanations [Military] (AABC)
SCOCLIS ...... Standing Conference of Co-Operative Library and Information Services [British]
Sco Costs .... Scott's Costs in the High Court [4th ed.] [1880] [A publication] (DLA)

SCOD .... Societe Cooperative Oecumenique de Developpement [Ecumenical Development Cooperative Society - EDCS] [Netherlands] (EAIO)
SCOD .... South Coast One Design [Cruising boat]
SCOD .... Specific Chemical Oxygen Demand Value [for Complete Oxidation]
SCOD .... Surface Crack Opening Displacement (PDAA)
SCODA .... Scan Coherent Doppler Attachment
SCODA .... Standing Conference on Drug Abuse (BUAC)
SCODHE .... Standing Conference on Dance in Higher Education [British] (DBA)
SCODL .... Scan Conversion Object Description Language [Computer science] (PCM)
SCODS .... Study Commission on Ocean Data Stations [Marine science] (MSC)
SCOE .... Special Checkout Equipment [NASA] (NASA)
SCOEG .... Standing Conference of Employers of Graduates [British]
SCOFA .... Shipping Control Office, Forward Area [Navy]
SCOFF .... Simplified Combustion Form Function (MCD)
ScoFF .... Southern Counties Folk Federation (BUAC)
SCOFOR .... Scottish Forces [World War II]
SCOFOR .... Scouting Force [Navy]
SCOH .... Staff Corporal of Horse [British military] (DMA)
SCOHLZA ..... Standing Committee of Head Librarians of Zambia (BUAC)
SCOHR .... Students Committee on Human Rights
Sco Int .... Scott's Intestate Laws [A publication] (DLA)
SCOL .... School (NVT)
SCOL .... Scottish Committee on Open Learning (AIE)
SCOLA .... Second Consortium of Local Authorities
SCOLAG .... Scottish Legal Action Group (BUAC)
SCOLAG Bull... Scottish Legal Action Group. Bulletin [A publication] (DLA)
Scol Anon ... Scolia Anonyma [Classical studies] (OCD)
SCOLAR .... Schools and Colleges Online Accounting and Registration System (NITA)
SCOLAR .... Standard Costing of Laboratory Resources
Scol Att ...... Scolia Attica [Classical studies] (OCD)
SCOLAVNMED... School of Aviation Medicine [Later, School of Aerospace Medicine]
SCOLCAP ..... Scottish Libraries Cooperative Automation Project
SCOLD .... Small Company Online Data [Computer science] (PDAA)
SCOLE .... Spacecraft Control Laboratory Experiment (MCD)
SCOLE .... Standing Committee on Library Education [American Library Association]
SCOLMA .... Standing Conference on Library Materials on Africa [British]
SCOLSHIP... Schoolship [Navy] (NVT)
SCOLT .... Southern Conference on Language Teaching, Inc. (EDAC)
SCOM .... Scientific Committee [NATO] (NATG)
SCOM .... Site Cutover Manager [Telecommunications] (TEL)
SCOM .... Spacecraft Communicator
SCOM .... Supervisory Communication Relations Test
SCOM .... System Communication (MHDI)
SCOMA .... Shipping Control Office, Marianas [Navy]
SCOMC .... SCS/Compute, Inc. [NASDAQ symbol] (SAG)
ScoMIA .... Scottish Marine Industries Association (DBA)
SCOMO .... Satellite Collection of Meteorological Observations
SCOMP .... Secure Communications Processor (NITA)
S/COMPT ..... Side Compartment [Automotive engineering]
SCON .... Quellon/Ad Quellon [Chile] [ICAO location identifier] (ICLI)
SCON .... Santiago/Quinta Normal [Chile] [ICAO location identifier] (ICLI)
SCON .... Superconductor Technologies [NASDAQ symbol] (SAG)
Sco NR .... Scott's New English Common Pleas Reports [A publication] (DLA)
SCONRES ..... Senate Concurrent Resolution (AFIT)
SConRes ...... Senate Concurrent Resolution (WPI)
SCONS .... Shipment Control System [Military]
SCONT .... Ship Control
SCONUL .... Standing Conference on National and University Libraries [British]
SCOOP .... Scientific Computation of Optimal Programs (IEEE)
SCOOP .... Scientific Computation of Optimum Procurement [Air Force]
SCOOP .... Self-Coupled Optical Pickup (NITA)
SCOOP .... Strategic Confirmation of Optical Phenomenology
SCOOP .... Support Plan to Continuity of Operations Plan [Military]
SCOOP .... System for Computerization of Office Processes (MHDI)
SCOOT .... Split Cycle and Offset Optimization Technique [FHWA] (TAG)
SCOOT .... Support Cambodia Out of Thailand [Military operation] (VNW)
SCOP .... Ferrocarril del Sureste [AAR code]
SCOP .... Scopolamine [Anticholinergic compound]
SCOP .... Scopus Technology [NASDAQ symbol] (TTSB)
SCOP .... Scopus Technology, Inc. [NASDAQ symbol] (SAG)
SCOP .... Single Copy Order Plan [Later, STOP] [Bookselling]
SCOP .... Steering Committee on Pilotage (DS)
SCOP .... Structural Classification of Proteins [Database of protein structures]
SCOPE .... Microscopic (DAVI)
SCOPE .... San Clemente Ocean Probing Experiment [Marine science] (OSRA)
SCOPE .... Schedule-Cost-Performance (IEEE)
SCOPE .... Scholarly Communication: Online Publishing and Education (NITA)
SCOPE .... Scientific Committee on Problems of the Environment [ICSU] (EA)
Scope .... Scope Industries [Associated Press] (SAG)
SCOPE .... Scripps Cooperative Oceanic Productivity Expedition [1956]
SCOPE .... Second Chance Opportunities and Education for Women (AIE)
SCOPE .... Select Council on Post-High-School Education
SCOPE .... Selected Contents of Periodicals for Educators (AEBS)
SCOPE .... Senior Citizens' Opportunities for Personal Enrichment [Federal antipoverty program]
SCOPE .... Sequential Customer Order Processing Electronically
SCOPE .... Service Center of Private Enterprise
SCOPE .... Simple Checkout-Oriented Program Language
SCOPE .... Simple Communications Programming Environment [Computer science]
SCOPE .... Smart Contract Preparation Environment [Computer science] (RDA)

SCOPE .... Southern Coastal Plains Expedition [*National Oceanic and Atmospheric Administration*] (MSC)
SCOPE .... Special Committee on Paperless Entries [*California interbank group*]
SCOPE .... Special Committee on Problems of the Environment [*of International Council of Scientific Unions*]
SCOPE .... Specifiable Coordinating Positioning Equipment (PDAA)
SCOPE .... Standardized Curriculum Oriented Pupil Evaluation (EDAC)
SCOPE .... Standing Committee on Professional Education (NITA)
SCOPE .... Standing Conference of Institutions of Printing Education (DGA)
SCOPE .... State Commission on Public Education
SCOPE .... Stromberg Central Operations Panel - Electric
SCOPE .... Student Council on Pollution and the Environment [*Association conceived in late 1969 by then Secretary of the Interior Walter J. Hickel*]
SCOPE .... Subsystem for the Control of Operations and Plan Evaluation
SCOPE .... Summer Community Organization and Political Education Program
SCOPE .... Supervisory Control of Program Execution (MCD)
SCOPE .... Supportive Council on Preventive Effort [*Ohio*]
SCOPE .... System for Capacity and Orders Planning and Enquiries (PDAA)
SCOPE .... System to Coordinate the Operation of Peripheral Equipment
SCOPES .... Squad Combat Operations Exercise, Simulation [*Military*]
SCOPLT .... Scope Plot (IAA)
SCOPP .... School-College Orientation Program of Pittsburgh
SCOPS .... Select Committee on Ocean Policy Study [*Federal Council for Science and Technology*]
SCOPT .... Subcommittee on Programming Technology (NITA)
Scopus......... Scopus Technology, Inc. [*Associated Press*] (SAG)
ScOr............ Orangeburg County Free Library, Orangeburg, SC [*Library symbol*] [*Library of Congress*] (LCLS)
SCOR .... Scientific Committee on Oceanic Research [*ICSU*] [*Halifax, NS*] (EAIO)
Scor............. Scorpius [*Constellation*]
SCOR .... Self-Calibrating Omnirange
SCOR .... Small Cycle Observation Recording
SCOR .... Special Center of Research [*HEW*]
SCOR .... Special Committee on Oceanographic Research
SCOR .... Specialized Center of Research in Atherosclerosis [*University of Chicago*] [*Research center*] (RCD)
SCOR .... Specialized Center of Research in Ischemic Heart Disease [*University of Alabama at Birmingham*] [*Research center*] (RCD)
SCOR .... Standing Conference on Refugees [*British*]
SCOR .... Status Control of Rejections (MCD)
SCOR .... Syncor International Corp. [*NASDAQ symbol*] (NQ)
SCOR .... Syncor Int'l [*NASDAQ symbol*] (TTSB)
SCORAN ..... Scorer and Analyzer [*Computerized educational testing*]
ScOrC .... Claflin College, Orangeburg, SC [*Library symbol Library of Congress*] (LCLS)
SCORDES .... Sferics Correlation Detection System
SCORE .... Satellite Computer-Operated Readiness Equipment [*SSD*]
SCORE......... Scenario-Oriented Recurring Evaluation (PDAA)
SCORE .... Scientific Cooperative Operational Research Expedition [*National Oceanic and Atmospheric Administration*] (MSC)
SCORE .... Select Concrete Objectives for Research Emphasis (PDAA)
SCORE......... Selection Copy and Reporting (IEEE)
SCORE......... Selective Conversion and Retention [*Navy*]
SCORE .... Service Corps of Retired Executives (NADA)
SCORE .... Service Corps of Retired Executives Association [*Washington, DC*] (EA)
SCORE .... Short Course Off-Road Event [*Off-road vehicle racing*]
SCORE .... Signal Communication by Orbiting Relay Equipment [*Radio*]
Score .... Simulated Combat Operations Range Equipment (MCD)
SCORE .... Solving Community Obstacles and Restoring Employment [*Occupational therapy*]
SCORE .... Southern California Off-Road Event [*An association*]
SCORE .... Space Communications for Orbiting Relay Equipment (MCD)
SCORE .... Special Claim on Residual Equity
SCORE .... Spectral Combinations for Reconnaissance Exploitation [*Photography*]
SCORE .... Standing Committee on Regulatory Effectiveness [*Nuclear Regulatory Commission*] (NRCH)
SCORE .... Stratified Charge, Omnivorous Rotary Engine [*Automotive engineering*]
SCORE .... Street Corner Offense Reduction Experiment
SCORE .... Student Competitions on Relevant Engineering
SCORE .... Subsystem Control of Required Equipment (MCD)
SCORE .... Supervisory Coaching Relations Test
SCORE .... Supplier Cost Reduction Effort [*Auto industry, project management*]
SCORE .... Systematic Communications of Range Effectiveness (MUGU)
SCORE .... Systematic Control of Range Effectiveness (IAA)
SCORE .... System Cost and Operational Resource Evaluation (MCD)
SCORE .... System for Computerized Olympic Results and Events [*Texas Instruments, Inc.*]
SCORE .... Systems Coordinative Reporting (MCD)
ScoreBd .... Score Board, Inc. [*Associated Press*] (SAG)
SCORES .... Scenario-Oriented Recurring Evaluation System [*Military*]
SCORES .... Standard Combat Oriented Recurring Evaluation System [*Military*]
SCORES .... Steering Column and Occupant Response Simulation [*Automotive safety*] [*Computer-aided design*]
SCOREx .... Supply Chain Optimization and Realtime Extended Execution
SCORN......... Special Committee Opposing Resurgent Nazism
SCORON ..... Scouting Squadron
SCOROR ..... Secretary's Committee on Research on Reorganization [*Navy*]
S/Corp .... Staff Corporal [*British military*] (DMA)
SCORP .... Statewide Comprehensive Outdoor Recreation Plan

SCORPI....... Subcritical Carbon-Moderated Reactor Assembly for Plutonium Investigations (MCD)
SCORPIO ..... Sub Critical Carbon-Moderated Reactor Assembly for Plutonium Investigations [*British*] (NUCP)
SCORPIO ..... Subject-Content-Oriented Retriever for Processing Information On-Line [*Congressional Research Service*]
SCORPIO ..... Submarine Craft for Ocean Repair, Positioning, Inspection, and Observation (PDAA)
ScOrS .... South Carolina State College, Orangeburg, SC [*Library symbol Library of Congress*] (LCLS)
ScOrSM .... Southern Methodist College, Orangeburg, SC [*Library symbol*] [*Library of Congress*] (LCLS)
ScOrTC .... Orangeburg-Calhoune Technical College, Orangeburg, SC [*Library symbol*] [*Library of Congress*] (LCLS)
SCOR U .... SCOR US Corp. [*Associated Press*] (SAG)
SCORU......... Statistical Control and Operations Records Unit [*Air Force*]
SCOS .... Scottish Certificate in Office Studies
SCOS .... Small Computer and Office Systems [*Honeywell, Inc.*]
SCOS .... Subsystem Computer Operating System [*NASA*] (NASA)
scos .... Subsystem Computer Operating System (NAKS)
SCOSA......... Spastic Centres of South Australia
SCOSE .... Standing Committee on Submarine Escape [*British military*] (DMA)
SCOSS .... Senior Chief Officer, Shore Signal Service (IAA)
SCOST .... Special Committee on Space Technology (KSC)
SCOSTEP...... Scientific Committee on Solar Terrestrial Physics (EA)
SCOSWS..... Senior Chief Officer, Shore Wireless Service (IAA)
SCOT .... Satellite Communications Overseas Transmission
SCOT .... Satellite Communication Terminal [*Navy British*] (MCD)
SCOT .... Scotland [*or Scottish*] (EY)
Scot .... Scotland (CMD)
Scot .... Scotland [*or*] Scottish (ODBW)
SCOT .... Scott & Stringfellow Financial, Inc. [*Richmond, VA*] [*NASDAQ symbol*] (NQ)
SCOT .... Scottish [*or Scotsman*] (ROG)
SCOT .... Scottish Canadian Oil & Transportation (WDAA)
SCOT .... Scottish Confederation of Tourism (DBA)
SCOT .... Scott/Stringfellow Finl [*NASDAQ symbol*] (TTSB)
SCOT .... Semi-Automated Computer-Oriented Text (PDAA)
SCOT .... Shaken and Circulatory Oxidation Test (PDAA)
SCOT .... Shell Claus Offgas Treating [*Chemical engineering*]
SCOT .... Shipborne SATCOM Terminal [*British*]
SCOT .... Shippers for Competitive Ocean Transportation [*Washington, DC*] (EA)
SCOT .... Standby Compatible One-Tape [*System*]
SCOT .... Steel Car of Tomorrow
SCOT .... Stepper Central Office Tester (NITA)
SCOT .... Subcostal Right Ventricle Outflow View [*Medicine*] (DMAA)
SCOT .... Supplementary Checkout Trailer
SCOT .... Support-Coated Open-Tubular [*Column*] [*Chromatography*]
SCOT .... Surface Coated Open Tubular (EDCT)
SCOTA .... Scottish Offshore Training Association (DBA)
SCOTAC ...... Speech-Compatible Tactile Communicant (MCD)
SCOTAPLL... Standing Conference on Theological and Philosophical Libraries in London
Scot App Rep... Scottish Appeal Reports [*A publication*] (DLA)
ScotBcp .... Scotland Bancorp, Inc. [*Associated Press*] (SAG)
SCOTBEC .... Scottish Business Education Council (DCTA)
SCOTBUILD... Scottish Building and Public Works Exhibition [*Scottish Exhibitions Ltd.*] (TSPED)
SCOTCAT .... Scottish Credit Accumulation and Transfer (AIE)
SCOTCH...... Summer Cultural Opportunities for Teams and Children [*National music program*]
SCOTEC ...... Scottish Technical Education Council [*British*]
SCOTENG.... Scottish Engineering Exhibition for Design, Production, and Automation [*Scottish Exhibitions Ltd.*] (TSPED)
SCOTHOT.... Scottish Hotel, Catering, and Licensed Trade Exhibition [*Scottish Exhibitions Ltd.*] (TSPED)
SCOTICE ..... Scotland Iceland (IAA)
SCOTICE ..... Scotland to Iceland Submarine Cable System [*Telecommunications*] (TEL)
Scot Jur....... Scottish Jurist [*A publication*] (DLA)
SCOTL .... Scotland (ROG)
Scot Law J... Scottish Law Journal [*Glasgow*] [*A publication*] (DLA)
ScotLiq........ Scotts Liquid Gold Co. [*Associated Press*] (SAG)
Scot LJ .... Scottish Law Journal and Sheriff Court Record [*A publication*] (DLA)
Scot LM....... Scottish Law Magazine and Sheriff Court Reporter [*A publication*] (DLA)
Scot L Mag... Scottish Law Magazine [*Edinburgh, Scotland*] [*A publication*] (DLA)
Scot LR....... Scottish Law Reporter [*A publication*] (DLA)
Scot L Rep... Scottish Law Reporter [*A publication*] (DLA)
Scot LT .... Scots Law Times [*A publication*] (DLA)
SCOTMET .... Scottish Metropolitan [*Property developer*]
Scotmn .... Scotsman Industries, Inc. [*Associated Press*] (SAG)
ScotNAE...... Scottish National Antarctic Expedition [*1902-04*]
SCOTNATS... Scottish Nationalists
Scot Parl Acts... Acts of the Parliaments of Scotland (DLA)
SCOTRACEN... Scouting Training Center [*Navy*]
SCOTS .... Surveillance and Control of Transmission Systems [*Bell Laboratories*]
SCOTS .... System Checkout Test Set (MCD)
Scots LTR.... Scots Law Times Reports [*A publication*] (DLA)
Scots RR ..... Scots Revised Reports [*1707-1873*] [*A publication*] (DLA)
ScotSt......... Scott & Stringfellow Financial, Inc. [*Associated Press*] (SAG)
ScotStrng..... Scott & Stringfellow Financial [*Associated Press*] (SAG)
Scott........... Scott's English Common Pleas Reports [*A publication*] (DLA)

Scott .... Scott's Reports [25, 26 New York Civil Procedure] [A publication] (DLA)
SCOTT .... Single Channel Objective Tactical Terminal [Army] (RDA)
SCOTT .... Synchronous Continuous Orbital Three-Dimensional Tracking
Scott (Eng)... Scott's English Common Pleas Reports [A publication] (DLA)
Scott J .... Reporter, English Common Bench Reports [A publication] (DLA)
Scott NR ...... Scott's New English Common Pleas Reports [A publication] (DLA)
ScottP .... Scott Paper Ltd. [Associated Press] (SAG)
SCOTT-R ...... Super-Critical, Once-Thru Tube Reactor [Experiment] [General Electric Co.]
Scotts .... Scotts Co. [Associated Press] (SAG)
SCOTTSU ..... Scottish Open Tech Training Support Unit (AIE)
SCOTUS .... Supreme Court of the United States (WDAA)
SCOTVEC ..... Scottish Technician and Vocational Educational Council (ACII)
SCOTVEC ..... Scottish Vocational Education Council (ODBW)
SCOTVIC ...... Standing Conference of Principals of Tertiary and Sixth Form Colleges [British] (AIE)
SCOU .... Ship Course
SC Oudh ...... Oudh Select Cases [India] [A publication] (DLA)
SCOUG .... Southern California Online User Group (NITA)
SCOUS .... Spectrum Clear of Unknown Signals (MUGU)
SCOUT .... Shared Currency Option Under Tender (ODBW)
SCOUT .... Surface-Controlled Oxide Unipolar Transistor
SCOW .... Scottish Convention of Women (DI)
SCOWAH....... Schmulowitz Collection of Wit and Humor [San Francisco Public Library]
SCOWR .... Special Committee on Water Research [International Council of Scientific Unions]
SCOYO .... Standing Conference of Youth Organisations (AIE)
SCP.............. Brotherhood of Sleeping Car Porters [Later, BRAC] (EA)
SCP.............. SAGE [Semiautomatic Ground Environment] Change Proposal (IAA)
SCP.............. SAGE [Semiautomatic Ground Environment] Computer Program
SCP.............. SAGE [Semiautomatic Ground Environment] Computer Project [Military] (IAA)
SCP.............. Satellite Cloud Photograph
SCP.............. Satin Chrome Plated
SCP.............. Scanner Control Power (MCD)
SCP.............. Scanning Phased Array
SCP.............. Schematic Change Proposal
SCP.............. Scope Indus [AMEX symbol] (TTSB)
SCP.............. Scope Industries [AMEX symbol] (SPSG)
SCP.............. Scottish Conservative Party [Political party]
SCP.............. Scrip (ROG)
SCP.............. Script [Films, television, etc.]
SCP.............. Secondary Control Point
SCP.............. Secondary Cross-Connection Point (NITA)
SCP.............. Sector Command Post [Military]
SCP.............. Secure Conferencing Project
SCP.............. Security Classification Procedure [Military]
SCP.............. Self-Consistent Phonon
SCP.............. Semiconductor Products (IAA)
SCP.............. Senior Companion Program (EA)
SCP.............. Serial Character Printer (OA)
SCP.............. Sertoli-Cell Protein [Immunology]
SCP.............. Service Control Point [DoD] (AFIT)
SCP.............. Servo-Controlled Positioner
SCP.............. Session Control Properties [Computer science]
SCP.............. Set Coverage Problem [Mathematical modelling]
SCP.............. Sheep Choroid Plexus
SCP.............. Short-Circuit Protection
SCP.............. Silver Cup Resources Ltd. [Vancouver Stock Exchange symbol]
SCP.............. Simplified Clearance Procedure [Customs] (DS)
SCP.............. Simulation Control Program [Military] (CAAL)
SCP.............. Simulator Control Panel [NASA]
SCP.............. Sindbis Core Protein [Virology]
SCP.............. Single-Cell Protein
SCP.............. Single Chip Package (AAEL)
SCP.............. Single Component Peak [Spectra]
SCP.............. Sleeping Car Porters Union (MHDB)
SCP.............. Small Cardioactive Peptide [Biochemistry]
SCP.............. Small Computer Program [Army] (RDA)
SCP.............. Smaller Communities Program [Department of Labor]
SCP.............. Social Credit Party (NADA)
SCP.............. Social Credit Party of Canada [Parti Credit Social du Canada] (PPW)
SCP.............. Societe Canadienne de la Population [Canadian Population Society - CPS]
SCP.............. Societe Canadienne de Pedatrie [Canadian Paediatric Society] (EAIO)
SCP.............. Societe Culinaire Philanthropique [New York, NY] (EA)
SCP.............. Society for Czechoslovak Philately (EA)
SCP.............. Society of California Pioneers (EA)
SCP.............. Society of Christian Philosophers (EA)
SCP.............. Sodium Cellulose Phosphate [Kidney-stone drug]
SCP.............. Software Change Proposal (MCD)
SCP.............. Solar Cell Panel
SCP.............. Soluble Cytoplasmic Protein (DB)
SCP.............. Sonobuoy Control Panel
SCP.............. Spacecraft Platform [NASA]
SCP.............. Spanish Communist Party
SCP.............. Special Category Patient [Aeromedical evacuation]
SCP.............. Specialist Component Producer
SCP.............. Specific Candlepower (NASA)
SCP.............. Specific Cleavage Product [Biochemistry]
SCP.............. Spherical Candlepower
SCP.............. Spiritual Counterfeits Project (EA)

SCP.............. Standard Corporate Protocol [Telecommunications]
SCP.............. Standardized Care Plans [for hospitals]
SCP.............. Standards Completion Program [Analytical method procedure, OSHA and NIOSH requirements]
SCP.............. State College [Pennsylvania] [Seismograph station code, US Geological Survey] (SEIS)
SCP.............. Stationary Combustion Process [Automotive engineering]
SCP.............. Station Communications Processor
SCP.............. St. Catharines Public Library [UTLAS symbol]
SCP.............. Sterol Carrier Protein
SCP.............. Storage-Command Pulse [Computer science] (ECII)
SCP.............. Storage Control Processor (NOAA)
SCP.............. Stromberg-Carlson Practices [Telecommunications] (TEL)
SCP.............. Structural Ceramic Panel
SCP.............. Subcontract Proposal (AAG)
SCP.............. Sudanese Communist Party [Political party] (PD)
SCP.............. Sulfachloropyridazine [Antibacterial]
SCP.............. Supervisor's Control Panel
SCP.............. Supervisory Control Program [Burroughs Corp.]
SCP.............. Supplier Change Proposal (MCD)
SCP.............. Supplier's Contract Property (MCD)
SCP.............. Supply Cataloging Program
SCP.............. Supply Control Plan [World War II]
SCP.............. Support Control Program (IAA)
SCP.............. Surrounding Combustion Process [Automotive engineering]
SCP.............. Surveillance Communication Processor [Aviation] (OA)
SCP.............. Survey Control Point [Military]
SCP.............. Symbol Conversion Program (NITA)
SCP.............. Symbolic Conversion Program (BUR)
SCP.............. Synthetic Fuels Commercialization Program [Also, SFCP] [Energy Resources Council]
SCP.............. Syrian Communist Party [Political party] (PPW)
SCP.............. System Change Package
SCP.............. System Change Proposal (COE)
SCP.............. System Communication Pamphlet (IEEE)
SCP.............. System Concept Paper [Army] (RDA)
SCP.............. System Control Panel (IAA)
SCP.............. System Control Processor [Honeywell, Inc.]
SCP.............. System Control Program (NITA)
SCP.............. System Control Programming [Computer science]
SCP.............. Systems Change Proposal (AFM)
SCP.............. Waukegan Avionics, Inc. [ICAO designator] (FAAC)
sCP.............. Without Chest Pain [Medicine]
SCPA .... Scottish Cashmere Producers Association (DBA)
SCPA .... Scottish Clay Pigeon Association (DBA)
SCPA .... Semiconductor Chip Protection Act of 1984
SCPA .... Societe Canadienne de Peintres en Aquarelle (AC)
SCPA .... Solar Cell Panel Assembly
SCPA .... Southern Coal Producers Association [Defunct] (EA)
SCPA .... Southern College Personnel Association (AEBS)
SCPA .... Spacecraft Payload Adapter (MCD)
SCPA .... Stabilization and Control System Control Panel (IAA)
SCPC .... Signal Corps Pictorial Center [Obsolete Army]
SCPC .... Single-Channel-per-Carrier [Telecommunications]
SCPCE .... Societe Canadienne pour la Prevention de Cruaute aux Enfants
SCPCU .... Society of Chartered Property and Casualty Underwriters (EA)
SCPD .... Scratch Pad [Computer science]
Sc-PD .... Silicon Photodiode
SCPD .... Staff Civilian Personnel Division [Army]
SCPDCIHE..... Standing Conference of Principals and Directors of Colleges and Institutes of Higher Education (AIE)
SCPD OCSA... Staff Civilian Personnel Division, Office, Chief of Staff, Army (AABC)
SCPE .... Simplified Chemical Protective Equipment [Army] (DOMA)
SCPE .... Simplified Collective Protection Equipment [Military] (RDA)
SCPE .... Societe Canadienne de Physiologie de l'Exercice [Formerly, Canadian Association of Sport Sciences] (AC)
SCPE .... Specialized Customer Premises Equipment [for the handicapped]
SCPE .... Square Corners Plain Edges [Bookbinding] (DGA)
SCPEA .... Standard City Planning Enabling Act (PA)
SCPF .... Sacra Congregatio de Propaganda Fide [Sacred Congregation for the Propagation of the Faith] [Latin]
SCPH .... Societe Canadienne des Pharmaciens d'Hopitaux [Canadian Society of Hospital Pharmacists] (EAIO)
SCPI.............. Scientists' Committee for Public Information [Defunct]
SCPI.............. Sequential Central Port Injection
SCPI.............. Small Computer Program Index [No longer published] [ALLM Books] (IID)
SCPI.............. Standard Commands for Programmable Controllers (ACII)
SCPI.............. Standing Committee on Professional Institutions (ACII)
SCPI.............. Structural Clay Products Institute [Later, BIA] (EA)
SCPK .... Serum Creatine Phosphokinase [An enzyme] (AAMN)
SCPL .... Senior Commercial Pilot's Licence [British] (DBQ)
SCPL .... Signal Corps Photographic Laboratory [Obsolete Army]
S/Cpl .... Staff Corporal [British military] (DMA)
SCPL .... Staff of Chief of Personnel and Logistics [British military] (DMA)
SCPL/H .... Senior Commercial Pilot's Licence/Helicopters [British] (AIA)
SCPM............ Sample Collection and Preparation Module [X-ray spectrometry]
SCPM............ Scanning Chemical Potential Microscope
SCPM............ Semiautomatic Circuit Performance Monitor [Navy] (MCD)
SCPM............ Silwood Centre for Pest Management [Imperial College] [British] (CB)
SCPMT......... Southern California Perceptual Motor Tests
SCPNT .... Southern California Postrotary Nystagmus Test
SCPO .... Second-Class Post Office
SCPO .... Senior Chief Petty Officer [Navy rating]

SCPP	Seasonal-to-Interannual Climate Prediction Program [*Marine science*] (OSRA)
SCPP	Sierra Cooperative Pilot Project [*Department of the Interior*]
SCPP	Supreme Court, Preliminary Prints
SCPP	Surveyor Command Preparation Program [*Aerospace*]
SCPPool	SCP Pool Corp. [*Associated Press*] (SAG)
SCPPS	Secondary Containment Purge and Pressure Control System [*Nuclear energy*] (NRCH)
SCPR	Semiconductor Parameter Retrieval [*Information Handling Services*] [*Database*]
SCPR	Social & Community Planning Research [*British*]
SCPR	Sri Chinmoy Oneness-Home Peace Run [*An association*] (EA)
SCPR	Standard Cardiopulmonary Resuscitation
SCPRF	Structural Clay Products Research Foundation [*BIA*] [*Absorbed by*] (EA)
SCPS	Servo-Controlled Positioning System
SCPS	Society of Civil and Public Servants [*A union*] [*British*] (DCTA)
SCP(S)	Subscribers' Call Processing (Subsystem) [*Telecommunications*] (TEL)
SCPS	Survivable Collective Projected System
SCPS	Survivable Collective Protection System [*Air Force*] (DOMA)
SCPS	Survivable Collision Protection System (DWSG)
SCPSC	South Carolina Public Service Commission Reports [*A publication*] (DLA)
SCPT	SAGE [*Semiautomatic Ground Environment*] Computer Programming Training
SCPT	Schizophrenic Chronic Paranoid Type [*Medicine*] (DMAA)
SCPT	Security Control Point [*Military*] (MUGU)
SCPT	Self-Consistent Perturbation Theory [*Physics*]
S-CPT	Swanson-Cognitive Processing Test (TMMY)
ScPT	Tri-County Technical College, Pendleton, SC [*Library symbol*] [*Library of Congress*] (LCLS)
SCPTR	Standing Committee on Personnel Training and Readiness [*Navy*]
SCPV	Silkworm Cytoplasmic Polyhedrosis Virus (PDAA)
SCPV	Societe Canadienne de Physiologie Vegetale (AC)
SCQ	Hanscom Air Force Base, Base Library, Hanscom AFB, MA [*OCLC symbol*] (OCLC)
SCQ	Saco Resources [*Vancouver Stock Exchange symbol*]
SCQ	Santiago De Compostela [*Spain*] [*Airport symbol*] (OAG)
SCQ	Sisters of Charity of Quebec [*Grey Nuns*] [*Roman Catholic religious order*]
SCQ	Sociedad Chilena de Quimca
SCQ-39	Situational Confidence Questionnaire (TMMY)
SCQC	Scout Crew Qualification Course [*Army*]
SCQE	Squad Combat Qualification Exercise [*Army*] (INF)
SCR	Cape Colony Supreme Court Reports [*A publication*] (DLA)
SCR	Chinook Regional Library, Swift Current, Saskatchewan [*Library symbol National Library of Canada*] (NLC)
SCR	Juta's Supreme Court Cases [*1880-1910*] [*Cape Of Good Hope, South Africa*] [*A publication*] (DLA)
SCR	Law Reports of Supreme Court of Sarawak, North Borneo, and Brunei [*A publication*] (DLA)
SCR	San Cristobal [*Chile*] [*Seismograph station code, US Geological Survey Closed*] (SEIS)
SCR	Scan Control Register (NITA)
SCR	Scanning Control Register
SCR	Schedule Change Report
SCR	Schedule Change Request [*NASA*] (NASA)
SCR	Score (ROG)
SCR	Scourer [*s*] [*or Scouring Freight*]
SCR	Scranton [*Diocesan abbreviation*] [*Pennsylvania*] (TOCD)
SCR	Scranton Public Library, Scranton, PA [*OCLC symbol*] (OCLC)
Scr	Scrapie [*Animal pathology*]
SCR	Scratch
SCR	Screen (WGA)
SCR	Screw (AAG)
scr	Scribe [*MARC relator code*] [*Library of Congress*] (LCCP)
SCR	Scrip (ADA)
Scr	Scripture (BJA)
SCR	Scruple [*Pharmacology*] (DAVI)
SCR	Scurry-Rainbow Oil Ltd. [*Toronto Stock Exchange symbol*]
SCR	Sea Containers Ltd. [*NYSE symbol*] (SPSG)
SCR	Section Cross Reference (MCD)
SCR(S)	Security Change Request [*Military*] (GFGA)
SCR	Selective Catalytic [*or Catalyst*] Reduction
SCR	Selective Chopper Radiometer
SCR	Selenium Control Rectifier [*Nuclear energy*] (NRCH)
SCR	Self-Consistent Renormalization Theory [*Quantum mechanics*]
SCR	Semiconductor
SCR	Semiconductor-Controlled Rectifier
SCR	Senate Concurrent Resolution (CDAI)
SCR	Senior Common Room [*in British colleges and public schools*]
SCR	Senior Contractor Representative
SCR	Sequence Checking Routine
SCR	Sequence-Control Register [*Computer science*] (EECA)
scr	Serbo-Croatian (Roman) [*MARC language code Library of Congress*] (LCCP)
SCR	Series Control Relay
SCr.	Serum Creatinine [*Hematology*]
SCR	Set Complete Radio
SCR	Shift Count Register
SCR	Shipboard Census Report [*FHWA*] (TAG)
SCR	Ship to Component Record [*Navy*]
SCR	Short-Circuit Ratio
SCR	Short Consensus Repeat [*Biochemistry*]

SCR	Si-Chang Flying Service Co. Ltd. [*Thailand*] [*ICAO designator*] (FAAC)
SCR	Signal Conditioner (IAA)
SCR	Signal Conditioning Rack
SCR	Signal Conversion Relay [*Telecommunications*] (TEL)
SCR	Signal Corps Radio [*Followed by model number*] [*Obsolete Army*]
SCR	Silicon-Controlled Rectifier [*Electronics*]
SCR	Simulation and Control Rack
SCR	Single Card Reader [*Computer science*] (IAA)
SCR	Single-Channel Reception (DEN)
SCR	Single Character Recognition
SCR	Skin Conductance Reading [*on Biofeedback*] [*Psychiatry*] (DAVI)
SCR	Skin Conductance Response
SCR	Sneak Circuit Report [*NASA*] (NASA)
SCR	Societe Collective de Retransmission du Canada (AC)
SCR	Society for Cultural Relations between the Peoples of the British Commonwealth and the USSR
SCR	Society of Cardiovascular Radiology [*Later, SCVIR*] (EA)
SCR	Sodium-Cooled Reactor [*Nuclear energy*]
SCR	Software Change Request [*NASA*]
SCR	Software Correction Report (CAAL)
SCR	Software Cost Reduction [*Computer science*]
SCR	Solar Corpuscular Radiation (IAA)
SCR	Solar Cosmic Radiation [*or Ray*]
SCR	SONAR Control Room
SCR	South Carolina Reports [*A publication*] (DLA)
SCR	Space Charge Recombination (IAA)
SCR	Spacecraft Received Time
SCR	Spanish Communication Region [*Air Force*] (MCD)
SCR	Spares Coordination Record (SAA)
SCR	Special Certification Roster
SCR	Specification Clarification Request (MCD)
SCR	Specific Commodity Rates (DS)
SCR	Speed Change Rate
SCR	Spondylitic Caudal Radiculopathy [*Medicine*] (DMAA)
SCR	Stable Continental Region [*Geology*]
SCR	Standard Class Rate
SCR	Static Card Reader
SCR	Stock Car Racing [*A publication*]
SCR	Strip Chart Recorder [*NASA*]
SCR	Structurally Conserved Region [*Biochemistry*]
SCR	Styrene-Chloroprene Rubber (EDCT)
SCR	Sub-Chief Ranger [*Ancient Order of Foresters*]
SCR	Subcontractor (SAA)
SCR	Summary Control Report [*Planning and Production*] [*Navy*]
SCR	Supersonic Combustion Ramjet
SCR	Support Control Room [*NASA*] (KSC)
SCR	Supreme Court Reports [*India*] [*A publication*] (DLA)
SCR	Supreme Court Reports [*Canada Department of Justice*] [*Information service or system*] (CRD)
SCR	Supreme Court Reports [*1928-41, 1946-51*] [*Sarawak*] [*A publication*] (DLA)
SCR	Surface Contour RADAR
SCR	Syrene-Chloroprene Rubber
SCR	System Change Request
SCR	System Conceptual Requirement (SSD)
SCR	System Control Record (NITA)
SCR	System Control Registers [*Computer science*]
SCR	System Control Routine
SCRA	Scottish Countryside Rangers Association (DBA)
SCRA	Sea Containers Ltd CI'A' [*NYSE symbol*] (TTSB)
SCRA	Single Channel Radio Access Subsystem (MCD)
SCRA	Specialized Carriers & Rigging Association
SCRA	Stanford Center for RADAR Astronomy
SCRA	Steel Can Recycling Association (EA)
SCRA	Supreme Council of the Royal Arcanum [*Boston, MA*] (EA)
SCRAA	Standing Conference of Regional Arts Associations [*British*] (DI)
SCRAC	Standing Conference of Regional Advisory Councils for Further Education
SCRAG	Senior Civilian Representative, Attorney General [*Department of Justice civil disturbance unit*]
SCRAM	Safety Control Rod Axe Man [*Nuclear energy*] (IEEE)
SCRAM	Scottish Campaign to Resist the Atomic Menace
SCRAM	Selective Combat Range Artillery Missile
SCRAM	Self-Corrected Remedial Aid and Media [*Teaching method*]
SCRAM	Service Change Release and Manufacture (MCD)
SCRAM	Several Compilers Reworked and Modified
SCRAM	Short-Range Attack Missile
SCRAM	Signal Corps Random-Access Memory (DNAB)
SCRAM	Space Capsule Regulator and Monitor
SCRAM	Spares Components Reidentification and Modification [*Program*] [*DoD*]
SCRAM	Spares Control, Release, and Monitoring
SCRAM	Special Criteria for Retrograde of Army Materiel (AABC)
SCRAM	Speech-Controlled Respirometer for Ambulation Measurement [*Medicine*] (DMAA)
SCRAM	Static Column Dynamic Random-Access Memory [*Computer science*] (EECA)
SCRAM	Supersonic Combustion Ramjet Missile
SCRAM	Synanon Committee for Responsible American Media [*Later, SCRAP*]
SCRAMJET	Supersonic Combustion Ramjet
SCRAMM	System Calibration, Repair, and Maintenance Model [*Military*] (CAAL)
SCRAP	Selective Curtailment of Reports and Paperwork [*Navy*]
SCRAP	Series Computation of Reliability and Probability [*Computer science*]

SCRAP .... Simple Complex Reaction-Time Apparatus
SCRAP .... Society for Completely Removing All Parking Meters
SCRAP .... South Coast Recycled Auto Project [*Air pollution controls credits from mobile sources for stationary sources*]
SCRAP .... Students Challenging Regulatory Agency Proceedings [*Student legal action organization*]
SCRAP .... Super-Caliber Rocket-Assisted Projectile (IEEE)
SCRAP .... Synanon Committee for a Responsible American Press (EA)
SCRAPE ...... Screening Country Requirements Against Plus Excess [*DoD*]
SCRATA ...... Steel Castings Research and Trade Association [*Sheffield, England*] (EAIO)
Scrat & Bra... Scratchley and Brabook's Building Societies [*2nd ed.*] [*1882*] [*A publication*] (DLA)
Scrat Bdg Soc... Scratchley's Building Societies [*5th ed.*] [*1883*] [*A publication*] (DLA)
Scrat Life Ass... Scratchley's Life Assurance [*13th ed.*] [*1887*] [*A publication*] (DLA)
SCR B .... Sea Containers Ltd Cl'B' [*NYSE symbol*] (TTSB)
SC-RB .... Separable Costs-Remaining Benefits (PDAA)
SCRB .... Software Configuration Review Board (CAAL)
SCRB .... Structured Case Review Blank
SCRBA .... Student Committee for the Right to Bear Arms [*Defunct*] (EA)
SCRC .... Spanish Colonial Research Center [*University of New Mexico*] [*Research center*] (RCD)
SCRC .... Study Circles Resource Center (EA)
SCRC .... Superfund Community Relations Coordinator [*Environmental Protection Agency*] (GFGA)
SCRD .... Secondary Control Rod Driveline [*Nuclear energy*] (NRCH)
SCRD .... Student Coalition for the Right to Drink [*Defunct*] (EA)
SCRD .... Vina Del Mar/Rodelillo [*Chile*] [*ICAO location identifier*] (ICLI)
SCRDB .... Screwed Bonnet
SCRDC .... Silicon Controlled Rectifier Regulated Direct Current (PDAA)
SCRDE .... Stores and Clothing Research and Development Establishment [*British*]
SCR dimmer... Silicon-Controlled Rectifier [*Dimmer*] [*Television*] (WDMC)
SCRDM .... Secondary Control Rod Drive Mechanism [*Nuclear energy*] (NRCH)
SCRDN .... Screw Down
SCRE .... Scottish Council for Research in Education
SCrE........... South Carolina Electric & Gas Co. [*Associated Press*] (SAG)
SCRE .... Stratified Charge Rotary Engine (DWSG)
SCRE .... Supreme Cossack Representation in Exile (EA)
SCREAM ..... Society for the Registration of Estate Agents and Mortgage Brokers (MHDB)
SCREEN ...... Screening Children for Related Early Educational Needs (TES)
SCREENEX... Screening Exercise [*Military*] (NVT)
SC Regs ...... South Carolina State Register [*A publication*] (AAGC)
SCREN .... Screen [*Laboratory science*] (DAVI)
SC Rep .... Juta's Supreme Court Cases [*1880-1910*] [*Cape Of Good Hope, South Africa*] [*A publication*] (DLA)
SC Res .... Senate Concurrent Resolution (DLA)
Sc Rev Rept... Scots Revised Reports [*A publication*] (DLA)
SCREWS ..... Solar Cosmic Ray Early Warning System (MUGU)
SCRF .... Small Craft Repair Facility [*Navy*] (NVT)
SCRF .... Stanford Center for Reservoir Forecasting [*Stanford University*] [*Research center*] (RCD)
SCRF .... Surface Coil Rotating Frame [*Medicine*] (DMAA)
SCRG .... Rancagua/De La Independencia [*Chile*] [*ICAO location identifier*] (ICLI)
SCRG .... Societe Canadienne de Recherche en Geriatrie
SCRG .... Stationary Cosmic Ray Gas
SCRG .... System Change Review Group [*George C. Marshall Space Flight Center*] (NASA)
SCRH .... Sisters of Charity of Rolling Meadows (TOCD)
ScRh.......... York County Library, Rock Hill, SC [*Library symbol*] [*Library of Congress*] (LCLS)
ScRhM........ Clinton Junior College, Rock Hill, SC [*Library symbol*] [*Library of Congress*] (LCLS)
ScRhW........ Winthrop College, Rock Hill, SC [*Library symbol Library of Congress*] (LCLS)
ScRhY......... York Technical College, Rock Hill, SC [*Library symbol*] [*Library of Congress*] (LCLS)
SCRI .... Science Court and Research Institute (EA)
SCRI .... Scientists' Committee for Radiation Information (EA)
SCRI .... Scottish Crop Research Institute [*Research center*] (IRC)
SCRI .... South Central Reservoir Investigation [*Department of the Interior*] (GRD)
SCRI .... Southern Center for Research and Innovation, Inc. [*University of Southern Mississippi*] [*Research center*] (RCD)
SCRI .... Supercomputer Computations Research Institute [*Florida State University*] [*Research center*] (RCD)
Scrib Dow.... Scribner on the Law of Dower [*A publication*] (DLA)
SCRIBE .... System for Computerized Reporting of Information for Better Education (MHDI)
SCRIBE .... System for Correspondence Recording and Interrogation by EDP [*Electronic Data Processing*]
SCRICI .... Selected Reagent Ion Chemical Ionization [*Spectroscopy*]
SCRID .... Silicon-Controlled Rectifier Indicator Driver (IAA)
SCRIM .... Sideway Force Coefficient Routine Investigating Machine [*Department of Transport*] [*British*]
SCRIM .... Supersonic Cruise Intermediate Range Missile (MCD)
SCRIMP ...... Save Cash, Reduce Immediately Meat Prices [*Boston, MA, group protesting high cost of food, 1973*]
SCRIMP ...... Seeman Composite Resin Infusion Molding Process
SCRIP .... Scriptum [*Something Written*] [*Latin*] (ROG)
SCRIP .... Scripture

SCRIP .... Select Commission on Immigration and Refugee Policy (NADA)
SCRIP .... Single-Chain Ribosome-Inactivating Protein [*Biochemistry*]
SCRIP .... Statine Congener of Renin Inhibitory Peptide [*Biochemistry*]
SCRIP .... System for Controlling Returns in Inventory and Production Data [*IRS*]
Scripps .... Scripps [*E. W.*] Co. [*Associated Press*] (SAG)
SCRIPPS ...... Scripps Coronary Radiation to Inhibit Proliferation Post-Stenting
SCRIPT .... Scientific and Commercial Interpreter and Program Translator (IAA)
SCRIPT .... Scientific and Commercial Subroutine Interpreter and Program Translator
SCRIPT .... Screenwriting Coalition for Industry Professionals and Teachers (EDAC)
SCRIPT .... Scripture
script .... Scripture (VRA)
SCRIPT .... Support for Creative Independent Production Talent [*EC*] (ECED)
SCRIPT .... System Controlling Research Image Processing Tasks (MCD)
SCRIS .... Southern California Regional Information Study [*Bureau of Census*]
Scriv Cop .... Scriven on the Law of Copyholds [*7th ed.*] [*1896*] [*A publication*] (DLA)
Scriven .... Scriven on the Law of Copyholds [*A publication*] (DLA)
SCRJ.......... Supersonic Combustion Ramjet
SCRL .... Sensory Communication Research Laboratory [*Gallaudet College*] [*Research center*] (RCD)
SCRL .... Signal Corps RADAR Laboratory [*Obsolete Army*]
SCRL .... Signal Corps Radio Laboratory [*Army*] (IAA)
SCRL .... Skill Components Research Laboratory [*Air Force*] (MCD)
SCRL .... Split-Level Charge-Recovery Logic [*Computer science*]
SCRL .... Station Configuration Requirement List [*NASA*] (MCD)
SCRLC .... South Central Research Library Council [*Library network*] (IID)
Scr LT .... Scranton Law Times [*Pennsylvania*] [*A publication*] (DLA)
SCRLV .... Subterranean Clover Red Leaf Virus
SCRM .... Isla Rey Jorge/Base Aerea Teniente R. Marsh Martin [*Chile*] [*ICAO location identifier*] (ICLI)
SCRM .... Secondary Certified Reference Material [*Nuclear energy*] (NRCH)
SCRMV .... Scrophularia Mottle Virus [*Plant pathology*]
SCRN .... Screen [*s*] [*or Screening Freight*]
scrn .... Screen (VRA)
scRNA........ Small Cytoplasmic RNA [*Ribanucleic Acid*] (BARN)
scRNP........ Ribonucleoprotein, Small Cytoplasmic
scrnpr .... Screenprint (VRA)
SCRNSW...... New South Wales Supreme Court Reports [*A publication*] (DLA)
SCRO .... Scottish Criminal Records Office [*Office of Population Census and Surveys*] [*British*]
SCRO .... Societe Canadienne de la Recherche Operationnelle
SCROLL....... String and Character Recording Oriented Logogrammatic Language [*1970*] [*Computer science*] (CSR)
SC ROM ...... Scotch Roman [*Typography*] (DGA)
SCROOGE .... Society to Curtail Ridiculous, Outrageous, and Ostentatious Gift Exchange (EA)
SCROPT....... Scientific and Commercial Subroutine Interpreter and Program Translator (IAA)
SC/ROSTENA... Bureau Regional de Science et de Technologie pour l'Europe et l'Amerique du Nord [*Regional Office for Science and Technology for Europe and North America*] (EAIO)
SCRP .... Small Card Release Processing [*Computer science*] (IAA)
SCRP .... Societe Canadienne des Relations Publiques
SCRP .... Superfund Community Relations Program [*Environmental Protection Agency*] (GFGA)
SCRP .... Supplemental Conventional Reading Program [*Education*]
SCRPC .... Societe de Physiotherapie Cardiorespiratoire du Canada (AC)
SCRPr......... Sea Cont Ltd $1.46 1/4cmPfd [*NYSE symbol*] (TTSB)
SCRPrC....... Sea Cont Ltd. $2.10'82 Pfd [*NYSE symbol*] (TTSB)
SCRPrD....... Sea Cont Ltd. $4.125cm Cv Pfd [*NYSE symbol*] (TTSB)
SCRPrE....... Sea Cont Ltd. $4 cm Cv Pfd [*NYSE symbol*] (TTSB)
Sc RR .... Scotch Revised Reports [*A publication*] (DLA)
SCRR .... Solar Central Receiver Reformer (PDAA)
SCRR .... Standard Compliance Review Report (AAGC)
SCRR .... Supercircular Reentry Research (IAA)
SCRS .... Secondary Control Rod System [*Nuclear energy*] (NRCH)
SCRS .... Self-Control Rating Scale
SCRS .... Serialized Control and Reporting System (NAKS)
SCRS .... Service Center Replacement System [*Computer science*]
SCRS .... Short Clinical Rating Scale [*Medicine*] (DB)
SCRS .... Society of Collision Repair Specialists (EA)
SCRS .... Strip Chart Recorder System [*NASA*]
SCRSY .... Serialized Control and Record System (NAKS)
SCRT .... Sealed Cathode Ray Tube
SCRT .... Subscribers' Circuit Routine Tester [*Telecommunications*] (TEL)
SCRTA .... Steel Castings Research and Trade Association [*British*]
SCRTC .... Signal Corps Replacement Training Center [*Obsolete Army*]
SCRTERM ..... Screw Terminal
SCRTY .... Security
SCRUMPie.... Socially Concerned Upwardly Mobile Professional [*Lifestyle classification*]
Scrut Charter... Scrutton on Charter-Parties [*18th ed.*] [*1974*] [*A publication*] (DLA)
Scrutton....... Scrutton on Charter-Parties [*16 eds.*] [*1886-1955*] [*A publication*] (DLA)
SCRV .... Spill Control Recovery Valve (PDAA)
SCRWC .... Sierra Club Radioactive Waste Campaign [*Later, RWC*] (EA)
ScS........... Reflected S Wave [*Earthquakes*]
SCS........... Safety Control Switch
SCS........... Safety-Critical Systems/Software [*British*]
SCS........... Saint Charles Seminary [*Later, SCBS*] [*Pennsylvania*]
SCS........... Santa Clara Systems, Inc. [*San Jose, CA*] [*Telecommunications service*] (TSSD)

SCS............	Satellite Communications Subsystem
SCS............	Satellite Control Satellite [*Telecommunications*] (TEL)
SCS............	Satellite Control Section (SSD)
SCS............	Satellite Control Squadron
SCS............	Satellite Test Center Communications Subsystem (MCD)
SCS............	Scan Converter [*or Counter*] System
SCS............	Scheduled Cargo Service (IIA)
SCS............	Scientific Certification Systems (EA)
SCS............	Scientific Civil Service [*British*]
SCS............	Scientific Control Systems (DIT)
SCS............	Scottish Combined Societies [*Australia*]
SCS............	Screening and Costing Staff [*NATO*] (NATG)
SCS............	Sea Control Ship [*Navy*] (NVT)
SCS............	Secondary Control Ship [*Navy*] (NVT)
SCS............	Secondary Control System (MCD)
SCS............	Secondary Coolant System [*Nuclear energy*] (NRCH)
scs............	Secondary Coolant System (NAKS)
SCS............	Secret Control Station [*NASA*] (KSC)
SCS............	Secret Cover Sheet (AAG)
SCS............	Section Control Station [*RADAR*]
SCS............	Secure Communications System [*Military*] (CAAL)
SCS............	Security Container System [*Army*] (AABC)
SCS............	Security Control System (IAA)
SCS............	Selected Cancers Study [*Centers for Disease Control*]
SCS............	Selected Classification Service (NITA)
SCS............	Semiconductor Controlled Switch (MSA)
SCS............	Senior Citizen's Services [*A publication*]
SCS............	Separate Channel Signalling (NITA)
SCS............	Septuagint and Cognate Studies (BJA)
SCS............	Sequence Coding System (IAA)
SCS............	Sequence Control System (KSC)
SCS............	Sequencing and Command Systems Specialist [*NASA*]
SCS............	Serious Crime Squad (WDAA)
SCS............	Shaken Child Syndrome (CPH)
SCS............	Ship Control Station [*Navy*] (CAAL)
SCS............	Short-Circuit-Stable
SCS............	Shutdown Cooling System [*Nuclear energy*] (NRCH)
SCS............	Sicasica [*Bolivia*] [*Seismograph station code, US Geological Survey Closed*] (SEIS)
SCS............	Sidewinder Control System (DWSG)
SCS............	Sigmacom Systems [*Vancouver Stock Exchange symbol*]
SCS............	Signal Center and School [*Army*] (MCD)
SCS............	Signal Communications System [*Air Force*]
SCS............	Signal Conditioning System (KSC)
SCS............	Silicon-Controlled Switch
SCS............	Simulation Control Subsystem (KSC)
SCS............	Simultaneous Color System (IAA)
SCS............	Single Change of Station (IAA)
SCS............	Single Channel Simplex
SCS............	Single Composition Spherical [*Dental alloy*]
SCS............	Single Control Support (BUR)
SCS............	Single Crystal Silicon (AAEL)
SCS............	Slovak Catholic Sokol [*An association*] (EA)
SCS............	Slow Code Scanner
SCS............	Small Components Structural
SCS............	Small Computer System
SCS............	Social Competence Scale
SCS............	Societe Canadienne du Sida (AC)
SCS............	Societe Canadienne du Sommeil (AC)
SCS............	Societe en Commandite Simple [*Simple Partnership*] [*Belgium*]
SCS............	Society for Carribean Studies (EAIO)
SCS............	Society for Ch'ing Studies (EA)
SCS............	Society for Cinema Studies (EA)
SCS............	Society for Computer Simulation [*Later, SCSI*] (EA)
SCS............	Society for Conservative Studies [*Later, YAF*] (EA)
SCS............	Society of Civil Servants [*British*]
SCS............	Society of Clinical Surgery [*Defunct*] (EA)
SCS............	Society of Construction Superintendents (EA)
SCS............	Society of Cosmetic Scientists (EAIO)
SCS............	Society of County Secretaries [*British*]
SCS............	Sodium Cellulose Sulfate [*Organic chemistry*]
SCS............	Sodium Characterization System [*Nuclear energy*] (NRCH)
SCS............	Software Communications Service
SCS............	Soil Conservation Service [*Department of Agriculture*]
SCS............	Solar Collector Subassembly (MCD)
SCS............	Solent Container Service [*British*] (DS)
SCS............	Solid Combustion Synthesis [*Physics*]
SCS............	SONAR Calibration Set
SCS............	SONAR Communications Set
SCS............	Soybean Corn Silage (OA)
SCS............	Space Cabin Simulator (IEEE)
SCS............	Space Command Station (AAG)
SCS............	Space Communication System (IAA)
SCS............	Spacecraft Control System (NASA)
scs............	Spacecraft Control System [*NASA*] (NAKS)
SCS............	Spacecraft System [*NASA*] (KSC)
SCS............	Spanish Colonial Style [*Cigars*]
SCS............	Special Communications System (MCD)
SCS............	Special Computer Service (IAA)
SCS............	Special Contingency Stockpile [*Military*] (AABC)
ScS............	Specialist in Science (GAGS)
SCS............	Speed Class Sequencing
SCS............	Speed-Controlled Spark [*Automotive engineering*]
SCS............	Speed Control System (PDAA)
SCS............	Spinal Cord Society (EA)

SCS............	Stabilization and Control System [*or Subsystem*] [*NASA*]
scs............	Stabilization and Control System [*NASA*] (NAKS)
SCS............	Standard Coordinate System (KSC)
SCS............	Stationing Capability System [*Army*] (AABC)
SCS............	Statistical Control System
SCS............	Stiffened Cylindrical Shell
SCS............	Stimulated Compton Scattering [*Spectroscopy*]
SCS............	Stop Control Braking System [*Lucas Girling*]
SCS............	Storage Computer Corp. [*AMEX symbol*] (SAG)
SCS............	Student's Confidential Statement [*Education*]
SCS............	Suit Communication System [*for spacesuits*] [*NASA*]
SCS............	Superintendent of Car Service
SCS............	Supervisory Control System (MCD)
SCS............	Supplementary Control Strategy [*System*] [*Environmental*] (GNE)
SCS............	Supplementary Control System (COE)
SCS............	Supply Control Study
SCS............	Surface Composition Strengthened
SCS............	Surface Connecting System (DB)
SCS............	Suspect Chemicals Sourcebook [*Roytech Publications*] [*Information service or system*] (CRD)
SCS............	Sussex Cattle Society (EAIO)
SCS............	Swedish Colonial Society (EA)
SCS............	Sweeping Current Supply
SCS............	Sweetens Computer Services [*British*]
SCS............	System Conformance Statement [*Telecommunications*]
SCS............	University of South California, School of Library Science, Los Angeles, CA [*OCLC symbol*] (OCLC)
SCSA	Secondary Colleges Staff Association [*Tasmania, Australia*]
SCSA	Ship Constructive and Shipwrights' Association [*A union*] [*British*]
SCSA	Siamese Cat Society of America (EA)
SCSA	Signal Computing System Architecture [*Computer science*] (IGQR)
SCSA	Soil Conservation Society of America (EA)
SCSA	Spastic Centres of South Australia
SCSA	Sports Car Collectors Society of America [*Later, SCCSA*] (EA)
SCSA	Standard Consolidated Statistical Area [*Census Bureau*]
SCSA	Steering Committee for Sustainable Agriculture [*Later, CSA*] (EA)
SCSA	Supreme Council for Sport in Africa [*See also CSSA*] [*Yaounde, Cameroon*] (EAIO)
SCSB	Standard Capital Superannuation Benefit [*British*]
SCSBCVG.....	Suore di Carita delle Sante Bartolomea Capitanio e Vincenza Gerosa [*Sisters of Charity of Saints Bartholomew Capitanio And Vincent Gerosa*] [*Italy*] (EAIO)
SCSBDE	Square Corners Silver Bevelled Deckle Edges [*Bookbinding*] (DGA)
SCSBE	Square Corners Silver-Bevelled Edges [*Bookbinding*] (DGA)
SCSBM	Society for Computer Science in Biology and Medicine
SCSC	Santiago/Ciudad [*Chile*] [*ICAO location identifier*] (ICLI)
SCSC	ScanSource, Inc. [*NASDAQ symbol*] (SAG)
SCSC	Secondary Curriculum Study Center [*of NASSP*]
SCSC	Sorores a Caritate Sanctae Crucis [*Sisters of Mercy of the Holy Cross*] [*Roman Catholic religious order*]
SCSC	South Carolina State College
Sc-SC.........	South Carolina Supreme Court, Columbia, SC [*Library symbol Library of Congress*] (LCLS)
SCSC	Southern Connecticut State College [*New Haven*]
SCSC	Strategic Conventional Standoff Capability (MCD)
SCSC	Summer Computer Simulation Conference
SCSCB	Sisters of Charity of St. Charles Borromeo [*See also LCB*] (EAIO)
SCSCCL	Sellin Center for Studies in Criminology and Criminal Law (EA)
SCSCLC	Single-Carrier Space-Charge-Limited Current
SCSCmp	SCS Compute, Inc. [*Associated Press*] (SAG)
SCSCO	Secure Submarine Communications (KSC)
SC (Scot).....	Scottish Court of Session Cases, New Series [*A publication*] (DLA)
SCSCP	System Coordination for SAGE [*Semiautomatic Ground Environment*] Computer Programming [*Military*] (IAA)
SCSCW	Scancource Inc. Wrrt [*NASDAQ symbol*] (TTSB)
Sc SD	Doctor of Social Sciences
SCSD	School Construction Systems Development [*Project*] [*of Educational Facilities Laboratories*]
SCSD	Simulation and Control Systems Division [*General Electric Co.*] (MCD)
SCSE..........	La Serena/La Florida [*Chile*] [*ICAO location identifier*] (ICLI)
SCSE..........	Smooth Curve - Smooth Earth
SCSE..........	Society of Casual Safety Engineers
SCSE..........	Square Corners Silver Edges [*Bookbinding*] (DGA)
SCSE..........	State Commission for Space Exploration [*Former USSR*]
SCSEP	Senior Community Service Employment Program (EA)
Sc Sess Cas...	Scotch Court of Session Cases [*A publication*] (DLA)
SCSFA	Sunset Coast Sub-tropical Fruits Association [*Queensland, Australia*]
SCSFX	Seligman Com. Stock Cl.A [*Mutual fund ticker symbol*] (SG)
SCSG	SAGE [*Semiautomatic Ground Environment*] Computer Support Group [*Military*] (IAA)
SCSG	Scottish Churches' Sudan Group Newsletter [*A publication*]
SCSG	Signal Conditioning Subsystem Group (MCD)
SCSG	Superior Cervical Sympathetic Ganglia [*Anatomy*]
SCSGIG........	Supreme Council Sovereign Grand Inspectors General [*Freemasonry*]
SCSH	Scottish Council for Single Homeless (DBA)
SCSH	Sisters of Charity of St. Hyacinthe [*Grey Nuns*] [*Roman Catholic religious order*]
SCSH	Structural Carbon Steel Hard
SCSH	Survey of the Chronic Sick and Handicapped [*British*]
SCSHX	Shutdown Cooling System Heat Exchange [*Nuclear energy*] (NRCH)
SCSI..........	Sensors and Control Systems Institute [*Beltsville, MD*] [*Department of Agriculture*] (GRD)
SCSI..........	Small Computer System Interface [*Pronounced "scuzzy"*]

SCSI.............	Societe Canadienne de la Surete Industrielle
SCSI.............	Society for Computer Simulation International (EA)
SCSIT.........	Southern California Sensory Integration Test [Ayres] [Education]
SCSJA.......	Sisters of Charity of St. Joan Antida (TOCD)
SCSJAT.......	Sisters of Charity of St. Jeanne Antide Thouret [Italy] (EAIO)
SCSL.............	Sandia Corporation, Sandia Laboratory (AABC)
SCSL.............	Scientific Continuous Simulation Language (IAA)
SCSL.............	Sisters of Charity of St. Louis [Roman Catholic religious order]
SCSL.............	Suncoast S & L Assn FSA [NASDAQ symbol] (TTSB)
SCSL.............	Suncoast Savings & Loan Association [Hollywood, FL] [NASDAQ symbol] (NQ)
SCSLP........	Smithsonian Center for Short-Lived Phenomena
SCSLP........	Suncoast S&L 8% Cv Pfd [NASDAQ symbol] (TTSB)
SCS(LS).......	Sea Control Ship (Lead Ship) [Navy] (MCD)
SCSM...........	Small Caliber Smart Munition [Army] (RDA)
SCSM...........	Spacecraft Systems Monitor (IAA)
SCSM...........	Structural Carbon Steel Medium
SCSMHPS....	Special Constituency Section for Mental Health and Psychiatric Services (EA)
SCSMHPS....	Special Constituency Section for Psychiatric and Substance Abuse Services [Formerly, Special Constituency Section for Mental Health and Psychiatric Services] (EA)
SCSN...........	Santo Domingo/Santo Domingo [Chile] [ICAO location identifier] (ICLI)
SCSN...........	Southern California Seismic Network
SCSN...........	Standard Computer Software Number
SCSO...........	Space Communications Station Operation
SCSO...........	Superconducting Cavity Stabilized Oscillator [For clocks]
ScSocD.......	Doctor of Social Science
ScSocL.......	Licence in Social Science [British]
SCSP..........	Schools Cultural Studies Project (AIE)
SCSP..........	Scottish Council for Single Parents (DBA)
SCSP..........	Secretariat of the Council for Scientific Policy [British]
SCSP..........	Serum Cancer-Suppressive Peptide [Oncology]
SCSP..........	Smaller Communities Services Program [Department of Labor]
SCSP..........	Solid Cast Steel Propeller (DS)
SCSP..........	South China Sea Fisheries Development and Coordinating Program [Marine science] (OSRA)
ScSp...........	Spartanburg County Public Library, Spartanburg, SC [Library symbol Library of Congress] (LCLS)
SCSP..........	Storm and Combined Sewer Program (GNE)
SC/SP.........	Supracondylar/Suprapatellar [Prosthesis]
SCSP..........	System Calibration Support Plan [Air Force] (CET)
ScSpC........	Converse College, Spartanburg, SC [Library symbol Library of Congress] (LCLS)
ScSpM........	Milliken Research Corp., Research Library, Spartanburg, SC [Library symbol Library of Congress] (LCLS)
ScSpS.........	Sherman College of Straight Chiropractic, Spartanburg, SC [Library symbol] [Library of Congress] (LCLS)
SCSPS........	Standing Committee on the Safeguard of the Pursuit of Science [International Council of Scientific Unions]
ScSpSM.......	Spartanburg Methodist College, Spartanburg, SC [Library symbol] [Library of Congress] (LCLS)
ScSpTC.......	Spartanburg Technical College, Spartanburg, SC [Library symbol] [Library of Congress] (LCLS)
ScSpW........	Wofford College, Spartanburg, SC [Library symbol Library of Congress] (LCLS)
ScSpW-MHi...	Methodist Historical Society, South Carolina Conference of the Methodist Church,Wofford College, Spartanburg, SC [Library symbol Library of Congress] (LCLS)
SCSR..........	Segundo Corral/Segundo Corral Alto [Chile] [ICAO location identifier] (ICLI)
SCSR..........	Self-Contained Self-Rescuer [Breathing device]
SCSR..........	Ship Construction Subsidy Regulations [Canada]
SCSRMA.......	Surface Coating Synthetic Resin Manufacturers Association [British] (BI)
SCSRS........	Shoe Cove Satellite Receiving Station [Canada]
SCSRS-S.......	Standard Command Supply Review System - SAILS
SCSS..........	Satellite Communications System Control (NATG)
SCSS..........	School Child Stress Scale [Child development test] [Psychology]
SCSS..........	Scottish Council of Social Service (DI)
SCSS..........	Self-Contained Starting System [NASA]
SCSS..........	Sequence Coding and Search System
SCSS..........	Specialist Computer Systems and Software [British] (TELE)
SCSS..........	State Controller and System Services [NASA]
SCSS..........	Structural Carbon Steel Soft
SCSSA........	School and Community Safety Society of America (EA)
SCSST........	Standing Conference on School Science and Technology [British]
SCST...........	Castro/Gamboa [Chile] [ICAO location identifier] (ICLI)
SCST...........	Scan Converter Storage Tube
SCST...........	Society of Commercial Seed Technologists (EA)
SCSTC........	Senior Citizen Ski Touring Committee (EA)
Sc St Crim...	Scandinavian Studies in Criminology [1965] [A publication] (DLA)
ScStg..........	Dorchester County Library, St. George, SC [Library symbol] [Library of Congress] (LCLS)
Sc St L........	Scandinavian Studies in Law [A publication] (DLA)
ScStm..........	Calhoun County Public Library, St. Matthews, SC [Library symbol] [Library of Congress] (LCLS)
SCSTR........	Segregated Continuous Stirred Tank Reactor [Chemical engineering]
Sc Stud Criminol...	Scandinavian Studies in Criminology [1965] [A publication] (DLA)
SCSU...........	St. Cloud State University
ScSu...........	Sumter County Library, Sumter, SC [Library symbol Library of Congress] (LCLS)
SCSU...........	System Control Signal Unit (NITA)

ScSuM........	Morris College, Sumter, SC [Library symbol Library of Congress] (LCLS)
ScSum.........	Timrod Library, Summerville, SC [Library symbol Library of Congress] (LCLS)
ScSumL.......	Timrod Library, Summerville, SC [Library symbol] [Library of Congress] (LCLS)
ScSuTC.......	Sumter Technical College, Sumter, SC [Library symbol] [Library of Congress] (LCLS)
SCSW.........	Stolt Comex Seaway SA [NASDAQ symbol] (SAG)
SCSW.........	Super-Chilled Seawater
SCSWF.......	Stolt Comex Seaway [NASDAQ symbol] (TTSB)
SCT.............	Air Force Institute of Technology, Wright-Patterson AFB, OH [OCLC symbol] (OCLC)
SCT.............	Saab Aircraft AB [Sweden ICAO designator] (FAAC)
SCT.............	Sacrococcygeal Teratoma [Oncology]
S-C-T...........	Salinity-Conductivity-Temperature
SCT.............	Salmon Calcitonin [Endocrinology]
SCT.............	Sample Control Tape [Computer science]
SCT.............	Satellite Communication Terminal (MCD)
SCT.............	S-Band Cassegrain Transmit
SCT.............	Scan Conversion Tube
SCT.............	Scanning Telescope (KSC)
SCT.............	Scattered
SCT.............	Schottky Clamped Transistor
SCT.............	Scintrex Ltd. [Toronto Stock Exchange symbol]
SCT.............	SciTex Continuous Tone [Image format] (AAEL)
SCT.............	Scorpion Toxin [Immunology]
SCT.............	Scotsman Industries [NYSE symbol] (TTSB)
SCT.............	Scotsman Industries, Inc. [NYSE symbol] (SPSG)
SCT.............	Scotty Lake [Alaska] [Seismograph station code, US Geological Survey] (SEIS)
SCT.............	Scout (AABC)
SCT.............	Screen Capture Test [Computer science]
Sct.............	Scutum [Constellation]
SCT.............	Semiconductor Curve Tracer
SCT.............	Sentence Completion Technique [or Test]
SCT.............	Sequence Checking Tape
SCT.............	Service Counter Terminal [Banking]
SCT.............	Sex Chromatin Test (MAE)
SCT.............	Sickle Cell Trait (AAMN)
SCT.............	Signal Corps Training [Military] (IAA)
SCT.............	Single-Cell Test (MCD)
SCT.............	Single Channel Transponder (MCD)
SCT.............	Sioux City Terminal Railway [AAR code]
SCT.............	Skylab Communication Terminal [NASA] (KSC)
SCT.............	Societe Canadienne de Theologie [Canadian Theological Society - CTS]
SCT.............	Society for Clinical Trials (EA)
SCT.............	Society of Cardiological Technicians [British]
SCT.............	Society of Cleaning Technicians (EA)
SCT.............	Society of Commercial Teachers (EAIO)
SCT.............	Society of County Treasurers [British]
SCT.............	Soldier Crew Tent [Army] (INF)
SCT.............	SONAR Certification Test
SCT.............	Source Coding Team (SAA)
SCT.............	Sous-Commission des Cartes Tectoniques [Subcommittee for Tectonic Maps of the Commission for the Geological Map of the World - STMCGMW] (EAIO)
SCT.............	Space Combat Tactics (SAA)
SCT.............	Special Characters Table [Computer science] (IBMDP)
SCT.............	Special Committee on Trade
SCT.............	Special Crew Time (DNAB)
SCT.............	Spectral Control Technique
SCT.............	Spectrographic Telescope
SCT.............	Spill Control Technology [Environmental science] (COE)
SCT.............	Staphylococcal Clumping Test [Medicine] (AAMN)
SCT.............	Step Control Table (CMD)
SCT.............	Structural Clay Tile [Technical drawings]
SCT.............	Student Coalition for Truth (EA)
SCT.............	Subroutine Call Table [Computer science]
SCT.............	Subscriber Carrier Terminal [Telecommunications] (TEL)
SCT.............	Sugar-Coated Tablet
S Ct.............	Supreme Court Reporter [A publication] (DLA)
SCt.............	Supreme Court Reports
SCT.............	Surface Charge Transistor [Electronics] (OA)
SCT.............	Surface-Controlled Transistor (IAA)
SCT.............	Swap Control Table [Computer science] (BYTE)
SCT.............	System Circuit Test
SCT.............	System Compatibility Tests
SCT.............	System Component Test (IAA)
SCT.............	System Configuration Table (IAA)
SCT.............	Systems and Computer Technology (IAA)
S Ct.............	US Supreme Court Reporter [West] [1882-present] [A publication] (AAGC)
SCTA...........	Scottish Commercial Travellers Association (DBA)
SCTA...........	Scottish Corn Trade Association (DBA)
SCTA...........	Secondary Container Transfer Area [Nuclear energy] (NRCH)
SCTA...........	Ships' Clerk Trade Association [A union] [British]
SCTA...........	Southern California Timing Association
SCTA...........	Steel Carriers Tariff Association, Inc. [Riverdale, MD]
SCTA...........	Stone Carvers Trade Association [A union] [British]
SCTA...........	Syndicat Canadien des Travailleurs Agricoles (AC)
SC (T & C)...	Thompson and Cook's New York Supreme Court Reports [A publication] (DLA)
SCTAT.........	Sex Cord Tumor with Annular Tubules [Medicine] (DMAA)

SCTB............. Santa Cruz Test Base (MCD)
SCTB............. Santiago/Eulogio Sanchez [Chile] [ICAO location identifier] (ICLI)
ScTB............. Scottish Tourist Board (DCTA)
SCTB............. Soprano, Contalto, Tenor & Bass (WDAA)
S Ct Bull (CCH)... United States Supreme Court Bulletin (Commerce Clearing House) [A publication] (DLA)
SCTC............. Self-Contained Training Capability (DNAB)
SCTC............. Signal Corps Training Center [Military] (IAA)
SCTC............. Small Craft Training Center
SC/TC........... Spacecraft Test Conductor (SAA)
SCTC............. Submarine Chaser Training Center [Navy]
SCTC............. Systems & Computer Tech [NASDAQ symbol] (TTSB)
SCTC............. Systems & Computer Technology Corp. [NASDAQ symbol] (NQ)
SCTC............. Temuco/Maquehue [Chile] [ICAO location identifier] (ICLI)
SCTCA......... SAC [Strategic Air Command] Channel and Traffic Control Agency (SAA)
SCTCA......... Strategic Air Command Channel and Traffic Control Agency (IAA)
SctCHt......... Scout Car, Half Track [Army]
SCTD........... Scattered
SCTD........... Scottish Centre for the Tuition of the Disabled [Queen Margaret College] (CB)
SCTD........... Subcaliber Training Device [Military] (AABC)
SCTE........... Puerto Montt/Internacional El Tepual [Chile] [ICAO location identifier] (ICLI)
SCTE........... Society of Cable Telecommunications Engineers (NTPA)
SCTE........... Society of Cable Television Engineers (EA)
SCTE........... Society of Carbide and Tool Engineers (EA)
SCTE........... Spacecraft Central Timing Equipment [NASA]
SCTF........... Santa Cruz Test Facility (SAA)
SCTF........... SHAPE [Supreme Headquarters Allied Powers Europe] Centralized Training Facility [NATO] (NATG)
SCTF........... Sodium Chemical Technology Facility [Nuclear energy] (NRCH)
SCTFR......... Short-Contact-Time Fluidized Reactors [Chemical engineering]
SCTH........... Service Center for Teachers of History (EA)
SCTI............. Santiago/Internacional Los Cerillos [Chile] [ICAO location identifier] (ICLI)
SCTI............. SC&T Intl [NASDAQ symbol] (TTSB)
SCTI............. Sodium Components Test Installation [Nuclear energy]
SCTI............. Solid Carbide Tool Institute (EA)
SCTI............. University of Southern California Tax Institute (DLA)
SCTIW......... SC&T Intl Wrrt [NASDAQ symbol] (TTSB)
SCTL........... Schottky Coupled Transistor Logic (IAA)
SCTL........... Short-Circuited Terminating Line (IAA)
SCTL........... Short-Circuited Transmission Line
SCTL........... Small Components Test Loop [Nuclear energy]
SCTL........... Societe Canadienne des Technologistes de Laboratoire [Canadian Society of Laboratory Technologists] (EAIO)
SCTN........... Chaiten/Chaiten [Chile] [ICAO location identifier] (ICLI)
SCTN........... Service Center Taxpayer Notice [IRS]
SCTO........... Societe Canadienne des Technologistes en Orthopedie [Canadian Society of Orthopaedic Technologists] (EAIO)
SCTO........... Soft Carrier Turn Off (HGAA)
SCTOC........ Satellite Communications Test Operations Center
SCTP........... Ship Construction Test Plan [Navy] (CAAL)
SCTP........... Straight Channel Tape Print [Computer science] (KSC)
SCTP........... Syndicat Canadien des Travailleurs du Papier [Canadian Paperworkers Union - CPU]
SCTP........... Systems and Control Technology Panel (ACII)
SCTPLS........ Society for Chaos Theory in Psychology and Life Sciences (NTPA)
SCTPP......... Straight Channel Tape Print Program [Computer science] (KSC)
SCTR........... Scooter (AAG)
SCTR........... Secretin Receptor [Medicine] (DMAA)
SCTR........... Sector (MSA)
Sctr............. Sector (TBD)
SCTR........... Signal Corps Technical Requirements (MCD)
SCTR........... Single Channel Transponder (DWSG)
SCTR........... [La] Societe Canadienne des Therapeutes Respiratoires (AC)
SCTR........... Specialty Teleconstructioners [NASDAQ symbol] (SAG)
SCTR........... Specialty Teleconstructors [NASDAQ symbol] (TTSB)
SCTR........... Standing Conference on Telecommunications Research (IAA)
SCTRACEN ... Submarine Chaser Training Center [Navy]
SCTRW........ Specialty Telecnstrctrs Wrrt [NASDAQ symbol] (TTSB)
SCTS........... SFOF [Space Flight Operations Facility] Communications Terminal Subsystem [NASA]
SCTS........... System Components Test Station (MCD)
SCTT........... Scotts Co. [NASDAQ symbol] (SAG)
SCTTA......... Scott Technologies [NASDAQ symbol] [Formerly, Figgie International]
SCTTU......... Scottish Council of Textile Trade Unions (DCTA)
SCTV........... Second City Television [Television program, the title of which was later changed to its initialism]
SCTV........... Standing Conference on Television Viewing [British]
ScTvC......... North Greenville College, Tigerville, SC [Library symbol] [Library of Congress] (LCLS)
SCTV-GDHS... Spacecraft Television - Ground Data Handling System [NASA]
scty............. Secretary (BARN)
SCTY........... Security (AFM)
SCTY........... Society
SCTYG......... Security Group [Military]
SCTYPOLICESq... Security Police Squadron [Air Force]
SCTYSERSCH... Security Service School [Air Force]
SCTYSq....... Security Squadron [Air Force]
SCTZ........... Puerto Montt [Chile] [ICAO location identifier] (ICLI)
SCU............. Santiago [Cuba] [Airport symbol] (OAG)
SCU............. S-Band Cassegrain Ultra

SCU .... Scan Control Unit (IAA)
SCU .... Scanner Control Unit
SCU .... Scottish Church Union
SCU .... Scottish Cricket Union (DBA)
SCU .... Scottish Crofters Union (DBA)
SCU .... Scottish Cyclists Union (DBA)
SCU .... Secondary Control Unit [Aerospace] (AAG)
scu .... Secondary Control Unit [NASA] (NAKS)
SCU .... Selector Checkout Unit
SCU .... Sensor Control Unit (MCD)
SCU .... Sequence Control Unit [Aerospace] (KSC)
scu .... Sequence Control Unit [NASA] (NAKS)
scu .... Service and Cooling Umbilical (NAKS)
SCU .... Service and Cooling Umbilical [Aerospace] (MCD)
SCU .... Service Command Unit
SCU .... Servicing Control Unit [Telecommunications] (TEL)
SCU .... Sheep Canyon [Utah] [Seismograph station code, US Geological Survey Closed] (SEIS)
SCU .... Signal Conditioning Unit (NASA)
scu .... Signal Conditioning Unit (NAKS)
scu .... Signal Control Unit (NAKS)
SCU .... Signal Control Unit (NASA)
SCU .... Single Conditioning Unit
scu .... South Carolina [MARC country of publication code Library of Congress] (LCCP)
SCU .... Special Care Unit
SCU .... Stable Control Unit
SCU .... Stand-Alone Computer Unit
SCU .... Static Checkout Unit (KSC)
SCU .... Station Control Unit
SCU .... Statistical Control Unit [Military]
SCU .... Steering Control Unit
SCU .... Storage Control Unit
SCU .... Street Crime Unit [Criminology] (LAIN)
SCU .... Subscriber Channel Unit (IAA)
SCU .... Subscribers' Concentrator Unit [Telecommunications] (TEL)
SCU .... Suit Cooling Unit (IAA)
SCU .... Sulfur-Coated Urea [Chemical technology]
SCU .... Surface Control Unit
SCU .... Switch Control Unit (MCD)
SCU .... Synchronous Controller Unit
SCU .... System Configuration Unit (MCD)
SCU .... System Control Unit
SCU .... System/Memory Control Unit (NITA)
ScU............. University of South Carolina, Columbia, SC [Library symbol Library of Congress] (LCLS)
SCUA .... Suez Canal Users Association (NATG)
SCUAE .... State Committee on the Utilization of Atomic Energy [Former USSR]
ScU-Ai .... University of South Carolina-Alken, Aiken, SC [Library symbol] [Library of Congress] (LCLS)
SCUAS .... Standing Conference of University Appointments Services [British]
ScU-B .... University of South Carolina-Beaufort, Beaufort, SC [Library symbol] [Library of Congress] (LCLS)
SCUBA .... Self-Contained Underwater Breathing Apparatus
scuba.......... Self-Contained Underwater Breathing Apparatus (ODBW)
SCUBA......... Submillimeter Common-User Bolometer Array [Instrumentation]
SCUBADIV ... Scuba Diver Badge [Military decoration] (GFGA)
SCUC .... Satellite Communications Users Conference [Convention] (TSSD)
ScU-C .... University of South Carolina-Coastal Carolina, Conway, SC [Library symbol] [Library of Congress] (LCLS)
SCUCC Dec... South Carolina Unemployment Compensation Commission Decisions [A publication] (DLA)
SCUCCR....... South Carolina Unemployment Compensation Commission Reports of Hearings [A publication] (DLA)
SCUD .... Scunner [Missile]
SCUD .... Subsonic Cruise Unarmed Decoy [Air Force] (MCD)
SCUDD......... Standing Conference of University Drama Departments (AIE)
ScudNA....... Scudder New Asia Fund [Associated Press] (SAG)
SCUDS........ Simplification, Clarification, Unification, Decimalization, Standardization
ScudWld....... Scudder World Income Opportunities Ltd. [Associated Press] (SAG)
SCUE .... Standing Conference on University Entrance [British] (DI)
SCUF .... Slow Continuous Ultrafiltration [Medicine] (DMAA)
SCUG .... Smart Card Users Group (CIST)
SCUGA........ Schools, Curriculum, Unusual, Geography, and Alumni [University admisssion rating system]
SCUIO .... Standing Conference of University Information Officers [British]
Scul .... Sculptor [Constellation]
SCUL .... Simulation of the Columbia University Libraries [Data processing research]
ScU-L .... University of South Carolina, Law School, Columbia, SC [Library symbol Library of Congress] (LCLS)
ScU-Lan...... University of South Carolina-Lancaster, Lancaster, SC [Library symbol] [Library of Congress] (LCLS)
SCULL .... Serial Communication Unit for Long Links
SCULP .... Sculpsit [He, or She, Engraved It] [Latin]
SCULP .... Sculptor
SCULP .... Sculpture (ROG)
sculp........... Sculpture (VRA)
SCULPS ...... Sculpsit [He, or She, Engraved It] [Latin]
SCULPT ...... Sculptor [or Sculpture]
Sculpt Hellenist Age... Sculpture of the Hellenistic Age [A publication] (OCD)
Sculpt R ...... Sculpture Review [A publication] (BRI)
SCUM .... Society for Cutting Up Men

ScU-M .... University of South Carolina, School of Medicine, Columbia, SC [*Library symbol Library of Congress*]

SCUMRA ...... Societe Central de l'Uranium et des Minerals et Metaux Radioactifs [*France*]

SC(UN) .... Security Council of the United Nations

ScUn .... Union County Library, Union, SC [*Library symbol*] [*Library of Congress*] (LCLS)

SCUP .... School, College, and University Partnerships Program [*Department of Education*] (GFGA)

SCUP .... School Computer Use Plan (IEEE)

SCUP .... Scupper

SCUP .... Service Center Unpostable [*IRS*]

SCUP .... Society for College and University Planning (EA)

SCUPA .... Single-Chain Urokinase-Like Plasminogen Activator [*Anticlotting agent*]

SCUPU .... Self-Contained Underwater Pinger Unit [*SONAR*]

SCUR .... Secure Computing [*NASDAQ symbol*] (TTSB)

SCUR .... Secure Computing Corp. [*NASDAQ symbol*] (SAG)

SCUR .... Selected Command Unit Review (MCD)

SCUS .... Supreme Court of the United States

ScU-S .... University of South Carolina, Science Library, Columbia, SC [*Library symbol Library of Congress*] (LCLS)

SCUSA .... Student Conference on United States Affairs

ScU-Sa .... University of South Carolina-Salkehatchie, Allendale, SC [*Library symbol*] [*Library of Congress*] (LCLS)

SCUSE .... Special Committee for United States Exports [*Washington, DC*] (EA)

ScU-Sp .... University of South Carolina-Spartanburg, Spartanburg, SC [*Library symbol*] [*Library of Congress*] (LCLS)

ScU-Su .... University of South Carolina at Sumter, Sumter, SC [*Library symbol Library of Congress*] (LCLS)

SCUT .... Schizophrenia, Chronic Undifferentiated Type [*Psychiatry*] (DAVI)

Scut .... Scutum [*of Hesiod*] [*Classical studies*] (OCD)

Scut .... Scutum [*Constellation*]

SCUTG .... Signal Corps Unit Training Group [*Military*] (IAA)

SCUTREA ..... Standing Conference on University Teaching and Research in the Education of Adults [*British*] (DI)

SCUU .... Southern College University Union

ScU-Un .... University of South Carolina-Union, Union, SC [*Library symbol*] [*Library of Congress*] (LCLS)

SCV .... Eglin Regional Hospital Library, Eglin AFB, FL [*OCLC symbol*] (OCLC)

SCV .... Saguaro Cactus Virus [*Plant pathology*]

SCV .... Scania AB [*NYSE symbol*] (SAG)

SCV .... Seaclutter Visibility [*Navy*] (CAAL)

SCV .... Selective Control Valve [*Hydraulics*]

SCV .... Side Control Valves

SCV .... Simultaneous Chest Compression and Ventilation [*Medicine*]

SCV .... Smooth, Capsulated, Virulent [*Bacteriology*]

SCV .... Solar Constant Variations

SCV .... Sons of Confederate Veterans (EA)

SCV .... South Atlantic Ltd. [*Vancouver Stock Exchange symbol*]

SCV .... Speed-Controlled Volume

SCV .... Speed Control Valve

SCV .... St. Croix [*Virgin Islands*] [*Seismograph station code, US Geological Survey*] (SEIS)

SCV .... Steam-Conditioning Valve

SCV .... Steel Containment Vessel [*Nuclear energy*] (NRCH)

SCV .... Stock Change Voucher [*Military*] (AFIT)

SCV .... Strip Chart Viewer

SCV .... Sub Center Visibility (MCD)

SCV .... Subclavian Vein [*Medicine*] (DB)

SCV .... Sub Clutter Visibility

SCV .... Subcutaneous Vaginal [*Block*] [*Anesthesiology*] (DAVI)

SCV .... Submesoscale Coherent Vortic [*Oceanography*]

SCV .... Suceava [*Romania*] [*Airport symbol*] (OAG)

SCV .... Supersonic Cruise Missile

SCV .... Swirl Control Valve [*Automotive engine design*]

SCV .... System Compatibility Vehicle

SCV .... System Component Verification

SCV.A .... Scania AB'A'ADS [*NYSE symbol*] (TTSB)

SCV.B .... Scania AB'B'ADS [*NYSE symbol*] (TTSB)

SCVD .... Valdivia/Pichoy [*Chile*] [*ICAO location identifier*] (ICLI)

SCVE .... Spacecraft Vicinity Equipment (IAA)

SCVF .... Single Channel Voice Frequency [*Telecommunications*] (OSI)

SCVIR .... Society of Cardiovascular and Interventional Radiology (EA)

SCVL .... Shoe Carnival [*NASDAQ symbol*] (TTSB)

SCVL .... Shoe Carnival, Inc. [*NASDAQ symbol*] (SAG)

SCVM .... Shuttle Command and Voice Multiplexer (MCD)

SCVO .... Scottish Council for Voluntary Organisations (DBA)

SCVP .... Society of Clerks of Valuation Panels [*British*] (DBA)

SCVS .... Society for Clinical Vascular Surgery (NTPA)

SCVT .... Suzuki Continuously-Variable Transmission [*Automotive powertrain*]

SCVTR .... Scan Converting Video Tape Recorder (MCD)

SCVWD .... Santa Clara Valley Water District

SCW .... AFWAL [*Air Force Wright Aeronautical Laboratories*] Technical Information Center, Wright-Patterson AFB, OH [*OCLC symbol*] (OCLC)

ScW .... Collection County Memorial Library, Walterboro, SC [*Library symbol*] [*Library of Congress*] (LCLS)

SCW .... Malmo Aviation AB [*Sweden ICAO designator*] (FAAC)

SCW .... Service Clarified Water [*Environmental science*] (COE)

SCW .... Sherman Crater - Mount Baker [*Washington*] [*Seismograph station code, US Geological Survey Closed*] (SEIS)

SCW .... Silicone Carbide Whisker

SCW .... Silk-Covered Wire (IAA)

SCW .... Single-Chromosome Workshop (HGEN)

SCW .... Slow Cyclotron Wave (IAA)

SCW .... Society of Colonial Wars

SCW .... Southern California Water Co. [*NYSE symbol*] (SAG)

SCW .... Southern Cal Water [*NYSE symbol*] (TTSB)

SCW .... Space Charge Wave (PDAA)

SCW .... State College of Washington

SCW .... St. Clair Paint & Wallpaper Corp. [*Toronto Stock Exchange symbol*]

SCW .... Substorm Current Wedge

SCW .... Supercritical Water

SCW .... Super-Critical Wing

SCW .... Superintendent of Contract Work [*Navy*]

SCWA .... South Carolina Waterfowl Association

SCWA .... Supreme Court of Western Australia

SCWAC .... Scenic West Athletic Conference (PSS)

ScWal .... Oconee County Library, Walhalla, SC [*Library symbol Library of Congress*] (LCLS)

SCWC .... Special Commission on Weather Modification

SC/WCA ...... Sneak Circuit/Worst Case Analysis (MCD)

SCWCU .... Supreme Council of the Western Catholic Union [*Later, Western Catholic Union*] (EA)

SCWDS .... Southeastern Cooperative Wildlife Disease Study [*University of Georgia*] [*Research center*] (RCD)

SCWEP .... Spinnable Cotton Waste Equalization Program

SCWG .... Satellite Communications Working Group [*NATO*] (NATG)

SCWGA .... Sonoma County Wineries Association [*Sonoma County Wine Growers Associatio n*] [*Acronym is based on former name,*] (EA)

ScWL .... Single-Comb White Leghorn [*Poultry*]

SCWM .... Subcortical White Matter [*Medicine*] (DMAA)

ScWn .... Fairfield County Library, Winnsboro, SC [*Library symbol*] [*Library of Congress*] (LCLS)

SCWO .... Supercalendered Web-Offset [*Paper*] (DGA)

SCWO .... Supercritical Water Oxidation [*Waste disposal technology*]

SCWPH .... Students Concerned with Public Health [*Defunct*] (EA)

SCWPLR ..... Special Committee for Workplace Product Liability Reform (EA)

SCWR .... Standing Committee on Water Resources [*Australia*]

SCWR .... Supercritical Water Reactor

SCWS .... Scottish Co-Operative Wholesale Society

SCWS .... Space Combat Weapon System (IAA)

SCWSL .... Small Caliber Weapon Systems Laboratory (MCD)

SCWT .... Stroop Color-Word Test [*Psychology*] (DAVI)

SCWT .... System Cold Wire Tests

SCX .... Oneida, TN [*Location identifier FAA*] (FAAL)

SCX .... Selector Channel Executive (CIST)

SCX .... Single-Charge Exchange

SCX .... Solar Coronal X-Ray

SCX .... Starrett [*L. S.*] Co. [*NYSE symbol*] (SPSG)

SCX .... Starrett (L.S.)'A' [*NYSE symbol*] (TTSB)

SCX .... Strong Cation Exchanger [*Chemistry*]

SCX .... Sun Country Airlines, Inc. [*ICAO designator*] (FAAC)

SCY .... Scan Converter Yoke

SCY .... Scurry, TX [*Location identifier FAA*] (FAAL)

SCY .... Sports Club [*AMEX symbol*] (TTSB)

SCY .... Sports Club Co., Inc. [*AMEX symbol*] (SAG)

SCYL .... Single-Cylinder

Scyt .... Scythia (VRA)

SCZ .... Santa Cruz [*Solomon Islands*] [*Airport symbol*] (OAG)

SCZ .... Schwitzer, Inc. [*NYSE symbol*] (SPSG)

SCZ .... State Coastal Zone (NOAA)

SD .... Decisions of the Sadr Court [*1845-62*] [*Bengal, India*] [*A publication*] (DLA)

SD .... Diamant [*France*] [*Research code symbol*]

SD .... Diploma in Statistics (WDAA)

SD .... Dirksen Senate Office Building [*Washington, D.C.*]

SD .... Doctor of Science (PGP)

SD .... Safe Deposit [*Business term*]

SD .... Safety Destructor (NG)

SD .... Said (ROG)

SD .... Sailed

S/D .... Sailing Date (DS)

SD .... Sailing Directions [*British*]

S/D .... Salaried Direct [*Ratio*]

SD .... Salt Depletion

SD .... Salutem Dicit [*Sends Greetings*] [*Latin*]

SD .... Same Day

SD .... Sample Data (NG)

SD .... Sample Delay

SD .... Sand (WGA)

SD .... Sandhoff Disease [*Medicine*] (DB)

SD .... San Diego [*Diocesan abbreviation*] [*California*] (TOCD)

SD .... Sash Door

SD .... Saturation Deficit

SD .... Scaling and Display (NASA)

SD .... Scan Data (IAA)

SD .... Scandinavian Delegation [*British*]

SD .... Scanning Densitometer [*Instrumentation*]

SD .... Schematic Diagram

SD .... Schottky Diode (IAA)

SD .... Scientiae Doctor [*Doctor of Science*] (ADA)

SD .... Scientific Design [*Group*]

SD .... Scleroderma [*Medicine*] (DAVI)

SD .... Scottish District [*Council*]

SD .... Scram Discharge [*Nuclear energy*] (NRCH)

SD .... Scrip Department (MHDB)

SD .... Sea Damaged

S/D...............	Seadrome
SD...............	Search Date (NITA)
SD...............	Search Depth [Navy] (NVT)
SD...............	Seasonal Derating (IEEE)
SD...............	Seasoned (WGA)
SD...............	Secchi Disk
SD...............	Secondary Distribution [Investment term]
SD...............	Second Defense [Men's lacrosse position]
SD...............	Second Difference [Statistics] (OA)
SD...............	Secretary of Defense
SD...............	Section Definition (IAA)
SD...............	Security Disconnect [Computer science] (ECII)
SD...............	Sedan
SD...............	Seed (WGA)
SD...............	Segregation Distorter [Genetics]
SD...............	Segregation Distortion (DOG)
SD...............	Sehr Dringend [Very urgent, used preceding German coded messages]
SD...............	Seismic Detector (MCD)
SD...............	Seize Detector
SD...............	Selenium Diode
SD...............	Selenoid Driver (IAA)
SD...............	Self-Destroying [Projectile]
SD...............	Self-Destruct
SD...............	Self Dual (IAA)
SD...............	Semantic Differential
SD...............	Semiconductor Device (IAA)
SD...............	Semi-Darkness (DNAB)
SD...............	Semidetached (ADA)
SD...............	Semidiameter
SD...............	Seminars Directory [A publication]
SD...............	Senate Document
SD...............	Senatus Decreto [By Decree of the Senate] [Latin]
SD...............	Send Data [Computer science]
SD...............	Send Digits [Telecommunications] (TEL)
SD...............	Senile Dementia [Medicine]
SD...............	Senior Deacon [Freemasonry]
SD...............	Septal Defect [Medicine]
SD...............	Sequential Disk (IAA)
SD...............	Serializer/Deserializer
SD...............	Serine Dehydratase [An enzyme]
SD...............	Serologically Defined [Immunology]
SD...............	Serologically Determined [Medicine]
SD...............	Serum Defect [Medicine] (MAE)
SD...............	Service Dated (ROG)
SD...............	Service Dress
SD...............	Servicing Diagram
SD...............	Servus Dei [Servant of God] [Latin]
SD...............	Settlement Date [Business] (MHDB)
SD...............	Several Dates
SD...............	Severe Duty [Truck]
SD...............	Severely Diabetic
SD...............	Sewed
SD...............	Sewer Drain
SD...............	Shakedown [Nuclear energy] (NRCH)
SD...............	Share Distribution (ECII)
S/D...............	Sharp/Dull (STED)
SD...............	Shell-Destroying [Device]
SD...............	Shelter Deck (DNAB)
SD...............	Shield of David (BJA)
SD...............	Ship Destination Test [Intelligence test]
SD...............	Shop Drawing (AAG)
SD...............	Short Day [Botany]
SD...............	Short Delay
SD...............	Short Delivery
sd...............	Short Delivery (ODBW)
SD...............	Short Duration
SD...............	Shoulder Disarticulation [Medicine] (MAE)
SD...............	Shoulder Dislocation
SD...............	Shower Drain (AAG)
S/D...............	Shut Down
SD...............	Shy-Drager [Syndrome] [Medicine] (DB)
SD...............	Sicherheitsdienst [Police Duty] [NAZI Germany]
S-D...............	Sickle Cell Hemoglobin D [Disease] [Medicine]
SD...............	Side Deck
SD...............	Side Door
SD...............	Side Drum
SD...............	Siegfried AG [Switzerland] [Research code symbol]
SD...............	Sight Draft [Business term]
SD...............	Signal Digit (IAA)
SD...............	Signals Division [British military] (DMA)
SD...............	Signal-to-Distortion (IAA)
SD...............	Signed (WGA)
SD...............	Signed Digit (IAA)
SD...............	Significant Digit [Mathematics]
SD...............	Simple Design
SD...............	Simplex Drop Out (IAA)
SD...............	Sine Dato [Undated book] [Latin]
SD...............	Sine Die [Without Day] [Latin]
SD...............	Single Deck [Navigation]
SD...............	Single Density [Computer science] (IAA)
SD...............	Single Determination
SD...............	Single Diaphragm [Automotive engineering]
SD...............	Single Distilled
SD...............	Single Domain [Grains in rocks] [Geophysics]

S/D...............	Sit and Dangle [Orthopedics] (DAVI)
SD...............	Site Defense [Military] (AABC)
SD...............	Situation Display
SD...............	Skid
SD...............	Skin Destruction [Medicine]
SD...............	Skin Dose
SD...............	Sleep Deprivation (PDAA)
SD...............	Sliding Door
SD...............	Slope Distribution [Statistics]
SD...............	Slowdown
s/d...............	Small Damage (DS)
SD...............	Small Dual [In-line Package] (AAEL)
SD...............	Small-Scale Disturbance Field
SD...............	Smoke Detector (NASA)
SD...............	Social Democratic Party [Germany]
SD...............	Socialdemokratiet i Danmark [Social Democratic Party of Denmark] [Political party] (PPE)
SD...............	Societas Docta (EA)
SD...............	Soft Drawn
SD...............	Soft Drug [One that is metabolized to an inactive compound]
SD...............	Software Dynamics [Buena Park, CA] (TSSD)
SD...............	Solar Dynamic (SSD)
SD...............	Solenoid Driver (IAA)
SD...............	Solicitation Document
SD...............	Solid Drawn
SD...............	Sort File Description [Computer science]
SD...............	Sorties per Day [Air Force] (AFIT)
SD...............	Sound [Films, television, etc.]
SD...............	Sound [Board on Geographic Names]
sd...............	Sound (WDMC)
SD...............	Sounding Doubtful [Nautical charts]
SD...............	Source/Destination [Inspection/Acceptance Point] (MCD)
SD...............	Source Document [Computer science]
S/D...............	Source/Drain (AAEL)
SD...............	South Dakota [Postal code]
SD...............	South Dakota Compiled Laws, Annotated [A publication] (DLA)
SD...............	South Dakota Reports [A publication] (DLA)
Sd...............	South Dakota State Library Commission, Pierre, SD [Library symbol Library of Congress] (LCLS)
SD...............	South Division (ROG)
SD...............	Southern District (DLA)
SD...............	Spaced Doublet (IAA)
SD...............	Space Division [Los Angeles, CA] [Air Force]
SD...............	Spare Disposition (MCD)
SD...............	Special Delivery
SD...............	Special District (COE)
SD...............	Special Document
SD...............	Special Duty [Military]
SD...............	Specialist Degree (PGP)
SD...............	Specially Denatured
SD...............	Specification Document [NASA] (NASA)
SD...............	Specification for Design
SD...............	Spectacle Dispenser [Navy technician]
SD...............	Spectral Distribution
SD...............	Speech Plus Duplex (IAA)
SD...............	Speed Density
SD...............	Speed Disk [Computer program] (PCM)
SD...............	Sphere Drake Holdings [NYSE symbol] (SPSG)
SD...............	Spin Device
SD...............	Spin-Dipolar [Physics]
SD...............	Splice Donor [Genetics]
SD...............	Splitter Damper (OA)
SD...............	Spontaneous Delivery [Obstetrics]
SD...............	Sporadic Depression [Medicine] (DMAA)
SD...............	Sprague-Dawley [Rat] (DB)
SD...............	Spreading Depression [Medicine] (DMAA)
SD...............	Square Law Detector [Telecommunications] (OA)
SD...............	Staff Development (ADA)
SD...............	Staff Duties [Military British]
SD...............	Stage Direction
SD...............	Stage Door [Theatrical slang]
SD...............	Stamp Duty
sd...............	Stamped [Stocks] (MHDW)
SD...............	Standard Decision (MCD)
SD...............	Standard Deduction
SD...............	Standard Definition [Electronics]
SD...............	Standard Design [of a vessel] (DS)
SD...............	Standard Deviation [Also, s]
SD...............	Standard Dress [Military British]
SD...............	Standardization Data
SD...............	Standardization Directory
SD...............	Standards Development (IEEE)
SD...............	Stands Detached [Freight]
SD...............	Stars of David (EA)
SD...............	Start Date (NITA)
SD...............	Start Delimiter [Computer science] (TNIG)
SD...............	State Department
SD...............	State Director
SD...............	State Disability (DAVI)
S/D...............	Statement of Differences
SD...............	Station Director [Deep Space Instrumentation Facility, NASA]
SD...............	Statutory Declaration
SD...............	Steel Deck (ADA)
SD...............	Stein & Day [Publishers]
SD...............	Stereo Directional

SD .... Sterile Dressing [*Medicine*] (MEDA)
SD .... Stern Discharge
SD .... Steward [*Navy rating*]
Sd .... Stimulus, Discriminative (MAE)
Sd .... Stimulus Drive (MAE)
SD .... Stock Dividend [*Investment term*]
SD .... Stone Disintegration [*Urology*]
S/D .... Storage or Distribution
SD .... Stores Depot [*British military*] (DMA)
SD .... Storm Deck [*Naval engineering*]
SD .... Storm Detection [*RADAR*]
SD .... Storm Drain [*Technical drawings*]
SD .... Stowage Drawer
SD .... Straight Drainage [*Medicine*] (MEDA)
SD .... Straight Duty
SD .... Strength Differential [*Steel*]
S-D .... Strength-Duration (STED)
SD .... Strength-Duration (Curve) [*Prosthesis*]
SD .... Streptodornase [*An enzyme*]
SD .... Stronnictwo Demokratyczne [*Democratic Party*] [*Poland Political party*] (PPE)
SD .... Structural Detail (AAG)
SD .... Structural Dynamics (KSC)
SD .... Structured Design (AAEL)
SD .... Studia et Documenta ad Iura Orientis Antiqui Pertinenta [*Leiden*] [*A publication*] (BJA)
SD .... Study Director (MCD)
SD .... Subcontractor Data
SD .... Subdural [*Anatomy*]
SD .... Submarine Detector (ADA)
SD .... Subtotal Discectomy [*Medicine*]
SD .... Sudan [*ANSI two-letter standard code*] (CNC)
SD .... Sudan Airways [*ICAO designator*] (AD)
S-D .... Sudden Death [*Tiebreaking in sports*]
SD .... Sudden Death [*Medicine*]
SD .... Sugar Determination
SD .... Sum of Digits (SAA)
SD .... Sun's Declensions [*Astronomy*] (ROG)
SD .... Super Density [*Computer science*]
SD .... Super Diesel [*Automotive engineering*]
SD .... Super Duty [*Automotive engineering*]
SD .... Superintendent of Documents [*US Government Printing Office*]
SD .... Superoxide Dismutase (DB)
SD .... Supplier Documentation (NASA)
SD .... Supply Department [*Navy*]
SD .... Supply Depot
SD .... Supply Detachment [*British military*] (DMA)
SD .... Supply Duct [*Nuclear energy*] (NRCH)
SD .... Support Directive (KSC)
SD .... Support [*or Supporting*] Document (KSC)
SD .... Support Dogs, Inc. [*An association*] (EA)
SD .... Surface Duct [*Navy*] (CAAL)
SD .... Surgical Drain (DAVI)
SD .... Surridge Dawson [*Commercial firm British*]
SD .... Surveillance Drone [*Air Force*]
SD .... Survival Dose
Sd .... Suspended [*Regulation or order suspended*] [*Used in Shepard's Citations*] [*Legal term*] (DLA)
SD .... Suspended Dust (DICI)
SD .... Swaziland
SD .... Sweep Driver
SD .... Switch Driver
SD .... Syllable Duration [*Entomology*]
SD .... Synchronous Detector [*Electronics*] (OA)
SD .... Synthetic Dextrose [*Biochemistry*]
SD .... System Demonstration [*Military*]
SD .... System Description
SD .... System Designator (AFIT)
SD .... System Drawer
SD .... Systems Designers [*Software manufacturer*] [*British*]
SD .... Systems Development (MCD)
SD .... Systems Directorate [*Army*] (RDA)
SD .... Systems Division [*Department of Commerce*] [*Information service or system*] (IID)
SD .... Systolic Discharge [*Cardiology*]
S/D .... Systolic to Diastolic [*Cardiology*] (MAE)
SD1 .... Steward, First Class [*Navy rating*]
SD2 .... Steward, Second Class [*Navy rating*]
SD3 .... Steward, Third Class [*Navy rating*]
SDA .... Augustana College, Sioux Falls, SD [*OCLC symbol*] (OCLC)
SDA .... Baghdad-Saddam [*Iraq*] [*Airport symbol*] (OAG)
SDA .... Sabouraud Dextrose Agar (STED)
SDA .... Sacrodextra Anterior [*A fetal position*] [*Obstetrics*]
SDA .... Sadr Diwani Adalat Reports [*India*] [*A publication*] (DLA)
SDA .... Salt-Dependent Agglutinin (STED)
SDA .... Satellite Data Area (IAA)
SDA .... Saw Diamond Abrasive (PDAA)
SDA .... Schweizerische Depeschenagentur AG [*Swiss News Agency*] (EY)
SDA .... Scottish Darts Association (DBA)
SDA .... Scottish Development Agency (DS)
SDA .... Scottish Diploma in Agriculture
SDA .... Screen Design Aid [*Computer science*] (HGAA)
SDA .... Screw Displacement Axis
SDA .... Section Department Authority
SDA .... Seismic Data Analysis

SDA .... Self-Defence Agency [*Japan*] (ECON)
SDA .... Semidehydroascorbate [*Biochemistry*]
SDA .... Sequential Degradation Analysis
SDA .... Service Delivery Area [*Job Training and Partnership Act*] (OICC)
SDA .... Seventh-Day Adventist
SDA .... Sex Discrimination Act [*1975*] [*British*] (DCTA)
SDA .... Shaft Drive Axis [*Aerospace*] (KSC)
SDA .... Shenandoah, IA [*Location identifier FAA*] (FAAL)
SDA .... Ship's Destination Authority (NVT)
SDA .... Shoulder Disarticulation [*Medicine*]
SDA .... Shut Down Amplifier (IAA)
SDA .... Sialodacryoadenitis [*Virus*] (STED)
SDA .... Significant Digit Arithmetic
SDA .... Simple Doublet Antenna
SDA .... Sleeve Dipole Antenna
SDA .... Slowdown Area
SDA .... Soap and Detergent Association (EA)
SDA .... Social Democratic Alliance [*British*]
SDA .... Social-Democratic Association [*Political party*] (EAIO)
SDA .... Solvent Deasphalting
SDA .... Somali Democratic Alliance [*Political party*] (EY)
SDA .... Source Data Acquisition (BUR)
SDA .... Source Data Automation [*Military*]
SDA .... Special Disbursing Agent, Bureau of Indian Affairs [*United States*] (DLA)
SDA .... Special Duty Assignment (AFM)
SDA .... Specially Denatured Alcohol
SDA .... Specific Dynamic Action [*of foods*] [*Physiology*]
SDA .... Spectral Distribution Analyzer
SDA .... Spontaneous Divergent Academic [*Test*] [*Education*]
SDA .... Stacked Dipole Array
SDA .... Standard Gold Mines Ltd. [*Vancouver Stock Exchange symbol*]
SDA .... St. Andrews Ltd. [*Canada ICAO designator*] (FAAC)
SDA .... Statistical Distribution Analyzer
SDA .... Step Down Amplifier
SDA .... Stepwise Discriminant Analysis
SDA .... Stereo Dimensional Array
SDA .... Steroid-Dependent Asthmatic [*Medicine*]
SDA .... Stevens-Duryea Associates (EA)
SDA .... Stirrer Drive Assembly
SDA .... Stranka Demokratske Akcije [*Party of Democratic Action*] [*Bosnia-Herzegovina*] [*Political party*] (EY)
SDA .... Structure-Directing Agent [*Organic chemistry*]
SDA .... Students for Democratic Action
SDA .... Studies in the Decorative Arts [*A publication*] (BRI)
SDA .... Subcarrier Demodulator Assembly [*Deep Space Instrumentation Facility, NASA*]
SDA .... Succinic Dehydrogenase Activity
SDA .... Sulfadiazine [*Antibiotic*]
SDA .... Superficial Distal Axillary [*Lymph node*]
SDA .... Supplier Data Approval [*Nuclear energy*] (NRCH)
SDA .... Supporting Data Analysis
SDA .... Surface Design Association (EA)
SDA .... Sweet Damn All [*Nothing At All*] [*Slang*]
SDA .... Symbolic Device Address
SDA .... Symbolic Disk Address (AFM)
SDA .... Symbols-Digits-Alphabetics
SDA .... System Design Agency [*Bell Telephone Laboratory*] (MCD)
SDA .... Systems Data Analysis
SDA .... Systems Dynamic Analyzer
SDAA .... Salt Distributors Association of America (EA)
SDAA .... Scottish Dancing Association of Australia
SDAA .... Servicemen's Dependents Allowance Act
SDAA .... Skein Dyers Association of America [*Later, SRPDAA*] (EA)
SDAA .... Stacked Dipole Aerial Array
SdAbA .... Alexander Mitchell Library, Aberdeen, SD [*Library symbol Library of Congress*] (LCLS)
SdAbN .... Northern State College, Aberdeen, SD [*Library symbol Library of Congress*] (LCLS)
SdAbP .... Presentation College, Aberdeen, SD [*Library symbol Library of Congress*] (LCLS)
SDAC .... Seismic Data Analysis Center
SDAC .... Shelby Dodge Automobile Club [*Defunct*] (EA)
SDAC .... Shipping Defence Advisory Committee [*General Council of British Shipping*] (DS)
SDACMG .... Seventh-Day Adventist Church Musicians Guild [*Defunct*] (EA)
SDAD .... Satellite Digital and Analog Display
SDAD .... Special Domestically Available Documents [*NASA*] (KSC)
SDADA .... Seventh-Day Adventist Dietetic Association (EA)
SD Admin R... .... Administrative Rules of South Dakota [*A publication*] (DLA)
SD Admin Reg... .... South Dakota Register [*A publication*] (DLA)
SDADS .... Satellite Digital and Display System
SDAE .... San Diego & Arizona Eastern Railway Co. [*AAR code*]
SDAE .... Source Data Automation Equipment
SDAEA .... Shop, Distributive and Allied Employees' Association [*Australia*]
SDAF .... Solid-Rocket Booster Disassembly Facility [*NASA*] (NASA)
SDAF .... Special Defense Acquisition Fund [*Military*]
SDAF .... Special Development Assistance Fund
SDAFRS .... Source Data Automated Fitness Report System [*Military*] (DNAB)
SDAID .... System Debugging Aids (NITA)
S DAK .... South Dakota
S Dak .... South Dakota Reports [*A publication*] (DLA)
SDAKC .... Seventh-Day Adventist Kinship Canada [*Defunct*] (EAIO)
SDAKI .... Seventh Day Adventist Kinship International (EA)

SdAl............ Alcester Public Library, Alcester, SD [*Library symbol Library of Congress*] (LCLS)
SDAL.......... Switched Data Access Line
SD Ala......... United States District Court for the Southern District of Alabama (DLA)
SdAle.......... Alexandria Public Library, Alexandria, SD [*Library symbol Library of Congress*] (LCLS)
SDAM .... Social Democratic Alliance of Macedonia [*Political party*] (EY)
SDAM .... Standard Deviation above the Mean [*Statistics*]
SDA Mad ..... Madras Sadr Diwani Adalat Reports [*India*] [*A publication*] (DLA)
SDAML........ Send by Airmail (NOAA)
SDANA........ Shrine Directors Association of North America (EA)
SD & A .... San Diego & Arizona Railway
SD & B .... Shaw, Dunlop, and Bell's Scotch Court of Session Reports, First Series [*1821-38*] [*A publication*] (DLA)
SD & BBA .... Soft Drink and Beer Bottlers Association [*British*] (DBA)
SD & B Sup... Shaw, Dunlop, and Bell's Supplement, Containing House of Lords Decisions [*A publication*] (DLA)
SD & B Supp... Shaw, Dunlop, and Bell's Supplement, Containing House of Lords Decisions [*Scotland*] [*A publication*] (DLA)
SD & I .... System Development and Integration (MCD)
SD & T .... Staff Development and Training
SD & T .... Staff Duties and Training [*British military*] (DMA)
SDANG........ South Dakota Air National Guard (MUSM)
SDAP.......... Sociaal-Democratische Arbeiders Partij [*Social Democratic Workers' Party*] [*Netherlands Political party*] (PPE)
SDAP.......... Special Duty Assignment Pay [*Army*] (INF)
SDAP.......... System Development and Performance
SDAP.......... Systems Development Analysis Program
SDAP.......... Systems Development and Acquisition Plan (MCD)
SDAPP........ Special Duty Assignment Proficiency Pay [*Air Force*]
SdAr............ Arlington Public Library, Arlington, SD [*Library symbol Library of Congress*] (LCLS)
SDAR.......... Submarine Departure Approval Request (DNAB)
SdArm .... Armour Public Library, Armour, SD [*Library symbol Library of Congress*] (LCLS)
SDAS .... Scientific Data Automation System (IEEE)
SDAS .... Shared Demand Assignment Signaling (MCD)
SDAS .... Simplified Directional Approach System [*Aviation*]
SDAS .... Sound Data Acquisition System [*Automotive engineering*]
SDAS .... Source Data Automation System [*Military*] (AABC)
SDA-S .... System Design Agency-Subcontractor Design Direction (MCD)
SDAS .... Systems Data Analysis Section
SDAT .... Safe Driver Attitude Test [*Educational test*]
SDAT .... Sector Design and Analysis Tool [*FAA*] (TAG)
SDAT .... Senile Dementia of the Alzheimer Type [*Medicine*]
SDAT .... Spacecraft Data Analysis Team [*NASA*]
SDAT .... Stanford Diagnostic Arithmetic Test
SDAT .... Stationary Digital Audio Tape
SDAU .... Safety Data and Analysis Unit [*British*] (DA)
SDAU .... Subscriber Digital Access Unit [*Telecommunications*]
SDAUG........ SDA [*Software Design Associates*] Users' Groups [*Later, IUG*] (EA)
SDAV .... Sialodacryoadenitis [*Virology*]
SDAVF .... Spinal Dural Arteriovenous Fistula [*Medicine*] (DMAA)
SDAVP........ Sinsinawa Dominican Apostolic Volunteer Program (EA)
SDB .... Sa Da Bandeira [*Angola*] [*Seismograph station code, US Geological Survey*] (SEIS)
SDB .... Safe Deposit Box (MHDB)
SDB .... Salesians of Don Bosco [*Roman Catholic men's religious order*]
sdb.............. Salesians of Don Bosco (TOCD)
SDB .... Sandberg, CA [*Location identifier FAA*] (FAAL)
SDB .... Seaward Defence Boat [*British military*] (DMA)
SDB .... Securities Data Base System [*Information service or system*] (IID)
SDB .... Segment Descriptor Block
SDB .... Self-Defeating Behavior [*Psychology*] (DHP)
SDB .... Shakespeare Data Bank, Inc. [*Information service or system*] (IID)
SDB .... Shallow Draft Barge (MCD)
SDB .... Shallow Draft Board (NASA)
SDB .... Silver-Dye-Bleach (PDAA)
SDB .... Skill Development Base [*Army*] (AABC)
SDB .... Sleep-Disordered Breathing [*Medicine*] (DMAA)
SDB .... Small Disadvantaged Business [*Department of Commerce*]
SDB .... Sociaal-Democratische Bond [*Social Democratic League*] [*Netherlands Political party*] (PPE)
SDB .... Society for Developmental Biology (EA)
SDB .... Software Development Board [*Computer science*] (MHDI)
SdB .... South Dakota State University, Brookings, SD [*Library symbol Library of Congress*] (LCLS)
SDB .... Spacecraft Design Book
SDB .... Special District Bond
SDB .... Square Die Bushing
SDB .... Standard Device Byte (IAA)
SDB .... Standard Dress Blue [*Navy*] (DOMA)
SDB .... State Development Bank [*Hungary*]
SDB .... Storage Data Bus
SDB .... Strength and Dynamics Branch [*Air Force*]
SDB .... Sulfur-Disproportionating Bacteria
sdb.............. Symbolic Debugger [*Also, SOLD, SYMDEB*] [*Computer science*] (BYTE)
SDB .... System Database
SDB .... System Data Buffer (MCD)
SDB .... Systems Development Branch [*Space Environmental Laboratory*] (USDC)
SDBC .... Small Disadvantaged Business Concerns
SDBCS .... Steam Dump Bypass Control System [*Nuclear energy*] (NRCH)

SDBD .... Software Data Base Document [*Computer science*] (MHDI)
SdBer.......... Beresford Public Library, Beresford, SD [*Library symbol Library of Congress*] (LCLS)
SdBf............ Belle Fourche Public Library, Belle Fourche, SD [*Library symbol Library of Congress*] (LCLS)
SDBF .... System Development Breadboard Facility
SDBGC .... Seventh Day Baptist General Conference (EA)
SDBHS .... Seventh Day Baptist Historical Society (EA)
SDBI .... Specifications Drawing Baseline Index (DNAB)
SDBI .... Storage Data Bus-In [*Computer science*] (MHDB)
SDB Jo .... South Dakota Bar Journal [*A publication*] (DLA)
SDBL .... Sight Draft Bill of Lading Attached [*Business term*]
SdB-M .... South Dakota State University, Minuteman Graduate Center Library, Ellsworth AFB,Rapid City, SD [*Library symbol Library of Congress*] (LCLS)
SDBMS .... Seventh Day Baptist Missionary Society (EA)
SDBN .... Software-Defined Broadbank Network (CDE)
SdBo............ Bonesteel Public Library, Bonesteel, SD [*Library symbol Library of Congress*] (LCLS)
SDBO .... Societe de Banque Occidentale [*France*] (EY)
SDBO .... Storage Data Bus-Out [*Computer science*] (MHDB)
SDBP .... Small Database Project (NITA)
SDBP .... Society for Developmental and Behavioral Pediatrics (EA)
SDBP .... Supine Diastolic Blood Pressure [*Medicine*]
Sd-BPH .... South Dakota State Library for the Handicapped, Pierre, SD [*Library symbol Library of Congress*] (LCLS)
SdBro.......... Brookings Public Library, Brookings, SD [*Library symbol Library of Congress*] (LCLS)
SdBrS .... Bristol Independent School District Library, Bristol, SD [*Library symbol Library of Congress*] (LCLS)
SDBS .... Samson Database Services (NITA)
SDBS .... Sodium Dodecylbenzene Sulfonate [*Organic chemistry*]
SdBu........... Burke Public Library, Burke, SD [*Library symbol Library of Congress*] (LCLS)
SDBUP .... Small Disadvantaged Business Utilization Program (DOMA)
SDBUS .... Small and Disadvantaged Business Utilization Specialist (COE)
SDBWF .... Seventh Day Baptist World Federation (EA)
SDBY .... Standby
SDC .... Chief Steward [*Later, MSC*] [*Navy rating*]
SDC .... National Service Dog Center (EA)
SDC .... SAGE [*Semiautomatic Ground Environment*] Direction Center [*Military*] (IAA)
SDC .... SAGE [*Semiautomatic Ground Environment*] Division Commander [*Military*] (IAA)
SDC .... Salivary Duct Carcinoma [*Oncology*]
SDC .... Salt Data Centre [*British*]
SDC .... Same Distribution Center Service Area [*US Postal Service*]
SDC .... Sample Data Collection
SDC .... San Diego Conference [*California*] (HGEN)
SDC .... San Diego - Robinson [*California*] [*Seismograph station code, US Geological Survey Closed*] (SEIS)
SDC .... Sands Minerals [*Vancouver Stock Exchange symbol*]
SDC .... Scientific Data Center (MCD)
SDC .... Scientific Documentation Center Ltd. [*Dunfermline, Fife, Scotland*]
SDC .... Seaward Defense Craft (NATG)
SDC .... Secondary Distribution Center (AAG)
SDC .... Secure Data Cartridge (BYTE)
SDC .... Seismological Data Center [*Environmental Science Services Administration*]
SDC .... Seize Detector Control
SDC .... Self-Defense Corps [*Vietnam*]
SDC .... Self-Destruct Circuit (SAA)
SDC .... Semiconductor Devices Council [*Joint Electronic Device Engineering Council*] (MCD)
SDC .... September Days Club (EA)
SDC .... Serum Digoxin Concentration [*Clinical chemistry*]
SDC .... Setpoint Digital Control (IAA)
SDC .... Several Dancers Core [*Houston, TX and Atlanta, GA*]
SDC .... Shaft-Driven Compressor (DOMA)
SDC .... Shaft-Driven Counter
SDC .... Shield Design Code [*Nuclear energy*] (NRCH)
SDC .... Shipment Detail Card [*Military*]
SDC .... Shutdown Cooling [*Nuclear energy*] (NRCH)
SDC .... Signal Data Converter
SDC .... Single Drift Correction
SDC .... Situation Display Console (DOMA)
SDC .... Situation Display Converter
SDC .... Society of Daily Communicants [*Defunct*] (EA)
SD-C .... Society of Designer-Craftsmen [*British*] (EAIO)
SDC .... Society of Dyers and Colourists (EAIO)
SDC .... Society of the Divine Compassion [*Anglican religious community*]
SDC .... Sodium Deoxycholate [*Organic chemistry*]
SDC .... Software Development Computer [*NASA*] (NASA)
SDC .... Solenoidal Detector Collaboration [*Particle detection*]
SDC .... Solenoid Detector Collaboration [*Physics*]
SDC .... Solid Dielectric Cable
SDC .... SONAR Data Computer [*Navy*] (CAAL)
SDC .... South Dakota Conference (PSS)
SDC .... Southern Defense Command [*Army*]
SDC .... Spacecraft Data Simulator [*NASA*] (KSC)
SDC .... Space Data Corp.
SDC .... Space Defense Center [*Military*] (MCD)
SDC .... Space Defense Corp. (MCD)
SDC .... Space Development Corp.
SDC .... Spares Disposition Code [*NASA*] (NASA)

SDC	Special Day Class [Education]
SDC	Special Devices Center [Navy]
SDC	Specific Damping Capacity [Metals]
SDC	Spiral-Defect Chaos [Physics]
SDC	Square Dance Callers Club [British] (DBA)
SDC	Stabilization Data Computer
SDC	Standard Data Chain
SDC	State Data Center [Bureau of the Census] (GFGA)
SDC	State Defense Council
SDC	State Development Company (AAGC)
SDC	State Disasters Committee [Australia]
SDC	Static Dielectric Constant
SDC	Station Directory Control (SAA)
SDC	Strategic Defense Command [Military] (SDI)
SDC	Strategic Direction Center (MCD)
SDC	Structural Design Criteria [Nuclear energy]
SDC	Studebaker Driver's Club (EA)
SDC	Subcontractor's Data Catalog (MCD)
SDC	Submersible Decompression Chamber [Underwater tank]
SDC	Submersible Diving Capsule [Oceanography]
SDC	Succinyldicholine [Biochemistry] (MAE)
SDC	Supply Distribution Center [Military] (AFIT)
SDC	Support Design Change
SDC	Swedish Airforce [ICAO designator] (FAAC)
SDC	System Designator Code (AFM)
SDC	System Design Confirmation
SDC	System Development Corp. [Information service or system] (IID)
SDC	System for Data Calculation [Information retrieval]
SDC	Systems Development District (AAG)
SDC	Yankton College, Yankton, SD [OCLC symbol] (OCLC)
SdCa	Canton Carnegie Public Library, Canton, SD [Library symbol Library of Congress] (LCLS)
SDCA	Scottish Deerhound Club of America (EA)
SDCA	Square Dance Callers Association [Australia]
SD Cal	United States District Court for the Southern District of California (DLA)
SdCan	Canova Public Library, Canova, SD [Library symbol Library of Congress] (LCLS)
SdCar	Carthage Public Library, Carthage, SD [Library symbol Library of Congress] (LCLS)
SDCC	Simulation Data Conversion Center [Space Flight Operations Facility, NASA]
SDCC	Small-Diameter Component Cask [Nuclear energy] (NRCH)
SDCC	Society of the Descendants of the Colonial Clergy (EA)
SDCE	Scientific Data Collection Exercise
SDCE	Society of Die Casting Engineers (EA)
SDCF	Sampled Data Channel Filter
SDCF	Software Development Computer Facility
SdCh	Chamberlain Public Library, Chamberlain, SD [Library symbol Library of Congress] (LCLS)
SDCH	Society of Descendants of Colonial Hispanics (EA)
SDCI	Singles and Doubles Configuration Interaction [Quantum chemistry] (MCD)
SDCIS	Supplier Data Control Information System (MCD)
SdCl	Clark Public Library, Clark, SD [Library symbol Library of Congress] (LCLS)
SDCL	South Dakota Codified Laws [A publication]
SDCL	Supplier Documentation Checklist (NASA)
SDCL	Symptom Distress Check List [Medicine] (MAE)
SdCla	Claremont Public Library, Claremont, SD [Library symbol Library of Congress] (LCLS)
SDCM	Master Chief Steward [Later, MSCM] [Navy rating]
SdCo	Colome Public Library, Colome, SD [Library symbol Library of Congress] (LCLS)
SD CO	Safe Deposit Company (MHDW)
SDCo	Safe Deposit Company (EBF)
SD Codified Laws	South Dakota Codified Laws [A publication] (DLA)
SD Codified Laws	South Dakota Codified Laws Annotated [A publication] (AAGC)
SD Codified Laws Ann	South Dakota Codified Laws, Annotated [A publication] (DLA)
SDCOI	Sector Direction Center Operating Instruction (SAA)
SD Comm	Doctor of Science in Commerce
SD Compiled Laws Ann	South Dakota Compiled Laws, Annotated [A publication] (DLA)
SD Comp Laws Ann	South Dakota Compiled Laws, Annotated [A publication] (DLA)
SDCP	Sample Data Collection Plan (MCD)
SDCP	Slug Discharge Control Plan [Pollution prevention]
SDCP	Summary Development Cost Plan [NASA] (NASA)
SDCP	Supply Demand Control Point [Military]
SDCR	Source Data Communication Retrieval
SDCS	SAIL [Shuttle Avionics Integration Laboratory] Data Communications System [NASA] (NASA)
SDCS	Sample Data Control System (MCD)
SDCS	Science Data Conditioning System
SDCS	Senior Chief Steward [Later, MSCS] [Navy rating]
SDCS	Shutdown Cooling System [Nuclear energy] (NRCH)
SDCS	Simulation Data Conversion System [Space Flight Operations Facility, NASA]
SDCS	Single Differential Cross Section
SDCS	Space Borne Data-Conditioning System (IAA)
SDCS	Station Digital Command System (IAA)
SDCT	Slosson Drawing Coordination Test
SdCu	Custer County Library, Custer, SD [Library symbol Library of Congress] (LCLS)

SDCU	Satellite Delay Compensation Unit [Telecommunications] (LAIN)
SDCW	San Diego College for Women [California]
SDD	Lubango [Angola] [Airport symbol] (OAG)
SDD	RIC, Inc. [ICAO designator] (FAAC)
SDD	Sa da Bandiera [Angola] [Airport symbol] (AD)
SDD	Santo Domingo [Ciudad Trujillo] [Dominican Republic] [Seismograph station code, US Geological Survey] (SEIS)
SDD	School of Dressmaking & Design (WDAA)
SDD	Scientific Discoveries and Discoverers [A publication]
SDD	Scottish Development Department- (DCTA)
SDD	Scottish Diploma in Dairying
SDD	Second Development Decade [United Nations]
SDD	Selected Dissemination of Documents
SDD	Selective Dissemination of Documentation (NITA)
SD/D	Service Deputy/Director (MUGU)
SDD	Shuttle Design Directive [NASA] (NASA)
SDD	Sierra Nevada Gold [Vancouver Stock Exchange symbol]
SDD	Signal Data Demodulator
SDD	Silicon Disk Drive [Computer science]
SDD	Single Diaphragm Distributor [Automotive engineering]
SDD	Sioux Falls Public Library, Sioux Falls, SD [OCLC symbol] (OCLC)
SDD	Slowdown Density
SDD	Sodium Dimethyldithiocarbamate [Also, SDDC] [Organic chemistry]
SDD	Software Description Document [NASA] (NASA)
SDD	Software Design Description [Computer science] (IEEE)
SDD	Software Design Document [NASA] (NASA)
SDD	Spark Delay Device [Automotive engineering]
SDD	Specially Designated Distributor [Liquor]
SDD	Speed-Dependent Damping [Automotive engineering]
SDD	Spin-Dependent Delocalization [Physical chemistry]
SDD	Sporadic Depressive Disease [Medicine] (DMAA)
SDD	Stacy Design and Development, Inc. [Telecommunications service] (TSSD)
SDD	Standard Delivery Date [Military]
SDD	Sterile Dry Dressing [Surgery] (DAVI)
SDD	Stored Data Description
SDD	Store Door Delivery
SDD	Stress Degree Day [Crop inventory]
SDD	Subchannel Data Distributor (KSC)
SDD	Subsystem Design Description (MCD)
SDD	Synthetic Dynamic Display [Aviation] (OA)
SDD	System Design Description [Nuclear energy] (NRCH)
SDD	System Design Document [NASA] (MCD)
SDD	System for Distributed Databases [Computer science] (CIST)
SDD	Systems Definition Directive [Military] (AFM)
SDD	Systems Development Department [David W. Taylor Naval Ship Research and Development Center]
SDD	Systems Development Dictionary (NITA)
SDD	Systems Development Division [Marine science] (OSRA)
SDDAA	School Dropout Demonstration Assistance Act
SDDC	Self Determination for DC [District of Columbia] (EA)
SDDC	Silver Diethyldithiocarbamate [Organic chemistry]
SDDC	Sodium Dimethyldithiocarbamate [Also, SDD] [Organic chemistry]
SDDC	Speed-Dependent Damping Control [Automotive engineering]
SDDC	Sterile Disposable Device Committee [Defunct]
SDDD	Software Detailed Design Document [Army]
SDDE	Surface Demand Diving Equipment
SDDE	System Design and Development Environment
SdDel	Dell Rapids Carnegie Public Library, Dell Rapids, SD [Library symbol Library of Congress] (LCLS)
SDDL	Stored Data Definition Language
SDDM	Secretary of Defense Decision Memorandum
SDDP	Sight Draft Documents Against Payment [Business term]
SdDr	Draper Public Library, Draper, SD [Library symbol Library of Congress] (LCLS)
SDDR	Standard Digital Data Recorder (DWSG)
SDDRL	Self-Loading Disk Dump and Reload (IAA)
SdDs	De Smet Public Library, De Smet, SD [Library symbol Library of Congress] (LCLS)
SDDS	Satellite Data Distribution System
SDDS	Scientific Document Delivery System
SDDS	Secondary Data Display System (MCD)
SDDS	Signal Data Demodulator Set [or System]
SDDS	Single-Dimensional Deflection System (IAA)
SDDS	Sleep Disorders Dental Society (EA)
SDDS	Solid Discharge Data System [Environmental Protection Agency] (GFGA)
SDDS	Sony Dynamic Digital Sound [Surround-sound technology] (PS)
SDDS	Switched Digital Data Service [Southern New England Telephone]
SD/DS	Synchro-Digital/Digital-Synchro (CAAL)
SDDTTG	Stored Data Definition and Translation Task Group
SDDU	Simplex Data Distribution Unit
SDE	Santiago Del Estero [Argentina] [Airport symbol] (OAG)
SDE	Self-Disinfecting Elastomer
SDE	Simple Designational Expression
SDE	Simultaneous Distillation-Extraction [Chemical engineering]
SDE	Societe de Droits d'Execution du Canada [Performing Rights Organization of Canada - PROC]
SDE	Society of Data Educators (EA)
SDE	Software Development Environment [NCR Corp.]
SDE	Source Data Entry
SDE	Space Division Evaluator [NASA] (NASA)
SDE	Spatial Database Engine
SDE	Specific Dynamic Effect [Medicine]
SDE	Spin-Density Excitation [Physics]

SDE..............	Standard Data Element [*Army*] (AABC)
SDE..............	Standard-Dose Epinephrine [*Medicine*]
SDE..............	Standard Etac Corp. [*Toronto Stock Exchange symbol*]
SDE..............	State Department of Education (DAVI)
SDE..............	State Difference Equation (IAA)
SDE..............	Steam Distillation Extracton
SDE..............	Students for Data Education (IEEE)
SDE..............	Subdural Empyema [*Medicine*] (DMAA)
SDE..............	Submission and Delivery Entity [*Telecommunications*] (OSI)
SDE..............	Support Data Engineering (MCD)
SDE..............	Syntax Directed Editor (NITA)
SDE..............	System Development Engine (NITA)
SDEA..............	Shop and Display Equipment Association [*British*] (EAIO)
SDE & C....	Standard Data Element and Codes [*Air Force*]
SDEC..........	Sequential Detection of Emerging Competitive Target
SDECE........	Service de Documentation Exterieure et de Contre-Espionnage [*Pronounced "suh-deck"*] [*Intelligence organization France Later, DGSE*]
SdEd..........	Edgemont Public Library, Edgemont, SD [*Library symbol Library of Congress*] (LCLS)
SdEdH..........	Edgemont High School, Edgemont, SD [*Library symbol Library of Congress*] (LCLS)
S/DEFL........	Stone Deflector [*Automotive engineering*]
SDEG..........	Special Doctrine Equipment Group [*Army*]
SDE/GWIS....	Sigma Delta Epsilon, Graduate Women in Science (EA)
SDE-IS.........	State Department of Education-Information System [*Minnesota*] (EDAC)
SdEI..........	Elkton Public Library, Elkton, SD [*Library symbol Library of Congress*] (LCLS)
S de M	Sisters Servants of Mary [*Roman Catholic religious order*]
SDEO..........	Second Division of Executive Officers [*A union*] [*British*]
SdeP..........	Sister Servants of the Poor (TOCD)
SDEP..........	Source Data Entry Package [*Computer science*] (MHDI)
SDER..........	Standardized Distributed Energy Release (MCD)
SdEs..........	Estelline Public Library, Estelline, SD [*Library symbol Library of Congress*] (LCLS)
S de S	Simon de Southwell [*Flourished, 1184-1209*] [*Authority cited in pre-1607 legal work*] (DSA)
SDES..........	Submarine Data Extraction System [*Navy*] (CAAL)
SDES..........	Symptomatic Diffuse Esophageal Spasm [*Medicine*] (DMAA)
SDESG........	Strapdown Electrically Suspended Gyro (KSC)
SdEu..........	Eureka Public Library, Eureka, SD [*Library symbol Library of Congress*] (LCLS)
SDEV..........	Sequential Deviation
S de V	Sicardus Fabri de Vauro [*Deceased, 1323*] [*Authority cited in pre-1607 legal work*] (DSA)
SDEV..........	Software Developers [*NASDAQ symbol*] (TTSB)
SDEV..........	[*The*] Software Developer's Co., Inc. [*NASDAQ symbol*] (NQ)
SDF..............	Louisville [*Kentucky*] [*Airport symbol*] (OAG)
SDF..............	Safing and Deservicing Facility [*NASA*] (NASA)
SDF..............	Sanatana Dharma Foundation [*Defunct*] (EA)
SDF..............	Sans Domicile Fixe [*No Fixed Address*] [*French*]
SDF..............	Satellite Distribution Frame [*Telecommunications*] (TEL)
SDF..............	Scottish Decorators Federation (EAIO)
SDF..............	Screen Definition Facility [*Computer science*]
SDF..............	Seasonal Derating Factor (IEEE)
SDF..............	Self-Defense Force [*Vietnam*] (VNW)
SDF..............	Self-Defense Force [*Japan*]
SDF..............	Ship Description File (DNAB)
SDF..............	Ship Design File (OA)
SDF..............	Simplified Directional Facility [*Aviation*]
SDF..............	Simultaneous Double Fire [*Automotive engineering*]
SDF..............	Single Degree of Freedom [*Also, SDOF*] [*Acoustics*]
SDF..............	Sioux Falls College, Sioux Falls, SD [*OCLC symbol*] (OCLC)
SDF..............	Slow Death Factor [*Medicine*]
SDF..............	Social Democratic Federation [*Japan Political party*] (PPW)
SDF..............	Social Democratic Federation [*Later, SDP*] [*Early British political party, members of which were sometimes referred to as "Silly Damn Fools"*]
SDF..............	Social Democratic Federation [*Iceland*] [*Political party*] (PPW)
SDF..............	Social Democratic Front [*Ghana*] [*Political party*] (PPW)
SDF..............	Social Democratic Front [*Cameroon*] [*Political party*] (EY)
SDF..............	Software Development Facility [*Military*] (CAAL)
SDF..............	Software Development File
SDF..............	Software Development Folder (MCD)
SDF..............	Software Development Framework (RDA)
SDF..............	Sonic Depth Finder
SDF..............	Source Development Fund [*Supply and Services Canada*]
SDF..............	Source Document Folders [*IRS*]
SDF..............	Southern Development Foundation (EA)
SDF..............	Spatial Distribution Functions [*Of molecules*]
SDF..............	Special Denatured Formula [*Applied to alcohol*]
SDF..............	Spectral Density Function
SDF..............	Standard Data Format [*Computer science*] (CDE)
SDF..............	Standard Distance File (DOMA)
SDF..............	Standard Distribution Format [*Computer science*]
SDF..............	Standard Drug File [*Derwent Publications Ltd.*] [*Database*]
SDF..............	Standiford Field [*FAA*] (TAG)
SDF..............	Static Design Factor
SDF..............	Static Direction Finder
SDF..............	Step Down Fix [*Aviation*] (DA)
SDF..............	Stopping Distance Factor (MCD)
SDF..............	Stowe-Day Foundation (EA)
SDF..............	Strategic Defensive Forces [*Army*] (AABC)
SDF..............	Stress Distribution Factor [*Medicine*] (DMAA)
SDF..............	Stromal Cell-Derived Factor [*Biochemistry*]
SDF..............	Structural Dynamics Malfunction
SDF..............	Student Description Form [*Psychology*]
SDF..............	Sudan Defence Force [*British*]
SDF..............	Sundorph Aeronautical, Corp. [*ICAO designator*] (FAAC)
SDF..............	Supergroup Distribution Frame [*Telecommunications*] (TEL)
SDF..............	Surface Direct Fire [*Navy*] (CAAL)
SDF..............	Swedish Defense Forces
SDF..............	System Data Format [*Computer science*]
SDF..............	System Development Facility [*NASA*] (KSC)
SDFAUS.......	State Defense Force Association of the United States (EA)
SDFC	Space Disturbance Forecast Center [*Environmental Science Services Administration*] (IEEE)
SDFC	Standardized Discriminant Function Coefficient
SDFD	System Data Flow Diagram (IAA)
SDFG	Single-Degree-of-Freedom Gyroscope (SAA)
SDFL	Schottky Diode FET [*Field Effect Transistor*] Logic
SD Fla	United States District Court for the Southern District of Florida (DLA)
SDFN	SONAR Dome Flow Noise
SDFOV........	Simultaneous Dual Field of View
SD-FP	Solvent Detergent Treated Frozen Plasma
SdFr............	Freeman Public Library, Freeman, SD [*Library symbol Library of Congress*] (LCLS)
SDFS	Same-Day Funds Settlement [*Securities and Exchange Commission*]
SD/FS	Smoke Detector/Fire Suppression (GFGA)
SDFS	Standard Disk Filing System
SDFSNM......	Sons and Daughters of the First Settlers of Newbury, Massachusetts (EA)
SDFT...........	Schottky Diode Field Effect Transistor Logic (MHDI)
SDFT...........	System Demonstration Flight Test [*DoD*]
SDFTN	Soda Fountain
SDFU	Sanitary Drainage Fixture Unit (DAC)
SDG	Aerosierra de Durango [*Mexico ICAO designator*] (FAAC)
SDG	Sacred Dance Guild (EA)
SDG	San Diego [*California*] (GAAI)
SDG	Sao Domingos [*Brazil*] [*Airport symbol*] (AD)
SDG	Scan Display Generator
SDG	Scenario Development Group (COE)
SDG	Screen Directors' Guild of America [*Later, DGA*]
SDG	Siding (AAG)
Sdg	Siding (WPI)
SDG	Signed, Directed Graph [*Mathematics*]
SDG	Simulated Data Generation (IAA)
SDG	Simulated Data Generator
SDG	Situation Display Generator
SDG	Sofamor Danek Group [*NYSE symbol*] (SPSG)
SDG	Soli Deo Gloria [*Glory to God Alone*] [*Latin*]
SDG	Special Development Groups [*Navy*]
SDG	Special District Government (COE)
SDG	Stormont, Dundas and Glengarry Highlanders [*British military*] (DMA)
SDG	Strapdown Gyroscope (SAA)
SDG	Subminiature Displacement Gyroscope
SDG	Sucrose Density Gradients
SDG	Sudan Democratic Gazette [*A publication*]
SDG	Sundance Gold Mining Ltd. [*Vancouver Stock Exchange symbol*]
SDG	Supplier Documentation Group [*NASA*] (NASA)
SDG	System Design Group (MCD)
SDGA	Single Conductor, Degaussing, Armored (IAA)
SDGA	Single Degaussing Cable
SDGA	Sucrose Density Gradient Analysis [*Clinical chemistry*]
SD GA	United States District Court for the Southern District of Georgia (DLA)
SDGC	Simulated Distillation Gas Chromatography
SDGC	Sun-Diamond Growers of California (EA)
SDGE	Situation Display Generator Element
SdGe	Sully-Potter County Library, Gettysburg, SD [*Library symbol Library of Congress*] (LCLS)
SDGF	Schwannoma-Derived Growth Factor [*Biochemistry*]
SDGH	Sweet Dough
SDgo...........	San Diego Gas & Electric Co. [*Associated Press*] (SAG)
SDGW	Structural Design Gross Weight
SDH	Scottish Diploma in Horticulture
SDH	Seasonal Derated Hours (IEEE)
SDH	Serine Dehydrase [*An enzyme*] (MAE)
SDH	Servicio de Helicopteros SL [*Spain ICAO designator*] (FAAC)
SDH	Single Dad's Hotline [*Defunct*] (EA)
SDH	Software Development Handbook [*NASA*] (NASA)
SDH	Sorbitol Dehydrogenase [*Also, Sorb D*] [*An enzyme*]
SDH	South Dakota Historical Resource Center, Pierre, SD [*OCLC symbol*] (OCLC)
SDH	Spinal Dorsal Horn [*Anatomy*]
SDH	Structured Document Handbook [*Computer science*]
SDH	Styling Data Handling
SDH	Subdural Hematoma [*Medicine*]
SDH	Subjacent Dorsal Horn (DB)
SDH	Succinic Dehydrogenase [*An enzyme*]
SDH	Support Dogs for the Handicapped (EA)
SDH	Synchronous Digital Hierarchy [*Computer science*]
SDH	System Development Handbook [*NASA*] (NASA)
SDHACU......	Sodium-Dependent High-Affinity Choline Uptake [*Biochemistry*]
SDHBS	South Devon Herd Book Society [*British*] (DBA)
SDHD..........	Society of Daughters of Holland Dames (EA)
SDHD..........	Sudden-Death Heart Disease [*Medicine*]
SDHE	Spacecraft Data Handling Equipment
SdHi...........	South Dakota Department of Cultural Affairs, Historical Resources Center, Pierre, SD [*Library symbol Library of Congress*] (LCLS)

SdHig.......... Hyde County Library, Highmore, SD [*Library symbol Library of Congress*] (LCLS)

SDHIRS........ Subdistrict Headquarters Induction and Recruiting Station [*Navy*]

SdHM.......... Minnehaha County Rural Library, Hartford, SD [*Library symbol Library of Congress*] (LCLS)

SdHow........ Howard Public Library, Howard, SD [*Library symbol Library of Congress*] (LCLS)

SDHP.......... Sosyal Demokrasi Halkci Partisi [*Social Democratic Populist Party*] [*Turkey Political party*] (MENA)

SDHS.......... Satellite Data Handling System

SDHS.......... Society of Dance History Scholars (EA)

SdHsV........ United States Veterans Administration Center, Hot Springs, SD [*Library symbol Library of Congress*] (LCLS)

SDHT.......... Selectively Doped Heterojunction Transistor (NITA)

SDHT.......... Selectively Doped Heterostructure Transistor

SdHuro....... Huron Public Library, Huron, SD [*Library symbol Library of Congress*] (LCLS)

SdHuroC..... Huron College, Huron, SD [*Library symbol Library of Congress*] (LCLS)

SDHW.......... Solar Domestic Hot Water

SDHX.......... Shutdown Heat Exchanger [*Environmental science*] (COE)

SDHyg......... Doctor of Science in Hygiene (GAGS)

SDI.............. Saab Direct Ignition [*Automotive engineering*]

SDI.............. Saidor [*Papua New Guinea*] [*Airport symbol*] (OAG)

SDI.............. Saudi Arabian

SDI.............. Saudi Arabian Airlines

SDI.............. Selected Descriptive Item

SDI.............. Selective Dissemination of Information [*System*] [*Computer science*]

SDI.............. Self-Description Inventory [*Vocational guidance test*]

SDI.............. Serial Data Interface [*Computer science*] (CDE)

SDI.............. Serial Dilution Indicator [*Clinical chemistry*]

SDI.............. Service de Documentation Interministerielle [*Interministerial Documentation Service*] [*National Telecommunications Research Center*] [*Information service or system*] (IID)

SDI.............. Ship's Drawing Index (DNAB)

SDI.............. Single Document Interface [*Computer science*] (CDE)

SDI.............. Situation Display Indicator [*Aviation*] (OA)

SDI.............. Size/Date Inconsistency (STED)

SDI.............. Society of Designers in Ireland (EAIO)

SDI.............. Source Data Information

SDI.............. Specifications Drawing Index (DNAB)

SDI.............. Standard Data Interface [*Computer science*]

SDI.............. Standard Deviation Interval [*Medicine*]

SDI.............. Standard Drive Interface [*Computer science*] (CDE)

SDI.............. Standardized Discharge Instructions [*for hospital patients*]

SDI.............. Stars of David International (EAIO)

SDI.............. State Disability Insurance

SDI.............. Steel Deck Institute (EA)

SDI.............. Steel Door Institute (EA)

SDI.............. Strategic Defense Initiative [*Commonly known as "Starwars"*] [*Facetiously translated as "Silly Damn Idea"*]

SDI.............. Subcontractor Data Item

SDI.............. Submarine Detector Instructor [*British military*] (DMA)

SDI.............. Super Data Interchange [*Computer science*] (HGAA)

SDI.............. Supplier Data Item (MCD)

SDI.............. Support Directive Instruction (KSC)

SDI.............. Surtees Difficulties Index (STED)

SDI.............. Switched Digital International [*AT&T*] (CDE)

SDI.............. Symbolic Displays, Inc. (MCD)

SDI.............. System Diagram Index (IAA)

SDI.............. Systems Designers International Ltd. [*British*] (IRUK)

SDIA.......... Small Defense Industries Association [*Later, Strategic Industries Association*]

SDIA.......... Soap and Detergent Industry Association [*British*] (DBA)

SDIAC.......... Strategic Defense Initiative Advisory Council [*Military*] (SDI)

SDIC.......... South Dakota-Iowa Conference (PSS)

SDIC.......... STC Communications Subsystem Distribution Interface Cabinet (MCD)

SDICC.......... Societe de Developpement de l'Industrie Cinematographique Canadienne [*Canadian Film Development Corp. - CFDC*]

SDICC.......... South Dakota Intercollegiate Conference (PSS)

SDID.......... Supplier Data Item Description (MCD)

SDIE.......... Special Defense Intelligence Estimate (MCD)

SDieGs....... San Diego Gas & Electric Co. [*Associated Press*] (SAG)

SDIF.......... Schistosome-Derived Immunosuppressive Factor [*Immunology*]

SDIF.......... Software Development and Integration Facility [*NASA*] (NASA)

SDIF.......... Standard Document Interchange Format [*Telecommunications*]

SDIG.......... Screen Directors International Guild [*Absorbed by Directors Guild of America*] (EA)

SDIHD......... Sudden-Death Ischemic Heart Disease [*Medicine*]

SDII.......... Special Devices [*NASDAQ symbol*] (TTSB)

SDII.......... Special Devices, Inc. [*NASDAQ symbol*] (SPSG)

SDII.......... Strategic Defense Initiative Institute [*Military*] (SDI)

SDI-KWOC ... Selected Dissemination of Information - Key Word Out of Context (DNAB)

SDILINE...... Selective Dissemination of Information Online [*National Library of Medicine*] [*Bethesda, MD Bibliographic database*]

SD III......... United States District Court for the Southern District of Illinois (DLA)

SDIM.......... System for Documentation and Information in Metallurgy [*Fachinformationszentrum Werkstoffe eV*] [*Information service or system*] (IID)

SDIMU......... Strapdown Inertial Measuring Unit (MCD)

SDIN.......... Special Defence Intelligence Notice (MCD)

SD Ind .... United States District Court for the Southern District of Indiana (DLA)

SDIO.......... Serial Digit Input/Output [*Computer science*]

SDIO.......... Strategic Defense Initiative Office [*DoD*]

SDIO.......... Strategic Defense Initiative Organization [*Washington, DC DoD*] (GRD)

SD Iowa....... United States District Court for the Southern District of Iowa (DLA)

SDIP.......... Specifically Designated Intelligence Position (AFM)

SDIP.......... Strengthening Developing Institutions Program [*HEW*]

SDIP.......... System Description and Implementation Plan [*Navy*]

SDIS.......... Ship Distance

SDIS.......... Ship Draft Indicating System (MSA)

SDISEM........ Strategic Defense Initiative System Evaluation Model

SDISM........ Strategic Defense Initiative System Effectiveness Model [*Military*]

SDIT.......... Service de Documentation et d'Information Techniques de l'Aeronautique

SDIT.......... Ship Draft Indicator Transmitter (MSA)

SDIT.......... Sons and Daughters in Touch [*An association*]

SDI/UC......... State Disability Insurance - Unemployment Compensation

SDIX.......... Strategic Diagnostics, Inc. [*NASDAQ symbol*] (SAG)

SDIZ.......... Submarine Defense Identification Zone

SDJ.......... Greensboro, NC [*Location identifier FAA*] (FAAL)

SDJ.......... Sanada [*Japan*] [*Seismograph station code, US Geological Survey*] (SEIS)

SDJ.......... Sendai [*Japan*] [*Airport symbol*] (OAG)

SDJ.......... Senn d'Or [*Vancouver Stock Exchange symbol*]

SDJ.......... Society of the Devotees of Jerusalem (EA)

SDK.......... Grupo Sidek SA de CV [*NYSE symbol*] (SAG)

SDK.......... Grupo Sidek S.A.'L'ADS [*NYSE symbol*] (TTSB)

SDK.......... Sandakan [*Malaysia*] [*Airport symbol*] (OAG)

SDK.......... Seljacko-Demokratska Koalicija [*Peasant-Democratic Coalition*] [*Former Yugoslavia*] [*Political party*] (PPE)

SDK.......... Shelter Deck

SDK.......... Si De Ka Quarterly [*Ann Arbor, MI*] [*A publication*] (DLA)

SDK.......... Sigma Delta Kappa [*Fraternity*]

SDK.......... Sociedad Aerea del Caqueta Ltd. [*Colombia*] [*ICAO designator*] (FAAC)

SDK.......... Software Developer's Kit [*Computer science*] (BYTE)

SDK.......... Software Development Kit [*Computer science*] (PCM)

SDK.......... Studebaker's Resource Development Ltd. [*Formerly, Rio Blanco Resources Ltd.*] [*Vancouver Stock Exchange symbol*]

SDK.......... System Design Kit

SDK.......... System Developers' Kit [*Computer hardware*] [*Microsoft, Inc.*] (PCM)

SDK.B.......... Grupo Sidek S.A.'B' ADS [*NYSE symbol*] (TTSB)

SdKJ.......... Jackson-Washabaugh County Library, Kadoka, SD [*Library symbol Library of Congress*] (LCLS)

SdL.......... Hearst Free Library, Lead, SD [*Library symbol Library of Congress*] (LCLS)

SDL.......... National Council, Sons and Daughters of Liberty (EA)

SDL.......... Saddle (MSA)

SDL.......... Scenario Development Language [*Military*] (CAAL)

SDL.......... Scientific DataLink [*Comtex Scientific Corp.*] [*Information service or system*] (IID)

SDL.......... Scottie Gold Mines Ltd. [*Vancouver Stock Exchange symbol*]

SDL.......... Scottsdale, AZ [*Location identifier FAA*] (FAAL)

SDL.......... Screw Dislocation Line [*Crystallography*]

SDL.......... Security Devices Laboratory (SAA)

SDL.......... Seedling (WGA)

SDL.......... Seismic Data Laboratory [*Teledyne Geotech*]

SDL.......... Self-Directed Learning (ADA)

SDL.......... Semiconductor Diode LASER [*Also, TDL*]

SDL.......... Sensory Distal Latency [*Medicine*]

SDL.......... Serum Digoxin Level [*Cardiology*] (DAVI)

SDL.......... Serum Drug Level (STED)

SDL.......... Shaft Driver, Left

SDL.......... SHORAD [*Short Range Air Defense*] Data Link [*Army*]

SDL.......... Side Discharge Loader [*Mining*]

SDL.......... Simulation Data Language

SDL.......... Single Driver's License [*Law*]

SDL.......... Slowdown Length

SDL.......... Software Design Language

SDL.......... Software Development Laboratory [*NASA*] (NASA)

SDL.......... Software Development Language [*Burroughs Corp.*]

SDL.......... Software Development Library

SDL.......... Sonic Delay Line

SDL.......... Space Disturbances Laboratory [*Boulder, CO*]

SDL.......... Space Dynamics Laboratories [*Utah State University*] [*Research center*] (RCD)

SDL.......... Specification and Description Language [*Telecommunications*] (TEL)

SDL.......... Speech Discrimination Loss (STED)

SDL.......... Standard Deviation of the Logarithm [*Statistics*]

SDL.......... Standard Distribution List [*NASA*]

SDL.......... Stark County District Library, Canton, OH [*OCLC symbol*] (OCLC)

SDL.......... State-Dependent Learning [*Psychology*]

SDL.......... Strip Delay Line

SDL.......... Sundsvall [*Sweden*] [*Airport symbol*] (OAG)

SDL.......... Supporting Document List

SDL.......... Surplus Distribution List (AAG)

SDL.......... Systematic Design Language [*Computer science*]

SDL.......... System Descriptive Language [*Computer science*] (IEEE)

SDL.......... System Design Language

SDL.......... System Development Language [*1971*] [*Computer science*] (CSR)

SDL.......... System Directory List [*Computer science*] (BUR)

SDL.......... Systems Designers Ltd. [*Research center British*]

SDL.......... Systems Design Laboratory (IAA)

SDL.......... Systems Development Laboratories (MCD)

SDLA.......... South Dakota Library Association

SDLC.......... Single-Level Data Link Control (IAA)

SDLC .... Synchronous Data Link Control [*Telecommunications*]
SDLC .... System Data Link Control [*Telecommunications*]
SDLC .... System Development Life Cycle
SDLCM .... Systems Development Life Cycle Methodology [*Environmental Protection Agency*] (AEPA)
SdLeH .... Lennox High School Library, Lennox, SD [*Library symbol Library of Congress*] (LCLS)
SdLem .... Lemmon Public Library, Lemmon, SD [*Library symbol Library of Congress*] (LCLS)
SdLemH .... Lemmon High School Library, Lemmon, SD [*Library symbol Library of Congress*] (LCLS)
SDLI .... SDL, Inc. [*NASDAQ symbol*] (SAG)
SDL Inc .... SDL, Inc. [*Associated Press*] (SAG)
SDLM .... Scheduled Depot Level Maintenance [*Navy*]
SDLM .... Special Depot Level Maintenance
SDLM .... Standard Depot Level Maintenance (MCD)
SDLO .... State, Defense Liaison Office [*Federal government*] (AABC)
SDLP .... Social Democratic and Labour Party [*Northern Ireland*] [*Political party*] (PPW)
SDLP .... Social Democratic and Liberal Party [*British Political party*]
SDLP .... Societe de Developpement du Livre et du Periodique [*Society for the Development of Books and Periodicals*] [*Canada*]
SDLRS .... Self-Directed-Learning Readiness Scale (MEDA)
SDLS .... Satellite Data Link Standard (DOMA)
SDLT .... Static/Dynamic Load Technology (SSD)
SDLTS .... Scanning Deep-Level Transient Spectroscopy (AAEL)
SDLV .... Shuttle-Derived Launch Vehicle [*NASA*] (SSD)
sdly .... Sidelying (STED)
SdM .... Mitchell Public Library, Mitchell, SD [*Library symbol Library of Congress*] (LCLS)
SDM .... National Association of Special Delivery Messengers [*Later, APWU*] [*AFL-CIO*]
SDM .... Samsonov Density Meter [*Gravimetrics*]
SDM .... San Diego, CA [*Location identifier FAA*] (FAAL)
SDM .... Santiago De Maria [*El Salvador*] [*Seismograph station code, US Geological Survey*] (SEIS)
SDM .... School in District Management [*LIMRA*]
SDM .... Schwarz Differential Medium (OA)
SDM .... Selective Dissemination of Microfiche
SDM .... Semiconductor Disk Memory
SDM .... Sensory Detection Method [*for measuring blood pressure*]
SDM .... Sequency-Division Multiplexing (IEEE)
SDM .... Ship Design Manager
SDM .... Short-Delay Monostable [*Circuitry*]
SDM .... Shutdown Margin [*Nuclear energy*] (NRCH)
SDM .... Shutdown Mode (IEEE)
SDM .... Shuttle Data Management [*NASA*] (MCD)
SDM .... Signal Density Model (MCD)
SDM .... Simulated Dynamic Missile [*Military*] (CAAL)
SDM .... Single, Divorced, Married (STED)
SDM .... Site Defense of Minutoman [*Missiles*] (MCD)
SDM .... Site-Directed Mutagenesis [*Biochemistry*]
SDM .... Situation Display Matrix (IAA)
SDM .... Slowdown Model
SDM .... Software Development Methodology (IAA)
SDM .... Soma Dendrite Membrane
SDM .... Somali Democratic Movement [*Political party*] (EY)
SDM .... Sons and Daughters of Malta (EA)
SDM .... Space Division Multiplexing [*Physics*]
SDM .... Spares Determination Method [*Bell System*]
SDM .... Sparse Distributed Memory [*Computer science*]
SDM .... Specially Designated Merchant [*Liquor sales*]
SDM .... Specific Device Model for Sensor Actuator Bus (AAEL)
SDM .... Standard Deviation of the Mean (AAMN)
SDM .... Standardization Design Memoranda (IEEE)
SDM .... STARAN Debug Module
SDM .... Statistical Delta Modulation
SDM .... Statistical-Dynamical Model
SDM .... Structural Development Model
SDM .... Structural Dynamics Modification
SDM .... Structures, Structural Dynamics, and Materials (MCD)
SDM .... Subdivision Manager
SDM .... Subsystem Design Manual [*NASA*] (MCD)
SDM .... Sugar Cane Downy Mildew [*Plant pathology*]
SDM .... Sulfadimethoxine [*Antibacterial*] [*Veterinary medicine*]
SDM .... Synchronous Digital Machine
SDM .... System Data Module (IAA)
SDM .... System Decision Manager (IAA)
SDM .... System Definition Manual [*NASA*] (NASA)
SDM .... Systems Design Methodology [*Computer science*] (HGAA)
SDM .... Systems Development Methodology [*Computer science*] (HGAA)
SdMa .... Bennett County Library, Martin, SD [*Library symbol Library of Congress*] (LCLS)
SDMA .... Sam Davis Memorial Association (EA)
SDMA .... Shared Direct Memory Access [*Sperry UNIVAC*]
SDMA .... Sodium Dihydrobis(methoxyethoxy)aluminate [*Organic chemistry*]
SDMA .... Space Division Multiple Access
SDMA .... Surgical Dressing Manufacturers Association [*British*] (BI)
SDMAC .... Shared Direct Memory Access Contoller [*Computer science*] (MHDI)
SdMadT .... Dakota State College, Madison, SD [*Library symbol Library of Congress*] (LCLS)
SdMar .... Dakota Wowapipahi Library, Marty, SD [*Library symbol Library of Congress*] (LCLS)
SDMA/SS-TDMA ... Space Division Multiple Access/Spacecraft Switched-Time Division Multiple Access (PDAA)
SDMD .... Sequential Decision Making Device (IAA)
SDME .... Synchronous Data Modern Equipment
SdMeS .... Menno Public School Library, Menno, SD [*Library symbol Library of Congress*] (LCLS)
SD (Met) ...... Doctor of Science in Metallurgy
SDMH .... Symmetrical-Dimthylhydrazine [*Organic chemistry*]
SdMi .... Hand County Library, Miller, SD [*Library symbol Library of Congress*] (LCLS)
SDMI .... Secure Digital Music Initiative
S-DMICC ...... State-Defense Military Information Control Committee (AFM)
SdMil .... Milbank Carnegie Library, Milbank, SD [*Library symbol Library of Congress*] (LCLS)
SDMIS .... Standard Depot Management Information System [*Army*]
SDMIS .... Standardization Data Management Information System
SD Miss .... United States District Court for the Southern District of Mississippi (DLA)
SDMIX .... South Dakota Medical Information Exchange [*University of South Dakota*] [*Sioux Falls*] [*Telecommunications*] (TSSD)
SDMJ .... Quarterly Payments of Interest or Dividends in September, December, March and June (EBF)
SDMJ .... September, December, March, and June [*Denotes quarterly payments of interest or dividends in these months*] [*Business term*]
SdMo .... A. H. Brown Public Library, Mobridge, SD [*Library symbol Library of Congress*] (LCLS)
SDMO .... Specifications and Data Management Office [*Military*]
SDMO .... Subcommand Data Management Office [*Military*] (AFIT)
SDMS .... Shipboard Data Multiplex System (MCD)
SDMS .... Society of Diagnostic Medical Sonographers (EA)
SDMS .... Spatial Data Management System (MCD)
SDMS .... Staff Development Management System (AIE)
SDMS .... Supplier Data Management System (MCD)
SDMSS .... Software Development and Maintenance Suppport System [*Computer science*] (MHDI)
SDMT .... Stanford Diagnostic Mathematics Test [*Education*]
SDMT .... Stress and Degraded Mode Test (CAAL)
SDMT .... Symbol Digit Modalities Test (STED)
SdMW .... Dakota Wesleyan University, Mitchell, SD [*Library symbol Library of Congress*] (LCLS)
SDN .... North American Baptist Seminary, Sioux Falls, SD [*OCLC symbol*] (OCLC)
SDN .... Sandane [*Norway*] [*Airport symbol*] (OAG)
SDN .... Satellite Data Network [*AgriData Resources, Inc.*] [*Telecommunications service Defunct*] (TSSD)
SDN .... Secret Document Number
SDN .... Separation Designation Number
SDN .... Service Dealer's Newsletter [*Lynott Associates*] [*A publication*] (IID)
SDN .... Sexually Dimorphic Nucleus [*Brain anatomy*]
SDN .... Societe Demographique Nordique [*Nordic Demographic Society - NDS*] (EAIO)
SDN .... Societe des Nations [*League of Nations*]
SDN .... Sodisco, Inc. [*Toronto Stock Exchange symbol*]
SDN .... Software Defined Network [*Telecommunications*]
SDN .... Software Development Note [*NASA*] (NASA)
SDN .... Solution-Dyed Nylon
SDN .... Strapdown Navigator
SDN .... Subdeacon
SDN .... Subscriber's Directory Number [*Telecommunications*] (TEL)
SDN .... Sudan [*ANSI three-letter standard code*] (CNC)
SDN .... Swindon [*British depot code*]
SDN .... Synchronized Digital Network [*Telecommunications*] (TEL)
SDN .... System Development Notification
SDN & SU ... Step-Down and Step-Up (MSA)
SDNB .... SDNB Financial [*Associated Press*] (SAG)
SDNB .... SDNB Financial [*NASDAQ symbol*] (TTSB)
SDNB .... SDNB Financial Corp. [*NASDAQ symbol*] (NQ)
SDNCO .... Staff Duty Noncommissioned Officer [*Army*]
SdNe .... Newell Public Library, Newell, SD [*Library symbol Library of Congress*] (LCLS)
SdNeu .... New Underwood Public Library, New Underwood, SD [*Library symbol Library of Congress*] (LCLS)
SDNF .... Shortened Disjuctive Normal Form (PDAA)
SDNI .... Software-Defined Network International [*AT&T*] (CIST)
SDNM .... Sampled-Data Nonlinearity Matrix (PDAA)
SDNR .... Screw Down Non-Return Valve (DS)
SDNRIU .... Secure Digital Net Radio Interface Unit [*Army*] (RDA)
SDNS .... Scottish Daily Newspaper Society (DBA)
SDNS .... Secure Data Network System [*Computer science*]
SDNT .... Student
SDNY .... United States District Court for the Southern District of New York (DLA)
SDO .... Oglala Sioux Community College, Learning Resources Center, Pine Ridge, SD [*OCLC symbol*] (OCLC)
SdO .... Onida Public Library, Onida, SD [*Library symbol Library of Congress*] (LCLS)
SDO .... Salado [*Chile*] [*Seismograph station code, US Geological Survey Closed*] (SEIS)
SDO .... San Diego Gas & Electric Co. [*AMEX symbol*] (SPSG)
SDO .... San Diego Gas & Electric Co. [*NYSE symbol*] (SAG)
SDO .... Scan Data Out (IAA)
SDO .... Schedules Duty Officer (KSC)
SDO .... Senior Divisional Officer (WDAA)
SDO .... Senior Duty Officer [*Air Force British*]
SDO .... Shielded Diatomic Orbitals [*Atomic physics*]
SDO .... Shipboard Distribution Only [*Navy*] (CAAL)

SDO	Ship Development Objective [*Navy*]
SDO	Signal Distributing Office [*British military*] (IAA)
SDO	Signal Distribution Officer [*British military*] (DMA)
SDO	Singlet Delta Oxygen
SDO	Sod House, NV [*Location identifier FAA*] (FAAL)
SDO	Software Distribution Operation (IAA)
SDO	SONAR Detection Opportunity [*Navy*] (CAAL)
SDO	Source Data Operation (MDG)
SDO	Spatial Data Option
SDO	Special Duty Officer (MCD)
SDO	Special Duty Only [*Military*]
SDO	Specialist Duty Only [*Navy personnel designation*]
SDO	Squadron Duty Officer [*Navy*] (NVT)
SDO	Staff Duty Officer [*Army*]
SDO	Standards Developing Organization
SDO	Standards Development Organization
SDO	Station Duty Officer [*Navy*]
SDO	Synthetic Drying Oil
SDO	Systems Development Office [*National Weather Service*]
SDOB	Scaled Depth of Burst (MCD)
S Doc	Senate Document (DLA)
SDOC	Specific Direct Operating Costs
S DOC	State Document (WDAA)
SDOE	State Department of Education (OICC)
SDOF	Single Degree of Freedom [*Also, SDF*] [*Acoustics*]
SD Ohio	United States District Court for the Southern District of Ohio (DLA)
SDOM	Society of Dirty Old Men [*Defunct*] (EA)
SDOM	Standard Deviation of Means [*Statistics*]
SDOP	Ship Doppler (IAA)
SDOP	Sons and Daughters of Oregon Pioneers (EA)
SDOPR	Sound Operator [*Navy*]
SDOPrA	San Diego G&E 5% Pfd [*AMEX symbol*] (TTSB)
SDOPrB	San Diego G&E 4.50% Pfd [*AMEX symbol*] (TTSB)
SDOPrC	San Diego G&E 4.40% Pfd [*AMEX symbol*] (TTSB)
SDOPrH	San Diego Gas & El $1.82 Pref [*AMEX symbol*] (TTSB)
SDOS	Source Data Operating System (IAA)
SDOSD	Standard Deviation of Standard Deviation [*Statistics*]
SDP	Aero Sudpacifico SA [*Mexico ICAO designator*] (FAAC)
SDP	National Society of Sons and Daughters of the Pilgrims (EA)
SDP	Sacrodextra Posterior [*A fetal position*] [*Obstetrics*]
SDP	Sand Point [*Alaska*] [*Airport symbol*] (OAG)
SDP	Sand Point, AK [*Location identifier FAA*] (FAAL)
SDP	School Development Plan [*British*] (DET)
SDP	Scottish Diploma in Poultry Husbandry
SDP	Sea Duty Pay [*Navy*]
SDP	Selective Data Processing (IAA)
SDP	Sentry Dog Patrol (AFM)
SDP	Serb Democratic Party [*Croatia*] [*Political party*] (EY)
SDP	Serbian Democratic Party [*Bosnia-Herzegovina*] [*Political party*] (EY)
SDP	Set-Down Pool [*Nuclear energy*] (NRCH)
SDP	Seychelles Democratic Party
SDP	Shelf Dynamics Program [*CUE*] (MSC)
SDP	Ship Development Plan [*Navy*]
SDP	Ship Discharge Package [*Military*] (INF)
SDP	Short-Day Plant [*Botany*]
SDP	Shuttle Data Processor [*NASA*] (MCD)
SDP	Signal Data Processor
SDP	Signal Dispatch Point [*Telecommunications*] (TEI.)
SDP	Silicon Diode Pellet
SDP	Singapore Democratic Party [*Political party*] (PPW)
SDP	Single Department Purchasing [*Agency*] [*Military*]
SDP	Single Dry Plate (IAA)
SDP	Sirotherm Demineralization Process
SDP	Site Data Processor
SDP	Site Development and Facilities Utilization Plan [*Oak Ridge National Laboratory*]
SDP	Skill Development Program [*Australia*]
SDP	Slowdown Power
SDP	Small Distribution Phenomena
SDP	Smoke Dispersion Pod
SDP	Social Democratic Party [*Albania*] [*Political party*] (EY)
SDP	Social Democratic Party [*Hungary*] [*Political party*]
SDP	Social Democratic Party [*Nigeria*] [*Political party*]
SDP	Social Democratic Party [*Germany Political party*]
SDP	Social Democratic Party [*Philippines*] [*Political party*] (PPW)
SDP	Social Democratic Party [*Trinidad and Tobago*] [*Political party*] (PPW)
SDP	Social Democratic Party [*Thailand*] [*Political party*] (PPW)
SDP	Social Democratic Party [*Australia Political party*]
SDP	Social Democratic Party [*Iceland*] [*Political party*] (PPW)
SDP	Social Democratic Party [*British Political party*]
SDP	Social-Democrat Party [*Zambia*] [*Political party*] (EY)
SDP	Social, Domestic, Pleasure [*Private car classification*] (WDAA)
SDP	Socialist Democratic Party [*South Korea Political party*] (EY)
SDP	Society of Decorative Painters (NTPA)
SDP	Software Development Plan [*NASA*] (NASA)
SDP	Software Development Processor (NITA)
SDP	Solar Desalination Plant
SDP	Sosyal Demokrat Partisi [*Social Democratic Party*] [*Turkish Cyprus*] [*Political party*] (EY)
SDP	Source Data Processing
SDP	Sozial Demokratesch Partei [*Social Democratic Party*] [*Luxembourg*] [*Political party*] (PPE)
SDP	Spectral Dependence Photocurrent
SDP	Sports Development Program [*Australia*]
SDP	Standard Data Processor (SSD)
SDP	Standard Distance Package (DOMA)
SDP	State Data Program [*Information service or system*] (IID)
SDP	Station Data Processing
SDP	Steyr-Daimler-Puch [*Manufacturing firm*] [*Automotive engineering*]
SDP	Storage and Distribution Point [*Military*] (AFM)
SDP	Stornaway Central Development [*Vancouver Stock Exchange symbol*]
SDP	Stranka Democratskih Reformi [*Party of Democratic Reform*] [*Slovenia*] [*Political party*] (EY)
SDP	Stratospheric Dust Particle
SDP	Streaming Data Procedure [*Computer science*] (CDE)
SDP	Sub-Seabed Disposal Program [*National Science Foundation*] (NUCP)
SdP	Sudetendeutsche Partei [*Sudeten German Party*] [*Former Czechoslovakia*] [*Political party*] (PPE)
SDP	Sulfonyldiphenol [*Organic chemistry*]
SDP	Sun Distributors Ltd. Class A [*NYSE symbol*] (SPSG)
SDP	Sunsource L.P. [*NYSE symbol*] (SAG)
SDP	Sunsource L.P.'A' [*NYSE symbol*] (TTSB)
SDP	Suomen Sosialidemokraattinen Puolue [*Finnish Social Democratic Party*] [*Political party*] (EAIO)
SDP	Supplementary Development Plan
SDP	Supplier Data Package (NASA)
SDP	Supply Distribution Point
SDP	Surface Deformation Pattern
SDP	Survey Data Processing
Sdp	Suspended in Part [*Regulation or order suspended in part*] [*Legal term*] (DLA)
SDP	Swaziland Democratic Party
SDP	System Decision Paper
SDP	System Design Proposal [*Navy*]
SDP	Systems Development Package [*or Plan*] [*Military*] (NG)
SdPa	Parker Public Library, Parker, SD [*Library symbol Library of Congress*] (LCLS)
SDPA	Small Defense Plants Administration [*Terminated, 1953*]
SDP.B	Sunsource L.P.'B' [*NYSE symbol*] (TTSB)
SDPC	Shuttle Data Processing Complex [*NASA*] (NAKS)
SDPC	Social Democratic Party of Canada
SDPC	Social Democratic Party of Croatia [*Political party*]
SDPD	Special Defense Projects Department
SDPDA	Special Defense Property Disposal Account [*DoD*]
SdPEC	South Dakota Department of Education and Cultural Affairs, Historical Resources Center, Pierre, SD [*Library symbol Library of Congress*] (LCLS)
SDPF	Science Data Processing Facility (SSD)
SDPF	Sensor Data Processing Facility (MCD)
SDPF	Social-Democratic Party of Finland
SDPH	Social Democratic Party of Hungary [*Political party*] (EAIO)
SdPiO	Oglala Sioux Community College, Pine Ridge, SD [*Library symbol Library of Congress*] (LCLS)
SDPJ	Social Democratic Party of Japan [*Political party*] (EAIO)
SdPl	Plankinton City Library, Plankinton, SD [*Library symbol Library of Congress*] (LCLS)
SDPL	Safeguard Data Processing Laboratory [*Army*] (AABC)
SDPL	Sensor Data Processing Laboratory (MCD)
SDPL	Servomechanisms and Data Processing Laboratory [*Massachusetts Institute of Technology*] (MCD)
SDPO	Site Defense Project Office [*Military*] (AABC)
SDPO	Space Defense Project Office [*AMC*]
SDPP	Social Democracy Popularist Party [*Turkey Political party*]
SDPP	Succinimidyl Diphenyl Phosphate [*Organic chemistry*]
SDP-PDR	Social Democratic Party - Party of Democratic Reform [*Croatia*] [*Political party*]
SdPr	Presho Public Library, Presho, SD [*Library symbol Library of Congress*] (LCLS)
SDPR	Sons and Daughters of Pioneer Rivermen (EA)
SDPR	System Design and Performance Requirements
SDPS	Signal Data Processing System
SDPS	Social Democratic Party of Slovenia [*Political party*] (EY)
SDPT	Structured Doll Play Test [*Psychology*]
SDPU	Socialist and Democratic People's Union [*Mauritania*] [*Political party*] (EY)
SDQ	Santo Domingo [*Dominican Republic*] [*Airport symbol*] (OAG)
SDQ	Self-Description Questionnaire
SDQ	Student Description Questionnaire
SDQA	SAFSCOM [*Safeguard System Command*] Document Quality Audit (MCD)
SDQFC	Sir Douglas Quintet Fan Club (EA)
SDR	New York State Department Reports [*A publication*] (DLA)
SdR	Rapid City Public Library, Rapid City, SD [*Library symbol Library of Congress*] (LCLS)
SDR	Santander [*Spain*] [*Airport symbol*] (OAG)
SDR	Schlumberger-Doll Research Center, Ridgefield, CT [*OCLC symbol*] (OCLC)
SDR	Scientific Data Recorder
SDR	Search Decision Rule [*Computer science*]
SDR	Search, Detection and Recognition [*Military*]
SDR	Seismic Detection and Ranging
SDR	Self-Decoding Readout
SDR	Sender (KSC)
SDR	Sensor Data Record [*For spacecraft*]
SDR	Service Difficulty Report (MCD)
SDR	Shaft Driver, Right
SDR	Sheffield District Railway (ROG)

SDR	Ship Destination Room (NATG)
SDR	Ship Diversion Room (NATG)
SDR	Shipment Document Release [*Military*] (AFIT)
SDR	Signal Data Recorder [*or Reproducer*] (MCD)
SDR	Signal Distribution Room [*NASA*] (KSC)
SDR	Signal to Distortion Ratio (NITA)
SDR	Significant Deficiency Report [*Nuclear energy*] (IEEE)
SDR	Simple Detection Response
SDR	Single-Drift Region (IEEE)
SDR	Single Drug Resistance
SDR	Sisters of the Divine Redeemer [*Roman Catholic religious order*]
SDR	Site Defense RADAR
SDR	Sloane, Donald R., New York NY [*STAC*]
SDR	Small Development Requirement [*Military*]
SDR	SNAP [*Systems for Nuclear Auxiliary Power*] Development Reactor
SDR	Snyder, TX [*Location identifier FAA*] (FAAL)
SDR	Society for Drug Research (EAIO)
SDR	Society of Dance Research [*British*] (DBA)
SDR	Sodium Deuterium Reactor
SDR	Software Design Requirement [*NASA*] (NASA)
SDR	Software Design Review [*NASA*] (MCD)
SDR	Solid Ducted Rocket (MCD)
SDR	Solution Development Record
SDR	SONAR Data Recorder
SDR	Sophisticated Data Research, Inc. [*Information service or system*] (IID)
SDR	Sounder (MSA)
SDR	South Dakota Register [*A publication*] (AAGC)
SDR	South Devon Railway (ROG)
SDR	Space Division Regulation [*NASA*] (NASA)
SDR	Spacelab Disposition Record [*NASA*] (NASA)
SDR	Spatial Delayed-Response [*Ophthalmology*]
SDR	Special Dispatch Rider
SDR	Special Drawing Rights (TDOB)
SDR	Spin Dependent Resonance [*Physics*]
SDR	Splash Detection RADAR [*Military*]
SDR	Spontaneously Diabetic Rat (DB)
SDR	Standard Deviation of the Regression [*Statistics*]
SDR	Standard Dimension Ratio (DAC)
SDR	Standardized Disease Ratio (LDT)
SDR	State-Dependent Retrieval [*Psychology*]
SDR	Statistical Data Recorder [*Computer science*] (MDG)
SDR	Storage Data Recorder (NITA)
SDR	Storage Data Register (MCD)
SDR	Strip Domain Resonance
SDR	Stroud Resources Ltd. [*Toronto Stock Exchange symbol*]
SDR	Subcontract Data Requirement
SDR	Succession Duties Reports [*A publication*] (ILCA)
SDR	Successive Discrimination Reversal
SDR	Suddeutscher Rundfunk [*South German Radio Network*]
SDR	Surgical Dressing Room (DAVI)
SDR	Survey of Doctorate Recipients [*National Research Council*] [*Database*]
SDR	Syder [*Bulgaria*] [*ICAO designator*] (FAAC)
SDR	System Data Record
SDR	System Definition Record [*Computer science*] (IBMDP)
SDR	System Definition Requirements
SDR	System Design Report [*NATO*] (NATG)
SDR	System Design Review [*NASA*] (NASA)
SDR	System Development Requirement [*Air Force*]
SDR	System Discrepancy Report
SDR	System for Data Retrieval [*Information retrieval*]
S DRAKE	Second Dynamic Response and Kinematics Experiment [*Marine science*] (MSC)
SDRAM	Synchonous Dynamic Random Access Memory [*Computer science*]
SDR & C	Shipment Document Release and Control [*Military*] (AFIT)
SDRB	Software Design Review Board [*NASA*] (NASA)
SDRB	Supplier Documentation Review Board [*NASA*] (NASA)
SDRC	Structural Dynamics Res [*NASDAQ symbol*] (TTSB)
SDRC	Structural Dynamics Research Corp. [*NASDAQ symbol*] (NQ)
SDRC Ops	South Dakota Board of Railroad Commissioners Opinions [*A publication*] (DLA)
SDRD	Supplier Data Requirements Description (NASA)
SDRD	Supplier Documentation Review Data (NASA)
SdRe	Redfield Carnegie Library, Redfield, SD [*Library symbol Library of Congress*] (LCLS)
SDRL	Seller Data Requirements List (MCD)
SDRL	Subcontractor Data Requirements List
SDRL	Supplier Data Requirements List (NASA)
SDRM	San Diego Railroad Museum (EA)
SdRM	South Dakota School of Mines and Technology, Rapid City, SD [*Library symbol Library of Congress*]
SdRN	National College of Business, Rapid City, SD [*Library symbol Library of Congress*] (LCLS)
SDRN	Supplier Data Review Notice (DNAB)
SDRNG	Sound Ranging (MUGU)
SDRP	Simulated Data Reduction Program
SDRP	Socjaldemokracja Rzeczypospolitej Polskiej [*Social Democracy of the Republic of Poland*] [*Political party*] (EY)
SdRS	Saint Martins Academy, Rapid City, SD [*Library symbol Library of Congress*] (LCLS)
SDRS	Signal Data Recording Set (MCD)
SDRS	Social Dysfunction Rating Scale [*Psychology*] (DB)
SDRS	Spache's Diagnostic Reading Scales (EDAC)
SDRS	Splash Detection RADAR System (MCD)

SDRS	Standardized Delay Reporting System [*FAA*] (TAG)
SDRT	Slot Dipole Ranging Test (OA)
SDRT	Spadafore Diagnostic Reading Test [*Educational test*]
SDRT	Stanford Diagnostic Reading Test [*Education*]
SDRT	Technical Research Sub-Department [*French Acronym is based on foreign phrase*]
SD Rulings	Stamp Duties Rulings [*Australia A publication*]
SDRW	SONAR Dome Rubber Window (NVT)
S-DRY	Surfaced Dry [*Lumber*]
SDS	CAA Training Standards [*British ICAO designator*] (FAAC)
SDS	Safety Data Sheet (KSC)
SDS	Same Day Surgery [*Medicine*]
SDS	Samostalna Demokratska Stranka [*Independent Democratic Party*] [*Former Yugoslavia*] [*Political party*] (PPE)
SDS	Sample Display Service [*Department of Commerce*]
SDS	Samson Data Systemen
SDS	Samsung Data Systems Co., Ltd. (EFIS)
SDS	Sanatorio Duran [*Costa Rica*] [*Seismograph station code, US Geological Survey*] (SEIS)
SDS	Satellite Data System [*Air Force*]
SDS	School Dental Service
SDS	Scientific Data System [*Later, XDS*]
SDS	Scientific Data Systems Corporation (NITA)
SDS	Secret Delivery Station (SAA)
SDS	Select Drive System [*Automotive engineering*]
SDS	Self-Defense Suite [*Air Force*] (DOMA)
SDS	Self-Directed Search
SDS	Self-Rating Depression Scale [*Psychology*]
SDS	Senior Direction Station (SAA)
SDS	Sensory Deprivation Syndrome [*Medicine*]
SDS	Serondela [*Botswana*] [*Airport symbol*] (AD)
SDS	Servo Drive System
SDS	Sexual Differentiation Scale [*Psychometrics*]
SDS	Shared Data Set (OA)
SDS	Ship Defense System
SDS	Shop Distribution Standards (KSC)
SDS	Short Distance Swimmer
SDS	Shutdown Sequencer [*Environmental science*] (COE)
SDS	Shuttle Dynamic Simulation [*NASA*] (NASA)
SDS	Side Detection System [*Delco*] (RDA)
SDS	Signal Distribution System
SDS	Signals Dispatch Service (IAA)
SDS	Sign-Digit Subtractor
SDS	Significant Digit Scanner (IAA)
SDS	Simulating Digital Systems
SDS	Simulation Data Subsystem (KSC)
SDS	Sisters of the Divine Saviour [*Roman Catholic religious order*]
SDS	Slowing Down Spectrometer (PDAA)
SDS	Small Digital Switch (NITA)
SDS	Smart Distributed Systems (AOII)
SDS	Smoke Destruction System
SDS	Social Desirability Scale (EDAC)
SDS	Society for Disability Studies (NTPA)
SDS	Society of the Divine Savior (TOCD)
sds	Society of the Divine Savior (TOCD)
SDS	Sodium Dodecyl Sulfate [*Also, SLS*] [*Organic chemistry*]
SDS	Software Design Specification [*NASA*] (NASA)
SDS	Software Development Specification (IAA)
SDS	Software Development System
SDS	Solar Disk Simulator
SDS	Sons and Daughters of the Soddies (EA)
SDS	Sound-Deadened Steel (PDAA)
SDS	South Dakota State Library Commission, Pierre, SD [*OCLC symbol*] (OCLC)
SDS	Sozialistischer Deutscher Studentenbund [*Student political organization*] [*Germany*]
SDS	Spacecraft Design Specification
SDS	Space Defense System (AAG)
SDS	Space Division Switching [*Telecommunications*]
SDS	Space Documentation Service [*NASA/ESRO*] (DIT)
SDS	Special Distress Signal (DEN)
SDS	Special Docking Simulator [*NASA*] (KSC)
SDS	Specific Diagnosis Service [*Medicine*] (DMAA)
SDS	Spectrometer Digital System
SDS	Splash Detection System
SDS	Srpska Demokratska Stranka [*Serb Democratic Party*] [*Political party*]
SDS	Standard Depot System [*Army*]
SDS	State Disability Service (DAVI)
SDS	Status Display Support (MCD)
SDS	St. David's Society of the State of New York (EA)
SDS	Steam Dump System [*Nuclear energy*] (NRCH)
SDS	Steering Damping System [*Aerospace*] (MCD)
SDS	Stimulator of DNA Synthesis [*Immunochemistry*]
SDS	Strategic Defense System [*DoD*]
SDS	Structured Design Strategy (NITA)
SDS	Structured Development Strategy (NITA)
SDS	Students for a Democratic Society [*Defunct*] (EA)
SDS	Submerged Demineralizer System [*Water purification*]
SDS	Subvent Datenbank Systeme [*Innovationstechnik GmbH & Co.*] [*Hamburg, Federal Republic of Germany*] [*Information service or system*] (IID)
SDS	Sudden Death Syndrome [*in children*] [*Medicine*]
SDS	Sudden Drowning Syndrome
SDS	Supplemental Data Sheet
SDS	Supplier Data Sheet

SDS .... Supplier Delivery Schedules [*Chrysler Corp.*]
SDS .... Support Data Sheet [*Military*]
SDS .... Surveillance Direction System (DOMA)
SDS .... Sweet Dough Stabilizer [*Brand of bakery product from H. C. Brill Co., Inc.*]
SDS .... Swimmer Distress Signal [*Navy*] (CAAL)
SDS .... Synchronous Data Set (NOAA)
SDS .... Syntactic Density Score (EDAC)
SDS .... Systematic Design Language [*Computer science*]
SDS .... System Data Synthesizer (KSC)
SDS .... System Design Specification
SDS .... Systems and Data Service (IAA)
SDSAM .... Specifically Designated Special Air Mission [*Aircraft*] [*Air Force*]
SDS & RU ... Soil Data Storage and Retrieval Unit [*Department of Agriculture*] (IID)
SDSBE .... San Diego Symposium for Biomedical Engineering
SDSC .... San Diego State College [*California*]
SDSC .... San Diego Supercomputer Center [*California*] [*National Science Foundation*]
Sd-SC .... South Dakota Supreme Court Library, Pierre, SD [*Library symbol Library of Congress*] (LCLS)
SDSD .... Saco Defense Systems Division [*Maremont Corp.*] (RDA)
SDSD .... Satellite Data Services Division [*National Oceanic and Atmospheric Administration Information service or system*] (IID)
SDSD .... Single Disk Storage Device [*Computer science*] (BUR)
SDSE .... Society of the Descendants of the Schwenkfeldian Exiles (EA)
SDSEM .... Spinocerebellar Degeneration-Slow Eye Movements Syndrome [*Medicine*] (DMAA)
SD Sess Laws... South Dakota Session Laws [*A publication*] (DLA)
SDSH .... Society Devoted to the Sacred Heart [*Roman Catholic women's religious order*]
SDSI .... Shared Data Set Integrity
SdSi............. Sisseton Library, Sisseton, SD [*Library symbol Library of Congress*] (LCLS)
SDSI .... Staff Development for School Improvement Program (EDAC)
SdSif........... Sioux Falls Carnegie Free Public Library, Sioux Falls, SD [*Library symbol Library of Congress*] (LCLS)
SdSifA .... Augustana College, Sioux Falls, SD [*Library symbol Library of Congress*] (LCLS)
SdSifB .... North American Baptist Seminary, Sioux Falls, SD [*Library symbol Library of Congress*] (LCLS)
SdSifC .... Sioux Falls College, Sioux Falls, SD [*Library symbol Library of Congress*] (LCLS)
SdSifH .... Coolidge High School Library, Sioux Falls, SD [*Library symbol Library of Congress*] (LCLS)
SdSifV .... United States Veterans Administration Center, Sioux Falls, SD [*Library symbol Library of Congress*] (LCLS)
SDSK .... Softdesk, Inc. [*NASDAQ symbol*] (SAG)
SD-SK .... Streptodornase-Streptokinase (DB)
SDSL .... Sail Dynamics Simulation Laboratory (MCD)
SDSL .... Site-Directed Spin Labeling [*Physical chemistry*]
SDSL .... Subject Directory of Special Libraries and Information Centers [*A publication*]
SDSL .... Symmetrical Digital Single Line (DMAA)
SDSM .... Socijaldemokratski Savez Makedonije [*Social Democratic Alliance of Macedonia*] [*Political party*] (EY)
SD SMS CLSD... Side Seams Closed [*Freight*]
SDSP .... Space Defense Systems Program (DNAB)
SDS/PAGE.... Sodium Didecylsulfate-Poly-Acrylamide Gel Electrophoresis [*Medicine*] (DMAA)
SdSpe .... Grace Balloch Memorial Library, Spearfish, SD [*Library symbol Library of Congress*] (LCLS)
SdSpen........ Hanson-McCook County Regional Library, Spencer, SD [*Library symbol Library of Congress*] (LCLS)
SdSpeT .... Black Hills State College, Spearfish, SD [*Library symbol Library of Congress*] (LCLS)
SdSpU .... University of South Dakota at Springfield, Springfield, SD [*Library symbol Library of Congress*] (LCLS)
SDSRS......... Subcontractor Data Status Reporting System (MCD)
SDSS .... San Diego Shrinkers Society (EA)
SDSS .... Satellite Data System Spacecraft [*Air Force*]
SDSS .... Satellite Data System Study [*Air Force*] (SSD)
SDSS .... Self-Deploying Space Station
SDSS .... Single and Double Simultaneous Stimulation [*Neuropsychology test*]
SDSS .... Sloan Digital Sky Survey [*Astronomy*]
SDSS .... Space Division Shuttle Simulator [*NASA*] (NASA)
SDSS .... STS [*Space Transportation System*] Data Select Switch (MCD)
SDSSE .... Science Data System Support Equipment
SDSST .... Single and Double Simultaneous Stimulation Test [*Neuropsychology test*]
SdSt............. Sturgis Public Library, Sturgis, SD [*Library symbol Library of Congress*] (LCLS)
SD St BJ...... South Dakota State Bar Journal [*A publication*] (DLA)
SDSU .... San Diego State University [*California*]
SDSU .... South Dakota State University [*Brookings, SD*]
SDSU .... Switched Data Service Unit [*Computer science*] (MHDI)
SDSVF .... State Dependent State Variable Feedback [*Rocket engine*] [*NASA*]
SDSW .... Sense Device Status Word
SDT............. National College Library, Rapid City, SD [*OCLC symbol*] (OCLC)
SDT............. Sacrodextra Transversa [*A fetal position*] [*Obstetrics*]
SDT............. Saidu Sharif [*Pakistan*] [*Airport symbol*] (OAG)
SDT............. Sanderson Tech, Inc. [*Vancouver Stock Exchange symbol*]
SDT............. Sandy Point [*Great Abaco Island, Bahamas*] [*Airport symbol*] (AD)
SDT............. Satellite Development Trust (NITA)
SDT............. Saturated Discharge Temperature [*Refrigeration*]
SDT............. Scaling and Display Task (NASA)

SDT............. Science Data Team
SDT............. Scientific Distribution Technique
SDT............. Sea Depth Transducer
SDT............. Second Destination Transportation (MCD)
SDT............. Self-Development Test [*Military*] (INF)
SDT............. Senior Director Technician (SAA)
SDT............. Serial Data Transmission
SDT............. Serum Dilution Test [*Clinical chemistry*]
SDT............. Shell-Destroying Tracer [*Ammunition*]
SDT............. Shipboard Data Terminal (MCD)
SDT............. Shock-to-Detonation Transition (MCD)
SDT............. Shoot Down Test (SAA)
SDT............. Shuttle Data Tape (NASA)
SDT............. Side Door Trim [*Automotive engineering*]
SDT............. Side Tank [*on a ship*] (DS)
SDt............. Sifre on Deuteronomy [*A publication*] (BJA)
SDT............. Signal Detection Theory
SDT............. Simplified Drive Train [*Navistar International Corp.*] [*Truck engineering*]
SDT............. Simulated Data Tape
SDT............. Simulated Dynamic Target [*Military*] (CAAL)
SDT............. Skylab Data Task [*NASA*]
SDT............. Society of Dairy Technology [*British*]
SDT............. Soldier Data Tag
SDT............. Source Distribution Technique
SDT............. Space Detection and Tracking (IAA)
SDT............. Spache Diagnostic Test [*Psychiatry*] (DAVI)
SDT............. Spatial Disorientation Trainer [*Military*]
SDT............. Speech Detection Threshold [*Otorhinolaryngology*] (DAVI)
SDT............. Speedy Drill Template (MCD)
SDT............. Standard Data Terminal
SDT............. Start-Data-Traffic [*Computer science*] (IBMDP)
SDT............. Steered Directional Transmission (MCD)
SDT............. Step-Down Transformer
SDT............. Stromberg Dexterity Test [*Education*]
SDT............. Structural Dynamic Test [*NASA*] (NASA)
SDT............. Subpoena Duces Tecum [*Legal term Latin*] (HGAA)
SDT............. Supplier Data Transmittal (MCD)
SD/T........... Surface Detector/Tracker [*Navy*] (CAAL)
SDT............. Surveillance Data Transmission
SDT............. Syntax-Directed Translation [*Computer science*] (MHDI)
SDT............. System Dynamic Tester
SDTH .... Terrain SDP SA [*Spain ICAO designator*] (FAAC)
SDTA .... Scottish Dance Teacher's Alliance [*Glasgow, Scotland*] (EAIO)
SDTA .... Stewardsman Apprentice, Steward, Striker [*Navy rating*]
SDTA .... Structural Dynamic Test Article [*NASA*] (NASA)
SDTAQ........ Speech and Drama Teachers Association of Queensland [*Australia*]
SDTDL .... Saturated-Drift Transistor-Diode Logic (IAA)
SD Tex........ United States District Court for the Southern District of Texas (DLA)
SDTF .... Scottish Dairy Trade Federation (DBA)
SDTI.......... Security Dynamics Technologies [*NASDAQ symbol*] (TTSB)
SDTI.......... Security Dynamics Technologies, Inc. [*NASDAQ symbol*] (SAG)
SDTI.......... Selective Dissemination of Technical Information [*Computer science*]
SDTI.......... Student Developmental Task Inventory [*Educational test*]
SDTIM .... Society for the Development of Techniques in Industrial Marketing [*British*]
SDTK .... Supported Drift Tube Klystron
SDTL.......... Schottky Diode Transistor Logic (IAA)
SDTLI......... Student Developmental Task and Lifestyle Inventory [*Test*] (TES)
SDTN .... Space and Data Tracking Network (SSD)
SDTN .... Stewardsman, Steward, Striker [*Navy rating*]
SDTP .... Startover Data Transfer and Processing [*Program*]
SDTP PROGRM... Startover Data Transfer and Processing Program
SDTR .... Serial Data Transmitter/Receiver [*Telecommunications*] (TEL)
SDTS .... Satellite Data Transmission System (DIT)
SDTS .... Self-Defense Test Ship
SDTS .... Spatial Data Transfer Standard [*Computer science*]
SDTS .... Syntax-Directed Translation Scheme [*Computer science*] (MHDI)
SDTT .... Silicon Diode Target Tube
SDTU .... Sign and Display Trades Union [*British*] (BI)
SDTV .... Standard Definition Television (IGQR)
SDU .... Huron College, Huron, SD [*OCLC symbol*] (OCLC)
SDU .... Memphis, TN [*Location identifier FAA*] (FAAL)
SDU .... Rio De Janeiro-Dumont [*Brazil*] [*Airport symbol*] (OAG)
SDU .... Satellite Data Unit (DA)
SDU .... Self-Destruct Unit
SDU .... Service Data Unit (TNIG)
SDU .... Shelter Decontamination Unit
SDU .... Short Double Upright Brace [*Orthopedics*] (DAVI)
SDU .... Signal Distribution Unit (AAG)
SDU .... Source Data Utility
sdu............. South Dakota [*MARC country of publication code Library of Congress*] (LCCP)
SDU .... Soziale Demokratische Union [*Social Democratic Union*] [*Germany Political party*] (PPW)
SDU .... Spectrum Display Unit
SDU .... Stand-Alone Display Unit
SDU .... Standard Deviation Unit [*Statistics*] (MAE)
SDU .... Station Display Unit
SDU .... Step Down Unit [*Medicine*] (CPH)
SDU .... Students for a Democratic University [*Canada*]
SDU .... Subcarrier Delay Unit
SDU .... Surface Drone Unit [*Navy*] (CAAL)
SdU............. University of South Dakota, Vermillion, SD [*Library symbol Library of Congress*] (LCLS)

SDU	Westair Commuter Airlines, Inc. [ICAO designator] (FAAC)
SDUB	Short Double Upright Brace [Medicine] (DMAA)
SDUK	Society for the Diffusion of Useful Knowledge
SdU-L	University of South Dakota, Law Library, Vermillion, SD [Library symbol Library of Congress] (LCLS)
SdU-M	University of South Dakota, Medical School, Vermillion, SD [Library symbol Library of Congress] (LCLS)
SDU-NDP	Slovenian Democratic Union - National Democratic Party [Political party] (EY)
SD Uniform Prob Code	South Dakota Uniform Probate Code [A publication] (DLA)
SDUSA	Social Democrats, USA (EA)
SDV	Santo Domingo [Venezuela] [Seismograph station code, US Geological Survey] (SEIS)
SDV	Satsuma Dwarf Virus [Plant pathology]
SDV	Scram Discharge Volume [Nuclear energy] (NRCH)
SDV	Servicios Aereos del Vaupes Ltd. [Colombia] [ICAO designator] (FAAC)
SDV	Shuttle Derived Vehicle (MCD)
SDV	Slowed-Down Video [RADAR]
SDV	Society of Divine Vocations [Vocationist Fathers] [Roman Catholic religious order]
SDV	Solar Daily Variation
SDV	Soybean Dwarf Virus [Plant pathology]
SDV	Spark Delay Valve [Automotive engineering]
SDV	Specially Designated Vehicle
SDV	Specific Desensitizing Vaccine [Medicine] (ADA)
SDV	Start Device (IAA)
SDV	Swimmer Delivery Vehicle [Navy symbol Obsolete] (MCD)
SDV	Tel Aviv/Yafo [Israel] [Airport symbol] (OAG)
SdV	Vermillion Public Library, Vermillion, SD [Library symbol Library of Congress] (LCLS)
SDV	Vocationist Fathers (TOCD)
sdv	Vocationist Fathers, Society of the Divine Vocations (TOCD)
SDV	Vocationist Sisters (TOCD)
S-DVB	Styrene-Divinylbenzene [Organic chemistry]
SDVF	Software Development and Verification Facilities [NASA] (NASA)
SDVI	Service Disabled Veterans Insurance
SDW	Dakota Wesleyan University, Layne Library, Mitchell, SD [OCLC symbol] (OCLC)
SDW	Sandwip [Bangladesh] [Airport symbol] (AD)
SDW	S. D. Warren [Paper manufacturer]
SDW	Segment Descriptor Word
SDW	Side Wheel (DS)
SDW	Six-Day War [Arab-Israeli War, 1967] (BJA)
SDW	Southdown, Inc. [NYSE symbol] (SPSG)
SDW	Spin-Density Wave [Physics]
SDW	Spin Density-Weighted (DMAA)
SDW	Standing Detonation Wave
SDW	Sterile Distilled Water
SDW	Swept Delta Wing
SdW	Watertown Regional Library, Watertown, SD [Library symbol Library of Congress] (LCLS)
SDWA	Safe Drinking Water Act [1974]
SdWa	Wagner Public Library, Wagner, SD [Library symbol Library of Congress] (LCLS)
SdWau	Waubay Public Library, Waubay, SD [Library symbol Library of Congress] (LCLS)
SdWe	Webster Public Library, Webster, SD [Library symbol Library of Congress] (LCLS)
SdWes	Wessington Springs Carnegie Public Library, Wessington Springs, SD [Library symbol Library of Congress] (LCLS)
SdWinT	Tripp County Library, Winner, SD [Library symbol Library of Congress] (LCLS)
SDWPrD	Southdown $2.875cm Cv'D' Pfd [NYSE symbol] (TTSB)
SDWRF	Stochastic Dominance with Respect to Function [Statistics]
SD W Va	United States District Court for the Southern District of West Virginia (DLA)
SDX	Satellite Data Exchange
SDX	Sedona [Arizona] [Airport symbol] (OAG)
SDX	Sigma Delta Chi [Fraternity] (NTCM)
S + DX	Speech with Duplex Telegraph
SDX	Stampeder Exploration Ltd. [NYSE symbol] (SAG)
SDX	Storage Data Acceleration [Computer science] (IGQR)
SDY	Mount Marty College, Yankton, SD [OCLC symbol] (OCLC)
SDY	Safe Air International, Inc. [ICAO designator] (FAAC)
SDY	Sandy Corp. [AMEX symbol] (SPSG)
SDY	Sidney [Montana] [Airport symbol] (OAG)
SDY	Sidney, MT [Location identifier FAA] (FAAL)
sdy	Study (VRA)
SdY	Yankton Community Library, Yankton, SD [Library symbol Library of Congress] (LCLS)
SdYC	Yankton College, Yankton, SD [Library symbol Library of Congress] (LCLS)
SdYM	Mount Marty College, Yankton, SD [Library symbol Library of Congress] (LCLS)
SDYN	Staodyn, Inc. [NASDAQ symbol] (NQ)
SDYNZ	Staodyn Inc. Wrrt'II' [NASDAQ symbol] (TTSB)
SDYS	Simpson Dysmorphia Syndrome [Medicine] (DMAA)
SDZ	Southern Pines, NC [Location identifier FAA] (FAAL)
SDZ	Stardust Ventures [Vancouver Stock Exchange symbol]
SDZ	Stimmen der Zeit (BJA)
SDZ	Surface Danger Zone [Military] (INF)
SE	British Charter [British ICAO designator] (ICDA)
SE	Ferrocarriles Unidos del Sureste, SA de CV [AAR code]

SE	Herself (DAVI)
SE	Himself (DAVI)
SE	Safety Equipment [British military] (DMA)
SE	Safety Evaluation (NRCH)
SE	Sales Engineer
SE	Saline Enema [Medicine]
SE	Sanford & Eastern Railroad [AAR code Terminated]
SE	Sanitary Engineer [Academic degree]
SE	Santos Dumont Experimental [British military] (DMA)
SE	Saorstat Eireann [Irish Free State]
SE	Saponification Equivalent [Analytical chemistry]
SE	Schleicher-Bruns [Germany ICAO aircraft manufacturer identifier] (ICAO)
SE	Schneider Engineers (EFIS)
SE	School of Engineering (MCD)
SE	Science, Mathematics, and Environmental Education [Educational Resources Information Center (ERIC) Clearinghouse] [Ohio State University] (PAZ)
SE	Scouting Experimental [British] (DMA)
SE	Sea [Maps and charts]
SE	Seasonal Employee [Business term] (MHDB)
SE	Secondary Education (AIE)
SE	Secondary Electron (MCD)
SE	Secondary Electron Multiplier (IAA)
SE	Secondary Emission (IAA)
SE	Second Entrance [Theatrical slang]
SE	Secretarial, Word Processing, and/or Medical Office Assistant Programs [Association of Independent Colleges and Schools specialization code]
SE	Securities Transaction [Banking]
SE	Seeing Eye [An association] (EA)
SE	Selenium [Chemical element]
Se	Selenium [Chemical element] (DOG)
SE	Seleucid Era (BJA)
SE	Self (DAVI)
SE	Self Employment [Social Security Administration] (OICC)
SE	Self-Evident Statement [Used in correcting manuscripts, etc.]
SE	Self-Extinguishing (IAA)
SE	Selling Expense (AAGC)
SE	Senegal [IYRU nationality code] (IYR)
SE	Senior Editor [Publishing]
SE	September (ADA)
SE	Sequence of Events
SE	Series
SE	Series Statement [Online database field identifier]
SE	Service Element (TNIG)
SE	Service Engineer
SE	Service Entrance (IAA)
SE	Service Equipment (AAG)
SE	Set
se	Seychelles [bi (British Indian Ocean Territory) used in records cataloged before January 1978] [MARC country of publication code Library of Congress] (LCCP)
SE	Shareholders' Equity [Business term]
SE	Shelter Equipment
SE	Sherritt Gordon Mines Ltd. [Toronto Stock Exchange symbol]
SE	Shielding Effectiveness (IEEE)
SE	Shift Engineer (NRCH)
SE	Shoot Emergence [Botany]
SE	Side Effect [Medicine]
SE	Signal Excess (NVT)
SE	Sign Extended (IAA)
SE	Silver Edge [Bookbinding] (DGA)
SE	Simultaneous Engineering
SE	Single End
SE	Single-Ended, Cylindrical Boiler [Navy]
SE	Single Engine
SE	Single Entry [Bookkeeping]
SE	Sisters of Emanuel (TOCD)
SE	Site Engineer (NITA)
S-E	Skandinaviska Enskilda Banken [Scandinavian Private Bank] [Sweden]
SE	Slip End (OA)
SE	Small End (OA)
SE	Smoke Extract
SE	Social Education [A publication] (BRI)
SE	Social Emotional
SE	Society of Engineers
SE	Society of Ethnobiology (EA)
SE	Socioeconomic
SE	Software Engineering (MCD)
SE	Soil Extract
SE	Solanaceae Enthusiasts [Defunct] (EA)
SE	Solar Ecliptic
SE	Solar Explorer [NASA]
SE	Solidaridad Espanola [Spanish Solidarity] [Political party] (PPW)
SE	Solid Extract [Pharmacy]
SE	Sonic Extract [Cytology]
SE	Sound Effect (NTCM)
SE	Sounding Equipment (IAA)
SE	Southeast
SE	Southeastern Reporter [National Reporter System] [A publication] (DLA)
SE	Southeast Skyways [ICAO designator] (AD)
SE	Southern Europe (NATG)

SE	Space Equivalent (IAA)
SE	Space Exploration (AAG)
SE	Spatial Emotional (Stimuli)
SE	Special Edition [Car model designation]
SE	Special Equipment
SE	Specialized Exhibition (IMH)
SE	Spectral Edge [Cardiology]
SE	Spectroscopic Ellipsometry (AAEL)
SE	Sphenoethmoidal [Suture] [Medicine]
SE	Spherical Equivalent
SE	Spherical Eyeball [Aviation] (OA)
SE	Spin-Echo Scan [Roentgenology]
SE	Split End [Football]
SE	Sprinkled Edge [Bookbinding] (DGA)
SE	Spurway-Eddowes [Syndrome] [Medicine] (DB)
SE	Stable Element
SE	Stack Empty (MHDI)
SE	Staff Engineer [Navy British] (ROG)
SE	Stage of Exhaustion [of gas] [Medicine]
SE	Stamped Envelope
SE	Standard English
SE	Standard Error
S/E	Standardization/Evaluation (AFM)
SE	Starch Equivalent
S-E	Starr-Edwards [Prosthesis] (AAMN)
SE	Starter Electrode
SE	Stationary Eddy
SE	Status Enquiry [British]
SE	Status Epilepticus [Medicine]
SE	Steam Emulsion
SE	Sterling Commerce [NYSE symbol] (TTSB)
SE	Sterling Electronics (IAA)
SE	Stock Exchange
SE	Stop Element [Computer science] (EECA)
SE	Storage Element (MCD)
SE	Straight Edge [Philately]
SE	Subcontract Engineers (MCD)
SE	Subcritical Experiment [Nuclear energy]
SE	Successful Effort (DICI)
se	Sugary Enhancer [A gene in sweet corn]
SE	Summer Emergency [Vessel load line mark]
SE	Sun Electric Corp. (EFIS)
SE	Super Einspritz [Super, Injection] [Mercedes-Benz automotive model designation]
SE	Superintending Engineer (ADA)
SE	Superior Electric (IAA)
SE	Support Equipment (AFM)
SE	Sustainer Engine (AAG)
SE	Sustaining Engineering
SE	Sweden [ANSI two-letter standard code] (CNC)
SE	Switching Element (IAA)
SE	Synthetic Environment
SE	System Effectiveness [Army] (AABC)
SE	System Element (NASA)
SE	System Engineering (IAA)
SE	System Equalizer (IAA)
SE	System Expansion [In "Macintosh SE"] [Apple Computer, Inc.]
SE	Systems Engineer (NITA)
SE	Wings of Alaska [ICAO designator] (AD)
SE2	Scientists and Engineers for Secure Energy (EA)
SE2d	South Eastern Reporter, Second Series [West] [A publication] (AAGC)
SEA	Clemson University, Clemson, SC [OCLC symbol] (OCLC)
SEA	Marine Manufacturers Safety Equipment Association (EA)
SEA	Safety Engineering Analysis (AFM)
SEA	Sailing Education Association
SEA	Scandinavian Endodontic Association [Sweden] (EAIO)
SEA	Scanning Electrostatic Analysis (NASA)
SEA	Science and Education Administration [Department of Agriculture]
SEA	Scientific Exchange Agreement
SEA	Screening Experiment Analysis [Medicine] (DB)
SEA	Seaboard World Airlines, Inc. (MCD)
SEA	Sea Echelon Area [Navy] (NVT)
SEA	Sea Education Association (EA)
SEA	Seashore Environmental Alliance
SEA	Seasonal Employees in Agriculture
SEA	Seattle [Washington] [Seismograph station code, US Geological Survey Closed] (SEIS)
SEA	Seattle/Tacoma [Washington] [Airport symbol] (OAG)
SEA	Securities Exchange Act [1934]
SEA	Selective Early Annuity [Army]
SEA	Selective Enforcement Audit [Automotive engineering]
SEA	Self-Extracting Archive [Computer science] (DOM)
SEA	Senior Enlisted Academy [Navy]
SEA	Senior Enlisted Advisor [Navy]
SEA	Senior Executives Association (EA)
SEA	Service Educational Activities [Military] (AABC)
SEA	Service Employers Association (EA)
SEA	Sheep Erythrocyte Agglutination [Test]
SEA	Shipbuilding Exports Association [British] (BI)
SEA	Ship/Equipment/Alterations [Navy] (NG)
SEA	Ships Editorial Association [Navy]
SEA	Shock Elicited Aggression (STED)
SEA	Silicon Elastimeter Ablator (NASA)
SEA	Sindicato de Escritores y Artistas [Ecuador]

SEA	Single European Act [EEC]
SEA	Slag Employers Association [British] (DBA)
SEA	Small Earth-Approacher [Asteroid]
SEA	Socialist Educational Association [British]
SEA	Societe d'Electronique et d'Automatique [Became part of Compagnie Internationale d'Informatique]
SEA	Society for Education in Anesthesia (NTPA)
SEA	Society for Education through Art [British]
SEA	Society for Engineering in Agriculture [Australia]
SEA	Society for the Elimination of Acronyms
SEA	Society of Electronics and Automation (IAA)
SEA	Society of Engineering Associates [Australia]
SEA	Society of Equestrian Artists [British] (DBA)
SEA	Society of Evangelical Agnostics [Defunct] (EA)
SEA	Sociology of Education Association (EA)
SEA	Soluble Egg Antigen [Medicine] (DMAA)
SEA	SONAR Evaluation and Assistance [Teams]
SEA	Sound Effects Amplifier (IIA)
SEA	Southeast Air, Inc. [ICAO designator] (FAAC)
SEA	Southeast Asia
SEA	Southern Economic Association (EA)
SEA	Space Energy Association (EA)
SEA	SPALT [Special Projects Alterations] Evaluation Area
SEA	Special Equipment Authorization (AAG)
SEA	Specific Energy Absorption
SEA	Spherical Electrostatic Analyzer
SEA	Spontaneous Electrical Activity [Physiology] (AAMN)
SEA	Standard Electronic Assembly
SEA	Staphylococcal Enterotoxin A [Medicine]
SEA	State Earthquake Administration [China] [Marine science] (OSRA)
SEA	State Economic Area [Bureau of Economic Analysis] [Department of Commerce]
SEA	State Education Agency [Department of Education]
SEA	State Enforcement Agreement [Environmental Protection Agency] (GFGA)
SEA	State-EPA [Environmental Protection Agency] Agreements (EG)
SEA	Static Error Analysis
SEA	Statistical Energy Analysis [or Approach] [Vibration analysis]
SEA	Storage Trust Realty [NYSE symbol] (SAG)
SEA	Students for Ecological Action
SEA	Styrene and Ethylbenzene Association (EA)
SEA	Subterranean Exploration Agency
SEA	Sudden Enhancement of Atmospherics [NASA]
SEA	Sulfated Ethoxylated Alcohol [Surfactants]
SEA	Sulphur Extended Asphalt [Paving material]
SEA	Support Electronics Assembly [Military]
SEA	Survival Education Association [Defunct] (EA)
SEA	Susquehanna Environmental Advocates (NRCH)
SEA	System Engineering Analysis
SEA	System Error Analysis
SEA	Systems Effectiveness Analyzer (IEEE)
SEAAC	Southeast Asian Art and Culture [Foundation]
SEAADSA	Sea Automated Data Systems Activity [Navy]
Sea & Sm	Searle and Smith's English Probate and Divorce Reports [A publication] (DLA)
SEAB	Seaboard Bancorp [NASDAQ symbol] (NQ)
SEA/B	Sea Energy Absorber/Bumper Barge (SAA)
SEAB	Secretary of Energy Advisory Board [Department of Energy] (EGAO)
SEABASS	Ships Emergency Automatic Buoyancy and Stability System [Seabass Ltd.]
SeabdOil	Seaboard Oil Co. [Associated Press] (SAG)
SEABEE	Construction Battalion [CB] [Acronym is a phonetic reference to a member of this Naval unit]
SEABEE	Sea Barge Carrying Ships [MARAD] [MTMC] (TAG)
SEABIRD	Ship-Design Engineering-Aided by Interactive Remote Display (PDAA)
SEABOARD	Seaboard World Airways (MHDB)
SEABT	SEABEE Team [Navy] (NVT)
SEABU	Southeast Asia Buildup (CINC)
Seab Vend	Seaborne on Vendors and Purchasers [9th ed.] [1926] [A publication] (DLA)
SEAC	School Examination & Assessment Council (WDAA)
SEAC	Schools Examination and Assessment Council [British] (DET)
SEAC	Seacoast
SeaC	Sea Containers Ltd. [Associated Press] (SAG)
SEAC	Single-Engined Aircraft (IAA)
SEAC	Social and Economic Archive Centre [British]
SEAC	Society for Economic, Social, Cultural Study and Expansion in Central Africa
SEAC	Society for Electroanalytical Chemistry
SEAC	Southeast Archeological Center [US Department of the Interior] [Research center] (RCD)
SEAC	Southeast Asia Center (EA)
SEAC	Southeast Asia Command
SEAC	Southern Examining Accreditation Council (AIE)
SEAC	Specialized Employability Assistance to Claimants (OICC)
SEAC	Spongiform Encephalopathy Advisory Committee [British]
SEAC	Standard Electronic Automatic Computer (IAA)
SEAC	Standards Eastern [or Electronic] Automatic Computer [National Institute of Standards and Technology]
SEAC	Submarine Exercise Area Coordinator [Navy] (NVT)
SEACAD	Sea Cadet Cruise [Navy] (NVT)
SEACALMIS	Sea Systems Calibration Management Information System (DNAB)
SEACAT	SeaBird Conductivity and Temperature Recorder [Marine science] (OSRA)

SeacBk .... Seacoast Banking Corp. Florida [*Associated Press*] (SAG)
SEACDT .... Southeast Asia Collective Defense Treaty (AABC)
SEACF .... Support Equipment Assembly and Checkout Facility [*NASA*] (NASA)
SEACO .... Senior Enlisted Advisor, Communications/Operations [*Navy*] (DNAB)
SEACOM ...... Southeast Asia Commonwealth
SEACOM ...... South-East Asia Commonwealth Cable (NITA)
SEACOM ...... Southeast Asia Communications (MCD)
SEACON .... Seafloor Construction Experiment [*Navy*]
SeaCont .... Sea Containers Ltd. [*Associated Press*] (SAG)
SEACOORD ... Southeast Asia Coordination Council [*Military*]
SEACOP .... Strategic Sealift Contingency Planning System [*Army*] (AABC)
Seacor .... Seacor Holdings [*Associated Press*] (SAG)
SEACOR .... Systems Engineering Associates Corp. (EFIS)
SEACORE ..... Southeast Asia Communications Research (MCD)
SEACOST ..... Systematic Equipment Analysis and Cost Optimization Scanning Technique (MHDB)
SEACS .... Search of Enemy Air Defense (MCD)
SEACS .... Ship Equipment Accounting System (MCD)
SeaCt .... Sea Containers Ltd. [*Associated Press*] (SAG)
SE/ACT .... Southern Europe - ACTISUD [*Authority for the Coordination of Inland Transport in Southern Europe*] [*NATO*] (NATG)
SEAD .... Scottish Education and Action for Development (EAIO)
SEAD .... Seneca Army Depot [*New York*] (AABC)
SEAD .... Suppression of Enemy Air Defenses (AABC)
SEAD .... Survivable Electronic Air Defense
SEADAB .... Southeast Asia DataBase (MCD)
SEADAC .... Seakeeping Data Analysis Center [*Navy*]
SEADAG .... Southeast Asia Development Advisory Group [*Department of State*]
SeaDas .... SeaWiFS [*Sea-Viewing Wide Field-of-View Sensor*] Data Analysis System (USDC)
SEADCUG .... NAVSEA Data Communications Users Group [*Navy*]
SEADD .... South-East Asia Development Division [*Overseas Development Administration*] [*British*] (DS)
SEADEX .... Seaward Defense Exercise [*NATO*] (NATG)
SEADRM ...... Seadrome [*Aviation*] (FAAC)
SEADROP .... Small Expendable Air-Dropped Remote Ocean Platform [*Marine science*] (MSC)
SEADS .... Shuttle Entry Air Data Sensor [*NASA*] (MCD)
SEADS .... Shuttle Entry Air Data System [*or Subsystem*] (NASA)
SEADS .... Survivable and Effective Airbreathing Defense [*Study*] (MCD)
SEADU .... Sea Duty
SEA-EX .... Sealift Express [*Military*]
SEAFAC .... System Engineering Analysis Facility (MCD)
SEAFAR .... Search and Automatic Track Fixed Array RADAR
SEAFD .... Seafood
SEAFDC .... South East Asian Fisheries Development Centre (EAIO)
SEAFDEC ..... South East Asian Fisheries Development Centre
SEAFIS .... South-East Asian Fisheries Information System [*Marine science*] (OSRA)
Seafld .... Seafield Capital Corp. [*Associated Press*] (SAG)
SEAFLOE ...... Southeast Florida Outfalls Experiment [*Marine science*] (OSRA)
SEAFRON ..... Sea Frontier
SeaFront ...... Sea Frontiers [*A publication*] (BRI)
Seagate .... Seagate Technology, Inc. [*Associated Press*] (SAG)
SEAgel .... Safe Emulsion Agar Gel [*Organic chemistry*]
Seag Parl Reg ... Seager on Parliamentary Registration [*A publication*] (DLA)
Seagram ...... [*The*] Seagram Co. Ltd. [*Associated Press*] (SAG)
Sea Grant L & Pol'y J ... Sea Grant Law and Policy Journal [*A publication*] (DLA)
Sea Grant LJ ... Sea Grant Law Journal [*A publication*] (DLA)
SEAGS .... Southeast Asian Geotechnical Society (EAIO)
SeagullE ...... Seagull Energy Corp. [*Associated Press*] (SAG)
Sea H .... Sea History [*A publication*] (BRI)
SEAI .... Station Employee Applicant Inventory [*Test*] (TES)
SEAIC .... Southeast Asia Information Center (NG)
SEAID .... Support Equipment Abbreviated Items Description [*NASA*] (NASA)
SEAIG .... Southeast Asia Information Group (AFM)
SEAIMP .... Solar Eclipse Atmospheric and Ionospheric Measurements Project (IEEE)
SEAIR .... Southeast Asia Airlift System [*Vietnam*] [*Also, SEAAS*] [*Air Force*] (VNW)
SEAISI .... South East Asia Iron and Steel Institute (EA)
SEAITACS .... Southeast Asia Integrated Tactical Air Control System (CINC)
SEAJ .... Semiconductor Equipment Association of Japan (AAEL)
SEAL .... Los Alamos [*Ecuador*] [*ICAO location identifier*] (ICLI)
SEAL .... Sea, Air, and Land
SEAL .... Sea, Air, and Land Team [*Refers to Navy personnel trained in unconventional warfare*]
SEAL .... Ship's Electronics Allowance List [*Navy*]
SEAL .... Signal Evaluation Airborne Laboratory [*FAA*]
SEAL .... Society of English and American Lawyers [*British*] (DBA)
SEAL .... Solar Energy Applications Laboratory [*Colorado State University*] [*Research center*] (RCD)
SEAL .... South-East Area Libraries (NITA)
SEAL .... Southeast Asian Learners (MEDA)
SEAL .... Standard Electronic Accounting Language [*Computer science*] (BUR)
SEAL .... Subsea Equipment Associates Ltd. [*Bermuda*]
SEALAB .... Sea Laboratory
SealdAir ...... Sealed Air Corp. [*Associated Press*] (SAG)
SEALF .... Semiempirical Absorption Loss Formula [*Radio*]
SEALF .... Southeast Asia Land Forces [*British*]
SEALITE .... Systematic Evaluation and Analysis of a LASER in a Test Environment (MCD)
SEALLINC .... Southeast Louisiana Library Network Cooperative [*Library network*]
SEALOB .... Sealift Obligation Report [*Army*]
SEALOCK ..... Search, Locate, Communications, or Kill (MCD)
SEALR .... Southeast Asia Logistic Requirement (AFM)
Sealrgt .... Sealright Co., Inc. [*Associated Press*] (SAG)
SEALS .... Severe Environmental Air Launch Study (KSC)
SEALS .... Stored Energy Actuated Lift System
SEAM .... Ambato [*Ecuador*] [*ICAO location identifier*] (ICLI)
SEAM .... Saber Enterprise Applications Manager [*Computer software*] [*Saber Software Corp.*] (PCM)
SEAM .... Scanning Electro-Acoustic Microscopy (MCD)
SEAM .... Seaman Furniture [*NASDAQ symbol*] (TTSB)
SEAM .... Seaman Furniture Co., Inc. [*Uniondale, NY*] [*NASDAQ symbol*] (NQ)
SEAM .... Sidewinder Expanded Acquisition Mode (MCD)
SEAM .... Society for the Emancipation of the American Male
SEAM .... Sociology and Economic Aspects of Medicine [*American Medical Association Information service or system*] (CRD)
SEAM .... Software Engineering and Management
SEAM .... Software Enhancement and Maintenance [*Contract*]
SEAM .... Southeast Asia Microfilm Project [*Library network*]
SEAM .... Subset Extraction and Association Measurement
SEAM .... Surface Environment and Mining Program
SEAMA .... Small Electrical Appliance Marketing Association [*British*] (DBA)
SeamanF ...... Seaman Furniture Co., Inc. [*Associated Press*] (SAG)
SEAMAP ...... Southeast Area Monitoring and Assessment Program [*Marine science*] (OSRA)
SEAMAP ...... Systematic Exploration and Mapping Program [*National Oceanic and Atmospheric Administration*] (MSC)
SeaMARCI ... Sea Mapping and Remote Characterization I [*Oceanography*]
SEAMARF .... Southeast Asia Military Air Reservation Facility (CINC)
SEAMES .... South East Asian Ministers of Education Secretariat [*Australia*]
SEAMEX .... Seamanship Exercise (NVT)
SEAMIC .... Southeast Asia Management Information Center [*Navy*]
SEAMINFO ... Surface Mining and Environment Information System [*University of Arizona*] (IID)
SEAMIST ...... Seavan Management Information System
SEAMO .... Southeast Asian Ministers of Education Organization
SEAMOD ...... Sea Systems Modification and Modernization by Modularity [*Program*] (DNAB)
SEAMORE .... Southeast Asia Mohawk Revision Program [*Army aviation*]
SEAMS .... Southeast Asian Mathematical Society [*Singapore, Singapore*]
SEAMS .... Special Electronics Air Mobility System [*Army*]
SEAMS .... Support Equipment Asset Management Subsystem (MCD)
SEAMS .... System Effectiveness Assurance Management System (MCD)
SEAMUS .... Society for Electro-Acoustic Music in the United States (EA)
SEAN .... Ana Maria [*Ecuador*] [*ICAO location identifier*] (ICLI)
SEAN .... Scientific Event Alert Network [*Smithsonian Institution*] [*Washington, DC*] (MCD)
SEAN .... Senior Enlisted Advisor, Navy (DNAB)
SEAN .... Strapdown Electrically Suspended Gyro Aerospace Navigation [*System*]
SEAN .... Syndicat des Enseignants Africains du Niger [*African Union of Teachers of Niger*]
SEANC .... Southeast Asia NOTAM [*Notice to Airmen*] Center [*Military*]
SE & CR ...... Southeastern & Chatham Railway [*Nickname: Seldom Ever Caught Running*]
SE & I .... Systems Engineering and Integration
SE & O .... Salvo Errore et Omission [*Errors or Omissions Excepted*] [*Latin*]
SE & T .... Supplies, Equipment, and Training [*Civil Defense*]
SE & TD .... Systems Engineering and Technical Direction (AAG)
SE & W .... Start Early and Walk [*Fictitious railroad initialism used to indicate one of the most reliable modes of rural transportation*]
SEANITEOPS ... Southeast Asia Night Operations [*Army*]
SEANWFZ .... Southeast Asian Nuclear Weapons Free Zone
SEANZ .... Small Enterprise Association of Australia and New Zealand
SEAOC .... Structural Engineers Association of California (EA)
SEAOPS .... Safe Engineering and Operations [*Program*] [*Marine Corps*] (DOMA)
SEAOPSS ..... Southeast Asia Operational Sensor System (MCD)
SEAOR .... Southeast Asia Operational Requirements (MCD)
SEAP .... Arapicos [*Ecuador*] [*ICAO location identifier*] (ICLI)
SEAP .... SEATO [*Southeast Asia Treaty Organization*] Administrative Publication
SEAP .... Secreted Alkaline Phosphatase [*Biochemistry*]
SEAP .... Southeast Asia Program [*Cornell University*] [*Research center*] (RCD)
SEAP .... Special Economic Acquisition Provision [*Procurement*]
SEAPA .... Spectrothermal Emission Aerosol Particle Analyzer
SEAPAC .... Sea Activated Parachute Automatic Crew Release (MCD)
SEAPADS .... Sea Planning Automated Data System
SEAPEX .... Southeast Asia Petroleum Exploration Society
SEAPG .... Support Equipment Acquisition Planning Group [*NASA*] (NASA)
SEAPRO .... Southeast Asia Programs Directorate
SEAPT .... Seaport
SEAQ .... Stock Exchange Automated Quotation (NITA)
SEAQ .... Stock Exchange Automated Quotation System [*British*]
SEAQ System ... Stock Exchange Automated Quotations System
SEAR .... Arajuno [*Ecuador*] [*ICAO location identifier*] (ICLI)
SEAR .... Safeguard Emergency Action Report [*Army*] (AABC)
SEAR .... Safety Evaluation Audit Report [*Nuclear energy*] (NRCH)
SEAR .... Southeast Asian Refugees (MEDA)
SEAR .... Summary Engineering Assessment Report (MCD)
SEAR .... Systematic Effort to Analyze Results
SEAR .... System Engineering Analysis Report
SEARA .... Stockpile Evaluation and Reliability Assessment Program
SEARAC .... Southeast Asia Resource Action Center (EA)
SEARAM ...... Semiactive RADAR Missile
SEA RARE .... Sea Reinforcement and Resupply of Europe (MCD)
SEARC .... Southeast Asia Regional Council

SEARCA...... SEAMEO [*Southeast Asia Ministers of Education Organization*] Regional Center for Graduate Study and Research in Agriculture [*Philippines*] [*Research center*] (IRC)
SEARCA...... Southeast Asia Regional Centre for Agriculture
SEARCC...... Southeast Asia Regional Computer Confederation (EA)
SEARCH...... Science, Engineering, and Related Career Hints [*Scientific Manpower Commi ssion*] [*A publication*] (EA)
SEARCH...... Scientific Evaluation and Research of Charismatic Healing [*An association*]
SEARCH...... Search for Justice and Equality in Palestine/Israel (EA)
SEARCH...... Search Group, Inc. [*An association*] (EA)
SEARCH...... Searching for Shapes [*Test*] (TES)
SearcH...... Siberian Husky Eye Anomaly Research Committee (EA)
SEARCH...... System Evaluation and Reliability Checker
SEARCH...... System for Electronic Analysis and Retrieval of Criminal Histories [*Project succeeded by National Crime Information Center*] [*Department of Justice*]
SEARCH...... System for Exploring Alternative Resource Commitments in Higher Education [*Computer science*]
SEARCH...... Systemized Excerpt Abstracts and Reviews of Chemical Headlines (NITA)
Search & Seizure Bull... Search and Seizure Bulletin [*A publication*] (DLA)
SEARCHEX... Sea/Air Search Exercise [*NATO*] (NATG)
SEARCHS..... Shuttle Engineering Approach/Rollout Control Hybrid Simulation (NASA)
SEAREQ...... Sea Requirement [*Canadian Navy*]
SEAREX ...... Sea/Air Chemical Exchange [*Marine science*] (MSC)
SEAREX ...... Study on Sea-Air Exchanges [*USA*] [*Marine science*] (OSRA)
Searle.......... Searle's Supreme Court Reports [*1850-67*] [*Cape Colony*] [*A publication*] (DLA)
Searle & Sm... Searle and Smith's English Probate and Divorce Reports [*1859-60*] [*A publication*] (DLA)
Searle Dig... Searle's Minnesota Digest [*A publication*] (DLA)
Searle Sm ... Searle and Smith's English Probate and Divorce Reports [*A publication*] (DLA)
SEARNG...... South East Asian Region Network for Geosciences [*International Council of Scientific Unions*]
Sears.......... Sears, Roebuck & Co. [*Associated Press*] (SAG)
SEAS............ Ascazubi [*Ecuador*] [*ICAO location identifier*] (ICLI)
SEAS............ Centre of South-East Asian Studies [*University of Hull*] [*British*] (CB)
SEAS............ Sea School [*Marine Corps*]
SEAS............ Selected Effects Armament Subsystem [*Army*] (RDA)
SEAS............ Share European Association (HGAA)
SEAS............ Shipboard Environmental Data Acquisition System [*National Oceanic and Atmospheric Administration*] (MSC)
SEAS............ Ship/Equipment/Alterations Summary [*Navy*] (NG)
SEAS............ Shoreline Erosion Advisory Service [*Bureau of Flood Protection*]
SEAS............ Spiral-Ecological Approach to Supervision (EDAC)
SEAS............ State Estimation Algorithm for Small-Scale System (PDAA)
SEAS............ Strategic Environmental Assessment System [*Environmental Protection Agency*]
SEAS............ Support Equipment Avionics System
SEAS............ Surveillance Environmental Acoustic Support [*Military*] (CAAL)
SEAS............ Surveillance Environmental Acoustic Support Project [*Naval Ocean Research and Development Activity*] [*Mississippi*]
SEAS............ System Enhancement and Support [*Military*] (CAAL)
SEASA.......... Science and Engineering Academy of South Africa
SEASAME ... Southeast Asian Science and Mathematics Experiment [*RECSAM*]
SEASAR...... Sea Synthetic Aperture RADAR
SEASAT........ Sea Satellite [*NASA*]
SEASC .... Scientific Exploration of the Atlantic Shelf Committee
SEASCO...... Southeast Asia Science Cooperation Office
SEASEE....... Southeast Asia Association on Seismology and Earthquake Engineering
SEASET....... Separate Effects and Systems Effects Tests [*Nuclear energy*] (NRCH)
SEASIA .... Southeast Asia (NG)
SEASS .... Southeast Asia Airlift System [*Vietnam*] [*Also, SEAIR*] [*Air Force*] (VNW)
SEASTAG .... Southeast Asia Treaty Organization Standardization Agreement
SEAT........... Atacames [*Ecuador*] [*ICAO location identifier*] (ICLI)
SEAT........... Sheep Erythrocyte Agglutination Test [*Medicine*] (DMAA)
SEAT........... Sociedad Espanol de Automoviles de Turismo [*Spanish automobile manufacturer; acronym used as name of its cars*]
SEAT........... Standardization and Evaluation Assistance Team [*Military*]
SEAT........... Stock Exchange Automated Trading
SEA/TAC....... Seattle/Tacoma International Airport (GAVI)
SEATAC....... Southeast Asian Agency for Regional Transport and Communications Development (EAIO)
SEATAF....... Southern European Atomic Task Force [*Military*]
SEATAR ...... Search and Automatic Track Array RADAR
SEATAR ...... Studies on East Asia Tectonics and Resources [*Marine science*] (MSC)
SEATEC....... Sea Test and Evaluation Capability [*Navy*] (CAAL)
SEATELCOM... Southeast Asia Telecommunications System [*Military*] (AABC)
Seat F Ch ... Seaton's Forms in Chancery [*A publication*] (DLA)
SEATIC....... Southeast Asia Translation and Interrogation Center [*Navy*]
SEATICC ..... Southeast Asia Tactical Information Communications Center (DNAB)
SeatlF.......... Seattle Film Works, Inc. [*Associated Press*] (SAG)
SEATO .... Southeast Asia Treaty Organization [*International organization formed to combat the spread of Communism*] (VNW)
SEATRAD ..... Southeast Asia Tin Research and Development Center [*Malaysia*] (IRC)
SEATS......... Shubert Entertainment and Arts Ticketing System [*National computerized theatre-ticket selling system*]

SEATS.......... Special Education Administration Task Simulation Game
SeattleF....... Seattle Film Works [*Associated Press*] (SAG)
Seattle Pac U... Seattle Pacific University (GAGS)
Seattle U ..... Seattle University (GAGS)
SEA-URICA... South East Asia Universal Realtime Information Cataloging and Administration System
Sea Vend..... Seaborne on Vendors and Purchasers [*9th ed.*] [*1926*] [*A publication*] (DLA)
SEAVEY....... Sea-to-Shore Rotation Survey (DNAB)
SEAWARS.... Seawater Activated Release System [*Navy*] (CAAL)
SEAWBS..... Southeast Asia Wideband System [*Military*]
SEAWEA ..... Sea and Weather Observations [*Navy*] (NVT)
SeawFd....... Seaway Food Town, Inc. [*Associated Press*] (SAG)
SeaWiFS..... Sea-Viewing Wide Field-of-View Sensor [*Marine science*] (OSRA)
SeaWiFS..... Sea-Viewing Wide-Field Sensor [*Oceanography*] (ECON)
SEA/W/O MEPS... South Eastern Alaska/Washington/Oregon Minimum Earned Premium Scale [*Aviation*] (AIA)
SEAX........... Span East Airlines, Inc. [*Air carrier designation symbol*]
SEB............. Scale for Emotional Blunting (STED)
SEB............. Scientific Equipment Bay [*NASA*] (KSC)
SEB............. Scottish Examining Board (DCTA)
SEB............. Seaboard Corp. [*AMEX symbol*] (SPSG)
SEB............. Sebenico [*Yugoslavia*] [*Seismograph station code, US Geological Survey Closed*] (SEIS)
SEB............. Sebha [*Libya*] [*Airport symbol*] (OAG)
Seb............. Sebir [*or Sebirin*] (BJA)
SEB............. Secondary Education Board
SEB............. Security Equipment Building
SEB............. Selective Enlistment Bonus [*Navy*] (NVT)
SEB............. Single-Ended Boiler (DS)
SEB............. Skandinaviska Enskilda Banken [*Sweden*]
SEB............. Social and Emotional Behavior
SEB............. Societe des Etudes Bloyennes [*France*] (EAIO)
SEB............. Society for Economic Botany (EA)
SEB............. Society for Experimental Biology (EAIO)
SEB............. Socio-Economic Benefit
SEB............. Software Engineering Bibliographic Database [*Air Force Systems Command*] [*Information service or system*] (CRD)
SEB............. Solo Events Board [*Auto racing*]
SEB............. Source Evaluation Board [*NASA*]
SEB............. Southeastbound [*ICAO designator*] (FAAC)
SEB............. South Equatorial Belt [*Planet Jupiter*]
SEB............. Southern European Broadcasting Service [*DoD*] (GFGA)
SEB............. Special Enlistment Bonus (MCD)
SEB............. Staphylococcal Enterotoxin B [*Medicine*]
SEB............. Strip Electron Beam
SEB............. Structural Engineering Bulletin [*Department of Housing and Urban Development*] [*A publication*] (GFGA)
SEB............. Support Equipment Building [*NASA*] (NASA)
SEB............. Support Equipment Bulletin (MCD)
SEB............. System Error Bridge
SEB............. Systems Engineering Branch [*NASA*] (NASA)
SEBA........... Babahoyo [*Ecuador*] [*ICAO location identifier*] (ICLI)
SEBA........... Staphylococcal Enterotoxin B Antisera [*Medicine*]
SEBA........... Staphylococcal Enterotoxin B Antiserum (STED)
Sebast Med... Sebastianus Medices [*Flourished, 16th century*] [*Authority cited in pre-1607 legal work*] (DSA)
Sebast Sap... Sebastianus Sapia [*Deceased, 1523*] [*Authority cited in pre-1607 legal work*] (DSA)
Sebast Vant... Sebastianus Vantius [*Flourished, 16th century*] [*Authority cited in pre-1607 legal work*] (DSA)
SEBBETSI .... Serikat Buruh Beras dan Seluruh Indonesia [*Rice and Tapioca Workers' Union of Indonesia*]
SEBC........... Bahia De Caraquez [*Ecuador*] [*ICAO location identifier*] (ICLI)
SEBC........... Societe des Eleveurs de Bovins Canadiens (AC)
SEBC........... South-Eastern Bible College [*Florida*]
SEBD .... Bola De Oro [*Ecuador*] [*ICAO location identifier*] (ICLI)
SEBD .... Software Engineering Bibliographic Data Base [*Data and Analysis Center for Software*] [*Information service or system*]
SEBDA .... Serikat Buruh Daehrah Autonoom [*Civil Servants' Union*] [*Indonesia*]
seb derm..... Seborrheic Dermatitis (STED)
SEBE........... La Beata [*Ecuador*] [*ICAO location identifier*] (ICLI)
SEbE........... Southeast by East
SEBECC...... Scanning Electron Beam Excited Charge Collection (IAA)
SEBH .... Balao Chico [*Ecuador*] [*ICAO location identifier*] (ICLI)
SEBI .... Boliche [*Ecuador*] [*ICAO location identifier*] (ICLI)
SEBI .... Securities and Exchange Board of India (ECON)
SEBIC......... Sustained Electron Bombardment-Induced Conductivity
seb ker .... Seborrheic Keratosis (STED)
SEBL........... Self-Emptying Blind Loop [*Gastroenterology*]
SEBL........... Siebel Systems, Inc. [*NASDAQ symbol*] (SAG)
SEBL........... Single European Banking Licence
SEBM.......... Society for Experimental Biology and Medicine (EA)
SEBQ.......... Senior Enlisted Bachelor Quarters [*Army*] (AABC)
SEBS.......... Single-Ended Boiler Survey (DS)
SEbS.......... Southeast by South
SEBS.......... Submarine Emergency Buoyancy System
Seb Sapi..... Sebastianus Sapia [*Deceased, 1523*] [*Authority cited in pre-1607 legal work*] (DSA)
SEBSCC ...... Southeast Bering Sea Carrying Capacity [*Study*] [*Marine science*] (OSRA)
SEBT........... El Batan [*Ecuador*] [*ICAO location identifier*] (ICLI)
Seb Trade-Marks... Sebastian on Trade-Marks [*A publication*] (DLA)
Seb Tr M ..... Sebastian on Trade-Marks [*5th ed.*] [*1911*] [*A publication*] (DLA)

SEBUMI .... Serikat Buruh Minjak, Stanvac [*Oil Workers' Union, Stanvac*] [*Indonesia*]
SEBV .... Solder End Ball Valve
Seb Vant ...... Sebastianus Vantius [*Flourished, 16th century*] [*Authority cited in pre-1607 legal work*] (DSA)
s-ec-- .... Ecuador [*MARC geographic area code Library of Congress*] (LCCP)
SEC .... Safeguards Equipment Cabinet (IEEE)
SEC .... Sanitary Engineering Center
SEC .... Scientific and Engineering Computation
SEC .... Scientific Estimates Committee [*Military*] (AABC)
SEC .... Scottish Evangelistic Council (DBA)
sec .... Secant (IDOE)
SEC .... Secant
SEC .... Second (AFM)
sec .... Second (IDOE)
sec .... Secondary (IDOE)
Sec .... Secondary [*Chemistry*]
SEC .... Secondary
SEC .... Secondary Electron Conduction [*Television camera system*]
SEC .... Secondary Emission Conductivity
SEC .... Secret (AFM)
SEC .... Secretariat
SEC .... Secretary (EY)
Sec .... Secretary (ODBW)
sec .... Secretary (DD)
SEC .... Secretin [*Biochemistry*]
SEC .... Section
sec .... Section (IDOE)
Sec .... Section (AAGC)
SEC .... Sector
SEC .... Secular
SEC .... Secundum [*According To*] [*Latin*]
SEC .... Secure (KSC)
Sec .... Secured (EBF)
SEC .... Securities [*or Security*] (AAG)
SEC .... Securities and Exchange Commission
SEC .... Securities and Exchange Commission Decisions and Reports [*A publication*] (DLA)
SEC .... Securities and Exchange Commission, Washington, DC [*OCLC symbol*] (OCLC)
SEC .... Security
Sec .... Security (EBF)
Sec .... Secus [*Otherwise*] [*Latin*] (ILCA)
SEC .... Sensor and Engagement Controller [*Army*]
SEC .... Sensormatic Canada Ltd. [*Toronto Stock Exchange symbol*]
SEC .... Sequential Events Controller [*NASA*] (NASA)
SEC .... Series Elastic Component [*Medicine*] [*Muscles*] (DB)
SEC .... Shaftless Expander-Compressor
SEC .... Simple Electronic Computer [*Birkbeck College*] [*London, England*] (DEN)
SEC .... Single-Edge Contact (PCM)
SEC .... Single Error Correcting
SEC .... Sisters of the Eucharistic Covenant (TOCD)
SEC .... Size Exclusion Chromatography
SEC .... Social Economic Council [*Sociaal Economische Raad*] [*Netherlands*]
SEC .... Social Education Centre (AIE)
SEC .... Societe des Ecrivains Canadiens [*Society of Canadian Writers*]
SEC .... Societe Europeenne de Culture [*European Society of Culture - ESC*] (EAIO)
SEC .... Society for Educative Communication (EA)
SEC .... Society of Exchange Counselors (EA)
SEC .... Soft Elastic Capsule [*Pharmacy*]
SEC .... Solar Energy Collector
SEC .... Solar Energy Concentrator
SEC .... Solid Electrolyte Capacitor
SEC .... Source Evaluation Committee [*NASA*] (NASA)
sec .... Source Evaluation Committee [*NASA*] (NAKS)
SEC .... South East College of Air Training [*British ICAO designator*] (FAAC)
SEC .... Southeast Environmental Contractors, Inc. (EFIS)
SEC .... Southeastern Command
SEC .... Southeastern Conference (EA)
SEC .... South Equatorial Current [*Oceanography*] (MSC)
SEC .... Southern Electronics Corp. (IAA)
SEC .... Space Environmental Chamber (AAG)
SEC .... Space Environment Center [*Marine science*] (OSRA)
SEC .... Special Emergency Campaign [*Red Cross fund-raising*]
SEC .... Special Event Charter Flight [*Aviation*] (DA)
SEC .... Specialty Equipment [*Stock market symbol*]
SEC .... Specialty Equipment [*NYSE symbol*]
SEC .... Specific Energy Consumption [*Automotive engineering*]
SEC .... Spectroelectrochemistry
SEC .... Squamous Epithelial Cells [*Medicine*] (MEDA)
SEC .... Staff Evaluation Coordinators (MCD)
SEC .... Standard Error of Calibration
SEC .... Standard Evaluation Cylinder (MCD)
SEC .... Standards and Ethics Commission [*American Occupational Therapy Association*]
SEC .... Standing with Eyes Closed [*Equilibrium test*]
SEC .... Sterling Electronics [*NYSE symbol*] (TTSB)
SEC .... Sterling Electronics Corp. [*NYSE symbol*] (SAG)
SEC .... Stevens Creek [*California*] [*Seismograph station code, US Geological Survey*] (SEIS)
SEC .... Stock Exchange Council [*British*]
SEC .... Strong Exchange Capacity (DB)
SEC .... Structural Engineers Councils (KSC)

SEC .... Submarine Element Coordinator (NVT)
SEC .... Sulfite Evaporator Condensate [*Pulp and paper technolgy*]
SEC .... Sulphur Export Corp. [*An association*] (EA)
SEC .... Supply Executive Committee [*NATO*] (NATG)
SEC .... Support Equipment Change (MCD)
SEC .... Supr Einspritz Coupe [*Super, Fuel Injection, Coupe*] [*Mercedes-Benz automotive model designation*]
SEC .... Switch Element Controller [*Telecommunications*]
SEC .... Switching Equipment Congestion [*Telecommunications*] (TEL)
SEC .... Sydney Entertainment Centre [*Australia*]
SECA .... Catarama [*Ecuador*] [*ICAO location identifier*] (ICLI)
SECA .... Self-Employment Contributions Act of 1954 [*under which self-employed persons contribute to OASDI coverage for themselves*]
SECA .... Shiatsu Education Center of America [*Later, Ohashi Institute - OI*] (EA)
SECA .... Societe d'Eco-Amenagement [*Commercial firm France*] (ECON)
SECA .... Solar Energy Construction Association [*Defunct*] (EA)
SECA .... Southern Early Childhood Association
SECA .... Southern Educational Communications Authority [*Television network*] [*Obsolete*]
SECA .... Sportbike Enthusiast Club of America (EA)
SECA .... Survey of Early Childhood Abilities [*K. Codding*] (TES)
SECAB .... Secretaria Ejecutiva Permanente del Convenio Andres Bello [*Permanent Executive Secretariat of the Andres Bello Convention*] (EAIO)
SECAC .... Sectional Aeronautical Chart
SECAD .... Services Engineering Computer-Aided Design [*Pierce Management Services*] [*Software package*] (NCC)
SECAD .... Support Equipment Concept Approval Data
SECAL .... Sectoral Adjustment Loan [*World Bank*]
SECAL .... Selected Calling System [*Military*] (AFM)
SECAL .... Separate Engineering Control Air Limits [*Environmental science*]
SECAM .... Sequence Electronique Couleur avec Memoire [*Color Sequence with Memory*] [*French color television system*]
SECAM .... Sequential Color and Memory (IAA)
SECAM .... Systeme Electronique Couleur avec Memoire [*French broadcast color standard*]
SECAN .... Science and Engineering Committee on Advisory to NOAA [*National Oceanic and Atmospheric Administration*] [*Marine science*] (OSRA)
SECAN .... Standing Group Communication Security and Evaluation Agency Washington
Sec & Ex C... Securities and Exchange Commission (DLA)
SECANT .... Separation and Control of Aircraft Using Nonsynchronous Techniques [*Collision avoidance*] [*RCA*]
SECAP .... System Experience Correlation and Analysis Program (IAA)
SECAP .... Systems Experiment Correlation and Analysis Program (MCD)
SECAR .... Secondary RADAR (IEEE)
SECARMY ... Secretary of the Army
SEC ART ...... Secundum Artem [*According to the Art*] [*Latin*]
SECAS .... Ship Equipment Configuration Accounting System (NVT)
SECB .... Security Bancorp (EFIS)
SECBASE ..... Section Base [*Navy*] (DNAB)
SecBcp .... Security Bancorp [*Associated Press*] (SAG)
SecBHld .... Security Bank Holding Co. [*Associated Press*] (SAG)
Sec Bk Judg... Second Book of Judgments (Huxley) [*England*] [*A publication*] (DLA)
SecBn .... Second Bancorp, Inc. [*Associated Press*] (SAG)
SECC .... Condorcocha [*Ecuador*] [*ICAO location identifier*] (ICLI)
SECC .... Safe Energy Communication Council (EA)
SECC .... Scientific and Engineering Computing Council (MCD)
SECC .... South Equatorial Countercurrent [*Oceanography*] (MSC)
SECC .... State Emergency Communications Committee [*National Oceanic and Atmospheric Administration*] (GFGA)
SECC .... Sun Electric Corp. (EFIS)
SECC .... Survivable Enduring Command and Control
SECCA .... Southeastern Center for Contemporary Art [*North Carolina*]
SecCap .... Security Capital Corp. [*Associated Press*] (SAG)
SecCapA ...... Security Capital Atlantic, Inc. [*Associated Press*] (SAG)
SecCaPT ...... Security Capital Pacific Trust [*Associated Press*] (SAG)
SecCapTr ..... Security Capital Industrial Trust Co. [*Associated Press*] (SAG)
SecComp ...... Secure Computing Corp. [*Associated Press*] (SAG)
SEC Compl (P-H)... Securities and Exchange Commission Compliance (Prentice-Hall, Inc.) [*A publication*] (DLA)
SECD .... Secondary (AABC)
SECD .... Second Bancorp [*NASDAQ symbol*] (TTSB)
SECD .... Second Bancorp, Inc. [*NASDAQ symbol*] (SPSG)
SECDA .... Secured (ROG)
SECDA .... Southeastern Community Development Association [*Defunct*] (EA)
SECDED .... Single-BIT [*Binary Digit*] Error Correction and Double-BIT Error Detection [*Binary Digit*]
SecDef .... Secretary of Defense [*DoD*] (VNW)
SECDEF .... Secretary of Defense
SEC DEL ...... Secretary of Delgation
SEC Docket... Securities and Exchange Commission Docket [*A publication*] (DLA)
SECDP .... Second Bncp $1.50 Cv Pfd'A' [*NASDAQ symbol*] (TTSB)
Secd Pt Edw III... Year Books, Part III [*England*] [*A publication*] (DLA)
Secd Pt H VI... Year Books, Part VIII [*England*] [*A publication*] (DLA)
SECDY .... Secondary
SecDyn .... Security Dynamics Technologies, Inc. [*Associated Press*] (SAG)
SECE .... Santa Cecilia [*Ecuador*] [*ICAO location identifier*] (ICLI)
SECE .... Selfhelp of Emigres from Central Europe (EA)
SECED .... Society for Earthquake and Civil Engineering Dynamics [*British*]
SECEM .... Support Equipment Cost Effectiveness Model (MCD)
SECEX .... Security Equity Cl.A [*Mutual fund ticker symbol*] (SG)

SECF.......... Somali Eastern and Central Front [*Political party*] (EY)
SECF.......... Surface Effect Cruiser Escort (DNAB)
SECFLT........ Second Fleet [*Atlantic*] [*Navy*]
SecFstNt...... Security First Network Bank [*Associated Press*] (SAG)
SECFT......... Second Foot (IAA)
SECG.......... Stress Electrocardiography [*Cardiology*] (DMAA)
SEC GEN....... Secretary General (WDAA)
SECGRUHQ... Security Group Headquarters
SECH.......... Chone [*Ecuador*] [*ICAO location identifier*] (ICLI)
sech........... Hyperbolic Secant (IDOE)
SECH.......... Secant, Hyperbolic
SECHT........ Scoping Emergency Cooling Heat Transfer [*Nuclear energy*] (KSC)
SECI.......... Support Equipment Critical Item (MCD)
SECIMP........ Secondary Impedance (IAA)
SECINSP...... Security Inspection [*Military*] (NVT)
Sec Int....... Secretary of the Interior (DLA)
SECIR......... Semiautomatic Encoding of Chemistry for Information Retrieval (DIT)
SECIS......... Selenocysteine Insertion Sequence [*Biochemistry*]
SECIT......... Syndicat des Employes Indigenes du Commerce du Togo [*Union of Indigenous Employees of Commerce of Togo*]
SECIX......... Security Growth & Income Cl.A [*Mutual fund ticker symbol*] (SG)
SEC Jud Dec... Securities and Exchange Commission Judicial Decisions [*A publication*] (DLA)
SECL.......... Chiles [*Ecuador*] [*ICAO location identifier*] (ICLI)
secl........... Secretarial (WGA)
SECL.......... Secretarial
SECL.......... Sequential Emitter Coupled Logic (IAA)
SECL.......... Ship Equipment Configuration List (MCD)
SECL.......... Symmetrical Emitter Coupled Logic (IAA)
SECL.......... Symmetrically-Operated Emitter Coupled Logic (IAA)
SECLA........ Southeastern Connecticut Library Association [*Library network*]
SEC LEG....... Secundum Legem [*According to Law*] [*Latin*]
SECLT......... Second Lieutenant [*Army*]
SECM.......... Clementina [*Ecuador*] [*ICAO location identifier*] (ICLI)
SECM.......... Scanning Electrochemical Microscope
SECM.......... School of English Church Music [*Later, RSCM*]
SECM.......... Secom General [*NASDAQ symbol*] (TTSB)
SECM.......... Secom General Corp. [*NASDAQ symbol*] (NQ)
SECMA........ Stock Exchange Computer Managers Association (MHDW)
SECMID....... Scanning Electrochemical Microscope-Induced Desorption
Sec Mkt...... Secondary Market [*Banking*] (TBD)
SECN.......... Section (ROG)
SECNA........ Secretary of the Navy (NOAA)
SEC NAT..... Secundum Naturam [*According to Nature*] [*Latin*]
SECNAV....... Secretary of the Navy
SECNAVINST... Secretary of the Navy Instruction
SecndB........ Second Bancorp, Inc. [*Associated Press*] (SAG)
SecNtl......... Security National Financial Corp. [*Associated Press*] (SAG)
SECNY......... Sales Executives Club of New York (EA)
SECO .... Coca [*Ecuador*] [*ICAO location identifier*] (ICLI)
SECO .... Securities and Exchange Commission
SECO .... Securities and Exchange Commission Organization
SECO .... Self-Regulating Error-Correct Coder-Decoder
SECO .... Sequential Coding
SECO .... Sequential Control [*Teletype*] [*Computer science*]
SECO .... Sequential Encoder-Decoder (IAA)
SECO .... Station Engineering Control Office [*Telecommunications*] (TEL)
SECO .... Steam and Electric Cogeneration [*Power source*]
SECO .... Sustainer-Engine Cutoff [*Aerospace*]
SECOBI....... Servicio de Consulta a Bancos de Informacion [*Database Consultation Service*] [*Information service or system Mexico*] (IID)
SECOF .... Shipboard Environmental Checkout Facility (DNAB)
SECOFF....... Section Office
SECOFI .... Secretaria de Comercio y Fomento Industrial [*Secretariat of Trade and Industrial Promotion*] [*Mexico*] (CROSS)
SECOIN....... Security Consultants International
SECOL........ Southeastern Conference on Linguistics
SECOLAS...... Southeastern Conference on Latin American Studies [*United States*]
SECOM .... School Emergency Communication
Secom .... Secom General Corp. [*Associated Press*] (SAG)
SECOM .... Security Committee
SECOM .... System Engineering Communication (IAA)
SECOMO...... Software [*or System*] Engineering Cost Model
SECON .... Secondary Electron Conduction [*Television camera system*]
Second Ed ... Secondary Education [*A publication*]
Second Teach... Secondary Teacher [*A publication*]
SECONNS .... Satellite ECCM [*Electronics Counter Countermeasure*] Communications Neural Network Syster
SECOR........ Sequential Collation [*or Collection*] of Ranges [*Army*]
SECOR........ Sequential Correlation
SECOR........ Sequential Correlation of Range (IAA)
SECOR........ Sequential Cosine Ranging [*System*] (MUGU)
SECOR........ Southeast Coastal Ocean Research [*Georgia*]
SECORD....... Secure Voice Cord Board [*Telecommunications*] (TEL)
SECP.......... Security Capital [*NASDAQ symbol*] (TTSB)
SECP.......... Security Capital Corp. [*NASDAQ symbol*] (SAG)
SECP.......... Software Engineering Change Proposal (MCD)
SECP.......... Solar Energy Conservation Program [*Department of Energy*]
SECP.......... State Energy Conservation Program
SECP.......... Subcontractor Engineering Change Proposal (MCD)
SecPac .... Security Pacific [*Bank*] (ECON)
SecPac .... Security Pacific Bank [*Hong Kong*]
SECPDED...... Single Error Correcting and Partial Double Error Detecting [*Computer science*] (MHDI)

SECPR........ Standard External Cardiopulmonary Resuscitation
SECPS........ Secondary Propulsion System [*NASA*] (KSC)
SECPS........ SEC Practice Section (TDOB)
SECR .... Curaray [*Ecuador*] [*ICAO location identifier*] (ICLI)
SECR .... Secretariat
SECRA........ Secondary RADAR [*RADAR beacon*]
SECRAC....... System Engineering Cost Reduction Assistance Contractor (PDAA)
SEC REG...... Secundum Regulam [*According to Rule*] [*Latin*]
Sec Reg Guide... Securities Regulation Guide [*Prentice-Hall, Inc.*] [*A publication*] (DLA)
SECREP .... Regional Representative of the Secretary of Transportation
SECRG........ Securing
SECRL........ Secretarial
SECS.......... Seagrass Ecosystems Component Study [*Marine science*] (MSC)
SECS.......... Selective Electron-Capture Sensitization [*Analytical chemistry*]
SECS.......... Semiconductor Equipment Communications Standard (NITA)
SECS.......... Sequential Events Control System [*NASA*] (KSC)
SECS.......... Shuttle Events Control Subsystem [*NASA*] (NASA)
SECS.......... Simulation and Evaluation of Chemical Synthesis [*Computer science*]
SECS.......... Single-Electron Capacitance Spectroscopy
SECS.......... Single-Engine Control Speed (DNAB)
SECS.......... Solar Electric Communication Satellite
SECS.......... Space Environmental Control System (AAG)
SECS.......... Stem Elevated Camera System
SECSA........ Single Engine Control System Application (MCD)
SECSTA....... Naval Security Station
SECSTATE.... Secretary of State (COE)
SECSW....... Science and Engineering Committee for a Secure World (EA)
SECSY....... Spin-Echo Correlated Spectroscopy
SECT.......... Firing Field Equipment Service [*French Acronym is based on foreign phrase*]
SECT.......... Secretariat
SECT.......... Section (KSC)
sect.......... Section (VRA)
Sect.......... Section (AL)
SECT.......... Skin Electric Tracing (IAA)
SECT.......... South East Cultural Trust [*South Australia*]
SECT.......... Submarine Emergency Communications Transmitter
SECTAM...... Sterile Environmental Control Technology Applications to Medicine
SECTASKFLT... Second Task Fleet
SECTBASE ... Section Base [*Navy*]
SECTL........ Secretarial
SECTL........ Sectional
SECTLZD...... Sectionalized
Sectn........ Section (TBD)
SECTRANS.... Secretary of Transportation (DOMA)
sec-treas ..... Secretary-Treasurer (DD)
SEC-TREAS... Secretary-Treasurer (DNAB)
SECTY....... Secretary
SECU .... Cuenca [*Ecuador*] [*ICAO location identifier*] (ICLI)
SECU .... Slave Emulator Control Unit
SecuBk .... Security Bank Corp. [*Associated Press*] (SAG)
SEC(UN) ..... Secretariat of the United Nations
Secur.......... Security (TBD)
SecurCT....... Security Connecticut Corp. [*Associated Press*] (SAG)
SECURE....... Systems Evaluation Code Under Radiation Environment
SecurFst...... Security First Corp. [*Associated Press*] (SAG)
SECUS........ Sex Information and Education Council of the United States
SECUS .... Supreme Emblem Club of the United States (EA)
SECUTC ...... Southeastern Consortium of University Transportation Centers [*MTMC*] (TAG)
SECUX .... Security Ultra [*Mutual fund ticker symbol*] (SG)
SECWAR...... Secretary of War [*Obsolete*]
SECWND...... Secondary Winding (IAA)
SECX.......... SED International Holdings [*NASDAQ symbol*] [*Formerly, Southern Electronics*] (SG)
SECX.......... Southern Electronics [*NASDAQ symbol*] (TTSB)
SECX.......... Southern Electronics Corp. [*Tucker, GA*] [*NASDAQ symbol*] (NQ)
SECY......... Secretary
Secy.......... Secretary (TBD)
SECY......... Security
SED........... Said [*Amateur radio shorthand*] (WDAA)
SED........... Sale/Engineering/Development [*Honda*] [*Automotive engineering*]
SED........... Sanitary Engineering Division [*MIT*] (MCD)
SED........... Saturn Electrostatic Discharges [*Planetary science*]
SED........... Scarborough Board of Education [*Professional Education Library*] [*UTLAS symbol*]
SED........... Scottish Education Department
SED........... Sedan (AAG)
SED........... Sedative [*Medicine*] (ROG)
SED........... Seddin [*German Democratic Republic*] [*Later, NGK*] [*Geomagnetic observatory code*]
Sed .... Sedes [*A Stool*] [*Medicine*]
SED........... Sediment [*or Sedimentation*]
Sed .... Sedimentation (DB)
SED........... Sedition [*FBI standardized term*]
SED........... Sedona Air Center, Inc. [*ICAO designator*] (FAAC)
SED........... Segmented Expanding Die (MCD)
SED........... Semiequilibrium Dialysis [*Physical chemistry*]
SED........... Sensor Evolutionary Development (MCD)
SED........... Sentence Expiry Date (WDAA)
SED........... Sequence Event Diagram (DNAB)
SED........... Seriously [*or Severely*] Emotionally Disturbed
SED........... SFS Bancorp, Inc. [*NASDAQ symbol*] (SAG)
SED........... Shipper's Export Declaration [*Customs Service*]

SED............. Shipper's Export Document [*FHWA*] (TAG)
SED............. Shore Establishments Division [*Navy*]
SED............. Side-Effects of Drugs (DB)
SED............. Signal Equipment Depot (IAA)
SED............. Simulative Electronic Deception [*Army*] (ADDR)
SED............. Skin Erythema Dose [*Medicine*]
SED............. Smoke-Emitting Diode [*Computer hacker terminology*] (NHD)
SED............. Software Engineering Data [*Data and Analysis Center for Software*] [*Information service or system*]
SED............. Software Engineering Design [*Army*]
SED............. Software Engineering Directorate [*Army*] (RDA)
SED............. Solar Energy Density
SED............. Sound Energy Density
SED............. Sozialistische Einheitspartei Deutschlands [*Socialist Unity Party of Germany*] [*Political party*] (PPW)
SED............. Soziolistische Linheitspartei Deutschlands [*Socialist Unity Party*] [*German*] (BARN)
SED............. Space Engineering Document [*NASA*] (IAA)
SED............. Space Environment Division [*NASA*]
SED............. Special Electrical Devices (AABC)
SED............. Special Expanded Display (IAA)
SEd............. Specialist in Education (GAGS)
SED............. Spectral Energy Distribution
SED............. Spondyloepiphysial Dysplasia [*Medicine*]
SED............. Staphylococcal Enterotoxin D [*Medicine*]
SED............. State Executive Director
SED............. Status Entry Device [*Telecommunications*] (TEL)
SEDT............ Stochastic Electrodynamics [*Quantum physics*]
SED............. Stray Energy Detector
sed............. Stream Editor [*Computer science*] (CDE)
SED............. Strong Exchange Degeneracy [*Physics*] (OA)
SED............. Students for Economic Democracy (EA)
SED............. Sun Entertainment [*Vancouver Stock Exchange symbol*]
SED............. Suppressed Electrical Discharge (IAA)
SED............. Swansea East Dock [*Welsh depot code*]
SED............. System Engineering Division [*Apollo Spacecraft Program Office*]
SED............. System Entry Date [*Military*] (AFIT)
SED............. Systems Effectiveness Demonstration (NG)
SEDA .... Safety Equipment Distributors Association (EA)
SEDA .... South Eastern Discotheque Association [*British*] (DBA)
SEDA .... Staff and Educational Development Association (AIE)
SEDA .... State Emergency Defense Airlift
SEDA .... Structured Exploratory Data Analysis
SEDACS ...... Support Equipment Data Acquisition and Control System (MCD)
SEDAR .... Shipborne Electronic Deflection Array RADAR (MCD)
SEDAS .... Spurious Emission Detection Acquisition System (MCD)
SedaSpc ...... Seda Speciality Packaging [*Commercial firm Associated Press*] (SAG)
SEDC .... Society for Emotional Development in Children [*Canada*]
SEDC .... Steam Engine Direct Connootod (MOA)
SEDCOR...... Specialty Electronics Development Corp.
SEDD .... Sensors and Electron Devices Directorate [*Army*]
SEDD .... Special Extra Deep Drawing (MCD)
SEDD .... Systems Evaluation and Development Division [*NASA*]
SEDEPAC ..... Servicio, Desarrollo y Paz [*Service, Development, and Peace*] [*An association Mexico*] (CROSS)
SEDES .... Societe d'Etudes pour le Developpement Economique et Social [*Society for the Study of Economic and Social Development*] [*Information service or system France*] (IID)
SEDFC .... Steve Earle and Dukes Fan Organization (EA)
SEDFRE .... Scholarship, Education, and Defense Fund for Racial Equality
Sedg & W Tit... Sedgwick and Wait on the Trial of Title to Land [*A publication*] (DLA)
Sedg & W Tr Title Land... Sedgwick and Wait on the Trial of Title to Land [*A publication*] (DLA)
Sedg Dam ... Sedgwick on the Measure of Damage [*A publication*] (DLA)
SEDGE .... SAGE [*Semiautomatic Ground Environment*] Experimental Display Generator [*Military*] (IAA)
SEDGE .... Special Experimental Display Generation (IAA)
SEDGE .... Special Experimental Display Generation Program (SAA)
Sedg L Cas... Sedgwick's Leading Cases on Damages [*A publication*] (DLA)
Sedg L Cas... Sedgwick's Leading Cases on Real Property [*A publication*] (DLA)
Sedg St & Const Law... Sedgwick on Statutory and Constitutional Law [*A publication*] (DLA)
Sedg Stat Law... Sedgwick on Statutory and Constitutional Law [*A publication*] (DLA)
SEDI............. Semi-Empirical Design of Impellers [*Hydraulics*] [*Computer-aided design*]
SEDI............. Software Engineering Demonstrator Initiative [*British*]
SEDI............. Spondyloepiphyseal Dysplasia, Late [*Medicine*] (DMAA)
SEDIC .... Sociedad Espanola de Documentacion e Informacion Cientifica [*Spanish Society for Documentation and Information Sciences*] [*Information service or system*] (IID)
SEDIS .... Service Information-Diffusion [*Information Dissemination Office*] [*National Institute for Research in Informatics and Automation*] [*Information service or system*] (IID)
SEDIS .... Surface Emitter Detection, Identification System [*Navy*]
SEDIT.......... Sophisticated String Editor (IEEE)
SEDIT.......... Source Program Editor (MHDB)
SEDL .... Southwest Educational Development Laboratory (EA)
SEDM.......... Society for Experimental and Descriptive Malacology (EA)
SEDM.......... State EPA Data Management Program [*Environmental Protection Agency*] (AEPA)
SEDM.......... Status Entry Device Multiplexer [*Telecommunications*] (TEL)
SEDME.......... Survey Electronics Distance Measuring Equipment (MCD)

SEDME........ Surveying Equipment Distance Measuring Electronic (MCD)
SEDOC .... European System for the International Clearing of Vacancies and Applications forEmployment [*EC*] (ECED)
SEDOR........ Spin Echo Double Resonance [*Physics*]
SEDP .... Site Evacuation and Decontamination Plan [*Environmental science*] (COE)
SEDP .... Support for Engineer Development Priorities (MCD)
SedPAC....... Sediment Priority Action Committee [*Water Quality Board*]
SEDPC........ Scientific and Engineering Data Processing Center
SEDR .... Science Education Development and Research Division [*National Science Foundation*] (GRD)
SEDR .... Service Engineering Department Report
SEDR .... Supplementary Experiment Data Record [*Aerospace*]
SEDR .... System Effective Data Rate (BUR)
SEDR .... Systems Engineering Department Report (IEEE)
sed rt.......... Sedimentation Rate [*Hematology*] (DAVI)
SEDS .... Social and Economic Development Strategy
SEDS .... Social-Emotional Dimension Scale [*Behavior problems test*]
SEDS .... Society for Educational Data Systems [*Later, SDE*]
SEDS .... Space Electronics Detection System (KSC)
SEDS .... State Energy Data System [*Department of Energy*] [*Database*]
SEDS .... Students for the Exploration and Development of Space (EA)
SEDS .... Support Equipment Data System
SEDS .... System Effectiveness Data System [*Air Force*]
SEDS .... Systems Engineering Detailed Schedule
SEDSCAF .... Standard ELINT Data System Codes and Format (NVT)
SEDSDR....... Support Equipment Delivery Schedule Delinquency Report (MCD)
SEDT........... Spondyloepiphyseal Dysplasia Tarda [*Medicine*] (DMAA)
SEE............. SAGE [*Semiautomatic Ground Environment*] Evaluation Exercise [*Military*] (IAA)
SEE............. San Diego/Santee, CA [*Location identifier FAA*] (FAAL)
SEE............. Sealed Air [*NYSE symbol*] (TTSB)
SEE............. Sealed Air Corp. [*NYSE symbol*] (SPSG)
SEE............. Secondary Electron Emission
SEE............. Seeing Essential English [*Sign language system for the hearing impaired*]
SEE............. Senior Electronic Engineer (IAA)
SEE............. Senior Environmental Employment
SEE............. Senior Environmental Employment Program [*Environmental Protection Agency*]
SEE............. Signals Experimental Establishment [*British military*] (DMA)
SEE............. Signed Exact English
SEE............. Significant Emotional Events
SEE............. Signing Exact English [*Sign language system for the hearing impaired*]
SEE............. Small Emplacement Excavations [*or Excavator*] [*Army*]
SEE............. Societe d'Etudes et d'Expansion [*Studies and Expansion Society - SES*] [*Later, Et Ex*] (EAIO)
SEE............. Societie pour l'Expansion des Exportations [*Export Development Corp.*] [*Canada*]
SEE............. Society for Excellence in Eyecare (NTPA)
SEE............. Society of Earthbound Extraterrestrials (EA)
SEE............. Society of Electronics Engineers
SEE............. Society of Environmental Engineers [*Later, Institute of Environmental Sciences*]
SEE............. Society of Explosives Engineers (EA)
SEE............. South East Air [*British ICAO designator*] (FAAC)
SEE............. Southeastern Electric Exchange
SEE............. Space Environmental Experiment [*NASA*] (IAA)
SEE............. Special Purpose End Effector (MCD)
SEE............. Standard End Effector (NASA)
SEE............. Standard Error of Estimate
SEE............. Staphylococcal Enterotoxin E [*Medicine*]
SEE............. Stop Everything Environmentalists
SEE............. Summer Educational Enrichment
SEE............. Sun Earth Explorer [*Satellite*] [*NASA*]
SEE............. Support Equipment Exhibit (MCD)
SEE............. Surgical Eye Expeditions International (EAIO)
SEE............. Survival, Evasion, and Escape [*Military*]
SEE............. Systems Effectiveness Engineering (MCD)
SEE............. Systems Effectiveness Evaluation (NG)
SEE............. Systems Efficiency Expert
SEE............. Systems Equipment Engineer [*Telecommunications*] (TEL)
SEEA.......... Societe Europeenne d'Energie Atomique
SEEA.......... Software Error Effects Analysis
SEEA.......... Southeast European Airlines [*Greece*] [*ICAO designator*] (FAAC)
SEE/AN .... Systems Effectiveness Evaluation/Analyzer (DNAB)
SEEAPAC .... Shore Electronic Engineering Activity, Pacific
SEEB.......... Seeburg Industries, Inc. [*NASDAQ symbol*]
SEECA......... Solar Energy and Energy Conservation Act of 1980
SEECA......... State Environmental Education Coordinators Association [*Defunct*] (EA)
SEECCIASDI... Standing EEC [*European Economic Community*] Committee of the International Association of the Soap and Detergent Industry [*See also CPCEAISD*] [*Brussels, Belgium*] (EAIO)
SEECL......... Solar Energy and Energy Conversion Laboratory [*University of Florida*] [*Research center*] (RCD)
SEED.......... DeKalb Genetics [*NASDAQ symbol*] (SAG)
SEED.......... Safe Eye Exposure Distance [*Air Force*]
SEED.......... Schoolhouse Energy Efficiency Demonstration Project (EDAC)
SEED.......... Scientists and Engineers in Economic Development [*National Science Foundation*]
SEED.......... Self-Electro-Optic Effect [*Computer imaging*]
SEED.......... Self Electrooptic Effect Device [*Optical analog of a transistor*]
SEED.......... Sewall Early Education Developmental Profiles

SEED............	Skill Escalation Employment Development (EA)
SEED............	Special Elementary Education for the Disadvantaged
SEED............	Structured Environment for the Emotionally Disturbed Project (EDAC)
SEED............	Strumech Engineering Electronic Developments (NITA)
SEED............	Supply of Essential Engineering Data
SEED............	Support for East European Democracies Act [1989]
SEED............	Sustainable Energy and Environment Division [United Nations]
SEEDB........	DEKALB Genetics'B' [NASDAQ symbol] (TTSB)
SEEDC.........	South East Economic Development Council [Australian Capital Territory]
SEEDIS........	Socio-Economic Demographic Information System [Lawrence Berkeley Laboratory] [Database]
SEEDS.........	Shipboard Equipments Environmental Design Study (PDAA)
SEEDS.........	Ship's Electrical and Electronic Data System (DNAB)
SEEDS.........	Space Exposed Experiment Developed for Students
SEEEE.........	Societe Europeenne d'Etudes et d'Essais d'Environnment [France] (PDAA)
SEEF............	Scientists and Engineers Emigrant Fund
SEEHRL.......	Sanitary Engineering and Environmental Health Research Laboratory [Research center] (RCD)
SEEI............	Special Essential Elements of Information (MCD)
SEEI............	Support Equipment End Item (MCD)
SEE-IN........	Significant Events Evaluation and Information Network
SEE Int'l......	Surgical Eye Expeditions International (EA)
SEEK............	Infoseek Corp. [NASDAQ symbol] (SAG)
SEEK............	Search for Education, Elevation, and Knowledge [Program]
SEEK............	Sooner Exchange for Educational Knowledge [Oklahoma] (EDAC)
SEEK............	Survival, Escape, and Evasion Kit [Navy] (NG)
SEEK............	Systems Evaluation and Exchange of Knowledge [Computer science]
SEEL............	Sex Equity in Educational Leadership Project [Oregon] (EDAC)
SEEL............	Singapore Electronic and Engineering, Ltd. (IAA)
SEEN............	Seeing-Eye Elephant Network [A computer-assisted instruction program] (EDAC)
SEEN............	Syndicat d'Etudes de l'Energie Nucleaire [Belgium]
SEEO............	Salvis Erroribus et Omissis [Errors and Omissions Excepted] [Latin]
SEEO............	Shore Electronic Engineering Office [Navy]
SEEP............	Sex Equity in Education Program (EA)
SEEP............	Shelf Edge Exchange Processes [Oceanography] (NOAA)
SEEP............	Sixth Fleet Escort Evaluation Program [Navy]
SEEP............	Small End-Expiratory Pressure [Medicine] (DAVI)
SEEP............	Stimulated Emission of Energetic Particles [Experiment for study of radio waves]
SEEPZ.........	Santacruz Electronics Export Processing Zone
SEEQ............	SEEQ Technology [NASDAQ symbol] (TTSB)
SEEQ............	SEEQ Technology, Inc. [NASDAQ symbol] (NQ)
SEEQ............	Side-Effects Expectancy Questionnaire [Psychology]
SEER............	Seasonal Energy Efficiency Rating (AAGC)
SEER............	Seasonal Energy-Efficiency Ratio [of heat pumps, air conditioners, etc.]
SEER............	Seer Tech [NASDAQ symbol] (TTSB)
SEER............	Seer Technologies, Inc. [NASDAQ symbol] (SAG)
SEER............	Sensor Experimental Evaluation and Review [Strategic Defense Initiative]
SEER............	Service des Etudes Ecologiques Regionales [Canada]
SEER............	Steam Electric Evaluating and Recording (IAA)
SEER............	Student Exposition on Energy Resources [Project]
SEER............	Submarine Explosive Echo Ranging
SEER............	Supervisory Electronic Engineer [Radio]
SEER............	Surveillance, Epidemiology, and End-Results [Program] [National Cancer Institute]
SEER............	Sustainable Equilibrium Exchange Rate [Economics]
SEER............	System for Electronic Evaluation and Retrieval [Computer science]
SEER............	Systems Engineering, Evaluation, and Research (MCD)
SEEREP.......	Ships' Essential Equipment Requisition Expediting Program [Navy] (NVT)
SEERS.........	Senior Enlisted Evaluation Reports [Military] (INF)
SeerTc.........	Seer Technologies, Inc. [Associated Press] (SAG)
SEES............	Esmeraldas/General Rivadeneira [Ecuador] [ICAO location identifier] (ICLI)
SEES............	Slavic and East European Section [Association of College and Research Libraries]
SEES............	Standard Entry/Exit System [Army]
SEES............	System Effectiveness Engineering Section
SEET............	Science End-to-End Test [Space]
SEET............	Scottish, English, and European Textiles [Commercial firm]
SEETB.........	South East England Tourist Board (DCTA)
SEETEC.......	Sight Enhancement, Education, and Technology
SEEX............	Systems Evaluation Experiment (MCD)
SEF............	Aero Servicios Ejecutivas del Pacifico, SA de CV [Mexico] [FAA designator] (FAAC)
SEF............	SALT Education Fund [Defunct] (EA)
SEF............	Sebring, FL [Location identifier FAA] (FAAL)
SEF............	Self-Extinguishing Fiber [Monsanto Co. trademark]
SEF............	Sequential Excitation Fluorescence [Aviation Navy]
SEF............	Shielding Effectiveness Factor
SEF............	Shock Excited Filter (IAA)
SEF............	Simple Environment Factor
SEF............	Simulated Engine Failure (ADA)
SEF............	Single Equivalent Formant (IAA)
SEF............	Small-End Forward [of command module]
SEF............	Software Engineering Facility
SEF............	Solar Energy Flux
SEF............	Somatically Evoked Field [Neurophysiology]
SEF............	Sound Energy Flux
SEF............	Southern Education Foundation (EA)
SEF............	Space Education Foundation [Later, AEF]
SEF............	Space Environmental Facility (SAA)
SEF............	Special Entry Flying List [Navy British]
SEF............	Stability Enhancement Function [Aviation] (GFGA)
SEF............	Standard External File
SEF............	Staphylococcus Aureus Enterotoxin F [Toxic shock toxin]
SEF............	Storage Extension Frame (NITA)
SEF............	Surface Effect Ship
SEF............	Systems Engineering Facility [Defense Communications Agency] (RDA)
SEFA............	Scientific Equipment and Furniture Association (NTPA)
SE/FAC........	Support Equipment/Facility [NASA] (NASA)
SEFACAN.....	Segregator, Facer, Canceller Machine
SEFAR.........	Sonic End Fire for Azimuth and Range
SEFC...........	Southeast Fisheries Center [Miami, FL] [National Marine Fisheries Service] (MSC)
SEFCAR.......	Southeast Florida and Caribbean Recruitment [Marine science] (OSRA)
SEFCL.........	Southeastern Fish Control Station [Department of the Interior] (GRD)
SEFD...........	Solar Energy Flux Density
SEFE...........	Societe Europenne pour la Formation des Ingenieurs (ACII)
SEFE...........	Standardization Evaluation Flight Examiner
SEFEL.........	Secretariat Europeen des Fabricants d'Emballages Metalliques Legers [European Secretariat of Manufacturers of Light Metal Packages] (EA)
SEFES.........	Southeastern Forest Experiment Station [Asheville, NC] [Department of Agriculture] (GRD)
SEFEWS......	Scientists and Engineers Field Experience with Soldiers (RDA)
SEFF...........	Snakeye Free-Fall [Navy] (DNAB)
SEFI...........	Sequential Electric Fuel Injection [Automotive engineering]
SEFI...........	Societe Europeenne pour la Formation des Ingenieurs [European Society for Engineering Education] (EA)
SEFIC.........	Seventh Fleet Intelligence Center [Navy]
SEFIC.........	Spoken English for Industry and Commerce (AIE)
SEFIP.........	Statistical Estimation Fault Isolation Procedure (MCD)
SEFIS.........	Small Engine Fuel Injection System
SEFLIN.......	Southeast Florida Library Information Network
SEFLO........	Sequence Flow [Tracing technique]
SEFM..........	Support Equipment Field Modification (AAG)
SEFOR........	Southwest Experimental Fast Oxide Reactor [Nuclear energy]
SEFR..........	Shielding Experiment Facility Reactor [Nuclear energy]
SEFR..........	Support Equipment for Robot (DWSG)
SEFR..........	System Effectiveness Forecast Report
SEFRL........	Southeastern Field Research Laboratory [Pennsylvania State University]
SEFS..........	Special Elite Forces Society (EA)
SefT...........	Sefer Torah. Post-Talmudic Tractate (BJA)
SEFT..........	Single Engine Flight Training
SEFT..........	Society for Education in Film and Television [British]
SEFT..........	Spin-Echo Fourier Transform [Physics]
SEG............	Saturday Evening Girls [Decorators of Arts and Crafts pottery]
SEG............	Scientific Ecology Group Inc. (GAAI)
SEG............	Screen Extras Guild (EA)
SEG............	Seagate Technology [NYSE symbol] (TTSB)
SEG............	Seagate Technology, Inc. [NYSE symbol] (SAG)
SEG............	Sealing
SEG............	Segment (AAG)
SEG............	Segno [Sign] [Music]
seg............	Segregation Block (WDAA)
SEG............	Segue [Follows] [Music]
SEG............	Selective Epitaxial Growth [Semiconductor technology]
SEG............	Selinsgrove, PA [Location identifier FAA] (FAAL)
SEG............	Sequence of Events Generator
SEG............	Side Entry Goniometer
SEG............	Skyline [Norway ICAO designator] (FAAC)
SEG............	Sliding Electron Gun
SEG............	Society of Economic Geologists (EA)
SEG............	Society of Exploration Geophysicists (EA)
SEG............	Socio-Economic Grade (ODBW)
SEG............	Soft Elastic Gelatin [Medicine] (DMAA)
SEG\...........	Solartron Electronic Group (IAA)
SEG............	Sonoencephalogram (AAMN)
SEG............	Special Effect Generator [Video technology]
SEG............	Special-Effects Generator [Filmmaking] (WDMC)
SEG............	Standardization Evaluation Group (AFM)
SEG............	Subesophageal Ganglion [Anatomy]
SEG............	System Engineering Groundrule [NASA] (NASA)
SEG............	Systems Engineering Group [Air Force]
SEG............	Systems Evaluation Group
SEGAX........	SunAmerica Small Co. Growth Cl.A [Mutual fund ticker symbol] (SG)
SEGBA........	Servicios Electricos del Gran Buenos Aires, SA [Electrical utility] [Argentina]
SEGD..........	Society of Environmental Graphics Designers (EA)
SEGE..........	Guale [Ecuador] [ICAO location identifier] (ICLI)
SEGH..........	Society for Environmental Geochemistry and Health (EA)
SEGL..........	Gul [Ecuador] [ICAO location identifier] (ICLI)
SEGM..........	Segment
SEGMOS......	Service Goods Movement System (IAA)
SEGR..........	Guarumal [Ecuador] [ICAO location identifier] (ICLI)
SEG/R & T...	Systems Engineering Group/Research and Technology [Air Force]
SEGS..........	Galapagos (Baltra) [Ecuador] [ICAO location identifier] (ICLI)
segs...........	Segmented Neutrophils [Also, polymorphonuclear leukocytes and segmented white cells] [Immunochemistry] (DAVI)
SEGS	Solar Electric Generating System
SEGS	Solar Energy Generating System (IAA)

SEGSYS.......	Segmentation System (IAA)
SEGU..........	Guayaquil/Simon Bolivar [Ecuador] [ICAO location identifier] (ICLI)
SEGU..........	Segue Software [NASDAQ symbol] (TTSB)
SEGU..........	Segue Software, Inc. [NASDAQ symbol] (SAG)
SegueS.......	Segue Software, Inc. [Associated Press] (SAG)
SEGV..........	Segmentation Violation [Computer science] (NHD)
SEGZ..........	Gualaquiza [Ecuador] [ICAO location identifier] (ICLI)
SEH............	Sehore [India] [Seismograph station code, US Geological Survey] (SEIS)
SEH............	Seriously Emotionally Handicapped [Psychology] (DHP)
SEH............	Shuttle Electronic Hardware [NASA]
SEH............	Single-Engined Helicopter (MCD)
SEH............	Societe Europeenne d'Hematologie
SEH............	Solar Equivalent Hours
SEH............	Spartech Corp. [NYSE symbol] (SAG)
SEH............	Standard Electrik Hellas (NITA)
SEH............	Star/Earth Horizon Sightings
SEH............	Strobel, E. H., Saint Louis MO [STAC]
SEH............	Subependymal Hemorrhage [Medicine]
SEH............	Waglisla Air, Inc. [Canada ICAO designator] (FAAC)
SEHAB	Sea Rehabilitation [Navy] (NVT)
SEHI...........	Cotacachi [Ecuador] [ICAO location identifier] (ICLI)
SEHI...........	Southern Energy Homes [NASDAQ symbol] (TTSB)
SEHI...........	Southern Energy Homes, Inc. [NASDAQ symbol] (SAG)
SEHK..........	Stock Exchange of Hong Kong (NUMA)
SEHK	Swedish Export Credit Corp. [Associated Press] (SAG)
SE-HPLC......	Size Exclusion-High Performance Liquid Chromatography
SEHPP........	Science and Environmental Health Policy Project
SEHSC........	Silicones Environmental Health and Safety Council of North America (NTPA)
SEHT..........	Hacienda Taura [Ecuador] [ICAO location identifier] (ICLI)
SEI............	Safety Equipment Institute (EA)
SEI............	Seitel, Inc. [NYSE symbol] (SPSG)
SEI............	Self Employment Income [Social Security Administration] (OICC)
SEI............	Self-Esteem Inventory [Coopersmith] (EDAC)
SEI............	Senhor Do Bonfim [Brazil] [Airport symbol] (OAG)
SEI............	Shane Resources [Vancouver Stock Exchange symbol]
SEI............	Sign and Engraving Institute (NTPA)
SEI............	Sisson Enterprises, Inc. (EFIS)
SEI............	Societa Editrice Internazionale [Italy] [Publisher]
SEI............	Societas Ergophthalmologica Internationalis [International Ergophthalmological Society] [Stockholm, Sweden] (EAIO)
SEI............	Society of Engineering Illustrators (EA)
SEI............	Society of Environmental Improvement [British] (DBA)
SEI............	Software Engineering Institute [DoD]
SEI............	Solid Electrolyte Interphase [Battery technology]
SEI............	Southeast Institute for Group and Family Therapy (EA)
SEI............	Space Exploration Initiative [NASA]
SEI............	Special Engineering Investigation (MCD)
SEI............	Special Equipment Item (MCD)
SEI............	Special Experience Identifier [Military]
SFI............	Statistical Engineering Institute (MCD)
SEI............	Stern Environment Indexes [Psychology]
SEI............	Stockholm Environment Institute
SEI............	Stockpile Entry Inspection [Navy] (NG)
SEI............	Stray Energy Indicator
SEI............	Stress Evaluation Inventory [Test]
SEI............	Sumitomo Electric Industries [Auto industry supplier]
SEI............	Superficial Epithelial Infiltrates [Ophthalmology] (DAVI)
SEI............	Support Equipment Illustration (MCD)
SEI............	Support Equipment Installation [NASA] (NASA)
SEI............	Sykes Enterprises, Inc. (PCM)
SEI............	System Engineering Instrumentation (NASA)
SEI............	System/Equipment Inventory
SEIA..........	Security Equipment Industry Association (EA)
SEIA..........	Socioeconomic Impact Analysis (COE)
SEIA..........	Solar Energy Industries Association (EA)
SEIA..........	Solar Energy Institute of America [Later, SEINAM] (MCD)
SEIAC.........	Science Education Information Analysis Center [ERIC]
SEIB..........	Ibarra [Ecuador] [ICAO location identifier] (ICLI)
SEIB..........	Service des Etudes et Inventaires Bio-Physiques [Quebec]
SEIB..........	Statistical and Economic Information Bulletin for Africa [A publication]
Seibel........	Seibels [Bruce] Group, Inc. [Associated Press] (SAG)
SEIC...........	SEI Corp. [NASDAQ symbol] (NQ)
SEIC...........	SEI Investments Co. [NASDAQ symbol] (SAG)
SEIC...........	Solar Energy Information Center
SEIC...........	Syndicat de l'Emploi et de l'Immigration du Canada
SEIC...........	System Effectiveness Information Central
SEICO	Science and Engineering Information Center Co. (IID)
SEICO	Support Equipment Installation and Checkout [NASA] (NASA)
SEICorp.......	SEI Corp. [Associated Press] (SAG)
SEID..........	Support Equipment Illustration Data (MCD)
SEIDB........	Solar Energy Information Data Bank [Department of Energy]
SEIE..........	Submarine Escape Immersion Equipment
SEIF...........	Speak Easy International Foundation (EA)
SEIFR.........	Support Equipment End Item Funding Report (MCD)
SEIG..........	Intag [Ecuador] [ICAO location identifier] (ICLI)
Seign Rep ...	Lower Canada Seignorial Questions Reports [A publication] (DLA)
SEI Inv	SEI Investments Co. [Associated Press] (SAG)
SEIL..........	Science Experiments Integration Laboratories
SEIL..........	Southeastern Educational Improvement Laboratory [Research Triangle Park, NC] [Department of Education] (GRD)
SEIM..........	Isla San Miguel [Ecuador] [ICAO location identifier] (ICLI)
SEIM..........	Software Engineering Improvement Method (AAEL)
SEIMC.........	Special Education Instructional Materials Centers [Office of Education] [Database producer] (IID)
SEIMS.........	State Economic Information Management System [State Department] [Database]
SEINAM	Solar Energy Institute of North America [Defunct] (EA)
SEIOD........	Spogli Elettronici dell'Italiano delle Origini e del Duecento [A lexical, morphological, and syntactical inventory of Old Italian texts]
SEIP..........	Strategy for Exploration of the Inner Planets (IAA)
SEIP..........	System Engineering Implementation Plan
SEIR...........	Solar Energy Intelligence Report [Business Publishers Inc.] [No longer available online] [Information service or system] (CRD)
SEIR...........	Southeast Indian Ridge [Antarctica] [Geology]
SEIR...........	Susceptible, Exposed, Infected or Immune, Recovered [Epidemiological model]
SEIRS	Suppliers and Equipment Information Retrieval System [International Civil Aviation Organization] [Databank] [Information service or system] (IID)
SEIS...........	Solar Energy Information Services (IID)
SEIS...........	Submarine Emergency Identification Signal (NG)
SEIS...........	Supplemental Environmental Impact Statement [Department of Agriculture]
SEISA..........	South Eastern Intercollegiate Sailing Association
SEISMOG.....	Seismographic
SEISMOL	Seismologic
SEIT...........	Satellite Educational and Informational Television
SEIT...........	Supervisory Electronic Installation Technician
SEIT...........	System Engineering Integration and Test (MCD)
SEIT...........	System Evaluation, Integration, and Test (MCD)
Seitel........	Seitel, Inc. [Associated Press] (SAG)
SEIU..........	Service Employees International Union (EA)
SEIWG........	Security Equipment Integration Working Group
SE/IWT.......	Southern Europe - Inland Waterways Transport [NATO] (NATG)
SEJ...........	Sliding Expansion Joint [Technical drawings]
SEJ...........	Society of Environmental Journalists (NTPA)
SEJ...........	Southeastern Jurisdictional Conference [United Methodist Church]
SEJA..........	Jaramillo [Ecuador] [ICAO location identifier] (ICLI)
SEJCR........	Societe Europeenne des Jeunes de la Croix-Bleue [European Society for Blue Cross Youth - ESBCY] (EAIO)
SEJI...........	Jipijapa [Ecuador] [ICAO location identifier] (ICLI)
SEK...........	Salomon, Inc. [AMEX symbol] (SAG)
SEK...........	Salomon Inc. 7.625% SNPL'ELKS' [AMEX symbol] (TTSB)
SEK...........	Standard Electric Kirk (NITA)
SEK...........	Synomospondia Ergaton Kyprou [Cyprus Workers' Confederation] ["Free Labour Syndicats"]
SEKE..........	Sosialistikon Ergatikon Komma tis Elladas [Socialist Labor Party of Greece] [Forerunner of Greek Communist Party (KKE)] (PPE)
SEKF..........	Sister Elizabeth Kenny Foundation [Later, SKI]
SEKLS.........	Southeast Kansas Library System [Library network]
SEKRLC	Southeastern Kentucky Regional Library Cooperative [Library network]
Sel..............	Ducretet-Thomson [Formerly, Ducretet Selmer] [Record label] [France]
SEL............	Safety Engineering Laboratory [British] (IRUK)
SEL............	Satellite Experiment Laboratory [National Oceanic and Atmospheric Administration] (GRD)
SEL............	School of Electric Light [British military] (DMA)
SEL............	Scouts' Esperanto League (EA)
SEL............	Select [or Selection] (AAG)
Sel............	Select (WPI)
SEL............	Selectair Ltd. [British ICAO designator] (FAAC)
SEL............	Selected Equipment List (NVT)
sel............	Selection [Literature]
Sel............	Selection (AL)
SEL............	Selective (IAA)
SEL............	Selector (IAA)
Sel............	Seleucid Era (BJA)
SEL............	Seligman Select Municipal Fund [NYSE symbol] (SPSG)
SEL............	Seligman Select Muni Fund [NYSE symbol] (TTSB)
SEL............	Selkirk College Library [UTLAS symbol]
sel............	Selkup [MARC language code Library of Congress] (LCCP)
SEL............	Semi-Effective List [British military] (DMA)
SEL............	Semlyachik [Former USSR Seismograph station code, US Geological Survey] (SEIS)
SEL............	Sensitized-Erythrocyte-Lysis (PDAA)
SEL............	SENTEL Corp. [FAA designator] (FAAC)
SEL............	Seoul [South Korea] [Airport symbol] (OAG)
SEL............	Signal Engineering Laboratories (AAG)
SEL............	Single Engine Land [Pilot rating] (AIA)
SEL............	Skolta Esperanto-Ligo [Scouts' Esperanto League] (EAIO)
SEL............	Socialist Electoral League [Norway] (PPW)
SEL............	Software Engineering Laboratory [NASA] (MCD)
SEL............	Solar Environmental Laboratory [National Oceanic and Atmospheric Administration]
SEL............	Southeastern Educational Laboratory
SEL............	Space Environment Laboratory [Boulder, CO] [Department of Commerce National Oceanic and Atmospheric Administration]
SEL............	Spontaneously Emitted Light
SEL............	Standard Elektrik Lorenz AG [Germany]
SEL............	Stanford Electronics Laboratory [Stanford University] [Research center] (MCD)
SEL............	Star/Earth Landmark Sightings
SEL............	Super Einspritz Lang [Fuel-injection, long wheelbase] [As in 450 SEL, the model number of a Mercedes-Benz automobile]
SEL............	Support Equipment List [Navy]
SEL............	Surface Emitting LASER

SEL	System Electronics Laboratory (MCD)
SEL	System Engineering Laboratories (MCD)
SELA	Lago Agrio [Ecuador] [ICAO location identifier] (ICLI)
SELA	Select Appointments Holdings [NASDAQ symbol] (SAG)
SELA	Southeastern Library Association (AEBS)
SELA	Systeme Economique Latino-Americain [Latin American Economic System - LAES] [French]
SELACJ	Secretariado Latinoamericano de la Compania de Jesus [Latin American Bureau of Society of Jesus] (EAIO)
SELANE	Secure Local-Area Network [Computer science]
Sel App Beng	Selected Appeals, Sadr Diwani Adalat [Bengal, India] [A publication] (DLA)
Selas	Selas Corp. of America [Associated Press] (SAG)
SELAVIP	Servicio Latinoamericano y Asiatico de Vivienda Popular [Latin American and Asian low Income Housing Service] [Chile] (EAIO)
SELB	Sel-Leb Marketing [NASDAQ symbol] (TTSB)
SELB	Sel-Leb Marketing, Inc. [NASDAQ symbol] (SAG)
SELB	Southern Education and Library Board [Northern Ireland] (AIE)
SelBab	Babylonian Seleucid Era (BJA)
SELBUS	Systems Engineering Laboratories Data Bus (NITA)
SELBW	Sel-Leb Marketing Wrrt [NASDAQ symbol] (TTSB)
SELC	La Cecilia [Ecuador] [ICAO location identifier] (ICLI)
SELC	South East London College [London, England]
SELC	Southern Environmental Law Center (WPI)
SELC	Synod of Evangelical Lutheran Churches (IIA)
SELCAL	Selective Calling [Radio]
Sel Cas	Select Cases, Central Provinces [India] [A publication] (DLA)
Sel Cas Ch	Select Cases in Chancery [England] [A publication] (DLA)
Sel Cas Ch (T King)	Select Cases in Chancery Tempore King [25 English Reprint] [1724-33] [A publication] (DLA)
Sel Cas DA	Select Cases, Sadr Diwani Adalat [India] [A publication] (DLA)
Sel Cas Ev	Select Cases in Evidence (Strange) [England] [A publication] (DLA)
Sel Cas KB Edw I	Select Cases in King's Bench under Edward I (Sayles) [England] [A publication] (DLA)
Sel Cas NF	Select Cases, Newfoundland [A publication] (DLA)
Sel Cas NWP	Select Cases, Northwest Provinces [India] [A publication] (DLA)
Sel Cas NY	Yate's Select Cases [1809] [New York] [A publication] (DLA)
Sel Cas SDA	Select Cases, Sadr Diwani Adalat [Bengal, Bombay, India] [A publication] (DLA)
Sel Cas T King	Select Cases in Chancery Tempore King [England] [A publication] (DLA)
Sel Cas T Nap	Select Cases Tempore Napier [Ireland] [A publication] (DLA)
Sel Cas with Opin	Select Cases with Opinions by a Solicitor [A publication] (DLA)
Sel Ca T King	Select Cases in Chancery Tempore King [25 English Reprint] [1724-33] [A publication] (DLA)
SELCH	Selector Channel
Sel Ch Cas	Select Cases in Chancery Tempore King, Edited by Macnaghten [England] [A publication] (DLA)
SELCIR	Systems Engineering Laboratory Circuit-Drawing Program (PDAA)
Sel Col Cas	Select Collection of Cases [England] [A publication] (DLA)
SELCOM	Select Committee [Army Materiel Command]
Selctln	Selective Insurance Group [Associated Press] (SAG)
SELCTV	Selected Television [Commercial firm British]
Seld	Selden's New York Reports [5-10 New York] [A publication] (DLA)
SELD	Snakeye Low-Drag [Navy] (DNAB)
SELDADS	SEL [Space Environmental Laboratory] Data Acquisition and Display System (USDC)
SELDADS	Space Environment Laboratory Data Acquisition and Display System [National Oceanic and Atmospheric Administration]
SELDAM	Selective Data Management System (MHDI)
Sel Dec Bomb	Select Cases, Sadr Diwani Adalat [Bombay, India] [A publication] (DLA)
SEL DECK	Select Decking [Lumber]
Sel Dec Madr	Select Decrees, Sadr Adalat [Madras, India] [A publication] (DLA)
Selden	Selden's New York Court of Appeals Reports [A publication] (DLA)
Selden Notes	Selden's New York Court of Appeals Notes of Cases [1st ed.] [1853] [A publication] (DLA)
Seld Fl	Selden's Dissertatio ad Fletam [A publication] (ILCA)
Seld J	Selden's Jani Anglorum [A publication] (ILCA)
Seld JP	Selden's Judicature in Parliaments [1681] [A publication] (ILCA)
Seld Mar Cl	Selden's Mare Clausum [A publication] (ILCA)
Seld Mare Claus	Selden's Mare Clausum [A publication] (DLA)
Seld Notes	Selden's New York Court of Appeals Notes [A publication] (DLA)
Seld Off Ch	Selden's Office of Lord Chancellor [1671] [A publication] (DLA)
SELDOM	Selected Dissemination of MARC (NITA)
Seld R	Selden's New York Court of Appeals Reports [A publication] (DLA)
Seld Soc	Selden Society (DLA)
Seld Soc Yrbk	Selden Society Yearbook [United States] [A publication] (DLA)
Seld Tit Hon	Selden's Titles of Honor [A publication] (DLA)
SELEC	Select (ROG)
SElec	Society of Electroscience [British] (DBA)
SELEC	Superelastic LASER Energy Conversion (MCD)
SELECTAVISION	Selected Television Video Disc System (NITA)
SELENE	Selenological and Engineering Explorer
SELEX	Systematic Evolution of Ligands by Exponential Enrichment [Genetics]
SELF	National Citizens Committee to Save Education and Library Funds
SELF	Self-Eject Launch Facility [NASA] (MCD)
SELF	Short Expeditious Landing Field (CINC)
SELF	Simplicity, Efficiency, Lower Rates, and Fairness Tax Plan
SELF	Societe des Ecrivains Luxembourgeois de Langue Francaise
SELF	Student Education Loan Fund [Minnesota]
SELF	Submarine Extremely Low Frequency Radio [Navy]
Selfcare	Selfcare, Inc. [Associated Press] (SAG)

Selfix	Selfix, Inc. [Associated Press] (SAG)
SELFOC	Self Focusing [Optics] (EECA)
SELFTAV	Self-Conducted Tender Availability [Navy] (NVT)
Self Tr	Selfridge's Trial [A publication] (DLA)
SELGEM	Self-Generating Master [Information management system] [Computer science]
SELI	Limoncocha [Ecuador] [ICAO location identifier] (ICLI)
SeligQual	Seligman Quality Municipal Fund [Associated Press] (SAG)
SeligSel	Seligman Select Municipal Fund [Associated Press] (SAG)
SELJ	La Julia [Ecuador] [ICAO location identifier] (ICLI)
SELK	Selkirkshire [County in Scotland]
SELL	Llurimaguas [Ecuador] [ICAO location identifier] (ICLI)
SELL	Sales Environment Learning Laboratory [Computer-based marketing game]
SELL	Suomi, Eesti, Latvija, Lietuva [Finland, Estonia, Latvia, Lithuania]
Sel L Cas	Select Law Cases [England] [A publication] (DLA)
Sel-Leb	Sel-Leb Marketing, Inc. [Associated Press] (SAG)
Sell Pr	Sellon's Practice in the King's Bench [A publication] (DLA)
Sell Prac	Sellon's Practice in the King's Bench [A publication] (DLA)
SellrPol	Seller Pollution Control [Associated Press] (SAG)
SELM	Loma Larga [Ecuador] [ICAO location identifier] (ICLI)
SE/LM	Systems Engineering/Logistics Management (MCD)
SELMA	Southeastern Lumber Manufacturers Association (WPI)
SelMac	Macedonian Seleucid Era (BJA)
SEL MERC	Select Merchantable [Lumber]
SELMOUS	Special English Language Materials for Overseas University Students
SELN	Limon [Ecuador] [ICAO location identifier] (ICLI)
SELN	Selection (AAG)
Sel NP	Selwyn's Law of Nisi Prius [A publication] (DLA)
SELO	Loja (La Toma) [Ecuador] [ICAO location identifier] (ICLI)
SELO	Some Essential Learner Outcomes [Minnesota] (EDAC)
Sel Off Ch	Selden's Office of Lord Chancellor [1671] [A publication] (DLA)
SELOR	Ship Emitter Location Report [Navy] (CAAL)
SELP	Senior Executive Leadership Program [Australia]
SELPA	Special Eduation Local Planning Agency (EDAC)
Sel Pr	Sellon's Practice [A publication] (DLA)
S/ELPS	Spanish/English Language Performance Screening (EDAC)
SELR	Saturn Engineering Liaison Request [NASA] (KSC)
SELR	Selector (AAG)
SELR	Support Equipment List Requirement (MCD)
SELRAS	SEL [Space Environmental Laboratory] Research and Analysis System (USDC)
SELREC	Shore Electronics Reconnaissance System
SELRECT	Selenium Rectifier (IAA)
SELREFTRA	Selected Refresher Training [Navy] (NVT)
SEL REL	Selective Release (COE)
SELRES	Selected Reserve [Military]
SELRFT	Selected Refresher Training [Navy] (NVT)
SELS	Selective Service
sels	SELSYN [Military] (BARN)
SELS	Severe Local Storm [National Weather Service]
SELS	Space Environment Laboratory Simulation [NASA]
SELSA	Southeast Library Service Area [Library network]
Sel Serv L Rep	Selective Service Law Reporter [A publication] (DLA)
Sel Serv L Rptr	Selective Service Law Reporter [A publication] (DLA)
SEL STR	Select Structural [Lumber]
SELSW	Selector Switch (MCD)
SELSYN	Self-Synchronizing [or Synchronous] (IAA)
SELSYN	Self-Synchronous [Trade name] [Motor]
sel-sync	Selective Synchronization (WDAA)
SELT	Latacunga [Ecuador] [ICAO location identifier] (ICLI)
SELT	SAGE [Semiautomatic Ground Environment] Evaluation Library Tape
SELT	Self-Eject Launch Technique [NASA] (KSC)
SELT	Sheet Explosive Loading Technique
SELTA	Swedish-English Literary Translators Association [British] (DBA)
SELTEC	South East London Technical College [British] (DI)
SELV	Safety Extra Low Voltage (IAA)
Selvac	Selvac Corp. [Associated Press] (SAG)
SELW	Selwyn College [Cambridge] [British] (ROG)
Selw	Selwyn's Law of Nisi Prius [England] [A publication] (DLA)
Selw & Barn	Barnewall and Alderson's English King's Bench Reports [1st part] [A publication] (DLA)
Selw NP	Selwyn's Law of Nisi Prius [England] [A publication] (DLA)
SEM	Cape Central Airways, Inc. [ICAO designator] (FAAC)
SEM	Satellite to Earth Missile
SEM	Scanning Electron Microscope [or Microscopy]
SEM	Scanning Electron Microscopy [Later, SMI] [An association] (EA)
SEM	Schedule Evaluation Model
SEM	Secondary Electron Multiplier [Detector]
SEM	Secondary Emission Material (IAA)
SEM	Secondary Emission Microscope
SEM	Secondary Emission Monitor
SEM	Secondary Enrichment Medium [Microbiology]
SEM	Security Environmental Systems, Inc. [Vancouver Stock Exchange symbol]
SEM	Seller's Engineering Memo [NASA] (NASA)
SEM	Selma, AL [Location identifier FAA] (FAAL)
Sem	Semahoth (BJA)
SEM	Semaphore
SEM	Semble [It Seems]
SEM	Semel [Once]
SEM	Semen (WGA)
SEM	Semester
SEM	Semi [One-Half] [Pharmacy]
SEM	Semicolon

sem	Semicolon (WDMC)
SEM	Semiconductor Electronic Memory (IAA)
SEM	Semiconductor Packaging Materials [*AMEX symbol*] (SAG)
SEM	Semienriched Minimal [*Agar*]
SEM	Semimobile (WGA)
SEM	Seminal (WGA)
SEM	Seminary
Sem	Seminary (AL)
SEM	Semipalatinsk [*Former USSR Seismograph station code, US Geological Survey*] (SEIS)
sem	Semitic [*MARC language code Library of Congress*] (LCCP)
SEM	Semitic [*Language, etc.*]
SEM	Sempre [*Throughout*] [*Music*]
SEM	Shared Equity Mortgage
SEM	Single European Market
SEM	Singularity Expansion Method (IEEE)
SEM	Society for Ethnic Missions [*Australia*]
SEM	Society for Ethnomusicology (EA)
SEM	Society for Experimental Mechanics (EA)
SEM	Society of Engineers and Machinists [*A union*] [*British*]
SEM	Soft Ejection Murmur [*Cardiology*] (DAVI)
SEM	Software Encapsulation Methodologies
SEM	Solar Environment Monitor
SEM	Solvent Extraction Milling (BARN)
SEM	Somatosensory Evoked Potential [*Neurology*] (DAVI)
SEM	Sortie Effectiveness Model [*NASA*] (MCD)
SEM	Southeast Missouri State University, Cape Girardeau, MO [*OCLC symbol*] (OCLC)
SEM	Southeast Monsoon
SEM	Southern Illinois University at Carbondale Center for Electron Microscopy [*Research center*] (RCD)
SEM	Space Environment Monitor [*NASA*]
SEM	Special Electric Motors [*Manufacturing company*] [*British*]
SEM	Standard Electronic Module (CAAL)
SEM	Standard Equipment Modules [*Navy*] (DOMA)
SEM	Standard Error of Measurement [*Testing*]
SEM	Standard Error of the Mean
SEM	Standard Estimating Module (IEEE)
SEM	State-Event Matrix [*Computer science*]
SEM	Station Engineering Manual [*Telecommunications*] (TEL)
SEM	Stereoscan Electron Microscope
SEM	Stray Energy Monitor
SEM	Structural Econometric Model [*Statistics*]
SEM	Structural Equation Modeling
SEM	Stupid Error Message [*Computer science*]
SEM	Subarray Electronics Module [*Computer science*]
SEM	Subcontractor Engineering Memorandum (MCD)
SEM	Supplimental Education Material
SEM	System Effectiveness Measure (IAA)
SEM	System Effectiveness Model (CAAI)
SEM	System Engineering Management [*NASA*]
S-E-M	Systems/Equipment/Munitions [*Army*] (AFIT)
SEM	Systolic Ejection Murmur [*Cardiology*]
SEMA	Macara [*Ecuador*] [*ICAO location identifier*] (ICLI)
SEMA	Semiotic Abstracts [*A publication*]
SEMA	Societe d'Etudes de Mathematiques Appliquees [*France*]
SEMA	Special Electronic Mission Aircraft (RDA)
SEMA	Specialty Equipment Manufacturers Association
SEMA	Specialty Equipment Market Association [*Later, SFI*] (EA)
SEMA	Spray Equipment Manufacturers' Association [*British*] (BI)
SEMA	Storage Equipment Manufacturers Association [*British*] (DBA)
SEMAA	Safety Equipment Manufacturers Agents Association (EA)
SEMANOL	Semantics-Oriented Language [*Computer science*] (PDAA)
SEMAT	Ship Electronic Module Assembly Test (DNAB)
SEMATECH	Semiconductor Manufacturing Technology (DOMA)
SEMATECH	Semiconductor Manufacturing Technology Consortium
SEMBEGS	Simply Extended and Modified Batch Environmental Graphical System (MHDI)
SEMBRAT	Single Echelon Multi-Base Resource Allocation Technique (PDAA)
SEMC	Macas [*Ecuador*] [*ICAO location identifier*] (ICLI)
SEMC	Semi-Tech Corp. [*NASDAQ symbol*] (SAG)
SEMC	State Emergency Management Committee [*New South Wales, Australia*]
SEMCA	Shipboard Electromagnetic Computability Analysis (DNAB)
SEMCC	Southeastern Massachusetts Health Sciences Libraries Consortium [*Library network*]
SEMCF	Semi-Tech Corp. 'A' [*NASDAQ symbol*] (TTSB)
SEMCIP	Shipboard Electromagnetic Capability Improvement Program [*Navy*] (NVT)
SEMCOG	Southeast Michigan Council of Governments [*Detroit, MI*]
SEMCOR	Semantic Correlation [*Machine-aided indexing*]
SEMD	Spondyloepimetaphyseal Dysplasia [*Medicine*] (DMAA)
SEMD	Stray Energy Monitor Device
SEMDJL	Spondylo-Epimetaphyseal Dysplasia with Joint Laxity [*Medicine*] (DMAA)
SEMDP	Senior Executive/Management Development Plan (DNAB)
SEM-E	Standard Electronic Module-E Format (MCD)
SEMEL in D	Semel in Die [*Once a Day*] [*Pharmacy*]
SEMET	Self-Evident Meteorological Code (NATG)
SEMG	Scanning Electron Micrograph
SEMG	Semenogelin (DMAA)
SEMH	Machala [*Ecuador*] [*ICAO location identifier*] (ICLI)
SEMH	Service Engineering Man-Hours
SEMHI	Southeastern Manufactured Housing Institute [*Later, Manufactured Housing Institute*] (EA)

SEMI	All American Semiconductor, Inc. [*NASDAQ symbol*] (NQ)
SEMI	All Amer Semiconductor [*NASDAQ symbol*] (TTSB)
SEMI	Self-Evacuating Multilayer Insulation [*System*]
SEMI	Semiconductor Equipment and Materials Institute (EA)
SEMI	Semiconductor Equipment and Materials Institute, Inc.
SEMI	Semiconductor Equipment and Materials International (AAEL)
semi	Semis [*One-Half*] [*Latin Pharmacy*] (MAE)
semi	Semitrailer [*Truck and trailer rigs*] (DAVI)
SEMI	Shipboard Electromagnetic Interference [*Navy*] (CAAL)
SEMI	Societe d'Etudes de Marche et d'Informatique [*Society for the Study of Marketing and Informatics*] [*Information service or system Defunct*] (IID)
SEMI	Special Electromagnetic Interference (MCD)
SEMI	Subendocardial Myocardial Infarction [*Cardiology*] (MAE)
SEMI	Subendorcardial Myocardial Injury [*Cardiology*] (MAE)
SEMIAUT	Semiautomatic (IAA)
SEMICON	Semiconductor (IAA)
SEMICOND	Semiconductor
semid	Semidrachma [*Half a Drachm*] [*Latin Pharmacy*] (MAE)
SEMIDR	Semidrachma [*Half a Drachma*] [*Pharmacy*]
SEMIH	Semihora [*Half an Hour*] [*Pharmacy*]
SEMIKON	Seminare/Konferenzen [*Seminars/Conferences*] [*Society for Business Information*] [*Information service or system*] [*Defunct*] (IID)
SemiLas	Semiconductor Laser International Corp. [*Associated Press*] (SAG)
SEMINEX	Seminary in Exile [*Liberal-oriented Lutheran seminary*]
SEMIRA	System of Electronic Marks' Interrogation, Registration, and Administration [*Database*] [*WIPO*] [*United Nations*] (DUND)
SEMIRAD	Secondary Electron-Mixed Radiation Dosimeter (IEEE)
SEMIROX	Semi-Recessed Oxide (PDAA)
SEMIS	Solar Energy Monitor in Space [*NASA*] (MCD)
SEMIS	State Extension Management Information System [*Department of Agriculture*]
SEMISPIN	Semiconductor Software Process Improvement Network (AAEL)
SemiTch	Semi-Tech Corp. [*Associated Press*] (SAG)
Semitool	Semitool, Inc. [*Associated Press*] (SAG)
SEML	Manglaralto [*Ecuador*] [*ICAO location identifier*] (ICLI)
SEMLAM	Semiconductor LASER Amplifier
SEMLAT	Semiconductor LASER Array Techniques
SEMLSB	Systolic Ejection Murmur, Left Sternal Border [*Cardiovascular*] (DAVI)
SEMM	Scanning Electron Mirror Microscope (IAA)
SEMM	Single Electron MOS [*Metal Oxide Semiconductor*] Memory
SEMM	Smoke Effectiveness Manual Model (MCD)
SEMM	Societe Europeenne de Materials Mobiles [*France*] (PDAA)
SEMM	Solar Electric Multiple-Mission (MCD)
SEMMS	Solar Electric Multiple-Mission Spacecraft
SEMN	Slow Extension Motoneuron [*Neurology*]
SEMN	Superficial Extensor Motoneuron [*Neurology*]
SEMO	Montalvo [*Ecuador*] [*ICAO location identifier*] (ICLI)
SEMO	State Emergency Management Organisation [*New South Wales, Australia*]
SEMO	Supply and Equipment Management Officer (AAGC)
SEMO	Systems Engineering and Management Operations [*Military*]
Semon	Semonides [*Seventh century BC*] [*Classical studies*] (OCD)
SEMOPS	Sequential Multiobjective Problem Solving
SEMP	Mopa [*Ecuador*] [*ICAO location identifier*] (ICLI)
SEMP	Self-Erecting Marine Platform (PDAA)
SEMP	Sempre [*Throughout*] [*Music*]
SEMP	Simplified Early Maturities Participation Plan [*Small Business Administration*]
SEMP	Societe d'Editions Medico-Pharmaceutiques [*Medical-Pharmaceutical Publishing Co.*] [*France*] [*Information service or system*] (IID)
SEMP	Socioeconomic Military Program (CINC)
SEMP	Standard Electronics Module Program (MCD)
SEMP	Superconducting Electromagnetic Propulsion (ECON)
SEMP	System Engineering Management Plan
SEMPA	Scanning Electron Microscope and Particle Analyzer
SEMPA	Scanning Electron Microscopy with Polarization Analysis
SEMPB	Schiffli Embroidery Manufacturers Promotion Board (EA)
SemPck	Semiconductor Packaging Materials [*Associated Press*] (SAG)
SEMPE	Socio-Economic Model of the Planet Earth (PDAA)
SEMR	Standard Electronic Module RADAR (PDAA)
SEMR	Support Equipment Management Report (MCD)
SEMRE	SPRINT Electromagnetic Radiation Evaluation [*Army*] (AABC)
SEMRFL	Michigan Regional Libraries Film Program at Monroe [*Library network*]
SEMS	Monjas Sur [*Ecuador*] [*ICAO location identifier*] (ICLI)
SEMS	Science and Education Management Staff [*Department of Agriculture*] (GFGA)
SEMS	Severe Environment Memory Series [*or System*] [*Computer science*]
SEMS	Space Environment Monitor System [*NASA*] (NASA)
SEMS	Steam Engine Makers' Society [*A union*] [*British*]
SEMS	Stray Energy Monitor System
SEMS	Support Engineering Manhour Summary (MCD)
SEMS	System Engineering Management Standard
SEMS	Systems Engineering and Management Support [*Air Force*]
SEMS	Systems Engineering Master Schedule
SEMT	Manta [*Ecuador*] [*ICAO location identifier*] (ICLI)
SEMT	SIGINT/EW [*Signal Intelligence/Electronic Warfare*] Maintenance Trainer [*Army*]
Semtch	Semtech Corp. [*Associated Press*] (SAG)
SEMTEC	Southeastern Marine Trades Exhibit and Conference [*National Marine Manufacturers' Association*] (TSPED)
SEMTR	SPRINT Early Missile Test RADAR [*Army*] (AABC)
SEMTR	Supervisory Electronic Maintenance Technician [*Relief*]
SEMTSA	Structural Econometric Modeling Time Series Analysis [*Statistics*]

sem ves.......	Seminal Vesicle [*Anatomy*] (WGA)
SEMX..........	Semiconductor Pkg Materials [*NASDAQ symbol*] (TTSB)
SEMY..........	Seminary
Sen..........	De Senectute [*of Cicero*] [*Classical studies*] (OCD)
SEN..........	Lexington, KY [*Location identifier FAA*] (FAAL)
SEN..........	Sacred Earth Network [*An association*] (EA)
SEN..........	Scanning Encoding [*Computer science*] (MHDI)
SEN..........	Science Engineering News [*National Oceanic and Atmospheric Administration*]
SEN..........	Semienclosed
SEN..........	Senair Charter Ltd. [*British ICAO designator*] (FAAC)
SEN..........	Senate
SEN..........	Senator
Sen..........	Senator (ODBW)
SEN..........	Sendai [*Mukaiyama*] [*Japan*] [*Seismograph station code, US Geological Survey*] (SEIS)
Sen..........	Seneca [*the Elder*] [*First century BC*] [*Classical studies*] (OCD)
Sen..........	Seneca [*the Younger*] [*First century AD*] [*Classical studies*] (OCD)
SEN..........	Senegal [*ANSI three-letter standard code*] (CNC)
Sen..........	Senior (EY)
Sen..........	Senior (WDAA)
SEN..........	Senlac Resources, Inc. [*Toronto Stock Exchange symbol*]
SEN..........	Sennae [*Of Senna*] [*Pharmacy*] (ROG)
SEN..........	Sense (IAA)
SEN..........	Sensitive
SEN..........	Sensor (AAG)
SEN..........	Senza [*Without*] [*Music*]
SEN..........	Single Edge Notched
SEN..........	Small Extension Node [*Telecommunications*] (LAIN)
SEN..........	Societe Europeenne de Neuro+radiologie [*European Neuroradiological Association*] [*France*] (EAIO)
SEN..........	Societe Europeenne de Neuroscience [*European Neuroscience Association - ENA*] (EA)
SEN..........	Software Error Notification [*Computer science*]
SEN..........	Southend [*Scotland*] [*Airport symbol*] (AD)
SEN..........	Southern European Network (DNAB)
SEN..........	Space Engagement Node
SEN..........	Special Educational Needs (AIE)
SEN..........	Spiritual Emergence Network (EA)
SEN..........	Sports Exchange Network [*Cable TV programming service*]
SEN..........	State Enrolled Nurse [*British*]
SEN..........	Statement of Essential Need (AAGC)
SEN..........	Steam Emulsion Number
SEN..........	Strike Energy, Inc. [*Vancouver Stock Exchange symbol*]
SEN..........	Successor Event Number (DNAB)
SEN..........	System Error Notification [*Computer science*]
SEN..........	Systems Engineering Notice
Sen..........	United States Senate (AAGC)
SENA..........	Nor Antizana [*Ecuador*] [*ICAO location identifier*] (ICLI)
SENA..........	Seaport Navigation Co. [*Later, SNCO*] [*AAR code*]
SENA..........	Societe d'Energie Nucleaire Franco-Belge des Ardennes [*Belgian-French power consortium*]
SENA..........	Sympathetic Efferent Nerve Activity
SENAV..........	Senior Naval Aviator (NVT)
SENAVAV.....	Senior Naval Aviator
SENAVOMAC...	Senior Naval Officer, Military Airlift Command (MCD)
SENB..........	Single Edge Notched Beam [*Materials science and technology*]
SENC..........	Nor Cayambe [*Ecuador*] [*ICAO location identifier*] (ICLI)
S en C..........	Sociedad en Comandita [*Limited partnership company*] [*Spanish*]
SenCh..........	Senior Chaplain [*Navy British*]
SENCX..........	Sentinel Group: Com. Stk [*Mutual fund ticker symbol*] (SG)
SEND..........	Scientists and Engineers for National Development [*Scholarship program*]
SEND..........	Securities and Exchange Commission News Digest [*A publication*]
SEND..........	Shared Equipment Need Date (NASA)
SEND..........	Southend [*County borough in England*]
SENDENTALO...	Senior Dental Officer [*Navy*] (DNAB)
Sen Doc.......	Senate Document (DLA)
SENE..........	Seneca Foods Corp. [*NASDAQ symbol*] (NQ)
SENEA..........	Seneca Foods Cl'A' [*NASDAQ symbol*] (TTSB)
SENEAM......	Servicios a la Navegacion en el Espacio Aereo Mexicano [*Mexico ICAO designator*] (FAAC)
SENEB..........	Seneca Foods Cl'B' [*NASDAQ symbol*] (TTSB)
SENECA.......	Semantic Networks for Conceptual Analysis (NITA)
Seneca........	Seneca Foods Corp. [*Associated Press*] (SAG)
Seneg........	Senegal
SENEGAMBIA...	Senegal and Gambia
SENEL..........	Single Noise Exposure Level
SENET..........	Scientific and Engineering Computer Network (MCD)
SENET..........	Slotted Envelope Network (MHDI)
Senetek.......	Senetek PLC [*Associated Press*] (SAG)
SENG..........	Single Engine
SEngFInstSMM...	Qualified Sales Engineer of the Institute of Sales and Marketing Management [*British*] (DBQ)
SenHgh.......	Senior High Income Portfolio [*Associated Press*] (SAG)
SenHgh2.......	Senior High Income Portfolio II [*Associated Press*] (SAG)
SENI..........	Nor Iliniza [*Ecuador*] [*ICAO location identifier*] (ICLI)
SENIC..........	Study on the Efficacy of Nosocomial Infection Control (MEDA)
SeniorTP.......	Senior Tour Players Development [*Associated Press*] (SAG)
Sen J........	Senate Journal [*A publication*] (DLA)
SENJIT........	Special Educational Needs Joint Initiative for Training (AIE)
Sen Jo........	Senate Journal [*A publication*] (DLA)
SENL..........	Standard Equipment Nomenclature List [*Military*]
SENLOG.......	Sentinel Logistics Command
SEN(M)........	State Enrolled Nurse (Mental Nursing) [*British*] (DBQ)

SENMEDO....	Senior Medical Officer [*Military*] (DNAB)
SENMEM......	Senior Member (DNAB)
SEN(MS)....	State Enrolled Nurse (Mental Subnormal Nursing) [*British*] (DBQ)
Senn..........	Sennaherib (BJA)
SE'NNIGHT...	Seven Nights [*A week*] (ROG)
SENO..........	Steam Emulsion Number
SENPO..........	Sentinel Project Office [*Army*] (MCD)
SENR..........	Senior
Sen Rep	Senate Report [*A publication*] (DLA)
Sen Rep	United States Senate Committee Report [*A publication*] (DLA)
SenrStrat......	Senior Strategic Income Fund [*Associated Press*] (SAG)
Sens..........	De Sensu [*of Aristotle*] [*Classical studies*] (OCD)
SENS..........	Sensitive (MSA)
SENS..........	Sensitivity (IAA)
SENS..........	Sensor [*Automotive engineering*]
SENS..........	Sensorium [*Neurology*] (DAVI)
SENS..........	Sensory
SENS..........	Sentex Sensing Technologies [*NASDAQ symbol*] (TTSB)
SENS..........	Sentex Sensing Technology, Inc. [*Ridgefield, NJ*] [*NASDAQ symbol*] (NQ)
SENS..........	Social England Series [*A publication*]
SENS..........	Stewart Evaluation of Nursing Scale (DMAA)
SENSCOM....	Sentinel Systems Command [*Army*] (MCD)
SENSE..........	Society for Ending Needless and Silly Expenditure [*British*] (DI)
SENSE..........	Sommers' Equivocation Network for Significant Expressions (SAA)
SENSEA......	Sentinel System Evaluation Agency [*DoD*]
SENSIM......	Sensor System Simulation
SENSO........	Sensor Operator (MCD)
SENSO........	Sentinel Systems Office [*Military*]
SENSOR......	Sentinel Event Notification System for Occupational Risks [*Medicine*]
Sensormt....	Sensormatic Electronics Corp. [*Associated Press*] (SAG)
SENT..........	Sentence (AABC)
Sent..........	Sentenza [*Decision, Judgment*] [*Italian*] (ILCA)
SENTA........	Societe d'Etudes Nucleaires et de Techniques Avancees [*France*]
SENTAC......	Society for Ear, Nose, and Throat Advances in Children (EA)
SENT CONF...	Sentence to be Confined [*Navy*] (DNAB)
SENTD........	Sentenced (WGA)
SenTechWeldI...	Senior Technician of the Welding Institute [*British*] (DBQ)
Sentex........	Sentex Sensing Technologies [*Associated Press*] (SAG)
SENT LP	Sentence to Lose Pay [*Navy*] (DNAB)
SENTOS......	Sentinel Operating System (IEEE)
SentoTch	Sento Technical Innovations Corp. [*Associated Press*] (SAG)
SenTP........	Senior Tour Players Development [*Associated Press*] (SAG)
SENTRAB....	Syndicat des Travailleurs des Entreprises, Privees, Travaux Publics et Batiments [*Union of Workers of Private Enterprises, Public Works and Buildings*] [*Togo*]
SENTRE	Sensor of Tail Region Emitters (MCD)
SENTRY	Survey Entry
SENU..........	Neuvo Rocafuerte [*Ecuador*] [*ICAO location identifier*] (ICLI)
SENU..........	Spectrum Efficient Network Unit (MCD)
SENUSNAVOFFNAVBALTAP...	Senior United States Naval Officer, Commander Allied Naval Forces, Baltic Approaches (DNAB)
SenWO........	Senior Warrant Officer [*British*] (DI)
SENYLRC.....	Southeastern New York Library Resources Council [*Highland, NY*] [*Library network*]
SEO..........	Salvage Engineering Order (MCD)
SEO..........	Satellite for Earth Observation
SEO..........	Seguela [*Ivory Coast*] [*Airport symbol*] (OAG)
SEO..........	Senior Engineer Officer [*Navy*]
SEO..........	Senior Executive Officer [*Civil Service*] [*British*]
SEO..........	Senior Experimental Officer [*Also, SExO, SXO*] [*Ministry of Agriculture, Fisheries, and Food*] [*British*]
SEO..........	Seoul [*Keizyo*] [*South Korea*] [*Seismograph station code, US Geological Survey*] (SEIS)
SEO..........	Serial Engineering Order (MCD)
SEO..........	Shoulder-Elbow Orthosis [*Medicine*]
SEO..........	Sin Errores y Omisiones [*Errors and Omissions Excepted*] [*Business term Spanish*]
SEO..........	Society of Education Officers [*British*]
SEO..........	Special Engineering Order [*NASA*] (NASA)
SEO..........	Special Equipment Option [*Automotive assembly*]
SEO..........	State Energy Office
SEO..........	Surgical Emergency Officer (MEDA)
SEO..........	Synchronous Equatorial Orbit [*or Orbiter*] [*NASA*] (KSC)
SEOA..........	Pasochoa [*Ecuador*] [*ICAO location identifier*] (ICLI)
SEOC..........	State Emergency Operations Centre [*New South Wales, Australia*]
SEOC..........	Submarine Extended Operating Cycle (NVT)
SEOC..........	Sudan Emergency Operations Consortium
SEOCS........	Sun-Earth Observatory and Climatology Satellite
SEODSE......	Special Explosive Ordnance Disposal Supplies and Equipment [*Army*] (AABC)
SEOG..........	Supplemental Educational Opportunity Grant [*Department of Education*]
SEOL..........	Olmedo [*Ecuador*] [*ICAO location identifier*] (ICLI)
SEON..........	Solar Electro-Optical Network (MCD)
SEON..........	Solar Electro-Optical Observing Network [*Marine science*] (OSRA)
SEOO..........	Sauf Erreur ou Omission [*Errors and Omissions Excepted*] [*French*]
SEOO..........	State Economic Opportunity Office
SEOP..........	Secondary Operand Unit (IAA)
SEOP..........	Segment End of Pulse
SEOP..........	SHAPE [*Supreme Headquarters Allied Powers Europe*] Emergency Operating Procedures [*NATO*] (NATG)
SEOP..........	Siecor Electro-Optic Products [*Research Triangle Park, NC*] (TSSD)
SEOP..........	State Emergency Operations Plan [*Environmental science*] (COE)
SEOP..........	System Employment and Organizational Plan [*Army*]

SEOPSN......	Select-Operate-Sense
SEOR	Oro [Ecuador] [ICAO location identifier] (ICLI)
SEOS	SIGINT Equipment Operator Simulator [Military]
S/EOS	Standard Earth Observation Satellite (MCD)
SEOS	Strategic Earth Orbit System (IAA)
SEOS	Symmetric Exchange of Symmetry [Spectrometry]
SEOS	Synchronous Earth Observatory Satellite [NASA]
SEOSS	Slewable Electro-Optical Sensor System
Seoul LJ.....	Seoul Law Journal [A publication] (DLA)
SEOW	Society of Engineering Office Workers (EA)
SEP.............	Salmonid Enhancement Program [Canada]
SEP.............	Samenwerkende Elektriciteit Produktie Bedrijven [Electric utility] [Netherlands]
SEP.............	Saturday Evening Post [A publication] (BRI)
SEP.............	Scientific and Engineering Personnel [Military]
SE(P)...........	Security Executive, Control at Ports [British World War II]
SEP.............	Segment End Pulse
SEP.............	Selective Employment Payments [British]
SEP.............	Selective Employment Plan
SEP.............	Self-Elevating Platform
SEP.............	Self-Employed Pension [British]
SEP.............	Semi-Engineered Prototype [Automotive engineering]
SEP.............	Sensory Evoked Potential [Neurophysiology]
SEP.............	Sepal [Botany] (WGA)
SEP.............	Separate (AFM)
sep.............	Separate (WDMC)
sep.............	Separation (WDMC)
SEP.............	Separation (IAA)
SEP.............	Separation Parameter
SEP.............	Sepia [Stamp collecting] (ROG)
sep.............	Sepia (VRA)
SEP.............	September (AFM)
SEP.............	Septuagint [Version of the Bible]
SEP.............	Sepultus [Buried] [Latin]
SEP.............	Serial Entry Printer
SEP.............	Shepherd Products Ltd. [Toronto Stock Exchange symbol]
SEP.............	Simplified Employee Pension
SEP.............	Simplified Employee Pension Plan (DFIT)
SEP.............	Site Emergency Plan [Nuclear energy] (NRCH)
SEP.............	Slow Electrical Process [Human brain]
SEP.............	Slug Ejector Punch
SEP.............	Society for Exact Philosophy (EA)
SEP.............	Society of Engineering Psychologists [Later, DAEEP] (EA)
SEP.............	Society of Experimental Psychologists (EA)
SEP.............	Software End Product [Army]
SEP.............	Software Engineering Practice
SEP.............	Software Engineering Process (AAEL)
SEP.............	Software Enhancement Proposal
SEP.............	Solar Electric Power [or Propulsion]
SEP.............	Solar Energetic Particle
SEP.............	Soldier Enhancement Program [Army] (INF)
SEP.............	Solid Electrolyte Potentiometry
SEP.............	Somatically Evoked Potential [Neurophysiology]
SEP.............	Somatosensory Evoked Potential [Neurology] (DAVI)
SEP.............	SOSUS Estimated Position (NVT)
SEP.............	Source Evaluation Panel [NASA] (NASA)
SEP.............	Southern Education Program [Defunct] (EA)
SEP.............	Space Electronic Package
SEP.............	Special Education Programs [Department of Education] [Formerly, BEH]
SEP.............	Special Emphasis Program [DoD]
SEP.............	Special Enrollment Period [Department of Health and Human Services] (GFGA)
SEP.............	Specific Excess Power (MCD)
SEP.............	Sperm Entry Point [into egg]
SEP.............	Spherical Error Precision [or Probability]
SEP.............	Stable Element Panel
SEP.............	Standard Electric Puhelinteollisius (NITA)
SEP.............	Standard Electronic Package
SEP.............	Standard Engineering Practice (AAG)
SEP.............	Standard Error of Prediction
SEP.............	Standard Evaluation Procedure [Environmental Protection Agency]
SEP.............	Star Epitaxial Planar (MSA)
SEP.............	Stephenville, TX [Location identifier FAA] (FAAL)
SEP.............	Stimulated Emission Pumping [Spectroscopy]
SEP.............	Strong Equivalence Principle [Thermodynamics]
SEP.............	Student Enhancement Program [Army]
SEP.............	Student Expense Program [Civil Defense]
SEP.............	Studiegroup voor Europese Politiek (EA)
SEP.............	Supervisor Executive Program [NASA] (KSC)
SEP.............	Supplemental Environmental Projects [Policy] [Environmental Protection Agency]
SEP.............	Support Equipment Package [NASA] (NASA)
SEP.............	Surface Electrical Property [Apollo] [NASA]
SEP.............	Surface Experiments [NASA]
SEP.............	Surrendered Enemy Personnel
SEP.............	Survey of Eastern Palestine [A publication] (BJA)
SEP.............	Swedish Export Credit Corp. [NYSE symbol] (SAG)
SEP.............	Symbolic Equations Program (IAA)
SEP.............	Syringe Exchange Program [To prevent infectious disease]
SEP.............	Systematic Evaluation Program [Nuclear Regulatory Commission]
SEP.............	Systems Effectiveness Plan
SEP.............	Systems Engineering Process
SEP.............	Systems Extension Plan
SEP.............	Systolic Ejection Period [Cardiology]

SEPA...........	Pastaza [Ecuador] [ICAO location identifier] (ICLI)
SEPA...........	Soft Enhancement of Percutaneous Absorption [Pharmacy]
SEPA...........	Southeastern Power Administration [Department of Energy]
SEPA...........	Southeastern Psychological Association (MCD)
SEPA...........	Southeast Pacific Area
SEPA...........	Soviet Extended Planning Annex (MCD)
SEPA...........	Spanish Evangelical Publishers Association (EA)
SEPA...........	State Environmental Protection Act (PA)
SEPA...........	System Evaluation Planning and Assessment Model (MCD)
SEPA...........	Systems Engineering, Policy Analysis and Management [Delft University of Technology, Netherlands]
SEPAA	Sheepskin Export Packers' Association of Australia
SEPAC	Space Experiments with Particle Accelerators [Spacelab mission]
SEPACFOR...	Southeast Pacific Force [later, Command] [Navy]
SEPACS	Sheltered Employment Procurement and Consultancy Service (AIE)
SEPAK	Suspension of Expendable Penetration Aids by Kite [Military]
SEP & A	Special Equipment Parts and Assemblies Section (AAG)
SEPAP	Shuttle Electrical Power Analysis Program [NASA]
separ..........	Separatum [Separately] [Latin] (MAE)
SEPAR	Shuttle Electrical Power Analysis Report [NASA] (NASA)
SEPARON ...	Separation (ROG)
SEPAWG......	Save EPA [Environmental Protection Agency] Working Group (EA)
SE/PB.........	Southern Europe - Ports and Beaches [NATO] (NATG)
SEP Btry	Separate Battery [Army]
SEPC...........	Seiler Pollution Ctl Sys [NASDAQ symbol] (TTSB)
SEPC...........	Seller Pollution Control [NASDAQ symbol] (SAG)
SEPC...........	Space Exploration Program Council [NASA]
SEPC...........	State Emergency Planning Committee (PA)
SEPCEN	Separation Center [Navy]
SEPCOR	Separate Correspondence (MCD)
SEPD	Scottish Economic Planning Department [British]
SEPD	Separated
SEPD	Special-Environment Powder Diffractometer [Crystallography]
SEPD	State Emergency Planning Director [Civil Defense]
SEPDC	Southern Ethiopian Peoples Democratic Coalition
SEPE...........	Pechichal [Ecuador] [ICAO location identifier] (ICLI)
SEPE...........	Seattle Port of Embarkation
SEPE...........	Separate (ROG)
SEPE...........	Single Escape Peak Efficiency [Nuclear science] (OA)
SEPE...........	Societe d'Edition et de Publications en Exlusivite
SEPEA........	Societe Europeene de Psychiatrie de l'Enfant et de l'Adolescent [European Society of Child and Adolescent Psychiatry - ESCAP] (EAIO)
SEPEL.........	Southeastern Plant Environment Laboratories [Duke University and North Carolina State University]
SEPEMIAG ...	Societe d'Etudes pour l'Equipement Miniere, Agricole, et Industrial du Gabon [Gabon Society for Study of Mining, Agricultural, and Industrial Equipment]
SEPESCA	Secretariat of Fisheries [Mexico] [Marine science] (OSRA)
SEPFA.........	South East Professional Fishermen's Association [Australia]
SEPG	Separating
SEPG	Software Engineering Process Group (AAEL)
SEPGA	Southeastern Pecan Growers Association (EA)
Seph	Sephardic [Jews from Spain, Portugal, North Africa, and the Mediterranean] (BJA)
SEPHA........	Special Emergency Programme for the Horn of Africa [World Food Programme] [United Nations]
SEPI...........	Pichincha [Ecuador] [ICAO location identifier] (ICLI)
SEPI...........	Society for the Exploration of Psychotherapy Integration (EA)
SEPI...........	Sylvania Electric Products, Inc. (KSC)
SEPIL.........	Selective Excitation of Probe Ion Luminescence [Analytical chemistry]
SEPL...........	Playas [Ecuador] [ICAO location identifier] (ICLI)
SEPL...........	South European Pipeline [Oil]
SEPLIS........	Secretariat Europeen des Professions Liberales, Independantes et Sociales [European Secretariat of the Liberal, Independant and Social Professions] [EC] (ECED)
SEPM...........	Society for Sedimentary Geology [Formerly, Society of Economic Paleontologists a nd Mineralogists] (EA)
SEPMAG	Separate Magnetic (NTCM)
SEPN	Separation (AAG)
SEPO	Posorja [Ecuador] [ICAO location identifier] (ICLI)
SEPO	Space Electric Power Office [AEC]
SEPOL	Settlement Problem-Oriented Language [Computer science] (IEEE)
SEPOL	Soil Engineering Problem-Oriented Language [Computer science]
SEPORT	Supply and Equipment Report [Army] (AABC)
SEPOS	Selected Enlisted Personnel for Overseas Service [Military] (AABC)
SEPP...........	Safety Engineering Program Plan [Military] (DNAB)
SEPP...........	Secure Electronic Payments Protocol [Telecommunications]
SEPP...........	Secure Encryption Payment Protocol [Computer science]
SEPP...........	Simplified Employee Pension Plan
SEPPA	Single Employer Pension Plan Amendments Act of 1986 (WYGK)
SEPPAA	Single-Employer Pension Plan Amendments Act [1986] (GFGA)
SEPPr.........	AB Svensk Exp Cap Sec [NYSE symbol] (TTSB)
SEPQUES	Separation Questionnaire [Military] (DNAB)
SEPR...........	Sepracor, Inc. [NASDAQ symbol] (SPSG)
Sepracr.......	Sepracor, Inc. [Associated Press] (SAG)
Sepragn.......	Sepragen Corp. [Associated Press] (SAG)
SEPRL	Southeast Poultry Research Laboratory [University of Georgia] [Research center] (RCD)
SEPROS........	Separation Processing (IAA)
SEPS...........	Pasaje [Ecuador] [ICAO location identifier] (ICLI)
SEPS...........	Secondary Electric Power System (IAA)
SEPS...........	Selenium-Containing Protein Saccharide (DB)
SEPS...........	Service Environment Power System (IAA)
SEPS...........	Service Module Electrical Power System [NASA] (KSC)

SEPS............ Severe Environment Power System (IEEE)
SEPS............ Shortstop Electronic Protection System [*Army*]
SEPS............ Smithsonian Earth Physics Satellite
SEPS............ Solar Electric Propulsion System [*NASA*]
SEPS............ System/Equipment Population Summary
SEPSA .... Society of Educational Programmers and Systems Analysts [*Later, SDE*]
SEPSC .... Spontaneous Excitatory Postsynaptic Current [*Neurophysiology*]
SEPSIT........ Solar Electric Propulsion Integration Technology (PDAA)
SEPSME...... Social Economic and Political Studies of the Middle East [*A publication*] (BJA)
SEPST......... Solar Electric Propulsion System Technology
SEPSU .... Science and Engineering Policy Studies Unit (AIE)
SEPT............ Putumayo [*Ecuador*] [*ICAO location identifier*] (ICLI)
SEPT............ Separate
sept .... Septem [*Seven*] [*Latin*] (MAE)
SEPT............ September (EY)
sept .... Septembre [*September*] [*French*] (ASC)
Sept............ Septem Contra Thebas [*of Aeschylus*] [*Classical studies*] (OCD)
Sept............ Septuagint [*Version of the Bible*] (BJA)
sept .... Septum [*Medicine*] (CPH)
SEPT............ Signaling End-Point Translator [*Telecommunications*] (ITD)
SEPT............ Silicon Epitaxial Planar Transistor (IAA)
SEPTA......... Southeastern Pennsylvania Transportation Authority
SEPTAR ...... Seaborne Powered Target [*Navy*] (NVT)
SEPTD......... Separated
SEPTEL....... Separate Telegram
Septel.......... Separate Telegram
SEPTG .... Separating
SEPTLA....... Southeastern Pennsylvania Theological Library Association [*Library network*]
SEPTR .... Separator
SEPTR .... September (ROG)
SEPU .... Puna [*Ecuador*] [*ICAO location identifier*] (ICLI)
SEPULT....... Sepultus [*Buried*] [*Latin*] (ROG)
SEPUP .... Science Education for Public Understanding Project [*Australia*]
SEPV .... Portoviejo [*Ecuador*] [*ICAO location identifier*] (ICLI)
SEPWC .... Senate Environment and Public Works Committee (COE)
SEPY............ Puyo [*Ecuador*] [*ICAO location identifier*] (ICLI)
SEQ............. Scientific Equipment (KSC)
SEQ............. Seguin, TX [*Location identifier FAA*] (FAAL)
SEQ............. Self-Esteem Questionnaire [*Personality development test*] [*Psychology*]
SEQ............. Sequel
seq............. Sequel (WDMC)
seq............. Sequence (WDMC)
SEQ............. Sequence (NAKS)
SEQ............. Sequencer (IAA)
SEQ............. Sequens [*Sequence*] [*Latin*] (AABC)
SEQ............. Sequente [*And in What Follows*] [*Latin*]
Seq............. Sequential (DB)
SEQ............. Sequential Pulse Counting [*Spectrometry*]
seq............. Sequestration [*Orthopedics*] (DAVI)
SEQ............. Sequestrum [*Medicine*]
SEQ............. Sequitur [*It Follows*] [*Latin*]
SEQ............. Side Effects Questionnaire [*Medicine*] (DMAA)
SEq............. Spatial Equalization
SEQ............. Storage Equities (EFIS)
SEQA........... State Environmental Quality Act (PA)
SEQDB........ Semiconductor Equipment Database (AAEL)
SEQ DEV EX... Sequential Developmental Exercises [*Occupational therapy*] (DAVI)
SEQE........... Quevedo [*Ecuador*] [*ICAO location identifier*] (ICLI)
SEQ-IC........ Sequencer-Iteration Control [*Computer science*] (MHDI)
SEQL........... Sequential (IAA)
SEQ LUCE ... Sequenti Luce [*The Following Day*] [*Latin*] (ADA)
SEQN.......... Quininde [*Ecuador*] [*ICAO location identifier*] (ICLI)
SEQOPT....... Sequential Optimization (MCD)
SEQQ .... Sequentes [*or Sequentia*] [*The Following Plural form*] [*Latin*]
SEQQ .... Sequentibus [*In the Following Places*] [*Latin*] (ADA)
SEQR .... Sequencer (AAG)
SEQREC....... Sequence Recall [*Neuropsychology test*]
SEQS .... Sequoia Systems [*NASDAQ symbol*] (TTSB)
SEQS .... Sequoia Systems, Inc. [*NASDAQ symbol*] (SAG)
SEQS .... Simultaneous Equation Solver [*Computer program*]
SEQT........... System Environment Qualification Test
SEQU .... Quito/Mariscal Sucre [*Ecuaor*] [*ICAO location identifier*] (ICLI)
sequ........... Sequitur [*It Follows*] [*Latin*] (WGA)
SEQU .... Sequoia and Kings Canyon National Parks
SEQU .... SEQUUS Pharmaceuticals [*NASDAQ symbol*] (TTSB)
SEQU .... Sequus Pharmaceuticals, Inc. [*NASDAQ symbol*] (SAG)
Sequa......... Sequa Corp. [*Associated Press*] (SAG)
SequaA....... Sequa Corp. [*Associated Press*] (SAG)
SequaB....... Sequa Corp. [*Associated Press*] (SAG)
SEQUAL...... Seasonal Equatorial Atlantic Experiment
SEQUEL ...... Structured English Query Language [*1974*] [*Computer science*] (CSR)
SEQUIN....... Sequential Quadrature Inband [*Television system*] (DEN)
SEQUIP....... Study of Environmental Quality Information Programs (KSC)
Sequnt........ Sequent Computer Systems, Inc. [*Associated Press*] (SAG)
Sequoi........ Sequoia Systems, Inc. [*Associated Press*] (SAG)
SEQUR .... Safety Equipment Requirements
SequTh....... Sequana Therapeutics, Inc. [*Associated Press*] (SAG)
Sequus .... Sequus Pharmaceuticals, Inc. [*Associated Press*] (SAG)
SEQUX........ Sequoia Fund [*Mutual fund ticker symbol*] (SG)
SER............. Aerocalifornia SA [*Mexico ICAO designator*] (FAAC)

SER............. Cataloging Services Department, OCLC [*Online Computer Library Center*], Inc., Columbus, OH [*OCLC symbol*] (OCLC)
SER............. Safety Evaluation Report [*Nuclear energy*] (NRCH)
SER............. Sandia Engineering Reactor [*Nuclear energy*]
SER............. Sebum Excretion Rate (OA)
SER............. Seder Eliyahu Rabbah (BJA)
SER............. Selective Early Retirement [*Army*]
SER............. Sensory Evoked Response [*Medicine*] (DMAA)
SER............. Sequential Events Recorder
SER............. Serial (AFM)
Ser............. Serial (EBF)
ser............. Serial (WDMC)
ser............. Series (IDOE)
Ser............. Series (EBF)
SER............. Series (AAG)
Ser............. Serine [*Also, S*] [*An amino acid*]
ser............. Serine [*An amino acid*] (DOG)
SER............. Sermon
Ser............. Serpens [*Constellation*]
SER............. Servant
SER............. Service (NATG)
SER............. Service, Employment, Redevelopment [*Operation for Mexican-Americans*] [*Later, SER - Jobs for Progress*]
SER............. Servico Inc. [*AMEX symbol*] (TTSB)
SER............. Seymour, IN [*Location identifier FAA*] (FAAL)
SER............. Shore Establishment Realignment [*Navy*] (NVT)
SER............. Significant Event Report (IEEE)
SER............. Sikorsky Engineering Report
SER............. Silver Eagle Resources [*Vancouver Stock Exchange symbol*]
SER............. Simultaneous Evoked [*Cortical*] Response [*Neurophysiology*]
SER............. Single Electron Response [*Electronics*] (OA)
SER............. Site Evaluation Report (MCD)
SER............. Smooth [*Surfaced*] Endoplasmic Reticulum [*Cytology*]
SER............. SNAP [*Systems for Nuclear Auxiliary Power*] Experimental Reactor
SER............. Sociedad Espanola de Radiodifusion [*Broadcasting organization*]
SER............. Society for Ecological Restoration (EA)
SER............. Society for Educational Reconstruction (EA)
SER............. Society for Epidemiologic Research (EA)
SER............. Software Engineering Requirement [*Army*]
SER............. Somatosensory Evoked Response [*Neurophysiology*]
SER............. South-Eastern Railway [*British*]
SER............. Space Electric [*or Electronic*] Rocket (DNAB)
SER............. Stem End Rot [*Plant pathology*]
SER............. Student Eligibility Report (EDAC)
SER............. Sua Eccellenza Reverendissima [*His Eminence*] (EY)
SER............. Summary Earnings Record [*Social Security Administration*] (GFGA)
SER............. Support Equipment Requirement
SER............. Surface Electrical Resistivity
SER............. System Environment Recording (BUR)
SER............. Systolic Ejection Rate [*Cardiology*] (MAE)
SERA .... Sequential Electrochemical Reduction Analysis (AAEL)
SERA .... Sierra Railroad Co. [*AAR code*]
SERA .... Sierra Semiconductor [*NASDAQ symbol*] (SPSG)
SERA .... Society for Entrepreneurship Research and Application [*Defunct*] (EA)
SERA .... Solar and Electric Racing Association
SERA .... Special Emphasis Reliability Area (MCD)
SERA .... Stop Equal Rights Amendment [*An association Defunct*] (EA)
SERAC .... Southeastern Regional Arts Council
SERAC .... State Energy Research Advisory Committee [*Australia*]
Seragen....... Seragen, Inc. [*Associated Press*] (SAG)
SERANAK..... Serge and Natalie Koussevitzky [*Acronym was name of summer home of Boston Symphony Orchestra conductor and his first wife*]
SERANDA .... Service Record, Health Record, Pay Account, and Personal Effects [*Military*]
SERAPE .... Simulator Equipment Requirements for Accelerating Procedural Evolution
SERAPHIM... Systems Engineering Respecting Acquisition and Propagation of Heuristic Instructional Materials [*Chemistry*]
SERB .... Riobamba [*Ecuador*] [*ICAO location identifier*] (ICLI)
SERB .... Selective Early Retirement Board [*Army*] (INF)
SERB .... Serbia
SERB .... Shuttle Engineering Review Board [*NASA*] (NASA)
SERB .... Societe Europeene de Radiobiologie [*European Society for Radiation Biology - ESRB*] (EAIO)
SERB .... Study of the Enhanced Radiation Belt [*NASA*]
SERB .... Systems Engineering Review Board [*NASA*] (NASA)
SERBAUD .... Serikat Buruh Angkutan Udara [*Airways' Union*] [*Indonesia*]
SERBB .... State Employees' Retirement Benefits Board [*Australia*]
SERBEP .... Southeastern Regional Biomass Energy Program (WPI)
SERBIS .... Southeastern Regional Biomedical Information System (AEBS)
SERBIUM...... Serikat Buruh Industri dan Umum [*Industrial and General Workers' Union*] [*Indonesia*]
SERBU........ Serikat Buruh Umum [*General Workers' Union*] [*Indonesia*]
SERBUHI...... Serikat Buruh Harian Indonesia [*Newspaper Employees' Union of Indonesia*]
SERBUMAMI... Serikat Buruh Makanan dan Minuman [*Food Workers' Union*] [*Indonesia*]
SERBUMIKSI... Serikat Buruh Minjak Kelapa Seluruh [*Coconut Oil Workers' Union*] [*Indonesia*]
SERBUMIT ... Serikat Buruh Minjak dan Tambang [*Oil and Minerals Workers' Union*] [*Indonesia*]
SERBUMUSI... Serikat Buruh Muslimin Indonesia [*Moslem Workers' Union of Indonesia*]

SERBUNI...... Serikat Buruh Unilever Indonesia [*Unilever Employees' Union of Indonesia*]

SERBUPI...... Serikat Buruh Perkebunan Indonesia [*Plantation Workers' Union of Indonesia*]

SERBUPRI ... Serikat Buruh Pertambangan Indonesia [*Mining Workers' Union of Indonesia*]

SERC .... Industry/University Cooperative Research Center for Software Engineering [*University of Florida, Purdue University*] [*Research center*] (RCD)

SERC .... Science and Engineering Research Council [*British Defunct*]

SERC .... Smithsonian Environmental Research Center

SERC .... Southeastern Electric Reliability Council [*Regional power council*]

SERC .... Special Education in the Regular Classroom Project [*U.S. Office of Special Educ ation and Rehabilitation Services*] (EDAC)

SERC .... State Emergency Response Commission [*Environmental science*]

SERC .... State Emergency Response Committee [*Environmental Protection Agency*]

SERC .... Sussex European Research Centre [*Research center British*] (IRC)

SERCA .... Servicios de Carga Aerea [*National Airlines*] [*Costa Rica*] (EY)

SERCH .... State Education Research Clearinghouse [*California*] (EDAC)

SERCNET .... SERC Network (NITA)

SERCS .... South-East Regional Crime Squad (WDAA)

SERD .... Stored Energy Rotary Drive

SERD .... Support Equipment Recommendation Data [*NASA*] (KSC)

SERD .... Support Equipment Requirements Data

SERDA .... Signals and Electronic Warfare Research and Development Act

SERDES ...... Serializer/Deserializer

SERDES CRC... Serializer-Deserializer Cyclic Redundancy Check (PDAA)

SERDF .... State Energy Research and Development Fund [*New South Wales, Australia*]

SERDP .... Strategic Environmental Research and Development Program [*National Center for Atmospheric Research*]

SERE .... Services Electronic Research Establishment [*British*] (DEN)

SERE .... Solar Electromagnetic Radiation Flux [*Model*] (USDC)

SERE .... Survival, Evasion, Resistance, and Escape [*Military*] (AFM)

SERENDIP... Search for Extraterrestrial Radio Emission from Nearby Developed Intelligent Populations

SERENE ...... Special Engineering Review of Events Nobody Envisioned

Serenpet...... Serenpet, Inc. [*Associated Press*] (SAG)

Serenpt........ Serenpet, Inc. [*Associated Press*] (SAG)

SEREP .... System Environment Recording and Edit Program [*Computer science*] (IAA)

SEREP .... System Environment Recording, Editing, and Printing [*Computer science*]

SEREP .... System Error Record Editing Program [*Computer science*]

SERER .... Survival, Evasion, Resistance, Escape, Recovery [*Environmental science*] (COE)

SERET .... Snakeye Retarded [*Navy*] (DNAB)

SERF........... Sandia Engineering Reactor Facility [*Nuclear energy*]

SERF........... Solar and Energy Research Facility [*University of Arizona*] [*Research center*] (RCD)

SERF........... Solar Electromagnetic Radiation Flux [*Model*] [*Marine science*] (OSRA)

SERF........... Space Environmental Research Facility

SERF........... Special Emergency Reaction Team Facility

SERF........... Special Environmental Radiometallurgy Facility [*Nuclear energy*] (NRCH)

SERF........... Special Extensive Routine Functions (NITA)

SERF........... Study of Energy Release in Flares [*International Council of Scientific Unions*]

SERF........... System for Equipment Requirements Forecasting (MHDB)

SERFACE ..... South East Regional Forum for Adult and Continuing Education [*British*] (DI)

SERFE......... Selection of Exempt Organization Returns for Examination [*IRS*]

SERFORSOPACSUBCOM... Service Force, South Pacific, Subordinate Command

SERG .... Sergeant

SERG .... Serving (MSA)

Serg & Lowb... English Common Law Reports, Edited by Sergeant and Lowber [*A publication*] (DLA)

Serg & Lowb Rep... English Common Law Reports, Edited by Sergeant and Lowber [*A publication*] (DLA)

Serg & R .... Sergeant and Rawle's Pennsylvania Reports [*A publication*] (DLA)

Serg & Raw... Sergeant and Rawle's Pennsylvania Reports [*A publication*] (DLA)

Serg & Rawl... Sergeant and Rawle's Pennsylvania Supreme Court Reports [*1814-28*] [*A publication*] (DLA)

Serg Att....... Sergeant on Attachment [*A publication*] (DLA)

Serg Const L... Sergeant's Constitutional Law [*A publication*] (DLA)

SERGE .... Socially and Ecologically Responsible Geographers [*Defunct*] (EA)

SERGG .... Southeast Regional Genetics Group (HGEN)

Serg Land Laws PA... Sergeant on the Land Laws of Pennsylvania [*A publication*] (DLA)

Serg LL........ Sergeant's Land Laws of Pennsylvania [*A publication*] (DLA)

Serg Mech L... Sergeant on Mechanics' Lien Law [*A publication*] (DLA)

SERGRAD .... Selected and Retained Graduate (DNAB)

SERGT .... Sergeant

SERH .... Secretaria de Estado de Recursos Hidricos [*Argentina*]

SERHL .... Southeastern Radiological Health Laboratory (SAA)

SERI........... Aguarico [*Ecuador*] [*ICAO location identifier*] (ICLI)

seri............ Serigraph (VRA)

SERI........... Society for the Encouragement of Research and Invention [*Defunct*] (EA)

SERI........... Solar Energy Research Institute [*Golden, CO*] [*Department of Energy*]

SER-IV........ Supination, External Rotation - Type IV Fracture

SERIX .... Swedish Environmental Research Index [*Swedish National Environmental Protection Board*] [*Database*] (IID)

SERJ........... Serjeant [*Military British*]

SERJ........... Space Electric Ramjet [*Air Force*]

SERJ........... Supercharged Ejector Ramjet [*Aircraft engine*]

Serjt........... Serjeant [*Military British*] (DMA)

SERJT-MAJ... Serjeant-Major [*Military British*] (ROG)

SERL.......... Sanitary Engineering Research Laboratory [*University of California*] (MCD)

SERL.......... Services Electronic Research Laboratory [*British*]

SERLANT..... Service Forces, Atlantic [*Navy*]

SERLINE ..... Serials On-Line [*National Library of Medicine*] [*Bethesda, MD Database*]

SERM.......... Selective Estrogen Peceptor Modulator

SERM.......... Selective Estrogen Receptor Modulator [*Genetics*]

SERM.......... Sermon (ROG)

SERM.......... Society of Early Recorded Music (EA)

SERM.......... Solar and Earth Radiation Monitor (NOAA)

SERMCE ..... Amalgamated Association of Street, Electric Railway, and Motor Coach Employees of America [*Later, ATU*]

SERME........ Sign Error Root Modulus Error

SERMIS .... Support Equipment Rework Management Information System [*Navy*] (GFGA)

SERMLP .... Southeastern Regional Medical Library Program [*Emory University*] [*Library network*] (IID)

SERMS .... Selective Estrogen Receptor Modulators

SERNO......... Serial Number

SERNO......... Service Number [*Military*]

SERO .... Santa Rosa [*Ecuador*] [*ICAO location identifier*] (ICLI)

sero .... Serological [*Examination*] [*Immunology*] (DAVI)

SERO .... Serologicals Corp. [*NASDAQ symbol*] (SAG)

SERO .... Serologicals Inc. [*NASDAQ symbol*] (TTSB)

SERO .... Service Employment Redevelopment Operation (OICC)

SERO .... System Engineering Release Order (MCD)

SERODS...... Surface-Enhanced Raman Optical Data Storage Technology [*Developed at Oak Ridge National Laboratory*]

Serolog........ Serologicals Corp. [*Associated Press*] (SAG)

SERON......... Service Squadron [*Navy*]

SERP .... Self-Employed Retirement Plan [*Keogh plan*]

Serp............ Serpens [*Constellation*]

SERP .... Simulated Ejector Ready Panel

SERP .... Software Engineering Research Projects [*Data and Analysis Center for Software*] [*Database*]

SERP .... Standardization/Evaluation Review Panel (AFIT)

SERP .... Strategic Environmental Research Program [*DoD Department of Energy*]

SERP .... Supervisor's Evaluation of Research Personnel (AEBS)

SERP .... Supplemental Executive Retirement Plan [*Human resources*] (WYGK)

SERPA .... Southeastern Resource Policy Association (EA)

SERPAC .... Service Forces, Pacific [*Navy*]

SERPIN .... Serine Proteinase Inhibitor [*Biochemistry*]

SERPN .... Society for Education and Research in Psychiatric Mental Health Nursing (NTPA)

SERPS .... Service Propulsion System [*or Subsystem*] [*NASA*] (KSC)

SERPS .... State Earnings-Related Pension Scheme [*British*]

SERR .... Semiannual RADWASTE [*Radioactive Waste*] Effluent Release (GFGA)

Ser R .... Serials Review [*A publication*] (BRI)

SERR .... Serrate (MSA)

SERRON ...... Service Squadron [*Navy*]

SERRS .... Surface-Enhanced Resonance Raman Scattering [*Spectroscopy*]

SE/RRT .... Southern Europe - Railroad Transport [*NATO*] (NATG)

SERS .... Rio Saloya [*Ecuador*] [*ICAO location identifier*] (ICLI)

SERS .... Seaborne Environmental Reporting System

SERS .... Shuttle Equipment Record System [*NASA*] (NASA)

SERS .... Southern Education Reporting Service

SERS .... Special Emergency Radio Service [*Telecommunications*] (OTD)

SERS .... State Employees Retirement System

SERS .... Stimulus Evaluation/Response Selection Test [*Medicine*] (DMAA)

SERS .... Support Equipment Requirements Sheet

SERS .... Surface-Enhanced Raman Scattering [*Spectroscopy*]

ser sect .... Serial Sections [*Pathology*] (DAVI)

Sert............. Sertorius [*of Plutarch*] [*Classical studies*] (OCD)

SERT........... Shipboard Electronic Readiness Team [*Navy*] (CAAL)

SERT........... Shipboard Electronic Repair Team [*Navy*] (DOMA)

SERT........... Single-Electron Rise Time [*Scintillation counting*] (IEEE)

SERT........... Society of Electronic and Radio Technicians (IAA)

SE/RT.......... Southern Europe - Road Transport [*NATO*] (NATG)

SERT........... Space Electric [*or Electronic*] Rocket Test

SERT........... Special Education Resource Teacher

SERT........... Special Education Review Team

SERT........... Special Emergency Reaction Team

SERT........... Spinning Satellite for Electric Rocket Test

SERT........... Sustained Ethanol Release Tube [*Pharmacology*]

SERTEL........ Servicios Telereservacios SA de CV [*ICAO designator*] (FAAC)

SERTH .... Satisfactory Evidence Received This Headquarters

SERTOG........ Space Experiment on Relativistic Theories of Gravitation (PDAA)

SERTOMA ..... Service to Mankind [*Meaning of name of Sertoma International Organization*]

SERTS .... Screaming Eagle Replacement Training School [*Vietnam*] [*Army*] (VNW)

SERTS .... Solar Extreme Ultraviolet Telescope and Spectrograph (MCD)

SERUG......... SII [*Systems Integrators, Incorporated*] Eastern Regional Users Group [*Defunct*] (EA)

SERV .... Serva [*Preserve*] [*Latin*] (WGA)

SERV	Servant
SERV	Servian (ROG)
SERV	Service (AAG)
Serv	Service (CMD)
SERV	Simian Endogenous Retrovirus
SERV	Single-Stage Earth-Orbital Reusable Vehicle (MCD)
SERV	Space Emergency Reentry Vehicle [NASA]
SERV	Surface Effect Rescue Vessel [Coast Guard]
ServC	Service Command [Army]
SERVCOMFMFPAC	Service Command, Fleet Marine Force, Pacific
SERVDIV	Service Division [Navy]
SERVE	Serve and Enrich Retirement by Volunteer Experience [Staten Island, NY, project]
SERVE	Service (ROG)
SERVFOR	Service Force [Navy]
SERVHEL	Service and Health Record (DAVI)
SERVHEL	Service Record and Health Record [Military]
Servico	Servico, Inc. [Associated Press] (SAG)
SERVIVENSA	Empresa Servicicious Avensa SA [Venezuela] [ICAO designator] (FAAC)
SERVLANT	Service Force, Atlantic Fleet
SERVLANTSUBORDCOMD	Service Force, Atlantic Fleet, Subordinate Command
SERVMART	Service Mart
SERVNO	Service Number [Navy]
SERVO	Service Office
SERVO	Servomechanism
SERVON	Service Squadron [Navy]
Servotr	Servotronics, Inc. [Associated Press] (SAG)
SERVPA	Service Record and Pay Record [Military]
SERVPAC	Service Force, Pacific Fleet
SERVPAHEL	Service Record, Pay Record, and Health Record [Military]
SERVREC	Service Record
SERVS	Spanish/English Reading and Vocabulary Screening Test
SERVSCOLCOM	Service School Command [Navy]
SERVSCOLCOMDET	Service Schools Command Detachment [Navy] (DNAB)
SERVSOWESPAC	Service Force, Southwest Pacific Fleet
SERVT	Servant
SERY	Sarayacu [Ecuador] [ICAO location identifier] (ICLI)
SES	Group Psychotherapy Suitability Evaluation Scale [Psychology]
SES	Samarbetsorganisationen for Emballagefragor i Skandinavien [Scandinavian Packaging Association] [Sweden] (EA)
SES	Satellite Earth Station
SES	Science Ethic Society (EA)
SES	Scientific Exploration Society (EA)
SES	Scottish Economic Society [British]
SES	Seafarers Education Service [British]
SES	Seagrass Ecosystem Study [Marine science] (MSC)
SES	Seasonal Energy Syndrome [Psychology] (DAVI)
SES	Seaward Extension Simulator (SAA)
SES	Secondary Electron Scattering
SES	Secondary Electron Spectroscopy (AAEL)
SES	Secondary Emissions Standard (COE)
SES	Section d'Eclaireurs-Skieurs [of Chasseurs Alpins, French Army]
SES	Seismic Electric Signal
SES	Selma [Alabama] [Airport symbol] (AD)
SES	Senior Executive Service [Civil Service]
SES	Senior Executive Staff (AAGC)
SES	Sequential Environmental Stress
SES	Service Engine Soon [Automotive engineering]
SES	Service Evaluation System [Telecommunications] (TEL)
SES	Sesone [Herbicide] [Trademark of Union Carbide Corp.]
SES	Shared Energy Savings
SES	Ship Earth Station [INMARSAT]
SES	Shorted Emitter Switch (IAA)
SES	Shuttle Engineering Simulation [NASA] (NASA)
SES	Shuttle Engineering System [NASA] (SSD)
SES	Sight Erection Support
SES	Signal Enhancement Seismograph
SES	Signals Exploitation Space (MCD)
SES	Singapore Stock Exchange (ODBW)
SES	Single Engine Sea [Pilot rating] (AIA)
SES	Small Edison Screw
SES	Smart Energy System [IBM Corp.] [Computer science] (PCM)
SES	Societe des Etudes Socialistes [Society for Socialist Studies - SSS]
SES	Society for Environmental Stabilization [Defunct] (EA)
SES	Society of Educators and Scholars (EA)
SES	Society of Engineering Science (EA)
SES	Society of Eye Surgeons (EA)
SES	Socioeconomic Status [or Strata]
SES	Soil Erosion Service [Became Soil Conservation Service, 1935]
SES	Solar Eclipse Sensor (MCD)
SES	Solar Energy Society [Later, International Solar Energy Society] (EA)
SES	Solar Environment Simulator
SES	SONAR Echo Simulator
SES	Space Environment Simulator [NASA]
SES	Space Erectable Structure
SES	Special Emphasis Study (NASA)
SES	Special Exchange Service [Telecommunications] (TEL)
SES	Special Exploitation Service [South Vietnamese studies and observations group] [Military] (VNW)
SES	SPRINT Engagement Simulation [Missile system evaluation] [Army] (RDA)
SES	Standards Engineering Society (EA)
SES	State Experiment Stations Division [of ARS, Department of Agriculture]
SES	Stationary Engine Society (EA)
SES	Steam Electric Station [Nuclear energy] (NRCH)
SES	Steam Engine Systems Corp.
SES	Stimulated Emission Spectroscopy
SES	Story of Exploration Series [A publication]
SES	Strategic Engineering Survey [Navy]
SES	Student Evaluation Scale [Student attitudes test]
SES	Studies and Expansion Society [See also SEE] (EAIO)
SES	Study of Education at Stanford [Stanford University]
SES	Subendothelial Space [Medicine] (DMAA)
SES	Suffield [Alberta] [Seismograph station code, US Geological Survey] (SEIS)
SES	Suffield Experimental Station [Canada]
SES	Superexcited Electronic State [Chemistry] (OA)
SES	Supervisory Electronics Specialist
SES	Support Equipment Subsystem
SES	Surface Effects Ship [Navy symbol]
SES	Sustaining Engineering Services
SES	Sydney Esperanto Society [Australia]
SES	Sylvania Electronic Systems (SAA)
SES	Symptom Evaluation Survey (EDAC)
SES	Synergist Erection System [Medicine]
SES	System Evaluation System (MCD)
SES	System External Storage
SES	Systems Engineering Study
SES	Systems Engineering Support
SES	Systems Engineering Work Statement
SES	Systems Evaluation Squadron [Air Force]
SESA	Salinas [Ecuador] [ICAO location identifier] (ICLI)
SESA	Signal Equipment Support Agency
SESA	Single End Strip Adhesion (PDAA)
SESA	Social and Economic Statistics Administration [Terminated, 1975] [Department of Commerce]
SESA	Society for Environmental Stress Analysis (IAA)
SESA	Society for Experimental Stress Analysis [Later, SEM] (EA)
SESA	Solar Energy Society of America (EA)
SESA	Southeast Singles Association
SESA	Standard Electrica, Sociedad Anonima [Brazilian affiliate of ITT]
SESA	State Employment Security Agency
SESA	Story of the Empire Series [A publication]
SESAC	Society of European Stage Authors and Composers
SESAC	Space and Earth Science Advisory Committee [NASA]
SESAC Inc	Society of European Stage Authors and Composers [Nashville, TN] (WDMC)
SESAM	System for Electronic Support of Academic Material (TELE)
SESAM	System for Emission Sampling and Measurement [Automotive engineering]
SESAME	Search for Excellence in Science and Mathematics Education [Graduate program at University of California at Berkeley]
SESAME	Selected Essential Stockage Availability Method
SESAME	Service, Sort and Merge [Computer science]
SESAME	Severe Environmental Storms and Mesoscale Experiment [National Science Foundation/National Oceanic and Atmospheric Administration]
SESAME	Systems Engineering Study on Atmospheric Measurements and Equipment (NOAA)
SESAMS	Strategic Electric Sector Assessment Methodology under Sustainability Conditions [Project]
SESAT	Stanford Early School Achievement Test [Educational test]
SESB	Sibambe [Ecuador] [ICAO location identifier] (ICLI)
SESC	Selective Elution Solvent Chromatography
SESC	Sequential Elution Solvent Chromatography
SESC	Shuttle Events Sequential Control [NASA] (MCD)
SESC	South Eastern State College [Oklahoma]
SESC	Space Environment Services Center [Boulder, CO] [National Oceanic and Atmospheric Administration] (KSC)
SESC	Special Environmental Sample Container [NASA] (PDAA)
SESC	Sucua [Ecuador] [ICAO location identifier] (ICLI)
SESC	Surface Environmental Sample Container [Apollo] [NASA]
SESCI	Solar Energy Society of Canada, Inc. [Societe d'Energie Solaire du Cana da]
SESCO	Secure Submarine Communications
SESD	Santo Domingo De Los Colorados [Ecuador] [ICAO location identifier] (ICLI)
SESD	Space Electronic Security Division [Military]
SESDA	Scottish Electro-Static Discharge Association (EAIO)
SESDA	Serikat Sekerdja Departemen Agama [Brotherhood of Employees of Department of Religious Affairs] [Indonesia]
SESDA	Small Engine Servicing Dealers Association (EA)
SESDAQ	Stock Exchange of Singapore Dealing and Automated Quotation System
SE Sdg	Square-Edge Siding (DAC)
SESE	Search for Excellence in Science Education [National Science Teacher Association] (EDAC)
SESE	Secadal [Educador] [ICAO location identifier] (ICLI)
SESE	Secure Echo-Sounding Equipment [SONAR] [Navy]
SESE	Shuttle Experiment Support Equipment
SE/SE	Single Entry/Single Exit
SESEF	Space Electronics Support Equipment (MCD)
SESEF	Ship Electronics System Evaluation Facility [Navy] (CAAL)
SESG	Sangay [Ecuador] [ICAO location identifier] (ICLI)
SESG	Southern Europe Shipping Group [NATO] (NATG)
SESGA	Show of Equipment and Supplies for the Graphic Arts (DGA)
SESH	San Honorato [Ecuador] [ICAO location identifier] (ICLI)
SESI	Socio-Economic-Status-Indicator (WDMC)

SESI............ Soils Engineering Services, Inc. (EFIS)
SESI............ Solar Energy Society of Ireland [*International Solar Energy Society*]
SESI............ Stock Exchange of Singapore Index (ODBW)
SESI............ Superior Energy Services, Inc. [*NASDAQ symbol*] (SAG)
SESI............ Superior Energy Svcs [*NASDAQ symbol*] (TTSB)
SESI............ Sur Iliniza [*Ecuador*] [*ICAO location identifier*] (ICLI)
SE/SI.......... Systems Engineering/Systems Integration (SDI)
SESIP......... Systems Engineering Summary of Installation and Program Planning (IAA)
SESIW........ Superior Energy Svcs Wrrt [*NASDAQ symbol*] (TTSB)
SESIZ......... Superior Energy Svcs Wrrt'B' [*NASDAQ symbol*] (TTSB)
SESJ........... San Jose [*Ecuador*] [*ICAO location identifier*] (ICLI)
SESK........... Silok [*Ecuador*] [*ICAO location identifier*] (ICLI)
SESL........... San Lorenzo [*Ecuador*] [*ICAO location identifier*] (ICLI)
SESL........... Self-Erecting Space Laboratory (AAG)
SESL........... Space Environment Simulation Laboratory [*NASA*]
SESLP........ Sequential Explicit Stochastic Linear Programming [*Computer science*]
SESM.......... Samborondon [*Ecuador*] [*ICAO location identifier*] (ICLI)
SESM.......... Strategies and Errors in Secondary Mathematics [*Project*] (AIE)
SESMA....... Special Event Search and Master Analysis (GAVI)
SESMI........ Systems Engineering Support and Management Integration (MCD)
SESN .... San Carlos [*Ecuador*] [*ICAO location identifier*] (ICLI)
SESO .... La Estrella [*Ecuador*] [*ICAO location identifier*] (ICLI)
SESO .... Senior Equipment Staff Officer [*Air Force British*]
SESOC........ Surface Effect Ship for Ocean Commerce
SESOME ...... Service, Sort, and Merge [*Computer science*] (IEEE)
SESP.......... Society of Experimental Social Psychology [*Defunct*] (EA)
SESP.......... Space Experimental Satellite Program [*NASA*] (SSD)
SESP.......... Space Experiment Support Program (MCD)
SESPA .... Scientists and Engineers for Social and Political Action [*Later, SFTP*] (EA)
SESPENDO... Serikat Buruh Pegawai Negeri dan Daeran Otonom [*Civil Servants Workers' Union*] [*Indonesia*]
SESPO .... Surface Effect Ships Project Office [*Navy*]
SESPROJ ..... Surface Effect Ship Project [*Navy*] (DNAB)
SESQUIH..... Sesquihora [*An Hour and a Half*] [*Pharmacy*] (ROG)
SESQUIHOR... Sesquihora [*An Hour and a Half*] [*Pharmacy*]
SESR .... San Rafael [*Ecuador*] [*ICAO location identifier*] (ICLI)
SESR .... Segment Entry Save Register [*Computer science*] (MHDI)
SESR .... Selected Equipment Status Report [*Navy*] (NG)
SESR .... Societe Europeenne de Sociologie Rurale [*European Society for Rural Sociology*]
SESR .... Special Environmental Storage Requirements (MCD)
SESRTCIC ... Statistical, Economic, and Social Research and Training Center for Islamic Countries [*Research center Turkey*] (IRC)
SESS........... Session
SESS........... Society of Ethnic and Special Studies (EA)
SESS........... Space Environmental Support System
SESS........... Summer Employment for Science Students
Sess Ca .... Scotch Court of Session Cases [*A publication*] (DLA)
Sess Ca .... Sessions Cases, King's Bench [*1710-48*] [*England*] [*A publication*] (DLA)
Sess Cas .... Scotch Court of Session Cases [*A publication*] (DLA)
Sess Cas .... Session Cases, High Court of Justiciary Section [*1906-16*] [*Scotland*] [*A publication*] (DLA)
Sess Cas .... Sessions Cases, King's Bench [*England*] [*A publication*] (DLA)
Sess Cas KB... Sessions Settlement Cases, King's Bench [*England*] [*A publication*] (DLA)
Sess Cas Sc... Scotch Court of Session Cases [*A publication*] (DLA)
Sess N........ Session Notes [*Scotland*] [*A publication*] (DLA)
Sess Pap CC... Central Criminal Court Cases, Sessions Papers [*1834-1913*] [*England*] [*A publication*] (ILCA)
Sess Pap CCC... Central Criminal Court Cases, Sessions Papers [*1834-1913*] [*England*] [*A publication*] (DLA)
Sess Pap OB... Old Bailey's Sessions Papers [*A publication*] (DLA)
Sest........... Pro Sestio [*of Cicero*] [*Classical studies*] (OCD)
SEST.......... San Cristobal (Galapagos) [*ICAO location identifier*] (ICLI)
SEST.......... Swedish-ESO Submillimetre Telescope [*Observatory*]
SESTF......... Surface Effect Ship Test Facility [*Navy*] (DNAB)
SESTM........ Societe Europeenne de la Science et de la Technologie des Membranes [*European Society of Membrane Science and Technology - ESMST*] (EA)
SestThr....... Southeastern Thrift and Bank Fund [*Associated Press*] (SAG)
SESUNC....... Sesuncia [*An Ounce and a Half*] [*Pharmacy*] (ROG)
SESUPP....... Safety Evaluation Supplement (IAA)
SESY.......... Sur Cayambe [*Ecuador*] [*ICAO location identifier*] (ICLI)
SESZ.......... Sur Antizana [*Ecuador*] [*ICAO location identifier*] (ICLI)
Set............. English Settlement and Removal Cases [*Burrow's Settlement Cases*] [*A publication*] (DLA)
SET............ Safety Education and Training
SET............ San Esteban [*Honduras*] [*Airport symbol*] (AD)
SET............ Satellite Experimental Terminal (NATG)
SET............ Scales for Effective Teaching [*Test*] (TMMY)
SET............ Scaling Erythema and Thickness [*Dermatology*]
SET............ Scientists, Engineers, Technicians
SET............ Secure Electronic Transactions [*Computer science*]
SET............ Secure Exchange Technology
SET............ Securities Exchange of Thailand
SET............ Security Escort Team [*Military*]
SET............ Selective Electronic Training [*Navy*] (NG)
SET............ Selective Employment Tax [*British*]
SET............ Self-Employment Tax [*IRS*]
SET............ Self-Extending Translator (IEEE)
SET............ Senior Electronic Technician [*National Weather Service*]

SET............ Sensory Evaluation Test [*Army*]
SET............ Serial Endosymbiotic Theory [*Evolution*]
SET............ Service Evaluation Telemetry (AAG)
SET............ Setif [*Algeria*] [*Seismograph station code, US Geological Survey*] (SEIS)
SET............ Setting (MSA)
SET............ Settlement (ROG)
SET............ Settling
SET............ Sheraton Executive Traveler [*Sheraton Corp.*]
SET............ Short Employment Tests [*Bennett and Gelink*] (TES)
SET............ Siemont Resources, Inc. [*Vancouver Stock Exchange symbol*]
SET............ Simplified Engineering Technique
SET............ Simulated Emergency Test
SET............ Single-Electron-Transfer [*Organic chemistry*]
SET............ Single Electron Transistor [*Physics*]
SET............ Single-Electron Tunneling [*Physics*]
SET............ Single Electron Tunneling/TransPort (AAEL)
SET............ Single Escape Tower
SET............ Skin Endpoint Titration [*Medicine*] (MEDA)
SET............ Sociedad Ecuatoriana de Transportes Aereos Ltda. [*Ecuador*] [*ICAO designator*] (FAAC)
SET............ Society for Environmental Therapy [*British*]
SET............ Society for Environmental Truth (EA)
SET............ Society for the Eradication of Television (EA)
SET............ Software Encapsulation Template
SET............ Software Engineering Technology
SET............ Software Engineering Terminology [*Computer science*] (IEEE)
SET............ Solar Energy Thermionic [*Program*] [*NASA*]
SET............ Source Evaluation Team [*Army*]
SET............ Spacecraft Elapsed Time
SET............ Space Electronics and Telemetry (MCD)
SET............ Special Engineering Test (IAA)
SET............ Sports Emotion Test [*Research test*] [*Psychology*]
SET............ Stack Entry Time [*Aviation*] (FAAC)
SET............ Standard d'Exchange et de Transfert [*Computer graphics*] [*French*]
SET............ Stepped Electrode Transistor
SET............ Stock Exchange of Thailand [*Thailand*]
SET............ Stored-Energy Transmission (PDAA)
SET............ Student Empowerment Training Project (EA)
SET............ Submarine Engineering Technical
SET............ Suitability Evaluation Team (MCD)
SET............ Supported Employment & Training (WDAA)
SET............ Surrogate Embryo Transfer [*Gynecology*] (CPH)
SET............ Symbol Elaboration Test [*Psychology*]
SET............ Synchro Error Tester
SET............ Syndicat des Enseignants du Togo [*Union of Togolese Teachers*]
SET............ System Evaluation Technique (IAA)
SET............ System Extension Test
SET............ Systems Effects Test [*Nuclear energy*] (GFGA)
SET............ Systems Engineering Test (CET)
SET............ Systolic Ejection Time [*Cardiology*] (MAE)
SETA.......... Satellite Electrostatic Triaxial Accelerometer
SETA.......... Scottish Egg Trade Association (DBA)
SETA.......... Simplified Electronic Tracking (IAA)
SETA.......... Simplified Electronic Tracking Apparatus [*Air Force*]
SETA.......... Systems Engineering and Technical Assistance (MCD)
SETA.......... Taura [*Ecuador*] [*ICAO location identifier*] (ICLI)
SETAB........ Sets Tabular Material [*Phototypesetting computer*]
SETAC........ Sector TACAN [*Tactical Air Navigation*] System
SETAC........ Society of Environmental Toxicology and Chemistry (EA)
SETAC........ Specially Equipped Traffic Accident Car [*British police*]
SETAC........ Systems Engineering and Technical Assistance Contract
SETAD........ Secure Encryption of Tactical Analog Data
SETAD........ Secure Transmission of Acoustic Data (NVT)
SETAF........ Southern European Task Force [*NATO*]
SETAR........ Serial Event Timer and Recorder
SETA-UITA ... Syndicat Europeen des Travailleurs de l'Alimentation, de l'Hotellerie, et des Branches Connexes dans l'UITA [*European Committee of Food, Catering, and Allied Workers' Unions within the IUF - ECF-IUF*] (EAIO)
SETB.......... Secondary Education Text-Books [*A publication*]
SETB.......... Set Theoretic Language - BALM [*1973*] [*Computer science*] (CSR)
SETB.......... Timbre [*Ecuador*] [*ICAO location identifier*] (ICLI)
SETBGT...... Set Ballistic Gain Table
SETC.......... Solid Electrolyte Tantalum Capacitor
SETC.......... Southeastern Theatre Conference (EA)
SETC.......... Submarine Escape Training Centre [*British military*] (DMA)
SETD.......... Scheduled Estimated Time of Departure [*Aviation*] (DA)
SETD.......... Sledborne Event Time Digitizer
SETD.......... Space Environment Test Division [*NASA*]
SE/TD......... Systems Engineering and Technical Direction (AAGC)
SETE.......... Secretariat for Electronic Test Equipment [*DoD*]
SETE.......... Status of Electronic Test Equipment (MCD)
SETE.......... Supersonic Expendable Turbojet Engine (MCD)
SETE.......... Support and Electronic Test Equipment
SETE.......... System Evaluation Test Equipment [*Military*] (CAAL)
SETE.......... Tena [*Ecuador*] [*ICAO location identifier*] (ICLI)
SETEC........ Semiconductor Equipment Technology Center (AAEL)
SETEL........ Societe Europeenne de Teleguidage [*Five European firms organized in 1958 under French law to act as European prime contractor for production of HAWK missiles*] [*NATO*]
SETEP........ Science and Engineering Technician Education Program [*National Science Foundation*]
SETF.......... SNAP [*Systems for Nuclear Auxiliary Power*] Experimental Test Facility

SETF............ STARAN Evaluation and Training Facility
SETFIA......... South East Trawl Fishing Industry Association [*Australia*]
SETG............ Tenguel [*Ecuador*] [*ICAO location identifier*] (ICLI)
SET-GO........ Support and Encouragement for Talent - Gateway to Opportunity [*Project*] (EA)
SETH............ Taisha [*Ecudaor*] [*ICAO location identifier*] (ICLI)
SETI............. Search for Extraterrestrial Intelligence
SETI............. Societe Europeenne pour le Traitement de l'Information [*European Society for the Processing of Information*]
SETI............. Tiputini [*Ecuador*] [*ICAO location identifier*] (ICLI)
SETID.......... Set Identification
SETINA........ Southeast Texas Information Network Association
SETIS.......... Societe Europeenne pour l'Etude et l'Integration des Systemes Spatiaux
SETL............ Science Experiment Test Laboratory [*NASA*]
SETL............ Set Theoretic Language [*1971*] [*Computer science*] (CSR)
SETLG......... Settling (MSA)
SETO............ Pacto [*Ecuador*] [*ICAO location identifier*] (ICLI)
SETOLS........ Surface Effect Takeoff and Land System [*Naval aviation*]
Seton........... Seton's Forms of Decrees, Judgments, and Orders in Equity [*7 eds.*] [*1830-1912*] [*A publication*] (DLA)
Seton Dec.... Seton's Forms of Decrees, Judgments, and Orders in Equity [*7th ed.*] [*1912*] [*A publication*] (DLA)
Seton Hall U... Seton Hall University (GAGS)
SETP............ Society of Experimental Test Pilots (EA)
SETP............ Tandapi [*Ecuador*] [*ICAO location identifier*] (ICLI)
SETR............ Setter (MSA)
SETR............ Tarapoa [*Ecuador*] [*ICAO location identifier*] (ICLI)
SETS............ Scottish Electrical Training Scheme Ltd. [*British*]
SETS............ Seeker Evaluation Test System [*Military*]
SETS............ Set Equation Transformation System [*1970*] [*Computer science*] (CSR)
SETS............ Site Enforcement Tracking System [*Environmental Protection Agency*] (GFGA)
SETS............ Skylab End-to-End Test System [*NASA*]
SETS............ Solar Electric Test Satellite
SETS............ Solar Energy Thermionic Conversion System [*NASA*]
SETS............ Special Electron Tube Section
SETS............ Squad Engagement Training System [*Army*] (INF)
SETS............ Standardized Environmental Technical Specifications [*Nuclear energy*] (NRCH)
SETS............ Statistical Export and Tabulation System (COE)
SETS............ Stereo Electro-Optical Tracking System (MCD)
SETSE.......... Single-Electron Transistor Scanning Electrometer [*Microscope*]
SETT............ School Readiness Evaluation by Trained Testers [*1984*] (TES)
Sett............. Settlement Cases [*A publication*] (DLA)
SETT............ Submarine Escape Training Tank
SETT............ Teniente Ortiz [*Ecuador*] [*ICAO location identifier*] (ICLI)
SETTA.......... Southeastern Test and Training Area [*Military*] (MCD)
Sett & Rem... Settlement and Removal Cases in English King's Bench [*A publication*] (DLA)
Sett Cas...... Burrow's English Settlement Cases [*A publication*] (DLA)
Sett Cas...... Settlement and Removal Cases in English King's Bench [*A publication*] (DLA)
SETTL......... Settler [*Genealogy*]
SETTLET...... Settlement (ROG)
SETTT......... Settlement (ROG)
SETU........... Tulcan [*Ecuador*] [*ICAO location identifier*] (ICLI)
SETWEG ...... Statistical Engine Test Work Group [*Lubricants testing*] [*Automotive engineering*]
SEU............. Saint Edward's University [*Texas*]
SEU............. Sales Education Units
SEU............. Scottish European Airways Ltd. [*British ICAO designator*] (FAAC)
SEU............. Seronera [*Tanzania*] [*Airport symbol*] (AD)
SEU............. Single Event Upset (SSD)
SEU............. Small End-Up (IAA)
SEU............. Solar Energy Update [*A publication*]
SEU............. Source Entry Utility
SEU............. Southeastern University [*Washington, DC*]
SEU............. Spiral Optics [*Vancouver Stock Exchange symbol*]
SEU............. Subjective Expected Utility [*Concept*] [*Theory used for decision making*]
SEU............. Surgery Expandable Unit (SAA)
SEUG .... Screaming Eagles Users Group [*Defunct*] (EA)
SEUL........... Servicio Europeo de Universitarios Latinoamericanos [*Belgium*]
SEUL........... Support Equipment Utilization List (NASA)
SEURE .... Systems Evaluation Code Under Radiation Environment (IEEE)
SEUS .... Southeastern United States
SEUSSN....... Southeastern United States Seismic Network (NRCH)
SEUY .... Chanduy [*Ecuador*] [*ICAO location identifier*] (ICLI)
SEV............. Scout Evaluation Vehicle
SEV............. Sensor Equivalent Visibility
SEV............. Service City, AK [*Location identifier FAA*] (FAAL)
SEV............. Sevastopol [*Former USSR Seismograph station code, US Geological Survey Closed*] (SEIS)
SEV............. Seven
SEV............. Several
SEV............. Severe [*Used to qualify weather phenomena*]
SEV............. Severed
Sev............. Severus [*of Scriptores Historiae Augustae*] [*Classical studies*] (OCD)
SEV............. Sevres [*China*] (ROG)
SEV............. Shelter Equipment Vault
SEV............. Ship Exercise Vehicle
SEV............. Simcoe Erie Investors Ltd. [*Toronto Stock Exchange symbol*]
SEV............. Small Earlywood Vessel [*Tree-ring property*]

SEV............. Societe d'Ethologie Veterinaire [*Society for Veterinary Ethology - SVE*] [*Edinburgh, Scotland*] (EAIO)
SEV............. Special Equipment Vehicle [*Military*]
SEV............. Split End Vector [*System for plant cell transformation*]
SEV............. SRAM Equivalent Volume (MCD)
SEV............. State Equalized Value [*Real estate*]
SEV............. Stockpile Emergency Verification [*DoD*]
SEV............. Surface Effects Vehicle [*Military*]
SEVA........... Skylab Extravehicular Visor Assembly [*NASA*]
SEVA........... Standup Extravehicular Activity [*Aerospace*]
SEVA........... Surface Extravehicular Activity [*Lunar exploration*]
SEVA........... System Evaluation Program (IAA)
SEVA........... Valdez [*Ecuador*] [*ICAO location identifier*] (ICLI)
SEVAC........ Secure Voice Access Console [*Army*] (AABC)
SEVAL........ Senior Evaluator (MCD)
Sev App Cas... Sevestre's Bengal High Court Appeal Cases [*1864-68*] [*India*] [*A publication*] (DLA)
SEVAS......... Secure Voice Access Systems [*Army*] (AABC)
Sev Cent N... Seventeenth-Century News [*A publication*] (BRI)
SEVEC......... Society for Educational Visits and Exchanges in Canada [*Societe Educative de Visites et d'Echanges au Canada*]
SEVENTHFLT... Seventh Fleet [*Navy*]
SevEnv....... Sevenson Environmental Services, Inc. [*Associated Press*] (SAG)
Sevestre ..... Calcutta Reports of Cases in Appeal [*A publication*] (DLA)
SEVFLT....... Seventh Fleet [*Pacific*] [*Navy*]
Sev HC .... Sevestre's Bengal High Court Reports [*India*] [*A publication*] (DLA)
SEVI........... Villano [*Ecuador*] [*ICAO location identifier*] (ICLI)
SEVL.......... 7th Level Inc. [*NASDAQ symbol*] (TTSB)
SEVL.......... Seventh Level, Inc. [*NASDAQ symbol*] (SAG)
SEVL.......... Several (ROG)
SEVN .... Sevenson Environmental Services, Inc. [*NASDAQ symbol*] (NQ)
SEVN .... Sevenson Enviro Svcs [*NASDAQ symbol*] (TTSB)
SEVN .... Vinces [*Ecuador*] [*ICAO location identifier*] (ICLI)
SevnHil....... Seven Hills Financial Corp. [*Associated Press*] (SAG)
SEVOCOM... Secure Voice Communications (AFM)
SEVP.......... Severance Pay [*Military*]
Sev SDA ...... Sevestre's Sadr Diwani Adalat Reports [*Bengal, India*] [*A publication*] (DLA)
SEVT.......... Ventanas [*Ecuador*] [*ICAO location identifier*] (ICLI)
SEW........... Sewage [*or Sewer*] (AAG)
SEW........... Seward [*Alaska*] [*Seismograph station code, US Geological Survey*] (SEIS)
SEW........... Sewing
SEW........... Shipboard Electronics Warfare [*Navy*]
SEW........... Silicon Epitaxial Wafer
SEW........... Singer Co. NV [*NYSE symbol*] (SPSG)
SEW........... SONAR Early Warning
SEW........... Sozialistische Einheitspartei Westberlins [*Socialist Unity Party of West Berlin*] [*Germany Political party*] (PPW)
SEW........... Space and Electronic Warfare (DOMA)
SEW........... Special Effects Warhead (MCD)
SEW........... Surface Electromagnetic Wave
SEWA......... Self-Employed Women's Association [*India*]
SEWAC .... South East Wales Access Consortium (AIE)
SEWACO..... Sensor Weapons Control and Command
SEWC........ SIGINT/Electronic Warfare Coordination Element (MCD)
S/EWCC ..... Signal Intelligence/Electronic Warfare Coordination Center (NVT)
Sew Cor...... Sewell on Coroners [*1843*] [*A publication*] (DLA)
Sewell Sheriffs... Sewell on the Law of Sheriffs [*A publication*] (DLA)
SEWG......... Sewing (WGA)
SEWHO....... Shoulder-Elbow-Wrist-Hand Orthosis [*Medicine*]
SEWL......... Southeast Water Laboratory [*Environmental Protection Agency*]
SEWMA...... Simple Exponentially-Weighted Moving-Average (PDAA)
SEWMRPG... Southern European Western Mediterranean Regional Planning Group [*NATO*] (NATG)
SEWO........ Shoulder-Elbow-Wrist Orthosis [*Medicine*]
SEWPS....... Safety Weather Probability Study (MCD)
Sew R......... Sewanee Review [*A publication*] (BRI)
SEWS........ Satellite Early Warning System
SEWS........ Sun-End Work Station [*NASA*] (KSC)
SEWS........ Surface Electromagnetic Wave Spectroscopy
Sew Sh....... Sewell on the Law of Sheriffs [*1842*] [*A publication*] (DLA)
SEWT......... Simulated Electronic Warfare Training [*Army*]
SEWT......... Simulator for Electronic Warfare Training
SEWY........ Seaway Food Town [*NASDAQ symbol*] (TTSB)
SEWY........ Seaway Food Town, Inc. [*NASDAQ symbol*] (NQ)
Sex........... Sextans [*Constellation*]
sex........... Sexual (DAVI)
SEX........... Shipment Exception Code [*Military*] (AFIT)
SEX........... Sign Extend [*Computer science*] (NHD)
SEX........... Size Exclusion [*Analytical chemistry*]
SEX........... Sodium Ethyl Xanthate [*Organic chemistry*]
SEX........... Software Exchange [*Computer science*] (NHD)
SEX........... Summer Experiment Group [*Summer work for engineering undergraduates*]
SEXAFS....... Surface-Extended X-Ray Absorption Fine Structure
S Exec Doc... Senate Executive Document [*A publication*] (DLA)
S Exec Rep... Senate Executive Report [*A publication*] (DLA)
S/EXH....... Single Exhaust [*Automotive engineering*]
Sex LR .... Sexual Law Reporter [*A publication*] (DLA)
Sex L Rep ... Sexual Law Reporter [*A publication*] (DLA)
SExO......... Senior Experimental Officer [*Also, SEO, SXO*] [*Ministry of Agriculture, Fisheries, and Food*] [*British*]
SeXO .... Serum Xanthine Oxidase [*Clinical chemistry*] (AAMN)

Sex Pomp....	Sextus Pomponius [Flourished, 2nd century] [Authority cited in pre-1607 legal work] (DSA)
SEXPOT	SPRINT [Solid-Propellant Rocket Intercept] Extra Pulse Out of Tail [Army]
s expr..........	Sine Expressione [Without Expressing] [Latin] (MAE)
Sex Prob Ct Dig...	Sex Problems Court Digest [A publication] (DLA)
SEXR	Shoulder External Rotation [Sports medicine]
SEXRAT	Sex Ratio [Biology]
Sext	Liber Sextus Decretalium [A publication] (DSA)
Sext	Sextans [Constellation]
SEXT	Sextant (WDAA)
SEXT	Shoulder Extension [Sports medicine]
Sext Emp	Sextus Empiricus [Third century AD] [Classical studies] (OCD)
SEY	Air Seychelles [ICAO designator] (FAAC)
SEY	Block Island, RI [Location identifier FAA] (FAAL)
SEY	Secondary Electron Yield
SEY	Selibaby [Mauritania] [Airport symbol] (OAG)
SEY	Seymchan [Former USSR Seismograph station code, US Geological Survey] (SEIS)
SEY	Southeastern Yiddish (BJA)
SEY	Starlight Energy [Vancouver Stock Exchange symbol]
SEY	Summer Employment Youth [DoD]
SEYA	Yaupi [Ecuador] [ICAO location identifier] (ICLI)
Seych LR	Seychelles Law Reports [A publication] (DLA)
SEYF	Scottish Episcopal Youth Fellowship
SEYM	Secondary Electron Yield Measurement
Sey Merch Sh...	Seymour's Merchant Shipping Acts [2nd ed.] [1857] [A publication] (DLA)
SEYMS	Secondary Electron Yield Measurement System
SEYS	Secondary Electron Yield System
SEZ	Mahe Island [Seychelles Islands] [Airport symbol] (OAG)
SEZ	Sedona, AZ [Location identifier FAA] (FAAL)
SEZ	Servicio Especializado de Carga Aerea [Columbia] [FAA designator] (FAAC)
Sez	Sezione [Division] [Italian] (ILCA)
SEZ	Special Economic Zone
SEZA	Zamora [Ecuador] [ICAO location identifier] (ICLI)
SEZP	Zumba-Pucupamba [Ecuador] [ICAO location identifier] (ICLI)
SF	E. R. Squibb & Sons [Research code symbol]
SF	Fleet Submarine [Navy symbol Obsolete]
SF	Meiji Seika Kaisha Ltd. [Japan] [Research code symbol]
SF	Provisional Sinn Fein [Northern Ireland] [Political party] (PPW)
SF	Royal Scots Fusiliers [Military unit] (DMA)
SF	Sabin-Feldman [Test] [Medicine] (DB)
SF	Sabre Foundation (EA)
SF	Sacrifice Fly [Baseball]
SF	Safe (NASA)
SF	Safety (IAA)
SF	Safety Factor
SF	Safety, Reliability, and Quality Assurance, and Protective Services [Kennedy Space Center] [NASA] (NASA)
SF	Salt Free [Diet]
SF	Sampled Filter (IEEE)
SF	San Francisco [California]
sf	Sao Tome and Principe [MARC country of publication code Library of Congress] (LCCP)
SF	Satiety Factor [Physiology]
SF	Saw Fixture (MCD)
SF	Scale Factor
SF	Scarlet Fever [Medicine]
SF	Scheduling Forecast
SF	Scheibe-Flugzeugbau GmbH [Germany ICAO aircraft manufacturer identifier] (ICAO)
SF	School of Chiropody Full Time [British]
SF	Science Fiction [Also, SCI-FI]
sf	Science Fiction (WDMC)
SF	Science Frontiers [An association] (EA)
SF	Scleroderma Federation (EA)
SF	Scouting Force [Navy]
SF	Scruse Air [ICAO designator] (AD)
SF	Sea Flood
SF	Seasonal Fluctuation (MHDB)
SF	Seasonal Food [Department of Employment] [British]
SF	Secondary Failure [NASA] (KSC)
SF	Secure Facility (MCD)
SF	Security Forces [Japanese army]
SF	Security Forecast [Control Risks Information Services - CRIS] [British Information service or system] (IID)
SF	Sefire Inscriptions (BJA)
SF	Select Frequency
SF	Selection Filter (MCD)
SF	Selous Foundation (EA)
SF	Semifinished [Steel or other material]
SF	Semifixed [Ammunition] (NATG)
SF	Semi-Floating [Automotive engineering]
SF	Semi-Fowler's [Position] [Surgery] (DAVI)
SF	Seminal Fluid [Medicine]
SF	Senate File (OICC)
SF	Senior Fellow
SF	Separation Factor [Chemical analysis]
SF	Serosal Fluid (DB)
SF	Serum Fibrinogen [Medicine] (MAE)
SF	Service Factor (MSA)
SF	Services to Families [Public human service program] (PHSD)
SF	Servicing Flight [British military] (DMA)
SF	Seva Foundation (EA)
SF	Sexagesimo-quarto [Book up to 7-1/2 centimeters in height] [Bibliography]
Sf	Sforzando [With Additional Accent] [Music]
SF	Sham Feeding [Medicine] (DMAA)
SF	Shell Fragment (MAE)
SF	Sherwood Foresters [Military unit] [British]
SF	Shift Forward
SF	Shipfitter [Navy]
SF	Shock Front (SAA)
SF	Shortening Fraction [Cardiology]
SF	Short Format
SF	Shrapnel Fragment (MAE)
SF	Side Frequency (DEN)
SF	Signal Frequency
SF	Signaling Frequency (NAKS)
SF	Significant Figure (IAA)
SF	Silicia Fume [Inorganic chemistry]
SF	Simian Foam-Virus [Medicine] (DMAA)
S/F	Single Face
SF	Single Family (PA)
SF	Single Feeder
S/F	Single Flow (NASA)
SF	Single Frequency [Telecommunications]
SF	Single-Fronted (ADA)
SF	Sinking Fund [Finance]
SF	Sinn Fein [Political front of the Irish Republican Army]
SF	Skin Fibroblast [Clinical chemistry]
SF	Skip Flag [Computer science] (MDG)
SF	Sliding Filter (NASA)
SF	Slip Factor
SF	Slip Fit (MSA)
SF	Slot Format [Microfiltration]
SF	Slow Fire [Military]
SF	Slow Initial Function (AAMN)
SF	Social Forces [A publication] (BRI)
SF	Society Farsarotul (EA)
SF	Sodium Azide, Fecal [Medium] [Microbiology] (DAVI)
SF	Soft [Horse racing]
SF	Soft Focus [Cinematography] (NTCM)
SF	Solar Flare [Astronomy]
SF	Soldiers of Freedom (EA)
SF	Solid Fuel (ADA)
SF	Soluble Factor (DAVI)
SF	SONAR Frequency [Military] (CAAL)
SF	Sons of the Holy Family [Roman Catholic men's religious order]
sf	Sons of the Holy Family (TOCD)
SF	Sosialistisk Folkepartiet [Socialist People's Party] [Norway Political party] (PPE)
SF	Sound and Flash [Military]
SF	Source and Fissionable [Material] [Obsolete; see SS] [Nuclear energy]
SF	Source Factor [Nuclear energy] (NRCH)
SF	Southern Forest Products Association
SF	South Following [Astronomy]
SF	Space Filler [Philately]
SF	Space Flight [A publication]
SF	Spacial Factor
SF	Sparing Fitting [Cargo battens] [Shipping] (DS)
SF	Special Facilities
SF	Special Features (NITA)
SF	Special Fixtures (MCD)
SF	Special Forces [Military]
SF	Special Fraction [Typography] (WDMC)
SF	Spent Fuel [Nuclear energy] (NRCH)
SF	Spinal Fluid [Medicine]
SF	Spin-Flip [Solid state physics]
SF	Spiritus Frumenti [Whisky] [Pharmacy] (ROG)
SF	Splicing Factor [Genetics]
SF	Spontaneous Fission [Radioactivity]
SF	Sports Foundation (EA)
SF	Spot Face
SF	Sprocket Feed (ECII)
SF	Spruce-Fast [Forestry]
SF	Squadron or Flotilla Flag [Navy British]
SF	Square Foot
SF	Stable Factor [Medicine] (DMAA)
SF	Stack Full (MHDI)
SF	Stainless Steel Fastenings
SF	Standard Form
SF	Standard Frequency
SF	Stanton Foundation [Later, KCSF] (EA)
SF	Star Field (MCD)
SF	Starlight Foundation (EA)
SF	Startled Falcon [Book written by Thomas Dunn English (1844)]
SF	State Forces [India] [Army]
SF	Statement of Functions (NATG)
sF	Statfarad [Also, statF] [Unit of capacitance]
SF	Static Firing [NASA] (NASA)
S/F	Statute of Frauds [Business term]
SF	Stepfamily Foundation (EA)
SF	Sterile Females [Genetics]
SF	Stifel Financial [NYSE symbol] (TTSB)
SF	Stifel Financial Corp. [NYSE symbol] (SPSG)
SF	Still-Felty [Syndrome] [Medicine] (DB)

SF	Stock Fund (AFM)
SF	Stopped-Flow [Spectroscopy]
S/F	Store-and-Forward [Data communications]
SF	Stowage Factor [Shipping]
SF	Streptococcus faecilis [Microbiology]
SF	Stress Formula
SF	Stripping Film (DGA)
SF	Structural Foam [Plastics] (DICI)
SF	Structure Function
SF	Subcontractor Furnished [NASA] (NASA)
SF	Subfile (NITA)
SF	Sub Finem [Near the End] [Latin]
SF	Subframe
SF	Substitute Fragment (NITA)
SF	Success Factor
SF	Successful Flight (MCD)
SF	Su Favor [Your Favor] [Spanish]
SF	Sufficient Funding (MCD)
SF	Sugar Flotation [Soil testing]
SF	Sugar-Free [Pharmacy]
SF	Sulfation Factor [of blood serum]
SF	Sun Factor (ADA)
SF	Sunk Face [Construction]
SF	Sunshine Foundation (EA)
SF	Supercritical Field (MEC)
SF	Super Fluorescence (AAEL)
SF	Superfund [Environmental Protection Agency] (GFGA)
SF	Supply Fan (AAG)
SF	Surface Foot
SF	Surfrider Foundation (EA)
SF	Sustained Fire [Military] (INF)
SF	Sustaining Fiber
Sf	Svedberg Flotation Unit (AAMN)
SF	Swedenborg Foundation (EA)
SF	Swiss Franc [Monetary unit]
SF	Symbral Foundation (EA)
SF	Symptom-Free [Medicine] (DAVI)
SF	Syndicat des Fonctionnaires [Lao Civil Servants' Union]
SF	Synovial Fluid [Medicine]
SF1	Shipfitter, First Class [Navy]
SF2	Shipfitter, Second Class [Navy]
Sf3	SAAB-Fairchild 340 [Airplane code]
SF3	Shipfitter, Third Class [Navy]
SF3	Society for the Furtherance and Study of Fantasy and Science Fiction (EA)
SF-4	Shipping Fever [An influenza serotype]
SF-6	Sulfur Hexafluoride [Used in fluid-gas exchange] [Ophthalmology] (DAVI)
SFA	Aerotransportes Entre Rios SRL [Argentina ICAO designator] (FAAC)
SFA	Sachs/Freeman Associates, Inc. [Telecommunications service] (TSSD)
SFA	Sadr Foujdaree Adalat Reports [India] [A publication] (DLA)
SFA	Saks Fifth Avenue [Retail department store]
SFA	Saturated Fatty Acid [Cardiology] (DAVI)
SFA	Scandinavian Fraternity of America (EA)
SFA	Scientific-Atlanta [NYSE symbol] (TTSB)
SFA	Scientific-Atlanta, Inc. [NYSE symbol] (SPSG)
SFA	Scientific Film Association (IAA)
SFA	Scottish Football Association (DI)
SFA	Screw Focusing Adjustment [Optical] (ROG)
SFA	Scruggs Family Association (EA)
SFA	Sears Family Association (EA)
SFA	Securities and Futures Authority [Finance British] (ECON)
SFA	Segmented Flow Analysis
SFA	Segment Frequency Algorithm
SFA	Selected Financial Assistance [British] (DCTA)
SFA	Semantic Feature Analysis (EDAC)
SFA	Seminal Fluid Assay (STED)
SFA	Sempervivum Fanciers Association (EA)
SFA	Sequential Functional Analysis (IAA)
SFA	Serum Folic Acid (STED)
SFA	Service-Factor Amperes (MSA)
SFA	Seven Falls [Quebec] [Seismograph station code, US Geological Survey Closed] (SEIS)
SFA	Sfax [Tunisia] [Airport symbol] (OAG)
SFA	Shanks Family Association (EA)
SFA	Short Field Aircraft
SFA	Show Folks of America (EA)
SFA	Sigmund Freud Archives (EA)
SFA	Simulated Flight - Automatic
SFA	Single Failure Analysis [Nuclear energy] (NRCH)
SFA	Single-Frequency Amplifier [Electronics] (ECII)
SFA	Single Frequency Approach [FAA] (TAG)
SFA	Slide Fastener Association [Defunct] (EA)
SFA	Slow Flying Aircraft
SFA	Small Farmers Association [British] (DBA)
SFA	Snack Food Association (EA)
SFA	Societe Francaise d'Acoustique [French Society of Acoustics - FSA] (EAIO)
SFA	Society of Filipino Accountants (EA)
SFA	Soil-Derived Fulvic Acid
SFA	Solid Fuels Administration [Terminated, 1954]
SFA	Soroptimist Federation of the Americas [Later, Soroptimist International of theAmericas] (EA)
SFA	Southeastern Fabric Association (EA)

SFA	Southeastern Fisheries Association (EA)
SFA	Southern Freight Association
SFA	Spatial Frequency Analyzer
SFA	Special Forces Association (EA)
SFA	Special Forces Auxiliary [Military]
SFA	Special Foreign Activities [Military] (AABC)
SFA	Spectral Flame Analyzer [Environmental science] (COE)
SFA	Speech Foundation of America (EA)
SFA	Spurlock Family Association (EA)
SFA	Standard Fuel Assembly [Nuclear energy] (NRCH)
SFA	Stimulated Fibrinolytic Activity [Medicine] (DMAA)
SFA	Stopped-Flow Analyzer [Chemical analysis]
SFA	Stovall Family Association (EA)
SFA	Streeter Family Association (EA)
SFA	Students for America (EA)
SFA	Stuttering Foundation of America
SFA	Subcommittee on Frequency Allocations
SFA	Sumner Family Association (EA)
SFA	Sun Finder Assembly [NASA]
SFA	Superficial Femoral Angioplasty (STED)
SFA	Superficial Femoral Artery [Anatomy]
SFA	Supplementary Failure Analysis [NASA] (KSC)
SFA	Support Facility Annex [Army]
SFA	Surface Fibroblast Antigen [Cytochemistry]
SFA	Surface Force Apparatus [Physical chemistry]
SFA	Surface Forces Apparatus [For study of bilayers] [Physical chemistry]
SFA	Symphony Foundation of America (EA)
SFAA	Society for Applied Anthropology (EA)
SfAA	Society for Applied Anthropology (NTPA)
SFAA	Society for French-American Affairs [Defunct] (EA)
SFAA	Strong Family Association of America (EA)
SFAAP	Sunflower Army Ammunition Plant (AABC)
SFAAW	Stove, Furnace, and Allied Appliance Workers International Union of North America [AFL-CIO]
SFAC	Solid Fuel Advisory Council [British] (DI)
SFAC	Statement of Financial Accounting Concepts
SFACA	Solid Fuel Advisory Council of America [Defunct] (EA)
SFACI	Software Flight Article Configuration Inspection [NASA] (NASA)
SFAD	Society of Federal Artists and Designers [Later, FDC] (EA)
SFADCO	Shannon Free Airport Development Company (ACII)
SFADS	San Francisco Air Defense Sector (ADC)
SFAF	San Francisco AIDS Foundation (EA)
SFAHD	Society of the Friends of Ancient and Historical Dubrovnik [Croatia] (EAIO)
SFAL	Samuel Feltman Ammunition Laboratory [Army]
SFAL	Stanley Airport [Falkland Islands] [ICAO location identifier] (ICLI)
SFAM	SpeedFam International, Inc. [NASDAQ symbol] (SAG)
SFAM	Speedfam Intl [NASDAQ symbol] (TTSB)
SF & FW	Science Fiction and Fantasy Workshop (EA)
SF & S	Supporting Facilities and Services
SF & T	Sawyer, Finn & Thatcher [Advertising agency]
SFAOD	Superficial-Femoral Artery Occlusive Disease [Medicine]
SFAP	Single-Fiber Action Potential (DMAA)
SFAP	Society for Folk Arts Preservation (EA)
SFA-PP	Slovenian Farmers' Association - People's Party (EY)
SFAPS	Space Flight Acceleration Profile Simulator [NASA]
SFAR	Sound Fixing and Ranging
SFAR	Special Federal Aviation Regulation [FAA]
SFAR	Special Flight Area Rule [Aviation]
SFAR	System Failure Analysis Report (IEEE)
SFAR-38	Special Federal Aviation Regulation 38 [FAA] (TAG)
SFARG	SIOP [Single Integrated Operations Plan] Force Application Review Group (CINC)
SFARP	Strike Fighter Advanced Readiness Program [Navy] (DOMA)
SFAS	Safety Features Actuation Signal [Nuclear energy] (NRCH)
SFAS	Self-Feeling Awareness Scale [Psychology] (EDAC)
SFAS	Special Forces Assessment and Selection [Military] (INF)
SFAS	Special Forces Association [Fraternal group of discharged military personnel who returned to live in Saigon] (VNW)
SFAS	Statement of Financial Accounting Standards
SFAT	Scott, Foresman Achievement Test (EDAC)
S F Austin St U	Stephen F. Austin State University (GAGS)
SFAV	Surrogate Fast Attack Vehicle [Two-passenger wheeled vehicle] (INF)
SFAW	Solid Fuel Administration for War [Terminated, 1947] [World War II]
SFAW	Stove, Furnace, and Allied Appliance Workers International Union of North America [AFL-CIO]
SFB	Air Sofia [Bulgaria] [ICAO designator] (FAAC)
SFB	Sanford, FL [Location identifier FAA] (FAAL)
SFB	San Francisco [California] [Seismograph station code, US Geological Survey Closed] (SEIS)
SFB	San Francisco Ballet
SFB	Segmented Filamentous Bacteria
SFB	Semiconductor Functional Block (IEEE)
SFB	Sender Freies Berlin [Radio network] [West Germany]
SFB	Sir Francis Bacon
SFB	Society for Biomaterials (NTPA)
SFB	Society of Friendly Boilermakers [A union] [British]
SFB	Society of Furnace Builders [British] (BI)
SFB	Solid Fiberboard
SFB	Solid-State Functional Block (IAA)
SFB	Southwestern Freight Bureau, St. Louis MO [STAC]
SFB	Spinning Form Block (MCD)
SFB	Standard Federal Bank [NYSE symbol] (SPSG)
SFB	Standard Fedl Bancorp'n [NYSE symbol] (TTSB)

SFB	Structural Feedback
SFB	Surgical Foreign Body (STED)
SFB	Symmetry Breaking Force (AAEL)
SFBA	Steamship Freight Brokers Association
SFBARTD	San Francisco Bay Area Rapid Transit District
SFBCS	Special Forces Burst Communications Systems [Army] (RDA)
SFBF	Standard Forms Bureau Form [Insurance] (IIA)
SFBI	Self-Filling Blind Loop (DMAA)
SFBI	Spent Fuel Building Isolation [Nuclear energy] (NRCH)
SFBL	Self-Filling Blind Loop [Gastroenterology]
SFBM	Security Bancorp [Formerly, Security Federal Savings Bank] [NASDAQ symbol] (NQ)
SFBNS	San Francisco Bay Naval Shipyard
SFBNSY	San Francisco Bay Naval Shipyard (DNAB)
SFBP	Siberian Flood Basalt Province [Geology]
SFBRI	Science Fiction Book Review Index 1923-1973 [A publication]
SFC	Chief Shipfitter [Navy rating]
SFC	Colorado Springs, CO [Location identifier FAA] (FAAL)
SFC	Saint Francis College [Indiana; Maine; New York; Pennsylvania; Wisconsin]
SFC	San Francisco [California] [Seismograph station code, US Geological Survey] (SEIS)
SFC	S-Band Frequency Converter
SFC	School Facilities Council of Architecture, Education, and Industry [Later, ASBO] (EA)
SFC	Scottish Film Council
SFC	Sculptured Flexible Circuit [Electronics]
SFC	Sectored File Channel (NITA)
SFC	Sectored File Controller
SFC	Securities and Futures Commission [Hong Kong]
SFC	Selection Filter Control (MCD)
SFC	Selector File Channel
SFC	Sequential Function Chart (ACII)
SFC	Sergeant First Class
SFC	Serial Frame Camera (CAAL)
SFC	Serum Fungicidal (STED)
SFC	Shipborne Fighter Control [Navy] (CAAL)
SFC	Ship Fire Control (AAG)
SFC	Shoes Fan Club (EA)
SFC	Short Form Catalog (IAA)
SFC	Shuswap Flight Centre Ltd. [Canada ICAO designator] (FAAC)
SFC	Sight Fire Control
SFC	Simon Foundation for Continence (EA)
SFC	Sioux Falls College [South Dakota]
SFC	Sis Fan Club [Later, RFC] (EA)
SFC	Societe Francaise de Chimie [French Chemical Society - FCS] (EAIO)
SFC	Societe Frederic Chopin [International Frederic Chopin Foundation] (EAIO)
SfC	Society for Calligraphy (EA)
SFC	Society of Flavor Chemists (EA)
sfc	Society of the Brothers of Charity (TOCD)
SFC	Solar Forecast [Air Force] (IAA)
SFC	Solar Forecast Center [Air Force] (IEEE)
SFC	Solid Fat Content [Food analysis]
SFC	Soluble Fibrin-Fibrinogen Complex [Hematology]
SFC	Southern Pacific Funding Corp. [NYSE symbol] (SAG)
SFC	Space Flight Center [NASA]
SFC	Space Forecast Center [Air Force] (GFGA)
SFC	Special Flight Charts [Air Force]
SFC	Special Foreign Currency [US counterpart funds]
SFC	Specific Fuel Consumption
SFC	Spinal Fluid Count [Medicine]
SFC	Sports Fans Connection [A publication]
SFC	Sports Federation of Canada (EAIO)
SFC	Star Field Camera [NASA]
SFC	Starfleet Command (EA)
SFC	State Fund Chairmen [Red Cross]
SFC	St. Francis Center (EA)
SFC	Subcritical Fluid Chromatography
SFC	Sub-Functional Code (DNAB)
SFC	Supercritical Fluid Chromatography
SFC	Superficial Fluid Chromatography (DB)
SFC	Superior Fine Cognac
SFC	Surefire Fan Club [Defunct] (EA)
SFC	Surface (AFM)
SFC	Switching Filter Connector
SFC	Sylvia Fan Club (EA)
SFC	Synchronized Framing Camera
SFC	Synthetic Fuels Corp. [Sponsored by the federal government]
SFCB	Services de Formation et de Consultation aux Bandes [Department of Indian and Inuit Affairs] [Canada]
SFCB	Shipfitter, Construction Battalion [Navy]
SFCBB	Shipfitter, Construction Battalion, Blacksmith [Navy]
SFCBM	Shipfitter, Construction Battalion, Mechanical Draftsman [Navy]
SFCBP	Shipfitter, Construction Battalion, Pipe Fitter and Plumber [Navy]
SFCBR	Shipfitter, Construction Battalion, Rigger [Navy]
SFCBS	Shipfitter, Construction Battalion, Steelworker [Navy]
SFCBW	Shipfitter, Construction Battalion, Welder [Navy]
SFCC	Sisters for a Christian Community
SFCD	Stopped-Flow Circular Dichroism [Spectroscopy]
SFCE	Surface
SFCES	Survivable Flight Control Electronic Set [Aviation] (PDAA)
SFCH	Society of Freight Car Historians (EA)
SF Chr	Science Fiction Chronicle [A publication] (BRI)

SFCI	Spirit of the Future Creative Institute [Commercial firm] (EA)
SFCM	Master Chief Shipfitter [Later, HTCM] [Navy rating]
SFCM	Slurry-Fed Ceramic Matter [Nuclear energy] (NUCP)
SFCMP	Self-Rising Flour and Corn Meal Program [Later, HBA] (EA)
SFCO	Safety Fund [NASDAQ symbol] (TTSB)
SFCO	Special Forces Co. [Military] (CINC)
SFCOp	Senior Fire Control Operator (WDAA)
SFCP	Shore Fire Control Party [Military]
SFCP	Special Foreign Currency Program [National Institute of Standards and Technology]
SFCP	Synthetic Fuels Commercialization Program [Also, SCP] [Energy Resources Council]
SFCPTNG	Shore Fire Control Party Training [Navy] (NVT)
SFCR	Storage Facility Control Room [Nuclear energy] (NRCH)
SFCRS	State-Federal Crop Reporting Service
SFCS	Saint Fidelis College and Seminary [Pennsylvania]
SFCS	Secondary Flow Control System [Nuclear energy] (NRCH)
SFCS	Senior Chief Shipfitter [Later, HTCS] [Navy rating]
SFCS	Shop Floor Control System (AAEL)
SFCS	Slats and Flaps Control System [Aerospace technology] (EECA)
SFCS	Spent Fuel Cooling System [Nuclear energy] (NRCH)
SFCS	Surveyor Flight Control Section
SFCS	Survivable Flight Control System [Military]
SFCSI	Special Foreign Currency Science Information [Program] [National Science Foundation]
SFCS I/F	Shop Floor Control System Interface (AAEL)
SFCSIP	Special Foreign Currency Science Information Program [National Science Foundation]
SFCSR	Storage Facility Cable Spreading Room [Nuclear energy] (NRCH)
SFCT	State Fire Commission of Tasmania [Australia]
SFCU	State and Function Control Unit [Computer science] (MHDI)
SFCV	State Film Centre of Victoria [Australia]
SFCW	San Francisco College for Women [California]
SFCW	Search for Critical Weakness [Aerospace] (AAG)
SFCW	Sweep Frequency, Continuous Wave
SFCW(I)	Swept Frequency Continuous Wave Illumination (MCD)
SFD	Florence-Darlington Technical College Library, Florence, SC [OCLC symbol] (OCLC)
SFD	San Fernando [Venezuela] [Airport symbol] (OAG)
SFD	Severe Fuel Damage (GAAI)
SFD	Sheep Factor Delta (DB)
SFD	Short Food Drape [Dietetics] (DAVI)
SFD	Signal Flow Diagram (MCD)
SFD	Simple Formattable Document [Telecommunications] (OSI)
SFD	Single Family Detached [Real estate terminology] (EMRF)
SFD	Single Family Dwelling [Economics]
SFD	Skin-Film Distance [Medicine] (MAE)
SFD	Small-for-Dates [Medicine] (MEDA)
SFD	Smith's Food & Drug'B' [NYSE symbol] (TTSB)
SFD	Smith's Food & Drug Centers [NYSE symbol] (SPSG)
SFD	Society of Film Distributors [British]
SFD	Software Functional Description [Computer science] (MHDI)
SFD	Solar Flux Density
SFD	Source-to-Film Distance [Radiology]
SFD	Soy-Free Diet (STED)
SFD	Spectral Frequency Distribution (STED)
SFD	Springfield [Diocesan abbreviation] [Illinois] (TOCD)
SFD	Stacking Fault Density (AAEL)
SFD	Start Frame Delimiter (TNIG)
SFD	Sudden Frequency Deviation
SFD	Suore Francescane di Dillingen [Sisters of St. Francis of Dillingen - SSFD] [Italy] (EAIO)
SFD	Supercritical Fluid Desorption [Chemical engineering]
SFD	Sydney Fire District [Australia]
SFD	Symbolic File Directory [Computer science] (HGAA)
SFD	Sympathetic Firing Device [Military] (CAAL)
SFD	System Functional Diagram [or Drawing] (KSC)
SFD	System Function Description (IEEE)
SFD	Systems Flexowriter Double Case
SFDA	Sale of Food and Drugs Act [British]
SFDA	Shakey's Franchised Dealers Association (EA)
SFDA	Special Forces Direct Action [Army]
SFDA	Sulfofluorescein Diacetate [Biological stain]
SFDALGOL	System Function Description Algorithmic Language (IAA)
SFDE	Staff and Faculty Development Elements
SFDI	Solar Facility Design Integration (MCD)
SFDip	Society of Floristry Diploma [British] (DI)
SFDLR	Stock Funding Depot - Level Repairables [Army]
SFDP	Societe Francophone de Primatologie [Francophone Primatological Society - FPS] [France] (EAIO)
SFDP	Software/Firmware Development Plan
SFDR	Single-Feeder
SFDR	Standard Flight Data Recorder
SFDS	Shipboard Fire Detection System (DWSG)
SFDS	Smithfield Foods [NASDAQ symbol] (TTSB)
SFDS	Smithfield Foods, Inc. [NASDAQ symbol] (NQ)
SFDS	Standby Fighter Director Ship [Navy]
SFDS	Strike Force Data System (NVT)
SFDS	System Functional Design Specification (MCD)
SFDT	Signal Format Development Team [France]
SFDT	Site Format Dump Tape (MCD)
SFDW	Special Friends of Dottie West (EA)
SFE	Safeguard Scientifics [NYSE symbol] (TTSB)
SFE	Safeguard Scientifics, Inc. [NYSE symbol] (SPSG)
SFE	Santa Fe [Diocesan abbreviation] [New Mexico] (TOCD)

SFE	Scale Factor Error (KSC)
SFE	Secondary Feedback Element (IAA)
SFE	Seismic Feature Extraction (MCD)
SFE	Seller-Furnished Equipment (MCD)
SFE	Slipped Femoral Epiphysis [Medicine] (DMAA)
SFE	Smart Front End
SFE	Societe Financiere Europeenne
SFE	Society of Financial Examiners (EA)
SFE	Society of Fire Engineers
SFE	Solar Flare Effect [Physics]
SFE	Solid Fuel Engine
SFE	Solution [or Solvent] Free Energy [Physical chemistry]
SFE	Southern Financial Exchange (TBD)
SFE	Soviet Far East (FEA)
SFE	Space Frequency Equivalence (MCD)
SFE	Special Furnished Equipment (MCD)
SFE	Stacking Fault Energy [Alloy]
SFE	Staged Field Experiment [Gas production]
SFE	Student-Faculty Evaluation
SFE	Students in Free Enterprise (EA)
SFE	Supercritical Fluid Extraction [Also, SCFE] [Chemical engineering]
SFE	Surface-Free Energy
SFE	Surf Inlet Mines [Vancouver Stock Exchange symbol]
SFE	Sustainable Forestry Education [Michigan]
SFE	Sydney Futures Exchange [Australia] (NUMA)
SFE	Synthetic Fermented Egg [Animal repellent]
SFEA	Scottish Further Education Association [British]
SFEA	Space and Flight Equipment Association (IAA)
SFEA	Squib Fuse Electrical Assembly (KSC)
SFEA	Survival [formerly, Space] and Flight Equipment Association [Later, SAFE Association]
SFEC	Standard Facility Equipment Card [Electronics]
SFED	SFS Bancorp [NASDAQ symbol] (TTSB)
SFeEnTr	Santa Fe Energy Trust [Associated Press] (SAG)
SFEF	Santa Fe Financial [NASDAQ symbol] (TTSB)
SFEF	Santa Fe Financial Corp. [NASDAQ symbol] (SAG)
SFeGam	Santa Fe Gaming Corp. [Associated Press] (SAG)
SFEL	Standard Facility Equipment List [Electronics]
SFEM	Segner's Fortified Edd Meat [Growth medium for phage]
SFEM	Southern Farm Equipment Manufacturers (EA)
SFEMG	Single Fiber Electromyography [Neurophysiology]
SFENA	Societe Francaise d'Equipements pour la Navigation Aerienne (MCD)
SFEP	Society of Freelance Editors & Proofreaders (WDAA)
SFePGld	Santa Fe Pacific Gold Corp. [Associated Press] (SAG)
SFePP	Santa Fe Pacific Pipeline Partners Ltd. [Associated Press] (SAG)
SFER	Santa Fe Energy Resources [Associated Press] (SAG)
SFER	Siata/Fiat 8V Register (EA)
SFERC	San Francisco Energy Research Center [Energy Research and Development Administration]
SFERICS	Atmospherics [NWS] (FAAC)
SFERT	Spinning Satellite for Electric Rocket Test (IAA)
SFERT	Systeme Fundamental Europeen de Reference pour la Transmission Telephonique [European master telephone reference system]
SFES	Small Firms Employment Subsidy (MHDB)
SFET	Surface Field Effect Transistor (IAA)
SFEX	Solar Flare X-Ray Polarimeter (NASA)
SFF	Santa Fe Energy Tr 'SPERs' [NYSE symbol] (TTSB)
SFF	Santa Fe Energy Trust Co. [NYSE symbol] (SAG)
SF/F	Science Fiction and Fantasy [Literary genre]
SFF	Science Fiction Foundation (EA)
SFF	Sea Frontier Force [Navy]
SFF	Self-Forging Fragment [Warhead] (MCD)
SFF	Senior Firefighter [Australia]
SFF	Sheffield [Tasmania] [Seismograph station code, US Geological Survey] (SEIS)
SFF	Silicone Rubber-Insulated Fixture Wire, Flexible Stranding (IAA)
SFF	Site Field Force [Army] (AABC)
SFF	Slocan Forest Products Ltd. [Toronto Stock Exchange symbol Vancouver Stock Exchange symbol]
SFF	Slovene Franciscan Fathers (EA)
SFF	Small Formation Flyer (SSD)
SFF	Small Form Factor [Computer science]
SFF	Solar Forecast Facility [Air Force] (MCD)
SFF	Solid Freeform Fabrication [Metallurgy]
SFF	Speaking Fundamental Frequency (STED)
SFF	Spiritual Frontiers Fellowship [Later, SFFI] (EA)
SFF	Spokane, WA [Location identifier FAA] (FAAL)
SFF	Standard File Format
SFF	Step Family Foundation (EA)
SFF	Supplementary Financing Facility [International Monetary Fund]
SFFA	Fireman Apprentice, Shipfitter [Navy rating]
SFFA	Serum Free Fatty Acid [Medicine] (DMAA)
SFFAS	Superfund Financial Assessment System [Environmental Protection Agency] (GFGA)
SFFB	Southern Financial Bancorp [NASDAQ symbol] (SAG)
SFFB	Southern Financial Federal Savings Bank [NASDAQ symbol] (SAG)
SFFB	Southern Finl Bancorp [NASDAQ symbol] (TTSB)
SFFC	Scottish Federation of Fishermen's Co-Operatives (DBA)
SFFC	StateFed Financial [NASDAQ symbol] (TTSB)
SFFC	Statefed Financial Corp. [NASDAQ symbol] (SAG)
SFFD	SFFed Corp. [Formerly, San Francisco Federal Savings & Loan Association] [NASDAQ symbol] (SPSG)
SFFed	SFFED Corp. [Associated Press] (SAG)
SFFF	Scandinavian Association of Zone-Therapeutists [Denmark] (EAIO)
SFFF	Sedimentation Field Flow Fractionation [For separation of colloids]

SFFF	Summary Format of Family Functioning
SFFI	Spiritual Frontiers Fellowship International (EA)
SF/FIA	Stock Fund/Financial Inventory Accounting
SFFMP	State/Federal Fisheries Management Program [National Marine Fisheries Service]
SFFN	Fireman, Shipfitter, Striker [Navy rating]
SFFNC	Society of the Founders and Friends of Norwich, Connecticut (EA)
SFFS	Satellite Frost Forecast System [Department of Agriculture]
SFFS	Save the Flags of Fort Sumter [Defunct] (EA)
SFFT	Superconducting Flux-Flow Transistor [Physics]
SFFUR	Safety and Flight Failure/Unsatisfactory Report
SFFV	Spleen Focus Formation Virus
SFFV	Spleen Focus Friend Virus (STED)
SFFV-F	Spleen Focus-Forming Virus in Friend Virus Complex [Medicine] (DB)
s-fg--	French Guiana [MARC geographic area code Library of Congress] (LCCP)
SFG	Screen Format Generator (IAA)
SFG	Serial Publications of Foreign Governments [A bibliographic publication]
SFG	Signal Flow Graph
SFG	Signal Frequency Generator [Telecommunications] (OA)
SFG	South Pacific Gold [Vancouver Stock Exchange symbol]
SFG	Special Forces Group [Military]
SFG	Staircase Function Generator
SFG	St. Maarten [Netherlands Antilles] [Airport symbol] (OAG)
SFG	Subglottic Foreign Body [Medicine] (DMAA)
SFG	Sudflug Suddeutsche Fluggesellschaft MbH [Germany ICAO designator] (FAAC)
SFG	Sum Frequency Generation
SFGA	Single Floating-Gate Amplifier [Electronics] (PDAA)
SFGA	Steel Fork Grinders' Association [A union] [British]
SFGD	Safeguard (AABC)
SFGD	Safeguard Health Enterpr [NASDAQ symbol] (TTSB)
SFGD	Safeguard Health Enterprises, Inc. [NASDAQ symbol] (NQ)
SFGD	Shell Flue Gas Desulfurization [Air pollution control]
SfgdSc	Safeguard Scientifics, Inc. [Associated Press] (SAG)
SFGE	San Francisco Grain Exchange [Defunct] (EA)
SFGEP	Space Flight Ground Environment Panel [NASA] (KSC)
SFGF	Shope Fibroma Growth Factor [Biochemistry]
SFGL	Safety Glass [Technical drawings]
SFGS	Southwestern Federation of Geological Societies
SFH	Simple Forwarding Header [Computer science] (CIST)
SFH	Simulated Flight Hour (MCD)
SFH	Slow Frequency Hopping (MCD)
SFH	Standard Fading Hour [National Institute of Standards and Technology]
SFH	Stroma-Free Hemoglobin [Medicine] (DB)
SFH	Super Flux Harness
SFHA	Scottish Federation of Housing Associations (DBA)
SFHA	Special Flood Hazard Area [Information service or system] (EMRF)
SFHb	Stroma-Free Hemoglobin [Hematology]
SFHC	Society of Folk Harpers and Craftsmen (EA)
SFHEA	Scottish Further and Higher Education Association (DBA)
SFHF	Society of the Friends of the Holy Father
SF/HGF	Scatter Factor Hepatocyte Growth Factor [Biochemistry]
SFH-P	Stroma-Free Hemoglobin Pyridoxylated [Clinical chemistry]
SFHR	Soclety for Film History Research [British] (BI)
SFHS	Society for French Historical Studies (EA)
SFI	Savannah Foods & Ind [NYSE symbol] (TTSB)
SFI	Savannah Foods & Industries, Inc. [NYSE symbol] (SPSG)
SFI	Sequential Fuel Injection [Automotive engineering]
SFI	Sexual Function Index [Medicine] (DMAA)
SFI	SFI Foundation (EA)
SFI	Shop-Fixed Interface (DNAB)
SFI	Sindacato Ferrovieri Itallani [Union of Italian Railroad Workers]
SFI	Sky Freighters NV [Belgium ICAO designator] (FAAC)
SFI	Small Flow Indicator
SFI	Social Function Index [Medicine] (DMAA)
SFI	Societe Financiere Internationale [International Finance Society]
SFI	Society of Friends of Icons [Germany] (EAIO)
SFI	Solid Fat Index [Food analysis]
SFI	Southern Forest Institute [Defunct] (EA)
SFI	Space Flight Instrumentation (AAG)
SFI	Sport Fishing Institute (EA)
SFI	Sports Fishing Initiative [Marine science] (OSRA)
SFI	Starfire Resources Ltd. [Vancouver Stock Exchange symbol]
SFI	Step Function Input
SFI	Strategic Facilities Initiative [Oak Ridge National Laboratory]
SFI	Support for Industry (NITA)
SFI	Sustainable Forestry Initiative [Michigan]
SFI	Synovial Fluid Lymphocyte [Medicine] (DMAA)
SFIA	School Fees Insurance Agency Ltd. [British]
SFIA	Sea Fish Industry Authority [British]
SFIB	Southern Freight Inspection Bureau
SFIC	San Francisco Information Center [Army Air Warning Service]
SFIC	Societe et Federation Internationale de Cardiologie [International Society and Federation of Cardiology] [Switzerland] (EAIO)
SFICEC	State-Federal Information Clearinghouse for Exceptional Children
SFID	Section Francaise de l'Internationale Ouvriere [French Section of the Workers International]
SFID	Self-floating Integrated Deck (PDAA)
SFID	Set Format Identifier
SFID	Supplementary Flight Information Documentation (IAA)
SFIMR	Stock Fund Inventory Management Record [Military] (AFIT)

S-FIN	Semi-Finished [*Automotive engineering*]
SFIN	Statewide Financial [*NASDAQ symbol*] (TTSB)
SFIN	Statewide Financial Corp. [*NASDAQ symbol*] (SAG)
SFInstE	Senior Fellow of the Institute of Energy [*British*] (DBQ)
SFInstF	Senior Fellow of the Institute of Fuel [*British*] (DI)
SFIO	Section Francaise de l'Internationale Ouvriere [*French Socialist Party*]
SFIR	Specific Force Integrating Receiver [*Air Force*]
SFIREG	State FIFRA [*Federal Insecticide, Fungicide, and Rodenticide Act*] Issues Research and Evaluation Group [*Environmental Protection Agency*] (EGAO)
SFIS	Selective Fisheries Information Service (IID)
SFIT	Simplified Fault Isolation Test (MCD)
SFIT	Standard Family Interaction Test [*Psychology*]
SFIT	Swiss Federal Institute of Technology (IAA)
SFJ	Sondre Stromfjord [*Greenland*] [*Airport symbol*] (OAG)
SFJ	Standforward Jamming [*Military*] (LAIN)
SFJ	Swept Frequency Jamming
SFK	Safia [*Papua*] [*Airport symbol*] (AD)
SFK	Special Function Key [*Calculators*]
SFK	Stonyfork, PA [*Location identifier FAA*] (FAAL)
SFL	Salt Flat, TX [*Location identifier FAA*] (FAAL)
SFL	San Felipe [*California*] [*Seismograph station code, US Geological Survey*] (SEIS)
SFL	Santa Fe Pacific Pipeline Ltd. [*NYSE symbol*] (SPSG)
SFL	Santa Fe Pac Pipeline [*NYSE symbol*] (TTSB)
SFL	Sao Filipe [*Cape Verde Islands*] [*Airport symbol*] (OAG)
SFL	Scholarships, Fellowships, and Loans [*A publication*]
SFL	Scientists for Life (EA)
SFL	Scottish Football League (DBA)
SFL	Secondary Freon Loop (NASA)
SFL	Sequence Flash Lights [*FAA*]
SFL	Sexual Freedom League (EA)
SFL	Short Flashing Light [*Navigation signal*]
SFL	Silver Falls Resources [*Vancouver Stock Exchange symbol*]
SFL	Sizing Float Level
SFL	Slip Full Load (IAA)
SFL	Society of Federal Linguists (EA)
SFL	Southflight Aviation Ltd. [*New Zealand*] [*ICAO designator*] (FAAC)
SFL	Southland Football League (PSS)
SFL	Substrate Fed Logic
SFL	Surinam Florin [*Monetary unit in Surinam*]
SFL	Symbolic Flowchart Language (IAA)
SFLC	San Francisco Laser Center [*Research center*] (RCD)
SFLD	Seafield Capital Corp. [*NASDAQ symbol*] (SPSG)
SFLIS	Sloga Fraternal Life Insurance Society [*Milwaukee, WI*] (EA)
SFLJ	San Francisco Law Journal [*A publication*] (DLA)
SFLOC	Synopic Reporting of the Location of Sources of Atmospherics [*Aviation*] (DA)
SFLRP	Society of Federal Labor Relations Professionals (EA)
3FLS	Semiflush
SFLS	Stress Fiber-Like Structure [*Biology*]
SFLX	Shoulder Flexion [*Sports medicine*]
SFLX	Smartflex Systems [*NASDAQ symbol*] (SAG)
SFM	Francis Marion College, Florence, SC [*OCLC symbol*] (OCLC)
SFM	Sanford, ME [*Location identifier FAA*] (FAAL)
SFM	San Francisco - Josephine D. Randall Junior Museum [*California*] [*Seismograph station code, US Geological Survey*] (SEIS)
SFM	San Francisco Movers Tariff Bureau, San Francisco CA [*STAC*]
SFM	Scanning Force Microscope
SFM	Scanning Force Mode [*Microscopy*]
sfm	Scarboro Foreign Missions (TOCD)
SFM	Scarboro Foreign Missions (TOCD)
SFM	Secure File Manager [*Telecommunications*] (OSI)
SFM	Serum Free Medium
SFM	SFM Corp. [*Later, EXX, Inc.*] [*AMEX symbol*] (SPSG)
sfm	Sfumato (VRA)
SFM	Shepherds Fold Ministries (EA)
SFM	Shipfitter, Metalsmith [*Navy*]
SFM	Signal Flow Matrix (IAA)
SFM	Simulated Flight - Manual
SFM	Simulated Flow Method
SFM	Sinai Field Mission [*US government*]
SFM	Sinusoidal Frequency Modulation [*Physics*]
SFM	Ski-Free Marine [*Vancouver Stock Exchange symbol*]
SFM	Society for Foodservice Management (EA)
SFM	Society for the Family of Man (EA)
SFM	Spectrophotofluorometer
SFM	Split Field Motor (IAA)
SFM	Storage Facility Manual (MCD)
SFM	Sum Frequency Mixer (CIST)
SFM	Surface Feet per Minute
SFM	Sustainable Forest Management
SFM	Swept Frequency Modulation
SFM	Switching Mode Frequency Multipliers
SFMA	Franciscan Missionary Sisters of Assisi (TOCD)
SFMA	School Furniture Manufacturers' Association [*British*] (BI)
SFMA	Scottish Furniture Manufacturers Association (DBA)
SFMA	Soda Fountain Manufacturers Association
SFMA	Southern Furniture Manufacturers Association [*Later, AFMA*] (EA)
SFMA	Steel Fork Makers' Association [*A union*] [*British*]
SFMA	Subscription Fulfillment Managers Association [*Later, FMA*] (EA)
SFMANSW	Stock Feed Manufacturers' Association of New South Wales [*Australia*]
SFMAQ	Stock Feed Manufacturers' Association of Queensland [*Australia*]
SFMASA	Stock Feed Manufacturers' Association of South Australia
SFMAV	Stock Feed Manufacturers' Association of Victoria [*Australia*]
SFMAWA	Stock Feed Manufacturers' Association of Western Australia
SFME	Storable Fluid Management Experiment (NASA)
SFMF	Scottish Fish Merchants Federation (DBA)
SFMF	Student Foreign Missions Fellowship [*Later, IVMF*] (EA)
SFMG	Franciscan Missionary Sisters of Assisi [*Roman Catholic religious order*]
SFMHS	San Francisco Men's Health Study [*Aids study*]
SFMI	Soft Fibre Manufacturers' Institute [*Defunct*] (EA)
SFMJF	Satoko and Franz M. Joseph Foundation (EA)
SFML	Standard Facility Material List [*Electronics*]
SFMN	Slow Flexor Motoneuron [*Neurology*]
SFMN	Superficial Flexor Motoneuron [*Neurology*]
SFMOMA	San Francisco Museum of Modern Art
SFMP	Surplus Facilities Management Program [*Department of Energy*]
SFMR	Stepped-Frequency Microwave Radiometer [*For measuring rain rate and wind speed*]
SFMS	Shipwrecked Fishermen and Mariners Royal Benevolent Society [*British*] (BI)
SFMT	Scottish Federation of Merchant Tailors (DBA)
SFMTA	Scottish Federation of Meat Traders Associations (DBA)
SF-MX	Stopped-Flow Multimixing Spectroflourimeter
SFN	Grupo Financiero Serfin [*NYSE symbol*] (SPSG)
SFN	Grupo Financiero Serfin ADS [*NYSE symbol*] (TTSB)
SFN	Safiran Airlines [*Iran*] [*ICAO designator*] (FAAC)
SFN	San Francisco Naval Shipyard
SFN	Santa Fe [*Argentina*] [*Airport symbol*] (OAG)
SFN	Seattle First National Bank, Seattle, WA [*OCLC symbol*] (OCLC)
SFN	See Footnote (ROG)
SFN	Ships and Facilities, Navy (NG)
SFN	Society for Neuroscience (NTPA)
SFN	Stefan Resources, Inc. [*Vancouver Stock Exchange symbol*]
SFN	Strategic Facsimile Network (IAA)
SFNA	Stabilized Fuming Nitric Acid
SFNB	Security First Network Bank [*NASDAQ symbol*] (SAG)
SFNC	Simmons First National Corp. [*Pine Bluff, AK*] [*NASDAQ symbol*] (NQ)
SFNC	Society of the Founders of Norwich, Connecticut (EA)
SFNCA	Simmons First Natl [*NASDAQ symbol*] (TTSB)
SFNCTU	Swiss Federation of National-Christian Trade Unions
SFNFC	Sally Field National Fan Club (EA)
SFNG	Safety Based Negative (VRA)
SFNS	San Francisco Naval Shipyard (DNAB)
SFNSY	San Francisco Naval Shipyard
SFO	Defense Solid Fuels Order [*United States*] [*A publication*] (DLA)
SFO	San Fernando Observatory [*Research center*] (RCD)
SFO	San Francisco/Oakland [*California*] [*Airport symbol*] (OAG)
SFO	Santa Fe Opera [*New Mexico*]
SFO	Satellite Field Office [*Marine science*] (OSRA)
SFO	Sector Frequency Only [*Military*] (CAAL)
SFO	Secular Franciscan Order [*Formerly, TOSF*] [*Roman Catholic religious order*]
SFO	Senior Flag Officer [*British military*] (DMA)
SFO	Serious Fraud Office [*Proposed*] [*British government*].
SFO	Service Fuel Oil
SFO	Servicing Finance Office (COE)
SFO	SFO [*San Francisco and Oakland*] Helicopter Airlines, Inc. [*Air carrier designation symbol*]
SFO	Simulated Flame Out [*Aviation*]
SFO	Single-Frequency Oscillator (IDOE)
SFO	Single-Frequency Outlet
SFO	Solicitation for Offers [*A publication*] (AAGC)
SFO	Space Flight Operations [*NASA*]
SFO	Spot Face Other Side [*Technical drawings*] (MSA)
SFO	Standard-Frequency Oscillator (IDOE)
SFO	Sterling Forest [*New York*] [*Seismograph station code, US Geological Survey*] (SEIS)
SFO	Strathfield Oil & Gas Ltd. [*Toronto Stock Exchange symbol*]
SFO	Subfornical Organ [*Brain anatomy*]
SFO	Submarine Fog Oscillator [*Maps and charts*]
SFO	Superannuation Funds Office [*Inland Revenue*] [*British*]
SFO	Superannuation Funds Officer (WDAA)
SFOB	Special Forces Operational Base [*Army*]
SFOBB	San Francisco-Oakland Bay Bridge
SFOC	Space Flight Operations Complex [*NASA*]
SFOD	San Francisco Ordnance District [*Military*]
SFOD	Space Flight Operations Director [*NASA*]
SFOD	Special Forces Operational Detachment [*Army*] (AABC)
SFOF	Space Flight Operations Facility [*NASA*]
SFOLDS	Ship Form Online Design System [*British Ship Research Association*] [*Software package*] (NCC)
SFOM	Shuttle Flight Operations Manual [*NASA*] (MCD)
SFOM	Space Flight Operations Memorandum [*NASA*]
SFOM	Special Furnish Off Machine [*Paper*] (DGA)
SFOM	Stabilized Flight Operations Manual
SFOMS	Ships Force Overhaul Management Systems [*Navy*]
SFOO	San Francisco Operations Office [*Energy Research and Development Administration*]
SFOP	Safety Operating Procedure [*Kennedy Space Center*] [*NASA*] (NASA)
SFOP	Space Flight Operations Plan [*NASA*]
SFor	Stabilisation Force [*Military*] (WDAA)
Sforz	Sforzando [*With Additional Accent*] [*Music*]
SFOSRC	South Florida Oil Spill Research Center [*Marine science*] (OSRA)

SFP............ Franciscan Sisters of the Poor [*Roman Catholic religious order*]
SFP............ Salton [*Stock market symbol*]
SFP............ San Felipe [*Mexico*] [*Seismograph station code, US Geological Survey*] (SEIS)
SFP............ Santa Fe Public Library, Santa Fe, NM [*OCLC symbol*] (OCLC)
SFP............ Screen Filtration Pressure [*Clinical chemistry*] (AAMN)
SFP............ Security Filter Processor
SFP............ Sforzato Piano [*Sudden change from forte to piano*] [*Music*] (ROG)
SFP............ Sherbrooke Forest Park [*Victoria, Australia*] [*Airport symbol*] (AD)
SFP............ Shipfitter, Pipefitter [*Navy*]
SFP............ Shungwayah Freedom Party [*Kenya*]
SFP............ Simultaneous Foveal Perception [*Ophthalmology*]
SFP............ Single Failure Point [*NASA*] (MCD)
SFP............ Sintered Ferrous Part
SFP............ Skeleton Flight Plan
SFP............ Slack Frame Program
SFP............ Slow Filling Period [*Cardiology*]
SFP............ Solar Flare Proton
SFP............ Spartan-Furnished Property [*Missiles*] (MCD)
SFP............ Special Film Project
SFP............ Special Furnished Property (MCD)
SFP............ Spent Fuel Pit [*Nuclear energy*] (NRCH)
SFP............ Spent Fuel Pool [*Nuclear energy*] (NRCH)
SFP............ Spinal Fluid Pressure [*Medicine*]
SFP............ Stopped Flow Pressure
SFP............ Straight Fixed Price
SFP............ Strike for Peace [*Later, WDFP*] (EA)
SFP............ Students for Peace (EA)
SFP............ Summary Financial Program
SFP............ Summary Flight Plan (MCD)
SFP............ Super Flat Pack
SFP............ Supplementary Feeding Program
SFP............ Surface Fixed Priority
SFP............ Sustainer Firing Package
SFP............ Svenska Folkpartiet [*Swedish People's Party*] [*Finland Political party*] (PPE)
SFPA............ Science Fiction Poetry Association (EA)
SFPA............ Single Failure Point Analysis [*NASA*] (KSC)
SFPA............ Southern Forest Products Association (EA)
SFPA............ Structural Fire Protection Association [*British*]
SFP-ANGS ... Standardization Field Panel for Artillery and Naval Gunfire Support [*Army*] (AABC)
SFPAVS ...... Spent Fuel Pool Area Ventilation System [*Nuclear energy*] (NRCH)
SFPC............ Society of Family Practitioner Committees [*British*] (DBA)
SFPCCS ...... Spent Fuel Pool Cooling and Cleanup System [*Nuclear energy*] (NRCH)
SFPCS .... Spent Fuel Pool Cooling System [*Nuclear energy*] (NRCH)
SFPE............ San Francisco Port of Embarkation [*Military*]
SFPE............ Society of Fire Protection Engineers (EA)
SFPF............ Special Federal Project Funds [*Medicaid Program*] (GFGA)
SFPL............ San Francisco Public Library [*California*]
SFPM............ Surface Feet per Minute
SFPO............ Senior Fire Prevention Officer (WDAA)
SFPO............ Senior Functional Policy Official (AAGC)
SFPOE .... San Francisco Port of Embarkation [*Military*]
SFPOMMPAB... Society for the Prevention of Married Men Posing as Bachelors
SFPP............ Spruce Fall Power & Paper [*AAR code*]
SFPP............ Stored Flight Plan Program [*Aviation*] (FAAC)
SFPPC .... Science Fiction Pen Pal Club (EA)
SFPPL........... Short Form Provisioning Parts List [*NASA*] (NASA)
SFPPS .... Shore Facilities Planning and Programming System [*Navy*]
SFPRF.......... Semifireproof (MSA)
SFPRL .... Spartan-Furnished Property Request List [*Missiles*] (MCD)
SFPS............ Secure Fast Packet Switching [*Telecommunications*]
SFPS............ Single Failure Point Summary [*NASA*] (NASA)
SFPT............ Society of Fire Protection Technicians (EA)
SFPT............ Standard Fixation Preference Test [*Laboratory science*] (DAVI)
SFPTU .... Swiss Federation of Protestant Trade Unions
SFQ............. Single Flux Quantum [*Pulse*] [*Physics*]
SFQ............. Suffolk, VA [*Location identifier FAA*] (FAAL)
SFQC .... Special Forces Qualification Course [*Military*] (INF)
SFQI............ Structured Full-Text Query Language [*Computer science*] (TELE)
SFR............. Safair Freighters (Pty) Ltd. [*South Africa ICAO designator*] (FAAC)
SFR............. Safety of Flight Requirements (AFM)
SFR............. San Fernando, CA [*Location identifier FAA*] (FAAL)
SFR............. San Francisco [*Diocesan abbreviation*] [*California*] (TOCD)
SFR............. San Francisco Review [*A publication*] (BRI)
SFR............. San Francisco - Rincon [*California*] [*Seismograph station code, US Geological Survey*] (SEIS)
SFR............. Santa Fe Energy Res [*NYSE symbol*] (TTSB)
SFR............. Santa Fe Energy Resources [*NYSE symbol*] (SPSG)
SFR............. Santa Fe Regional Library [*Gainsville Public Library*] [*UTLAS symbol*]
SfR............. Scholars' Facsimiles & Reprints, Inc., Delmar, NY [*Library symbol Library of Congress*] (LCLS)
SFR............. Screen Filtration Resistance [*Clinical chemistry*] (AAMN)
SFR............. Selective File Retrieval
SFR............. Semi-Fire-Resistive Construction
SFR............. Sequenced Flashing Lights
SFR............. Sequential Filter Regeneration [*Automotive engineering*]
SFR............. Serial Flechette Rifle (PDAA)
SFR............. Signal Frequency Receiver [*Telecommunications*] (OA)
SFR............. Simon Fraser Resources [*Vancouver Stock Exchange symbol*]
SFR............. Sinking Fund Return [*Finance*] (MHDW)

SFR............. Small Fluidal Round Colonies [*Moko disease of Banana*] [*Plant pathology*]
SFR............. Solar Flare Radiation
SFR............. Space Frame RADOME
SFR............. Special Federal Responsibilities (OICC)
SFR............. Special Forces Reconnaissance [*Army*]
SFR............. Spin Flip Raman [*LASER*]
SFR............. Star Formation Rate [*Astronomy*]
SFR............. Star-Forming Regions [*Astronomy*]
SFR............. Starved Feed Reactor [*for Polymerization*]
SFR............. Stroke with Full Recovery [*Neurology*] (DAVI)
SFR............. Submarine Fleet Reactor
SFR............. Supervisory Field Representative [*Department of Commerce*] (GFGA)
S FR........... Swiss Franc [*Monetary unit*]
SFRA........... Science Fiction Research Association (EA)
SFRA........... System Fielding Readiness Analysis [*Army*]
SFRA........... System Fielding Readiness Assessment [*Army*]
SFRB .... [*The*] Atchison, Topeka & Santa Fe Railway Co. - DF Loaders [*AAR code*]
SFRB .... San Francisco Review of Books [*A publication*] (BRI)
SFRC .... Short Form Research Contract (AAGC)
SFRC .... Soya Food Research Council
SFRCS .... Steam and Feedwater Line Rupture Control System [*Nuclear energy*] (NRCH)
SFRD .... [*The*] Atchison, Topeka & Santa Fe Railway Co. - Refrigerator Cars [*AAR code*]
SFRD .... Safe Functional Requirements Document (MCD)
SFRD .... Secret Formerly Restricted
SFRF .... Sport Fishery Research Foundation [*Later, SFRP*] (EA)
SFRJ .... Solid Fuel Ramjet
SFRL .... Spin-Flip Raman LASER (PDAA)
SFRP .... Sport Fishery Research Program (EA)
SFRPr .... Santa Fe Energy Res 7% Pfd [*NYSE symbol*] (TTSB)
SFRPrA .... Santa Fe Ener Res 8.25%'DECS' [*NYSE symbol*] (TTSB)
SFRS .... Search for Random Success [*Aerospace*] (AAG)
SFRS .... Swept Frequency Radiometer System
SFRT .... Science Fiction and Fantasy RoundTable [*GE Information Services*] [*Information service or system*] (CRD)
SFRY .... Socialist Federal Republic of Yugoslavia
SFS .... Free Software Foundation (EA)
SFS .... Saint Francis Seminary [*Wisconsin*]
SFS .... San Fernando [*Spain*] [*Seismograph station code, US Geological Survey*] (SEIS)
SFs .... Saybolt Furol Seconds [*Oil viscosity*]
SFS .... S-Band Feed System
SFS .... School Focused Secondment (AIE)
SFS .... School of Field Studies [*Beverly, MA*]
SFS .... Science-Fiction Studies [*A publication*] (BRI)
SFS .... Seamen's and Firemen's Society [*A union*] [*British*]
SFS .... Secure File System [*Telecommunications*] (OSI)
SFS .... Sektion fuer Systementwicklung [*GID*] [*Information retrieval*]
SFS .... Senior Flight Surgeon [*Army*] (AABC)
SFS .... Serial Focal Seizures [*Medicine*]
SFS .... Shakespeare for Students [*A publication*]
SFS .... Shared File System [*Telecommunications*]
SFS .... Sharm es-Sheikh [*Israel*] [*Airport symbol*] (AD)
SFS .... Shoot-Fail-Shoot [*Military*]
SFS .... Shuttle Flight Status [*NASA*] (MCD)
SFS .... Simplified Firing System
SFS .... Sine Fraude Sua [*Without Fraud on His Part*] [*Latin*] (DLA)
SFS .... Sioux Falls [*Diocesan abbreviation*] [*South Dakota*] (TOCD)
SFS .... Skin and Facial Stapler [*Surgery*] (DAVI)
SFS .... Small Firms Service [*British*]
SFS .... Smith's Flight System [*Aviation*] (AIA)
SFS .... Society for Foodservice Systems (EA)
SFS .... Society for Freedom in Science
SFS .... Society for French Studies [*British*]
SFS .... Sodium Formaldehyde Sulfoxylate [*Organic chemistry*]
SFS .... Software Facilities and Standards [*Computer science*] (TEL)
SFS .... Solicitors' Financial Services [*British*]
SFS .... Sonic Frequency System
SFS .... Southern Frontier Air Transport Ltd. [*Canada ICAO designator*] (FAAC)
SFS .... South San Francisco, CA [*Location identifier FAA*] (FAAL)
SFS .... Space Flight Systems (SAA)
SFS .... Space Futures Society (EA)
SFS .... Split Function Study (MAE)
SFS .... Star Field Sensor
SFS .... Start of Frame Sequence (CIST)
SFS .... State Fleet Services [*New South Wales, Australia*]
SFS .... Statistical Fine Structure [*Physics*]
SFS .... Steam and Feedwater System [*Nuclear energy*] (NRCH)
SFS .... Suomen Standardisomisliitto [*Finnish Standards Association*] [*Information service or system*] (IID)
SFS .... Super Food Services [*NYSE symbol*] (TTSB)
SFS .... Super Food Services, Inc. [*NYSE symbol*] (SPSG)
SFS .... Surfaced Four Sides [*Technical drawings*]
SFS .... Surface Effect Fast Sea Lift Ship [*MTMC*] (TAG)
SFSPr .... Symbolic File Support
SFS .... System Failure Summaries [*NASA*] (KSC)
SFSA.......... Scottish Federation of Sea Anglers (DBA)
SFSA.......... Scottish Field Studies Association [*British*]
SFSA.......... Steel Founders' Society of America (EA)
SFSAFBI ...... Society of Former Special Agents of the Federal Bureau of Investigation (EA)

SFSAS	Standard Fuel Savings Advisor System
SFSB	Suburbfed Financial Corp. [*NASDAQ symbol*] (SAG)
SFSB	Suburbfed Finl [*NASDAQ symbol*] (TTSB)
SFS Bcp	SFS Bancorp, Inc. [*Associated Press*] (SAG)
SFSC	San Francisco State College [*Later, California State University*]
SFSC	Southeast Fisheries Science Center [*Marine science*] (OSRA)
SFSCL	Shunt Feedback Schottky Clamped [*Electronics*]
SFSCPD	San Francisco Signal Corps Procurement District
SFSCT	Smooth-Face Structural Clay Tile [*Technical drawings*]
SFSD	Star Field Scanning Device
SFSE	San Francisco Stock Exchange
SFSK	Safeskin Corp. [*NASDAQ symbol*] (SAG)
SFSL	Security First Corp. [*NASDAQ symbol*] (NQ)
SFSMD	Studia Fransisci Scholten Memorial Dicata (BJA)
SFSN	Society of French-Speaking Neurosurgeons (EA)
SFSO	San Francisco Symphony Orchestra
SFSP	Spent Fuel Storage Pool [*Nuclear energy*] (NRCH)
SFSP	Summer Food Service Program [*Department of Agriculture*] (GFGA)
SFSR	Senior Field Service Representative [*DoD*]
SFSR	Shipfitter, Ship Repair [*Navy*]
SFSRC	Shipfitter, Ship Repair, Chipper-Caulker [*Navy*]
SFSRD	Shipfitter, Ship Repair, Diver [*Navy*]
SFSRF	Shipfitter, Ship Repair, Steelworker-Anglesmith [*Navy*]
SFSRL	Shipfitter, Ship Repair, Driller-Reamer [*Navy*]
SFSRP	Shipfitter, Ship Repair, Pipe Fitter-Plumber [*Navy*]
SFSRR	Shipfitter, Ship Repair, Riveter [*Navy*]
SFSRS	Shipfitter, Ship Repair, Shipfitter [*Navy*]
SFSRW	Shipfitter, Ship Repair, Welder [*Navy*]
SFSS	Satellite Field Services Stations [*National Weather Service*]
SFSS	Satellite Field Service Station [*Marine science*] (OSRA)
SFST	Scherenfernrohrstand [*Emplacement of battery commander's telescope*] [*German military - World War II*]
SFST	Standardized Field Sobriety Test [*NHTSA*] (TAG)
SFSU	San Francisco State University
SFSU	Singapore Federation of Services' Unions
SFSU	Single Frequency Signaling Unit
SFSU-35	San Francisco State University Videotex Cable Service [*Telecommunications service*] (TSSD)
SFSW	State Financial Services Corp. [*NASDAQ symbol*] (SAG)
SFSW	State Financial Svcs'A' [*NASDAQ symbol*] (TTSB)
SFSZ	Sulfasalazine [*Medicine*] (TAD)
S-FT	Second-Foot (WDAA)
SFT	Serum-Free Thyroxine (DB)
SFT	Shaft (MSA)
SFT	Shift
SFT	Simulated Flight Tests
SFT	Skelleftea [*Sweden*] [*Airport symbol*] (OAG)
SFT	Skinfold Thickness [*Medicine*]
SFT	Skyfreight, Inc. [*ICAO designator*] (FAAC)
sft	Soffit (VRA)
sft	Soft [*Quality of the bottom*] [*Nautical charts*]
SFT	Soft Top [*Automotive advertising*]
SFT	Software [*Computer science*] (RDA)
SFT	Special Flight Test
SFT	Specific Financial Transactions
SFT	Spiral Fin Tubing
SFT	Squeeze Film Test
SFT	Stacking Fault Tetrahedra [*Metals*]
SFT	Stanford [*California*] [*Seismograph station code, US Geological Survey*] (SEIS)
SFT	Static Firing Test [*NASA*] (NASA)
SFT	Stockpile Flight Tests
SFT	Stop for Tea [*British*]
SFT	Structural Firing Test [*Military*] (CAAL)
SFT	Submerged Floating Tunnell
SFT	Sudanese Flight [*Sudan*] [*ICAO designator*] (FAAC)
SFT	Sufficient Feasibility Test
SFT	Superfast Train
SFT	Supplemental Flight Test
SFT	System Fault Tolerant [*Novell, Inc.*] [*Orem, UT*] [*Telecommunications*]
SFTA	Society of Film and Television Arts Ltd. [*British*] (BI)
SFTA	Spent Fuel Transportation Accident [*Nuclear energy*] (NRCH)
SFTA	Structural Fatigue Test Article [*NASA*] (NASA)
SFTAA	Short Form Test of Academic Aptitude (EDAC)
SFTab	Special Forces Tab [*Military*] (GFGA)
SFTAR	Subsystem Fault Tree Analysis Report
SftArt	Software Artistry [*Associated Press*] (SAG)
SFTB	Southern Freight Tariff Bureau
SFTC	Sherman Fairchild Technology Center (MCD)
SFTC	Standard Freight Trade Classification [*Council for Mutual Economic Assistance*] (DS)
SFTCD	Senior Fellow, Trinity College, Dublin (ROG)
SFTE	Society of Flight Test Engineers (EA)
SFTE	Space Full Time Equivalent (AIE)
SFTF	Static Firing Test Facility [*NASA*] (NASA)
SFTFC	Search for Tomorrow Fan Club [*Defunct*] (EA)
SFTI	Special Flight Test Instrumentation (MCD)
SFTIP	Special Flight Test Instrumentation Pool (NG)
SFTK	Single Fiber Tensile Kinetic [*Method for studying permanent hair waving*]
SFTL	Small Firms' Trading Loan (WDAA)
SFTL	Sonic Fatigue Test Laboratory (AAG)
SFTO	San Diego Field Test Operations [*Aerospace*] (AAG)
SFTP	Science for the People (EA)

SftProf	Software Professionals, Inc. [*Associated Press*] (SAG)
SftQuad	SoftQuad International, Inc. [*Associated Press*] (SAG)
SFTR	Shipfitter (AAG)
SFTR	Summary Flight Test Report (MCD)
SFTRC	Small Firms' Training Resource Centre (WDAA)
SFTS	San Francisco Theological Seminary [*San Anselmo, CA*]
SFTS	Scale Factor Temperature Sensitivity
SFTS	Service Flying Training School [*British*]
SFTS	Sickle Forgers' Trade Society [*A union*] [*British*]
SFTS	Society of Friends of the Touro Synagogue (EA)
SFTS	Space Flight Test System (MCD)
SFTS	Standard Frequency and Time Signals (IEEE)
SFTS	Swept Frequency Topside Sounder (SAA)
SFTS	Swinburne Film and Television School [*Australia*]
SFTS	Synthetic Flight Training Simulator
SFTS	Synthetic Flight Training System [*Army*]
SFTT	Spent Fuel Transfer Tubes [*Nuclear energy*] (NRCH)
SFTW	Enlighten Software Solutions [*NASDAQ symbol*] (SAG)
SFTW	Software Professionals [*NASDAQ symbol*] (TTSB)
SFTW	Software Professionals, Inc. [*NASDAQ symbol*] (SAG)
SFTW	Stamps for the Wounded (EA)
SFTWD	Softwood (WGA)
SFTWE	Software (NASA)
SftwPb	Software Publishing Corp. [*Associated Press*] (SAG)
SFTWR	Software [*Computer science*] (MCD)
SFTY	Safety
Sfty1st	Safety 1st, Inc. [*Associated Press*] (SAG)
SftyCmp	Safety Components International, Inc. [*Associated Press*] (SAG)
SFU	Furman University, Greenville, SC [*OCLC symbol*] (OCLC)
SFU	Safia [*Papua New Guinea*] [*Airport symbol*] (OAG)
SFU	Signals Flying Unit [*British*]
SFU	Simon Fraser University [*Canada*]
SFU	Simon Fraser University Library [*UTLAS symbol*]
SFU	Societe de Fluoration de l'Uranium [*An international nuclear fuel company*]
SFU	Space Flyer Unit (SSD)
SFU	Special Function Unit
SFU	Standard Firing Unit [*NASA*] (NASA)
SFU	Status Fill-In Unit [*Telecommunications*] (TEL)
SFU	Suitable for Upgrade (WDAA)
SFU	Surfdale [*Waiheke Island, New Zealand*] [*Airport symbol*] (AD)
SFU	Suriname Freedom Union (EA)
SFU	Syncytium-Forming Units [*Biochemistry*]
SFU	Synthetic Fuels Update [*A publication*]
SFUDS	Simplified Federal Urban Driving Schedule [*Electric vehicle testing*]
SFUGE	Singapore Federation of Unions of Government Employees
SF/UIS	Space Frame and Unit Integrating System
SFUN	Standard Fdg Corp. [*NASDAQ symbol*] (TTSB)
SFUN	Standard Funding Corp. [*NASDAQ symbol*] (SAG)
SFUS	Statistical Forecasts of the United States [*A publication*]
SF/USA	Stopped-Flow/Unsegmented Storage Analyzer [*Chemical analysis*]
SFV	Saybolt Furol Viscosity (BARN)
SFV	Schizophrenia Fellowship of Victoria [*Australia*]
SFV	Semliki Forest Virus
SFV	Shipping Fever Virus [*Medicine*] (DMAA)
SFV	Shope Fibroma Virus [*Medicine*] (DMAA)
SFV	Sight Feed Valve
SFV	Simian Foamy Virus
SFV	Sports Federation of Victoria [*Australia*]
SFV	Squirrel Fibroma Virus [*Medicine*] (DMAA)
SFVC	State Fund Vice Chairmen [*Red Cross*]
SFVCS	San Francisco Vocational Competency Scale
SFW	Sante Fe [*Panama*] [*Airport symbol*] (OAG)
SFW	Sensor Fuzed Weapon
SFW	Sexual Function of Women [*Medicine*] (DMAA)
SFW	Shell Fragment Wound [*Medicine*]
SFW	Shrapnel Fragment Wound (MAE)
SFW	Software (NASA)
SFW	Special Filter Wheel [*Military*] (CAAL)
SFW	Swept Forward Wing [*Aviation*] (PDAA)
SFW	Williston, ND [*Location identifier FAA*] (FAAL)
SFWA	Science Fiction and Fantasy Writers of America (NTPA)
SFWA	Science Fiction Writers of America (EA)
SFWA	Sierra Foothill Winery Association (EA)
SFWA	Soccer Federation of Western Australia
SFWA	Southern Fleece Washers Association [*British*] (DBA)
SFWB	Single Fronted Weatherboard (ADA)
SFWC	Supreme Forest Woodmen Circle [*Later, Woodmen of the World Life Insurance Society*] (EA)
SFWEM	Static Feed Water Electrolysis Module [*NASA*]
SFWI	Ship's Force Work Item (DNAB)
SFWLI	Ship's Force Worklist Instruction
SFWM	Swiss Federation of Watch Manufacturers (EA)
SFWMD	South Florida Water Management District
SFWR	Software 2000 [*NASDAQ symbol*] (TTSB)
SFWR	Software 2000, Inc. [*NASDAQ symbol*] (SAG)
SFWR	Stewardesses for Women's Rights
SFWS	Stopped-Flow Wavelength Scanning [*Spectrometry*]
SFX	San Felix [*Venezuela*] [*Airport symbol*] (AD)
SFX	Santa Fe Pacific (EFIS)
SFX	SFX Entertainment 'A' [*NYSE symbol*]
SFX	Sound Effects [*Script code*]
SFX	Special Effects
SFX	St. Francis Xavier University Library [*UTLAS symbol*]
SFXB	SFX Broadcasting, Inc. [*NASDAQ symbol*] (SAG)

SFXBA	SFX Broadcasting'A' [*NASDAQ symbol*] (TTSB)
SFX Brd	SFX Broadcasting, Inc. [*Associated Press*] (SAG)
SFXD	Semifixed
SFXR	Super Flash X-Ray (MCD)
SFY	Gulf Flite Center, Inc. [*ICAO designator*] (FAAC)
SFY	Savanna, IL [*Location identifier FAA*] (FAAL)
SFY	Special Fund for Youth [*UNESCO*] (EAIO)
SFY	Standard Facility Years [*FAA*]
SFY	Swift Energy [*NYSE symbol*] (TTSB)
SFY	Swift Energy Co. [*NYSE symbol*] (SPSG)
SFYMHS	San Francisco Young Mens Health Study [*AIDS study*]
SFZ	Pawtucket, RI [*Location identifier FAA*] (FAAL)
SFZ	Pawtucket-Woonsocket [*Rhode Island*] [*Airport symbol*] (AD)
SFZ	Scott & Fetzer Co. (EFIS)
Sfz	Sforzando [*With Additional Accent*] [*Music*]
SG	Atlantis [*ICAO designator*] (AD)
SG	Command Surgeon [*AFSC*]
SG	Goldwyn [*Samuel*] Co. [*AMEX symbol*] (SPSG)
SG	Royal South Gloucestershire Light Infantry Militia [*British military*] (DMA)
SG	Sachs-Georgi [*Test for syphilis*] [*Also, S-GT*] [*Obsolete*]
SG	Safety Guide (NRCH)
SG	Sa Grace [*His or Her Grace*] [*French*]
SG	Sa Grandeur [*His or Her Highness*] [*French*]
SG	Salisbury Group (EAIO)
SG	Salutis Gratia [*For the Sake of Safety*] [*Latin*]
SG	Sample Gas
SG	Sawtooth Generator
SG	Scanning Gate
SG	Schedule Generator
SG	School for Girls (ADA)
SG	Schutzgemeinschaft Gegen Meinungsterror [*Guard Society Against Opinion Terror*] [*Germany*]
SG	Scots Guards [*Military unit*] [*British*]
SG	Screen Grid [*Electrode or vacuum tube*]
SG	Sculptors Guild (EA)
SG	Seabird Group (EAIO)
Sg	Seaborgium [*Chemistry*] (MEC)
SG	Sea Grant
SG	Seaman Gunner [*British Obsolete*]
SG	Secretary-General [*United Nations*]
SG	Security Group [*Military*] (DNAB)
SG	Security Guard (SAA)
SG	Segment (IAA)
SG	Selling [*Exchange rate marking*] [*British*]
sg	Senegal [*MARC country of publication code Library of Congress*] (LCCP)
SG	Senior Gleaners (EA)
SG	Senior Grade
SG	Sergeant (WGA)
SG	Serum Globulin [*Medicine*] (MAE)
SG	Serum Glucose [*Medicine*] (DAVI)
SG	Service Group (MUGU)
SG	Set Gate
SG	Sheller-Globe Corp.
SG	Shell Gland
SG	Shell Gun
SG	Sherrgold, Inc. [*Toronto Stock Exchange symbol*]
SG	Ship and Goods [*British*] (ROG)
SG	Shipcraft Guild (EA)
SG	Siebelwerke ATG GmbH [*Germany ICAO aircraft manufacturer identifier*] (ICAO)
SG	Sign (MAE)
SG	Signal Generator
SG	Signal Ground (BUR)
SG	Signed (WGA)
SG	Silica Gel [*Analytical chemistry*]
SG	Singapore [*ANSI two-letter standard code*] (CNC)
SG	Singing
SG	Single Gourmet (EA)
SG	Single Groove [*Insulators*]
Sg	Singular (BJA)
SG	Skin Graft [*Medicine*]
S/G	Slaved Gyro (MCD)
S/G	Smith/Greenland [*Advertising agency*]
SG	Smoke Generator
SG	Snow Grains [*ICAO*] (FAAC)
SG	Society of Genealogists (EA)
SG	Society of Gilders (EA)
SG	Soft Gelatin [*Pharmacy*]
SG	Solar Generator (IAA)
SG	Sol-Gel [*Materials science*]
SG	Solicitor General
SG	Soluble Gelatin
SG	Solution of Glucose (OA)
Sg	Song of Songs [*Old Testament book*] [*Roman Catholic canon*] (BJA)
SG	Sort Generator (BUR)
SG	Sound Generation (MCD)
SG	South Georgia Railway Co. [*AAR code Terminated*]
SG	Sozialgericht [*Social Security Court*] [*German*] (ILCA)
SG	Spark Gap (DEN)
SG	Special Grade (DNAB)
SG	Special Group [*NATO*]
SG	Specific Gravity [*Also, SPG, SPGR*]
SG	Spheroidal Graphite [*Metallurgy*]

SG	Stacking Gel [*Biochemistry*]
SG	Stained Glass
SG	Standardization Group [*Air Force*] (AFM)
SG	Standing Group
SG	Steam Generator (NRCH)
SG	Steel Girder [*Bridges*]
SG	Steering Group (MCD)
SG	Stellate Ganglion [*Neuroanatomy*]
SG	Stern-Gerlach [*Experiment for measuring atomic magnetism*]
S/G	Strain Gage (NAKS)
SG	Strain Gauge (KSC)
SG	Strandberg-Groenblad [*Syndrome*] [*Medicine*] (DB)
SG	Strategic Group [*Military*]
SG	Structural Gene
SG	Structural Glass
SG	Student Guide
S-G	Subgeneric (WDAA)
S-G	Subgenus (WDAA)
SG	Substantia Gelatinosa [*Anatomy*]
S/G	Su Giro [*Your Draft*] [*Spanish Business term*]
SG	Summation Gallop [*Cardiology*]
SG	Sun Gate
SG	Sunkist Growers (EA)
SG	Sunset Gun [*Military ceremonial*]
SG	Sunsweet Growers (EA)
SG	Super Group (NATG)
SG	Super Guppy (KSC)
Sg	Supplementing [*New matter added to an existing regulation or order*] [*Used in Shepard's Citations*] [*Legal term*] (DLA)
SG	Surgeon
SG	[*The*] Surgeon General [*Army, Air Force*]
SG	Swamp Glider
SG	Swan-Ganz [*Catheter*] [*Cardiology*] (DAVI)
SG	Sweep Generator
SG	Sydney Greens [*Political party Australia*]
SG	Symbol Generator
SG	Synchronous Generator (IAA)
SG	Syringe (DNAB)
SG	System Gain
SG43 MMG...	Stankovyi Goryunova 1943 Medium Machine Gun [*Soviet made*] (VNW)
SGA	Air Saigon [*Vietnam*] [*ICAO designator*] (FAAC)
SGA	Saga Communications [*AMEX symbol*] (SPSG)
SGA	Saga Communications'A' [*AMEX symbol*] (TTSB)
SGA	Saga Resources [*Vancouver Stock Exchange symbol*]
SGA	Savoonga, AK [*Location identifier FAA*] (FAAL)
SGA	Scientific Glass Apparatus Co., Inc.
SGA	Scottish Games Association (EAIO)
SGA	Scottish Glass Association (DBA)
SGA	Screened Granulated Aluminate [*Inorganic chemistry*]
SGA	Sea Grant Association (EA)
SGA	Self-Gating and Shipboard, General Use, Armored (IAA)
SGA	Shirtsleeve Garment Assembly [*NASA*]
SGA	Showmen's Guild of Australia
SGA	Sickle Grinders' Association [*A union*] [*British*]
SGA	Sigma Security, Inc. [*Vancouver Stock Exchange symbol*]
SGA	Single-Monitor Graphic Adaptor [*Computer graphics*]
SGA	Slave Gyro Assembly
SGA	Slavic Gospel Association (EA)
SGA	Small for Gestational Age [*Pediatrics*]
SGA	Societe de Geologie Appliquee aux Gites Mineraux [*Society for Geology Applied to Mineral Deposits*] [*ICSU*] (EAIO)
SGA	Societe Generale Australia
SGA	Society of Gastrointestinal Assistants [*Later, SGNA*] (EA)
SGA	Society of Governmental Appraisers [*Later, Association of Governmental Appraisers*] (EA)
SGA	Society of Graphic Art [*British*]
SGA	Society of Graphic Art, Toronto [*1912, founded c.1903 as GAC, CSGA from 1923*] [*Canada*] (NGC)
SGA	Solanaceous Glycoalkaloid [*Compound*]
SGA	Solar Greenhouse Association (EA)
SGA	Songwriters Guild of America (EA)
SGA	Soybean Growers of America (EA)
SGA	Spectrometric Gas Analysis
SGA	Split Group Aperture
SGA	Spouses of Gays Association [*Defunct*] (EA)
SGA	Standards of Grade Authorization [*Military*]
SGA	State Guaranteed Agency (GFGA)
SGA	Stephens Glacier [*Alaska*] [*Seismograph station code, US Geological Survey Closed*] (SEIS)
SGA	Substantial Gainful Activity [*Social Security Administration*] (OICC)
SGA	Superior Geniculate Artery [*Anatomy*]
SGA	Switch Group Assembly
SGAA	Sporting Goods Agents Association (EA)
SGAA	Stained Glass Association of America (EA)
SGAC	Secretariat General for Civil Aviation [*French*]
SGAC	Silvermine Guild Arts Center (EA)
SGAC	State Governmental Affairs Council (EA)
SGACC	Secretariat General de l'Aviation Civile et Commerciale [*France*]
SGAD	Safeguard Army Depot (AABC)
SGAE	Studiengesellschaft fuer Atomenergie [*Implements Austria's nuclear program*] (NRCH)
SGAHRS	Steam Generator Auxiliary Heat Removal System [*Nuclear energy*] (NRCH)
SGAIG	Scholars Group Against the Invasion of Grenada (EA)

SG & A	Selling, General, and Administrative Expenses
SGA of M-A	Sod Growers Association of Mid-America (EA)
SGAS	Asuncion/Presidente General Stroessner [*Paraguay*] [*ICAO location identifier*] (ICLI)
SGAS	Society for German-American Studies (EA)
SGAS	Space Geodesy Altimetry Study [*Raytheon Co.*]
SGAS	Star Gas Partners L.P. SBI [*NASDAQ symbol*] (SAG)
SGAS	Steam Generator Available Signal [*Nuclear energy*] (NRCH)
SGASZ	Star Gas Ptnrs L.P. [*NASDAQ symbol*] (TTSB)
SGAUA	Scitex Graphic Arts Users Association (EA)
SGAUG	Scitex Graphic Arts Users Group [*Later, SGAUA*] (EA)
SGAUS	State Guard Association of the United States (NTPA)
SGAUSA	St. George Association of the USA (EA)
sGAW	Specific Airway Conductance
SGAW	Specific Airway Conductance (STED)
SGAW	Subgroup on Assessment of Weapons [*NATO*] (NATG)
SGAY	Ayolas [*Paraguay*] [*ICAO location identifier*] (ICLI)
SGB	Santa Fe, NM [*Location identifier FAA*] (FAAL)
SGB	Schweizerischer Gewerkschaftsbund [*Swiss Federation of Trade Unions*]
SGB	Societe Generale de Banque [*Bank Society*] [*Information service or system*] (IID)
SGB	Southern Gas Basin [*British*]
SGB	Southwest Georgia Financial Corp. [*AMEX symbol*] (SAG)
SGB	Steam Generator Blowdown [*Nuclear energy*] (NRCH)
SGB	Steam Generator Building [*Nuclear energy*] (NRCH)
SGB	Steam Gunboat [*British military*] (DMA)
SGB	Stellate Ganglion Blockade [*Anesthesiology*]
SGB	Strain Gauge Bridge
SGB	Switchgear Block (MSA)
SGBA	Societe Generale de Banque aux Antilles [*Guadeloupe*] (EY)
SGBD	Steam Generator Blowdown [*Nuclear energy*] (NRCH)
SGBI	Santa Gertrudis Breeders International (EA)
SGBI	Schoolmistresses' and Governesses' Benevolent Institution [*British*] (BI)
SGBIP	Subject Guide to Books in Print [*A publication*]
SGBPS	Steam Generator Blowdown Processing System [*Nuclear energy*] (NRCH)
SGBS	Steam Generator Blowdown System [*Nuclear energy*] (NRCH)
SGBS	Strathelyde Graduate Business School [*Toulouse, France*] (ECON)
SGBV	Bella Vista [*Paraguay*] [*ICAO location identifier*] (ICLI)
SGC	Saint Gregory College [*Oklahoma*]
SGC	Salivary Gland Choristoma [*Medicine*]
SGC	Sample Gas Cell [*Instrumentation*]
SGC	Screen Grid Current
SG-C	Serum Gentamicin Concentration (STED)
SGC	Simulated Generation Control
SGC	Software Generation Center (MCD)
SGC	Solicitor General Canada
SGC	Southern Governors Conference
SGC	South Georgia College [*Douglas*]
SGC	Space General Corp. (MCD)
SGC	Spartan Guidance Computer [*Missiles*] (AABC)
SGC	Specialist in Guidance and Counseling (GAGS)
SGc	Specific Conductance (STED)
SGC	Spermicide-Germicide Compound [*Medicine*] (DMAA)
SGC	Spherical Gear Coupling
SGC	Stabilized Ground Cloud [*NASA*] (NAKS)
SGC	Stabilizer Gyro Circuit
SGC	Standard Geographical Classification [*Canada*]
SGC	Starburst Giant Cells [*Cytology*]
SGC	State Grants Commission [*Tasmania, Australia*]
SGC	Strata Energy Corp. [*Vancouver Stock Exchange symbol*]
SGC	Students Guide to Childcare [*British*]
SGC	Supergroup Connector [*Telecommunications*] (TEL)
SGC	Superior Geocentric Conjunction
SGC	Superior Surgical [*AMEX symbol*] (TTSB)
SGC	Superior Surgical Manufacturing Co., Inc. [*AMEX symbol*] (SPSG)
SGC	Superior Uniform Group [*AMEX symbol*] [*Formerly, Superior Surgical*]
Sg C	Surgeon-Captain [*British military*] (DMA)
SGC	Swan-Ganz Catheter (STED)
SGC	Swept Gain Control (DA)
SGC	Washington, DC [*Location identifier FAA*] (FAAL)
SGCA	Silvermine Guild Center for the Arts [*Later, SGAC*] (EA)
SGCA	Spacecraft Ground Controlled Approach (IAA)
SGCA	Subependymal Giant Cell Astrocytoma [*Medicine*] (DMAA)
SGCC	Safety Glazing Certification Council (EA)
SGCD	Society of Glass and Ceramic Decorators (EA)
SGCE	Ship Gyrocompass Equipment [*Navy*] (CAAL)
SGCEC	Standing Group Communications-Electronics Committee [*Later, MCEWG*] [*NATO*] (NATG)
SGCF	SNAP [*Systems for Nuclear Auxiliary Power*] Generalized Critical Facility
SGCMG	Single Gimbal Control Moment Gyro [*Navigation*]
SGCO	Concepcion [*Paraguay*] [*ICAO location identifier*] (ICLI)
SGCP	Shipboard Gauge Calibration Program (DNAB)
Sg Cr	Surgeon-Commander [*British military*] (DMA)
SGCS	Silicon Gate-Controlled Switch
SGCS	Slave Gyro Control System
SGD	Napa, CA [*Location identifier FAA*] (FAAL)
SGD	Scott's Liquid Gold [*NYSE symbol*] (TTSB)
SGD	Scotts Liquid Gold Co. [*NYSE symbol*] (SAG)
SGD	Seafloor Geosciences Division (EA)
SGD	Self-Generating Dictionary

SGD	Senior Grand Deacon [*Freemasonry*]
SGD	Shogun Developments Corp. [*Vancouver Stock Exchange symbol*]
SGD	Signaling Ground [*Telecommunications*] (TEL)
SGD	Signed
sgd	Signed (WDMC)
Sgd	Signed (EBF)
SGD	Silicon Grown Diffused (IAA)
SGD	Sliding Glass Door (ADA)
SGD	Society of Geniuses of Distinction [*Defunct*] (EA)
SGD	Society of Glass Decorators [*Later, SGCD*] (EA)
SGD	Sonderborg [*Denmark*] [*Airport symbol*] (OAG)
SGD	Sparks-Goosen-Drake Engine [*Auto racing*]
SGD	Special Government Design (DNAB)
SGD	Specific Granule Deficiency [*Physiology*]
SGD	Sperry Gyroscope Division [*Sperry Rand Corp.*] (MCD)
SGD	Straight Gravity Drainage [*Surgery*] (DAVI)
SGD	Sui Generis Degree
SGDE	Steering Gear Dual Emergency (MSA)
SGDE	System Ground Data Equipment [*RADAR*]
SGDF	Supergroup Distribution Frame [*Telecommunications*] (TEL)
SGDHF	Sodium Glycodihydrofusidate [*Hemolytic*]
SGDI	Swaging Die [*Tool*]
SGDI	Switched Ground Discrete Input (MCD)
SGDO	Switched Ground Discrete Output (MCD)
SGDPS	Second Generation Data Processing System (MCD)
SGDS	Supergroup Distribution Frame [*Telecommunications*] (OSI)
Sge	Sagitta [*Constellation*]
SGE	Secondary Generalized Epilepsy (STED)
SGE	Secondary Grid Emission
SGE	Selfish Genetic Elements
SGE	Severable Government Equipment
SGE	Sigma Gamma Epsilon [*Society*]
SGE	Significant Glandular Enlargement [*Endocrinology*] (DAVI)
SGE	Slow Glass Etch (IAA)
SGE	Society of Government Economists (EA)
SGE	Solutions Generation Environment [*Computer science*] (BTTJ)
SGE	Starch Gel Electrophoresis (OA)
SGE	Student Goals Exploration [*Test*] (TMMY)
SGE	Subscriber Group Equipment [*Telecommunications*]
SGE	Super-Critical Gas Extraction [*Chemical engineering*]
SGE	Support Group Europe [*Military*]
SGEM	Study Group on Environmental Monitoring [*National Research Council*]
SGEMP	System-Generated Electromagnetic Pulse [*Army*]
SGEN	Encarnacion [*Paraguay*] [*ICAO location identifier*] (ICLI)
SGENX	SoGen Intl. Fund [*Mutual fund ticker symbol*] (SG)
SGEP	Socialist Group in the European Parliament [*See also GSPE*] (EAIO)
SGES	Society of Grain Elevator Superintendents [*Later, GEAPS*]
SGET	Spacecraft Ground Elapsed Time
SGEU	Singapore General Employees' Union
SGF	Sample Gas Flow
SGF	Sarcoma Growth Factor
SGF	Seventh Generation Fund for Indian Development (EA)
SGF	Silica Gel Filter (STED)
SGF	Singapore Fund [*NYSE symbol*] (SPSG)
SGF	Skeletal Growth Factor [*Genetics*]
SGF	Small Gene Fragment [*Genetics*]
SGF	Smoke Generating Fuel (IAA)
SGF	Southern Group of Forces [*Former USSR*] (NATG)
SGF	Spermiogenesis Growth Factor [*Biochemistry*]
SGF	Springfield [*Missouri*] [*Airport symbol*] (OAG)
SGF	Springfield, MO [*Location identifier FAA*] (FAAL)
SGF	Steam Generator Feedwater (DNAB)
SGF	Sydney Garden Festival [*Australia*]
SGFA	Asuncion [*Paraguay*] [*ICAO location identifier*] (ICLI)
SGFA	Society of Graphic Fine Art [*British*] (DBA)
SGFC	Sharon Gless Fan Club (EA)
SGFI	Filadelfia [*Paraguay*] [*ICAO location identifier*] (ICLI)
SGFID	Seventh Generation Fund for Indian Development (EA)
SGFNT	Significant (FAAC)
SGFP	Steam Generator Feed Pump (IEEE)
SGFR	Single-Nephron Glomerular Filtration Rate [*Medicine*] (MAE)
SGG	Saint George Island, AK [*Location identifier FAA*] (FAAL)
SGG	Signatures (WGA)
SGG	Simanggang [*Malaysia*] [*Airport symbol*] (AD)
SGG	South Georgia [*United Kingdom*] [*Geomagnetic observatory code*]
SGG	St. George Minerals [*Vancouver Stock Exchange symbol*]
SGG	Sustainer Gas Generator
SGGP	Seller's Guide to Government Purchasing [*A publication*]
SGGR	Guaira [*Paraguay*] [*ICAO location identifier*] (ICLI)
SGH	Serum Growth Hormone [*Endocrinology*]
SGH	Servisair Ltd. [*British ICAO designator*] (FAAC)
SGH	Seth G. Huntington [*Designer's mark on US bicentennial half dollar*]
SGH	Signal Hill Energy Corp. [*Vancouver Stock Exchange symbol*]
SGH	Springfield [*Ohio*] [*Airport symbol*] (AD)
SGH	Springfield, OH [*Location identifier FAA*] (FAAL)
SGH	Stable-Type Glycated Hemoglobin [*Medicine*] (DB)
SGH	Sterling House [*AMEX symbol*] (TTSB)
SGH	Sterling House Corp. [*AMEX symbol*] (SAG)
SGH	Sud-Ghoubbet [*Djibouti*] [*Seismograph station code, US Geological Survey*] (SEIS)
SGH	Surgical Hospital [*Medicine*]
SGHT	StarSight Telecast [*NASDAQ symbol*] (TTSB)
SGHT	StarSight Telecast, Inc. [*NASDAQ symbol*] (SAG)

SGHW .... Steam-Generating, Heavy-Water [*Reactor*] [*British Nuclear energy*] (NRCH)

SGHWR .... Steam-Generating, Heavy-Water Reactor [*British Nuclear energy*] (NRCH)

SGI .... Sea Grant Institute [*University of Wisconsin*] [*Research center*] (RCD)

SGI .... Search Group, Inc. [*An association*] (EA)

SGI .... Senior Gleaners, Inc. [*An association*] (EA)

SGI .... Servers, Supercomputers, and Graphics Workstations that Enable Breakthrough Insights

SGI .... Servicio Geodesico Interamericano [*Inter-American Geodetic Survey - IAGS*] [*United States*]

SGI .... Sheriff Guards International [*Nigeria*] (EAIO)

SGI .... Silicon Graphics [*NYSE symbol*] (SPSG)

SGI .... Silicon Graphics Incorporated [*Computer science*]

SGI .... Small Group Instructor [*or Instruction*] [*Army*] (INF)

SGI .... Society for Gynecologic Investigation (EA)

SGI .... Soka Gakkai International [*An association*]

SGI .... Specific Gravity Indicator

SGI .... Spring Garden Institute

SGI .... Standard Graphic Interface [*XOR Systems*]

SGI .... Systems Group, Inc. [*Telecommunications service*] (TSSD)

SGIA .... Screenprinting and Graphic Imaging Association International (NTPA)

SGIA .... Sun Glass Institute of America [*Defunct*] (EA)

SGIB .... Itaipu [*Paraguay*] [*ICAO location identifier*] (ICLI)

SGIC .... Silicon Graphics (MHDW)

SGIG .... Sovereign Grand Inspector-General [*Freemasonry*] (ROG)

SGIH .... Scientific Games Hldgs [*NASDAQ symbol*] (TTSB)

SGIH .... Scientific Games Holding Corp. [*NASDAQ symbol*] (SAG)

SGIM .... Society of General Internal Medicine (EA)

SGINDEX ..... System Generation Cross-Reference Index [*NASA*]

SGIS .... Safeguards Initiation Signal [*Nuclear energy*] (NRCH)

SGIS .... Steam Generator Isolation Signal (IEEE)

SGIS .... Student Government Information Service (EA)

SGIT .... Special Group Inclusive Tour [*Airline fare*]

SGITS .... Spacecraft Ground Operational Support System Interface Test System (IAA)

SGI-USA ..... Soka Gakkai International - United States of America (EA)

SGJ .... Sagarai [*Papua New Guinea*] [*Airport symbol*] (OAG)

SGJ .... St. Augustine, FL [*Location identifier FAA*] (FAAL)

SGJ .... Supersonic Gas Jet

SGJA .... Sporting Goods Jobbers Association [*Later, NASGW*]

SGJKT .... Society of Goldsmiths, Jewellers, and Kindred Trades [*A union*] [*British*]

SGJN .... San Juan Nepomuceno [*Paraguay*] [*ICAO location identifier*] (ICLI)

SGJP .... Satellite Graphic Job Processor [*Computer science*]

SGK .... Hsinkong [*Republic of China*] [*Also, HSI*] [*Seismograph station code, US Geological Survey*] (SEIS)

SGK .... Knoxville, TN [*Location identifier FAA*] (FAAL)

SGK .... Schawk, Inc. [*Formerly, Filtertek Inc.*] [*NYSE symbol*] (SAG)

SGK .... Schawk Inc.'A' [*NYSE symbol*] (TTSB)

SGKA .... Skyward Aviation Ltd. [*Canada ICAO designator*] (FAAC)

SGKA .... Studien zur Geschichte und Kultur des Alterums [*A publication*] (BJA)

SGKB .... Societe Generale-Komercni Banka [*Former Czechoslovakia*] (EY)

SGKF .... Susan G. Komen Breast Cancer Foundation (EA)

SGKF .... Susan G. Komen Foundation (EA)

SGL .... Mount Signal [*California*] [*Seismograph station code, US Geological Survey*] (SEIS)

s gl .... Sans Correction [*Without correction*] [*Ophthalmology*] (DAVI)

SGL .... Senegalair [*Senegal*] [*ICAO designator*] (FAAC)

SGL .... Signal

Sgl .... Signalman [*Military*] (WDAA)

SGL .... Single (MSA)

SGL .... Sleeping Gold Ltd. [*Vancouver Stock Exchange symbol*]

SGL .... Slightly-Grounded Lightplane (PDAA)

SGL .... Society of Gas Lighting (EA)

SGL .... South State Cooperative Library System, Los Angeles, CA [*OCLC symbol*] (OCLC)

SGL .... Space-Ground Link (MCD)

SGL .... Staff Group Leader [*Army*]

SGL .... Strategic Global Income Fd [*NYSE symbol*] (TTSB)

SGL .... Strategic Global Income Fund [*NYSE symbol*] (SPSG)

SGL .... Sumerisches Glossar [*A publication*] (BJA)

SGL .... Sunglasses

SGL .... Superannuation Guarantee Levy

SGL .... System Generation Language (IAA)

S GLAM .... South Glamorgan [*County in Wales*]

SGLC .... Strain Gauge Load Cell

Sg L Cr .... Surgeon Lieutenant-Commander [*British military*] (DMA)

SGLE .... Single (AAG)

SGLF .... Scottish Grand Lodge of Freemasons

SGLI .... Service Government Life Insurance (DOMA)

SGLI .... Servicemen's Group Life Insurance [*Military*]

SGLI .... Slave Gyro Leveling Integrator

SGLIC .... Steam Generator Level Instrumentation Cabinet [*Nuclear energy*] (NRCH)

SGLLI .... Section on Gay and Lesbian Legal Issues [*Association of American Law Schools*] (EA)

SGLO .... Lobrego, Fortin [*Paraguay*] [*ICAO location identifier*] (ICLI)

SGLO .... Standing Group Liaison Officer to the North Atlantic Council

SGLP .... Standing Group Representative Liaison Paper to the International Staff [*Obsolete NATO*] (NATG)

SGLS .... Satellite Ground Link System (NATG)

SGLS .... Space-Ground Link Station [*NASA*] (NASA)

SGLS .... Space-Ground Link System (IAA)

SGLS .... Space-to-Ground Link Subsystem [*NASA*]

SGLSY .... Space Ground Link System [*NASA*] (NAKS)

SGLV .... La Victoria (Ex Casado) [*Paraguay*] [*ICAO location identifier*] (ICLI)

SGLWCH ..... Study Group on Labor and Working Class History (EA)

SGM .... College Mathieu, Gravelbourg, Saskatchewan [*Library symbol National Library of Canada*] (NLC)

SGM .... Sahara Gaming [*AMEX symbol*] (SPSG)

SGM .... Santa Fe Gaming [*AMEX symbol*] [*Formerly, Sahara Gaming*] (SG)

SGM .... Santa Fe Gaming Corp. [*AMEX symbol*] (SAG)

SGM .... Screen Grid Modulation

SGM .... Sea Gallantry Medal [*Navy British*]

SGM .... Sergeant Major (AABC)

SGM .... Silver Gate [*Montana*] [*Seismograph station code, US Geological Survey*] (SEIS)

SGM .... Single Geometric Model [*Computer-assisted design*]

SGM .... Sisters of Charity of Montreal (Grey Nuns) (TOCD)

SGM .... Society for General Microbiology [*British*]

SGM .... Society for General Music (EA)

SGM .... Soeurs Grises de Montreal [*Sisters of Charity, Grey Nuns of Montreal*] [*Roman Catholic religious order*]

SGM .... Spark Gap Modulation

SGM .... Standing Group Memorandum [*Obsolete NATO*] (NATG)

SGM .... Stationary Gaussian Markov [*Telecommunications*] (IAA)

SGM .... Strategic Guidance Memo [*Navy*]

SGM .... Strict Good Middling (IAA)

SGMA .... Sigmatron International [*NASDAQ symbol*] (SAG)

SGMA .... Soup and Gravy Manufacturers Association [*British*] (DBA)

SGMA .... Sporting Goods Manufacturers Association [*North Palm Beach, FL*] (EA)

SGMAA .... Sporting Goods Manufacturers Agents Association [*Later, SGRA*]

SGMAS .... Sea Grant Marine Advisory Services (COE)

SGMC .... Standing Group Meteorological Committee [*Obsolete NATO*] (NATG)

SGMCI .... Sporting Goods Manufacturers' Credit Interchange [*Defunct*] (EA)

SGMD .... Swaging Mandel

SGME .... Mariscal Estigarribia [*Paraguay*] [*ICAO location identifier*] (ICLI)

SGME .... Service Generale des Moyens de l'Enseignement [*Canada*]

SGML .... Standard Generalized Markup Language [*Also, GSML*] [*International Standards Organization*]

SGML .... Study Group for Mathematical Learning (EA)

SGMM .... Semiconductor Generic Manufacturing Model (AAEL)

SGMN .... Signalman [*Military British*]

SGMP .... Society of Government Meeting Planners (EA)

SGMPr .... Santa Fe Gaming 8% Ex Pfd [*AMEX symbol*] (TTSB)

SGMS .... Shipboard Gravity Measuring System

SGMSR .... Steam Generator Maximum Steam Rate [*Nuclear energy*] (NRCH)

SGMT .... Simulated Greenwich Mean Time (MCD)

SGMT .... Subgroup Modern Terminal

SGM/USA ..... Scripture Gift Mission/USA (EA)

SGM/USA ..... SGM International/United States of America [*Formerly, Scripture Gift Mission/United States of America*] (EA)

SGN .... Ho Chi Minh [*Vietnam*] [*Airport symbol*] (OAG)

SGN .... Saigon [*South Vietnam*] [*Airport symbol*] (AD)

SGN .... Sartigan Granite [*Vancouver Stock Exchange symbol*]

SGN .... Scan Gate Number

SGN .... Seamless Garment Network (EA)

SGN .... Self-Generated Noise [*Oceanography*]

SGN .... Service Geologique National [*National Geological Survey*] [*Bureau of Geological and Mining Research*] [*Information service or system*] (IID)

sgn .... Signer [*MARC relator code*] [*Library of Congress*] (LCCP)

SGN .... Standing Group, North Atlantic Treaty Organization

SGN .... Surgeon [*Military British*]

SGN .... Surgeon General of the Navy

SGNA .... Nueva Asuncion [*Paraguay*] [*ICAO location identifier*] (ICLI)

SGNA .... Society of Gastroenterology Nurses and Associates (EA)

SGNET .... Sea Grant Network [*National Oceanic and Atmospheric Administration Information service or system*] (IID)

SGNIS .... Sea Grant Non-Indigenous Species

SgnlApl .... Signal Apparel Co., Inc. [*Associated Press*] (SAG)

SGNLD .... Signalled (ROG)

SGNLS .... Sequential Generalized Nonlinear Least Squares [*Statistics*]

SgnlTech ...... Signal Technology Corp. [*Associated Press*] (SAG)

SGNMOS ...... Screen-Grid N-Channel Metal Oxide Semiconductor

SGNR .... Signature (AABC)

SGNS .... Signature Inns, Inc. [*NASDAQ symbol*] (SAG)

SGO .... Saint George [*Australia Airport symbol*] (OAG)

SGO .... Sea Gold Oil Corp. [*Vancouver Stock Exchange symbol*]

SGO .... Seagull Energy [*NYSE symbol*] (TTSB)

SGO .... Seagull Energy Corp. [*NYSE symbol*] (SPSG)

SGO .... Society of Geriatric Ophthalmology (EA)

SGO .... Society of Gynecologic Oncologists (EA)

SGO .... Solicitor-General's Office [*Australia*]

SGO .... Sports & Games Officer (WDAA)

SGO .... Squadron Gunnery Officer

SGO .... Stained Glass Overlay [*Commercial firm British*]

SGO .... Strict Good Ordinary (IAA)

SGO .... Subgenual Organ [*Entomology*]

SGO .... Surgeon General's Office

SGO .... Surgery, Gynecology, and Obstetrics (MAE)

SGO .... Sydney Godolphin Osborne [*Literary signature of 19th-century British writer*]

SGOG .... Steam Generators Owners Group [*Nuclear energy*] (NRCH)

SGOG .... Suppressor Grid Orbitron Gauge

SGOL .... Olimpo [*Paraguay*] [*ICAO location identifier*] (ICLI)

SGOL .... Saint Helena Gold Mines [*NASDAQ symbol*] (SAG)

SGOL	St. Helena Gold Mines Ltd. [*NASDAQ symbol*] (NQ)
SGOLY	St. Helena Gold Mines ADR [*NASDAQ symbol*] (TTSB)
SGOMSEC	Scientific Group on Methodologies for the Safety Evaluation of Chemicals [*International Council of Scientific Unions*]
SGOR	Solution Gas-Oil Ratio
SGOS	Shuttle Ground Operations Simulator [*NASA*] (NASA)
SGOT	Serum Glutamic Oxaloacetic Transaminase [*An enzyme*]
SGP	San Gregorio [*Peru*] [*Seismograph station code, US Geological Survey Closed*] (SEIS)
SGP	Schering-Plough [*NYSE symbol*] (TTSB)
SGP	School Guarantee Program (DNAB)
SGP	Secondary Gun Pointer [*Navy*]
SGP	Seminiferous Growth Factor [*Biochemistry*]
SGP	Serine Glycerophosphatide [*Biochemistry*] (MAE)
SGP	Sialoglycoprotein (DB)
SGP	Simulated Ground Plane [*Automotive engineering*]
SGP	Singapore [*ANSI three-letter standard code*] (CNC)
SGP	Single Ground Point [*NASA*] (MCD)
SGP	Society of General Physiologists (EA)
SGP	Society of Ghana Philatelists [*Defunct*] (EA)
SGP	Solicitor General, Prairies [*UTLAS symbol*]
SGP	Soluble Glycoprotein [*Medicine*] (MAE)
SGP	Southern Galactic Pole
SGP	Southern Great Plains [*Marine science*] (OSRA)
SGP	South Galactic Pole
SGP	Specialty Glass Products, Inc.
SGP	Staatkundig Gereformeerde Partij [*Netherlands Political party Benelux*]
SGP	Stabilized Gyro Platform
SGP	Standard Guidance Package
SGP	Stephen Greene Press
SGP	Subscriber Group Plant (IAA)
SGP	Sudeten German Party
SGP	Sulfated Glycoprotein [*Biochemistry*]
SGPA	Stained Glass Professionals Association [*Inactive*] (EA)
SGPB	Southern Growth Policies Board
SGPC	Soviet Government Purchasing Commission [*World War II*]
SGPDO	Sodo Gordena People's Democratic Organisation [*Ethiopia*]
SGPF	Spencer Gulf Prawn Fishery [*Australia*]
SGPI	Pilar [*Paraguay*] [*ICAO location identifier*] (ICLI)
SGPI	Superintendent of Government Printing, India (ROG)
SGPM	Saint-Gobain-Pont-A-Mousson [*French industrial giant*]
SgpNL	National Library, Singapore, Singapore [*Library symbol Library of Congress*] (LCLS)
SgpNU	Nangang University, Singapore, Singapore [*Library symbol Library of Congress*] (LCLS)
SGPO	Puerto Pinasco [*Paraguay*] [*ICAO location identifier*] (ICLI)
SGPO	Speed-Gate-Pull-Off (PDAA)
SGPO	Standing Group Representative Communication to the Private Office of the NATO Secretary General [*Obsolete*] (NATG)
SGPS	Ciudad Presidente Stroessner [*Paraguay*] [*ICAO location identifier*] (ICLI)
SGPT	Gelatin Silver Print (VRA)
SGPT	Serum Glutamic-Pyruvic Transaminase [*An enzyme*]
SGPT	Silver Gelatin Print (VRA)
SgpU	University of Singapore, Singapore, Singapore [*Library symbol Library of Congress*] (LCLS)
SGR	Greenville County Library, Greenville, SC [*OCLC symbol*] (OCLC)
SGR	Houston, TX [*Location identifier FAA*] (FAAL)
SGR	Sachs-Georgi Reaction [*On test for syphilis*] [*Infectious diseases*] (DAVI)
Sgr	Sagittarius [*Constellation*]
SGR	Saturn Energy & Resources Ltd. [*Vancouver Stock Exchange symbol*]
SGR	School of General Reconnaissance [*Air Force British*]
SGR	Scientists for Global Responsibility (WDAA)
SGR	Seismic Group Recorder [*Geophysics*]
SGR	Self-Generation Reactor [*Nuclear energy*] (NRCH)
SGR	Seminal Groove
SGR	Set Graphics Rendition [*Computer science*] (PCM)
SGR	Short Growth Rate (OA)
SGR	Singer [*Music*]
SGR	Sodium Graphite Reactor [*Nuclear energy*]
SGR	Soft Gamma-Ray Repeater [*Astrophysics*]
SGR	Stack Gas Reheat [*Air pollution control*]
SGR	Steam Gas Recycle [*Shale oil process*]
S/GR	Steering Gear [*Automotive engineering*]
SGR	Submandibular Gland Renin [*Endocrinology*]
SGR	Substantia Gelatinosa Rolandi [*Medicine*] (DMAA)
SGR	Sugar Land [*Texas*] [*Airport symbol*] (OAG)
SGRA	Sporting Goods Representatives Association [*of SIRA*] [*Later, SGAA*] (EA)
Sg RA	Surgeon Rear-Admiral [*British military*] (DMA)
SGRAC	Supreme Grand Royal Arch Chapter [*Freemasonry*] (ROG)
SGRAE	Scientists' Group for Reform of Animal Experimentation (EA)
SGRAM	Synchronous Graphics RAM [*Random Access Memory*] (PCM)
SGRCA	Sodium Graphite Reactor Critical Assembly (IEEE)
SGRD	Signal Ground (AAG)
SGRD	State Government Research Directory [*A publication*]
SGREP	Standing Group Representative [*NASA*]
sgrf	Sgraffito (VRA)
SGRFX	Seligman Growth Cl.A [*Mutual fund ticker symbol*] (SG)
S-GRN	Surfaced Green [*Lumber*]
SGRO	Rosario [*Paraguay*] [*ICAO location identifier*] (ICLI)
SGRP	Seating Reference Point [*49CFR571*] (TAG)
SGRS	Stockton Geriatric Rating Scale [*Psychology*]
SGRU	Sawyers' General Representative Union [*British*]
SGS	Hermanas del Buen Pastor (TOCD)
SGS	Sage Resources Ltd. [*Vancouver Stock Exchange symbol*]
SGS	Salem Generating Station [*Nuclear energy*] (GFGA)
SGS	Scottish Guild of Servers [*Episcopalian*]
SGS	Secondary Grammar School (ADA)
SGS	Secretary of the General Staff [*Army*]
SGS	Seeley Genealogy Society (EA)
SGS	Segmented Gamma Scanner [*Nuclear energy*] (NRCH)
SGS	Signal Generating Station (CET)
SGS	Single Green Silk-Covered [*Wire insulation*]
SGS	Sisters of the Good Samaritan (ADA)
SGS	Society of Graduate Surgeons (NTPA)
SGS	Society of the Golden Section [*Defunct*] (EA)
SGS	Society of the Good Shepherd [*Anglican religious community*]
SGS	Software Generation System
SGS	Solution Gas Drive [*Petroleum engineering*]
SGS	Song of Songs [*Old Testament book*] [*Roman Catholic canon*]
SGS	Stactic Gel Strength [*Well drilling technology*]
SGS	Stage Golfing Society [*British*] (BI)
SGS	Statistics Gathering System [*NASA*]
SGS	Steam Generator System [*Nuclear energy*] (NRCH)
SGS	Steep Glide Slope (NASA)
SGS	St. George [*South Carolina*] [*Seismograph station code, US Geological Survey*] (SEIS)
SGS	Strategy Gaming Society (EA)
SGS	Stream Generation Statement [*Computer science*]
SGS	Stretch Glass Society (EA)
SGS	Swiveling Gunner's Station
SGS	Symbol Generation and Storage [*Computer science*]
SGSC	Samuel Gompers Stamp Club (EA)
SGSC	Standing Group Security Committee [*Obsolete NATO*] (NATG)
SGSC	Strain Gauge Signal Conditioner [*NASA*] (MCD)
SGSE	Standard Ground Support Equipment
SGSFU	Salt-Glazed Structural Facing Units [*Technical drawings*]
SGSG	Scandinavian Glioma Study Group [*Medicine*] (DMAA)
SGSI	Stabilized Glide Slope Indicator (NVT)
SGSN	Skylab Ground Support Network [*NASA*]
SGSNY	St. George's Society of New York (EA)
SGSO	Space Ground Support Operations [*NASA*] (KSC)
SGSP	Salt Gradient Solar Ponds [*Energy source*]
SGSP	Single Groove, Single Petticoat [*Insulators*]
SGSP	Society for Glass Science and Practices (EA)
SGSR	Society for General Systems Research (EA)
SGSS	Stokes/Gordon Stress Scale [*Test*] (TMMY)
SGSS	Study Group on Social Security [*Defunct*] (EA)
SGS TM	SGS Thomson Microelectronics, NV [*Associated Press*] (SAG)
SGSU	Society of Government Service Urologists (NTPA)
SGSUB	Salt-Glazed Structural Unit Base [*Technical drawings*]
SGSVDV	Steam Generator Stop Valve Dump Valve (IEEE)
S-GT	Sachs-Georgi Test [*for syphilis*] [*Also, SG*] [*Obsolete*]
SGT	Satellite Ground Terminal
SGT	Seagram's Gin and Tonic
SGT	Section Gunnery Trainer [*Army*]
SGT	Segment Table [*Computer science*] (IBMDP)
SGT	Sergeant (AABC)
Sgt	Sergeant (WDAA)
SGT	Silicon Gate Transistor (IAA)
SGT	Small Gas Turbine
SGT	Small Group Therapy
SGT	Small Group Trial
SGT	Societa' Aerotaxi SUD [*Italy ICAO designator*] (FAAC)
SGT	Society of Glass Technology (EAIO)
SGT	Soligen Technologies, Inc. [*AMEX symbol*] (SAG)
SGT	Special Gas Taper [*Thread*]
SGT	Speculative Gains Tax
SGT	Starter or Ground, Thermoplastic [*Automotive engineering*]
SGT	Stuttgart, AR [*Location identifier FAA*] (FAAL)
SGT	Subsystem Ground Test (MCD)
SGT	Surface Ground Temperature [*Climatology*]
SGTA	Servo Gear Train Assembly
SGTBX	SunAmerica U.S. Govt. Secs. Cl.B [*Mutual fund ticker symbol*] (SG)
Sgte	Sagitta [*Constellation*]
SGT EC	Soligen Technologies [*ECM Symbol*] (TTSB)
SGTF	Steam Generator Test Facility [*Nuclear energy*] (NRCH)
SGTI	SATCOM [*Satellite Communications*] Ground Terminal Interoperability
SGTI	Surgical Technologies [*NASDAQ symbol*] (TTSB)
SGTI	Surgical Technologies, Inc. [*NASDAQ symbol*] (SAG)
SGTIA	Standing Group Technical Intelligence Agency [*NATO*] (NATG)
SGTM	Strain Gauge Thrust Meter
SGTM	Titanium Dioxide Manufacturers Sector Group (EAIO)
SGTMAJ	Sergeant Major
Sgt Maj	Sergeant Major (WDAA)
SGTPS	Saw Grinders' Trade Protective Society [*A union*] [*British*]
Sgtr	Sagittarius [*Constellation*]
SGTR	Standard Government Travel Request
SGTR	Standardized Government Travel Regulations
SGTR	Steam Generator Test Rig [*Nuclear energy*] (NRCH)
SGTR	Steam Generator Tube Rupture [*Nuclear energy*] (NRCH)
SGTS	Satellite Ground Terminal System
SGTS	Scottish Gaelic Texts Society (DBA)
SGTS	Second Genration Tank Sight [*Army*]
SGTS	Standby Gas Treatment System [*Nuclear energy*] (NRCH)

SGTS	Swing Grip Thermal Stripper
SGTT	Standard Glucose Tolerance Test [*Medicine*] (DB)
SGTX	Surugatoxin [*Toxicology*] (LDT)
SGU	Saint George [*Utah*] [*Airport symbol*] (OAG)
SGU	Saint George, UT [*Location identifier FAA*] (FAAL)
SGU	Sammelbuch Griechischer Urkunden aus Aegypten [*A publication*] (BJA)
SGU	Scottish Gliding Union (DBA)
SGU	Scottish Golf Union (DBA)
SGU	Sidewinder Generator Unit (NG)
SGU	Single Gun Unit [*British military*] (DMA)
SGU	Standard Geographical Unit (WDMC)
SGU	Sveriges Geologiska Undersokning [*Geological Survey of Sweden*] [*Uppsala*] [*Information service or system*] (IID)
S-G(UN)......	Secretary-General of the United Nations
SGUS	Slovak Gymnastic Union Sokol of the USA (EA)
SGV	Saint Genevieve Resources Ltd. [*Toronto Stock Exchange symbol*]
SGV	Salivary Gland Virus
SGV	Screen Grid Voltage (IAA)
SGV	Selective Gastric Vagotomy [*Medicine*] (DB)
SGV	Self-Guided Vehicle
SGV	Sierra Grande [*Argentina*] [*Airport symbol*] (OAG)
SGV	Small Granular Vesicle [*Cytology*]
Sg VA	Surgeon Vice-Admiral [*British military*] (DMA)
SGV & P	Selective Gastric Vagotomy and Pyloroplasty [*Medicine*] (CPH)
SGVB	SGV Bancorp [*NASDAQ symbol*] (TTSB)
SGVB	SGV Bancorp, Inc. [*NASDAQ symbol*] (SAG)
SGV BC	SGV Bancorp, Inc. [*Associated Press*] (SAG)
SGVHD.......	Syngeneic Graft-Versus-Host Disease [*Medicine*] (DMAA)
SGW	Salt-Glazed Ware
SGW	Security Guard Window (AAG)
SGW	Senior Grand Warden [*Freemasonry*]
SGW	Simulated Ground Water [*Analytical chemistry*]
SGW	South Carolina State College, Orangeburg, SC [*OCLC symbol*] (OCLC)
SGW	Stone Groundwood [*Pulp and paper technology*]
SGW	Stratospheric Gravity Waves [*Planetary science*]
SGWD........	Submarine Ground Water Discharge [*Geophysics*]
SGWLC	Steam Generator Water Level Control [*Nuclear energy*] (NRCH)
SGWM	Standing Group Working Memorandum [*NATO*] (NATG)
SGWS	Shared Graphics Work Space
SGWS	Stove Grate Workers' Society [*A union*] [*British*]
SGX	Selector Group Matrix [*Telecommunications*] (TEL)
SGX	Songea [*Tanzania*] [*Airport symbol*] (OAG)
SGX	Synergistics Industries Ltd. [*Toronto Stock Exchange symbol*]
s-gy--	Guyana [*MARC geographic area code Library of Congress*] (LCCP)
SGY	Skagway [*Alaska*] [*Airport symbol*] (OAG)
SGY	Skagway Air Service, Inc. [*ICAO designator*] (FAAC)
SGY	Skagway, AK [*Location identifier FAA*] (FAAL)
SGY	Sooner Energy Corp. [*Vancouver Stock Exchange symbol*]
SGY	Stone Energy [*NYSE symbol*] (TTSB)
SGY	Stone Energy Corp. [*NYSE symbol*] (SPSG)
SGYR	Yasyreta [*Paraguay*] [*ICAO location identifier*] (ICLI)
SGZ............	Green Bay, WI [*Location identifier FAA*] (FAAL)
SGZ............	Signet Resources, Inc. [*Vancouver Stock Exchange symbol*]
SGZ............	Singora [*Thailand*] [*Airport symbol*] (AD)
SGZ............	Surface Ground Zero
SH.............	Air-Cushion Vehicle built by Sealand Hovercraft [*England*] [*Usually used in combination with numerals*]
SH.............	Hart Senate Office Building [*Washington, D.C.*]
SH.............	Sacred Heart (ROG)
SH.............	Sacrifice Hit [*Baseball*]
Sh.............	Safe Hit [*Baseball*]
SH.............	Sa Hautesse [*His, or Her, Highness*] [*French*]
SH.............	Samaritan Free Hospital [*British*] (ROG)
S/H.............	Sample and Hold (IEEE)
SH.............	Sash (WGA)
SH.............	Schering AG [*Germany*] [*Research code symbol*]
SH.............	Schistosoma Hematobium [*A parasitic fluke*]
SH.............	Schonlein-Henoch Purpura [*Medicine*] (DMAA)
SH.............	Schoolhouse
SH.............	Scinde Horse [*British military*] (DMA)
SH.............	Scleroscope Hardness
SH.............	Scottish Horse [*British military*] (DMA)
SH.............	Scratch Hardness [*Aerospace*]
SH.............	Scripophila Helvetica (EA)
SH.............	Scripta Hierosolymitana (BJA)
SH.............	Scrum Half [*Rugby*] (WGA)
SH.............	Secondary Hypertension [*Medicine*] (DHP)
SH.............	Secondhand (ADA)
SH.............	Second Harmonic (PDAA)
SH.............	Second Harvest [*An association*] (EA)
SH.............	Second Harvest, the National Food Bank Network (EA)
SH.............	Section Heading (NITA)
SH.............	Section Heading Code [*Online database field identifier*]
SH.............	Sefer ha-Shanah (BJA)
SH.............	Sekira Hodshit [*Tel Aviv*] (BJA)
SH.............	Semester Hour
SH.............	Send Hub [*Telegraphy*] (TEL)
SH.............	Senior Hunter [*Purebred canine award*]
SH.............	Sephardic House [*An association*] (EA)
SH.............	Sequence History
SH.............	Serum Hepatitis [*Medicine*]
SH.............	Service Hours [*Electronics*] (IEEE)
SH.............	Session Handler

SH.............	Severely Handicapped
SH.............	Severn House [*Publisher*] [*British*]
SH.............	Sex Hormone (MAE)
SH.............	Sexual Harassment
SH.............	Shackle (AAG)
SH.............	Shale [*Lithology*]
SH.............	Shall
Sh.............	Shallow
SH.............	Shandong Huaneng Power Development ADR [*NYSE symbol*] (SAG)
Sh.............	Shandong Huaneng Pwr ADS [*NYSE symbol*] (TTSB)
SH.............	Shand's Reports [*11-41 South Carolina*] [*A publication*] (DLA)
SH.............	Shanghai
SH.............	Share
sh.............	Share (WDAA)
Sh.............	Shauri (BJA)
Sh.............	Shaw's Scotch Appeal Cases [*A publication*] (DLA)
Sh.............	Shaw's Scotch Justiciary Cases [*A publication*] (DLA)
Sh.............	Shaw's Scotch Session Cases [*A publication*] (DLA)
Sh.............	Shaw's Scotch Teind [*Tithe*] Court Reports [*A publication*] (DLA)
SH.............	Sheathing [*Technical drawings*]
SH.............	Sheep (ROG)
SH.............	Sheep Skin [*Bookbinding*] (ROG)
SH.............	Sheet (AAG)
Sh.............	Sheldon's Superior Court Reports [*Buffalo, New York*] [*A publication*] (DLA)
SH.............	Shelf [*Technical drawings*]
sh.............	Shell [*Computer science*] (CDE)
SH.............	Shell Development Co. [*Research code symbol*]
sh.............	Shells [*Quality of the bottom*] [*Nautical charts*]
Sh.............	Shepherd's Alabama Reports [*A publication*] (DLA)
Sh.............	Shepley's Reports [*13-18, 21-30 Maine*] [*A publication*] (DLA)
Sh.............	Sheriff (DLA)
SH.............	Sherwood Number
SH.............	Shield (MSA)
Sh.............	Shiel's Cape Times Law Reports [*South Africa*] [*A publication*] (DLA)
SH.............	Shigella [*Bacteriology*] (AAMN)
SH.............	Shilling [*Monetary unit in Britain*] [*Obsolete*]
SH.............	Ship
S/H.............	Shipping/Handling (WGA)
SH.............	Shipp's Reports [*66-67 North Carolina*] [*A publication*] (DLA)
SH.............	Ship's Head [*Heading*] [*Navigation*]
SH.............	Ship's Serviceman [*Navy rating*]
Sh.............	Shipwright
Sh.............	Shire
Sh.............	Shirley's Reports [*49-55 New Hampshire*] [*A publication*] (DLA)
SH.............	Shoal (ROG)
SH.............	Shock (WGA)
SH.............	Shooting [*FBI standardized term*]
SH.............	Shop (WGA)
SH.............	Short (ROG)
sh.............	Short (STED)
SH.............	Short Brothers & Harland Ltd. [*ICAO aircraft manufacturer identifier*] (ICAO)
S/H.............	Shorthand
sh.............	Shoulder
SH.............	Show (WGA)
SH.............	Showers (AAG)
SH.............	Shower's English King's Bench Reports [*A publication*] (DLA)
SH.............	Shower's English Parliamentary Cases [*A publication*] (DLA)
SH.............	Shunt [*Electricity*]
SH.............	Shuttle (MCD)
SH.............	Sick in Hospital
SH.............	Single Heterostructure (MCD)
SH.............	Single-Hung [*Door*] (DAC)
SH.............	Sinus Histiocytosis [*Medicine*]
SH.............	Sleeve Housings (COE)
SH.............	Small Heavy Seeds [*Botany*]
SH.............	Social History
S/H.............	Socialization and Handling [*Pet-adoption terminolgy*]
SH.............	Socially Housed [*Experimental animals*]
SH.............	Society for HematoPathology (EA)
SH.............	Society for the Humanities (EA)
S/H.............	Software/Hardware [*Cost*]
SH.............	Soldiers' Home [*Later, US Soldiers' and Airmen's Home*] [*Government agency*]
SH.............	Somatotrophic [*Growth*] Hormone [*Also, GH, STH*] [*Endocrinology*]
SH.............	Source Handshake
SH.............	Southern Hemisphere
SH.............	Southland Hussars [*British military*] (DMA)
SH.............	Spanish Heritage (EA)
sh.............	Spanish Territories in Northern Morocco [*Spanish North Africa*] [*MARC country of publication code Library of Congress*] (LCCP)
SH.............	Special Hazards
SH.............	Special Honor
SH.............	Specified Hours
SH.............	Spontaneously Hypertensive [*Medicine*]
SH.............	State Hospital (MAE)
sH.............	Stathenry [*Also, statH*] [*Unit of inductance*]
SH.............	Stationary High-Power [*Reactor*] (NRCH)
SH.............	Station Hospital [*Military*]
SH.............	Station House
SH.............	Steel Heads
SH.............	Steelton & Highspire Railroad Co. [*AAR code*]
SH.............	St. Helena [*ANSI two-letter standard code*] (CNC)
SH.............	Stockholder

SH............... Stored Heading (MCD)
SH............... Stoy Hayward [Venture capital group] [British]
SH............... Student Handout [Military training document] (INF)
SH............... Student Health (MAE)
SH............... Subharmonic (IAA)
SH............... Subject Heading (NITA)
S/H............. Suicidal/Homicidal [Ideation] [Psychiatry] (DAVI)
SH............... Sulfhydryl [Chemistry]
SH............... Super-High-Frequency [Radio wave] (NG)
SH............... Superstructure Heater (DS)
SH............... Support Hospital (COE)
SH............... Surgical Hernia [Medicine] (WDAA)
SH............... Surgical History [Medicine]
SH............... Switch Handler [Telecommunications] (TEL)
SH............... Switch Hook (HGAA)
SH1............. Ship's Serviceman, First Class [Navy rating]
SH2............. Ship's Serviceman, Second Class [Navy rating]
sh2............. Shrunken-2 Gene [In sweet corn]
SH2............. Supercritical Hydrogen [NASA] (NASA)
SH3............. Ship's Serviceman, Third Class [Navy rating]
Sh3............. Shorts 330 [Airplane code]
Sh6............. Shorts 360 [Airplane code]
SHA........... Ozark, AL [Location identifier FAA] (FAAL)
SHA .... Safety Hazard Analysis (MCD)
SHA .... Sailplane Homebuilders Association (EA)
SHA .... Sample and Hold Amplifier
SHA .... Scottish Hockey Association (DBA)
SHA .... Scriptores Historiae Augustae [Classical studies] (OCD)
SHA .... Secondary Heads Association [British] (DBA)
SHA .... Secretariat for Hispanic Affairs (National Conference of Catholic Bishops) (EA)
SHA .... Servicio Aereo de Honduras SA [ICAO designator] (FAAC)
SHA .... Shakwak Exploration Co. [Vancouver Stock Exchange symbol]
SHA .... Shanghai [China] [Airport symbol] (OAG)
ShA........... Shulhan 'Arukh (BJA)
SHA .... Sidereal Hour Angle
SHA .... Site Hazard Assessment [Environmental science] (BCP)
SHA .... Smith-Hughes Act (MHDW)
SHA .... Smith-Hurd's Illinois Annotated Statutes [A publication] (DLA)
SHA .... Socialist Health Association [British] (DBA)
SHA .... Societe Historique Acadienne [Acadian Historical Society] (EA)
SHA .... Society for Historical Archaeology (EA)
SHA .... Society for Humane Abortion (EA)
SHA .... Society for Humanistic Anthropology (EA)
SHA .... Sodium Hydroxide Addition [Nuclear energy] (NRCH)
SHA .... Software Hazard Analysis [Military]
SHA .... Software Houses Association (IAA)
SHA .... Solid Homogeneous Assembly [Nuclear energy]
SHA .... Southern Historical Association (EA)
SHA .... Special Handling Area (EECA)
SHA .... Special Health Authority [Government body] [British]
SHA .... Spherical Harmonic Analysis [Geophysics]
SHA .... Spring Hill [Alabama] [Seismograph station code, US Geological Survey] (SEIS)
SHA .... Staphylococcal Hemagglutinating Antibody [Medicine] (DMAA)
SHA .... State Highway Agency [MOCD] (TAG)
SHA .... Station Housing Allowance [Military] (MCD)
sHa........... Suckling Hamster [Medicine] (DMAA)
SHa........... Sulgi Hymn A (BJA)
SHA .... Superheated Aerosol (DAVI)
SHA .... Support Harness Assembly
SHA .... System Hazard Analyses [NASA] (NASA)
SHAA .... Sealed Head Access Area [Nuclear energy] (NRCH)
SHAA .... Serum Hepatitis Associated Antigen [Hematology]
SHAA .... Society of Hearing Aid Audiologists [Later, NHAS] (EA)
SHAA-Ab..... Serum Hepatitis Associated Antigen-Antibody [Hematology]
SHA-Ab....... Serum Hepatitis Associated Antibody [Hematology]
Shab........... Shabbath (BJA)
SHAB .... Soft and Hard Acid and Base (PDAA)
SHABS........ Shock Absorber
SHAC......... School Heads Advisory Committee [National Association of Independent Schools] (EDAC)
SHAC......... Small Hydrofoil Aircraft Carrier (DNAB)
SHAC......... Society for the History of Alchemy and Chemistry (EA)
SHAC......... Solar Heating and Air Conditioning
Sh Acc....... Hale's Sheriff's Account [A publication] (DLA)
SHACC........ Servicing Hotels and the Caribbean Community
SHACO........ Shorthand Coding
SHACOB....... Solar Heating and Cooling of Buildings [Energy Research and Development Administration]
SHACV........ Second Harmonic AC [Alternating Current] Voltammetry [Instrumentation]
SHAD .... Shallow Habitat Air Dive [Navy]
SHAD .... Sharpe Army Depot [California]
SHAD .... Shipboard Hazards Appraisal and Defense (CINC)
SHADCOM.... Shipping Advisory Committee [NATO]
SHADE........ Shielded Hot-Air-Drum Evaporator [Concentrator for hazardous wastes]
SHADO........ Supreme Headquarters, Alien Defense Organization [in television program "UFO"]
SHADRAC .... Shelter Housed Automatic Digital Random Access [Computer science]
SHAEF .... Supreme Headquarters, Allied Expeditionary Force [Europe] [World War II]
SH-AF .... Shelter-Afrique (EAIO)

SHAF .... Staying Healthy after Fifty [Project] [AARP]
SHAFB .... Sheppard Air Force Base [Texas] (AAG)
SHAFFT....... Second Husbands Alliance for Fair Treatment
SHAFR .... Society for Historians of American Foreign Relations (EA)
SHAFT .... Sad, Hostile, Anxious, Frustrating, Tenacious Patient Syndrome [Medicine] (DMAA)
SHAFT .... Second Home All-Inclusive First Trust [Real estate]
SHAFT .... Shaftsbury [England]
SHAG .... Share Holder Action Group [Australia]
SHAG .... Simplified High-Accuracy Guidance [NASA] (NASA)
SHAK .... Shakespeare
Shakes Q.... Shakespeare Quarterly [A publication] (BRI)
Shaks........... Shakespeare (BARN)
SHAL .... Subject Heading Authority List [Computer science]
Shale .... Decrees and Judgments in Federal Anti-Trust Cases [United States] [A publication] (DLA)
SHALE .... Stand-off, High Altitude, Long Endurance (PDAA)
Shalm......... Shalmaneser (BJA)
SHALOM...... Synchronous Halo Monitor [NASA]
SHALTA ...... Skin, Hide, and Leather Trades Association [British] (DBA)
SHAM .... Salicylhydroxamic Acid [Chelating agent]
Shaman...... Shaman Pharmaceuticals, Inc. [Associated Press] (SAG)
SHAME .... Save, Help Animals Man Exploits [Connecticut organization]
SHAME .... Society to Humiliate, Aggravate, Mortify, and Embarrass Smokers
SHAME .... Stop Hospital and Medical Errors
SHAMP .... Ship Acquisition Project Manager [Navy] (DOMA)
SHAMS .... Smart Howitzer Automated Management System [US Army Human Engineering Laboratory] (RDA)
SHAMYR..... Shomrei Mitzvot Yotzei Russia (BJA)
Shan .... Shannon's Unreported Tennessee Cases [A publication] (DLA)
Shan Cas ... Shannon's Tennessee Cases [A publication] (DLA)
Shand .... Shand's Reports [11-41 South Carolina] [A publication] (DLA)
Sh & Dunl ... Shaw and Dunlop's Scotch Court of Session Reports, First Series [A publication] (DLA)
Sh & Macl... Shaw and Maclean's Scotch Appeal Cases [A publication] (DLA)
Shand Pr .... Shand's Practice, Scotch Court of Sessions [A publication] (DLA)
Sh & R Neg... Shearman and Redfield on the Law of Negligence [A publication] (DLA)
SH & T .... Shower and Toilet (AAG)
SHANE........ Steerable Hydrophone Array, Nonlinear Element
ShangPt...... Shanghai Petrochemical Co. [Associated Press] (SAG)
ShanHua...... Shandong Huaneng Power Development ADR [Associated Press] (SAG)
SHANICLE.... Short-Range Navigation Vehicle [System] [Air Force]
Shankland's St... Shankland's Tennessee Public Statutes [A publication] (DLA)
Shannon Cas (Tenn)... Shannon's Unreported Tennessee Cases [A publication] (DLA)
Shannon's Code... Shannon's Tennessee Annotated Code [A publication] (DLA)
SHANT......... Shantung [Province in China] (ROG)
SHAOB........ Strategic High-Altitude Orbital Bomber (IAA)
SHAP .... Ship Acquisition Plan [Navy] (CAAL)
SHAPA........ Solids Handling and Processing Association (EAIO)
SHAPE........ SAGE [Semiautomatic Ground Environment] High Altitude Prototype Environment [Military] (IAA)
SHAPE .... Simulated Hospital Administration and Planning Exercise
SHAPE .... Supersonic High-Altitude Parachute Experiment [NASA]
SHAPE .... Supreme Headquarters, Allied Powers Europe [NATO]
SHAPES ...... Spatial, High-Accuracy Position Encoding Sensor (SSD)
SHAPEX....... SHAPE [Supreme Headquarters Allied Powers Europe] Annual Command Exercise [NATO] (NATG)
SHAPM .... Shear Horizontal Acoustic Plate Model [Instrumentation]
SHAPM .... Ship Acquisition Project Manager [Navy]
Sh App....... Shaw's Scotch Appeal Cases, House of Lords [A publication] (DLA)
SHAPX........ SMBS Appreciation CI.A [Mutual fund ticker symbol] (SG)
ShAr.......... Shulhan 'Arukh (BJA)
SHAR .... Simplified Hourly Absence Reporting (MCD)
SHAR .... Sriharikota Island Launch Complex [India]
SHARC........ Super Harvard Architecture Computer
SHARE........ Schoolboys Harness Aid for the Relief of the Elderly (AIE)
SHARE........ Share: Building a New El Salvador Today [An association] (EA)
SHARE........ Shared Area Resources Exchange [Library network]
SHaRE......... Shared Research Equipment Collaborative Research Program [Oak Ridge, TN] [Oak Ridge National Laboratory] [Department of Energy] (GRD)
SHARE........ SHARE Foundation (EA)
SHARE........ Share Happily and Reap Endlessly [Hollywood women's charity organization]
SHARE........ Siblings Helping Persons with Autism through Resources and Energy (MEDA)
SHARE........ Society to Help Avoid Redundant Effort [in data processing]
SHARE........ Software Help in Applications, Research and Education [International program to develop meteorological analysis and display software for developing countries] (USDC)
SHARE........ So Handicapped All Read Easily
SHARE........ Soldier Housing and Retirement Equity
SHARE........ Systems for Heat and Radiation Energy [Nuclear energy]
SHAREM...... Ship ASW [Antisubmarine Warfare] Readiness Effectiveness Measuring Program
SHARES...... Shared Acquisitions and Retention System
Shark Elec... Sharkey's Practice of Election Committees [2nd ed.] [1866] [A publication] (DLA)
SHARNB....... Sharnbrook [England]
SHARP........ School Health Additional Referral Program [Public Health Service]
SHARP........ Self-Healing Alternate Route Protection [Telecommunications] (ITD)
SHARP........ Senior High Assessment of Reading Performance [Educational test]

SHARP........ Ships Analysis and Retrieval Program [*Navy*]
SHARP........ Ships and Analysis and Retrieval Project (NITA)
SHARP........ Small Histidine-Alanine-Rich Protein (DB)
SHARP........ Society for the History of Authorship, Reading and Publishing (EA)
SHARP........ Sperry Heading and Attitude Reference Platform (SAA)
SHARP........ Stationary [*or Strategic*] High-Altitude Relay Platform [*Microwave airplane*] [*Canada*]
SHARP........ Strategic High Altitude Relay Platform [*Aviation*]
Sharp Cong Ct... Sharp on Congregational Courts [*A publication*] (DLA)
Sharpe........ Calendar of Coroners Rolls of the City of London [*A publication*] (DLA)
SHARPE........ Symbolic Hierarchical Automated Reliability and Performance Evaluator
Sharp Ins Dig... Sharpstein's Insurance Digest [*A publication*] (DLA)
SHARPS........ Ship/Helicopter Acoustic Range-Prediction System [*Navy*] (NVT)
SHARPS........ Sonic High-Accuracy Ranging and Positioning System
Shars & B Lead Cas Real Prop... Sharswood and Budd's Leading Cases on Real Property [*A publication*] (DLA)
Shars Black... Sharswood's Edition of Blackstone's Commentaries [*A publication*] (DLA)
Shars Bl Comm... Sharswood's Edition of Blackstone's Commentaries [*A publication*] (DLA)
Shars Comm L... Sharswood's Commercial Law [*A publication*] (DLA)
Shars Law Lec... Sharswood's Lectures on the Profession of the Law [*A publication*] (DLA)
Shars Leg Eth... Sharswood's Legal Ethics [*A publication*] (DLA)
Shars Tab Ca... Sharswood's Table of Cases, Connecticut [*A publication*] (DLA)
SHAS .... Self Help Association for Stammerers [*British*] (DI)
SHAS .... Shared Hospital Accounting System [*Computer science*]
SHaS .... Shishah Sedarim (BJA)
SHATA .... Saddle, Harness, and Allied Trade Association (NTPA)
SHATC .... SHAPE [*Supreme Headquarters Allied Powers Europe*] Technical Center [*Formerly, SADTC*] [*NATO*] (NATG)
SHATCPS..... St. Helena, Ascension, and Tristan da Cunha Philatelic Society (EA)
SHAU .... Subject Heading Authority Unit (NITA)
SHAV .... Superior Hemiazygos Vein (STED)
SHAVE........ Sugar Hotel Alpha Victor Echo [*Apollo 10 astronauts' code for shaving operation*]
SHAVIB....... Shaft Alignment and Vibration (DNAB)
SHAW .... Shaw Group [*NASDAQ symbol*] (NQ)
Shaw .... Shaw Industries, Inc. [*Associated Press*] (SAG)
Shaw .... Shaw's Scotch Appeal Cases [*A publication*] (DLA)
Shaw .... Shaw's Scotch Court of Session Cases, First Series [*A publication*] (DLA)
Shaw .... Shaw's Scotch Justiciary Cases [*A publication*] (DLA)
Shaw .... Shaw's Scotch Teind [*Tithe*] Court Reports [*A publication*] (DLA)
Shaw & D.... Shaw and Dunlop's Scotch Court of Session Reports, First Series [*A publication*] (DLA)
Shaw & Dunl... Shaw and Dunlop's Scotch Court of Session Reports, First Series [*A publication*] (DLA)
Shaw & M ... Shaw and Maclean's Scotch Appeal Cases [*A publication*] (DLA)
Shaw & Macl... Shaw and Maclean's Scotch Appeal Cases [*A publication*] (DLA)
Shaw & M Sc App Cas... Shaw and Maclean's Scotch Appeal Cases [*1835-38*] [*A publication*] (DLA)
Shaw App .... Shaw's Scotch Appeal Cases, English House of Lords [*A publication*] (DLA)
SHAWCO...... Students' Health and Welfare Centers Organization
Shaw Crim Cas... Shaw's Criminal Cases, Scotch Justiciary Court [*A publication*] (DLA)
Shaw D & B... Shaw, Dunlop, and Bell's Scotch Court of Session Reports, First Series [*A publication*] (DLA)
Shaw D & B Supp... Shaw, Dunlop, and Bell's Supplement, Containing House of Lords Decisions [*Scotland*] [*A publication*] (DLA)
Shaw Dec.... Shaw's Decisions in Scotch Court of Sessions, First Series [*A publication*] (DLA)
Shaw Dig..... Shaw's Digest of Decisions [*Scotland*] [*A publication*] (DLA)
Shaw Dunl & B... Shaw, Dunlop, and Bell's Scotch Court of Session Cases, First Series [*1821-38*] [*A publication*] (DLA)
ShawGp....... Shaw Group [*Associated Press*] (SAG)
Shaw HL...... Shaw's Scotch Appeal Cases, House of Lords [*1821-24*] [*A publication*] (DLA)
Shaw J .... John Shaw's Justiciary Cases [*1848-52*] [*Scotland*] [*A publication*] (DLA)
SHAWL........ Special Hard-Target Assault Weapon LAW (RDA)
ShawN........ Shawmut National Corp. [*Associated Press*] (SAG)
ShawNt....... Shawmut National Corp. [*Associated Press*] (SAG)
Shaw P........ Patrick Shaw's Justiciary Cases [*1819-31*] [*Scotland*] [*A publication*] (DLA)
Shaw PL...... Shaw's Parish Law [*A publication*] (DLA)
Shaw Sc App Cas... Shaw's Scotch Appeal Cases, House of Lords [*1821-24*] [*A publication*] (DLA)
Shaw TC..... Shaw's Scotch Teind [*Tithe*] Cases [*1821-31*] [*A publication*] (DLA)
Shaw T Cas... Shaw's Scotch Teind [*Tithe*] Court Reports [*A publication*] (DLA)
Shaw Teind... Shaw's Scotch Teind [*Tithe*] Court Decisions [*1821-31*] [*A publication*] (DLA)
Shaw W & C... Shaw, Wilson, and Courtenay's Scotch Appeals Reports, House of Lords [*A publication*] (DLA)
SHAZ .... Spirohydantoin Aziridine [*Biochemistry*]
SHB .... Nakashibetsu [*Japan*] [*Airport symbol*] (OAG)
SHB .... Second-Harmonic Band
SHB .... Sequential Hemibody [*Irradiation*] [*Medicine*] (DMAA)
SHB .... Shabair [*Zaire*] [*ICAO designator*] (FAAC)
SHB .... Shark Bay [*Western Australia*] [*Airport symbol*] (AD)
SHB .... Shelbyville, IN [*Location identifier FAA*] (FAAL)
SHb............ Sickle Hemoglobin [*Screen*] [*Hematology*] (DAVI)

SHB .... Silhouette Harness Board (MCD)
SHB .... Sodium Hydroxybutyrate [*Organic chemistry*]
SHB .... Subacute Hepatitis with Bridging [*Medicine*]
S Hb .... Sulfhemoglobin [*Medicine*] (MAE)
SHB .... Sulfhemoglobin (STED)
SHB .... Super Highband [*Radio frequency*] (NTCM)
SHBD .... Serum Hydroxybutyrate Dehydrogenase [*An enzyme*]
SHBD INT .... Shipboard Intelligence (DOMA)
SHBE .... Southern Hemisphere Balloon Experiment (SAA)
SHBG .... Sex-Hormone-Binding Globulin [*Endocrinology*]
SHBLDR...... Shipbuilder (MSA)
SHBTh .... Society of Health and Beauty Therapists [*British*] (DBA)
SHBZ .... ShowBiz Pizza Time [*NASDAQ symbol*] (TTSB)
SHBZ .... ShowBiz Pizza Time, Inc. [*NASDAQ symbol*] (CTT)
SHC .... Chief Ship's Serviceman [*Navy rating*]
SHC .... Mount St. Helena [*California*] [*Seismograph station code, US Geological Survey*] (SEIS)
SHC .... Sacred Heart College [*Cullman, AL*]
SHC .... Schult Homes Corp. [*AMEX symbol*] (SPSG)
SHC .... Self-Help Crafts [*An association*] (EA)
SHC .... Sensitized Human Cell (PDAA)
SHC .... SENTRY [*Survey Entry*] Hazard Control
SHC .... Seton Hill College [*Greensburg, PA*]
SHC .... Shape and Hamiltonian Consistent [*Physics*]
SHC .... Shell Canada'A'vtg [*TS Symbol*] (TTSB)
SHC .... Shell Canada Ltd. [*Toronto Stock Exchange symbol Vancouver Stock Exchange symbol*]
SHC .... Shipping Coordinating Committee [*Coast Guard*]
SHC .... Shire Indaselassie [*Ethiopia*] [*Airport symbol*] (OAG)
SHC .... Siena Heights College [*Adrian, MI*]
SHC .... Silicones Health Council (EA)
SHC .... Sky Harbor Air Service, Inc. [*ICAO designator*] (FAAC)
SHC .... Societe Heraldique du Canada [*Heraldry Society of Canada*] (EAIO)
SHC .... Societe Historique du Canada [*Canadian Historical Association - CHA*]
SHC .... Sodium Hypochlorite [*Inorganic chemistry*]
SHC .... Southern Hemisphere Cap [*on Triton*]
SHC .... Southern Humanities Conference (EA)
SHC .... Special Handling Code
SHC .... Spherical Harmonic Coefficient [*Geophysics*]
SHC .... Spontaneous Human Combustion
SHC .... Spring Hill College [*Mobile, AL*]
SHC .... Stanford Humanities Center [*Stanford University*] [*Research center*] (RCD)
SHC .... Superheat Control [*Boilers*]
SHC .... Superhybrid Composite [*Laminate*]
SHC .... Superior Heliocentric Conjunction
SHC .... Surveillance Helicopter Co. [*Army*] (AABC)
SHC .... Synthesized Hydrocarbon (PDAA)
SHC .... Synthetic Hydrocarbons [*Lubricants*]
SHCA .... Safety Helmet Council of America (EA)
SHCA .... Siberian Husky Club of America (EA)
SHCA .... Solid Homogeneous Critical Assembly [*Nuclear reactor*] [*Japan*]
Sh/Cat......... Sheaf Catalogue [*Library term*] (DGA)
SHC-BRC .... Small Homes Council-Building Research Council [*University of Illinois*] [*Research center*] (RCD)
SHCC .... Shriners Hospitals for Crippled Children (EA)
SHCC .... Statewide Health Coordinating Council
SHCC .... Susan Hayward Collectors Club (EA)
SHCG .... Social History Curators Group [*British*] (DBA)
SHCGSAS .... Shrimp Harvesters Coalition of the Gulf and South Atlantic States (EA)
SHCI .... Salick Health Care, Inc. [*Beverly Hills, CA*] [*NASDAQ symbol*] (NQ)
SHCID......... Salick Health Care(New) [*NASDAQ symbol*] (TTSB)
SHCJ.......... Society for the History of Czechoslovak Jews (EA)
SHCJ.......... Society of the Holy Child Jesus [*Roman Catholic women's religious order*]
SHCM .... Master Chief Ship's Serviceman [*Navy rating*]
SHCO .... Schult Homes Corp. (MHDW)
SHCO .... Sulfated Hydrogenated Castor Oil (MAE)
SHCON........ Shore Connection (IAA)
SHCOS........ Supreme Headquarters, Chief of Staff [*World War II*]
SHCPP........ Sanitation Handbook of Consumer Protection Programs
SHCR .... Sheridan Healthcare [*NASDAQ symbol*] (TTSB)
SHCR .... Sheridan Healthcare, Inc. [*NASDAQ symbol*] (SAG)
SHCR .... Sheridian Healtcare, Inc. [*NASDAQ symbol*] (SAG)
SHCR .... Shipping Container
SHCR .... Skyline Hikers of the Canadian Rockies (EA)
Sh Crim Cas... Shaw's Justiciary Court, Criminal Cases [*Scotland*] [*A publication*] (DLA)
SHCRT .... Short Circuit (AAG)
SHCS .... Senior Chief Ship's Serviceman [*Navy rating*]
SHCS USAF... School of Health Care Sciences, United States Air Force (AFM)
SHCT .... Sheriff Court [*Legal*] [*British*]
SHCT .... Studies in the History of Christian Thought [*A publication*] (BJA)
Sh Ct of Sess... Shaw's Scotch Court of Session Cases [*A publication*] (DLA)
Sh Ct Rep... Sheriff Court Reports [*Scotland*] [*A publication*] (DLA)
SHCW .... Scottish History from Contemporary Writers [*A publication*]
SHD .... Sandhill Decline [*Citrus blight*]
SHD .... Scottish Home Department (ILCA)
SHD .... Second Harmonic Distortion (IAA)
SHD .... Shade
SHD .... Shahrud [*Iran*] [*Seismograph station code, US Geological Survey*] (SEIS)
SHD .... Sherwood Group [*NYSE symbol*] (SAG)

SHD .... Shield Development [Vancouver Stock Exchange symbol]
SHD .... Ship's Diver [Navy British]
SHD .... Shode
SHD .... Should (ROG)
SHD .... Shroud (AAG)
SHD .... Silo Hardsite Defense
SHD .... Slant Hole Distance [Nuclear energy] (OA)
SHD .... Society for the History of Discoveries (EA)
SHD .... Special Handling Designator (MCD)
SHD .... State Highway Departments [A publication] (AAGC)
SHD .... Staunton [Virginia] [Airport symbol] (OAG)
SHD .... Staunton/Waynesboro/Harrisonburg, VA [Location identifier FAA] (FAAL)
SHD .... Sudden Heart Death [Medicine] (DMAA)
SHd .... Sulgi Hymn D (BJA)
SHDA .... Selenaheptadecanoic Acid [Organic chemistry]
SHDC .... Sacred Heart Dominican College [Texas]
SHDC .... Subject Headings Used in the Dictionary Catalog [Later, LCSH] [A publication]
SHDCD .... Shore Duty Commencemnt Date [Navy] (DNAB)
SHDI .... Supraoptic-Hypophyseal Diabetes Insipidus [Endocrinology]
Sh Dig .... Shaw's Digest of Decisions [Scotland] [A publication] (DLA)
SHDN .... Shutdown (NASA)
SHDP .... Supportive Housing Demonstration Program [Department of Housing and Urban Development] (GFGA)
SHDPS .... St. Helena and Dependencies Philatelic Society (EA)
SHDR .... Service and Hardware Difficulty Reports (MCD)
SHDS .... Safety and Health Data Sheet [Army]
SHDS .... Second-Harmonic Discrimination System (MCD)
ShdTech ...... Shared Technologies, Inc. [Associated Press] (SAG)
SHE .... Safety, Health and Environment (ACII)
SHE .... Scheffield Explorations [AMEX symbol] (SAG)
SHE .... Securities Hazards Expert [In film title]
SHE .... Self-Help Enterprises (EA)
SHE .... Semihomogeneous Experiment [Nuclear energy]
SHE .... Sheba Copper Mines [Vancouver Stock Exchange symbol]
SHE .... Shell Aircraft Ltd. [British ICAO designator] (FAAC)
SHE .... Shemkha [Former USSR Seismograph station code, US Geological Survey] (SEIS)
SHE .... Shenyang [China] [Airport symbol] (OAG)
SHE .... Siderphile Superheavy Element [Physics]
SHE .... Signal Handling Equipment (AAG)
SHE .... Society for History Education (EA)
SHE .... Society for Human Ecology (EA)
SHE .... Society for the Health Education [British]
SHE .... Sodium Heat Engine
SHE .... Spares Handling Expense
SHE .... Special Handling Equipment
SHE .... Standard Hydrogen Electrode [Electrochemistry]
SHE .... Subject Headings for Engineering [A publication]
SHE .... Substrate Hot Electron (IAA)
S/HE .... Sundays and Holidays Excepted
SHE .... Supercritical Helium (KSC)
SHE .... Superheavy Element [Nuclear physics]
SHE .... Support, Help, and Empowerment
SHE .... Syrian Hamster Embryonic [Cells]
SHEA .... Society for Healthcare Epidemiology of America (NTPA)
SHEA .... Society for Hospital Epidemiology of America
SHEA .... Society of Heathcare Executive Assistants (NTPA)
SHEAL .... Shuttle High-Energy Astrophysics Laboratory [NASA] (SSD)
SHEAR .... Society for Historians of the Early American Republic (EA)
Shear & R Neg... Shearman and Redfield on the Law of Negligence [A publication] (DLA)
Shear Bar Ex... Shearwood's Bar Examinations [A publication] (DLA)
Shear Cont... Shearwood on Contract [1897] [A publication] (DLA)
Shearm & Red Neg... Shearman and Redfield on the Law of Negligence [A publication] (DLA)
Shear Pers Pr... Shearwood on Personal Property [1882] [A publication] (DLA)
Shear R Pr... Shearwood on Real Property [3rd ed.] [1885] [A publication] (DLA)
SHEB .... Shebear [England]
Sheb .... Shebi'it (BJA)
SHEBA .... Surface Heat Budget of the Arctic [Marine science] (OSRA)
SHEBA .... Surface Heat Budget of the Arctic Ocean
Shebi .... Shebi'it (BJA)
Shebu .... Shebu'oth (BJA)
SHED .... Sealed Housing for Evaporative Determinations [EPA engine test]
SHED .... Settlement Houses Employment Development [Large group of settlement houses]
SHED .... SMT Health Services, Inc. [NASDAQ symbol] (SAG)
SHED .... SMT Health Svcs [NASDAQ symbol] (TTSB)
SHED .... Solar Heat Exchanger Drive (IAA)
SHEDA .... Storage and Handling Equipment Distributors Association [British] (DBA)
SHEDS .... Ship Helicopter Extended Delivery System [Navy] (NVT)
SHEDW .... SMT Health Svcs Wrrt [NASDAQ symbol] (TTSB)
SHEE .... Safe High-Energy Explosive
SHE EC .... Sheffield Exploration [ECM Symbol] (TTSB)
SHEENT .... Skin, Head, Eyes, Ears, Nose, and Throat [Medicine] (DMAA)
SHEEO .... State Higher Education Executive Officers Association (EA)
SHEF .... Sandwich Chef (EFIS)
Shef .... Sheffield [England] (BARN)
SHEF .... Sheffield, IL [Commercial waste site] (GAAI)
SHEFD .... Sheffield [England]
SHEFF .... Shefford [England]
ShefldMd ..... Sheffield Medical Technologies [Associated Press] (SAG)

SHEG .... Scottish Health Education Group (DI)
SHEG .... Superfluid-Helium Gyroscope
SHEIA .... Steric Hindrance Enzyme Immunoassay [Clinical chemistry]
Sheil Ir Bar... Sheil's Sketches of the Irish Bar [A publication] (DLA)
SHEK .... Schweizer Hilfswerk fuer Emigrationskinder (BJA)
Shek .... Shekalim (BJA)
SHEL .... Sheldahl, Inc. [NASDAQ symbol] (NQ)
SHEL .... Shore ELINT [Electromagnetic Intelligence] System [Navy] (NG)
Shel Bank ..... Shelford's Bankrupt and Insolvency Law [3rd ed.] [1862] [A publication] (DLA)
Shelby .... Shelby Williams Industries, Inc. [Associated Press] (SAG)
Shel Ca .... Shelley's Cases in Vol. 1 of Coke's Reports [A publication] (DLA)
Sheld .... Sheldon's Superior Court Reports [Buffalo, New York] [A publication] (DLA)
Sheldl .... Sheldahl Co. [Associated Press] (SAG)
Sheldon .... Sheldon's Superior Court Reports [Buffalo, New York] [A publication] (DLA)
Sheld Subr... Sheldon on Subrogation [A publication] (DLA)
SHELF .... Super-Hard Extremely-Low Frequency (MCD)
Shelf J St Cos... Shelford on Joint-Stock Companies [A publication] (DLA)
Shelf Lun ..... Shelford on Lunacy [A publication] (DLA)
Shelf Mar & Div... Shelford on Marriage and Divorce [A publication] (DLA)
Shel High .... Shelford on Highways [4th ed.] [1869] [A publication] (DLA)
Shel J St Com... Shelford on Joint Stock Companies [2nd ed.] [1870] [A publication] (DLA)
SHELLREP ... Shelling Report [Military] (NATG)
ShellTr .... Shell Transport & Trading Co. Ltd. [Associated Press] (SAG)
Shel Lun ..... Shelford on Lunacy [2nd ed.] [1847] [A publication] (DLA)
Shel M & D... Shelford on Marriage and Divorce [1841] [A publication] (DLA)
Shel Mort .... Shelford on Mortmain and Charitable Uses [1836] [A publication] (DLA)
Shel Prob .... Shelford on Probate, Legacy, Etc. [2nd ed.] [1861] [A publication] (DLA)
SHELREP ..... Shelling Report [Military]
SHELREPT ... Shelling Report [Military] (MUGU)
Shel R Pr St... Sheldon's Real Property Statutes [9th ed.] [1893] [A publication] (DLA)
Shel Ry .... Shelford on Railways [4th ed.] [1869] [A publication] (DLA)
SheltCm ...... Shelter Components Corp. [Associated Press] (SAG)
Shel Will .... Shelford on Wills [1838] [A publication] (DLA)
Shel Wills ... Shelford on Wills [A publication] (DLA)
SHEM .... Hemolyzed - Unable to Do Test [laboratory science] (DAVI)
SHEMA .... Steam Heating Equipment Manufacturers Association [Defunct] (EA)
S-HEMP .... System - Hydraulic, Electrical, Mechanical, Pneumatic
SHEN .... First Shenango Bancorp [NASDAQ symbol] (TTSB)
SHEN .... First Shenango Bancorp, Inc. [NASDAQ symbol] (SAG)
SHEN .... Shenandoah [A publication] (BRI)
SHEN .... Shenandoah National Park
Shep .... Select Cases [37-39 Alabama] [A publication] (DLA)
Shep .... Shepard's Citations [A publication] (AAGC)
Shep .... Shepherd's Alabama Reports [A publication] (DLA)
Shep .... Shepley's Reports [13-18, 21-30 Maine] [A publication] (DLA)
SHEP .... Shock Hydrodynamic Elastic Plastic (MCD)
SHEP .... Solar High-Energy Particles
SHEP .... Systolic Hypertension in the Elderly Program [Medicine]
Shep Abr .... Sheppard's Abridgment [A publication] (DLA)
Shep Act .... Sheppard's Action on the Case [A publication] (DLA)
Shep Cas .... Sheppard's Cases of Slander, Etc. [A publication] (DLA)
Shepherd..... Shepherd's Reports [19-21, 24-41, 60, 63, 64 Alabama] [A publication] (DLA)
Sheph Sel Cas... Shepherd's Select Cases [Alabama] [A publication] (DLA)
Shepley ...... Shepley's Reports [13-18, 21-30 Maine] [A publication] (DLA)
Shep Prec.... Sheppard's Precedent of Precedents [9th ed.] [1825] [A publication] (DLA)
Shep Sel Cas... Shepherd's Select Cases [Alabama] [A publication] (DLA)
SHER .... Sheriff
SHERB .... Sandia Human Error Rate Bank [NASA] (NASA)
SHERB .... Sherborne [Urban district in England]
SHERCI .... Safety, Health, and Environmental Resource Center International (EA)
Sher Ct Rep... Sheriff Court Reports [Scotland] [A publication] (DLA)
Sheridan ..... Sheridan Healthcare, Inc. [Associated Press] (SAG)
SHERK .... [The] New Schaff-Herzog Encyclopaedia of Religious Knowledge [A publication] (BJA)
SHERLOC..... Something to Help Everyone Reduce Load on Computers [Army]
Sher Mar Ins... Sherman's Marine Insurance [A publication] (DLA)
Sher Pr....... Sheridan's Practice, King's Bench [A publication] (DLA)
SHERVICK.... Sherman Tanks Converted into Tractors by Vickers Armstrong
Sherwin....... Sherwin-Williams Co. [Associated Press] (SAG)
Shet .... Shetland (WGA)
Shev .... Shevi'it (BJA)
SHEVE .... Southern Hemisphere VLBI [Very-Long-Baseline Interferometry] Experiment [For observing intergalactic radio components]
Shevu .... Shevu'ot (BJA)
SHEX .... Sundays and Holidays Excepted [Business term]
SHF .... Schiffner Oilfield & Technology Corp. [Vancouver Stock Exchange symbol]
SHF .... Schroder Asian Growth [NYSE symbol] (SAG)
SHF .... Schroder Asian Growth Fd [NYSE symbol] (TTSB)
SHF .... Sea Heritage Foundation (EA)
SHF .... Self Help Foundation (EA)
SHF .... Sensible Heat Factor (IAA)
SHF .... Shawinigan Falls [Quebec] [Seismograph station code, US Geological Survey Closed] (SEIS)
SHF .... Shift (MSA)

SHF	Simian Hemorrhagic Fever [*Medicine*] (DMAA)
SHF	Sisters of the Holy Faith [*Roman Catholic religious order*]
SHF	Sisters of the Holy Family [*Roman Catholic religious order*]
SHF	Soil and Health Foundation [*Later, RI*] (EA)
SHF	Storage-Handling Facility [*Nuclear energy*] (NRCH)
SHF	Structures Heating Facility
SHF	Super High Frequency [*Radio wave*]
shf	Superhigh Frequency (WDMC)
SHF	Support Helicopter Flight NI [*British ICAO designator*] (FAAC)
SHF	Supra-High Frequency [*Radio wavelength*] (IAA)
SHF	Synthesized Hydrocarbon Fluid [*Petroleum engineering*]
SHF	Syper HyperFine [*Interaction*] (AAEL)
SHF	University of Sheffield, Postgraduate School of Librarianship, Sheffield, England [*OCLC symbol*] (OCLC)
SHFA	Single Conductor, Heat and Flame Resistant, Armor [*Cable*]
SHFA	Societe Historique Franco-Americaine [*French*]
SHFC	Seven Hills Financial Corp. [*NASDAQ symbol*] (SAG)
SHFC	Seven Hills Finl [*NASDAQ symbol*] (TTSB)
SHFCC	Shriners Hospitals for Crippled Children (EA)
SHFD	Split Hand/Foot Deformity [*Medicine*] (DMAA)
SHF/EHF	Super-High Frequency/Extremely-High Frequency (MCD)
SHFF	Societe Historique et Folklorique Francaise [*Defunct*] (EA)
SHFG	Society for History in the Federal Government (EA)
SHF-GMFSC	Super-High-Frequency - Ground Mobile Forces Satellite Communications (MCD)
SHFL	Shoulder Horizontal Flexion [*Sports medicine*]
SHFL	Shuffle Master [*NASDAQ symbol*] (TTSB)
SHFL	Shuffle Master, Inc. [*NASDAQ symbol*] (SAG)
SHFS	Superhyperfine Structure
SHFT	Shift
SHF-TDMA-MODEM	Super-High-Frequency - Time Division Multiple Access - MODEM (MCD)
SHFTG	Shafting [*Freight*]
SHFTGR	Shaft Gear
SHFTR	Shift Register (NITA)
SHFV	Simian Haemorrhagic Fever Virus
SHG	Sauerbruch, Herrmannsdorfer, Gerson Diet [*For tuberculosis*] (DAVI)
SHG	Second-Harmonic Generation [*LASER*]
SHG	Selected Honor Guards (MCD)
SHG	Sexual Harassment Guidelines
SHG	Sharpe Energy and Resources Ltd. [*Vancouver Stock Exchange symbol*]
SHG	Shipping (WGA)
SHG	Shirttail Gulch [*California*] [*Seismograph station code, US Geological Survey*] (SEIS)
SHG	Shoprite Group Ltd. [*British ICAO designator*] (FAAC)
SHG	Short-Handed Goal [*Hockey*]
SHG	Shorthand Typist (Higher Grade) [*British military*] (DMA)
SHG	Shungnak [*Alaska*] [*Airport symbol*] (OAG)
SHG	Shungnak, AK [*Location identifier FAA*] (FAAL)
SHG	Sister Servants of the Holy Ghost and Mary Immaculate [*Roman Catholic religious order*]
SHG	Special High Grade [*Zinc metal*]
SHG	Sun Healthcare Group [*NYSE symbol*] (SPSG)
SHG	Synthetic Human Gastrin [*Medicine*] (MAE)
SHGAPE	Society for Historians of the Gilded Age and Progressive Era (NTPA)
SHGF	Scottish Hang Gliding Federation (DBA)
SHGM	Society for the History of the Germans in Maryland (EA)
SHGR	Self-Heating Group Ration [*Military*] (INF)
SHH	Shenandoah Resources Ltd. [*Vancouver Stock Exchange symbol*]
SHH	Shishmaref [*Alaska*] [*Airport symbol*] (OAG)
SHH	Shishmaref, AK [*Location identifier FAA*] (FAAL)
SHH	Sociedad Honoraria Hispanica (EA)
SHHD	Scottish Home and Health Department (ILCA)
SHHH	Self-Help for Hard of Hearing People (EA)
SHHP	Semihorizontal Heart Position (MAE)
SHHV	Society for Health and Human Values (EA)
SHI	Scenic Hudson (EA)
SHI	Shanghai Petrochemical [*NYSE symbol*] (SPSG)
SHI	Shanghai Petrochemical ADS [*NYSE symbol*] (TTSB)
SHI	Sheet Iron
SHI	Shimojishima [*Japan*] [*Airport symbol*] (OAG)
SHI	Shiraz [*Iran*] [*Seismograph station code, US Geological Survey*] (SEIS)
SHI	Substance Hazard Index [*Environmental science*]
S-HI	System-Human Interaction
SHID	Spartan Hardware Inspection Discrepancy [*Missiles*] (MCD)
SHIEF	Shared Information Elicitation Facility [*Computer science*]
Shiel	Cape Times Law Reports, Edited by Shiel [*A publication*] (DLA)
Shiel	Shiel's Cape Colony Reports [*A publication*] (DLA)
SHIELD	Supreme Headquarters, International Espionage Law-Enforcement Division [*Organization in comic book "Nick Fury, Agent of SHIELD"*]
SHIELD	Sylvania High-Intelligence Electronic Defense (MCD)
Shig	Shigella [*Bacteriology*]
SHIIP	Senior Health Insurance Information Program
SHIL	Shillelagh [*Army surface-to-surface missile*] (AABC)
SHIL	Shiloh National Military Park
Shill WC	Shillman's Workmen's Compensation Cases [*Ireland*] [*A publication*] (DLA)
Shiloh	Shiloh Industries, Inc. [*Associated Press*] (SAG)
SHIM	Self-Heating Individual Meal [*Military*] (INF)
SHIMM	Self-Heating Individual Meal Module [*Army*] (RDA)
SHIMMS	Shipboard Integrated Man-Machine System (SAA)
SHIN BET	Israel General Security Service [*Acronym represents Hebrew phrase*]
SHINC	Sundays and Holidays Included [*Business term*]
SHINCOM	Ship Integrated Communications System [*Canadian Navy*]
SHINE	Self-Help is Necessary Everywhere [*Navy*] (DNAB)
Shingle	[*The*] Shingle. Philadelphia Bar Association [*A publication*] (DLA)
SHINMACS	Shipborne Integrated Machinery Control System [*Canadian Navy*]
Shinn Repl	Shinn's Treatise on American Law of Replevin [*A publication*] (DLA)
SHIN PADS	Shipboard Integrated Processing Display System [*Military*]
SHIOER	Statistical Historical Input/Output Error Rate Utility [*Sperry UNIVAC*]
SHIP	Search-Height Integration Program (SAA)
SHIP	Self-Help Improvement Program
SHIP	Self-Help Issue Point [*Army*]
SHIP	Separator for Heavy Ion Reaction Products
SHIP	Shipment
SHIP	Slater Hall Information Products [*Database producer*] (IID)
SHIP	Special Handling Inventory Procedure (MCD)
SHIP	Standard Hardware Interface Program
SHIPACS	Ship Acquisition Study [*Navy*]
SHIPALT	Ship Alteration [*Navy*]
SHIPBLDG	Shipbuilding
SHIPCON	Shipping Control [*NATO*] (NATG)
SHIPDA	Shipping Data [*Military*]
SHIPDAFOL	Shipping Data Follows
SHIPDAT	Shipping Date
SHIPDES	Ship Descriptions (NITA)
SHIPDTO	Ship on Depot Transfer Order [*Military*]
SHIPG	Shipping
Ship Gaz	Shipping Gazette [*London*] [*A publication*] (DLA)
SHIPGO	Shipping Order [*Military*]
SHIPIM	Ship Immediately [*Military*]
SHIPMT	Shipment (DNAB)
SHIPOPS	Ship(board) Operations [*Navy*] (DNAB)
SHIPOSI	Ship Operational Support Inventory [*Navy*] (DNAB)
Shipp	Shipp's Reports [*66-67 North Carolina*] [*A publication*] (DLA)
Shippensburg U	Shippensburg University of Pennsylvania (GAGS)
SHIPREPTECH	Ship Repair Technician [*Navy*] (DNAB)
SHIPREQ	Ship to Apply on Requisition [*Military*]
SHIPS	Shipment Planning System [*Military*]
SHIPS	Statistical Hurricane Intensity Prediction Scheme [*Marine science*] (OSRA)
SHIPS	Super-High Impact Polystyrene (EDCT)
SHIPSTO	Ship Store Office [*Navy*] (DNAB)
SHIPSUM	Shipping Summary
SHIPSYSCOM	Ship Systems Command [*Navy*]
SHIPT	Shipment
Shipt	Shipment (EBF)
SHIR	Self-Heating Individual Ration [*Army*] (RDA)
SHIR	Ship History and Inventory Record [*Navy*] (NG)
SHIRAN	S-Band High-Accuracy Ranging and Navigation
SHIRAN	S-Band High Presicion Short Range Navigation (IAA)
Shir Cr L	Shirley's Sketch of the Criminal Law [*2nd ed.*] [*1889*] [*A publication*] (DLA)
Shir DC Ca	Shirley's Dartmouth College Case [*A publication*] (DLA)
SHIRL	Serial Holdings in Irish Libraries [*Library science*] (TELE)
Shirl	Shirley's Reports [*49-55 New Hampshire*] [*A publication*] (DLA)
Shirley	Shirley's Reports [*49-55 New Hampshire*] [*A publication*] (DLA)
Shirl LC	Shirley's Leading Crown Cases [*England*] [*A publication*] (DLA)
Shir Mag L	Shirley on Magisterial Law [*2nd ed.*] [*1896*] [*A publication*] (DLA)
SHIRTDIF	Storage, Handling, and Retrieval of Technical Data in Image Formation [*Computer science*] (IEEE)
SHIRTS	Smith-Houghton Infrared Temperature Sounder (NOAA)
SHIRW	Shirwell [*England*]
SHIU	Steering Hover Indicator Unit (MCD)
Shiva	Shiva Corp. [*Associated Press*] (SAG)
SHIVA	Super-High-Intensity Vulnerability Assessor
SHJ	Shamrock Resources, Inc. [*Vancouver Stock Exchange symbol*]
SHJ	Sharjah [*United Arab Emirates*] [*Airport symbol*] (OAG)
SHJ	Sharjah Ruler's Flight [*United Arab Emirates*] [*ICAO designator*] (FAAC)
SHJ	Shionomisaki [*Japan*] [*Seismograph station code, US Geological Survey*] (SEIS)
SHJ	Society for Humanistic Judaism (EA)
SHJC	Sacred Heart Junior College [*North Carolina; Pennsylvania*]
SHJM	Sisters of the Sacred Hearts of Jesus and Mary [*Roman Catholic religious order*]
SHJP	[*A*] History of the Jewish People in the Time of Jesus Christ [*Emil Schurer*] [*A publication*] (BJA)
SHJR	Senate-House Joint Reports [*A publication*] (DLA)
Sh Jus	Shaw's Scotch Justiciary Cases [*A publication*] (DLA)
SHK	Sehonghong [*Lesotho*] [*Airport symbol*] (OAG)
SHK	Shank (AAG)
Shk	Shikimic Acid [*Biochemistry*]
SHK	Shiraki [*Japan*] [*Seismograph station code, US Geological Survey*] (SEIS)
SHK	SHL Systemhouse, Inc. [*Toronto Stock Exchange symbol*]
SHK	Shock (MSA)
SHK	Shorouk Air [*Egypt*] [*ICAO designator*] (FAAC)
SHK	Speaker of the House of Keys [*British*] (ROG)
SHK	Systems Housekeeping
SHKDN	Shakedown (AABC)
SHKDNCRU	Shakedown Cruise [*Navy*] (ANA)
SHL	Sacred Heart League (EA)
SHL	Samson Aviation Services [*British ICAO designator*] (FAAC)
SHL	Sensorineural Hearing Loss [*Medicine*]
SHL	Shaw Industries Ltd. [*Toronto Stock Exchange symbol*]
SHL	Sheldon, IA [*Location identifier FAA*] (FAAL)

SHL.............	Shell (AAG)
shl	Shell (VRA)
SHL.............	Shellac (MSA)
SHL.............	Shell Canada Ltd. [*UTLAS symbol*]
SHL.............	Shillong [*India*] [*Seismograph station code, US Geological Survey*] (SEIS)
Sh L	Shipwright Lieutenant [*British military*] (DMA)
SHL.............	Shoal
SHL.............	Southall [*British depot code*]
SHL.............	Southern Hockey League
SHL.............	Student Homophile League [*Superseded by Gay People at Columbia*] (EA)
SHL.............	Studio-to-Headend Link [*Transmitter site relay*] (NTCM)
SHL.............	Subject Heading Language [*Classification and indexing*] [*Association for Library Collections and Technical Services*]
SHLB	Simulation Hardware Load Boxes (NASA)
SHLD	Sheild
SHLD	Shield (AAG)
SHLD	Shift Left Double [*Computer science*] (PCM)
SHLD	Shoulder (AAG)
SHLDR.........	Shoulder (MSA)
ShLH	Shne Luhot Ha-Berit (BJA)
Sh Lit..........	Shortt on Works of Literature [*2nd ed.*] [*1884*] [*A publication*] (DLA)
Sh Litt	Shortt on Works of Literature [*2nd ed.*] [*1884*] [*A publication*] (DLA)
SHLL...........	Shells Seafood Restaurants [*NASDAQ symbol*] (TTSB)
SHLL...........	Shells Seafood Restaurants, Inc. [*NASDAQ symbol*] (SAG)
ShllsS.........	Shells Seafood Restaurants, Inc. [*Associated Press*] (SAG)
ShllsSea	Shells Seafood Restaurants, Inc. [*Associated Press*] (SAG)
SHLLW	Shells Seafood Rest Wrrt [*NASDAQ symbol*] (TTSB)
SHLM...........	Schulman (A.) [*NASDAQ symbol*] (TTSB)
SHLM...........	Schulman [*A.*], Inc. [*NASDAQ symbol*] (NQ)
SHLM...........	Society of Hospital Laundry Managers [*British*] (BI)
SHLMA	Southern Hardwood Lumber Manufacturers Association [*Later, HMA*] (EA)
SHLN	Shoreline (MSA)
SHLO	Shiloh Industries [*NASDAQ symbol*] (TTSB)
SHLO	Shiloh Industries, Inc. [*NASDAQ symbol*] (SAG)
SHLP	Shiplap (WGA)
SHLR	Schuler Homes [*NASDAQ symbol*] (TTSB)
SHLR	Schuler Homes, Inc. [*NASDAQ symbol*] (SAG)
SHLRC.........	Speech and Hearing Language Research Centre [*Macquarie University, Australia*]
SHLS	Shawnee Library System [*Library network*]
SHLS	Shoals (MCD)
SHLTA	Skin, Hide, and Leather Traders Association [*British*] (EAIO)
SHLTR	Shelter (WGA)
SHLW	Simulated High-Level Waste [*Nuclear engineering*]
SHM...........	Nanki Shirahama [*Japan*] [*Airport symbol*] (OAG)
SHM...........	Security Home Mortgage Investment Corp [*Toronto Stock Exchange symbol*]
SHM...........	Sheffield Medical Technologies, Inc. [*AMEX symbol*] (SPSG)
SHM...........	Sheffield Medl Tech [*AMEX symbol*] (TTSB)
SHM...........	Sheffield Pharmaceuticals [*AMEX symbol*] [*Formerly, Sheffield Medical Tech*] (SG)
SHM...........	Shimizu [*Japan*] [*Seismograph station code, US Geological Survey*] (SEIS)
SHM...........	Ship Heading Marker [*Navigation*]
SHM...........	Simple Harmonic Motion
SHM...........	Sinusoidal Hydrodynamic Modulation [*Electrochemistry*]
SHM...........	Society for Hybrid Microelectronics (IAA)
SHM...........	Stage Handling Manual [*NASA*] (KSC)
SHMD	Safety and Health Management Division [*Department of Agriculture*] (GFGA)
SHMD	Shore Manning Document [*Navy*] (NVT)
SHMED	State Hazardous Materials Enforcement Development [*Nuclear energy*] (NRCH)
SHMGX.........	SMBS Managed Govt. Cl.A [*Mutual fund ticker symbol*] (SG)
SHMI	Saddlery Hardware Manufacturers Institute [*Defunct*] (EA)
SHMIS	Society of Headmasters of Independent Schools [*British*]
SHMKR.........	Shoemaker (MSA)
SHMMX	SMBS Managed Municipals Cl.A [*Mutual fund ticker symbol*] (SG)
SHMN	Shaman Pharmaceuticals [*NASDAQ symbol*] (TTSB)
SHMN	Shaman Pharmaceuticals, Inc. [*NASDAQ symbol*] (SAG)
SHMN	Subacute Hepatitis with Multilobular Necrosis [*Medicine*]
SHMO	Senior Hospital Medical Officer [*British*]
SHMO	Shadow Mountain National Recreation Area
SHMO	Social/Health Maintenance Organization [*Department of Health and Human Services*]
SHMP	Sodium Hexametaphosphate [*Inorganic chemistry*]
SHMT	Serine Hydroxymethyltransferase (DB)
SHMV	Sunn-Hemp Mosaic Virus [*Plant pathology*]
SHN	Sclerosing Hyaline Necrosis [*Medicine*]
SHN	Scripps-Howard News Service [*Washington, DC*] (WDMC)
SHN	Shaheen Airport Services [*Pakistan*] [*ICAO designator*] (FAAC)
shn.............	Shan [*MARC language code Library of Congress*] (LCCP)
SHN	Shandon Resources, Inc. [*Vancouver Stock Exchange symbol*]
SHN	Shelton, WA [*Location identifier FAA*] (FAAL)
SHN	Shimonoseki [*Japan*] [*Seismograph station code, US Geological Survey*] (SEIS)
SHN	Shoney's, Inc. [*NYSE symbol*] (SPSG)
SHN	Shorthand Note
SHN	Shown (AAG)
SHN	Sisterhood of the Holy Nativity [*Episcopalian religious order*]
SHN	Spontaneous Hemorrhagic Necrosis [*Medicine*]
SHN	St. Helena [*ANSI three-letter standard code*] (CNC)

SHN	Subacute Hepatic Necrosis [*Medicine*] (DMAA)
SHNA.........	SHARAF Name Authority [*UTLAS symbol*]
SHNC.........	Scottish Higher National Certificate
SHND.........	Scottish Higher National Diploma
SHNFZ	Southern Hemisphere Nuclear Free Zone [*Australia*]
SHNG.........	Shingle
SHNH.........	Society for the History of Natural History [*British*] (EAIO)
S/HNP.........	Skagit/Hanford Nuclear Project (NRCH)
SHNP.........	Sydney Harbour National Park [*Australia*]
SHNPP.........	Shearon Harris Nuclear Power Plant (GFGA)
SHNS.........	Society of Head and Neck Surgeons (EA)
SHO	North Shore Aero Club, Inc. [*New Zealand*] [*ICAO designator*] (FAAC)
SHO	Schedule Order (MCD)
SHO	Secondary Hypertrophic Osteoarthropathy [*Medicine*]
SHO	Senate Historical Office
SHO	Senior House Officer [*British*]
SHO	Serious Habitual Offender [*Criminology*]
SHO	Shikotan [*Former USSR Seismograph station code, US Geological Survey*] (SEIS)
sho.............	Shona [*MARC language code Library of Congress*] (LCCP)
SHO	Shore
SHO	Show [*Automotive advertising*]
SHO	Showing [*Technical drawings*]
SHO	Shutout [*Sports*]
SHO	Starrett Corp. [*AMEX symbol*] (TTSB)
SHO	Starrett Housing Corp. [*AMEX symbol*] (SPSG)
SHO	Student Health Organizations [*Defunct*]
SHO	Super High Output [*Model of Ford automobile*]
SHOA.........	Superannuation, Home, and Overseas Allowances [*Civil Service*] [*British*]
SHOAL.........	Shoal [*Commonly used*] (OPSA)
SHOALS......	Scanning Hydrographic Operational Airborne Lidar Survey [*Army*]
SHOALS......	Shoals [*Commonly used*] (OPSA)
SHOAP.........	Symbolic Horribly Optimizing Assembly Program (IAA)
SHOAR.........	Shore [*Commonly used*] (OPSA)
SHOARS......	Shores [*Commonly used*] (OPSA)
SHOB.........	Shore-Based (CINC)
SHOBOM......	Shore Bombardment [*Navy*] (NVT)
SHOBOMTNG...	Shore Bombardment Training [*Navy*] (NVT)
SHOC............	Self-Help Opportunity Center [*Department of Labor*] [*Washington, DC*] (AEBS)
SHOC............	SHAPE [*Supreme Headquarters Allied Powers Europe*] Operations Center [*NATO*] (NATG)
SHOC............	Software/Hardware Operational Control
SHOCK.........	Students Hot on Conserving Kilowatts [*Student legal action organization*]
SHODOP	Short-Range Doppler
ShoeCarn.....	Shoe Carnival, Inc. [*Associated Press*] (SAG)
SHOF.........	Shipboard Cable, Heat and Oil Resistant, Flexible (IAA)
SholodgE	Sholodge, Inc. [*Associated Press*] (SAG)
SHOLS.........	Single-Hoist Ordnance Loading System [*Navy*] (DNAB)
SHOM.........	Sequencing by Hybridization on Matrices (HGEN)
SHOMADS ...	Short-to-Medium-Range Air Defense System [*Army*] (RDA)
Sho-Me......	Sho-Me Financial Corp. [*Associated Press*] (SAG)
Shome LR ...	Shome's Law Reporter [*India*] [*A publication*] (DLA)
Shoney......	Shoney's, Inc. [*Associated Press*] (SAG)
S'HONG......	Souchong [*Tea trade*] (ROG)
SHOO.........	Madden Steven Ltd. [*NASDAQ symbol*] (SAG)
SHOO.........	Stephen Madden Ltd. [*NASDAQ symbol*] (SAG)
SHOOZ.........	Madden (Steven) Wrrt'B' [*NASDAQ symbol*] (TTSB)
SHOP.........	Sequential Heuristic Optimization Programming [*Computer science*] (CIST)
SHOP.........	Shell Higher Olefin Process [*Petrochemistry*]
SHOPA.........	School and Home Office Products Association (EA)
SHOPAIR	Short Path Infrared (MCD)
SHOPAT.......	Shore Patrol [*Navy*] (NVT)
Shopco.........	Shopco Laurel Centre Ltd. [*Associated Press*] (SAG)
ShopHm......	Shop at Home, Inc. [*Associated Press*] (SAG)
Shopko......	Shopko Stores [*Associated Press*] (SAG)
ShopTV	Shopping by Television [*British Telecom*]
SHOR.........	Shore
SHOR.........	Shorewood Packaging [*NASDAQ symbol*] (TTSB)
SHOR............	Shorewood Packaging Corp. [*NASDAQ symbol*] (NQ)
SHORAD......	Short-Range Air Defense [*Army*] (NATG)
SHORAD C²...	Short-Range Air Defense Command and Control
SHORADS......	Short-Range Air Defense System [*Army*] (RDA)
SHORAN	Short-Range Aid to Navigation (IAA)
SHORAN	Short-Range Navigation
SHORD.........	Short-Range Air Defense
SHORDU......	Shore Duty [*Navy*]
SHORE.........	Shore [*Commonly used*] (OPSA)
SHOREALT...	Shore Alteration
SHORES.......	Shores [*Commonly used*] (OPSA)
ShorInFn......	Shoreline Financial [*Associated Press*] (SAG)
SHORN.........	Short-Range Navigation System (FAAC)
SHOROC......	Shore-Required Operational Capability [*Navy*]
SHOROUTPUBINST...	Shore Duty Beyond the Seas Is Required by the Public Interest [*Navy*]
SHORPUBINT...	Shore Duty Is Required by the Public Interest [*Navy*]
SHORSTAMPS...	Shore Requirements, Standards, and Manpower Planning System [*Navy*]
SHORSTAS...	Short-Range Surveillance and Target Acquisition System (PDAA)
SHORSTRAMPS...	Shore Requirements Strength and Manpower Planning System [*Navy*] (ANA)

SHORT.........	Shard Hospital Online Real-Time Time-Sharing (PDAA)
SHORT.........	Short Stature, Hyperextensibility of Joints or Hernia or Both, Ocular Depression, Rieger Anomaly, Teething Delayed [Medicine] (DMAA)
SHORTD......	Shortened (ROG)
SHORTIE......	Short Range Thermal Imaging Equipment (PDAA)
Shortt Inf	Shortt on Informations, Criminal, Quo Warranto, Mandamus, and Prohibition [1887] [A publication] (DLA)
Shortt Inform...	Shortt on Informations, Criminal, Quo Warranto, Mandamus, and Prohibition [A publication] (DLA)
Shortt Lit	Shortt on Literature and Art [2nd ed.] [1884] [A publication] (DLA)
SHORTZ......	Short-Term Terrain Model (COE)
SHORVEY	Shore Duty Survey
Shorwd........	Shorewood Packaging Corp. [Associated Press] (SAG)
SHOSJ........	Sovereign Hospitaller Order of St. John (EA)
SHOT........	Shooting, Hunting, Outdoor Trade Show
SHOT........	Society for the History of Technology (EA)
Show	Shower's English King's Bench Reports [A publication] (DLA)
Show	Shower's English Parliamentary Cases [A publication] (DLA)
SHOW........	Showscan Entertainment [NASDAQ symbol] (TTSB)
SHOW........	Showscan Entertainment, Inc. [NASDAQ symbol] (SAG)
SHOW.........	Showtime [Cable television channel]
Showbiz......	ShowBiz Pizza Time, Inc. [Associated Press] (SAG)
Showbt........	Showboat, Inc. [Associated Press] (SAG)
Shower KB...	Shower's English King's Bench Reports [89 English Reprint] [1678-95] [A publication] (DLA)
Shower KB (Eng)...	Shower's English King's Bench Reports [89 English Reprint] [A publication] (DLA)
Shower PC (Eng)...	Shower's English Parliamentary Cases [1 English Reprint] [A publication] (DLA)
Show KB	Shower's English King's Bench Reports [A publication] (DLA)
Show Parl Cas...	Shower's English Parliamentary Cases [1 English Reprint] [A publication] (DLA)
Show PC......	Shower's English Parliamentary Cases [1 English Reprint] [A publication] (DLA)
SHP	Santa Helena [Peru] [Seismograph station code, US Geological Survey Closed] (SEIS)
SHP	Schonlein-Henoch Purpura [Medicine] (MEDA)
SHP	Schools History Project (AIE)
SHP	Secondary Hyperparathyroidism [Medicine] (DB)
SHP	Securities Shipped as Instructed
SHP	Seeker Head Position
SHP	Service Aerien Francais [France ICAO designator] (FAAC)
SHP	Shaft Horsepower
SHP	Shaker Heights Public Library, Shaker Heights, OH [OCLC symbol] (OCLC)
SHP	Shape (MSA)
SHP	Shearon Harris Plant [Nuclear energy] (NRCH)
SHP	Shoal Petroleum [Vancouver Stock Exchange symbol]
SHP	Shoppe
SHP	Shreveport [Diocesan abbreviation] [Louisiana] (TOCD)
SHP	Single Highest Peak [Aerospace]
SHP	Society for Hospital Planning of the American Hospital Association [Later, SHPM] (EA)
SHP	Society for Hungarian Philately (EA)
SHP	Sosyal Demokrasi Halkci Partisi [Social Democratic Populist Party] [Turkey Political party] (EAIO)
SHP	Southern Hardwood Producers [Later, HMA]
ShP............	Southern Historical Press, Easley, SC [Library symbol Library of Congress] (LCLS)
SHP	Standard Hardware Program [Military]
SHP	Standard Holding Pattern [Aviation]
SHP	Standard Holding Procedure [Aviation]
SHP	State Health Plan [Generic term] (DHSM)
SHP	[The] Stop & Shop Companies, Inc. [NYSE symbol] (SPSG)
SHP	Stop & Shop Cos. [NYSE symbol] (TTSB)
SHP	Surgical Hypoparathyroidism [Medicine] (MAE)
SHP	Wichita Falls, TX [Location identifier FAA] (FAAL)
SHPA	Prairie Agricultural Machinery Institute, Humboldt, Saskatchewan [Library symbol National Library of Canada] (NLC)
SHPBD........	Shipboard (MSA)
SHPC..........	Scenic Hudson Preservation Conference [Later, SHI] (EA)
SHPCL.........	Ship Class
SHPD..........	Seeker Head Position Display [Military] (CAAL)
SHPD..........	Super High-Performance Diesel [Fuel]
SHPDA........	State Health Planning and Development Agency
SHPE	Society of Hispanic Professional Engineers (EA)
SHPG	Shipping
shpg..........	Shipping (ODBW)
SHPHG........	Shipment of Household Goods (NOAA)
SHPI	Specialized Health Prods Intl [NASDAQ symbol] (TTSB)
SHPI	Specialized Health Products International, Inc. [NASDAQ symbol] (SAG)
SHPM	Society for Hospital Planning and Marketing of the American Hospital Association (EA)
SHPMT	Shipment (AABC)
SHPMX.......	World Funds: Sand Hill Manager [Mutual fund ticker symbol] (SG)
SHPNG........	Shipping
Shpng.........	Shopping (TBD)
SHPO.........	State Historic Preservation Office
SHPO	State Historic Preservation Officer
SHPO	Subharmonic Parametric Oscillator (IAA)
SHPOL........	Supplemental Health Manpower Shortage Area Placement Opportunity List [Department of Health and Human Services] (GFGA)

SHPR	Shipper
SHPRB.........	State Historic Preservation Review Board (COE)
SHPRF	Shakeproof (MSA)
SHPS	Seahead Pressure Simulator
SHPS	Sodium Hydroxide Purge System (IEEE)
SHPSD.........	Shipside (AABC)
SHPT	Shipment (AAG)
shpt	Shipment (ODBW)
SHPTARBY..	Ship to Arrive By _____ [Military]
SHQ	Shasper Industries Ltd. [Toronto Stock Exchange symbol]
SHQ	Squadron Headquarters [British military] (DMA)
SHQ	Station Headquarters
SHQ	Supreme Headquarters
SHR	Scherer [R.P.] Corp. [NYSE symbol] (SPSG)
SHR	Scherer (R.P.) [NYSE symbol] (TTSB)
SHR	Semi-Homogeneous Fuel Reactor (IAA)
SHR	Share [Stock exchange term]
shr	Share (WDAA)
SHR	Shear
SHR	Shepard Insurance Group [Vancouver Stock Exchange symbol]
SHR	Sheridan [Wyoming] [Airport symbol] (OAG)
SHR	Sheridan, WY [Location identifier FAA] (FAAL)
SHR	Shift Register [Computer science] (IAA)
SHR	Shirakawa [Japan] [Seismograph station code, US Geological Survey] (SEIS)
SHR	Shooter Air Courier Corp. [Canada ICAO designator] (FAAC)
SHR	Shore (MCD)
SHR	Shower
SHR	Single High-Resolution File [Computer science]
SHR	Sisters of the Holy Redeemer [Roman Catholic religious order]
SHR	Society for Historical Research (EA)
SHR	Solar Heat Reflecting (KSC)
SHR	Spontaneously Hypertensive Rats
SHR	Standard Hourly Rate
SHR	Step-Height Ratio [Crystallography]
SHR	Student Homelessness Rate [Australia]
SHR	Supervisory Human Relations Test
SHR	Synchronous Hubbing Regeneration (MHDI)
Shr	[The] Taming of the Shrew [Shakespearean work]
SHRA	Rain Showers [ICAO] (FAAC)
SHRAM	Short-Range Air-to-Surface Missile
SHRAP	Shrapnel
SHRC	Safety and Health Regulations for Construction [Bureau of Reclamation]
SHRC	Shared Housing Resource Center [Later, NSHRC] (EA)
SHRC	Shopping Hours Reform Council [British] (DBA)
SHRCX........	SMBS Calif. Munic. Cl.A [Mutual fund ticker symbol] (SG)
SHRD	Shift Right Double [Computer science] (PCM)
SHRD	Shredded [Freight]
SHRD	Shroud [Engineering]
SHRD	Supplemental Heat Rejection Devices (NASA)
SHRDF	Shroud Fin [Engineering]
SHRDR	Shredder (MSA)
ShrdTch	Shared Technologies Cellular, Inc. [Associated Press] (SAG)
SHREAD......	Share Registration and Dividend Warrants (MHDB)
SHREWD......	System for Holding and Retrieving Wanted Data (IAA)
SHRF	Ship Regular Freight [Military] (AABC)
SHRG	Scottish Homosexual Rights Group (DBA)
SHRI	Sciences and Humanities Research Institute [Iowa State University] [Research center] (RCD)
SHRIMP	Sensitive High Mass Resolution Ion Microprobe
SHRIMP	Super-High Resolution Ion Microprobe [Analytical chemistry]
SHRIV	Shrivenham [England]
SHRM	Society for Human Resource Management (EA)
ShrMed........	Shared Medical Systems Corp. [Associated Press] (SAG)
SHRNG	Shearing (MSA)
SHROC........	Shore-Required Operational Capability [Navy] (DNAB)
SHROPS	Shropshire [County in England]
SHRP	Sharpener (MSA)
SHRP	Sharper Image [NASDAQ symbol] (TTSB)
SHRP	Sharper Image Corp. [NASDAQ symbol] (NQ)
SHRP	Society for History, Research, and Preservation (EA)
SHRP	Strategic Highway Research Program [National Research Council]
SHRP	Subcommittee on Health Risk Assessment [World Health Organization]
ShrpIm.........	Sharper Image Corp. [Associated Press] (SAG)
SHRS	Shores
SHRS	Shutdown Heat Removal System [Nuclear energy] (NRCH)
SHRS	Supplementary Heat Removal System (IEEE)
SHRSDV	Scottish Historic and Research Society of Delaware Valley (EA)
Shr Sui	Shrady on Suicide and Intemperance in Life Insurance [A publication] (DLA)
SHRTG........	Shortage (AABC)
SHRTWV......	Shortwave (FAAC)
SHRV	Sudan Human Rights Voice [A publication]
SHS	Galveston, TX [Location identifier FAA] (FAAL)
SHS	Sacred Heart Seminary [Detroit, MI]
SHS	Sample Handling System [Chemistry]
SHS	Sayer Head Sling [Medicine]
SHS	Scandinavian Herpetological Society [Denmark] (EAIO)
SHS	Scottish History Society (EA)
SHS	Secure Hash Standard [Electronic Commerce]
SHS	Self-Propagating High-Temperature Synthesis [Ceramic technology]
SHS	Senior High School
SHS	Shares [Stock exchange term]

Shs	Shares (EBF)
SHS	Shashi [China] [Airport symbol] (OAG)
SHS	Shasta Dam [California] [Seismograph station code, US Geological Survey Closed] (SEIS)
SHS	Sheep Hemolyzate Supernatant
SHS	Sheet Steel (IAA)
SHS	Shipley-Hartford Scale [Psychology] (DAVI)
SHS	Ship's Heading Servo
SHS	Shire Horse Society [British] (DI)
SHS	Shop Television Network [Vancouver Stock Exchange symbol]
SHS	Simulation Hardware System [NASA] (MCD)
SHS	Sisters of the Holy Spirit (TOCD)
SHS	Small Hydro Society [Defunct] (EA)
SHS	Smoothing Heading Spot (SAA)
SHS	Social History Society of the United Kingdom
SHS	Societatis Historiae Socius [Fellow of the Historical Society] [Latin]
SHS	Sod House Society (EA)
SHS	Sodium Hexadecyl Sulfate [Organic chemistry]
SHS	Soil and Health Society [Later, RI] (EA)
SHS	Soviet Hydrometeorological Service
SHS	Spartan Homing Sensor [Missiles]
SHS	Spherical Harmonic Series (SAA)
SHS	Sports Hall of Shame [Defunct] (EA)
SHS	Square Hollow Section [Metal industry]
SHS	Standard Heavy Spanwire [Military] (CAAL)
SHS	Student Health Service (DAVI)
SHS	Sunshine Aviation SA [Switzerland ICAO designator] (FAAC)
SHS	Superheated Steam
SHS	Surveyors Historical Society (EA)
SHS	Systemhouse Ltd. [Toronto Stock Exchange symbol]
SHS	University of Sheffield, Postgraduate Librarianship, Sheffield, England [OCLC symbol] (OCLC)
SHSA	Saint Hubert Society of America (EA)
SHSA	Scottish Harp Society of America (EA)
SHSA	Seaman Apprentice, Ship's Serviceman, Striker [Navy rating]
SHSA	Southern Hardwood Square Association (EA)
SHSA	State Highway Safety Agencies [NHTSA] (TAG)
SHSAC	Supreme Headquarters, Supreme Allied Commander [World War II]
SHSC	Sierra Home Services [NASDAQ symbol] (SAG)
SHSC	Sierra Home Svc Cos. [NASDAQ symbol] (TTSB)
Sh Sc App	Shaw's Scotch Appeal Cases, House of Lords [A publication] (DLA)
SHS/DC	Social and Human Sciences Documentation Centre [UNESCO] (DUND)
SHSGS	Supreme Headquarters, Secretary General Staff [World War II]
ShSh	Shomer Shabbat [BJA)
SHSLB	Street and Highway Safety Lighting Bureau [Defunct] (EA)
SHSLC	Siouxland Health Sciences Consortium [Library network]
SHSMB	Safety and Health Standards Management Board (IAA)
SHSN	Seaman, Ship's Serviceman, Striker [Navy rating]
SHSN	Snow Showers [ICAO] (FAAC)
SHSN	Sod House Society of Nebraska [Later, SHS] (EA)
SHSO	Southshore Corp. [NASDAQ symbol] (SAG)
SHSp	Sisters of the Holy Spirit and Mary Immaculate (TOCD)
SHSP	Spontaneously Hypertensive Stroke-Prone Rat [Medicine] (DMAA)
SHSR	Society for Humanity and Social Reform [British]
SHSS	Stanford Hypnotic Susceptibility Scale [Psychology]
SHSS	Superhigh Speed Steel (IAA)
SHSTF	Scout Helicopter Special Task Force (MCD)
SHSTS	Ship Status
SHSV	Superstructure Heater Safety Valve (DS)
SHSWD	Society for Hospital Social Work Directors (EA)
SHT	British Airways Shuttle [ICAO designator] (FAAC)
SHT	Salvo Honoris Titulo [Latin]
SHT	Scottish Heritable Trust
SHT	Seal Head Tank (COE)
SHT	Sheet (AAG)
sht	Sheet (VRA)
SHT	Sholia Resources Ltd. [Vancouver Stock Exchange symbol]
SHT	Short (MSA)
SHT	Sidi Hakoma Tuff [Geology]
SHT	Simple Hypocalcemic Tetany [Medicine]
SHT	Society for the History of Technology (EA)
SHT	Society of the Most Holy Trinity [Anglican religious community]
SHT	Space Hand Tool [NASA]
SHT	Subcutaneous Histamine Test [Medicine] (MAE)
SHT	Swansea Harbour Trust [Wales]
SHTC	Short Time Constant (MSA)
Sh Teind Ct	Shaw's Scotch Teind [Tithe] Court Decisions [A publication] (DLA)
SHTG	Sheeting [Freight]
SHTG	Shortage (AFM)
SHTH	Sheath (IAA)
SHTHG	Sheathing (MSA)
SHT IRN	Sheet Iron [Freight]
SHT IRN STL	Sheet Iron or Steel [Freight]
SHTIX	AIM Limited Maturity Treas. Shs. [Mutual fund ticker symbol] (SG)
SHTL	Shuttle (MSA)
SHTL	Small Heat-Transfer Loop [Nuclear energy] (NRCH)
SHT MTL	Sheet Metal [Freight]
SHTN	Short Ton [2000 lbs.]
SHTPB	Saturated Hydroxy-Terminated Polybutadiene
SHTR	Shutter (AAG)
SHTSD	Short Side
SHT STL WRE	Sheet Steel Ware [Freight]
SHTT	Sequential Headturn Test
S-HTTP	Secure Hypertext Transfer Protocol [Computer science]

SHTTP	Secure Hyper Text Transport Protocol [Computer science] (IGQR)
SHU	Sacred Heart University, Library, Bridgeport, CT [OCLC symbol] (OCLC)
SHU	Sakhalinskie Aviatrassy [Former USSR] [FAA designator] (FAAC)
SHU	Seton Hall University [South Orange, NJ]
SHU	Shurgard Storage Centers [NYSE symbol] (SAG)
SHU	Shute Harbour [Queensland] [Airport symbol] (AD)
SHU	Shuyak Island [Alaska] [Seismograph station code, US Geological Survey] (SEIS)
SHU	Skyhigh Resources Ltd. [Vancouver Stock Exchange symbol]
ShufMst	Shuffle Master, Inc. [Associated Press] (SAG)
SHUR	Selected History Update and Reporting (MCD)
SHUR	System for Hospital Uniform Reporting
Shurgard	Shrugard Storage Centers [Associated Press] (SAG)
SHUSA	Scottish Heritage USA (EA)
SHUT	Shuttle (SSD)
SHUTDN	Shutdown (NASA)
SHV	Series Hybrid Vehicle
SHV	Shavano Air, Inc. [ICAO designator] (FAAC)
SHV	Sheave (MSA)
SHV	Shreveport [Louisiana] [Airport symbol] (OAG)
SHV	Shreveport, LA [Location identifier FAA] (FAAL)
SHV	Simian Herpes Virus (DB)
SHV	Solenoid Hydraulic Valve
SHV	Sub Hoc Voce [or Sub Hoc Verbo] [Under This Word] [Latin]
SHVA	Scottish Health Visitors Association (DBA)
SHVA	Shiva Corp. [NASDAQ symbol] (SAG)
SHVG	Shaving [Freight]
SHVHS	Sandy Hook Veterans Historical Society (EA)
SHVSCE	Shuttle Versus Current Expendable Launch Vehicle [NASA] (KSC)
SHVSNE	Shuttle Versus New Expendable Launch Vehicle [NASA] (KSC)
SHW	Air South, Inc. [ICAO designator] (FAAC)
SHW	Mount St. Helens [Washington] [Seismograph station code, US Geological Survey] (SEIS)
SHW	Sharurah [Saudi Arabia] [Airport symbol] (OAG)
SHW	Sherwin-Williams [NYSE symbol] (TTSB)
SHW	Sherwin-Williams Co. [NYSE symbol] (SPSG)
SHW	Short Wave (IAA)
Sh W & C	Shaw, Wilson, and Courtenay's Scotch Appeals Reports [Wilson and Shaw's Reports] [A publication] (DLA)
SHWCS	Showcase
ShwdGp	Sherwood Group [Associated Press] (SAG)
SHWL	Seasonal High Water Level (GNE)
SHWL	Solidified High Waste Level [Nuclear energy] (NUCP)
SHWR	Saturated Hydrocarbon Weathering Ratio [Ecology] (DAVI)
SHWRM	Showroom [Automotive advertising]
Shwscn	Showscan Entrtainment, Inc. [Associated Press] (SAG)
shwy	Showy [Horticulture]
SHWY	Super Highway (TEL)
SHX	Shageluk [Alaska] (OAG)
SHX	Shageluk, AK [Location identifier FAA] (FAAL)
SHX	Shaw Indus [NYSE symbol] (TTSB)
SHX	Shaw Industries, Inc. [NYSE symbol] (SPSG)
SHx	Social History (DAVI)
SHY	Kaiser, MO [Location identifier FAA] (FAAL)
SHY	Sharon Energy Ltd. [Vancouver Stock Exchange symbol]
SHY	Shinyanga [Tanzania] [Airport symbol] (OAG)
SHY	Syllable Hyphen Character [Computer science]
SHZ	Seshute's [Lesotho] [Airport symbol] (OAG)
SHZ	Shizuoka [Japan] [Seismograph station code, US Geological Survey] (SEIS)
SHZ	Steelhead Resources Ltd. [Vancouver Stock Exchange symbol]
SI	ACM Government Spectrum Fund [NYSE symbol] (SPSG)
SI	ACM Gvt Spectrum Fund [NYSE symbol] (TTSB)
SI	Air Sierra [ICAO designator] (AD)
SI	International System [FHWA] (TAG)
SI	International System of Units (ACII)
SI	Sacroiliac [Medicine]
SI	Safety Injection [Nuclear energy] (NRCH)
SI	Safety Inspection (IEEE)
SI	Sailmakers Institute (EA)
SI	Saintpaulia International (EA)
SI	Saline Infusion (DB)
SI	Saline Injection [Abortion technique]
SI	Salinity Indicator
SI	Salmon Institute [Formerly, CSI] (EA)
SI	Salt Institute (EA)
SI	Sample Interval
SI	Sandwich Islands
SI	Sanitary Inspector [British] (ROG)
SI	Saturation Index [Chemistry]
SI	Saturday Inspection [Slang]
SI	Save It [Energy-saving campaign] [British]
SI	Scholastic, Inc. (EFIS)
SI	School Inventory [Psychology]
SI	Scientific Instrument (NASA)
si	Scientific Instrument (NAKS)
SI	Screen Grid Input
SI	Seal In (IAA)
SI	Seasonal Industry (MHDW)
SI	Secondary Injection
SI	Secondary Item [Army]
SI	Security Identity
SI	Seine Island [Island off the coast of France] (ROG)
SI	Selected Item (MCD)

SI	Selective Identification
SI	Self Incompatible
SI	Self-Induction (IAA)
SI	Self Inflicted (MAE)
si	Self Inking (DGA)
SI	Semi-Insulating
S-I	Sensation-Intuition [Jungian psychology]
SI	Sense Indicator (IAA)
SI	Sensitive Index (STED)
SI	Sensitive Information (MCD)
SI	Sensory Integration
SI	Septic Inflammation [Medicine]
SI	Sergeant Instructor [Military British]
SI	Serial Input [Computer science] (EECA)
SI	Serious Illness (STED)
SI	Seriously Ill [Military] (AABC)
SI	Serra International (EA)
SI	Sertoma International (EA)
SI	Serum Insulin (STED)
SI	Serum Iron [Serology]
SI	Servas International (EA)
SI	Service Index (STED)
SI	Service Indicator [Telecommunications] (TEL)
SI	Service Instruction
SI	Service Interruption
SI	Severity Index (STED)
SI	Sex Inventory [Psychology]
SI	Sexual Intercourse (ADA)
SI	Shared Information (PCM)
SI	Shetland Isles
SI	Shift In [Transistor] (IAA)
SI	Shift-In Character [Keyboard] [Computer science]
SI	Ship Item (MCD)
SI	Shipping Instructions (AFM)
SI	Ship's Installation [Navy]
SI	Short Interest [Brokerage]
SI	Signal Intelligence (MCD)
SI	Signal Interface
S/I	Signal-to-Interference
SI	Signal-to-Intermodulation [Ratio]
S/I	Signal-to-Intermodulation Ratio (IDOE)
SI	Sign Code (IAA)
SI	Signed Integer [Computer science]
SI	Silence [Navigation]
SI	Silicon [Chemical element]
SI	Silicone [Organic chemistry]
Si	Silty Soil [Agronomy]
si	Silver (VRA)
SI	Silver Institute (EA)
SI	Similarity Index
Si	Simon de Bisignano [Flourished, 1174-79] [Authority cited in pre-1607 legal work] (DSA)
SI	Simple Interest [Banking]
SI	Simulation Routine (IAA)
SI	Simulator Initiation (MCD)
SI	Sinai (BJA)
si	Singapore [MARC country of publication code Library of Congress] (LCCP)
SI	Singh Index (STED)
SI	Single Injection (STED)
SI	Single Instruction
SI	Single Silk [Wire insulation] (AAG)
SI	Sinus Iridum [Bay of Rainbows] [Lunar area]
SI	Sirach [Ecclesiasticus] [Old Testament book]
SI	Site Identification [Environmental science] (COE)
SI	Site, Inc. (EA)
SI	Site Inspection [Environmental Protection Agency] (AEPA)
SI	Site Investigation
SI	Skill Identifier [Career development] [Army] (RDA)
SI	Slaved Illuminator [Military] (CAAL)
SI	Slovenia [Internet country code]
SI	Small Inclusions [Diamond clarity grade]
SI	Small Intestine [Anatomy]
S/I	Smectite-Illite [Clay mineral]
SI	Smith International, Inc. (EFIS)
SI	Smiths Industries, Inc. (EFIS)
SI	Smithsonian Institution
SI	Social Independiente [Netherlands Antilles] [Political party] (EY)
SI	Social Introversion (STED)
SI	Socialist International [Political party] (EAIO)
SI	Society of Illustrators (EA)
SI	Society of Indexers (EAIO)
SI	Software Implementation
SI	Solar Inertial (MCD)
si	Solar Inertial (NAKS)
SI	Solidarity International (EA)
SI	Solomon Islands (BARN)
SI	Solubility Index [Water]
SI	Soluble Insulin
SI	Soroptimist International [Cambridge, England] (EAIO)
SI	Sound Investment (MHDW)
SI	Source Impedance
SI	Southeast Institute for Group and Family Therapy (EA)
SI	South Island [New Zealand] (BARN)
SI	Southpaw's International [Defunct] (EA)
SI	Space Institute [University of Tennessee] [Research center] (RCD)
SI	Space Intelligence [Parapsychology]
SI	Spark Ignition
SI	Speaker Intercom
SI	Special Inquiry [Classification system used by doctors on Ellis Island to detain, re-examine, and possibly deny entry to certain immigrants]
SI	Special Inspection (MCD)
SI	Special Instruction
SI	Special Intelligence [Army] (AABC)
SI	Special Intervention [Medicine]
SI	Specialist Insectivore
SI	Specific Impulse (IAA)
SI	Specific Inventory (OA)
SI	Spectrum Index
SI	Speech Intelligibility (RDA)
SI	Speech Interpolation [Telecommunications] (TEL)
SI	Speed Indicator (IAA)
SI	Spirachaetosis Icterohaemorrhagica (DB)
SI	Spirochetosis Icterohaemorrhagica (STED)
SI	Spokane International Railroad Co. [AAR code]
SI	Sponsor Identification [Television]
SI	Spot Inspection [Military] (AFM)
SI	Spot Inventory
SI	Spratly Islands [ANSI two-letter standard code] (CNC)
SI	Square Inch (MCD)
SI	Staff Inspector
SI	Standard International Unit (IAA)
SI	Standardization and Interoperability
SI	Standards Institution [Telecommunications]
SI	Standex International Corp. (EFIS)
SI	Standing Instruction (MSA)
SI	Star of India
SI	Staten Island
SI	Station Identification
SI	Status Indicator (IAA)
SI	Steer, Inc. [An association] (EA)
SI	Steering Intelligence (MCD)
SI	Step Index [Nuclear energy] (NUCP)
SI	Stereo Imaging (SSD)
SI	Stimulation Index [Cytochemistry]
SI	Storage Immediate
SI	Straight-In Approach [Aviation]
SI	Straight, Inc. (EA)
SI	Strathclyde Institute [Glasgow, Scotland]
SI	Streptozotocin Induced (STED)
SI	Stress Incontinence [Urology] (DAVI)
SI	Stretch-Inactivated Ion Channel
SI	Stretch Inhibitor
SI	Strict Isolation (STED)
S/I	Strike/Interdiction (MCD)
SI	Stroke Index
SI	Structure-of-Intellect [Model]
SI	Student Investigator (KSC)
S/I	Subject Issue
SI	Subscription Item
S/I	Sucrose to Isomaltase [Ratio] (STED)
SI	Suicidal Ideation [Psychiatry] (DAVI)
SI	Suitability Index [Fishery science]
SI	Sulfated Insulin (STED)
SI	Sulphur Institute (EA)
si	Sum Insured (ODBW)
SI	Sundance Institute (EA)
SI	Superimpose (MDG)
SI	Superintendent of Document/Item (NITA)
SI	Supply Instruction [Marine Corps]
SI	Support Installation (MCD)
SI	Suppression Index (STED)
SI	Surface Impoundment (EG)
SI	Surface Integrity
SI	Surface Ionization [Physics]
SI	Surveillance Inspection [Nuclear energy] (NRCH)
SI	Survival International [British] (EAIO)
SI	Suspect Index [British]
SI	Swap-In [Computer science]
SI	Switch Interpretation (IAA)
SI	Symbolic Input [Computer science]
SI	Syncytium Inducing [Cytology]
SI	Systeme International (NITA)
SI	Systeme International d'Unites [International System of Units] [Also, SIU]
SI	System Information [Computer science] (PCM)
SI	System Integration
SI	System International (IAA)
SI	System Inventory [or Review of Systems] (DAVI)
SI	Systolic Index (STED)
SI	U.S. Servas [An association] (EA)
SIA	Sailing Industry Association (EA)
SIA	San Francisco, CA [Location identifier FAA] (FAAL)
SIA	Sanitary Institute of America [Later, IAWCM]
SIA	Sasquatch Investigations of Mid-America (EA)
SIA	Satellite Industry Association (DDC)
SIA	Scaffold Industry Association (EA)
SIA	Science Information Association
SIA	Scottish Island Area [Council]

SIA............. Securities Industry Association (EA)
SIA............. Security Industry Association (NTPA)
SIA............. Self-Insurers Association
SIA............. Self-Interstitial Atom
SIA............. Semiconductor Industry Association (EA)
SIA............. Sensor Interface Assembly
SIA............. Serial Input Adapter
SIA............. Service Industry Accounting [*Sybiz International, Inc.*] [*Computer program*] (PCM)
SIA............. Service in Information and Analysis [*Host*] [*British*] (BUR)
SIA............. Shelter Oil & Gas Ltd. [*Toronto Stock Exchange symbol*]
SIA............. Shuttle Induced Atmosphere (NASA)
SIA............. Sialic Acid [*Biochemistry*]
SIA............. Sian [*Republic of China*] [*Seismograph station code, US Geological Survey Closed*] (SEIS)
SIA............. Sian [*China*] [*Airport symbol*] (AD)
SIA............. Sigma Immunoassay [*Test for rubella*]
SIA............. Signal Apparel [*NYSE symbol*] (TTSB)
SIA............. Signal Apparel Co., Inc. [*NYSE symbol*] (SPSG)
SIA............. Singapore Airlines
SIA............. Singapore Airlines Ltd. [*ICAO designator*] (FAAC)
SIA............. Singles in Agriculture [*An association*] (EA)
SIA............. Ski Industries America (EA)
SIAON......... Societa Italiana di Agopuntura [*Italy*]
SIA............. Societe Internationale Arthurienne, [*International Arthurian Society*] North American Branch (EA)
SIA............. Societe Internationale d'Acupuncture [*International Society of Acupuncture*]
SIA............. Society for Industrial Archeology (EA)
SIA............. Society of Industrial Accountants of Canada
SIA............. Society of Insurance Accountants [*Crozet, VA*] (EA)
SIA............. Software Impact Assessment [*NASA*] (NASA)
SIA............. Software Industry Association (IAA)
SIA............. Software Institute of America [*Andover, MA*] [*Telecommunications*] (TSSD)
SIA............. Solar Inertial Attitude (NASA)
SIA............. Solvents Industry Association [*British*] (DBA)
SIA............. Soroptimist International of the Americas (EA)
SIA............. Speaker Intercom Assembly [*NASA*]
SIA............. Special Interest Automobiles [*A publication*]
SIA............. Special Investor Account [*Stock purchasing*]
SIA............. Spinal Injuries Association [*British*]
SIA............. Sprinkler Irrigation Association [*Later, IA*] (EA)
SIA............. Standard Instrument Approach [*RADAR*] [*Aviation*]
SIA............. Standard Interface Adapter
SIA............. Station Interface Adapter (SSD)
SIA............. Station of Initial Assignment
SIA............. Stereo-Image Alternator (PDAA)
SIA............. Stimulation-Induced Analgesia (DB)
SIA............. Storage Instantaneous Audimeter [*Measures television viewing*]
SIA............. Strategic Industries Association (EA)
SIA............. Stress-Induced Analgesia [*Medicine*]
SIA............. Strip Immunoblot Assay [*Immunology*]
SIA............. Structural Inventory and Appraisal [*Of roads and bridges*]
SIA............. Subacute Infectious Arthritis [*Medicine*] (DMAA)
SIA............. Subaru-Isuzu Automotive
SIA............. Subminiature Integrated Antenna
SIA............. Survivors of Incest Anonymous (EA)
SIA............. Swiss Society of Engineers and Architects (IAA)
SIA............. Synalbumin-Insulin Antagonism [*Medicine*]
SIA............. Syncytia Induction Assay (DB)
SIA............. System Integration Area (MCD)
SIA............. Xian [*China*] [*Airport symbol*] (OAG)
SIAA........... Seed Industry Association of Australia
SIAAP......... Sugar Industry Adjustment Assistance Program [*Australia*]
SIABA......... Sindacato Italiano Artisti Belle Arti [*Italian Union of Fine Arts*]
SIABC......... Sociedad Iberoamericana de Biologia Celular [*Ibero-American Society for Cell Biology - IASCB*] (EAIO)
SIAC........... Secretariat International des Artistes Catholiques
SIAC........... Securities Industry Automation Corp. [*NYSE/ASE*] [*New York, NY*]
SIAC........... Shock Isolator Air Compressor (DWSG)
SIAC........... Societe Internationale des Artistes Chretiens [*International Society for Christian Artists*] [*Lydiate, Merseyside, England*] (EAIO)
SIAC........... Southeastern Intercollegiate Athletic Association (MCD)
SIAC........... Southern Intercollegiate Athletic Conference (PSS)
SIAC........... Special Interest Auto Club [*Defunct*] (EA)
SIAC........... State Industry Advisory Committee [*Civil Defense*]
SIAC........... Submarine Integrated Attack Center (MCD)
SIAC........... Support List Allowance Card
SIACE......... Scottish Institute of Adult and Continuing Education (DBA)
SIACI......... Societe Intercontinental d'Assurances pour le Commerce et l'Industrie [*Intercontinental Assurance Company of Commerce and Industry*] [*France*]
SIAD.......... Sierra Army Depot [*California*] (AABC)
SIAD.......... Society of Industrial Artists and Designers [*British*] (DI)
SIADH........ Syndrome of Inappropriate Antidiuretic Hormone [*Endocrinology*]
SIADS........ Sensor Integration and Display Sharing [*Military*] (CAAL)
SIAE.......... Scottish Institute of Adult Education (DI)
SIAE.......... Scottish Institute of Agricultural Engineering [*Research center*] (IRC)
SIAF.......... Service Indicator Associated Field [*Telecommunications*] (TEL)
SIAF.......... Small Independent Action Force [*Military*]
SIAGL........ Survey Instrument, Azimuth Gyroscope, Lightweight (MCD)
SIAL.......... Salon International de l'Alimentation [*World Food Fair*]
SIAL.......... Sialagogue [*Promoting Flow of Saliva*] [*Medicine*] (ROG)
SIAL.......... Sigma-Aldrich [*NASDAQ symbol*] (TTSB)

SIAL............ Sigma-Aldrich Corp. [*NASDAQ symbol*] (NQ)
SIAL............ Southeast Iowa Academic Libraries [*Library network*]
SIALON....... Silicon, Aluminum, Oxygen, and Nitrogen [*A ceramic*]
SIAM......... Scanning Interferometric Apertureless Microscope
SIAM......... Self-Initiating Antiaircraft Munition [*ARPA*]
SIAM......... Separate Index Access Method [*Computer science*] (BUR)
SIAM......... Signal Information and Monitoring Service [*American radio monitoring service*]
SIAM......... Society for Industrial and Applied Mathematics (EA)
SIAM......... Strategic Impact and Assumptions Identification Method
SIAM......... System for Improved Acquisition of Material (MCD)
SIAM......... System Integrated Access Method (IAA)
SIAMA....... Society for Interests of Active Missionaries in Asia, Africa, and America (EAIO)
SIAM Rev ... SIAM Review [*A publication*] (BRI)
SIAMS .... Secondary Ion Accelerator Mass Spectrometry
SIAN .... Societe Industrielle et Agriculturelle du Niari [*Industrial and Agricultural Society of Niari*]
SI & CTF..... Scottish Industry and Commerce Trade Fair (ITD)
SI & F........ Spinal Instrumentation and Fusion [*Neurology*] (DAVI)
Si & So...... Sight and Sound [*A publication*] (BRI)
SIANM....... Special Inspection, Army Nuclear Matters (MCD)
SI/AO........ Smithsonian Institution/Astrophysical Observatory (KSC)
SIAON....... Silicon-Aluminum Oxynitride
SIAP.......... Sociedad Interamericana de Planeficacion [*Inter-American Planning Society*] [*Mexico*]
SIAP.......... Standard Instrument Approach Procedure [*Aviation*]
SIAP.......... Standard-Italo Americana Petroli
SIAP.......... Statistical Institute for Asia and the Pacific [*United Nations*] (ECON)
SIAP.......... Straight-In Approach [*Aviation*]
SIAP.......... System for Improved Acoustic Performance
SIAR.......... Small, Irregular, Agglutinated Rooms [*Architecture*]
SIAS.......... Safety Injection Actuation Signal [*Nuclear energy*] (NRCH)
SIAS.......... Scandinavian Institute of Asian Studies [*See also CINA*] [*Later, NIAS*] (EAIO)
SIAS.......... Signals Intelligence Analysis System (MCD)
SIASP........ Submarine Integrated Antenna System (MCD)
SIASP........ Society for Italian-American Scientists and Physicians (EA)
SIAT.......... Single Integrated Attack Team
SIAT.......... Synthesis of Impact Acceleration Technology (MCD)
SIATE-MTS... Simulated Intermediate Automatic Test Equipment-Maintenance Training System [*Air Force*]
SIAU .... Seminario Internacional de Administracao Universitaria
SIAWS .... Satellite-Interrogated Automatic Weather Station (NOAA)
SIB............. Satellite Integrated Buoy
SIB............. Satellite Ionospheric Beacons [*Military*]
SIB............. Saudi International Bank
SIB............. Scale plus Index plus Base
SIB............. Scales of Independent Behavior [*Occupational therapy*]
SIB............. Screen Image Buffer [*Computer science*]
SIB............. Securities and Investments Board [*British*]
SIB............. Selection Interview Blueprint [*LIMRA*]
SIB............. Self-Injurious Behavior [*Abnormal psychology*]
SIB............. Serial Interface Board
SIB............. Severe Impairment Battery [*Neuropsychological test*]
SIB............. Shipbuilding Industry Board [*British*]
SIB............. Ship Information Booklet [*Navy*]
SIB............. Siberia
Sib............. Siberia (VRA)
SIB............. Sibiti [*Congo*] [*Airport symbol*] (OAG)
Sib............. Sibling
sib .... Sibling (DOG)
SIB............. Sibola Mines Ltd. [*Vancouver Stock Exchange symbol*]
Sib............. Sibyllines (BJA)
SIB............. SIDPERS [*Standard Installation/Division Personnel System*] Interface Branch [*Military*] (INF)
SIB............. Simulation Interface Buffer (SSD)
SIB............. Sistema de Informacion Bursatil [*Stock Exchange Information System*] [*Madrid Stock Exchange*] [*Information service or system*] (IID)
SIB............. Situation Intelligence Brief (DNAB)
SIB............. Snake in the Box (IAA)
SIB............. Societa' Siba Aviation [*Italy ICAO designator*] (FAAC)
SIB............. Societe Internationale de Biometeorologie [*International Society of Biometeorology*] (EAIO)
SIB............. Society for Industrial Biology (HGEN)
SIB............. Special Intelligence Brief (MCD)
SIB............. Special Investigation Branch [*Army British*]
SIB............. Standard Index Base (DNAB)
SIB............. Standard Iron Bar (MSA)
SIBI........... Subject Interface Box (KSC)
SIB............. System Integration Board (SSD)
SIB............. System Interconnect Bus [*Computer science*]
SIB............. Systems Information Bulletin [*Computer science*]
SIBA.......... Scottish Indoor Bowling Association (DBA)
SIBA.......... Small Independent Brewers' Association [*British*] (ECON)
SIBC.......... Saudi Investment Banking Corp.
SIBC.......... Societe Internationale de Biologie Clinique [*World Association of Anatomic and Clinical Pathology Societies*]
SIBC.......... Southern Intercollegiate Bowling Conference (PSS)
SIBD.......... Soviet Independent Business Directory [*A publication*]
SIBE.......... Sustainable Business Entity
SIBEX........ Second International BIOMASS Experiment
SIBEX........ Singapore International Building Exhibition
SIBH .... Salicylideniminobenzohydroxamic Acid [*Biochemistry*]

SIBH .... Society of Interpretation of Britain's Heritage (DBA)
SIBI .... SIBIA Neurosciences [NASDAQ symbol] (TTSB)
SIBI .... SIBIA Neurosciences, Inc. [NASDAQ symbol] (SAG)
SIBI .... Survivor Income Benefit Insurance (DICI)
SIBIA .... SIBIA Neurosciences, Inc. [Associated Press] (SAG)
SIBIL .... Systeme Integre pour les Bibliotheques Universitaires de Lausanne [Integrated System for the University of Lausanne Libraries] [Switzerland] (IID)
SIBIL .... System Informatise pour Biblitheques [Information System for Libraries] (EAIO)
SIBIS .... Self-Injurious Behavior Inhibiting System [Psychology]
SIBIS .... Smithsonian Institution Bibliographic Information System
SIBL .... Science, Industry, and Business Library [New York, NY]
SIBL .... Separate Infantry Brigade Light (INF)
SIBM .... Societe Internationale de Biologie Mathematique [International Society of Mathematical Biology] (EAIO)
SIBMAS ...... Societe Internationale des Bibliotheques et Musees des Arts du Spectacle [International Association of Libraries and Museums of the Performing Arts] (EAIO)
SIB-MIBOC... Securities and Investments Board and the Marketing of Investments Board Organisation Commission [British]
SIBOL .... Sweden Integrated Banking On-Line (IAA)
SibOr .... Sibylline Oracles (BJA)
SIBOR .... Singapore Interbank Offered Rate
SIBP .... Self-Insured Benefits Plan [Human resources] (WYGK)
SIBR .... Styrene-Isoprene-Butadiene Rubber [Materials science]
SI/BRC .... Strategic Intelligence/Business Research Corp.
SIBS .... Salk Institute for Biological Studies
SIBS .... Semiconductor Industry & Business Survey [Database] [HTE Management Resources] [Information service or system] (CRD)
SIBS .... Specially Important Brothers and Sisters (of Our Patients) [Medicine]
SIBS .... Stellar Inertial Bombing System
sib-ship ...... Sibling Relationship (DAVI)
SIBTN .... Something Is Better than Nothing
SIC .... Air Sicilia, SRL [Italy] [FAA designator] (FAAC)
SIC .... Covington/Cincinnati, OH [Location identifier FAA] (FAAL)
SIC .... High School Student Information Center (EA)
SIC .... Safety Information Center [National Safety Council] (IID)
SIC .... Sakharov International Committee (EA)
SIC .... San Antonio do Ica [Brazil] [Airport symbol] (AD)
SIC .... Science Information Council [National Science Foundation]
SIC .... Scientific Information Center
SIC .... Security Intelligence Centre [British World War II]
SIC .... Security Intelligence Corps
SIC .... Semiconductor (IAA)
SIC .... Semiconductor Integrated Circuit
SIC .... Senior Intelligence Committee (DOMA)
SIC .... Sept-Iles [Quebec] [Seismograph station code, US Geological Survey] (SEIS)
SIC .... Serial Interface Chip
SIC .... Serum Insulin Concentration [Medicine] (DMAA)
SIC .... Service, Inc., Omaha NE [STAC]
SIC .... Servicio Informativo Continental [Press agency] [Argentina]
SIC .... Siccus [Dry] [Latin] (ADA)
SIC .... Sicily
Sic .... Sicily (VRA)
SIC .... Sico, Inc. [Toronto Stock Exchange symbol]
SIC .... Silicon Carbide (IDOE)
SIC .... Silicon Coated (IAA)
SIC .... Silicon-Insulating Compound
SIC .... Silicon Integrated Circuit
SIC .... Simulated Interface Calibration
SIC .... Skills Inventory Coordinator
SIC .... Social Implications of Computers (IAA)
SIC .... Social Interaction Code
SIC .... Societe Internationale de Cardiologie [International Society of Cardiology]
SIC .... Societe Internationale de Chirurgie [International Society of Surgery - ISS] [Basel, Switzerland] (EA)
SIC .... Societe Internationale de Criminologie [International Society of Criminology] (EA)
SIC .... Society of Inkwell Collectors (EA)
SIC .... SONAR Information Center (NVT)
SIC .... Sorties per Inspection Cycle [Air Force] (AFIT)
SIC .... Southeastern Independent Conference (PSS)
SIC .... Special Information Center (MCD)
SIC .... Special Interest Committee
SIC .... Specific Inductive Capacitance
SIC .... Specific Inductive Capacity (IDOE)
SIC .... Split Investment Company [Generic term]
SIC .... Sports Industries Commission [New South Wales, Australia]
SIC .... Standard Industrial Classification [File indexing code] [Also, an information service or system]
SIC .... Standard Industrial Code [Wood industry] (WPI)
SIC .... Standard Industry Code (PCM)
SIC .... Standard Inspection Criteria
SIC .... Standard Interface Connector (SSD)
SIC .... States Information Center [Council of State Governments] (IID)
SIC .... Status of Implementation Chart
SIC .... Stock Item Catalog (MCD)
SIC .... Structural Influence Coefficient
SIC .... Subscriber Interface Control (DOMA)
SIC .... Sudbury Igneous Complex [Geology]
SIC .... Supervisory Inventory on Communication [Test]
SIC .... Support Identification Code (SSD)

SIC .... Survey Information Center [Military]
SIC .... Systeme Informatique pour la Conjoncture [Information System for the Economy] [INSEE] [France] [Information service or system] (IID)
SIC .... System Integration Computer (MCD)
SIC .... Systems Integration Contractor
SIC 72 .... Standard Industrial Classification 72 (NITA)
SICA .... Secondary Inventory Control Activity (MCD)
SICA .... Securities Industry Committee on Arbitration (DFIT)
SICA .... Soccer Industry Council of America (EA)
SICA .... Society of Industrial and Cost Accountants of Canada
SICA .... Subud International Cultural Association (EA)
SICAC .... Society of Inter-Celtic Arts and Culture (EA)
SICAM .... Sex Information Council of America [Later, CSIE] (EA)
SIC & DH.... Scientific Instrument Computer and Data Handling (SSD)
SICB .... Senior Interservice Control Board (DNAB)
SICB .... Society for Integrative and Comparative Biology (NTPA)
SICBM .... Single-Warhead Intercontinental Ballistic Missile (MCD)
SICBM .... Small Intercontinental Ballistic Missile (MCD)
SICBM .... Super Intercontinental Ballistic Missile (IAA)
SICC .... Safeguard Inventory Control Center [Army] (AABC)
SICC .... Secondary Item Control Center
SICC .... Secours International de Caritas Catholica [Belgium] (EAIO)
SICC .... Service Inventory Control Center [DoD]
SICC .... Standards Information Center of China [Library]
SICC .... State Interagency Coordinating Council
SICCI .... Schools Information Centre on the Chemical Industry (AIE)
SICCM .... Supervisor Information on Civilian Career Management [Navy] (DNAB)
SICCS .... Social Interaction and Creativity in Communication System [Educational test]
SICD .... Sequenced Inventory of Communication Development (EDAC)
SICD .... Sequenced Inventory of Communicative Development [Speech and language therapy] (DAVI)
SICD .... Serum Isocitric Dehydrogenase (MAE)
SICD .... Supplier Interface Control Drawing (MCD)
SICDO .... Society of Industrial Civil Defence Officers [British] (BI)
SICDOC....... Special Interest Committee on Program Documentation [Association for Computing Machinery]
SICE .... Standard Interface Control Electronics (ECII)
SICEA .... Steel Industry Compliance Extension Act of 1981
SICEJ .... Society of Instrument and Control Engineers of Japan (IAA)
SICF .... Societe des Ingenieurs Civils de France
SICF .... Societe Ivoirienne des Chemins de Fer [Railway system] [The Ivory Coast] (EY)
SICI .... Serial Item and Contribution Identifier [Library science] (TELE)
SICIS .... Strategic Issue Competitive Information System (PDAA)
SIC/JIC....... Secondary Injection Control/Jet Interaction Control
Sick .... Sickels' Reports [46-85 New York] [A publication] (DLA)
SICK .... Sickle Cells [Hematology] (DAVI)
Sick .... Single Income, Couple of Kids [Lifestyle classification]
Sick Min Dec... Sickels' United States Mining Laws and Decisions [A publication] (DLA)
Sick Op........ Sickels' Opinions of the New York Attorneys-General [A publication] (DLA)
SICL .... Sampling Inspection Checklist
SICL .... Selected Item Configuration Log
SICL .... Self-Interview Checklist [Navy] (NVT)
SICL .... Supplier Item Control List (MCD)
SICLOPS ..... Simplified Interpretive COBOL Operating System (PDAA)
SICM .... Scanning Ion-Conductance Microscope
SICM .... Scheduled Input Control Method (MCD)
SICM .... Small Intercontinental Ballistic Missile (MCD)
SICM .... Soybean Integrated Crop Management Model
SICMA .... Special Initial Clothing Monetary Allowance [Military] (DNAB)
SICMA-CIV... Special Initial Clothing Monetary Allowance - Civilian [Military] (DNAB)
SICMA-NAOC... Special Initial Clothing Monetary Allowance - Naval Aviation Officer Candidate [Navy] (DNAB)
SICMA-NAVCAD... Special Initial Clothing Monetary Allowance - Naval Aviation Cadet [Navy] (DNAB)
SICN .... Statewide Instructional Computing Network [New York] (EDAC)
SICN .... Syndicate for Fabrication of Fuel Elements [French Acronym is based on foreign phrase]
SICO .... Signal Control (DEN)
SICO .... Switched in for Checkout [NASA] (KSC)
SICO .... Systems Integration and Checkout
SICOB .... Salon International de l'Informatique, de la Communication, et de l'Organisationdu Bureau [Business equipment exhibition]
SICOM .... Securities Industry Communication [Western Union Corp.] [Information service or system]
SI COMMS... Special Intelligence Communications (MCD)
SICOMP ...... Siemens Computer (NITA)
SICOT .... Societe Internationale de Chirurgie Orthopedique et de Traumatologie [International Society of Orthopaedic Surgery and Traumatology] [Brussels, Belgium] (EAIO)
SICOVAM..... Societe Interprofessionnelle pour la Compensation des Valeurs Mobilieres [French depository body]
SICP .... Selected Ion Current Profile [Spectrometry]
SICP .... Shut-in Casing Pressure [Well drilling technology]
SICP .... Society of Indochina Philatelists (EA)
SICP .... Society of Invasive Cardiovascular Professionals (EA)
SICPS .... Standardized Integrated Command Post System [Army] (INF)
SICR .... Selected Item Configuration Record (MCD)
SICR .... Specific Intelligence Collection Requirements [Military] (AFM)

SICR	Supply Item Change Record
SICRI	Substances Immunologically Cross-Reactive with Insulin
SICRYS	Sydney Indochinese Refugee Youth Support Group [*Australia*]
SICS	Safety Injection Control System [*Nuclear energy*] (NRCH)
SICS	Secondary Infrared Calibration System
SICS	Ships Integrated Communications System (MCD)
SICS	Source Information Control System (NITA)
SICS-PACK...	Screw Integrated Control System - Pontoon Air Cushion Kit [*Army*] (RDA)
SICSVA	Sequential Impaction Cascade Sieve Volumetric Air (MAE)
SICT	Scientific Inventory Control Technique (IAA)
SICT	Selective Intracoronary Thrombolysis [*Cardiology*] (DAVI)
SICTLM	Solomon Islands Cultural Traditional Leaders Movement
SICU	Surgical Intensive Care Unit [*Medicine*]
Sicu Ab	Abbas Siculus [*Deceased, 1445*] [*Authority cited in pre-1607 legal work*] (DSA)
SID	Doctor of Industrial Science
SID	ICP [*International Computer Programs, Inc.*] Software Information Database [*Information service or system*] (CRD)
SID	Ilha do Sal [*Cape Verde Islands*] [*Airport symbol*] (AD)
SID	Sal Island [*Cape Verde Islands*] [*Airport symbol*] (OAG)
SID	Scale of Institutional Differentiation (AEBS)
SID	Scheduled Issue Date [*Telecommunications*] (TEL)
SID	Seal-In Device (MSA)
SID	Security and Intelligence Service [*Army*]
SID	Seismic Intrusion Detector [*or Device*] [*Army*]
SID	Selected Item Drawing (MCD)
sid	Semel in Die [*Once a Day*] [*Pharmacy*]
SID	Sequence Information Data
SID	Serial Input Data [*Computer science*]
SID	Servizio Informazioni Difesa [*Defense Intelligence Service*] [*Italy*]
SID	Shuttle Integration Device [*NASA*] (NASA)
SID	Sida [*Iceland*] [*Seismograph station code, US Geological Survey*] (SEIS)
sid	Sidamo [*MARC language code Library of Congress*] (LCCP)
SID	Side-Impact Dummy [*Collision testing device*]
Sid	Siderfin's King's Bench Reports [*82 English Reprint*] [*A publication*] (DLA)
SID	Sidfin Air Ltd. [*Zambia*] [*ICAO designator*] (FAAC)
SID	Signal Identification (NITA)
SID	Silicon Imaging Device (IEEE)
SID	Silver Iodine Generator
SID	Simulator Interface Device (MCD)
SID	Situation Display
SID	Situation Information Display
SID	Sketch-in-Depth [*Parthorn*] [*Software package*] (NCC)
SID	Skin Inserted Detonator (MCD)
SID	Slew-Induced Distortion
SID	Society for Information Display (EA)
SID	Society for International Development (EA)
SID	Society for Investigative Dermatology (EA)
SID	Sodium Ionization Detector [*Nuclear energy*] (NRCH)
SID	Software Interface Document (MCD)
SID	Solid Ink Density (DGA)
SID	Solubilization by Incipient Development (OA)
SID	Sound Ideas, Inc. [*Vancouver Stock Exchange symbol*]
SID	Sound Interface Device [*Computer chip*]
SID	Sound Interference Device
SID	Source Image Distortion
SID	Space and Information Systems Division [*NASA*]
SID	Space Intruder Detector [*Burglar alarm*]
SID	Special Intelligence Detachment [*Military*] (CINC)
SID	Specification Interpretation Documentation (MCD)
SID	Specific Infrared Detector
SID	Speech Input Device (IAA)
SID	Spiritus in Deo [*Spirit Rests in God*] [*Latin*]
SID	Sports Information Director
SID	Standard Instrument Departure [*RADAR*] [*Aviation*]
SID	Standard Interface Document (NASA)
SID	Strategic Intelligence Digests [*Military*] (AABC)
SID	Structure Isolation Dynamics [*Vehicle development*] [*Automotive engineering*]
SID	Subcontract Item Definition
SID	Subject Identification Module [*NASA*]
SID	Subscriber Identification (CAAL)
SID	Subsystem Identification [*Electronics*]
SID	Sucrase-Isomaltase Deficiency [*Medicine*] (DB)
SID	Sudden Infant Death [*Syndrome*] [*Medicine*]
SID	Sudden Ionospheric Disturbance [*Geophysics*]
SID	Suprathermal Ion Detector (PDAA)
SID	Surface-Induced Dissociation [*Physics*]
SID	Surface Ionization Detector [*Instrumentation*]
SID	SWIFT [*Society for Worldwide Interbank Financial Telecommunications*] Interface Device
SID	Synchronous Identification System (DNAB)
SID	Syntax Improving Device (IEEE)
SID	System Identification Numbers [*Telecommunications*] (OTD)
SID	System Integrational Diagnostic (IAA)
SID	System Interface Document [*NASA*] (NASA)
SID	Systems Integration and Deployment [*Program*] [*Department of Transportation*]
SID	Systems Integration Demonstrator [*Aircraft*]
SIDA	7th Infantry Division Association (EA)
SIDA	Acquired Immunodeficiency Syndrome [*Medicine*] [*French, Spanish and other Romance languages*] (TAD)

SIDA	SIOP [*Single Integrated Operations Plan*] Integrated Data Base (MCD)
SIDA	Societe Internationale Fernand de Vischer pour l'Histoire des Droits de l'Antiquite (EA)
SIDA	Stable Isotope Dilution Assay [*Analytical chemistry*]
SIDA	Swedish International Development Agency
SIDAAC	Snow and Ice Distributed Active Archive Center (USDC)
SIDAC	Single Integrated Damage Anaysis Capability (MCD)
SIDAC	Supportability Investment Decision Analysis Center [*Air Force*]
Sid Apoll	Sidonius Apollinaris [*Fifth century AD*] [*Classical studies*] (OCD)
SIDAR	Selective Information Dissemination and Retrieval [*Computer science*] (DIT)
SIDAR	Symposium on Image Display and Recording
SIDASE	Significant Data Selection
SIDC	Slaved Illuminator Data Converter [*Military*] (CAAL)
SIDC	Supply Item Design Change [*Navy*] (NG)
SIDC	Support Issue Development Committee [*Military*] (CAAL)
SIDC	Systems Identification Data Cost
SIDD	Scientific Information and Documentation Division [*Later, ESIC*]
SIDD	Standard Inside Diameter Dimension Ratio (DAC)
SIDE	Siding
SIDE	Suprathermal-Ion-Detector Experiment [*Apollo*] [*NASA*]
SIDEC	Stanford International Development Education Center [*Stanford University*]
SIDEFCOOP...	Sociedad Interamericana de Desarrollo de Financiamiento Cooperativo [*Inter-American Society for the Development of Cooperative Financing*] [*Buenos Aires, Argentina*] (EAIO)
Sid (Eng)	Siderfin's King's Bench Reports [*82 English Reprint*] [*A publication*] (DLA)
SIDER	Siderocytes [*In Differential*] [*Hematology*] (DAVI)
SIDES	Source Input Data Edit System
SIDF	Sinusoidal Input Describing Function [*Computer science*]
SIDF	Standard Independent Data Format Association
SIDF	Standard Interchange Data Form [*Computer science*] (MHDI)
SIDF	System Independent Data Format [*Computer science*] (PCM)
SIDFA	Senior Industrial Development Field Adviser [*United Nations*]
SIDFA	System Independent Data Format Association (NTPA)
Sid Gov	Sidney on Government [*A publication*] (DLA)
SI Diam	SI Diamond Technology [*Commercial firm Associated Press*] (SAG)
SIDL	System Identification Data List [*Navy*] (NG)
SIDLOB	Side Lobe [*Entomology*]
SIDM	Shipboard Identification Demolition Model [*Navy*]
SIDM	Solar Internal Dynamics Mission (SSD)
SIDM	Syndicat International des Debardeurs et Magasiniers [*International Longshoremen's and Warehousemen's Union ILWU*] [*Canada*]
SIDMS	Status Inventory Data Management System (MCD)
SIDN	Small Industry Development Network [*Georgia Institute of Technology*]
SIDO	Societe Internationale pour le Developpement des Organisations [*International Society for the Development of Organizations*] (EAIO)
SIDOR	Siderurgica del Orinoco [*Government steel company*] [*Venezuela*]
SIDOS	Site Document Order Section (SAA)
SIDP	Seed Industry Development Program [*UN Food and Agriculture Organization*]
SIDP	Sheep Industry Development Program (EA)
SIDP	Society of Infectious Diseases Pharmacists (EA)
SIDP	Sputter Ion Depth Profiling (AAEL)
SIDPE	Sensing, Identifying, Deciding, Predicting, and Executing
SIDPERS	Standard Installation/Division Personnel System [*Military*] (AABC)
SIDS	Satellite Imagery Dissemination System (MCD)
SIDS	Screening Information Data Set [*Environmental science*]
SIDS	Secondary Imagery Dissemination System (DOMA)
SIDS	Sensor Interface Data System [*Military*] (CAAL)
SIDS	Ships Integrated Defense System
SIDS	Shrike Improved Display System [*Military*] (NVT)
SIDS	Societe Internationale de Defense Sociale [*International Society for Social Defence - ISSD*] [*Paris, France*] (EAIO)
SIDS	Societe Internationale de Droit Sociale
SIDS	Space Investigations Documentation System [*NASA*]
SIDS	Spares Integrated Data System (MCD)
SIDS	Specification Interpretation Documents (MCD)
SIDS	Speech Identification System (IAA)
SIDS	Standard Information Display System [*Military*] (CAAL)
SIDS	Stellar Inertial Doppler System
SIDS	Strike Improved Display System (MCD)
SIDS	Sudden Infant Death Syndrome [*Medicine*]
SIDS	Sulfo-Iduronate Sulfatase (DMAA)
SIDS	Support Integrated Data System (MCD)
SIDSA	Sudden Infant Death Syndrome Act of 1974
SIDS Alliance...	Sudden Infant Death Syndrome Alliance (PAZ)
SIDT	SI Diamond Technology [*Commercial firm NASDAQ symbol*] (SAG)
SIDT	Silicon Integrated Device Technology (IAA)
SIDTC	Single Integrated Development Test Cycle
SIDTEC	Single Integrated Development Test Cycle (MCD)
SIDTS	Single Integrated Development Test System
SIDY	Science Dynamics [*NASDAQ symbol*] (TTSB)
SIDY	Science Dynamics Corp. [*NASDAQ symbol*] (NQ)
SIE	Science Information Exchange [*Later, SSIE*] [*Smithsonian Institution*]
SIE	Sea Isle, NJ [*Location identifier FAA*] (FAAL)
SIE	Selected Inertial Equipment
SIE	Selected Item Exchange (MCD)
SIE	Select Information Exchange [*Information service or system*] (IID)
SIE	Sensory Isolation Experiment (SAA)
SIE	Serum Immunoreative Erythropoietin [*Immunochemistry*]

SIE..............	Servizio Informazioni Esercito [*Italy*] [*Forces Intelligence Service*]
SIE..............	Shanell International Energy Corp. [*Vancouver Stock Exchange symbol*]
SIE..............	Shuttle Interface Equipment [*NASA*] (NASA)
Sie..............	Siemens [*Unit of electric conductance*]
SIE..............	Siena [*Italy*] [*Seismograph station code, US Geological Survey*] (SEIS)
SIE..............	Sierra Express, Inc. [*ICAO designator*] (FAAC)
SIE..............	Sierra Health Services [*NYSE symbol*] (TTSB)
SIE..............	Sierra Health Services, Inc. [*NYSE symbol*] (SAG)
SIE..............	Single Instruction Execute
SIE..............	Societe Internationale d'Electrochimie [*International Society of Electrochemistry*]
SIE..............	Society of Industrial Engineers [*Later, SAM*]
SIE..............	Soroptimist International d'Europe [*Soroptimist International of Europe*] (EAIO)
SIE..............	Special Inspection Equipment
SIE..............	Start Interpretive Execution (HGAA)
SIE..............	Stroke in Evolution [*Medicine*] (MEDA)
SIE..............	Suicide Information and Education [*Suicide Information and Education Center*] [*Canada Information service or system*] (CRD)
SIE..............	Surface Ionization Engine
SIE..............	System Integration Equipment (KSC)
SIE..............	System Investigation Equipment (KSC)
SIEA...........	Sensor Interface Electronics Assembly (MCD)
SIEB...........	Satellite-Interrogated Environmental Buoy
SIEB...........	Siebert Financial Corp. [*NASDAQ symbol*] (SAG)
SiebelS.......	Siebel Systems, Inc. [*Associated Press*] (SAG)
Siebert.......	Siebert Financial Corp. [*Associated Press*] (SAG)
SIEC...........	Societe Internationale pour l'Enseignement Commercial [*International Society for Business Education*] [*Lausanne, Switzerland*] (EAIO)
SIEC...........	Suicide Information and Education Centre [*Canadian Mental Health Association*] [*Information service or system*] (IID)
SIECCAN.....	Sex Information and Education Council of Canada
SIECD.........	Societe Internationale d'Education Continue en Dentisterie [*International Society of Continuing Education in Dentistry - ISCED*] [*Brussels, Belgium*] (EAIO)
SIECOP.......	Scientific Information and Education Council of Physicians (EA)
SIECUS.......	Sex Information and Education Council of the US (EA)
SIECUS.......	Sexuality Information and Education Council of the United States (EA)
SIED...........	Supplier Item Engineering Order (MCD)
SIEDS.........	Societe Internationale d'Etude du Dix-Huitieme Siecle [*International Society for Eighteenth-Century Studies - ISECS*] (EAIO)
SIEF...........	Societe Internationale d'Ethnographie et de Folklore [*International Society for Ethnology and Folklore*]
SIEFA.........	Source Inventory and Emission Factor Analysis [*Environmental Protection Agency*]
SIEGE.........	Simulated EMP [*Electromagnetic Pulse*] Ground Environment [*Air Force*]
Siego.........	Single, Intelligent, and Educated and Growing Old [*Lifestyle classification*]
SIEL...........	Superficial Image Emphasis Lithography (NITA)
SIEM..........	Society of Insurance Financial Management (NTPA)
sien...........	Sienna [*Philately*]
Siena Heights C...	Siena Heights College (GAGS)
SIEP...........	Screening Inspection for Electronic Parts [*NASA*]
SIEP...........	State Implementation and Enforcement Program [*Environmental Protection Agency*]
SIEPM........	Societe Internationale pour l'Etude de la Philosophie Medievale [*International Society for the Study of Medieval Philosophy*] (EAIO)
SIER..........	Sierra On-Line [*NASDAQ symbol*] (TTSB)
SIER..........	Sierra On-Line, Inc. [*NASDAQ symbol*] (CTT)
SieraHm......	Sierra Home Services [*Commercial firm Associated Press*] (SAG)
SierH.........	Sierra Home Services [*Commercial firm Associated Press*] (SAG)
SierHS.......	Sierra Health Services, Inc. [*Associated Press*] (SAG)
SIERNEV.....	Sierra Nevada (FAAC)
SierOn.......	Sierra On-Line, Inc. [*Associated Press*] (SAG)
SierPac......	Sierra Pacific Resources [*Associated Press*] (SAG)
Sierra Leone LR...	Law Reports, Sierra Leone Series [*A publication*] (ILCA)
Sierra Leone L Rec...	Law Recorder (Sierra Leone) [*A publication*] (ILCA)
SierraP......	Sierra Pac Pw [*Associated Press*] (SAG)
SierraSem ...	Sierra Semiconductor Corp. [*Associated Press*] (SAG)
SierSm.......	Sierra Semiconductor Corp. [*Associated Press*] (SAG)
SierTah......	Sierra Tahoe Bancorp [*Associated Press*] (SAG)
SierWst......	SierraWest Bancorp [*Associated Press*] (SAG)
SIES..........	Ship Integrated Electronic System
SIES..........	Sobek's International Explorer's Society [*Commercial firm*] (EA)
SIES..........	Society of the Incarnation of the Eternal Son [*Anglican religious community*]
SIES..........	Supervision, Inspection, Engineering, and Services (NASA)
SIESC........	Secretariat International des Enseignants Secondaires Catholiques [*International Secretariat of Catholic Secondary School Teachers*] [*Acronym used in association name, SIESC Pax Romana Nijmegen, Netherlands*] (EAIO)
SIESO........	Society of Industrial Emergency Services Officers [*British*] (DBA)
SIESTA.......	Silent Energy Sources for Tactical Applications (MCD)
SIETAR/INTL...	International Society for Intercultural Education, Training, and Research (EA)
SIEUSE.......	Secretariat International de l'Enseignement Universitaire des Sciences de l'Education
SI/EW........	Special Intelligence/Electronic Warfare (MCD)
SIF............	Reidsville, NC [*Location identifier FAA*] (FAAL)
SIF............	Salvo in Flight [*Military*] (CAAL)

SIF............	School Interoperability Framework
SIF............	Science Information Facility [*FDA*]
SIF............	Scleroderma International Foundation (EA)
SIF............	Scotch-Irish Foundation (EA)
SIF............	Scott Industrial Foam
SIF............	Secure Identification Feature
SIF............	Security and Intelligence Foundation [*Later, CIS*] (EA)
Sif............	Segment Inferior (STED)
SIF............	Selective Identification Feature [*Military decoder modification*]
SIF............	Selective Interrogation Feature (MCD)
SIF............	Serum-Inhibition Factor [*Medicine*] (DMAA)
SIF............	Serum Inhibitory Factor (STED)
SIF............	Service Incroyance et Foi [*Canadian Catholic Conference*]
SIF............	Short-Intrusion Fuze (RDA)
SIF............	SIFCO Indus [*AMEX symbol*] (TTSB)
SIF............	SIFCO Industries, Inc. [*AMEX symbol*] (SPSG)
SIF............	Signaling Information Field [*Telecommunications*] (TEL)
SIF............	Simra [*Nepal*] [*Airport symbol*] (OAG)
SIF............	Single Face
SIF............	Skycy Freighters International Ltd. [*Kenya*] [*ICAO designator*] (FAAC)
SIF............	Small Intensely Fluorescent [*Cytology*]
SIF............	Social Investment Forum (EA)
SIF............	Sociedad Iberoamericana de Filosofia [*Spain*] (EAIO)
SIF............	Society of International Friendship (EA)
SIF............	Solvent-Induced Force [*Physical chemistry*]
SIF............	Sound Intermediate Frequency
SIF............	Source Image Format (DOM)
SIF............	Source Input Format [*Computer science*]
SIF............	Standard Image Format [*Computer science*]
SIF............	Standard Interchange Format
SIF............	Standard Interface (IAA)
SIF............	Storage Interface Facility
SIF............	Stress Intensity Factor (MCD)
SIF............	Suncorp Insurance and Finance [*Commercial firm Australia*]
SIF............	Switched In-Flight (KSC)
SIF............	Synthetic Interstitial Fluid [*Biochemistry*]
SIFA..........	Society of Independent Financial Advisors [*Englewood, CO*] (EA)
SIFAD........	Separate Ion Formation and Drift
SIFAR........	Surveillance Imagery Fast Access Recording (MCD)
SIFAT........	Servants in Faith and Technology (EA)
SIFC..........	Saskatchewan Indian Federated College [*University of Regina*]
SIFC..........	Sparks International Official Fan Club (EAIO)
SIFCC........	Senate Interstate and Foreign Commerce Committee
Sifco.........	SIFCO Industries, Inc. [*Associated Press*] (SAG)
SIFCO........	Steel Improvement & Forge Co. (EFIS)
SIFCON.......	Slurry-Infiltrated Fiber-Concrete (BARN)
SIFCS........	Sideband Intermediate Frequency Communications System (AAG)
SifDeut	Sifrei Deuteronomy (BJA)
SIFE..........	Sanitation Inspection Fish Establishment [*National Marine Fisheries Service*] (NOAA)
SIFE..........	Students in Free Enterprise [*Bolivar, MO*] (EA)
SIFEM........	Side-Impact Finite Element Model [*Automotive safety*] [*Computer-assisted design*]
SIFF..........	Stock Index Futures Fund
SIFI..........	Starlog Franchise [*NASDAQ symbol*] (TTSB)
SIF/IFF.......	Selective Identification Feature/Identification Friend or Foe [*Military*] (AFM)
SifNum	Sifrei Numbers (BJA)
SIFO..........	Societa Italiana di Farmacia Ospedaliera [*Italy*]
SIFO..........	Svenska Institutet foer Opinionsundersoekningar
Si-Fo-An-Di...	Silica-Forsterite-Anorthite-Diopside [*Lunar geology*]
Si-Fo-Di.....	Silica-Forsterite-Diopside [*Lunar geology*]
SIFPPS	Shore Installations and Facilities Planning and Programming System [*Navy*] (MCD)
SIFR..........	Serious Injury Frequency Rate
SIFR..........	Simulated Instrument Flight Rules (AAG)
SIFR..........	Sun-Improved Frequency Response
SIFT..........	Selected-Ion Flow Tube [*Instrumentation*]
SIFT..........	Share Internal FORTRAN Translator [*Computer science*] (IEEE)
SIFT..........	Simplified Input for TIROS Operational Satellite System (IAA)
SIFT..........	Simplified Input for Toss [*Computer science*]
SIFT..........	Skills Inventory for Teams [*Test*] (TMMY)
SIFT..........	Software Implemented Fault Tolerance [*NASA*]
SIFT..........	Summary of Information on Film and Television [*British*]
SIFT..........	System Identification from Tracking (MCD)
SIFTER........	ScIntillating Fiber Telescope for Energetic Radiation [*Proposed, 1996*]
SIFTOR	Sifting of Information for Technology of Reactors [*MIT-AEC study*]
SIFX..........	Simulated Installation Fixture (AAG)
SifZut.........	Sifrei Zuta (BJA)
SIG...........	San Juan/Isla Grande [*Puerto Rico*] [*Airport symbol*] (OAG)
SIG...........	San Juan, PR [*Location identifier FAA*] (FAAL)
SIg............	Secretory Immunoglobin [*Immunology*]
SIG...........	Self-Insurance Group (WYGK)
SIG...........	Senior Interagency Group [*Federal government*]
SIG...........	Senior Interdepartmental Group [*Department of State*]
SIG...........	Serum Immune Globulin [*Immunochemistry*]
Sig............	Serum Immune Globulin [*Medicine*] (STED)
SIG...........	Ship Improvement Guide
SIG...........	SIGCORP, Inc. [*NYSE symbol*] [*Formerly, Southern Indiana Gas & Electric*] (SG)
SIG...........	Sigmoidoscope [*or Sigmoidoscopy*] [*Medicine*] (AAMN)
SIG...........	Signa [*Write*] [*Pharmacy*]
SIG...........	Signal
sig............	Signal (WDMC)

SIG..............	Signalman [Navy rating British]
SIG..............	Signature (AFM)
sig	Signature (WDMC)
Sig..............	Signature (STED)
SIG..............	Signetur [Let It Be Labelled] [Pharmacy]
sig	Significant
SIG..............	Significant Testing (IAA)
SIG..............	Signifying (ROG)
Sig..............	Signor (WA)
SIG..............	Signore [or Signora] (EY)
SIG..............	Silicon-Insulated Gate
SIG..............	Silver-Intensified Gold [Biological stain]
SIG..............	Silver Ridge Resources, Inc. [Vancouver Stock Exchange symbol]
SIG..............	Simplicity Is Greatness [See also GIS]
SIG..............	Simplified Inertial Guidance
SIG..............	Society for Integrative Graphology [Defunct] (EA)
SIG..............	Southern Indiana Gas & Electric Co. [NYSE symbol] (SPSG)
SIG..............	South Ingalls [Colorado] [Seismograph station code, US Geological Survey Closed] (SEIS)
SIG..............	Special Interest Group
SIG..............	Special Investigative Group [DoD]
SIG..............	Starfield Image Generator
SIG..............	State Implementation Grant
SIG..............	Stellar Inertial Guidance Signal
SIG..............	Strapdown Inertial Guidance
SIG..............	Street Index Guide (PA)
SIG..............	Sub-Interface Generator (NITA)
Sig	Surface Immunoglobulin [Medicine] (STED)
sIg	Surface Immunoglobulin [Immunochemistry]
SIG..............	Three Sigma Market Newspaper Audiences [Three Sigma Research Center, Inc.] [Information service or system] (CRD)
SIG3C	Special Interest Group on Computing at Community Colleges (NTPA)
S-IgA	Secretory Immunoglobulin A [Immunology]
SIGA	Sigma Circuits [NASDAQ symbol] (TTSB)
SIGA	Sigma Circuits, Inc. [NASDAQ symbol] (SAG)
Siga	Signora [Madam] [Italian]
SigA..........	Surface Immunoglobulin A (STED)
SIGACT	Special Interest Group for Algorithm and Computation Theory (NTPA)
SIGACT	Special Interest Group on Automata and Computability Theory (EA)
SIGADA.......	Special Interest Group on Ada (EA)
SIGAda	Special Interest Group on Ada Programming Language (NTPA)
SIGAGCY.....	Signal Agency (IAA)
SIG/AH	Special Interest Group/Arts and Humanities [of the American Society for Information Science]
SIGAIRDEFENGRAGCY...	Signal Air Defense Engineering Agency (IAA)
SIG/ALP	Special Interest Group/Automated Language Processing [American Society for Information Science]
SIGAP	Surrey Investigation Group into Aerial Phenomena [British]
SIGAPL.......	Special Interest Group on APL Programming Language (EA)
SIGAPP.......	Special Interest Group on Applied Computing (NTPA)
SIGARCH	Special Interest Group for Architecture of Computer Systems (EA)
SIGART	Special Interest Group on Artificial Intelligence (EA)
SIGAVNCO ...	Signal Aviation Company (IAA)
SIGBAT	Signal Battalion [Army]
SIG/BC	Special Interest Group/Biological and Chemical Information Systems [of the American Society for Information Science]
SIGBDP.......	Special Interest Group for Business Data Processing and Management (EA)
SIGBI	Soroptimist International of Great Britain and Ireland (EAIO)
SIGBIO........	Special Interest Group on Biomedical Computing (EA)
SIGBN	Signal Battalion (IAA)
SIG/BSS.......	Special Interest Group/Behavioral and Social Sciences [of the American Society for Information Science]
SIGC	Signal Corps [Later, Communications and Electronics Command] [Army]
SIGC	Signal Corps Engineering Laboratories [Fort Monmouth, NJ]
SIGCAPH......	Special Interest Group for Computers and the Physically Handicapped (EA)
SIGCAS........	Special Interest Group for Computers and Society (EA)
SIGCAT	Special Interest Group on CD-ROM Applications and Technology (AAGC)
SIGCAT ACM...	Special Interest Group on CD-ROM Applications and Technology (DDC)
SIG/CBE	Special Interest Group/Costs, Budgeting, and Economics [of the American Society for Information Science]
Sig CD	Signature Card [Banking] (MHDW)
SIGCEN	Signal Center [Military] (AABC)
SIGCHI........	Special Interest Group on Computer and Human Interaction (EA)
SIGCO.........	Signal Company (IAA)
SIGCOA........	Signal Company, Airline (IAA)
SIGCOC........	Signal Company, Cable (IAA)
SIGCOM.......	Signal Communication (IAA)
SIGCOMM....	Special Interest Group on Data Communication (EA)
SIGCOMM ACM...	Special Interest Group on Data Communications (DDC)
SIGCOMMAGCY...	Signal Communication Agency (IAA)
SIGCOMMSECAGCY...	Signal Communication Security Agency (IAA)
SIGCONDNET...	Signal Conditioning Network (IAA)
SIGCONDR...	Signal Conditioner (MCD)
SIGCONSBN...	Signal Construction Battalion (IAA)
SIGCOR.......	Signal Corps [Later, Communications and Electronics Command] [Army]
SIGCOSIM....	Special Interest Group on Computer Systems, Installation Management [Association for Computing Machinery]
SIGCOW.......	Signal Company, Wireless (IAA)
SIGCOWG	Signal Company, Wing (IAA)

SIGCOY.......	Signal Company (IAA)
SIGCPR.......	Special Interest Group for Computer Personnel Research (EA)
SIG/CR........	Special Interest Group/Classification Research [of the American Society for Information Science]
SIGCS	Special Interest Group for Computers and Society [Association for Computing Machinery] (EA)
SIG CSE......	Special Interest Group for Computer Science Education (EA)
SIGCUE.......	Special Interest Group for Computer Uses in Education (EA)
SIG-D.........	Simplified Inertial Guidance-Demonstration [Army] (RDA)
SIGDA........	Special Interest Group for Design Automation (EA)
SIG/DAT......	Signal/Data (MHDI)
SIGDEP.......	Signal Depot (IAA)
SIGDEPCO ...	Signal Depot Company [Military] (IAA)
SIGDIV.......	Signal Division [SHAPE] (NATG)
SIGDOC.......	Special Interest Group for Systems Documentation (EA)
SIGDOC.......	Special Interest Group on Documentation (NTPA)
SIGE...........	Silicon Germanium
SIGE...........	Societe Internationale de Gastro-Enterologie
SIGEFT.......	Special Interest Group on Electronic Funds Transfer (MHDI)
SIGENGRAGCY...	Signal Engineering Agency (IAA)
SIGEQUIP...	Signal Equipment (IAA)
SIG/ES	Special Interest Group/Education for Information Science [of the American Society for Information Science]
SIGEX	Signal Exercise (NATG)
SIGFET........	Silicon Gate Field Effect Transistor (IAA)
SIGFIDET	Special Interest Group on File Description and Translation [Association for Computing Machinery] [Later, Special Interest Group on the Management of Data]
sig fig.........	Significant Figures [Mathematics] (BARN)
SIG/FIS	Special Interest Group/Foundations of Information Science [of the American Society for Information Science]
SIGFORTH ...	Special Interest Group for Forth Programming Language (NTPA)
SIGG	Signatures (WGA)
SIGGEN.......	Signal Generator (IEEE)
SIGGND	Signal Ground (IAA)
SIGGRAPH...	Special Interest Group on Computer Graphics (EA)
SIGGRAPH...	Special Interest Group on Graphics (NITA)
SIGGRAPH ACM...	Special Interest Group on Computer Graphics (DDC)
SIGGY	Signet Group [NASDAQ symbol] (SPSG)
SIGGY	Signet Group ADR [NASDAQ symbol] (TTSB)
SIGGZ	Signet Grp $1.06 Cv Pfd [NASDAQ symbol] (TTSB)
SightRes......	Sight Resources Corp. [Associated Press] (SAG)
SIGHVCONSTBN...	Signal Heavy Construction Battalion (IAA)
SIGI	Selective Insurance Gr [NASDAQ symbol] (TTSB)
SIGI	Selective Insurance Group, Inc. [Branchville, NJ] [NASDAQ symbol] (NQ)
SIGI	System for Interactive Guidance and Information [Computerized career-counseling service offered by the Educational Testing Service] [Princeton, NJ]
SIG/IAC........	Special Interest Group/Information Analysis Centers [of the American Society for Information Science]
SIGICE	Special Interest Group on Individual Computing Environments (NTPA)
SIGILL........	Sigillum [Seal] [Latin] (WGA)
SIGINT........	Signal Intelligence [Military] (AABC)
SIGINTELAGCY...	Signal Intelligence Agency (IAA)
SIGINT/EW...	Signal Intelligence/Electronic Warfare (MCD)
SIGIPS........	Signals Information Processing System [Navy] (DOMA)
SIGIR.........	Special Interest Group on Information Retrieval (EA)
SIGIRD........	Systeme Integre de Gestion Informatise des Ressources Documentaires [Integrated System for the Management of Documentary Resources] [University of Quebec, Montreal] [Information service or system] (IID)
SIG/IRG.......	Senior Interdepartmental Group / Interdepartmental Regional Group (DNAB)
SIG/ISE	Special Interest Group/Information Services to Education [of the American Society for Information Science]
Sig L	Signal Lieutenant [British military] (DMA)
SIG/LA........	Special Interest Group/Library Automation and Networks [of the American Society for Information Science]
SIGLASH......	Special Interest Group on Language Analysis and Studies in the Humanities [Association for Computing Machinery]
SIGLE.........	System for Information on Grey Literature in Europe [European Association for Grey Literature Exploitation] [Commission of the European Communities] [Information service or system] (IID)
SIGLEX	Special Interest Group on Lexicography [National Security Agency]
SIGLINK......	Special Interest Group on Hypertext (NTPA)
SIGLINK ACM...	Special Interest Group on Hypertext and Hypermedia (DDC)
SIGLINT.......	Signal Intelligence [US surveillance satellite]
SIGM	Sigma Designs [NASDAQ symbol] (TTSB)
SIGM	Sigma Designs, Inc. [Fremont, CA] [NASDAQ symbol] (NQ)
SIGM	Syndicat International des Gens de Mer du Canada
SIGMA	Science in General Management [British] (DI)
SIGMA	Sealed Insulating Glass Manufacturers Association (EA)
SIGMA	Shielded Inert Gas Metal Arc (IAA)
SIGMA	Site Information Generation and Material Accountability Plan [Army] (AABC)
SIGMA	Society of Independent Gasoline Marketers of America [Washington, DC] (EA)
SIGMA	Society of In-Plant Graphics Management Associations
SIGMA	Society of Inventors of Games and Mathematical Attractions [British]
SIGMA	Standardized Inertial Guidance Multiple Application
SigmaC........	Sigma Circuits, Inc. [Associated Press] (SAG)
SigmAI........	Sigma-Aldrich Corp. [Associated Press] (SAG)
SIGMALOG....	Simulation and Gaming Method for Analysis of Logistics [Army]
SIGMAP	Special Interest Group for Mathematical Programming [Defunct] (EA)

SIGMAS	Signal Measurement and Analysis System
Sigmatr	Sigmatron International [*Associated Press*] (SAG)
SigmDg	Sigma Designs, Inc. [*Associated Press*] (SAG)
SIGMET	Significant Meteorological Conditions
SIGMET	Significant Meteorological Information [*FAA*] (TAG)
SIGMETRICS	Special Interest Group on Measurement and Evaluation (EA)
SIGMICRO	Special Interest Group on Microprogramming and Microarchitecture (EA)
SIGMINI	Special Interest Group on Minicomputers [*Later, SIGSMALL*] [*Association for Computing Machinery*] (CSR)
Sig Mis	Signature Missing
SIGMIS	Special Interest Group on Management Information Systems (NTPA)
SIGMM	Special Interest Group on Multimedia (NTPA)
SIGMM ACM	Special Interest Group on Multimedia Systems (DDC)
SIGMN	Signalman
sigmo	Sigmoidoscopy [*Medicine*]
SIGMOBILE	Special Interest Group on Mobility of Systems, Users, Data, and Computing (NTPA)
SIGMOD	Special Interest Group on Management of Data (EA)
sigmoid	Sigmoidoscopy [*Medicine*] (DAVI)
SIGMR	Signal Master (IAA)
SIGMS	Signal Material Support (DNAB)
SIGMSGCEN	Signal Message Center (IAA)
SIGMSLSPTAGCY	Signal Missile Support Agency (IAA)
SIGN	Plasti-Line [*NASDAQ symbol*] (TTSB)
SIGN	Plasti-Line, Inc. [*NASDAQ symbol*] (NQ)
SIGN	Signa [*Label*] [*Pharmacy*] (ROG)
SIGN	Signal (IAA)
sign	Signature (DAVI)
SIGN	Strapdown Inertial Guidance and Navigation (MCD)
SIGNA	Signora [*Madam*] [*Italian*] (ROG)
Signa	Signorina [*Miss*] [*Italian*]
SIGNA	Species Iris Group of North America (EA)
SIGNCE	Significance (ROG)
SIGNE	Signature
SIGNET	Signal Network
SIGNET	Supplies Invoice Generation Network (PDAA)
SignetB	Signet Banking Corp. [*Associated Press*] (SAG)
SignetGp	Signet Group [*Associated Press*] (SAG)
SIGNF	Signify (ROG)
SignInns	Signature Inns, Inc. [*Associated Press*] (SAG)
SIGN N P	Signetur Nomine Proprio [*Let It Be Written Upon with the Proper Name*] [*Pharmacy*] (ROG)
SIGNO	Signal Officer (IAA)
Signor de Homod	Signorolus de Homodeis de Mediolano [*Flourished, 14th-15th century*] [*Authority cited in pre-1607 legal work*] (DSA)
SIG/NPM	Special Interest Group/Nonprint Media [*of the American Society for Information Science*]
Sig N Pro	Signa Nomine Proprio [*Label with the Proper Name*] [*Pharmacy*]
SIGNRE	Signature (ROG)
Signs	Signs: Journal of Women in Culture and Society [*A publication*] (BRI)
SigntG	Signet Group [*Associated Press*] (SAG)
SIGNUM	Special Interest Group on Numerical Control [*Military*]
SIGNUM	Special Interest Group on Numerical Mathematics (EA)
SIGO	Signal Officer
Sigo	Signorolus de Homodeis de Mediolano [*Flourished, 14th-15th century*] [*Authority cited in pre-1607 legal work*] (DSA)
SIGOA	Special Interest Group on Office Automation [*Later, SIGOIS*]
SIGOFFR	Signal Officer (IAA)
SIGOIS	Special Interest Group on Office Information Systems (EA)
SIGOP	Signal Optimization Program [*Federal Highway Administration*]
SIGOPNBN	Signal Operation Battalion (IAA)
SIGOPS	Special Interest Group on Operating Systems (EA)
SIGOUT	Signal Output (MHDI)
SIGPC	Special Interest Group on Personal Computing [*Association for Computing Machinery*]
SIGPLAN	Special Interest Group on Programming Languages (EA)
SIGPRAD	Special Interest Group on Phobias and Related Anxiety Disorders (EA)
SIGPROCOFC	Signal Procurement Office (IAA)
SIGR	Signature Resorts, Inc. [*NASDAQ symbol*] (SAG)
SIGRAM	Sound Intensity Diagram (MCD)
SIGREAL	Special Interest Group on Real Time Processing [*Association for Computing Machinery*]
SIGREPCO	Signal Repair Company [*Military*] (IAA)
SIGRES	Signal Corps Reserve [*Military*] (IAA)
SigRsrts	Signature Resorts, Inc. [*Associated Press*] (SAG)
SIG/RT	Special Interest Group/Reprographic Technology [*of the American Society for Information Science*]
SIGRTN	Signal Return [*Electronics*]
SIGS	Sandia Interactive Graphics System
SIGS	Simplified Inertial Guidance System (MCD)
SIGS	Stellar Inertial Guidance System [*Air Force*] (AAG)
SIGSAC	Special Interest Group on Security, Audit, and Control (EA)
SIGSAM	Special Interest Group for Symbolic and Algebraic Manipulation (EA)
SIGSCH	Signal School (IAA)
SIGSCSA	Special Interest Group on Small Computing Systems and Applications [*Later, SIGSMALL*] [*Association for Computing Machinery*] (EA)
SIG/SDI	Special Interest Group/Selective Dissemination of Information [*American Society for Information Science*]
SIGSEC	Signal Section (IAA)
SIGSEC	Signal Security [*Military*] (AABC)
SIG SEL	Signal Selector (DNAB)
SIGSERVCO	Signal Service Company [*Military*] (IAA)

SIGSIM	Special Interest Group for Simulation and Modeling (NTPA)
SIGSIM	Special Interest Group on Simulation (EA)
SIGSMALL	Special Interest Group on Small Computing Systems and Applications [*Formerly, SIGSCSA*] [*Association for Computing Machinery*] (EA)
SIGSMALL/PC	[*A*] Special Interest Group on Small and Personal Computing Systems and Applications [*An association for Computing Machinery*] (HGAA)
SIGSOC	Special Interest Group on Social and Behavioral Science Computing [*Association for Computing Machinery*]
SIGSOFT	Special Interest Group on Software Engineering (EA)
SIGSOP	Signals Operator (ADA)
SIGSOUND	Electronic Forum on Sound Technology (NTPA)
SIGSPAC	Special Interest Group on Urban Data Systems, Planning, Architecture, and Civil Engineering [*Association for Computing Machinery*]
SIGSPACE	Senior Interagency Group (Space)
SIGSPCSA	Special Interest Group on Small and Personal Computing Systems Applications (EA)
SIGSPTBN	Signal Support Battalion [*Military*] (IAA)
Sig Sta	Signal Station [*Nautical charts*]
SIGSTN	Signal Station [*Navigation*]
SIGSTR	Signal Strength (IAA)
SIGSUPAGNCY	Signal Supply Agency (IAA)
SIGSUPBN	Signal Supply Battalion [*Military*] (IAA)
SIGSVCBN	Signal Service Battalion [*Military*] (IAA)
SIGTC	Signal Training Center (IAA)
SIGTNG	Signal Training (IAA)
SIGTNGCEN	Signal Training Center (IAA)
SIGTNGDET	Signal Training Detachment (IAA)
SIGTRAN	Special Interest Group on Translation [*National Security Agency*]
SIGTTO	Society of International Gas Tanker and Terminal Operators (EAIO)
SIGUCC	Special Interest Group on University Computing Centers (IAA)
SIGUCCS	Special Interest Group for University and College Computing Services (EA)
Sig Unk	Signature Unknown (EBF)
SIG/UOI	[*A*] Special Interest Group on User Online Interaction [*An association for Computing Machinery*] (HGAA)
SIGVOICE	Special Interest Group on Voice [*National Security Agency*]
SIG-WEB	Special Interest Group on the WWW
SIGWX	Significant Weather [*Aviation*] (FAAC)
SIG/ZBB/ADP	Special Interest Group on Zero-Based Budgeting and Automated Data Processing (MHDI)
SIH	Schweizerisches Institut fuer Hauswirtschaft
SIH	Scinde Irregular Horse [*British military*] (DMA)
SIH	Seafarers and International House (EA)
SIH	Silgarhi Doti [*Nepal*] [*Airport symbol*] (OAG)
SIH	Societe Internationale d'Hematologie [*International Society of Hematology - ISH*] [*Buenos Aires, Argentina*] (EA)
SIH	Society for Italic Handwriting (EA)
SIH	South Irish Horse [*British military*] (DMA)
SIH	Stimulation-Induced Hypalgesia [*Medicine*] (DMAA)
SIH	Sun Ice Ltd. [*Toronto Stock Exchange symbol*]
SIH	Sun International Hotels
SIH	Sun Intl Hotels Ord [*NYSE symbol*] (TTSB)
SIH	Superstar Ice Hockey [*Computer game*]
SiH4	Silane (AAEL)
SIHAG	Experimental Farm, Agriculture Canada [*Ferme Experimentale, Agriculture Canada*], Indian Head, Saskatchewan [*Library symbol National Library of Canada*] (BIB)
SI Hand	SI Handling Systems [*Associated Press*] (SAG)
SIHBF	Sun International [*NASDAQ symbol*] (SAG)
SIHGO	Sour, Imported Heavy Gas Oil [*Petroleum chemistry*]
SIHL	Sun International [*NASDAQ symbol*] (SAG)
SIHP	Stress Indicator & Health Planner [*Test*] (TMMY)
SIhPTH	Serum Immunoractive Human Parathormone [*Immunology*] (DAVI)
SIHR	Supervisory Inventory on Human Relations [*Test*]
SIHS	Scottish Industrial Heritage Scoeity (DBA)
SIHS	S.I. Handling Sys [*NASDAQ symbol*] (TTSB)
SIHS	SI Handling Systems, Inc. [*NASDAQ symbol*] (NQ)
SIHS	Society for Italian Historical Studies (EA)
SIHT	Space Impact Hand Tool [*NASA*]
SIHW	Society for Italic Handwriting (EA)
SII	School Interest Inventory [*Psychology*]
SII	Security-Insecurity Inventory [*Psychology*]
SII	Self-Inflicted Injury [*Medicine*] (DMAA)
SII	Self-Interview Inventory [*Psychology*]
SII	Severity of Illness Index [*Health insurance*] (GHCT)
SII	Sexual Interaction Inventory [*DHP*]
SII	Short Interval Identification
SII	Sidi Ifni [*Morocco*] [*Airport symbol*] (AD)
SII	Siimes Aviation AB [*Finland ICAO designator*] (FAAC)
SII	Sitkinak Island [*Alaska*] [*Seismograph station code, US Geological Survey*] (SEIS)
SII	Smith International, Inc. [*NYSE symbol*] (SPSG)
SII	Smith Intl [*NYSE symbol*] (TTSB)
SII	Software and Information Industry Association
SII	Soldier-Information Interface (RDA)
SII	Space Industries, Inc.
SII	Special Instruction Indicator (AAGC)
SII	Special Interest Items (MCD)
SII	Sponsor Identification Index [*Advertising*] (NTCM)
SII	Standard Identification for Individuals [*Social security*] [*American National Standards Institute*]
SII	Statement of Intelligence Interest [*Army*] (RDA)

SII	Strategic Impediments Initiative (MHDW)
SII	Structural Impediments Initiative [US-Japan trade negotiations]
SII	Sugar Information, Inc. [Defunct] (EA)
SII	Supervisory Immigrant Inspector [Immigration and Naturalization Service]
SIIA	Self-Insurance Institute of America (EA)
SIIAEC	Secretariat International des Ingenieurs, des Agronomes, et des Cadres Economiques Catholiques [International Secretariat of Catholic Technologists, Agriculturists, and Economists] [Paris, France] (EAIO)
SIIC	Secretariat International des Groupements Professionnels des Industries Chimiques des Pays de la CEE
SIIC	Special Interest Item Code [Military] (AABC)
SIIFT	Sociedad Internacional de Ingenieros Forestales Tropicales [International Society of Tropical Foresters] (EAIO)
SIII	S3, Inc. [NASDAQ symbol] (SAG)
SIIL	Schottky Integrated Injection Logic (IAA)
SIINC	Scientific Instrumentation Information Network and Curricula [National Science Foundation]
SIIR	Spares Item Inventory Record (MCD)
SIIRS	Smithsonian Institution Information Retrieval System (DIT)
SIITO	Standard Installation Instruction Technical Order (SAA)
SIJ	Minneapolis, MN [Location identifier FAA] (FAAL)
SIJ	Sacroiliac Joint
SIJ	Siglufjordur [Iceland] [Airport symbol] (OAG)
SIJADEP	International Secretariat of Jurists for an Amnesty and Democracy in Paraguay [Paris, France] (EAIO)
SIJAU	Secretariat International des Juristes pour l'Amnistie en Uruguay [France]
SI/JI	Secondary Injection/Jet Interaction
SIJIC	Senior International Joint Intelligence Course (MCD)
SIJt	Sacroiliac Joint [Anatomy] (DAVI)
SIK	Sikeston, MO [Location identifier FAA] (FAAL)
SIK	Silknit Ltd. [Toronto Stock Exchange symbol]
Sik	Single Income, Kids [Lifestyle classification]
SIL	Ile a la Crosse Public Library, Saskatchewan [Library symbol National Library of Canada] (NLC)
SIL	Safety Information Letter (IEEE)
SIL	Safety Integrity Level (ACII)
SIL	Sao Hill [Tanzania] [Airport symbol] (AD)
SIL	Scanner Input Language
SIL	Schedule Interface Log
SIL	SCN [Stock Control Number] Index and Log
SIL	Sea Island Air Ltd. [Canada ICAO designator] (FAAC)
SIL	Selected Item List
SIL	Semiconductor Injector LASER
SIL	Seriously Ill List [Military]
SIL	Service Information Letter
SILSP	Set Indicators of the Left Half (SAA)
SIL	Shift Indicator Light [Automotive engineering]
SIL	Silcorp Ltd. [Toronto Stock Exchange symbol]
SIL	Silence (MSA)
SIL	Silent (NTCM)
SIL	Silicate
Sil	Silius Italicus [First century AD] [Classical studies] (OCD)
Sil	Sillimanite [Mineralogy]
Sil	Silurian [Period, era, or system] [Geology]
Sil	Silver (AAG)
Sil	Silver Tax Division (Internal Revenue Bulletin) [A publication] (DLA)
Sil	Silvester Godinho [Deceased, 1244] [Authority cited in pre-1607 legal work] (DSA)
SIL	Single in Line [Electronics] (EECA)
SIL	Slidel, LA [Location identifier FAA] (FAAL)
SIL	Smart Integral Linearizer [Instrumentation]
SIL	Smithsonian Institution Information Leaflets
SIL	Smithsonian Institution Libraries
SIL	SNOBOL Implementation Language Reimplemented [1974] [Computer science] (CSR)
SIL	Societas Internationalis Limnologiae Theoreticae et Applicae [International Association of Theoretical and Applied Limnology]
SIL	Societe Internationale de la Lepre [International Leprosy Association]
SIL	Society for Individual Liberty (EA)
SIL	Solid Immersion Lens [Computer science] (PCM)
SIL	Sound Intensity Level
SIL	Sound Interference Level [NASA] (NASA)
SIL	Special Interest Launch [Military] (AFIT)
SIL	Specific Individual Licence [Importing] [British] (DS)
SIL	Speech Interference Level
SIL	Squamous Intraepithelial Lesion [Medicine]
SIL	Steam Isolation Line (IEEE)
SIL	Store Interface Link
SIL	Summer Institute of Linguistics
SIL	Supply Information Letter (MCD)
SIL	Support Items List (MCD)
SIL	Surge Impedance Loading
SIL	System Implementation Language [Computer science]
SIL	System Information Library [Computer science] (CIST)
SIL	Systems Integration Laboratory [NASA] (MCD)
SILAF	Sindacato Italiano Lavoratori Appalti Ferroviari [Italian Union of Railroad Contract Workers]
SILAP	Sindacato Nazionale Dipendenti Ministero del Lavori Pubblici [National Union of Employees in the Ministry of Public Welfare] [Italy]
SILAT	Society for Iberian and Latin American Thought (EA)
SILAT	Subionospheric Latitude

SILC	Sheep Industry Liaison Committee [New South Wales, Australia]
SILC	Silicon Ltd. [NASDAQ symbol] (SAG)
SILCA	Sindacato Italiano Lavoratori Cappellai ed Affini [Italian Federation of Hat and Allied Workers]
SILCF	Silicon Ltd [NASDAQ symbol] (TTSB)
SilcLtd	Silicon Ltd. [Associated Press] (SAG)
SiICLV	Silicon Liquid Crystal Light Valve [NASA]
SilcnGph	Silicon Graphics [Associated Press] (SAG)
Sil (Ct of Ap)	Silvernail's New York Court of Appeals Reports [A publication] (DLA)
SILF	Societe Internationale de Linguistique Fonctionelle [International Society of Functional Linguistics] (EAIO)
SILG	Silencing (MSA)
SILI	Siliconix, Inc. [NASDAQ symbol] (NQ)
SILI	Sindacato Nazionale Lavoratori Italcable [National Union of Cable Workers] [Italy]
SILI	Standard Item Location Index
SILICA	System for International Literature Information on Ceramics and Glass [Fachinformationszentrum Werkstoffe] [Database]
SilicnVl	Silicon Valley Group, Inc. [Associated Press] (SAG)
Silicnx	Siliconix, Inc. [Associated Press] (SAG)
SiliconS	Silicon Storage Technology, Inc. [Associated Press] (SAG)
SilicVly	Silicon Valley Bancshares [Associated Press] (SAG)
SiliValR	Silicon Valley Research, Inc. [Associated Press] (SAG)
SILJ	Survey of Inmates of Local Jails [Department of Justice] (GFGA)
SILK	Single Income, Lots of Kids
Sill Comp	Sill on Composition in Bankruptcy [A publication] (DLA)
SilLtd	Silicon Ltd. [Associated Press] (SAG)
SILM	Single In-Line Module [Computer science]
SILMOD	Silhouette Model [Military] (INF)
SILO	Schools Industry Liaison Officer (AIE)
SILO	Security Intelligence Liaison Office [Central Mediterranean Forces] [Navy]
SILON	Subionospheric Longitude
SILP	Saskatchewan International Labour Program [Canada] (CROSS)
SILP	Section of International Law and Practice (EA)
SILP	Sindacato Italiano Lavoratori del Petrolio [Italian Union of Oil Workers]
SILP	Sindacato Italiano Lavoratori Postelegrafonici [Italian Union of Postal and Telegraph Workers]
SILP	Solomon Islands Liberal Party [Political party] (EY)
SILPT	Silhouette Print (VRA)
SiLPTG	Silverplating
SILPWS	Sheet Iron and Light Plate Workers' Society [A union] [British]
SILS	Shipboard Impact Locator System
SILS	Shipley-Institute of Living Scale for Measuring Intellectual Impairment [Psychology]
SILSP	Silver Solder
SILSP	Safeguard Integrated Logistics Support Plan [Army] (AABC)
Sil (Sup Ct)	Silvernail's New York Supreme Court Reports [A publication] (DLA)
SILT	Stored Information Loss Tree
SILTF	System Integration Laboratory and Test Facility
SILTS	Shuttle Infrared Leeside Temperature Sensing [NASA] (NASA)
Silv	Silvae [of Statius] [Classical studies] (OCD)
SILV	Silver (ROG)
Silv	Silvernail's New York Criminal Reports [9-14 New York] [A publication] (DLA)
Silv	Silvernail's New York Reports [1886-92] [A publication] (DLA)
Silv	Silvernail's New York Supreme Court Reports [1889-90] [A publication] (DLA)
SILV	Sunshine Mining & Refining Co. [NASDAQ symbol] (SAG)
Silv A	Silvernail's New York Court of Appeals Reports [A publication] (DLA)
Silv App	Silvernail's New York Court of Appeals Reports [A publication] (DLA)
Silv Cit	Silvernail's New York Citations [A publication] (DLA)
Silv Ct App	Silvernail's New York Court of Appeals Reports [A publication] (DLA)
Silv Ct App (NY)	Silvernail's New York Court of Appeals Reports [A publication] (DLA)
Silve	Silvester Godinho [Deceased, 1244] [Authority cited in pre-1607 legal work] (DSA)
SilverFds	Silverado Foods, Inc. [Associated Press] (SAG)
Silvernail's NY Rep	Silvernail's New York Court of Appeals Reports [A publication] (DLA)
SILVIC	Silviculture
Silvr	Silvester Godinho [Deceased, 1244] [Authority cited in pre-1607 legal work] (DSA)
Silv Sup	Silvernail's New York Supreme Court Reports [A publication] (DLA)
Silv (Sup Ct)	Silvernail's New York Supreme Court Reports [A publication] (DLA)
SILVTR	Silent Videotape Recording (DOAD)
Silv Unrep	Silvernail's New York Unreported Cases [A publication] (DLA)
SILVW	Sunshine Mng & Refining Wrrt [NASDAQ symbol] (TTSB)
SILWR	Silverware
SILZ	Silicon Ltd. [NASDAQ symbol] (SAG)
SILZF	Silicon Ltd Wrrt [NASDAQ symbol] (TTSB)
SIM	Grupo Simec [AMEX symbol] (SPSG)
SIM	Grupo Simec ADS [AMEX symbol] (TTSB)
SIM	Missionaries of the Kingship of Christ (TOCD)
SIM	SACLANT [Supreme Allied Commander, Atlantic] Staff Instruction Manual (NATG)
SIM	SAM [Surface-to-Air Missile] Intercept Missile (DNAB)
SIM	Scanning Ion Microscope
SIM	Schedule of Implementation Procedures [FAA] (TAG)
SIM	School of Industrial Management [MIT] (MCD)
sim	Scientific Instrumentation Module [NASA] (NAKS)
SIM	Scientific Instrument Module [NASA]
SIM	Sclerite-Inducing Membrane [Entomology]

SIM.............. Selected Inventory Management [*Military*] (CAAL)
SIM.............. Selected Ion Monitoring [*Chromatography*]
SIM.............. Selected Item Management
SIM.............. Sequential Inference Machine [*Computer science*]
SIM.............. Sergeant Instructor of Musketry
SIM.............. Service Instructions Message [*Telecommunications*] (TEL)
SIM.............. Service International de Microfilm, Paris, France [*Library symbol Library of Congress*] (LCLS)
SIM.............. Servicio Intelligencia Militar [*Military Intelligence Service*] [*Dominican Republic*]
SIM.............. Servizio Informazioni Militaro [*Military Intelligence Service*] [*Italy*]
SIM.............. Set Interrupt Mask [*Computer science*]
SIM.............. Shima Resources [*Vancouver Stock Exchange symbol*]
SIM.............. Ship Instrumentation Manager (KSC)
SIM.............. Simbai [*Papua New Guinea*] [*Airport symbol*] (OAG)
SIM.............. Simferopol [*Former USSR Seismograph station code, US Geological Survey*] (SEIS)
SIM.............. Similar (AAG)
SIM.............. Simile [*In a Similar Manner*] [*Music*]
sim.............. Simile (WDMC)
Sim.............. Simmons' Reports [*95-97, 99 Wisconsin*] [*A publication*] (DLA)
Sim.............. Simons' English Chancery Reports [*57-60 English Reprint*] [*1826-50*] [*A publication*] (DLA)
SIM.............. Simplex
SIM.............. Simposio Internacional de Macromoleculas [*International Symposium on Macromoleculas*]
SIM.............. Simulated [*or Simulation*] (AABC)
sim.............. Simulated (VRA)
SIM.............. Simulated Approach [*Aviation*] (FAAC)
SIM.............. Simulated Flight Training Ltd. [*British ICAO designator*] (FAAC)
SIM.............. Simulation (IAA)
sim.............. Simulation (NAKS)
SIM.............. Simulator [*Computer science*]
SIM.............. Single Interface Module [*Telecommunications*] (ITD)
SIM.............. Single Rotation Machine (IAA)
SIM.............. Small Intestine Metaplasia [*Medicine*]
SIM.............. Societa di Intermediazione Mobiliare [*Finance Italy*] (ECON)
SIM.............. Societa Italiana di Metapsichica [*Italy*]
SIM.............. Societe Internationale de la Moselle [*International Moselle Co.*]
SIM.............. Societe Internationale de Musicologie [*International Musicological Society*]
SIM.............. Society for Industrial Microbiology (EA)
SIM.............. Society for Information Management [*Chicago, IL*] (EA)
SIM.............. Solar Interplanetary Model
SIM.............. Somali Islamic Movement [*Political party*]
SIM.............. Space Interceptor Missile (MCD)
SIM.............. Spatial Information Management
SIM.............. Specific Ion Monitoring (DB)
SIM.............. Stage Inert Mass
SIM.............. Standard Injection Method [*Laboratory science*]
SIM.............. Steatite Insulation Material
SIM.............. Stellar Image Monitor
SIM.............. Structural Integrity Monitoring (MCD)
SIM.............. Student Interracial Ministry [*Defunct*]
SIM.............. Submarine Intended Movement (NVT)
SIM.............. Subsystem Interface Module
SIM.............. Subtotal Integration Mode
SIM.............. Sucrose-Isomaltose Deficiency [*Medicine*]
SIM.............. Sudan Interior Mission
SIM.............. Sulfide Production, Indole Production, and Motility [*Growth medium*]
SIM.............. Surveillance Intelligence and Reconnaissance Mission [*Military*] (CAAL)
SIM.............. Symbolic Integrated Maintenance (IAA)
SIM.............. Synchronous Interface Module
SIM.............. Systems Integration Model (MCD)
SIMA.............. Salon International de la Machine Agricole
SIMA.............. Scientific Instrument Manufacturers' Association [*British*]
SIMA.............. Ships Intermediate Maintenance Activity (DOMA)
SIMA.............. Shore Intermediate Maintenance Activity [*Navy*] (NVT)
SIMA.............. Single Internal Mammary Artery [*Medicine*] (DMAA)
SIMA.............. Sonics & Materials [*NASDAQ symbol*] (TTSB)
SIMA.............. Sonics & Materials, Inc. [*NASDAQ symbol*] (SAG)
SIMA.............. Stanford Integrated Manufacturing Association [*Stanford University*] [*Research center*] (RCD)
SIMA.............. Steel Industry Management Association [*Trade union*] [*British*]
SIMAC.............. Sonic Instrument Measurement and Control (AAG)
SIMAJ.............. Scientific Instrument Manufacturers' Association of Japan
SIMAL.............. Simplified Accountancy Language (PDAA)
SIMAL.............. Simulated All-Purpose Language (PDAA)
Sim & C ...... Simmons and Conover's Reports [*99-100 Wisconsin*] [*A publication*] (DLA)
Sim & S ...... Simons and Stuart's English Chancery Reports [*57 English Reprint*] [*A publication*] (DLA)
Sim & St .... Simons and Stuart's English Chancery Reports [*57 English Reprint*] [*A publication*] (DLA)
Sim & Stu .... Simons and Stuart's English Vice-Chancery Reports [*57 English Reprint*] [*A publication*] (DLA)
Sim & Stu (Eng)... Simons and Stuart's English Chancery Reports [*57 English Reprint*] [*A publication*] (DLA)
SIMANNE.... Simulation of Analogical Network (IAA)
SIMAP .... Satellite Image Mapping
SIMAS .... Shuttle Information Management Accountability System [*NASA*] (NASA)
SIMAS .... SONAR In-Situ Mode Assessment System (MSC)
SIMATS........ Supplementary Interim Medium Antitank System [*Army*] (INF)

SIMAW .... Sonics & Materials Wrrt [*NASDAQ symbol*] (TTSB)
SIMBAD ...... Simulation as a Basis for Social Agents' Decisions [*Computer science*]
SIMBAY ...... Scientific Instrumentation Module Bay [*NASA*] (KSC)
SIMBOL ...... Simulated Boolean-Oriented Language (IAA)
SIMC .... Silicon Integrated Monolithic Circuit
SIMC .... Societe Internationale de Medecine Cybernetique [*International Society of Cybernetic Medicine*]
SIMC .... Societe Internationale de Medecine de Catastrophe [*International Society for Disaster Medicine - ISDM*] [*Switzerland*] (EA)
SIMC .... Societe Internationale pour la Musique Contemporaine [*International Society for Contemporary Music*]
SIMC .... Spacetec IMC [*NASDAQ symbol*] (TTSB)
SIMC .... Spacetec IMC Corp. [*NASDAQ symbol*] (SAG)
SIMC .... Syndicat International des Marins Canadiens [*Seafarers' International Union of Canada - SIU*]
SIMCA .... Simple Modelling of Class Analogy [*Data analysis*] [*Computer science*]
SIMCA .... Societe Industrielle de Mecanique et de Carrosserie Automobile [*French automobile manufacturer; acronym used as name of its cars*]
SIMCA .... Soft Independent Modeling of Class Analogy [*Analytical chemistry technique*]
SIMCA .... Statistical Isolinear MultiCategory Analysis [*Data analysis*] [*Computer science*]
SIMCANSOC... Simulated Canadian Society [*Simulation game*]
SIMCAP ...... Simulation, Corps Automated Procedures (MCD)
SIMCE .... Simulation Communications Electronics [*Group of computer programs*] [*Army*]
SIMCEN ...... Simulation Center [*Deep Space Network, NASA*]
SIMCERT .... Simulator Certification
SIMCHE ...... Simulation and Checkout Equipment [*NASA*] (KSC)
SIMCO .... Sea Ice Microbial Colony
SIMCOM ...... Simulation and Computer [*Computer science*]
SIMCOM ...... Simulation Complex (NASA)
SIMCOM ...... Simulator Compiler [*Computer*]
SIMCON ...... Scientific Inventory Management and Control
SIMCON ...... Simplified Control
SIMCON ...... Simulation Controller
Sim Ct M .... Simmons on Courts-Martial [*A publication*] (DLA)
SIMD .... Single Input Multiple Data Stream (IAA)
SIMD .... Single Instruction, Multiple Data (IEEE)
SIMD .... Single Instruction Multiple Data Stream (NITA)
SIMDEP ...... Simulation Development Program [*DASA*]
Sim Des Pat... Simonds' Law of Design Patents [*A publication*] (DLA)
Sim Dig ...... Simmons' Wisconsin Digest [*A publication*] (DLA)
Sim Dig Pat Dec... Simonds' Digest of Patent Office Decisions [*United States*] [*A publication*] (DLA)
SIMDS .... Single Instruction Multiple Data Stream (IAA)
SIME .... Security Intelligence, Middle East [*Navy*]
Sim Elect.... Simeon on Elections [*A publication*] (DLA)
Sim (Eng).... Simons' English Chancery Reports [*57-60 English Reprint*] [*A publication*] (DLA)
Simes & S Future Interests... Simes and Smith on the Law of Future Interests [*A publication*] (DLA)
SIMEX........ Secondary Item Materiel Excess [*DoD*]
SIMEX........ Singapore International Metals Exchange
SIMEX........ Singapore International Monetary Exchange (WDAA)
SIMEX........ Singapore Monetary Exchange (ECON)
SIMFAC........ Simulation Facility [*NASA*]
SIMFAR ...... Simulated Frequency Analysis and Recording (MCD)
SIMFIRE ...... Simulated Fire
SIMFIRE ...... Simulated Mission Firing
SIMG .... Societas Internationalis Medicinae Generalis [*International Society of General Practice*] [*Klagenfurt, Austria*] (EAIO)
SIMGCA ...... Similarity Graft Clustering Analysis [*Plant phylogeny*]
SIMGEN ...... Simulation Generating System (MHDI)
SIMHA .... Societe Internationale de Mycologie Humaine et Animale [*International Society for Human and Animal Mycology - ISHAM*] [*British*] (EA)
SIMI .... Sea Ice Mechanics Initiative [*Marine science*] (OSRA)
SIMICOR...... Simultaneous Multiple Image Correlation
SIMILE........ Simulator of Immediate Memory in Learning Experiments
Sim Int ...... Simons' Law of Interpleader [*A publication*] (DLA)
SIMIS........ SAIC [*Science Applications International Corp.*] Integrated Management Information System (MCD)
Simkin .... Simulation Kinetics [*Analysis*] [*Toxicology*] (DAVI)
SIML........ Similar (AAG)
SIML........ Simulation Language [*Computer science*] (MHDI)
Simla........ All India Reporter, Simla [*1951*] [*A publication*] (DLA)
SIMLR........ Similar (ROG)
SIMM........ Simmons Outdoor Corp. [*Chicago, IL NASDAQ symbol*] (NQ)
SIMM........ Single In-Line Memory Module [*Computer science*]
SIMM........ Symbolic Integrated Maintenance Manual (MCD)
SIMMOD...... Airport and Airspace Simulation Model [*FAA*] (TAG)
Simmons C.... Simmons College (GAGS)
SIM M-R.... Simulation Monitor-Recorder (SAA)
SIMMS........ Single Inline Computer Memory Modules (COE)
SIMN........ Simon Transportation Services, Inc. [*NASDAQ symbol*] (SAG)
SIMN........ Simon Transportation Svcs'A' [*NASDAQ symbol*] (TTSB)
SimnD .... Simon DeBartolo Group, Inc. [*Associated Press*] (SAG)
SIMNET...... Simulation Network
SIMNEX...... Simulation Net Executor (NITA)
SimnFt........ Simmons First National Corp. [*Associated Press*] (SAG)
SimnOut ...... Simmons Outdoor Corp. [*Associated Press*] (SAG)

Sim NS....... Simons' English Vice-Chancery Reports, New Series [*61 English Reprint*] [*A publication*] (DLA)
SIMNS......... Simulated Navigation Systems
Sim NS (Eng)... Simons' English Vice-Chancery Reports, New Series [*61 English Reprint*] [*A publication*] (DLA)
SIMO .... Simultaneously (NASA)
simo .... Simultaneously (NAKS)
SIMO .... Single Input, Multi Output (AAEL)
SIMO .... Special Items Management Office
SIMOBS........ Simultaneous Observations [*RADAR and optical*]
SIMOC .... Simulated Occupant [*People Machine*] [*Office of Civil Defense*]
SIMON .... Shell Inventory Managed Order Network
Simon.......... Simonides [*Fifth century BC*] [*Classical studies*] (OCD)
SIMON .... Software Implementation Monitor [*Computer science*] (MHDI)
SimonDeB .. Simon DeBartolo Group, Inc. [*Associated Press*] (SAG)
SimonPr ...... Simon Property [*Associated Press*] (SAG)
Simon's TC... Simon's Tax Cases [*United Kingdom*] [*A publication*] (DLA)
SimonT .... Simon Transportation Services, Inc. [*Associated Press*] (SAG)
SIMOP .... Simultaneous Operation
SIMOS .... Space Imbalanced Military Occupational Specialty
SIMOS .... Stacked Gate Injection Metal-Oxide Semiconductor [*Computer science*] (IAA)
SIMOX .... Separation by Implantation of Oxygen [*Semiconductor technology*]
SIMP............ Satellite Information Message Protocol
SIMP........... Satellite Interface Message Processor (IAA)
SIMP........... Schmele Instrument to Measure the Process of Nursing Care [*Medicine*] (DMAA)
SIMP .... Shipboard Integrated Maintenance Program [*Navy*] (NG)
simp .... Simple (DAVI)
SIMP........... Simpleton (DSUE)
simp .... Simplex (MAE)
SIMP........... Simulation Program (IAA)
Simp .... Single Income, Money Problems [*Lifestyle classification*]
SIMP........... Societa Italiana di Medicina Psicosomatica [*Italy*]
SIMP........... Specific Impulse (MSA)
SIMPAC ...... Simplified Programming for Acquisition and Control (IEEE)
SIMPAC ...... Simulation Package [*Computer science*]
SIMPARAG... Simultaneous Parallel Array Grammers (MHDI)
Sim Pat L ... Simond's Patent Law [*A publication*] (DLA)
SimpInd ...... Simpson Industries, Inc. [*Associated Press*] (SAG)
Simp Inf ...... Simpson on Infants [*4th ed.*] [*1926*] [*A publication*] (DLA)
SIMPL.......... Simulation Implementation Machine Programming Languages (KSC)
SIMPL/1....... Simulation Language Based on Programming Language, Version One
SIMPLAN .... Simple Modeling and Planning [*SIMPLAN Users Group*] [*New York, NY*] (CSR)
SIMPLAN .... Simplified Modeling and Planning [*Programming language*] [*1973*] (CSR)
SIMPLE....... Savings Incentive Match Plan for Employees [*Business term*]
SIMPLE....... Semi-Implicit Pressure-Linked Equation [*Algorithm*]
SIMPLE....... Simulation of Industrial Management Problems [*Program*] [*1958*] [*Computer science*] (CSR)
SIMPLE....... Solver for Implicit Equations [*Computer language*]
SIMPLE....... System for Integrated Maintenance and Program Language Extension
SIMPLER ..... System for Information Management and Program Logic for Education and Research (IAA)
SIMPO .... Simulation of Personnel Operations [*Army Research Institute for the Behavioral and Social Sciences*] (RDA)
SIMPP .... Simple Image-Processing Package (BYTE)
SIMPP .... Society of Independent Motion Picture Producers
SimpsnMf... Simpson Manufacturing Co., Inc. [*Associated Press*] (SAG)
SIMPU .... Simulation Punch
SIMR .... Schenley Instant Market Reports
SIMR .... Simulator (AAG)
SIMR .... Societe Internationale de Mecanique des Roches [*International Society for Rock Mechanics - ISRM*] (EAIO)
SIMR .... Systems Integration Management Review [*NASA*] (MCD)
SIMRAND .... Simulation of Research and Development
Sim Ry Acc... Simon's Law Relating to Railway Accidents [*1862*] [*A publication*] (DLA)
SIMS........... Schools Information Management System (AIE)
SIMS........... Secondary Ion Mass Spectrometry [*or Spectroscopy*]
SIMS........... Second International Mathematics Study
SIMS........... Sedna Information Management System [*Sedna Corp.*] [*Information service or system*] (IID)
SIMS........... Selected Item Management System [*Military*] (AABC)
SIMS........... Selective Interference Modulation Spectrometer
SIMS........... Services Information Management System [*DoD*] (GFGA)
SIMS........... Shuttle Imaging Microwave System [*NASA*] (NASA)
SIMS........... Shuttle Inventory Management System [*NASA*] (NASA)
SIMS........... SIAM [*Society for Industrial and Applied Mathematics*] Institute for Mathematics and Society
SIMS........... SIMS Communications [*NASDAQ symbol*] (TTSB)
SIMS........... Sims Communications, Inc. [*NASDAQ symbol*] (SAG)
SIMS........... Single Item, Multisource (IEEE)
SIMS........... Skandinaviska Simuleringssaellskapet [*Scandinavian Simulation Society*] [*Also, SSS*] (EA)
SIMS........... Societal Institute of the Mathematical Sciences [*Research center*] (RCD)
SIMS........... Socio-Economic Information Management System (NITA)
SIMS NS...... Stable Isotope Mass Spectrometer
SIMS........... Standards Information Management System (COE)
SIMS........... Station Infomation Management System [*Navy*] (DOMA)
SIMS......... Stellar Inertial Measurement System [*NASA*]

SIMS........... Strategic Integrated Management System [*American Occupational Therapy Association*]
SIMS........... Students' International Meditation Society
SIMS........... Supply Information Management System [*Air Force*] (GFGA)
SIMS........... Symbolic Integrated Maintenance System
SIMSA......... Savings Institutions Marketing Society of America
SimsC......... Sims Communications, Inc. [*Associated Press*] (SAG)
SimsCm....... Sims Communications, Inc. [*Associated Press*] (SAG)
SIMSCRIPT... Simulation High-Level Programming Language [*Computer science*] (BARN)
SIMSEP....... Simulation of Solar Electric Propulsion [*NASA*]
SIMSER....... Simple Serial (MHDI)
SIMSGA....... Sugar Industry Manufacturers and Service Group of Australia
SIMSHO ...... Simulation Scheduled Order (SSD)
SIMSI......... Selective Inventory Management of Secondary Items [*Navy*]
SIMSIN .... Simulated Strapdown Inertial Navigation (MCD)
SIMSLIN ..... Safety in Mines Scattered Light Instrument (ADA)
SIMSOC ...... Simulated Society
SIMSTF....... Societe Internationale de Mecanique des Sols et de Travaux de Fondations [*International Society for Soil Mechanics and Foundation Engineering - ISSMFE*]
SIMSU .... SIMS Communications Unit [*NASDAQ symbol*] (TTSB)
SIMSUP ...... Simulation Supervisor
SIMSW .... Sims Communications Wrrt'A' [*NASDAQ symbol*] (TTSB)
SIMS-X .... Selected Items Management System - Expanded (MCD)
SIMSYS ...... Simulated System (CAAL)
SIMSZ........ Sims Communications Wrrt'B' [*NASDAQ symbol*] (TTSB)
SIMTC......... Southwest Center for Manufacturing Technology [*University of New Mexico*] [*Research center*] (RCD)
SIMTOP ...... Silicon Nitride-Masked Thermally-Oxidized Post-Diffused Mesa Process (PDAA)
SIMTOS ...... Simulated Tactical Operations Systems [*Army*] (RDA)
SIMTRACC... Simulator Trainer Command and Control
SIMTS......... Scientific Instrument Makers Trade Society [*A union*] [*British*]
SIMU .... Simulated Inertial Measurement Unit (NASA)
simu .... Simulated Inertial Measurement Unit (NAKS)
SIMU .... Stellar Inertial Measuring Unit (IAA)
SIMU .... Suspended from Issue, Movement, and Use [*Army*] (ADDR)
SIMUL .... Simultaneous (AABC)
Simula .... Simula, Inc. [*Associated Press*] (SAG)
SIMULA ...... Simulation Language [*1964*] [*Computer science*]
SIMUPOL..... Simulative Procedure Oriented Language (MCD)
SIMV .... Synchronized Intermittent Mandatory Ventilation [*Medicine*] (DAVI)
SIMWF .... Simware, Inc. [*NASDAQ symbol*] (SAG)
SIN............. Salpingitis Isthmica Nodosum
SIN............. Security Information Network
SIN............. Sensitive Information Network
SIN............. Simultaneous Interpenetrating Networks [*Organic chemistry*]
SIN............. Sinagawa [*Japan*] [*Seismograph station code, US Geological Survey Closed*] (SEIS)
SIN............. Sinair [*France ICAO designator*] (FAAC)
SIN............. Sinclair Community College, Dayton, OH [*OCLC symbol*] (OCLC)
SIN............. Sine [*Without*] [*Latin*]
SIN............. Sine [*Mathematics*]
sin .... Sine (IDOE)
SIN............. Sinecure (ROG)
Sin.:........... Sinemurian [*Geology*]
SIN............. Singapore [*Airport symbol*] (OAG)
SIN............. Single Identifying Number
SIN............. Sinistra [*Left Hand*] [*Music*]
Sin............. Sinter [*Record label*] [*Brazil*]
SIN............. Social Insurance Number [*Canada*]
SIN............. Society for International Numismatics (EA)
SIN............. Sonically-Induced Narrowing [*Physics*]
SIN............. [*The*] Spanish Information Network [*Later, Spanish International Network*] [*Cable- television system*] (WDMC)
SIN............. Spanish International Network [*Cable-television system*]
SIN............. Special Item Number (AAGC)
SIN............. Squamous Intraepithelial Neoplastic [*Oncology*]
SIN............. Stop Inflation Now [*Variation on the anti-inflation WIN slogan of President Gerald Ford*]
SIN............. Study Item Number [*Army*] (AABC)
S IN .... Sub Initio [*At the Beginning*] [*Latin*] (ROG)
SIN............. Subject Indication Number
SIN............. Support Information Network
SIN............. Swedish Ionosonde Network
SIN............. Symbolic Integrator [*Computer science*] (CIST)
SIN............. Syngold Exploration, Inc. [*Toronto Stock Exchange symbol*]
SINA .... Scheduling Information Not Available (KSC)
SINA .... Shellfish Institute of North America [*Also known as Oyster Growers and Dealers Association of North America*] (EA)
SINA .... Society for Indecency to Naked Animals [*A hoax association*]
SINA .... Sports Injury Nurses Association [*Australia*]
SINACMA..... Sindacato Nazionale Dipendenti Corte dei Conti e Magistrature Amministrare [*National Union of General Accounting Office Employees*] [*Italy*]
SINAD......... Signal Plus Noise and Distortion
SINAD......... Signal-to-Noise Ratio and Distortion (IAA)
SINADIMID... Sindacato Nazionale Dipendenti Ministero Difesa [*National Union of Ministry of Defense Employees*] [*Italy*]
SINAF .... Sindacato Nazionale Dipendenti Ministero Agricoltura e Foreste [*National Union of Ministry of Agriculture and Forestry Employees*] [*Italy*]
SINAMAI..... Sindacato Nazionale e Dipendenti Ministero Africa Italiana [*National Union of Former Italian Employees of African Ministry*] [*Italy*]

SINAMIL ...... Sindacato Nazionale Dipendenti Ministero del Lavoro e Previdenza Sociale [*National Union of Ministry of Labor and Social Security Employees*] [*Italy*]
SINAMN .... Sindacato Nazionale Dipendenti Marina Mercantile [*National Union of Merchant Marine Workers*] [*Italy*]
SINAP .... Satellite Input to Numerical Analysis and Prediction [*National Weather Service*]
SINAP .... Sinapis [*Mustard*] [*Pharmacology*] (ROG)
SINAPI .... Sindacato Nazionale Ministero Pubblica Istruzione [*National Union of Ministry of Public Instructors*] [*Italy*]
SINASCEL .... Sindacato Nazionale Scuola Elementare [*National Union of Elementary School Teachers*] [*Italy*]
SINB .... Southern Interstate Nuclear Board
SINC .... Nicaraguan International Rescue from Communism (PD)
SinC .... Sisters in Crime [*An association*]
S in C .... Surgeon-in-Chief (WDAA)
SINCGARS ... Single-Channel Ground and Airborne Radio System [*or Subsystem*] (MCD)
SINCGARS-V... Single-Channel Ground and Airborne Radio System, Very High Frequency
Sinclair .... Sinclair Broadcast Group, Inc. [*Associated Press*] (SAG)
Sinclair .... Sinclair's Manuscript Decisions, Scotch Session Cases [*A publication*] (DLA)
SINCOE .... Sindacato Nazionale Dipendenti Ministero Industria e Commercio Estero [*National Union of Ministry of Industry and Foreign Commerce Employees*] [*Italy*]
SINCTRAC ... Single Channel Tactical Radio Communications [*Army*] (RDA)
Sind .... All India Reporter, Sind [*1914-50*] [*A publication*] (DLA)
Sind .... Indian Rulings, Sind Series [*A publication*] (DLA)
SIND .... Satellite Inertial Navigation Determination (MCD)
SIND .... Southern Indiana Railway, Inc. [*AAR code*]
SIND .... Strobe Intersection Deghoster
SINDA .... Systems Improved Numerical Differencing Analyses [*Database*]
SINDAF .... Sindacato Nazionale Dipendenti Amministrazioni Finanziarie [*National Union of Financial Administration Employees*] [*Italy*]
SINE .... Short Interspersed Nucleotide Element [*Genetics*]
sine .... Sinusoidal [*Otorhinolaryngology*] (DAVI)
SINES .... Short Interspaced Repeated Segments [*of Deoxyribonucleic Acid*] [*Genetics*] (DAVI)
SIN-ETH ...... Swiss Institute of Nuclear Research - Eidgenoessische Technische Hochschule
SINEWS .... Ship Integrated Electronic Warfare System
SINF .... Sinfonia [*Symphony*] [*Music*]
SINFDOK ..... Statens Rad for Vetenskaplig Information och Dokumentation [*Swedish Council for Scientific Information and Documentation*] (IID)
SINFX .... Seligman Income Cl.A [*Mutual fund ticker symbol*] (SG)
SING .... Singapore
SING .... Singing Machine Company, Inc. [*NASDAQ symbol*] (SAG)
SING .... Singular
sing .... Singular (WDMC)
SING .... Singulorum [*Of Each*] [*Pharmacy*]
SINGAN .... Singularity Analyzer [*Computer science*]
Singap .... Singapore Fund [*Associated Press*] (SAG)
Singer .... Singer Co. NV [*Associated Press*] (SAG)
Singer Prob Cas (PA)... Singer's Probate Cases [*Pennsylvania*] [*A publication*] (DLA)
Singers .... Singer's Probate Court [*Pennsylvania*] [*A publication*] (DLA)
Singing .... Singing Machine Co., Inc. [*Associated Press*] (SAG)
SingM .... Singing Machine Co., Inc. [*Associated Press*] (SAG)
SINGR .... Singular
SINH .... Sine, Hyperbolic
Sinh .... Sinhalese [*Language*] (BARN)
SINIE .... Sistema Nacional de Informacion Documental en Educacion [*National System of Documentary Information on Education*] [*Information service or system*] (IID)
SINIST .... Sinister [*Left*] [*Latin*]
Sink .... Single Income, No Kids [*Lifestyle classification*]
SIno .... Thioinosine [*Also, Sno, M*] [*A nucleoside*]
Si Non Val ... Si Non Valeat [*If It Is Not Effective*] [*Pharmacy*]
SINPO .... Strength, Interference, Noise, Propagation, and Overall Merit Code [*Signal reception quality rating*] (NTCM)
SINR .... Shoulder Internal Rotation [*Sports medicine*]
SINR .... Signal to Interference plus Noise Ratio (MCD)
SINR .... Swiss Institute for Nuclear Research
SINS .... Satellite Interceptor Navigation System [*Navy*] (CAAL)
SINS .... Ship Inertial Navigational System
SINS .... Ship's Inertial Marine Navigational System (IAA)
SINS .... Ship's Inertial Navigation System
SINS .... Sindacato Scuola non Statale [*Union of Private Schools' Employees*] [*Italy*]
SINS .... Stellar Inertial Navigation System (IAA)
SINS .... Submarine Inertial Navigation System (IAA)
SInstBB .... Student of the Institute of British Bakers (DBQ)
SInstPet ...... Student of the Institute of Petroleum [*British*] (DBQ)
SINSW .... Security Institute of New South Wales [*Australia*]
S INT .... Senza Interruzione [*Without Interruption or Pause*] [*Music*]
S INTER .... Senza Interruzione [*Without Interruption or Pause*] [*Music*] (ROG)
SinterMtl ...... Sinter Metals Co. [*Associated Press*] (SAG)
SINTO .... Sheffield Interchange Organization (NITA)
SI N VAL ...... Si Non Valeat [*If It Is Not Effective*] [*Pharmacy*] (ROG)
SIO .... Sacroiliac Orthosis [*Medicine*]
SIO .... Satellite in Orbit (WDAA)
SIO .... Scripps Institution of Oceanography [*La Jolla, CA*] [*Research center*]
SIO .... Senior Information Officer (DCTA)

SIO .... Senior Instructor Operator [*Military*] (INF)
SIO .... Senior Intelligence Officer (MCD)
SIO .... Serial Input/Output (MCD)
sio .... Serial Input/Output (NAKS)
SIO .... Ship's Information Officer [*Navy*]
SIO .... Simultaneous Interface Operation [*Printer technology*] [*Computer science*] (PCM)
SIO .... Sindacato Italiano Ostetriche [*Italian Union of Midwives*]
sio .... Siouan [*MARC language code Library of Congress*] (LCCP)
SIO .... Skidway Institute of Oceanography [*Georgia*] (NOAA)
SIO .... Smithton [*Australia Airport symbol*] (OAG)
SIO .... Smithtown [*Tasmania*] [*Airport symbol*] (AD)
SIO .... Sorting It Out [*An association Defunct*] (EA)
SIO .... Southern Union Resources [*Vancouver Stock Exchange symbol*]
SIO .... Special Inquiry Officer
SIO .... Special Intelligence Officer [*Military*] (NVT)
SIO .... Staged in Orbit
SIO .... Standard Input/Output (MCD)
SIO .... Start Input/Output
SIO .... Step Input/Output (NITA)
sio .... Systems Integration Office (NAKS)
SIO .... Systems Integration Office [*NASA*] (NASA)
SIOA .... Surface Induced Optical Anisotropy (AAEL)
SIOA .... System Input/Output Adapter (CAAL)
SIOATH .... Source Identification and Ordering Authorization [*DoD*]
SIOC .... Serial Input/Output Channel
SIOD .... Sindacato Italiano Odonototecnici Diplomati [*Italian Union of Odontotechnicians*]
SIOE .... Special Issue of Equipment
SIO/EIA .... Ship Intelligence Officer/Enlisted Intel Assistant (DOMA)
SIOFC .... Sparks International Official Fan Club (EA)
SIOG .... Societe Internationale d'Ophtalmologie Geographique [*International Society of Geographic Opthalmology*] (EAIO)
SIOH .... Supervision, Inspection, and Overhead (AFM)
SIOMS .... Surface Ionization Organic Mass Spectrometry
SIOP .... Secure Identification Operating Procedure
SIOP .... Selector Input/Output Processor [*Computer science*] (IEEE)
SIOP .... Single Integrated Operational [*or Operations*] Plan [*Military*] (AFM)
SIOP .... Societe Internationale d'Oncologie Pediatrique [*International Society of Pediatric Oncology*] [*Leeds, England*] (EAIO)
SIOP .... Strategic Integrated Operational Plan [*Nuclear warfare*]
SIOP-ESI ..... Single Integrated Operational Plan - Extremely Sensitive Information [*Security level above Top Secret*]
SI OP SIT ..... Si Opus Sit [*If There Be Occasion*] [*Pharmacy*] (ROG)
SIOR .... Society of Industrial and Office Realtors (EA)
SIOS .... Spectrophotometer Input-Output System
SIOSA .... Sicula Oceanicas SA [*Shipping line*] [*Italy*] (EY)
SIOUX .... Sequential and Iterative Operation Unit X (IEEE)
SIOV .... Siemens Metal Oxide Varistor (IAA)
SIP .... Air Spirit, Inc. [*ICAO designator*] (FAAC)
SIP .... Safety Injection Pump (IEEE)
SIP .... Safety Instrumentation Package (MCD)
SIP .... SAGE [*Semiautomatic Ground Environment*] Improvement Program (IAA)
SIP .... Sample Item Portion
SIP .... Sampling Inspection Procedures
SIP .... Saskatchewan Institute of Pedology [*University of Saskatchewan*] [*Research center*] (RCD)
SIP .... Satellite Information Processor
SIP .... Satellite Inspector Program (AAG)
SIP .... Satellite Interceptor Program (IAA)
SIP .... SCANS [*Scheduling and Control by Automated Network Systems*] ImplementationPlan (SAA)
SIP .... Schedule-Induced Polydipsia [*Psychology*]
SIP .... Schedule of Investment Projects
SIP .... Scientific Information [*or Instruction*] Processor [*Honeywell, Inc.*]
SIP .... Scientific Instrument Package [*NASA*] (KSC)
SIP .... Sea Ice Penetrometer (PDAA)
SIP .... Seat Index Point [*Automotive design*]
SIP .... Securities Investor Protection Corp.
SIP .... Segment Inertial Properties (STED)
SIP .... Selma [*Alabama*] Interreligious Project (EA)
SIP .... Senior Intensified Program [*Education*]
SIP .... Separation Instrument Package [*NASA*] (MCD)
SIP .... Sharebuilder Investment Plan [*Banking*]
SIP .... Sheet Metal Insert Process
SIP .... Shinkiari [*Pakistan*] [*Seismograph station code, US Geological Survey*] (SEIS)
SIP .... Ship Improvement Program
SIP .... Ship in Production
SIP .... Short Interval Plan [*Management principles*]
SIP .... Short Irregular Pulses
SIP .... Sickness Impact Profile [*National Institutes of Health*]
SIP .... Side Impact Protection [*Automotive safety system*] (PS)
SIP .... Silicon-on-Insulator and Polysilicon (PDAA)
SIP .... Simferopol [*Former USSR Airport symbol*] (OAG)
SIP .... Simple Internet Protocol (TNIG)
SIP .... Simulated Input Processor [*Computer science*]
SIP .... Sindacato Italiano Pescatori [*Italian Union of Fishermen*]
SIP .... Single In-Line Package [*Computer science*]
SIP .... Single In-Line PIN [*Computer science*] (PCM)
SIP .... Single In-Line Plastic (IAA)
SIP .... Sipald Resources [*Vancouver Stock Exchange symbol*]
SIP .... Skill Improvement Program [*Bureau of Apprenticeship and Training*] [*Department of Labor*]

SIP	Slow Inhibitory Potential [Electrophysiology]
SIP	Small Interplanetary Probes (SAA)
SIP	Smithsonian Institution Press [Publisher]
SIP	Sociedad Interamericana de Prensa [Inter-American Press Association]
SIP	Sociedad Interamericana de Psicologia [Interamerican Society of Psychology] (EAIO)
SIP	Societa Italiana per l'Esercizio Telefonico [Italian Society for Telephone Use] [Information service or system] (IID)
SIP	Society for Invertebrate Pathology (EA)
SIP	Society of Independent Producers (NTCM)
SIP	Society of Indiana Pioneers (EA)
SIP	Society of Israel Philatelists (EA)
SIP	Sodium Iron Pyrophosphate
SIP	Software in Print [Technique Learning] [Information service or system] (IID)
SIP	Software Instrumentation Package [Sperry UNIVAC] [Computer science]
SIP	Solar and Interplanetary Programme [International Council of Scientific Unions]
SIP	Solar Instrument Probe (MUGU)
SIP	SONAR Instrumentation Probe (IAA)
SIP	SPALT [Special Projects Alterations] Improvement Program
SIP	Special Impact Program (OICC)
SIP	Standard Initial Provisioning System (MCD)
SIP	Standard Inspection Procedure [Military]
SIP	Standard Interest Profile
SIP	Standardization Instructor Pilot [Military] (AABC)
SIP	State Implementation Plan [Environmental Protection Agency]
SIP	Station Independence Program [Public television project] (NTCM)
SIP	Steam-In-Place [Sterilization process]
SIP	Step in Place
SIP	Stewardship Incentive Program [Forestry]
SIP	Strain Isolator Pad [Aerospace]
SIP	Strategic Information Plan (SSD)
SIP	Strongly Implicit Procedure
SIP	Structural Insulated Panel
SIP	Student Insurance Producers Association (EA)
SIP	Studies in Process [Jet Propulsion Laboratory, NASA]
SIP	Submerged Injection Process [Steelmaking]
SIP	Supermolecular Information Processor
SIP	Supersonic Infantry Projectile
SIP	Supplemental Income Plan
SIP	Supply Improvement Program
SIP	Support for Innovation Project (AIE)
SIP	Surface Impulsion Propulsion (PDAA)
SIP	Surface Inductive Plethysmography (STED)
SIP	Svensk-Internationella Pressbyran [Swedish-International Press Bureau] (EY)
SIP	Symbolic Input Program [Computer science] (BUR)
SIP	System Improvement Plan (INF)
SIP	System Initialize Program (IAA)
SIP	Systems Implementation Plan [Military]
SIPA	Secondary Item Procurement Appropriation [Army]
SIPA	Securities Investor Protection Act [1970]
SIPA	Silicon Valley Indian Professionals Association (DDC)
SIPA	Structural Insulated Panel Association (NTPA)
SIPA	Systems Information Processing Analysis (EDAC)
SIPAMA	Servico de Inspecao dos Produtos Agropecuarios e Materiais Agricolas [Brazil]
SIPB	Safety Injection Permissive Block (IEEE)
SIPC	Securities Investor Protection Corp. [Government insurance agency for brok erage accounts] [Pronounced "sipic"]
SIPC	Securities Investor Protection Corporation (EBF)
SIPC	Simply Interactive PC (PCM)
SIPC	Stationing and Installations Planning Committee [Military]
SIPCO	Signal Processor Checkout (CAAL)
SIPD	Supply Item Provisioning Document [Navy] (NG)
SIPDE	Sensing, Identifying, Predicting, Deciding, and Executing
SIPE	Scientific Information Program on Eutrophication [University of Wisconsin]
SIPE	Societe Internationale de Psychopathologie de l'Expression [International Society of Art and Psychopathology]
SIPE	Soldier Integrated Protective Ensemble [Army]
SIPE	System Internal Performance Evaluator (IAA)
SIPES	Society of Independent Professional Earth Scientists (EA)
SipexCp	Sipex Corp. [Associated Press] (SAG)
SIPG	Societe Internationale de Pathologie Geographique [International Society of Geographical Pathology] [Australia] (EAIO)
SIPG	Special Intercept Priorities Group [Armed Forces Security Agency]
SIPI	Scientists' Institute for Public Information (EA)
SIPI	Short Imaginal Process Inventory [Personality development test] [Psychology]
SIPI	Sisterhood Is Powerful Institute (EA)
SIPI	Southwestern Indian Polytechnic Institute [New Mexico]
SIPI	Supervisory Immigration Patrol Inspector [Immigration and Naturalization Service]
SIPL	Seeley's Illustrated Pocket Library [A publication]
SIPLA	Student Intellectual Property Law Association (AAGC)
SIPM	Star Identification Program, Mariner [NASA]
SIPMOS	Single In-Line Package Metal-Oxide Semiconductor (CIST)
SIPN	Semi-Interpenetrating Polymer Network [Organic chemistry]
SIPO	Serial-In, Parallel-Out [Telecommunications] (TEL)
SIPO	Sicherheitspolizei [Security Police] [NAZI] (BJA)
SIPO	Spacecraft Integration Project Office

SIPO	Swiss Intellectual Property Office [Bern] [Information service or system] (IID)
SIPOA	Servico de Inspecao de Produtos de Origem Animal [Brazil]
SIPOP	Satellite Information Processor Operational Program (AFM)
SIPOS	Semi-Insulating Polycrystalline Silicon [Photovoltaic energy systems]
SIPP	Simple Internet Protocol Plus [Computer science] (DDC)
SIPP	Sodium Iron Pyrophosphate
SIPP	Standard Interline Passenger Procedures Manual [Air Traffic Conference of America] [IATA] (DS)
SIPP	Survey on Income and Program Participation [Census Bureau, Department of Health and Human Services]
SIPP	System Information Processing Program (MCD)
SIPPAP	Survey of Income and Program Participation Awareness Program [Bureau of the Census] (GFGA)
SIPPS	System of Information Processing for Professional Societies
Sippy	Senior Independent Pioneer [Lifestyle classification]
SIPR	Special In-Process Review (MCD)
SIPRA	Societa Italiana Pubblicita Per Azioni [Italian radio and television advertising company]
SIPRE	Snow, Ice, and Permafrost Research Establishment
SIPRI	Stockholm International Peace Research Institute [Solna, Sweden] (EAIO)
SIPRNET	Secret Internet Protocol Router Network [Military]
SIPRO	Servicios Informativos Procesados [Processed Information Services] [Mexico] (CROSS)
SIPROS	Simultaneous Processing Operation System [Control Data Corp.] [Computer science]
SIPS	SAC [Strategic Air Command] Intelligence Data Processing System (IAA)
SIPS	Science Innovation Program [Australia]
SIPS	Shipbuilding Industries Pension Scheme [British]
SIPS	Side-Impact Protection System [Automotive safety]
SIPS	Simulated Input Preparation System (IEEE)
SIPS	Simulated Interpersonal Problem Situation (EDAC)
SIPS	Small Instrument Pointing System (MCD)
SIPS	Societa Internazionale de Psicologia della Scrittura [International Society of Psychology of Handwriting - ISPH] (EAIO)
SIPS	Societe Internationale de Psychologie des Sports [International Society of Sports Psychology] (EAIO)
SIPS	Spartan Improved Performance Study [Missiles] (AABC)
SIPS	Sputter-Induced Photon Spectroscopy (MCD)
SIPS	State Implementation Plan System [Environmental Protection Agency]
SIPS	Statistical Interactive Programming System
sIPSC	Spontaneous Inhibitory Postsynaptic Current [Neurophysiology]
SIPSDE	Society of Independent and Private School Data Education [Later, SDE] (EA)
SIPSF	Space Invariant Point Spread Function (PDAA)
SIPSP	Slow-Inhibitory Postsynaptic Potential (DB)
SIPT	Sensory Integration and Praxis Test [Occupational therapy]
sipt	Silverpoint (VRA)
SIPT	Simulating Part (AAG)
SIPTH	Serum Immunoreactive Parathyroid Hormone [Endocrinology]
sIPTH	Serum Immunoreactive Parathyroid Hormone [Medicine] (STED)
SIPTU	Services Industrial Professional Technical Union [Ireland] (EAIO)
SIPU	Selective Inactivation Photodynamic Unit
SIPX	Sipex Corp. [NASDAQ symbol] (SAG)
SIQ	Sick in Quarters
SIQ	Singkep Island [Indonesia] [Airport symbol] (AD)
SIQ	Social Intelligence Quotient [In book title]
SIQ	Student Interests Quarterly [A publication]
SIQ	Suicidal Ideation Questionnaire (TES)
SIQ	Superior Internal Quality (WDAA)
SIQ	Symptom Interpretation Questionnaire [Medicine] (DMAA)
SIQR	Semi-Interquartile Range [Medicine] (DMAA)
SIR	Safari International Resources [Vancouver Stock Exchange symbol]
SIR	Safeguards Implementation Report [Nuclear energy] (NRCH)
SIR	Safe Integral Reactor [Nuclear energy]
SIR	Salair, Inc. [ICAO designator] (FAAC)
SIR	Scientific Information Retrieval (NITA)
SIR	Scientific Information Retrieval, Inc. [Database management system] [Information service or system] (IID)
SIR	Search, Inspection, and Recovery (NVT)
SIR	Secondary-Image-Registration [Photography]
SIR	Segment Identification Register
SIR	Selected Item Reporting
SIR	Selected Item Review (MCD)
SIR	Selective Information Retrieval [Computer science]
SIR	Selective Ion Recording [Spectrometry]
SIR	Self-Indication Ratio
SIR	Self-Insured Retention [Insurance]
SIR	Semantic Information Retrieval [Massachusetts Institute of Technology] [Computer science] (DIT)
SIR	Semiannual Inventory Report [Navy] (NVT)
SIR	Serial Infrared Communications Interface [Hewlett Packard Co.] (PCM)
SIR	Serial Infrared Specification [Computer science] (PCM)
SIR	Serious Incident Report [Military] (AFM)
SIR	Serum Inducible Repeat [Genetics]
SIR	Service International de Recherches [International Tracing Service] [Red Cross]
SIR	Set Indicators of the Right Half (SAA)
SIR	Shipboard Intercept Receiver [Navy]
SIR	Shuttle Imaging RADAR [of earth's surface] [NASA]
SIR	Signal-to-Interference Ratio

SIR............. Silent Information Regulator [*Genetics*]
SIR............. Silo Installation Refurbish (SAA)
SIR............. Simulated Robot (NITA)
SIR............. Simultaneous Impact Rate (AFM)
SIR............. Sinclair, WY [*Location identifier FAA*] (FAAL)
SIR............. Single Imaging RADAR
SIR............. Single Isomorphous Replacement [*Crystallography*]
SIR............. Single Item Release
SIR............. Single Item Removal [*Maintenance*]
SIR............. Sion [*Switzerland*] [*Airport symbol*]
Sir............. Sirach [*Old Testament book*] [*Roman Catholic canon*]
SIR............. Siria [*Venezuela*] [*Seismograph station code, US Geological Survey*] (SEIS)
Sir............. Sirius [*Record label*] [*Sweden*]
SIR............. Sirrom Capital [*NYSE symbol*]
SIR............. Size Up, Interview, Rate [*Mnemonic used by Responsible Beverage Service in its bartender training program*]
SIR............. Small Intestine Rinse [*Physiology*]
SIR............. Snow and Ice on Runway [*NWS*] (FAAC)
SIR............. Societa Italiana Resine [*Italy*]
SIR............. Societe Rorschach Internationale [*International Rorschach Society*] [*Originally, Societe Internationale du Test de Rorschach et Autres Methodes Projectives*]
SIR............. Society for Individual Responsibility [*Defunct*] (EA)
SIR............. Society of Industrial Realtors [*Association name and designation awarded by this group*] [*Washington, DC*] (EA)
SIR............. Society of Insurance Research [*Appleton, WI*] (EA)
SIR............. Software Incident Report (MCD)
SIR............. Software Initiated Restart (NASA)
SIR............. Sound Isolation Room
SIR............. Spaceborne Imaging RADAR
SIR............. Speaker Independent Recognition (IAA)
SIR............. Special Information Retrieval
SIR............. Special Inspection Requirement
SIR............. Special Investigative Requirement (AFM)
SIR............. Specification Information Retrieval System [*Computer science*] (MCD)
SIR............. Specific Immune Release (STED)
SIR............. Specific Information Requirement [*Military*] (INF)
SIR............. Specific Insulation Resistance
SIR............. Stable Isotopes Resource
SIR............. Standardized Incidence Ratio (STED)
SIR............. Standarization, Interoperability, and Readiness [*NATO*] (MCD)
SIR............. Staten Island Rapid Transit Railway Co. [*Later, SIRC*] [*AAR code*]
SIR............. Statistical Information Retrieval
SIR............. Statutory Invention Registration [*Patents*]
SIR............. Strategic Information Review (NITA)
SIR............. Stratified Indexing and Retrieval [*Japan Computer science*]
SIR............. Struthers Industries [*AMEX symbol*] (SPSG)
SIR............. Student Instructional Report [*Test of teacher performance*]
SIR............. Styrene-Isoprene Rubber
SIR............. Subcontractor Information Request
SIR............. Submarine Intermediate Reactor [*Nuclear energy*]
SIR............. Subsurface Interface RADAR [*A trademark*]
SIR............. Supersonic Infantry Rocket
SIR............. Suppliers Information Request
SIR............. Surface Insulation Resistance [*Electronics*] (AAEL)
SIR............. Symbolic Input Routine [*Computer science*] (DIT)
SIR............. Synthetic-Aperture Imaging RADAR [*System*]
SIR............. System Initialization Routine
SIR............. System Integration Receiver [*System*]
SIR............. System Interface Requirements (NASA)
SIR............. Systems Integration Review [*NASA*] (NASA)
SIRA .... Safety Investigation Regulations (IEEE)
SIRA .... Scientific Instrument Research Association [*British*]
SIRA .... Social Issues Research Associates (EA)
SIRA .... Sports Industries Representatives Association (EA)
SIRA .... Stable Isotope Ratio Analysis
SIRA .... Strapdown Inertial Reference Assembly (MCD)
SIRA .... Strategic Intelligence Research and Analysis
SIRA .... System for Instructional Response Analysis
SIRAP .... System of Information Retrieval and Analysis, Planning [*Army Information service or system*] (IID)
SIRAS .... Single Isomorphous Replacement, Anomalous Scattering [*Crystallography*]
SIRB .... Sintered Iron Rotating Band
SIRC .... Science Information Resource Center [*Harper & Row*] [*Information service or system*]
SIRC .... Sirco International Corp. [*NASDAQ symbol*] (NQ)
SIRC .... Sirco Intl [*NASDAQ symbol*] (TTSB)
SIRC .... Socialist International Research Council [*British*]
SIRC .... Spares Integrated Reporting and Control [*System*]
SIRC .... Sport Information Resource Centre [*Coaching Association of Canada*] [*Database*] (IID)
SIRC .... [*The*] Staten Island Railroad Corp. [*AAR code*]
SIRC .... Styrene Information and Research Center (EA)
SIRCH .... Scientific Instrumentation & Research Division (ACII)
SIR(CICR) .... Service International de Recherches (du Comite International de la Croix-Rouge) [*International Tracing Service of the International Committee of the Red Cross*]
Sirco........... Sirco International Corp. [*Associated Press*] (SAG)
SIRCS .... Shipboard Intermediate Range Combat System [*Navy*]
SIRCULS...... San Bernardino-Inyo-Riverside Counties United Library Services [*Library network*]
SIRCUS........ Standard Information Retrieval Capability for Users [*Army*]

SIRD .... Shore-Based Interfare Requirement Date
SIRD .... Support Instrumentation Requirements Document [*NASA*]
SIRE .... Satellite Infrared Experiment (MCD)
SIRE .... Society for the Investigation of Recurring Events (EA)
SIRE .... Symbolic Information Retrieval (IAA)
SIRE .... Syracuse Information Retrieval Experiments (NITA)
SIREF .... Specific Immune Response Enhancing Factor [*Medicine*] (DMAA)
SIREN .... Sanders Intact Reentry Encapsulation (MCD)
SIREN .... SIGSEC Resources and Equipment Needs (MCD)
SirenaA........ [*The*] Sirena Apparel Group [*Associated Press*] (SAG)
SIREWS .... Shipboard Infrared Electronic Warfare System
SIRF .... Severely Impaired Renal Function [*Medicine*] (DMAA)
SIRF .... System Information Reports Formatting (MCD)
SIRI .... Societe Internationale pour la Readaptation des Invalides
SIRI .... Stieglitz Informal Reading Inventory: Assessing Reading Behaviors from Emergent to Advanced Levels (TMMY)
SIRI .... Suicide Intervention Response Inventory [*Test*] [*Robert A. Neimeyer*] (TES)
SIRIC .... Soybean Insect Research Information Center [*University of Illinois*] [*Champaign, IL*]
SIRIJ.......... Semiconductor Industry Research Institute of Japan (AAEL)
SIRIN .... Single Readiness Information System [*NORRS*]
SIRIS .... Sputter-Initiated Resonance Ionization Spectrometry
SIRIS .... Sylloge Inscriptionum Religionis Isiacae et Sarapiacae [*A publication*] (BJA)
SIRIVS .... Spaceborne Intensified Radiometer for Imaging Vetroviolet Spectroscopy (MCD)
SIRL.......... Site Installation Requirements List (AAG)
SIRL.......... Support Item Requirement List (MCD)
SIRLEJ........ Societe Internationale de Recherche en Litterature d'Enfance et de Jeunesse [*International Research Society for Children's Literature - IRSCL*] (EA)
Sir L Jenk.... Wynne's Life of Sir Leoline Jenkins [*1724*] [*A publication*] (DLA)
SIRLS .... Information Retrieval System for the Sociology of Leisure and Sport [*University of Waterloo*] [*Information service or system*] (IID)
SIRLS .... Southwest Idaho Regional Library System [*Library network*]
SIRLS .... Specialized Information Retrieval and Library Services (IID)
SIRM .... Saturation Isothermal Remanent Magnetization [*Paleomagnetics*]
SIRM .... Sterile Insect Release Method
SIRMA .... Small Independent Record Manufacturers Association [*Stanford, CT*] (EA)
SIRMCE ...... Societe Internationale pour la Recherche sur les Maladies de Civilisation et l'Environment [*International Society for Research on Civilization Diseases and Environment*] [*Brussels, Belgium*] (EAIO)
SIRMS .... Stable Isotope Ratio Mass Spectrometer [*or Spectrometry*]
SIRN .... [*The*] Sirena Apparel Group [*NASDAQ symbol*] (SAG)
SIRO .... Service in Random Order (IAA)
SIROF .... Sputtered Iridium Oxide Film (PDAA)
SIROS......... Specialized Operating System (DNAB)
SIROW........ Southwest Institute for Research on Women [*University of Arizona*] [*Research center*] (RCD)
SIRP .... Signal-Regulatory Protein [*Biochemistry*]
SIRR .... Section on Individual Rights and Responsibilities (EA)
SIRR .... Small Integral Rocket/Ramjet (MCD)
SIRR .... Software Integration Readiness Review [*NASA*] (NASA)
SIRR .... Southern Industrial Railroad, Inc. [*AAR code*]
SIRRA .... Sleep-Induction/Rapid Reawakening System [*Military*] (RDA)
Sirrom .... Sirrom Capital Corp. [*Associated Press*] (SAG)
SIRS .... Salary Information Retrieval System (IEEE)
SIRS .... Satellite Infrared Spectrometer [*NASA*]
SIRS .... Scheduled Issue Release System
SIRS .... School Information and Research Service (EDAC)
SIRS .... Ship Installed RADIAC [*Radiation Detection, Indication, and Computation*] System (NATG)
SIRS .... Skills Inventory Retrieval System (MCD)
SIRS .... Small Independent Radio Stations [*An association British*]
SIRS .... Social Issues Resources Series [*A publication*]
SIRS .... Soils Information Retrieval Systems [*Database*] [*Army Corps of Engineers*]
SIRS .... Soluble Immune Response Suppressor [*Immunology*]
SIRS .... Special Issue Rating System [*Veterans Administration*]
SIRS .... Specification, Instrumentation, and Range Safety
SIRS .... Statewide Individual Referral System (OICC)
SIRS .... Structure of Instruction Rating Scale (EDAC)
SIRS .... Student Information Record System (AEBS)
SIRS .... Supplemental Inflatable Restraint System [*Automotive engineering*]
SIRS .... Systemic Inflammatory Response Syndrome [*Medicine*]
SIRS .... System Integration Receiver System (MCD)
SIRSA .... Special Industrial Radio Service Association (EA)
SIRT........... Signaling Information Receiver/Transmitter (MCD)
SIRT........... Staten Island Rapid Transit Railway Co. [*Later, SIRC*]
SIRTF......... Space [*formerly, Shuttle*] Infrared Telescope Facility [*NASA*]
Sir T Ray.... Sir T. Raymond's English King's Bench Reports [*A publication*] (DLA)
SIRU .... Strapdown Inertial Reference Unit [*Navigation*]
SIRVES .... SIGINT [*Signal Intelligence*] Requirements Validation and Evaluation Subcommittee
SIRW .... Safety Injection and Refueling Water [*Nuclear energy*] (NRCH)
SIRW .... Stuffed Indirect Reference Word [*Computer science*] (MHDI)
SIRWT .... Safety Injection and Refueling Water Tank [*Nuclear energy*] (NRCH)
SIRWT .... Safety Injection Reserve Water Tank (IEEE)
SIS............. Canadian Security and Intelligence Service [*UTLAS symbol*]
SIS............. Naval Intelligence Service [*Italy*]
SIS............. Paine Webber Gp Stk Index Sec [*AMEX symbol*] (TTSB)
SIS............. Paine Webber Group [*AMEX symbol*] (SAG)

SIS...............	Safety Information System [Department of Transportation]
SIS...............	Safety Injection Signal [Nuclear energy] (IAA)
SIS...............	Safety Injection System [Nuclear energy] (NRCH)
SIS...............	Safety Instrumented System (ACII)
SIS...............	SAGE [Semiautomatic Ground Environment] Interceptor Simulator
SIS...............	SAIL [Shuttle Avionics Integration Laboratory] Interface System [NASA] (NASA)
SIS...............	Saline Infusion Sonohysterography [Gynecological procedure]
SIS...............	Sample Inlet System [Automotive exhaust emission testing]
SIS...............	Satellite Infrared Spectrometer [NASA]
SIS...............	Satellite Interceptor System [Military] (AFM)
SIS...............	Savage Information Services (IID)
SIS...............	Scale for the Identification of School Phobia [Test]
SIS...............	Scanning Image Spectrometer
sis...............	Scanning Imaging Spectrometer (NAKS)
SIS...............	Science Information Service (EA)
SIS...............	Science Information Services [Franklin Institute]
SIS...............	Scientific Instruction Set
SIS...............	Scientific Instrument Society (EA)
SIS...............	Scotch-Irish Society of the United States of America (EA)
SIS...............	Screening/Inspection System (DNAB)
SIS...............	Secondary Injection System
SIS...............	Secretarial Information System (EPA)
SIS...............	Secret Intelligence Service [British]
SIS...............	Security Intelligence Service [New Zealand] (WDAA)
SIS...............	Selected Inventor Service (NITA)
SIS...............	Selected Ion Storage [For spectometry]
SIS...............	Semiautomatic Imagery Screening Subsystem (MCD)
SIS...............	Semiconductor-Insulator-Semiconductor
SIS...............	Seminar Information Service Database [Seminar Information Service, Inc.] [Information service or system] (CRD)
SIS...............	Senior Intelligence Service [CIA personnel]
SIS...............	Sensor Image Simulator (MCD)
SIS...............	Sensor Integration System (DWSG)
sis...............	Serial Input Special (NAKS)
SIS...............	Serial Input System (MCD)
SIS...............	Serving the Indigent Sick
SIS...............	Settlement Information Strategy [Australia]
SIS...............	Seychelles International Safari Air Ltd. [ICAO designator] (FAAC)
SIS...............	Shared Information Service (CMD)
SIS...............	Share Information Service [British] (DCTA)
SIS...............	Shipping Instruction Sheet
SIS...............	Shock-Isolation Support
SIS...............	Shock-Isolation System
SIS...............	Shorter Interval Scheduling [Quality control] (IAA)
SIS...............	Short Interval Scheduling [Quality control]
SIS...............	Shut-In Society
SIS...............	Shuttle Information System [NASA] (MCD)
sis...............	Shuttle Information System [NASA] (NAKS)
sis...............	Shuttle Interface Simulator [NASA] (NAKS)
SIS...............	Shuttle Interface Simulator [NASA] (NASA)
SIS...............	Signaling Interworking Subsystem [Telecommunications] (TEL)
SIS...............	Signal Intelligence Service [Later, Army Security Agency]
SIS...............	Significant Indications Summary
SIS...............	Silicon of Insulating Substrate (MCD)
SIS...............	Silkridge Resources [Vancouver Stock Exchange symbol]
SIS...............	Simian Sarcoma Virus [Oncology]
SIS...............	Simulation Interface Subsystem (KSC)
SIS...............	Single Item Squawk Sheet
SIS...............	Singles in Service (EA)
SIS...............	Sion [Switzerland] [Seismograph station code, US Geological Survey Closed] (SEIS)
SIS...............	Sishen [South Africa] [Airport symbol] (OAG)
SIS...............	Sisomicin (STED)
SIS...............	Sister
SIS...............	Social Information System [Medicine] (DMAA)
SIS...............	Societa Internazionale Scotista [International Scotist Society - ISS] (EAIO)
SIS...............	Society for Iranian Studies (EA)
SIS...............	Society for Italian Studies (AIE)
SIS...............	Society of International Secretaries
sis...............	Software Implementation Specification (NAKS)
SIS...............	Software Implementation Specifications [NASA] (NASA)
SIS...............	Software Integrated Schedule [NASA] (NASA)
sis...............	Software Integrated Schedule (NAKS)
SIS...............	Solid-State Imaging Spectrometer
SIS...............	Somatic Inkblot Series [Personality development test] [Psychology]
SIS...............	Sound in Sync (IAA)
SIS...............	Soviet Intelligence Services
SIS...............	Space and Information System
SIS...............	SPALT [Special Projects Alterations] Information Shut
SIS...............	SPALT [Special Projects Alterations] Information System
SIS...............	Spark Ignition System
SIS...............	Speaker Intercom System (KSC)
SIS...............	Special Industrial Services [United Nations Industrial Development Organization]
SIS...............	Special Information System (MCD)
SIS...............	Special Intelligence Service
SIS...............	Special Interest Sessions
SIS...............	Special Isotope Separation [Physics]
SIS...............	Special Isotope Separator (COE)
SIS...............	Specification Information System
SIS...............	Spectral Imaging Sensor
SIS...............	Spectral Index of Sample [Experimentation]
SIS...............	Spontaneous Interictal Spike [Medicine] (DMAA)
SIS...............	Spuria Iris Society (EA)
SIS...............	Stage Interface Simulator (IAA)
SIS...............	Stage Interface Substitute
SIS...............	Stall Inhibitor System [Aviation] (GFGA)
SIS...............	Stand-Alone Information System [National Library of Medicine]
SIS...............	Standard Indexing System [DoD]
SIS...............	Standard Instruction Set (MSA)
SIS...............	Standard Interface Specification [NASA] (GFGA)
sis...............	Standard Interface Specification (NAKS)
SIS...............	Standards Information Service [National Institute of Standards and Technology] (IID)
SIS...............	State Information Service [Australia]
SIS...............	Station Identification Store [Bell Laboratories]
SIS...............	Stator Interstage Seal
SIS...............	STEP [Scientific and Technical Exploitation Program] Information Subsystem
SIS...............	Sterile Injectable Solution (STED)
SIS...............	Sterile Injectable Suspension
SIS...............	Stored Information System (IAA)
SIS...............	Strategic Intelligence School [Military]
SIS...............	Strategic Intelligence Summary [Military] (NATG)
SIS...............	Strategic Intelligence Systems, Inc. [Also, an information service or system] (IID)
SIS...............	Streamlined Inspection System [USDA meat standards]
SIS...............	Student Instruction Sheet [Military]
SIS...............	Student International Service [Foundation]
SIS...............	Styrene-Isoprene-Styrene [Organic chemistry]
SIS...............	Submarine Integrated SONAR
SIS...............	Successor Instruction Set (IAA)
SIS...............	Superconductivity Information System [Department of Energy] [Information service or system] (IID)
SIS...............	Superconductor-Insulator-Superconductor [Transistor technology]
SIS...............	Supervisory Inventory on Safety [Test]
SIS...............	Supplier Identification System [London Enterprise Agency] [Information service or system] (IID)
SIS...............	Supplies Information System (NITA)
SIS...............	Supply Item Status
SIS...............	Surgical Infection Society (EA)
SIS...............	Sveriges Standardiseringskommission [Swedish Standards Institution] [Also, an information service or system] (IID)
SIS...............	Swedish Inteplanetary Society (IAA)
SIS...............	Swedish Standards Institution (IID)
SIS...............	Synchronous Identification System (MCD)
SIS...............	Synopsis Information System (AAGC)
SIS...............	System Integration Schedule [NASA] (NASA)
SIS...............	System Integration Support
SIS...............	System Interrupt Supervisor
sis...............	Systems Integration Schedule (NAKS)
SISA............	Supporters of Interoperable Systems in Australia (DDG)
3Isabel........	Santa Isabel SA [Associated Press] (SAG)
SISAC.........	Serials Industry Systems Advisory Committee [Book Industry Study Group] [Information service or system] (IID)
SISAM........	Spectrometer with Interference Selective Amplitude Modulation [Physics]
SI/SAO.......	Special Intelligence/Special Activities Office (MCD)
SISB...........	SIS Bancorp, Inc. [NASDAQ symbol] (SAG)
SISB...........	Springfield Instit'n for Svgs [NASDAQ symbol] (TTSB)
SISB...........	Springfield Institution for Savings [NASDAQ symbol] (SAG)
SIS Bncp.....	SIS Bancorp, Inc. [Associated Press] (SAG)
SISC...........	Sentry Interceptor Subsystem Contractor [DoD]
SISC...........	Single Screw
SISC...........	Statewide Information Steering Committee [California]
SISCIS........	Subject Index to Sources of Comparative International Statistics [A publication]
SISCO.........	Singer Information Services Co. (IAA)
SISCO.........	Special Inter-Departmental Selection Committee [UN Food and Agriculture Organization]
SISCON.......	Science in Social Context
SISD...........	Scientific Information Systems Department [Information service or system] (IID)
SISD...........	Single Instruction, Single Data (IEEE)
SISD...........	Single Instruction Single Data Stream (IAA)
SISD	Standards and Interface Specification Document
SISDATA.....	Single Instruction Single Data Stream (NITA)
SISDATA.....	Statistical Information System Data (NITA)
SISDG........	Shipboard Information System Development Group [Maritime Transportation ResearchBoard] (PDAA)
SISEX........	Satellite Imaging Spectrometer Experiment (USDC)
SISEX........	Shuttle Imaging Spectrometer Experiment [NASA]
SISFET.......	Semiconductor-Insulator-Semiconductor Field Effect Transistor (AAEL)
SISG	ISG International Software Group [NASDAQ symbol] (SAG)
SISGF	ISG Intl Software Group [NASDAQ symbol] (TTSB)
SISH	Societe Internationale de la Science Horticole [International Society for Horticultural Science - ISHS] (EAIO)
SISI...........	Short Increment Sensitivity Index [Medicine]
SISI...........	S I Technologies [NASDAQ symbol] (TTSB)
SISI...........	SI Technologies, Inc. [NASDAQ symbol] (SAG)
SISI...........	Structural Instrumentation, Inc. [NASDAQ symbol] (SAG)
SISI...........	Surveillance and In-Service Inspection [Nuclear energy] (NRCH)
SI-SIC........	Siliconized Silicon Carbide (SAA)
SISIR.........	Singapore Institute of Standards and Industrial Research
SISK...........	Siskon Gold 'A' [NASDAQ symbol] (TTSB)
SISK...........	Siskon Gold Corp. [NASDAQ symbol] (SAG)
Siskon	Siskon Gold Corp. [Associated Press] (SAG)

S Isl	Sandwich Islands
SISL	Sons of Italy Supreme Lodge (EA)
SIS-MDS	Single Instruction Stream, Multiple Data Stream [Computer science] (MHDI)
SISMP	Site Integrated Stabilization Plan
SISMS	Standard Integrated Support Management System [Joint Chiefs of Staff]
SISO	Science Information Services Organization [Franklin Institute] (IID)
SISO	Shift In, Shift Out (IEEE)
SISO	Single-Input, Single-Output [Process engineering]
SISOR	Supply Item Status Order Reporting [Army]
SISORS	Supply Item Status and Order Reporting System
SISP	Sudden Increase of Solar Particles
SISP	Surface Imaging and Sounding Package
SISPA	Sequence-Independent Single Primer Amplification [Genetics]
SISR	Selected Items Status Report [Army] (AABC)
SISS	Second International Science Study [International Association for the Evaluation of Educational Achievement]
SISS	Semiconductor-Insulator-Semiconductor System
SISS	Sensory Integration Special Interest Section [American Occupational Therapy Association]
SIS-S	SENTRY [Survey Entry] Interceptor System Simulator
SISS	Serum Inhibitor of Streptolysin S (STED)
SISS	Single Item, Single Source (IEEE)
SISS	Societe Internationale de la Science du Sol
SISS	Sources of Information on Social Security [British]
SISS	Standoff Imaging Sensor System (MCD)
SISS	Submarine Integrated SONAR System
SISS	Synchronous Identification System Study
SISS	System Integration Support Service
SISSC	Special Interest Sections Steering Committee [American Occupational Therapy Association]
SIS-SDS	Single Instruction Stream, Single Data Stream [Computer science] (MHDI)
SIST	Self-Inflating Surface Target
SIST	Sentence Imitation Screening Test [Speech and language test]
SIST	Sister
SISTER	Special Institution for Scientific and Technological Education and Research [In proposal stage, 1964, in Great Britain]
SISTM	Simulation by Incremental Stochastic Transition Matrices (MCD)
SISTMS	Standard Integrated Supply/Transportation Manifest System [Military] (AABC)
SISTRAN	System for Information Storage and Retrieval and Analysis
SISU	Schools In-Service Unit [University of Birmingham] [British] (AIE)
SISUL	Serials in Swaziland University Libraries [A publication]
SISUSA	Scotch-Irish Society of the United States of America (EA)
SiSV	Simian Sarcoma Virus [Also, SSV]
SISWG	STS [Shuttle Test Station] Integrated Schedule Working Group [NASA] (GFGA)
SISWP	Soroptimist International of the South West Pacific [Sydney, NSW, Australia] (EAIO)
SIT	Safety Injection Tank [Nuclear energy] (NRCH)
SIT	Safety Injection Transmitter [Nuclear energy] (NRCH)
SIT	Satellite Inspector Target (MCD)
SIT	Self-Ignition Temperature
SIT	Self-Induced Transparency (IAA)
SIT	Sensory Integration Training
SIT	Separation-Initiated Timer
SIT	Sequential Interval Timer
SIT	Serum Inhibitory Titer [Clinical chemistry]
SIT	Shorr Imagery Test [Personality development test] [Psychology]
SIT	Shuttle Integrated Test [NASA] (NASA)
SIT	Shuttle Interface Test [NASA] (NASA)
SIT	Silicon Intensified Target (NITA)
SIT	Silicon Intensifier Target
SIT	Silicon Intensifier Tube
SIT	Simulation Input Tape
sit	Sino-Tibetan [MARC language code Library of Congress] (LCCP)
SIT	Sitka [Alaska] [Airport symbol] (OAG)
SIT	Sitka, AK [Location identifier FAA] (FAAL)
SIT	Situation (AFM)
SIT	Slosson Intelligence Test
SIT	Social Intelligence Test [Psychology]
SIT	Societe International de Telecommunications Aeronautiques [Belgium ICAO designator] (FAAC)
SIT	Society of Industrial Tutors [British]
SIT	Society of Instrument Technology [British]
SIT	Society of International Treasurers (EAIO)
SIT	Software Integrated Test [NASA] (KSC)
SIT	Software Integration Test (IAA)
SIT	Spaceborne Infrared Tracker
SIT	Space Impact Tool [NASA]
SIT	Special Information Tones [Telecommunications]
SIT	Sperm Immobilization Test [Clinical chemistry]
SIT	Spontaneous Ignition Temperature
SIT	SSV [Space Shuttle Vehicle] Integrated Test [NASA] (NASA)
SIT	Stand-Alone Intelligent Terminal (MHDI)
SIT	State Income Tax (AAGC)
SIT	State Information Technology [Western Australia]
SIT	Statement of Inventory Transaction [Military]
SIT	Static Induction Transistor [Telecommunications] (TEL)
SIT	Stepped Impedance Transformer (IAA)
SIT	Sterile Insect Technology
SIT	Stevens Institute of Technology [Hoboken, NJ]
SIT	Stop Immorality on Television [An association]
SIT	Stopping in Transit
SIT	Storage Inspection Test [Navy] (NG)
SIT	Storage in Transit
SIT	Structurally Integrated Thruster (MCD)
SIT	Sugar Industry Technologists (EA)
SIT	Swinburne Institute of Technology [Australia]
SIT	System Initialization Table [Computer science] (CIST)
SIT	System Integration Test
SIT	Systems Interface Test (NVT)
SITA	Sociedade Internacional de Trilogia Analitica [International Society of Analytical Trilogy - ISAT] [Sao Paulo, Brazil] (EAIO)
SITA	Societe Internationale des Telecommunications Aeronautiques [International Society of Aeronautical Telecommunications] [London, England]
SITA	Students' International Travel Association
SITA	System International Tinplate Area
SITAP	Simulator for Transportation Analysis and Planning (DNAB)
SITAR	Societa Incremento Turismo Aereo [Italy]
SITAR	System for Interactive Test Editing, Analysis, and Retrieval (IAA)
SITB	Shipbuilding Industrial Training Board [British]
SITC	Salford Information Technology Centre (NITA)
SITC	Satellite International Television Center [Telecommunications] (TEL)
SITC	Single Integrated Test Cycle [Army]
SITC	Standard Industrial Trade Classification [United Nations]
SITC	Standard International Trade Classification
SITCA	Secretaria de Integracion Turistica Centroamericana
SITCEN	Situation Center [NATO] (NATG)
SITCOM	Situation Comedy [Television]
Sit-Comm	Situation Commercial [Advertisement imitating a TV sitcom]
SITE	Sample Instruction Test Exercise (MCD)
SITE	Satellite Instructional Television Experiment [NASA/Indian Space Research Organization, 1974]
SITE	Sculpture in the Environment [In Best by SITE, Inc.]
SITE	Search Information Tape Equipment
SITE	Securities-Investment Trust Enterprise
SITE	Shipboard Information, Training, and Education [System] [Navy] (NVT)
SITE	Site Holdings, Inc. [NASDAQ symbol] (SAG)
SITE	Situate (ROG)
SITE	Snow and Ice Traversing Equipment [Army]
SITE	Society of Incentive Travel Executives [New York, NY] (EA)
SITE	Society of Insurance Trainers and Educators (EA)
SITE	Spacecraft Instrumentation Test Equipment
SITE	Space Influences on the Terrestrial Environment [Space Enviromental Laboratory] (USDC)
SITE	Stockholm Institute of Transition Economics and East European Economics
SITE	Suction Infusion Tissue Extractor [Ophthalmology]
SITE	Superfund Innovative Technologies Evaluation Program [Environmental Protection Agency]
SITE	Superfund Innovative Technology Evaluation
SI Tech	SI Technologies, Inc. [Associated Press] (SAG)
S-ITED	Superimposed Integrated Trajectory Error [Aviation]
SiteHld	Site Holdings, Inc. [Associated Press] (SAG)
Sitel	Sitel Corp. [Associated Press] (SAG)
SITEL	Societe des Ingenieurs do Telecommunication [Belgium]
SITES	Smithsonian Institution Traveling Exhibition Service
Sithe	Sithe Energies, Inc. [Associated Press] (SAG)
SITI	Swiss Institute for Technical Information [Information service or system] (IID)
SITIM	Societe Internationale des Techniques d'Imagerie Mentals [International Society for Mental Imagery Techniques in Psychotherapy and Psychology] [Paris, France] (EAIO)
SITIP	School Improvement Through Instructional Process [Maryland] (EDAC)
SITK	Sitka National Monument
SITL	Sitel Corp. [NASDAQ symbol] (SAG)
SITL	Southwestern Industrial Traffic League (EA)
SITL	Static Induction Transistor Logic (NITA)
SITLILM	Subcontractor Interceptor Transporter/Loader Intermediate Level Maintenance Course
SITMAP	Situation Map (MCD)
SITN	Situation (ROG)
SITO	Senior Information Technology Officer
SITOR	Simplex TELEX over Radio
SITP	Scheduled into Production
SITP	Shipyard Installation Test Procedure [or Program]
SITP	Site Inspection and Test Procedure [Nuclear energy] (NRCH)
SITP	System Integration Test Program
SITP	Systems Integrated Test Plan [Military] (CAAL)
SITPB	System Integration Test Program Board
SITPRO	Simplification of International Trade Procedures [Committee or Board] [British]
SITRAM	Societe Ivoirienne de Transport Maritime [The Ivorian national shipping industry]
SITREP	Situation Report
Sitrep	Situation Report [Military] (WDAA)
SITS	IEEE Social Implications of Technology Society (EA)
SITS	SAGE [Semiautomatic Ground Environment] Intercept Target Simulation
SITS	Scientists in the Sea Program [National Oceanic and Atmospheric Administration] (MSC)
SITS	Secondary Influent Treatment System
SITS	Secure Imagery Transmission System [Military] (CAAL)

SITS.............	Societe Internationale de Transfusion Sanguine [*International Society of Blood Transfusion - ISBT*] [*Paris, France*] (EA)
SITS.............	Still in the Seventies [*Lifestyle classification*]
SITS.............	Student Interactive Training System
SITS.............	System Integration Test Service
SITS.............	System Integration Test Site [*Military*] (CAAL)
SITSUM.........	Situation Summary [*Military*] (NVT)
SITT.............	System Integration of Triad Technology (IAA)
SITTS...........	Small-Inventory Top-Tier Site [*Industrial hazard designation*] [*British*]
SITU.............	Society for the Investigation of the Unexplained (EA)
SITU.............	South India Teachers' Union
SITU.............	Surgical Intensive Therapy Unit
SITV.............	System Integration Test Vehicle
SITVC..........	Secondary Injection Thrust Vector Control
SITW...........	State Income Tax Withheld
SITYS..........	See, I Told You So [*Rush Limbaugh's mantra and book title*] (ECON)
Sitz.............	Sitzungsberichte [*Proceedings*] [*German*] (OCD)
Sitz Wien....	Sitzungsberichte der Akademie der Wissenschaften in Wien [*A publication*] (OCD)
SIU.............	Saturn Instrumentation [*NASA*]
SIU.............	Seafarers' International Union of North America [*AFL-CIO*]
SIU.............	Sequence Initiate Update
SIU.............	Sets in Use [*Television rating*] (WDMC)
SIU.............	Shiloh Resources Ltd. [*Vancouver Stock Exchange symbol*]
SIU.............	Signal Interface Unit (MCD)
siu.............	Signal Interface Unit (NAKS)
SIU.............	Significant Industrial Use
SIU.............	Simushir [*Former USSR Seismograph station code, US Geological Survey*] (SEIS)
SIU.............	Slide-In Unit [*Telecommunications*] (TEL)
SIU.............	Societe Internationale d'Urologie [*International Society of Urology - ISU*] [*Paris, France*] (EAIO)
SIU.............	Sonobuoy Interface Unit [*Navy*] (CAAL)
SIU.............	Southern Illinois University
SIU.............	Special Investigations Unit [*Insurance*]
SIU.............	Station Interface Unit [*Computer science*] (ECII)
SIU.............	Systeme International d'Unites [*International System of Units*] [*Also, SI*]
SIU.............	System Integration Unit (IAA)
SIU.............	System [*or Subsystem*] Interface Unit
SIU-AGLI......	Seafarers' International Union of North America [*AFL-CIO*]; Atlantic, Gulf,Lakes, and Inland Waters District
SIU-AGLIW...	Seafarers' International Union of North America [*AFL-CIO*]; Atlantic, Gulf,Lakes, and Inland Waters District
SIUC	Southern Illinois University, Carbondale
SIUCB	Societa Italiana della Union Chimique Belge [*Italy*]
SIUFL..........	Suspend Issue and Use of Following Lots
SIU-IUP.......	Seafarers' International Union of North America [*AFL-CIO*]; Inlandboatmen'sUnion of the Pacific
SIU-IUPW	Seafarers' International Union of North America [*AFL-CIO*]; International Union of Petroleum Workers
SIU-MCS......	Seafarers' International Union of North America [*AFL-CIO*]; Marine Cooks and Stewards' Union
SIU-MFOW...	Seafarers' International Union of North America [*AFL-CIO*]; Pacific Coast Marine Firemen, Oilers, Watertenders, and Wipers Association
SIUNA.........	Seafarers' International Union of North America (EA)
SIUP	Southern Illinois University Press
SIUPA	Solomon Islands United Party [*Political party*] (PPW)
SIUSA	Survival International, USA [*Defunct*] (EA)
SIUSM	Suspend from Issue and Use as Suspect Material
SIU-SUP	Seafarers' International Union of North America [*AFL-CIO*]; Sailors' Union of the Pacific
SIU-TSAW....	Seafarers' International Union of North America [*AFL-CIO*]; Transporation Services and Allied Workers
SIV.............	Sensors in Vacuum (AAEL)
siv.............	Sieve (NAKS)
SIV.............	Sieve (NASA)
SIV.............	Silicon Videcon [*TV system*]
SIV.............	Silver Cloud Mines [*Vancouver Stock Exchange symbol*]
SIV.............	Simian Immunodeficiency Virus
SIV.............	Solar and Interplanetary Variability [*Meteorology*]
SIV.............	Special Interest Vessel [*Navy*]
SIV.............	Spectrum Identification Voltage [*Military*] (CAAL)
SIV.............	Sprague-Dawley-Ivanovas [*Rat*] (DB)
SIV.............	Sprague-Dawley-Ivanovas Rat [*Medicine*] (DMAA)
SIV.............	Sullivan, IN [*Location identifier FAA*] (FAAL)
SIV.............	Survey of Interpersonal Values [*Psychology*]
SIVAN	Sistema de Vigilancia de Amazonia [*Amazon Surveillance System*] [*Brazil*]
SIVB...........	Silicon Valley Bancshares [*NASDAQ symbol*] (NQ)
SIVB...........	Silicon Valley Bancshrs [*NASDAQ symbol*] (TTSB)
SIVB...........	Society for In Vitro Biology (NTPA)
SIVD	Spacecraft Information Viewing Device
SIVE...........	Shuttle Interface Verification Equipment [*NASA*] (NASA)
SI VIR PERM.	Si Vires Permittant [*If the Strength Will Bear It*] [*Pharmacy*] (ROG)
SIVOMAR.....	Societe Ivoirenne de Navigation Maritime [*Ivory Coast*] (EY)
SIVZV..........	Sunshine Mining & Refining Wrrt [*NASDAQ symbol*] (TTSB)
SIW.............	Congregation of the Incarnate Word and the Blessed Sacrament [*Roman Catholic women's religious order*]
SIW.............	Samaria [*Papua*] [*Airport symbol*] (AD)
SIW.............	Schmitt Industries, Inc. [*Vancouver Stock Exchange symbol*]
SIW.............	Self-Inflicted Wound [*Military*]
SIW.............	Serum Samples from Infertile Women [*Immunochemistry*]
SIW.............	Socialist International Women (EA)
SIW.............	Strassburger Israelitisch Wochenschrift [*A publication*] (BJA)
SIW.............	Strategic Intelligence Wing (MCD)
SIW.............	Subpolar Intermediate Water [*Oceanography*]
SIWA	Scottish Inland Waterways Association (DBA)
SIWDR.........	Sidewinder [*Naval ordnance*]
SIWIP	Self-Induced Water Intoxication and Psychosis [*Medicine*] (DMAA)
SIWL	Single Isolated Whell Load [*ICAO*] (FAAC)
SIX.............	Singleton [*Australia Airport symbol*] (OAG)
SIXATAF	Sixth Allied Tactical Air Force, Southeastern Europe [*NATO*] (NATG)
Six Circ......	Cases on the Six Circuits [*1841-43*] [*Ireland*] [*A publication*] (DLA)
Six Ct J......	Sixteenth Century Journal [*A publication*] (BRI)
SIXEP.........	Site Ion Exchange Effluent Plant [*Nuclear energy*]
SIXES.........	Selectively-Induced X-Ray Emission Spectroscopy
SIXFLT........	Sixth Fleet [*Atlantic*] [*Navy*]
SIXP..........	Sixpenny [*England*]
SIXPAC........	System for Inertial Experiment Priority and Attitude Control (MCD)
SIXT...........	Sixth-Plate (VRA)
SIXTHFLT.....	Sixth Fleet [*Atlantic*] [*Navy*]
SIXX..........	Sixx Hldgs [*NASDAQ symbol*] (TTSB)
SIXX..........	Sixx Holdings, Inc. [*NASDAQ symbol*] (SAG)
Sixx..........	Sixx Holdings, Inc. [*Associated Press*] (SAG)
SIY...........	Aerosiyusa, SA [*Mexico*] [*FAA designator*] (FAAC)
SIY...........	Montague, CA [*Location identifier FAA*] (FAAL)
SIY...........	Shropshire Imperial Yeomanry [*British military*] (DMA)
SIY...........	South of Ireland Yeomanry [*British military*] (DMA)
SIY...........	Staffordshire Imperial Yeomanry [*British military*] (DMA)
SIY...........	Sussex Imperial Yeomanry [*British military*] (DMA)
SIZ...........	Security Identification Zone
SIZ...........	Sizeler Property Investors, Inc. [*NYSE symbol*] (SPSG)
SIZ...........	Sizeler Property Inv operty Inv [*NYSE symbol*] (TTSB)
SizelerP......	Sizeler Property Investors, Inc. [*Associated Press*] (SAG)
Sizzler	Sizzler International, Inc. [*Associated Press*] (SAG)
SJ.............	Jesuit Fathers and Brothers (TOCD)
sj.............	Jesuit Fathers and Brothers, Society of Jesus (TOCD)
SJ.............	Sales Journal [*Accounting*]
SJ.............	Samuel Johnson [*Initials used as pseudonym*]
SJ.............	San Jose [*Diocesan abbreviation*] [*California*] (TOCD)
SJ.............	San Juan [*Puerto Rico*]
SJ.............	Schistosoma Japonicum [*Parasitic fluke*]
SJ.............	Scottish Jurist [*1829-73*] [*A publication*] (DLA)
SJ.............	Servants of Jesus (TOCD)
SJ.............	Service Junior
SJ.............	Show Jumper [*or Jumping*] [*Horsemanship*] [*British*] (DI)
SJ.............	Side Judge [*Football*]
SJ.............	Single Jewish [*Classified advertising*]
SJ.............	SJ Huvudkontor [*Swedish State Railways*] (DCTA)
SJ.............	Slip Joint [*Technical drawings*]
SJ.............	Sloppy Joe [*Sandwich*]
SJ.............	Societas Jesu [*Society of Jesus*] [*Jesuits*] [*Roman Catholic men's religious order*]
SJ.............	Solicitors' Journal [*A publication A publication*] (DLA)
SJ.............	Source Jamming
SJ.............	Statens Jaernvaegar [*Sweden*]
S-J...........	Stevens-Johnson Syndrome [*Medicine*] (AAMN)
SJ.............	Stewart Island [*ICAO designator*] (AD)
SJ.............	Sub Judice [*Under Consideration*] [*Latin*]
sj.............	Sudan [*MARC country of publication code Library of Congress*] (LCCP)
SJ.............	Supersonic Jet [*Gas stream*]
SJ.............	Support Jamming [*Military*] (LAIN)
SJ.............	Svalbard and Jan Mayen Islands [*ANSI two-letter standard code*] (CNC)
SJ.............	Swirl Jet
SJ24NACA ...	San Juan 24 North American Class Association (EA)
SJA...........	San Juan de Arama [*Colombia*] [*Airport symbol*] (AD)
SJA...........	Service Job Analysis [*A publication*]
SJA...........	Servicios Aereos Especiales de Jalisco SA de CV [*Mexico ICAO designator*] (FAAC)
SJA...........	Sisters of Ste. Jeanne D'Arc (TOCD)
SJA...........	Staff Judge Advocate [*Military*]
SJA...........	St. John Ambulance (WDAA)
SJAA..........	Swedish Journalists Association of America (EA)
SJAE..........	Steam Jet Air Ejector [*Nuclear energy*] (NRCH)
SJAL..........	School Journal Association of London [*British*] (AIE)
SJAOI.........	Staff Judge Advocate Office Institute (SAA)
SJART.........	San Jacinto Army Terminal
SJB...........	San Joaquin [*Bolivia*] [*Airport symbol*] (AD)
SJB...........	Sisters of St. John Bosco (Taylor, TX) (TOCD)
SJB...........	Society of Jewish Bibliophiles (EA)
SJB...........	Society of Journeymen Brushmakers [*A union*] [*British*]
SJB...........	St. Joseph Belt Railway Co. [*AAR code*]
SJB...........	Westfield, MA [*Location identifier FAA*] (FAAL)
SJBA..........	Sephardic Jewish Brotherhood of America (EA)
SJBC..........	Saint John the Baptist, Clewer
SJC...........	Avastar Jet Charter and Management Services, Inc. [*FAA designator*] (FAAC)
SJC...........	Saint John's College [*California; Kansas; Maryland*]
SJC...........	Saint Joseph College [*West Hartford, CT*]
SJC...........	Saint Joseph's College [*California; Indiana; Maine; New Jersey; New York, Pennsylvania*]
SJC...........	San Javier [*Chile*] [*Seismograph station code, US Geological Survey Closed*] (SEIS)
SJC...........	San Jose [*California*] [*Airport symbol*] (OAG)
SJC...........	San Jose, CA [*Location identifier FAA*] (FAAL)
SJC...........	Sayre Junior College [*Oklahoma*]

SJC	Sisters of St. Joseph of Cluny (TOCD)
SJC	Snead Junior College [Boaz, AL]
SJC	Society of Jews and Christians
SJC	Southend Jet Centre Ltd. [British ICAO designator] (FAAC)
SJC	Southerland, J. C., Dearborn, MI [STAC]
SJC	Standing Joint Committee
SJC	Supreme Judicial Court
SJC	Sydney Journalists' Club [Australia]
SJCC	Cayey [Puerto Rico] [Seismograph station code, US Geological Survey] (SEIS)
SJCC	Saint John College of Cleveland [Ohio]
SJCC	San Jose City College [California]
SJCC	Scott Joplin Commemorative Committee (EA)
SJCC	Social Justice Consultative Council [Victoria, Australia]
SJCC	Spring Joint Computer Conference [American Federation of Information Processing Societies]
SJCC	Sydney Junior Chamber of Commerce [Australia]
SJCL	Standardized Job Control Language (PDAA)
SJCPS	Society of Jewish Composers, Publishers, and Songwriters [Defunct] (EA)
SJCS	Secretary Joint Chiefs of Staff (MCD)
SJCW	Saint Joseph's College for Women [Later, SJC] [New York]
SJD	Doctor of Judicial Science (GAGS)
SJD	Doctor of Juridical Science [or Doctor of the Science of Jurisprudence or Doctor of the Science of Law]
SJD	Los Cabos [Mexico] [Airport symbol] (OAG)
SJD	Silicon Junction Diode (IDOE)
SJD	St. Joseph's College, Philadelphia, PA [OCLC symbol] (OCLC)
SJD	Supervisory Job Discipline Test
SJDAOIIA	Saint John of Damascus Association of Orthodox Iconographers, Iconologists, and Architects (EA)
SJDFC	Spirit, John Denver Fan Club (EA)
SJDM	Society for Judgement and Decision Making (EA)
SJE	San Jose Del Guaviaro [Colombia] [Airport symbol] (OAG)
SJE	Standard Jewish Encyclopedia [A publication]
SJE	St. Jude Express [An association] (EA)
SJE	Swiveling Jet Engine
SJF	Saint John [Virgin Islands] [Airport symbol] (OAG)
SJF	Shortest Job First [Computer science]
SJF	Single Jewish Female [Classified advertising]
SJF	Sonny James and Friends [An association Defunct] (EA)
SJF	Soros Justice Fellowships
SJF	Supersonic Jet Flow
SJFC	Saint John Fisher College [Rochester, NY]
SJFC	Skidrow Joe Fan Club (EA)
SJFZ	San Jacinto Fault Zone [Geology]
SJG	San Juan [Puerto Rico] [Seismograph station code, US Geological Survey] (SEIS)
SJGE	St. Joseph Grain Exchange (EA)
SJH	San Juan Del Cesar [Colombia] [Airport symbol] (OAG)
SJH	St. Johns [Antigua, Leeward Islands, West Indies] [Airport symbol] (AD)
SJH	St. Joseph Seminary [California] [Seismograph station code, US Geological Survey] (SEIS)
SJI	Mobile, AL [Location identifier FAA] (FAAL)
SJI	San Jose [Philippines] [Airport symbol] (OAG)
SJI	Society for Japanese Irises (EA)
SJI	South Jersey Industries, Inc. [NYSE symbol] (SPSG)
SJI	State Justice Institute
SJI	Steel Joist Institute (EA)
SJI	Sun Jet International Airlines, Inc. [ICAO designator] (FAAC)
SJI	Supervisory Job Instruction Test
SJIA	Saint Joan's International Alliance [See also AIJA] (EAIO)
SJIA-USA	St. Joan's International Alliance U.S. Section (EA)
SJIFC	Spike Jones International Fan Club (EA)
SJIS	State Judicial Information System (OICC)
SJJ	Sarajevo [Former Yugoslavia] [Airport symbol] (OAG)
SJJC	Sheldon Jackson Junior College [Sitka, AK] [Later, Sheldon Jackson College]
SJJR	Societe Jean-Jacques Rousseau [Switzerland] (EAIO)
SJJR	Standard Jack and Jennet Registry of America (EA)
SJK	Saint John Knits, Inc. [NYSE symbol] (SAG)
SJK	Sao Jose Dos Campos [Brazil] [Airport symbol] (OAG)
SJK	Steam-Jacketed Kettle
SJK	St. John Knits [NYSE symbol] (TTSB)
SJK	St. John Knits, Inc. [NYSE symbol] (SPSG)
SJL	San Joaquin Valley Library System, Fresno, CA [OCLC symbol] (OCLC)
SJL	South Jersey Indus [NYSE symbol] (TTSB)
SJL	St. Jude League (EA)
SJLAC	Soviet Jewry Legal Advocacy Center (EA)
SJLB	Selected Judgments, Lower Burma [A publication] (DLA)
SJLC	Single Junction Latching Circulator
SJLC	St. Johnsbury & Lamoille County R. R. [AAR code]
SJM	San Jose De Maipo [Chile] [Seismograph station code, US Geological Survey Closed] (SEIS)
SJM	Single Jewish Male [Classified advertising]
SJM	Smucker [J. M.] Co. [NYSE symbol] (SPSG)
SJM	Southern Air Transport, Inc. [ICAO designator] (FAAC)
SJM	Special Joint Meeting
SJM	Svalbard and Jan Mayen Islands [ANSI three-letter standard code] (CNC)
SJM	System Junction Module [Deep Space Instrumentation Facility, NASA]
SJM.A	Smucker (J.M.) CI'A' [NYSE symbol] (TTSB)
SJM.B	Smucker (J.M.) CI'B' [NYSE symbol] (TTSB)
SJMC	Signed Judgments of the Military Courts in the Administered Territories [Israel] (BJA)
SJMJ	Societe de Jesus, Marie et Joseph [Society of Jesus, Mary and Joseph] [Netherlands] (EAIO)
SJMO	Smithsonian Jazz Masterworks Orchestra
SJN	Chartair, Inc. [ICAO designator] (FAAC)
SJN	San Juan [Peru] [Seismograph station code, US Geological Survey Closed] (SEIS)
SJN	San Juan [Diocesan abbreviation] [Puerto Rico] (TOCD)
S/J + N	Signal-to-Jamming - plus Noise Ratio
SJN	St. Johns, AZ [Location identifier FAA] (FAAL)
SJN	Supersonic Jet Noise
SJNB	San Jose National Bank (EFIS)
SJNB	SJNB Financial Corp. [Associated Press] (SAG)
SJNB	SJNB Financial Corp. [NASDAQ symbol] (NQ)
SJNB	SJNB Finl [NASDAQ symbol] (TTSB)
SJO	San Jose [Costa Rica] [Airport symbol] (OAG)
SJO	Service Junior - Oil-Resistant
SJOJ	Savez Jevrejskih Opstina Jugoslavije (BJA)
SJP	Saint Joe Co. [NYSE symbol] [Formerly, Saint Joe Corp.]
SJP	Saint Joe Corp. [NYSE symbol] (SAG)
SJP	San Jose Public Library, San Jose, CA [OCLC symbol] (OCLC)
SJP	San Juan [Puerto Rico] [Seismograph station code, US Geological Survey Closed] (SEIS)
SJP	San Juan [Peru] [Airport symbol] (AD)
SJP	Sao Jose Do Rio Preto [Brazil] [Airport symbol] (OAG)
SJP	Serialized Job Processor
SJP	Singapore Justice Party [Political party] (PPW)
SJP	Socialist Janata Party [India] [Political party] (ECON)
SJP	Special Job Procedure [Navy] (NG)
SJP	Stacked Job Processing (IAA)
SJP	Standard Jet Penetration [Aviation]
SJP	St. James Press [Publisher]
SJP	St. Joe Corp. [NYSE symbol] [Formerly, St. Joe Paper] (SG)
SJP	St. Joe Paper [NYSE symbol] (TTSB)
SJP	St. Joe Paper Co. [NYSE symbol] (SPSG)
SJP	St. Josaphat in Parma [Diocesan abbreviation] [Ohio] (TOCD)
SJP	Sun-Jupiter-Probe [Angle]
SJPC	Standing Joint Pacifist Committee [Defunct] (EAIO)
SJPS	Saint John's Provincial Seminary [Plymouth, MI]
SJQ	San Joaquin Reservoir [California] [Seismograph station code, US Geological Survey Closed] (SEIS)
SJQ	Selected Job Queue (IAA)
SJQ	Sesheke [Zambia] [Airport symbol] (AD)
SJR	San Jose [Costa Rica] [Seismograph station code, US Geological Survey Closed] (SEIS)
SJR	San Juan de Uraba [Colombia] [Airport symbol] (AD)
SJR	Senate Joint Resolution
SJR	Shinowara-Jones-Reinhard Unit [Medicine] (MAE)
SJRB	Soviet Jewry Research Bureau (EA)
SJRES	Senate Joint Resolution (AFIT)
SJRes	Senate Joint Resolution (WPI)
SJRF	Scott Joplin Ragtime Festival (EA)
SJRMF	Senator Joseph R. McCarthy Foundation (EA)
SJRT	St. Johns River Terminal [AAR code]
SJS	Saint John's Seminary [Brighton, MA]
SJS	Saint Joseph's Seminary [Illinois; New York]
SJS	San Jose [Costa Rica] [Seismograph station code, US Geological Survey] (SEIS)
SJS	San Jose [Bolivia] [Airport symbol] (AD)
SJS	Search Jam System
SJS	Secretary, Joint Staff [Military] (CINC)
SJS	Servants of the Blessed Sacrament (TOCD)
SjS	Sjogren Syndrome [Medicine] (DMAA)
SJS	Society of Jewish Science (EA)
SJS	Stevens-Johnson Syndrome [Medicine] (DMAA)
SJS	St. Johns Tracking Station [Newfoundland]
SJS	Sunshine-Jr Stores (EFIS)
SJS	Supervisory Job Safety Test
SJSB	SJS Bancorp [NASDAQ symbol] (TTSB)
SJSB	SJS Bancorp, Inc. [NASDAQ symbol] (SAG)
SJS Bcp	SJS Bancorp, Inc. [Associated Press] (SAG)
SJSC	San Jose State College [California] [Later, San Jose State University]
SJSD	Soviet Jewry Solidarity Day (BJA)
SJSM	Sisters of St. Joseph of St. Mark (TOCD)
SJSS	Saint Joseph's Seraphic Seminary [New York]
SJSU	San Jose State University [California]
SJT	San Angelo [Texas] [Airport symbol] (OAG)
SJT	San Angelo, TX [Location identifier FAA] (FAAL)
SJT	San Juan Basin Royalty Trust [NYSE symbol] (SPSG)
SJT	San Juan Basin Rty Tr [NYSE symbol] (TTSB)
Sjt	Serjeant [Military British] (DMA)
SJT	Service Junior - Thermoplastic
SJT	Stephen Joseph Theatre (WDAA)
SJT	St. Joseph Terminal Railroad Co. [AAR code]
SJT	Subsonic [or Supersonic] Jet Transport
SJT	Yorkshire European Airways Ltd. [British ICAO designator] (FAAC)
SJTCA	San Juan 21 Class Association (EA)
SJTCC	State Job Training Coordinating Council (OICC)
SJTh	Scottish Journal of Theology [A publication] (BJA)
SJU	Luiz Munoz Marin International Airport [FAA] (TAG)
SJU	San Juan [Puerto Rico] [Airport symbol] (OAG)
SJU	St. John's University [Minnesota; New York]

SJU	St. John's University, Division of Library and Information Science, Jamaica, NY [*OCLC symbol*] (OCLC)
SJuanB	San Juan Basin Royalty Trust [*Associated Press*] (SAG)
SJUF	Skandinavisk Jodisk Ungdomsforbund (BJA)
SJUMPS	Shipboard Joint Uniform Military Pay System [*Navy*] (DNAB)
S Jur	Sirey. Jurisprudence [*France*] [*A publication*] (DLA)
S Just	Shaw's Scotch Justiciary Cases [*A publication*] (DLA)
SJV	San Javier [*Bolivia*] [*Airport symbol*] (AD)
SJV	Sharing Joint Venture
SJV	Societe Jules Verne [*France*] (EAIO)
SJV	St. John [*Virgin Islands*] [*Seismograph station code, US Geological Survey*] (SEIS)
SJVLS	San Joaquin Valley Library System [*Library network*]
SJVWGA	San Joaquin Valley Wine Growers Association (EA)
SJW	Single Jewish Woman [*Classified advertising*]
SJW	Sisters of St. Joseph the Worker (TOCD)
SJW	SJW Corp. [*AMEX symbol*] (SPSG)
SJW	St. Louis, MO [*Location identifier FAA*] (FAAL)
SJWCP	Skid Jacket Water Cooling Pump [*Nuclear energy*] (NRCH)
SJWVUSA	Sons of Jewish War Veterans of the United States of America (EA)
SJX	Sartaneja [*Belize*] [*Airport symbol*] (OAG)
SJX	St. James, MI [*Location identifier FAA*] (FAAL)
SJY	San Jacinto, CA [*Location identifier FAA*] (FAAL)
SJZ	Angola, IN [*Location identifier FAA*] (FAAL)
SJZ	Sao Jorge Island [*Azores*] [*Airport symbol*] (OAG)
SJZ	Selected Judgments, Zambia [*A publication*] (DLA)
SJZ	Sueddeutsche Juristenzeitung [*German*] (ILCA)
SK	Sack
SK	Safekeeping
SK	Safety-Kleen [*NYSE symbol*] (TTSB)
SK	Safety-Kleen Corp. [*NYSE symbol*] (SPSG)
S-K	Saltonstall-Kennedy [*Promote and Develop American Fisheries*] (USDC)
S-K	Saltonstall-Kennedy Promote and Develop American Fisheries [*Marine science*] (OSRA)
S K	S & K Famous Brands, Inc. [*Associated Press*] (SAG)
SK	Sanitaetskompanie [*Medical company*] [*German military - World War II*]
SK	Santa Klaus (ROG)
SK	Saskatchewan [*Canadian province, postal code*]
SK	Scandinavian Airlines System [*Sweden*] [*ICAO designator*] (OAG)
SK	Sealed Knot [*An association*] (EAIO)
SK	Seek Command (IAA)
SK	Senile Keratosis [*Dermatology*] (DAVI)
SK	Service Kit
SK	Sick
sk	Sikkim [*ii (India) used in records cataloged after January 1978*] [*MARC country of publication code Library of Congress*] (LCCP)
SK	Sikorsky Aircraft Division [*United Aircraft Corp.*] [*ICAO aircraft manufacturer identifier*] (ICAO)
SK	Sinclair-Koppers Co. [*Later, Arco Polymers, Inc.*]
SK	Sink (AAG)
CK	Okein
sk	Skeletal [*Orthopedics*] (DAVI)
SK	Skeletals (DCTA)
SK	Sketch (AAG)
sk	Sketch (VRA)
sk	Skewbald [*Color of a horse*] (BARN)
Sk	Skewness (WGA)
SK	Skimmed
SK	Skin (DAVI)
SK	Skinned (MSA)
SK	Skin Test [*Medicine*] (DB)
SK	Skip
Sk	Skiver [*Leather bookbinding*] (DGA)
sk	Skot [*Unit of luminance*]
SK	Sky Condition [*Aviation*] (FAAC)
SK	Sloan-Kettering [*Cancer-treatment compound*] (MAE)
SK	Slovak Republic [*Internet country code*]
SK	Smack (ROG)
SK	Smith Kline Diagnostics (DAVI)
SK	Socket (DEN)
SK	Solar Keratosis [*Dermatology*] (DAVI)
SK	Sonic Key (MCD)
SK	South Kensington [*District of London*] (ROG)
SK	South Korea
SK	Sovetskyaya Kolonia [*Soviet Colony*]
SK	Spontaneous Killer [*Cells*] [*Immunology*] (DAVI)
SK	Station-Keeping
SK	Stockport [*Postcode*] (ODBW)
SK	Storekeeper [*Navy rating*]
SK	Streptokinase [*An enzyme*]
SK	Striae Keratopathy [*Ophthalmology*] (DAVI)
Sk	Strike [*or Stroke*]
SK	Substance K [*Biochemistry*]
SK	Sumerische Kultlieder aus Altbabylonischer Zeit [*A publication*] (BJA)
SK1	Storekeeper, First Class [*Navy rating*]
SK2	Storekeeper, Second Class [*Navy rating*]
SK3	Storekeeper, Third Class [*Navy rating*]
SKA	Aupracondylar Knee-Ankle[*Orthosis*] [*Orthopedics*] (DAVI)
SKA	Rio Air Express, SA [*Brazil*] [*FAA designator*] (FAAC)
SKA	Scottish Knitwear Association (DBA)
SKA	Skalstugan [*Sweden*] [*Seismograph station code, US Geological Survey*] (SEIS)
SKA	Skegair [*British ICAO designator*] (FAAC)
SKA	Skill, Knowledge, and Ability [*or Attitude*] [*Employment*]
SKA	Spokane, WA [*Location identifier FAA*] (FAAL)
SKA	Station-Keeping Assistance (DS)
S/KA	Submarine Kit Allowance [*British military*] (DMA)
SKA	Switchblade Knife Act
SKAD	Survival Kit Air-Droppable [*Military Canada*]
SKAI	Skylink America (EFIS)
SKAI	Square Kilometer Array Interferometer [*A proposed international collaboration*]
SKAMP	Station-Keeping and Mobile Platform [*Robot sailboat*]
SKAN	Solidariteits Komitee Argentiniee [*Netherlands*]
SK&F	SmithKline Beecham ADS (EFIS)
SKAND SF	Skandinaviska Seglarforbundet [*Scandinavian Yachting Association - SYA*] (EAIO)
SKAP	Armedia/El Elden [*Colorado ICAO location identifier*] (ICLI)
SKAP	Skills, Knowledge, Abilities, and Personnel [*Attributes*] (MCD)
SKAS	Puerto Asis [*Colorado ICAO location identifier*] (ICLI)
SKAT	Kommentar zum Alten Testament [*A publication*] (BJA)
SKAT	Sex Knowledge and Aptitude [*Test*]
SKAT	Skysat Communications Network Corp. [*NASDAQ symbol*] (SAG)
SKATA	Skysat Commun Network'A' [*NASDAQ symbol*] (TTSB)
SKATI	Skills, Knowledges, Aptitudes, Temperaments, Interests (OICC)
SKATW	Skysat Communicns Ntwk Wrrt'A' [*NASDAQ symbol*] (TTSB)
SKATZ	Skysat Communicns Ntwk Wrrt'B' [*NASDAQ symbol*] (TTSB)
SKB	Saint Kitts [*Leeward Islands*] [*Airport symbol*] (OAG)
SKB	Skew Buffer
SKB	Skybridge International, Inc. [*Vancouver Stock Exchange symbol*]
SKB	Skyfreighters Corp. [*ICAO designator*] (FAAC)
SKB	Wichita Falls, TX [*Location identifier FAA*] (FAAL)
SKBC	El Banco/Los Flores [*Colorado ICAO location identifier*] (ICLI)
SKBF	Schweizerische Koordinationsstelle fuer Bildungsforschung [*Swiss Coordination Center for Research in Education*] [*Information service or system*] (IID)
SKBG	Bucaramanga/Palo Negro Sur [*Colorado ICAO location identifier*] (ICLI)
SKBO	Bogota/Eldorado [*Colorado ICAO location identifier*] (ICLI)
SKBQ	Barranquilla/Ernesto Cortissoz [*Colorado ICAO location identifier*] (ICLI)
SKBS	Bahia Solano/Jose Celestino Mutis [*Colorado ICAO location identifier*] (ICLI)
SKBU	Buenaventura [*Colorado ICAO location identifier*] (ICLI)
SKC	Scottish Kennel Club (BARN)
SKC	Services Kinema Corp. [*British military*] (DMA)
SKC	Skycare Management Services Ltd. [*British ICAO designator*] (FAAC)
SKC	Sky Clear [*ICAO*] (FAAC)
SKC	Suki [*Papua New Guinea*] [*Airport symbol*] (OAG)
SKC	Waukesha, WI [*Location identifier FAA*] (FAAL)
SKCATL	South Korea Conventional Air Target List (MCD)
SKCB	Skylands Cmnty Bk NJ [*NASDAQ symbol*] (TTSB)
SKCB	Skylands Community Bank [*NASDAQ symbol*] (SAG)
SKCB	Storekeeper, Construction Battalion, Stevedore [*Navy rating*]
SKCC	Cucuta/Camilo Daza [*Colorado ICAO location identifier*] (ICLI)
SKCD	Condoto/Mandinga [*Colorado ICAO location identifier*] (ICLI)
SKCG	Cartagena/Rafael Nunez [*Colorado ICAO location identifier*] (ICLI)
SKCH	Skyline Chili [*NASDAQ symbol*] (TTSB)
SKCH	Skyline Chili, Inc. [*Cincinnati, OH*] [*NASDAQ symbol*] (NQ)
SKCL	Cali/Alfonso Bonilla Aragon [*Colorado ICAO location identifier*] (ICLI)
SKCM	Master Chief Storekeeper [*Navy rating*]
SKCM	Society of King Charles the Martyr (EA)
SKCMA	Steel Kitchen Cabinet Manufacturers Association (EA)
SKCO	Tumaco/La Florida [*Colorado ICAO location identifier*] (ICLI)
SKCS	Senior Chief Storekeeper [*Navy rating*]
SKCZ	Corozal/Las Brujas [*Colorado ICAO location identifier*] (ICLI)
SKD	Samarkand [*Former USSR Airport symbol*]
SKD	Selve-Kornbegel-Dornheim [*Name of a German small arms ammunition factory*] [*World War II*]
SKD	Semi Knocked Down [*Shipping*] (DS)
SKD	Singer, Kearfott Division [*NASA*] (NAKS)
SKD	Sitkalidak Island [*Alaska*] [*Seismograph station code, US Geological Survey*] (SEIS)
SKD	Skid
SKD	Skilled (MSA)
SKD	Skirted
SKD	Skyguard Ltd. [*British ICAO designator*] (FAAC)
SKD	Skyworld Resources & Development Ltd. [*Vancouver Stock Exchange symbol*]
SKD	Smith Kline Diagnostics (DAVI)
SKD	Station-Keeping Distance [*British military*] (DMA)
SKD	St. Katherine's Dock [*Shipping*] [*British*] (ROG)
SKD	Storekeeper, Disbursing [*Navy rating*]
SKDH	Shikimate Dehydrogenase [*An enzyme*]
SKDL	Suomen Kansan Demokraattinen Liitto [*Finnish People's Democratic League*] [*Political party*] (PPW)
SKDN	Shakedown [*Navy*] (NVT)
SKDNC	Shakedown Cruise [*Navy*]
SKDNCRU	Shakedown Cruise [*Navy*] (NVT)
SKDP	Sambungan Komunikasi Data Packet [*Indonesia*] [*Telecommunications service*] (TSSD)
SKDR	Skydoor Media & Entmt [*NASDAQ symbol*] (TTSB)
SKDU	Ship's Keyboard Display Unit
SKE	Belleville, IL [*Location identifier FAA*] (FAAL)
SKE	Skeena Resources Ltd. [*Vancouver Stock Exchange symbol*]
SKE	Skien [*Norway*] [*Airport symbol*] (OAG)
SKE	Sky Tours, Inc. [*ICAO designator*] (FAAC)
SKE	Station-Keeping Equipment

SKEC .... Barranquilla [*Colorado ICAO location identifier*] (ICLI)
SKED .... Bogota [*Colorado ICAO location identifier*] (ICLI)
SKED .... Schedule (NG)
SKED .... Sort Key Edit [*Library of Congress*]
SKEDCON .... Schedule Conference [*Military*] (NVT)
SKEEC .... Southern Central Kansas Environmental Education Center (EDAC)
SKEJ .... Barrancabermeja/Yariguis [*Colorado ICAO location identifier*] (ICLI)
SKEL .... Skeletal (AAG)
SKET .... Skeleton Key (DSUE)
SKEY .... Softkey International [*NASDAQ symbol*] (TTSB)
SKEY .... Softkey International, Inc. [*NASDAQ symbol*] (SAG)
SKEYW .... Softkey Intl Wrrt [*NASDAQ symbol*] (TTSB)
SKF .... San Antonio, TX [*Location identifier FAA*] (FAAL)
SKF .... SKF AB [*Associated Press*] (SAG)
SKF .... Skycraft, Inc. [*ICAO designator*] (FAAC)
SKF .... SmithKline Corp. [*Formerly, Smith, Kline & French Co.*] [*Research code symbol*]
SKF .... Svenska Kullagerfabriken AB [*Swedish manufacturer, especially of ball bearings; active in many countries*]
SKF .... Svenska Kullager Frabikon [*Swedish Ball Bearing Manufacturing*]
SKFA .... Scottish Keep Fit Association (DBA)
SKFB .... S & K Famous Brands [*NASDAQ symbol*] (TTSB)
SKFB .... S & K Famous Brands, Inc. [*NASDAQ symbol*] (NQ)
SKFL .... Florencia/Capitolio [*Colorado ICAO location identifier*] (ICLI)
SKFR .... SKF AB [*Goteborg, Sweden*] [*NASDAQ symbol*] (NQ)
SKFRY .... SKF AB ADR [*NASDAQ symbol*] (TTSB)
SkFx .... Skull Fracture [*Medicine*]
Skg .... Safekeeping
SKG .... Salonika [*Greece*] [*Airport symbol*] (AD)
SKG .... Sikaman Gold Resources Ltd. [*Toronto Stock Exchange symbol*]
SKG .... Skycraft Air Transport, Inc. [*Canada ICAO designator*] (FAAC)
SKG .... Thessaloniki [*Greece*] [*Airport symbol*] (OAG)
SKGI .... Girardot/Santiago Vila [*Colorado ICAO location identifier*] (ICLI)
SKGP .... Guapi [*Colorado ICAO location identifier*] (ICLI)
SKH .... Selkirk Communications Ltd. [*Toronto Stock Exchange symbol*]
SKH .... Skywatch Ltd. [*British ICAO designator*] (FAAC)
SKH .... Surkhet [*Nepal*] [*Airport symbol*] (OAG)
SKHS .... Sri Kapila Humanitarian Society (EAIO)
SKI .... Sac City, IA [*Location identifier FAA*] (FAAL)
SKI .... Sex Knowledge Inventory [*Premarital and marital relations test*]
SKI .... Sister Kenny Institute (EA)
SKI .... Skiff, Ice [*Coast Guard*] (DNAB)
SKI .... Skilda [*Algeria*] [*Airport symbol*] (AD)
SKI .... SKI Ltd. [*Associated Press*] (SAG)
SKI .... Skin (DAVI)
SKI .... Skylink Airlines [*Canada ICAO designator*] (FAAC)
SKI .... Sloan-Kettering Institute for Cancer Research
SKI .... Spinal Kinematic Instrument [*Medicine*]
SKI .... St. Kitts [*St. Kitts*] [*Seismograph station code, US Geological Survey*] (SEIS)
SKIA .... Secure Key-Issuing Authority [*Computer science*]
SKIB .... Ibague/Perales [*Colorado ICAO location identifier*] (ICLI)
Skid Min ...... Skidmore's Mining Statutes [*A publication*] (DLA)
SKIF .... Social Security Number Key Index File [*IRS*]
SKIF .... Sotsyalistisher Kinder Farband (BJA)
SKII .... S-K-I Ltd. [*Killington, VT*] [*NASDAQ symbol*] (NQ)
SKIL .... Scanner Keyed Input Language
SKILA .... Southern Korean Interim Legislative Assembly
SKILL .... Satellite Kill
Skill Pol Rep... Skillman's New York Police Reports [*A publication*] (DLA)
Skin .... Skinner's English King's Bench Reports [*A publication*] (DLA)
Skinker .... Skinner's Reports [*65-79 Missouri*] [*A publication*] (DLA)
Skinner .... Skinner's English King's Bench Reports [*90 English Reprint*] [*1681-98*] [*A publication*] (DLA)
Skinner (Eng)... Skinner's English King's Bench Reports [*90 English Reprint*] [*A publication*] (DLA)
SKINS .... Supplemental Knowledge Incentive Notes [*Scrip offered to students for good performance*] [*Experimental learning program*]
SKINY .... Pharma Patch plc [*NASDAQ symbol*] (TTSB)
SKIP .... Ipiales/San Luis [*Colorado ICAO location identifier*] (ICLI)
SKIP .... Sick Kids Need Involved People (EA)
SKIP .... Skill/Knowledge Improvement Program [*Navy*] (DNAB)
SKIP .... Skinner Investigation Platform
SKIPI .... Super Knowledge Information Processing Intelligence [*Computer science*]
Skippies ...... School Kids with Income, Purchasing Power [*Lifestyle Classification*]
SKJ .... Sitkinak Island, AK [*Location identifier FAA*] (FAAL)
SKJ .... Skyjet, Inc. [*Antigua and Barbuda*] [*ICAO designator*] (FAAC)
SKK .... Shaktoolik [*Alaska*] [*Airport symbol*] (OAG)
SKK .... Shaktoolik, AK [*Location identifier FAA*] (FAAL)
SKK .... Sikka [*Former USSR Seismograph station code, US Geological Survey Closed*] (SEIS)
SKK .... Skylane Air Charter [*British ICAO designator*] (FAAC)
SKK .... Sowjetische Kontrollkommission
SKKCA .... Supreme Knight of the Knights of Columbus of America
SKL .... Isle Of Skye [*Scotland*] [*Airport symbol*] (OAG)
SKL .... Serum-Killing Level [*Pharmacology*] (DAVI)
SKL .... Skiff, Light [*Coast Guard*] (DNAB)
SKL .... Skilak [*Cooper Landing*] [*Alaska*] [*Seismograph station code, US Geological Survey*] (SEIS)
SKL .... Skill Level
SKL .... Skycharter (Malton) Ltd. [*Canada ICAO designator*] (FAAC)
SKL .... Skylight [*Technical drawings*]
SKL .... Smith, Kline & French Laboratories [*Canada*] (IIA)
SKL .... Stackpool Resources Ltd. [*Vancouver Stock Exchange symbol*]

SKL .... Suomen Kristillinen Liitto [*Finnish Christian League*] [*Political party*] (PPE)
SKLC .... Los Cedros/Uraba [*Colorado ICAO location identifier*] (ICLI)
SKLL .... Skill
SKLM .... La Mina/Riohacha [*Colorado ICAO location identifier*] (ICLI)
SKLP .... South Korean Labor Party
SKLT .... Leticia/Alfredo Vasquez Cobo [*Colorado ICAO location identifier*] (ICLI)
SKLT .... Station Keeping Light (NFPA)
SKM .... Fayetteville Flying Service & Scheduled Skyways System [*ICAO designator*] (FAAC)
SKM .... Korea Mobile Telecommunications [*NYSE symbol*] (SAG)
SKM .... Schuster-Kubelka-Munk [*Optics*]
SKM .... Sine-Kosine Multiplier
SKM .... Skiff, Medium [*Coast Guard*] (DNAB)
SKMC .... Sickness due to Misconduct [*Military*] (DNAB)
SKMG .... Magangue/Baracoa [*Colorado ICAO location identifier*] (ICLI)
SkMg .... Sulfate of Potash Magnesia Export Association (EA)
SKMG .... Sulfate of Potash Magnesia Export Association (NTPA)
SKMQ .... Mariquita/Mariquita [*Colorado ICAO location identifier*] (ICLI)
SKMR .... Monteria/Los Garzones [*Colorado ICAO location identifier*] (ICLI)
SKMU .... Mitu/Mitu [*Colorado ICAO location identifier*] (ICLI)
SKMZ .... Manizales/La Nubia [*Colorado ICAO location identifier*] (ICLI)
SKN .... Skaneateles [*New York*] [*Seismograph station code, US Geological Survey*] (SEIS)
SKN .... Skein (ROG)
SKN .... Skyline Aviation Services, Inc. [*ICAO designator*] (FAAC)
SKN .... Smithville, TN [*Location identifier FAA*] (FAAL)
SKN .... Stokmarknes [*Norway*] [*Airport symbol*] (OAG)
SKNTO .... St. Kitts-Nevis Tourist Office (EA)
S/KNU .... Steering Knuckle [*Automotive engineering*]
SKNV .... Neiva/La Manguila [*Colorado ICAO location identifier*] (ICLI)
SKO .... Deadhorse, AK [*Location identifier FAA*] (FAAL)
SKO .... Saskatchewan Oil & Gas Corp. [*Toronto Stock Exchange symbol*]
SKO .... Scottish Airways Flyers Ltd. [*ICAO designator*] (FAAC)
SKO .... Sets, Kits, and Outfits (MCD)
SKO .... Shopko Stores [*NYSE symbol*] (SPSG)
SKO .... Skopje [*Yugoslavia*] [*Seismograph station code, US Geological Survey*] (SEIS)
SKO .... Society of Kastorians "Omonoia" (EA)
SKO .... Sokoto [*Nigeria*] [*Airport symbol*] (OAG)
SKOC .... Ocana/Aguas Claras [*Colorado ICAO location identifier*] (ICLI)
SKOI .... Suomen Konsulttitoimistojen Liitto [*Finnish Association of Consulting Firms*] (EY)
SKOL .... Suomen Konsulttitoimistojen Liitto [*Finnish Association of Consulting Firms*] (EY)
SKOLD .... Screening Kit of Language Development [*Child development test*]
SKOR .... Sperry Kalman Optical Reset [*Ship's Inertial Navigation System*] [*Navy*] (DNAB)
SKOT .... Otu/Otu [*Colorado ICAO location identifier*] (ICLI)
Skoteys .... Spoiled Kids of the Eighties [*Offspring of the Yuppies*] [*Lifestyle classification*]
SKP .... Aero North Aviation Services [*Canada ICAO designator*] (FAAC)
SKP .... Skip (BUR)
SKP .... Skip Line Printer [*Computer science*] (ECII)
SKP .... Skopje [*Former Yugoslavia*] [*Airport symbol*] (OAG)
SKP .... Station-Keeping Position
SKP .... Suomen Kommunistinen Puolue [*Communist Party of Finland*] [*Political party*] (PPW)
SKP .... Sveriges Kommunistiska Partiet [*Communist Party of Sweden*] [*Political party*] (PPE)
SKPB .... Puerto Bolivar/Riohacha [*Colorado ICAO location identifier*] (ICLI)
SKPC .... Puerto Carreno [*Colorado ICAO location identifier*] (ICLI)
SKPE .... Pereira/Matecana [*Colorado ICAO location identifier*] (ICLI)
SKPI .... Pitalito [*Colorado ICAO location identifier*] (ICLI)
SKPI .... Super Knowledge, Processing Interaction [*Concept advanced by Timothy Leary*]
SK-PJ .... Savez Komunista - Pokret za Jugoslaviju [*League of Communists - Movement for Yugoslavia*] [*Political party*]
SKPL .... Sketch Pad Layout (MCD)
skpo .... Slip One, Knit One, Pass Slipped Stitch Over [*Knitting*] (BARN)
SKPP .... Popayan/Guillermo Leon Valencia [*Colorado ICAO location identifier*] (ICLI)
S-K-P's .... Escapees, Inc. (EA)
SKPS .... Pasto/Antonio Narino [*Colorado ICAO location identifier*] (ICLI)
skpsso .... Slip One, Knit One, Pass Slipped Stitch Over [*Knitting*] (BARN)
SKPV .... Providencia/Providencia [*Colorado ICAO location identifier*] (ICLI)
SKQ .... Sekakes [*Lesotho*] [*Airport symbol*] (OAG)
SKQ .... Sexual Knowledge Questionnaire
SKR .... Bedford, MA [*Location identifier FAA*] (FAAL)
SKR .... Sanskrit [*Language, etc.*]
Skr .... Sanskrit (WDAA)
SKR .... Saskatchewan Regional Libraries [*UTLAS symbol*]
SKR .... Saturn Kilometer-Wave Radiation [*Planetary science*]
SKR .... Sea King Replacement [*Naval aircraft*] [*British*]
SKR .... Seeker
SKR .... Separator-Key Generator-Recombiner (MCD)
SKR .... Severo-Kurilsk [*Former USSR Seismograph station code, US Geological Survey*] (SEIS)
SKR .... Shaker Heights City School District, Shaker Heights, OH [*OCLC symbol*] (OCLC)
Skr .... Skipper [*Navy British*]
SKR .... Skogar [*Iceland*] [*Airport symbol*] (AD)
SKR .... Skylark Resources Ltd. [*Vancouver Stock Exchange symbol*]
SKR .... Skyrover Ltd. [*British ICAO designator*] (FAAC)

SKR	South Korea Republic
SKR	Station-Keeping RADAR
SKR	Substance-K Receptor [*Biochemistry*]
S KR	Swedish Krona [*Monetary unit*]
Skr	Swedish Krona [*Monetary unit*] (ODBW)
SKRG	Rio Negro/Jose Maria Cordova [*Colorado ICAO location identifier*] (ICLI)
SKRH	Rio Hacha, Guajira [*Colorado ICAO location identifier*] (ICLI)
SKRI	Striker Industries [*NASDAQ symbol*] (SAG)
SKRSU	Sikouras Pictures Unit [*NASDAQ symbol*] (TTSB)
Skrt	Sanskrit [*Language*] (BARN)
SKS	Career Development Center, Shaker Heights, OH [*OCLC symbol*] (OCLC)
SKS	Saks Holdings [*NYSE symbol*] (TTSB)
SKS	Samozaryadnyi Karabin Simonova Carbine [*Soviet made semiautomatic rifle*] (VNW)
SKS	Savezna Komisija za Standardizacija [*Federal Commission for Standardization*] [*Yugoslavia*]
SKS	Scanning Kinetic Spectroscopy
SKS	Schichtlade Kammer System [*Stratified Combustion Chamber System*] [*Automotive engineering German*]
SKS	Skrydstrup [*Denmark*] [*Airport symbol*] (OAG)
SKS	Sky Service [*Belgium ICAO designator*] (FAAC)
SKS	Soren Kierkegaard Society [*Copenhagen, Denmark*] (EA)
SKS	Specialist Knowledge Services [*British organization for occult research*]
SKS	Station-Keeping Ship
SKS	Svetoveho Kongresu Slovakov [*Canada*] (EAIO)
SKSA	Saravena/Saravena El Eden [*Colorado ICAO location identifier*] (ICLI)
SKSA	Seaman Apprentice, Storekeeper, Striker [*Navy rating*]
SKSD	Streptokinase Streptodornase [*An enzyme mixture*] [*Medicine*]
SKSG	Santagueda/Santagueda [*Colorado ICAO location identifier*] (ICLI)
SKSJ	San Jose Del Guaviare/S. J. Del Guaviore [*Colorado ICAO location identifier*] (ICLI)
SKSL	Skaneateles Short Line Railroad Corp. [*Later, SSL*] [*AAR code*]
SKSM	Santa Marta/Simon Bolivar [*Colorado ICAO location identifier*] (ICLI)
SKSN	Seaman, Storekeeper, Striker [*Navy rating*]
SKSP	San Andres/Sesquicentenario, San Andres [*Colorado ICAO location identifier*] (ICLI)
SKSS	Stoleczny Komitet Samopomocy Spolecznej [*Warsaw*] (BJA)
SKSV	San Vicente Del Caguan [*Colorado ICAO location identifier*] (ICLI)
SKT	Dyad Services Ltd. [*British ICAO designator*] (FAAC)
SKT	Sanskrit [*Afrikaans*]
Skt	Sanskrit (WDAA)
SKT	Saskatchewan Trust Co. [*Toronto Stock Exchange symbol*]
SKT	Skill Knowledge Tests
SKT	Skiptrace (LAIN)
SKT	Skirt (MSA)
SKT	Skwentna [*Alaska*] [*Seismograph station code, US Geological Survey*] (SEIS)
SKT	Socket (MSA)
SKT	Specialty Knowledge Test [*Military*] (AFM)
SKT	Storekeeper, Technical [*Navy rating*]
SKT	Tanger Factory Outlet Centers, Inc. [*NYSE symbol*] (SPSG)
SKT	Tanger Factory Outlet Ctrs [*NYSE symbol*] (TTSB)
SKTA	Shetland Knitwear Trades Association [*British*] (DBA)
SKTD	Trinidad [*Colorado ICAO location identifier*] (ICLI)
SKTF	Spring Knife Trade Federation [*A union*] [*British*]
SKTM	Tame [*Colorado ICAO location identifier*] (ICLI)
SKTPrA	Tanger Fac Outlt Cv Dep Pfd [*NYSE symbol*] (TTSB)
sk tr	Skeletal Traction [*Orthopedics*] (DAVI)
SKTU	Turbo, Gonzalo Mejia [*Colorado ICAO location identifier*] (ICLI)
SKTV	Silver King Communic [*NASDAQ symbol*] (TTSB)
SKTV	Silver King Communications [*NASDAQ symbol*] (SAG)
sk tx	Skeletal Traction [*Orthopedics*] (DAVI)
SKU	Newburgh, NY [*Location identifier FAA*] (FAAL)
SKU	Sakura [*Japan*] [*Seismograph station code, US Geological Survey 'Closed'*] (SEIS)
SKU	Stock Keeping Unit [*Merchandising system*]
SKUC	Arauca/Santiago Perez [*Colorado ICAO location identifier*] (ICLI)
SKUI	Quibdo/El Carano [*Colorado ICAO location identifier*] (ICLI)
SKUL	Seeker-Killer-Utility Lasers (DOMA)
SKV	Santa Katarina [*Egypt*] [*Airport symbol*] (OAG)
SKV	Skewing the Pitch Angle
SKV	Skukum Gold [*Vancouver Stock Exchange symbol*]
SKV	Storekeeper, Aviation [*Navy rating*]
SKVP	Valledupar/Alfonso Lopez [*Colorado ICAO location identifier*] (ICLI)
SKVV	Schweizerischer Katholischer Volksverein
SKVV	Villavicencio/Vanguardia [*Colorado ICAO location identifier*] (ICLI)
SKW	Shichikawa [*Japan*] [*Seismograph station code, US Geological Survey*] (SEIS)
SKW	Skwentna, AK [*Location identifier FAA*] (FAAL)
SKW	Sky West, Inc. [*ICAO designator*] (FAAC)
SKW	Sturge-Kalische-Weber [*Syndrome*] [*or Sturge-Weber Syndrome*] [*Medicine*] (DAVI)
SKW	Sueddeutsche Kalkstickstoffwerke [*AG*]
SKW	Syndicate of North Germany Electric Utilities [*Germany*] [*Acronym is based on foreign phrase*]
SKWC	Sky Way Conference (PSS)
SKWOC	Structured Keyword Out of Context (NITA)
SKWY	Skyway [*Postal Service standard*] (OPSA)
SKX	Skechers U.S.A. Cl'A' [*NYSE symbol*]
SKX	Skyline Explorations Ltd. [*Vancouver Stock Exchange symbol Toronto Stock Exchange symbol*]

SKX	Skyways AB [*Sweden ICAO designator*] (FAAC)
SKX	Taos, NM [*Location identifier FAA*] (FAAL)
SKY	Cooper Skybird Air Charters Ltd. [*Kenya*] [*ICAO designator*] (FAAC)
SKY	Sandusky, OH [*Location identifier FAA*] (FAAL)
SKY	Skyline Corp. [*NYSE symbol*] (SPSG)
SKY	Skyrocket Exploration [*Vancouver Stock Exchange symbol*]
SKYBET	Skylab Best Estimate of Trajectory [*NASA*]
SKYC	American Mobile Satellite Corp. [*NASDAQ symbol*] (SAG)
SKYC	Amer Mobile Satellite [*NASDAQ symbol*] (TTSB)
SKYCAV	Sky Cavalry
SkyChili	Skyline Chili, Inc. [*Associated Press*] (SAG)
SKYCOM	Skylab Communications Engineer [*NASA*]
SKYFC	Sky Games International Ltd. [*NASDAQ symbol*] (SAG)
SKYG	Sky Games International Ltd. [*NASDAQ symbol*] (SAG)
SKYGF	Sky Games Intl [*NASDAQ symbol*] (TTSB)
SkyGms	Sky Games International, Ltd. [*Associated Press*] (SAG)
SKYL	Skyline Multimedia Entertainment [*NASDAQ symbol*] (SAG)
SKYL	Skyline Multimedia Entmt [*NASDAQ symbol*] (TTSB)
SKYLAC	Skyline Athletic Conference (PSS)
SkylandP	Skylands Park Management [*Associated Press*] (SAG)
SkylCBk	Skylands Community Bank [*Associated Press*] (SAG)
Skyline	Skyline Corp. [*Associated Press*] (SAG)
SkyInd	Skylands Park Management [*Associated Press*] (SAG)
SKYLW	Skyline Multimeida Entmt Wrrt'A' [*NASDAQ symbol*] (TTSB)
SKYLZ	Skyline Multimedia Entmt Wrrt'B' [*NASDAQ symbol*] (TTSB)
SkyM	Skyline Multimedia Entertainment [*Associated Press*] (SAG)
SKYM	SkyMall, Inc. [*NASDAQ symbol*] (SAG)
SkyMall	SkyMall, Inc. [*Associated Press*] (SAG)
SkyMI	Skyline Multimedia Entertainment [*Associated Press*] (SAG)
SkyMult	Skyline Multimedia Entertainment [*Associated Press*] (SAG)
SKYP	Skylands Park Management [*NASDAQ symbol*] (SAG)
SKYP	Skylands Park Mgmt [*NASDAQ symbol*] (TTSB)
SKYP	Suomen Kansan Yhtenaeisyyden Puolue [*People's Unity Party*] [*Finland Political party*] (PPW)
SKYP	Yopal/Yopal [*Colorado ICAO location identifier*] (ICLI)
SKYPW	Skylands Pk Mgmt Wrrt [*NASDAQ symbol*] (TTSB)
SKYS	Sky Scientific [*NASDAQ symbol*] (TTSB)
Skysat	Skysat Communications Network Corp. [*Associated Press*] (SAG)
SkysatC	Skysat Communications Network Corp. [*Associated Press*] (SAG)
skyscr	Skyscraper (VRA)
Skyst	Skysat Communications Network Corp. [*Associated Press*] (SAG)
SKYT	Skytel Communications [*NASDAQ symbol*] [*Formerly, Mobile Telecommunications Tech.*]
SKYW	SkyWest, Inc. [*St. George, UT*] [*NASDAQ symbol*] (NQ)
SKYWAY	Skyway [*Commonly used*] (OPSA)
SkyWest	SkyWest, Inc. [*Associated Press*] (SAG)
SKZ	Sukkur [*Pakistan*] [*Airport symbol*] (OAG)
SL	Large-Scale Disturbance Field
SL	Lloydminster Public Library, Saskatchewan [*Library symbol National Library of Canada*] (NLC)
SL	Rio Sul [*ICAO designator*] (AD)
SL	Safe Locker (AAG)
SL	Safety Level [*Army*]
SL	Safety Limit [*Nuclear energy*] (NRCH)
SL	Sales Letter
SL	Salt Loading
SL	Salvage Loss
SL	Sample Laboratory (MCD)
SL	Sand-Loaded [*Technical drawings*]
SL	San Luis Obispo [*Mexican state; city and county in California*]
SL	Sarcolemma (DB)
SL	Satellite-Like Virus
SL	Saturated Logic (IAA)
SL	Save Lebanon (EA)
sl	Scale Leaf [*Botany*]
SL	Scanning Slit (MCD)
SL	School Leavers [*Department of Employment*] [*British*]
SL	Schutte Lanz [*World War I German aircraft designation*]
SL	Scientists for Life [*An association Defunct*] (EA)
SL	Sclerosing Leukoencephalopathy [*Medicine*] (DMAA)
SL	Scottish Liturgy [*Episcopalian*]
SL	Scout Leader (WDAA)
SL	Seal (NASA)
SL	Sea Level
SL	Searchlight
SL	Second Lieutenant
SL	Section Leader [*Nuclear energy*] (NRCH)
SL	Section List (MCD)
SL	Secundum Legem [*According to Law*] [*Latin*]
SL	Security List (WDAA)
SL	Seditious Libeler
SL	Sendero Luminoso [*Shining Path*] [*Peru*] (PD)
SL	Send Leg [*Telegraphy*] (TEL)
SL	Sensation Level [*Audiometry*]
SL	Sensu Lato [*In a Broad Sense*] [*Latin*]
SL	Separate Lead [*Cables*]
SL	Sergeant-at-Law
SL-	Serious List [*Hospital administration*] (DAVI)
S-L	Serosa to Lumen [*Anatomy*] (DAVI)
SL	Service Letter (MCD)
SL	Servomechanisms Laboratory [*MIT*] (MCD)
SL	Session Laws (DLA)
SL	Shear Layer [*or Load*]
SL	Shelf Life (NASA)
SL	Shelf List [*A card catalog arranged in call number order*]

SL	Shift Left
S/L	Shiplap (DAC)
SL	Ship Library [*Maritime Data Network, Inc.*] [*Information service or system*] (CRD)
SL	Ship-of-the-Line
SL	Shipowner's Liability [*Business term*]
S/L	Shops and Labs [*NASA*] (NASA)
SL	Short Landed [*Tea trade*] (ROG)
SL	Short Lengths [*Construction*]
SL	Short Letter (DCTA)
S-L	Short-Long [*as of a signal light's flash cycle*]
SL	Sibley-Lehninger [*Unit*] (MAE)
SL	Sick Leave (AFM)
S/L	Side Lay [*Printing machine*] (DGA)
S/L	Sidelever [*Rifles*] (DICI)
SL	Side Load (AAG)
SL	Sidelobe (CAAL)
SL	Sierra Leone [*ANSI two-letter standard code*] (CNC)
sl	Sierra Leone [*MARC country of publication code Library of Congress*] (LCCP)
SL	Sigillo Locus [*Place for the Seal*] [*Latin*] (ROG)
SL	Signal Level
SL	Significance Level
SL	Silicon Lacquer
SL	Silvaire [*ICAO aircraft manufacturer identifier*] (ICAO)
SL	Silver Library [*A publication*]
SL	Simulation Language [*Computer science*] (BUR)
SL	Sinding Larsen [*disease*] [*or Larsen's disease, or Larsen-Johansson disease*] [*An association known as Larsen's Disease, or Larsen-Johansson Disease*] [*Orthopedics*] (DAVI)
SL	Sine Loco [*Without Place*] [*Latin*]
SL	Single Lead [*Cables*] (IAA)
SL	Single Ledger [*Accounting*]
SL	Single Line
SL	Single-Locus [*Light flashes*]
SL	Sisters of Loretto at the Foot of the Cross [*Roman Catholic religious order*]
SL	Sjogren-Larsson [*Syndrome*] [*Medicine*] (DAVI)
SL	Skilled Labor (MHDW)
SL	Skill Level
SL	Skylab [*NASA*] (KSC)
SL	Slain (ROG)
SL	Slate (AAG)
SL	Sleeve [*Technical drawings*]
SL	Slesvigske Parti [*Schleswig Party*] [*Denmark Political party*] (PPE)
SL	Slide (AAG)
SL	Slightly
sl	Slightly (WDMC)
SL	SL Industries [*NYSE symbol*] (TTSB)
SL	SL Industries, Inc. [*NYSE symbol*] (SPSG)
SL	Slip [*Knitting*]
SL	Slit Lamp [*Instrumentation*]
SL	Slough [*Postcode*] (ODBW)
SL	Slovenia [*International civil aircraft marking*] (ODBW)
SL	Slow [*Track condition*] [*Thoroughbred racing*]
SL	Small Light Seeds [*Botany*]
SL	Small Lymphocytes [*Hematology*]
SL	Small Lymphoma [*Oncology*]
SL	Societas Liturgica (EA)
SL	Society of Limerents (EA)
SL	Sockellafette [*Pedestal mount*] [*German military - World War II*]
SL	Sodium Lactate (MAE)
S/L	Soft Landing (MCD)
SL	Soft LASER
SL	Solar Lobby [*An association*] (EA)
SL	Sold
SL	Solicitor-at-Law
SL	Solidified Liquid (MAE)
SL	Solid Logic (IAA)
SL	Somatolactin [*Biochemistry*]
SL	Sonic Log
SL	Sonoluminescence [*Physics*]
SL	Sons of Liberty (EA)
SL	Sortie Lab [*NASA*]
SL	Sound Level (NASA)
SL	Sound Locator [*Military*]
SL	Source Language [*Computer science*] (BUR)
SL	Source Level
SL	Source Library (IAA)
SL	Southeast Airlines, Inc. [*ICAO designator Obsolete*] (OAG)
SL	South Latitude
SL	Spacelab [*NASA*] (NASA)
S/L	Space Laboratory (KSC)
SL	Spartacist League (EA)
SL	Special Layout (MCD)
SL	Special Letter (WDAA)
SL	Special Libraries [*A publication*] (BRI)
SL	Special Linear [*Group theory, mathematics*]
SL	Specification Limit (AAEL)
S/L	Speed/Length [*Boating*]
S/L	Speedletter
SL	Speed Lock [*Computer science*] (PCM)
SL	Split Level [*Home*] [*Classified advertising*]
SL	Spool
SL	Sport Leicht [*Sports Lightweight (Car)*] [*German*]
SL	Sprinkler Leakage [*Insurance*]
SL	Squadron-Leader [*Military*]
SL	Stage Left [*A stage direction*]
SL	Stagnation Line
SL	Standard Label [*Computer science*]
SL	Standard Length
SL	Standard Load [*Automotive engineering*]
SL	Standard Location [*Civil Defense*]
SL	Standard of Living
SL	Star Line
SL	Start Line
SL	Stationary Low-Power [*Reactor*] [*Dismantled*] (NRCH)
SL	Statistical List
S/L	Statute of Limitations (OICC)
SL	Stein-Leventhal [*Syndrome*] [*Medicine*] (DB)
SL	Stern Loading
SL	Stock Length [*Construction or manufacturing materials*]
SL	Stock Level (AFM)
SL	Stock List (MCD)
SL	Stomodeal Lip [*Endocrinology*]
SL	Stoplamp [*Automotive engineering*]
SL	Storage Location
SL	Straight Line
SL	Streamline
SL	Streptolysin [*Hematology*]
SL	Stronnictwo Ludowe [*Peasant Party*] [*Poland Political party*] (PPE)
SL	Structures Laboratory [*Army*] (GRD)
SL	Struempell-Lorain [*Disease*] [*Medicine*] (DB)
SL	Student Load
SL	Studio Location
SL	Suberin Lamella [*Botany*]
SL	Sub-Lieutenant [*British military*]
SL	Sublingual [*Medicine*]
SL	Submarine Lightwave Cable [*AT & T*] [*Telecommunications*]
SL	Submarine Qualification Lapsed [*Navy*]
SL	Subscriber's Loop [*Telecommunications*] (TEL)
S:L	Sucrase to Lactase Ratio (DAVI)
SL	Sue and Labor Charges [*Insurance*]
SL	Sumerian Laws (BJA)
SL	Summary Language (NITA)
SL	Sunday League (EA)
sl	Suo Loco [*In Its Place*] [*Latin*] (WGA)
SL	Superlattice [*Solid state physics*]
SL	Superluminal [*Galaxy*]
SL	Supplementary List [*Navy British*]
SL	Supplier Letter (MCD)
SL	Support Line [*Military*]
SL	Surface Launch (MUGU)
SL	Surveillance Licence [*Importing*] [*British*] (DS)
SL	Sydney & Louisburg Railway Co. [*AAR code*]
SL	Symmetrizing Line (IAA)
SL	Synchronous Line Medium Speed (BUR)
SL	Syria and Lebanon
SL	System Language
S-L 9	Shoemaker-Levy 9 [*Comet or asteroid that crashed into Jupiter in 1994*]
SLA	American Select Portfolio [*NYSE symbol*] (SPSG)
SLA	La Ronge Public Library, Saskatchewan [*Library symbol National Library of Canada*] (NLC)
SLA	Left Sacroanterior Position [*of the fetus*] [*Obstetrics*]
SLA	Sacrolaeva Anterior [*A fetal position*] (AAMN)
SLA	Salta [*Argentina*] [*Airport symbol*] (OAG)
SLA	Sandia Laboratories, Albuquerque (AABC)
SLA	San Lorenzo [*Argentina*] [*Seismograph station code, US Geological Survey*] (SEIS)
SLA	Saturn LM [*Lunar Module*] Adapter [*NASA*]
SLA	Scanning LASER Altimeter (SSD)
SLA	School Leaving Age (AIE)
SLA	School Lecturers' Association [*British*]
SLA	School Library Association
SLA	Scottish Library Association
SLA	Scott Library [*A publication*]
SLA	Sealed Lead Acid [*Battery*] [*Automotive engineering*]
SLA	Second Language Acquisition
SLA	Security Lock Association [*British*] (DBA)
SLA	Sequential Launch Adapter [*Missiles*] (RDA)
SLA	Shared Line Adapter
SLA	Short and Long Arm [*Automotive engineering*]
SLA	Showmen's League of America (EA)
SLA	Side-Looking LASER Altimeter (RDA)
SLA	Sierra Leone Airlines
SLA	Sierra National Airlines [*Sierra Leone*] [*ICAO designator*] (FAAC)
SLA	Single-Line Approach
sla	Slate (VRA)
sla	Slavic [*MARC language code Library of Congress*] (LCCP)
SLA	Sleep-Learning Association (EA)
SLA	Slide Latex Agglutination [*Clinical chemistry*] (AAMN)
SLA	Slovak League of America (EA)
SLA	Small Landlord's Association [*British*] (DBA)
SLA	Society for Linguistic Anthropology (EA)
SLA	Soluble Leishmania Antigen [*Immuno chemistry*]
SLA	Somali Liberation Army
SLA	Southeastern Library Association (AEBS)
SLA	South Lebanon Army
SLA	Southwestern Library Association (AEBS)

SLA	Spacecraft LM [*Lunar Module*] Adapter [*NASA*]
SLA	Special Libraries Association (EA)
SLA	Specific Leaf Area [*Botany*]
SLA	Sports Lawyers Association (EA)
SLA	Square Loop Antenna
SLA	Stable Lads' Association [*British*] (ECON)
SLA	Standard Life Association (EA)
SLA	Standard Location Area [*Civil Defense*]
SLA	State Liquor Authority
SLA	Statutory Licensing Authority [*Embryology*] [*British*]
SLA	Stereolithography [*Desktop manufacturing*]
SLA	Stored Logic Array
SLA	Strategic Logistics Agency [*Army*] (RDA)
SLA	Stripline
SLA	Sulfur-Lead Analyzer
SLA	Supplies in Liberated Areas [*British World War II*]
SLA	Supply Loading Airfield
SLA	Support and Logistics Areas [*NASA*] (MCD)
SLA	Switching Linear Amplifier
SLA	Symbionese Liberation Army [*Defunct*] (EA)
SLA	Synchronous Line Adapter
SLA-212	Cyclophosphamide, Vincristine, Methotrexate, Daunomycin, and Predinisone Consolidation and Maintenance [*Antineoplastic drug regimen*] (DAVI)
SLAA	Sex and Love Addicts Anonymous (EA)
SLAA	Society for Latin American Anthropology (EA)
SLAA	State and Local Assistance Act
SLAAP	St. Louis Army Ammunition Plant
SLAAS	Supersonic Low-Altitude Attack Aircraft System (MCD)
SLAB	Abopo [*Bolivia*] [*ICAO location identifier*] (ICLI)
SLAB	Sage Laboratories, Inc. [*NASDAQ symbol*] (NQ)
SLAB	Sage Labs [*NASDAQ symbol*] (TTSB)
SLAB	Students for Labeling of Alcoholic Beverages [*Student legal action organization*]
SLABCON	Slab Construction
SLAC	Scapholunate Advanced Collapse [*Wrist*] [*Medicine*] (DMAA)
SLAC	Special Committee on Latin American Coordination
SLAC	Stanford Linear Accelerator Center [*Stanford, CA*] [*Department of Energy*]
SLAC	Stanford Linear Accelerator Computer [*Stanford University*] [*Department of Energy*] (IAA)
SLAC	Stowage Launch Adapter Container
SLAC	Straight-Line (Linear) Accelerator [*Nuclear energy*]
SLAC	Subscriber Line Audio Processing Circuit [*Telecommunications*] (EECA)
SLAC	Subscriber Line Audio Processor Circuit (NITA)
SLAC	Support List Allowance Card (MCD)
SLAD	Salon Litteraire, Artistique, et Diplomatique
SLAD	Shipboard Landing Assist Device
SLAD	SONAR Locator, Altimeter, and Depthometer
SLAD	System Logic and Algorithm Development
Slade	Slade's Reports [*15 Vermont*] [*A publication*] (DLA)
SLADE	Society of Lithographic Artists, Designers, and Engineers [*British*]
SLAE	Standard Lightweight Avionics Equipment [*Army*] (RDA)
SLAE	Supplementary Leak Collection and Release System [*Nuclear energy*] (IAA)
SLAET	Society of Licensed Aircraft Engineers and Technologists (EAIO)
SLAFRS	Southwestern Livestock and Forage Research Station [*Oklahoma State University*] [*Research center*] (RCD)
SLAG	Monteagudo [*Bolivia*] [*ICAO location identifier*] (ICLI)
SLAG	Safe Launch Angle Gate
SLAG	Scottish Legal Action Group (ILCA)
SLAG	Side-Looking Air-to-Ground [*RADAR*]
SLAHF	Slovak League of America Heritage Foundation (EA)
SLAHTS	Stowage List and Hardware Tracking System [*NASA*] (MCD)
SLAIS	School of Library, Archival, and Information Studies [*University of British Columbia, Vancouver*] [*Canada*]
SLAIT	Study Group on Legal Aspects of Intermodal Transportation [*National Research Council*]
SLAK	Spacelab Late Access Kit [*NASA*] (NASA)
SLAKSJ	Supreme Ladies Auxiliary Knights of St. John (EA)
SLAL	Stowage Launch Adapter, Lower
SLALOM	Scalable, Language-Independent, Ames Laboratory, One-Minute Measurement [*Computer technology*]
SLAM	Samuel Lyman Atwood Marshall [*American general and author, 1900-1977*]
SLAM	Scanning Interferometric Apertureless Microscope
SLAM	Scanning LASER Acoustic Microscope
SLAM	Sea-Launched Air Missile (NVT)
SLAM	Seeking, Locating, Annihilating, Monitoring [*Army project, Vietnam*]
SLAM	Semiconductor Transistor (IAA)
SLAM	Short LOFAR [*Low-Frequency Acquisition and Ranging*] Alerting Message (NVT)
SLAM	Shoulder-Launched Antitank Missile [*Army*]
SLAM	Side Load Arresting Mechanism (KSC)
SLAM	Sierra Leone Alliance Movement (PD)
SLAM	Signalling Lymphocyte-Activation Molecule [*Immunology*]
SLAM	Simulation Language for Alternative Modeling [*Computer science*] (CSR)
SLAM	Single Layer Metallization (IAA)
SLAM	Society's League Against Molestation (EA)
SLAM	Space-Launched Air Missile (MCD)
SLAM	Spares Level Activity Model (MCD)
SLAM	Standoff Land Attack Missile [*Military*]
SLAM	Stored Logic Adaptable Metal Oxide (IAA)

SLAM	Stowage Launch Adapter, Middle
SLAM	Strategic Low Attitude Missile
SLAM	Stress Wave in Layered Arbitrary Media (SAA)
SLAM	Submarine-Launched Air Missile
SLAM	Suburban Lodges America [*NASDAQ symbol*] (TTSB)
SLAM	Suburban Lodges of America, Inc. [*NASDAQ symbol*] (SAG)
SLAM	Supersonic Low-Altitude Missile [*Later, LASV*] [*NATO*] (NATG)
SLAM	Support List Allowance Master
SLAM	Surface-Launched Air Missile
SLAM	Surface Look-Alike Mine
SLAM	Symbolic Language Adapted for Microcomputers
SLAMEX	Systemic Lupus Erythematosus Activity Measure [*Medicine*] (DMAA)
SLAMEX	Submarine-Launched Assault Missile Exercise (NVT)
SLAMMR	Side Looking Modular Multi-Mission RADAR (PDAA)
SLAMMR	Sideways-Looking Airborne Multi-Mode Radar (DOMA)
SLAMS	Simplified Language for Abstract Mathematical Structures [*Computer science*] (IEEE)
SLAMS	State and Local Air Monitoring Stations [*Environmental Protection Agency*]
SLAMS	Successive Linear Approximation at Minimum Step (SAA)
SLAMS	Surface Look-Alike Mine System (MCD)
SLAN	Angora [*Bolivia*] [*ICAO location identifier*] (ICLI)
SLAN	Shock Landing Analysis (MCD)
SLAN	Sine Loco, Anno, vel Nomine [*Without Place, Year, or Name*] [*Latin*]
SLAN	Slander [*or Slanderous*] [*FBI standardized term*]
SL & A	Sine Loco et Anno [*Without Place and Year*] [*Latin*]
SL & C	Shipper's Load and Count [*Bills of lading*]
SL & I	System Load and Initialization [*NASA*] (NASA)
SL & R	Shop Order Load Analysis and Reporting [*IBM Corp.*]
SL & T	Shipper's Load and Tally [*Bills of lading*]
SLANG	Selected Letter and Abbreviated Name Guide [*Environmental Protection Agency A publication*] (GFGA)
SLANG	Systems Language
SLANT	Simulator Landing Attachment for Night Landing Training
SLAO	Committee on Supply Questions in Liberated Areas (Official) [*World War II*]
SLAP	Apolo [*Bolivia*] [*ICAO location identifier*] (ICLI)
SLAP	Office of State and Local Assistance Programs [*Department of Energy*]
SLAP	Saboted Light Armor Penetrator [*Weaponry*] (MCD)
SLAP	Sandia-Livermore Aeroheating Program
SLAP	Serum Leucine Aminopeptidase [*An enzyme*] (MAE)
SLAP	Service Life Assessment Program [*Military*]
S/LAP	Shiplap (DAC)
SLAP	Simplified Labor and Performance (MCD)
SLAP	Slot Allocation Procedure [*Aviation*] (DA)
SLAP	Subscriber Line Access Protocol (IAA)
SLAP	Symbolic Language Assembly Program [*Computer science*] (KSC)
SLAPN	Succinyl-L-alanyl-L-alanyl-L-alanine-p-nitroanilide [*Biochemistry*]
SLAPP	Strategic Lawsuit Against Public Participation [*Term coined by George Pring and Penelope Canan*]
SLAPS	Serious Literary, Artistic, Political, or Scientific Value [*Obscenity law*] (NTCM)
SLAPS	Subscriber Loop Analysis Program System [*Bell System*]
SLAQ	Aiquile [*Bolivia*] [*ICAO location identifier*] (ICLI)
SLAR	Select ADC [*Analog-to-Digital Converter*] Register [*Computer science*] (MDG)
SLAR	Senior Logistics Aviation Representative (MCD)
SLAR	Side-Looking Aerial [*or Airborne*] RADAR [*Military*]
SLAR	Side-Looking Airborne Radar [*Marine science*] (OSRA)
SLAR	Slant Range
SLAR	Slargando [*Slackening*] [*Music*] (ROG)
SLAR	Steerable LASER Radiometer (MCD)
SLARF	Slant Range Fuze (NG)
SLARG	Slargando [*Slackening*] [*Music*]
SLA/RP	Stereolithography / Rapid Prototyping [*Design*] (RDA)
SLAS	Ascencion De Guarayos [*Bolivia*] [*ICAO location identifier*] (ICLI)
SLAS	Society for Latin American Studies [*British*]
SLAS	State Library Agency Section [*Association of Specialized and Cooperative Library Agencies*]
SLASC	St. Louis Area Support Center [*Military*] (MCD)
SLASER	Space LASER (SSD)
SLASH	Second Edition List of Australian Subject Headings [*A publication*]
SLASH	Seiler Laboratory ALGOL Simulated Hybrid [*Computer science*]
SLASH	Small Light Antisubmarine Helicopter
SLAST	Submarine-Launched Antiship Torpedo
SLASX	Selected Amer. Shares [*Mutual fund ticker symbol*] (SG)
SLAT	Sample Lot Acceptance Testing
s lat	Sensu Lato [*In a Wide Sense*] [*Latin*]
SLAT	Ship-Launched Air Targeting (MCD)
SLAT	Simultaneous Laryngoscopy and Abdominal Thrusts [*Medicine*] (DMAA)
SLAT	Sindacato Lavoratori Amministrativi e Technichi [*Union of Administration and Technical Workers*] [*Somalia*]
SLAT	South Latitude
SLAT	Special Logistics Actions, Thailand (AABC)
SLAT	Strike Leader Attack Training [*Navy*] (DOMA)
SLAT	Supersonic Low Activities Target (MCD)
SLAT	Supersonic Low-Altitude Target [*Navy*]
SLAT	Support List Allowance Tape (MCD)
SLAT	Surface Launcher Air-Targeted [*Weapon*] (MCD)
SLATE	Ship-Launched ASW [*Antisubmarine Warfare*] Two-Way Expendable [*Buoy*] [*Navy*] (CAAL)
SLATE	Small, Lightweight Altitude-Transmission Equipment [*FAA*]
SLATE	Stimulated Learning by Automated Typewriter Environment

SLATO .... Secretariado Latinamericano de Trotskismo Orthodoxo [*Peru*]
SLATS.......... Strike Leader Attack Training School [*Navy*] (DOMA)
SLAU .... San Aurelio [*Bolivia*] [*ICAO location identifier*] (ICLI)
SLAU .... Stowage Launch Adapter, Upper
SLAUGH....... Slaughter [*England*]
SLAV........... Avicaya [*Bolivia*] [*ICAO location identifier*] (ICLI)
SLAV........... Slavonic [*Language, etc.*]
SLAV........... Special Logistics Actions, South Vietnam (CINC)
SLAVCA ...... Sindacato Nazionale Lavoratori Vetro e Ceramica [*National Union of Glass and Ceramics' Workers*] [*Italy*]
SlavEnoch.... Slavic Book of Enoch (BJA)
Slav R .... Slavic Review [*A publication*] (BRI)
SLAW.......... Conference on the Sociology of the Languages of American Women [*1976*]
SLAW.......... St. Lawrence Railroad [*Division of National Railway Utilization Corp.*] [*AAR code*]
SLAX.......... Ay-Luri [*Bolivia*] [*ICAO location identifier*] (ICLI)
SLB........... Schlumberger Ltd. [*NYSE symbol*] (SPSG)
SLB........... Self-Lubricating Bearing
SLB........... Shallow Land Burial [*Environmental science*] (COE)
SLB........... Short Leg Brace [*Medicine*]
SLB........... Side-Lobe Blanking [*RADAR*]
SLB........... Signal Light Bare (MSA)
SLB........... Sintered Lead Bronze
SLB........... Society for Leukocyte Biology (NTPA)
SLB........... Society for Leukocyte Biology (A Reticuloendothelial Society) (EA)
SLB........... Solomon Islands [*ANSI three-letter standard code*] (CNC)
SLB........... Steam Line Break (NRCH)
SLB........... St. Louis Blueliners (EA)
SLB........... Storm Lake, IA [*Location identifier FAA*] (FAAL)
SLB........... Superannuation Law Bulletin [*A publication*]
SLBC.......... Boca Chapare [*Bolivia*] [*ICAO location identifier*] (ICLI)
SLBD .... Sea Lite Beam Director [*Navy*] (DOMA)
SLBF.......... Blanca Flor [*Bolivia*] [*ICAO location identifier*] (ICLI)
SLBH .... Buena Hora [*Bolivia*] [*ICAO location identifier*] (ICLI)
SLBI........... Sidelobe Blanking Indicator
SLBJ........... Bermejo [*Bolivia*] [*ICAO location identifier*] (ICLI)
SLBL.......... Soluble (MSA)
SLBM.......... Sea [*or Submarine or Surface*]-Launched Ballistic Missile [*Navy*] (CAAL)
SLBM.......... Space-Launched Ballistic Missile (IAA)
SLBMD & W... Sea-Launched Ballistic Missile Detection and Warning
SLBMDWS .... Submarine-Launched Ballistic Missile Detection and Warning System (IEEE)
SLBMW........ Submarine-Launched Ballistic Missile Warning (IAA)
SLBN .... Bella Union [*Bolivia*] [*ICAO location identifier*] (ICLI)
SLBP.......... Spring-Loaded Ball Plunger
SLBS.......... Sierra Leone Broadcasting Service
SLBtry......... Searchlight Battery [*Army*]
SLBU.......... Baures [*Bolivia*] [*ICAO location identifier*] (ICLI)
SLBV.......... Villa Vista [*Bolivia*] [*ICAO location identifier*] (ICLI)
SLBW.......... Buena Vista [*Bolivia*] [*ICAO location identifier*] (ICLI)
SLBY.......... Boyuibe [*Bolivia*] [*ICAO location identifier*] (ICLI)
SLC........... Salt Lake City [*Utah*] [*Seismograph station code, US Geological Survey*] (SEIS)
SLC........... Salt Lake City, UT [*Location identifier FAA*] (FAAL)
SLC........... [*The*] San Luis Central Railroad Co. [*AAR code*]
SLC........... Sarah Lawrence College [*Bronxville, NY*]
SLC........... Satellite LASER Communication [*Military*]
SLC........... Schools and Libraries Corp.
SLC........... Schoool Leaving Certificate [*British*] (BARN)
SLC........... Scottish Land Court Reports [*A publication*] (DLA)
SLC........... Scottish Leaving Certificate
SLC........... Sea-Level Canal Study (IID)
SLC........... Searchlight Control [*Military*]
SLC........... Secretarial Language Certificate [*British*] (DI)
SLC........... Selector (NITA)
SLC........... Selector Channel
SLC........... Set Location Counter (CMD)
SLC........... Shelf Life Code (MCD)
SLC........... Shift Left and Count Instructions [*Computer science*] (MDG)
SLC........... Short-Leg Cast [*Orthopedics*] (DAVI)
SLC........... Shuttle Launch Center [*Vandenberg Air Force Base, CA*] [*NASA*]
SLC........... Side-Lobe Cancellation [*RADAR*]
SLC........... Side-Lobe Clutter
SLC........... Signal Level Converter (DWSG)
SLC........... Simulataneous-Lobe Comparison [*RADAR*] (IAA)
SLC........... Simulated Linguistic Computer
SLC........... Single Launch Contractor (KSC)
SLC........... Single Lead Covered (IAA)
SLC........... Single Line Control (BUR)
SLC........... Single-Loop Controller (ACII)
SLC........... Slice (MSA)
SLC........... Slicer (IAA)
SLC........... Small Library Computing, Inc. [*Information service or system*] (IID)
SLC........... Smith's Leading Cases [*A publication*] (DLA)
SLC........... Society of Antique Label Collectors (EA)
SLC........... Songwriters and Lyricists Club (EA)
SLC........... Sonobuoy Launch Container (NVT)
SLC........... Southland Conference (PSS)
SLC........... South London College [*London, England*]
SLC........... Southwestern Life Corp. [*Formerly, ICH Corp.*] [*AMEX symbol*] (SAG)
SLC........... Space Launch Complex [*NASA*]
SLC........... Spanish Literature Committee (EA)

SLC........... Special Libraries Cataloguing, Inc. [*Information service or system*] (IID)
SLC........... Specific-Line Capacitance [*or Capacity*] (IAA)
SLC........... Sport Leicht Coupe [*Sports Lightweight Coupe*] [*German*]
SLC........... Standard Launch Complex (KSC)
SLC........... Standard Location Codes
SLC........... Standby Letter of Credit (EBF)
SLC........... Standby Liquid Control [*Nuclear energy*] (NRCH)
SLC........... Standing Liaison Committee
SLC........... Stanford Linear Collider [*High-energy physics*]
SLC........... State Legislative Committee
SLC........... State Library of Ohio, Catalog Center, Columbus, OH [*OCLC symbol*] (OCLC)
SLC........... Stockage List Code [*Military*] (AABC)
SLC........... Stock Ledger Control
SLC........... Straight-Line Capacitance [*or Capacity*]
SLC........... Straight-Line Capacitor (IAA)
SLC........... Strategic LASER Communications [*Military*] (CAAL)
SLC........... Stuart's Lower Canada Appeal Cases [*1810-35*] [*A publication*] (DLA)
SLC........... Sublingual Cleft [*Medicine*]
SLC........... Submarine LASER Communications
SLC........... Subscriber Line Circuit [*Telecommunications*] (IAA)
SLC........... Subscriber Line Concentrator [*Telecommunications*]
SLC........... Subscriber Loop Carrier [*Telecommunications*] (TEL)
SLC........... Sue and Labor Clause [*Business term*]
SLC........... Surface Laminar Circuit (AAEL)
SLC........... Surgeon Lieutenant-Commander [*British military*]
SLC........... Susquehanna Library Cooperative [*Library network*]
SLC........... Sustained Load Crack [*Titanium alloy*]
SLC........... Swiftlines Ltd. [*Kenya*] [*ICAO designator*] (FAAC)
SLC........... Synchro Loop Closure
SLC........... Synchronous Line Medium Speed with Clock (BUR)
SLC........... Synchronous Link Control [*Computer science*]
SLC........... System Life Cycle
SLCA.......... Camiri [*Bolivia*] [*ICAO location identifier*] (ICLI)
SLC App ...... Stuart's Lower Canada Appeal Cases [*A publication*] (DLA)
SLCB.......... Cochabamba/Jorge Wilsterman [*Bolivia*] [*ICAO location identifier*] (ICLI)
SLCB.......... Single-Line Color Bar (IEEE)
SLCBMA ...... Solid Leather Case and Bag Makers' Association [*A union*] [*British*]
SLCC.......... Copacabana [*Bolivia*] [*ICAO location identifier*] (ICLI)
SLCC.......... Lincoln Cent Collectors Society (EA)
SLCC.......... Saturn Launch Control Computer [*NASA*] (KSC)
SLCC.......... Saturn Launcher Computer Complex (IAA)
SLCC.......... Society of Local Council Clerks [*British*]
SLCC.......... Soft Launch Control Center (IAA)
SLCC.......... Store Level Communications Controller (MHDI)
SLCD.......... Surplus Land for Community Development
SLCG.......... Charagua [*Bolivia*] [*ICAO location identifier*] (ICLI)
SLCH.......... Chapacura [*Bolivia*] [*ICAO location identifier*] (ICLI)
SLCI........... Clara Rios [*Bolivia*] [*ICAO location identifier*] (ICLI)
SLCJ........... Cavinas [*Bolivia*] [*ICAO location identifier*] (ICLI)
SLCL.......... Collpani [*Bolivia*] [*ICAO location identifier*] (ICLI)
SLCL.......... Shop/Lab Configuration Layout [*NASA*] (MCD)
SLCL.......... Sierra Leone Council of Labour
SLCL.......... Small Lymphocyte Cell Lymphoma [*Oncology*]
SLCM.......... Camiare [*Bolivia*] [*ICAO location identifier*] (ICLI)
SLCM.......... Sea-Launched Cruise Missile [*Pronounced "slick-em"*] (AABC)
SLCM.......... Ship Life-Cycle Management
SLCM.......... Software Life Cycle Management
SLCM.......... Southland Corp. [*NASDAQ symbol*] (TTSB)
SLCM.......... Structural Liquid Composite Molding [*Plastics technology*]
SLCM.......... Submarine-Launched Cruise Missile (IEEE)
SLCM.......... Surface Launch Cruise Missile
SLCMP........ Software Life Cycle Management Plan (DNAB)
SLCN.......... Charana [*Bolivia*] [*ICAO location identifier*] (ICLI)
SL Co.......... Appendices of Proceedings of the Scottish Land Court [*A publication*] (DLA)
SLCO .... Cobija [*Bolivia*] [*ICAO location identifier*] (ICLI)
SL Co R...... Appendices of Proceedings of the Scottish Land Court [*A publication*] (DLA)
SLCP.......... Concepcion [*Bolivia*] [*ICAO location identifier*] (ICLI)
SLCP.......... Saturn Launch Computer Program (OA)
SLCP.......... Ship's Loading Characteristics Pamphlet [*Navy*] (NVT)
SLCP.......... Standing Liaison Committee of Physiotherapists within the EEC [*European Economic Community*] [*See also CPLK*] [*Copenhagen, Denmark*] (EAIO)
SLCQ.......... Copaquilla [*Bolivia*] [*ICAO location identifier*] (ICLI)
SLCR.......... Comarapa [*Bolivia*] [*ICAO location identifier*] (ICLI)
SLCR.......... Scottish Land Court Reports [*A publication*] (DLA)
SLCRM........ Ship Life-Cycle Reference Matrix [*Navy*]
SLCRS........ Supplementary Leak Collection and Release System [*Nuclear energy*] (NRCH)
SLCS.......... Cerdas [*Bolivia*] [*ICAO location identifier*] (ICLI)
SLCS.......... Standby Liquid Control System [*Nuclear energy*] (NRCH)
SLCSAT....... Submarine LASER Communications Satellite (MCD)
SLCT.......... Choretl [*Bolivia*] [*ICAO location identifier*] (ICLI)
SLCT.......... Select Software Tools [*NASDAQ symbol*] (SAG)
Slct ADR.... Select Software Tools [*Associated Press*] (SAG)
SlctApp....... Select Appointments Holdings [*Associated Press*] (SAG)
SLCTTS....... Soft-Load Closed Transition Transfer Switch
SLCU.......... Standard Landing Craft Unit [*Military*]
SLCU.......... Synchronous Line Control Unit
SLCV.......... Cavinas [*Bolivia*] [*ICAO location identifier*] (ICLI)

SLCV............	Squash Leaf Curl Virus
SLCY............	Collpa [*Bolivia*] [*ICAO location identifier*] (ICLI)
SLCZ............	Santa Cruz/El Trompillo [*Bolivia*] [*ICAO location identifier*] (ICLI)
SLD............	Sailed
SLD............	San Luis Dam [*California*] [*Seismograph station code, US Geological Survey*] (SEIS)
SLD............	Schools and Libraries Division [*National Center of Education Statistics*]
SLD............	Sea Landing Division [*NATO*]
SLD............	Sealed
SLD............	Secretarial Language Diploma [*British*] (DI)
SLD............	Serum Lactate Dehydrogenase [*Also, SLDH*] [*An enzyme*]
SLD............	Severe Learning Difficulties (WDAA)
SLD............	Shelf Life Data [*Army*]
SLD............	Shutdown Logic Diagram [*Nuclear energy*] (NRCH)
SLD............	Simplified Logic Diagram (IAA)
SLD............	Simulated Launch Demonstration [*NASA*] (KSC)
SLD............	Sliac [*Former Czechoslovakia*] [*Airport symbol*] (OAG)
SLD............	Slide
SLD............	Sliding Door (AAG)
SLD............	Slim Line Diffuser (OA)
SLD............	Slowdown (AAG)
SLD............	Slumber Lodge Development Corp. Ltd. [*Vancouver Stock Exchange symbol*]
SLD............	Social and Liberal Democrats [*British Political party*] (ECON)
SLD............	Society of Loyalist Descendants (EA)
SLD............	Sold
Sld............	Sold (EBF)
SLD............	Solder
SLD............	Solid
SLD............	Solid Logic Dense (BUR)
SLD............	Sonic Layer Depth (NVT)
SLD............	Source Language Debug [*Computer science*] (IEEE)
SLD............	Source-Level Debugger [*Motorola, Inc.*]
SLD............	Special Litigation Division [*Environmental Protection Agency*] (GFGA)
SLD............	Special Low-Dispersion [*Optics*]
SLD............	Specific Language [*or Learning*] Disability [*Education*]
SLD............	Square Law Detection
SLD............	Stiff-Leg Derrick (NASA)
SLD............	Straight Line Depreciation [*Telecommunications*] (TEL)
SLD............	Strong Lattice Deformation (AAEL)
SLD............	Superluminescent Diode [*Tomography*]
SLD............	Symmetrized Logarithmic Derivative (IAA)
SLD............	Synchronous Line Driver
SLDA............	Solid Logic Design Automation (IAA)
SLDAA............	SACLANT [*Supreme Allied Commander, Atlantic*] Distributing and Accounting Agency (NATG)
SLD CARB DI...	Solidified Carbon Dioxide [*Freight*]
SLDD............	Scientific Library and Documentation Division [*National Science and Technology Authority*] [*Philippines*] [*Information service or system*] (IID)
SLDG............	Sliding
SLDH............	Serum Lactate Dehydrogenase [*Also, SLD*] [*An enzyme*]
SLDI............	Sector List Drop Interval [*FAA*] (TAG)
SLDN............	El Desengano [*Bolivia*] [*ICAO location identifier*] (ICLI)
SLDP............	Loma Del Porvenir [*Bolivia*] [*ICAO location identifier*] (ICLI)
SLDP............	Sierra Leone Democratic Party [*Political party*] (EY)
SLDPF............	Spacelab Data Processing Facility (MCD)
SLDR............	Solder (MSA)
SLDR............	Soldier
S/Ldr............	Squadron Leader [*British military*] (DMA)
SLDR............	Sublethal Damage Repair [*Medicine*] (DMAA)
SLDR............	System Loader [*Computer science*]
SLDRAM......	Sync-link DRAM [*Display Random Access Memory*] [*Computer science*]
SLDS............	Scanning LASER Doppler System [*NASA*]
SLDS............	Single-Level Dynamic Scan [*Radiology*] (DAVI)
SLDS............	Skylab Launch Data System [*NASA*] (KSC)
SLDSX............	SMBS Diversified Strategic Inc. Cl.B [*Mutual fund ticker symbol*] (SG)
SLDTF............	State and Local Documents Task Force [*Government Documents Round Table*] [*American Library Association*]
SLDTSS.......	Single Language Dedicated Time-Sharing System
SLDVS.......	Scanning LASER Doppler Vortex System [*NASA*]
SLE............	Salem [*Oregon*] [*Airport symbol*] (OAG)
SLE............	Salem, OR [*Location identifier FAA*] (FAAL)
SLE............	Sara Lee Corp. [*NYSE symbol*] (SPSG)
SLE............	Segment Limits End (NITA)
SLE............	Service Life Evaluation
SLE............	Sierra Leone [*ANSI three-letter standard code*] (CNC)
SLE............	Slit Lamp Examination [*Medicine*] (DMAA)
SLE............	Small Lattice Experiment
SLE............	Small Local Exchange [*Telecommunications*] (TEL)
SLE............	Smith, Leland C., Oakland CA [*STAC*]
SLE............	Snap Lock Environmental [*Electrical engineering*]
SLE............	Societas Linguistica Europaea [*Linguistic Society of Europe*] [*Austria*] (EAIO)
SLE............	Society of Land Economists [*Australia*]
SLE............	Society of Logistics Engineers (MCD)
SLE............	Spacelab Engineering [*European Research National Organization*] (MCD)
SLE............	Sport Luxury Edition [*Automobile classification*]
SLE............	Station Liaison Engineer [*NASA*]
SLE............	St. Louis Encephalitis [*Medicine*]
SLE............	Stochastic Liouville Equation [*Statistical mechanics*]
SLE............	Student Letter Exchange (EA)
SLE............	Studio Lighting Equipment
SLE............	Sulphurets Gold [*Vancouver Stock Exchange symbol*]
SLE............	Superheat Limit Explosion
SLE............	Systemic Lupus Erythematosus [*Medicine*]
SLEA............	Sheep Erythrocyte Antibody [*Medicine*] (DMAA)
SLEAT............	Society of Laundry Engineers and Allied Trades (IAA)
SLEAT............	Society of Licensed Aircraft Engineers and Technologists (DA)
SLEC............	El Cairo [*Bolivia*] [*ICAO location identifier*] (ICLI)
SLED............	El Dorado [*Bolivia*] [*ICAO location identifier*] (ICLI)
SLED............	Single Large Expensive Disk [*Computer science*] (PCM)
SLED............	State Level Electricity Demand [*Model*] [*Nuclear Regulatory Commission*]
SLED............	Surface Light Emitting Diode [*Electronics*]
SLED............	System-Level Engineering Document (SSD)
SledDogs.....	Sled Dogs Co. [*Associated Press*] (SAG)
SLEDGE......	Simulating Large Explosive Detonable Gas Experiments
SLEEC............	Shingle Lap Extendable Exit Cone (MCD)
SLEED............	Spin-Polarized Low Energy Electron Diffraction (AAEL)
SLEEP............	Scanning Low-Energy Electron Probe (IEEE)
SLEEP............	Silent, Lightweight, Electric Energy Plant (RDA)
SLEEP............	Swedish Low-Energy Experimental Pile [*Nuclear energy*]
SLEF............	El Triunfo [*Bolivia*] [*ICAO location identifier*] (ICLI)
SLEF............	Short-Lived Large Energy Fluctuation [*Physics*]
SLEH............	Stage Loose Equipment Hardware (SAA)
SLEICC............	Statue of Liberty - Ellis Island Centennial Commission (EA)
SLEIF............	Statue of Liberty - Ellis Island Foundation (EA)
SLEJ............	El Jovi [*Bolivia*] [*ICAO location identifier*] (ICLI)
SLEKE............	Sabot-Launched Electric Gun Kinetic Energy [*DoD*]
SLEL............	El Roseda [*Bolivia*] [*ICAO location identifier*] (ICLI)
SLEM............	Solution of Linearized Equations of Motion
SLEMA............	Schiffli Lace and Embroidery Manufacturers Association (EA)
SLEMU............	Spacelab Engineering Model Unit [*NASA*] (MCD)
SLENT............	Slentando [*Slackening*] [*Music*] (ROG)
SLEO............	El Paraiso [*Bolivia*] [*ICAO location identifier*] (ICLI)
SLEP............	El Peru [*Bolivia*] [*ICAO location identifier*] (ICLI)
SLEP............	Secondary Level English Proficiency Test
SLEP............	Second Large ESRO [*European Space Research Organization*] Project
SLEP............	Service Life Extension Program [*Military*] (MCD)
SLEP............	Short Latent Evoked Potential [*Medicine*] (DMAA)
SLEP............	State Line End Point (DNAB)
SLES............	Espiritu [*Bolivia*] [*ICAO location identifier*] (ICLI)
SLES............	Semilinear Erection System (SAA)
sleta............	Sine Loco et Anno [*Without Place and Year*] [*Latin*] (DGA)
SLEU............	Eucaliptos [*Bolivia*] [*ICAO location identifier*] (ICLI)
SLEUTH.......	System for Locating Eruptive Underwater Turbidity and Hydrography [*Marine science*] (OSRA)
SLEV............	El Salvador [*Bolivia*] [*ICAO location identifier*] (ICLI)
SLEV............	Salaried Legal Expense Voucher
SLEV............	St. Louis Encephalitis Virus
SLEW............	Standby Local Early Warning and Control Center (PDAA)
SLEW............	Static Load Error Washout
SLEZ............	La Esperanza [*Bolivia*] [*ICAO location identifier*] (ICLI)
SLF............	Saturn Launch Facility [*NASA*]
SLF............	Savings and Loan Foundation [*Later, FSI*] (EA)
SLF............	Scientific Laboratory Facility
SLF............	Scottish Landowners Federation (DBA)
SLF............	Selfcare, Inc. [*AMEX symbol*] (SAG)
SLF............	Shuttle Landing Facility [*NASA*] (MCD)
SLF............	Skandinaviska Lackteknikers Forbund [*Federation of Scandinavian Paint and Varnish Technologists*] [*Sweden*] (EAIO)
SLF............	Society of the Little Flower (EA)
SLF............	South Luzon Force [*Army World War II*]
SLF............	Southwestern Legal Foundation (DLA)
SLF............	Special Landing Forces [*Marine Corps*]
SLF............	Steel Locus Factor [*Genetics*]
SLF............	Straight-Line Frequency
SLF............	Strategic Leadership Forum (NTPA)
SLF............	Stress Loading Facility [*Fort Huachuca, AZ*] [*United States Army Electronic Proving Ground*] (GRD)
SLF............	Suction Line Filter
SLF............	Sulayel [*Saudi Arabia*] [*Airport symbol*] (AD)
SLF............	Super-Low-Frequency (MCD)
SLF............	System Library File [*Computer science*] (BUR)
SLFA............	Fatima [*Bolivia*] [*ICAO location identifier*] (ICLI)
SLFAA............	State and Local Fiscal Assistance Amendments of 1972 (COE)
SLFB............	Solid-Liquid Fluidized Bed [*Chemical engineering*]
SLFC............	Shoreline Financial [*NASDAQ symbol*] (TTSB)
SLFC............	Shoreline Financial Corp. [*NASDAQ symbol*] (NQ)
SLFC............	Sierra Leone Full Court Reports [*A publication*] (DLA)
SLFC............	Steve Long Fan Club [*Defunct*] (EA)
SLFC............	Supervisor of Loan Fund Companies [*New South Wales, Australia*]
SLFC............	Survivable Low-Frequency Communications [*Air Force*]
SLFCLN............	Self-Cleaning [*Engineering*]
SLFCS............	Survivable Low-Frequency Communications System [*Air Force*]
SLFD............	Steam Lava Flow Deflector (MCD)
SLFGEN......	Self-Generating
SLFIA............	Substrate-Labeled Fluorescent Immunoassay
SLFIND......	Self-Indicating
S-LFL............	Short-Long Flashing Light [*Navigation signal*]
SLFLKG.......	Self-Locking [*Engineering*]
SLFOEAMTMTS...	St. Louis Field Office, Eastern Area, Military Traffic Management and Terminal Service [*Army*] (AABC)
SLFP............	Sri Lanka Freedom Party [*Political party*] (PPW)

SLFSE.......... Self-Sealing [*Engineering*]
SLFTPG........ Self-Tapping [*Screw*] [*Design engineering*]
SLFX............. Selfix, Inc. [*NASDAQ symbol*] (CTT)
SLG.............. Community of the Sisters of the Love of God [*Anglican religious community*]
SLG.............. Lander College, Larry A. Jackson Library, Greenwood, SC [*OCLC symbol*] (OCLC)
SLG.............. Sailing (WGA)
SLG.............. Saskatchewan Government Air Ambulance Service [*Canada*] [*FAA designator*] (FAAC)
SLG.............. Satellite Landing Ground [*British military*] (DMA)
SLG.............. Scott's Liquid Gold, Inc. (EFIS)
SLG.............. Self-Launching Glider
SLG.............. Shorthand Typist (Lower Grade) [*British military*] (DMA)
SLG.............. Siloam Springs, AK [*Location identifier FAA*] (FAAL)
SLG.............. Single Line to Ground (IAA)
SLG.............. Sludge (MSA)
SLG.............. Slugger [*Percentage*] [*Baseball*]
SLG.............. Soda Lime Glass
SLG.............. Solid-Liquid-Gas [*Phase diagram line*]
SLG.............. Southern Lights [*Vancouver Stock Exchange symbol*]
SLG.............. State or Local Government
SLG.............. Synchronous Line Group (BUR)
SLGA............ Scottish Ladies Golfing Association (DBA)
SLGB............ Society of Local Government Barristers [*British*] (DLA)
SLGJ............. Guadalajara [*Bolivia*] [*ICAO location identifier*] (ICLI)
SLGM........... Surface-Launched Guided Missile
SLGP............ Student Loan Guaranty Program
SLGR............ Slinger
SLGR............ Small Lightweight GPS [*Global Positioning System*] Receivers [*Army*] (RDA)
SLGRU.......... State Local Government Relations Unit [*South Australia*]
SLGW........... Salt Lake, Garfield & Western Railway Co. [*AAR code*]
SLGXT.......... Symptom-Limited Graded Exercise Test [*Cardiology*] (DAVI)
SLGY............ Guayaramerin [*Bolivia*] [*ICAO location identifier*] (ICLI)
SLH.............. Sociedade Latinoamericana de Hepatologia [*Latin American Society of Hepatology - LASH*] (EAIO)
SLH.............. Sola [*Vanuatu*] [*Airport symbol*] (OAG)
SLHA............ Small Luxury Hotel Association (EA)
SLHJ............. Huacaraje [*Bolivia*] [*ICAO location identifier*] (ICLI)
SLHN............ Chane Bedoya [*Bolivia*] [*ICAO location identifier*] (ICLI)
SLHN............ Stearns & Lehman, Inc. [*NASDAQ symbol*] (SAG)
SLHR............ Sex-Linked Hypophosphatemic Rickets [*Medicine*] (DB)
SLHR............ Society for Life History Research (EA)
SLHRP.......... Society for Life History Research in Psychopathology [*Later, SLHR*] (EA)
SLHT............ Colquechaca [*Bolivia*] [*ICAO location identifier*] (ICLI)
SLHT............ Spatialight, Inc. [*NASDAQ symbol*] (SAG)
SLHU............ Huachi [*Bolivia*] [*ICAO location identifier*] (ICLI)
SLHY............ Caquiaviri [*Bolivia*] [*ICAO location identifier*] (ICLI)
SLI............... Los Alamitos, CA [*Location identifier FAA*] (FAAL)
SLI............... Sandia Laboratory Instruction (COE)
SLI............... Seal and Label Institute
SLI............... Sea-Level Indicator (KSC)
SLI............... Servicios Aeroes Litoral SA de CV [*Mexico ICAO designator*] (FAAC)
SLI............... Shelf Life Item [*Military*] (AABC)
SLI............... Shropshire Light Infantry [*British military*] (DMA)
SLI............... Signal Line Isolator
SLI............... Sikh Local Infantry [*British military*] (DMA)
SLI............... Silver Hill Mines [*Vancouver Stock Exchange symbol*]
SLI............... Slick Airways, Inc.
SLI............... Slide Lobe Indicator
SLI............... SLI, Inc. [*NYSE symbol*] [*Formerly, Chicago Miniature Lamp*]
SLI............... Society for Louisiana Irises (EA)
SLI............... Somatostatin-Like Immunoreactivity
SLI............... Somerset Light Infantry [*Military unit*] [*British*]
SLI............... Sound Level Indicator
SLI............... Spacelab Integration (MCD)
SLI............... Specific Language Impairment
SLI............... Splenic Localization Index [*Medicine*] (MAE)
SLI............... Starting, Lighting, and Ignition [*Automobile system*]
SLI............... Stations Legers d'Infrastructures [*Light infrastructures*] [*French*]
SLI............... Steam Line Isolation [*Nuclear energy*] (NRCH)
SLI............... St. Lucia [*Seismograph station code, US Geological Survey Closed*] (SEIS)
SLI............... Suppress Length Indication (BUR)
SLI............... Synchronous Line Interface
SLIA............. Spiritual Life Institute of America (EA)
SLIAC........... St. Louis Intercollegiate Athletic Conference (PSS)
SLIAG.......... State Legalization Impact Assistance Grant [*Department of Health and Human Services*]
SLIB............. Source Library [*Computer science*]
SLIB............. Subsystem Library [*Computer science*] (IBMDP)
SLIC............. Coroico [*Bolivia*] [*ICAO location identifier*] (ICLI)
SLIC............. Search of the Library Information Collection [*Search system*]
SLIC............. Selected Listing in Combination (NITA)
SLIC............. Selective Letters [*or Listing*] in Combination
SLIC............. Semiconductor Laser International Corp. [*NASDAQ symbol*] (SAG)
SLIC............. Semiconductor Laser Intl [*NASDAQ symbol*] (TTSB)
SLIC............. Signature Library Intelligence Catalogue
SLIC............. Silent Liquid Integral Cooler (MHDI)
SLIC............. Silicon Language for Integrated Circuit (NITA)
SLIC............. Simulation Linear Integrated Circuit [*Electronics*] (OA)
SLIC............. Standard-Function Linear Integrated Circuit [*Electronics*] (AAEL)
SLIC............. Subscriber Loop Interface Circuit (NITA)

SLIC............. Subscriber's Line Interface Circuit [*Telecommunications*] (TEL)
SLIC............. System Line Image Composer
SLICB........... Sea-Launched Intercontinental Ballistic Missile (MUGU)
SLICBM........ Sea-Launched Intercontinental Ballistic Missile (SAA)
SLICE........... Source Label Indicating and Coding Equipment
SLICE........... Southwestern Library Interstate Cooperative Endeavor
SLICE........... Students Litigating Against Injurious Can Edges [*Student legal action organization*]
SLICE........... Surrey Library Interactive Circulation Experiment (NITA)
SLICE........... System Life Cycle Estimation
SLICW.......... Semiconductor Laser Wrrt [*NASDAQ symbol*] (TTSB)
SLID............. Scanning Light Intensity Device
SLID............. Solid-Liquid Interdiffusion (IAA)
SLID............. Students League for Industrial Democracy [*Later, Students for a Democratic Society*]
SLIDE........... Source Library Image Delivery Expeditor [*Computer science*] (MHDI)
SLIF............. Student Loan Insurance Fund [*Department of Health and Human Services*] (GFGA)
SLIG............. Inglaterra [*Bolivia*] [*ICAO location identifier*] (ICLI)
SLIG............. Sucker, Low-Brow, Idiot, Goodwill-Buster [*Acronym used as word meaning "act of discourtesy or stupid criticism"*] [*World War II*]
SLIGO.......... Sand Lake Irish Gatherings Organization
SLIH............. Samaihuate [*Bolivia*] [*ICAO location identifier*] (ICLI)
SLIH............. Second Level Interrupt Handler (CMD)
SLIJ............. Iniguazu [*Bolivia*] [*ICAO location identifier*] (ICLI)
SLIM............ Saint Louis Institute of Music
SLIM............ Side Line Indexing Method [*Spectrometry*]
SLIM............ Simplified Logistics and Improved Maintenance (MCD)
SLIM............ Slewed-Launch Interceptor Missile
SLIM............ Special Language Interpreting Matrix (IAA)
SLIM............ Standards Laboratory Information Manual (NG)
SLIM............ Stock Line Inventory Management (MHDW)
SLIM............ Store Labor and Inventory Management (MHDW)
SLIM............ Submarine-Launched Inertial Missile
SLIMS.......... Supply Line Inventory Management System [*Bell System*]
SLIN............ Standard Library Identification Number
SLIN............ Standard Line Item Number [*Army*] (AABC)
SLIN............ Sub-Line Item Number (MCD)
SLIN............ System Line Item Number (MCD)
SL Ind.......... SL Industries, Inc. [*Associated Press*] (SAG)
Slink............. Single, Lots of Income, No Kids [*Lifestyle classification*]
SLIP............. Self Leisure Interest Profile
SLIP............. Serial Line Interface Protocol (DMAA)
SLIP............. Serial Line Intermit Protocol
SLIP............. Serial Line Internet Protocol [*Telecommunications*] (PCM)
SLIP............. Singer Loomis Inventory of Personality (DHP)
SLIP............. Single Line Internet Protocol [*Telecommunications*] (DOM)
SLIP............. Skills Level Improvement Program
SLIP............. Symbolic List Processor
SLIP............. Symmetric List Interpretive Program [*Computer science*]
SLIP............. Symmetric List Processor [*FORTRAN extension*]
Slip op......... Slip Opinion (AAGC)
SLIPP........... Second Language Learning in the Primary Classroom (AIE)
Slippery Rock U... Slippery Rock University of Pennsylvania (GAGS)
SLIPR........... Source Language Input Program
SLIQ............. Special Libraries in Queensland [*Australia A publication*]
SLIR............. Ibori [*Bolivia*] [*ICAO location identifier*] (ICLI)
SLIR............. School of Labor and Industrial Relations [*Michigan State University*] [*Research center*] (RCD)
SLIR............. Somatostatin-Like Immunoreactivity (STED)
SLIRBM........ Sea-Launched Intermediate-Range Ballistic Missile (MUGU)
SLIS............. Shared Laboratory Information System
SLIS............. Social Legislation Information Service (EA)
SLISP........... Symbolic List Processing (NITA)
SLIT............. Itaguazurenda [*Bolivia*] [*ICAO location identifier*] (ICLI)
SLIT............. Little S Positive [*Laboratory science*] (DAVI)
SLIT............. Serial/Lot Item Tracking (DNAB)
SLIV............. Isla Verde [*Bolivia*] [*ICAO location identifier*] (ICLI)
S Liv............ Southern Living [*A publication*] (BRI)
SLIV............. Steam Line Isolation Valve [*Nuclear energy*] (NRCH)
SLIX............. Ixiamas [*Bolivia*] [*ICAO location identifier*] (ICLI)
SLIZ............. Izozog [*Bolivia*] [*ICAO location identifier*] (ICLI)
SLJ.............. Hattiesburg, MS [*Location identifier FAA*] (FAAL)
SLJ.............. School Library Journal [*A publication*] (BRI)
SLJ.............. Scottish Law Journal [*Edinburgh*] [*A publication*] (DLA)
S/LJ............. Semiconductor/Liquid Junction
SLJ.............. Silly Little Job (DSUE)
SLJ.............. Straits Law Journal [*1888-92*] [*Malasia*] [*A publication*] (DLA)
SLJD............ El Jordan [*Bolivia*] [*ICAO location identifier*] (ICLI)
SLJE............ San Jose [*Bolivia*] [*ICAO location identifier*] (ICLI)
SLJM........... San Juan De Fribal [*Bolivia*] [*ICAO location identifier*] (ICLI)
SLJN............ San Juan (Estancias) [*Bolivia*] [*ICAO location identifier*] (ICLI)
SLJO............ San Joaquin [*Bolivia*] [*ICAO location identifier*] (ICLI)
SLJR............ Sudan Law Journal and Reports [*A publication*] (DLA)
SLJT............ Santa Juanita [*Bolivia*] [*ICAO location identifier*] (ICLI)
SLJV............ San Javier [*Bolivia*] [*ICAO location identifier*] (ICLI)
SLK.............. Kitsaki School/Public Library, La Ronge, Saskatchewan [*Library symbol National Library of Canada*] (BIB)
SLK.............. Lake Placid-Saranac Lake [*New York*] [*Airport symbol*] (AD)
SLK.............. Saranac Lake [*New York*] [*Airport symbol*] (OAG)
SLK.............. Saranac Lake, NY [*Location identifier FAA*] (FAAL)
slk............... Silk (VRA)
SLK.............. Silkair (Singapore) Pte Ltd. [*ICAO designator*] (FAAC)
SLK.............. Slick (MCD)
SLK.............. Superior Limbic Keratoconjunctivitis [*Ophthalmology*]

SLk .... Surface Linking Number [*Genetics*]
SLKC .... Superior Limbic Keratoconjunctivitis [*Ophthalmology*] (MAE)
SLKP .... Supreme Lodge Knights of Pythias (EA)
SLKPEN ..... Slack and Penalty
SLKQ .... San Miguel [*Bolivia*] [*ICAO location identifier*] (ICLI)
slksc .... Silkscreen (VRA)
SLKT .... Survivability, Lethality, and Key Technologies (SDI)
SLKY .... Puerto Yuca [*Bolivia*] [*ICAO location identifier*] (ICLI)
SLL .... La Loche Public Library, Saskatchewan [*Library symbol National Library of Canada*] (NLC)
SLL .... Saarland Airlines AG [*Germany ICAO designator*] (FAAC)
SLL .... Salalah [*Oman*] [*Airport symbol*] (OAG)
SLL .... Sandia Laboratories, Livermore (AABC)
SLL .... Sandwell Swan Wooster, Inc. [*Toronto Stock Exchange symbol*]
SLL .... Shelf Life Limit (MCD)
SLL .... Signal Long Lines
SLL .... Small Lymphocytic Lymphoma [*Medicine*] (DMAA)
SLL .... Society for Libertarian Life [*Defunct*] (EA)
SLL .... Station List Publishing Co., St. Louis MO [*STAC*]
SLL .... Sterling Lord Literistic, Inc. [*Literary agency*] [*British*]
SLL .... Stollet [*Sweden*] [*Seismograph station code, US Geological Survey*] (SEIS)
SLL .... Suffolk University, Law Library, Boston, MA [*OCLC symbol*] (OCLC)
SLLA .... La Asunta [*Bolivia*] [*ICAO location identifier*] (ICLI)
SLLC .... La China [*Bolivia*] [*ICAO location identifier*] (ICLI)
SLLE .... La Ele [*Bolivia*] [*ICAO location identifier*] (ICLI)
SLLI .... La India [*Bolivia*] [*ICAO location identifier*] (ICLI)
SLLJ .... Laja [*Bolivia*] [*ICAO location identifier*] (ICLI)
SLLL .... Laguna Loa [*Bolivia*] [*ICAO location identifier*] (ICLI)
SLLL .... Synchronous Line, Low, Load (BUR)
SLLP .... La Paz/Kennedy Internacional [*Bolivia*] [*ICAO location identifier*] (ICLI)
SLLR .... Sierra Leone Law Recorder [*A publication*] (DLA)
SLLS .... Snap Lock Limit Switch
SLLS .... Solid-State LASER Light Source
SLLT .... Los Tajibos [*Bolivia*] [*ICAO location identifier*] (ICLI)
SLLU .... San Lorenzo [*Cordillera*] [*ICAO location identifier*] (ICLI)
SLLV .... La Selva [*Bolivia*] [*ICAO location identifier*] (ICLI)
SLLZ .... San Lorenzo [*Bolivia*] [*ICAO location identifier*] (ICLI)
SLM .... Salesian Lay Missioners (EA)
SLM .... Samaritan Lay Missioners [*An association*] (EA)
SLM .... School for Latin America [*Military*]
SLM .... Sea-Launched Missile
SLM .... Senior Level Management
SLM .... Ship Launched Missile (IAA)
SLM .... Signal Level Meter (NTCM)
SLM .... Silver Life-Saving Medal [*Military decoration*] (GFGA)
SLM .... Simulated Laboratory Module
SLM .... Single Longitudinal Mode
SLM .... SLM Holding [*NYSE symbol*] [*Formerly, Student Loan Marketing*] (SG)
SLM .... Snow Lake Mines Ltd. [*Vancouver Stock Exchange symbol*]
SLM .... Sound Level Meter
SLM .... Space Laboratory Module (IAA)
SLM .... Spatial Light Modulator [*Computer imaging*]
SLM .... Standard Laboratory Module
SLM .... Statistical Learning Model (IEEE)
SLM .... St. Louis [*Missouri*] [*Seismograph station code, US Geological Survey*] (SEIS)
SLM .... Student Loan Marketing Association [*NYSE symbol*] (SPSG)
SLM .... Student Loan Mktg [*NYSE symbol*] (TTSB)
SLM .... Submarine-Launched Missile
SLM .... Subscriber Loop Multiplex [*Bell System*]
SLM .... Supported Liquid Membrane [*Separation science and technology*]
SLM .... Surface-Launched Missile [*Navy*] (CAAL)
SLM .... Surinaamse Luchtvaart Maatschappij NV [*Surinam*] [*ICAO designator*] (FAAC)
SLM .... Surrey Local Militia [*British military*] (DMA)
SLM .... Synchronous Line Module
SLMA .... Shoe Lace Manufacturers Association [*Defunct*] (EA)
SLMA .... Southeastern Lumber Manufacturers Association (EA)
SLMA .... Steel Lintel Manufacturers Association [*British*] (DBA)
SLMA .... Student Loan Marketing Association [*Government-chartered private corporation*] [*Nickname: "Sallie Mae"*]
SLMAB .... Single-Line Missile Assembly Building
SLMC .... Spanish Literature Ministries Committee (EA)
SLMC .... Spontaneous Lymphocyte-Mediated Cytotoxicity [*Medicine*] (DB)
SLMCX .... Seligman Communic. & Info. Cl.A [*Mutual fund ticker symbol*] (SG)
SLMD .... Madidi [*Bolivia*] [*ICAO location identifier*] (ICLI)
SLMD .... SpaceLabs Medical [*NASDAQ symbol*] (TTSB)
SLMD .... SpaceLabs Medical, Inc. [*NASDAQ symbol*] (SAG)
SLMD(RA) ... Searchlight Militia Depot (Royal Artillery) [*British military*] (DMA)
SLME .... Select Manual Entry Switch
SLMES .... School Library Media Educators Section [*AASL*] (AL)
SLMFD .... Sterile Low Midforceps Vaginal Delivery (STED)
SLMG .... Magdalena [*Bolivia*] [*ICAO location identifier*] (ICLI)
SLMG .... Self-Launching Motor Glider [*Aviation*] (DA)
SL-MICRO ... Statistical Language for Microcomputers (IID)
SLML .... La Madre [*Bolivia*] [*ICAO location identifier*] (ICLI)
SLMM .... Simultaneous Compass Locator at Middle Marker [*Aviation*] (FAAC)
SLMM .... Submarine-Launched Mobile Mine (MCD)
SLMP .... Mapiri [*Bolivia*] [*ICAO location identifier*] (ICLI)
SLMP .... School Library Manpower Project [*American Association of School Librarians*] (IAA)
SLMP .... Self-Loading Memory Print (IAA)

SLMP .... Since Last Menstrual Period [*Medicine*] (STED)
SLMPrA ...... Student Ln Mktg Adj Rt A Pfd [*NYSE symbol*] (TTSB)
SLMQ .... School Library Media Quarterly [*American Association of School Librarians*] [*A publication*]
SLMR .... Memore [*Bolivia*] [*ICAO location identifier*] (ICLI)
SLMR .... Sailmaker [*Navy British*]
SLMS .... Saturn-Launched Meteoroid Satellite (IAA)
SLMS .... Scanning LASER Mass Spectrometry
SLMS .... Ship-Based Long-Range Missile System (DNAB)
SLMS .... Ship-Launched Missile System (IAA)
SLMS .... Society for Luminescent Microscopy and Spectroscopy (NTPA)
SLMS .... Sound Level Measuring Set
SLMS .... Surface-Launched Missile System
SLMSC .... South London (Volunteers) Medical Staff Corps [*British military*] (DMA)
SLMV .... Monte Verde [*Bolivia*] [*ICAO location identifier*] (ICLI)
SLMW .... Matequa [*Bolivia*] [*ICAO location identifier*] (ICLI)
SLMX .... Monos Arana [*Bolivia*] [*ICAO location identifier*] (ICLI)
SLN .... Salena Research Corp. [*Vancouver Stock Exchange symbol*]
SLN .... Salina [*Kansas*] [*Airport symbol*] (OAG)
SLN .... Salina, KS [*Location identifier FAA*] (FAAL)
SLN .... Salinas [*Chile*] [*Seismograph station code, US Geological Survey*] (SEIS)
SLN .... Salon
SLN .... Santiago Library System, Orange, CA [*OCLC symbol*] (OCLC)
SLN .... Secretariat Linguistiques Nordiques [*Nordic Language Secretariat - NLS*] [*Oslo, Norway*] (EAIO)
SLN .... Section List Number (MCD)
SLN .... Selena Research [*Vancouver Stock Exchange symbol*]
SLN .... Sense Lights On (SAA)
SLN .... Sequence Line Number [*Army*]
SLN .... Service Link Network [*Bell Laboratories*]
SLN .... Sloane Aviation Ltd. [*British ICAO designator*] (FAAC)
SLN .... Solution
SLN .... Southeastern Library Network [*Library network*]
SLN .... Sri Lanka Navy
SLN .... Statement of Logistical Needs [*Air Force*]
SLN .... Sublentiform Nucleus (DMAA)
SLN .... Subsidiary Learning Net (IAA)
SLN .... Superior Laryngeal Nerve [*Neuroanatomy*]
SLNC .... Service Life Not Completed (DNAB)
SLND .... Sine Loco Nec Data [*Without Place or Date of Printing*] [*Latin*]
SLNE .... Nueva Era [*Bolivia*] [*ICAO location identifier*] (ICLI)
SLNK .... SpectraLink Corp. [*NASDAQ symbol*] (TTSB)
SLNO .... Nuevo Mundo [*Bolivia*] [*ICAO location identifier*] (ICLI)
SLNP .... Nueva Esperanza [*Bolivia*] [*ICAO location identifier*] (ICLI)
SLNQ .... Nueva Esperanza (Marban) [*Bolivia*] [*ICAO location identifier*] (ICLI)
SLNS .... Department of Northern Saskatchewan, La Ronge, Saskatchewan [*Library symbol National Library of Canada*] (NLC)
SLNTG .... Sublingual Nitroglycerin (STED)
SLNV .... Nieve [*Bolivia*] [*ICAO location identifier*] (ICLI)
SLNWBC ..... Short Leg Non-Weight-Bearing Cast [*Medicine*] (STED)
SLNWC .... Short Leg Nonwalking Cast [*Medicine*] (DMAA)
SLO .... Edgartown Air, Inc. [*ICAO designator*] (FAAC)
SLO .... Salem, IL [*Location identifier FAA*] (FAAL)
SLO .... Santa Ana [*Columbia*] [*Airport symbol*] (AD)
SLO .... Scanning LASER Ophthalmoscope
SLO .... Searchlight Operator [*British military*] (DMA)
SLO .... Segment Limits Origin
SLO .... Senior Loan Officer [*Banking*] (TBD)
SLO .... Sensitive Lands Ordinance (PA)
SLO .... Shark Liver Oil
SLO .... Ship Liaison Officer [*Navy*] (CAAL)
SLO .... Single Loop Operation [*Nuclear energy*] (NRCH)
SLO .... Sligo [*County in Ireland*] (ROG)
SLO .... Sloan's Supermarkets [*AMEX symbol*] (TTSB)
SLO .... Sloan's Supermarkets, Inc. [*Formerly, Designcraft Industries, Inc.*] [*AMEX symbol*] (SPSG)
SLO .... Slocan Development [*Vancouver Stock Exchange symbol*]
SLO .... Slough [*British depot code*]
slo .... Slovak [*MARC language code Library of Congress*] (LCCP)
SLO .... Slow [*Aviation*] (DA)
SLO .... Slow Lift-Off (MCD)
SLO .... Space Laboratory Operations
SLO .... Staff Legal Officer [*Navy*] (DNAB)
SLO .... State Liaison Officer
SLO .... State Library of Ohio
SLO .... Stop-Limit Order [*Business term*]
SLO .... Stop-Loss Order [*Business term*]
SLO .... Streptolysin O [*Hematology*]
SLO .... Submarine Liaison Officer [*Navy*] (NVT)
SLO .... Swept Local Oscillator (IEEE)
Sloan L & T... Sloan on Landlord and Tenant [*New York*] [*A publication*] (DLA)
Sloan Leg Reg... Sloan's New York Legal Register [*A publication*] (DLA)
SloanSup ..... Sloans Supermarkets [*Associated Press*] (SAG)
SLOB .... Satellite Low-Orbit Bombardment
SLOB .... Secured Lease Obligation Bond (EBF)
SLOB .... Strategic Low-Orbit Bomber (AAG)
SLOB .... Supplemental Layoff Benefits (MCD)
SLOB .... Supply Left of Baseline (MCD)
SLOC .... Sea Lines of Communication [*NATO*] (NATG)
SLOC .... Source Lines of Code (SSD)
SLOCOP ...... Specific Linear Optimal Control Program [*Hydrofoil*] [*Grumman Aerospace Corp.*]
SLOE .... Save Life on Earth (EA)

SLOE............ Special List of Equipment [*Air Force*]
SLOH............ Skylab Operations Handbook [*NASA*] (MCD)
SLOI............. Orialsa [*Bolivia*] [*ICAO location identifier*] (ICLI)
SLOM........... Simultaneous Compass Locator at Outer Marker [*Aviation*] (FAAC)
SLOMAR...... Space Logistics Maintenance and Repair (IAA)
SLOMAR...... Space Logistics, Maintenance, and Rescue
SLO MO....... Slow Motion (NTCM)
SLON........... Saloon
SLOP........... Self-Selected Listener Oriented Poll
SLOP........... Small Lot Optimum Procurement (PDAA)
SLOP........... Standard Listen Output Program (IAA)
SLOPE........ Study of Lunar Orbiter Photographic Evaluation (MCD)
SLOR........... Oruro [*Bolivia*] [*ICAO location identifier*] (ICLI)
SLOR........... Simultaneous Line Over-Relaxation [*Nuclear energy*]
SLOR........... Successive Line Overrelaxation (IAA)
SLOR........... Swept Local Oscillator Receiver (NG)
SLORC........ State Law and Order Restoration Council [*Myanmar*]
SLORV........ Structural Loads on Reentry Vehicles (MCD)
SLOS........... Scanning Line of Sight (KSC)
SLOS........... Secondary Line of Sight [*Sextants*]
SLOS........... Sierra Leone Organization Society
SLOS........... Smith-Lemli-Opitz Syndrome [*Medicine*]
SLOS........... Star Line-of-Sight (MCD)
SLOS........... Sun Line-of-Sight
SLOS........... Swept Local Oscillator
SLOSH........ Sea, Lake, and Overland Surge Hurricane
SLOSH........ Sea Lake and Overland Surges from Hurricanes [*Model*] (USDC)
SLOSH........ Sea Level and Overland Surge from Hurricanes [*National Oceanic and Atmospheric Administration*]
SLOSJ......... State and Local Officials for Soviet Jews (EA)
SLO/SRI...... Shift Left Out/Shift Right In
SLOSYN....... Slow Synchronization (IAA)
SLOT........... Anchor Gaming [*NASDAQ symbol*] (SAG)
SLOT........... Sinaota [*Bolivia*] [*ICAO location identifier*] (ICLI)
SLOT........... Slotted (IAA)
SLOT........... Stabilized Line-of-Sight Tracker
SLOT........... Submarine-Launched One-Way Tactical [*Buoy*] (NVT)
SLOT........... Submarine Launched One-Way Transmitter [*AN/BRT-1*] (DOMA)
SLOTE......... Second Language Oral Test of English [*A. Fathman*] (TES)
SLOTH......... Suppressing Line Operands and Translating to Hexadecimal [*Telecommunications*] (TEL)
Slov .... Slovenia
SLOWPOKE... Safe Low-Power Critical Experiment [*Nuclear energy*]
SLP............. Left Sacroposterior Position [*of the fetus*] [*Obstetrics*]
SLP............. Sacrolaeva Posterior [*A fetal position*] (AAMN)
SLP............. Safe Leeward Position
SLP............. Salpa Aviation Co. Ltd. [*Sudan*] [*ICAO designator*] (FAAC)
SLP............. San Luis Potosi [*Mexico*] [*Airport symbol*] (AD)
SLP............. School Lunch Program
SLP............. Scintilore Explorations Ltd. [*Toronto Stock Exchange symbol*]
SLP............. Scottish Labour Party [*Political party*] (PPW)
SLP............. Scottish Liberal Party [*Political party*]
SLP............. Scouting Landplane
SLP............. Sea-Level Pressure
SLP............. Secretary for Logistics Planning [*Air Force*]
SLP............. Sectional Linear Programming [*Computer science*]
SLP............. Segmental Limb Systolic Pressure [*Medicine*] (DMAA)
SLP............. Segmented Level Programming [*Computer science*] (IEEE)
SLP............. Selective Line Printing (IAA)
SLP............. Service Location Protocol [*Computer science*]
SLP............. Sex-Limited Protein [*Immunology*]
SLP............. Shelby, NC [*Location identifier FAA*] (FAAL)
SLP............. Short Luteal Phase [*Medicine*] (DMAA)
SLP............. Silicon Light Pulser
SLP............. Sine Legitima Prole [*Without Lawful Issue*] [*Latin*]
SLP............. Single Langmuir Probe (IAA)
SLP............. Single Layer Polysilicon (IAA)
SLP............. Single Linear Polarization
SLP............. Single Link Procedures (TNIG)
SLP............. Sleep
SLP............. Slip (ADA)
SLP............. Sloop
SLP............. Slope (MSA)
SLP............. Socialist Labor Party [*Egypt*] [*Political party*] (PPW)
SLP............. Socialist Labor Party of America [*Political party*] (EA)
SLP............. Soft Lander Probe [*Aerospace*]
SLP............. Sound Level Plot [*Military*] (CAAL)
SLP............. Source Language Processor [*Computer science*] (BUR)
SLP............. Spacelab Program Office [*European Research National Organization*] (MCD)
SLP............. Specific Line of Precipitin [*Immunology*]
SLP............. Speech Language Pathologist
SLP............. Speed Limiting Point [*Aviation*] (FAAC)
SLP............. Spring-Loaded Pulley
SLP............. Standard Long Play [*VHS recorder playing time mode*] (NTCM)
SLP............. St. Lucie Plant [*Nuclear energy*] (NRCH)
SLP............. Stock List Price [*Military*] (AFIT)
S/LP........... Stop Lamp [*Automotive engineering*]
SLP............. Strategic Locations Planning [*Information service or system*] (IID)
SLP............. Strategic Logistic Program [*Army*] (RDA)
SLP............. Street Legal Performance [*Auto model designation*]
SLP............. Subluxation of Patella (STED)
SLP............. Sun Energy Partners LP [*NYSE symbol*] (SPSG)
SLP............. Sun Energy Ptnrs L.P. [*NYSE symbol*] (TTSB)
SLP............. Super Long Play [*Video technology*]

SLP............. Supersonic Local Pressure
SLP............. Supplier Loaned Property (MCD)
SLP............. Surface Launch Platform (NVT)
SLP............. Symbol Location Point (NITA)
SLP............. Systematic Layout Planning [*Industrial engineering*]
SLPA........... Selected Legally Protected Animals [*Marine science*] (MSC)
SLPA........... Silicon Light Pulser Array
SLPA........... Solid Logic Process Automation (IAA)
SLPA........... State Lamb Producers' Association [*Queensland, Australia*]
SLPB........... Spacelab Program Board [*NASA*] (NASA)
SLPC........... Signal Lines Pair Combination (IAA)
SLPC........... Single Loop Programmable Indicating Controller (NITA)
SLPC........... Socialist Labour Party of Canada
SLPC........... St. Louis Production Center
SLPC........... Supported Liquid Phase Catalyst [*Chemical engineering*]
SLPD........... Skylab Program Directive [*NASA*] (KSC)
SLPD........... State and Local Planning Division [*Environmental Protection Agency*] (GFGA)
SLPH........... Seat Lock Pin Handle
SLPHR........ Sulphur
SLPI........... Secretory Leukocyte Protease Inhibitor [*Medicine*] (TAD)
SLPI........... Secretory Leukoprotease Inhibitor [*Biochemistry*]
SLPL........... Sea Loading Pipe Line [*Technical drawings*]
SLPL........... St. Louis Public Library [*Missouri*]
SLPM.......... Palmira [*Bolivia*] [*ICAO location identifier*] (ICLI)
SLPM.......... Scanned-LASER Photoluminescence Microscope (PDAA)
SLPM.......... Selected List of Published Material [*Her Majesty's Stationery Office*] [*British*]
SLPM.......... Silicon Light Pulser Matrix
SLPMS........ Short Leg Posterior Molded Splint [*Medicine*] (MEDA)
SLPMS........ Single Level Power Management System
SLPO........... Potosi [*Bolivia*] [*ICAO location identifier*] (ICLI)
SLPO........... Skylab Program Office [*NASA*] (KSC)
SLPP........... Paraparau [*Bolivia*] [*ICAO location identifier*] (ICLI)
SLPP........... Serum Lipophosphoprotein [*Serology*]
SLPP........... Sierra Leone People's Party [*Political party*] (PD)
SLPP........... Sri Lanka People's Party [*Political party*] (PPW)
SLPR........... Puerto Rico [*Bolivia*] [*ICAO location identifier*] (ICLI)
SLPR........... Sidelobe Pulse Rejection [*Military*] (CAAL)
SLPR........... Supplier Loaned Property Request (MCD)
SLPRF........ Northern Teacher Education Program, Inc., La Ronge, Saskatchewan [*Library symbol National Library of Canada*] (NLC)
SLPS........... Puerto Suarez [*Bolivia*] [*ICAO location identifier*] (ICLI)
SLPS........... Sonobuoy Launcher Pneumatic System
SLPS........... State and Local Program Support [*Nuclear energy*] (NRCH)
SLPSS........ Semiconductor LASER Pumped Solid State (AAEL)
SLPT........... Peta [*Bolivia*] [*ICAO location identifier*] (ICLI)
SLPT........... Salted Paper Print (VRA)
SLPT........... Socialist Labor Party of Turkey [*Turkiye Sosyalist Isci Partisi*] [*Political party*] (PPW)
SLPTC......... Solid-Liquid Phase-Transfer Catalysis
SLPU........... Puchuni [*Bolivia*] [*ICAO location identifier*] (ICLI)
SLPV........... Puerto Villa-Roel [*Bolivia*] [*ICAO location identifier*] (ICLI)
SLPW.......... Sloop-of-War
SLQ............. Sleetmute [*Alaska*] [*Airport symbol*] (OAG)
SLQ............. Sleetmute, AK [*Location identifier FAA*] (FAAL)
SLQ............. Surface Layer Quality
SLQY........... Curichi [*Bolivia*] [*ICAO location identifier*] (ICLI)
SLR............. Radcliffe College, Schlesinger Library, Cambridge, MA [*OCLC symbol*] (OCLC)
SLR............. Sales Letter Report
SLR............. Saskatchewan Law Reports [*A publication*] (DLA)
SLR............. Satellite LASER Ranging [*For geodetic and geophysical measurements*]
SLR............. Scanning Laser Rangefinder
SLR............. Scottish Land Court Reports [*A publication*] (DLA)
SLR............. Scottish Law Reporter [*Edinburgh*] [*A publication*] (DLA)
SLR............. Scottish Law Review and Sheriff Court Reports [*1885-1963*] [*A publication*] (DLA)
SLR............. Sealer
SLR............. Sea-Level Rise [*Climatology*]
SLR............. Self-Loading Rifle (MCD)
SLR............. Sense Line Register
SLR............. Service Level Reporter [*IBM Corp.*]
SLR............. Seychelles Law Reports [*1921-23*] [*A publication*] (DLA)
SLR............. Short Latency Response [*Neurology*]
SLR............. Side-Looking RADAR (AFM)
SLR............. Sierra Leone Railway (MHDB)
SLR............. Simple Left to Right [*Computer science*]
SLR............. Simple Linear Regression [*Statistics*]
SLR............. Sind Law Reporter [*India*] [*A publication*] (DLA)
SLR............. Singapore Law Reports [*1946-49, 1953-56*] [*A publication*] (DLA)
SLR............. Single-Lens Reflex [*Camera*]
SLR............. Skylab Rescue [*NASA*] (KSC)
SLR............. Slush on Runway [*NWS*] (FAAC)
SLR............. Small Lattice Relaxation (AAEL)
SLR............. SOBELAIR [*Societe Belge de Transport Aeriens*] [*Belgium ICAO designator*] (FAAC)
SLR............. Solar (AAG)
SLR............. Solectron Corp. [*NYSE symbol*] (SPSG)
SLR............. Sound Level Recorder
SLR............. Southern Law Review [*St. Louis, MO*] [*A publication*] (DLA)
SLR............. South Lancashire Regiment [*British*]
SLR............. Special Leave Refused
SLR............. Special Light Rifle (NATG)

SLR	Specific Lung Resistance
SLR	Spin Lattice Relaxation
SLR	Sport Leicht Renn [*Sports Lightweight Racing (Car)*] [*German*]
SLR	Stabell Resources [*Vancouver Stock Exchange symbol*]
SLR	Static Line Regulation
SLR	Static Loaded Radius [*Automotive engineering*]
SLR	Statute Law Revision [*A publication*] (DLA)
SLR	Storage Limits Register
SLR	Straight Leg Raising [*Medicine*]
SLR	Streptococcus Lactis, Resistant [*Immunology*] (DAVI)
SLR	Streptococcus lactis R Factor [*Biochemistry*]
SLR	Sulphur Springs, TX [*Location identifier FAA*] (FAAL)
SLR	Surface Layout Release
SLR	System Level Requirement [*Military*] (CAAL)
SLRA	San Ramon [*Bolivia*] [*ICAO location identifier*] (ICLI)
SLRA	Sierra Leone Royal Artillery [*British military*] (DMA)
SLRA	Soviet Long-Range Air (MCD)
SLRA	Suede and Leather Refinishers of America [*Defunct*] (EA)
SLRAP	Standard Low-Frequency Range Approach
SLRB	Robore [*Bolivia*] [*ICAO location identifier*] (ICLI)
SLRB	State Labor Relations Board
SLRB	Steel Labor Relations Board [*New Deal*]
SLRC	San Luis Rey College [*California*]
SLRC	Short Length Record (IAA)
SLRC/MILO...	State Library Resource Center - Maryland Interlibrary Organization [*Library network*]
SLRD	Searchlight RADAR
SLRE	El Remate [*Bolivia*] [*ICAO location identifier*] (ICLI)
SLRE	Self-Loading Random Access Edit (IAA)
SLREG	Stepwise Linear Regression (IAA)
SL Rev	Scottish Law Review and Sheriff Court Reports [*A publication*] (DLA)
SLRH	Rancho Alegre [*Bolivia*] [*ICAO location identifier*] (ICLI)
SLRI	Riberalta [*Bolivia*] [*ICAO location identifier*] (ICLI)
SLRI	Shipboard Long-Range Input
SLR Leic	Leicester's Straits Law Reports [*Malaya*] [*A publication*] (DLA)
SLR Leicester...	Leicester's Straits Law Reports [*Malaya*] [*A publication*] (DLA)
SLRN	Select Read Numerically
SL RNG	Slope Range
SLRNS	Straits Law Reports, New Series [*Malasia*] [*A publication*] (DLA)
SLRP	Rosapata [*Bolivia*] [*ICAO location identifier*] (ICLI)
SLRP	Society for Strategic and Long Range Planning [*Later, Strategic Planning Society - SP*] (EAIO)
SLRP	State Loan Repayment Program [*Department of Health and Human Services*] (GFGA)
SLRP	Survey, Liaison, and Reconnaissance Party [*Navy*] (ANA)
SLRQ	Rurrenabaque [*Bolivia*] [*ICAO location identifier*] (ICLI)
SLRR	Retiro [*Bolivia*] [*ICAO location identifier*] (ICLI)
SLRRB	Senior Logistics Readiness Review Board [*Fort Lewis*] (MCD)
SLRS	Rio Seco [*Bolivia*] [*ICAO location identifier*] (ICLI)
SLRS	Satellite LASER Ranging System
SLRS	Sexual Law Reform Society [*British*]
SLRT	Santa Rita [*Bolivia*] [*ICAO location identifier*] (ICLI)
SLRT	Straight Leg Raising Test [*or Tenderness*] [*Medicine*]
SLRTB	Saskatchewan Department of Tourism and Small Business, La Ronge, Saskatchewan [*Library symbol National Library of Canada*] (NLC)
SLRUM	Simple Least Recently Used Stack Model (MHDI)
SLRV	Shuttle Launched Research Vehicle [*NASA*] (NASA)
SLRV	South London Regiment of Volunteers [*British military*] (DMA)
SLRV	Standard Light Rail Vehicle [*Mass transit*]
SLRV	Strawberry Latent Ringspot Virus [*Plant pathology*]
SLRV	Surveyor Lunar Roving Vehicle [*Aerospace*] (MCD)
SLRY	Reyes [*Bolivia*] [*ICAO location identifier*] (ICLI)
SLS	Aeroservicios Ejecutivos Sinaloenses SA [*Mexico ICAO designator*] (FAAC)
SLS	Saint Lawrence Seaway Development Corp. [*Department of Transportation*]
SLS	Saint Lawrence Seminary [*Wisconsin*]
SLS	Sales
SLS	Santiago Library System [*Library network*]
SLS	Saskatchewan Land Surveyor [*Canada*] (ASC)
SLS	Sassafras Loamy Sand [*Type of soil*]
SLS	Saturn Longitude System [*Planetary science*]
SLS	Scanning LASER System
SLS	School of Library Service [*Columbia University*] [*Defunct*]
SLS	School of Logistics Science [*Army*]
SLS	Scots Language Society [*British*] (DBA)
SLS	Sea-Land Service, Inc. [*AAR code*]
SLS	Sea Level, Standard Day
SLS	Sea-Level Static
SLS	Secondary Landing Site [*NASA*] (NASA)
SLS	Securities Lending Service [*Australian Stock Exchange*]
SLS	Segment Long-Spacing Collagen Fiber
SLS	Selas Corp. of Amer [*AMEX symbol*] (TTSB)
SLS	Selas Corp. of America [*AMEX symbol*] (SPSG)
SLS	Selective LASER [*Light Amplification by Stimulated Emission of Radiation*] Sintering [*Desktop manufacturing*]
SLS	Serra Cooperative Library System, San Diego, CA [*OCLC symbol*] (OCLC)
SLS	Shore Labourers Society [*A union*] [*British*]
SLS	Short-Leg Splint [*Orthopedics*] (DAVI)
SLS	Side-Lobe Suppression RADAR
SLS	Side-Looking SONAR
SLS	Signaling Link Selection [*Telecommunications*] (TEL)
SLS	Silicon Light Source
SLS	Silistra [*Bulgaria*] [*Airport symbol*] (OAG)
SLS	Sindacato Lavoratori della Somalia [*Workers Union of Somalia*]
SLS	Skylab Simulator [*NASA*] (KSC)
SLS	Slightly Soluble
SLS	Slovenska Ljudska Stranka [*Slovene People's Party*] [*Former Yugoslavia*] [*Political party*] (PPE)
SL'S	Slovenska L'Udova Strana [*Slovak People's Party*] [*Also, HSL'S*] [*Political party*] (PPE)
SLS	Society for Laparoendoscopic Surgeons (NTPA)
SLS	Society for Libyan Studies (EAIO)
SLS	Society for Literature and Science
SLS	Society of Landscape Studies [*British*] (DBA)
SLS	Society of Laparoendoscopic Surgeons (EA)
SLS	Sodium Lauryl Sulfate [*Also, SDS*] [*Organic chemistry*]
SLS	Soengei Langka [*Sumatra*] [*Seismograph station code, US Geological Survey Closed*] (SEIS)
SLS	Software Loadable System [*Computer science*] (PCM)
SLS	So-Luminaire Systems [*Vancouver Stock Exchange symbol*]
SLS	Solution-Liquid-Solid [*Chemistry*]
SLS	Sonobuoy Localization System (NVT)
SLS	Sortie Lab Simulator [*NASA*] (NASA)
SLS	Sound Learning Society [*British*]
SLS	Source Library System [*Computer science*]
SLS	Spacecraft Landing Strut
SLS	Space Laboratory Simulator [*NASA*]
SLS	Space Launch System
SLS	Specialist in Library Science (PGP)
SLS	Specific Living Space (AAG)
SLS	Spoken Language Services, Inc.
SLS	Standard Light Spanwire [*Military*] (CAAL)
SLS	Start Launch Sequence [*Military*]
SLS	Statement Level Simulator [*NASA*] (NASA)
SLS	Stein-Leventhal Syndrome [*Medicine*] (DMAA)
SLS	Stephenson Locomotive Society [*British*] (BI)
SLS	Stores Locator System (MCD)
SLS	Strained-Layer Superlattices [*Crystalline materials*]
SLS	Strategic Lunar System (IAA)
SLS	Student Lesson Sheets
SLS	Students for a Libertarian Society (EA)
SLS	Styles of Leadership Survey [*Test*]
SLS	Suburban Library System [*Library network*]
SLS	Sun-Load Sensor [*Automotive engineering*]
SLS	Supplemental Loans for Students [*Department of Education*]
SLS	Surface Laboratory System [*NASA*] (KSC)
SLS	SWALCAP Library Services Ltd. [*Information service or system*] (IID)
SLS	Symbolic Layout System (MCD)
SLSA	Santa Ana De Yacuma [*Bolivia*] [*ICAO location identifier*] (ICLI)
SLSA	Seamen's Loyal Standard Association [*A union*] [*British*]
SLSA	Secondary Lead Smelters Association (FA)
SLSA	Shuttle Logistics Support Aircraft [*NASA*] (MCD)
SLSA	Slotting Saw
SLSA	St. Lawrence Seaway Authority [*See also AVMS*] [*Canada*]
SLSAC	Saint Lawrence Seaway Authority of Canada
SLSADJ	Stores Locator System Adjustment (MCD)
SLSB	San Borja [*Bolivia*] [*ICAO location identifier*] (ICLI)
SLSC	Santa Clara (Moxos) [*Bolivia*] [*ICAO location identifier*] (ICLI)
SLSD	San Carlos Gutierrez [*Bolivia*] [*ICAO location identifier*] (ICLI)
SLSDC	Saint Lawrence Seaway Development Corp. [*Department of Transportation*]
SLSF	San Francisco (Moxos) [*Bolivia*] [*ICAO location identifier*] (ICLI)
SLSF	Sodium Loop Safety Facility [*Nuclear energy*]
SLSF	St. Louis-San Francisco Railway Co. [*AAR code*]
SLSG	Sipuati [*Bolivia*] [*ICAO location identifier*] (ICLI)
SLSG	S-Locus-Specific Glycoprotein [*Botany*]
SLSH	Santa Ana De Huachi [*Bolivia*] [*ICAO location identifier*] (ICLI)
SLSH	Short Length Super HIPPO [*High Internal Pressure Producing Orifice*] (MCD)
SLSI	San Ignacio De Velasco [*Bolivia*] [*ICAO location identifier*] (ICLI)
SLSI	Super Large-Scale Integration
SLSJ	Salinas [*Bolivia*] [*ICAO location identifier*] (ICLI)
SLSK	Sauces [*Bolivia*] [*ICAO location identifier*] (ICLI)
SLSL	Santa Lucia (Cliza) [*Bolivia*] [*ICAO location identifier*] (ICLI)
SLSL	Statutory Long Service Leave (ADA)
SLSM	San Ignacio De Moxos [*Bolivia*] [*ICAO location identifier*] (ICLI)
SLSM	Silver Life-Saving Medal [*Military decoration*]
SLSM	Simple Line Source Model [*Environmental Protection Agency*] (GFGA)
SLSMGR	Sales Manager (WGA)
SLSMN	Salesman
SLSMS	Spacelab Support Module Simulator [*NASA*] (MCD)
SLSN	Sanandita [*Bolivia*] [*ICAO location identifier*] (ICLI)
SLSO	Santa Barbara De Parra [*Bolivia*] [*ICAO location identifier*] (ICLI)
SLSO	Shipyard Labour Supply Officer [*British*]
SLSP	SACLANT Scheduled Program (MCD)
SLSP	Slow Speed
SLSQ	Saahaqui [*Bolivia*] [*ICAO location identifier*] (ICLI)
SLSR	Santa Rosa De Yacuma [*Bolivia*] [*ICAO location identifier*] (ICLI)
SLSS	Sasasama [*Bolivia*] [*ICAO location identifier*] (ICLI)
SLSS	Secondary Life Support System [*NASA*]
SLSS	Shuttle Launch Support System (MCD)
SL-SS	Spacelab Subsystem [*NASA*] (NASA)
SLSS	Swimmer Life Support System [*Navy*] (CAAL)
SLSS	Systems Library Subscription Service [*Computer science*] (IBMDP)
SLSSM	Submerged Launched Surface-to-Surface Missile (MCD)
SL-SSS	Spacelab Subsystem Segment [*NASA*] (NASA)

SLST............ San Antonio [*Bolivia*] [*ICAO location identifier*] (ICLI)
SI St .... Slade's Compilation of the Statutes of Vermont [*A publication*] (DLA)
SLST............ Slightly Staining
SLST............ Slip Stitch [*Knitting*]
SLST............ St. Louis, San Francisco & Texas Railway Co. [*AAR code*]
SLSU............ Sucre [*Bolivia*] [*ICAO location identifier*] (ICLI)
SLSUX.......... SMBS Utilities Fund Cl.B [*Mutual fund ticker symbol*] (SG)
SLSW.......... Santa Barbara (Versalles) [*Bolivia*] [*ICAO location identifier*] (ICLI)
SLSW.......... St. Louis Southwestern Railway Co. (IIA)
SLSX............ San Ramon De Senac [*Bolivia*] [*ICAO location identifier*] (ICLI)
SLT .... Pious Society of Our Lady of the Most Holy Trinity (TOCD)
SLT .... Sacrolaeva Transversa [*A fetal position*] (AAMN)
SLT .... Salant Corp. [*AMEX symbol*] (SAG)
SLT .... Salant Corp. [*NYSE symbol*] (SPSG)
SLT .... Salta [*Argentina*] [*Seismograph station code, US Geological Survey Closed*] (SEIS)
SLT .... Saltair Ltd. [*British ICAO designator*] (FAAC)
SLT .... Searchlight
SLT .... Second Law of Thermodynamics
SLT .... Self-Loading Tape (AFM)
SLT .... Sellectek Industries, Inc. [*Vancouver Stock Exchange symbol*]
SLT .... Sense Light Test (SAA)
slt .... Servants of Our Lady of the Most Holy Trinity (TOCD)
SLT .... Shiga-Like Toxin [*Biochemistry*]
SLT .... Ship Letter Telegram
SLT .... Shuttle Loop Transit [*NASA*]
SLT .... Signaling Link Termination [*Telecommunications*]
SLT .... Simulated LASER Target
SLT .... Simulated Launch Test [*NASA*] (KSC)
SLT .... Skylight (AAG)
SLT .... Slate (MSA)
SLT .... Slate Run, PA [*Location identifier FAA*] (FAAL)
SLT .... Slight (DAVI)
SLT .... Slit
SLT .... Solid Logic Technique [*Computer science*] (IEEE)
SLT .... Solid Logic Technology
SLT .... Soluble Lytic Transglycosylase [*An enzyme*]
SLT .... Sonobuoy Launch Tube [*Navy*] (CAAL)
SLT .... Spacelab Technology [*NASA*] (NAKS)
SLT .... Special [*or Specific*] Launch Trajectory (AFM)
SLT .... Speech Language Therapist
SLT .... Spontaneous Lymphocyte Transportation (PDAA)
SLT .... Spotlight (MSA)
SLT .... Squadron Landing Team [*Marine Corps*] (DOMA)
SLT .... Sri Lanka Telecom Ltd.
SLT .... Standard Light Source (IAA)
SLT .... Stockpile Laboratory Tests
SLT .... Stress Limit Tests
SLT .... Structured Learning Therapy
S Lt .... Sub-Lieutenant [*British military*] (DMA)
SLT .... Swing [*Parachute*] Landing Trainer [*Military*] (INF)
SLT .... Switchman's Local Test [*Telecommunications*] (TEL)
SLTA .... Scottish Lawn Tennis Association (DBA)
SLTA .... Scottish Licensed Trade Association (DBA)
SLT & SDL... Searchlight and Sound Locator [*Navy*]
SLTB .... Society for Low Temperature Biology (EA)
SLTB .... St. Lucia Tourist Board (EA)
SLTBR .... Society for Light Treatment and Biological Rhythms
SLTC .... Society of Leather Technologists and Chemists [*British*]
SLTD .... Salted
SLTD .... Slotted (MSA)
SLTDP .... Special LASER Technology Development Program
SLTE .... Self-Loading Tape Edit (IAA)
SLTE .... Teoponte [*Bolivia*] [*ICAO location identifier*] (ICLI)
SLTEA .... Sheffield Lighter Trades Employers' Association [*British*] (DCTA)
SLTF .... San Telmo (Cordillera) [*Bolivia*] [*ICAO location identifier*] (ICLI)
SLTF .... Shortest Latency Time First
SLTF .... Silo-Launch Test Facility
SLTG .... Santiago [*Bolivia*] [*ICAO location identifier*] (ICLI)
sltgz .... Saltglaze (VRA)
SLTH .... Tumichucua [*Bolivia*] [*ICAO location identifier*] (ICLI)
SLTI .... San Matias [*Bolivia*] [*ICAO location identifier*] (ICLI)
SLTI .... Surgical Laser Tech [*NASDAQ symbol*] (TTSB)
SLTI .... Surgical Laser Technologies, Inc. [*NASDAQ symbol*] (NQ)
SLTJ .... Tarija [*Bolivia*] [*ICAO location identifier*] (ICLI)
SLT (Lyon Ct)... Scots Law Times (Lyon Court Reports) [*A publication*] (DLA)
SLTM .... Short Lead Time Material (DNAB)
SLTM .... Standard Lap Turn Method (NVT)
SLTM .... Structural Lander Test Model
SLTN .... Solution
SLT (Notes)... Scots Law Times (Notes of Recent Decisions) [*A publication*] (DLA)
SLTO .... Sea-Level Takeoff
SLTP .... Tipuani [*Bolivia*] [*ICAO location identifier*] (ICLI)
SLTR .... Service Life Test Report (AAG)
SlTr .... Silent Treatment [*Psychology*] (DAVI)
Sl Tr .... Slight Trace (CPH)
SLTR .... Trinidad [*Bolivia*] [*ICAO location identifier*] (ICLI)
SLTS .... Todos Santos [*Bolivia*] [*ICAO location identifier*] (ICLI)
SLT (Sh Ct)... Scots Law Times Sheriff Court Reports [*A publication*] (DLA)
sLTSV .... Satellite Lucerne Transient Streak Virus
SLTT .... Total Bolivia [*Bolivia*] [*ICAO location identifier*] (ICLI)
SLTU .... Sierra Leone Teachers' Union
SLTU .... Tucavaca [*Bolivia*] [*ICAO location identifier*] (ICLI)
SLTUF .... Sri Lanka Trade Union Federation [*Sri Lanka Vurthiya Samithi Sammelanaya*]

SLTV............ St. Lucia Television Service
SLT.WS........ Salant Corp. Wrrt [*AMEX symbol*] (TTSB)
SLTX............ Sales Tax
SLTY............ Tiguipa [*Bolivia*] [*ICAO location identifier*] (ICLI)
SLTZ............ Tupiza [*Bolivia*] [*ICAO location identifier*] (ICLI)
SLU .... Pavlovsk [*Later, LNN*] [*Former USSR Geomagnetic observatory code*]
SLU .... Saint Lawrence University [*Canton, NY*]
SLU .... Secondary Logic Unit
SLU .... Serial Line Unit
Slu .... Slough [*Maps and charts*]
SLU .... Slutsk [*Later, LNN*] [*Former USSR Geomagnetic observatory code*]
SLU .... Source Library Update [*Computer science*]
SLU .... Southern Labor Union
SLU .... Special Liaison Unit [*Military intelligence*] [*World War II*]
SLU .... Special Line Unit (NITA)
SLU .... St. Louis University [*Missouri*]
SLU .... St. Louis University, Law Library, St. Louis, MO [*OCLC symbol*] (OCLC)
SLU .... St. Lucia [*West Indies*] [*Airport symbol*] (OAG)
SLU .... Subscriber Line Unit [*Telecommunications*] (IAA)
SLU .... Subscriber Line Use [*Telecommunications*]
SLU .... Switching Logic Unit (CAAL)
SLUC .... Standard Level User Charge
SLUC .... Uncia [*Bolivia*] [*ICAO location identifier*] (ICLI)
SLUD .... Salivation, Lacrimation, Urination, Defecation [*Medicine*] (DMAA)
SLUDGE...... Salivation, Lacrimation, Urination, Defecation, Gastrointestinal Upset, Emesis [*Medicine*] (DMAA)
SLUF.......... Short Little Ugly Feller [*Nickname for A-7 aircraft*] (MCD)
SLUFAE....... Surface-Launched Unit, Fire Area Equipment (MCD)
SLUFAE....... Surface-Launched Unit, Fuel-Air Explosive Mine Neutralizer [*Army*] (RDA)
SLUG .... Superconducting Low-Inductance Undulatory Galvanometer
SLUMINE .... Surface-Launched Unit, Mine Layer (MCD)
SLUMT........ Slacked Unconstrained Minimization Technique (PDAA)
SLUR .... Share Library User Report [*Computer science*] (OA)
SLURB........ Slovenly Suburb
SLURP........ Self Leveling Unit for Removing Pollution [*Marine science*] (MSC)
SLURP........ Spiny Lobster Undersea Research Project
SLURREX.... Slurry Reactor Experiment
SLUS .... Subscriber's Line Use System [*AT & T*] [*Telecommunications*] (TEL)
SLUV .... Uvas Verdes [*Bolivia*] [*ICAO location identifier*] (ICLI)
SLUY .... Uyuni [*Bolivia*] [*ICAO location identifier*] (ICLI)
SLV .... El Salvador [*ANSI three-letter standard code*] (CNC)
SLV .... Salivate (KSC)
SLV .... San Jose, CA [*Location identifier FAA*] (FAAL)
SLV .... Sao Paulo de Olivenca [*Brazil*] [*Airport symbol*] (AD)
SLV .... Satellite Launching Vehicle [*Air Force*]
SLV .... Satellite-Like Virus
SLV .... Saturn Launch Vehicle [*NASA*] (KSC)
SLV .... Seldovia [*Alaska*] [*Seismograph station code, US Geological Survey*] (SEIS)
SLV .... Shallot Latent Virus [*Plant pathology*]
SLv .... Sifra on Leviticus [*A publication*] (BJA)
SLV .... Silverado Foods [*AMEX symbol*] (TTSB)
SLV .... Silverado Foods, Inc. [*AMEX symbol*] (SAG)
SLV .... Silver Lady Resources [*Vancouver Stock Exchange symbol*]
SLV .... Simulated Launch Vehicle (MCD)
SLV .... Single Lamellar Vesicle (MEC)
SLV .... Sleeve (AAG)
slv .... Slovenian [*MARC language code Library of Congress*] (LCCP)
SLV .... Small Launch Vehicle [*Air Force*] (DOMA)
SLV .... Soft Landing Vehicle [*NASA*]
S-L-V.......... Solid-Liquid-Vapour (DB)
SLV .... Solvent (WGA)
SLV .... Southern Launch Vehicle [*Australia*]
SLV .... Space Launch Vehicle [*NASA*]
SLV .... Space-Like Vector
SLV .... Sport-Luxury Vehicle
SLV .... Standardized Launcher Vehicle (IAA)
SLV .... Standard Launch Vehicle
SLVA.......... Villa Aroma [*Bolivia*] [*ICAO location identifier*] (ICLI)
SLVC.......... Selvac Corp. [*NASDAQ symbol*] (NQ)
SLVC.......... Super Linear Variable Capacitor (PDAA)
SLVD.......... Covendo [*Bolivia*] [*ICAO location identifier*] (ICLI)
SLVE.......... Venecia [*Bolivia*] [*ICAO location identifier*] (ICLI)
SLVG .... Salvage
SLVG .... Sleeving [*Electricity*]
SLVG .... Special Launch Vehicle Group [*NASA*] (KSC)
SLVG .... Valle Grande [*Bolivia*] [*ICAO location identifier*] (ICLI)
SLVI.......... Caranavi [*Bolivia*] [*ICAO location identifier*] (ICLI)
SlvKing ...... Silver King Communications [*Associated Press*] (SAG)
SLVM.......... Villa Montes [*Bolivia*] [*ICAO location identifier*] (ICLI)
SlvMin .... Silverado Mines Ltd. [*Associated Press*] (SAG)
SLVN .... Sylvan Learning Systems [*Montgomery, AL*] [*NASDAQ symbol*] (NQ)
SLVN .... Valencia [*Bolivia*] [*ICAO location identifier*] (ICLI)
SLVR .... Silver [*Automotive advertising*]
SLVR .... Silver Diner Dvlpmt [*NASDAQ symbol*] (TTSB)
SLVR .... Viru Viru [*Bolivia*] [*ICAO location identifier*] (ICLI)
SLVRJ.......... Surface-Launched Low-Volume Ramjet
SLVS .... San Luis Valley Southern Railroad (IIA)
SLVT .... Solvent (MSA)
SLVTN........ Salvation
SLW............ Saltillo [*Mexico*] [*Airport symbol*] (AD)
SLW............ Silversword Corp. [*Vancouver Stock Exchange symbol*]

SLW............	Single Line Working [Railway engineering term] (DCTA)
SLW............	Sisters of the Living Word [Roman Catholic religious order]
SLW............	Slow
SLW............	Space-Based LASER Weapon (MCD)
SLW............	Specific Leaf Weight [Botany]
SLW............	Spectral Line Width
SLW............	St. Laurent Paperboard [NYSE symbol]
SLW............	Store Logical Word
SLW............	Straight-Line Wavelength
SLW............	Supercooled Liquid Water [Marine science] (OSRA)
SLW............	Wooster, OH [Location identifier FAA] (FAAL)
SLWA..........	Santa Rosa De Abuna [Bolivia] [ICAO location identifier] (ICLI)
SLWC..........	Short-Leg Walking Cast [Orthopedics] (DAVI)
SLWD..........	Seis De Agosto [Bolivia] [ICAO location identifier] (ICLI)
SLWL..........	Straight-Line Wavelength (MSA)
SLWMS........	Secondary Liquid Waste Management System [Nuclear energy] (NRCH)
SL-Wola Ludu...	Stronnictwo Ludowe-Wola Ludu [Peasant Party-People's Will] [Poland Political party] (PPE)
SLWOP	Special Leave Without Pay
SLWT..........	Side Loadable Warping Tug [Navy] (CAAL)
SLX............	Salt Cay [British West Indies] [Airport symbol] (OAG)
SLX............	Self-Lubricating Exterior (IAA)
SLX............	Siltronics Ltd. [Toronto Stock Exchange symbol]
SLX............	Slate Creek, AK [Location identifier FAA] (FAAL)
SLY............	Hayward, WI [Location identifier FAA] (FAAL)
SLY............	Safety, Liquidity, Yield
SLY............	Skelly Resources Ltd. [Vancouver Stock Exchange symbol]
SLY............	Sky Line for Air Services Ltd. [Sudan] [ICAO designator] (FAAC)
SLY............	Sloppy [Horse racing]
SLY............	Southerly
SLYA..........	Yacuiba [Bolivia] [ICAO location identifier] (ICLI)
SLYB..........	El Bato [Bolivia] [ICAO location identifier] (ICLI)
SLYI...........	Yapacani [Bolivia] [ICAO location identifier] (ICLI)
SLYP..........	Muyupampa [Bolivia] [ICAO location identifier] (ICLI)
SLYP..........	Short Leaf Yellow Pine [Lumber]
SLYY..........	San Yo Yo [Bolivia] [ICAO location identifier] (ICLI)
SLZ............	Sao Luiz [Brazil] [Airport symbol] (OAG)
SLZ............	Solidor Resources, Inc. [Vancouver Stock Exchange symbol]
SLZ............	Suppress Leading Zero [Computer science]
SLZA..........	Scandinavian Lead Zinc Association [Stockholm, Sweden] (EAIO)
SLZB..........	San Pedro [Bolivia] [ICAO location identifier] (ICLI)
SLZF..........	San Francisco (Naciff) [Bolivia] [ICAO location identifier] (ICLI)
SLZG..........	San Agustin [Bolivia] [ICAO location identifier] (ICLI)
SLZJ..........	San Pedro (Richard) [Bolivia] [ICAO location identifier] (ICLI)
SLZK..........	San Lucas [Bolivia] [ICAO location identifier] (ICLI)
SLZR..........	San Rafael (Isidoro) [Bolivia] [ICAO location identifier] (ICLI)
SLZX..........	San Pedro (Salvatierra) [Bolivia] [ICAO location identifier] (ICLI)
SM............	Aberdeen Airways [Airline flight code] (ODBW)
SM............	Dr. Schwarz Arzneimittolfabrik GmbH [Germany] [Research code symbol]
SM............	Geographic Information System-Mobile
sm............	Marist Fathers (TOCD)
SM............	Marist Sisters Congregation of Mary (TOCD)
SM............	Master of Science
SM............	Medal of Service of the Order of Canada
SM............	Meteorological Aids Station [ITU designation]
SM............	Misericorde Sisters [Roman Catholic religious order]
SM............	Sacred to the Memory of -- [Epitaphs] (ROG)
SM............	Sales Manager
SM............	Salvage Mechanic [Navy]
Sm............	Samarium [See Sa] [Chemical element]
Sm............	Samuel [Old Testament book]
SM............	Sanctae Memoriae [Of Holy Memory] [Latin]
SM............	San Marco [Satellite] [NASA/Italy]
sm............	San Marino [IYRU nationality code] [MARC country of publication code Library of Congress] (LCCP)
SM............	San Marino [ANSI two-letter standard code] (CNC)
SM............	Scheduled Maintenance (MCD)
SM............	Scheuthauer-Marie [Syndrome] (DAVI)
SM............	Schistosoma Mansoni [A parasitic fluke]
S-M............	Schuetzenmine [Antipersonnel mine] [German military - World War II]
SM............	Schwarz/Mann [Supply company in biochemistry and chemistry]
SM............	Scientific Memorandum
Sm............	Sclerotinia minor [A fungus]
SM............	Screw Motorship (IAA)
SM............	Seamen [British military] (DMA)
SM............	Search Month (NITA)
SM............	Seat Mile
SM............	Secondary Market [Investment term]
SM............	Secondary Memory [Computer science] (BUR)
SM............	Second Mortgage [Banking]
SM............	Secretary's Memorandum [Military]
SM............	Security Manual (AAG)
SM............	Security Monitor (AAG)
SM............	Seed Mass [Botany]
SM............	Segment Mark (IAA)
SM............	Self-Monitoring (DAVI)
Sm............	Semahot (BJA)
SM............	Semiconductor Memory
SM............	Semimat (IAA)
SM............	Semimembranous [Anatomy] (DAVI)
SM............	Semimonthly
SM............	Senate Memorial (WPI)

SM............	Senior Magistrate
SM............	Senior Manager
S/M............	Sensory-to-Motor [Ratio]
SM............	Sentence Modifier [Linguistics]
SM............	Sequence Monitor
SM............	Sergeant Major
SM............	Serious Music [Canadian Broadcasting Corp. record series prefix]
SM............	Serratia Marcescens [Bacterium]
S/M............	Service/Maintenance (NASA)
SM............	Service Manual
SM............	Service Mark [Trademarks]
SM............	Service Member [Military] (AABC)
SM............	Service Module [NASA]
SM............	Service Monitoring [Telecommunications] (TEL)
SM............	Servomotor (IAA)
SM............	Set Mode (BUR)
SM............	Sewage Microparticulates [Oceanography]
SM............	Sewing Machine
SM............	Sexual Myths [Scale]
SM............	Shape Memory [Metallurgy]
SM............	Shared Memory [Computer science] (BUR)
SM............	Share of Market (NITA)
SM............	Sheet Metal
SM............	Shell Model
SM............	Shelter Management [Civil Defense]
SM............	Shigella Mutant [A bacterium] (DAVI)
SM............	Shine Mould [Medium] (DB)
SM............	Shipment Memorandum [Navy]
SM............	Ship Movement Library [Maritime Data Network, Inc.] [Information service or system] (CRD)
SM............	Shipping Monthly Data [Department of Commerce] (GFGA)
SM............	Ship's Manifest (ADA)
SM............	Shock Mount
SM............	Shop Manual [Air Force] (AAG)
SM............	Short Meter [Music]
SM............	Short Module [NASA] (NASA)
sm............	Short Module (NAKS)
sm............	Shuttle Management [Kennedy Space Center] (NAKS)
SM............	Shuttle Management [Kennedy Space Center] [NASA] (NASA)
SM............	SIAI-Marchetti SpA [Italy ICAO aircraft manufacturer identifier] (ICAO)
SM............	Siam
S/M............	Siemens per Meter
SM............	Signaling Module [Telecommunications] (TEL)
SM............	Signalman [Navy rating]
SM............	Silver Medalist
SM............	Silver Methenamine [Biological stain]
SM............	Silver Mica [Capacitor]
SM............	Simple Maintenance
SM............	Simple Mastectomy [Medicine]
SM............	Simpson's Multipliers [Naval architecture]
SM............	Simulated Missile (AAG)
SM............	Simulators [JETDS nomenclature] [Military] (CET)
SM............	Single Manager [Military]
SM............	Single Mode
SM............	Sinistra Mano [Left Hand]
SM............	Sinus Medii [Central Bay] [Lunar area]
SM............	Sisters of Mercy [Roman Catholic religious order]
SM............	Sisters of Mercy (Cork and Ross) (TOCD)
SM............	Sisters of Mercy of Tralee (TOCD)
SM............	Sisters Servants of Mary (TOCD)
SM............	Skim Milk (MAE)
SM............	Slime Mold [Biochemistry] (DAVI)
SM............	Slow Moving
SM............	Small (AAG)
sm............	Small (VRA)
SM............	Small Pica
SM............	Smectic Phase [Physical chemistry]
Sm............	Smectite [Agronomy]
Sm............	Smith Antigen [Immunology]
Sm............	Smith Collection. British Museum [London] (BJA)
SM............	SMM Enterprises Ltd. [Vancouver Stock Exchange symbol]
SM............	Smoker (DAVI)
SM............	Smooth (MSA)
SM............	Smooth Muscle [Medicine] (DMAA)
SM............	Snell Motorcycle
SM............	Socially Maladjusted
SM............	Societa Altair [Italy ICAO designator] (ICDA)
SM............	Societas Mariae [Congregation of Mary] [Marists] [Roman Catholic religious order]
SM............	Society of Mary (Marianists) (TOCD)
SM............	Society of Medalists
SM............	Society of Miniaturists (EA)
sm............	Socity of Mary, Marianists (TOCD)
SM............	Soft Manual (NASA)
sm............	Soft Manual (NAKS)
SM............	Soil Mechanics
SM............	Solar Magnetic [System] [NASA]
SM............	Solar Magnetospheric
SM............	Soldier's Manual
SM............	Soldier's Medal [Military decoration]
SM............	Solicitor's Memorandum [IRS] (AAGC)
SM............	Solicitor's Memorandum, United States Internal Revenue Bureau [A publication] (DLA)
SM............	Solid Measure (ROG)

SM	Somatomedin [*Biochemistry*]
SM	Song of Moses (BJA)
SM	Sons of Malta
S/M	Sort/Message (NITA)
SM	Sound Management [*Radio Advertising Bureau*] [*A publication*]
SM	Southern Minnesota Railroad
SM	Space Medicine (SAA)
SM	Spanish Moss
SM	Spawning Mark
SM	Special Memorandum
SM	Specification Memo (AAG)
SM	Spectrum Management (NTCM)
SM	Speculative Masonry [*Freemasonry*]
SM	SpenderMenders [*An association*] (EA)
SM	Sphingomyelin [*Also, Sph*] [*Biochemistry*]
SM	Square Meter
SM	Stability Margin
SM	Stabilized Member [*NASA*] (KSC)
sm	Stable Member (NAKS)
SM	Stack Mark (IAA)
SM	Staff Manager [*Insurance*]
SM	Staff Memorandum
SM	Stage Manager
SM	Standard Matched
SM	Standard Memoranda (AAG)
SM	Standard Methods
SM	Standard Missile
SM	Standards Manual
SM	Stapedius Muscle [*Anatomy*] (DAVI)
SM	Staphylococcus Medium [*Microbiology*]
SM	State Militia [*e.g., NJSM - New Jersey State Militia*]
SM	Static Margin
SM	Stationary Media (GAAI)
SM	Stationary Medium-Power [*Reactor*] [*Nuclear energy*]
SM	Station Manager [*Broadcasting*] (NTCM)
SM	Station Manager [*Deep Space Instrumentation Facility, NASA*]
SM	Station Master (WDAA)
SM	Statistical Multiplexer (MCD)
SM	Statistiske Meddelelser [*Denmark*]
SM	Status Monitor
SM	Statute Mile
SM	Stipendiary Magistrate
SM	St. Marys Railroad Co. [*AAR code*]
SM	Stock Market
SM	Stock Material (SAA)
SM	Storage Mark [*Computer science*] (OA)
SM	Strategic Missile (NATG)
SM	Streptomycin [*An antibiotic*]
SM	Stress Migration (AAEL)
SM	Stria Medullaris [*Neuroanatomy*]
SM	Strict Middling (IAA)
SM	Strip Mine
SM	Structural Mechanical (MCD)
S/M	Structural/Mechanical (NAKS)
SM	Structure Memory
SM	Structures Memorandum
SM	Strumpell-Marie [*Disease*] [*Also, Rheumatoid Spondylitis*] [*Medicine*] (DAVI)
SM	Student Manual [*Civil Defense*]
SM	Studio SM [*Record label*] [*France*]
SM	Submandibular [*Anatomy*] (DAVI)
S/M	Submarine [*British*]
SM	Submarine Flag [*Navy British*]
SM	Submarine, Minelaying [*Obsolete*]
S/M	Submarine Pay
sm	Submetacentric [*Botany*]
SM	Subminiature (IAA)
SM	Submucosal [*Anatomy*] (DAVI)
SM	Submucous [*Medicine*] (MAE)
SM	Substituted Metabolites [*Biochemistry*] (DAVI)
SM	Substitute for Morphine [*Pharmacology*] (DAVI)
SM	Substitute Materials [*British*]
SM	Suckling Mice
sM	Suckling Mouse (STED)
SM	Sucrose Medium [*Microbiology*] (DAVI)
SM	Suction Method [*Medicine*] (MAE)
SM	Sulphurized Mineral Oil (IAA)
SM	Sumerian Mythology [*S. N. Kramer*] [*A publication*] (BJA)
SM	Summary Memorandum
SM	Superimpose (IAA)
SM	Superior Mesenteric [*Anatomy*] (DAVI)
SM	Super Maneuverable Aircraft
S/M	Super Mare [*On Sea*] [*In place names*] [*Latin*] (ROG)
SM	Supermarket (WDMC)
SM	Supply Manual [*Military*]
SM	Supply Module (SSD)
SM	Support Module [*NASA*] (NASA)
sm	Support Module (NAKS)
SM	Supramamillary [*Neurology*] (DAVI)
SM	Surface Measure
SM	Surface Missile (AAG)
SM	Surface Mount [*Electronics*] (EECA)
SM	Surgeon Major
SM	Suspended Matter [*Chemistry*]
SM	Sustained Medication [*Pharmacology*]

SM	Sutton [*Postcode*] (ODBW)
SM	Symbolic Manipulation [*Computer science*]
SM	Symptom [*Medicine*] (MAE)
SM	Synaptic Membrane [*Medicine*] (DMAA)
SM	Synchronous MODEM
SM	Synovial Membrane [*Anatomy*] (DAVI)
SM	Synthetic Medium [*Microbiology*]
SM	Systema Malykh [*Small System*] [*Russian Computer science*]
SM	Systemic Mastocytosis [*Medicine*]
SM	System Manager [*Military*] (AFM)
SM	System Manual (IAA)
SM	System Mechanics
SM	System Monitor
SM	Systems Management [*NASA*] (MCD)
SM	Systems Memory [*Computer science*] (BUR)
SM	Systolic Mean [*Cardiology*]
SM	Systolic Murmur [*Cardiology*]
SM	Syzygy Mathematics (WDAA)
SM1	Signalman, First Class [*Navy rating*]
SM-1	Singh's Mosquito [*Tissue culture medium*] [*Microbiology*] (DAVI)
SM2	Signalman, Second Class [*Navy rating*]
SM3	Signalman, Third Class [*Navy rating*]
SMA	Andreafsky/St. Marys, AK [*Location identifier FAA*] (FAAL)
SMA	Atlas Aviation Simera (Pty) Ltd. [*South Africa*] [*FAA designator*] (FAAC)
SMA	Safe Manufacturers' Association
SMA	Saigon Mission Association (EA)
SMA	Salad Manufacturers Association (EA)
SMA	Salt Manufacturing Association [*British*]
SMA	Sa Majeste Aulique [*His, or Her, Austrian Majesty*] [*French*] (ROG)
SMA	San Manuel Arizona Railroad Co. [*AAR code*]
SMA	Santa Maria [*Azores*] [*Airport symbol*] (OAG)
SMA	Saw Manufacturers' Association [*British*] (BI)
SMA	Scale Manufacturers Association (EA)
SMA	Scheduled Maintenance Action
SMA	Schedule of Maximal Allowance (STED)
SMA	Schools Music Association [*British*] (BI)
SMA	Science Masters Association (IAA)
SMA	Screen Manufacturers Association (EA)
SMA	Scythe Makers' Association [*A union*] [*British*]
SMA	Search Mode Acquisition [*Telecommunications*] (LAIN)
SMA	Seasoning Manufacturers Association [*British*] (DBA)
SMA	Self-Managed Account (WYGK)
SMA	Semimajor Axis
SMA	Senior Marine Advisor
SMA	Senior Military Attache
SMA	Sequential Multichannel Autoanalyzer (STED)
SMA	Sequential Multiple Analysis [*or Analyzer*] [*Clinical chemistry*]
SMA	Sequential/Serial Multiple Analysis (STED)
SMA	Sergeant Major Academy [*Army*]
SMA	Sergeant Major of the Army (AABC)
SMA	Serum Muramidase Activity (STED)
SMA	Service Merchandisers of America [*Later, NASM*] (EA)
SMA	Shape Memory Alloy (RDA)
SMA	Shelving Manufacturers Association (EA)
SMA	Shielded Metal Arc [*Nickel and alloy welding*]
SMA	Ship's Material Account
SMA	Simulated Machine Analysis (IAA)
SMA	Simultaneous Multichannel Autoanalyzer [*Laboratory science*] (DAVI)
SMA	Simultaneous Multiphasic Analysis [*Medicine*]
SMA	Single Manager Approach
SMA	Single Manager for Ammunition [*DoD*] (MCD)
SMA	Site Maintenance Area (AAG)
SMA	Slave Manipulator Arm [*Astronautics*]
SMA	Small Arms (NATG)
SMA	Smooth Muscle Antibody (AAMN)
SMA	Socialist Medical Association [*British*]
SMA	Social Maturity Age
SMA	Societe des Missionnaires d'Afrique [*Society of Missionaries of Africa*] (EA)
SMA	Society for Medical Anthropology (EA)
SMA	Society for Medieval Archaeology (EA)
SMA	Society of African Missions [*Roman Catholic men's religious order*]
sma	Society of African Missions (TOCD)
SMA	Society of Make-up Artists (NTCM)
SMA	Society of Management Accountants
SMA	Society of Manufacturer's Agents [*Later, SMR*] (EA)
SMA	Society of Marine Artists [*British*]
SMA	Society of Maritime Arbitrators (EA)
SMA	Society of Medical Administrators (EA)
SMA	Society of Mineral Analysts (EA)
SMA	Society of Municipal Arborists (EA)
SMA	Society of Museum Archaeologists [*British*] (DBA)
SMA	Software Maintenance Association (EA)
SMA	Software Manufacturing Association (NTPA)
SMA	Solar Maximum Analysis [*Meteorology*]
SMA	Solder Makers' Association [*British*] (BI)
SMA	Somatomedin A [*Biochemistry*]
SMA	Soviet Military Administration
SMA	Special Management Areas [*Environmental science*] (COE)
SMA	Special Market Area (NTCM)
SMA	Special Miscellaneous Account
SMA	Special Mission Aircraft (DOMA)
SMA	Special Mission Alteration
SMA	Spectral Map Analysis

SMA.............	Spinal Muscular Atrophy [Medicine]
SMA.............	Spiritual Ministry [An association] (EA)
SMA.............	Spiritual Ministry for Adults (EA)
SMA.............	Spontaneous Motor Activity [Neurophysiology]
SMA.............	Squadron Maintenance Area
SMA.............	Stabilized Member Assembly [NASA]
SMA.............	Stadium Managers Association (NTPA)
SMA.............	Stage Management Association [British]
SMA.............	Standard Maintenance Allowance
SMA.............	Standard Methods Agar [Microbiology]
SMA.............	State Meteorlogy Administration [China] [Marine science] (OSRA)
SMA.............	State Mutual Life Assurance Co. of America
SMA.............	Statutory Marketing Authority
SMA.............	Steatite Manufacturers Association [Later, DPCSMA] (EA)
SMA.............	Steel Manufacturers Association (EA)
SMA.............	Stichting Mondiaal Alternatief [Foundation for Ecological Development Alternatives] [Netherlands] (EAIO)
SMA.............	Stoker Manufacturers Association (EA)
SMA.............	Strategic Management Accounting (ADA)
SMA.............	Strategic Mobility Analysis [Military]
SMA.............	Structured Markov Algorithm (MHDI)
SMA.............	Stucco Manufacturers Association (EA)
SMA.............	Stylomastoid Artery [Anatomy]
SMA.............	Styrene-Maleic Anhydride [Organic chemistry]
SMA.............	Styrene-Maleic Anhydride Copolymer (EDCT)
SMA.............	Subject Matter Area (AFM)
SMA.............	Submerged Metal Arc Welding
SMA.............	Submillimeter Array [Telescope]
SMA.............	Subsequent Maintenance Assessment
SMA.............	Suggested for Mature Audiences [Motion pictures]
SMA.............	Sukuma Exploration [Vancouver Stock Exchange symbol]
SMA.............	Summerton [South Carolina] [Seismograph station code, US Geological Survey Closed] (SEIS)
SMA.............	Superior Mesenteric Artery [Anatomy]
SMA.............	Superphosphate Manufacturers' Association [British] (BI)
SMA.............	Superplastic Metal Alloy
SMA.............	Supplemental Maintenance Appraisal
SMA.............	Supplementary Motor Area [Anatomy]
SMA.............	Support Management Area [Mission Control Center] [NASA]
SMA.............	Surface Modulating Assembly [Cytology]
SMA.............	Surface Mount Assembly (AAEL)
SMA.............	Surface Mounting Applicator (NITA)
SMA.............	Surplus Marketing Administration [New Deal]
SMA.............	Switch, Modular, Attenuator (IAA)
SMA-6..........	Sydney Metropolitan Area [Australia]
SMA-6..........	Sequential Multiple Analysis-Six Different Serum Tests (STED)
SMA 6/60.....	Sequential Multiple Analysis-Six Tests in Sixty Minutes (STED)
SMA-12........	Sequential Multiple Analysis-Twelve-Channel Biochemical Profile (STED)
SMA 12/60...	Sequential Multiple Analysis-Twelve Different Serum Tests in Sixty Minutes (STED)
SMA-20........	Sequential Multiple Analysis of Twenty Chemical Constituents (STED)
SMA-60........	Sequential Multiple Analysis of Sixty Chemical Constituents (STED)
SMAA..........	Secretaries and Managers' Association of Australia
SMAA..........	Submarine Movement Advisory Authority (NVT)
Sma & Giff...	Smale and Giffard's English Vice-Chancellors' Reports [A publication] (DLA)
SMAB..........	Solid Motor Assembly Building [for Missiles]
SMAB..........	Spartan Management Action Board [Missiles] (MCD)
SMABF........	Superior Mesenteric Artery Blood Flow [Medicine] (DMAA)
SMAC..........	Scene Matching Area Correlator [Navy] (MCD)
SMAC..........	Science and Mathematics Analysis Center [ERIC]
SMAC..........	Scientific Machine Automation Corp.
SMAC..........	Senate Military Affairs Committee [British] (DAS)
SMAC..........	Sequential Multiple Analysis Plus Computer (PDAA)
SMAC..........	Sequential Multiple Analyzer Computerized [Laboratory science] (DAVI)
SMAC..........	Serial Memory Address Counter [Computer]
SMAC..........	Shielded Metal Arc Cutting [Welding]
SMAC..........	Simulation, Manual and Computerized
SMAC..........	Simulation Model of Automobile Collisions (IAA)
SMAC..........	Single Manager for Ammunition, Conventional [DoD]
SMAC..........	Society of Management Accountants of Canada
SMAC..........	Space Maintenance Analysis Center (IAA)
SMAC..........	Spartan Material Availability Control [Army]
SMAC..........	Special Mission Attack Computer
SMAC..........	State Minerals Advisory Council [Australia]
SMAC..........	Store Multiple Access Control (MHDI)
SMAC..........	Striated Microtubule-Associated Components [Botanical cytology]
SMAC..........	Submicron Aerosol Collector
SMAC..........	System Management and Control
SMACC........	Scheduling, Manpower Allocation, and Cost Control (MHDB)
SMAC/CRC..	Surface Modification and Characterization Collaborative Research Center [Oak Ridge, TN] [Oak Ridge National Laboratory] [Department of Energy] (GRD)
SMACH........	Sounding Machine [Engineering]
SMACK........	Society of Males Who Appreciate Cute Knees [Group opposing below-the-knee fashions introduced in 1970]
SMACNA......	Sheet Metal and Air Conditioning Contractors' National Association (EA)
SMACRATRACEN...	Small Craft Training Center
SMACS........	Serialized Missile Accounting and Control System
SMACS........	Simulated Message Analysis and Conversion Subsystem
SMACS........	Small Missions to Asteroids/Comets [NASA, proposed]
Sm Act.........	Smith's Action at Law [12th ed.] [1876] [A publication] (DLA)

SMACTRACEN...	Small Craft Training Center [Navy] (DNAB)
SMAD.........	Scaled Median Absolute Deviation [Mathematics]
SMAD.........	Solvated Metal Atom Dispersion [Chemistry]
SMAD.........	Sowjetische Militaeradministration
Sm Adm Pr...	Smith's Admiralty Practice [4th ed.] [1892] [A publication] (DLA)
SMADS.......	Sault Sainte Marie Air Defense Sector (SAA)
SMAE.........	Sbornik Muzeia Antropologii i Etnografii [A publication] (BJA)
SMAE.........	Society of Model Aeronautical Engineers [British]
SMAE.........	Superior Mesenteric Artery Embolus [Medicine]
SMAE.........	System Management Application Entity
SMAF.........	Afobaka [Surinam] [ICAO location identifier] (ICLI)
SMAF.........	Shipboard Maintenance Action Form (DNAB)
SMAF.........	Smooth Muscle Activating Factor
SMAF.........	Special Mission Aircraft Flights (NATG)
SMAF.........	Specific Macrophage Arming Factor [Hematology]
SMAF.........	Superior Mesenteric Artery Flow
SMAG.........	Simulator Missile Airborne and Ground (MCD)
SMAG.........	Special Medical Advisory Group (DMAA)
SMAG.........	Star Magnitude (NASA)
SMAG.........	Systems Management Analysis Group (MCD)
SMAGOL.....	Small Computer Algorithmic Language (DNAB)
SMAI..........	Solvated Metal Atom Impregnation [Chemistry]
SMAI..........	Station Manager Applicant Inventory [Test] [London House, Inc.] (TES)
SMAIL........	Source Mail [Electronic mail]
SMAJ.........	Sergeant Major
SMAL.........	Serum Methyl Alcohol Level [Medicine] (DMAA)
SMAL.........	Single Mode Alignment (CAAL)
SMAL.........	Society for Musteline Arts and Literature (EA)
SMAL.........	Storage Multiple Access Control (NITA)
SMAL.........	Structural Macroassembly Language
SMAL.........	System Material Analysis List
SMALC.......	Sacramento Air Logistics Center (MCD)
Smale & G...	Smale and Giffard's English Vice-Chancellors' Reports [A publication] (DLA)
SMALGOL....	Small Computer Algorithmic Language
SMALL........	Selenium Diode Matrix Alloy Logic (IAA)
Smallww......	Smallworldwide PLC [Associated Press] (SAG)
SMAM........	Amotopo [Surinam] [ICAO location identifier] (ICLI)
SMAM........	Single Mission Air Medal (DNAB)
SMAMA.......	Sacramento Air Materiel Area (KSC)
SMAME.......	Society of Marine Architects and Marine Engineers (EA)
Sm Amt.......	Small Amount (CPH)
sm an.........	Small Animal (DAVI)
SMAN........	Standard Management [NASDAQ symbol] (TTSB)
SMAN........	Standard Management Corp. [NASDAQ symbol] (SAG)
SMAN........	Standard Medium-Accuracy Navigator
SMANCS.....	Styrene Maleic Acid Neocarzinostatin [Antineoplastic drug]
Sm & Bat....	Smith and Batty's Irish King's Bench Reports [A publication] (DLA)
Sm & BRR Cas...	Smith and Bates' American Railway Cases [A publication] (DLA)
SM & DSL....	Sector Management and Direct Support Logistics Center [Navy] (DNAB)
Sm & G.......	Smale and Giffard's English Vice-Chancery Reports [A publication] (DLA)
Sm & G.......	Smith and Guthrie's Missouri Appeal Reports [81-101 Missouri] [A publication] (DLA)
Sm & M......	Smedes and Marshall's Mississippi Reports [9-22 Mississippi] [A publication] (DLA)
Sm & M Ch...	Smedes and Marshall's Mississippi Reports [9-22 Mississippi] [A publication] (DLA)
Sm & S.......	Smith and Sager's Drainage Cases [Canada] [A publication] (DLA)
SM & S.......	Systems Management and Sequencing (NASA)
SM&S.........	Systems Management and Sequencing (NAKS)
Sm & Sod L & T...	Smith and Soden on Landlord and Tenant [2nd ed.] [1878] [A publication] (DLA)
SMANP.......	Standard Mgmt 11% Cv 'S' Pfd [NASDAQ symbol] (TTSB)
SMAO.........	Society of Management Accountants of Ontario [Canada] (DD)
SMAO.........	Superior Mesenteric Artery Occlusion [Medicine] (DMAA)
Smap..........	Surprised Middle-Aged Person [Lifestyle classification]
SMAP.........	System Management Application Process [or Protocol] [Telecommunications]
SMAP.........	Systems Management Analysis Project (MCD)
SMAQ.........	Stipendiary Magistrates Association, Queensland [Australia]
SMAR.........	Sheet Metal Assembler Riveter (MCD)
SMAR.........	Summary of Monthly Aerological Reports [Navy] (DNAB)
SMARC.......	Survivable-MOS [Metal-Oxide Semiconductor] Array Computer [Air Force]
SM Arch S...	Master of Science in Architectural Studies (PGP)
SMART.......	Salton's Magical Automatic Retriever of Texts [Computer science]
SMART.......	Satellite Maintenance and Repair Techniques [Air Force]
SMART.......	Satellite Monitoring and Remote Tracking
SMART.......	Scheduled Maintenance and Reliability Team (MCD)
SMART.......	Scheduling Management and Allocating Resources Technique (CIST)
SMART.......	Science, Mathematics, and Related Technologies
SMART.......	Secondary Materials and Recycled Textiles Association (NTPA)
SMART.......	Selected Methods for Attracting the Right Targets [Bombing system] (AFM)
SMART.......	Self-Monitoring, Analysis and Reporting Technology [Computer science]
SMART.......	Sensitive-Membrane-Antigen-Rapid-Test
SMART.......	Sequential Mechanism for Automatic Recording and Testing
SMART.......	Shuttle Meeting Action - Item Review Tracking [NASA] (NASA)
SMART.......	Simplified Method to Achieve Regulated Training
SMART.......	Simulation and Modeling for Acquisition, Requirements, and Training [Army]

SMART	Simultaneous Multiple Angle Reconstruction Technique [*Medicine*] (DMAA)
SMART	Small Firms Merit Award for Research and Technology [*British*]
SMART	Socony Mobil Automatic Real Time (DIT)
SMART	Software Metering and Resource Tracking [*Computer science*]
SMART	Sort Merge and Reduction Tapes (CAAL)
SMART	Source Management of Resources and Time (DNAB)
SMART	Space Maintenance and Repair Techniques
SMART	Space Management and Retail Tracking System [*Information Resources, Inc.*]
SMART	Spacesaver Material Accounting Resource Terminal [*Spacesaver Corp.*]
SMART	Specific, Measurable, Agreed-To, Reachable, Time-Specific [*Management technique*]
SMART	State and Metropolitan Analyses of Regional Transportation [*BTS*] (TAG)
SMART	Stop Merchandising Alcohol on Radio and Television
SMART	Structural Maintenance and Repair Team (MCD)
SMART	Supermarket Allocation and Recorder Technique (IAA)
SMART	Supersonic Military Air Research Track
SMART	Supersonic Missile and Rocket Track
SMART	Supply and Maintenance Assessment and Review Team [*Army*]
SMART	System for Management and Allocation of Resources Technique [*Computer science*]
SMART	System for Manipulation and Retrieval of Text
SMART	System for the Mechanical Analysis and Retrieval of Text
SMART	System Malfunction Analysis Reinforcement Trainer
SMART	System Management and Review Technique (HGAA)
SMART	System Monitoring and Reporting Tool (HGAA)
SMART	Systems Management Analysis, Research, and Testing (MCD)
SMART	Systems Managers Administrative Rating Test [*Simulation game*]
SMART	University of Saskatchewan Libraries Machine-Assisted Reference Teleservices [*University of Saskatchewan Library*] [*Information service or system*] (IID)
SMARTee	Smart End-Effector [*Robotics*] (ECON)
Smartel	Smartel Communications Corp. [*Associated Press*] (SAG)
SMARTIE	Simple-Minded Artificial Intelligence (PDAA)
SMARTIE	Submarine Automatic Remote Television Inspection Equipment (PDAA)
SMARTII	Simple-Minded Artificial Intelligence (IAA)
SmarTlk	SmarTalk TeleServices, Inc. [*Associated Press*] (SAG)
SMARTS	Selective Multiple Addresses Radio and Television Service [*A program delivery service introduced by RCA*]
SMARTS	Sport Management Art and Science Society [*Defunct*] (EA)
SMARTS	Status Memory and Real Time System [*AT & T*]
SMARTS	Submarine Advanced Reactive Tactical Training System
SMART-T	Secure Mobile, Anti-Jam, Reliable Tactical Trainer [*Army*]
SMAS	Society for the Maintenance of the Apostolic See (DICI)
SMAS	Subcontract Material Availability Schedule
SMAS	Submuscular Aponeurotic System [*Medicine*]
SMAS	Superficial Musculoaponeurotic System [*Plastic surgery*]
SMAS	Switched Maintenance Access System [*Bell System*]
SMASE	Systems Management Application Service Element [*Telecommunications*] (OSI)
SMASF	Servicemen's Mutual Aid and Savings Fund [*South Vietnam*]
SMASH	Small Manned Anti-Submarine Helicopter (SAA)
SMASH	Southeast Asia Multisensor Armed Surveillance Helicopter
SMASH	Steeple Morden After School & Holiday Club (WDAA)
SMASH	Step-by-Step Monitor and Selector Hold [*Telecommunications*] (TEL)
SMASH	Students Mobilizing on Auto Safety Hazards [*Student legal action organization*] (EA)
SMASHEX	Search for Simulated Submarine Casualty Exercise [*Navy*] (NVT)
SMASHT	Simple-Minded Approach to Squeezed Hollerith Text (SAA)
SMASS	Small Main-Belt Asteroid Spectroscopic Survey
SMAST	Short Michigan Alcoholism Screening Test (EDAC)
SMAT	School Motivation Analysis Test [*Personality development test*] [*Psychology*]
SMAT	Superior Mesenteric Artery Thrombosis [*Medicine*]
SMATH	Satellite Materials Hardening (MCD)
SMATS	Speed-Modulated Augmented Thrust System (NG)
SMATV	Satellite Master Antenna Television
SMATV	Satellite Master Antenna Television Service [*Telecommunications*] (OTD)
SMATV	Satellite Master Antenna Television Systems (NITA)
SMAW	Second Marine Aircraft Wing
SMAW	Shielded Metal Arc Welding
SMAW	Shoulder-Launched Multipurpose Assault Weapon (MCD)
SMAW	Shoulder-Mounted Assault Weapon (DWSG)
SMAW	Submerged Metal Arc Weld [*Nuclear energy*] (NRCH)
SMAWT	Short-Range Man-Portable Antitank Weapons Technology
SMB	Bachelor of Sacred Music
SMB	Cerro Sombrero [*Chile*] [*Airport symbol*] (AD)
SMB	Samaipata [*Bolivia*] [*Seismograph station code, US Geological Survey Closed*] (SEIS)
SMB	Sa Majeste Britannique [*His or Her Britannic Majesty*] [*French*]
SMB	Selected Mucosal Biopsy [*Medicine*] (DMAA)
SMB	Server Message Blocks (PCM)
SMB	Simba Resources, Inc. [*Vancouver Stock Exchange symbol*]
SMB	Simulated Moving Bed [*Chemical engineering*]
SMB	Single-Mask Bumping (AAEL)
SMB	Small and Medium-Sized Businesses
SMB	Space Meteorology Branch [*NASA*]
SMB	Standard Merchants Bank [*British*]
SMB	Standard Mineral Base [*Medium*] [*Medicine*]
SMB	Static Memory Board [*Computer science*] (BYTE)

SMB	Steve Miller Band [*Pop music group*]
SMB	Stock Medicines Board [*Australia*]
sMb	Suckling Mouse Brain [*Microbiology*] (DMAA)
SMB	System Message Block [*Telecommunications*] (PCM)
SMB	System Monitor Board
SMB	Systems Management Branch [*Space Environmental Laboratory*] (USDC)
SMBA	Scottish Marine Biological Association [*British*] (IRUK)
SMBA	Slovenian Mutual Benefit Association [*Later, AMLA*] (EA)
SMBC	Santuario Madre del Buon Consiglio [*Pious Union of Our Mother of Good Counsel - PUMGC*] [*Genazzano, Italy*] (EAIO)
SMBC	SouMOBc [*NASDAQ symbol*] (SAG)
SMBC	Southern Missouri Bancorp [*NASDAQ symbol*] (TTSB)
SMBDB	Structural Margin Beyond Design Basis [*Nuclear energy*] (NRCH)
SMBF	Superior Mesenteric Blood Flow [*Physiology*]
SMBFT	Small Bowel Follow-Through [*Medicine*]
SMBG	Bakhuys [*Surinam*] [*ICAO location identifier*] (ICLI)
SMBG	Self-Monitoring of Blood Glucose [*Medicine*]
SMBJ	Style Manual for Biological Journals
SMBL	Semimobile
SMBL	Stratocumulus-Topped Boundary Layer [*Marine science*] (OSRA)
SMBN	Albina [*Surinam*] [*ICAO location identifier*] (ICLI)
SMBO	Botopasie [*Surinam*] [*ICAO location identifier*] (ICLI)
SMBS	Safeguard Material Balance Simulator
SMBSA	Stock Medicines Board of South Australia
SMBT	Master of Science in Building Technology (PGP)
Sm Bus Rep	Small Business Reports [*A publication*] (BRI)
SMBW	Bronsweg [*Surinam*] [*ICAO location identifier*] (ICLI)
SMC	Chief Signalman [*Navy rating*]
SMC	Medical University of South Carolina Library, Charleston, SC [*OCLC symbol*] (OCLC)
SMC	Sabang Merauke Raya Air Charter PT [*Indonesia*] [*ICAO designator*] (FAAC)
SMC	SAGE [*Semiautomatic Ground Environment*] Maintenance Control
SMC	Saint Martin's College [*Washington*]
SMC	Saint Mary's College [*Indiana; Kansas; Michigan; Minnesota*]
SMC	Saint Michael's College [*Vermont*]
SMC	Sa Majeste Catholique [*His or Her Catholic Majesty*] [*of Spain*] [*French*]
SMC	Save the Manatee Club (EA)
SMC	Science Management Corp. (EFIS)
smc	Scientific Manpower Commission (NAKS)
SMC	Scientific Manpower Commission (EA)
SMC	Scottish Mountaineering Club (BARN)
SMC	Sealant Manufacturers Conference [*Federation of British Rubber and Allied Manufacturers*] (BI)
SMC	Secondary Mesenchyme Cell [*Cytology*]
SMC	Segmented Maintenance Cask [*Nuclear energy*] (NRCH)
SMC	Selection and Monitoring Chassis (COE)
SMC	Selective Market Coverage [*Advertising*] (WDMC)
SMC	Senior Management Committee (AIE)
SMC	Senior Medical Consultant
SMC	Senior Mission Controller (MCD)
SMC	Sensory Mother Cell [*Genetics*]
SMC	Sensory Organ Mother Cell [*Genetics*]
SMC	Sequential Machine Controller [*Programming language*] [*1977-78*] (CSR)
SMC	Service Men's Center [*World War II*]
SMC	Sheet Molding Compound [*Plastics technology*]
SMC	Short-Run Marginal Cost Curve [*Economics*]
SMC	Shunt Mounted Chip (IAA)
SMC	Silicon Monolithic Circuit
SMC	Silva Mind Control [*Psychic system*]
SMC	Single Mothers by Choice (EA)
smc	Small Capitals [*Typography*] (BARN)
SMC	Small Magellanic Cloud [*Astronomy*]
SMC	Smith [*A. O.*] Corp. [*AMEX symbol*] (SPSG)
SMC	Smooth Muscle Cell [*Cytology*]
SMC	Societe Mediterraneenne de Chimiotherapie [*Mediterranean Society of Chemotherapy - MSC*] [*Italy*] (EAIO)
SMC	Society of Marine Consultants (EA)
SMC	Soil and Moisture Conservation
SMC	Solar Monitor Constant (SSD)
SMC	Somatomedin C [*Biochemistry*]
SMC	Somerset [*Colorado*] [*Seismograph station code, US Geological Survey*] (SEIS)
SmC	Southern Microfilm Corporation, Houston, TX [*Library symbol Library of Congress*] (LCLS)
SMC	Southern Missionary College [*Tennessee*]
SMC	Southern Motor Carriers Rate Conference, Atlanta GA [*STAC*]
SMC	Space and Missile Systems Center [*Air Force*] (AAGC)
SMC	Spanish Music Center [*Commercial firm*] (EA)
SMC	Special Monthly Compensation (MAE)
SMC	Special Mouth Care [*Medicine*]
S-M-C	Sperm [*or Spore*] Mother-Cell
SMC	Spin Muon Collaboration [*Nuclear research*]
SMC	Squared Multiple Correlation [*Psychology*]
SMC	Squawk Mode Code [*Aviation*] (FAAC)
SMC	Staff Message Control [*Military*]
SMC	Standard Mean Chord [*Aviation*] (AIA)
SMC	Standard-Modern Technologies Corp. [*Toronto Stock Exchange symbol*]
SMC	Standard Molding Corp.
SMC	Standard Motorists Centre [*Automotive sales and service chain*] [*British*]

SMC........... Station-Control and Monitor Console Subsystem [*Deep Space Instrumentation Facility, NASA*]
SMC........... Steady Magnetospheric Convection
SMC........... Stepper Motor Control
SMC........... Storage Module Controller
SMC........... Structural Maintenance of Chromosome [*Cytology*]
SMC........... Student Mobilization Committee [*to End the War in Vietnam*] [*Defunct*] (EA)
SMC........... Sub-Machine Carbine [*British military*] (DMA)
SMC........... Substances Misuse Coordinator (WDAA)
SMC........... Succinylmonocholine [*Biochemistry*] (MAE)
SMC........... Sunnybrook Medical Centre, Toronto [*UTLAS symbol*]
SMC........... Super-Multi-Coating [*Camera lenses*]
SMC........... Supply and Maintenance Command [*Army*]
SMC........... Surface Mount Component [*Environmental science*]
SMC........... Surface-Mounted Component (AAEL)
SMC........... Surface Movement Control [*Aviation*]
SMC........... Switch Maintenance Center [*Telecommunications*] (TEL)
SMC........... Synchronized Maneuver Countermeasures Model (MCD)
SMC........... System Monitor Console (CAAL)
SMC........... System Monitor Controller (NITA)
SMC........... Systems, Man, and Cybernetics (MCD)
SMCA......... Cayana [*Surinam*] [*ICAO location identifier*] (ICLI)
SMCA......... Single Manager for Conventional Ammunition [*DoD*]
SMC.A........ Smith (A.O.) CI'A' [*AMEX symbol*] (TTSB)
SMCA......... Smooth Muscle Contracting Agent (DB)
SMCA......... Sodium Monochloroacetate [*Organic chemistry*]
SMCA......... Suckling Mouse Cataract Agent [*Microbiology*]
SMCAA....... Sheet Molding Compound Automotive Alliance [*An association*]
SMCAF....... Society of Medical Consultants to the Armed Forces (EA)
sm cap....... Small Capitals [*Typography*] (WGA)
SMCC........ Saint Mary's College of California
SMCC........ Santa Monica City College [*California*]
SMCC........ Show-Me Collegiate Conference (PSS)
smcc......... Shuttle Mission Control Center [*NASA*] (NAKS)
SMCC........ Shuttle Mission Control Center [*NASA*] (NASA)
SMCC........ Simulation Monitor and Control Console (KSC)
SMCC........ SMC Corp. [*NASDAQ symbol*] (SAG)
SMCC........ Society of Memorial Cancer Center
SMCC........ Sport Medicine Council of Canada
SMCC........ Standard Machinery Control Console [*Canadian Navy*]
SMCC........ State Manpower Coordinating Committee [*Department of Labor*]
SMCC........ Succinimidyl (Maleimidomethyl)cyclohexanecarboxylate [*Organic chemistry*]
SMCC........ System Monitoring and Coordinating Center [*National Weather Service*] (USDC)
SMC-CF...... Smooth Muscle Cell-Chemotactic Factor [*Oncology*]
Sm CCM..... Smith's Circuit Courts-Martial Reports [*Maine*] [*A publication*] (DLA)
SMC Cp...... SMC Corp. [*Associated Press*] (SAG)
SMC(Disp)... Spectacle Makers Co. (Dispenser) [*British*] (DI)
SMCE......... Master of Science in Civil Engineering
SMCE......... Sociedad Mexicana de Computacion Electronica [*Mexico*]
SMCH........ Standard Mixed Cargo Harness (NASA)
SMchG........ Southeastern Michigan Gas Enterprises, Inc. [*Associated Press*] (SAG)
SMCHMA.... Supreme Master Ching Hai Meditation Association (EA)
Sm Ch Pr.... Smith's Chancery Practice [*7th ed.*] [*1862*] [*A publication*] (DLA)
SMCI......... Coeroeni [*Surinam*] [*ICAO location identifier*] (ICLI)
SM-C/IGF.... Somatomedin C/Insulin-Like Growth Factor (STED)
Smckr....... Smucker [*J.M.*] Co. [*Associated Press*] (SAG)
SMCL......... Secondary Maximum Contaminant Level [*Environmental science*] (BCP)
SMCL......... Southeastern Massachusetts Cooperating Libraries [*Library network*]
SMCLN....... Semicolon (AABC)
SMCM........ Master Chief Signalman [*Navy rating*]
SMCM........ Surface Mine Countermeasures [*Navy*] (DOMA)
SMCN........ Selective Myocardial Cell Necrosis [*Cardiology*]
SMCO........ Coronie [*Surinam*] [*ICAO location identifier*] (ICLI)
SMCO........ SAGE [*Semiautomatic Ground Environment*] Maintenance Control Office
SMCO........ Simpson Manufacturing [*NASDAQ symbol*] (TTSB)
SMCO........ Simpson Manufacturing Company, Inc. [*NASDAQ symbol*] (SAG)
Sm Com L... Smith's Manual of Common Law [*12th ed.*] [*1905*] [*A publication*] (DLA)
Sm Con...... Smith on Contracts [*8th ed.*] [*1885*] [*A publication*] (DLA)
Sm Cond Ala... Smith's Condensed Alabama Reports [*A publication*] (DLA)
Sm Const Cons... Smith on Constitutional and Statutory Construction [*A publication*] (DLA)
Sm Conv..... Smith on Conveyancing [*A publication*] (DLA)
SMCP......... San Marino Communist Party
SMCP......... Supply and Maintenance Career Program
SMCP......... Supply and Maintenance Control Point
SMCPA....... System of Multi-Cultural Pluralistic Assessment [*Psychiatry*] (DAVI)
SMCPCF..... Fort Walsh National Historic Park, Parks Canada [*Parc Historique National Fort Walsh, Parcs Canada*] Maple Creek, Saskatchewan [*Library symbol National Library of Canada*] (NLC)
SMCPSTC... Supply and Maintenance Command Packaging Storage and Transportability Center [*Army*]
SMCR........ Selected Marine Corps Reserve
SMCR........ Smith-Magenis Chromosome Region [*Medicine*] (DMAA)
SMCR........ Society for Menstrual Cycle Research (EA)
SMCRA....... Surface Mining Control and Reclamation Act [*1977*]
SMCRC...... Southern Motor Carriers Rate Conference
SMCS........ IEEE Systems, Man, and Cybernetics Society (EA)
SMCS........ Senior Chief Signalman [*Navy rating*]

SMCS......... Separation Monitor and Control System [*NASA*] (MCD)
smcs......... Separation Monitor and Control System (NAKS)
SMCS......... Simulation Monitor and Control System (CAAL)
SMCS......... Star Multi Care Services, Inc. [*NASDAQ symbol*] (SAG)
SMCS......... Star Multi Care Svcs [*NASDAQ symbol*] (TTSB)
SMCS......... Structural Mode Control System (MCD)
SMCSG....... Special Military Construction Study Group (AABC)
SMCT......... Cottica [*Surinam*] [*ICAO location identifier*] (ICLI)
SMCT......... Soldier's Manual of Common Tasks [*A publication*] (ADDR)
SMCTG...... Standard Missile Correlation Task Group [*Military*]
SMCTG...... Surface Missile Compatibility Test Group [*Military*]
SMCU........ Separation Monitoring Control Unit [*NASA*] (MCD)
smcu........ Separation Monitoring Control Unit (NAKS)
SMD......... Doctor of Sacred Music
SMD......... Fort Wayne, IN [*Location identifier FAA*] (FAAL)
SMD......... Saint Michael's College, Library, Winooski, VT [*OCLC symbol*] (OCLC)
SMD......... Sauter Mean Diameter (KSC)
SMD......... Sauter Mean Droplet [*Diesel engine fuel injection*]
SMD......... Scheduling Management Display
SMD......... Scottish Malt Distillers [*British*]
SMD......... Semiconductor Magnetic Field Detector (IAA)
SMD......... Senile Macular Degeneration [*Medicine*]
SMD......... Serum Malic Dehydrogenase [*An enzyme*]
SMD......... Service and Methods Demonstration [*Program*] [*TRB*] (TAG)
SMD......... Ship Manning Document [*Navy*]
SMD......... Short Meter Double [*Music*]
SMD......... Silicon Multiplier Detector
SMD......... Single Molecule Detection [*Analytical chemistry*]
SMD......... Singular Multinomial Distribution [*Statistics*]
SMD......... Society of Medical-Dental Management Consultants (EA)
SMD......... Soil Moisture Deficit (PDAA)
SMD......... Spacelab Mission Development [*NASA*] (MCD)
SMD......... Special Measuring Device (NASA)
SMD......... Specific Material Designation
SMD......... Speed Measuring Device (PDAA)
SMD......... Spondylometaphyseal Dysplasias [*Medicine*]
SMD......... Standardized Military Drawing Program (AAGC)
SMD......... Standardized Military Drawings [*Army*]
SMD......... Statistical Methods Division [*Bureau of the Census*] (OICC)
SMD......... Sternocleidomastoid Diameter (STED)
SMD......... Stop Motion Detector
SMD......... Storage Module Device [*Computer science*]
SMD......... Storage Module Drive
SMD......... Structures and Mechanics Division [*NASA*]
SMD......... Submanubrial Dullness [*Medicine*]
SMD......... Submarine Mine Depot
SMD......... Submersible Mining Device
SMD......... Sunrise Medical [*NYSE symbol*] (TTSB)
SMD......... Sunrise Medical, Inc. [*NYSE symbol*] (SPSG)
SMD......... Superintendent of Mine Design (WDAA)
SMD......... Super Market Distributors, Inc. (FFIS)
SMD......... Surface Mountable Device (NITA)
SMD......... Surface Mount Device (AAEL)
SMD......... Surface Mounted Device [*Microelectronics*]
SMD......... Surplus Materials Division (AAGC)
SMD......... Susceptor Meus Dominus [*God Is My Protector*] [*Motto of Jacob, Margrave of Baden-Hochberg (1562-90); Georg Friedrich, Margrave of Baden-Hochberg (1573-1638)*] [*Latin*]
SMD......... Symptom Medication Diary [*Medicine*]
SMD......... Synchronous Modulator-Demodulator (MCD)
SMD......... System Management Directive (AFM)
SMD......... Systems Display [*Vancouver Stock Exchange symbol*]
SMD......... Systems Manufacturing Division [*IBM Corp.*]
SMD......... Systems Measuring Device (KSC)
SMD......... Systems Monitor Display
SMDA......... Drietabbetje [*Surinam*] [*ICAO location identifier*] (ICLI)
SMDA......... Safe Medical Devices Act of 1990
SMDA......... Second Marine Division Association (EA)
SMDA......... Sewing Machine Dealers Association Ltd. [*British*] (BI)
SMDA......... Sixth Marine Division Association [*Later, 6th MAR DIV*] (EA)
SMDA......... Starch Methylenedianiline (STED)
SMDA......... State Medicaid Directors Association (EA)
SMDC......... Saint Mary's Dominican College [*Louisiana*]
SMDC......... Shielded Mild Detonating Cord
SMDC......... Sisters of Mercy, Daughters of Christian Charity of St. Vincent de Paul [*Roman Catholic religious order*]
SMDC......... Sisters of Mercy of Christian Charity of St. Vincent de Paul of Hungary (TOCD)
SMDC......... Sodium Methyldithiocarbamate [*Fungicide*]
SMDC......... Superconductive Materials Data Center (KSC)
SMDE......... Static Mercury Drop Electrode [*Electrochemistry*]
SMD-E....... Storage Module Drive - Enhanced [*Computer science*] (BTTJ)
SM Dendrol... Master of Science in Dendrology
SMDF......... SCATS [*Simulation, Checkout, and Training System*] Main Distributing Frame
SMDG......... Standoff Mine Detection Ground [*Army*] (DOMA)
SMDI......... Surface Miss Distance Indicator [*Navy*] (CAAL)
SMDJ......... Djoemoe [*Surinam*] [*ICAO location identifier*] (ICLI)
SMDK......... Donderskamp [*Surinam*] [*ICAO location identifier*] (ICLI)
SMDL......... Spares Master Data Log (IAA)
SMDL......... Standard Music Description Language [*Computer science*]
SMDL......... Subminiature Microwave Delay Line
SMDM......... Society for Medical Decision Making (NTPA)
SMDMC...... Society of Medical-Dental Management Consultants (EA)

SMDO	Ladoeanie [*Surinam*] [*ICAO location identifier*] (ICLI)
SMDO	Special Microwave Devices Operation [*Raytheon Co.*]
SMD, OCOFS	Staff Management Division, Office, Chief of Staff [*Army*]
SMD OC of SA	Staff Management Division, Office, Chief of Staff, Army (AABC)
SMD OCSA	Staff Management Division, Office, Chief of Staff, Army (AABC)
SMDP	Scottish Microelectronics Development Programme (NITA)
SMDP	Stock Management Description Pattern
SMDPL	Supply Management Date and Price List [*Navy*]
SMDPS	Service Module Deluge Purge System [*NASA*] (KSC)
SMDPS	Strategic Mission Data Preparation System [*Air Force*] (DOMA)
SMDR	Selected Management Data Report [*DoD*]
SMDR	Station Message Detail Recorder (NITA)
SMDR	Station Message Detail Recording [*Formerly, MDR*] [*Telecommunications*]
SMDR	Station Message-Detail Reporting [*Computer science*] (ITD)
SMDR	Structure Manning Decision Review
SMDR	Summary Management Data Report [*DoD*]
SMDS	Switched Multimegabit Data Service [*Telecommunications*] (PCM)
SMDS	Switched Multimegabit Digital Service [*Telecommunications*] (ITD)
SMDT	Shore Mode Data Transmitter (MCD)
SME	Sales and Marketing Executives-International (EA)
SME	Sancta Mater Ecclesia [*Holy Mother Church*] [*Latin*]
SME	Scale Model Engineering [*Initialism is brand name of tone arm*]
SME	School of Military Engineering
SME	Science, Mathematics, and Engineering (RDA)
SME	Semiconductor Manufacturing Equipment [*Sumitomo Metals*]
SME	Service Merchandise [*NYSE symbol*] (TTSB)
SME	Service Merchandise Co., Inc. [*NYSE symbol*] (SPSG)
SME	Shape Memory Effect [*Metal alloy property*]
SME	Sheet Metal Enclosure
SME	Shell Metal Extractant
SME	Shipbuilding and Marine Engineering [*Department of Employment*] [*British*]
SME	SHOWME [*VERALEX, Inc.*] [*Information service or system*] (CRD)
SME	Singleton Materials Engineering Laboratories [*Tennessee Valley Authority*] (GRD)
SME	Small and Medium-Size Enterprises
SME	Small-to-Medium Enterprise
SME	SM Exports Ltd. [*British ICAO designator*] (FAAC)
SME	Society for Mining, Metallurgy, and Exploration, Inc. [*In association name, SME , Inc.*] (EA)
SME	Society of Manufacturing Engineers (EA)
SME	Society of Military Engineers (KSC)
SME	Soil and Materials Engineers, Inc. (EFIS)
SME	Soil Mechanics Experiment [*NASA*]
SME	Solar Mesosphere Explorer (MCD)
SME	Somerset, KY [*Location identifier FAA*] (FAAL)
SME	Sony Music Entertainment (ECON)
SME	Spartan Missile Equipment [*Missiles*] (MCD)
SME	Squadron Medical Element
SME	Stalk Median Eminence [*Anatomy*]
SME	Standard Medical Examination [*Military*]
SME	Static Mission Equivalent (IAA)
SME	Stellar Mass Ejection
SME	Subject Matter Expert (NVT)
SME	Surface Measuring Equipment
SME	Surface Movement Element (AFIT)
SME	Suriname [*International vehicle registration*] (ODBW)
SMEA	Sun Marine Employees Association (EA)
SMEAC	Science, Mathematics, and Environmental Education Information Analysis Center
SMEADO	Selected Major Exploratory Advanced Development Objective (MCD)
SMEAG	Research Station, Agriculture Canada [*Station de Recherches, Agriculture Canada*], Melfort, Saskatchewan [*Library symbol National Library of Canada*] (BIB)
SMEAR	SPAN [*Spacecraft Analysis*] Mission Evaluation Action Request [*NASA*] (GFGA)
SMEAT	Skylab Medical Experiments Altitude Test [*NASA*]
SMEC	Single Module Engine Control [*Automotive engineering*]
SMEC	Strategic Missile Evaluation Committee [*Air Force*]
Sm Ecc Cts	Smith on Ecclesiastical Courts [*7th ed.*] [*1920*] [*A publication*] (DLA)
SMECTYMNUS	Steven Marshall, Edward Calamy, Thomas Young, Matthew Newcomen, William Spurstow [*Collective author of 17th-century antiepiscopal tract*]
SMED	Shared Medical Sys [*NASDAQ symbol*] (TTSB)
SMED	Shared Medical Systems Corp. [*NASDAQ symbol*] (NQ)
SMED	Single Minute Exchange of Die [*Manufacturing*]
Sm Ed	Smith's Education for the English Bar [*A publication*] (DLA)
Smed & M	Smedes and Marshall's Mississippi Reports [*A publication*] (DLA)
Smed & M Ch	Smedes and Marshall's Mississippi Chancery Reports [*A publication*] (DLA)
Smedes and Marshall's Chy Repts	Smedes and Marshall's Mississippi Chancery Reports [*A publication*] (DLA)
Smedes & M Ch	Smedes and Marshall's Mississippi Chancery Reports [*A publication*] (DLA)
Smedes & M (Miss)	Smedes and Marshall's Mississippi Reports [*A publication*] (DLA)
SMEDI	Stillbirth-Mummification, Embryonic-Death, Infertility Syndrome [*Medicine*] (DMAA)
SmedvA	Smedvig Asa [*Associated Press*] (SAG)
SmedvB	Smedvig Asa [*Associated Press*] (SAG)
Smee	Collection of Abstracts of Acts of Parliament [*A publication*] (DLA)
SMEE	Master of Science in Electrical Engineering
SMEE	Society of Model and Experimental Engineers [*British*] (BI)
SMEF	Smooth Muscle-Derived Elastogenic Factor [*Biochemistry*]

SMEI	Sales and Marketing Executives International [*An association*] [*Cleveland, OH*]
SMEI	Severe Myoclonic Epilepsy of Infancy [*Medicine*] (DMAA)
SMEK	Summary Message Enable Keyboard
Sm El	Smith's Elements of Law [*A publication*] (DLA)
SMELT	Smelting
SMEM	Serial Memory (NITA)
SMEM	Supplemented Eagle's Minimum Essential Medium [*Medicine*] (DMAA)
SMEMA	Surface Mount Equipment Manufacturers Association (EA)
Sm Eng	Smith's English King's Bench Reports [*A publication*] (DLA)
SME of AIME	Society of Mining Engineers of American Institute of Mining, Metallurgical, and Petroleum Engineers [*Later, SME, Inc.*] (EA)
SMEP	Society of Multivariate Experimental Psychology (EA)
SMEPP	Subminiature End-Plate Potential (STED)
Sm Eq	Smith's Principles of Equity [*A publication*] (DLA)
SMER	Skylab Mission Evaluation Report [*NASA*] (MCD)
SM-ER	Surface Missile, Extended Range
SMERC	San Mateo Educational Resources Center [*San Mateo County Office of Education*] [*Information service or system*] (IID)
SMERE	SPRINT Missile Electromagnetic Radiation Evaluation [*Army*] (AABC)
SMERF	Social, Military, Ethnic, Religious, and Fraternal Groups [*Market segment*]
SMERFS	Statistical Modeling and Estimation Review of Functioning Software [*Science Applications International Corp.*]
SMERP	Supplemental Medical Expense Reimbursement Plan
SMERSH	Smert' Shpionam [*Death to the Spies*] [*Former Soviet Union state security organization, often referred to in the popular James Bond espionage stories*]
SMES	Shuttle Mission Engineering Simulator [*NASA*] (NASA)
SMES	Shuttle Mission Evaluation Simulation [*NASA*] (NASA)
SMES	Strategic Missile Evaluation Squadron
SMES	Superconducting Magnetic Energy Storage (NASA)
SMESA	Special Middle East Sealift Agreement (DOMA)
SME/SC	SPRINT Missile Engineering/Service Course [*Army*] (AABC)
SMET	Science Mathematics Engineering and Technology
SMET	Simulated Mission Endurance Test (MCD)
SMET	Spacecraft Maneuver Engine Transients [*Apollo program*] [*NASA*]
SMETC	Swiss Mouse Embryo Tissue Culture
SMETDS	Standard Message Trunk Design System [*Telecommunications*] (TEL)
Smeth LS	Smethurst on Locus Standi [*1867*] [*A publication*] (DLA)
SMETO	Staff Meteorological Officer [*NATO*] (NATG)
SMEX	Singapore International Monetary Exchange
Sm Ex Int	Smith on Executory Interest [*A publication*] (DLA)
SMF	Sacramento [*California*] [*Airport symbol*] (OAG)
SMF	Sacramento, CA [*Location identifier FAA*] (FAAL)
SMF	Sales Manpower Foundation (EA)
SMF	Sample Management Facility
SMF	S & M Photolabels, Inc. [*Toronto Stock Exchange symbol*]
SMF	Saticon Mixed-Field [*Video technology*]
SMF	Saw Machine Fixture (MCD)
SMF	S-Band Multifrequency
SMF	Schumann Memorial Foundation [*Defunct*] (EA)
SMF	Scientific Marriage Foundation (EA)
SMF	Screw Machine Feeder
SMF	Senior Management Forum [*Information Industry Association*]
SMF	Service to Military Families [*Red Cross*]
SMF	Shaker Museum Foundation (EA)
SMF	Signal De Mont [*France*] [*Seismograph station code, US Geological Survey*] (SEIS)
SMF	Single-Mode Fiber [*Optics*] (CDE)
SMF	Site Modification Facility
SMF	Smart & Final, Inc. [*NYSE symbol*] (SPSG)
SMF	Snell Memorial Foundation, Inc.
SMF	Society for the Maintenance of the Faith [*British*]
SMF	Software Maintenance Function [*Computer science*] (TEL)
SMF	Solar Magnetic Field
SMF	Space Manufacturing Facility
SMF	Spar Material Factor [*Yacht racing regulation*]
SMF	Special Modifying Factor (DEN)
SMF	Spectral Multilayer Filter
SMF	Stable Matrix Form
SMF	Standard Messaging Format [*Computer science*] (CDE)
SMF	Standard MIDI [*Musical Instrument Digital Interface*] File
SMF	Static Magnetic Field
SMF	Streptozocin, Mitomycin C, Fluorouracil [*Antineoplastic drug regimen*]
SMF	Student Missions Fellowship [*Later, IVMF*] (EA)
SMF	Swift Museum Foundation (EA)
SMF	Switchable Matched Filter
SMF	Synthetic Mineral Fiber
SMF	System Management Facility [*IBM Corp.*]
SMF	System Measurement Facility [*Computer science*] (IEEE)
SMFA	Simplified Modular Frame Assignment System [*Telecommunications*] (TEL)
SMFA	Specific Management Functional Area [*Telecommunications*] (OSI)
SMFAS	Simplified Mainframe Administration System (MCD)
SMFAS	Simplified Modular Frame Assignment System [*Bell System*]
SMFC	Shellee Morris Fan Club (EA)
SMFC	Sho-Me Financial [*NASDAQ symbol*] (TTSB)
SMFC	Sho-Me Financial Corp. [*NASDAQ symbol*] (SAG)
sm-FeSV	McDonough Feline Sarcoma Virus [*Veterinary medicine*] (MEDA)
SMFF	Script Mathematical Formula Formatter [*IBM Corp.*]
SMFL	Science, Mathematics, Foreign Languages
SmFlts	Small Faults [*Philately*]

SMFMA .... Sprayed Mineral Fiber Manufacturers Association (EA)
Sm For Med... Smith on Forensic Medicine [*10th ed.*] [*1955*] [*A publication*] (DLA)
Sm Forms.... Smith's Forms of Procedure [*A publication*] (DLA)
SMFP........... State Medical Facilities Plan [*Generic term*] (DHSM)
SMFR........... Service to Military Families Representative [*Red Cross*]
SMFR........... Summit Family Restaurants [*NASDAQ symbol*] (TTSB)
SMFR........... Summit Family Restaurants, Inc. [*NASDAQ symbol*] (SAG)
SMFT........... Semitrailer-Mounted Fabric Tank [*for water distribution*] [*Army*]
SMFUA........ Silk and Man-Made Fibre Users' Association [*British*] (BI)
SMFVD........ Sterile Midforceps Vaginal Delivery (STED)
SMFW........... Society of Medical Friends of Wine (EA)
SMG............. Megilot Genuzot [*E. L. Sukenik*] [*A publication*] (BJA)
SMG............. San Miguel [*Portugal*] [*Geomagnetic observatory code*]
SMG............. School of Military Government [*World War II*]
SMG............. Science Management Corp. [*AMEX symbol*] (SPSG)
SMG............. Scotts Co.'A' [*NYSE symbol*] (TTSB)
SMG............. Screen Management Guide (AAEL)
SMG............. Seismocardiogram
SMG............. Senior Master Sergeant (MCD)
SMG............. Sisters Poor Servants of the Mother of God [*Roman Catholic religious order*]
SMG............. Software Message Generator [*Computer science*] (TEL)
SMG............. Solids Moisture Gauge
SMG............. Sort Merge Generator (IAA)
SMG............. Spacecraft Meteorology Group (KSC)
SMG............. Spaceflight Meteorology Group [*NASA*] (NASA)
SMG............. Space Missions Group [*Ford Aerospace & Communications Corp.*] [*Detroit, MI*] [*Telecommunications service*] (TSSD)
SMG............. Specialty Medical Group (DMAA)
SMG............. Speed Made Good [*Navy*] (NVT)
SMG............. Submachine Gun
SMG............. Submandibular Gland [*Anatomy*]
SMGC........... Sun-Maid Growers of California (EA)
SMGC........... Surface Movement Guidance and Control [*FAA*] (TAG)
SMGD........... Supply Management Grouping Designator [*Navy*] (NG)
SM Geol...... Master of Science in Geology
SMGO........... Senior Military Government Officer [*World War II*]
SMGP........... Strategic Missile Group [*Air Force*]
SMGPC......... Small Molecule Gel Permeation Chromatography
SMGS........... Southeastern Mich Gas Ent [*NASDAQ symbol*] (TTSB)
SMGS........... Southeastern Michigan Gas Enterprises, Inc. [*NASDAQ symbol*] (NQ)
SMH............. Scheduled Man-Hours (MCD)
SMH............. Section for Metropolitan Hospitals (EA)
SMH............. Semtech Corp. [*AMEX symbol*] (SPSG)
SMH............. Simple Harmonic Motion (IAA)
SMH............. Smith Air, Inc. [*ICAO designator*] (FAAC)
SMH............. Societe Suisse de Microelectronique et d'Horlogerie [*Commercial firm*] (ECON)
SMH............. Society for Military History (NTPA)
SMH............. Standard Mirror Hybrid (MCD)
SMH............. State Mental Hospital (STED)
SMH............. St. Michael's Hospital, Toronto [*UTLAS symbol*]
SMH............. Strongyloidiasis with Massive Hyperinfection [*Medicine*] (DMAA)
SMH............. Sydney Morning Herald [*Database*]
SMHA........... Southern Mutual Help Association (EA)
SMHA........... State Mental Health Agency (DMAA)
SMHC........... Sarcomeric Myosin Heavy Chain [*Muscle physiology*]
SMHE........... Selected Material Handling Equipment [*Army*] (RDA)
SMHMO........ Staff Model Health Maintenance Organization [*Insurance*] (WYGK)
Sm Homest... Smyth on the Law of Homesteads and Exemptions [*A publication*] (DLA)
SMHS........... Superstition Mountain Historical Society (EA)
SMI.............. Aero Sami SA de CV [*Mexico ICAO designator*] (FAAC)
SMI.............. Masonry and Concrete Saw Manufacturers Institute (NTPA)
SMI.............. Sales Method Index [*LIMRA*]
SMI.............. Sa Majeste Imperiale [*His or Her Imperial Majesty*] [*French*]
SMI.............. Samos Island [*Greece*] [*Airport symbol*] (OAG)
SMI.............. Scanning Microscopy International (EA)
SMI.............. Science Management Corp. (EFIS)
SMI.............. Secondary Metal Institute (EA)
SMI.............. Self-Metering Instrumentation
SMI.............. Senior Medical Investigator
SMI.............. Sergeant-Major Instructor [*British military*] (DMA)
SMI.............. Service at Military Installations [*Red Cross*]
SMI.............. Severely Mentally Ill (GFGA)
SMI.............. Shelter Management Instructor [*Civil Defense*]
SMI.............. Ship Missile Interface
SMI.............. Silent Myocardial Ischemia [*Medicine*] (DB)
SMI.............. Simla [*India*] [*Seismograph station code, US Geological Survey Closed*] (SEIS)
SMI.............. Simple Mail Interface [*Computer science*] (CDE)
SMI.............. Simulation of Machine Indexing
SMI.............. Sisters of Mary Immaculate (TOCD)
SMI.............. Slipped Mutagenic Intermediate [*Biochemistry*]
SMI.............. Small Volume Infusion [*Pharmacology*] (DAVI)
SMI.............. Smithsonian Institution, Washington, DC [*OCLC symbol*] (OCLC)
SMI.............. Society for Machine Intelligence [*Defunct*] (EA)
SMI.............. Soldier-Machine Interface [*Army*] (RDA)
SMI.............. Sorptive Minerals Institute (EA)
SMI.............. Special Manufacturing Instruction
SMI.............. Special Multiperil Insurance
SMI.............. Spectrametrics, Inc.
SMI.............. SpenderMenders International [*Defunct*] (EA)
SMI.............. Spring Manufacturers Institute (EA)
SMI.............. Springs Industries'A' [*NYSE symbol*] (TTSB)
SMI.............. Springs Industries, Inc. [*Formerly, Springs Mills, Incorporated*] [*NYSE symbol*] (SPSG)
SMI.............. Standardized Incidence Ratio
SMI.............. Standard Measuring Instrument
SMI.............. Start Manual Input (IAA)
SMI.............. Static Memory Interface [*Computer science*] (MDG)
SMI.............. Statute Miles
SMI.............. Stress Myocardial Image [*Medicine*] (DB)
SMI.............. Structure of Management Information
SMI.............. Style of Mind Inventory [*Psychology*]
SMI.............. Styles of Management Inventory [*Test*]
SMI.............. Success Motivation Institute
SMI.............. Super Market Institute [*Later, FMI*] (EA)
SMI.............. Supplementary Medical Insurance
SMI.............. Supply Management Inspection (NVT)
SMI.............. Sustained Maximal Inspiration [*Physiology*]
SMI.............. Swiss Market Index (ECON)
SMI.............. Synthetic Multiple-Interaction [*For chiral separation*]
SMI.............. System Management Interrupt [*Computer science*] (PCM)
SMI.............. System Memory Interface [*Computer science*]
SMI.............. Systems Measurement Instrument [*Computer science*]
SMI^{2}LE......... Space Migration, Intelligence Increase, Life Extension [*Idea advanced by Timothy Leary, 1960's counterculture figure*]
SMIA........... Serial Multiplexer Interface Adapter (NASA)
SMIA........... Sheet Metal Industries Association [*British*] (BI)
SMIA........... Social Marketing International Association [*Queretaro, Mexico*] [*Defunct*] (EAIO)
SMIA........... Steel Management in Action [*Bethlehem Steel Co.*]
SMIAC......... Soil Mechanics Information Analysis Center [*Army Corps of Engineers*] (IID)
SMIAL.......... Software Manufacturing Industry in Australia [*Database*]
Smi & Bat... Smith and Batty's Irish King's Bench Reports [*A publication*] (DLA)
SMIAT.......... Special Military Intelligence Activities Team (CINC)
SMIC........... Missionary Sisters of the Immaculate Conception of the Mother of God [*Roman Catholic religious order*]
SMIC........... Sorghum and Millets Information Center [*ICRISAT*] [*India*]
SMIC........... Special Material Identification Code
SMIC........... Study of Man's Impact on Climate
SMIC........... Submarine Material Identification and Control [*Navy*] (DNAB)
SMIC........... Supply Management Information Center [*Military*] (CAAL)
SMIC........... Surveying and Mapping Industry Council (EERA)
SMICBM...... Semimobile Intercontinental Ballistic Missile
SMID........... Semiconductor Memory Integrated Device (MCD)
SMID........... Single Instruction Multiple Data (AAEL)
SMID........... Smith-Midland [*NASDAQ symbol*] (TTSB)
SMID........... Smith-Midland Corp. [*NASDAQ symbol*] (SAG)
SMIDA......... Small Business Innovation Development Act [*1982*]
SMIDW........ Smith-Midland Wrrt [*NASDAQ symbol*] (TTSB)
SMIEEE........ Senior Member of Institute of Electrical and Electronic Engineers
SMIER......... Societe Medicale Internationale d'Endoscopie et de Radiocinematographie [*International Medical Society for Endoscopy and Radiocinematography*]
SMIF........... Standard Mechanical Interface (NITA)
SMIG........... Sergeant-Major Instructor of Gunnery [*British military*] (DMA)
SmIg........... Surface Membrane Immunoglobulin [*Immunochemistry*]
SMIIS.......... Solar Microwave Interferometer Imaging System
SMIL........... Solidaritet med Israel
SMIL........... Statistics and Market Intelligence Library [*Department of Trade*] [*British*] (DCTA)
SMIL........... Synchronized Multimedia Integration Language [*Computer science*]
SMILAC........ Society for Music in the Liberal Arts College (AEBS)
SMILE.......... Safe Military Infrared LASER Equipment
SMILE.......... Ship's Master Index Listing of Equipment (MCD)
SMILE.......... Significant Milestone Integration Lateral Evaluation [*Computer science*]
SMILE.......... Society for Microcomputers in Life and Education (EDAC)
SMILE.......... South Central Minnesota Interlibrary Exchange [*Library network*]
SMILE.......... Spherical Micro Integrated Lens
SMILE.......... Surface Mixed Layer Experiment (NOAA)
SMILES........ Simplified Molecular Input Line Editor [*or Entry*] System [*Computer science*]
SMILI.......... Synthetic Model Interferometric LASER Imaging (PDAA)
SMILS.......... Sonobuoy Missile Impact Location System [*Navy*] (CAAL)
SM/IM......... System Manager or Item Manager (AFIT)
SMIMD........ Switched Multiple Instruction, Multiple Data Stream [*Computer science*] (MHDI)
S/MIME........ Secure Multimedia Internet Mail Extensions [*Computer science*]
SMIN........... Southern Mineral [*NASDAQ symbol*] (TTSB)
SMIN........... Southern Mineral Corp. [*NASDAQ symbol*] (NQ)
Sm Ind......... Smith's Reports [*1-4 Indiana*] [*A publication*] (DLA)
SM in Hyg... Master of Science in Hygiene
SMIO........... Search and Rescue Mission Information Officer (COE)
SMIO........... Spares Multiple Item Order (AAG)
SMIP........... Ship's 3-M Improvement Plan [*Navy*] (NVT)
SMIP........... Spares Management Improvement Program (DOMA)
SMIP........... Specific Management Information Protocol [*Telecommunications*] (OSI)
SMIP........... Structure Memory Information Processor
SMIPE......... Small Interplanetary Probe Experiment (DNAB)
SMIPP......... Sheet Metal Industry Promotion Plan (EA)
SMIPS......... Small Interactive Image Processing System [*NASA*]
SMIR........... Shuttle Multispectral Infrared Radiometer [*NASA*] (GFGA)
SMIRE......... Senior Member of the Institution of Radio Engineers
SMIRR......... Shuttle Multispectral Infrared Radiometer [*NASA*]

SMIRS .... School Management Information Retrieval Service [*University of Oregon*] [*Eugene, OH*]
SMIS .... Safeguard Management Information System [*Army*] (AABC)
SMIS .... School of Management Information Systems [*Army*]
SMIS .... Section of Medical Information Science (IAA)
SMIS .... Ship Management Information System (MCD)
SMIS .... Society for Management Information Systems (EA)
SMIS .... Specific Management Information Service [*Telecommunications*] (OSI)
SMIS .... Supply Management Information System
SMIS .... Survey Methodology Information System [*Inter-University Consortium for Political & Social Research*] [*Database*]
SMIS .... Symbolic Matrix Interpretation System
SMIS INC ..... Societe de Microelectronique Industrielle de Sherbrooke, Inc. [*University of Sherbrooke*] [*Canada Research center*] (RCD)
SMISOP .... Safeguard Management Information System Operating Program [*Army*] (AABC)
SMIT .... Schmit Industries, Inc. [*NASDAQ symbol*] (SAG)
SMIT .... Schmitt Industries [*NASDAQ symbol*] (TTSB)
SMIT .... Sherman Mental Impairment Test [*Psychology*]
SMIT .... Simulated Midcourse Interaction Test [*NASA*]
SMIT .... Spin Motor Interruption Technique
SMIT .... Submit (ROG)
SMIT .... System Management Interface Tool [*IBM Corp.*]
SMITE .... Simulated Mechanical Impact Test Equipment (MCD)
SMITE .... Simulation Model of Interceptor Terminal Effectiveness
SMITES .... State-Municipal Income Tax Evaluation System (PDAA)
Smith .... Smith on English Registration [*A publication*] (DLA)
Smith .... Smith, Reporter (7, 12 Heiskell's Tennessee Reports) [*A publication*] (DLA)
Smith .... Smith's Indiana Reports [*A publication*] (DLA)
Smith .... Smith's New Hampshire Reports [*A publication*] (DLA)
Smith .... Smithsonian [*A publication*] (BRI)
Smith .... Smith's Reports [*81-83 Missouri Appeals*] [*A publication*] (DLA)
Smith .... Smith's Reports [*2-4 South Dakota*] [*A publication*] (DLA)
Smith .... Smith's Reports [*1-11 Wisconsin*] [*A publication*] (DLA)
Smith .... Smith's Reports [*54-62 California*] [*A publication*] (DLA)
Smith .... Smith's Reports [*61-84 Maine*] [*A publication*] (DLA)
Smith Act .... Smith's Actions at Law [*A publication*] (DLA)
Smith & B ... Smith and Bates' American Railway Cases [*A publication*] (DLA)
Smith & B ... Smith and Batty's Irish King's Bench Reports [*A publication*] (DLA)
Smith & Bat... Smith and Batty's Irish King's Bench Reports [*A publication*] (DLA)
Smith & BRRC... Smith and Bates' American Railway Cases [*A publication*] (DLA)
Smith & G ... Smith and Guthrie's Missouri Appeal Reports [*81-101 Missouri*] [*A publication*] (DLA)
Smith & H ... Smith and Heiskell [*Tennessee*] [*A publication*] (DLA)
SmithAO ...... Smith AO Corp. [*Associated Press*] (SAG)
Smith C .... Smith College (GAGS)
Smith CCM... Smith's Circuit Courts-Martial Reports [*Maine*] [*A publication*] (DLA)
Smith Ch Pr... Smith's Chancery Practice [*A publication*] (DLA)
Smith Com Law... Smith's Manual of Common Law [*A publication*] (DLA)
Smith Cond... Smith's Condensed Alabama Reports [*A publication*] (DLA)
Smith Cond Rep... Smith's Condensed Alabama Reports [*A publication*] (DLA)
Smith Cong Election Cases... Smith's Election Cases [*United States*] [*A publication*] (DLA)
Smith Cont... Smith on Contracts [*A publication*] (DLA)
Smith Dict Antiq... Smith's Dictionary of Greek and Roman Antiquities [*A publication*] (DLA)
SmithEnv ..... Smith Environmental Technologies Corp. [*Associated Press*] (SAG)
Smith Ext Int... Smith on Executory Interest [*A publication*] (DLA)
Smith-Hurd... Smith-Hurd's Illinois Annotated Statutes [*A publication*] (DLA)
Smith-Hurd Ann St... Smith-Hurd's Illinois Annotated Statutes [*A publication*] (DLA)
SmithIn .... Smith International, Inc. [*Associated Press*] (SAG)
Smith Ind ..... Smith's Indiana Reports [*A publication*] (DLA)
Smith Inst .... Smithsonian Institution (BARN)
Smith KB ..... Smith's English King's Bench Reports [*A publication*] (DLA)
Smith Laws PA... Smith's Laws of Pennsylvania [*A publication*] (DLA)
Smith LC ..... Smith's Leading Cases [*A publication*] (DLA)
Smith Lead Cas... Smith's Leading Cases [*A publication*] (DLA)
Smith LJ ...... Smith's Law Journal [*A publication*] (DLA)
SmithM .... Smith-Midland Corp. [*Associated Press*] (SAG)
Smith Man Eq Jur... Smith's Manual of Equity Jurisprudence [*A publication*] (DLA)
Smith ME ..... Smith's Reports [*61-84 Maine*] [*A publication*] (DLA)
Smith Merc Law... Smith on Mercantile Law [*A publication*] (DLA)
SmithMic ..... Smith Micro Software, Inc. [*Associated Press*] (SAG)
SmithMid ..... Smith-Midland Corp. [*Associated Press*] (SAG)
SmithMo ...... Smithway Motor Xpress Corp. [*Associated Press*] (SAG)
Smith NH ..... Smith's New Hampshire Reports [*A publication*] (DLA)
Smith NY ..... Smith's Court of Appeals Reports [*15-27, 147-162 New York*] [*A publication*] (DLA)
Smith Rec ... Smith's Law of Receivers [*A publication*] (DLA)
Smith Repar... Smith's Law of Reparation [*A publication*] (DLA)
SmithRR ...... Smith [*Charles E.*] Residential Realty, Inc. [*Associated Press*] (SAG)
Smith Rules... Smith's Chancery Rules [*A publication*] (DLA)
Smith's (Ind) R... Smith's Indiana Reports [*A publication*] (DLA)
Smith's Laws... Smith's Laws of Pennsylvania [*A publication*] (DLA)
Smith's Lead Cas... Smith's Leading Cases [*A publication*] (DLA)
Smith's R ... Smith's Indiana Reports [*A publication*] (DLA)
Smith Wealth Nat... Smith's Inquiry into the Nature and Causes of the Wealth of Nations [*A publication*] (DLA)
Smith Wis ... Smith's Reports [*1-11 Wisconsin*] [*A publication*] (DLA)
SMIU .... Stove Mounters International Union of North America [*Later, Stove, Furnace, Allied Appliance Workers International Union of North America*]
SMJ .... Moose Jaw Public Library, Saskatchewan [*Library symbol National Library of Canada*] (NLC)
SMJ .... Santa Margherita [*Italy*] [*Airport symbol*] (AD)
SMJ .... Santa Marina Gold [*Vancouver Stock Exchange symbol*]
SMJ .... Services Missionnaires des Jeunes [*Canada*]
SMJ .... Sim [*Papua New Guinea*] [*Airport symbol*] (OAG)
SMJ .... Society of Malawi. Journal [*A publication*]
SMJ .... Society of Medical Jurisprudence (EA)
SMJAB .... State Medical Journal Advertising Bureau (DAVI)
SMJAEM ...... Saskatchewan Department of Advanced Education and Manpower, Moose Jaw, Saskatchewan [*Library symbol National Library of Canada*] (NLC)
SMJC .... Saint Mary's Junior College [*Minnesota; Missouri; North Carolina*]
SMJC .... Service Module Jettison Controller [*NASA*] (MCD)
SM-JDCC .... Sunshine Music - Jan and Dean Collectors Club (EA)
SMJK .... Njoeng Jakob Kondre [*Surinam*] [*ICAO location identifier*] (ICLI)
SMJP .... Palliser Regional Library, Moose Jaw, Saskatchewan [*Library symbol National Library of Canada*] (NLC)
Sm J St Comp... Smith on Joint-Stock Companies [*A publication*] (DLA)
SMJT .... Saskatchewan Technical Institute, Moose Jaw, Saskatchewan [*Library symbol National Library of Canada*] (NLC)
SMK .... Smack [*Ship*]
SMK .... Smoke (AAG)
SMK .... Software Migration Kit [*Microsoft, Inc.*] [*Computer science*] (PCM)
SMK .... St. Michael [*Alaska*] [*Airport symbol*] (OAG)
SMK .... St. Michael, AK [*Location identifier FAA*] (FAAL)
SMK .... System Monitor Kernal (MHDI)
SMKA .... Kabalebo [*Surinam*] [*ICAO location identifier*] (ICLI)
Sm KB .... Smith's English King's Bench Reports [*A publication*] (DLA)
SMKD .... Smoked (WGA)
SMKE .... Kayser [*Surinam*] [*ICAO location identifier*] (ICLI)
SMKLS .... Smokeless (AAG)
SMKSTK ...... Smokestack [*s*] [*Freight*]
SMKW .... Paramaribo/Kwatta [*Surinam*] [*ICAO location identifier*] (ICLI)
SML .... CV Sportsmark International, Inc. [*Vancouver Stock Exchange symbol*]
SML .... Montreal Lake Library, Saskatchewan [*Library symbol National Library of Canada*] (NLC)
SML .... Saluda Motor Lines [*AAR code*]
SML .... Sawmill [*Alaska*] [*Seismograph station code, US Geological Survey*] (SEIS)
SML .... Search Mode Logic
SML .... Security Market Line
SML .... Semantic-Meta-Language
SML .... Serials Master List
SML .... Silent Mating Loci [*Genetics*]
SML .... Simulate [*or Simulation*] (WDAA)
SML .... Simulator Load
SM-L .... Singh's Mosquito [*Tissue culture medium*] (BABM)
SML .... Single Macro Language [*Computer science*]
SML .... Skylab Mobile Laboratory [*NASA*] (KSC)
SML .... Smith Air (1976) Ltd. [*Canada ICAO designator*] (FAAC)
SML .... Smouldering Leukemia [*Medicine*] (DMAA)
SML .... Software Master Library [*Computer science*] (TEL)
SML .... Solicitation Mailing List (AAGC)
SML .... Southern Maine Library District, Portland, ME [*OCLC symbol*] (OCLC)
SML .... Spartan Material List [*Missiles*] (MCD)
SML .... Spectrum Management Licence [*Telecommunications British*]
SML .... Spool Multileaving [*Computer science*] (IBMDP)
SML .... Standard Markup Language [*Computer science*]
SML .... States Marine Lines
SML .... Stella Maris [*Bahamas*] [*Airport symbol*] (OAG)
SML .... Strategies for Media Literacy [*An association*] (EA)
SML .... Structure Mold Line (MCD)
SML .... Subacute Myeloid Leukemia [*Oncology*]
SML .... Support Material List
SML .... Symbolic Machine Language [*Computer science*]
SMLA .... Kamala Soela [*Surinam*] [*ICAO location identifier*] (ICLI)
Sm L & T .... Smith's Landlord and Tenant [*A publication*] (DLA)
Sm Lawy ..... Smith's Lawyer and His Profession [*A publication*] (DLA)
SMLC .... Scottish Mountain Leadership Certificate (DI)
Sm LC .... Smith's Leading Cases [*A publication*] (DLA)
SMLC .... Southwest Michigan Library Cooperative [*Library network*]
Sm L Cas Com L... Smith's Leading Cases on Commercial Law [*A publication*] (DLA)
SMLCC .... Synchronous Multiline Communications Coupler (NITA)
SMLD .... Suckling Mouse Mean Lethal Dose [*Microbiology*]
SMLE .... Short Magazine Lee-Enfield Rifle
SMLE .... Small-Medium Local Exchange [*Telecommunications*] (TEL)
Sm LJ .... Law Journal (Smith) [*England*] [*A publication*] (DLA)
SMLM .... Simple-Minded Learning Machine (IEEE)
SMLM .... Soviet Military Liaison Mission [*Army*]
SMLO .... Senior Military Liaison Officer
SmlOil .... Smalls Oilfield Services [*Associated Press*] (SAG)
SMLR .... Stepwise Multiple Linear Regression [*Mathematics*]
SMLS .... Saint Mary of the Lake Seminary [*Mundelein, IL*]
SMLS .... Sea-Based Mobile Logistics Supply [*Navy*] (CAAL)
SMLS .... Seamless (AAG)
SMLS .... Skye Main Lava Succession [*Geology*]
SMLS .... Small and Medium-Sized Libraries Section [*Public Library Association*]
SMLT .... Langatabbetje [*Surinam*] [*ICAO location identifier*] (ICLI)
SMLV .... Standard Memory Loader Verifier (DWSG)
SMM .... Master of Sacred Music (BJA)

SMM............. Montfort Missionaries (TOCD)
smm .... Montfort Missionaries (TOCD)
SMM............. Safeguards and Materials Management [AEC]
SMM............. Saigon Military Mission [Vietnam]
SMM............. Sancta Mater Maria [Holy Mother Mary] [Latin]
SMM............. Scanning Multichannel Microwave
SMM............. Scattering Matrix Method [Materials research]
SMM............. Secondary Mortgage Market (ADA)
SMM............. Semiconductor Memory Module
SMM............. Semporna [Malaysia] [Airport symbol] (OAG)
SMM............. Shared Main Memory (NITA)
SMM............. Shared Multiport Memory
SMM............. Ship, Machinery, Marine Technology International Exhibition
SMM............. Smoldering Multiple Myeloma [Medicine] (DMAA)
SMM............. Smooth-Muscle Myosin [Biology]
SMM............. Societas Mariae Montfortana [Missionaries of the Company of Mary]
                 [Montfort Fathers] [Roman Catholic religious order]
SMM............. Solar Maximum Mission [NASA] (MCD)
smm .... Solar Maximum Mission [NASA] (NAKS)
SMM............. Sooty Mangabey Monkey
SMM............. Specially Meritorious Medal
SMM............. Spectral Matrix Method (KSC)
SMM............. Standard Method of Measurement (IEEE)
SMM............. Start of Manual Message (BUR)
SMM............. Stress Memo Manual
SMM............. Study of Media & Markets [Simmons Market Research Bureau, Inc.]
                 [Information service or system] (CRD)
SMM............. Submarine Miners [British military] (DMA)
SMM............. Subsystem Measurement Management [NASA] (NASA)
smm .... Subsystem Measurement Management (NAKS)
SMM............. Summit Airlines [ICAO designator] (FAAC)
SMM............. Supervisory Middle Management
SMM............. Supplemental Minimal Medium [Microbiology]
SMM............. System Maintenance Manual
SMM............. System Maintenance Monitor [Telecommunications] (IAA)
SMM............. System Management Mode [Computer science] (PCM)
SMM............. Systems Maintenance Management [Computer science]
SMMA........... Small Motor Manufacturers Association [Libertyville, IL] (EA)
SMMA........... Social Mapping Matrix Assessment (EDAC)
Sm M & S ... Smith on Master and Servant [8th ed.] [1931] [A publication] (DLA)
SMMAS........ Shipboard Maintenance Manpower Analysis System [Navy] (DNAB)
SMMB.......... Scottish Milk Marketing Board (DI)
SMMB.......... Stores Management Multiplex Bus [Computer science] (MCD)
SMMC.......... Standard Monthly Maintenance Charge (NITA)
SMMC.......... System Maintenance Monitor Console [FAA]
SMMCEQ ..... Standard Method of Measurement for Civil Engineering Quantities
                 (PDAA)
SMMD.......... Specimen Mass Measurement Device [NASA] (KSC)
SMMDA........ Smaller Manufacturers Medical Device Association [Inactive] (EA)
Sm ME......... Smith's Reports [01-04 Maine] [A publication] (DLA)
SMME.......... Society for Mining, Metallurgy, and Exploration [In association name,
                 SMME, Inc.] (EA)
Sm Merc L... Smith on Mercantile Law [13th ed.] [1931] [A publication] (DLA)
SMMG.......... Sisters of Mary, Mother of God (TOCD)
SMMH .... Scheduled Maintenance Man-Hours (MCD)
SMMHC........ Smooth Muscle Myosin Heavy Chain [Biochemistry]
SMMI........... El Senoussi Multiphasic Marital Inventory [Psychology]
SMMI........... Salesian Missionaries of Mary Immaculate [See also SSMMI]
                 [Gentilly, France] (EAIO)
SMMI........... Sisters Minor of the Mary Immaculate (TOCD)
SMMIP......... Strategic Material Management Information Program (PDAA)
SM MLCK ... Smooth Muscle Form of Myosin Light Chain Kinase [An enzyme]
SMMO.......... Moengo [Surinam] [ICAO location identifier] (ICLI)
SMMO.......... Soluble Methane Monooxygenase [Biochemistry]
SMMP.......... Screw Machine Metal Part
SMMP.......... Standard Methods of Measuring Performance (IEEE)
SMMP.......... System MANPRINT [Manpower and Personnel Integration]
                 Management Plan [Army]
SMMR .... Scanning Multichannel [or Multifrequency or Multispectral] Microwave
                 Radiometer
SMMR .... Simmons Major Market Research, Inc. [New York, NY Information
                 service or system] (IID)
SMMR .... Specific Mobilization Material Requirement [Military] (AFIT)
SMMR .... Standard Missile Medium-Range (SAA)
SM-MR .... Surface Missile, Medium Range
SMMS.......... Shipbuilding Material Management Systems [Navy] (NG)
SMMS.......... Society of Mary Missionary Sisters (TOCD)
SMMS.......... Standard Maintenance Management System [Military] (CAAL)
SMMS.......... Support Maintenance Management System [Army]
SMMT.......... Society of Motor Manufacturers and Traders [Defunct] (EA)
SMMT.......... Strategic Missiles Materials Technology (MCD)
SMMT.......... Summit Design, Inc. [NASDAQ symbol] (SAG)
SMMW......... Submillimeter Wave (MCD)
SMN............. Nazi Texts in the Semitic Museum [Harvard] (BJA)
SMN............. Salmon, ID [Location identifier FAA] (FAAL)
SMN............. Satellite Music Network (NTCM)
SMN............. Seaman
SMN............. Second Malignant Neoplasm [Medicine] (DMAA)
SMN............. Single Wire Multiplex Network [Automotive engineering]
SMN............. Sleeping Mountain [Nevada] [Seismograph station code, US
                 Geological Survey Closed] (SEIS)
SMN............. Spain-Morocco Network [Armed Forces Radio-Television] (DNAB)
SMN............. Survival Motor Neuron [Genetics]
SMNA .... Safe Manufacturers' National Association (EA)
SMNC .... Self-Monitoring Negative Checklist (EDAC)

SMNC .... Splenic Mononuclear Cell [Cytology]
Sm Neg .... Smith on Negligence [2nd ed.] [1884] [A publication] (DLA)
SMNI .... New Nickerie/Nickerie [Surinam] [ICAO location identifier] (ICLI)
SMNK .... Smooth Neck
SMNO .... Singapore Malays National Organization [Pertubohan Kebangsaan
                 Melayu Singapore] [Political party] (PPW)
SMNRY........ Seminary
SMO............. Medical Officer of Schools (DAVI)
SMO............. Santa Maria Resources Ltd. [Toronto Stock Exchange symbol]
SMO............. Santa Monica [California] [Airport symbol] (AD)
SMO............. Santa Monica Bank [AMEX symbol] (SAG)
SMO............. Santa Monica, CA [Location identifier FAA] (FAAL)
SMO............. Science Management Office (USDC)
SMO............. Secondary Market Operation
SMO............. Senior Medical Officer [Military]
SMO............. Senior Meteorological and Oceanograhic Officer (COE)
SMO............. Service Module Oxidizer [NASA]
SMO............. Slip Made Out (MAE)
SMO............. Slowly Moving Object [Astronomy]
SMO............. Small Machine Organizer (IAA)
SMO............. Small Magnetospheric Observatory [Satellite] [NASA]
SMO............. Smoke
SMO............. Society of Military Ophthalmologists (EA)
SMO............. Society of Military Otolaryngologists [Later, SMO-HNS] (EA)
SMO............. So Much Of
SMO............. Sovereign Military Order [British]
SMO............. Special Military Operation
SMO............. Squadron Medical Officer
SMO............. Stabilized Master Oscillator
SMo............. Stainless Steel with Molybdenum [Devices] [Orthopedics] (DAVI)
SMO............. State Maintenance Office [or Officer] [Military]
SMO............. Statistical Model of Overlap
SMO............. Stock Material Order (SAA)
SMO............. Strategic Mobility Office (COE)
SMO............. Supermassive Object [Cosmology]
SMO............. Supplemtary Meteorological Office (BARN)
SMO............. Supply Management Office [Air Force] (AFM)
SMO............. Surface Mining Office [Department of the Interior] (OICC)
SMO............. Survivability Management Office [Adelphi, MD] [Army]
SMO............. Survivability Management Operation
SMO............. System Management Office (AFIT)
SMO............. Systems Methodology Office
SMOA .... Ships Material Office, Atlantic
SMOA .... Single-Manager Operating Agency [Military]
SMOA .... Superfund Memorandum of Agreement [Environmental Protection
                 Agency]
SMOBC........ Solder Mask Over Bare Copper [Electronics]
SMOBE .... Surveys of Minority-Owned Business Enterprises [Bureau of the
                 Census] (GFGA)
SMOBSMOD... Strategic Mobility Simulation Model
SMOC .... Simulation Mission Operation Computer [NASA] (MCD)
smoc .... Simulation Mission Operation Computer (NAKS)
SMOC .... Submodule and Operator Controller [For sequence of telephonic
                 operations]
SMOCTA ...... Service Members Occupational Conversions and Training Acts
SMOD .... SMART Modular Tech [NASDAQ symbol] (TTSB)
SMOD .... SMART Modular Technologies, Inc. [NASDAQ symbol] (SAG)
SMODOS...... Self-Modulating Derivative Optical Spectrometer (IAA)
SMOG .... Sales Management Organization Game
SMOG .... Save Me, Oh God
SMOG .... Smoke and Fog
SMOG .... Special Monitor Output Generator (IEEE)
SMOG .... Sprite-Midget Owners Group (EA)
SMOG .... Structural Modeling Oriented Graphics [Module]
SMOH .... Senior Medical Officer of Health [British] (DAVI)
SMOH .... Since Major Overhaul (DA)
SMOH .... Society of Medical Officers of Health [British]
SMOHI......... Sheet Metal Occupational Health Institute (EA)
SMO-HNS .... Society of Military Otolaryngologists - Head and Neck Surgeons (EA)
SmOi .... Smalls Oilfield Services [Associated Press] (SAG)
SMOKE .... Surface Magnetooptic Kerr Effect [Surface analysis]
SMOL.......... Oelemari [Surinam] [ICAO location identifier] (ICLI)
SMOLANT ..... Ships Material Office, Atlantic (MCD)
SMOM .... Sovereign Military Order of Malta (EA)
SMON .... Subacute Myelo-Optic Neuropathy [Medicine]
SMonBk ...... Santa Monica Bank [Associated Press] (SAG)
SMOOSA ...... Save Maine's Only Official State Animal [Moose]
SMOOTH...... Spectra Mode of Operation through Hardware (IAA)
SMOP .... Ships Material Office, Pacific
SMOP .... Simple [or Small] Matter of Programming (NHD)
SMOP .... So Much of Paragraph
SMOPAC ...... Ships Material Office, Pacific (MCD)
SMOPS .... School of Maritime Operations [British]
SMORE .... Self-Heating Meal, Ordered Ready-to-Eat [Army] (RDA)
SMORG .... Senior Marketing Officers Research Group [LIMRA]
SMORZ .... Smorzando [Slower and Softer] [Music]
SMOS .... Secondary Military Occupational Specialty
SMOS .... Senior Marketing Officers Seminar [LIMRA]
SMOS .... Society of Military Orthopaedic Surgeons (EA)
SMOS .... Submicrometer Metal-Oxide Semiconductor (IAA)
SMOSC .... Secondary Military Occupational Specialty Code (AABC)
SMOTE .... Simulation of Turbofan Engine [Air Force]
SMOTEC ...... Special Missions Operational Test and Evaluation Center [Hurlburt
                 Field, FL]

Smoult.........	Notes of Cases in Smoult's Collection of Orders [*Calcutta, India*] [*A publication*] (DLA)
SMOW	Standard Mean Ocean Water
SMOWOG	Simulation Model Object Working Group
SMP.............	Daughters of Our Mother of Peace (TOCD)
SMP.............	Sacred Music Press (BJA)
SMP.............	Saint Mary's Press [*Record label*] [*New York*]
SMP.............	Salinity Management Plan [*Australia*]
SMP.............	Sampler (DEN)
SMP.............	Santa Monica Public Library, Santa Monica, CA [*OCLC symbol*] (OCLC)
SMP.............	Scanning and Measuring Projector
SMP.............	Scanning Microscope Photometer (OA)
SMP.............	Scheduled Maintenance Program (MCD)
SMP.............	School Mathematics Project [*British*]
SMP.............	See Me Please
SMP.............	Self-Maintenance Period [*British military*] (DMA)
SMP.............	Self-Management Program (DAVI)
SMP.............	Sempati Air Transport PT [*Indonesia*] [*ICAO designator*] (FAAC)
SMP.............	Sensitized Material Print (MSA)
SMP.............	Servo Meter Panel (AAG)
SMP.............	Shipboard Microfilm Program [*Navy*] (DNAB)
SMP.............	Ship's Mission Profile [*Navy*] (CAAL)
SMP.............	Silicon-Modified Polyether [*Organic chemistry*]
SMP.............	Simple Management Protocol [*Computer science*] (DOM)
SMP.............	Simplon Resources Ltd. [*Vancouver Stock Exchange symbol*]
SMP.............	Simulation Management Plan
SMP.............	Simultaneous Macular Perception [*Ophthalmology*]
SMP.............	Simultaneous Membership Program [*Military*]
SMP.............	Sine Mascula Prole [*Without Male Issue*] [*Latin*]
SMP.............	Sisters of St. Mary of the Presentation [*Roman Catholic religious order*]
SMP.............	Skimmed Milk Powder (ADA)
SMP.............	Slow-Moving Protease
SMP.............	Smith, Miller, and Patch [*Commercial firm*] (DAVI)
SMP.............	Smudge Pot
SMP.............	Social Marginal Productivity
SMP.............	Society of Miniature Painters [*British*] (ROG)
SMP.............	Society of Our Mother of Peace (TOCD)
smp.............	Society of Our Mother of Peace (TOCD)
SMP.............	Sodium Mercaptopyruvate [*Organic chemistry*]
SMP.............	Software Management Plan [*NASA*] (MCD)
SMP.............	Soil Management Program [*of Tasmania*] [*State*] (EERA)
SMP.............	Soldier Modernization Plan [*Army*] (INF)
SMP.............	Somplago [*Italy*] [*Seismograph station code, US Geological Survey Closed*] (SEIS)
SMP.............	Sound Motion Picture Technician [*Navy*]
SMP.............	Soviet Military Power [*A publication 1981-1991; changed in 1992 to Forces in Transition*] (DOMA)
SMP.............	Special Maintenance Project [*FAA*]
SMP.............	Special Manufacturing Procedure
SMP.............	Special Marketing Program [*Business*]
SMP.............	Special Monthly Pension (DAVI)
SMP.............	Special Multiperil [*Insurance*]
SMP.............	Stampede Pass, WA [*Location identifier FAA*] (FAAL)
SMP.............	Standard Maintenance Procedure
SMP.............	Standard Motor Prod [*NYSE symbol*] (TTSB)
SMP.............	Standard Motor Products, Inc. [*NYSE symbol*] (SPSG)
SMP.............	Standard Motor Pump
SMP.............	Standards, Methods, and Planning
SMP.............	Statutory Maternity Pay [*British*]
SMP.............	St. Martin's Press
SMP.............	Stores Management Process (MCD)
SMP.............	Submitochondrial Particle [*Cytology*]
SMP.............	Sulfamethoxypyridazine [*Antimicrobial compound*]
SMP.............	Summary Maneuver Plan
SMP.............	Suomen Maaseudun Puolue [*Finnish Rural Party*] [*Political party*] (PPW)
SMP.............	Supply Master Plan
SMP.............	Symbolic Mathematics Program
SMP.............	Symmetric Multiprocessing
SMP.............	Symmetric Multiprocessor [*Computer science*]
SMP.............	Synthesis Measurement Plan (IAA)
SMP.............	Syrtis Major Plantia [*A filamentary mark on Mars*]
SMP.............	System Maintenance Program (IAA)
SMP.............	System Management Plan
SMP.............	System Mechanical Performance
SMP.............	System Memory Pool (PCM)
SMP.............	System Modification Program [*Computer science*]
SMP.............	Systems and Management Panel (ACII)
SMP.............	Systems Maintenance Procedure (MCD)
SMP.............	Systems Management Processor (IAA)
SMP.............	Systems Modernization Plan [*Social Security Administration*]
SMP.............	Systems Monitoring Panel (NVT)
SMPA.........	Paloemeu/Vincent Fajks [*Surinam*] [*ICAO location identifier*] (ICLI)
SMPA.........	Saskatchewan Motion Pictures Association [*Canada*] (WWLA)
SMPA.........	Scottish Master Plasterers Association (DBA)
SMPA.........	Solid Motor Processing Area [*NASA*] (KSC)
SMPA.........	Switch Mode Power Amplifier (DWSG)
SMPAD	Society of Motion Picture Art Directors [*Later, SMPTAD*] (EA)
Sm Pat	Smith on Patents [*2nd ed.*] [*1854*] [*A publication*] (DLA)
SMPB.........	Paramaribo [*Surinam*] [*ICAO location identifier*] (ICLI)
SMPB.........	Succinimidyl (Maleimidophenyl)butyrate [*Organic chemistry*]
SMPC.........	Saint Mary of the Plains College [*Dodge City, KS*]
SMPC.........	Simplified Model Predictive Control [*Chemical engineering*] [*Computer science*]
SMPC.........	Sum of Magnitudes of Pitch Matrix - Correlator
SMPD	Ship Maintenance Planning Data (MCD)
SMPD	Surface Missile Processing Description (MCD)
SMPDU	Service Message Protocol Data Unit [*Telecommunications*] (OSI)
SMPE	Society of Marine Port Engineers (EA)
SMPE	Society of Motion Picture Engineers [*Later, SMPTE*] (NTCM)
SMPF.........	Scientific & Medical Publications of France, Inc.
SMPG.........	Poesoegroenoe [*Surinam*] [*ICAO location identifier*] (ICLI)
SMPG.........	Seat Miles per Gallon [*BTS*] (TAG)
SMPG.........	Small Magazine Publishers Group (EA)
SMPG.........	Standardization Management Policy Group
SMPG.........	Successful Magazine Publishers Group [*Defunct*] (EA)
SMPI.........	Sequential Multipoint Injection [*Automotive engineering*]
SMPI.........	Surface Missile Proficiency Inspection (MCD)
SMPL.........	Sample
Sm Pl	Somersetshire Pleas (Civil and Criminal), Edited by Chadwyck-Healey and Landon [*Somerset Record Society Publications, Vols. 11, 36, 41, 44*] [*A publication*] (DLA)
SMPLG	Sampling (MSA)
SMPM.........	Paramaribo [*Surinam*] [*ICAO location identifier*] (ICLI)
SMPM.........	Structural Materials Property Manual [*NASA*] (NASA)
SM/PM.........	System Management/Performance Monitor [*NASA*] (NASA)
SMPMA	Sausage and Meat Pie Manufacturers Association [*British*] (BI)
SMPO	SEATO [*Southeast Asia Treaty Organization*] Military Planning Office (CINC)
SMPO	Sound Motion Picture Operator [*Navy*]
Sm Poor L ...	Smith's Scotch Poor Law [*A publication*] (DLA)
SMPP.........	Sintered Metal Powder Process (MCD)
S-MPR	Semimonthly Progress Reports [*Navy*]
Sm Pr	Small Press [*A publication*] (BRI)
SMPR	Supply and Maintenance Plan and Report [*Army*] (AABC)
Sm Pr Eq ...	Smith's Principles of Equity [*A publication*] (DLA)
Sm Prob L ...	Smith's Probate Law and Practice [*A publication*] (DLA)
Sm Pr R ...	Small Press Review [*A publication*] (BRI)
SMPS.........	Simplified Message Processing Simulation (IEEE)
SMPS.........	Simpson Indus [*NASDAQ symbol*] (TTSB)
SMPS.........	Simpson Industries, Inc. [*NASDAQ symbol*] (NQ)
SMPS.........	Simultaneous Multiple Peptide Synthesis [*Biochemistry*]
SMPS.........	Society for Marketing Professional Services [*Alexandria, VA*] (EA)
SMPS.........	Society of Master Printers Scotland (DBA)
SMPS.........	Special Mobile Provost Section [*British military*] (DMA)
SMPS.........	Sum of Magnitudes of Pitch Matrix - Skin
SMPS.........	Switched-Mode Power Supply (PDAA)
SMPS.........	Switch Mode Power Supply (EECA)
SMPSA	Solid Motor Processing and Storage Car
SMPT.........	Apentina [*Surinam*] [*ICAO location identifier*] (ICLI)
SMPT.........	Shuttle Main Propulsion Test (SSD)
SMPT.........	Sound Movie Projector Technician [*Navy*] (DNAB)
SMPTAD	Society of Motion Picture and Television Art Directors (EA)
SMPTE	Society of Motion Picture and Television Engineers (EA)
SMPTRB	Shuttle Main Propulsion Test Requirement Board [*NASA*] (MCD)
SMPVS	Central Resource Centre, Prairie View School Division No. 74, Milestone, Saskatchewan [*Library symbol National Library of Canada*] (NLC)
SMPY.........	Study of Mathematically Precocious Youth (EDAC)
SMQ.........	Silvermaque Mining Ltd. [*Toronto Stock Exchange symbol*]
SMQ.........	Social Maturity Quotient
SMQ.........	Source One Mortgage Services [*NYSE symbol*] (SAG)
SMQ.........	Source One Mtg 9.375%'QUICS' [*NYSE symbol*] (TTSB)
SMQ.........	Structure Module Qualification Test (MCD)
SMQ.........	Surface Metastable Quenching [*Surface analysis*]
SMQC.........	Sunport Medical Corp. [*NASDAQ symbol*] (SAG)
SMQCF	Sunport Med [*NASDAQ symbol*] (TTSB)
SMR.........	Great Falls, MT [*Location identifier FAA*] (FAAL)
SMR.........	Midrash Rabbah [*H. Freedman and Maurice Simon*] [*A publication*] (BJA)
SMR.........	Sa Majeste Royale [*His, or Her, Royal Majesty*] [*French*]
SMR.........	Samaritan Health Services [*ICAO designator*] (FAAC)
SMR.........	San Marino [*ANSI three-letter standard code*] (CNC)
SMR.........	Santa Marta [*Colombia*] [*Airport symbol*] (OAG)
SMR.........	Saskatchewan Mounted Rifles (DMA)
SMR.........	Scheduled Maintenance Replacement
SMR.........	School of Materiel Readiness [*Formerly, SAM*] [*Army*] (RDA)
SMR.........	Secret Marriage Rite (BJA)
SMR.........	Semeru [*Java*] [*Seismograph station code, US Geological Survey Closed*] (SEIS)
SMR.........	Semiconductor Mask Representation (AAEL)
SMR.........	Seminarians for Ministerial Renewal [*Later, NFCS*] (EA)
SMR.........	Senior Maintenance Rating [*British military*] (DMA)
SMR.........	Senior Medical Resident (DAVI)
SMR.........	Sensorimotor Rhythm [*Neurophysiology*]
SMR.........	Series Mode Rejection
SMR.........	Severely Mentally Retarded
SMR.........	Shared Mobile Radio [*Telecommunications*]
SMR.........	Sheffield and Midland Railway [*British*] (ROG)
SMR.........	Shield Mock-Up Reactor
SMR.........	Shiftout Modular Redundancy (MHDI)
SMR.........	Side-Looking Mapping RADAR
SMR.........	Signal Master (IAA)
SMR.........	Signal Memory Recorder (NITA)
SMR.........	Skeletal Muscle Relaxant [*Drug*]
SMR.........	Small Missile Range (MCD)
SMR.........	Society of Magnetic Resonance (NTPA)

SMR............	Society of Manufacturers' Representatives (EA)
SMR............	Society of Mary Reparatrix [Roman Catholic women's religious order]
SMR............	Solid Moderated Reactor [Nuclear energy]
SMR............	Somnolent Metabolic Rate [Medicine]
SMR............	Source, Maintenance, and Recoverability (MCD)
SMR............	Spanish Mustang Registry (EA)
SMR............	Specialized Mobile Radio
SMR............	Special Money Requisition [Military]
SMR............	Standardised Minimum Rules [For the treatment of prisoners] [Australia]
SMR............	Standardized Mortality Ratio
SMR............	Standard Malaysian Rubber [Grade of natural rubber]
SMR............	Standard Morbidity Ratio (MAE)
SMR............	Standard Mortality Rate
SMR............	Stanmar Resources Ltd. [Vancouver Stock Exchange symbol]
SMR............	Statement of Material Requirements
SMR............	Status Monitoring Routine
SMR............	Statutory Minimum Remuneration [British] (DI)
SMR............	Steam-Methane Reforming [Chemical engineering]
SMR............	St Mark's Review [A publication] (APTA)
SMR............	Stock Management Report [Military]
Smr.............	Streptomycin Resistance [Genetics]
SMR............	Stroke with Minimum Residuum [Medicine] (DMAA)
SMR............	Structure-Metabolism Relationship [For drug design prediction]
SMR............	Submucous Resection [Medicine]
SMR............	Super-Metal Rich [Astronomy]
SMR............	Supplemental Medical Report
SMR............	Supply, Maintenance, and Recoverability Code [Army]
SMR............	Supply Management Report
SMR............	Supportability, Maintainability, and Repairability (SSD)
SMR............	Surface Movement RADAR
SMR............	Switching Mode Regulator
SMR............	System Malfunction Report
SMR............	Systems Management Responsibility (SAA)
SMRA	Raleighvallen [Surinam] [ICAO location identifier] (ICLI)
SMRA	Scottish Milk Records Association (DBA)
SMRA	Simultaneous Multicomponent Rank Annihilation [Mathematics]
SMRA	Spare Module Replacement Analysis
Sm R & P Prop...	Smith on the Law of Real and Personal Property [A publication] (DLA)
SMRAS	Safeguard Maintenance and Reporting Analysis System [Army] (AABC)
SMRB :.........	Simmons Market Research Bureau, Inc. [Database producer] [New York, NY]
SMRC	Scottish Motor Racing Club (DBA)
SMRC	Silver Marten Rabbit Club (EA)
SMRC	Society of Miniature Rifle Clubs [British] (ROG)
SMRCS	Service Module Reaction Control System [NASA] (KSC)
SMRD	Spin Motor Rate Detector (IAA)
SMRD	Spin Motor Rotation [or Running] Detector (MCD)
SMRD	Spin Motor Run Discrete (NASA)
SMRD	Stress-Related Mucosal Damage [Medicine] (DMAA)
SMRE	Safety in Mines Research Establishment [British]
SMRE	Societe de Marie Reine d'Ecosse [Mary Queen of Scots Society] (EAIO)
SMRE	Submerged Repeater Monitoring Equipment [RADAR]
SMRF	Salvadoran Medical Relief Fund (EA)
SMRF	Series Mode Rejection Factor (IAA)
SMRF	Small Materials Recovery Facility [for recycling of glass, plastics, etc.]
SMRGC	Sun-Maid Raisin Growers of California (EA)
SMRI	Society for Magnetic Resonance Imaging (EA)
SMRI	Solution Mining Research Institute (EA)
SMRIS	Soviet Missile Range Instrumented Ship (CINC)
SMRL..........	Stanford Magnetic Resonance Laboratory [Stanford University] [Research center] (RCD)
SMRL..........	Submarine Medical Research Laboratory
SMRLA	Southern Maryland Regional Library Resource Center [Library network]
SMRLH	Soldier's Mail, Rush Like Hell [On correspondence]
SMRM	Solar Maximum Repair Mission [NASA] (NASA)
SMR/MIS	Supply, Maintenance and Readiness Management Information System [Logistics Management Information System] [Military] (AABC)
SMRP	Society for Medieval and Renaissance Philosophy (EA)
SMRP	Strategic Mobilization Requirements and Program (MCD)
SMRP	Surface Mining and Reclamation Program (COE)
SMRR	Submucous Resection and Rhinoplasty [Medicine] (MAE)
SMRR	Supplier Material Review Record (MCD)
SMRRF	Strategic Metals Recovery Research Facility [University of Arizona] (RCD)
SMRS	Specialized Mobile Radio System
SMRS	Specific Mobilization Reserve Stock [Military] (AFIT)
SM/RSF	Ammunition Stores Management and Remote Set Fuzing (MCD)
SMRSF	Special Moment Resisting Space Frame (COE)
SMRT	Scheduled Maintenance Replacement Time
SMRT	Single Message Rate Timing
SMRT	Stein Mart [NASDAQ symbol] (TTSB)
SMRT	Stein Mart, Inc. [NASDAQ symbol] (SAG)
SMRTB	Ship and Marine Requirements Technology Board [British] (ODBW)
Smrtflx........	Smartflex Systems [Associated Press] (SAG)
SmrtFn........	Smart & Final, Inc. [Associated Press] (SAG)
SmrtSr	SmartServ Online, Inc. [Associated Press] (SAG)
SmrtSrv	SmartServ Online, Inc. [Associated Press] (SAG)
SMRU	Sea Mammal Research Unit [British] (ARC)
SMRV	South Middlesex Rifle Volunteers [British military] (DMA)
SMRV	Squirrel Monkey Retravirus
SMRVS	Small Modular Recovery Vehicle System [Nuclear energy]
SMRY	Seminary
SMRY	Summary (FAAC)
SMS............	Marine Service Squadron
SMS............	Safety Management System [NHTSA] (TAG)
SMS............	Safety Manual Supplement
SMS............	Saint Marie [Madagascar] [Airport symbol] (OAG)
SMS............	Saint Mary's Seminary [Connecticut; Missouri; Ohio; Vermont]
SMS............	Sales Motivation Survey [Test]
SMS............	Sa Majeste Suedoise [His, or Her, Swedish Majesty] [French] (ROG)
SMS............	Samos [Greece] [Seismograph station code, US Geological Survey Closed] (SEIS)
SMS............	Sample Management System [Laboratory science]
SMS............	Satellite Motion Simulator
SMS............	Satellite Multiservice System (NITA)
SMS............	Scandinavian Migraine Society (EA)
SMS............	Scheuthauer-Marie-Sainton [Syndrome] [Medicine] (DB)
SMS............	School of Mathematical Sciences (EERA)
SMS............	Scientific Microsystems Inc. (NITA)
SMS............	Scientific Mission Support
SMS............	Screen Management System [Computer technology]
SMS............	Security Management System [Computer science]
SMS............	Semiconductor-Metal-Semiconductor
SMS............	Senior Medical Student (DAVI)
SMS............	Sensor Monitoring Set (MCD)
SMS............	Separation Mechanism Subsystem [NASA] (NASA)
sms............	Separation Mechanism Subsystem [NASA] (NAKS)
SMS............	Sequence Milestone System
SMS............	Serial Motor Seizures [Medicine]
SMS............	Service Management System [Telecommunications]
SMS............	Service Manipulator System (SSD)
SMS............	Service Module Simulator (IAA)
SMS............	Servicios Aerolineas Mexicanas SA de CV [Mexico ICAO designator] (FAAC)
SMS............	Shared Mass Storage
SMS............	Sheet-Metal Screw (DAC)
SMS............	Ship Motion Simulator
SMS............	Ship's Missile System (MCD)
SMS............	Shoreline Modeling System [US Army Corps of Engineers]
SMS............	Short Message Service
SMS............	Shuttle Mission Simulator [NASA] (NASA)
sms............	Shuttle Mission Simulator [NASA] (NAKS)
SMS............	Signal Messenger Service (NATG)
SMS............	Signal Missile Support [Air Force] (MUGU)
SMS............	Silane to Molten Silane [Photovoltaic energy systems]
SMS............	Silico-Manganese Steel
SMS............	Simulation Modeling System [FAA] (TAG)
SMS............	Sinatra Music Society (EAIO)
SMS............	Single Molecule Spectroscopy
SMS............	Skandinavisk Migraeneselskab [Scandinavian Migraine Society] (EAIO)
SMS............	Small Magnetospheric Satellite [NASA]
SMS............	Small Mass Store (IAA)
SMS............	Smithsonian Institution's Marine Station
SMS............	Snowy Mountains Scheme [Australia]
SMS............	Socioeconomic Monitoring Survey (DAVI)
sms............	Solar Maximum Satellite [NASA] (NAKS)
SMS............	Solar Maximum Satellite [NASA] (MCD)
SMS............	Sonics & Materials, Inc. [AMEX symbol] (SAG)
SMS............	Spanish Market Selection [Cigars]
SMS............	Spares Management System
SMS............	Special Mint Set [Numismatics]
SMS............	Spectronics Micro Sytems [Computer science]
SMS............	Spin Motor Supply
SMS............	SPRINT [Solid-Propellant Rocket Intercept] Missile Subsystem [Army]
SMS............	Standard Material Specification (MCD)
SMS............	Standard Meteorological Station (SAA)
SMS............	Standard Modular System
SMS............	Standard Molecular System
SMS............	State Medical Society (MAE)
SMS............	Stationary Meteorological Satellite [NASA]
SMS............	Status Monitor Software
SMS............	Stiff-Man Syndrome [Medicine]
SMS............	Storage Management Service [Telecommunications] (PCM)
SMS............	Storage Management System (IAA)
SMS............	Stores Management Sea [Navy]
SMS............	Stores Management System (MCD)
SMS............	Strategic Management Society [British]
SMS............	Strategic Missile Squadron [Air Force]
SMS............	Structures and Mechanical System [Skylab] [NASA]
SMS............	Student Monitoring System [Vocational guidance]
SMS............	Styrene Methylstyrene [Organic chemistry]
SMS............	Subject Matter Specialist
SMS............	Success Management System
SMS............	Sucrose Monostearate (WDAA)
SMS............	Sumter, SC [Location identifier FAA] (FAAL)
SMS............	Surface Missile Ship (MUGU)
SMS............	Surface Missile System [NASA]
SMS............	Surface-Water Modeling System
SMS............	SURTASS Measurement System [Navy] (CAAL)
SMS............	Suspended Maneuvering System [McDonnell Douglas Corp.] (MCD)
SMS............	Switching and Maintenance Set

SMS............ Synchronous Altitude Meteorological Satellite (IAA)
SMS............ Synchronous Meteorological Satellite [NASA]
sms............ Synchronous Meteorological Satellite (NAKS)
SMS............ Synoptic Meteorological Sounding
SMS............ Syro-Mesopotamian Studies [Malibu, CA] [A publication] (BJA)
SMS............ System Measurement Software (IAA)
SMS............ System Migration Section [Social Security Administration]
SMS............ Systems Maintenance Service (MCD)
SMS............ Systems Management Server [Microsoft Corp.] (PCM)
SMS/360PPE... Software Management System/360 Problem Program Efficiency
SMSA.......... Seaman Apprentice, Signalman, Striker [Navy rating]
SMSA.......... Selected Metropolitan Statistical Area [FHWA] (TAG)
SMSA.......... Shop Missile Assembly and Maintenance
SMSA.......... Signal Missile Support Agency [Air Force] (AAG)
SMSA.......... Standard Metropolitan Statistical Area [Later, MSA] [Census Bureau]
SMSA.......... Super-Cooled Infrared Multispectral Survey and Analysis [Traces
                  mineral deposits]
SMSAE........ Surface Missile System Availability Evaluation [NASA] (KSC)
SMSanE....... Master of Science in Sanitary Engineering
SMSB.......... Strategic Missile Support Base [Air Force] (AFM)
SMSC.......... Service Module Sequence Controller [NASA]
SMSC.......... Southeastern Missouri State College
SMSC.......... Standard Microsystems [NASDAQ symbol] (TTSB)
SMSC.......... Standard Microsystems Corp. [NASDAQ symbol] (NQ)
SMSC.......... Standard Modular System Card [Computer science] (BUR)
SMSC.......... State Manpower Service Council [Department of Labor]
SMSC.......... Sum of Magnitudes of Sum [Channel Matrix] Correlator
SMSCC....... Shuttle Mission Simulator Computer Complex [NASA] (MCD)
SMSD.......... Ship Magnetic Submarine Detector
SMSF.......... Special Maintenance Support Facility (MCD)
SMSF.......... Special Mission Support Force [Navy] (DOMA)
SMSG .... School Management Study Group (EA)
SMSG .... School Mathematics Study Group (IIA)
SMSG .... Self-Mutilators Support Group (EA)
SMSG .... Survivability Management Steering Group [DoD]
SMSGT .... Senior Master Sergeant
SMSH .... Sisters of Sainte Marthe [of St. Hyacinthe] [Roman Catholic religious
                  order]
SMSI.......... Sipaliwini [Surinam] [ICAO location identifier] (ICLI)
SMSI.......... Smith Micro Software [NASDAQ symbol] (TTSB)
SMSI.......... Smith Micro Software, Inc. [NASDAQ symbol] (SAG)
SMSI.......... Standard Manned Space Flight Initiator [Later, NSI-I] [NASA] (NASA)
SMSI.......... State Microscopical Society of Illinois (EA)
SMSI.......... Strong Metal-Support Interaction [Catalysis]
SMSIP .... Space Mission Survivability Implementation Plan
SMSIP .... Surface Missile Ship Improvement Program (MCD)
SMSJ.......... Scott's Monthly Stamp Journal [A publication]
SMSLP........ Smithsonian Marine Station at Link Port
SMSM.......... Kwamalasoemoetoe [Surinam] [ICAO location identifier] (ICLI)
SMSM.......... Marist Missionary Sisters (TOCD)
SMSM.......... Missionary Sisters of the Society of Mary - Marist Missionary
                  Sisters (EA)
SMSM.......... Soeurs Missionnaires de la Societe de Marie [Missionary Sisters of
                  the Society of Mary] (EAIO)
SMSMS....... Strategic Missile Squadron Munitions Section [Air Force] (AAG)
SMSN .... Seaman, Signalman, Striker [Navy rating]
SMSO .... Subcontract Material Sales Order
SMSP........ Security Military Space Program (MUGU)
SMSP........ Soil Moisture Strength Prediction [Army]
SMSP.......... St. Peter's Abbey and College, Muenster, Saskatchewan [Library
                  symbol National Library of Canada] (NLC)
SMSq.......... Strategic Missile Squadron [Air Force]
SMSR .... Society of Master Shoe Repairers [British] (DBA)
SMSRL .... Sarah Mellon Scaife Radiation Laboratory [University of Pittsburgh]
                  (MCD)
SMSRS .... Shipboard Meteorological Satellite Readout Station
SMSS.......... School of Management and Strategic Studies [Founded 1982 by
                  Richard Farson, offers a two-year management program through
                  GTE Telenet]
SMSS.......... Strategic Mission Support Study [DoD]
SMSS.......... Sum of Magnitudes of Sum [Channel Matrix] Skin
SMST.......... Stoelmanseiland [Surinam] [ICAO location identifier] (ICLI)
Sm Stat Law... Smith's Statute Law [A publication] (DLA)
SMSTR .... Signal Master (IAA)
SMSTRS .... Seamstress (WGA)
SMSU .... Southwest Missouri State University (PDAA)
SMSV.......... San Miguel Sea Lion Virus
SMT............. Professional Society for Sales and Marketing Training (NTPA)
SMT............. Sacred Marriage Texts (BJA)
SMT............. Sample Mix Table [Musical instrument digital interface]
SMT............. Samuel Manu-Tech, Inc. [Toronto Stock Exchange symbol]
SMT............. Satellite Media Tour [Journalism] (WDMC)
SMT............. Saturn Missile Test [NASA]
SMT............. S-Band Megawatt Transmit
SMT............. Scheduled Maintenance Time [Automotive engineering]
SMT............. Segmented Mirror Telescope [Astronomy]
SMT............. Selective Message Transaction (NASA)
SMT............. Self-Managed Team
SMT............. Senior Management Team (AIE)
SMT............. Senior Medical Technician
SMT............. Service Module Technician [NASA] (KSC)
SMT............. Sexual Medicine Today [A publication]
SMT............. Shelter Management Training [Civil Defense]
SMT............. Shipboard Marriage Test
SMT............. Ship Maintenance Test

SMT............. Ship Mean Time (IAA)
SMT............. Ship's Mean Time [Navigation]
SMT............. Shop Mechanic's Test
SMT............. Small Missile Telecamera
SMT............. SMT Health Services [Associated Press] (SAG)
SMT............. Snider Match Test (DB)
SMT............. Snow Monitoring Tire [Automotive engineering]
SMT............. Societe de Micro-informatique et de Telecommunications (NITA)
SMT............. Society of Metropolitan Treasurers [British]
SMT............. South Dakota School of Mines and Technology, Rapid City, SD
                  [OCLC symbol] (OCLC)
SMT............. Spontaneous Mammary Tumor [Medicine] (DB)
SMT............. Square Mesh Tracking [Air Force]
SMT............. Stabilized March Technique
SMT............. Standard Mean Time (CIST)
SMT............. Standard Measurement Technique [Navy]
SMT............. Station Management
SMT............. Steiner Minimum Tree [Mathematics] (BARN)
SMT............. Storage Management Task [Computer science] (CIST)
SMT............. Student Medical Technologist (MEDA)
SMT............. Subject Matter Trainer (SAA)
SMT............. Sultan-Mazar [Former USSR Seismograph station code, US
                  Geological Survey Closed] (SEIS)
SMT............. Summit (MCD)
SMT............. Summit Properties [NYSE symbol] (TTSB)
SMT............. Summit Properties, Inc. [NYSE symbol] (SAG)
SMT............. Supermedial Thigh [Flap for plastic surgery]
SMT............. Supplementary Monophonic Transmission (ADA)
SMT............. Supply, Maintenance, and Transportation [Directorate] [Army] (RDA)
SMT............. Surface Missile Test [Navy] (CAAL)
SMT............. Surface Mounted Technology (NITA)
SMT............. Surface-Mount Technology [Electronics]
SMT............. System Maintenance Test
SMT............. System Maintenance Trainer (MCD)
SMT............. System Master Tape (IAA)
SMT............. System Modulation Transfer [Acutance] [Photography]
SMT............. Systems Management Team (CIST)
SMT............. Systems Manufacturing Technology [San Marcos, CA]
SMTA.......... Scottish Motor Trade Association (DBA)
SMTA.......... Sewing Machine Trade Association (EA)
SMTA.......... Surface Mount Technology Association (EA)
SMTA.......... Tabiki [Surinam] [ICAO location identifier] (ICLI)
SMTAS........ Shuttle Model Test and Analysis System [NASA] (NASA)
SMTB.......... Tafelberg/Rudi Kappel [Surinam] [ICAO location identifier] (ICLI)
SmtBc........ Smithkline Beecham Ltd. [Associated Press] (SAG)
SmtBGA....... Summit Bank Corp. (GA) [Associated Press] (SAG)
SmtBIn........ Smith Barney Intermediate Quality Municipal Fund [Associated
                  Press] (SAG)
SmtBrnM....... Smith Barney Municipal Fund [Associated Press] (SAG)
SmtBTX....... Summit Bancshares Texas [Associated Press] (SAG)
SMTC.......... Sa Majeste Tres Chretienne [His, or Her, Most Christian Majesty]
                  [French]
SMTC.......... Semtech Corp. [NASDAQ symbol] (SAG)
SMTD.......... Short Take-Off and Landing and Maneuvering Technology
                  Demonstrator [Air Force]
SMTE .... Segment Map Table Entry (IAA)
SMTE .... Society for Music Teacher Education (EA)
SMTES........ Small Firms Technical Enquiry Service [British]
SMTF.......... Sa Majeste Tres Fidele [His, or Her, Most Faithful Majesty] [French]
SMTF.......... Spacecraft Magnetic Test Facility [Goddard Space Flight Center]
                  [NASA]
SMTF.......... Spectrum Management Task Force [Electromagnetic spectrum
                  regulation] (NTCM)
SmtFD......... Smith's Food & Drug Centers, Inc. [Associated Press] (SAG)
SMTG.......... Solid-State and Molecular Theory Group [MIT] (MCD)
SMTG.......... Somatogen, Inc. [NASDAQ symbol] (SPSG)
Smth.......... Smith [A.O.] Corp. [Associated Press] (SAG)
SMTH.......... Smith Environmental Tech [NASDAQ symbol] (TTSB)
SMTH.......... Smith Environmental Technologies Corp. [NASDAQ symbol] (SAG)
SMTH.......... Smooth [NWS] (FAAC)
SmthAO....... Smith [A.O.] Corp. [Associated Press] (SAG)
SmthAOA....... Smith AO Corp. [Associated Press] (SAG)
SmthBc........ SmithKline Beecham Ltd. [Associated Press] (SAG)
SmthF......... Smithfield Foods, Inc. [Associated Press] (SAG)
Smthfld........ Smithfield Co., Inc. [Associated Press] (SAG)
SMT Hlt ...... SMT Health Services, Inc. [Associated Press] (SAG)
SMTI.......... Selective Moving Target Indicator (IEEE)
SMTI.......... Sodium Mechanisms Test Installation [Nuclear energy] (NRCH)
SMTI.......... Southeastern Massachusetts Technological Institute [Later,
                  Southeastern Massachusetts University]
SMTI.......... Tibiti [Surinam] [ICAO location identifier] (ICLI)
SMTK.......... SmarTalk TeleServices, Inc. [NASDAQ symbol] (SAG)
SMTK.......... Sump Tank
SMTL.......... Semitool, Inc. [NASDAQ symbol] (SAG)
SmtMod....... SMART Modular Technologies, Inc. [Associated Press] (SAG)
SMTN.......... Smoky Mountain R. R. [AAR code]
SMTO.......... Senior Mechanical Transport Officer [British military] (DMA)
SMTO.......... St. Maarten Tourist Office (EA)
SMTOE........ Sets My Teeth on Edge
SMTP.......... Simple Mail Transfer Protocol [Computer science] (PCM)
SMTP.......... Tepoe [Surinam] [ICAO location identifier] (ICLI)
SMTR.......... Scheduled Maintenance Time Ratio [Automotive service]
SMTRB........ Ship and Marine Technology Requirements Board [British]
SMTS.......... Simulated Maintenance Training System [Air Force]
SMTS.......... Somanetics Corp. [NASDAQ symbol] (SAG)

SMTS	Southern Manufacturing Technology Show and Conference (ITD)
SMTS	Special Machine Tool Standard (IAA)
SMTS	Strategic Material Transport System (AAEL)
SMTS	Synchronous Meteorological Test Satellite [*NASA*]
SMTSZ	Somanetics Corp. Wrrt'B' [*NASDAQ symbol*] (TTSB)
SMTT	Small Bowel Transit Time [*Gastroenterology*]
SMU	Scottish Mothers' Union [*Episcopalian*]
SMU	Secondary Multiplexing Unit
SMU	Self-Maneuvering Unit [*Air Force*]
SMU	Sheep Mountain, AK [*Location identifier FAA*] (FAAL)
SMU	Simula, Inc. [*AMEX symbol*] (SPSG)
SMU	Single Motor Unit
SMU	Soft Mock-Up [*NASA*] (MCD)
smu	Soft Mockup (NAKS)
SMU	Southeastern Massachusetts University [*North Dartmouth*]
SMU	Southeastern Massachusetts University, North Dartmouth, MA [*OCLC symbol*] (OCLC)
SMU	Southern Methodist University [*Texas*]
SMU	Speaker/Microphone Unit (NAKS)
SMU	Spectrum Monitoring Unit
SMU	Statement Match Unit (IAA)
SMU	St. Mary's University Library [*UTLAS symbol*]
SMU	Store Monitor Unit
SMU	Sunnyside Mine [*Utah*] [*Seismograph station code, US Geological Survey Closed*] (SEIS)
SMU	Super-Module Unit [*Telecommunications*] (TEL)
SMU	System Maintenance Unit [*Computer science*]
SMU	System Monitoring Unit
SMUAP	Simple Motor Unit Action Potential [*Medicine*]
SMUC	Societe de Musique des Universites Canadiennes [*Canadian University Music Society - CUMS*]
SMUD	Sacramento Municipal Utility District [*Photovoltaic energy systems*]
SMUD	Smudge Cell [*hematology*] (DAVI)
SMUD	Standoff Munitions Disrupter System (MCD)
SMUG	Smuggling [*FBI standardized term*]
SMuLV	Scripps Murine Leukemia Virus [*Medicine*] (DB)
SMUN	Soviet Mission to the United Nations (LAIN)
SMUS	Soviet Mission to the United States (WDAA)
S Mus D	Doctor of Sacred Music
SMUSE	Socialist Movement for the United States of Europe
SMUT	Shrink Mock-Up Template (MSA)
SMUT	Special Mission Utility Transport [*Aviation*]
SMV	Samovar Hills, AK [*Location identifier FAA*] (FAAL)
SMV	Samsville [*Illinois*] [*Seismograph station code, US Geological Survey*] (SEIS)
SMV	Santa Maria Valley Railroad Co. [*AAR code*]
SMV	Satellite Mutual Visibility
SMV	Science Museum of Victoria [*State*] (EERA)
SMV	Short Market Value [*Investment term*]
SMV	Sinusoidal Membrane Vesicle [*Anatomy*]
SMV	Skeletal Muscle Ventricle [*Medicine*]
SMV	Slow Moving Vehicle [*Emblem to prevent rear-end collisions*]
SMV	Small Volume (STED)
SMV	Smedvig Asa [*NYSE symbol*] (SAG)
SMV	Soybean Mosaic Virus [*Plant pathology*]
SMV	Special Mobility Vehicle
SM/V	Squared-Mean to Variance
SMV	Submento-Vertex [*View*] [*Radiology*] (DAVI)
SMV	Submentovertical (STED)
SMV	Superior Mesenteric Vein [*Anatomy*]
SMV	Surveying and Mapping Victoria [*Australia*]
SMVH	Service in Military and Veterans Hospitals [*Red Cross*]
SM Vis S	Master of Science in Visual Studies (PGP)
SMVLF	Shipboard Mobile Very Low Frequency [*Navy*] (DNAB)
SMVO	Avanavero [*Surinam*] [*ICAO location identifier*] (ICLI)
SMVP	Shuttle Master Verification Plan [*NASA*] (NASA)
SMVRD	Shuttle Master Verification Requirements Document [*NASA*] (NASA)
SMVT	Sustained Monomorphic Ventricular Tachycardia [*Cardiology*] (DAVI)
SMVU	Survey of Motor Vehicle Use (EERA)
SMW	Second Main Watch
SMW	Sheet Metal Workers' International Association (EA)
SMW	Simpatico Wines [*Vancouver Stock Exchange symbol*]
SMW	Slotted Metal Window
SMW	Smara [*Morocco*] [*Airport symbol*] (OAG)
SMW	Society of Magazine Writers [*Later, ASJA*] (EA)
SMW	Society of Military Widows (EA)
SMW	South Mountain [*Washington*] [*Seismograph station code, US Geological Survey*] (SEIS)
SMW	Standard Materials Worksheet [*NASA*] (NASA)
smw	Standard Materials Worksheet (NAKS)
SMW	Standard Metal Window (WDAA)
SMW	Strategic Missile Wing [*Air Force*]
SMWA	Wageningen [*Surinam*] [*ICAO location identifier*] (ICLI)
Smware	Simware, Inc. [*Associated Press*] (SAG)
SMWBA	Scottish Master Wrights and Builders Association (DBA)
SMWC	Saint Mary-Of-The-Woods College [*Indiana*]
SMWC	Society for the Ministry of Women in the Church [*British*] (BI)
SMWDSEP	Single, Married, Widowed, Divorced, Separated
SMWG	Space Shuttle Structures and Materials Working Group [*NASA*] (PDAA)
SMWG	Strategic Missile Wing [*Air Force*]
SMWG	Synthesis and Modeling Working Group [*Marine science*] (OSRA)
SMWG	System Management Work Group
SMWHT	Somewhat (DNAB)
SMWIA	Sheet Metal Workers' International Association (EA)

SMWO	Society of Mental Welfare Officers [*British*] (BI)
SMWP	Strategic Mobility Work Project [*Army*] (AABC)
SMWS	Scotch Malt Whisky Society (DBA)
SMWS	Washabo [*Surinam*] [*ICAO location identifier*] (ICLI)
SMX	Santa Maria [*California*] [*Airport symbol*] (OAG)
SMX	Santa Maria, CA [*Location identifier FAA*] (FAAL)
SMX	Semi-Micro Xerography
SMX	Server Macro Expansion [*Computer science*]
SMX	Submultiplex (IAA)
SMX	Submultiplexer Unit
SMX	Sulfamethoxazole [*Also, S, SMZ*] [*Antibacterial compound*]
SMXC	Smithway Motor Xpress Corp. [*NASDAQ symbol*] (SAG)
SMY	Marianna, FL [*Location identifier FAA*] (FAAL)
SMY	Scientist-Man Year
SMY	Shemya [*Alaska*] [*Seismograph station code, US Geological Survey*] (SEIS)
SMY	Simenti [*Senegal*] [*Airport symbol*] (OAG)
SMY	Smyrna Public Library, Smyrna, DE [*OCLC symbol*] (OCLC)
Smy	Smythe's Irish Common Pleas Reports [*1839-40*] [*A publication*] (DLA)
SMY	Solar Maximum Year [*August, 1979-February, 1981*]
SMY	Summary (MSA)
Smy & B	Smythe and Bourke's Irish Marriage Cases [*1842*] [*A publication*] (DLA)
Smy Home	Smyth on the Law of Homestead and Exemptions [*A publication*] (DLA)
SMYS	Specified Minimum Yield Strength
Smythe	Smythe's Irish Common Pleas Reports [*1839-40*] [*A publication*] (DLA)
SMZ	Sonmez Airlines [*Turkey*] [*ICAO designator*] (FAAC)
SMZ	Southern Maritime Zone (DNAB)
SMZ	Stoelmanseiland [*Surinam*] [*Airport symbol*] (OAG)
SMZ	Streamside Management Zone [*Forest industry*] (WPI)
SMZ	Sulfamethazine [*Antibacterial*] [*Veterinary medicine*]
SMZ	Sulfamethoxazole [*Also, S, SMX*] [*Antibacterial compound*]
SMZ	Sulphamethoxazole (DB)
SMZO	Paramaribo/Zorg en Hoop [*Surinam*] [*ICAO location identifier*] (ICLI)
SMZTMP	Sulamethoxazole and Trimethoprim [*Antibiotics*] (DAVI)
SMZY	Paramaribo/Zandery [*Surinam*] [*ICAO location identifier*] (ICLI)
sn----	Andean Area [*MARC geographic area code Library of Congress*] (LCCP)
SN	Parke, Davis & Co. [*Research code symbol*]
SN	Sacramento Northern Railway [*AAR code*]
SN	Safety Notice (MCD)
SN	Sample Name
SN	SAN [*Societe Aeronautique Normande*] [*France ICAO aircraft manufacturer identifier*] (ICAO)
Sn	Sanitary
Sn	Santa [*Saint*] [*Italian*]
SN	Santo
SN	Saponification Number [*Analytical chemistry*]
SN	Saturday Night [*A publication*] (BRI)
SN	Saturn Nuclear [*NASA*] (IAA)
SN	School of Nursing (AAMN)
SN	Sciatic Notch (STED)
SN	Scientific Note
SN	Sclerema Neonatorum (STED)
SN	Scrub Nurse (STED)
SN	Seaman [*Navy rating*]
SN	Season
SN	Second Nucleotide (DB)
SN	Secretary of the Navy
SN	Sector Number (MUGU)
SN	Secundum Naturam [*According to Nature*] [*Latin*]
SN	See Note (ROG)
SN	Semiconductor Network (IEEE)
SN	Senegal [*ANSI two-letter standard code*] (CNC)
SN	Senior Navigator [*Air Force*]
SN	Sensorineural (STED)
SN	Sensory Neuron [*Anatomy*] (DAVI)
SN	Sequence Number [*Computer science*] (DDC)
SN	Sergeant Navigator [*British*]
SN	Serial Note (EBF)
SN	Serial Number
SN	Serum Neutralization Test
SN	Service Note (MSA)
SN	Service Number [*Military*]
SN	Session Notes [*Scotland*] [*A publication*] (DLA)
SN	Shalom Network (EA)
SN	Shaping Network (MCD)
Sn	Shingle [*Quality of the bottom*] [*Nautical charts*]
SN	Shipping Note [*Business term*]
S/N	Shipping Number
SN	Side Note
SN	Sigma Nu [*A national fraternity*]
SN	Sign (BUR)
SN	Signal Node
S/N	Signal to Noise Ratio [*Unweighted*] (CMD)
SN	Silicon Nitrate
SN	Sine [*Without*] [*Latin*]
sn	Sine Nomine [*Without Name*] [*Latin*] (WGA)
sn	Sine Numero [*Without Number*] [*Latin*]
SN	Sine of the Amplitude (IEEE)
SN	Single Nephron (STED)
SN	Sinoatrial Node [*Medicine*]

SN..............	Sinus [or Sinoatrial] Nerve [Anatomy] (DAVI)
SN..............	Sinus Node (STED)
SN..............	Siren
sn..............	Small Nuclear
SN..............	Small-Probe Nephelometer [NASA]
SN..............	Smoke Number [Emissions measurement] (EG)
SN..............	Snellen [Test types] [Ophthalmology]
SN..............	Society for Neuroscience (EA)
SN..............	Solid Neutral
S/N..............	Sons of Norway (EA)
SN..............	Soon [Amateur radio shorthand] (WDAA)
SN..............	Sound Negative (IAA)
SN..............	Source Name (NITA)
SN..............	Special Nuclear [Material]
S/N..............	Speech/Noise [Ratio] [Electronics]
SN..............	Spinal Needle (STED)
SN..............	Sponsoring Agency [Online database field identifier]
SN..............	Spontaneous Nystagmus (STED)
SN..............	SSIE Number (NITA)
SN..............	Staff Nurse (MEDA)
SN..............	Standard Nomenclature
Sn..............	Stannum [Tin] [Chemical element]
SN..............	Stationing Flag [Navy British]
SN..............	Statutes of Newfoundland [A publication] (ILCA)
SN..............	Steam Navigation
sn..............	Stereospecifically Numbered [Biochemistry]
SN..............	Sterling Nuclear Plant (NRCH)
SN..............	Sternal Notch [Anatomy] (DAVI)
sn..............	Sthene [Absolute unit of force]
SN..............	Stock Number (MCD)
SN..............	Story of the Nations [A publication]
SN..............	Streptonigrin [Antineoplastic drug] (DAVI)
S-N..............	Stress Number (NASA)
SN..............	Stronnictwo Narodowe [Nationalist Party] [Poland Political party] (PPE)
SN..............	Strouhal Number [Sound]
SN..............	Student Nurse
SN..............	Subject Name (NITA)
SN..............	Sub Nanosecond (IAA)
SN..............	Subnetwork (IAA)
SN..............	Subnormal
SN..............	Substantia Nigra [Brain anatomy]
SN..............	Sudan Embassy News [A publication]
SN..............	Sun Coast Indus [NYSE symbol]
SN..............	Sun Coast Industries [Formerly, Sun Coast Plastics] [NYSE symbol] (SPSG)
SN..............	Sunday Nation [A publication]
SN..............	Supernatant [Chemistry]
SN..............	Supernormal (STED)
SN..............	Supernova
SN..............	Suprasternal Notch [Anatomy]
SN..............	Survey Number
SN..............	Syllable Number [Entomology]
SN..............	Synchronizers [JETDS nomenclature] [Military] (CET)
Sn..............	Tin [Chemical element] (DOG)
SNA..............	Laguna Beach-Santa Ana [California] [Airport symbol] (AD)
SNA..............	Orange County [California] [Airport symbol] (OAG)
SNA..............	Sadr Nizamut Adalat Reports [India] [A publication] (DLA)
SNA..............	Sanae [Antarctica] [Seismograph station code, US Geological Survey] (SEIS)
SNA..............	Santa Ana, CA [Location identifier FAA] (FAAL)
SNA..............	Santana Petroleum [Vancouver Stock Exchange symbol]
SNA..............	Satellite Networking Associates, Inc. [New York, NY] [Telecommunications] (TSSD)
SNA..............	Schlaraffia Nordamerika (EA)
SNA..............	Scottish Netball Association (DBA)
SNA..............	Sella, Nasion, A [Anthropometric landmark]
SNA..............	Senator Aviation Charter GmbH, Koln [Germany] [FAA designator] (FAAC)
S_{Na}..............	Serum Sodium [Organic chemistry] (DAVI)
SNA..............	Shaping Network Assembly (SSD)
SNA..............	Snap-On Tools Corp. [NYSE symbol] (SPSG)
SNA..............	Sodium Naphthalene Acetate (IIA)
SNA..............	Soil Nutrient Availability
SNA..............	Somalia National Alliance
SNA..............	Soviet Naval Aviation
SNA..............	Specimen Not Available [Medicine] (DMAA)
SNA..............	Standard National Account [Economics]
SNA..............	Steel Nail Association [British] (BI)
SNA..............	Stern Air, Inc. [ICAO designator] (FAAC)
SNA..............	Student Naval Aviator
SNA..............	Student Nurses' Association (DAVI)
SNA..............	Suburban Newspapers of America (EA)
SNA..............	Sudan News Agency (BJA)
SNA..............	Surface Navy Association (DOMA)
SNA..............	Surinaams Nieuws Agentschap [Surinam News Agency] (EY)
SNA..............	Syrian News Agency (BJA)
SNA..............	System Numerical Attributes (IAA)
SNA..............	System of National Accounts [United Nations]
SNA..............	Systems Network Architecture [IBM Corp.] [Computer science]
SNAA..............	Syndicat National des Travailleurs de l'Amiante d'Asbestos [Canada]
SNAAQS..............	Secondary National Ambient Air Quality Standards [Environmental Protection Agency] (GFGA)
SNAB..............	Staff Nurse Advisory Board (MEDA)
SNAB..............	Stock Number Action Bulletin

SNA Beng....	Sadr Nizamut Adalat Reports [India] [A publication] (DLA)
SNA Beng (NS)...	Sadr Nizamut Adalat Reports, New Series [1851-59] [Bengal, India] [A publication] (DLA)
SNAC..............	S-Nitroso-N-Acetylcysteine [Biochemistry]
SNAC..............	SONAR Automatic Controller (IAA)
SNACC..............	Society of Neurosurgical Anesthesia and Critical Care (EA)
SNACMA..............	Snack, Nut, and Crisp Manufacturers' Association [British]
SNACP..............	Subnetwork Access Protocol [Telecommunications] (OSI)
SNACS..............	Share News on Automatic Coding Systems [Computer science]
SNACS..............	Single Nuclear Attack Case Study [DoD]
SNACS..............	Stock Number Assignment Control System [Air Force] (AFM)
SNADIGC..............	Sindacato Nazionale Dipendenti Ministero Grazia e Giustizia [National Union of Ministry of Justice Employees] [Italy]
SNADS..............	Systems Network Architecture Distributed Services [Computer science] (CIST)
SNADS..............	Systems Network Architecture Distribution Services [Computer science] (DDC)
SNAE..............	Society of Norwegian American Engineers (IAA)
SNAF..............	Soviet Naval Air Force
SNAFS..............	Systems Network Architecture File Services [Computer science] (CIST)
SNAFU..............	Situation Normal, All Fouled Up [Military slang] [Bowdlerized version]
SNAG..............	Sensitive New-Age Guy
SNAG..............	Society of North American Goldsmiths (EA)
SNagg..............	Serum Normal Agglutinator [Hematology]
SNAI..............	Standard Nomenclature of Athletic Injuries [Medicine] (MAE)
SNAIAS..............	Ship's Navigation and Aircraft Inertial Alignment System [Navy] (NG)
SNAICC..............	Secretariat of National Aboriginal and Islander Child Care [Australia]
SNAKE..............	Stochastic Network Adaptive Kinematics Evaluator
SNAKE..............	Super-Normal Attitude Kinetic Enhancement [Later, Enhanced Fighter Maneuverability] [X-31 experimental aircraft under development by Rockwell International Corp. and Messerschmitt-Boelkow-Blohm GmbH]
SNAL..............	Site Number Assignment List (SAA)
SNA/LEN..............	Systems Network Architecture/Local Entry Networking (NITA)
SNAME..............	Society of Naval Architects and Marine Engineers (EA)
SNaN..............	Signaling Not a Number [Computer programming] (BYTE)
Sn & W Ch...	Snow and Winstanley's Chancery Practice [A publication] (DLA)
SNANSC..............	Society of Neurosurgical Anesthesia and Neurological Supportive Care [Later, SNACC] (EA)
SNAO/CWC...	Sustained Naval Aviation Operations in Chemical, Biological, and Radiological Warfare Conditions [Military]
SNAP..............	Sarawak National Party [Malaysia] [Political party] (PPW)
SNAP..............	Satellite Navigation Alert Plotter (PDAA)
SNAP..............	Satellite Nuclear Auxiliary Power [Military] (CAAL)
SNAP..............	Selective Niobium Anodization Process [Semiconductor technology]
SNAP..............	Senior Naval Aviator Present
SNAP..............	Sensory Nerve Action Potential [Neurophysiology]
SNAP..............	Sharp National Account Program [Sharp Electronics Corp.]
SNAP..............	Sharp Numeric Assembler Program [Sharp Electronics Corp.] (IAA)
SNAP..............	Shelter Neighborhood Action Project
SNAP..............	Shielded Neutron Assay Probe [Nuclear energy] (NRCH)
SNAP..............	Shipboard Nontactical ADP [Automatic Data Processing] Program [Navy] (CAAL)
SNAP..............	Short Notice Annual Practice [Military]
SNAP..............	Significant New Alternatives Policy [Environmental science]
SNAP..............	Significant Noncompliance Action Program [Environmental Protection Agency] (GFGA)
SNAP..............	Simplified Needs Assessment Profile System [Developed by Texas Instruments, Inc.]
SNAP..............	Simplified Numerical Automatic Programmer [Computer science]
SNAP..............	Simulated Network Analysis Program (SAA)
SNAP..............	Single Number Access Plan [Telecommunications] (TEL)
SNAP..............	Six Node Averaging Program [Computer science]
SNAP..............	Small Nuclear Adapted Power Source
SNAP..............	Small Nuclear Auxiliary Power
snap..............	Snapdragon [Horticulture]
SNAP..............	S-Nitroso-N-Acetylpenicilamine [Biochemistry]
SNAP..............	Society of National Association Publications (EA)
SNAP..............	Soluble N-Ethylmaleimide-Sensitive Fusion Attachment Proteins [Biochemistry]
SNAP..............	Soviet Nuclear Artillery Projectile (MCD)
SNAP..............	Space Nuclear Auxiliary Power
SNAP..............	Special Needs Action Programme [Education] (AIE)
SNAP..............	Special Night Answer Position [Telecommunications]
SNAP..............	Specifications for Non-Heat-Set Advertising Printing
SNAP..............	Staffing Needs Assessment Process
SNAP..............	Standard Navy Accounting Procedures
SNAP..............	Standard Network Access Protocol [Computer science]
SNAP..............	Static Nibble Access Path [Computer science]
SNAP..............	Steerable Null Antenna Processor (RDA)
SNAP..............	Stereonet Analysis Program (PDAA)
SNAP..............	Sterile Nitrogen Atmosphere Processing
SNAP..............	Strong No-Trump After Passing [Bridge card games] (BARN)
SNAP..............	Structural Network Analysis Program
SNAP..............	Student Naval Aviation Pilot
SNAP..............	Student Nursing Assistant Program
SNAP..............	Subnetwork Access Point (TNIG)
SNAP..............	Summary of Navy Approved Programs
SNAP..............	Supersonic Nonequilibrium Analysis Program (MCD)
SNAP..............	Survivors of Those Abused by Priests [An association]
SNAP..............	Switching Network Analysis Program [Bell System]
SNAP..............	Synaptic Pharmaceutical [NASDAQ symbol] (TTSB)
SNAP..............	Synaptic Pharmaceutical Corp. [NASDAQ symbol] (SAG)
SNAP..............	Synaptosomal-Associated Protein [Biochemistry]

SNAP .... Systematic National Acquisitions Programme [*Public Archives of Canada*]
SNAP .... System for Nuclear Auxiliary Power (IAA)
SNAP .... System Net Activity Program (NITA)
SNAP .... System Network Activity Program [*Sperry UNIVAC*]
SNAP .... Systems for Nuclear Auxiliary Power
SNAP .... Systems Network Analysis Process [*Computer science*] (AEBS)
SNAP(G) ...... Student Naval Aviation Pilot (Glider)
SnapOn........ Snap-On Tools Corp. [*Associated Press*] (SAG)
SNAPPS........ Short-Term Nuclear Annual Power Production Simulation Model [*Department of Energy*] (GFGA)
SNAPS .... Standard Notes and Parts Selection (TEL)
SNAPS .... State and National Apprenticeship Program Statistics [*Bureau of Apprenticeship and Training*] [*Department of Labor*]
SNAPS .... Switching Node and Processing Sites [*ITT*] (TEL)
SNAPTRAN... Systems for Nuclear Auxiliary Power Transient
SNARC........ Short Nickel Line Accumulating Register Calculator (PDAA)
SNARD........ Special Notification Anticipating Receipt of Direction
SNARE........ Sandia Nuclear Assembly for Reactor Experiments
SNARE........ SNAP [*Soluble NAF Attachment Protein*] Receptor [*Medicine*]
SNARE........ Soluble NSF [*N-Ethylmaleimide-Sensitive Fusion Protein*] Receptors [*Biochemistry*]
SNARK........ Snake-Shark (SAA)
SNARL........ Significant No Adverse Reaction Level [*Environmental science*] (COE)
SNARL........ Suggested No Adverse Response Level [*Environmental science*] (COE)
SNARL........ Suggested No Adverse Risk Levels [*Environmental Protection Agency*]
SNAS .... Student Need Analysis System
SNase.......... Staphylococcal Nuclease [*An enzyme*]
SNASOR ...... Static Nonlinear Analysis of Shells of Revolution [*Computer program*]
SNAT .... Serotonin N-Acetyltransferase [*An enzyme*]
SNATCH...... Systems Network Architecture and Transdata Coupling of Hosts [*IBM Corp.*] (IAA)
SNAU .... Society for North American Union (EA)
SNAV .... Sindacato Nazionale Attrazionisti Viaggianti [*National Union of Traveling Entertainers*] [*Italy*]
SNAX .... Lincoln Snacks [*NASDAQ symbol*] (TTSB)
SNAX .... Lincoln Snacks Co. [*NASDAQ symbol*] (SAG)
SNB .... Lakeland Library Region, North Battleford, Saskatchewan [*Library symbol National Library of Canada*] (NLC)
SNB .... Scalene Node Biopsy [*Medicine*]
SNB .... Sella, Nasion, B [*Anthropometric landmark*]
SNB .... Sierra Nevada Batholith [*Geology*]
SNB .... Silverman Needle Biopsy [*Pathology*] (DAVI)
SNB .... Small Navigation Buoy (DNAB)
SNB .... Snake Bay [*Australia Airport symbol*] (OAG)
SNB .... Southern National [*NYSE symbol*] (TTSB)
SNB .... Southern National Corp. [*NYSE symbol*] (SAG)
SNB .... Soviet News Bureau
SNB .... Spinal Nucleus of the Bulbocavernosus [*Neuroanatomy*]
SNB .... Statutes of New Brunswick [*Database*] [*Department of Justice*] [*Information service or system*] (CRD)
SNB .... Swiss National Bank
SNBA .... Societe Nationale des Beaux-Arts, Paris [*1890*] [*French*] (NGC)
SNBH .... Battleford Union Hospital Memorial Library, North Battleford, Saskatchewan [*Library symbol National Library of Canada*] (BIB)
SNBL .... Sioux City & New Orleans Barge Line [*AAR code*]
SNBNK........ Snowbank [*NWS*] (FAAC)
SNBR .... Snubber [*Mechanical engineering*]
SNBRTU....... Screw, Nut, Bolt, and Rivet Trade Union [*British*]
SNBS .... Slovene National Benefit Society (EA)
SNBS .... Sodium Nitrobenzene Sulfonate [*Organic chemistry*]
SNBU .... Switched Network Backup [*Computer science*] (IBMDP)
SNC .... Air Cargo Carriers, Inc. [*ICAO designator*] (FAAC)
SNC .... , and Chassigny [*Egypt*] [*Pronounced "snick" Classification for a group of meteorites recovered from these sites*] [*French*]
SNC .... Saint Norbert College [*Wisconsin*]
SNC .... San Antonio College, San Antonio, TX [*OCLC symbol*] (OCLC)
SNC .... Sanitary Corps [*Army*]
SNC .... San Nicolas Island [*California*] [*Seismograph station code, US Geological Survey Closed*] (SEIS)
snc.............. Saskatchewan [*MARC country of publication code Library of Congress*] (LCCP)
SNC .... Satellite News Channel [*Cable-television system*] [*Went off the air October, 1983*]
S/NC .... Satisfactory/No Credit [*University grading system*]
SNC .... School of Naval Co-Operation [*Air Force British*]
SNC .... Scottish National Certificate
SNC .... Servo Nozzle Control (MCD)
SNC .... Shawmut National Corp. [*NYSE symbol*] (SPSG)
SNC .... Shipped Not Credited [*Military*] (AFIT)
SNC .... Significant Noncomplier [*Environmental Protection Agency*] (GFGA)
SNC .... Skilled Nursing Care
SNC .... Snyder Communications
SNC .... Snyder Communications, Inc. [*NYSE symbol*] (SAG)
SNC .... Standard Navigation Computer
SNC .... Stored Program Numeric Control [*Computer science*] (IAA)
SNC .... Submarine Net Controller (MCD)
SNC .... Substantia Nigra [*pars*] Compacta [*Brain anatomy*]
SNC .... Sunatco Development Corp. [*Vancouver Stock Exchange symbol*]
SNC .... Supreme National Council [*Cambodia*]
SNC .... Swiss Nonvaleurs Club [*Later, Scripophila Helvetica - SH*] (EAIO)
SNC .... Syndicat National du Cinema [*National Syndicate of Motion Pictures*]

SNCA .... Scottish National Camps Association (DBA)
SNCC .... Selected Non-Communist Countries
SNCC .... Student National Coordinating Committee [*Pronounced "snick"*] (EA)
SNCC .... Student Non-Violent Coordinating Committee (WDAA)
SNCC .... System Network Computer Center [*Louisiana State University*] [*Research center*] (RCD)
SNCCDIPP ... Selected Non-Communist Countries Defense Intelligence Projection for Planning (MCD)
SN cell .... Sequence Number Cell (DDC)
SNCF .... SECOMO [*Software Engineering Cost Model*] Non-COCOMO Factor [*Constructive Cost Model*]
SNCF .... Societe Nationale des Chemins de Fer Francais [*French National Railways*]
SNCFA .... Societe Nationale des Chemins de Fer Algeriens [*Algerian Railways*]
SN-CIE .... Statement of Need - Clothing and Individual Equipment [*Military*]
SNCL .... Serial Number Configuration List (MCD)
SNCL .... Serial Number Conversion List
SNCLAR....... University of Santa Clara School of Law (DLA)
SNCLF .... Societe de Neuro-Chirurgie de Langue Francaise [*Society of French-Speaking Neurosurgeons - SFSN*] (EA)
SNCM .... Second Nicaraguan Campaign Medal
SNCO .... Seaport Navigation Co. [*AAR code*]
SNCO .... Senior Noncommissioned Officer
SNCO .... Staff Noncommissioned Officer [*Military*]
SNCOC........ Senior Noncommissioned Officer Course
SNCP .... Special Navy Control Program (MCD)
SNCR .... Selective Noncatalytic Reduction [*Combustion technology*]
SNCUNESCO... Swedish National Commission for UNESCO (EAIO)
SNCV .... Sensory Nerve Conduction Velocity [*Neurology*] (DAVI)
SND .... San Diego - College [*California*] [*Seismograph station code, US Geological Survey*] (SEIS)
SND .... Sanford, FL [*Location identifier FAA*] (FAAL)
SND .... Sanfred Resources [*Vancouver Stock Exchange symbol*]
SND .... Sap No Defect
snd.............. Sap No Defect [*Wood industry*] (WPI)
SND .... Scottish National Dictionary [*A publication*]
SND .... Scottish National Diploma
SND .... Second Class Passengers [*Shipping*] [*British*]
SND .... Selected Natural Diamond
SND .... Self-Powered Neutron Detector
SND .... Semiconductor Neutron Dosimeter
SND .... Seno [*Laos*] [*Airport symbol*] (AD)
snd.............. Sindhi [*MARC language code Library of Congress*] (LCCP)
SND .... Sinus Node Disease [*Cardiology*] (CPH)
SND .... Sinus [*or Sinoatrial*] Node Dysfunction [*Cardiology*] (DAVI)
SND .... Sisters of Notre Dame [*Roman Catholic religious order*]
SND .... Sisters of Notre Dame de Namur [*Roman Catholic religious order*]
SND .... Society of Newspaper Design (EA)
SND .... Sound (AAG)
SND .... Standardized Normal Distribution
SND .... Standard Normal Distribution [*Mathematics*]
SND .... Static No Delivery
SNDA .... Scottish National Dancing Association [*Australia*]
SNDA .... Scottish National Dictionary Association
SNDA .... Student National Dental Association (EA)
SNDA .... Sunday Newspaper Distibutors' Association (DGA)
SNDC .... Sand Technology Systems International, Inc. [*NASDAQ symbol*] (NQ)
SNDC .... Serbian National Defense Council (EA)
SNDCF .... Sand Technology Sys'A' [*NASDAQ symbol*] (TTSB)
SNDCF .... Subnetwork Dependent Convergence Function [*Telecommunications*] (OSI)
SNDCP......... Subnetwork Dependent Convergence Protocol [*Telecommunications*] (OSI)
SNDdeN....... Sisters of Notre Dame de Namur (TOCD)
SNDG.......... Sending (MSA)
SNDG.......... Sounding (MSA)
SNDK.......... SanDisk Corp. [*NASDAQ symbol*] (SAG)
SNDL.......... Sandale R. R. [*AAR code*]
SNDL.......... Special Navy Distribution List (DOMA)
SNDL.......... Standard Navy Distribution List
SNDL.......... Standard Nomenclature List [*Military*]
SNDLF .... Societe de Nutrition et de Dietetique de Langue Francaise [*French-Language Society of Nutrition and Dietetics - FLSND*] [*France*] (EAIO)
sndlwd........ Sandalwood (VRA)
SNDM.......... Secretary of Navy Decision Memorandum
SND-MB....... Selected Natural Diamond - Metal Bond
SNDN.......... Sisters of Notre Dame de Namur [*Roman Catholic religious order Rome, Italy*] (EAIO)
SNDO.......... Standard Nomenclature of Diseases and Operations [*Medicine*]
SNDP.......... Sustainable National Domestic Product (EERA)
SNDPLG....... Sandwich Plug (IAA)
SNDPRF....... Soundproof (MSA)
SNDRY........ Sundry
SNDS .... [*The*] Sands Regent [*Reno, NV*] [*NASDAQ symbol*] (NQ)
SNDS .... Stillbirth and Neonatal Death Society [*British*] (EAIO)
SNDS .... Stock Number Data Section (MCD)
SNDS .... Supplementary New Drug Submission [*Medicine*] (DB)
SndSrce....... Sound Source Interactive, Inc. [*Associated Press*] (SAG)
SNDT .... Shreemati Nathibai Domodar Thackersey Women's University [*India*]
SNDT .... Society for Nondestructive Testing [*Later, ASNT*] (KSC)
SNDT .... Sundata Corp. [*NASDAQ symbol*] (SAG)
SNDT .... SunGard Data Systems [*NASDAQ symbol*] (TTSB)
SNDU.......... Somali National Democratic Union

SNDV	Strategic Nuclear Delivery Vehicle [*Army*] (AABC)
SNDWCH	Sandwich
SndySpr	Sandy Spring Bancorp, Inc. [*Associated Press*] (SAG)
SNE	Santa Elena, TX [*Location identifier FAA*] (FAAL)
SNE	Sao Nicolau [*Cape Verde Islands*] [*Airport symbol*] (OAG)
SNE	Servicios Aereos Norte Sur SA de CV [*Mexico ICAO designator*] (FAAC)
SNE	Severe Noise Environment
SNE	Single Nylon Enamelled (IAA)
SNE	Sinus Node Electrogram [*Medicine*] (DMAA)
SNE	Society for Nutrition Education (EA)
SNE	Sony Corp. ADR [*NYSE symbol*] (TTSB)
SNE	Sony Corp. America [*NYSE symbol Toronto Stock Exchange symbol Vancouver Stock Exchange symbol*] (SPSG)
SNE	Spatial Nonemotional (Stimuli)
SNE	Strategic Network Environment (NITA)
SNE	Subacute Necrotizing Encephalomyelopathy [*Medicine*]
SNE	Suppress Normal End (IAA)
SNE	Syndicat National de l'Edition [*French publishers' association*]
SNEA	Student National Education Association (EA)
SNEAC	Southern New England Athletic Conference (PSS)
SNEC	Saxton Nuclear Engineering Corp.
SNEC	Secondary Navy Enlisted Classification (DNAB)
SNEC	Staff Nurse Executive Committee (MEDA)
SNEC	Subgroup on Nuclear Export Coordination [*Nuclear Regulatory Commission*] (GFGA)
SNECI	Sindicato Nacional dos Empregados do Comercio e da Industria da Provincia de Mocambique [*National Union of Commercial and Industrial Workers of Mozambique*]
Sneed	Sneed's Kentucky Decisions [*2 Kentucky*] [*A publication*] (DLA)
Sneed	Sneed's Tennessee Reports [*33-37 Tennessee*] [*A publication*] (DLA)
Sneed Dec.	Sneed's Kentucky Decisions [*2 Kentucky*] [*A publication*] (DLA)
Sneed Tenn	Sneed's Tennessee Reports [*A publication*] (DLA)
Sneed (Tenn) Rep	Sneed's Tennessee Reports [*A publication*] (DLA)
SN(EF)	Seaman (Electronics Field) [*Navy rating*] (DNAB)
SNEF	Skilled Nursing Extended Care Facility (DAVI)
SNEFU	Situation Normal - Everything Fouled Up [*Bowdlerized version Obsolete*] (DSUE)
SNEG	Syndicat National des Enseignants de Guinee [*National Union of Guinean Teachers*]
SNEI	Societe Nouvelle d'Editions pour l'Industrie [*Industrial News Publishing Company*] (IID)
SNEIL	Secretariat for the Nordic Energy Information Libraries (IID)
SNEL	Societe Nationale d'Electricite
SNEL	Special Nuclear Effects Laboratory
Snell Eq	Snell's Principles in Equity [*A publication*] (DLA)
SNELPIF	Sindacato Nazionale Esperti Laureati Propagandisti Industrie Farmaceutiche [*National Union of University Graduated Experts for Propaganda in Pharmaceutical Industries*] [*Italy*]
SNEMSA	Southern New England Marine Sciences Association
SNEP	Saudi Naval Expansion Program (MCD)
SNEP FIT	Saudi Naval Expansion Program, Fleet Introduction Team (DNAB)
SNEP PMT	Saudi Naval Expansion Program, Project Management Team (DNAB)
SNEP PROJMGR	Saudi Naval Expansion Program, Project Manager (DNAB)
SNEP PROJMGRT AFT	Saudi Naval Expansion Program, Project Manager, Technical Assistance Field Team (DNAB)
SNEPT	Space Nuclear Electric Propulsion Test
SNES	Super Ninendo Entertainment System
SNES	Syndicat National de l'Enseignement Secondaire [*National Union of Secondary Schoolteachers*] [*France*]
SNET	Southern New England Telecommunications Corp. [*New Haven, CT*] (TSSD)
SNET	Syndicat National de l'Enseignement Technique [*National Union of Technical School Teachers*] [*France*]
SNETel	Southern New England Telecommunications Corp. [*Associated Press*] (SAG)
SNF	Sampled N-Path Filter (PDAA)
SNF	San Felipe [*Venezuela*] [*Airport symbol*] (AD)
SNF	Secret - No Foreigners [*Security classification*]
SNF	Serb National Federation (EA)
SNF	Short-Range Nuclear Forces
SNF	Sierra Nevada Fault [*Geology*]
SNF	Silicon Nitride Film
SNF	Sinus Node Formation (DB)
SNF	Skilled Nursing Facility
SNF	Solids Not Fat
SNF	Somali National Front [*Political party*] (EY)
SNF	Spain Fund [*NYSE symbol*] (SPSG)
SNF	Spent Nuclear Fuel
SNF	Spot Noise Figure
SNF	Sudanese National Front [*Political party*] (PD)
SNF	System Noise Figure
SNFC	Security National Financial Corp. [*NASDAQ symbol*] (SAG)
SNFCA	Security Natl Finl 'A' [*NASDAQ symbol*] (TTSB)
SNFCC	Shippers National Freight Claim Council [*Later, TCPC*] (EA)
SNFH	Schizophrenia Nonfamily History (STED)
SNFL	Standing Naval Force, Atlantic (MCD)
SNFLD	Secret - Limited Distribution - Not Releasable to Foreigners [*Security classification*]
SNFLK	Snowflake [*NWS*] (FAAC)
SNFO	Student Naval Flight Officer
SNFPP	Syndicat National de la Fonction Publique Provinciale [*National Union of Provincial Government Employees - NUPGE*] [*Canada*]
SNFR	Small-Probe Net Flux Radiometer [*NASA*]

SNFRC	Seattle National Fisheries Research Center [*Seattle, WA*] [*Department of the Interior*] (GRD)
SNFS	Student Naval Flight Surgeon
SNFU	Scottish National Farmers' Union
SNG	San Ignacio De Velasco [*Bolivia*] [*Airport symbol*] (OAG)
SNG	Sans Notre Garantie [*Without Our Guarantee*] [*French Business term*]
SNG	Satellite News Gathering [*Trademark*] (NTCM)
SNG	Scottish Neuroscience Group (DBA)
SNG	Sending [*Electronics*] (ECII)
SNG	Singapore (WDAA)
SNG	Solidified Nitroglycerol [*or Nitroglycerin*] [*Explosive*]
SNG	Songkhla [*Thailand*] [*Seismograph station code, US Geological Survey*] (SEIS)
SNG	Southern New England Telecommunications Corp. [*NYSE symbol*] (SPSG)
SNG	Southern New Eng Telecom [*NYSE symbol*] (TTSB)
SNG	Stabilization Network Group
SNG	Sterling Energy Corp. [*Vancouver Stock Exchange symbol*]
SNG	Substitute [*or Synthetic*] Natural Gas
Sng	Synagogue (BJA)
SNG	Synthetic Natural Gas (IEEE)
SNGA	Sodium N-Glycoloylarsanilic [*or N-Glycolylarsanilic*] Acid [*Pharmacology*]
SNGBF	Single Nephron Glomerular Blood Flow [*Medicine*] (STED)
SNGFR	Single Nephron Glomerular Filtration Rate
sngl	Senegal (VRA)
SNGL	Single
SNGN	Segmental Necrotizing Glomerulonephritis [*Medicine*]
SNGOD	Special NGO [*Nongovernmental Organization*] Committee on Disarmament (EA)
SNGPF	Single Nephron Glomerular Plasma Flow [*Medicine*] (STED)
SNGS	Salem Nuclear Generating Station (NRCH)
SNH	Savannah, TN [*Location identifier FAA*] (FAAL)
SNH	Signtech, Inc. [*Toronto Stock Exchange symbol*]
snh	Sinhalese [*MARC language code Library of Congress*] (LCCP)
SNH	Skilled Nursing Home
SNH	Snatch [*Block*] [*Design engineering*]
SNH	Society for Nursing History [*Defunct*] (EA)
SNH	South Nottinghamshire Hussars [*British military*] (DMA)
SNH	Sunshine Point [*Alaska*] [*Seismograph station code, US Geological Survey*] (SEIS)
SNHA	Shenandoah Natural History Association (EA)
SNHL	Sensorineural Hearing Loss [*Medicine*] (MAE)
SNHY	Sun Hydraulics Corp. [*NASDAQ symbol*] (SAG)
SNI	National Intelligence Service [*Zaire*] (PD)
SNI	San Nicolas Island
SNI	Selective Notification of Information
SNI	Seneca Nation of Indians (DOGT)
SNI	Sequence Number Indicator
SNI	Serial Network Interface (PDAA)
SNI	Signal-to-Noise Improvement [*Data transmission*] (IEEE)
S/N + I	Signal-to-Noise plus Interference Ratio
SNI	Sinoe [*Liberia*] [*Airport symbol*] (OAG)
SNI	Sistema Nacional de Informacion [*National Information System*] [*Colorado*] (IID)
SNI	Societe Nigerienne de Transports Aeriens [*Niger*] [*ICAO designator*] (FAAC)
SNI	Sonor Investments Ltd. [*Toronto Stock Exchange symbol*]
SNI	Soviet Naval Infantry (DOMA)
SNI	Sports Network, Inc. [*Later, HSN*]
SNI	Standard Network Interconnection [*Telecommunications*]
SNI	Subscriber Network Interface [*Computer science*] (CDE)
SNI	Sun City Indus [*AMEX symbol*] (TTSB)
SNI	Sun City Industries, Inc. [*AMEX symbol*] (SPSG)
SNI	Syndicat National des Instituteurs [*National Union of Teachers*] [*France*]
SNIC	Singapore National Institute of Chemistry
SNIC	Sonic Solutions [*NASDAQ symbol*] (SAG)
SNICP	Subnetwork Independent Convergence Protocol [*Telecommunications*] (OSI)
SNIE	Sindacato Nazionale Insegnanti Elementari [*National Union of Elementary Teachers*] [*Italy*]
SNIE's	Special National Intelligence Estimates [*Summaries of foreign policy information and advice prepared for the president*] [*Known informally as "sneeze"*]
SNIF	American Sensors, Inc. [*NASDAQ symbol*] (SAG)
SNIF	Short-Term Note-Issuance Facility [*Banking*]
SNIF	Signal-to-Noise Improvement Factor (IAA)
SNIF	Site-Specific Natural Isotope Fractionation [*Analytical chemistry*]
SNIF	Standard Neutron Irradiation Facility [*Department of Energy*]
SNIF	Standby Note Issuance Facility [*Finance*]
SNIF	Syndicated Note-Issuance Facility [*Banking*] (ADA)
SNIFF	Amer Sensors [*NASDAQ symbol*] (TTSB)
SNIFFEX	Sniffer [*Exhaust trail indicator*] Exercise [*Military*] (NVT)
SNIFTIRS	Subtractively Normalized Interfacial FTIR [*Fourier Transform Infrared*] Spectroscopy
SNIG	Sustainable Non-Inflationary Growth (ODBW)
SNIMOG	Sustained Noninflationary Market-Oriented Growth
SNIOS	Special Needs in the Ordinary School (AIE)
SNIP	Single Net Information and Position [*Reporting procedures*] [*Navy*] (NVT)
SNIP	Single Net Integrated Procedure [*Military*] (CAAL)
SNIPA	Seronegative Inflammatory Polyarthritis [*Medicine*] (DMAA)

SNIPE	SDI [*Strategic Defense Initiative*] Network Interface Processor Engine (SDI)
SNIPE	Simple Network Interacting Program Executive (PDAA)
SNIPE	Soviet Naval Interdiction Possibilities, Europe
SNIPS	Skillshare National Information Processing System [*Australia*]
SNIR	Signal-to-Noise Plus Interference Ratio
SNIRD	Supposedly Noiseless Infrared Detector
SNIT	Stock Number Identification Table
SNIVT	Society of Non-Invasive Vascular Technology (EA)
SNJ	Everett, WA [*Location identifier FAA*] (FAAL)
SNJ	Sinj [*Yugoslavia*] [*Seismograph station code, US Geological Survey Closed*] (SEIS)
SNJ	Switching Network Junction [*Telecommunications*] (OA)
SN(JC)	Seaman (Junior College) [*Navy rating*] (DNAB)
SN(JCE)	Seaman (Junior College Technical Electrician) [*Navy rating*] (DNAB)
SN(JCNE)	Seaman (Junior College Nuclear Field Electronics) [*Navy rating*] (DNAB)
SN(JCNSET)...	Seaman (Junior College Nuclear Submarine Engineering Technician) [*Navy rating*] (DNAB)
SN(JCPE)	Seaman (Junior College Polaris Field Electronics) [*Navy rating*] (DNAB)
SN(JCPL)	Seaman (Junior College Polaris Field Launcher) [*Navy rating*] (DNAB)
SN(JCT)	Seaman (Junior College Technical) [*Navy rating*] (DNAB)
SNJM	Sisters of the Holy Names of Jesus and Mary [*Roman Catholic religious order*]
SNK	Shannock Corp. [*Vancouver Stock Exchange symbol*]
SNK	Snyder [*Texas*] [*Airport symbol*] (AD)
SNK	Snyder, TX [*Location identifier FAA*] (FAAL)
SNK	Soviet Narodnykh Komissarov [*Council of People's Commissars*] [*Former USSR*] (LAIN)
SNK	Student-Newman-Keuls [*Statistical procedure*]
SNK	Survey of Next of Kin [*Department of Health and Human Services*] (GFGA)
SNKE	Golf Technology Holding, Inc. [*NASDAQ symbol*] (SAG)
SNKI	Swank, Inc. [*NASDAQ symbol*] (NQ)
SNKIE	Swank Inc. [*NASDAQ symbol*] (TTSB)
SNKL	Snorkel (MSA)
SNKORL	Subject to No Known or Reported Losses [*Insurance*] (AIA)
SNL	Department of State. Newsletter [*A publication*]
SNL	Sample Noise Level
SNL	Sand Creek [*Guyana*] [*Airport symbol*] (AD)
SNL	Sandia National Laboratories [*Department of Energy*] [*Albuquerque, NM*] (GRD)
SNL	Saturday Night Live [*Television program*]
SNL	Selected Nodes List [*Telecommunications*] (TEL)
SNL	Seminole Resources, Inc. [*Vancouver Stock Exchange symbol*]
SNL	Sevenhill [*Australia Seismograph station code, US Geological Survey Closed*] (SEIS)
SNL	Shawnee, OK [*Location identifier FAA*] (FAAL)
SNL	Snout Length [*Pisciculture*]
SNL	Somali National League
SNL	Soonair Lines, Inc. [*ICAO designator*] (FAAC)
SNL	Spore Newsletter [*A publication*]
SNL	Springfields Nuclear Laboratories [*British*] (NUCP)
SNL	Standard Name Line [*Military*]
SNL	Standard Nomenclature List [*Military*]
SNL	State Narcotic Law
SNL	Stock Not Listed (AAG)
SNLA	Sandia National Laboratory (Albuquerque)
SNLB	Second National Bancorp (EFIS)
SNLC	Senior NATO Logistician Conference (NATG)
SNLC	Service National des Liberations Conditionnelles [*Canada*]
SNL/CA	Sandia National Laboratories/California (GAAI)
SNL/CA	Sandia National Laboratory/California (DOGT)
SNLG	Signaling (MSA)
SNLL	Sandia National Laboratories-Livermore (COE)
SNL/NM	Sandia National Laboratories/New Mexico (GAAI)
SNL/NM	Sandia National Laboratory/New Mexico
SNLR	Services No Longer Required
SNLS	Society for New Language Study (EA)
SNLV	Strategic Nuclear Launch Vehicle
SNM	Saint Mary's University, San Antonio, TX [*OCLC symbol*] (OCLC)
SNM	San Ignacio de Moxos [*Bolivia*] [*Airport symbol*] (AD)
SNM	Satellite Navigation Map
SNM	Senior Naval Member
SNM	Sensitive Nuclear Material (NUCP)
SNM	Signal-to-Noise Merit
SNM	Sinter Metals 'A' [*NYSE symbol*] (TTSB)
SNM	Sinter Metals Co. [*NYSE symbol*] (SAG)
SNM	SNAM SpA [*Italy ICAO designator*] (FAAC)
SNM	Society of Nuclear Medicine (EA)
SNM	Socorro [*New Mexico*] [*Seismograph station code, US Geological Survey*] (SEIS)
SNM	Somali National Movement [*Political party*] (PD)
SNM	Special Nuclear Material
SNM	Spent Nuclear Material (IEEE)
SNM	Square Nautical Mile (NVT)
SNM	Subject Named Member (NVT)
SNM	Sulfanilamide [*Antimicrobial compound*]
SNM	Sunmask Petroleum [*Vancouver Stock Exchange symbol*]
SNM	System Notification Message (COE)
SNMA	Student National Medical Association (EA)
SNMC	Service Provider's Network Management Center

SNMCB	Scheduled Not Mission Capable Both [*Maintenance and supply*] (MCD)
SNMCM	Scheduled Not Mission Capable Maintenance (MCD)
SNMDCS	Standard Navy Maintenance Data Collection System
SNMMMIS ...	Standard Navy Maintenance and Material Management Information System
SNMMMS	Standard Navy Maintenance and Material Management System
SNMP	Simple Network Management Protocol [*Computer science*]
SNMP	Small Network Management Packet (USDC)
SNMP	Spent Nuclear Material Pool (IEEE)
SNMS	Secondary Neutrals Mass Spectrometry
SNMS	Sputtered Neutral Mass Spectrometry [*Surface analysis*]
SNMT	Society of Nuclear Medical Technologists [*Defunct*] (EA)
SNM-TS	Society of Nuclear Medicine - Technology Section (DAVI)
SNMV	Solanum Nodiflorum Mottle Virus [*Plant pathology*]
SNN	Sha Na Na [*An association Defunct*] (EA)
SNN	Shannon [*Ireland*] [*Airport symbol*] (OAG)
SNN	Shared Nearest Neighbor (MCD)
SNN	Sienna Resources Ltd. [*Toronto Stock Exchange symbol*]
SNN	Signal Plus Noise-to-Noise (IAA)
SNN	Sining [*Republic of China*] [*Seismograph station code, US Geological Survey*] (SEIS)
SNN	Smith College, Northampton, MA [*OCLC symbol*] (OCLC)
SNN	Structure-Nomenclature Notation [*Chemistry*]
SNNE	Sustainable Net National Expenditure (EERA)
SNNEB	Scottish Nursery Nurses Examination Board (DI)
SNO	Delta Air Charter Ltd. [*Canada ICAO designator*] (FAAC)
SNO	Scottish National Opera (WDAA)
SNO	Seasonal Net Outgassing [*Oceanography*]
SNO	Semiempirical Natural Orbital [*Physical chemistry*]
SNO	Senior Naval Officer
SNO	Senior Navigation Officer [*Air Force British*]
SNO	Senior Nursing Officer [*British*]
SNO	Serial Number (MDG)
SNO	Special Naval Operations (NVT)
SNO	Stock Number (MSA)
SNO	Sudbury Neutrino Observatory [*Proposed joint US-Canadian project*]
Sno	Thioinosine [*Also, SIno, M*] [*A nucleoside*]
SNOAD	Senior Naval Officer Adriatic [*British*]
SNOB	Senior Naval Officer on Board
S Nob	Sine Nobilitate [*Without Nobility*] [*Notation used at Oxford University to indicate that a student was untitled*] [*Latin*]
SNOBOL	String-Oriented Symbolic Language [*1963*] [*Computer science*]
SNOBS	Sodium Nonanoyloxybenzene Sulfonate [*Detergent formulation*]
SNODO	Standard Nomenclature of Diseases and Operations [*Medicine*] (DHSM)
SNOE	Smart Noise Equipment [*RADAR jammer*] [*Air Force*]
SNOINCR	Snow Depth Increase in Past Hour [*NWS*] (FAAC)
SNOK	Secondary Next of Kin [*Army*] (AABC)
SNOL	Senior Naval Officer, Landings [*British*]
SNOM	Scanning Near-Field Optical Microscope (ECON)
SNOM	Scanning Nearfield Optical Microscopy (AAEL)
SNOM	Scanning Near-Field Optical Microscope
SNOMED	Standardized Nomenclature of Medicine (STED)
SNOMed	Systematized Nomenclature of Medicine
SNOO	Small Nonoverlapping Offset [*Oceanography*]
SNOOP	Students Naturally Opposed to Outrageous Prying [*Student legal action organization*] (EA)
SNOOP	Systematic Nursing Observation of Psychopathology (STED)
SNOOPE	System for Nuclear Observation of Possible Explosives [*Science Applications International Corp.*] [*Aviation*]
SNOOPI	System Network Online Operations Information [*Suggested name for the Library of Congress computer system*]
SNOP	Senior Naval Officer Present
SNOP	Standard Nomenclature of Pathology [*College of American Pathologists*]
SNOP	Systematized Nomenclature of Pathology [*NCI*]
SNOPG	Senior Naval Officer, Persian Gulf [*British military*] (DMA)
SNORE	Self-Noise Reduction
SNORE	Signal-to-Noise Ratio Estimator
SNORKEX	Snorkel Detection Exercise [*Military*] (NVT)
SNORT	Supersonic Naval Ordnance Research Track [*China Lake, CA*]
SNOS	Scottish National Orchestra Society
SNOS	Silicon Nitride Oxide Silicon (IAA)
SNOTEL	Snow Survey Telemetry Network [*Department of Agriculture*]
SNOW	Sled Dogs Co. [*NASDAQ symbol*] (SAG)
Snow	Snow's Reports [*3 Utah*] [*A publication*] (DLA)
SNOW	Standard Normal Ocean Water
SNOWCAT ...	Support of Nuclear Operations with Conventional Air Tactics (NATG)
SNOWFLEX...	Field Exercise under Snow Conditions [*Military*] (NVT)
SNOWI	Senior Naval Officer, West Indies [*British*]
SNOW TIME...	SAC-NORAD [*Strategic Air Command - North American Air Defense*] OperationalWeapons Test Involving Military Electronics
S-N-P	Salt and Pepa [*Rap recording group*]
SNP	Samnordisk Planteforedling [*Internordic plant breeding*] [*An association Sweden*] (EAIO)
SNP	School Nurse Practitioner
SNP	Scottish National Party [*Political party*] (PPW)
SNP	Single Nucleotide Polymorphism [*Genetics*]
SNP	Sinus Node Potential (STED)
SNP	Skagit Nuclear Project (NRCH)
SNP	Slovak National Party [*Former Czechoslovakia*] [*Political party*] (EY)
SNP	Society for Natural Philosophy (EA)
SNP	Sodium Nitroprusside [*A vasodilator*]
SNP	Soluble Nonreactive Phosphorus [*Marine science*]

SNP .... Soluble Nucleoprotein
SNP .... Sonepat [India] [Seismograph station code, US Geological Survey Closed] (SEIS)
SNP .... Space Nuclear Propulsion
SNP .... Statistical Network Processor
SNP .... St. Paul Island [Alaska] [Airport symbol] (OAG)
SNP .... St. Paul Island, AK [Location identifier FAA] (FAAL)
SNP .... Sudanese National Party [Political party] (EY)
SNP .... Suspected, Not Proved
SNP .... Synchronous Network Processor
SNP .... Synchro Null Pulse
SNP .... System Network Processor
SNPA .... Scottish Newspaper Publishers' Association (DBA)
snpa .... Sinopia (VRA)
SNPA .... Southern Newspaper Publishers Association
SNPA .... Subnetwork Point of Attachment [Telecommunications] (OSI)
SNPDL .... Springfields Nuclear Power Development Laboratories [British] (NUCP)
SN(PFE) ...... Seaman (Polaris Field Electronics) [Navy rating] (DNAB)
SN(PFL) ...... Seaman (Polaris Field Launcher) [Navy rating] (DNAB)
SNPJ .... Slovene National Benefit Society (EA)
S-N (Plane)... Sella Turcica-Nasion [Plane that passes through these points] [Cephalometrics]
SNPM .... Standard and Nuclear Propulsion Module
SNPMA .... Student National Podiatric Medical Association (EA)
SNPO .... Society for Nonprofit Organizations (EA)
SNPO .... Space Nuclear Propulsion Office [Later, Division of Space Nuclear Systems, of Energy Research and Development Administration] [AEC-NASA]
SNPOA .... Space Nuclear Propulsion Office, Albuquerque [See SNPO]
SNPOC .... Space Nuclear Propulsion Office, Cleveland [See SNPO]
SNPON .... Space Nuclear Propulsion Office, Nevada [See SNPO]
SNPP .... Sequoyah Nuclear Power Plant (NRCH)
SNPR .... Screen Print (AAG)
SNPRI .... Selected Nonpriority List Item [Military]
SNPRM .... Supplemental Notice of Proposed Rulemaking
SNPS .... Satellite Nuclear Power Station (OA)
SNPS .... Shoreham Nuclear Power Station (NRCH)
SNPS .... Synopsys, Inc. [NASDAQ symbol] (SAG)
SNQ .... Sea-1 Aquafarms Ltd. [Vancouver Stock Exchange symbol]
SNQ .... Shared Enqueue (MHDI)
SNR .... Aero Sonora SA de CV [Mexico ICAO designator] (FAAC)
SNR .... Saint Nazaire [France] [Airport symbol] (OAG)
SNR .... Schaffner Ranch [California] [Seismograph station code, US Geological Survey] (SEIS)
SNR .... Schenectady Naval Reactors Office [Energy Research and Development Administration]
SNR .... Selective Nitrogen Oxide Reduction [Combustion technology]
SNR .... Selective Noncatalytic Reduction [Combustion technology]
SNR .... Senior
Snr .... Senior (ODBW)
SNR .... Senior National Representatives SONAR [Four Power Army] (MCD)
SNR .... Senor [Mister] [Spanish]
SNR .... Service Not Required
SNR .... Signal-to-Noise Ratio
SNR .... Slow Neutron Reactor [Nuclear energy] (NRCH)
SNR .... Society for Nautical Research [British] (EAIO)
SNR .... SONAR
SNR .... Subject to Non-Renewal [Advertising] (DOAD)
SNr .... Substantia Nigra Pars Reticulata [Brain anatomy]
SNR .... Sudan Notes and Records [A publication]
SNR .... Sunair Electronics [AMEX symbol] (TTSB)
SNR .... Sunair Electronics, Inc. [AMEX symbol] (SPSG)
SNR .... Supernova Remnant [Astronomy]
SNR .... Supplier Nonconformance Report [Nuclear energy] (NRCH)
SNRA .... Sawtooth National Recreation Area [Idaho]
SNRA .... Senora [Mrs.] [Spanish]
SNRAFU .... Situation Normal, Really All Fouled Up [Military slang] [Bowdlerized version]
SNRC .... Sudanese National Research Council
SNRCN .... Signal-to-Noise Ratio Due to Channel Noise (IAA)
SNRE .... Small Nuclear Rocket Engine
SNRLTCS .... Skilled Nursing and Related Long Term Care Services (EA)
SNRM .... Set Normal Response Mode [Telecommunications] (OSI)
SNRME .... Set Normal Response Mode Extended [Telecommunications] (OSI)
snRNA .... Ribonucleic Acid, Small Nuclear [Biochemistry, genetics]
snRNP .... Ribonucleoprotein, Small Nuclear [Biochemistry]
snRNP .... Small Nuclear Ribonucleo Protein Particle (HGEN)
SNRO .... Schenectady Naval Reactors Office [Department of Energy] [Schenectady, NY] (GAAI)
SNRS .... Sunrise
SNRT .... Sinus Node Recovery Time [Cardiology]
SNRTA .... Symms National Recreational Trails Act of 1991 (COE)
SNRTC .... Sinus Node Recovery Time Corrected [Cardiology]
SNRTi .... Sinus Node Recovery Time, Indirect Measuring [Medicine] (DMAA)
SNRZ .... Sunrise Assisted Living [NASDAQ symbol] (TTSB)
SNRZ .... Sunrise Assisted Living, Inc. [NASDAQ symbol] (SAG)
SNS .... Salinas [California] [Airport symbol] (AD)
SNS .... Salinas, CA [Location identifier FAA] (FAAL)
SNS .... Samarbeidsnemden for Nordisk Skogforskning [Nordic Forest Research Cooperation Committee - NFRCC] [Finland] (EAIO)
SNS .... San Onofre [California] [Seismograph station code, US Geological Survey] (SEIS)
SNS .... Scandinavian Neurosurgical Society (EA)
SNS .... Seabrook Nuclear Station (NRCH)

SNS .... Selected Numeric Service (NITA)
SNS .... Senior Nursing Sister [Navy British]
SNS .... Sensorstat System [Vancouver Stock Exchange symbol]
SNS .... Service National des Sauveteurs [Canada]
SNS .... Simulated Network Simulations (KSC)
SNS .... Skyline Network Service [Satellite Business Systems] [McLean, VA] [Telecommunications] (TSSD)
SNS .... Slovak National Party [Political party] (ECON)
SNS .... Small Nuclear Stage (KSC)
SNS .... Societe Centrafricaine de Transport Aerien [Central African Republic] [ICAO designator] (FAAC)
SNS .... Society of Neurological Surgeons (EA)
SNS .... Software Notification Service (NITA)
SNS .... Somatic Nervous System
SNS .... Space Navigation System (OA)
SNS .... Space Nuclear System
SNS .... Spallation Neutron Source
SNS .... Special Night Squads [Palestine] (BJA)
SNS .... Stabilized Night Sight
SNS .... Standard National Scale [British] (DET)
SNS .... Sundstrand Corp. [NYSE symbol] (TTSB)
SNS .... Superconductor/Normal Metal/Superconductor [Physics]
SNS .... Switched Network Server [Tylink Corp.]
SNS .... Sympathetic Nervous System [Physiology]
SN/SC .... Stock Number Source Code (MCD)
SNSCNY ...... St. Nicholas Society of the City of New York (EA)
SNSE .... Society of Nuclear Scientists and Engineers [Defunct]
SNSH .... Snow Showers [Meteorology]
SNSHN .... Sunshine
SNSL .... Standard Navy Stock List
SNSL .... Stock Number Sequence Listing (MSA)
SNSM .... Sindacato Nazionale Scuola Media [National Union of Intermediate School Teachers] [Italy]
SNSN .... Standard Navy Stock Number
SNSO .... Space Nuclear Systems Office [AEC/NASA]
SNSO .... Superintending Naval Stores Officer [British military] (DMA)
SNSR .... Control Devices, Inc. [NASDAQ symbol] (SAG)
SNSR .... Sensor (AAG)
SNSRY .... Sensory
SNSS .... School Natural Science Society [British]
SNST .... Sonesta International Hotels Corp. [NASDAQ symbol] (NQ)
SNST .... Special Needs Support Team [Education] (AIE)
SNST .... Sunset
SNSTA .... Sonesta Intl Hotels [NASDAQ symbol] (TTSB)
SNT .... Saint
SNT .... [The] Scrolls and the New Testament [K. Stendahl] [A publication] (BJA)
SNT .... Sealant [Technical drawings]
SNT .... Sears Point [California] [Seismograph station code, US Geological Survey] (SEIS)
SNT .... Secretaria Nacional de Transportes [Brazil] (EY)
SNT .... Selective Nuclear Transfer
SNT .... Serial Number Tracking
SNT .... Sign on Table (IAA)
SNT .... Silicon Needle Transducer
SNT .... Sindacato Nazionale Tabacchine [National Union of Women Tobacco Workers] [Italy]
SNT .... Single Negotiating Text [UN Law of the Sea Conference]
SNT .... Sinuses, Nose, and Throat [Anatomy] (DAVI)
SNT .... Society for Nondestructive Testing [Later, ASNT] (EA)
SNT .... Sonat, Inc. [NYSE symbol] (SPSG)
SNT .... Suncoast Aviation, Inc. [ICAO designator] (FAAC)
SNT .... Synthetic Navigation Trainer
SNT .... System Noise Temperature
SNTA .... Sodium Nitrilotriacetate
SNTC .... Syndicat National des Transporteurs de Cameroun [National Union of Cameroonese Transportation Workers]
SNTC .... Syndicat National des Travailleurs Congolais [National Union of Congolese Workers] [Leopoldville]
SNTC .... Synetic, Inc. [NASDAQ symbol] (NQ)
SNTCC .... Simplified Neutron Transport Computer Code
SNTF .... Special Navy Task Force (MUGU)
SNTFC .... Special Navy Task Force Commander
SNTF(SMS)... Special Navy Task Force for Surface Missile Systems (MUGU)
SNTK .... Senetek Ltd. [NASDAQ symbol] (NQ)
Sntk .... Senetek PLC [Associated Press] (SAG)
SNTKY .... Senetek Plc ADS [NASDAQ symbol] (TTSB)
SNTL .... Superior National Insurance Group, Inc. [NASDAQ symbol] (SAG)
SNTL .... Superior Natl Insurance Grp [NASDAQ symbol] (TTSB)
SntO .... Santander Overseas Bank, Inc. [Associated Press] (SAG)
SNTO .... Sento Technical Innovations Corp. [NASDAQ symbol] (SAG)
SNTO .... Swiss National Tourist Office (EA)
SntOv .... Santander Overseas Bank, Inc. [Associated Press] (SAG)
SNTPC .... Scottish National Town Planning Council (DAS)
SNTR .... Sinter [Metallurgy]
SNTS .... Short-Length, Nonbuoyant Torpedo System
SNTS .... Society for New Testament Study [Exeter, Devonshire, England] (EA)
SNTV .... Sun Television & Appliances [NASDAQ symbol] (SAG)
SNTW .... Senetek Ltd. [NASDAQ symbol] (SAG)
SNTWF .... Senetek Plc Wrrt'A' [NASDAQ symbol] (TTSB)
SNTZ .... Senetek Ltd. [NASDAQ symbol] (SAG)
SNTZD .... Sensitized (MSA)
SNTZF .... Senetek Plc Wrrt'B' [NASDAQ symbol] (TTSB)
SNTZG .... Sensitizing (MSA)

SNU	Santa Clara [Cuba] [Airport symbol] (AD)
SNU	Seoul National University [Korea]
SNu	Sifre on Numbers (BJA)
SNU	SNC Group, Inc. [Toronto Stock Exchange symbol]
SNU	Snunit Aviation [Israel] [ICAO designator] (FAAC)
SNU	Solar Neutrino Unit [Astrophysics]
SNU	Somalia News Update [A publication]
SNU	Somali National Union
SNU	Spiritualists National Union [British] (DBA)
SNU	Street Narcotics Unit [Criminology] (LAIN)
SNUB	Show Nothing Unless Bad
SNUD	Stock Number User Directory [Air Force] (AFM)
SNUJ	Singapore National Union of Journalists
SNUM	Special Nuclear Material
SNUN	Significant New Use Notice [Government emissions regulations]
SNUPPS	Standardized Nuclear Unit Power Plant System [Nuclear reactor combine]
SNUR	Significant New Use Rule [Government emissions regulations]
SNUR	Significant New Use Rules [Environmental Protection Agency]
SNURP	Small Nuclear Ribonucleoprotein Particle [Genetics]
SNUS	SONUS Pharmaceuticals [NASDAQ symbol] (TTSB)
SNUS	Sonus Pharmaceuticals, Inc. [NASDAQ symbol] (SAG)
SNV	Aero Servicio del Norte SA de CV [Mexico ICAO designator] (FAAC)
SNV	Santa Elena [Venezuela] [Airport symbol] (OAG)
SNV	Satellite Newsgathering Vehicle (WDMC)
SNV	Satellite News Vehicle (NTCM)
SNV	Spleen Necrosis Virus
SNV	Suneva Resources [Vancouver Stock Exchange symbol]
SNV	Synovus Financial [NYSE symbol] (TTSB)
SNV	Synovus Financial Corp. [NYSE symbol] (SPSG)
SNV	Systema Nervosum Vegetativo [Obsolete term for the autonomic nervous system] [Medicine]
SNV	Systemic Necrotizing Vasculitis [Medicine] (CPH)
SNVB	Society for Northwestern Vertebrate Biology (EA)
SNVPP	Simulated Night Vertical Pinpoint
SNVT	Short No-Voltage Tester [Ground surveillance RADAR system] (MCD)
SNW	Sandoway [Myanmar] [Airport symbol] (OAG)
SNW	Scottsdale Charter, Inc. [ICAO designator] (FAAC)
S/Nw	Signal-to-Noise, Weighted
SNW	Slow Negative Wave [Medicine] (DMAA)
SNW	Snowwater Resources Ltd. [Vancouver Stock Exchange symbol]
SNW	Strategic Nuclear Weapon
SNWFL	Snowfall [NWS] (FAAC)
SNWS	Shipboard Nuclear Weapon Security [Navy] (CAAL)
SNWT	Steel Non-Watertight [Shipfitting]
SNX	Sun Air Aviation Services [Canada ICAO designator] (FAAC)
SNX	Sunburst Exploration Ltd. [Toronto Stock Exchange symbol]
SNY	Air Sandy, Inc. [Canada ICAO designator] (FAAC)
SNY	Sidney [Nebraska] [Airport symbol] (OAG)
SNY	Snyder Oil Corp. [NYSE symbol] (SPSG)
SNY	Southern New York Railway [AAR code]
SNY	Spanish Navy
SNY	Sunny (MSA)
SNYC	South Nottinghamshire Yeomanry Cavalry [British military] (DMA)
Snyder	Snyder Oil Corp. [Associated Press] (SAG)
SnyderC	Snyder Communications, Inc. [Associated Press] (SAG)
Snyder Mines	Snyder on Mines and Mining [A publication] (DLA)
SnyderOil	Snyder Oil Corp. [Associated Press] (SAG)
Snydr	Snyder Oil Corp. [Associated Press] (SAG)
Sny Not Man	Snyder's Notaries' and Commissioners' Manual [A publication] (DLA)
SNYPO	Sold, Not Yet Paid Out
SNYPrA	Snyder Oil cm Dep Ex Pfd [NYSE symbol] (TTSB)
Sny Rel Corp	Snyder on Religious Corporations [A publication] (DLA)
SNZ	Senzan [Japan] [Seismograph station code, US Geological Survey] (SEIS)
SNZ	Shipping Corp. of New Zealand (CDA) [Toronto Stock Exchange symbol]
SNZO	South Karori [New Zealand] [Seismograph station code, US Geological Survey] (SEIS)
SO	Austrian Air [ICAO designator] (AD)
SO	Austrian Air Services [Austria ICAO designator] (ICDA)
SO	Safety Observer [Environmental science] (COE)
SO	SAI Ambrosini SpA [Italy ICAO aircraft manufacturer identifier] (ICAO)
SO	Sail Only (CINC)
SO	Sales Office (MHDW)
SO	Sales Order
SO	Salpingo-Oophorectomy [Medicine]
SO	Salvis Omissis [Omissions Excepted] [Latin]
SO	Saturdays Only [British railroad term]
SO	Saturn Orbiter [NASA]
SO	Schenectady Operation [Energy Research and Development Administration] (MCD)
SO	Schlatter-Osgood [Disease] [Medicine] (DB)
SO	Scientific Officer [Ministry of Agriculture, Fisheries, and Food] [Also, ScO] [British]
SO	Scottish [Communion] Office [Episcopalian]
SO	Scouting-Observation Plane [When prefixed to Navy aircraft designation]
S(O)	Seaman (Operator) [British military] (DMA)
SO	Second Class Open [Train ticket] (DCTA)
SO	Second Opinion [An association Defunct] (EA)
SO	Secretary's Office [Navy]

SO	Secretary's Order
SO	Section Officer [British military] (DMA)
SO	Secure Operations (MCD)
SO	Security Office
SO	Seder 'Olam (BJA)
SO	Select Order (IAA)
SO	Seller's Option [Stock exchange term]
so	Seller's Option (ODBW)
SO	Sell-Off (AAG)
SO	Send Only
SO	Senior Officer [Military, police]
SO	Sensory Organ [Anatomy]
SO	Serial Output
SO	Serviceability Objective
SO	Service Order
SO	Sex Offender
SO	Sheriff's Office [or Officer] (ROG)
SO	Shift-Out [Computer science] (IAA)
SO	Shift-Out Character [Keyboard] [Computer science]
SO	Shipment [or Shipping] Order
SO	Shipping Order (WGA)
so	Shipping Order (ODBW)
SO	Ships-on-Order Library [Maritime Data Network, Inc.] [Information service or system] (CRD)
SO	Ship's Option
SO	Shop Order
SO	Shot
S-0	Shut-Off (AAG)
S/0	Shutoff (NAKS)
SO	Shutout [Sports]
SO	Signal Officer
SO	Signal Oscillator (OA)
SO	Significant Other [Term for members of unmarried couples]
S/0	Sign Off
SO	Silvered Optics
SO	Sleepout (ADA)
SO	Slope Occurrence
SO	Slow Operate [Relay]
SO	Slow Oxidative [Fibers] [Neuroanatomy]
SO	Small Oocyte
SO	Small Outline (NITA)
SO	Social Studies/Social Science Education [Educational Resources Information Center (ERIC) Clearinghouse] [Indiana University] (PAZ)
SO	Society (ROG)
SO	Socket (IAA)
SO	Sold Out (ADA)
SO	Solicitor's Opinion [Legal term] (DLA)
so	Somalia [MARC country of publication code Library of Congress] (LCCP)
SO	Somalia [ANSI two-letter standard code] (CNC)
SO	SONARman [Navy]
S/0	Son Of [Genealogy]
SO	Sorrel Resources Ltd. [Toronto Stock Exchange symbol]
SO	Sorting Office [British] (ROG)
S/0	Sound Off
SO	Source [Online database field identifier]
SO	South [or Southern]
SO	Southern Airways [ICAO designator]
SO	Southern Co. [NYSE symbol] (SPSG)
SO	Southern Oscillation [Meteorology]
So	Southern Reporter [National Reporter System] [A publication] (DLA)
S/0	South Of [In outdoor advertising] (WDMC)
SO	Special Olympics [Later, SOI] (EA)
SO	Special Operations
SO	Special Orders [Military]
SO	Spheno-Occipital [Synchondrosis] [Medicine]
SO	Spin-Orbital (IAA)
SO	Spiracular Organ [Fish anatomy]
SO	Spring Opening
SO	Staff Office [Marine science] (OSRA)
SO	Staff Officer
SO	Stamp Office [British] (ROG)
SO	Standing Order
SO	State Officer
SO	Stationary Orbit (IAA)
SO	Stationery Office [British]
SO	Station Officer [British police]
SO	Statutes of Ontario [QL Systems Ltd.] [Information service or system] (CRD)
SO	Stay Out [Official leave from Eton College] [British]
SO	Stockage Objectives [Military]
SO	Stock Option [Investment term]
SO	Stock Order (AAG)
SO	Stock Outboard [Powerboat]
SO	Stop Order (MCD)
SO	Stopover [Slang]
SO	Stores Officer [British military] (DMA)
SO	Strategic Outline Chart [Air Force]
SO	Strikeouts [Baseball]
SO	Submarine Oscillator (DEN)
SO	Suboffice
S/0	Substance Of
SO	Substitution Oscillator (IAA)
SO	Superior Oblique [Muscle] [Anatomy]

SO...............	Superior Old [*Spirits*]
SO...............	Supply Officer
SO...............	Support Operations
SO...............	Supraoptic [*Nucleus*] [*Ophtalmology*] (DAVI)
SO...............	Surface Operations [*Navy*] (CAAL)
SO...............	Surveillance Officer
SO...............	Switching Oscilloscope
SO...............	Switchover
SO...............	Symbolic Output [*Computer science*]
SO...............	Sympathetic Ophthalmia [*Medicine*]
SO...............	Symphony Orchestra
SO...............	System Override (AAG)
SO...............	Systems Orientation
SO1.............	SONARman First Class [*Navy*]
SO$_2$.............	Arterial Oxygen Saturation [*Medicine*] (DAVI)
SO2.............	SONARman Second Class [*Navy*]
SO$_2$.............	Sulfur Dioxide [*Organic chemistry*] (DAVI)
SO2.............	Sulfur Dioxide
So 2d...........	Southern Reporter, Second Series [*West*] [*A publication*] (AAGC)
SO3.............	SONARman Third Class [*Navy*]
SO4.............	Science on 4 [*Radio program*] [*British*]
SO$_4$.............	Sulfate (GNE)
SOA.............	Aupraorbita Artery [*Anatomy*] (DAVI)
SOA.............	Safe Operating Area (IEEE)
SOA.............	Sales Order Authority (AAG)
SOA.............	Scandinavian Orthopaedic Association (EA)
SOA.............	School of the Air [*Army*] (TSSD)
SOA.............	Secondary Organic Aerosol [*Atmospheric science*]
SOA.............	Self-Optimizing and Adaptive
SOA.............	Senate Operating Agency (MCD)
SOA.............	Separate Operating Agency [*Air Force*] (AFM)
SOA.............	Serial Output Adapter
SOA.............	Shelby Owners of America (EA)
SOA.............	Ship Operating Automation
SOA.............	Shipyard Overhaul Availability
SOA.............	Shuttle Orbital Application [*NASA*]
SOA.............	Skoda Air [*Czechoslovakia*] [*ICAO designator*] (FAAC)
SOA.............	Smithsonian Office of Anthropology
SOA.............	Society of Actuaries (EA)
SOA.............	Society of Authors [*British*] (EAIO)
SOA.............	Soc Trang [*South Vietnam*] [*Airport symbol*] (AD)
SOA.............	Sonora, TX [*Location identifier FAA*] (FAAL)
SOA.............	Sorata Development, Inc. [*Vancouver Stock Exchange symbol*]
SOA.............	Soundness of Approach (MCD)
SOA.............	Source of Assignment (MCD)
SOA.............	Southern Africa Fund [*NYSE symbol*] (SAG)
SOA.............	Southern Airways (MCD)
SOA.............	Specially-Oriented Advertisements [*Consumer Protection Packet - US Post Office*]
SOA.............	Special Olympics Australia
SOA.............	Special Open Allotment [*Military*] (AABC)
SOA.............	Special Operating Agency [*Military*] (AABC)
SOA.............	Special Operations Aircraft
SOA.............	Speed of Advance [*Military*]
SOA.............	Speed of Approach
SOA.............	Spirit of Adventure (EA)
SOA.............	Staff Officer, Administration [*British military*] (DMA)
SOA.............	Standardbred Owners Association (EA)
SOA.............	Start of Address
SOA.............	Statement of Assurance
SOA.............	Statements of Attainment [*British*] (DET)
SOA.............	State Oceanic Administration [*China*] [*Marine science*] (OSRA)
SOA.............	State of Alert
SOA.............	State of the Art
SOA.............	Stimulus Onset Asynchrony [*Psychology*]
SOA.............	Student Orientation Assistant
SOA.............	Superoxide Anion [*Chemistry*]
SOA.............	Supplement on Aging [*to the 1984 National Health Interview Survey*] [*Department of Health and Human Services*] (GFGA)
SOA.............	Supraorbital Artery Test [*Neurological evaluation*] (CPH)
SOA.............	Swelling of Ankles [*Medicine*] (DMAA)
SOA.............	Switch Off Assembly (MCD)
SOAA..........	Signed Out Against Advice [*Medicine*]
SOAA..........	Staff Officers Association of America (EA)
SOAC..........	State-of-the-Art Car [*Transit*] [*Department of Transportation*]
SOAC..........	Submarine Officer Advanced Course [*Navy*] (DNAB)
SOACMS.....	Special Operations Aviation Combat Mission Simulator [*Military*]
SOAD..........	Spectrometric Oil Analysis Device
SOAD..........	Staff Officer, Air Defence [*British military*] (DMA)
SoAF..........	Soviet Air Force
SOAF..........	Sultanate of Oman Air Force
So Afr.........	South Africa
So Afr LT....	South African Law Times [*A publication*] (DLA)
So Afr Prize Cas...	South African Prize Cases (Juta) [*A publication*] (DLA)
SOAI...........	Service des Organisations Aeronautiques Internationales [*France*]
SOAL..........	Search Optical Augmentation LASER (MCD)
SOALM.......	Scanned Optically Addressed Light Modulators (IAA)
SOA-MCA.....	Superficial Occipital Artery to Middle Cerebral Artery [*Medicine*] (MAE)
SOAMUS......	Study of One-Atmosphere Manned Underwater Structures
SO & S........	Scouting, Observation, and Sniping [*British military*] (DMA)
SOAP..........	Sarnia Olefins and Aromatics Project [*Canadian ethylene project*]
SOAP..........	Self-Optimizing Automatic Pilot
SOAP..........	Shaft Optimum Alignment Procedure (DNAB)
SOAP..........	Ship Overhaul Assistance Program (MCD)

SOAP..........	Silicate-Oxy-Apatite (PDAA)
SOAP..........	Simplify Obscure ALGOL [*Algorithmic Language*] Programs (MCD)
SOAP..........	Society for Obstetric Anesthesia and Perinatology (EA)
SOAP..........	Society of Airway Pioneers (EA)
SOAP..........	Society of Office Automation Professionals [*Later, AMS*] [*Telecommunications service Willow Grove, PA*] (TSSD)
SOAP..........	Spectrochemical [*or Spectrographic, Spectrometric, or Spectroscopic*] Oil Analysis Program [*Air Force*]
SOAP..........	Standing Order Advance Payment
SOAP..........	Students Opposed to Advertised Pollutants [*Student legal action organization*]
SOAP..........	Subjective, Objective, Assessment, and Plan [*Medicine*]
SOAP..........	Submarine Overhaul Allowance Parts [*Navy*] (DNAB)
SOAP..........	Sunflower Seed Oil Assistance Program [*Department of Agriculture*]
SOAP..........	Supply Operations Assistance Program [*Military*]
SOAP..........	Symbolic Optimum Assembly Programming [*IBM Corp.*] [*Computer science*]
SOAP..........	Symptoms, Observations, Assessment, Plan
SOAP..........	Systems Operational Analysis Plan
SOAPD........	Southern Air Procurement District
SOAPIE.......	Subjective, Objective, Assessment, Plan, Implementation, and Evaluation [*Medicine*] (DMAA)
SOAPS........	Suction, Oxygen, Apparatus, Pharmaceuticals, Saline [*Mnemonic device for anesthetists*] (AAMN)
soapst........	Soapstone (VRA)
SOAR..........	Safe Operating Area
SOAR..........	Satellite Ocean Analysis for Recruitment [*Marine science*] (OSRA)
SOAR..........	Save Our American Resources [*Boy Scout project*]
SOAR..........	Seminars on Aeroanxiety Relief
SOAR..........	Shuttle Orbital Applications and Requirements [*NASA*]
SOAR..........	Simulation of Airlift Resources [*Air Force*]
SOAR..........	Simulation of Apollo Reliability [*NASA*] (KSC)
SOAR..........	Smalltalk on a RISC (NITA)
SOAR..........	Special Operations Aviation Regiment [*Military*]
SOAR..........	Staff Organization and Regulation
SOAR..........	State-of-the-Art Report [*Navy*]
SOAR..........	State Operator and Result [*Computer program*]
SOAR..........	Stress on Analytical Reasoning
SOAR..........	Support Our Aging Religious, Inc.
SOARS........	Satellite On-Board Attack Reporting System (MCD)
SOARS........	Second Order Attitude Reference Set (MCD)
SOARS........	Shuttle Operations Automated Reporting System [*NASA*] (NASA)
SOAS..........	School of Oriental and African Studies [*University of London*]
SOAS..........	Special Operations ADP [*Automatic Data Processing*] System (DOMA)
SOASC(I)....	Senior Officer Assault Ships and Craft (India) [*British*]
SOase.........	Sulfite Oxidase [*An enzyme*]
SOATS........	Support Operations Automated Training System [*NASA*] (NASA)
SOAV..........	Solenoid-Operated Air Valve (IAA)
Sob.............	De Sobrietate [*of Philo*] (BJA)
SOB.............	Second Overtone Band
SOB.............	See Order Blank [*Laboratory science*] (DAVI)
SOB.............	Senate Office Building
SOB.............	Service Observance Bureau [*A telephone-monitoring section of the Bell System*]
SOB.............	Sexually Oriented Business (PA)
SOB.............	Shipped on Board a Specified Vessel (DS)
SOB.............	Shortness of Breath [*Cardiology*]
SOB.............	Silly Old Bugger [*Officer over the age of 39*] [*British*] (DSUE)
SOB.............	Sobral [*Brazil*] [*Airport symbol*] (AD)
SOB.............	Society of Bookmen (DGA)
SOB.............	Son of a Bitch
SOB.............	Souls on Board (BARN)
SOB.............	Soviet Order of Battle (DOMA)
SOB.............	Space Orbital Bomber (AAG)
SOB.............	Special Obligation Bond (FBF)
SOB.............	Start of Block
SOB.............	Sub-Occipito Bregma [*Medicine*] (ROG)
SOB.............	Sudost-Bahn [*Swiss Southeastern Railway*]
SOB.............	Sulfur Oxidizing Bacteria
SOB.............	Superior Official Bureaucrat [*Satirical bureaucracy term*]
SOBA..........	605th Ordnance Battalion Association (EA)
SOBA..........	System of Operational Buoys in the North Atlantic [*Marine science*] (OSRA)
SOBASSPIFTAGE...	Society of Beer and Sordid Sex Professional Invitational Fishing Tournament and Gastronomical Extravaganza
SOBC..........	Save Our Barns Committee (EA)
SOBC..........	Submarine Officer Basic Course [*Navy*] (DOMA)
SOBECOV....	Societe de Stockage et de Commercialisation des Produits Vivriers [*Development organization*] [*Burundi*] (EY)
SOBELAIR....	Societe Belge de Transports Pan Air [*Airline*] [*Belgium*]
SOBEP........	Scale of Beliefs in Extraordinary Phenomena [*Research test*] [*Psychology*]
SOBI...........	Sobieski Bancorp [*NASDAQ symbol*] (TTSB)
SOBI...........	Sobieski Bancorp, Inc. [*NASDAQ symbol*] (SAG)
Sobieski......	Sobieski Bancorp, Inc. [*Associated Press*] (SAG)
SOBIGM......	Sign Off Brother, I've Got Mine [*Remark used by seamen who avoided risky assignments during World War II*] [*Also used as hoax by National Maritime Union for name of organization issuing pamphlet about low state of merchant marine service*]
SOBLIN........	Self-Organizing Binary Logical Network [*OTS*]
SOBND........	Southbound (WGA)
SOBP...........	Sentral Organisasi Buruh Pantjasila [*Central Organization of Pantjasila Labor*] [*Indonesia*]
SOBP...........	Society of Biological Psychiatry (NTPA)

SOBS	Scanning Ocean Bottom SONAR
SOBS	Society for Office-Based Surgery [*Later, ASOS*] (EA)
SOB's	Sons of Bosses International [*Later, NFBC*] [*An association*] (EA)
SOB's	South of Broad Street [*Reference is to residents of the historic and aristocratic section of Charleston, South Carolina*]
SOBU	Student Organization for Black Unity
SOC	Chief SONARman [*Navy rating Obsolete*]
SOC	Saint Olaf College [*Northfield, MN*]
SOC	Satellite Operations Center [*Cape Kennedy*]
SOC	Satellite Operations Complex
SOC	Satellite Orbit Control
SOC	Save Our Constitution [*An association*] (EA)
SOC	Scene of Crime
SOC	Schedule of Compliance [*Environmental science*] (COE)
SOC	Schedule of Organizational Change [*Air Force*] (AFM)
SOC	Scottish Ornithologists' Club [*British*]
SOC	Sector Operations Center [*Air Force*]
SOC	Security on Campus [*An association*] (EA)
SOCAC	Sedimentary Organic Carbon [*Marine science*]
SOC	Self-Organized Criticality [*Physics*]
SOC	Self-Organizing Control
SOC	Separated Orbit Cyclotron (IEEE)
SOC	Sequence of Controls
SOC	Sequential Oral Contraceptive (HGAA)
SOC	Service and Overhaul Change (MSA)
SOC	Servicemen's Opportunity College [*DoD*]
SOC	Set Overrides Clear (IEEE)
SOC	Severity of Ozone Cracking (PDAA)
SOC	Sexual Over-Seriousness [*Attitude disorder*]
SOC	Shop Order Control
SOC	Signal Officer (IAA)
SOC	Silicon on Ceramic [*Technique for producing solar cells*]
SOC	Simulated Operational Computer (KSC)
SOC	Simulation Operation Computer (IAA)
soc	Simulation Operation Computer (NAKS)
soc	Simulation Operations Center [*NASA*] (NAKS)
SOC	Simulation Operations Center [*NASA*] (KSC)
SOC	Singer Owners Club (EA)
SOC	Single Orbit Computation
SOC	Sochi [*Former USSR Seismograph station code, US Geological Survey*] (SEIS)
SOC	Social
Soc	Social (PHSD)
Soc	Socialist (ODBW)
SOC	Socialist (EY)
SOC	Socialist Objectives Committee [*Australian Labor Party*]
SOC	Society
Soc	Society [*A publication*] (BRI)
SOC	Society of Cinematologists [*Later, SCS*] (EA)
SOC	Sociology
Soc	Sociology (DD)
SOC	Socket (AAG)
SOC	Socrates [*Greek philosopher, 470-399BC*] (ROG)
SOC	Soil Organic Carbon
SOC	Solo [*Indonesia*] [*Airport symbol*] (OAG)
SOC	Somerset County College, Somerville, NJ [*OCLC symbol*] (OCLC)
SOC	Southampton Oceanography Centre [*British*]
So C	South Carolina Reports [*A publication*] (DLA)
SOC	Southern Oregon College
SOC	Spacecraft-Orientation-Control [*NASA*] (IAA)
SOC	Space Operations Center
SOC	Space Operations Controller
SOC	Specialised Oceanographic Centre (EERA)
SOC	Specialized Oceanographic Center [*National Oceanic and Atmospheric Administration*] (MSC)
SOC	Special Operations Capability [*Marine Corps*] (DOMA)
SOC	Special Operations Capable [*Military*] (MUSM)
SOC	Special Operations Command [*Military*] (AABC)
SOC	Specific Optimal Control
SOC	Spin-Orbit Coupling [*Physical chemistry*]
SOC	Spouse Observation Checklist
SOC	Squadron Operations Center [*Air Force*]
SOC	Standard Occupational Classifications (OICC)
SOCD	Standard Oil Co.
SOC	Standards of Official Conduct [*A publication*] (DLA)
SOC	Standing Order Confirmation [*Publishing*]
SOC	Standing Orders Committee [*British*] (DCTA)
SOC	Start of Climb [*Aviation*] (DA)
SOC	Start of Construction [*Military*] (AFIT)
SOC	Start of Conversion [*Navy*]
SOC	Start-of-Cycle [*Engineering*]
SOC	Statement of Capability (MCD)
SOC	Statement of Charges
SOC	Statement of Conditions
SOC	State of Charge
SoC	State of Consciousness
SOC	State-Operated Contracts
SOC	State-Owned Corporation
SOC	Statewide Operations Center
SOC	Station Operations Console (MCD)
SOC	Strike Operations Coordinator [*Navy*] (NVT)
SOC	Strike Options Comparison (MCD)
SOC	Struck off Charge [*British military*] (DMA)
SOC's	Sunbeam Corp. [*NYSE symbol*] (SAG)
SOC	Superposition of Configuration [*Atomic physics*]

SOC	Supply Overhaul Coordinator (MCD)
SOC	Support Operations Center
SOC	Suspended Organic Carbon [*Chemistry*]
SOC	Synthetic Organic Chemical
SOC	Syphilitic Osteochondritis [*Medicine*] (DB)
SOC	System on Chip (AAEL)
SOC	System Operational Complex
SOC	System Operational Concept
SOC	System Operations Control [*Canadian Airlines International*]
SOC	System Option Controller [*NASA*] (NASA)
soc	System Option Controller (NAKS)
SOC	Systems Operation Center
SOCA	Cayenne/Rochambeau [*French Guiana*] [*ICAO location identifier*] (ICLI)
SOCA	Soul and Calypso [*Music*]
SOCA	Staff Officer for Civil Affairs [*British World War II*]
SOCA	Submariners Old Comrades Association (WDAA)
SOCABU	Societe du Caoutchouc Butyl [*France*]
SOCAC	Southern California Athletic Conference (PSS)
SOCACHA ...	South Carolina Automated Clearing House Association (TBD)
Soc Action & L...	Social Action and the Law [*A publication*] (DLA)
SOCAD	Serviceman's Opportunity for College Associate Degree [*Military*] (MCD)
SOCAL	Southern California [*Military*] (NVT)
SOCAL	Standard Oil Co. of California
So Cal C Optometry...	Southern California College of Optometry (GAGS)
So Calif Tax Inst...	University of Southern California School of Law Tax Institute (DLA)
SOCALSEC...	Southern California Sector, Western Sea Frontier
Soc Alt	Social Alternatives [*A publication*]
SOCAN	Society of Composers, Authors and Music Publishers of Canada [*Canada*] (WWLA)
SOCAP	Society of Consumer Affairs Professionals in Business [*Alexandria, VA*] (EA)
SOCAR	Shuttle Operational Capability Assessment Report [*NASA*] (MCD)
So Car	South Carolina Reports [*A publication*] (DLA)
SOCAR	Statement of Condition and Recommendation [*Military*] (AABC)
SOCAR	Systems Operational Compatibility Assessment Review [*NASA*]
So Car BA Rep...	South Carolina Bar Association Reports [*A publication*] (DLA)
So Car Const...	South Carolina Constitutional Reports (Treadway, Mill, or Harper) [*A publication*] (DLA)
So Car LJ ...	South Carolina Law Journal [*Columbia*] [*A publication*] (DLA)
So Car R	South Carolina Law Reports [*A publication*] (DLA)
So Car St U...	South Carolina State University (GAGS)
SOCAS	Subcommittee on Chemical Abstracts Service [*American Chemical Society*]
SOCAT	Student Occupational Competency Achievement Testing [*Educational test*]
SOCATOUR...	Societe Camerounaise de Tourisme (EY)
SOCATS	Scenario Oriented Corps Area Training System (MCD)
SOCB	Shop Order Control Board
SOCBRO	Society of Chief Building Regulation Officers [*British*] (DBA)
SOCC	Salvage Operational Control Center [*On submarine rescue ship during salvage operation*]
SOCC	Satellite Oceanic Control Center
SOCC	Satellite Operations Control Center [*NASA*] (NASA)
socc	Satellite Operations Control Center [*NASA*] (NAKS)
SOCC	Sector Operations Control Center [*NORAD*] (FAAC)
SOCC	Self-Orthogonal Convolutional Code (PDAA)
SOCC	South Coast Conference (PSS)
SOCC	Spacecraft Operations Control Center
SOCC	Special Opportunities Counties and Cities Program [*Tennessee Valley Authority*]
SOCC	Submarine Operations Control Center [*Navy*] (CAAL)
SOCC	Subordinate Operations Control Center
SOCCE	Special Operations Command and Control Element
SOCCENT	Special Operations Command, Central Command [*Military*]
SOCCER	SMART's Own Concordance Constructor, Extremely Rapid [*Cornell University*] [*Computer science*]
SoCCS	Study of Cataloguing Computer Software (AIE)
SOCCS	Study of Computer Cataloguing Software (NITA)
SOCCS	Summary of Component Control Status [*Nuclear energy*] (NRCH)
SOCCT	Special Operations Combat Control Team (DOMA)
SOCD	Source Control Document (MCD)
SOCD	Source Control Drawing
SOCDS	Source Codes (MCD)
SOCE	Staff Officer Construction Engineering
Soc Econ Wetgeving...	Social Economisch Wetgeving. Tijdschrift voor Europees en Economisch Recht [*A publication*] (DLA)
SOCELEX	Society Against Elephant Exploitation (EA)
SOCEUR	Special Operations Command, Europe [*Military*] (DOMA)
SOCEX	Southern Ocean Cloud Experiment (EERA)
SOCEX	Special Operations Capable Exercise (DOMA)
SOCF	Spacecraft Operations and Checkout Facility (AAG)
SocGen	Societe Generale [*France*] [*Banking*]
SOCGPA	Seed, Oil, Cake, and General Produce Association [*British*] (BI)
SOCH	Spacelab Orbiter Common Hardware [*NASA*] (MCD)
SOCHINAFOR...	South China Force [*World War II*]
SOCIAL SCISEARCH...	Social Science Citation Index Search [*Database*]
SOCIM	Society of Connoisseurs in Murder (EA)
Socin Sen ...	Marianus Socinus, the Elder [*Deceased, 1467*] [*Authority cited in pre-1607 legal work*] (DSA)
SOCIOL	Sociology
Socio R	Sociological Review [*A publication*] (BRI)
Soc Is	Society Islands (BARN)

Soc Isl........ Society Islands
SOCist......... Cistercian Monks of the Strict Observance (TOCD)
socist.......... Cistercian Monks of the Strict Observance (TOCD)
SO Cist........ Sacer Ordo Cisterciensis [Order of Cistercians] [Roman Catholic men's religious order]
Socket........ Socket Communications, Inc. [Associated Press] (SAG)
SocketC....... Socket Communications, Inc. [Associated Press] (SAG)
SOCL........... Social
Soc Lab Bull... Social and Labour Bulletin [A publication] (ILCA)
Soc Labour Bull... Social and Labour Bulletin [A publication]
SOCLGY...... Sociology
SOCM........ Master Chief SONARman [Navy rating]
SOCM........ Standoff Cluster Munitions
SOCMA....... Scottish Operative Coach Makers' Association [A union]
SOCMA....... Second Order Coherent Multiple Access (PDAA)
SOCMA....... Synthetic Organic Chemical Manufacturers Association (EA)
SOCMAC..... Socially-Oriented Comprehensive Memory-Assist Computer (IIA)
SOCMC....... Special Order of the Commandant of the Marine Corps
Soc Mean Leg Con... Social Meaning of Legal Concepts [A publication] (ILCA)
SOCMI......... Synthetic Organic Chemical Manufacturing Industry [Environmental Protection Agency]
SOCN.......... Source Control Number
SOCO.......... Scenes-of-the-Crime Officer [Scotland Yard]
SOCO.......... Snyder Oil Corp. (EFIS)
SOCO.......... Source Code (NITA)
SOCO.......... Standard Oil Co. of California
SOCO.......... Standards of Conduct Office (AAGC)
SOCO.......... Switched out for Checkout [NASA] (KSC)
SOCOCO..... Symposium of Software for Computer Control (MHDI)
SOCOM....... Society and Commerce Publications
SOCOM....... Solar Communications
SOCOM....... Solar Optical Communications System (IAA)
SOCOM....... Solar-Orbital Communications (IAA)
SOCOM....... Southern Command (MCD)
SOCOM....... Special Operations Command [Military]
SOCON........ Southern Conference (PSS)
So Conn St U... Southern Connecticut State University (GAGS)
SOCONY...... Standard Oil Co. of New York [Socony Mobil is now official name of firm]
SOCOORD.... Special Operations Coordination [DoD]
So C Optometry... Southern College of Optometry (GAGS)
SOCORICO... Society of Costa Rica Collectors (EA)
SOCP.......... Satellite Orbit Control Program (IAA)
SOCPAC...... Special Operations Center, Pacific Command (CINC)
SOCPO......... Society of Chief Personnel Officers [British]
SOCQ.......... Stages of Concern Questionnaire [Educational test]
SocQuim...... Sociedad Quimica [Associated Press] (SAG)
SOCR.......... Scan-Optics [NASDAQ symbol] (TTSB)
SOCR.......... Scan-Optics, Inc. [NASDAQ symbol] (NQ)
SOCR.......... Special Operational Contract Requirements (AAG)
SOCR.......... Sustained Operations Control (IAA)
SOCR.......... Sustained Operations Control Room [NASA] (KSC)
SOCR.......... Synchronous Orbit Communication Relay (MCD)
SOCRATES... Service Order, Customer Records, and Terminal Entry System
SOCRATES... Simulation of Closure and Rendezvous Approach Techniques for Early Spacecraft (IAA)
SOCRATES... Simulator or Creative Reasoning Applied to Education Systems (IAA)
SOCRATES... Special Operations Command Research, Analysis, and Threat Evaluation System (DOMA)
SOCRATES... Strategy for Organisations Concerned in Rural Advanced Telecommunications Experiments [Computer science] (TELE)
SOCRATES... System for Organizing Content to Review and Teach Educational Subjects
SOCRATES... System for Organizing Current Reports to Aid Technologists and Scientists (NITA)
SOCRATES... System for Organizing Current Reports to Aid Technology and Science
SOCRATES... System of Cellular Radio for Traffic Efficiency and Safety [FHWA] (TAG)
SOCRED...... Social Credit Party [British]
SOCREDO.... Societe pour le Credit et le Developpement en Oceanie [Commercial bank] [French Polynesia] (EY)
SOC ROS..... Societas Rosicruciana [Freemasonry]
SOCS.......... Satellite Operations Control System
SOCS.......... School of Corresponding Studies [Military] (INF)
SOCS.......... Senior Chief SONARman [Navy rating]
SOCS.......... Ship Operational Characteristics Study (DOMA)
SOCS.......... Society of County Secretaries [British] (DBA)
SOCS.......... Spacecraft-Orientation-Control System
SOCS.......... Space Operation Command System [NASA] (IAA)
SOCS.......... Subsystem Operating and Checkout System [NASA] (MCD)
socs.......... Subsystem Operation and Checkout System (NAKS)
SOCS.......... Suppressor of Cytokine Signalling [Genetics]
SOCS.......... Survey of Clerical Skills (AEBS)
SocSc......... Social Science (DD)
SocSciComR... Social Science Computer Review [A publication] (BRI)
SOCSE........ Special Operations Communications Elements [Military] (GFGA)
SocSec........ Social Security (DAVI)
Soc Sec J..... Social Security Journal [A publication]
Soc Sec Q ... Social Security Quarterly [A publication]
Soc Ser R.... Social Service Review [A publication] (BRI)
Soc Services Rev... Social Services Review [A publication]
S-OCT.......... Serum Ornithine Carbamyltransferase [Medicine] (DMAA)
SOCTAP....... Sulfur Oxide Control Technology Assessment Panel [Federal interagency committee]

Soc W.......... Social Work [A publication] (BRI)
SOCY.......... Society (ROG)
SOCY.......... Sociology (ROG)
SOD........... Secretary of Defense [DoD] (VNW)
SOD........... Sediment Oxygen Demand [of water bodies]
SOD........... Seller's Option to Double [Stock exchange term]
SOD........... Sell-Off Date (AAG)
SOD........... Septo-Optic Dysplasia [Medicine] (DMAA)
SOD........... Serial Output Data [Computer science]
SOD........... Shorter Oxford Dictionary [A publication]
SOD........... Shuttle Operational Data (MCD)
SOD........... Silicon on Diamond (AAEL)
SOD........... Small Object Detector
SOD........... Small Oriented Diode (IAA)
SOD........... Societas Docta [An association] (EA)
SOD........... Society of Dismas (EA)
SOD........... Sodalite [A zeolite]
SOD........... Sodankyla [Finland] [Seismograph station code, US Geological Survey] (SEIS)
SOD........... Sodium (DHSM)
SOD........... Sodomy [FBI standardized term]
SOD........... Soldier Orientation and Development (MCD)
SOD........... Solitron Devices (EFIS)
SOD........... Sons of the Desert (EA)
SOD........... Sound-on-Disk (DEN)
SOD........... Space Operation Directorate (SSD)
SOD........... Special Operations Detachment [Military] (AABC)
SOD........... Special Operations Division [Office of Preparedness, General Services Administration]
SOD........... Special Order Discharge
SOD........... Spin-on-Dielectric (AAEL)
SOD........... Staff Operations Division [NASA] (MCD)
SOD........... Start-Over Dad
SOD........... Statute of Distribution [Legal shorthand] (LWAP)
SOD........... Student Organization Development (EDAC)
SOD........... Sudden-Dosage Onset [Pharmacology] (DAVI)
SOD........... Sum-of-the-Years Digit [Statistics] (IAA)
SOD........... Superintendent of Documents [US Government Printing Office]
SOD........... Superoxide Dismutase [Also, SODI] [An enzyme]
SOD........... Surface-Oriented Diode (IAA)
SOD........... Surgical Officer of the Day (DAVI)
SOD........... Surgical Operations Database [Medicine]
SOD........... Sustained Operational Date (AFM)
SOD........... Systems Operational Description [or Design]
SODA.......... Salmonella Outbreak Detection Algorithm [Medicine]
SODA.......... Source Oriented Data Acquisition
SODA.......... Sportsplex Owners and Directors of America
SODA.......... Stamp Out Drug Addiction
SODA.......... System Optimization and Design Algorithm (HGAA)
SODAC........ Source Data Collection
sod acid phos... Sodium Acid Phosphatase [or Sodium Biphosphate] [Pharmacology] (DAVI)
Sodak.......... Sodak Gaming, Inc. [Associated Press] (SAG)
So Dak B Jo... South Dakota Bar Journal [A publication] (DLA)
So Dak Sch M&T... South Dakota School of Mines and Technology (GAGS)
So Dak St U... South Dakota State University (GAGS)
SODAR........ Sound Detecting and Ranging
SODAS........ Sandia Optical Disk Archival System [Online map database] [Developed by Sandia National Laboratories for the USGS]
SODAS........ Spheroidal Oral Drug Absorption System [Medicine] (DMAA)
SODAS........ Structure-Oriented Description and Simulation (IEEE)
SODAS........ Synoptic Oceanographic Data Acquisition System [Marine science] (MSC)
SODB.......... Science Organization Development Board [National Academy of Sciences]
SODB.......... Shuttle [or Spacecraft] Operational Data Book [NASA]
SODB.......... Sodbury [England]
SODB.......... Start of Data Block (MCD)
sod bicarb ... Sodium Bicarbonate [Inorganic chemistry] (MAE)
SODC.......... Siblings of Disabled Children (EA)
SODC.......... Sporting Owner Drivers' Club Ltd. [British] (BI)
SODDS........ Submarine Oceanographic Digital Data System [Navy] (DNAB)
Sodep......... Social Democratic Party [Turkey Political party] (PPW)
SODEPALM... Societe pour le Developpement et l'Exploitation du Palmier a Huile [Ivory Coast]
SODEPAX..... Committee on Society, Development, and Peace [of the Roman Catholic Church and the World Council of Churches] [Defunct] (EA)
SODEX........ Social Data Exchange Association [Council for Community Services] [Information service or system] (IID)
SODF.......... Sperm Outer Defense Fiber [Medicine] (DMAA)
SODH.......... Sorbitol Dehydrogenase (DMAA)
SODI........... Superoxide Dismutase [SOD] [Absorbed by An enzyme]
SO DIMM..... Small Outline Dual-in-Line Memory Module (AAEL)
SODIMM...... Small-Outline Dual In-Line Memory Module [Computer science]
SODIS........ Soluble Ophthalmic Drug Insert (DB)
SODITAL...... Societe de Developpement de l'Industrie Touristique en Algerie (EY)
SODK.......... Sodak Gaming [NASDAQ symbol] (TTSB)
SODK.......... Sodak Gaming, Inc. [NASDAQ symbol] (SAG)
SODPAL...... Social Democrat Party and Liberal [British]
SODRE........ Servicio Oficial de Difusion Radio Electrica [Radio and television network] [Uruguay]
SODRS........ Synchronous Orbit Data Relay Satellite
SODS.......... Saturn Operational Display System [NASA]
SODS.......... Shuttle Operational Data System [NASA] (MCD)

SODS	Skylab Orbit-Deorbit System [*NASA*] (MCD)
SODS	Strategic Offensive Delivery Systems (DOMA)
SODS	Subordinate Operations Data System (NVT)
SODT	Scope Octal Debugging Tape
SODTICIOAP	Special Ordnance Depot Tool Identification, Classification, Inventory, and Obsolescence Analysis Program [*Popularly called "Soda Cap"*]
SODU	Screen Oriented Disk Utility [*Computer science*]
SODW	Simulation Object Domain Working Group
SOE	Senior Officer Escort [*British military*] (DMA)
SOE	Sequence of Events
SOE	Short of Exchange [*Economics*]
SOE	Significant Operating Experience (IEEE)
SOE	Silicon Overlay Epitaxial (IAA)
SOE	Silver Oxide Electrode
SOE	Skylab Operational Environment [*NASA*]
SOE	Slater Orbital Exponents [*Atomic physics*]
SOE	Society of Editors (DGA)
SOE	Souanke [*Congo*] [*Airport symbol*] (OAG)
SOE	Special Operations Executive [*British research unit corresponding to OSS*] [*World War II*]
SOE	Specific Optimal Estimation (PDAA)
SOE	Stage Operations Engineer
SOE	Standard Option Equipment (DOMA)
SOE	Start of Entry [*Computer science*]
SOE	State of Environment [*Australia*]
SOE	State of the Environment (EERA)
SOE	State-Owned Enterprise
SOE	Stationary Operating Engineer (COE)
SOE	Status of Equipment [*Army*] (AABC)
SOE	Stripline Opposed Emitter (IAA)
SOE	Summary of Engagements (MCD)
SOE	Super Orbit Entry
SOEAP	Summary of Effective Allowance Parts List [*Navy*]
SOEAPL	Summary of Effective Allowance Parts List [*Navy*] (DNAB)
SOEASTPAC	Southeast Pacific Command [*Navy*]
So East Rep	Southeastern Reporter [*A publication*] (DLA)
SOEBT	Stationery and Office Equipment Board of Trade (EA)
SOEC	Statistical Office of the European Communities (DCTA)
SOED	Scottish Office Education Department (DET)
SOED	Shorter Oxford English Dictionary [*A publication*]
SOEH	Society for Occupational and Environmental Health (EA)
SoElec	Southern Electronics Corp. [*Associated Press*] (SAG)
SOEMC	Senior Officer Executive Management Course [*Naval War College*]
SOEP	Solar-Oriented Experimental Package [*NASA*]
SOER	Significant Operating Event Report (IEEE)
SOER	State of the Environment Report (EERA)
SOERO	Small Orbiting Earth Resources Observatory (IEEE)
SOES	Small Order Execution System [*Business term*]
SOES	Special Operations Evaluation System (DNAB)
SOES	Station Operations and Engineering Squadron [*Marine Corps*]
SOE/SO	Special Operations Executive, Special Operations [*British World War II*]
SOF	Safety of Flight [*NASA*] (NASA)
SOF	Satisfactory Operation Factor [*Telecommunications*] (TEL)
SOF	Secretary's Open Forum (EA)
SOF	Shortest Operation First
SOF	Signal Officer (IAA)
SOF	Single Oriental Female [*Classified advertising*]
SoF	Society of Floristry [*British*] (DBA)
Sof	Soferim (BJA)
SOF	Sofia [*Bulgaria*] [*Seismograph station code, US Geological Survey*] (SEIS)
SOF	Softnet Systems [*Formerly, Vader Group, Inc.*] [*AMEX symbol*] (SPSG)
SOF	Soldier of Fortune (MUSM)
SOF	Soluble Organic Fraction [*Environmental chemistry*]
SOF	Soluble Organic Fractions
SOF	Sound on Film
SOF	Special Operations Force [*Military*]
SOF	Spillover Factor
SOF	Spreading Ocean Floor
SOF	Start-of-Format Control [*Computer science*]
SOF	Start of Frame
SOF	Status of Forces
SOF	Statute of Fraud [*Legal shorthand*] (LWAP)
SOF	Storage Oscilloscope Fragments
SOF	Strategic Offensive Forces [*Army*] (AABC)
SOF	Sub-Occipito Frontal [*Medicine*] (ROG)
SOF	Superior Orbital Fissure [*Eye anatomy*]
SOF	Supervisor of Flying (MCD)
SOFA	Krause's Furniture [*NASDAQ symbol*] (TTSB)
SOFA	Krauses Furniture, Inc. [*NASDAQ symbol*] (SAG)
S of A	School of Artillery [*British military*] (DMA)
SOFA	Status of Forces Agreement [*International treaty*]
SOFA	Student Overseas Flights for Americans
SOFAA	Society of Fine Art Auctioneers [*British*] (DBA)
Sofamor	Sofamor Danek Group [*Associated Press*] (SAG)
SOFAR	Sound Fixing and Ranging [*Navy underground sound system*]
SOFAR	Sound Fusing and Ranging
SOFAR/BF	Sound Fixing and Ranging/Bomb Fuze [*Navy underground sound system*] (SAA)
SOFAS	Suitable Occupation for a Sloane [*British Slang*]
SOFAS	Survivable Optical Forward Acquisition Sensor
SOFAS	Survivable Optical Forward Acquisition System (MCD)
SOF ATS	Special Operations Force Aircrew Training System [*Military*]
SOFC	Saturn Operational Flight Control [*NASA*]
SOFC	Solid Electrolyte Fuel Cell [*Chemistry*]
SOFC	Solid Oxide Fuel Cell [*Energy source*]
S of C	Statutes of Canada [*A publication*] (DLA)
SOFCS	Self-Organizing Flight Control System
SofD	Sons of David (BJA)
SOFE	Society of Financial Examiners (EA)
SOFEX	Southern Ocean Float Experiment [*Marine science*] (MSC)
S/OFF	Sign Off [*Computer science*] (MDG)
SOFFEX	Swiss Options and Financial Futures Exchange
S of G	School of Gunnery [*British military*] (DMA)
S of I	School of Infantry [*British military*] (DMA)
SOFI	Software Information (IAA)
SOFI	Spray-On Foam Insulation (NASA)
S of I	Superintendent of Instruction [*British military*] (DMA)
SOFI	Supersearch-Online Friendly Interface [*Computer science*]
SOFIA	Stratospheric Observatory for Infrared Astronomy [*NASA*]
SOFIE	Sources de Financement des Entreprises [*CCMC Informatique de Gestion*] [*Database*]
SOFIS	Sophicated Optimized Fuel Injection System
SOFIS	Sophisticated Optimized Fuel Injection System [*Automotive engineering*]
SOFIX	Software Fix [*NASA*]
S-of-L	Ship-of-the-Line
SOFLAM	Special Operations Force LASER Marker [*Military*] (RDA)
S of M	School of Musketry [*Military British*] (ROG)
S of M	Society of Metaphysicians (EA)
SOFNET	Solar Observing and Forecasting Network [*Air Force*]
S of P	Sons of Phoenix [*Freemasonry*] (ROG)
SOFPAC	Special Operating Forces, Pacific [*Military*]
SOFR	State of the Forests Report (EERA)
SOFRES	Societe Francaise d'Enquetes par Sondages [*French opinion-polling organization*]
S of S	Secretary of State
S of S	Secretary of State for Defence [*British*] (RDA)
S of S	Song of Solomon [*Old Testament book*]
S of Sol	Song of Solomon [*Old Testament book*] (ROG)
SOFT	Signature of Fragmented Tanks
SOFT	Simple Output Format Translator (IEEE)
SOFT	Society of Forensic Toxicologists (EA)
SOFT	SofTech, Inc. [*NASDAQ symbol*] (NQ)
SOFT	Software [*Computer science*]
S of T	Sons of Temperance
SOFT	Space Operations and Flight Techniques [*NASA*] (NASA)
SOFT	Special Operational Forces Taiwan (CINC)
SOFT	Status of Forces Treaty
S of T	Superintendent of Transportation
SOFT	Support Organization for Trisomy 18, 13 and Related Disorders (DAZ)
SOFT 18/13	Support Organization for Trisomy 18/13 (EA)
SOFTA	Shippers Oil Field Traffic Association (EA)
SOFTCON	Software Conference [*Trademark*]
Softdesk	Softdesk, Inc. [*Associated Press*] (SAG)
Softech	SofTec, Inc. [*Associated Press*] (SAG)
Softkey	Softkey International, Inc. [*Associated Press*] (SAG)
SOFTMARK	Software Marketing (IAA)
Softnet	Softnet Systems [*Associated Press*] (SAG)
SoftSpc	Software Spectrum, Inc. [*Associated Press*] (SAG)
Software	Software 2000, Inc. [*Associated Press*] (SAG)
SoftwrDv	Software Developers [*Commercial firm Associated Press*] (SAG)
SOFTY	Southern Federation of Temple Youth
SOG	Same Output Gate [*Computer science*] (AAG)
SOG	Satellite Operations Group [*Military*]
SOG	Seat of Government [*Washington, DC*]
SOG	Second-Order Gradient
SOG	Senior Officials Group on Telecommunications (OSI)
SOG	Small Outline Gullwing [*Electronics*] (CDE)
sog	Sogdian [*MARC language code Library of Congress*] (LCCP)
SOG	Sogenannt [*So-Called*] [*German*]
SOG	Sogndal [*Norway*] [*Airport symbol*] (OAG)
SOG	Special Operations Group [*Navy*]
SOG	Speed Made Good Over the Ground (NATG)
SOG	Spin On Glass [*Microlithography*]
SOG	Statement of Guidance
SOG	Straits Oil & Gas [*Vancouver Stock Exchange symbol*]
SOG	Studies and Observations Group [*Military*]
SOG	Supraoesophageal Ganglion [*Invertebrate nuerology*]
SOGA	Spouses of Gays Association (EA)
SOGAT	Society of Graphical and Allied Trades [*British*]
SOGEAC	Societe de Gestion et d'Exploitation de l'Aeroport de Conakry [*Guinea*] (EY)
SOGEKO	Korean-French Banking Corp. [*Acronym is based on foreign phrase*] (EY)
SOGITS	Senior Officials Group on IT [*Information Technologies*] Standardisation [*British*]
SOGp	Special Operations Group [*Air Force*] (AFM)
SOGS	Saudi-Oriented Guide Specifications (NITA)
SOGS	Science Operations Ground System [*Space telescope software*]
SOGWPIP	Silly Old Grandmother with Pictures in Purse
SOH	Skylab Operations Handbook [*NASA*]
SOH	SONARman Harbor Defense [*Navy*] (IAA)
SOH	Southern Ohio Aviation Sales Co. [*ICAO designator*] (FAAC)
SOH	Start of Header [*or Heading*] [*Transmission control character*] [*Computer science*]

SOH	Stichting Oecumenische Hulp aan Kerken en Vluchtelingen [Netherlands]
SOH	Supply Overhaul (MCD)
SOH	Sympathetic Orthostatic Hypotension [Medicine] (DMAA)
SOHAH	Society in Opposition to Human-Animal Hybridization
SOHAM	Southampton [City in England] (ROG)
SOHC	Single Overhead Camshaft [Automotive engineering]
SOHF	Sense of Humor Failure [British Slang]
SOHI	Sponsors of Open Housing Investment [Later, Fund for an Open Society] (EA)
SOHIC	Stress-Oriented Hydrogen-Induced Cracking [Metallurgy]
SOHIO	Standard Oil Co. (Ohio)
SOHN	Society of Otorhinolaryngology and Head/Neck Nurses (EA)
SOHN	Supraoptic Hypothalamic Nucleus [Medicine] (DMAA)
SOHO	Small Office, Home Office (PCM)
SOHO	Solar and Heliospheric Observatory [European Space Agency]
SOHO	Solar Heliospheric Observatory
SoHo	South of Houston Street [See also NoHo, SoSo, TriBeCa] [Artists' colony in New York City]
SOHR	Solar Hydrogen Rocket Engine
SOI	Scientific and Optical Instruments
SOI	Security and Operational Inspection [Army]
SOI	Severity of Illness [Medicine] (DMAA)
SOI	Shoshoni Gold [Vancouver Stock Exchange symbol]
SOI	Signal Operation [or Operating] Instructions
SOI	Silicon-on-Insulator
SOI	Simulating Oriented Language
SOI	SOI Industries, Inc. [AMEX symbol] (SPSG)
SOI	S.O.I Industries(New) [AMEX symbol] (TTSB)
SOI	Solar Oscillations Imager [Instrumentation]
SOI	Southern Illinois University at Carbondale, Carbondale, IL [OCLC symbol] (OCLC)
SOI	Southern Indiana Railway, Inc. [Later, SIND] [AAR code]
SOI	Southern Oscillation Index
SOI	South Molle Island [Australia Airport symbol] (OAG)
SOI	Space Object Identification (AFM)
SOI	Special Olympics International (EA)
SOI	Special Olympics Ireland (EAIO)
SOI	Specific Operating Instruction (AFM)
SOI	SPEEDEX [Systemwide Project for Electronic Equipment at Depots Extended] Operating Instructions
SOI	Sphere of Influence
SOI	Staff Officer Intelligence (WDAA)
SOI	Standard Operating Instruction (KSC)
SOI	Start of Injection [Fuel systems] [Automotive engineering]
SOI	Statement of Intent
SOI	State of Stimulus Overinclusion [Schizophrenia]
SOI	Statistics of Income [IRS]
SOI	Stimulus Onset Interval
SOI	Structure of Intellect [Education] (AEE)
SOI	Surety and Operational Inspection [Military] (AFIT)
SOI	Survey of India [India] (EERA)
SOIC	Small Outline Integrated Circuit [Computer science]
SOIC	Supply Officer-in-Command [Military]
SOICAS	Space Object Identification Central Analysis System
SOICC	State Occupational Information Coordinating Committee
SOICS	Special Operations Improved Cryptographic System (CIST)
SOICS	Special Operations Improved Crypto System [Military] (RDA)
SOICS	Summary of Installation Control Status [Nuclear energy] (NRCH)
SOID	Shipboard Ordnance Infrared Decoy (MCD)
SOIF	Summary Object Interchange Format [Computer science] (TELE)
SOIG	Special Operations Industry Group [Army]
SOI Ind	SOI Industries, Inc. [Associated Press] (SAG)
SOI-LA	Structure of Intellect-Learning Abilities Test (EDAC)
So III U	Southern Illinois University (GAGS)
So III U (Edwardsville)	Southern Illinois University at Edwardsville (GAGS)
SOILVENT	Soil Venting Model [Environmental Protection Agency] (AEPA)
SO-in-C	Signal Officer-in-Chief [British military] (DMA)
SOINC	Supply Officer-in-Charge [Navy]
SoIndGs	Southern Indiana Gas & Electric Co. [Associated Press] (SAG)
SOIP	Sell-Off Impact Prognosticator [Aerospace] (AAG)
SOIP	Ship Overhaul Improvement Program [Navy]
SOIP	Sphere of Influence People
SOIR	Simultaneous Operations on Intersecting Runways [FAA] (TAG)
SOIS	Shipping Operations Information System (OA)
SOIS	Silicon on Insulating Substrate (PDAA)
SOIS	Spacelab/Orbiter Interface Simulator [NASA] (NASA)
SOIS	Space Object Identification System
SOIS	Student Outcomes Information Service (TES)
SOISCUM	Space Object Identification Summary (MCD)
SOITLM	Subcontractor Organizational Intermediate Level Maintenance
SOIWR	Simultaneous Operations on Intersecting Wet Runways [FAA] (TAG)
SOJ	Sea of Japan (NVT)
SOJ	Small Outline J Leaded (NITA)
SOJ	Sorkjosen [Norway] [Airport symbol] (OAG)
SOJ	Standoff Jammer (NVT)
SoJerIn	South Jersey Industries, Inc. [Associated Press] (SAG)
So Jersey LS Dictum	South Jersey Law School Dictum [A publication] (DLA)
SOJIM	Standoff Jammer Interceptor Missile (MCD)
SOJS	Standoff Jammer Suppression (MCD)
SOJS	Standoff Jammer System (MCD)
SOJSM	Standoff Jammer Suppression Missile (MCD)
SOJT	Structured On-the-Job Training (MCD)
SOJT	Supervised On-the-Job Training
SOJTA	State On-the-Job Training Agencies [Department of Labor]

SOK	American Sokol Educational and Physical Culture Organization
SOK	Semongkong [Lesotho] [Airport symbol Obsolete] (OAG)
SOK	Slovo o Knige [A publication]
SOK	South Kauai, HI [Location identifier FAA] (FAAL)
SOK	Supply OK [i.e., Authorized]
SOKS	Sport of Kings Society (EA)
SOKSI	Sentral Organisasi Karyawan Sosialis Indonesia [Central Organization of Indonesian Socialist Workers]
SOL	Safe Operating Limit
SOL	Sasko Oil & Gas Ltd. [Toronto Stock Exchange symbol Vancouver Stock Exchange symbol]
SOL	Saturation Output Level [Recording tapes]
SOL	School of Living (EA)
SOL	Second Order Logic
SOL	Secretary of Labor (OICC)
SOL	Senior Operator License [Nuclear energy] (NRCH)
SOL	Sequence Operated Lock (IAA)
SOL	Shipowner's Liability [Business term]
SOL	Short Octal Load (IAA)
SOL	Short of Luck (DSUE)
SOL	Shut-Off Lights (SAA)
SOL	Simulation Oriented Language [Computer science]
SOL	Sisters of Our Lady [Roman Catholic religious order]
SOL	Social Organisation Limited
SOL	Sola International [NYSE symbol] (TTSB)
SOL	Solar (AAG)
SOL	Solder
sol	Soldier
SOL	Soldier out of Luck [Military slang]
SOL	Solenoid (AAG)
SOL	Soleus Muscle [Anatomy]
SOL	Soliciting [FBI standardized term]
SOL	Solicitor
Sol	Solicitor (PHSD)
SOL	Solicitor of Labor [Department of Labor]
SOL	Solid (MSA)
SOL	Soliloquy [Theater term]
SOL	Solitaire [Jewelry] (ROG)
Sol	Soloman's Court of Request Appeals [Ceylon] [A publication] (DLA)
SOL	Solomon [Biblical king] (ROG)
SOL	Solomon Airlines Ltd. [Solomon Islands] [ICAO designator] (FAAC)
SOL	Solomon, AK [Location identifier FAA] (FAAL)
Sol	Solon [of Plutarch] [Classical studies] (OCD)
SOL	Solubilis [Soluble] [Pharmacy]
SOL	Soluble
sol	Soluble (IDOE)
SOL	Solutio [Solution] [Pharmacy]
SOL	Solution
Sol	Solution [Medicine] (DB)
sol	Solution (IDOE)
SOL	Solve [or Solutus] [Dissolve or Dissolved] [Pharmacy] (ROG)
SOL	Sons of Light [An association]
SOL	Source/Object Library (NITA)
SOL	Southern Illinois University, School of Law Library, Carbondale, IL [OCLC symbol] (OCLC)
SOL	Space-Occupying Lesion [Medicine]
SOL	Standard of Living
SOL	Statute of Limitations [Legal shorthand] (LWAP)
Sol	Still Out of Luck [Army Slang]
SOL	Strictly Out of Luck (IIA)
SOL	Substitute Optical Landing System (NG)
SOL	Sure out of Luck [Bowdlerized version]
SOL	System Oriented Language
SOLA	Selected Objects for Living Actively [Commercial firm specializing in home furnishings for the elderly]
Sola	Sola International, Inc. [Associated Press] (SAG)
SOLA	Student Organization for Latin America [University of Notre Dame] [Research center] (RCD)
SOLACE	School of Librarianship Automatic Cataloguing Experiment (NITA)
SOLACE	Society of Local Authority Chief Executives [British] (DBA)
SOLAGRAL	Solidarites Agricoles et Alimentaires [France] (EERA)
SOLAIR	Solomon Islands Airways Ltd. (FEA)
SOLAN	Solid Angles
SOLANT	South Atlantic Force [Later, Command] [Navy World War II]
SOLANTFOR	South Atlantic Force [Later, Command] [Navy World War II]
SOLAR	Sandel On-Line Automated Reference [Information service or system]
SOLAR	Semantically Oriented Lexical Archive
SOLAR	Serialized On-Line Automatic Recording [Computer science] (IEEE)
SOLAR	Shared On-Line Airline Reservations (IAA)
SOLAR	Shop Operations Load Analysis Reporting
SOLAR	Sociedad Latinoamericana de Estudios sobre America Latina y el Caribe [Mexico] (EAIO)
SOLAR	Society of Loose Actors Revolving [SOLAR Theater, Inc.]
SOLAR	Storage Online Automatic Retrieval (NITA)
SOLARIS	Submerged Object Locating and Retrieving Identification System
SOLAR MAX	Solar Maximum Mission Satellite
SolarMt	Solar-Mates, Inc. [Associated Press] (SAG)
SOLAS	International Convention for the Safety of Life at Sea (EERA)
SOLAS	Safety of Life at Sea [An international agreement requiring operators of cruise ships to meet certain standards of construction and fire safety]
SOLAS	Safety of Life at Sea Conference [Intergovernmental Maritime Consultative Organization] (MSC)
SOLAS	Safety of Life at Sea Convention (BARN)

SOLAS 74 .... International Convention for the Safety of Life at Sea
SOLAT .... Style of Learning and Thinking [*Occupational therapy*]
So Law .... Southern Lawyer [*A publication*] (DLA)
So Law T ...... Southern Law Times [*A publication*] (DLA)
SOLB .... Start of Line Block (CET)
SOLCGS .... Sisters of Our Lady of Charity of the Good Shepherd [*Roman Catholic religious order Rome, Italy*] (EAIO)
SOLCHEM ..... Solar-Chemical [*Energy conversion process*]
Sol Cl Gaz ... Solicitors' Clerks' Gazette [*1921-40*] [*A publication*] (DLA)
SOLCR .... Solicitor
SOLD .... Simulation of Logic Design
SOLD .... Soldering
SOLD .... Symbolic Debugger [*Also, sdb, SYMDEB*] [*Computer science*]
SOLDIER ...... Solution of Ordinary Differential Equations Routine (IAA)
SOLE .... Society of Logistics Engineers (EA)
SOLE .... Special Operations Liaison Element (COE)
SOLEC .... Stand on Leg, Eyes Closed [*Equilibrium test*]
Solectron ..... Solectron Corp. [*Associated Press*] (SAG)
SOLERS22 ... Solar Electromagnetic Radiation Study for Solar Cycle 22 (USDC)
SOLF .... Southern Oregon Library Federation [*Library network*]
SOLFEAS ..... Solar Energy System Economic Feasibility Program [*Army*] (RDA)
Sol G .... Solicitor General [*Legal term*] (DLA)
Sol-Gel .... Solution-Gelatin (SDI)
Sol Gen .... Solicitor General [*Legal term*] (DLA)
SOLI .... Symphony Orchestra Library Information [*Sinfonia Software*] [*Piedmont, CA*]
SOLIC .... Solicitation
SOLIC .... Special Operations/Low Intensity Conflict [*Army*]
SOLICO .... Sorenson Lighted Controls, Inc.
SOLIC PREP... Solicitation Preparation
SOLID .... Self-Organizing Large Information Dissemination System (IEEE)
SOLID .... Simulation of Life Insurance Decisions [*Game*]
solidif .... Solidification (BARN)
Soligen .... Soligen Technologies, Inc. [*Associated Press*] (SAG)
SOLIMPEX ... Societe Lao Import-Export (EY)
SOLINET ...... Southeastern Library Network [*Atlanta, GA*] [*Library network*]
SOLION .... Solution of Ions [*Office of Naval Research*]
Sol Is .... Solomon Islands
SOLIS .... Sozialwissenschaftliches Literaturlnformationssystem [*Database*] [*Informationszentrum Sozialwissenschaften Social Sciences Literature Information System*] [*German*] [*Information service or system*] (CRD)
SOLIS .... Symbionics On-Line Information System [*Computer science*]
SOLISTRON... Solid-State Klystron
So LJ .... Southern Law Journal and Reporter [*A publication*] (DLA)
Sol J & R ..... Solicitors' Journal and Reporter [*A publication*] (DLA)
SOLL .... Special Operations, Low Level (MCD)
Sol Labor Op... Opinion of the Solicitor of Labor (AAGC)
SOLLAR .... Soft Lunar Landing and Return (SAA)
SOLM .... Sisters of Our Lady of Mercy [*Mercedarians*] [*Roman Catholic religious order*]
SOLM .... Soldier's Medal [*Military decoration*]
Sol Man Cl Gaz Solicitor's Managing Clerks' Gazette [*1941-62*] [*A publication*] (DLA)
SOLMC .... Senior Officer Logistics Management Course [*Military*] (INF)
SOLMIS .... Supply Online Management Information System [*Computer science*] (PDAA)
SOLN .... Solution
SOLO .... SAMI Online Operations (NITA)
SOLO .... Selective Optical Lock-On [*Sighting device*]
SOLO .... Senior Officer Legal Orientation (MCD)
SOLO .... Southeastern Ohio Library Organization [*Library network*]
SOLO .... Status of Logistics Offensive [*Military*] (AABC)
SOLO .... Super Oak Leaf Online [*Santa Rosa Junior College online conference*]
SOLO .... Supply On-Line Option [*IMS America Ltd.*] [*Database*]
SOLO .... System for Online Optimization [*Computer science*] (PDAA)
SOLO .... System for Ordinary Life Operations [*Insurance*]
SOLOC .... Southern Line of Communications [*World War II*]
SOLOG .... Standardization of Certain Aspects of Operations and Logistics [*Military*]
SOLOMON ... Simultaneous Operation Limited Ordinal Modular Network (NITA)
SOLOMON ... Simultaneous Operation Linked Ordinal Modular Network
Sol Op .... Solicitor's Opinion [*Especially of Internal Revenue Bureau*] [*United States*] (DLA)
SOLOQ .... Solo Serve Corp. [*NASDAQ symbol*] (SAG)
SOLP .... Salomon Page Group Ltd. [*NASDAQ symbol*] (SAG)
SOLP .... Solomon Page Group Ltd. [*NASDAQ symbol*] (SAG)
SolPage .... Solomon Page Group Ltd. [*Associated Press*] (SAG)
SOLPH .... Sisters of Our Lady of Perpetual Help (TOCD)
SOLPW .... Solomon-Page Grp Wrrt [*NASDAQ symbol*] (TTSB)
Sol Q .... Solicitor Quarterly [*1962-65*] [*A publication*] (DLA)
So LQ .... Southern Law Quarterly [*A publication*] (DLA)
SOLR .... Sidetone Objective Loudness Rating [*of telephone connections*] (IEEE)
SOLR .... Solar-Mates [*NASDAQ symbol*] (TTSB)
SOLR .... Solar-Mates, Inc. [*NASDAQ symbol*] (SAG)
SOLR .... Solicitor
So LR .... Southern Law Review [*Nashville, TN*] [*A publication*] (DLA)
SOLRAD .... Solar Radiation [*Satellite system*] [*Navy*]
SOLRAD-HI... Solar Radiation - High-Altitude [*Satellite system*] [*Navy*]
SOL Rev ...... School of Law. Review [*Canada*] [*A publication*] (DLA)
So L Rev ..... Southern Law Review [*A publication*] (DLA)
So L Rev NS... Southern Law Review, New Series [*St. Louis, MO*] [*A publication*] (DLA)
SolrMt .... Solar-Mates, Inc. [*Associated Press*] (SAG)
So LRNS ...... Southern Law Review, New Series [*St. Louis, MO*] [*A publication*] (DLA)
SOLRU .... Solar-Mates Inc. Unit [*NASDAQ symbol*] (TTSB)
SOLRW .... Solar-Mates Wrrt [*NASDAQ symbol*] (TTSB)
SOLS .... Substitute Optical Landing System (MCD)
SOL-SAL ...... Solar Scientific Airlock
SOLT .... Our Lady of the Most Holy Trinity Convent (TOCD)
SOLT .... Society of London Theatres [*England*] (WDAA)
SOLT .... Society of Our Lady of the Most Holy Trinity (TOCD)
solt .... Society of Our Lady of the Most Holy Trinity (TOCD)
So LT .... Southern Law Times [*A publication*] (DLA)
SOLTIP .... Solar Connections to Transient Interplanetary Processes [*Program*] (USDC)
Soltr .... Solutrean (VRA)
SOLTRAN ..... Solar Spectrum and Transmittance [*Solar energy research*]
SOLU .... Solute (AAMN)
SOLUB .... Aqueous Solubility Database [*Chemical Information Systems, Inc.*] [*Information service or system*] (CRD)
SOLUG .... San Antonio On Line User Group (NITA)
SOL U/T .... Solicitor's Undertaking (DCTA)
SOLUT .... Solutus [*Dissolved*] [*Pharmacy*] (ROG)
SOLV .... Solenoid Valve [*Mechanical engineering*]
SOLV .... Solve [*Dissolve*] [*Pharmacy*]
SOLV .... Solvent
SOLV .... Solv-Ex Corp. [*NASDAQ symbol*] (NQ)
SOLV .... Super-Open-Frame Low Voltage (IEEE)
SOLVD .... Studies of Left Ventricular Dysfunction [*National Heart, Lung, and Blood Institute*]
SOLVE C CAL... Solve Cum Calore [*Dissolve by Heating*] [*Pharmacy*]
SolvEx .... Solv-Ex Corp. [*Associated Press*] (SAG)
SOLW .... Society of Our Lady of the Way (EA)
SOLY .... Solubility
Som .... De Somniis [*of Philo*] (BJA)
SOM .... SACLANT [*Supreme Allied Commander, Atlantic*] Staff Organization Manual (NATG)
SOM .... San Tome [*Venezuela*] [*Airport symbol*] (OAG)
SOM .... Saskatchewan Order of Merit [*Decoration*] [*Canada*] (CMD)
SOM .... Scanning Optical Microscope
SOM .... Secretory Otitis Media [*Medicine*] (MAE)
SOM .... Securities Order Matching [*Computer science*]
SOM .... See Our Message
SOM .... Self-Organizing Machine
SOM .... Self-Organizing Map [*Computer science*] (CDE)
SOM .... Send-Only-Multipoint (DNAB)
SOM .... Sensitivity-of-Method [*FDA*]
SOM .... Serous Otitis Media [*Ear inflammation*]
SOM .... Share of Market [*Advertising*]
SOM .... Share of Market [*Lundberg Survey, Inc.*] [*Information service or system*] (CRD)
SOM .... Shift Operations Manager (NRCH)
SOM .... Ship Operations Manager [*NASA*] (KSC)
som .... Ship Operations Manager [*NASA*] (NAKS)
SOM .... Simulator Operation and Maintenance Program (MCD)
SOM .... Single Oriental Male [*Classified advertising*]
SOM .... Skidmore, Owings & Merrill [*Architectural firm*]
SOM .... Small Office Microfilm
SOM .... Small Office Microfilm Systems (NITA)
SOM .... Society of Medalists [*Defunct*] (EA)
SOM .... Society of Metaphysicians [*British*] (DBA)
SOM .... Society of Occupational Medicine [*British*]
SOM .... Soil Organic Matter
som .... Somalia [*MARC language code Library of Congress*] (LCCP)
SOM .... Somalia [*ANSI three-letter standard code*] (CNC)
SOM .... Somali Airlines [*Somalia*] [*ICAO designator*] (FAAC)
SOM .... Somatostatin [*Biochemistry*]
SOM .... Somatotrophin [*Endocrinology*]
SOM .... Sombrero [*Chile*] [*Seismograph station code, US Geological Survey*] (SEIS)
SOM .... Somerset [*County in England*]
SOM .... Somerset County Library, Bridgewater, NJ [*OCLC symbol*] (OCLC)
Som .... Somerset Legal Journal [*Pennsylvania*] [*A publication*] (DLA)
SOM .... Somersetshire [*County in England*]
SOM .... Somnolent [*A metabolic test*] (DAVI)
SOM .... Somnus [*Sleep*] [*Latin*] (ROG)
SOM .... SONARman [*Navy*]
SOM .... Soundman (IAA)
SOM .... Sound of Music [*Dolls by Alexander*] [*Doll collecting*]
SOM .... Source One Mortgage Services [*NYSE symbol*] (SAG)
SOM .... Spacecraft Operations Manual
SOM .... Spares Optimization Model [*NASA*] (NASA)
som .... Spares Optimization Model (NAKS)
SOM .... Stage Operating Manual [*NASA*] (KSC)
SOM .... Standard Online Module (NITA)
som .... Standard Operating Manual (NAKS)
SOM .... Standard Operating Manual [*NASA*] (NASA)
SOM .... Standoff Missile (MCD)
SOM .... Start of Message [*Telecommunications*]
SOM .... State Operations Manual [*Home Health Agency Program*] [*Department of Health and Human Services*] (GFGA)
SOM .... Steward of Meeting [*Auto racing*]
SOM .... Storage Operations Module [*SAILS*] (MCD)
SOM .... Strap-On Motor
SOM .... Suborbital Mission [*NASA*] (SAA)
SOM .... Sulfomethoxine [*Medicine*] (MAE)

SOM............	Superior Oblique Muscle [*Eye anatomy*]
SOM............	Superior Old Marsala
SOM............	Survivability Optimization Model (MCD)
SOM............	Sustained Operations Manual
SOM............	Sustained Operations Model
SOM............	System Object Model [*Computer science*] (PCM)
SOM............	System Operator Manual [*Military*] (CAAL)
SOMA	Services to Ongoing Mature Aging [*Counseling group*]
SOMA	Sharing of Missionaries Abroad [*Church of England*]
SOMA	Signed Out Against Medical Advice
SOMA	Society of Medical Administrators (NTPA)
Soma	Somanetics Corp. [*Associated Press*] (SAG)
SOMA	Somatix Therapy [*NASDAQ symbol*] (TTSB)
SOMA	Somatix Therapy Corp. [*NASDAQ symbol*] (SAG)
SoMa	South of Market [*District of San Francisco*]
SOMA	Student Osteopathic Medical Association (EA)
SOMA	Survey of Market Absorption [*Department of Housing and Urban Development*] (GFGA)
SOMADA......	Self-Organizing Multiple-Access Discrete Address [*Computer science*] (IEEE)
Somanetc ...	Somanetics Corp. [*Associated Press*] (SAG)
SOMART......	Conseil des Metiers d'Art du Quebec (AC)
somat	Somatic [*Pertaining to the body or the body wall*] (DAVI)
Somatgn......	Somatogen, Inc. [*Associated Press*] (SAG)
SOMC	Shadow Open Market Committee
SOM/DSOM...	System Object Model/Distributed System Object Model [*Computer science*]
SOME..........	Secretary's Office, Management Engineer [*Navy*]
SOME..........	Senior Ordnance Mechanical Engineer [*British military*] (DMA)
SOMEG to ADV...	Something to Advantage [*Advertising*] [*Legal term*]
SOMER	State of the Marine Environment Reporting [*Commonwealth*] (EERA)
Somerset LJ...	Somerset Legal Journal [*A publication*] (DLA)
SOMET.........	Sometimes
So Meth U ...	Southern Methodist University (GAGS)
SOMF..........	SIDPERS [*Standard Installation/Division Personnel System*] Organization Master File [*Military*] (AABC)
SOMF..........	Start of Minor Frame (MCD)
SOMH	SONARman Harbor Defense [*Navy*]
SOM-H	Start-of-Message - High Precedence (CET)
SOMI	Skull Occipital Mandibular Immobilization [*Orthosis*] [*Dentistry*] (DAVI)
SOMI	Sternal-Occipital-Mandibular Immobilization [*Medicine*]
SOMIEX	Societe Malienne d'Importation et d'Exportation [*Malian Import Export Co.*]
SoMinrl........	Southern Mineral Corp. [*Associated Press*] (SAG)
SOMISA	Sociedad Mixta Siderurgia Argentina [*Steel producer in Argentina*]
SOMISS	Study of Management Information Systems Support [*Army*]
SOM-L.........	Start-of-Message - Low Precedence (CET)
Som Leg J (PA)...	Somerset Legal Journal [*Pennsylvania*] [*A publication*] (DLA)
SOM-LI	Somatostatin-Like Immunoreactivity
Som LJ	Somerset Legal Journal [*Pennsylvania*] [*A publication*] (DLA)
Som LR	Somalia Law Reports [*A publication*] (DLA)
SOMM	Commission
SOMM	Shift Operations Maintenance Manager (SSD)
SOMM	Stand-Off Modular Missile (PDAA)
Somn on Gav...	Somner on Gavelkind [*A publication*] (DLA)
SOMO	Semioccupied Molecular Orbital [*Physical chemistry*]
SOMO	Senior Officer Management Office [*Army*] (INF)
SOMOS........	Society of Military Orthopedics Surgeons (DAVI)
SOM-P	Start-of-Message - Priority
SOMP	Sydney Ocean Meeting Point [*Navy*]
SOMPA	System of Multicultural Pluralistic Assessment [*Psychological and educational testing*]
SOMPF	Special Operations Mission Planning Folder (COE)
Som Pl	Somersetshire Pleas (Civil and Criminal), Edited by Chadwyck-Healey and Landon [*Somerset Record Society Publications, Vols. 11, 36, 41, 44*] [*A publication*] (DLA)
SOMPrA.......	Source One Mtg 8.42%'A'Pfd [*NYSE symbol*] (TTSB)
SOMPRSS....	Compress
SOMR	Somerset Group [*NASDAQ symbol*] (TTSB)
SOMR	[*The*] Somerset Group, Inc. [*Indianapolis, IN*] [*NASDAQ symbol*] (NQ)
SOMRB	Senior Officers Materiel Review Board [*Army*] (AABC)
SomrGp	Somerset Group, Inc. [*Associated Press*] (SAG)
SOMS	Senior Officer, Minesweepers [*British military*] (DMA)
SOMS	Service Order Mechanization [*or Mechanized*] System [*AT & T*]
SOMS	Shuttle Orbiter Medical System [*NASA*] (MCD)
soms...........	Shuttle Orbiter Medical System [*NASA*] (NAKS)
Soms	Somerset County [*England*] (BARN)
SOMS	Space Operations Management System (PDAA)
SOMS	Standard Operations and Maintenance Squadron (DNAB)
SOMS	Synchronous, Operational Meteorological Satellite
SOMS	Systems Optimization and Monitoring Services (MHDI)
SOMSG........	See Our Message [*Aviation*] (FAAC)
SOMSS	Submarine Off-Board Mine Search System (DOMA)
SOMST	Somersetshire [*County in England*] (ROG)
SomstSv	Somerset Savings Bank [*Associated Press*] (SAG)
SOMT..........	Soldier Operator Maintainer Testing (MCD)
SOMTE.........	Soldier-Operator-Maintainer-Tester-Evaluator [*Military*] (PDAA)
Somtix	Somatix Therapy Corp. [*Associated Press*] (SAG)
SOMTO	Subversive Operations, Mediterranean Theatre of Operations [*World War II*]
SOMTS	Division of Ship Operations and Marine Technical Support [*Research center*] (RCD)
SoMV...........	Sowbane Mosaic Virus

SON	Espiritu Santo [*Vanuatu*] [*Airport symbol*] (OAG)
SON	Linea Aerea Aerosanta [*Chile*] [*ICAO designator*] (FAAC)
SON	Northwest Jet Sales & Leasing, Inc. [*FAA designator*] (FAAC)
S/ON	Sign On [*Computer science*] (MDG)
SON	Snijders-Oomen Non-Verbal Intelligence Scale (AEBS)
SON	Society of Nematologists (EA)
SON	Sonata [*Music*] (WGA)
son.............	Songhai [*MARC language code Library of Congress*] (LCCP)
SON	Sonneberg [*Federal Republic of Germany*] [*Seismograph station code, US Geological Survey Closed*] (SEIS)
Son	Sonnets [*Shakespearean work*]
SON	Sonoco Products [*NYSE symbol*] (TTSB)
SON	Sonoco Products Corp. [*NYSE symbol*] (SAG)
Son	Sonora [*Record label*] [*Sweden*]
SON	Sonora Gold Corp. [*Toronto Stock Exchange symbol Vancouver Stock Exchange symbol*]
SON	Southern (WGA)
SON	Statement of Operational Need
SON	Submitting Office Number [*Navy*] (DNAB)
SON	Support of Other Nations [*Military support furnished certain nations and funded by the Air Force*]
SON	Supraoptic Nucleus [*Brain anatomy*]
SONA	School of Naval Administration, Leland Stanford University
SONA	Sonic Environmental Systems, Inc. [*NASDAQ symbol*] (SAG)
SonA...........	Stratford-on-Avon [*British*]
S on A	Stratford-On-Avon, England
SONAC........	SONAR Nacelle [*Sonacelle*]
SONAD........	Sonic Azimuth Detector (MCD)
SONAD........	Sound-Operated Noise Attenuation Device (IAA)
SONAD........	Speech-Operated Noise Adjusting Device [*Telecommunications*] (TEL)
SONAR........	Sonic Azimuth and Ranging [*British military*] (DMA)
SONAR........	Sound Navigation and Ranging
SONARRAY...	SONAR Array [*Sounding system*] [*Navy*]
Sonat	Sonat, Inc. [*Associated Press*] (SAG)
SoNat..........	Southern National Corp. [*Associated Press*] (SAG)
SoNatCp	Southern National Corp. [*Associated Press*] (SAG)
SonatOff	Sonat Offshore Drilling, Inc. [*Associated Press*] (SAG)
SONATRACH...	Societe Nationale de Transport et de Commercialisation des Hydrocarbures
So Nazarene U...	Southern Nazarene University (GAGS)
SONB	Sonobuoy
Sonc	Soncino (BJA)
SONC	Sonic Corp. [*NASDAQ symbol*] (SPSG)
SoncinoB	[*The*] Soncino Books of the Bible (Bornemouth) [*A publication*] (BJA)
SONCM........	SONAR Countermeasures and Deception [*Military*]
SONCR.........	SONAR Control Room (MSA)
SOND..........	Secretary's Office, Navy Department
Sonesta	Sonesta International Hotels Corp. [*Associated Press*] (SAG)
SONET	Synchronous Optical Network [*Computer science*]
SONG	Satellite for Orientation, Navigation, and Geodesy (IAA)
SONG	Seeking of Noetic Goals Test [*Personality development test*] [*Psychology*]
Song	Song of Songs [*Old Testament book*] [*Roman Catholic canon*]
Song 3 Childr...	Song of the Three Children [*Old Testament book*] [*Apocrypha*]
SongCh........	Song of the Three Children [*Old Testament book*] [*Apocrypha*] (BJA)
Song of Three Childr...	[*The*] Song of the Three Holy Children [*Apocrypha*]
SongR.........	Song of Songs Rabbah (BJA)
SONGS........	San Onofre Nuclear Generating Station (NRCH)
Song Sol......	Song of Solomon [*Old Testament book*]
SONH..........	Supraopticoneurohypophysial (DB)
SONI	Staff Officer Navigation Instructor (IAA)
SONIBANQUE...	Societe Nigerienne de Banque (EY)
Sonic	Sonic Corp. [*Associated Press*] (SAG)
Sonic	Sonic Environmental Systems, Inc. [*Associated Press*] (SAG)
SONIC.........	SPAN [*Space Physics Analysis Network*] Ocean Network Information Center [*Database*]
SONIC.........	System-Wide On-Line Network for Information Control [*Computer science*]
SonicEnv......	Sonic Environmental Systems, Inc. [*Associated Press*] (SAG)
SonicM........	Sonics & Materials, Inc. [*Associated Press*] (SAG)
SonicSol......	Sonic Solutions Co. [*Associated Press*] (SAG)
SONITA........	Societe Nigerienne de Transports Aeriens [*Niger*] [*ICAO designator*] (FAAC)
SONK..........	Spontaneous Osteonecrosis of the Knee [*Orthopedics*] (DAVI)
SONMET	Special Operations Naval Mobile Environment Team (COE)
SONN	Sonning [*England*]
SONNA........	Somali National News Agency
SONNF........	Sonora Gold Corp. (MHDW)
SONO..........	Satellite Object Number (MUGU)
SONO..........	Sonobuoy
SONO..........	Sonogram [*Medicine*] (DHSM)
SONOAN	Sonic Noise Analyzer
Sonoco	Sonoco Products Corp. [*Associated Press*] (SAG)
SonocoP	Sonoco Products Corp. [*Associated Press*] (SAG)
SONOSW	Sonoswitch
SONP	Solid Organs Not Palpable [*Medicine*]
SONPrA........	Sonoco Prd $2.25 Sr'A'Cv Pfd [*NYSE symbol*] (TTSB)
SONRD.........	Secretary's Office, Office of Research and Development [*Navy*]
SONRES.......	Saturated Optical Nonresonant Emission Spectroscopy
SONS	Seek Out New Suppliers
SONS	Society of Non-Smokers (EA)
SONS	Statistics of Naval Shipyards
SonusP........	Sonus Pharmaceuticals, Inc. [*Associated Press*] (SAG)
SONV	Sonchus Virus [*Plant pathology*]

SonyCp .... Sony Corp. America [*Associated Press*] (SAG)
SOO .... Sault Meadows Energy [*Vancouver Stock Exchange symbol*]
SOO .... Schenectady Operations Office [*Energy Research and Development Administration*]
SOO .... Senior Operating Officer (TBD)
SOO .... Songo [*Mozambique*] [*Airport symbol*] (OAG)
SOO .... Soo Line Corp. [*NYSE symbol and AAR code*] (SPSG)
SOO .... Specialty Occupational Outlook [*A publication*]
SOO .... Staff Officer Operations [*British*]
SOO .... Statement of Objectives (AAGC)
SOOA .... State of Origin [*Soccer*]
SOOA .... Solus Outdoor Advertising Association [*British*] (BI)
SOOAC .... Sooner Athletic Conference (PSS)
SOOE .... Study of Odors and Odorous Emissions [*Environmental science*] (COE)
SOOG .... Saint-Georges-De-L'Oyapock [*French Guiana*] [*ICAO location identifier*] (ICLI)
SOOM .... Saigon Officers Open Mess [*Vietnam*]
SOOM .... Saint-Laurent du Maroni [*French Guiana*] [*ICAO location identifier*] (ICLI)
SOON........... Sequence for Opportunities and Negatives [*Rand Corp.*]
SOON........... Solar Observing Optical Network [*Air Force*]
SOONS........ Scientific Opportunities Offered by a Nuclear Submarine [*A publication*]
SOONSPOT... SOON's [*Solar Observing Optical Network*] Solar Patrol on Tape (USDC)
SOOP .... Ship of Opportunity Program [*National Oceanic and Atmospheric Administration*] (GFGA)
SOOP .... Special Old Oil Price
SOOP .... Submarine Oceanographic Observation Program
SOOR .... Regina [*French Guiana*] [*ICAO location identifier*] (ICLI)
So Ore St C... Southern Oregon State College (GAGS)
SOOS .... Saul [*French Guiana*] [*ICAO location identifier*] (ICLI)
SOOSE .... Suborbital Offense Systems Group [*NASA*] (SAA)
SOOY .... Sinnamary [*French Guiana*] [*ICAO location identifier*] (ICLI)
SOP .... Pinehurst [*North Carolina*] [*Airport symbol*] (OAG)
SOP .... Safety Operating Plan
SOP .... Sales Order Processing [*Manufacturing management*]
SOP .... Saturn Orbiter Probe [*NASA*]
SOP .... Scavenging, Oil Pump (MSA)
SOP .... Scented Orange Pekoe [*Tea trade*] (ROG)
SOP .... Sea of Peace (IAA)
SOP .... Seat of the Pants
SOP .... Secondary Operation
SOP .... Secondary Oxygen Pack [*NASA*]
SOP .... Second Opinion Program [*Later, NSOP*] (EA)
SOP .... Selective Oxidation Process (PDAA)
SOP .... Semiopen Position [*Dancing*]
SOP .... Semiorganic Polymer
SOP .... Senior Officer Present
SOP .... Sensory Organ Precursor [*Cytology*]
SOP .... Shift Operating Procedures (COE)
SOP .... Ship-of-Opportunity Program [*Marine science*] (OSRA)
SOP .... Ship's Operational Program [*Navy*] (NVT)
SOP .... Shop Overload Parts (AAG)
SOP .... Signal Operating Procedure (IAA)
SOP .... Simulated Output Program [*Computer science*]
SOP .... Simulation Operations Plan [*NASA*] (KSC)
SOP .... Sleeping-Out Pass [*British armed forces*]
SOP .... Society of Protozoologists (NTPA)
SOP .... Solution Output Processor (PDAA)
SOP .... Soprano
SOP .... Sopron [*Hungary*] [*Seismograph station code, US Geological Survey*] (SEIS)
SOP .... Southern Pines [*North Carolina*] [*Airport symbol*] (AD)
SOP .... Southern Pines, NC [*Location identifier FAA*] (FAAL)
SOP .... Spacelab Opportunity Payload [*NASA*] (MCD)
SOP .... Spares Order Processing (MCD)
SOP .... Special Operating Procedure (IEEE)
SOP .... Special Order Price
SOP .... Sphere of Positon (SAA)
SOP .... Staff Officer of Pensioners [*Army British*] (ROG)
SOP .... Standard Operating Plan (OICC)
SOP .... Standard Operating Power (COE)
SOP .... Standard [*or Standing*] Operating Procedure
SOP .... Statement of Policy [*SEC*]
SOP .... Statement of Position (EBF)
SOP .... State of Polarization
SOP .... State-Operated Program [*Department of Education*] (GFGA)
SOP .... Statewide Operating Plan
SOP .... Station Operating Plan (AAG)
SOP .... Stock Option Plan
SOP .... Strategic Objectives Plan
SOP .... Strategic Orbit Point (KSC)
SOP .... Study Organization Plan (BUR)
SOP .... Subsystem Operating Program (NASA)
SOP .... Subsystems Operating Procedure [*NASA*] (NASA)
SOP .... Successive Organization of Perception [*Pilot behavior*]
SOP .... Sulfate of Potash [*Fertilizer*]
SOP .... Sum-of-Products [*Computer science*] (OA)
SOP .... Supplemental Oxygen Package (MCD)
SOP .... Supplier Operating Procedure (MCD)
SOP .... Supplier-Outside-Price [*Automobile content legislation*]
SOP .... Surface Oil Pickup
SOP .... Surgical Outpatient [*Medicine*]

SOP .... Survey of Use Permits [*Bureau of the Census*] (GFGA)
SOP .... Symbolic Optimum Program
SOP .... System Operations Panel (SSD)
SOP .... Systems Operation Plan [*NASA*] (KSC)
SOPA .... Senior Officer Present Afloat [*Navy*]
SOP(A)........ Senior Officer Present (Ashore) [*Navy*]
SOPA .... Society of Professional Archeologists (EA)
SOPA .... Standard Operating Procedure Amplified (GAVI)
SOPA .... Standoff Precision Attack [*Military*] (CAAL)
SOPA .... Syndrome of Primary Aldosteronism [*Medicine*] (DMAA)
SOPAC .... Joint CCOP/IOC Program of Research on the South Pacific [*Marine science*] (MSC)
SOPAC .... Southern Pacific Railroad Co.
SOPAC .... South Pacific Applied Geoscience Commission (EERA)
SOPAC .... South Pacific Command [*Navy*]
SOPAC .... South Pacific Countries (EERA)
SOPACBACOM... South Pacific Base Command [*Navy World War II*]
SOPACCOMS... South Pacific Communications [*Navy*]
SoPacPet...... Southern Pacific Petroleum [*Associated Press*] (SAG)
SOPAD .... SOPA [*Senior Officer Present Afloat*] Administrative Duties [*Military*] (NVT)
SOPAD .... Summary of Proceedings and Debate [*of House of Representatives*]
SOPAG .... Societe des Participations Gardinier [*French fertilizer firm*]
SOPAT .... South China Patrol [*Navy World War II*]
SOPC .... Sales Operations Planning and Control [*Management*]
SOPC .... Selected Outpatient Psychiatric Clinic [*Health insurance*] (GHCT)
SOPC .... Shuttle Operations and Planning Center [*NASA*] (MCD)
SOPC .... Shuttle Operations Planning Complex [*NASA*]
SOPCA .... Sporadic Olivopontocerebellar Ataxia [*Medicine*] (DMAA)
SoPcPt......... Southern Pacific Petroleum [*Associated Press*] (SAG)
SOPDOSS .... Submersible Oriented Platform for Deep Ocean Sediment Studies [*Marine science*] (MSC)
SOPE .... Simulated Off-the-Pad Ejection [*NASA*]
SO-PE .... Sodium Pentathol [*Nickname*]
Soph .... Sopherim (BJA)
Soph .... Sophista [*of Plato*] [*A publication*] (OCD)
SOPH .... Sophister [*British*] (ROG)
SOPH .... Sophocles [*Greek poet, 496-406BC*] [*Classical studies*] (ROG)
SOPH .... Sophomore
Soph .... Sophonias [*Old Testament book*] [*Douay version*]
SOPH .... Starboard Out, Port Home [*Variation of POSH*]
SOPHE .... Society for Public Health Education (EA)
Soph El ...... Sophistici Elenchi [*of Aristotle*] [*Classical studies*] (OCD)
SOPHIA....... Society of Philosophers in America (NTPA)
SOPI .... Service Object Pair Instance (DMAA)
SOPI .... Superintendent of Public Instruction (OICC)
SOPLASCO... Southern Plastics Co.
SOPLC .... Senior Officer Preventive Logistics Course (MCD)
SOPM .... Standard Orbital Parameter Message [*NASA*] (KSC)
SOPMET...... Standing Operating Procedure - Meteorological Plan (NATG)
SOP/MR....... Standard Operating Procedure/Maintenance Requirement (MCD)
SOPN .... First Savings Bancorp [*NASDAQ symbol*] (TTSB)
SOPN .... First Savings Bank of Moore County [*NASDAQ symbol*] (SAG)
SOPO .... Society of Oral Physiology and Occlusion
SOPODA ...... Social Planning, Policy & Development Abstracts [*Sociological Abstracts, Inc.*] [*Database*]
SOPP .... Sodium Ortho-Phenylphenoxide [*Organic chemistry*]
SOPP .... Special Order Perfect Price [*for undamaged merchandise*]
SOPP .... Statement of Provisioning Policy [*Military*] (AFIT)
SOPP .... State Operating Permit Program [*Environmental Protection Agency*]
SOPPC......... Special Operations Photo Processing Cell (MCD)
SOPR .... South Pierce Railroad [*AAR code*]
SOPR .... Spanish Open Pool Reactor
SOPR .... Special Officer Personnel Requirements [*Military*]
SOPR .... Standing Operating Procedure Regulation [*Navy*] (MCD)
SOPS .... Select Committee on Ocean Policy [*Interagency Committee on Marine Science and Engineering*] (USDC)
SOPS .... Shot Noise Optical Optimization Communication System with Stops [*NASA*]
S Op S........ Si Opus Sit [*If Needed*] [*Pharmacy*]
SOPS .... Spacecraft Operations Planning Section
SOPS .... Special Operations Power Source [*Military*] (RDA)
SOPSA........ Shuttle Orbit-Injection Propulsion System Analysis [*NASA*]
SOPT .... Science Operations Planning Team
SOPTX .... SMBS Premium Total Return Cl.B [*Mutual fund ticker symbol*] (SG)
SOPUS........ Senior Officer Present, United States Navy
SOPUSN...... Senior Officer Present, United States Navy (SAA)
SOPWA....... Survivors of a Person with AIDS [*An association*] (CPII)
SOPY .... Support of Positive Youth [*Australia*]
SOQ .... Senior Officers' Quarters
SOQ .... Sick Officer Quarters
Soq .... Soqotri (BJA)
SOQ .... Sorong [*Indonesia*] [*Airport symbol*] (OAG)
SOQ .... Star One Resources, Inc. [*Vancouver Stock Exchange symbol*]
SOQ .... Suicide Opinion Questionnaire (STED)
SOQ .... System Optical Quality (MCD)
SOQAS........ Statement of Quality and Support (MCD)
SOQE .... Society for Optical and Quantum Electronics
SOQUEM...... Societe Quebecoise d'Exploration Miniere [*Quebec Mining Exploration Co.*]
SOQUIJ........ Societe Quebecoise d'Information Juridique [*Quebec Society for Legal Information*] [*Information service or system*] (IID)
SOR .... Air Stord AS [*Norway ICAO designator*] (FAAC)
SOR .... Sale or Return [*Business term*] (ADA)
SOR .... Sampling Oscilloscope Recorder

SOR .... Saxon Owners Registry (EA)
SOR .... Schedule Outlook Report (SAA)
SOR .... Seder 'Olam Rabbah (BJA)
SOR .... Sensor Operation Room (AFM)
SOR .... Service Operational Requirement
sor .... Short Open Reading [*Frame*] [*Genetics*] (DAVI)
SOR .... Sign Own Release [*Medicine*] (STED)
SOR .... Single Operation Responsibility (IAA)
SOR .... Single Order Release (MCD)
SOR .... Slow Operate Relay (IAA)
SoR .... Society of Radiographers (WDAA)
SOR .... Society of Rheology (EA)
SoR .... Society of Roadcraft [*British*] (DBA)
SOR .... Sonor Petroleum Corp. [*Toronto Stock Exchange symbol*]
Sor .... Soria [*Record label*]
SOR .... Soroa [*Cuba*] [*Seismograph station code, US Geological Survey*] (SEIS)
SOR .... Source Capital [*NYSE symbol*] (TTSB)
SOR .... Source Capital, Inc. [*NYSE symbol*] (SPSG)
SOR .... Source of Repair (MCD)
SOR .... Specification Operational Requirement (NAKS)
SOR .... Specific Operational Requirement [*Military*]
SOR .... Spilled Oil Research Team [*National Oceanic and Atmospheric Administration*] (MSC)
SOR .... Squadron Operational Report
SOR .... Stable Orbit Rendezvous [*NASA*] (NAKS)
SOR .... Standard Operating Report
SOR .... Standard Operating Rules
SOR .... Standoff Range (MCD)
sor .... Starboard (DS)
SOR .... Starfire Optical Range [*Air Force*]
SOR .... Start of Record (MUGU)
SOR .... Start-of-Run [*Engineering*]
SOR .... Statement of Requirement [*Military*] (AFIT)
SOR .... State of Readiness (MCD)
SOR .... Status or Operating Resources (MCD)
SOR .... Statutory Orders and Regulations (NITA)
SOR .... Statutory Orders and Regulations of Canada [*Canada Department of Justice*] [*Information service or system*]
SOR .... Stearic/Oleic Acid Ratio [*Clinical chemistry*]
SOR .... Stephens Owners Registry [*Defunct*] (EA)
SOR .... Stimulus-Organism Response (STED)
SOR .... Stockholder of Record
SOR .... Strategy and Options Review (DOMA)
SOR .... Students for Origins Research (EA)
SOR .... Subcarrier Oscillator Rack
SOR .... Successive Overrelaxation
SOr .... Supraorbitale (STED)
SOR .... Synchrotron Orbital Radiation [*High-energy physics*]
SOR .... Systems Operational Requirement
SOR .... Winfield/Arkansas City, KS [*Location identifier FAA*] (FAAL)
SORA .... Secretary's Office, Records Administration [*Navy*]
SORA .... Sodium-Cooled Research Reactor [*Nuclear energy*] (NUCP)
SORA .... Sorgento Rapido [*Reactor*] (NRCH)
SORAD .... Sonic Ranging and Detection (KSC)
SORAFOM .... Societe de Radiodiffusion de la France d'Outre-Mer [*Society for Radio Broadcasting of Overseas France*]
SORAK .... Special Operation Radio Antenna Kit [*Military*] (RDA)
SORAP .... Signature Overlap Range Prediction
SORAP .... Standard Omnirange Approach
SORAT .... Submarine Operational Readiness Assessment and Training
sorb .... Sorbitol (STED)
Sorb .... Soritol [*Biochemistry*] (DAVI)
SORB .... Submarine Overhaul and Refueling Building [*Navy*] (DNAB)
SORB .... Subsistence Operations Review Board [*Military*] (AABC)
Sorb D .... Sorbitol Dehydrogenase [*Also, SDH*] [*An enzyme*]
SORC .... Serious Offenders Review Council [*New South Wales, Australia*]
SORC .... Signal Officers' Reserve Corps
SORC .... Simultaneous Oxidation-Reduction Catalyst [*Automotive engineering*]
SORC .... Sound Ranging Control
SORC .... Source Co. [*NASDAQ symbol*] (TTSB)
SORC .... Southern Ocean Racing Conference
SORC .... Station Operations Review Committee [*Nuclear energy*] (NRCH)
SORCS .... Shipboard Ordnance Requirement Computer System [*Navy*]
SORD .... Society of Record Dealers of America
SORD .... Southwestern Order Retrieval and Distribution [*Southwest Bell Telephone Co.*]
SORD .... Special Operations and Research Division [*Air Resources Laboratory*] (USDC)
SORD .... Statement of Operational Requirements Document (AAGC)
SORD .... Submerged Object Recovery Device
SORD .... Submerged Ordnance Recovery Device [*Navy*]
SORD .... Systematic Organizational Design
SORD .... System of Operational Requirements Document [*Air Force*] (DOMA)
SORDAC ..... Special Operations Research, Development, and Acquisition Center [*Military*]
SORDC .... Southwest Ohio Regional Data Center [*University of Cincinnati*] [*Research center*] (RCD)
SORDID ...... Summary of Reported Defects, Incidents and Delays (MHDB)
SORE .... Stamp Out Regulatory Excesses [*An association*] (EA)
SOREL .... Sun-Orbiting Relativity Experiment Satellite
SOREM .... Sleep-Onset REM [*Rapid Eye Movement*]
SOREMP ..... Sleep-Onset Rapid Eye Movement Period (STED)
So Rep .... Southern Reporter [*A publication*] (DLA)
So Repr ...... Southern Reporter [*A publication*] (DLA)

SORFO .... Society of Rural Financial Officers [*British*] (BI)
SORG .... Stratospheric Ozone Review Group [*British*] (DBA)
SORG .... Submarine Operations Research Group [*Navy*]
SORI .... Southern Research Institute (AAG)
SORI .... Staff Officer Radio Instructor (IAA)
SORIN .... Societa Ricerche Impianti Nucleari [*Italy*]
SORIS .... Specialised Organics Information Service [*British*] (DBA)
SORM .... Set-Oriented Retrieval Module
SORM .... Ships Organization Manual (DOMA)
SORNE(I) .... Senior Officer, Royal Naval Establishment (India) [*British World War II*]
SORNG .... Sound Ranging
SORO .... Scan on Receive Only (MCD)
SORO .... Sort Program, Sort Routine [*Computer science*] (IAA)
SORO .... Special Operations Research Office
SORP .... Signature Overlay Range Prediction (MCD)
SORP .... Statement of Recommended Practice [*Accounting*] [*British*]
SORPr .... Source Capital $2.40 Pfd [*NYSE symbol*] (TTSB)
SORPTR ..... South Repeater [*NASA*] (MCD)
SORR .... SIGINT [*Signal Intelligence*] Operations Readiness Review [*Military*] (AABC)
SORR .... Submarine Operations Research Report [*Navy*]
SORRA .... Somali Relief and Rehabilitation Agency
SORRAT ...... Society for Research on Rapport and Telekinesis [*Defunct*] (EA)
SORS .... Shipboard Operational Readiness System [*Navy*] (CAAL)
SORS .... Spacecraft Oscillograph Recording System
SORSA .... Spatially Orientated Referencing Systems Association (EERA)
SORSI .... Sacro Occipital Research Society International (EA)
SORT .... Gunther International, Ltd. [*NASDAQ symbol*] (SAG)
SORT .... Self-Observation and Report Technique
SORT .... Senior Officer Refresher Training
SORT .... Shippers of Recycled Textiles [*An association*] (EA)
SORT .... Ship's Operational Readiness Test
SORT .... Simulated Optical Range Target (MCD)
SORT .... Slosson Oral Reading Tests
SORT .... Spanish Oral Reading Text (EDAC)
SORT .... Special Operations Response Team [*Prison management*]
SORT .... Spilled Oil Response Team [*Marine science*] (MSC)
SORT .... Staff Organizations Round Table [*American Library Association*]
SORT .... Structured-Objective Rorschach Test [*Psychology*]
SORT .... Structures for Orbiting Radio Telescope (MCD)
SORT .... Supply Corps Officer Refresher Training [*Navy*] (DNAB)
SORT .... System Operational Readiness Test (MCD)
SORTE .... Summary of Radiation Tolerant Electronics
SORTEC ...... Synchrotron Orbital Radiation Technology [*High-energy physics*]
SORTI .... Satellite Orbital Track and Intercept [*ARPA*]
SORTI .... Star-Oriented Real-Time Teaching Instrument (AAG)
SORTI .... Star-Oriented Real-Time Tracking Instrument [*Aerospace*] (IAA)
SORTIE .... Simulation of Reentry Target Interceptor Endgame (MCD)
SORTIE .... Suborbital Reentry Test Integrated Environment [*NASA*] (IAA)
SORTIE .... Supercircular Orbital Reentry Test Integrated Environment [*NASA*] (IAA)
SORTIE .... Super-Orbital Reentry Test Integrated Environment (MUGU)
SORT-R .... Slosson Oral Reading Test-Revised (TES)
SORTRAN ... Syntax-Oriented Translator (PDAA)
SORTS .... Shipboard Organizational Troubleshooting System (MCD)
SORTS .... Status Of Readiness and Training System (DOMA)
SORTS .... Status of Resources and Training System [*Environmental science*] (COE)
SORTS .... Status of Resources and Training System Report [*Military*]
SORV .... Stuck-Open Relief Valve (COE)
SORWUC .... Service, Office, and Retail Workers Union of Canada
SOS .... Coalition to Protect Social Security (EA)
SOS .... Congress of Scientists on Survival [*Inactive*]
SOS .... Safety Observation Station
SOS .... Safety on the Streets [*Project of National Safety Council*]
SOS .... Same Old Sludge [*Slang phrase used to describe television programming*]
SOS .... Same Old Stew [*Military slang*] [*Bowdlerized version*]
SOS .... Same Old Stuff [*Reference to the weather*]
SOS .... Same Only Softer [*Band leader's signal*] [*Slang*]
SOS .... Sanity on Sex [*Group opposing sex education in schools*]
SOS .... Satellite Observation System
SOS .... Satellite Observing System [*Marine science*] (OSRA)
SOS .... Save Our Schools (EA)
SOS .... Save Our Security (EA)
SOS .... Save Our Security Coalition (EA)
SOS .... Save Our Ship [*or Souls*] [*Popular explanation of Morse code letters used as a signal for extreme distress*]
SOS .... Save Our Shires [*British*] [*An association*] (DBA)
SOS .... Save Our Shores (EA)
SOS .... Save Our Snails [*An association*]
SOS .... Save Our Sons [*Cancer information service*] [*British*]
SOS .... Save Our Souls
SOS .... Save Our Strays (EA)
SOS .... Save Outdoor Sculpture [*Database producer*] (IID)
SOS .... Scheduled Oil Sampling [*Automotive engineering*]
SOS .... Science of Survival
SOS .... Scientists for Sakharov, Orlov, and Shcharansky (EA)
SOS .... Secretary of State
SOS .... Secular Organizations for Sobriety (EA)
SOS .... Self-Observation Scales [*Test*] (TES)
SOS .... Self-Obtained Smear [*Medicine*] (DMAA)
SOS .... Self-Opening Sack [*Paper bag*]
SOS .... Self-Organizing System

SOS	Send Out Succor
SOS	Senior Officer Service
SOS	Senior Officer Structure
SOS	Senior Opportunities and Services [*OEO*]
SOS	Sentinel on Station
SOS	Serial Output Special (MCD)
SOS	Serial Output Special (NAKS)
SOS	Service off the Shelf (IAA)
SOS	Service of Supply [*Later, ASF*] [*Army*]
SOS	Service on Sight [*Computer warranty program offered by Hyundai Electronics*] (PCM)
SOS	Service Order System [*Telecommunications*] (TEL)
SOS	Shakespeare Oxford Society (EA)
SOS	Share Operating System [*Computer science*]
SOS	Share Our Strength (EA)
SOS	Ship Our Ships Program [*Navy*] (DNAB)
SOS	Ships Operational Safety [*A publication*]
SOS	Ships Ordnance Summary
SOS	Shock-on-Shock
SOS	Shop Order Shop (SAA)
SOS	Shop Out of Stock (SAA)
SOS	Signed-Off Sick
SOS	Silicon-on-Sapphire [*Integrated circuit*]
SOS	Silicon-on-Spinel (IAA)
SOS	Simulator Operating System (IAA)
SOS	Simultaneous Oral Spelling [*Gillingham method*] [*Education*]
SOS	Si Opus Sit [*If Needed*] [*Pharmacy*]
SOS	Si Opus Sit [*If Necessary*] [*Latin*] (WDAA)
SOS	Sisters of Service [*Roman Catholic religious order*]
SOS	Slip on Show [*Indicates a woman's slip is showing*] (DSUE)
SOS	Slum on a Shingle [*Army breakfast dish*] [*Bowdlerized version*]
SOS	Sniping, Observation, and Scouting [*Course*] [*World War I*] [*Military British*]
SOS	Society for Occlusal Studies (EA)
SOS	Society of Operative Stonemasons [*A union*] [*British*]
SOS	Society of Scribes (EA)
SOS	Society of Separationists (EA)
SOS	Society of Shuttlemakers [*A union*] [*British*]
SOS	Society of Signalmen (EA)
SoS	Song of Songs [*Old Testament book*] [*Roman Catholic canon*] (BJA)
SOS	Sophisticated Operating System [*Apple III microcomputer*] [*Computer science*]
SOS	Sostenuto [*Sustained*] [*Music*]
SOS	Sound on Sound (NTCM)
SOS	Sound on Sync (IAA)
SOS	Source of Supply
SOS	Source of Supply (NAKS)
SOS	Southern Oxidant Study [*Marine science*] (OSRA)
SOS	Soviet Oceanographic Surveillance (MCD)
SOS	Space Ordnance Systems, Inc. (MCD)
SOS	Spare Operation Support
SOS	Special Operations Squadron [*Air Force*]
SOS	Special Organizational Services [*An association*] (EA)
SOS	Speed of Service [*Telecommunications*] (TEL)
SOS	Speed of Sound
SOS	SPRINT Operations Shelter [*Army*]
SOS	Squadron Officers School [*Air Force*]
SOS	Squadron Operational Support [*Military*] (AFIT)
SOS	Stabilized Optical Sight
SOS	Stabilized Optical Sight (NAKS)
SOS	Stamp Out Stupidity [*Student group opposing drug abuse*]
SOS	Stars Organisation for Spastics [*British television awards program*]
SOS	Starthrowers [*An association*] (EA)
SOS	Start of Significance [*Computer science*] (BUR)
SOS	Statement of Service [*Military*]
SOS	Statement of Supply
SOS	Station Operating Supervisor (IEEE)
SOS	Stimulation of Senses (STED)
SOS	Stock Order Shipment
SOS	Storage Computer [*AMEX symbol*] (TTSB)
SOS	Storage Computer Corp. [*AMEX symbol*] (SAG)
SOS	Storage-on-Site [*Grolier Electronic Publishing, Inc.*]
SOS	Store Overstocked [*Inventory*]
SOS	Strategic Orbital System (AAG)
SOS	Strongpoint Obstacle System [*Military*] (VNW)
SOS	Struck off Strength [*British military*] (DMA)
SOS	Student Orientations Survey [*Student attitudes test*]
SOS	Student-Originated Studies [*National Science Foundation*]
SOS	Studies on Smoking, Inc. [*Research center*] (RCD)
SOS	Suborbital Sequence [*NASA*]
SOS	Sum-of-the-Squares
SOS	Sum over States [*Physics*]
SOS	Supervisor of Shipbuilding [*Navy*]
SOS	Supplemental Oxygen System (MCD)
SOS	Supplementary Ophthalmic Service [*Medicine*]
SOS	Supporters of Silkwood [*Defunct*] (EA)
SOS	Support on Site [*Computer science*]
SOS	Support Our Soldiers [*Network of antiwar-oriented coffee houses located near military bases*] (EA)
SOS	Survivors of Sacrifice [*Defunct*] (EA)
SOS	Survivors of Stalking
SOS	Survivors of Suicide
SOS	Suspend Other Service [*Business term*]
SOS	Suspension of Service [*Pilots' strike*]
SOS	Sustain Our Schools
SOS	Symbolic Operating System [*Computer science*]
SOS	Symmetry, Orbitals, and Spectra [*Atomic physics*]
SOS	Synchronous Orbit Satellite (AAG)
SOS	System Operational Specification [*Military*] (CAAL)
SOSA	Sell Overseas America, the Association of American Export [*Redondo Beach, CA*] (EA)
SOSA	Somerset Savings Bank [*NASDAQ symbol*] (SAG)
SOSA	Starfleet Operations [*An association*] (EA)
SOSA	State Opera of South Australia
SOSA	Sustained Operations Support Area [*NASA*] (KSC)
SOSAL	School of Systems and Logistics [*Military*]
SOSAS	Severe Obstructive Sleep Apnoea Syndrome [*Medicine*] (WDAA)
SOSAT	Submarine One-Way Satellite [*Navy*] (CAAL)
SOSB	Special Operations Signal Battalion (DOMA)
SOSB	Special Operations Support Battalion (DOMA)
SOSC	Safety Observation Station Display Console
SOSC	Smithsonian Oceanographic Sorting Center
SOSC	Source of Supply Code
SOSC	Suburban Ostomy Supply Co., Inc. [*NASDAQ symbol*] (SAG)
SOSCAR	Supervisor of Shipbuilding, Conversion, and Repair [*Navy*] (DNAB)
SoScLfe	Southern Security Life Insurance Co. [*Associated Press*] (SAG)
SOSCMOS	Silicon-on-Sapphire Complementary Metal Oxide Semiconductor (IAA)
SOSCU	Stamps on Stamps - Centenary Unit (EA)
SOSD	Spatial Operational Sequence Diagram
SOSD	System Ordnance Safing Device [*Military*]
SOSE	Science Operations Support Equipment
SOSE	Silicon-on-Something-Else [*Telecommunications*] (TEL)
SOSE	Special Operations Support Element [*Military*] (GFGA)
SOSEC	Satellite Ocean Surveillance Evaluation Center
SOSED	Secretary's Office, Shore Establishments Division [*Incorporated into SECP, 1944*] [*Navy*]
SOSF	Single Organ System Failure [*Medicine*] (DMAA)
SOSFET	Silicon-on-Sapphire Field Effect Transistor (IAA)
SOSH	Search for the Odd Shape [*Neuropsychology test*]
SO SH	Somali Shilling [*Monetary unit*]
SOS:HRG	SOS: Human Rights for Guyana (EA)
SOS Intl	Society of Saunterers, International (EA)
SOSIS	Status of Support Information System
SOSK	Squadron Operational Support Kit (MCD)
SO/SL	Saturn Orbiter Satellite Lander [*NASA*]
SOSM	Ship Overhaul Schedule Milestone [*Navy*]
SOSM	Source of Supply Modifier
SOSO	Safety and Operating Systems Office [*NASA*]
SoSo	South of SoHo [*See also NoHo, SoHo, TriBeCa*] [*Artists' colony in New York City*]
SOSO	Synchronous Orbiting Solar Observatory
SOSP	Squadron Operational Support Package [*Military*] (AFIT)
SOSQ	Special Operations Squadron
SOSR	Spin on Straight Rail
SOSR	Suppress, Obscure, Secure, and Reduce [*Military*] (INF)
SOSRAM	Silicon-on-Sapphire Random Access Memory (IAA)
SOSS	Satellite Ocean Surveillance System
SOSS	Satellite Optical Surveillance Station (MCD)
SOSS	Shipboard Oceanographic Survey System
SOSS	SONAR Schoolship [*Navy*] (NVT)
SOSS	SOS Staffing Services, Inc. [*NASDAQ symbol*] (SAG)
SOSS	SOS Staffing Svcs [*NASDAQ symbol*] (TTSB)
SOSS	Sound Search Station
SOSS	Soviet Ocean Surveillance System (MCD)
SOSS	Strategic Orbital System Study (AAG)
SOSS	Structurally Oriented Simulation System [*NASA*]
SOSSI	Scouts on Stamps Society International (EA)
SOSSI	SOS Sahel International (EAIO)
SOSSPA	Service of Supply, South Pacific Area [*Navy World War II*]
SOS Stf	SOS Staffing Services, Inc. [*Associated Press*] (SAG)
SOSSUS	Sound Surveillance System [*Navy*]
SOSSUS	Study on Surgical Services in the United States [*Medicine*]
SOST	Sostenuto [*Sustained*] [*Music*]
SOST	Special Operator Service Traffic [*Telecommunications*] (TEL)
SOSTEL	Solid-State Electric Logic (NG)
SOSTEN	Sostenuto [*Sustained*] [*Music*]
SOSU	Scout Observation Service Unit [*Navy*]
SOSU	Seattle Ocean Services Unit [*National Oceanic and Atmospheric Administration*] (GFGA)
SOSU	Ships on Stamps Unit (EA)
SOSUS	SONAR Surveillance System [*Military*]
SOSUS	Sound Surveillance System (MSA)
SOSUS	Sound Surveillance Undersea (MCD)
SOSUS	Sound Surveillance Underwater System [*Navy*]
SOSVS	Sound Surveillance System
SOT	Same Old Thing [*Slang*]
SOT	Scanning Oscillator Technique (IAA)
SOT	Secretary of Transportation (NATG)
SOT	Sensation of Transcendence
SOT	Shower over Tub [*Real estate*]
SOT	Simulated Operational Training [*Navy*] (DNAB)
SOT	Sky Wave Observation Timer (IAA)
SOT	Small Outline Transistor [*Electronics*] (AAEL)
SOT	Snowbird, TN [*Location identifier FAA*] (FAAL)
SOT	Society of Ornamental Turners (EA)
SOT	Society of Toxicology (EA)
SOT	Solar Optical Telescope
SOT	Son of Temperance [*A heavy drinker*] [*Slang*]
Sot	Sotah (BJA)

SOT............. Sound on Tape [*Videotape*]
SOT............. Sounds of Our Times, Cook Studio [*Record label*]
SOT............. Southeast Correct Craft, Inc. [*ICAO designator*] (FAAC)
SOT............. South Omaha Terminal Railway Co. [*AAR code*]
SOT............. Soviet Orientation Team (MCD)
SOT............. Spatial Orientation Trainer [*Air Force*]
SOT............. Special Operations Team (ADA)
SOT............. Specified Organ Transplant [*Health insurance*] (GHCT)
SOT............. SRO Entertainment [*Vancouver Stock Exchange symbol*]
SOT............. Start of Tape
SOT............. Start of Text
SOT............. State of Termination [*Telecommunications*] (TEL)
S-O-T........... Stoke-On-Trent [*City in England*]
SOT............. Strap-On Tank [*NASA*] (NASA)
SOT............. Stream of Thought
SOT............. Structural Operations Technology Group (SSD)
SOT............. Subscriber Originating Trunk [*Telecommunications*] (TEL)
SOT............. Syntax-Oriented Translator (IEEE)
SOT............. Systemic Oxygen Transport (STED)
SOT............. Systems Operating Test
SOTA........... SIGINT [*Signal Intelligence*] Operational Tasking Authority [*Military*]
SOTA........... State of the Art
SOTA........... State of the Art, Inc. [*NASDAQ symbol*] (SPSG)
SOTA........... Students Older than Average
SOTAC......... State-of-the-Art Car [*Transit*] [*Department of Transportation*]
SOTACA....... State-of-the-Art Contingency Analysis System [*Science Applications International Corp.*] (MCD)
SOTAP......... Sophisticated Training Program
SOTARSS..... Standoff Target Acquisition Reconnaissance Surveillance System (MCD)
SOTAS......... Standoff Target Acquisition/Attack System
SOTASS....... Standoff Target Acquisition and Surveillance System [*Army*]
SOTB.......... Secretary's Office, Transportation Branch [*Navy*]
SOTD.......... Stabilized Optical Tracking Device (SAA)
SOTDAT....... Source Test Data [*Environmental science*] (COE)
SOTDAT....... Source Test Data System [*Environmental Protection Agency*]
SOTE.......... Standard Optical Test Equipment
SOTE.......... System Operational Test Evaluation (SAA)
SOTEAG....... Shetland Oil Terminal Environmental Advisory Group
SOTER......... Soil and Terrain Database [*USA*] (EERA)
So Tex C Law... South Texas College of Law (GAGS)
So Tex LJ .... Southern Texas Law Journal [*A publication*] (DLA)
SOTF.......... Special Operations Task Force [*Military*] (GFGA)
SOTFE......... Special Operations Task Force, Europe [*Military*]
SOTG.......... Sales Other than Gasoline [*Business term*]
SOTG.......... Special Operations Training Group [*Marine Corps*] (DOMA)
Sothbys........ Sotheby's Holdings, Inc. [*Associated Press*] (SAG)
SOTI............. [*A*] Survey of Old Testament Introductions [*Gleason L. Archer*] [*A publication*] (BJA)
SOTIM .... Sonic Observation of the Trajectory and Impact of Missiles
SOTP.......... Saturn Orbiter/Titan Probe (MCD)
SOTP.......... Ship Overhaul Test Program
SOTP.......... Shipyard Overhaul Test Program
SOTP.......... System Overhaul Test Program
SOTR.......... Single Object Tracking RADAR (MCD)
SOTR.......... SouthTrust Corp. [*NASDAQ symbol*] (NQ)
SOTS.......... Society of Old Testament Study [*British*] (DBA)
SOTS.......... Suborbital Tank Separation [*NASA*] (MCD)
SOTS.......... Synchronous Orbiting Tracking Stations (MCD)
SOTT........... Second-Order Transition Temperature
SOTT........... Synthetic Medium Old Tuberculin Trichloroacetic Acid Precipitated [*Later, PPD, Purified Protein Derivative*] [*Immunology*]
SOTUS......... Sequentially Operated Teletypewriter Universal Selector
SOU .... Flight Line, Inc. [*ICAO designator*] (FAAC)
SOU .... Scandinavian Ornithological Union [*Lund, Sweden*] (EAIO)
SOU .... Souchong [*Tea trade*] (ROG)
SOU .... Sources Public Library [*UTLAS symbol*]
SOU .... South (ROG)
SOU .... Southampton [*England*] [*Airport symbol*] (OAG)
SOU .... Southern Airways [*Air carrier designation symbol*]
SOU .... Southern Petroleum Corp. [*Vancouver Stock Exchange symbol*]
SOU .... Southern Railway System [*AAR code*]
SOU .... Statens Offentliga Utredningar [*Sweden*]
SOU .... Statute of Uses [*Legal shorthand*] (LWAP)
SouAfrica..... Southern Africa Fund [*Associated Press*] (SAG)
SouAla........ South Alabama Bancorp [*Associated Press*] (SAG)
So U & A&M C... Southern University and Agricultural and Mechanical College (GAGS)
SouBnc .... Southside Bancshares [*Associated Press*] (SAG)
SoUCo .... Southern Union Co. [*Associated Press*] (SAG)
Soudw .... Southdown, Inc. [*Associated Press*] (SAG)
Soudwn....... Southdown, Inc. [*Associated Press*] (SAG)
SouFncl ...... Southern Financial Bancorp [*Associated Press*] (SAG)
SouFncl ...... Southern Financial Federal Savings Bank [*Associated Press*] (SAG)
SOUL .... Studies of Ocean Upper Layers (MSC)
Soule Syn .... Soule's Dictionary of English Synonymes [*A publication*] (DLA)
SouMoBc ..... SouMOBc Co. [*Associated Press*] (SAG)
SoUnCo .... Southern Union Co. [*Associated Press*] (SAG)
SoundA........ Sound Advice, Inc. [*Associated Press*] (SAG)
SoUnF......... Southern Union Financing [*Associated Press*] (SAG)
So Univ....... Southern University (GAGS)
SOUP .... Software Updating Package [*Computer science*] (CIST)
SOUP .... Software Utility Package (NITA)
SOUP .... Solar Optical Universal Polarimeter
SOUP .... Solid Uncured Propellant (MCD)

SOUP .... Students Opposed to Unfair Practices [*in advertising*] [*Student legal action organization*]
SOUP .... Submarine Operational Update Program [*Canadian Navy*]
SouPacR....... Southern Pacific Rail Corp. [*Associated Press*] (SAG)
SouPoint...... South Pointe Enterprises [*Associated Press*] (SAG)
SOUPr......... South'n Cal Gas cm6%PfdA vtg [*PC symbol*] (TTSB)
SOUQAR ...... Section d'Oceanographie d'Universite de Quebec a Rimouski [*Canada*] (MSC)
SOUR.......... Specific Oxygen Uptake Rate [*In wastewater*]
SourcC........ Source Capital, Inc. [*Associated Press*] (SAG)
SOURCE...... Simulation of Utilization, Resources, Cost, and Efficiency
SOURS........ Subcommittee on Use of Radioactivity Standards [*National Research Council*]
SOUSAFE..... Status of United States Air Force Equipment
SOUSSA...... Steady, Oscillatory, and Unsteady, Subsonic, and Supersonic Aerodynamics [*NASA*]
SOUT .... Swap-Out [*Computer science*]
SOUTC .... Satellite Operators and Users Technical Committee [*Defunct*] (EA)
South .... Southern Reporter [*National Reporter System*] [*A publication*] (DLA)
Southard...... Southard's New Jersey Law Reports [*4-5 New Jersey*] [*A publication*] (DLA)
South Car ... South Carolina Reports [*A publication*] (DLA)
SOUTHCOM... Southern Command [*Military*] (AFM)
SouthCp....... Southshore Corp. [*Associated Press*] (SAG)
South CR ..... South Carolina Review [*A publication*] (BRI)
South Cul..... Southern Cultures [*A publication*] (BRI)
Southeastern La U... Southeastern Louisiana University (GAGS)
Southeastern Okla St U... Southeastern Oklahoma State University (GAGS)
Southeastern Rep... South Eastern Reporter [*A publication*] (DLA)
Southeast Mo St U... Southeast Missouri State University (GAGS)
Southern...... Southern Reporter [*A publication*] (DLA)
Southern Rep... Southern Reporter [*A publication*] (DLA)
SOUTHFORNET... Southern Forestry Information Network [*Forest Service*] (IID)
South HR ..... Southern Humanities Review [*A publication*] (BRI)
South Law J... Southern Law Journal [*Tuscaloosa, AL*] [*A publication*] (DLA)
South Law J & Rep... Southern Law Journal and Reporter [*A publication*] (DLA)
South Law Rev... Southern Law Review [*A publication*] (DLA)
South Law Rev NS... Southern Law Review, New Series [*A publication*] (DLA)
SouthldCp.... Southland Corp. [*Associated Press*] (SAG)
South LJ...... Southern Law Journal [*A publication*] (DLA)
South LJ & Rep... Southern Law Journal and Reporter [*A publication*] (DLA)
South L Rev... Southern Law Review [*A publication*] (DLA)
South L Rev NS... Southern Law Review, New Series [*A publication*] (DLA)
SOUTHN ...... Southampton [*City in England*] (ROG)
SouthnCo..... Southern Co. [*Associated Press*] (SAG)
South R ...... Southern Review [*A publication*] (BRI)
Southtrst..... Southtrust Corp. [*Associated Press*] (SAG)
SOUTHW...... Southwell [*City in England*] (ROG)
Southwestern Okla St U... Southwestern Oklahoma State University (GAGS)
Southwestern U Law... Southwestern University School of Law (GAGS)
Southwest Mo St U... Southwest Missouri State University (GAGS)
Southwest Tex St U... Southwest Texas State University (GAGS)
Southw LJ ... Southwestern Law Journal and Reporter [*A publication*] (DLA)
SouUnCo...... Southern Union Co. [*Associated Press*] (SAG)
Souwal .... Southwall Technologies, Inc. [*Associated Press*] (SAG)
SOV .... Sammons' Opuntia Virus [*Plant pathology*]
SOV .... Saratov Aviation Division [*Former USSR*] [*FAA designator*] (FAAC)
SOV .... Seldovia, AK [*Location identifier FAA*] (FAAL)
SOV .... Sham Ovariectomy [*Endocrinology*]
SOV .... Share of Voice [*Advertising*]
SOV .... Shut-Off Valve
sov............. Shut-Off Valve (NAKS)
SOV .... Simulated Operational Vehicle (MCD)
SOV .... Single-Occupancy Vehicle (ECON)
SOV .... Solenoid-Operated Valve
sov............. Solenoid Operated Valve (NAKS)
SOV .... Somerset County Vocational and Technical School, Bridgewater, NJ [*OCLC symbol*] (OCLC)
SOV .... Sound on Vision (IAA)
SOV .... Sovereign
SOV .... Soviet
SOV .... Study of Values
SOV .... Styles on Video [*AMEX symbol*] (TTSB)
SOV .... Styles on Video, Inc. [*AMEX symbol*] (SPSG)
SOV .... Subjective Optical Vertical
SOVA .... Society of Voluntary Associates [*British*] (DBA)
SOVAC........ Software Validation and Control System (MCD)
SovAE......... Soviet Antarctic Expedition [*1955-*]
Sov & E Eur For Tr... American Review of Soviet and Eastern European Foreign Trade [*A publication*] (DLA)
SOVAS......... Scanning Optical Vibration Analysis System (IAA)
SovBcp........ Sovereign Bancorp, Inc. [*Associated Press*] (SAG)
SOVD.......... Stabilized Optical Viewing Device
SOVE.......... Society for Vector Ecology (NTPA)
Soviet Jewry L Rev... Soviet Jewry Law Review [*A publication*] (DLA)
Soviet Stat & Dec... Soviet Statutes and Decisions [*A publication*] (DLA)
Soviet YB Int'l L... Soviet Year-Book of International Law [*A publication*] (DLA)
SOVIII......... Third Survey of Veterans [*Veterans Administration*] (GFGA)
SOVIN......... Samenwerkingsverband voor Opleiding en Vorming op het Terrein van de Informatieverzorging via Netwerken [*Collective for Training and Education in Connection with Information Provision via Networks*] [*Ceased operation*] [*Netherlands Information service or system*] (IID)
SOVIX .... Hancock(J) Sovereign Investors Cl.A [*Mutual fund ticker symbol*] (SG)

SOVMEDRON...	Soviet Mediterranean Squadron [*NATO*] (NATG)
SOVNARKOM...	Soviet Narodnykh Komissarov [*Council of People's Commissars*] [*Former USSR*] (LAIN)
SOVNROF	State of Vietnam Ribbon of Friendship [*Presidential unit commendation*]
SOVOG.........	Sozialistische Volksorganisation [*Socialist National Community*] [*Lithuania*] [*Political party*] (PPE)
SovranSS....	Sovran Self Storage, Inc. [*Associated Press*] (SAG)
SoVrnSS	Sovran Self Storage, Inc. [*Associated Press*] (SAG)
SOVS	Sovereigns [*Monetary unit*] [*Obsolete British*]
SOVX.........	Sham Ovariectomized [*Endocrinology*]
SOW	Scope of Work (MCD)
SOW	Scramble-on-Warning
SOW	Show Low [*Arizona*] [*Airport symbol Obsolete*] (OAG)
SOW	Skylab Orbital Workshop [*NASA*]
SOW	Sowind Air Ltd. [*Canada ICAO designator*] (FAAC)
SOW	Special Operations Wing [*Military*] (MCD)
SOW	Standoff Weapons (MCD)
SOW	Start of Word
sow	Start of Word (NAKS)
SOW	Start of Work
SOW	Statement of Work (MCD)
sow	Statement of Work (NAKS)
sow	Subdivision of Work (NAKS)
SOW	Subdivision of Work [*NASA*] (NASA)
SOW	Sunflower Ordnance Works [*Military*]
SOW	Synthetic Ocean Water
SOWA.........	Stock Option Writers Association [*Defunct*] (EA)
SOWC.........	Senior Officers' War Course [*British*]
SOWESPAC...	Southwest Pacific Command [*Navy*]
SOWESSEAFRON...	Southwest Sea Frontier [*Navy*]
SOWESTDIVDOCKS...	Southwest Division, Bureau of Yards and Docks [*Navy*] (MUGU)
SOWESTPACCOM...	Southwest Pacific Command [*Navy*] (DNAB)
So West Rep...	South Western Reporter [*A publication*] (DLA)
SOWETO	Southwestern Townships [*South Africa*]
SOWEX	Southern Ocean Waves Experiment [*Marine science*] (OSRA)
SOWg	Special Operations Wing [*Air Force*] (AFM)
SOWIDOK	Sozialwissenschaftliche Dokumentation [*Social Sciences Documentation Center*] [*Vienna Chamber of Labor*] [*Information service or system*] (IID)
SOWM	Special Ocean Wave Model
SOWN.........	Supportive Older Women's Network [*An association*]
SOWP	Society of Wireless Pioneers (EA)
SOWR.........	Submarine Overhaul Work Requirement [*Navy*] (DNAB)
SOWRA.......	Submarine Overhaul Work Requirement Authorization [*Navy*] (DNAB)
SOWRBALL...	Southwest RADAR Balloon [*for illegal drug interdiction*]
SOW/S & D...	Statement of Work/Specifications and Design
SOWT/TE ...	Special Operations Weather Team/Tactical Element (COE)
SOX	Sentry Resources Corp. [*Formerly, Sentry Oil & Gas*] [*Vancouver Stock Exchange symbol*]
SOX	Solid Oxygen
SOX	Sound Exchange [*A sound conversion program*] (PCM)
SOX	Sulfur Oxide
SOX...........	Sulphur Oxides [*Chemical*] (EERA)
SOX	Supercritical Oxygen [*NASA*] (KSC)
SOY	Sioux Center, IA [*Location identifier FAA*] (FAAL)
SOY	SO Resources [*Vancouver Stock Exchange symbol*]
SOY	Stronsay [*Scotland*] [*Airport symbol*] (OAG)
SOYD	Sum of the Years' Digits Method [*Finance*]
SOYDV........	Soybean Dwarf Virus [*Plant pathology*]
SOYMV	Soybean Mosaic Virus [*Plant pathology*]
SOYO	Society of Orthodox Youth Organizations (EA)
SOZ...........	Seder 'Olam Zuta (BJA)
SOZ...........	Solo International Resources Ltd. [*Vancouver Stock Exchange symbol*]
SOZ...........	Somerset, PA [*Location identifier FAA*] (FAAL)
SOZ...........	Soviet Occupied Zone (NATG)
Sp	Biblioteca Nacional, Madrid, Spain [*Library symbol Library of Congress*] (LCLS)
SP.............	Error in Spelling [*Used in correcting manuscripts, etc.*]
SP.............	International Society of Philology
sp----	La Plata River and Basin [*MARC geographic area code Library of Congress*] (LCCP)
SP.............	Motor Patrol Boat [*Navy symbol Obsolete*]
Sp	[*The*] New Testament of Our Lord and Saviour Jesus Christ (1937) (Francis Aloysius Spencer) [*A publication*] (BJA)
SP.............	Office of State Programs [*Nuclear energy*] (NRCH)
SP.............	Poland [*International civil aircraft marking*] (ODBW)
SP.............	Sacra Pagina [*Paris-Gembloux*] [*A publication*] (BJA)
Sp.............	Sacropubic [*Anatomy*] (AAMN)
SP.............	Sacrum Posterior [*A fetal position*] (DAVI)
SP.............	Sacrum to Pubis [*Medicine*] (DMAA)
SP.............	Safety Panel
SP.............	Sailing Plan Report
SP.............	Salisbury [*Postcode*] (ODBW)
SP.............	Salivary Progesterone [*Medicine*] (DMAA)
SP.............	Samajwadi Party [*Italy Political party*] (ECON)
SP.............	Same Point (ILCA)
SP.............	Same Principle (ILCA)
SP.............	Sample Part
SP.............	Sampling Point (NRCH)
SP.............	Sanctissime Pater [*Most Holy Father*] [*Latin*]
SP.............	San Pedro [*California*]
SP.............	Satellite Processor [*Data transmission*]

SP.............	Scalable Processing [*Northgate*] [*Computer science*]
SP.............	Scan Programmer (DGA)
SP.............	Schering-Plough Corp. [*Commercial firm*]
SP.............	Schizotypal Personality [*Medicine*] (DMAA)
SP.............	Schools of Philosophy [*A publication*]
SP.............	Schwangerschaftsprotein [*Biochemistry*] (DAVI)
SP.............	Science Pilot
SP.............	Science Press [*Information service or system*] (IID)
SP.............	Scientific Paper
SP.............	Scientific Processor (BUR)
S/P.............	Scientific Products
SP.............	Scottish Peer (ROG)
SP.............	Scratch Pad [*Computer science*]
S/P.............	Seaplane
SP.............	Sea Platform (MCD)
SP.............	Secretory Piece [*Superseded by SC, Secretory Component*] [*Immunology*]
SP.............	Secretory Protein [*Endocrinology*]
SP.............	Section Patrol [*Navy*]
SP.............	Security Pacific Corp. (EFIS)
SP.............	Security Police [*Air Force*] (AFM)
SP.............	Security Procedure (NRCH)
SP.............	Security Publication [*Navy*]
SP.............	Seed Production [*Agriculture*]
SP.............	Seeing Problems [*Research test*] [*Psychology*]
SP.............	Selective Purchases
SP.............	Self Potential [*Log*]
SP.............	Self-Powered [*Gun*] (MCD)
SP.............	Self-Propelled [*Military*]
SP.............	Selling Price
SP.............	Seminar Press
SP.............	Semipostal
S/P.............	Semiprivate [*Room*]
SP.............	Semipublic [*Telecommunications*] (TEL)
SP.............	Send Processor
sP.............	Senile Parkinsonism [*Medicine*] (DMAA)
SP.............	Senile Plaque [*Neurology*]
SP.............	Senior Partner
SP.............	Senior Pilot [*Air Force*]
SP.............	Sensor Processor (BUR)
Sp.............	Senterpartiet [*Center Party*] [*Norway Political party*] (PPE)
SP.............	Senza Pedale [*Without Pedals*] [*Music*]
SP.............	Separate Element Pricing (IAA)
SP.............	Septum Pellucidum [*Brain anatomy*]
SP.............	Sequence Programmer [*Computer science*] (AAG)
S-P.............	Sequential-Phase (CET)
SP.............	Sequential Processor
SP.............	Sequential Pulse [*Medicine*] (DAVI)
S/P.............	Serial to Parallel (KSC)
SP.............	Series Parallel [*Computer science*] (IAA)
SP.............	Serum Protection (DB)
SP.............	Serum Protein (DB)
SP.............	Servants of the Holy Paraclete [*Roman Catholic men's religious order*]
sp.............	Servants of the Paraclete (TOCD)
sP.............	Servants of the Paraclete (TOCD)
SP.............	Service Package (OA)
SP.............	Service Panel
SP.............	Service Phase (MCD)
SP.............	Service Police [*British military*] (DMA)
SP.............	Service Processor (IEEE)
SP.............	Service Publications (AAG)
SP.............	Serving Point [*Telecommunications*]
SP.............	Session of Peace [*Legal*] [*British*] (ROG)
SP.............	Set Pattern (IAA)
SP.............	Set Point
SP.............	Severely, Profoundly Handicapped (OICC)
SP.............	Sewer Pipe [*Telecommunications*] (TEL)
SP.............	Shanti Project (EA)
SP.............	Shear Plate [*Technical drawings*]
SP.............	Shick-Positive (DB)
SP.............	Shift Pulses
SP.............	Shipping Port
SP.............	Shoreline Protection [*Type of water project*]
SP.............	Shore Party [*Navy*]
SP.............	Shore Patrol [*Navy*]
SP.............	Shore Police [*Navy*]
SP.............	Shortest Path
SP.............	Short Page
SP.............	Short Perforation [*Philately*]
SP.............	Short Period
SP.............	Short Persistence
SP.............	Short Position [*Investment term*]
SP.............	Short Pulse
SP.............	Shoulder Pitch (MCD)
SP.............	Shunt Pressure (DB)
SP.............	Shunt Procedure [*Medicine*] (MAE)
SP.............	Shuttle Projects Office [*Kennedy Space Center*] [*NASA*] (NASA)
SP.............	Sic Porro [*So Forth*] [*Latin*]
SP.............	Sidepull [*Bicycle*] (DICI)
SP.............	Sieve Pore [*Botany*]
SP.............	Signaling Projector [*British*]
S/P.............	Signal Processor (NASA)
SP.............	Signal Publication [*British*]
SP.............	Signed Photograph

SP.............	Sign Post
SP.............	Sikkim Parishad [*India*] [*Political party*] (PPW)
SP.............	Silver Plate
SP.............	SilverPlatter Information, Inc. [*Commercial firm*]
SP.............	Silver Protein [*An antiseptic*]
SP.............	Simple Printing
sp.............	Sine Prole [*Without Issue*] [*Latin*] (WA)
SP.............	Singing Point [*Telecommunications*] (TEL)
SP.............	Single Particle
SP.............	Single Payment (ILCA)
SP.............	Single-Peaked (IAA)
SP.............	Single-Phase
SP.............	Single-Pole [*Switch*]
sp.............	Single-Pole (IDOE)
SP.............	Single Precision (NASA)
SP.............	Single Programmer
SP.............	Single Purpose
SP.............	Sisters of Providence [*Roman Catholic religious order*]
SP.............	Sisters of Providence of Saint Mary-of-the-Woods, IN (TOCD)
SP.............	Sisters of the Presentation of Mary [*Roman Catholic religious order*]
SP.............	Skin Painting [*Method of administering experimental chemicals*]
SP.............	Skin Potential (MAE)
SP.............	Skin Prick [*Immunology*]
SP.............	Sloop (ROG)
SP.............	Slugging Percentage [*Baseball*]
SP.............	Small Packet
SP.............	Small Paper [*Printing*]
SP.............	Small Pica
SP.............	Small Plaque
SP.............	Small Premises [*Hairdressers, doctors, dentists, etc.*] [*Public-performance tariff class*] [*British*]
SP.............	Smith Predictor [*Process control*]
SP.............	Smoke Control and Pressurization Panel [*NFPA pre-fire planning symbol*] (NFPA)
SP.............	Smokeless Powder
SP.............	Smokeless Propellant (NATG)
SP.............	Smoki People [*An association*] (EA)
SP.............	Sniper's Post [*British military*] (DMA)
SP.............	Socialistische Partij [*Socialist Party*] [*Belgium Political party*] (PPW)
SP.............	Socialist Party
SP.............	Society of Philaticians [*Defunct*] (EA)
SP.............	Society of Protozoologists (EA)
SP.............	Sociolinguistics Program (EA)
SP.............	Softening Point (MCD)
SP.............	Soil Pipe
SP.............	Soil Pit
SP.............	Soil Psychrometer
SP.............	Solar Panel
SP.............	Solar Physics (NASA)
SP.............	Soldiers for Peace (EA)
SP.............	Sole Proprietor (MHDW)
SP.............	Solid Phase (DB)
SP.............	Solid Propellant
SP.............	Soluble Powder (GNE)
SP.............	Solution Provider [*Microsoft workgroup*] (PCM)
SP.............	Sort Program [*Computer science*] (IAA)
SP.............	Sosyalist Parti [*Socialist Party*] [*Turkey Political party*] (EY)
S/P.............	Sotto Protesto [*Under Protest*] [*Italian*]
SP.............	Sound Positive (IAA)
SP.............	Sound Powered (CAAL)
SP.............	Soundproof [*Technical drawings*]
SP.............	Source Program [*Computer science*] (IAA)
SP.............	Southern Pacific Transportation Co. [*AAR code*]
SP.............	Southern Pine [*Utility pole*] [*Telecommunications*] (TEL)
SP.............	South Pacific
SP.............	South Pole [*Also, PS*]
SP.............	South Proceeding [*Astronomy*]
sp.............	Space [*Crocheting*]
SP.............	Space (ECII)
SP.............	Space and Power
SP.............	Space Character [*Keyboard*] (AAG)
SP.............	Space Patrol (AAG)
SP.............	Space Platform (SSD)
SP.............	Space Probe (IAA)
Sp.............	Spacers [*Electron transfer*]
SP.............	Spain
sp.............	Spain [*MARC country of publication code Library of Congress*] (LCCP)
Sp.............	Spaniard (WDAA)
Sp.............	Spanish (ODCC)
Sp.............	Spare (AAG)
SP.............	Spare Part
SP.............	Spares Planning (AAG)
Sp.............	Spark (AAG)
SP.............	Spark Plug (IAA)
SP.............	Spartan Program [*Missiles*] (MCD)
SP.............	Spasmolytic Polypeptide [*Biochemistry*]
Sp.............	Spears' South Carolina Law Reports [*1842-44*] [*A publication*] (DLA)
SP.............	Special (AFM)
sp.............	Special (IDOE)
Sp.............	Special Branch [*Navy British*]
SP.............	Speciale Prototipo [*Special Prototype*] [*Italy*]
SP.............	Specialist (ADA)
sp.............	Specialist (WDMC)
SP.............	Specialist Degree (PGP)
SP.............	Special Paper
SP.............	Special Performance
SP.............	Special Planning (AAG)
SP.............	Special Product (MCD)
SP.............	Special Proficiency [*British military*] (DMA)
SP.............	Special Program
SP.............	Special Progress [*Program*] [*Education*]
SP.............	Special Projects
SP.............	Special Propellants
SP.............	Special Provisions (AAGC)
SP.............	Special Publication
SP.............	Special Purchase (ADA)
SP.............	Special Purpose
SP.............	Species [*Also, sp*]
sp.............	Species (LDT)
SP.............	Specific (AAG)
SP.............	Specific Performance [*Legal shorthand*] (LWAP)
SP.............	Specific Power
SP.............	Specimen
SP.............	Speck (WGA)
SP.............	Spectral Pitch [*Neurophysiology*]
SP.............	Speech (WGA)
SP.............	Speech Pathologist
SP.............	Speed (MSA)
SP.............	Spelling
sp.............	Spelling (WDMC)
SP.............	Spelling Entertainment Group [*Formerly, Charter Co.*] [*NYSE symbol*] (SPSG)
SP.............	Spelling Entertainment Grp [*NYSE symbol*] (TTSB)
sp.............	Spell Out [*Proofreading*] (WDMC)
SP.............	Spherical [*Buoy*]
SP.............	Spherical Polar
sp.............	Spherical Tank [*Liquid gas carriers*]
SP.............	Sphingomyelin [*Also, SM, Sph*] [*Biochemistry*] (DAVI)
S/P.............	Spikes Plant [*Wheat*]
SP.............	Spine [*or Spinal*]
sp.............	Spinel [*CIPW classification*] [*Geology*]
SP.............	Spine Point Bullet
Sp.............	Spinks' English Admiralty Prize Cases [*164 English Reprint*] [*1854-56*] [*A publication*] (DLA)
Sp.............	Spinks' English Ecclesiastical and Admiralty Reports [*A publication*] (DLA)
SP.............	Spin Polarized [*Physics*]
Sp.............	Spirillum (MAE)
SP.............	Spirit
SP.............	Spiritus [*Spirit*] [*Latin*] [*Pharmacy*] (DAVI)
SP.............	Spirometry
SP.............	Spitze [*Point*] [*Music*]
SP.............	Splash Plate
SP.............	Splashproof (MSA)
SP.............	Spleen (DB)
SP.............	Splinting [*Dentistry*]
SP.............	Splitting [*Electronics*]
SP.............	Sponge (WGA)
SP.............	Sponsor (NITA)
SP.............	Sponsoring Program (NITA)
Sp.............	Spontaneous
SP.............	Spontaneous Potential [*Log*]
SP.............	Spool (MSA)
SP.............	Spoon (WGA)
SP.............	Spore Plasma [*Botany*]
SP.............	Sport
SP.............	Sportavia Puetzer GmbH & Co. KG [*Germany ICAO aircraft manufacturer identifier*] (ICAO)
SP.............	Sports for the People [*Defunct*] (EA)
SP.............	Spot Price [*Investment term*]
SP.............	Spouse
SP.............	Sprague-Dawley [*Rat variety*]
SP.............	Spray Pressure [*Agriculture*]
Sp.............	Spring Tide
Sp.............	Square Planar [*Organic chemistry*]
SP.............	Square Punch
SP.............	Stable Platform
SP.............	Stack and Play Hub [*Intellicom, Inc.*] [*Telecommunication switching device*] (PCM)
SP.............	Stack Pointer [*Computer science*]
SP.............	Stack Pool [*Computer memory*] (PCM)
SP.............	Staff Paymaster [*Navy British*] (ROG)
SP.............	Staff Planner [*DoD*]
SP.............	Stained Pollen [*Botany*]
SP.............	Standard Holding Pattern [*Aviation*]
SP.............	Standard or Peculiar (NASA)
SP.............	Standard Peripherals (IAA)
SP.............	Standard Pile [*Nuclear reactor*]
SP.............	Standard Play [*Video technology*]
SP.............	Standard Practice [*or Procedure*]
SP.............	Standard Pressure (IAA)
SP.............	Standard Price
SP.............	Standard Program [*Computer science*] (BUR)
SP.............	Standby Power
SP.............	Standing Procedure (NATG)
SP.............	Standpipe (MSA)
SP.............	Staphylococcal Protease [*Medicine*] (DMAA)
SP.............	Staphylococcal Protein A [*Biochemistry*] (DAVI)
SP.............	Starting Point

SP	Starting Price
SP	Start Permission (KSC)
SP	State Park [State] (EERA)
SP	State Plan (OICC)
SP	State Primary (OTD)
SP	Static Pointer [Computer science]
SP	Static Pressure
SP	Station Police [British military] (DMA)
SP	Status Panel (CAAL)
SP	Status Positive [Medicine] (CPH)
S/P	Status Post [Medicine]
SP	Steady Potential (MAE)
SP	Stern Post
SP	Stipule [Botany]
SP	Stirrup Pump
SP	Stool Preservative [Medicine]
SP	Stop Payment [Banking]
SP	Stop Press (ADA)
SP	Storage Protection (IAA)
SP	Storage Protein [Food industry]
SP	St. Petersburg [Diocesan abbreviation] [Florida] (TOCD)
SP	Straight Partners [Defunct] (EA)
SP	Strategic Planning Chart [Air Force]
SP	Strategic Planning Society [See also SPS] [London, England] (EAIO)
SP	Street Price (ROG)
SP	Stretcher Party
SP	Stronnictwo Pracy [Labour Party] [Poland Political party] (EY)
SP	Structured Programming [Computer science] (BUR)
S-P	Studebaker-Packard [Automobile manufacturer]
SP	Study Plan
SP	Subject-Predicate
SP	Subliminal Perception
SP	Submarine Patrol [Navy]
S/P	Submarine Pay [British military] (DMA)
SP	Subplate [Neurology]
SP	Subprofessional [Civil Service employees designation]
SP	Subprogram (IAA)
SP	Substance P [A peptide] [Biochemistry]
SP	Successive Planometric [A discrimination task]
SP	Sugar Phosphate [Biochemistry]
SP	Suicide Precaution (MAE)
SP	Sulfopropyl [Organic chemistry]
SP	Sumerian Proverbs (BJA)
SP	Summary Plotter [RADAR]
SP	Summary Punch [Computer science] (OA)
SP	Summating Potential [Hearing]
SP	Summus Pontifex [Supreme Pontiff, Pope] [Latin]
SP	Sundries Pack [Field troops military issue] (VNW)
SP	Sunlit Period
SP	Sun's Parallax [Astronomy] (ROG)
SP	Superficial Pineal Organ [Neuroanatomy]
SP	Superparamagnetic [Fraction in rock] [Geophysics]
SP	Superseded in Part [New matter substituted for part of an existing regulation or order] [Used in Shepard's Citations] [Legal term] (DLA)
SP	Supervisory Package (OA)
SP	Supervisory Printer [Computer science] (OA)
SP	Supervisory Process [Telecommunications] (TEL)
SP	Supplement
SP	Supplemental Pack [Field troops military issue] (VNW)
SP	Supply Point [Military] (NATG)
SP	Support
SP	Support Plan (MCD)
SP	Support Publications (AAG)
SP	Suppression Pool [Environmental science] (COE)
SP	Supraprotest
SP	Suprapubic [Medicine]
SP	Surveillance Procedure (NRCH)
SP	Surviving Propagules [Botany]
SP	Suspicious Person
SP	Sustainer Pitch (AAG)
SP	Swelling Power [Food technology]
SP	Switch Panel
SP	Switch Port [Telecommunications]
SP	Syllable Period [Entomology]
SP	Symbol Programmer (MUGU)
SP	Symphonic Popular [Armed Forces Radio-Televsion] (DNAB)
SP	Symphysis Pubica [Anatomy]
SP	Synperiplanar [Chemistry]
SP	System Parameter (KSC)
SP	System Processor (IEEE)
S-P	Systems and Procedures
SP	Systolic Pressure [Cardiology]
SP	Teaching and Teacher Education [Educational Resources Information Center (ERIC) Clearinghouse] [American Association of Colleges for Teacher Education] (PAZ)
Sp3c	Specialist, Third Class (GFGA)
SP3T	Single-Pole, Triple-Throw [Switch] (IEEE)
SP4	Specialist 4 [Army]
SP4T	Single-Pole, Quadruple-Throw [Switch] (IEEE)
SP5	Specialist 5 [Obsolete Army]
SP6	Specialist 6 [Obsolete Army]
SP7	Specialist 7 [Army]
SP8	Specialist 8 [Obsolete Army]
SP9	Specialist 9 [Obsolete Army]
SPA	Greenville/Spartanburg [South Carolina] Downtown [Airport symbol] (OAG)
SPA	Sacrum Palatium Apostolicum [Sacred Apostolic Palace, Vatican, Quirinal] [Latin]
SPA	Salaried Pharmacists' Association [Australia]
SPA	Salt-Poor Albumin [Medicine]
SPA	Salt Producers Association [Later, SI] (EA)
SPA	Sample Preparation Accessory [Laboratory analysis]
SPA	Satellite Personnel Activity [Military]
SPA	Saudi Press Agency
SPA	S-Band Power Amplifier
SPA	Scalable Processing Architecture [Computer hardware] [Northgate] (PCM)
SPA	Scatter Propagation Antenna
SPA	Schedules Planning and Analysis [Aviation] (DA)
SPA	Schizophrenia with Premorbid Asociality [Psychology] (DB)
SPA	Science and Public Affairs [A publication]
SPA	Scintillation Proximity Assay [Analytical biochemistry]
SPA	Scottish Paraplegic (Spinal Injury) Association [British]
SPA	Scottish Pistol Association (DBA)
SPA	Scottish Publishers Association (DBA)
SPA	Screen Producers' Association [Australia]
SPA	Sea Photo Analysis [Navy]
SPA	Seaplane Pilots Association (EA)
SPA	Self-Phasing Array
SPA	Self Publishing Association [British] (DBA)
SPA	Semipermanently Associated [Telecommunications] (TEL)
SPA	Service for Photographic Art [Canada] (ASC)
SPA	Service Pay and Allowances [Military British]
SPA	Servo Power Amplifier (NASA)
SPA	Servo Power Assembly (MCD)
SPA	Servo Preamplifier
SPA	Shared Peripheral Area (NASA)
SPA	Sheep Pulmonary Adenomatosis [Medicine] (DMAA)
SPA	Shore Protection Act of 1988 (COE)
SPA	Sierra Pacific Airlines [ICAO designator] (FAAC)
SPA	Signal Processor Assembly [NASA]
SPA	Silicon Pulser Array
SPA	Singapore People's Alliance
SPA	Single Parameter Analysis
SPA	Single Photon Absorptiometry [Analytical chemistry]
SPA	Single Position Automatic [Tester]
SPA	Singles Press Association (EA)
SPA	Skill Performance Aid [Army] (RDA)
SPA	Small-Particle Aerosol
SPA	Socialist Party of Albania [Political party] (EY)
SPA	Socialist Party of Australia [Political party]
SPA	Society for Pediatric Anesthesia (NTPA)
SPA	Society for Personality Assessment (EA)
SPA	Society for Personnel Administration [Later, IPMA] (EA)
SPA	Society for Psychological Anthropology (EA)
SPA	Society for Public Administration
SPA	Society of Participating Artists [Record label]
SPA	Society of Philatelic Americans [Defunct] (EA)
SPA	Society of Philosophers in America (EA)
SPA	Society of Professional Assessors [Address unknown]
SPA	Sociological Practice Association (EA)
SPA	Sodium Polyacrylate [Organic chemistry]
SPA	Software Producers' Association (NITA)
SPA	Software Product Assurance (SSD)
SPA	Software Publishers Association (EA)
SPA	Solar Power Array
SPA	Songwriters Protective Association [Later, AGAC]
SPA	SOSUS Probability Area (NVT)
SPA	Southeastern Peanut Association (EA)
SPA	Southern Pine Association [Later, SFPA] (EA)
SPA	South Pacific Area [World War II]
SPA	South Pole [Antarctica] [Seismograph station code, US Geological Survey] (SEIS)
SPA	Southwestern Power Administration [Department of Energy]
SPA	Southwestern Psychological Association (IAA)
SPA	Southwest Placement Association (AEBS)
SPA	Space Processing Applications [Program] [NASA]
SPA	Spade [Freight]
Spa	Spain (VRA)
SPA	Spanish
spa	Spanish [MARC language code Library of Congress] (LCCP)
SPA	Spartanburg, SC [Location identifier FAA] (FAAL)
SPA	Sparton Corp. [NYSE symbol] (SPSG)
SpA	Specialist in Art (GAGS)
SPA	Specialist in Public Administration (GAGS)
SPA	Specialist, Physical Training Instructor [Navy rating]
SPA	Specially Protected Area (EERA)
SPA	Special Project Activities (MCD)
SPA	Special Public Assistance
SPA	Special Purchase Allowance (DOAD)
SPA	Special-Purpose Aircraft [Drone vehicle] [Military]
SPA	Special Purpose Alteration (MCD)
SPA	Specifically Planned Area (PA)
SPA	Specification Preparing Activity (AAGC)
SPA	Spectair Industry [Vancouver Stock Exchange symbol]
SPA	Spectrum Analyzer
SPA	Spinal Progressive Amyotrophy [Medicine] (DMAA)
SPA	Splice Plug Assembly
SPA	Spondyloarthropathy [Medicine] (MEDA)

SPA............ Sportsman Pilots Association
SPA............ Standard Plate Agar [Microbiology] (OA)
SPA............ Standard Practice Amendment (AAG)
SPA............ Staphylococcal Protein A [Immunochemistry]
SPA............ State Planning Agency [Department of Justice]
SPA............ State Ports Authority [South Carolina]
SPA............ State Power Authority (IAA)
SPA............ State Property Agency [Hungary] (ECON)
SPA............ Steering Position Amplifier [NASA] (NAKS)
SPA............ Sterile Preparation Area (MCD)
SPA............ Stimulation-Produced Analgesia
SPA............ St. Maarten Patriotic Alliance [Netherlands Antilles] [Political party] (EY)
SPA............ Strategic Posture Analysis [Army] (AABC)
SPA............ Subject to Particular Average [Insurance]
SPA............ Submarine Patrol Area [Navy] (NVT)
SPA............ Subpoena [Legal term]
SPA............ Substance P Antagonist [Biochemistry]
SPA............ Substitute Part Authorization (AAG)
SPA............ Sudden Phase Anomaly [Radio engineering]
SPA............ Suicide Prevention Association [Australia]
SPA............ Sundry Persons' Account [Banking]
SPA............ Superphosphoric Acid [Fertilizer]
SPA............ Supervisory Performance Appraisal [Civil Service]
SPA............ Supplemental Preclaims Assistance [Department of Education] (GFGA)
SPA............ Suprapubic Aspiration [Medicine]
SPA............ Supreme People's Assembly [Political party North Korea] (FEA)
SPA............ Surface Vehicle Power Adapter
SPA............ Surinaamse Partij van de Arvid [Suriname Labour Party] [Political party] (EY)
SPA............ SURTASS Probability Area [Navy] (CAAL)
SPA............ Survey of Personal Attitude [Psychology]
SPA............ Symbolic Processing Array [Computer science]
SPA............ Syndicated Program Analysis (NTCM)
SPA............ System Performance Analyzer [Motorola, Inc.]
SPA............ System Problem Area (SAA)
SPA............ Systems and Procedures Association [Later, ASM] (EA)
SPAA............ Caraz [Peru] [ICAO location identifier] (ICLI)
SPAA............ Scottish Passenger Agents Associaiton (DBA)
SPAA............ Spacecraft Performance Analysis Area
SPAA............ Systems and Procedures Association of America (IAA)
SPAAC......... Syndicat du Personnel Africain de l'Aeronautique Civile [African Union for Civil Aviation Employees]
SPA ad TEST... Subpoena ad Testificandum [Subpoena to Testify] [Latin] (ROG)
SPAAG........ Self-Propelled Anti-Aircraft Gun [Former Soviet Union]
SPAALAL ..... Society for the Promotion of African, Asian, and Latin American Literature [See also GFLAAL] [Germany] (EAIO)
SPAAMFAA... Society for the Preservation and Appreciation of Antique Motor Fire Apparatus inAmerica (EA)
SPAAN .... Societe Protectrice des Animaux en Afrique du Nord [Society for the Protection of Animals in North Africa - SPANA] (EAIO)
SPAASS ...... Synod Office, Diocese of Saskatchewan, Anglelican Church of Canada, Prince Albert, Saskatchewan [Library symbol National Library of Canada] (NLC)
SPAB .... Huancabamba [Peru] [ICAO location identifier] (ICLI)
SPAB .... Security Pacific Asian Bank
SPAB .... Society for the Protection of Ancient Buildings (EA)
SPAB .... Society of Psychologists in Addictive Behaviors [Later, PAB] (EA)
SPAB .... SPACEHAB Inc. [NASDAQ symbol] (TTSB)
SpAb........... Specifically Purified Antibody (DB)
SPAB .... Supply, Priorities, and Allocations Board [World War II]
SPABH .... Society for the Preservation of American Business History (EA)
SPAC .... Ciro Alegria [Peru] [ICAO location identifier] (ICLI)
SPAC .... Salinity Program Advisory Council (EERA)
SPAC .... Saratoga Performing Arts Center [Summer home of NYCB] [Saratoga Springs, NY]
SPAC .... Secretary's Pesticide Advisory Committee [HEW]
SPAC .... Sectionally Processed Antibody Coated [Medicine] (STED)
SPAC .... Signal Programmer and Conditioner [Air Force Eastern Test Range]
SPAC .... Soil and Plant Analysis Council (NTPA)
SPAC .... Spacecraft Performance Analysis and Command [NASA]
SPAC .... Space Program Advisory Council [Terminated, 1977] [NASA]
SPAC .... Spacious (ADA)
SPAC .... Spatial Computer
SPACC .... Space Control Center (DOMA)
SPACCS ...... Space Command and Control System
SPACE .... Council of AFL-CIO Unions for Scientific, Professional, and Cultural Employees [Later, Department for Professional Employees, AFL-CIO]
SPACE .... Sales Profitability and Contribution Evaluator [Computer science]
SPACE .... Satellite Precipitation and Cloud Experiment [National Oceanic and Atmospheric Administration]
SPACE .... Satellite Project for Adult and Continuing Education (AIE)
SPACE .... Self-Programming Automatic Circuit Evaluator
SPACE .... Sequential Position and Covariance Estimation (IEEE)
SPACE .... Settlement, Payment, Accounting, Credit Extension (MHDB)
SPACE .... Shuttle/Payload Contamination Evaluation Program (MCD)
SPACE .... Sidereal Polar Axis Celestial Equipment
SPACE .... Single Potential Analysis of Cavernous Electrical Activity [Medicine] (DMAA)
SPACE .... Society for Private and Commercial Earth Stations [Telecommunications information service or system] (EA)
SPACE .... Spacecraft Prelaunch Automatic Checkout Equipment [NASA]
SPACE .... Space Program American Citizens' Effort

SPACE .... Special Political Agricultural Community Education [Milk cooperative trust fund]
SPACE .... Speech Analog Compression and Editing [Loop] (IAA)
SPACE .... Sperry Program for Advancing Careers through Education
SPACE .... Support Package for Aerospace Computer Emulation (MCD)
SPACE .... Symbolic Programming Anyone Can Enjoy
SPACECOM... Space Command [Military]
SPACECOM... Space Communications
SPACECOMPS... Spacecraft Components (NITA)
SpaceLb ...... SpaceLabs Medical, Inc. [Associated Press] (SAG)
SPACES .... Saving and Preserving Arts and Cultural Environments (EA)
SPACES .... Solving Problems of Access to Careers in Engineering and Science (EDAC)
SPACETAC ... Space and Tactical System Corp. (MCD)
Spacetec...... Spacetec IMC Corp. [Associated Press] (SAG)
SPACETRACK... Space Tracking System [Air Force] (MCD)
SPacFd .... Southern Pacific Funding Corp. [Associated Press] (SAG)
SPacFdg ...... Southern Pacific Funding Corp. [Associated Press] (SAG)
SPACG .... Syndicat du Personnel de l'Aeronautique Civile du Gabon [Union of Civil Aviation Employees of Gabon]
SPACHEE..... South Pacific Action Committee for Human Ecology and Environment (EERA)
SPACLALS ... South Pacific Association for Commonwealth Literature and Language Studies (EAIO)
SPACON...... Space Control
SPACS .... Sodium Purification and Characterization System [Nuclear energy] (NRCH)
SPAD .... Satellite Position Prediction and Display
SPAD .... Satellite Protection for Area Defense [ARPA]
SPAD .... Scratch Pad Memory [Computer science]
SPAD .... Seaway Port Authority of Duluth
SPAD .... Shuttle Payload Accommodation Document [NASA] (MCD)
SPAD .... Simplified Procedures for Analysis of Data (OA)
SPAD .... Societe pour Aviation et ses Derives [France] [World War I airplane]
SPAD .... Space Patrol Active Defense
SPAD .... Space Patrol for Air Defense
SPAD .... Space Principles, Applications, and Doctrine [Air Force Systems Command]
SPAD .... Special Programs and Analysis Division [Environmental Protection Agency] (GFGA)
SPAD .... SPRINT Air-Directed Defense [Army]
SPAD .... Stenosing Peripheral Arterial Disease [Medicine] (DMAA)
SPAD .... Subcutaneous Peritoneal Access Device [Nephrology] (DAVI)
SPAD .... Submarine Patrol Area Definition (MCD)
SPAD .... Subsystem Postioning Aid Device (NASA)
SPADATS ..... Space Detection and Tracking System [Military]
SPADATSC... Space Detection and Tracking System Center [Air Force]
SPADATSIMP... Space Detection and Tracking System Improved [Air Force] (IAA)
SPADATSS... Space Detection and Tracking System Sensors [Air Force]
SPADCCS..... Space Defense Command and Control System (MCD)
SPADE .... Signal Processing and Display Equipment
SPADE .... Single Channel Per Carrier Multiple Access Demand Assignment Equipment (NITA)
SPADE .... Single-Channel-per-Carrier, Pulse-Code-Modulation, Multiple-Access, Demand-Assignment Equipment [Telecommunications]
SPADE .... Small Portable Analysis and Diagnostic Equipment [Aircraft maintenance]
SPADE .... Spare Parts Analysis, Documentation, and Evaluation
SPADE .... Sparta Acquisition Digital Equipment (MCD)
SPADE .... Sperry Air Data Equipment
SPADE .... Stratospheric Photochemistry Aerosols, and Dynamics Expedition [Meteorology]
SPADE .... Strike Planning and Damage Estimator [Military]
SPADES .... Solar Perturbation and Atmospheric Density Measurement Satellite
SPADETS ..... Space Detection Network [Military]
SPADL .... Spare Parts Application Data List
SPADNS...... (Sulfophenylazo)dihydroxynaphthalene-disulfonate [Organic chemistry]
SPADOC...... Space Defense Operations Center [DoD]
SPADS........ Satellite Position and Display System
SPADS........ Shuttle Problem Action [or Analysis] Data System [NASA] (NASA)
SPADS........ SPRINT Air-Directed Defense System [Army] (AABC)
SPADS........ STRATCOM Program Automated Data System [Army]
SPA DT........ Subpoena Duces Tecum [Legal] [Latin] (ROG)
SPAE.......... Societe Planetaire pour l'Assainissement de l'Energie [Planetary Association for Clean Energy] (EAIO)
SPAEF........ Societe des Petroles d'Afrique Equatoriale Francaise [French Equatorial African Petroleum Co.]
SPAEF........ Southern Public Administration Education Foundation (EA)
SPAEI......... South Pacific Association of Environmental Institutions
SPAF.......... Forestry Branch, Saskatchewan Department of Natural Resources, Prince Albert, Saskatchewan [Library symbol National Library of Canada] (NLC)
SP-AF .... Shuttle Projects - Air Force Liaison Office [Kennedy Space Center] [NASA] (NASA)
SPAF.......... Simulation Processor and Formatter (MCD)
SPAF.......... Spontaneous Paroxysmal Atrial Fibrillation [Medicine] (DMAA)
SPAF.......... Stroke in Patients with Atrial Fibrillation
SPAF.......... Student Product Assessment Form (EDAC)
SPAG.......... Small-Particle Aerosol Generator (DAVI)
SPAG.......... South Plains Association of Governments
SPAG.......... Space Radiation Analysis Group [NASA]
SPAG.......... Spaghetti (DSUE)
SPAG.......... Special Program/Analysis Guidance [DoD]
SPAG.......... Spelling, Pronunciation & Grammar (WDAA)

SPAG	Sphenopalatine Ganglion [*Neurology*] (DAVI)
SPAG	Standards and Practices Action Group (TELE)
SPAG	Standards Promotion Application Group [*Telecommunications*]
SPAH	Society for the Preservation and Advancement of the Harmonica (EA)
SPAH	Spacelab Payload Accommodations Handbook [*NASA*] (MCD)
SPAI	Screen Printing Association International (EA)
SPAI	Steroid Protein Activity Index [*Medicine*] (MAE)
SPAID	Sheffield Package Analysis and Identification of Data [*Commercial & Industrial Development Bureau*] [*Software package*] (NCC)
SPAID	Society for the Prevention of Asbestosis and Industrial Diseases [*British*] (DI)
SPAIN	Indian and Northern Affairs Canada [*Affaires Indiennes et du Nord Canada*] Prince Albert, Saskatchewan [*Library symbol National Library of Canada*] (NLC)
Spain	Spain Fund [*Associated Press*] (SAG)
SPAL	Simulator, Projectile, Airburst, Liquid [*Chemical defense device*] [*Military*] (RDA)
SPAL	Stabilized Platform Airborne LASER (RDA)
SPAL	Succinyl-poly-DL-alanine Poly-L-lysine [*Biochemical analysis*]
SPALDA	Scottish Peat and Land Development Association (DBA)
Spald Cop	Spalding on Copyright [*A publication*] (DLA)
Spalding C	Spalding College (GAGS)
SPALT	Single-Point Articulated Loading Tower [*Engineering*]
SPALT	Special Projects Alterations [*Navy*]
SPALTRA	Special Projects Alterations, Training [*Navy*]
SPAM	Camana [*Peru*] [*ICAO location identifier*] (ICLI)
SPAM	Satellite Processor Access Method
SPAM	Scanning Photoacoustic Microscopy
SPAM	Scratch Pad Memory Address [*Computer science*] (IAA)
SPAM	Search Pattern Assessment Model [*Military*] (CAAL)
SPAM	Shipment Planning and Movement [*Army*]
SPAM	Ship Position and Attitude Measurement (IEEE)
SPAM	Shop Portable Aircraft Maintenance [*Army*]
SPAM	Society for the Publication of American Music [*Record label*]
SPAM	Soil-Plant-Atmosphere [*Computer simulation model*]
SPAM	Sonobuoy Placement Assortment Model (MCD)
SPAM	S-Parameter Acquisition and Manipulation [*Computer software program*] [*General Motors Corp.*]
SPAM	Special Aeronautical Material [*Navy*] (NG)
SPAM	Special Personal Attack Message [*Internet-delivered direct mail*] [*Computer science*]
SPAM	Spiced Ham [*Hormel (George A.) & Co.*]
SPAMA	Spanish Air Materiel Area
SPAMAG	Space Medicine Advisory Group (MCD)
SpamEx	Spam Exterminator [*Unisyn*] [*Computer science*]
SPAMF	Seychelles Popular Anti-Marxist Front [*Political party*] (PD)
SPAMM	Spatial Modulation of Magnetization [*Medicine*] (DMAA)
SPAMMER	Space Hammer
SPAMS	Ship Position and Altitude Measurement System (MOD)
SPAN	Serials, Periodicals, and Newspapers
SPAN	Single Payer Across the Nation [*Health insurance*]
SPAN	Small Publishers Association of North America (NTPA)
SPAN	Social Planning Around Neighbourhoods [*Australia*]
SPAN	Social Policy and Administration Network [*A publication*]
SPAN	Social Studies Priorities, Practices, and Needs (EDAC)
SPAN	Society of Philatelists and Numismatists (EA)
SPAN	Solar Particle Alert Network [*National Oceanic and Atmospheric Administration*]
SPAN	Solar Proton Alert Network
SPAN	Solid Phase Alloy Nucleation (PDAA)
SPAN	South Pacific Action Network
SPAN	Space Communications Network
SPAN	Spacecraft Analysis (KSC)
SPAN	Space Navigation
SPAN	Space Physics Aeronautics Network (USDC)
SPAN	Space Physics Analysis Network [*Database*]
SPAN	Space Plasma Analysis Network [*NASA*]
SPAN	Span-America Medical Systems, Inc. [*NASDAQ symbol*] (NQ)
SPAN	Span-America Med Sys [*NASDAQ symbol*] (TTSB)
SPAN	Span Analysis (NITA)
SPAN	Spaniard (ROG)
SPAN	Spanish
span	Spansule (STED)
Span	Spansule [*Pharmacology*] (DAVI)
SPAN	Standard Portfolio Analysis of Margin [*Finance*] (NUMA)
SPAN	Statistical Processing and Analysis [*Computer science*]
SPAN	Storage Planning and Allocation [*Computer science*]
SPAN	Stored Program Alphanumerics [*FAA*]
SPAN	Submarine Piloting and Navigation [*Navy*]
SPAN	Successive, Proportionate, Additive Numeration [*Decision making*]
SPAN	Sullana [*Peru*] [*ICAO location identifier*] (ICLI)
SPAN	System for Projection and Analysis
SPANA	Society for the Protection of Animals Abroad [*British*] (EAIO)
SPANA	Society for the Protection of Animals in North Africa [*See also SPAAN*] (EAIO)
SpanAm	Span-America Medical Systems, Inc. [*Associated Press*] (SAG)
SPANAT	Systems Planning Approach - North Atlantic [*FAA*]
SPANC	Wapiti Regional Library, Prince Albert, Saskatchewan [*Library symbol National Library of Canada*] (NLC)
SPAND	Solar Proton Albedo Neutron Decay
SPANDAR	Space and Range RADAR [*NASA*]
SP & O	Special Plans and Operation [*Military*]
SP & S	Special Processes and Sequencing (NASA)
Sp & Sel Cas	Special and Selected Law Cases [1648] [*England*] [*A publication*] (DLA)
Spanet	Secure Prioritized ATM [*Asynchronous Transfer Mode*] Network [*Telecommunications*]
SPANGLISH	Spanish and English
SPANI	Northern Institute of Technology, Prince Albert, Saskatchewan [*Library symbol National Library of Canada*] (NLC)
Spanlink	Spanlink Communications, Inc. [*Associated Press*] (SAG)
SPANNER	Special Analysis of Net Radio [*Study*]
SPANNET	Space Navigation Network (IAA)
SPANPAC	Sales, Purchases and Nominal Package (MHDB)
SPANRAD	Superimposed Panoramic RADAR Display
SPANRAD	Superposed Panoramic RADAR Display (IAA)
SPANS	Sealift Procurement and National Security [*Study*]
SPANS	Small Passive Navigation System (DNAB)
spans	Spansules [*Pharmacology*] (CPH)
SPANS	Spectral Processing Analysis System (PDAA)
SPANSULE	Space Plus Capsule (WDAA)
SPAO	San Juan Aposento [*Peru*] [*ICAO location identifier*] (ICLI)
SPAOPSUP	Space Operations Support (NVT)
SPAP	Picota [*Peru*] [*ICAO location identifier*] (ICLI)
SPAP	Serum Prostatic Acid Phosphatase [*An enzyme*]
SPAP	Special Package Auto Policy [*Insurance*]
SpAppBiol	Specialist in Applied Biology (GAGS)
SPAQUA	Sealed Package Quality Assurance (IEEE)
SPAR	Alerta [*Peru*] [*ICAO location identifier*] (ICLI)
SPAR	SAC [*Strategic Air Command*] Peacetime Airborne Reconnaissance
SPAR	Satellite Position Adjusting Rocket (SAA)
SPAR	Seagoing Platform for Acoustic Research [*NOL*]
SPAR	Semper Paratus [*Always Ready*] [*Coast Guard motto*]
SPAR	Sensitivity Prediction by Acoustic Reflex (STED)
SPAR	Sensitivity Prediction from the Acoustic Reflex [*Audiometry*]
SPAR	Society of Photographers and Artist Representatives (EA)
SPAR	Soil-Plant-Atmosphere-Research [*Agriculture*]
SPAR	Space Precision Altitude Reference System (MCD)
SPAR	Space Processing Applications Rocket [*NASA*]
SPAR	SPALT [*Special Projects Alterations*] Planning and Authorization Report
Spar	Spartan
SPAR	Spartan Motors [*NASDAQ symbol*] (TTSB)
SPAR	Spartan Motors, Inc. [*Charlotte, MI*] [*NASDAQ symbol*] (NQ)
SPAR	Special Prelaunch Analysis Request [*NASA*] (KSC)
SPAR	Special Progressive Aircraft Rework
SPAR	Spelling and Reading Tests
SPAR	Staff Payroll Allocation and Record (OA)
SPAR	Staff Planning & Reporting System (WDAA)
SPAR	Staff Procurement Activity Requirement [*Military*]
SPAR	Stock Point ADP [*Automatic Data Processing*] Replacement Program [*Navy*] (GFGA)
SPAR	Store Port Allocation Register (PDAA)
SPAR	Student Profile and Assessment Record [*Student attitudes test*]
SPAR	Submersible Pipe Alignment Rig [*Deep-sea diving*]
SPAR	Super-Precision Approach RADAR
SPAR	Surveillance and Precision Approach RADAR (NATG)
SPAR	Symbolic Program Assembly Routine [*Computer science*]
SPAR	Synchronous Position Altitude Recorder
SPAR	System Program Assessment Review [*Air Force*]
SPARC	Scalable Performance Architecture [*Computer science*] (IGQR)
SPARC	Scalar Processor Architecture Reduced-Instruction-Set Computer (DOM)
SPARC	Scaleable Processor Architecture [*Computer science*]
SPARC	Scholarly Publishing & Academic Resources Coalition
SPARC	Secreted Protein Acidic and Rich in Cysteine [*Biochemistry*]
SPARC	Shore-Establishment Planning Analysis and Review Cooperation [*or Coordination*] [*Navy*] (NG)
SPARC	Short Planning Analysis and Review Cooperation
SPARC	Slab Penetration and Reflection Calculation
SPARC	Space Air Relay Communications (MCD)
SpARC	Space Automation and Robotics Center [*University of Michigan*] [*Research center*] (RCD)
SPARC	Space Program Analysis and Review Council [*Air Force*]
SPARC	Space Research Capsule [*or Conic*] [*NASA*]
SPARC	Spare Parts Provisioning for Combat
SPARC	Spectral Analysis and Recognition Computer [*NASA*]
SPARC	Standards Planning and Requirements Committee [*ANSI*]
SPARC	Steam Plant Automation and Results Computer
SPARC	Stratospheric Processes and their Role in Climate [*Marine science*]
SPARC	Support Planning Analysis Reporting and Control [*Navy*] (NG)
SPARC	Sustainability Predictions for Army Spare Component Requirements for Combat (RDA)
SPARC	System Parametric Allocation of Resources and Cost (MCD)
SPARCS	Solar Pointing Aerobee Rocket Control System
SPARCS	Statewide Planning and Research Cooperative System [*New York State Department of Health*] [*Albany*] [*Information service or system*] (IID)
SPARE	Save Pound Animals from Research Experiments (EA)
SPARE	System for Projecting Ammunition Repairable End Items [*Military*]
SPAREM	Spares Provisioning and Requirements Effectiveness Model (PDAA)
SPARES	Space Radiation Evaluation System [*NASA*] (KSC)
SPAREX	Canada Regional Industrial Expansion [*Expansion Industrielle Regionale*], Prince Albert, Saskatchewan [*Library symbol National Library of Canada*] (BIB)
SPARK	Saboteurs for a Philistine America Redeemed from Kultur [*From book, "Bringing Down the House," by Richard P. Brickner*]
SPARK	Screen Pattern Analyzer and Rescreening Key [*Printing process*]

SPARK .... Seminars on Practical Applications of Research Knowledge [*Advertising Research Foundation*]
SPARK .... Solid Propellant Advanced Ramjet Kinetic Energy (MCD)
SPARK .... Systematic Pulmono/Cardiac Anaphylaxis Resusitation Kit (MCD)
Sparks .... Sparks' Reports [*British Burma*] [*A publication*] (DLA)
SPARM .... Solid-Propellant Augmented Rocket Motor [*Navy*]
SPARM .... Sparrow Antiradiation Missile (MCD)
SPARMIS ..... Standard Police Automated Resource Management Information System
SPARMO ...... Solar Particles and Radiations Monitoring Organization
SPARPS .... Spares and Repair Parts Support [*Navy*] (NG)
SPARR .... Self-Contained Perspective Approach Rotor Blade RADAR (IAA)
SPARR .... Steerable Paraboloid Azimuth Radio Reflector (IAA)
SPARS .... Semper Paratus [*US Coast Guard Women's Auxiliary; name taken from Coast Guard motto*]
SPARS .... Site Production and Reduction System
SPARS .... Society of Professional Audio Recording Services (EA)
SPARS .... Space Precision Altitude [*or Attitude*] Reference System
SPARS .... Women's Coast Guard Reserves [*From Coast Guard motto "Semper Paratus-Always Ready"*] (EBF)
SPARSA .... Sferics, Position [*or Pulse*], Azimuth, Rate, and Spectrum Analyzer
SPARSIM ..... Spartan Simulation [*Missile system evaluation*] (RDA)
SPART .... Space Research and Technology [*Report*] [*NASA*] (KSC)
SPART .... Sunny Point Army Terminal
SPARTA .... Sequential Programmed Automatic Recording Transistor Analyzer
SPARTA .... Spatial Antimissile Research Test in Australia (IAA)
SPARTA .... Special Antimissile Research Tests in Australia
SPARTA .... System for Private Access for Reservations and Travel Agents [*British*] (DI)
SpartaFd ...... Sparta Foods [*Commercial firm Associated Press*] (SAG)
SPARTAN ..... Shuttle-Pointed Autonomous Research Tool for Astronomy [*NASA*]
SPARTAN ..... Special Proficiency at Rugged Training and Nation Building [*Training program for Green Berets*] [*Army*]
SPARTAN ..... System for Personnel Automated Reports, Transactions, and Notices [*Census Bureau, NASA*]
SpartaPh ..... Sparta Pharmaceutical, Inc. [*Associated Press*] (SAG)
Spartch .... Spartech Corp. [*Associated Press*] (SAG)
SpartMot ..... Spartan Motors, Inc. [*Associated Press*] (SAG)
Sparton .... Sparton Corp. [*Associated Press*] (SAG)
SPAS .... Safety Performance Analysis System [*FAA*] (TAG)
SPAS .... Security Police Automated System [*Air Force*] (GFGA)
SPAS .... Serial Poll Active State (IAA)
SPAS .... Shipboard Pollution Abatement System [*Navy*] (CAAL)
SPAS .... Shuttle Pallet Satellite [*NASA*]
SPAS .... Skill Performance Aids
SPAS .... Social Service Department, Prince Albert, Saskatchewan [*Library symbol National Library of Canada*] (NLC)
SPA-S .... Societa Prodotti Antibiotici [*Italy*] [*Research code symbol*]
SPAS .... Societatis Philosophicae Americanae Socius [*Member of the American Philosophical Society*] [*Latin*]
SPAS .... Solar Proton Alpha Spectrometer
SPAS .... Student's Perception of Ability Scale (EDAC)
SPASA .... Servicios Politecnicos Aereos SA [*Spain ICAO designator*] (FAAC)
SPASE .... South Pole Air Shower Experiment [*Astronomy*]
SPASEC .... Space Track Sensor Computer (IAA)
SPASEP .... Secretaria Permanente del Acuerdo Sudamericano de Estupefacientes y Psicotropicos [*Permanent Secretariat of the South American Agreement on Narcotic Drugs and Psychotropic Substances - PSSAANDPS*] [*Argentina*] (EAIO)
SPASM .... Self-Propelled Air-to-Surface Missile (MCD)
SPASM .... Smithsonian Package for Algebra and Symbolic Mathematics (MCD)
SPASM .... Space Propulsion Automated Synthesis Modeling [*Program*]
SPASM .... Specific Person with Authority to Spend Money (WDAA)
SPASM .... System Performance and Activity Software Monitor [*Computer science*] (IEEE)
SPAST .... Special Assistant [*Navy*]
SPASUR .... Space Surveillance System [*Navy*]
SPASYN .... Space-Syncromesh
SPAT .... Aguas Calientes [*Peru*] [*ICAO location identifier*] (ICLI)
SPAT .... Self-Propelled Antitank Gun (MCD)
SPAT .... Silicon Precision Alloy Transistor
SPAT .... Slow Paroxysmal Atrial Tachycardia [*Medicine*] (DMAA)
SPAT .... Spleen Antigen [*Complement Fixation*] Test [*Immunology*]
SPAT .... Supplementary Pay Appeals Tribunal [*British*] (DI)
SPAT .... Systems Programming Aptitude Test
SPATA .... Society of Polish-American Travel Agents (EA)
SPATA .... Swimming Pool and Allied Trades Association [*British*] (DBA)
SPATE .... Sergeant Production Automatic Test Equipment
SPATE .... South Pacific Association for Teacher Education [*Later, ATEA*] (EA)
SPATE .... Student Personnel Association for Teacher Education [*Later, AHEAD*] (EA)
Spatialght .... Spatialight, Inc. [*Associated Press*] (SAG)
SpatialT .... Spatial Technology, Inc. [*Associated Press*] (SAG)
Spatlzr .... Spatializer Audio Labs, Inc. [*Associated Press*] (SAG)
SPATS .... South Pacific Air Transportation Service [*Navy*]
SPAU .... Signal Processing [*or Processor*] Arithmetic Unit [*Navy*]
SPAU .... Stable Platform Alignment Unit
Spaulding .... Spaulding's Reports [*71-73 Maine*] [*A publication*] (DLA)
SPAW .... Learning Resource Centre, Woodland Campus, Saskatchewan Institute of Applied Science and Technology, Prince Albert, Saskatchewan [*Library symbol National Library of Canada*] (BIB)
SPAWAR ...... Space and Naval Warfare Systems Command [*Washington, DC Navy*] (GRD)
SPAWG .... Special Activity Wing (MUGU)
SPAWN .... Salmon Protection Association of Western Newfoundland [*Canada*] (ASF)
SPAYZ .... Spatial Property Analyzer
SPAZ .... Spatializer Audio Labs [*NASDAQ symbol*] (TTSB)
SPAZ .... Spatializer Audio Labs, Inc. [*NASDAQ symbol*] (SAG)
SPB .... ASA [*Former USSR ICAO designator*] (FAAC)
SPB .... Scottish Prayer Book [*Episcopalian*]
SPB .... Seaplane Base
SPB .... Shergottite Parent Body [*Planetary science*]
SPB .... Ship's Plotting Board
SPB .... Silver-Plated Bronze
SPB .... Society of the Precious Blood [*Anglican religious community*]
SPB .... Solar Particle Beams
SPB .... Sotheby Parke Bernet [*Formerly, PB*] [*Manhattan art auction house*]
SPB .... Special Pathogens Branch [*Centers for Disease Control*]
SPB .... Spindle Pole Body [*Cell biology*]
SPB .... Springboard Resources Ltd. [*Vancouver Stock Exchange symbol*]
SPB .... Standardized Performance Battery [*Acoustics*]
SPB .... Standard Practice Bulletin (MCD)
SPB .... Stored Program Buffer
SPB .... St. Thomas [*Virgin Islands*] Seaplane Base [*Airport symbol*] (OAG)
SPB .... Summary Plot Board (SAA)
SPB .... Surplus Property Board
SPB .... Systems Personnel Branch (SAA)
SPBA .... Society of Professional Benefit Administrators [*Washington, DC*] (EA)
SPBA .... Specialty Paper and Board Affiliates [*Later, API*] (EA)
SpBaU .... Universidad de Barcelona, Biblioteca Universitaria y Provincal, Barcelona, Spain [*Library symbol Library of Congress*] (LCLS)
SpBaU-SQ .... Universidad de Barcelona, Facultad de Quimica y Fisica, Barcelona, Spain [*Library symbol*] [*Library of Congress*] (LCLS)
SPBB .... Moyobamba [*Peru*] [*ICAO location identifier*] (ICLI)
SPBC .... Caballococha [*Peru*] [*ICAO location identifier*] (ICLI)
SPBC .... Saint Paul Bible College [*Saint Bonifacius, MN*]
SPBC .... Society of Professional Business Consultants [*Chicago, IL*] (EA)
SPBC .... South Pacific Base Command [*Navy World War II*]
SPBC .... St. Paul Bancorp [*NASDAQ symbol*] (TTSB)
SPBC .... St. Paul Bancorp, Inc. [*NASDAQ symbol*] (NQ)
SPBD .... Springboard (NVT)
SPBE .... Service de Presse Baptiste Europeen [*European Baptist Press Service - EBPS*] (EAIO)
SPBE .... Society of Parrot Breeders and Exhibitors (EA)
SPBEC .... South Pacific Bureau for Economic Cooperation in Developing Uniform Maritime Standards for the Pacific Area [*Suva, Fiji*] (EAIO)
SPBI .... Serikat Buruh Pertjetakan Indonesia [*Printing Workers' Union of Indonesia*]
SPBI .... Serum Protein-Bound Iodine [*Clinical chemistry*] (AAMN)
SPBI .... Society for Proclaiming Britain in Israel
SPBI .... Speciality Paperboard, Inc. [*NASDAQ symbol*] (SAG)
SPBI .... Specialty Paperboard [*NASDAQ symbol*] (TTSB)
SPBI .... Specialty Paperboard, Inc. [*NASDAQ symbol*] (SAG)
S-PBigG .... Serum-Platelet Bindable Immunoglobulin G (STED)
SPBK .... Speed Brake (NASA)
SPBL .... Bellavista/Huallaga [*Peru*] [*ICAO location identifier*] (ICLI)
SPBM .... Single Point Buoy Mooring [*Oil platform*]
SPBOT .... Stationers and Publishers Board of Trade [*Later, Stationery and Office Equipment Board of Trade*]
SPBP .... Society for the Preservation of Birds of Prey (EA)
SPBR .... Iberia [*Peru*] [*ICAO location identifier*] (ICLI)
SPBR .... Speed Brake (MCD)
SPBS .... Jeberos/Bellavista [*Peru*] [*ICAO location identifier*] (ICLI)
SPBS .... Schweizerische Partei der Behinderten und Sozialbenachteiligten [*Swiss Party of the Handicapped and Socially Disadvantaged*] [*Political party*] (PPW)
SPBS .... Standard Property Book System [*Army*]
SPBS-R .... Standard Property Book System - Redesign [*or Redesigned*] [*Army*]
SPBT .... Obenteni [*Peru*] [*ICAO location identifier*] (ICLI)
SPBT .... Suprapubic Bladder Tap [*Medicine*] (MEDA)
SPBT .... Suprapublic Bladder Tap [*Urology*] (DAVI)
SPBU .... Vista Breau [*Peru*] [*ICAO location identifier*] (ICLI)
SPBW .... Society for the Preservation of Beers from the Wood [*British*] (EAIO)
SPC .... Institute for Studies of Destructive Behaviors and the Suicide Prevention Centerof Los Angeles [*California*] (EA)
SPC .... Political Committee at Senior Level [*NATO*] (NATG)
SPC .... Saint Paul Companies, Inc. [*NYSE symbol*] (SAG)
SPC .... Saint Paul's College [*Missouri; Virginia; Washington, DC*]
SPC .... Saint Paul's College, Lawrenceville, VA [*OCLC symbol*] (OCLC)
SPC .... Saint Peter College [*Maryland; New Jersey*]
SPC .... Saint Procopius College [*Illinois*]
SPC .... Salicylamide, Phenacetin [*Acetophenetidin*], and Caffeine [*Pharmacy*]
SPC .... Salkowski Positive Compound (OA)
SPC .... Santa Cruz La Palma [*Canary Islands*] [*Airport symbol*] (OAG)
SPC .... Saratoga Processing Co. Ltd. [*Vancouver Stock Exchange symbol*]
SPC .... Satellite Processing Center [*Military*]
SPC .... Schick-Positive Compound (DB)
SPC .... School Psychology Certificate (PGP)
SPC .... Seattle Pacific College [*Washington*]
SPC .... Self-Polishing Copolymer [*Anti-fouling paint*] (DS)
SPC .... Self-Programming Compiler [*Software*] [*Computer science*]
SPC .... Sequence Parameter Checking (SAA)
SPC .... Set Point Control [*Computer science*] (ECII)
SPC .... Set Point Controller
SPC .... Shanghai Petrochemical Co. [*Commercial firm*] [*China*]
SPC .... Shipping and Packing Cost (NASA)
SPC .... Shop Process Card [*Navy*] (DNAB)

SPC	Shuttle Pin Clutch
SPC	Shuttle Processing Contractor [NASA]
SPC	Sickle-Shaped Particle Cell (DB)
spc	Silicon Point-Contact (IDOE)
spc	Silver-Plated Copper (IDOE)
SPC	Silver-Plated Copper
SPC	Simple Prose Coefficient [Publishing]
SPC	Simultaneous Prism and Cover (Test) [Ophthalmology]
SPC	Single Palmar Crease [Medicine] (DMAA)
SPC	Single Paper Covered [Wire insulation] (IAA)
SPC	Single Prime Contractor [Weapon system procurement] [Air Force] (AAG)
SPC	Sisters of St. Paul of Chartres (TOCD)
SPC	Site Programmer Course
SPC	Size-Press Coated [Publishing]
SPC	Skalnate-Pleso [Czechoslovakia] [Seismograph station code, US Geological Survey] (SEIS)
SPC	Skyworld Airlines, Inc. [ICAO designator] (FAAC)
SPC	Small Peripheral Controller
SPC	Soap Perfumery and Cosmetics [A publication]
SPC	Socialist Party of Canada [Political party]
SPC	Socialist Party of Chile
SPC	Socialist Party of Croatia [Political party] (EY)
SPC	Socialist Party of Cyprus [Political party] (EAIO)
SPC	Society for Philosophy of Creativity (EA)
SPC	Society for the Prevention of Crime [Defunct] (EA)
SPC	Software Productivity Consortium (MCD)
SPC	Software Publishing Corp.
SPC	Solar Pointing Control
SPC	Solid-Propellant Combustion
SPC	Solid-Propellant Conference
S/P/C	Sotto Protesto per Mettere in Conto [Under Protest to Place to Account] [Italian]
SPC	Southern Pacific Communications (NITA)
SPC	Southern Pacific Communications Corp.
SPC	Southern Ports Foreign Committee, Chicago IL [STAC]
SPC	South Pacific Commission [See also CPS] (EAIO)
SPC	South Polar Cap [A filamentary mark on Mars]
SPC	Soy Protein Council (EA)
SPC	Space
SPC	Space Development Conference
SPC	Space Polymer Chemistry (SSD)
SPC	Space Projects Center [NASA]
SPC	Spacer [Technical drawings]
SpC	Spanish Columbia, San Sebastian [Record label] [Spain]
SPC	Spare Parts Catalog
SPC	Special Code
Sp C	Special Commissioner (DLA)
SPC	Special Common [Projectile]
SPC	Specialist, Classification Interviewer [Navy rating]
Sp C	Specialist in Counseling (PGP)
SPC	Special Political Committee [Australia]
SPC	Special Premiers Conference (EERA)
SPC	Special Program Code [Navy]
SPC	Special Project Code [IRS]
SPC	Special Purpose Chaff [Navy] (CAAL)
SPC	Special Purpose Computer
SPC	Specification
SPC	Specific Propellant Consumption
SPC	Speech Processing Chip (NITA)
SPC	Spleen Cell (DB)
SPC	Springfield-Cape Girardeau [Diocesan abbreviation] [Missouri] (TOCD)
SPC	Standard Plate Count [Microbiology]
SPC	Standard Products Committee [Navy]
SPC	Standby Pressure Control [Nuclear energy] (NRCH)
SPC	Starting Point Code (NASA)
SPC	Starting Point Counter [NASA] (IAA)
SPC	Static Power Conservers (MCD)
SPC	Static Power Converter (IAA)
SPC	Static Pressure Compensation
SPC	Station Program Cooperative [Public television]
SPC	Statistical Process Control
SPC	Sterilizable Potting Compound
SPC	Stigmastanyl(phosphorylcholine) [Biochemistry]
SPC	Still-Picture Camera (DNAB)
SPC	Stockage Priority Code [Military] (AFIT)
SPC	Storage Planning Centre [Shipping]
SPC	Storage Program Computer (IAA)
SPC	Stored Program Command [or Control] [Computer science]
SPC	Stored Program Control [Telecommunications] (IAA)
SPC	Storm Prediction Center [Marine science] (OSRA)
SPC	Storms Prediction Center (USDC)
SPC	St. Paul Cos. [NYSE symbol] (TTSB)
SPC	St. Paul's Cathedral [London, England]
SPC	Strategy and Planning Committee [Military]
SPC	Subcontract Plans Committee
SPC	Sucrose-Phosphate-Citrate [A culture medium]
SPC	Sugar Packet Club (EA)
SPC	Suicide Prevention Center (IIA)
SPC	Summary Punch Control [Computer science] (IAA)
SPC	Supplemental Planning Card (AAG)
SPC	Supplementary Patent Certificate [European Community]
SPC	Supplementary Protection Certificates [For European patents]
SPC	Suppression Pool Cooling [Environmental science] (COE)
SPC	Suspended Plaster Ceiling [Technical drawings]
SPC	Sweet Potato Council of the United States (NTPA)
SPC	Switching and Processing Center [EFTS] [Banking]
SPC	Syndicat des Postiers du Canada [Canadian Union of Postal Workers - CUPW]
SPC	Synoptic Properties Code (MCD)
SPC	Synthesizing Protein Complex (DB)
SPC	Synthetic Polymer Complement [Biochemistry]
SPC	System Professional Computer (HGAA)
SPC	Systemwide Program Committee [Individually-guided education] (AEE)
SPCA	Barraca [Peru] [ICAO location identifier] (ICLI)
SPCA	School Projectionist Club of America [Defunct] (EA)
SPCA	Serum Prothrombin Conversion Accelerator [Factor VII] [Also, PPCA Hematology]
SPCA	Society for the Prevention of Cruelty to Animals
SPCA	Southern Pulpwood Conservation Association [Later, SFI] (EA)
SPCA	Spark Plug Collectors of America (EA)
SPCA	Special-Purpose Cable Assembly
SPCAP	Society of Professors of Child and Adolescent Psychiatry (EA)
SPCAT	Special Category (MSA)
SPCB	Aguas Blancas [Peru] [ICAO location identifier] (ICLI)
SPCB	Single-Pole Circuit Breaker (IAA)
SPCC	Sample Polarity Coincidence Correlator (IAA)
SPCC	Servo Pressure Control Console
SPCC	Ship's Parts Control Center
SPCC	Society for the Prevention of Cruelty to Children
SPCC	Southern Pacific Communications Corp.
SPCC	Space Parts Control Center (MUGU)
SPCC	Spill Prevention, Containment, and Countermeasures [Environmental science] (COE)
SPCC	Spill Prevention Control and Countermeasure [Petroleum industry]
SPCC	Staggered Phase Carrier Cancellation
SPCC	Standardization, Policy, and Coordination Committee [NATO] (NATG)
SPCC	State Pollution Control Commission [of New South Wales] [State] (EERA)
SPCC	Stored Program CAMAC [Computer-Aided Measurement and Control] Channel [Computer science]
SPCC	Strength Power and Communications Cable
SPCC	STS [Shuttle Test Station] Processing Control Center [NASA] (GFGA)
SPCC	Study Planning and Coordinating Committee [Army]
SPCC	Sugar Packet Collectors Club (EA)
SPCC	Super-Packed Capillary Column [Spectroscopy]
SPCC	System Performance Check Compound
SpcChm	Specialty Chemical Resources, Inc. [Associated Press] (SAG)
SPCCP	Spill Prevention, Control, and Countermeasures Plan [Environmental science] (COE)
SPCD	Space Communications Division [Military]
SPCD	Specification Control Drawing (MCD)
sp cd	Spinal Cord [Medicine] (MAE)
SPCD	Syndrome of Primary Ciliary Dyskinesia [Medicine] (DMAA)
SPCDS	Small Permanent Communications and Display Segment (MCD)
SPCEC	Stereo Photographers, Collectors, and Enthusiasts Club (EA)
SPCF	Special Project Control File [IRS]
SPCFCTN	Specification
Sp Ch	Spears' South Carolina Chancery Reports [A publication] (DLA)
SPCH	Speech
SPCH	Sport Chalet [NASDAQ symbol] (TTSB)
SPCH	Sport Chalet, Inc. [NASDAQ symbol] (SAG)
SPCH	Tocache [Peru] [ICAO location identifier] (ICLI)
SPCHG	Supercharge
SPCHGR	Supercharger (AAG)
SPCHR	Supercharger (IAA)
SPCK	Society for Promoting Christian Knowledge [Publisher] [British]
SPCL	Pucallpa [Peru] [ICAO location identifier] (ICLI)
SPCL	Single Product Cost Leadership (MHDB)
SPCL	Special (MSA)
SPCLASGN	Special Assignment [Military] (NVT)
SpclDv	Special Devices, Inc. [Associated Press] (SAG)
SpclEqp	Speciality Equipment [Associated Press] (SAG)
SpclEqp	Specialty Equipment [Commercial firm Associated Press] (SAG)
SPCLN	Special Cleaning
SpclPap	Speciality Paperboard, Inc. [Associated Press] (SAG)
SpclPap	Specialty Paperboard, Inc. [Associated Press] (SAG)
SPCLST	Specialist
SPCLTY	Specialty
SPCLY	Especially (FAAC)
SPCM	Contamana [Peru] [ICAO location identifier] (ICLI)
SPCM	Master Chief Steam Propulsionman [Navy rating]
SPCM	Spanish Campaign Medal
SPCM	Special Court-Martial
SPCMO	Special Court-Martial Order
SPCMWOMJ	Special Court-Martial without a Military Judge (AFM)
SPCN	Silver-Plated Copperweld Conductor (IAA)
SPCN	Specially Constructed Vehicle [Automotive engineering]
SPCN	Stored Program Controlled Network [Telecommunications]
SPCNI	Society for Pacific Coast Native Irises (EA)
SPCO	Allegro New Media, Inc. [NASDAQ symbol] (SAG)
SPCO	Software Publishing [NASDAQ symbol] (TTSB)
SPCO	Software Publishing Corp. [Mountain View, CA] [NASDAQ symbol] (NQ)
SPCO	Southern Pacific Co.
SPCOA	Spark Plug Collectors of America (EA)
SPCONV	Speed Converter

SPCP	Pucacaca [Peru] [ICAO location identifier] (ICLI)
SPCP	Single Prime Contractor Policy [Air Force] (AAG)
SPCP	Society of Professors of Child Psychiatry [Later, SPCAP] (EA)
SPCP	Standardization and Parts Control Program
SPCP	Steam Propulsion Control Panel (DNAB)
SPCPrM	St. Paul Cos. LLC 6%Cv'MIPS' [NYSE symbol] (TTSB)
SPCR	Scratch Pad Control Register [Computer science] (IAA)
SPCR	Silicon Planar Controlled Rectifier (IAA)
SPCR	Spacer
SPCR	Spare Parts Change Request
Spcr	Spectinomycin Resistance
Sp Cr Ct	Special Criminal Court (DLA)
SPCS	Schedule Planning and Control System (MCD)
SPCS	Selective Paging Communications System
SPCS	Ship Production Control System (PDAA)
SPCS	Standard and Poor's Compustat Services (NITA)
SPCS	Standard & Poor's COMPUSTAT Services, Inc. [Also, an information service or system] (IID)
SPCS	State Plane Coordinate System [National Geodetic Survey Division] [National Oceanic and Atmospheric Administration]
SPCS	Static Power Conversion System
SPCS	Statistical Process Control Society (EA)
SPCS	Storage and Processing Control System
SPCS	Surgical Postcaval Shunt [Medicine]
SPC/SQC	Statistical Process/Statistical Quality Control
SPCT	Chota [Peru] [ICAO location identifier] (ICLI)
SPCT	Science Process Competency Test (EDAC)
SPCT	Spectrian Corp. [NASDAQ symbol] (SAG)
SPCT	Statistical Process Control Toolbox (RDA)
SPCTG	Spherical Cartridge
Spctran	SpecTran Corp. [Associated Press] (SAG)
Sp Ct RRRA	Special Court Regional Railroad Reorganization Act [A publication] (DLA)
SpctSig	Spectrum Signal Processing [Commercial firm Associated Press] (SAG)
SPCTYS	Society for the Prevention of Cruelty to Young Singers
SPCU	Simulation Process Control Unit (MCD)
SPCU	Skylab Process Control Unit [NASA]
SPCUS	Sweet Potato Council of the United States (EA)
SPCW	Specialist, Chemical Warfare [Navy rating]
SPCW	Stored Program Command Word [Computer science] (NASA)
SPCZ	South Pacific Convergence Zone (MCD)
SPD	Airspeed Aviation, Inc. [Canada ICAO designator] (FAAC)
SPD	Doctor of Political Science
SPD	Safety Program Directive [NASA]
SPD	Saidpur [Bangladesh] [Airport symbol] (OAG)
SPD	Salmon Poisoning Disease [Medicine] (AAMN)
SPD	Salutem Plurimam Dicit [He Wishes Much Health] [Latin]
SPD	Sampled [Tea trade] (ROG)
SPD	Sample Preparation and DNA [Deoxyribonucleic Acid] Probe
SPD	S-Band Polarization Diversity
SPD	Scientific Passenger Pod (MCD)
SPD	Seaplane Depot Ship
SPD	Sedona Industries Ltd. [Toronto Stock Exchange symbol]
SPD	Semipermeable Dressing [Medicine]
SPD	Separation Program Designator [Military] (AABC)
SPD	Serial Poll Disable (IAA)
SPD	Service Project Drawing
SPD	Shearing, Piling, and Disking [Forest management]
SPD	Ship Performance Department [David W. Taylor Naval Ship Research and Development Center]
SPD	Ship Planning Document (DNAB)
SPD	Ship Project Directive [Navy]
SPD	Sigma Phi Delta (EA)
SPD	Silicon Photodiode
SPD	Single Path Doppler [RADAR] (AAG)
SPD	Situation Projected Display
SPD	Skylab Program Directive [NASA] (KSC)
SPD	Smokeless Powder, Diphenylamine (DNAB)
SPD	Social Democratic Party [Germany] [Political party]
SPD	Society for Pediatric Dermatology (EA)
SPD	Society of Professional Drivers (EA)
SPD	Society of Publication Designers (EA)
SPD	Sociopathic Personality Disorder [Psychiatry] (DAVI)
SPD	Software Product Description [Computer science] (MHDI)
SPD	Southern Procurement Division [Navy]
SPD	South Pacific Division [Army World War II]
SPD	South Polar Distance
SPD	Sozialdemokratische Partei Deutschlands [Social Democratic Party of Germany] [West Germany]
SpD	Spanish Decca, San Sebastian [Record label] [Spain]
SPD	Specific Paroxysmal Discharge (DB)
SPD	Spectral Power Density [Electronics]
SPD	Spectral Power Distribution (MCD)
SPD	Speech Processing Device
SPD	Speed (AABC)
Spd	Spermidine [Biochemistry]
SPD	Sprayed (WGA)
SPD	Standard Design Platform
SPD	Standard Peak Dilution (DB)
SPD	Standard Periodical Database [Oxbridge Communications, Inc.] [Information service or system] (CRD)
SPD	Standard Periodical Directory [A publication]
SPD	Standard Practice Directive [NASA] (NASA)
SPD	Standard Products [NYSE symbol] (TTSB)

SPD	Standard Products Co. [NYSE symbol] (SPSG)
SPD	Standard Program Device (NITA)
SPD	State Programs Division [Environmental Protection Agency] (GFGA)
SPD	Static Pressure Distribution
SPD	Statistical Policy Division [Office of Management and Budget]
SPD	Steamer Pays Dues [Shipping]
SPD	Stick Positioning Device (MCD)
SPD	Storage Pool Disease
SPD	Stored Program Decoder [or Decommutation]
SPD	St. Peter's Dome Lookout [New Mexico] [Seismograph station code, US Geological Survey] (SEIS)
SPD	Strategic Posture Display (MCD)
SPD	Student Pilot Disposition (DNAB)
SPD	Subcorneal Pustular Dermatosis [Sneddon-Wilkinson disease] [Dermatology]
SPD	Subjective Probability Distribution
SPD	Subject to Permission to Deal [Finance] (WDAA)
SPD	Summary Plan Description
SPD	Superheater Protection Device (DNAB)
SPD	Supplemental Program Directive (AFIT)
SPD	Supplementary Petroleum Duty [Tax] [British]
SPD	Surge Protective Device (MCD)
SPD	Suspended-Particle Display [Glazing technology]
SPD	Synchronized Parallel Displacement [Automotive engineering]
SPD	Synchronizer for Peripheral Devices
SPD	Synchronous Phase Demodulator
SPD	Synpolydactyly [Medicine]
SPD	System Performance Demonstration
SPD	System Program Directive (AFIT)
SPD	System Program Director [Air Force] (MCD)
SPD	Systems Parameters Document (AAG)
SPD	Systems Program Documentation
SPDA	Sea Photo Diffraction Analysis (PDAA)
SPDA	Single-Premium Deferred Annuity [Insurance]
SPDAC	Societe de Perception de Droit d'Auteur du Canada (AC)
SPDB	Subsystem Power Distribution Box (MCD)
SPDBK	Speed Brake (MCD)
SPDC	Spare Parts Distributing Center [Navy]
SPDC	Stored Program Data Compressor [Computer science] (IAA)
SPDC	Strio-Pallido-Dentate Calcinosis [Medicine] (DMAA)
SPDCI	Standard Payload Display and Control Interface (NASA)
SPDCU	Subsurface Probe Data and Control Unit
SP DEL	Special Delivery (WDAA)
SPDF	Smokeless Powder, Diphenylamine, Flashless (DNAB)
SPDF	Special Projects Data Facility
SPDF	Swedish Post Defense Forces
SpdFam	SpeedFam International, Inc. [Associated Press] (SAG)
SPDG	Spiral Point Drill Geometry
SPDHF	Special Pay for Duty Subject to Hostile Fire [Military]
SPDI	Special Discriminant (CAAL)
SPDL	Spin-Dependent Luminescence [Physics]
SPDL	Spindle (MSA)
SPDL	Standard Page Description Language [ISO/IEC] [Computer science]
SPDLTR	Speedletter
SPDM	Special Purpose Dexterous Manipulator
SPDM	Subprocessor with Dynamic Microprogramming
SPDMS	Shuttle Program Data Management System [NASA] (SSD)
SPDMTR	Speedometer
SPDN	Screen Printing and Display News [A publication] (DGA)
SPDN	Smokeless Powder, Diphenylamine, Nonvolatile (DNAB)
SPD NAV	Speed Navigation (MCD)
SPDO	Mollendo [Peru] [ICAO location identifier] (ICLI)
SPDO	Sidama People's Democratic Organisation [Ethiopia]
SPDOM	Speedometer (MSA)
SPDP	Society of Professional Data Processors (IAA)
SPDP	Stored Program Data Processor (KSC)
SPDP	Succinimidyl(pyridyldithio)propionate [Organic chemistry]
SPDR	Software Preliminary Design Review [NASA] (NASA)
SPDR	Special Drill [Tool] (AAG)
SPDR	Spider [Engineering acoustics]
SPDR	Standard & Poors Depositary Receipts [Associated Press] (SAG)
SP/DR	Systems Performance/Design Requirements
SPDRAB	Society for the Prevention of Disparaging Remarks about Brooklyn
SPDS	Safe-Practice Data Sheet (MSA)
SPDS	Safety Parameter Display System [Instrumentation]
SPDS	Self-Power Density Spectrum (IAA)
SPDS	Sequential Payload Delivery System (MCD)
SPDS	Strategic Platform Defense Study [DoD]
SPDS	Suggestion Program Data System [Military]
SPDT	Single-Pole, Double-Throw [Switch]
SPDTDB	Single-Pole, Double-Throw, Double-Break [Switch]
SPDTNCDB	Single-Pole, Double-Throw, Normally-Closed, Double-Break [Switch]
SPDTNO	Single-Pole, Double-Throw, Normally-Open [Switch]
SPDTNODB	Single-Pole, Double-Throw, Normally-Open, Double-Break [Switch]
SPDTSW	Single-Pole, Double-Throw Switch
SPDU	Session Protocol Data Unit [Telecommunications] (OSI)
SPDW	Smokeless Powder, Diphenylamine, Reworked (DNAB)
SPDW	South Pacific Deep Water
SPDWY	Speedway
SPDY	Speedy
Spe	Durandi. Speculum Judiciale [A publication] (DSA)
s-pe--	Peru [MARC geographic area code Library of Congress] (LCCP)
SPE	Secondary Particulate Emissions [Environmental Protection Agency] (GFGA)
SPE	Senior Project Engineer

SPE............	Sepulot [*Malaysia*] [*Airport symbol*] (AD)
SPE............	Serial Passage Experiment [*Experimental evolution*]
SPE............	Serial Poll Enable (IAA)
SPE............	Serum Protein Electrolytes [*Biochemistry*] (DAVI)
SPE............	Serum Protein Electrophoresis
SPE............	Service Propulation Engine (IAA)
SPE............	Shaft Position Encoder
SPE............	Sian [*Republic of China*] [*Seismograph station code, US Geological Survey*] (SEIS)
SPE............	Signal Processing Element [*Navy*]
SPE............	Silicon Planar Epitaxial (IAA)
SPE............	Simultaneous Purging Extraction [*Chemistry*]
SPE............	Sliding Padeye (MCD)
SPE............	Small Processing Element [*Computer science*]
SPE............	Society for Photographic Education (EA)
SPE............	Society for Pure English
SPE............	Society of Petroleum Engineers (EA)
SPE............	Society of Plastics Engineers (EA)
SPE............	Society of Professors of Education (EA)
SPE............	Solar Proton Event [*Geophysics*]
SPE............	Solid Phase Epitaxy
SPE............	Solid-Phase Extraction
SPE............	Solid Polymer Electrolysis (NAKS)
SPE............	Solid Polymer Electrolyte
SPE............	Sony Pictures Entertainment [*Commercial firm*] (ECON)
SPE............	Space Processing Equipment [*Astronautics*]
SPE............	Special Purpose Electronics (MCD)
SPE............	Special-Purpose Equipment
SPE............	Sperry UNIVAC Information Center, Blue Bell, PA [*OCLC symbol*] (OCLC)
SPE............	Spherical Probable Error
SPE............	Sprague Electric Co. [*ICAO designator*] (FAAC)
SPE............	Standard Polishing Index
SPE............	Static Phase Error [*NASA*]
SPE............	Station Project Engineer [*NASA*]
SPE............	Stepped Potential Electrode [*Electrode chemistry*]
SPE............	Stop Project ELF [*Extremely Low Frequency system*] [*Defunct*] (EA)
SPE............	Stored Program Element
SPE............	Streptococcal Enterotoxin [*Medicine*]
SPE............	Studies in Philosophy and Education [*A publication*] (AEBS)
SPE............	Subport of Embarkation
SPE............	Sucrose Polyester [*Pharmacology*]
SPE............	Sun-Planet-Earth [*Astronomy*]
SPE............	Superficial Punctate Erosions [*Ophthalmology*] (DAVI)
SPE............	Switch Processing Element (NITA)
SPE............	System Performance Evaluation (KSC)
SPE............	Systems Performance Effectiveness
SPE............	Unilabo [*France*] [*Research code symbol*]
SPEA............	Panamanian Society of Engineers and Architects (IAA)
SPEA............	Sales Promotion Executives Association [*Later, MCFI*] (FA)
SPEA............	Scottish Physical Education Association [*British*]
SPEA............	Southeastern Poultry and Egg Association (EA)
SPEA............	Streptococcal Pyrogenic Exotoxin A [*Immunochemistry*]
SPEAC.........	Selma Project Education Alternatives Center [*Alabama*] (EA)
SPEAC.........	Solar Photovoltaic Energy Advisory Committee [*Terminated, 1986*] (EGAO)
SPEAC.........	Special Purpose Electronic Area Correlator (MHDI)
SPEAHR.......	Society for the Protection of East Asians' Human Rights/USA (EA)
SPEAK.........	Society for Promoting and Encouraging the Arts and Knowledge of the Church (EA)
SPEAL.........	Special-Purpose Engineering Analysis Language (MCD)
SPEAR........	Selective Parenteral and Enteral Anti-Sepsis Regimen [*Medicine*] (DMAA)
SPEAR........	Signal Processing, Evaluation, Alert, and Report [*Navy*] (NVT)
SPEAR........	SLAC Positron-Electron Asymmetric Ring
SPEAR........	Small Payload Ejection and Recovery for the Space Shuttle [*NASA*] (MCD)
SPEAR........	Source Performance Evaluation and Reporting
SPEAR........	Spaceborne Earth Applications Ranging System (MCD)
Spear..........	Spears' South Carolina Law Reports [*1842-44*] [*A publication*] (DLA)
SPEAR........	Special Project Evaluation and Anti-War Warfare Research (DOMA)
SPEAR........	Squadron Performance Effectiveness Analysis Representation (MCD)
SPEAR........	Stanford Positron-Electron Axisymmetric Ring
SPEAR........	Statistical Property Estimation and Regeneration (MCD)
SPEAR........	Strike Projection Evaluation and Anti-War Warfare Research (DOMA)
SPEAR........	Supplier Performance Evaluation and Reporting [*or Review*] [*General Motors quality award*]
Spear Ch	Spears' South Carolina Chancery Reports [*A publication*] (DLA)
Spear Eq......	Spears' South Carolina Equity Reports [*A publication*] (DLA)
Spear Ext.....	Spear's Law of Extradition [*A publication*] (DLA)
Spear High....	Spearman on Highways [*1881*] [*A publication*] (DLA)
SPEARS.......	Satellite Photoelectric Analog Rectification System
SPEARS.......	Satellite Photo Electronic Analog Rectification System (IAA)
SPEARS.......	Screener Proficiency Evaluation and Report System [*FAA*] (TAG)
SPEARS.......	Spaceborne Earth Applications Ranging System [*NASA*]
Spears........	Spears' South Carolina Equity Reports [*1842-44*] [*A publication*] (DLA)
Spears........	Spears' South Carolina Law Reports [*A publication*] (DLA)
SPEARS.......	Spill Planning Exercise and Response System [*USCG*] (TAG)
Spears Eq....	Spears' South Carolina Equity Reports [*A publication*] (DLA)
SPEB..........	Pebas [*Peru*] [*ICAO location identifier*] (ICLI)
SPEB..........	Streptococcal Pyrogenic Exotoxin B [*Immunochemistry*]
SPEBSQSA...	Society for the Preservation and Encouragement of Barber Shop Quartet Singing inAmerica (EA)
Spec	De Specialibus Legibus [*of Philo*] (BJA)

SPEC........	Scientific Pollution and Environmental Control Society
SPEC........	Simulation of Propulsion Engine Cycle [*NASA*]
SPEC........	Society for Pollution and Environmental Control (COE)
SPEC........	Society of Professional Engineering Checkers
SPEC........	South Pacific Bureau for Economic Cooperation (EERA)
Spec	Special (TBD)
SPEC........	Special [*or Specialist*] (KSC)
Spec	Specialist (CMD)
SPEC........	Species (WGA)
SPEC........	Specific
SPEC........	Specification (AFM)
spec........	Specification (IDOE)
Spec	Specification (AAGC)
SPEC........	Specificity (DMAA)
SPEC........	Specimen (AAG)
Spec	Spectacle [*or Spectacular*] (WGA)
Spec	Spectator [*A publication*] (BRI)
spec........	Spectrum (IDOE)
SPEC........	Spectrum
SPEC........	Spectrum Control [*NASDAQ symbol*] (TTSB)
SPEC........	Spectrum Control, Inc. [*NASDAQ symbol*] (NQ)
SPEC........	Speculation (WGA)
Spec	Speculator [*Guillelmus Durandi*] [*Deceased, 1296*] [*Authority cited in pre-1607 legal work*] (DSA)
spec........	Speculum [*Obstetrics*] (DAVI)
SPEC........	Speech Predictive Encoded Communications [*Telephone channels*]
SPEC........	Speech Predictive Encoding System [*Telephone channels*] (IAA)
SPEC........	Staff of the Production Executive Committee [*of the WPB*] [*Obsolete*]
SPEC........	Standard Performance Evaluation Corp. (DDC)
SPEC........	Stored Program Educational Computer
SPEC........	Streptococcal Pyrogenic Exotoxin C [*Immunochemistry*]
SPEC........	Studies in the Political Economy of Canada [*Society*]
SPEC........	Systems and Procedures Exchange Center [*Association of Research Libraries*]
SPECA	Society for the Preservation and Enjoyment of Carriages in America [*Defunct*] (EA)
SPECA	Supplier Performance Evaluation and Corrective Action (PDAA)
SPECAN......	Spectral Analysis
spec an......	Spectrum Analyzer (IDOE)
SPECASTSECNAV...	Special Assistant to the Secretary of the Navy (DNAB)
SPECAT......	Special Category (AABC)
Sp Ecc & Ad...	Spinks' English Ecclesiastical and Admiralty Reports [*164 English Reprint*] [*1853-55*] [*A publication*] (DLA)
SpecCata.....	Specialty Catalog Corp. [*Associated Press*] (SAG)
SpecCtl.......	Spectrum Controls, Inc. [*Associated Press*] (SAG)
SPECD	Specification Correlation Data Base
SPECDEVCEN...	Special Devices Center [*Navy*]
Spec Ed	Special Education (DAVI)
SPECFORCOM...	Special Forces Command [*Navy*] (DNAB)
spec grav....	Specific Gravity (DAVI)
SpecHlth......	Specialized Health Products International, Inc. [*Associated Press*] (SAG)
SPECHNDLG...	Special Handling (MCD)
SpecHol.......	Spectrum HoloByte, Inc. [*Associated Press*] (SAG)
SPECI........	Selected Special Weather Report [*Aviation*] (FAAC)
SPECI........	Special Weather Report [*Aviation*] (DA)
SPECI........	Specimen (DSUE)
SPECIF.......	Specific (WGA)
specif........	Specification (DAVI)
SPECIFD	Specified (ROG)
SPECIFN	Specification (ROG)
SPECINVESDIST...	Special Investigations District [*Air Force*]
SPECK.......	Safety, Pride, Efficiency, Compatibility, Knowledge (DNAB)
SPECL.......	Special (ROG)
SPECL.......	Specialize
SPECLE......	Specification Language [*Computer science*] (MHDI)
SpecLink.....	SpectraLink Corp. [*Associated Press*] (SAG)
SPECLST.....	Specialist
SPECMAP....	Spectral Mapping
SpecMu	Spec's Music, Inc. [*Associated Press*] (SAG)
SPECO	Steel Products Engineering Co.
SPECOL	Special Customer-Oriented Language
SPECOM	Special Command
SPECOMALT...	Special Communications Alteration
SPECOMDIV...	Special Communications Division [*Navy*] (DNAB)
SPECOMME...	Specified Command Middle East [*Military*]
SPECON......	Systems Performance Effectiveness Conference
SPECOPNSSq...	Special Operations Squadron [*Air Force*]
SPECOPS.....	Special Operations [*Navy*] (NVT)
SPECOR	Spectral Correlation RADAR (MCD)
SPECPROJOUK...	Special Projects Liaison Offices, United Kingdom [*Navy*] (DNAB)
SpecRetl.....	Specialty Retail Group [*Commercial firm Associated Press*] (SAG)
specs..........	Specifications (IDOE)
SPECS	Spectacles (ROG)
SPECS	Switched Proton Electron Challeltron Spectrometer (BARN)
SpecSci	SpectraScience, Inc. [*Associated Press*] (SAG)
SPECT........	Single Photon Emission Computed Tomography
Spect	Spectacula [*of Martial*] [*Classical studies*] (OCD)
SPECT........	Spectrograph
SPECT........	Spectrometer (NASA)
SPECT........	Spectrum
SPECTA......	Structure-Preserved Error-Correcting Tree Automata (MHDI)
SpecTelec....	Specialty Teleconstructioners [*Associated Press*] (SAG)
SPECTNG.....	Specialist Training [*Navy*] (NVT)

SPECTOR..... Single Path Error Correcting Teleprinter over Radio [*Telecommunications*] (IAA)

Spectra....... [*The*] Spectranetics Corp. [*Associated Press*] (SAG)

Spectral...... Spectral Diagnostics, Inc. [*Associated Press*] (SAG)

SPECTRE ..... Special Executive for Counterintelligence, Terrorism, Revenge, and Extortion [*Fictitious organization whose agents were characters in the late Ian Fleming's "James Bond" mysteries*]

SPECTRE ..... Special Radiation Experiment [*Marine science*] (OSRA)

SPECTRE ..... Spectral Radiation Experiment (USDC)

Spectrian .... Spectrian Corp. [*Associated Press*] (SAG)

SPECTROL... Scheduling, Planning, Evaluation, and Cost Control [*Air Force*]

SpectV .... Spectra Vision, Inc. [*Formerly, SPI Holdings, Inc.*] [*Associated Press*] (SAG)

SpectVis ...... Spectra Vision, Inc. [*Formerly, SPI Holdings, Inc.*] [*Associated Press*] (SAG)

Specu .... Speculator [*Guillelmus Durandi*] [*Deceased, 1296*] [*Authority cited in pre-1607 legal work*] (DSA)

Specu .... Speculum [*A publication*] (BRI)

Specula ...... Speculator [*Guillelmus Durandi*] [*Deceased, 1296*] [*Authority cited in pre-1607 legal work*] (DSA)

SPECVER.... Specification Verification [*Computer science*] (IEEE)

SPECWAR.... Special Warfare (DOMA)

SPED .... Society of Piping Engineers and Designers (NTPA)

SPED .... Special Education

SPED .... Special Education Director

Sp Ed.......... Specialist in Education [*Academic degree*]

SPED .... Sulfur, Phosphorus, Emission Detector [*Chromatograph accessory*]

SPED .... Supersonic Planetary Entry Decelerator (KSC)

SPEDAC...... Solid-State, Parallel, Expandable, Differential Analyzer Computer

SPEDCO...... Southeastern Pennsylvania Development Corp.

SPEDE .... System for Processing Educational Data Electronically

SPEDIAT ..... Special Diary Transcript [*Military*]

Sp Ed S ...... Special Education Specialist (PGP)

SPEDTAC .... Stored Program Educational Transistorized Automatic Computer

SPEDY .... Summer Program for Economically Disadvantaged Youth [*Department of Labor*]

SPEE .... Society for the Promotion of Engineering Education [*Later, ASEE*]

SPEE .... Society of Petroleum Evaluation Engineers (IAA)

SPEE .... Special Purpose End Effector (MCD)

SPEECS ...... Speech Parameter Extraction Experimental Comparison System (IAA)

SPEED .... Scheduled Procurement of Essential Equipment Deliveries [*US Postal Service*]

SPEED .... Self-Programmed Electronic Equation Delineator

SPEED .... Signal Processing in Evacuated Electronic Devices

SPEED .... Single-Point Emergency Equipment Divestment

SPEED .... Special Procedures for Expediting Equipment Development (MCD)

SPEED .... Study and Performance Efficiency in Entry Design

SPEED .... Subsistence Preparation by Electronic Energy Diffusion

SPEED .... Systematic Plotting and Evaluation of Enumerated Data [*National Institute of Standards and Technology Computer science*]

SPEED .... Systems Planning and Effectiveness Evaluation Device (MCD)

SPEED .... Systemwide Project for Electronic Equipment at Depots [*Military*] (AABC)

SPEEDEX ..... Systemwide Project for Electronic Equipment at Depots Extended [*Military*] (AABC)

SpeedM .... Speedway Motorsports, Inc. [*Associated Press*] (SAG)

SPEEDO ...... Speedometer [*Automotive engineering*]

SPEEDS ...... System for Pinpointed, Exhaustive and Expeditious Dissemination of Subjects (PDAA)

SPEEDX ..... Society to Preserve the Engrossing Enjoyment of DXing (EA)

SPEEL......... Shore Plant Electronic Equipment List (MUGU)

SPEER .... Scientists and Professional Engineers Employment Registry [*Career Technologies Corp. - CTC*] [*Andover, MA*] [*Information service or system*] (IID)

SPEERA ...... Secretarial Panel For the Evaluation of Epidemiologic Research Activities for the Department of Energy (EGAO)

SPEEREBRA... Speech Research Branch [*Navy*] (DNAB)

Speers........ Speers' [*or Spears'*] South Carolina Law Reports [*A publication*] (DLA)

Speers Eq.... Speers' [*or Spears'*] South Carolina Equity Reports [*A publication*] (DLA)

Speers Eq (SC)... Speers' [*or Spears'*] South Carolina Equity Reports [*A publication*] (DLA)

Speers L (SC)... Speers' [*or Spears'*] South Carolina Law Reports [*A publication*] (DLA)

SPEF.......... Single Program Element Funding [*Military*] (AABC)

SPEF.......... Student Performance Evaluation Form

SPEFC......... Solid Polymer Electrolyte Fuel Cell (EDCT)

SPEG .... Serum Protein Electrophoretogram [*Clinical chemistry*]

SPEG .... Solid Phase Epitaxy Growth (AAEL)

SPEG .... Spencerville & Elgin Railroad Co. [*AAR code*]

SPEG .... Staff Planning Evaluation Group (AAG)

SPEGL .... Short-Term Public Exposure Guidance Level [*Environmental science*] (COE)

SPEH .... May & Speh Inc. [*NASDAQ symbol*] (TTSB)

SPEI........... Savoy Pictures Entertainment [*NASDAQ symbol*] (TTSB)

SPEI........... Savoy Pictures Entertainment, Inc. [*NASDAQ symbol*] (SAG)

Speizmn ..... Speizman Industries, Inc. [*Associated Press*] (SAG)

SPEK .... Spec's Music [*NASDAQ symbol*] (TTSB)

SPEK .... Spec's Music, Inc. [*Miami, FL*] [*NASDAQ symbol*] (NQ)

SPELD........ Specific Learning Disability (ADA)

SPELEOL.... Speleological

Spel Feuds... Spelman on Feuds [*A publication*] (DLA)

Spel Gl .... Spelman's Glossarium Archaiologicum [*A publication*] (DLA)

SPELL......... Society for the Preservation of English Language and Literature (EA)

SpellEnt...... Spelling Entertainment, Inc. [*Associated Press*] (SAG)

Spell Extr Rel... Spelling on Extraordinary Relief in Equity and in Law [*A publication*] (DLA)

Spell Extr Rem... Spelling's Treatise on Injunctions and Other Extraordinary Remedies [*A publication*] (DLA)

Spel LT....... Spelman's Law Tracts [*A publication*] (DLA)

Spelm........ Spelman's Glossarium Archaiologicum [*3 eds.*] [*1626-87*] [*A publication*] (DLA)

Spelman .... Spelman's Glossarium Archaiologicum [*3 eds.*] [*1626-87*] [*A publication*] (DLA)

SPELPAT...... Spelling Patterns

Spel Rep ..... Spelman's Reports, Manuscript, English King's Bench [*A publication*] (DLA)

SPEM......... Semispectral Primitive Equation Model [*Marine science*] (OSRA)

SPEM......... Sindacato Petrolieri e Methanieri [*Union of Oil and Methane Gas Workers*] [*Italy*]

SPEMS........ Self-Propelled Elevated Maintenance Stand (MCD)

SPEMU....... Stable-Price Economic and Monetary Union [*Europe*]

SPEN .... Iscozacin [*Peru*] [*ICAO location identifier*] (ICLI)

SPENAVO.... Special Naval Observer

Spenc .... Spencer's Law Reports [*20 New Jersey*] [*A publication*] (DLA)

Spenc .... Spencer's Reports [*10-20 Minnesota*] [*A publication*] (DLA)

Spence Ch .. Spence's Equitable Jurisdiction of the Court of Chancery [*A publication*] (DLA)

Spence Cop... Spence on Copyright of Designs [*A publication*] (DLA)

Spence Eq Jur.. Spence's Equitable Jurisdiction of the Court of Chancery [*A publication*] (DLA)

Spence Or L... Spence's Origin of Laws [*A publication*] (DLA)

Spence Pat Inv... Spence on Patentable Inventions [*1851*] [*A publication*] (DLA)

Spencer...... Spencer's Law Reports [*20 New Jersey*] [*A publication*] (DLA)

Spencer...... Spencer's Reports [*10-20 Minnesota*] [*A publication*] (DLA)

Spencer-M... Spencer-Mead [*Commercial firm*] (DAVI)

Spen (NJ) .... Spencer's Law Reports [*20 New Jersey*] [*A publication*] (DLA)

Spens Sel Cas... Spens' Select Cases [*Bombay, India*] [*A publication*] (DLA)

SPEO......... Chimbote [*Peru*] [*ICAO location identifier*] (ICLI)

SPE of AIME... Society of Petroleum Engineers of American Institute of Mining, Metallurgical, and Petroleum Engineers (EA)

SPEOPT....... Special Optical Tracking System [*NASA*]

SPEP.......... Puerto Esperanza [*Peru*] [*ICAO location identifier*] (ICLI)

SPEP.......... Serum Protein Electrophoresis [*Clinical chemistry*]

SPEP.......... Society for Phenomenology and Existential Philosophy (EA)

SPEPD .... Space Power and Electric Propulsion Division [*Formerly, Nuclear Systems and Space Power Division*] [*NASA*]

SPEPOS .... Society of Petroleum Engineers Production Operations Symposium and Exhibition (ITD)

SPEPS......... Specialist, Motion Picture Service - Booker [*Navy rating*]

SPEQ .... Moquegua [*Peru*] [*ICAO location identifier*] (ICLI)

Sp Eq.......... Spears' South Carolina Equity Reports [*A publication*] (DLA)

SPEQ .... Special Equipment (AAG)

SPEQ .... Speciality Equipment [*NASDAQ symbol*] (SAG)

SPEQ .... Specialty Equipment [*NASDAQ symbol*] (SAG)

SPERDVAC... Society to Preserve and Encourage Radio Drama, Variety, and Comedy (EA)

SPERM .... Secret Paper Reconstitution Mechanism [*Device to reclaim documents that have been inadvertently shredded*]

sperm .... Spermatozoa (DOG)

sperm .... Spermatozoan (DOG)

SPERMFLOW... Society for the Preservation and Enhancement of the Recognition of Millard Fillmore, Last of the Whigs (EA)

SPERT .... Schedule Performance Evaluation and Review Technique

SPERT .... Schedule Program Evaluation and Review Technique (IAA)

SPERT .... Short Pulse Experimental RADAR Techniques (MCD)

SPERT .... Simplified Program Evaluation and Review Technique [*Trademark*]

SPERT .... Special Power Excursion Reactor Test [*US reactor facilities*]

SPERTTT...... Society for Promotion of Educational Reform through Teacher Training [*British*]

SPeruC .... Southern Peru Copper Corp. [*Associated Press*] (SAG)

SPERW .... Specialist, Recreation and Welfare Assistant [*Navy rating*]

SPES.......... Servico de Propaganda e Educacao Sanitaria [*Brazil*]

SPES.......... Short Psychiatric Evaluation Scale (CPH)

SPES.......... South Place Ethical Society [*British*]

SpES.......... Special Education Specialist (GAGS)

SPES.......... Stored Program Element System [*Computer science*] (IEEE)

SPESA .... Sewn Products Equipment Suppliers Association (NTPA)

SPESS .... Stored Program Electronic Switching System [*Telecommunications*] (TEL)

SPET .... Single Photon Emission Tomography

SPET .... Solid-Propellant Electric Thruster [*Aerospace*]

SPET .... Super Power Electron Tube

SPETE .... Special Purpose Electronic Test Equipment [*Military*] (CAAL)

SPETERL..... Ship Portable Electrical/Electronic Test Equipment Requirement List [*Navy*] (CAAL)

SPEX .... Small and Specialists Publishers Exhibition

SPEX .... Sozialwissenschaftliche Experten und Gutachter [*Social Science Experts*] [*NOMOS Datapool Database*] (IID)

SPEX .... Space Plasma Experiment [*NASA*] (SSD)

SPEX .... Special Exercise [*Navy*] (NVT)

spex .... Specifications (WDMC)

SPEZ .... Puerto Bermudez [*Peru*] [*ICAO location identifier*] (ICLI)

SPF .... Science Policy Foundation [*Later, ISPF*] [*British*]

SPF .... Scottish Pharmaceutical Federation [*British*]

SPF .... Security Police Flight [*Air Force*]

SPF .... Service Publication Form (AAG)

SPF .... Shortest Path First (TNIG)

SPF	SIDPERS [*Standard Installation/Division Personnel System*] Personnel File [*Military*] (AABC)
SPF	Single Point Failure (NASA)
SPF	Single Project Funding (MCD)
SPF	Site Population Factor [*Nuclear energy*] (NRCH)
SPF	Skin Protection Factor [*Medicine*]
SPF	Society for the Propagation of the Faith (EA)
SPF	Society of Phantom Friends (EA)
SPF	Software Production Facility [*NASA*] (NASA)
SPF	Somali Patriotic Front [*Political party*] (EY)
SPF	South Pacific Airline SA [*Chile*] [*ICAO designator*] (FAAC)
SPF	South Pacific Forum [*Australia*]
SPF	Soy Protein Flour [*Food technology*]
SPF	Spacelab Processing Facility [*NASA*] (NASA)
SPF	Space Power Facility
SPF	Spaero JSP [*Ukraine*] [*FAA designator*] (FAAC)
SPF	Spearfish [*South Dakota*] [*Airport symbol*] (AD)
SPF	Spearfish, SD [*Location identifier FAA*] (FAAL)
SPF	Specialist, Firefighter [*Navy rating*]
SPF	Special Production Fund [*Australian Film Commission*]
SPF	Special Purpose Force (MCD)
SPF	Specific-Pathogen Free [*Medicine*]
SPF	Spectrophotofluorometer
S-PF	S Phase Fraction
SPF	Spinning Form (MCD)
SPF	Split Product of Fibrin (MAE)
SPF	Springfield Resources [*Vancouver Stock Exchange symbol*]
SPF	Standard Pacific [*NYSE symbol*] (TTSB)
SPF	Standard-Pacific Corp. [*NYSE symbol*] (SPSG)
SPF	Standard Perfusion Fluid [*Medicine*] (DMAA)
SPF	Standard Pesticide File [*Derwent Publications Ltd.*] [*Database*]
SPF	Standard Program Facility (NITA)
SPF	Standard Project Flood [*Nuclear energy*] (NRCH)
SPF	Start-Promoting Factor [*Cytology*]
SPF	St. Paul-En-Foret [*France*] [*Seismograph station code, US Geological Survey*] (SEIS)
SPF	St. Photios Foundation (EA)
SPF	Strategic Protection Force
SPF	Stressed Panel Fasteners
SPF	Structured Programming Facility [*Computer science*]
SPF	Studded Panel Fastener (DNAB)
SPF	Subscriber Plant Factor [*Telecommunications*]
SPF	Sun-Protection Factor [*Cosmetics industry*]
SPF	Superabsorbent Polymer Formulation
SPF	Super Plastic Formed [*Metal fabrication*]
SPF	Superplastic Forming [*Materials science*]
SPF	Surrogate Parent Foundation (EA)
SPF	Survival Probability Function
SPF	Synthesis-Phase Fraction [*Medicine*] (CDI)
SPF	Synthetic Phenolic Foam
SPF	System Performance Factor [*Telecommunications*] (TEL)
SPF	System Productivity Facility [*Computer science*]
SPFA	Scottish Pelagic Fishermen's Association (DBA)
SPFA	Single Point Failure Analysis (KSC)
SPFA	Societe des Professeurs Francais et Francophones en Amerique (EA)
SPFA	Steel Plate Fabricators Association (EA)
SPFC	Site Peculiar Facility Change (AAG)
SPFC	Society for the Parents of Fugitive Children [*Fictional organization in film "Taking Off"*]
SPFC	Solid Polymer Fuel Cell [*Energy source*]
SPFD	Solid-Particle Filter Dye [*Color film technology*]
SPF/DB	Superplastic Forming/Diffusion Bonding [*Materials science*]
SpFest	Spanish Festival [*Record label*]
SPFFA	South Pacific Forum Fisheries Agency [*Honiara, Solomon Islands*] (EAIO)
SPFFC	Southern Ports Foreign Freight Committee
SP-FGS	Shuttle Projects - Flight and Ground Systems Office [*Kennedy Space Center*] [*NASA*] (NASA)
SPFI	Solid-Phase Fluorescent Immunoassay [*Oncology*] (DAVI)
SPFL	Southern Philippines Federation of Labor
sp fl	Spinal Fluid [*Medicine*] (MAE)
SPFM	Society for the Preservation of Film Music (EA)
SPFM	Society of Priests for a Free Ministry (EA)
SPFM	Spinning Form [*Tool*] (AAG)
SPFMV	Sweet Potato Feather Mottle Virus
SPFO	Sparta Foods [*Commercial firm NASDAQ symbol*] (SAG)
SPFP	Single Pass Fit Program (MCD)
SPFP	Single Point Failure Potential (KSC)
SPFP	Single-Precision Floating Point [*Computer science*]
SPFP	Sudanese People's Federal Party [*Sudan*] [*Political party*] (MENA)
SPFPAD	Spacecraft Performance and Flight Path Analysis Directorate [*NASA*]
SPFS	Soldier Physical Fitness School [*Army*] (INF)
SPFT	Single-Pedestal Flat-Top [*Desk*]
SPFT	Sixteen Personality Factors Test [*Psychology*] (DAVI)
SPFW	Single-Phase Full Wave
SPFWBR	Single-Phase Full-Wave Bridge (DWSG)
SPFX	Special Effects [*Filmmaking*]
SPG	Saint Paul Guild (EA)
SPG	Salicyl Phenolic Glucuronide [*Organic chemistry*]
SPG	Saxifrage Publications Group (EA)
SPG	Scan Pattern Generator
SPG	Schizophyllum Polyglucosan (DB)
SPG	Screen Producers Guild [*Later, PGA*] (EA)
SPG	Security Police Group [*Air Force*]
SPG	Seed Pea Group [*Defunct*] (EA)
SPG	Self-Propelled Gun [*British military*] (DMA)
SPG	Shift Pattern Generator [*Automotive engineering*]
SPG	Short Pulse Generator
SPG	Signal Point Ground (NASA)
SPG	Signal Processor Group
SPG	Silver Spring Mining [*Vancouver Stock Exchange symbol*]
SPG	Simon DeBartolo Group [*NYSE symbol*] [*Formerly, Simon Property Group*] (SG)
SPG	Simon DeBartolo Group, Inc. [*NYSE symbol*] (SAG)
SPG	Simon Property Group [*NYSE symbol*] (SPSG)
SPG	Simple Phrase Grammar
SPG	Single-Point Ground (MCD)
SPG	Sinusoidal Pressure Generator
SPG	Society for the Propagation of the Gospel [*Later, USPG*] [*British*]
SPG	Sort Program Generator [*Computer science*] (BUR)
SPG	Source Power Gain
SPG	Spastic Paraplegia [*Medicine*]
SPG	Specialist, Gunnery [*Navy rating*]
SPG	Special Patrol Group [*of the London Metropolitan Police, providing protection for public figures*]
SPG	Special Performance Group [*In automobile name SAAB 900 Turbo SPG*]
SPG	Special Planning Group [*Special Operations Force*] (DOMA)
SPG	Special Project Group [*DoD*]
SPG	Special Purpose Grant
SPG	Specific Gravity [*Also, SP, SPGR*]
SPG	Spiroglycol [*Organic chemistry*]
Spg	Sponge [*Quality of the bottom*] [*Nautical charts*]
SPG	Spooling (MSA)
SPG	Spring (AAG)
SPG	Springdale Air Services, Inc. [*ICAO designator*] (FAAC)
SPG	Statistical Paper Group (NTPA)
SPG	Stereophotogrammetry [*Medicine*]
SPG	St. Petersburg, FL [*Location identifier FAA*] (FAAL)
SPG	Study Planning Guide (MCD)
SPG	Sucrose, Phosphate, Glutamate [*A culture medium*]
SPG	Symmetrical Perpheral Gangrene [*Medicine*] (DB)
SPG	Synchronization Pulse Generator (IAA)
SPG	System Phasing Group (MCD)
SPGA	Scottish Professional Golfers Association (BARN)
SPGA	Southeastern Pecan Growers Association
SPGA	Southwestern Peanut Growers Association (EA)
SPGA	Staggered Pin-Grid Array [*Computer science*]
SPGB	Socialist Party of Great Britain (PPW)
SPGCPS	Senior Policy Group for Canadian Production Sharing
SPGD	Self-Powered Gamma Detector [*Nuclear energy*] (NRCH)
SPGE	Steam Plant Gauge (DNAB)
SPGFP	Society for the Propagation of the Gospel in Foreign Parts [*British*] (DA3)
SPGG	Solid-Propellant Gas Generator (AAG)
SPGH	Society for the Preservation of the Greek Heritage (EA)
SPGJ	Society for the Propagation of the Gospel among the Jews [*British*]
SPGJ	Stomach-Partitioning Gastrojejunostomy [*Surgery*]
SPGL	Spiegel, Inc. [*NASDAQ symbol*] (NQ)
SPGLA	Spiegel Cl'A' [*NASDAQ symbol*] (TTSB)
Sp Glos	Spelman's Glossarium Archaiologicum [*A publication*] (DLA)
SPGM	Specialist, Gunnery, Aviation Free Gunnery Instructor [*Navy rating*]
SPGM	Tingo Maria [*Peru*] [*ICAO location identifier*] (ICLI)
SPGN	Specialist, Gunnery, Antiaircraft Gunnery Instructor [*Navy rating*]
SPGN	Sympathetic Post-Ganglionic Neurone [*Neurology*]
SPGNA	Sepragen Cop. [*NASDAQ symbol*] (SAG)
SPGNA	Sepragen Corp. 'A' [*NASDAQ symbol*] (TTSB)
SPGNU	Sepragen Corp. Unit [*NASDAQ symbol*] (TTSB)
SPGNW	Sepragen Corp. Wrrt'A' [*NASDAQ symbol*] (TTSB)
SPGNZ	Sepragen Corp. Wrrt'B' [*NASDAQ symbol*] (TTSB)
SPGPM	Shots per Gun per Minute [*Military*] (NVT)
SPGR	Specialist Personal GPS Receiver
sp gr	Specific Gravity (IDOE)
SPGR	Specific Gravity [*Also, SG, SPG*]
SP GRV	Specific Gravity [*Also, SP, SPGR, SPG*] (DAVI)
SPGS	Lagunas [*Peru*] [*ICAO location identifier*] (ICLI)
SPGS	Secondary Power-Generating Subsystem (IAA)
SPGS	Spare Guidance System
SPGS	Springs (MCD)
SPGT	Puerto Victoria [*Peru*] [*ICAO location identifier*] (ICLI)
SPGT	Springfield Terminal Railway Co. [*Later, ST*] [*AAR code*]
SPGTA	Signal Processor Group Test Assembly
SPGU	Bagua [*Peru*] [*ICAO location identifier*] (ICLI)
SpgWre	Spaghetti Warehouse, Inc. [*Associated Press*] (SAG)
SPGX	Spastic Paraplegia, X-Linked [*Medicine*] (DMAA)
SPH	San Pedro Hill [*California*] [*Seismograph station code, US Geological Survey Closed*] (SEIS)
SPH	Scans per Hour [*Photocopying, Microfilming*]
SPH	Secondary Pulmonary Hemosiderosis [*Medicine*] (MAE)
SPH	Self-Propelled Howitzer (MCD)
SPH	Severely and Profoundly Handicapped
SPH	Sheets per Hour (WDMC)
SPH	Singapore Press Holdings (ECON)
S-Ph	Single-Phase
SPH	Smoothed-Particle Hydrodynamics [*Statistical mechanics*]
SPH	Smooth Particle Hydrodynamic
SPH	Sociedade Portuguesa de Helicopteros Lda. [*Portugal*] [*FAA designator*] (FAAC)
SPH	Society of Public Health (EAIO)

SPH .... Sound Protective Helmet [*Military*]
SPH .... Soy Protein Hydrolyzate
SPH .... Space Heater (KSC)
SPH .... Special Psychiatric Hospital [*Former USSR*]
SPH .... Spherical (ROG)
SPH .... Spherical Lens [*Ophthalmology*]
Sph .... Sphingomyelin [*Also, SM, SP*] [*Biochemistry*] (DAVI)
Sph .... Sphingosine [*Also, SM*] [*Biochemistry*]
SPH .... Springhill, LA [*Location identifier FAA*] (FAAL)
SPH .... Stable Platform Housing
SPH .... Statement of Personal History [*Military*]
SPH .... Suburban Propane Ptnrs L.P. [*NYSE symbol*] (TTSB)
SPH .... Superphantom (IAA)
SPHA .... Chincha [*Peru*] [*ICAO location identifier*] (ICLI)
SPHC .... Chala [*Peru*] [*ICAO location identifier*] (ICLI)
SPHCT .... Simplified Perturbed Hard Chain Theory [*Equation of state*]
SPHD .... Special Pay for Hostile Duty [*Military*] (AFM)
SP/Hd .... Spool Piece Head [*Nuclear energy*] (NRCH)
SPHE .... Society of Packaging and Handling Engineers [*Later, IoPP*] (EA)
SPHE .... Society of Public Health Educators (DAVI)
SPHE .... Spherocytes [*Also, SPHER*] [*Hematology*] (DAVI)
SPHER .... Small-Particle Heat-Exchange Receiver [*Solar energy technology*]
SPHER .... Spherical
SPHER .... Spherocytes [*Also, SPHE*] [*Hematology*] (DAVI)
SPHERE .... Scientific Parameters for Health and the Environment, Retrieval and Estimation [*Database*] [*Environmental Protection Agency Washington, DC*]
SPHF .... Spin-Polarized Hartree-Fock [*Atomic wave-function*]
SPHF .... Spontaneous Hole Filling [*Spectrometry*]
SPHG .... Speed and Heading [*Navy Navigation and Satellite System*] (DNAB)
SPHI .... Chiclayo/Cap. Jose Abelardo Quinones Gonzalez [*Peru*] [*ICAO location identifier*] (ICLI)
SPHI .... Studio Plus Hotels [*NASDAQ symbol*] (TTSB)
SPHI .... Studio Plus Hotels, Inc. [*NASDAQ symbol*] (SAG)
SPHINX .... Space Plasma High-Voltage Interaction Experiment [*Spacecraft*] [*NASA*]
SPHINX .... Survival Probability Hazard in a Nuclear Exchange
SPHL .... Self-Propelled Hyperbaric Lifeboat (DS)
SP-HL .... Sun Present - Horizon Lost
SPHN .... Siphon (MSA)
SPHO .... Ayacucho/Coronel FAP Alfredo Mendivil Duarte [*Peru*] [*ICAO location identifier*] (ICLI)
SPHQ .... Shore Patrol Headquarters
SphrDrk .... Sphere Drake Holdings [*Associated Press*] (SAG)
SPHS .... Society for the Promotion of Hellenic Studies (EA)
SPHS .... Swedish Pioneer Historical Society (EA)
SP/HT .... Specific Heat
SPHT .... Super Pressure - High Temperature
SPHU .... Huancayo [*Peru*] [*ICAO location identifier*] (ICLI)
SPHV .... Huanuco Viejo [*Peru*] [*ICAO location identifier*] (ICLI)
SPHW .... Single-Phase Half Wave
SPHY .... Andahuaylas [*Peru*] [*ICAO location identifier*] (ICLI)
SPHZ .... Anta/Comdte. FAP German Arias Grazziani [*Peru*] [*ICAO location identifier*] (ICLI)
SPI .... Die Sprache der Palmyrenischen Inschriften [*Leipzig*] [*A publication*] (BJA)
SPI .... Illinois State Library, Springfield, IL [*OCLC symbol*] (OCLC)
SPI .... Scanning Pulse Immobilization
SPI .... Schedule Performance Index (MCD)
SPI .... Scottish Provident Institution [*Commercial firm*]
SPI .... Secondary Protocol Identifier (TNIG)
SPI .... Secretariats Professionnels Internationaux
SPI .... Security Parameters Index
SPI .... Selected Period Investment [*Finance*] (WDAA)
SPI .... Selective Population Inversion [*Physics*]
SPI .... Self-Paced Instruction (IEEE)
SPI .... Self-Perception Inventory [*Personality development test*] [*Psychology*]
SPI .... Semi Process Inc. (NITA)
SPI .... Senior Patrol Inspection [*Immigration and Naturalization Service*]
SPI .... Septum-Equipped Programmable Injector [*Gas chromatography*]
SPI .... Sequence of Pulse Intervals
SPI .... Serial Peripheral Interface [*Electronics*]
SPI .... Series-Parallel Interface [*Computer science*]
SPI .... Serum Precipitable Iodine [*Serology*]
SPI .... Service Pedalogique Interafricain
SPI .... Service Provider Interface [*Computer science*]
SPI .... Service Publication Instruction (AAG)
SPI .... Severely and Profoundly Impaired
SPI .... Shared Peripheral Interface
SPI .... Share Price Index (ADA)
SPI .... Shipley Personal Inventory [*Medicine*] (DMAA)
SPI .... Ship's Plan Index
SPI .... Signal Point Identification (IAA)
SPI .... Signal Presence Indicator (CAAL)
SPI .... Single Point Injection [*Automotive engineering*]
SPI .... Single Processor Interface
SPI .... Single Program Initiated [*Computer science*] (IAA)
SPI .... Single Program Initiation [*Computer science*]
SPI .... Single Program Initiator [*Computer science*] (ECII)
SPI .... Site Peculiar Interference (AAG)
SPI .... Site Population Index [*Nuclear energy*] (NRCH)
SPI .... Smoke Point Improvement [*Petroleum refining*]
SPI .... Smoking Policy Institute (EA)

SPI .... Societe pour l'Informatique [*Company for Informatics*] [*Information service or system Defunct*] (IID)
SPI .... Society for Prevention of Infertility (EA)
SPI .... Society of Photographic Illustrators (EA)
SPI .... Society of Practitioners of Insolvency (BUAC)
SPI .... Society of Professional Investigators (EA)
SPI .... Society of the Plastics Industry (EA)
SPI .... Software Process Improvement (AAEL)
SPI .... Solid Propellant Information
SPI .... South Pacific Island Airways, Inc. [*ICAO designator*] (FAAC)
SPI .... Soy Protein Isolate [*Food technology*]
SPI .... Spanish Paprika Institute (EA)
SPI .... Specialist, Punched Card Accounting Machine Operator [*Navy rating*]
SPI .... Special Position Identification
SPI .... Specific Productivity Index (IEEE)
SPI .... Spectrophotometric Process Ink (DGA)
Spi .... Spicules [*Quality of the bottom*] [*Nautical charts*]
SPI .... SPI Holdings, Inc. [*Later, SpectraVision, Inc.*] [*AMEX symbol*] (SPSG)
SPI .... Sports Philatelists International (EA)
SPI .... Sports Promotion International (BUAC)
SPI .... Springfield [*Illinois*] [*Airport symbol*] (OAG)
SPI .... Standard Performance Indicator [*Army*]
SPI .... Standard Practice Instructions (MCD)
SPI .... Standard Protective Item
SPI .... Statement of Policy or Interpretation [*Food and Drug Administration*]
SPI .... Station Program Identification [*Telecommunications*] (TEL)
SPI .... Storage Protein Isolate [*Food industry*]
SPI .... St. Paul Island [*Alaska*] [*Seismograph station code, US Geological Survey Closed*] (SEIS)
SPI .... Strategic Planning Initiative [*Environmental Protection Agency*] (GFGA)
SPI .... Strategic Planning Institute [*Cambridge, MA*]
SPI .... Stuttering Prediction Instruction [*Speech and language therapy*] (DAVI)
SPI .... Sun Position Indicator (IAA)
SPI .... Superintendent of Public Instruction (DNAB)
SPI .... Supervisory Practices Inventory [*Test*]
SPI .... Surface Position Indicator (NASA)
SPI .... Symbolic Pictorial Indicator (MCD)
SPI .... Synergy Power Institute [*Defunct*] (EA)
SPI .... Synthetic Phase Isolation [*Telemetry*]
SPI .... System Performance Indicator
SPI .... System Programming Interface [*Computer science*]
SPIA .... Ica [*Peru*] [*ICAO location identifier*] (ICLI)
SPIA .... Single Premium Immediate Annuities [*Insurance*]
SPIA .... Solid-Phase Immunoabsorption [*Medicine*] (DMAA)
SPIA .... Solid Propellant Information Agency [*Air Force*]
SPIAM .... Sodium Purity In-Line Analytical Module [*Nuclear energy*] (NRCH)
SPIAP .... Shuttle/Payload Integration Activities Plan (NASA)
SPIB .... Scripta Pontificii Instituti Biblici [*A publication*] (BJA)
SPIB .... Shetland Pony Identification Bureau
SPIB .... Social and Prevocational Information Battery
SPIB .... Society of Power Industry Biologists (EA)
SPIB .... Southern Pine Inspection Bureau (EA)
SPIBS .... Satellite Positive-Ion-Beam System [*Air Force*] (MCD)
SPIC .... Ship Position Interpolation Computer
SPIC .... Sisters of Providence and of the Immaculate Conception [*Roman Catholic religious order*]
SPIC .... Society of the Plastics Industry of Canada
SPIC .... Southern Petrochemical Industries Corp. [*India*] (BUAC)
SPIC .... Spare Parts Inventory Control (MHDB)
SPIC .... Standard and Poor's Index - Composite [*Stock market*]
SPIC .... Students for Promotion of Identity on Campus [*New York group promoting ethnic pride among Latin American students*]
SPIC .... Summary Punch IBM [*International Business Machines*] Collector
SPICBM .... Solid Propellant Intercontinental Ballistic Missile
SPICE .... Sales-Point Information Computing Equipment [*Merchandising*]
SPICE .... Self-Paced Instruction for Competency Education (EDAC)
SPICE .... Simplified Procurement in a Competitive Environment (AAGC)
SPICE .... Simulation Program with Integrated Circuit Emphasis (MCD)
SPICE .... Solar Particle Intensity Composition Experiment [*NASA*]
SPICE .... Space Integrated Controls Experiment (DOMA)
SPICE .... Spacelab Payload Integration and Coordination in Europe [*NASA*] (NASA)
SPICE .... Space Power Internal Combustion Engine (MCD)
SPICE .... Special Programs Incorporating Custom Elective
SPICE .... Special Programs Increasing Counseling Effectiveness [*Pennsylvania State Department of Public Instruction*]
SPICE .... Stanford Program on International and Cross Cultural Education [*Stanford University*] [*Research center*] (RCD)
SpiceEnt ...... Spice Entertainment Companies, Inc. [*Associated Press*] (SAG)
SPICI .... SPI [*Society of the Plastics Industry*] Composites Institute (EA)
SPICMA .... Special Projects in Christian Missionary Areas (BUAC)
SPIC-MACAY... Society for Promotion of Indian Classical Music and Culture Amongst the Young (BUAC)
SPID .... Seismic Personnel Intrusion Detector (PDAA)
SPID .... Service Profile Identifier [*Computer science*]
SPID .... Service Provider ID (PCM)
SPID .... SIS [*Superconductivity Information System*] Published Information Database [*Office of Scientific and Technical Information*] [*Department of Energy*]
SPID .... Standard Performance Indicator Dictionary [*Army*]
SPID .... Submersible Portable Inflatable Dwelling
SPID .... Summed Pain Intensity Difference [*Medicine*] (DMAA)

SPID	Sum of Pain Intensity Differences
SPIDAC	Specimen Input to Digital Automatic Computer
SPIDE	Short Planning Identification File
SPIDER	Smokeless Propellant in Demonstration Experimental Rocket (KSC)
SPIDER	Sonic Pulse-Echo Instrument Designed for Extreme Resolution (IEEE)
SPIDER	Systematic Planning for the Integration of Defense Engineering and Research [*Program*]
SPIDF	Support Planning Identification File [*NASA*] (MCD)
Spidir	Spiritual Direction (WDAA)
SPIDO	Shuttle Payload Integration and Development Program Office [*NASA*]
SPIDOT	Self-Propelled Immersible Drive-Off Trolley [*British*] (DI)
SPIDPO	Shuttle Payload Integration and Development Program Office [*Johnson Space Center*] (NASA)
SPIDR	Society of Professionals in Dispute Resolution (EA)
SPIE	International Society of Photo-Optical Instrumentation Engineers (BUAC)
SPIE	Scavenging-Precipitation-Ion Exchange (IEEE)
SPIE	Secretariat Professionnel International de l'Enseignement [*International Federation of Free Teachers' Unions - IFFTU*] [*Amsterdam, Netherlands*] (EAIO)
SPIE	Self-Programmed Individualized Education (IEEE)
SPIE	Ships Precise Identification Emitter (MCD)
SPIE	Simulated Problem Input Evaluation
SPIE	Society of Photo-Optical Instrumentation Engineers [*International Society for Optical Engineering*]
SPIE	Society of Political Item Enthusiasts (EA)
SPIE	Special Patrol Insertion/Extraction (MCD)
SPIE	SPIE - the International Society for Optical Engineering (EA)
Spiegel	Spiegel, Inc. [*Associated Press*] (SAG)
SpiekerP	Spieker Properties [*Associated Press*] (SAG)
Spiekr	Spieker Properties [*Associated Press*] (SAG)
SPIES	Specialized Professional Information Expeditors
SPIES	Stanford Preschool Internality-Externality Scale (EDAC)
SPIF	Sales Performance Incentive Fund [*Business term*]
SPIF	School Practices Information File [*BRS Information Technologies*] [*Information service or system Defunct*]
SPIF	Sequential Prime Implicant Form
SPIF	Shuttle Payload Integration Facility [*NASA*] (MCD)
SPIF	Standard Payload Interface Facility [*NASA*] (MCD)
SPIFC	Southern Pacific International Fan Club (EA)
SPIFDA	South Pacific Islands Fisheries Development Agency [*Noumea, New Caledonia*] (EAIO)
SPIFR	Single Pilot Instrument Flight Rules [*Program*]
SPIH	Superimposed Pregnancy-Induced Hypertension [*Obstetrics*] (DMAA)
SPII	Scottish Pig Industry Initiative (BUAC)
SPII	Seed and Plant Improvement Institute [*Iran*] (BUAC)
SPII	Shuttle Program Implementation Instruction [*NASA*] (NASA)
SPII	Standard and Poor's Index - Industrials [*Stock market*]
SPIIC	Societe de Protection des Infirmieres et Infirmiers du Canada (AO)
SPIIN	Supplemental Procurement Instrument Identification Number [*DoD*]
SPIKE	Science Planning Interactive Knowledge Environment System [*NASA*] (CIST)
SPIKE	Specially Prepared Individuals for Key Events [*Paramilitary training*] (ECON)
Spike M & S	Spike on Master and Servant [*3rd ed.*] [*1872*] [*A publication*] (DLA)
SPIL	Quincemil [*Peru*] [*ICAO location identifier*] (ICLI)
SPIL	Self-Rating Psychiatric Inventory List [*Personality development test*] [*Psychology*]
SPIL	Sensitive Projects and Installation List (MCD)
SPIL	Ship's Parts Integration List
SPIL	Society for the Promotion and Improvement of Libraries [*India*] (BUAC)
SP-ILS	Shuttle Projects - Integrated Logistics Support [*Kennedy Space Center*] [*NASA*] (NASA)
SPIM	Lima-Callao/Internacional Jorge Chavez [*Peru*] [*ICAO location identifier*] (ICLI)
SPIM	Service de Previsions Ionospherique Militaire
SPIMS	Shuttle Program Information Management System [*NASA*]
SPIN	School Practices Information Network [*Bibliographic Retrieval Services*] [*Information service or system*] (IID)
SPIN	Science for Peace International Network [*Canada*] (BUAC)
SPIN	Science Procurement Information Network [*Canada*]
SPIN	Searchable Physics Information Notes (NITA)
SPIN	Searchable Physics Information Notices [*American Institute of Physics*] [*New York, NY Bibliographic database*]
SPIN	Separation Program Number [*DoD*] (VNW)
SPIN	Service Parts Information Notice
SPIN	Software Process Improvement Network (AAEL)
SPIN	Space Inspection
SPIN	Space Intercept (SAA)
SPIN	Special Inquiry [*FBI term*]
SPIN	Spinster (ADA)
SPIN	Standard & Poor's 500 Index Subordinated Notes
SPIN	Standard and Poor's Indexed Note (TDOB)
SPIN	Standard and Poor's Indexed Notes (EBF)
SPIN	Standard Prescriber Identification Number [*Insurance*]
SPIN	Standard Procedure Instructions (KSC)
SPIN	Strategies and Policies for Informatics [*Intergovernmental Bureau for Informatics*]
SPIN	Submarine Program Information Notebook
SPIN	Superconductive Precision Inertial Navigation
Spinakr	Spinnaker Industries [*Associated Press*] (SAG)
SPINAL	Stimulator, Planetary Instrument Alignment
SPINAR	Spinning Star [*Astronomy*]

sp indet	Species Indeterminata [*Species Indeterminate*] [*Latin*] (MAE)
SPINDEX	Selective Permutation Indexing [*Library of Congress*]
SPINDEX	Subject Profile Index [*Computer-based*]
SPINE	Simulated Program for Investigation of Nuclear Effects
SPINE	Space Informatics Network Experiment [*European Space Agency*]
SPINES	Science and Technology Policies Information Exchange System [*UNESCO*] [*Bibliographic database*] (IID)
SpineT	Spine-Tech, Inc. [*Associated Press*] (SAG)
SpineTch	Spine-Tech, Inc. [*Associated Press*] (SAG)
Spinks	Spinks' English Ecclesiastical and Admiralty Reports [*164 English Reprint*] [*A publication*] (DLA)
Spinks Eccl & Adm (Eng)	Spinks' English Ecclesiastical and Admiralty Reports [*164 English Reprint*] [*A publication*] (DLA)
Spinks PC	Spinks' English Admiralty Prize Cases [*A publication*] (DLA)
Spinks Prize Cas	Spinks' English Admiralty Prize Cases [*164 English Reprint*] [*A publication*] (DLA)
Spinks Prize Cas (Eng)	Spinks' English Admiralty Prize Cases [*164 English Reprint*] [*A publication*] (DLA)
SPINOE	Spin Polarization-Induced Nuclear Overhauser Effect [*Physics*]
sp inquir	Species Inquirendae [*Species of Doubtful Status*] [*Latin*] (MAE)
SPINS	Ship Passive Integrated Navigation System (DNAB)
SPINS	South Pacific Information Network System [*Australia*]
SPINS	Special Instruction (DOMA)
SPINSTRE	Spencer Information Storage and Retrieval System (DIT)
SPINT	Special Intelligence (MCD)
SPINTAC	Special Interest Aircraft (NVT)
SPINTCOM	Special Intelligence Communications [*Later, DIN/DSSCS*]
SPINTCOMM	Special Intelligence Communications [*Later, DIN/DSSCS*] (CET)
SPINVESWG	Special Investigation Wing (MUGU)
SPIO	Systems Planning and Integration Office [*NASA*]
SPIP	Satipo [*Peru*] [*ICAO location identifier*] (ICLI)
SPIP	Software Process Improvement Plan (AAGC)
SPIP	Special Position Identification Pulse (CET)
S'PIPE	Spin-Polarized Inverse Photoemission [*Physics*]
S'PIPE	Standpipe
SPIPES	Spin-Polarized Inverse Photoemission Spectroscopy
SPI-PUD	Society of the Plastics Industry - Polyurethane Division (NTPA)
SPIR	Patria [*Peru*] [*ICAO location identifier*] (ICLI)
SPIR	School Performance Information Regulations (AIE)
SPIR	Search Program for Infrared Spectra [*Canada Institute for Scientific and Technical Information*] [*Information service or system*]
SPIR	Sears Point International Raceway [*California*]
SPIR	Single Pilot Instrument Rating [*Aviation*] (DA)
SPIR	Spiral
SPIR	Spire Corp. [*NASDAQ symbol*] (NQ)
SPIR	Spiritoso [*With Animation*] [*Music*]
SPIR	Spiritual (DAVI)
SPIR	Spiritus [*Spirit*] [*Pharmacy*]
SPIR	Standard and Poor's Index - Rails [*Stock market*]
SPIR	Standardized Proportional Incidence Ratio [*Epidemiology*]
SPIR	Student Project for International Responsibility
SPIRAL	Sperry Inertial RADAR Altimeter
3PIRAS	Setpoint Precision Infrared Angular Scanner (PDAA)
SPIRAT	Strategic Program for Innovative Research on AIDS Treatment [*The National Institute of Allergy and Infectious Diseases*]
SPIRBM	Solid-Propellant Intermediate Range Ballistic Missile (AAG)
SPIRE	South Pacific Institute for Renewable Energy [*Polynesia, Tahiti*] (BUAC)
SPIRE	Spatial Inertial Reference Equipment
SPIRE	Spatial Paradigm for Information Retrieval and Exploration [*Computer science*]
Spire	Spire Corp. [*Associated Press*] (SAG)
SPIREP	Spot Intelligence Report [*Air Force*]
SPIRES	Single-Photon Infrared Emission Spectroscopy
SPIRES	Standard Personnel Information Retrieval System [*Military*]
SPIRES	Stanford Public Information Retrieval System [*Stanford University Libraries*] [*Stanford, CA Bibliographic database management system*] [*Information service or system*]
SPIREX	South Pole Infrared Explorer [*University of Chicago*] [*Research center*] (RCD)
SPIRIT	Sales Processing Interactive Real-Time Inventory Technique [*NCR Corp. trademark*]
SPIRIT	School for Postgraduate Interdisciplinary Research on Interculturalism and Transnationality [*Aalborg University, Denmark*]
SPIRIT	Sensible Policy in Information Resources and Information Technology [*Defunct*] (EA)
SPIRIT	Spiritoso [*With Animation*] [*Music*]
SPIRIT	Spiritus [*Spirit*] [*Latin*] (ROG)
SPIRIT	Systematic Productivity Improvement Review In TRADOC [*Training and Doctrine Command*] [*Army*]
SPIRO	Students Protesting Illegal Real Estate Operators [*Student legal action organization*] (EA)
SPIRS	Silver-Platter Information Retrieval System [*Computer science*]
SPIRT	Short Path Infrared Tester (KSC)
SPIRT	Stock Point Interrogation/Requirements Technique
SPIS	Pias [*Peru*] [*ICAO location identifier*] (ICLI)
SPIS	Senate Permanent Investigating Subcommittee (AAG)
SPIS	Serial Poll Idle State (IAA)
SPIS	Space Philatelists International Society (EA)
SPIS	Standard Production Information Systems (NITA)
SPIS	State Plantations Impact Study [*Victoria, Australia*]
SPISE	Special Projects in Science Education
SPISS	Spissus [*Dried*] [*Pharmacy*]
SPIT	Paita [*Peru*] [*ICAO location identifier*] (ICLI)
SPIT	Secondary Power Integration Test (MCD)

SPIT .... Selective Printing of Items from Tape [*Computer science*]
SPITS .... Scan Platform Inertial Thermal Simulator
SPIU .... Ship Position Interpolation Unit
SPIU .... Standard and Poor's Index - Utilities [*Stock market*]
SPIW .... ESCAP [*Economic and Social Commssion for the Asia and Pacific*] Division for Shipping, Ports, and Inland Waterways (EAIO)
SPIW .... Special-Purpose Individual Weapon [*A rifle that fires flechettes or darts*] [*Pronounced "spew"*]
SPIY .... Yauri [*Peru*] [*ICAO location identifier*] (ICLI)
SPIZ .... Uchiza [*Peru*] [*ICAO location identifier*] (ICLI)
SPJ .... Austria (Republic) SIGNs [*NYSE symbol*] (TTSB)
SPJ .... Austria [*Republic of*] Stock Index Growth Notes [*NYSE symbol*] (SPSG)
SPJ .... Saphenopopliteal Junction [*Medicine*] (DMAA)
SPJ .... Senior Puisne Judge [*British*] (ILCA)
SPJ .... Socialist Party of Japan [*Nikon Shakaito*] [*Political party*] (PPW)
SPJ .... Society of Professional Journalists [*Also, SDX*] (NTCM)
SPJ .... Socijalisticka Partija Jugoslavije [*Socialist Party of Yugoslavia*] [*Political party*] (PPE)
SPJ .... Sparta [*Greece*] [*Airport symbol Obsolete*] (OAG)
SPJ .... Special Purpose Jammer [*Military*] (CAAL)
SPJA .... Rioja [*Peru*] [*ICAO location identifier*] (ICLI)
SPJB .... Cajabamba/Pampa Grande [*Peru*] [*ICAO location identifier*] (ICLI)
SPJC .... St. Petersburg Junior College [*Clearwater, FL*]
SP-JFI .... School Principal Job Functions Inventory [*Test*]
SPJI .... Juanjui [*Peru*] [*ICAO location identifier*] (ICLI)
SPJJ .... Jauja [*Peru*] [*ICAO location identifier*] (ICLI)
SPJL .... Juliaca [*Peru*] [*ICAO location identifier*] (ICLI)
SPJN .... San Juan [*Peru*] [*ICAO location identifier*] (ICLI)
SPJR .... Cajamarca/Mayor General FAP Armando Revoredo Iglesias [*Peru*] [*ICAO location identifier*] (ICLI)
SPJ SDX .... Society of Professional Journalists, Sigma Delta Chi (EA)
SPJTG .... Secondary Plant Joint Test Group (DNAB)
SPK .... Diamond Aviation, Inc. [*ICAO designator*] (FAAC)
SPK .... Reno, NV [*Location identifier FAA*] (FAAL)
SPK .... Saporamean Kampuchea News Agency [*Cambodia*]
SPK .... Sapporo [*Japan*] [*Airport symbol*] (OAG)
SPK .... Scotts Peak [*Tasmania*] [*Seismograph station code, US Geological Survey*] (SEIS)
SPK .... Serum Pyruvate Kinase (DB)
SPK .... Silver Tusk Mines [*Vancouver Stock Exchange symbol*]
SPK .... Socialist Party of Kazakhstan [*Political party*] (BUAC)
SPK .... Socialist Party of Kurdistan [*Iraq*] [*Political party*] (MENA)
SPK .... Spare Parts Kit
SPK .... Spark (MSA)
spk .... Speckled [*Quality of the bottom*] [*Nautical charts*]
SPK .... Spieker Properties [*NYSE symbol*] (SPSG)
SPK .... Spike (MSA)
SPK .... Spinnbarkheit [*With reference to cervical mucus*] [*Medicine*]
SPK .... Spokane [*Diocesan abbreviation*] [*Washington*] (TOCD)
SPK .... Storage Protection Key [*Computer science*] (IAA)
SPK .... Superficial Punctate Keratitis [*Ophthalmology*]
SPKC .... Small Pig Keepers' Council [*British*] (BI)
SPKL .... Spreckels Industries, Inc. [*NASDAQ symbol*] (SAG)
SPKL .... Sprinkle [*NWS*] (FAAC)
SPKP .... Suomen Perustuslaillinen Kansanpuolue [*Finnish Constitutional People's Party*] [*Political party*] (PPW)
SPKPrB .... Spieker Prop 9.45%'B' Pfd [*NYSE symbol*] (TTSB)
SPKPRF .... Spark Proof (IAA)
SPKR .... Speaker (AAG)
spkr .... Speaker (IDOE)
Spkr .... Speaker (TBD)
SPKR .... Sprinkler (WGA)
Spksmn .... Spokesman (TBD)
SPKT .... Sprocket
SPL .... San Pedro de Jagua [*Colombia*] [*Airport symbol*] (AD)
SPL .... Saskatoon Public Library [*UTLAS symbol*]
SPL .... Scan-Pol Ltd. [*Poland ICAO designator*] (FAAC)
SPL .... Scott Paper Ltd. [*Toronto Stock Exchange symbol Vancouver Stock Exchange symbol*]
SPL .... Scratch Pad Line [*NASA*] (MCD)
SPL .... Self-Propelled Launcher [*British military*] (DMA)
SPL .... Separate Parts List (MSA)
SPL .... Serialized Parts List [*NASA*] (MCD)
SPL .... Service Priority List (BUR)
SPL .... Set Priority Level [*Computer science*] (NHD)
SPL .... Short-Pulse LASER
SPL .... Signal Processing Language [*Computer science*] (CSR)
SPL .... Signature and Propagation Laboratory [*Army*] (RDA)
SPL .... Simple Phrase Language [*Computer science*]
SPL .... Simple Programming Language [*Computer science*]
SPL .... Simulation Programming Language [*Computer science*]
SPL .... Sine Prole Legitima [*Without Legitimate Issue*] [*Latin*]
SPL .... Single Pet Lover
SPL .... Single-Premium Life [*Insurance*]
SPL .... Single-Premium Whole Life [*Insurance*]
SPL .... Single Propellant Loading (AFM)
SPL .... Skin Potential Level
SPL .... Sloane Physics Laboratory [*Yale*] (MCD)
SPL .... Smoke Puff Limiter [*Automotive engineering*]
SPL .... Socialist Party of Labour [*Romania*] [*Political party*] (BUAC)
SPL .... Software Parts List [*Computer science*] (TEL)
SPL .... Software Programming Language [*Computer science*] (IEEE)
SPL .... Solar Pumped LASER (SSD)
SPL .... Sound Power Level [*Acoustics*]
SPL .... Sound Pressure Level [*Acoustics*]
SPL .... Source Program Library
SPL .... Spaceborne Programming Language [*Computer science*] (IAA)
SPL .... Space Physics Laboratory [*Aerospace corporation*]
SPL .... Space Programming Language [*Computer science*]
SPL .... Space Programs Laboratory [*Fort Belvoir, VA*] [*United States Army Engineer Topographic Laboratories*] (GRD)
SPL .... Spare Parts List
SPL .... Spartanburg County Public Library, Spartanburg, SC [*OCLC symbol*] (OCLC)
SPL .... Special (AAG)
SPL .... Special-Purpose Language [*Computer science*]
SPL .... Speed Phase Lock
SPL .... Spermatophore Length
SPL .... Spiral (MSA)
SPL .... Spiridon Lake [*Alaska*] [*Seismograph station code, US Geological Survey*] (SEIS)
SPL .... Splanchnic (DB)
SPL .... Splice [*Telecommunications*] (TEL)
SPL .... Splice Junction Mutation [*Genetics*]
SPL .... Spontaneous Lesion [*Medicine*] (MAE)
SPL .... Sporulation per Lesion [*Plant pathology*]
SPL .... Spritsail [*Ship's rigging*] (ROG)
SPL .... Standard Programming Logic [*Computer science*] (IAA)
SPL .... Standard Pulse LASER
SPL .... Standards Parts Listing (MCD)
SPL .... Staphylococcal Phage Lysate [*Biochemistry*]
SPL .... Student Pilot's Licence (AIA)
SPL .... Succinyl-Poly-L-Lysine [*Biochemical analysis*]
SPL .... Summary Parts List
SPL .... Sun Pumped LASER (MCD)
SPL .... Superior Parietal Lobule [*Neuroanatomy*]
Spl .... Supplement (BJA)
SPL .... Supplementary Flight Plan Message [*Aviation code*]
SPL .... Support Platoon Leader [*Military*] (INF)
SPL .... Swiss Party of Labour
SPL .... Symbolic Programming Language [*Computer science*] (IAA)
SPL .... System Program Loader
SPL .... System Programming Language [*Computer science*] (NASA)
SPL .... Systems Programming Ltd. (IAA)
SPLA .... Louisiana [*Peru*] [*ICAO location identifier*] (ICLI)
SPLA .... Scottish Poetry Library Association (DBA)
SPLA .... Special-Purpose Lead Azide (MCD)
SPLA .... Sudan People's Liberation Army
SPLAASH .... Spacecraft Protective Landing Area for the Advancement of Science and Humanities [*Landing zone for flying saucers near Mt. Rainier, WA*]
Splaj .... Socialist People's Libyan Arab Jamahiriya [*Gathering of the masses*] [*Muammar Qaddafi's name for his country*]
SPLAN .... Support Plan (MCD)
SPLANCH .... Split-Level Ranch [*House*]
SPLASH .... Shipboard Platforms for Landing and Servicing Helicopters
SPLASH .... Single Parent Links and Special Holidays (BUAC)
SPLASH .... Special Program to List Amplitudes of Surges from Hurricanes
SplashT .... Splash Technology Holdings, Inc. [*Associated Press*] (SAG)
SPLAT .... Simplified Programming Language for Artists [*1978*] [*Computer science*] (CSR)
SPLAT .... Student Potential Life Achievement Test [*Parody of Scholastic Aptitude Test preparation books*]
SPLATT .... Single Pedestrians League Against Taxes and Traffic [*British*] (DI)
SPLATT .... Split Anterior Tibial Tendon [*Medicine*] (DMAA)
SPLATT .... Split Anterior Tibial Transfer [*Orthopedics*] (DAVI)
SPLATT TALTFR ... Split Anterior Tibial Transfer, Tendo Achillis Lengthening, and Toe Flexor Release [*Orthopedics*] (DAVI)
Sp Laws .... Spirit of the Laws (Montesquieu) [*A publication*] (DLA)
SPLC .... Ship Program Life Cycle [*Navy*]
SPLC .... Short Product Life Cycle [*Business term*] (MHDB)
SPLC .... Simulated Planetary Landing Capsule (DNAB)
SPLC .... Southern Poverty Law Center (EA)
SPLC .... Spare Parts List for Codification
SPLC .... Splice
SPLC .... Standard Point Location Code [*American Trucking Association and Association of American Railroads*]
SPLC .... Student Press Law Center (EA)
SPLCF .... Sustained Peak Low-Cycle Fatigue (PDAA)
SPLD .... Celendin [*Peru*] [*ICAO location identifier*] (ICLI)
SPLEEM .... Spin-Polarized Low-Energy Electron Microscopy
SPLF .... Society for the Preservation of Life from Fire (BUAC)
S/PLF .... Station/Platform LIDAR Facility (SSD)
SPLH .... Splash Technology Holdings, Inc. [*NASDAQ symbol*] (SAG)
SPLHC .... Sgt. Pepper's Lonely Hearts Club [*Defunct*] (EA)
SPLI .... Lima [*Peru*] [*ICAO location identifier*] (ICLI)
SPLI .... Single-Premium Life Insurance (MHDW)
SPLI .... Spermatophore Length Index
SPLI .... Substance P-Like Immunoreactivity
SPLICE .... Shorthand Programming Language in COBOL [*Common Business-Oriented Language*] Environment [*Computer science*] (MHDI)
SPLICE .... Stock Point Logistics Integrated Communications Environment Project [*Navy*]
SPLICS .... Special-Purpose Linear Integrated Circuits [*Electronics*] (AAEL)
SPLIT .... Space Program Language Implementation Tool (KSC)
SPLIT .... Spent Pot Lining Insolubilisation Technology [*Metallurgy*]
SPLIT .... Sundstrand Processing Language Internally Translated
SPLK .... Spanlink Communications [*NASDAQ symbol*] (TTSB)
SPLK .... Spanlink Communications, Inc. [*NASDAQ symbol*] (SAG)

SPLL............	Self-Propelled Launcher Loader (MCD)
SPLL............	Standard Phase-Locked Loop
SPLLG..........	Stable Production Low Leach Glass [For nuclear wastes]
SPLM...........	Space Programming Language Machine
SPLM...........	Sudan People's Liberation Movement [Political party]
SPLMD.........	Soil-Pore Liquid Monitoring Device (GNE)
SP-LMO........	Shuttle Projects - Logistics Management Office [NASA] (GFGA)
SPLN...........	Rodriguez de Mendoz/San Nicolas [Peru] [ICAO location identifier] (ICLI)
SPLN...........	Spline [Engineering]
SPLNS.........	South Plains (FAAC)
SPLO...........	Ilo [Peru] [ICAO location identifier] (ICLI)
SPLP...........	Las Palmas [Peru] [ICAO location identifier] (ICLI)
SPLS...........	Staples, Inc. [NASDAQ symbol] (NQ)
SPLS...........	Zorrillos [Peru] [ICAO location identifier] (ICLI)
SPLT...........	Lobitos [Peru] [ICAO location identifier] (ICLI)
SPLT...........	Specialist, Link Trainer Instructor [Navy rating]
SPLTR.........	Splitter
SPLTRK.......	Special Tracker [Military] (CAAL)
SPLTY.........	Specialty (WGA)
S-Plus.........	Statistical Software Package [Computer science] (EERA)
SPLV...........	Lago Verde [Peru] [ICAO location identifier] (ICLI)
SPLV...........	Serum Parvovirus-Like Virus [Medicine] (DMAA)
SPLV...........	Spinach Latent Virus [Plant pathology]
SPLV...........	Stable Plurilamellar Vesicle [Pharmacology]
SPLX...........	Simplex [Mathematics]
SPLY...........	Supply (MSA)
SPM............	Air Saint-Pierre SA [France ICAO designator] (FAAC)
SPM............	Saga Petroleum AS [NYSE symbol] (SAG)
SPM............	Scanned Probe Microscopy
SPM............	Scanning Photoemission Microscope
SPM............	Scanning Probe Microscopy
SPM............	Scratch Pad Memory [Computer science] (BUR)
SPM............	Scratch Pad Module [Computer science] (IAA)
SPM............	Scripture Press Ministries (EA)
SPM............	Security Program Manager [Military] (GFGA)
SPM............	Sedimentary Phosphate Method
SPM............	Self-Propelled Mount [Military]
SPM............	Semipermeable Membrane
SPM............	Senior Project Manager
SPM............	Sequential Processing Machine (DIT)
SPM............	Serial Parallel Multiplier (IAA)
SPM............	Session Protocol Machine [Telecommunications] (OSI)
SPM............	Shore Protection Manual [Army]
SPM............	Short Particular Metre [Music]
SPM............	Shots per Minute [Military] (RDA)
SPM............	Significant Probability Mapping
SPM............	Sine Prole Mascula [Without Male Issue] [Latin]
SPM............	Single-Point Management
SPM............	Single-Point Mooring [Oil platform]
SPM............	Single Program Manager [Air Force]
SPM............	Six Point Mooring [Oil platform]
SPM............	Smaller Profit Margin
SPM............	Socialist Party of Macedonia [Political party] (BUAC)
SPM............	Socialist Party of Montenegro [Political party] (BUAC)
SPM............	Societas Patrum Misericordiae [Fathers of Mercy] [Roman Catholic religious order]
SPM............	Society for Policy Modeling (EA)
SPM............	Society of Pharmaceutical Medicine (BUAC)
SPM............	Society of Pragmatic Mysticism (EA)
SPM............	Society of Prospective Medicine (EA)
SPM............	Software Programmer's Manual
SPM............	Solar Polar Mission (MCD)
SPM............	Solar Power Module
SPM............	Solar Proton Monitor
SPM............	Somali Patriotic Movement [Political party] (EY)
SPM............	Sound-Powered Microphone
SPM............	Source Program Maintenance [IBM Corp.]
SPM............	Specialist, Mail Clerk [Navy rating]
SPM............	Special-Purpose Materials (MCD)
SPM............	Spectrophosphorimeter
SPM............	Spectrum Industrial Resources [Vancouver Stock Exchange symbol]
SpM............	Spiriformis Medialis Nucleus [Brain anatomy]
SPM............	Split Phase Motor
SPM............	SP Ministries [Formerly, Scripture Press Ministries] (EA)
SPM............	Standard Payload Module (MCD)
SPM............	Standard Practice Memo (MCD)
SPM............	Standard Preparation Method
SPM............	Standard Procedure Manual (AAG)
SPM............	Standard Process Manual
SPM............	Standard Progressive Matrices [Also, Raven's Coloured Progressive Matrices] [A type of intelligence test] (PAZ)
SPM............	Standard Prototype Microcomputer (NITA)
SPM............	Static Presentation Mode
SPM............	Stationary Plasma Motor
SPM............	Statistical Parametric Mapping [Data treatment]
SPM............	St. Philips Marsh [Bristol] [British depot code]
SPM............	St. Pierre and Miquelon [ANSI three-letter standard code] (CNC)
SPM............	Strokes per Minute
SPM............	Subhuman Primate Model [Medicine] (DMAA)
SPM............	Subscriber's Private Meter [Telecommunications] (TEL)
SPM............	Subsystem Project Manager [NASA] (NASA)
SPM............	Sun Probe-Mars [NASA]
SPM............	Superparamagnetic [Fraction in rock] [Geophysics]
SPM............	Support Program Management

SPM............	Surface Plasmon Microscopy [Physics]
SPM............	Suspended Particulate Matter
SPM............	Symbol Processing Machine (IEEE)
SPM............	Synaptic Plasma Membrane [Neurophysiology]
SPM............	Synaptosomal Plasma Membrane [Neurobiology]
SPM............	Synthetic Plasma Membrane [Biochemistry]
SPM............	System Performance Model
S/PM...........	System/Project Management
SPM............	Systems Program Manager
SPMA..........	Rio Maranon [Peru] [ICAO location identifier] (ICLI)
SPM.A.........	Saga Petroleum ADS'A' [NYSE symbol] (TTSB)
SPMA..........	Scottish Modern Pentathlon Association (BUAC)
SPMA..........	Sewage Plant Manufacturers' Association [British] (BI)
SPMA..........	Shoe Pattern Manufacturers Association [Defunct] (EA)
SPMA..........	Society for Post-Medieval Archaeology [British]
SPMA..........	Soda Pulp Manufacturers Association [Defunct] (EA)
SPMA..........	Southwest Parks and Monuments Association (EA)
SPMA..........	Spinal Progressive Muscular Atrophy [Medicine] (AAMN)
SPMA..........	Sterilization Packaging Materials Association (BUAC)
SPMA..........	String Polling Multiple Access (PDAA)
SPMA..........	Sump Pump Manufacturers Association [Later, SSPMA] (EA)
SPMAGTF.....	Special Purpose Marine Air Ground Task Force (DOMA)
SPMAR........	Scratch Pad Memory Address Register [Computer science] (MHDI)
SPM.B.........	Saga Petroleum ADS'B' [NYSE symbol] (TTSB)
SPMB..........	Strong Partial Maternal Behavior [Psychology]
SPMBNI.......	Seed Potato Marketing Board for Northern Ireland (BUAC)
SPMC..........	Shannon Park Marine Center [West Washington University] [Anacortes, WA]
SPMC..........	Society of Paper Money Collectors (EA)
SPMC..........	Society of Professional Management Consultants [Association name and designation awarded by this group] [Englewood, NJ] (EA)
SPMC..........	Southern Pine Marketing Council (WPI)
SPMC..........	Special Machine [Tool] (AAG)
SPMC..........	Standard Procedure Monitor Chart (PDAA)
SPMD..........	Silicon Planar Multiple Diode (IAA)
SPME..........	Solar Proton-Monitoring Experiment (PDAA)
SPME..........	Solid Phase Microextraction [Chemistry]
SPME..........	Spectroscopic Phase-Modulated Ellipsometry
SPME..........	Tumbes/Pedro Canga [Peru] [ICAO location identifier] (ICLI)
SPMEA........	Sulfate of Potash Magnesia Export Association (EA)
SPMG..........	Scottish Primary Mathematics Group (AIE)
SPMG..........	Societe pour le Patrimoine Musical Canadien (AC)
SPMI...........	Status Post Myocardial Infarction [Cardiology] (DAVI)
SPMid.........	Standard & Poor's MidCap 400 Depository Receipts [Associated Press] (SAG)
SPML..........	Special Meal [Diabetic, low-cholesterol, low-calorie, hypoglycemic, or gluten-free] [Airline notation] (ADA)
SPMLF........	Societe de la Psychologie Medicale de Langue Francaise [French-Language Society of Medical Psychology - FLSMP] (EA)
SPMM.........	Society for the Promotion of Mohammedan Missions [Defunct] (EA)
SPMMV.......	Sweet Potato Mild Mottle Virus [Plant pathology]
SPMO..........	SAMMS [Standard Automated Materiel Management System] Program Management Office [DOD]
SPMO..........	Senior Principal Medical Officer [British] (DI)
SPMOL........	Source Program Maintenance Online
SPMP..........	Special-Purpose Multiprocessor [Computer science]
SP-MPC.......	Shuttle Projects - Management Planning and Control Office [Kennedy Space Center] [NASA] (NASA)
SPMR..........	Southern Provinces Mounted Rifles [British military] (DMA)
SPMR..........	Standard Proportionate Mortality Ratio [Medicine] (DMAA)
SPMR..........	Sub Postmaster [British] (DCTA)
SPMRL........	Sulphite Pulp Manufacturers' Research League (EA)
SPMS..........	Safety Performance Measurement System [Environmental science] (COE)
SPMS..........	Serial Poll Mode State (IAA)
SPMS..........	Sine Prole Mascula Superstite [Without Surviving Male Issue] [Latin] (ADA)
SPMS..........	Solar Particle Monitoring System [NASA] (KSC)
SPMS..........	Special-Purpose Manipulator System [NASA] (NASA)
SPMS..........	Special-Purpose Monitoring Station [Environmental Protection Agency]
SPMS..........	Strategic Planning and Management System [Environmental Protection Agency] (GFGA)
SPMS..........	Suppression Pool Makeup System [Nuclear energy] (NRCH)
SPMS..........	Surveyor Payload Mechanism Section
SPMS..........	System Program Management Surveys [Air Force]
SPMS..........	Yurimaguas [Peru] [ICAO location identifier] (ICLI)
Sp Msgr......	Special Messenger [Army]
SPMSQ........	Short Portable Mental Status Questionnaire (EDAC)
SPMT..........	Sportmart, Inc. [NASDAQ symbol] (SAG)
SPMTA........	Sportmart Inc.'A' [NASDAQ symbol] (TTSB)
SPMTS........	Simplified Predetermined Motion Time System (MHDB)
SPMV..........	Satellite Panicum Mosaic Virus
SPMW........	Subpolar Mode Water [Marine science] (OSRA)
SPMY..........	Dos De Mayo [Peru] [ICAO location identifier] (ICLI)
SPN............	Cape Shipunski [Former USSR Seismograph station code, US Geological Survey] (SEIS)
SPN............	Pelican Narrows Public Library, Saskatchewan [Library symbol National Library of Canada] (NLC)
SPN............	Saipan [Mariana Islands] [Airport symbol] (OAG)
SPN............	Satellite Programming Network [Cable-television system]
SPN............	Satellite Program Network (NITA)
SPN............	Savanna Pastoral Neolithic [Archeology]
SPN............	Scrabble Players News
SPN............	Secretariado da Propaganda Nacional [Portugal]

SPN .... Semiconductor Productivity Network (NITA)
SPN .... Senior Plan Network [*Information service or system*] (HCT)
SPN .... Separation Program Number [*Military*]
SPN .... Series Parallel Network (IAA)
SPN .... Service Part Number
SPN .... Service Protection Network (NITA)
SPN .... Shared Processing Network (USDC)
SPN .... Shipment/Performance Notification [*DoD*]
SPN .... Shuttle Project Notice [*Kennedy Space Center*] [*NASA*] (NASA)
SPN .... Skorpion Air [*Bulgaria*] [*ICAO designator*] (FAAC)
spn .... Society of Pediatric Nurses (NTPA)
SPN .... Solitary Pulmonary Nodule [*Medicine*] (DAVI)
SPN .... Sparton Resources, Inc. [*Toronto Stock Exchange symbol*]
SPN .... Special Program Number (MUGU)
sp n .... Species Novum [*New Species*] [*Also, sp nov*] [*Biology*] (DAVI)
SPN .... Specimen (WGA)
SPN .... Sponsor Program Number [*Military*]
SPN .... Standard Precision Navigator
SPN .... Student Practical Nurse (AAMN)
SPN .... Subscriber Premises Network [*Telecommunications*]
SPN .... Supplementary Parenteral Nutrition (STED)
SPN .... Switched Public Network [*Telecommunications*] (IAA)
SPN .... Sympathetic Preganglionic Neuron [*Anatomy*]
SPNA .... Punta De Lomas [*Peru*] [*ICAO location identifier*] (ICLI)
SPNB .... Security Pacific National Bank (NITA)
SPNC .... Huanuco/Alferez FAP David Figuerao Fernandini [*Peru*] [*ICAO location identifier*] (ICLI)
SPNC .... [*The*] Spectranetics Corp. [*NASDAQ symbol*] (SPSG)
SPND .... Self-Powered Neutron Detector [*Nuclear energy*] (NRCH)
SPND .... Suspend (NASA)
SPNEA .... Society for the Preservation of New England Antiquities (EA)
SPNF .... Shot Peening Fixture (MCD)
SPNFT .... South Pacific Nuclear Free Treaty
SPNFZ .... South Pacific Nuclear Free Zone (EERA)
SPNFZT ...... South Pacific Nuclear Free Zone Treaty
SPNG .... Society for Provincial Notaries General [*British*]
SPNG .... Sponge
SPNG .... Spring [*Commonly used*] (OPSA)
SPN/GEANS... Standard Precision Navigator/Gimbaled Electrostatic-Gyro Aircraft Navigation System (MCD)
SPN/GEANS... Standard Precision Navigator/Gimballed Electrostatic Aircraft Navigation System
SPNGS .... Springs [*Commonly used*] (OPSA)
SPNH .... Laguna Choclococha [*Peru*] [*ICAO location identifier*] (ICLI)
SPNH .... Special Purpose Nursing Home [*Australia*]
SPNHC .... Society for the Preservation of Natural History Collections (EA)
SPNI .... Societe pour la Protection de la Nature en Israel [*Society for the Protection of Nature in Israel*] [*Tel Aviv*] (EAIO)
SPNI .... Society for the Protection of Nature [*Israel*] (BUAC)
SPNI .... Spinnaker Inds [*NASDAQ symbol*] (SAG)
SPNI .... Spinnaker Industries [*NASDAQ symbol*] (TTSB)
S/PNL .... Side Panel [*Automotive engineering*]
SPNM .... Society for the Promotion of New Music [*British*]
SPNO .... Ancon [*Peru*] [*ICAO location identifier*] (ICLI)
sp nov .... Species Nova [*New Species*] [*Biology*]
SPNP .... Puno [*Peru*] [*ICAO location identifier*] (ICLI)
SPNR .... Ricran [*Peru*] [*ICAO location identifier*] (ICLI)
SPNR .... Society for the Promotion of Nature Reserves [*British*] (BI)
SPNR .... Spanner (AAG)
SPNR .... System Peculiar Non-Repairable
SPNS .... Sapiens International Corp. [*NASDAQ symbol*] (SAG)
SPNS .... Spoons (ROG)
SPNS .... Standard Product Numbering System (PDAA)
SPNS .... Standards of Performance for New Sources [*Power*] (DICI)
SPNS .... Switched Private Network Service [*ITT service mark*]
SPNSF .... Sapiens Intl N.V. [*NASDAQ symbol*] (TTSB)
SPNSN .... Suspension (MSA)
SPNT .... Intuto [*Peru*] [*ICAO location identifier*] (ICLI)
SPNT .... Society for the Promotion of Nutritional Therapy (BUAC)
SPNU .... Manu [*Peru*] [*ICAO location identifier*] (ICLI)
SPNZ .... Santa Cruz [*Peru*] [*ICAO location identifier*] (ICLI)
SPNZ .... Socialist Party of New Zealand [*Political party*] (PPW)
SPO .... Aeroservicios Ejecutivos del Pacifico SA [*Mexico ICAO designator*] (FAAC)
SPO .... Denver, CO [*Location identifier FAA*] (FAAL)
SPO .... Sacramento Peak Observatory
SPO .... Sandia Pulse Reactor
SPO .... Saturn Program Office [*NASA*] (KSC)
SPO .... Saturn Project Office [*NASA*] (IAA)
SPO .... Sausages, Potatoes, and Onions [*Meaning a cheap restaurant that specializes in these*] [*British slang*]
SPO .... Sea Post Office
SPO .... Senate Post Office
SPO .... Senior Probation Officer (WDAA)
SPO .... SENTRY [*Survey Entry*] Project Office
SPO .... Separate Partition Option
SPO .... Shore Patrol Officer [*Navy*]
SPO .... Short Period Oscillation
SPO .... Shuttle Project Office [*NASA*] (KSC)
SPO .... Signal Property Office [*Military*]
SPO .... Single Pickle Ordinary [*Metal industry*]
SPO .... Slaving Pick-Off
SPO .... Society of Perinatal Obstetricians (EA)
SPO .... Society of Planning Officials

SPO .... Sozialdemokratische Partei Oesterreichs [*Social Democratic Party of Austria*] [*Political party*]
SPO .... Spacelab Program Office [*NASA*]
SPO .... Spare Parts Order [*NASA*] (NASA)
SPO .... Specialist, Inspector of Naval Material [*Navy rating*]
SPO .... Special Placement Officer (ADA)
SPO .... Special Projects Office [*Navy*]
SPO .... Spokane [*Washington*] [*Seismograph station code, US Geological Survey Closed*] (SEIS)
SPO .... Sponsoring Organization (NITA)
SPO .... Spooner Mines & Oils Ltd. [*Toronto Stock Exchange symbol*]
SPO .... Srpski Pokret Obnove [*Serbian Renaissance Movement*] [*Political party*] (EY)
SPO .... Status Postoperative [*Surgery*] (DAVI)
SPO .... Stoker Petty Officer [*Navy British*] (DSUE)
SPO .... Subpurchase Order (AAG)
SPO .... Supplemental Production Order (AAG)
SPO .... Surplus Property Office [*Transferred to War Assets Administration, 1947*]
SPO .... Synchronized Power On (MHDI)
SPO .... System Program [*or Project*] Office [*Military*]
SPOA .... Les Sagesses du Proche-Orient Ancien. Colloque de Strasbourg [*1962*]. Travaux du Centre d'Etudes Superieurs Specialise d'Histoire des Religions de Strasbourg [*Paris*] [*A publication*] (BJA)
SPOA .... Saposoa [*Peru*] [*ICAO location identifier*] (ICLI)
SPOA .... Scottish Plant Owners Association (DBA)
SPOA .... Scottish Prison Officers' Association (BUAC)
SPOAV .... Specialist, Inspector of Aviation Material [*Navy rating*]
SPOBS .... Special Observer [*US Army group in London*] [*World War II*]
SPOC .... Search and Rescue Points of Contact [*Environmental science*] (COE)
SPOC .... Shuttle Payload Operations Contractor (NASA)
SPOC .... Shuttle Payload Opportunity Carrier
SPOC .... Shuttle Portable Onboard Computer [*NASA*]
SPOC .... Single Point of Contact (GFGA)
SPOC .... Single-Point Orbit Calculator
SPOC .... Solid Phase Organic Chemistry
SPOC .... Solid-Propulsion Optimization Code (MCD)
SPOC .... Spacecraft Oceanography Project [*Navy*]
SPOC .... Special Projects Operations Center [*Allied Force Headquarters*] [*World War II*]
SPOC .... Splicing of Cross Correlation Function (IAA)
SPOC .... Sydney Paralympic Organising Committee [*Australia*]
SPOC .... Systems Program Office Cadre (MCD)
SPOCC .... South Pacific Organizations Coordinating Committee (EERA)
SPOCK .... Simulated Procedure for Obtaining Common Knowledge
SPOCK .... Special Purpose Operational Computing Kernel [*Pilot training device developed at Georgia Institute of Technology*]
SPOCM .... Society for the Preservation of Old Mills (EA)
SPOCN .... Subpurchase Order Change Notice (AAG)
SPOD .... Association to Aid the Sexual and Personal Relationships of People with a Disability (BUAC)
SPOD .... Seaports of Debarkation (MCD)
SPOD .... Sexual and Personal Relationships of the Disabled (AIE)
SPOD .... Ship's Plan of the Day [*Navy*] (DNAB)
SpOd, ... Spanish Odeon, Barcelona [*Record label*] [*Spain*]
SPOD .... Spouse's Perception of Disease (STED)
SPODA .... Society for the Prevention of Drug Addiction
SPODAC ...... SITS [*SAGE Intercept Target Simulation*] Probability of Detection and Conversion (MCD)
SPODP .... Single Precision Orbit Determination Program [*NASA*]
SPOE .... Sea Port of Export [*MTMC*] (TAG)
SPOE .... Seaports of Embarkation (MCD)
SPOE .... Society of Post Office Engineers [*Pronounced "spowee"*] [*British*] (DCTA)
SPOE .... Sozialistische Partei Oesterrelchs [*Socialist Party of Austria*]
SPOEN .... Specialist, Engineering Inspector [*Navy rating*]
S/P-OF .... Secretary's Open Forum [*An association*] (EA)
SP OFF .... Special Offering [*Stocks*] (MHDW)
SPOFOR ...... Sportwissenschaftliche Forschungsprojekte [*Bundesinstitut fuer Sportwissenschaft*] [*Germany Information service or system*] (CRD)
SPOG .... Sales of Products Other than Gasoline
SPOH .... Society for the Preservation of Oral Health (NTPA)
SPOL .... Collique [*Peru*] [*ICAO location identifier*] (ICLI)
SPOLIT .... Sportliteratur [*Bundesinstitut fuer Sportwissenschaft*] [*Germany Information service or system*] (CRD)
SPOM .... Society of Post Office Managers [*A union*] [*British*]
SPOM .... STS [*Shuttle Test Station*] Planning and Operations Management [*NASA*] (GFGA)
SPOM .... Suspended Particulate Organic Material [*Environmental chemistry*]
SPOMCUS .... Selective Prepositioning of Materiel Configured to Unit Sets [*Army*] (AABC)
S Pomp .... Sextus Pomponius [*Flourished, 2nd century*] [*Authority cited in pre-1607 legal work*] (DSA)
SPON .... Sponsor (AFM)
SPON .... Spontaneous (WGA)
spon .... Spontaneous (STED)
SPON .... Statistical Profile of Old Norse
SPONG .... Sponsoring
spont .... Spontaneous (STED)
SPONT .... Spontaneous
Spont Ab ...... Spontaneous Abortion [*Medicine*] (MAE)
SPOOF .... Society for the Perpetration of Outrageous Farces (BUAC)
SPOOF .... Society for the Protection of Old Fishes (EA)

SPOOF......... Structure and Parity Observing Output Function
SPOOFS....... Society for the Promotion of Otherwise Overlooked Football Scores
SPOOK........ Supervisor Program Over Other Kinds [Computer science]
SPOOL........ Simultaneous Peripheral Operation Online [Computer science] (MCD)
SPOOL........ Simultaneous Processing of Off-Line Item
SPOOL........ Simultaneous Production Operation Online
SPOOL......... Spontaneous Peripheral Operations Online Spooling [Computer science] (IAA)
spooling ...... Simultaneous Peripheral Operations Online [Computer science] (IGGR)
SPOOM........ Society for the Preservation of Old Mills (EA)
Spoon........ Spooner's Reports [12-15 Wisconsin] [A publication] (DLA)
Spooner...... Spooner's Reports [12-15 Wisconsin] [A publication] (DLA)
SPOOR........ Specialist, Ordnance Inspector [Navy rating]
SPOP .... Poto [Peru] [ICAO location identifier] (ICLI)
SPOP .... Scan Platform Operations Program
SPOPE .... Specialist, Petroleum Technician [Navy rating]
SP-OPI........ Shuttle Projects - Operations Planning and Integration [NASA] (GFGA)
SP-OPN....... Shuttle Projects - Operations Planning Office [Kennedy Space Center] [NASA] (NASA)
SPO-PO....... System Program Office/Project Office [Air Force] (AFIT)
SPOPS........ Special Operations
SPOR .... Sport-Haley [NASDAQ symbol] (TTSB)
SPOR .... Sport Haley, Inc. [NASDAQ symbol] (SAG)
SPORE........ Society for the Preservation of the Rain-Forest Environment (BUAC)
SPORK........ Spoon and Fork
SPORO........ Sporotrichosis [A fungal infection] (DAVI)
SPORS........ Slosson Pre-Observational Record Screen [Educational test]
SPORT........ Soldier Portable On-System Repair Tool [Military]
SPORT........ Space Probe Optical Recording Telescope [Army]
SPORT........ Sporting (ROG)
SPORT........ St. Petersburg [Florida] Olympic Regatta Training
SPORTFOR.... Support Force
SportM....... Sports Media, Inc. [Associated Press] (SAG)
Spor Tr........ Sporting Traditions [A publication]
SportRec...... Sports & Recreation, Inc. [Associated Press] (SAG)
SPORT-SCAN... Sports Sponsorship Computer Analysis (BUAC)
SportsClb..... Sports Club Company, Inc. [Associated Press] (SAG)
Sports Med... Sports Medicine (MEC)
SportSup...... Sport Supply Group [Associated Press] (SAG)
SPORTSWR... Sportswear
SPOS .... Strong Point/Obstacle System [Military] (NVT)
SPOS .... System Program Offices (IAA)
SPOS .... Zorritos [Peru] [ICAO location identifier] (ICLI)
SP-OSO....... Shuttle Projects - Off-Site Offices [NASA] (GFGA)
SPOSS........ Society for the Promotion of Science and Scholarship (EA)
SPOT .... Earth Observation Satellite [France] [Marine science] (OSRA)
SPOT .... PanAmSat Corp. [NASDAQ symbol] (SAG)
SPOT .... Satellite and Physicians Office Testing
SPOT .... Satellite Positioning and Tracking
SPOT .... Simulated Pave Penny Omnidirectional Target (MCD)
SPOT .... Skill in Personnel through On-Site Training [Department of Labor]
SPOT .... Small Portable Operational Terminal (LAIN)
SPOT .... Smithsonian Precision Optical Tracking
SPOT .... Spectral Pattern-Oblique Transillumination (RDA)
SPOT .... Speed Position and Track (MCD)
Spot........... Spotlight [Record label] [Australia]
SPOT .... Spot Wind [Meteorology] (DA)
SPOT .... Steel Plate Ordering Technique (IAA)
SPOT .... Symptom Pattern Observation Technique [Aviation]
SPOT .... System Probatoire d'Observation de la Terre [of France] [Instrument] (EERA)
SPOTR........ Special Projects Officer, Technical Representative [Navy] (DNAB)
SPOTREP..... Spot Report [Military] (NVT)
SPOTS .... Sikorsky Program Operations Tracking System (MCD)
SPOTS .... Slosson Post-Observational Testing Screen [Educational test]
Spott........... Spottiswoode's Equity [Scotland] [A publication] (DLA)
Spott Eq Rep... Spottiswoode's English Equity Reports [A publication] (DLA)
Spottis CL & Eq Rep... Common Law and Equity Reports, Published by Spottiswoode [A publication] (DLA)
Spottis Eq.... Spottiswoode's Equity [Scotland] [A publication] (DLA)
Spottis Pr.... Spottiswoode's Practices [Scotland] [A publication] (DLA)
Spottis St.... Spottiswoode's Styles [Scotland] [A publication] (DLA)
Spottisw..... Spottiswoode's Equity [Scotland] [A publication] (DLA)
Spottisw Eq... Spottiswoode's Equity [Scotland] [A publication] (DLA)
SPOTY .... Single Parent of the Year
SPOUT........ System Peripheral Output Utility [Nuclear energy] (NRCH)
SPOV .... Leon Velarde/Shiringayoc O Hda. Mejia [Peru] [ICAO location identifier] (ICLI)
SPOY .... Atico [Peru] [ICAO location identifier] (ICLI)
SPP............. Menongue [Angola] [Airport symbol] (OAG)
SPP............. New York Society for the Prevention of Pauperism
SPP............. Peace Corps School Partnership Program [Later, PCPP] (EA)
SPP............. Safe-Practice Procedure (MCD)
SPP............. Samoa-Pago Pago [Diocesan abbreviation] (TOCD)
SPP............. Scalable Parallel Processor [Computer science] (CDE)
SPP............. Scientific Passenger Pod [NASA]
SPP............. Sclerosing Papillomatous Pattern [Medicine]
SPP............. Scott Paper Co. [NYSE symbol] (SPSG)
SPP............. Secular Periodic Perturbation
SPP............. Seed Potato Promotions of Northern Ireland (BUAC)
SPP............. Sensor-Pointing Platform (SSD)
SPP............. Sequenced Packet Protocol [Computer science] (PCM)
SPP............. Serpa [Portugal] [Airport symbol] (AD)

SPP............. Severe Parental Punishment
SPP............. Sexuality Preference Profile
SPP............. Signal Processing Peripheral
SPP............. Signal Processing Program [BV Engineering] [Computer science]
SPP............. Simulation Planning Panel [NASA] (NASA)
SPP............. Single-Phase Printing (AAEL)
SPP............. Skin Perfusin Pressure [Medicine] (DMAA)
SPP............. Slovene People's Party [Political party] (BUAC)
SPP............. Society for Pediatric Psychology (EA)
SPP............. Society of Private Printers [Middlesex, England]
SPP............. Society of Professional Pilots (EA)
SPP............. Sodium Pentachlorophenoxide [Insecticide]
SPP............. Soeurs de la Providence de Portieux (EAIO)
SPP............. Solar Photometry Probe (AAG)
SPP............. Solar Physics Payload [NASA] (MCD)
SPP............. Solar Pumped Plasma (SSD)
SPP............. Sole Parent's Pension
SPP............. Soluble Protein Preparation [Biochemistry]
SPP............. Song Position Pointer [Computer science] (PCM)
SPP............. Sound Powered Phone (IAA)
SPP............. Southwest Power Pool [Regional power council]
SPP............. Spainair [Spain ICAO designator] (FAAC)
SPP............. Spare Parts Provisioning
SPP............. Specialist, Photographic Specialist [Navy rating]
SPP............. Specially Promoted Programme [British]
SPP............. Special Proficiency Pay [British military] (DMA)
SPP............. Special Purpose Processor
SPP............. Species [Plural form] [Also, spp]
SPP............. Species Plantarum Project (EERA)
SPP............. Specific Purpose Payment
SPP............. Speed Power Product (IAA)
SPP............. Sponsor Program Proposal (MCD)
SPP............. Spot Product Prices [Database] [Petroleum Intelligence Weekly] [Information service or system] (CRD)
SPP............. Standard Parallel Port [Computer science] (CDE)
SPP............. Standard Practice Procedures (MCD)
SPP............. Standards Policy Panel (ACII)
SPP............. Still Picture Projector (MSA)
SPP............. Stock Purchase Plan [Offered by a company to its employees]
SPP............. St. Paul [Alaska] [Seismograph station code, US Geological Survey Closed] (SEIS)
SPP............. St. Paul Public Library, St. Paul, MN [OCLC symbol] (OCLC)
SPP............. St. Philips Resources [Vancouver Stock Exchange symbol]
SPP............. Straight Path Penetration
SPP............. Structured Programming Processor [Computer science] (IAA)
SPP............. Suprapubic Prostatectomy [Medicine]
SPP............. Surplus Personal Property
SPP............. Swaziland Progressive Party
SPP............. System Package Plan [or Program] [Military]
SPPA .... Puerto Ocopa [Peru] [ICAO location identifier] (ICLI)
SPPA .... Scottish Pre-School Play Association (DBA)
SPPA .... Scottish Pre-School Playgroup Association (BUAC)
SPPA .... Screen Process Printing Association [Later, SPAI] (EA)
SPPA .... Singapore Planned Parenthood Association (BUAC)
SPPA .... Social Development Program for Poor Areas [UNICEF] (ECON)
SPPA .... Society for Philosophy and Public Affairs (EA)
SPPA .... Society for the Preservation of Poultry Antiquities (EA)
SPPA .... South Pacific Ports Association (BUAC)
SPPAC .... Salinity Pilot Program Advisory Council (EERA)
SP-PAI........ Shuttle Projects - Project Assessment and Integration Staff [NASA] (GFGA)
Sp Path....... Speech Pathology (DAVI)
SPPAY .... Semipost-Pay, Pay-Station [Telecommunications] (TEL)
SP-PAY....... Shuttle Projects - Payload Integration Office [Kennedy Space Center] [NASA] (NASA)
SPPB .... Sodium Pyrophosphate Buffer [Analytical chemistry]
SPPB .... Statens Psykologisk-Pedagogiska Bibliotek [National Library for Psychology and Education] [Sweden] [Information service or system] (IID)
SPPC .... Self-Pumped Phase Conjugator [Optics]
SPPC .... Society of Plant Protection of China (BUAC)
SPPC .... Spare Parts Provisioning Card
SP-PCO....... Shuttle Projects - Program Control Office [NASA] (GFGA)
SPPD .... Space Propulsion and Power Division [NASA]
SPPD .... Spin-Polarized Photoelectron Diffraction [Physics]
SPPE .... State per Pupil Expenditure [Education] (GFGA)
SPPED .... System for Pupil and Program Evaluation and Development (EDAC)
SPPES .... Spin-Polarized Photoemission Spectroscopy
SPPF.......... Seychelles People's Progressive Front (PPW)
SPPF.......... Solid-Phase Pressure Forming [Shell Chemical Co.]
SPPG .... Paramonga [Peru] [ICAO location identifier] (ICLI)
SPPG .... Space Plasma Physics Payload Group [NASA] (SSD)
SP-PG......... Sulfated Polysaccharide-Peptoglycan [Biochemistry]
SPPH .... Split Phase [Electronics] (IAA)
SPPI........... Southern Production Program, Inc.
SPPI........... Structured Pediatric Psychosocial Interview (EDAC)
SPPI........... Symposium on the Preventability of Perinatal Injury
SPPIL .... Shuttle Preferred Pyrotechnic Items List [NASA] (NASA)
SPPK .... Studien zur Palaeographie und Papyruskunde [C. Wessely] [A publication] (BJA)
SPPL.......... Spare Parts Provisioning List [NASA] (NASA)
SPPL.......... Spark Plug
SPPL.......... Statewide Public Library Interlibrary Loan and Reference Network [Library network]
SPPLB .... Specialist, Photographer, Laboratory [Navy rating]

SPPLITT....... Southern Pacific Pipelines and International Tank Terminals [*Two companies jointly building deepwater port to accommodate outsize oil carriers*]
SpPm........... Biblioteca Publica, Palma De Mallorca, Spain [*Library symbol Library of Congress*] (LCLS)
SPPM........... Pomacocha [*Peru*] [*ICAO location identifier*] (ICLI)
SPPM........... Safe Passage Path Map (SAA)
SPPM........... Serial Parallel Pipeline Multiplier (IAA)
SPPMP........ Specialist, Motion Picture Production [*Navy rating*]
SP-PMS ...... Shuttle Projects - Performance Management Systems Office [*NASA*] (GFGA)
SPPN .... Society of Private and Pioneer Numismatics (EA)
SPPO .... Scheduled Program Printout (NATG)
SPPO .... Spacelab Payload Project Office [*NASA*]
SPPO .... Special Projects Program Order (AAG)
SPPP .... Huanacopampa [*Peru*] [*ICAO location identifier*] (ICLI)
SPPP .... Spacelab Payloads Processing Project (NASA)
SPPP .... Superior Performance Proficiency Pay (MCD)
SPPPA .... Spartan Potential Production Problem Analysis [*Missiles*] (MCD)
SPPPA .... Spartan Production Program Producibility Analysis [*Missiles*] (MCD)
SPPPG .... Specialist, Photogrammetry [*Navy rating*]
SPPPM .... Surveyor Project Policy and Procedure Manual [*NASA*]
SPPR .... Specialist, Public Relations [*Coast Guard*]
SPPR .... Special Peacetime Program Requirements [*DoD*]
SPPR .... Special Program Review [*Army*] (RDA)
SPPR .... Supertel Hospitality [*NASDAQ symbol*] (TTSB)
SPPR .... Supertel Hospitality, Inc. [*NASDAQ symbol*] (SAG)
Sp Pr Cas .... Spinks' English Admiralty Prize Cases [*1854-56*] [*A publication*] (DLA)
SPPRI......... Sichuan Pulp and Paper Research Institute (BUAC)
SPPRT .... Support
SPPS .... Semipost-Pay, Pay-Station [*Telecommunications*] (TEL)
SPPS .... Solid-Phase Peptide Synthesis [*Biochemistry*]
SPPS .... Solid State Peptide Synthesis (EDCT)
SPPS .... Specialist, Port Security [*Coast Guard*]
SPPS .... Special Products and Program Support
SPPS .... Stable Plasma Protein Solution [*Medicine*]
SPPS .... Subsystem Program Preparation Support [*Programming language*] [*Computer science*]
SPPT .... Southern Pacific Petroleum NL [*NASDAQ symbol*] (NQ)
SPPT.......... Superprecipitation Response [*Medicine*] (DMAA)
SPPTY .... Southern Pac Petrol NL [*NASDAQ symbol*] (TTSB)
SPPVM .... Specialist, V-Mail [*Navy rating*]
SPPY .... Chachapoyas [*Peru*] [*ICAO location identifier*] (ICLI)
SPQ .... Memphis, TN [*Location identifier FAA*] (FAAL)
SPQ .... Sandpiper Oil & Gas [*Vancouver Stock Exchange symbol*]
SPQ .... San Pedro [*California*] [*Airport symbol Obsolete*] (OAG)
SPQ .... Special Product Quotation (IAA)
SPQ .... Stanford Parent Questionnaire [*Psychology*]
SPQ .... Student Progress Questionnaire (AIE)
SPQ .... Study Process Questionnaire [*J. Biggs*] (TES)
SPQBX .... Hancock(J) Special Equities Cl.B [*Mutual fund ticker symbol*] (SG)
SPQCR........ Specialist, Communications Specialist, Cryptographer [*Navy rating*]
SPQE .... Subpool Queue Element (MHDI)
SPQIN .... Specialist, Communications Specialist, Radio Intelligence [*Navy rating*]
SPQJ........... Jaqui [*Peru*] [*ICAO location identifier*] (ICLI)
SPQN .... Requena [*Peru*] [*ICAO location identifier*] (ICLI)
SPQR .... Selected Product Quality Review [*DoD*]
SPQR .... Senatus Populusque Romanus [*The Senate and People of Rome*] [*Latin*]
SPQR .... Small Profits, Quick Returns
SPQR.......... Speed, Power, Quietness, and Reliability [*Automotive engineering*]
SPQRP........ Specialist, Communications Specialist, Registered Publication Clerk [*Navy rating*]
SPQS .... Self Profile Q-Sort [*Child development test*]
SPQT .... Iquitos/Coronel FAP Francisco Secada Vignetta [*Peru*] [*ICAO location identifier*] (ICLI)
SPQTE .... Specialist, Communications Specialist, Technician [*Navy rating*]
SPQU .... Arequipa/Rodriguez Ballon [*Peru*] [*ICAO location identifier*] (ICLI)
SPR .... Eastern Flying Service Ltd. [*Canada ICAO designator*] (FAAC)
SPR .... Puerto Rico Reports, Spanish Edition [*A publication*] (DLA)
SPR .... Sampling with Partial Replacement
SPR .... Sandia Pulsed Reactor [*Nuclear energy*]
SPR .... San Pedro [*Belize*] [*Airport symbol*] (OAG)
SPR .... Sapper [*Military*]
SPR .... Satellite Parametric Reduction
SPR .... S-Band Planetary RADAR
SPR .... Scientific Process & Research, Inc. [*Information service or system*] (IID)
SPR .... Seal Pressure Ratio
SPR .... Seconds per Revolution [*or Rotation*] (NVT)
SPR .... Secretarial Performance Review [*DoD*] (DOMA)
SPR .... Secretary of the Air Force Program Review (MCD)
SPR .... Selective Parallel Running (NITA)
SPR .... Semiconductor Process Representation (AAEL)
SPR .... Semipermanent Repellent (ADA)
SPR .... Send Priority and Route Digit [*Telecommunications*] (TEL)
SPR .... Sense Printer
SPR .... Sequential Probability Ratio [*Statistics*]
SPR .... Serial Printer (IAA)
SPR .... Serial Probe Recognition [*Psychometrics*]
SPR .... Shock Position Ratio
SPR .... Shortest Possible Route (MCD)
SPR .... Short Pulse RADAR (IAA)
SPR .... Silicon Power Rectifier

SPR .... Simplified Practice Recommendation
SPR .... Single-Ply Roofing
SPR .... Single-Point Refueling (MCD)
SPR .... Skin Potential Response [*Physiology*]
SPR .... Society for Pediatric Radiology (EA)
SPR .... Society for Pediatric Research (EA)
SPR .... Society for Philosophy of Religion (EA)
SPR .... Society for Physical Research [*British*] (BI)
SPR .... Society for Prevention Research (EA)
SPR .... Society for Psychical Research [*British*]
SPR .... Society for Psychophysiological Research (EA)
SPR .... Society for Psychosomatic Research (EAIO)
SPR .... Society of Patient Representatives [*Later, NSPR*] (EA)
SPR .... Society of Property Researchers (BUAC)
SPR .... Software Problem Report [*NASA*] (NASA)
SPR .... Solid-Phase Reactor
SPR .... Solid Phase Receptacle [*Laboratory testing*]
SPR .... Solid-Propellant Rocket
SPR .... South Polar Region
SPR .... Spacer (AAG)
SPR .... Spare [*Telecommunications*] (TEL)
SPR .... Specialist, Recruiter [*Navy rating*]
SPR .... Special Program Requirement (AFM)
SPR .... Special Program Review [*Army*] (RDA)
SPR .... Special Project Report
SPR .... Special-Purpose RADAR
SPR .... Special-Purpose Requirements [*Army*]
SPR .... Specific Price Reduction
SPR .... Specific Resistance (IAA)
SPR .... Spinster
SPR .... Sponsor
SPR .... Sponsor's Program Review [*Navy*] (DOMA)
Spr .... Sprague's United States District Court (Admiralty) Decisions [*A publication*] (DLA)
SPR .... Spratly Islands [*ANSI three-letter standard code*] (CNC)
SPR .... Spring (MSA)
SPR .... Springer Resources [*Vancouver Stock Exchange symbol*]
SPR .... Springfield [*Diocesan abbreviation*] [*Massachusetts*] (TOCD)
Spr .... Sprinkled [*Bookbinding*] (DGA)
SPR .... Sprinkler (AAG)
spr .... Spruce (VRA)
SPR .... Statement of Procedural Rules [*A publication*] (DLA)
SPR .... Statisitcal Pattern Recognition [*Computer science*]
SPR .... Sterling Capital [*AMEX symbol*] (TTSB)
SPR .... Sterling Capital Corp. [*AMEX symbol*] (SPSG)
SPR .... Stop Prisoner Rape [*An association*] (EA)
SPR .... Storage Protection Register
SPR .... St. Pierre [*Quebec*] [*Seismograph station code, US Geological Survey Closed*] (SEIS)
SPR .... Strategic Petroleum Reserve [*Department of Energy*]
SPR .... Strategic Planning Review (SSD)
SPR .... Stroposcopic Pulse Radiolysis [*Physical chemistry*]
SPR .... Structure-Property Relationship [*Chemistry*]
SPR .... Subcontractor Performance Review [*NASA*] (NASA)
SPR .... Sub Petito Remissionis [*With Request for Return*] [*Latin*]
SPR .... Substance P Receptor [*Biochemistry*]
SPR .... Sudden Pressure Relay
SPR .... Sun Protection Required [*Identification system for heat-sensitive cargo*] [*Shipping*] (DCTA)
SPR .... Super
SPR .... Supervisory Printer Read [*Computer science*] (OA)
SPR .... Supervisory Profile Record [*Test*] [*Richardson, Bellows, Henry, and Co. Inc.*] (TES)
SPR .... Supplementary Progress Report
SPR .... Supply Performance Report (CINC)
SPR .... Support Period Requirement
SPR .... Support Plans and Requirements
SPR .... Surface Plasmon Resonance [*Physics*]
SPR .... Symmetrical Phase Recording [*Computer science*]
SPR .... System Parameter Record [*Computer science*] (IBMDP)
SPR .... System Performance Rating
SPR .... System Problem Report (MCD)
SPR .... System Program Review [*Military*] (AABC)
SPrA .... Sears, Roebuck 8.88% Dep Pfd [*NYSE symbol*] (TTSB)
SPRA .... Semi-Permanet Release Agent
SPRA .... Space Probe RADAR Altimeter (KSC)
SPRA .... Special-Purpose Reconnaissance Aircraft [*Navy*]
SPRA .... Sponsor's Profit and Risk Allowance [*Department of Housing and Urban Development*] (GFGA)
SPRAA........ Strategic Plans and Resource Analysis Agency (DOMA)
SPRACAY.... Society for Prevention of Rock and Roll and Corruption of American Youth [*Organization in 1956 movie "Shake, Rattle and Roll"*]
SPRAG........ Spray Arrester Gear (MCD)
SPRAG........ STS Payload Requirements and Analysis Group [*NASA*] (NASA)
Sprague....... Sprague's United States District Court (Admiralty) Decisions [*A publication*] (DLA)
SPRANS...... Special Projects of Regional and National Significance [*HHS*]
SPRAT .... Small Portable RADAR Torch
SPRB .... Senior Performance Review Board (MHDB)
SPR BOG .... Springender Bogen [*Bouncing Bow*] [*Music*]
SPRC .... Seafood Products Research Center [*Public Health Service*] (GRD)
SPRC .... Self-Propelled Robot Craft (IEEE)
SPRC .... Society for Prevention and Relief of Cancer (BUAC)
SPRC .... Society of Public Relations Counsellors
SPRC .... Star Petroleum Refinery Complex [*Thailand*]

SPRCA	Scottish Public Relations Consultants Association (BUAC)
SPRCAC	South Pacific Regional Civil Aviation Council [*Fiji*] (BUAC)
SPRCHTB	Senior Parachutist Badge [*Military decoration*] (GFGA)
SPRCS	Safe Passage Route Creation Sheet (SAA)
SPRD	Science Policy Research Division [*of Congressional Research Service, Library of Congress*]
SPRD	Subsurface Protection and Remediation Division of the National Risk Library [*Environmental Protection Agency*] (AEPA)
SPRD	Survey of Primary Reading Development (AEBS)
SPRDA	Solid Pipeline Research and Development Association (HGAA)
SPRDNG	Spreading [*Freight*]
SPRDR	Spreader (MSA)
SPRDS	Steam Pipe Rupture Detector System (IEEE)
SPRE	Society of Park and Recreation Educators (EA)
SPRE	Solid-Propellant Rocket Engine
SPRE	Special Prefix Code [*Northern Telecom*] [*Telecommunications*]
SPREAD	Spring Evaluation Analysis and Design (MCD)
SPREAD	Supercomputer Project Research Experiment in Advanced Development [*Lawrence Livermore Laboratory, Los Alamos National Laboratory, and SRI*]
SPREAD	Support Program for Remote Entry of Alphanumeric Displays (NITA)
SPREC	Specular Reflection Computer Program (MCD)
Spreckel	Spreckels Industries, Inc. [*Associated Press*] (SAG)
SPREd	Society of Picture Researchers and Editors [*British*] (DBA)
SPRED	Society of Picture Researchers and Editors (BUAC)
SPREE	Solid-Propellant Exhaust Effects (MCD)
SPREE	Structure Preserving Estimation (ADA)
SPREG	Speed Regulator
SPREP	South Pacific Environment Protection Convention (EERA)
SPREP	South Pacific Regional Environment Program (EERA)
SPREP	South Pacific Regional Environment Programme [*of the South Pacific Commission*] [*New Caledonia*]
SPRES	Star Present (NASA)
SPRF	Sandia Pulsed Reactor Facility [*Nuclear energy*]
SPRF	Schweizer Public-Relations-Forum (BUAC)
SPRF	Space Propulsion Research Facility (AAG)
SPRF	Special-Purpose Receiving Facility
SprfldSv	Springfield Institution for Savings [*Associated Press*] (SAG)
SPRG	San Regis [*Peru*] [*ICAO location identifier*] (ICLI)
SPRG	Social Policy Research Group, Inc. [*Information service or system*] (IID)
SPRG	Spring
SPRG	Sprinkling (MSA)
Sprgn	Sepragen Corp. [*Associated Press*] (SAG)
SPRI	Scott Polar Research Institute [*Cambridge, England*]
SPRI	Single Ply Roofing Institute (EA)
SPRI	Social Problems Research Institute [*University of South Carolina at Columbia*] [*Research center*] (RCD)
SPRI	Social Process Research Institute [*Research center*] (RCD)
SPRI	Social Psychiatry Research Institute (EA)
SPRI	Sperm Reservoir Length Index
SPRI	Sugar Processing Research, Inc.
SPRIA	Solid-Phase Radioimmunoassay [*or Radioimmunoprecipitation Assay*] [*Clinical medicine*]
SPR III	Sandia Pulse Reactor III (COE)
SPRING	Spring [*Commonly used*] (OPSA)
Springfield C	Springfield College (GAGS)
Springs	Spring Industries, Inc. [*Associated Press*] (SAG)
SPRINGS	Springs [*Commonly used*] (OPSA)
SPRINT	Selective Printing [*Computer science*]
SPRINT	Solid-Propellant Rocket Intercept Missile [*ARPA/AMC*]
SPRINT	Southern Pacific Communications' Switched Long Distance Service [*Telecommunications*] (TEL)
SPRINT	Spare Parts Review Initiatives [*Army*] (RDA)
SPRINT	Special Police Radio Inquiry Network [*New York City*]
Sprint	Sprint Corp. [*Associated Press*] (SAG)
SPRINT	Strategic Programme for Innovation and Technology Transfer [*European Commission*]
SPRINTEL	Speedy Retrieval of Information on the Telephone (TELE)
SPRINTER	Specification of Profits with Interaction under Trial and Error Response
Spr Int L	Sprague on International Law [*A publication*] (DLA)
Sprint00	Sprint Corp. [*Associated Press*] (SAG)
SPRITE	Sequential Polling and Review of Interacting Teams of Experts (PDAA)
SPRITE	Sheffield People's Resource for Information Technology [*British*] (AIE)
SPRITE	Signal Processing in the Element (MCD)
SPRITE	Solid-Propellant Rocket Ignition Test and Evaluation (KSC)
SPRITE	Surveillance, Patrol, Reconnaissance, Intelligence Gathering, Target Designation, and Electronic Warfare [*Unmanned aircraft*] [*Military*]
SPRJ	Self-Powered Reference Junction
SPRKLG	Sprinkling [*Freight*]
SPRKT	Sprocket (MSA)
SPRL	Society for the Promotion of Religion and Learning (BUAC)
SPRL	Space Physics Research Laboratory [*University of Michigan*] [*Research center*] (RCD)
SPRM	San Ramon/Capitan Alvarino [*Peru*] [*ICAO location identifier*] (ICLI)
SPRM	Special Reamer [*Tool*] (AAG)
SPRM	Spermatozoa (DAVI)
SPRM	Supreme
SPRMRKT	Supermarket
SPRNG	Spring [*Commonly used*] (OPSA)
SPRNGS	Springs [*Commonly used*] (OPSA)

SPRO	Services Public Relations Officer [*British military*] (DMA)
S-P/ROM	Slave Programmable Read-Only Memory
SPROM	Slave Programmable ROM (NITA)
SPROM	Spontaneous Premature Rupture of Membrane [*Medicine*] (DMAA)
SPROM	Spontaneous Rupture of Membranes [*Obstetrics*] (DAVI)
SPROM	Switched Programmable Read-Only Memory
SPROM NIL	Spontaneous Rupture of Membranes, Not In Labor [*Obstetrics*] (DAVI)
SPROPS	Section Properties [*Camutek*] [*Software package*] (NCC)
SPROSS	Simulation Program for Sequential System (PDAA)
SPRP	Signalling Preprocessing Program (PDAA)
SPRR	Selective Paramagnetic Relaxation Reagent [*Chemistry*]
SPRR	Self-Propelled Recoilless Rifle [*British military*] (DMA)
SPRRS	Southern Plains Range Research Station [*Oklahoma State University*] [*Research center*] (RCD)
SPRS	Single Passenger Reservation System [*DoD*]
SPR's	Small Parcels and Rolls [*Postal Service*]
SPRS	Society for the Promotion of Roman Studies (EAIO)
SPRS	Special-Purpose RADAR Set
SPRS	Student Proficiency Rating Scale
SPRS	Sublime Power of the Royal Secret [*Freemasonry*] (ROG)
SPRT	Rio Tigre [*Peru*] [*ICAO location identifier*] (ICLI)
SPRT	Sequential Probability Ratio Test [*Statistics*]
SPRT	Sport
SPRT	Standard Platinum Resistance Thermometer
SPRT	Support (MSA)
SPRT	System Performance and Repeatability Test [*Military*] (CAAL)
SprtaP	Sparta Pharmaceutical, Inc. [*Associated Press*] (SAG)
SPRTAP	Specially Prepared Tape Program (SAA)
SprtaSur	Sparta Surgical Corp. [*Associated Press*] (SAG)
SprtHaley	Sport Haley, Inc. [*Associated Press*] (SAG)
Sprtmrt	Sportmart, Inc. [*Associated Press*] (SAG)
SprtP	Sparta Pharmaceutical, Inc. [*Associated Press*] (SAG)
SprtS	Sparta Surgical Corp. [*Associated Press*] (SAG)
SprtS	Sports Sciences, Inc. [*Associated Press*] (SAG)
SprtS96	Sparta Surgical Corp. [*Associated Press*] (SAG)
SprtSci	Sports Sciences, Inc. [*Associated Press*] (SAG)
SPRU	Science Policy Research Unit [*Research center British*] (IRC)
SPRU	Trujillo/Capitan Carlos Martinez de Pinillos - Huanchaco [*Peru*] [*ICAO location identifier*] (ICLI)
SPRUCE	Special Programs and Rehabilitation under Unemployment Compensation [*Department of Labor*]
SPS	Safety Precedence Sequence [*Environmental science*] (COE)
SPS	Saint Patrick's Seminary [*Menlo Park, CA*]
SPS	Saint Patrick's Society for the Foreign Missions (BUAC)
SPS	Samples per Second
SPS	San Pedro De Poas [*Costa Rica*] [*Seismograph station code, US Geological Survey*] (SEIS)
SPS	Satellite and Production Services [*Tallahassee, FL*] [*Telecommunications*] (TSSD)
SPS	Satellite Power System (MCD)
SPS	Saturn Parts Sales [*NASA*]
SPS	Saturn Propulsion System [*NASA*]
SPS	Scene per Second (MCD)
SPS	Scheduled Passenger Service (IIA)
SPS	Schedule Promulgated Separately [*Navy*] (NVT)
SPS	School of Practical Science
SPS	School Psychology Specialist (PGP)
SPS	Scientific Power Switching
SPS	Scottish Prison Service (BUAC)
SPS	Seamen's Protection Society [*A union*] [*British*]
SPS	Secondary Plant System [*Nuclear energy*] (NRCH)
SPS	Secondary Power Source
SPS	Secondary Power System [*or Subsystem*] (MCD)
SPS	Secondary Propulsion System [*NASA*]
SPS	Second Preferred Stock [*Investment term*]
SPS	Security Police Squadron [*Air Force*]
SPS	Sekcja Pracy Spolecznej [*A publication*] (BJA)
SPS	Self Protection System (MCD)
SPS	Senior Private Secretary
SPS	Sensor Processing Subsystem (GAVI)
SPS	Sequential Partition System (IAA)
SPS	Serial Parallel Serial (NITA)
SPS	Serial-Parallel-Serial Structure (IAA)
SPS	Series-Parallel-Serial Configuration [*Electronics*] (MDG)
SPS	Service Propulsion System [*or Subsystem*] [*NASA*]
SPS	Servo Parameter Shift
SPS	Set Point Station
SpS	Sharpshooter [*Military decoration*] (AABC)
SPS	Sheltered Placement Scheme (AIE)
SPS	Shipping/Production Scheduling
SPS	Ship Planning System
SPS	Ship Program Schedule
SPS	Shuttle Procedures Simulator [*NASA*] (NASA)
SPS	Signal Pre-emption System
SPS	Signal Processing System (KSC)
SPS	Silent Propulsion System (MCD)
SPS	Simple Phrase System
SPS	Simplified Processing Station (MCD)
SPS	Simulated Parts Sketch (MCD)
SPS	Simulator Panel Set (MCD)
SPS	Sine Prole Superstite [*Without Surviving Issue*] [*Latin*]
SPS	Single-Pole Switch
SPS	Socialistische Partij Suriname [*Surinam Socialist Party*] [*Political party*] (PPW)

SPS.............. Socialist Party of Serbia [*Political party*] (BUAC)
SPS.............. Socialist Party of Slovenia [*Political party*] (EY)
SPS.............. Social Problems Series [*A publication*]
SPS.............. Society for Pentecostal Studies (EA)
SPS.............. Society of Pelvic Surgeons (EA)
SPS.............. Society of Physics Students (EA)
SPS.............. Society of Portrait Sculptors [*British*] (BI)
SPS.............. Socijalisticka Partija Srbije [*Socialist Party of Serbia*] [*Political party*] (EY)
SPS.............. Sodium Polyanetholesulfonate [*Analytical biochemistry*]
SPS.............. Sodium Polystyrene Sulfonate [*Organic chemistry*]
SPS.............. Soft Particle Spectrometer [*Geophysics*]
SPS.............. Software Procurement Specification
SPS.............. Software Product Specification
SPS.............. Software Products Scheme [*Computer science*] (DCTA)
SPS.............. Solar Panel Substrate
SPS.............. Solar Power Satellite [*NASA*]
SPS.............. Solar Power System (MCD)
SPS.............. Solar Probe Spacecraft [*Pioneer satellite*]
SPS.............. Solar Proton Stream [*Geophysics*] (SAA)
SPS.............. Solid Phase Synthesis [*Chemistry*]
SPS.............. Soluble Polysaccharide of Soybean [*Food technology*]
SPS.............. SONAR Phase Shifter
SPS.............. Sound Production Sample [*Medicine*] (DMAA)
SPS.............. South Pole Station [*National Weather Service*]
SPS.............. Southwestern Public Service Co. [*NYSE symbol*] (SPSG)
SPS.............. Southwestern Publishing Service (EFIS)
SPS.............. Southwestern PubSv [*NYSE symbol*] (TTSB)
SPS.............. Sozialdemokratische Partei der Schweiz [*Social Democratic Party of Switzerland*] [*Political party*] (PPE)
SPS.............. Sozialdemokratische Partei Suedtirols [*Social Democratic Party of South Tirol*] [*Political party*] (PPE)
SPS.............. Spacecraft Propulsion System (AAG)
SPS.............. Space Planning System [*Applied Research of Cambridge Ltd.*] [*Software package*] (NCC)
SPS.............. Space Power System (CET)
SPS.............. SPASA Servicios Politecnicos Aereos SA [*Spain ICAO designator*] (FAAC)
SPS.............. Special Education Specialist (PGP)
SpS.............. Specialist in Science (GAGS)
SPS.............. Specialist, Personnel Supervisor [*Women's Reserve*] [*Navy rating*]
SPS.............. Specialist, Shore Patrol and Security [*Navy rating*]
SPS.............. Special-Purpose SONAR (MCD)
SPS.............. Special Services [*Military*]
SPS.............. Specific Pavement Studies [*FHWA*] (TAG)
SPS.............. Spectrum Planning Subcommittee [*FCC*]
SPS.............. Speed Switch (IEEE)
SPS.............. Spokane, Portland & Seattle Railway System [*AAR code*]
SPS.............. SPS Technologies, Inc. [*Formerly, Standard Pressed Steel Co.*] (MCD)
SPS.............. Stabilized Platform Subsystem (KSC)
SPS.............. Standard Pipe Size
SPS.............. Standard Port System (MCD)
SPS.............. Standard Positioning Service
SPS.............. Standard Pressed Steel Co. (EFIS)
SPS.............. Standard Process Specification (MCD)
SPS.............. Standard Procurement System (AAGC)
SPS.............. Standard Project Storm [*Nuclear energy*] (NRCH)
SPS.............. Standby Power Source [*Electronics*]
SPS.............. Standby Power Supply (PCM)
SPS.............. Standby Power System (IGQR)
SPS.............. Statement of Prior Submission (NASA)
SPS.............. State Permit System [*Environmental Protection Agency*] (GFGA)
SPS.............. Static Power System
SPS.............. Static Pressure System
SPS.............. Statistical Performance Standards [*Navy*] (NG)
SPS.............. Stator Pivot Seal
SPS.............. Status Projection System
SPS.............. Steady Potential Shift
SPS.............. Steampipe Survey
SPS.............. Steering Pressure Sensor [*Automotive engineering*]
SPS.............. Stereo Photographic System
SPS.............. Stichting Plurale Samenlevingen [*Foundation for the Study of Plural Societies - FSPS*] (EAIO)
SPS.............. Stimulated Protein Synthesis [*Medicine*] (DMAA)
SPS.............. Stored Program Simulator
SPS.............. St. Patrick's Missionary Society [*Roman Catholic men's religious order*]
sps.............. St. Patrick's Missionary Society (TOCD)
SPS.............. Strategical Planning Section [*Joint Planning Staff*] [*World War II*]
SPS.............. Strategic Planning Society [*Formerly, Society for Strategic and Long Range Planning*] (EA)
SPS.............. Strategic Planning Staff [*Social Security Administration*]
SPS.............. String Processing System [*Word processing software*]
SPS.............. String Process System (NITA)
SPS.............. Student Profile Section [*of the American College Testing Test Battery*]
SPS.............. Submarine Piping System
SPS.............. Submerged Production System [*Deepwater platform*] [*Humble Oil*]
SPS.............. Subsea Production System [*Petroleum technology*]
SPS.............. Sucrose-Phosphate Synthase [*An enzyme*]
SPS.............. Suicide Probability Scale [*Personality development test*] [*Psychology*]
SPS.............. Sulfadiazine [*Microbiology*] (DAVI)
SPS.............. Sulfite-Polymyxin-Sulfadiazine [*Agar*] [*Microbiology*]
SPS.............. Summit Power Station [*Nuclear energy*] (NRCH)

SPS.............. Super Proton Synchrotron [*Particle physics*]
SPS.............. Supplementary Power Supply (IAA)
SPS.............. Supplementary Protection System [*Nuclear energy*] (NRCH)
SPS.............. Supply Point Simulation (MCD)
SPS.............. Surface Preparation System (AAEL)
SPS.............. Symbolic Programming System [*Computer science*]
SPS.............. Symbolic Program System (NITA)
SPS.............. Symbols per Second [*Computer science*]
SPS.............. Synchronous Program Supervisor (IAA)
SPS.............. Syndiotactic Polystyrene [*Organic chemistry*]
SPS.............. Systemic Progressive Sclerosis [*Medicine*] (AAMN)
SPS.............. System Performance Score [*Telecommunications*] (TEL)
SPS.............. System Performance Simulation
SPS.............. Wichita Falls [*Texas*] [*Airport symbol*] (OAG)
SPSA.......... Casma [*Peru*] [*ICAO location identifier*] (ICLI)
SPSA.......... Senate Press Secretaries Association (EA)
SPSA.......... Society of Philippine Surgeons in America (EA)
SPSA.......... Special Projects School for Air
SPSA.......... Standard Page Specification Association (BTTJ)
SPSAA........ Swimming Pool and Spa Association of Australia
SpSAG........ Archivo General de Indias [*Archives of the Indies*], Seville, Spain [*Library symbol Library of Congress*] (LCLS)
SPSBS........ Shetland Pony Stud Book Society (BUAC)
SPSBS........ Shetland Pony Study Book Society [*British*] (DBA)
SPSC.......... Saharan People's Support Committee (EA)
SPSC.......... Seventy Plus Ski Club (EA)
SP/SC........ Shield Plug/Support Cylinder [*Nuclear energy*] (NRCH)
SPSC.......... Signal Processing and Spectral Control
SPSC.......... Space Power Systems Conference
SPSC.......... Standard Performance Summary Charts (AAG)
SPSC.......... System Planning and System Control (COE)
SPSCR........ Special Screw
SPSD.......... Shipboard Passive Surveillance and Detection System (PDAA)
SPSD.......... Space Power Systems Division [*NASA*]
SPSD.......... State Purchasing and Sales Division [*Tasmania, Australia*]
SP-SDF........ Socialist Party - Social Democratic Federation [*Later, Socialist Party of the United States of America*] (EA)
SPSDM........ Society for the Philosophical Study of Dialectical Materialism (EA)
SPSDS........ Ship's Passive Surveillance and Detection System [*Navy*] (CAAL)
SPSE.......... Society of Photographic Scientists and Engineers (EA)
SPSE.......... Special Purpose Support Equipment
SPSF.......... Self-Propagating-Star Formation [*Galactic science*]
SPSF.......... Society of the President Street Fellows (EA)
SPSF.......... Spent Fuel Storage Pool [*Nuclear energy*] (NUCP)
SPSFM........ St. Patrick's Society for the Foreign Missions [*See also SSPME*] [*Kiltegan, County Wicklow, Republic of Ireland*] (EAIO)
SPSFV .... State Public Services Federation Victoria [*Australia*]
SPSG.......... Sparta Surgical [*NASDAQ symbol*] (TTSB)
SPSG.......... Sparta Surgical Corp. [*NASDAQ symbol*] (SAG)
SPSGU........ Sparta Surgical Unit [*NASDAQ symbol*] (TTSB)
SPSGW........ Sparta Surgical Wrrt [*NASDAQ symbol*] (TTSB)
SP/SHLD.... Splash Shield [*Automotive engineering*]
SPSHP........ Special Shaped
SPSHS........ Stanford Profile Scales of Hypnotic Susceptibility [*Psychology*]
SPSI.......... Serikat Pelajaran Seluruh Indonesia [*Sailors' Union of Indonesia*]
SPSI.......... Society for the Promotion of Scientific Industry [*British*]
SPSI.......... SpectraScience, Inc. [*NASDAQ symbol*] (SAG)
SPSJ.......... San Jose De Sisa [*Peru*] [*ICAO location identifier*] (ICLI)
SPSL.......... Lamas [*Peru*] [*ICAO location identifier*] (ICLI)
SPSL.......... Socialist Party of Sri Lanka
SPSL.......... Society for the Philosophy of Sex and Love (EA)
SPSL.......... Society for the Protection of Science and Learning [*British*]
SPSL.......... Spare Parts Selection List
SPSLGI........ Society for the Psychological Study of Lesbian and Gay Issues (EA)
SPSM.......... Socialist Party of San Marino [*Political party*] (EAIO)
SPSM.......... Society for the Philosophical Study of Marxism (EA)
SPSM.......... Supply Point Simulation Model (MCD)
SPSME........ Spacelab Payload Standard Modular Electronics (MCD)
SP-SMO...... Shuttle Projects - Site Management Office [*NASA*] (GFGA)
SPSN.......... Submitted Package Sequence Number (MCD)
SPSO.......... Pisco [*Peru*] [*ICAO location identifier*] (ICLI)
SPSO.......... Senior Personnel Staff Officer [*Air Force British*]
SPSO.......... Senior Principal Scientific Officer [*Ministry of Agriculture, Fisheries, and Food*] [*British*]
SPSP.......... Small Power System Program (IAA)
SPSP.......... Solid-Propellant Surveillance Panel [*Military*]
SPSP.......... Somali Revolutionary Socialist Party [*Political party*] (BUAC)
SPSP.......... Spare Parts Support Package
SPSP.......... St. Peter and St. Paul [*The Papal seal*]
SPSP-AGE.... Spare Parts Support Package for Aerospace Ground Equipment (MCD)
SPSPS........ Specialist, Personnel Supervisor, V-10 [*Navy rating*]
SPSQ.......... Satisfaction with Performance Scaled Questionnaire
SpsQualBad... Sharpshooter Qualification Badge [*Military decoration*] (AABC)
SPSS.......... Masisea [*Peru*] [*ICAO location identifier*] (ICLI)
SPSS.......... Shield Plug Storage Station [*Nuclear energy*] (NRCH)
SPSS.......... Single-Pole Snap Switch (IAA)
SPSS.......... Single Pulse Selection System
SPSS.......... Society of the Priests of St. Sulpice [*See also CPSS*] [*Paris, France*] (EAIO)
SPSS.......... SPSS, Inc. [*NASDAQ symbol*] (SAG)
SPSS.......... Statistical Package for the Social Sciences [*Programming language*] [*1970*]
SPSS.......... Supplementary Power Supply Set (IAA)

SPS-SCWG...	Spanish Philatelic Society Spanish Civil War Study Group [Defunct] (EA)
SPSSI	Society for the Psychological Study of Social Issues (EA)
Sp St	Private and Special Laws [A publication] (DLA)
SPST	Single-Pole, Single-Throw [Switch]
SPST	Social Problem-Solving Test (EDAC)
SPST	Spent Resin Storage Tank [Nuclear energy] (IAA)
SPST	Symonds Picture-Story Test [Psychology]
SPST	Tarapoto [Peru] [ICAO location identifier] (ICLI)
SPSTec	SPS Technologies, Inc. [Associated Press] (SAG)
SPSTNC	Single-Pole, Single-Throw, Normally-Closed [Switch]
SPSTNO	Single-Pole, Single-Throw, Normally-Open [Switch]
SPSTNODM...	Single-Pole, Single-Throw, Normally-Open, Double-Make [Switch]
SPSTP	Solid-Propellant Rocket Static Test Panel [Military]
SPS Trns	SPS Transaction Services, Inc. [Associated Press] (SAG)
SPSTSW	Single-Pole, Single-Throw Switch
SP SURF	Specific Surface (WDAA)
SPSW	Single-Pole Switch
S/PSWO	Service/Parts Sales Work Order (MCD)
SPSWO	Spare Parts Sales Work Order
S Psy S	Specialist in Psychological Services (PGP)
SPT	Albuquerque, NM [Location identifier FAA] (FAAL)
SPT	Bengis Aviation (Pty) Ltd. [South Africa] [FAA designator] (FAAC)
SPT	Piedmont Technical College, Greenwood, SC [OCLC symbol] (OCLC)
SPT	Scaled-Particle Theory
SPT	School of Physical Training [British]
SPT	Scientist-Pilot [NASA] (KSC)
SPT	Seaport
SPT	Sectors per Track
SPT	Selective Population Transfer [Physics]
SPT	Sense Printer Test (SAA)
Spt	September (CDAI)
SPT	Septic [Classified advertising] (ADA)
SPT	Septuple (MSA)
SPT	Shaft Position Transducer
SPT	Shared Page Table [Computer science] (OA)
SPT	Shipper Pays Taxes
SPT	Ship Position Transmitter
SPT	Shortest Processing Time (AAEL)
SPT	Short-Period Tremors [Volcanology]
SPT	Silicon Planar Transistor
SPT	Silicon-Powered Transistor
SPT	Skin Prick Test [Immunology]
SPT	Slowest Processing Time
SPT	Small Perturbation Theory
SPT	Socialist Party of Thailand [Political party] (FEA)
SPT	Society for Philosophy and Technology (EA)
SPT	Society of Painters in Tempera (EA)
SPT	Society of Photo-Technologists (FA)
SPT	Society of Projective Techniques [Later, SPA] (EA)
SPT	Sodium Pyridinethione [Organic chemistry]
SPT	Sogepet Ltd. [Toronto Stock Exchange symbol]
SPT	Solar Panel Technology (SSD)
SPT	Sound-Powered Telephone
SPT	Sound Production Tasks (DB)
SPT	South Point [Hawaii] [Seismograph station code, US Geological Survey] (SEIS)
SPT	Space Power Tool
SpT	Spanish Telefunken [Record label]
SPT	Spare Parts Transfer
Spt	Specialist Degree (PGP)
SPT	Specialist, Teacher [Navy rating]
SPT	Special Perishable Tool (MCD)
SPT	Special Purpose Test [Nuclear energy] (NRCH)
SP T	Special Term [Legal term] (DLA)
SPT	Spirit
spt	Spiritus [Spirit] [Latin Pharmacy] (MAE)
SPT	Split (MSA)
SPT	Spondee Picture Test (DB)
SPT	Spraytight
Spt	Spritsail [Ship's rigging] (DS)
SPT	Sputum
SPT	Standard Penetration Test [Nuclear energy] (NRCH)
SPT	Star Point Transfer [Photography] (OA)
SPT	Static Pressure Transducer
SPT	Steering Position Transducer [NASA] (NAKS)
SPT	Streptomycin Phosphotransferase [An enzyme]
SPT	Structural Programming Technique
SPT	Supervisory Potential Test
SPT	Support (AFM)
SPT	Symbolic Play Test [Child development test]
SPT	Symbolic Program Tape [Computer science] (IEEE)
SPT	Symbolic Program Translator [Computer science] (IEEE)
SPT	System Page Table [Telecommunications] (TEL)
SPT	System Parameter Table [Computer science] (IBMDP)
SPT	System Planning Team [Military] (AFIT)
SPTA	Nauta [Peru] [ICAO location identifier] (ICLI)
SPTA	Scottish Provision Trade Association
SPTA	Small Potteries Trade Association (BUAC)
SPTA	Southern Paper Trade Association [Defunct] (EA)
SPTA	Southern Pressure Treaters Association (EA)
SPTA	Sparta Pharmaceutical, Inc. [NASDAQ symbol] (SAG)
SPTA	Sparta Pharmaceuticals [NASDAQ symbol] (TTSB)
SPTA	Spectrin Alpha (DMAA)
SPTAN	Spectrin Alpha, Nonerythroid (DMAA)
SPT & PA	Society for Projective Techniques and Personality Assessment [Later, SPA]
SptaP	Sparta Pharmaceutical, Inc. [Associated Press] (SAG)
SptAuth	[The] Sports Authority, Inc. [Associated Press] (SAG)
SPTAW	Sparta Pharmaceuticals Wrrt'A' [NASDAQ symbol] (TTSB)
Sp Tax Rul	Special Tax Ruling [Internal Revenue Service] [United States] [A publication] (DLA)
SPTAZ	Sparta Pharmaceuticals Wrrt'B' [NASDAQ symbol] (TTSB)
SPTC	Septic
SPTC	Share-Purchase Tax Credit [Canada]
SPTC	Single Parent Travel Club (BUAC)
SPTC	South Pacific Trade Commission [Australia]
SPTC	Specified Period of Time Contract
SPTCA	Swimming Pool Trades and Contractors Association (NTPA)
SPTCEN	Support Center [Army]
SptChalt	Sport Chalet, Inc. [Associated Press] (SAG)
SPTCS	South Pacific Trade Commissioner Service [Australia]
SPTD	Signal Processor Techniques Department
SPTD	Supplemental Provisioning Technical Documentation [NASA] (NASA)
SPTDP	South Pacific Telecommunications Development Programme [Fiji] (BUAC)
SPTE	Special Purpose Test Equipment (MCD)
SPTE	Teresita [Peru] [ICAO location identifier] (ICLI)
SPTEA	Single Persons for Tax Equality Association (EAIO)
SpTelc	Specialty Teleconstructioners [Associated Press] (SAG)
SPTF	Screen Printing Technical Foundation (EA)
SPTF	Shortest Processing Time First [Computer science] (MHDI)
SPTF	Shortest Programming Time First (NITA)
SPTF	Signal Processing Test Facility
SPTF	Social Progress Trust Fund [Inter-American Development Bank]
SPTF	Sodium Pump Test Facility [Energy Research and Development Administration]
SPTF	Support Flight [Military]
SPTG	Sporting (WDAA)
SPTG	Support Group [Military]
SPTH	Systolic Threshold Pressure [Cardiology]
SPT-HP	Scholastic Proficiency Test - Higher Primary Level [Educational test] [South Africa]
SPTI	Puerto Inca [Peru] [ICAO location identifier] (ICLI)
SPTI	Senior Physical Training Instructor [British military] (DMA)
SPTI	Systolic Pressure Time Index [Cardiology] (DAVI)
SPTL	Society of Public Teachers of Law [British] (DLA)
SPTL	Society of Public Teachers of Law in Great Britain and Northern Ireland (BUAC)
SPTL	Superconducting Power Transmission Line (PDAA)
SPTL	Support Line [Military]
SptM	Sports Media, Inc. [Associated Press] (SAG)
SPTN	Tacna [Peru] [ICAO location identifier] (ICLI)
SPTP	Spatial Peak Temporal Peak (STED)
SPTP	Special-Purpose Test Program (MCD)
SPTP	Talara/El Pato [Peru] [ICAO location identifier] (ICLI)
SP(TR)	Specialist (Transportation) [Coast Guard]
SPTR	SpecTran Corp. [NASDAQ symbol] (NQ)
SPTR	Tournavista [Peru] [ICAO location identifier] (ICLI)
SPTRJ	Self-Powered Thermocouple Reference Junction
Sp Trs	Special Troops [Army]
SPTS	Spirits
SPTS	Sports Media [NASDAQ symbol] (TTSB)
SPTS	Sports Media, Inc. [NASDAQ symbol] (SAG)
SPTS	Stock Positioning and Transportation Study [DoD]
SPTS	Subjective Posttraumatic Syndrome [Medicine] (DMAA)
SPTS	Support Squadron [Air Force]
SPTSL	Sports Media Wrrt'C' [NASDAQ symbol] (TTSB)
SPTSq	Support Squadron [Air Force]
SptSu	Sparta Surgical Corp. [Associated Press] (SAG)
SptSup	Sport Supply Group [Associated Press] (SAG)
SPTSZ	Sports Media Wrrt'B' [NASDAQ symbol] (TTSB)
SPTT	Single-Pole, Triple-Throw [Switch] (CET)
SPTU	Puerto Maldonado/Padre Aldamiz [Peru] [ICAO location identifier] (ICLI)
SPTUF	South Pacific Trade Union Forum [14-nation group opposed to nuclear testing and dumping in the Pacific]
SPTURP	Status Post Transurethral Resection of the Prostate [Medicine] (DAVI)
SPTV	Supersonic Parachute Test Vehicle (IAA)
SPTW	Single-Pedestal Typewriter [Desk]
SPTW	Society for Promoting the Training of Women (BUAC)
SPTW	Society Promoting Training Women [British] (DBA)
SPTWC	Salle Palasz and Tri-Weapon Club (EA)
SPTx	Static Pelvic Traction [Medicine] (STED)
SPU	Mount Spur [Alaska] [Seismograph station code, US Geological Survey] (SEIS)
SPU	Salinas Public Library, Salinas, CA [OCLC symbol] (OCLC)
SPU	S-Band Polar Ultra
SPU	School Personnel Utilization
SPU	Scientific Programs Unit [Commonwealth] (EERA)
SPU	Sekretno-Politicheskoye Upravleniye [Secret Political Directorate] [Former USSR] (LAIN)
SPU	Self-Propelled Underwater Missile (IAA)
SPU	Sense Punch [Computer science] (IAA)
SPU	Service Propulsion Unit
SPU	Short Procedure Unit [Medicine] (CPH)
SPU	Signal Processing Unit
SPU	Slave Processing Unit

SPU .... Smallest Publishable Unit
SPU .... Small Peripheral Unit (IAA)
SPU .... Society for Pediatric Urology (EA)
SPU .... Southeast Airmotive Corp. [*ICAO designator*] (FAAC)
SPU .... Specialist, Utility [*Women's Reserve*] [*Navy rating*]
SPU .... Special Power Unit (NTCM)
SPU .... Split [*Former Yugoslavia*] [*Airport symbol*] (OAG)
SPU .... Standard Propulsion Unit (IAA)
SPU .... Student Peace Union [*Defunct*] (EA)
SPU .... Subsurface Propulsion Unit
SPU .... Supertech Industries [*Vancouver Stock Exchange symbol*]
SPU .... System Partitioning Unit [*Computer science*]
SPU .... System Power Unit
SPU .... System Power Up
SPUC .... Huamachuco [*Peru*] [*ICAO location identifier*] (ICLI)
SPUC .... Society for the Protection of Unborn Children (EA)
SPUD .... Salary Policy Under Discussion (WDAA)
SPUD .... Sniff, Paw, Urinate, and Defecate [*Ungulate territorial marking procedure*]
SPUD .... Society for Prevention of Unwholesome Diet [*National Potato Council*]
SPUD .... Solar Power Unit Demonstrator
SPUD .... Soon to be Pushing Up Daisies [*Lifestyle classification*] (ECON)
SPUD .... Stored Program Universal Demonstrator
SPUD .... St. Paul Union Depot Co. [*AAR code*]
SpU/In .... Supertrust Trust Index Trust [*Associated Press*] (SAG)
SPUK .... Special Projects, United Kingdom
SpU/MM ...... Supertrust Trust Money Market Trust [*Associated Press*] (SAG)
SPUMS .... South Pacific Underwater Medicine Society (BUAC)
SPUN .... Society for the Protection of the Unborn through Nutrition (EA)
SPUP .... School of Public and Urban Policy [*Pennsylvania University*] (PDAA)
SPUP .... Seychelles People's United Party [*Political party*] (PPW)
SPUR .... Piura/Capitan Concha [*Peru*] [*ICAO location identifier*] (ICLI)
SPUR .... San Francisco Planning and Urban Research Association [*California*] [*Information service or system*] (IID)
SPUR .... Singapore Planning Urban Research Group (BUAC)
SPUR .... Single Precision Unpacked Rounded [*floating-point package*] [*Computer program system Sperry Rand Corp.*]
SPUR .... Software Package for Unique Reports (GFGA)
SPUR .... Source Program Utility Routine
SPUR .... Space Power Unit Reactor [*Air Force*]
SPUR .... Special Purchase Office [*DoD*]
SPUR .... Spur [*Postal Service standard*] (OPSA)
SPUR .... Support for Projects Under Research [*British*]
SPUR .... Support for Promoting the Utilization of Resources [*Esso Education Foundation*]
SPUR .... Symbolic Processing Using RISC [*Reduced Instruction Set Computer*]
SPURM .... Special Purpose Unilateral Repetitive Modulation (IEEE)
SPURS .... Special Program for Urban and Regional Studies of Developing Areas (BUAC)
SPURS .... Spurs [*Commonly used*] (OPSA)
SPURT .... Simulation Package for University Research and Teaching (PDAA)
SPURT .... Small Primate Unrestrained Test
SPURT .... Spinning Unguided Rocket Trajectory
SPURV .... Self-Propelled Underwater Research Vehicle
SP-USA .... Socialist Party of the United States of America (EA)
SP-USA .... Student Pugwash USA [*An association*] (EA)
SPUT .... Sputum [*Medicine*] (DAVI)
SPUTNIC ...... Synchronously Programmed User Terminal and Network Interface Control [*Computer science*] (MHDI)
SPV .... Sa-Pa [*Vietnam*] [*Seismograph station code, US Geological Survey*] (SEIS)
SPV .... Selective Proximal Vagotomy [*Medicine*] (DMAA)
SPV .... Sensor Payload Vehicle
SPV .... Shope Papilloma Virus
SPV .... Slow-Phase Velocity [*Ophthalmology*]
SPV .... Space Position Value [*Outdoor advertising*] (NTCM)
SpV .... Spanish RCA Victor [*Record label*]
SPV .... Spark Port Vacuum [*Automotive engineering*]
SPV .... Specialist, Transport Airman [*Navy rating*]
SPV .... Special-Purpose Vehicle [*Military*]
SPV .... Specification Performance Validation [*Military*] (CAAL)
SPV .... Split-Product Vaccine [*Immunology*]
SPV .... Sterile Process Validation [*Drug evaluation*]
SPV .... STN Shop Television Network Ltd. [*Vancouver Stock Exchange symbol*]
SPV .... Storage Process Vent [*Nuclear energy*] (NRCH)
SPV .... Storage Protect Violation (CMD)
SPV .... Sulfophosphovanillin (Reaction) [*Clinical chemistry*]
SPV .... Sun Probe near Limb of Venus [*Angle*]
SPV .... Supervisor (ECII)
SPV .... Surface Photovoltage [*Photovoltaic energy systems*]
SPV .... Surface Photovoltage Spectroscopy (AAEL)
SPV .... Survey of Personal Values [*Psychology*]
SPVA .... Society for the Preservation of Variety Arts (EA)
SPVEA .... Superintendencia do Plano de Valorizacao Economica da Amazonia [*Brazil*]
SPVL .... Caraveli [*Peru*] [*ICAO location identifier*] (ICLI)
SPVLI .... Single Premium Variable Life Investment [*Insurance*]
SPVN .... Society of Peripheral Vascular Nursing (EA)
SPVN .... Supervision (MSA)
SPVOL .... Specific Volume (DEN)
SPVPF .... Shuttle Payload Vertical Processing Facility [*NASA*] (MCD)
SPVR .... Storage Process Vent Room [*Nuclear energy*] (NRCH)

SPVR .... Systemic Peripheral Vascular Resistance [*Cardiology*] (DAVI)
SPVR .... Vitor/San Isidro [*Peru*] [*ICAO location identifier*] (ICLI)
SPVS .... Society of Practising Veterinary Surgeons (BUAC)
SPVS .... Supervisors Section [*American Association of School Librarians*]
Spvsr .... Supervisor
SPW .... Self-Protection Weapon
SPW .... Seward Park [*Washington*] [*Seismograph station code, US Geological Survey*] (SEIS)
SPW .... Shipment Planning Worksheet
SPW .... Spare Parts Withdrawal (MCD)
SPW .... Specialist, Chaplain's Assistant [*Navy rating*]
SPW .... Special Warfare (NVT)
SPW .... Speedwings SA [*Switzerland ICAO designator*] (FAAC)
SPW .... Spencer [*Iowa*] [*Airport symbol*] (OAG)
SPW .... SPX Corp. [*Formerly, Sealed Power Corp.*] [*NYSE symbol*] (SPSG)
SPW .... Stock Purchase Warrant (MHDW)
SPW .... Subxiphoid Pericardial Window [*Medicine*] (DMAA)
SPW .... Surface Plasma Wave
SPW .... Wofford College, Spartanburg, SC [*OCLC symbol*] (OCLC)
SPWA .... Southern Peanut Warehousemen's Association (EA)
SPWA .... Steel Products Warehouse Association
SPWAO .... Small Press Writers and Artists Organization (EA)
SPWAR .... Special Warfare
SPWC .... Society for the Punishment of War Criminals (EA)
SPWG .... Space Parts Working Group
SPWL .... Single Premium Whole Life Insurance Policy
SPWLA .... Society of Professional Well Log Analysts (EA)
SPWM .... Single-Sided Pulse Width Modulation [*Telecommunications*]
SPWP .... Society of Prayer for World Peace (EAIO)
SPWR .... Small Pressurized Water Reactor
SPWS .... Self-Protection Weapon System
SPWS .... Shipment Planning Worksheet (MCD)
SPWSM .... Spanish War Service Medal
SPWT .... SSM/I [*Special Sensor Microwave/Imager*] Land Products Working Team [*Marine science*] (OSRA)
SPWWIII ...... Society for the Prevention of World War III [*Defunct*]
SPWY .... Penske Motorsports [*NASDAQ symbol*] (TTSB)
SPWY .... Penske Motorsports, Inc. [*NASDAQ symbol*] (SAG)
SPX .... League City, TX [*Location identifier FAA*] (FAAL)
SPX .... San Pedro [*Colombia*] [*Airport symbol*] (AD)
SPX .... Sequenced Packet Exchange [*Telecommunications*] (PCM)
SPX .... Simplex Circuit
SPX .... Simplex Instrument [*Telegraphy*]
Spx .... Spirex [*Wire binding*] (DGA)
SPX .... Spirit Petroleum [*Vancouver Stock Exchange symbol*]
SPX .... Stepped Piston Crossover (PDAA)
SPX .... Superheat Power Experiment [*Nuclear energy*]
SPXAC .... Specialist, Archivist [*Navy rating*]
SPXAR .... Specialist, Artist [*Navy rating*]
SPXBL .... Specialist, Ballistics [*Navy rating*]
SPXCC .... Specialist, Cable Censor [*Navy rating*]
SPXCG .... Specialist, Crystal Grinder [*Navy rating*]
SPX Cp .... SPX Corp. [*Formerly, Sealed Power Corp.*] [*Associated Press*] (SAG)
SPXCT .... Specialist, Cartographer [*Navy rating*]
SPXDI .... Specialist, Discharge Interviewer [*Navy rating*]
SPXED .... Specialist, Engineering Draftsman [*Navy rating*]
SPXFP .... Specialist, Fingerprint Expert [*Navy rating*]
SPXGU .... Specialist, Gauge Specialist [*Navy rating*]
SPXID .... Specialist, Intelligence Duties [*Navy rating*]
SPXIR .... Specialist, Interpreter [*Navy rating*]
SPXJO .... Specialist, Journalist [*Navy rating*]
SPXKP .... Specialist, Key Punch Operator and Supervisor [*Navy rating*]
SPXNC .... Specialist, Naval Correspondent [*Navy rating*]
SPXOP .... Specialist, Special Project [*Navy rating*]
SPXPC .... Specialist, Position Classifier [*Navy rating*]
SPXPI .... Specialist, Pigeon Trainer [*Navy rating*]
SPXPL .... Specialist, Plastic Expert [*Navy rating*]
SPXPR .... Specialist, Public Information [*Navy rating*]
SPXQM .... Specialist, Operations - Plotting and Chart Work [*Navy rating*]
SPXRL .... Specialist, Research Laboratory [*Navy rating*]
SPXRS .... Specialist, Armed Forces Radio Service and Special Naval Radio Units [*Navy rating*]
SPXSB .... Specialist, Telephone Switchboard Operator and Supervisor [*Navy rating*]
SPXST .... Specialist, Strategic Services [*Navy rating*]
SPXTD .... Specialist, Topographic Draftsman [*Navy rating*]
SPXTS .... Specialist, Air Stations Operations Desk - Time Shack [*Navy rating*]
SPXVA .... Specialist, Visual Training Aids [*Navy rating*]
s-py-- .... Paraguay [*MARC geographic area code Library of Congress*] (LCCP)
SPY .... Saint Paul Island, AK [*Location identifier FAA*] (FAAL)
SPY .... San Pedro [*Ivory Coast*] [*Airport symbol*] (OAG)
spy .... Spray (VRA)
SPY .... Square Pyramidal [*Organic chemistry*]
SPY .... Standard & Poor's Deposit Receipts [*AMEX symbol*] (SPSG)
SPY .... Standard & Poor's Dep Receipts [*AMEX symbol*] (TTSB)
SPYA .... Luya [*Peru*] [*ICAO location identifier*] (ICLI)
SPYC .... Yarinacocha [*Peru*] [*ICAO location identifier*] (ICLI)
SPYG .... Spyglass, Inc. [*NASDAQ symbol*] (SAG)
Spyglss ...... Spyglass, Inc. [*Associated Press*] (SAG)
SPYL .... Talara/Capitan Montes [*Peru*] [*ICAO location identifier*] (ICLI)
SPYN .... Spine-Tech, Inc. [*NASDAQ symbol*] (SAG)
SPYO .... Pacasmayo [*Peru*] [*ICAO location identifier*] (ICLI)
SPYR .... Sprayer (MSA)
SPYU .... Yauca [*Peru*] [*ICAO location identifier*] (ICLI)

SPZ............. Secretin Pancreozymin (STED)
SPZ............. Spar Aerospace Ltd. [Toronto Stock Exchange symbol]
SPZ............. Springdale [Arkansas] [Airport symbol] (OAG)
SPZ............. Submarine Patrol Zone [Navy] (NVT)
SPZ............. Sulfinpyrazone [Uricosuric compound]
SPZA........... Nazca [Peru] [ICAO location identifier] (ICLI)
SPZE........... Spice Entertainment Companies, Inc. [NASDAQ symbol] (SAG)
SPZH........... Pachiza [Peru] [ICAO location identifier] (ICLI)
SPZK........... Sotziki [Peru] [ICAO location identifier] (ICLI)
SPZN........... Speizman Ind [NASDAQ symbol] (TTSB)
SPZN........... Speizman Industries, Inc. [NASDAQ symbol] (SAG)
SPZO........... Cuzco/Velazco Astete [Peru] [ICAO location identifier] (ICLI)
SPZT........... Chazuta [Peru] [ICAO location identifier] (ICLI)
SQ............... E. R. Squibb & Sons [Research code symbol]
SQ............... Safety Quotient
SQ............... Sequens [Following] [Latin]
SQ............... Sick Quarters [Navy British]
SQ............... Singapore Airlines [Airline flight code] (ODBW)
SQ............... Situation Questionnaire
SQ............... Social Quotient [Psychology]
SQ............... Specialist Qualifications [British military] (DMA)
SQ............... Squadron
SQ............... Squalene (STED)
SQ............... Squall [Meteorology]
SQ............... Squamous [Cell] [Oncology]
sq............... Squamous (STED)
Sq............... Squamous (STED)
Sq............... Square (DD)
sq............... Square (IDOE)
SQ............... Square (EY)
sq............... Square Tank [Liquid gas carriers]
SQ............... Squawk (DA)
SQ............... Squeezed Files [Computer science]
SQ............... Squint Quoin [Construction] (IAA)
Sq............... Squire (WGA)
SQ............... Staff Qualified [Military British]
SQ............... State Question (WPI)
SQ............... Status Quo (STED)
SQ............... Stereoquadraphonic [Record playing system] [CBS]
S-Q............. Stock Quality [Pisciculture]
SQ............... Subcutaneous [Beneath the Skin] [Medicine]
SQ............... Superquick [Fuse]
SQ............... Survey Question (STED)
SQ............... Survival Quotient (ADA)
sq............... Swaziland [MARC country of publication code Library of Congress] (LCCP)
SQ............... Symptom Questionnaire [Medicine] (STED)
SQ3R.......... Survey, Question, Read, Review, Recite [Psychology]
SQA............ Sequa Corp. [NYSE symbol] (SPSG)
SQA............ Simple, Quick & Affordable [Office furniture]
SQA............ Society for Quality Assurance
SQA............ Society of Quality Assurance (NTPA)
SQA............ Society of Quantitative Analysts (NTPA)
SQA............ Software Quality Assurance [Computer science] (IEEE)
SQA............ South Queensland Airways [Australia]
SQA............ Sparrevohn, AK [Location identifier FAA] (FAAL)
SQA............ SQA, Inc. [Associated Press] (SAG)
SQA............ Squaring Amplifier
SQA............ Stina Resources Ltd. [Vancouver Stock Exchange symbol]
SQA............ Supplier Quality Assurance
SQA............ Surveyor Quality Assurance
SQA............ System Queue Area [Computer science] (BUR)
SQA.A........ Sequa Corp. CI'A' [NYSE symbol] (TTSB)
SQAA.......... Supplier Quality Assurance Assistance
SQA.B........ Sequa Corp. 'B' [NYSE symbol] (TTSB)
SQAB.......... Society for Quantitative Analyses of Behavior (BUAC)
SQAD.......... Surveyor Quality Assurance Directive
SQAI........... Square Industries [NASDAQ symbol] (TTSB)
SQAI........... Square Industries, Inc. [NASDAQ symbol] (NQ)
SQAP.......... Software Quality Assurance Procedure (CIST)
SQAP.......... Supplemental Quality Assurance Provision [Military]
SQAP.......... Swedish Question Answering Project (NITA)
SQAPP........ Software Quality Assurance Program Plan [Computer science]
SQAPr........ Sequa $5cm Cv Pfd [NYSE symbol] (TTSB)
SQAR.......... Supplier Quality Assurance Representative
SQAT.......... Ship's Qualification Assistance Team [Navy]
SQAX.......... SQA Inc. [NASDAQ symbol] (TTSB)
SQB............ Space Qualified Booster
SQBC.......... Space Qualified Booster Charger
SQBE.......... Small Quantity Burner Exemption [Environmental Protection Agency] (EPA)
Sq Bk........ Square Back [Bookbinding] (DGA)
SQBLA........ Scotch Quality Beef and Lamb Association [British] (DBA)
SQC............ Self-Quenching Control
SQC............ Sierra Madre Resources [Vancouver Stock Exchange symbol]
SQC............ Southern Cross [Australia Airport symbol] (OAG)
Sq C.......... Square Corners [Bookbinding] (DGA)
SQC............ Station Quality Control [RADAR]
SQC............ Statistical Quality Control
Sq Ca........ Squamous Cell Carcinoma [Endocrinology] (CPH)
SqCCA........ Squamous-Cell Carcinoma [Medicine] (MEDA)
Sq CCa...... Squamous-Cell Carcinoma [Oncology] (DAVI)
sq cell ca.... Squamous Cell Carcinoma [Medicine] (MAE)
SQCG.......... Squirrel Cage [Electricity]
sq ch.......... Square Chain (BARN)

SQCM.......... Square Centimeter (MSA)
SQCP.......... Statistical Quality Control Procedure
SQCS.......... Statement of Quality Control Standards (EBF)
SQCS.......... Statements on Quality Control Standards (TDOB)
SQD............ Self-Quenching Detector
SQD............ Signal Quality Detector
SQD............ Silicone Quadrant Detector (MCD)
SQD............ Social Questions of Today [A publication]
SQD............ Squad (AABC)
SQD............ Squadron (NVT)
SQDC.......... Special Quick Disconnect Coupling
SQ-DEL....... Superquick and Delay [Fuse] (SAA)
SQDN.......... Squadron (AAG)
Sqdn Ldr..... Squadron-Leader [British military] (DMA)
SQE............ Signal Quality Error [Computer science] (PCM)
SQE............ Software Quality Evaluation (MCD)
SQE............ Startec Marketing [Vancouver Stock Exchange symbol]
SQE............ Supplier Quality Engineering (MCD)
SqE & S...... Square-Edge and Sound (DAC)
SQEP.......... Software [Firmware] Quality Evaluation Plan
Sq Epith...... Squamous Epithelium [Medicine] (CPH)
SQF............ Cleveland, OH [Location identifier FAA] (FAAL)
SQF............ Seligman Quality Municipal Fund [NYSE symbol] (SPSG)
SQF............ Seligman Quality Muni Fd [NYSE symbol] (TTSB)
SQF............ Semiquantitative Fibrinogen [Hematology]
SQF............ Slovak Air Force [FAA designator] (FAAC)
SQF............ Subjective Quality Factor (OA)
sq ft.......... Square Feet (NAKS)
sq ft.......... Square Foot
SQFT.......... Square Foot (MSA)
SQG............ Small Quantity Generator [Automotive engineering Environmental Protection Agency]
SQH............ Square Head [Bolt]
SQ/H.......... Square of the Hatch [Stowage] (DNAB)
SQHA.......... Standard Quarter Horse Association (EA)
SQI............ Skill Qualification Identifier [Army] (INF)
SQI............ Special Qualifications Identifiers [Army] (AABC)
SQI............ Sterling/Rock Falls [Illinois] [Airport symbol] (OAG)
SQI............ Submerged Quench Incinerator (BCP)
SQI............ Supplier Quality Improvement
SQIC.......... Suppliers Quality Identification Classification
SQIN.......... Sequential Quadrature Inband [Television system] (IAA)
SQIN.......... Square Inch (MSA)
sq in.......... Square Inch
SQK............ Squawk [Aviation] (FAAC)
SQKM.......... Square Kilometer (MSA)
SQL............ San Carlos, CA [Location identifier FAA] (FAAL)
SQL............ School Quota Letter
SQL............ Servicious de Alquiler Aereo SA de CV [Mexico ICAO designator] (FAAC)
SQL............ Space Qualified LASER
SQL............ Squelch
SQL............ Standard High-Level Query Language
SQL............ Standard Quantum Limit [Physics]
SQL............ Standard Query Language [Computer science]
SQL............ Strand Resources [Vancouver Stock Exchange symbol]
SQL............ Structured Query Language [IBM Corp.]
SQL/DS....... Structured Query Language/Data System [IBM Corp.]
SQM........... Level Island, AK [Location identifier FAA] (FAAL)
SQM........... Sao Miguel Do Araguaia [Brazil] [Airport symbol] (OAG)
SQM........... Sociedad Quimica y Minera [NYSE symbol] (SPSG)
SQM........... Sociedad Quimica Y Minera ADS [NYSE symbol] (TTSB)
SQM........... Square Meter
SQM........... Strategic Quality Management (AIE)
SQMC.......... Squadron Quartermaster-Corporal [British military] (DMA)
SQMD.......... Squadron Manning Document (NVT)
sq mi.......... Square Mile (CDAI)
sq mm........ Square Millimeter (MAE)
SQMP.......... Strategic Quality Management Process [National Court Reporters Association]
SQMS.......... Squadron Quartermaster-Serjeant [Military British] (ROG)
SQMS.......... Staff Quartermaster Sergeant
SQMV.......... Squash Mosaic Virus
SQN............ Sanana [Indonesia] [Airport symbol] (OAG)
SQN............ School Quota Number
SQN............ Spin Quantum Number [Atomic physics]
SQN............ Squadron (NATG)
SQNA.......... Sequana Therapeutics [NASDAQ symbol] (TTSB)
SQNA.......... Sequana Therapeutics, Inc. [NASDAQ symbol] (SAG)
SQNA.......... Squadron Airfield (NATG)
Sqn Ldr....... Squadron Leader (WDAA)
Sqn Obs...... Squadron Observer [British military] (DMA)
Sqn Offr...... Squadron-Officer [British military] (DMA)
SQNT.......... Sequent Computer Sys [NASDAQ symbol] (TTSB)
SQNT.......... Sequent Computer Systems, Inc. [NASDAQ symbol] (NQ)
SQO............ Senior Quarters Officer [British military] (DMA)
SQO............ Squadron Officer
SQORD........ Separation, Quality Analysis of RADAR Data (SAA)
SQP............ Secret Pass Mine [Vancouver Stock Exchange symbol]
SQP............ Shippensburg State College, Shippensburg, PA [OCLC symbol] (OCLC)
SQP............ Successive Quadratic Programming [Algorithm] [Computer science]
SQPCM........ Slope Quantized Pulse Code Modulation [Telecommunications] (IAA)
SQPD.......... Super Quick Point Detonating
SQPMM....... Software Quality and Process Maturity Model (AAEL)

SQPN	Staggered Quadriphase Pseudorandom Noise (MCD)
SQPP	Software Quality Program Plan
SQPSK	Staggered Quadraphase Phase Shift Key Modulation [*Computer science*] (PDAA)
SQPSK	Staggered Quadriphase Shift Keying [*Computer science*] (CIST)
SQQ	San Quentin Quail [*A minor female*] [*Slang*]
SQQ	Sequentibus [*In the Following Places*] [*Latin*]
SQR	Sequence Relay (KSC)
SQR	Sequoia Resources Ltd. [*Vancouver Stock Exchange symbol*]
SQR	Soroako [*Indonesia*] [*Airport symbol*] (OAG)
SQR	Square
SQR	Square Root [*Computer science*]
SQR	Square Rooter (IDOE)
SQR	Square-Root Function (IDOE)
SQR	Supplier Quality Rating
SQR	Supplier Quality Representative [*Nuclear energy*] (NRCH)
SQRA	Singapore Quality and Reliability Association (BUAC)
sq rd	Square Rod (CDAI)
SQRE	Square [*Commonly used*] (OPSA)
SQRS	Squares [*Commonly used*] (OPSA)
SQRT	Seismic Qualification Review Team [*Nuclear energy*] (NRCH)
SQRT	Square Root
SQS	Skill Qualification Score [*Military*] (AABC)
SQS	Squares [*Postal Service standard*] (OPSA)
SQS	Statistische Quellenwerke der Schweiz [*Switzerland*]
SQS	Stochastic Queuing System
SQS	Stratford American Corp. [*Vancouver Stock Exchange symbol*]
SQS	Superquick Sensor (MCD)
SQ/SD	Special Qualifications/Special Designation (NVT)
SQSPM	Software Quality Standards and Procedures Manual
SQSSE	Supplier Quality System Survey Evaluations (MCD)
SQT	Melbourne, FL [*Location identifier FAA*] (FAAL)
SQT	Queensland State Reports [*A publication*] (DLA)
SQT	Ship Qualification Test [*or Trial*] [*Navy*]
SQT	Silverquest Resources [*Vancouver Stock Exchange symbol*]
SQT	Skill Qualification Test [*Army*]
SQT	Soldier Qualification Test (MCD)
SQT	Sterilization Qualification Tests
SQT	System Qualification Tests
SQTIPT	Ship Qualification Trials in Port [*Navy*] (NVT)
SQTNG	Squadron Training (NVT)
SQTP	System Qualification Test Phase
SQTT	Ship Qualification Trial Team [*Navy*] (NG)
SQT(WC)	Skill Qualification Test (Written Component) [*Army*] (INF)
SQU	E. R. Squibb & Sons, Princeton, NJ [*OCLC symbol*] (OCLC)
SQU	Squamous [*Cell*] [*Oncology*] (DAVI)
Squ	Square (BJA)
SQU	Squaw Peak [*Utah*] [*Seismograph station code, US Geological Survey*] (SEIS)
SQUAD	Squadron
SQUADEX	Squadron Exercises [*Canadian Navy*]
SQUAF	Sonobuoy Qualification Facility [*Navy*] (CAAL)
SQUALL	Salary Quotient at Lower Limits [*Business term*]
SQUAM	Squamous [*Cell*] [*Oncology*] (DAVI)
SQUANK	Simpson Quadrature Used Adaptively - Noise Killed (PDAA)
SQUAP	Supplementary Quality Assurance Provisions
SQUAPP	Software Quality Assurance Program Plan
SQUARE	Specifying Queries as Relational Expressions [*Programming language*] [*1973*] [*Computer science*] (CSR)
SQUARE	Square [*Commonly used*] (OPSA)
SQUARE	Statistical Quality Analysis Report (MHDB)
Squarel	Square Industries, Inc. [*Associated Press*] (SAG)
SQUARES	Squares [*Commonly used*] (OPSA)
SQUASH	Squatters Action for Secure Homes [*An association*] (BUAC)
Squibb Auc	Squibb on Auctioneers [*2nd ed.*] [*1891*] [*A publication*] (DLA)
SQUID	Semiconducting Quantum Interference Device (MCD)
SQUID	Sperry Quick Updating of Internal Documentation (IEEE)
SQUID	Submerged Quick Intervention Device [*Human-powered submarine*]
SQUID	Superconducting Quantum Interference Detector [*or Device*] [*For study of magnetic fields*]
SQUID	Superconducting Quantum Interference Device [*Physics*]
SQUIRE	Submarine Quickened Response
SQUIRE	System for Quick Ultra-Fiche-Based Information Retrieval [*Computer science*] (PDAA)
SQUO	Squadron-Officer [*British military*] (DSUE)
SQUOD	Selected Quantile Output Device [*Electronics*]
SQUOFF	Squadron-Officer [*British military*] (DSUE)
SQUP	Software Quality Assurance Plan [*Computer science*] (IAA)
SQW	Single Quantum Well [*Physics*]
SQW	Squarewave (MSA)
SQWV	Squarewave
SQX	Sulfaquinoxaline [*or (Sulfanilamido)quinoxaline*] [*Animal antibiotic*]
sq yd	Square Yard (CDAI)
SQZE	Stark Quadratic Zeeman Effect [*Physics*]
SQZGR	Squeeze Grip
SR	Air-Cushion Vehicle built by Saunders Roe [*England*] [*Usually used in combination with numerals*]
SR	Air Search RADAR Receiver [*Shipborne*]
SR	General Society, Sons of the Revolution (EA)
SR	New York State Reporter [*A publication*] (DLA)
SR	Partiia Sotsialistov Revolyutsionerov [*Socialist Revolutionary Party*] [*Russian Political party*] (PPE)
SR	Regina Public Library, Saskatchewan [*Library symbol National Library of Canada*] (NLC)
SR	Russell Senate Office Building [*Washington, D.C.*]
SR	Saarlandischer Rundfunk [*Radio network*] [*West Germany*]
SR	Safety Recommendation (AAG)
SR	Safety Release [*Army*]
S/R	Safety Relief Valve [*Nuclear energy*] (NRCH)
S/R	Safety Representative [*Insurance*]
SR	Safety Rod [*Nuclear energy*] (NRCH)
SR	Salva Ratificatione [*On Condition of Ratification*] [*Latin*]
SR	Sample Rate
SR	Sanctioned Ritual [*British Slang*]
SR	Santa Rosa [*Diocesan abbreviation*] [*California*] (TOCD)
SR	Sarcoplasmic Reticulum [*Anatomy*]
SR	Saturable Reactor
SR	Saturation Recovery [*NMR imaging*]
SR	Saudi Riyal [*Monetary unit*] (BJA)
SR	Savannah River Operations Office (DOGT)
SR	Savannah River Test Pile [*Nuclear energy*] (NRCH)
SR	Sawyer Rifle
SR	Scanning Radiometer
SR	Scan Radius
SR	Scan Rate
SR	Scan Ratio (MCD)
SR	Schmidt-Ruppin [*Strain*] [*Medicine*] (DB)
SR	Schooner [*Shipping*] (ROG)
SR	Schumann Runge [*Spectral region*]
SR	Scientific Report
SR	Scientific Research
SR	Scoring Reliability (MCD)
SR	Scottish Regional [*Council*]
SR	Scottish Rifles [*Military unit*] [*British*]
SR	Screen (DAVI)
SR	Scripture Reader (ROG)
SR	Seaman Recruit [*Navy*]
SR	Seaplane Reconnaissance Aircraft
SR	Search and Reconnaissance [*Air Force*]
SR	Search and Recovery [*Military*]
SR	Search and Rescue
SR	Search and Retrieve [*Computer science*] (TELE)
SR	Search RADAR
SR	Secondary RADAR (IAA)
SR	Second-Harmonic Resonance (MCD)
SR	Second Routing (MCD)
SR	Secretion Rate [*Endocrinology*]
SR	Section Report
SR	Sedimentation Rate
SR	Seer (WGA)
SR	Segment Root (IAA)
SR	Seizure Resistant [*Neurology*] (DAVI)
SR	Selective Ringing
SR	Selenium Rectifier [*Electronics*]
SR	Self Raising (WDAA)
SR	Self-Rectifying
SR	Semantic Reaction
SR	Senate Recedes
SR	Senate Report
SR	Senate Resolution
SR	Send and Receive
SR	Send Receive (NITA)
Sr.	Senior (TBD)
SR	Senior
sr	Senior (DD)
SR	Senior Registrar
SR	Senior Reviewer
SR	Senor [*Mister*] [*Spanish*]
SR	Sensibility Reciprocal (WGA)
SR	Sensitivity Ratio
SR	Sensitivity Response [*Cell*] [*Radiology*]
SR	Sensitization Response
SR	Sensory Rhodopsin [*Biochemistry*]
SR	Separate Rations [*Military*]
SR	Series Number [*Online database field identifier*]
SR	Series Relay [*Electronics*] (IAA)
SR	Service Record [*Military*]
SR	Service Report
SR	Service Rifle [*British military*] (DMA)
S-R	Set-Reset [*Flip-Flop*] [*Computer science*]
SR	Settlement Register [*Computer science*]
SR	Severe, Right-Moving [*Thunderstorm*]
SR	Sex Ratio [*Biology*]
SR	Shaft Rate (NVT)
SR	Sharpened Romberg [*Equilibrium*]
SR	Shift Register
SR	Shift Reverse
SR	Shift Right
SR	Shipment [*or Shipping*] Request
S/R	Shipper/Receiver [*Difference*]
SR	Shipping Receipt [*Business term*]
SR	Ship Repair Ratings
SR	Ships Records (MCD)
SR	Ship-to-Shore RADAR [*or Radio*] (DEN)
SR	Shock Related
SR	Shock Resistance
SR	Shorthair Guinea Pig [*Medicine*] (DMAA)
SR	Short Range
SR	Short Rate
SR	Short Run [*Economics*]

SR	Shunt Reactor [*Electricity*] (IAA)
SR	Shutdown Request [*NASA*] (KSC)
SR	Side Rails [*On a bed*] [*Medicine*]
SR	Sierra Railroad Co. (IIA)
SR	Sigma Reaction
SR	Signal Regulation (IAA)
S/R	Signal-to-Noise Ratio [*Radio*] (WDMC)
SR	Signor [*Mister*] [*Italian*]
SR	Silicon Rectifier
SR	Silicon Rubber
SR	Simian Rotavirus [*Pathology*]
SR	Simla Rifles [*British military*] (DMA)
SR	Simple Reaction (DB)
SR	Simulation Report
SR	Single Reduction
SR	Sinus Rhythm [*Medicine*]
SR	Sinus Roris [*Bay of Dew*] [*Lunar area*]
SR	Sir
SR	Sister
SR	Sisters of Reparation of the Sacred Wounds of Jesus (TOCD)
SR	Skagit River Railroad (IIA)
SR	Skeleton Records [*Army*]
SR	Skin Resistance [*Physiology*] (MAE)
SR	Skywave Synchronization (DEN)
SR	Slant Range
SR	Slew Rate
SR	Sling Ring
SR	Slip Ring [*Electricity*]
SR	Sloane Ranger [*Member of a British social set satirized in "The Official Sloane Ranger Handbook, The First Guide to What Really Matters in Life"*] [*Name is derived from Sloane Square in Chelsea*]
SR	Slow Release [*Electronics*]
SR	Slow Release Relay [*Electronics*] (IAA)
SR	Slow Running (IAA)
SR	Small Ring
S-R	Smooth-Rough Variation [*Medicine*] (MAE)
SR	Socialist Revolutionary [*Former USSR*]
SR	Social Register
SR	Society of Radiographers (EAIO)
SR	Society of Rheology [*Later, SoR*] (EA)
SR	Society of Rosicrucians (EA)
SR	Soft Radiation (IAA)
SR	Solar Radiation
SR	Solar Reference
SR	Solicitor's Recommendation [*Internal Revenue Bureau*] [*United States*] [*A publication*] (DLA)
SR	Solid Rocket
SR	Soluble, Repository [*With reference to penicillin*]
SR	Soror [*Sister*]
SR	Sorter Reader
SR	Sortie Rate (MCD)
SR	Sound Ranging
SR	Sound Rating (IEEE)
SR	Sound Recordings [*US Copyright Office class*]
SR	Sound Reinforcement (NTCM)
SR	Sound Report
SR	Source Range [*Nuclear energy*] (NRCH)
SR	Southern Railway (EFIS)
SR	Southern Rhodesia [*Later, Zimbabwe*]
SR	Southern Rhodesia High Court Reports [*A publication*] (DLA)
SR	Sparebanken Rogaland [*Rogaland Savings Bank*] [*Norway*]
S/R	Spares Requirement
SR	Special Reconnaissance [*Special Operations Force*] (DOMA)
SR	Special Register
SR	Special Regulations [*Military*]
SR	Special Report
SR	Special Reserve
SR	Specification Requirement
SR	Specific Range
SR	Specific Reactivity [*Exhaust emissions*] [*Automotive engineering*]
SR	Specific Release (DB)
SR	Specific Resistance (IAA)
SR	Spec Racer [*Automotive classification*]
SR	Spectral Recording [*Trademark of Dolby Laboratories Licensing Corp.*]
SR	Speculative Resource [*Minerals*]
SR	Speech Recognition
SR	Speed Recorder (IEEE)
SR	Speed Regulator
SR	Spelling Reform (ADA)
SR	Spencer Rolls Direct
SR	Spin-Rotation [*Physics*]
SR	Split Ring [*Technical drawings*]
SR	Spontaneous Discharge Rate [*Audiology*]
SR	Sports Racer [*Automotive classification*]
S/R	Spotter Reconnaissance [*Air Force British*]
S-R	Spring Inflow-River Inflow [*Geology*]
SR	Square [*Ship's rigging*] (ROG)
SR	Stable Recipient [*Medicine*]
SR	Staff Report
SR	Stage of Resistance [*in General-Adaptation Syndrome*]
SR	Stage Right [*A stage direction*]
SR	Standardization Report
SR	Standard Range Approach [*Aviation*]
SR	Standard Register [*NYSE symbol*] (TTSB)
SR	Standard Repair (AAG)
SR	Standard Requirement
SR	Standard Resistor (IAA)
SR	Standard Speed Radial [*Automobile tires*]
SR	Star Route [*A type of rural postal delivery route*]
SR	Starting Relay (DEN)
SR	Starting Resistor (IAA)
SR	Statement of Requirements [*NASA*] (MCD)
SR	State Register
SR	State Relay [*Telecommunications*] (OTD)
SR	Stateroom (MSA)
SR	Stationery Request (MCD)
SR	Station Radio [*British*]
SR	Station Regulation
SR	Statstjanstemannens Riksforbund [*National Association of Salaried Employees in Government Service*] [*Sweden*]
SR	Status Register [*Computer science*]
SR	Status Report
SR	Status Review [*NASA*] (NASA)
SR	Statutes Revised [*A publication*] (DLA)
SR	Statutory Rule (ADA)
SR	Steep Rock Resources, Inc. [*Toronto Stock Exchange symbol*]
sr	Steradian [*Symbol*] [*SI unit of solid angle*]
Sr	Steradians (COE)
SR	Steroid Receptor [*Endocrinology*]
SR	Stimulation Ratio (DB)
S-R	Stimulus-Response
SR	Stirred-Tank Reactor (IAA)
SR	Stochastic Resonance [*Dynamical systems*]
SR	Stock Replacement (AAG)
SR	Stock Report
SR	Stoichiometric Ratio [*Chemistry*]
SR	Stomach Rumble [*Medicine*] (AAMN)
SR	Storage and Repair (MCD)
SR	Storage Rack
SR	Storage Register
SR	Storage Room
SR	Stove or Range
SR	Stransky-Regala [*Syndrome*] [*Medicine*] (DB)
SR	Strategic Reconnaissance [*Military*]
SR	Strategic Research (MCD)
SR	Street Rod [*Automobile modification*]
SR	Stress-Rupture (MCD)
SR	Stretch Reflex (MAF)
SR	Strike Rate (ADA)
SR	Stripe Rot [*Plant pathology*]
SR	Strong Reactive [*Laboratory science*] (DAVI)
Sr	Strontium [*Chemical element*]
Sr	Strouhal Number [*IUPAC*]
SR	Study Regulation (MCD)
SR	Study Requirement [*Air Force*]
SR	Styrene Rubber
SR	Subject Ratio
SR	Submarine Recorder [*British military*] (DMA)
SR	Subroutine [*Computer science*] (AAG)
SR	Subscriber Register
SR	Sugar Requirements and Quotas
SR	Sulfonamide-Resistant [*Microbiology*]
SR	Summary Report
SR	Sunrise (NAKS)
SR	Superficial Reflex [*Neurology*] (DAVI)
SR	Superior Rectus [*Ophthalmology*] (MAE)
SR	Supervisor (TEL)
SR	Supplemental Report
SR	Supplementary Regulation
SR	Supplementary Reserve [*British military*] (DMA)
SR	Supply Room
SR	Supporting Research [*Military*]
SR	Support Reaction Load (NRCH)
SR	Support Request [*or Requirement*] (KSC)
SR	Support Room (MCD)
SR	Suppressor Receptor [*Embryology*]
SR	Supreme Court of Quebec, Reports [*A publication*] (DLA)
SR	Su Remesa [*Your Remittance*] [*Spanish Business term*]
SR	Surface Roughness
SR	Surgical Removal (DAVI)
SR	Surinam [*ANSI two-letter standard code*] (CNC)
sr	Surinam [*MARC country of publication code Library of Congress*] (LCCP)
SR	Surtax Rate (MHDW)
SR	Surveillance RADAR [*Air Force*]
SR	Surveillance Requirement [*Nuclear Regulatory Commission*] (GFGA)
SR	Surveying Recorder [*Navy rating British*]
SR	Surveyor [*British military*] (DMA)
SR	Sustained Release [*Pharmacy*]
SR	Suture Removal [*Surgery*] (DAVI)
SR	Sveriges Radio
SR	Swissair [*Airline*] [*ICAO designator*]
SR	Switched Reluctance
SR	Switch Register
SR	Synchrotron Radiation [*High-energy physics*]
SR	Systemic Resistance [*Medicine*] (MAE)
SR	System Requirement (SSD)
SR	Systems Research (DAVI)

SR.............	Systems Review [*Medicine*]
SR.............	Union of Soviet Socialist Republics [*IYRU nationality code*] (IYR)
SR-11.........	Sapporo Rat (Virus)
SRA............	Sair Aviation [*Canada ICAO designator*] (FAAC)
SRA............	San Ramon [*Costa Rica*] [*Seismograph station code, US Geological Survey*] (SEIS)
SRA............	Santo Rosa [*Brazil*] [*Airport symbol*] (AD)
SRA............	Saskatchewan Archives, Regina, Saskatchewan [*Library symbol National Library of Canada*] (NLC)
SRA............	Satanic Ritual Abuse
SRA............	Satellite RADAR Altimetry [*Instrumentation*]
SRA............	Scanning Radar Altimeter [*Marine science*] (OSRA)
SRA............	Science Research Associates (AEBS)
SRA............	Scottish Records Association (DBA)
SRA............	Scottish Rifle Association (DI)
SRA............	Screw Research Association (EA)
SRA............	Scuba Retailers Association (EA)
SRA............	Sea Rangers' Association [*British*] (DI)
SRA............	Selected Reserve Augmentee (DOMA)
SRA............	Selective Restricted Availability (MCD)
SRA............	Self-Regulatory Agency [*Securities*] [*British*]
SrA.............	Senior Airman
SRA............	Senior Residential Appraiser [*Society of Real Estate Appraisers*] [*Designation awarded by*]
SRA............	Separate Reporting Activities [*Army*]
SRA............	Service and Regulatory Announcement, Department of Agriculture [*A publication*] (DLA)
SRA............	Servicemen's Readjustment Act
SRA............	Shift Register Available
SRA............	Ship Radio Authorization [*Army*] (AABC)
SRA............	Ship Repair Agreement [*MARAD*] (TAG)
SRA............	Ship Replaceable Assembly (MCD)
SRA............	Shipyard Restricted Availability [*Navy*] (CAAL)
SRA............	Shooters' Rights Association [*British*] (DBA)
SRA............	Shop-Replaceable Assembly [*NASA*]
SRA............	Short-Range Acquisition (MCD)
SRA............	Short Range Aids [*USCG*] (TAG)
SRA............	Short Reflex Arc
SRA............	Significant Regulatory Action [*Office of Management and Budget*] (GFGA)
SRA............	Simultaneous Range Adcock Antenna [*Military RADAR*]
SRA............	Singapore Robot Association (BUAC)
SRA............	Small, Replaceable Assembly (RDA)
SRA............	Smoker's Rights Alliance (EA)
SRA............	Snail Racing Association (BUAC)
SRA............	Social Research and Applications [*Research center*] (RCD)
SRA............	Social Research Association [*British*]
SRA............	Social Responsibility Auditing (ADA)
SRA............	Society for Research on Adolescence (NTPA)
SRA............	Society for Risk Analysis (NTPA)
SRA............	Society of Research Administration (BUAC)
SRA............	Society of Research Administrators (EA)
SRA............	Society of Residential Appraisers [*Later, AI*]
SRA............	Sociological Research Association (EA)
SRA............	Software Requirements Analysis
SRA............	Southern Rhodesia Artillery [*British military*] (DMA)
SRA............	Southern Rural Action, Inc.
SRA............	Spanish Refugee Aid (EA)
SRA............	Specialized Repair Activity
SRA............	Specially Reserved Area [*Australia*]
SRA............	Special Refractories Association [*Defunct*] (EA)
SRA............	Special Repair Activity (MCD)
SRA............	Special Rules Area
SRA............	Specular Reflectance Accessory [*Spectrophotometry*]
SRA............	Speedway Riders Association [*British*] (DBA)
SRA............	Spherical Radiation Absorber (MCD)
SRA............	Spin Reference Axis (KSC)
SRA............	Spleen Repopulating Activity [*Medicine*] (DMAA)
SRA............	Squash Rackets Association [*British*]
SRA............	Stabilization Reserve Account [*Health insurance*] (GHCT)
SRA............	Standard Reference Aerosol (PDAA)
SRA............	Standards of Readiness and Availability (NATG)
SRA............	State and Regional Associations of the United States [*A publication*]
SRA............	State Rail Authority [*Australia*] (BUAC)
SRA............	State Recreation Area [*State*] (EERA)
SRA............	Station Representatives Association (EA)
SRA............	Stearman Restorers Association (EA)
SRA............	Stock Record Account
SRA............	Strategic Resource Area (PDAA)
SRA............	Stratus Computer [*NYSE symbol*] (TTSB)
SRA............	Stratus Computer, Inc. [*NYSE symbol*] (SPSG)
SRA............	Stress Relieved Annealed [*Metallurgical engineering*]
SRA............	Structures Research Associates
SRA............	Subminiature Rotary Actuator
SRA............	Sugar Rationing Administration [*Department of Agriculture*] [*Ceased functions, 1948*]
SRA............	Sulforicinoleic Acid [*Organic chemistry*]
SRA............	Sun's Right Ascension [*Astrology*] (ROG)
SRA............	Supplemental Retirement Annuities
SRA............	Support Requirements Analysis [*NASA*] (NASA)
SRA............	Surgeon Rear-Admiral [*British military*]
SRA............	Surveillance RADAR Approach
SRA............	System Reaction Analysis [*Bell System*]
SRA............	System Reliability Analysis
SRA............	System Requirements Analysis

SRA	Systems Research and Applications Corp. [*Arlington, VA*] (TSSD)
SRAA	Scholastic Rowing Association of America (EA)
SRAA	Senior Army Advisor (AABC)
SRAA	Statistical Record of Asian Americans [*A publication*]
SRAAG	Senior Army Advisor, Army National Guard (AABC)
SRAAM	Short-Range Air-to-Air Missile (MCD)
SRAAR	Senior Army Advisor, Army Reserve (AABC)
SRAB	Allan Blair Memorial Clinic, Regina, Saskatchewan [*Library symbol National Library of Canada*] (NLC)
SRAC	Alcoholism Commission of Saskatchewan, Regina, Saskatchewan [*Library symbol National Library of Canada*] (NLC)
SRAC	Safe Return Amnesty Committee (EA)
SRAC	Sears Roebuck Acceptance Corp.
SRAC	Second Regional Assistance Command [*US advisory command*] [*Vietnam*] (VNW)
SRAC	Short Run Average Costs
SRAC	Societe Royale d'Astronomie du Canada
SRAC	Supplier Relations Action Council (AAEL)
SRACCMB....	Senior Aircraft Crewman Badge [*Military decoration*] (GFGA)
SrAcftCrmnBad...	Senior Aircraft Crewman Badge [*Military decoration*] (AABC)
SR-ACK.......	Service Request Acknowledgment [*Air Force*] (CET)
SRACR.......	Southern Rhodesia Armoured Car Regiment [*British military*] (DMA)
SRAD	Ship's Restricted Availability Date [*Navy*] (DNAB)
SRAD	Solar Radiation (NOAA)
SRAD	Steerable Right-Angle Drive (DNAB)
SR/AD........	Supporting Research and Advanced Development
SRAD	Surveillance RADAR (MCD)
SRAE	Solar Radio Astronomy Experiment
SRAEL........	Labour Market Planning and Information Resource Centre, Saskatchewan Department of Advanced Education and Manpower, Regina, Saskatchewan [*Library symbol National Library of Canada*] (NLC)
SRAEN	Systeme de Reference pour la Determination de l'Affaiblissement Equivalent pour la Nettete [*Master telephone transmission reference system*]
SRAEW	Women's Services Branch, Saskatchewan Department of Advanced Education and Manpower, Regina, Saskatchewan [*Library symbol National Library of Canada*] (NLC)
SRAF	Archibald Foundation, Regina, Saskatchewan [*Library symbol National Library of Canada*] (NLC)
SRAF	Social Revolutionary Anarchist Federation (EA)
SRAF	Standby Reserve of the Armed Forces
SRAFO	Senior Royal Air Force Officer [*British military*] (DMA)
SRAG..........	Saskatchewan Department of Agriculture, Regina, Saskatchewan [*Library symbol National Library of Canada*] (NLC)
SRAG..........	Semiactive RADAR Antiair Guidance System
SRAG..........	Space Radiation Analysis Group [*NASA*] (NASA)
SRAG..........	Sydney Rainforest Action Group (EERA)
SRAGE........	Shared Services, Agriculture Canada [*Services en Commun, Agriculture Canada*], Regina, Saskatchewan [*Library symbol National Library of Canada*] (NLC)
SRAGR........	Research Station, Agriculture Canada [*Station de Recherches, Agriculture Canada*] Regina, Saskatchewan [*Library symbol National Library of Canada*] (NLC)
SRAI	Social Role Adjustment Instrument (DB)
SRAI	Soybean Research Advisory Institute [*Terminated, 1984*] (EGAO)
SRAI	Supercat Race Association International (EA)
SRAIS	Statewide Resource Information and Accounting System [*State*] (EERA)
SRAM	Semirandom Access Memory
SRAM	Short-Range Attack Missile [*Military*]
SRAM	Skill Qualification Test Requirements Alert Message
SRAM	Some Remarks on Abstract Machines [*Computer science*]
SRAM	Sort Reentrant Access Method [*Computer science*] (CIST)
SRAM	SQT [*Ship's Qualification Trial*] Requirements Alert Message
SRAM	Static Random Access Memory [*Computer science*]
SRAM	System Rehabilitation and Modernization (MCD)
SRAMA	Spring Research and Manufacturers' Association (EAIO)
SRAMS	Short-Range Attack Missile System (IAA)
SRAM(T)......	Short-Range Attack Missile (Tactical) [*Military*]
SRAN	Short-Range Aids to Navigation [*Navy*]
SRAN	Skill Qualification Test Requirements Alert Notice
SRAN	Stock Record Account Number (AFM)
SRAN	Surgical Resident's Admission Note (DAVI)
SRANA	Shrine Recorders Association of North America (EA)
SRANC	Southern Rhodesia African National Congress
SR & A	Strategy, Research & Action [*Commercial firm British*]
SR & F	Selection, Referral, and Followup
SR & O	Statutory Rules and Orders [*England*] [*A publication*] (DLA)
SR & O and SI Rev...	Statutory Rules and Orders and Statutory Instruments Revised [*England*] [*A publication*] (DLA)
SR & P	Station Resources and Planning [*Navy*] (DNAB)
SR & PO	Station Resources and Planning Office [*Navy*] (DNAB)
SR & Q	Safety, Reliability, and Quality (NASA)
SR&Q.........	Safety, Reliability, and Quality (NAKS)
SR&QA.......	Safety, Reliability, and Quality Assurance (NAKS)
SR & QA	Safety, Reliability, and Quality Assurance (NASA)
SR&T	Supporting Research and Technology (AAGC)
SRAO	Supplemental Recreational Activities Overseas [*Red Cross*]
SRAP	Service Record and Allied Papers [*Military*]
SRAP	Slow Response Action Potentials [*Neurophysiology*]
SRAP	Standard Range Approach [*Aviation*]
SRAPI	Speech Recognition API [*All-Purpose Interface*] (PCM)
SRAPI	Speech Recognition Application Programming Interface Committee [*Microsoft Corp.*]

SRAPMA......	Science Research Associates Primary Mental Abilities [*Psychology*] (AEBS)
SRARAV......	Senior Army Aviator (AABC)
SRARAVB	Senior Army Aviator Badge [*Military decoration*] (GFGA)
SrArAvBad ...	Senior Army Aviator Badge [*Military decoration*]
SRARM........	Short-Range Antiradiation Missile
SRAS	Albert South Library, Regina, Saskatchewan [*Library symbol National Library of Canada*] (NLC)
SRAS	Southern Riverina Advisory Service [*Australia*]
SRAS	State Rural Assistance Scheme [*New South Wales*] [*State*] (EERA)
SRASA........	Small Retailers Association of South Australia
SRASM........	Short-Range Air-to-Surface Missile (MCD)
SRAT	Search RADAR Alignment Test [*Military*] (CAAL)
SRAT	Short-Range Applied Technology
SRAT-B.......	Self-Report Assertiveness Test for Boys
SRATC	Short-Run Average Total Cost [*Economics*]
SRATS	Solar Radiation and Thermospheric Structure [*Japanese satellite*]
SRATUC......	Southern Rhodesian African Trade Union Congress
SRAVC	Short-Run Average Variable Cost [*Economics*]
SRAW	Short-Range Antitank Weapon
SRaw	Specific Resistance, Airway [*Medicine*]
SRAX	Southern Air Transport, Inc. [*Air carrier designation symbol*]
SRB	Safety Review Board [*Nuclear energy*] (NRCH)
SRB	Schilpp, Reed B., Los Angeles CA [*STAC*]
SRB	Scientific Review Board [*Intergovernmental Oceanographic Commission*] (GFGA)
SRB	Seaplane Repair Base
SRB	Selective Reenlistment Bonus [*Military*] (AABC)
SRB	Self-Retaining Bolt
SRB	Send Receive Bomb (IAA)
SRB	Senior Review Board
SRB	Service Record Book [*Military*]
SRB	Service Request Block [*Computer science*] (BUR)
SRB	Sex Ratio at Birth [*Demographics*]
SRB	Sheftall Record Book [*A publication*] (BJA)
SRB	Sky Ranch for Boys (EA)
SRB	Software Release Bulletin [*A publication*] (COE)
SRB	Solar Reflectory Beacon
SRB	Solid-Rocket Booster [*NASA*]
SRB	Sorter Reader Buffer
SRB	Sorter Reader Buffered (NITA)
SRB	Source-Route Bridge [*Computer science*] (PCM)
SRB	Sparta, TN [*Location identifier FAA*] (FAAL)
SRB	Special Research Bureau [*Department of External Affairs*] [*Canada*]
SRB	Special Review Board [*Military*] (INF)
SRB	Specification Review Board [*Navy*] (DNAB)
SRB	Spherical Roller Bearing
SRB	State Research Bureau [*Secret police*] [*Uganda*]
SRB	State Revenue Board [*Victoria, Australia*]
SRB	Styrono Rubber Butadiene (NQ)
SRB	Subspecialty Requirements Board [*Navy*] (DNAB)
SRB	Suburban Air Freight, Inc. [*ICAO designator*] (FAAC)
SRB	Sulfate Reducing Bacteria
SRB	Sulfur Reducing Bacteria [*Diesel fuels*]
SRB	Support Research Branch [*Springfield Armory*]
SRB	Surface Radiation Budget [*Marine science*] (OSRA)
SRB	Survey and Reports Branch [*Division of Biometry and Applied Sciences, National Institute of Mental Health*] (GFGA)
SRB	System Review Board (MCD)
SRBA	Statistical Record of Black America [*A publication*]
SRBA	Students for the Right to Bear Arms (EA)
SRBAB	Solid-Rocket Booster Assembly Building [*NASA*] (NASA)
SRBC	Serum-Treated Red Blood Cell [*Clinical chemistry*]
SRBC	Sheep Red Blood Cell [s] [*Also, SRC*]
SRBC	Sickle Red Blood Cells [*Hematology*] (DAVI)
SRBC	Sunrise Bancorp [*NASDAQ symbol*] (NQ)
SRBC	Susquehanna River Basin Commission [*Federal government*] (EGAO)
SRBC	Susquehanna River Basin Compact [*Maryland, Pennsylvania, New York*]
SRBCP	Satellite Radiation Budget Climatology Project [*Marine science*] (OSRA)
SRBCSS.......	Scales for Rating the Behavioral Characteristics of Superior Students [*Educational test*]
SRBD	Sleep-Related Breathing Disorder [*Medicine*] (DMAA)
SRBDF	Solid-Rocket Booster Disassembly Facility [*NASA*] (NASA)
SRBDM	Short-Range Bomber Defense Missile
SRBM	Short-Range Ballistic Missile
SRBMI	BMI Finance, Regina, Saskatchewan [*Library symbol National Library of Canada*] (NLC)
SRBOC........	Super Rapid Bloom Off Board Chaff [*Navy*] (NVT)
SRBOW.......	Spontaneous Rupture of Bag of Water [*Obstetrics*] (DAVI)
SRBOW.......	Spontaneous Rupture of Bag of Waters [*Medicine*] (MEDA)
SRBP	Synthetic Resin Bonded Paper (IAA)
SRBPF	Solid-Rocket Booster Processing Facility [*NASA*] (NASA)
SRBR	Storage and Retrieval of Bibliographic References Program (EDAC)
SRBR	Surface Reflected Bottom Reflected (IAA)
SRBT	Single-Rod Burst Test [*Nuclear energy*] (NRCH)
SRBTRY.......	Sound Ranging Battery (IAA)
SRBUC........	Scientific Research in British Universities and Colleges [*Later, RBUPC*] [*British Library*]
SRC	AMF Sunfish Racing Class Association (EA)
SRC	Richland County Library, Columbia, SC [*OCLC symbol*] (OCLC)
SRC	Sacra Rituum Congregatio [*Sacred Congregation of Rites*] [*Latin*]
SRC	Safety Research Center [*Bureau of Mines*]
SRC	Safety Review Committee (COE)
SRC	Salinas Road [*California*] [*Seismograph station code, US Geological Survey*] (SEIS)
SRC	Sample Recovery Container [*NASA*] (KSC)
SRC	Sample Return Container [*NASA*] (NASA)
SRC	Sample Rock Container [*NASA*]
SRC	Sarcoma
SRC	Saskatchewan Research Council [*University of Saskatchewan*] [*Research center*] (RCD)
SRC	Saturable Reactor Coil
SRC	Scheduled Removal Component (MCD)
SRC	Schedule Request Confirmation (SSD)
SRC	Science Research Council [*Later, SERC*] [*British*]
SRC	Scientific Research Committee [*Australia*]
SRC	Scleroderma Renal Crisis [*Medicine*]
SRC	Scott's Hospitality, Inc. [*Toronto Stock Exchange symbol*]
SRC	Searcy, AR [*Location identifier FAA*] (FAAL)
SRC	Secured Returns Code [*IRS*]
SRC	Securities Research Co.
SRC	Security Connecticut Corp. [*NYSE symbol*] (SAG)
SRC	Sedimented Red Cell [*Hematology*] (MAE)
SRC	Selective Ride Control [*Suspension systems*] [*Automotive engineering*]
SRC	Semiconductor Research Cooperative
SRC	Semiconductor Research Corp.
SRC	Senate Rail Caucus (EA)
SRC	Send Register Control [*Computer science*]
SRC	Se Ruega Contestacion [*The Favor of a Reply Is Requested*] [*Spanish*]
SRC	Servants of Our Lady Queen of the Clergy [*Roman Catholic women's religious order*]
SRC	Sheep Red Cell [s] [*Also, SRBC*]
SRC	Shop Resident Control (SAA)
SRC	Shutdown Reactor Cooling [*Nuclear energy*] (NRCH)
SRC	Signal Reserve Corps
SRC	Silicon Readout Cell
SRC	Silicon Rectifier Column
SRC	Single Round Container [*for toxic chemicals*] [*Army*]
SRC	Ski Retailers Council [*Inactive*] (EA)
SRC	Slow-Recovery Capsules [*Pharmacy*]
SRC	Snyder Research Co. [*Information service or system*] (IID)
SRC	Social Rehabilitation Center [*Psychology*] (DAVI)
SRC	Social Rehabilitation Clinic (EA)
SRC	Societe Royale du Canada [*Royal Society of Canada - RSC*]
SRC	Society of Friends Community Relations Committee [*British*]
SRC	Solvent-Refined Coal
SRC	Sound Ranging Central (IAA)
SRC	Sound Ranging Control
SRC	Sound Recording Co. [*Record label*]
SRC	Source
SRC	Source Range Channel (IEEE)
SRC	Southeast Asia Resource Center (EA)
SRC	Southern Regional Council (EA)
SRC	Southwest Radio Church [*An association*]
SRC	Southwest Research Corp.
SRC	Space Research Council [*British*]
SRC	Spares Receiving Checklist (NRCH)
SRC	Special Regular Commissions [*Army British*]
SRC	Special Release Card (IAA)
SRC	Special Research Contract (AAGC)
SRC	Specific Reactant Consumption [*Engine*]
SRC	Specimen Research Centrifuge (SSD)
SRC	Specimen Return Container (SAA)
SRC	Specimen Return Control (SAA)
SRC	Speech Recognition Computer
SRC	Standard Requirements Code [*Military*]
SRC	Standards Review Committee [*American Occupational Therapy Association*]
SRC	Station Reliability Coordinator
SRC	Statistical Record of Children [*A publication*]
SRC	Statuts Revises du Canada [*Revised Statutes of Canada*] [*Database Federal Department of Justice*] [*Information service or system*] (CRD)
SRC	Stereo Radio Cassette
SRC	Sterility Research Center [*Public Health Service*] (GRD)
SRC	Steroid Receptor Coactivator [*Endocrenalogy*]
SRC	Stock Record Card [*Military*]
SRC	Stored Response Chain [*Computer science*] (BARN)
SRC	Strasburg Railroad Co. [*AAR code*]
SRC	Strategic Reconnaissance Center [*Air Force*] (DOMA)
SRC	Stray Radiation Chamber
SRC	Stuart's Lower Canada Reports [*A publication*] (DLA)
SRC	Student Reaction to College [*Student attitudes test*]
SRC	Students' Representative Council [*British*]
SRC	Subject-Field Reference Code (ADA)
SRC	Submarine Rescue Chamber (MCD)
SRC	Subrenal Capsule (DB)
SRC	Subsidiary Record Categories [*Telecommunications*] (OTD)
SRC	Support Review Code (MCD)
SRC	Survey Research Center [*Oregon State University*] [*Research center*] (RCD)
SRC	Survey Research Center [*University of Kentucky*] [*Research center*] (RCD)
SRC	Survival Recovery Center (COE)
SRC	Sustained-Release Capsule [*Pharmacology*]
SRC	Swiss Red Cross

SRC	Synchronous Remote Control
SRC	Synchrotron Radiation Center [*University of Wisconsin - Madison*] [*Research center*] (RCD)
SRC	Syracuse Research Corp. [*New York*] [*Information service or system*] (IID)
SRC	Systems Release Certification [*Social Security Administration*]
SRC	Systems Research Configuration
SRC/2	Student Reactions to College: Two Year College Edition [*Research Staff of Educational Testing Service*] (TES)
SRC/4	Student Reactions to College: Four Year College Edition [*Researchh Staff of Educational Testing Service*] (TES)
SRCA	Saskatchewan Department of Consumer Affairs, Regina, Saskatchewan [*Library symbol National Library of Canada*] (NLC)
SRCA	Slovenian Research Center of America (EA)
SRCA	Specific Red Cell Adherence [*Test*] [*Clinical chemistry*]
SRCA	Subrenal Capsule Assay (DB)
SRCAS	Safety-Related Control Air System [*Nuclear energy*] (NRCH)
SRCB	Canadian Bible College, Regina, Saskatchewan [*Library symbol National Library of Canada*] (NLC)
SRCB	Software Requirements Change Board [*NASA*] (NASA)
SRCB	Software Requirements Control Board [*NASA*] (NASA)
SRCBC	Serum Reserve Cholesterol Binding Capacity [*Medicine*] (DMAA)
SRCBD	Software Requirements Change Board Directive [*NASA*] (NASA)
SRCBD	Software Requirements Control Board Directive [*NASA*] (NASA)
SRCC	Senior Control Center [*Air Force*]
SRCC	Sensor Referenced and Computer Controlled [*For remote manipulators*]
SRCC	Shift, Rotate, Check, Control (IAA)
SRCC	Simplex Remote Communications Central
SRCC	Solar Rating and Certification Corp. (EA)
SRCC	Strikes, Riots, and Civil Commotions [*Insurance*]
SrcCp	Source Capital, Inc. [*Associated Press*] (SAG)
SRCD	Set-Reset Clocked Data [*Computer science*]
SRCD	Society for Research in Child Development (EA)
SRCD	Society of Richmond County Descendants (EA)
SRCE	First Source Corp. [*NASDAQ symbol*] (NQ)
SrceCap	Source Capital Corp. [*Associated Press*] (SAG)
SR-CEF	Schmidt-Ruppin Chick Embryo Fibroblast [*s*]
SrceMed	Source Media, Inc. [*Associated Press*] (SAG)
SrceOne25 ...	Source One Mortgage Services [*Associated Press*] (SAG)
SrceSrv	Source Services Corp. [*Associated Press*] (SAG)
SRCG	Safety Razor Collectors Guild (EA)
SRCH	Search (AAG)
SRCI	Safety-Related Controls and Instrumentation [*Nuclear energy*] (NRCH)
SRCI	Survey Research Consultants International, Inc. [*Information service or system*] (IID)
SRCL	Security Requirements Check List (MCD)
SRCL	Stericycle, Inc. [*NASDAQ symbol*] (SAG)
SRCM	Savonius Rotor Current Meter
SRCM	Sisters of Reparation of the Congregation of Mary [*Roman Catholic religious order*]
SRCM	Source Media [*NASDAQ symbol*] (TTSB)
SRCM	Source Media, Inc. [*NASDAQ symbol*] (SAG)
SRCMA	Steel Radiator and Convector Manufacturers' Association [*British*] (BI)
SRCMLT	Standing Representative Committee for Medical Laboratory Technology in the EEC [*European Economimc Community*] [*England*] (EAIO)
SRCMP	Southern Rhodesia Corps of Military Police [*British military*] (DMA)
SRCN	State Registered Children's Nurse (WDAA)
SRCNET	Science and Engineering Research Council Network [*Later, SERCNET*]
SRCNET	SRC Network (NITA)
SRCO	Sealright Co. [*NASDAQ symbol*] (TTSB)
SRCO	Sealright Co., Inc. [*Kansas City, MO*] [*NASDAQ symbol*] (NQ)
SRCO	Selected Regardless of Race, Color, Creed, or National Orgin (SAA)
SrcOne	Source One Mortgage Services [*Associated Press*] (SAG)
SRCP	Short Range Construction Program [*Military*]
SRCP	Society of Retired Catholic Persons (EA)
SRCP	Special Reserve Components Program [*Military*]
SRCPP	Solvent Refined Coal Pilot Plant (BCP)
SRCR	Saskatchewan Culture and Recreation, Regina, Saskatchewan [*Library symbol National Library of Canada*] (NLC)
SRCR	SONAR Control Room
SRCR	Stability Regulated Controlled Rectifier
SRCR	System Run Control Record
SRCRA	Shipowners Refrigerated Cargo Research Association [*Research center British*] (IRUK)
SRCRC	Snake River Conservation Research Center [*University of Idaho*] [*Research center*] (RCD)
SRCS	Service (IAA)
SRCS	Special Reverse Charge (IAA)
SRCT	Standard Recovery Completion Time
SRCTG	Sales Representatives and Commercial Travellers Guild [*Australia*]
SRCU	Credit Union Central, Regina, Saskatchewan [*Library symbol National Library of Canada*] (NLC)
SRCU	Secretary's Records Correspondence Unit [*Department of Labor*]
SRD	Safety and Reliability Directorate [*England*] (IID)
SRD	San Andres [*Colombia*] [*Seismograph station code, US Geological Survey*] (SEIS)
SRD	Satellite Racing Development [*British*]
SRD	Scheduled Release Date (MCD)
SRD	Search & Rescue 22 [*British ICAO designator*] (FAAC)
SRD	Secret - Restricted Data [*Security classification*]

SRD	Seldom Reaches Destination
SRD	Selective Radiation Detector
SRD	Self-Reading Dosimeter (IEEE)
SRD	Self-Reported Delinquency (EDAC)
SRD	Serous Retinal Detachment [*Ophthalmology*]
SRD	Service Revealed Deficiency [*or Difficulty*]
SRD	Service Rum Diluted [*British military*] (DMA)
SRD	Shift Register Drive
S-RD	Shipper-Receiver Difference (NRCH)
SRD	Shuttle Requirements Definition [*NASA*] (NASA)
SRD	Shuttle Requirements Document [*NASA*] (NASA)
SRD	Silver Drake Resources [*Vancouver Stock Exchange symbol*]
SRD	Single Radial Diffusion [*or Immunodiffusion*] [*Analytical biochemistry*]
SRD	Small Rigid Dome
SRD	Society for the Relief of Distress [*British*]
SRD	Society for the Right to Die (EA)
SRD	Sodium Restricted Diet [*Medicine*] (DMAA)
SRD	Software Requirements Document [*Computer science*]
SRD	Soluble, Repository, Plus Dihydrostreptomycin [*Referring to penicillin*] [*Pharmacology*] (DAVI)
SRD	Special Research Detachment [*Army*]
SR-D	Spectral Recording-Digital [*Sound Technology*] (PS)
SRD	Stafford Road [*Wolverhampton*] [*British depot code*]
SRD	Standard Rate and Data (IAA)
SRD	Standard Reference Data
SRD	Standard Repair Design [*Navy*] (MCD)
SRD	Standard Reporting Designator (MCD)
SRD	State Registered Dietician [*British*] (WDAA)
SRD	State Registered Dietitian
SRD	Statistical Research Division [*Census*] (OICC)
SRD	Step Recovery Diode
SRD	Studio Reference Disc [*Prosonus*] [*Electronic music*]
SRD	Super-Radiant Diode
SRD	Surplus Release Date (AAGC)
SRD	Sutherland Resources [*Vancouver Stock Exchange symbol*]
SRD	Swing Rate Discriminator (IAA)
SRD	Systems Requirements Document [*NASA*]
Srd	Thiouridine [*Also, S, SU*] [*A nucleoside*]
SRDA	Dunlop Art Gallery, Regina, Saskatchewan [*Library symbol National Library of Canada*] (NLC)
SRDA	Search RADAR Designation Alignment (MCD)
SRDA	Sodium Removal Development Apparatus [*Nuclear energy*] (NRCH)
SRDAS	School Retrofit Design Analysis System (EDAC)
SRDAS	Service Recording and Data Analysis System (IEEE)
SRDB	Scientific Research and Development Branch [*Home Office*] [*British*] (IRUK)
SRDC	Shopfitting Research and Development Council [*British*] (BI)
SRDC	Southern Rural Development Center (WPI)
SRDC	Standard Reference Data Center
SRDC	State Rural Development Councils (USGC)
SRDC	Sugar Research and Development Corp. (EERA)
SRDCS	Simulation Reconfiguration Data Collection Subsystem (SSD)
SRDD	Sorbent Regenerated Dialysate Delivery (DB)
SRDE	Signals Research and Development Establishment [*British*]
SRDE	Smallest Replaceable Defective Element
SRDG	Software Research and Development Group [*University of Calgary*] [*Research center*] (RCD)
SRDH	Subsystems Requirements Definition Handbook [*NASA*] (NASA)
SRDI	Safety-Related Display Instrumentation [*Nuclear energy*] (NRCH)
SRDL	Saskatchewan Department of Labour, Regina, Saskatchewan [*Library symbol National Library of Canada*] (NLC)
SRDL	Semiconductor Research and Development Laboratory (IAA)
SRDL	Signals Research and Development Laboratory [*Army British*]
SRDM	Subrate Data Multiplexer [*Telecommunications*] (TEL)
SRDP	Sulawesi Regional Development Project [*Coordinated by Indonesian and Canadian governments*] (ECON)
SRDS	Shop Repair Data Sheets
SRDS	Single Requirements Determination System
SRDS	Standard Rate and Data Service, Inc. [*Information service or system*] (MCD)
SRDS	Standard Reference Data System (DIT)
SRDS	Systems Research and Development Service [*FAA*] (MCD)
SRDT	Single Radial Diffusion Test [*Medicine*] (DMAA)
SRDT	Single Rotating Directional Transmission [*Military*] (CAAL)
SRE	Sanctae Romanae Ecclesiae [*Of the Most Holy Roman Church*] [*Latin*]
SRE	Sancta Romana Ecclesia [*Most Holy Roman Church*] [*Latin*]
SRE	Saskatchewan Department of the Environment, Regina, Saskatchewan [*Library symbol National Library of Canada*] (NLC)
SRE	Scanning Reference Electrode (MCD)
SRE	Schedule of Recent Experience [*Psychometrics*]
SRE	Search RADAR Element (IAA)
SRE	Seminole, OK [*Location identifier FAA*] (FAAL)
SRE	Sending Reference Equivalent (NITA)
SRE	Send Reference Equivalent, Search RADAR [*Telecommunications*] (TEL)
SRE	Senior-Reliability Engineer (IAA)
SRE	Series Relay [*Electronics*]
SRE	Serum Response Element [*Genetics*]
SRE	Serum-Response Enhancer [*Genetics*]
SRE	Shelby's Rabbit Eater [*In model name Omni SRE, proposed for Dodge car designed by Carroll Shelby*]
SRE	Signaling Range Extender [*Telecommunications*] (TEL)
SRE	Single Region Execution
SRE	Single Rotation Engine (IAA)

SRE	Single Round Effectiveness (NATG)
SRE	Single Rural Eligible [Classified advertising]
SRE	Site Resident Engineer [Telecommunications] (TEL)
SRE	Society for Reproductive Surgeons (EA)
SRE	Society of Recreation Executives (EA)
SRE	Society of Relay Engineers [British]
SRE	Society of Reliability Engineers (EA)
SRE	Society of Reproduction Engineers [Later, IAVCM] (EA)
SRE	Society of Reproductive Endocrinologists (EA)
SRE	Sodium Reactor Experiment [Nuclear energy]
SRE	Sound Reproduction Equipment (DEN)
SRE	Special Re-Education
SRE	Srednekan [Later, MGD] [Former USSR Geomagnetic observatory code]
SRE	Standard RADAR Environment
SRE	Statistical Record of the Environment [A publication]
SRE	STDN [Space Tracking and Data Network] Ranging Equipment [NASA] (GFGA)
SRE	Sterol Regulatory Element [Genetics]
SRE	Stray Radiant Energy
SRE	Sucre [Bolivia] [Airport symbol] (OAG)
SRE	Surveillance RADAR Element
SRE	Surveillance RADAR Equipment
SREA	Senior Real Estate Analyst [Society of Real Estate Appraisers] [Designation awarded by]
SREA	Society of Real Estate Appraisers [Later, AI] (EA)
SREA	Street Rod Equipment Association (EA)
SREA	Supplier Request for Engineering Approval
SREAE	AES Regina Weather Office, Environment Canada [Bureau Meteorologique du SEA de Regina, Environnement Canada] Saskatchewan [Library symbol National Library of Canada] (NLC)
SREB	Southern Regional Educational Board
SREB	Southern Regional Examinations Board [Education] (AIE)
SREBP	Sterol Regulatory Element Binding Protein [Biochemistry]
SREC	Executive Council, Regina, Saskatchewan [Library symbol National Library of Canada] (NLC)
SREC	Southern Rice Export Corp. (EA)
SRED	Saskatchewan Department of Education, Regina, Saskatchewan [Library symbol National Library of Canada] (NLC)
SREEP	Environmental Protection Service, Environment Canada [Service de la Protection de l'Environnement, Environnement Canada] Regina, Saskatchewan [Library symbol National Library of Canada] (NLC)
SR(EF)	Seaman Recruit (Electronics Field) [Navy rating] (DNAB)
SREG	[The] Standard Register Co. [NASDAQ symbol] (NQ)
SREG	Standing Register [Civil Service]
SREH	Storm-Relative Environmental Helicity [Marine science] (OSRA)
SREHP	Serine-Rich Entamoeba Histolytica Protein [Biochemistry]
SREI	Student Role Expectation Inventory
SREIW	Inland Waters Directorate, Environment Canada [Direction Generale des Eaux Interieures, Environnement Canada] Regina, Saskatchewan [Library symbol National Library of Canada] (NLC)
SREJ	Selective Reject [Computer science] (MHDI)
SREL	Savannah River Ecology Laboratory [Department of Energy] [Aiken, SC]
SREL	Southwest Regional Educational Laboratory (AEBS)
SREL	Space Radiation Effects Laboratory [Langley, VA] [NASA]
SREM	Scanning Reflection Electron Microscopy
SREM	School of Resource and Environmental Management (EERA)
S-REM	Sleep with Rapid Eye Movement
SREM	Software Requirements Engineering Methodology
SREM	Sound Ranging Evaluation Model (MCD)
SREMP	Source Region Electromagnetic Pulse
SREODB	Senior Explosive Ordnance Disposal Badge [Military decoration] (GFGA)
S Rep	Senate Reports [A publication] (DLA)
S Rep	Southern Reporter [A publication] (DLA)
SREP	State Rivers and Estuaries Policy [New South Wales] (EERA)
SREP	Sydney Regional Environmental Plan [Australia]
SREPT	Senate Committee Report (AFIT)
SRES	School for Resource and Environmental Studies [Dalhousie University] [Canada] (IRC)
SRES	Senate Resolution (AFIT)
S Res	Senate Resolution (AAGC)
SRes	Senate Resolution (WPI)
SRES	Senores [Sirs, Gentlemen] [Spanish]
SRES	Sex-Role Egalitarianism Scale [Test] (TMMY)
SRES	Southern Railway Employees' Sangh [India]
S Res	United States Senate Resolution [A publication] (DLA)
SRET	Satellite de Recherches et d'Environment Technique [Satellite for Environmental and Technical Research] [France]
SRET	Scanning Reference Electrode [Corrosion testing]
SRET	Subroutine Recipe Entry Pointer Table
SRETL	Screened Resistor Evaporated Transistor Logic (IAA)
SRE(V)	Singapore Royal Engineers (Volunteers) [British military] (DMA)
SRF	Salmonellosis-Resistance Factor
SRF	Sam Rayburn Foundation
SRF	San Rafael, CA [Location identifier FAA] (FAAL)
SRF	S-Band Receiver Filter
SRF	Scleroderma Research Foundation (EA)
SRF	Seal Rescue Fund (EA)
SRF	Secondary Refrigerant Freezing (PDAA)
SRF	Secure Reserve Forces [Military] (MCD)
SRF	Selected Reserve Force [Units] [of Army National Guard Discontinued, 1969]

SRF	Self-Realization Fellowship (EA)
SRF	Self-Referenced Fringe (MCD)
SRF	Self-Resonant Frequency
SRF	Semireinforcing Furnace [Carbon black manufacture]
SRF	Serum Response Factor [Biochemistry]
SRF	Ship Repair Facility [Navy] (NVT)
SRF	Short Rotary Furnace [Metallurgy]
SRF	Shuttle Refurbish Facility [NASA] (NASA)
SRF	Sido, Robert F., Edwardsville IL [STAC]
SRF	Signal Strength Radio Frequency (IAA)
SRF	Skin Reactive Factor [Immunochemistry]
SRF	Skin Respiratory Factor [Physiology]
SRF	Sliding Roof [Automotive advertising]
SRF	Slovak Relief Fund (EA)
SRF	Smithsonian Research Foundation (BARN)
SRF	Snake Ranch Flats [New Mexico] [Seismograph station code, US Geological Survey Closed] (SEIS)
SRF	Software Recording Facility
SRF	Software Recovery Facility [Computer science] (IBMDP)
SRF	Solar Radiation Flux
SRF	Somatotrophin-Releasing Factor [Endocrinology]
SRF	Sorter Reader Flow
SRF	Spacecraft Research Foundation [Defunct] (EA)
SRF	Space Requirement Forms (AAG)
SRF	Special Reporting Facility [Department of State]
SRF	Spectral Redistribution Function (IAA)
SRF	Sperm-Release Pheromone [Biology]
SRF	Split Renal Function [Medicine] (MAE)
SRF	Stable Radio Frequency
SRF	State Revolving Fund [Environmental Protection Agency] (GFGA)
SRF	Strategic Reserve Forces (MCD)
SRF	Strategic Retaliatory Forces (AAG)
SRF	Strategic Rocket Forces (MCD)
SRF	Strength of Radio Frequency (IAA)
SRF	Submarine Range-Finder
SRF	Submarine Repair Facility
SRF	Subretinal Fluid [Ophthalmology] (MAE)
SRF	Summary Reference File (DOMA)
SRF	Sun River Gold Corp. [Vancouver Stock Exchange symbol]
SRF	Supported Ring Frame
SRF	Surface Roughness Factor [Telecommunications] (TEL)
SRF	Survival Research Foundation (EA)
SRF	System Recovery Factor
SRF-A	Slow-Reacting Factor of Anaphylaxis [Medicine] (MEDA)
SRF-A	Slow Releasing Factor of Anaphylaxis [Immunology] (DAVI)
SRFB	Space Research Facilities Branch [National Research Council of Canada]
SRFblack	Semireinforcing Black (EDCT)
SRFBX	SteinRoe Balanced Fund [Mutual fund ticker symbol] (SG)
SRFC	Sheep Red Cell Rosette Forming Cells (AAMN)
SRFC	Shotgun Red Fan Club (EA)
SRFCS	Self-Repairing Flight Control System
SRFCX	SteinRoe Capital Opport. [Mutual fund ticker symbol] (SG)
SRFD	Society for the Rehabilitation of the Facially Disfigured [Later, National Foundation for Facial Reconstruction] (EA)
SRFF	Set-Reset Flip-Flop [Computer science]
SRFI	Self-Rising Flour Institute [Later, HBA]
SRFI	Sugar Research Foundation, Inc. [Later, ISRF] (EA)
SRFLANT	Ships Repair Facility, Atlantic (DNAB)
SRFLSBAD	Senior Flight Surgeon Badge [Military decoration] (GFGA)
SrFltSurgBad	Senior Flight Surgeon Badge [Military decoration] (AABC)
SRFM	Source Range Flux Monitoring [Nuclear energy] (NRCH)
SRFO	Society of Rural Financial Officers [British] (BI)
SRFPAC	Ships Repair Facility, Pacific (DNAB)
SRFS	Split Renal Function Study [Medicine] (MAE)
SRFSX	SteinRoe Growth Stock [Mutual fund ticker symbol] (SG)
SRFT	Shortest Remaining First Time (HGAA)
SRFTL	Secure Resource Force Target List (MCD)
SRFU	Seal Research and Fisheries Unit [British]
SRG	Regina General Hospital, Saskatchewan [Library symbol National Library of Canada] (NLC)
SRG	Santa Sarita Mining [Vancouver Stock Exchange symbol]
SRG	Schering-Plough Corp. [Research code symbol]
SRG	Search & Rescue 202 [British ICAO designator] (FAAC)
SRG	Semarang [Indonesia] [Airport symbol] (OAG)
SRG	Servomotor Rate Generator
SRG	Shift Register Generator [Computer science] (IAA)
SRG	Sine-Random Generator
SRG	Social Research Group [George Washington University] [Research center] (RCD)
SRG	Society of Remedial Gymnasts (EA)
SRG	Sound Ranging
SRG	Specialty Review Group [Medicine] (DMAA)
SRG	Spectrum Roentgen-Gamma [Proposed international space observatory]
SRG	Statistical Research Group [Princeton University] (MCD)
SRG	Steel Research Group [National Science Foundation]
SRG	Stimulated Raman Gain [Spectroscopy]
SRG	Stock Removal Grinding (MCD)
SRG	Surge (MSA)
SRG	System Routing Guide [Military] (CAAL)
SRG	Systems Research Group (CINC)
SRGA	Stable Reactor, General, Atomic
SRGC	Specialty Retail Group [NASDAQ symbol] (SAG)

SRGD.......... Gabriel Dumont Institute, Regina, Saskatchewan [*Library symbol National Library of Canada*] (NLC)
SRGE.......... Saskatchewan Government Employees Association, Regina, Saskatchewan [*Library symbol National Library of Canada*] (NLC)
SRGE.......... Surge Components, Inc. [*NASDAQ symbol*] (SAG)
SRGH.......... Pasqua Hospital, Regina, Saskatchewan [*Library symbol National Library of Canada*] (NLC)
SRGI.......... Saskatchewan Government Insurance, Regina, Saskatchewan [*Library symbol National Library of Canada*] (NLC)
SRGM.......... Super Rapid Gun Mounting [*Military*]
SRGN.......... Seragen, Inc. [*NASDAQ symbol*] (SAG)
SRGN.......... Surgeon
SRGR.......... Short-Range Guided Rocket
SRGR.......... Sound Ranging Group (IAA)
SRGS.......... Saskatchewan Genealogical Society, Regina, Saskatchewan [*Library symbol National Library of Canada*] (NLC)
SRGS.......... Scottish Rock Garden Club (DBA)
SRGS.......... Stimulated Raman Gain Spectroscopy (PDAA)
SRGS.......... St. Rosalie Generating Station [*Nuclear energy*] (NRCH)
SRGS.......... Survivable Radio Guidance System [*Military*]
SRGSC.......... Southern Rhodesia General Service Corps [*British military*] (DMA)
SRH.......... Safra Republic Holdings
SRH.......... Saskatchewan Housing Corp., Regina, Saskatchewan [*Library symbol National Library of Canada*] (BIB)
SRH.......... Secretaria de Recursos Hidraulicos [*Mexico*]
SRH.......... Sequential Rough Handling (MCD)
SRH.......... Single Radial Hemolysis [*Immunochemistry*]
SRH.......... Single Radical Hemolysis [*Hematology*] (DAVI)
SRH.......... Smith, R. H., Minneapolis MN [*STAC*]
SRH.......... [*A*] Social and Religious History of the Jews [*S. W. Baron*] [*A publication*] (BJA)
SRH.......... Somatotropin-Releasing Hormone [*Endocrinology*] (MAE)
SRH.......... Spontaneously Responding Hyperthyroidism [*Endocrinology*]
SRH.......... Stigmata of Recent Hemorrhage [*Medicine*]
SRH.......... Strathcona Resources Industries Ltd. [*Toronto Stock Exchange symbol*]
SRH.......... Structural Repair Handbook (DNAB)
SRH.......... Subsystems Requirements Handbook [*NASA*] (NASA)
SRH.......... Sue Ryder Home (WDAA)
SRH.......... Supply Railhead
SRH.......... Switchyard Relay House [*Nuclear energy*] (NRCH)
SRHA.......... Statistical Record of Hispanic Americans [*A publication*]
SRHB.......... Society for Research into Hydrocephalus and Spina Bifida (EA)
SRHC.......... Shutdown Reactor Head Cooling [*Nuclear energy*] (NRCH)
SR HCR....... Southern Rhodesia High Court Reports [*1911-55*] [*A publication*] (DLA)
SRHE.......... Society for Religion in Higher Education [*Later, SVHE*] (EA)
SRHE.......... Society for Research into Higher Education [*Guildford, Surrey, England*] (EAIO)
SRHIT.......... Small RADAR-Homing Interceptor Technology
SRHJ.......... [*A*] Social and Religious History of the Jews [*S. W. Baron*] [*A publication*] (BJA)
SRHL.......... Small RADAR Homing Interceptor
SRHL.......... Southwestern Radiological Health Laboratory [*HEW*]
SRHM.......... Statistical Record of Health and Medicine [*A publication*]
SRHP.......... Planning Branch, Saskatchewan Department of Highways and Transportation, Regina, Saskatchewan [*Library symbol National Library of Canada*] (NLC)
SRHP.......... Section for Rehabilitation Hospitals and Programs [*American Hospital Association*] (EA)
SRHQ.......... Subregional Headquarters [*Military British*]
SRHS.......... Health Sciences Library, Plains Health Centre, Regina, Saskatchewan [*Library symbol National Library of Canada*] (NLC)
SR(HS)....... Seaman Recruit (High School) [*Navy rating*] (DNAB)
SRHSB......... Society for Research into Hydrocephalus and Spina Bifida (FA)
SRI.......... Air Safaris & Services (NZ) Ltd. [*New Zealand*] [*ICAO designator*] (FAAC)
SRI.......... Emotional Problems Scales [*Test*] (TMMY)
SRI.......... Sacrum Romanum Imperium [*The Holy Roman Empire*] [*Latin*]
SRI.......... Samarinda [*Indonesia*] [*Airport symbol*] (OAG)
SRI.......... Satellite RADAR Interferometry
SRI.......... Scholarly Resources, Incorporated, Wilmington, DE [*Library symbol Library of Congress*] (LCLS)
SRI.......... Sefid-Roud [*Iran*] [*Seismograph station code, US Geological Survey*] (SEIS)
SRI.......... Selective Retention Indicators (NVT)
SRI.......... Senior Resident Inspector [*Nuclear energy*] (NRCH)
SRI.......... Serenpet, Inc. [*AMEX symbol*] (SPSG)
SRI.......... Serotin Reuptake Inhibitor [*Pharmacology*]
SRI.......... Servo Repeater Indicator
SRI.......... Severe Renal Insufficiency [*Medicine*]
SRI.......... Signal Routing and Interface (MCD)
SRI.......... Silicon Rubber Insulation
SRI.......... Ski Retailers International (EA)
SRI.......... Social Research Institute [*University of Utah*] [*Research center*] (RCD)
SRI.......... Society for Rational Individualism [*Later, SIL*] (EA)
SRI.......... Sorry [*Communications operator's procedural remark*]
SRI.......... Southeastern Reservoir Investigation [*Department of the Interior*] (GRD)
SRI.......... Southern Research Institute
SRI.......... Southwest Research Institute
SRI.......... Space Research Institute [*Defunct*] (EA)
SRI.......... Spalling Resistance Index (IEEE)
SRI.......... Special Recreation, Inc. (EA)

SRI.......... Spectrum Resolver Integrator
SRI.......... Spectrum Resources, Inc. [*St. Charles, MO*] [*Telecommunications*] (TSSD)
SRI.......... Speech Rehabilitation Institute (EA)
SRI.......... Spring Research Institute (EA)
SRI.......... Standardized Reading Inventory [*P. Newcomer*] (TES)
SRI.......... Standard Research Institute (MCD)
SRI.......... Standby Request for Information [*Military*] (AABC)
SRI.......... Standing Request for Information (MCD)
SRI.......... Stanford Research Institute [*Later, SRI International*] [*Databank originator*]
SRI.......... Stanford Resources, Inc.
SRI.......... Statistical Reference Index [*A publication*]
SRI.......... Steel Recycling Institute (NTPA)
SRI.......... Stick to Rudder Interconnect (MCD)
SRI.......... Storeroom Item (DNAB)
SRI.......... Successful Retirement Institute (NTPA)
SRI.......... Sugar Research Institute [*Australia*]
SRI.......... Sulfate Reduction Index [*Environmental chemistry*]
SRI.......... Supply Requisition Inquiry
SRI.......... Surface Roughness Indicator
SRI.......... Surveillance, Reconnaissance, and Intelligence [*Marine Corps*] (DOMA)
SRI.......... Swiss Radio International
SRI.......... Syllable Repetition Interval [*Entomology*]
SRI.......... System of Reinforcement-Inhibition (PDAA)
SRIA.......... Saskatchewan Intergovernmental Affairs, Regina, Saskatchewan [*Library symbol National Library of Canada*] (NLC)
SRIA.......... Society of Rosicrucians in America (EA)
SRIA.......... State and Regional Indicators Archive [*University of New Hampshire*] [*Information service or system*] (IID)
SRIAER....... Scientific Research Institute for Atomic Energy Reactors [*Former USSR*]
SRIB.......... Strike Route Information Book [*Strategic Air Command*] (AABC)
SRIC.......... Short-Run Incremental Cost (ADA)
SRIC.......... Southwest Research and Information Center (EA)
SRIC.......... Subsurface Remediation Information Center [*Environmental Protection Agency*] (AEPA)
SRID.......... Search RADAR Input Device (MCD)
SRID.......... Single Radial Immunodiffusion [*Medicine*] (DMAA)
SRIF.......... Somatotrophin-Releasing Inhibiting Factor [*Also, GH-RIF, GH-RIH, GRIF, SS*] [*Endocrinology*]
SRIF.......... Somatotropin-Release Inhibiting Factor (DB)
SRIF.......... Special Risk Insurance Fund [*Federal Housing Administration*]
SRIFC.......... Saskatchewan Indian Federated College, Regina, Saskatchewan [*Library symbol National Library of Canada*] (NLC)
SRIG.......... Surveillance, Reconnaissance, and Intelligence Group [*Marine Corps*] (DOMA)
SRIH.......... Somatostatin [*Biochemistry*]
SRIH.......... Somatotropin Release Inhibiting Hormone [*Biochemistry*]
SRILTA........ Stanford Research Institute Lead Time Analysis
SR-IM.......... Office of Strategic Research, Intelligence Memoranda [*CIA*]
SRIM.......... Short-Range Intercept Missile (MCD)
SRIM.......... Standing Order Microfiche Service
SRIM.......... Structural Reaction Injection Molding [*Plastics*]
SRIM.......... Structural Reinforced Injection Molding (COE)
SRIMO......... Senior Radio Installation and Manufacture Officer (IAA)
SRIN.......... Indian and Northern Affairs Canada [*Affaires Indiennes et du Nord Canada*],Regina, Saskatchewan [*Library symbol National Library of Canada*] (BIB)
SRINF.......... Shorter Range Intermediate-Range Nuclear Forces (DOMA)
SRIO.......... Systems Research Integration Office [*Army Air Mobility Research and Development Laboratory*] [*St. Louis, MO*]
SRIP.......... Selected Reserve Incentive Program [*Army*]
SRIP.......... Ship Readiness Improvement Plan [*Navy*] (NG)
SRIP.......... Short-Range Impact Point (MUGU)
SRIP.......... Soldier/Robot Interface Program Vehicle [*Military*] (RDA)
SRIP.......... Specification Review and Improvement Program [*Navy*] (NG)
SRIP.......... Supplier Rating Incentive Program
SRIS.......... Safety Recommendation Information System [*Database*]
SRIS.......... Safety Research Information Service [*National Safety Council*] (IID)
SRIS.......... Science Reference and Information Service (IID)
SRIS.......... Surplus Record Information Services (IID)
SRISP.......... Interprovincial Steel & Pipe Corp. Ltd., (IPSCO), Regina, Saskatchewan [*Library symbol National Library of Canada*] (NLC)
SRIT.......... Service and Repair Identification Tag (MCD)
Srita.......... Senorita [*Miss*] [*Spanish*]
SRIY.......... Sherwood Rangers Imperial Yeomanry [*British military*] (DMA)
SRJ.......... San Borja [*Bolivia*] [*Airport symbol*] (OAG)
SRJ.......... Scorcorp Industries, Inc. [*Vancouver Stock Exchange symbol*]
SRJ.......... Self-Restraint Joint
SRJ.......... Short Run Job (MCD)
SRJ.......... Standard-Range Juno [*Survey meter for radiation*]
SRJ.......... Static Round Jet
SRJC.......... Communications Policy Branch, Saskatchewan Department of Justice, Regina, Saskatchewan [*Library symbol National Library of Canada*] (NLC)
SRJC.......... Santa Rosa Junior College [*California*]
SRK.......... Skywork SA [*Switzerland ICAO designator*] (FAAC)
SRK.......... Soave-Redlich-Kwong [*Equation of state*]
SRK.......... Spirit Lake, IA [*Location identifier FAA*] (FAAL)
SRK.......... S-Receptor Kinase [*An enzyme*]
SRK.......... Sredniy Kalar [*Former USSR Seismograph station code, US Geological Survey*] (SEIS)
SRK.......... Stralak Resources [*Vancouver Stock Exchange symbol*]

SRKN............	Single Rotating Knife
SRL...............	HRIN [*Human Resource Information Network*] Special Reports Library [*Executive Telecom System, Inc.*] [*Information service or system*] (CRD)
SRL...............	Legislative Library of Saskatchewan, Regina, Saskatchewan [*Library symbol National Library of Canada*] (NLC)
SRL...............	Santa Rosalia [*Mexico*] [*Seismograph station code, US Geological Survey Closed*] (SEIS)
SRL...............	Savannah River Laboratory [*Department of Energy*] [*Aiken, SC*]
SRL...............	Save-the-Redwoods League (EA)
SRL...............	Sceptre Resources [*AMEX symbol*] (TTSB)
SRL...............	Sceptre Resources Ltd. [*AMEX symbol Toronto Stock Exchange symbol*] (SPSG)
SRL...............	Schema Representation Language (NITA)
SRL...............	Scheme Representation Language [*Artificial intelligence*]
SRL...............	Science Reference Library (NITA)
SRL...............	Scientific Research Laboratory (AAG)
SRL...............	Screwworm Research Laboratory [*Department of Agriculture*] (GRD)
SRL...............	Seiler Research Laboratory [*Air Force*] (MCD)
SRL...............	Send-Receive Logic (ECII)
SRL...............	Service Rights Layer [*Computer science*]
SRL...............	Shift Register Label (NITA)
SRL...............	Shift Register Latch [*Computer science*] (CIST)
SRL...............	Singing Return Loss [*Telecommunications*] (TEL)
SRL...............	Skin Resistance Level [*Physiology*]
SRL...............	Sleep Research Laboratory [*Loughborough University*] (WDAA)
SRL...............	Society of Romance Linguistics [*Nancy, France*] (EAIO)
SRL...............	Sonobuoy Receiver Logic [*Navy*] (CAAL)
SRL...............	Sound Reference Laboratory [*Orlando, FL*] [*Navy*]
SRL...............	Sound Research Laboratories Ltd. [*Research center British*] (IRUK)
SRL...............	Space Radar Laboratory [*NASA*]
SRL...............	Spares Recommendation List (MCD)
SRL...............	Stability Return Loss [*Telecommunications*] (TEL)
SRL...............	Standard Reference Library
SRL...............	Strangeways Research Laboratory [*British*] (IRUK)
SRL...............	Stress Relieving Liner (KSC)
SRL...............	Structural Return Loss [*Telecommunications*] (TEL)
SRL...............	Student Religious Liberals [*Later, SRL, A Free Religious Fellowship*] [*Defunct*]
SRL...............	Study Reference List (AFM)
SRL...............	Summary Requirements List (MCD)
SRL...............	Support Requirements Letter (CET)
SRL...............	Survey Research Laboratory [*University of Illinois*] [*Information service or system*] (IID)
SRL...............	System Reference Library (HGAA)
SRL...............	Systems Research Laboratory
SRL...............	Varmlandsflyg AB [*Sweden ICAO designator*] (FAAC)
SRLA............	Scottish Recreational Land Association (DBA)
SRLC............	Luther College, Regina, Saskatchewan [*Library symbol National Library of Canada*] (NLC)
SRLD............	Small Rocket Lift Device
SRLP............	Leader-Post Ltd., Regina, Saskatchewan [*Library symbol National Library of Canada*] (NLC)
SRLP............	Socialist and Revolutionary Labour Party [*Gambia*] [*Political party*] (PD)
SRLS............	Law Society of Saskatchewan Libraries, Regina [*Library symbol National Library of Canada*] (BIB)
Sr LS............	Senior Life Saving [*Red Cross*]
SRLS............	Starved Rock Library System [*Library network*]
SRLY............	Series Relay (IEEE)
SRLZ............	Southern Rock Lobster Zone [*Australia*]
SRM.............	Flying Swiss Ambulance Maldives (Pvt) Ltd. [*ICAO designator*] (FAAC)
SRM.............	Safety, Reliability, and Maintainability (SSD)
SRM.............	Schedule Request Message (MCD)
SRM.............	Scrim-Reinforced Material [*Nonwoven sheets*]
SRM.............	Seatbelt Retractor Module [*Automotive engineering*]
SRM.............	Secretory Rate Maximum [*Physiology*]
SRM.............	Selected-Reaction Monitoring [*Spectrometry*]
SRM.............	Sensomatic Elect [*NYSE symbol*] (TTSB)
SRM.............	Sensor Response Model
SRM.............	Serbian Renaissance Movement [*Political party*] (EY)
SRM.............	Server Requewst Manager [*Computer science*]
SRM.............	Service Repair Manual
SRM.............	Shared Resource Management [*Computer science*]
SRM.............	Shift Register Memory
SRM.............	Ship Repair and Maintenance [*National Shipping Authority*]
SRM.............	Shock Remanent Magnetization (OA)
SRM.............	Short-Range Missile [*Projected; not to be confused with SRAM*]
SRM.............	Short-Range MODEM
SRM.............	Single Register Machine
SRM.............	Smokeless Rocket Motor (MCD)
SRM.............	Snowmelt-Runoff Model [*Hydrology*]
SRM.............	Society for Range Management (EA)
SRM.............	Sociomoral Reflection Measures (EDAC)
SRM.............	Socorro - La Joya [*New Mexico*] [*Seismograph station code, US Geological Survey Closed*] (SEIS)
SRM.............	Solid-Rocket Motor
SRM.............	Source Range Monitor [*Nuclear energy*] (NRCH)
SRM.............	Specification Requirements Manual [*NASA*] (NASA)
SRM.............	Specific Repair Methods [*Boeing*]
SRM.............	Speed of Relative Movement
SRM.............	Spiritual Regeneration Movement [*Foundation of America*] (EA)
SRM.............	Square Root Mode [*Computer science*]
SRM.............	Standard Reference Material [*National Institute of Standards and Technology*]
SRM.............	Standard Reference Method (COE)
SRM.............	Standard Reference Module
SRM.............	Standard Repair Manual (MCD)
SRM.............	Strategic Reconnaissance Missile
SRM.............	Structural Repair Manual
SRM.............	Subarea Routing Manager (IAA)
SRM.............	Subsystem Response Message [*Military*]
SRM.............	Superior Rectus Muscle [*Eye anatomy*]
SRM.............	Switched Reluctance Motor (ECON)
SRM.............	System for Resources Management [*Jet Propulsion Laboratory, NASA*]
SRM.............	System Resource Manager [*IBM Corp.*] (BUR)
SRMA..........	Silk and Rayon Manufacturers Association [*Defunct*] (EA)
SRMA..........	Ski Resort Marketing Association [*Defunct*] (EA)
SRMA..........	Split-Channel Reservation Multiple Access (PDAA)
SRM & QA...	Safety, Reliability, Maintainability, and Quality Assurance [*NASA*] (SSD)
SRMBR........	Senior Member (DNAB)
SRMC..........	Short Run Marginal Cost (MHDB)
SRMC..........	Society of Risk Management Consultants [*Baton Rouge, LA*] (EA)
SRMC..........	Specification Requirements Manual (MCD)
SRMC..........	Stimulus/Response Measurements Catalog (NASA)
SRMCASE....	Symmetry-Restricted-Multiconfiguration Annihilation of Single Excitations [*Physics*]
SRMD..........	Slow Release Matrix Device [*US Army Corps of Engineers*]
SRMD..........	Stress-Related Mucosal Damage [*Medicine*]
SRMF..........	Short-Run Manufacturing Facility (MCD)
SRMH..........	Single Role Mine-Hunter [*Military*] (PDAA)
SRMI...........	Swissray International, Inc. [*NASDAQ symbol*] (SAG)
SRMI...........	SWISSRAY Intl [*NASDAQ symbol*] (TTSB)
SR-MIR........	Specific Reactivity - Maximum Incremental Reactivity [*Exhaust emissions*] [*Automotive engineering*]
SRML..........	Short-Range Missile Launcher
SRMP..........	Supply Readiness Milestone Plan [*Military*] (CAAL)
SRMR..........	Saskatchewan Department of Mineral Resources, Regina, Saskatchewan [*Library symbol National Library of Canada*] (NLC)
SRMS..........	Scheduling and Resource Management System [*Tymshare UK*] [*Software package*] (NCC)
SRMS..........	Ships Records Management System (MCD)
SRMS..........	Shuttle Remote Manipulator System (SSD)
SRMS..........	Sociomoral Reflection Maturity Score (EDAC)
SRMS..........	Strategic Research and Management Service
SRMS..........	Structure Resonance Modulation Spectroscopy
SRMT..........	Southern Rock Mountain Trench [*Geology*]
SRMU..........	Signal RADAR Maintenance Unit (IAA)
SRMU..........	Solid Rocket Motor Upgrade [*Air Force*]
SRN.............	Sabine River & Northern Railroad Co. [*AAR code*]
3RN.............	Saskatchewan Registered Nurses Association, Regina, Saskatchewan [*Library symbol National Library of Canada*] (NLC)
SRN.............	Satellite Radio Navigation (DNAB)
SRN.............	Serial Reference Number
SRN.............	Simulation Reference Number
SRN.............	Slurry Response Number [*Well drilling technology*]
SRN.............	Software Release Notice [*NASA*] (NASA)
SRN.............	Southern
SRN.............	Southern Air Transport, Inc.
SRN.............	Southern Banc(AL) [*AMEX symbol*] (TTSB)
SRN.............	Southern Banc Co., Inc. [*AMEX symbol*] (SAG)
SRN.............	Specification Revision Notice (MCD)
SRN.............	State Registered Nurse [*British*]
SRN.............	Strathearn House Group Ltd. [*Toronto Stock Exchange symbol*]
SRN.............	Stretch Receptor Neuron
SRN.............	Student Registered Nurse (MAE)
SRN.............	Subcommittee on Research Needs [*World Health Organization*]
SRN.............	Subretinal Neovascularization [*Ophthalmology*] (DAVI)
sRNA...........	Ribonucleic Acid, Soluble [*Replaced by tRNA*] [*Biochemistry, genetics*]
SRNA..........	Shipbuilders and Repairers' National Association [*British*] (BI)
SRNC..........	Severn River Naval Command
SR/NE.........	Sinus Rhythm, No Ectopy [*Cardiology*] (DAVI)
SRNFC........	Source Range Neutron Flux Channel (IEEE)
SR(NFE)......	Seaman Recruit (Nuclear Field Electronics) [*Navy rating*] (DNAB)
SRNG..........	Sustained Release Nitroglycerin (DMAA)
SRNG..........	Syringe
SRNH..........	Service Request Not Honored (IAA)
SRNLS........	Northern Library Services, Saskatchewan Library, Regina, Saskatchewan [*Library symbol National Library of Canada*] (NLC)
SRNNA........	Statistical Record of Native North Americans [*A publication*]
SRNR..........	Stock Request Number
SRNS..........	Steroid-Responsive Nephrotic Syndrome [*Medicine*]
SRNS..........	Surveyor Retro Nozzle Structure
SR(NSET)....	Seaman Recruit (Nuclear Submarine Engineering Technician) [*Navy rating*] (DNAB)
SRNT..........	Society for Research on Nicotine and Tobacco (NTPA)
SRNV..........	Subretinal Neovascularization [*Ophthalmology*]
SRO.............	Safety Recall Order (MCD)
SRO.............	Sales Release Order
SRO.............	Saskatchewan Oil Co., Regina, Saskatchewan [*Library symbol National Library of Canada*] (NLC)
SRO.............	Savannah River Operation [*Office*] [*Energy Research and Development Administration*]
SRO.............	S-Band RADAR Operational
SRO.............	Scarboro Resources Ltd. [*Toronto Stock Exchange symbol*]

SRO	Scottish Record Office
SRO	Seismological Research Observatory [Australia]
SRO	Self-Regulatory Organisation [Financial Services Act of 1986] [British]
SRO	Senior Range Officer
SRO	Senior Ranking Officer [Army] (ADDR)
SRO	Senior Reactor Operator [Nuclear energy] (NRCH)
SRO	Senior Research Officer [Ministry of Agriculture, Fisheries, and Food] [British]
SRO	Servicios Aereos Rutas Oriente SA de CV [Mexico ICAO designator] (FAAC)
SRO	Sex-Ratio Organism [Entomology]
SRO	Sharable and Read Only [Computer science] (PCM)
SRO	Shop Readiness Objective
SRO	Shop Repair Order
SRO	Short-Range Order [Solid state physics]
SRO	Shrobarova [Czechoslovakia] [Seismograph station code, US Geological Survey] (SEIS)
SRO	Single-Room Occupancy [Housing]
SRO	Singly Resonant Oscillator (IEEE)
SRO	Society of Radio Operators
SRO	Society of Registration Officers - Births, Deaths, and Marriages [British] (DBA)
SRO	Solar Radio Observatory
SRO	Spares Requirement Order
SRO	Special Rate Order [Business term]
SRO	Special Regional Operations (NATG)
SRO	Specification Release Order [Nuclear energy] (NRCH)
SRO	Squadron Recreation Officer [Navy British]
SRO	Standing Room Only [Theater]
SRO	Standing Route Order [Army] (AABC)
SRO	State Recycling Organizations [Environment] (GNE)
SRO	Station Routine Order (IAA)
SRO	Statutory Rules and Orders
SRO	Steele-Richardson-Olszewski Syndrome [Medicine]
SRO	Stock Record Officer
SRO	Strategic Research Objective [Military]
SrO	Strontium Oxide
SRO	Strontium Ruthenate [Inorganic chemistry]
SRo	Studia Rosenthaliana [A publication] (BJA)
SRO	Superintendent [or Supervisor] of Range Operations [NASA]
SRO	Supervisor Range Operations (MCD)
SRO	Supplementary Reserve of Officers [Military British]
SRO	System Readiness Objective
SRO	Systems Reproduction Order (MCD)
SROA	Safety-Related Operator Action [Nuclear energy] (NRCH)
SROA	Society for Radiation Oncology Administrators (EA)
SROA	Statistical Record of Older Americans [A publication]
SROB	Short-Range Omnidirectional Beacon [Aerospace]
SROD	Stove Rod
SROE	Statistical Record of the Environment [A publication]
SROEQ	Selected References on Environmental Quality as It Relates to Health [A publication]
SROF	Self-Renewal Occupational Field
SROF	Sustained Rate of Fire [Military] (INF)
SROH	Societe de Recherche en Orientation Humaine [Canada]
SROKA	Second Republic of Korea Army
SROM	Sirrom Capital [NASDAQ symbol] (TTSB)
SROM	Sirrom Capital Corp. [NASDAQ symbol] (SAG)
SROM	Sociomoral Reflection Objective Measure (EDAC)
SROM	Spontaneous Rupture of Membrane [Medicine] (DMAA)
SRON	Space Research Organization Netherlands
SROP	Senior Registered Options Principal [Investment term]
SROS	Seybold Report on Office Systems (HGAA)
SROS	Special Run Operations Sheet (IAA)
SROTC	Senior Reserve Officers' Training Corps [Military] (AABC)
SROTS	Superficial Rays of the Sun [In reference to suntanning, supposedly occuring before 10am and after 2pm] [See also BROTS]
SROWW	Statistical Record of Women Worldwide [A publication]
SRP	Safeguard Readiness Posture [Army] (AABC)
SRP	Salary Reduction Plan [Business term]
SRP	Saskatchewan Library and Union Catalogue, Regina, Saskatchewan [Library symbol National Library of Canada] (NLC)
SRP	Saskatchewan Provincial Library [UTLAS symbol]
SRP	Savannah River Plant [Department of Energy]
SRP	Savings and Retirement Plan
SRP	Scientific Research Proposal (AAG)
SRP	Sealift Readiness Program [Military]
SRP	Seat Reference Point
SRP	Seismic Reflection Profile [Marine science] (MSC)
SRP	Selected Reference Point (GAVI)
SRP	Selective Reenlistment Program [Air Force]
SRP	Self-Recording Penetrometer
SRP	Sensor Reporting Post
SRP	Sequential Range Policy (PDAA)
SRP	Serbian Radical Party [Political party]
SRP	Shags Rocks Passage [Oceanography]
SRP	Shared Resources Processing [Computer science] (CIST)
SRP	Shared Resources Programmming (NITA)
SRP	Shark Research Panel [Navy] (DNAB)
SRP	Shift Register Partition (IAA)
SRP	Ship's Repair Party [Navy British]
SRP	Short Ragweed Pollen [Immunology]
SRP	Sierra Pacific Resources [NYSE symbol] (SPSG)
SRP	Sierra Pac Pw [NYSE symbol] (SAG)
SRP	Signal Recognition Particle [Biochemistry]
SRP	Signal Recognition Protein (DB)
SRP	Sink Resistant Plastic (PDAA)
SRP	SIOP Reconnaissance Plan (MCD)
SRP	Slot Reference Point (DA)
SRP	Slow-Release Pellet
SRP	Small Rotating Plug [Nuclear energy] (NRCH)
SRP	Socialisticka Radnicka Partija Jugoslavije [Socialist Workers' Party of Yugoslavia] [Political party] (PPE)
SRP	Socialist Revolutionary Party [India] [Political party] (PPW)
SRP	Socialist Revolutionary Party [Former USSR Political party]
SRP	Socialist Revolution Party [Turkey Political party] (PPW)
SRP	Society for Radiological Protection [British] (DEN)
SRP	Society of Recorder Players [British] (DBA)
SRP	Software Renewal Program [Food and Nutrition Service] [Department of Agriculture] (GFGA)
SRP	Solar Radiation Pressure
SRP	Soldier Readiness Processing [Military]
SRP	Solicitation Review Panel [Air Force]
SRP	Soluble Reactive Phosphorus [Marine science] (OSRA)
SRP	Sonobuoy Referenced Position [Navy] (NG)
SRP	Source Record Punch
SRP	Sozialistische Reichspartei [Socialist Reich Party] [Germany Political party] (PPE)
SRP	Space Requirement Program (MCD)
SRP	Spin Recovery Parachute
SRP	Spreading Resistance Probe (AAEL)
SRP	Stabilization Reference Package (MCD)
SRP	Standard Relative Power
SRP	Standard Repair Procedures
SRP	Standard Review Plan [Nuclear energy] (NRCH)
SRP	Start Rendezvous Point (MCD)
SRP	State Registered Physiotherapist [British]
SRP	Status Report Panels (SAA)
SRP	Stern Reference Point [Navy] (DNAB)
SRP	Stratospheric Research Program
SRP	Stray Radiant Power
SRP	Stress Resiliency Profile [Test] (TMMY)
SRP	Styrene-Rubber Plastics (EDCT)
SRP	Suggested Retail Price (WDMC)
SRP	Supply and Repair Parts (DNAB)
SRP	Supply Readiness Program [Air Force]
SRP	Supply Refuelling Point [Air Force British]
SRP	Traverse City, MI [Location identifier FAA] (FAAL)
SRPA	Senior Real Property Appraiser [Society of Real Estate Appraisers] [Designation awarded by]
SRPA	Small Reclamation Projects Act of 1956 (COE)
SRPA	Spherical Retarding Potential Analyzer (MCD)
SRPA	Squash Rackets Professionals Association [British] (DBA)
SRPA	Sydney Regional Planning Authority [Proposed] [Australia]
SRPARABAD	Senior Parachutist Badge [Military decoration]
SRPB	Scottish River Purification Board
SRPBA	Scottish River Purification Boards Association
SRPC	SaskPower, Regina, Saskatchewan [Library symbol National Library of Canada] (NLC)
SRPC	Sulphate Resisting Portland Cement
SRPC	Supplier Request for Product Change
SRPCRD	Research and Development Center Library, SaskPower, Regina, Saskatchewan [Library symbol National Library of Canada] (NLC)
SRPD	System Research and Planning Division [NASA]
SRPDAA	Silk and Rayon Printers and Dyers Association of America (EA)
SRPE	Senior Rater Potential Evaluation [Army]
SRPEX	SteinRoe Growth & Income [Mutual fund ticker symbol] (SG)
SR(PFE)	Seaman Recruit (Polaris Field Electronics) [Navy rating] (DNAB)
SR(PFL)	Seaman Recruit (Polaris Field Launcher) [Navy rating] (DNAB)
SRPG	Scraping
SRPH	Saskatchewan Department of Health, Regina, Saskatchewan [Library symbol National Library of Canada] (NLC)
srph	Seraph (VRA)
SRPI	Scrap Rubber and Plastics Institute (EA)
SRPI	Server Requester Programming Interface [Computer science] (CDE)
SRPI	Silk and Rayon Print Institute [Defunct] (EA)
SRPIS	Southern Regional Plant Introduction Station [University of Georgia] [Research center] (RCD)
SRPJ	Self-Restraining Pipe Joint
SRPM	Shaft Revolutions per Minute (DNAB)
SRPM	Single Reversal Permanent Magnet (IAA)
SRPM	Standard Raven's Progressive Matrix [Psychiatry] (DAVI)
SRPM	Stated Redemption Price at Maturity [of debt instruments]
SRPMME	Society for Research in the Psychology of Music and Music Education [British]
SRPN	Special Requisition Priority Number
SRPNSE	State Required Public Notification of Standards Exceedances [Environmental Protection Agency]
SRPO	Science Resources Planning Office [National Science Foundation]
SRPP	Public Participation Library, Regina, Saskatchewan [Library symbol National Library of Canada] (BIB)
SRPP	Skeletal Rod of Palp
SRP/PDS	Stabilization Reference Package / Position Determination System [Military]
SRPR	Saskatchewan Parks and Renewable Resources, Regina, Saskatchewan [Library symbol National Library of Canada] (NLC)
SRPR	Scraper
SRPR	Signal Recognition Particle Receptor (DMAA)
SRPR	Stray Radiant Power Ratio

SrPrchtBad...	Senior Parachutist Badge [*Military decoration*]
SRPS	Saskatchewan Public Service Commission, Regina, Saskatchewan [*Library symbol National Library of Canada*] (NLC)
SRPS	Scientific Research Project Support [*National Science Foundation*]
SRPS	Scottish Railway Preservation Society (DBA)
SRPS	Secure Record and Playback System (MCD)
SRPS	Sensor-Referenced Positioning System
SR/PS	Shipping Request/Packing Sheet (MCD)
SRPS	Short Rib-Polydactyly Syndrome [*Medicine*] (DMAA)
SRPS	Supply and Repair Parts Specification (DNAB)
SRPT	Shortest Remaining Processing Time (PDAA)
SRPT	Small Repair Parts Transporter
SRPT	Statements of Responsibilites in Tax Practice (TDOB)
SRPT	Statements on Responsibilites in Tax Practice (EBF)
SRPT	Stress Relaxation Processability Tester (PDAA)
SRPV	Stationary Remotely Piloted Vehicle (MCD)
SRPW	Savannah River Plant - Well DRB-10 [*South Carolina*] [*Seismograph station code, US Geological Survey*] (SEIS)
SRQ	Sarasota/Bradenton [*Florida*] [*Airport symbol*]
SRQ	Self-Reporting Questionnaire [*Medicine*] (DMAA)
SRQ	Self-Righteousness Questionnaire [*Psychology*] (EDAC)
SRQ	Service Request
SRQ	Status Request Field [*Computer science*] (IAA)
SRQS	Service Request State (IAA)
SRR	Central New York Library Resources Council, Syracuse, NY [*OCLC symbol*] (OCLC)
SRR	Scots Revised Reports [*A publication*] (DLA)
SRR	Search and Range RADAR
SRR	Seastar Resource Corp. [*Vancouver Stock Exchange symbol*]
SRR	Security Rules and Regulations
srr	Serer [*MARC language code Library of Congress*] (LCCP)
SRR	Serially Reusable Resource [*Computer science*]
SRR	Service Representative Report (MCD)
SRR	Shift Register Recognizer (IEEE)
SRR	Short-Range RADAR
SRR	Short-Range Recovery (IEEE)
SRR	Shuttle Requirements Review [*NASA*] (MCD)
SRR	Site Readiness Review [*NASA*] (NASA)
SRR	Skin Resistance Response [*Physiology*]
SRR	Slow Rotation Room [*NASA*]
SRR	Socialist Republic of Romania
SRR	Society for Reformation Research (EA)
SRR	Software Requirements Review [*NASA*] (NASA)
SRR	Sorreisa [*Norway*] [*Airport symbol*] (AD)
SRR	Sound Recorder-Reproducer (MSA)
SRR	Source-Receptor Relation [*Environmental chemistry*]
SRR	Special Reimbursement Rate (AFM)
SRR	Special Report Writer [*NASA*]
SRR	Spot Radio Report (WDMC)
SRR	Spurious Response Rejection
SRR	Stain Release Rating [*Textile technology*]
SRR	Standardized Rate Ratio (DMAA)
SRR	Star Air IS [*Denmark ICAO designator*] (FAAC)
SRR	State Regulation Report: Toxics [*Business Publishers, Inc.*] [*Information service or system*] (CRD)
SRR	Steering Reversal Rate
SRR	Stimulus Response Ratio (DB)
SRR	Strategic Ready Reserve [*Military*]
SRR	Stride Rite [*NYSE symbol*] (TTSB)
SRR	Stride Rite Corp. [*NYSE symbol*] (SPSG)
SRR	Subsystem Requirements Review
SRR	Supplementary Reserve Regulations [*Army British*]
SRR	Supplier Rating Report (SAA)
SRR	Support Requirements Records [*Navy*] (NG)
SRR	Surgery Recovery Room [*Medicine*] (DMAA)
SRR	Surplus Review Record (SAA)
SRR	Survival, Recovery, and Reconstitution [*Military*] (AFM)
SRR	System Readiness Review (MCD)
SRR	System Requirements Review [*NASA*]
SRRA	Statistical Record of Religion in America [*A publication*]
SRRB	Search and Rescue Radio Beacon
SRRB	Solar Radiation Research Branch [*Air Resources Laboratory*] (USDC)
SRRC	Resource Centre, RCMP [*Royal Canadian Mounted Police*] Academy, Regina, Saskatchewan [*Library symbol National Library of Canada*] (NLC)
SRRC	Scottish Reactor Research Centre (DEN)
SRRC	Southern Regional Research Center [*Department of Agriculture*] [*New Orleans, LA*] (GRD)
SRRC	Sperry Rand Research Center (MCD)
SRRC	Standing Results Review Committee [*Nuclear energy*] (NRCH)
SRRC	Star Resources Corp. [*NASDAQ symbol*] (SAG)
SRRCP	Petroleum Division, Saskatchewan Research Council, Regina [*Library symbol National Library of Canada*] (BIB)
SRRCS	Surface Raid Reporting Control Ship [*Navy*] (NVT)
SRRE	Prairie Farm Rehabilitation Administration, Agriculture Canada [*Administration du Retablissement Agricole des Prairies, Agriculture Canada*] Regina, Saskatchewan [*Library symbol National Library of Canada*] (NLC)
SRRI	School Related Resources Index [*Australia*]
SRRI	Wascana Campus, Saskatchewan Institute of Applied Science and Technology, R egina, Saskatchewan [*Library symbol National Library of Canada*] (NLC)
SRRP	Source Reduction Review Program [*Environmental science*]
SRRS	Social Readjustment Rating Scale [*Psychometrics*]
SR-RSV........	Rous Sarcoma Virus, Schmidt-Ruppin Strain
SRRT	Simultaneous Rotating and Reciprocating Technique (DNAB)
SRRT	Social Responsibilities Round Table [*American Library Association*] (EA)
SRS	Sales Relations Survey [*Test*]
SRS	San Marcos [*Colombia*] [*Airport symbol*] (AD)
SRS	Saskoil, Regina, Saskatchewan [*Library symbol National Library of Canada*] (NLC)
SRS	Satellite RADAR Station (NATG)
SRS	Satellite Readout Station (MCD)
SRS	Satellite Receiving Station
SRS	Savannah River Site [*Department of Energy*] [*Aiken, SC*] (GAAI)
SRS	Saved Registers Stack (ECII)
SRS	Scandinavian Radiological Society (EA)
SRS	Schizophrenic Residual State [*Psychology*] (DB)
SRS	Science Requirements Strategy [*Viking lander mission*] [*NASA*]
SRS	Scientific Reference Service [*HEW*]
SRS	Scientific Research Society of America [*Later, Sigma XI, The Scientific Research Society of America*] (AAG)
SRS	Scoliosis Research Society (NTPA)
SRS	Scottish Record Society [*Glasgow*] (EA)
SRS	Scottish Reformation Society (DBA)
SRS	Search and Rescue Ship (KSC)
SRS	Seat Reservation System (IAA)
SRS	Secondary RADAR System
SRS	Secondary Recovery Ships [*NASA*] (KSC)
SRS	Second Readiness State (AAG)
SRS	Secure Range Safety [*NASA*] (KSC)
SRS	Segment Ready Storage
SRS	Seismic Recording System
SRS	Selective Record Service (NITA)
SRS	Selenium Rectifier Stack
SRS	Self-Rating Scale [*Psychology*]
SRS	Selkirk Remote Sensing Ltd. [*Canada ICAO designator*] (FAAC)
SRS	Senate Recording Studio
SRS	Send Receive Switch [*Telecommunications*] (IAA)
SRS	Septal Rage Syndrome (DB)
SRS	Series [*Deltiology*]
SRS	Sex Reassignment Surgery (STED)
SRS	Shakespeare Reading Society [*British*] (DBA)
SRS	Shakespeare Recording Society [*Commercial firm*] (EA)
SRS	Shared Registry System [*Computer science*]
SRS	Shipboard RADAR System
SRS	Shorter Range Scheduling
SRS	Short-Range Search (MCD)
SRS	Side Looking RADAR System
SRS	Sight Restoration Society (EA)
SRS	Silent Running Society (EA)
SRS	Silver-Russell Syndrome [*Medicine*]
SRS	Simple Random Sample [*Statistics*]
SRS	Simulated Raman Scattering
SRS	Simulated Remote Sites [*NASA*] (KSC)
SRS	Simulated Remote Station [*NASA*]
SRS	Skeletal Repair System [*Medicine*]
SRS	Slave Register Set
SRS	Sleep Research Society (EA)
SRS	Slippery Rock State College, Slippery Rock, PA [*OCLC symbol*] (OCLC)
SRS	Slow-Reacting Substance [*of anaphylaxis*] [*Leukotriene C Immunology*]
SRS	Small Research Satellite (KSC)
SRS	Small Ring Sparger [*Engineering*]
SRS	Social and Rehabilitation Service [*Abolished, 1977*] [*HEW*]
SRS	Social Reticence Scale (TES)
SRS	Societatis Regiae Socius [*or Sodalis*] [*Fellow of the Royal Society*] [*Latin*] (GPO)
SRS	Society for Reproductive Surgeons (NTPA)
SRS	Society for Romanian Studies (EA)
SRS	Sodium Removal Station [*Nuclear energy*] (NRCH)
SRS	Software Requirements Specification [*NASA*] (NASA)
SRS	Solar Radiation Satellite (IAA)
SRS	Solar Radiation Simulator
SRS	Solid RADWASTE [*Radioactive Waste*] System [*Nuclear energy*] (NRCH)
SRS	Solvents Recovery Service (EFIS)
SRS	Songwriters Resources and Services [*Later, NAS*] (EA)
SRS	Sonobuoy Reference System [*Navy*] (CAAL)
SRS	Sounding Rocket System
SRS	Sound Ranging Section (IAA)
SRS	Sound Ranging Set
SRS	Sound Recordings Specialists [*Record label*]
SRS	Sound Retrieval System [*Hughes Aircraft Co.*]
SRS	Southern Railway System (MCD)
SRS	Space and Reentry System (IAA)
SRS	Spaceborne Reconnaissance System
SRS	Space Recovery Systems (KSC)
SRS	Spares Recommendation Sheet (MCD)
SRS	Spares Requirement Schedule (MCD)
SRS	Spatial Reference System [*Mapping*] (EERA)
SRS	Special Revenue Sharing (OICC)
SRS	Specification Requirement Sheet (RDA)
SRS	Specification Revision Sheet [*NASA*] (NASA)
SRS	Speech Reinforcement System
SRS	Splenorenal Shunt [*Medicine*]
SRS	Spontaneous Reporting System [*Food and Drug Administration*]
SRS	Squad Radio Set

SRS	Srpska Radikalna Stranka [*Serbian Radical Party*] [*Former Yugoslavia*] [*Political party*] (PPE)
S/RS	Staff Returns [*Marine Corps*]
SRS	Standard Random Sample
SRS	Standard Reference Section
SRS	Standard Repair Specification (MCD)
SRS	State Revenue Society (EA)
SRS	Statistical Reporting Service [*Later, ESCS*] [*Department of Agriculture*]
SRS	Stimulated Raman Scattering [*Spectrometry*]
SRS	Stimulated Rayleigh Scattering (IAA)
SRS	Strategic Reconnaissance Squadron (MCD)
SRS	Strike Reporting System
SRS	Structural Research Series
SRS	Student Record System [*Australia*]
SRS	Student Response System [*Automated group instruction*]
SRS	Submarine Reactor Small
SRS	Subscriber-Response System [*Study of cable television*] [*Hughes Aircraft Co.*]
SRS	Substitute Route Structure
SRS	Sum of All Repairable Subassemblies
SRS	Sunrise Metals [*Vancouver Stock Exchange symbol*]
SRS	Supplemental Restraint System [*Automotive engineering*]
SRS	Supply Response Section [*Navy*]
SRS	Support Requirement System [*NASA*] (NASA)
SRS	Surgical Research Society [*British*]
SRS	Surveillance RADAR Station
SRS	Survey Research Service [*National Opinion Research Center, University of Chicago*] [*Research center*]
SRS	Survey Research Singapore (Pte) Ltd. [*Information service or system*] (IID)
SRS	Swiss Railways Society [*British*] (DBA)
SRS	Symptom Rating Scale (STED)
SRS	Synchronous Relay Satellite [*Telecommunications*] (TEL)
SRS	Synchrotron Radiation Source [*High-energy physics*]
SRS	System Requirements Specification (MCD)
SRS	Systems Reliability Service (NUCP)
SRSA	Saskatchewan Arts Board, Regina, Saskatchewan [*Library symbol National Library of Canada*] (NLC)
SRSA	Scientific Research Society of America [*Later, Sigma XI, The Scientific Research Society of America*]
SRS-A	Slow-Reacting Substance of Anaphylaxis [*Immunology*]
SRSAGM	Short-Range Surface-to-Air Guided Weapon (IAA)
SR SATSIM	Search RADAR Satellite Simulation [*Military*] (CAAL)
SRSC	Slippery Rock State College [*Pennsylvania*]
SRSC	Space Remote Sensing Center
SRSC	Sul Ross State College [*Later, SRSU*] [*Texas*]
SRSC	System Centre, Saskatchewan Revenue Supply and Services, Regina, Saskatchewan [*Library symbol National Library of Canada*] (NLC)
SRSCC	Simulated Remote Station Control Center
SRSCC	Simulated Remote Station Control Console [*NASA*] (IAA)
SRSCCD	Saskatchewan Co-Operation and Co-Operative Development, Regina, Saskatchewan [*Library symbol National Library of Canada*] (NLC)
SRSCU	Saskatchewan Computer Utility Corp. [*SaskComp*], Regina, Saskatchewan [*Library symbol National Library of Canada*] (NLC)
SRSEM	Saskatchewan Department of Energy and Mines, Regina, Saskatchewan [*Library symbol National Library of Canada*] (NLC)
SRSEMG	Geological Laboratory, Saskatchewan Department of Energy and Mines, Regina, Saskatchewan [*Library symbol National Library of Canada*] (NLC)
SRSF	and Subassembly Facility [*or Refurbishment*] [*NASA*] (NASA)
SRSF	Saskatchewan Finance, Regina, Saskatchewan [*Library symbol National Library of Canada*] (NLC)
SRSG	Search RADAR Simulation Group [*Military*] (CAAL)
SRSG	Special Representatives of the Secretary General [*United Nations*]
SRSG	Subsurface Geological Laboratory, Regina, Saskatchewan [*Library symbol National Library of Canada*] (NLC)
SRSH	Wascana Hospital, Regina, Saskatchewan [*Library symbol National Library of Canada*] (NLC)
SRSK	Short-Range Station Keeping (NG)
SRSL	SRS Labs, Inc. [*NASDAQ symbol*] (SAG)
SRS Lbs	SRS Labs, Inc. [*Associated Press*] (SAG)
SRSM	Special Research Study Memorandum
SRSNY	Stockholder Relations Society of New York (EA)
SRSO	Scoliosis Research Society (EA)
SRSO	Silicon-Rich Silicon Oxide [*Inorganic Chemistry*]
SR-SOM	Short-Range Stand-Off Missile [*Military*] (MUSM)
SRSP	Stockpile Reliability/Survivability Program
SRSPMC	Saskatchewan Property Management Corp., Regina, Saskatchewan [*Library symbol National Library of Canada*] (NLC)
SRSPX	SteinRoe Special [*Mutual fund ticker symbol*] (SG)
SRSQ	Sex Role Stereotype Questionnaire (DHP)
SR Sq	Strategic Reconnaissance Squadron
SRSR	Schedule and Resources Status Report [*NASA*] (NASA)
SRS-RSV	Schmidt-Ruppin Strain Rous Sarcoma Virus [*Oncology*] (DAVI)
SRSS	Resource Centre, Saskatchewan Department of Social Services, Regina, Saskatchewan [*Library symbol National Library of Canada*] (NLC)
SRSS	Shuttle Range Safety System [*NASA*] (NASA)
SRSS	Simulated Remote Sites Subsystem [*NASA*] (KSC)
SRSS	Sociological Resources for Secondary Schools (AEBS)
SRSS	Sociological Resources for Social Studies [*Project of American Sociological Association*]

SRSS	Solar Radiation Simulator System
SRSS	Square Root of the Sum of the Squares (NRCH)
SR-SS	Sunrise-Sunset (DA)
SRST	SASK TEL Corporate Library, Regina, Saskatchewan [*Library symbol National Library of Canada*] (NLC)
SRST	Speed Reading Self-Taught [*Learning International*]
SRST	System Resource and Status Table [*Computer science*] (IAA)
SRSTA	Society of Roller Skating Teachers of America (EA)
SRSU	Satellite Readout Station Upgrade (DWSG)
SRSU	Sul Ross State University [*Texas*]
SRSV	Small Round-Structured Virus [*Medicine*]
SRSV	Source Services Corp. [*NASDAQ symbol*] (SAG)
SRT	Sagittal Ray Trace
SRT	Sarafotoxin [*Biochemistry*]
SRT	Sarutani [*Japan*] [*Seismograph station code, US Geological Survey*] (SEIS)
SRT	S-Band Radio Transmitter
SRT	Scarlet Energy, Inc. [*Vancouver Stock Exchange symbol*]
SRT	School Readiness Test [*Child development test*]
SRT	School Response Team
SRT	Science Recommendation Team
SRT	Science, Research, and Technology
SRT	Search RADAR Terminal
SRT	Security Response Team [*Military*]
SRT	Sedimentation Rate Test
SRT	Self-Repair Technique
SRT	Serials Round Table [*Later, RTSD*] [*American Library Association*]
SRT	Set Reset Trigger [*Flipflop*] [*Computer science*] (IAA)
SRT	Shift-Register Transfer [*Computer science*]
SRT	Short-Range Transport [*Aircraft*] (NATG)
SRT	Short Residence Time [*Chemical engineering*]
SRT	Shuttle Requirements Traceability [*NASA*] (MCD)
SRT	Sick Role Tendency [*Medicine*] (STED)
SRT	Silica RADOME Technique
SRT	Simple Reaction Time [*Psychometry*]
SRT	Single Requesting Terminal [*Computer science*] (IBMDP)
SRT	Single Run Time (IAA)
SRT	Sinus Node Recovery Time [*Medicine*] (DMAA)
SRT	Slow-Run-Through Trials [*Navy*] (NG)
SRT	Sludge Retention Time [*Wastewater treatment*]
SRT	Smoke Removal tube [*Used in laser therapy*] [*Gynecology*] (DAVI)
SRT	Social Relations Test [*Psychology*]
SRT	Society of Romanian Air Transports [*ICAO designator*] (FAAC)
SRT	Solar Radiation Test
SRT	Solar Radio Telescope
SRT	Solids Retention Time [*Water pollution*]
SRT	Soroti [*Uganda*] [*Airport symbol*] (OAG)
SRT	Source Routing Transparent [*Telecommunications*]
SRT	Special Rated Thrust [*Aerospace*] (MCD)
SRT	Special Real-Time Command (MCD)
SRT	Special Response Team [*Marine Corps*] (MUSM)
SRT	Special Review Team [*Nuclear energy*] (NRCH)
SRT	Specification Requirements Table [*NASA*] (NASA)
SRT	Speech Reception Test [*Audiometry*] (MAE)
SRT	Speech Reception Thresholds [*Audiometry*]
SRT	Speech Recognition Technology [*Computer science*] (CDE)
SRT	Spent Resin Tank [*Nuclear energy*] (NRCH)
SRT	Spontaneously Resolving Thyrotoxicosis (STED)
SRT	Spousal Remainder Trust [*Banking*]
SRT	Standard Radio & Telefon (NITA)
SRT	Standard Rate Turn (NVT)
SRT	Standard Remote Terminal
SRT	Station Readiness Test
SRT	Step Recovery Transistor
SRT	Strategic Relocatable Target [*DoD*]
SRT	Strategic Rocket Troops (NATG)
SRT	Stress Relief Tool
SRT	Stroke Rehabilitation Technician (MAE)
SRT	Subcaliber Rocket Trainer [*Army*] (INF)
SRT	Supply Response Time
SRT	Supporting Research and Technology (MCD)
SRT	Surface Recording Terminal (MCD)
SRT	Sustained Release Theophylline [*Medicine*]
SRT	Symptom Rating Test [*Medicine*] (STED)
SRT	Synchro and Resolver Transmission
SRT	System Reaction Time (KSC)
SRT	System Reliability Test
SRT	Systems Readiness Test (KSC)
SRTA	Senorita [*Miss*] [*Spanish*]
SRTA	Single Relaxation Time Approximation [*Physics*]
SRTA	Stationary Reflector/Tracking Absorber [*Solar power*] (DICI)
SRTB	Source Routing-Transparent Bridge [*IBM Corp.*] (CIST)
SRTBM	Short-Range Tactical Ballistic Missile
SRTBX	Mgn. Stanley D. Witter Strategist Cl.B [*Mutual fund ticker symbol*] (SG)
SRTC	Savannah River Technology Center [*Department of Energy*]
SRTC	Scientific Research Tax Credit [*Canada*]
SRTC	Search RADAR Terrain Clearance (NG)
SRTC	Signal Replacement Training Center (IAA)
SRTC	Society of Ration Token Collectors (EA)
SRTC	Southern Rhodesia Transport Corps [*British military*] (DMA)
SRTC	Special Real-Time Command (KSC)
SRTC	Stored Program Real-Time Commands (MCD)
SRTCA	Senate Radio-Television Correspondents Association (NTCM)
SRTD	Sorted (MCD)

SRTE............	Sound Receiving/Transmitting Equipment
SRTF............	Shortest Remaining Time First [*Computer science*]
SRTF............	Short-Range Task Force
SRTM............	Shuttle Radar Topography Mission [*NASA*]
SRTM............	Simplified Real-Time Monitor [*Computer science*] (MHDI)
SRTN............	Sensor Return [*Automotive engineering*]
SRTN............	Solar Radio Telescope Network
SRTN............	Special Representative for Trade Negotiations [*Later, USTR*] [*Executive Office of the President*]
SRTOS........	Special Real-Time Operating System (PDAA)
SRTP..........	Sensitized Room Temperature Phosphorescence
SRTR..........	Senior Tour Players Development [*NASDAQ symbol*] (SAG)
SRTR..........	Senior Tour Players Dvlmt [*NASDAQ symbol*] (TTSB)
SRTR..........	Short-Range Training Round [*Army*] (INF)
SRTRW........	Senior Tour Players Dev Wrrt [*NASDAQ symbol*] (TTSB)
SRTS..........	Scaled Range Target System (MCD)
SRTS..........	Science Research Temperament Scale [*Psychology*]
SRTS..........	Short-Range Thermal Sight [*Army*] (INF)
SRTS..........	Steam Railway Traction Society [*British*] (BI)
SRTS..........	Strategic Reconnaissance Training Squadron
SRTS..........	Surveillance RADAR Test Set
SRTSB........	Business Library, Saskatchewan Department of Tourism and Small Business, Regina,Saskatchewan [*Library symbol National Library of Canada*] (NLC)
SRTT............	Serial Reaction Time Task [*Physiology*]
SRTU	Ship Repair Training Unit
SRTUC........	Southern Rhodesian Trade Unions Congress
SRTV	Soldiers Radio and Television [*Information service or system Military*]
SRTVM........	Short-Range Track via Missile [*Military*] (CAAL)
SRU	Santa Cruz, CA [*Location identifier FAA*] (FAAL)
SRU	Scottish Rugby Union (DAS)
SRU	Seaplane Reconnaissance Unit
SRU	Search and Rescue Unit (COE)
SRU	Secondary Replaceable Unit
SRU	Selective Reserve Unit [*Navy*] (NVT)
SRU	Self-Recording Unit (IAA)
SRU	Self-Representing Unit (GFGA)
SRU	Sensor Readout Unit (MCD)
SRU	Servo Repeater Unit
SRU	Ship Repair Unit
SRU	Shop-Replaceable Unit [*NASA*] (NASA)
SRU	Side Rails Up [*On a bed*] (DAVI)
SRU	Signal Responder Unit (AAG)
SRU	Silver Recovery Unit
SRU	Smallest Replaceable Unit (MCD)
SRU	Societe de Raffinage d'Uranium [*France*]
SRU	Solitary Rectal Ulcer [*Medicine*] (DMAA)
SRU	Space Replaceable Unit (MCD)
SRU	Structural Repeating Unit [*Polymer nomenclature system*]
SRU	Student Response Unit
SRU	Subassembly Repairable Unit (MCD)
SRU	Submarine Repair Unit
SRU	Subscriber-Response Unit (IAA)
SRU	Sulfur Recovery Unit [*Chemical engineering*]
SRU	Support Resource Unit (MCD)
SRU	Suspension and Release Units (AFM)
SRU	System Replaceable Unit
SRU	System Resource Unit [*Environmental Protection Agency*] (GFGA)
SRU	University of Regina, Saskatchewan [*Library symbol National Library of Canada*] (NLC)
SRU	University of Scranton, Scranton, PA [*OCLC symbol*] (OCLC)
SRUA..........	Saskatchewan Urban Affairs, Regina, Saskatchewan [*Library symbol National Library of Canada*] (NLC)
SRUC..........	Regina Campus, Campion College, University of Saskatchewan, Saskatchewan [*Library symbol National Library of Canada*] (NLC)
SRUE..........	Education Library, University of Regina, Saskatchewan [*Library symbol National Library of Canada*] (BIB)
SRUFA........	Faculty of Fine Arts, University of Regina, Saskatchewan [*Library symbol National Library of Canada*] (NLC)
SRUG..........	Department of Geography, University of Regina, Saskatchewan [*Library symbol National Library of Canada*] (NLC)
SRUNM.......	Norman MacKenzie Art Gallery, University of Regina, Saskatchewan [*Library symbol National Library of Canada*] (NLC)
SRUS..........	Solitary Rectal Ulcer Syndrome [*Medicine*] (STED)
SRV	Safety Relief Valve [*Nuclear energy*] (NRCH)
SRV	Saline Retention Value
SRV	Satellite Reentry Vehicle
SRV	Schmidt-Ruppin Virus [*Medicine*] (DB)
SRV	Service Corp. International [*NYSE symbol*] (SPSG)
SRV	Service Corp. Intl [*NYSE symbol*] (TTSB)
SRV	Shark River Virus [*Medicine*] (DB)
SRV	Short-Range Viewer
SRV	Simian Retrovirus [*Medicine*] (TAD)
SRV	Simulated Reentry Vehicle
SRV	Sirius Resources [*Vancouver Stock Exchange symbol*]
SRV	Socialist Republic of Vietnam
SRV	Society of Russian Veterans of the World War (EA)
SRV	Space Recovery [*or Rescue*] Vehicle
SRV	Step Recovery Varactor
SRV	Stony River [*Alaska*] [*Airport symbol*] (OAG)
SRV	Styling Research Vehicle [*Automotive engineering*]
SRV	Submerged Research Vehicle
SRV	Superior Radicular Vein (STED)
SRV	Surface Recombination Velocity (DEN)
SRV	Surface Roving Vehicle [*NASA*] (KSC)

SRV	Surrogate Research Vehicle [*Army Tank-Automotive Command*]
SRV	Surveillance (DA)
SRV	System Readiness Verification
SRVAMPL....	Servo Amplifier (IAA)
S-R variation...	Smooth-Rough Variation (STED)
Srvc............	Service
SRVC	Sine-Random Vibration Control
SRVC	SunRiver Corp. [*NASDAQ symbol*] (TTSB)
SRVCD........	Serviced [*Automotive advertising*]
SRVCLG......	Service Ceiling [*Aerospace engineering*]
SRVCW.......	SunRiver Corp. Wrrt [*NASDAQ symbol*] (TTSB)
SRVDL........	Safety/Relief Valve Discharge Line [*Nuclear energy*] (NRCH)
Srve............	Service
SRVEILOPS...	Surveillance Operations [*Military*] (NVT)
SRVIN..........	Servo Inlet (IAA)
SRVL	Survival (MSA)
SRVLSCH....	Survival School [*Air Force*]
SRVPrT........	SCI Fin $3.125'TECONS' [*NYSE symbol*] (TTSB)
SRVRET.......	Servo Return (IAA)
Srvs............	Services (PHSD)
SRVT	Sustained Re-Entrant Ventricular Tachyarrhythmia [*Cardiology*] (DMAA)
SrvTch	Serv-Tech, Inc. [*Associated Press*] (SAG)
SRVY	Survey
SRW	Salisbury, NC [*Location identifier FAA*] (FAAL)
SRW	Saskatchewan Wheat Pool, Regina, Saskatchewan [*Library symbol National Library of Canada*] (NLC)
SRW	Savannah River Water (COE)
SRWM..........	Search & Rescue HQ [*British ICAO designator*] (FAAC)
SRW	Short Ragweed [*Immunology*]
SRW	Silenced Reconnaissance Weapon (MCD)
SRW	Smith(Charles E.)Res Rlty [*NYSE symbol*] (TTSB)
SRW	Smith [*Charles E.*] Residential Realty, Inc. [*NYSE symbol*] (SAG)
SRW	Strategic Reconnaissance Wing [*Air Force*] (MCD)
SRWA..........	Swiss Review of World Affairs [*A publication*]
SRWBR........	Short-Range Wideband Radio (MCD)
SRWD..........	South Saskatchewan Committee for World Development, Regina, Saskatchewan [*Library symbol National Library of Canada*] (NLC)
SRWG..........	Software Review Working Group [*Computer science*] (MHDI)
SRWg	Strategic Reconnaissance Wing [*Air Force*] (AFM)
SRWL	Speeded Reading of Word List [*Neuropsychology test*]
SRWR..........	Saskatchewan Water Resources Commission, Regina, Saskatchewan [*Library symbol National Library of Canada*] (NLC)
SRWS..........	Simplified and Regularized Writing System
SRWS..........	Solid Radioactive Waste System [*Nuclear energy*] (NRCH)
SRWS..........	Standard Reference Water Sample [*US Geological Survey*]
SRX	Sert [*Libya*] [*Airport symbol Obsolete*] (OAG)
SRX	SR Telecom, Inc. [*Toronto Stock Exchange symbol*]
SRY	Secondary [*ICAO designator*] (FAAC)
SRY	Sherwood Rangers Yeomanry [*Military unit*] [*British*]
SRY	Ship Repair Yard (CINC)
SRY	Shiroyama [*Japan*] [*Seismograph station code, US Geological Survey*] (SEIS)
SRY	Stryker Resources Ltd. [*Vancouver Stock Exchange symbol*]
SRY	Surety Capital [*AMEX symbol*] (TTSB)
SRY	Surety Capital Corp. [*AMEX symbol*] (SAG)
SRZ	San Marcos, TX [*Location identifier FAA*] (FAAL)
SRZ	Santa Cruz [*Bolivia*] [*Airport symbol*] (OAG)
SRZ............	Satz Rechen Zentrum [*Computer Composition Center*] [*Hartmann & Heenemann*] [*Information service or system*] (IID)
SRZ............	Special Rules Zone
SRZ............	Stratas Corp. [*Vancouver Stock Exchange symbol*]
SRZ............	Surveillance RADAR Zone (DA)
SRZF	Synchro Resolver Zeroing Fixture
SRZLO........	Supreme Royal Zuanna, Ladies of the Orient [*Defunct*] (EA)
SS................	Faulty Sentence Structure [*Used in correcting manuscripts, etc.*]
SS................	Passing Stop Sign [*Traffic offense charge*]
SS................	Royal Statistical Society [*British*]
SS................	Saccharin Sodium [*Sweetening agent*]
SS................	Sacred Scripture
SS................	Safer Sex
SS................	Safe Shutdown [*Nuclear energy*] (NRCH)
SS................	Safety Services [*Red Cross*]
SS................	Safety Supervisor (MUGU)
SS................	Safety Supplements [*Air Force*]
SS................	Sagittal Sinus [*Anatomy*]
SS................	Saints [*as in "SS Peter and Paul"*]
SS................	Saint-Sacrement [*Blessed Sacrament*] [*French*]
SS................	Saline Soak
SS................	Saline Solution [*Pharmacology*] (DAVI)
SS................	Saliva Sample (MAE)
SS................	Salmonella-Shigella [*Microbiology*]
SS................	Salt-Sensitive
SS................	Salt Substitute (DAVI)
s/s................	Same Size [*Publishing*] (WDAA)
SS................	Same Size [*Photography, publishing*]
SS................	Sampled Servo [*Formatting scheme*] [*Computer science*] (PCM)
SS................	Sample Sink [*Nuclear energy*] (NRCH)
SS................	Sample Size (EDAC)
S/S................	Samples per Second (KSC)
SS................	Sample Station [*Nuclear energy*] (NRCH)
SS................	Sampling System (NRCH)
SS................	Sanarelli-Schwartzman [*Reaction*] [*Medicine*] (DAVI)
SS................	Sancti [*Saints*] [*Latin*]
SS................	Sanctissimus [*Most Holy*] [*Latin*]

SS .... Sanctum Sanctorum [Holy of Holies] [Freemasonry] [Latin]
SS .... Sand Springs Railway Co. [AAR code]
SS .... Sandstone [Lithology]
SS .... Sans [Without] [Latin] (DAVI)
SS .... Sans Serif [Typeface] [Printing] (NTCM)
SS .... Sartre Society (EA)
SS .... Sa Saintete [His Holiness] [The Pope] [French]
SS .... Sa Seigneurie [His Lordship] [French]
SS .... Saskatoon Public Library, Saskatchewan [Library symbol National Library of Canada] (NLC)
SS .... Satellite Space System (IAA)
SS .... Satellite-Switched
SS .... Satellite System
SS .... Saturated Solution [Pharmacy]
SS .... Sawin Society [Defunct] (EA)
SS .... Scandinavian Seminar (EA)
SS .... Scanning Slit
SS .... Schempp-Hirth KG [Germany ICAO aircraft manufacturer identifier] (ICAO)
SS .... Schizophrenia Spectrum [Psychiatry] (DAVI)
SS .... Schutzstaffel [Elite Guard] [NAZI Germany]
SS .... Science Service
SS .... Scilicet [Namely] [Legal term Latin]
SS .... Scintiscanning [Medicine]
SS .... Sclerotinia sclerlatiorum (Causative Agent of Peanut Blight)
SS .... Screw Steamer
SS .... Sculptors' Society [Australia]
SS .... Sea Scout - Nonrigid Airship [Royal Naval Air Service] [British]
SS .... Sea Service [British military] (DMA)
SS .... Sea State
SS .... Secondary School
SS .... Secondary Sources
SS .... Secondary Surveillance
SS .... Second Stage
SS .... Secretary for Scotland
SS .... Secretary of State
SS .... Secretary of State Department [Canada]
SS .... Secret Service
SS .... Sections (ADA)
SS .... Security Service
SS .... Security Systems, Inc. [In TV series "Max Headroom"]
SS .... See a Solicitor [British]
S/S .... See Safe [Bookselling] (DGA)
SS .... Seingalt Society (EA)
SS .... Seizure Sensitive [Neurology] (DAVI)
SS .... Selden Society (EA)
SS .... Selective Service
SS .... Selective Signaling
SS .... Selector Switch (IEEE)
SS .... Select Standby
S/S .... Self Shank (WDAA)
SS .... Self Simulation
SS .... Selling Short [or Short Sale] [Investment term]
SS .... Semifinal Splice [Telecommunications] (TEL)
SS .... Semis [One-Half] [Pharmacy]
SS .... Semisteel
SS .... Semisubmersible [Drilling unit]
SS .... Sempervivium Society [Burgess Hill, West Sussex, England] (EAIO)
SS .... Senior Scholars (EA)
SS .... Senior Security [Investment term]
SS .... Sensor [Genetics]
SS .... Sensor Supervisor [Military] (CAAL)
SS .... Sensu Stricto [In a Narrow Sense] [Latin]
SS .... Sentence Suspended
SS .... Senza Sordini [Without Mutes] [Music]
SS .... Sequentia [What Follows] [Latin] (ROG)
SS .... Sequential Switch
SS .... Serials Section [Resources and Technical Services Division] [American Library Association]
SS .... Series Separate
Ss .... Serum Serologic [Immunochemistry]
SS .... Serum Sickness [Medicine]
SS .... Service Sink (MSA)
SS .... Service Squadron (AAG)
SS .... Service Structure (KSC)
SS .... Sessions
SS .... Session Service [Telecommunications] (OSI)
SS .... Set Screw [Technical drawings]
SS .... Set Steering
SS .... Sezary Syndrome [Dermatology]
SS .... Shackamaxon Society (EA)
SS .... Sharpshooter [Marine Corps]
SS .... Shear Strength (AAG)
SS .... Shelf Stock
SS .... Shell Shock
SS .... Shift Superintendent (COE)
SS .... Shift Supervisor (IEEE)
SS .... Shigella Sonnei [A bacterium] (DAVI)
SS .... Shimmy Showing [From one girl to another, in reference to dress disarrangement]
SS .... Shiplovers' Society [Australia]
SS .... Shipmasters' Society [A union] [British]
SS .... Shipping Situation [British]
SS .... Ship Service
SS .... Shipside

SS .... Ship Station
SS .... Ship System
S/S .... Ship-to-Shore (MUGU)
SS .... Shock Society (NTPA)
SS .... Shomrim Society (EA)
SS .... Shoot Tip Abscission Scar [Botany]
SS .... Shop Steward
SS .... Short Sight (ADA)
SS .... Short Sleeves
SS .... Short Stay (DAVI)
SS .... Shortstop
SS .... Shosin Society (EA)
SS .... Showroom Stock [Automotive classification]
SS .... Shrinking Stock [Corporate investment]
SS .... Shuttle System [NASA] (MCD)
SS .... Siblings (DAVI)
SS .... Side by Side (AAG)
SS .... Side Scatter
SS .... Side Seam
SS .... Side Slip (MCD)
SS .... Sidestream Smoke [from cigarettes]
SS .... Side-to-Side [Anastomosis] [Cardiology] (DAVI)
SS .... Signaling System [Telecommunications] (TEL)
SS .... Signal Selector (DEN)
SS .... Signal Strength [Broadcasting] (KSC)
SS .... Signed and Sealed
S/S .... Sign Signature (AAG)
S/S .... Silk Screen (ADA)
SS .... Silvernail's New York Supreme Court Reports [A publication] (DLA)
SS .... Silver Spur Resources [Vancouver Stock Exchange symbol]
SS .... Silver Standard [Vancouver Stock Exchange symbol]
SS .... Silver Star [Military decoration]
SS .... Simmonds-Sheehan [Syndrome] [Medicine] (DB)
SS .... Simple Spike
SS .... Simplified Spelling
SS .... Simulated Strike (SAA)
SS .... Simulation Supervisor (SAA)
SS .... Single Scan
SS .... Single Scattering [Photonics]
SS .... Single Seated
SS .... Single Shot
SS .... Single Sideband
SS .... Single Signal
SS .... Single Silk [Wire insulation] (IAA)
SS .... Single Stage (EDCT)
SS .... Single Stout [Beer] (ROG)
SS .... Single-Stranded [or ss] [Genetics]
SS .... Single Strength [Citrus juices]
SS .... Single String (MCD)
SS .... Sinistral Sig (EA)
SS .... Sinner Saved [Pseudonym used by William Huntington]
SS .... Site Safety [Nuclear energy] (NRCH)
SS .... Site Suitability [Nuclear energy] (NRCH)
SS .... Sjoegren's Syndrome [Medicine]
SS .... Skid Strip (KSC)
SS .... Skinners' Society [A union] [British]
SS .... Skull Series [Radiology] (DAVI)
SS .... Slaters' Society [A union] [British]
SS .... Sliding Scale (AAG)
SS .... Slip Sent [Laboratory science] (DAVI)
SS .... Slocum Society (EA)
SS .... Slop Sink
SS .... Slowdown Strike (MHDB)
SS .... Slow Setting [Asphalt grade]
SS .... Slow (Wave) Sleep [Neurology] (DAVI)
SS .... Smallest Subunit [Genetics]
SS .... Small Signal
SS .... Small Subcompact [Car size]
SS .... Smoke Stand (MSA)
SS .... Soap Solution
SS .... Soapsuds
SS .... Social Science
SS .... Social Security
SS .... Social Security Number [Followed by numerals] (DAVI)
SS .... Social Service
SS .... Social Shopper
SS .... Social Studies [A publication] (BRI)
SS .... Social Surveys
SS .... Society for Strings (EA)
SS .... Society of Separationists (EA)
SS .... Society of Shuttlemakers [A union] [British]
SS .... Society of Signalmen (EA)
SS .... Society of St. Sulpice [Sulpicians] [Roman Catholic men's religious order]
SS .... Society of the Priest of Saint Sulpice, Sulpician Fathers (TOCD)
SS .... Society of the Silurians (EA)
SS .... Socioeconomic Status (COE)
SS .... Socket Service [Computer science] (PCM)
SS .... Sodium Salicylate [Organic chemistry] (OA)
SS .... Sodium Sulfite [Inorganic chemistry]
SS .... Soft Sarcoma [Oncology]
SS .... SoftSearch, Inc. [Information service or system] (IID)
SS .... Soft Sized [Paper] (DGA)
SS .... Software Systems
SS .... Solar Simulator (MCD)

SS	Solar System (IAA)
SS	Sole Source (SAA)
SS	Solid Shield (MCD)
SS	Solid Solution (OA)
SS	Solid State
SS	Soluble Solids [Chemistry]
SS	Solution Space
SS	Somatics Society [Commercial firm] (EA)
SS	Somatostatin [Also, GH-RIF, GH-RIH, GRIF, SRIF] [Endocrinology]
SS	Songsmith Society (EA)
SS	Song Sparrow [Ornithology]
SS	Sonneck Society (EA)
SS	Soprano Saxophone
SS	Sound System
SS	Source and Special [Material] [Nuclear energy]
SS	Source of Supply (AFM)
SS	Source Selection (MCD)
S/S	Source/Sink [Computer science] (IBMDP)
SS	Source/Source [Inspection/Acceptance point] (MCD)
SS	South Coast Airlines [ICAO designator] (AD)
SS	South Saxon (ROG)
S/S	South Side [In outdoor advertising] (WDMC)
SS	Souvenir Sheet [Philately]
SS	Space Sciences (IAA)
SS	Space Segment (SSD)
SS	Space Shuttle [NASA] (KSC)
SS	Space Simulator (IEEE)
SS	Space Station (AAG)
SS	Space Switch [Telecommunications] (TEL)
SS	Space System (IAA)
ss	Spanish Sahara [Western Sahara] [MARC country of publication code Library of Congress] (LCCP)
SS	Sparingly Soluble
SS	Special Senses [Medicine] (DAVI)
SS	Special Series
SS	Special Service [Vessel load line mark]
SS	Special Services [Military] (DAVI)
SS	Special Session
SS	Special Settlement [Business term]
SS	Special Source Materials [Nuclear energy] (NRCH)
SS	Special Staff
SS	Special Strike (NATG)
SS	Special Study
SS	Special Subjects
SS	Special Survey [Lloyd's Register of Shipping] (DS)
SS	Specification for Structure
S/S	Spectrum Signature (NG)
SS	Speed Sensor (NRCH)
SS	Spenser Society (EA)
SS	Spherical Symmetry
SS	Spillinger-Stock [Disease] [Medicine] (DB)
SS	Spin-Stabilized [Rockets]
SS	Spiral to Spiral
SS	Spore Surface [Immunology]
SS	Spread Spectrum (CET)
SS	Squawk Sheet (KSC)
S/S	Stabilization/Solidification (FFDE)
SS	Stabilization System (AAG)
SS	Stabilized Screen (IAA)
SS	Stable Sarcoidosis [Medicine] (DAVI)
SS	Staccato Syndrome [Medicine] (DAVI)
SS	Stack Segment [Computer science]
SS	Staff Sergeant [Military British] (ROG)
SS	Staff Specialist [Military]
SS	Staff Surgeon
SS	Stainless Steel
ss	Stainless Steel (VRA)
SS	Standard Frequency Station [ITU designation]
SS	Standardized Solution [Pharmacy]
SS	Standard Score [Psychology]
SS	Standard Size (ADA)
SS	Starlight Scope
S/S	Start/Stop
S/S	Statement of Service [Military]
SS	State School (ADA)
SS	Statesman Series [A publication]
SS	State Supervisor
SS	Static Stretching [Medicine]
SS	Stationary Satellite (IAA)
SS	Stationary Source [Environmental Protection Agency]
SS	Station Set [NASA] (NASA)
SS	Station Supervision
SS	Statistically Significant (MAE)
SS	Statistical Standards
SS	Statistics Section [LAMA] (AL)
SS	Statistics Sources [A publication]
ss	Statsiemens [Also, statS] [Unit of electric conductance, admittance, and susceptance]
SS	Steady State
SS	Steamship
SS	Steel Sash
SS	Steering Safety
SS	Steering.System
SS	Step Size (IAA)
SS	Stereoscopic Society [Chessington, Surrey, England] (EAIO)
SS	Stereoscopic Society - American Branch (EA)
SS	Sterile Solution
SS	Steroid Score [Immunology]
SS	Steroid Sulfurylation (AAMN)
SS	Stickler Syndrome [Medicine] (DMAA)
SS	Stimulator Substance [Liver regeneration]
SS	Stock Shot (NTCM)
SS	Stopped Stock (MHDB)
SS	Stop Scan (IAA)
SS	Storage to Storage (MCD)
SS	Strachan-Scott [Syndrome] [Medicine] (DAVI)
SS	Straight Shank [Screw]
SS	Straight Sided
SS	Straits Settlements [in Malaya]
SS	Strategic Squadron
SS	Strategic Study [Military]
Ss	Striped Shiner [Ichthyology]
SS	Strong Safety [Football]
SS	Structure-Superstructure [Economics]
SS	Student at Staff College [Army British] (ROG)
SS	Stumpwork Society (EA)
SS	Style Sac
SS	Subaortic Stenosis [Medicine] (MAE)
Ss	Subjects in a Study
SS	Subject-Subject [Education of the hearing-impaired]
SS	Subliminal Self [Psychical research]
SS	Submarine [Navy symbol]
SS	Submarine Qualification [Navy]
SS	Submarine Scout
SS	Submarine Studies [SORG]
SS	Subsagittal [Medicine]
SS	Subscale
SS	Subscapularis [Muscle] [Anatomy] (DAVI)
SS	Subscriber Switching [Telecommunications] (TEL)
SS	Subsegmental [Medicine] (DAVI)
SS	Subsequent Sibling (DAVI)
SS	Subsolar [NASA] (KSC)
SS	Substernal [Anatomy] (DAVI)
SS	Substitutes [Sports]
ss	Substructure [Computer science]
SS	Subsystem (AAG)
SS	Suburban Service (DD)
SS	Successive Stereometric [A discrimination task]
SS	Suction Socket (AAMN)
SS	Sugar Snap [Peas] (DICI)
SS	Sulfasalazine (MEDA)
SS	Summary Sheet
SS	Summation Sound
SS	Summing Selector (MSA)
SS	Summono (NOQ)
SS	Sum-of-the-Squares
SS	Sunday School
SS	Sunday Sport [A publication]
SS	Sun Seeker (AAG)
SS	Sun Sensor
SS	Sunset (NAKS)
SS	Sun Simulator (MCD)
SS	Superfund Surcharge [Environmental Protection Agency] (GFGA)
SS	Superintending Scientist [British] (ADA)
SS	Superintending Sister [Navy British]
SS	Supersaturated (MAE)
SS	Super Search (MCD)
SS	Supersensitive (AAG)
SS	Supersonic
SS	Super Speed
SS	Super Sport [In automobile model name]
SS	Super Stock [Automotive classification]
SS	Super Symmetric [Particle physics]
SS	Supervisors Section [American Association of School Librarians]
SS	Supply Ship (MCD)
SS	Supportive Service (OICC)
SS	Support System [Air Force]
SS	Supra Scriptum [Written Above] [Latin]
SS	Surface Ship
SS	Surface-Sized [Paper]
SS	Surface-to-Surface (NATG)
SS	Surging Sine [Mathematics] (DAVI)
SS	Surratt Society (EA)
SS	Surveillance Station [RADAR]
SS	Survivability System [Military]
SS	Suspended Sentence
ss	Suspended Sentence [Legal term] (WDAA)
SS	Suspended Solids [Wastewater treatment]
SS	Swallow Sidecar [Automobile manufacturer] [Forerunner to Jaguar]
SS	Swedish Society, Discofil [Record label] [Sweden]
SS	Sweet Syndrome [Medicine] (DMAA)
SS	Switch Selector (KSC)
SS	Sworn Statement
SS	Symmetrical Strength [Neurology] (DAVI)
SS	Sympathetically Stimulated [Physiology]
SS	Synchro Standard
SS	Synergetic Society (EA)
SS	Synopsis Series of the United States Treasury Decisions [A publication] (DLA)
SS	System Sclerosis [or Scleroderma] [Rheumatology] (DAVI)

SS..............	System Segment (MCD)
SS..............	System Sensitivity
SS..............	System Software [*NASA*] (MCD)
SS..............	Systems Specifications [*NASA*] (NG)
SS..............	System Summary [*NASA*] (MCD)
SS..............	System Supervisor
SS7..............	Signaling System 7 [*Telecommunications*] (OTD)
SSA..............	Associate in Secretarial Science
SSA..............	Cargo Submarine [*Navy symbol Obsolete*]
SSA..............	First Soprano, Second Soprano, and Alto [*in all-women choral groups*]
SSA..............	Safe Sector Altitude [*Aviation*] (DA)
SSA..............	Sagittal Split Advancement (STED)
SSA..............	Salicylaslicylic Acid [*Later, salsalate*] (DAVI)
SSA..............	Salicylsalicylic Acid [*Organic chemistry*] (MAE)
SSA..............	Salisbury Sound Association (EA)
SSA..............	Salsalate [*Anti-inflammatory drug*]
SSA..............	Salvador [*Brazil*] [*Airport symbol*] (OAG)
SSA..............	Saskatchewan Archives Office, Saskatoon, Saskatchewan [*Library symbol National Library of Canada*] (NLC)
SSA..............	SATCOM [*Satellite Command*] Signal Analyser (DWSG)
SSA..............	Sauna Society of America (EA)
SSA..............	S-Band Single Access (MCD)
SSA..............	Scandinavian Society of Anaesthesiologists (EA)
SSA..............	Scandinavian Sociological Association (EA)
SSA..............	School Secretaries Association (DBA)
SSA..............	Schools Sailing Association [*British*]
SSA..............	Scottish Schoolmasters Association [*British*]
SSA..............	Scottish Shipmasters' Association [*A union*]
SSA..............	Secretary of State for Air [*British*]
SSA..............	Security Support Activity
SSA..............	Security Supporting Assistance [*US government program for promoting economic and political stability in areas of strategic interest*]
SSA..............	Segment Search Argument [*Computer science*] (BUR)
SSA..............	Seismological Society of America (EA)
SSA..............	Selective Service Act
SSA..............	Self Storage Association (NTPA)
SSA..............	Semiconductor Industry Association (AAEL)
SSA..............	Semiconductor Safety Association (EA)
SSA..............	Semiotic Society of America (EA)
SSA..............	Senior Scientific Assistant [*Ministry of Agriculture, Fisheries, and Food*] [*British*]
SSA..............	Sensat Technologies Ltd. [*Vancouver Stock Exchange symbol*]
SSA..............	Sequential Spectrometer Accessory [*Instrumentation*]
SSA..............	Serial Storage Architecture [*Computer science*] (CDE)
SSA..............	Series of Standard Additions
SSA..............	Service Specialists Association (NTPA)
SSA..............	Service Support Arrangement
SSA..............	Shakespeare Society of America (EA)
SSA..............	Shan State Army [*Myanmar*] [*Political party*] (EY)
SSA..............	Shaw Society of America [*Defunct*] (EA)
SSA..............	Sheath of Skeletal Axis
SSA..............	Ship's Stores Ashore [*Navy*]
SSA..............	Shuttle Simulation Aircraft [*NASA*] (NASA)
SSA..............	Side-Saddle Association [*British*] (DBA)
SSA..............	Side-to-Side Anastamosis [*Medicine*] (CPH)
SSA..............	Signal Security Agency [*Later, Army Security Agency*]
SSA..............	Signal Supply Agency
SSA..............	Silo Subassembly (SAA)
SSA..............	Simian Society of America (EA)
SSA..............	Simpler Spelling Association [*Later, PSC*] (EA)
SSA..............	Sinatra Society of America (EA)
SSA..............	Single Line Synchronous Adapter (MCD)
SSA..............	Single-Strand Annealing [*Genetics*]
SSA..............	Singular-Spectrum Analysis [*Meteorology*]
SSA..............	Sisters of St. Ann (TOCD)
SSA..............	Sisters of St. Anne (TOCD)
SSA..............	Sisters of St. Ann of Providence [*Roman Catholic religious order*]
SS-A..............	Sjogren's Syndrome A [*Medicine*]
SSA..............	Skin Sensitizing Antibody (AAMN)
SSA..............	Skin Sympathetic Activity [*Medicine*] (DMAA)
SSA..............	Slave Service Area [*Telecommunications*] (IAA)
SSA..............	Slaving Signal Amplifier
SSA..............	Sleeve Stub Antenna
SSA..............	Slovak Studies Association (EA)
SSA..............	Small Search Area (SAA)
SSA..............	Smith Surface Antigen [*Medicine*] (DMAA)
SSA..............	Soaring Society of America (EA)
SSA..............	Social Security Act [*1935*] [*Also, SSACT*]
SSA..............	Social Security Administration [*Department of Health and Human Services*]
SSA..............	Society for the Study of Addiction to Alcohol and Other Drugs (EAIO)
SSA..............	Society of Scottish Artists (DBA)
SSA..............	Society of Security Analysts
SSA..............	Society of Study Addiction [*British*] (DBA)
SSA..............	Software Support Activity (SSD)
SSA..............	Sole-Source Aquifer (GNE)
SSA..............	Solid-State Abstracts
SSA..............	Solid-State Amorphization [*Metallurgy*]
SSA..............	Solid State Amplifier (NTCM)
SSA..............	Somali Salvation Alliance
SSA..............	Sommelier Society of America (EA)
SSA..............	Source Selection Activity [*or Authority*] [*Military*]
SSA..............	Space Structure Assembly (SSD)
SSA..............	Space Suit Assembly (KSC)
SSA..............	Spanish-Surnamed American
SSA..............	Spatial Sound Around [*Acoustics*]
SSA..............	Specialist in School Administration (GAGS)
SSA..............	Special Service Agreement [*UN Food and Agriculture Organization*]
SSA..............	Special Service Authorization [*FCC*] (NTCM)
SSA..............	Special Somatic Afferent (STED)
SSA..............	Special Support Activity [*National Security Agency*] (DOMA)
SSA..............	Special Survey Automated Controls [*Lloyd's Register of Shipping*] (DS)
SSA..............	Specialty Sleep Association (NTPA)
SSA..............	Sperm-Specific Antigen (STED)
SSA..............	Sperm-Specific Antiserum (STED)
SSA..............	Sportswear Salesmen's Association (EA)
SSA..............	Staff Supply Assistant [*Military*] (AABC)
SSA..............	Staff Support Agencies [*Military*]
SSA..............	Staging and Support Area [*NASA*] (KSC)
SSA..............	Standard Single Account (INF)
SSA..............	Standard Spending Assessment [*Department of the Environment*] [*British*]
SSA..............	Standard System Applications [*Military*]
SSA..............	Star of Asia [*Kyrgyzstan*] [*FAA designator*] (FAAC)
SSA..............	Stars of the Stage [*A publication*]
SSA..............	Steel Sleeper Association [*British*] (BI)
SSA..............	Steuben Society of America (EA)
SSA..............	Stick Sensor Assembly (MCD)
SSA..............	Stratford Public Library, Stratford, CT [*OCLC symbol*] (OCLC)
SSA..............	Stratosphere Sulfate Aerosol [*Meteorology*]
SSA..............	Streptococcal Superantigen [*Immunochemistry*]
SSA..............	Structured Systems Analysis (NITA)
SSA..............	Student Ski Association (EA)
SSA..............	Studio Suppliers Association (EA)
SSA..............	Style Sac Artery
ssa..............	Sub-Saharan African [*MARC language code Library of Congress*] (LCCP)
SSA..............	Sub-Saharan African Country
SSA..............	Subsegmental Airway (STED)
SSA..............	Subsegmental Atelectasis (STED)
SSA..............	Subterranean Sociological Association (EA)
SSA..............	Sulfite Sensitive Asthmatic
SSA..............	Sulfosalicylic Acid [*Organic chemistry*]
SSA..............	Sumi-E Society of America (EA)
SSA..............	Supply Support Activity [*Military*] (AABC)
SSA..............	Supply Support Arrangements [*A bilateral agreement between the United States and a friendly foreign government*]
SSA..............	Support Services Alliance [*Schoharie, NY*] (EA)
SSA..............	Survey of School Attitudes [*Student attitudes test*]
SSA..............	Survival Surface-to-Air (MCD)
SSA..............	Suspension Specialists Association (EA)
SSA..............	Symbol Synchronizer Assembly [*NASA*]
SSA..............	Synchro Signal Amplifier
SSA..............	System Safety Assessment [*Army*]
SSAA..............	Saskatchewan Institute of Applied Arts, Saskatoon, Saskatchewan [*Library symbol National Library of Canada*] (NLC)
SSAA..............	Self Storage Association of Australia
SSAA..............	Shoe Suppliers Association of America (EA)
SSAA..............	Skate Sailing Association of America (EA)
SSAA..............	Social Security Acts Amendments [*A publication*] (DLA)
SSAA..............	Space Science Analysis Area [*Space Flight Operations Facility, NASA*]
SSAAII..............	Ses Altesses Imperiales [*Their Imperial Highnesses*] [*French*] (ROG)
SSAANSW..............	Stock and Station Agents' Association of New South Wales [*Australia*]
SSAAT..............	Sun Sensor Attitude Angle Transducer
SSAB..............	Site-Specific Advisory Board
SS-Ab..............	Sjogren's Syndrome Antibody [*Immunology*] (DAVI)
SSAB..............	Source Selection Advisory Board (USDC)
SSAB..............	Special Surveys and Analysis Branch [*National Center for Education Statistics*] [*Department of Education*] (GFGA)
SSAC..............	Armak Chemicals, Saskatoon, Saskatchewan [*Library symbol National Library of Canada*] (NLC)
SSAC..............	Auxiliary Submarine [*Navy symbol*]
SSAC..............	Scottish Society of Autistic Children (DBA)
SSAC..............	Scottish Sub-Aqua Club (DBA)
SSAC..............	Secondary School Admissions Center [*Defunct*] (EA)
SSAC..............	Signalling System Alternating Current (NITA)
SSAC..............	Social Security Advisory Committee [*British*]
SSAC..............	Social Security Advisory Council [*Australia*]
SSAC..............	Society for the Study of Architecture in Canada [*Established 1974*]
SSAC..............	Soil Site Assimilated Capacity [*Environmental science*] (COE)
SSAC..............	Solid-State Audio Clock (DWSG)
SSAC..............	Source Selection Advisory Council [*Military*] (AFM)
SSAC..............	Space Science Advisory Committee [*European Space Agency*]
SSAC..............	Space Science Analysis and Command [*Team*] [*NASA*]
SSAC..............	Sponsors' Standards Advisory Committee [*American National Standards Institute*]
SSAC..............	Standing State Advisory Committee [*Terminated, 1977*] [*of Water Resources Council*] (EGAO)
SSAC..............	Suprasellar Arachnoid Cyst [*Medicine*]
SSAC..............	Suspended Sprayed Acoustical Ceiling [*Technical drawings*]
SSACT..............	Social Security Act [*1935*] [*Also, SSA*]
SSADARS..............	Social Security Administration Data Acquisition and Response System
SSADC..............	Solid-State Air Data Computer (MCD)
SSADH..............	Succinate-Semialdehyde Dehydrogenase [*An enzyme*]

SSADM	Structured Systems Analysis and Design Method [*British*]
SSADP	Soldier's, Sailor's, and Airmen's Deposit Program (DNAB)
SSADP	Support Site Activation Data Package (MCD)
SSAE	Society of Senior Aerospace Executives (EA)
SSAE	Stamped Self-Addressed Envelope (WDMC)
SSAEC	Society for the Study of Alchemy and Early Chemistry [*British*]
SSAEPL	Space Station Approved EEE [*Electrical, Electronic, and Electromechanical*]Parts List (SSD)
SSAF	S-Band, Single Access Forward (SSD)
SSAF	Standard Single Account File [*Number*] (MCD)
SSAFA	Soldiers, Sailors, and Airmen's Family Association [*British*]
SSAG	Single-Step Acidulation Granulation [*Fertilizer technology*]
SSAG	Strategic Studies Advisory Group [*Army*] (AABC)
SSAGA	Animal Pathology Laboratory, Food Production and Inspection Branch, Agriculture Canada [*Laboratoire de Pathologie Veterinaire, Direction Generale de la Production et de l'Inspection des Aliments, Agriculture Canada*], Saskatoon, Saskatchewan [*Library symbol National Library of Canada*] (BIB)
SSAGR	Research Station, Agriculture Canada [*Station de Recherches, Agriculture Canada*] Saskatoon, Saskatchewan [*Library symbol National Library of Canada*] (NLC)
SSAIA	Serial Storage Architecture Industry Association (NTPA)
SSAIS	Senior South African Individual Scale [*Intelligence test*]
SSAJ	Sweep Stop Alarm Jam (MCD)
SSAL	Sequenced Flashing Lights [*Aviation*] (DA)
SSAL	Simplified Short Approach Light [*Aviation*]
S-SAL	Solar Scientific Airlock
SSALF	Simplified Short ALS [*Approach Light System*] with Sequenced Flashers [*Aviation*]
SSALR	Simplified Short ALS [*Approach Light System*] with Runway Alignment Indicator Lights [*Aviation*]
SSALR	Simplified Short Approach Light System with Rail [*FAA*] (TAG)
SSALS	Simplified Short Approach Light System [*Aviation*]
SSALSR	Simplified Short Approach Light System with Runway Alignment Indicator Lights [*Aviation*]
SSAM	Seismic Spectral Amplitude Measurement
SSAMA	Sailors, Soldiers and Airmen's Mothers' Association of Australia
SSAMR	John Dolan Resource Library, Saskatchewan Association for the Mentally Retarded,Saskatoon, Saskatchewan [*Library symbol National Library of Canada*] (NLC)
SSAMX	State St. Research Managed Assets Cl.A [*Mutual fund ticker symbol*] (SG)
SSAN	Social Security Account Number
SS & A	Space Systems and Applications [*NASA*] (NASA)
SS & C	Same Sea and Country [*or Coast*] [*Shipping*] (DS)
SS & C	Supersized and Calendered [*Paper*]
SS & CS	Ship's Stores and Commissary Stores [*Navy*]
SS & D	Synchronization Separator and Digitizer
SS & FO	Specialized Safety and Flight Operations
SS & P	Service, Supply, and Procurement [*Military*]
SSAO	Semicarbazide-Sensitive Amine Oxidase [*Biochemistry*]
SSAO	Solid-State Audio Oscillator
SSAP	Source Service Access Point
SSAP	Statement of Standard Accounting Practice
SSAP	Survival Stabilator Actuator Package [*Hydraulic power*]
SSAPEA	Swedish Society Against Painful Experiments on Animals (EAIO)
SSAR	S-Band, Single Access Return (SSD)
S-SAR	Secret - Special Access Required [*Security classification*] (MCD)
SSAR	Site Safety Analysis Report [*Nuclear energy*] (NRCH)
SSAR	Social Security Acquisition Regulation [*A publication*] (AAGC)
SSAR	Society for the Study of Amphibians and Reptiles (EA)
SSAR	Special Save Register [*Computer science*] (IAA)
SSAR	Spin-Stabilized Aircraft Rocket
SSAR	Standard Safety Analysis Report [*Nuclear energy*] (NRCH)
SSAR	Steady State Adiabatic Reactor [*Chemical engineering*]
SSAR	Stereo Synthetic Aperture RADAR (SSD)
SSARR	Streamflow Synthesis and Reservoir Regulation [*Computer science*]
SSARS	Statement on Standards for Accounting and Review Services (EBF)
SSAS	Salzburg Seminar in American Studies (EA)
SSAS	Searchless Self-Adjusting System
SSAS	Self-Scoring Answer Sheet (DNAB)
SSAS	Signal Security Assessment System [*Military*] (CAAL)
SSAS	Small Sample Assay System [*Nuclear energy*] (NRCH)
SSAS	Small Self-Administered Scheme [*Pensions*] [*British*]
SSAS	Society for South Asian Studies (EAIO)
SSAS	Special Signal Analysis System [*Electronic countermeasures system*]
SSAS	Stable Super-Active Scavenger [*Color film technology*]
SSAS	Static Stability Augmentation System [*Aviation*]
SSAS	Station Signaling and Announcement Subsystem [*Telecommunications*] (TEL)
SSAS	Surface Ship Advance Sonar [*Navy*] (LAIN)
SSAS	Synthetic Sodium Aluminosilicate [*Inorganic chemistry*]
SSAT	Screening Speech Articulation Test [*Educational test*]
SSAT	Secondary School Admission Test Board (EA)
SSAT	Shuttle Service and Access Tower [*NASA*] (NASA)
SSAT	Society for Surgery of the Alimentary Tract (EA)
SSAT	Space Shuttle Access Tower [*NASA*] (MCD)
SSAT	Space Station Assembly Technology (SSD)
SSAT	State Student Assessment Test [*Florida*] (EDAC)
SSAT	Steady-State Advanced TOKAMAK [*Toroidal Kamera Magnetic*] [*Plasma physics*]
SSAT	Sweep Stop Alarm Target [*Military*] (CAAL)
SSATB	Secondary School Admission Test Board (EA)
SSATX	State St. Research Tax Exempt Cl.A [*Mutual fund ticker symbol*] (SG)

SSAU	Submarine Search Attack Unit (NVT)
SSAV	Self-Sealing Aerospace Vehicle (IAA)
SSAV	Simian Sarcoma Associated Virus
SSAVE	Special Student Access to Vocational Education Project (EDAC)
SSAW	Saatchi & Saatchi Advertising Worldwide (ECON)
SSAW	Sea-Salt Aerosol Water [*Oceanography*]
SSAWS	Single Seat Attack Weapon System [*Military*]
SSAWS	Spring, Summer, Autumn, Winter, and Snow [*Pronounced "zausu"*] [*Another name for Skidome, an indoor ski center*] (ECON)
SSAWV	Sons of Spanish American War Veterans (EA)
SSAX	System Software [*NASDAQ symbol*] (TTSB)
SSAX	System Software Associates, Inc. [*NASDAQ symbol*] (NQ)
SSB	Ballistic Missile Submarine [*Navy symbol*]
SSB	Cave Junction, OR [*Location identifier FAA*] (FAAL)
SSB	Fleet Ballistic Submarine [*Navy symbol*]
SSB	Salvo Squeezebore (PDAA)
SSB	Scotland Bancorp [*AMEX symbol*] (TTSB)
SSB	Scotland Bancorp, Inc. [*AMEX symbol*] (SAG)
SSB	Scots Styles Book [*A publication*] (ILCA)
SSB	Scottish Society of Boilermakers [*A union*]
SSB	Security Screening Board [*Army*]
SSB	Selective Service Board
SSB	Short Spike Burst [*Medicine*] (DMAA)
SSB	Signal Sight Back (SAA)
SSB	Single Sideband
ssb	Single Sideband
SSB	Single-Strand Break [*Genetics*]
SSB	Single-Stranded DNA [*Deoxyribonucleic Acid*] Binding Protein [*Biochemistry*]
SSB	Sino-Soviet Bloc
SSB	Size of Spawning Stock [*Fishery management*]
SS-B	Sjogren's Syndrome B [*Medicine*]
SSB	Social Security Bank [*Ghana*] (EY)
SSB	Social Security Board [*Abolished, 1946*]
SSB	Society for the Study of Blood (EA)
SSB	Society of Systematic Biologists (NTPA)
SSB	Soft Service Building (SAA)
SSB	Source Selection Board [*NASA*]
SSB	Space Science Board [*National Research Council*]
SSB	Special Separation Benefit [*DoD*]
SSB	Special Service Battalion [*British military*] (DMA)
SSB	Special Studies Branch [*Supreme Headquarters Allied Powers Europe*] (NATG)
SSB	Spontaneous Symmetry Breaking [*Physics*]
SSB	Standard Software Base (MCD)
SSB	State Seismological Bureau [*China*]
SSB	State Supply Board [*South Australia*]
SSB	St. Croix [*Virgin Islands*] Seaplane Base [*Airport symbol*] (OAG)
SSB	Stereospecific Binding (STED)
SSB	Strategic Standardization Board
SSB	St. Sauveur Badole [*France*] [*Seismograph station code, US Geological Survey*] (SEIS)
SSB	Submarine, Ballistic Missile [*Diesel*] [*NATO*]
SSB	Subscriber Busy [*Telecommunications*] (TEL)
SSB	Subsystem Status Block (MCD)
SSB	Supersonic Balloon (IAA)
SSB	Swimmer Support Boat
SSBA	Scottish Spina Bifida Association (DBA)
SSBA	Shropshire Sheep Breeders Association and Flock Book Society [*British*] (DBA)
SSBA	Sons of Scotland Benevolent Association (EA)
SSBA	Surface Supplied Breathing Apparatus
SSBAM	Single Sideband Amplitude Modulation (KSC)
SSBARA	Single Sideband Amateur Radio Association (IAA)
SSBC	Solar System Barycenter [*Astronomy*]
SSBC	Stock Status Balance Card (NG)
SSBC	Summary Sheet Bar Chart [*NASA*] (NASA)
SSBD	American Society of Breast Disease [*Formerly, Society for the Study of Breast Disease*] (EA)
SSBD	Single-Sideboard (IEEE)
SSBD	Society for the Study of Breast Disease (EA)
SSBD	Systematic Screening for Behavior Disorders [*Test*] (TMMY)
SSB/DPUT	Serikat Sekerdja Biro/Dinas Pembangunan Usaha Tani [*Agricultural Development Service Workers' Union*] [*Indonesia*]
SSBE	Saskatoon Board of Education, Saskatchewan [*Library symbol National Library of Canada*] (NLC)
SSBF	Single Sideband Filter
SSBF	Solid Surface Burning Facility (SSD)
SSBFH	Star-Spangled Banner Flag House Association (EA)
SSBFM	Single Sideband Frequency Modulation (IEEE)
SSBG	Sex Steroid Binding Globulin [*Endocrinology*]
SSBG	Single Sideband Generator
SSBG	Social Services Block Grant [*Department of Health and Human Services*]
SSB/GP	Source Selection Board/General Procurement (MCD)
SSBH	Self-Aligned Strip Buried Heterostructure (NITA)
SSBIC	Specialized Small Business Investment Company
SSBK	Strongsville Savings Bank [*NASDAQ symbol*] (SAG)
SSBK	Strongsville Svgs Bk Ohio [*NASDAQ symbol*] (TTSB)
SSBKD	Serikat Sekerdja/Buruh Ketapradja Djakarta Raja [*General Union of Government Officials of Greater Djakarta*] [*Indonesia*]
SSBKTN	Serikat Sekerdja Bank Koporasi, Tani dan Nelajan Disingkat [*Cooperative, Farmers and Fishers Bank Employees' Union*] [*Indonesia*]
SSB/L	Steamship Bill of Lading [*Shipping*]

SS B/L	Steamship Bill of Lading (EBF)
SSBM	Single Sideband Amplitude Modulation [*Telecommunications*] (IAA)
SSBM	Single Sideband Angle Modulation [*Telecommunications*] (IAA)
SSBM	Single Sideband Modulation
SSBMA	Students to Save Baltic and Mediterranean Avenues [*Defunct*] (EA)
SSBN	Fleet Ballistic Missile Submarine (Nuclear powered) [*Navy symbol*]
SSBN	Ships Submersible Ballistic Nuclear [*British military*] (DMA)
SSBO	Single Swing Blocking Oscillator (MSA)
SSBPI	Serikat Sekerdja Bank Pembangunan Indonesia [*Indonesian Development Bank Employees' Union*]
SSBPS	Social Security Benefit Protection Service (EA)
SSBPT	Serikat Sekerdja Balai Penelitian Tekstil [*Textile Research Institute Workers' Union*] [*Indonesia*]
SSBR	See Separate Bacteriology Report (DAVI)
SSBR	Smooth-Surface Built-Up Roof [*Technical drawings*]
SSBR	Solid Strand Burning Rate (KSC)
SSBR	Solution-Based Styrene-Butadiene Rubber [*Materials science*]
SSBS	School Social Behavior Scales [*Test*] (TMMY)
SSBS	Sisters Servants of the Blessed Sacrament [*Roman Catholic religious order*]
SSBS	Surface-to-Surface Strategic Ballistic Missile System (IAA)
SSBSC	Single Sideband Suppressed Carrier [*Telecommunications*]
SSBSC	Single Switched Suppressed Carrier [*Telecommunications*] (IAA)
SSB-SC/AM...	Single Sideband Suppressed Carrier Amplitude Modulation (NITA)
SSBSCAM	Single Sideband with Suppressed Carrier, Amplitude Modulated [*Telecommunications*] (IAA)
SSBSCOM....	Single Sideband Suppressed Carrier Optical Modulator
SSBUS	South Slavic Benevolent Union Sloga [*Later, Sloga Fraternal Life Insurance Society*] (EA)
SSBUV	Shuttle SBUV [*Solar Backscatter Ultraviolet*] (USDC)
SSBUV	Shuttle Solar Backscatter Ultraviolet Instrument (MCD)
SSBWC	Single Sideband with Carrier [*Telecommunications*] (IAA)
SSBWM	Society of Scale Beam and Weighing Machinists [*A union*] [*British*]
SSC	Coastal Submarine [*Navy symbol*]
SSC	Co-Operative College of Canada, Saskatoon, Saskatchewan [*Library symbol National Library of Canada*] (NLC)
SSC	Cruiser Submarine [*Navy symbol Obsolete*]
SSC	Missionary Sisters of St. Columban [*Roman Catholic religious order*]
SSC	Naval Service School Command
SSC	Safeguard System Command [*Obsolete Army*] (MCD)
SSC	Saline Sodium Citrate [*Clinical chemistry*]
SSC	Salisbury State College, Salisbury, MD [*OCLC symbol*] (OCLC)
SSC	Samantha Smith Center (EA)
SSC	Sandford's New York Superior Court Reports [*A publication*] (DLA)
SSC	Sarawak Supreme Court Reports [*A publication*] (DLA)
SSC	Satellite Situation Center
SSC	Satellite Systems Corp. [*Virginia Beach, VA*] [*Telecommunications*] (TSSD)
SSC	Savannah State College [*Georgia*]
SSC	SCANNET Service Centre (NITA)
SSC	Scan-to-Scan Correlation
SSC	School of the Salt Creek [*Ballet*]
SSC	Scientific Support Coordinator (FFDE)
SSC	Scotch Session Cases [*A publication*] (DLA)
SSC	Scottish Ski Club (DBA)
SSC	Sculptors Society of Canada
SSC	Sea-State Correction [*Doppler navigation*] (DEN)
SSC	Sea Surveillance and Coordination [*Navy*] (DOMA)
SSC	Sea Systems Command [*Also, NSSC*] [*Navy*]
SSC	Secondary School Certificate [*India*] (WDAA)
SSC	Second Search Character [*Computer science*] (IAA)
SSC	Second-Stage Conduit
SSC	Secretarial Studies Certificate (AIE)
SSC	Sector Switching Center [*Telecommunications*] (TEL)
SSC	Secure Systems Corp. [*Manassas, VA*] [*Telecommunications Defunct*] (TSSD)
SSC	Security Classification Code (MCD)
SSC	Selector Subchannels
SSC	Senate Staff Club (EA)
SSC	Senate Steel Caucus (EA)
SSC	Senior Service College [*Army*] (AABC)
SSC	Sensor Signal Conditioner
SSC	Sequential Subsystem Controllers (MCD)
SSC	Serendipitous Survey Catalog [*Infrared Astronomical Satellite*] [*Astronomy*]
SSC	Serial Shift Counter [*Computer science*]
SSC	Service Schools Command (MCD)
SSC	Servicing Support Center (SSD)
SSC	Seton Shrine Center (EA)
SSC	Seven Springs Center [*An association*] (EA)
SSC	Shape Selective Cracking (PDAA)
SSC	Shipbuilding Stabilization Committee [*World War II*]
SSC	Shipment Status Correlation
SSC	Ship's Speed Converter (MCD)
SSC	Ship Structure Committee (EA)
SSC	Ship Systems Command [*Navy*]
SSC	Short Segmented Cask [*Nuclear energy*] (NRCH)
SSC	Short Service Commissions [*Army British*]
SSC	Short Story Criticism [*A publication*]
SSC	Shuttle System Contractor [*NASA*] (NASA)
ssc	Shuttle System Contractor [*NASA*] (NAKS)
SSC	Siblings for Significant Change (EA)
SSC	Side-Stick Controller
SSC	Signaling and Supervisory Control
SSC	Sikh Study Circle (EA)

SSC	Silver Star Citation [*Military award*]
SSC	Simulated Spacecraft [*NASA*]
SSC	Single Silk-Covered [*Wire insulation*]
ssc	Single Silk Enameled (IDOE)
SSC	Single-Site Catalyst [*Chemistry*]
SSC	Single-Stage Command (NASA)
ssc	Single-Stage Command [*NASA*] (NAKS)
SSC	Sintered Silicon Carbide (MCD)
SSC	Sisters of St. Casimir [*Roman Catholic religious order*]
SSC	Site Selection Criteria (AAG)
SSC	Skill Specialty Code (MCD)
SSC	Small Saver Certificate [*Banking*]
SSC	Small Scientific Computer (IAA)
SSC	Socialist Scholars Conference (EA)
SSC	Social Sciences Center [*University of Nevada*] [*Research center*] (RCD)
SSC	Societas Sanctae Crucis [*Society of the Holy Cross*] [*Latin*]
SSC	Society for the Study of Caucasia (EA)
SSC	Society of Silver Collectors (EA)
SSC	Society of St. Columban (TOCD)
ssc	Society of St. Columban, St. Columban's Foreign Mission Society (TOCD)
SSC	Society of the Sacred Cross [*Anglican religious community*]
SSC	Society of the Sisters of the Church (TOCD)
SSC	Sodium Chloride-Sodium Citrate [*Analytical chemistry*]
SSC	Software Steering Committee (LAIN)
SSC	Software Support Center [*Army*] (RDA)
SSC	Software System Change (MCD)
SSC	Solar Stabilization Computer
SSC	Soldier Support Center
SSC	Solicitor, Supreme Court
SSC	Solid-Solution CERMET [*NASA*] (NASA)
SSC	Solid-State Circuit
SSC	Solid-State Computer
SSC	Solid-State Culture [*Biology*]
SSC	Solid State Frequency Converter (DA)
SSC	Soluble Solids Content [*Analytical chemistry*]
SSC	Southeastern Simulation Council
SSC	Southeastern State College [*Later, Southeastern Oklahoma State University*]
SSC	Southern Seaplane, Inc. [*ICAO designator*] (FAAC)
SSC	Southern State College [*Arkansas; South Dakota*]
SSC	Southern States Conference (PSS)
SSC	Space Communications Corp. [*Japan*] (ECON)
SSC	Spacecraft System Console
SSC	Space Science Committee [*Formerly, Provisional Space Science Advisory Board for Europe*] [*of the European Science Foundation*] (EA)
SSC	Space Suit Communicator [*Apollo*] [*NASA*]
SSC	Space Systems Center
SSC	Speciality Shopping Centre [*British*]
SSC	Special Service Center [*Bell System*]
SSC	Special Service Clergyman [*Church of England*]
SSC	Species Survival Commission (EERA)
SSC	Spectroscopy Society of Canada [*Societe de Spectroscopie du Canada*]
SSC	Spin Synchronous Clock
SSC	Spontaneous Synaptic Current [*Neuroscience*]
SSC	Squadron Supervisory Console [*Air Force*]
SSC	Squadron Support Center (AAG)
SSC	Squib Simulator Console
SSC	Staff Selection Committee [*UN Food and Agriculture Organization*]
SSC	Staff Service Center (MCD)
SSC	Stainless Steel Crown [*Dentistry*] (DAVI)
SSC	Standardization Status Code [*DoD*]
SSC	Standard Saline Citrate
SSC	Standards Steering Committee [*ANSI*]
SSC	Standard Systems Center [*Military*]
SSC	Standard Systems Command (AAGC)
SSC	State Sports Council [*Victoria, Australia*]
SSC	State Superfund Contract [*Environmental Protection Agency*]
SSC	State Supply Commission [*Western Australia*]
SSC	Static Standby Computer [*Mission Control Center*] [*NASA*]
SSC	Station Selection Code [*Western Union*] (BUR)
SSC	Statistical Society of Canada [*Societe Statistique du Canada*]
SSC	Stein Sentence Completion (DB)
SSC	Stellar Simulation Complex (OA)
SSC	Stepping Switch Counter (AAG)
SSC	Stock Shortage Control (SAA)
SSC	Stores Stock Catalog
SSC	Strategic Systems Committee [*DoD*] (DOMA)
SSC	Structures, Systems, and Components [*Nuclear energy*] (NRCH)
SSC	St. Sauveur De Carouges [*Seismograph station code, US Geological Survey*] (SEIS)
SSC	Submarine Supply Center
SSC	Subspecialty Codes (DOMA)
SSC	Subsystem Computer (MCD)
ssc	Subsystem Computer (NAKS)
ssc	Subsystem Sequence Controller (NAKS)
SSC	Subsystem Sequence Controller [*NASA*] (NASA)
SSC	Sudden Storm Commencement [*Physics*]
SSC	Sumter, SC [*Location identifier FAA*] (FAAL)
SSC	Sunshine Mining & Refining [*Formerly, Sunshine Mining*] Co. [*NYSE symbol*] (SPSG)
SSC	Superconducting Super Collider [*Particle accelerator*]

SSC............. Super Serial Card [Apple Computer, Inc.]
SSC............. Super Star Cluster [Astronomy]
SSC............. Super System Code (NRCH)
SSC............. Supply and Services Canada
SSC............. Supply Status Code [Army] (AABC)
SSC............. Supply Support Center [Navy]
SSC............. Supply System Command [Navy] (MCD)
SSC............. Support Software Center
SSC............. Survey Science Centre [A consortium of European oranizations]
SSC............. Synchrotron Self-Compton [X-ray emission]
SSC............. Syngeneic Spleen Cells (DB)
SSC............. System Simulation Center
SSC............. System/Site Control (DOMA)
SSC............. Systems Science and Cybernetics (MCD)
SSC............. Systems Support Center (BUR)
SSC............. System Support Controller (NITA)
SSCA .... Scottish Ship Chandlers Association (DBA)
SSCA .... Scottish Stone Cutters' Association [A union]
SSCA .... Seven Seas Cruising Association (EA)
SSCA .... Single Shoulder Contrast Arthrography [Radiology] (DAVI)
SSCA .... Single-Strand Conformational Analysis [Analytical biochemistry]
SSCA .... Southern Speech Communication Association (EA)
SSCA .... Spontaneous Suppressor Cell Activity [Medicine] (DMAA)
SSCA .... Spray System Compressed Air [Nuclear energy] (NRCH)
SSCA .... Standard Schnauzer Club of America (EA)
SSCA .... Strobed Single Channel Analyzer [Electronics] (OA)
SSCA .... Super Sunfish Class Association [Defunct] (EA)
SSCA .... Surface Sampler Control Assembly [NASA] (NASA)
SSCAEU ...... Social Service Commission of the American Ethical Union (EA)
SSCAEU ...... Social Services Commission of the American Ethical Union (EA)
SSCAG .... Research Station, Agriculture Canada [Station de Recherches, Agriculture Canada] Swift Current, Saskatchewan [Library symbol National Library of Canada] (NLC)
SSCATS ...... Skylab Simulation, Checkout, and Training System [NASA]
SSCAVC ...... Senate Select Committee on Agricultural and Veterinary Chemicals [Australia]
SSCB .... Space Station Control Board (SSD)
SSCB .... Super Small-Scale Cook-Off Bomb (MCD)
SSCB(B)....... Submarine Safety Certification Boundary (Book) [Navy] (DNAB)
SSCBD........ Space Station Control Board Directive (SSD)
SSCBM........ Shipping and Storage Container Ballistic Missile (IAA)
SSCC .... Common Channel Signaling System [Telecommunications] (TEL)
SSCC .... Congregation of the Sacred Hearts and of Perpetual Adoration (TOCD)
sscc .... Congregation of the Sacred Hearts of Jesus and Mary (TOCD)
SSCC .... Congregation of the Sacred Hearts of Jesus and Mary [Rome, Italy] (EAIO)
SSCC .... Salt Shaker Collectors Club [Later, AAGSSCS] (EA)
SSCC .... SATCOM System Control Center (KSC)
SSCC .... Scottish Sporting Car Club (DBA)
SSCC .... Sea Surface Chlorophyll Concentration
SSCC .... Second-Stage Conduit Container
SSCC .... Smurfit-Stone Container [Formerly, Jefferson Smurfit] [NASDAQ symbol]
SSCC .... Solid-State Circuits Council [IEEE] (EA)
SSCC .... Sound Surveillance System Control Center (MCD)
SSCC .... Space Surveillance Control Center
SSCC .... Spin-Scan Cloud Camera [NASA]
SSCC .... State Stewardship Coordinating Committee (WPI)
SSCC .... Sulfide Stress Corrosion Cracking (MCD)
SSCC .... Support Services Control Center [NASA] (MCD)
sscc .... Support Services Control Center (NAKS)
SSCCB .... Safeguard System Configuration Control Board [Army] (AABC)
SSCCS .... Slow Spinal Cord Compression Syndrome [Medicine] (DMAA)
SSCCS .... Solid State Component Control System [Nuclear energy] (NRCH)
S SC D .... Doctor of Social Science (WDAA)
SSCD .... Society of Small Craft Designers (EA)
SSCD .... Start Sample Command Delayed
SSCD .... Stationary Source Compliance Division [Environmental Protection Agency] (GFGA)
SSCD .... Superheated Superconducting Colloid Detector [Particle physics]
SSCD .... Support System Concept Document
SSCDR........ Subsystem Critical Design Review
SSCDS .... Small Ship Combat Data System
SSCE............. Silver/Silver Chloride Electrode
SSCE............. Sodium Chloride Calomel Electrode
SSCE............. Squadron Supervisory and Control Equipment (SAA)
SSCE............. Study Skills Counseling Evaluation Reading (AEBS)
SSCERA .... Senate Standing Committee on the Environment, Recreation, and the Arts [Australia]
SS/CF........... Signal Strength, Center Frequency [Broadcasting]
SSCF........... Sleep Stage Change Frequency [Medicine] (DMAA)
SSCF........... Space Subsystem Control Facility (NATG)
SSCF........... Stress/Strain Controlled Fatigue (MCD)
SSCFADT ..... Senate Standing Committee on Foreign Affairs, Defence, and Trade [Australia]
SSCFP .... Senior Service College Fellowship Program [Army] (RDA)
SSCH .... Sisters of Ste. Chretienne [Roman Catholic religious order]
SSCHS .... Space Shuttle Cargo Handling System [NASA] (NASA)
SSCI............. Sanitation Suppliers and Contractors Institute [Defunct] (EA)
SSCI............. Saskatoon Collegiate Institute, Saskatchewan [Library symbol National Library of Canada] (NLC)
SSCI............. Senate Select Committee on Intelligence (MCD)
SSCI............. Sports Sciences [NASDAQ symbol] (TTSB)
SSCI............. Sports Sciences, Inc. [NASDAQ symbol] (SAG)

SSCI............. Steel Service Center Institute (EA)
SSCI............. Steel Shipping Container Institute (EA)
SSCIA .... Scottish Spinal Cord Injury Association (DBA)
SSCIST .... Senate Standing Committee on Industry, Science, and Technology [Australia]
SSCIW .... Sports Sciences Wrrt [NASDAQ symbol] (TTSB)
SSCJ........... Sisters of the Sacred Heart of Jesus of Saint Jacut (TOCD)
SSCJ........... Sorores a Sacro Corde Jesus [Sisters of the Sacred Heart of Jesus] [Roman Catholic religious order]
SSCK .... Sister Servants of Christ the King [Roman Catholic religious order]
SSCL........... Shuttle System Commodity List [NASA]
SSCL........... Shuttle System Commonality List [NASA] (NASA)
SSCL........... Social Science Computing Laboratory [University of Western Ontario] [Information service or system] (IID)
SSCM........... Scattering Structural Contour Map [Surface analysis]
SSCM........... Servants of the Holy Heart of Mary [Roman Catholic women's religious order]
SSCM........... Sisters of Saints Cyril and Methodius [Roman Catholic religious order]
SSCMA .... Special Supplementary Clothing Monetary Allowance [Military]
SSCN .... Nuclear Cruise Missile Submarine (MCD)
SSC-NCR ..... Soldier Support Center - National Capitol Region [Army]
SSCND........ Senate Special Committee on National Defence [Canada]
SSCNS .... Ship's Self-Contained Navigation System
SSCO .... Shipper Service Control Office [Military] (AABC)
SSCO .... System Security Control Officer [Military] (GFGA)
SSCOM .... Soldier Systems Command [Army] (INF)
SSCP .... School Science Curriculum Project
SSCP .... Single-Strand Conformation Polymorphism [Genetics]
SSCP .... Small Self-Contained Payload (NASA)
SSCP .... Standard Saline Citrate Phosphate [A buffer]
SSCP .... State Service Center Program (OICC)
SSCP .... System Services Control Point [Computer science]
SSCPE .... Single-Strand Conformational Polymorphism Electrophoresis [Analytical biochemistry]
SSCQT .... Selective Service College Qualifying Test
SSCR .... Scottish Society of Crop Research (DBA)
SSCR .... Set Screw
SSCR .... Sind Sadr Court Reports [India] [A publication] (DLA)
SSCR .... Space Station Change Request (SSD)
SSCR .... Spectral Shift Control Reactor [Nuclear energy]
SSCr .... Stainless Steel Crown [Dentistry]
SSCRA .... Soldiers' and Sailors' Civil Relief Act [1940]
SSCRI......... Social Science Computer Research Institute [University of Pittsburgh] [Pennsylvania] [Information service or system] (IID)
SSCRN......... Silkscreen (MSA)
SSCS .... Sea Shepherd Conservation Society (EA)
SSCS .... Shipboard Satellite Communications System
SSCS .... Side-Stick Control System
SSCS .... Single Sideband Communications System
SSCS .... Southern Signal Corps School
SSCS .... Space Station Communication System (SSD)
SSCS .... Space Suit Communications System (MCD)
SSCS .... Spatial Spectrum Center Shifting (PDAA)
SSCS .... Standards and Security Compliance Section [Social Security Administration]
SSCS .... Steep-Spectrum Compact Sources [of galactic radio waves]
SSCS .... Student Self-Concept Scale [Test] (TMMY)
SSCS .... Submarine SONAR Calibration Set
SSCS .... Synchronous Satellite Communications System
SSCSP .... Space Shuttle Crew Safety Panel [NASA] (NASA)
SSCT........... Sacks Sentence Completion Test [Psychology] (DAVI)
SSCT........... Shipboard Communications Terminal
SSCT........... Solid-State Celestial Tracker
SSCT........... Solid State Circuit (IAA)
SSCT........... Solid-State Control Transformer
SSCT........... Stereotactic Subcaudate Tractotomy [Medicine] (DMAA)
SSCTC .... Senate Standing Committee on Trade and Commerce [Australia]
SSCTS .... Space Station Communication and Tracking System (SSD)
SSCU .... Segregation Security & Care Unit (WDAA)
SSCU .... Soil Sampler Control Unit
SSCU .... Spacecraft Systems Controller Unit [NASA] (KSC)
SSCU .... Special Signal Conditioning Unit
SSCU .... Store Station Control Unit (MCD)
SSCV .... Semisubmersible Crane Vessel
SSCVYO .... Scottish Standing Conference of Voluntary Youth Organisations (AIE)
SSCW .... Single Silk-Covered Wire [Insulation] (IAA)
SSCW .... Slow Space Charge Wave (IAA)
SSCX .... Solid-State Control Transformer
SSD .... Doctor of Sacred Scripture
SSD .... Institute of the Sisters of St. Dorothy [Roman Catholic religious order]
SSD .... Safe Separation Device
SSD .... Sanctissimus Dominus [Most Holy Lord] [Latin]
SSD .... Satellite System Development (IAA)
SSD .... Saturted Surface Dry (DICI)
SSD .... Scientific Support Division [National Severe Storms Laboratory] (USDC)
SSD .... Scrap Salvage Division [Navy]
SSD .... SDC Sydney Development Corp. [Toronto Stock Exchange symbol Vancouver Stock Exchange symbol]
SSD .... Second-Degree Stochastic Dominance [Statistics]
SSD .... Security Support Detachment (MCD)
SSD .... Seize Signal Detector
SSD .... Semiconductor Silicon Detector

SSD .... Separation Systems Division [*Energy Research and Development Administration*]
SSD .... Sequence Switch Driver
SSD .... Short Sequence Deinking [*Recycling*]
SSD .... Signal Seeking Device
SSD .... Silicon Single Diffused (IAA)
SSD .... Silver Sulfadiazine [*An anti-infective used in burn therapy*] (DAVI)
SSD .... Single Saturating Dose [*Medicine*] (DB)
SSD .... Single Station Doppler (IAA)
SSD .... Single-Station DOVAP [*Doppler, Velocity, and Position*]
SSD .... Smoothing by Spectral Dispersion [*LASER technology*]
SSD .... Social Security Disability
SSD .... Social-Services Department [*British*]
SSD .... Software System Design [*Computer science*]
SSD .... Soldiers Service Dress [*British military*] (DMA)
SSD .... Soldier Support Division [*US Army Training and Doctrine Command*] (INF)
SSD .... Solid-State Detector
SSD .... Solid State Devices (IAA)
SSD .... Solid-State Disk [*Computer science*]
SSD .... Solid-State Dosimeter
SSD .... Solid-State Storage Device [*Computer science*]
SSD .... Source-to-Skin [*or -Surface*] Distance [*Radiology*]
SSD .... Spacecraft Software Division [*NASA*] (NASA)
SSD .... Space Sciences Division [*Jet Propulsion Laboratory*]
SSD .... Space Shuttle Display [*NASA*]
SSD .... Space Systems Division [*Air Force*]
SSD .... Specialized Storage Depot
SSD .... Specialized Support Department [*Air Force*] (AFM)
SSD .... Specialized Support Depot [*Army*] (AABC)
SSD .... Special Service Division [*Army Services Forces*] [*World War II*]
SSD .... Specific Surface Diameter
SSD .... Speech-Sound Discrimination (DB)
SSD .... Split-Screen Display
SSD .... Split Stage Demonstrator (MCD)
SSD .... Squared Successive Differences [*Computer science*]
SSD .... Staatssicherheitsdienst [*State Security Service*] [*Germany*]
SSD .... Stabilized Ship Detector [*Navy*]
SSD .... Standards Support Document [*Environmental Protection Agency*] (GFGA)
SSD .... Star Service International [*France ICAO designator*] (FAAC)
SSD .... Static Sensitive Device [*Electronics*] (EECA)
SSD .... Station Selected Display [*Electronics*] (ECII)
SSD .... Statistical Subdivision (EERA)
SSD .... Steady State Distribution (IAA)
SSD .... Stock Split-Down [*Investment term*]
SSD .... Structured Systems Design (NITA)
SSD .... Subsoil Drain [*Technical drawings*]
SSD .... Succinate Semialdehyde Dehydrogenase (DB)
SSD .... Sudden Sniffing Death (DAVI)
SSD .... Sum of Square Deviation (MAE)
SSD .... Sum-of-the-Squares of the Differences [*Mathematics*]
SSD .... Sun Shadow Device
SSD .... Supplementary Special Deposit [*British*]
SSD .... Support Software Documentation (MCD)
SSD .... Surface Sampler Device [*NASA*]
SSD .... Surveillance Situation Display
SSD .... Survival Support Device (NVT)
SSD .... Sydney Statistical Division [*Australia*]
SSD .... Systems Support Division [*Air Force*]
SSD .... System Status Display
SSD .... System Summary Display [*NASA*] (MCD)
SSDA .... Sequential Similarity Detection Algorithm
SSDA .... Service Station Dealers of America (EA)
SSDA .... Social Science Data Archive [*University of Iowa*] [*Iowa City*] [*Information service or system*] (IID)
SSDA .... Social Science Data Archive [*Carleton University*] [*Canada Information service or system*] (IID)
SSDA .... Stainless Steel Development Association [*British*] (BI)
SSDA .... Synchronous Serial Data Adapter
SSDA-AT...... Service Station Dealers of America and Allied Trades (NTPA)
SSDB .... Shore Station Development Board
SSDC .... Sclerosing Sweat Duct Carcinoma [*Oncology*]
SSDC .... Signalling System-Direct Current (NITA)
SSDC .... Signal Source Distribution Center (AAG)
SSDC .... Social Science Data Center [*University of Connecticut*] [*Research center*] (IID)
SSDC .... Social Science Data Center [*University of Pennsylvania*] [*Philadelphia*] [*Information service or system*] (IID)
SSDC .... Social Science Documentation Centre [*Indian Council of Social Science Research*] [*Information service or system*] (IID)
SSDC .... Society of Stage Directors and Choreographers (EA)
SSDC .... Space and Strategic Defense Command [*Army*] (RDA)
SSDC .... Space Science Data Center [*NASA*] (MCD)
SSDC .... Synoptic-Scale Subprogramme Data Centre [*Marine science*] (MSC)
SSDC .... System Safety Development Center (IAA)
SSDD .... Single-Sided Double Density (NITA)
SSDD .... Single-Sided, Double-Density Disk [*Magnetic disk*] [*Computer science*]
SSDD .... Software System Design Document (MCD)
SSDD .... Steroid Sulfatase Deficiency Disease [*Medicine*] (DMAA)
SSDD .... System Segment Design Document
SSDF .... Somali Salvation Democratic Front
SSDF .... Space Science Development Facility (SAA)
SSD(F)........ Submarine Support Division (Fleet Support) [*Navy*] (DNAB)

SSDF-NAA ... Space Science Development Facility-North American Aviation (SAA)
SSDG .... Ship Service Diesel Generator [*Navy*] (CAAL)
SSDG .... Society for the Study of Development and Growth [*Later, SDB*] (EA)
SSDH .... Subsystem Data Handbook [*NASA*] (NASA)
SSDHPER .... Society of State Directors of Health, Physical Education, and Recreation (EA)
SSDI .... Social Security Disability Income (DAVI)
SSDI .... Social Security Disability Insurance
SSDI .... Support System Design Integration (AAG)
SSDK .... Savannah State Docks Railroad Co. [*AAR code*]
SSDL .... Secondary Standard Dosimetry Laboratory
SSDL .... Social Science Data Library [*University of North Carolina*] [*Chapel Hill*] [*Information service or system*] (IID)
SSDL .... Society for the Study of Dictionaries and Lexicography [*Later, DSNA*] (EA)
SSDM .... Shielding Standard Design Method (MCD)
SSDM .... Systematic Software Development and Maintenance [*Computer science*] (MHDI)
SSDMIC ...... Secretariat State-Defense Military Information Control Committee
SSDMS .... Space Station Data Management System [*NASA*] (SSD)
SSDN .... Sanctissimus Dominus Noster [*Our Most Holy Lord, Jesus Christ*] [*Latin*]
SSD/N .... Sun Synchronous Day/Night (SSD)
ssDNA .... Deoxyribonucleic Acid, Single-Stranded [*Biochemistry, genetics*]
SSDP .... Standard Source Data Package (AFIT)
SSDP .... Suomen Sosialidemokraattinen Puolue [*Finnish Social Democratic Party*] [*Political party*] (PPW)
SSDPA .... Soft-Serv Dairy Products Association [*Later, NSSFFA*] (EA)
SSDPE .... Society for the Systematic Documentation of Paranormal Experiments (EA)
SSDPS .... Solar System Data Processing System
SSDR .... Satellite Situation Display Room
SSDR .... SIGINT/SIGSEC Facilities Data Reporting System (MCD)
SSDR .... Species Specific Defense Reaction
SSDR .... Steady State Determining Routine
SSDR .... Subsystem Design Review
SSDR .... Subsystem Development Requirement (AFM)
SSDR .... Supermarket Subsystem Definition Record [*Computer science*] (IBMDP)
SSDRS .... Safeguard System Design Release Schedule [*Army*] (AABC)
SSDS .... Ship Self Defense System
SSDS .... Single Ship Deep Sweep (DOMA)
SSDS .... Small Ship Data System (MUGU)
SSDS .... Space Shuttle Display and Simulation [*NASA*]
SSDS .... Space Station Data System (NASA)
SSD(S)........ Submarine Support Division (Shore Facilities) [*Navy*] (DNAB)
SSDS .... Surface-Supported Diving System (CAAL)
SSDS .... System of Social and Demographic Statistics (EERA)
SSDSA .... Solomon Schecter Day School Association (EA)
SSDSG .... Special State Defense Study Group [*Military*]
SSD(ST)...... Submarine Support Division (Staff Support) [*Navy*] (DNAB)
SSDT .... Society of Soft Drink Technologists (EA)
SSDU .... Session Service Data Unit [*Telecommunications*] (OSI)
SSDVOR ...... Single Sideband Doppler Very-High-Frequency Omnidirectional Range [*FAA*]
SSE .... Safe Shutdown Earthquake [*Nuclear energy*] (NRCH)
SSE .... Safety System Engineering (MCD)
SSE .... Saline Solution Enema [*Medicine*]
SSE .... Salvador Society of Engineers
SSE .... Satellite Systems Engineering, Inc. [*Bethesda, MD*] [*Information service or system*] (TSSD)
SSE .... Scale of Socio-Egocentrism [*Psychology*]
SSE .... Schick Shaving Experience [*Advertising slogan*]
SSE .... Scuola de Sviluppo Economico [*Italy*]
SSE .... Sector Scan Engagement [*Military*] (CAAL)
SSE .... Security and Safety Equipment (IMH)
SSE .... Seed Savers Exchange (EA)
SSE .... Self-Sustained Emission
SSE .... Separated Statistical Ensemble [*Physical chemistry*]
SSE .... Servicios Aereos Sunset, SA de CV [*Mexico*] [*FAA designator*] (FAAC)
SSE .... SIGINT Support Element (MCD)
SSE .... Signal Security Element [*Military*] (AABC)
SSE .... Single Sideband Exciter
SSE .... Single Silk Covering over Enamel Insulation [*Telecommunications*] (TEL)
SSE .... Sisters of St. Elizabeth [*Roman Catholic religious order*]
SSE .... Site Server [*Microsoft Corp.*] [*Computer science*]
SSE .... Skin Self Examination [*Medicine*]
SSE .... Soap Suds Enema [*Medicine*]
SSE .... Society for Scientific Exploration (EA)
SSE .... Society for the Study of Evolution (EA)
sse............ Society of Saint Edmund (TOCD)
SSE .... Society of Shipping Executives [*British*] (BI)
SSE .... Society of St. Edmund [*Roman Catholic men's religious order*]
SSE .... Software Support Environment (SSD)
SSE .... Solid-State Electrolyte (IAA)
SSE .... Solid-State Electronics
SSE .... South by South East (EERA)
SSE .... Southeastern Stock Exchange
SSE .... South-Southeast
SSE .... Southwest Semiconductor and Electronics Exposition (TSPED)
SSE .... Space Shuttle Engines [*NASA*] (MCD)
SSE .... Special Support Equipment
SSE .... Spokane Stock Exchange [*Washington*]

SSE	Squared Sum of Errors [*Statistics*]
SSE	Stage Systems Engineer
SSE	Stateside Energy Corp. [*Vancouver Stock Exchange symbol*]
SSE	Stockholm Stock Exchange
SSE	Straight to Services Economy
SSE	Submarine Scout Experimental [*British military*] (DMA)
SSE	Subsystem Element [*NASA*] (NASA)
SSE	Subsystem Support Equipment [*NASA*] (MCD)
SSE	Summary Status Entry (SAA)
SSE	Sum of Squared Errors [*Statistics*]
SSE	Supplemental Support Evaluation
SSE	Support System Evaluation
SSE	Support Systems Engineering [*Boeing*]
SSE	Surface Support Equipment
SSE	Switching System Engineer (IAA)
SSE	Sydney Stock Exchange [*Australia*] (ADA)
SSE	Systemic Side Effects [*Pharmacology*] (DAVI)
SSE	System Safety Engineering (AFM)
SSE	System Status Evaluation [*Army*] (AABC)
SSE	System Support Engineering
SSE	System Support Equipment
SSEA	Sentinel System Evaluation Agency [*DoD*]
SSEA	Separate Sampling and Excitation Analysis [*Spectroscopy*]
SSEA	Stage-Specific Embryonic Antigen [*Immunology*]
SSEA	System Safety Engineering Analysis (MCD)
SSEAM	Ship Systems Equipment Acquisition Manual (MCD)
SSEAT	Surveyor Scientific Evaluation Advisory Team [*NASA*]
SSEB	Source Selection Evaluation Board [*Military*] (AFM)
SSEB	South of Scotland Electricity Board (ECON)
SSEB	Swiss Societies for Experimental Biology
SSEC	Secondary School Examinations Council [*British*] (BI)
SSEC	Selective Sequence Electronic Calculator [*Computer science*]
SSEC	Social Science Education Consortium (EA)
SSEC	Society for the Study of Early China (EA)
SSEC	Solar System Exploration Committee [*NASA*]
SSEC	Solid-State Electronic Chronograph
SSEC	Sound Surveillance Evaluation Center [*Navy*] (NVT)
SSEC	Space Science and Engineering Center [*University of Wisconsin - Madison*] [*Research center*] (RCD)
SSEC	Static Source Error Correction
SSEC	Subsystem Executive Control Program (IAA)
SSECO	Second-Stage Engine Cutoff
SSECS	Space Station Environmental Control System
SSECW	Prairie Migratory Bird Research Centre, Canadian Wildlife Service, Environment Canada [*Centre de Recherches sur les Oiseaux Migrateurs des Prairies, Service Canadien de la Faune, Environnement Canada*] Saskatoon, Saskatchewan [*Library symbol National Library of Canada*] (NLC)
SSEDF	Software Support Environment Development Facility (SSD)
SSEE	Standing-Shock Equilibrium Expansion
S-SEED	Symmetric Self Electrooptic Effect Device [*Optical Computing*]
SSE/EWE	SIGINT [*Signal Intelligence*] Support Element/Electronic Warfare Element [*Military*] (AABC)
SSEF	Solid-State Electro-Optic Filter
SSEF	Support Squadron Eastern Flank [*British military*] (DMA)
SSEG	Scottish Solar Energy Group (DBA)
SSEG	Ship System Engineering Group [*British*]
SSEG	System-Segment [*Computer science*]
SSEH	National Hydrology Research Centre, Environment Canada [*Centre National de Recherche en Hydrologie, Environnement Canada*] Saskatoon, Saskatchewan [*Library symbol National Library of Canada*] (NLC)
SSEIF	Software Support Environment Integration Facility (SSD)
SSEIP	Special Stockpile Engineering Investigation Program (MCD)
SSEIS	Standard Support and Environmental Impact Statement [*Environmental Protection Agency*] (GFGA)
SSEIS	Stationary Source Emissions and Inventory System [*Environmental Protection Agency*] (GFGA)
SSEKP	Single Shot Engagement Kill Probability (MCD)
SSEL	Solid-State Electronics Laboratory [*Stanford University*] (MCD)
SSEL	Space Science and Engineering Laboratory [*Pennsylvania State University*]
SSEL	Standard Statistical Establishment List [*Bureau of the Census*]
SSELA	Standing Committee on Social Sciences, Economic, and Legal Aspects [*Great Lakes Research Advisory Board*]
SSEM	Serial-Section Electron Microscopy
SSEM	Solid State Extended Memory (MCD)
SSEM	Space System Effectiveness Model
SSEM	Stepper Specific Equipment Model (AAEL)
SSEM	Supply Support Element Manager
SSEO	SEABEE Support and Equipment Office [*Navy*]
SSEOF	Software Support Environment Operation Facility (SSD)
SSEOS	Space Shuttle Engineering and Operations Support [*NASA*] (MCD)
SSEP	Somatosensory Evoked Potential [*Neurophysiology*]
SSEP	Source Selection Evaluation Plan
SSEP	Steady State Evoked Potential [*Neurophysiology*]
SSEP	Submarine Surveillance Equipment Program (NVT)
SSEP	System Safety Engineering Plan (AFM)
SSEPA	Society of Spanish Engineers, Planners, and Architects (EA)
SSEPF	Software Support Environment Production Facility (SSD)
SSER	Site Safety Evaluation Report [*Nuclear energy*] (NRCH)
SSER	Somatosensory Evoked Response [*Neurophysiology*]
SSER	Supplement to Safety Evaluation Report [*Nuclear energy*] (NRCH)
SSES	Sexual Self-Efficacy Scale [*Medicine*] (DMAA)
SSES	Shipboard Signal Exploration System (MCD)
SSES	Ship Signals Exploitation Space [*Navy*] (CAAL)
SSES	Single Strip Engine System
SSES	Special Signal Exploitation Spaces (NVT)
SSES	Susquehanna Steam Electric Station [*Nuclear energy*] (NRCH)
SSESC	College of Emmanuel and St. Chad, Saskatoon, Saskatchewan [*Library symbol National Library of Canada*] (NLC)
SSESI	Statistical and Social Enqiry Society of Ireland
SSESM	Spent Stage Experimental Support Module (KSC)
SSESPF	Software Support Environment Software Production Facility (SSD)
SSESS	Soviet Space Event Support Ships (CINC)
SSET	Source Selection Evaluation Team (AAGC)
SSET	Source Selection Evaluation Test
SSET	SSE Telecom [*NASDAQ symbol*] (TTSB)
SSET	SSE Telecom, Inc. [*NASDAQ symbol*] (SAG)
SSET	State Science, Engineering, and Technology Program [*National Science Foundation*]
SSE TI	SSE Telecom, Inc. [*Associated Press*] (SAG)
SSEU	System Selector Extension Unit
SS EVAL	Skill Specialty Evaluation Code [*Army*]
SSF	Congregation of the Sisters of the Family [*Roman Catholic religious order*]
SSF	Congregation of the Sisters of the Holy Family (TOCD)
SSF	Safe Shutdown Facility [*Nuclear energy*] (NRCH)
SSF	Saint Saulge [*France*] [*Seismograph station code, US Geological Survey*] (SEIS)
SSF	Samantha Smith Foundation (EA)
SSF	San Antonio, TX [*Location identifier FAA*] (FAAL)
SSF	Saybolt Seconds Furol [*Oil viscosity*]
SSF	S-Band Shuttle Forward (SSD)
SSF	Scottish Spring Fair (ITD)
SSF	Scottish Surfing Federation (DBA)
SSF	Seconds Saybolt Furol [*Oil viscosity*] (IAA)
SSF	Semi-Lagrangian and Semi-Geostrophic Finite Element [*Model*] [*Marine science*] (OSRA)
SSF	Service Storage Facility [*Military*]
SSF	Service Support Force [*Military*]
SSF	Ship's Service Force [*Navy*]
SSF	Short Stature Foundation (EA)
SSF	Simulated Spinal Fluid [*Medicine*]
SSF	Simultaneous Saccharification and Fermentation [*Chemical engineering*]
SSF	Single-Seated Fighter
SSF	Single Sideband Filter
SSF	Single Sided Frame [*Telecommunications*] (TEL)
SSF	Single Solar Flare
SSF	Single-Stage Fan
SSF	Single Stock Fund [*DoD*]
SSF	Sjogren's Syndrome Foundation (EA)
SSF	Smallest Serving Factor (PDAA)
SSF	Small, Shelly Fauna [*Paleontology*]
SSF	Society for the Study of Fertility [*British*]
SSF	Society of State Filers (NTPA)
SSF	Society of St. Francis [*Anglican religious community*]
SSF	Sodium Silicofluoride [*Inorganic chemistry*]
SSF	Software Support Facility (MCD)
SSF	Solid-State Fermentation
SSF	Solid Substrate Fermentation
SSF	Soluble Suppressor Factor [*Immunology*]
SSF	Somali Salvation Front (PD)
SSF	Sona Systems Ltd. (Canada) [*Vancouver Stock Exchange symbol*]
SSF	Southern Shark Fishery [*Australia*]
SSF	Space Simulation Facility (AAG)
SSF	Special Security Facility
SSF	Special Security Force (DOMA)
SSF	Special Service Force [*Canadian and US troops under combined command*] [*World War II*]
SSF	Spin Stretch Factor [*Textile technology*]
SSF	Spun Soy Fiber [*Food technology*]
SSF	SRB [*Solid-Rocket Booster*] Storage Facility [*NASA*] (NASA)
SSF	Stainless Steel Fiber
SSF	Standard Saybolt Furol [*Oil viscosity*]
SSF	Standby Shutdown Facility [*Nuclear energy*] (NRCH)
SS/F	Starboard Side/Forward [*Stowage*] (DNAB)
SSF	Straight Filament [*Biochemistry*]
SSF	Structured Surfactant Formulation [*Solvent technology*]
SSF	Studies in Short Fiction [*A publication*] (BRI)
SSF	Style Sac Flap
SSF	Supersonic Frequency (IAA)
SSF	Supply Status File (MCD)
SSF	Symmetrical Switching Function
SSF	System Support Facility
SSFA	Stainless Steel Fabricators' Association of Great Britain (BI)
SSFC	Sequential Single Frequency Code System [*Telecommunications*] (TEL)
SSFC	Severe Storm Forecast Center [*U.S. Weather Service*] (BARN)
SSFC	Social Science Federation of Canada [*Research center*] (IRC)
SSFC	Solid State Frequency Changer [*Military*] (CAAL)
SSFC	South Street Financial Center [*NASDAQ symbol*] (SAG)
SSFC	Susanne Severeid Fan Club (EA)
SSFD	Sisters of St. Francis of Dillingen [*See also SFD*] [*Rome, Italy*] (EAIO)
SSF-DC	Solid State Floppy Disk Card (PCM)
SSFDR	Solid-State Flight Data Recorder (GAVI)
SSFE	Scandinavian Society of Forest Economics (EAIO)
SSFF	Scholastic Science Fiction Federation [*Defunct*] (EA)

SSFF............ Solid Smokeless Fuels Federation [British] (BI)
SSFF............ Space Shuttle Furnace Facility [NASA] (SSD)
SSFGSS....... Space Shuttle Flight and Ground System Specification [NASA] (NASA)
SSFI............ Safety System Functional Inspection [Environmental science] (COE)
SSFI............ Scaffolding, Shoring, and Forming Institute (EA)
SSFL............ Santa Susana Field Laboratory [NASA] (NASA)
SSFL............ Steady-State Fermi Level
SSFLC.......... Surface Stabilized Ferroelectric Liquid Crystal [Physical chemistry]
SSFM.......... Single Sideband Frequency Modulation
SSFMAC .... Southern Shark Fishery Management Advisory Committee (EERA)
SSFMP......... Southern Shark Fishery Management Plan [Australia]
SSFN........... Solidarity: A Socialist-Feminist Network [Defunct] (EA)
SSFnTA........ Stet Societa Finaziaria Telefonica PA [Associated Press] (SAG)
SSFnTel........ Stet Societa Finaziaria Telefonica PA [Associated Press] (SAG)
SSFO........... Scandinavian Society of Forensic Odontology (EA)
SSFO........... Simultaneous Single Frequency Outlet
SSFP........... Steady-State Free Precession [Magnetic resonance imaging] [Radiology] (DAVI)
SSFR........... Safety Services Field Representative [Red Cross]
SSFS........... Space Shuttle Functional Simulator [NASA] (KSC)
SSFS........... Special Services Forecasting System [Telecommunications] (TEL)
SSFS........... Steven Spielberg Film Society (EA)
SSFT........... Self-Sealing Fuel Tank
SSFT........... Self-Service Financial Terminal [Computer science] (MHDI)
SSFU........... Scottish Sea Fishers' Union
SSFVT.......... Subsystems Functional Verification Test [NASA]
SSG .... Guided Missile Submarine [Navy symbol]
SSG .... Malabo [Equatorial Guinea] [Airport symbol] (OAG)
SSG .... Safety Study Group (MCD)
SSG .... Santa Isabel [Spanish Guinea] [Airport symbol] (AD)
SSG .... Science Steering Group [NASA]
SSG .... Scientific Steering Group [Tropical Ocean-Global Atmosphere] (USDC)
SSG .... Scleroderma Support Group (EA)
SSG .... Search Signal Generator
SSG .... Security Service Guide (SAA)
SSG .... Senior Savers Guide Publishing, Inc. [Vancouver Stock Exchange symbol]
SSG .... Ships Service Generator (DOMA)
SSG .... Shuttle Support Group (MCD)
SSG .... Single Sideband Generator
SSG .... Slovak Government Flying Service [FAA designator] (FAAC)
SSG .... Small Signal Gain (IEEE)
SSG .... Society of Saint Gregory [British] (DBA)
SSG .... Software Support Group (NITA)
SSG .... Solution-Sol-Gel [Materials science]
SSG .... Southern Society of Genealogists (EA)
SSG .... South Sydney Greens [Political party Australia]
SSG .... Special Security Group (MCD)
SSG .... Special Studies Group [Joint Chiefs of Staff] [Military]
SSG .... Special Support Group [FBI] (CINC)
SSG .... Staff Sergeant [Army] (AABC)
SSG .... Standard Signal Generator (IAA)
SSG .... Standard Systems Group [Air Force]
SSG .... State Services Group [Information service or system] (IID)
SSG .... Stonehenge Study Group (EA)
SSG .... Strategic Studies Group [Naval War College] (DOMA)
SSG .... Subscriber Switching Grid (IAA)
SSG .... Subsystem Software Group
SSG .... Supply Spectrum Generator
SSG .... Surface Discharge Spark Gap (IAA)
SSG .... Sweep Signal Generator
SSG .... Symbolic Stream Generator [Computer science]
SSG .... System Safety Group [Air Force]
SSGA .... Scottish Salmon Growers' Association
SSGA .... Single Conductor, Shipboard General Use, Armored (IAA)
SSGA .... Society of St. Gregory of America [Later, CMAA] (EA)
SSGA .... Sterling Silversmiths Guild of America (EA)
SSGA .... Swordsmen and Sorcerers' Guild of America (EA)
SSGB .... Suore di San Giovanni Baptista [Sisters of St. John the Baptist - SSJB] [Rome, Italy] (EAIO)
SSGC .... Saskatoon Gallery and Conservatory, Saskatchewan [Library symbol National Library of Canada] (NLC)
SSGC .... Short System Ground Check
SSGD .... Smoke Screen Generative Device
SSGIX .... State St. Research Govt. Income Cl.A [Mutual fund ticker symbol] (SG)
SSGJ........... Single Strength Grapefruit Juice
SSGJ........... Supersonic Gas Jet
SSGM.......... Service Station & Garage Management [Canada A publication]
SSGN.......... Guided Missile Submarine (Nuclear Propulsion) [Navy symbol]
SSGP .... Spin Stabilized Guided Projectile (MCD)
SSGp .... System Safety Group [Air Force] (AFM)
SSGS .... Solid-State Gamma Switch
SSGS .... Standard Space Guidance System
SSGT .... Ship Service Gas Turbine [Navy] (CAAL)
SSGT .... Small-Scale Gap Test [Explosive]
SSGT .... Staff Sergeant [Military]
SSGT .... Subsystem Ground Test (MCD)
SSGTG .... Ship's Service Gas Turbine Generator [Navy] (NVT)
SSGW .... Surface-to-Surface Guided Weapon (NATG)
SSH .... S-Band Shuttle (SSD)
SSH .... Schwartz-Slawsky-Herzfeld [Theory] [Chemical kinetics]
SSH .... Sea Surface Height [Oceanography]

SSH .... Second-Stage Hydraulics
SSH .... Sharm E Sheikh [Israel] [Airport symbol] (OAG)
SSH .... Sisters Servants of the Most Sacred Heart (TOCD)
SSH .... Small-Scale Hydroelectric Project
SSH .... Snowshoe Hare
SSH .... Social Sciences and Humanities Research Council of Canada [UTLAS symbol]
SSH .... Social Service Handbooks [A publication]
SSH .... South Shore [AAR code]
SSH .... Special Survey of the Hull [Lloyd's Register of Shipping] (DS)
SSH .... Stationary-State Hypothesis [Chemistry]
SSH .... Student Semester Hours (EDAC)
SSH .... Substantial Stockholder
SSH .... Sunshine [Alaska] [Seismograph station code, US Geological Survey] (SEIS)
SSHA .... Scottish Special Housing Association (WDAA)
SSHA .... Social Science History Association (NTPA)
SSHA .... Subsystem Hazard Analysis
SSHA .... Survey of Study Habits and Attitudes [Education]
SSHA .... System Safety Hazard Analysis [Military]
SSHACS .... Small Ships Accounting System (DNAB)
SSHAX .... State St. Research High Income Cl.A [Mutual fund ticker symbol] (SG)
SSHb .... Homozygous for Sickle Cell Hemoglobin [Medicine] (STED)
SSHB .... Society for the Study of Human Biology (EA)
SSHB .... Stainless Steel Helium Bottle
SSHB .... Station Set Handbook [NASA] (NASA)
SSHC .... Single-Stage Hydrocracker [Chemical engineering]
SSHC .... Society to Support Home Confinement [British] (DBA)
SSHCG .... Students' Series of Historical and Comparative Grammars [A publication]
SSHD .... Single-Silo Hardsite Defense
SSHE .... Scraped-Surface Heat Exchanger [Process engineering]
SSHI .... Sunstone Hotel Investors [NASDAQ symbol] (TTSB)
SSHI .... Sunstone Hotel Investors, Inc. [NASDAQ symbol] (SAG)
SSHJM .... Sisters of the Sacred Hearts of Jesus and Mary [Roman Catholic religious order]
SSHJP .... Servants of the Sacred Heart of Jesus and of the Poor [Roman Catholic women's religious order]
SSHL .... Severe Sensorineural Hearing Loss (STED)
S/SHLD .... Side Shield [Automotive engineering]
SSHM .... Scottish Society of History Medicine (DBA)
SSHM .... Society for the Social History of Medicine [Oxford, England] (EAIO)
SSHMA .... Senior Secondary Headmasters' Association [British]
SSHP .... Single-Shot Hit Probability
SSHPF .... Space Station Hazardous Processing Facility (SSD)
SSHR .... Social Systems and Human Resources [National Science Foundation] (MCD)
SSHR .... Spartan Safety Hazard Report [Missiles] (MCD)
SSHRC .... Social Sciences and Humanities Research Council of Canada
SSHRCC ...... Social Sciences and Humanities Research Council of Canada [Pronounced "sherk"] [See also CRSHC]
SSHS .... Stainless Steel Helium Sphere
SSHSA .... Steamship Historical Society of America (EA)
S/Shtg .... Slipsheeting (DGA)
SSI .... Brunswick [Georgia] [Airport symbol] (AD)
SSI .... Brunswick, GA [Location identifier FAA] (FAAL)
SSI .... Safecard Services (EFIS)
SSI .... Safe Shutdown Impoundment [Nuclear energy] (NRCH)
SSI .... Safeway Stores, Inc.
SSI .... Sale Satisfaction Index [Business term]
SSI .... Sales Styles Indicator [Test] (TMMY)
SSI .... Satellite Sequential Imaging
SSI .... Satellite Services, Inc. [Houston, TX] [Telecommunications] (TSSD)
SSI .... Scaffolding and Shoring Institute [Later, SSFI] (EA)
SSI .... Scientific Systems, Inc.
SSI .... Screening Site Inspection [Environmental science] (BCP)
SSI .... Seacor Services, Inc. (EFIS)
SSI .... Second-Stage Ignition
SSI .... Sector Scan Indicator
SSI .... Security Systems, Inc. [In TV series "Max Headroom"]
SSI .... Security Systems Inspectorate [Established in 1987] [British]
SSI .... Segmental Sequential Irradiation (AAMN)
SSI .... Seismic Survival Indicator [Earthquake analysis program] [Computer science]
SSI .... Semiconductor Specialists, Inc. (IAA)
SSI .... Semisopochnoi Island [Alaska] [Seismograph station code, US Geological Survey Closed] (SEIS)
SSI............. Service Social International [International Social Service - ISS] [Geneva, Switzerland] (EAIO)
SSI .... Shaft Speed Indicator
SSI .... Ship and Shore Installation (MCD)
SSI .... Shoulder Sleeve Insignia [Military] (AABC)
SSI .... Signed Short Integer [Computer science]
SSI .... Significant Structural Item (NASA)
ssi .... Significant Structural Item (NAKS)
SSI .... Single Scale Integration (IAA)
SSI .... Single Service Institute [Later, FPI] (EA)
SSI .... Single System Image
SSI .... Site of Special Scientific Interest [Great Britain]
SSI .... Size Selective Inlet [Environmental Protection Agency] (GFGA)
SSI .... Skill Speciality Identifier (MCD)
SSI .... Sky Survey Instrument
SSI............. Slater Industries, Inc. [Toronto Stock Exchange symbol]

SSI .... Slater Steels Corp. [*Formerly, Slater Steel Industries*] [*Toronto Stock Exchange symbol*]
SSI .... Small-Scale Integration
SSI .... Smart Set International [*Program to discourage drug abuse*] [*Defunct*] (EA)
SSI .... Social Science Institute [*Washington University*] [*Research center*] (RCD)
SSI .... Social Security Income (DAVI)
SSI .... Social Security Information
SSI .... Society for Siberian Irises (EA)
SSI .... Society for the Study of Internationalism (EA)
SSI .... Society of Saunterers, International (EA)
SSI .... Society of Scribes and Illuminators (EA)
SSI .... Society of Strip Illustration [*British*] (DBA)
SSI .... Software Sciences Institute (NITA)
SSI .... Solid-State Imaging [*Physics*]
SSI .... Solid-State Inverter
SSI .... Spacecraft System Integration
SSI .... Space Studies Institute (EA)
SSI .... Spares Status Inquiry (AAG)
SSI .... Special Secretariat for Informatics (NITA)
SSI .... Special Subject for Inspection [*DoD*]
SSI .... Special Surveillance Inspection (MCD)
SSI .... Specialty Skill Identifier [*Military*] (AABC)
SSI .... Specific Searching Image [*Tendency of birds to select prey of the color to which they have been accustomed*]
SSI .... Staff Sergeant Instructor [*Military British*]
SSI .... Standards Starts Index [*Horse racing*] (DICI)
SSI .... Standing Signal Instructions [*Military*]
SSI .... Start Signal Indicator [*Telecommunications*] (TEL)
SSI .... Steady-State Irradiation [*Nuclear energy*] (NRCH)
SSI .... Stockpile Surveillance Inspection
SSI .... Storage-to-Storage Instruction (IEEE)
SSI .... Strategic Studies Institute (MCD)
SSI .... Structural Significant Item (MCD)
SSI .... Student/Supervisor Instructions [*Army Training Extension Course*] (INF)
SSI .... Stuttering Severity Index [*Speech and language therapy*] (DAVI)
SSI .... Stuttering Severity Instrument (STED)
SSI .... Subshock Insulin [*Pharmacology*] (DAVI)
SSI .... Subsod Injection [*Waste treatment*] (DICI)
SSI .... Subunit-Subunit Interface (DB)
SSI .... Sucro-Sac-Ologists Society International [*Defunct*] (EA)
SSI .... Sunstone Hotel Investors, Inc. [*NYSE symbol*] (SAG)
SSI .... Supplemental Security Income [*Social Security Administration*]
SSI .... Supplemental Security Income Program (USGC)
SSI .... Supplemental Security Insurance [*Program*]
SSI .... Supply Support Index (CAAL)
SSI .... Surprise Security Inspection [*Navy*] (NVT)
SSI .... Survey Sampling, Inc. [*Information service or system*] (IID)
SSI .... Sustaining Support Increment [*Military*]
SSI .... Symptom Sign Inventory [*Psychology*]
SSI .... Synchronous Serial Interface [*Computer science*] (CIST)
SSI .... Synchronous Systems Interface
SSI .... Synthetic Sentence Indentification [*Speech and language Therapy*] (DAVI)
SSI .... System Science Institute [*IBM Corp.*]
SSI .... System Sign Inventory (DAVI)
SSI .... System Status Index (IAA)
SSI .... System Status Indicator [*Bell System*]
SSIA .... Scottish Society for Industrial Archaeology (EA)
SSIA .... Shiprepairers and Shipbuilders Independent Association [*British*] (DS)
SSIA .... Shoe Service Institute of America (EA)
SSIA .... Specification Serial of Individual Assigned
SSIAM .... Structured and Scaled Interview to Assess Maladjustment [*Psychometrics*]
SSIB .... Shop Stock Items Bin (MCD)
SSIBD .... Shuttle System Interface Block Diagram [*NASA*] (NASA)
SSIC .... Saskatchewan Indian Cultural College, Saskatoon, Saskatchewan [*Library symbol National Library of Canada*] (NLC)
SSIC .... Small-Scale Integrated Circuit
SSIC .... Southern States Industrial Council [*Later, USIC*] (EA)
SSIC .... Standard Subject Identification Code (NVT)
SSIC .... Stressed-Skin Insulated-Core Panels [*Construction technology*] (PS)
SSICM .... Spin-Stabilized Impulsively Controlled Missile (MCD)
SSID .... Ship Systems Integration Data (MCD)
SSID .... Shuttle Stowage Installation Drawing (NASA)
SSIDA .... Steel Sheet Information and Developement Association [*British*] (BI)
SSIDS .... Siblings of Sudden Infant Death Syndrome Victims [*Medicine*]
SSIE .... Skylab Systems Integration Equipment [*NASA*] (MCD)
SSIE .... Smithsonian Science Information Exchange [*National Technical Information Service*] [*Later, FEDRIP*]
SSIE .... Smithsonian Science Information Exchange, Inc. (EBF)
SSIE .... Solid Surface Interaction Experiment
SSIEM .... Society for the Study of Inborn Errors of Metabolism [*Middleway, England*] (EAIO)
SSIFC .... Saskatoon Campus, Saskatchewan Indian Federated College, Saskatchewan [*Library symbol National Library of Canada*] (BIB)
SSIFC .... Sharon Smith International Fan Club (EA)
SSIG .... Single Signal (IEEE)
SSIG .... State Student Incentive Grant [*Department of Education*]
SSIGS .... Special Survey of Inert Gas System [*Lloyd's Register of Shipping*] (DS)
S Sig Sta .... Storm Signal Station [*Nautical charts*]
SSII .... Safran Student' Interest Inventory (STED)
SSII .... Solid-State Image Intensifier
SSII .... Sound Source Interactive, Inc. [*NASDAQ symbol*] (SAG)
SSIK .... Shipboard SONAR Bouy Interface Kit (DWSG)
SSIL .... Supply Significant Items List (MCD)
SSILA .... Society for the Study of Indigenous Languages of the Americas (EA)
SSILS .... Solid State Instrument Landing System (MCD)
S-SIM .... S-Band Simulator (SSD)
SSIM .... Southern Sudan Independence Movement [*Political party*]
SSIM .... Static Secondary Ion Mass Spectroscopy
SSIM .... Statistical, Sampling Inventory Method [*Military*] (AABC)
SSIMS .... Static Secondary Ion Mass Spectroscopy
SSINA .... Specialty Steel Industry of North America (NTPA)
SSINI .... System Input Unit I [*Computer science*] (AEBS)
SSIO .... Southern Subtropical Indian Ocean
SSIP .... Ship Support Improvement Program [*DoD*]
SSIP .... Shuttle Student Involvement Project [*NASA*]
SSIP .... Solvent-Separated Ion-Pair [*Physical chemistry*]
SSIP .... Specific, Sincere, Immediate, Private, and Personal [*Management technique*]
SSIP .... Standard Systems Improvement Program
SSIP .... Subsystem Integration Plan (IAA)
SSIP .... Subsystems Integration Program [*or Project*] [*NATO*] (NATG)
SSIP .... System Setup Indicator Panel
SSIP .... Systems Software Interface Processing [*NASA*] (MCD)
SSIPL .... Support and Sustaining Implications of Increased POMCUS Levels [*Military*]
SSIR .... Soil Survey Investigations Report
SSIR .... Special Security Investigation Requirement (AFM)
SSIRT .... Support Staff Interests Round Table [*American Library Association*]
SSIS .... Social Security Information System [*ILO*] [*United Nations*] (DUND)
SSIS .... Society for South India Studies (EA)
SSIS .... Spacecraft System Integration Support
SSIS .... Space Station Information System (NASA)
SSIS .... Space Station Information System [*NASA*] (NAKS)
SSI/S .... Supplemental Security Income Program for the Aged, Blind, and Disabled/State Supplementation [*Public human service program*] (PHSD)
SSISI .... Statistical and Social Inquiry Society of Ireland (DBA)
SSISS .... Spacecraft System Integration Support Service
SSI/SSP .... Supplemental Security Income/State Supplemental Payment (DAVI)
SSIT .... Semi-Submarine Ice-Breaking Tanker (PDAA)
SSIT .... Subscapularis, Supraspinatus, Infraspinatus, Teres Minor [*Muscle*] (STED)
SSITF .... Standard Shipboard Inspection and Testing Form [*Navy*] (DNAB)
SSITKA .... Steady-State Isotopic Transient Kinetic Analysis [*Chemical physics*]
SSITP .... Shuttle System Integrated Test Plan [*NASA*] (NASA)
SSIT-R .... Slosson Screening Intelligence Test-Revised (TES)
SSIU .... Subsystem Interface Unit (MCD)
SSIUL .... Social Sciences Information Utilization Laboratory
SSIUS .... Specialty Steel Industry of the United States (EA)
SSIWA .... Shipwrights' and Shipwrights Iron Workers' Association [*A union*] [*British*]
SSIX .... Submarine Satellite Information Exchange [*Geosynchronous communications satellite*]
SSIXS .... Submarine Satellite Information Exchange System (MCD)
SSJ .... Sandnessjoen [*Norway*] [*Airport symbol*] (OAG)
SSJ .... Savez Sindikata Jugoslavije [*Yugoslavia Federation of Trade Unions*]
SSJ .... Self-Aligning Swivel Joint
SSJ .... Self-Screening Jammer (MCD)
SSJ .... Sequential Spot Jamming [*Military*] (CAAL)
SSJ .... Servants of St. Joseph (TOCD)
SSJ .... Servo Summing Junction
SSJ .... Shinshu-Shinmachi [*Japan*] [*Seismograph station code, US Geological Survey*] (SEIS)
SSJ .... Side-Support Jack
SSJ .... Sinatra Society of Japan [*Tokyo*] (EAIO)
SSJ .... Single Subsonic Jet
SSJ .... Sisters of Saint Joseph of Chestnut Hill, Philadelphia (TOCD)
SSJ .... Sisters of St. Joseph [*Roman Catholic religious order*]
SSJ .... Sisters of St. Joseph (Buffalo) (TOCD)
SSJ .... Sisters of St. Joseph (Burlington) (TOCD)
SSJ .... Sisters of St. Joseph (Erie) (TOCD)
SSJ .... Sisters of St. Joseph (Kalamazoo, Nazareth) (TOCD)
SSJ .... Sisters of St. Joseph of St. Augustine, Florida (TOCD)
SSJ .... Sisters of St. Joseph of the Third Order of St. Francis [*Roman Catholic religious order*]
SSJ .... Sisters of St. Joseph (Ogdensburg) (TOCD)
SSJ .... Sisters of St. Joseph (Rochester) (TOCD)
SSJ .... Sisters of St. Joseph (Springfield, MA) (TOCD)
SSJ .... Sisters of St. Joseph (Wheeling) (TOCD)
SSJ .... Societas Sancti Joseph Sanctissimi Cordis [*St. Joseph's Society of the Sacred Heart*] [*Josephites*] [*Roman Catholic men's religious order*]
SSJ .... Socijalisticka Stranka Jugoslavije [*Yugoslav Socialist Party*] [*Political party*] (EAIO)
SSJ .... Solid-State Jammer
ssj .... St. Joseph's Society of the Sacred Heart, Jospehite Fathers (TOCD)
SSJB .... Sisters of St. John the Baptist [*See also SSGB*] [*Roman Catholic religious order Rome, Italy*] (EAIO)
SSJC .... Sisters of St. Joseph Benedict Cottolengo (TOCD)
SSJC .... Southern Seminary and Junior College [*Virginia*]
SSJD .... Society of St. John the Divine [*Anglican religious community*]
SSJE .... Society of St. John the Evangelist [*Anglican religious community*]
SS-JFI .... School Superintendent Job Functions Inventory [*Test*]

SSJG............ Sisters of St. John of God [*Wexford, Republic of Ireland*] (EAIO)
SSJSM......... Sisters of St. Joseph of St. Mark [*Roman Catholic religious order*]
SSJ-TOSF .... Sisters of St. Joseph of the Third Order of St. Francis (TOCD)
SSK............. Antisubmarine Submarine [*Navy symbol*]
SSK............. Keethanou School/Public Library, Stanley Mission, Saskatchewan [*Library symbol National Library of Canada*] (BIB)
SSK............. Service Sink [*Technical drawings*]
SSK............. Skystar International [*ICAO designator*] (FAAC)
SSK............. Slip, Slip, Knit [*Knitting*] (BARN)
SSK............. Sociology of Scientific Knowledge
SSK............. Softkey Software Products, Inc. [*Toronto Stock Exchange symbol*]
SSK............. Soil Stack
SSK............. Super Sport Kurz [*Super, Sport, Short chassis*] [*Mercedes-Benz automotive model designation*]
SSKAT .... Socio-Sexual Knowledge and Attitudes Test [*Psychology*]
SSKDN......... Serikat Sekerdja Kementerian Dalam Negeri [*Union of Workers in the Department of Interior*] [*Indonesia*]
SSKI............ Saturated Solution of Potassium Iodide [*Medicine*]
SSKIL........... Library Technician Program, Kelsey Institute of Applied Arts & Sciences, Saskatoon, Saskatchewan [*Library symbol National Library of Canada*] (NLC)
SSKP .... Serikat Sekerdja Kementerian Pertaganan [*Ministry of Defense Workers' Unions*] [*Indonesia*]
SSKP .... Single-Shot Kill Probability
SSKPS .... Solid-State Klystron Power Supply
SSKTP .... Society for Spreading the Knowledge of True Prayer [*British*] (BI)
SSL............. Congregation of the Sisters of St. Louis, Juilly-Monaghan (TOCD)
SSL............. Licentiate of Sacred Scripture
SSL............. Safety Systems Laboratory [*Formerly, Office of Vehicle Systems Research*] [*Department of Transportation*]
SSL............. School of Systems and Logistics [*Military*]
SSL............. Scientific Subroutine Library
SSL............. Scientific Support Laboratory [*CDEC*] (MCD)
SSL............. Seattle, WA [*Location identifier FAA*] (FAAL)
SSL............. Secure Sockets Layer [*Computer science*] (PCM)
SSL............. Seismograph Service Ltd. [*British*]
SSL............. Selected Source List (AAG)
SSL............. Self-Aligned Superintegration Logic (IAA)
SSL............. Self Serve Laundry [*Military*] (INF)
SSL............. Serpentine Superlattice [*Physics*]
SSL............. Service Security Layer [*Computer science*]
SSL............. Shift and Select [*Computer science*] (MDG)
SSL............. Ship Shortage Log (AAG)
SSL............. Shop Stock List (MCD)
SSL............. Signal Selectro Logic (ECII)
SSL............. Skaneateles Short Line Railroad Corp. [*AAR code*]
SSL............. Skin Surface Lipid [*Physiology*]
SSL............. Social Security Administration Library, Baltimore, MD [*OCLC symbol*] (OCLC)
SSL............. Sociosystem Laboratory
SSL............. Sodium Stearoyl Lactylate
SSL............. Soeurs de Saint Louis [*Sisters of Saint Louis*] (EAIO)
SSL............. Software Sciences Ltd. [*British*]
SSL............. Software Slave Library [*Computer science*] (TEL)
SSL............. Software Specification Language
SSL............. Solid State Lamp (MCD)
SSL............. Solid-State LASER
SSL............. Solid Statement Library (HGAA)
SSL............. Source Statement Library [*Computer science*]
SSL............. Southern Star Resources Ltd. [*Vancouver Stock Exchange symbol*]
SSL............. Space Sciences Laboratory [*University of California, Berkeley*] [*Research center NASA*] (MCD)
SSL............. Space Simulation Laboratory
SSL............. Special Sensor-Lightning
SSL............. Spent Sulfite Liquor [*Papermaking*]
SSL............. Spicilegium Sacrum Lovaniense [*A publication*] (ODCC)
SSL............. Storage Structure Language
SSL............. Sunset Lake [*Pennsylvania*] [*Seismograph station code, US Geological Survey Closed*] (SEIS)
SSL............. Super Speed Logic [*Computer science*] (IAA)
SSL............. Support Status List (MCD)
SSL............. Support System Language [*Computer science*] (IAA)
SSL............. Synthetic Sentence List (STED)
SSL............. System Software Loader (NASA)
SSL............. System Specification Language
SSL............. System Stock List (NATG)
SSLC........... Ship System Life Cycle [*Navy*]
SSLC........... Society of Savings and Loan Controllers [*Later, Financial Managers Society*] (EA)
SSLC........... Synchronous Single-Line Controller
SSLE........... Subacute Sclerosing Leukoencephalitis [*Medicine*]
SSLF........... Southern Sudan Liberation Front (BJA)
SSLH .... Society for the Study of Labour History [*Sheffield, England*] (EA)
SSLI............ Serum Sickness-Like Illness [*Medicine*]
SSLI............ Society of School Librarians International (EA)
SSLI............ Southern Sec Life Ins [*NASDAQ symbol*] (TTSB)
SSLI............ Southern Security Life Insurance Co. [*NASDAQ symbol*] (NQ)
SSLM.......... Solid-Supported Liquid Membrane [*Chemical engineering*]
SSLO .... Solid-State Local Oscillator
SSLOG .... Seton Sisters of Our Lady of Guadalupe, Tucson (TOCD)
SSLORAN ... Skywave Synchronized Long-Range Aid to Navigation
SSLP........... Simple-Sequence Length Polymorphism [*Genetics*]
SSLP........... Single-Sequence Length Polymorphism (HGEN)
SSLP........... Transport Submarine (MCD)

SSL-POW/MIA... Seaside Support League - POW/MIA [*Prisoner of War/Missing in Action*] (EA)
SSLPS .... Solid-State Logic Protection System [*Nuclear energy*] (NRCH)
SSLR .... Straits Settlements Law Reports [*A publication*] (DLA)
SSLR Supp... Straits Settlements Law Reports, Supplement [*1897-99*] [*Malasia*] [*A publication*] (DLA)
SSLS........... Solid-State LASER System
SSLS........... Standard Space Launch System [*BSD*]
SSLSM......... Single Service Logistics Support Manager (MCD)
SSLT........... Solid-State Logic Timer
SSLT........... Starboard Side Light (MCD)
SSLT........... Stock Status Lag Time (AABC)
SSLV........... Southern San Luis Valley Railroad Co. [*AAR code*]
SSLV........... Standard Small Launch Vehicle (DOMA)
SSLV........... Standard Space Launch Vehicle
SSM............ Aero 1 Prop-Jet, Inc. [*Canada ICAO designator*] (FAAC)
SSM............ Midget Submarine [*Navy symbol*]
SSM............ Satellite Stratospheric Monitor (NOAA)
SSM............ Sault Ste. Marie [*Michigan*] [*Airport symbol*] (OAG)
SSM............ Scanning SQUID [*SuperConducting Quantum Interference Device*] Microscope [*Physics*]
SSM............ School in Sales Management [*LIMRA*]
SSM............ Scientific Survey Module (IAA)
SSM............ Second-Stage Motor
SSM............ Second Surface Mirror
SSM............ Second-Tier Securities Market [*Investment term*]
SSM............ Self-Sterilizing-Material [*Pharmacology*]
SSM............ Semiconductor Storage Model (NITA)
SSM............ Semiconductor Storage Module
SSM............ Seminaire St. Martial [*Haiti*] [*Seismograph station code, US Geological Survey Closed*] (SEIS)
SSM............ Semisolid Material [*Metallurgy*]
SSM............ Serum-Supplemented Medium [*Microbiology*]
SSM............ Sesquiterpenoid Stress Metabolite [*Plant physiology*]
SSM............ Set Sign Minus (SAA)
SSM............ Set System Mask (HGAA)
SSM............ Ship Simulation Model [*Navy*]
SSM............ Signal Strength Monitor [*Broadcasting*]
SSM............ Sign Status Matrix (GAVI)
SSM............ Silver Star Medal [*Military decoration*]
SSM............ Simplified Storage Management [*Computer science*]
SSM............ Simulation Support Module
SSM............ Single Sideband Modulation
SSM............ Single Sideband Signal Multiplier [*Telecommunications*]
SSM............ Sisters of St. Mary of the Third Order of St. Francis [*Roman Catholic religious order*]
SSM............ Sisters of the Sorrowful Mother [*Third Order of St. Francis*] [*Roman Catholic religious order*]
SSM............ Small Semiconductor Memory
SSM............ Society of St. Margaret [*Anglican religious community*]
SSM............ Society of St. Monica (EA)
SSM............ Society of the Sacred Mission [*Anglican religious community*]
SSM............ Society of the Servants of Mary [*Anglican religious community*]
SSM............ Solar Simulation Module
SSM............ Solar Stereoscopic Mission [*NASA*]
SSM............ Solid-State Materials (CET)
SSM............ Southlands Mining [*Vancouver Stock Exchange symbol*]
SSM............ Spacecraft Systems Monitor [*NASA*] (MCD)
ssm............ Spacecraft Systems Monitor [*NASA*] (NAKS)
SSM............ Space Station Module [*NASA*] (KSC)
SSM............ Spark Source Mass Spectroscopy
SSM............ Special Safeguarding Measures [*Telecommunications*] (TEL)
SSM............ Special Survey of the Machinery [*Lloyd's Register of Shipping*] (DS)
SSM............ Spread Spectrum Modulation (NATG)
SSM............ Squadron Sergeant Major
SSM............ Staff Sergeant Major [*Military*]
SSM............ Staff Squadron Major [*Military British*]
SSM............ Stage Scanning Microscope
SSM............ Standard Schedule Message (DA)
SSM............ Standard Surfacing Mat [*Fiberglass*]
SSM............ Stochastic Sequential Machine (IAA)
SSM............ Stone Street Bancorp [*AMEX symbol*] (TTSB)
SSM............ Stone Street Bancorp, Inc. [*AMEX symbol*] (SAG)
SSM............ Strategic Sourcing Methodology (AAEL)
SSM............ St. Thomas More College, Saskatoon, Saskatchewan [*Library symbol National Library of Canada*] (NLC)
SSM............ Subsynaptic Membrane [*Anatomy*]
SSM............ Subsystem Manager [*NASA*] (NASA)
ssm............ Subsystem Manager (NAKS)
SSM............ Superficial Spreading Melanoma [*Oncology*]
SSM............ Supply Support Management
SSM............ Support Subsystem Manager
ssm............ Support System Module (NAKS)
SSM............ Support Systems Module [*NASA*]
SSM............ Surface-to-Surface Missile
SSM............ Sync-Stream Manager (PCM)
SSM............ System Security Manager [*Military*] (GFGA)
SSM............ System Software Message [*Computer science*] (IAA)
SSM............ Systems Support Module [*NASA*] (MCD)
ssm............ Systems Support Module (NAKS)
SSM............ System Supply Manager
SSM-POW/MIA... System Support Machine [*Telecommunications*]
SSM............ System Support Management [*or Manager*] [*Military*] (AFM)
SSMA........... School Science and Mathematics Association (EA)
SSMA........... Soldiers, Sailors, Marines, and Airmen's Club [*Washington, DC*]

SSMA	Solid-State Microwave Amplifier
SSMA	Southwest Spanish Mustang Association (EA)
SSMA	Spread-Spectrum Multiple Access [Satellite communications]
SSMA	State Servants and Allied Motoring Association [British] (DBA)
SSMA	Sterilised Suture Manufacturers Association [British] (DBA)
SSMAS	Standards for Management Advisory Services (TDOB)
SSMB	Ship's Serviceman, Barber [Navy rating]
SSMB	Space Shuttle Maintenance Baseline [NASA] (MCD)
SSMB	Special Services Management Bureau [Telecommunications] (TEL)
SSMC	Second-Stage Motor Container
SSMC	Ship's Serviceman, Cobbler [Navy rating]
SSMC	Silver Spring Metro Complex (USDC)
SSMC	Silver Spring Metropolitan Complex [Marine science] (OSRA)
SSMC	Singer Sewing Machine Co. (EFIS)
SSMCC	Space Shuttle Mission Control Center [NASA] (SSD)
SSMCIS	Secondary School Mathematics Curriculum Improvement Study [National Science Foundation]
SSMCNP	Safeguard System Management Communications Network Program [Army] (AABC)
SSMCO	SPARTAN Santa Monica Checkout [NASA]
SSMCS	Synchronous Satellite Military Communication System
SSMD	Saskatchewan Mining Development Corp., Saskatoon, Saskatchewan [Library symbol National Library of Canada] (NLC)
SSMD	Silicon Stud-Mounted Diode
SSME	Satellite System Monitoring Equipment
SSME	Society for the Study of Medical Ethics [British]
SSME	Space Shuttle Main Engine [NASA]
SSME	Spread Spectrum Modulation Equipment [NATO] (MCD)
SSMEC	Space Shuttle Main Engine Controller [NASA] (MCD)
SSMECA	Space Shuttle Main Engine Controller Assembly [NASA] (NASA)
SSMES	Systems Support Module Equipment Section [NASA] (SSD)
SSMF	Signalling System Multi-Frequency (NITA)
SSMF	Symbol Sink - Matched Filter
SSMG	Satellite Systems Monitoring Group [INTELSAT]
SSMG	Ship's Service Motor Generator [Navy] (NVT)
SSMH	Scottish Society for the Mentally Handicapped (EAIO)
SSMH	Scottish Society of Mentally Handicapped (DBA)
SSMHRC	Spanish Speaking Mental Health Research Center [Public Health Service] [Research center] (RCD)
SSM/I	Sensor System Microwave/Imager
SSMI	Sister Servants of Mary Immaculate [Roman Catholic religious order]
SSMI	Special Sensor Microwave Imager [Marine science] (OSRA)
SSMI	Special Sensor Microwave Imagery (COE)
SSMIF & G	Squadron Sergeant-Major Instructor in Fencing and Gymnastics [Military British] (ROG)
SSMI/I	Special Sensor Microwave/Imager [Marine science] (OSRA)
SSM/IM	System Support Manager/Inventory Manager (MCD)
SSMIMA	Scissor, Shear, and Manicure Implement Manufacturers Association [Later, National Association of Scissors and Shears Manufacturers] (EA)
SSMIS	Support Services Management Information System [Army]
SSML	Shaped Substrata Meanderline (MCD)
SSML	Ship's Serviceman, Laundryman [Navy rating]
SSML	Society for the Study of Midwestern Literature (EA)
SSMLL	Society for the Study of Medieval Languages and Literature [British]
SSMM	Space Station Mathematical Model
SSMMA	Staple and Stapling Machine Manufacturers Association [Defunct]
SSMMI	Soeurs Salesiennes Missionnaires de Marie Immaculee [Salesian Missionaries of Mary Immaculate - SMMI] [Gentilly, France] (EAIO)
SSMN	Sisters of St. Mary of Namur [Roman Catholic religious order]
SSMO	Sisters of St. Mary of Oregon [Roman Catholic religious order]
SSMO	Summary of Synoptic Meteorological Observations [National Oceanic and Atmospheric Administration] (MSC)
SSMOB	Surface-to-Surface Missile Order of Battle (MCD)
SSMP	Safeguard System Master Plan [Army] (AABC)
SSMP	Supply Support Management Plan [Military] (CAAL)
SSM PEIS	Stockpile Stewardship and Management Programmatic Environmental Impact Statement
SSMPP	Society for the Study of Male Psychology and Physiology (EA)
SSMRP	Seismic Safety Margins Research Program [Nuclear Regulatory Commission]
SSMS	Solid-State Mass Spectrometer
SSMS	Sons of Sherman's March to the Sea (EA)
SSMS	Spark Source Mass Spectroscopy
SSMS	Submarine Safety Monitoring System
SSMSN	Surface-to-Surface Mission [Military] (AABC)
S SMS N CLSD	Side Seams Not Closed [Freight]
SSMT	Salvage Sales Material Transfer
SSM/T	Sensor System Microwave/Temperature
SSMT	Ship's Serviceman, Tailor [Navy rating]
SSMT	Site Security Maintenance Team
SSMT	Society for the Study of Myth and Tradition (EA)
SSMT	Stress Survival Matrix Test (PDAA)
SSMTG	Solid-State and Molecular Theory Group [MIT] (MCD)
SSMTS	Spade and Shovel Makers' Trade Society [A union] [British]
SSMUX	Spread-Spectrum Multiplexing [Telecommunications] (IAA)
SSMV	Single-Shot Multivibrator
SSMVP	Space Station Master Verification Plan [NASA] (SSD)
SSMVR	Space Station Master Verification Requirement [NASA] (SSD)
SSN	Auburn [New York] [Airport symbol] (AD)
SSN	Romulus, NY [Location identifier FAA] (FAAL)
SSN	Samson Gold Corp. [Vancouver Stock Exchange symbol]
SSN	San Juan Del Sur [Nicaragua] [Seismograph station code, US Geological Survey] (SEIS)

SSN	Season and Sunspot Number (DNAB)
SSN	Segment Stack Number
SSN	Senior Security Network (EA)
SSN	Senior Strategic Income Fund [NYSE symbol] (SAG)
SSN	Severely Subnormal
SSN	Ship, Submersible (Nuclear-Powered)
SSN	Social Security Number (AABC)
SSN	Soviet Sciences in the News [A publication]
SSN	Space Surveillance Network
SSN	Specification Serial Number [Military]
SSN	Standard Serial Numbers (DIT)
SSN	Standard Study Number [Military]
SSN	Station Serial Number (CET)
SSN	Stock Segregation Notice [DoD]
SSN	Submarine (Nuclear-Powered) [Navy symbol] (NVT)
SSN	Switched Service Network [Telecommunications]
SSN	Sykepleiernes Samarbeid i Norden [Northern Nurses Federation - NNF] (EAIO)
SSNAP	Single Seat Night Attack Program (MCD)
SSNCHK	Social Security Number Check
SSND	School Sisters of Notre Dame (IIA)
SSND	Solid-State Neutral Dosimeter
SSN(DS)	Submarine (Nuclear-Powered) in Direct Support [Navy symbol] (NVT)
SSNDT	Scottish School of Non-Destructive Testing [Research center] (IRUK)
SSNF	Source Spot Noise Figure
SSNJ	Self-Screening Noise Jammer (MCD)
SSNLO	Shan State Nationalities Liberation Organization [Myanmar] (PD)
SSNM	Southern Somali National Movement
SSNM	Strategic Special Nuclear Materials
SSNMH	Scipio Society of Naval and Military History (EA)
SSNNP	Sustainable Social Net National Product (EERA)
SSNPP	Small-Size Nuclear Power Plant
SSNS	Scottish Society for Northern Studies
SSNS	Standard Study Numbering System [Military] (AABC)
SSNS	Steroid-Sensitive Nephrotic Syndrome [Medicine] (DMAA)
SSNTD	Solid-State Nuclear Track Detection (PDAA)
SSNW	Social Scientists Against Nuclear War (EA)
SSNY	Swiss Society of New York (EA)
SSO	Safety/Security Officer [Military] (AABC)
SSO	Safety Significant Operation [Aerospace]
SSO	Safety Signification Operation [NASA] (NAKS)
SSO	Sanitary Sewer Overflow [Environmental Protection Agency]
SSO	San Simon, AZ [Location identifier FAA] (FAAL)
SSO	Saturn Systems Office [NASA] (SAA)
SSO	Second Surgical Opinion [Insurance] (WYGK)
SSO	Security System Organization
SSO	Senior Safety Officer [Navy] (CAAL)
SSO	Senior Scientific Officer [Ministry of Agriculture, Fisheries, and Food] [British]
SSO	Senior Staff Officer [Military British]
SSO	Senior Supply Officer [Military British]
SSO	Sequence-Specific Oligonucleotide [Probe] [Medicine] (DMAA)
SSO	Ship Safety Officer
SSO	Simosato [Japan] [Later, HTY] [Geomagnetic observatory code]
SSO	Single Sweep Operation
SSO	Single System Operator (WDMC)
SSO	Society of Surgical Oncology (EA)
SSO	Solid-State Oscillator
SSO	Source Selection Official (NASA)
SSO	Source Selection Official (NAKS)
SSO	Southern Sotho [MARC language code Library of Congress] (LCCP)
SSO	Spacecraft Systems Officer (SAA)
SSO	Space Sciences Office (IAA)
SSO	Space Shuttle Orbiter [NASA] (RDA)
SSO	Space Shuttle Orbiter [NASA] (NAKS)
SSO	Space Station Office [NASA] (SSD)
SSO	Spares Shipping Order
SSO	Special Security Office [or Officer] [Military] (CINC)
SSO	Special Sense Organ [Medicine] (DMAA)
SSO	Special Service Officer [Military]
SSO	Spindle Speed Override (IAA)
SSO	Squadron Signals Officer [Navy British]
SSO	Staff Security Officer (AAG)
SSO	Staff Signals Officer [British military] (DMA)
SSO	Station Staff Officer [British military] (DMA)
SSO	Statistical Service Office [Military]
SSO	Steady-State Oscillation
SSO	Submarine Oiler [Navy ship symbol]
SSO	Submarine Supply Office
SSO	Subsystem Operation [in Spacelab] [NASA] (MCD)
SSO	Sunflower Seed Oil
SSO	Support Services Office [Environmental Protection Agency] (GFGA)
SSO	Support System for OEX [Orbiter Experiments] (NASA)
SSO	System Security Officer
SSO	System Service Order [Bell System]
SSO	System Staff Office
SSOA	Submarine Operating Area [Navy]
SSOA	Subsurface Ocean Area (NVT)
SSOB	Senior Scientist on Board [Navy]
SSOC	Southern Student Organizing Committee [Defunct]
SSOC	Space Station Operations Center [NASA] (SSD)
SSOC	Space Surveillance Operations Center (SAA)
SSOC	Switching Service Operations Center [Telecommunications]
SSOCA	Senior Staff Officer for Civil Affairs [British World War II]
SSOCC	Space Station Operations and Control Center [NASA] (SSD)

SSOD .... Solid-State Optical Detector
SSOD .... Special Session on Disarmament [*A special session of the UN General Assembly held from May 23 to June 28, 1978*]
SSODCM ...... Space Systems Operational Design Criteria Manual [*NASA*]
SSODIA .... Special Security Office, Defense Intelligence Agency (CINC)
SSOE .... Special Subject Operational Evaluation
SSOEC .... Ship Suppliers' Organization of the European Community [*Hague, Netherlands*] (EAIO)
SS of A .... Secular Society of America [*Defunct*]
SSOFS .... Smiling Sons of the Friendly Shillelaghs
SSOG .... Satellite Systems Operations Guide [*INTELSAT*]
SSOG .... Scandinavian Association of Obstetricians and Gynaecologists (EA)
SSOG .... Spur Stepover Gear
SSOJ .... Savez Socialisticke Omladine Jugoslavije [*League of Socialist Youth of Yugoslavia*] [*Political party*] (PPE)
SSOJ .... Single Strength Orange Juice
SSOL .... SmartServ Online [*NASDAQ symbol*] (TTSB)
SSOL .... SmartServ Online, Inc. [*NASDAQ symbol*] (SAG)
SSOL .... Space Station Operations Language [*NASA*] (SSD)
SSOLW .... SmartServ Online Wrrt [*NASDAQ symbol*] (TTSB)
SSOM .... Solid-State Optical MASER
SSOM .... [*The*] Space Shuttle Operator's Manual
SSOMI .... Safety System Outage Modification Inspection [*Environmental science*] (COE)
SSOO .... Satellite Supply Operations Officer [*Military*] (AFIT)
SSOP .... Satellite Systems Operations Plan [*INTELSAT*]
SSOP .... Second Surgical Opinion Program (MEDA)
SSOP .... Shrink Small Outline Package (AAEL)
SSOP .... Space Systems Operating Procedures [*NASA*] (MCD)
SSOP .... Standard Security Operating Procedure (SSD)
SSOR .... Ship Systems Operational Requirements
SSOR .... Slice Successive Overrelaxation
S SORD ...... Senza Sordini [*Without Mutes*] [*Music*]
SSORM .... Standard Ship's Organization and Regulations Manual [*Navy*] (NVT)
SSORM .... Standard Submarine Operations and Regulations Manual (DOMA)
SSORM .... Standing Submarine Operations and Repair Manual [*Navy*] (DNAB)
SSORT .... Ship's Systems Operational Readiness Test (MCD)
SSORT .... Ships Systems Operational Requirements
SSOS .... One Sky, the Saskatchewan Cross Cultural Centre, Saskatoon, Saskatchewan [*Library symbol National Library of Canada*] (NLC)
SSOS .... Single Source of Supply (MCD)
SSOSMFC .... Simply Simon - The Official Simon MacCorkindale Fan Club (EA)
SSOT .... Special Session of Oyer and Terminer [*Legal*] [*British*] (ROG)
SSOTC .... Skinner's School Officers Training Corps [*British military*] (DMA)
SSOU1 .... System Output Unit 1 [*IBM Corp.*] (MDG)
SSOW .... Subcontractor Statement of Work (MCD)
SSOWSJ ...... Supreme Shrine of the Order of the White Shrine of Jerusalem (EA)
SSP .... Association of the Sons of Poland (EA)
SSP .... Pauline Fathers and Brothers (TOCD)
ssp .... Pauline Fathers and Brothers, Society of St. Paul for the Apostolate of Communications (TOCD)
SSP .... Plant Biotechnology Institute, National Research Council Canada [*Institut de Biotechologie des Plantes, Conseil National de Recherches Canada*], Saskatoon, Saskatchewan [*Library symbol Obsolete National Library of Canada*] (NLC)
SSP .... SACEUR [*Supreme Allied Commander, Europe*] Schedule Program [*Army*] (AABC)
SSP .... Safer Society Program and Press [*An association*] (EA)
SSP .... Sagittal Sinus Pressure [*Medicine*]
SSP .... Salt Soluble Protein [*Food industry*]
SSP .... Sanarelli-Shwartzman Phenomenon [*Medical research*] (DAVI)
SSP .... Schwartzman-Sanarelli Phenomenon [*Medicine*] (MAE)
SSP .... Scientific Services Program [*Army Research Office*] (RDA)
SSP .... Scientific Software Products, Inc. [*Information service or system*] (IID)
SSP .... Scientific Subroutine Package [*Computer science*]
SSP .... Scouting Seaplane
SSP .... Scripps EW [*NYSE symbol*] (SAG)
SSP .... Scripps(E.W.)'A' [*NYSE symbol*] (TTSB)
SSP .... Secondary Stock Point (DNAB)
SSP .... Seguro Resources [*Vancouver Stock Exchange symbol*]
SSP .... Seismic Section Profiler
SSP .... Semi-Annual Service Program [*Army*] (INF)
SSP .... Sensor Select Panel (MCD)
SSP .... Sentence Synthesizing Program
SSP .... Serbian Socialist Party [*Political party*]
SSP .... Set Sign Plus (SAA)
SSP .... Ship Speed
SSP .... Ship's Stores Profit [*Navy*]
SSP .... Shortage Specialty Pay [*Navy*] (NVT)
SSP .... Shoshone Peak [*Nevada*] [*Seismograph station code, US Geological Survey*] (SEIS)
SSP .... SIGINT Support Plan (MCD)
SSP .... Signalling and Switching Processor (NITA)
SSP .... Silo Support Plan (SAA)
SSP .... Simulation Support Processor
SSP .... Single-Shot Probability [*Military*]
SSP .... Single Stock Point [*Military*] (AFIT)
SSP .... Single-Stranded Polypeptide (DB)
SSP .... Site Survey Payload (MCD)
SSP .... Size-Selective Precipitation [*Physics*]
SSP .... Skylab Student Project [*NASA*]
SSP .... Small Sortie Payload [*NASA*] (NASA)
SSP .... Society for Scholarly Publishing (EA)
SSP .... Society of Satellite Professionals [*Later, SSPI*] (EA)

SSP .... Society of St. Paul for the Apostolate of Communications [*Pauline Fathers*] [*Roman Catholic religious order*]
SSP .... Sodium Sampling Package [*Nuclear energy*] (NRCH)
SSP .... Sole Supporting Parent
SSP .... Solid-State Photodiode
SSP .... Solid-State Pneumatic
SSP .... Solid-State Preamplifier
SSP .... Solid-State Products [*Electronics*] (IAA)
SSP .... SONAR Signal Processor
SSP .... Sorghum Soy Pellet (OA)
SSP .... Source Selection Plan
SSP .... South Simpson, AK [*Location identifier FAA*] (FAAL)
SSP .... Space Shuttle Program [*NASA*] (NASA)
SSP .... Space Station Program [*NASA*] (SSD)
SSP .... Specialist in School Psychology (GAGS)
SSP .... Specialist Skills Practitioner (WDAA)
SSP .... Special Services Protection [*Telecommunications*] (TEL)
SSP .... Special Session of Peace [*Legal*] [*British*] (ROG)
SSP .... Special Studies Program [*Australia*]
SSP .... Species Survival Plans [*Program sponsored by the American Association of Zoological Parks and Aquariums to protect certain endangered species*]
SSP .... Sporozoite Surface Protein [*Biochemistry*]
SSP .... Staff Site Position [*Nuclear energy*] (NRCH)
SSP .... Stainless Steel Propeller (DS)
SSP .... Standard Shop Practice (MCD)
SSP .... Standard Stability Prediction (MCD)
SSP .... Standard Subroutine Package
SSP .... Standard Switch Panel (MCD)
SSP .... Standby Status Panel
SSP .... Starspeed Ltd. [*British ICAO designator*] (FAAC)
SSP .... State Supplementary Payment [*Department of Health and Human Services*]
SSP .... Static Sodium Pot [*Nuclear energy*] (NRCH)
SSP .... Static Spontaneous Potential (IAA)
SSP .... Statutory Sick Pay [*British*]
SSP .... Steady-State Pulse [*Telecommunications*] (IAA)
SSP .... Steam Service Pressure
SSP .... Stores Select Panel (SAA)
SSP .... Stores Stressed Platform [*Military British*]
SSP .... St. Philip's College, San Antonio, TX [*OCLC symbol*] (OCLC)
SSP .... Strategic Systems Project [*Office*] [*Navy*]
SSP .... Subacute Sclerosing Panencephalitis [*Medicine*] (DAVI)
SSP .... Submarine Scout Patrol (DMA)
SSP .... Submarine Transport [*Navy symbol Obsolete*]
SSP .... Subsatellite Point [*Telecommunications*] (TEL)
SSP .... Subsolar Point [*Aerospace*]
SSP .... Subspecies [*Also, ssp*]
ssp .... Subspecies
S/SP .... Subsystem Software Program (MCD)
SSP .... Supersensitivity Perception
SSP .... Supervisory Surveillance Program [*DoD*]
SSP .... Supplemental Standard Practice (AAG)
SSP .... Support Software Package (MCD)
SSP .... Surgical Specialist
SSP .... Sustained Superior Performance [*Military*]
SSP .... System Safety Plan (MCD)
SSP .... System Security Plan
SSP .... System Service Program [*Computer science*] (IAA)
SSP .... System Status Panel
SSP .... System Support Processor (NITA)
SSP .... System Support Program (AFM)
SSPA .... Senescent-Soybean-Pod Agar [*Microbiology*]
SSPA .... Social Security Pensions Act [*1975*] [*British*] (DCTA)
SSPA .... Society of St. Peter Apostle (EA)
SSPA .... Solid State Phased Array (MCD)
SSPA .... Solid State Power Amplifier (DA)
SSPA .... Southern Sudanese Political Association [*Sudan*] [*Political party*] (MENA)
SSPA .... Specialist in Speech Pathology and Audiology (GAGS)
SSPA .... Student Support and Parent Awareness [*Australia*]
SSPANC .... Society of St. Peter the Apostle for Native Clergy [*Later, SSPA*] (EA)
SSPB .... Socket Screw Products Bureau [*Defunct*] (EA)
SSPB .... Swedish State Power Board [*Nuclear energy*]
SSPC .... Missionary Sisters of St. Peter Claver (TOCD)
SSPC .... Seda Speciality Packaging [*NASDAQ symbol*] (SAG)
SSPC .... Solid-State Power Controller [*NASA*]
SSPC .... Spacelab Stored Program Command [*NASA*] (MCD)
SSPC .... Steel Structures Painting Council (EA)
SSPCA .... Scottish Society of Prevention of Cruelty to Animals (DBA)
SSPCL .... System Software Package Component List (MCD)
SSPCL .... System Support Package Component List (MCD)
SSPCP .... Service-Specific Practice Cost Percentage [*Medicine*] (DMAA)
SSPCP .... Shipboard Signal Processing Control Program [*Navy*] (CAAL)
SSPCT .... Technical Library, Potash Corp. of Saskatchewan, Saskatoon, Saskatchewan [*Library symbol National Library of Canada*] (NLC)
SSPD .... Shuttle System Payload Data [*NASA*] (NASA)
SSPD .... Shuttle System Payload Definition Study [*NASA*] (NASA)
SSPD .... Shuttle System Payload Description [*NASA*] (NASA)
S/SPD .... Single Speed [*Automotive engineering*]
SSPDA .... Space Shuttle Payload Data Activity [*NASA*] (NASA)
SSPDA .... Surface Sampler Processing and Distribution Assembly
SSPDB .... Subsystem Power Distribution Box (MCD)
SSPDR .... Subsystem Preliminary Design Review
SSPDS .... Space Shuttle Payload Data Study [*NASA*] (NASA)

SSPE............ Software Spectrum [*NASDAQ symbol*] (TTSB)
SSPE............ Software Spectrum, Inc. [*NASDAQ symbol*] (SPSG)
SSPE............ Space Station Program Element [*NASA*] (SSD)
SSPE............ Subacute Sclerosing Panencephalitis [*Medicine*]
SSPE............ Support System Project Engineer
SSPF............ Signal Structure Parametric Filter [*Telecommunications*] (OA)
SSPF............ Software Support Production Facility (SSD)
SSPF............ Space Station Processing Facility [*NASA*] (SSD)
SSPF............ Structured Soy Protein Fiber [*Food industry*]
SSPFC........... Stainless Steel Plumbing Fixture Council [*Defunct*] (EA)
SSPG............ Steady State Plasma Glucose [*Medicine*] (DMAA)
SSPGSE........ Space Shuttle Program Ground Support Equipment [*NASA*] (GFGA)
SSPHS.......... Society for Spanish and Portuguese Historical Studies (EA)
SSPI............ Sight System Passive Infrared [*Sensor*] [*Army*]
SSPI............ Society of Satellite Professionals International (TSSD)
SSPI............ Spectrum Signal Processing [*NASDAQ symbol*] (SAG)
SSPI............ Steady State Plasma Insulin [*Medicine*] (DMAA)
SSP-ICF....... System Support Program-Interactive Communication Feature [*Computer science*] (MHDI)
SSPIF........... Software Support Production Integration Facility (SSD)
SSPIF........... Spectrum Signal Processing [*NASDAQ symbol*] (TTSB)
SSPK .... Single Shot Probability of Kill [*Military*]
SSPL .... Saturation Sound Pressure Level
SSPL .... Solid-State Pneumatic Logic
SSPL .... Steady-State Power Level (IEEE)
SSPL .... System Support Package List (MCD)
SSPM........... Schedule Statusing and Performance Measurement (SSD)
SSPM........... Single Sideband Phase Modulation [*Telecommunications*] (IAA)
SSPM........... Single Strokes per Minute (MSA)
SSPM........... Software Standards and Procedures Manual (SSD)
SSPM........... Space Shuttle Program Manager [*NASA*] (NASA)
SSPMA........ Sump and Sewage Pump Manufacturers Association (EA)
SSPME......... Societa di San Patrizio per le Missioni Estere [*St. Patrick's Society for the Foreign Missions - SPSFM*] [*Kiltegan, County Wicklow, Republic of Ireland*] (EAIO)
SSPMO .... SONAR Systems Project Management Office
SSPN .... Satellite System for Precise Navigation [*Air Force*]
SSPN .... Ship's Stores and Profit, Navy
SSPN .... System for Precise Navigation [*Later, DNSS*] (MCD)
ssp nov ...... Subspecies Nova [*New Subspecies*] [*Biology*]
SSPO .... Space Shuttle Program Office [*NASA*] (KSC)
SSPO .... Strategic Systems Project Office [*Navy*]
SSPO .... Survey of Student Personnel Objectives (EDAC)
SSPOTR........ Strategic Systems Project Office, Technical Representative [*Navy*] (DNAB)
SSPP .... POS Pilot Plant Corp., University of Saskatchewan Campus, Saskatoon, Saskatchewan [*Library symbol National Library of Canada*] (NLC)
SSPP .... Sancti Patres [*Holy Fathers*] [*Latin*]
SSPP .... Schedule Status Preprocessor (MCD)
SSPP .... Serikat Sekerdja Pamong Pradja [*Public Officials' Union*] [*Indonesia*]
SSPP .... Shan State Progressive Party [*Myanmar*] [*Political party*] (EY)
SSPP .... Society for Service Professionals in Printing (NTPA)
SSPP .... Society for the Study of Process Philosophies (EA)
SSPP .... Solar Sea Power Plant [*NASA*]
SSPP .... Space Station Program Participant [*NASA*] (SSD)
SSPP .... Static Strength Prediction Program [*Ergonometrics*]
SSPP .... Subspecies [*Plural form*] [*Also, sspp*]
SSPP .... Subsynaptic Plate Perforation [*Neurophysiology*]
SSPP .... System Safety Program Plan [*Navy*]
SSPPSG....... Space Shuttle Payload Planning Steering Group [*NASA*] (NASA)
SSPQ .... Science Studies' Perception Questionnaire (AIE)
SSPR .... Subcontract Schedule and Procurement Request
SSPRO......... Space Shuttle Program Resident Office [*NASA*] (NASA)
SSpS........... Missionary Sisters Servants of the Holy Spirit (TOCD)
SSPS .... Satellite Solar Power Station [*or System*] [*NASA*]
SSPS .... Sheffield Sawmakers' Protection Society [*A union*] [*British*] (DCTA)
SSPS .... Side-to-Side Portacaval Shunt [*Medicine*] (DMAA)
SSPS .... Silver/Somatostatin Positive Structure [*Anatomy*]
SSP-S .... Single Source Processor-SIGINT [*Signal Intelligence*]
SSPS .... Small Solar-Power System [*Energy source*]
SSPS .... Solar-Based Solar Power Satellite
SSPS .... Solar Satellite Power Station
SSPS .... Solid-State Protection System [*Nuclear energy*] (IEEE)
SSPS .... Spacecraft Support Planning Section
SSPS .... Space Shuttle Program Schedule [*NASA*] (NASA)
SSPS .... Sunflower Space Power System (IAA)
SSPSA......... Seabrook Station Probabilistic Safety Assessment [*Environmental science*] (COE)
SSpSdeAP ... Sister Servants of the Holy Spirit of Perpetual Adoration (TOCD)
SSPSF......... Stochastic Self-Propagating Star Formation
SSPSG........ Science and Public Policy Studies Group [*Newsletter*]
SSPSM .... Serikat Sekerdja Pabrik Sendjata dan Mesiu [*Armaments' Union*] [*Indonesia*]
SSPT............ Speech Sounds Perception Test (EDAC)
SSPTF.......... Santa Susana Propulsion Test Facility [*NASA*] (NASA)
SSPTS .... Security Support Squadron
SSPTT.......... Serikat Sekerdja Pos, Telegraph dan Telepon [*National Postal, Telegraph and Telephone Employees' Union*] [*Indonesia*]
SSPU .... Ship's Service Power Unit [*Navy*] (CAAL)
SSPV .... Scottish Society of Prevention of Vivisection (DBA)
SSPW .... Sun Sportswear [*NASDAQ symbol*] (TTSB)
SSPW .... Sun Sportswear, Inc. [*NASDAQ symbol*] (NQ)
SSPWB .... Studium Spraw Polskich (Wielka Brytania) [*Information Centre for Polish Affairs*] (EAIO)

SSPWR........ Small-Size Pressurized Water Reactor [*Nuclear energy*]
SSQ .... Noosa Air Sunstate Airlines [*Australia ICAO designator*] (FAAC)
SSQ .... Shell Lake, WI [*Location identifier FAA*] (FAAL)
SSQ .... Simple Sinusoidal Quantity
SSQ .... Social Science Quarterly [*A publication*] (BRI)
SSQ .... Society for Software Quality (EA)
SSQ .... Station Sick Quarters
SSQ .... Sum of the Squares (IAA)
SSQA .... Standardize Supplier Quality Assessment (AAEL)
SSR .... RADAR Picket Submarine [*Navy symbol*]
SSR .... SACEUR [*Supreme Allied Commander, Europe*] Strategic Reserve [*Army*] (NATG)
SSR .... Safe Secure Railcar [*Army*]
SSR .... Safety Services Representative [*Red Cross*]
SSR .... Saskatchewan Research Council, Saskatoon, Saskatchewan [*Library symbol National Library of Canada*] (NLC)
SSR .... SATCOM Station Reports (MCD)
SSR .... Satellite Situation Report (AAG)
SSR .... S-Band Shuttle Return
SSR .... Schedule Shipment Record (MCD)
SSR .... Scratched Surface Recording (IAA)
SSR .... Seal Steam Regulator [*Nuclear energy*] (NRCH)
SSR .... Secondary Surveillance RADAR
SSR .... Secondary System Relief [*Environmental science*] (COE)
SSR .... Security Services [*Vancouver Stock Exchange symbol*]
SSR .... Security Survey Report [*Nuclear energy*]
SSR .... Seek-Storm RADAR
SSR .... Selective Serotonin Re-ceptake Indicator [*Medicine*]
SSR .... Selenium Stack Rectifier
SSR .... Self-Sufficiency Ratio [*Business term*]
SSR .... Sempati Air PT [*Indonesia*] [*ICAO designator*] (FAAC)
SSR .... Separate Superheater Reactor [*Nuclear energy*]
SSR .... Shipbuilding and Ship Repair [*Department of Employment*] [*British*]
SSR .... Shop Support Request [*NASA*] (NASA)
SSR .... SIA [*Semiconductor Industry Association*] Statistical Review [*A publication*] (EAAP)
SSR .... Signal-Sequence Receptor [*Biochemistry*]
SSR .... Simple Sequence Repeat [*Genetics*]
SSR .... Simple Sequence Repeats [*Genetics*]
SSR .... Single Signal Receiver [*Telecommunications*] (IAA)
SSR .... Sink to Source Relation
SSR .... Sisters Island, AK [*Location identifier FAA*] (FAAL)
SSR .... Site Suitability Report [*Nuclear energy*] (NRCH)
SSR .... Slate-Shingle Roof [*Technical drawings*]
SSR .... Slow Strain Rate [*Tensile test*]
SSR .... Societe Suisse de Radiodiffusion et Television [*Radio and television network*] [*Switzerland*]
SSR .... Society for the Study of Reproduction (EA)
SSR .... Software Specification Review
SSR .... Solid State Relay (IEEE)
SSR .... South Staffordshire Regiment [*Military unit*] [*British*]
SSR .... Soviet Socialist Republic
SSR .... Special Scientific Report
SSR .... Special Services Request [*Travel industry*]
SSR .... Special Survey of Refrigerated Machinery [*Lloyd's Register of Shipping*] (DS)
SSR .... Specification Status Report [*Nuclear Regulatory Commission*] (GFGA)
SSR .... Spin-Stabilized Rockets
SSR .... Spotted Swine Record [*Later, National Spotted Swine Record*] (EA)
SSR .... Staff-Student Ratio (DET)
SSR .... Staff Support Room [*NASA*]
SSR .... Standby Supply Relay [*Telecommunications*] (IAA)
SSR .... Static Shift Register
SSR .... Static Squelch Range
SSR .... Station Set Requirement [*NASA*] (NASA)
SSR .... Statistical Summary Report (AAG)
SSR .... Steady-State Rate [*of production*] [*Medicine*]
SSR .... Stock Status Report
SSR .... Students for Social Responsibility (EA)
SSR .... Subsynchronous Resonance (IEEE)
SSR .... Summarized Spares Requirement
SSR .... Sum of the Squared Residuals [*Econometrics*]
SSR .... Supplemental Security Record [*Social Security Administration*] (GFGA)
SSR .... Supplementary Statement Required [*Civil Service*]
SSR .... Supply Support Request [*or Requirement*] [*Military*] (AFM)
SSR .... Support Staff Rooms (SAA)
SSR .... Surface Search RADAR (SAA)
SSR .... Surface Slip Resistance
s-sr-- .... Surinam [*MARC geographic area code Library of Congress*] (LCCP)
SSR .... Susara [*Romania*] [*Seismograph station code, US Geological Survey*] (SEIS)
SSR .... Sustained Silent Reading [*Education*] (AEE)
SSR .... Switching Selector Repeater (PDAA)
SSR .... Synchronous Stable Relaying (IEEE)
SSR .... System Status Report
SSR .... System Status Review
SSR .... System Study Requirement (AAG)
SSR .... System Subroutines (SAA)
SSR .... System Support Record
SSRA .... Scottish Squash Rackets Association (EAIO)
SSRA .... Spread Spectrum Random Access System [*Telecommunications*] (TEL)
SSRA .... System Safety Risk Analysis [*Army*]

SSRAM .... Synchronous Static Ramdom Access Memory (AAEL)
SSRB .... Sole Source Review Board (MCD)
SSRB .... Supply Systems Redevelopment Branch [*Australian Defence Force*]
SSRBD .... Solid State RADAR Beacon Decoder (DWSG)
SSRC .... Single Sideband Reduced Carrier [*Telecommunications*] (IAA)
SSRC .... Social Science Research Center [*Mississippi State University*] [*Research center*] (RCD)
SSRC .... Social Science Research Council (EA)
SSRC .... Social Systems Research Center [*California State University, Dominguez Hills*] [*Research center*] (RCD)
SSRC .... Society for the Study of Religion and Communism (EA)
SSRC .... Structural Stability Research Council (EA)
SSRC .... Swedish Space Research Committee
SSRCA .... Super Sunfish Racing Class Association (EA)
SSRCC .... Social Sciences Research Council of Canada [*See also CCRSS*] [*Later, SSHRCC*]
SSRCR .... Suggested State Regulations for the Control of Radiation [*Nuclear Regulatory Commission*] (NRCH)
SSRD .... Secondary Surveillance RADAR Digitizer (IAA)
SSRD .... Station Set Requirements Document [*NASA*] (NASA)
SSRE .... Shear-Stress Responsive Element [*Biochemistry*]
SSRE .... Society for Social Responsibility in Engineering (EERA)
SSREIU .... Shipbuilding, Ship Repairing, and Engineering Industrial Union [*British*]
SSREX .... Canada Department of Regional Industrial Expansion [*Ministere de l'Expansion Industrielle Regionale*] Saskatoon, Saskatchewan [*Library symbol National Library of Canada*] (NLC)
SSRF .... Shell-Supported Ring Frame
SSRF .... Small-Scale Raiding Force [*Military*]
SSR-F .... Special Scientific Report - Fisheries
SSRFC .... Social Science Research Facilities Center [*University of Minnesota*] [*Research center*] (RCD)
SSRG .... Selective Service Regulations
SSRG .... Simple Shift Register Generator
SSRH .... General Constituency Section for Small or Rural Hospitals (EA)
SSRI .... Selective Serotonin Re-uptake Inhibitor [*Antidepressant*]
SSRI .... Serotonum-Specific Reuptake Inhibitor [*Medicine*] (WDAA)
SSRI .... Social Science Research Institute [*of CRESS*] [*University of Hawaii at Manoa*] [*Research center*] (RDA)
SSRI .... Social Science Research Institute [*University of Maine at Orono*] [*Research center*] (RCD)
SSRI .... Social Systems Research Institute [*University of Wisconsin - Madison*] [*Research center*] (RCD)
SSRI .... Specific Serotonin Reuptake Inhibitor [*Antidepressant*]
SSRL .... Stanford Synchrotron Radiation Laboratory [*Stanford, CA*] [*Department of Energy*]
SSRL .... Systems Simulation Research Laboratory
SSRM .... Sealectro Small Reliable Miniature (IAA)
SSRM .... Second-Stage Rocket Motor
SSRMS .... Space Station Remote Manipulator System [*NASA*] (SSD)
SSRN .... RADAR Picket Submarine (Nuclear Powered) [*Navy symbol Obsolete*]
SSRN .... Service Shop Requirement Notice
SSRN .... System Software Reference Number [*NASA*] (NASA)
SSRNJ .... Socijalisticka Savez Radnog Naroda Jugoslavije [*Socialist Alliance of Working People of Yugoslavia - SAWPY*] [*Political party*] (PPE)
SSRO .... Sector Scan Receive Only [*Military*] (LAIN)
SSRP .... Single Shot Kill Probability (MCD)
SSRP .... Somali Socialist Revolutionary Party
SSRP .... Stanford Synchrotron Radiation Project
SSRP .... Structure-Specific Recognition Protein [*Biochemistry*]
SSRPOS .... Space Station Rendezvous and Proximity Operations Simulator [*NASA*] (SSD)
SSRQ .... Steep-Spectrum Radio Quasar [*Galaxy*]
SSRR .... Social Service Reporting Requirements [*HEW*]
SSRR .... Station Set Requirements Review [*NASA*] (NASA)
SSRR .... System Software Requirement Review (MCD)
SSRS .... SIGINT Surveillance and Reporting System (MCD)
SSRS .... Society for Social Responsibility in Science (EA)
SSRS .... Source Storage and Retrieval System [*Computer science*] (MHDI)
SSRS .... Start-Stop-Restart System [*NASA*] (KSC)
SSRS .... Submarine Sand Recovery System
SSRSB .... Safety and Special Radio Services Bureau [*of FCC*]
SSRSJC .... Saudi-Sudanese Red Sea Joint Commission [*Commercial firm Jeddah, Saudi Arabia*] (EAIO)
SSRT .... Slow Strain Rate Technique [*Nuclear energy*] (NUCP)
SSRT .... Subsystem Readiness Test (KSC)
SSRTP .... Solid Substrate Room Temperature Phosphorescence
SS-RTP .... Solid-Surface, Room-Temperature Phosphorescence [*Physics*]
SSRU .... Scottish Schools Rugby Union (AIE)
SSS .... Compania de Servicios Aereos SA [*Spain ICAO designator*] (FAAC)
SSS .... Congregation of the Blessed Sacrament (TOCD)
SSS .... Congregation of the Blessed Sacrament (TOCD)
SSS .... Safeguard Spartan System [*Aerospace*] (MCD)
SSS .... Safe Shutdown System [*Environmental science*] (COE)
SSS .... San Salvador [*El Salvador*] [*Seismograph station code, US Geological Survey*] (SEIS)
SSS .... Satellite Surveillance System (MCD)
SSS .... Satellite Syndicated Systems [*Douglasville, GA*] [*Cable TV programming service*] [*Telecommunications*]
SSS .... Sauna - Swimming Pool - Storage Area [*Key fitting those locks in apartment complex*]
SSS .... Scalded Skin Syndrome [*Medicine*] (MAE)
SSS .... Scaled Skin Syndrome [*Dermatology*] (DAVI)
SSS .... Scandinavian Surgical Society (FAIO)

SSS .... Scene Storage System (MCD)
SSS .... School of Social Studies [*British*]
SSS .... Scientific Subroutine System [*Computer science*] (BUR)
SSS .... Sea Surface Salinity
SSS .... Secondary Sampling System [*Nuclear energy*] (NRCH)
S/SS .... Sector/Subsector
SSS .... Selective Service System
SSS .... Self-Service Store
SSS .... Self-Shifting Synchronizing (PDAA)
SSS .... Semitic Study Series [*A publication*] (BJA)
SSS .... Senior Service School [*Military*] (AFM)
SSS .... Sensitized Stainless Steel (NRCH)
SSS .... Sentinel-Spartan System (MCD)
SSS .... Sequential Scheduling System (IAA)
SSS .... Serial Signalling Scheme (PDAA)
SSS .... Servants of the Blessed Sacrament (TOCD)
SSS .... Shevchenko Scientific Society (EA)
SSS .... Shield and Seismic Support [*Nuclear energy*] (NRCH)
SSS .... Shift Ship Superintendent [*Navy*] (DNAB)
SSS .... Ship's Service Stores
SSS .... Ship Stamp Society [*British*] (DBA)
SSS .... Shnat Sherut Scheme (BJA)
SSS .... Shore Signal Service [*British Royal Navy*]
SSS .... Siassi [*Papua New Guinea*] [*Airport symbol*] (OAG)
SSS .... Sick Sinus Syndrome [*Medicine*]
SSS .... Signal Switching System
SSS .... Signature Security Service [*DoD*]
SSS .... Silicon-Symmetrical Switch (CET)
SSS .... Simplified Spelling Society (EA)
SSS .... Simulation Study Series (KSC)
SSS .... Single Screw Ship
SSS .... Single Signal Superhet (IAA)
SSS .... Single Signal Supersonic [*Heterodyne*] (DEN)
SSS .... Sisters of Social Service [*Roman Catholic religious order*]
SSS .... Sisters of Social Service of Los Angeles, Inc. (TOCD)
SSS .... Site Security Supervisor (AFM)
SSS .... Skills Support System [*Education*]
SSS .... Small Scientific Satellite [*NASA*]
SSS .... Small Solar Satellite [*NASA*]
SSS .... Small Starlight Scope [*Light-intensifying device*]
SSS .... Small Structures Survey [*Civil Defense*]
SSS .... Social Science Series [*A publication*]
SSS .... Social Status Study [*Psychology*]
SSS .... Societas Sanctissimi Sacramenti [*Congregation of the Blessed Sacrament*] [*Roman Catholic men's religious order*]
SSS .... Societe Scandinave de Simulation [*Scandinavian Simulation Society*] [*Finland*] (EAIO)
SSS .... Society for Slovene Studies (EA)
SSS .... Society for Socialist Studies [*See also SES*] [*Canada*]
SSS .... Society for the Second Self (EA)
SSS .... Society for the Suppression of Speculative Stamps [*Defunct*]
SSS .... Society of St. Stephen (EA)
SSS .... Sodium Styrenesulfonate [*Organic chemistry*]
SSS .... Software/Segment Specification
SSS .... Software Service System [*Anti-piracy device invented by Ryoichi Mori of the Japan Electronics Industry Development Association*] (BYTE)
SSS .... Software Specification Sheet [*Computer science*] (IAA)
SSS .... Software Staging Section [*Social Security Administration*]
SSS .... Solid-State Scientific (IAA)
SSS .... Solid-State Spectrometer
SSS .... Solid-State Switching (NG)
SSS .... Solid-State System
SSS .... SONAR Signal Simulator
SSS .... Sortie Support System (MCD)
SSS .... Sound Suppression System (NASA)
SSS .... Sound Suppression System (NAKS)
SSS .... Southern Satellite Systems, Inc. [*Tulsa, OK*] [*Telecommunications*] (TSSD)
SSS .... Sovran Self Storage [*NYSE symbol*] (TTSB)
SSS .... Sovran Self Storage, Inc. [*NYSE symbol*] (SAG)
SSS .... Spacecraft System Support
SSS .... Space Settlers' Society [*Defunct*] (EAIO)
SSS .... Space Shuttle Simulation [*NASA*]
SSS .... Space Shuttle System [*NASA*] (KSC)
SSS .... Space Shuttle System [*NASA*] (NAKS)
SSS .... Space Station Simulator
SSS .... Space Surveillance System [*Navy*] (MCD)
SSS .... Special Safeguards Study [*Nuclear energy*] (NRCH)
SSS .... Special Safety Safeguards (NRCH)
SSS .... Special Security Squadron
SSS .... Special Source Survey (AAGC)
SSS .... Special Support Services
SSS .... Specific Soluble Substance [*Polysaccharide hapten*]
SSS .... Speed-Sensitive Steering [*Automotive engineering*]
SSS .... Spinning Space Station
SSS .... Spin-Stabilized Spacecraft
SSS .... Stability and Safety Screening [*Sailing terminology*]
SSS .... Stabilized Sighting System
SSS .... Staff Summary Sheet (MCD)
SSS .... Stage Separation Subsystem [*NASA*] (NASA)
SSS .... Stage Separation Subsystem (NAKS)
SSS .... Stainless Steel Sink [*Classified advertising*] (ADA)
SSS .... Standard Scratch Score [*Golf*]
SSS .... Standard Seawater Service [*British*]

SSS	Standard Supply System [*Army*] (AABC)	
SSS	Stanford Sleepiness Scale	
SSS	Starlight Scope [*Night sighting device*] [*Military*] (VNW)	
SSS	State Supply Service [*Victoria, Australia*]	
SSS	Station Set Specification [*NASA*] (NASA)	
sss	Station Set Specification (NAKS)	
SSS	Stepping Switch Scanner	
SSS	Sterile Saline Soak	
SSS	Stockholders Sovereignty Society [*Later, FFSR*] (EA)	
SSS	STOL Support Ship [*Navy*] (CAAL)	
SSS	Storage Serviceability Standard [*Army*]	
SSS	Strategic Satellite System (MCD)	
SSS	Strategic Studies Staff [*Environmental Protection Agency*] (GFGA)	
SSS	Strategic Support Squadron [*Air Force*]	
SSS	Stratum Super Stratum [*Layer Over Layer*] [*Latin*]	
SSS	Strict Suicide Supervision (WDAA)	
SSS	Strike Support Ship [*Navy*] (NVT)	
SSS	Strong Soap Solution	
SSS	Structures Subsystem (KSC)	
SSS	Student Support Services Program [*Department of Education*] (GFGA)	
SSS	Study Skills Surveys [*Educational test*]	
SSS	Subjective Stress Scale	
SSS	Subject Specialists Section [*Association of College and Research Libraries*]	
SSS	Subscribers' Switching Subsystem [*Telecommunications*] (TEL)	
SSS	Substructure Search System [*Later, SANSS*] [*NIH/EPA*]	
SSS	Subsystem Segment [*NASA*] (NASA)	
sss	Subsystem Segment (NAKS)	
SSS	Subsystem Support Service (BUR)	
SSS	Sunday Shakespeare Society [*British*]	
SSS	Superior Shore Systems [*An association*] (EA)	
SSS	Supplementary Safety System [*Environmental science*] (COE)	
SSS	Supply Screening Section [*Navy*]	
SSS	Survivable Satellite System (MCD)	
SSS	Symbolic Shorthand System	
SSS	System Safety Society (EA)	
SSS	System Segment Specification (MCD)	
SSS	Systems, Science, and Software	
SSS	Trois Fois Salut [*Thrice Greeting*] [*Freemasonry*] [*French*] (ROG)	
SSSA	Scottish Salmon Smokers Association (DBA)	
SSSA	Self-Service Storage Association [*Later, SSA*] (EA)	
SSSA	Soil Science Society of America (EA)	
SSSA	Sotos Syndrome Support Association (EA)	
SSSA	St. Andrew's College, Saskatoon, Saskatchewan [*Library symbol National Library of Canada*] (NLC)	
SSSA	Submarine SONAR Subjective Analysis (NVT)	
SSSAS	Society of Spanish and Spanish-American Studies (EA)	
SSSAS	Space Station Systems Analysis Study [*NASA*] (SSD)	
SSSB	Sagittal Split Setback (STED)	
SSSB	Society for the Study of Social Biology (EA)	
SSSB	System Source Selection Board [*Air Force*]	
SSSBCR	Star, Starling, Stuart, and Briton Car Register (EA)	
SSSBP	System Source Selection Board Procedure [*Air Force*]	
SSSC	Self Service Supply Center [*Military*] (AFIT)	
SSSC	Single Sideband Suppressed Carrier	
SSSC	Soft-Sized Super-Calendered [*Paper*]	
SSSC	Solid-State Sciences Committee [*National Research Council*] [*Physics*]	
SSSC	Space Science Steering Committee	
SSSC	Space Station Support Center [*NASA*] (SSD)	
SSSC	Special Spectrum Study Committee	
SSSC	Stainless Steel Sink Council [*Defunct*] (EA)	
SSSC	Surface/Subsurface Control [*Navy*] (CAAL)	
SSSC	Surface/Subsurface Surveillance Center [*Navy*] (NVT)	
SSSC	Surface/Subsurface Surveillance Coordinator [*Navy*]	
SSSCP	Single Supply Support Control Point (MCD)	
SSSD	Second-Stage Separation Device	
SSSD	Single-Sided, Single-Density Disk [*Magnetic disk*] [*Computer science*]	
SSSD	Solid-State Solenoid Driver	
SSSD	Space Shuttle Simulation Display [*NASA*]	
SSSEDA	Aerospace Products Division, SED Systems Ltd., Saskatoon, Saskatchewan [*Library symbol National Library of Canada*] (NLC)	
SSSERC	Scottish Schools Science Equipment Research Centre (CB)	
SSSF	School Sisters of St. Francis (TOCD)	
SSSF	Stationary Source Simulator Facility [*Environmental science*]	
SSSG	SLCM [*Sea-Launched Cruise Missile*] Survivability Steering Group [*Navy*] (CAAL)	
SSSI	Kelsey Institute of Applied Arts and Sciences, Saskatoon, Saskatchewan [*Library symbol National Library of Canada*] (NLC)	
SSSI	Siegel Scale of Support for Innovation (DMAA)	
SSSI	Site of Special Scientific Interest [*British*]	
SSSI	Society for the Study of Symbolic Interaction (EA)	
SSSI	Special Steel Summary Invoice [*International Trade Administration*]	
SSSI	Steel Scaffolding and Shoring Institute [*Later, SSFI*] (EA)	
SSSJ	Single Subsonic Jet	
SSSJ	Student Struggle for Soviet Jewry (EA)	
SSSL	Society for the Study of Southern Literature (EA)	
SSSL	Supersonic Split Line (KSC)	
SSSLF	South Slavonian Socialist Labor Federation [*Defunct*] (EA)	
SSSM	Site Space Surveillance Monitor (AFM)	
SSSM	South Street Seaport Museum (EA)	
SSSM	Subset-Specified Sequential Machine [*Air Force*]	
SSSM	Systems Support Service Module (SSD)	
SSSMC	Sports Science and Sports Medicine Centre [*Australia*]	

SSSMP	Surface Ship SONAR Modernization Program (MCD)	
SSSN	Secondary Social Security Number	
S/S/SN	System/Subsystem/Subject Number (MCD)	
SSSO	Specialized Satellite Service Operators [*British*]	
SSSO	Specialized Surplus Sales Office [*Military*]	
SSSO	Special Service Satellite Operator [*Telecommunications*]	
SSSP	Secondary School Science Project [*Princeton University*] (AEE)	
SSSP	Society for the Study of Social Problems (EA)	
SSSP	Space Settlement Studies Program (EA)	
SSSP	Space Shuttle Synthesis Program [*National Academy of Sciences*]	
SSSP	Station to Station Send Paid [*Telecommunications*] (TEL)	
SSSP	System Source Selection Procedure [*Air Force*]	
SSSQ	McCarron-Dial Street Survival Skills Questionnaire [*Occupational therapy*]	
SSSQ	Street Survival Skills Questionnaire (DHP)	
SS/SR	Safety Standdown/Safety Review (MCD)	
SSSR	SAGE [*Semiautomatic Ground Environment*] System Status Report	
SSSR	Smallest Set of Smallest Rings [*Organic chemistry*]	
SSSR	Social Sciences Services and Resources (EA)	
SSSR	Society for the Scientific Study of Religion (EA)	
SSSR	Soyuz Sovetskikh Sotsialisticheskikh Respublik [*Union of Soviet Socialist Republics*]	
SSSR	Syracuse Scales of Social Relations [*Education*]	
SSSS	Shallow Spherical Sandwich Shell	
SSSS	Society for Social Studies of Science (NTPA)	
SSSS	Society for the Scientific Study of Sex (EA)	
SSSS	Spaceborne Software Systems Study (DNAB)	
SSSS	Space Shuttle System Segment (MCD)	
SSSS	Space Shuttle System Specification [*NASA*] (NASA)	
ssss	Space Shuttle System Specification [*NASA*] (NAKS)	
SSSS	Space Systems Support Squadron	
SSSS	Staphylococcal Scalded Skin Syndrome [*Medicine*]	
SSSS	Stewart & Stevenson [*NASDAQ symbol*] (TTSB)	
SSSS	Stewart & Stevenson Services, Inc. [*NASDAQ symbol*] (NQ)	
SSSSC	Surface/Subsurface Surveillance Coordinator [*Navy*] (CAAL)	
SSSSS	Searched, Silenced, Safeguarded, Segregated, and Sped Out of the Area [*US POW hadling practice*] (VNW)	
SSSST	Subscale Subsonic Targets (MCD)	
SSST	S-Band Spread Spectrum Transponder (MCD)	
SSST	Simulated Social Skills Training (AIE)	
SSST	Site Suitability Source Term [*Nuclear energy*] (NRCH)	
SSST	Solid-State Silicon Target	
SSST	Space Station Simulator Trainee [*or Trainer*] [*NASA*] (SSD)	
SSST	Spectroscopic Survey Telescope [*Proposed*] [*Joint project of the University of Texas and Pennsylvania State University*]	
SSST	Superior Sagittal Sinus Thrombosis (STED)	
SSStJ	Serving Sister, Order of St. John of Jerusalem [*British*]	
SSSU	Scottish Speed Skating Union (DBA)	
SSSV	Superior Sagittal Sinus Blood Velocity [*Medicine*] (AAMN)	
SSSV	Superior Sagittal Sinus Velocity (STED)	
SSSW	Surface/Subsurface Warfare [*Navy*] (CAAL)	
SST	Missionary Society of St. Thomas the Apostle (TOCD)	
sst	Missionary Society of St. Thomas the Apostle (TOCD)	
SST	Safe Secure Trailer [*For transporting nuclear materials*]	
SST	Safe Separate/Timing (CINC)	
SST	Sagittal Sinus Thrombosis (STED)	
SST	Sample Sound Technology [*Computer science*]	
SST	Saskatchewan Teachers' Federation Saskatoon, Saskatchewan [*Library symbol National Library of Canada*] (NLC)	
SST	Satellite Servicing Technology (SSD)	
SST	Satellite-to-Satellite Tracking	
SST	Saturated Suction Temperature [*Refrigeration*]	
SST	Saturn Systems Test [*NASA*]	
SST	Scroll Symbolic Tracer (IAA)	
SST	Seaplane Shuttle Transport [*New York-Philadelphia air-link*]	
SST	Sea Surface Temperature [*Oceanography*]	
SST	Secondary Surge Tank [*Nuclear energy*] (NRCH)	
SST	Semi-Submerged Trimaran [*Tri-hull ship design invented by Calvin Gongwer*]	
SST	Serviceability Self-Test (MCD)	
SST	Set Strobe Time [*Computer science*] (OA)	
SST	Shelter Components Corp. [*AMEX symbol*] (SPSG)	
SST	Shipboard [*Weapon*] Suitability Test [*Navy*] (NG)	
SST	Ships Service Turbine (MCD)	
SST	Shore Survey Team (DNAB)	
SST	Sideways-Spinning Tube [*Spectrometry*]	
SST	Sight, Sound, and Touch [*Ways to identify proper belt tension*] [*Automotive engineering*]	
SST	Silicon Storage Technology (PCM)	
SST	Silver Sceptre Resources [*Vancouver Stock Exchange symbol*]	
SST	Simulated Structural Test (KSC)	
SST	Single Shell Tank (COE)	
SST	Single Sideband Transmission [*Telecommunications*] (TEL)	
SST	Single Step (IAA)	
SST	Single Subscriber Terminal [*Army*] (RDA)	
SST	Single Systems Trainer [*NASA*] (MCD)	
SST	Slide, Script, and Tape	
SST	Social Security Tax Ruling [*Internal Revenue Bulletin*] [*A publication*] (DLA)	
SST	Society for the Study of Theology [*British*]	
SST	Society of Surveying Technicians (EAIO)	
SST	Sodium Sulfite Titration (STED)	
SST	Software Sciences Teleordering (NITA)	
S/S/T	Solid-State Technology (IAA)	
SST	Solid-State Transmitter (MCD)	

SST............... Somatosensory Thalamus (STED)
SST............... Somatostatin (STED)
SST............... SONAR Signaling (NVT)
SST............... Source Selection Team (AAGC)
SST............... Soviet Science and Technology [*IFI/Plenum Data Corp.*] [*Information service or system*] (IID)
SST............... Spacecraft System Test [*NASA*]
SST............... Space Selector Terminal (SAA)
SST............... Space Surveillance Technology
SST............... Special Strike Teletype (NATG)
SST............... Spectroscopic Survey Telescope [*Proposed*] [*Joint project of the University of Texas and Pennsylvania State University*]
SST............... Split Second Timing
SST............... Stainless Steel
SST............... Station Service Transformer [*Nuclear energy*] (NRCH)
SS/T............. Steady-State/Transient Analysis [*Nuclear energy*] (NRCH)
SST............... Step-by-Step Test (IAA)
SST............... Stiffened Super-Tough [*Polymer technology*]
SST............... Stock Size Template (MCD)
SST............... Stream Support Team (MCD)
SST............... Structural Static Test [*NASA*] (NASA)
SST............... Student Science Training [*Program*] [*National Science Foundation*] [*Defunct*]
SST............... Subject Standardized Test
SST............... Submarine Scout Twin-Type [*British military*] (DMA)
SST............... Subscriber Transferred [*Telecommunications*] (TEL)
SST............... Subsystems Test (KSC)
SST............... Subsystem Terminal on Spacelab [*NASA*] (MCD)
SST............... Sunwest Airlines Ltd. [*Canada ICAO designator*] (FAAC)
SST............... Superficial Spreading Type (Melanoma) [*Oncology*]
SST............... SuperSerial Technology [*Equinox Systems, Inc.*] [*Telecommunications*]
SST............... Super Show & Tell [*Ask Me Multimedia Center software*] [*Computer science*] (PCM)
SST............... Super Smoothing Technology [*Apple Computer, Inc.*]
SS/T............. Supersonic Telegraphy [*British military*] (DMA)
SST............... Supersonic Transport
SST............... Super Surface Treatment (IAA)
SST............... Supplementary Service Tariff [*British*] (DCTA)
SST............... Susitna [*Alaska*] [*Seismograph station code, US Geological Survey Closed*] (SEIS)
SST............... Synchronous System Trap
SST............... System Segment Table
SST............... Systems Support Tape
SST............... System Survey Team [*Military*] (AFIT)
SST............... Target and Training Submarine [*Self-propelled*] [*Navy symbol*]
SST............... Training Submarine [*Navy symbol*]
SSTA............ Scottish Secondary Teachers' Association (DI)
SSTA............ Sea-Service Temperature Anomaly [*Marine science*] (OSRA)
SSTA............ Secondary School Theatre Association [*Defunct*] (EA)
SSTA............ Support System Task Analysis (AAG)
SSTADS........ Small Ship Typhoon Air Defense System (MCD)
SSTAR.......... Society for Sex Therapy and Research (EA)
SSTC............ Secondary School Theatre Conference [*Later, SSTA*] (EA)
SSTC............ Ship System Test Contractor (MCD)
SSTC............ Single-Sideband Transmitted Carrier (IEEE)
SSTC............ Solid-State Timer-Controller
SSTC............ Spacecraft System Test Console [*NASA*]
SSTC............ Space Shuttle Test Conductor [*NASA*] (NASA)
SSTC............ Specialized System Test Contractor
SSTC............ State Science and Technology Commission [*China*]
SSTC............ Summary of Supplemental Type Certificates
SSTCWN...... Specifications Subject to Change without Notice
SSTD........... Solid State Track Detector [*Instrumentation*]
SSTD........... Surface Ship Torpedo Defense [*Navy*] (CAAL)
SSTDC......... Society of Stage Directors and Choreographers (EA)
SSTDMA...... Satellite Switched Time Division Multiple Access (NITA)
SSTDMA...... Spacecraft Switched Time Division Multiple Access [*Telecommunications*]
SS/TDMA..... Spread Spectrum/Time Division Multiple Access (MCD)
SSTDS........ Small Ship Tactical Data System [*Navy*] (CAAL)
SSTEP........ System Support Test Evaluation Program
SSTF........... Saturn Static Test Facility [*NASA*]
SSTF........... Shortest Seek Time First
SSTF........... Space Shuttle Task Force [*NASA*]
SSTF........... Space Simulation Test Facility (AAG)
SSTF........... Space Station Task Force [*NASA*]
SSTF........... Space Station Training Facility [*NASA*] (SSD)
SSTF........... Subject Summary Table File [*US Census Bureau*]
SSTG .... Ship Service Turbo Generator (MSA)
SSTG .... Space Shuttle Task Group [*NASA*] (KSC)
SSTG .... Special Service Training Group [*World War II*]
SSTI............ Serikat Sekerdja Topografi Indonesia [*Indonesian Topography Employees' Union*]
SSTI............ Silicon Storage Tech [*NASDAQ symbol*] (TTSB)
SSTI............ Silicon Storage Technology, Inc. [*NASDAQ symbol*] (SAG)
SSTIR.......... Sea Surface Temperature Imaging Radiometer
SSTIXS........ Small Ship Teletype Information Exchange System [*or Subsystem*] (MCD)
SSTL........... Sector System Training Leader (SAA)
SSTL........... Solid State Track Link [*TOW*] (MCD)
SSTLA......... Strip Shunt Transmission Line Antenna [*Aviation*] (AIA)
SSTM........... SAGE [*Semiautomatic Ground Environment*] System Training Mission
SSTM........... Single Service Training Manager (MCD)

SSTM........... Solid-State Target Monoscope (PDAA)
SSTM........... System Support Technical Manager [*Navy*] (NG)
SSTMS........ Standard Supply Transportation Manifest System
SSTN .... Sandostain [*Antineoplastic drug*] (CDI)
SSTO .... Second-Stage Tail Off (IAA)
SSTO .... Single Stage to Orbit [*NASA*]
SSTO .... Superintending Sea Transport Officer [*British military*] (DMA)
SSTP .... Software Support Transition Plan [*Army*]
SSTP .... Student Science Training Program [*National Science Foundation Defunct*]
SSTP .... Subsystems Test Procedure (KSC)
SSTP .... Supersonic Transport Panel [*International Civil Aviation Organization*]
SSTR .... Senior Staff Technical Representative (MCD)
s str............ Sensu Stricto [*In a Narrow Sense*] [*Latin*] (MAE)
SSTR .... Solid-State Track Recorder (PDAA)
SSTRA........ Successive Subtraction with Total Recognition Accuracy [*Algorithm*]
SSTS .... School Student Transport Scheme [*Australia*]
SSTS .... Sight Switch Technology System (PDAA)
SSTS .... Signaling and Supervision Techniques Study
SSTS .... Solid State Transfer Switch
SSTS .... Space Surveillance and Tracking System [*Military*]
SSTS .... Sub-System Technical Specification
SSTT .... Specialized Systems Test Teams (SAA)
SSTT .... Subsea Test Tree (PDAA)
SST-T-T ...... Sound, Sense, Today, Tomorrow, Thereafter [*Teacher's Guide, published by Department of Transportation, for promoting supersonic travel*]
SSTU .... SAGE [*Semiautomatic Ground Environment*] System Training Unit
SSTU .... Seamless Steel Tubing
SSTV .... Congregation of Sisters of St. Thomas of Villanova [*Roman Catholic religious order*]
SSTV .... Sea Skimming Test Vehicles
SSTV .... Slow-Scan Television
SSTV .... Submarine Shock Test Vehicle
SStW .... Synoptische Studien fuer A. Wikenhauser [*1953*] [*A publication*] (BJA)
SSU .... Safety Sequence Unit (MCD)
SSU .... Sangamon State University (PDAA)
SSU .... San Pedro Sula [*Honduras*] [*Seismograph station code, US Geological Survey*] (SEIS)
SSU .... Saybolt Seconds Universal [*Oil viscosity*]
SSU .... Self-Service Unit
SSU .... Semiconductor Storage Unit [*Computer science*]
SSU .... Sensor Simulator Unit
SSU .... Sight Survey Unit
SSU .... Signal Summing Unit [*Aviation*]
SSU .... Single Signaling Unit [*Telecommunications*] (TEL)
SSU .... Small Subunit [*Genetics*]
SSU .... Solvent Service Unit
SSU .... Source Resources Ltd. [*Vancouver Stock Exchange symbol*]
SSU .... Spacecraft Support Unit
SSU .... Special Service Unit [*Military*]
SSU .... Species Services Unit [*of the Bureau of Meteorology*] (EERA)
SSU .... Squadron Service Unit [*Aircraft*]
SSU .... Stabilized Sight Unit (MCD)
SSU .... Standard Saybolt Universal [*Oil viscosity*]
SSU .... Statistical Service Unit [*Military*]
SSU .... Sterile Supply Unit (MAE)
SSU .... Strategic Services Unit [*Formerly, OSS*]
SSU .... Stratospheric Sounding Unit [*Telecommunications*] (TEL)
SSU .... Study Skills Unit (AIE)
SSU .... Subscriber Switching Unit [*Telecommunications*] (TEL)
SSU .... Subsequent Signal Unit [*Group of BITS*] [*Telecommunications*] (TEL)
SSU .... Sunday School Union
SSU .... Surface Screen Unit [*Navy*] (NVT)
SSU .... Switch Selector Update
SSU ,.......... System Selector Unit
SSU .... System Support Unification (MCD)
SSU .... University of Saskatchewan, Saskatoon, Saskatchewan [*Library symbol National Library of Canada*] (NLC)
SSU .... White Sulphur Springs, WV [*Location identifier FAA*] (FAAL)
SSUEM .... Uranerz Exploration & Mining Ltd., Saskatoon, Saskatchewan [*Library symbol National Library of Canada*] (NLC)
SSUFT .... Single Station Unit Fielding Training [*Air Force*] [*Navy*] (DOMA)
SSUGP........ Government Publications, University of Saskatchewan, Saskatoon, Saskatchewan [*Library symbol National Library of Canada*] (NLC)
SSUIS .... Space Station User Information System [*NASA*] (SSD)
SSUJD .... [*The*] Right Honourable John G. Diefenbaker Centre, University of Saskatchewan, Saskatoon, Saskatchewan [*Library symbol National Library of Canada*] (NLC)
SSUL .... Law Library, University of Saskatchewan, Saskatoon, Saskatchewan [*Library symbol National Library of Canada*] (NLC)
SSULS .... Lutheran Seminary, University of Saskatchewan, Saskatoon, Saskatchewan [*Library symbol National Library of Canada*] (NLC)
SSUM .... Medical Library, University of Saskatchewan, Saskatoon, Saskatchewan [*Library symbol National Library of Canada*] (NLC)
SSUMC .... Ukrainian Museum of Canada, Saskatoon, Saskatchewan [*Library symbol National Library of Canada*] (NLC)
SSURADS .... Shipboard Surveillance RADAR System (MCD)
SSURO........ Stop Sale, Use and Removal Order [*Environmental Protection Agency*] (GFGA)
SSUS .... Spinning Solid Upper Stage (RDA)
ssus .... Spinning Solid Upper Stage [*NASA*] (NAKS)
SSUS .... Spin-Stabilized Upper Stage [*NASA*] (NASA)
SSUS .... System Support Unification Subsystem (MCD)

SSUSA.........	Special Staff, United States Army
SSUS-A......	Spinning Solid Upper Stage - Atlas Class Spacecraft (MCD)
SSUS-D......	Spinning Solid Upper Stage - Delta Class Spacecraft (MCD)
SSUSN........	Society of Sponsors of the United States Navy (EA)
SSUSP........	Spinning Solid Upper Stage Project (MCD)
SSUTC........	Special Service Unit Training Center [World War II]
SSV.............	Satellite Servicing Vehicle
SSV.............	Schoolman-Schwartz Virus [Medicine] (DMAA)
SSV.............	Seraphic Society for Vocations [Defunct] (EA)
SSV.............	Sheep Seminal Vesicle
SSV.............	Ship-to-Surface Vessel
SSV.............	Simian Sarcoma Virus [Also, SiSV]
SSV.............	Skyservice FBO, Inc. [Canada] [FAA designator] (FAAC)
SSV.............	Small Synaptic Vesicle [Neurobiology]
SSV.............	Solid-Surfacing Veneer
SSV.............	Southern Sudan Vision [A publication]
ssv.............	Space Shuttle Vehicle [NASA] (NAKS)
SSV.............	Space Shuttle Vehicle [NASA]
SSV.............	Spastic Society of Victoria [Australia]
SSV.............	Special Surveillance Vehicle [Navy] (DNAB)
SSV.............	Spool Selector Valve
SSV.............	SPRINT [Solid-Propellant Rocket Intercept] Service Vehicle [Army]
SSV.............	Static Self-Verification
SSV.............	Stock-Spielmeyer-Vogt [Syndrome] [Medicine] (DB)
SSV.............	Subjective Scale Value
SSV.............	Sub Signo Veneni [Under a Poison Label] [Pharmacy]
SSV.............	Sumac Ventures, Inc. [Vancouver Stock Exchange symbol]
SSV.............	Supersatellite Vehicle
SSV.............	Supersonic Test Vehicles
SSV.............	Sydslesvigsk Vaelgerforening [South Schleswig Voters' Association] [Also, SSW] [Germany] [Political party] (PPW)
SSVA	Signal Susceptibility and Vulnerability Assessment [Military] (CAAL)
SSVC	Selective Service [Military]
SSVC	Services Sound and Video Corp. [British]
SSVE	Subacute Spongiform Virus Encephalopathies [Medicine]
SSVF..........	Straits Settlements Volunteer Force [British military] (DMA)
SSV/GC & N...	Space Shuttle Vehicle/Guidance, Control, and Navigation [NASA]
SSVM..........	Self-Scaling Variable Metric [Algorithms] [Computer science]
SSVN..........	Subsystem and Vehicle Number (SAA)
SSVP	Society of St. Vincent De Paul [Paris, France] (EAIO)
SSVP	Soviet Ship Vulnerability Program
SSVS	Slow-Scan Video Simulator
SSVS	Super Smart Vehicle System [FHWA] (TAG)
SSV-SSAV...	Simian Sarcoma Virus-Simian Sarcoma Associated Virus [Complex]
SSW.............	Safety Switch
SSW.............	Satellite-Switched [Telecommunications] (CIST)
SSW.............	Save the Strippers Wells (EA)
SSW.............	Scramble Status and Weather (SAA)
SSW.............	Secretary of State for War [British]
SSW.............	Senior Social Worker (ADA)
SSW.............	Sense Switch [Military] (AFIT)
SSW.............	Shipboard Safety Watch [Navy] (DNAB)
SSW.............	Siemens-Schuckert Werke [Germany]
SSW.............	Solid-State Welding
SSW.............	South by South West (EERA)
SSW.............	South-Southwest
SSW.............	Space Support Wing [Military]
SSW.............	Space Switch [Telecommunications] (TEL)
SSW.............	Staggered Spondaic Word
SSW.............	Staggered Spondiac World Test [Speech and language therapy] (DAVI)
SSW.............	Standby Service Water [Nuclear energy] (NRCH)
SSW.............	Sterling Software [NYSE symbol] (TTSB)
SSW.............	Sterling Software, Inc. [NYSE symbol] (SPSG)
SSW.............	St. Louis Southwestern Railway Co. [AAR code]
SSW.............	Sudden Stratospheric Warming (EERA)
SSW.............	Suedschleswigscher Waehlerverband [South Schleswig Voter's League] [Also, SSV] [Germany] [Political party] (PPE)
SSW.............	Support Software (MCD)
SSW.............	Surface Science Western [University of Western Ontario] [Research center] (RCD)
SSW.............	Surface Strike Warfare [Navy] (CAAL)
SSW.............	Swept Square Wave (MCD)
SSW.............	Synchro Switch [Electronics]
SSW.............	Systems West Consultants Ltd. [Vancouver Stock Exchange symbol]
SSW.............	Wheatland Regional Library, Saskatoon, Saskatchewan [Library symbol National Library of Canada] (NLC)
SSWA	Sanitary Supply Wholesalers Association (EA)
SSWA	Scottish Society of Women Artists (DBA)
SSWAHC.....	Society for Social Work Administrators in Health Care (EA)
SSWAHC.....	Society Social Work Administrators in Health Care (EA)
SSWAM	Single-Sided Wideband Analog Modulation [Telecommunications] (IAA)
SSWC	Surface/Subsurface Warfare Coordinator [Navy] (CAAL)
SSWD	Single, Separated, Widowed, or Divorced
SSWD	Western Development Museum, Saskatoon, Saskatchewan [Library symbol National Library of Canada] (NLC)
SSWF	Sudden Shortwave Fade
SSWG	Supplementary Strategies Working Group (EERA)
SSWG	System Safety Working Group
SSWLH	Society for the Study of Women in Legal History (EA)
SSWM	Standing Spin Wave Mode (MCD)
SSWM	Superimposed Surface Wave Modes
SSWO	Special Service Work Order [Telecommunications] (TEL)
SSWP	Space Station Work Package [NASA] (SSD)

SSWP	Station Service Water Pump [Nuclear energy] (NRCH)
SSWQC.......	Site-Specific Water Quality Criteria (WPI)
SSWS	Standby Service Water System [Nuclear energy] (NRCH)
SSWU	Singapore Sawmill Workers' Union
SSWWS	Seismic Sea-Wave Warning System
SSX.............	Samsun [Turkey] [Airport symbol] (OAG)
SSX.............	Small Systems Executive (IAA)
SSX.............	Space Ship Experimental
SSX.............	SS1 [Nevada] [Seismograph station code, US Geological Survey Closed] (SEIS)
SSX.............	Submarines, Experimental
SSX.............	Sulfisoxazole [An antibiotic]
SSX.............	Supplementary Service Exchange (NITA)
SSXBT	Submarine Expendable Bathythermograph [Marine science] (MSC)
SSY.............	M'Banza Congo [Angola] [Airport symbol] (OAG)
SSY.............	Sao Salvador [Angola] [Airport symbol] (AD)
SSY.............	Sharpshooters Yeomanry [British military] (DMA)
SSY.............	Silver Strike Resources [Vancouver Stock Exchange symbol]
SSY.............	South Somerset Yeomanry [British military] (DMA)
SSYAC	Selective Service Youth Advisory Committee [Military] (VNW)
SSYS	Stratasys, Inc. [NASDAQ symbol] (SAG)
S/SYS	Subsystem (NASA)
SSZ.............	Pocket Submarine (NATG)
SSZ.............	Saigon Special Zone [Military]
SSZ.............	Samos Resources, Inc. [Vancouver Stock Exchange symbol]
SSZ.............	Santos [Brazil] [Airport symbol] (AD)
SSZ.............	Sea Scout Zero - Nonrigid Airship [Royal Naval Air Service] [British]
SSZ.............	Society of Systematic Zoology (EA)
SSZ.............	Specified Strike Zone [Army] (AABC)
SSZ.............	Supra-Subduction Zone [Geology]
ST.............	Belize Airways [ICAO designator] (AD)
St.............	C. H. Boehringer Sohn, Ingelheim [Germany] [Research code symbol]
St.............	E. Merck AG [Germany] [Research code symbol]
ST.............	Esotropia [Ophthalmology] (MAE)
ST.............	Missionarii Servi Sanctissimae Trinitatis [Missionary Servants of the Most Holy Trinity] [Roman Catholic men's religious order]
st.............	Missionary Servants of the Most Holy Trinity (TOCD)
ST.............	Saddle Tank [Trains] [British]
ST.............	Safety Tool (MCD)
ST.............	Saint (EY)
St.............	Saint (DD)
ST.............	Sainte
ST.............	Sales Tax
ST.............	Sales Tax Branch, United States Internal Revenue Bureau (DLA)
ST.............	Sales Tax Rulings, United States Internal Revenue Bureau [A publication] (DLA)
ST.............	Salmonella Typhi (DB)
ST.............	Sample Tube
ST.............	Sanitary Towel [British] (USUE)
ST.............	Sao Tome and Principe [ANSI two-letter standard code] (CNC)
ST.............	Save the Theaters [Defunct] (EA)
ST.............	Sawtooth [Architecture]
ST.............	Scalar Totalizer
ST.............	Scalloped Tinned [Configuration] (MCD)
ST.............	Schmidt Telescope
ST.............	Schmitt Trigger [Electronics]
ST.............	Schuler Tuning
ST.............	Science Train
ST.............	Sclerotherapy [Medicine]
ST.............	Screw Terminal
ST.............	Seaman Torpedoman [Obsolete Navy]
S/T.............	Search/Track
ST.............	Seat
ST.............	Secretary/Treasurer [or Secretary and Treasurer]
ST.............	Sedimentation Time
ST.............	Segment Table [Computer science] (OA)
ST.............	Select Time (WDAA)
ST.............	Self-Test
ST.............	Self-Toning [Paper] [Photography] (ROG)
ST.............	Semitendinosus [Muscle]
ST.............	Senior Teacher (ADA)
ST.............	Sensitivity Training
ST.............	Senza Tempo [Without Regard to Time] [Music]
ST.............	Sequence Timer
ST.............	Serial Tasking [Computer science] (IAA)
ST.............	Service Tabulating (AAG)
ST.............	Service Test [Military]
ST.............	Service Tools (AAG)
ST.............	Set Trigger
ST.............	Severance Tax (MHDB)
ST.............	Shares Time With [Broadcasting term]
S/T.............	Shelter Taxi [NASA] (KSC)
ST.............	Shipping Ticket [Military]
ST.............	Ship Trial (MCD)
ST.............	Shock Troops [Military] (WDAA)
ST.............	Shock Tube
ST.............	Shock Tunnel
ST.............	Shoot Tip [Botany]
ST.............	Shop Telegraph (IAA)
ST.............	Shorthand Writer [British military] (DMA)
ST.............	Short-Term Stay [in hospital] [British]
ST.............	Short Time (IAA)
ST.............	Short Ton [2000 lbs.]
ST.............	Short Tour [Military]

ST..............	Shrink Template
S-T..............	Sickle-Cell Thalassemia [*Hematology*] (DAVI)
ST..............	Side Tank [*on a ship*] (DS)
ST..............	Sidetone [*Telecommunications*] (TEL)
ST..............	Sigma Tau [*Later, Tau Beta Pi Association*]
ST..............	Silent [*Films, television, etc.*]
ST..............	Silicon Tube
ST..............	Silicotungstate [*Inorganic chemistry*]
ST..............	Simhat Torah (BJA)
ST..............	Simplification Task (MCD)
ST..............	Simulator Training
st..............	Sine Tempore [*At the Time Announced*] [*Latin*]
ST..............	Single Throw [*Switch*]
st..............	Single-Throw (IDOE)
ST..............	Single Tire
ST..............	Single Turn (MSA)
ST..............	Sinus Tachycardia [*Cardiology*]
ST..............	Skill Technical (INF)
ST..............	Skin Temperature (OA)
ST..............	Skin Test
ST..............	Skin Thickness [*Medicine*] (DMAA)
ST..............	Skin Track (MUGU)
ST..............	Sleeping Time
ST..............	Sleeve Target (COE)
ST..............	Slide and Tape
St..............	Slight (DAVI)
ST..............	Slight Trace
ST..............	Slow-Twitch [*Muscular fiber*] [*Medicine*] (DB)
ST..............	Small Tug [*Army*]
ST..............	Societe Theosophique [*Theosophical Society*]
ST..............	Society for Theriogenology (EA)
ST..............	Solar Thermal [*Energy source*]
ST..............	SONAR Technician [*Navy rating*]
S/T..............	Sonic Telegraphy
ST..............	Sons of Temperance
ST..............	Sounding Tube
ST..............	Sound Telegraphy [*Telecommunications*] (IAA)
ST..............	Sound Trap (OA)
ST..............	Source and Time Frame (NITA)
ST..............	Southern Tablelands [*New South Wales*] [*Region*] (EERA)
ST..............	Spaced Triplet (SAA)
ST..............	Spacelab Technology [*NASA*] (NASA)
ST..............	Space Telescope [*NASA*]
ST..............	Space-Time
ST..............	Spanlang-Tappeiner [*Syndrome*] [*Medicine*] (DB)
ST..............	Spasmodic Torticollis [*Medicine*]
ST..............	Special Test
ST..............	Special Text [*Military*]
ST..............	Special Tooling (GFGA)
ST..............	Special Translation
ST..............	Speech Therapist
ST..............	Speech Therapy (DAVI)
ST..............	Speech Threshold [*Speech and language therapy*] (DAVI)
ST..............	Speed Transmitter (NRCH)
ST..............	Sphincter Tone [*Medicine*] (MAE)
ST..............	Spin Transition [*Physics*]
ST..............	Split Thickness [*Skin Graft*] [*Plastic surgery*] (DAVI)
ST..............	Springfield Terminal Railway Co. [*AAR code*]
ST..............	Spring Tide (WDAA)
ST..............	SPS Technologies [*NYSE symbol*] (TTSB)
ST..............	SPS Technologies, Inc. [*Formerly, Standard Pressed Steel Co.*] [*NYSE symbol*] (SPSG)
ST..............	Stable
ST..............	Stable Toxin (DB)
st..............	Stage [*of Disease*] (DAVI)
ST..............	Stage
ST..............	Stain (WGA)
St..............	Stair's Decisions, Scotch Court of Session [*A publication*] (DLA)
St..............	Stair's Institutes [*5th ed.*] [*1832*] [*A publication*] (DLA)
St..............	Stamen [*Botany*]
S-T..............	Stamped [*Stock exchange term*] (SPSG)
ST..............	Stand (WGA)
ST..............	Standard
ST..............	Standardized Test [*Psychology*]
ST..............	Standard Temperature (IAA)
ST..............	Standard Time
ST..............	Standby Time (MCD)
St..............	Stanton Number [*IUPAC*]
ST..............	Stanza
st..............	Stanza (WDMC)
ST..............	Starboard Flag [*Navy British*]
ST..............	Starsky Operupolnomochennyy [*Senior Case Officer*] [*Soviet military rank*]
ST..............	Start
st..............	Start (WDMC)
ST..............	Starter (MCD)
ST..............	Star Tracker [*NASA*] (AAG)
S/T..............	Start Tank (AAG)
ST..............	Start Timing
ST..............	State
st..............	State (WDMC)
ST..............	Statement (WDAA)
S-T..............	State Trials [*Legal*] [*British*]
ST..............	Static (KSC)
ST..............	Static Test

ST..............	Static Thrust
ST..............	Statim [*Immediately*] [*Latin*] (ROG)
ST..............	Station [*Medicine*]
ST..............	Statue (WDMC)
st..............	Statue (WDMC)
ST..............	Status
ST..............	Statute
ST..............	Steam (AAG)
ST..............	Steamer (ROG)
ST..............	Steam Tanker
ST..............	Steam Trawler
ST..............	Steam Tug
ST..............	Steam Turbine (MCD)
ST..............	Steel [*Technical drawings*]
ST..............	Steel Truss [*Bridges*]
ST..............	Stem [*Linguistics*] [*Botany*]
ST..............	Stencil
ST..............	Stenographer [*British military*] (DMA)
st..............	Stent [*Let Them Stand*] [*Latin*] (MAE)
st..............	Stere [*Metric measure of volume*]
ST..............	Stereochemical Descriptor (NITA)
ST..............	Stereocilia [*Zoology*]
ST..............	Sternothyroid [*Anatomy*]
ST..............	Sternotomy [*Medicine*]
ST..............	Stern Thruster [*Type of ship*] (DS)
ST..............	Stet [*Let It Stand*] [*Latin*]
ST..............	Stewart-Treves [*Syndrome*] [*Medicine*] (DB)
ST..............	Stichting Tool [*Tool Foundation - TF*] [*Amsterdam, Netherlands*] (EAIO)
ST..............	Sticky Type [*Bomb*]
ST..............	Stigma [*Botany*]
ST..............	Stimulus [*Medicine*]
ST..............	Stinson [*ICAO aircraft manufacturer identifier*] (ICAO)
ST..............	Stitch
ST..............	St. Lawrence Cement, Inc. [*Toronto Stock Exchange symbol*]
ST..............	Stock Transfer
ST..............	Stoke (IAA)
ST..............	Stoke-on-Trent [*Postcode*] (ODBW)
St..............	Stokes [*Unit of kinematic viscosity*]
St..............	Stomach (MAE)
ST..............	Stone [*Unit of weight*]
st..............	Stone [*Unit of weight*] (ODBW)
ST..............	Stone Roller [*Ichthyology*]
St..............	Stones [*Quality of the bottom*] [*Nautical charts*]
ST..............	Stony Soil [*Agronomy*]
st..............	Stool [*Gastroenterology*] (DAVI)
ST..............	Stop Tap
ST..............	Stop-Transfer [*Genetics*]
ST..............	Storage Tube
ST..............	Store (AAG)
ST..............	Stored Time
ST..............	Store Transfer (IAA)
ST..............	Story (ROG)
St..............	Story's United States Circuit Court Reports [*A publication*] (DLA)
ST..............	Stotinki [*Monetary unit*] [*Bulgaria*]
st..............	Straight (AAMN)
S/T..............	Straight Time
ST..............	Straight Tip [*Fiber connector for coaxial cable*] [*Telecommunications*] (PCM)
ST..............	Strainer (DAC)
ST..............	Strait
ST..............	Straps [*JETDS nomenclature*] [*Military*] (CET)
ST..............	Strategic Transport [*Aircraft*] [*Military*]
St..............	Stratosphere
ST..............	Stratosphere-Troposphere [*Radar*] [*Marine science*] (OSRA)
ST..............	Stratus [*Meteorology*]
ST..............	Street (EY)
st..............	Street (WDMC)
St..............	Street (DD)
ST..............	Stress Testing [*Medicine*]
ST..............	Strict [*Medicine*]
S-T..............	Strip-Tin (MSA)
ST..............	Stroma [*Medicine*]
ST..............	Strophe [*Poetry*] (ROG)
ST..............	Structural (NASA)
ST..............	Structure Tee (AAG)
St..............	Stuart, Milne, and Peddie's Scotch Court of Session Cases [*A publication*] (DLA)
ST..............	Student's t-Test [*Statistical mathematics*]
ST..............	Studies in Theology [*A publication*]
ST..............	Studi e Testi [*A publication*] (ODCC)
ST..............	Studio to Transmitter (IAA)
St..............	Stumped [*Cricket*]
St..............	Styrene [*Also, Sty*] [*Organic chemistry*]
ST..............	Sublingual Tablet [*Medicine*] (MEDA)
ST..............	Substitution Theorem [*Logic*]
ST..............	Subtalar [*Medicine*] (MAE)
st..............	Subtelocentric [*Botany*]
ST..............	Subtentacular [*Zoology*]
ST..............	Subtotal (MAE)
ST..............	Sub Tuner (IAA)
St..............	Subtype (MAE)
ST..............	Sucrose Tallowate (OA)
ST..............	Sulfotransferase [*An enzyme*]
ST..............	Summa Theologica [*A publication*] (ODCC)

ST	Summer Time [Daylight saving time]
ST	Superintendent of Transportation
ST	Superior Turbinate [Otorhinolaryngology] (DAVI)
ST	Super Tampella [Explosive] (INF)
ST	Supplementary Term [Online database field identifier]
ST	Supporting Technologies [Military] (RDA)
ST	Surface Target [Navy] (CAAL)
ST	Surface Tension
ST	Surface Tracker [Navy] (CAAL)
ST	Surgical Technician
ST	Surgical Technologist (DAVI)
ST	Surtax (WDAA)
ST	Surveillance Test (NATG)
ST	Survival Time
ST	Swept Tone
ST	Symbol Table (IAA)
ST	Symmetrical TOKAMAK
ST	Synchroniztion Table (IAA)
ST	Syncopated Time (WDAA)
ST	Syndrome of the Trephined [Medicine] (DMAA)
ST	Synthesis Telescope
ST	System Response Time [Computer order entry]
ST	Systems Technology (IAA)
ST	System Table (IAA)
ST	System Test
ST	Szondi Test [Psychology]
St.	United States Statutes at Large [A publication] (DLA)
ST1	SONAR Technician, First Class [Navy rating]
ST2	SONAR Technician, Second Class [Navy rating]
ST3	SONAR Technician, Third Class [Navy rating]
ST 37	Hexylresorcinol [An antiseptic] [Pharmacology] (DAVI)
STA	Japanese Science and Technology Agency (USDC)
STA	Sail Training Association (EA)
STA	Sales Transaction Audit [Test]
STA	Santa [Saint] [Italian]
STA	Satara [India] [Seismograph station code, US Geological Survey Closed] (SEIS)
STA	Satellite Test Annex (SAA)
STA	Satellite Tracking Annex (MUGU)
STA	S-Band Test Antenna
STA	Science and Technology Agency
STA	Science and Technology Agent (SDI)
STA	Scottish Trampoline Association (DBA)
STA	Securities Transfer Association (EA)
sta	Security Traders Association (EA)
STA	Segment Table Address [Computer science] (IAA)
STA	Semiconductor Trade Agreement [US and Japan] (ECON)
STA	Serum Thrombotic Accelerator [Serology]
STA	Serum Thymic-Like Activity [Biochemistry]
STA	Servico des Transportes Aereos [Portuguese West Africa]
STA	Shift Technical Adviser [Nuclear energy] (NRCH)
STA	Shipboard Transmitting Antenna
STA	Shore-Based Transmitting Antenna
STA	Short-Term Arrangements [Department of State]
STA	Short-Term Averaging (CAAL)
STA	Short-Terms Abroad
STA	Shuttle Training Aircraft [NASA]
STA	Sialyltransferase Activity [Medicine]
STA	Single Tape Armored (IAA)
STA	Single Target Attack
STA	Skills Training Agency [British]
STA	Slaving Torquer Amplifier
STA	Slurry Technology Association [Later, CSTA] (EA)
STA	Small Tactical Airlifter [Military British]
STA	Small Tracts Act (COE)
STA	Society of Typographic Arts [Later, ACD] (EA)
STA	Softening Temperature of Ash
STA	Solar Trade Association [British] (DBA)
STA	Solution Treat and Age [Metals]
STA	Southern Textile Association (EA)
STA	Space Technology Applications
STA	Space Transportation Association (EA)
STA	Spanning Tree Algorithm [Computer science] (PCM)
STA	Spark Thrust Augmentor (SAA)
STA	Specialist Teacher Assistant [British] (DET)
STA	Special Temporary Allowance
STA	Special Temporary Authorization [FCC]
STA	Spice Trade Association [British] (DBA)
STA	Stacia Ventures [Vancouver Stock Exchange symbol]
STA	Staff Training Assistant [Army] (AABC)
STA	Stagger Tuned Antenna
STA	Stamped
STA	Stara Dala [Czechoslovakia] [Later, HRB] [Geomagnetic observatory code]
STA	Star Aviation [British ICAO designator] (FAAC)
STA	Starter Corp. [NYSE symbol] (SPSG)
STA	State Technical Assistance (OICC)
Sta	Statham's Abridgment [A publication] (DSA)
STA	Static Test Article (NASA)
STA	Station [Telecommunications]
Sta	Station (AL)
sta	Station (IDOE)
sta	Stationary (IDOE)
STA	Stationary (MSA)
STA	Stator (WGA)

STA	Status [Online database field identifier] (AABC)
STA	Statute (WGA)
STA	St. Augustine [Diocesan abbreviation] [Florida] (TOCD)
STA	Stauning [Denmark] [Airport symbol] (OAG)
STA	Steel Carriers Tariff Association, Inc., East Riverdale MD [STAC]
STA	Steel Tape Armored [Cables]
STA	Stock Transfer Association [New York, NY] (EA)
STA	Store Accumulator
STA	Store Address (SAA)
STA	Store Answer (NITA)
STA	Straight in Approach [Aviation] (DA)
STA	Strategic Transportation Analysis [MTMC] (TAG)
STA	Structural Test Article (NASA)
STA	Subcontractors Trade Association (NTPA)
STA	Submarine Tender Availability
STA	Subscription Television Association (NTCM)
STA	Superficial Temporal Artery [Anatomy]
STA	Superior Temporal Artery [Anatomy]
STA	Supersonic Tunnel Association (EA)
STA	Surveillance and Target Acquisition [Marine Corps] (DOMA)
STA	Survival in Target Area (MCD)
STA	Swedish Telecommunications Administration [Telecommunications]
STA	Swimming Teachers' Association [British]
STA	Swimming Teachers of America (NTPA)
STA	Systems Test Area
STA	University of Santa Clara, Orradre Library, Santa Clara, CA [OCLC symbol] (OCLC)
STAA	Signal Training, All Arms (IAA)
STAA	Soldiers Total Abstinence Association [British military] (DMA)
STAA	STAAR Surgical [NASDAQ symbol] (TTSB)
STAA	Staar Surgical Co. [NASDAQ symbol] (NQ)
STAA	Surface Transportation Assistance Act [1978]
STAA	Survey Test of Algebraic Aptitude [Education] (AEBS)
StAAA	Saint Andrew's Ambulance Association [British] (DBA)
STAAD	Submarine Tender Availability Arrival/Departure [Obsolete]
STAAF	Study to Align AMC [Now DAR COM] Functions (MCD)
STAAG	Standard Tachymetric Anti-Aircraft Gun [British military] (DMA)
StaarSur	Staar Surgical Co. [Associated Press] (SAG)
STAAS	Surveillance and Target Acquisition Aircraft System (AFM)
Staatsverw	Roemische Staatsverwaltung [A publication] (OCD)
STAB	SEAL [Sea, Air, and Land] Team Assault Boat [Navy] (VNW)
STAB	Space, Time, and Beyond [Dance work choreographed by Marie Chouinard]
STAB	Squadron Tactical Analysis Board [Military] (CAAL)
stab	Stability (IDOE)
stab	Stabilization (IDOE)
STAB	Stabilization [or Stabilizer] (IAA)
STAB	Stabilize [or Stabilizer] [Aviation] (AAG)
stab	Stabilizer (IDOE)
Stab	Stable [Army]
STAB	Standby Advisory Board [Army] (INF)
St Ab	Statham's Abridgment [A publication] (DLA)
STAB	Strike Assault Boat [Navy symbol]
STAB	Supersonic Tests of Aerodynamic Bombs (MUGU)
STAB	Supersonic Transport Advisory Board
STABAMP	Stabilizing Amplifier [Telecommunications] (IAA)
STAB AUG	Stability Augmentation [Aviation] (MCD)
STABE	Second-Time-Around-Beacon-Echo (PDAA)
STABEX	Stabilization of Export Earnings [Program of the EEC]
STABIS	State Boarding Information Service [British] (DET)
StAbs	Status Absolutus
STABS	Suinn Test Anxiety Behavior Scale [Psychology]
STABY	Stability (MSA)
STAC	Science and Technology Advisory Committee [NASA] (MCD)
STAC	Software Timing and Control
STAC	Southern Technology Applications Center [University of Florida] [Gainesville] [NASA] [Information service or system] (IID)
STAC	Staccato [Detached, Distinct] [Music]
STAC	Stac Electronics [NASDAQ symbol] (SAG)
STAC	Stac Inc. [NASDAQ symbol] (TTSB)
STAC	Standard Tariff Agents Code
STAC	Stop the Act Coalition [An association]
STAC	Submarine Tactical Acoustic Communications [Navy] (ANA)
STAC	Submarine-to-Aircraft Communications
STAC	Surface Target Attack Comparison Model (MCD)
STACAP	Status and Capability (SAA)
STACC	Staccato [Detached, Distinct] [Music]
STACCS	Standard Theater Army Command and Control System (RDA)
Staceys	Staceys Buffet [Commercial firm Associated Press] (SAG)
STACK	Start Acknowledge [Computer science] (MHDI)
STACO	Standing Committee for the Study of Scientific Principles of Standardization [ISO]
STACOM	Standard Army Commissary Operating Manual
STACOM	Standard Computer Output Microform [Army]
STACOM	State Criminal Justice Communications
Sta Com	Station Complement [Army]
STACRES	Standing Committee on Research and Statistics [UN Food and Agriculture Organization]
STACS	Subtropical Atlantic Climate Studies [National Oceanic and Atmospheric Administration]
STACWV	Standing Technical Advisory Committee on Water Quality [Department of the Environment] [British]
Stacys	Staceys Buffet [Commercial firm Associated Press] (SAG)
STAD	Start Address [Telecommunications] (TEL)
STAD	Student Teams-Achievement Division (AEE)

STAD .... Student Teams-Achievement Divisions (EDAC)
STAD .... Submarine Tender Availability Document
STADAC .... Station Data Acquisition and Control [*NASA*] (NASA)
STADACOL... Statistical Data Collection Program
STADAD .... Satellite Tracking and Data Acquisition Department
STADAN .... Satellite Tracking and Data Acquisition Network [*Later, STDN*]
STADAN .... Space Tracking and Data Acquisition Network
STADAR .... Servo Tester With Automatic Data Acquisition and Reduction (IAA)
STADB .... Chinese Scientific and Technological Periodical Abstracts [*Information service or system*] (IID)
STADD .... Ship-Towed Acoustic Deception Device (MCD)
STADES .... Standard Army Data Elements Systems (MCD)
STADES .... Standard Data Elements System (MCD)
STADIN .... Standing Administrative Instruction for Army Attaches (AABC)
STADINAIR... Standing Administrative Instruction for Air Attaches (AFM)
St Adm NS... Stuart's Lower Canada Vice-Admiralty Reports, New Series [*A publication*] (DLA)
STADMR .... Station Administrator (FAAC)
STADN .... Space Tracking and Acquisition Data Network
STADSS .... Strategic Transportation Analysis Decision Support System [*MTMC*] (TAG)
STADU .... System Termination and Display Unit (MCD)
STA-DYNULSIMU... Static-Dynamic Ullage Simulation Unit
STAE .... Second Time Around Echo
STAE .... Specify Task Asynchronous Exit [*Computer science*]
Sta Eng ...... Stationary Engineer
STAEP .... Scientific and Technical Assessment of Environmental Pollutants [*Marine science*] (MSC)
STAESA .... Society of Turkish Architects, Engineers, and Scientists in America (EA)
STAF .... Science Teachers' Authoring Facility (AIE)
STAF .... Science Team Analysis Facility [*NASA*]
STAF .... Scientific and Technical Application Forecasts
STAF .... Simulation/Test Acceptance Facility [*Army*] (RDA)
STAF .... Staff
STA/F .... Standard Access and Format [*Reference Technology, Inc. software*]
STAF .... Standard Test and Administrative Form (SAA)
STAF .... Statistical Analysis of Files (IAA)
STAF .... St. Thomas Aquinas Foundation (EA)
StafBld ...... Staff Builders, Inc. [*Associated Press*] (SAG)
STAFDA .... Specialty Tools and Fasteners Distributors Association (EA)
STAFEX .... Staff Exercises [*NATO*] (NATG)
STAFF .... Smart Target-Activated Fire and Forget [*Antitank weapon system*] (RDA)
STAFF .... Society for Techno-Innovation of Agriculture, Forestry and Fisheries [*Japan*]
STAFF .... Staffordshire [*County in England*]
STAFF .... Stellar Acquisition Flight Feasibility
Stafford ...... Stafford's Reports [*69-71 Vermont*] [*A publication*] (DLA)
STAFFS .... Staffordshire [*County in England*]
Staffs .... Staffordshire [*County in England*] (ODBW)
STAFS .... Standard Automated Financial System [*Navy*] (GFGA)
STAFS .... Sugar, Tobacco, Alcohol, Fat, and Salt
STAFS .... Supportable Technology for Affordable Fighter Structures [*Air Force*] (DOMA)
STAFT .... Steerable Antenna Focusing Technique
STAG .... Sharper-than-the-Average-Gook [*American POW slang*] (VNW)
STAG .... Shuttle Turnaround Analysis Group [*NASA*] (NASA)
STAG .... Skills Training Adjustment Group [*Educational project sponsored by The Hartford*]
STAG .... Slow Target-Attaching Globulin [*Medicine*] (DB)
STAG .... Society of Travel Agents in Government (NTPA)
STAG .... Soils, Trees, and Grass Program (EERA)
STAG .... Special Task Air Group
STAG .... Split Thickness Autogenous Graft [*Plastic surgery*] (DAVI)
STAG .... Standards Technical Advisory Group
STAG .... Steam and Gas [*Turbine*]
STAG .... Straight-Talking American Government [*Comedian Pat Paulsen's political party*]
STAG .... Strategy and Tactics Analysis Group [*Later, Concepts Analysis Agency*] [*Army*] (KSC)
STAG .... Student Agitation [*FBI*]
STAG .... Submarine-Rocket Technical Advisory Group
STAG .... Survivable Tactical Army Generator (RDA)
STAGD .... Syndicat des Travailleurs de l'Administration Generale du Dahomey [*Dahomean Union of General Administration Workers*]
STAGE .... Simulated Total Atomic Global Exchange [*DoD*]
Stage .... Stage II Apparel Corp. [*Associated Press*] (SAG)
STAGG .... Small-Turbine Advanced Gas Generator
STAGING...... Stuctural Analysis via Generalized Interactive Graphics (PDAA)
STAG-MAG... Stage Manager [*Theater term*] (DSUE)
STAGN .... Stagnation [*NWS*] (FAAC)
STAGS .... Simulated Tank and Antiarmor Gunnery System (INF)
STAGS .... Sterling Transferable Accruing Government Securities (TDOB)
STAGS .... Structural Analysis of General Shells
STAGS .... Swedish Tank Agility/Survivability Test (MCD)
STAGS-D...... Simulated Tank Antiarmor Gunnery System - Dragon [*Army*] (INF)
STAI .... Simulation Tape Alarm Indicator (SAA)
STAI .... Speilberger's Trait-Anxiety Inventory (EDAC)
STAI .... State-Trait Anxiety Inventory [*Psychology*]
STAI .... Subtask ABEND [*Abnormal End*] Intercept [*Computer science*] (BUR)
STAIC .... State-Trait Anxiety Inventory for Children [*Psychology*]
STAID .... Station Identification
STAI-I .... State-Trait-Anxiety Index-I (STED)

Stair............ Stair's Decisions of the Lords of Council and Session [*1661-81*] [*Scotland*] (DLA)
STAIR .... Structural Analysis Interpretive Routine
Stair I .... Stair's Institutes [*5 eds.*] [*1681-1832*] [*A publication*] (DLA)
Stair Inst .... Stair's Institutes [*5 eds.*] [*1681-1832*] [*A publication*] (DLA)
Stair Prin.... Stair's Principles of the Laws of Scotland [*A publication*] (DLA)
Stair Rep .... Stair's Decisions, Scotch Court of Session [*A publication*] (DLA)
STAIRS .... Standard Advanced Infrared Sensor [*Military*]
STAIRS .... Storage and Information Retrieval System [*Computer science*] (CDE)
STAIRS/VS... Storage and Information Retrieval System/Virtual Storage [*IBM Corp.*]
STAJ .... Science and Technology Agency of Japan (EERA)
STAJ .... Short-Term Anti-Jam (MCD)
STAK .... Austins Steak & Saloon, Inc. [*NASDAQ symbol*] (SAG)
STAK .... Austins Steaks & Saloon [*NASDAQ symbol*] (TTSB)
StakeTc ...... Stake Technology Ltd. [*Associated Press*] (SAG)
STAL .... Screening Test of Adolescent Language [*Educational test*]
STAL .... Stalactite/Stalagmite Formation (DSUE)
STALAG .... Stammlager [*Prisoner-of-war camp*] [*German*]
STALAGLUFT... Stammlagerluft [*Prisoner-of-war camp for airmen*] [*German*]
STALAPCO ... State and Local Air Pollution Control Official [*Environmental Protection Agency*] (ERG)
STALAS........ Stationary LASER Site [*NASA*]
Stal Elect.... Stalman on Election and Satisfaction [*1827*] [*A publication*] (DLA)
STALO .... Stabilized Local Oscillator [*RADAR*]
stalo .... Standardized Oscillator (IDOE)
STALOC .... Self-Tracking Automatic Lock-On Circuit (PDAA)
STALOG .... Study of Automation of the Logistic System [*Military*]
STALOS .... Stabilized Tunable Local Oscillator
STALPETH ... Steel, Aluminum, Polyethylene [*Components of a type of telecommunications cable*]
STaM .... Sefer Torah. Tefillin. Mezuzah
STAM .... Sequential Thermal Anhysteric Magnetization [*Helical scan videotape duplicating system*] (NTCM)
STAM .... Shared Tape Allocation Manager
STAM .... Statistical Analog Monitor (PDAA)
STAM .... Submarine Tactical Advanced Missile (MCD)
STAM .... Superintendent of Technical Applications of Metals [*Ministry of Supply*] [*British World War II*]
STAM .... Surface Target Acquisition Model (MCD)
STAM .... System Telecommunications Access Method [*NCR Corp.*]
STAMAT....... Schaie-Thurstone Adult Mental Abilities Test [*Intelligence test*] [*Psychology*]
STA-MCA ..... Superficial Temporal Artery to Middle Cerebral Artery [*Anatomy*] (MAE)
StamEx .... Stampeder Exploration Ltd. [*Associated Press*] (SAG)
Sta Mi .... Statute Mile
STAMIC .... Set Theory Analysis and Measure of Information Characteristics
STAMIDS ..... Standoff Minefield Detection System [*Military*] (INF)
STAMINRQ... Status During Minimize Required (MCD)
STAMIS........ Standard Army Management Information System
STAMM........ Systematic Teaching and Measuring Mathematics [*Education*]
STAMMIS .... Standard Army Multicommand Management Information System (MCD)
STAMNI .... Sonic True Airspeed and Mach Number Indicator
STAMO .... Stable Master Oscillator
STAMOCAP... State Monopoly Capitalism
STAMOS ...... Sortie Turn Around Maintenance Operations Simulation [*NASA*] (KSC)
STAMP........ Satellite Telecommunications Analysis and Modeling Program
STAMP........ Small Tactical Aerial Mobility Platform [*Proposed*] [*Marine Corps*]
STAMP........ Space Technology Analysis and Mission Planning (MCD)
STAMP........ Standard Air Munitions Package
STAMP........ Systems Tape Addition and Maintenance Program [*Computer science*] (IEEE)
STAMPED ... Size, Temperature, Application, Material, Pressure, Ends, and Delivery [*To aid selection of industrial hose*]
STAMPEX .... National Stamp Exhibition [*British*] (ITD)
STAMPG ...... Stamping
STAMPS ...... Spectrophotometric Transient Analysis Method for Multiple Positions and Species
STAMPS ...... Stabilized Translation and Maneuvering Propulsion System (IAA)
STAN .... Selectable Two-Area Nozzle (MCD)
STAN .... Stanchion
STAN .... Standard (WGA)
STAN .... Standish Care [*NASDAQ symbol*] (TTSB)
STAN .... Standish Care Co. [*NASDAQ symbol*] (SAG)
STAN .... Stanstead [*England*]
STAN .... Sum Total and Nosegear (MCD)
STANA .... Statistics on the North Atlantic [*Fisheries*] [*UN Food and Agriculture Organization*]
STANAG....... Standardization Agreement [*NATO*]
STANAVFORCHAN... Standing Naval Force, Channel [*NATO*] (NATG)
STANAVFORLANT... Standing Naval Force, Atlantic (ANA)
STANAVFORMED... Standing Naval Force Mediterranean [*NATO*] (DOMA)
STANAVITO... Syndicat des Travailleurs de Transport et de la Navigation du Togo [*Union of Transport and Navigation Workers of Togo*]
STANB .... Stanborough [*England*]
STANCAL .... Standard Oil Co. of California
STANCHART... Standard Chartered [*International bank*] [*British*]
STANCIB ..... State-Army-Navy Communications Intelligence Board [*Later, USCIB*]
STAND .... Standard
Stand .... Standard (AAGC)
Stand .... Stand Magazine [*A publication*] (BRI)
STANDAN ..... Space Tracking and Data Acquisition Network (IAA)
standard ...... Standardization [*or Standardized*] (DAVI)

ST & E......... Security Test and Evaluation [*Military*] (GFGA)
Standex....... Standex International Corp. [*Associated Press*] (SAG)
Stand Ex Prof Tax Rep... Standard Excess Profits Tax Reporter [*Commerce Clearing House*] [*A publication*] (DLA)
Stand Fed Tax Rep... Standard Federal Tax Reporter [*Commerce Clearing House*] [*A publication*] (DLA)
Stand GA Prac... Standard Georgia Practice [*A publication*] (DLA)
St & H Abor... Storer and Heard on Criminal Abortion [*A publication*] (DLA)
Stan Dig...... Stanton's Kentucky Digest [*A publication*] (DLA)
St & Loc Taxes (BNA)... State and Local Taxes (Bureau of National Affairs) [*A publication*] (DLA)
St & Loc Tax Serv (P-H)... State and Local Tax Service (Prentice-Hall, Inc.) [*A publication*] (DLA)
St & P......... Stewart and Porter's Alabama Reports [*A publication*] (DLA)
Stand PA Prac... Standard Pennsylvania Practice [*A publication*] (DLA)
St and Port... Stewart and Porter's Alabama Reports [*A publication*] (DLA)
StAndr......... Saint Andrews Golf Corp. [*Associated Press*] (SAG)
StAndrew..... Saint Andrews Golf Corp. [*Associated Press*] (SAG)
Standsh....... Standish Care Co. [*Associated Press*] (SAG)
ST & SP........ Start and Stop
STAN/EVAL... Standardization/Evaluation
STANFINS.... Standard Financial System [*Military*] (AABC)
STANFINS-R... Standard Finance System Redesign [*DoD*] (GFGA)
STANFLT....... Standardization Flight [*Naval Air Training and Operating Procedures Standardization*] (DNAB)
Stanford....... Stanford's English Pleas of the Crown [*A publication*] (DLA)
Stanford 9... Stanford Achievement Test, Ninth Edition (TMMY)
Stanford U... Stanford University (GAGS)
StanfTl......... Stanford Telecommunications, Inc. [*Associated Press*] (SAG)
Stanhm......... Stanhome, Inc. [*Associated Press*] (SAG)
STANHOME... Stanley Home Products, Inc. (EFIS)
STANINE...... Standard Nine Score [*Military*]
STANLANCRU... Standard Landing Craft Unit [*Military*]
StanlFrn....... Stanley Furniture Co. [*Associated Press*] (SAG)
StanlWk....... [*The*] Stanley Works [*Associated Press*] (SAG)
STANO......... Surveillance, Target Acquisition, and Night Observation [*DoD*]
STANOC....... Surveillance, Target Acquisition, Night Observation, and Counter - Surveillance [*British*] (MCD)
STANOLIND... Standard Oil Co. (Indiana)
STANORD.... Standardization Order [*Navy*] (NG)
STANPAC.... Standard Pacific Corp. (EFIS)
Stan PA Prac... Standard Pennsylvania Practice [*A publication*] (DLA)
StanPsych.... Standard Psychiatric [*Medicine*] (DMAA)
STANS........ Soviet Tactical Nuclear Study (MCD)
STANS......... Standard Aircraft Navigation System
STANS......... Standard Army Nonappropriated System (MCD)
StAns.......... Studia Anselmiana [*Rome*] [*A publication*]
STANSM...... STANO [*Surveillance, Target Acquisition, and Night Observation*] System Manager [*Army*] (RDA)
Stant........... Stant Corp. [*Associated Press*] (SAG)
STANTEC...... Standard Telephones Electronic Computer (MCD)
Stanton...... Stanton's Reports [*11-13 Ohio*] [*A publication*] (DLA)
Stanton's Rev St... Stanton's Revised Kentucky Statutes [*A publication*] (DLA)
STANVAC..... Standard Vacuum Oil Co.
STANY......... Security Traders Association of New York
Staody......... Staodyn, Inc. [*Associated Press*] (SAG)
Staodyn....... Staodyn, Inc. [*Associated Press*] (SAG)
STAP............ Science and Technology Advisory Panel
STAP............ Scientific and Technical Analysis and Programs Directorate
STAP............ Screening Test for Auditory Perception
STAP............ Shipbuilding Temporary Assistance Program
STAP............ Ships Towed Acoustic Project (DWSG)
STAP............ Special Technical Assistance Program (EA)
STAP............ Stapleton [*England*]
STAP............ Staploe [*England*]
STAP............ State Transit Authority Plan [*Victoria, Australia*]
STAP............ Survivability Test Advisory Panel [*Military*] (CAAL)
Sta P C........ Staundeforde's Pleas of Crown [*A publication*] (DSA)
STAPFUS..... Stable Axis Platform Follow-Up System
STAPH......... Staphylococcus [*Medicine*]
staph........... Staphylococcus [*Medicine*] (STED)
Staph........... Staphylococcus [*Medicine*] (DB)
Staph Epi..... Staphylococcus Epidermidis [*A bacterium*] (DAVI)
STAPL.......... Ship Tethered Aerial Platform (PDAA)
STAPL.......... SIGPLAN Technical Committee on APL [*A Programming Language*] [*Association for Computing Machinery*] (CSR)
STAPLAN..... Status, Time, Attrition, Planning Methodology
Staples....... Staples, Inc. [*Associated Press*] (SAG)
STAPP.......... Short-Term Anxiety-Provoking Psychotherapy (PDAA)
STAPP.......... Simulation Tape Print Program
STAPP.......... Single-Thread All-Purpose Program
STAPP.......... Standard Tape Print Program [*Computer science*] (IAA)
STAPP.......... State and Territorial Air Pollution Program (COE)
STAPPA....... State and Territorial Air Pollution Program Administrators (EA)
Sta Pr.......... Staundeforde's Exposition of the King's Prerogative [*A publication*] (DSA)
STAPRC....... Scientific and Technical Association of the People's Republic of China
STAQ........... Security Traders Automated Quotation [*System*]
STAQ........... Student Teachers' Attitude Questionnaire
STAQC......... Statistical Quality Control System [*Military*]
STAR........... Lone Star Steakhouse & Saloon, Inc. [*NASDAQ symbol*] (SAG)
STAR........... Lone Star Steakhouse/Saloon [*NASDAQ symbol*] (TTSB)
STAR........... Safe Teenage Rocketry
STAR........... San Clemente 3-D Acoustic Range (MCD)
STAR........... Satellites for Telecommunications, Applications, and Research [*Consortium*]
STAR........... Satellite Telecommunications Automatic Routing
STAR........... Satellite Television Asia Region [*Hong Kong*]
STAR........... Satellite Transponder Addressable Receiver
STAR........... Scheduled Theater Airlift Route [*Air Force*] (DOMA)
STaR........... School Technology and Readiness Report
STAR........... Science and Technology Aerospace Reports (NITA)
STAR........... Science Teaching Achievement Recognition
STAR........... Score, Teach, and Record [*Teaching machine*]
STAR........... Screening Test of Academic Readiness [*Child development test*]
STAR........... Screening Tracking and Retrieval
STAR........... Second Time Around Racers [*Car racing*]
STAR........... Segment Table Address Register [*Computer science*] (IAA)
STAR........... Selective Training and Retention [*Navy*]
STAR........... Self-Steering Array Repeater (IAA)
STAR........... Self-Test Antenna Radiation [*Military*] (CAAL)
STAR........... Self-Test Automatic Readout
STAR........... Self-Testing and Repairing [*Computer self-repair*]
STAR........... Self-Training and Assessment of Readiness
STAR........... Serials Titles Automated Records [*US National Agricultural Library*] [*Beltsville, MD*] [*A publication*]
STAR........... Set-Theoretic Approach to Relations (PDAA)
STAR........... Shell Transient Asymmetric Response
STAR........... Shield Test Air Reactor [*Nuclear energy*]
STAR........... Shipboard Tactical Airborne Remote Piloted Vehicle [*Navy*] (CAAL)
STAR........... Ship-Tended Acoustic Relay [*Military*]
STAR........... Shock Thermodynamics Applied Research [*Department of Energy*]
STAR........... Shuttle Turnaround Analysis Report [*NASA*] (NASA)
STAR........... Simple Test Approach for Readability [*General Electric*]
STAR........... Simulation of Tactical Alternative Responses (MCD)
STAR........... Simultaneous Tansmitted and Reflected (AAEL)
STAR........... Simultaneous Temperature Alarm Readout
STAR........... Simultaneous Transmission and Reception RADAR [*DoD*] (ECON)
STAR........... Sled Towed Array (MCD)
STAR........... Society for Technological Advancement of Reporting (NTPA)
STAR........... Society for Test Anxiety Research (EA)
STAR........... Society of Romanian Air Transports [*ICAO designator*] (FAAC)
STAR........... Space Technology and Advanced Research
STAR........... Space Technology and Research Center [*Research center*] (RCD)
STAR........... Space Terminal Auxiliary Reactor (IAA)
STAR........... Space Thermionic Auxiliary Reactor [*Nuclear energy*]
STAR........... Space-Time Autoregressive [*Statistics*]
STAR........... Specialized Training and Reassignment [*Military*]
STAR........... Specialized Training for Army Readiness [*Army Reserve*]
STAR........... Special Treatment and Review [*Navy*] (NG)
STAR........... Special Tube Analyzing Recorder
STAR........... Spectral Technology and Applied Research
STAR........... Speed through Aerial Resupply [*Air Force*]
STAR........... Sport, Travel, Art, and Recreation
STAR........... Standard Routine (IAA)
STAR........... Standard Telecommunications Automatic Recognizer [*Computer science*]
STAR........... Standard Tensioned Alongside Receiver [*Navy*] (NVT)
STAR........... Standard Terminal Arrival Route [*Aviation*]
STAR........... Standard Test Authorization and Report System [*Navy*]
Star............ Starkie's English Nisi Prius Reports [*A publication*] (DLA)
STAR........... State Acid Rain Projects [*Environmental Protection Agency*] (GFGA)
STAR........... Statistical Analysis Routine (IAA)
STAR........... Statistical Table Assembly and Retrieval System [*Proposed for Social Security Administration*]
STAR........... Statistical Treatment of Aircraft Returns (MCD)
STAR........... Status Application Resource (HGAA)
STAR........... Steerable Array RADAR
STAR........... Stellar Attitude Reference
STAR........... Steps to Abstract Reasoning
STAR........... STING [*Swift Target Identification Notification Grid*] Array [*Computer system*]
STAR........... Stock Technical Analysis Reports [*Innovest Systems, Inc.*] [*Database*]
STAR........... Stop the Arms Race [*Women's International League for Peace and Freedom*]
STAR........... Storage Address Register [*Telecommunications*] (IAA)
STAR........... Strategic Action in Rural Areas (WDAA)
STAR........... Strategic Technologies for the Army
STAR........... Streamlined Acquisition Requirements System [*DoD*]
STAR........... Stream Tension Actuated Remotely [*Navy*] (DOMA)
STAR........... Stress and Anxiety Research Society (EA)
STAR........... Strike, Transfers, Acquisitions, or Removals [*Navy*] (NG)
STAR........... String Array [*Computer system*] (MCD)
STAR........... String Array Processor
STAR........... Structural Testing, Analysis, and Reporting
STAR........... Students Taking Action with Recognition [*Kentucky*] (EDAC)
STAR........... Students Taught Awareness and Resistance [*An association*]
STAR........... Study of Tamoxifen and Raloxifene [*U.S. and Canadian research program*]
STAR........... Submarine Test and Research (MCD)
STAR........... [*The*] Sunday Times Atlantic Riband [*Award offered by a London newspaper to any sailboat beating the 1905 record for a transatlantic crossing*]
STAR........... Supplementary Teaching Assistance in Reading (AEBS)
STAR........... Supplier Transmittal and Approval Request (MCD)
STAR........... Support to Aftermarket Repairs [*Toyota automobile service repair program*]
STAR........... Surface-to-Air Recovery

STAR	Surveillance, Target Acquisition, and Reconnaissance
STAR	Swedish Tactical Attack RADAR
STAR	System for Telephone Administrative Response [*Computer science*]
STAR	System for Time and Accomplishment Reporting (MCD)
STAR	Systems Test Bed for Avionics Research
STAR	System Threat Assessment Report [*Army*]
STAR	System to Automate Records (NITA)
STAR	System Training Application Requirements
STARA	Scientific and Technical Aerospace Reports Administrator (AAGC)
STARAD	Starfish Radiation [*Satellite*] [*NASA*]
STARAN	Stellar Attitude Reference and Navigation
Starbase	Starbase Corp. [*Associated Press*] (SAG)
StarBc	Star Banc Corp. [*Associated Press*] (SAG)
Starbcks	Starbucks Corp. [*Associated Press*] (SAG)
STARC	Solar Thermal Advanced Research Center [*University of Houston*] [*Research center*] (RCD)
STARC	State Area Commands (MCD)
STARC	State Area Coordinator (COE)
Star Ch Ca	Star Chamber Cases [*1477-1648*] [*England*] [*A publication*] (DLA)
Star Ch Cas	Star Chamber Cases [*1477-1648*] [*England*] [*A publication*] (DLA)
STARCIPS	Standard Army Civilian Pay System
STARCIPS-R	Standard Army Civilian Pay System Redesign (GFGA)
STARCOM	Strategic Army Command Network
STARCOM	Strategic Army Communications System
Starcraft	Starcraft Automotive Corp. [*Associated Press*] (SAG)
STARE	Scandinavian Twin Auroral RADAR Experiment [*Ionospheric science*]
STARE	Steerable Telemetry Antenna Receiving Equipment
STARFIARS	Standard Army Financial Inventory Accounting and Reporting System
STARFIRE	System to Accumulate and Retrieve Financial Information with Random Extraction [*Computer science*]
StarGas	Star Gas Partners L.P. SBI [*Associated Press*] (SAG)
STARIMAR	Space-Time Autoregressive Integrated Moving Average [*Statistics*]
Stark	Starkie's English Nisi Prius Reports [*1815-22*] [*A publication*] (DLA)
Stark CL	Starkie's Criminal Law [*A publication*] (DLA)
Stark Cr Pl	Starkie's Criminal Pleading [*A publication*] (DLA)
Stark Ev	Starkie on Evidence [*A publication*] (DLA)
Starkie	Starkie's English Nisi Prius Reports [*A publication*] (DLA)
Starkie (Eng)	Starkie's English Nisi Prius Reports [*171 English Reprint*] [*A publication*] (DLA)
Starkie Ev	Starkie on Evidence [*A publication*] (DLA)
Starkie's	English Nisi Prius Reports [*171 English Reprint*] [*A publication*] (DLA)
Starkie Sland & L	Starkie on Slander and Libel [*A publication*] (DLA)
Stark Jury Tr	Starkie on Trial by Jury [*A publication*] (DLA)
Stark Lib	Starkie on Libel [*A publication*] (DLA)
Stark NP	Starkie's English Nisi Prius Reports [*A publication*] (DLA)
Stark Sl & L	Starkie on Slander and Libel [*A publication*] (DLA)
STARLAB	Space Technology Applications and Research Laboratory [*NASA*]
STARLab	Space, Telecommunications, and Radioscience Laboratory [*Stanford University*] [*Research center*] (RCD)
Starl I Cr Law	Starling's East India Criminal Law and Procedure [*A publication*] (DLA)
STARLO	Special Test Army Reserve Limited Objective
StarMC	Star Multi Care Services, Inc. [*Associated Press*] (SAG)
St Arm Leg Pow	St. Armand on the Legislative Power of England [*A publication*] (DLA)
STARNET	Sustaining Base Army Network (GFGA)
STARP	Supplemental Training and Readiness Program
STARPAHC	Space Technology Applied to Rural Papago Advanced Health Care (SSD)
STARPUBS	Standard Army Publications System
STARR	Schedule, Technical, and Resources Report [*NASA*] (NASA)
STARR	Staff Assessment of Readiness Report (MCD)
STARR	Study Techniques for Advanced RADAR Requirements
Starr & C Ann St	Starr and Curtis' Annotated Statutes [*Illinois*] [*A publication*] (DLA)
StarRes	Star Resources Corp. [*Associated Press*] (SAG)
Starret	Starrett [*L.S.*] Co. [*Associated Press*] (SAG)
StarrtCp	Starrett Corp. [*Associated Press*] (SAG)
STARS	Satellite Telemetry Automatic Reduction System [*NASA*]
STARS	Satellite Transmission and Reception Specialists [*Houston, TX*] [*Telecommunications*] (TSSD)
STARS	Seaborne Tracking and Ranging Station
STARS	Sealink Ticket and Reservation System [*Sealink UK Ltd.*] [*Information service or system*] (IID)
STARS	Secondary Training for Alaskan Rural Students (EDAC)
STARS	Services and Techniques for Advanced Real-Time Systems [*Computer science*] (IAA)
STARS	Shell Theory Automated for Rotational Structures
STARS	Ship Tracking and Retrieval System [*MARAD*] (TAG)
STARS	Short-Term Auction Rate Cumulative Preferred Stock (EBF)
STARS	Short-Term Auction-Rate Stock [*Investment term*]
STARS	Short-Term Auditory Retrieval and Storage Test
STARS	Short Track Auto Racing Series [*Car racing*]
STARS	Short Track Auto Racing Stars [*An association*]
STARS	Silent Tactical Attack Reconnaissance System
STARS	Simmons Teen-Age Research Study [*Simmons Market Research Bureau, Inc.*] [*Information service or system*] (CRD)
STARS	Simplified Three Axes Reference System (IAA)
STARS	Simulation and Training Advanced Research System [*Air Force*]
STARS	Software Technology for Adaptable, Reliable Systems [*Military*]
STARS	Soot Trap and Regeneration System [*Diesel engine exhaust emission controls*]
STARS	Spaulding Teacher Activity Rating Schedule (EDAC)
STAR(S)	Specialized Training and Reassignment (Student) [*Military*]
STARS	Stabilized Twin-Gyro Attitude Reference System
STARS	Standard Accounting and Reporting Systems (MCD)
STARS	Standard Terminal Arrival Routes [*Aviation*] (MCD)
STARS	Standard Terminal Automation Replacement System [*FAA*] (TAG)
STARS	Standard Time and Rate Setting (MHDB)
STARS	Standard, TRADOC Automated Retrieval System (MCD)
STARS	Star Shot (SAA)
STARS	Stationary Automotive Road Simulator
STARS	Stellar Tracking Attitude Reference System
STARS	Strategically Targeted Activities for Results System
STARS	Strategic Target System [*Rocket*]
STARS	Study of Tactical Airborne RADAR System
STARS	Support Tracking Analysis Reporting Systems (MCD)
STARS	Surface-to-Air Recovery System
STARS	Surveillance Target Attack RADAR System
STARS	Synchronized Time, Automated Reporting System
STARS	System Test and Astronaut Requirement Simulation
STARS	System Thermal Air Platform Reconnaissance Signature (MCD)
Star SC	Star Session Cases [*1824-25*] [*A publication*] (DLA)
STARS II	Shell Theory Automated for Rotational Structures - II (MCD)
START	Safety Technology Applied to Rapid Transit [*Committee*] [*American Public Transit Association*]
START	Selection to Activate Random Testing [*Module*] [*NASA*]
START	Service Technician Advancement, Recruitment, and Training
START	Small Tight Aspect Ratio Tokamak [*Plasma physics*]
START	Spacecraft Technology and Advanced Reentry Tests [*Air Force*]
START	Space Test and Reentry Technology
START	Space Transport and Reentry Tests
START	Special Treatment and Rehabilitative Training [*Prisons project*]
START	Spend Today and Retire Tomorrow [*Consumer pension plan*]
START	Sports Technique and Reaction Trainer [*Computerized training program for baseball and tennis*]
START	State of the Total Army Report Team
START	Story-Telling Automatic Reading Tutor
START	Strategic Arms Reduction Talks (USGC)
START	Strategic Arms Reduction Treaty
START	Summary Tape Assistance, Research, and Training
START	Superfund Technical Assessment and Response Team (COE)
START	Systematic Tabular Analysis of Requirements Technique (IEEE)
START	System for Analysis, Research, and Training (USDC)
START	System of Transportation Applying Rendezvous Technique (MCD)
StarTc	Star Technologies, Inc. [*Associated Press*] (SAG)
StarTel	StarSight Telecast, Inc. [*Associated Press*] (SAG)
Starter	Starter Corp. [*Associated Press*] (SAG)
STARTEX	Start of the Exercise (MCD)
STARTLE	Surveillance and Target Acquisition RADAR for Tank Location and Engagement [*Army*] (MCD)
STARTS	Software Tools for Application to Real Time Systems [*British*]
STARUTE	Stable Parachute
Starwd	Starwood Lodging Trust [*Associated Press*] (SAG)
StarwdLT	Starwood Lodging Trust [*Associated Press*] (SAG)
STAS	Safe-to-Arm Signal
STAS	Safe-to-Arm System (MUGU)
STAS	Short Term Analysis Services [*Scientific Services Program*] [*Army*] (RDA)
STAS	Space Transportation Architecture Study [*1985*]
STAS	Sporadic Testicular Agenesis Syndrome [*Medicine*] (DMAA)
STAS	Statutes
STAS	Strategic Transportation Analysis System [*MTMC*] (TAG)
STASH	Student Association for the Study of Hallucinogens [*Defunct*] (EA)
STASHIP	Station Ship [*Navy*] (NVT)
STASS	Special Tactical Air Surveillance System (IAA)
STASS	Submarine Tactical Array SONAR System
STASS	Submarine Towed Array SONAR System [*Navy*]
STASS	Submarine-Towed Array Surveillance System (NVT)
STASS	Surveillance Target Acquisition Support System (IAA)
StaSTBos	State Street Boston, Inc. [*Associated Press*] (SAG)
stat-	Electrostatic (IDOE)
STAT	i-STAT [*NASDAQ symbol*] (TTSB)
STAT	I-Stat Corp. [*NASDAQ symbol*] (SAG)
STAT	Photostat (NTCM)
STAT	SEABEE Technical Assistance Team [*Navy*]
STAT	SEABEE Training Advisory Team [*Navy*]
STAT	Seeing through Arithmetic Tests (AEBS)
STAT	Signal Transducer and Activator of Transcription [*Biochemistry*]
STAT	Signal Transducers and Activators of Transcription [*Biochemistry*]
STAT	Small Transport Aircraft Technology (MCD)
STAT	Society of Teachers of the Alexander Technique (EAIO)
STAT	State
STAT	Static (AAG)
STAT	Statim [*Immediately*] [*Latin*]
STAT	Station
STAT	Stationary [*Chemistry*]
STAT	Stationery Office [*British*]
STAT	Statistic (AFM)
Stat	Statistic (TBD)
Stat	Statistical (AL)
Stat	Statistics (AL)
Stat	Statius [*First century AD*] [*Classical studies*] (OCD)
Stat(	Stative (BJA)
STAT	Statuary
STAT	Status (MSA)
STAT	Status Request (CIST)
STAT	Statute

stat .... Statute (WDAA)
Stat .... [*United States*] Statutes at Large (USGC)
STAT .... Statutory Tenant (DSUE)
STAT .... Stop Teen-Age Addiction to Tobacco (EA)
STAT .... Stratospheric Tracers of Atmospheric Transport [*Marine science*] (OSRA)
STAT .... Suprathreshold Adaptation Test (STED)
Stat .... United States Statutes at Large (EBF)
statA .... Statampere [*Also, sA*] [*Unit of electric current*]
STAT AN ...... Statistical Annals (DLA)
Stat at L .... United States Statutes at Large [*A publication*] (DLA)
StatAut .... State Auto Financial Corp. [*Associated Press*] (SAG)
statC .... Statcoulomb [*Also, sC*] [*Unit of electric charge*]
StatCan .... Statistics Canada [*Statistics Canada Library*] [*Information service or system*]
StatCas .... Station Casinos, Inc. [*Associated Press*] (SAG)
STATCAT .... Statistical Context-Aided Testing [*North-Holland Publishing Co.*] [*Software package*] (NCC)
STATCO .... Statistical Passenger Data Collection System [*MTMC*] (TAG)
StatConst .... Status Constructus (BJA)
Stat Def .... Statutory Definition [*Legal term*] (DLA)
STATDSB .... Status Disable [*Computer science*] (MHDI)
STATE .... Simplified Tactical Approach and Terminal Equipment
STATE .... Simulation for Tank/Antitank Evaluation (NATG)
STATE .... Space Transportation Air-Breathing Technology Evaluation [*DoD*]
StateBcp .... State Bancorp, Inc. [*Associated Press*] (SAG)
State Dept Bull... United States State Department. Bulletin [*A publication*] (DLA)
StateF .... Statewide Financial Corp. [*Associated Press*] (SAG)
StateFn .... Statefed Financial Corp. [*Associated Press*] (SAG)
STATEM .... Shipment Status System [*Military*] (AABC)
State Mot Carr Guide... State Motor Carrier Guide [*Commerce Clearing House*] [*A publication*] (DLA)
State R .... New York State Reporter [*A publication*] (DLA)
State Rep ...... New York State Reporter [*A publication*] (DLA)
STATES .... Simplified Tactical Approach and Terminal Equipment System
states .... Statesman [*or Stateswoman*]
State Tax Cas Rep... State Tax Cases Reporter [*Commerce Clearing House*] [*A publication*] (DLA)
State Tr .... State Trials (Howell) [*England*] [*A publication*] (DLA)
State Tr NS... State Trials, New Series, Edited by Macdonell [*England*] [*A publication*] (DLA)
StatewdeF ... Statewide Financial Corp. [*Associated Press*] (SAG)
statF .... Statfarad [*Also, sF*] [*Unit of capacitance*]
Stat Glo .... Statute of Gloucester [*First statute to give costs in actions*] [*A publication*] (DLA)
statH .... Stathenry [*Also, sH*] [*Unit of inductance*]
STATH .... Statherin (DMAA)
Stath Abr ...... Statham's Abridgment [*A publication*] (DLA)
StatHlt .... Stat Healthcare, Inc. [*Associated Press*] (SAG)
StatHlth .... Stat Healthcare, Inc. [*Associated Press*] (SAG)
STATIC .... Student Taskforce Against Telecommunication Information Concealment [*Student legal action organization*]
Stat ICJ .... Statute of the International Court of Justice [*A publication*] (DLA)
STATINDFX .... Stationery Industry Exhibition [*British*] (ITD)
STATINF ...... Statistical Information System [*Bundesamt fuer Statistik*] [*Switzerland Information service or system*] (CRD)
Stat Inst ...... Statutory Instruments [*A publication*] (DLA)
STATION ...... Station [*Commonly used*] (OPSA)
STATIS .... Statistics
StatI .... Statistical [*Army*]
St at Large... Statutes at Large [*A publication*] (DLA)
STATLIB .... Statistical Computing Library [*Bell System*]
Stat Local .... Governments Statute of Local Governments [*A publication*] (DLA)
Stat Marl ...... Statute of Marlbridge [*A publication*] (DLA)
Stat Mer ..... Statute of Merton [*A publication*] (DLA)
Stat Mert ..... Statute of Merton [*A publication*] (DLA)
STATMUX ...... Statistical Multiplexer [*Computer science*]
STATN .... Station [*Commonly used*] (OPSA)
StatnCas ...... Station Casinos, Inc. [*Associated Press*] (SAG)
STATNET ...... Statistical Analysis of Network
STATNR .... Stationer
STATNRY ..... Stationary
Stat NZ .... Statutes of New Zealand [*A publication*] (DLA)
Stat O & R... Statutory Orders and Regulations [*Canada*] [*A publication*] (DLA)
statOe .... Statoersted (IDOE)
STATPAC .... Statistics Package [*Computer program*] (IEEE)
STAT-PACK... Statistical Package (MHDI)
STATRAFO... Standard Transfer Order
Stat R & O... Statutory Rules and Orders [*1890-1947*] [*England*] [*A publication*] (DLA)
Stat R & O & Stat Inst Rev... Statutory Rules and Orders and Statutory Instruments Revised [*England*] [*A publication*] (DLA)
Stat R & ONI... Statutory Rules and Orders of Northern Ireland [*A publication*] (DLA)
Stat Realm... Statutes of the Realm [*England*] [*A publication*] (DLA)
Stat Reg NZ... Statutory Regulations [*New Zealand*] [*A publication*] (DLA)
STATREP ..... Advise Present Grade, Status, Physical Condition, and Mailing Address of Following Named [*Military*]
STATS .... Simulated Tax and Transfer System [*Social Security Administration*] (GFGA)
STATS .... Stationary Tank Automatic Target System (MCD)
Stats .... Statistics (DD)
statS .... Statsiemens [*Also, sS*] [*Unit of electric conductance, admittance, and susceptance*]
STATS .... Strategic/Tactical Area Test System (MCD)

STATSBOBP... Scale of Teacher Attitudes toward Selective Behavior of Boy Pupils [*Satirical*]
Stats Can..... Statistics Canada
STAT-SEL .... Status Select [*Army*]
STATSERVOFF... Statistical Service Office [*Supreme Headquarters Allied Powers Europe*] (NATG)
STATSVS ...... Statistical Services (MUGU)
STATT .... Statement
statT .... Stattesla [*Unit of magnetic flux density*]
STATTS .... Stationary Automatic Tank Target System (MCD)
statV .... Statvolt [*Also, sV*] [*Electrostatic unit of potential difference*]
statWb .... Statweber [*Unit of magnetic flux*]
Stat Westm... Statute of Westminster [*A publication*] (DLA)
Stat Winch... Statute of Winchester [*A publication*] (DLA)
STATY .... Stationary (WGA)
STATY .... Statutory (ROG)
Staundef ...... Staundeforde's Exposition of the King's Prerogative [*A publication*] (DLA)
Staundf Prerog... Staundeforde's Exposition of the King's Prerogative [*A publication*] (DLA)
Staund Pl..... Staundeforde's Pleas of Crown [*A publication*] (DLA)
Staunf Pr .... Staundeforde's Exposition of the King's Prerogative [*A publication*] (DLA)
STAVRA ...... Supreme High Command of the Soviet Armed Forces [*Russian*] (MCD)
STAX........... Sludge Tracking Acoustical Experiment [*Marine science*] (MSC)
STAXI .... State-Trait Anger Expression Inventory [*Test*] (TMMY)
STAY .... Extended Stay Amer [*NASDAQ symbol*] (TTSB)
STAY .... Extended Stay America [*NASDAQ symbol*] (SAG)
STB .... Bachelor of Sacred Theology (NADA)
STB .... Bachelor of the Science of Theology
StB .... Kommentar zum Neuen Testament aus Talmud und Midrasch (H. L. Strack - F. Billerbeck) [*A publication*] (BJA)
STB .... Sacrae Theologiae Baccalaureus [*Bachelor of Sacred Theology*] [*Latin*] (GPO)
STB .... Santa Barbara [*Venezuela*] [*Airport symbol*] (OAG)
STB .... Save the Bush Project [*Commonwealth*] (EERA)
STB .... Scandinavian Tourist Boards (EA)
STB .... Scan True Bearing (NVT)
STB .... Science and Technology Branch [*United Nations*] (EA)
STB .... Scottish Tourist Board (EAIO)
STB .... Segment Table Base [*Computer science*] (IAA)
STB .... Segment Tag BITS [*Binary Digits*]
STB .... September Resources Ltd. [*Vancouver Stock Exchange symbol*]
STB .... Shore Terminal Box (MSA)
STB .... Signal Training Brigade (MCD)
STB .... Snci-Tours Benin Inter Regional [*ICAO designator*] (FAAC)
STB .... Soprano, Tenor, Bass
STB .... Southern Tourist Board [*British*] (DCTA)
STB .... Special Tax Bond
Stb .... Staatsblad [*Official Bulletin*] [*Netherlands*] (ILCA)
STB .... Stable (MSA)
STB .... Staged Turbulent Bed Process [*Chevron Corp.*] [*Oil shale pyrolysis*]
STB .... Standard Torsion Bar (MCD)
STB .... Star Banc Corp. [*NYSE symbol*] (SAG)
STB .... State Tender Board [*Victoria, Australia*]
STB .... St. Blazey [*British depot code*]
STB .... Steinbach [*Federal Republic of Germany*] [*Seismograph station code, US Geological Survey*] (SEIS)
STB .... Stillborn [*Medicine*]
Stb .... Stillborn (STED)
STB .... Stock-Tank Barrel [*Petroleum industry*]
STB .... Stop Bar (DA)
STB .... Stourbridge [*British depot code*]
STB .... Strata Titles Board [*New South Wales, Australia*]
STB .... Streaming Tape Backup Unit
STB .... Stretch Block (MCD)
STB .... Subsystems Test Bed (MCD)
STB .... Sun's True Bearing [*Navigation*]
STB .... Supertropical Bleach [*Sanitizing agent*]
STB .... Surface Transportation Board [*Formerly, the ICC - Interstate Commerce Commission, 1996*]
STB .... Systems Testing Branch [*Social Security Administration*]
STB .... System [*or Subsystem*] Test Bed [*NASA*] (KSC)
STBA........... S & T Bancorp [*NASDAQ symbol*] (SAG)
STBA........... Selective Top-to-Bottom Algorithm (DIT)
STBAL........ Standing Balance (STED)
St Bar Rev... State Bar Review [*A publication*] (DLA)
STBC........... School Readiness Tests for Blind Children
STBC........... State Bancorp, Inc. [*NASDAQ symbol*] (SAG)
STBC........... State Bancorp NY [*NASDAQ symbol*] (TTSB)
STBD........... Starboard
STBDQ........ Supervising Teacher Behavior Description Questionnaire (EDAC)
STBE........... Society of Teachers in Business Education [*British*] (EAIO)
STBE........... Space Transportation Booster Engine
STBF........... Southeastern Thrift & Bank Fund [*NASDAQ symbol*] (SAG)
sTBG........... Slow Thyroxine-Binding Globulin [*Endocrinology*]
STBI........... STB Systems [*NASDAQ symbol*] (TTSB)
STBI........... STB Systems, Inc. [*NASDAQ symbol*] (SAG)
STBL........... Stable
STBLN........ Stabilization (MSA)
STBLZ........ Stabilize (AABC)
STBM........... Shaft-to-Bore Misalignment
St Bonaventure U... St. Bonaventure University (GAGS)
StBPt .... Standard Brands Paint Co. [*Associated Press*] (SAG)

STBRIAV......	Saint Briavels [*England*]
St Brown......	Stewart-Brown's Cases in the Court of the Star Chamber [*1455-1547*] [*A publication*] (DLA)
STBS............	Sierra Tahoe Bancorp [*NASDAQ symbol*] (SAG)
STBSCP	Stroboscope [*Engineering*]
STB Sy........	STB Systems, Inc. [*Associated Press*] (SAG)
STBT............	Steamboat (ADA)
STBT............	Subcaliber Tracer Bullet Trainer [*Army*] (INF)
STBU............	Statistical Bulletin
STBY............	Standby (AAG)
STC.............	Chief SONAR Technician [*Navy rating*]
STC.............	Sacramento Test Center (MCD)
STC.............	Said to Contain [*Cargo manifest description*]
STC.............	Samuel Taylor Coleridge [*Nineteenth-century British poet*]
STC.............	Satellite Television Corp. [*Washington, DC*] [*Telecommunications*] (TSSD)
STC.............	Satellite Test Center [*Air Force*]
STC.............	Satellite Tracking Center [*Sunnyvale, CA*]
STC.............	Satellite Tracking Committee [*Military*]
STC.............	Scandinavian Travel Commission [*Later, Scandinavian National Travel Offices*] (EA)
STC.............	Science and Technology Center [*National Science Foundation*]
STC.............	Science and Technology Corp. (RDA)
STC.............	Security Time Control
STC.............	Security Trade Control
STC.............	Security Training Center
STC.............	Senate Tourism Caucus (EA)
STC.............	Senior Training Corps [*British*]
STC.............	Sensitivity-Time Control [*RADAR*]
STC.............	Sequence-Tagged Connector [*Genetics*]
STC.............	Serum Theophylline Concentration [*Clinical chemistry*]
STC.............	Service Technology Corp. [*of Ling-Temco-Vought, Inc.*]
STC.............	Service to Chapters [*Red Cross*]
STC.............	Service to Claimants [*Unemployment Insurance Service*] [*Department of Labor*]
STC.............	Serving Test Center [*Bell System*]
STC.............	Set Carry
STC.............	[*The*] Seven Tablets of Creation [*L. W. King*] [*A publication*] (BJA)
STC.............	Sexually Transmitted Condition (STED)
STC.............	SHAPE [*Supreme Headquarters Allied Powers Europe*] Technical Center [*Formerly, SADTC*] [*The Hague, Netherlands*] [*NATO*]
STC.............	Short Time Constant
STC.............	Short Title Catalog [*A publication*]
STC.............	Short Training Courses (AIE)
STC.............	Signal Training Centre [*British military*] (DMA)
STC.............	Silicon Transistor Corp. (IAA)
STC.............	Simulation Tape Conversion
STC.............	Single Strip Container (COE)
STC.............	Single-Trip Container
STC.............	Ski Touring Council [*Defunct*] (EA)
STC.............	Slow Time Constant (MCD)
STC.............	Smokeless Tobacco Council (EA)
STC.............	Societe de Transports et de Tourisme [*Mali*] [*ICAO designator*] (FAAC)
STC.............	Society for Technical Communication (EA)
STC.............	Society of Telecommunications Consultants (EA)
STC.............	Society of Theatrical Carpenters [*A union*] [*British*]
STC.............	Society of Town Clerks [*British*] (BI)
STC.............	Soft Tissue Calcification [*Medicine*]
STC.............	Solar Thermal Commission (PDAA)
STC.............	Solidaridad de Trabajadores Cristianos [*Nicaragua*] [*Political party*] (EY)
STC.............	Solid Tantalum Capacitor (PDAA)
STC.............	Sound Transmission Class [*Followed by number, indicates FHA rating of sound insulating quality of a partition construction*].
STC.............	Source Telecomputing Corp. [*McLean, VA*] [*Telecommunications*] (TSSD)
STC.............	South Thames College [*London, England*]
STC.............	Spacecraft Test Conductor [*NASA*] (KSC)
STC.............	Space Technology Center
STC.............	Space Test Center [*Air Force*]
STC.............	Space-Time Continuum
STC.............	Spatiotemporal Chaos [*Physics*]
STC.............	Specialists Training Center
STC.............	Specialty Tobacco Council (NTPA)
STC.............	Specific Taste Changes
STC.............	Specific Thermal Capacity
STC.............	Spectral Transfer Coefficient
STC.............	Standard Telephone and Cable [*IT & T affiliate*] [*Research center British*]
STC.............	Standard Test Chamber (MCD)
STC.............	Standard Test Configuration [*NASA*] (NASA)
STC.............	Standard Transmission Code [*Computer science*]
STC.............	Standing Technical Committee [*British*] (DCTA)
STC.............	State Tax Cases [*Commerce Clearing House*] [*A publication*] (DLA)
STC.............	State Teachers College
STC.............	State Total Cost [*Bookselling*] (DGA)
STC.............	State Trading Co. (WDAA)
STC.............	Station Technical Control [*Telecommunications*] (TEL)
STC.............	Station Test and Calibration
StC.............	Status Constructus (BJA)
STC.............	St. Cloud, MN [*Location identifier FAA*] (FAAL)
STC..........	Stepchild
St C	Stephen's Commentaries on the Laws of England [*21st ed.*] [*1950*] [*A publication*] (DLA)
STC............	Step Timing Control [*Truck engineering*]
STC.......	Stereo Tape Club of America
STC.........	Stern Telecommunications Corp. [*New York, NY*] [*Telecommunications*] (TSSD)
STC............	Stewart Information Services Corp. [*NYSE symbol*] (SPSG)
STC............	Stewart Information Sv [*NYSE symbol*] (TTSB)
STC............	Stewart, Tabori & Chang [*Publisher*]
STC............	Still Traffic Camera
STU............	Stimulate to Cry (STED)
STC............	Stock Trust Certificate [*Investment term*]
STC............	Stone Canyon Observatory [*California*] [*Seismograph station code, US Geological Survey*] (SEIS)
STC............	Storage Container (MCD)
STC............	Storage Technology Corp. (IAA)
STC............	Stored Time Command
STC............	Straight Cactus [*Horticulture*]
STC............	Streamtube Curvature
STC............	Stroke Treatment Center (STED)
STC............	Subtotal Colectomy (STED)
STC............	Subtropical Convergence [*Oceanography*]
STC............	Sugar Tongue Cast (STED)
STC............	Summit Technical Center [*Celanese Research Co.*]
STC............	Supplemental Type Certificate
STC............	Surgical Textiles Conference [*British*] (DBA)
STC............	Symbol Table Counter [*Computer science*] (IAA)
STC............	Synaptic Transporter Current [*Neurochemistry*]
STC............	Synthetic Turf Conference [*Defunct*] (EA)
STC............	Systems Test Complex [*NASA*]
STC............	System Technical Control
STC............	System Test Complex (IAA)
STC............	System Test Configuration
STC............	System Test Console
STC............	System Transfer Constant
STCA............	Scottish Terrier Club of America (EA)
STCA............	Short Term Conflict Alert System [*Aviation*] (DA)
STCA............	Short Tests of Clerical Ability
STCA............	Silky Terrier Club of America (EA)
STCA............	Skye Terrier Club of America (EA)
STCA............	Sodium Trichloroacetate [*Organic chemistry*]
STCA............	Staffordshire Terrier Club of America (EA)
S/TCAC	Scientific/Technical Careers Advisory Committee [*Environmental Protection Agency*] (GFGA)
STCAC	Sydney Transport Coordination Advisory Council [*New South Wales, Australia*]
STCAN/FOM...	Services Techniques des Construction et Armes Navales / France Outre Mer [*French river patrol boat used in Vietnam*] (VNW)
St Cas.........	Stillingfleet's English Ecclesiastical Cases [*A publication*] (DLA)
StCath.........	Studia Catholica [*Nijmegen*] [*A publication*] (BJA)
STCB............	Subtask Control Block [*Computer science*] (IBMDP)
STCC............	Spacecraft Technical Control Center (MDG)
STCC............	Springfield Technical Community College [*Massachusetts*]
STCC............	Standards Council of Canada [*See also CCNO*]
STCC............	Standard Transportation Commodity Classification [*or Code*]
STCC............	Syndicat des Travailleurs en Communication du Canada
STCC............	Syndicat des Travailleurs en Communication, Electronique, Electricite, Techniciens, et Salaries du Canada [*Communications, Electronic, Electrical, Technical, and Salaried Workers of Canada - CWC*]
STCCF..........	Smartel Communications [*NASDAQ symbol*] (TTSB)
STCCF..........	Smartel Communications [*NASDAQ symbol*] (SAG)
STCDHS......	Spacecraft Telemetry Command Data Handling System
STCDS	System Test Complex Data System
STCDSS	Standing Technical Committee on Disposal of Sewage Sludge [*British*] (DCTA)
STCE............	System Test Complex Equipment
STCFEO........	Science and Technology Center, Far East Office [*Army*] (AABC)
STCG	Super Tension Cables Group [*British*] (DBA)
STCH	Shared Tech Fairchild [*NASDAQ symbol*] (TTSB)
STCH	Shared Technologies Fairchild [*NASDAQ symbol*] [*Formerly, Shared Technologies*] (SG)
STCH	Shared Technologies, Inc. [*NASDAQ symbol*] (NQ)
STCH	Stitch (MSA)
St Ch Cas	Star Chamber Cases [*England*] [*A publication*] (DLA)
STCI............	Siebert Telecommunications Consulting, Inc. [*Cincinnati, OH*] [*Telecommunications*] (TSSD)
STCI............	Station Casinos [*NASDAQ symbol*] (TTSB)
STCI............	Station Casinos, Inc. [*NASDAQ symbol*] (SAG)
STCICS	Strike Command Integrated Communications System [*British*]
STCIP..........	Station Casinos $3.50 Cv Pfd [*NASDAQ symbol*] (TTSB)
STCK............	Stock
STCK............	Store Clock (CIST)
STCKHLDR...	Stockholder
STCL............	Shared Tech Cellular [*NASDAQ symbol*] (TTSB)
STCL............	Shared Technologies Cellular, Inc. [*NASDAQ symbol*] (SAG)
STCL............	Source-Term Control Loop [*Nuclear energy*] (NRCH)
STCL............	Standardized Test of Computer Literacy [*Montag and Simonson*] (TES)
STCLB..........	Start Climb [*Aviation*] (FAAC)
St Clem	St. Clement's Church Case [*Philadelphia, PA*] [*A publication*] (DLA)
St Cloud St U...	St. Cloud State University (GAGS)
STCM..........	Master Chief SONAR Technician [*Navy rating*]
STCN	Short Title Catalogue Netherlands (TELE)
STCO	Strata and Tenancy Commissioner's Office [*New South Wales, Australia*]
STCO	Supervisor Training Conference Outline [*Air Force*] (MCD)

STCOL	Steel Column [*Camutek*] [*Software package*] (NCC)
STCP	Short-Term Cost Plan [*NASA*] (NASA)
STCP	Society of Tympanuchus Cupido Pinnatus (EA)
STCR	Solar Thermal Central Receiver
STCR	Starcraft Automotive Corp. [*NASDAQ symbol*] (SAG)
STCR	Starcraft Corp. [*NASDAQ symbol*] (TTSB)
STCR	Systems, Test, and Checkout Report (DICI)
STCRS	Solar Thermal Central Receiver System
STCS	Science and Technology Center for Superconductivity [*National Science Foundation*]
STCS	Senior Chief SONAR Technician [*Navy rating*]
STCS	Society of Technical Civil Servants [*British*] (BI)
STC'S	Stock Trust Certificates (EBF)
STCS	Surveyor Thermal Control Section
STCST	Second Telecommunications Carrier Selection Team [*Australia*]
STCT	Small Transportable Communications Terminal
STCT	System Technical Coordinator Technician (SAA)
StCu	Stratocumulus [*Cloud*] [*Meteorology*] (AIA)
STCV	Strawberry Crinkle Virus [*Plant pathology*]
STCVS	Society of Thoracic and Cardiovascular Surgeons [*British*] (DBA)
STCW	Standard of Training, Certification, and Watchkeeping Convention (DS)
STCW	Stichting Technisch Centrum Waalsteen [*Research center Netherlands*] (IRC)
STCW	System Time Code Word
STD	Banco de Santander SA [*NYSE symbol*] (SPSG)
STD	Banco Santander ADS [*NYSE symbol*] (TTSB)
STD	Doctor of Sacred Theology (NADA)
STD	Doctor of the Science of Theology
STD	Sacrae Theologiae Doctor [*Doctor of Sacred Theology*] [*Latin*]
STD	Safety Topic Discussion (AAG)
STD	Salinity, Temperature and Depth [*Probe*] [*Marine science*] (OSRA)
STD	Salinity/Temperature/Density [*or Depth*] [*Oceanography*]
STD	Santo Domingo [*Venezuela*] [*Airport symbol*] (AD)
std	Saturated (MAE)
STD	Schools of Theology in Dubuque [*Library network*]
STD	Seated (WGA)
STD	Sea Transport Department [*British military*] (DMA)
STD	Seismic Tunnel Detector [*DoD*] (VNW)
STD	Semiconductor on Thermoplastic on Dielectric [*Technology*] (IAA)
STD	Servo Tape Display
STD	Set Driver (SAA)
STD	Sexually Transmitted Disease [*Medicine*]
STD	Ship Training Detachment
STD	Short-Term Debt (MHDW)
STD	Short-Term Disability
STD	Short Time Duty (IAA)
STD	Shuttle Test Director [*NASA*] (MCD)
STD	Silicon Triple Diffused (IAA)
STD	Skin Test Dose
STD	Skin to Tumor Distance [*Medicine*] (MAE)
STD	Skytrak Aeronautical Systems Ltd. [*British*] [*FAA designator*] (FAAC)
STD	Sledborne Time Digitizer
STD	Society for Theological Discussion [*Defunct*] (EA)
STD	Society of Typographic Designers [*British*] (EAIO)
STD	Sodium Tetradecyl Sulfate [*Pharmacology*] (DAVI)
STD	Sodium Thermionic Detector (SAA)
STD	Software Test Description [*DoD*]
STD	South Tibetan Detachment [*Geology*]
STD	South Tropical Disturbance [*of the planet Jupiter*] (BARN)
STD	Spacecraft Technology Division [*NASA*] (KSC)
STD	Spectral Theory of Diffraction (IAA)
STD	Sports Trainers Digest [*A publication*]
STD	Standard (AFM)
std	Standard (COE)
STD	Standard Test Dose
STD	Standard Trustco Ltd. [*Toronto Stock Exchange symbol*]
STD	Standing (AABC)
STD	Started (ADA)
STD	State Taxation Department [*Western Australia*]
STD	State-Transition Diagram [*Computer science*]
STD	Stepwise Thermal Desorption [*Surface analysis*]
STD	Steward [*British*]
ST D	Stopped Diapason [*Organ stop*] [*Music*]
STD	Storage Target Date
STD	Storage Tube Display
STD	Store Decrement (SAA)
STD	Strain Gauge Transient Dosimetry
STD	Strategic Technical Directorate [*South Vietnamese studies and observations group*] (VNW)
STD	Stream Tree Data (PDAA)
STD	Stripline Tunnel Diode
STD	Studio
STD	Subscriber Toll Dialing [*Telecommunications*] (TSSD)
STD	Subscriber Trunk Dialing [*Telephone communications*]
STD	Sunbeam-Talbot-Darracq [*Automobile manufacturer*]
STD	Superconductive Tunneling Device (IAA)
STD	Supporting Technology Development (KSC)
STD	Suspension Technology Demonstrator [*Army*] (RDA)
STD	Synopsis Series of the United States Treasury Decisions [*A publication*] (DLA)
STD	System Technology Demonstration Program (RDA)
S-TDA	Selenium-Tellurium Development Association (EA)
STDA	Steward's Assistant [*Navy*]
STDA	StreetTalk Directory Assistance [*VINES*] [*Computer science*] (PCM)
STDA	Stripline Tunnel Diode Amplifier
ST-DACL	State Trait-Depression Adjective Check Lists [*Test*] (TMMY)
STDB	Steward's Branch [*Marine Corps*]
STDBY	Standby (NVT)
STDC	Society of Typographic Designers of Canada (DGA)
STDC	Southern Travel Directors Council
STDC	Standards Council of Canada [*See also CCNO*]
STDCF	Space Telescope Data Capture Facility [*NASA*] (SSD)
StdCm	Standard Commercial Corp. [*Associated Press*] (SAG)
STD/DEV	Standard Deviation (MCD)
STDDS	Submarine Tactical Data Display Subsystem (MCD)
St Dept	State Department Reports [*A publication*] (DLA)
STDF	Sodium Taurodihydrofusidate [*Organic chemistry*]
STDF	Standoff
StdFdBcp	Standard Federal Bancorp [*Associated Press*] (SAG)
StdFincl	Standard Financial Co. [*Associated Press*] (SAG)
StdFndg	Standard Funding Corp. [*Associated Press*] (SAG)
STDFT³	Standard Cubic Feet (WDAA)
stdgls	Stained Glass (VRA)
STDH	Skin Test for Delayed Hypersensitivity [*Medicine*] (DMAA)
ST DIAP	Stopped Diapason [*Organ stop*] [*Music*]
STDL	Standard Distribution List [*NASA*] (NASA)
STDL	Submarine Tactical Data Link (NVT)
StdM	Standard Matched (DAC)
STDM	Statistical Time Division Multiplexer [*or Multiplexing*]
STDM	Synchronous Time-Division Multiplexing [*Computer science*] (MDG)
STDMA	Slotted Time-Division Multiple Access [*Computer science*] (CIST)
StdMgt	Standard Management Corp. [*Associated Press*] (SAG)
StdMic	Standard Microsystems Corp. [*Associated Press*] (SAG)
STDN	Set the Date Now [*Association supporting the end of US military involvement in Indochina*] [*Defunct*] (EA)
STDN	Spacecraft Tracking and Data Network (NITA)
STDN	Space Flight Tracking and Data Network [*Formerly, STADAN*] [*NASA*]
STDN	Space Tracking and Data Network [*NASA*] (NAKS)
STDN	Standardization (AFM)
STDNT	Student
STDP	Short-Term Dynamic Psychotherapy
STDP	Special Training Devices Program (AFM)
StdPac	Standard-Pacific Corp. [*Associated Press*] (SAG)
StdProd	Standard Products Co. [*Associated Press*] (SAG)
STDR	Science and Technology Desk Reference [*A publication*]
STDR	Space Technology Data Report
STDR	Standard
StdReg	Standard Register Co. [*Associated Press*] (SAG)
STDS	Set Theoretic Data Structure (IAA)
STDS	Snake Torpedo Destruction System
STDS	South Tibetan Detachment System [*Geology*]
STDS	Standards [*Timbor measurement*] (EY)
STDS	Strategic Target Data System (SSD)
STDS	Submarine Tactical Data System (MCD)
STDS	Survey of Teacher Demand and Shortage [*Department of Education*] (GFGA)
STDS	System for Thermal Diagnostic Studies
STDST	Start Descent [*Aviation*] (FAAC)
STDT	Standard Tone-Decay Test (DB)
STD TF	Standard Tube Feeding [*Gastroenterology*] (DAVI)
STDV	Start Tank Discharge Valve (KSC)
STDVG	Stern Diving
STDW	Standard Deviation Waveform [*Physics*]
STDWN	Stand Down (MCD)
STDY	Saturday
STDY	Steady (MSA)
STDZN	Standardization (AABC)
STE	Sainte [*French*] (EY)
Ste	Sainte (WDAA)
STE	Scholars for Teaching Excellence (DMAA)
STE	Segment Table Entry [*Computer science*] (MDG)
STE	Self-Trapped Exciton [*Physical chemistry*]
STE	Semitool Europe Ltd. [*British ICAO designator*] (FAAC)
STE	Service Technique Externe (IAA)
STE	Shield Test Experiment [*Nuclear energy*] (NRCH)
STE	Shift Technical Engineer [*Nuclear energy*] (NRCH)
STE	Signalling Terminal Equipment [*Telecommunications*] (OSI)
STE	[*The*] Simplified Test Equipment [*Army*] (INF)
STE	Single Threshold Element [*Computer science*] (IAA)
Ste	Societe [*Company*] [*French Business term*]
STE	Society of Telecom Executives [*Trade union*] [*British*]
STE	Society of Telecommunications Executives (NITA)
STE	Society of Test Engineers [*British*] (DBA)
STE	Society of Tractor Engineers [*Later, SAE*]
STE	Spacecraft Test Engineering [*NASA*] (KSC)
STE	Spanning Tree Explorer [*Computer science*] (DDC)
STE	Span Terminating Equipment [*Telecommunications*] (TEL)
STE	Special Temporary Enlistment [*Coast Guard*]
STE	Special Test Equipment
STE	Special-Type Ellipsometer
STE	Specific Temperature Excursion
STE	Standard Terminal Equipment [*Computer science*] (HGAA)
STE	Star Tracker Electronics [*Apollo*] [*NASA*]
STE	Station Test Equipment [*Deep Space Instrumentation Facility, NASA*]
STE	Statute
STE	Stelco, Inc. [*Toronto Stock Exchange symbol Vancouver Stock Exchange symbol*]

STE .... Stepanavan [*Former USSR Seismograph station code, US Geological Survey Closed*] (SEIS)
Ste .... Stephanus Provincialis [*Flourished, 1290-97*] [*Authority cited in pre-1607 legal work*] (DSA)
Ste .... Stephanus Tornacensis [*Deceased, 1203*] [*Authority cited in pre-1607 legal work*] (DSA)
STE .... STERIS Corp. [*NYSE symbol*]
STE .... Stet Societa Finaziaria Telefonica PA [*NYSE symbol*] (SAG)
STE .... STET-Societa Fin Tel Ord ADS [*NYSE symbol*] (TTSB)
STE .... Stevens Point [*Wisconsin*] [*Airport symbol Obsolete*] (OAG)
STE .... Stockton Terminal & Eastern Railroad [*AAR code*]
STE .... Stop Transfer Effector [*Genetics*]
STE .... Suitability Test Evaluation (AAG)
STE .... Suite
Ste .... Suite (TBD)
STE .... Supergroup Translation Equipment
STE .... Support Test Equipment (MCD)
STE .... Syrian Telecommunications Establishment [*Syrian Arab Republic*] (TSSD)
STE .... System Test and Evaluation
STE .... System Test Engineer [*NASA*] (NASA)
STE .... System Timing Element (ECII)
STE .... System Training Exercise (SAA)
STEA .... Short-Term Emergency Assistance
STE.A .... Stelco Inc.'A' [*TS symbol*] (TTSB)
STE A .... STET-Societa Fin Tele Svg ADS [*NYSE symbol*] (TTSB)
STEA .... Surveyor Test Equipment Assembly
STEA .... System Test, Evaluation, and Assembly
STEADY .... Simulation Tables - Environment and Dynamic (SAA)
STEAG .... Steinkohlen-Elektrizitaet AG [*West Germany*]
STEAM .... Department of Science, Technology, Energy, and Materials [*Proposed Cabinet department*]
STEAM .... Schema Tuning, Evaluation, and Analytical Model (PDAA)
STEAM .... Sensor Technology as Applied to the Marine Corps
STEAM .... Standard Towing Equipment for Aircraft Maintenance (MCD)
STEAM .... Stimulated Echo Acquisition Mode [*Medicine*] (DMAA)
STEAM .... Stochastic Evolutionary Adoption Model (PDAA)
STEAM .... Streptonigrin, Thioguanine, Endoxan [*Cyclophosphamide*], Actinomycin, Mitomycin C [*Antineoplastic drug regimen*]
STEAP .... Simulated Trajectories Error Analysis Program [*NASA*]
Stearns RA .... Stearn's Real Actions [*A publication*] (DLA)
Stearns Real Act .... Stearn's Real Actions [*A publication*] (DLA)
SteArt .... State of the Art, Inc. [*Associated Press*] (SAG)
steat .... Steatite (VRA)
STEC .... Serv-Tech, Inc. [*NASDAQ symbol*] (NQ)
STEC .... Solar Thermal Electric Conversation (MCD)
STEC .... Surface Treatment Enhancement Council [*Metallurgy*]
STEC .... Syndicat des Travailleurs de l'Energie et de la Chimie [*Energy and Chemical Workers Union - ECWU*] [*Canada*]
St Eccl Cas .... Stillingfleet's English Ecclesiastical Cases [*A publication*] (DLA)
Stecher Agency & Partnership .... Stecher's Cases on Agency and Partnership [*A publication*] (DLA)
SteckVn .... Steck-Vaughn Publishing Corp. [*Associated Press*] (SAG)
STECR .... Ships Tactical Environmental Control Receiver
STECS .... Software Technology and Engineering Center Staff [*Social Security Administration*]
STED .... Science, Technology, and Economic Development
STED .... Science Technology and Education Division [*British Council*] (AIE)
STED .... Solar Turboelectric Drive (IAA)
STED .... Standard Technical Equipment Development Division [*National Security Agen cy*] [*Obsolete*]
STEDBAC .... Stearyldimethylbenzylammonium Chloride [*Organic chemistry*]
STEDI .... Space Thrust Evolution and Disposal Investigation [*Air Force*]
STEDI .... Student Explorer Demonstration Initiative [*NASA*]
STEDMIS .... Ships Technical Data Management Information System [*Navy*]
STEDMIS .... Standard Technical Data Management Information System (CAAL)
St Edward's U .... St. Edward's University (GAGS)
STEEG .... Scanned Topographic Electroencephalograph
STEEL .... Simulation Test Environment to Evaluate Team Load (SAA)
STEELFACTS .... Materials Database Steel and Iron [*German Iron and Steel Engineers Association*] [*Ceased operation*] [*Information service or system*] (IID)
SteelTch .... Steel Technologies, Inc. [*Associated Press*] (SAG)
Steenth .... Sixteenth [*Stock and commodity price quotes*]
STEEP .... Safety Training for the Execution of Emergency Procedures [*NASA*]
STEEP .... Shock Two-Dimensional Eulerian Elastic Plastic [*Computer code*]
STEEP .... Solution to Environmental and Economic Problems
Steer PL .... Steer on Parish Law [*6th ed.*] [*1899*] [*A publication*] (DLA)
STEG .... Staatliche Gesellschaft zur Erfassung von Ruestungsgut [*German Public Corporation for the Collection and Distribution of War Materials*]
STEG .... Supersonic Transport Evaluation Group
STEI .... Stewart Enterprises'A' [*NASDAQ symbol*] (TTSB)
STEI .... Stewart Enterprises, Inc. [*NASDAQ symbol*] (SPSG)
STE/ICE .... Simplified Test Equipment for Internal Combustion Engines (RDA)
STE/ICE .... Standard Test Equipment / Internal Combustion Engine
STE/ICEPM .... Simplified Test Equipment for Internal Combustion Engine Powered Material (MCD)
STEIN .... System Test Environment Input
S Teind .... Shaw's Scotch Teind [*Tithe*] Cases [*A publication*] (DLA)
SteinMrt .... Stein Mart, Inc. [*Associated Press*] (SAG)
STEK .... Steck-Vaughn Publishing [*NASDAQ symbol*] (TTSB)
STEK .... Steck-Vaughn Publishing Corp. [*NASDAQ symbol*] (SAG)
STEL .... SA Holdings [*NASDAQ symbol*] (SAG)
STEL .... SA Telecommunications [*NASDAQ symbol*] (TTSB)

STEL .... SA Telecommunications, Inc. [*NASDAQ symbol*] (SAG)
STEL .... Short-Term Exposure Limit [*Environmental chemistry*]
STEL .... Society of Telegraphic Engineers [*British*]
STEL .... Structure Tests, English Language [*Educational test*]
STEL .... Studenta Tutmonda Esperantista Liga [*World League of Esperanto-Speaking Students*]
STELCO .... Steel Co. of Canada
STELLA .... Satellite Transmission Experiment Linking Laboratories [*European Space Agency*]
STELLA .... Structural Thinking Experiential Learning Laboratory with Animation [*Software*]
STELLA .... System Ten European Language Ledger Accounting (PDAA)
STELLAR .... Star Tracker for Economical Long Life Attitude Reference [*NASA*]
STEM .... Scanning Transmission Electron Microscope
STEM .... Scanning Transmission Electron Microscopy
STEM .... Science and Technology Employment [*Longman Cartermill Ltd.*] [*Scotland*] [*Information service or system*] (CRD)
STEM .... Science, Technology and Mathematics [*Adult Literacy Project*] [*Australia*]
STEM .... SEABEE Tactical Equipment Management [*Navy*]
STEM .... Searching Together Educational Ministries (EA)
STEM .... Self-Storing Tubular Extensionable Member (IAA)
STEM .... Shaped Tube Electrolytic Machining [*GE*]
STEM .... Shoplifters Take Everybody's Money
STEM .... Short-Term Energy Monitoring [*Colorado State University*]
STEM .... Situated Atop an Extendable Mast (SAA)
STEM .... Society of Teachers of Emergency Medicine (EA)
STEM .... Socio-Technological-Economic-Military [*DoD*]
STEM .... Solar-Terrestrial Environment Model [*to predict the terrestrial effects of solar events*]
STEM .... Special Technical and Economic Mission
STEM .... Special Telemetry Equipped Missile
STEM .... Statistically-Tensioned Extension Mast (DNAB)
STEM .... Stay Time Extension Module [*NASA*]
STEM .... Stellar Tracker Evaluation Missile
STEM .... Storable Tubular Extendable Member
STEM .... Systems for Tools and Equipment Management [*Military*] (AFIT)
STEM .... Systems Training and Exercise Module (MCD)
STEM .... System Test Equipment Mission [*NASA*] (KSC)
STEMBOR .... Supervision Through Educational Management by Objectives and Results (EDAC)
STEMFAB .... Storable Tubular Extendable Member Fabrication
STEMPRA .... Science, Technology, Engineering, Medicine Public Relations Association [*Great Britain*]
STEMS .... Small Terminal Evasive Missile System (MCD)
STEMS .... Society to Encourage Miniskirts [*New York group opposing below-the-knee fashions introduced in 1970*]
STEMS .... Structural Tracking and Engine Monitoring System (MCD)
STEM-TEM .... Scanning Transmission Electron Microscopy - Transmission Electron Microscopy
STEN .... Sheppard-Turpin-England [*Machine carbine codesigned by Sheppard and Turpin*]
STEN .... Stencil
STEN .... Stenographer
Sten .... Submachine Gun [*Named after Sheppard, Turpin and England, its Inventors*] (BARN)
STENCH .... Society to Exterminate Neo-Communist Harbingers
ST-ENDOR .... Special Triple-Electron Nuclear Double Resonance [*Spectroscopy*]
STENO .... Stenographer (MUGU)
STENS .... Standard Terrestrial Navigation System (MCD)
STENS .... STD Terrestrial Navigation System (MCD)
Stenton .... Stenton. Rolls of the Justices in Eyre [*A publication*] (ILCA)
Stenton G .... Rolls of the Justices in Eyre for Gloucestershire, Worcestershire, and Staffordshire [*A publication*] (ILCA)
Stenton Y .... Rolls of the Justices in Eyre in Yorkshire [*A publication*] (ILCA)
STEO .... Special Test Equipment Order (MCD)
STEP .... Safeguard Test and Evaluation Program [*Army*] (AABC)
STEP .... Safety Test Engineering Program [*AEC*]
STEP .... Sales Tax Exemption Processing System [*Software*]
STEP .... School to Employment Program
STEP .... Science and Technology for Environmental Protection Program [*Australia*]
STEP .... Scientific and Technical Exploitation Program (AFM)
STEP .... Selective Traffic Enforcement Program [*Department of Transportation*]
STEP .... Self-Teaching Exportable Package
STEP .... Sensitivity Temperature Error Program (MCD)
STEP .... Sequentially Timed Events Plotting [*In publication title, "Investigating Accidents with STEP"*] [*Marcel Decker, Inc.*]
STEP .... Sequentially Timed Events Process [*Engineering*]
STEP .... Sequential Test of Educational Programs (DMAA)
STEP .... Sequential Tests of Educational Progress [*of ETS; given in 10th and 12th grades*]
STEP .... Service Technician Education Program
STEP .... Service Test and Evaluation Program [*FAA*] (TAG)
STEP .... Shell Technology Enterprise Programme [*British*]
STEP .... Ship Type Electronics Plan [*Navy*] (NG)
STEP .... Short Term Enrichment Program [*of US Information Agency*]
STEP .... Simple Transition to Economical Processing (IEEE)
STEP .... Simple Transition to Electronic Processing
STEP .... Simulated Tracking Evaluation Program (SAA)
STEP .... Software T & E Panel (RDA)
STEP .... Software Test and Evaluation Process [*DoD*]
STEP .... Solar-Terrestrial Energy Program

STEP........... Solutions to Employment Problems [*A program of National Association of Manufacturers*]
STEP........... Space Technology Experiments Platform
STEP........... Space Terminal Evaluation Program
STEP........... Space Thermoelectric Power (IAA)
STEP........... Special Temporary Employment Program (WDAA)
STEP........... Special Temporary Employment Programme (AIE)
STEP........... Special Training Enlistment Program
STEP........... Special Training Equipment Program Document (AFIT)
STEP........... Specificaiton Technology Evaluation Program (MHDI)
STEP........... Staff Training Extramural Programs [*National Institutes of Health*]
STEP........... Standard Equipment Practice (IAA)
STEP........... Standard for the Exchange of Product Data [*Materials science*]
STEP........... Standard Tape Executive Package [*or Program*] [*NCR Corp.*]
STEP........... Standard Tape Executive System (NITA)
STEP........... Standard Terminal Program [*Computer science*] (IEEE)
STEP........... Standard Test Equipment Procedure (NG)
STEP........... Stand for Exchange of Product Model Data [*Computer-assisted engineering*]
STEP........... State Technology Extension Program [*National Institute of Standards and Technology*]
STEP........... Statistical Trajectory Estimation Program [*NASA*]
STEP........... Strategies for Today's Environmental Partnership
STEP........... Stratosphere-Troposphere Exchange Project [*NASA*]
STEP........... Stripes for Exceptional Performers [*Air Force*] (DOMA)
STEP........... Structures Technology Experiments Platform (MCD)
STEP........... Student Education Program
STEP........... Students toward Environmental Participation [*UNESCO and National Park Service*]
STEP........... Student Transfer Education Plan [*National Urban League*] [*Defunct*]
STEP........... Summer Training Employment Program (MCD)
STEP........... Supervisory Tape Executive Program [*Computer science*]
STEP........... Supplemental Training and Employment Program (OICC)
STEP........... Systematic Test and Evaluation Process (CIST)
STEP........... Systematic Training for Effective Parenting
STEP........... System for Testing Evaluation of Potential [*Employee evaluation software*] [*London House, Inc.*]
STEP........... Systems Test Equipment Program (MCD)
Stepan......... Stephan Co. [*Associated Press*] (SAG)
STEPCLB...... StepClimb (GAVI)
Steph........... Stephanus Pragensis [*Flourished, 14th century*] [*Authority cited in pre-1607 legal work*] (DSA)
Steph........... Stephanus Tornacensis [*Deceased, 1203*] [*Authority cited in pre-1607 legal work*] (DSA)
Steph........... Stephens' Supreme Court Decisions [*1774-1923*] [*Jamaica*] [*A publication*] (DLA)
Stepha Bertrand... Stephanus Bertrandus [*Flourished, 16th century*] [*Authority cited in pre-1607 legal work*] (DSA)
Stephan....... Stephan Co. [*Associated Press*] (SAG)
Steph Cl...... Stephens on Clergy [*1848*] [*A publication*] (DLA)
Steph Com... Stephen's Commentaries on the Laws of England [*A publication*] (DLA)
Steph Comm... Stephen's Commentaries on the Laws of England [*A publication*] (DLA)
Steph Const... Stephens on the English Constitution [*A publication*] (DLA)
Steph Cr...... Stephen's Digest of the Criminal Law [*A publication*] (DLA)
Steph Crim Dig... Stephen's Digest of the Criminal Law [*A publication*] (DLA)
Steph Cr L... Stephen's General View of the Criminal Law [*9 eds.*] [*1877-1950*] [*A publication*] (DLA)
Steph Cr Law... Stephen's General View of the Criminal Law [*A publication*] (DLA)
Steph Dig.... Stephen's Digest, New Brunswick Reports [*A publication*] (DLA)
Steph Dig Cr L... Stephen's Digest of the Criminal Law [*A publication*] (DLA)
Steph Dig Cr Law... Stephen's Digest of the Criminal Law [*A publication*] (DLA)
Steph Dig Ev... Stephen's Digest of the Law of Evidence [*A publication*] (DLA)
Steph Elect... Stephens on Elections [*1840*] [*A publication*] (DLA)
Stephen HCL... Stephen's History of Criminal Law [*A publication*] (DLA)
Stephens..... Supreme Court Decisions, by J. E. R. Stephens [*A publication*] (DLA)
Steph Ev...... Stephen's Digest of the Law of Evidence [*A publication*] (DLA)
Steph Gen View... Stephen's General View of the Criminal Law [*2nd ed.*] [*1890*] [*A publication*] (DLA)
Steph J St Comp... Steph's Joint-Stock Companies in Canada [*A publication*] (DLA)
Steph Lect... Stephen's Lectures on the History of France [*A publication*] (DLA)
Steph NP..... Stephen's Law of Nisi Prius [*A publication*] (DLA)
Steph Pl...... Stephen on Pleading [*A publication*] (DLA)
Steph Proc... Stephens on Procurations [*A publication*] (DLA)
Steph Slav... Stephens on Slavery [*A publication*] (DLA)
STEPO......... Self-Contained, Toxic Environment, Protective Outfit [*Army*] (INF)
STEPP.......... Society of Teachers in Education of Professional Photography (EA)
STEPPS........ Some Tools for Evaluating Parallel Programs [*Computer science*] (MHDI)
STEPR......... Saturation Transfer Electron Paramagnetic Resonance [*Physics*]
STEPS.......... School-Leavers' Training and Employment Preparation Scheme [*New Zealand Labor Department*] (BARN)
STEPS.......... Science and Technology Evaluation and Prioritization System [*Program*] (RDA)
STEPS.......... Ships Technical Publication System [*Navy*]
STEPS.......... Solar Thermionic Electrical Power System
STEPS.......... Solar Thermionic Electrical Propulsion System (IAA)
STEPS.......... Staff Training Exercise for Programming Supervisor (SAA)
STEPS.......... Stored Thermal Energy Propulsion System
STEPS.......... Strategy Evaluator and Planning-Production System (PDAA)
STEPS.......... Surviving Today's Experiences and Problems Successfully Curriculum [*West Virginia*] (EDAC)
STEP-W....... Sequential Test of Educational Progress-Writing Test (EDAC)
STER........... Seater
STER........... Steradian
ster............. Stereo (VRA)
STER........... Stereo
STER........... Stereotype
STER........... Stereoview (VRA)
STER........... Sterilize (AABC)
STER........... Sterling
ster............. Sterling (ODBW)
STER........... Sterling Healthcare Group [*NASDAQ symbol*] (SAG)
STER........... Successively Truncated Expectation of the Reciprocal [*Statistics*]
STER........... System Training Equipment Requirement
Stereo......... Solar-Terrestrial Relations Observatory [*NASA mission*]
Stereo......... Stereogram [*Radiology*] (DAVI)
STEREO....... Stereophonic (MSA)
Stereo......... Stereo Review [*A publication*] (BRI)
STEREO....... Stereoscope [*or Stereoscopic*]
STEREO....... Stereotype [*Refers to old news*] [*Slang*] (DSUE)
STERF......... Special Test Equipment Repair Facility
SterileC....... Sterile Concepts Holdings, Inc. [*Associated Press*] (SAG)
Steris.......... Steris Corp. [*Associated Press*] (SAG)
STERL......... Sterling (ADA)
SterlEl......... Sterling Electronics Corp. [*Associated Press*] (SAG)
SterlHlth..... Sterling Healthcare Group [*Associated Press*] (SAG)
SterlHous.... Sterling House Corp. [*Associated Press*] (SAG)
SterlHs........ Sterling House Corp. [*Associated Press*] (SAG)
SterlSft........ Sterling Software, Inc. [*Associated Press*] (SAG)
STERNLITE... Sterner Lighting Systems (EFIS)
STERNUT..... Sternutamentum [*Snuff*] [*Pharmacy*]
SterRecv...... Sterile Recoveries, Inc. [*Associated Press*] (SAG)
STES............ Solar Thermal Energy System
STESD......... Software Tool for Evaluating System Designs [*Computer science*] (MHDI)
STESS.......... Subject's Treatment Emergent Symptom Scale [*Medicine*] (DMAA)
S (Test)....... Suitability Test [*Military*] (CAAL)
STESTG........ Space Test Group [*Military*]
STE-T.......... Simplified Test Equipment - Transitional [*Army*]
STET........... Specialized Technique for Efficient Typesetting
STET........... Steward, Technical [*Marine Corps*]
STET........... Submaximal Treadmill Exercise Test (AAMN)
STET........... System Test Experiments Tape
STETF.......... Solar Total Energy Test Facility [*Energy Research and Development Administration*]
STETS.......... Solar-Terrestrial Energy Transfer Studies [*Meteorology*]
Stetson U..... Stetson University (GAGS)
STEV........... Spinach Temperate Virus [*Plant pathology*]
STEV........... Stevedore
Stev & Ben Ins... Stevens and Benecke on Insurance [*A publication*] (DLA)
Stev & G...... Stevens and Graham's Reports [*98-139 Georgia*] [*A publication*] (DLA)
Stev Arb...... Stevens on Arbitration [*2nd ed.*] [*1835*] [*A publication*] (DLA)
Stev Av........ Stevens on Average [*5th ed.*] [*1835*] [*A publication*] (DLA)
Stev Dig...... Stevens' New Brunswick Digest [*A publication*] (DLA)
STEVE.......... Space Tool for Extravehicular Emergencies
Stevens & G... Stevens and Graham's Reports [*98-139 Georgia*] [*A publication*] (DLA)
Stevens Inst Tech... Stevens Institute of Technology (GAGS)
StevInt......... Stevens International, Inc. [*Associated Press*] (SAG)
STEVS.......... Spartan Tactical Equipment Verification Site [*Missiles*] (MCD)
STEVS.......... Subsystem Tactical Equipment Verification Site
Stew............ Stewart's Alabama Reports [*1827-31*] [*A publication*] (DLA)
Stew............ Stewart's Equity Reports [*28-45 New Jersey*] [*A publication*] (DLA)
Stew............ Stewart's Nova Scotia Admiralty Reports [*A publication*] (DLA)
Stew............ Stewart's Reports [*1-10 South Dakota*] [*A publication*] (DLA)
Stew Adm.... Stewart's Nova Scotia Vice-Admiralty Reports [*1803-13*] [*A publication*] (DLA)
Stew Admr... Stewart's Nova Scotia Admiralty Reports [*A publication*] (DLA)
Stew (Ala)... Stewart's Alabama Reports [*A publication*] (DLA)
Stew & P..... Stewart and Porter's Alabama Supreme Court Reports [*1831-34*] [*A publication*] (DLA)
Stew and Porter... Stewart and Porter's Alabama Reports [*A publication*] (DLA)
Stew & P Rep... Stewart and Porter's Alabama Reports [*A publication*] (DLA)
Stew Ans..... Stewart's Answers to Dirleton's Doubts [*2 eds.*] [*1715, 1762 Scotland*] [*A publication*] (DLA)
Stewart........ Stewart's Alabama Reports [*1827-31*] [*A publication*] (DLA)
Stewart........ Stewart's Equity Reports [*28-45 New Jersey*] [*A publication*] (DLA)
Stewart........ Stewart's Nova Scotia Admiralty Reports [*A publication*] (DLA)
Stewart........ Stewart's Reports [*1-10 South Dakota*] [*A publication*] (DLA)
Stewart (Ala)... Stewart's Alabama Reports [*A publication*] (DLA)
Stewart-Brown... Stewart-Brown's Lancashire and Cheshire Cases in the Court of Star Chamber [*A publication*] (DLA)
Stewart R.... Stewart's Alabama Reports [*A publication*] (DLA)
Stew Dig...... Stewart's Digest of Decisions of Law and Equity [*New Jersey*] [*A publication*] (ILCA)
Stew Eq....... Stewart's Equity Reports [*28-45 New Jersey*] [*A publication*] (DLA)
StewInfo...... Stewart Information Services [*Associated Press*] (SAG)
Stew N Sc... Stewart's Nova Scotia Admiralty Reports [*A publication*] (DLA)
STEWS......... Shipboard Tactical Electronic Warfare System [*Navy*]
STEWS......... Standardized Test of Essential Writing Skills (EDAC)
Stewt Rep.... Stewart's Alabama Reports [*A publication*] (DLA)
Stew VA....... Stewart's Nova Scotia Vice-Admiralty Reports [*A publication*] (DLA)
STE-X.......... Simplified Test Equipment-Expandable [*Army*] (RDA)
STEX........... Statute Expired [*IRS*]
St Ex............ Stock Exchange (WDAA)
STeZ............ South Temperate Zone

STF	Safety Test Facility [*Nuclear energy*]
STF	Satellite Tracking Facility [*Air Force*]
STF	S-Band Temperature Fahrenheit
STF	S-Band Transmit Filter
STF	Serum Thymus Factor (DB)
STF	Service Tabulating Form (AAG)
STF	Setif [*Algeria*] [*Airport symbol*] (AD)
STF	SFT-Sudanese Flight [*ICAO designator*] (FAAC)
STF	Shield Test Facility [*Nuclear energy*] (GFGA)
STF	Shock-Induced Thermal Fragmentation [*Astrophysics*]
STF	Short Title File (NITA)
STF	Signal Tracking Filter
STF	Signal Transducing Factor [*Biochemistry*]
STF	Snap Shield Test Facility Reactor [*Nuclear energy*] (IAA)
STF	Sociedad Colombiana de Transporte Ferroviario SA [*Public rail services*] (EY)
STF	Software Test Facility [*NASA*] (MCD)
STF	Soil Transport and Fate Database and Model Management System [*Environmental Protection Agency*] (AEPA)
STF	Spacecraft Test Facility
STF	Space Track Facility
STF	Specialized Treatment Facility [*Medicine*] (MEDA)
STF	Special Task Force [*Army*]
STF	Special Technical Factors (MCD)
STF	Special Tube Feeding [*Medicine*]
STF	Spin Test Facility [*NASA*]
STF	Staff (AFM)
STF	Stamford Ukrainian [*Diocesan abbreviation*] [*Connecticut*] (TOCD)
STF	Standardized Test of Fitness [*Canadian Association of Sports Sciences*]
STF	Stanford Resources Ltd. [*Toronto Stock Exchange symbol*]
St F	Starch-Free [*Pharmacy*]
STF	Starkville, MS [*Location identifier FAA*] (FAAL)
STF	Static Test Facility (KSC)
STF	Stereochemistry Fragment (NITA)
stf	Stiff [*Quality of the bottom*] [*Nautical charts*]
STF	Stirred-Tank Fermentors [*Chemical engineering*]
STF	Structural Fatigue Test (MCD)
STF	Subjective Transfer Function (MCD)
STF	Subject to Finance (ADA)
STF	Summary Tape File [*Bureau of the Census*] (GFGA)
STF	Supervisory Time Frame
STF	Systemic Transformation Facility [*Former USSR*] (ECON)
STF	Systems Technology Forum [*Fairfax, VA*] [*Telecommunications*] (TSSD)
STF	System Test Facility
STFA	Step-Father (DAVI)
STFAS	Support to Total Force Analysis [*TRADOC*] (MCD)
STFC	State Auto Financial [*NASDAQ symbol*] (TTSB)
STFC	State Auto Financial Corp. [*NASDAQ symbol*] (SPSG)
STF DDC	System Test Facility Data Display Control (SAA)
ST-FeSv	Snyder-Thielen Feline Sarcoma Virus [*Veterinary medicine*] (MEDA)
STFF	Safeguard Tactical Field Force [*Army*] (AABC)
STFF	Stuff
STFG	Staffing Guides [*Army*] (AABC)
STFG	Stuffing (MSA)
STFM	Society of Teachers of Family Medicine (EA)
STFM	Stretcher Form [*Tool*] (AAG)
StFncl	State Financial Services Corp. [*Associated Press*] (SAG)
STFR	Saint Francis Capital Corp. [*NASDAQ symbol*] (SAG)
STFR	St. Francis Capital [*NASDAQ symbol*] (TTSB)
StFrancis	Saint Francis Capital Corp. [*Associated Press*] (SAG)
St Francis C (Ind)	St. Francis College (Indiana) (GAGS)
St Francis C (Penn)	St. Francis College (Pennsylvania) (GAGS)
STFRM	Stratiform [*NWS*] (FAAC)
STFSGT	Staff Sergeant [*Marine Corps*]
STFT	Short-Time Fourier Transform (DMAA)
STFT	Stray Field Test (NVT)
STG	Saint George Island [*Alaska*] [*Airport symbol*] (OAG)
STG	Santiago [*Brazil*] [*Airport symbol*] (AD)
STG	Satellite Terminal Guidance
Stg	Sea-Tangle [*Nautical charts*]
STG	Seating [*Technical drawings*]
STG	Sedalia-Marshall-Booville Stage Line, Inc. [*ICAO designator*] (FAAC)
STG	Short-Term Goal (DAVI)
STG	SONAR Technician, Ground [*Navy rating*] (DNAB)
STG	Souther Gold Resources [*Vancouver Stock Exchange symbol*]
STG	Space Task Group [*Later, Manned Spacecraft Center*] [*NASA*]
STG	Space Telescope Guidance [*NASA*]
STG	Special Technology Group [*National Technical Information Service*] (MCD)
STG	Special Training Group [*Military*]
STG	Split Thickness Graft [*Medicine*]
STG	Stage (NAKS)
STG	Staging (AABC)
STG	Standing [*Numismatics*]
STG	Starting (MSA)
STG	Steering Task Group
STG	Sterling
stg	Sterling (ODBW)
Stg	Sterling (EBF)
STG	Stomatogastric Ganglion [*Neuroanatomy*]
STG	Storage
Stg	Storage (AAGC)
STG	Storage Properties, Inc. [*AMEX symbol*] (SAG)
STG	Storage Triacylglycerol [*Biochemistry*]
STG	Strathgordon [*Tasmania*] [*Seismograph station code, US Geological Survey*] (SEIS)
STG	Study Group [*NATO*]
STG	Sturmgewehr [*Storm Rifle*] [*German military - World War II*]
STGA	Saratoga Brands [*NASDAQ symbol*] (TTSB)
STGA	Saratoga Brands, Inc. [*NASDAQ symbol*] (NQ)
STGA	Scottish Tourist Guides Association (DBA)
STGA	Shrub and Tree Growers of Australia
STGAA	Shade Tobacco Growers Agricultural Association (EA)
STGAR	Staging Area [*Military*]
STGB	Staging Base [*Military*]
StGB	Strafgesetzbuch [*Penal Code*] [*German*]
STGC	Secure Task Group, Common (MCD)
STGE	Stage
STGE	Stage Stores, Inc. [*NASDAQ symbol*] (SAG)
stge	Storage (WDAA)
STGE	Storage
STGEN	Steam Generator
St Ger D & S	St. German's Doctor and Student [*A publication*] (DLA)
StgeStrs	Stage Stores, Inc. [*Associated Press*] (SAG)
STGG	Staging (AAG)
STGHT	Straight
St Gloc	Statute of Gloucester [*First statute to give costs in actions*] [*A publication*] (DLA)
STGP	Subcontract Task Group Procurement
STGR	Stringer (AAG)
STGSA	SONAR Technician, Ground, Seaman Apprentice [*Navy rating*] (DNAB)
STGSN	SONAR Technician, Ground, Seaman [*Navy rating*] (DNAB)
STG/STF	Special Task Group/Special Task Force [*Army*] (MCD)
STGT	Secondary Target [*Military*]
STGT	Stargardt Disease [*Medicine*]
STGWG	State and Tribal Government Working Group (COE)
STH	Satellite to Host [*Telecommunications*] (CIST)
S Th	Scholar in Theology [*British*]
STH	Seton Hall University, South Orange, NJ [*OCLC symbol*] (OCLC)
STH	Short-Term Holiday (MHDB)
STH	Soft tissue Hematoma [*Hematology*] (DAVI)
STH	Somatotrophic [*Growth*] Hormone [*Also, GH, SH*] [*Endocrinology*]
STH	South
STH	Southern Airlines Ltd. [*British ICAO designator*] (FAAC)
STH	Stanhome, Inc. [*NYSE symbol*] (SPSG)
STH	Stoney Hill [*Jamaica*] [*Seismograph station code, US Geological Survey*] (SEIS)
STH	Stray Horse Resources, Inc. [*Vancouver Stock Exchange symbol*]
STH	Student in Theology [*British*]
STh	Subthalamus [*Anatomy*]
STH	Subtotal Hysterectomy [*Medicine*]
STH	Supplemental Thyroid Hormone (DB)
STH	Toronto School of Theology Library, University of Toronto [*UTLAS symbol*]
Sth Afr Rep	South African Republic High Court Reports [*A publication*] (DLA)
SThB	Sacrae Theologiae Baccalaureus [*Bachelor of Sacred Theology*]
SthCoB	Southern Community Bancshares, Inc. [*Associated Press*] (SAG)
SThD	Sacrae Theologiae Doctor [*Doctor of Sacred Theology*]
STHE	Special Tools and Handling Equipment
Sthen	Stheneboea [*of Euripides*] [*Classical studies*] (OCD)
STHEST	Southeast
STHESTN	Southeastern
Sthfst	Southfirst Bancshares, Inc. [*Associated Press*] (SAG)
SthfstB	Southfirst Bancshares, Inc. [*Associated Press*] (SAG)
S ThL	Sacrae Theologiae Lecentiatus [*Licentiate in Sacred Theology*]
StHlGd	Saint Helena Gold Mines Ltd. [*Associated Press*] (SAG)
STHLY	Southerly [*A publication*]
STHM	Scanning Thermal Microscope (AAEL)
STHMPN	Southampton [*England*]
STHN	Southern
Sthn	Southern (TBD)
SthnBnc	Southern Banc Co., Inc. [*Associated Press*] (SAG)
SthnEH	Southern Energy Homes, Inc. [*Associated Press*] (SAG)
SthnEnH	Southern Energy Homes, Inc. [*Associated Press*] (SAG)
StHR	Stress Hypertensive Rats
STHRF	Somatotropin-Releasing Factor (DB)
STHRN	Southern
STHS	Scottish Thoracic Society
STHSD	Southside
SthStrF	South Street Financial Center [*Associated Press*] (SAG)
SthwestB	Southwest Banks, Inc. [*Associated Press*] (SAG)
STHWST	Southwest
STHWSTN	Southwestern
STI	Mountain Home, ID [*Location identifier FAA*] (FAAL)
STI	Santiago [*Dominican Republic*] [*Airport symbol*] (OAG)
STI	Saskatoon Technical Institute [*UTLAS symbol*]
STI	Saxton Industries [*Vancouver Stock Exchange symbol*]
STI	Scientific and Technical Information [*System*] [*Canada*]
STI	Scientific and Technical Information [*Facility*] [*NASA*]
STI	Screw Thread Insert
STI	Self-Test Input [*Electronics*]
STI	Serum Trypsin Inhibitor [*Serology*]
STI	Server Technology, Inc. [*Information service or system*] (IID)
STI	Service Tools Institute [*Later, HTI*] (EA)
STI	Sexually-Transmitted Infection [*Medicine*] (DI)
STI	Shallow Trench Isolation (AAEL)
STI	Shear Thinning Index (PDAA)

STI.............	Shielding Technologies Inc.
STI.............	Short-Term Integration (CAAL)
STI.............	Silicon Target Intensifier
STI.............	Single Tooth Indexer
STI.............	Skin Test Index [Chemical medicine]
STI.............	Small Towns Institute (EA)
STI.............	Societa Servizi Trasporti [Italy] [FAA designator] (FAAC)
STI.............	Software Tool Information Database [Air Force Systems Command] [Information service or system] (CRD)
STI.............	Soybean Trypsin Inhibition [Biochemistry]
STI.............	Space Technology, Inc. (MCD)
STI.............	Special Test Instructions (SAA)
STI.............	Specifications Technology, Inc.
STI.............	Speech Transmission Index
STI.............	Standard Technical Institute (SSD)
STI.............	Star Valley [Idaho] [Seismograph station code, US Geological Survey] (SEIS)
STI.............	State Technical Institute
STI.............	Steel Tank Institute (EA)
STI.............	Steel Tube Institute
STI.............	Steel Tube Institute of North America (NTPA)
STI.............	Stem Tolerance Index [Botany]
sti.............	Stich (VRA)
STI.............	Stilbite [A zeolite]
Sti.............	Stinson [Record label]
STI.............	Store Indicators (SAA)
STI.............	Straight Times Index [Singapore Stock Exchange]
STI.............	St. Thomas Institute [Research center] (RCD)
STI.............	SunTrust Banks [NYSE symbol] (TTSB)
STI.............	SunTrust Banks, Inc. [NYSE symbol] (SPSG)
STI.............	Surface Targets of Interest (MCD)
STI.............	Surveillance Test Interval [Environmental science] (COE)
STI.............	Survive Tomorrow, Inc. [Commercial firm] (EA)
STI.............	Systems Technology Inc.
STI.............	Systolic Time Interval [Cardiology]
STIA.............	Satellite Television Industry Association [Formerly, SPACE] (NTCM)
STIA.............	Scientific, Technological, and International Affairs Directorate [National Science Foundation]
STIAC.............	Science Technology and Innovation Advisory Council [Ireland]
STIAP.............	Standard Instrument Approach [RADAR] [Aviation]
STIB.............	Stimulus Train-Induced Bursting [Neuroscience]
STIB.............	Stratosphere-Troposphere Interactions and the Biosphere (EERA)
STIC.............	Scientific and Technical Intelligence Center [DoD]
STIC.............	SEAL [Sea, Air, Land] Tactical Insertion Craft [Navy] (DOMA)
STIC.............	Security Threat Intelligence Cell (LAIN)
STIC.............	Serum Trypsin Inhibition Capacity (DB)
STIC.............	Solid-State Transducer Intercompartmental Catheter [Instrumentation]
STIC.............	Space Technical Information Control (MCD)
STIC.............	Space Toy Information Center [Defunct] (EA)
STICAP.............	Stiff Circuit Analysis Program [Computer science]
STICEC.............	Special Travel Industry Council on Energy Conservation
ST/ICERD.............	Suntory Toyota International Centre for Economics and Related Disciplines [London School of Economics and Political Science] [British] (CB)
Stich.............	Stichus [of Plautus] [Classical studies] (OCD)
STICO.............	Standard Interpretation and Compilation System (IAA)
STICTION.............	Static Friction
STID.............	Scientific and Technical Information Dissemination [NASA]
STID.............	Scientific and Technical Information Division [NASA] (IEEE)
STID.............	Ship's Test and Inspection Department [Navy] (DNAB)
STIDAS.............	Speech Transmission Index Device [Using] Artificial Signals
STIDC.............	Scientific and Technical Information and Documentation Committee (CIST)
STIF.............	Scientific and Technical Information Facility [NASA]
STIF.............	Search Track Intermediate Frequency [Military]
STIF.............	Short-Term Irradiation Facility [Nuclear energy] (NRCH)
STIF.............	Short-Term Issuance Facility [Finance]
STIF.............	Spectral Transmission Interference Filter
STIF.............	Stiffener [Civil engineering]
STIFC.............	Space Track Interim Fire Control
Stifel.............	Stifel Financial Corp. [Associated Press] (SAG)
STIFS.............	Short-Term Integrated Forecasting System [Department of Energy] (GFGA)
STIG.............	Steam-Injected Gas Turbine
STII.............	Science and Technology Information Institute [Information service or system] (IID)
STII.............	Stanford Telecommun [NASDAQ symbol] (TTSB)
STII.............	Stanford Telecommunications, Inc. [NASDAQ symbol] (NQ)
STIL.............	Short-Term Inhalation Limits [of air pollutants]
STIL.............	Software Test and Integration Laboratory [NASA] (NASA)
STIL.............	Statistical Interpretive Language [Computer science] (MDG)
Stil.............	Stillingfleet's English Ecclesiastical Cases [1702-04] [A publication] (DLA)
STILE.............	Students' and Teachers' Integrated Learning Environment (AIE)
Stiles.............	Stiles' Reports [22-29 Iowa] [A publication] (DLA)
Stiles (IA).............	Stiles' Reports [22-29 Iowa] [A publication] (DLA)
STILLAT.............	Stillatim [By Drops or In Small Quantities] [Pharmacy]
STILLB.............	Stillborn [Medicine]
Still Ecc Law.............	Stillingfleet's Discourse on Ecclesiastical Law [A publication] (DLA)
Still Eccl Cas.............	Stillingfleet's English Ecclesiastical Cases [A publication] (DLA)
StillwtrM.............	Stillwater Mining Co. [Associated Press] (SAG)
STILO.............	Scientific and Technical Intelligence Liaison Officer (MCD)
STILS.............	Stinger Launch Simulator (MCD)
STIM.............	Scanning Transmission Ion Microscopy
STIM.............	Sensitivity Training Impact Model

STIM.............	Stimsonite Corp. [NASDAQ symbol] (SAG)
STIM.............	Stimulant (DSUE)
STIM.............	Stimulating (ROG)
stim.............	Stimulus
STIM.............	Subsystem: Short-Term Integrating Model [Department of Energy] (GFGA)
S Times.............	Sunday Times [A publication]
Stim Gloss.............	Stimson's Law Glossary [A publication] (DLA)
Stim Law Gloss.............	Stimson's Law Glossary [A publication] (DLA)
Stim L Gl.............	Stimson's Law Glossary [A publication] (DLA)
stimn.............	Stimulation (DAVI)
STIMS.............	Scientific and Technical Information Modular System [NASA] (MCD)
Stimson.............	Stimsonite Corp. [Associated Press] (SAG)
Stimson.............	Stimson's Law Glossary [A publication] (DLA)
STIMSUP.............	Stimulant to Sustain Performance (RDA)
STIN.............	Science Teacher Inventory of Need (EDAC)
STIN.............	Scientific and Technical Information Network (COE)
STINA.............	Steel Tube Institute of North America (EA)
STINCOM.............	Scientific and Technical Information and Communication (SAA)
Stiness.............	Stiness' Reports [20-34 Rhode Island] [A publication] (DLA)
STINET.............	Scientific and Technical Information Network [Internet] (AAGC)
STINFO.............	Scientific and Technical Information Office [Army]
STINFO.............	Scientific and Technical Information Officers (NITA)
STINFO.............	Scientific/Technical Information (AAGC)
STING.............	Swift Target Identification Notification Grid (MCD)
STINGER.............	SEABEE Tactically Installed, Navy Generated, Engineer Resources [System] [Navy] (NVT)
STINGS.............	Stellar Inertial Guidance System [Air Force]
St Inst.............	Stair's Institutes [5th ed.] [1832] [A publication] (ILCA)
STIO.............	Scientific and Technical Information Office [NASA]
STIO.............	Store Input-Output [Computer science] (IAA)
STIP.............	Basophilic Stippling [Biochemistry] (DAVI)
STIP.............	Scientific and Technical Information Program (MCD)
STIP.............	Short Term Industrial Paper [Finance]
STIP.............	Skill Training Improvement Program [Department of Labor]
STIP.............	Solar Technical Information Program [Solar Energy Research Institute] [Information service or system] (IID)
STIP.............	Statewide Transportation Improvements Program [MOCD] (TAG)
STIP.............	Stipend [or Stipendiary]
Stip.............	Stipites [Stalk] [Latin]
STIP.............	Stipulation (DAS)
STIP.............	Study of Travelling Interplanetary Phenomena [Meteorology]
STIPE.............	Stipendiary Magistrate [British] (DSUE)
stipe.............	Stipendiary Magistrate [British] (WDAA)
STIPIS.............	Scientific, Technical, Intelligence, and Program Information System [HEW]
STIQ.............	Survival Technology [NASDAQ symbol] (TTSB)
STIQ.............	Survival Technology, Inc. [NASDAQ symbol] (SAG)
STIR.............	Scientific and Technical Intelligence Register (AFM)
STIR.............	Separate Track and Illumination RADAR [Military] (CAAL)
STIR.............	Shield Test and Irradiation Reactor [Nuclear energy]
STIR.............	Short Tau Inversion Recovery [Medicine] (DMAA)
STIR.............	Signal Track and Illuminating RADAR [Canadian Navy]
STIR.............	SNAP [Systems for Nuclear Auxiliary Power] Shield Test Irradiation Reactor
STIR.............	Statistics Indexing and Retrieval Project (NITA)
STIR.............	Stirrup (WGA)
STIR.............	Surplus to Immediate Requirements (ADA)
STIRD.............	SAIL [Shuttle Avionics Integration Laboratory] Test Implementation Requirements Document [NASA] (NASA)
STIRS.............	Self-Training Interpretive Retrieval System
STIS.............	Science and Technology Information System [National Science Foundation]
STIS.............	Scientific & Technical Information Services, Inc. [Information service or system] (IID)
STIS.............	Silicon Target Image Sensor
STIS.............	Space Telescope Imaging Spectrograph
STIS.............	Specialized Textile Information Service
STIS.............	Sumika Technical Information Service, Inc. [Information service or system] (IID)
STISP.............	Science and Technology Information Service for Parliament [British] (IAA)
STI/SS.............	Scientific and Technical Information System and Service (PDAA)
STIT.............	Scientific and Technical Information Team [Army] (GFGA)
STIT.............	Signal Technical Intelligence Team [Army] (AABC)
STIT.............	Simulated Time in Turn (SAA)
STIT.............	Sweet's Technical Information Test [Vocational guidance test]
STIT-CONUS.............	Scientific and Technical Information Team, Continental United States [Army] (AABC)
STIT-EUR.............	Scientific and Technical Information Team, Europe [Army] (AABC)
STIT-FE.............	Scientific and Technical Information Team, Far East [Army] (AABC)
STIV.............	Silicon Target Intensifier Vidicon
StIves.............	Saint Ives Laboratories, Inc. [Associated Press] (SAG)
STIZ.............	Scientific Technologies [NASDAQ symbol] (TTSB)
STIZ.............	Scientific Technology, Inc. [NASDAQ symbol] (NQ)
StiZ.............	Stimmen der Zeit [A publication] (BJA)
STIZ.............	Submarine Transit Identification Zones (NVT)
STJ.............	Saint Joseph College, West Hartford, CT [OCLC symbol] (OCLC)
STJ.............	Saint Jude Medical, Inc. [NYSE symbol] (SAG)
STJ.............	Series Tee Junction
STJ.............	Severn Tunnel Junction [British depot code]
STJ.............	Society of St. Teresa of Jesus (TOCD)
STJ.............	Special Trial Judge [US Tax Court]
STJ.............	St. John's [Newfoundland] [Seismograph station code, US Geological Survey] (SEIS)

STJ	St. Joseph [*Missouri*] [*Airport symbol*] (AD)
STJ	St. Joseph, MO [*Location identifier FAA*] (FAAL)
StJ	St. Joseph Railway
STJ	Subtalar Joint [*Anatomy*] (DAVI)
STJ	Subtropical Jet Stream (ADA)
STJ	Superconducting Tunnel Junction [*Physics*]
STJA(NC)	St. John Ambulance (Nursing Cadets) [*British*]
STJM	St. Jude Medical [*NASDAQ symbol*] (TTSB)
STJM	St. Jude Medical, Inc. [*NASDAQ symbol*] (NQ)
St J MO PUC	St. Joseph, Missouri, Public Utilities Commission Reports [*A publication*] (DLA)
StJoe	Saint Joe Corp. [*Associated Press*] (SAG)
StJoe	St. Joe Paper Co. [*Associated Press*] (SAG)
StJohn	Saint John Knits, Inc. [*Associated Press*] (SAG)
StJohn	St. John Knits, Inc. [*Associated Press*] (SAG)
St John's C	St. John's College (Sante Fe) (GAGS)
St John's U (Minn)	St. John's University (Minnesota) (GAGS)
St John's U (NY)	St. John's University (New York) (GAGS)
StJoLP	Saint Joseph Light & Power [*Associated Press*] (SAG)
StJoLP	St. Joseph Light & Power Co. [*Associated Press*] (SAG)
St Joseph C (Conn)	St. Joseph College (Connecticut) (GAGS)
St Joseph's U (Penn)	St. Joseph's University (Pennsylvania) (GAGS)
STJU	St. John's University [*Minnesota; New York*]
StJude	Saint Jude Medical, Inc. [*Associated Press*] (SAG)
STJW	Stretcher Jaws [*Tool*] (AAG)
STK	Satellite Tool Kit
stk	Scotland [*MARC country of publication code Library of Congress*] (LCCP)
STK	Serine-Threonine Kinase [*An enzyme*]
STK	Single Tone Keying
STK	Situation Track Display .
STK	Soiuz Trudovogo Krest'ianstva [*Union of Working Peasantry*] [*Russian*]
STK	Stack (MSA)
STK	Stakes Race [*Horse racing*]
STK	Standard Test Key [*Computer science*]
STK	Steak
STK	Stephens Creek [*Australia Seismograph station code, US Geological Survey*] (SEIS)
STK	Sterling, CO [*Location identifier FAA*] (FAAL)
STK	Stick Shift [*Automotive advertising*]
stk	Sticky [*Quality of the bottom*] [*Nautical charts*]
STK	Stock (AAG)
Stk	Stock (EBF)
stk	Stock (VRA)
STK	Storage Technology [*NYSE symbol*] (TTSB)
STK	Storage Technology Corp. [*NYSE symbol*] (SPSG)
STK	Strake [*Mining engineering*]
STK	Streptokinase [*An enzyme*] (AAMN)
STK	Strike [*Navy*] (DOMA)
STK	Sturmkanone [*Self-propelled assault gun*] [*German military - World War II*]
STKD	Stockade (AABC)
STK EX	Stock Exchange
Stk Exch	Stock Exchange (EBF)
STKF	Stock Fund [*Military*]
STKFA	Stock Fund Accounting [*Military*]
STKFS	Stock Fund Statement [*Military*]
STKG	Sturzkampfgeschwader [*Dive-bomber wing*] [*German military - World War II*]
STKL	Stake Technology Ltd. [*Oakville, ON*] [*NASDAQ symbol*] (NQ)
STKLF	Stake Technology Ltd [*NASDAQ symbol*] (TTSB)
STK NO	Stock Number
STKR	Stocker & Yale [*NASDAQ symbol*] (TTSB)
STKR	Stockroom (AABC)
STKR	Stoker [*Navy British*]
STKS	Stakes (ROG)
StkVC	Stokely-Van Camp, Inc. [*Associated Press*] (SAG)
StkVC	Stokley Van Camp [*Associated Press*] (SAG)
STKY	Stokely USA [*NASDAQ symbol*] (TTSB)
STKY	Stokely USA, Inc. [*Oconomowoc, WI*] [*NASDAQ symbol*] (NQ)
STKYD	Stockyard
STL	Bibliotheque Municipale de Saint-Laurent [*UTLAS symbol*]
STI	Esotropia, Left [*Ophthalmology*] (DAVI)
STL	Licentiate in Sacred Theology (GAGS)
STL	Sacrae Theologiae Lector [*Reader in Sacred Theology*] [*Latin*]
STL	Sacrae Theologiae Licentiatus [*Licentiate in Sacred Theology*] [*Latin*]
STL	Safe Tow Length
STL	Santa Lucia [*Chile*] [*Seismograph station code, US Geological Survey Closed*] (SEIS)
STL	Satellite
STL	Schottky Transistor Logic (IEEE)
STL	Seatrain Lines, Inc. [*AAR code*]
STL	Secondary Target Line [*Army*]
STL	Selective Tape Listing [*Computer science*] (IAA)
STL	Self-Test Logic [*Navy Navigation Satellite System*] (DNAB)
STL	Sequential Table Lookup
STL	Short Term Leaflet. Ministry of Agriculture, Fisheries, and Food [*A publication*]
STL	Short-Term Loan (ADA)
STL	Simulated Tape Load
STL	Site Team Leader [*Nuclear energy*] (NRCH)
STL	Southern Traffic League
STL	Southern Transportation League (EA)
STL	Space Technology Laboratories [*of TRW Group*]

STL	Special Tool List
STL	Stall (WGA)
STL	Standard Telecommunications Laboratory (IAA)
STL	Standard Telegraph Level [*Telecommunications*] (TEL)
STL	Stapleford Flight Center [*British ICAO designator*] (FAAC)
STL	Station Transmission Link [*Telecommunications*] (IAA)
STL	Status and Telling (SAA)
STL	Steel (KSC)
stl	Steel (VRA)
STL	Step-Through Latencies
STL	Stereo Lithography
STL	Sterling Bancorp [*NYSE symbol*] (SPSG)
STL	Stile (WGA)
STL	St. Louis [*Missouri*] [*Airport symbol*]
STL	St. Louis [*Diocesan abbreviation*] [*Missouri*] (TOCD)
STL	Stockage List [*Military*]
STLI	Stock, Time Limitation (DNAB)
STL	Storage Time Limit (DNAB)
STL	Strategic Technology Leveraging
STL	Studio-Transmitter Link
STLL	Supersonic Transition Locus [*Galactic winds*]
STL	Support Table Load
STL	Suppressor T Lymphocyte [*Immunology*]
STL	Swelling, Tenderness, Limitation of Movement [*Medicine*]
STL	Symmetrizing and Transformation Line (IAA)
STL	Synchronous Transistor Logic (MDG)
STL	Systems Techniques Laboratory [*Stanford University*] (MCD)
STL	System Test Loop (IEEE)
STLA	Southern Transportation Logistics Association (NTPA)
STLA	Strip Transmission Line Adapter [*or Assembly*]
StL & OR	St. Louis & Ohio River Railroad
StL & SW	St. Louis & South Western Railway
StLAR	St. Lawrence & Atlantic Railway
St Law	Loughborough's Digest of Statute Law [*Kentucky*] [*A publication*] (DLA)
St Lawrence U	St. Lawrence University (GAGS)
STLB & M	St. Louis, Brownsville & Mexico [*Railway*]
STLBY	Stolt-Nielsen S.A. ADS [*NASDAQ symbol*] (TTSB)
STLC	Sequence Thin-Layer Chromatography
STLC	Short-Term Lethal Concentration [*of air pollutants*]
STLC	Soluble Threshold Limit Concentration [*Environmental chemistry*]
STLC	StreamLogic Corp. [*NASDAQ symbol*] (TTSB)
STLD	Support Teacher Learning Difficulties
STLD	Surface Transport Loading Data [*MTMC*] (TAG)
STLDD	Software Top Level Design Document [*Army*]
STLE	Senior Test Laboratory Engineer (IAA)
STLE	Society of Tribologists and Lubrication Engineers (EAIO)
STLF	Southern Troops and Landing Force
STLG	Sterling (WGA)
STLI	Statue of Liberty National Monument
STLI	Stockage List Item [*Military*]
STLI	Subtotal Lymphoid Irradiation [*Medicine*] (DMAA)
St Lim	Statute of Limitations [*A publication*] (DLA)
StLIM & S	St. Louis, Iron Mountain & Southern Railway
STLL	Submarine Tender Load List
STLM	Safeguard Tactical Logistics Management
STLO	Scientific and Technical Liaison Office [*AFSC*]
STLOS	Star Line-of-Sight (KSC)
St Louis L Rev	St. Louis Law Review [*A publication*] (DLA)
St Louis U	Saint Louis University (GAGS)
STLR	Semitrailer
STLS	Ship's Transducer Location System (DNAB)
STLS	Southern Tier Library System [*Library network*]
STLS	South Texas Library System [*Library network*]
STLS	Stinger Training Launch Simulator (MCD)
STL-SF	St. Louis-San Francisco Railway Co.
STL-SF & T	St. Louis, San Francisco & Texas Railway Co.
STL STL and WD	Steel or Steel and Wood [*Freight*]
STLSW of T	St. Louis Southwestern Railway Co. of Texas
STLT	Small Transportable Link Terminal
STLT	Stellite [*Metallurgy*]
STLT	Studio-Transmitter Link-Television
STLTF	Stolt Nielson SA [*NASDAQ symbol*] (SAG)
STLTF	Stolt Tankers & Terminals SA (MHDW)
STLU	St. Louis University [*Missouri*]
St LU Intra L Rev	St. Louis University. Intramural Law Review [*A publication*] (DLA)
STLV	Simian T-Cell Lymphotropic Virus
STL WD	Steel or Wood [*Freight*]
STL WI	Steel or Wire [*Freight*]
StlWVa	Steel West Virginia, Inc. [*Associated Press*] (SAG)
STLY	Stanley Furniture [*NASDAQ symbol*] (TTSB)
STLY	Stanley Furniture Co. [*NASDAQ symbol*] (SAG)
STM	Groupement International d'Editeurs Scientifiques, Techniques, et Medicaux [*International Group of Scientific, Technical, and Medical Publishers*] (EAIO)
STM	International Group of Scientific, Technical, and Medical Publishers (EAIO)
STM	Master of Arts in Theology
STM	Master of Sacred Theology (NADA)
STM	Master of the Science of Theology
STM	Sacrae Theologiae Magister [*Master of Sacred Theology*]
STM	Safety Test Missile (MCD)
STM	Santarem [*Brazil*] [*Airport symbol*] (OAG)

STM............ Satellite Technology Management, Inc. [*Torrance, CA*] [*Telecommunications*] (TSSD)
STM............ Save the Manatee Club (EA)
STM............ Scanning Tunneling Microscope
STM............ Scientific, Technical, and Medical
STM............ Screened through Matching [*Parapsychology*]
STM............ Section Technical Manual [*Jet Propulsion Laboratory, NASA*]
STM............ Self-Test Mode
STM............ Send Test Message (AAG)
STM............ Service Technique Militaire [*Switzerland*]
STM............ Service Test Model (NG)
STM............ SGS Thomson Microelectronics, NV [*NYSE symbol*] (SAG)
STM............ SGS-THOMSON N.V. [*NYSE symbol*] (TTSB)
STM............ Shielded Tunable Magnetron
STM............ Short Term Measure (BCP)
STM............ Short-Term Memory
STM............ Signal Termination Module [*NASA*] (NASA)
STM............ Signature-Tagged Transposon Method [*Genetics*]
STM............ Significant Technical Milestone (SDI)
STM............ Simply Transformed Manufacture
STM............ Simulated Test Markets [*Market research*] (WDMC)
STM............ Slate Mountain [*Nevada*] [*Seismograph station code, US Geological Survey Closed*] (SEIS)
STM............ Society for Traditional Music (EA)
STM............ Sonet Transmission Manager [*Adaptive Corp.*]
STM............ Southam, Inc. [*Toronto Stock Exchange symbol Vancouver Stock Exchange symbol*]
STM............ Specialized Trade Mission [*Department of Commerce*]
STM............ Special Test Missile
STM............ Specification Test Material (MCD)
STM............ Spin Tuned Magnetron
STM............ Spore Tip Mucilage [*Mycology*]
STM............ Stack Tritium Monitor [*Environmental science*] (COE)
STM............ Standards Tool Master (MCD)
STM............ Standard Test Methods Bulletins [*A publication*] (EAAP)
STM............ Standard Type Material (MCD)
STM............ Statement (ECII)
STM............ State Transition Matrix
STM............ Static Test Model (MCD)
STM............ Statistical Multiplexing [*Telecommunications*]
STM............ Statute Mile
STM............ Steam
STM............ Steward's Mate [*Navy rating*]
STM............ St. Martin Hospitals Group [*British*]
STM............ STMicroelectronics NV [*NYSE symbol*] [*Formerly, SGS Thomson NV*]
STM............ STM Publishers (NITA)
STM............ Store Multiple [*Computer command*] (PCM)
STM............ Straddle the Market [*Investment term*] (MHDW)
STM............ Stream [*Board on Geographic Names*]
STM............ Streamline Aviation [*British ICAO designator*] (FAAC)
STM............ Streptomycin [*An antibiotic*] (AAMN)
STM............ Structural Test Model
STM............ Subject to Mortgage (ADA)
STM............ Supersonic Tactical Missile (MCD)
STM............ Supplementary Technical Manual [*Military*]
STM............ Support Test Manager (NASA)
STM............ Surface-to-Target-to-Missile
STM............ Synchronous Transfer Module [*Computer science*] (DDC)
STM............ Synthetic Timing Mode
STM............ System Training Mission (AFM)
STMA........... Space-Time Moving Average [*Statistics*]
STMA........... Sports Turf Managers Association [*Defunct*] (EA)
STMA........... Stuffed Toy Manufacturers Association
St Mark........ St. Mark's Church Case [*Philadelphia, PA*] [*A publication*] (DLA)
St Marlb....... Statute of Marlbridge [*A publication*] (DLA)
StMary........ Saint Mary Land & Exploration [*Associated Press*] (SAG)
St Mary's C... St. Mary's College of Minnesota (GAGS)
St Mary's U... St. Mary's University (GAGS)
STMC.......... Scrap Tire Management Council (NTPA)
STMCCMW... Subcommission for Tectonic Maps of the Commission for the Geological Map of the World (EAIO)
STMD.......... Stormedia 'A' [*NASDAQ symbol*] (TTSB)
STMD.......... Stormedia, Inc. [*NASDAQ symbol*] (SAG)
STME.......... Space Transportation Main Engine
STME.......... Stellar Television Monitor Equipment
St Mert........ Statute of Merton [*A publication*] (DLA)
STMEV........ Storm Evasion [*Navy*] (NVT)
STMFR........ Steamfitter (WGA)
STMG......... Steaming (MSA)
STMGR........ Station Manager (FAAC)
STMI.......... Satellite Technology Management [*NASDAQ symbol*] (SAG)
St Mi .... Statute Mile [*Nautical charts*]
STMI.......... STM Wireless [*NASDAQ symbol*] (TTSB)
STMI.......... STM Wireless, Inc. [*NASDAQ symbol*] (SAG)
St Michael's C... St. Michael's College (GAGS)
STMIS......... System Test Manufacturing Information System (IEEE)
STML.......... Separate Transporter and Mobile Launcher
STML.......... Sindicato de Trabajadores Mineros de Llallagua
STML.......... Stimulate (MSA)
STMM......... Short-Term Money Market
STMNT........ Statement (IAA)
STMO......... Step-Mother (DAVI)
St Mot Carr Guide (CCH)... State Motor Carrier Guide (Commerce Clearing House) [*A publication*] (DLA)

StMotr .... Standard Motor Products, Inc. [*Associated Press*] (SAG)
STMP.......... Ship Test Management Plan [*Navy*] (CAAL)
STMP.......... Single Track Master Operational Recording Tape Processing (IAA)
STMP.......... Stamp
STMP.......... System Training Management Plan (MCD)
STMR.......... Steamer
S/T-MR .... Surplus Termination Material Requisition (MCD)
STMS.......... Scientific and Technical Modular System
STMS.......... Scottish Tramway Museum Society (DCTA)
STMS.......... Short-Term Monetary Support [*Finance*]
STMS.......... Spring Trap Makers' Society [*A union*] [*British*]
STMS.......... State Tax Management System [*Price Waterhouse & Co.*] (PCM)
STMS.......... St. Thomas More Society (EA)
STMT.......... Starmet Corp. [*NASDAQ symbol*] [*Formerly, Nuclear Metals*] (SG)
STMT.......... Statement (AFM)
STMT of SVC... Statement of Service [*Military*]
STMU.......... Special Test and Maintenance Unit
STMV.......... Satellite Tobacco Mosaic Virus [*Immunology*]
STMV.......... Stump-Tailed Macaque Virus (PDAA)
STMW......... Subtropical Mode Water [*Oceanography*]
STMWire ..... STM Wireless, Inc. [*Associated Press*] (SAG)
STMX.......... SyStemix, Inc. [*NASDAQ symbol*] (SPSG)
STN............ SAC [*Strategic Air Command*] Telephone Net
STN............ Satellite Television Network [*Telecommunications Defunct*] (TSSD)
STN............ Satellite Theater Network [*Falls Church, VA*] (TSSD)
STN............ Satellite Tracking Network (MCD)
STN............ Saturn Airways, Inc. (MCD)
STN............ Scientific and Technical Information Network
STN............ Seatoun [*New Zealand*] [*Seismograph station code, US Geological Survey Closed*] (SEIS)
S tn........... Short Ton (EBF)
STN............ Society of Trauma Nurses
STN............ Software Trouble Note [*NASA*] (NASA)
STN............ Solar Telescope Network
STN............ Solitary Tract Nucleus [*Also, NST*] [*Anatomy*]
STN............ Special Traffic Notice [*British*] (DCTA)
STN............ Specification Transmittal Notice (MCD)
STN............ Stain [*Deltiology*]
STN............ Stainless
STN............ Stansted [*England*] [*Airport symbol*] (OAG)
STN............ Statement of Technology Needs [*Air Force*]
STN............ St. Athan MU [*British ICAO designator*] (FAAC)
STN............ Station
stn............. Station (IDOE)
Stn .... Station (ASC)
STN............ Station Casinos, Inc. [*NYSE symbol*] (SAG)
STN............ St. Nicholas in Chicago Ukrainian [*Diocesan abbreviation*] [*Illinois*] (TOCD)
STN............ Stomatogastric Nerve [*Neuroanatomy*]
STN............ Stone [*Unit of weight*] (AAG)
STN............ Strategic Air Command Telephone Network (IAA)
STN............ Subthalamic Nucleus [*Neurobiology*]
STN............ SuperTwisted Nematic [*Electronics*] (CDE)
STN............ Switched Telecommunications Network
STNA.......... Scottish Teachers Nursing Association (DBA)
STNA.......... Sons of Temperance of North America [*Defunct*] (EA)
STNAG........ Standardization Agreement [*NATO*]
STnC.......... Skeletal Troponin C [*Biochemistry*]
stncl.......... Stencil (VRA)
STND.......... Stained (WGA)
STND.......... Standard [*Legal shorthand*] (LWAP)
STND.......... Standard Financial [*NASDAQ symbol*] (SAG)
StneWb....... Stone & Webster, Inc. [*Associated Press*] (SAG)
STNG.......... Sustaining
STNI.......... Subtotal Nodal Irradiation [*Oncology*]
STNLS .... Stainless
sTNM.......... Surgical-Evaluative Staging of Cancer [*Classification of malignant tumors*] [*T refers to the size of the tumor, N refers to the status of the nodes, and M refers to metastases*] (DAVI)
Stn O .... Station Officer (WDAA)
STNR.......... Stationary
STNR.......... Symmetric Tonic Neck Reflex [*Medicine*] (DMAA)
STNT.......... Stant Corp. [*NASDAQ symbol*] (SAG)
STNV .... Satellite Tobacco Necrosis Virus
STNWRE...... Stoneware [*Freight*]
STO............ Aero Santos SA de CV [*Mexico ICAO designator*] (FAAC)
STO............ Science and Technology Objectives (MCD)
STO............ Sea Transport Officer
STO............ Segment Table Origin
STO............ Self-Test Output [*Automotive engineering*]
STO............ Senior Technical Officer (WDAA)
STO............ Senior Training Officer
STO............ Senior Trust Officer [*Banking*] (TBD)
STO............ Service du Travail Obligatoire [*French labor force*] [*World War II*]
STO............ Ship Test Organization (DNAB)
STO............ Short Takeoff (MCD)
STO............ Short-Term Objective
STO............ Slater-Type Orbital [*Atomic structure*]
STO............ Small-Time Operator [*Slang*]
STO............ Soft Target of Opportunity [*Terrorism*] (DI)
STO............ Sojourner Truth Organization (EA)
STO............ Solar Terrestrial Observatory (SSD)
STO............ Source Translation and Optimization [*Computer science*]
STO............ Standard Transfer Order
STO............ Standing Order [*Business term*] (DCTA)

STO............. Standing Orders (NITA)
STO............. Standing Tool Order (KSC)
STO............. State Taxation Office [Australia]
StO............. Steuerordnung [Tax Law] [German] (ILCA)
STO............. Stockholm [Sweden] [Airport symbol] (OAG)
STO............. Stockton [Diocesan abbreviation] [California] (TOCD)
STO............. Stoker [Navy British]
StO............. St. Olaf [Record label]
STO............. Stone Container [NYSE symbol] (TTSB)
STO............. Stone Container Corp. [NYSE symbol] (SPSG)
STO............. Stonehill College, North Easton, MA [OCLC symbol] (OCLC)
STO............. Stonyhurst [Blackburn] [England] [Seismograph station code, US Geological Survey] [Closed] (SEIS)
STO............. Storage (IDOE)
STO............. Storage Processor
STO............. Store (IDOE)
STO............. Storekeeper [Coast Guard]
Sto.............. Storey's Delaware Reports [A publication] (DLA)
STO............. Story (WGA)
Sto............. Story's United States Circuit Court Reports [A publication] (DLA)
STO............. Stow (NASA)
STO............. Strategic Technology Office [Arlington, VA] [DoD] (GRD)
STO............. Strontium, Titanium, Oxygen [Inorganic chemistry]
STO............. Swedish Trade Office (EA)
STO............. System Test Objective (IAA)
STO............. System Test Objectives
STO............. System Test Operator (IAA)
STOA........... Shock Time-of-Arrival [Marine science] (OSRA)
Sto Abr Const... Story's Abridgment of the Constitution [A publication] (DLA)
STOAD......... Scientific and Technical Organizations and Agencies Directory [A publication]
Sto Ag .... Story on Agency [A publication] (DLA)
STOAL......... Short Takeoff Arrested Landing (MCD)
Sto & G .... Stone and Graham's Private Bills Decisions [1865] [A publication] (DLA)
Sto & H Cr Ab... Storer and Heard on Criminal Abortion [A publication] (DLA)
Sto Att Lien... Stokes on Lien of Attorneys and Solicitors [1860] [A publication] (DLA)
Sto Bailm .... Story on Bailments [A publication] (DLA)
Sto Bills ...... Story on Bills [A publication] (DLA)
STobRV....... Satellite Tobacco Ringspot Virus
STOC .... Spontaneous Transient Outward Current [Physiology]
STOC .... Standard Tactical Operating Condition
STOC .... Systems for Test Output Consolidation [Computer science]
STOCC .... Space Telescope Operations Control Center [NASA] (NASA)
Sto CC .... Story's United States Circuit Court Reports [A publication] (DLA)
Stock .... Stockton's New Brunswick Vice-Admiralty Reports [1879-91] [A publication] (DLA)
Stock .... Stockton's New Jersey Equity Reports [A publication] (DLA)
Stock Adm ... Stockton's New Brunswick Vice-Admiralty Reports [A publication] (DLA)
Stockett .... Stockett's Reports [27-53 Maryland] [A publication] (DLA)
STOCKH....... Stockholmia [Stockholm] [Imprint] (ROG)
Stock Non Com... Stock on Non Compotes Mentis [A publication] (DLA)
Stockt .... Stockton's New Jersey Equity Reports [9-11 New Jersey] [A publication] (DLA)
Stockt Ch ..... Stockton's New Jersey Equity Reports [9-11 New Jersey] [A publication] (DLA)
Stockton ...... Stockton's New Brunswick Vice-Admiralty Reports [A publication] (DLA)
Stockton Adm (New Br)... Stockton's New Brunswick Vice-Admiralty Reports [A publication] (DLA)
Stockt Vice-Adm... Stockton's New Brunswick Vice-Admiralty Reports [A publication] (DLA)
Sto Comm ... Story's Commentaries on the Constitution of the United States [A publication] (DLA)
Sto Con........ Story on Contracts [A publication] (DLA)
Sto Conf Law... Story on Conflict of Laws [A publication] (DLA)
Sto Const..... Story's Commentaries on the Constitution of the United States [A publication] (DLA)
Sto Const Cl B... Story's Constitutional Class Book [A publication] (DLA)
Sto Cont ...... Story on Contracts [A publication] (DLA)
STOCS .... Small Terminal-Oriented Computer System (IAA)
STOCS .... South Texas Outer Continental Shelf
STOC-TV ..... Satellite Technical and Operational Committee - Television (NTCM)
STOD .... Special Technical Operations Division (COE)
STOD .... Stodden [England]
Sto Eq Jur ... Story on Equity Jurisprudence [A publication] (DLA)
Sto Eq Pl ..... Story on Equity Pleadings [A publication] (DLA)
STOG .... Science and Technology Objectives Guide (MCD)
STOG .... State/Territorial Operational Guidelines [Australia]
STOGW....... Short Takeoff Gross Weight [Aviation]
STOIAC........ Static Technology Office Information Analysis Center (NITA)
STOIAC........ Strategic Technology Office Information Analysis Center [Battelle Memorial Institute] (MCD)
STOIC......... Stack-Oriented Interactive Compiler [Computer science] (MHDI)
STOIIP......... Stock Tank Oil Initially in Place [Petroleum technology]
Stokely .... Stokely USA, Inc. [Associated Press] (SAG)
STOKEN....... Space Token [IBM Corp.] (CIST)
Stokes L of Att... Stokes on Liens of Attorneys [A publication] (DLA)
STOKPAC..... Stock Control Package (IAA)
STOL........... Saturn Test Oriented Language [NASA]
STOL........... Short Takeoff and Landing [Aviation]
STOL........... Slow Takeoff and Landing (IAA)
STOL........... Standing Operating and Landing

STOL........... Systems Test and Operation Language
STOLAND.... STOL Navigation and Landing System (MCD)
Sto Laws ..... Story's Laws of the United States [A publication] (DLA)
Stolport....... Short Takeoff and Landing Airport [London, England]
Stolt........... Stolt Nielsen SA [Associated Press] (SAG)
StoltCmx..... Stolt Comex Seaway SA [Associated Press] (SAG)
StoltNiel ..... Stolt-Nielsen, SA [Associated Press] (SAG)
STOM......... Safe Transport of Munitions (MCD)
STOM......... Shot through Obscuration MILES [Multiple Integrated LASER Engagement System] [Army]
STOM......... Stomachic [To Strengthen the Stomach] [Medicine] (ROG)
STOM......... Stomatocytes [Hematology] (DAVI)
STOM......... System Test and Operations Manual
Sto Miscel Writ... Story's Miscellaneous Writings [A publication] (DLA)
STOMPER.... Soil Test Ordnance Multipurpose Exploration Rocket (SAA)
STON Indus... GreenStone Indus [NASDAQ symbol] (TTSB)
STON .... GreenStone Industries, Inc. [NASDAQ symbol] (SAG)
STON .... Short Ton [2000 lbs.] (AABC)
StonC.......... Stone Container Corp. [Associated Press] (SAG)
Stone.......... Stone's Justices' Manual (Annual) [A publication] (DLA)
Stone Ben Bdg Soc... Stone's Benefit Building Societies [1851] [A publication] (DLA)
StoneC........ Stone Container Corp. [Associated Press] (SAG)
StoneEn....... Stone Energy Corp. [Associated Press] (SAG)
STONEH....... Stonehouse [England]
Stone Just Man... Stone's Justices' Manual (Annual) [A publication] (DLA)
StoneStB..... Stone Street Bancorp, Inc. [Associated Press] (SAG)
STONW....... GreenStone Inds Wrrt [NASDAQ symbol] (TTSB)
STOP .... Safe Tables Our Priority [Protest organization compreised of parents and friends of E. coli victims] (ECON)
STOP .... Save the Oppressed People Committee [Defunct] (EA)
STOP .... Security Trading of Office Property
STOP .... Selected Test Optimization Program (MCD)
S/TOP .... Selective Tubal Occlusion Procedure [Medicine]
STOP .... Ship's Toxicological Protective System
STOP .... Single Title Order Plan [Formerly, SCOP] [ABA]
STOP .... Society that Opposes Pornography
STOP .... Software Theft Opposition Project [Project STOP] [Information service or system] (CRD)
STOP .... Stable Ocean Platform
STOP .... Stable Tubule Only Polypeptide [Biochemistry]
STOP .... Start Tromping on Pedal [Facetious interpretation of the traffic sign]
STOP .... Stop forced busing; Teach children, not bus them; Operate neighborhood schools for those in the neighborhood wishing to attend them; Put an end to government interference in the parent-child relationship [An association] (EA)
STOP .... Stopped Bonds [Stock exchange term] (MHDB)
STOP .... Stop the Oil Profiteers [Antioil price slogan]
STOP .... Stop the Olympic Prison [Lake Placid Olympics, 1980] [Opposed possible later use of an Olympic building as a prison] [Defunct]
STOP .... Stop This Outrageous Purge [Group opposed to extremist measures used by segregationists in Arkansas; opposed by CROSS]
STOP .... Storage Protector [Computer science] (IAA)
STOP .... Strategic Orbit Point (AFM)
STOP .... Strategic Talks on Prevention [of accidental atomic war and nuclear weapons proliferation] [Proposed by Sen. Gary Hart, 1982]
STOP .... Students Tackle Ocean Plastics
STOP .... Student/Teacher Organization to Prevent Nuclear War [Defunct] (EA)
STOP .... Sudden Tetanus of Prey [Biology]
STOP .... Supersonic Transport Optimization Program [NASA]
STOP ABC ... Stop Abuse by Counselors (EA)
Sto Part....... Story on Partnership [A publication] (DLA)
STOP-H....... Swedish Trial in Old Patients with Hypertension
Sto Pl .... Story's Civil Pleading [A publication] (DLA)
STOP-NSA ... Students to Oppose Participation in the National Student Association (EA)
STOPP .... Society of Teachers of Professional Photography [Later, STEPP] (EA)
STOPP .... Society of Teachers Opposed to Physical Punishment
STOPP .... Stop Planned Parenthood [An association] (EA)
STOPPS ...... Standard Transportation Operations Personnel Property (MCD)
Sto Pr .... Story on Prize Courts [A publication] (DLA)
STOPrE........ Stone Container Cv Ex Pfd [NYSE symbol] (TTSB)
Sto Pr Notes... Story on Promissory Notes [A publication] (DLA)
STOPS .... Shipboard Toxicological Operational Protective System [Navy]
STOPS .... Stability Operations
STOPS .... Stabilized Terrain Optical Position Sensor [Army]
STOPS .... Standard Transportation Operations Property System (MCD)
STOPS .... Supreme Temple Order Pythian Sisters (EA)
StopSh........ [The] Stop & Shop Companies, Inc. [Associated Press] (SAG)
STOQ .... Storage Queue
STOR .... Scripps Tuna Oceanographic Research
STOR .... Segment Table Origin Register [Computer science] (BUR)
STOR .... Storage (AFM)
STOR .... Summary Tape Operations Rental [Bureau of the Census]
STOR .... System Test and Operations Report
STORAD....... Stored Address [Computer science]
STORADS ..... Site Tactical Optimized Range Air Defense System
Stor & H Abor... Storer and Heard on Criminal Abortion [A publication] (DLA)
STORC......... Self-Ferrying Trans-Ocean Rotary-Wing Crane [Helicopter]
STORCH....... Syphilis, Toxoplasmosis, Other Agents Rubella, Cytomegalovirus, and Herpes [Medicine] (DAVI)
STORCH....... Syphilis, Toxoplasmosis, Rubella, Cytomegalovirus, and Herpesvirus [Medicine] (DMAA)
Stor Dict ..... Stormouth's Dictionary of the English Language [A publication] (DLA)

STORE	Storage Technology for Operational Readiness
STORE	Student's Own Record of Education (AIE)
STORE	Students to Observe Retail Establishments [*Student legal action organization*] (EA)
STORES	Syntactic Tracer Organized Retrospective Enquiry System [*Instituut voor Wiskunde, Informatiewerk, en Statistiek*] [*Computer science*] [*Netherlands*]
STORET	Storage and Retrieval [*Computer science*]
STORET	Storage and Retrieval for Water Quality Data [*Databank*] [*Environmental Protection Agency*] (MSC)
STORET	Storage and Retrieval of U.S. Waterways Parametric Data [*Environmental Protection Agency*] (AEPA)
STORLAB	Space Technology Operations and Research Laboratory (IEEE)
STORM	Safe Transport of Munitions Project (MCD)
STORM	Sensor, Tank, Off-Route Mine (MCD)
STORM	Somali, Tigray, and Ormo Resistance Monitor [*British*]
STORM	Statistically Oriented Matrix Program (IEEE)
STORM	Stormscale Operational and Research Meteorology [*National Oceanic and Atmospheric Administration*]
Stormda	Stormedia, Inc. [*Associated Press*] (SAG)
STORM-FEST	STORM [*Stormscale Operational and Research Meteorology*] Fronts Experiment Systems Test [*Marine science*] (OSRA)
STORMS	Standardized Operation Research Management System (MCD)
STORMSAT	Storm Satellite (MCD).
StorPr	Storage Properties, Inc. [*Associated Press*] (SAG)
STORS	Sludge to Oil Reactor System [*Battelle Memorial Institute*]
StorTc	Storage Technology Corp. [*Associated Press*] (SAG)
StorTch	Storage Technology Corp. [*Associated Press*] (SAG)
StorTRlt	Storage Trust Realty [*Associated Press*] (SAG)
Story	Story on Equity Jurisprudence [*1836-1920*] [*A publication*] (DLA)
Story	Story's United States Circuit Court Reports [*A publication*] (DLA)
Story Ag	Story on Agency [*A publication*] (DLA)
Story Bailm	Story on Bailments [*A publication*] (DLA)
Story Comm Const	Story's Commentaries on the Constitution of the United States [*A publication*] (DLA)
Story Confl Laws	Story on Conflict of Laws [*A publication*] (DLA)
Story Const	Story's Commentaries on the Constitution of the United States [*A publication*] (DLA)
Story Cont	Story on Contracts [*A publication*] (DLA)
Story Eq Jur	Story on Equity Jurisprudence [*A publication*] (DLA)
Story Eq Pl	Story's Equity Planning [*A publication*] (DLA)
Story Laws	Story's Laws of the United States [*A publication*] (DLA)
Story Merchants	Abbott's Merchant Ships and Seamen, by Story [*A publication*] (DLA)
Story Partn	Story on Partnership [*A publication*] (DLA)
Story Prom Notes	Story on Promissory Notes [*A publication*] (DLA)
Story R	Story's United States Circuit Court Reports [*First Circuit*] [*A publication*] (DLA)
Story Sales	Story on Sales of Personal Property [*A publication*] (DLA)
Story's Circuit CR	Story's United States Circuit Court Reports [*First Circuit*] [*A publication*] (DLA)
Story's Laws	Story's United States Laws [*A publication*] (DLA)
Story's Rep	Story's United States Circuit Court Reports [*A publication*] (DLA)
Story US Laws	Story's Laws of the United States [*A publication*] (DLA)
STOS	Santos Ltd. [*NASDAQ symbol*] (NQ)
STOS	Space Test Operations Section
S to S	Station to Station
Sto Sales	Story on Sales of Personal Property [*A publication*] (DLA)
STOSY	Santos Ltd ADR [*NASDAQ symbol*] (TTSB)
STOT	Scheduled Time over Target (AFM)
STOT	Stockpile-to-Target (AFM)
STOTINS	Standoff Techniques for Parachute Insertion (MCD)
StOTPr	Studies in Old Testament Prophecy Presented to T. H. Robinson [*A publication*] (BJA)
StOU	Stimmen Orient und Uebersee [*A publication*] (BJA)
STOU	Super Tractor Oil-Universal [*Lubricants*]
Sto US Laws	Story's Laws of the United States [*A publication*] (DLA)
STOV	State Theatre of Victoria [*Australia*]
Stov Hors	Stovins' Law Respecting Horses [*A publication*] (DLA)
STOVL	Short Takeoff and Vertical Landing (MCD)
STOW	Side Transfer Optimum Warehousing
STOW	Stowage (AAG)
STOW	Swim the Ontario Waterways [*Personal incentive program for fitness swimmers*] [*Ontario Masters Swimming Club*]
STOW	Synthetic Theater of War [*Army*]
STOW	System for Takeoff Weight
STOW-SKID	Synthetic Theater of War-Systems Engineering, Integration, and Demonstration [*Military*] (RDA)
STP	2,5-Dimethoxy-4-Methylamphetamine [*Also, Methyldimethoxy-Amphetamine and DOM*] [*An illicit hallucinogenic drug*] (DAVI)
STP	Holidair Airways [*Canada ICAO designator*] (FAAC)
STP	Sacrae [*or Sacrosanctae*] Theologiae Professor [*Professor of Sacred Theology*]
STP	SAGE [*Semiautomatic Ground Environment*] System Training Program
STP	Saint Peter's College, Jersey City, NJ [*OCLC symbol*] (OCLC)
STP	Sao Tome and Principe [*ANSI three-letter standard code*] (CNC)
STP	Satellite Ticket Printer [*Travel industry*]
STP	Satellite Tracking Program [*of the Smithsonian Institution's Astrophysical Observatory*]
STP	Save the Tallgrass Prairie [*An association*] (EA)
STP	Science and Technology Policy [*Marine science*] (OSRA)
STP	Scientifically Treated Petroleum [*A motor fuel oil additive*] [*Initials reported, by extension of meaning, also to stand for a hallucinogenic drug, DOM*]

STP	Seal to Parents [*Genealogy*] (PCM)
STP	Sea Test Phase [*Navy*] (CAAL)
STP	Secure Transfer Protocol [*Computer science*] (DOM)
STP	Selective Tape Print
STP	Self-Test Program (MCD)
STP	Sent to Printer [*Publishing*]
STP	Separation Transfer Point [*Army*] (ADDR)
STP	Serenity, Tranquility, Peace [*Experimental hallucinogen developed by DOW Chemical Co.*] (IIA)
STP	Sewage Treatment Plant
STP	Shielded Twisted-Pair [*Computer science*] (PCM)
STP	Short-Term Potentiation [*Neurology*]
STP	Short-Term Program [*Nuclear energy*] (NRCH)
STP	Short Term Projections [*Townsend, Greenspan & Co., Inc.*] [*No longer available online*] [*Information service or system*]
STP	Shuttle Technology Panel [*NASA*] (NASA)
STP	Signal Transfer Point [*Telecommunications*] (TEL)
STP	Simultaneous Test Procedure [*Statistics*]
STP	Simultaneous Track Processor
STP	Singing Tree Press [*Publisher's imprint*]
STP	Site Treatment Plan (DOGT)
STP	Skills Training Program
ST-P	Small Transmitter Coated with Paraffin
STP	Socialism: Theory and Practice [*A publication*]
STP	Society for Thai Philately (EA)
STP	Society of Telecommunications Professionals (TSSD)
STP	Society of Television Pioneers (EA)
STP	Society of Toxicologic Pathologists (EA)
STP	Sodium Thiopental [*A general anesthetic*] (DAVI)
STP	Sodium Triphosphate [*or Sodium Tripolyphosphate*] [*Also, STPP Inorganic chemistry*]
STP	Software Test Plan [*DoD*]
STP	Solar-Terrestrial Physics (IID)
STP	Solar-Terrestrial Probe [*NASA*]
STP	Soldier Training Publications [*Military*] (INF)
STP	South Texas Project [*Nuclear energy*] (NRCH)
STP	Space Technology Payload [*NASA*] (MCD)
STP	Space Technology Products [*NASA*] (IAA)
STP	Space Test Program [*Air Force*]
STP	Specialised Tender Panel [*Finance*]
STP	Special Technical Publication (MCD)
STP	Special Tool Production
STP	Special Trade Passenger Ship (PDAA)
STP	Spectrum of Time Project [*Astronomy*]
STP	Stamp (MSA)
STP	Standardized Test Program
STP	Standard Program [*Computer science*] (IAA)
STP	Standard Temperature and Pressure
stp	Standard Temperature and Pressure (WA)
STP	Standard [*Normal*] Temperature and Pulse [*Medicine*]
STP	Standard Test Procedure
STP	Standard Thermal Profile
STP	Standard Type Process (MCD)
St P	State Papers [*A publication*] (DLA)
STP	Stepping (WGA)
STP	Sterilization Test Program
STP	Steroidogenesis-Stimulating Protein [*Physiology*]
STP	Stop Character [*Computer science*]
STP	Stoppage (AABC)
STP	Stop the Pentagon/Serve the People (EA)
STP	Storage Tube Processor
STP	Storm Track Prediction (MCD)
STPr	St. Paul and Minneapolis [*Diocesan abbreviation*] [*Minnesota*] (TOCD)
STP	St. Paul, MN [*Location identifier FAA*] (FAAL)
STP	Strength, Toughness, Pride
STP	Strip
STP	Structural Test Plan (ACII)
STP	Submarine Technology Program [*Defense Advanced Research Projects Agency*] (DOMA)
STP	Subsystem Test Plan [*NASA*] (NASA)
STP	Supracondylar Tibial Prosthesis [*Medicine*]
STP	Surface Transportation Program [*MOCD*] (TAG)
STP	Sustainment Training Program [*Army*] (INF)
STP	Sycamore Test Procedure [*Aerospace*] (AAG)
STP	Systems Technology Program (MCD)
STP	Systems Training Program [*RADAR*]
STP	System Test Plan
STP	System Test Procedure [*Nuclear energy*] (GFGA)
STP	System Test Program [*Navy*] (CAAL)
STPA	Statistical Training Programme for Africa [*United Nations*] (EY)
StP & D	St. Paul & Duluth Railroad
StP & P	St. Paul & Pacific Railroad
StP & SC	St. Paul & Sioux City Railroad
StPaul	Saint Paul Companies, Inc. [*Associated Press*] (SAG)
StPaul	[*The*] St. Paul Companies, Inc. [*Associated Press*] (SAG)
StPaulBc	Saint Paul Bancorp, Inc. [*Associated Press*] (SAG)
StPaulC	Saint Paul Capital LLC [*Associated Press*] (SAG)
StPaulC	St. Paul Capital LLC [*Associated Press*] (SAG)
STPC	Southern Timber Purchasers Council (WPI)
StPCyRy	St. Paul City Railway
STPD	Stamped (ROG)
Stpd	Stamped (EBF)
STPD	Standard Temperature and Pressure, Dry
STPD	Stripped (MSA)

STPD	Stumped (WGA)
STPD	System Training Production Department (SAA)
STPDN	Stepdown
STPDS	Scientific and Technical Personnel Data System [National Science Foundation] (GFGA)
STPF	Shield Test Pool Facility [Nuclear energy]
STPF	Stabilized Temperature Platform Furnace
STPFM	Subsystem: Short-Term Price Forecasting Model [Department of Energy] (GFGA)
STPG	Sequential Test Plan Generator (PDAA)
STPG	Spare-Time Production for Gain [FAO]
STPG	Stamping (ROG)
STPG	Stepping (MSA)
STPH	Static Phase Error [NASA] (NASA)
STPI	Science and Technology Policy Implementation [Project]
STPI	Software Technology Parks of India (DDC)
STPI	Static Power Inverter (DWSG)
STPL	Short-Term Public Exposure Limit (MCD)
STPL	Sidetone Path Loss [Telecommunications] (TEL)
STPL	Standard Test Processing Language (NITA)
STPL	Steeple (DS)
STPL	Stern Plane
St Pl Cr	Staundeforde's Pleas of Crown [A publication] (DLA)
STP-M	Solar-Terrestrial Physics - Meteorology
STPM	Syndicat Togolais du Personnel de la Meteorologie [Togolese Union of Meteorological Personnel]
StPM & M	St. Paul, Minneapolis & Manitoba Railway
STP-MET	Solar-Terrestrial Physics - Meteorology [International Council of Scientific Unions]
STPN	South Pointe Enterprises [NASDAQ symbol] (SAG)
STPNG	Stopping (MSA)
STPO	Science and Technology Policy Office [Supersedes OST] [National Science Foundation]
STPO	Strategic Targets Product Office [Army] (RDA)
STPO	Systems Technology Project Office
STPP	Sodium Tripolyphosphate [Also, STP] [Inorganic chemistry]
STPP	Student Teacher Performance Profile
STPP	Surface Transportation Policy Project [Military]
STPR	Semiannual Technical Progress Report
STPR	Software Test Procedure
St Pr	Staundeforde's Exposition of the King's Prerogative [A publication] (DLA)
STPR	Stepper [Motor] [Electronics]
STPR	Stripper
STPR	Stumper [Freight]
St Pr Reg	Style's Practical Register [England] [A publication] (DLA)
STPS	S-Band Tracking Processor System
STPS	Series-Tuned Parallel-Stabilized [Computer science] (IAA)
STPS	Solar Thermal Power System
STPS	Specific Thalamic Projection System [Medicine] (DMAA)
STPS	Stern Teacher Preference Schedule
STPS	Summary Task Planning Sheet
STPS	Systems Test Planning Section (SAA)
STPST	Stop-Start [Telecommunications] (TEL)
STPT	Society of Town Planning Technicians [British]
STPTC	Standardization of Tar Products Test Committee
STPUB	Stem Pubescence [Botany]
StPUD	St. Paul Union Depot
StPUSY	St. Paul Union Stock Yards Co.
STPV	Semitrailer Petroleum Van (DWSG)
STPX	Systems Training Program Exercise (AABC)
STQ	Society of Translators of Quebec [Canada]
STQ	Streator, IL [Location identifier FAA] (FAAL)
STQ	Superior Temporal Quadrant [Medicine] (DMAA)
STr	Esotropia, Right [Ophthalmology] (DAVI)
STR	Questar Corp. [NYSE symbol] (SPSG)
STR	Scientific and Technological Research (DEN)
STR	Scientific Technical Report
STR	Search and Track RADAR
STR	Seater (ADA)
STR	Sea Test Range (MUGU)
STR	Segment Table Register
STR	Senior Technical Representative
STR	Service Test Review
STR	Service Trouble Report
STR	Short Term Reinitialization [Army]
STR	Short-Term Returns
STR	Sidetone Reduction [Telecommunications] (TEL)
STR	Simple Tandem Repeat [For genotype determination]
STR	Single Token Ring [Telecommunications] (OSI)
STR	Society for Theatre Research (EA)
STR	Society of Thoracic Radiology (EA)
STR	Software Test Report
STR	Software Trouble Report (MCD)
STR	Software Trouble Reporting Service (NITA)
STR	Solar Transition Region [Solar physics]
STR	Spacecraft Telemetry Regenerator (MCD)
STR	Special Theory of Relativity
STR	Special Trade Representative
STR	Special Treatment Room [Medicine] (DAVI)
STR	Speed Tolerant Recording [Electronic Processors, Inc.]
STR	Staff Technical Representative
STR	Standard Broadcasting Corp. Ltd. [Toronto Stock Exchange symbol]
STR	Standard Taxiway Routing
STR	Standard Telephon und Radio [Switzerland] (NITA)

STR	Standard Tool Request
STR	Standard Training Requirements [Navy] (NVT)
STR	Start Address Register [Telecommunications] (IAA)
STR	Status Register [Computer science]
STR	Steamer
STR	Stellair [France ICAO designator] (FAAC)
STR	Stirred-Tank Reactor [Chemical engineering]
STR	Storage Rack (MCD)
STR	Store
STR	Straight (AAG)
STR	Strainer (AAG)
STR	Strait [Maps and charts]
Str	Strange's Cases of Evidence [1698-1732] [England] [A publication] (DLA)
Str	Strange's English King's Bench Reports [1716-49] [A publication] (DLA)
STR	Strasbourg [France] [Seismograph station code, US Geological Survey] (SEIS)
STR	Strasse [Street] [German]
Str	Strategemata [of Frontinus] [Classical studies] (OCD)
STR	Strategic Training Range (MCD)
STR	Streak
str	Streaky [Quality of the bottom] [Nautical charts]
STR	Stream [Maps and charts]
STR	Stream Routing [Computer science]
STR	Street
STR	Streichinstrumente [Stringed Instruments] [Music]
STR	Strength (AFM)
STR	Streptococcus [Medicine]
Str	Streptococcus [Medicine] (DB)
STR	Stretch [Horse racing]
Str	Striatum [Brain anatomy] [Also, ST]
STR	Striking (WGA)
STR	String
str	String (WDAA)
str	Stringed (WDAA)
STR	Stringendo [Hastening] [Music]
STR	Strings [of an orchestra]
STR	Strip (AAG)
STR	Strobe [NASA] (IAA)
STR	Stroke
STR	Strophe [Classical studies] (OCD)
STR	Structural [Lumber]
STR	Structure (NAKS)
St R	Stuart's Lower Canada Appeal Cases [Quebec] [A publication] (DLA)
STR	Stuttgart [Germany Airport symbol] (OAG)
STR	Submarine Test Reactor
STR	Submarine Thermal Reactor [Nuclear energy]
STR	Submersible Test Rack
STR	Summary Technical Report
STR	Super Transportable RADAR
STR	Surplus to Requirements (ADA)
STR	Symbol Time Recovery (NITA)
STR	Synchronous Transmit Receive (NITA)
STR	Synchronous Transmitter Receiver [Computer science]
STR	Systems Technology RADAR (MCD)
STR	Systems Technology Report (MCD)
STR	System Test Report [Military]
STR	System Test Review [NASA] (NASA)
STRA	Stravenue [Postal Service standard] (OPSA)
STRA	Strayer Education, Inc. [NASDAQ symbol] (SAG)
STRA	Supply and Training Mission [Military] (CINC)
STRAAD	Special Techniques Repair Analysis Aircraft Damage [Navy] (NVT)
STRAB	Strabismus [Medicine]
Strab	Strabo [First century BC] [Classical studies] (OCD)
STRABAD	Strategic Base Air Defense [Military] (AABC)
STRAC	Standards in Training Commission [Army] (INF)
STRAC	Strategic Army Corps [Acronym has come to mean "ordered" or "neat"]
STRACNET	Strategic Rail Corridor Network [MTMC] (TAG)
STRACOS	Strategic Air Combat Operations Staff
STRACS	Small Transportable Communications Stations
STRACS	Surface Traffic Control System (MCD)
STRAD	Signal Transmission Reception and Distribution (IEEE)
Strad	Stradivari [Record label]
STRAD	Stradivarius Violin [Music] (DSUE)
STRAD	Strategic Aerospace Division [Air Force] (AFM)
STRAD	Switching, Transmitting, Receiving, and Distribution
STRADAP	Storm RADAR Data Processor [ESD]
STRADIS	Structured Analysis, Design and Implementation of Information Systems (MHDI)
STRAF	Special Therapeutic and Rehabilitation Activities Fund [Department of Veterans Affairs]
STRAF	Strategic Army Forces
STRAFE	Students Resisting Aerosol Flurocarbon Emissions [Student legal action organization] (EA)
Strafford	Smith's New Hampshire Reports [A publication] (DLA)
STRAFIP	Strategic Army Forces Readiness Improvement Program (AABC)
STRAFLO	Straight-Flow [Water turbine]
STRAFPOA	Strategic Air Force, Pacific Ocean Area
STRAG	Straggler
STRAGL	Straggler Line [Military]
Strahan	Strahan's Reports [19 Oregon] [A publication] (DLA)
Strah Domat	Strahan's Domat's Civil Law [A publication] (DLA)
STRAHNET	Strategic Highway Corridor Network [BTS] [MTMC] (TAG)

STRAIN........ Structural Analytical Interpreter
STRAIRPOA... Strategic Air Force, Pacific Ocean Area
Straits LJ & Rep... Straits Law Journal and Reporter [*A publication*] (DLA)
STRAM .... Synchronous Transmit Receive Access Method (CMD)
Str & HC...... Streets and Highways Code [*A publication*] (DLA)
STRANGE..... SAGE [*Semiautomatic Ground Environment*] Tracking and Guidance Evaluation System
Strange........ Strange's English Court Reports [*A publication*] (DLA)
Strange (Eng).. Strange's English Courts Reports [*93 English Reprint*] [*A publication*] (DLA)
Strange Madras... Strange's Notes of Cases, Madras [*A publication*] (DLA)
STRAP .... SCAR Team Report Analysis Program (MCD)
STRAP .... Simplified Transient Radiation Analysis Program (MCD)
STRAP .... Simultaneous Transmission and Recovery of Alternating Pictures [*TV system*]
STRAP .... Sonobuoy Thinned Random Array Program [*Navy*] (CAAL)
STRAP .... Star [*or Stellar*] Tracking Rocket Attitude Positioning [*System*] [*NASA*]
STRAP .... Stretch Assembly Program [*IBM Corp.*]
STRAP .... Structural Analysis Package
STRAP .... System Training Plan
STRAPP....... Standard Tanks, Racks, Adapter, and Pylon Packages (MCD)
STRAPS....... Stated Rate Auction Preferred Stock (EBF)
STRASB....... Strasbourg [*Imprint*] (ROG)
STRAT .... Strategic (AFM)
STRAT .... Stratigraphic
STRAT .... Stratton [*England*]
STRATA .... Short-Term Reconaissance and Target Acquisition Team [*US Special Forces*] (VNW)
STRATAD ..... Strategic Aerospace Division [*Air Force*]
STRATANALSUPPGRU... Strategic Analysis Support Group [*Navy*] (DNAB)
Stratasys ...... Stratasys, Inc. [*Associated Press*] (SAG)
Stratcm........ Stratacom, Inc. [*Associated Press*] (SAG)
STRATCOM... Strategic Air Command [*Air Force*]
STRATCOM... Strategic Communications [*Army*] (IAA)
STRATCOM... Strategic Communications Command [*Army*] (RDA)
STRATCOM... Stratospheric Composition (MCD)
STRATCOMMEX... Strategic Communications Military Exchange [*Army*] (IAA)
StratCp........ Stratosphere Corp. [*Associated Press*] (SAG)
STRATF....... Stratford [*England*]
STRATMAS... Strategic Mobility [*Planning and*] Analysis System [*Military*] (NVT)
STRATMID... Strategic Military Intelligence Detachment [*Army*] (MCD)
STRATO .... Stratosphere (AFM)
STRATOSCOPE... Stratosphere Telescope (IAA)
STRATSAT... Strategic Satellite System [*Air Force Telecommunications*] (TEL)
Strattec........ Strattec Security Corp. [*Associated Press*] (SAG)
Stratton........ Stratton's Reports [*12-14 Oregon*] [*A publication*] (DLA)
Stratus......... Stratus Computer, Inc. [*Associated Press*] (SAG)
STRATWARM... Stratospheric Warming
STRAV .... Stravenue [*Commonly used*] (OPSA)
STRAVE .... Stravenue [*Commonly used*] (OPSA)
STRAVEN..... Stravenue [*Commonly used*] (OPSA)
STRAVENUE... Stravenue [*Commonly used*] (OPSA)
STRAVN ...... Stravenue [*Commonly used*] (OPSA)
STRAW .... Simultaneous Tape Read and Write
Strayer......... Strayer Education, Inc. [*Associated Press*] (SAG)
STRB .... Strobe (NASA)
STRB .... Strober Organization [*NASDAQ symbol*] (TTSB)
STRB .... [*The*] Strober Organization, Inc. [*Brooklyn, NY*] [*NASDAQ symbol*] (NQ)
STRBK .... Strongback
STRb M .... Grupo Situr'B' [*ME symbol*] (TTSB)
STRC .... Science and Technology Research Center [*North Carolina*] (MCD)
STRC .... Scientific, Technical, and Research Commission (EY)
STRC .... Society of Traditional Roman Catholics (EA)
STRC .... Sterile Recoveries, Inc. [*NASDAQ symbol*] (SAG)
STRC .... Switch Tail Ring Counter
Str Cas Ev ... Strange's Cases of Evidence ("Octavo Strange") [*A publication*] (DLA)
STRCH........ Stretch (AAG)
StrchMb....... Streicher Mobile Fueling, Inc. [*Associated Press*] (SAG)
STRC-IVS..... STRC [*Science and Technology Research Center*] Inverted File Search System [*Search system*]
StrCmp .... Storage Computer Corp. [*Associated Press*] (SAG)
StrctIns........ Structural Instrumentation, Inc. [*Associated Press*] (SAG)
STRCTRD..... Structured
STRD .... Short Tour Return Date [*Military*]
STRD .... Stored
STRD .... Strand [*Engineering*]
STRD .... Strategic Distribution [*NASDAQ symbol*] (SAG)
STRE.......... Specialist Teams Royal Engineers [*Military British*]
STRE.......... Stress Response Element [*Genetics*]
STREAM ...... Standard Tensioned Replenishment Alongside Method [*Military*] (NVT)
STREAM ...... Stream [*Commonly used*] (OPSA)
S Treaty Doc... Senate Treaty Documents [*A publication*] (DLA)
STREET....... Street [*Commonly used*] (OPSA)
Street Ry Rep... Street Railway Reports [*A publication*] (DLA)
STREETS...... Streets [*Commonly used*] (OPSA)
STREME....... Stream [*Commonly used*] (OPSA)
STREMIC ..... Securitized Real Estate Mortgage Investment Conduit (EBF)
STRENGTHD... Strengthened (ROG)
STREP .... Ship's Test and Readiness Evaluation Procedure
STREP .... Space Trajectory Radiation Exposure Procedure
St Rep .... State Reporter [*A publication*] (DLA)

St Rep .... State Reports [*A publication*] (DLA)
STREP .... Status Report [*IRS*]
Strep........... Strepsiptera [*Entomology*]
STREP .... Streptococcus [*Medicine*]
STREP .... Systems Technology Reentry Experiment Program [*Military*]
strept.......... Streptococcus [*A bacterium*] [*Medicine*] (DAVI)
STREPTO...... Streptomycin [*An antibiotic*] (DSUE)
StRes .... Sight Resources Corp. [*Associated Press*] (SAG)
STRES .... Store Release Evaluation System (MCD)
STRESS .... Satellite Transmission Effects Simulation (MCD)
STRESS .... Stop the Robberies, Enjoy Safe Streets [*Detroit police unit*] [*Disbanded*]
STRESS .... Structural Engineering Systems Solver [*Programming language*] [*1962*]
STRET......... Street
stret........... Stretcher (VRA)
STRETCH .... Space Technology Requirements Engineering Test of Component Hardware [*NASA*] (KSC)
Str Ev.......... Strange's Cases of Evidence [*1698-1732*] [*England*] [*A publication*] (DLA)
STRF........... Sea Turtle Rescue Fund (EA)
STRF........... Spectrotemporal Receptive Field [*Neuroscience*]
STRFLD .... Star Field (MCD)
STRFX .... Strong Total Return [*Mutual fund ticker symbol*] (SG)
STRG .... Steering (AAG)
STRG .... String (NASA)
strg .... String (VRA)
STRG .... Strong (MSA)
StrgCmp ...... Storage Computer Corp. [*Associated Press*] (SAG)
strgcr.......... Stringcourse (VRA)
StrGlob .... Strategic Global Income Fund [*Associated Press*] (SAG)
STRG WND... String or Wind [*Freight*]
Str HL .... Strange's Hindoo Law [*A publication*] (DLA)
STRI .... Smithsonian Tropical Research Institute [*Miami, FL*]
STRI .... Sports Turf Research Institute [*British*] (IRUK)
STRI .... Stones River National Battlefield
Strick Ev ...... Strickland on Evidence [*1830*] [*A publication*] (DLA)
STRICOM..... Simulation, Training, and Instrumentation Command [*Army*] (RDA)
STRICOM..... Strike Command [*Military*]
Stricycle ...... Stericycle, Inc. [*Associated Press*] (SAG)
STRIDE .... Science and Technology for Regional Innovation and Development in Europe [*EC*] (ECED)
STRIDE .... Standard Reactor Island Design [*Nuclear energy*] (NRCH)
STRIDE .... Strategically Tiered Regionally Integrated Data Environment [*Computer science*] (CIST)
STRIDE .... System to Retrieve Information from Drug Evidence [*Drug Enforcement Administration*]
StrideRt....... Stride Rite Corp. [*Associated Press*] (SAG)
STRIKEOPS... Strike Operations [*Military*] (NVT)
Striker .... Striker Industries [*Associated Press*] (SAG)
STRIKEX ...... Strike Exercise [*Navy NATO*] (NATG)
STRIKFLTLANT... Striking Fleet Atlantic [*Military*]
STRIKFORSOUTH... Striking and Support Forces Southern Europe [*Navy*]
STRIKFTLANTREPEUR... Striking Fleet Atlantic Representative in Europe [*NATO*] (NATG)
STRIKWARN... Strike Warning Message [*Army*] (ADDR)
STRING....... Stringendo [*Hastening*] [*Music*]
Stringf .... Stringfellow's Reports [*9-11 Missouri*] [*A publication*] (DLA)
Stringfellow... Stringfellow's Reports [*9-11 Missouri*] [*A publication*] (DLA)
STRINGS...... Stellar Inertial Guidance System (DNAB)
STRINO........ Stringendo [*Hastening*] [*Music*] (ROG)
STRIP .... Select Technical Requirements Information Program
STRIP .... Specification Technical Review and Improvement Program [*Navy*] (NG)
STRIP .... Standard Requisition and Issue Procedures [*Military*] (CINC)
STRIP .... Standard Taped Routines for Image Processing [*National Institute of Standards and Technology*]
STRIP .... Stock Turn-In and Replenishment Invoicing Procedures
STRIP .... Strategic Intermediate Planner (PDAA)
STRIP .... String Processing Language [*Computer science*] (DIT)
STRIPE .... Stress-Induced Pseudoelasticity (PDAA)
STRIPE .... Swap Transferring Risk with Participating Element [*Finance*]
STRIPS........ Separate Trading of Registered Interest and Principal of Securities [*Investment term*]
STRIPS .... Stanford Research Institute Problem Solver [*Computer system*]
STRIVE .... Society for the Preservation of Rural Industries and Village Enterprises [*British*] (ODBW)
STRIVE .... Standard Techniques for Reporting Information on Value Engineering
STRJ........... Self-Powered Thermocouple Reference Junction
STRK .... Star Tracker (NASA)
STRK .... Stroke (MSA)
STRKP .... Storekeeper
STRKR........ Striker [*Automotive engineering*]
STRL.......... Schottky Transistor Resistor Logic [*Electronics*] (IAA)
STRL........... Sea Trials [*Navy*] (NVT)
STRL........... Steris Corp. [*NASDAQ symbol*] (SAG)
STR L .... Straight Line [*Freight*]
STRL.......... Structural
StrlBcp........ Sterling Bancorp [*Associated Press*] (SAG)
StrlBnc........ Sterling Bancshares, Inc. [*Associated Press*] (SAG)
StrlCap .... Sterling Capital Corp. [*Associated Press*] (SAG)
StrlCh .... Sterling Chemicals, Inc. [*Associated Press*] (SAG)
STRLEN .... String Length [*Computer science*] (PCM)
StrlF........... Sterling Financial Corp. [*Associated Press*] (SAG)
StrlFnWA .... Sterling Financial Corp. [*Associated Press*] (SAG)

STR LGTHS...   Straight Lengths [Freight]
StrLhmn.......   Stearns & Lehman, Inc. [Associated Press] (SAG)
STRLN.........   Streamline (MSA)
STRLNG.......   Sterling
strl si..........   Sterling Silver (VRA)
StrlVis........   Sterling Vision, Inc. [Associated Press] (SAG)
StrlWst.......   Sterling West Bancorp [Associated Press] (SAG)
STRM.........   Storeroom (MSA)
strm...........   Store Room (VRA)
STRM.........   Stratacom, Inc. [NASDAQ symbol] (SAG)
STRM.........   Stream
StrMb........   Streicher Mobile Fueling, Inc. [Associated Press] (SAG)
STRMD.......   Strategic Missile Division [Military]
StrmLog.......   StreamLogic Corp. [Associated Press] (SAG)
STRN.........   Standard Technical Report Number
STRN.........   Strength (AAG)
STRNG.......   Steering
STRNR........   Strainer (AAG)
STRO.........   Scandinavian Tire and Rim Organization (EA)
STRO.........   Stereo Routes [Aviation] (FAAC)
STRO.........   Strouds, Inc. [NASDAQ symbol] (SAG)
Strob.........   Strobhart's South Carolina Law Reports [1846-50] [A publication] (DLA)
Strob Ch .....   Strobhart's South Carolina Equity Reports [A publication] (DLA)
STROBE.......   Satellite Tracking of Balloons and Emergencies
STROBE.......   Stroboscopic (MSA)
Strob Eq ......   Strobhart's South Carolina Equity Reports [1846-50] [A publication] (DLA)
Strober ....   Strober Organization, Inc. [Associated Press] (SAG)
STROBES.....   Shared-Time Repair of Big Electronic Systems [Computer science]
Strobh Eq (SC)...   Strobhart's South Carolina Equity Reports [A publication] (DLA)
Strobh L (SC)...   Strobhart's South Carolina Law Reports [A publication] (DLA)
STROFAC.....   Stabilized Routing for Afloat Commands (MCD)
STR OFF FIXT...   Store or Office Fixture [s] [Freight]
STROG........   Strait of Gibraltar (DOMA)
Strom.........   Stromateis [of Clemens Alexandrinus] [Classical studies] (OCD)
STROM.......   Stromberg [Automotive engineering]
StrongSv......   Strongsville Savings Bank [Associated Press] (SAG)
STROP........   Stock Ratio Optimizing (MHDB)
Strouds.......   Strouds, Inc. [Associated Press] (SAG)
Stroud Sl.....   Stroud on Slavery [A publication] (DLA)
StroUSA......   Storage USA, Inc. [Associated Press] (SAG)
STRP ....   Short Tandem Repeat Polymorphisms [Genetics]
STRP ....   Strap
STRR ....   Star Technologies [NASDAQ symbol] (TTSB)
STRR ....   Star Technologies, Inc. [Sterling, VA] [NASDAQ symbol] (NQ)
STRS ....   SAGE [Semi-Automatic Ground Equipment] Training Requirements Section (SAA)
STRS ....   Stimulated Thermal Rayleigh Scattering (PDAA)
STRS ....   Strategic Transportation Research Study [FHWA] (TAG)
STRS ....   Submarine Technical Repair Standard [Navy] (DNAB)
STRSPH.......   Stratosphere (WGA)
STRT..........   Skin Temperature Recovery Time [Medicine] (DMAA)
STRT..........   Start
STRT..........   [The] Stewartstown Railroad Co. [AAR code]
STRT..........   Strait [Board on Geographic Names]
STRT..........   Strattec Security [NASDAQ symbol] (TTSB)
STRT..........   Strattec Security Corp. [NASDAQ symbol] (SAG)
STRT..........   Street [Commonly used] (OPSA)
StrtCp ....   Stratosphere Corp. [Associated Press] (SAG)
StrtDiag ......   Strategic Diagnostics, Inc. [Associated Press] (SAG)
STRTGC ......   Strategic
StrtgDist .....   Strategic Distribution [Associated Press] (SAG)
STRTL.........   Structural
STRTR ....   Starter [Automotive engineering]
STRU ....   Styrelserepresentationsutredningen [Sweden]
STRUBAL.....   Structured Basic Language [Computer science] (CSR)
STRUC........   Structure (AABC)
StrucD ....   Structural Dynamics Research Corp. [Associated Press] (SAG)
STRUCT.......   Structure (AAG)
STRUDL.......   Structural Design Language [Computer science] (MCD)
STRUDLDYNAL...   Structural Design Language Dynamic Analysis [Computer science]
STRUDLPLOTS...   Structural Design Language Output Plots
STRUDLTOWER...   Structural Design Language for Transmission Tower
STRUFO......   Structural Formula [Chemistry] [Computer science]
ST Rulings...   Sales Tax Rulings [Australia A publication]
Struther ......   Struthers Industries [Associated Press] (SAG)
Struve.........   Struve's Washington Territory Reports [1854-88] [A publication] (DLA)
STRV ....   Short Tons Raw Value
STRVN ....   Stravenue [Commonly used] (OPSA)
STRVNUE....   Stravenue [Commonly used] (OPSA)
STRW ....   Straw [Colored] [Laboratory science] (DAVI)
STRW ....   Strawbridge & Clothier [NASDAQ symbol] (NQ)
STRWA ....   Strawbridge/Clothier'A' [NASDAQ symbol] (TTSB)
StrwbCl.......   Strawbridge Clothier [Associated Press] (SAG)
STRY ....   Stryker Corp. [NASDAQ symbol] (NQ)
STRYCH......   Strychnina [Strychnine] [Pharmacy] (ROG)
Stryker.......   Stryker Corp. [Associated Press] (SAG)
St Ry Rep...   Street Railway Reports [United States] [A publication] (DLA)
STrZ..........   South Tropical Zone [Planet Jupiter]
STS............   Office of State Technical Services [Also, OSTS] [Abolished, 1970 Department of Commerce]
STS............   SAGE [Semi-Automatic Ground Equipment] Training Specialist (SAA)

Sts.............   Saints (ODBW)
STS............   Saint Thomas Seminary [Colorado; Connecticut; Kentucky]
STS............   Santa Rosa [California] [Airport symbol] (OAG)
STS............   Santiago [Spain] [Seismograph station code, US Geological Survey] (SEIS)
STS............   Satellite-to-Satellite (CET)
STS............   Satellite Tracking Station
STS............   Satellite Transmission Systems, Inc. [Hauppauge, NY] [Telecommunications] (TSSD)
STS............   S-Band Transmitter System
STS............   Scanning Tunneling Spectroscopy
STS............   Scheduled Truck Service [Army]
STS............   School Television Service
STS............   School-to-School [Red Cross Youth]
STS............   Science and Technology Section [Association of College and Research Libraries]
STS............   Science of To-Day Series [A publication]
STS............   Science Talent Search (EA)
STS............   Science, Technology, and Society
STS............   Scientific Terminal System (IAA)
STS............   Scottish Tartans Society (EA)
STS............   Sea Training Staff [Canadian Navy]
STS............   Security Termination Statement [Military] (AFM)
STS............   Self-Test Select
STS............   Seminex [Concordia Seminary in Exile] Library, St. Louis, MO [OCLC symbol] (OCLC)
STS............   Sequence-Tagged Site [Genetics]
STS............   Serological Test for Syphilis [Medicine]
STS............   Servicios Auxiliares de Transportes Aereos [Brazil] [ICAO designator] (FAAC)
STS............   Servocylinder Test Set (MCD)
STS............   Servo Test System
STS............   Seville Touring Sedan [General Motors Corp.]
STS............   Sewage Treatment System [Navy] (CAAL)
STS............   Shared Tenant Services [Telecommunications] (TSSD)
STS............   Ship-to-Shore
STS............   Shuttle Test Station (NASA)
STS............   Shuttle Transportation System (MCD)
STS............   Siltstone [Lithology]
STS............   Simulator Test Set (CAAL)
STS............   Single Thread System
STS............   Skaggs Telecommunications Service [Salt Lake City, UT] [Telecommunications] (TSSD)
STS............   Skylab Terminal System [NASA]
STS............   Society for Textual Scholarship (EA)
STS............   Society of Thoracic Surgeons (EA)
STS............   Socio-Technical Systems [Management technique]
STS............   Sodium Tetradecyl Sulfate [Organic chemistry]
STS............   Sodium Thiosulfate [Inorganic chemistry, biochemistry]
STS............   Soft Tissue Sarcoma [Oncology]
STS............   Soft-Tissue Swelling [Radiology] (DAVI)
STS............   Solar Tracking System
STS............   SONAR Technician, Submarine [Navy rating] (DNAB)
STS............   SONAR Test System
STS............   Sonic Telex System [Sonicair] [Phoenix, AZ] [Telecommunications] (TSSD)
STS............   Spacecraft Telecommunications System
STS............   Spacecraft Tracking Station [NASA] (KSC)
STS............   Space Technology Satellite (IAA)
STS............   Space-Time-Space [Digital switching structure] [Telecommunications] (TEL)
STS............   Space Transportation System
STS............   Special Task Stores [Military British]
STS............   Special Test System [Air Force] (AFM)
STS............   Special Training Standard [Air Force] (AFM)
STS............   Special Treatment Steel
STS............   Specialty Training System
STS............   Specific Tensile Strength
STS............   Spring Trapmakers' Society [British] (DCTA)
STS............   Stabilized Telescope System
StS............   Stamp Seal (BJA)
STS............   Standard (Galilean) Telescopes [Instrumentation]
STS............   Standard Technical Specifications [Nuclear energy] (NRCH)
STS............   Standard Test for Syphilis [Medicine]
STS............   Standard Threshold Shift
STS............   State Technical Services [Abolished, 1970]
STS............   Static Test Stand
STS............   Stationary Time Series
STS............   Station to Station
STS............   Status [ICAO designator] (FAAC)
STS............   Sterol-sulphatase [An enzyme]
STS............   Stimulated Thermal Scattering [Photonics]
STS............   Stockpile-to-Target Sequence [Military]
STS............   Stock Trading System
STS............   Stomatogastric Nervous System [Neuroanatomy]
STS............   Strategic Technical Service (CINC)
STS............   Strategic Training Squadron (MCD)
STS............   Streets [Postal Service standard] (OPSA)
STS............   Structural Transition Section [NASA] (MCD)
STS............   Student Travel School
STS............   Sugar-Tong Splint [Medicine] (MEDA)
STS............   Superior Temporal Sulcus [Brain anatomy]
STS............   Supernatant Treatment System [Nuclear energy] (NUCP)
STS............   Supersonic Target System
STS............   Supplementary Test Site [Nuclear energy] (IID)

STS..............	Suprasonic Transport [*Aviation*] (DAVI)
STS..............	Supreme Industries [*Formerly, ESI Industries Corp.*] [*AMEX symbol*] (SPSG)
STS..............	Supreme Industries'A' [*AMEX symbol*] (TTSB)
STS..............	Surface Target Simulator [*Navy*] (DNAB)
STS..............	Surveillance Test Set (MCD)
STS..............	Survey Tabulation Services, Inc. [*Information service or system*] (IID)
STS..............	Synchronous Transport Signal [*Computer science*]
STS..............	Synchrony Service and Transport System [*Ascom Timeplex, Inc.*]
STS..............	System Technical Services
STS..............	System Test Set
STS..............	System Test Software (CAAL)
STS..............	System Test Station (SAA)
STS..............	System Training Section (SAA)
STS..............	System Training Specialist (SAA)
STS..............	System Trouble Shooting
STS..............	System Trouble Survey (CET)
STSA.............	Seaman Apprentice, SONAR Technician, Striker [*Navy rating*]
STSA.............	Southern Thoracic Surgical Association (EA)
STSA.............	State Technical Services Act
STSA.............	Sterling Financial Corp. [*NASDAQ symbol*] (SAG)
STSA.............	Sterling Finl (WA) [*NASDAQ symbol*] (TTSB)
STSA.............	Sub-tropical Seedgrowers' Association [*Australia*]
STSALV.........	Standby Salvage Ship [*Navy*] (NVT)
STSAP	Sterling Finl $1.8125 Cv Pfd [*NASDAQ symbol*] (TTSB)
ST-SAS	Septic Tank-Subsurface Absorption System
STSC.............	Scientific Time Sharing Corp. [*Host*] [*Information service or system*] (IID)
STSC.............	Scottish Teachers Salaries Committee [*British*]
STSC.............	Shipboard Tactical Satellite Communications (DNAB)
ST SCI..........	Space Telescope Science Institute [*Johns Hopkins University*] [*Research center*] (RCD)
STScI...........	Space Telescope Science Institute
STSCM.........	Space Transportation System Cost Model [*NASA*] (KSC)
STSD............	Society of Teachers of Speech and Drama [*British*]
STSE............	Split-Thickness Skin Excision [*Medicine*] (DMAA)
STSF............	Spatial Transformation of Sound Fields
STSFCTN	Satisfaction
STSFSC........	Scarf Trailers Science Fiction Social Club [*Defunct*] (EA)
STSG	Screening Test of Spanish Grammar (EDAC)
STSG	Shuttle Test Group [*NASA*] (NASA)
STSG	Space Topics Study Group (EA)
STSG	Split Thickness Skin Graft
STSH	Stabilized Shunt [*Electricity*]
STSI.............	Scientific Technical and Societal Information (NITA)
STSI.............	Space Telescope Science Institute [*NASA*]
STSJHA........	St. Thomas - St. John Hotel Association [*Virgin Islands*] (EAIO)
STSK............	Scandinavian Committee for Satellite Communications [*Telecommunications*] (TEL)
STSL.............	Sea Turtle Survival League
STSM............	Statesman (WGA)
STSM............	Surface-to-Target-to-Surface-to-Missile
STSN............	Seaman, SONAR Technician, Striker [*Navy rating*]
STSN............	Set-and-Test-Sequence-Number [*Computer science*] (IBMDP)
STSO	Senior Technical Staff Officer [*British*]
STSOC.........	Space Transportation System Operations Contact [*NASA*] (SSD)
STSOPO.......	Shuttle Transportation Systems Operations Program Office [*Johnson Space Center*] (NASA)
STS-QN........	Serological Test for Syphilis-Quantitation [*Medicine*] (DAVI)
ST-SR	Small Transmitter Coated with Silicon Rubber
STSR	Stepped-Temperature Stress-Rupture [*Ceramics*] (DICI)
STSR	System Test Summary Report [*NASA*] (NASA)
STSS	Sensitive Thrust Stand System
STSS	Series-Tuned Series-Stabilized [*Computer science*] (IAA)
STSS	Society for Traumatic Stress Studies (EA)
STSS	Staphylococcal Toxic Shock Syndrome [*Medicine*] (DMAA)
STSSA	SONAR Technician, Submarine, Seaman Apprentice [*Navy rating*] (DNAB)
STSSN	SONAR Technician, Submarine, Seaman [*Navy rating*] (DNAB)
STSSPF.......	Space Transportation System Spacelab Processing Facility [*NASA*] (SSD)
STSTA.........	Small Aerial Surveillance and Target Acquisition (PDAA)
STSTB.........	Status Strobe (MHDI)
ST/STE........	Special Tooling / Special Test Equipment [*Navy*] (DNAB)
Sts Tog........	Saints Together [*Library cataloging*] (DGA)
STSTX.........	State St. Research Invest. Trust Cl.S [*Mutual fund ticker symbol*] (SG)
STSV............	Satellite-to-Space Vehicle (SAA)
STS.WS	Supreme Indus Wrrt [*AMEX symbol*] (TTSB)
STSX...........	Synchronous Transport Signal Cross-Connect [*Telecommunications*] (CIST)
STT	Air St. Thomas [*ICAO designator*] (FAAC)
STT	Charlotte Amalie, VI [*Location identifier FAA*] (FAAL)
STT	Cyril E. King Airport [*FAA*] (TAG)
STT	Saigon Transportation Terminal Command [*Republic of Vietnam Armed Forces*]
STT	Save the Theatres (EA)
STT	Scaphotrapeziotrapezoid [*Joint*] [*Anatomy*] (DAVI)
STT	School of Tank Technology [*British military*] (DMA)
STT	School of Technical Training [*British military*] (DMA)
STT	SEAL [*Sea, Air, Land*] Tactical Training (DOMA)
STT	Seattle - Marshall [*Washington*] [*Seismograph station code, US Geological Survey Closed*] (SEIS)
STT	Secure Transaction Technology [*Telecommunications*]
STT	Seek Time per Track

STT	Semitendinosus Tendon [*Anatomy*]
STT	Sensitization Test
STT	Sent to Typesetter [*Publishing*]
STT	Serial Thrombin Time [*Medicine*] (MAE)
STT	Ship Turn Transmitter
STT	Shock Tube Test
STT	Shore Targeting Terminal [*Navy*] (CAAL)
STT	Short-Term Test [*Toxicology*]
STT	Short Time Test (IAA)
STT	Signal Tracing Tester
STT	Single Target Track [*Navy*] (NG)
STT	Single Transition Time (IAA)
STT	Single Transmission Time (NITA)
STT	Skid-to-Turn
STT	Skin Temperature Test [*Physiology*]
STT	Small Tactical Terminal [*Marine science*] (OSRA)
STT	Spacecraft Terminal Thrust
STT	Spacelab Transfer Tunnel (NASA)
STT	Spade Tongue Terminal
STT	Spinothalamic Tract [*Brain anatomy*]
STT	Standard Triple Therapy [*For hypertension*]
STT	Start Time (IAA)
STT	State Str Boston [*NYSE symbol*] (TTSB)
STT	State Street Boston, Inc. [*NYSE symbol*] (SAG)
STT	Stenographer, Medical [*Navy*]
STT	Store Tag (SAA)
STT	Strain-Transport-Time [*Geology*]
STT	St. Thomas [*Virgin Islands*] [*Airport symbol*]
STT	Superior Teletec (EFIS)
STT	Sutton Resources Ltd. [*Vancouver Stock Exchange symbol*]
STT	Syndicat des Travailleurs en Telecommunications [*Telecommunications Workers Union - TWU*] [*Canada*]
STTA............	Scottish Table Tennis Association (DBA)
STTA............	Scottish Timber Trade Association (DBA)
St Tax Cas Rep (CCH)...	State Tax Cases Reporter (Commerce Clearing House) [*A publication*] (DLA)
St Tax Rep (CCH)...	State Tax Reporter (Commerce Clearing House) [*A publication*] (DLA)
STTC............	Schottky Transistor-Transistor Logic (NITA)
STTC............	Scottish Textile and Technical Centre Ltd. [*British*] (IRUK)
STTC............	Sheppard Technical Training Center (AFM)
StTDJ...........	Studies on the Texts of the Desert of Judah [*J. Van Der Ploeg*] [*Leiden*] [*A publication*] (BJA)
STTE............	Society of Travel and Tourism Educators (EA)
STTE............	Special Tools and Test Equipment
STTF............	Service to the Fleet [*A publication*] (DNAB)
STTF............	SONAR Test Tower Facility
STTF............	Special Tank Task Force (MCD)
STTF............	System Technology Test Facility (MCD)
STT-FNB	Suomen Tietotoimisto-Finska Notisbyran [*Press agency*] [*Finland*]
STTL............	Schottky Clamped Transistor-Transistor Logic [*Electronics*] (IAA)
S/TTL..........	Schottky Transistor-Transistor Logic
STTL............	Sit Tibi Terra Levis [*May the Earth Lie Light on Thee*] [*Letters found on Roman tombs*] [*Latin*]
STTM...........	Stabilized Tracking Tripod Module (RDA)
STTMA.........	Screw Thread Tool Manufacturers Association [*British*] (DBA)
STTNG	Star Trek, the Next Generation [*Television program*]
STTO	Sawtooth Timing Oscillator (DEN)
STTO	Staking Tool (AAG)
STTOL..........	Standing Tolerance (STED)
STTOT..........	Single Target Track on Target [*Navy*]
STTP............	Space Test and Transportation Program (DOMA)
St Tr	Howell's English State Trials [*1163-1820*] [*A publication*] (DLA)
STTR............	Small Business Technology Transfer Resources (GAVI)
STTR............	Stator
St Tri	State Trials [*A publication*] (DLA)
St Tr NS	Macdonell's State Trials [*1820-58*] [*A publication*] (DLA)
STTS	S-Band Transponder Test Set (MCD)
STTS	Scottish Tramway and Transport Society (DBA)
STTS	Shipboard Target Tracking System
STTSRA	Scoot-Tours Touring Scooter Riders Association (EA)
STTT............	Space Telescope Task Team [*NASA*]
STTX...........	Steel Technologies [*NASDAQ symbol*] (TTSB)
STTX...........	Steel Technologies, Inc. [*Louisville, KY*] [*NASDAQ symbol*] (NQ)
STTZ...........	Sutton Resource Ltd. [*NASDAQ symbol*] (SAG)
STTZF..........	Sutton Resources [*NASDAQ symbol*] (TTSB)
STU.............	Secure Telephone Unit [*Computer science*]
STU.............	Seeker Test Unit (MCD)
STU.............	Service Trials Unit
STU.............	Servo Test Unit
STU.............	Shock Trauma Unit [*Emergency medicine*] (DAVI)
STU.............	Short Ton Unit
STU.............	Signal Transfer Unit
STU.............	Skin Test Unit
STU.............	Space-Time Unit [*Computer*]
STU.............	Special Test Unit (CET)
STU.............	Special Training Unit
STU.............	Star Tracker Unit [*NASA*] (MCD)
STU.............	Static Test Unit (KSC)
STU.............	Step Up
STU.............	Steubenville [*Diocesan abbreviation*] [*Ohio*] (TOCD)
STU.............	Stuart (ROG)
STU.............	Stuart [*D. A.*] Ltd. [*Toronto Stock Exchange symbol*]
stu.............	Stucco (VRA)
Stu.............	Student (AL)

STU..............	Student (AFM)
STU..............	Student Loan Corp. [NYSE symbol] (SPSG)
STU..............	Stuttgart [Federal Republic of Germany] [Seismograph station code, US Geological Survey] (SEIS)
STU..............	Styrelsen foer Teknisk Utveckling [Swedish Board for Technical Development]
STU..............	Submarine Test Unit
STU..............	Submersible Test Unit [Navy]
STU..............	Subscribers' Trunk Unit [Telecommunications] (TEL)
STU..............	Systems Test Unit (KSC)
STU..............	System Time Unit (NITA)
STU..............	System Timing Unit
STU..............	System Transition Unit [Computer science]
STU..............	System Transmission Unit (NITA)
STU..............	Transportes Aereos Fueguino [Argentina ICAO designator] (FAAC)
STU..............	University of Steubenville, Steubenville, OH [OCLC symbol] (OCLC)
STUA..........	Stuart Entertainment [NASDAQ symbol] (SPSG)
Stu Adm	Stuart's Lower Canada Vice-Admiralty Reports [A publication] (DLA)
Stu Adm NS...	Stuart's Lower Canada Vice-Admiralty Reports, New Series [A publication] (DLA)
Stu Ap	Stuart's Lower Canada King's Bench Reports, Appeal Cases [A publication] (DLA)
Stuart..........	Stuart, Milne, and Peddie's Scotch Court of Session Cases
Stuart..........	Stuart's Lower Canada Reports [A publication] (DLA)
Stuart..........	Stuart's Lower Canada Vice-Admiralty Reports [A publication] (DLA)
Stuart Adm NS...	Stuart's Lower Canada Vice-Admiralty Reports, New Series [A publication] (DLA)
Stuart & Por...	Stuart [or Stewart] and Porter's Alabama Reports [A publication] (DLA)
Stuart & Porter...	Stuart [or Stewart] and Porter's Alabama Reports [A publication] (DLA)
Stuart Beng...	Stuart's Select Cases [1860] [Bengal, India] [A publication] (DLA)
Stuart KB.....	Stuart's Lower Canada King's Bench Reports [1810-25] [Quebec] [A publication] (DLA)
Stuart KB (Quebec)...	Stuart's Lower Canada King's Bench Reports [Quebec] [A publication] (DLA)
Stuart LCKB...	Stuart's Lower Canada King's Bench Reports [A publication] (DLA)
Stuart LCVA...	Stuart's Lower Canada Vice-Admiralty Reports [A publication] (DLA)
Stuart M & P...	Stuart, Milne, and Peddie's Scotch Court of Session Cases [1851-53] [A publication] (DLA)
Stuart's Adm...	Stuart's Lower Canada Vice-Admiralty Reports [A publication] (DLA)
Stuart's R	Stuart's Lower Canada King's Bench Reports, Appeal Cases [Quebec] [A publication] (DLA)
Stuart Vice-Adm...	Stuart's Lower Canada Vice-Admiralty Reports [A publication] (DLA)
STUB	Stadt- und Universitaetsbibliothek Frankfurt [Database producer]
Stubbs CH ...	Stubb's Constitutional History [A publication] (DLA)
Stubbs Sel Ch...	Stubb's Select Charters [A publication] (DLA)
STUC..........	Sarawak Trade Union Congress
STUC..........	Scottish Trades Union Congress
STUC..........	Singapore Trade Union Congress
STUCENFL ...	Student Census-Date Report File (EDAC)
STUD	Standard Tractor, Universal with Dozer [Army]
STUD	Student
STUD	Studies
STUD	Study
Stud Anc Technol...	Studies in Ancient Technology [A publication] (OCD)
Stud Cont Ed...	Studies in Continuing Education [A publication]
Stud Doc Hist Iur...	Studia et Documenta Historiae et Iuris [Rome] [A publication] (OCD)
STUDE..........	Studebaker [Automotive engineering]
StudtIElecIE...	Student of the Institution of Electrical and Electronic Incorporated Engineers [British] (DBQ)
StudtIWHTE...	Student of the Institution of Works and Highways Technician Engineers [British] (DBQ)
Student Law J...	Student Lawyer Journal [A publication] (DLA)
Student L Rev...	Student Law Review [A publication] (DLA)
Stud Etr	Studi Etruschi [Firenze] [A publication] (OCD)
Stud Gesch Kult Alt...	Studien zur Geschichte und Kultur des Altertums [A publication] (OCD)
Stud Gr Rom Hist...	Studies in Greek and Roman History [A publication] (OCD)
Stud Hist	Studies in History, Economics, and Public Law [A publication] (DLA)
Studies Crim L...	Studies in Criminal Law and Procedure [A publication] (DLA)
StudIManf...	Student Member of the Institute of Manufacturing [British] (DBQ)
StudIMS.......	Student of the Institute of Management Specialists [British] (DBQ)
StudInstBTM...	Student Member of the Institute of Business and Technical Management [British] (DBQ)
Stud Int'l Fiscal L...	Studies on International Fiscal Law [A publication] (DLA)
StudioP........	Studio Plus Hotels, Inc. [Associated Press] (SAG)
StudioPH	Studio Plus Hotels, Inc. [Associated Press] (SAG)
Studi Stor	Studi Storici per l'Antichita Classica [A publication] (OCD)
Stud Ital	Studi Italiani di Filologia Classica [A publication] (OCD)
Stud L & Econ Dev...	Studies in Law and Economic Development [A publication] (DLA)
Stud Law Lex...	Students' Pocket Law Lexicon [A publication] (DLA)
StudSCP	Student of the Society of Certified Professionals [British] (DBQ)
StudSE........	Student of the Society of Engineers [British] (DBQ)
StudSLAET...	Student of the Society of Licensed Aircraft Engineers and Technologists [British] (DBQ)
Stud Urb	Studi di Urbanistica Antica [A publication] (OCD)
Stud W Aust Hist...	Studies in Western Australian History [A publication]
StudWeldI....	Student of the Welding Institute [British] (DBQ)
STUF............	Short-Term Underwriting Facility [Finance]

STUF............	Student Flight [Military]
STUFF..........	System to Uncover Facts Fast
STUFT..........	Ships Taken Up from Trade
STUG	Student Group [Military]
STUG	Sturmgeschuetz [Self-propelled assault gun] [German military - World War II]
STUH	Stuart Hall (EFIS)
STU-IIM	Secure Terminal Unit-II Militarized
STUK	Sturmkanone [Self-propelled assault gun] [German military - World War II]
STUKA	Sturzkampfflugzeug [Dive bomber] [German military - World War II]
Stu KB	Stuart's Lower Canada King's Bench Reports [1810-35] [A publication] (DLA)
Stu LC	Stuart's Lower Canada King's Bench Reports [1810-35] [A publication] (DLA)
StuLnCp......	Student Loan Corp. [Associated Press] (SAG)
Stu M & P ...	Stuart, Milne, and Peddie's Scotch Court of Sessions Reports [A publication] (DLA)
Stu Mil & Ped...	Stuart, Milne, and Peddie's Scotch Court of Sessions Reports [A publication] (DLA)
STUMP	Submersible, Transportable Utility, Marine Pump (PDAA)
Stun............	Serial Tunneling [Computer science]
STUP	Spinning Tubular Projectile (MCD)
STUPID........	Simulation of the Underlying Processes in Decisions (MCD)
STURAA.......	Surface Transportation and Uniform Relocation Assistance Act [1987]
Stur & Porter...	Stuart [or Stewart] and Porter's Alabama Reports [A publication] (DLA)
S Turb	Steam Turbine (DS)
Sturg BL	Sturgeon. Bankrupt Acts [A publication] (ILCA)
Sturg Ins D...	Sturgeon's Insolvent Debtors Act [1842] [A publication] (DLA)
STURM	Sturminster [England]
SturmR	Sturm Ruger & Co. [Associated Press] (SAG)
STURP	Shroud of Turin Research Project (EA)
SturtEn........	Stuart Entertainment, Inc. [Associated Press] (SAG)
STUS	Student Squadron
STUTIS	Secondary, Technical, and University Teachers' Insurance Society [British] (BI)
STUTNG.......	Student Training [Navy] (DNAB)
Stu VA	Stuart's Lower Canada Vice-Admiralty Reports [A publication] (ILCA)
STUW	Subtropical Underwater [Marine science] (OSRA)
STV.............	Santa Anna Di Valdieri [Italy] [Seismograph station code, US Geological Survey] (SEIS)
STV.............	Satellite Test Vehicle (IAA)
STV.............	Scottish Television (DI)
STV.............	Separation Test Vehicle
STV.............	Short-Term Variability (STED)
STV.............	Short-Tube Vertical [Evaporator]
STV.............	Single Transferable Vote
STV.............	Small Test Vessel [Nuclear energy] (NRCH)
STV.............	Soft-Tissue View [Radiology] (DAVI)
STV.............	Solar Thermal Vacuum
STV.............	Solidaridad de Trabajadores Vascos [Solidarity of Basque Workers] [In exile Spain]
STV.............	Southern Aviation Ltd. [Ghana] [ICAO designator] (FAAC)
STV.............	Southern Television [British] (DI)
STV.............	Space Test Vehicle [NASA] (KSC)
STV.............	Special Test Vehicle
STV.............	Standard Test Vehicle
STV.............	Staverton [England] [Airport symbol] (AD)
STV.............	Steam Tank Vessel (DNAB)
STV.............	Steerable Low-Light-Level Television (PDAA)
STV.............	Stikine Silver [Vancouver Stock Exchange symbol]
STV.............	Stonewall, TX [Location identifier FAA] (FAAL)
STV.............	Stove [Classified advertising] (ADA)
STV.............	Structural Test Vehicle [NASA] (KSC)
STV.............	St. Thomas [Diocesan abbreviation] [Virgin Islands] (TOCD)
STV.............	STV Group, Inc. [Associated Press] (SAG)
STV.............	Submarine Target Vessel (NVT)
STV.............	Subscription Television
STV.............	Subscription Television Authority [FCC] (NTCM)
STV.............	Subscription TV, Inc. (NTCM)
STV.............	Superior Temporal Vein [Medicine] (DMAA)
STV.............	Supersonic Test Vehicle (AAG)
STV.............	Surveillance Television (AFM)
STVA..........	Self-Tuning Vibration Absorber [Navy] (CAAL)
STVA..........	Subscription Television Association [Defunct] (EA)
STVA..........	Subtotal Villose Atrophy [Medicine] (MAE)
STVC..........	Space Thermal Vacuum Chamber (SAA)
STVC..........	Sumerian Texts of Varied Context [E. Chiera] [A publication]
STVD..........	Spacecraft Television Video Data
stvdr..........	Stevedore (DS)
STVI...........	STV Group [NASDAQ symbol] (TTSB)
STVI...........	STV Group, Inc. [NASDAQ symbol] (SAG)
STVM..........	Semitrailer Van Mount
STVP..........	Salinity, Temperature, Sound-Velocity and Pressure-Sensing System (PDAA)
STVP..........	Short-Term Vehicle Park (DS)
STVS..........	Short-Term Visual Storage [or Store] [Psychophysiology]
STVS..........	Surinaamse Televisie Sichting [Television network] [Surinam]
STVS..........	Surinaamse Televisie Stichtig (EY)
STW...........	Save the Whales (EA)
STW...........	Sewage Treatment Works
STW...........	Short-Term Waviness [Surface finish]
STW...........	Southwest Tech [Vancouver Stock Exchange symbol]
STW...........	Speed Made Good Through the Water (NATG)

STW.............	Standard Commercial [*NYSE symbol*] (TTSB)
STW.............	Standard Commercial Corp. [*NYSE symbol*] (SPSG)
STW.............	Star Trek Welcommittee (EA)
STW.............	Starways SA [*Switzerland ICAO designator*] (FAAC)
STW.............	Stern Wheel [*of a ship*] (DS)
STW.............	Stillwater, NJ [*Location identifier FAA*] (FAAL)
STW.............	Stillwater Public Library, Stillwater, OK [*OCLC symbol*] (OCLC)
STW.............	Store Word [*Computer science*] (IAA)
STW.............	Storm Water
STW.............	Striped Peak [*Washington*] [*Seismograph station code, US Geological Survey*] (SEIS)
STW.............	Subtropical Water
STW.............	System Tape Writer [*Computer science*] (IAA)
STWA...........	School to Work Association (EA)
ST. WAPNIACL...	State, Treasury, War, Attorney General, Postmaster General, Navy, Interior, Agriculture, Commerce, Labor [*Pre-1947 mnemonic guide to names of the departments in the President's Cabinet, in order of creation*] [*Obsolete*]
STWBRD......	Strawboard [*Shipping*]
STWE.........	Society of Technical Writers and Editors [*Later, STWP, STC*]
St Westm.....	Statute of Westminster [*A publication*] (DLA)
STWG	Stowage (MSA)
STWL.........	Stopway Light [*Aviation*] (FAAC)
STWO	Staff Tactical Watch Officer (DOMA)
STWP.........	Society of Technical Writers and Publishers [*Formerly, STWE*] [*Later, STC*] (EA)
STWP.........	Steam Working Pressure (MSA)
stwr	Stoneware (VRA)
StwStv	Stewart & Stevenson Services, Inc. [*Associated Press*] (SAG)
STWY..........	Stairway (AAG)
STX.............	Aerocharter [*Czechoslovakia*] [*ICAO designator*] (FAAC)
STX.............	Christiansted, St. Croix, VI [*Location identifier FAA*] (FAAL)
STX.............	Saxitoxin [*A neurotoxin*]
STX.............	Situational Training Exercise [*Army*] (INF)
STX.............	Spherical Torus Experiment [*Oak Ridge National Laboratory*]
STX.............	Starrex Mining Corp. Ltd. [*Toronto Stock Exchange symbol*]
STX.............	Start of Text [*Telecommunications*] (OSI)
STX.............	Start of Text Character [*Keyboard*] [*Computer science*]
STX.............	Station 2 [*Nevada*] [*Seismograph station code, US Geological Survey Closed*] (SEIS)
STX.............	St. Croix [*Virgin Islands*] [*Airport symbol*]
STX.............	Sterling Chemicals [*NYSE symbol*] (TTSB)
STX.............	Sterling Chemicals, Inc. [*NYSE symbol*] (CTT)
STX.............	Structure (STED)
St Xavier U...	St. Xavier University (GAGS)
STXM..........	Scanning Transmission X-Ray Microscopy (MCD)
STXRF	Source-Tuned X-Ray Fluorescence [*Spectroscopy*]
STY.............	Salto [*Uruguay*] [*Airport symbol*] (OAG)
STY.............	Space-Time Yield [*Chemical engineering*]
STY.............	Spatial Technology, Inc. [*AMEX symbol*] (SAG)
3IY.............	Standard Yiddish (BJA)
STY.............	Stony River [*Alaska*] [*Seismograph station code, US Geological Survey*] (SEIS)
Sly	Story [*Journalism*]
Sty	Style's English King's Bench Reports [*1646-55*] [*A publication*] (DLA)
sty..............	Stylus (VRA)
Sty	Styrene [*Also, St*] [*Organic chemistry*]
STYCAR	Screening Tests for Young Children and Retardates (MAH)
STYL..........	Style
Style	Style's English King's Bench Reports [*A publication*] (DLA)
Style Pr Reg...	Style's Practical Register [*A publication*] (DLA)
StyleVid.......	Styles On Video, Inc. [*Associated Press*] (SAG)
STYLG	Styling
STYLST.......	Stylist
STYP..........	Styptic [*Stopping Bleeding*] [*Medicine*] (ROG)
Sty Pr Reg...	Style's Practical Register [*1657-1710*] [*A publication*] (DLA)
STZ.............	Santa Terezinha [*Brazil*] [*Airport symbol*] (OAG)
STZ.............	Schweizerische Theologische Zeitschrift [*Zurich*] [*A publication*] (BJA)
STZ.............	Serum-Treated Zymosan [*Clinical chemistry*]
STZ.............	Signal Technology [*AMEX symbol*] (TTSB)
STZ.............	Signal Technology Corp. [*AMEX symbol*] (SAG)
STZ.............	Southern Transgressive Zone [*Geology*]
STZ.............	Stallion Resources Ltd. [*Vancouver Stock Exchange symbol*]
STZ.............	Store Zero [*Computer science*] (IAA)
STZ.............	Stratford [*New Zealand*] [*Seismograph station code, US Geological Survey Closed*] (SEIS)
STZ.............	Streptozocin [*Antineoplastic drug*]
STZ.............	Streptozyme (STED)
Su	Ciba-Geigy Corp. [*Research code symbol*]
SU.............	Egypt [*International civil aircraft marking*] (ODBW)
SU.............	Optical Device [*JETDS nomenclature*] [*Military*] (CET)
SU.............	Salicyluric Acid [*Also, SUA*] [*Biochemistry*]
SU.............	Salmon Unlimited (EA)
su	Saudi Arabia [*MARC country of publication code Library of Congress*] (LCCP)
SU.............	Savings Unit
SU.............	Scorable Unit
SU.............	Scripture Union [*British*]
SU.............	Seamen's Union [*British*]
SU.............	Search Unit (COE)
SU.............	Seasonal Unemployment (MHDW)
SU.............	Secular Unemployment [*Business term*] (MHDW)
SU.............	Selectable Unit (BUR)
SU.............	Sensation Units
SU.............	Sensory Urgency [*Neurology*] (DAVI)
SU.............	Separation Ullage
SU.............	Service Unit [*Military*]
SU.............	Set Up [*Freight*]
SU.............	Shipment Unit [*Army*]
SU.............	Siemens Unit
SU.............	Sigma Units
SU.............	Signaling Unit
SU.............	Single Uptake [*Boilers*]
SU.............	Single User [*The military activity that has the sole interest in an item of supply*] [*DoD*]
SU.............	Society of St. Ursula (TOCD)
SU.............	Society of the Sisters of St. Ursula of the Blessed Virgin [*Roman Catholic religious order*]
SU.............	Solar Urticaria (STED)
SU.............	Somogyi Unit [*of amylase*] [*Clinical chemistry*]
SU.............	Sonics and Ultrasonics (MCD)
SU.............	Sorbent Unit (STED)
SU.............	Sosialistisk Ungdom [*Norway*]
SU.............	Soviet Union [*The USSR*]
SU.............	Space Unit (EA)
SU.............	Special Unitary [*Algebra*]
SU.............	Spectrophotometric Unit (DB)
S/U.............	Squared Up [*Typography*] (DGA)
SU.............	Standard Upkeep
SU.............	Stanford University [*California*]
SU.............	Start Up [*of a relay, power switchgear*] (IEEE)
SU.............	Station Unit [*Telecommunications*] (OA)
SU.............	Statistical Unit [*UNRISD*] [*United Nations*] (DUND)
SU.............	Storage Unit [*Computer science*]
SU.............	Stress Ulcer [*Medicine*] (DB)
SU.............	Stripers Unlimited (EA)
SU.............	Strontium Units [*Nuclear energy*]
SU.............	Structural Unemployed [*Business term*] (MHDW)
SU.............	Student Union
SU.............	Stunts Unlimited (EA)
SU.............	Subject [*Online database field identifier*]
SU.............	Submarine School Graduate [*Navy*] (DNAB)
SU.............	Subresolution Attenuated (AAEL)
SU.............	Subscriber Unit [*RADA*] [*Army*] (RDA)
SU.............	Sub-Unit (DNAB)
SU.............	Sudan Update [*A publication*]
Su	Sufentanil [*or Sulfentanyl*] [*An analgesic*]
su	Sugary [*A gene in sweet corn*]
SU.............	Suit (DNAB)
Su	Suite
SU.............	Sukhoy [*Aircraft*]
Su	Sulcus [*Brain anatomy*]
SU.............	Sulfonamide [*An antibiotic*] (DAVI)
SU.............	Sulfonylurea (STED)
Su	Sulphonamide (DB)
SU.............	Sulphonylurea (DB)
Su	Sumet [*Let Him, or Her, Take*] [*Pharmacy*]
SU.............	Suncor, Inc. [*Toronto Stock Exchange symbol AMEX symbol*]
SU.............	Sunday
Su	Superb [*Philately*]
SU.............	Supercommutation (SAA)
Su	Superior Court (DLA)
SU.............	Super Unleaded (Gasoline)
SU.............	Supine (STED)
SU.............	Supply [*Business term*]
SU.............	Support (IAA)
SU.............	Support Unit [*NASA*] (NASA)
su	Support Unit (NAKS)
SU.............	Suppressor [*Electronics*] (MDG)
SU.............	Surface to Underwater (IAA)
SU.............	Surgery (DAVI)
SU.............	Switching Unit
SU.............	Sydney University [*State*] (FFRA)
SU.............	Symbolic Unit (IAA)
SU.............	Syne Unit [*Telecommunications*] (OA)
SU.............	Syracuse University [*New York*]
SU.............	Thiouridine [*Two-letter symbol; see Srd*]
SU.............	Union of Soviet Socialist Republics [*ANSI two-letter standard code*] (CNC)
SUA............	Aviation Associates, Inc. [*St. Croix*] [*ICAO designator*] (FAAC)
SUA............	Salicyluric Acid [*Also, SU*] [*Biochemistry*]
SUA............	Satellite Unfurlable Antenna
SUA............	Sedative Urinary Antibiotic (DAVI)
SUA............	Serum Uric Acid [*Clinical chemistry*]
SUA............	Shipped Unassembled (MHDW)
SUA............	Silver Users Association (EA)
SUA............	Single Umbilical Artery [*Medicine*] (MAE)
SUA............	Small Unit Action [*Military*] (CINC)
SUA............	Society for Urban Anthropology (EA)
SUA............	Special Use Airspace [*FAA*] (TAG)
SUA............	Standard Unit of Accounting [*Computer science*]
SUA............	State Universities Association [*Later, NASULGC*]
SUA............	Stuart [*Florida*] [*Airport symbol*] (OAG)
SUA............	Stuart, FL [*Location identifier FAA*] (FAAL)
SUA............	Summit Tax Exempt Bond [*AMEX symbol*] (TTSB)
SUA............	Summit Tax Exempt Bond Fund Ltd. [*AMEX symbol*] (SPSG)
SUA............	Superior Acceptance Corp. Ltd. [*Toronto Stock Exchange symbol*]
SUA............	Supplemental Unemployment Assistance

SUA	Supply/Utilization Accounts [FAO] [Information service or system United Nations] (DUND)
SUA	Susitna [Alaska] [Seismograph station code, US Geological Survey] (SEIS)
SUA	Sweetener Users Association (EA)
SUAA	Montevideo/Angel S. Adami [Uruguay] [ICAO location identifier] (ICLI)
SUAB	Svenska Utvecklingsaktiebolaget [Swedish Corporation for Development]
SUAC	Scottish Universities Accommodation Consortium (AIE)
SUADPS	Shipboard Uniform Automatic Data Processing System [Navy]
SUAEWICS..	Soviet Union Airborne Early Warning and Interceptor Control System (MCD)
SUAG	Artigas/Aeropuerto Deptal [Uruguay] [ICAO location identifier] (ICLI)
SUALM	Submerged Anchor Leg Mooring [Engineering]
SUAR	Start Unload Address Register
Suas	Suasoriae [of Seneca the Elder] [Classical studies] (OCD)
SUAS	System for Upper Atmosphere Sounding (MCD)
SUAVE	Submersible System Used to Assess Vented Emissions (USDC)
SUAVE	Submersible [System] Used to Assess Vented Emissions [Marine science] (OSRA)
SUAWACS....	Soviet Union Airborne Warning and Control System (MCD)
SUB	Skene's, Urethral, and Bartholin's [Glands] [Anatomy] (DAVI)
SUB	Student Union Building [Canada]
SUB	Subaddressing [Telecommunications] (DOM)
SUB	Subaltern
SUB	Subaud [Understand] [Latin]
Sub	Subcommittee (DLA)
SUB	Subcontractor (WGA)
SUB	Subdrift (IAA)
SUB	Subeditor
sub.............	Subeditor (WDAA)
sub.............	Subfloor (BARN)
SUB	Subject
SUB	Subjunctive [Grammar]
SUB	Sublevel (IAA)
SUB	Submarine (AFM)
SUB	Submerged
SUB	Subordinate (DSUE)
SUB	Subroutine
Sub	Subscriber [Finance]
SUB	Subscription [Finance]
Sub	Subsidary (TBD)
SUB	Subsidiary [Business term]
SUB	Subsistence (WDAA)
SUB	Substantive (WDAA)
SUB	Substation (IAA)
SUB	Substitute
SUB	Substitute Character [Keyboard] (AFM)
SUB	Substitution (IAA)
SUB	Substratum
SUB	Subtract
SUB	Subtract Binary Number [Computer science]
SUB	Suburban
SUB	Subway (AAG)
SUB	Summit Bancorp [NYSE symbol] (TTSB)
SUB	Supplemental Unemployment Benefits
SUB	Surabaya [Indonesia] [Airport symbol] (OAG)
Subac	Subacute [Medicine] (DMAA)
SUBACLANT..	Submarine Allied Command, Atlantic [NATO] (NATG)
SUBACS	Submarine Advanced [or Active] Combat System
SUBAD........	Submarine Air Defense
SUBAD........	Submarine Force, Pacific Fleet Administration
SUBADMI	Submarine Force, Pacific Fleet Administration, Mare Island
SUBASE.......	Submarine Base [Navy]
SUBASELANT...	Submarine Bases, Atlantic [Navy]
SUBASEPAC...	Submarine Bases, Pacific [Navy]
SUBASSY....	Subassembly
SUBASWEX...	Submarine-Antisubmarine Warfare Exercise (NVT)
SUBB	Suburban Bancorp (EFIS)
SUB-BELL	Submarine Fog Bell [Mechanical]
Sub Bk	Subscription Book (DGA)
SubBn	Suburban Bancshares, Inc. [Associated Press] (SAG)
SubBnc	Suburban Bancshares, Inc. [Associated Press] (SAG)
SubBncp	Suburban Bancorp [Associated Press] (SAG)
SubBncsh	Suburban Bancshares, Inc. [Associated Press] (SAG)
SUBC	Subler, Carl, Agent, Versailles OH [STAC]
SUBCAL	Subcaliber
SUBCERT.....	Submarine Safety Certification [Navy] (DNAB)
SUBCH........	Subchapter (DNAB)
SUBCOM.....	Subcommittee
Subcom	Subcommittee (AL)
SUBCOM......	Subordinate Command, Service Force, Pacific Fleet
SUBCOMNELM...	Subordinate Command, [US] Naval Forces, Eastern Atlantic and Mediterranean
subconj.......	Subconjunctival [Ophthalmology] (DAVI)
SUBCOR	Subject to Correction (DNAB)
subcrep.......	Subcrepitant [Medicine]
SUBCU........	Subcutaneous [Beneath the Skin] [Medicine]
subcu..........	Subcuticular [Medicine] (DAVI)
subcut.........	Subcutaneous [Beneath the Skin] [Medicine]
Subd	Subdivision (DLA)
SUBDEVGRUONE...	Submarine Development Group One [San Diego]
SUBDEVGRUTWO...	Submarine Development Group Two [New York]
Subdiv	Subdivision (TBD)
SUBDIV........	Submarine Division [Navy]
SUBDIZ	Submarine Defense Identification Zone
SUBEASTLANT...	Submarine Force, Eastern Atlantic [NATO]
SUBED	Submarine Electromagnetic Deception System
SUBEX	Submarine Exercise (NATG)
SUBFIN COCT...	Sub Finem Coctionis [When the Boiling Is Nearly Finished] (ROG)
SUBFLOT	Submarine Flotilla [Navy]
subg............	Subgenus
SUBGEN.......	Subgenus
SUBGRU	Submarine Group
SUBH	Scripta Universitatis atque Bibliotecae Hierosolymitanarum Jerusalem [A publication] (BJA)
Sub Hdg	Subsidiary Heading (DGA)
SUBI	Sun Bancorp [NASDAQ symbol] (TTSB)
SUBI	Sun Bancorp, Inc. [NASDAQ symbol] (SAG)
SUBIC	Submarine Integrated Control Systems
Sub Init	Sub Initio [At the Beginning] [Latin]
SUBINSURV...	Inspection and Survey Board Sub Board [Navy]
SUBINSURV (LANT) (PAC)...	Sub Board of Inspection and Survey of Atlantic and Pacific [Navy] (ANA)
SUBJ...........	Subject (AFM)
Subj............	Subject (AL)
SUBJ...........	Subjective (ROG)
SUBJ...........	Subject To [ICAO designator] (FAAC)
SUBJ...........	Subjunctive [Grammar]
SUBJV	Subjunctive [Grammar] (WGA)
SUBK	Suffolk Bancorp [Riverhead, NY] [NASDAQ symbol] (NQ)
SUBL	Sublimation Point (IAA)
SUBL	Sublime [or Subliming]
SUBLANT	Submarine Force, Atlantic Fleet
SubLdgs	Suburban Lodges of America, Inc. [Associated Press] (SAG)
subling	Sublingual [Medicine]
Sub-Lt.........	Sub-Lieutenant [British military] (DMA)
SUBM	Submarine (WGA)
SUBM	Submerged
SUBM	SubMicron Systems [NASDAQ symbol] (TTSB)
SUBM	SubMicron Systems Corp. [NASDAQ symbol] (SAG)
SUBM	Submission [or Submit] (AFM)
SUBMACOM...	Major Army Subcommand (AABC)
submand......	Submandibular [Medicine]
SUBMED	Submarines Mediterranean [NATO] (NATG)
SUBMEDCEN...	Submarine Medical Center [Navy]
SUBMEDNOREAST...	Submarines Northeast Mediterranean [NATO] (NATG)
SUBMG........	Submerged (MSA)
SubMicr.......	SubMicron Systems Corp. [Associated Press] (SAG)
SUBMIN	Subminiature
SUBMISS.....	Submarine Missing [Navy] (NVT)
SUBMIS/SUBSUNK...	Submarine Missing/Presumed Sunk [Navy]
SUBMON......	Submission (ROG)
Subm W	Submerged Well [Nautical charts]
SubN...........	Subthalamic Nucleus (DB)
SUBN	Suburban
SUBN	[The] Summit Bancorporation [NASDAQ symbol] (NQ)
SUBNAVPERS...	Submit to Naval Personnel (DNAB)
SUBNEWSTA...	Submit New Duty Station [Navy] (DNAB)
SUBNO........	Substitutes Not Desired [Military]
sub nom	Sub Nomine [Under the Name] [Latin] (DLA)
SUBNOT......	Submarine Notice (MCD)
SUBNOTE.....	Submarine Notice [Navy] (NVT)
Sub O	Sub Officer (WDAA)
SUBOK	Substitution Acceptable [Military]
SUBOPAUTH...	Submarine Operating Authority [Navy] (NVT)
sub opn	Subsequent Opinion (HGAA)
SUBOR........	Subordinate (AFM)
SUBORCOM...	Subordinate Command
SUBORCOMDSERVLANT...	Subordinate Command, Service Force, Atlantic Fleet
SUBORCOMDSERVPAC...	Subordinate Command, Service Force, Pacific Fleet
SUBORD	Subordinate [Linguistics]
SUB-OSC	Submarine Oscillator
SubOstm......	Suburban Ostomy Supply Co., Inc. [Associated Press] (SAG)
SUBP	Subpoena [Legal shorthand] (LWAP)
SUBPA	Antisubmarine Warfare Barrier Submarine Patrol Area [Navy] (NVT)
SUBPAC.......	Submarine Force, Pacific Fleet
SUBPACAD...	Submarine Force, Pacific Fleet, Administrative Command
SUBPACSUBORDCOM...	Submarine Force, Pacific Fleet, Subordinate Command
Subpar........	Subparagraph (DLA)
SUBPARA	Subparagraph
SUBPrB........	Summit Bcp Adj B Pfd [NYSE symbol] (TTSB)
SUBPT.........	Subpart (WDAA)
SUBPZ	Antisubmarine Warfare Barrier Submarine Patrol Zone [Navy] (NVT)
SUB Q.........	Subcutaneous [Beneath the Skin] [Medicine]
Sub-Q	Subcuticular [Medicine] (DAVI)
SUBQ	Subsequent (AABC)
SUBRAP.......	Submarine Range Prediction System [Navy] (NVT)
Subrfed.......	Suburbfed Financial Corp. [Associated Press] (SAG)
SUBRO........	Subrogation
SUBROC	Submarine Rocket
SUBROCK	Submarine Rocket (IAA)
SUBRON......	Submarine Squadron [Navy]
SUBRPIO.....	Sub-Registered Publications Issuing Office
SUBRQMT....	Subrequirement
SUBRU	Submarine Repair Unit
SUBS	Miami Subs [NASDAQ symbol] (TTSB)
SUBS	Miami Subs Corp. [NASDAQ symbol] (SAG)
SUBS	Salford University Business Services [British]

Subs	Subscribing (AL)
SUBS	Subscription (WGA)
SUBS	Subsidiary [*Business term*]
SUBS	Subsistence (AABC)
SUBS	Substantive [*Grammar*]
SUBS	Substitute
SUBSAFE	Submarine Safety [*Program*]
SUBSAFECEN...	Submarine Safety Center [*Navy*]
SUBSALVEX...	Submarine Salvage Exercise [*Navy*] (DNAB)
SUBSAM	Submarine Surface-to-Air Missile [*Military*] (LAIN)
Subsc..........	Subscription (DLA)
SUBSCD.......	Subscribed (ROG)
SUBSCOFOR...	Submarines Scouting Force [*Pacific Fleet*]
SUBSCR........	Subscription
SUBSCRON...	Subscription [*Finance*] (ROG)
SUBSEC........	Subsection
SUBSECT.......	Subsection [*Legal shorthand*] (LWAP)
SUBSELS	Subsisting Elsewhere
SUBSEQ.......	Subsequent (ROG)
SUBSET	Subscriber Set (CET)
SUBSID.......	Subsidiary [*Business term*] (ROG)
SUBSIS........	Subsistence (AFM)
SUBSLANT...	Submarines, Atlantic Fleet
SUBSLY........	Subsequently (ROG)
SUBSP.........	Subspecies
SUBSPAC.....	Submarines, Pacific Fleet
subspp.........	Subspecies [*Plural form*]
SUBSQ........	Subsequently (ADA)
SUB-SRA	Sub-Shop Replaceable Assembly
SUBSS	Submarine Schoolship [*Navy*] (NVT)
SUBSSOWESPAC...	Submarines, Southwest Pacific Force
SUBST	Substance (ROG)
SUBST	Substantive (ROG)
SUBST	Substitute (AAG)
SUBSTA	Substation
SubstAb	Substance Abuse Technology, Inc. [*Associated Press*] (SAG)
SubstAbus ...	Substance Abuse Technology, Inc. [*Associated Press*] (SAG)
Substand	Substandard (WGA)
substd.........	Substandard (DAVI)
SUBSTD.......	Substituted (ROG)
SUB-STD.......	Substitute Standard [*Army*]
SUBSTG.......	Substituting (AAG)
SUBSTN.......	Substitution
Substn	Substitution (EBF)
SUBSTR.......	Substructure (AAG)
SUBSTTD.......	Substituted
SUBSUNK.....	Submarine Sunk [*Navy*] (NVT)
SUBSYS.......	Subsystem (AAG)
SUBTACGRU...	Submarine Tactical Group [*NATO*] (NATG)
SUBTAG.......	Submarine Tactics Analysis Group
SUBTEL.......	Submarine Telegraph [*Military*] (IAA)
SUBTEL.......	Submarine Telephone [*Military*] (IAA)
SUBTIL	Synthesized User-Based Terminology Index Language (NITA)
SUBTR.........	Subtraction (MSA)
SUBTRAFAC...	Submarine Training Facility
SUBTRAP.....	Submersible Training Platform [*Marine science*] (MSC)
subtrop	Subtropical
SUBV	Subversion (AABC)
Sub Vol........	Submarine Volcano [*Nautical charts*]
SUBWESTLANT...	Submarine Force, Western Atlantic Area [*NATO*] (NATG)
Suby	Subsidiary [*Business term*]
SUBY	Subsidiary
SUC	Small Unit Coward [*Military*] (MUSM)
SUC	Society of University Cartographers [*British*]
SUC	Society of Urologic Cryosurgeons (NTPA)
SUC	Southern Union College [*Wadley, AL*]
SUC	Start-Up Costs [*Business term*] (MHDB)
SUC	Succeeding (MSA)
SUC	Successor (ADA)
Suc	Succinoyl [*Biochemistry*]
SUC	Succus [*Juice*] [*Pharmacy*]
SUC	Sucre [*Bolivia*] [*Seismograph station code, US Geological Survey Closed*] (SEIS)
SUC	Sucrose [*Organic chemistry*]
SUC	Suction (ADA)
SUC	Suncoast Petroleum [*Vancouver Stock Exchange symbol*]
SUC	Sundance, WY [*Location identifier FAA*] (FAAL)
SUC	University of South Carolina, Columbia, SC [*OCLC symbol*] (OCLC)
SUCA	Colonia/Aeropuerto Deptal. [*Uruguay*] [*ICAO location identifier*] (ICLI)
SUCAP.........	Surface Combat Air Patrol (DOMA)
SUCC	State University Computation Center [*Iowa State University*] [*Research center*] (RCD)
SUCC	Succentor [*Ecclesiastical*] (ROG)
SUCC	Successor (ROG)
SUCC	Succinate
SUCC	Succinum [*Amber*] [*Latin*] (ROG)
Succ...........	Succursale [*Station*] [*French*] (ASC)
succ............	Succursale (DD)
SUCCESS	Sources to Upgrade the Career Counseling and Employment of Special Students [*Florida*] (EDAC)
Success.......	Successories, Inc. [*Associated Press*] (SAG)
SUCCESS	Sulfonium Compounds Containing Expellable Sophisticated Sidegroups [*Photoresists*]
SUCCN.........	Succession (ROG)
SUCCON	Succession

SUCCR........	Successor
SUCE.........	South Universal Commodity Exchange [*Ukraine*] (EY)
SUCEE	Socialist Union of Central and Eastern Europe (PD)
SUCHTRANS...	Such Transportation as Command Indicated Designates
SUCHTRANSAVAIL...	Such Transportation as Available
SUCI	Socialist Unity Center of India [*Political party*] (PPW)
SUCKER.......	Society for Understanding Cats, Kangaroos, Elks, and Reptiles [*Slang*]
SUCL	Set Up in Carloads [*Freight*]
SUCL	Stetson University College of Law (DLA)
SUCO..........	Service Universitaire Canadien Outre-Mer [*Canadian University Service Overseas - CUSO*]
SUCR..........	Successor (WGA)
SUCR..........	Sunset Crater National Monument
SUCT	Suction (AAG)
Su Ct Rev ...	Supreme Court Review [*A publication*] (ILCA)
SUD	Skin Unit Dose [*Medicine*] (DMAA)
SUD	Stretched Upper Deck (AIA)
SUD	Stroud, OK [*Location identifier FAA*] (FAAL)
SUD	Sudan Airways [*ICAO designator*] (FAAC)
SUD	Sudbury [*Ontario*] [*Seismograph station code, US Geological Survey*] (SEIS)
SUD	Sudbury Board of Education [*UTLAS symbol*]
SUD	Sudbury Contact Mines Ltd. [*Toronto Stock Exchange symbol*]
SUD	Sudden Unexpected [*or Unexplained*] Death [*Medicine*]
SUD	Sudorific [*Causing Sweat*] [*Pharmacy*] (ROG)
SUDAAN	Survey Data Analysis [*Computer science*]
SUDAER......	Stanford University, Department of Aeronautics and Astronautics (MCD)
SUDAM........	Sunk or Damaged [*Navy*]
Sudan LJ & Rep...	Sudan Law Journal and Reports [*Khartoum*] [*A publication*] (DLA)
SUDAP........	Superintendencia da Agricultura e Producao [*Brazil*]
Sudbury.......	Sudbury, Inc. [*Associated Press*] (SAG)
Sud Dew Ad...	Sudder Dewanny Adawlut [*or Sadr Diwani Adalat*] Reports [*India*] [*A publication*] (DLA)
Sud Dew Rep...	Sudder Dewanny [*or Sadr Diwani*] Reports, Northwest Province [*India*] [*A publication*] (DLA)
SUDDS........	Substance Use Disorder Diagnosis Schedule [*Test*] (TMMY)
SUDEC........	Superintendencia do Desenvolvimento Economico e Cultural [*Brazil*]
SUDEL........	Groupe Regional pour la Coordination de la Production et du Transport de l'Energie Electrique entre l'Autriche, la Grece, l'Italie et la Yougoslavie (EA)
SUDENE.......	Superintendencia do Desenvolvimento do Nordeste [*Brazil*]
SUDEP........	Sudden Unexplained Death in Epilepsy [*Medicine*]
SUDH.........	Succinyldehydrogenase (DMAA)
SUDI	State Unemployment Disability Insurance (AAG)
SUDI	Sudden Unexpected Death in Infancy [*Medicine*] (DMAA)
SUDIC........	Sulfur Development Institute of Canada
SUDIC........	Sulphur Development Institute of Canada
SUDM.........	Single User Drive Module [*Computer science*] (MHDI)
Sudoc.........	Superintendent of Documents [*Government Printing Office*]
Su Doc........	Superintendent of Documents, Government Printing Office (DLA)
SUDOSAT.....	Sudanian Satellite
SUDS..........	Satellite Undetected Duds
SUDS..........	Silhouetting Underwater Detecting System
SUDS..........	Single-Use Diagnostic System [*Trademark of the Murex Corp.*]
SUDS..........	Small Unit Delivery System (MCD)
SUDS..........	Software Update Distribution System [*Computer software*] [*Frye Computer Systems, Inc.*] (PCM)
SUDS..........	State's Urban Development Something-or-Other [*Slang for Urban Development Corporation, New York*]
SUDS..........	Steps Up Developmental Screening Program [*Child development test*] [*Psychology*]
SUDS..........	Subjective Units of Disturbance
SUDS..........	Submarine Detecting System
SUDS..........	Sudbury, Inc. [*NASDAQ symbol*] (NQ)
SUDT..........	Silicon Unilateral Diffused Transistor
SUDU..........	Durazno/Santa Bernardina Internacional de Alternativa [*Uruguay*] [*ICAO location identifier*] (ICLI)
SUE	Aerolineas del Sureste SA [*Mexico ICAO designator*] (FAAC)
SUE	Sahara Upwelling Experiment [*US, Spain*] (MSC)
SUE	Seismic Underwater Explorer
SUE	Servants' United Effort [*Lemonade*] [*Slang British*] (DSUE)
SUE	Shuttle Unique Equipment (MCD)
SUE	Signal Underwater Exploding [*British military*] (DMA)
SUE	Significantly Underutilized Employee Program [*DoD*]
SUE	Skylab Upwelling Experiment [*Marine science*] (MSC)
SUE	Strontium Unit Equivalent
SUE	Sturgeon Bay, WI [*Location identifier FAA*] (FAAL)
SUE	Sub-Unit Evaluation (MCD)
SUE	Sudden Expansion
SUE	Suzie Mining Exploration [*Vancouver Stock Exchange symbol*]
SUE	System User Engineered (IAA)
SUEDE	Surface Evaluation and Definition
SUEL..........	Sperry Utah Engineering Laboratory (MCD)
SUEM..........	Syndicat Unique des Enseignants de Mauritanie [*Unitary Union of Mauritanian Teachers*]
SUEO..........	Montevideo [*Uruguay*] [*ICAO location identifier*] (ICLI)
SUEOTU......	Supreme Unsurpassable Engineers of the Universe [*Rank in Junior Woodchucks organization mentioned in Donald Duck comic by Carl Barks*]
SUERF........	Societe Universitaire Europeenne de Recherches Financieres (EAIO)
SUET..........	Small Unit Evaluation and Training (MCD)
Suet..........	Suetonius [*First century AD*] [*Classical studies*] (OCD)

SUF............ Lametia-Terme [*Italy*] [*Airport symbol*] (OAG)
SUF............ Scottish Union of Fishermen
SUF............ Sequential Ultrafiltration [*Nephrology*] (DAVI)
SUF............ Socialist Unity Front [*Romania*] [*Political party*] (PPW)
SUF............ Southernera Resources Ltd. [*Toronto Stock Exchange symbol*]
SUF............ Sufficient (AFM)
SUF............ Suffolk University, Boston, MA [*OCLC symbol*] (OCLC)
SUF............ Sunflower Airlines Ltd. [*Fiji*] [*ICAO designator*] (FAAC)
SUF............ Swaziland United Front
SUFF.......... Sufficient
SUFF.......... Sufficit [*Suffices*] [*Latin*]
SUFF.......... Suffix (AAG)
SUFF.......... Suffolk [*County in England*]
SUFF.......... Suffragan [*Ecclesiastical*] (ROG)
Suff............ Suffragan (WDAA)
SuffBnc...... Suffolk Bancorp [*Associated Press*] (SAG)
SUFFER...... Save Us from Formaldehyde Environmental Repercussions [*Later, CURE FormaldehydePoisoning Association*] (EA)
SUFFER...... System Utility Facility for Easy Recovery [*NASA*]
Suffolk U ... Suffolk University (GAGS)
SUFFR........ Suffragan [*Ecclesiastical*] (WGA)
SUFFT........ Sufficient
SUFFTY...... Sufficiently (ROG)
SUFPAC...... Surface Force Pacific (MCD)
SUFSW....... Small Unit Fire Support Weapon (MCD)
SUG .... Asheville, NC [*Location identifier FAA*] (FAAL)
SUG .... Sell Under the Guise of Market Research [*Marketing*] [*British*]
SUG .... Smartmac User Group (EA)
SUG .... Southern Union [*NYSE symbol*] (TTSB)
SUG .... Southern Union Co. [*NYSE symbol*] (SAG)
SUG .... Southern Union Financing [*NYSE symbol*] (SAG)
SUG .... Sugar
SUG .... Sugar Island [*Michigan*] [*Seismograph station code, US Geological Survey Closed*] (SEIS)
SUG .... Suggest (AFM)
SUG .... Sun User Group [*An association*]
SUG .... Surigao [*Philippines*] [*Airport symbol*] (OAG)
SUGAR........ Software Users Guide to Available Resources [*Australia A publication*]
Sugd Powers... Sugden on Powers [*A publication*] (DLA)
Sugd Vend... Sugden on Vendors and Purchasers [*A publication*] (DLA)
SUGEN........ SUGEN, Inc. [*Associated Press*] (SAG)
SUGEND ...... Sugendus [*To Be Sucked*] [*Pharmacy*]
Sug Est........ Sugden on the Law of Estates [*A publication*] (DLA)
SUGG.......... Suggestion (ROG)
Sug Hd Bk ... Sugden's Hand-Book of Property Law [*A publication*] (DLA)
SUGI .... SAS [*Statistical Analysis System*] Users Group International (EA)
SUGN.......... SUGEN, Inc. [*NASDAQ symbol*] (SAG)
Sug Pow...... Sugden on Powers [8 eds.] [1808-61] [*A publication*] (DLA)
Sug Pr .... Sugden on the Law of Property [*A publication*] (DLA)
SUGPrA........ So Union Financing 9.48%'TOPrS' [*NYSE symbol*] (TTSB)
Sug Prop ..... Sugden on the Law of Property as Administered by the House of Lords [*A publication*] (DLA)
Sug Pr St.... Sugden on Property Statutes [*A publication*] (DLA)
SUGR.......... Summagraphics [*NASDAQ symbol*] (TTSB)
SUGR.......... Summagraphics Corp. [*NASDAQ symbol*] (NQ)
Sug V & P ... Sugden on Vendors and Purchasers [14 eds.] [1805-62] [*A publication*] (DLA)
Sug Vend.... Sugden on Vendors and Purchasers [*A publication*] (DLA)
SUH............ Rockland, ME [*Location identifier FAA*] (FAAL)
SUHL.......... Sylvania Ultrahigh-Level Logic (IEEE)
SUHL.......... Sylvania Universal High-Level Logic (IAA)
SUHT.......... Squared Up Halftone [*Typography*] (DGA)
SUI.............. Bundesamt fur Militarflugplatze [*Switzerland ICAO designator*] (FAAC)
SUI.............. Safe Use Instructions [*General Motors Corp.*]
SUI.............. Speleological Union of Ireland (EAIO)
SUI.............. Standard Universal Identifier (NITA)
SUI.............. Standard Universal Identifying Number
SUI.............. Stanford University Institute for Plasma Research
SUI.............. State University of Iowa [*Later, University of Iowa*]
SUI.............. Stress Urinary Incontinence [*Medicine*] (DMAA)
SUI.............. Suihwa [*Republic of China*] [*Seismograph station code, US Geological Survey*] (SEIS)
SUI.............. Sukhumi [*USSR*] [*Airport symbol*] (AD)
SUI.............. Summit Resources Ltd. [*Toronto Stock Exchange symbol*]
SUI.............. Sun Communities [*NYSE symbol*] (SPSG)
SUIAP......... Simplified Unit Invoice Accounting Plan
SUIC .... Salford University Industrial Centre Ltd. [*British*] (IRUK)
SUID .... Sudden Unexpected Infant Death [*Medicine*]
SUID .... Sudden Unexplained Infant Death [*Neonatology*] (DAVI)
SUIH .... State University of Iowa Hospitals (DAVI)
SUIP .... Support Unit Improvement Program (MCD)
SUIS .... Ship Upkeep Information System [*Ministry of Defense*] [*British*] (PDAA)
SUIS .... Smoloskyp, Ukrainian Information Service (EA)
SUIT........... Mens Warehouse [*NASDAQ symbol*] (SAG)
SUIT........... Sight Unit Infantry Trilux [*British*]
SUIT........... Simple User Interface Toolkit [*University of Virginia*]
SUITS .... Scottish and Universal Investments
SUIV .... Suivant [*Following*] [*French*]
SuizaF........ Suiza Foods Corp. [*Associated Press*] (SAG)
SUJ............. Satu Mare [*Romania*] [*Airport symbol*] (OAG)
SUJ............. Side Upset Jaw (MSA)
SUJ............. Suntac Minerals [*Vancouver Stock Exchange symbol*]

SUJB........... Southern Universities Joint Board [*for school examinations*] [*British*] (DCTA)
SUK .... Suckling Hill [*Alaska*] [*Seismograph station code, US Geological Survey*] (SEIS)
Suk .... Sukkah (BJA)
suk .... Sukuma [*MARC language code Library of Congress*] (LCCP)
SUKLO .... Senior United Kingdom Liaison Officer [*Later, BJSM*] [*British*]
SUL............ Helisul Linhas Aereas, SA [*Brazil*] [*FAA designator*] (FAAC)
SUL............ Simplified User Logistics [*Military*] (AABC)
SUL............ Small University Libraries
SUL............ Sophia University [*UTLAS symbol*]
SUL............ Standard User Labels [*Computer science*]
SUL............ State University of New York, Union List of Serials, Albany, NY [*OCLC symbol*] (OCLC)
SUL............ Sui [*Pakistan*] [*Airport symbol*] (OAG)
SUL............ Sulcus Computer [*AMEX symbol*] (TTSB)
SUL............ Sulcus Computer Corp. [*AMEX symbol*] (SPSG)
SUL............ Sulcus Hospitality Tech [*AMEX symbol*] [*Formerly, Sulcus Computer*] (SG)
SUL............ Sulpetro Ltd. [*Toronto Stock Exchange symbol*]
SUL............ Sulphur Creek [*New Britain*] [*Seismograph station code, US Geological Survey*] (SEIS)
SULC.......... Sulcus Computer (EFIS)
SULCL......... Set Up in Less than Carloads [*Freight*]
Sulcus .... Sulcus Computer Corp. [*Associated Press*] (SAG)
SuLEXCo..... Sulphur Export Corp. [*An association*] (EA)
SULF.......... Speedball Up-Range Launch Facility [*Army*] (AABC)
sulf .... Sulfate [*or Sulphate*] [*Chemistry*] (DAVI)
SULF.......... Sulfur [*Chemical element*] (DAVI)
SULFHB....... Sulfhemoglobin [*Also, Sulfmethemoglobin*] [*Biochemistry*] (DAVI)
SULF-PRIM... Sulfamethoxazole and Trimethoprim [*Medicine*] (DMAA)
SULINAC...... Super Linear Accelerator [*Space flight simulator*]
SULIRS........ Syracuse University Libraries' Information Retrieval System (NITA)
SULIS .... Syracuse University Libraries Information System [*Syracuse University Libraries*] [*New York*] [*Information service or system*] (IID)
Sull .... Pro Sulla [*of Cicero*] [*Classical studies*] (OCD)
Sull .... Sulla [*of Plutarch*] [*Classical studies*] (OCD)
SULL.......... Sullivan Dental Products [*NASDAQ symbol*] (SAG)
Sull Dnt...... Sullivan Dental Products [*Associated Press*] (SAG)
Sullivan ..... Smith's New Hampshire Reports [*A publication*] (DLA)
Sull Ld Tit ... Sullivan's Land Titles in Massachusetts [*A publication*] (DLA)
Sull Lect..... Sullivan's Lectures on Constitution and Laws of England [*A publication*] (DLA)
sulph .... Sulphate [*or Sulfate*] [*Chemistry*] (DAVI)
sulpha .... Sulphonamide [*or Sulfonamide*] [*An antibacterial*] (DAVI)
Sul Ross St U... Sul Ross State University (GAGS)
SULS .... Maldonado/Base Aeronaval C/C Carlos A. Curbelo [*Uruguay*] [*ICAO location identifier*] (ICLI)
SULS .... Suffolk University Law School [*England*] (HGEN)
SULT........... Sultan
Sum .... Hale's Summary of the Pleas of the Crown [*England*] [*A publication*] (DLA)
SUM........... San Juan de Cesar [*Colombia*] [*Airport symbol*] (AD)
SUM........... Saturn Umbilical Maintenance [*NASA*]
SUM........... Save Uganda Movement
SUM........... Servicio Universitario Mundial [*World University Service*]
SUM........... Set-Up [*Control*] Module [*Telecommunications*] (TEL)
SUM........... Shallow Underwater Missile
SUM........... Shallow Underwater Mobile (IAA)
SUM........... Socialist Unionist Movement [*Al Haraka at Tawhidiyya al Ishtirakiyya*] [*Syria*] [*Political party*] (PPW)
SUM........... Software User's Manual [*Army*]
SUM........... Solar Ultraviolet Monitor (MCD)
SUM........... Some [*Amateur radio shorthand*] (WDAA)
SUM........... Sullivan Mines, Inc. [*Toronto Stock Exchange symbol*]
SUM........... Sumantur [*Let It Be Taken*] [*Latin*] [*Pharmacy*] (DAVI)
SUM........... Sumat [*Let Him Take, Let the Person Take*] [*Latin*] [*Pharmacy*] (DAVI)
Sum .... Sumatra
SUM........... Sume [*Take*] [*Pharmacy*]
SUM........... Sumendum [*To Be Taken*] [*Latin*] [*Pharmacy*] (DAVI)
Sum .... Sumerian (BJA)
SUM........... Summary (AABC)
sum .... Summary (NAKS)
SUM........... Summation (AAMN)
SUM........... Summator (IAA)
SUM........... Summer
SUM........... Summing
Sum .... Summit: Journal of the Liturgical Commission [*of the Archdiocese of Melbourne*] [*A publication*] (APTA)
SUM........... Summoned
Sum .... Sumner's United States Circuit Court Reports [*A publication*] (DLA)
SUM........... Sumoto [*Japan*] [*Seismograph station code, US Geological Survey*] (SEIS)
SUM........... Sumter [*South Carolina*] [*Airport symbol*] (OAG)
SUM........... Surface-to-Underwater Missile
SUM........... Symantec Utilities for Macintosh [*Computer software*] (CDE)
SUM........... System Check and Utility Master (MCD)
SUM........... Systems Unit Method [*Medical transcription*]
SUM........... System Utilization Monitor [*Computer science*]
SUMF.......... University of South Carolina, School of Medicine, Columbia, SC [*OCLC symbol*] (OCLC)
SUMA .... Sporadic Ulcerating and Mutilating Acropathy [*Medicine*] (DMAA)
SUMA .... Suma Four [*NASDAQ symbol*] (TTSB)

SUMA	Summa Four, Inc. [*NASDAQ symbol*] (SAG)
SUMAC	Sheffield University Metals Advisory Centre [*British*] (IRUK)
SUMARPI	Supplemental Maintenance and Repair Parts Instruction
Sumat	Sumatra (VRA)
sumc	Space Ultrareliable Modular Computer (NAKS)
SUMC	Space Ultrareliable Modular Computer
SUMC	Stanford University Medical Center
SUMC	Summit Care [*NASDAQ symbol*] (TTSB)
SUMC	Summit Care Corp. [*NASDAQ symbol*] (SAG)
SUMCM	Summary Court-Martial
SUMCMO	Summary Court-Martial Order
Sum Dec	Summary Decisions [*Bengal, India*] [*A publication*] (DLA)
SUME	Mercedes/Ricardo de Tomasi [*Uruguay*] [*ICAO location identifier*] (ICLI)
SUMED	Suez-Mediterranean [*Pipeline*]
SUMER	Solar Ultraviolet Measurements of Emitted Radiation [*Instrumentation*]
SUMEX	Stanford University Medical Experimental Computer Project [*Stanford University*] [*Research center*] (RCD)
SUMEXAIM	Stanford University Medical Experiment-Applications of Artificial Intelligence to Medical Research (NITA)
Sumgph	Summagraphics Corp. [*Associated Press*] (SAG)
SUMI	Sumitomo Bank (CA) [*NASDAQ symbol*] (TTSB)
SUMI	Sumitomo Bank of California [*NASDAQ symbol*] (NQ)
SUMIT	Single-Concept User-Adaptable Microcomputer-Based Instructional Technique (EDAC)
SUMIT	Standard Utility Means for Information Transformation [*Computer science*]
SUMIT	Streptokinase-Urokinase Myocardial Infarction Trial (STED)
SUMIT	Summit [*Commonly used*] (OPSA)
SumitB	Summit Bancorp New Jersey [*Associated Press*] (SAG)
SumitFR	Summit Family Restaurants, Inc. [*Associated Press*] (SAG)
Sumito	Sumitomo Bank of California [*Associated Press*] (SAG)
SUMITT	Summit [*Commonly used*] (OPSA)
SumitTc	Summit Technology, Inc. [*Associated Press*] (SAG)
SUMIZ	Sumitomo Bank CA Dep'A'Pfd [*NASDAQ symbol*] (TTSB)
SUMM	Summarize (IAA)
SUMM	Summary
summ	Summary (NAKS)
SUMM	Summer
SUMM	Summitatis [*Summits or Tops*] [*Pharmacy*] (ROG)
SUMM	Summit Financial [*NASDAQ symbol*] (SAG)
SUMM	Summons [*Legal shorthand*] (LWAP)
Summa	Summa Industries [*Associated Press*] (SAG)
SUMMA	Superconducting Magnetic Mirror Apparatus
SUMMAC	Stanford University Modified Markers and Cell Method
SummaF	Summa Four, Inc. [*Associated Press*] (SAG)
Summa Theol	Summa Theologica [*A publication*] (ODCC)
SUMMCO	Summary Court-Martial Order
Summ Dec	Summary Decisions [*Bengal, India*] [*A publication*] (IICA)
Summerfield	Summerfield's Reports [*21 Nevada*] [*A publication*] (DLA)
Summerfield S	S. Summerfield's Reports [*21 Nevada*] [*A publication*] (DLA)
SUMMIT	Sperry UNIVAC Minicomputer Management of Interactive Terminals
SUMMIT	Summit [*Commonly used*] (OPSA)
SUMMIT	Supervisor of Multiprogramming, Multiprocessing, Interactive Time Sharing [*Computer science*] (IEEE)
Summ NP	Summary of the Law of Nisi Prius [*A publication*] (DLA)
Sumn	Sumner's United States Circuit Court Reports [*A publication*] (DLA)
Sumner	Sumner's United States Circuit Court Reports [*A publication*] (DLA)
SUMNS	Summons (ROG)
Sumn Ves	Sumner's Edition of Vesey's Reports [*A publication*] (DLA)
SUMO	Melo/Aeropuerto Deptal de Cerro Largo [*Uruguay*] [*ICAO location identifier*] (ICLI)
SUMPAC	Southampton University Man-Powered Aircraft [*British*]
SUMPM	Summary Performance Measure (MCD)
sumpt	Sumptuary (VRA)
Sum Rep	Sumner's United States Circuit Court Reports [*A publication*] (DLA)
SUMS	Shuttle Upper-Atmosphere Mass Spectrometer [*NASA*] (MCD)
sums	Shuttle Upper-Atmosphere Mass Spectrometer (NAKS)
SUMS	Southern Universities' Management Services (AIE)
SUMS	Specialized Unit Maintenance Support (MCD)
SUMS	Sperry UNIVAC Material System
SUMS	Standard USAREUR Munitions System
SUMS	Summons (ROG)
SUMSTAT	Summary Statistical Data [*Federal government*]
SUMT	Sequential Unconstrained Minimization Technique
SUMT	Summit Medical System [*NASDAQ symbol*] (TTSB)
SUMT	Summit Medical Systems, Inc. [*NASDAQ symbol*] (SAG)
SUM TAL	Sumat Talem [*Take One Like This*] [*Pharmacy*]
SumtBTX	Summit Bancshares TX [*Associated Press*] (SAG)
SumtCre	Summit Care Corp. [*Associated Press*] (SAG)
SumtDsg	Summit Design, Inc. [*Associated Press*] (SAG)
SumtFn	Summit Financial [*Associated Press*] (SAG)
SumtMd	Summit Medical Systems, Inc. [*Associated Press*] (SAG)
SumtPrp	Summit Properties, Inc. [*Associated Press*] (SAG)
SumtTx	Summit Tax Exempt Bond Fund Ltd. [*Associated Press*] (SAG)
SUMU	Montevideo/Carrasco Internacional [*Uruguay*] [*ICAO location identifier*] (ICLI)
Sum UCCR	Sumner's United States Circuit Court Reports [*A publication*] (DLA)
Sum Ves	Sumner's Edition of Vesey's Reports [*A publication*] (DLA)
SUMX	Suma Industries [*NASDAQ symbol*] (SAG)
SUMX	Summa Industries [*NASDAQ symbol*] (TTSB)
SUN	Antillana de Nevegacion Aerea SA [*Dominican Republic*] [*ICAO designator*] (FAAC)
SUN	Hailey, ID [*Location identifier FAA*] (FAAL)
SUN	OPTEVFOR [*Operational Test and Evaluation Force*] Detachment, Sunnyvale, CA [*Navy*] (CAAL)
SUN	Serum Urea Nitrogen [*Clinical medicine*]
SUN	Spanish Universal Network [*Cable-television system*]
SUN	SPINDEX Users' Network (NITA)
SUN	Spiritual Unity of Nations [*An association*]
SUN	Standard Units and Nomenclature (MCD)
SUN	State University of Nebraska
SUN	Sun Co. [*NYSE symbol*] (TTSB)
SUN	Sun Co., Inc. [*NYSE symbol*] (SPSG)
sun	Sundanese [*MARC language code Library of Congress*] (LCCP)
SUN	Sunday (AFM)
Sun	Sunday (ODBW)
SUN	Sundstrand-Turbo Division (AAG)
SUN	Sun Life Assurance Co. of Canada [*UTLAS symbol*]
SUN	Sunnyside [*Utah*] [*Seismograph station code, US Geological Survey Closed*] (SEIS)
SUN	Sunoco, Inc. [*Formerly, Sun Co.*] [*NYSE symbol*]
SUN	Sunset Railway Co. [*AAR code*]
SUN	Suntech Library and Information Center, Marcus Hook, PA [*OCLC symbol*] (OCLC)
SUN	Suntec Ventures Ltd. [*Vancouver Stock Exchange symbol*]
SUN	Sun Valley [*Idaho*] [*Airport symbol*] (OAG)
SUN	Switching Unit
SUN	Symbolic Unit Number [*Computer science*] (WDAA)
SUN	Symbols, Units, and Nomenclature [*Commission*] [*IUPAC*]
SUN	Symphony for United Nations (EA)
SUN	Union of Soviet Socialist Republics [*ANSI three-letter standard code*] (CNC)
SUNA	Seafarers' International Union of North America [*AFL-CIO*] (EA)
SUNA	Society of Urologic Nurses and Associates (NTPA)
SUNA	Sudan News Agency
Suna	Sunamerica, Inc. [*Associated Press*] (SAG)
SUNA	Switchmen's Union of North America [*Later, United Transportation Union*]
SunaC	Sunamerica Capital Trust [*Associated Press*] (SAG)
SunaC	Sunamerica Capital Trust II [*Associated Press*] (SAG)
SunaC	Sunamerica Capital Trust III [*Associated Press*] (SAG)
Sunair	Sunair Electronics, Inc. [*Associated Press*] (SAG)
Sunamer	Sunamerica, Inc. [*Associated Press*] (SAG)
SUNAT	Scandinavian Union for Non-Alcoholic Traffic (EA)
SunBanc	Sun Bancorp, Inc. [*Associated Press*] (SAG)
SunBCA	Sunrise Bancorp [*Associated Press*] (SAG)
SunBcNY	Sunrise Bancorp, Inc. NY [*Associated Press*] (SAG)
SunBcp	Sun Bancorp, Inc. [*Associated Press*] (SAG)
Sunbeam	Sunbeam Corp. [*Associated Press*] (SAG)
Sunbelt	Sunbelt Companies [*Associated Press*] (SAG)
SUnBH	Scripta Universitatis atque Bibliotecae Hierosolymitanarum Jerusalem [*A publication*] (BJA)
SUNCC	Sunocoat Conference (PSS)
SunCmts	Sun Communities [*Associated Press*] (SAG)
SunCo	Sun Co., Inc. [*Associated Press*] (SAG)
SunCoast	Sun Coast Industries, Inc. [*Associated Press*] (SAG)
Suncor	Suncor, Inc. [*Associated Press*] (SAG)
SUNCOR	Sun Oil Co. of Radnor [*Pennsylvania*]
SunCty	Sun City Industries, Inc. [*Associated Press*] (SAG)
SUND	Sound Advice [*NASDAQ symbol*] (TTSB)
SUND	Sound Advice, Inc. [*NASDAQ symbol*] (NQ)
SUND	Sunday
SUND	Sundries
SUNDAE	Stanford University Division of Aero Engineering (AAG)
Sunday Rev	Sunday Review [*A publication*]
Sund H	Sunday Herald [*Melbourne*] [*A publication*]
SundHme	Sundance Homes, Inc. [*Associated Press*] (SAG)
SunDis	Sun Distributors Ltd. [*Associated Press*] (SAG)
SunDist	Sun Distributors Ltd. [*Associated Press*] (SAG)
SUNDS	Sudden Unexpected Nocturnal Death Syndrome [*Medicine*] (ECON)
SUNDS	Sundries (ROG)
SUNEC	Seaborne Supply of the Northeast Command (DNAB)
SunEng	Sun Energy Partners Ltd [*Associated Press*] (SAG)
SUNET	[*The*] Swedish University Network (TNIG)
SUNF	Sunstar Foods, Inc. (MHDW)
SUNFED	Special United Nations Fund for Economic Development
Sunglss	Sunglass Hut International, Inc. [*Associated Press*] (SAG)
SunGrd	Sundata Corp. [*Associated Press*] (SAG)
SUNH	Sundance Homes [*NASDAQ symbol*] (TTSB)
SUNH	Sundance Homes, Inc. [*NASDAQ symbol*] (SAG)
SunHltcr	Sun Healthcare Group, Inc. [*Associated Press*] (SAG)
SunHydr	Sun Hydraulics Corp. [*Associated Press*] (SAG)
SUNI	Southern Universities Nuclear Institute
SUN III	Sydney UNIX Network (TNIG)
SunInt	Sun International [*Associated Press*] (SAG)
SunIntl	Sun International [*Associated Press*] (SAG)
SUNIST	Serveur Universitaire National de l'Information Scientifique et Technique [*Online service*]
Sunk	Single, Unemployed, No Kids [*Lifestyle classification*]
SUNL	Sunrise Resources [*NASDAQ symbol*] (TTSB)
SUNL	Sunrise Resources, Inc. [*NASDAQ symbol*] (SAG)
SunM	Sunshine Mining & Refining Co. [*Associated Press*] (SAG)
SunMed	Sunrise Medical, Inc. [*Associated Press*] (SAG)
SunMic	Sun Microsystems, Inc. [*Associated Press*] (SAG)
SunMn	Sunshine Mining & Refining Co. [*Associated Press*] (SAG)
SunNur	Sunbelt Nursery Group, Inc. [*Associated Press*] (SAG)
SUNO	Southern University in New Orleans
SUNOCO	Sun Oil Co. [*Later, Sun Co., Inc.*]

SUNP..........	SunPharm Corp. [*NASDAQ symbol*] (SAG)
SunPh........	SunPharm Corp. [*Associated Press*] (SAG)
SunPhm.......	SunPharm Corp. [*Associated Press*] (SAG)
Sunport.......	Sunport Medical Corp. [*Associated Press*] (SAG)
SUNPrD	Sun Co.'A'Dep'TARGETS' [*NYSE symbol*] (TTSB)
SUNPW.........	Sunpharm Corp. Wrrt [*NASDAQ symbol*] (TTSB)
SUNQ.........	Sunquest Information Sys [*NASDAQ symbol*] (TTSB)
SUNQ.........	Sunquest Information Systems, Inc. [*NASDAQ symbol*] (SAG)
Sunquest	Sunquest Information Systems, Inc. [*Associated Press*] (SAG)
SUNR........	Sunrise Preschools [*NASDAQ symbol*] (TTSB)
SUNR........	Sunrise Preschools, Inc. [*NASDAQ symbol*] (SAG)
SunrAss......	Sunrise Assisted Living, Inc. [*Associated Press*] (SAG)
SunResc	Sunrise Resources, Inc. [*Associated Press*] (SAG)
Sunrise........	Sunrise Preschools, Inc. [*Associated Press*] (SAG)
SunRiver......	SunRiver Corp. [*Associated Press*] (SAG)
SUNRP........	Sunrise Preschools Cv'C' Pfd [*NASDAQ symbol*] (TTSB)
Sunrst.........	Sunresorts Ltd. NV [*Associated Press*] (SAG)
SUNS	New Day Beverage, Inc. [*NASDAQ symbol*] (SAG)
SUNS	Small Unit Navigation System
SUNS	Sonic Underwater Navigation System (WDAA)
SUNS	SunStar Healthcare [*NASDAQ symbol*] (TTSB)
SUNS	SunStar Healthcare, Inc. [*NASDAQ symbol*] (SAG)
SUNSAT......	Sun-Energy Collecting Satellite
SunSav	Suncoast Savings & Loan Association [*Associated Press*] (SAG)
SunshJr	Sunshine-Jr Stores, Inc. [*Associated Press*] (SAG)
SunsMn	Sunshine Mining & Refining Co. [*Associated Press*] (SAG)
Sunsource ...	Sunsource LP [*Associated Press*] (SAG)
SUNSPOT	Study of Utilization Systems, Policies, and Techniques (MCD)
SunSpt........	Sun Sportswear, Inc. [*Associated Press*] (SAG)
SunsrceB	Sunsource LP [*Associated Press*] (SAG)
SUNSTAR	Stanford University Network for Space Telescience Applications Research [*Research center*] (RCD)
SunStar.......	SunStar Healthcare, Inc. [*Associated Press*] (SAG)
Sunstat	Sunstates Corp. [*Associated Press*] (SAG)
Sunstate	Sunstates Corp. [*Associated Press*] (SAG)
SunstH........	Sunstone Hotel Investors, Inc. [*Associated Press*] (SAG)
SunstoneH....	Sunstone Hotel Investors, Inc. [*Associated Press*] (SAG)
Sunstrnd	Sundstrand Corp. [*Associated Press*] (SAG)
SunSv	Suncoast Savings & Loan Association [*Associated Press*] (SAG)
SUNTC........	Sunward Technologies (EFIS)
SunTrst.......	SunTrust Banks, Inc. [*Associated Press*] (SAG)
SunTV	Sun Television & Applicances, Inc. [*Associated Press*] (SAG)
SUNW.........	Sun Microsystems [*NASDAQ symbol*] (TTSB)
SUNW.........	Sun Microsystems, Inc. [*Mountain View, CA*] [*NASDAQ symbol*] (NQ)
SUNWACD ...	Swaleureniddwharfeairecalderdon [*British town*]
SUNY..........	State University of New York [*Computer retrieval and control projects*] [*Albany, NY*]
SUNY	State University of New York Athletic Conference (PSS)
SUNY..........	Sunrise Bancorp, Inc. New York [*NASDAQ symbol*] (SAG)
SUNYA........	State University of New York at Albany
SUNYAB.......	State University of New York at Buffalo
SUNY (Albany)...	State University of New York at Albany (GAGS)
SUNY BCN ...	State University of New York Biomedical Communication Network (EA)
SUNY (Binghampton)...	State University of New York at Binghampton (GAGS)
SUNY (Buffalo)...	State University of New York at Buffalo (GAGS)
SUNYC (Brockport)...	State University of New York College at Brockport (GAGS)
SUNYC (Buffalo)...	State University of New York College at Buffalo (GAGS)
SUNYC (Cortland)...	State University of New York College at Cortland (GAGS)
SUNYC Environ Sci & For (Syracuse)...	State University of New York College of Environmental Science and Forestry at Syracuse (GAGS)
SUNYC (Fredonia)...	State University of New York College at Fredonia (GAGS)
SUNYC (Geneseo)...	State University of New York College at Geneseo (GAGS)
SUNYC (New Paltz)...	State University of New York College at New Paltz (GAGS)
SUNYC (Oneonta)...	State University of New York College at Oneonta (GAGS)
SUNYC (Oswego)...	State University of New York College at Oswego (GAGS)
SUNYC (Plattsburg)...	State University of New York College at Plattsburg (GAGS)
SUNYC (Potsdam)...	State University of New York College at Potsdam (GAGS)
SUNY H Sci Cent...	State University of New York Health Science Center at Brooklyn (GAGS)
SUNY H Sci Cent...	State University of New York Health Science Center at Syracuse (GAGS)
SUNY/OCLC...	State University of New York Online Computer Library Center [*Library network*]
SunyP	State University of New York Press, Albany, NY [*Library symbol Library of Congress*] (LCLS)
SUNY (Stony Brook)...	State University of New York at Stony Brook (GAGS)
SUO	Senior Under-Officer [*Royal Military Academy*] [*British*] (ROG)
SUO	Shell Oil Co. [*Toronto Stock Exchange symbol*] (SPSG)
SUO	Society of University Otolaryngologists [*Later, SOU-HNS*] (EA)
SUO	Sun River [*Oregon*] [*Airport symbol Obsolete*] (OAG)
SUO	Syncope of Unknown Origin (DB)
SUO-HNS.....	Society of University Otolaryngologists - Head and Neck Surgeons (EA)
SUOT	Spacelab Ultraviolet Telescope
SUP	Aerosuper AS de CV [*Mexico ICAO designator*] (FAAC)
SUP	Sabah United Party [*Malaysia*] [*Political party*]
SUP	Sailors' Union of the Pacific (EA)
SUP	Single Unit Pack [*for vehicles*]
SUP	Single Unit Package [*Pharmacy*]
SUP	Single Unit Parameter
SUP	Southern University Press (DGA)
SUP	Special Utility Program [*NASA*] (KSC)
SUP	Standard Unit of Processing [*Computer science*]
SUP	Stanford University Press (DGA)
SUP	Statistical Utility Program
SUP	Super
sup............	Super (WDMC)
SUP	Superannuation
SUP	Superficial (AAMN)
SUP	Superfine
SUP	Superior (AFM)
sup............	Superior (WDMC)
SUP	Superior Indus Intl [*NYSE symbol*] (TTSB)
SUP	Superior Industries International, Inc. [*NYSE symbol*] (SPSG)
SUP	Superior Oil Co., Exploration Library, Houston, TX [*OCLC symbol*] (OCLC)
SUP	Superlative
SUP	Supersede (WGA)
SUP	Supervisor (IAA)
sup............	Supervisor (WDMC)
SUP	Supination [*or Supinator*] [*Medicine*] (DAVI)
SUP	Supine
SUP	Supplement (AFM)
sup............	Supplement (WDMC)
SUP	Supply [*Business term*] (AFM)
sup............	Supply (WDAA)
SUP	Supply Contract (AAGC)
SUP	Support
SUP	Suppresor [*Electronics*] (ECII)
SUP	Suppress (DEN)
sup............	Suppression (IDOE)
sup............	Suppressor (IDOE)
SUP	Supra [*Above*] [*Latin*]
Sup............	Supraphon [*Record label*] [*Former Czechoslovakia*]
SUP	Supreme
SUP	Supreme Resources, Inc. [*Vancouver Stock Exchange symbol*]
SUP	Sydney University Press [*Australia*] (ADA)
SUP	Symptomatic Uterine Prolapse [*Medicine*] (STED)
SUP	Syracuse University Press (DGA)
SUP	System Utilization Procedure
sup............	What's Up? [*Internet language*] [*Computer science*]
SUPA	Society of University Patent Administrators (EA)
SUPAC........	Scale-Up and Post Approval Changes [*Food and Drug Administration*]
SUPAD........	Supplementary Address (MCD)
SUPADS......	Suppression of Air Defense System (MCD)
SUPANX......	Supply Annex
SUPARCO	Space and Upper Atmospheric Research Committee [*Pakistan*]
SUPARS.......	Supply Acquisition Regulation Supplement [*Navy*]
SUPARS.......	Syracuse University Psychological Abstracts Retrieval Service (NITA)
sup ben	Supplementary Benefit (WDAA)
SUPC	Superior Consultant Holdings Corp. [*NASDAQ symbol*] (SAG)
Sup C.........	Superior Court (BARN)
Sup C.........	Supreme Court (BARN)
Sup C.........	Supreme Court Reporter (BARN)
SUPCE........	Syracuse University Publications in Continuing Education (EA)
SUPCEN......	Supply Center
SUPCHG	Supercharge (FAAC)
SUPCOM......	Support Command [*Army*]
SUPCOM......	Supreme Command
SUPCON	Superintending Constructor
SupConsl	Superior Consultant Holdings Corp. [*Associated Press*] (SAG)
SUPCOSTINS...	Supervisory Cost Inspector [*Navy*]
Sup Court Rep...	Supreme Court Reporter [*A publication*] (DLA)
SUPCRIT......	Super Critical (MCD)
Sup Ct	Supreme Court (DLA)
Sup Ct	Supreme Court Reporter [*National Reporter System*] [*A publication*] (DLA)
Sup Ct App...	Supreme Court Appeals [*India*] [*A publication*] (DLA)
Sup Ct J	Supreme Court Journal [*India*] [*A publication*] (DLA)
Sup Ct MR...	Supreme Court Monthly Review [*India*] [*A publication*] (DLA)
Sup Ct Pr....	Supreme Court Practice [*A publication*] (DLA)
Sup Ct R.....	Supreme Court Reports [*India*] [*A publication*] (DLA)
Sup Ct R.....	United States Supreme Court Rule [*A publication*] (DLA)
Sup Ct Rep...	Supreme Court Reporter [*A publication*] (DLA)
Sup Ct Repr...	Supreme Court Reporter [*A publication*] (DLA)
Sup Ct R (NY)...	New York Supreme Court Reports [*A publication*] (DLA)
SUPCUR	Superimposed Current
SUPDEP......	Supply Depot
SUPDIV.......	Supervisor of Diving [*Navy*]
SUPDIVE......	Supervisor of Diving [*Navy*]
SUPDOC......	Superintendent of Documents-Government Printing Office (TAG)
SUPDT........	Superintendent (ADA)
SUPE	Punta Del Este/Aeropuerto Deptal de Maldonado [*Uruguay*] [*ICAO location identifier*] (ICLI)
SUPE	Super Eight [*Motion picture*] (VRA)
SupE..........	Superior Energy Services, Inc. [*Associated Press*] (SAG)
SupEnrgy.....	Superior Energy Services, Inc. [*Associated Press*] (SAG)
SUPER........	Superannuation
SUPER........	Supercalendered (NTCM)
SUPER........	Superficial
SUPER........	Superfine
SUPER........	Superimpose
SUPER........	Superimposition (NTCM)
SUPER........	Superintendent
SUPER........	Superior
Super..........	Superior Court (DLA)
Super..........	Superior Court Reports [*A publication*] (DLA)

SUPER.........	Supernumerary
SUPER.........	Supersede (MUGU)
SUPER.........	Supervisor (DSUE)
SUPER.........	System Used for Prediction and Evaluation of Reliability [Computer science] (MHDI)
Super Ct	Superior Court (DLA)
Super Ct App Div...	Superior Court, Appellate Division (DLA)
Super Ct Ch Div...	Superior Court, Chancery Division (DLA)
Super Ct Law Div...	Superior Court, Law Division (DLA)
Super Ct Rep...	Superior Court Reports [New York, Pennsylvania, etc.] [A publication] (DLA)
Super Ct (RI)...	Rhode Island Superior Court (DLA)
Supercut........	Supercuts, Inc. [Associated Press] (SAG)
SUPERFL.......	Superficial (ROG)
SuperG	SuperGen, Inc. [Associated Press] (SAG)
SuperGn	SuperGen, Inc. [Associated Press] (SAG)
SUPERHET.....	Superheterodyne
SuperInd......	Superior Industries International, Inc. [Associated Press] (SAG)
SuperJANET...	Super Joint Academic Network [UK] (EERA)
SUPERL	Superlative
SUPERMAG....	Superconducting Magnet (SSD)
SUPERSTR....	Superstructure
Supertel.......	Supertel Hospitality, Inc. [Associated Press] (SAG)
SUPG	SuperGen Inc. [NASDAQ symbol] (TTSB)
SUPG	System Utilization Procedural Guide
SUP GOSSYP...	Super Gossypium [On Cotton Wool] [Pharmacy]
SUPGW........	SuperGen Inc. Wrrt [NASDAQ symbol] (TTSB)
SUPHTD......	Superheated (AAG)
SUPHTR......	Superheater (AAG)
SUPI	Supreme International [NASDAQ symbol] (TTSB)
SUPI	Supreme International Corp. [NASDAQ symbol] (SAG)
SUPIER........	Supply Pier [Navy]
supin	Supination [Medicine] (DMAA)
SupIn	Supreme Industries [Associated Press] (SAG)
SUPINSMAT...	Supervising Inspector of Naval Material
SUPINSP......	Supply Inspection [Navy] (NVT)
SupIntl........	Supreme International Corp. [Associated Press] (SAG)
SUPINTREP...	Supplementary Intelligence Report [Military] (AABC)
SUPIR.........	Supplementary Photographic Interpretation Report [Military]
Sup Jud Ct...	Supreme Judicial Court [Massachusetts] (DLA)
SUPL	Supply
SUP LINT.....	Super Linteum [On Lint] [Pharmacy]
SUPLO.........	Scottish Union of Power Loom Overlookers
SUPLS	Supplies (WGA)
SUPMG	Southern University Press Marketing Group [Acronym is pronounced "soupmug"]
SUPMTL......	Supplemental
SupNatl.......	Superior National Insurance Group, Inc. [Associated Press] (SAG)
SUPNZ.........	Socialist Unity Party of New Zealand
SUPO..........	Super Power [Water boiler] [Nuclear reactor]
SUPO..........	Supply Officer
SUPOH DI....	Supply on Hand or Due In
SUPOHDU....	Supply from Stock on Hand or Due In
SUPOPS......	Supply Operations [DoD]
Supp	New York Supplement Reports [A publication] (DLA)
SUPP	Sarawak United People's Party [Malaysia] [Political party] (PPW)
Supp	Supplement (KSC)
Supp	Supplement (AAGC)
Supp	Supplices [of Euripides] [Classical studies] (OCD)
Supp	Supplices Contra Thebas [of Aeschylus] [Classical studies] (OCD)
SUPP	Supply
SUPP	Support (AAG)
Supp	Support (AL)
SUPP	Suppositorium [Suppository] [Pharmacy]
supp...........	Suppository (STED)
supp...........	Suppurative [Medicine]
SUPPACT.....	Support Activity
Supp Aesch...	Supplementum Aeschyleum [A publication] (OCD)
SUPP BAS ...	Supplemental Basic Allowance for Subsistence [Military] (DNAB)
SUPPL	Supplement (AABC)
Suppl	Supplementary (DLA)
SUPPLOT....	Supplemental Plot (MCD)
SUPPLT	Supply Platoon [Military] (DNAB)
SUPPORT	Study to Understand Prognoses and Preferences for Outcomes and Risks of Treatments
SUPPOS.......	Suppository [Pharmacy]
suppos.........	Suppository (STED)
SUPPR.........	Suppression (MSA)
SUPPREP.....	Supplemental Reporting Code
Supp Rev.....	Supplement to the Revision [A publication] (DLA)
Supp Rev St...	Supplement to the Revised Statutes [A publication] (DLA)
Supp Rev Stat...	Supplement to the Revised Statutes [A publication] (GFGA)
SUPPS	Regional Supplementary Procedures [Aviation code]
SUPPT	Supply Point [Military]
Supp Ves Jun...	Supplement to Vesey, Junior's, Reports [A publication] (DLA)
SUPR	Superintendent (ROG)
SUPR	Superior (AABC)
SUPR	Superior Services [NASDAQ symbol] (TTSB)
SUPR	Superior Services, Inc. [NASDAQ symbol] (SAG)
SUPR	Supervisor
SUPR	Suppress
SUPR	Supreme
SUPRA	Suppression Pool Retention Analysis [Nuclear energy]
supra cit......	Supra Citato [Cited Above] [Latin] (DAVI)
SUPRAD	Supplementary Radio (NG)

Supr Ct	Pennsylvania Superior Court Reports [A publication] (DLA)
Supr Ct Rep...	Supreme Court Reporter [A publication] (DLA)
SuprFd........	Super Food Services, Inc. [Associated Press] (SAG)
SuprmInd.....	Supreme Industries [Associated Press] (SAG)
SUPRN.........	Suppression
SUPROX.......	Successive Approximation (IEEE)
SuprSrg	Superior Surgical Manufacturing Co., Inc. [Associated Press] (SAG)
SUPRSTR	Superstructure (AAG)
Suprtex........	Suprtex, Inc. [Associated Press] (SAG)
SUPRVRADSTA...	Supervisory Radio Station (IAA)
SUPRVSN	Supervision
SUPS	Seamen's United Protection Society [A union] [British]
SUPS	Services to User Populations Section [Disbanded by the Board at the Midwinter meeting]
SUPS	Supply Squadron
SUPSAL........	Supervisor of Salvage [Navy]
SUPSALREPWCOAST...	Supervisor of Salvage Representative, West Coast [Navy] (DNAB)
SUPSALV.....	Supervisor of Salvage [Navy]
SUPSD........	Supersede (AFM)
SUPSENS.....	Supersensitive
SupServ......	Superior Services, Inc. [Associated Press] (SAG)
SUPSGT.....	Supply Sergeant [Marine Corps]
SUPSHIP.....	Supervisor of Shipbuilding [Navy]
SUPSHIPS ...	Superintendent of Shipbuilding [Navy] (AAGC)
SupSpcl......	Suprema Specialities, Inc. [Associated Press] (SAG)
SUPSTARS....	Supply Selective Treatment and Review System
SUPSYSCOM...	Supply System Command [Navy]
SUPSYSECGRU...	Supply System, Security Group [Navy] (DNAB)
SUPT	Specialized Undergraduate Pilot Training [Air Force]
SUPT	Superintendent (EY)
supt	Superintendent (DD)
Supt...........	Superintendent (AL)
SUPT	Support (CINC)
SupTech	Superconductor Technologies [Commercial firm Associated Press] (SAG)
SUPTG	Supporting (AAG)
SUPTNAVOBSY...	Superintendent, Naval Observatory
SUPU	Paysandu/Aeropuerto Deptal [Uruguay] [ICAO location identifier] (ICLI)
Supv	Supervising (AL)
SUPV	Super Vision International [NASDAQ symbol] (SAG)
SUPV	Supervisor (AAG)
Supv	Supervisor (AL)
Supv	Supervisory (AL)
SUPVA	Super Vision Intl'A' [NASDAQ symbol] (TTSB)
Supval	Supervalu, Inc. [Associated Press] (SAG)
SUPVG........	Supervising
supvr	Supervisor (DD)
SUPVRY......	Supervisory
supvry.........	Supervisory (MHDW)
SupVs	Super Vision International [Associated Press] (SAG)
SUPVSN......	Supervision
SupVsn	Super Vision International [Associated Press] (SAG)
SUPVSR......	Supervisor
SUPVW.......	Super Vision Intl Wrrt'A' [NASDAQ symbol] (TTSB)
SUPVZ........	Super Vision Intl Wrrt'B' [NASDAQ symbol] (TTSB)
SUPWB	Socialist Unity Party of West Berlin [Germany]
SUP X	Super Extra [Bookbinding] (DGA)
SUPX	Supertex, Inc. [NASDAQ symbol] (NQ)
SUPY	Supervisory (DEN)
SUR	SCOR US Corp. [NYSE symbol] (SPSG)
SUR	Seemingly Unrelated Regression [Statistics]
SUR	Small Unit Radio [Military] (INF)
SUR	Speech Understanding Research
SUR	Starcke [Queensland] [Airport symbol] (AD)
SUR	Start-Up Rate (NRCH)
SUR	State University Railroad Co. [AAR code]
SUR	Sufonylurea Receptor [Biochemistry]
SUR	Sul Ross State University, Library, Alpine, TX [OCLC symbol] (OCLC)
SUR	Supervisory Union Relations Test
Sur.............	Sural Nerve
SUR	Suramin [Antineoplastic drug] (CDI)
SUR	Surcharge [Business term] (ROG)
Sur.............	Surety (DLA)
SUR	Surface (AABC)
sur.............	Surface (WDMC)
SUR	Surgery
SUR	Surinam [ANSI three-letter standard code] (CNC)
SUR	Surlari [Romania] [Geomagnetic observatory code]
Sur.............	Surplus (EBF)
SUR	Surrender (DNAB)
SUR	Surrendered (WGA)
SUR	Surround
SUR	Survivor (DNAB)
SUR	Sutherland [South Africa] [Seismograph station code, US Geological Survey] (SEIS)
Sur.............	Thiouracil [Also, SUra] [Biochemistry]
SURA..........	Shan United Revolutionary Army [Myanmar] (PD)
SURA..........	Southeastern Universities Research Association
SUra	Thiouracil [Also, Sur] [Biochemistry]
SURAnet.......	[The] Southeastern Universities Research Association Network (TNIG)
SURANO	Surface RADAR and Navigation Operation

SURBAT.......	Simultaneous Unlimited Rigorous Block Analytical Triangulation [*Apollo program*] [*NASA*]
SURC..........	Syracuse University Research Corp.
SURCAL.......	Surveillance Calibration Satellite
SURCAP.......	Surviving Capability Plan [*Military*]
SURCO.........	State University Research Center at Oswego [*State University College at Oswego*] [*Research center*] (RCD)
Sur Ct	Surrogate's Court (DLA)
SURE	Safeguards Upgrade Rule Evaluation (PDAA)
SURE	Sensor Upgrade and Refurbishment Effort [*Marine Corps*] (MCD)
SURE	Shuttle Users Review and Evaluation [*NASA*] (NASA)
SURE	Simplicity, Useability, Reliability, Economy
SURE	Space Ultraviolet Radiation Environment (MCD)
SURE	Subsystem Replacement
SURE	Sulfate Regional Experiment Program [*Environmental science*] (COE)
SURE	Sulphate Regional Experiment [*Electric Power Research Institute*]
SURE	Symbolic Utilities Revenue Environment [*IBM Corp.*]
SUREA	Syracuse University Resources for Educators of Adults (EDAC)
SUREJ	Surface Ship Electromagnetic Jammer
SUREPI	Surface Ship Electromagnetic Passive Intercept System
SUREQ..........	Submit Requisition (NOAA)
SureSh.........	Sure Shot International, Inc. [*Associated Press*] (SAG)
SuretyC........	Surety Capital Corp. [*Associated Press*] (SAG)
SURF	Antisubmarine Warfare Barrier Surface Patrol Ship [*Navy*] (NVT)
SURF	Single Unit Retrieval Format
SURF	Space Ultravacuum Research Facility (LAIN)
SURF	Standard UNREP [*Underway Replenishment*] Receiving Fixture [*Navy*] (NVT)
SURF	Support of User Records and Files [*Computer science*]
SURF	Surface
surf	Surfactant
SURF	Synchrotron Ultraviolet Radiation Facility [*National Institute of Standards and Technology*]
SURF	Synthetic Unrandomization of Randomized Fragments [*Chemistry*]
SURF	System Utilization Reporting Facility (HGAA)
SURFAC.......	Surveillance Facility [*Navy*]
Surface DJ...	Surface Design Journal [*A publication*] (BRI)
SURFC.........	Surface
SURFCO.......	Surf Code (DNAB)
SURF DET TRKR...	Surface Detector/Tracker [*Navy*] (CAAL)
SURF EWO...	Surface Electronic Warfare Officer [*Course*] (DOMA)
SUR/FIN.......	American Electroplaters' and Surface Finishers Society Exposition (ITD)
SURFLANT...	Surface Forces Atlantic Fleet [*Navy*]
SURFPA.......	Antisubmarine Warfare Barrier Surface Patrol Area [*Navy*] (NVT)
SURFPAC.....	Surface Forces Pacific Fleet [*Navy*]
SURFPZ.......	Antisubmarine Warfare Barrier Surface Patrol Zone [*Navy*] (NVT)
SURFRAD	Surface Radiation [*Marine science*] (OSRA)
SURFSIDE....	Small Unified Reactor Facility Systems for Isotopes, Desalting, and Electricity [*Nuclear energy*]
SURFWARDEVGRU...	Surface Warfare Development Group [*Also, SWDG*] [*Navy*]
SURG..........	Surgeon [*or Surgery or Surgical*] (AFM)
Surg..........	Surgeon (AL)
SURG..........	Surgery
SurgAf	Surgical Care Affiliates, Inc. [*Nashville, TN*] [*Associated Press*] (SAG)
Surg Cdr	Surgeon-Commander [*British military*]
SURGCL.......	Surgical
SURGE........	SEASAT Users Group of Europe (MSC)
SURGE........	Sorting, Updating, Report Generating, Etc. [*IBM Corp.*] [*Computer science*]
SurgeC........	Surge Components, Inc. [*Associated Press*] (SAG)
SurgeCm......	Surge Components, Inc. [*Associated Press*] (SAG)
SURGEN......	[*The*] Surgeon General [*Army, Air Force*]
Surg Gen	Surgeon General (GFGA)
SurgLsr.......	Surgical Laser Technologies, Inc. [*Associated Press*] (SAG)
Surg Lt	Surgeon Lieutenant [*British military*]
SURGN	Surgeon
SurgTc	Surgical Technologies, Inc. [*Associated Press*] (SAG)
SURI	Syracuse University Research Institute (MCD)
SURIC.........	Surface Integrated Control (MCD)
SURIC.........	Surface Ship Integrated Control System [*Obsolete Navy*]
SURISS........	Sheffield Urban and Regional Instructional Simulation System [*British*]
surj............	Surjet [*Knitting*] [*French*] (BARN)
SURM	Standard Usage Rate Modifier
SURMAC......	Surface Magnetic Confinement (MCD)
SUROB.........	Surf Observation Report [*Navy*] (NVT)
SURORDTECH...	Surface Ordnance Technician [*Navy*] (DNAB)
SURP	Service and Unit Record Processor [*Computer science*] (CIST)
SURP	Submerged Unmanned Recovery Platform (NVT)
SURPIC........	Surface Picture [*AMVER*] [*Coast Guard*]
SURPL	Surplus
SURPO........	Survey of Pupil Opinion (EDAC)
Surps..........	Surplus
SURR	Surrender (AABC)
SURR	Surrey [*County in England*]
SURR	Surrogate
SURRC........	Scottish Universities Research and Reactor Centre [*Research center*] (IRC)
Surr Ct Proc Act...	Surrogate's Court Procedure Act [*A publication*] (DLA)
SURRD	Surrendered (ROG)
SURRO	Surrogate (ADA)
SURS	Solitary Ulcer of Rectum Syndrome [*Medicine*] (DMAA)
SURS	Standard Umbilical Retraction System (NASA)
SURS	Surface Export Cargo System [*Military*] (AABC)
SURS	Surveillance Squadron
SURSAN	Superintendencia de Urbanizacao e Saneamento [*Brazil*]
SURSAT.......	Satellite Surveillance Program [*Canada*] (MSC)
SURSAT.......	Survey Satellite [*NASA*]
SUR/SATCOM...	Survivable Satellite Communications
SURSHIP......	Suretyship [*Legal shorthand*] (LWAP)
SurShot.......	Sure Shot International, Inc. [*Associated Press*] (SAG)
SURT	Sarcoidosis of Upper Respiratory Tract [*Medicine*] (CPH)
SURTAC.......	NORAD Surveillance and Tactical Network (MCD)
SURTAC.......	Surveillance Tactical (MCD)
SURTASS.....	Surveillance Towed Array Sensor System [*Marine science*] (OSRA)
SURTASS.....	Surveillance Towed Array SONAR System
SURTEMS.....	Surface Temperature Measuring System
SURTOPS	Surveillance Training and Operating Procedures Standardization [*Military*] (CAAL)
SURV	Rivera/Aeropuerto Deptal [*Uruguay*] [*ICAO location identifier*] (ICLI)
SURV	Standard Underwater Research Vehicle
SURV	Surveillance (AAG)
SURV	Surveillance Aircraft Company [*Army*] (VNW)
SURV	Survey (AABC)
SURV	Surveyor
SURV	Survival (AFM)
SURV	Surviving
Surv	Survivor
SURVAL.......	Simulator Universal Radio Variability Library
Survey Calif L..	Survey of California Law [*A publication*] (DLA)
SURVFOR	Surveillance Force (DNAB)
SURVI.........	Surveillance
SURVIAC......	Survivability/Vulnerability Information Analysis Center [*Wright-Patterson Air Force Base, OH*] [*DoD*] (MCD)
SURVL	Surveillance (AFM)
SURVM........	Surveillance and Maintenance [*Army*] (AABC)
SURVOPS	Survey Operations [*Navy*] (NVT)
SURVOR	Survivor
SURVR	Surveyor
SURVR	Survivor (AAG)
SURVRAP	Surveillance Range Acoustics Prediction System (MCD)
SURVSA.......	Survivable Satellite Communications System (MCD)
SURVSAT.....	Survivable Satellite
SURVSATCOM...	Survivable Satellite Communications System
SURVSUM	Surveillance Summary Reports (NVT)
SurvTc	Survival Technology, Inc. [*Associated Press*] (SAG)
SURVYR	Surveyor
SURWAC......	Surface Water Automatic Computer (AAG)
SUS	Samband Ungra Sjalfstaedismanna [*National Youth Organization of the Independence Party*] [*Iceland*] [*Political party*] (EAIO)
SUS	Saybolt Universal Seconds [*Oil viscosity*]
SUS	Scottish Union of Students (AEBS)
SUS	Second User Systems Ltd. (NITA)
SUS	Semiconductor Unilateral Switch (MSA)
SUS	Signal Underwater Sound
SUS	Silicon Unidirectional Switch (IAA)
SUS	Silicon Unilateral Switch
SUS	Single Underwater Sound (MCD)
SUS	Small Ultimate Size [*Telecommunications*] (TEL)
SUS	Society for Utopian Studies (EA)
SUS	Society of University Surgeons (EA)
SUS	Solitary Ulcer Syndrome [*Medicine*] (DMAA)
SUS	Sound Underwater Source [*Navy*] (CAAL)
SUS	Special Urban Survey 1987 [*Bureau of the Census*] (GFGA)
SUS	Speech Understanding System
SUS	Stained Urinary Sediment [*Medicine*] (MAE)
SUS	Startup System [*Nuclear energy*] (NRCH)
SUS	Steel User Service [*British*] (BI)
SUS	St. Louis [*Missouri*] Spirit of St. Louis Airport [*Airport symbol Obsolete*] (OAG)
SUS	Stop Unnecessary Spending
SUS	Storage USA [*NYSE symbol*] (TTSB)
SUS	Storage USA, Inc. [*NYSE symbol*] (SAG)
SUS	Suit Umbilical System (MCD)
SUS	Sun-Air of Scandinavia AS [*Denmark ICAO designator*] (FAAC)
SUS	Sunshine Columbia [*Vancouver Stock Exchange symbol*]
SUS	Suppressor Sensitive [*Laboratory scienc*] (DAVI)
SUS	Surkhet [*Nepal*] [*Airport symbol*] (AD)
SUS	Susaki [*Mitsui*] [*Japan*] [*Seismograph station code, US Geological Survey*] [*Closed*] (SEIS)
Sus	Susanna [*Apocrypha*] (BJA)
SUS	Suspect
SUS	Suspended [*Technical drawings*]
SUS	Suspicion Law [*Statute permitting policemen to detain individuals suspected of criminal activity*] [*British*]
SUS	Susquehanna University, Selinsgrove, PA [*OCLC symbol*] (OCLC)
SUS	Sustainer (AAG)
sus............	Susu [*MARC language code Library of Congress*] (LCCP)
SUSA	Service Industries USA [*A publication*]
SUSA	Seventh United States Army
SUSAFFS	Society of United States Air Force Flight Surgeons
SUSAI........	SIAMA [*Society for Interest of Active Missionaries Abroad*] USA, Inc. [*Defunct*] (EA)
SUSAN........	System Utilizing Signal-Processing for Automatic Navigation (MCD)
SUSAT	Sight Unit Small Arms Trilux [*British*]
SUSC	Religieuses de la Sainte-Union des Sacres-Coeurs de Jesus et Marie [*Religious of the Holy Union of the Sacred Hearts*] [*Roman Catholic women's religious order*]

SUSC	Sisters of the Holy Union (TOCD)
SUSC	Sunshine State Conference (PSS)
SUSD	State University of South Dakota
SUSDP	Standard for the Uniform Scheduling of Drugs and Poisons (EERA)
SUS DUP	Suspected Duplicate
SUSEME	Superintendencia de Servicos Medicos [Brazil]
SUSF	Scottish Universities Sports Federation (AIE)
SUSF	State University System of Florida (NOAA)
SUSFU	Situation Unchanged, Still Fouled Up [Military slang] [Bowdlerized version]
SUSGR	Southwestern Union for the Study of Great Religions (EA)
SUSH	Set-Up Sheet (AAG)
SUSI	Superb Seeing Imager [Astronomy]
SUSIE	Sequential Unmanned Scanning and Indicating Equipment (IAA)
SUSIE	Stock Updating Sales Invoicing Electronically (IEEE)
SUSIE	Surface/Underwater Ship Intercept Equipment (DNAB)
SUSIM	Solar Ultraviolet Spectral Irradiance Monitor (MCD)
susim	Solar Ultraviolet Spectral Irradiance Monitor (NAKS)
SUSIO	State University System of Florida Institute of Oceanography (NOAA)
SUSIS	Sport und Sportwissenschaftliche Informationssystem [Sport and Sports-Scientific Information System] [West Germany] (IID)
SUSIX	Security Capital U.S. Real Estate Cl.I [Mutual fund ticker symbol] (SG)
Sus Leg Chron	Susquehanna Legal Chronicle [Pennsylvania] [A publication] (DLA)
SUSLO	Senior United States Liaison Officer [National Security Agency]
SUSM	Scottish United Services Museum [British military] (DMA)
SUSMOP	Senior United States Military Observer Palestine
SUSNO	Senior United States Naval Officer
SUSO	Salto/Aeropuerto Deptal [Uruguay] [ICAO location identifier] (ICLI)
SUSOPS	Sustained Operations [Study of soldier performance in extended combat situation] [Army]
SUSP	Suspected [Passage or line of a work] [Literary criticism] (ROG)
SUSP	Suspend [or Suspension] (AFM)
SUSP	Suspicion [FBI standardized term]
SUSPD	Suspended
SUSPDNG	Suspending [Freight]
Sus Per Col	Suspensio per Collum [Execution by Hanging] [Latin]
Sus Per Coll	Suspendatur per Collum [Let Him Be Hanged by the Neck] [Latin]
SUS per COLL	Suspensio per Collum [Hanged by the Neck] [Latin]
SUSP L	Suspecta Lectio [Double Reading] [Latin] (ROG)
SUSPNSN	Suspension
SUSQ	Susquehanna Bancshares, Inc. [Lititz, PA] [NASDAQ symbol] (NQ)
SusqBnc	Susquehanna Bancshares, Inc. [Associated Press] (SAG)
Susq LC	Susquehanna Leading Chronicle [Pennsylvania] [A publication] (DLA)
Susq L Chron	Susquehanna Legal Chronicle [Pennsylvania] [A publication] (DLA)
Susq Legal Chron	Susquehanna Legal Chronicle [Pennsylvania] [A publication] (DLA)
Susq Leg Chron	Susquehanna Legal Chronicle [Pennsylvania] [A publication] (DLA)
SUSQU	Susquehanna Bancshares [NASDAQ symbol] (TTSB)
Susquehanna Leg Chron (PA)	Susquehanna Legal Chronicle [Pennsylvania] [A publication] (DLA)
SUSREP	Senior United States Representative to Defense Production Board [NATO] (NATG)
SUSRX	Security Capital U.S. Real Estate Cl.R [Mutual fund ticker symbol] (SG)
SUSS	Shuttle Upper-Stage System (SSD)
SUSS	Signalmen's United and Sick Society [A union] [British]
SUSS	Sound Underwater Signal Source (MCD)
SUSS	Submarine Schoolship [Navy] (NVT)
SUSS	Sussex [County in England]
SUST	Sunstates Corp. [NASDAQ symbol] (SAG)
SUST	Sustainer
SUSTA	Southern United States Trade Association (WPI)
SUSTD	Sustained [Legal] (ROG)
SUSTE	Sunstates Corp. [NASDAQ symbol] (TTSB)
SUSTN	Sustain [Legal] (ROG)
SUSTN	Sustentation [Ecclesiastical] (ROG)
SUSTP	Sunstates $3.75 cm Pfd [NASDAQ symbol] (TTSB)
SUSV	Small Unit Support Vehicle [Military] (RDA)
SUSY	Subsystem (IAA)
SUSY	Such Systems (NITA)
SUSY	Survey System (IAA)
SUSY's	Supersymmetric Theories [Particle physics]
SUT	Satellite under Test
SUT	Set-Up Time
SUT	Small Unit Transceiver [Military] (INF)
SUT	Society for Underwater Technology (EA)
SUT	Southport, NC [Location identifier FAA] (FAAL)
SUT	Start-Up Transformer (NRCH)
SUT	State Unemployment Tax (MCD)
SUT	Subunit Test
SUT	Surface and Underwater Target (MCD)
SUT	Suttsu [Japan] [Seismograph station code, US Geological Survey] (SEIS)
SUT	Swinburne University of Technology [Australia]
SUT	Syndicat Uni du Transport [United Transportation Union - UTU] [Canada]
SUT	System under Test (AAG)
SUTAGS	Shuttle Uplink Text and Graphics Scanner (NASA)
SUTARS	Search Unit Tracing and Recording System
SUTB	Tacuarembo [Uruguay] [ICAO location identifier] (ICLI)
SUTEC	Seneca Underwater Test and Evaluation Center
SUTH	Sutherland [County in Scotland]
Suth	Sutherland's Calcutta Reports [India] [A publication] (DLA)
Suth App	Sutherland's Appeal Reports, Small Causes Court [1861-65] [Bengal, India] [A publication] (DLA)
Suth Bengal	Sutherland's Bengal High Court Reports [India] [A publication] (DLA)
Suth Dam	Sutherland on the Law of Damages [A publication] (DLA)
Suth FBR	Sutherland's Bengal Full Bench Reports [India] [A publication] (DLA)
Suth Mis	India Weekly Reporter, Miscellaneous Appeals [A publication] (DLA)
Suth PCA	Sutherland's Privy Council Appeals [A publication] (DLA)
Suth PCJ	Sutherland's Privy Council Judgments [A publication] (DLA)
Suth Sp N	Full Bench Rulings [Calcutta] [A publication] (DLA)
Suth Sp N	Sutherland's Special Number of Weekly Reporter [A publication] (DLA)
Suth Stat Const	Sutherland on Statutes and Statutory Construction [A publication] (DLA)
Suth St Const	Sutherland on Statutes and Statutory Construction [A publication] (DLA)
Suth WR	Sutherland's Weekly Reporter, Calcutta [1864-76] [A publication] (DLA)
Suth WR Mis	Sutherland's Weekly Reports, Miscellaneous Appeals [India] [A publication] (DLA)
SUTI	Symptomatic Urinary Tract Infection [Medicine] (DMAA)
SUTR	Treinta Y Tres [Uruguay] [ICAO location identifier] (ICLI)
SUTRA	Saturated-Unsaturated Transport [Ground-water modeling]
SUTRASFCO	Sindicato Unificado de Trabajadores de la Standard Fruit Co. [Honduras]
SUTT	Small Unit Training Team [Military]
Sutton	Sutton on Personal Actions at Common Law [A publication] (DLA)
SuttRsc	Sutton Resource Ltd. [Associated Press] (SAG)
SUU	Fairfield, CA [Location identifier FAA] (FAAL)
SUU	Santaquin Canyon [Utah] [Seismograph station code, US Geological Survey] (SEIS)
SUU	Society of University Urologists (EA)
SUU	Suspended Underwing Unit [Military] (MUSM)
SUU	Suspension Unit (AFM)
SUU	Suspension Unit Universal [Weaponry] [Air Force] (INF)
SUUD	Sudden, Unexpected, Unexplained Death (DAVI)
SUV	Saybolt Universal Viscosity (IAA)
SUV	Small Unilamellar Vesicle [Pharmacy Biochemistry]
SUV	Small Unilamellar Vessel [Medicine] (DMAA)
SUV	Sociated Unilamellar Vesicles
SUV	Souvenir
SUV	Sport-Utility Vehicle [Type of truck]
SUV	Sumpter Valley Railway [AAR code]
SUV	Suva [Fiji] [Airport symbol] (OAG)
SUVAT	Support Unit Vehicle Automatic Tester
SUVCW	Sons of Union Veterans of the Civil War (EA)
SUVI	Strong Ultraviolet Index
SUW	Superior, WI [Location identifier FAA] (FAAL)
SUW	Surface Warfare (NVT)
SUWC	Surface Warfare Coordinator [Also, SWC] (NVT)
SUWU	Skilled and Unskilled Workers' Union [Somali Republic]
SUX	Sioux City [Iowa] [Airport symbol] (OAG)
SUX	Succinylcholine [A muscle relaxant] (DAVI)
sux	Sumerian [MARC language code Library of Congress] (LCCP)
SUY	Aerial Surveys (1980) Ltd. [New Zealand] [ICAO designator] (FAAC)
SUY	State University Railroad Co. [Later, SUR] [AAR code]
SUY	Sudureyri [Iceland] [Airport symbol] (OAG)
s-uy--	Uruguay [MARC geographic area code Library of Congress] (LCCP)
SUYR	Southampton University Yacht Research Group [British]
SUZ	Suez Petroleum Corp. [Vancouver Stock Exchange symbol]
SUZ	Suria [Papua New Guinea] [Airport symbol] (OAG)
SV	El Salvador [ANSI two-letter standard code] (CNC)
SV	Safety Valve (AAG)
sv	Safety Valve (NAKS)
SV	Sailing Vessel
SV	Sales Voucher [Business term] (DCTA)
SV	Sampling Visit (GNE)
SV	Sancta Virgo [Holy Virgin] [Latin]
SV	Sanctitas Vestra [Your Holiness] [Latin]
SV	Saponification Value [Organic analytical chemistry]
SV	Sapper Vehicle [Military]
SV	Sarcoma Virus [Medicine] (MAE)
SV	Satellite Vehicle [Instrument] (EERA)
SV	Satellite Virus
SV	Saudi Arabian Airlines [ICAO designator] (AD)
SV	Saudia-Saudi Arabia Airlines [Airline flight code] (ODBW)
SV	Saves [Baseball]
SV	Savings Transfer [Banking]
SV	Scalp Vein [Medicine]
SV	Schedule Variance (MCD)
SV	Schweizerische Volkspartei [Swiss People's Party] [Political party]
SV	Scientific Visualization (CDE)
SV	Secondary Valve
SV	Secular Variation [Geophysics]
SV	Security Violation (AAG)
SV	Selecta Vision [RCA brand name for tape cartridges of TV programs]
SV	Selective Volunteer [Navy]
SV	Selenoid Valve (MCD)
sv	Selenoid Valve (NAKS)
SV	Self-Ventilated (MSA)
SV	Self Verification
SV	Seminal Vesicle [Anatomy]

SV	Service
SV	Service Vehicle
S/V	Servovalve
SV	Set Value
SV	Severe (MAE)
SV	Shutter Value [*Photography*]
SV	Shuttle Vehicle [*NASA*] (NASA)
sv	Shuttle Vehicle (NAKS)
SV	Side Valve [*Automotive engineering*]
SV	Side View (MSA)
SV	Sieve
Sv	Sievert [*SI unit for radioactive dose equivalent*]
SV	Sigmoid Volvulus [*Gastroenterology*] (DAVI)
SV	Silicone Varnish
SV	Silvercraft SpA [*Italy ICAO aircraft manufacturer identifier*] (ICAO)
SV	Simian Virus
SV	Simulated Video (MCD)
SV	Single Silk Varnish [*Wire insulation*] (AAG)
SV	Single Value
SV	Single Valve [*Automobile model, Stutz Motors*]
SV	Single Ventricle [*Cardiology*] (DAVI)
SV	Single Vessel (DB)
SV	Single Vibrations [*Half cycles*]
SV	Sinus Venosus [*Anatomy*]
SV	Siste, Viator [*Stop, Traveller*] [*Latin*] (ROG)
SV	Slide Valve
SV	Slowed-Down Video [*RADAR*] (CET)
SV	Sluice [*or Stop*] Valve
SV	Snake Venom [*Medicine*]
SV	Sodium Vapor
SV	Soft Valve
SV	Solenoid Valve (KSC)
SV	Solicited Volunteer [*In drug studies*]
SV	Sons of Veterans
SV	Sophisticated Vocabulary (AAG)
SV	Sosialistisk Valgforbund [*Socialist Electoral Alliance*] [*Norway Political party*] (PPE)
SV	Sosialistisk Venstreparti [*Socialist Left Party*] [*Norway Political party*] (PPE)
SV	Sotto Voce [*In an Undertone*] [*Music*]
SV	Space Vehicle
sv	Space Vehicle (NAKS)
SV	Space Velocity [*Chemical engineering*]
SV	Space Visualization [*Visual perception*]
SV	Spatial Velocity (DB)
SV	Specified Value (MCD)
SV	Spillmeyer-Vogt [*Disease*] [*Medicine*] (DB)
sv	Spiritus Vini [*Alcoholic Spirit*] [*Latin*]
SV	Spiritus Vinosus [*Ardent Spirit*] [*Pharmacy*] (ROG)
SV	Splenic Vein [*Medicine*] (DB)
SV	Spoken Voice (MEDA)
SV	Spontaneous Ventilation [*Medicine*] (MEDA)
SV	Star of Valour [*British*] (ADA)
SV	State Vector (KSC)
sv	State Vector (NAKS)
SV	Status Valid
sV	Statvolt [*Also, statV*] [*Electrostatic unit of potential difference*]
SV	Steam Valve
SV	Stimulation Value [*Psychology*]
SV	Stimulus Valve [*Medicine*] (DAVI)
SV	Stock Volume (DAVI)
SV	Stop Valve (IAA)
SV	Storm Vulcan
SV	Stripping Voltammetry [*Electroanalytical chemistry*]
SV	Stroke Volume [*Physiology*]
SV	Study of Values [*Psychology*]
SV	Subclavian Vein [*Cardiology*]
SV	Subdivision Flag [*Navy British*]
SV	Subjective Vertical [*Neurology*]
SV	Subject-Verb [*Education of the hearing-impaired*]
SV	Subventricular (DB)
SV	Sub Verbo [*or Sub Voce*] [*Under the Word*] [*Latin*]
sv	Sub Vi [*Under Compulsion*] [*Latin*]
SV	Supervisor (IAA)
SV	Super Volkswagen [*Auto racing*]
S/V	Supply Valve (MCD)
SV	Support Vehicle [*British military*] (DMA)
SV	Supraventricular [*Cardiology*]
SV	Supravital [*Medicine*] (MAE)
SV	Surface Vessel
S/V	Surface/Volume [*Ratio*]
sv	Surrender Value (ODBW)
S/V	Survivability/Vulnerability [*Applied to ability of weapon systems to survive attacks*] [*Military*]
sv	Swan Islands [*used in records cataloged after January 1978*] [*MARC country of publication code Library of Congress*] (LCCP)
SV	Swept Volume
SV	Symptomatic Volunteer [*In drug studies*]
SV	Synaptic Vesicle [*Neurobiology*]
SV	Synchronous Voltage (OA)
SV 40	Simian Virus 40 [*A DNA virus in non-human primates*] (DOG)
SVA	Sample Valve Assembly
SVA	Saudi Arabian Airlines [*ICAO designator*] (FAAC)
SVA	Savoonga [*Alaska*] [*Airport symbol*] (OAG)
SVA	School of Visual Arts [*New York, NY*]
SVA	Scottish Volleyball Association (DBA)
SVA	SEABEE Veterans of America (EA)
SVA	Sectionalized Vertical Antenna
SVA	Security and Vulnerability Analysis (MCD)
SVA	Selective Vagotomy with Antrectomy [*Medicine*] (DB)
SVA	Selective Visceral Angiography [*Medicine*] (AAMN)
SVA	Severe Thunderstorm Watch [*Telecommunications*] (OTD)
SVA	Shared Virtual Area [*Computer science*]
SVA	Shareholder Valuation Analysis
SVA	Singapore Volunteer Artillery [*British military*] (DMA)
SVA	Single-Valve First-Actuation [*Nuclear energy*] (NRCH)
SVA	Single Vehicle Accident [*Automotive safety*]
SVA	Singular-Value Analysis [*Industrial control*]
SVA	Society for Visual Anthropology (EA)
SVA	Solar Vane Actuators
SVA	Statistical Vibration Analysis
SVA	Stock Valuation Adjustment [*Business term*] (ADA)
SVA	Suva [*Fiji*] [*Seismograph station code, US Geological Survey*] (SEIS)
SVAA	Super Vernier Auto Alert [*Military*] (CAAL)
SVAB	Shuttle Vehicle Assembly Building [*NASA*] (NASA)
SVAC	Acarigua, Portuguesa [*Venezuela ICAO location identifier*] (ICLI)
SVAC	Senate Veterans Affairs Committee
SVAC	Shuttle Vehicle Assembly and Checkout [*NASA*] (GFGA)
SVAC	Singapore Volunteer Artillery Corps [*British military*] (DMA)
SVAD	Savanna Army Depot [*Illinois*] (AABC)
SVADA	Savanna Army Depot Activity (AABC)
SVAF	South Vietnamese Armed Forces (VNW)
SVAFB	South Vandenberg Air Force Base [*California*] (NASA)
SVALC	Sangamon Valley Academic Library Consortium [*Library network*]
SV-AMC	Suspect-Variant Anomalous Mental Condition
SVAN	Anaco, Anzoategui [*Venezuela ICAO location identifier*] (ICLI)
SVAO	Service at Veterans Administration Offices [*Red Cross*]
SVAR	Sequential Variance
SVAR	Stuart's Lower Canada Vice-Admiralty Reports [*A publication*] (DLA)
SVAS	Supravalvular Aortic Stenosis [*Cardiology*] (MAE)
SVAS	Supraventricular Aortic Stenosis [*Medicine*] (DMAA)
SVAT	San Fernando De Atabapo, T. F. Amazonas [*Venezuela ICAO location identifier*] (ICLI)
SVAT	Soil Vegetation Atmosphere Transfer (EERA)
SVAT	Standard Version Acceptance Test (MCD)
SVAT	Synaptic Vesicle Amine Transporter [*Biochemistry*]
SVB	Sambava [*Madagascar*] [*Airport symbol*] (OAG)
SVB	Saphenous Vein Bypass [*Cardiology*] (DMAA)
SVB	Shuttle Vehicle Booster [*NASA*] (NASA)
SVB	Space Vehicle Booster [*NASA*] (MCD)
SVB	Sterivet Laboratories Ltd. [*Toronto Stock Exchange symbol*]
SV:B	Study of Values: British Edition [*Psychology*]
SVBC	Barcelona/Gral. Jose Antonio Anzoategui Internacional Anzoategui [*Venezuela ICAO location identifier*] (ICLI)
SVBEEQV	Si Vales, Bene Est; Ego Quoque Valeo [*I Hope You're Well; I Am*] [*Latin*]
SVBI	Barinas, Barinas [*Venezuela ICAO location identifier*] (ICLI)
SVBL	Maracay/El Libertador, Base Aerea Aragua [*Venezuela ICAO location identifier*] (ICLI)
SVBM	Barquisimeto/Internacional, Lara [*Venezuela ICAO location identifier*] (ICLI)
SVBP	Single-Variable Bypass Program [*DoD*]
SVBPG	Saphenous Vein Bypass Graft [*Cardiology*] (DAVI)
SVBS	Maracay/Mariscal Sucre, Base Aerea Aragua [*Venezuela ICAO location identifier*] (ICLI)
SVBT	Space Vehicle Booster Test (AAG)
SVBV	Strawberry Vein Banding Virus [*Plant pathology*]
SVBZ	Bruzual, Apure [*Venezuela ICAO location identifier*] (ICLI)
SVC	Saint Vincent College [*Latrobe, PA*]
SVC	Selective Venous Catheterization [*Cardiology*]
SVC	Service (AFM)
Svc	Service (TBD)
SVC	Service Command [*Army*]
SVC	Service Message [*Aviation code*]
SVC	Silver City [*New Mexico*] [*Airport symbol*] (OAG)
SVC	Silver Creek [*California*] [*Seismograph station code, US Geological Survey*] (SEIS)
SVC	Sine Vibration Control
SVC	Singapore Volunteer Corps [*British military*] (DMA)
SVC	Single Variable Control
SVC	Slow Vital Capacity [*Medicine*] (MAE)
SVC	Society of Vacuum Coaters (EA)
SVC	Space Vehicle Code
svc	Space Vehicle Operations [*Kennedy Space Center*] (NAKS)
SVC	Special Verification Commission (DOMA)
SVC	Spiroplasmavirus citri [*Bacteriology*]
SVC	Spring Viremia of Carp
SVC	Still Video Camera
SVC	Stokely-Van Camp, Inc. [*NYSE symbol*] (SPSG)
SVC	Stokley Van Camp [*NYSE symbol*] (SAG)
SVC	Superior Vena Cava [*Anatomy*]
SVC	Supervisor Call (NASA)
svc	Supervisor Call (NAKS)
SVC	Suprahepatic Vena Cava [*Medicine*] (AAMN)
SVC	Switched Virtual Call [*Telecommunications*] (NITA)
SVC	Switched Virtual Circuit
SVCA	Caracas Maiquetia Distrito Federal [*Venezuela ICAO location identifier*] (ICLI)
SVCAB	Saphenous Vein Coronary Artery Bypass [*Cardiology*]
SVCB	Ciudad Bolivar, Bolivar [*Venezuela ICAO location identifier*] (ICLI)

SVCBL	Serviceable
SVCBV	Solenoid Valve-Carburetor Bowl Vent [*Automotive engineering*]
SVCC	Caracas Ciudad Distrito Federal [*Venezuela ICAO location identifier*] (ICLI)
SVCD	Caicara De Orinoco, Bolivar [*Venezuela ICAO location identifier*] (ICLI)
SVCE	Service
SvceCp	Service Corp. International [*Associated Press*] (SAG)
SVCG	Servicing (IAA)
SVCG	Spatial Vectorcardiogram [*Cardiology*]
SVCH	Achaguas, Apure [*Venezuela ICAO location identifier*] (ICLI)
SVCI	Cachipo, Monagas [*Venezuela ICAO location identifier*] (ICLI)
SVCJ	San Carlos, Cojedes [*Venezuela ICAO location identifier*] (ICLI)
SVCL	Calabozo, Guarico [*Venezuela ICAO location identifier*] (ICLI)
SvcMer	Service Merchandise Co., Inc. [*Associated Press*] (SAG)
SVCMN	Service Man (NVT)
Svcmst	Servicemaster Ltd. Partnership [*Associated Press*] (SAG)
Svcmstr	ServiceMaster Ltd. [*Associated Press*] (SAG)
SVCN	Canaima, Bolivar [*Venezuela ICAO location identifier*] (ICLI)
SVCO	Carora, Lara [*Venezuela ICAO location identifier*] (ICLI)
SVCO	Superior Vena Cava Obstruction [*Cardiology*] (DAVI)
SVCP	Carupano/Gral. en Jefe Jose Francisco Bermudez, Sucre [*Venezuela ICAO location identifier*] (ICLI)
SVCP	Special Virus Cancer Program [*National Cancer Institute*]
SVC-PA	Superior Vena Cava-Pulmonary Artery [*Shunt*] [*Medicine*] (STED)
SVCPr	Stokely-Van Camp 5% Pref [*NYSE symbol*] (TTSB)
SVCR	Coro/Internacional, Falcon [*Venezuela ICAO location identifier*] (ICLI)
SVCR	Segmented Venous Capacitance Ratio (STED)
SVC-RPA	Superior Vena Cava - Right Pulmonary Artery Shunt [*Anatomy*] (MAE)
SVCS	Caracas/Internacional del Centro Miranda [*Venezuela ICAO location identifier*] (ICLI)
SVCS	Star Vector Calibration Sensor [*Aviation*] (OA)
SVCS	Superior Vena Caval Syndrome [*Medicine*]
SvcStrs	Service Stars [*Military decoration*]
SVCT	Supervisor Call Address Table (IAA)
SVCU	Cumana, Sucre [*Venezuela ICAO location identifier*] (ICLI)
SVCU	Space Visualization Contralateral Use [*Occupational therapy*]
SVD	Seismic Velocity Discontinuity [*Geology*]
SVD	Share Valuation Division [*Inland Revenue*] [*British*]
SVD	Silver Talon Mines Ltd. [*Vancouver Stock Exchange symbol*]
SVD	Simple Vertex Delivery [*Medicine*]
SVD	Simplified Vapor Detector
SVD	Simultaneous Voice/Data
SVD	Single Vessel Disease [*Medicine*] (STED)
SVD	Singular Value Decomposition [*Mathematics*]
SVD	Small Vessel Disease [*Medicine*] (STED)
SVD	Societas Verbi Divini [*Society of the Divine Word*] [*Roman Catholic men's religious order*]
SVD	Society of the Divine Word (TOOD)
svd	Society of the Divine Word (TOCD)
SVD	Space Vehicles Division [*NASA*] (MCD)
SVD	Spontaneous Vaginal Delivery [*Gynecology*]
SVD	Spontaneous Vetex Delivery [*Obstetrics*] (DAVI)
SVD	St. Vincent [*Windward Islands*] [*Airport symbol*] (OAG)
SVD	Surveyor Vehicle Department
SVD	Sverdlovsk [*Former USSR Geomagnetic observatory code*]
SVD	Swine Vesicular Disease [*Medicine*] (DMAA)
SVDA	Savanna Depot Activity [*Army*]
SVDF	Segmented Virtual Display File
SVDP	La Divina Pastora, Bolivar [*Venezuela ICAO location identifier*] (ICLI)
SVDP	Saint Vincent de Paul (ADA)
SVDP	Skylab Video Documentation Project [*NASA*] (KSC)
SVDS	Space Vehicle Dynamic Simulator [*NASA*] (NASA)
SVE	Aero Servicios Especializados SA de CV [*Mexico ICAO designator*] (FAAC)
SVE	Secure Voice Equipment (NATG)
SVE	Seminal Vesicle Epithelium [*Anatomy*]
SVE	Severide Resources, Inc. [*Vancouver Stock Exchange symbol*]
SVE	Slow Volume Encephalography (STED)
SVE	Society for Vector Ecology (EA)
SVE	Society for Veterinary Ethology [*See also SEV*] [*Edinburgh, Scotland*] (EAIO)
SVE	Society for Visual Education, Inc. (AEBS)
SVE	Soil Vacuum Extraction [*Computer science*]
SVE	Soil Vapor Extraction [*Environmental science*]
SVE	Soluble Viral Extract (STED)
SVE	Space Vehicle Electronics (SAA)
SVE	Special Vehicle Engineering [*Ford Motor Co.*]
SVE	Special Visceral Efferent (STED)
SVE	Sterile Vaginal Examination [*Obstetrics*] (DAVI)
SVE	Streptococcus Viridans Endocarditis [*Medicine*] (DB)
SVE	Sum of Vector Elements (IAA)
SVE	Supraventricular Ectopic [*Beat*] [*Cardiology*]
SVE	Susanville, CA [*Location identifier FAA*] (FAAL)
SVE	Sverdlovsk [*Ekaterinburg*] [*Former USSR Seismograph station code, US Geological Survey*] (SEIS)
SVE	Swept Volume Efficiency [*Air Force*]
SVE	System Valve Engineering
s-ve--	Venezuela [*MARC geographic area code Library of Congress*] (LCCP)
SVEA	Schweizerischer Verband Evangaelischer Arbeitnehmer [*A union*] [*Switzerland*] (DCTA)
SVEA	Slowly Varying Envelope Approximation [*Computer science*] (IAA)
SVEA	Supplemental Vocational Education Assistance (OICC)
SVEAA	Schweizerischer Verband Evangelischer Arbeiter und Angestellter [*Swiss Federation of Protestant Trade Unions*]
SVEAD	State Variable Estimation and Accuracy Determination
SVECF	ScanVec Co. [*NASDAQ symbol*] (TTSB)
SVECF	ScanVec Co. Ltd. [*NASDAQ symbol*] (SAG)
SVED	El Dorado, Bolivar [*Venezuela ICAO location identifier*] (ICLI)
SVEN	Shipboard Voice-Enhanced Navigation System [*for blind sailors*]
SVER	Spatial Visual Evoked Response (OA)
SVER	State Veterans Employment Representative [*Department of Labor*]
SVERT	Subvert (ROG)
SVES	Satellite Video Exchange Society [*Canada*] (EAIO)
SVEZ	Elorza, Apure [*Venezuela ICAO location identifier*] (ICLI)
SVF	Save [*Benin*] [*Airport symbol*] (OAG)
SVF	Services Flight [*Military*]
SVF	Set Vertical Format (IAA)
SVF	Silverleaf Resources Ltd. [*Vancouver Stock Exchange symbol*]
SVF	Simple Vector Format [*Proposed Standard*] (EERA)
SVF	Standard Vented Furnace
SVF	Standard Volume Flow (IAA)
SVF	State Variable Filter
SVF	Stoicorum Veterum Fragmenta [*A publication*] (OCD)
SVFM	Caracas/Generelisimo Francisco De Miranda Base Aerea La Carlota, Miranda [*Venezuela ICAO location identifier*] (ICLI)
SVFR	Special Visual Flight Rules [*Aviation*]
SVG	Saphenous Vein Graft [*Cardiology*]
SVG	Sauvagine [*A polypeptide*]
SVG	Saving (WDAA)
Svg	Saving (TBD)
SVG	Servicing
SVG	Serving (FAAC)
SVG	Spiritus Vini Gallici [*Brandy*] [*Pharmacy*] (ROG)
SVG	Stavanger [*Norway*] [*Airport symbol*] (OAG)
SVG	Stevens International, Inc. [*AMEX symbol*] (SPSG)
SVG	Sun Valley Gold Mines Ltd. [*Vancouver Stock Exchange symbol*]
SVG.A	Stevens Intl CI'A' [*AMEX symbol*] (TTSB)
SVGA	Super Video Graphics Array [*Computer science*]
SVG.B	Stevens Intl CI'B' [*AMEX symbol*] (TTSB)
SVGC	Secure Voice and Graphic Conferencing (MCD)
SVGD	Guasdualito, Apure [*Venezuela ICAO location identifier*] (ICLI)
SVGI	Guiria, Sucre [*Venezuela ICAO location identifier*] (ICLI)
SVGI	Silicon Valley Group [*NASDAQ symbol*] (TTSB)
SVGI	Silicon Valley Group, Inc. [*NASDAQ symbol*] (NQ)
SVGL	Silicon Valley Group Lithography (ECON)
SVGS	Savings
SVGT	Guasipati, Bolivar [*Venezuela ICAO location identifier*] (ICLI)
SVGU	Guanare, Portuguesa [*Venezuela ICAO location identifier*] (ICLI)
SVH	Seven Mile High Resources, Inc. [*Vancouver Stock Exchange symbol*]
SVH	Severely Handicapped
SVH	Solar Vacuum Head [*Astronomy*] (OA)
SVH	Statesville, NC [*Location identifier FAA*] (FAAL)
SVHE	Society for Values in Higher Education (EA)
SVHG	Higuerote, Miranda [*Venezuela ICAO location identifier*] (ICLI)
SVHS	Super Video Home System [*Japan Victor Co.*]
SVI	San Vincente Del Caguan [*Colombia*] [*Airport symbol*] (OAG)
SVI	Service Interception [*Telecommunications*]
SVI	Servicios de Transporte Aereo, SA de CV [*Mexico*] [*FAA designator*] (FAAC)
SVI	Singapore Volunteer Infantry [*British military*] (DMA)
SVI	Single Vendor Integrity (MCD)
SVI	Single Vibrational Level [*Physics*]
SVI	Sludge Volume Index [*Wastewater treatment*]
SVI	Sound Velocity Indicator
SVI	Spiritus Vini Industrialis [*Industrial Alcohol*] [*Pharmacy*]
SVI	Stroke Volume Index [*Medicine*]
SVI	St. Vincent [*St. Vincent*] [*Seismograph station code, US Geological Survey Closed*] (SEIS)
SVI	System Verification Installation
SVIA	Specialty Vehicles Institute of America (EA)
SVIB	Strong Vocational Interest Blank [*Psychology*]
SVIC	Icabaru, Bolivar [*Venezuela ICAO location identifier*] (ICLI)
SVIC	Shock and Vibration Information Center [*Terminated Navy*] (MCD)
SVIC	Silicon Valley Information Center [*Database producer*] (IID)
SVICLC	Shenandoah Valley Independent College Library Cooperative [*Library network*]
SVID	System V Interface Definition (NITA)
SVIE	Isla De Coche, Nueva Esparta [*Venezuela ICAO location identifier*] (ICLI)
SVIF	Svenski Indianska Foerbundet [*Sweden*]
SVIMR	St. Vincent's Institute of Medical Research [*Australia*]
SVIMS	Short Vehicle Integrated Management System
SVIO	Superintending Veterinary Investigation Officer [*Ministry of Agriculture, Fisheries, and Food*] [*British*]
SVIP	Secure Voice Improvement Program [*DoD*]
SVIPA	Swiss Videotex Industry Association [*Information service or system*] (IID)
SVIPA	Swiss Viewdata Information Providers Association [*Zurich*] [*Telecommunications*]
SVJ	Lompoc, CA [*Location identifier FAA*] (FAAL)
SVJ	Steed Ventures Corp. [*Formerly, Poney Explorations Ltd.*] [*Vancouver Stock Exchange symbol*]
SVJ	Solvaer [*Norway*] [*Airport symbol*] (OAG)
SVJC	Paraguana/Josefa Camejo Internacional, Falcon [*Venezuela ICAO location identifier*] (ICLI)
SVK	Air Slovakia BWJ Ltd. [*FAA designator*] (FAAC)

SVK............ Secure Voice Kit (DWSG)
SVKA........ Kavanayen, Bolivar [*Venezuela ICAO location identifier*] (ICLI)
SVKM........ Kamarata, Bolivar [*Venezuela ICAO location identifier*] (ICLI)
SVL............ Saak [*Russian Federation*] [*ICAO designator*] (FAAC)
SVL............ Sapphire Vacuum Lens
SVL............ Savonlinna [*Finland*] [*Airport symbol*] (OAG)
SVL............ Scripps Visibility Laboratory
SVL............ Set-Valued Logic [*Computer science*]
SVL............ Silver Lake Resources, Inc. [*Toronto Stock Exchange symbol*]
SVL............ Snout-to-Vent Length [*Biometry*]
SVL............ Star Valley Resources [*Vancouver Stock Exchange symbol*]
SVL............ Support Validation Laboratory [*Army*]
SVLA.......... Steered Vertical Line Array [*Military*] (CAAL)
SVLB.......... Sapphire Vacuum Lens Blank
SVLF.......... La Fria, Tachira [*Venezuela ICAO location identifier*] (ICLI)
SVLF.......... Shipboard Very Low Frequency [*Navy*] (NG)
SVLH.......... Surma Valley Light Horse [*British military*] (DMA)
SVLL.......... Short Vertical Lower Left
SVLO.......... La Orchila - Dependencia Federal [*Venezuela ICAO location identifier*] (ICLI)
SVLOG........ Servicing Log [*Telecommunications*] (TEL)
SVLP.......... Special Virus Leukemia Program [*National Cancer Institute*]
SVLR.......... Short Vertical Lower Right
SVLTE........ Services Valve Life Test Establishment [*British*] (MCD)
SVLW.......... Sectoraal Verband Landbouwwetenschappen [*Committee on International Education in Agricultural Sciences*] [*Netherlands*] (EAIO)
SVM............ Aeroservicios Monterrey SA de CV [*Mexico ICAO designator*] (FAAC)
SVM............ Salem, MI [*Location identifier FAA*] (FAAL)
SVM............ Seminal Vesicle Mesenchyme [*Anatomy*]
SVM............ Seminal Vesicle Microsome [*Anatomy*]
SVM............ Semitrailer Van Mount
SVM............ ServiceMaster Co. [*NYSE symbol*] [*Formerly, ServiceMaster L.P.*] (SG)
SVM............ ServiceMaster L.P. [*NYSE symbol*] (TTSB)
SVM............ ServiceMaster Ltd. [*NYSE symbol*] (SPSG)
SVM............ Service Volontaire Mennonite [*Mennonite Voluntary Service*]
SVM............ Ship's Value Manual (DNAB)
SVM............ Ship Vulnerability Model (MCD)
SVM............ Silicon Video Memory
SVM............ Silver City [*New Mexico*] [*Seismograph station code, US Geological Survey*] (SEIS)
SVM............ Silver Hart Mines Ltd. [*Vancouver Stock Exchange symbol*]
SVM............ Sisters of the Visitation of the Congregation of the Immaculate Heart of Mary [*Roman Catholic religious order*]
SVM............ Special Vehicle Management [*Automotive engineering*]
SVM............ Spiritus Vini Methylatus [*Methylated Spirit*] [*Pharmacy*]
SVM............ Stamp Vending Machine (DCTA)
SVM............ Standard Volvox Medium (DB)
SVM............ Syncytiovascular Membrane [*Medicine*] (MAE)
SVM............ System Validation Model (NVT)
SVMA.......... Space Vehicle Mission Analysis
SVMB.......... Society for Vascular Medicine and Biology (EA)
SVMC.......... Maracaibo/La Chinita Internacional, Zulia [*Venezuela ICAO location identifier*] (ICLI)
SVMD.......... Merida/Alberto Carnevalli, Merida [*Venezuela ICAO location identifier*] (ICLI)
SVMG.......... Margarita/Internacional del Caribe Gral Santiago Marino, Neuva Esparta [*Venezuela ICAO location identifier*] (ICLI)
SVMI.......... Caracas/Simon Bolivar Internacional Maiquetia Distrito Federal [*Venezuela ICAO location identifier*] (ICLI)
SVML.......... Standard Vehicle Mounted Launcher [*Army*]
SVMP.......... Caracas/Metropolitano Internacional, Miranda [*Venezuela ICAO location identifier*] (ICLI)
SVMPCG...... Grasslands National Park, Parks Canada [*Parc National Grasslands, Parcs Canada*] Val Marie, Saskatchewan [*Library symbol National Library of Canada*] (NLC)
SVMR.......... Maracay/Centro Nacional de Comunicaciones/Meteorologicos, Aragua [*Venezuela ICAO location identifier*] (ICLI)
SVMT.......... Maturin/Internacional, Monagas [*Venezuela ICAO location identifier*] (ICLI)
SVMTR........ Servomotor [*Control systems*]
SVN............ Saravena [*Colombia*] [*Airport symbol*] (AD)
SVN............ Savanair (Angola) Lda. [*FAA designator*] (FAAC)
SVN............ Savannah, GA [*Location identifier FAA*] (FAAL)
SVN............ Small Volume Nebulizer [*Pharmacology*] (DAVI)
SVN............ Society for Vascular Nursing (NTPA)
SVN............ South Vietnam (CINC)
SVN............ Space Vehicle Number [*Aviation*] (FAAC)
SVN............ Spectra Vision, Inc. [*Formerly, SPI Holdings, Inc.*] [*AMEX symbol*] (SAG)
SVN............ SpectraVision Inc. 'B' [*AMEX symbol*] (TTSB)
SVNAF........ South Vietnamese Air Force (VNW)
SVNESE...... South Vietnamese
SVNG.......... Seventh Generation [*NASDAQ symbol*] (TTSB)
SVNGS........ Savings
SVNLA........ South Vietnamese Liberation Army (VNW)
SVNM.......... St. Vincent National Movement [*Political party*] (PPW)
SVNMC........ South Vietnamese Marine Corps (VNW)
SVNN.......... South Vietnamese Navy (VNW)
SVNNP........ South Vietnamese National Police Force (VNW)
SVNRF........ State of Vietnam Ribbon of Friendship [*Military decoration*] (AABC)
SVNSF........ South Vietnamese Special Forces (VNW)
SVNVAC...... Sunny Von Bulow National Victim Advocacy Center [*Later, NVC*] (EA)

SVO .... Moscow Sheremetyevo Airport [*Former USSR Airport symbol*] (OAG)
SVO .... Scottish Variety Orchestra (DI)
SVO .... Senior Veterinary Officer [*British military*] (DMA)
SVO .... Servo (KSC)
SVO .... Space Vehicle Operations (MCD)
SVO .... Special Vehicle Operation [*Ford Motor Co.*]
SVO .... Special Vehicle Option [*Automobile production*]
SVO .... Subject-Verb-Object [*Education of the hearing-impaired*]
SVOC .... Semivolatile Organic Compound (BCP)
SVOIR .... Specification Verification Open Item Report
SVOM .... Sequential Volitional Oral Movement (DB)
SVP .... Bie [*Angola*] [*Airport symbol*] (OAG)
SVP .... Saturated Vapor Pressure (IAA)
SVP .... Security Vehicle Patrol [*Air Force*] (AFM)
SVP .... Selective Vagotomy with Pyloroplasty [*Medicine*] (DB)
SVP .... Seminal Vesicle Protein [*Biochemistry*]
SVP .... Senior Vice President
SVP .... Service Processor (BUR)
SVP .... Services Vegetable Production [*British military*] (DMA)
SVP .... Sewer Vent Pipe
SVP .... Silver Princess Resources [*Vancouver Stock Exchange symbol*]
SVP .... S'il Vous Plait [*If You Please*] [*French*]
SVP .... Single-Voyage Permit
SVP .... Small Volume Parenteral [*Pharmacy*]
SVP .... Snake Venom Phosphodiesterase [*Also, SVPD, SVPDE*] [*An enzyme*]
SVP .... Social Venture Partners
SVP .... Societe pour Vaincre la Pollution [*Canada*]
SVP .... Society of St. Vincent de Paul
SVP .... Society of Vertebrate Paleontology (EA)
SVP .... Software Verification Plan [*Computer science*] (IAA)
SVP .... Sound Velocity Profile
SVP .... Special Visitors Program [*Australia*]
SVP .... Specific Vocational Preparation [*US Employment Service*] [*Department of Labor*]
SVP .... Star-Vaporizing Millisecond Pulsar [*Cosmology*]
SVP .... Steam Vacuum Pulse
SVP .... St. Louis Public Library, St. Louis, MO [*OCLC symbol*] (OCLC)
SVP .... Sudtiroler Volkspartei [*South Tyrolean People's Party*] [*Italy Political party*] (EAIO)
SVP .... Supplemental Vacation Plan
SVP .... Surface Velocity Program [*Marine science*] (OSRA)
SVP .... Surface Velocity Programme (USDC)
SVP .... Surge Voltage Protection (IAA)
S/VP .... Surveillance/Vantage Point [*Military*] (INF)
SVPA .... Puerto Ayacucho, T. F. Amazonas [*Venezuela ICAO location identifier*] (ICLI)
SVPB .... Supraventricular Premature Beats [*Cardiology*]
SVPC .... Puerto Cabello/Gral. Bartolome Salom Internacional, Carabobo [*Venezuela ICAO location identifier*] (ICLI)
SVPD .... Snake Venom Phosphodiesterase [*Also, SVP, SVPDE*] [*An enzyme*]
SVPDE .... Snake Venom Phosphodiesterase [*Also, SVP, SVPD*] [*An enzyme*]
SVPM .... San Cristobal/Paramillo, Tachira [*Venezuela ICAO location identifier*] (ICLI)
SVPM .... Small Vehicles, Program Manager
SVPP .... Schweizerische Vereinigung fuer Parapsychologie
SVPR .... Guayana/Puerto Ordaz Internacional, Bolivar [*Venezuela ICAO location identifier*] (ICLI)
SVPT.......... Palmarito, Apure [*Venezuela ICAO location identifier*] (ICLI)
SVPT.......... Supraventricular Paroxysmal Tachycardia [*Cardiology*] (DAVI)
SVQ .... Scottish Vocational Qualification (WDAA)
SVQ .... Seville [*Spain*] [*Airport symbol*] (OAG)
SVR .... Sequential Vascular Response (DB)
SVR .... Severe Thunderstorm Warning [*Telecommunications*] (OTD)
SVR .... Shop Visit Rate (DOMA)
SVR .... Singapore Volunteer Rifles [*British military*] (DMA)
SVR .... Slant Visual Range
SVR .... Society of Vietnamese Rangers (EA)
SVR .... Software Verification Report [*Computer science*] (IAA)
SVR .... Spiritus Vini Rectificatus [*Rectified Spirit of Wine*] [*Pharmacy*]
SVR .... Spirit Varnish Resistance Ink (DGA)
SVR .... Super Video Recorder
SVR .... Supply-Voltage Rejection (IEEE)
SVR .... Surface/Volume Ratio
SVR .... Sverdlovsk Airline [*Russian Federation*] [*ICAO designator*] (FAAC)
SVR .... Systemic Vascular Resistance [*Medicine*]
SVR .... Ural Airlines [*Former USSR*] [*FAA designator*] (FAAC)
SVRA .... Sportscar Vintage Racing Association (EA)
SVRA .... State Vehicular Recreation Area
SVRB .... Supervisor Request Block [*Computer science*] (BUR)
SVRC .... Short-Range Vehicle to Roadside Communication [*FHWA*] (TAG)
SVRC .... Social/Vocational Rehabilitation Clinic (EA)
SVRD .... Silicon Voltage Reference Diode
SVREP .... Southwest Voter Registration Education Project (EA)
SVRI .... Silicon Valley Research [*NASDAQ symbol*] (TTSB)
SVRI .... Silicon Valley Research, Inc. [*NASDAQ symbol*] (SAG)
SVRI .... Southwest Voter Research Institute [*San Antonio, TX*] (CROSS)
SVRI .... Systemic Vascular Resistance Index
SVRN .... Sovereign Bancorp [*NASDAQ symbol*] (TTSB)
SVRN .... Sovereign Bancorp, Inc. [*NASDAQ symbol*] (NQ)
SVRNP .... Sovereign Bancorp 6.25% Cv Pfd [*NASDAQ symbol*] (TTSB)
SVRR .... Software Verification Readiness Review [*NASA*] (NASA)
SVRS .... Los Roques, Dependencia Federal [*Venezuela ICAO location identifier*] (ICLI)
SVS............ Schedule Visibility System (AAG)

SVS............	Secure Voice Switch
SVS............	Secure Voice System [*Telecommunications*]
SVS............	Service School [*Military*]
SVS............	Services Squadron
SVS............	Severe Weather Statement [*Telecommunications*] (OTD)
SVS............	Silverside Resources, Inc. [*Toronto Stock Exchange symbol*]
SVS............	Single Virtual Storage [*IBM Corp.*] [*Computer science*]
SVS............	Slandsville [*South Carolina*] [*Seismograph station code, US Geological Survey*] (SEIS)
SVS............	Society for Vascular Surgery (EA)
SVS............	Society for Visiting Scientists Ltd. [*British*] (BI)
SVS............	Soil Vapor Survey [*Environmental chemistry*]
SVS............	Sound Velocity Structure
SVS............	Space Vehicle Simulator (AAG)
SVS............	Space Vehicle System (IAA)
SVS............	Spectroradiometer Visible System
SVS............	Spinning Vehicle Simulator
SVS............	Stabilized Viewing System
SVS............	Stamp Ventures [*Printer of U.S. postage stamps*] (BARN)
SVS............	Stationary Control Variable Speed (IAA)
SVS............	Stevens Village [*Alaska*] [*Airport symbol*] (OAG)
SVS............	Still-Camera Video System [*Canon, Inc.*]
SVS............	Suit Ventilation System [*Aerospace*] (MCD)
svs............	Suit Ventilation System (NAKS)
SVS............	Supervisory Signal (IAA)
SVS............	Synthetic Vision Systems, Inc.
SVSA............	San Antonio, Tachira [*Venezuela ICAO location identifier*] (ICLI)
SVSB............	Santa Barbara De Barinas, Barinas [*Venezuela ICAO location identifier*] (ICLI)
SVSC	San Carlos De Rio Negro, T. F. Amazonas [*Venezuela ICAO location identifier*] (ICLI)
SVSC............	Space Vehicle Sectoring Code
SVSE............	Santa Elena de Uairen, Bolivar [*Venezuela ICAO location identifier*] (ICLI)
SVSO	Santo Domingo/Mayor Buenaventura Vivas A. B., Tachira [*Venezuela ICAO location identifier*] (ICLI)
SVSO	Superintending Victualling Stores Officer [*British*]
SVSP	San Felipe/Subteniente Nestor Arias, Yaracuy [*Venezuela ICAO location identifier*] (ICLI)
SVSP	School Volunteer Services Program
SV-SP	Spray Volume - Spray Pressure
SVSPT	Single Virtual Storage Performance Tool [*Computer science*] (CIST)
SVSR	San Fernando De Apure, Apure [*Venezuela ICAO location identifier*] (ICLI)
SVSS............	Sprague Voltage-Sensitive Switch
SVST............	San Tome, Anzoategui [*Venezuela ICAO location identifier*] (ICLI)
SVSZ............	Santa Barbara Del Zulia, Zulia [*Venezuela ICAO location identifier*] (ICLI)
SVT............	Sakhaviatrans [*Former USSR*] [*FAA designator*] (FAAC)
SVT............	Secure Voice Terminal (MCD)
SVT............	Self Valuation Test [*Psychology*]
SVT............	Servotronics, Inc. [*AMEX symbol*] (SPSG)
SVT............	Silicon Vidicon Target
SVT............	Silverton Resources Ltd. [*Toronto Stock Exchange symbol*]
SVT............	Sinoventricular Tachycardia [*Medicine*] (DB)
SVT............	Society of Vascular Technology (EA)
SVT............	Solar Vacuum Telescope
SVT............	Space Vehicle Test
SVT............	Space Visualization Test
SVT............	Special Vehicle Team [*Automotive engineering*]
SVT............	Spiritus Vini Tenuis [*Proof Spirit of Wine*] [*Pharmacy*]
SVT............	Stray Voltage Tester
SVT............	St. Vincent [*St. Vincent*] [*Seismograph station code, US Geological Survey*] (SEIS)
SVT............	Subclavian Vein Thrombosis [*Medicine*] (DMAA)
SVT............	Supralaryngeal Vocal Tract [*Anatomy*]
SVT............	Supraventricular Tachyarrhythmia [*Cardiology*] (DAVI)
SVT............	Supraventricular Tachycardia [*Cardiology*]
SVT............	System Validation Testing
SVT............	System Verification Test [*Automotive engineering*]
SVTC............	Surrey Volunteer Training Corps [*British military*] (DMA)
SVTC............	Tucupita, T. F. Delta Amacuro [*Venezuela ICAO location identifier*] (ICLI)
SVTG	Savior Technology Group [*NASDAQ symbol*] [*Formerly, Western Micro Technology*] (SG)
SVTL............	Semivital
SVTL............	Services Valve Test Laboratory [*British*] (NATG)
SVTM............	Shielded Voltage Tunable Magnetron
SVTM............	Tumeremo, Bolivar [*Venezuela ICAO location identifier*] (ICLI)
S/VTOL	Short/Vertical Takeoff and Landing [*Aviation*] (NATG)
SVTP............	Sound, Velocity, Temperature, Pressure
SVT(S).........	Space Vehicle Test (Supervisor)
SVTSV	Space-Vehicle-to-Space-Vehicle (SAA)
SVTT............	Surface Vessel Torpedo Tube (NVT)
SVU............	Savusavu [*Fiji*] [*Airport symbol*] (OAG)
S/VU............	Sound/Video Unlimited
SVU	Spur Ventures [*Vancouver Stock Exchange symbol*]
SVU............	Supervalu Inc. [*NYSE symbol*] (TTSB)
SVU............	Surface Vehicular Unit
SVU............	System Verification Unit
SVUL	Short Vertical Upper Left
SVUL	Suomen Valtakunnan Uhreiluliitto [*Finnish Central Sports Federation*]
SVUM	Uriman, Bolivar [*Venezuela ICAO location identifier*] (ICLI)
SVUQ..........	Uonquen, Bolivar [*Venezuela ICAO location identifier*] (ICLI)
SVUR	Short Vertical Upper Right

SVV............	Empresa Servicicious Avensa SA [*Venezuela*] [*ICAO designator*] (FAAC)
SVV............	Sit Venia Verbo [*Forgive the Expression*] [*Latin*]
SVV............	Solenoid Vent Valve [*Automotive engineering*]
svv............	Sub Vocibus [*Latin*]
SVVA	Valencia/Internacional, Carabobo [*Venezuela ICAO location identifier*] (ICLI)
SVVL...........	Valera/Dr. Antonio Nicolas Briceno, Trujillo [*Venezuela ICAO location identifier*] (ICLI)
SVVP..........	Valle De La Pascua, Guarico [*Venezuela ICAO location identifier*] (ICLI)
SVW...........	Silverhawk Resources [*Vancouver Stock Exchange symbol*]
SVW...........	Sparrevohn [*Alaska*] [*Seismograph station code, US Geological Survey*] (SEIS)
SVW...........	Sparrevohn, AK [*Location identifier FAA*] (FAAL)
SVX............	Socanav, Inc. [*Toronto Stock Exchange symbol*]
SVY............	Cooper Aerial Surveys Ltd. [*British*] [*FAA designator*] (FAAC)
SVY............	GCA Surveys [*British ICAO designator*] (FAAC)
SVY............	Survey
SVZ............	San Antonio [*Venezuela*] [*Airport symbol*] (OAG)
SVZ............	Sisters of Charity of St. Vincent de Paul [*Roman Catholic religious order*]
SVZ............	Subventricular Zone [*Anatomy*]
SVZM..........	Maiquetia [*Venezuela ICAO location identifier*] (ICLI)
SVZZ..........	Maiquetia [*Venezuela ICAO location identifier*] (ICLI)
SW............	Methylphosphonous Dichloride [*Toxic compound*] [*Army symbol*]
SW............	Namib Air [*ICAO designator*] (AD)
Sw............	Royal Swedish Library (Kungl. Biblioteket), Stockholm, Sweden [*Library symbol Library of Congress*] (LCLS)
SW............	Sadler's Wells Theatre [*London*]
SW............	Salt Water
SW............	Sandwich-Wound (DEN)
SW............	Sapwood [*Botany*]
SW............	Satan Worship
SW............	Schwartz-Watson Test [*Medicine*] (MAE)
SW............	Seaboard World Airlines, Inc.
SW............	Seawater
sw............	Sea Water (NAKS)
S/W............	Seaworthy (ADA)
SW............	Secretary of War [*Obsolete*]
SW............	Secret Writing [*Espionage*]
SW............	Security Watch
SW............	Semiweekly
SW............	Senior Warden [*Freemasonry*]
SW............	Senior Wolf [*An accomplished philanderer*] [*Slang*]
SW............	Senior Woodward [*Ancient Order of Foresters*]
SW............	Sent Wrong [*i.e., misdirected*]
SW............	Series Winding [*Wiring*] (DNAB)
SW............	Seriously Wounded (DAVI)
SW............	Service Water [*Nuclear energy*] (NRCH)
SW............	Sewing Machine Repair Program [*Association of Independent Colleges and Schools specialization code*]
SW............	Shallow Water (DOMA)
SW............	Shallow Water Attack Craft [*Navy symbol*]
SW............	Shallow Water Diver [*British military*] (DMA)
SW............	Shelter Warden [*British Home Defence*] [*World War II*]
SW............	Shipper's Weights [*Bills of lading*]
SW............	Ship's Warrant [*Marine Corps*]
SW............	Shirl J. Winter [*Designer's mark when appearing on US coins*]
SW............	Shock Wave (IAA)
SW............	Shorter Workweek [*Business term*] (MHDB)
SW............	Shortwave [*Electronics*]
sw............	Short Wave (NAKS)
SW............	Short Weight
SW............	Shotgun Wedding [*Forced marriage*] [*Slang*]
SW............	Side Wheel
SW............	Sidewinder
SW............	Simple Wear
SW............	Single Wall (AAG)
SW............	Single Weight
SW............	Single Wheel [*Landing gear*] [*Aviation*] (DA)
SW............	Slow Wave [*Electroencephalograph*]
SW............	Smith's Weekly [*A publication*]
SW............	Snow [*Ship's rigging*] (ROG)
SW............	Snow Shower [*Meteorology*] (BARN)
SW............	Social Work [*or Worker*]
SW............	Socket Weld
SW............	Software [*Computer science*]
sw............	Software (NAKS)
SW............	Softwood
SW............	Solar Wind [*Astronomy*]
SW............	Solar Wing (MCD)
sw............	Solar Wing (NAKS)
SW............	Solid Waste
SW............	Son of a Witch (EA)
SW............	Sound Whistle [*British railroad term*]
SW............	Sound Wormy [*Wood industry*] (WPI)
SW............	South Wales
SW............	Southwest
SW............	Southwest Africa (MCD)
S-W............	South-Western Educational Publishing [*International Thomson Publishing Co.*]
SW............	South Western Reporter [*National Reporter System*] [*A publication*] (DLA)
SW............	Special Warfare

SW	Special Weapon
SW	Specification of Wiring (IAA)
SW	Specific Weight
SW	Sperm Whale
SW	Spike Wave [*Medicine*] (DMAA)
SW	Spiral Wound [*Medicine*] (MAE)
SW	Spontaneous Swallows [*Gastroenterology*]
SW	Spores Injected into Wounded Kernels [*Plant pathology*]
SW	Spore Wall [*Botany*]
SW	Spotweld [*Technical drawings*]
SW	Stab Wound [*Medicine*] (MAE)
SW	Stall Warning System (MCD)
SW	Standard Winter
SW	Standby Service Water [*Nuclear energy*] (NRCH)
SW	Standing Wave (IAA)
SW	Stationary Wave (IAA)
SW	Station Wagon [*Car*]
SW	Status of Women [*Canada*]
SW	Status Word
sw	Status Word (NAKS)
SW	Steam Wagon [*British*]
SW	Steel Wire (IAA)
SW	Steelworker [*Navy rating*]
SW	Stenciled Weight
SW	Sterile Water
SW	Stewart-Warner Corp.
SW	Stock Width [*Construction or manufacturing materials*]
SW	Stone & Webster [*NYSE symbol*] (TTSB)
SW	Stone & Webster, Inc. [*NYSE symbol*] (SPSG)
SW	Strategic Warning (MCD)
SW	Strategic Wing [*Military*]
SW	Strike-Warn [*Army*]
SW	Stroke Work [*Cardiology*]
SW	Struthers Wells Corp. (IAA)
SW	Stud-Arc Welding
SW	Sturge-Weber [*Disease*] [*Medicine*] (DB)
SW	Subjective Weakness [*Medicine*]
SW	Subject Word (NITA)
SW	Surface Warfare (MCD)
S/W	Surface Wind [*Meteorology*] (DA)
Sw	Swabey's English Admiralty Reports [*A publication*] (DLA)
Sw	Swabey's English Ecclesiastical Reports [*1855-59*] [*A publication*] (DLA)
sw	Swamp [*Maps and charts*]
Sw	Swann [*Blood group*]
Sw	Swan's Tennessee Reports [*31, 32 Tennessee*] [*A publication*] (DLA)
Sw	Swanston's English Chancery Reports [*A publication*] (DLA)
SW	Swash
SW	Swatch (WGA)
SW	Swear
SW.	Swearingen Aircraft [*ICAO aircraft manufacturer identifier*] (ICAO)
sw	Sweden [*MARC country of publication code Library of Congress*] (LCCP)
Sw	Sweden (ODBW)
Sw	Swedish (ODBW)
Sw	Sweeney's New York Superior Court Reports [*A publication*] (DLA)
SW	Swell Organ
Sw	Swine [*Veterinary medicine*] (DAVI)
Sw	Swinton's Scotch Justiciary Cases [*A publication*] (DLA)
SW	Swiss
SW	Swiss Webster Mouse [*Medicine*] (DMAA)
SW	Switch (AAG)
sw	Switch (IDOE)
SW	Switchband Wound [*Relay*]
SW	Switcher [*Broadcasting*] (WDMC)
sw	Switcher (NAKS)
SW	Switzerland
SW1	Steelworker, First Class [*Navy rating*]
SW2	Steelworker, Second Class [*Navy rating*]
SW 2d	South Western Reporter, Second Series [*A publication*] (DLA)
SW2d	South Western Reporter, Second Series [*West*] [*A publication*] (AAGC)
SW3	Steelworker, Third Class [*Navy rating*]
SWA	Namibia [*International vehicle registration*] (ODBW)
SWA	Reports of the High Court of South-West Africa [*1920-46*] [*A publication*] (DLA)
SWA	Scheduler Work Area [*Computer science*] (IBMDP)
SWA	Scope of Word Addendum (MCD)
SWA	Scotch Whisky Association [*British*] (DBA)
SWA	Seaboard World Airlines (MHDW)
SWA	Seriously Wounded in Action [*Military*]
SWA	Shallow Water Acoustics
SWA	Shantou [*China*] [*Airport symbol*] (OAG)
SWA	Shayna International Industry [*Vancouver Stock Exchange symbol*]
SWA	Single Wire Armored [*Cables*]
SWA	SLow-Wave Activity [*Medicine*] (DMAA)
SWA	Society of Women Artists [*British*] (DBA)
SWA	Solo Wargamers Association (EAIO)
SWA	Southern Water Authority [*British*] (DCTA)
SWA	Southern Wholesalers Association [*Atlanta, GA*] (EA)
SWA	Southern Woodwork Association [*Defunct*] (EA)
SWA	Southwest Africa
SWA	Southwest Airlines Co. [*ICAO designator*] (FAAC)
SWA	Southwest Approach (DNAB)
SWA	Southwest Asia

SWA	Specialty Wire Association [*Later, AWPA*]
SWA	Sports Writers' Association [*British*] (BI)
SWA	Standing Wave Apparatus
SWA	State Welfare Agency [*Social Security Administration*] (OICC)
SWA	Steel Window Association [*British*] (DBA)
SWA	Straight Wire Antenna
SWA	Stunt Women of America [*Later, SAMP*] (EA)
SWA	Superwomen's Anonymous (EA)
SWA	Support Work Authorization [*NASA*] (MCD)
swa	Swahili [*MARC language code Library of Congress*] (LCCP)
SWA	Swan Island [*Seismograph station code, US Geological Survey Closed*] (SEIS)
SWA	Swedish Warmblood Association (EA)
SWA	Swissair [*Airline*] (MCD)
SWA	System Work Area
SWAA	Slovak Writers and Artists Association (EA)
SWAA	Spacelab Window Adapter Assembly (NASA)
SWAAA	Scottish Women's Amateur Athletic Association (DBA)
Swaacs	Small Waterplane Air Cushion Ship
SWAAG	Solidarity with Aboriginal Australians Group
SWAAT	Sea-Water Acetic Acid Test (PDAA)
Swab	Swabey's English Ecclesiastical Reports [*1855-59*] [*A publication*] (DLA)
SWAB	Swap Byte [*Computer science*] (NHD)
Swab Admr	Swabey's English Admiralty Reports [*166 English Reprint*] [*A publication*] (DLA)
Swab & T	Swabey and Tristram's Probate and Divorce Reports [*164 English Reprint*] [*A publication*] (DLA)
Swab & Tr	Swabey and Tristram's Probate and Divorce Reports [*164 English Reprint*] [*A publication*] (DLA)
Swab Div	Swabey on Divorce and Matrimonial Causes [*3rd ed.*] [*1859*] [*A publication*] (DLA)
Swabey Adm	Swabey's English Admiralty Reports [*166 English Reprint*] [*1855-59*] [*A publication*] (DLA)
Swabey Adm (Eng)	Swabey's English Admiralty Reports [*166 English Reprint*] [*A publication*] (DLA)
Swabey & T (Eng)	Swabey and Tristram's Probate and Divorce Reports [*164 English Reports*] [*A publication*] (DLA)
SWAC	Shallow Water Attack Craft, Light (MCD)
SWAC	Southwestern Athletic Conference (PSS)
SWAC	Special Warhead Arming Control (AFM)
SWAC	Specification Writers Association of Canada
SWAC	Spotweld Accessory [*Tool*] (AAG)
SWAC	Standards Western Automatic Computer [*National Institute of Standards and Technology*]
SWACHA	Southwestern Automated Clearing House Association
SWACS	Space Warning and Control System [*NORAD*]
SWAD	Special Warfare Aviation Detachment [*Army*]
SWAD	Subdivision of Work Authorization Document [*NASA*] (NASA)
SWADE	Second Wives of America Demanding Equality
SWADS	Scheduler Work Area Data Set [*IBM Corp.*] (MCD)
SW Af	South-West Africa
SWAFAC	Southwest Atlantic Fisheries Advisory Commission [*FAO*]
SWAG	Scientific Wild Aim Guess [*Bowdlerized version*]
SWAG	Standard Written Agreement [*Military*]
SWAG	Systems Work Assignment Group (SAA)
SWAGS	Scientific Wild-Aim Guess System [*Bowdlerized version*] (MCD)
SWAH	Studies in Western Australian History [*A publication*]
SWAJB	South and Western Australia Judgements Bulletin [*A publication*]
SWAK	Sealed with a Kiss [*Correspondence*]
SWAK	Spinners and Weavers Association of Korea [*Defunct*] (EA)
SWAL	Shallow Water Attack Craft, Light [*Navy symbol*] (NVT)
SWALC	Southwest Academic Library Consortium [*Library network*] (IID)
SWALCAKWS	Sealed with a Lick 'Cause a Kiss Won't Stick [*Correspondence*] (DSUE)
SWALCAP	South West Academic Libraries Cooperative Automation Project (NITA)
SWALK	Sealed with a Loving Kiss [*Correspondence*]
SWALM	Switch Alarm (AAG)
SWAM	Shallow Water Attack Craft, Medium [*Navy symbol*] (NVT)
SWAM	Sine Wave Amplitude Modulation
SWAMI	Software-Aided Multiform Input [*Software*] [*Computer science*]
SWAMI	Speech with Alternating Masking Index [*Discrimination test*]
SWAMI	Stall Warning and Margin Indicator
SWAMI	Standing Wave Area Monitor Indicator (MUGU)
SWAMI	Stanford Worldwide Acquisition of Meteorological Information [*Weather prediction system*]
SWAMP	Southwest Area Monsoon Project (USDC)
SWAMP	Stuntwomen's Association of Motion Pictures (NTPA)
SWAMP	Swine-Associated Mucoprotein (STED)
SWAN	School of Women Artists Network [*Australia*]
SWAN	Second Wives Association of North America (EA)
SWAN	Severe Weather Avoidance Nationwide [*National Oceanic and Atmospheric Administration*]
SWAN	Society of Wildlife Art Nations [*British*] (DBA)
SWAN	Study of Women's Health Across the Nation
Swan	Swan's Tennessee Supreme Court Reports [*1851-53*] [*A publication*] (DLA)
Swan	Swanston's English Chancery Reports [*A publication*] (DLA)
SWANA	Solid Waste Association of North America (NTPA)
Swan & CR St	Swan and Critchfield's Revised Statutes [*Ohio*] [*A publication*] (DLA)
Swan & S St	Swan and Sayler's Supplement to the Revised Statutes [*Ohio*] [*A publication*] (DLA)
Swan Ch	Swanston's English Chancery Reports [*A publication*] (DLA)

Sw & Tr...... Swabey and Tristram's Probate and Divorce Reports [*164 English Reprint*] [*A publication*] (DLA)
Swan Eccl C... Swan's Ecclesiastical Courts [*1830*] [*A publication*] (DLA)
Swan Just.... Swan's Justice [*Ohio*] [*A publication*] (DLA)
SWANK....... Sealed with a Nice Kiss [*Correspondence*]
Swank........ Single Woman and No Kids [*Lifestyle classification*]
Swank......... Swank, Inc. [*Associated Press*] (SAG)
Swan Pl & Pr... Swan on Pleading and Practice [*Ohio*] [*A publication*] (DLA)
Swan Pr....... Swan on Practice [*Ohio*] [*A publication*] (DLA)
Swan's....... Swan's Tennessee Reports [*A publication*] (DLA)
Swans........ Swanston's English Chancery Reports [*A publication*] (DLA)
Swan's R..... Swan's Tennessee Reports [*A publication*] (DLA)
Swan's St..... Swan's Ohio Statutes [*A publication*] (DLA)
Swanst........ Swanston's English Chancery Reports [*36 English Reprint*] [*A publication*] (DLA)
Swanst (Eng)... Swanston's English Chancery Reports [*36 English Reprint*] [*A publication*] (DLA)
Swan Tr....... Swan's Ohio Treatise [*A publication*] (DLA)
SWANU....... South West Africa National Union [*Namibia*] [*Political party*] (PPW)
SWAP .... Section on Women and Psychology [*Canadian Psychology Association*]
SWAP .... Severe Weather Avoidance Plan (FAAC)
SWAP .... Severe Weather Avoidance Program (GAVI)
SWAP .... Shared Wireless Access Protocol [*Computer science*]
SWAP .... Smith-Winnick-Abrams-Prausnitz [*Vapor pressure correlation equation*]
SWAP .... Society for Wang Applications and Programs (CSR)
SWAP .... Standard Wafer Array Programming
SWAP .... Stewart-Warner Array Program [*Electronics*] (EECA)
SWAP .... Stress Wave Analyzing Program
SWAP .... Student Woodlawn Area Project [*Chicago, IL*]
SWAP .... Surface Water Acidification Project [*Joint venture involving Norway, Sweden, and Great Britain*]
SWAP .... SWAP [*Salesmen with a Purpose*] Club International [*Arvada, CO*] (EA)
SWAP .... Sydney Wastewater Action Program [*Australia*]
SWAP .... Systems Worthiness Analysis Program [*FAA*]
SWAPDOP ... Southwest Asia Petroleum Distribution Operation Project [*Army*]
SWAPO .... South West African People's Organisation (EERA)
SWAPO .... South West Africa People's Organization [*Namibia*] (PD)
SWAPS .... Ship Workload and Priority Systems [*Navy*]
SWAPS .... Special Wire Assembly Planning System (MCD)
SWAPS .... Standing-Wave Acoustic Parametric Source (PDAA)
SWARK....... Southwark [*Borough of London*] (ROG)
SWARM....... Southwestern and Rocky Mountain Division [*AAAS division*]
SWARMS.... Small Warhead and Reentry Multiple System
SWAS .... Slim Whitman Appreciation Society of the United States (EA)
SWAS .... Submillimeter Wave Astronomy Satellite [*Military*]
SWASG....... Submarine Sensor to Weapon Alignment Steering Group
SWASGB..... Slim Whitman Appreciation Society of Great Britain (EAIO)
Swash......... Small Waterplane Area Single Hull Ship
SWASS .... Screwworm Adult Suppression System [*Medicine*]
SWASS .... Slim Whitman Appreciation Society of Scotland (EAIO)
SWAT......... Secure Wire Access Terminal (MCD)
SWAT......... Service Weapons Acceptability Tests
SWAT......... Sidewinder Acquisition Track (IEEE)
SWAT......... Sidewinder Angle Tracking [*Missiles*] (NG)
SWAT......... Simultaneous Wide Area Telecommunications Service (TSSD)
SWAT......... Sipay Word Analysis Test [*Educational test*]
SWAT......... Sodium-Water Reaction Test [*Nuclear energy*] (NUCP)
SWAT......... Software Action Team (AAEL)
SWAT......... Solid Waste Assessment Test
SWAT......... Special Warfare Armored Transporter [*A vehicle*]
SWAT......... Special Weapons and Tactics [*Police*]
SWAT......... Special Wrenches and Techniques [*Automotive repair*]
SWAT......... Squad Weapon Analytical Trainer (MCD)
SWAT......... Steering Wheel Anti-Theft [*Device*] [*Auto Alarm*]
SWAT......... Strengths, Weaknesses, Alternatives, Threats [*Analysis*] (ADA)
SWAT......... Stress Wave Analysis Technique
SWAT......... Students Working Against Tobacco [*An association*]
SWAT......... Study With a Teacher Program [*Ohio*] (EDAC)
SWATCH...... Swiss Watch
SWATH....... Small Waterplane Area Twin Hull [*Ship*] [*Navy*]
SWATH....... Space Weather and Terrestrial Hazards [*Proposed satellite*]
SWATM....... Shallow Water Antitraffic Mine [*Military*]
SWATS .... Sea-Based Weapons and Advance Tactics School (DOMA)
SWATS .... Shallow Water Acoustic Tracking System [*Navy*] (CAAL)
SWATT........ Simulator for Antitank Tactical Training [*Army*] (INF)
SWAX .... Southwest Airlines Co. [*Air carrier designation symbol*]
SWAZ .... Swaziland (WDAA)
Swazil......... Swaziland
SWB........... Sandia Wind Balloon (MUGU)
SWB........... Short Wheelbase
SWB........... Single Weight Baryta [*Photography*] (OA)
SWB........... Single with Bath [*Hotel room*]
SWB........... South Wales Borderers [*Military unit*] [*British*]
SWB........... Southwestbound [*ICAO designator*] (FAAC)
SWB........... South Westchester BOCES [*Boards of Cooperative Educational Services*] [*UTLAS symbol*]
SWB........... Southwestern Motor Freight Bureau, Dallas TX [*STAC*]
SWB........... Subjective Well-Being [*Psychology*]
SWB........... Summary of World Broadcasts [*British Broadcasting Corporation*]
SWB........... Sweden Airways [*ICAO designator*] (FAAC)
SWB........... Switchboard (NATG)
SWBA .... Southwest Banks [*NASDAQ symbol*] (TTSB)

SWBA .... Southwest Banks, Inc. [*NASDAQ symbol*] (SAG)
SWB & IE .... South West Business and Industry Exhibition [*British*] (ITD)
SWBC......... Sterling West Bancorp [*NASDAQ symbol*] (SAG)
SwBcsh........ Southwest Bancshares, Inc. [*Associated Press*] (SAG)
SWBD......... Switchboard (AAG)
SWBDOP...... Switchboard Operator (IAA)
SWBHD....... Swash Bulkhead
SWBI .... Southwest Bancshares [*NASDAQ symbol*] (TTSB)
SWBI .... Southwest Bancshares, Inc. [*NASDAQ symbol*] (SAG)
SWBM .... Still-Water Bending Moment (PDAA)
SWBP......... Service Water Booster Pump [*Nuclear energy*] (IEEE)
SWBS .... Ship Work Breakdown Structure [*Navy*] (CAAL)
SWBS .... SierraWest Bancorp. [*NASDAQ symbol*] [*Formerly, Sierra Tahoe Bancorp.*] (SG)
SWBS .... Software Work Breakdown Structure (MCD)
SWBS .... Solid Waste Barrel Storage [*Nuclear energy*] (NRCH)
SWbS......... Southwest by South
SWBS .... Subcontract Work Breakdown Structure (MCD)
SWbW......... Southwest by West
SWC........... Chief Steelworker [*Navy rating*]
SWC........... Omaha, NE [*Location identifier FAA*] (FAAL)
SWC........... Safe Water Coalition (EA)
SWC........... Saline Water Conversion (MCD)
SWC........... Scanning with Compensation
SWC........... Scan-with-Composition (MCD)
SWC........... Second Wives Coalition (EA)
SWC........... Semi-Wadcutter [*Ammunition*]
SWC........... Senate Wine Caucus (EA)
SWC........... Settlement with Conditions [*Environmental Protection Agency*] (GFGA)
SWC........... Share the Work Coalition [*Defunct*] (EA)
SWC........... Ship Weapon Coordinator (NVT)
SWC........... Shock Wave Control
SWC........... Shortwave Converter
SWC........... Signals Warfare Center [*Warrenton, VA*] [*Army*]
SWC........... Simon Wiesenthal Center (EA)
SWC........... Single Wire Connector
SWC........... Skywave Correction [*Aircraft navigation*]
SWC........... Slovak World Congress (EAIO)
SWC........... Soft Wired Control (IAA)
SWC........... Soil and Water Conservation Research Division [*of ARS, Department of Agriculture*]
SWC........... Solar Wind Compensator [*or Composition*] [*Apollo 11*] [*NASA*]
SWC........... Solid Wastes Cask [*Nuclear energy*] (NRCH)
SWC........... South West Air Ltd. [*Canada ICAO designator*] (FAAC)
SWC........... Southwest Conference [*College sports*]
SWC........... Southwestern Connecticut Library Council, Bridgeport, CT [*OCLC symbol*] (OCLC)
SWC........... Special Warfare Center [*Later, J. F. Kennedy Center for Special Warfare*] [*Army*]
SWC........... Special Warfare Craft [*Navy*] (CAAL)
SWC........... Special Weapons Center [*or Command*]
SWC........... Sportscar World Championship [*Auto racing*]
SWC........... Stall Warning Computer (MCD)
SWC........... Stawell [*Australia Airport symbol*] (OAG)
SWC........... Step-Wise Cracking (MCD)
SWC........... Stormwater Channel
SWC........... Submaximal Working Capacity (DMAA)
SWC........... Submersible Work Chamber
SWC........... Superior White Crystal [*Sugar*]
SWC........... Supreme War Council [*World War II*]
SWC........... Surewin Resources Corp. [*Vancouver Stock Exchange symbol*]
SWC........... Surface Warfare Coordinator [*Also, SUWC*] (NVT)
SWC........... Surface Weapons Control
SWC........... Surface Weapons Coordinator [*Navy*] (CAAL)
SWC........... Surge Withstand Capability (IEEE)
SWC........... Switching Control [*Telecommunications*] (IAA)
SWC........... System Weapons Coordinator [*Navy*] (CAAL)
SWCA .... Constructionman Apprentice, Steelworker, Striker [*Navy rating*]
SWCA .... Silver Wyandotte Club of America (EA)
SWCAA .... Soil and Water Conservation Association of Australia (EERA)
SWCB .... [*The*] Sandwich Co-Operative Bank [*Sandwich, MA*] [*NASDAQ symbol*] (NQ)
SWCC .... Second World Climate Conference (EERA)
SWCC .... Southwest Christian Conference (PSS)
SWCD .... Solar Wind Composition Detector (PDAA)
SWCE......... Solar Wind Composition Experiment (PDAA)
SWCEL....... Southwestern Cooperative Educational Laboratory
SWCENT....... Switching Central [*Telecommunications*] (AABC)
SWCH .... Switch (MCD)
SWCHMN....... Switchman (WGA)
SWCL .... Seawater Conversion Laboratory (KSC)
SWCL .... Special Warfare Craft, Light [*Navy symbol*]
SWCL .... State Worker's Compensation Law (OICC)
SWCLR....... Southwest Council of La Raza [*Mexican-American organization*] (EA)
SWCM .... Master Chief Steelworker [*Navy rating*]
SWCM .... Social Work Case Manager (DMAA)
SW/CM .... Software Configuration Management (MCD)
SWCM .... Special Warfare Craft, Medium [*Navy symbol*]
SWCN......... Constructionman, Steelworker, Striker [*Navy rating*]
SWCP......... Saline Water Conversion Program [*Department of the Interior*]
SWCP......... Salt-Water Circulating Pump (MSA)
SWCP......... Society of the War of 1812 in the Commonwealth of Pennsylvania (EA)
SWCPI....... Solid Waste Council of the Paper Industry [*Defunct*] (EA)

SWCS .... SAC Warning and Control System (MCD)
SWCS .... Salt-Water Cooling System [*Nuclear energy*] (NRCH)
SWCS .... Senior Chief Steelworker [*Navy rating*]
SWCS .... Soil and Water Conservation Society (NTPA)
SWCS .... Space Warning and Control System [*NORAD*] (IAA)
SWCST .... Saturn Workshop Cockpit Simulation Trainer [*NASA*]
SWD .... Self-Wiring Data [*Telecommunications*] (TEL)
SWD .... Senior Weapon Director [*Air Force*]
SWD .... Seward, AK [*Location identifier FAA*] (FAAL)
SWD .... Sewed
SWD .... Short-Wave Diathermy [*Medicine*]
SWD .... Sideward (WGA)
SWD .... Side Water Depth
SWD .... Single Word Dump
SWD .... Sliding Watertight Door
SWD .... Smaller Word
SWD .... Softwood
SWD .... Soil Water Deficit [*Soil science*]
SWD .... Southwestern Division [*Army Corps of Engineers*]
SWD .... Special Water Dispenser [*British military*] (DMA)
SWD .... Standing Wave Detector
SWD .... Stormwater Drain
SwD .... Students with Disabilities
SWD .... Submarine Wire Dispenser
SWD .... Sun, Wind, Dust [*Goggles*] (MCD)
SWD .... Surface Wave Dielectrometer
SWD .... Swaziland [*Swaziland*] [*Seismograph station code, US Geological Survey*] (SEIS)
SWD .... Swinderby FTU [*British ICAO designator*] (FAAC)
SWD .... Synchronous Wave Device
SWDA .... Scottish Wholesale Druggist Association (DBA)
SWDA .... Solid Waste Disposal Act [*1965*]
SWDA .... South West Development Authority [*Western Australia*]
SWDA .... Step-Wise Discriminant Analysis
SWDB .... Special Weapons Development Board
SWDC .... Shock Wave Data Center [*Lawrence Radiation Laboratory*]
SwdEC .... Swedish Export Credit Corp. [*Associated Press*] (SAG)
SWDG .... Sun, Wind, Dust Goggles [*Military*] (INF)
SWDG .... Surface Warfare Development Group [*Also, SURFWARDEVGRU*] [*Navy*]
SWDL .... Safe Winter Driving League [*Defunct*] (EA)
SWDL .... Surface Wave Delay Line
SwdMtch ...... Swedish Match [*Associated Press*] (SAG)
SWDS .... Scrolls from the Wilderness of the Dead Sea. Smithsonian Institution Exhibit Catalogue [*Washington, DC*] (BJA)
SWDS .... Software Development System (MCD)
SWDVS .... Software Development and Verification System [*NASA*]
SWDYN .... Single-Wheel Dynamometer
SWE .... Scalar Wave Equation
SWE .... Shift Word, Extracting
SWE .... Simulated Work Experience
SWE .... Single Wafer Etching (NITA)
SWE .... Slow-Wave Encephalography [*Neurology*] (DAVI)
SWE .... Society of Wine Educators (EA)
SWE .... Society of Women Engineers (EA)
SWE .... Solar Wind Experiment [*NASA*] (KSC)
SWE .... Spherical Wave Expansion [*Telecommunications*] (TEL)
SWE .... Status Word Enable
SWE .... Steelworker Erector [*Navy rating*]
SWE .... Stress Wave Emission
SWE .... Swedair AB [*Sweden ICAO designator*] (FAAC)
SWE .... Sweden [*ANSI three-letter standard code*] (CNC)
Swe .... Sweden (VRA)
swe .... Swedish [*MARC language code Library of Congress*] (LCCP)
SWEA .... Swensen's, Inc. [*Vancouver Stock Exchange symbol*]
SWEA .... Swedish Women's Educational Association, International (EA)
SWEAT .... Standard Wafer-Level Electromigration Accelerated (AAEL)
SWEB .... SoftQuad International, Inc. [*NASDAQ symbol*] (SAG)
SWEB .... South West Electricity Board (WDAA)
SWEBF .... SoftQuad Intl [*NASDAQ symbol*] (TTSB)
SWECS .... Small Wind Energy Conversion Systems
SWED .... Sweden [*or Swedish*]
SwedAE .... Swedish Antarctic Expedition [*1901-04*]
SWEDIS .... Swedish Drug Information System [*Swedish National Board of Health and Welfare*] [*Databank*] (IID)
SWEDL .... Southwest Educational Development Laboratory
SWEDTEL ...... Swedish Telecoms International AB [*Telecommunications*]
SWEE .... Southwest Electronic Exhibit
Sween .... Sweeney's New York Superior Court Reports [*31-32 New York*] [*1869-70*] [*A publication*] (DLA)
Sweeney (NY)... Sweeney's New York Superior Court Reports [*31-32 New York*] [*A publication*] (DLA)
Sweeny........ Sweeney's New York Superior Court Reports [*31-32 New York*] [*A publication*] (DLA)
SWEEP........ Structures with Error Expurgation Program
SWEET......... Stay at Work, Earn Extra Time [*United Auto Workers*]
Sweet .... Sweet on the Limited Liability Act [*A publication*] (DLA)
Sweet .... Sweet on Wills [*A publication*] (DLA)
Sweet .... Sweet's Law Dictionary [*A publication*] (DLA)
Sweet .... Sweet's Marriage Settlement Cases [*A publication*] (DLA)
Sweet .... Sweet's Precedents in Conveyancing [*A publication*] (DLA)
Sweet LD ..... Sweet's Dictionary of English Law [*1882*] [*A publication*] (DLA)
Sweet LL ..... Sweet on the Limited Liability Act [*A publication*] (DLA)
Sweet M Sett Cas... Sweet's Marriage Settlement Cases [*England*] [*A publication*] (DLA)

Sweet Pr Conv... Sweet's Precedents in Conveyancing [*4th ed.*] [*1886*] [*A publication*] (DLA)
SweetW .... SweetWater, Inc. [*Associated Press*] (SAG)
SWEFCO ...... Special Weapons Ferry Control Office [*or Officer*]
SWEHAC ...... Statewide Ear Health Advisory Committee [*Australia*]
SWEJDFC .... Sing with the Earth John Denver Fan Club (EA)
SWEL.......... Special Weapons Equipment List
Swell.......... Single Woman Earning Lots in London [*Lifestyle classification*]
SWELSTRA... Special Weapons Equipment List Single Theater Requisitioning Agency
SWEMED ..... Swedish Medical Literature [*Database*] [*Karolinska Institute Library and Information Center/Medical Information Center*] [*Information service or system*] (CRD)
SWEMS........ Soil, Water, Estuarine Monitoring [*Environmental Protection Agency*] (GFGA)
Swen .... Sweeney's New York Superior Court Reports [*31-32 New York*] [*A publication*] (DLA)
SWEPS .... Safety Weather Probability Study
SWERD........ Solid Waste and Emergency Response [*Environmental Protection Agency*] (GFGA)
SWERD........ Solid Waste and Emergency Response Division [*Office of General Counsel*] (COE)
SWESS .... Special Weapons Emergency Separation System (AFM)
SWESSAR.... Stone and Webster Standard Safety Analysis Report [*Nuclear energy*] (NRCH)
SWET .... Simulated Water Entry Test [*Nuclear energy*]
SWET .... Society of West End Theatre [*British*] (DBA)
SWET .... Society of West End Theatres [*England*] (WDAA)
SWET .... Special Weapon Equipment Test (SAA)
SWETS .... Solid Waste Engineering Transfer System
SWETTU ...... Special Weapons Experimental Tactical Test Unit
SWExB .... South Western Examinations Board [*Education*] (AIE)
SWF .... Air Swift [*British ICAO designator*] (FAAC)
SWF .... Newburgh [*New York*] [*Airport symbol*] (OAG)
SWF .... Screw Worm Fly
SWF .... Seawater Feed
SWF .... Shortwave Fadeouts
SWF .... Silver Wings Fraternity (EA)
SWF .... Single White Female [*Classified advertising*]
SWF .... Small Winemakers' Forum [*Australia*]
SWF .... Special Warning Function (MCD)
SWF .... Special Weapons Facility [*Navy*]
SWF .... Steelworker Fabricator [*Navy rating*]
SWF .... Stelway Food [*Vancouver Stock Exchange symbol*]
SWF .... Still Waters Foundation (EA)
SWF .... Sturge-Weber Foundation (EA)
SWF .... Sudden Wave Fade Out (IAA)
SWF .... Suedwestfunk [*Radio network*] [*West Germany*]
SWFB .... Southwestern Freight Bureau
SWFC.......... Southwest Fisheries Center [*La Jolla, CA*] [*Department of Commerce*]
SWFC.......... Surface Weapons Fire Control
SWFG .... Secondary Waveform Generator [*Telecommunications*] (TEL)
SWFI.......... Sterile Water for Injection [*Pharmacology*] (DAVI)
SWFI.......... Stratified Fuel-Water Injection [*Automotive engineering*]
SWFM .... Standing-Wave Fluorescence Microscopy
SWFPA .... Scottish White Fish Producers Association (DBA)
SWFPA .... Structural Wood Fiber Products Association [*Later, SCFPA*] (EA)
SWFR .... Slow Write, Fast Read [*Computer science*] (IEEE)
SWFSC .... Southwest Fisheries Science Center [*San Diego, CA*]
SWFT.......... Swift Transportation [*NASDAQ symbol*] (TTSB)
SWFT.......... Swift Transportation Co. [*NASDAQ symbol*] (SAG)
SwftEng ...... Swift Energy Co. [*Associated Press*] (SAG)
SWFX .... Spotweld Fixture [*Tool*]
SWG .... Ground Air Transfer, Inc. [*ICAO designator*] (FAAC)
SWG .... Salam-Weinberg-Glashow [*One unified field theory in physics*]
SWG .... Science Working Group (EERA)
SWG .... Scientific Working Group [*EXAMETNET*]
SWG .... Screen Writers Guild (WDMC)
SWG .... Seabed Working Group [*Nuclear energy*] (NUCP)
SWG .... Shock Wave Generator
SWG .... Shuttle Working Group [*NASA*] (MCD)
SWG .... Sine Wave Generator
SWG .... Slotted Waveguide
SWG .... Society of Woman Geographers (EA)
SWG .... Software Working Group [*NASA*] (NASA)
SWG .... Songwriters Guild of Great Britain
SWG .... South-West Gold Corp. [*Vancouver Stock Exchange symbol*]
SWG .... Space Wing [*Military*]
SWG .... Special Wireless Group [*World War II British*]
SWG .... Special Working Group
SWG .... Spirit Airlines, Inc. [*FAA designator*] (FAAC)
SWG .... Squarewave Generator
SWG .... Staff Working Group
SWG .... Standard Wire Gauge [*Telecommunications*]
SWG .... Standard/Working Group (MCD)
SWG .... Strictly Wild Guess (SAA)
SWG .... Stubs Wire Gauge
SWG .... Sub-Working Group
SWG .... Swing (MSA)
SWG .... Swing-N-Slide Corp. [*AMEX symbol*] (SAG)
SWG .... Switching (WGA)
SwGAFn ...... Southwest Georgia Financial Corp. [*Associated Press*] (SAG)
SwGas .... Southwest Gas Capital I [*Associated Press*] (SAG)
SWGD......... Swinging Door

SWGM .... Spanish World Gospel Mission (EA)
SWGR .... Switchgear
SWGR .... Switchgear Room (COE)
SWGS .... Surface Wire Grounding System [*Electronics*] (RDA)
SwGU.......... Goteborgs Universitetsbibliotek, Goteborg, Sweden [*Library symbol Library of Congress*] (LCLS)
SWH .... Scottish Women's Hospital [*British military*] (DMA)
SWH .... Seaway Multi-Corp Ltd. [*Toronto Stock Exchange symbol*]
SWH .... Significant Wave Height [*Oceanography*]
SWH .... Solar Water Heating
SWH .... Spaghetti Warehouse [*NYSE symbol*] (TTSB)
SWH .... Spaghetti Warehouse, Inc. [*NYSE symbol*] (SPSG)
SWH .... Standard Working Home [*Pet-adoption terminology*]
SWH .... Swan Hill [*Victoria, Australia*] [*Airport symbol*] (AD)
SWHA .... Social Welfare History Archives Center [*University of Minnesota*] [*Research center*] (RCD)
SwHelv .... Swiss Helvetia Fund, Inc. [*Associated Press*] (SAG)
SWHG .... Social Welfare History Group [*Western Michigan University*] [*Kalamazoo*] (EA)
SWHS .... Scissor Workboard Hands' Society [*A union*] [*British*]
SWI .... Salt-Water Igniter
SWI .... Scottish Woollen Industry
SWI .... Scudder World Income Opportunities Ltd. [*NYSE symbol*] (SAG)
SWI .... Scudder World Inc. Oppt Fd [*NYSE symbol*] (TTSB)
SWI .... Sealant and Waterproofers Institute (EA)
SWI .... Seawind Resources, Inc. [*Vancouver Stock Exchange symbol*]
SWI .... Seaworthiness Impairment (NVT)
SWI .... Self Worth Inventory [*Test*] (TMMY)
SWI .... Sherman [*Texas*] [*Airport symbol*] (OAG)
SWI .... Shock Wave Interaction
SWI .... Short-Wave Interference [*Telecommunications*] (IAA)
SWI .... Sidewall Indentation [*Tire manufacturing*]
SWI .... Sine Wave Inverter
SWI .... Skin and Wound Isolation (STED)
SWI .... Software Interrupt [*Computer science*]
SWI .... Special Weather Intelligence (MCD)
SWI .... Special World Intervals
SWI .... Stall Warning Indicator
SWI .... Standing Wave Indicator
SWI .... Static Walkthrough/Inspection (AAEL)
SWI .... Steel Window Institute (EA)
SWI .... Sterile Water for Injection [*Pharmacology*] (DAVI)
SWI .... Stroke Work Index [*Neurology*]
SWI .... Sunworld International Airways, Inc. [*ICAO designator*] (FAAC)
SWI .... Surgical Wound Infection (STED)
SWIA .... Southwest Association of Indian Arts (BARN)
SWIBA .... Scottish Women's Indoor Bowling Association (DBA)
SWICA .... Self Winding Clock Association (EA)
SWICS .... Solar Wind Ion Composition Spectrometer (MCD)
SWIDOC....... Sociaal-Wetenschappelijk Informatie on Dooumontatiocentrum [*Social Science Information and Documentation Center*] [*Netherlands Information service or system*] (IID)
SWIE.......... Southern Waste Information Exchange (GNE)
SWIFT........ Selected Words in Full Title (NITA)
SWIFT........ Sequential Weight Increasing Factor Technique (IAA)
SWIFT........ Significant Word in the Full Title [*Computer science*] (DIT)
SWIFT........ Society for Worldwide Interbank Financial Telecommunication [*Banking netw ork*] [*Belgium*]
SWIFT........ Society for Worldwide Interbank Financial Transactions (NITA)
SWIFT........ Software Implemented Friden Translator [*Computer science*]
SWIFT........ Stored Wave Inverse Fourier Transform [*Spectrometry*]
SWIFT........ Strength of Wings Including Flutter
SWIFT........ Swept Wing with Inboard Flap for Trim [*Hang glider*] (PS)
SWIFT........ System Workshops in Forecasting Techniques [*Bell System*]
SWIFT-ANSWER... Special Word Indexed Full Text Alpha Numeric Storage with Easy Retrieval [*Software*]
Swift Dig ..... Swift's Connecticut Digest [*A publication*] (DLA)
Swift Ev ...... Swift on Evidence, and Bills and Notes [*A publication*] (DLA)
SWIFT LASS... Signal Word Index of Field and Title - Literature Abstract Specialized Search (DIT)
SWIFT SIR... Signal Word Index of Field and Title - Scientific Information Retrieval (DIT)
Swift Sys ..... Swift's System of the Laws of Connecticut [*A publication*] (DLA)
SwiftT......... Swift Transportation Co. [*Associated Press*] (SAG)
SWIG .... Southwestern Irrigated Cotton Growers Association
SWIM .... Sea Warfare Interim Model (CINC)
SWIM .... Semiconductor Workbench for Integrated Modeling (AAEL)
SWIM .... Ship Weapons Installation Manual (MCD)
SWIM .... Soil-Water Infiltration & Movement
SWIM .... Sperm-Washing Insemination Method
SWIM .... Standard Wozniak Integrated Machine [*Computer science*]
SWIM .... Super Wozniak Integrated Machine [*Computer science*]
SWIM .... Surface Water Improvement and Management (MCD)
SWIM .... Switch Tail Interceptor Missile (MCD)
SWIMCRIT... Swim Criteria
SWIMS .... Serialized Weapons Information Management System [*Navy*]
SWIMS .... Skills for Working in a Multicultural Society [*Australia*]
SWIMS .... Solid Waste Information Management System (GAAI)
Swin .... Swinburne on Wills [10 eds.] [*1590-1803*] [*A publication*] (DLA)
SWIN .... Swinehead [*England*]
Swin .... Swinton's Scotch Justiciary Reports [*1835-41*] [*A publication*] (DLA)
Swinb Desc... Swinburne on Descents [*1825*] [*A publication*] (DLA)
Swinb Mar... Swinburne on Married Women [*1846*] [*A publication*] (DLA)
Swinb Spo ... Swinburne on Spousals [*A publication*] (DLA)
Swinb Wills... Swinburne on Wills [*A publication*] (DLA)

SWINC .... Soft Wired Integrated Numerical Controller (IAA)
SWINE .... Students Wildly Indignant about Nearly Everything [*Group in "L'il Abner" comic strip*]
SWING........ Sterling Warrant into Gilt-Edged Stock [*British*]
SwingNSI..... Swing-N-Slide [*Associated Press*] (SAG)
SWINGR ...... Sweep Integrator (AAG)
SwingSI ...... Swing-N-Slide Corp. [*Associated Press*] (SAG)
Swin Jus Cas... Swinton's Scotch Justiciary Cases [*A publication*] (DLA)
Swin Reg App... Swinton's Scotch Registration Appeal Cases [*1835-41*] [*A publication*] (DLA)
Swint .... Swinton's Scotch Justiciary Cases [*A publication*] (DLA)
SWINTER ..... Service Women in Non-Traditional Environmental Roles [*Canadian armed forces*]
SWIO .... SACLANT [*Supreme Allied Commander, Atlantic*] War Intelligence Organization (NATG)
SWIP .... Secret Work in Process (MCD)
SWIP .... Shared Whois Project
SWIP .... Shared Working in Prisons (WDAA)
SWIP .... Society for Women in Philosophy (EA)
SWIP .... Soil-Wheel Interaction Performance
SWIP .... Standing Wave Impedance Probe [*Geophysical instrument*]
SWIP .... Stichting Werkgroep Indianen Projekt [*Netherlands*]
SWIP .... Super-Weight Improvement Program [*Navy*] (NG)
SWIP .... Systems Weapon Improvement Program [*A-6 Intruder*] (DOMA)
SWIPMD ..... Society for Women in Philosophy, Midwest Division (EA)
SWIPS .... Soil Water Information Processing System
SWIR .... Shortwave Infrared
SWIR .... Southwest Indian Ridge [*Geology*]
SWIR .... Special Weapons Inspection Report
SWIRL .... South Western Industrial Research Ltd. [*British*] (ARC)
SWIRLS ...... Southwest Regional Library System [*Library network*]
SWIRS .... Solid Waste Information Retrieval System [*Environmental Protection Agency*]
SWIS .... Satellite Weather Information System [*National Oceanic and Atmospheric Administration*]
SWIS .... Sensitive Wildlife Information System [*Army*] (IID)
SWIS .... Special Weapons Integration Subcommittee (SAA)
SWIS .... St. Ives Laboratories, Inc. [*NASDAQ symbol*] (NQ)
SWIS .... Swiss Wildlife Information Service [*Zurich*] [*Information service or system*] (IID)
Swish........ Swisher International [*Commercial firm Associated Press*] (SAG)
Swisher...... Swisher International [*Commercial firm Associated Press*] (SAG)
Swissray...... Swissray International, Inc. [*Associated Press*] (SAG)
SWIT .... Switzerland
SWITCH ...... Swiss Academic and Research Network (TELE)
SWITL .... Southwestern Industrial Traffic League (EA)
SWITT .... Surface Wave Independent Tap Transducer (IEEE)
SWITZ........ Switzerland
Switz.......... Switzerland (VRA)
SWJ .... Single Wire Junction
SWJ .... Society of Women Journalists (DGA)
SWJ .... Socket Wrench Joint
SWJ .... StatesWest Airlines, Inc. [*ICAO designator*] (FAAC)
SWK .... General Aerospace, Inc. [*Canada ICAO designator*] (FAAC)
SWK .... Southwark [*England*]
SWK .... [*The*] Stanley Works [*NYSE symbol*] (SPSG)
SWK .... Stewart Lake Resources, Inc. [*Toronto Stock Exchange symbol*]
SWKO .... Sawako Corp. [*NASDAQ symbol*] (SAG)
SWKOY .... Sawako Corp. ADR [*NASDAQ symbol*] (TTSB)
SW KR........ Swedish Krona [*Monetary unit*]
SWL .... Safe Working Load [*Shipping*]
SWL .... Short Wavelength LASER
SWL .... Short Wavelength Limit
SWL .... Shortwave Listener [*Radio*]
SWL .... Signals Warfare Laboratory [*Army*] (RDA)
SWL .... Single-Wheel Loading [*Aviation*]
SWL .... Snow Hill, MD [*Location identifier FAA*] (FAAL)
SWL .... Software Writer's Language [*Computer science*] (CIST)
SWL .... Solid Waste Litter
SWL .... Southwest Realty Ltd. [*Later, Southwestern Property Trade*] AM (SPSG)
SWL .... Spanish Wells [*Bahamas*] [*Airport symbol*] (AD)
SWL .... Special Weapons Loading (SAA)
SWL .... Still Water Level
SWL .... Strategic Weapons Loader (DWSG)
SWL .... Sulfite Waste Liquor
SWL .... Surface Wave Line
SWLA .... Southwestern Library Association
SWLC .... Southwestern Connecticut Library Council [*Library network*]
SWLC .... South West London College [*London, England*]
SWLD .... Smallworldwide PLC [*NASDAQ symbol*] (SAG)
SWLDG .... Socket Welding
SWLF .... Southwestern Legal Foundation (EA)
SWLG .... Scottish Wild Land Group (DBA)
SWLIN .... System Work List Item Number (DNAB)
SWL Rev ..... Southwestern Law Review [*A publication*] (DLA)
SwLU .... Lunds Universitet [*University of Lund*], Lund, Sweden [*Library symbol Library of Congress*] (LCLS)
SwLuH .... Hogskolan i Lulea [*Lulea University*], Lulea, Sweden [*Library symbol*] [*Library of Congress*] (LCLS)
Swm .... Metro Prop-Jet [*Airplane code*]
SWM .... Sawmill [*California*] [*Seismograph station code, US Geological Survey Closed*] (SEIS)
SWM .... Schweitzer Mauduit International Inc. [*NYSE symbol*] (SAG)
SWM .... Schweitzer-Mauduit Intl [*NYSE symbol*] (TTSB)

SWM............ Segmental Wall Motion [*Medicine*] (DMAA)
SWM............ Serber-Wilson Method [*Nuclear energy*] (NRCH)
SWM............ Shipboard Wave Meter
SWM............ Single White Male [*Classified advertising*]
SWM............ Society of Women Musicians, Inc. [*British*] (BI)
SwM............ Southwest Microfilm, Inc., El Paso, TX [*Library symbol Library of Congress*] (LCLS)
SWM............ Special Warfare Mission (AABC)
SWM............ Spotweld Machine [*Tool*]
SWM............ Stan West Mining Corp. [*Toronto Stock Exchange symbol*]
SWM............ Stewart Warner Microcircuits (IAA)
SWM............ Suia-Missu [*Brazil*] [*Airport symbol*] (OAG)
SWM............ Surface Wave Mode
SWMA......... Scottish Wirework Manufacturers Association (DBA)
SWMA......... Society of Women in Military Aviation (EA)
SWMA......... Solid Waste Management Association
SWMA......... Southwestern Monuments Association [*Later, SPMA*] (EA)
SWMA......... Steel Wool Manufacturers' Association [*British*] (BI)
SWMA......... Swedish Match [*NASDAQ symbol*] (SAG)
SWMAT........ Switch Matrix (MCD)
SWMAY .... Swedish Match AB ADR [*NASDAQ symbol*] (TTSB)
SWMC......... Sanctuary Wood Multimedia [*NASDAQ symbol*] (SAG)
SWMCCS..... Standard Weather Messages Command and Control System (MCD)
SWMCF....... Sanctuary Woods Multimedia [*NASDAQ symbol*] (TTSB)
SWMCM...... Shallow-Water Mine Countermeasures (DOMA)
SWMF........ South Wales Miners' Federation (DAS)
SWMFB........ Southwestern Motor Freight Bureau
SWMM......... Storm Water Management Model [*Environmental Protection Agency*] (AEPA)
SWMO .... Solid Waste Management Office [*Later, Office of Solid Waste Management Programs*] [*Environmental Protection Agency*]
SWMS .... Solid Waste Management System [*Nuclear energy*] (NRCH)
SWMTEP...... System-Wide Medium-Term Environment Programme (GNE)
SWMU .... Solid Waste Management Unit [*Environmental science*]
SWN .... Leadville, CO [*Location identifier FAA*] (FAAL)
SWN .... Notre Dame College, Wilcox, Saskatchewan [*Library symbol National Library of Canada*] (NLC)
SWN .... Southwestern Energy [*NYSE symbol*] (TTSB)
SWN .... Southwestern Energy Co. [*NYSE symbol*] (SPSG)
SWN .... Sworn (ROG)
SWNCC........ State, War, Navy Coordinating Committee [*Later, SANAAC*]
SWND .... Social Workers for Nuclear Disarmament (EA)
SwnEnrg ...... Southwestern Energy Co. [*Associated Press*] (SAG)
SWNJ.......... Southwest New Jersey Consortium for Health Information Services [*Library network*]
SwnLfe .... Southwestern Life Corp. [*Formerly, ICH Corp.*] [*Associated Press*] (SAG)
SwnLife .... Southwestern Life Corp. [*Formerly, ICH Corp.*] [*Associated Press*] (SAG)
SWNT .... Single-Wall Nanotube [*Materials science*]
SWO .... Second Wind Organization (EA)
SWO .... Senior Watch Officer [*Navy*] (NVT)
SWO .... Shallow Resources, Inc. [*Vancouver Stock Exchange symbol*]
SWO .... Signal Wireless Officer (IAA)
SWO .... Solid Waste Office [*Later, Office of Solid Waste Management Programs*] [*Environmental Protection Agency*]
SWO .... Southwestern Oregon Community College, Coos Bay, OR [*OCLC symbol*] (OCLC)
SWO .... Squadron Wireless Officer [*Navy British*]
SWO .... Squarewave Oscillator
SWO .... Staff Watch Officer (NVT)
SWO .... Staff Weather Officer [*Military*]
SWO .... Station Warrant Officer [*Air Force British*]
SWO .... Stillwater [*Oklahoma*] [*Airport symbol*] (OAG)
SWO .... Stop Work Order
SWO .... Stud Welding Outfit
SWO .... Superficial White Onychomycosis (STED)
SWO .... Support Work Order (AAG)
SWO .... Surface Warfare Officer [*Navy*] (NVT)
SW/O .... Switchover
SWOAPQS ... Surface Warfare Officer, Personnel Qualification Standards [*Navy*] (DNAB)
SWOB .... Salaries, Wages, Overhead, and Benefits (NASA)
SWOB .... Ship Waste Off-Loading Barge [*Navy*] (CAAL)
SWOC .... Special Weapons Operation Center [*Army*] (AABC)
SWOC .... Steel Workers Organizing Committee [*Became United Steelworkers of America*]
SWOC .... Subject Word out of Context [*Computer science*] (DIT)
SWOD .... Special Weapons Ordnance Devices
SWOE .... Smart Weapons Operability Enhancement (RDA)
SWOG .... Special Weapons Overflight Guide (AFM)
SWOP .... Service Weapons Operational Procedures (MCD)
SWOP .... Special Leave Without Pay
SWOP .... Special Weapons Ordnance Publication [*Navy*] (NVT)
SWOP .... Specifications for Web Offset Publications [*Printing technology*]
SWOP .... Standard Web Offset Press [*Computer science*] (PCM)
SWOP .... Stereo Wave Observation Project (IAA)
SWOP .... Stop without Pay
SWOP .... Structural Weight Optimization Program [*NASA*] (KSC)
SWOP .... Switchboard Operator [*British military*] (DMA)
SWOP AMP... Switchable-Input Operational Amplifier [*Electronics*] (EECA)
SWOPS .... Single Well Oil Production Ship [*British*]
SWOPSI....... Stanford Workshop on Political and Social Issues [*Stanford University*]
SWORD........ Separated, Widowed, or Divorced [*New York City association*]

SWORD....... Shallow Water Oceanographic Research Data [*System*] [*Naval Ordnance Laboratory and Naval Oceanographic Office*]
SWORD....... Small Wars Operational Research Division [*Military*] (INF)
SWORD....... Software Optimization for the Retrieval of Data [*Computer science*] (MHDI)
SWORD....... Submarine Warfare Operations Research Department (DOMA)
SWORDS ..... Standard Work Ordering and Reporting Data System [*Army*]
SWORL .... Southwestern Ohio Rural Libraries [*Library network*]
SwOrM........ Regionsjukhuset, Medicinska Biblioteket [*Regional Hospital, Medical Library*], Orebro, Sweden [*Library symbol Library of Congress*] (LCLS)
SWOS .... Surface Warfare Officer's School [*Navy*] (NVT)
SWOSCOLCOM... Surface Warfare Officer's School Command [*Navy*] (NVT)
SWOSCOLCOMDET... Surface Warfare Officer's School Command Detachment [*Navy*] (DNAB)
SWOSU .... Southwestern Oklahoma State University
SWOT .... Strengths, Weaknesses, Opportunities, Threats [*Analysis for organizations*]
SWOV .... Switchover (MSA)
SWP .... Safety Work Permit [*Environmental science*] (COE)
SWP .... Safe Working Pressure
SWP .... Salt-Water Pump (MSA)
SWP .... Science Working Panel [*NASA*]
SWP .... Scientific Word Processor [*Computer science*]
SWP .... Sector Working Party [*British*] (DCTA)
SWP .... Semi-Tech Microelectronics, Inc. [*Toronto Stock Exchange symbol*]
SWP .... Service Water Pump [*Nuclear energy*] (NRCH)
SWP .... Shock Wave Profile
SWP .... Short Wavelength Prime [*Camera for spectra*]
SWP .... Single Wafer Processing (AAEL)
SWP .... Small Whirlpool (STED)
SWP .... Socialist Workers' Party [*British Political party*] (PPW)
SWP .... Society for Women in Plastics (EA)
SWP .... Society of Wedding Photographers [*British*] (DBA)
SWP .... Society of Wireless Pioneers
SWP .... Soil-Test Water Probe
SWP .... Solid Waste Packaging [*Nuclear energy*] (NRCH)
SWP .... Solid Waste Processing [*Nuclear energy*] (NRCH)
SWP .... Southwestern Property Trust, Inc. [*Later, South West Property Trust*] [*NYSE symbol*] (SPSG)
SWP .... Southwest Pacific
SWP .... South West Prop Tr [*NYSE symbol*] (TTSB)
SWP .... Space, Weight, and Power
SWP .... Special Weapons Project [*Military*]
SWP .... Special Working Party [*Military*]
SWP .... Standard Work Procedure (SAA)
SWP .... Standby Warning Panel (MCD)
SWP .... State Water Project [*California*] (ECON)
SWP .... Stichting Waakzaamheid Persoonregistratie [*Netherlands*]
SWP .... Stiftung Wissenschaft und Politik [*Foundation for Science and Politics*] [*Information service or system*] (IID)
SWP.......... Submersible Water Pump
SWP.......... Summer Work Program
SWP.......... Supply Working Party of Official Committee on Armistice Terms and Civil Administration [*World War II*]
SWP.......... Surface Warfare Plan [*Navy*] (CAAL)
SWP.......... Surface Wave Phenomena
SWP.......... Survey of Western Palestine [*C. R. Conder et al*] [*A publication*] (BJA)
SWP.......... Swakopmund [*South-West Africa*] [*Airport symbol*] (AD)
SWP.......... Swamp (ADA)
SWP.......... Swamp Creek [*Montana*] [*Seismograph station code, US Geological Survey Closed*] (SEIS)
SWP.......... Sweep
SWPA .... Section for Women in Public Administration (EA)
SWPA .... Southwestern Power Administration [*Department of Energy*]
SWPA .... Southwestern Psychological Association (MCD)
SWPA .... Southwest National [*NASDAQ symbol*] (TTSB)
SWPA .... Southwest National Corp. [*Greensburg, PA*] [*NASDAQ symbol*] (NQ)
SWPA .... Southwest Pacific Area [*World War II*]
SWPA .... Southwest Placement Association (AEBS)
SWPA .... Spotweld Pattern [*Tool*] (AAG)
SWPA .... Steel Works Plant Association [*British*] (BI)
SWPA .... Submersible Wastewater Pump Association (EA)
SWPA .... Surplus War Property Administration [*Terminated, 1944*]
SWPAN .... Special Weapons Project Analysis (SAA)
SWPB .... Surplus War Property Board [*Terminated, 1945*]
SWPC .... Short Wing Piper Club (EA)
SWPC .... Smaller War Plants Corp. [*World War II*]
SWPC .... Southern Water Polo Conference (PSS)
SWPC .... Southwest Pacific Command [*Navy*]
SWPCP .... Prince Albert National Park, Parks Canada [*Parc National Prince Albert, ParcsCanada*] Waskesiu Lakes, Saskatchewan [*Library symbol National Library of Canada*] (NLC)
SWPF......... Southwest Pacific Force [*Later, Southwest Pacific Command*] [*Navy*]
SWPIA .... Southwest Pacific Island Arc [*Oceanography*]
SWPJ......... Study of Western Palestine: Jerusalem [*C. Warren and C. R. Conder*] [*A publication*] (BJA)
SWPlan....... Solid Waste Management Planning Software
SWPM .... Survey of Western Palestine: Memoirs [*C. R. Conder*] [*A publication*] (BJA)
SW/PM .... System Management/Performance Monitor
SW Pol Sci Q... Southwestern Political Science Quarterly [*A publication*] (DLA)
SWPP .... Service Water Pressurization Pump [*Nuclear energy*] (IEEE)
SWPP .... Southwest Power Pool [*Regional power council*] (NRCH)

SWPP	State Wellhead Protection Program (COE)
SWPPD	Society for Women in Philosophy, Pacific Division (EA)
SWPPP	Storm Water Pollution Prevention Plan [*Environmental science*]
SwPropT	Southwestern Property Trust, Inc. [*Associated Press*] (SAG)
SWP(S)	Solid Waste Processing System [*Nuclear energy*] (NRCH)
SWPS	Strategic War Planning System [*Air Force*]
SWPSA	Southwestern Peanut Shellers Association (EA)
SWPSD	Society for Women in Philosophy, Southwest Division (EA)
SWPSP	Survey of Western Palestine: Special Papers [*A publication*] (BJA)
SWPT	Service Weapons Test (NVT)
SWQ	Sumbawa [*Indonesia*] [*Airport symbol*] (AD)
SWQI	South West Queensland Initiative (EERA)
SWR	Semiconductor Wafer Representation (AAEL)
SWR	Serum Wassermann Reaction [*Clinical chemistry*]
SWR	Service Water Reservoir [*Nuclear energy*] (NRCH)
SWR	Sewer
SWR	Short Wavelength Radiation (KSC)
SWR	Shortwave Ratio (DEN)
SWR	Sine Wave Response
SWR	Siphon Withdrawal Response
SWR	Sodium-Water Reaction [*Nuclear energy*] (NRCH)
SWR	Sons of the Whiskey Rebellion (EA)
SWR	Southwestern Railway [*British*] (ROG)
SWR	South Western Reporter [*A publication*] (DLA)
SWR	Southwest Review [*A publication*] (BRI)
SWR	Special Warning Receiver (MCD)
SWR	Sperm Wassermann Reaction [*Urology*] (DAVI)
SWR	Standing Wave Ratio [*Voltage*] [*Electronics*]
SWR	State Wildlife Reserve [*State*] (EERA)
SWR	Steel Wire Rope
SWR	Stepwise Refinement (IAA)
SWR	Stonewall Resources [*Vancouver Stock Exchange symbol*]
SWR	Stress Wave Riveter [*Metal forming*]
SWR	Submarine Water Reactor [*Nuclear energy*] (NRCH)
SWR	Swisher International Group
SWR	Swissair (Societe Anonyme Switzerland pour la Navigation Aerienne) [*ICAO designator*] (FAAC)
SWR	Switch Rails
SWR2	Scaled Weapons Radius Squared (SAA)
SWRA	Selected Water Resources Abstracts [*US Geological Survey*] [*Information service or system*] (CRD)
SWRA	Stepwise Regression Analysis (PDAA)
SWRB	Sadler's Wells Royal Ballet [*British*]
SWRB	Standing Wave Ratio Bridge [*Electronics*]
SWRCB	State Water Resources Control Board (DOGT)
SW Rep	South Western Reporter [*A publication*] (DLA)
SW Repr	South Western Reporter [*A publication*] (DLA)
SWRF	Sine Wave Response Filter [*Program*]
SWRHL	Southwestern Radiological Health Laboratory [*HEW*]
SWRI	Scottish Women's Rural Institutes (DI)
SWRI	Sealant, Waterproofing, and Restoration Institute (NTPA)
SWRI	Sea World Research Institute [*Marine science*] (GNE)
SWRI	Southwestern Research Institute [*San Antonio, TX*] [*Research contor*]
SWRJ	Split Wing Ramjet
SWRL	Southwest Regional Laboratory [*Research center*] (RCD)
SWRL	Southwest Regional Laboratory for Educational Research and Development
SWRLSS	Southwest Regional Library Service System [*Library network*]
SWRM	Standing Wave Ratio Meter [*Electronics*]
SWRMPAC...	Southwestern Regional Manpower Advisory Committee [*Terminated, 1974*] [*Department of Labor*] (EGAO)
SWROM	Standing Wave Read-Only Memory [*Computer science*]
SWROSS	Southwest Regional Office for Spanish Speaking (EA)
SWRP	Satellite Wildlife Research Project
SWRP	Sectionalized Work Requirements Package (MCD)
SWRPRS	Sodium-Water Reaction Pressure Relief Subsystem [*Nuclear energy*] (NRCH)
SWRSIC	Southern Water Resources Scientific Information Center [*Raleigh, NC*]
SWRT	Software Artistry [*NASDAQ symbol*] (SAG)
SWS	Lindquist Investment Co., Inc. [*ICAO designator*] (FAAC)
SWS	Salt Water System [*Environmental science*] (COE)
SWS	Sargent-Welch Scientific Co. (EFIS)
SWS	Saturn Workshop [*NASA*]
SWS	Seam Welding System
SWS	Service Water System [*Nuclear energy*] (NRCH)
SWS	Service-Wide Supply
SWS	Shallow Water SONAR
SWS	Shift Word, Substituting
SWS	Shock Wave Sensor (RDA)
SWS	Shore Wireless Service [*British military*] (DMA)
SWS	Short Wavelength Spectrometer
SWS	Short-Wave Sleep (OA)
SWS	Single White Silk-Covered [*Wire insulation*]
SWS	Slow-Wave Sleep
SWS	Slow Wave Structure [*Satellite delay tube*] (NTCM)
SWS	Smart Weapons Systems [*Army*] (RDA)
SWS	Sniper Weapon Sight (INF)
SWS	Sniper Weapon System [*Army*]
SWS	Social World Service (DAVI)
SWS	Sociologists for Women in Society (EA)
SWS	Solar Wind Spectrometer
SwS	Solidarity with Solidarity [*See also SzS*] [*Defunct*] (EAIO)
SWS	Solid Waste System [*Nuclear energy*] (NRCH)
SWS	Space Weapon Systems [*Air Force*]
SWS	Special Weapon Systems [*Military*]
SWS	Spike-Wave Stupor [*Medicine*] (DMAA)
SWS	Standard Weapon Station [*Nuclear arms control*]
SWS	Static Water Supply (ADA)
SWS	Steroid Wasting Syndrome [*Medicine*] (DB)
SWS	Still Water Surface
SWS	Strategic Warning Staff
SWS	Strategic Weapon System [*Military*] (CAAL)
SWS	Stripline with Stud (IAA)
SWS	Student Ward Secretary [*Hospital administration*] (DAVI)
SWS	Sturge-Weber Syndrome [*Medicine*] (DAVI)
SWS	Survey of Works Styles [*Test*] (TMMY)
SWS	Swansea [*Wales*] [*Airport symbol*] (OAG)
SWS	Swift Minerals Ltd. [*Vancouver Stock Exchange symbol*]
SWS	Switch Scan (MCD)
sws	Switch Scan (NAKS)
SWS	Switch Stand
SWS	Systolic Wall Stress [*Cardiology*]
SWSA	Scottish Water Ski Associaton (DBA)
SWSA	Solid Waste Storage Area [*Environmental science*] (COE)
SWSA	Southern Wood Seasoning Association
SWSD	Special Weapons Supply Depot
SWSE	Southeast Regional Library, Weyburn, Saskatchewan [*Library symbol National Library of Canada*] (NLC)
SWSF	Society for a World Service Federation [*Defunct*] (EA)
SWSG	Security Window Screen and Guard
SWSH	Swisher International [*NASDAQ symbol*] (SAG)
SWSHW	Swisher Intl Wrrt [*NASDAQ symbol*] (TTSB)
SWSI	Single Width, Single Inlet (OA)
SWSI	Surface Water Supply Index [*to measure drought*]
SWSIR	Ship Weapons System Integration Requirements [*Navy*]
SwSK	Kungliga Tekniska Hoegskolan [*Royal Institute of Technology*], Stockholm, Sweden [*Library symbol Library of Congress*] (LCLS)
SwSKB	Kungliga Biblioteket, Bibliotheca Regia Holmiensis, Stockholm, Sweden [*Library symbol Library of Congress*] (LCLS)
SwSKM	Kungliga Karolinska Mediko-Kirurgiska Institutes, Stockholm, Sweden [*Library symbol Library of Congress*] (LCLS)
SwSL	Latinamerika-Institutet, Stockholm, Sweden [*Library symbol Library of Congress*] (LCLS)
SWSL	Supplemental Weather Service Location [*Aviation*] (FAAC)
SWSM	Special Weapons Supply Memorandum [*Army*] (AABC)
SWSR	Solid Waste Shipping Room [*Nuclear energy*] (NRCH)
SWSR	Standing Wave Signal Ratio (IAA)
SWSRAAA...	Sipsey Wild and Scenic River and Alabama Addition Act (COE)
SWS/SUM PTS...	Selection Work Sheets/Summary Parts
SWST	Service Water Storage Tank [*Nuclear energy*] (IEEE)
SWST	Society of Wood Science and Technology (EA)
SWST	Southwest Securities Group [*NASDAQ symbol*] (SPSG)
SWST	Southwest Securities Grp [*NASDAQ symbol*] (TTSB)
SwstAirl	Southwest Airlines Co. [*Associated Press*] (SAG)
SwstBc	Southwest Bancorp [*Associated Press*] (SAG)
SwstBcp	Southwest Bancorp [*Associated Press*] (SAG)
SwstNat	Southwest National Corp. [*Associated Press*] (SAG)
SwstSec	Southwest Securities Group [*Associated Press*] (SAG)
SwSU	Stockholms Universitetsbibliotheket, Stockholm, Sweden [*Library symbol Library of Congress*] (LCLS)
SwSU-T	University of Stockholm, Department of Physical Geography, Trafala Glaciological Station, Stockholm, Sweden [*Library symbol*] [*Library of Congress*] (LCLS)
SWSVC	Souris Valley Regional Care Center, Weyburn, Saskatchewan [*Library symbol National Library of Canada*] (NLC)
SW-SWIP	Society for Women in Philosophy, Southwestern Division (EA)
SWSWTU	Sheffield Wool Shear Workers' Trade Union [*British*] (DCTA)
SWSWU	Sheffield Wool Shear Workers Union [*British*] (WDAA)
SWT	Safe Women's Transport [*British*]
SWT	Scottish Wildlife Trust [*British*]
SWT	Scout Weapons Team [*Army*] (DOMA)
SWT	Search-while-Track (CAAL)
SWT	Seward, NE [*Location identifier FAA*] (FAAL)
SWT	Shortwave Transmitter
SWT	Silent Witness [*Vancouver Stock Exchange symbol*]
SWT	Sine-Wave Threshold (DB)
SWT	Single-Weight [*Paper*]
SWT	Special Weapons Test
SWT	Spiral Wrap Tubing
SWT	Spotweld Template (MCD)
SWT	Stab Wound of the Throat (DAVI)
SWT	Steel Watertight [*Shipfitting*]
SWT	Supersonic Wind Tunnel (MCD)
SWT	Sweat
SWT	Sweet
SWT	Swept Frequency Transform (CAAL)
SWT	Swiftair SA [*Spain ICAO designator*] (FAAC)
SWT	Switch Ties
SWT	System Work Team (MCD)
SWTA	Special Weapons Training Allowance
SWTC	Special Weapon Technical Command [*Navy*] (MCD)
SWTC	Stop War Toys Campaign (EA)
SWTG	Switching (WGA)
SwtGas	Southwest Gas Corp. [*Associated Press*] (SAG)
SWTI	Special Weapons Technical Instructions [*Army*] (AABC)
SWTL	Surface Wave Transmission Line
SWTMA	Scottish Woollen Trade Mark Association (DBA)
SwtPS	Southwestern Public Service Co. [*Associated Press*] (SAG)

SWTR .... Surface Water Treatment Rule [*Environmental Protection Agency*]
SWTS.......... Secondary Waste Treatment System [*Nuclear energy*] (NRCH)
SWTT.......... Single-Well Tracer Test [*Petroleum technology*]
SWTTEU ...... Special Weapons Test and Tactical Evaluation Unit
SWTX .... Southwall Technologies [*NASDAQ symbol*] (TTSB)
SWTX .... Southwall Technologies, Inc. [*NASDAQ symbol*] (NQ)
SWTZ .... Switzerland
SWU .... Idaho Falls, ID [*Location identifier FAA*] (FAAL)
SWU .... Sagami Women's University [*UTLAS symbol*]
SWU .... Separative Work Unit [*Measure of uranium enrichment capability*]
SWU .... Septic Workup [*Bacteriology*] (DAVI)
SWU .... Slovenian Women's Union (EA)
SWU .... Special Wash Up [*Printing*] (DGA)
SWU .... Standard Work Unit (EG)
SWU .... Steelhawk Resources Ltd. [*Vancouver Stock Exchange symbol*]
SWUCNET..... Southwest Universities Computer Network (NITA)
SWULANT..... Special Weapons Unit, Atlantic [*Navy*] (DNAB)
SWULSCP .... Southwest University Libraries Systems Cooperative Project (NITA)
SwUmU........ Umea Universitetsbibliotek, Umea, Sweden [*Library symbol Library of Congress*] (LCLS)
SWUPAC...... Special Weapons Unit, Pacific [*Navy*] (DNAB)
SWUS .... Southwest United States
SWUSL .... Southwestern University School of Law (DLA)
SwUU......... Universitet i Uppsala [*University of Uppsala*], Uppsala, Sweden [*Library symbol Library of Congress*] (LCLS)
SWV........... Squarewave Voltammetry [*Electrochemistry*]
SWV........... Swan View [*Australia Seismograph station code, US Geological Survey*] (SEIS)
SWV........... Swivel (AAG)
SWVA......... Scottish War Veterans of America (EA)
SWVA......... Shemya WWII Veterans Association (EA)
SWVA......... Steel of West Virginia [*NASDAQ symbol*] (TTSB)
SWVA......... Steel of West Virginia, Inc. [*NASDAQ symbol*] (NQ)
SWVA......... Steel West Virginia [*NASDAQ symbol*] (SAG)
SWVB......... Social Work Vocational Bureau (EA)
SWVL......... Swivel (MSA)
SWVR........ Standing Wave Voltage Ratio [*Electronics*] (IAA)
SWW........ Intersun Havacilik Anonim Sirketi [*Turkey*] [*FAA designator*] (FAAC)
SWW........ Severe Weather Warning (KSC)
SWW........ Society of Women Writers (DGA)
SWW........ Soft White Winter [*Wheat*] (OA)
SWW........ Stow Resources [*Vancouver Stock Exchange symbol*]
SWW........ Sweetwater [*Texas*] [*Airport symbol*] (AD)
SWW........ Sweetwater, TX [*Location identifier FAA*] (FAAL)
SWW........ Winthrop College, Rock Hill, SC [*OCLC symbol*] (OCLC)
SWWA........ South-West Water Authority [*British*] (DCTA)
SwWatr....... Southwest Water Co. [*Associated Press*] (SAG)
SWWBDS..... Software Work Breakdown Structure (MCD)
SWWBS ..... Software Work Breakdown Structure
SWWC .... Southwest Water Co. [*La Puente, CA*] [*NASDAQ symbol*] (NQ)
SWWF .... Speed-Welding Wire Feeder
SWWJ......... Society of Women Writers and Journalists (DGA)
SWWOAH..... Society of World War One Aero Historians [*Defunct*] (EA)
SWWT........ SweetWater, Inc. [*NASDAQ symbol*] (SAG)
SWWU .... Singapore Wood Workers' Union
SWX.......... Southwest Gas [*NYSE symbol*] (TTSB)
SWX.......... Southwest Gas Corp. [*NYSE symbol*] (SPSG)
SWXO........ Staff Weather Officer [*NASA*] (KSC)
SWXPrA...... So West Gas Cap 1 9.125%'TOPrS' [*NYSE symbol*] (TTSB)
SWY.......... Albemarle, NC [*Location identifier FAA*] (FAAL)
SWY.......... Safeway, Inc. [*NYSE symbol*] (SPSG)
SWY.......... Skyway Business Travel Ltd. [*British ICAO designator*] (FAAC)
SWY.......... Stopway
SWY.......... Stornaway Resources Corp. [*Vancouver Stock Exchange symbol*]
SWY.......... Swiss Yiddish (BJA)
SWY.WS...... Safeway Inc. Wrrts [*NYSE symbol*] (TTSB)
SWZ.......... Smyrna, TN [*Location identifier FAA*] (FAAL)
SWZ.......... Special Watch Zone [*Navy*] (NVT)
SWZ.......... Swaziland [*ANSI three-letter standard code*] (CNC)
SWZ.......... Swiss Helvetia Fund [*NYSE symbol*] (SPSG)
SWZA........ Suiza Foods [*NASDAQ symbol*] (TTSB)
SWZA........ Suiza Foods Corp. [*NASDAQ symbol*] (SAG)
Swzld........ Swaziland (VRA)
SX............ Christman Air System [*ICAO designator*] (AD)
SX............ Pia Societas Sancti Francisci Xaverii pro Exteris Missionibus [*St. Francis Xavier Foreign Mission Society*] [*Xaverian Missionary Fathers*] [*Roman Catholic religious order*]
SX............ Sacks
S-X............ SEC Regulations (EBF)
SX............ Sigma Xi [*Society*]
Sx............ Signs (DAVI)
SX............ Simplex [*Transmission direction*] (CET)
SX............ Simplex Signaling (IAA)
SX............ Society of St. Francis Xavier for the Foreign Missions [*Also known as Xaverian Missionaries*] (EAIO)
SX............ Solvent Extraction (DEN)
sx............ South West Africa [*Namibia*] [*MARC country of publication code Library of Congress*] (LCCP)
SX............ Stability Index (FAAC)
sx............ Suction [*Surgery*] (DAVI)
SX............ Surgeries (DAVI)
SX............ Sussex [*County in England*]
SX............ SXT Resources Ltd. [*Vancouver Stock Exchange symbol*]
Sx............ Symptoms [*Medicine*] (WGA)

SX............ Union of Soviet Socialist Republics [*Later, FC*] [*License plate code assigned to foreign diplomats in the US*]
SX............ Xaverian Missionary Fathers (TOCD)
sx............ Xaverian Missionary Fathers, St. Francis Xavier Mission Society (TOCD)
SX70.......... SX-70 (VRA)
SXA.......... Shannon Executive Aviation Ireland Ltd. [*ICAO designator*] (FAAC)
SXA.......... Stored Index to Address
SXAD......... Sioux Army Depot
SXAP .... Soft X-Ray Appearance Potential (IAA)
SXAPS........ Soft X-Ray Appearance Potential Spectrometer [*or Spectroscopy*]
SXB........... Strasbourg [*France*] [*Airport symbol*] (OAG)
SXBT......... Shipboard Expendable Bathythermograph [*System*] [*Naval Oceanographic Office*]
SXC........... Saint Xavier College [*Chicago, IL*]
SXC........... Santa Catalina, CA [*Location identifier FAA*] (FAAL)
SXC........... Santa Catalina Island [*California*] [*Airport symbol*] (AD)
SXCT......... Spiral X-Ray Computed Tomography [*Medicine*] (DMAA)
SXD........... Springfield, VT [*Location identifier FAA*] (FAAL)
SXD........... Store Index in Decrement (SAA)
SXE........... Sale [*Australia Airport symbol*] (OAG)
SXE........... Soft X-Ray Experiment [*Also, SXX*]
SXE........... Spencar Explorations Ltd. [*Vancouver Stock Exchange symbol*]
SXEW........ Solvent Extraction and Electrowinning [*Metallurgy*]
SXF........... Berlin [*Germany Airport symbol*] (OAG)
SXF........... Solvent Extraction Feed [*Nuclear energy*] (NRCH)
SXG........... Senanga [*Zambia*] [*Airport symbol*] (OAG)
SXH........... Sehulea [*Papua New Guinea*] [*Airport symbol*] (OAG)
SXI........... Software Extraordinaire, Inc. [*Telecommunications service*] (TSSD)
SXI........... Solar X-Ray Imager [*Marine science*] (OSRA)
SXI........... Standex International Corp. [*NYSE symbol*] (SPSG)
SXI........... Standex Intl [*NYSE symbol*] (TTSB)
SXI........... Synex International, Inc. [*Toronto Stock Exchange symbol*]
SXIS.......... Scattered X-Ray Internal Standard [*for surface analysis*]
SXL........... Sexless [*Connector*]
SXL........... Short-Arc Xenon Lamp
SXL........... Soft X-Ray LASER
SXL........... Summersville, WV [*Location identifier FAA*] (FAAL)
SXM.......... Scanning X-Ray Microscopy (MCD)
SXM.......... Sint Maarten [*Netherlands Antilles*] [*Airport symbol*] (AD)
SXM.......... Sphinx Mining Inc. [*Vancouver Stock Exchange symbol*]
SXM.......... St. Maarten [*Netherlands Antilles*] [*Airport symbol*]
SXML......... San Xavier Mining Laboratory [*University of Arizona*] [*Research center*] (RCD)
SXMTX........ SMBS Tax Exempt Cl.B [*Mutual fund ticker symbol*] (SG)
SXN.......... Sal Luftverkehrs GmbH, Flughafen Leipzig-Halle [*Germany*] [*FAA designator*] (FAAC)
SXN.......... Sao Jose Do Xingu [*Brazil*] [*Airport symbol*] (OAG)
SXN.......... Section (MDG)
SXO .... Senior Experimental Officer [*Also, SEO, SExO*] [*Ministry of Agriculture, Fisheries, and Food*] [*British*]
SXP........... Sheldon Point [*Alaska*] [*Airport symbol*] (OAG)
SXP........... Sunnyvale Public Library, Sunnyvale, CA [*OCLC symbol*] (OCLC)
SXPL......... Soft X-Ray Projection Lithography
SXPS .... Soft X-Ray Photoelectron Spectroscopy (AAEL)
SXQ........... Soldotna, AK [*Location identifier FAA*] (FAAL)
SXR........... Soft X-Ray Region
SXR........... Srinagar [*India*] [*Airport symbol*] (OAG)
SXRB......... Soft X-Ray Background [*Astronomy*]
SXRF......... Synchrotron X-Ray Fluorescence [*Spectrometry*]
SXRT......... Soft X-Ray Telescope (SSD)
SXS........... Gunes Ekspres Havacilik AS (Sunexpress) [*Turkey*] [*ICAO designator*] (FAAC)
SXS........... Sigma Xi Society
SXS........... Stellar X-Ray Spectra
SXS........... Step by Step Switch (NITA)
SxS........... Step-by-Step Switching System [*Telecommunications*]
SXS........... Surface X-Ray Scattering [*Physics*]
SXT........... Lehman Br G1 Tele'SUNS'2000 [*AMEX symbol*] (TTSB)
SXT........... Lehman Brothers, Inc. [*AMEX symbol*] (SAG)
SXT........... Sextant (NASA)
SXT........... Sexton Summit, OR [*Location identifier FAA*] (FAAL)
SXT........... Sextuple (MSA)
SXT........... Soft X-Ray Telescope [*Astronomy*] (PS)
SXT........... Stable X-Ray Transmitter
SXTF......... Sulfamethoxazole [*An antibacterial*] (DAVI)
SXTF......... Satellite X-Ray Test Facility
SXTN .... Sextant (MSA)
SXU........... Soddu [*Ethiopia*] [*Airport symbol*] (AD)
SXX........... Satellite Aero, Inc. [*ICAO designator*] (FAAC)
SXX........... Soft X-Ray Experiment [*Also, SXE*]
SXY........... Sidney [*New York*] [*Airport symbol*] (OAG)
SY............ Air Alsace [*ICAO designator*] (AD)
SY............ School Year (AABC)
SY............ Search Year (NITA)
SY............ Security
SY............ Sefer Yezirah (BJA)
SY............ Seychelles
SY............ Shelby Williams Ind [*NYSE symbol*] (TTSB)
SY............ Shelby Williams Industries, Inc. [*NYSE symbol*] (SPSG)
SY............ Shipyard
SY............ Shoulder Yaw (MCD)
SY............ Shropshire Yeomanry [*British military*] (DMA)
SY............ Sloppy [*Track condition*] [*Thoroughbred racing*]
SY............ Southern Yiddish (BJA)

SY	Spectroscopy [Medicine] (DMAA)
SY	Spring Yearling
SY	Square Yard
SY	Staff Years (OICC)
SY	Steam Yacht (ROG)
SY	Sticky (WGA)
SY	Stripping Yield [Agriculture] (OA)
SY	Supply [Business term]
SY	Surrey [County in England]
SY	Survey
SY	Sussex Yeomanry [British military] (DMA)
SY	Sustainer Yaw (AAG)
SY	Symbol (IAA)
Sy	Symmachus (BJA)
SY	Symmetry [or Symmetrical] (DAVI)
Sy	Symptoms [Medicine]
SY	Synchronized (MDG)
SY	Synchronoscope (IAA)
Sy	Synchronous System [on a ship] (DS)
SY	Synonyms (NITA)
SY	Syphilis [Medicine]
SY	Syphilitic [Medicine] (DMAA)
SY	Syracuse [Diocesan abbreviation] [New York] (TOCD)
SY	Syria [or Syrian Arab Republic] [ANSI two-letter standard code] (CNC)
sy	Syria [MARC country of publication code Library of Congress] (LCCP)
SY	Syrup (WGA)
SY	System
SYA	Save Your Afterdeck [Bowdlerized version]
SYA	Scandinavian Yachting Association [See also SKAN SF] (EAIO)
SYA	Shemya Island [Alaska] [Airport symbol] (OAG)
SYA	Subacute Yellow Atrophy (DB)
SYA	Subud Youth Association (EA)
SYADS	Syracuse Air Defense Sector (SAA)
SYAH	Aishalton [Guyana] [ICAO location identifier] (ICLI)
SYAN	Annai [Guyana] [ICAO location identifier] (ICLI)
SY & LI	Sherwood Yeomanry and Light Infantry [British military] (DMA)
SYAP	Apoteri [Guyana] [ICAO location identifier] (ICLI)
SYAW	Awaruwaunawa [Guyana] [ICAO location identifier] (ICLI)
SYB	Seal Bay [Alaska] [Airport symbol] (OAG)
SYB	Statesman's Yearbook [A publication]
SYB	Sybron International Co. [Formerly, Sybron Corp.] [NYSE symbol] (SAG)
SYB	Sybron Intl [NYSE symbol] (TTSB)
SYB	Symbol [Spain ICAO designator] (FAAC)
SYB	Syracuse University, Syracuse, NY [OCLC symbol] (OCLC)
SYBA	S.Y. Bancorp [NASDAQ symbol] (SAG)
Sybase	Sybase, Inc. [Associated Press] (SAG)
SY Bcp	S.Y. Bancorp [Associated Press] (SAG)
SYBF	Share Your Birthday Foundation [Defunct] (EA)
SyblTc	Symbol Technologies, Inc. [Associated Press] (SAG)
SYBR	Baramita [Guyana] [ICAO location identifier] (ICLI)
Svbron	Sybron Chemical Industries [Associated Press] (SAG)
SybronInt	Sybron International Co. [Formerly, Sybron Corp.] [Associated Press] (SAG)
SYBS	Sybase, Inc. [NASDAQ symbol] (SPSG)
SYBT	Bartica [Guyana] [ICAO location identifier] (ICLI)
SYC	Sanday [Scotland] [Airport symbol] (AD)
SYC	Seychelles [ANSI three-letter standard code] (CNC)
SYC	Small, Yellow, Constipated [Stool] [Gastroenterology] (DAVI)
SYC	Spartacus Youth Club (EA)
SYC	Swedish Export Credit Corp. [AMEX symbol] (SAG)
SYC	Sycamore (AAG)
SYC	Symbol Correspondence Element [Computer science] (PCM)
SYC	Symbolic Corrector (SAA)
SYC	Synco Development [Vancouver Stock Exchange symbol]
SYCATE	Symptom-Cause-Test
SYCLOPS	SYFA Concurrent Logic Operating System
SYCLOPS	SYFA Current Logic Operating System (NITA)
SYCM	Sybron Chemicals [NASDAQ symbol] (TTSB)
SYCM	Sybron Chemicals, Inc. [NASDAQ symbol] (SPSG)
SYCOM	Sydney Computerised Overnight Market [Australia]
SYCOM	Synchronous Communications [Satellite] [GSFC]
SYCOM	Systems Command
SYCOSPARE	Shipyard Checkout Spare
SYCOT	Shipyard Checkout Test
SYCR	Sychronize (IAA)
SYD	Air Yendis Ltd. [Zambia] [FAA designator] (FAAC)
SYD	Casper, WY [Location identifier FAA] (FAAL)
SYD	Release Subject Your Discretion (FAAC)
SYD	Scheer Energy Development Corp. [Vancouver Stock Exchange symbol]
SYD	Scotland Yard
SYD	Shipyard
SYD	South Yemen Dinar (BJA)
SYD	Sum of the Year's Digits [Statistics]
SYD	Sydney [Australia Seismograph station code, US Geological Survey Closed] (SEIS)
SYDAS	System Data Acquisition System
SYDEC	Selective Yield Delayed Coking [Foster Wheeler USA Corp. process]
SYDIA	System Developer Interface Activity [Computer science]
Syd Inst Crim Proc	University of Sydney Faculty of Law. Proceedings of the Institute of Criminology [A publication]
Sydney Univ Gaz	Sydney University. Gazette [A publication]
Sydney Univ Rev	Sydney University. Review [A publication]
SYDP	Six-Year Defense Plan [Used briefly from the late 1980s to 1991] (DOMA)
Syd R	Sydney Review [A publication]
SYE	Sa'Dah [Yemen Arab Republic] [Airport symbol] (OAG)
SYE	Sheba Aviation [Yemen] [FAA designator] (FAAC)
SYE	Square Yards Equivalent (DICI)
SYE	Symbol Element [Computer science] (PCM)
SYEB	Ebini [Guyana] [ICAO location identifier] (ICLI)
SYEP	Summer Youth Employment Program [Department of Labor]
SYEP	Symmetrical Disubstituted Ethoxy Propane [Organic chemistry] (MCD)
SYERS	Senior Year Electro-optical Reconnaissance System [Air Force] (DOMA)
SYF	Sky One Express Airlines, Inc. [ICAO designator] (FAAC)
SYF	Spiritualist Yoga Fellowship (EAIO)
SYF	St. Francis, KS [Location identifier FAA] (FAAL)
SYFA	System for Access [Computer science] (IAA)
SYFA	System for Application [Computer science]
SYFANET	System for Access Network [Wespac] (TSSD)
SYG	Arcola, TX [Location identifier FAA] (FAAL)
SYG	Secretary-General (NATG)
SYG	Symbol Graph [Computer science] (PCM)
SYG	Synergy International [Vancouver Stock Exchange symbol]
SYGA	Systems Gauge [Tool] (AAG)
SYGC	Georgetown [Guyana] [ICAO location identifier] (ICLI)
SYGH	Good Hope [Guyana] [ICAO location identifier] (ICLI)
SYGO	Ogle [Guyana] [ICAO location identifier] (ICLI)
SYGR	Synagro Technologies, Inc. [NASDAQ symbol] (SAG)
SYGRU	Synagro Tech Unit [NASDAQ symbol] (TTSB)
SYGRW	Synagro Technologies Wrrt [NASDAQ symbol] (TTSB)
SYGT	Georgetown [Guyana] [ICAO location identifier] (ICLI)
SYH	Scottish & York Holdings Ltd. [Toronto Stock Exchange symbol]
SYH	See You Home [Teen slang]
Syh	Syrohexapla (BJA)
SYHA	Scottish Youth Hostels Association
SYI	Shelbyville [Tennessee] [Airport symbol] (AD)
SYI	Shelbyville, TN [Location identifier FAA] (FAAL)
SYI	Symes Resources [Vancouver Stock Exchange symbol]
SYI	System Industries (EFIS)
SYIB	Imbaimadai [Guyana] [ICAO location identifier] (ICLI)
SYJ	Slate Falls Airways Ltd. [Canada ICAO designator] (FAAC)
SYK	Skyhawk Resources, Inc. [Vancouver Stock Exchange symbol]
SYK	Stykkisholmur [Iceland] [Airport symbol] (OAG)
SYKA	Kaieteur [Guyana] [ICAO location identifier] (ICLI)
SYKE	Sukes Enterprises [NASDAQ symbol] (TTSB)
SYKE	Sykes Enterprises Inc. [NASDAQ symbol] (SAG)
SykesEn	Sykes Enterprises Inc. [Associated Press] (SAG)
SYKI	Kaow Island [Guyana] [ICAO location identifier] (ICLI)
SYKK	Kurukabaru [Guyana] [ICAO location identifier] (ICLI)
SYKM	Kamarang [Guyana] [ICAO location identifier] (ICLI)
SYKR	Karanambo [Guyana] [ICAO location identifier] (ICLI)
SYKS	Karasabai [Guyana] [ICAO location identifier] (ICLI)
SYKT	Kato (Karto) [Guyana] [ICAO location identifier] (ICLI)
SYKW	Kwakwani [Guyana] [ICAO location identifier] (ICLI)
SYL	Salvation Army Youth Line [Australia]
SYL	San Miguel, CA [Location identifier FAA] (FAAL)
SYL	Somali Youth League [Political party] (AF)
SYL	Spartacus Youth League (EA)
Syl	[The] Syllabi [A publication] (DLA)
SYL	Syllable (ADA)
SYL	Syllabus (WDAA)
SYLCU	Synchronous Line Control Unit [Computer science] (MHDI)
SYLD	Linden [Guyana] [ICAO location identifier] (ICLI)
SYLK	Symbolic Link [Data format]
SYLK file	Symbolic Link File [Computer science]
SYLL	Syllable
SYLN	Sylvan, Inc. [NASDAQ symbol] (SAG)
SYLP	Lumid Pau [Guyana] [ICAO location identifier] (ICLI)
SYLP	Support Your Local Police
SYLT	Lethem [Guyana] [ICAO location identifier] (ICLI)
Sylvan	Sylvan Foods Holdings, Inc. [Associated Press] (SAG)
SylvnLrn	Sylvan Learning Systems [Commercial firm Associated Press] (SAG)
SYM	Salesian Youth Movement (EA)
SYM	Secondary Yield Measurement
SYM	Seymour Resources [Vancouver Stock Exchange symbol]
SYM	Simao [China] [Airport symbol] (OAG)
SYM	Symbiont
SYM	Symbol [or Symbolic] (AAG)
sym	Symbol (IDOE)
Sym	Symmachus' Greek Translation of the Bible [A publication] (BJA)
sym	Symmetrical [Also, s] [Chemistry]
SYM	Symmetry
sym	Symmetry (IDOE)
sym	Symphony (WDAA)
SYM	Symphony
Sym	Symphony Recording Co. [Record label]
sym	Symptom [Medicine] (CPH)
SYM	Syms Corp. [NYSE symbol] (SPSG)
SYM	System (MDG)
SYMAN	Symbol Manipulation [Computer science]
SYM/ANNOT	Symbology Annotation (MCD)
SYMAP	Synagraphic Mapping System [Computer-made maps]
SYMB	Mabaruma [Guyana] [ICAO location identifier] (ICLI)
SYMB	Symbol

Symb	Symbollon Corp. [*Associated Press*] (SAG)
SYMBA	Symbollon Corp. [*NASDAQ symbol*] (TTSB)
SYMBAL	Symbolic Algebraic Language [*Computer science*]
SYMBAS	Symbolization All Series (ADA)
Symbl	Symbollon Corp. [*Associated Press*] (SAG)
SYMBOL	System for Mass Balancing in Off-line (IAA)
SYMBOLANG	Symbolic Manipulation Language [*Computer science*] (CSR)
Symboln	Symbollon Corp. [*Associated Press*] (SAG)
Symb Philol Danielsson	Symbolae Philologicae [*O. A.*] Danielsson Octogenario Dicatae [*Uppsala*] [*A publication*] (OCD)
SYMBUG	Symbolic Debugger [*Computer science*] (MHDI)
SYMBW	Symbollon Corp. Wrrt'A' [*NASDAQ symbol*] (TTSB)
SYMBZ	Symbollon Corp. Wrrt'B' [*NASDAQ symbol*] (TTSB)
SYMC	Symantec Corp. [*NASDAQ symbol*] (NQ)
SyMC	Syracuse Microfilm Co., Syracuse, NY [*Library symbol*] [*Library of Congress*] (LCLS)
Sym Code	Syms' Code of English Law [*1870*] [*A publication*] (DLA)
SYMD	Mahdia [*Guyana*] [*ICAO location identifier*] (ICLI)
SYMDEB	Symbolic Debugger [*Also, sdb, SOLD*] [*Computer science*]
Syme	Syme's Scotch Justiciary Reports [*1826-30*] [*A publication*] (DLA)
SYMES	Systematic Machinery and Equipment Selection (PDAA)
Symetr	Symetrics Industries, Inc. [*Associated Press*] (SAG)
Symetric	Symmetricom, Inc. [*Associated Press*] (SAG)
SYMEVETOPHARSA	Syndicat des Medecins, Veterinaires, Pharmaciens, et Sages Femmes Africains du Mali [*Union of African Doctors, Pharmacists, Midwives, and Veterinarians of the Mali Federation*]
Symf	Symfoni & Artist [*Record label*] [*Sweden*]
SYMGR	Sympalmograph (VRA)
SYMGUG	Symbolic Debugger [*Computer science*] (CIST)
Symix	Symix Systems [*Associated Press*] (SAG)
SYMM	Monkey Mountain [*Guyana*] [*ICAO location identifier*] (ICLI)
SYMM	Symmetrical (MSA)
SYMM	Symmetricom, Inc. [*NASDAQ symbol*] (SAG)
SYMMOD	Symbolic Modeling [*Computer science*]
SYMMTRAC	Sylvania Multimode Tracking [*Aerospace*] (MCD)
SYMN	Manari [*Guyana*] [*ICAO location identifier*] (ICLI)
Symntc	Symantec Corp. [*Associated Press*] (SAG)
SYMP	Mountain Point [*Guyana*] [*ICAO location identifier*] (ICLI)
Symp	Symposium [*of Plato*] [*Classical studies*] (OCD)
SYMP	Symposium (MSA)
SYMP	Symptom [*Medicine*] (AAMN)
SYMPAC	Symbolic Program for Automatic Control
sympat	Sympathetic [*Neurology*]
sympath	Sympathetic [*Neurology*] (DAVI)
SYMPH	Symphony (ADA)
SYMPLE	Syntax Macro Preprocessor for Language Evaluation [*Computer science*] (PDAA)
Symposum Jun Bar	Symposium. Association de Jeune Barreau de Montreal [*A publication*] (DLA)
sympt	Symptom [*Medicine*]
SYMR	Matthews Ridge [*Guyana*] [*ICAO location identifier*] (ICLI)
SYMRO	System Management Research Operation (DIT)
SYMS	Secondary Yield Measurement System
SymsCp	Syms Corp. [*Associated Press*] (SAG)
SYMT	Symetrics Industries [*NASDAQ symbol*] (TTSB)
SYMT	Symetrics Industries, Inc. [*NASDAQ symbol*] (NQ)
SYMW	Maruranawa [*Guyana*] [*ICAO location identifier*] (ICLI)
SYMWAR	System for Estimating Wartime Attrition and Replacement Requirements (AABC)
SYMX	Symix Systems [*NASDAQ symbol*] (SPSG)
SYN	Stanton, MN [*Location identifier FAA*] (FAAL)
SYN	Synagogue
SYN	Synaptec, a Knowledge Engineering Corp. [*Vancouver Stock Exchange symbol*]
Syn	Synbiotics Corp.
SYN	Synchronize (IAA)
SYN	Synchronous (AAG)
SYN	Synchronous Idle [*Transmission control character*] [*Computer science*]
SYN	Syncrude Canada Ltd. [*ICAO designator*] (FAAC)
SYN	Syndicate (ROG)
SYN	Synergist (WGA)
SYN	Synod
SYN	Synonym
Syn	Synopsis (DLA)
syn	Synovial [*Fluid*] [*Medicine*]
syn	Synovitis [*Medicine*]
SYN	Syntex Corp., Palo Alto, CA [*OCLC symbol*] (OCLC)
SYN	Synthesizer
SYN	Synthetic (AAG)
SYN	Syntype
SYNA	New Amsterdam [*Guyana*] [*ICAO location identifier*] (ICLI)
SYNAC	Synthesis of Aircraft (MCD)
Synagro	Synagro Technologies, Inc. [*Associated Press*] (SAG)
Synaloy	Synalloy Corp. [*Associated Press*] (SAG)
SynapPhm	Synaptic Pharmaceutical Corp. [*Associated Press*] (SAG)
SYNAPSE	CUEA Synthesis and Publication Segment [*Marine science*] (MSC)
SYNBAPS	Synthetic Bathymetric Profiling System [*Naval Oceanographic Office*]
Synbio	Synbiotics Corp. [*Associated Press*] (SAG)
SYNC	Synalloy Corp. [*NASDAQ symbol*] (SAG)
SYNC	Synchromechanism
sync	Synchronism (IDOE)
sync	Synchronization (IDOE)
SYNC	Synchronize (AAG)
SYNC	Synchronizing Character [*Computer science*] (IAA)

sync	Synchrony
SYNCCODE	Synchronization Code (IAA)
SYNCD	Synchronized (AAG)
SYNCELL	Synthetic Cell [*Biological research*]
SYNCG	Synchronizing (AAG)
SYNCH	Synchronize
SYNCH	Synchronous Transmission [*Computer science*] (TSSD)
SYNCIN	Synchronization Input [*Computer science*] (IAA)
SYNCOM	Synchronous Communications [*Hughes Aircraft Co.*]
SYNCOM	Synchronous Communication Satellite [*Telecommunications*] (IAA)
SYNCOM	Synchronous-Orbiting Communications Satellite [*GSFC*]
Syncor	Syncor International Corp. [*Associated Press*] (SAG)
SYNCOUT	Synchronization Output (IAA)
SYNCR	Synchronizer (AAG)
SyncRes	Sync Research, Inc. [*Associated Press*] (SAG)
SYNCRO	Synchromesh [*Automotive engineering*]
SYNCRUDE	Synthetic Crude
SYNCS	Synchronous (AAG)
SYNCSCP	Synchronoscope (IAA)
SYND	Syndicate
Synd	Syndicate (EBF)
synd	Syndicate (WDMC)
Synd	Syndication (TBD)
synd	Syndrome [*Medicine*]
SYNDARC	Standard Format for Exchange of MAPMOPP Data among Data Centers (MSC)
syndet	Synthetic Detergent (BARN)
SYNDETS	Synthetic Detergents
SYNDEX	Syndicated Exclusivity [*FCC*]
SYNEC	Synecdoche (WDAA)
SYNEP	Syntech International, Inc. (MHDW)
SYNESCI	Syndicat National des Enseignants du Second Degre de Cote d'Ivoire
Synetic	Synetic, Inc. [*Associated Press*] (SAG)
syn fl	Synovial Fluid [*Medicine*] (MAE)
SYNFRQ	Synthesizer Frequency
synfuel	Synthetic Fuel (BARN)
SYNFUELS	Synthetic Fuels
syngas	Synthetic Gas (BARN)
SYNGLISH	Synthetic English (MHDI)
Syngro	Synagro Technologies, Inc. [*Associated Press*] (SAG)
SYNH	Synergistic Hldg [*NASDAQ symbol*] (TTSB)
SYNH	Synergistic Holding Corp. [*NASDAQ symbol*] (SAG)
SynHld	Synergistic Holding Corp. [*Associated Press*] (SAG)
SynHold	Synergistic Holding Corp. [*Associated Press*] (SAG)
SYNHW	Synergistic Hldg Wrrt [*NASDAQ symbol*] (TTSB)
SYNL	Syntellect, Inc. [*NASDAQ symbol*] (SAG)
SYNMAS	Synchronous Missile Alarm System
SYNON	Synonym (ROG)
SYNOP	Synopsis (AABC)
synop	Synopsis (WDAA)
SYNOP	Synoptic (FAAC)
Synopsy	Synopsys, Inc. [*Associated Press*] (SAG)
Synovus	Synovus Financial Corp. [*Associated Press*] (SAG)
Synpt	Synoptic [*or Synoptist*] (BJA)
SYNRAMS	Synoptic Random Access Measurement System (NOAA)
SYNROC	Synthetic Rock [*For storage of nuclear waste*]
SYNS	Synopsis (MSA)
SYNSCP	Synchroscope (KSC)
SYNSEM	Syntax and Semantics (IEEE)
Syn Ser	Synopsis Series of the United States Treasury Decisions [*A publication*] (DLA)
SYNSOC	Synergetic Society (EA)
SYNSPADE	Symposium on the Numerical Solution of Partial Differential Equations [*Book title, Academic Press*]
SYNT	Syntel [*Stock market symbol*]
synt	Synthetic (VRA)
SYNT	Synthetic
SYNTAC	Synthetic Tactics
SYNTEEDISETO	Syndicat des Travailleurs de l'Energie Electrique et de Distribution d'Eau du Togo [*Union of Electrical and Water Distribution Workers of Togo*]
SYNTH	Synthesizer
synth	Synthesizer (WDAA)
SYNTH	Synthetic
Synthe	Synthetech, Inc. [*Associated Press*] (SAG)
SYNTI	Synchro Tie
SYNTIRT	Syndicat des Travailleurs des Industries Reunies du Togo [*Union of Workers of United Industries of Togo*]
Syntlct	Syntellect, Inc. [*Associated Press*] (SAG)
SYNTOL	Syntagmatic Organization Language [*Computer science*]
SYNTRAN	Syntax Translation [*Computer science*] (DIT)
SYNV	Sonchus Yellow Net Virus [*Plant pathology*]
SYNX	Sync Research [*NASDAQ symbol*] (TTSB)
SYNX	Sync Research, Inc. [*NASDAQ symbol*] (SAG)
SYNZYMES	Synthetic Enzymes
SYO	Sayre, OK [*Location identifier FAA*] (FAAL)
SYO	Skygold Resources [*Vancouver Stock Exchange symbol*]
SYO	Syowa [*Ongul*] [*Antarctica*] [*Seismograph station code, US Geological Survey*] (SEIS)
SYO	Syowa Base [*Antarctica*] [*Geomagnetic observatory code*]
SYOR	Orinduik [*Guyana*] [*ICAO location identifier*] (ICLI)
SYP	Parkland Regional Library, Yorkton, Saskatchewan [*Library symbol National Library of Canada*] (NLC)
SYP	Santa Ynez Peak [*California*] [*Seismograph station code, US Geological Survey*] (SEIS)

SYP	Simplicity Pattern Co., Inc. (EFIS)
SYP	Society of Young Publishers (DGA)
SYP	Southern Yellow Pine
SYP	Suomen Yksityisyrittaejaein Puoluejaerjesto [*Finnish Private Entrepreneurs' Party*] [*Political party*] (PPE)
SYP	Swedish Export Credit Corp. [*AMEX symbol*] (SAG)
Syp	Syropalaestinum (BJA)
SYPH	Syphilis (DSUE)
Syph	Syphilology [*or Syphilologist*] [*Medicine*] (DAVI)
Sy PO	Supply Petty Officer [*British military*] (DMA)
SYPR	Paruima [*Guyana*] [*ICAO location identifier*] (ICLI)
SyQstTc	SyQuest Technology, Inc. [*Associated Press*] (SAG)
SYQT	SyQuest Technology [*NASDAQ symbol*] (TTSB)
SYQT	SyQuest Technology, Inc. [*NASDAQ symbol*] (SPSG)
syr	Sirop [*Syrup*] [*Pharmacy*]
SYR	Smyrna [*Washington*] [*Seismograph station code, US Geological Survey*] (SEIS)
SYR	South Yorkshire Railway [*British*] (ROG)
SYR	Syracuse [*New York*] [*Airport symbol*]
SYR	Syratech Corp. [*NYSE symbol*] (SPSG)
SYR	Syria [*or Syrian Arab Republic*] [*ANSI three-letter standard code*] (CNC)
Syr	Syria (VRA)
syr	Syriac [*MARC language code Library of Congress*] (LCCP)
SYR	Syrian [*Language, etc.*] (ROG)
Syr	Syrian (WDAA)
SYR	Syrian Arab Airlines [*ICAO designator*] (FAAC)
SYR	Syrian Hamster [*Medicine*] (DMAA)
SYR	Syringe [*Medicine*]
SYR	Syrupus [*Syrup*] [*Pharmacy*]
SYRACUSE	System of Radio Communications Using a Satellite [*Telecommunications*] (TSSD)
Syracuse J Int'l L	Syracuse Journal of International Law [*A publication*] (DLA)
Syracuse U	Syracuse University (GAGS)
Syratch	Syratech Corp. [*Associated Press*] (SAG)
Syr D	De Syria Dea [*of Lucian*] [*Classical studies*] (OCD)
SyrH	Hexaplaric Syriac (BJA)
SYRIUS	Symbolic Representations for Image Understanding System (MHDI)
SYRP	Summer Youth Recreation Program
SYRUCL	Syracuse University College of Law (DLA)
SyrW	Syriac Version in Walton's Polyglot (BJA)
SYS	See Your Service (FAAC)
SYS	Shawbury FTU [*British ICAO designator*] (FAAC)
SYS	Sobeys Stores Ltd. [*Toronto Stock Exchange symbol*]
SYS	Somerset, PA [*Location identifier FAA*] (FAAL)
SYS	Sterile Concepts [*NYSE symbol*] (TTSB)
SYS	Sterile Concepts Holdings, Inc. [*NYSE symbol*] (SAG)
SYS	Stretching-Yawning Syndrome [*Medicine*] (DMAA)
SYS	Sweet Yet Simple [*Computer science*]
SYS	Synthocowork Schwarzheide [*Former East German chemical company*] (ECON)
SYS	System (AFM)
Sys	System (AL)
sys	Systemic [*Medicine*] (DAVI)
SYSAD	Systems Adviser
SYSADMIN	System Administrator [*Computer science*]
SYSCAP	System of Circuit Analysis Program
SYSCMA	System Core Image Library Maintenance Program [*Computer science*] (IAA)
Sysco	Sysco Corp. [*Associated Press*] (SAG)
SYSCOM	System Communications
SYSCOM	Systems Command [*Navy*]
SYSCON	Systems Control [*Military*] (AABC)
SYSCTLG	System Catalog [*Computer science*] (ECII)
SYSDEV	Systems Development (NOAA)
SYSEC	System Synthesizer and Evaluation Center
SYSEX	System Executive (MHDB)
SYSF	Systemsoft Corp. [*NASDAQ symbol*] (SAG)
SYSGEN	System Generator Program (NITA)
SYSGEN	Systems Generator [*or Generation*] [*Computer science*]
SYSIN	System Input [*Computer science*] (MDG)
SYSIPT	System Input Stream [*or Unit*] [*Computer science*] (MHDI)
SYSLIB	System Library [*Computer science*] (MDG)
SYSLOG	System Log [*Computer science*]
SYSM	Systemed [*NASDAQ symbol*] (SAG)
SYSM	SysteMed Inc. [*NASDAQ symbol*] (TTSB)
SYSMIN	System for Mineral Products [*European Community*] (MHDB)
SYSMIN	System for Safeguarding and Developing Mineral Production [*EC*] (ECED)
SYSOP	System Operator [*Computer networking*]
SYSOP	Systems Operator (EERA)
SYSOPO	System Programmed Operator [*Computer science*] (MHDB)
SYSOUT	System Output [*Computer science*] (IBMDP)
SYSP	Sixth-Year Specialist Program [*Library science*]
SYSPCH	System Punch [*Computer science*] (MHDI)
SYSPLLTM	System Purchase of Long Lead Time Material
SYSPM	System Performance Measure (MCD)
SYSPOP	System Programmed Operators [*Computer science*] (MDG)
SYSRDR	System Reader [*Computer science*] (MHDI)
SysReg	System Request [*Computer science*] (CDE)
SYSRES	System Residence [*Computer science*]
SYST	System
syst	Systemic [*Medicine*]
syst	Systolic [*Cardiology*]
SystCpt	Systems & Computer Technology Corp. [*Associated Press*] (SAG)

Systemix	Systemix, Inc. [*Associated Press*] (SAG)
SYSTEP	Systems Test and Evaluation Plan [*Military*] (AABC)
SYSTID	System Time-Domain Simulation Program [*Computer science*] (PDAA)
SYSTIM	Systematic Interaction Model (PDAA)
SYST M	Systolic Murmur [*Cardiology*] (BABM)
syst m	Systolic Murmur [*Cardiology*] (DAVI)
Systmd	Systemed, Inc. [*Associated Press*] (SAG)
SystmSft	Systemsoft Corp. [*Associated Press*] (SAG)
SYSTO	System Staff Office [*or Officer*]
SYSTRAN	Systems Analysis Translator [*Computer science*]
SYSTRAN	System Transatlantic [*Foreign language translator*] (EECA)
SystSft	System Software Associates [*Associated Press*] (SAG)
SystSftw	System Software Associates, Inc. [*Associated Press*] (SAG)
SYSTSW	System Software [*Computer science*] (IAA)
SYSVER	System Specification Verification (IEEE)
SYSX	Systems Exchange [*Computer science*] (IAA)
SYT	Sithe Energies USA, Inc. [*NYSE symbol*] (SPSG)
SYT	Sweet Young Thing [*An attractive girl*] [*Slang*]
SYT	Synaptotagmin [*Neurochemistry*]
SYTA	Sustained-Yield Tropical Agroecosystem
SYTM	Georgetown/Timehri Internacional [*Guyana*] [*ICAO location identifier*] (ICLI)
SYU	Sudanese Youth Union
SYU	Synchronization Signal Unit [*Telecommunications*]
SYU	Syuhurei [*South Korea*] [*Seismograph station code, US Geological Survey Closed*] (SEIS)
SYUS	Specialized Youth Units [*Canada*]
SYV	Saynor Varah, Inc. [*Toronto Stock Exchange symbol*]
SYV	Society for Young Victims [*Later, SYV/MCC*] (EA)
SYV	Solanum Yellows Virus [*Plant pathology*]
SYV	Sylvester, GA [*Location identifier FAA*] (FAAL)
SYV	Symbol Value [*Computer science*] (PCM)
SYV	Syva Research Library, Palo Alto, CA [*OCLC symbol*] (OCLC)
SYV/MCC	Society for Young Victims, Missing Children Center (EA)
SYVV	Sowthistle Yellow Vein Virus
SYW	Skyway Resources Ltd. [*Vancouver Stock Exchange symbol*]
SYWI	Wichabai [*Guyana*] [*ICAO location identifier*] (ICLI)
SYX	Astral Aviation, Inc. d/b/a Skyway Airlines [*FAA designator*] (FAAC)
SYY	Stornoway [*Scotland*] [*Airport symbol*] (OAG)
SYY	Sysco Corp. [*NYSE symbol*] (SPSG)
SYZ	Shelbyville, IL [*Location identifier FAA*] (FAAL)
SYZ	Shiraz [*Iran*] [*Airport symbol*] (OAG)
SZ	China Southwest Airlines [*ICAO designator*] (AD)
SZ	ProAir Services [*ICAO designator*] (AD)
SZ	Sceptre Investment Counsel Ltd. [*Toronto Stock Exchange symbol*]
sz	Schizophrenia [*Psychology*]
Sz	Schweizerische Landesbibliothek [*Swiss National Library*], Bern, Switzerland [*Library symbol Library of Congress*] (LCLS)
SZ	Secondary Zone
SZ	Seizure [*Telecommunications*] (TEL)
sz	Seizure [*Medicine*]
SZ	Sha'arei Zedek (BJA)
SZ	Size (IAA)
sz	Size (VRA)
SZ	Sizzler International [*NYSE symbol*] (SPSG)
SZ	Skevas-Zerfus [*Disease*] [*Medicine*] (DB)
SZ	Skin Impedance [*Neurology*] (DAVI)
SZ	Splash Zone
SZ	Sponsoring Organization Zip Code (NITA)
SZ	Streptozocin [*Antineoplastic drug*]
SZ	Subduction Zone [*Geology*]
SZ	Suction [*Surgery*] (DAVI)
SZ	Surface Zero [*Navy*] (NVT)
SZ	Surf Zone (DOMA)
SZ	Swaziland [*ANSI two-letter standard code*] (CNC)
sz	Switzerland [*MARC country of publication code Library of Congress*] (LCCP)
SZA	Aerolineac do El Salvador SA [*ICAO designator*] (FAAC)
SZA	Santo Antonio do Zaire [*Angola*] [*Airport symbol*] (AD)
SZA	Solar Zenith Angle [*Geophysics*]
SZA	Soyo [*Angola*] [*Airport symbol*] (OAG)
SZB	Santa Barbara [*Honduras*] [*Airport symbol*] (AD)
SZB	Silver-Zinc Battery
SZB	Sintered Zinc Battery
SZB	SouthFirst Bancshares [*AMEX symbol*] (TTSB)
SZB	Southfirst Bancshares, Inc. [*AMEX symbol*] (SAG)
SzBaL	Lonza Aktiengesellschaft, Zentralbibliothek, Basel, Switzerland [*Library symbol Library of Congress*] (LCLS)
SzBaM	Museum fur Volkerkunde und Schweizerisches Museum fur Volkskunde, Basel, Switzerland [*Library symbol Library of Congress*] (LCLS)
SzBaU	Universitat Basel, Basel, Switzerland [*Library symbol Library of Congress*] (LCLS)
SzBaU-IO	Institut fur Organische Chemie der Universitat Basel, Basel, Switzerland [*Library symbol Library of Congress*] (LCLS)
SZC	Silver-Zinc Cell
SZD	Sovetski Zhelezno-Dorozhni [*Soviet railways*] [*Former USSR*]
SZD	St. George, SC [*Location identifier FAA*] (FAAL)
SzDP	Magyarorszagi Szocialdemokrata Part [*Hungarian Social-Democratic Party*] [*Political party*] (EY)
SZDSZ	Alliance of Free Democrats [*Hungary Political party*]
SzDSz	Szabad Demokratak Szovetsege [*Alliance of Free Democrats*] [*Hungary Political party*] (EY)

SZE .... Szeged [Hungary] [Seismograph station code, US Geological Survey Closed] (SEIS)
SZEA .... Standard Zoning Enabling Act (PA)
SZEC .... Silver-Zinc Electrochemical Cell
SZECC .... Silver-Zinc Electrochemical Cell
SZG .... Salzburg [Austria] [Airport symbol] (OAG)
SZG .... Soviet Zone Germany (NATG)
SzGB .... Bibliotheque Battelle, Centre de Recherche, Geneve, Switzerland [Library symbol Library of Congress] (LCLS)
SzGBNU .... Bibliotheque des Nations Unies, Geneve, Switzerland [Library symbol Library of Congress] (LCLS)
SzGE .... Ecole de Chimie, Geneva, Switzerland [Library symbol Library of Congress] (LCLS)
SzGPAr .... Archives Jean Piaget, Geneve, Switzerland [Library symbol Library of Congress] (LCLS)
SzGSI .... Societe Generale pour l'Industrie, Geneve, Switzerland [Library symbol Library of Congress] (LCLS)
SZI .... Seattle, WA [Location identifier FAA] (FAAL)
SZI .... Service Zone Indication [Computer science] (IAA)
SZI .... Soroti [Uganda] [Airport symbol] (AD)
SZI .... Subzonal Sperm Insertion [In-vitro fertilization] (PAZ)
SZJ .... Atlanta, GA [Location identifier FAA] (FAAL)
SZK .... Roanoke, VA [Location identifier FAA] (FAAL)
SZK .... Skukuza [South Africa] [Airport symbol] (OAG)
SZL .... Knob Noster, MO [Location identifier FAA] (FAAL)
SZL .... SZL Sportsight [Vancouver Stock Exchange symbol]
SzLaCU .... Bibliotheque Cantonal et Universitaire de Lausanne, Lausanne, Switzerland [Library symbol Library of Congress] (LCLS)
SzLaS .... Station Federale d'Essais Agricoles, Lausanne, Switzerland [Library symbol Library of Congress] (LCLS)
SZM .... Stereo Zoom Microscope
SZM .... Synthetic Zeolite Molecule
SZN .... Santa Barbara, CA [Location identifier FAA] (FAAL)

SZN .... Streptozocin [Antineoplastic drug]
SZO .... Student Zionist Organization [Defunct] (EA)
SZOG .... Soviet Zone of Occupation of Germany (NATG)
SZOR .... Sintered Zinc Oxide Resistor
SZOT .... Szakszervezetek Orszagos Tanacsa [National Trade Union Council] [Hungary]
SZP .... Santa Paula, CA [Location identifier FAA] (FAAL)
SZP .... Surf Zone Process
SZP .... Synchro Zeroing Procedure
SZR .... Sintered Zinc Resistor
SZR .... Stargazer Resources Ltd. [Vancouver Stock Exchange symbol]
SZR .... University of South Carolina, Regional Campus Processing Center, Columbia, SC [OCLC symbol] (OCLC)
SzS .... Solidarnosc z Solidarnoscia [Solidarity with Solidarity - SwS] [Defunct] (EAIO)
SZS .... Srpska Zemljoradnicka Stranka [Serbian Agrarian Party] [Former Yugoslavia] [Political party] (PPE)
SZS .... Staatliche Zentrale fuer Strahlenschutz Berlin [East Germany]
SZS .... Stewart Island [New Zealand] [Airport symbol] (OAG)
SZSB .... Silver-Zinc Secondary [or Storage] Battery
SzStg .... Stadtbibliothek Vadiana, St. Gallen, Switzerland [Library symbol Library of Congress] (LCLS)
SZT .... Sandpoint, ID [Location identifier FAA] (FAAL)
SZU .... Segou [Mali] [Airport symbol] (AD)
SZutNu .... Sifre Zuta on Numbers (BJA)
SZVR .... Silicon Zener Voltage Regulator
SZY .... Selmer, TN [Location identifier FAA] (FAAL)
SZZ .... Szczecin [Poland] [Airport symbol] (OAG)
SzZ .... Zentralbibliothek Zurich, Zurich, Switzerland [Library symbol Library of Congress] (LCLS)
SzZE .... Eidgenoessische Technische Hochschule, Zurich, Switzerland [Library symbol Library of Congress] (LCLS)
SzZU .... Universitat Zurich, Universitatsspital-Bibliothek, Kantonsspital, Zurich, Switzerland [Library symbol Library of Congress] (LCLS)

T

By Acronym

T .... Absolute Temperature [*Symbol*] [*IUPAC*]
T .... Aerotec [*Sociedade Aerotec Ltda.*] [*Brazil ICAO aircraft manufacturer identifier*] (ICAO)
T .... Air Temperature Correction
T .... American Telephone & Telegraph Co. [*Wall Street slang name: "Telephone"*] [*NYSE symbol*] (SPSG)
t------ .... Antarctic [*MARC geographic area code Library of Congress*] (LCCP)
T .... AT&T Corp. [*NYSE symbol*] (TTSB)
t .... Backhoe Trench [*Archaeology*]
t .... Celsius Temperature [*Symbol*] [*IUPAC*]
T .... Electrocardiographic Wave Corresponding to Repolarization of Ventricles (STED)
T .... Half-Life of a Radioactive Substance (BARN)
T .... Internal Transmittance [*Symbol*] [*IUPAC*]
T .... Kinetic Energy [*Symbol*] [*IUPAC*]
T .... Mardi [*French*] (ASC)
t .... Marginal Propensity to Tax [*Economics*]
T .... Meridian Angle
T .... Metric Ton
T .... Military Sealift Command Ship [*When precedes vessel classification*] [*Navy symbol*]
T .... Octodecimo [*Book from 12-1/2 to 15 centimeters in height*] [*Bibliography*]
T .... Ribothymidine [*One-letter symbol; see Thd*]
T .... Shape Descriptor [*T-bar and T-square, for example. The shape resembles the letter for which it is named*]
T .... Surface Tension [*Physics*] (WDAA)
T .... Table
T .... Tablespoon [*Measure*]
T .... Tablet (WGA)
T .... Tablet-Shaped [*As in "T-grains"*] [*Photography*]
t .... Tabula [*Plate*] [*Latin*]
T .... Tabulated [*or Charted*] LORAN Reading [*Long-Range Aid to Navigation*]
T .... Tace [*Be Silent*]
T .... Tackle [*Football*]
T .... Tactical Organization
T .... Tactual
T .... Taenia [*Medicine*] (MAE)
t .... Tag [*Computer science*] [*Telecommunications*]
T .... Taken
T .... Tala [*Monetary unit in Western Samoa*]
T .... Talc
T .... Talk/Monitor (NASA)
T .... Talon [*Heel of the Bow*] [*Music*]
T .... Tamoxifen [*Antineoplastic drug*]
T .... Tamper (NFPA)
T .... Tango [*Phonetic alphabet*] [*International*] (DSUE)
T .... Tanhuma (BJA)
T .... Tank [*Trains*] [*British*]
T .... Tanna (BJA)
T .... Tanycyte Ependymal Cell (STED)
T .... Taped Commentary [*On a bus tour*] [*British*]
T .... Taper
T .... Tapered Hatchway [*on a ship*] (DS)
T .... Tappan's Ohio Common Pleas Reports [*A publication*] (DLA)
T .... Tare [*Phonetic alphabet*] [*World War II*] (DSUE)
T .... Target
T .... Tasmania [*State*] (EERA)
T .... Tasto [*Touch, Key, Fingerboard*] [*Music*]
T .... Tau [*Nineteenth letter of the Greek alphabet*] (DAVI)
T .... Taxation [*Economics*]
T .... Taxes (DLA)
T .... T-Bandage (STED)
T .... T-Bar (STED)
T .... Teacher
T .... Tear [*Phonetic alphabet*] [*World War II*]
t .... Teaspoon [*Measure*]
T .... Technical [*or Technician*]
T .... Technical College [*British*]
T .... Technological Service [*Queen's Award*] [*British*]
T .... Tee [*Piping joint, etc.*] [*Technical drawings*]
T .... Teeth [*Technical drawings*]
T .... Teich [*Pond*] [*German military*]
T .... Telefunken [*Record label*] [*Germany, etc.*]
T .... Telegram (BJA)

T .... Telegraph (ROG)
T .... Telegrapher [*Navy*]
T .... Telemeter [*or Telemetry*] [*Telecommunications*] (IAA)
T .... Telephone
T .... Telephone Trunk Call [*British*] (ROG)
T .... Teletype
T .... Television [*FCC*] (NTCM)
T .... Telnet [*Internet*]
t .... Telocentric
T .... Temperance [*i.e., entitled to a daily rum ration but voluntarily not drawing it and receiving money instead*] [*See also G, UA*] [*Navy*] [*British*]
T .... Temperature
T .... Tempo
T .... Temporal
T .... Temporal Electrode Placement in Electroencephalography (STED)
T .... Temporary
T .... Tempore [*In the Time of*] [*Latin*]
T .... Tenant [*Legal shorthand*] (LWAP)
T .... Tender [*Horticulture*]
T .... Tendre [*Tender*] [*Music*]
T .... Tenero [*Tender*]
T .... Tennessee State Library and Archives, Nashville, TN [*Library symbol Library of Congress*] (LCLS)
T .... Tenor [*Genotype of Phlox paniculata*]
t .... Tenor (WDAA)
T .... Tense
T .... Tension [*Intraocular*] [*Opthalmology*] (DAVI)
T .... Tensor
T .... Tentative Target
T .... Ter [*Three Times*] [*Pharmacy*]
T .... Tera [*A prefix meaning multiplied by 10^{12}*] [*SI symbol*]
T .... Teracycle (BUR)
T .... Term [*Mathematics*] (WDAA)
T .... Term [*Medicine*]
T .... Terminal
T .... Terminal Area Chart [*Followed by Identification*] [*Aviation*]
T .... Terminal Banding (STED)
T .... Termination
T .... Terminator [*Genetics*]
T .... Terminus [*Biochemistry*]
T .... Terrain
T .... Terrain Clearance Altitude [*Aviation*] (DA)
T .... Territory
t .... Tertiary [*Also, tert*] [*Chemistry*]
T .... Tertiary (STED)
T .... Tesla [*Symbol*] [*SI unit of flux density*]
T .... Test (MSA)
T .... Testament (ROG)
T .... Testamentum [*Will*] [*Latin*]
T .... Testator [*Legal term*]
T .... Test Equipment (NG)
T .... Testicle (STED)
t .... Test of Significance [*Medicine*] (MAE)
T .... Testosterone (STED)
T .... Test Reactor
T .... Test Set
T .... Tetra [*Prefix meaning four*] (DAVI)
T .... Tetracycline [*Antibiotic compound*]
T .... T-Fiber (STED)
T .... Thaler [*or Talari*] [*Monetary unit Ethiopia*]
T .... Than
T .... That
T .... Theatres [*Public-performance tariff class*] [*British*]
T .... Theft
T .... Theophylline [*Pharmacology*]
T .... Thermodynamic Temperature [*Symbol*] [*IUPAC*]
T .... Thermometer
T .... Thermoplastic [*Also, TP*] [*Plastics technology*] (MSA)
T .... Thermostabilized (NASA)
T .... Thickness
T .... Thief
T .... Thioguanine [*Also, TG*] [*Antineoplastic drug*]
T .... Thiopental [*An anesthetic*]
T .... Third Word Designator [*Computer science*]

T................ Thomas Mieres [*Flourished, 1429-39*] [*Authority cited in pre-1607 legal work*] (DSA)
T................ Thoracic [*Anatomy*]
T................ Thorax [*Anatomy*] (MAE)
T................ Thread
T................ Threonine [*One-letter symbol; see Thr*] [*An amino acid*]
T................ Threshold Lighting [*Aviation*] (DA)
T................ Thrill [*Cardiology*] (DAVI)
T................ Thromboxane [*Also, TA, Tx, TX*] [*Biochemistry*]
T................ Throttle Command (NASA)
T................ Thrust (IAA)
T................ Thruster [*of a ship*] (DS)
T................ Thrust of Propeller [*Naval engineering*] (DAS)
T................ Thunderstorm [*Meteorology*]
T................ Thursday (WGA)
T................ Thymidine [*Medicine*] (MAE)
T................ Thymine [*Also, Thy*] [*Biochemistry*]
T................ Thymus [*Medicine*]
T................ Thymus Derived [*Hematology*]
T................ Thyroid [*Medicine*]
T................ Tidal Gas [*Respiration*] [*Medicine*]
T................ Tide Rips [*Navigation*]
T................ Tie [*Sports*]
T................ Tier [*Psychology*]
T................ Tiler [*Freemasonry*]
T................ Tilic Subgroup [*Ilmenite, titanite, perofskite, rutile*] [*CIPW classification Geology*]
t................ Time [*Symbol*] [*IUPAC*]
T................ Time
T................ Time Constant (IAA)
T................ Time Consumed in Playing Game [*Baseball*]
t................ Time in Seconds [*Aerospace*]
T................ Timekeeper [*Sports*]
T+............ Time Postintegration (NASA)
T................ Time Prior to Launch [*Usually followed by a number*] [*NASA*] (KSC)
T................ Timer (IAA)
T................ Time-Reversal [*Atomic physics*]
T................ Time Trial
T................ Tip [*Switchboard plug*] [*Telecommunications*] (TEL)
T................ Tipper [*Shipping*] (DS)
T................ Tithing [*Geographical division*] [*British*]
T................ Title [*Bibliography*]
T................ Toarcian [*Geology*]
T................ Tobacco Tax Ruling, Internal Revenue Bureau [*United States*] [*A publication*] (DLA)
T................ Toc [*Phonetic alphabet*] [*Pre-World War II*] (DSUE)
T................ Tocopherol [*Biochemistry*]
T................ Toe
T................ Toggle [*Telecommunications*] (IAA)
T................ Toilet (MSA)
T................ Toll
T................ Tommy [*Phonetic alphabet*] [*Royal Navy World War I*] (DSUE)
T................ Tomo [*Volume*] [*Italian*] (ILCA)
T................ Tomus [*Volume*]
T................ Ton
T................ Tone (IAA)
T................ Tonnage [*Shipping*]
t................ Tonne [*Metric*]
T................ Tonometer Reading [*Medicine*] (MEDA)
T................ Tooth
T................ Top
T................ Topical (ADA)
t................ Top [*or Truth*] (Quark) [*Atomic physics*]
T................ Top Secret
T................ Toronto Stock Exchange
T................ Torpedo [*Obsolete Navy British*] (ROG)
T................ Torpedoman [*Navy British*]
T................ Torque
T................ Tosefta (BJA)
T................ Total
T................ Total Temperature (NAKS)
T................ Tourist [*Rate*] [*Value of the English pound*]
T................ Toward [*Altitude difference*]
T................ Town
T................ Township
T................ Toxicity (MAE)
T................ Trace (DAVI)
T................ Trace of Precipitation [*Less than 0.005 inch of rain or 0.05 inch of snow*]
T................ Tracer [*Ammunition*] (NATG)
T................ Trachea [*Anatomy*]
T................ Tracheotomy Set (CPH)
T................ Track
T................ Tracker [*British military*] (DMA)
T................ Traded
T................ Tradesman [*British military*] (DMA)
T................ Traditional (BJA)
T................ Trafalgar [*On army list*] [*British*] (ROG)
T................ Traffic Cases [*A publication*] (DLA)
T................ Traffic Headquarters
T................ Trainer [*Designation for all US military aircraft*]
T................ Trainer Aircraft Designation [*MTMC*] (TAG)
T................ Training (FAAC)
t................ Trans [*Chemical conformation*]
T................ Transaction

T................ Transcription
T................ Transducer
t................ Transfer [*Genetics*]
T................ Transferred [*Navy*]
T................ Transferrin [*Also, TF, TRF*] [*Biochemistry*]
T................ Transformation Rule [*Linguistics*]
T................ Transformer
T................ Transfusion [*Medicine*]
T................ Transient [*Bureau of the Census*]
T................ Transistor [*Electronics*] (IAA)
T................ Transit
T................ Transition
T................ Transition point (DAVI)
T................ Transitive
T................ Translated (ROG)
T................ Translation
T................ Translocation
T................ Transmission [*Telecommunications*] (IAA)
T................ Transmission Stop (NTCM)
T................ Transmissivity (FFDE)
T................ Transmit [*or Transmitting*]
T................ Transmittance [*A symbol used in spectrophotometry*] (DAVI)
T................ Transmitter
T................ Transpiration [*Botany*]
T................ Transponder (IAA)
T................ Transport (NATG)
t................ Transport Number [*Symbol*] [*Electrochemistry*]
T................ Transport Number [*Chemistry*] (BARN)
T................ Transvaal Provincial Division Reports [*South Africa*] [*A publication*] (DLA)
T................ Transverse (AAMN)
T................ Transverse Tubule [*Muscle neurobiology*]
T................ Travel News [*Wire service code*] (NTCM)
T................ Trawling
T................ Tread [*Stair details*] [*Technical drawings*]
T................ Treasurer
T................ Treasury [*As in T-Bill, T-Bond, T-Note*]
T................ Treated
T................ Treatment
T................ Treaty [*Legal shorthand*] (LWAP)
T................ Treble [*Music*] (ROG)
t................ Trend Landing Forecast [*Aviation*] (DA)
T................ Treponema [*Microbiology*] (AAMN)
T................ Triangle
T................ Trichome [*Botany*]
T................ Trichomonas [*A parasite*] (DAVI)
T................ Trichophyton [*Medicine*] (MAE)
T................ Trigger (IAA)
T................ Triggered [*Cardiology*]
T................ Trillion [10^{12}]
T................ Trillo [*Trill*] [*Music*]
T................ Trimethoprim [*Also, TMP*] [*Antibacterial compound*]
T................ Trimmer (IAA)
T................ Trinitas [*The Trinity*]
T-0.......... Triode
T................ Triple
T................ Tritium [*Also, H_3*] [*Radioisotope of hydrogen*]
t................ Triton [*A nuclear particle*]
T................ Triton Industries, Inc. [*Toronto Stock Exchange symbol*]
T................ Tropical [*Load line mark, or air mass*]
T................ Trotter
T................ Troy [*A system of weights for precious metals*]
T................ Truce
T................ True [*Direction*]
T................ Trunk (IAA)
T................ Truss (AAG)
T................ Trypanosoma [*Medicine*] (MAE)
T................ Tube (IAA)
T................ Tubular (IAA)
T................ Tubulin [*A protein*]
T................ Tuesday
T................ Tufa [*Quality of the bottom*] [*Nautical charts*]
T................ Tug [*Navy*]
T................ Tumor [*Oncology*]
T................ Tun [*Unit of liquid capacity*]
T................ Turbocharged [*Automotive engineering*]
T................ Turkish
T................ Turn [*or Turning*]
T................ Turner [*Navy rating British*]
T................ Turnkey [*Medicine*] (DMAA)
T................ Turnover Index [*Botany*]
T................ Tutti [*Sing or Play Together*] [*Music*]
T................ Twentyfourmo [*Book up to 15 centimeters in height*]
T................ Twin Screw [*Shipping*] (DS)
T................ Type
T................ Typed [*Manuscript descriptions*]
T................ Typhlosole [*Biology*]
T................ Typhoid
T................ Wrong Tense of Verb [*Used in correcting manuscripts, etc.*]
T-0.......... Time Zero (MCD)
T1............ First Thoracic Nerve [*T2 Second Thoracic Nerve, etc., through T12*] [*Anatomy*] (DAVI)
T1............ First Thoracic Vertebra [*T2 Second thoracic vertebra, etc., through T12*] [*Anatomy*] (DAVI)
T1............ First Transcript [*Genetics*]

T1 .... Longitudinal Relaxation Time Constant [*Radiology*] (DAVI)
T1 .... Telecommunications [*An association*] (DDC)
T_1 .... Tricuspid First Heart Sound [*Cardiology*]
T_1 .... Tricuspid First Sound [*Cardiology*] (DAVI)
T_2 .... Diiodothyronine [*Endocrinology*]
T-2 .... Protocol [*A chemotherapy regimen including dactinomycin, doxorubicin, vincristine, cyclophosphamide, and radiation therapy*] (DAVI)
T2 .... Second Transcript [*Genetics*]
T2 .... Terminator 2 [*Motion picture*]
T2 .... Time of Flight to Intercept [*Military*] (CAAL)
T2 .... Transverse Relaxation Time Constant [*On magnetic resonance imaging (MRI) scans*] [*Also called spin-spin relaxation time constant*] [*Radiology*] (DAVI)
T_2 .... Tricuspid Second Heart Sound [*Cardiology*]
T2 .... Tuvalu [*International civil aircraft marking*] (ODBW)
T2G .... Technician, Second Grade [*Military*]
T^2L .... Transistor-Transistor Logic [*Also, TTL*]
T2S .... Technology Transfer Society (EA)
T2S2 .... Total Tank System Study [*Army*]
T3 .... Kiribati [*International civil aircraft marking*] (ODBW)
T3 .... Tank Track Test [*Army*]
T-3 .... Tocotrienol [*Biochemistry*]
T_3 .... Train-the-Trainer [*Army*]
T_3 .... Triiodothyronine [*Also, TITh*] [*Endocrinology*]
T_3(RIA) .... Serum Triiodothyronine Radioimmunoassay [*Endocrinology*] (DAVI)
T_3RIA .... Triiodothyronine Radioimmunoassay [*Endocrinology*] (DAVI)
T_3RU .... Triiodothyronine Resin Uptake [*Endocrinology*] (MAE)
T_3SU .... Triiodothyronine Serum Uptake [*Endocrinolgy*] (CPH)
T_3U .... Triiodothyronine Uptake [*Endocrinology*]
T_3UP.......... Tri-Iodothyronine Uptake [*Endocrinology*] (DAVI)
T_3UR .... Triiodothyronine Uptake Radio [*Endocrinology*] (DAVI)
T4 .... Thyroxine [*Also, Thx, Ty*] [*An amino acid Endocrinology*]
T_4(c) .... Serum Thyroxine [*Measured by column chromatographic technique*] [*Endocrinology*] (DAVI)
T4C .... Technology for Children [*Vocational program*]
T4C .... Termination for Convenience (AAGC)
T_4(D) .... Serum Thyroxine [*Measured by displacement analysis*] [*Endocrinology*] (DAVI)
T_4I .... Total Serum Thyroxine Iodine Also, called tri-iodothyronine [*Endocrinology*] (DAVI)
T_4(RIA) .... Serum Thyroxine Radioisotope Assay [*Endocrinology*] (DAVI)
T_4RIA .... Thyroxine Radioisotope Assay [*Endocrinology*] (DAVI)
T_4SA.......... Thyroxine-Specific Activity [*Medicine*] (MAE)
T/5 .... Technician Fifth Grade [*Army*]
T7 .... San Marino [*International civil aircraft marking*] (ODBW)
T-1824 .... Evans Blue Dye [*Radiology*] (DAVI)
T2000 .... Transport 2000 Ltd. (BUAC)
T2000I .... Transport 2000 International [*British*] (EAIO)
TA .... Chinese Taipei [*IYRU nationality code*] (IYR)
Ta .... Ta'anith (BJA)
TA .... Tabled Agreement [*in labor relations*]
TA .... Table of Allowances (MCD)
TA .... Table of Authorization
TA .... Tablet (ADA)
TA .... TACA International Airlines SA [*El Salvador*] [*ICAO designator*] (ICDA)
TA .... Tactical Aircraft
T/A .... Tactical Airlift [*Tactical Air Command*]
TA .... Tactical Air Missile
TA .... Tactile Afferent [*Medicine*] (DMAA)
TA .... Tailhook Association (EA)
TA .... Takayasu Arteritis (STED)
TA .... Talanta [*A publication*]
TA .... Talmudical Academy (BJA)
TA .... Talmudische Archaeologie [*A publication*] (BJA)
TA .... Tanabe Seiyaku Co. Ltd. [*Japan*] [*Research code symbol*]
TA .... Tangible Asset
TA .... Tank Army (MCD)
TA .... Tanker [*Shipping*] (DCTA)
TA .... Tank Tainers [*Shipping*] (DCTA)
TA .... Tannic Acid [*Urology*] (DAVI)
Ta .... Tantalum [*Chemical element*]
TA .... Tape (IAA)
TA .... Tape Adapter
TA .... Tape Advance (AAG)
TA .... Tape Armored [*Telecommunications*] (TEL)
TA .... Target (DEN)
TA .... Target Acquisition (MCD)
TA .... Target Aircraft (MUGU)
TA .... Target Area [*Military*] (AFM)
TA .... Targeting Agent [*Medicine*]
TA .... Tariff Act [*1930*]
TA .... Tartana [*Ship's rigging*] (ROG)
TA .... Task Analysis
TA .... Task Assignment (AAG)
TA .... Tax Abatement
TA .... Tax Agent
TA .... Tax Amortization [*Plan*]
TA .... Tea Association of the USA [*Defunct*] (EA)
TA .... Teacher Assessment (DET)
TA .... Teaching Assistant [*in a university*]
TA .... Technical Advisor (MCD)
TA .... Technical Analysis (NG)

TA .... Technical Applications [*Branch*] [*Forecast Systems Laboratory*] (USDC)
TA .... Technical Architecture [*Computer science*] (RDA)
TA .... Technical Assessor
TA .... Technical Assistance [*or Assistant*]
TA .... Technology Assessment Database [*Fachinformationszentrum Karlsruhe GmbH*] [*Germany Information service or system*] (CRD)
TA .... Technonet Asia (EA)
TA .... Teichoic Acids [*Biochemistry*]
TA .... Tel Aviv [*Israel*] (BJA)
TA .... Telecom Australia (BUAC)
TA .... Teleflora Australia
TA .... Telegraphic Address
TA .... Teleoperator Assembler (SSD)
TA .... Telephone Apparatus [*JETDS nomenclature*] [*Military*] (CET)
TA .... Telescope Assembly (KSC)
TA .... Television Associates [*Mountain View, CA*] (TSSD)
TA .... Telex Network Adapter (MHDB)
TA .... Tell-Amarna [*Egypt*] (BJA)
TA .... Tell Asmar [*Iraq*] (BJA)
TA .... Telluride Association (EA)
TA .... Temperature Alarm [*Engineering*]
TA .... Temperature, Axillary
TA .... Temple Autobiographies [*A publication*]
TA .... Temporal Arteritis [*Medicine*]
TA .... Temporal Average (STED)
T/A .... Temporary Assistant (WDAA)
TA .... Tendo Achilis Reflex [*Neurology*] (DAVI)
TA .... Tendon of Achilles (STED)
TA .... Tennis Australia
TA .... Tension Arterial (STED)
TA .... Tension Arterielle [*Blood Pressure*] [*Medicine*]
TA .... Tension by Applanation [*Ophthalmology*]
TA .... Tenuazonic Acid [*Biochemistry*]
TA .... Teologinen Aikakauskirja [*Helsinki*] [*A publication*] (BJA)
TA .... Terephthalic Acid [*Also, TPA*] [*Organic chemistry*]
TA .... Terminal Adapter [*Telecommunications*]
TA .... Terminal Address
TA .... Terminal Antrum (STED)
TA .... Terrain Avoidance [*Helicopter*]
TA .... Terrarium Association (EA)
TA .... Territorial Army
TA .... Test Access [*Telecommunications*] (TEL)
TA .... Test Accessory (AAG)
TA .... Test Age (STED)
TA .... Test Announcer (IAA)
TA .... Testantibus Actis [*As the Records Show*] [*Latin*]
TA .... Test Article (NASA)
TA .... Test Authorizations [*Environmental science*] (COE)
TA .... Theater Army
TA .... Theatre Authority (EA)
TA .... Therapeutic Abortion [*Medicine*]
TA .... Thermal Activation [*Physics*]
TA .... Thermal Analysis
TA .... Thermophilic Actinomyces [*Microbiology*]
TA .... Third Attack [*Men's lacrosse position, until 1933*]
TA .... Thoracoabdominal Stapler [*Surgery*] (DAVI)
TA .... Threat Analysis (MCD)
TA .... Threat Axis [*Military*] (NVT)
TA .... Thromboxane [*Also, T, Tx, TX*] [*Biochemistry*]
TA .... Thromboxane A [*Also, TxA, TXA*] [*Biochemistry*]
TA .... Throw Away
TA .... Thunderbirds of America (EA)
TA .... Thymocytotoxic Autoantibody (DB)
TA .... Thyroglobulin Auto-Precipitation [*Endocrinology*] (AAMN)
TA .... Thyroglobulin Autoprecipitin (STED)
TA .... Thyroid Antibody (STED)
TA .... Thyroid Autoantibody [*Endrocrinology*] (DAVI)
TA .... Tibialis Anterior [*A muscle*]
TA .... Time Actual (NASA)
T/A .... Time and Amount (DMAA)
TA .... Time and Attendance
TA .... Tippers Anonymous (EA)
TA .... Tithe Annuity
TA .... [*Journal*] Title Abbreviation (NITA)
TA .... Title Annotation (NITA)
TA .... Titratable Acid [*Clinical chemistry*]
TA .... Titration Alkalinity [*Oceanography*]
TA .... Tnu'at 'Aliyah (BJA)
TA .... Tobacco Associates (EA)
TA .... Tool Available
TA .... Top Assembly
TA .... Torah Atmosphere (BJA)
TA .... Total Aboard (FAAC)
TA .... Total Adenine [*Nucleotide pool*] [*Medicine*]
TA .... Total Alkaloids [*Medicine*]
TA .... Total Audience [*Television ratings*]
TA .... Toward
TA .... Toxic Adenoma (STED)
TA .... Toxin-Antitoxin [*Also, TAT*] [*Immunology*]
TA .... Tracers Association [*A union*] [*British*]
TA .... Tracheal Aspirate (STED)
TA .... Track Accelerator [*Missile simulator*]
TA .... Track Address (IAA)

TA .... Traction Assist [*Automotive engineering*]
TA .... Trade Acceptance [*Investment term*] (DFIT)
TA .... Trade Agreements Act
TA .... Trade Association (DCTA)
TA .... Trading As
ta .... Trading As (AAGC)
TA .... Traffic Accident (DAVI)
TA .... Traffic Agent [*or Auditor*]
T/A .... Traffic Analysis [*National Security Agency*]
TA .... Trained Aide [*Medicine*]
TA .... Training Advisor (WDAA)
TA .... Training Agency (EERA)
TA .... Training Allowance [*British military*] (DMA)
TA .... Training Analyst (HGAA)
T/A .... Training As
TA .... Transactional Analysis [*System of psychotherapy developed by Eric Berne, MD*]
TA .... Transaldolase [*An enzyme*] (AAMN)
TA .... Transalta Corp. [*TS symbol*] (TTSB)
TA .... Transalta Resources Corp. [*Toronto Stock Exchange symbol*]
TA .... Trans Am [*Model of automobile*]
TA .... Transamerica Corp. [*NYSE symbol*] (SPSG)
TA .... Transamerica Delaware Ltd. [*NYSE symbol*] (SAG)
TA .... Transantral [*Medicine*] (AAMN)
TA .... Transfer Agent [*Business term*]
TA .... Transfer Aisle (NRCH)
T/A .... Transfer of Accountability
TA .... Transfusion Associated
TA .... Transient Alert (MCD)
TA .... Transit Authority
TA .... Transition Agreement
TA .... Transition Altitude
TA .... Transition Area [*For chart use only*] [*Aviation*]
TA .... Transmission Authenticator [*Telecommunications*] (TEL)
TA .... Transplantation Antigen [*Medicine*]
TA .... Transportability Approval [*Army*]
TA .... Transport Association [*British*] (DBA)
TA .... Transportation Act of 1989 (WYGK)
TA .... Transportation Agent
TA .... Transportation Alternatives (EA)
TA .... Transportation Authorization (AAG)
TA .... Transverse Acoustic
TA .... Travel Allowance
TA .... Travel [*or Trip*] Authorization (MCD)
TA .... Traveler's Advisory [*Weather information*]
TA .... Triacetin [*Antifungal compound*] [*Organic chemistry*]
TA .... Triamcinolone Acetonide [*Also, TAA*] [*Synthetic steroidal drug*]
TA .... Tribunal Administratif [*Administrative Court*] [*French*] (ILCA)
TA .... Tricuspid Atresia [*Cardiology*]
TA .... Tricycle Association [*British*] (DBA)
TA .... Trinidad Artillery [*British military*] (DMA)
TA .... Trip Authorization
TA .... Triple Antigen [*Medicine*]
TA .... Triplex Annealed
TA .... Triumph Adler Computer Series (NITA)
TA .... Trophoblast Antigen [*Immunochemistry*]
TA .... Truck Assembly
TA .... True Altitude [*Height*] [*Navigation*]
TA .... True Anomaly
TA .... Truncus Arteriosus [*Medicine*] (DMAA)
TA .... Trunk Amplifier (IAA)
TA .... Trunnion Angle (KSC)
TA .... Trustee under Agreement [*Legal term*] (DLA)
TA .... Truth in Advertising [*An association Defunct*] (EA)
TA .... Tryptophane Acid (AAMN)
TA .... Tryptose Agar [*Medicine*] (DMAA)
TA .... Tube Agglutination [*Medicine*] (MAE)
TA .... Tuberculin, Alkaline [*Medicine*]
TA .... Tubular Atrophy [*Nephrology*]
TA .... Tumor Associated [*Medicine*] (DMAA)
T/A .... Turboalternator
TA .... Turbulence Amplifier
TA .... Turkish Army (NATG)
T/A .... Turnaround (NASA)
TA .... Turning Angle [*Automotive engineering*]
Ta .... T-wave Atrial [*Found on electrocardiograms*] (DAVI)
TA .... Type Americain [*World War I troop train in France made according to US specifications*]
TA .... Type Approval
TA .... Type Availability
TA .... Typographic Adviser (DGA)
TA .... VEB Fahlberg-List [*East Germany*] [*Research code symbol*]
TA1 .... Trophoblast Antigen One [*Immunochemistry*]
TA3DPT .... Twitchell-Allen Three-Dimensional Personality Test [*Psychology*]
TA₄ .... Tetraiodothyroacetic Acid [*Medicine*] (MAE)
TAA .... Aerotamatan SA de CV [*Mexico ICAO designator*] (FAAC)
TAA .... Tactical Air Army (NATG)
TAA .... Tactical Army Automation (MCD)
TAA .... Tactical Assembly Area [*Army*] (DOMA)
TAA .... Tactical Automation Appraisal (MCD)
TAA .... Taiwanese Association of America (EA)
TAA .... Tamburitza Association of America (EA)
TAA .... Tannic Acid Agar [*Culture media*]
TAA .... Taxpayers' Association of Australia
TAA .... Technical Assistance Administration [*United Nations*]

TAA .... Technical Assistance Agreement [*NASA*] (NASA)
TAA .... Technology Assessment Annex (MCD)
TAA .... Telephone Artifacts Association (EA)
TAA .... Television Appliance Association
TAA .... Temporary Access Authorization (NASA)
TAA .... Terre Adelie [*Antarctica*] [*Seismograph station code, US Geological Survey Closed*] (SEIS)
TAA .... Territorial Army Association [*British*]
TAA .... Tertiary-Amyl Alcohol [*Organic chemistry*]
TAA .... Texas Armadillo Association [*Commercial firm*] (EA)
TAA .... Text and Academic Authors Association (NTPA)
TAA .... Textbook Authors Association (EA)
TAA .... Thioacetamide [*Organic chemistry*]
TAA .... Thoracic Aortic Aneurysm [*Cardiology*]
TAA .... Three-Axis Accelerometer
TAA .... Ticket Agents' Association [*British*]
TAA .... Timber Arbitrators Association [*British*] (DBA)
TAA .... Timber Arbitrators Association of the United Kingdom (BUAC)
TAA .... Time and Attendance (IAA)
TAA .... Tobacconists' Association of America (EA)
TAA .... Total Aerospace Vehicle [*or Aircraft*] Authorization
TAA .... Total Aircraft Authorized (MCD)
TAA .... Total Ankle Arthroplasty [*Medicine*] (DMAA)
TAA .... Total Antioxidant Activity [*Chemistry*]
TAA .... Total Army Analysis (AABC)
TAA .... Total Army Authorization
TAA .... Trade Adjustment Act
TAA .... Trade Adjustment Assistance [*Department of Commerce*]
TAA .... Trade Agreements Act
TAA .... Trade Agreements Act of 1979 (AAGC)
TAA .... Trans-American Airline
TAA .... Trans-Antarctic Association [*British*]
TAA .... Trans-Atlantic Agreement (BUAC)
TAA .... Trans-Australia Airlines (ADA)
TAA .... Transcript of Absentee's Account
TAA .... Transferable Account Area [*Business term*] (DCTA)
TAA .... Transfer and Accountability (IAA)
TAA .... Transient Absorption Anisotropy [*Physics*]
TAA .... Transit Advertising Association [*Washington, DC*] (EA)
TAA .... Transportation Association of America (EA)
TAA .... Triamcinolone Acetonide [*Also, TA*] [*Synthetic steroidal drug*]
TAA .... Triticale Association of Australia
TAA .... Tropical Agriculture Association (BUAC)
TAA .... Tumor-Associated Antibody [*Medicine*] (DAVI)
TAA .... Tumor-Associated Antigen [*Immunology*]
TAA .... Turbine Alternator Assembly
TAA .... Turfgrass Association of Australia
TAA .... Turkish-American Associations (EA)
TAA .... Typical Address Access (NITA)
TAAA .... Teen-Age Assembly of America (EA)
TAAA .... Thoracoabdominal Aortic Aneurysm [*Cardiology*]
TAAA .... Total Active Aircraft Authorized (MCD)
TAAA .... Travelers Aid Association of America [*Defunct*] (EA)
TAAB .... Tasmanian Arts Advisory Board [*Australia*]
TAABS .... [*The*] Army Automated Budget System
TAAC .... [*The*] Association of American Cultures (EA)
TAAC .... Target Area Advisory Council (OICC)
TAAC .... Technology Assessment Advisory Council [*Washington, DC*] (EGAO)
TAAC .... Trade Adjustment Assistance Center [*Department of Commerce*]
TAAC .... Training Ammunition Authorization Committee (MCD)
TAAC .... Trans America Athletic Conference (PSS)
TAAC .... Troubles d'Apprentissage - Association Canadienne [*Learning Disabilities Association of Canada*] (EAIO)
TAACOM ..... Theater Army Area Command (AABC)
TAAD .... Task Assignment and Directive (MCD)
TAAD .... Terrain Avoidance Accessory Device
TAADC .... Theater Army Air Defense Command (AABC)
TAADCOM ... Theater Army Air Defense Command (AABC)
TAADS .... TOE [*Table of Organization and Equipment*] Army Authorization Document System
TAAF .... Test, Analyze, and Fix (AAGC)
TAAF .... Test, Analyze, and Fix Program [*Navy*] (MCD)
TAAF .... Thromboplastic Activity of Amniotic Fluid [*Medicine*]
TAAFA .... Territorial Army and Air Force Association [*British military*] (DMA)
TAAFFEE ...... Tactical Air Against First and Following Enemy Echelons (MCD)
TAAFLO .... Trans-Atlantic American Flag Liner Operations (NTPA)
TAAG .... Technical Analysis and Advisory Group [*Navy*] (MCD)
TAAG .... Tropical Africa Advisory Group [*British Overseas Trade Board*] (DS)
TAAI .... Total Active Aircraft Inventory (MCD)
TAALODS ...... [*The*] Army Automated Logistic Data System
TAALS .... [*The*] American Association of Language Specialists (EA)
TAALS .... [*The*] Judge Advocate General Automated Army Legal System
TAALS .... Tactical Army Aircraft Landing Systems
TAAM .... Terminal Area Altitude Monitoring (PDAA)
TAAM .... Theoretical and Applied Mechanics (IAA)
TAAM .... Tomahawk Air Field Attack Missile (MCD)
TAAM .... Transportation Army Aviation Maintenance
Ta'an .... Ta'anith (BJA)
TAAN .... Transporte Aereo Andino SA [*Venezuela*] [*ICAO designator*] (FAAC)
TAAN .... Transworld Advertising Agency Network [*Englewood, CO*] (EA)
TAANA .... [*The*] American Association of Nurse Attorneys (EA)
TAAP .... Three-Axis Antenna Positioner
TAAP .... Trade Adjustment Assistance Program [*Department of Commerce*]
TAAP .... Transient Analysis Array Program
TAAR .... Target Area Analysis-RADAR

TAAR .... Target Area Analysis-Repair (MCD)
TAARS .... [*The*] Army Ammunition Reporting System (AABC)
TAAS .... Tactical Air Armament Study (MCD)
TAAS .... Terminal Advanced Automation System [*Aviation*]
TAAS .... Texas Assessment of Academic Skills
TAAS .... Thorotrast-Associated Angiosarcoma [*Oncology*]
TAAS .... Three-Axis Attitude Sensor (IEEE)
TAAS .... Traffic Account Analysis System [*Military British*]
TAASC .... [*The*] Association of American Sword Collectors (EA)
TAASII .... Tianjin Academy of Agricultural Science Information Institute [*China*] (BUAC)
TAASP .... [*The*] Association for the Anthropological Study of Play (EA)
TAB .... Airborne Tanker, Boom (NVT)
TAB .... Tab-automated Bonded [*Computer science*] (PCM)
TAB .... Tabella [*Tablet*] [*Pharmacy*]
TAB .... Table
TAB .... Tablet (WDAA)
tab .... Tablet [*Medicine*] (WDAA)
TAB .... Tabloid (NTCM)
TAB .... Tabloncillo [*Race of maize*]
TAB .... Tabriz [*Iran*] [*Seismograph station code, US Geological Survey*] (SEIS)
TAB .... Tabular Language [*Computer science*] (IEEE)
TAB .... Tabulate (AAG)
tab .... Tabulate (WDAA)
TAB .... Tabulating Machine (IAA)
TAB .... Tabulation (NITA)
tab .... Tabulator (WDAA)
TAB .... Tactical Air Base (AFM)
TAB .... Tactical Analysis Branch [*Military*] (DNAB)
TAB .... Tamper Attempt Board
TAB .... Tape Automated Bonding [*Integrated circuit technology*]
TAB .... Target Acquisition Battalion [*Military*]
TAB .... Target Acquisition Battery (MCD)
TAB .... Tax Anticipation Bill [*Obligation*] [*Department of the Treasury*]
TAB .... Technical Abstract Bulletin [*ASTIA*] [*A publication*]
TAB .... Technical Activities Board (MCD)
TAB .... Technical Advisory Board (IAA)
TAB .... Technical Assistance Board [*United Nations*]
TAB .... Technical Assistance Bureau [*ICAO*] (DA)
TAB .... Technology Assessment Board [*Washington, DC*] (EGAO)
TAB .... Telecommunications Advisory Board
TAB .... Temporarily Able-Bodied
TAB .... Testing, Adjusting, and Balancing [*Heating and cooling technology*]
TAB .... Tetraaminobiphenyl [*Organic chemistry*]
T-AB .... Thai-American Business [*A publication*] (IMH)
TAB .... The Associated Blind (EA)
TAB .... Therapeutic Abortion [*Medicine*] (MEDA)
TAB .... Thermactor Air Bypass [*Automotive engineering*]
TAB .... Thiolacetoxybenzanilide [*Organic chemistry*]
TAB .... Title Abstract Bulletin (IAA)
TAB .... Title Announcement Bulletin
TAB .... Tobago [*Trinidad and Tobago*] [*Airport symbol*] (OAG)
TAB .... Tone Answer Back [*Telecommunications*] (IAA)
TAB .... Top and Bottom (IAA)
TAB .... Total Abstinence Brotherhood
TAB .... Total Annual Benzene-in-Waste [*Environmental Protection Agency*]
TAB .... Total Autonomic Blockage [*Medicine*] (DMAA)
TAB .... Totalizer Agency Board (IAA)
TAB .... Towed Assault Bridge [*Army*]
TAB .... Traffic Audit Bureau [*Later, TABMM*] (EA)
TAB .... Traffic Audit Bureau for Media Measurement (NTPA)
TAB .... Training Aid Bulletins [*Navy*]
TAB .... Transatlantic Broadcasting Co. [*In TV series "W.E.B."*]
TAB .... Transportes Aereos Boliviands [*Bolivia*] [*ICAO designator*] (FAAC)
TAB .... Transportes Aereos da Bacia Amazonica SA [*Brazil*] [*ICAO designator*] (FAAC)
TAB .... Transports Aeriens du Benin [*Benin*] (EY)
TAB .... Triple Antibiotic [*Bacitracin, neomycin, and polymyxin*] [*Pharmacology*] (DAVI)
TAB .... Truck, Airplane, Boat (SAA)
TAB .... Turned and Bored (IAA)
TAB .... Typhoid, Paratyphoid A and B [*Vaccine*]
TABA .... [*The*] American Book Award [*Later, ABA*]
TABA .... Timber Agents and Brokers Association of the United Kingdom (BUAC)
TABA .... Transcaribe [*Airline*] [*Colorado*]
TABA .... Transportes Aereos da Bacia Amazonica [*Airline*] [*Brazil*]
TABAMLN .... Tampa Bay Medical Library Network [*Library network*]
TABBSS .... Tactical Bare Base Support Study [*Air Force*]
TABC .... Tabulator Character (IAA)
TABC .... Total Aerobic Bacteria Counts
TABC .... Typhoid-Paratyphoid A, B and C [*Vaccine*] [*Medicine*] (BABM)
TABCASS ..... Tactical Air Beacon Command and Surveillance System (MCD)
TAB-CD .... Tabulating Card
TABD .... Trans-Atlantic Business Dialogue (TELE)
TABE .... Tests of Adult Basic Education [*Achievement test*]
TABE .... Texas Association for Bilingual Education (EDAC)
TABEL .... Tabella [*Tablet*] [*Pharmacy*] (ROG)
TABE-PS ...... Tests of Adult Basic Education Work-Related Problem Solving (TMMY)
TABE WF ..... Tests of Adult Basic Education Work-Related Foundation Skills (TMMY)
TABKO .... All Brit Karate Organisation (DBA)
TABL .... Tropical Atlantic Biological Laboratory

TABLASER ... Trace Element Analyzer Based on LASER Ablation and Selectivity (MCD)
TABMM .... Traffic Audit Bureau for Media Measurement (EA)
TABNSW ...... Totalisator Agency Board of New South Wales [*Australia*]
TABP .... Tetraaminobenzophenone [*Organic chemistry*]
TABP .... Type A Behavior Pattern [*Medicine*] (DMAA)
TABPM .... Transportation Authorized in Accordance with BUPERS Manual, Article ____
TabPrd .... Tab Products Co. [*Associated Press*] (SAG)
TABS .... Tabulator Stops (AAG)
TABS .... Tactical Airborne Beacon System (AFM)
TABS .... Tailored Abstracts (NITA)
TABS .... Tangential Bomb Suspension (MCD)
TABS .... Team Approach to Better Schools [*National Education Association program*]
TABS .... Technical and Business Service
TABS .... Telemetry Asynchronous Block Serial (CIST)
TABS .... Telephone Area Billing System
TABS .... Telephone Automated Briefing Service (DA)
TABS .... Terminal Access to Batch Service [*Computer science*] (BUR)
TABS .... Tests of Achievement in Basic Skills [*Educational test*]
TABS .... Texas Assessment of Basic Skills (EDAC)
TABS .... Theater Air Base Survivability [*Air Force*]
TABS .... Time Analysis and Billing System (BUR)
TABS .... Total Army Basing Study (DOMA)
TABS .... Total Automatic Banking System [*Trademark of Diebold, Inc.*]
TABS .... Transatlantic Book Service [*British*]
TABS .... TRIS-Acetate-Buffered Saline [*Clinical chemistry*]
TABSIM .... Table Simulation [*or Simulator*] (IAA)
TABSIM .... Tabulating Simulator (NITA)
TABSIM .... Tabulator Simulator
TABSOL .... Tabular Systems-Oriented Language [*General Electric Co.*] [*British*]
TABSTONE ... Target and Background Signal-to-Noise Evaluation (MUGU)
TABSTONE ... Target and Background Signal-to-Noise Experiment (IAA)
TABT .... Typhoid, Paratyphoid A, and Paratyphoid B, and Tetanus Toxoid Combined [*A vaccine*] (DAVI)
TABTD .... Typhoid, Paratyphoid A, and Paratyphoid B, Tetanus Toxoid, and Diptheria Toxoid Combined [*A vaccine*] (DAVI)
TABU .... Typical Army Ball-Up [*Slang for a military muddle*]
TABV .... Theater Air Base Vulnerability [*Air Force*] (AFM)
TAB VEE ..... Theater Air Base Vulnerability [*Air Force*]
TABWAG ...... Tank Battle War Game
TABWDS .... Tactical Air Base Weather Dissemination System [*Air Force*]
TABWE .... Tactical Air Base Weather Element [*Air Force*]
TABWS .... Tactical Airborne Weather Stations (MCD)
TABWX .... Tactical Air Base Weather
TAC .... [*The*] Aeroplane Collection [*British*]
TAC .... [*The*] Architects Collaborative [*Design firm*]
TAC .... [*The*] Athletics Congress [*Track*] [*An association*]
TAC ..,....... Austin Community College, Austin, TX [*OCLC symbol*] (OCLC)
Tac .... Tacitus [*First century AD*] [*Classical studies*] (OCD)
TAC .... Tacloban [*Philippines*] [*Airport symbol*] (OAG)
TAC .... Tacon [*Flamenco dance term*]
TAC .... Tactical (AAG)
TAC .... Tactical Air Command [*Air Force*]
TAC .... Tactical Air Controller (NVT)
TAC .... Tactical Air Coordinator (SAA)
TAC .... Tactical Air Cover
TAC .... Tactical Assignment Console
TAC .... Tactical Command Post [*Army*] (INF)
TAC .... Tactical Coordinator (NATG)
Tac .... Tactical Officer [*Military*] (MUSM)
TAC .... Tacubaya [*Mexico*] [*Seismograph station code, US Geological Survey*] (SEIS)
TAC .... Taiwan Aerospace Corp. (ECON)
TAC .... Tamoxifen, Adriamycin, Cyclophosphamide [*Antineoplastic drug regimen*]
TAC .... Tandycrafts, Inc. [*NYSE symbol*] (SPSG)
TAC .... Tape Adapter Cabinet (IAA)
TAC .... Target Acquisition Center [*Army*]
TAC .... Target Acquisition Console [*Military*] (CAAL)
TAC .... Targeted Amortization-Class Bond [*Investment term*]
TAC .... Targeting and Control (IAA)
TAC .... Tasmanian AIDS [*Acquired Immune Deficiency Syndrome*] Council [*Australia*]
TAC .... Taxable Adjustment Column (AAGC)
TAC .... Tax Court of the United States Reports [*A publication*]
TAC .... Team Activity Chart
TAC .... Technical Activities Committee (SAA)
TAC .... Technical Advisory Center [*National Bureau of Standards*]
TAC .... Technical Advisory Committee
TAC .... Technical Advisory Group (EERA)
TAC .... Technical and Agricultural College (AIE)
TAC .... Technical Applications Center [*Air Force*]
TAC .... Technical Area Coordinator
TAC .... Technical Assignment Control [*Nuclear energy*] (NRCH)
TAC .... Technical Assistance Center [*State University College at Plattsburgh*] [*Research center*] (RCD)
TAC .... Technical Assistance Center [*Operated by the Helen Keller National Center for Deaf-Blind Youths and Adults (HKNC)*] (PAZ)
TAC .... Technical Assistance Committee [*of the Economic and Social Council of the United Nations*]
TAC .... Technical Assistance Contract [*Nuclear energy*] (NRCH)
TAC .... Technology Application Center [*University of New Mexico*] [*Albuquerque, NM*]

TAC............	Teleconference Association of Canada [Toronto, ON] [Information service or system] (TSSD)
TAC............	Telemetry and Command (MCD)
TAC............	TELENET Access Controller
TAC............	Television Advertising Council [Australia]
TAC............	Television Advisory Committee [British] (DEN)
TAC............	Temperature Altitude Chamber
TAC............	Temporary Allocation Center (WDAA)
TAC............	Terminal Access Controller [Advanced Research Projects Agency Network] [DoD]
TAC............	Terminal Antrum Contraction (STED)
TAC............	Terminal Area Chart [Aviation] (FAAC)
TAC............	Terminal Atrial Contraction [Cardiology] (DAVI)
TAC............	Terrain Analysis Center [Army] (RDA)
TAC............	Test Access Control [Telecommunications] (TEL)
TAC............	Test Advisory Committee (MUGU)
TAC............	Test of Auditory Comprehension
TAC............	[Official] Texas Administrative Code (AAGC)
TAC............	Thai Airways Co. Ltd. [Later, Thai Airways International] [ICAO designator] (FAAC)
TAC............	Theatres Advisory Committee [British]
TAC............	Theoretical Astrophysics Centre
TAC............	Thermostatic Air Cleaner [Automotive engineering]
TAC............	Thyroid-Adrenocortical [Syndrome] [Medicine] (DB)
TAC............	Time Action Calendar [Management]
TAC............	Time-Activity Curve (STED)
TAC............	Time and Charges [Telecommunications] (IAA)
TAC............	Time at Completion (MCD)
TAC............	Time-to-Amplitude Converter
TAC............	Tobacco Advisory Council [British]
TAC............	Tokyo Automatic Computer (IAA)
TAC............	Total Aganglionosis Coli (STED)
TAC............	Total Alkaloids of Cinchona [Medicine]
TAC............	Total Allowable Catch [Fishing regulation proposed by EEC]
TAC............	Total Annualized Cost
TAC............	Total Automatic Color (IAA)
TAC............	Total Average Cost (KSC)
TAC............	Totally Accurate Clock
TAC............	Toxic Air Contaminant
TAC............	Toxicant Analysis Center (STED)
TAC............	Toyota Atlantic Championship [Auto racing]
TAC............	Tracking Accuracy Control
TAC............	Trade Agreements Committee [An interagency committee of the executive branch of US government] [Terminated, 1963]
TAC............	Traders and Contacts
TAC............	Trades Advisory Council [British]
TAC............	Trades Advisory Council of British Jewry (BUAC)
TAC............	Training Alarm Controller
TAC............	TRANSAC [Transistorized Automatic Computer] Assembler Compiler
TAC............	Trans-Aminocrotonic Acid [Also, TACA] [Organic chemistry]
TAC............	Transformer Analog Computer
TAC............	Transistor-Assisted Circuit (ADA)
TAC............	Transistorized Automatic Computer (IAA)
TAC............	Transistorized Automatic Control
TAC............	Transitional Authority in Cambodia [United Nations] (BUAC)
TAC............	Transkei Airways Corp. [South Africa] (BUAC)
TAC............	Translations Activities Committee [Special Libraries Association]
TAC............	Translator, Assembler, Compiler
TAC............	Transmitter Assembler Compiler [Telecommunications] (IAA)
TAC............	Transonic Aerodynamic Characteristics
TAC............	Transportation Account Code [Military] (AFM)
TAC............	Transportation Acquisition Circular (AAGC)
TAC............	Transportation Association of Canada (EAIO)
TAC............	Transportes, Aduanas, y Consignaciones SA [Shipping company] [Spain] (EY)
TAC............	Transportes Aereos Coyhaique [Chile] [ICAO designator] (FAAC)
TAC............	Trapped Air Cushion
TAC............	Traskei Airways Corp. [South Africa] (EY)
TAC............	Travel Air Club (EA)
TAC............	Travelcraft Ambassadors Club [Defunct] (EA)
TAC............	Trialkoxycitrate [Organic chemistry]
TAC............	Triallyl Cyanurate [Organic chemistry]
TAC............	Triamcinolone Acetonide Cream (STED)
TAC............	Triamcinolone Cream [Anti-inflammatory steroid]
TAC............	Trouble Analysis Chart
TAC............	True Airspeed Computer
TAC............	Turboalternator Compressor
TAC............	Type Address Code
TAC............	Type of Activity Code [Military]
TAC............	Types of Assistance Code [Army]
TACA............	[The] Association of Comedy Artists (EA)
TACA............	Tactical Airborne Controller Aircraft [Military] (CAAL)
TAC(A).........	Tactical Air Coordinator [or Controller] (Airborne) [Military] (NVT)
TACA............	TELECOMS Authorities Cryptographic Algorithm [Bell Telephone encryption chip]
TACA............	Test of Adult College Aptitude
TACA............	Trans-Aminocrotonic Acid [Also, TAC] [Organic chemistry]
TACA............	Tucker Automobile Club of America (EA)
TACAC.........	Theater Army Civil Affairs Command (AABC)
TACAC.........	Trans Atlantic Committee on Agricultural Change (BUAC)
TACAD.........	Tactical Advisory [Military] (CAAL)
TACAD.........	Traffic Alert and Collision Avoidance Detection [Aviation]
TACADE.........	Teachers' Advisory Council on Alcohol and Drug Education [British]
TACADS.........	Tactical Automated Data Processing System
TAC/AFSC	Tactical Air Command/Air Force Systems Command
TACAID	Tactical Airborne Information Document (NVT)
TACAIR	Tactical Air [Military] (AABC)
TACAIRLIFTSq...	Tactical Airlift Squadron [Air Force]
TACAIRLIFTTNGSq...	Tactical Airlift Training Squadron [Air Force]
TACAIR TED...	Tactical Air Threat Environment Description (MCD)
TACALS........	Tactical Air Control and Landing System [Military] (IAA)
TACAMO	Take Charge and Move Out Aircraft [Military]
TACAN	Tactical Air Command and Navigation [System] (NAKS)
TACAN	Tactical Air Navigation [System]
TACANCEN	Tactical Air Navigation Control Center (DNAB)
TACAN-DME...	Tactical Air Navigation Distance Measuring Equipment
TACAP	Tactical Air Command Aircraft Profiler Capability [Air Force]
TACAV	Linea Aerea TACA de Venezuela
TACAV	Tactical Aviation Model
TACAWS	[The] Army Combined Arms Weapons System
TACAWS	[The] Army Counter-Air Weapons System
TACAX	Hancock(J) Cal. Tax Free Inc. Cl.A [Mutual fund ticker symbol] (SG)
TACBOMBSq...	Tactical Bomb Squadron [Air Force]
TACC	Tactical Air Command and Control [Air Force]
TACC	Tactical Air Command Center [Air Force] (NVT)
TACC	Tactical Air Command, Central
TACC	Tactical Air Control Center [Air Force]
TACC	Tactical Air Coordination Center [Military] (CAAL)
TACC	Temporary Augmentation for Command and Control [Navy] (ANA)
TACC	Thorotrast-Associated Cholangiocarcinoma [Oncology]
TACC	Time Averaged Clutter Coherent (MCD)
TACC	Total Army Career Counselor [Inservice recruiter] (INF)
TACCAR	Time Averaged Clutter Coherent Airborne RADAR
TACCIMS	Theater Automated Command and Control Information Management System (MCD)
TACCO	Tactical Air Control Coordinator
TACCO	Tactical Control Officer [Army] (AABC)
TACCOM	Tactical Communications (MCD)
TACCOMSIM......	Tactical Communications Simulator
TACCONSq...	Tactical Control Squadron [Air Force]
TACCOPS	Tactical Air Control Center Operations (NVT)
TAC COUNT...	Tactical Countermeasure
TACCP	Tactical Command Post [Army]
TACCS	Tactical Airborne Command, Control, and Surveillance
TACCS	Tactical Air Command Control System (MCD)
TACCS	Tactical Air Control Center Squadron
TACCS	Tactical Army Combat Service Support Computer System
TACCSF......	Theater Air Command and Control Simulator Facility [Air Force]
TACCS-K......	Theater Automated Command and Control System - Korea
TACCTA.......	Tactical Commander's Terrain Analysis [Military] (AABC)
TAC-D	Tactical Deception (MCD)
TACD	Transport and Communications Division, United Nations ESCAP [Economic and Social Commission for Asia and the Pacific] [Thailand] (EAIO)
TACDA	[The] American Civil Defense Association (EA)
TACDACS.....	Target Acquisition and Data Collection System
TAC D & E...	Tactical Development and Evaluation [Military] (CAAL)
TACDAS	Target Acquisition and Data Collection System
TACDEN	Tactical Data Entry [Army] (IAA)
TACDEN	Tactical Data Entry Unit [Army]
TACDEP	(One-Day) Tactical Deception [Orientation] (DOMA)
TACDEW	Tactical Advanced Combat Direction and Electronic Warfare (MCD)
TACDEW/EGCS...	Tactical Advanced Combat Direction and Electronic Warfare Environmental Generation Control System [Navy]
TACDIFINSPRO...	Temporary Active Duty with Instruction in a Flying Status Involving ProficiencyFlying [Navy] (DNAB)
TACDIFPRO...	Temporary Active Duty in a Flying Status Involving Proficiency Flying [Navy] (DNAB)
TACE	Tactical Air Coordination Element
TAC-E.........	Tactical Emergency [Army]
TACE..........	Talos Conversion Equipment (MCD)
TACE..........	Teichoic Acid Crude Extract [Medicine] (DMAA)
TACE..........	Trianisylchloroethylene (STED)
TACE..........	Tri-para-anisylchloroethylene [Estrogen]
TACE..........	Turbine Automatic Control Equipment (IAA)
TACED	Tank Appended Crew Evaluation Device (MCD)
TACELECRON...	Tactical Electronic Warfare Squadron [Air Force] (DNAB)
TACELECRONDET...	Tactical Electronic Warfare Squadron Detachment [Air Force] (DNAB)
TACELINT	Tactical Electronic Intelligence [Navy] (ANA)
TACELIS.......	Tactical Communications Emitter Location and Identification System [Army] (MCD)
TACELRON...	Tactical Electronic Warfare Squadron [Navy] (ANA)
TACES.......	Tactical Electronics Squadron
TACESS.......	Tactical Communications-Electronics Simulation and Support System
TACEST	Tactical Test [Military] (NVT)
TACET........	Television Advisory Committee for Educational Television (NTCM)
TACEVAL......	Tactical Evaluation (MCD)
TACEXEC......	Tactical Executive
TACF.........	Temporary Alteration Control Form (IAA)
TACFAX	Tactical Digital Facsimile Equipment (MCD)
TACFDC	Tactical Fire Direction Center [Army] (AABC)
TACFIRE......	Tactical Fire [Military]
TACFO	TASAMS [The Army Supply and Maintenance System] Coordination Field Office (AABC)
TACFTRRSq...	Tactical Fighter Replacement Squadron [Air Force]
TACG	Tactical Air Control Group [Military]
TACG	Tactical Group [Military]
TACGP	Tactical Air Control Group [Military]
TACGRU......	Tactical Air Control Group [Military] (NVT)

TACH	Athens Community Hospital, Athens, TN [*Library symbol Library of Congress*] (LCLS)
TACH	Tachometer (AAG)
tach	Tachometer (IDOE)
TACH	Tachometer Generator (IAA)
tach	Tachycardia [*Cardiology*] (DAVI)
TACH	Turban Action Committee against Helmets (WDAA)
TACHA	Tennessee Automated Clearing House Association
TACHO	Tachometer (DSUE)
TACHY	Tachycardia [*Cardiology*] (AAMN)
tachy	Tachycardia [*Medicine*] (STED)
TACI	Tactical Initialization [*Computer software*] [*Military*]
TACI	Test Access Control Interface [*Telecommunications*] (TEL)
TACI	Transport Accident Commission Insurance [*Victoria, Australia*]
TACIES	Tactical Imagery Exploitation System [*Military*] (MUSM)
TACIMPS	Tactical Integrated Mission Planning Station (MCD)
TACIN	Town and Country Information Network (BUAC)
TACINTEL	Tactical Intelligence Information Exchange System (NVT)
TACIS	Technical Assistance to Commonwealth of Independent States
TACIT	Technical Advisory Committee on Inland Transport
TACIT	Time-Authenticated Cryptographic Identity Transmission [*Military*]
TACJAM	Tactical Jamming
TACL	Tactical Air Command Letter [*Air Force*]
TACL	Tactical Loader [*Preparation software*] [*Army*]
TACL	Tank-Automotive Concepts Laboratory [*Army*] (RDA)
TACL	Test for Auditory Comprehension of Language [*Speech and language therapy*] (DAVI)
TACL	Theater Authorized Consumption List [*Army*] (AABC)
TACL	Time and Cycle Log [*NASA*] (KSC)
TACLAND	Tactical Instrument Landing (MCD)
TACLET	Tactical Law Enforcement Teams [*Coast Guard*]
TACLINC	Tactical Communications Location Identification Navigation and Control System [*Military*] (ECON)
TACLO	Tactical Air Command Liaison Officer (FAAC)
TACLOG	Tactical-Logistical [*Army*] (AABC)
TACLOG GP	Tactical-Logistics Control Group [*Military*]
TACM	Tactical Air Command Manual [*Air Force*]
TACM	Transit Air Cargo Manifest
TACMA	Association of Control Manufacturers (BUAC)
TACMAN	Tactical Manuals [*Aircraft*] (MCD)
TACMAR	Tactical Memory Address Register [*Computer science*] (IAA)
TACMAR	Tactical Multifunction Array RADAR [*Air Force*]
TACMAS	Tactical Computer Modeling Analysis and Simulation (SSD)
TACMEMO	Tactical Memorandum [*Navy*] (ANA)
TACMIS	Tactical Management Information System [*Army*] (RDA)
TACMOD	Tactical Modular Display [*Army*] (PDAA)
TACMS	Tactical Missile System [*Provisional*] [*Army*] (RDA)
TACN	Triazacyclononane [*Organic chemistry*]
TACNAV	Tactical Navigation System
TACNAVMOD	Tactical/Navigational Modernization [*Navy*]
TACNNR	Turkish Association for the Conservation of Nature and Natural Resources (BUAC)
TACNOTE	Tactical Notice (NVT)
TACO	Taco Cabana 'A' [*NASDAQ symbol*] (TTSB)
TACO	Taco Cabana, Inc. [*NASDAQ symbol*] (SAG)
TACO	Tactical Coordinator (NG)
TACO	Tamoxifen, Adriamycin, Cyclophosphamide, Oncovin [*Vincristine*] [*Antineoplastic drug regimen*]
TACO	Technical Appliance Corp. (IAA)
TACO	Test and Checkout Operations [*NASA*] (NASA)
TAC-OA	Tactical Air Command Office of Operations Analysis [*Langley Air Force Base, VA*]
TACOC	Tactical Air Control Operation Center
TacoCab	Taco Cabana, Inc. [*Associated Press*] (SAG)
TACODA	Target Coordinate Data (IEEE)
TACOL	Thinned Aperture Computed Lens (IEEE)
TACOM	Tactical Area Communications System (MCD)
TACOM	Tactical Communications (AFM)
TACOM	Tank-Automotive Command [*Warren, MI*] [*Army*] (MCD)
TACOMA	Television Advisory Committee of Mexican Americans (NTCM)
TACOM-ARDEC	Tank-Automotive and Armaments Command's Armament Research Development and Engineering Center [*Army*]
TACOMM	Tactical Communications [*Military*] (AABC)
TACOMPLAN	Tactical Communications Plan [*NATO*]
TACOMSAT	Tactical Communications Satellite [*Also, TACSAT*] [*DoD*]
TACOM-TARDEC	Tank-Automotive and Armaments Command's Tank Automotive Reseach, Development, and Engineering Center [*Army*]
TACON	Tactical Control [*Military*] (CAAL)
TACOPNSSq	Tactical Operations Squadron [*Air Force*]
TACOPS	Tactical Air Combat Operations Staff (MCD)
TACOPS	Tactical Organization Paperless System [*Army*]
TACOR	Threat Assessment and Control Receiver [*Air Force*]
TACOS	Tactical Airborne Countermeasures or Strike [*Air Force*]
TACOS	Tactical Air Combat Operations Staff
TACOS	Tactical Air Combat Simulation (NATG)
TACOS	Tactical Communications System
TACOS	Talos Adaptable Computer System [*Navy*]
TACOS	Tool for Automatic Conversion of Operational Software
TACOS	Travel Agents Computer Society [*Defunct*] (EA)
TACOSS	Tactical Container Shelter System [*Rockwell International Corp.*]
TACP	Tactical Air Command Pamphlet [*Air Force*]
TACP	Tactical Air Command Post [*Air Force*] (MCD)
TACP	Tactical Air Control Party [*Air Force*]
TACP	Tactical Air Control Point
TACP	Technical Analysis of Cost Proposals [*DoD*]
TA/CP	Technology Assessment/Control Plan [*Environmental science*] (COE)
TACPACS	Tactical Packet Switching System [*Army*] (RDA)
TACPOL	Tactical Procedure Oriented Language [*Computer science*] (CSR)
TACPOL	Tactile Procedure-Oriented Language (CSR)
TACR	Tachykinin Receptor [*Medicine*] (DMAA)
TACR	Tactical Air Command Regulation [*Air Force*]
TAC/R	Tactical Reconnaissance
TACR	Time and Cycle Record [*NASA*] (KSC)
TAC/RA	TACAN [*Tactical Air Navigation*] RADAR Altimeter (NASA)
TACRAC	Tactical Warfare Research Advisory Committee [*Military*] (RDA)
TACRAC	Technical and Cost Reduction Assistance Contract
TACRAPS	Tactical Range Prediction System
TACREACT	Tactical Reconnaissance Reaction Aircraft (MCD)
TACREDD	Tactical Readiness Drill [*Military*] (DNAB)
TACREP	Tactical Report (DOMA)
TAC RISE	Tactical Reconnaissance Intelligence System Enhancement [*Air Force*]
TACRON	Tactical Air Control Squadron [*Military*]
TACRON	Tactical Air Squadron (DOMA)
TACRV	Tracked Air-Cushion Research Vehicle [*DoD*]
TACS	Auxiliary Crane Ship [*Navy symbol*]
TACS	Tactical Air Control System [*Air Force*]
TACS	Talker Active State [*Telecommunications*] (IAA)
TACS	Tasmanian Association of Children's Services [*Australia*]
TACS	Technical Assignment Control System [*Nuclear energy*] (NRCH)
TACS	Telemetry and Command System (MCD)
TACS	Test Assembly Conditioning Station [*Nuclear energy*] (NRCH)
TACS	Theater Area Communications Systems [*Military*]
TACS	Theater Army Communications System (MCD)
TACS	Thruster Attitude Control System [*NASA*]
TACS	Total Access Communications System [*Commercial firm British*]
TACSAT	Tactical Communications Satellite [*Also, TACOMSAT*] [*DoD*]
TACSAT	Tactical Satellite [*Military*] (IAA)
TACSATCOM	Tactical Satellite Communications [*Military*]
TACSCE	Texas Association for Community Service and Continuing Education (EDAC)
TACSI	Tactical Air Communications [*or Control*] System Improvements [*Air Force*] (MCD)
TACSIM	Tactical Simulation
TACSOP	Tactical Standing Operating Procedure [*Army*] (INF)
TACSQ	Tactical Air Control Squadron [*Air Force*]
TACSS	Tactical Army Combat Service Support (DOMA)
TACSS	Tactical Schoolship [*Navy*] (NVT)
TACSS	Takenaka Aqua-Reactive Chemical Soil-Stabilisation System [*Nuclear energy*] (NUCP)
TACS/TADS	Tactical Air Control System/Tactical Air Defense System
TACSYR	Tactical Communications Systems Requirements (MCD)
TACT	[*The*] Association of Corporate Trustees [*British*] (EAIO)
Tact	Tactica [*of Arrian*] [*Classical studies*] (OCD)
TACT	Tactical
TACT	Tactical Air Control Training
TACT	Tactical Transport [*Aircraft*]
TACT	Technological Aid to Creative Thought (PDAA)
TACT	Television Action Committee for Today and Tomorrow [*Later, American Council forBetter Broadcasts*] (AEBS)
TACT	Terminal Activated Channel Test
TACT	Tories Against Cruise and Trident [*Missiles*] [*British*] (DI)
TACT	Total Audit Concept Technique (PDAA)
TACT	Transactional Analysis Control Technique [*Training program*] [*American Airlines*]
TACT	TransAct Technologies
TACT	TransAct Technologies Inc. [*NASDAQ symbol*] (SAG)
TACT	Transistor and Component Tester
TACT	Transonic Aircraft Technology [*Program*] [*NASA and Air Force*]
TACT	Truth about Civil Turmoil [*An association Defunct*] (EA)
TAC/TADS	Tactical Air Control/Tactical Air Defense System [*Military*] (CAAL)
TACTAN	Tactical Air Control and Navigation
TACTAS	Tactical Towed Array Sensor [*Formerly, ETAS*] [*Navy*]
TACTAS	Tactical Towed Array SONAR [*Navy*]
TACTASS	Tactical Tone and Acoustic Surveillance System [*Military*] (CAAL)
TACTASS	Tactical Towed-Array Surveillance System (DOMA)
TACTEC	Tactical Technology Information Analysis Center [*Columbus, OH*] [*DoD*] (GRD)
TACTEC	Totally Advanced Communications Technology
TACTECS	Tables and Charts through Extended Character Sets [*Computer science*]
TACTIC	Technical Advisory Committee to Influence Congress [*Federation of American Scientists*]
TACTICS	Technical Assistance Consortium to Improve College Services [*Defunct*] (EA)
TACTL	Tactical (AAG)
TACTLASS	Tactical Towed Array Surveillance System [*Military*] (MCD)
TAC T MR	Tactical Transport Medium Range [*Aircraft*]
TACTOOL	Tactical [*Software*] Tools
TACTRAGRULANT	Tactical Training Group, Atlantic [*Military*] (DNAB)
TACTRAGRUPAC	Tactical Training Group, Pacific [*Military*] (DNAB)
TACTRI	Taiwan Agricultural Chemicals and Toxic Substances Research Institute (BUAC)
TACTRUST	[*The*] Athletics Congress/USA Trust Fund
TACTS	Tactical Aircrew Combat Training System (NVT)
TACTS/ACMI	Tactical Aircrew Combat Training System/Air Combat Maneuvering Instrumentation (NVT)
TAC T SR	Tactical Transport Short Range [*Aircraft*]
TAC/USA	[*The*] Athletics Congress/USA (EA)
TACV	Tracked Air-Cushion Vehicle [*High-speed ground transportation*]

TACV	Transportes Aereos de Cabo Verde [*Cape Verde*] [*ICAO designator*] (FAAC)
TACVA	Tactical Vulnerability Assessment [*Military*] (MCD)
TACVA/CEWIS	Tactical Communications Vulnerability Assessment of Combat Electronics Warfare Intelligence System (MCD)
TACV/LIM	Tracked Air Cushion Vehicle Powered by Linear Induction Motor (PDAA)
TACWAR	Tactical Warfare (Model) [*Army*]
TACWE	Tactical Weather System (MCD)
TAD	Airborne Tanker, Drogue (NVT)
TAD	Tactical Action Display [*SAGE*]
TAD	Tactical Air Defense (MCD)
TAD	Tactical Air Direction [*Military*]
TAD	Tactical Atomic Demolition [*Munitions*] [*Obsolete Military*] (NG)
TAD	Tadiran Limited [*NYSE symbol*] (SPSG)
TAD	Tadiran Limited ADS [*NYSE symbol*] (TTSB)
TAD	Tadotu [*Japan*] [*Seismograph station code, US Geological Survey Closed*] (SEIS)
TAD	Target Acquisition Data
TAD	Target Activation Date (AAG)
TAD	Target Area Designator [*Air Force*]
TAD	Target Audience Description [*Army*]
TAD	Task Assignment Directive (KSC)
TAD	Task Assignment Drawing (MCD)
TAD	Technical Acceptance Date (AAG)
TAD	Technical Acceptance Demonstration (IAA)
TAD	Technical Analysis Division [*National Bureau of Standards*]
TAD	Technical Approach Demonstration
TAD	Technical Approval Demonstration (AAG)
TAD	Technology Area Description (MCD)
TAD	Technology Availability Date (MCD)
TAD	Telecommunications Automation Directorate [*Army*] (RDA)
TAD	Telemetry Analog to Digital [*Information converter*]
TAD	Telemetry and Data [*Telecommunications*] (IAA)
TAD	Telephone Answering Device
TAD	Television Advertising Duty
TAD	Temperature and Dew Point (NASA)
TAD	Temporary Additional Duty [*Military*]
TAD	Temporary Assigned Duty [*Military*] (VNW)
TAD	Temporary Attached Duty
TAD	Terminal Address Designator
TAD	Test Acceptance Document [*Computer science*] (IAA)
TAD	Test and Development (MCD)
TAD	Theater Air Defense [*Military*]
TAD	Thermactor Air Diverter [*Automotive engineering*]
TAD	Thermal Analysis Data
TAD	Thioguanine, ara-C, Daunomycin [*Daunorubicin*] [*Antineoplastic drug regimen*]
TAD	Thomas Aloysius Dorgan [*Satirical cartoonist*]
TAD	Thoracic Asphyxiant Dystrophy [*Medicine*] (MAE)
TAD	Throw Away Detector [*Space shuttle*] [*NASA*]
TAD	Thrust-Augmented Delta [*NASA*]
TAD	Time Available for Delivery (CET)
TAD	Tobyhanna Army Depot, Library, Tobyhanna, PA [*OCLC symbol*] (OCLC)
TAD	Tooele Army Depot [*Utah*]
TAD	Top Assembly Drawing
TAD	Toward Affective Development [*Educational tool*]
TAD	Traffic Accident Data [*Project*] [*National Safety Council*]
TAD	Trailing-Arm-Drive
TAD	Training Aid and Device [*Military*]
TAD	Training Aids Division [*Navy*]
TAD	Traitement Automatique des Donnees [*Automatic Data Processing*] [*French*]
TAD	Transaction Application Drive [*Computer Technology, Inc.*]
TAD	Transmission and Distribution (IAA)
TAD	Transporte Aereo Dominicano SA [*Dominican Republic*] [*ICAO designator*] (FAAC)
TAD	Transverse Abdominal Diameter (DAVI)
TAD	Traveling Around Drunk
TAD	Tricyclic Antidepressant Drug [*Medicine*] (STED)
TAD	Trinidad [*Colorado*] [*Airport symbol Obsolete*] (OAG)
TAD	Trio Archean Developments [*Vancouver Stock Exchange symbol*]
TAD	Twin and Add (SAA)
TADA	Tasmanian Amateur Diving Association [*Australia*]
TADA	Terrorist and Disruptive Activities Act [*India*] (ECON)
TADA	Tracking and Data Acquisition (IAA)
TADAAS	TEMPEST Automated Data Acquisition and Analysis System
TADAC	Therapeutic Abortion, Dilation, Aspiration, Curettage [*Medicine*] (MAE)
TADAR	Tactical Area Defense Alerting RADAR (MCD)
TADARS	Target Acquisition/Designation Aerial Reconnaissance System (MCD)
TADAS	Tactical Air Defense Alerting System [*Army*]
TADC	Tactical Air Direction Center [*Military*]
TADC	Training and Distribution Center [*Navy*]
TaDD	Tactical Demilitarization Development Program [*Army*]
TADD	Tangential Abrasive Dehulling Device [*for grains*]
TADD	Target Alert Data Display Set (MCD)
TADD	Termite and Ant Detection Dog [*In TADD Services Corp.*]
TADD	Truckers Against Drunk Drivers [*Defunct*] (EA)
TADDS	Target Alert Data Display Set (RDA)
TADE	Tetraaminodiphenylether [*Organic chemistry*]
TADF	Thermally Activated Delayed Fluorescence [*Analytical chemistry*]
TADF	Thomas A. Dooley Foundation [*Later, Dooley Foundation/Intermed-USA*]
TADGC	Tactical Air Designation Grid System [*Tactical Air Command*]
TADI	Time Assigned Data Interpolation (HGAA)
TADIC	Telemetry Analog-Digital Information Converter
TADIL	Tactical Data Information Link [*DoD*]
TADIL	Tactical Digital Information Link
TADIL-J	Tactical Data Information Link-JTIDS [*Joint Tactical Information Distribution System*] [*DoD*]
TADIL-J	Tactical Digital Information Link - Joint
TADILS	Tactical Automatic Data Information Links (MCD)
Tadiran	Tadiran Ltd. [*Associated Press*] (SAG)
TADIX	Tactical Data Information Exchange Subsystem [*Navy*] (ANA)
TADIXS	Tactical Data Information Exchange Subsystem
TADJET	Transport Air Drop and Jettison Test [*Air Force, Army*]
TADLR	Tooling Automated Direct Labor Reporting (MCD)
TADM	Tactical Atomic Demolition Munitions [*Obsolete Military*] (AABC)
TADO	Tactical Airlift Duty Officer (AFM)
TADOR	Table Data Organization and Reductions
TADP	Tactical Air Direction Post [*Military*]
TAD/P	Terminal Area Distribution Processing
TADP	Toronto Anti-Draft Programme [*Defunct*] (EA)
TADR	Tabulated Drawing (MSA)
TADR	Test Answer Document Reader
TADREPS	Tactical Data Replay System (NVT)
TADRS	Target Acquisition/Designation Reconnaissance System (MCD)
TADS	Tactical Air Defense Systems (RDA)
TADS	Tactical Automatic Digital Switch [*Military*]
TADS	Target Acquisition and Data System [*Army*] (DOMA)
TADS	Target Acquisition and Designation System (MCD)
TADS	Target Acquisition Designation Sight [*Army*]
TADS	Target and Activity Display System [*Military*]
TADS	Target Designation System [*Navy*]
TADS	Technical Assistance Data
TADS	Teletypewriter Automatic Dispatch System
TADS	Test and Debug System (HGAA)
TADS	Thermal Analysis Data Station
TADS	Throw Away Detector (PDAA)
TADS	Tracking and Display System
TADS	Transportable Automatic Digital Switch (PDAA)
TADS	Type [*Command*] Automated Data System [*Navy*]
TADSIXS-B	Tactical Data Information Exchange System-B (DOMA)
TADSO	Tactical Digital Systems Office [*Navy*] (MCD)
TADS/PNVS	Target Acquisition Designation System/Pilot Night Vision System [*Army*] (RDA)
TADSS	Tactical Automatic Digital Switching System
TADSS	Training Aid, Device, Simulation and Simulator [*Military*]
TADSYS	Turbine Automated Design System
TADYL	Tom Dooley Youth League [*Defunct*]
TadzhSSR	Tadzhik Soviet Socialist Republic
TAE	Tactical Aeromed Evacuation (CINC)
TAE	Taegu [*South Korea*] [*Seismograph station code, US Geological Survey Closed*] (SEIS)
TAE	Taligent Application Environment [*Taligent, Inc.*] [*Computer science*]
TAE	Tallow Amine Ethoxylate
TAE	Tannic Acid Equivalent [*Analytical chemistry*]
TAE	Technician Aeronautical Engineering (IAA)
TAE	Test and Evaluation (MCD)
TAE	Textes Arameens d'Egypte [*A publication*] (BJA)
TAE	Time and Event (IAA)
TAE	Transantarctic Expedition (ADA)
TAE	Transcatheter Arterial Embolization [*Medicine*]
TAE	Transferable Atom Equivalent [*Chemical modeling*]
TAE	Transoceanic Airborne Environment
TAE	Transportes Aereos Militares Ecatorianos CA [*Ecuador*] [*ICAO designator*] (FAAC)
TAE	Tris-Acetate-EDTA [*Ethylenediaminetetraacetate*] [*Buffer*]
TAEA	Tangipahoa & Eastern [*AAR code*]
TAEAS	Tactical ASW [*Antisubmarine Warfare*] Environmental Acoustic Support [*Navy*] (CAAL)
TAEC	Thai Atomic Energy Commission for Peace (BUAC)
TAEC	Thailand Atomic Energy Commission for Peace
TAEC	Turkish Atomic Energy Commission
TAED	Tetraacetylethylenediamine [*Laundry bleaching agent*]
TAEDP	Total Army Equipment Distribution Program (AABC)
TAEDS	Texas Association for Educational Data Systems (EDAC)
TAEDS	Total Army Equipment Distribution System (MCD)
TAEE	Tertiary Amyl Ethyl Ether [*Gasoline*] [*Organic chemistry*]
TAEG	Training Analysis and Evaluation Group [*Navy*]
TAEG	Training and Evaluation Group [*Navy*] (MCD)
TAEM	Terminal Area Energy Management [*NASA*] (NASA)
TAEMS	Transportable Automated Electromagnetic Measurement System (MCD)
TAEO	Test Article Engineering Order (MCD)
TAER	Time, Azimuth, Elevation, and Range [*Aerospace*]
TAEREC	Time and Event Recorder (IAA)
TAERS	[*The*] Army Equipment Record System [*Later, TAMMS*]
TAES	Tactical Aeromedical Evacuation System
TAES	Techicas Aereas de Estudios y Servicios SA [*Spain ICAO designator*] (FAAC)
TAES	Texas Agricultural Experiment Station [*Texas A & M University*] [*Research center*] (RCD)
TAES	Transportes Aereos de El Salvador SA de CV [*ICAO designator*] (FAAC)
TAETGM	Test and Evaluation Task Group Manager (MCD)
TAF	Arnold Engineering Development Center, Arnold Air Force Station, TN [*OCLC symbol*] (OCLC)

TAF............	[*The*] Asia Foundation (EA)
TAF............	Oran-Tafaraoui [*Algeria*] [*Airport symbol*] (OAG)
TAF............	Stores Ship [*Military Sea Transportation Service*] (CINC)
TAF............	Tactical Air Force
TAF............	Tactical Area Files [*Military*] (CAAL)
TAF............	Taforalt [*Morocco*] [*Seismograph station code, US Geological Survey*] (SEIS)
TAF............	Task Analysis Form
TAF............	Taxpayers Against Fraud [*Washington, DC*] (AAGC)
TAF............	Taxpayers Against Fraud, the False Claims Act Legal Center (EA)
TAF............	Technology Access Fund [*Chrysler Corp.*]
TAF............	Terminal Aerodrome Forecast [*Also, TAFOR*]
TAF............	Test, Analyze, Fix (MCD)
TAF............	Third Air Force
TAF............	Thousand Acre-Feet [*Measurement*]
TAF............	Time Air Ltd. [*Canada ICAO designator*] (FAAC)
TAF............	Time and Frequency (MHDB)
TAF............	Tissue Angiogenesis Factor [*Medicine*] (DMAA)
TAF............	Top of Active Fuel [*Nuclear energy*] (NRCH)
TAF............	Toxoid-Antitoxin Floccules [*Immunology*]
TAF............	Traditional Acupuncture Foundation (EA)
TAF............	Training Analysis and Feedback (MCD)
TAF............	Transaction Facility
TAF............	Transaxel Fluid (IAA)
TAF............	Transcription Activation Function [*Genetics*]
TAF............	Trend Asignment File [*Computer science*] (ECII)
TAF............	Trim after Forming (MSA)
TAF............	Trypsin-Aldehyde-Fuchsin [*Medicine*] (MAE)
TAF............	Tuberculin Albumose-Frei [*Albumose-Free Tuberculin*] [*German Medicine*]
TAF............	Tumor-Angiogenesis Factor [*Medicine*]
TAF............	Turkish Air Force (NATG)
TAFA............	Territorial and Auxiliary Forces Association [*British military*] (DMA)
TAFAD	Task Force Air Defense (MUGU)
TAFB............	Travis Air Force Base [*California*]
TAFB............	Tyndall Air Force Base [*Florida*]
TAFCSD	Total Active Federal Commissioned Service to Date [*Military*]
TAFCV.........	Tobacco and Associated Farmers' Cooperative of Victoria [*Australia*]
TAFD	Test for Auditory Figure-Ground Discrimination
TAFDS	Tactical Airfield Fuel Dispensing System (NG)
TAFE..........	Technical and Further Education (ODBW)
TAFE..........	Telemetry Auto Following Equipment
TAFE..........	Transverse Alternating Field Electrophoresis
TAFECNSW...	Technical and Further Education Commission New South Wales [*Australia*]
TAFEDAB	Technical and Further Education Discipline Appeals Board [*Victoria, Australia*]
TAFEESC......	Technical and Further Education External Studies College [*Western Australia*]
TAFENCRD...	Technical and Further Education National Centre for Research and Development [*Australia*]
TAFERS........	Technical and Further Education Rural Studies [*South Australia*]
TAFETANSW...	Technical and Further Education Teachers' Association of New South Wales [*Australia*]
TAFETSAB....	Technical and Further Education Teaching Service Appeals Board [*Victoria, Australia*]
TAFF............	Take-Away and Fast Food Federation (BUAC)
TAFF............	Thermally Activated Flux Flow [*Physics*]
TAFF............	Timer, Actuator, Fin, Fuze (DWSG)
TAFFE..........	Tactical Air Against First and Follow-On Eschelon (MCD)
Taffie..........	Technologically Advanced Family [*Lifestyle classification*]
TAFFS..........	[*The*] Army Functional Files System
TAFFTS........	[*The*] Army Functional Files Test System (MCD)
TAFG..........	Two-Axis Free Gyro (AAG)
TAFHQ	Tactical Air Force Headquarters
TAFI............	Technical Association of the Fur Industry
TAFI............	Turnaround Fault Isolation [*Aviation*]
TAFIC..........	Tasmanian Fishing Industry Council (EERA)
TAFIES........	Tactical Air Forces Intelligence Exploitation System
TAFIG..........	Tactical Air Forces Interoperability Group [*Air Force*]
TAFIIS.........	Tactical Air Force Integrated Information Systems (MCD)
TAFIM..........	Technical Architecture Framework for Information Management [*Army*]
TAFIM..........	Turnaround Fault Isolation Manual
TAFIN..........	Tactical Air Force Initiative (MCD)
TAFIS..........	TCATA [*TRADOC Combined Arms Test Activity*] Automated Field InstrumentationSystem (MCD)
TAFIS..........	TEXCOM [*Test and Experimentation Command*] Automated Field Instrumentation System [*Army*]
TAFLE..........	Thornton Aviation Fuel Lubricity Evaluator [*Fuels and lubricants testing*]
TAFMM........	Tactical Air Force Maintenance Management (MCD)
TAFMS........	Total Active Federal Military Service (DNAB)
TAFMSD	Total Active Federal Military Service to Date
TAFNORNOR...	Allied Tactical Air Force, Northern Norway [*NATO*]
TAFO..........	Theater Accounting and Finance Office [*Military*] (AFM)
TAFOR	Terminal Aerodrome Forecast [*Also, TAF*]
TAFPD	Technical Assessment and Fraud Prevention Division [*Environmental Protection Agency*] (GFGA)
TAF QR	Taxpayers Against Fraud Quarterly Review (AAGC)
TAFR..........	Total Age-Specific Fertility Rate [*Population studies*]
TAFR..........	Trouble and Failure Report [*Army*]
TAFROC	Tactical Air Force Required Operational Capability (MCD)
TAFS..........	Stores Ship
TAFS............	Training Aid Feasibility Studies (AAG)
TAFSEA........	Technical Applications for Southeast Asia [*Air Force*]
TAFSEG........	Tactical Air Force Systems Engineering Group (MCD)
TAFSONOR...	Allied Tactical Air Force, South Norway [*NATO*] (NATG)
TAFSUS	Turkish American Friendship Society of the United States (EA)
TAFT............	Technical Assistance Field Team (MCD)
TAFUBAR	Things Are Fouled Up Beyond All Recognition [*Military slang*] [*Bowdlerized version*]
TAFVER........	Terminal Aerodrome Forecast Verification
TAFX............	Tapping Fixture
TAFY............	American Theatre Arts for Youth (EA)
TAFY............	Technically Advanced Family (PS)
TAG............	[*The*] Acronym Generator [*An RCA computer program*]
TAG............	[*The*] Acrylonitrile Group (EA)
TAG............	[*The*] Adjutant General [*Army*]
TAG............	Airborne Tanker, General (NVT)
TAG............	American Group of CPA Firms [*Lombard, IL*] (EA)
TAG............	[*The*] Association for the Gifted (EA)
TAG............	[*The*] Attorneys Group (EA)
TAG............	[*The*] Audiotex Group [*Princeton, NJ*] [*Telecommunications service*] (TSSD)
TAG............	Orion Air, Inc. [*ICAO designator*] (FAAC)
TAG............	Tactical Air Group [*MTMC*] (TAG)
TAG............	Tactical Airlift Group (MCD)
TAG............	Tactical Analysis Group [*Military*] (CAAL)
tag............	Tagalog [*MARC language code Library of Congress*] (LCCP)
TAG............	Tagbilaran [*Philippines*] [*Army*] (OAG)
TAG............	TAG International (NTPA)
TAG............	Talented and Gifted (EDAC)
TAG............	Talk Address Group (CIST)
TAG............	Target Attaching Globulin [*Medicine*] (AAMN)
TAG............	Target Attitude Group [*Advertising*]
TAG............	Tavern and Guild Association [*Division of Homophile Effort for Legal Protection*] (EA)
TAG............	Taxi Air Group, Inc.
TAG............	Technical Advisory Group (EERA)
TAG............	Technical Air-to-Ground (NASA)
TAG............	Technical Art Group
TAG............	Technical Assessment Group [*Navy*]
TAG............	Technical Assistance Grant
TAG............	Technical Assistance Group [*NASA*] (KSC)
TAG............	Technical Assistance Guides (OICC)
TAG............	Technician Affiliate Group [*of American Chemical Society*]
TAG............	Technology Applications Group [*Commercial firm*] (IID)
TAG............	Telecomputer Applications Group
TAG............	Telegraphist Air Gunner [*British military*] (DMA)
TAG............	Telemetry System Analysis Group
TAG............	Tennessee, Alabama & Georgia Railway Co. [*AAR code*]
TAG............	Terminal Applications Group, Inc.
TAG............	Terminating Amber Codon [*Genetics*]
TAG............	Terminating and Grounding
TAG............	Test Analysis Guide
TAG............	Test Assembly Grapple [*Nuclear energy*] (NRCH)
TAG............	Test Automation Growth
TAG............	Texas A & M University at Galveston, Galveston, TX [*OCLC symbol*] (OCLC)
TAG............	Thalassemia Action Group [*Organization concerned with Cooley's anemia*] (PAZ)
TAG............	Theatre about Glasgow [*Acting company*] (ECON)
TAG............	Thomson Advisory Group (EFIS)
TAG............	Thymine, Adenine, Guanine [*Laboratory science*] (DAVI)
TAG............	Time Arrive Guarantee (AAG)
TAG............	Time Automated Grid
TAG............	Tongue and Groove [*Lumber*] (IAA)
TAG............	Towpath Action Group (BUAC)
TAG............	Training Aids Guide [*Navy*]
TAG............	Transatlantic Geotraverse [*Geology*]
TAG............	Transfer Agent [*Business term*] (MHDB)
TAG............	Transient Analysis Generator
TAG............	Transport Air Group [*Joint Army, Navy, and Marine Corps*]
TAG............	Transportation Acronym Guide [*BTS*] (TAG)
TAG............	Transportation Alternatives Group [*Transportation 2000*] [*MTMC*] (TAG)
TAG............	Trauma Action Group [*Defunct*] (EA)
TAG............	Treatment Action Group [*for AIDS medication*] [*FDA*]
TAG............	Tree-Adjoining Grammar [*Artificial intelligence*]
TAG............	Triacylglycerol [*Food technology*]
TAG............	Tumor-Associated Glycoprotein [*Biochemistry*]
TAGA	Tasmanian Amateur Gymnastics Association [*Australia*]
TAGA	Technical Association of the Graphic Arts (EA)
TAGA	Telegraphist Air Gunner's Association [*Navy British*]
TAGA	Trace Atmospheric Gas Analyser [*Instrument*]
TAGA	Travel Agents Guild of America (EA)
TAGAMET......	Antagonist Cimetidine [*Ulcer medicine manufactured by SmithKline Beckman Corp.*]
TAGBDUSA...	[*The*] Adjutant General's Board, United States Army
TAGC..........	Tripped Automatic Gain Control
TAGCEN	[*The*] Adjutant General Center [*Army*] (AABC)
TAGER	[*The*] Association for Graduate Education and Research
TAGF..........	Tumor Angiogenetic Factor [*Medicine*] (DB)
TAGH..........	Triiodothyronine, Amino Acids, Glucagon, and Heparin [*Medicine*] (DMAA)
TagHeur.......	Tag Heuer International SA [*Associated Press*] (SAG)
TAGIS.........	Tracking and Ground Instrumentation System (DNAB)
TAGIU........	Tracking and Ground Instrumentation Unit [*NASA*]
TAGM..........	Range Instrumentation Ship

TAGM..........	Table and Art Glassware Manufacturers [*Defunct*] (EA)
TAGN	Triaminoguanidine Nitrate [*Propellant ingredient*]
TAGO	[*The*] Adjutant General's Office [*Army*]
TAGOTA	TACFIRE [*Tactical Fire*] Ad Hoc Group on Testing and Analysis (MCD)
TAGRDCUSA...	[*The*] Adjutant General's Research and Development Command, United States Army
TAGRET	Thermal Advanced Gas-Cooled Reactor Exploiting Thorium [*Nuclear energy*] (IAA)
TAGRX	Hancock(J) Growth & Inc. Cl.A [*Mutual fund ticker symbol*] (SG)
TAGS	FBM [*Fleet Ballistic Missile*] Support Ship
TAGS	Tactical Aircraft Guidance System [*Air Force*]
TAGS	Tarrant Apparel Group [*NASDAQ symbol*] (SAG)
TAGS	Technology for the Automated Generation of Systems (NITA)
TAGS	Teledyne Airborne Geophysical Services
TAGS	Text and Graphics System [*or Subsystem*] (NASA)
TAGS	Theater Air-Ground Warfare Simulation (MCD)
TAGS	Time-Automated Grid System (CIST)
TAGS	Total Associates Guest Satisfaction
TAGS	Tower Automated Ground Surveillance System (MCD)
TAGSRWC....	[*The*] Andy Griffith Show Rerun Watchers Club (EA)
TAGSS	Triple-A Guaranteed Secondary Securities (EBF)
TAGSUSA.....	[*The*] Adjutant General's School [*United States*], Army
TAH.............	Air Moorea [*France ICAO designator*] (FAAC)
TAH.............	Hospital Ship
Tah	Taehti [*Record label*] [*Finland*]
TAH.............	Tahiti [*Society Islands*] [*Seismograph station code, US Geological Survey Closed*] (SEIS)
TAH.............	Tanna Island [*Vanuata*] [*Airport symbol*] (OAG)
TAH.............	Tell Abu Huwam (BJA)
TAH.............	Total Abdominal Hysterectomy [*Medicine*]
TAH.............	Total Artificial Heart [*Cardiology*] (DMAA)
TAH.............	Transabdominal Hysterectomy [*Medicine*] (MAE)
TAH.............	Trans-African Highway Co-Ordinating Committee (BUAC)
TA/H............	Turn Altitude/Height [*Aviation*] (DA)
TAHA	Tapered Aperture Horn Antenna
TAHA	Trans-African Highway Authority (BUAC)
TAHBSO.......	Total Abdominal Hysterectomy Bilateral Salpingo-Oophorectomy [*Medicine*] (MAH)
TAHE...........	Thin Line Array Handling Equipment (DWSG)
TAHOE	TOW Against Helicopter Operational Equipment (RDA)
TAHOP.........	Tank/Attack Helicopter Operational Performance (MCD)
TAHPERD.....	Texas Association of Health, Physical Education, Recreation, and Dance (BUAC)
TAHQ	Theater Army Headquarters
TAI..............	National Organization for Travelers Aid Societies [*Also known as Travelers Aid International*] (EA)
TAI..............	TACA International Airlines SA [*El Salvador*] [*ICAO designator*] (FAAC)
TAI..............	Tactical Area of Interest [*Military*] (INF)
TAI..............	Tainan [*Republic of China*] [*Seismograph station code, US Geological Survey*] (SEIS)
Tai	Taiwan
TAI..............	Taiz [*Yemen Arab Republic*] [*Airport symbol*] (OAG)
TAI..............	Target Area of Interest [*Army intelligence matrix*] (INF)
TAI..............	Teacher Attitude Inventory [*Teacher evaluation test*]
TAI..............	Team-Assisted Individualization (EDAC)
TAI..............	Temps Atomique International [*International Atomic Time*] [*Telecommunications*]
TAI..............	Test Anxiety Inventory [*Educational test*]
TAI..............	Thai Airways International (MCD)
TAI..............	Therapy Attitude Inventory [*Test*] [*Psychology*]
TAI..............	Thermal Anti-Ice (GAVI)
TAI..............	Time-to-Autoignition [*NASA*] (KSC)
TAI..............	Total Active Inventory (MCD)
TAI..............	Total Aircraft Inventory
TAI..............	Traditionally Administered Instruction (BUR)
TAI..............	Trait Anxiety Inventory [*Psychology*] (DHP)
TAI..............	Transamerica Income Shares, Inc. [*NYSE symbol*] (SPSG)
TAI..............	TransAmerica Inc. Shrs [*NYSE symbol*] (TTSB)
TAI..............	Transport Africain International [*Togo*] (BUAC)
TAI..............	Transports Aeriens Intercontinentaux [*Privately owned French airline*]
TAI..............	Turnaround Index [*Computer science*]
TAI..............	Tuskegee Airmen, Inc. (EA)
TAIB............	Trans-Arabian Investment Bank (MENA)
TAIC............	Technical Air Intelligence Center [*Navy*]
TAIC............	Tokyo Atomic Industrial Consortium
TAIC............	Triallylisocyanurate [*Organic chemistry*]
TAICH	Technical Assistance Information Clearing House [*of ACVAFS*] [*Information service or system*] (EA)
TAID............	Thrust-Augmented Improved Delta [*Launch vehicle*] [*NASA*]
TAID............	Thunderbird American Indian Dancers (EA)
TAIDB..........	Tank-Automotive Integrated Database (MCD)
TAIDEC	Togo Agro Industrial Development Corp. (BUAC)
TAIDET........	Triple Axis Inertial Drift Erection Test
TAIDHS........	Tactical Air Intelligence Data Handling System (NATG)
TAIDSC........	Tasmanian AIDS [*Acquired Immune Deficiency Syndrome*] Council [*Australia*]
TAIF............	[*The*] Australasian Institute of Fundraising
TAIL............	Tail Wind [*Aviation*] (FAAC)
TAILRATS	Tail RADAR Acquisition and Tracking System (MCD)
TAILS..........	Tactical Automatic Landing System [*Aviation*] (NG)
TAIM...........	Technical Area Integration Manager (SSD)
TAIM...........	Total Army Inventory Management [*Army*]
TAIM...........	Trial of Antihypertensive Interventions and Management [*Medicine*]

TAINS	TERCOM [*Terrain Contour Mapping*]-Assisted Inertial Navigation System (MCD)
TAIP...........	Terminal Area Impact Point (MUGU)
TAIR...........	Terminal Area Instrumentation RADAR (MCD)
TAIR...........	Test Assembly Inspection Record [*NASA*] (NASA)
TAIRCF	Tactical Air Control Flight [*Military*]
TAIRCG	Tactical Air Control Group [*Military*] (AFIT)
TAIRCS	Tactical Air Control Squadron [*Air Force*]
TAIRCW	Tactical Air Control Wing [*Air Force*]
TAIS	Tactical Air Intelligence System [*Military*] (MCD)
TAIS	Technology Applications Information System
TAIS	Time Assessment Interview Schedule (DMAA)
TAISEL........	Taiwan International Standard Electronics Ltd. (NITA)
TAISSA	Travelers Aid - International Social Service of America [*Later, ISS/AB*]
TAIT	Taitron Components 'A' [*NASDAQ symbol*] (TTSB)
TAIT	Taitron Components, Inc. Class A [*NASDAQ symbol*] (SAG)
Tait	Tait's Index to Morison's Dictionary [*Scotland*] [*A publication*] (DLA)
Tait	Tait's Index to Scotch Session Cases [*1823*] [*A publication*] (DLA)
Tait	Tait's Manuscript Decisions, Scotch Session Cases [*A publication*] (DLA)
Tait Ev........	Tait on Evidence [*A publication*] (DLA)
Tait Ind.......	Tait's Index to Scotch Session Cases [*1823*] [*A publication*] (DLA)
Tait JP........	Tait's Justice of the Peace [*A publication*] (DLA)
Taitron........	Taitron Components, Inc. Class A [*Associated Press*] (SAG)
TAIU...........	Technical Aircraft Instrument Unit [*Navy*]
TAIU...........	Training Agency Intelligence Unit (AIE)
Taiw...........	Taiwan (VRA)
Taiwan........	Taiwan Fund, Inc. [*Associated Press*] (SAG)
TaiwanE.......	Taiwan Equity Fund, Inc. [*Associated Press*] (SAG)
TAJ	Tadji [*Papua New Guinea*] [*Airport symbol*] (OAG)
taj	Tajik [*MARC language code Library of Congress*] (LCCP)
TAJ	Tanegashima [*Ryukyu Islands*] [*Seismograph station code, US Geological Survey*] (SEIS)
TAJ	Taracua [*Brazil*] [*Airport symbol*] (AD)
TAJ	Thermal Arc Jet
TAJ	Tunisavia - Societe de Transport, Services et Travaux Aeriens [*Tunisia*] [*ICAO designator*] (FAAC)
TAJ	Turbulent Air Jet
TAJA	[*The*] Abibi Jazz Artists [*British*]
TAJA	[*The*] Australian Journal of Anthropology [*A publication*]
TAJAG.........	[*The*] Assistant Judge Advocate General [*Army*] (AABC)
TAJBIC........	The Arlin J. Brown Information Center (EA)
TAK............	Cargo Ship [*Military Sea Transportation Service*] (CINC)
TAK............	Takaka [*New Zealand*] [*Seismograph station code, US Geological Survey Closed*] (SEIS)
TAK............	Takamatsu [*Japan*] [*Airport symbol*] (OAG)
TAK............	Taken
TAK............	Trainer Appraisal Kit
TAK............	Transkel Airways [*South Africa ICAO designator*] (FAAC)
TAK............	Transparent Armor Kit
TAKC...........	Theological Associate, King's College [*London*]
TAKCAL.......	Tachometer Calibration (DNAB)
TAKIS	Tutmonda Asocio pri Kibernetiko, Informatiko, kaj Sistemiko [*World Association of Cybernetics, Computer Science, and System Theory*] (EAIO)
TAKIT.........	Teaching Aids Kit [*Red Cross Youth*]
TAKR	Vehicle Cargo Ship
TAKRX	Fast Sealift Ship
TAKV	Cargo Ship and Aircraft Ferry [*Military Sea Transportation Service*] (CINC)
TAKX...........	Maritime Prepositioning Ship
TAL	[*The*] Apocryphal Literature: A Brief Introduction [*1945*] [*A publication*] (BJA)
Tal	Cases Tempore Talbot, English Chancery [*1734-38*] [*A publication*] (DLA)
TAL	Tailor (MSA)
TAL	Talair Pty Ltd. [*New Guinea*] [*ICAO designator*] (FAAC)
TAL	Talara [*Peru*] [*Seismograph station code, US Geological Survey*] (SEIS)
Tal	Talbot's Cases in Equity [*1734-38*] [*A publication*] (DLA)
TAL	Talcorp Ltd. [*Toronto Stock Exchange symbol*]
TAL	Talis [*Such*] [*Pharmacy*]
TAL	Talladega College, Talladega, AL [*OCLC symbol*] (OCLC)
TAL	Talley Indus [*NYSE symbol*] (TTSB)
TAL	Talley Industries, Inc. [*NYSE symbol*] (SPSG)
TAL	Talmud
TAL	Tanana [*Alaska*] [*Airport symbol*] (OAG)
TAL	Target Acquisition Laboratory
TAL	Teacher Assessment of Leverage (EDAC)
TAL	Technische Akademie der Luftwaffe [*Germany*] (MCD)
TAL	Telecommunications Access Language
TAL	Tendo Achillis Lengthening [*Orthopedics*] (DAVI)
TAL	TEPI [*Technical Equipment Planning Information*] Approved Letter
TAL	Terminal Application Language
TAL	Territory Airlines [*Australia*]
TAL	Tetraalkyllead [*Organic chemistry*]
TAL	Thymic Alymphoplasia [*Medicine*] (MAE)
TAL	Timeslips III Accounting Link [*Computer science*]
TAL	Track Adjusting Link [*Army*] (RDA)
TAL	Training Aids Library [*Navy*]
TAL	Transaction Application Language [*Computer science*] (MHDB)
TAL	TransAlpine [*Pipeline*] [*Western Europe*]
TAL	Transatlantic (SSD)
TAL	Transatlantic Abort Landing [*NASA*] (NAKS)

TAL .... Transatlantic Landing
TAL .... Transocean Air Lines
TAL .... Transoceanic Abort Landing (NASA)
TAL .... Transporter Air Lock [Nuclear energy] (NRCH)
TALA .... Teacher Author League of America [Formerly, TALNY] (EA)
TALA .... Textile Association of Los Angeles
TALA .... Travel Agents' Licensing Authority [Victoria, Australia]
TALAFIT .... Tank, Laying, Aiming, and Firing Trainer (MCD)
TALANT .... Thiokol Nuclear Development Center; Allison Division, General
                       Motors; Linde Division, Union Carbide; and Nuclear Development
                       Corp. Team (SAA)
TALAR .... Tactical Approach and Landing RADAR [NASA]
TALAR .... Talos Activity Report (MCD)
Talb .... Cases Tempore Talbot, English Chancery [1734-38] [A publication]
                       (DLA)
Talb .... Talbot's Cases in Equity [1734-38] [A publication] (DLA)
TALB .... Travel Agents' Licensing Board [Australia]
TALBE .... Talk and Listen Beacon [Radio]
Talbots .... Talbots, Inc. [Associated Press] (SAG)
TALC .... Tactical Airborne Laser Communication (DOMA)
TALC .... Tactical Airborne Laser Communications [Military] (LAIN)
TALC .... Tactical Airlift Center (AFM)
TALC .... Take-a-Look-See (MCD)
TALC .... Tank-Automotive Logistics Command [Army]
TALC .... Territory Anti-Litter Committee [Northern Territory, Australia]
TALC .... Tutoring Adults through Literacy Councils (EDAC)
TALCM .... Tactical Air-Launched Cruise Missile (MCD)
TALC-OA .... Tactical Airlift Center Office of Operations Analysis [Pope Air Force
                       Base, NC]
TALCOR .... Transponder Array Location by Co-Planar Ranges [Oceanography]
                       (DICI)
TALD .... Tactical Air Launched Decoy (DOMA)
TALDT .... Total Administrative and Logistics Downtime (MCD)
TALF .... Take a Look Foundation (EA)
TALF .... Trial Attorney's Litigation File (AAGC)
TALFF .... Total Allowable Level of Foreign Fishing
TALFF .... Total Allowance Level of Foreign Fishing [Marine science] (OSRA)
TALH .... Thick Ascending Limb of Henle's Loop [Medicine] (DMAA)
TALIRO .... Tanzania Livestock Research Organisation (BUAC)
TALIS .... Topics in Australasian Library and Information Studies [A publication]
TALISMAN ... Transfer Accounting, Lodging for Investments, and Stock
                       Management for Jobbers [Stock exchange term British]
TALISSI .... Tactical Light Shot Simulation (MCD)
TALK .... Tel-Save Holdings [NASDAQ symbol] (TTSB)
TALK .... Tel-Save Holdings, Inc. [NASDAQ symbol] (SAG)
TALK .... Titles Alphabetically Listed by Keyword (KSC)
TAlk .... Total Alkalinity [Marine science] (OSRA)
TALK .... Transfer of African Language Knowledge [South Africa] (WDAA)
T-ALL .... T-Cell Acute Lymphoblastic Leukemia [Oncology]
Talley .... Talley Industries, Inc. [Associated Press] (SAG)
TALM .... Tactical Air Launched Missile (MCD)
TALM .... Temperature Alarm Monitor (COE)
TALMA .... Truck and Ladder Manufacturers Association (BUAC)
TALMIS .... Technology-Assisted Learning Market Information Services
                       [Educational Programming Systems, Inc.]
TALMS .... Tangier American Legation Museum Society (EA)
TALMS .... Tunable Atomic Line Molecular Spectroscopy
TALNY .... Teacher Author League of New York [Later, TALA] (EA)
TALO .... Tactical Air Liaison Officer [Air Force]
TALO .... Time after Lift-Off
TALO .... Total Audience Listening Output [Television ratings] (WDMC)
TALOG .... Theater Army Logistical Command
TALON .... South Central Regional Medical Library Program [Library network]
TALON .... Tactical Air-Land Operations (MCD)
TALON .... Testing and Analysis of Local Area Optical Networks (NITA)
TALON .... Texas Arkansas Louisiana Oklahoma, New Mexico (NITA)
TALONS .... Tactical Airborne LORAN Navigation System [Model] (MCD)
TALOP .... Terminology, Administrative, Logistical, and Operational Procedures
                       [Military]
TALPrB .... Talley Indus,$1.00 Cv B Pfd [NYSE symbol] (TTSB)
TALPS .... Transactional Analysis Life Position Survey [Psychology]
TAL QUAL .... Talis Qualis [Such As It Is] [Latin] (ROG)
TALR .... Law Reports of the District Court of Tel Aviv [A publication] (BJA)
TALS .... [The] American Lupus Society (EA)
TALS .... [The] Army Language School
TALS .... Barge Cargo Ship
TALS .... Test of Awareness of Language Segments [Diane J. Sawyer] (TES)
TALS .... Transport Approach and Landing Simulator
TALT .... Tracking Altitude (MCD)
TALTC .... Test Access Line Termination Circuit [Telecommunications] (TEL)
TALTER .... Teno [or Tendo] Achillis Lengthening and Toe Flexor Release
                       [Orthopedics] (DAVI)
TALTT .... Thrust Augmented Long Tank Thor (MCD)
TALUS .... Transportation and Land Use Study [Michigan]
TALX .... Talx Corp. [NASDAQ symbol] (SAG)
TalxCp .... Talx Corp [Associated Press] (SAG)
TAM .... [The] Access Method (IAA)
TAM .... [The] Associated Missions (EA)
TAM .... Tactical Airlift Modernization
TAM .... Tactical Air Missile
TAM .... Tactical Air Mission [Air Force]
TAM .... Tamanrasset [Algeria] [Seismograph station code, US Geological
                       Survey] (SEIS)
TAM .... Tamara Resources, Inc. [Vancouver Stock Exchange symbol]
TAM .... Tamerton [England]

Tam .... Tamid (BJA)
TAM .... Tamil [Language, etc.] (ROG)
tam .... Tamil [MARC language code Library of Congress] (LCCP)
Tam .... Tamlyn's English Rolls Court Reports [48 English Reprint]
                       [A publication] (DLA)
TAM .... Tamoxifen [Antineoplastic drug]
TAM .... Tampico [Mexico] [Airport symbol] (OAG)
TAM .... Tangent Approximating Manifold
TAM .... Target Acquisition Model [Military]
TAM .... Target Activated Munition [Air-delivered land mines]
TAM .... Technical Acknowledgment Message [Aviation]
TAM .... Technical Advice Memorandum
TAM .... Technical Ammunition
TAM .... Technical Area Manager
TAM .... Technical Association of Malaysia (BUAC)
TAM .... Techniques of Alcohol Management [Campaign, sponsored in part by
                       the National Licensed Beverage Association, to prevent drunk
                       driving]
TAM .... Telecommunications Access Method
TAM .... Telephone Answering Machine (IEEE)
TAM .... Teleprocessing Access Method [Telecommunications] (IAA)
TAM .... Television Audience Measurement
TAM .... Teresian Apostolic Movement [See also MTA] [Italy] (EAIO)
TAM .... Terminal Access Method
TAM .... Test Access Multiplexer [Telecommunications] (TEL)
TAM .... Texas A & M University [College Station, TX]
TAM .... Thermal Analytical Model [Apollo] [NASA]
TAM .... Thermoacidurans Agar Modified [Microbiology] (DAVI)
TAM .... Throw Away Maintenance
TAM .... Time and Materials (MCD)
TAM .... Tituli Asiae Minoris [Vienna] [A publication] (OCD)
TAM .... Total Active Motion [Orthopedics]
TAM .... Towed Acoustic Monitor (PDAA)
TAM .... Toxoid-Antitoxin Mixture [Immunology]
TAM .... Traction Asynchronous Motor (PDAA)
TAM .... Trajectory Application Method (MCD)
TAM .... Transantarctic Mountains
TAM .... Transistor-Amplifier-Multiplier (IIA)
TAM .... Transparent Anatomical Manikin [An exhibit at the Chicago Museum
                       of Science and Industry]
TAM .... Transportacion Aerea Mexicana [Mexico ICAO designator] (FAAC)
TAM .... Transportation Acquisition Manual [A publication] (AAGC)
TAM .... Transportes Aereos Regionals SA [Brazil] [ICAO designator] (FAAC)
TAM .... Trialkylamine [Organic chemistry]
TAM .... Triangle Amplitude Modulation
TAM .... Tubos de Acero de Mexico [AMEX symbol] (SPSG)
TAM .... TubosDeAceroMex ADR [AMEX symbol] (TTSB)
TAM .... Tumor-Associated Macrophages [Immunology]
TAM .... Twentieth Anniversary Mobilization (EA)
TAM .... Type-Approval Model
TAM .... Tyrosine Activation Motif [Biochemistry]
TAMA .... Technical Assistance and Manufacturing Agreement
TAMA .... Threat to Army Mission Areas
TAMA .... Training Aids Management Agency [Army] (AABC)
TAMAC .... Three-Axis Manual Attitude Controller
TAMAC .... Toxic Air Monitoring Technical Advisory Committee [Environmental
                       science] (COE)
TAMALAN .... Table Manipulation Language (MHDB)
Tamb .... Tambyah's Reports [Ceylon] [A publication] (DLA)
TAMBA .... Twins and Multiple Births Association [British] (DBA)
Tambd .... Tambrands, Inc. [Associated Press] (SAG)
TAMBX .... Hancock(J) Tax Free Bond CI.A [Mutual fund ticker symbol] (SG)
TAMC .... Tactical Aviation Maintenance Co. [Army]
TAMC .... Transportation Aircraft Maintenance Company [Army]
TAMC .... Tripler Army Medical Center (AABC)
TAMCO .... Training Aid for MOBIDIC Console Operations
TAMDA .... Timber and Allied Materials Development Association [South Africa]
                       (BUAC)
TAME .... Tactical Air-to-Air Mission Evaluation (MCD)
TAME .... Tactical Missile Encounter [Air Force] (KSC)
TAME .... Tertiary-Amyl Methyl Ether [Gasoline additive]
TAME .... Toluene-Sulfo-Trypsin Arginine Methyl Ester [Organic chemistry]
                       (MAE)
TAME .... Tosyl-L-arginine Methyl Ester [Also, TosArgOMe] [Biochemical
                       analysis]
TAMED .... Totally Automated Method Development [High-performance liquid
                       chromatography]
TAMF .... Tactical Automated Maintenance Facility
TAMI .... Tanks and Mechanized Infantry Experiment (MCD)
TAMI .... Television Accessory Manufacturers Institute (NTCM)
TAMI .... Thrombolysis and Angioplasty in Myocardial Infarction [Cardiology
                       study]
TAMI .... Tip Air Mass Injection [Helicopter]
TAMICSS ..... TAFIES [Tactical Air Force Intelligence Exploitation System] Microfilm
                       Subsystem (MCD)
TAMIRAD .... Tactical Mid-Range Air Defense Program [Army] (AABC)
TAMIS .... Telemetric Automated Microbial Identification System
TAMIS .... Training Ammunition Management Information System (MCD)
Taml .... Tamlyn's English Rolls Court Reports [48 English Reprint]
                       [A publication] (DLA)
TAML .... Taunton Municipal Lighting Plant [Nuclear energy] (NRCH)
TAMLA .... Technical Assistance and Manufacturing License Agreement
Taml Ev ...... Tamlyn's Evidence in Chancery [2nd ed.] [1846] [A publication]
                       (DLA)
Taml TY ...... Tamlyn's Terms of Years [1825] [A publication] (DLA)

Tamlyn	Tamlyn's English Rolls Court Reports [*48 English Reprint*] [*A publication*] (DLA)
Tamlyn Ch ...	Tamlyn's English Rolls Court Reports [*48 English Reprint*] [*A publication*] (DLA)
Tamlyn (Eng)...	Tamlyn's English Rolls Court Reports [*A publication*] (DLA)
TAMM	Tetrakis(acetoxymercuri)methane [*Organic chemistry*]
TAMMC	Theater Army Materiel Management Center
TAMMIS	Theater Army Medical Management Information System (GFGA)
TAMMIS-D ..	Theater Army Medical Management Information System - Division
TAMMS	[*The*] Army Maintenance Management System [*Formerly, TAERS*] (AABC)
TAMO	Tooling Advance Material Order (MCD)
TAMO	Training Aids Management Office [*Army*] (AABC)
TAMOR	Turkish Association of Marketing and Opinion Research (BUAC)
TAMOS	Terminal Automatic Monitoring System
TAMOS	Terminal Auto-Operator and Monitor System (NITA)
TAMP	Tactical Antimissile Measurement Program [*Military*] (IAA)
TAMP	Tactical Armament Master Plan (MCD)
TAMP	Tampering [*FBI standardized term*]
TAMP	Terminally (Guided) Anti-Armor Mortar Projectile [*Navy*] (DOMA)
TAMP	Tertiary-Amylphenol [*Disinfectant*]
TAMP	Thailand Ammunition Manufacturing Plant (CINC)
TAMP	Theater Aviation Maintenance Program [*Army*] (DOMA)
TAMP	Transition Assistance Management Program [*Army*]
TAMP	Tufts Assessment of Motor Performance [*Occupational therapy*]
TAMPA	Tender Assist Minimum Platform Arrangement (PDAA)
Tampa	Transportes Aereos Mercantiles Panamericanos [*National airlines*] [*Colorado*] (EY)
TAMPER	Tables for Approximation of Midpoints for Exponential Regression (MCD)
TAMPNL	Trigger and Monitor Panel (IAA)
TAMPS	Tactical Aircraft Mission Planning System (DOMA)
TAMPS	Teaming Analysis Model Personnel Selector (MCD)
TAMR	Teen Association of Model Railroading (EA)
TAMRA	Technical and Miscellaneous Revenue Act of 1988
TAMS	Defender Tank Antimissile System [*British*] [*Military*] (INF)
TAMS	Intime Systems International, Inc. [*NASDAQ symbol*] (SAG)
TAMS	Tactical Avionics Maintenance Simulation (KSC)
TAMS	Tandem Accelerator Mass Spectrometry
TAMS	Target Activated Munitions System
TAMS	Technical Assistance and Management Services [*General Services Administration*] (GFGA)
TAMS	Test and Monitoring System (MCD)
TAMS	Texas Assesment Modeling Systems (EDAC)
TA-MS	Thermal Analysis Mass Spectrometry
TAMS	Thruster-Assisted Mooring System [*of a ship*] (DS)
TAMS	Token and Medal Society (EA)
TAMS	Total Active Military Service (AFM)
TAMS	Total Automotive Management Service
TAMS	Toxic Air Monitoring System [*Environmental Protection Agency*] (GFGA)
TAMS	Trade Action Monitoring System [*Office of the United States Trade Representative*] (GFGA)
TAMS	Training Ammunition Management Study [*Army*] (MCD)
TAMSA	Intime Systems Intl'A' [*NASDAQ symbol*] (TTSB)
TAMSA	Transportes Aereos Mexicano, Sociedad Anonima
Tam Shr	[*The*] Taming of the Shrew [*Shakespearean work*] (BARN)
TAMSU	Intime Systems Intl Unit [*NASDAQ symbol*] (TTSB)
TAMSW	Intime Sys Intl Wrrt [*NASDAQ symbol*] (TTSB)
TAMT	[*The*] American Mime Theatre (EA)
TAMTAC	Toxic Air Monitoring Technical Advisory Committee [*Environmental Protection Agency*] (GFGA)
TAMTI	Textile Academy, Ministry of Textile Industry [*China*] (BUAC)
TAMTU	Tanzania Machinery Testing Unit (BUAC)
TAMU	Texas A & M University
TAMU	Texas A&M University, College Station (USDC)
TAMV	Tulare Apple Mosaic Virus [*Plant pathology*]
TAMVEC	Texas A & M University Variable Energy Cyclotron
TAMWA	Tanzania Media Women Association (BUAC)
TAN	Tananarive [*Madagascar*] [*Seismograph station code, US Geological Survey*] (SEIS)
Tan	Tancredus [*Deceased circa 1236*] [*Authority cited in pre-1607 legal work*] (DSA)
TAN	Tandem (AAG)
TAN	Tandy Corp. [*NYSE symbol*] (SPSG)
Tan	Taney's United States Circuit Court Reports [*A publication*] (DLA)
TAN	Tangent [*Mathematics*]
tan	Tangent [*Mathematics*] (ODBW)
TAN	Tangential Cell [*Neurology*]
TAN	Tanglewood Consolidated Resources, Inc. [*Toronto Stock Exchange symbol*]
Tan	Tanhuma (BJA)
TAN	Tanned (MSA)
TAN	Tanning
TAN	Tanzania (WDAA)
TAN	Task Authorization Notice
TAN	Tasman Air Services [*New Zealand*] [*FAA designator*] (FAAC)
TAN	Taunton, MA [*Location identifier FAA*] (FAAL)
TAN	Tax Administrators News [*Federation of Tax Administrators*] [*A publication*]
TAN	Tax Anticipation Note [*Obligation*] [*State or local government*]
TAN	Taxation Assessment Notice
TAN	Technische Arbeitsnorm
TAN	Technology Alert Network (GNE)
TAN	Telephone Answering Service (NITA)
TAN	Teletype Alert Network (NVT)
TAN	Test Area North [*AEC*]
TAN	Thiazolylazonaphthol [*An indicator*] [*Chemistry*]
TAN	Third Age Network (BUAC)
TAN	Title Analytic [*Bibliography*]
TAN	Tonically Active Neurons [*Neurobiology*]
TAN	Total Acid Number [*Oil analysis*]
TAN	Total Adenine Nucleotide [*Medicine*]
TAN	Total Ammonia Nitrogen
TAN	Trainable Adaptive Network
TAN	Transall-Normen (MCD)
TAN	Transonic Aerodynamic Nozzle
TAN	Transportes Aereos Nacionales, SA [*TAN Airlines*]
TAN	Transportes Aeros Nacionales [*National Air Line*] [*Honduras*] (PDAA)
TAN	Twilight All Night
TAN ALT	Tangent Altitude [*Photography*]
TANB	Trailerable Aids to Navigation Boat [*USCG*] (TAG)
Tanc	Tancredus [*Deceased circa 1236*] [*Authority cited in pre-1607 legal work*] (DSA)
TANC	Through-Axis Navigational Control
TANC	Total Absorption Nuclear Cascade
TANCA	Technical Assistance to Non-Commonwealth Countries (BUAC)
TANCAV	Tactical Navigation and Collision Avoidance [*Military*] (CAAL)
Tanc QW	Tancred. Quo Warranto [*A publication*] (ILCA)
Tancre	Tancredus [*Deceased circa 1236*] [*Authority cited in pre-1607 legal work*] (DSA)
Tancred	Tancredus [*Deceased circa 1236*] [*Authority cited in pre-1607 legal work*] (DSA)
TAND	Tandum (FAAC)
TanD	Towns and Development [*Netherlands*] (BUAC)
T&A	Taken and Accepted (CIST)
T & A	Test and Adjust (SSD)
T & A	Time and Allowance
T&A	Time and Attendance (USDC)
TANDA	Time and Attendance Report [*Aviation*] (FAAC)
T & A	Tonsillectomy and Adenoidectomy [*or Tonsils and Adenoids*] [*Medicine*]
T & A	Tops and Accessories [*Show business slang*] [*Bowdlerized version*]
T & A	Turnbull & Asser [*Men's fashions*]
T & AT	Tank and Antitank [*Artillery and ammunition*] (NATG)
T & AVR	Territorial and Army Volunteer Reserve [*British*]
T & B	Taylor and Bell's Calcutta Supreme Court Reports [*India*] [*A publication*] (DLA)
T&B	Thomas & Betts Corp. (EFIS)
T&B	Top and Bottom (COE)
T & B	Top and Bottom [*Technical drawings*]
T & B	Truck and Bus
T & B	Turn-and-Bank Indicators
T and B......	Turned and Bored
T & BB	Top and Bottom Bolt [*Technical drawings*]
T&C	Technology and Culture [*A publication*] (BRI)
T & C	Telemetry and Command (SSD)
T & C	Terms and Conditions
T & C	Test and Crossmatch [*Medicine*] (MAH)
T & C	Thompson and Cook's New York Supreme Court Reports [*A publication*] (DLA)
T & C	Time and Charges [*Telecommunications*] (TEL)
T & C	Touch and Concern [*Legal shorthand*] (LWAP)
T & C	Town & Country [*A publication*]
T & C	Turn and Cough [*Medicine*]
T & CCA	Turks and Caicos Canadian Association
T & CCP	Telecommunications and Command and Control Program [*Air Force*] (AFIT)
T & CD	Timing and Countdown [*NASA*] (NASA)
T&CP	Test and Checkout Procedure [*NASA*] (NAKS)
T & CTB	Thames and Chilterns Tourist Board [*British*] (DCTA)
T & D	Taps and Dies (WDAA)
T & D	Training and Detention (ADA)
T & D	Transmission and Distribution
T & D	Transportation and Docking [*NASA*] (NAKS)
T & D	Transposition and Docking [*NASA*] (KSC)
T & DC	Training and Distribution Center [*Navy*]
T&DE	Test and Diagnostic Equipment [*Environmental science*] (COE)
T & E	Test and Evaluation [*Navy*] (NG)
T&E	Threatened and Endangered [*Forest industry*] (WPI)
T&E	Threatened and Endangered Species (COE)
T & E	Time and Events (AAG)
T&E	Tired & Emotional [*Medicine*] (WDAA)
T & E	Training and Education
T & E	Travel and Entertainment [*IRS*]
T & E	Traverse and Elevation [*Weapons*] [*Army*] (INF)
T & EC	Test and Evaluation Command [*Army*]
T & EC	Trauma and Emergency Center [*Medicine*]
TANDEL	Temperature Autostabilizing Nonlinear Dielectric Element (IAA)
Tandem	Tandem Computers, Inc. [*Associated Press*] (SAG)
TANDEM	Tibi Aderit Numen Divinum, Expecta Modo [*God Will Help Thee - Only Wait*] [*Motto of Elisabeth Ernestine Antonie, Duchess of Saxony (1681-1766)*] [*Latin*]
T & EO	Training and Evaluation Outline
T & ETGM....	Test and Evaluation Task Group Manager
T & F	Ticknor & Fields [*Publisher*]
T & G	Tongue and Groove [*Lumber*]
T & G	Tonopah & Goldfield Railroad (IIA)
T & G	Touch and Go [*Landings*] [*Aviation*] (MCD)
T & G	Tremont & Gulf Railroad (IIA)

T & G......... Tyrwhitt and Granger's English Exchequer Reports [1835-36] [A publication] (DLA)
T & H......... Test and Handling [Equipment] (NG)
T & H......... Thames & Hudson [Publisher]
T&H.......... Track and Hold (CIST)
T & HCA.... Towboat and Harbor Carriers Association of New York and New Jersey (EA)
T & HP...... Transportation and Handling Procedure
T & H Prac.. Troubat and Haly's Pennsylvania Practice [A publication] (DLA)
T & I......... Tax and Insurance Payment [Banking]
T&I.......... Test and Integration (CIST)
T and I...... Trade and Industrial Education (AEE)
T & L........ Thrift & Loans [Industrial loan company]
T & M........ Temple and Mew's English Criminal Appeal Cases [A publication] (DLA)
T & M........ Temple and Mew's English Crown Cases [1848-51] [A publication] (DLA)
T & M........ Test and Maintenance (WDAA)
T & M........ Test and Measurement [Quality control]
T & M........ Test and Monitor (CAAL)
T & M........ Time and Materials
T & M........ Trichomonas and Monilia [cultures] (DAVI)
T & NC...... Tennessee & North Carolina [Railroad] (MHDB)
T & NC...... Tennessee & North Carolina Railroad (IIA)
T & O........ Taken and Offered [Sporting] [British]
T & O........ Test and Operation [NASA] (KSC)
T & O........ Training and Operations [Military]
TANDOC..... Tanzania National Documentation Centre [National Central Library] [Information service or system] (IID)
T & OE...... Tentage and Organizational Equipment B ranch [US Army Natick Research, Development, and Engineering Center]
T & OHI..... Truck & Off-Highway Industries [A publication]
T & P........ Tank and Pump Unit [Mechanized infantry battalion] (DWSG)
T and P..... [The] Texas & Pacific Railway Co. [Absorbed into Missouri Pacific System]
T and P..... Theft and Pilferage
T & P........ Turner and Phillips' English Chancery Reports [A publication] (DLA)
T & PI....... Totally and Permanently Incapacitated [Insurance] (ADA)
T & R........ Testing and Regulating Department [Especially, in a wire communications maintenance division]
T & R........ Training and Readiness [Marine Corps] (DOMA)
T&R.......... Transmit-Receive (CIST)
T & R........ Turner and Russell's English Chancery Reports [1822-25] [A publication] (DLA)
T and RA.... Tennis and Rackets Association [British] (DBA)
T & RNP..... Transportation and Recruiting Naval Personnel [Budget appropriation title]
T and S...... Technical and Scientific Information [United Nations Development Program]
T & S........ Thomson and Steger's Tennessee Statutes [A publication] (ILCA)
T and S...... Touch and Stay
T & S........ Type and Screen
T & SA....... Task and Skill Analysis (AAG)
T & SER..... Tilbury & Southend Railway [British] (NOQ)
T & S Pr..... Tillinghast and Shearman's New York Practice [A publication] (DLA)
T & SW...... Temperance and Social Welfare [Free Church] [British]
T & T........ Tanqueray [Gin] and Tonic
T & T........ Targets and Timetables
T & T........ Tax and Tip
T & T........ Technicals and Turnovers [Basketball]
T & T........ Tijuana & Tecate Railway Co. (IIA)
T & T........ Time and Temperature
T & T........ Touch and Tone [Neurology] (DAVI)
T & T........ Transportation and Transportability
T&T.......... Travel and Tourism (EERA)
T & T........ Tympanostomy with Tube Placement [Otorhinolaryngology] (DAVI)
T & TA....... Training and Technical Assistance (OICC)
T & TEC..... Trinidad & Tobago Electricity Commission
T & TP...... Terry and the Pirates [Pop music group]
T&TPC....... Trinidad and Tobago Management Development and Productivity Centre (BUAC)
T & T Sup... Trinidad and Tobago Supreme Court Judgments [A publication] (ILCA)
T&UG......... Telephone and Utilities Group (CIST)
T & V........ Test and Verify Programs [Computer science] (MDG)
T & X........ Type and Crossmatch [Clinical chemistry]
Tandy........ Tandy Corp. [Associated Press] (SAG)
TandyBr..... Tandy Brands Accessories, Inc. [Associated Press] (SAG)
TANE........ Transportes Aereos Nacionales Ecuatorianas [Airline] [Ecuador]
TANESCO.... Tanzania Electric Supply Co.
Taney........ Taney's United States Circuit Court Reports [A publication] (DLA)
TANEYCOMO... Taney County, MO [A lake at Branson, MO]
Taney's CC Dec... Taney's United States Circuit Court Reports [A publication] (DLA)
Taney's Dec (USCC)... Taney's United States Circuit Court Reports [A publication] (DLA)
TANF......... Temporary Assistance for Needy Families
TANF......... Temporary Assistance to Needy Families [An association]
TANF......... Transition Assistance for Needy Families [Welfare program]
TANG........ Tangential (AAG)
TangEnt...... Tangram Enterprise Solutions, Inc. [Associated Press] (SAG)
Tanger....... Tanger Factory Outlet Centers [Associated Press] (SAG)
TANGLE...... Angle at Tip of Leaf [Botany]
Tangr........ Tanger Factory Outlet Centers [Associated Press] (SAG)
tanh......... Hyperbolic Tangent (IDOE)

TANH......... Tangent, Hyperbolic
Tanh......... Tanhuma (BJA)
TANI......... Total Axial Lymph Node Irradiation [Medicine]
TANJUG...... Telegrafska Agencija Nove Jugoslavije [Press agency] [Yugoslavia]
TANK........ Floatation Tank Association (EA)
TANK........ Tanknology Environmental [NASDAQ symbol] (SPSG)
TANKBAT..... Tank Battalion [Army]
TANKD....... TEI, Inc. [NASDAQ symbol] [Formerly, Tanknology Environmental]
TANKEX...... Tank Field Exercise (NVT)
Tanklgy..... Tankology Environmental, Inc. [Associated Press] (SAG)
TANKOPINS... Tanker Operating Instructions (DNAB)
Tan LR...... Tanganyika Territory Law Reports [A publication] (DLA)
Tann......... Tanner's Reports [8-14 Indiana] [A publication] (DLA)
Tann......... Tanner's Reports [13-17 Utah] [A publication] (DLA)
Tanner...... Tanner's Reports [13-17 Utah] [A publication] (DLA)
Tanner...... Tanner's Reports [8-14 Indiana] [A publication] (DLA)
TANO........ Triacetoneamine Nitroxide [Organic chemistry]
TANREM...... Tactical Nuclear Weapons Requirements Methodology
TANS........ Tactical Air Navigation System [Helicopter]
TANS........ Tax Anticipation Notes
TANS........ Terminal Area Navigation System
TANS........ Territorial Army Nursing Service [British]
TA-NS....... Total Abstinence - No Smoking [On social invitations]
TANSE....... Transportes Aereos Neuquinos Sociedad de Estado [Argentina ICAO designator] (FAAC)
TANSTAAFL... There Ain't No Such Thing As a Free Lunch [Principle of economics indicating that one cannot get something for nothing] [See also TINSTAAFL]
TANSW....... Taxpayers' Association of New South Wales [Australia]
TANT........ Tennant Co. [NASDAQ symbol] (NQ)
TANU........ Tanganyika African National Union [Political party]
TANWERE.... Tactical Nuclear Weapons Requirements (CINC)
TANY........ Typographers Association of New York (EA)
Tanz......... Tanzania
TAN-ZAM.... Tanzania-Zambia [Railway]
TAO......... Auxiliary Oiler [Military Sea Transportation Service]
TAO......... Hammond, LA [Location identifier FAA] (FAAL)
TAO......... Qingdao [China] [Airport symbol] (OAG)
TAO......... Tactical Action Observer [Military] (CAAL)
TAO......... Tactical Action Officer [Navy] (NVT)
TAO......... Tactical Air Observation [or Observer] (NATG)
TAO......... Tactical Air Officer (NVT)
TAO......... Tactical Air Operations
TAO......... Technical Analysis Office (MCD)
TAO......... Technical Analysis Order
TAO......... Technical Assistance Office
TAO......... Technical Assistance Operations [United Nations]
TAO......... Technical Assistance Order (KSC)
TAO......... Technology Applications Office [NASA]
TAO......... Technology Assistance Officer [Small Business Administration]
TAO......... Telecommunications Advancement Organization [Japan] (DDC)
TAO......... Telephone Area Office [British]
TAO......... Terrain Avoidance Override (MCD)
TAO......... Test Analysis Outline
TAO......... Test and Operation (IAA)
TAO......... Thermal Array for the Ocean (USDC)
TAO......... Thromboangitis Obliterans [Cardiology]
TAO......... Time and Altitude Over [Aviation] (FAAC)
TAO......... Tokyo Astronomical Observatory
TAO......... Total Acid Output [Clinical chemistry]
TAO......... Transition Assistance Office [Army] (INF)
TAO......... Transportation Applications Office [Jet Propulsion Laboratory, NASA]
TAO......... Transportes Aeromar [Mexico ICAO designator] (FAAC)
TAO......... Triacetylole-Andomycin [Medicine] (DMAA)
TAO......... Troleandomycin [Formerly, Triacetyloleandomycin] [Antibacterial compound]
TAO......... Tropical Array Ocean
TAO......... Tropical Atmosphere-Ocean [Marine science] (OSRA)
TAO......... TSCA [Toxic Substances Control Act] Assistance Office [Environmental Protection Agency] (GFGA)
TAOBBATED... [The] Adventures of Buckaroo Banzai across the Eighth Dimension [1984 movie title]
TAOC........ [The] Army Operations Center
TAOC........ Tactical Air Operations Center
TAOC........ Train Axis Optical Cube
TAOCC....... Tactical Air Operations Control Center (NATG)
TAOG........ Gasoline Tanker [Military Sea Transportation Service] (CINC)
TAOI........ Tactical Area of Interest [Military]
TAOM/MCE... Tactical Air Operations Module/Modular Control Equipment [Military] (RDA)
TAOO........ Tactical Air Operations Officer [Tactical Air Command]
TAOR........ Tactical Area of Responsibility [Military] (AFM)
TAOS........ Taiwan-American Occultation Survey [Astronomy]
TAOS........ Taiwanese American Occultation Survey
TAOS........ Thrust-Assisted Orbiter Shuttle [NASA]
TAOS........ Travel Allowance on Separation [Military]
TA/OSD...... Task Analysis/Operational Sequence Diagram
TAOT........ Transport Oiler Ship
TAP......... [The] Ada Project [World Wide Web]
TAP......... Amarillo Public Library, Amarillo, TX [OCLC symbol] (OCLC)
TAP......... [The] Angel Planes (EA)
TAP......... [The] Antarctica Project [An association] (EAIO)
TAP......... [The] Army Plan
TAP......... Onitap Resources, Inc. [Toronto Stock Exchange symbol]
TAP......... Table of Authorized Personnel (NATG)

TAP	Tackled Attempting to Pass [Football]
TAP	Tactical Action Programs
TAP	Tactical Armament Plan (MCD)
TAP	Taipei [Taihoku] [Taiwan] [Seismograph station code, US Geological Survey] (SEIS)
TAP	Tapachula [Mexico] [Airport symbol] (OAG)
TAP	Tapestry (ADA)
tap	Tapestry (VRA)
Tap	Tappan's Ohio Common Pleas Reports [A publication] (DLA)
TAP	Tapping Achievement Potential Project (EDAC)
TAP	Target Aim Points
TAP	Target Analysis and Planning [Computer system] [Military]
TAP	Target and Penetration (IAA)
TAP	Target Angular Position [Photonics]
TAP	Target Assignment Panel
TAP	Task Area Plan
TAP	T-Cell-Activating Protein [Biochemistry]
TAP	Teacher's Aide Program
TAP	Technical Achievement Plan [NASA] (NASA)
TAP	Technical Action Panel [Department of Agriculture]
TAP	Technical Action Program (OICC)
TAP	Technical Advisory Panel [United Nations]
TAP	Technical Area Plan [Navy] (MCD)
TAP	Technical Assistance Program [Environmental Protection Agency] (GFGA)
TAP	Technical Assistance Project (EA)
TAP	Technological Adjustment Pay
TAP	Technological American Party (EA)
TAP	Technology Adaptation Program [Massachusetts Institute of Technology] [Research center] (RCD)
TAP	Technology Applications Program [University of Kentucky] [Lexington, KY] [NASA]
TAP	Technology Assistance Program [Army]
TAP	Telemetry Acceptance Pattern (KSC)
TAP	Telemetry Antenna Pedestal
TAP	Temporal Analysis of Products [System developed by Monsanto Chemical Co.]
TAP	Tension by Applanation [Ophthalmology]
TAP	Term Availability Plan (IAA)
TAP	Terminal Access Point [Telecommunications] (OSI)
TAP	Terminal Access Processor
TAP	Terminal Applications Package (IEEE)
TAP	Terminal Area Productivity (GAVI)
TAP	Terrain Analysis Program [Military]
TAP	Terrestrial Auxiliary Power
TAP	Test Access Port [Computer science] (CIST)
TAP	Test Administration Plan (NASA)
TAP	Test Anxiety Profile [Educational test]
TAP	Test Assistance Program [Sperry UNIVAC]
TAP	Test of Auditory-Perceptual Skills
TAP	Tests of Achievement and Proficiency [Educational test]
TAP	Theater of All Possibilities [International touring company of actor-authors]
TAP	Thermal Analysis Program [Nuclear energy]
TAP	Thermodynamics and Physical Properties Package (NITA)
TAP	Thermosiphoning Air Pan
TAP	Thermoviscoelastic Analysis Program (MCD)
TAP	Thesaurus at Play [Acronym is trademark for word game]
TAP	Thiol Alkaline Phosphatase [An enzyme]
TAP	Three-Axis Package
TAP	Tibetan Aid Project (EA)
TAP	Time-Sharing Accounting Package (MHDB)
TAP	Time-Sharing Assembly Program [Computer science] (DIT)
TAP	Tool Application Program (AAEL)
TAP	Total Action Against Poverty [A federal government program]
TAP	Total Air Pressure (NASA)
TAP	Total Annualized Profit
TAP	Total Assets Protection, Inc. (EFIS)
TAP	Total Audience Plan [Radio advertising] (NTCM)
TAP	Toxic Air Pollutant
TAP	Toxicological Agent Protective Item [or Suit] (MCD)
TAp	Tracheal Antimicrobial Peptide [Biochemistry]
TAP	Tracking Alarms Processor [Space Flight Operations Facility, NASA]
TAP	Training Access Point (WDAA)
TAP	Training Accreditation Program [Environmental science] (COE)
TAP	Trajectory Analysis Program (MCD)
TAP	Transaction Application Program [Computer science]
TAP	Trans-Alaska Pipeline
TAP	Transcription Activating Protein [Biochemistry]
TAP	Transferable Assets Program
TAP	Transformation-Associated Protein [Biochemistry]
TAP	Transition Assistance Program [Military]
TAP	Transmission Access Processor [Newbridge Networks, Inc.]
TAP	Transponder Access Program [Satellite Business Systems] [McLean, VA] [Telecommunications] (TSSD)
TAP	Transporter Associated with Antigen Processing [Biochemistry]
TAP	Transportes Aereos Portugueses EP [Portugal ICAO designator] (FAAC)
TAP	Transportes Aereos Portugueses, SARL [Portuguese Air Transport]
TAP	Transport Ship [Military Sea Transportation Service] (CINC)
TAP	Travelers/Aetna Prop Casual'A' [NYSE symbol] (TTSB)
TAP	Travelers Aetna Property Casualty Corp. [NYSE symbol] (SAG)
TAP	Travelers Corp. P & C Capital I [NYSE symbol] (SAG)
TAP	Travelers Corp. P & C Capital II [NYSE symbol] (SAG)

TAP	Trend Analysis Program [American Council of Life Insurance] [Washington, DC Information service or system] (IID)
TAP	Triaminopyrimidine [Organic chemistry]
TAP	Trickle Ammonia Process [for drying grain feedstuffs]
TAP	Trimethylaminoethylpiperazine [Organic chemistry]
TAP	Truck Assembly Plants
TAP	Trustee, Administration, and Physician's Institute [Seminar]
TAP	Tuition Assistance Program [New York] (EDAC)
TAP	Tunis-Afrique Presse [Press agency] [Tunisia]
TAPA	St. Johns/V. C. Bird [Antigua Island] [ICAO location identifier] (ICLI)
TAPA	Tanzania African Parents Association (BUAC)
TAPA	(Tetranitrofluorylideneaminooxy)propionic Acid
TAPA	Three-Dimensional Antenna Pattern Analyzer [Air Force]
TAPA	Total Army Personnel Agency (INF)
TAPA	Trade Assistance and Planning Office (AAGC)
TAPA	Trans-Alaska Pipeline Authorization Act
TAPA	Turkish American Physicians Association (EA)
TAPAC	Tape Automatic Positioning and Control
TAPAC	Transportation Allocations, Priorities, and Controls Committee [Military]
TAPAK	Tape-Pack
TAPAT	Tape Programmed Automatic Tester
TAPATS	Threat Artillery Preparation Against Thermal Sights (MCD)
TAPC	Total Army Personnel Command (DOMA)
TAPCC	Technology and Pollution Control Committee [Environmental Protection Agency]
TAPCHAN	Tapered Channel [Wave power technology]
TAPCIS	[The] Access Program for the CompuServe Information Service (PCM)
Tap CM	Tapping's Copyholder's Manual [A publication] (DLA)
TAPCO	Thompson Products, Inc. [Later, Thompson Ramo Wooldridge, Inc.]
TAP-D	Test of Articulation Performance - Diagnostic
TAPDB	Total Army Personnel Database (GFGA)
TAPDS	Toxic Air Pollutant Data System [Environmental Protection Agency] (GFGA)
TAPE	Tactical Air Power Evaluation [Air Force]
TAPE	Tape Automatic Preparation Equipment
TAPE	Target Profile Examination Technique [RADAR analysis concept] [Air Force]
TAPE	Technical Advisory Panel for Electronics [Air Force]
TAPE	Television Audience Program Evaluation
TAPE	Tentative Annual Planning Estimate (NVT)
TAPE	Timed Access to Pertinent Excerpts
TAPE	Total Application of Prerecorded Evidence
TAPE	Totally Automated Programming Equipment
TAPE	Transactional Analysis of Personality and Environment [Psychology] (AEBS)
TAPER	[The] Army Plan for Equipment Records
TAPER	Tailored Performance Test Vehicle (SAA)
TAPER	Temporary Appointment Pending Establishment of a Register [Civil Service]
TAPER	Theater Army Personnel (MCD)
TAPER	Turbulent Air Pilot Environment Research [NASA-FAA project]
TAPES	Total Army Personnel Evaluation System
TAPES	Transformer Analog Polynomial Equation Solver (PDAA)
TAPEX	Tape Executive Program (SAA)
TAPFOR	[The] Army Portion of Force Status and Identify Report [Force Status Report] (AABC)
TAPGA	Tasmanian Apple and Pear Growers' Association [Australia]
TAPGEN	Terminal Applications Program Generator [Computer science] (MHDI)
TAPH	Codrington [Barbuda Island] [ICAO location identifier] (ICLI)
TAPH	Toluic Acid Phenylhydrazide [Organic chemistry]
TAPI	Tapistron International, Inc. [NASDAQ symbol] (SAG)
TAPI	Tapistron Intl [NASDAQ symbol] (TTSB)
TAPI	Technology Application and Promotion Institution [Philippines] (BUAC)
TAPI	Telephony Application Programming Interface [Microsoft Corp.] (PCM)
TAPI	Tropical Agricultural Products Institute [Thailand] (BUAC)
TAPIO	Tape Input and Output [Computer science] (DNAB)
Tapist	Tapistron International, Inc. [Associated Press] (SAG)
Tapistrn	Tapistron International, Inc. [Associated Press] (SAG)
TAPIT	Tactical Photographic Image Transmission
TAPITS	Tactical Airborne Processing, Interpretation, and Transmission System [Military]
TAPITS	Tactical Photographic Image Transmission System
TAPIW	Tapistron Intl Wrrt [NASDAQ symbol] (TTSB)
TAPLF	Trans-Alaska Pipeline Liability Fund
TAPLINE	Trans-Alaska Pipeline
TAPLINE	Trans-Arabian Pipeline
TAPM	Technology Application Program Management [Air Force]
Tap Man	Tapping on the Writ of Mandamus [1848] [A publication] (DLA)
TAPO	Termination Accountable Property Officer
TAPO	Tris(I-aziridinyl) Phosphine Oxide [Organic chemistry]
TAPOC	Theater Army Personnel Operations Center
TAPOL	Comite de Defense des Prisonniers en Indonesie [France]
Tapp	Tappan's Ohio Common Pleas Reports [A publication] (DLA)
TAPP	Technical Assistance for Parents Program [Established under the EHC (Education for all Handicapped Children act)] (PAZ)
TAPP	Technical Assistance for Public Participation
TAPP	Tetragonal Almandine-Pyrope Phase [Geology]
TAPP	Time and Attendance, Payroll, and Personnel (GFGA)
TAPP	Trade Association of Proprietary Plants (EA)
TAPP	Tumor Acquisition, Processing, and Preservation [Oncology]
TAPP	Two-Axis Pneumatic Pickup (IEEE)

Tappan .... Tappan's Ohio Common Pleas Reports [*A publication*] (DLA)
Tappan (Ohio)... Tappan's Ohio Common Pleas Reports [*A publication*] (DLA)
Tappan's Ohio Rep... Tappan's Ohio Common Pleas Reports [*A publication*] (DLA)
Tappan's R... Tappan's Ohio Common Pleas Reports [*A publication*] (DLA)
TAPPI........... Technical Association of the Pulp and Paper Industry (EA)
Tapping .... Tapping on the Writ of Mandamus [*A publication*] (DLA)
Tapp M & Ch... Tapp on Maintenance and Champerty [*1861*] [*A publication*] (ILCA)
TAPPrA .... Travelers P&C Cap 1 8.08% Pfd [*NYSE symbol*] (TTSB)
TAPPrB .... Travelers P&C Cap II 8.00% Pfd [*NYS*] (TTSB)
TAPPS .... [*The*] Automated Procurement Planning System
TAPR .... Tactical Automation Program Review [*Military*]
TAPR .... Toxic Altitude Propulsion Research (MCD)
TAPR .... [*Department of*] Transportation Acquisition Procurement Regulation [*A publication*] (AAGC)
TAPR .... Treasury Acquisition/Procurement Regulation (AAGC)
TAPrA .... Transamerica Del L.P.'MIPS' [*NYSE symbol*] (TTSB)
TAPrD .... Transamerica 8.50% Dep Pfd [*NYSE symbol*] (TTSB)
TAPRE .... Tracking in an Active and Passive RADAR Environment
TAPRI .... Tampere Peace Research Institute [*Finland*] (BUAC)
TAPS........... Tactical Area Positioning System [*Military*]
TAPS........... Tactical Protective Structures (MCD)
TAPS........... Tarapur Atomic Power Station [*India*]
TAPS........... Teachers Audio Placement System
TAPS........... Technical Analysis Positions System
TAPS........... Teenage Attitudes and Practices Survey [*Centers for Disease Control*]
TAPS........... Telemetry Antenna Positions System [*Military*] (CAAL)
TAPS........... Television Arts Performance Showcase (WDAA)
TAPS........... TERCOM [*Terrain Contour Mapping*] Aircraft Positioning Systems [*Air Force*]
TAPS........... Terminal Application Processing System
TAPS........... Terminal Application Program System [*Computer science*]
TAPS........... Terminal Area Positive Separation [*FAA*]
TAP-S .... Test of Articulation Performance - Screen
TAPS........... Test of Auditory-Perceptual Skills (TMMY)
TAPS........... Time Analysis of Program Status
TAPS........... Total Atoll Production System (NOAA)
TAPS........... Traditional Arts Projects Ltd. (BUAC)
TAPS........... Training for Aboriginals Program Scheme [*Australia*]
TAPS........... Trajectory Accuracy Prediction System [*Air Force*]
TAPS........... Trans-Alaskan Pipeline [*Marine science*] (OSRA)
TAPS........... Trans-Alaska Pipeline System [*Department of Energy*]
TAPS........... Trial Assessment Procedure Scale [*Medicine*] (DMAA)
TAPS........... Tris(hydroxymethyl)methylamino Propanesulfonic Acid
TAPS........... Tropical Assimilation and Prognosis System (EERA)
TAPS........... Turboalternator Power System (IEEE)
TAPS........... Turret-Anchored Production System [*Petroleum engineering*]
TAPSC .... Trans-Atlantic Passenger Steamship Conference [*Later, IPSA*] (EA)
TAPSHA .... Technology and Physical Science History Associates (IID)
TAPSYS .... Total Army Personnel System
TAPU .... Tanganyika African Postal Union
TAPVC .... Total Anomalous Pulmonary Venous Connection [*Cardiology*]
TAPVD .... Total Anomalous Pulmonary Venous Drainage [*Cardiology*] (AAMN)
TAPVR .... Total Anomalous Pulmonary Venous Return [*Cardiology*]
TapZee .... Tappen Zee Financial, Inc. [*Associated Press*] (SAG)
TAQ............ Task Attribution Questionnaire (EDAC)
Taq .... Thermus Aquaticus [*Bacteria*]
TAQ............ Trans Asian Resources [*Vancouver Stock Exchange symbol*]
TAQ............ Transient Airman Quarters [*Air Force*] (AFM)
TAQA .... Test and Quality Assurance (IAA)
TAQT........... Task Assignment Queue Table (MCD)
TAQTD .... Task Assignment Queue Table Display (MCD)
TAQTU .... Task Assignment Queue Table Update (MCD)
TAQW .... Transient Abnormal Q Wave [*Medicine*] (DMAA)
TAQW .... Transient Abnormal Q Waves [*Medicine*] (AAMN)
TAR............ Tactical Aircraft Recovery (CINC)
TAR............ Tactical Air Reconnaissance (AFM)
TAR............ Tactical Air Request (NVT)
tar............. Tadzhik Soviet Socialist Republic [*MARC country of publication code Library of Congress*] (LCCP)
TAR............ Tansy Resources, Inc. [*Vancouver Stock Exchange symbol*]
TAR............ Tape Address Register [*Demography*]
TAR............ Tape Address Register File [*Bureau of the Census*] (GFGA)
tar............. Tape Archive [*Computer science*] (IGQR)
TAR............ Tape Archive [*Computer science*] (DOM)
TAR............ Tara Exploration & Development Co. Ltd. [*Toronto Stock Exchange symbol*]
TAR............ Taranto [*Italy*] [*Seismograph station code, US Geological Survey*] (SEIS)
TAR............ Target
tar............. Tatar [*MARC language code Library of Congress*] (LCCP)
TAR............ Tax Advance Rulings [*Database*] [*Taxation Canada*] [*Information service or system*] (CRD)
TAR............ Team Acceptance Review (SAA)
TAR............ Technical Action Request [*Army*] (AABC)
TAR............ Technical Amendment Regulation [*Federal government*] (EG)
TAR............ Technical Analysis Request [*NASA*] (KSC)
TAR............ Technical Assistance Request [*Nuclear energy*] (NRCH)
TAR............ Teen Age Republican [*Lifestyle classification*]
TAR............ Telefonica De Argentina ADS [*NYSE symbol*] (TTSB)
TAR............ Telefonica de Argentina SA [*NYSE symbol*] (SAG)
TAR............ Temporary Accumulator (IAA)
TAR............ Temporary Accumulator Register (IAA)
TAR............ Temporary Active Reserve (DNAB)
TAR............ Tennessee Administrative Register [*A publication*] (AAGC)
TAR............ Terminal Address Register
TAR............ Terminal Area Surveillance RADAR
TAR............ Terrain Avoidance RADAR
TAR............ Terrier Advanced RADAR (DNAB)
TAR............ Territorial Army Regulations [*British military*] (DMA)
TAR............ Test Action Requirement (NASA)
TAR............ Test Agency Report (NASA)
TAR............ Test Analysis Report
TAR............ Test and Return (IAA)
TAR............ Therm Advanced Research (SAA)
TAR............ Threat Avoidance Receiver (MCD)
TAR............ Thrombocytopenia with Absent Radii [*Medicine*]
TAR............ Thrust-Augmented Rocket [*NASA*]
TAR............ Total Accomplishment Requirement (DNAB)
TAR............ Total Ankle Replacement [*Orthopedics*] (DAVI)
TAR............ Total Assets Reporting (MCD)
TAR............ Towed Array RADAR
TAR............ Track Address Register
TAR............ Training and Administration of the Reserve
TAR............ Trajectory Analysis Room [*NASA*] (KSC)
TAR............ Trans-Acting Responsive Sequence [*Genetics*]
TAR............ Transaction Area (IAA)
TAR............ Trans-Activator Response Element [*Genetics*]
TAR............ Transactivator-Responsive Region [*Genetics*]
TAR............ Transformation-Associated Recombination [*Genetics*]
TAR............ Transmit and Receive (IAA)
TAR............ [*Department of*] Transportation Acquisition Regulation [*A publication*] (AAGC)
TAR............ Transportes Aereos Regionais [*Airline*] [*Brazil*]
TAR............ Treatment-Authorization Request [*Medicine*] (MEDA)
TAR............ Triannual Review (NATG)
TAR............ Truck and Rail
TAR............ Tunis Air-Societe Tunisienne de l'Air [*Tunisia*] [*ICAO designator*] (FAAC)
TAR............ Turnaround Ratio
TAR............ Two-Axis Rate (SAA)
TARA .... Teachers Anti-Racist Alliance (BUAC)
TARA .... Technical Assistant, Royal Artillery [*British military*] (DMA)
TA/RA .... Technical Availability/Restricted Availability [*Navy*] (NVT)
TARA .... Terrain Avoidance RADAR (IAA)
TARA .... Territorial Army Rifle Association [*British military*] (DMA)
TARA .... Total Articular Replacement Arthroplasty [*Orthopedics*]
TARA .... Truck-Frame and Axle Repair Association (EA)
TARA .... Tumor-Associated Rejection Antigen [*Immunology*] (MAE)
TARA .... Turmor-Associated Rejection Antigen [*Immunology*]
TARABS .... Tactical Air Reconnaissance and Aerial Battlefield Surveillance System [*Military*]
TARAC .... Terminology, Aids, References, Applications, and Coordination (IAA)
TARAD .... Tracking Asynchronous RADAR Data (DA)
TARADCOM... Tank-Automotive Research and Development Command [*Army*]
TARAN .... Tactical Attack RADAR and Navigation
TARAN .... Test and Repair [*or Replace*] as Necessary
Tarb .... Tarbiz. Jerusalem (BJA)
TARBIT .... Three-Axis Rout Byro Inertial Tracker (IAA)
TARC .... [*The*] Army Research Council
TARC .... Tactical Air Reconnaissance Center [*Shaw Air Force Base*]
TARC .... Television Allocation Research Committee [*or Council*]
TARC .... Theater Army Replacement Command
TARC .... Through Axis Rotational Control [*NASA*] (NAKS)
TARC .... Thru-Axis Rotational Control
TARC .... Total Available Residual Chlorine [*Water quality*]
TARC .... Toxics Testing and Assessment Research Committee [*Terminated, 1984*] [*Environmental Protection Agency*] (EGAO)
TARC .... Trace Analysis Research Centre [*Dalhousie University*] [*Canada*] (IRC)
TARC .... Transport Airworthiness Reports Committee [*AIA*] (MCD)
TARC .... Tropical Agricultural Research Center [*Japan*] (BUAC)
TARCAP .... Target Combat Air Patrol [*Navy*]
TARC-OA...... Tactical Air Reconnaissance Center Office of Operations Analysis [*Shaw Air Force Base, SC*]
TARCOG....... Top of Alabama Regional Council of Governments
TARCOM ...... Tank-Automotive Materiel Readiness Command [*Army*]
TARCOMSA... Tank-Automotive Materiel Readiness Command, Selfridge Activity (MCD)
TArDC .... Arlington Development Center, Arlington, TN [*Library symbol Library of Congress*] (LCLS)
TARDEC .... Tank-Automotive Research, Development, and Engineering Center [*Army*] (RDA)
TARDIS .... Time and Relative Dimensions in Space [*Acronym is name of spaceship in British TV series "Dr. Who"*]
TARDIS .... Titles Automated Register and Document Information System [*Australian*] (EERA)
TARDIS .... Tropical Analysis and Real-Time Display [*National Oceanic and Atmospheric Administration*]
TARE........... Telegraphic Automatic Relay [*or Routing*] Equipment (NG)
TARE........... Telemetry Automatic Reduction Equipment
TARE........... Transistor Analysis Recording Equipment
TAREA .... Terminal Leaf Area [*Botany*]
TAREF .... [*The*] Acronym Generator Reference [*RCA computer program*] (IAA)
TAREWS .... Tactical Air Reconnaissance and Electronic Warfare Support (MCD)
TAREX .... Target Exploitation [*Military*] (AABC)
TARF........... [*The*] Acid Rain Foundation (EA)
TARF........... Tracking and Reporting Format [*Military*] (CAAL)
TARFS .... Three Axis Rotational Flight Simulator [*Military*] (RDA)

TARFU	Things Are Really Fouled Up [*Military slang*] [*Bowdlerized version*]
TARFX	Tracking and Reporting Format Extended [*Military*] (CAAL)
Targ	Targum (BJA)
TARGA	Truevision Advanced Raster Graphics Adapter [*AT & T*]
TARGET	Team to Advance Research for Gas Energy Transformation [*Group of US gas and gas-electric companies*]
TARGET	Thames Action and Resources Group for Education and Training [*British*] (AIE)
TARGET	Thermal Advanced Reactor, Gas-Cooled, Exploiting Thorium [*Nuclear energy*]
TARGET	Trans-European Automated Real-Time Gross-Settlement Express Transfer [*Banking*]
TARGET	Transportability Analysis Reports Generator [*Military*] (MCD)
TARGET	Transportation Accident Research Graduate Education and Training
TargetT	Target Therapeutics, Inc. [*Associated Press*] (SAG)
TargGene	Targeted Genetics Corp. [*Associated Press*] (SAG)
TargJer	[*The*] Jerusalem Targum of the Pentateuch (BJA)
TargJon	Targum Jonathan (BJA)
TargOnk	Targum Onkelos (BJA)
TargTch	Target Technologies, Inc. [*Associated Press*] (SAG)
TargYer	Targum Yerusahlmi (BJA)
TARI	Taiwan Agricultural Research Institute (BUAC)
TARIF	Telegraphic Automatic Routing in the Field (MCD)
TARIT	Telegraph Automatic Routing in the Field (IAA)
TARL	Texas Archaeological Research Laboratory (BUAC)
TARL	Training Aids Research Laboratory [*Air Force*] (MCD)
Tarleton St U ...	Tarleton State University (GAGS)
TARLOCS	Target Locating System [*Military*] (MCD)
TARM	Telephone Answering and Recording Machine (NITA)
TARMAC	Tar Macadam
TARMAC	Terminal Area RADAR/Moving Aircraft (KSC)
TARMOCS	[*The*] Army Operations Center System
TARN	Tactical Air Request Net [*Army*] (DOMA)
TARN	Team Acceptance Review Notice (SAA)
TArnA	ARO, Inc., AEDC Library, Arnold Air Force Station, TN [*Library symbol Library of Congress*] (LCLS)
TARND	Turn Around [*Aviation*] (FAAC)
TARO	Taro Pharmaceutical Industries [*NASDAQ symbol*] (SAG)
TARO	Territorial Army Reserve of Officers [*British*]
TAROF	Taro Pharmaceutical Ind [*NASDAQ symbol*] (TTSB)
TAROM	Transporturi Aeriene Romane [*Romanian Air Transport*]
TaroPh	Taro Pharmaceutical Industries [*Associated Press*] (SAG)
TAROT	[*The*] Associated Readers of Tarot International (EA)
TARP	Tactical Airborne Reconnaissance Pod
TARP	Tactical Airborne Recording Package
TARP	Tarpaulin (AAG)
tarp	Tarpaulin (VRA)
TARP	Test and Repair Processor [*Computer science*]
TARP	Theater Army Repair Program
TARP	Total Army Requirements Program
TARP	Tour Advisory Review Panel [*Army National Guard*] (INF)
TARP	Transient Acoustic Radiation Program
TARP	Transportation Accounts Receivable and Payment System [*GSA*] (TAG)
TARP	Typical Airland Resupply Profile (MCD)
TARPAC	Television and Radio Political Action Committee [*National Association of Broadcasters*]
TARPS	Tactical Aerial Reconnaissance Pod System (MCD)
TARPS	True and Relative Motion Plotting System (IAA)
TARPTOLA ...	Theologiae Apud Remonstrantes Professorem, Tyrannidis Osorem, Limburgium Amstelodamensem [*Pseudonym used by John Locke*]
TARR	Time-Adjusted Rate of Return
Tarrant	Tarrant Apparel Group [*Associated Press*] (SAG)
TARS	[*The*] Arthur Ransome Society [*British*] (EAIO)
TARS	Tactical Air Reconnaissance School [*Air Force*]
TARS	Tactical Air Research and Survey Office [*Air Force*]
TARS	Target Acquisition Reconnaissance and Surveillance System (SAA)
TARS	Technical Aircraft Reliability Statistics (IAA)
TARS	Technical Assistance Recruitment Service [*United Nations*]
TARS	Teen Age Republicans
TARS	Terminal Automated RADAR Services [*Aviation*] (FAAC)
TARS	Terrain Analog RADAR Simulator
TARS	Terrain and RADAR Simulator (IAA)
TARS	Terrain Avoidance RADAR System (MCD)
TARS	Test and Repair Station
TARS	Tethered Aerostat RADAR System [*Aviation*] (FAAC)
TARS	Theater Army Replacement System (AABC)
TARS	Three-Axis Reference System [*Used in reference to Titan missile*]
TARS	Training and Administrative Reserves [*on permanent active duty*]
TARS	Transportation Aircraft Rebuild Shops [*National Guard*] (MCD)
TARS	Turnaround Ranging Station [*Telecommunications*] (TEL)
TARS-75	Tactical Reconnaissance and Surveillance - 1975 [*Army*]
TARSA	Transportes Aereos Ranquetes, Sociedad Anonima [*Argentina*]
TARSCC	Three-Axis Reference System Checkout Console [*Used in reference to Titan missile*]
TARSLL	Tender and Repair Ship Load List [*Navy*] (NG)
TARS OCUL ...	Tarsis Oculorum [*To the Eyelids*] [*Pharmacy*]
TARS/SEA	Theater Army Replacement System / Southeast Asia (SAA)
TART	Tactical Antiradiation Tracker [*Military*] (CAAL)
TART	Tartarum [*Tartar*] [*Pharmacy*] (ROG)
TART	Tartrate
TART	Task Analysis Reduction Technique [*Navy*]
TART	Theodore Army Terminal
TART	Transonic Armament Technology (MCD)

TART	Twin Accelerator Ring Transfer (IEEE)
TARTA	Tactical RADAR Target Analysis [*Military*] (CAAL)
TARTC	Theater Army Replacement and Training Command
TARVAN	Truck and Rail Van
TARWI	Target Weather Information
TAS	[*The*] Air Surgeon [*Army*]
TAS	[*The*] Army Staff
TAS	TACAN [*Tactical Air Navigation*] Antenna System (DWSG)
TAS	Tactical Advisory Service [*Department of Commerce*]
TAS	Tactical Airlift Squadron [*Air Force*]
TAS	Tactical Air Support [*Tactical Air Command*]
TAS	Tactical Area Switching
TAS	Tactical Automated System (MCD)
TAS	Tactical Automatic Switch [*Military*] (AABC)
TAS	Taiwanese-American Society (EA)
TAS	Tallow Alkyl Sulfate [*Surfactant*]
TAS	Tampa Southern Railroad [*AAR code*]
TAS	Taos, NM [*Location identifier FAA*] (FAAL)
TAS	Tape Alteration Subroutine
TAS	Target Acquisition System
TAS	Tashkent [*Former USSR Seismograph station code, US Geological Survey*] (SEIS)
TAS	Tasmania
Tas	Tasmania (ODBW)
TAS	Tasmanian Ambulance Service [*Australia*]
TAS	Tasu Resources Ltd. [*Vancouver Stock Exchange symbol*]
TAS	Tax Administration System [*Internal Revenue Service*]
TAS	Teacher Authoring System (EDAC)
TAS	Team Apache Systems [*Army*]
TAS	Technical Advisory Services [*Army*] (RDA)
TAS	Technological and Applied Studies
TAS	Telecom Analysis Systems, Inc.
TAS	Telecommunications Authority Singapore
TAS	Telegraphy with Automatic Switching [*Telecommunications*] (IAA)
TAS	Telemetry Antenna Subsystem (NASA)
TAS	Telephone Answering Service [*or System*]
TAS	Telephone Area Staff [*British*]
TAS	Teleprogrammer Assembly System [*Computer science*] (IAA)
TAS	Telomere-Associated Sequence [*Genetics*]
TAS	Tempelhof Automatic System (DWSG)
TAS	Temperature-Actuated Switch (IEEE)
TAS	Tenancy Advice Service [*Australia*]
TAS	Tennessee Academy of Science (BUAC)
TAS	Tenure Administration System [*Queensland*] [*State*] (EERA)
TAS	Terminal Access System (MCD)
TAS	Terminal Address Selector
TAS	Test Access Selector [*Telecommunications*] (TEL)
TAS	Test Analyzer System [*Electronics*]
TAS	Test and Set [*Computer science*]
TAS	Test Answer Sheets
TAS	Test Article Specification (NASA)
TAS	Test for Ascendance-Submission (DB)
TAS	Test of Attitude Toward School [*Guy Thibaudeau*] (TES)
TAS	Texture Analysis System [*Image analysis for biochemistry*]
TAS	Theatre Arts Society [*British*]
TAS	Therapeutic Activities Specialist [*Physical therapy*] (DAVI)
TAS	Three-Axis Stabilization (AAG)
TAS	Time Air Speed (NATG)
TAS	Torpedo and Antisubmarine [*Obsolete Navy British*]
TAS	Towed Array SONAR
TAS	Trace Analysis System (AAEL)
TAS	Tracking Adjunct System [*I-HAWK*] (MCD)
TAS	Tracking Antenna System
TAS	Traditional Acupuncture Society [*Stratford-Upon-Avon, Warwickshire, England*] (EAIO)
TAS	Traffic Analysis Survey (MCD)
TAS	Training Aids Section [*Navy*]
TAS	Transalsace [*France*] [*FAA designator*] (FAAC)
TAS	Transfer Alignment Set (DNAB)
TAS	Transportes Aereos Salvador [*Brazil*]
TAS	Transverse Air Spring
TAS	Tribunal Arbitral du Sport [*Court of Arbitration of Sport - CAS*] [*Switzerland*] (EAIO)
TAS	Triple Axis Spectrometer [*Biochemistry*]
TAS	Troop Airlift Squadron (CINC)
TAS	True Airspeed
TAS	TRW Advanced Steering [*Automotive components*]
TAS	Tychon's Assembler (MCD)
TAS3	Transportation Aviation Supply Support System
TASA	[*The*] Aircraft Service Association
TASA	[*The*] Antique Stove Association (EA)
TASA	[*The*] Assistant Secretary of the Army
TASA	Tactical Air Support Aircraft
TASA	Task and Skill Analysis [*Military*] (AABC)
TASA	Tasmanian Association for Sustainable Agriculture [*Australia*]
TASA	Taxpayers' Association of South Australia [*Australia*]
TASA	Technical Advisory Service for Attorneys [*Technical Advisory Service, Inc.*] [*Information service or system*]
TASA	Telecomunicacoes Aeronauticas SA [*Brazil*] [*ICAO designator*] (FAAC)
TASA	Television Audio Support Activity [*Army*]
TASA	Test Area Support Assembly
TASC	Touchstone Applied Science [*NASDAQ symbol*] (TTSB)
TASA	Touchstone Applied Sciences [*NASDAQ symbol*] (SAG)
TASA	Tumor-Associated Surface Antigen [*Immunology*]

TASAE......... Training and Audio-Visual Support Activity - Europe (MCD)
TASAG .... TACOM [*Tank Automotive Command*] Scientific Advisory Group [*DoD*] (EGAO)
TASAMS ...... [*The*] Army Supply and Maintenance System (AABC)
TASAP .... [*The*] Army Scientific Advisory Panel
TASAPS .... [*The*] Army Security Assistance Program Study Group
Tas Build ..... Tasmanian Builder [*A publication*]
Tas Build J... Tasmanian Building Journal [*A publication*]
TASC.......... [*The*] Analytic Sciences Corp.
TASC.......... Centre for Technology and Social Change (EERA)
TASC.......... Tabular Sequence Control
TASC.......... Tactical Air Support Center (CINC)
TASC.......... Tactical Articulated Swimmable Carrier (OA)
TASC.......... Target Area Sequential Correlator (MCD)
TASC.......... Teaching as a Career [*British*]
TASC.......... Technical Activity Steering Committee [*Nuclear energy*] (NRCH)
TASC.......... Technology and Social Change [*Australia*]
TASC.......... Tehran Area Support Center [*Military*] (MCD)
TASC.......... Telecommunication Alarm Surveillance and Control [*AT & T*]
TASC.......... Terminal Area Sequencing and Control
TASC.......... Test Anxiety Scale for Children [*Psychology*]
TASC.......... Total Absorption Shower Cascade
TASC.......... Total Avionic Support Capability
TASC.......... Training Aids Support Center [*Army*]
TASC.......... Training and Audiovisual Support Center [*Army*]
TASC.......... Treatment Alternatives to Street Crime [*Antidrug program*]
TASC.......... True Airspeed Computer
TASCA .... Training and Supervision in Counselling and Related Areas Association (BUAC)
TASCC .... Tactical Air Support Coordination Center (MCD)
TASCC .... Tandem Accelerator Superconducting Cyclotron Facility [*Canadian nuclear physics facility*]
TASCC .... Test Access Signaling Conversion Circuit [*Telecommunications*] (TEL)
TASCFORM... Technique for Assessing Comparative Force Modernization [*Army*]
Tasch Cr Acts... Taschereau's Criminal Law Acts [*Canada A publication*] (DLA)
TASCO .... Tactical Automatic Switch Control Office
TASCOM ...... Theater Army Support Command [*Terminated, 1975*] [*West Germany*] (AABC)
TASCOM(S)... Theater Army Support Command (Supply)
TASCON .... Television Automatic Sequence Control
TASCORP..... Tasmanian Public Finance Corp. [*Commercial firm Australia*]
TASCS .... Tactical Air Support Control System [*Military*] (PDAA)
TASC/SC ..... Training and Audiovisual Support Center/Subcommunity [*Army*]
TASD .... Tactical Action Situation Display
TASD .... Technical and Administrative Support Division [*Marine science*] (OSRA)
TASD .... Technical and Adminstrative Support Division [*Pacific Marine Environmental Laboratory*] (USDC)
TASD .... Terminal Railway, Alabama State Docks [*AAR code*]
TASDA .... [*The*] American Safe Deposit Association (EA)
TASDA .... Tactical Airborne SONAR Decision Aid
TASDAC .... Tactical Secure Data Communication [*Air Force*] (DOMA)
TASDC .... Tank-Automotive Systems Development Center [*Army*]
TASE.......... Tactical Air Support Element [*Military*] (AABC)
TASE.......... Tactical Support Equipment
TASE.......... Tel Aviv Stock Exchange [*Israel*] (IMH)
T'ASE.......... Tryptophane Synthetase [*An enzyme*] (DAVI)
Taseko......... Taseko Mines Ltd. [*Associated Press*] (SAG)
TASER .... Teleactive Shock Electronic Repulsion [*Nonlethal weapon*]
TASER .... Tom Swift and His Electric Rifle [*Electronic "stun gun"*] [*A trademark*]
TASES .... Tactical Airborne Signal Exploitation System (MCD)
TASF.......... Tactical Air Strike Force [*Air Force*]
TASF.......... Tactical Air Support Force [*Air Force*]
TASFMA....... Target Acquisition Systems Force Mix Analysis [*Military*]
TASFMEA..... Target Acquisition Systems Force Mix Evaluation Analysis
TASFUIRA.... Things Are So Fouled Up It's Really Amazing [*Military slang*] [*Bowdlerized version*]
TASG .... Tactical Air Support Group [*Air Force*] (AFIT)
TASH .... The Association for Persons with Severe Handicaps (PAZ)
TASH .... The Association for the Severely Handicapped [*Later, TASH: the Association for Persons with Severe Handicaps*] (EA)
TASHA .... Tranquilliser Anxiety Stress Help Association (BUAC)
TAS/I.......... Target Acquisition System / Integrated [*Military*] (DNAB)
TASI.......... Time Assignment Speech Interpolation [*Timesharing technique*] [*Telecommunications*]
TASI.......... Torpedo and Anti-Submarine Instructor [*British military*] (DMA)
TASI.......... Transactional Analysis Systems Institute
TASIC......... Thermal Analysis of Substrates and Intergrated Circuits (PDAA)
TAS/IRAS..... Target Acquisition System / Infrared Automatic System [*Military*] (DNAB)
Tas Irreg Notes... Tasmanian Irregular Notes [*A publication*]
TASIS......... [*The*] American School in Switzerland
TASK.......... Team of Advocates for Special Kids
TASK.......... Temporary Assembled Skeleton [*Computer science*] (IAA)
TASK.......... Temporary Assigned Skeleton [*Computer science*]
TASK.......... Test of Academic Skills [*Sanford University*] (EDAC)
TASK.......... Training and Skills Program
TASKFLOT.... Task Flotilla
TASKFORNON... Allied Task Force, North Norway [*NATO*] (NATG)
TASL.......... Theater Authorized Stockage List [*Military*] (AABC)
TASL.......... Toronto Art Students' League [*1886-1903*] [*Canada*] (NGC)
TASLAP....... Tasmanian Labour Adjustment Package [*Australia*]
Tas LN .... Tasmanian Law Newsletter [*A publication*]
TASM.......... Tactical Air-to-Surface Missile (NATG)

TASM.......... Tactical Antiship Missile (MCD)
TASM.......... Tasmania (ROG)
TASM.......... Tomahawk Antiship Missile (MCD)
TASM.......... Trialkylstannylmaleate [*Organic chemistry*]
TASM.......... Turbo Assembler [*Computer science*]
TASMA .... Tanzania Sisal Marketing Board (BUAC)
Tasm Acts ... Tasmania Acts of Parliament [*A publication*] (DLA)
Tasmania LR... University of Tasmania. Law Review [*A publication*] (DLA)
Tasmanian J... Tasmanian Journal of Natural Science [*A publication*]
TASME........ Tosyl-L-arginyl Sarcosine Methyl Ester [*Biochemistry*]
TASMGS ...... Tomahawk Antiship Missile Guidance Set (MCD)
TASMO .... Tactical Air Support for Maritime Operations [*Navy*] (NVT)
TASMOL ..... Tactical Aircraft Support Model (MCD)
TASNSW ...... Travellers' Aid Society of New South Wales [*Australia*]
TASO .... Television Allocations Study Organization [*Defunct*]
TASO .... Terminal Area Security Officer [*Military*] (AABC)
TASO .... Training Aids Service Office [*Army*] (AABC)
TASO .... Training and Audiovisual Support Officer [*Military*]
TASOS .... Towed Array SONAR System
TASOSC...... Theater Army Special Operations Support Command
TASP.......... [*The*] Army Studies Program (AABC)
TASP.......... Target Antisubmarine Patrol (NVT)
TASP.......... Telemetry Analysis and Simulation Program [*Spacecraft*] [*NASA*]
TASP.......... Template-Assisted Synthetic Protein [*Biochemistry*]
TASP.......... Tentative Acceptance Sampling Procedure [*Army*]
TASP.......... Texas Academic Skills Program
TASP.......... Toll Alternatives Studies Program [*Telecommunications*] (TEL)
TAS-PAC..... Total Analysis System for Production, Accounting, and Control [*Computer science*]
TASPAWS.... Tasmanian Parks and Wildlife Service [*State*] (EERA)
TASPR .... Technical and Schedule Performance Report [*NASA*] (NASA)
TASQ .... Tactical Airlift Squadron [*Air Force*]
TASQUE ...... University of Tasmania Consultative Unit [*State*] (EERA)
TASR .... Tactical Automated Situation Receiver [*Military*]
TASR .... Temperature Auto Stabilizing Regime (IAA)
TASR .... Terminal Area Surveillance RADAR
TASR .... Torque Arm Speed Reducer
TASRA .... Tabular System Reliability Analysis
TASRA .... Thermal Activation-Strain Rate Analysis
TAS/RAS ..... Target Acquisition System / RADAR Automatic System [*Military*] (DNAB)
TAS/RMS ..... Target Acquisition Sytem / RADAR Manual System [*Military*] (DNAB)
TASROCO ... Tactical Aerial Surveillance and Reconnaissance Operational Capability Objectives [*1995*] (MCD)
TASS.......... [*The*] Army Study System
TASS.......... Tactical Air Support Section [*Military*]
TASS.......... Tactical Air Support Squadron [*Military*]
TASS.......... Tactical Avionics System Simulator [*Army*] (MCD)
TASS.......... Tactical Signal Simulator [*Canadian Astronautics Ltd. RADAR threat simulation system*]
TASS.......... Technical, Administrative, and Supervisory Section [*Amalgamated Union of Engineering Workers - Engineering Section*] [*British*]
TASS.......... Technical Assembly System
TASS.......... Telegraphnoye Agentstvo Sovyetskovo Soyuza [*Telegraph Agency of the Soviet Union*] [*News agency*]
TASS.......... Teleprinter Automatic Switching System (NITA)
TASS.......... Terminal Air Surveillance System [*FAA*] (TAG)
TASS.......... Terminal Application Support System (MCD)
TASS.......... Terrain Analyst's Synthesizer Station [*Army*] (RDA)
TASS.......... Theater Army Signal System (IAA)
TASS.......... Tianjin Academy of Social Sciences [*China*] (BUAC)
TASS.......... Total Army School System (INF)
TASS.......... Towed Acoustic Surveillance System [*Marine science*] (MSC)
TASS.......... Towed Array SONAR System
TASS.......... Towed Array Surveillance System [*Navy*] (CAAL)
TASS.......... Trouble Analysis System or Subsystem [*Telecommunications*] (TEL)
TASSA .... [*The*] Army Signal Supply Agency
TASSC .... [*The*] American Specialty Surety Council [*Later, ASA*] (EA)
TASSEL....... Three-Astronaut Space System Experimental Laboratory (MCD)
TASSI .... Tactical Airborne SIGINT Support Improvement Acquisition Plan (MCD)
TASSO .... Tactical Special Security Office [*Army*] (AABC)
TASSO .... Transatlantic Air Safety Service Organization
TASSO .... Two-Arm Spectrometer Solenoid (MCD)
TASSq......... Tactical Air Support Squadron [*Military*] (AFM)
TASSRAP..... Towed Array Surveillance Range Prediction (MCD)
TASST .... Tentative Airworthiness Standards for Supersonic Transports
TAST.......... Tactical Assault Supply Transport (MCD)
TAST.......... Test Article Signal Translator (MCD)
TAST.......... Thermoacoustic Sensing Technique (IEEE)
TAST.......... Tracking Adjunct Systems Trainer
TASTA .... [*The*] Administrative Support Theaters Army
TASTE......... Thermal Accelerated Short Time Evaporator [*Facetious term used in orange juice industry*]
TASTG .... Tactical Air Support Training Group [*Air Force*]
TASTNGSq... Tactical Air Support Training Squadron [*Air Force*]
TASTS .... Tactical Air Support Training Squadron [*Air Force*]
Tasty.......... Tasty Baking Co. [*Associated Press*] (SAG)
T.A. SURVEY... Trustworthiness Attitude Survey [*Alan L. Strand*] (TES)
TASV.......... Travellers' Aid Society of Victoria [*Australia*]
TASWD .... Torpedo, Anti-Submarine, and Mine Warfare Division [*British military*] (DMA)
Tasw Lang Hist... Taswell-Langmead's English Constitutional History [*10th ed.*] [*1946*] [*A publication*] (DLA)
TASWM........ Test ASW [*Antisubmarine Warfare*] Missile [*Navy*] (CAAL)

TAT	[*The*] Absolute Truth [*In Julian Barnes' novel "Staring at the Sun"*]
TAT	[*The*] Associated Turtles [*Defunct*] (EA)
TAT	European Airlines [*France ICAO designator*] (FAAC)
TAT	Tactical Analysis Team [*Military drug interdiction program*]
TAT	Tactical Armament Turret (NG)
TAT	Target Abilities Test [*Psychometrics*]
TAT	Target Aircraft Transmitter
TAT	Task Assignment Table (MCD)
TAT	Tateyama [*Japan*] [*Seismograph station code, US Geological Survey*] (SEIS)
TAT	Tatry/Poprad [*Former Czechoslovakia*] [*Airport symbol*] (OAG)
TAT	Taxpayers' Association of Tasmania [*Australia*]
TAT	Technical Acceptance Team [*NASA*] (AAG)
TAT	Technical Approval Team
TAT	Technical Assistance and Training
TAT	Technical Assistance Team [*Air Force*] (AFM)
TAT	Technology Application Team [*NASA*]
TAT	Telephone and Telegraph (IAA)
TAT	Television Awareness Training
TAT	Temporary Ambulance Train [*British military*] (DMA)
TAT	Tensile Adhesion Test [*for coatings*]
TAT	Terrorist Action Team [*Military*] (MCD)
TAT	Tetanus Antitoxin [*Medicine*]
TAT	Thematic Apperception Test [*Psychology*]
TAT	Thinned Aperture Telescope
TAT	Thromboplastin Activation Test [*Clinical chemistry*]
TAT	Thromboplastin Activation Time [*Clinical chemistry*] (DAVI)
TAT	Thrust-Augmented Thor [*NASA*]
TAT	Till All Taken [*Pharmacy*] (DAVI)
TAT	Time and Attendance Terminal (MHDI)
TAT	To Accompany Troops
TAT	Tochas Affen Tish [*In television production company name "TAT Productions." Words are Yiddish and translate figuratively as "Let's Be Honest"*]
TAT	Torpedo Attack Teacher [*Navy*]
TAT	Total Aircraft Time (MCD)
TAT	Total Air Temperature (NASA)
TAT	Total Alert Time
TAT	Total Antitryptic Activity [*Medicine*] (MAE)
TAT	Touraine Air Transport [*Private airline*] [*French*] (EY)
TAT	Tourism Authority of Thailand (BUAC)
TAT	Tourist Authority of Thailand (ECON)
TAT	Toxin-Antitoxin [*Also, TA*] [*Immunology*]
TAT	Trace Acceptance Tester
TAT	Training and Technology
TAT	Trans-Activator [*Genetics*]
TAT	Trans Atlantic Resources, Inc. [*Vancouver Stock Exchange symbol*]
TAT	Transatlantic Telephone [*Cable*]
TAT	Transcontinental Air Transport
TAT	Transportes Aeroside Timor [*Portuguese Timor*]
TAT	Tree Advice Trust (BUAC)
TAT	Triaminotrinitrobenzene [*Organic chemistry*]
TAT	Triamterene [*Diuretic*]
TAT	True Air Temperature (AFM)
TAT	Tumor Activity Test [*Medicine*] (DMAA)
TAT	Tuned Aperiodic Tuned (IAA)
TAT	Turbine Trip and Throttle Valve [*Nuclear energy*] (IAA)
TAT	Turnaround Time
TAT	Two-Axis Tracking
TAT	Type-Approval Test
TAT	Tyrosine Aminotransferase [*An enzyme*]
TAT-3	Transactivator Gene [*Medicine*] (TAD)
TAT 8	Transatlantic Telecommunications 8 (NITA)
TATA	Tumor-Associated Transplantation Antigen [*Medicine*] (DMAA)
TATAC	Temporary Air Transport Advisory Committee [*NATO*] (NATG)
TATAC	Trans Atlantic Athletic Conference (PSS)
TATAWS	Tank, Antitank, and Assault Weapons Study [*or System*] [*Army*]
TATB	Theater Air Transportation Board
TATB	Triaminotrinitrobenzene [*Organic chemistry*]
TATC	Tactical Air Traffic Control (NVT)
TATC	Terminal Air Traffic Control
TATC	Transatlantic Telephone Cable (IEEE)
TATCA	Terminal Air Traffic Control Automation [*FAA*] (TAG)
TATCA	Trialkoxytricarballylate [*Organic chemistry*]
TATCE	Terminal Air Traffic Control Element
TATCF	Terminal Air Traffic Control Facility
TATCO	Tactical Automatic Telephone Central Office [*Military*]
TATCS	Terminal Air Traffic Control System
TATD	Task Assignment Table Display (MCD)
TATDL	Tabulated Assembly Technical Data List
TATE	Tank Arrangement Thermal Efficiency [*Computer program*] (KSC)
TATE	Traditional Aboriginal Teacher Education [*Australia*]
TATER	Talos-Terrier-Recruit [*Flight-test vehicle*]
Tate's Dig	Tate's Digest of Laws [*Virginia*] [*A publication*] (DLA)
TATG	Tactical Airlift Training Group [*Air Force*]
TATG	Tuned Anode Tuned Grid (DEN)
Tatham	Tatham Offshore, Inc. [*Associated Press*] (SAG)
TATHS	Tool and Trades History Society (EAIO)
TATI	Total Air Temperature Indicator
TATI	Tumor-Associated Trypsin Inhibitor [*Medicine*]
TATO	Taipei [*Taiwan*] [*Seismograph station code, US Geological Survey*] (SEIS)
TATP	TACFIRE [*Tactical Fire*] Advanced Training Program [*Army*]
TATP	Two-Axis Tracking Pedestal
TATR	Tactical Air Target Recommender

TATr	Tyrosine Aminotransferase Regulator
TATRC	Type-Approval Test Review Committee
TATS	Tactical Aerial Targets Squadron (MCD)
TATS	Tactical Airlift Training Squadron [*Air Force*]
TATS	Tactical Armament Turret System
TATS	Tactical Transmission System Summary (KSC)
TATS	Target Acquisition and Track System (MUGU)
TATS	Technical Assistance and Training Survey [*Department of Labor*] (OICC)
TATS	Test and Training Satellite [*Also, TETR, TTS*] [*NASA*]
TATSA	Transportation Aircraft Test and Support Activity [*Military*]
TATSC	Total Army Training System Course (INF)
TATST	Tetanus Antitoxin Skin Test [*Medicine*] (MAE)
TATSU	Transportation Aviation Test and Support
TATT	Technical Assistance and Technology Transfer (NOAA)
TAT Tch	TAT Technologies [*Associated Press*] (SAG)
TATTE	Talos [*Missile*] Tactical Test Equipment
TATTF	TAT Technologies [*NASDAQ symbol*] (SAG)
TATTF	TAT Technologies Ltd [*NASDAQ symbol*] (TTSB)
TATT syndrome	Tired All the Time Syndrome [*Medicine*] (WDAA)
TATU	Technical Advanced Training for Units (MCD)
TAU	Fort Meade, MD [*Location identifier FAA*] (FAAL)
TAU	Tape Adapter Unit [*Computer science*] (IAA)
TAU	Tasmania University [*Tasmania*] [*Seismograph station code, US Geological Survey*] (SEIS)
TAU	Tauramena [*Colombia*] [*Airport symbol*] (AD)
Tau	Taurus [*Constellation*]
TAU	Technical Advisory Unit (OICC)
TAU	Tel Aviv University [*Israel*]
TAU	Temporary Authorization [*Personnel*] (OICC)
TAU	Test Access Unit [*Telecommunications*] (TEL)
TAU	Thesaurus Alphabetical Up to Date (NITA)
TAU	Thousand Astronomical Units
TAU	Toros Airlines [*Turkey*] [*ICAO designator*] (FAAC)
TAU	Transalta Utilities Corp. [*Toronto Stock Exchange symbol*]
TAU	Triton Acid Urea
TAU	Trunk Access Unit
TAU	Twin Agent Unit [*Fire fighting*] (NVT)
Taubmn	Taubman Centers Co., Inc. [*Associated Press*] (SAG)
TauCA	Taurus Municipal California Holdings [*Associated Press*] (SAG)
TAUCH	Tauchnitz [*Bibliography*] (ROG)
TAUF	Test Assembly Unloading Fixture [*Nuclear energy*] (NRCH)
TAUM	Groupe de Recherches pour la Traduction Automatique [*Universite de Montreal*] [*Canada Research center*]
Taun	Taunton's English Common Pleas Reports [*A publication*] (DLA)
TAUN	Technical Assistance of the United Nations
Taunt (Eng)	Taunton's English Common Pleas Reports [*127, 129 English Reprint*] [*A publication*] (DLA)
TauNY	Taurus Municipal New York Holdings [*Associated Press*] (SAG)
Taur	Taurus [*Constellation*]
TAURUS	Transfer and Automated Registration of Uncertificated Stock [*London Stock Exchange computer project*] (ECON)
TAUS	Tobacco Association of United States (EA)
TAUSA	Trans-Atlantic Universities Speech Association
Taut	Taunton's English Common Pleas Reports [*A publication*] (DLA)
TAUT	Tautology (ADA)
TAUVEX	Tel Aviv University Ultra-Violet Explorer [*Israel*]
TAV	Compania de Servicios Aereos, TAVISA [*Spain ICAO designator*] (FAAC)
TAV	Tau [*American Samoa*] [*Airport symbol*] (OAG)
TAV	Tavern (ROG)
TAV	Tavistock [*England*]
TAV	Tavurvur [*New Britain*] [*Seismograph station code, US Geological Survey*] (SEIS)
TAV	Taxpayers' Association of Victoria [*Australia*]
TAV	Technical Assistance Visit (MCD)
TAV	Technical Availability [*Navy*] (NG)
TAV	Temperature-Activated Vacuum [*Automotive engineering*]
TAV	Tender Availability [*Navy*]
TAV	Test and Validation (KSC)
TAV	Thorn Apple Valley, Inc. (EFIS)
TAV	Tomato Aspermy Virus
TAV	Total Asset Visibility [*Army*]
TAV	Toward, Away, versus Selection System [*Psychology*] (AEBS)
TAV	Transatmospheric Vehicle [*Proposed futuristic plane capable of flying at hypersonic speeds*]
TAV	Trapped Air Volume [*Medicine*] (DMAA)
TAV	Triathlon Association of Victoria [*Australia*]
TAVC	Total Active Vitamin C [*Nutrition*]
TAVE	Average Temperature (NRCH)
TAVE	Thor-Agena Vibration Experiment [*NASA*]
TAVERNS	Test and Verification Environment for Remote Network Systems (SSD)
TAVET	Temperature Acceleration Vibration Environmental Tester
TAVG	Temperature Average (IAA)
TAVI	Thorn Apple Valley [*NASDAQ symbol*] (TTSB)
TAVI	Thorn Apple Valley, Inc. [*Southfield, MI*] [*NASDAQ symbol*] (NQ)
TAVIP	Tahun Vivere Pericoloso [*The Year of Living Dangerously*] [*President Sukarno's national policy in 1964 Indonesia*]
TAVRA	Territorial Auxiliary and Volunteer Reserve Association [*British Armed Forces*]
TAVS	Turbine Area Ventilation System [*Nuclear energy*] (NRCH)
TAVSC	Training and Audiovisual Support Center [*Army*]
TAVT	Terminal Airspace Visualization Tool [*FAA*] (TAG)
TAW	Tactical Air [*or Airlift*] Wing

TAW............	Tactical Assault Weapon
TAW............	Tawu [*Republic of China*] [*Seismograph station code, US Geological Survey*] (SEIS)
TAW............	Tennessee Wesleyan College, Athens, TN [*Library symbol Library of Congress*] (LCLS)
TAW............	Terrawest [*Vancouver Stock Exchange symbol*]
TAW............	Thrust-Augmented Wing [*NASA*] (MCD)
TAW............	[*The*] Toledo, Angola & Western Railway Co. [*AAR code*]
TAW............	Train America's Workforce [*An association*] (WYGK)
TAW............	Transway Air Services, Inc. [*Liberia*] [*ICAO designator*] (FAAC)
TAW............	Troop Airlift Wing (CINC)
TAW............	Twice a Week [*Advertising frequency*]
TAWACS......	Tactical Airborne Warning and Control System (AFM)
TAWAR	Tactical All Weather Attack Requirements [*Air Force*] (MCD)
TAWB..........	Through Air Waybill [*Shipping*] (DS)
TAWC	Tactical Air Warfare Center [*Air Force*]
TAWC	Tactical Armored Weapons Carrier (MCD)
TAWC	Tasmanian Amateur Walking Club [*Australia*]
TAWCS	Tactical Air Weapons Control System
TAWDS	Target Acquisition Weapon Delivery System [*Air Force*] (MCD)
TAWDS	Terminal Area Weapon Delivery Simulator (MCD)
TAWG	Tactical Air Warfare Group
TAWG	Target Acquisition Working Group [*Air Force*]
TAWOG	Travel Arrangements Without Government Expense (FAAC)
TAWPI	The Association for Work Process Improvement
TAWRS	Tower Aviation Weather Reporting Station (NOAA)
TAWS	Tactical Area Weather Sensor (MCD)
TAWS	Tactical Automatic Weather Station [*Buoy*] (MSC)
TAWS	Tactical Warfare Center [*Army*] (AABC)
TAWS	Technical Analysis Work Sheet (AAG)
TAWS	Terrain Analyst Work Station [*Army*] (RDA)
TAWS	Thomasville Aircraft and Warning Station (IAA)
TAWS	Total Airborne Weapon Systems (MUGU)
TAWS	Total Armament Weapons System (MUGU)
TAWS	Transonabuoy Automatic Weather System (SAA)
TA Wst........	TransAmerican Waste Industries, Inc. [*Associated Press*] (SAG)
TAWT..........	Tawton [*England*]
TAWU	Transport and Allied Workers' Union [*Kenya*] (BUAC)
TAX.............	Madison, WI [*Location identifier FAA*] (FAAL)
TAX.............	Tactical Air Exercise (CINC)
TAX.............	Tarxien International, Inc. [*Toronto Stock Exchange symbol*]
tax	Taxation (DD)
TAX.............	Taxiing [*Aviation*]
TAX.............	Taxol (DMAA)
TAX.............	Training Assessment Exercise
TAX.............	Travelair GmbH [*Germany ICAO designator*] (FAAC)
Tax ABC	Canada Tax Appeal Board Cases [*A publication*] (DLA)
Tax Acct	Taxation for Accountants [*A publication*] (DLA)
Tax Adm'rs News...	Tax Administrators News [*A publication*] (DLA)
Tax & Rev...	Taxation and Revenue (DLA)
Tax Aust	Taxation in Australia [*A publication*]
Tax Cas	Tax Cases [*A publication*] (DLA)
Tax Ct Mem Dec...	Tax Court Memorandum Decisions [*Commerce Clearing House*] [*A publication*] (DLA)
Tax Ct Rep...	Tax Court Reporter [*Commerce Clearing House*] [*A publication*] (DLA)
Tax Ct Rep & Mem Dec (P-H)...	Tax Court Reported and Memorandum Decisions (Prentice-Hall, Inc.) [*A publication*] (DLA)
Tax Ct Rep Dec...	Tax Court Reported Decisions [*Prentice-Hall, Inc.*] [*A publication*] (DLA)
TAXDX	Mgn. Stanley D. Witter Tax Exempt Secs. Cl.D [*Mutual fund ticker symbol*] (SG)
Taxes..........	Tax Magazine [*A publication*] (DLA)
TAXI............	Medallion Financial [*NASDAQ symbol*] (TTSB)
taxi	Taximeter Cabriolet
TAXI............	Transparent Asynchronous Transceiver Interface
TAXIR..........	Taxonomic Information Retrieval [*Computer science*] (DIT)
Tax Law Rep...	Tax Law Reporter [*A publication*] (DLA)
TAXLE.........	Tandem Cantilevered Axle
Tax LR........	Tax Law Reporter [*A publication*] (DLA)
Tax L Rep...	Tax Law Reporter [*A publication*] (DLA)
Tax Mag	Tax Magazine [*A publication*] (DLA)
Tax Man	Tax Management [*A publication*] (DLA)
Tax Mgmt (BNA)...	Tax Management (Bureau of National Affairs) [*A publication*] (DLA)
Tax Mgmt Int'l J...	Tax Management International Journal [*A publication*] (DLA)
Tax Mngm't...	Tax Management [*Bureau of National Affairs*] [*A publication*] (DLA)
TAXN	Taxation (ROG)
TAXON	Taxonomy
Tax Pl Int...	Tax Planning International [*A publication*] (DLA)
Tax Pl Rev...	Tax Planning Review [*A publication*] (DLA)
Tax Pract Forum...	Tax Practitioners Forum [*A publication*] (DLA)
Tax R..........	Taxation Reports [*England*] [*A publication*] (DLA)
t-ay--	Antarctica [*MARC geographic area code Library of Congress*] (LCCP)
TAY.............	Talia Airlines [*Turkey*] [*ICAO designator*] (FAAC)
TAY.............	Taylor, FL [*Location identifier FAA*] (FAAL)
Tay.............	Taylor's North Carolina Reports [*1 North Carolina*] [*1798-1802*] [*A publication*] (DLA)
Tay.............	Taylor's Supreme Court Reports [*1847-48*] [*Bengal, India*] [*A publication*] (DLA)
Tay.............	Taylor's Upper Canada King's Bench Reports [*1823-1827*] [*A publication*] (DLA)
Tay.............	Tayside [*Scotland*] (WGA)
TAY.............	Tule Lake Aster Yellows [*Plant pathology*]
Tay & B	Taylor and Bell's Bengal Reports [*India*] [*A publication*] (DLA)

Tay Bank L...	Taylor on the Bankruptcy Law [*A publication*] (DLA)
Tay Bk R....	Taylor's Book of Rights [*1833*] [*A publication*] (DLA)
Tay Civ L....	Taylor's Elements of Civil Law [*A publication*] (DLA)
TAYD	Taylor Devices [*NASDAQ symbol*] (TTSB)
TAYD	Taylor Devices, Inc. [*NASDAQ symbol*] (NQ)
Tay Eq Jur...	Taylor on Equity Jurisprudence [*A publication*] (DLA)
Tay Ev	Taylor on Evidence [*12th ed.*] [*1931*] [*A publication*] (DLA)
Tay Glos.....	Taylor's Law Glossary [*2nd ed.*] [*1823*] [*A publication*] (DLA)
Tay Gov......	Taylor on Government [*A publication*] (DLA)
Tay L & T...	Taylor's Landlord and Tenant [*A publication*] (DLA)
Tayl Civil Law...	Taylor on Civil Law [*A publication*] (DLA)
Tayl Corp....	Taylor on Private Corporations [*A publication*] (DLA)
Tayl Ev	Taylor on Evidence [*A publication*] (DLA)
Tay L Gl	Taylor's Law Glossary [*A publication*] (DLA)
Tayl Gloss...	Taylor's Law Glossary [*A publication*] (DLA)
Tayl Landl & Ten...	Taylor's Landlord and Tenant [*A publication*] (DLA)
Tayl Med Jur...	Taylor's Medical Jurisprudence [*A publication*] (DLA)
Tayl NC.......	Taylor's North Carolina Reports [*1 North Carolina*] [*A publication*] (DLA)
Taylor.........	Taylor's Customary Laws of Rembau [*1903-28*] [*Malaya*] [*A publication*] (DLA)
Taylor.........	Taylor's North Carolina Reports [*1 North Carolina*] [*A publication*] (DLA)
Taylor.........	Taylor's North Carolina Term Reports [*4 North Carolina*] [*A publication*] (DLA)
Taylor.........	Taylor's Reports [*Bengal, India*] [*A publication*] (DLA)
Taylor.........	Taylor's Upper Canada King's Bench Reports [*A publication*] (DLA)
Taylor KB (Can)...	Taylor's Upper Canada King's Bench Reports [*A publication*] (DLA)
Taylor (Malaya)...	Taylor's Customary Laws of Rembau [*1903-28*] [*Malaya*] [*A publication*] (DLA)
Taylor UC....	Taylor's Upper Canada King's Bench Reports [*A publication*] (DLA)
Tayl Priv Corp...	Taylor on Private Corporations [*A publication*] (DLA)
TaylrDv.......	Taylor Devices, Inc. [*Associated Press*] (SAG)
Tayl St........	Taylor's Revised Statutes [*Wisconsin*] [*A publication*] (DLA)
Tay Med Jur...	Taylor's Medical Jurisprudence [*12th ed.*] [*1966*] [*A publication*] (DLA)
TAYMEL......	Taylor Woodrow Management & Engineering Ltd. [*British*] (IRUK)
Tay NC........	Taylor's North Carolina Reports [*1 North Carolina*] [*A publication*] (DLA)
Tay Poi	Taylor on Poisons [*3rd ed.*] [*1875*] [*A publication*] (DLA)
Tay Rep......	Taylor's North Carolina Reports [*1 North Carolina*] [*A publication*] (DLA)
Tay Tit	Taylor on Tithe Commutation [*1876*] [*A publication*] (DLA)
Tay UC........	Taylor's Upper Canada King's Bench Reports [*1 vol.*] [*1823-27*] [*A publication*] (DLA)
Tay Wills.....	Taylor's Precedents of Wills [*A publication*] (DLA)
Tay Wis Stat...	Taylor's Wisconsin Statutes [*A publication*] (DLA)
TAZ.............	Tactical Alert Zone (NATG)
TAZ.............	Taylorville, IL [*Location identifier FAA*] (FAAL)
TAZ.............	Theater Administrative Zone [*Military*]
TAZ.............	Traffic Analysis Zone [*Bureau of the Census*] (GFGA)
TAZ.............	Transient Absorption Zener (CIST)
TAZ.............	Transportation Analysis Zone [*MM*] (TAG)
TAZ.............	Transporte Aereo de la Amazonia [*Colombia*] [*ICAO designator*] (FAAC)
TAZ.............	Triazolam [*Tranquilizer*]
TAZARA	Tanzania-Zambia Railway
TAZARA	Tanzania-Zambia Railway Authority (BUAC)
TB...............	Aerospatiale (SOCATA) Stark KG [*Germany ICAO aircraft manufacturer identifier*] (ICAO)
TB...............	Automotive Engine Rebuilders Association. Technical Bulletin [*A publication*] (EAAP)
Tb...............	Body Temperature [*Medicine*]
TB...............	Mycobacterium Tuberculosis [*A bacterium*] [*Medicine*] (DAVI)
tb...............	Tablespoon [*Measure*] (WGA)
TB...............	Tabulation Block (MSA)
TB...............	Tail Back [*Football*]
TB...............	Talk Back [*NASA*] (KSC)
TB...............	Talmud Bavli (BJA)
TB...............	Tangential Bracket
TB...............	Tank Battalion [*Army*]
TB...............	Tape Backup Unit
TB...............	Tapes for the Blind [*Defunct*] (EA)
TB...............	Tariff Bureau
TB...............	Tasmanian Bank [*Australia Commercial firm*]
TB...............	Taussig-Bing [*Syndrome*] [*Medicine*] (DB)
Tb...............	Tbilisi (DB)
TB...............	Techbyte, Inc. [*Vancouver Stock Exchange symbol*]
TB...............	Technical Bulletin [*Military*]
TB...............	Tejas Airlines [*ICAO designator*] (AD)
TB...............	Telegraph Bureau
TB...............	Temple Biographies [*A publication*]
TB...............	Temporary Buoy [*Nautical charts*]
TB...............	Tenor, Bass (CDAI)
Tb...............	TeraBIT [*Binary Digit*] [*10^{12} BITs*]
TB...............	Terabyte [*10^{12} bytes*]
Tb...............	Terabyte [*Computer science*] (EERA)
Tb...............	Terbium [*Chemical element*]
TB...............	Terminal Base (MCD)
TB...............	Terminal Block
TB...............	Terminal Board
TB...............	Terminal Bronchiole [*Medicine*] (MAE)
TB...............	Test Bed (MCD)
TB...............	Test Bulletin

TB	Thermobarometer
TB	Thexylborane [*Organic chemistry*]
T-B	Thomas-Binetti [*Test*] [*Laboratory science*] (DAVI)
TB	Thoroughbred
TB	Thromboxane B [*Also, TxB, TXB*] [*Biochemistry*]
TB	Throttle Body [*Automotive engineering*]
TB	Through Bolt (DAC)
T/B	Thunderbird [*Automobile*]
TB	Thymol Blue [*An indicator*]
TB	Ticket Board (DGA)
TB	Tight Binding (AAEL)
TB	Tile Base [*Technical drawings*]
T/B	Tile Block [*Technical drawings*]
TB	Time-Bandwidth
TB	Time Base
TB	Time between Points [*Experimentation*]
TB	Time Duration of Burn (MCD)
TB	Times at Bat [*Baseball*]
T/B	Title Block (SAA)
Tb	Tobit [*Old Testament book*] [*Roman Catholic canon*]
TB	Toggle Buffer (MCD)
TB	Toluidine Blue [*Organic chemistry*]
tb	Tomb (VRA)
TB	Tone Burst
TB	Top Boy [*British*] (DSUE)
T/B	Top to Bottom
TB	Torch Bible Commentaries [*A publication*] (BJA)
TB	Torch Brazing
TB	Torpedo Boat [*Navy symbol Obsolete*]
TB	Torpedo Bomber [*or Bombing*]
TB	Torsion Bar [*Automotive engineering*]
TB	Total Bases
TB	Total Bilirubin [*Clinical chemistry*]
TB	Total Blank [*Entertainment slang for poor show town*]
TB	Total Body [*Nuclear energy*] (NRCH)
TB	Total Body [*Medicine*] (DAVI)
TB	Total Bouts [*Boxing*]
TB	Total Burn
TB	Tourism Brisbane [*Australia*]
TB	Towel Bar [*Technical drawings*]
TB	Tracer Bullet
TB	Tracheal-Bronchiolar [*Region*] [*Medicine*]
TB	Tracheobronchitis [*Medicine*]
TB	Tractor Biplane
TB	Trading Bank
TB	Trafalgar Brookmount [*British*]
TB	Traffic Bureau
TB	Training Back [*Main parachute*]
TB	Training Battalion [*British military*] (DMA)
TB	Tranquility Base [*Moon landing site*]
TB	Transfer Building
TB	Transmitter-Blocker (DEN)
TB	Transmitter Buffer [*Telecommunications*] (IAA)
TB	Transparent Bridging [*Computer science*] (DDC)
TB	Trapezoid Body [*Audiometry*]
TB	Treasury Bill
TB	Treasury Board Secretariat [*Canada*]
TB	Trial Balance [*Bookkeeping*]
tb	Trial Balance [*Bookkeeping*] (ODBW)
TB	Trial Balloon
TB	Trigonal Bipyramid [*Medicine*] (DB)
TB	Triple-Braided (CET)
TB	Troop Basis [*Military*]
TB	True Bearing [*Navigation*]
TB	True Blue [*A fluorescent dye*]
TB	Trump Shuttle [*ICAO designator*] (AD)
TB	Trunk Barrier [*Telecommunications*] (IAA)
TB	Tryptone Broth [*Culture medium*]
TB	Tubercle Bacillus [*Bacteriology*]
TB	Tuberculin [*or Tuberculosis*] (AABC)
tb	Tuberculosis (STED)
TB	Tumor-Bearing [*Animal*]
TB	Tundra Biome [*Ecological biogeographic study*]
TB	Turbine Building [*Nuclear energy*] (NRCH)
TB	Turbulence [*Aviation*] (FAAC)
TB	Twin Branch Railroad Co. [*AAR code*]
TB	Twirly Birds (EA)
TBA	[*The*] Bettmann Archive [*A publication*]
TBA	[*The*] Black Agenda [*An association*]
TBA	Tabibuga [*Papua New Guinea*] [*Airport symbol*] (OAG)
TBA	Tables of Basic Allowances [*Previously, Basic Tables of Commissioning Allowances*] [*Navy*]
TBA	Task Budget Allocation (MCD)
TBA	Tasmanian Badminton Association [*Australia*]
TBA	Tasmanian Bar Association [*Australia*]
TBA	Tasmanian Basketball Association [*Australia*]
TBA	Tasmanian Beekeepers' Association [*Australia*]
TBA	Tasmanian Bookmakers' Association [*Australia*]
TBA	Tasmanian Bridge Association [*Australia*]
TBA	Taurine Bibliophiles of America (EA)
TBA	Tea Brokers' Association [*London*] (BUAC)
TBA	Tea Buyers' Association [*British*] (EAIO)
TBA	Teaching Brothers' Association (BUAC)
TBA	Television Bureau of Advertising
TBA	Terminal Board Assembly (MSA)

TBA	Tertiary Butyl Acetate [*Organic chemistry*]
TBA	Tertiary Butyl Alcohol [*Gasoline additive*]
TBA	Tertiary-Butylamine [*Organic chemistry*]
TBA	Tertiary-Butylarsine [*Organic chemistry*]
TBA	Test Bed Aircraft
TBA	Test Boring Association (EA)
TBA	Test of Basic Assumptions [*Psychology*]
TBA	Testosterone-Binding Affinity [*Endocrinology*] (MAE)
TBA	Thermo Bioanalysis Corp. [*AMEX symbol*] (SAG)
TBA	Thiobarbituric Acid [*Organic chemistry*]
TBA	Thoroughbred Breeders' Association [*British*] (BI)
TBA	Thyroxine-Binding Albumin [*Biochemistry*] (MAE)
TBA	Tires, Batteries, and Accessories
TBA	To Be Absorbed [*Pharmacology*] (DAVI)
TBA	To Be Activated [*Military*]
TBA	To Be Added (AAG)
TBA	To Be Administered (STED)
TBA	To Be Admitted [*Medicine*] (DAVI)
TBA	To Be Agreed (AIA)
TBA	To Be Announced
TBA	To Be Assigned
TBA	To Be Avoided [*Slang*]
TBA	Torsional Braid Analysis [*Instrumentation*]
TBA	Total Bile Acid (STED)
TBA	Total Body Surface Area (STED)
TBA	Towed Buoy Antenna
TBA	Traditional Birth Attendant
TBA	Transbrasil SA Linhas Aereas [*Brazil*] [*ICAO designator*] (FAAC)
TBA	Travel Buyers Association (NTPA)
TBA	Tributylamine [*Organic chemistry*]
TBA	Trichlorobenzoic Acid [*Herbicide*] [*Organic chemistry*]
TBA	Tropical Biology Association (BUAC)
TBA	Trypsin-Binding Activity (STED)
TBA	Tuba [*Music*]
TBA	Tubercle Bacillus (STED)
TBA	Tumor-Bearing Animal (AAMN)
TBA	Twin Bonanza Association (EA)
TBAB	Tetrabutylammonium Bromide [*Organic chemistry*]
TBAB	Theosophical Book Association for the Blind (EA)
TBAB	Tryptose Blood Agar Base [*Medicine*] (DMAA)
TBAC	Tandy Brands Accessories [*NASDAQ symbol*] (TTSB)
TBAC	Tandy Brands Accessories, Inc. [*NASDAQ symbol*] (SAG)
TBAC	Tertiary-Butylacetyl Chloride [*Organic chemistry*]
TBACC	Tetrabutylammonium Chlorochromate [*Organic chemistry*]
TBAC/FLM	Treasury Board Advisory Committee on Federal Land Management [*Canada*]
TBAD	To Be Advised (AIA)
TBAF	Tetrabutylammonium Fluoride [*Organic chemistry*]
TBAF	Tetrabutylammonium Fluoroborate [*Organic chemistry*]
TBAG	To Be Agreed (AIA)
TBAH	Tetrabutylammonium Hydroxide [*Organic chemistry*]
TBAHS	Tetrabutylammonium Hydrogen Sulfate [*Organic chemistry*]
TBAI	Temporary Base Activation Instruction (AAG)
TBAM	Tone Burst Amplitude Modulation
TBAN	To Be Announced [*Army*] (AABC)
TBAN	Transbronchial Aspiration Needle [*Medicine*] (DMAA)
TB & B	Tuberculosis and Brucellosis [*Medicine*] (ADA)
T banding	Telomere/Terminal Banding of Chromosomes (STED)
TB & M	Tracewell, Bowers, and Mitchell's United States Comptroller's Decisions [*A publication*] (DLA)
TB & S	Top, Bottom, and Sides [*Lumber*]
TBAP	Tetrabutylammoniumperchlorate [*Photovoltaic energy systems*]
TBARA	Trakehner Breed Association and Registry of America [*Defunct*] (EA)
TBARS	Thiobarbituric Acid Reactive Substance [*Analytical chemistry*]
TBAS	[*The*] Band Appreciation Society (EAIO)
TBAT	Tow/Bushmaster Armored Turret [*Military*]
TBAV	Tenpin Bowling Association of Victoria [*Australia*]
TBAV	ThunderBYTE Anti-Virus [*Computer software*] (PCM)
TBAVF	Translocated Basilic Vein Arteriovenous Fistula [*Surgery*]
TBAWRBA	Travel by Military Aircraft, Military and/or Naval Water Carrier, Commercial Rail and/or Bus Is Authorized [*Army*] (AABC)
TBAX	Tube Axial
TBAZFCA	Toledo Bird Association, Zebra Finch Club of America (EA)
TBB	Columbus, MS [*Location identifier FAA*] (FAAL)
TBB	Die Tempel von Babylon und Borsippa [*A publication*] (BJA)
TBB	Temporal Bone Banks [*Otology*] (EA)
TBB	Tenor, Baritone, Bass
TBB	Tobex Resources Ltd. [*Vancouver Stock Exchange symbol*]
TBB	Transbronchial Biopsy [*Medicine*]
TBB	Trolleybus Bulletin [*A publication*] (EAAP)
TBB	Tuy Hoa [*South Vietnam*] [*Airport symbol*] (AD)
TBBA	Tea Buying Brokers' Association [*British*] (DBA)
TBBA	Terephthalyl Bis(butylaniline) [*Organic chemistry*]
TBBA	Thai-British Business Association (BUAC)
TBBF	Top Baseband Frequency
TBBM	Total Body Bone Mineral
TBBPA	Tetrabromobisphenol-A [*Organic chemistry*]
TBBS	[*The*] Bread Board System [*eSoft, Inc.*] [*Computer science*] (PCM)
TBC	Belmont College, Nashville, TN [*OCLC symbol*] (OCLC)
TBC	Confederation College of Applied Arts and Technology [*UTLAS symbol*]
TBC	Taiwan Base Command (CINC)
TBC	Tanker and Bulk Carrier
TBC	Tasmanian Bowls Council [*Australia*]
TBC	Tasty Baking [*AMEX symbol*] (TTSB)

TBC	Tasty Baking Co. [*AMEX symbol*] (SPSG)
TBC	TBC Corp. [*Associated Press*] (SAG)
TBC	Technology & Business Centre (BUAC)
TBC	Technology & Business Communications, Inc. [*Information service or system*] (IID)
TBC	Television Briefing Console
TBC	Tembec Inc. [*Toronto Stock Exchange symbol*]
TBC	Terminal Buffer Controller (NASA)
TBC	Tertiary-Butylcatechol [*Organic chemistry*]
TBC	Theatre Ballet of Canada
TBC	Thermal Barrier Coating (RDA)
TBC	Thyroxine-Binding Capacity [*Biochemistry*]
TBC	Thyroxine-Binding Coagulin [*Biochemistry*] (MAE)
TBC	Tie Line Bias Control [*Telecommunications*] (IAA)
TBC	Time Base Corrector [*Videotape recording element*] [*Early processing device*]
TBC	Time-Based Competition [*Business term*]
TBC	Time-Based Competitiveness (AAEL)
TBC	To Be Cooked [*Food*]
TBC	Token Bus Controller [*Motorola, Inc.*]
TBC	Torch Bible Commentaries [*New York/London*] [*A publication*] (BJA)
TBC	Torrey Botanical Club (EA)
TBC	Toss Bomb Computer
TBC	Total Body Calcium
TBC	Total Body Carbon
TBC	Total Body Clearance (STED)
TBC	Total Body Counting (STED)
TBC	Trinidad Base Command [*World War II*]
TBC	Trunk Block Connector
TBC	Tuba City, AZ [*Location identifier FAA*] (FAAL)
TBC	Tube Bending Chart
TBC	Tubercidin (STED)
TBC	Tubercle Bacillus [*Bacteriology*]
TBC	Tuberculosis
TBC	Turbulent Bed Contactor [*Chemical engineering*]
TBCA	Test Boring Contractors Association [*Later, TBA*] (EA)
TBCA	Transportation Brokers Conference of America (EA)
TBCC	TBC Corp. [*NASDAQ symbol*] (NQ)
TBCC	Tom Baker Cancer Centre [*University of Calgary*] [*Formerly, Southern Alberta Cancer Centre*] [*Research center*] (RCD)
TBCCW	Turbine-Building Closed Cooling Water [*Nuclear energy*] (NRCH)
TBCE	Time Buffered Coarse Fine (IAA)
TBCITC	Tasmanian Building and Construction Industry Training Committee [*Australia*]
TBCOA	Triathalon Broadcasting Co. [*NASDAQ symbol*] (SAG)
TBCOA	Triathlon Broadcasting 'A' [*NASDAQ symbol*] (TTSB)
TBCOL	Triathlon Brdcst 9% Pfd [*NASDAQ symbol*] (TTSB)
TBCR	Times British Colonies Review [*London*] [*A publication*]
TBD	Tactical Battle Drill [*Army*] (INF)
TBD	Target Bearing Designator [*Navy*]
TBD	Terminal Bomber Defense [*Army*] (AABC)
TBD	Thibodaux, LA [*Location identifier FAA*] (FAAL)
TBD	Thousand Barrels per Day [*Also, KBD*]
TBD	Thunderbird Touro [*Canada*] [*FAA designator*] (FAAC)
TBD	To Be Declassified (AAG)
TBD	To Be Defined
TBD	To Be Designated (MCD)
TBD	To Be Determined (AFM)
TBD	To Be Developed (NASA)
TBD	To Be Disbanded
TBD	To Be Done (AAG)
TBD	Too Badly Decomposed
TBD	Torpedo-Boat Destroyer [*Obsolete*]
TBD	Total Body Density [*Medicine*] (MAE)
TBD	Trans Border Energy [*Vancouver Stock Exchange symbol*]
TBD	Triazabicydo-decene [*Organic chemistry*]
TBD	Troubleshooting Block Diagram
TBD	Tube Bending Data (MCD)
TBD	Twin Boundary Diffusion
TBDA	Thexylborane-N, N-Diethylaniline [*Organic chemistry*]
TBDD	Tetrabromodibenzo-p-dioxin [*Organic chemistry*]
TBDF	Transborder Data Flows [*Also, TDF*] [*Telecommunications*]
TBDI	TMBR/Sharp Drilling [*NASDAQ symbol*] (TTSB)
TBDI	TMBR Sharp Drilling, Inc. [*NASDAQ symbol*] (SAG)
TBDL	To Be Designated Later (CINC)
TBDL	Total Bile-Duct Ligation [*Medicine*]
TBDMIM	Tertiary-Butyldimethylsilylimidazole [*Organic chemistry*]
TBDMS	Tertiary-Butyldimethylsilyl [*Organic chemistry*]
TBDMSCI	Tertiary-Butyldimethylsilyl Chloride [*Also, TBSCI*] [*Organic chemistry*]
TBDPS	Tertiary-Butyldiphenysilyl [*Also, TBDMS, TBS*] [*Organic chemistry*]
TBDS	Test Base Dispatch Service (AAG)
TBD/TDA	Too Badly Decomposed/Technician Destroyed Animal [*Laboratory testing*]
TBE	Federation Europeenne des Fabricants de Tuiles et de Briques [*European Association of Brick and Tile Manufacturers*] (EAIO)
TBE	Tenant by the Entirety [*Legal shorthand*] (LWAP)
TBE	Tetrabromoethane [*Microscopy*]
TBE	Thread Both Ends (MSA)
TBE	Tiber Energy Corp. [*Toronto Stock Exchange symbol*]
TBE	Tick-Borne Encephalitis
TBE	Time Base Error
TBE	Tobe, CO [*Location identifier FAA*] (FAAL)
TBE	To Be Evaluated (NASA)
TBE	To Be Expended (AAG)
TBE	Toronto Board of Education, Professional Library [*UTLAS symbol*]

TBE	Total Binding Energy (IAA)
TBE	Total Body Ergometer
TBE	Total Breech Extraction [*Gynecology*]
TBE	Transmitter Buffer Empty [*Computer science*]
TBE	Tris-Borate Buffer Electrophoresis
TBE	Tris-Borate-EDTA [*Ethylenediaminetetraacetate*] [*Buffer*]
TBE	Tuberculin Bacillen Emulsion [*Medicine*]
TBEA	Tennessee Business Education Association (EDAC)
TBEA	Truck Body and Equipment Association [*Defunct*] (EA)
TBED	Time Base Error Difference [*Computer science*] (IAA)
TBEM	Terminal-Based Electronic Mail
TBeP	Polk County High School, Benton, TN [*Library symbol Library of Congress*] (LCLS)
TBEP	Technology Base Enhancement Project
TBEP	Tri(butoxyethyl) Phosphate [*Organic chemistry*]
TBES	Total Body Exchangeable Sodium (DB)
TBESC	Tech Base Executive Steering Committee [*Army*] (RDA)
TBESC	Technology Base Executive Steering Commitee [*Army*] (RDA)
TBESI	Turbine-Building Exhaust System Isolation [*Nuclear energy*] (NRCH)
TBEX	Tube Expander
TBF	Tabiteuea North [*Kiribati*] [*Airport symbol*] (OAG)
TBF	Tail Bomb Fuse (KSC)
TBF	Teachers' Benevolent Fund (AIE)
TBF	Technical and Biological Feasibility [*Environmental science*] (COE)
TBF	Test de Bon Fonctionnement [*Spacelab*] (MCD)
TBF	Testicular Blood Flow [*Physiology*]
TBF	Tie Bus Fault
TBF	Time between Failures [*Quality control*] (AFIT)
TBF	To Be Funded [*Contracting*] [*Military*]
TBF	Torpedo Bomber Fighter (NATG)
TBF	Total Body Fat
TBF	Tour Basing Fare [*Air travel term*]
TBF	Tributyl Phosphate [*Organic chemistry*]
TBF	Tuberculin Bouillon Filtrate [*Medicine*] (DB)
TBF	Two-Body Force
TBFC	Teresa Brewer Fan Club (EA)
TBFC	Tom Burford Fan Club (EA)
TBFC	Tony Booth Fan Club (EA)
TBFCA	Technical and Biological Facility and Cost Effectiveness of Alternatives [*Environmental science*] (COE)
TBFFU	Twin-Ball Fire Fighting Unit [*Military*] (PDAA)
TBFG	Tom Baker Friendship Group (EAIO)
TBFI	Throttle Body Fuel Injection [*Fuel systems*] [*Automotive engineering*]
TBFU	Twin-Ball Fire Fighting Unit [*Navy*] (DNAB)
TBFX	Tube Fixture [*Tool*] (AAG)
TBG	Tabubil [*Papua New Guinea*] [*Airport symbol*] (OAG)
TBG	Testosterone-Binding Globulin [*Endocrinology*]
TBG	Teubners Bibliotheca Scriptorum Graecorum et Romanorum (BJA)
TBG	Thermobarogravimetry (DB)
TBG	Thyroglobulin [*Endocrinology*] (DAVI)
TBG	Thyroxine-Binding Globulin [*Biochemistry*]
TBG	Thyssen-Bornemisza Group NV [*Netherlands*]
TBG	Tidy Britain Group [*An association*] (EAIO)
TBG	Tipping Bucket Gauge (NOAA)
TBG	Tris-Buffered Gey's Solution (DB)
TBG	Tubing (MSA)
TBGAA	Travel by Government Automobile Authorized
TBG cap	Thyroxine-Binding Capacity of Thyroxine-Binding Globulin Assays [*Endrocrinology*] (DAVI)
TBGP	Tactical Bomb Group [*Air Force*]
TBGP	Total Blood Granulocyte Pool [*Hematology*]
TBGR	Tropical Botanical Garden and Research Institute [*India*]
TBGTA	Travel by Government Transportation Authorized [*Military*] (AABC)
TBH	Tablas [*Philippines*] [*Airport symbol*] (OAG)
TBH	Technical Benzene Hexachloride [*Organic chemistry*]
TBH	Test Bed Harness (MCD)
TBH	Test Bench Harness (NG)
TBH	Total Body Hematocrit [*Medicine*] (MAE)
TBH	TourBase Hotel-/Unterkunftsdaten [*Jaeger-Verlag GmbH*] [*Germany Information service or system*] (CRD)
TBH	Trinidad [*Brigand Hill*] [*Trinidad-Tobago*] [*Seismograph station code, US Geological Survey*] (SEIS)
TBH	Trinity Air Bahamas [*ICAO designator*] (FAAC)
TBHB	Trisbicyclo Thexabenzene [*Organic chemistry*]
TBHBA	Tribromo(hydroxy)benzoic Acid [*Organic chemistry*]
TBHP	Tertiary-Butylhydroperoxide [*Organic chemistry*]
TBHP	Tertiary-Butyl Hydroperoxide [*Organic chemistry*]
TBHP	Trihydroxybutyrophenone [*Antioxidant*] [*Organic chemistry*]
TBHQ	Tertiary-Butylhydroquinone [*Also, MTBHQ*] [*Organic chemistry*]
TBI	Target Bearing Indicator [*Military*]
TBI	Teacher-Based Instruction (EDAC)
TBI	Telecom Broadcasting, Inc. [*Oceanside, CA*] [*Telecommunications service*] (TSSD)
TBI	Test Bed Installation (MCD)
TBI	Test Bench Installation (NG)
TBI	Theodor Bilharz Research Institute [*Egypt*] (BUAC)
TBI	Thomson Business Information [*The Thomson Corp.*] [*Publishing*]
TBI	Threaded Blind Insert
TBI	Throttle Body Fuel Injection [*Automotive engineering*]
TBI	Through-Bulkhead Initiator [*Military*] (MCD)
TBI	Thyroxine-Binding Index [*Biochemistry*] (MAE)
TBI	Time between Inspections [*Quality control*]
TBI	Time, Bulb, Instantaneous [*Initials on certain Kodak cameras*]
TBI	Tissue Banks International [*An association*] (EA)
TBI	To Be Inactivated

TBI	To Be Indicated (AIA)
TBI	To Be Initiated (IAA)
TBI	Toothbrushing Instruction [Dentistry] (DMAA)
TBI	Total Body Irradiation [Medicine]
TBI	Traditionally Black Institutions (EDAC)
TBI	Traumatic Brain Injury [Medicine]
TBI	Trinity Bible Institute, Ellendale, ND [OCLC symbol] (OCLC)
TBI	Tromboni [Trombones]
TBI	Tubuai [Tubuai Islands] [Seismograph station code, US Geological Survey] (SEIS)
TBIFC	Thom Bierdz International Fan Club (EA)
TbIG	Terbium Iron Garnet (IEEE)
TBII	[TSH] Thyroid-stimulating hormone Binding Inhibitory Immunoglobulin [Endocrinology] (DAVI)
TBII	Thyrotropin-Binding Inhibitor Immunoglobulin
TBIL	Total Bilirubin [Clinical chemistry]
T Bili	Total Bilirubin [Clinical chemistry] (MAE)
T-bill	Treasury Bill (TDOB)
TBIP	Tomahawk Baseline Improvement Program (DOMA)
TBIRD	Terrestrial Background Infrared Detection (SAA)
T-BIRD	Terrestrial Ballistic Infrared Development (SAA)
T (Bird)	Thunderbird [Automobile] (DSUE)
TBIS	Technology Base Investment Strategy [Army]
TBIT	Telebit Corp. [NASDAQ symbol] (SAG)
TBJ	Turbulent Bounded Jet
TBJT	Turbojet (FAAC)
TBK	TEFLON Bonding Kit
TBK	Tolland Bank [AMEX symbol] (SPSG)
TBK	ToolBook [Computer format] (PCM)
TBK	Total Body Potassium [Clinical chemistry]
T/BKL	Turn Buckle [Automotive engineering]
TBL	[The] Berline, Berlin-Brandenburgisches Luftfahrtunternehmen GmbH [Germany ICAO designator] (FAAC)
TBL	Tabele [Papua New Guinea] [Seismograph station code, US Geological Survey] (SEIS)
TBL	Table
TBL	Tableland [Western Australia] [Airport symbol] (AD)
tbl	Tablespoon [Measurement] (DAVI)
TBL	Tactical Bomb Line (NVT)
TBL	[The] Tamarind Book of Lithography
TBL	Tasmanian Baseball League [Australia]
TBL	Terminal Ballistics Laboratory [Army]
TBL	Thin Base Laminate
TBL	Thomas Branigan Memorial Library, Las Cruces, NM [OCLC symbol] (OCLC)
TBL	Through Back of Loop [Knitting]
TBL	Through Bill of Lading [Shipping]
TBL	Timberland Co. [NYSE symbol] (SPSG)
TBL	Timberland Co. Cl'A' [NYSE symbol] (TTSB)
TBL	Tombill Mines Ltd. [Toronto Stock Exchange symbol]
TBL	Tootal Broadhurst Lee [Textile testing] [Obsolete]
TBL	Trouble [Telecommunications] (TEL)
TBL	True Blood Loss
TBL	Turbulent Boundary Layer
TBLB	Transbronchial Lung Biopsy [Medicine] (DMAA)
TBLB	Transbronchial Lung Brush [Medicine] (DAVI)
TBLC	Term Birth, Living Child [Medicine]
TBLE	Top Blacks in Law Enforcement [Later, BLE] (EA)
TBLE	Trouble (IAA)
TBLI	Term Birth, Living Infant [Obstetrics] (DAVI)
T/BLK	Terminal Block [Automotive engineering]
TBLN	Tracheobronchial Lymph Node [Anatomy]
TBLR	Tumbler (MSA)
TBLS	Trail Blazer Library System [Library network]
TBLSP	Tablespoon
TBM	Morgan StanGp 6% Telebras'PERQS' [AMEX symbol] (TTSB)
TBM	School of Aerospace Medicine, Brooks AFB, TX [OCLC symbol] (OCLC)
TBM	Tactical Ballistic Missile [Military] (CAAL)
TBM	Tax Board Memorandum [Internal Revenue Bulletin] [United States] [A publication] (DLA)
TBM	TBM NT Corp. [Toronto Stock Exchange symbol]
TBM	Tell Beit Mirsim (BJA)
TBM	Temporary Bench Mark
TBM	TeraBIT [Binary Digit] Memory [Computer science]
TBM	Terrestrial Biogeochemical Model [for climate effects]
TBM	Tertiary Butyl Mercaptan [Organic chemistry]
TBM	Theater Ballistic Missile
TBM	Theater Battle Model (MCD)
TBM	Thyroxine-Binding Meningitis [Medicine] (DB)
TBM	Tone Burst Modulation
TBM	Trailokya Bauddha Mahasangha [Friends of the Western Buddhist Order] [British] (EAIO)
TBM	Transport Bandwidth Manager [Telecommunications] (ITD)
TBM	Treasury Board Manual [Canada] (AAGC)
TBM	Trophoblastic Basement Membrane (PDAA)
TBM	Tuberculous Meningitis [Medicine]
TBM	Tubular Basement Membrane
TBM	Tunnel Boring Machine
TBMA	Tetiary Butyl Methacrylate (EDCT)
TBMA	Textile Bag Manufacturers Association (EA)
TBMA	Timber and Building Materials Association [New South Wales, Australia]
TBMAA	Travel by Military Aircraft Authorized
TBMAC	Tributylmethylammonium Chloride [Organic chemistry]

TBMC	Test Bed Mode Control
TBMD	Tactical Ballistic Missile Defense (DOMA)
TBMD	Terminal Ballistic Missile Defense [Army] (AABC)
TBMD	Theater Ballistic Missile Defense (DOMA)
TBMN	Thin Basement Membrane Nephropathy [Medicine] (DMAA)
TBMO	Test Base Material Operation (AAG)
T B Mon	T. B. Monroe's Kentucky Supreme Court Reports [17-23 Kentucky] [1824-28] [A publication] (DLA)
T B Mon (KY)	T. B. Monroe's Kentucky Reports [17-23 Kentucky] [A publication] (DLA)
TBMOS	TeraBIT Memory Operating System (NOAA)
TBMS	Text-Based Management Systems [Computer science]
TBMSG	Trailokya Bauddha Mahasangha Sahayaka Gana [Friends of the Western Buddhist Order] [British] (EAIO)
TBMT	Transmitter Buffer Empty [Computer science]
TBMU	Transitional Butterworth Modified Ultraspherical Filter (PDAA)
TBMX	Tactical Ballistic Missile Experiment
TBN	Bacillus Emulsion [Medicine] (DAVI)
TBN	Banker's Note [AMEX symbol] (SAG)
TBN	Fort Leonard Wood [Missouri] [Airport symbol] (OAG)
TBN	Tertiary-Butylnaphthalene [Organic chemistry]
TBN	Tetrabenzonaphthalene [Organic chemistry]
TBN	The Baseball Network
TBN	Titratable Base Number [Analytical chemistry]
TBN	To Be Negotiated (NASA)
TBN	To Be Nominated
TBN	Total Base Number [Automotive engineering]
TBN	Total Body Nitrogen [Medicine] (DMAA)
TBN	Traveling Businesswomen's Network (EA)
TBN	Trinity Broadcasting Network [Cable-television system]
TBN	Turbine Helicopters Ltd. [British] [FAA designator] (FAAC)
TBNA	Total Body Neutron Activation (AAMN)
TBNA	Transbronchial Needle Aspiration [Medicine] (DMAA)
TBNA	Treated but Not Admitted [Medicine]
TBNAA	Total Body Neutron Activation Analysis
TBN.EC	Banker's Note [ECM Symbol] (TTSB)
TBNHL	Tippecanoe Battleground National Historical Landmark (EA)
TBNI	Technology Board for Northern Ireland (BUAC)
Tbnl	Tribunal
tbnle	Tabernacle (VRA)
TBO	Tabora [Tanzania] [Airport symbol] (OAG)
TBO	Thermal Bakeout
TBO	Time Between Oil Changes [Automotive servicing]
TBO	Time between Overhauls [of engine, or other equipment]
TBO	Total Blackout (IIA)
TBO	Total Blood Out [Medicine] (DMAA)
TBO	TourBase Ortsdaten [Jaeger-Verlag GmbH] [Germany Information service or system] (CRD)
TBO	Transactions by Others [Military]
TBO	Tropical Biennial Oscillation [Climatology]
TBOA	T-18 Builders and Owners Association (EA)
TBOA	Tuna Boat Owners' Association [Defunct] (EA)
TBOAA	Tuna Boat Owners' Association of Australia
TBOASA	Tuna Boat Owners' Association of South Australia
t-Boc	Butoxycarbonyl [or t-BOC] [Biochemistry]
t-BOC	tert-Butyloxycarbonyl [Also, t-Boc] [Organic chemistry]
TBOI	Tentative Basis of Issue [Army] (AABC)
TBOIP	Tentative Basis of Issue Plan [Army] (AABC)
TBOIPFD	Tentative Basis of Issue Plan Feedback Data [Army]
TBoIMH	Western Mental Health Institute, Boliver, TN [Library symbol Library of Congress] (LCLS)
TBON	[The] Bank of Nashville [NASDAQ symbol] (NQ)
TBOS	Telemetry Byte-Oriented Serial [Telecommunications] (ITD)
TBOS	Tracer Burst Obscuration System [Weaponry simulation] [Military] (INF)
TBP	Bithionol [A Bacteriostatic] [Pharmacology] (DAVI)
TBP	Tab Products [AMEX symbol] (TTSB)
TBP	Tab Products Co. [AMEX symbol] (SPSG)
TbP	Tampa Blue Print Co., Tampa, FL [Library symbol Library of Congress] (LCLS)
TBP	Target Benefit Plan [Human resources] (WYGK)
TBP	TATA Box-Binding Protein (DOG)
TBP	Tat-Binding Protein [Genetics]
TBP	Tau Beta Pi Association
TBP	Tertiary Butyl Phosphine [Organic chemistry]
TBP	Testosterone-Binding Protein [Endocrinology] (MAE)
TBP	Tethered Buoyed Platform [Petroleum engineering]
TBP	Tetraphenylboron [Analytical chemistry]
TBP	Thiobisdichlorophenol [Pharmacology]
TBP	Thyroxine-Binding Protein [Biochemistry]
TBP	Timing Belt Pulley
TBP	To Be Planned (MCD)
TBP	To Be Provided (NASA)
TBP	To be Published
TBP	Total-Body Photograph (STED)
TBP	Total Bypass (STED)
TBP	Trainable Bow Propeller
TBP	Tributyl Phosphate [Organic chemistry]
TBP	Tributyl Phosphate Task Force (NTPA)
TBP	Tributyl Phosphine [Organic chemistry]
TBP	Trigonal Bipyramidal [Geometry of molecular structure]
TBP	True Boiling Point
TBP	Tuberculous Peritonitis [Medicine] (DAVI)
TBP	Tumbes [Peru] [Airport symbol] (OAG)
TBP	Twisted Bonded Pair

TBP	Two-Body Problem
TBPA	Tenpin Bowling Proprietors Association (BUAC)
TBPA	Tetrabromophthalic Anhydride [Flame retardant] [Organic chemistry]
TBPA	Textile Bag and Packaging Association (EA)
TBPA	Thyroxine-Binding Prealbumin [Biochemistry]
TBPA	Torso Back Protective Armor (PDAA)
TBPA	Transatlantic Brides and Parents Association (EA)
TBPB	Bridgetown/Grantley Adams Internacional [Barbados] [ICAO location identifier] (ICLI)
TBPB	Tertiary-Butyl Perbenzoate [Organic chemistry]
TBPC	Tertbutyl-P-Cresol (DICI)
TBPC	Text-Books of Physical Chemistry [A publication]
TBPH	Tetrabutylperoxyhydroxide [Organic chemistry]
TBPI	Thigh Brachial Pressure Index
TBPO	Bridgetown [Barbados] [ICAO location identifier] (ICLI)
TBPS	Terabits per Second (EECA)
TBPS	Tert-Butylbicyclophosphorothionate [Biochemistry]
TBPT	Total Body Protein Turnover [Medicine] (DMAA)
TBPU	To Be Picked Up [Postal service marking] [British]
TBQ	Addison, TX [Location identifier FAA] (FAAL)
TBR	Advisory Tax Board Recommendation [Internal Revenue Bureau] [United States] [A publication] (DLA)
TBR	Statesboro, GA [Location identifier FAA] (FAAL)
TBR	Table Base Register
TBR	Table Rock [New York] [Seismograph station code, US Geological Survey] (SEIS)
TBR	Telecommunicacoes Brasilerias SA Telebras [NYSE symbol] (SAG)
TBR	Telecomun Brasil-Telbras ADS [NYSE symbol] (TTSB)
TBR	Temporary Base Register [Computer science] (IAA)
TBR	Test of Behavioral Rigidity [Psychology]
TBR	Tilt Board Reach [Test] [Occupational therapy]
TBR	To be Released (SAA)
TBR	To be Resolved (SSD)
TBR	Torpedo Bomber Reconnaissance Aircraft [Navy]
TBR	Total Bed Rest [Medicine] (MEDA)
TBR	Total Bilirubin [Gastroenterology] (DAVI)
TBR	Training Base Review (MCD)
TBR	Treasury Bill Rate (MHDW)
TBR	Trickle Bed Reactor [Chemical engineering]
TBR	Tubelair [Tunisia] [FAA designator] (FAAC)
TBR	Tumor-Bearing Rabbit (STED)
TBR	Tumor-Bearing Rabbit Serum [Immunology]
TBR	Turbo Resources Ltd. [Toronto Stock Exchange symbol]
TBRC	Time-Based Recurring Cost
TBRC	Top-Blown Rotary Converter [Nonferrous metallurgy]
TB-RD	Tuberculosis - Respiratory Disease (MAE)
TBRG	Thomson Book/Reference Group [The Thomson Corp.] [Publishing]
TBRI	Technical Book Review Index
TBriH	Bristol Memorial Hospital, Bristol, TN [Library symbol Library of Congress] (LCLS)
TBriK	King College, Bristol, TN [Library symbol Library of Congress] (LCLS)
TBRL	Timber Lodge Steakhouse [NASDAQ symbol] (TTSB)
TBRL	Timber Lodge Steakhouse, Inc [NASDAQ symbol] (SAG)
TBroH	Haywood Park General Hospital, Brownsville, TN [Library symbol Library of Congress] (LCLS)
TBRS	Timed Behavioral Rating Sheet (STED)
TBRV	Tomato Black Ring Virus [Plant pathology]
TBS	[The] Buddhist Society [British] (EAIO)
TBS	Sir Thomas Beecham Society (EA)
TBS	Tablespoon
TBS	Tactical Bomb Squadron [Air Force]
TBS	Talk-between-Ships [which are tactically maneuvering; also, the VHF radio equipment used for this purpose]
TBS	Tall Building Syndrome
TBS	Tanzanian Bureau of Standards (BUAC)
TBS	Tape and Buffer System [Computer science]
TBS	Tapered Bearing Simulator [Lubricant testing]
TBS	Task Breakdown Structure (NASA)
TBS	Taut Band Suspension (IAA)
TBS	Tbilisi [Former USSR Airport symbol] (OAG)
TBS	Temple, Barker & Sloane, Inc. [Lexington, MA] [Telecommunications service] (TSSD)
TBS	Tensile Bond Strength [Materials science]
TBS	Terminal Business System [Computer science] (IAA)
TBS	Tertiary-Butyldimethylsilyl [Also, TBDMS, TBDPS] [Organic chemistry]
TBS	Tertiary Butylphenyl Salicylate [Food packaging]
TBS	Tertiary-Butylstyrene [Organic chemistry]
TBS	Test Bench Set (MCD)
TBS	Tetrapropylene Alkylbenesulfonate [Surfactant] [Organic chemistry]
TBS	Text-Books of Science [A publication]
TBS	#The Basic School [Marine Corps] (DOMA)
TBS	Theta-Burst Stimulation [Neurophysiology]
TBS	Tight Building Syndrome [Air quality]
TBS	Tired Bureaucrat Syndrome
TBS	Tobacco Black-Shank Nematode [Plant pathology]
TBS	To Be Selected (KSC)
TBS	To Be Specified (NASA)
TBS	To Be Superseded (NASA)
TBS	To Be Supplied (KSC)
TBS	Tokyo Broadcasting System
TBS	Toronto Baptist Seminary
TBS	Toronto Board of Education, Secondary Schools [UTLAS symbol]
TBS	Torsion Bar Spring [Automotive engineering]
TBS	Total Body Solute [Biochemistry]

TBS	Total Body Surface [Medicine]
TBS	Total Burn Size [Medicine] (DMAA)
TBS	Tracheal Bronchial Submucosal [Gland] [Medicine] (DB)
TBS	Training and Battle Simulation [SAGE]
TBS	Translator Bail Switch
TBS	Treasury Board Secretariat [Canada]
TBS	Tribromosalicylanilide [or Tribromsalan] [Organic chemistry]
TBS	Triethanolamine-Buffered Saline [Organic chemistry] (MAE)
TBS	Trinitarian Bible Society [British]
TBS	TRIS-Buffered Saline [Solution]
TBS	Tubeshaft (DS)
TBS	Turbine Bypass System [Nuclear energy] (NRCH)
TBS	Turner Broadcasting System, Inc. [AMEX symbol] (SPSG)
TBS	Turner Broadcasting Systems (NITA)
TBSA	Total Body Surface Area [Medicine]
TBSA	Total Burn Surface Area (DAVI)
TBSA	Total Serum Bile Acid [Clinical chemistry]
TBSA	TRIS-Buffered Saline Azide [Culture media]
TBS.A	Turner Broadcast'A' [AMEX symbol] (TTSB)
TBS.B	Turner Broadcast'B' [AMEX symbol] (TTSB)
TBSCCW	Turbine Building Secondary Closed Cooling Water [Nuclear energy] (NRCH)
TBSCI	Tertiary-Butyldimethylsilyl Chloride [Also, TBDMSCI] [Organic chemistry]
TBSG	Test Base Support Group (AAG)
TBSL	To be Supplied Later (COE)
TBSM	Tributylstannylmaleate [Organic chemistry]
TBSP	Tablespoon
tbsp	Tablespoonful (ODBW)
TBSR	Total Business System Review (AAGC)
TBST'G	Troubleshooting
TBSV	Time between Scheduled Visits (MCD)
TBSV	Tomato Bushy Stunt Virus
TBSW	Turbine Building Service Water [Environmental science] (COE)
TBT	Mid American Baptist Theological Seminary, Memphis, TN [OCLC symbol] (OCLC)
TBT	Tabatinga [Brazil] [Airport symbol] (OAG)
TBT	Taburiente [Canary Islands] [Seismograph station code, US Geological Survey] (SEIS)
TBT	Target Bearing Transmitter
TBT	Tax-Benefit Transfer (WGA)
TBT	Terminal Ballistic Track
TBT	Tetrabutyl Titanate [Organic chemistry]
TBT	Thallium Beam Tube
TBT	Tilt Board Tip [Test] [Occupational therapy]
TBT	Tolbutamide - Tolerance Test [Clinical chemistry] (MAE)
TBT	Tracheobronchial Toilet [Medicine] (MAE)
TBT	Transitional Butterworth Thomson (IAA)
TBT	Tributyltin [Anitimicrobial agent]
TBT	Tributyl Tin [Chemical] (EERA)
TBT	Tulsa Ballet Theatre
TBTA	Thames Boating Trades' Association [British] (BI)
TBTC	Transportable Blood Transfusion Shipment Center (DWSG)
TBTC	Transportable Blood Transshipment Center (COE)
TBTD	Tetrabutylthiuram Disulfide [Organic chemistry]
TBTF	Tributyltin Fluoride [Antimicrobial agent]
TBTH	Tributyltin Hydride [Organic chemistry]
TBTNR	Toronto Biculture Test of Nonverbal Reasoning [Speech and language therapy] (DAVI)
TBTO	Bis(tri-n-butyltin) Oxide [Wood preservative] (WPI)
TBTO	Tributyltin Oxide [Organic chemistry]
TBTP	Tributyl Trithiophosphate [Defoliant] [Organic chemistry]
TBTS	Tributyltin Sulfide [Organic chemistry]
TBTT	Tuberculin Time Test [Medicine] (DMAA)
TBTU	Tributylthiourea [Organic chemistry]
TBU	Telemetry Buffer Unit (SSD)
TBU	Terminal Buffer Unit [Telecommunications] (TEL)
TBU	Test Before Using (MCD)
TBU	Time Base Unit
TBU	Tongatapu [Tonga Island] [Airport symbol] (OAG)
TBU	Transitional Butterworth Ultraspherical Filter (PDAA)
TBUD	Team Rental Group [NASDAQ symbol] (SAG)
TBUD	Team Rental Group'A' [NQS] (TTSB)
TBUP	Tributylphosphine [Organic chemistry]
TBUS	Digital Recorders [NASDAQ symbol] (TTSB)
TBUS	Digital Recorders, Inc. [NASDAQ symbol] (SAG)
TBUSW	Digital Recorders Wrrt [NASDAQ symbol] (TTSB)
TBV	Thermal Bypass Valve
TBV	Total Blood Volume [Physiology]
TBV	Trabecular Bone Volume
TBV	Transluminal Balloon Valvuloplasty [Cardiology] (DAVI)
TBV	Tubercle Bacillus Vaccine [Medicine]
TBV	Tulip Breaking Virus [Plant pathology]
TBV	Turbine Block Valve (COE)
TBV	Turbine Building Ventilation [Nuclear energy] (NRCH)
TBVD	Torsional-Bending Vibration Damper [Mechanical engineering]
TBVE	Two-Point Boundary Value Equation [Mathematics]
TB-Vis	Isoniazid [An Antibacterial] [Pharmacology] (DAVI)
TBVP	Total Blood Volume Predicted from Body Surface [Physiology] (MAH)
TBW	[The] Business World [A publication]
TBW	Tampa Bay-Ruskin, FL [Location identifier FAA] (FAAL)
TBW	T B Wood's [NYSE symbol] (TTSB)
TBW	TB Woods Corp. [NYSE symbol] (SAG)
TBW	That Bloody Woman [Nickname given to British Prime Minister Margaret Thatcher]

TBW.............	Time Band-Width (IAA)
TBW.............	Titanium Butt Weld
TBW.............	Tobacco Bud Worm [Agronomy]
TBW.............	To Be Withheld
TBW.............	Total Bandwidth
TBW.............	Total Body Water [Man]
TBW.............	Total Body Weight [Medicine]
TBWCA.......	Tracking Band Width (MCD)
TBWCA.......	Texas Barbed Wire Collectors Association (EA)
TBWEP.........	Trial Boll Weevil Eradication Program [Department of Agriculture]
TBWG	Tactical Bomb Wing [Air Force]
TBWO	Tuned Backward Wave Oscillator
TB Wood......	TB Woods Corp. [Associated Press] (SAG)
TBWP..........	Triple-Braid Weatherproof (IAA)
TBX.............	Tactical Ballistic Missile, Experimental
TBX.............	Tactical Range Ballistic Missile [Military] (IAA)
TBX.............	Thromboxane (DB)
TBX$_2$.........	Total Body Irradiation [Radiation therapy] (DAVI)
TBX$_2$.........	Thromboxane B$_2$ [Hematology] (DAVI)
TBY.............	Oxford, CT [Location identifier FAA] (FAAL)
TBY.............	TCBY Enterprises [NYSE symbol] (TTSB)
TBY.............	TCBY Enterprises, Inc. [NYSE symbol] (CTT)
TBY.............	Terrace Bay Resources [Vancouver Stock Exchange symbol]
Tbyte	Terabyte [Computer science] (EERA)
TBZ.............	Istanbul [Trabzon] [Turkey] [Seismograph station code, US Geological Survey] (SEIS)
TBZ.............	Tabriz [Iran] [Airport symbol] (OAG)
TBZ.............	Tetrabenazine [Tranquilizer]
TBZ.............	Thiabendazole [or Thiazolyl] Benzimidazole [Pesticide]
TBZ.............	Toy Biz'A' [NYSE symbol] (TTSB)
TBZ.............	Toy Biz, Inc. [NYSE symbol] (SAG)
TC................	Air Tanzania [ICAO designator] (AD)
TC................	All India Reporter, Travancore-Cochin [1950-57] [A publication] (DLA)
TC................	Chattanooga-Hamilton County Bicentennial Library, Chattanooga, TN [Library symbol Library of Congress] (LCLS)
TC................	Cold Leg Temperature [Nuclear energy] (NRCH)
Tc................	Core Temperature [Medicine]
TC................	[The] Courier [Code name for Robert W. Owen, participant in the Iran-Contra affair during the Reagan Administration]
Tc	Generation Time [Laboratory Science] (DAVI)
TC................	Neurotrauma Center [Medicine] (DAVI)
TC................	Order of the Trinity Cross [Trinidad and Tobago]
TC................	Table of Contents (IT)
TC................	Tablettes Cappadociennes [Paris] [A publication] (BJA)
TC................	Tabulating Card (AAG)
TC................	Tactical Command (NATG)
TC................	Tactical Communications [Military] (DWSG)
TC................	Tactical Computer (IEEE)
T/C..............	Tactical Coordinator (NVT)
TC................	Tactile Communicator [Device which aids the deaf by translating certain sounds into coded vibrations]
TC................	Tag Code (NITA)
TC................	Tail Clamp
TC................	Talk[ing] Club
TC................	Tall Copy [Publishing] (DGA)
TC................	Tandem Club (BUAC)
TC................	Tandy Corp. (EFIS)
TC................	Tank Car
TC................	Tank Circuit (IAA)
TC................	Tank Commander (RDA)
TC................	Tank Company [Military] (MCD)
TC................	Tank Corps
TC................	Tantalum Capacitor (IEEE)
TC................	Tape Command
TC................	Tape Core
TC................	Taraxacum Club [Netherlands] (BUAC)
TC................	Target Cell [Immunology]
TC................	Target Concentration [or Toxic] (GNE)
TC................	Target Control (MCD)
TC................	Tariff Circular
TC................	Tariff Commission [Later, International Trade Commission]
TC................	Taurocholate [Microbiology] (MAE)
TC................	Tax Cases [Legal] [British]
TC................	Tax Certificate
TC................	Tax Code [A publication] (AAGC)
TC................	Tax Council (EA)
TC................	Tax Court [of the United States] [Also, TCUS Later, United States Tax Court]
TC................	Taxiway Centerline Lighting [Aviation] (DA)
TC................	Taxonomic Code (NITA)
TC................	Taxpayers' Committee [Defunct] (EA)
TC................	Taylorcraft [ICAO aircraft manufacturer identifier] (ICAO)
TC................	Tayu Center (EA)
TC................	T-Carrier [Telecommunications] (TEL)
TC................	Teachers' Centre (AIE)
TC................	Teacher's Certificate [British]
TC................	Teachers College
TC................	Tea Council of the United States of America (EA)
TC................	Teardown Compliance
Tc................	Technetium [Chemical element]
TC................	Technical Center [Environmental Protection Agency] (GFGA)
TC................	Technical Characteristics [Military] (AABC)
TC................	Technical Circular
TC................	Technical College

TC	Technical Committee
TC	Technical Communication
TC	Technical Control (MSA)
TC	Technical Cooperation
TC	Technical Corrigendum [Correction] (OSI)
TC	Technically Classified (BARN)
TC	Technician's Certificate [British] (DI)
TC	Technicolor (KSC)
TC	Tekakwitha Conference National Center [Later, TCNC] (EA)
T/C	Telecine
TC	Telecommunications
TC	Telecommunications Counselor [Voice & Data Resources, Inc.] [Information service or system Defunct] (IID)
TC	TeleCommuting Report [Electronic Services Unlimited] [Information service or system] (CRD)
TC	Telecomputing Corp. (IAA)
TC	Telefunken Computer AG (IAA)
TC	Telegram to be Repeated (EBF)
TC	Telephone Center (IAA)
TC	Telephone Central Office (IAA)
TC	Telescoping Collar (OA)
TC	Temperament Comparator [Psychology]
TC	Temperature Capability
TC	Temperature Change [Refrigeration]
TC	Temperature Coefficient
TC	Temperature Compensating (MSA)
TC	Temperature Control
TC	Temperature Controller [Nuclear energy] (NRCH)
TC	Temperature in Degrees Centigrade (IAA)
TC	Temple Classics [A publication]
TC	Temporary Chaplain [British military] (DMA)
TC	Temporary Constable
TC	Temporary Correction
TC	Tennessee Central Railway Co. [AAR code]
TC	Tennis Club
TC	Teracycle
TC	Terciarios Capuchinos de Nostra Signora de los Dolores [Tertiary Capuchins of Our Lady of Sorrows] [Italy] (EAIO)
TC	Term Coordination (NITA)
TC	Terminal Computer (BUR)
TC	Terminal Concentrator
TC	Terminal Congestion [Telecommunications] (TEL)
TC	Terminal Control (NITA)
TC	Terminal Controller
TC	Terminating Contracting Officer (AAGC)
T/C	Termination Check [NASA] (NASA)
T/C	Termination for Convenience [DoD]
TC	Terra Cotta [Technical drawings]
TC	Terrain Clearance [Military] (NG)
T/C	Terrain Correlation (MCD)
TC	Test Case Specification (IAA)
TC	Test Chief
TC	Test Collection [Educational Testing Service] [Information service or system] (IID)
TC	Test Conductor (AAG)
TC	Test Console
TC	Test Controller
TC	Test Coordinator
TC	Testing Complete (CAAL)
Tc	Tetracycline [Medicine] (DB)
TC	Tetrahedral Cubic [Metallography]
TC	Texas Central Railroad Co.
TC	Thai Capital Fund [NYSE symbol] (TTSB)
TC	Thai Capital Fund, Inc. [NYSE symbol] (SPSG)
TC	Thames Conservancy [British] (BI)
TC	Therapeutic Category [Medicine] (DB)
TC	Therapeutic Concentration [Pharmacology]
TC	Thermal Conductivity
TC	Thermal Control (KSC)
TC	Thermal Cracker [Chemical engineering]
TC	Thermal Cutting [Welding]
T/C	Thermocompression (AAEL)
TC	Thermocouple
TC	Thermocurrent (IEEE)
TC	Thickness Chord Wing [Aviation] (AIA)
TC	Thinking Cap [Layman's term for neocortex]
TC	Thiokol Corp. (NAKS)
TC	Thomas C. Calvin [Character in TV series "Magnum, P.I."]
TC	Thoracic Cage [Medicine]
TC	Thread Cutting (MSA)
TC	Threshold Circuit [Telecommunications] (OA)
TC	Throat Culture [Clinical chemistry]
TC	Thrust Chamber [Air Force, NASA]
TC	Thyrocalcitonin [Endocrinology] (MAE)
TC	Tical [Monetary unit in Thailand]
TC	Tidal Constants [Marine science] (MSC)
TC	Tidal Current (COE)
TC	Tie Connector (MCD)
TC	Tierce [Unit of measurement]
TC	Till Cancelled [Press advertisements] (DGA)
T/C	Till Counterbalanced
TC	Till Countermanded
TC	Tilt Covered [Truck] (DCTA)
Tc	Time Called [Baseball]
TC	Time Certificate of Deposit [Banking]

T/C	Time Charter [*Shipping*]
TC	Time Check
TC	Time Clock
TC	Time Closing (MSA)
TC	Time Code (NTCM)
TC	Time Compensation
TC	Time Compression [*Computer science*] (IAA)
TC	Time Constant (MSA)
TC	Time-Constrained [*Computer science*]
TC	Time Controlled [*Computer science*] (IAA)
TC	Time to Circular (MCD)
TC	Time to Computation
TC	Timing Channel
TC	Timing Cover Gasket [*Automotive engineering*]
TC	Tinned Copper
TC	Tissue Culture [*Microbiology*]
TC	Title Card (NTCM)
TC	Tobramycin-Clindamycin [*Antibiotic compound*]
T/C	To Consider (DAVI)
T/C	To Contain [*Pipet calibration*]
TC	Today's Computers [*A publication*]
TC	Togoland Congress [*Ghana*] [*Political party*]
TC	Toilet Case (MSA)
TC	Toll Center [*Telecommunications*]
TC	Toll Completing [*Telecommunications*]
TC	Toluene-Cellosolve [*Scintillation solvent*]
TC	Tone Control [*Telecommunications*] (IAA)
TC	Top Cap (IAA)
TC	Top Carnivore
TC	Top Cat [*Cartoon character*]
TC	Top Center [*Valve position*]
TC	Top Chord
TC	Top Contact [*Valve*] (DEN)
T/C	Top-of-Climb (GAVI)
TC	Top of Column
TC	Topographic Center [*Defense Mapping Agency*]
TC	Torpedo Control [*British military*] (DMA)
TC	Torpedo Coxswain [*British military*] (DMA)
TC	Total Capacity [*Lung*]
TC	Total Carbon
TC	Total Chances
TC	Total Cholesterol [*Medicine*]
TC	Total Colonoscopy [*Proctoscopy*]
TC	Total Control (PCM)
TC	Total Cost
TC	Touring Club
TC	Towed Cable [*Telecommunications*] (IAA)
Tc	Towing Chock [*Shipfitting*]
TC	Town Clerk [*or Councillor*]
TC	Town Council (WDAA)
TC	Toxic Concentration (LDT)
TC	Toxicity Characteristic [*Environmental Protection Agency*]
TC	Traceability Code (NASA)
TC	Track Circuit (DCTA)
TC	Track Commander [*Army*] (INF)
TC	Tracking Camera
TC	Tracking Console
TC	Trade Cases [*Commerce Clearing House*] [*A publication*] (DLA)
TC	Traffic Collision
TC	Traffic Commissioner [*or Consultant*]
TC	Traffic Consultant (WGA)
TC	Traffic Controller (CAAL)
TC	Training Center [*Military*]
TC	Training Chest [*Emergency parachute*]
TC	Training Circular [*Military*]
TC	Training Command (AAG)
TC	Training Corps [*British military*] (DMA)
TC	Transaction Code [*Military*]
TC	Transceiver Code [*Navy*]
TC	Transcobalamin [*Biochemistry*]
Tc	Transcobalamin (DB)
TC	Transcontinental (DOAD)
TC	Transcutaneous
TC	Transfer Canal [*Nuclear energy*] (NRCH)
TC	Transfer Clerk
TC	Transfer Control [*or Controller*] (HGAA)
TC	Transfer Count (MHDB)
TC	Transistorized Carrier
TC	Transit Canal (NVT)
TC	Transitional Control (IAA)
TC	Translation Controller
TC	Transmission Control [*Telecommunications*] (IAA)
TC	Transmission Controller
TC	Transmitter Controller [*Electronics*] (ECII)
TC	Transmitter Tuning Circuit [*Telecommunications*] (IAA)
TC	Transmitting Circuit [*Telecommunications*] (OA)
TC	Transnational Corporation
TC	Transpersonal Consciousness [*Parapsychology*]
TC	Transponder Component (MCD)
TC	Transport and Communications [*Department of Employment*] [*British*]
T/C	Transportation Corps [*Military*]
TC	Transport Canada [*Government regulatory agency*]
TC	Transport Cargo (NATG)
TC	Transport Combine [*Combined Transport*] [*French Business term*]
TC	Transport Command [*British military*] (DMA)
TC	Transporte Combinado [*Combined Transport*] [*Spanish Business term*]
TC	Transporto Combinato [*Combined Transport*] [*Italian Business term*]
TC	Transvaal Cadets [*British military*] (DMA)
TC	Travellers Cheque [*British*] (ADA)
TC	Treacher Collins Syndrome [*Medicine*] (DMAA)
TC	Treasury Circular
T/C	Treated Versus Cured [*Medicine*]
T/C	Treatment Charge [*Metallurgy*]
TC	Treatment Code (NITA)
TC	Treatment Completed [*Medicine*] (MEDA)
TC	Tre Corde [*With Three Strings, or Release the Soft Pedal*] [*Music*]
TC	Trial Counsel [*Military*]
TC	Tribology Centre [*British*]
TC	Tribunal des Conflits [*Tribunal of Conflicts*] [*French*] (ILCA)
TC	Trichloroacetic Acid (EDCT)
TC	Tricuspid Closure [*Cardiology*]
TC	Tricycle Club [*British*]
TC	Triennial Cycle (BJA)
TC	Trilateral Commission (EA)
TC	Trim Coil (AAG)
TC	Trip Cell (IAA)
TC	Trip Coil
TC	Triplet Connection (EA)
TC	Triton Corp. (EA)
TC	Troop Carrier [*Air Force*]
TC	Tropical Continental [*American air mass*]
TC	Tropical Cyclone (ADA)
TC	Tropocollagen [*Genetics*] (DAVI)
TC	Truck Commander [*Military*] (INF)
TC	True Color (CDE)
T/C	True Complement
TC	True Conjugate [*Ophthalmology*] (DAVI)
TC	True Course
TC	Truncated Cone [*Golf balls*]
TC	Trunk Control
TC	Trusteeship Council [*of the United Nations*]
T/C	Trust or Complement (MHDI)
TC	Tuberculosis, Contagious [*Medicine*] (AAMN)
TC	Tubing Connector [*Instrumentation*]
TC	Tubocurarine [*Muscle relaxant*]
TC	Tumor Cell [*Medicine*] (DB)
TC	Tuned Circuit [*Telecommunications*] (IAA)
TC	Tungsten Carbide (IAA)
TC	Turbocharger [*Automotive engineering*]
TC	Turf Course [*Horse racing*]
TC	Turkey Coryza [*Pathology*]
TC	Turks and Caicos Islands [*ANSI two-letter standard code*] (CNC)
tc	Turks and Caicos Islands [*MARC country of publication code Library of Congress*] (LCCP)
TC	Turn-Cock (ROG)
TC	Turning Circle [*Automotive engineering*]
TC	Turnip Crinkle Virus
TC	Turret Captain [*Navy*]
TC	[*The*] Twentieth Century New Testament [*A publication*] (BJA)
TC	Twin Camshaft [*Automotive engineering*]
TC	Twin Carburetor [*Automotive engineering*]
TC	Two Cycle [*Mechanics*]
TC	Type and Crossmatch [*of blood*]
TC	Type Certificate
TC	Type Classification
TC	Typhoon Committee [*World Health Organization*] (BUAC)
TC	United States Tax Court Cases [*A publication*] (DLA)
TC	United States Tax Court Reporters [*A publication*] (AAGC)
TC	US Tax Court (EBF)
TC3	Telecommunications, Command, Control, and Computer System
Tc-99	Technetium-99
TCA	Adventist Network of Georgia, Cumberland Elementary Library, Collegedale, TN [*OCLC symbol*] (OCLC)
TCA	Tactical Combat Aircraft (IEEE)
TCA	Tactical Communications Area
TCA	Tahiti Conquest Airlines [*France ICAO designator*] (FAAC)
TCA	Taipei Computer Association [*Taiwan*]
TCA	Tandem Club of America (EA)
TCA	Tanner's Council of America [*Later, LIA*] (EA)
TCA	Tanzer 22 Class Association (EA)
TCA	Target Class Assignment
TCA	Task Control Area (IAA)
TCA	Tasmanian Canoe Association [*Australia*]
TCA	Tasmanian Council on the Ageing [*Australia*]
TCA	Tasmanian Croquet Association [*Australia*]
TCA	Tattoo Club of America (EA)
TCA	Taurocholic Acid [*Biochemistry*] (DB)
TCA	TCA Cable TV, Inc. [*Associated Press*] (SAG)
TCA	Teach Cable Assembly [*Robot technology*]
TCA	Teaching Curriculum Association [*A generic term; not the name of a specific organization*]
TCA	Technical Change Analysis (MCD)
TCA	Technical Contract Administrator
TCA	Technical Cooperation Administration [*Transferred to Foreign Operations Administration, 1953*]
TCA	Technician in Costing and Accounting [*British*] (DBQ)
TCA	Telecable Associates, Inc. (EFIS)
TCA	Tele-Communications Association (EA)
TCA	Telecomputing Corporation of America (NITA)

TCA	Telemarketing Corp. of America [*Phoenix, AZ*] (TSSD)
TCA	Telemetering Control Assembly (AAG)
TCA	Telephone Consultants of America [*Bergenfield, NJ*] [*Telecommunications*] (TSSD)
TCA	Teleservice Corp. of America (EFIS)
TCA	Television Critics Association (EA)
TCA	Tempelhof Central Airport [*West Berlin*]
TCA	Temperance Collegiate Association [*British*] (AEBS)
TCA	Temperature Control Amplifier (IAA)
TCA	Temperature Control Assembly (KSC)
TCA	Temperature-Controlled Animal
TCA	Temporary Care Arrangement
TCA	Ten Class Association (EA)
TCA	Tonnant Creek [*Australia Airport symbol*] (OAG)
TCA	Tennessee Code Annotated [*A publication*]
TCA	Terminal Cancer [*Medicine*]
TCA	Terminal Carcinoma [*Oncology*] (DAVI)
TCA	Terminal Communication Adapter
TCA	Terminal Control Area [*Aviation*] (AFM)
TCA	Tertiary Colleges Association [*British*] (DBA)
TCA	Test Calibration Assembly (AAEL)
TCA	Tetracyanoanthracene [*Organic chemistry*]
TCA	Textile Converters Association (EA)
TCA	Thalamocortical Axon [*Neurophysiology*]
TCA	Theater Commander's Approval [*Military*]
TCA	Therapeutic Communities of America (EA)
TCA	Thermal Critical Assembly [*Nuclear energy*]
TCA	Thermo Cardiosystems [*AMEX symbol*] (TTSB)
TCA	Thermo Cardio Systems, Inc. [*AMEX symbol*] (SAG)
TCA	Thermocentrifugometric Analysis [*Analytical chemistry*]
TCA	Thiocarbanilide [*Organic chemistry*]
TCA	Thistle Class Association (EA)
TCA	Thoroughbred Club of America (EA)
TCA	Thrust Chamber Assembly [*Missile technology*]
TCA	Thyrocalcitonin [*Also, CT, TCT*] [*Endocrinology*]
TCA	Tiger Cat Association [*Defunct*] (EA)
TCA	Tile Council of America (EA)
TCA	Tilt-Up Concrete Association (EA)
TCA	Time of Closest Approach [*Aerospace*]
TCA	Tissue Culture Association (EA)
TCA	Tithe Commutation Act [*British*]
TCA	To Come Again [*in a given number of days*] [*Medicine*]
TCA	TOKAMAK [*Toroidal Kamera Magnetic*] Chauffage Alfven [*Plasma physics instrumentation*]
TCa	Total Calcium [*Clinical chemistry*]
TCA	Total Cholic Acid [*Biochemistry*] (DB)
TCA	Total Circulating Albumin [*Medicine*] (DMAA)
TCA	Trace Contamination Analysis
TCA	Track Continuity Area (NATG)
TCA	Track Crossing Altitude [*or Attitude*]
TCA	Track Crossing Angle
TCA	Traffic Control Area [*Aviation*]
TCA	Trailer Coach Association [*Later, Manufactured Housing Institute*] (EA)
TCA	Train Collectors Association (EA)
TCA	Trans-Canada Airlines [*Facetious translation: "Two Crashes Apiece"*]
TCA	Trans-Caribbean Airways (IIA)
TCA	Transcontinental Control Area [*Aviation*] (DA)
TCA	Transfer Control A Register (SAA)
TCA	Translation Controller Assembly (NASA)
TCA	Transluminal Coronary Angioplasty [*Cardiology*]
TCA	Transportation Corridor Agencies
TCA	Travellers Cheque Association Ltd. [*British*]
TCA	Tricalcium Aluminate [*Inorganic chemistry*] (MAE)
TCA	Tricarboxylic Acid [*Cycle*] [*Biochemistry*]
TCA	Trichloroacetate [*Organic chemistry*]
TCA	Trichloroacetic Acid [*Also, TCAA*] [*Organic chemistry*]
TCA	Trichloroanisole [*Organic chemistry*]
TCA	Trichosanic Acid [*Biochemistry*]
TCA	Tricuspid Atresia [*Cardiology*] (DAVI)
TCA	Tricyclic Antidepressant [*Medicine*] (WDAA)
TCA	Turbulent Contacting Absorber
TCA	Turks and Caicos Islands [*ANSI three-letter standard code*] (CNC)
TCA	Two Hundred Contemporary Authors [*A publication*]
TCA	Typographic Communications Association (EA)
TCAA	Technical Communication Association of Australia (BUAC)
TCAA	Tile Contractors' Association of America (EA)
TCAA	Trichloroacetic Acid [*Also, TCA*] [*Organic chemistry*]
TCAA	Truck Cap and Accessory Association (NTPA)
TCAA	Trustee Companies' Association of Australia
TCAAP	Twin Cities Army Ammunition Plant (AABC)
TCAB	Temperature of Cabin [*Aerospace*] (MCD)
TCAB	Tetrachloroazobenzene [*Organic chemistry*]
TCABG	Triple Coronary Artery Bypass Graft [*Cardiology*]
TCAC	Technical Committee on Agricultural Chemicals (EERA)
TCAC	Technical Control and Analysis Center
TCAC	Tennessee Collegiate Athletic Conference (PSS)
TCAC	Tone-Count Audiometric Computer (PDAA)
TCAC	William V.S. Tubman Center of African Culture [*Liberia*] (BUAC)
TC ACCIS	Transportation Coordination [*or Coordinator*] Automated Command and Control Information System [*Military*]
TCAC-D	Technical Control and Analysis Center - Division
TCAD	Technology Computer-Aided Design [*Computer science*]
TCAD	Tetracyclic Antidepressant [*Medicine*] (DB)
TCAD	Traffic Alert and Collision Avoidance Device [*Aviation*] (DA)
TCAD	Tricyclic Antidepressant [*Pharmacology*] (DAVI)
TCADS	Truck Crash Analysis Data System [*FHWA*] (TAG)
TCAE	Technical Control and Analysis Element (INF)
TCAF	TEFLON-Coated Aluminum Foil
TCAI	Tutorial Computer-Assisted Instruction (IEEE)
TC-AIMS	Transportation Coordinator's Automated Information for Movement System (DOMA)
TCAL	Tasmanian Council for Adult Literacy [*Australia*]
T-cal	Thermal calibration (CDE)
TCAL	Total Calorimeter (KSC)
T-Cal	Triconix Control Application Language (NITA)
TCA LM	Tele-Communications Class A [*Associated Press*] (SAG)
TCAM	Telecommunications Access Method [*IBM Corp.*] [*Computer science*]
TCAM	Telegraph Construction and Maintenance (IAA)
TCAM	Thinking Creatively in Action and Movement [*Test*]
TCAM	Transport Corp. Amer [*NASDAQ symbol*] (TTSB)
TCAM	Transport Corp. of America, Inc. [*NASDAQ symbol*] (SAG)
TCaMH	Smith County Memorial Hospital, Carthage, TN [*Library symbol Library of Congress*] (LCLS)
TCAM-IMS/VS	TCAM-Information Management System/Virtual Storage (NITA)
TC & DB	Turn, Cough, and Deep Breathe [*Medicine*]
TC & M	Telemetry Control and Monitoring
TCAOB	Tetrachloroazoxybenzene [*Organic chemistry*]
T-CAP	Baker's Antifol, Cyclophosphamide, Adriamycin, and Cisplatin [*Antineoplastic drug regimen*] (DAVI)
TCAP	Tactical Channel Assignment Panel [*Military radio*]
T/CAP	Thermal Capacitor (MCD)
TCAP	Tricyanoaminopropene [*Organic chemistry*]
TCAP	Trimethylcetylammonium Pentachlorphenate [*Organic chemistry*]
TCAPE	Truck Computer Analysis of Performance and Economy
TCAR	T-Cell Antigen Receptor [*Medicine*] (DMAA)
TCARC	Technical Centre for Agricultural and Rural Cooperation (BUAC)
TCARC	Tropical Cyclone Aircraft Reconnaissance Coordinator [*Navy*] (DNAB)
T-carrier system	Telecommunications Carrier System (NITA)
TCARS	Test Call Answer Relay Set (PDAA)
TCaS	Smith County High School Library, Carthage, TN [*Library symbol Library of Congress*] (LCLS)
TCAS	T-Carrier Administration System [*Minicomputer*] [*Bell System*]
TCAS	Technical Control and Analysis System (MCD)
T/CAS	Threat Alert Collision Avoidance System
TCAS	Three Counties Agricultural Society [*British*]
TCAS	Traffic Alert and Collision Avoidance System [*Aviation*]
TCASNY	Turkish Cypriot Aid Society of New York (EA)
TCAT	Tape-Controlled Automatic Testing
TCAT	TCA Cable TV, Inc. [*NASDAQ symbol*] (NQ)
TCAT	Test Coverage Analysis Tool (IEEE)
TCAT	Thermal Catalyst Aging Tester [*Chemical engineering*]
TCAT	Transmission Computer-Assisted Tomography [*Medicine*] (DAVI)
TCAT	Type Commander Amphibious Training (DOMA)
TCATA	Textile Care Allied Trades Association (EA)
TCATA	TRADOC Combined Arms Test Activity [*Army*] (MCD)
TCATA	TRADOC [*Training and Doctrine Command*] Combined Arms Test Agency [*Army*]
TCAV	Tennis Coaches' Association of Victoria [*Australia*]
TCAWA	Tennis Coaches' Association of Western Australia
TCAX	Trans Continental Air Transport [*Air carrier designation symbol*]
TCB	[*The*] College Board (EA)
TCB	[*The*] Computer Bulletin (IAA)
TCB	[*The*] Conference Board (EA)
TCB	Fort Worth, TX [*Location identifier FAA*] (FAAL)
TCB	Take Care of Business [*Slang*]
TCB	Taking Care of Business [*Brand name of Alberto-Culver Co.*]
TCB	Tantalum Carbon Bond
TCB	Tape Control Block [*Computer science*] (IAA)
TCB	Target Control Box [*Army*]
TCB	Task Control Block [*Computer science*]
TCB	Task Force for Community Broadcasting (EA)
TCB	Tasmanian Convention Bureau [*Australia*]
TCB	Taylor-Carlisle Bookseller [*ACCORD*] [*UTLAS symbol*]
TCB	TCF Financial [*NYSE symbol*] (TTSB)
TCB	TCF Financial Corp. [*NYSE symbol*] (SAG)
TCB	Teachers' Certification Board [*Australia*]
TCB	Technical Coordinator Bulletin [*NASA*] (KSC)
TCB	TEN Private Cable Systems, Inc. [*Vancouver Stock Exchange symbol*]
TCB	Tent City Bravo [*Area near Tan Son Nhut Air Base, formerly site of USAR headquarters*]
TCB	Terminal Control Block [*Computer science*] (OA)
TCB	Tetracarboxy Butane (EDCT)
TCB	Tetrachlorobiphenyl [*Organic chemistry*]
TCB	Themes Concerning Blacks [*Personality development test*] [*Psychology*]
TCB	Thermal Compression Bond
TCB	Time Correlation Buffer (MCD)
TCB	Title Certificate Book [*A publication*] (DLA)
TCB	TMIS [*Technical and Management Information System*] Control Board [*NASA*] (SSD)
TCB	Total Cardiopulmonary Bypass [*Medicine*] (MAE)
TCB	TOW [*Tube-Launched, Optically-Tracked, Wire-Guided Weapon*] Control Box (INF)
TCB	Trans-Continental Freight Bureau, Chicago IL [*STAC*]
TCB	Transfer Control Block
TCB	Transporte del Caribe [*Colombia*] [*ICAO designator*] (FAAC)
TCB	Treasure Cay [*Bahamas*] [*Airport symbol*] (OAG)
TCB	Trichlorobenzene [*Organic chemistry*]

TCB.............	Tropical Chocolate Bar [*Military issue*] (VNW)
TCB.............	Trouble Came Back [*Computer hacker terminology*] (NHD)
TCB.............	Truss Connector Bulletin [*Department of Housing and Urban Development*] [*A publication*] (GFGA)
TCB.............	Trusted Computing Base
TCB.............	Tulare County Free Library System, Visalia, CA [*OCLC symbol*] (OCLC)
TCB.............	Tumor Cell Burden [*Oncology*]
TCBA............	Tesla Coil Builders Association (EA)
T-CBA..........	Transfluxor, Constant Board Assembly (AAG)
TCBC...........	Trichlorobenzyl Chloride [*Organic chemistry*]
TCBC...........	Twin Cities Biomedical Consortium [*Library network*]
TCBCO.........	Thallium Calcium Barium Copper Oxide [*Inorganic chemistry*]
TCBCS	Blue Cross and Blue Shield of Tennessee, Chattanooga, TN [*Library symbol Library of Congress*] (LCLS)
TCBE...........	Thermocompression Bonding Equipment
TCBEFC........	TCB [*Taking Care of Business*] for Elvis Fan Club (EA)
TCBG	Training Centre Brigade of Gurkhas [*British military*] (DMA)
TCBH	Time Consistent Busy Hour (NITA)
TCBHHA.......	The Church of the Brethren Homes and Hospitals Association [*Later, BHOAM*] (EA)
TCBI...........	Television Center for Business and Industry
TCBK...........	Trico Bancshares [*NASDAQ symbol*] (SAG)
TCB LM.......	Tele-Communications Class A [*Associated Press*] (SAG)
TCBM..........	Time-Consistent Busy Hour [*Telecommunications*] (EECA)
TCBM..........	Transcontinental Ballistic Missile [*Air Force*]
TCBO	Trichlorobutylene Oxide [*Organic chemistry*]
TCBS	Thiosulfate-Citrate-Bile Salt Sucrose [*Growth medium*]
TCBT	[*The*] Circuit Board Thermometer [*Computer science*]
TCBV..........	Temperature Coefficient of Breakdown Voltage
TCBY...........	[*The*] Country's Best Yogurt [*Store franchise*]
TCBY...........	TCBY Enterprises, Inc. [*Associated Press*] (SAG)
TCC.............	AT&T Capital [*NYSE symbol*] (TTSB)
TCC.............	AT & T Capital Corp. (SPSG)
TCC.............	Capita Preferred Trust [*NYSE symbol*] (SAG)
TCC.............	[*The*] Cesarean Connection (EA)
TCC.............	[*The*] Coin Coalition (EA)
TCC.............	[*The*] Cola Clan [*Later, Coca-Cola Collectors Club International*] (EA)
TCC.............	[*The*] Comedy Channel
TCC.............	[*The*] Computer Co. [*Information service or system*] (IID)
TcC	[*The*] Computer Co., Richmond, VA [*Library symbol*] [*Library of Congress*] (LCLS)
TCC.............	[*The*] Conservative Caucus (EA)
TCC.............	[*The*] Creative Coalition
TCC.............	[*The*] Curwood Collector [*A publication*] (EA)
TCC.............	New Mexico Institute of Mining and Technology Computer Center [*Research center*] (RCD)
TCC.............	Tactical Cell Controller (AAEL)
TCC.............	Tactical Command Center (DOMA)
TCC.............	Tactical Command Control (MCD)
TCC.............	Tactical Communications Center
TCC.............	Tactical Control Center [*Military*]
TCC.............	Tactical Control Computer (AAG)
TCC.............	Tactical Control Console (NATG)
TCC.............	Tactics Certification Course [*Army*] (INF)
TCC.............	Tag Closed Cup [*Flash point test*]
TCC.............	Tagliabue Closed Cup [*Analytical chemistry*]
TCC.............	Tank Car Committee [*RSPA*] (TAG)
TCC.............	Tara Collectors Club (EA)
TCC.............	Target Coordination Center
TCC.............	Task Control Character (CMD)
TCC.............	Tasmanian Cancer Committee [*Australia*]
TCC.............	Tasmanian Chamber of Commerce [*Australia*]
TCC.............	T-Cell Clone [*Cytology*]
TCC.............	Teachers College of Connecticut
TCC.............	Technical Change Centre [*British*] (CB)
TCC.............	Technical Computing Center (IEEE)
TCC.............	Technical Control Center
TCC.............	Technological Change Committee (EERA)
TCC.............	Technology Commercialization Center [*Minority Business Development Administration*]
TCC.............	Telecommunications Center (CET)
TCC.............	Telecommunications Consumer Coalition [*Defunct*] (EA)
TCC.............	Telecommunications Coordinating Committee [*Department of State*]
TCC.............	Telecommunications Corp. [*Jordan*] (BUAC)
TCC.............	Teleconcepts in Communications, Inc. [*New York, NY*] [*Telecommunications*] (TSSD)
TCC.............	Telegraph Condenser Co. (IAA)
TCC.............	Telemetry Standards Coordination Committee (HGAA)
TCC.............	Television Control Center
TCC.............	Temperature Coefficient of Capacitance
TCC.............	Temperature Control Circuit
TCC.............	Temporary Council Committee [*NATO*]
TCC.............	Terminal Control Corridor [*Aviation*]
TCC.............	Test Conductor Console (AAG)
TCC.............	Test Control Center [*NASA*]
TCC.............	Test Control Commission [*NATO*]
TCC.............	Test Controller Computer (MCD)
TCC.............	Test Controller Console (KSC)
TCC.............	Test Coordinating Center [*Army*]
TCC.............	Test Coordinator Console (CAAL)
TCC.............	Tethys Circumglobal Current [*Paleooceanography*]
TCC.............	Tetrachlorocatechol [*Organic chemistry*]
TCC.............	Textile Conservation Centre (BUAC)
TCC.............	Theater Communications Center (MCD)
TCC.............	Theater Communications Command (MCD)
TCC.............	Thermal Control Coating
TCC.............	Therofor Catalytic Cracking
TCC.............	Thiamine Cobalt Chlorophyllin [*Antiulcer*]
TCC.............	Thiokol Chemical Corp. [*Later, Thiokol Corp.*] (AAG)
TCC.............	Third Continental Congress (EA)
TCC.............	Thromboplastic Cell Component [*Hematology*]
TCC.............	Through-Connected Circuit [*Telecommunications*] (TEL)
TCC.............	Time Compression Coding
TCC.............	Tocix Chemicals Committee (EERA)
TCC.............	Toll Centre Code (NITA)
TCC.............	Toroidal Combustion Chamber
TCC.............	Torque Converter Clutch [*Automotive engineering*]
TCC.............	TOS [*TIROS Operational Satellite*] Checkout Center [*Goddard Space Flight Center*] (NOAA)
TCC.............	Total Car Coefficient [*Formula*] [*Automobile analysis*]
TCC.............	Total COBOL [*Common Business-Oriented Language*] Capability [*Computer science*] (IAA)
TCC.............	Total Comparative Costs [*Army*]
TCC.............	Toxic Chemicals Committee (BUAC)
TCC.............	Tracking and Communication Component
TCC.............	Tracking and Control Center
TCC.............	Tracking Computer Controls (MCD)
TCC.............	Tractor Computing Corp. (IAA)
TCC.............	Traffic Control Center
TCC.............	Traffic Control Complex (SAA)
TCC.............	TRANS-CIS Commodities [*Monte Carlo*] (ECON)
TCC.............	Transcontinental Corps [*Amateur radio*]
TCC.............	Transfer Channel Control (IEEE)
TCC.............	Transient Combustion Chamber [*Analysis*] (MCD)
TCC.............	Transit Control Center (SAA)
TCC.............	Transitional Cell Carcinoma
TCC.............	Transmission Control Character [*Telecommunications*] (TEL)
TCC.............	Transmit Carry and Clear
TCC.............	Transparent Conductive Coating [*Organic chemistry*]
TCC.............	Transportable Cassette Converter (IAA)
TCC.............	Transport and Communications Commission [*United Nations*] (WDAA)
TCC.............	Transportation Commodity Classification Code
TCC.............	Transportation Component Command (DOMA)
TCC.............	Transportation Component Compound (COE)
TCC.............	Transportation Control Card [*Military*]
TCC.............	Transportation Control Center
TCC.............	Transportation Control Committee [*Navy*]
TCC.............	Transport Control Center [*Air Force*]
TCC.............	Travel Classification Code
TCC.............	Travel Correction Calculator (MSA)
TCC.............	Travelers' Century Club (EA)
TCC.............	Triactor Resources Corp. [*Vancouver Stock Exchange symbol*]
TCC.............	Trichlorocarbanilide [*Organic chemistry*]
TCC.............	Triclocarban [*Pharmacology*]
TCC.............	Trilobita-Crustacea-Chelicerata [*Evolution history*]
TCC.............	Triple Cotton-Covered [*Wire insulation*]
TCC.............	Troop Carrier Command [*World War II*]
TCC.............	Tucumcari, NM [*Location identifier FAA*] (FAAL)
TCC.............	Turbine Close Coupled (MSA)
TCC.............	Turnbull Canyon [*California*] [*Seismograph station code, US Geological Survey Closed*] (SEIS)
TCC.............	Type of Changed Code [*Army*]
TCCA...........	Teachers' Committee on Central America (EA)
TCCA...........	Textile and Clothing Contractors' Association [*British*] (BI)
TCCA...........	Textile Color Card Association of the US [*Later, CAUS*]
TCCA...........	Thana Central Cooperative Association [*Bangladesh*] (BUAC)
TCCA...........	Thermometer Collectors Club of America (EA)
TCCA...........	Tin Container Collectors Association (EA)
TCCA...........	Trichloroisocyanuric Acid [*Organic chemistry*]
TCCA...........	Turkish Cypriot Cultural Association (BUAC)
TCCAV.........	Transitional-Cell Cancer-Associated Virus [*Medicine*] (DB)
TCCB...........	Test and County Cricket Board [*British*]
TCCBL.........	Transitional-Cell Carcinoma of Bladder [*Oncology*] (DAVI)
TCCBL.........	Tons of Cubic Capacity Bale Space [*Shipping*]
TCCC..........	3CI Complete Compliance [*NASDAQ symbol*] (TTSB)
TCCC..........	Three CI Complete Compliance Corp. [*NASDAQ symbol*] (SAG)
TCCC..........	Tower Control Computer Complex [*Aviation*]
TCCCS.........	Tactical Command, Control, and Communications System [*Canada*]
TCC/CT........	Telecommunications/Communications Terminal (MCD)
TCCD	Transcranial Color-Coded Doppler [*Medicine*] (DMAA)
TCCDC	Chattem Drug and Chemical Co., Chattanooga, TN [*Library symbol Library of Congress*] (LCLS)
TCCE...........	Turkish Chamber of Civil Engineers (BUAC)
TCCF...........	Tactical Communications Control Facility [*Air Force*] (MCD)
TCCFU.........	Typical Coastal Command Foul Up [*RAF slang*] [*World War II*]
TCCH	Tracer Control Chassis
TCC Inds......	TCC Industries, Inc. [*Formerly, Telecom Corp.*] [*Associated Press*] (SAG)
TCCKA.........	Tai Chi and Chi Kung Academy [*Australia*]
TCCL...........	T-Cell Chronic Lymphoblastic Leukemia [*Medicine*] (DMAA)
TCCM..........	Thermal Control Coating Material
TCCN..........	TransCanada Computer Communications Network (IAA)
TCCO..........	Technical Communications [*NASDAQ symbol*] (TTSB)
TCCO..........	Technical Communications Corp. [*NASDAQ symbol*] (NQ)
TCCO..........	Temperature-Compensated Crystal Oscillator (MCD)
TCCO..........	Temperature-Controlled Crystal Oscillator (IAA)
TC CO$_2$........	Transcutaneous Carbon Dioxide [*Monitor*] [*Medicine*] (DAVI)
TC-CON.......	Type Classification - Contingency

TCCP...........	Tissue Culture for Crops Project [*Colorado State University*] [*Research center*] (RCD)
TCCPSWG....	Tactical Command and Control Procedures Standardization Working Group [*Army*] (AABC)
TCCRAEF	[*The*] Conservative Caucus Research, Analysis, and Education Foundation (EA)
TCCS...........	Technical Committee on Communications Satellites
TCCS...........	Tide Communication Control Ship (NATG)
TCCS...........	Toyota's Computer-Controlled System (ADA)
TCCS...........	Trace Contaminant Control System
TCCS...........	Transcranial Color-Coded Sonography [*Medicine*] (DMAA)
TCC/SCA	Tai Chi Chuan/Shaolin Chuan Association (EA)
TCCT...........	Tactical Communications Control Terminal (MCD)
TCCT...........	Tooling Contour Check Tool (MCD)
TCCT...........	Type Commander Core Training (DOMA)
TCCU...........	Tribally Controlled Colleges and Universities
TCCWCA	Tasmanian Council of Churches World Christian Action [*Australia*]
TCD.............	Chad [*ANSI three-letter standard code*] (CNC)
TCD.............	Department of Technical Cooperation for Development [*United Nations*]
TCD.............	Tactical Communications Division [*Military*]
TCD.............	Tapetochoroidal Dystrophy [*Ophthalmology*]
TCD.............	Target Center Display
TCD.............	Task Completion Date (AAG)
TCD.............	Technical Contracts Department
TCD.............	Telemetry and Command Data (KSC)
TCD.............	Teletype Conversion Device (DWSG)
TCD.............	Temperature Control Device for Crystal Units (IAA)
TCD.............	Tentative Classification of Damage
TCD.............	Tentative Classification of Defects (NG)
TCD.............	Tentative Classification of Documents
TCD.............	Terminal Countdown Demonstration
TCD.............	Test Communications Division (SAA)
TCD.............	Test Completion Date (NASA)
TCD.............	Test Control Document [*NASA*] (MCD)
TCD.............	Test Control Drawings (MCD)
TCD.............	Thermal Conductivity Detector [*Analytical instrumentation*]
TCD.............	Thermochemical Deposition
TCD.............	Three-Channel Decoder
TCD.............	Thyratron Core Driver
TCD.............	Time Compliance Directive [*Air Force*] (MCD)
TCD.............	Time Correlation Data
TCD.............	Tissue Culture Dose (AAMN)
TCD.............	Tor-Cal Resources Ltd. [*Toronto Stock Exchange symbol*]
TCD.............	Total Cost Approach to Distribution
TCD.............	Tour Completion Date
TCD.............	TOXLINE Chemical Dictionary [*A publication*]
TCD.............	Traffic Control Devices [*MOCD*] (TAG)
TCD.............	Transistor Chopper Driver
TCD.............	Transistor-Controlled Delay (MCD)
TCD.............	Transportability Clearance Diagram (MCD)
TCD.............	Transportation Control Demonstration (COE)
TCD.............	Trinity College, Dublin [*Ireland*]
TCD.............	Tumor Cell Detection [*Medicine*]
TCD.............	Tumor Control Dose [*Oncology*]
TCD.............	Type Classification Date [*Army*]
TCD$_{50}$	Tissue Culture Dose, 50% Infectivity
TCDA	Touring Car Drivers Association [*Automobile racing*]
TCdaC.........	TransCanada Pipeline Ltd. Capital [*Associated Press*] (SAG)
TCDB	Turn, Cough, Deep Breathe [*Medicine*] (DMAA)
TCDC	Taurochenodeoxycholate [*Biochemistry*]
TCDC	Technical Cooperation among Developing Countries [*United Nations*]
TCDC/INRES...	Information Referral System for Technical Co-operation among Developing Countries [*United Nations Development Programme*] [*Information service or system*] (IID)
TCDD	Tetrachlorodibenzodioxin [*Organic chemistry*]
TCDD	Tower Cab Digital Display (PDAA)
TCDF...........	File [*Document Locator Number*] [*IRS*]
TCDF...........	Temporary Container Discharge Facility
TCDF...........	Tetrachlorodibenzofuran [*Organic chemistry*]
TCDL...........	Tasmanian Canine Defence League [*Australia*]
TCDMS	Telecommunication/Data Management System
TCDN	Techdyne, Inc. [*NASDAQ symbol*] (SAG)
TCDP	Transmitter Control and Display Panel
TCDRI	Tianjin Cement Industry Design and Research Institute [*China*] (BUAC)
TCDS	Tryptamine Chemical Delivery System [*Pharmacology*]
TCDU	Transport Command Development Unit [*British military*] (DMA)
TCE.............	[*The*] Chemical Engineer [*A publication*]
TCE.............	Taking Care of Elvis [*Motto of Elvis Presley fans*]
TCE.............	Talker Commission Error (MUGU)
TCE.............	Talker Communication Error (IAA)
TCE.............	Tax Counseling for the Elderly [*Internal Revenue Service*]
TCE.............	Teachers' Centers Exchange (EA)
TCE.............	Telemetry Checkout Equipment (KSC)
TCE.............	Telephone Co. Engineered [*Telecommunications*] (TEL)
TCE.............	Temperature Coefficient of Expansion
TCE.............	Terminal Control Element (CAAL)
TCE.............	Terminal Cretaceous Event [*Geology*]
TCE.............	Terrace (ROG)
TCE.............	Test Connection Equipment (IAA)
TCE.............	Tetrachloro-Diphenyl- Ethane [*An insecticide*] (DAVI)
TCE.............	Tetrachloroethylene [*Also, P*] [*Organic chemistry*]
TCE.............	Thermal Canister Experiment [*Space shuttle*] [*NASA*]
TCE.............	Thermal Coefficient of Expansion

TCE.............	Thomson's Loss-Making Consumer-Electronics [*France*] (ECON)
TCE.............	Tons of Coal Equivalent
TCE.............	Top Computer Executive (MHDB)
TCE.............	Total Composite Error
TCE.............	Total Concept Engineering
TCE.............	TOW [*Tube-Launched, Optically Tracked, Wire-Guided (Weapon)*] Crew Evaluator [*Military*] (INF)
TCE.............	Transaction Cost Estimator (MHDI)
TCE.............	Trans-Colorado Airlines, Inc. [*ICAO designator*] (FAAC)
TCE.............	Transportation-Communication Employees Union [*Later, TCIU*]
TCE.............	Trichloroethanol [*An anesthetic and hypnotic*] [*Pharmacology*] (DAVI)
TCE.............	Trichloroethene
TCE.............	Trichloroethylene [*Also, TRI*] [*Organic chemistry*]
TCE.............	Tubular Carbon Electrode
TCE.............	Tulcea [*Romania*] [*Airport symbol*] (OAG)
TCE.............	Tyumen Commodity Exchange [*Russian Federation*] (EY)
TCEA..........	Texas Computer Education Association (EDAC)
TCEA..........	Training Center for Experimental Aerodynamics [*NATO*]
TCEA..........	Trichloroethane [*Organic chemistry*]
TCEC..........	Erlanger Medical Center, Medical Library, Chattanooga, TN [*Library symbol Library of Congress*] (LCLS)
TCEC-N	Erlanger Medical Center, Nursing School, Chattanooga, TN [*Library symbol Library of Congress*] (LCLS)
TCEC-P	Erlanger Medical Center, I. C., Thompson's Children's Pediatric Library, Chattanooga, TN [*Library symbol Library of Congress*] (LCLS)
TCED..........	Thrust Control Exploratory Development (KSC)
TCEEA........	Tasmanian Catholic Education Employees' Association [*Australia*]
TCEL..........	T Cell Sciences [*NASDAQ symbol*] (TTSB)
TCEL..........	T Cell Sciences, Inc. [*Cambridge, MA*] [*NASDAQ symbol*] (NQ)
T Cell.........	T Cell Sciences, Inc. [*Associated Press*] (SAG)
T-cell..........	Thymus Cell (DB)
TCEO..........	Theatre Committee for Eugene O'Neill (EA)
TCEP..........	Tris(chloroethyl)phosphite [*Organic chemistry*]
TCEP..........	Tris(cyanoethoxy)propane [*Organic chemistry*]
TCEPA........	Tasmanian Commercial Egg Producers' Association [*Australia*]
TCert..........	Teacher's Certificate [*British*] (DBQ)
TCES..........	Time-Controlled Explosion System [*Galenics*] (DB)
TCES..........	Transcutaneous Cranial Electrical Stimulation [*Medicine*]
TCESOM	Trichlorethylene-Extracted Soybean Oil Meal
TCET..........	Transcerebral Electrotherapy
TCEU..........	Transportation-Communication Employees Union (MHDB)
TCF.............	[*The*] Charity Forum [*British*] (EAIO)
TCF.............	[*The*] Children's Foundation (EA)
TCF.............	[*The*] Compassionate Friends (EA)
TCF.............	Tactical Control Flight
TCF.............	Tank Checkout Facility [*NASA*] (NASA)
TCF.............	Tasmanian Cycling Federation [*Australia*]
TCF.............	TCF Financial Corp. [*Associated Press*] (SAG)
TCF.............	Technical Control Facility [*or Function*]
TCF.............	Technical Cooperation Fund (EERA)
TCF.............	Temporary Chaplain to the Forces [*British*]
TCF.............	Terminal Communication Facility [*Telecommunications*] (TSSD)
TCF.............	Terminal Configuration Facility [*Computer science*]
TCF.............	Territorial Cadet Force [*British military*] (DMA)
TCF.............	Test Control Fixture (MCD)
TCF.............	Time Correction Factor (ADA)
TCF.............	Tissue Coding Factor [*Medicine*] (DMAA)
TCF.............	T-Lymphocyte Chemotactic Factor
TCF.............	To Be Called For [*British Rail parcel service*] [*Obsolete*] (DI)
TCF.............	Total Coronary Flow [*Medicine*] (MAE)
TCF.............	Totally Chlorine-Free [*Pulp and paper processing*]
TCF.............	Toulx Ste. Croix [*France*] [*Seismograph station code, US Geological Survey*] (SEIS)
TCF.............	Training Check Frame [*Computer science*]
TCF.............	Transparent Computing Facility
TCF.............	Treacher Collins Foundation (EA)
TCF.............	Treacher-Collins-Franceschetti Syndrome (STED)
TCF.............	Trillion Cubic Feet
TCF.............	Troop Carrier Forces [*Military*]
TCF.............	Tunable Control Frequency
TCF.............	Twentieth Century Fund (EA)
TCFB..........	Trans-Continental Freight Bureau
TCFC..........	[*The*] Cars Fan Club (EA)
TCFC..........	Thom Christopher Fan Club (EA)
TCFC..........	Tom Cruise Fan Club (EA)
TCFC..........	Tommy Cash Fan Club [*Defunct*] (EA)
TCFC..........	Turkish Children Foster Care (EA)
TCFCA........	Textile Clothing and Footwear Council of Australia
TCFD..........	Technical Committee on Fish Diseases [*Australia*]
TCF Fn........	TCF Financial Corp. [*Associated Press*] (SAG)
TCFIC.........	Textile, Clothing, and Footwear Industries Committee [*British*] (DCTA)
TCFlt..........	Tactical Control Flight
TCFM.........	Teilhard Centre for the Future of Man (EAIO)
TCFM.........	Temperature Control Flux Monitor [*NASA*]
TCFNO	[*The*] Common Fund for Nonprofit Organizations [*Ford Foundation*]
TCFNSW.....	Teachers' Christian Fellowship of New South Wales [*Australia*]
TCFP..........	Thrust Chamber Fuel Purge (SAA)
TCFS..........	Turkish Cypriot Federated State
TCFU..........	Tumor Colony-Forming Unit [*Oncology*]
TCG.............	[*The*] Crimson Group [*Cambridge, MA*] [*Telecommunications*] (TSSD)
TCG.............	Tactical Control Group [*Air Force*]
TCG.............	Technical Coordination Group (MCD)

TCG.............	Telecommunications Consulting Group, Inc. [Washington, DC] (TSSD)
TCG.............	Telecommunications Group [Range Commanders Council] [NASA]
TCG.............	Territorial College of Guam
TCG.............	Test Call Generator [Telecommunications] (TEL)
TCG.............	Test Control Group [NASA] (NASA)
TCG.............	Theatre Communications Group (EA)
TCG.............	Threat Coordinating Group [DoD]
TCG.............	Time Code Generator
TCG.............	Time-Compensated Gain [Cardiology]
TCG.............	Time Controlled Gain (AAG)
TCG.............	Tooling Coordination Group (AAG)
TC/G.............	Total Fielding Chances per Game [Baseball]
TCG.............	Trans Canada Glass Ltd. [Toronto Stock Exchange symbol Vancouver Stock Exchange symbol]
TCG.............	Transponder Control Group
TCG.............	Tritocerebral Commissure, Giant [Zoology]
TCG.............	Tucson, Cornelia & Gila Bend Railroad Co. [AAR code]
TCG.............	Tune-Controlled Gain
TCGA.............	Tanzania Coffee Growers Association (BUAC)
TCGA.............	Tasmanian Chicken Growers' Association [Australia]
TCGE.............	Tool and Cutter Grinding Equipment (MCD)
TCGF.............	T-Cell Growth Factor [See also IL-2] [Biochemistry]
TCGF.............	Thymus Cell Growth Factor [Cytology]
TCGH.............	Downtown General Hospital, Chattanooga, TN [Library symbol Library of Congress] (LCLS)
TCGI.............	Teleport Communications Group, Inc. [NASDAQ symbol] (SAG)
TCGIX.............	DW TCW/DW North Amer. Govt. Income [Mutual fund ticker symbol] (SG)
TCGP.............	Girls' Prepatory School, Chattanooga, TN [Library symbol] [Library of Congress] (LCLS)
TCGp.............	Tactical Control Group [Air Force] (AFM)
TCGT.............	Georgia-Tennessee Regional Health Commission, Chattanooga, TN [Library symbol Library of Congress] (LCLS)
TCGT.............	Tool and Cutter Grinding Tool (MCD)
TCGU.............	Texaco Continuous Grease Unit
TCH.............	Chattanooga-Hamilton County Bicentennial Library, Chattanooga, TX [OCLC symbol] (OCLC)
TCH.............	Tanned Cell Hemagglutination (STED)
TCH.............	Tasmanian College of Hospitality [Australia]
TCH.............	Tchibanga [Gabon] [Airport symbol] (OAG)
TCH.............	Tchimkent [Former USSR Seismograph station code, US Geological Survey Closed] (SEIS)
TCH.............	Tchoupitoulas [Virus]
TCH.............	Tea Clearing House [British] (DBA)
TCH.............	Technologie-Centrum Hannover GmbH [Database producer] (IID)
TCH.............	Tec Tech [Vancouver Stock Exchange symbol]
TCH.............	Templeton China World Fd [NYSE symbol] (TTSB)
TCH.............	Templeton China World Fund [NYSE symbol] (SPSG)
TCH.............	Temporary Construction Hole [Technical drawings]
TCH.............	Tetrachlorohydroquinone [Organic chemistry]
TCH.............	Thiocarbohydrazide [Organic chemistry]
TCH.............	Threshold Crossing Height [Aviation] (FAAC)
TCH.............	Total Circulating Hemoglobin [Medicine] (MAE)
TCH.............	Touch
TCH.............	Trans-Canada Highway
TCH.............	Trans-Charter [Former USSR] [FAA designator] (FAAC)
TCH.............	Transfer in Channel
TCH.............	Trust Chamber [NASA] (KSC)
TCH.............	Turn, Cough, Hyperventilate [Medicine]
TCHA.............	Tasmanian Community Health Association [Australia]
TchA.............	Touchstone Applied Sciences [Associated Press] (SAG)
TchApld.............	Touchstone Applied Sciences [Associated Press] (SAG)
TCHCB.............	Chattanooga-Hamilton County Bicentennial Library, Chattanooga, TN [Library symbol Library of Congress] (LCLS)
TchCom.............	Technical Communications Corp. [Associated Press] (SAG)
TCHD.............	Threshold Crossing Height Downwind [Aviation] (FAAC)
Tchdyn.............	Techdyne, Inc. [Associated Press] (SAG)
Tchdyne.............	Techdyne, Inc. [Associated Press] (SAG)
TchE.............	Total Cholinesterase (DB)
TchElec.............	Tech Electro Industries, Inc. [Associated Press] (SAG)
TCHEP.............	Technical Committee on High Energy Physics [of the Federal Council for Science and Technology]
TCHG.............	Teaching
TCHHNLGCL...	Technological
TCHHW.............	Tropic Higher High Water [Tides]
TCHHWI.............	Tropic Higher High-Water Interval [Tides]
TcHIDA.............	Technetium Hepatoiminodiacetic Acid [Scan] [Radiology] (DAVI)
TCHIP.............	Town Campers' Housing and Infrastructure Program [Australia]
TCHK.............	Text Check [Computer science]
TCHLW.............	Tropic Higher Low Water [Tides]
Tchnal.............	Technalysis Corp. [Associated Press] (SAG)
TCHNG.............	Teaching
TChO.............	Olin Corp., D. B. Beene Technical Information Center, Charleston, TN [Library symbol Library of Congress] (LCLS)
TCHOG.............	Technical Operations Group [Air Force]
TCHOS.............	Technical Operations Squadron [Air Force]
TCHP.............	Telechips Corp. [NASDAQ symbol] (SAG)
TCHPW.............	Telechips Corp. Wrrt [NASDAQ symbol] (TTSB)
TCHR.............	Teacher
Tchr.............	Teacher (AL)
TchRsh.............	Technology Research Corp. [Associated Press] (SAG)
TchSym.............	Tech-Sym Corp. [Associated Press] (SAG)
TCHT.............	Tanned-Cell Hemagglutination Test [Immunology]
TCHTS.............	Technical Training Squadron [Air Force]
TCHTW.............	Technical Training Wing [Air Force]
TCHU.............	Threshold Crossing Height Upwind [Aviation] (FAAC)
TCI.............	Santa Cruz de Tenerife [Canary Islands] [Airport symbol] (AD)
TCI.............	Tall Clubs International (EA)
TCI.............	Tank Consultants, Inc. (EFIS)
TCI.............	Tasmanian Confederation of Industries [Australia]
TCI.............	T-Cell Immunity (DB)
TCI.............	TCI: The Business of Entertainment Technology and Design [A publication] (BRI)
TCI.............	TDRS Command Interface (MCD)
TCI.............	Technical Component Industries [Aerospace British]
TCI.............	Technical Critical Item (NASA)
TCI.............	Technology Catalysts, Inc. [Information service or system] (IID)
TCI.............	Technology Communications, Inc.
TCI.............	Technology Concepts, Inc. [Sudbury, MA] [Telecommunications] (TSSD)
TCI.............	Technology for Communications International
TCI.............	Technology for Communications International, Inc. (AAGC)
TCI.............	Tele-Communications, Inc. [Brookpark, OH] (TSSD)
TCI.............	Teleconferencing Systems International, Inc. [Elk Grove Village, IL] [Telecommunications] (TSSD)
TCI.............	Telemetry Components Information (KSC)
TCI.............	Telephone Collectors International (EA)
TCI.............	Temperature Control Instrument
TCI.............	Temporary Customs Impost [British]
TCI.............	Tenerife [Canary Islands] [Airport symbol] (OAG)
TCI.............	Tenneco, Inc. (EFIS)
TCI.............	Teracurie (STED)
TCI.............	Terminal Communications Interface
TCI.............	Terrain Clearance Indicator
TCI.............	Test Control Instruction (KSC)
TCI.............	Theoretical Chemistry Institute [University of Wisconsin - Madison] [Research center] (RCD)
TCI.............	Thermo Cardiosystems, Inc. (PS)
TCI.............	Thimble Collectors International (EA)
TCI.............	Thomson CEA Industries [France] (ECON)
TCI.............	Time Change Item (MCD)
TCI.............	To Come In [to hospital] [Medicine]
TCI.............	Torque Control Isolation [Automotive engineering]
TCI.............	Total Cerebral Ischemia
TCI.............	Totman's Change Index (STED)
TCI.............	Traffic Clubs International (EA)
TCI.............	Transcontinental Realty Investors [NYSE symbol] (SPSG)
TCI.............	Transcontinental Rlty [NYSE symbol] (TTSB)
TCI.............	Transient Cerebral Ischemia [Medicine]
TCI.............	Transportation Clubs International (EA)
TCI.............	Travel Consultants, Inc.
TCI.............	Tree Council of Ireland (BUAC)
TCI.............	Tricuspid Insufficiency [Medicine] (MEDA)
TCI.............	Trunk Cut In
TCI.............	Trust Companies Institute [South Africa] (BUAC)
TCI.............	Turbocharged Generation One [Automotive engine identification]
TCI.............	Turks & Caicos National Airlines [ICAO designator] (FAAC)
TCIA.............	Truck Cap Industry Association (FA)
TCIAS.............	Texas Council of Industrial Arts Supervisors (EDAC)
TCIATE.............	Texas Council on Industrial Arts Teacher Education (EDAC)
TCIC.............	Technical Committee on Industrial Classification [Office of Management and Budget] [Washington, DC] (EGAO)
TCI Cm.............	TCI Communications Financing I [Associated Press] (SAG)
TCICm.............	TCI Communications Financing II [Associated Press] (SAG)
TCID.............	Terminal Computer Identification (KSC)
TCID.............	Test Configuration Identifier (NASA)
TCID.............	Test Configuration Identifier Document (NAKS)
TCID.............	Tissue Culture Infectious [or Infective] Dose
TCID.............	Tissue-Culture Inoculated Dose [Medicine] (DB)
TCID50.............	Median Tissue Culture Infective Dose [Laboratory science] (DAVI)
Tc-IDA.............	Technetium Iminodiacetic Acid [Clinical chemistry]
TCIE.............	Transient Cerebral Ischemic Episode [Medicine] (MAE)
TCIF.............	Telecommunications Industry Forum (EA)
TCII.............	TCI International, Inc. [NASDAQ symbol] (NQ)
TCII.............	TCI Intl [NASDAQ symbol] (TTSB)
TCI Int.............	TCI International, Inc. [Associated Press] (SAG)
TCIL.............	Telecommunications Consultants India Ltd. (BUAC)
TCI Pac.............	TCI Pacific Communications [Associated Press] (SAG)
TCIR.............	Technical Command Informal Reports [Army] (MCD)
TCIS.............	TELEX Computer Inquiry Service
TCI Sat.............	TCI Satellite Entertainment, Inc. [Associated Press] (SAG)
TCITP.............	Terminal Communications Interface Test Program (MCD)
TCIU.............	Transportation Communications International Union (EA)
TCIV.............	Turbocharged Generation 4 [Automotive engine identification]
TCIX.............	Total Containment [NASDAQ symbol] (SAG)
TCJ.............	Tactical Communications Jamming [Military] (CAAL)
TCJ.............	Tarrant County Junior College, Hurst, TX [OCLC symbol] (OCLC)
TCJ.............	Thermocouple Junction
TCJ.............	Turbulent Confined Jet
TCJCC.............	Trades Councils' Joint Consultative Committee [British] (DCTA)
TCK.............	Test Clock (CIST)
TCK.............	Thermochemical-Kinetic
TCK.............	Thermo Ecotek [AMEX symbol] (TTSB)
TCK.............	Thermo Ecotek Corp. [AMEX symbol] (SAG)
TCK.............	Tilletia controversa Kuehn [Wheat fungus]
TCK.............	TOW [Tube-Launched, Optically-Tracked, Wire-Guided Weapon] Cooler Kit (DWSG)
TCK.............	Track [or Tracking] (AAG)
TCK.............	Two-Cavity Klystron

TCKL	Tackle
TCL	[*The*] Command Language [*Computer science*] (PCM)
TCL	Escape Aviation [*ICAO designator*] (FAAC)
TCL	Takeoff Cruise Landing [*Aviation*]
TCL	Tanzania Creameries Ltd. (BUAC)
TCL	Target Cleanup Level [*Environmental science*] (ERG)
TCL	Target Compound List [*Environmental science*] (COE)
TCL	Telecommunication Laboratories [*Taiwan*]
TCL	Telephone Cables Ltd. [*British*]
TCL	Terminal Command Language [*Applied Digital Data Systems*]
TCL	Terminal Control Language
TCL	Textes Cuneiformes. Departement des Antiquites Orientales. Musee du Louvre [*A publication*] (BJA)
TCL	Thin Charcoal Layer
TCL	Through-Camera-Lens
TCL	Time and Cycle Log [*NASA*] (KSC)
TCL	Toll Circuit Layout [*Telecommunications*] (TEL)
TCL	Tool Command Language [*Computer science*]
TCL	Tool Control List [*Military*] (AFIT)
TCL	Total Capacity of the Lung [*Medicine*] (DMAA)
TCL	Traction Control [*Mitsubishi*] [*Transmission systems*]
TCL	Transatlantic Carriers Ltd. [*Steamship line*] (MHDW)
TCL	TransCanada Pipeline Ltd. Capital [*NYSE symbol*] (SAG)
TCL	Transcon, Inc. (EFIS)
TCL	Transfer Chemical LASER (IEEE)
TCL	Transistor Contact Land
TCL	Transistor Coupled Logic
TCL	Transmit Clock (IAA)
TCL	Transportable Calibration Laboratory
TCL	Transport Canada Library, Ottawa [*UTLAS symbol*]
TCL	Trap Control Line
TCL	Trinity College, London
TCL	Trinity College of Music, London (BUAC)
TCL	Troposcatter Communications Link
TCL	Tsumet Corp. Ltd. (BUAC)
TCL	Tulane Computer Laboratory [*Tulane University*] [*Research center*] (RCD)
TCL	Tuscaloosa [*Alabama*] [*Airport symbol*] (OAG)
TCL	Tusculum College, Greenville, TN [*Inactive*] [*OCLC symbol*] (OCLC)
TCIA	Austin Peay State University, Clarksville, TN [*Library symbol Library of Congress*] (LCLS)
TCLA	T-Cell Line Adapted [*Cytology*]
TCLAS	Type Classification [*Military*] (AABC)
TCLBRP	Tank Cannon Launched Beam Rider Projectile (MCD)
TCLBS	Tropical Constant-Level Balloon System [*Meteorology*]
TCLC	Tri-State College Library Cooperative [*Rosemont College Library*] [*Rosemont, PA*] [*Library network*]
TCLC	Twentieth-Century Literary Criticism [*A publication*]
TC/LD	Thermocouple/Lead Detector [*Nuclear energy*] (NRCH)
TCle	Cleveland Public Library, Cleveland, TN [*Library symbol Library of Congress*] (LCLS)
TCLE	Temperature Coefficient of Linear Expansion (MED)
TCLE	Thermal Coefficient of Linear Expansion [*Rocket motor stress*]
TCleB	Bradley Memorial Hospital, Cleveland, TN [*Library symbol Library of Congress*] (LCLS)
TCleC	Cleveland State Community College, Cleveland, TN [*Library symbol Library of Congress*] (LCLS)
TCleL	Lee College, Cleveland, TN [*Library symbol Library of Congress*] (LCLS)
TCIH	Clarksville Memorial Hospital, Clarksville, TN [*Library symbol*] [*Library of Congress*] (LCLS)
TCLHW	Tropic Lower High Water [*Tides*]
TCLL	T-Cell Chronic Lymphocytic Leukemia [*Oncology*]
TCLLW	Tropic Lower Low Water [*Tides*]
TCLLWI	Tropic Lower Low-Water Interval [*Tides*]
TCLN	Techniclone International Corp. [*NASDAQ symbol*] (SAG)
TCLN	Techniclone Intl [*NASDAQ symbol*] (TTSB)
TCLNA	Tall Cedars of Lebanon of North America (EA)
TCLo	Toxic Concentration Low (ERG)
TCLP	Toxic Characteristic Leaching Procedure
TCLP	Toxic Characteristics Leaching Procedure [*Environmental Protection Agency*]
TCLP	Toxicity Characteristic Leachate Procedure [*Environmental science*] (COE)
TCLP	Toxicity Characteristic Leaching Procedure [*Environmental Protection Agency*]
TCLP	Toxicity Characteristic Leading Procedure [*Hazardous materials control*]
TCLP	Type Classification, Limited Procurement
TC-LP	Type Classification - Limited Production
TC-LPT	Type Classified - Limited Production Test
TC-LPU	Type Classification - Limited Production Urgent
TCLR	Toll Circuit Layout Record [*Telecommunications*] (TEL)
TCLSC	Theater COMSEC [*Communications Security*] Logistic Support Center [*Army*] (AABC)
TCLSC-E	Theater COMSEC Logistics Support Center - Europe (MCD)
TCLT	Tentative Calculated Landing Time [*FAA*] (TAG)
TCM	Tacoma, WA [*Location identifier FAA*] (FAAL)
TCM	Tactical Cruise Missile (MCD)
TCM	Tasmanian Chamber of Mines [*Australia*]
TCM	Tax Court Memorandum Decisions [*Commerce Clearing House or Prentice-Hall, Inc.*] [*A publication*] (DLA)
TCM	Teaching Career Month
TCM	Technical Committee Minutes [*Military*] (AFIT)
TCM	Technical Coordination Meeting (MCD)
TCM	Telecommunications Manager (MHDB)
TCM	Telecommunications Monitor
TCM	Teledyne Continental Motors [*ICAO designator*] (FAAC)
TCM	Telemetry Code Modulation
TCM	Telephone Channel Monitor
TCM	Temperature-Compensated Mask (IAA)
TCM	Temperature-Compensation (IAA)
TCM	Temperature Control Model
TCM	Terminal Capacity Matrix (OA)
TCM	Terminal-to-Computer Multiplexer
TCM	Termination of Centralized Management (MCD)
TCM	Terrain Clearance Measurement
TCM	Terrestrial Carbon Model [*Earth science*]
TCM	Test Call Module [*Telecommunications*] (TEL)
TCM	Tetrachloromercurate [*Inorganic chemistry*]
TCM	Texas Climatological Model [*Environmental Protection Agency*] (GFGA)
TCM	Theater Combat Model (NATG)
TCM	Thermal Conduction Module [*IBM Corp.*]
TCM	Thermocouple Meter (IDOE)
TCM	Thermoplastic Cellular Molding [*Plastics technology*]
TCM	Time Compression Multiplex (IAA)
TCM	Tissue Culture Medium
TCM	Tone Code Modulation (IAA)
TCM	Toroidal Carbohydrate Module [*i.e., doughnut*] [*Slang*]
TCM	Torpedo Countermeasures (NVT)
TCM	Total Catchment Management (EERA)
TCM	Total Downtime for Corrective Unscheduled Maintenance [*Quality control*] (MCD)
TCM	Toxic Chemical Munitions [*Army*]
TCM	Traditional Chinese Medicine
TCM	Trajectory Correction Maneuver
TCM	Transcutaneous [*Oxygen*] Monitoring [*Medicine*]
TCM	Transfluxor Constants Matrix (AAG)
TCM	Translator CAM [*Computer-Aided Manufacturing*] Magnet (IAA)
TCM	Translator Command Module [*Fluorescence technique*]
TCM	Transportation Control Measure [*Environmental Protection Agency*] (GFGA)
TCM	Travel Cost Method
TCM	Trellis-Coded Modulation [*Data transmission*] (BYTE)
TCM	Troop Corporal-Major [*British military*] (DMA)
TCM	Truck Components Marketing [*Eaton Corp.*]
TCM	T/SF Communications [*AMEX symbol*] (TTSB)
TCM	T/SF Communications Corp. [*AMEX symbol*] (SPSG)
TCM	Tubing Connector Manifold [*Instrumentation*]
TCM	Tucuman [*Argentina*] [*Seismograph station code, US Geological Survey Closed*] (SEIS)
TCM	Tunneling Current Microscopy (AAEL)
TCM	Turner Classic Movies [*Television*]
TCM	Twin-Cartridge Machine
TCMA	Tabulating Card Manufacturers Association [*Later, IOSA*] (EA)
TCMA	Telephone Cable Makers' Association [*British*] (BI)
TCMA	Textile Chemical Manufacturers Association [*Later, IOSA*] (EA)
TCMA	Theater Container Management Agency
TCMA	Third Class Mail Association (EA)
TCMA	Tooling Component Manufacturers Association (EA)
TCM/A	Toxic Chemical Munitions/Agents (MCD)
TCMA	Tufted Carpet Manufacturers' Association [*British*] (BI)
TCMB	Tomato and Cucumber Marketing Board (BUAC)
TCMB	Turkiye Cumhuriyet Merkez Bankasi [*The Central Bank of the Republic of Turkey*]
TCM (CCH)	Tax Court Memorandum Decisions (Commerce Clearing House) [*A publication*] (DLA)
TCMD	Transnational Corporations and Management Division (BUAC)
TCMD	Transportation Cargo Manifest Document
TCMD	Transportation Control and Movement Document [*Military*]
TC Memo	Memorandum Opinion of the United States Tax Court (AAGC)
TC Memo	Tax Court Memorandum Decisions [*Commerce Clearing House or Prentice-Hall, Inc.*] [*A publication*] (DLA)
TCMF	Touch Calling Multifrequency (IEEE)
TCMH	Memorial Hospital, Chattanooga, TN [*Library symbol Library of Congress*] (LCLS)
TCMH	Tumor-Direct Cell-Mediated Hypersensitivity [*Oncology*] (DAVI)
TCMI	Moccasin Bend Mental Health Institute, Chattanooga, TN [*Library symbol Library of Congress*] (LCLS)
TCMIS	Trade Control Measures Information System [*UNCTAD*] [*United Nations*] (DUND)
TCMIS	TRADOC [*Training and Doctrine Command*] Command Management Information System [*Military*]
T C MITS	[*The*] Common Man in the Street [*The average man*] [*See also MITS*]
TCMJA	Tasmanian Country Music Jamboree Association [*Australia*]
TCML	Target Coordinate Map Locator [*Military*] (PDAA)
TCMP	Taxpayer Compliance Measurement Program [*IRS*]
TCMP	Thematic Content Modification Program (DMAA)
TCM (P-H)	Tax Court Memorandum Decisions (Prentice-Hall, Inc.) [*A publication*] (DLA)
TCMR	Trafford Centre for Medical Research (BUAC)
TCMS	Technical Control and Management Subsystem (MCD)
TCMS	Telecommunications Management System (MHDI)
TC-MS	Thermal Chromatography/Mass Spectrometry
TCMS	Toll Centering and Metropolitan Sectoring [*AT & T*] [*Telecommunications*] (TEL)
TCMS	Track Combat Status (SAA)
TCMS	Training Certification Management System [*NASA*]

TCMS .... Turbocharger Management System [Automotive electronics]
TCMTB .... (Thiocyanomethylthio)benzothiazole [Fungicide] [Organic chemistry]
TCMZ .... Trichloromethiazide [Diuretic]
TCN .... Carson-Newman College, Jefferson City, TN [OCLC symbol] (OCLC)
TCN .... Teen Challenge National [An association] (EA)
TCN .... Telecommunications Cooperative Network (EA)
TCN .... Teleconference Network [University of Nebraska Medical Center] [Omaha, NE] [Telecommunications] (TSSD)
TCN .... Territorial Command Net
TCN .... Test Change Notice [NASA] (MCD)
TCN .... Tetracycline [Antibiotic]
TCN .... Texcan Technology Corp. [Vancouver Stock Exchange symbol]
TCN .... Third Country National (WDAA)
TCN .... Tobacco Cyst Nematode [Plant pathology]
TCN .... Toconce [Chile] [Seismograph station code, US Geological Survey] (SEIS)
TCN .... Tracing Change Notice
TCN .... Track Channel Number (SAA)
TCN .... Trade Commission of Norway (EA)
TCN .... Trans Continental Airlines [ICAO designator] (FAAC)
TCN .... Transfer on Channel Not in Operation (SAA)
TCN .... Transparent Content Negotiation (TELE)
TCN .... Transportation Control Number [Air Force] (AFM)
TCN .... Trolley Coach News [A publication] (EAAP)
TCNA .... Tube Council of North America (EA)
TCNB .... Tetracyanobenzene [Organic chemistry]
TC-NBT .... Thiocarbamyl-nitro-blue Tetrazolium [Organic chemistry]
TCNC .... Tekakwitha Conference National Center (EA)
TCNCO .... Test Control Noncommissioned Officer (AFM)
TCNE .... Tetracyanoethylene [Organic chemistry]
TCNEO .... Tetracyanoethylene Oxide [Organic chemistry]
TCNJ .... Trust Co. of New Jersey [NASDAQ symbol] (NQ)
TCNL .... Tecnol Medical Products [NASDAQ symbol] (SPSG)
TCNM .... Trimethylcyclopropenyl(nitrophenyl)malononitrile [Organic chemistry]
TCNO .... Tecnomatix Technologies Ltd. [NASDAQ symbol] (SAG)
TCNOF .... Tecnomatix Technologies Ltd [NASDAQ symbol] (TTSB)
TCNQ .... Tetracyanoquinodimethane [Organic chemistry]
TCNS .... Transcutaneous Nerve Stimulation [Medicine] (MAE)
TCNSW .... Travel Centre of New South Wales [Australia]
TCNT .... Transpiration-Cooled Nose Tip
TCNTL .... Trans-Continental [Aviation] (FAAC)
TCO .... Aerotranscolombiana de Carga Ltda. [Columbia] [FAA designator] (FAAC)
TCO .... Tactical Combat Operations
TCO .... Tactical Control Officer [Army]
TCO .... Taken Care Of (MCD)
TCO .... Taubman Centers [NYSE symbol] (TTSB)
TCO .... Taubman Centers, Inc. [NYSE symbol] (SPSG)
TCO .... Technical Checkout [Nuclear] (MCD)
TCO .... Technical Contracting Office [Navy]
TCO .... Technical Cooperation Officer [British]
TCO .... Telecommunications Certifying Officer [Air Force] (AFIT)
TCO .... Telemetry and Command Subsystem [Deep Space Instrumentation Facility, NASA]
TCO .... Temperature Coefficient of Offset (IAA)
TCO .... Terminal Control Office [or Officer]
TCO .... Termination Contracting Officer [Military]
TCO .... Test and Checkout [NASA] (GFGA)
TCO .... Test Control Officer [Military]
TCO .... Thrust Cutoff (NVT)
TCO .... Thunderstorm Census Organisation (BUAC)
TCO .... Tillamook County Library, Tillamook, OR [OCLC symbol] (OCLC)
TCO .... Time and Charges, Operate
TCO .... Tjaenstemaennens Centralorganisation [Central Organization of Salaried Employees] [Sweden]
TCO .... Tool Change Order (MCD)
TCO .... Torpedo Control Officer [British military] (DMA)
TCO .... Total Cost of Ownership (PCM)
TCO .... Traffic Camera Office [Victoria, Australia]
TCO .... Train Conducting Officer [British military] (DMA)
TCO .... Trans Canada Options [Stock exchange network of VSE, TSE, and MSE]
TCO .... Trans-Canada Resources Ltd. [Toronto Stock Exchange symbol]
TCO .... Transfer on Channel in Operation (IAA)
TCO .... Translational Control (SAA)
TCO .... Translocation Crossover [Geology]
TCO .... Transparent Conductive Oxide [Photovoltaic energy systems]
TCO .... Transportation Co. [Army]
TCO .... Transportation Control Officer [Air Force] (AFM)
TCO .... Trinity College, Oxford [British] (DAS)
TCO .... Triode Cavity Oscillator
TCO .... Trunk Cutoff
TCO .... Tumaco [Colombia] [Airport symbol] (OAG)
TCOA .... Telephone Contract Officers' Association [A union] [British]
TCOA .... Trustee Companies Officers' Association [Australia]
T-COAP .... Vincristine, Prednisone, Cytosine Arabinoside, Cyclophosphamide, and 6-Thioguanine [Antineoplastic drug regimen] (DAVI)
TCOBS .... Type Classification - Obsolete (MCD)
TCoC .... Columbia State Community College, Columbia, TN [Library symbol] [Library of Congress] (LCLS)
TCOC .... Transverse Cylindrical Orthomorphic Chart
TCOCD .... Thermocouple Open Circuit Detection (IAA)
TCOED .... Training Centre for Oil Exploration and Development [China] (BUAC)
T (Colds) ..... Toxic Colds [Medicine]

TColISM ...... Southern Missionary College, Collegedale, TN [Library symbol Library of Congress] (LCLS)
TCOM .... Tele-Communications Class A [NASDAQ symbol] (SAG)
TCOM .... Tele-Communications, Inc. [NASDAQ symbol] (NQ)
TCOM .... Terminal Communications [Aviation] (FAAC)
TCOM .... Terminal or Computer Originated Mail Systems, Inc. [Washington, DC] (TSSD)
TCOM .... Tethered Communications, Inc. [Westinghouse subsidiary]
TCOM .... Texas College of Osteopathic Medicine
TCOM .... Transcutaneous Oxygen Monitor [Laboratory Science] (DAVI)
TCOMA .... Tele-Communic'ATCI Group [NASDAQ symbol] (TTSB)
TCOMB .... Tele-Communic'B'TCI Group [NASDAQ symbol] (TTSB)
T-Comm .... Terret Communications [Whitehouse Station, NJ] (TSSD)
TCOMP .... Tape Compare Processor [Computer science]
TCOMP .... TeleComm TCI Grp 6% Exch Pfd [NASDAQ symbol] (TTSB)
T/COMP .... Trimmed Complete [Automotive engineering]
TCON .... Naval Telecommunications Command (AAGC)
TCON .... Trailer Container [MTMC] (TAG)
TCON .... Transportation Constructor [MTMC] (TAG)
T/CONT .... Throttle Control [Automotive engineering]
T/CONV .... Torque Converter [Automotive engineering]
TCoo .... Putnam County Public Library, Cookeville, TN [Library symbol Library of Congress] (LCLS)
TCooH .... Cookeville General Hospital, Stephen Farr Health Sciences Library, Cookeville, TN [Library symbol Library of Congress] (LCLS)
TCooP .... Tennessee Technological University, Cookeville, TN [Library symbol Library of Congress] (LCLS)
TCOP .... Test and Checkout Plan [NASA] (KSC)
TCOP .... Thrust Chamber Oxidizer Purge (SAA)
TCOR .... Chrysler Town and Country Owners Registry (EA)
TCOS .... The Canadian Orthoptic Society (AC)
TCOS .... Trunk Class of Service [Telecommunications] (TEL)
TCOSS .... Tasmanian Council of Social Service [Australia]
TCOT .... Tension Control Optimisation Theory [Tire manufacturing]
T-COUNT ..... Terminal Count [Flight readiness count] (MCD)
TCovH .... Tipton County Hospital, Covington, TN [Library symbol Library of Congress] (LCLS)
TCP .... [The] Acronym Generator Converter Program [RCA computer program] (IAA)
TCP .... Tactical Computer Processor
TCP .... Tactical Control Panel (MCD)
TCP .... Tactical Cryptologic Program [DoD]
TCP .... Tape Carrier Package (PCM)
TCP .... Tape Carrier Packaging [Computer science]
TCP .... Tape Conversion Program [Computer science] (MDG)
TCP .... Task Change Proposal (AAG)
TCP .... Task Control Packet (NASA)
TCP .... Task Control Program
TCP .... Teachers College Press
TCP .... Technical Change Proposal
TCP .... Technical Coordination Program [Military] (AFIT)
TCP .... Technical Cost Proposal (AAG)
TCP .... Technological Capabilities Panel (LAIN)
TCP .... Technology Coordinating Paper
TCP .... Telecommunications Processor (IAA)
TCP .... Telemetry and Command Processor Assembly [Deep Space Instrumentation Facility, NASA]
TCP .... Temple Cyclopaedic Primers [A publication]
TCP .... Temporary Change Procedure (AAG)
TCP .... Terminal Control Program
TCP .... Test and Checkout Procedure [NASA] (KSC)
TCP .... Test Change Proposal (CAAL)
TCP .... Test Checkout Panel
TCP .... Test Control Package (NASA)
TCP .... Test of Creative Potential
TCP .... Tetrachlorobiphenyl [Organic chemistry]
TCP .... Tetrachlorophenol [Organic chemistry]
TCP .... Tetracyanoplatinate [Inorganic chemistry]
TCP .... Tetracyanopyrazine [Organic chemistry]
TCP .... Texaco Combustion Process [Automotive engineering]
TCP .... Therapeutic Continuous Penicillin [Medicine] (MAE)
TCP .... Thermoform Continuous Percolation (IAA)
TCP .... Thienyl(cyclohexyl)piperidine [Biochemistry]
TCP .... Thrust Chamber Pressure [Aerospace] (IEEE)
TCP .... Time, Cost, and Performance
TCP .... Time Limited Correlation Processing
TCP .... Timing and Control Panel
TCP .... Tocopilla [Chile] [Seismograph station code, US Geological Survey Closed] (SEIS)
TCP .... Tool Center Point [Robotics]
TCP .... Torpedo Certification Program [Military] (CAAL)
TCP .... Total Cell Protein [Biochemistry]
TCP .... Total Circulating Protein [Medicine] (DMAA)
TCP .... Total Clottable Protein [Clinical chemistry]
TC + P .... Total Colonoscopy plus Polypectomy [Proctoscopy]
TCP .... Town and Country Planning Act [British]
TCP .... Toxin-Coregulated Pili [Biochemistry]
TCP .... Trading Corp. of Pakistan (BUAC)
TCP .... Traffic Control Point [or Post] [Military]
TCP .... Trainer Change Proposal [Military] (AFIT)
TCP .... Training Controller Panel
TCP .... Transcorp Airways [British ICAO designator] (FAAC)
TCP .... Transfer of Control Point [Aviation] (FAAC)
TCP .... Transformer-Coupled Plasma (AAEL)
TCP .... Transmission Control Program [Telecommunications] (OSI)

TCP............	Transmission Control Protocol [*Advanced Research Projects Agency Network*] [*DoD*]
TCP............	Transmitter Control Pulse (NITA)
TCP............	Transparent Conducting Polymers [*Photovoltaic energy systems*]
TCP............	Transportation Control Plan [*Environmental Protection Agency*] (GFGA)
TCP............	Transport Command Police [*British military*] (DMA)
TCP............	Transport Control Protocol [*Telecommunications*]
TCP............	Tranylcypromine [*Organic chemistry*]
TCP............	Tricalcium Phosphate [*Inorganic chemistry*]
TCP............	Trichlorophenol [*Organic chemistry*]
TCP............	(Trichlorophenoxy)acetic Acid [*Also known as 2,4,5-T*] [*Herbicide*]
TCP............	Trichloropropane [*Organic chemistry*]
TCP............	Tricresyl Phosphate [*Organic chemistry*]
TCP............	Tropical Canine Pancytopenia (RDA)
TCP............	Tropical Conservation Program (GNE)
TCP............	True Conservative Party [*British*] (ECON)
TCP............	Trust Chamber Pressure [*Missile technology*] (KSC)
TCPA...........	Tantawangalo Catchment Protection Association (EERA)
TCPA...........	Tetrachlorophthalic Anhydride [*Flame retardant*] [*Organic chemistry*]
TCPA...........	Time to Closest Point of Approach [*Navigation*]
TCPA...........	Town & Country Planning Act (WDAA)
TCPA...........	Town and Country Planning Association [*British*]
TCPA...........	Trichlorophenylacetic Acid [*Herbicide*] [*Organic chemistry*]
TCPAM........	Tentative CNO [*Chief of Naval Operations*] Program Analysis Memorandum (NVT)
TCPC..........	Tab Card Punch Control
TCPC..........	Telephone Cable Process Controller (MHDB)
TCPC..........	Time-Correlated Photon Counting [*Spectrometry*]
TCPC..........	Town and Country Planning Commission [*Tasmania, Australia*]
TCPC..........	Transportation Claims and Prevention Council (EA)
TCPC..........	Transportation Consumer Protection Council (NTPA)
TCP(CC)R	Town and Country Planning (Compensation and Certificates) Regulations [*British*]
TCP(CPRW)R...	Town and Country Planning (Churches, Places of Religious Worship, and Burial Grounds) Regulations [*British*]
TCP-E.........	Thermal Case Penetrator - External (MCD)
TCPGR........	Town and Country Planning General Regulations [*British*]
TCPH	Toluoyl Chloride Phenylhydrazine [*Drug for sheep*]
TCPI..........	Technical Chemicals & Products [*NASDAQ symbol*] (SAG)
TCP-I.........	Thermal Case Penetrator - Internal (MCD)
TCPI..........	"To Complete" Performance Index (MCD)
TCPI..........	Transportation Club of the Petroleum Industry (EA)
TCP/IP	Transmission Control Protocol [*or Program*] and Internet Protocol (PCM)
TCP/IP	Transmission Control Protocol/Internet Protocol [*Computer science*] (EERA)
Tc-PIPIDA	Technetium Pertechnetate/N-Paraisoproplyacetanilide-Iminodiacetic Acid Scan [*Radiology*] (DAVI)
TCPL..........	TransCanada Pipelines Ltd. [*Commercial firm*]
TCPLD	Tunable Compound Phase-Locked Demodulator (IAA)
TCP(M)R......	Town and Country Planning (Minerals) Regulations [*British*]
TCPO	bis(Trichlorophenyl) Oxalate [*Organic chemistry*]
TCPO	Third-Class Post Office
TC pO₂	Transcutaneous Partial Pressure of Oxygen [*Monitor*] [*Medicine*] (DAVI)
TCPP..........	(Tetrachlorophenyl)pyrrole [*Organic chemistry*]
TCPPA	(Trichlorophenoxy)propionic Acid [*Plant hormone*] [*Herbicide*]
TCPS..........	Texas Center for Policy Studies (CROSS)
TCPS..........	Total Cavopulmonary Shunt [*Medicine*] (DMAA)
TCPS..........	Trailerless Collective Protection Station [*Military*]
TCPS..........	Transportable Collective Protection System (DWSG)
TCPTF........	Target Cost plus Target Fee
TC Pub........	Tariff Commission Publications [*A publication*] (DLA)
TCpY..........	Transcarpathian Yiddish (BJA)
TCQ...........	Tacna [*Peru*] [*Airport symbol*] (OAG)
TCQ...........	Teacher Concerns Questionnaire (EDAC)
TCQ...........	Trichlorobenzoquinoneimine [*Reagent*]
TCQC	Tank Crew Qualification Course [*Army*]
TCQM.........	[*The*] Chief Quartermaster [*Military*]
TCQM.........	Tetracyanoquionodimethane [*Organic chemistry*] (SAA)
TCR...........	Laneas Aeraes Trans Costa Rica SA [*ICAO designator*] (FAAC)
TCR...........	Tab Card Reader
TCR...........	Tactical Control RADAR (IAA)
TCR...........	Tantalum-Controlled Rectifier
TCR...........	Tape Cassette Recorder
TCR...........	Task Change Request [*Army*]
TCR...........	T-Cell Reactivity
TCR...........	T-Cell Receptor [*Immunology*]
TCR...........	T-Cell Recovery Column [*Chromatography*]
TCR...........	T-Cell Rosette [*Medicine*] (DMAA)
TCR...........	Teacher Contact Ratio (AIE)
TCR...........	Teachers' Central Register [*Australia*]
TCR...........	Teachers College Record [*A publication*] (BRI)
TCR...........	Technical Change Request
TCR...........	Technical Characteristics Review
TCR...........	Technical Compliance Record
TCR...........	Technical Cost Review (SSD)
TCR...........	Telemetry Compression Routine
TCR...........	Television Cathode Ray (IAA)
TCR...........	Temperature Coefficient of Resistance
TCR...........	Temperature Control Reference
TCR...........	Tentative Cancellation Request
TCR...........	Terrain Clearance RADAR
TCR...........	Test Compare Results (MCD)

TCR...........	Test Condition Requirements [*Army*]
TCR...........	Test Conductor (MCD)
TCR...........	Test Constraints Review [*NASA*] (MCD)
TCR...........	Tetrachlororesourcinol [*Organic chemistry*]
TCR...........	Thalamocortical Relay [*Neurology*]
TCR...........	Thermal Coefficient of Resistance (IAA)
TCR...........	Thermal Concept Review (NASA)
TCR...........	Thermochemical Recuperator [*Proposed heat recovery system*]
TCR...........	Thitec Recovery [*Vancouver Stock Exchange symbol*]
TCR...........	Tie Control Relay (MCD)
TCR...........	Time Code Reader
TCR...........	Time Critical Requirements (MCD)
TCR...........	Tonecraft Realty, Inc. [*Toronto Stock Exchange symbol*]
TCR...........	Tool Completion Report
TCR...........	Tooling Change Request
TCR...........	Total Contractual Requirements (MCD)
TCR...........	Total Controlled Return (WDAA)
TCR...........	Total Control Racing [*Road-racing game*] [*Ideal Toy Corp.*]
TCR...........	Total Core Recovery [*Nuclear energy*] (NUCP)
TCr...........	Total Creatine [*Pool*]
TCR...........	Tracer (AAG)
TCR...........	Traffic Control RADAR
TCR...........	Trainer Change Request [*Military*]
TCR...........	Training/Conversion/Replacement (MCD)
TCR...........	Transaction Confirmation Report [*Computer science*] (ITD)
TCR...........	Transceiver (AABC)
TCR...........	Transcription-Coupled Repair [*Genetics*]
TCR...........	Transfer Control Register
TCR...........	Transistorized Car Radio (IAA)
TCR...........	Transit Commission Reports [*New York*] [*A publication*] (DLA)
TCR...........	Transmittal Control Record [*Computer science*]
TCR...........	Transportable Cassette Recorder (IAA)
TCR...........	Transportation Corps Release [*Military*]
TCR...........	Travaux. Centre de Recherche sur le Proche-Orient et la Grece Antiques. Universite de Sciences Humaines de Strasbourg [*A publication*] (BJA)
TCR...........	Tubing Connector Reducer [*Instrumentation*]
TCR...........	Two-Color Radiometer
TCrA..........	Art Circle Public Library, Crossville, TN [*Library symbol Library of Congress*] (LCLS)
TCRA..........	T-Cell Receptor Alpha (DMAA)
TCRA..........	Telegraphy Channel Reliability Analyzer [*Telecommunications*] (OA)
TCRB..........	T-Cell Receptor Beta (DMAA)
TCRC	Telecommunications Research Centre [*India*] (BUAC)
TCRC	Time and Cycle Record Card [*NASA*] (KSC)
TCRC	Tobacco Chemists Research Conference (BUAC)
TCRD	T-Cell Receptor Delta (DMAA)
TCRD	Test and Checkout Requirements Document [*NASA*] (KSC)
TCRE..........	Temperature-Compensated Reference Element
TCRE..........	Transcervical Endometrial Resection [*Medicine*]
TCREC........	Transportation Research Command [*Army*] (MCD)
TCRF..........	Toxic Chemical Release Form
TCRI..........	Tobacco and Cotton Research Institute [*South Africa*] (BUAC)
TCRI..........	Toxic Chemical Release Inventory (GNE)
TCRJ..........	Thermocouple Reference Junction
TCRM.........	Thermochemical Remanent Magnetization
TCRMG	Tripartite Commission for the Restitution of Monetary Gold [*Belgium*] (EAIO)
TCRN	Temporary Chaplain to the Royal Navy [*British*]
tcRNA	Translation Control Ribonucleic Acid (MAE)
TCRP	Tactical Command Readiness Program [*Army*]
TCRP	Total Cellular Receptor Pool (DMAA)
TCRP	Transit Cooperative Research Program [*FTA*] (TAG)
TCRPA	Trans-Continental Railroad Passenger Association [*Defunct*] (EA)
TCRPC	Tri-County Regional Planning Commission [*Information service or system*] (IID)
TCRSD	Test and Checkout Requirements Specification Documentation [*NASA*] (NASA)
TCRTA	Terracotta Roofing Tile Association [*Australia*]
TCRV	Total Red Cell Volume [*Medicine*] (DMAA)
TCRZ..........	T-Cell Receptor Z (DMAA)
TCS	[*The*] Classification Society (EA)
TCS	[*The*] Coastal Society (EA)
TCS	[*The*] Constant Society (EA)
TCS	[*The*] Cousteau Society (EA)
TCS	[*The*] Crustacean Society (EA)
TCS	[*The*] Cybele Society (EA)
TCS	Tactical Call Sign (IAA)
TCS	Tactical Computer System [*Army*] (MCD)
TCS	Tactical Control Squadron
TCS	Tanking Control System (AAG)
TCS	Tanscontinental Service
TCS	Target Control System
TCS	Target Cost System
TCS	Tasmanian Caledonian Society [*Australia*]
Tcs	T-Cell-Mediating Contact Sensitivity (STED)
TCS	T-Cell Supernatant (STED)
TCS	Teacher Characteristics Schedule
TCS	Teaching Company Scheme [*British*]
TCS	Technical Change Summary [*NASA*] (MCD)
TCS	Technical Classification of Soils [*For pine plantations*] [*Australia*]
TCS	Technical Concurrence Sheets [*NASA*] (NASA)
TCS	Technical Countdown Sequences (KSC)
TCS	Technology Club of Syracuse [*New York*] (BUAC)

TCS .... Telecommunications Consulting Services [*Richard A. Eisner & Co.*] [*New York, NY*] (TSSD)
TCS .... Telecommunications Control System [*Toshiba Corp.*] [*Computer science*]
TCS .... Telecommunications System
TCS .... Teleconference System [*Memorial University of Newfoundland*] [*St. John's, NF*] [*Telecommunications*] (TSSD)
TCS .... Telemetry and Command Station [*Aerospace*] (MCD)
TCS .... Telephone Conference Summary (NRCH)
TCS .... Television Camera Set (MUSM)
TCS .... Television Camera System
TCS .... Television Control Set
TCS .... Telex Communications Service (NITA)
TCS .... Temperature Coefficient of Sensitivity (IAA)
TCS .... Temperature Control Subsystem (KSC)
TCS .... Temporary Change of Station [*Military*]
TCS .... Temporary Conditioning Station [*Nuclear energy*] (NRCH)
TCS .... Temporary Correction Sheet (MCD)
TCS .... Terminal Communications Subsystem
TCS .... Terminal Computer System (BUR)
TCS .... Terminal Control System [*Hewlett-Packard Co.*]
TCS .... Terminal Countdown Sequencer [*or Sequences*] [*NASA*] (KSC)
TCS .... Terminal Count Sequence (IAA)
TCS .... Ternary Compound Semiconductor
TCS .... Test Call Sender (NITA)
TCS .... Test Control Supervisor (NASA)
TCS .... Test Control System (NASA)
TCS .... Test of Cognitive Skills [*Achievement test*]
TCS .... Texas Centennial Society (EA)
TCS .... Texts from Cuneiform Sources [*A publication*] (BJA)
TCS .... Theater Communications System (MCD)
TCS .... Thermal Conditioning Service (IAA)
TCS .... Thermal Conditioning System (KSC)
TCS .... Thermal Control System [*or Subsystem*]
TCS .... Thermally Stimulated Charge [*Analytical chemistry*]
TCS .... Timing Cover and Seal Set [*Automotive engineering*]
TCS .... Tin Can Sailors (EA)
TCS .... Tire Control System [*Automotive engineering*]
TCS .... Token Corresponding Society [*British*] (DBA)
TCS .... Tone Call Squelch [*Telecommunications*] (IAA)
TCS .... Tool Clearance Slip (AAG)
TCS .... Tool Coordinate System
TCS .... Total Cellular Score (STED)
TCS .... Total Commissioned Service (DOMA)
TCS .... Total Communication Systems [*Pittsburgh, PA*] [*Telecommunications service*] (TSSD)
TCS .... Total Coronary Score (STED)
TCS .... Total Current Spectroscopy
TCS .... Tracheal Cellular Score [*Medicine*]
TCS .... Trac Industries, Inc. [*Toronto Stock Exchange symbol Vancouver Stock Exchange symbol*]
TCS .... Traction Control System [*Alfred Teves GmbH*] [*Automotive engineering*]
TCS .... Trade Commission of Spain (EA)
TCS .... Traffic Control Satellite
TCS .... Traffic Control Station
TCS .... Traffic Control System [*Army*]
TCS .... Transaction Control System [*Hitachi Ltd.*]
TCS .... TransCanada Telephone System [*Later, Telecom Canada*] (TSSD)
TCS .... Transcutaneous Stimulation
TCS .... Transducer Calibration System
TCS .... Transfer Carry Subtract
TCS .... Transmission Controlled Spark (MCD)
TCS .... Transmission-Controlled Speed (IIA)
TCS .... Transmission Control System (IAA)
TCS .... Transportable Communications System
TCS .... Transportation and Communications Service [*of GSA*] [*Abolished, 1972*]
TCS .... Transportation Consulting & Service Corp., Chicago IL [*STAC*]
TCS .... Transportation Costing Service [*Database*] [*A. T. Kearney, Inc.*] [*Information service or system*] (CRD)
TCS .... Transportes de Carga Aerea Especializada y Servicios Aeronauticos [*Mexico ICAO designator*] (FAAC)
TCS .... Trichlorosilane [*Inorganic chemistry*]
TCS .... Trichosanthin [*Botany*]
TCS .... Trim Control System
TCS .... Tripanel, Convoluted, Y-Strap [*A knee immobilizer*] [*Orthopedics*] (DAVI)
TCS .... Troop Carrier Squadron [*Military*] (CINC)
TCS .... Troposcatter Communications System
TC's .... Trust Certificates (EBF)
TCS .... Truth Or Consequences, NM [*Location identifier FAA*] (FAAL)
TCS .... Tube Cooling Supply
TCS .... Turbine Control System [*Nuclear energy*] (NRCH)
TCS .... Two-Photon Coherent States (MCD)
TCSA .... Tetrachlorosalicylanilide [*Organic chemistry*]
TCSA .... Trunk Cross Sectional Area [*of a tree*]
TCSAA .... Twentieth Century Spanish Association of America (EA)
TCS-AF .... Telecommunications Control System-Advanced Function (MHDI)
TCS & D ...... Temperature Controlled Storage and Distribution Exhibition [*British*] (ITD)
TCSC .... Time-Critical Shipment Committee [*Defunct*] (EA)
TCSC .... Toyota Celica Supra Club (EA)
TCSC .... Trainer Control and Simulation Computer
TCSC .... Two-Channel Scan Camera (NOAA)

TCSCLC .... Two-Carrier Space-Charge-Limited Current
TCSD .... Telemetry and Communications Systems Division [*Apollo*] [*NASA*]
TCSEC .... Trusted Computer System Evaluation Criteria (MCD)
TCSEV .... Twin-Cushion Surface Effect Vehicle (PDAA)
TCSF .... T-Colony-Stimulating Factor (DMAA)
TCSF .... Thomson-CSF [*France NASDAQ symbol*]
TCSF .... Total Counts of Successive Fractions [*Chromatography*]
TCSFY .... Thomson-CSF ADS [*NASDAQ symbol*] (TTSB)
TCSG .... [*The*] Center for Social Gerontology (EA)
TCSI .... TCSI Corp. [*NASDAQ symbol*] (TTSB)
TCSI .... Teknekron Communications Systems [*NASDAQ symbol*] (SPSG)
TCSI Cp ...... TCSI Corp. [*Associated Press*] (SAG)
TCSL .... Transistor Current Switching Logic [*Electronics*] (IAA)
TCSM .... Test of Cognitive Style in Mathematics [*Educational test*]
TCSM .... Transportation Control Strategies and Measure (COE)
TCSM .... Tropospheric Chemistry Systems Model (MCD)
TCSM .... Twin Channel Substrate Mesa (NITA)
TCSMC .... Transportation Corps Supply Maintenance Command [*Army*]
TCSnet .... Thai Computer Science Network (TNIG)
TCSP .... Tactical Communications Satellite Program [*DoD*] (MCD)
TCSP .... Tandem Cross-Section Program [*Bell System*]
TCSP .... Test Checkout Support Plan (KSC)
TCSP .... Tourism Council of the South Pacific (EERA)
TCSP .... Tourist Council of the South Pacific (BUAC)
TCSPC .... Time-Correlated Single Photon Counting [*Analytical chemistry*]
TCSPr .... Second Presbyterian Church Library, Chattanooga, TN [*Library symbol Library of Congress*] (LCLS)
TCSq .... Troop Carrier Squadron [*Air Force*] (AFM)
TCSR .... Typographic Council for Spelling Reform (EA)
TCSS .... Tactical Control Surveillance System
TCSS .... Tasmanian Council of Social Service [*Australia*]
TCSS .... Tri-Cone Support Structure [*NASA*]
TCSSS .... Thermal Control Subsystem Segment [*NASA*] (NASA)
TCST .... Chattanooga State Technical Community College, Chattanooga, TN [*Library symbol Library of Congress*] (LCLS)
TC STD .... Type Classification - Standard (MCD)
TCSTE .... Triangle Coalition for Science and Technology Education (EA)
TCSUH .... Texas Center for Superconductivity, University of Houston [*Research center*] (RCD)
TCSW .... Thinking Creatively with Sounds and Words [*Educational test*]
TCT .... Tactical Communications Terminal
TCT .... Tactical Computer Terminal [*Army*] (MCD)
TCT .... Takotna [*Alaska*] [*Airport symbol*] (OAG)
TCT .... Takotna, AK [*Location identifier FAA*] (FAAL)
TCT .... Tasmanian Conservation Trust [*State*] (EERA)
T Ct .... Tax Court of the United States, Reports [*A publication*] (DLA)
TCT .... Telemetry-Computer Translator [*Bell Laboratories*]
TCT .... Tennessee Temple Schools, Chattanooga, TN [*Library symbol Library of Congress*] (LCLS)
TCT .... Tennessee Temple University, Chattanooga, TN [*OCLC symbol*] (OCLC)
TCT .... Terminal Control Table [*Computer science*] (IAA)
TCT .... Terracotta Tile [*Classified advertising*] (ADA)
TCT .... Texas City Terminal Railway Co. [*AAR code*]
TCT .... Thrombin Clotting Time [*Clinical chemistry*]
TCT .... Thyrocalcitonin [*Also, CT, TCA*] [*Endocrinology*]
TCT .... Time Code Translator
TCT .... Tin Can Tourists of the World (EA)
Tct .... Tinctura [*Tincture*] [*Latin*]
TCT .... Toll Connecting Trunk [*Telecommunications*] (TEL)
TCT .... Tool Change Time
TCT .... Tool Cost Transportation [*MTMC*] (TAG)
TCT .... Total Composite Tolerance
TCT .... Total Controlled Tabulation (WDAA)
TCT .... Town & Country Corporate Trust [*NYSE symbol*] (SPSG)
TCT .... Town & Country Trust [*NYSE symbol*] (TTSB)
TCT .... Traffic Control Transponder
TCT .... Translator and Code Treatment Frame (IEEE)
TCT .... Traveling Contact Team [*Military*]
TCT .... Trial Court [*Legal shorthand*] (LWAP)
TCT .... Trichloromethyltriazine
TCT .... True Centerline Tested
TCT .... Trunk Coin Telephone (OA)
TCT .... Tur Avrupa Havayollari AS [*Turkey*] [*ICAO designator*] (FAAC)
TCT .... Turbid Creamy Layer on Top [*Laboratory science*] (DAVI)
TCT .... Two-Component TOKAMAK
TcT .... Tympanostomy with Tube Placement [*Otorhinolaryngology*] (DAVI)
TCTA .... Teaching Certificate for Teachers of Art [*British*]
TCTC .... Temperature-Controlled Test Chamber [*EPA engine test*]
TCTC .... Tompkins City Trustco [*NASDAQ symbol*] (TTSB)
TCTC .... Tompkins County Trust Co. [*Ithaca, NY*] [*NASDAQ symbol*] (NQ)
TCTC .... Transportation Corps Technical Committee [*Army*]
TCTFE .... Trichlorotrifluoroethane [*Organic chemistry*]
TCTI .... Time Compliance Technical Instruction (NASA)
TCTL .... Tactical (AAG)
TCTM .... Aircraft Time Compliance Technical Manuals
T Ct Mem .... Tax Court of the United States, Memorandum [*A publication*] (DLA)
TCTNB .... Trichlorotrinitrobenzene [*Organic chemistry*]
TCTO .... Technical Changes to Technical Orders
TCTO .... Time Compliance Technical Order [*NASA*] (AAG)
TCTP .... Tetrachlorothiophene [*Organic chemistry*]
TCTP .... Tricapped Triangular Prism
TCTS .... Tactical Combat Training System [*Navy*]
TCTS .... Tactical Communications Systems Technical Standards [*Military*]
TCTS .... Tank Crew Turret Simulator (MCD)

TCTS	Trans-Canada Telephone System (MCD)
TCTU	Turkish Confederation of Trade Unions
TCTV 00	Tel-Com Wireless Cable TV [*NASDAQ symbol*] (TTSB)
TCTV 00	Tel-Com Wireless Cable TV Corp. [*NASDAQ symbol*] (SAG)
TCTV	Telemedia Communication Television [*Cable-television system*]
TCTV	Today's Child, Tomorrow's Victim [*Book title*]
TCTVA	Tennessee Valley Authority, Technical Library, Chattanooga, TN [*Library symbol Library of Congress*] (LCLS)
TCTVW	Tel-Com Wireless CATV Wrrt [*NASDAQ symbol*] (TTSB)
TCu	Copper T [*An intrauterine contraceptive device*] (DAVI)
TCU	Tactical Control Unit (MCD)
TCU	Taichung [*Taityu*] [*Republic of China*] [*Seismograph station code, US Geological Survey*] (SEIS)
TCU	Tape Control Unit
TCU	Target Control Unit (IAA)
TCU	Tecumseh, MI [*Location identifier FAA*] (FAAL)
TCU	Telecommunications Control Unit (NITA)
TCU	Teletype Communications Unit (NVT)
TCU	Teletypewriter Control Unit (CET)
TCU	Temperature Control Unit
TCU	Tentative Clean Up (MCD)
TCU	Terminal Cluster Unit
TCU	Terminal Control Unit (MCD)
TCU	Test Computer Unit
TCU	Test Control Unit
TCU	Test of Concept Utilization [*Psychometrics*]
TCU	Texas Christian University [*Fort Worth, TX*]
TCU	Thermal Control Unit
TCU	Threshold Control Unit (CET)
TCU	Thrust Control Unit
TCU	Tight Close-Up [*Cinematography*] (NTCM)
TCU	Time Change Unit (MCD)
TCU	Timing Control Unit
TCU	Topping Control Unit (AAG)
TCU	Torpedo Control Unit
TCU	Towering Cumulus [*Meteorology*]
TCU	Transmission Control Unit
TCU	Transportable Computer Unit
TCU	Transportation-Communication Employees Union [*Later, TCIU*]
TCU	Transportation, Communications, and Utilities
TCU	Transportation Communications International Union (NTPA)
TCU	Transportation Control Unit [*MTMC*] (TAG)
TCU	Transport Conversion Unit [*British military*] (DMA)
TCU	Trauma Care Unit [*Medicine*] (DMAA)
TCU	Treatment Control Unit [*Medicine*] (DMAA)
TCU	Tri-College University Library Consortium [*Library network*]
TCU	Turbine Control Unit
TCU	University of Tennessee at Chattanooga, Chattanooga, TN [*Library symbol Library of Congress*] (LCLS)
TCUA	[*The*] Committee to Unite America [*Defunct*] (EA)
TCUA	Time-Critical, Unspecified Area
TCUCC	Texas Christian University Computer Center [*Research center*] (RCD)
TCUL	Tap Changing Under Load (MSA)
TC(UN)	Trusteeship Council of the United Nations
TCUS	Tax Court of the United States [*Also, TC*] [*Later, United States Tax Court*]
TCUSA	Trans Am Club USA (EA)
TCV	Tank Cleaning Vessel (ADA)
TCV	Temperature Coefficient of Voltage
TCV	Temperature Control Valve (AAG)
TCV	Temperature Control Voltage (NAKS)
TCV	Terminal-Configured Vehicle [*NASA*]
TCV	Thoracic Cage Volume [*Medicine*]
TCV	Three Concept View [*Medicine*] (DMAA)
TCV	Throttle Control Valve
TCV	Thrust Chamber Valve (MCD)
TCV	Thrust Control Valve
TCV	TOKAMAK [*Toroidal Kamera Magnetic*] Chauffage Variable [*Plasma physics instrumentation*]
TCV	Total Containment Vessel (CAAL)
TCV	Tracked Combat Vehicle (MCD)
TCV	Transportes Aereos de Cabo Verde [*Cape Verde*] [*ICAO designator*] (FAAC)
TCV	Travelling Convection Vortices
TCV	Treasury Corp. Victoria [*Australia*]
TCV	Troop Carrying Vehicle
TCV	Turbine Control Valve [*Nuclear energy*] (NRCH)
TCV	Turnip Crinkle Virus
TCVA	Terminal-Configured Vehicles and Avionics [*Program*] [*NASA*]
TCVA	Thromboembolic Cerebral Vascular Accident (STED)
TCVA	Thromboembolic Cerebrovascular Accident [*Cardiology*] (DAVI)
TCVC	Tape Control via Console
TCVD	Technical Committee on Veterinary Drugs (EERA)
TCVR	Transceiver (CET)
TCW	Tactical Control Wing [*Air Force*]
TCW	TCW Convertible Security Fund [*Associated Press*] (SAG)
TCW	Time Code Word
TCW	Tinned Copper Weld
TCW	Tocumwal [*Australia Airport symbol*] (OAG)
TCW	Track Confirmation Word [*Computer science*]
TCW	Triple-Crown Resources [*Vancouver Stock Exchange symbol*]
TCW	Troop Carrier Wing [*Military*] (CINC)
TCW 00	TCW/DW Term Trust 2000 [*Associated Press*] (SAG)
TCW 02	TCW/DW Term Trust 2002 [*Associated Press*] (SAG)

TCW 03	TCW/DW Term Trust 2003 [*Associated Press*] (SAG)
T-CW & IB	Trans-Continental Weighing and Inspection Bureau
TCWC	Texas Cooperative Wildlife Collections [*Texas A & M University*] [*Research center*] (RCD)
TCWEM	TCW/DW Emerging Markets Opportunities Trust [*Associated Press*] (SAG)
TCWF	Tibetan Children's Welfare Fund (BUAC)
TCWG	Tasmanian Carpet Wool Growers' Ltd. [*Commercial firm Australia*]
TCWG	Telecommunication Working Group
TCWg	Troop Carrier Wing [*Air Force*] (AFM)
TCX	Transfer of Control Cancellation Message [*Aviation*]
TCXO	Temperature-Compensated Crystal Oscillator
TCXO	Temperature-Controlled Crystal Oscillator
TCXW	Tracer Petroleum Corp. [*NASDAQ symbol*] (SAG)
TCXWF	Tracer Pete Wrrt [*NASDAQ symbol*] (TTSB)
TCXXF	Tracer Petroleum [*NASDAQ symbol*] (TTSB)
TCXXF	Tracer Petroleum Corp. [*NASDAQ symbol*] (SAG)
TCYAW	Twentieth Century Young Adult Writers [*A publication*]
TCZD	Temperature-Compensated Zener Diode
TD	Area Training Director [*Red Cross*]
TD	Chad [*ANSI two-letter standard code*] (CNC)
Td	Dorsal Touch Neurons [*of a leech*]
TD	Table of Distribution [*Military*]
TD	Tabular Data (BUR)
TD	Tactical Director [*Military*] (GFGA)
TD	Tactical Division [*Air Force*]
TD	Takayasu's Disease (DAVI)
TD	Tank Destroyer [*Military*]
TD	Tank Division (MCD)
TD	Tansavio [*ICAO designator*] (AD)
TD	Tape Degausser
TD	Tape Distributor [*Computer science*] (IAA)
TD	Tape Drive
TD	Tardive Dyskinesia [*Medicine*]
TD	Target Designator (MCD)
TD	Target Discrimination
TD	Target Drone
TD	Task Description (AAG)
TD	Task Directive (AAG)
Td	T-Cell, Delayed Type [*Immunology*]
TD	T-cell Dependent (STED)
TD	T-Dependent [*Immunology*]
TD	Teacher's Diploma [*British*]
TD	Teachta Dala [*Member of Parliament*] [*Ireland*]
TD	Tealto Dail [*Member of the Dail*] [*Irish*] (ILCA)
TD	Technical Data
TD	Technical Demonstration (AAG)
TD	Technical Design (AAG)
TD	Technical Development (WDAA)
TD	Technical Direction [*or Directive*]
TD	Technical Director [*Television*]
TD	Technical Discussion
TD	Technical Division
TD	Technical Drawing
TD	Technician's Diploma [*British*] (DI)
TD	Technological Dependence
TD	Technology Demonstration [*NASA*] (RDA)
TD	Technology Document (KSC)
TD	Telegraph Department
TD	Telegraphist Detector [*British military*] (DMA)
TD	Telemetry Data
TD	Telephone Department
TD	Telephone Depot (IAA)
TD	Telephone Directory
T/D	Temperature Datum (NG)
TD	Temperature Differential (MSA)
TD	Temporarily Discontinued [*Fog signal*]
TD	Temporary Disability
TD	Temporary Duty
TD	Teratoma Differentiated (STED)
TD	Ter in Die [*Three Times a Day*] [*Pharmacy*]
TD	Terminal Device [*of a prosthesis*]
TD	Terminal Digit [*Telecommunications*] (TEL)
TD	Terminal Display (BUR)
TD	Terminal Distributor (KSC)
TD	Termination Date (NITA)
TD	Territorial Decoration [*Military British*]
TD	Territorial Efficiency Decoration (WDAA)
TD	Test and Diagnostics (IAA)
TD	Test Data
TD	Test Design Specification (IEEE)
TD	Test Directive (AAG)
TD	Test Director
TD	Test Distributor [*Telecommunications*] (TEL)
TD	Test Drawing (MCD)
TD	Testing and Development Division [*Coast Guard*]
TD	Testing Device (MSA)
TD	Tetanus and Diphtheria [*Toxoids*] [*Medicine*]
Td	Tetrahedral [*Molecular geometry*]
TD	Tetrodotoxin (STED)
TD	Thanatophoric Dysplasia [*Lethal dwarfism*]
TD	Theoretical Density [*Nuclear energy*] (NRCH)
TD	Therapeutic Dietitian (STED)
TD	Therapy [*or Treatment*] Discontinued [*Medicine*]
TD	Thermal Desorption [*from surfaces*]

TD............... Thermal Dilution (STED)
TD............... Thermal Donor (AAEL)
TD............... Thermodilution
TD............... Thiamine Deficient (OA)
TD............... Thioredoxin [Also, TR, Trx] [Biochemistry]
TD............... Third Defense [Men's lacrosse position, until 1933]
TD............... Thoracic Duct [Anatomy]
TD............... Thor-Delta [Satellite]
TD............... Thoria Dispersed [Nickel]
TD............... Threat Determination (MCD)
TD............... Three Times Per Day [Medicine] (STED)
TD............... Threshold Decoding [Computer science] (IAA)
TD............... Threshold Detection
TD............... Threshold Dose [Medicine]
TD............... Threshold of Discomfort [Medicine] (MAE)
TD............... Thymus Dependent [Cells] [Hematology]
TD............... Tibial Dyschondroplasia [Medicine]
TD............... Tidal [Volume] [Laboratory science] (DAVI)
TD............... Tidal Disruption [Astronomy]
TD............... Tied
TD............... Tilbury Docks (ROG)
TD............... Tile Drain [Technical drawings]
TD............... Timed Disintegration [Pharmacy]
TD............... Time Delay
TD............... Time Deposit [Banking]
TD............... Time Difference [or Differential]
TD............... Time Disintegration (MEDA)
TD............... Time Division (SAA)
TD............... Time Docket (DGA)
TD............... Time of Departure
TD............... Timing Device
TD............... Tinned
TD............... Tod [Unit of weight]
TD............... To Deliver [Pipet calibration]
TD............... Tolerance Detector
TD............... Tone Decay [Audiometry] (MAE)
TD............... Tons per Day
TD............... Tool Design
TD............... Tool Disposition
TD............... Tool Drawing (MCD)
TD............... Top Down
T/D............... Top-of-Descent (GAVI)
TD............... Topographic Draftsman [Navy]
TD............... Toronto Dominion Bank [Toronto Stock Exchange symbol Vancouver
                   Stock Exchange symbol]
TD............... Toronto-Dominion Bk [TS symbol] (TTSB)
TD............... Torpedo Dive Bomber Aircraft
TD............... Torsion Dystonia [Medicine] (AAMN)
TD............... Total Damage [Meteorology]
TD............... Total Denier [Textile technology]
TD............... Total Depth
TD............... Total Dictatorship
TD............... Total Disability [Medicine]
TD............... Total Discectomy [Medicine]
TD............... Total Dose [of radiation]
TD............... Total Drift (COE)
T/D............... Touchdown [NASA] (NASA)
TD............... Touchdown [Football]
TD............... Touring Diesel [Automobile model, Mercedes-Benz Motors]
TD............... Towns and Development [Netherlands] (BUAC)
TD............... Toxic Dose (EG)
TD............... Toyota Diffusion/Deposition
TD............... Tracing Dye (OA)
TD............... Track Data
TD............... Track Display
TD............... Track Dog [Dog show term]
TD............... Tracking Dog
TD............... Tractor-Drawn
TD............... Trade Development (AAGC)
TD............... Trade Dispute (OICC)
TD............... Trade Division [British military] (DMA)
TD............... Tradesman [British military]
TD............... TRADEVMAN [Training Devices Man] [Navy rating]
TD............... Traffic Decisions [Interstate Commerce Commission]
TD............... Traffic Department [Scotland Yard]
TD............... Traffic Director
TD............... Training Detachment
TD............... Training Developments
TD............... Training Device (MCD)
TD............... Training of Documentalists
TD............... Trajectory Diagram [Army] (MCD)
TD............... Transaction Diaries [Bureau of the Census] (GFGA)
TD............... Transaction Driven (IAA)
TD............... Transdermal (DAVI)
TD............... Transducer [Electronics] (IAA)
TD............... Transfer Dolly [Bottom-loading transfer cask] [Nuclear energy]
                   (NRCH)
TD............... Transform Domain
TD............... Transient Detector
TD............... Transmission Distributor (NITA)
TD............... Transmit Data (IEEE)
T-D............... Transmitter-Distributor
TD............... Transmitting Data [Modem status information light] [Computer
                   science] (IGQR)
TD............... Transportation and Docking (MCD)

TD............... Transportation Department
TD............... Transportation Disadvantaged [MOCD] (TAG)
TD............... Transport Driver (NOAA)
TD............... Transverse Diameter [Of heart] [Anatomy]
TD............... Transverse Direction
TD............... Transverse Division [Cytology]
TD............... Trapped Domain (IAA)
TD............... Traveler's Diarrhea [Medicine] (DMAA)
TD............... Treasury Decision [In references to rulings]
TD............... Treasury Department
TD............... Treatment Day
T/D............... Treatment Discontinued [Medicine]
TD............... Trinidad and Tobago
TD............... Tropical Depression [Meteorology]
TD............... Tropical Deterioration Committee Reports [of NDRC] [World War II]
TD............... Truck Driving Program [Association of Independent Colleges and
                   Schools specialization code]
TD............... True Depth [Diamond drilling]
TD............... Trust Deed
TD............... Tuberoinfundibular Dopaminergic [Neurons] [Neurology]
TD............... Tumor Dose [Radiation therapy] (DAVI)
TD............... Tunnel Diode
TD............... Turbine Direct
TD............... Turbine Drive [or Driven]
TD............... Turbodiesel [Automotive engineering]
TD............... Turning Diameter [Automotive engineering]
TD............... Turntable Desk (DEN)
TD............... Tyne Division [British military] (DMA)
TD............... Typhoid Dysentery (AAMN)
TD............... Typographic Draftsman [Navy]
TD1............... TRADEVMAN [Training Devices Man], First Class [Navy rating]
TD2............... TRADEVMAN [Training Devices Man], Second Class [Navy rating]
TD3............... TRADEVMAN [Training Devices Man], Third Class [Navy rating]
TD$_{50}$............... Median Toxic Dose [Pharmacology] [Radiation therapy] (DAVI)
TDA............... American Train Dispatchers Association
TDA............... [The] Disposables Association
TDA............... Table of Distribution and Allowances [Military] (AABC)
TDA............... Table of Distribution-Augmentation [Military]
TDA............... Tableware Distributors' Association (BUAC)
TDA............... Tactical Decision Aid
TDA............... Tactical Development Agent [Military] (CAAL)
TDA............... Taking and Driving Away [Motoring offense] [British] (DI)
TDA............... Target Docking Adapter [NASA] (KSC)
TDA............... Tax Deferred Annuity [Insurance]
TDA............... Tax Deposit Account [Banking] (MHDW)
TDA............... Taxi Drivers' Association [Australia]
TDA............... Taxpayer Delinquent Account [IRS]
TDA............... Technical Directing Agency
TDA............... Telecommunications Dealers Association (EA)
TDA............... Telemetric Data Analyzer
TDA............... Temporary Danger Area (DA)
TDA............... Test Development Activity [Army]
TDA............... Test Development Agent (CAAL)
TDA............... Tetradecenyl Acetate [Organic chemistry]
TDA............... Texas Department of Agriculture
TDA............... Textile Distributors Association (EA)
TDA............... Thermal Depolarization Analysis
TDA............... Thermodifferential Analysis
TDA............... Thyroid-Stimulating Hormone-Displacing Antibody [Medicine] (DMAA)
TDA............... Timber Development Association (BUAC)
TDA............... Timber Drying Association [British] (DBA)
TDA............... Time Delay Amplifier
TDA............... Timeshare Developers Association [British] (DBA)
TDA............... Titanium Development Association (EA)
TDA............... Today (FAAC)
TDA............... Toll Dial Assistance [Telecommunications] (TEL)
TDA............... Toluenediamine [Organic chemistry]
TDA............... Tornado Detection Algorithm [Marine science] (OSRA)
TDA............... Torpedo Danger Area (NVT)
TDA............... Total Dissolved Arsenic
TDA............... Town Development Act [Town planning] [British]
TDA............... Tracking and Data Acquisition
TDA............... Tracking Data Analysis
TDA............... Trade and Development Agency (USGC)
TDA............... Trade Development Authority [India] (BUAC)
TDA............... Training and Development Alert [Advanced Personnel Systems]
                   [Information service or system] (CRD)
TDA............... Training Development Advisors (MCD)
TDA............... Transcarga SA [Costa Rica] [ICAO designator] (FAAC)
TDA............... Transportation Development Agency [British]
TDA............... Transportation Development Association (NTPA)
TDA............... Transport Distribution Analysis (DCTA)
TDA............... Treatment Development and Assessment Committee [National
                   Institutes of Health] (EGAO)
TDA............... Trinidad [Colombia] [Airport symbol] (AD)
TDA............... Trunnion Drive Axis (SAA)
TDA............... Tundra Gold Mines [Vancouver Stock Exchange symbol]
TDA............... Tuning Device Assembly
TDA............... Tunnel-Diode Amplifier
TDA............... Tyrosine-D-Arginine [Biochemistry]
TDAA .... Airman Apprentice, TRADEVMAN [Training Devices Man], Striker
                   [Navy rating]
TDA/AE .... Tracking and Data Acquisition/Advanced Engineering
TDaB........... William Jennings Bryan University, Dayton, TN [Library symbol
                   Library of Congress] (LCLS)

TDAC	Training Data and Analysis Center
TDAC	Tropical Deterioration Administrative Committee [*of NDRC*] [*World War II*]
TDAC	Tumor-Derived Activated Cell [*Oncology*]
TDAD	Trade Development Assistance Division [*Bureau of East-West Trade*] [*Former USSR*] (IMH)
TDAE	Tactics Development and Evaluation [*Military*] (MCD)
TDAE	Test Design and Evaluation (MCD)
TDAE	Tetrakis(dimethylamino)ethylene [*Also, TKDE, TMAE*] [*Organic chemistry*]
TDAFP	Turbine-Driven Auxiliary Feed Pump [*Nuclear energy*] (NRCH)
TDAFWP	Turbine-Driven Auxiliary Feedwater Pump [*Nuclear energy*] (NRCH)
TDAG	Technology Development Advocacy Group [*NASA*] (SSD)
TDAIR	Taxpayer Delinquent Account Information Record [*IRS*]
TDAK	Tumor-Derived Activated Killer (DB)
TDAL	Tetradecenal [*Biochemistry*]
TDAMM	Training Device Acquisition Management Model (MCD)
TDAMTB	Tables of Distribution and Allowances Mobilization Troop Basis [*Army*] (AABC)
TDAN	Airman, TRADEVMAN [*Training Devices Man*], Striker [*Navy rating*]
TDANA	Time-Domain Automatic Network Analyzer [*National Institute of Standards and Technology*]
TD & E	Test Design and Evaluation
TD & E	Transposition, Docking, and Ejection [*NASA*] (KSC)
TD & G	Tall, Dark, and Gruesome [*Slang*]
TD & GS	Technical Documentation and Graphic Services
TD & H	Tall, Dark, and Handsome [*Slang*]
TD & I	Technology Development and Integration
TD & RA	Threat Determination and Resource Allocation
TD & RA	Twist Drill and Reamer Association [*British*] (DBA)
TD & SA	Telephone, Data, and Special Audio (NASA)
TDANSW	Timber Development Association (New South Wales) [*Australia*]
TDAP	Total Distribution Action Plan
TDAP	Training Development Action Plan (DOMA)
TDAR	Tactical Defense Alerting RADAR
TDARA	Threat Determination and Resource Allocation (MCD)
TDARDS	Truth Data Acquisition, Recording, and Display System
TDaRI	Tropical Development and Research Institute (PDAA)
TDAS	Tactical Data Automation System (IAA)
TDAS	Thermal Decomposition Analytical System [*For study of incineration*]
TDAS	Thermocouple Data Acquisition System
TDAS	Thickness Data Acquisition System [*Southwest Research Institute*]
TDAS	Tracking and Data Acquisition Satellite (SSD)
TDAS	Tracking and Data Acquisition System
TDAS	Traffic Data Administration System [*Bell System*]
TDAS	Training Device Acquisition Strategy
TDAS	Tunnel-Diode Amplifier System
TDASA	Timber Development Association of South Australia
TDASS	Tracking and Data Acquisition Satellite System (SSD)
TDAT	Technical Directorate Assistance Team [*South Vietnamese studies and observation group team*] (VNW)
TDAT	Teradata Corp. (EFIS)
TDATD	Total Distribution Advanced Technology Demonstration [*Army*]
TDAY	Today's Bancorp [*NASDAQ symbol*] (TTSB)
TDAY	Todays Bancorp, Inc. [*NASDAQ symbol*] (SAG)
T (Day)	Transition Day [*Based on the expected transition from a two-front to a one-front war*] [*World War II*]
T (Day)	Truce Day
TDB	Task Database [*Computer science*] (PCM)
TDB	Technical Directive Bulletin (MCD)
TDB	Temporary Disability Benefits [*Insurance*]
TDB	Temps Dynamique Barycentrique [*Barycentric Dynamical Time*] [*French*]
TDB	Terminological Data Bank
TDB	Terminology Database (NITA)
TDB	Terrain Data Base [*Army*] (RDA)
TDB	Terrestrial Dust Belt
TDB	Test Documentation Booklet [*Navy*] (CAAL)
TDB	Tetebedi [*Papua New Guinea*] [*Airport symbol*] (OAG)
TDB	Top Drawing Breakdown (AAG)
TDB	Total Disability Benefit (DLA)
TDB	Toxicology Data Bank [*National Library of Medicine*] [*Information service or system*] (IID)
TDB	Track Database (MCD)
TDB	Trade and Development Board [*United Nations Conference on Trade and Development*]
TDB	Trade Development Bank [*Subsidiary of American Express Bank*]
TDB	Transportable Database [*Telecommunications*]
TDB	Turbine-Driven Blower
TDB	Welch Aviation, Inc. [*ICAO designator*] (FAAC)
TDbE	Tanna di-be Eliahu (BJA)
TDBG	Training Depot Brigade of Gurkhas [*British military*] (DMA)
TDBI	Test During Burn-In (CIST)
TDBI	Training Directory for Business and Industry [*A publication*]
TDBM	Tactical Data Base Manager (DOMA)
TDBM	Technical Data Base Management [*Environmental science*] (COE)
TDBMS	Tactical Database Management System
TDBP	Tris(dibromopropyl) Phosphate [*Also, TDBPP, Tris, T ris-BP*] [*Flame retardant, mutagen*]
TDBPP	Tris(dibromopropyl) Phosphate [*Also, TDBP, Tris, Tris-BP*] [*Flame retardant, mutagen*]
TDBS	Texas Data Base System (EDAC)
TDC	Chief TRADEVMAN [*Training Devices Man*] [*Navy rating*]
TDC	Dallas Christian College, Dallas, TX [*OCLC symbol*] (OCLC)
TDC	[*The*] Discovery Channel [*Television*]

TDC	Tactical Data Converter
TDC	Tactical Digital Computer (MCD)
TDC	Tactical Document Copier (MCD)
TDC	Tadair SA [*Spain ICAO designator*] (FAAC)
TDC	Taiwan Defense Command (MCD)
TDC	Tank Destroyer Center [*Army*]
TDC	Tape Data Controller [*Computer science*] (CIST)
TDC	Target Data Collection
TDC	Target Data Communicator (DWSG)
TDC	Target Designator Control (MCD)
TDC	Tarif Douanier Commun [*Common Customs Tariff*]
TDC	Taurodeoxycholate [*or Taurodeoxycholic*] Acid [*Biochemistry*]
TDC	Technical Data Center [*Department of Labor*] [*Information service or system*] (IID)
TDC	Technical Development Capital (IAA)
TDC	Technical Development Center
TDC	Technical Development Contractor
TDC	Technical Directive Compliance (MCD)
TDC	Technical Document Center
TDC	Technical Document Change (MCD)
TDC	Technology Development Corp.
TDC	TEFLON Dielectric Capacitor
TDC	Tektronix Development Co. (NITA)
TDC	Teledyne Canada Ltd. [*Toronto Stock Exchange symbol*]
TDC	Temperature Density Computer
TDC	Temporary Detective Constable [*Scotland Yard*]
TDC	Terminal Data Corp. [*Information service or system*] (IID)
TDC	Termination Design Change
TDC	Test Director Console
TDC	Thermal Diffusion Chamber
TDC	Thermal Diffusion Coefficient [*Nuclear energy*] (NRCH)
TDC	Through Deck Cruisers [*British*]
TDC	Time Data Card (AAG)
TDC	Time Delay Closing
TDC	Time Distribution Card (AAG)
TDC	Time-Domain Coding
TDC	Time of Day Clock (IAA)
TDC	Time-to-Digital Converter [*Instrumentation*]
TDC	Tone Digital Command (IAA)
TDC	Tooling Design Change
TDC	Top Dead Center
TDC	Top Desk Computer (IAA)
TDC	Torpedo Data Computer [*Navy*] (NVT)
TDC	Total Design Concept [*Sarcastic reference to a completely coordinated wardrobe, decorating scheme, etc.*] [*Slang*]
TDC	Total Dietary Calories [*Dietetics*] (DAVI)
TDC	Total Distributed Control [*Computer science*]
TDC	Totally Decentralized Control (IAA)
TDC	Tourist Development Corp. of Malaysia
TDC	Track Data Center
TDC	Track Data Central
TDC	Track Data Corp. [*Software firm*] [*Information service or system*] (IID)
TDC	Track Detection Circuit [*Electronics*] (OA)
TDC	Trade Development Corp. [*South Australia*] [*Commercial firm*]
TDC	Trade Development Council [*Hong Kong*] (BUAC)
TDC	Training Device Center
TDC	Transferable Development Credit
TDC	Transistor Digital Circuit (IAA)
TDC	Transistor Digital Control (IAA)
TDC	Transmission Distribution Center (IAA)
TDC	Transportation Development Center [*Cambridge, MA*] [*Department of Transportation Formerly, NASA Electronic Research Center*]
TDC	Transportation Development Centre [*Transport Canada*] [*Research center*] (RCD)
TDC	Transportation Development Centre Library [*UTLAS symbol*]
TDC	Transport Code for Computer (IAA)
TDC	[*US*] Travel Data Center [*BTS*] (TAG)
TDC	Treasury Department Circular [*A publication*] (DLA)
TDC	Tridecylcyclohexane [*Organic chemistry*]
TDC	Trinidad [*Colorado*] [*Seismograph station code, US Geological Survey Closed*] (SEIS)
TDC	Tristate Data Consultants, Inc. [*Database producer*] (IID)
TDC	Tube Deflection Coil
TDC	Two-Dimensional Finite Cylinder (IAA)
TDC	Type Directors Club (EA)
TDC	Tyrosine Decarboxylase [*An enzyme*]
TDCA	Therapeutic Discovery Corp. [*NASDAQ symbol*] (SAG)
TDCB	Tapered Double Cantilever Beam (MCD)
TDCC	Tactical Data Communications Center
TDCC	Transportation Data Coordinating Committee [*Later, EDIA*]
TDCC/EDIA	TDCC [*Transportation Data Coordinating Committee*]: the Electronic Data Interchange Association [*Telecommunications service*] (TSSD)
TDCE	Technical Direction Contract Effort
TDCF	Technical Directive Compliance Form (NVT)
TDCH	Tridecylcyclohexane [*Organic chemistry*]
TDCK	Technisch Documentatie Centrum voor der Krijgsmacht [*Netherland Armed Services Technical Documentation and Information Center*] (MCD)
TDCM	Master Chief TRADEVMAN [*Training Devices Man*] [*Navy rating*]
TDCM	Transistor Driver Core Memory
TD/CMS	Technical Data/Configuration Management System (MCD)
TDCN	Technical Data Change Notice (MCD)
TDCN	Time Delay Compression Network

TDCO	Test Director Console Operator [*Navy*] (CAAL)
TDCO	Thermal Dilution Cardiac Output
TDCO	Torpedo Data Computer Operator [*Navy*]
TDCR	Teacher's Diploma of the College of Radiographers [*British*] (DBQ)
TDCR	Technical Data Change Request [*NASA*] (KSC)
TDCR	Technical Data Contract Requirement (MCD)
TDCR	Test Deficiency Change Request [*Nuclear energy*] (NRCH)
TDCS	Senior Chief TRADEVMAN [*Training Devices Man*] [*Navy rating*]
TDCS	Tactical Deployment Control Squadron
TDCS	Tape Data Control Sheet [*Computer science*]
TDCS	Target Detection-Conversion Sensor
TDCS	Time-Division Circuit Switching [*Telecommunications*]
TDCS	Traffic Data Collection System (MCD)
TDCSP	Tactical Defense Communications Satellite Program (MCD)
TDCT	Time-Domain Coding Technique
TDCT	Track Data Central Tables (SAA)
TDCT	Tunnel-Diode Charge Transformer
TDCTL	Tunnel-Diode Charge-Transformer Logic
TDCU	Target Data Control Unit (AAG)
TDCU	Target Designator Control Unit (MCD)
TDCU	Threat Display Control Unit (MCD)
TDCU	Tinned Copper
TDD	Tactical Data Display
TDD	Target Detecting Device
TDD	Task Description Document (NASA)
TDD	Teardown Deficiency (MCD)
TDD	Technical Data Digest [*Air Force*]
TDD	Technical Documents Division [*Naval Air Systems Command*]
TDD	Telecommunications Device for the Deaf
TDD	Telecommunications for the Deaf and Disabled
TDD	Telemetry Data Digitizer
TDD	Telephone Device for the Deaf
TDD	Test Data Division (SAA)
TDD	Test Definition Document
TDD	Test Design Description [*Nuclear energy*] (NRCH)
TDD	Test Development Director
TDD	Tetradecadiene [*Organic chemistry*]
TDD	Thedford, NE [*Location identifier FAA*] (FAAL)
TDD	Thoracic Duct Drainage [*Medicine*]
TDD	Three D Departments, Inc. [*AMEX symbol*] (SPSG)
TDD	Timing Data Distributor (IAA)
TDD	Timing Defense Depot (SAA)
TDD	Top Down Development (MHDB)
TDD	Total Digitalizing Dose [*Medicine*] (MEDA)
TDD	Tracy Defense Depot (SAA)
TDD	Transdermal Drug Delivery [*Medicine*]
TDD	Treasury Department Decision (AFIT)
TDD	Trinidad [*Bolivia*] [*Airport symbol*] (OAG)
TDD	Tuberculous Diseases Diploma [*British*]
TDDA	Tetradecadienyl Acetate [*Biochemistry*]
TDDA	Three Depts Cl'A' [*AMEX symbol*] (TTSB)
TDD.B	Three D Depts Cv Cl'B' [*AMEX symbol*] (TTSB)
TDDB	Time-Dependent Dielectric Breakdown (AAEL)
TDDD	ThreeD Labs, Inc. Ltd. [*NASDAQ symbol*] (SAG)
TDDL	Time-Division Data Link [*Radio*]
TDDLPO	Time-Division Data Link Print-Out [*Telecommunications*] (IAA)
TDDM	Time-Division Digital Multiplexer (MCD)
TDDM	Training Device Development Management [*Model*] (MCD)
TDDn	Tank Destroyers Division [*Army*]
TDDO	Time Delay Dropout [*Relay*] (AAG)
TDDR	Technical Data Department Report [*NASA*] (KSC)
TDDR	Transdermal Drug Delivery Research
TDDRA	Telephone Disclosure and Dispute Resolution Act (OTD)
TDDRS	Total Dose/Dose Rate Simulator
TDDS	Tactical Data Display System (MCD)
TDDS	Talking Directory Display System [*FTA*] (TAG)
TDDS	Teacher Development in Desegregating Schools [*Office of Education*]
TDDS	Television Data Display System (KSC)
TDDS	Two-Dimensional Deflection System (IAA)
TDE	Tactical Display Element (NVT)
TDE	Tactics Development Evaluation (MCD)
TDE	Technical Data Engineer (MCD)
TDE	Technical Data Evaluation
TDE	Testing Difficulty Estimator
TDE	Tetrachlorodiphenylethane [*Also, DDD*] [*Insecticide*]
TDE	Three Day Event [*Horseriding*] [*British*] (DI)
TDE	Time Displacement Error (IAA)
TDE	Toluene-Dioxane-Ethanol [*Scintillation solvent*]
TDE	Total Daily Energy [*Requirement*] [*Dietary*] (DAVI)
TDE	Total Data Entry
TDE	Total Differential Equation
TDE	Total Digestible Energy [*Nutrition*]
TDE	Transdermal Estradiol [*Pharmacology*]
TDE	Trans-Dominion Energy Corp. [*Toronto Stock Exchange symbol*]
TDE	Triethylene Glycol Diglycidyl Ether [*Medicine*]
TDE	Two-Dimensional Equilibrium
TDEC	Technical Development Evaluation Center
TDEC	Technical Division and Engineering Center [*FAA*] (MCD)
TDEC	Telephone Line Digital Error Checking
TDEC	Tennessee Department of Environmental Conservation
TDEC	Therapeutic Device Evaluation Committee [*Australia*]
TDECC	Tactical Display Engagement Control Console [*Military*] (RDA)
TDED	Trade Data Elements Directory (DS)
TDEFWP	Turbine-Driven Emergency Feedwater Pump [*Nuclear energy*] (NRCH)

TDEL	Time Delay (FAAC)
TDEM	Time-Domain Electromagnetics [*Technique for searching for underground water*]
TDEN	Total Density [*Ecology*]
TDEP	Tracking Data Editing Program [*NASA*]
TDES	[*The*] Duke Ellington Society (EA)
TDEV	Transport-Level Deviation (AAEL)
TDF	Tactical Digital Facsimile (MCD)
TDF	Tape Data Family
TDF	Target Development Facility [*Proposed, 1986, for fusion research*]
TDF	Task Deletion Form [*Nuclear energy*] (NRCH)
TDF	Telediffusion de France [*Broadcasting agency*] [*French*]
TDF	Templeton Dragon Fd [*NYSE symbol*] (TTSB)
TDF	Templeton Dragon Fund [*NYSE symbol*] (SAG)
TDF	Temporary Detention Facility
TDF	Testis-Determining Factor [*Genetics*]
TDF	Theatre Development Fund (EA)
TDF	Thin Dielectric Film
TDF	Thinking Disturbance Factor (STED)
TDF	Thoracic Duct Fistula [*Medicine*] (MAE)
TDF	Thoracic Duct Flow [*Medicine*] (MAE)
TDF	Time-Dependence Fluorescence [*Chemistry*]
TDF	Time-Domain Filter
TDF	Time Dose Fractionation Factor [*Roentgenology*]
TDF	Tissue-Damaging Factor (STED)
TDF	Tonga Defence Force [*British military*] (DMA)
TDF	Training Directors' Forum [*An association*] (EA)
TDF	Transborder Data Flows [*Also, TBDF*] [*Telecommunications*]
TDF	Transformer Differential (IAA)
TDF	Transitional Data Flow [*Computer science*] (DDC)
TDF	Transkei Defence Force [*South Africa*]
TDF	Trial-Dependent-Forgetting [*Process*] [*Psychology*]
TDF	Trim and Drill Fixture (MCD)
TDF	Trunk Distribution Frame (DEN)
TDF	Tumor Dose Fractionation [*Oncology*] [*Radiation therapy*] (DAVI)
TDF	Two Degrees of Freedom
TDFC	Thomas Dolby Fan Club (EA)
TDFCHB	Telemetry Data Format Control Handbook (KSC)
TDFL	Tanzania Development Finance Co. Ltd. (BUAC)
TDFL	Tunnel-Diode FET [*Field-Effect Transistor*] Logic (IAA)
TDFR	Total Duration-Specific Fertility Rate [*Population studies*]
TDFS	Terminal Digit Fitting System [*Military*] (AABC)
TDG	Tactical Decision Game [*Marine Corps*] (DOMA)
TDG	Tactical Development Group [*Military*] (CAAL)
TDG	Tactical Drone Group [*Military*]
TDG	Talladega, AL [*Location identifier FAA*] (FAAL)
TDG	Tandag [*Philippines*] [*Airport symbol*] (OAG)
TDG	Technical Design Guide
TDG	Technical Developing Group [*of the Publishers' Association*] [*British*]
TDG	Telemetry Data Generation
TDG	Test Data Generator (BUR)
TDG	Test Display Generator
TDG	Test Documentation Group
TDG	Tetradecanylglutarate [*Biochemistry*]
TDG	Textile Designers Guild (EA)
TDG	Thio(deaza)guanine [*Antineoplastic drug*]
TDG	Thiodigalactoside [*Organic chemistry*]
TDG	Thiodiglycol [*Organic chemistry*]
TDG	Time Delay Generator
TDG	Timesharer Developers' Group [*British*]
TDG	Toodoggone Gold [*Vancouver Stock Exchange symbol*]
TDG	Top-Down Greedy
TDG	TOTAL Energold Corp. [*Toronto Stock Exchange symbol*]
TDG	Trading (DCTA)
TDG	Transportation of Dangerous Goods [*International symposium*]
TDG	Transport Development Group Ltd. [*British*]
TDG	Twist Drill Gauge
TDGA	Tetradecylglycidate (DB)
TDGL	Test Data Generating Language (MHDB)
TDGO	3-D Geophysical [*NASDAQ symbol*] (TTSB)
TDGO	Three D Geophysical, Inc. [*NASDAQ symbol*] (SAG)
TDGS	Test Data Generation Section [*Social Security Administration*]
TDH	Terre des Hommes [*An international organization*]
TDH	Threonine Dehydrogenase (DB)
TDH	Threonine Dehyrogenase (STED)
TDH	Total Decreased Histamine (STED)
TDH	Total Dynamic Head (AAG)
TDH	Toxic Dose High (OA)
TDH	Tracking Data Handling
TDH	Transport Disengaging Height [*Fluidized beds of particles*]
TDHC	Thermadyne Holdings [*NASDAQ symbol*] (TTSB)
TDHC	Thermadyne Holdings Corp. [*NASDAQ symbol*] (SAG)
TDHGA	Travel of Dependents and Household Goods Authorized [*Military*] (AABC)
TDHL	Transdihydrolisuride [*Biochemistry*]
TDHS	Tape Data Handling System
TDHS	Time Domain Harmonic Scaling [*Telecommunications*] (LAIN)
TDI	[*The*] Democracy International (EA)
TDI	TACAN [*Tactical Air Navigation*] Distance Indicator
TDI	Target Data Inventory [*Military*] (AFM)
TDI	Target Doppler Indicator [*RADAR*]
TDI	Task Description Item (MCD)
TDI	Taxpayer Delinquent Investigation [*IRS*]
TDI	Teardown Inspection
TDI	Technical Data International [*Information service or system*] (IID)

TDI.............. Technology Dynamics Institute [*Telecommunications service*] (TSSD)
TDI.............. Telecommunications Data Interface
TDI.............. Telecommunications for the Deaf, Inc. (EA)
TDI.............. Telegraphist Detector Instructor [*British military*] (DMA)
TDI.............. Teletec Development, Inc. [*Vancouver Stock Exchange symbol*]
TDI.............. Temperature Difference Integrator (STED)
TDI.............. Temporary Disability Insurance [*Unemployment*]
TDI.............. Test Data Interpolation
TDI.............. Textile Dye Institute [*Later, American Dye Manufacturers Institute*]
TDI.............. Therapeutic Donor Insemination [*Obstetrics*]
TDI.............. Therapy Dogs International (EA)
TDI.............. Time Delay and Integration (MCD)
TDI.............. Tolerable Daily Intake [*Toxicology*]
TDI.............. Toluene [*or Tolylene*] Diisocyanate [*Organic chemistry*]
TDI.............. Tool and Die Institute (KSC)
TDI.............. Total Domestic Incomes [*Department of Employment*] [*British*]
TDI.............. Total Dose Infusion [*Medicine*] (MAE)
TDI.............. Trade Data Interchange (DS)
TDI.............. Training Development and Improvement Program [*Department of Education*]
TDI.............. Training Developments Institute [*Army*]
TDI.............. Transportation Displays, Inc. [*A company*] [*Advertising*] [*New York, NY*] (WDMC)
TDI.............. Trasport Device Interface [*Computer science*]
TDI.............. TSH [*Thyroid-Stimulating Hormone*] Displacing Immunoglobulin [*Endocrinology*]
TDI.............. Turbine Disk Integrity [*Nuclear energy*] (NRCH)
TDI.............. Twin Disc [*NYSE symbol*] (TTSB)
TDI.............. Twin Disc, Inc. [*NYSE symbol*] (SPSG)
TDI.............. Two-Wire Direct Interface (MHDB)
TDI.............. Tymnet DTS, Inc. [*San Jose, CA*] [*Telecommunications*] (TSSD)
TDIA............. Tasmanian Dairy Industry Authority [*Australia*]
TDIA............. Transient Data Input Area [*Computer science*] (IAA)
TDIC............. Target Data Input Computer
TDIC............. Total Dissolved Inorganic Carbon [*Environmental chemistry*]
TDIL............. Target Detection, Identification, and Location
TDINF .... Taxpayer Delinquency Investigation Notice File [*IRS*]
TDIO .... Timing Data Input-Output
TDIP .... Total Disability Income Provisions [*Military*] (AABC)
TDIPR .... Test Design In-Process Review (MCD)
TDIPRE .... Target Data Inventory Master Tape Preparation [*Military*] (IAA)
TDIS............. Technical Data Impact Summary (MCD)
TDIS............. Terminal Data Input System (MCD)
TDIS............. Terminal Defense Interceptor Subsystem [*DoD*]
TDIS............. Thai Development Information Service (EAIO)
TDIS............. Time Distance [*Military*] (AABC)
TDIS............. Time Distance Terminal Data Input System (MCD)
TDIS............. Training Development Information System [*Army*]
TDIS............. Travel Document and Issuance System [*US passport*] [*Department of State*]
TDISTR .... Tape Distributor (MSA)
TDIU .... Target Data Input Unit
TDJ.............. Dallas County Community College District, Dallas, TX [*OCLC symbol*] (OCLC)
TDJ.............. Tadjoura [*Djibouti*] [*Seismograph station code, US Geological Survey*] (SEIS)
TDJC .... Technical Data Justification Code [*Army*]
TDK.............. Tardive Dyskinesia [*Neurology*] (DAVI)
TDK.............. TDK Corp. [*NYSE symbol*] (SPSG)
TDK.............. TDK Corp. ADS [*NYSE symbol*] (TTSB)
TDK.............. Test of Diabetes Knowledge
TDK.............. Tokyo Denki Kagaku [*Tokyo Electronics and Chemical Co.*] [*Initialism is now name of recording tape manufacturer and brand name of its products*]
TDKF .... Fahrzeugtestdatenbank [*Dokumentation Kraftfahwesen eV*] [*Germany Information service or system*] (CRD)
TDKP .... Turkish Revolutionary Communist Party [*Political party*] (PD)
TDL.............. David Lipscomb College, Nashville, TN [*OCLC symbol*] (OCLC)
TDL.............. Tactical Data Link
TDL.............. Tandil [*Argentina*] [*Airport symbol*] (OAG)
TDL.............. Tapped Delay Line
TDL.............. Target Development Laboratory [*Eglin AFB*] (AAG)
TDL.............. Task-Directed Learning
TDL.............. Technical Data Laboratory [*National Weather Service*]
TDL.............. Technical Document List
TDL.............. Telemetry Data Link [*Telecommunications*] (IAA)
TDL.............. Test and Diagnostic Language (MCD)
TDL.............. Test Description Log (MCD)
TDL.............. Thoracic Duct Lymph [*Medicine*] (STED)
TDL.............. Thoracic Duct Lymphocyte [*Immunochemistry*]
TDL.............. Threshold Damage Level
TDL.............. Threshold Detection Level
TDL.............. Thymus-Dependent Lymphocyte [*Hematology*]
TDL.............. Topographic Developments Laboratory [*Fort Belvoir, VA*] [*United States Army Engineer Topographic Laboratories*] (GRD)
TDL.............. Toxic Dose Low (OA)
TDL.............. Transaction Definition Language
TDL.............. Transformation Definition Language [*Computer science*] (IBMDP)
TDL.............. Translation Definition Language
TDL.............. Transparent Data Link (SSD)
TDL.............. Tunable Diode LASER [*Also, SDL*]
TDL.............. Tunnel-Diode Logic
TDLAS .... Tunable Diode LASER Absorption Spectrometry
TDLB........... Training and Development Lead Body (AIE)
TDLCA .... Thoracic Duct Lining Cells Antigen [*Immunology*]

TDLo .... Toxic Dose Low (ERG)
TDLO .... Toxic Dose Low [*Environmental science*] (COE)
TDLOA .... Training Device Letter of Agreement
TDLR .... Terminal Descent and Landing RADAR
TDLR .... Training Device Letter Requirement [*Military*]
TDLS............ Topographic Data Library System
TDLS............ Tower Data-Link Services [*FAA*] (TAG)
TDLU .... Terminal Duct Lobular Unit [*Of mammary gland*]
TDM............. Mount Alvernia Friary, Wappingers Falls, NY [*Inactive*] [*OCLC symbol*] (OCLC)
TDM............. Palmyra [*Syria*] [*Airport symbol*] (AD)
TDM............. Tandem (AAG)
TDM............. Tandem Computers [*NYSE symbol*] (TTSB)
TDM............. Tandem Computers, Inc. [*NYSE symbol*] (SPSG)
TDM............. Tandem Resources [*Vancouver Stock Exchange symbol*]
TDM............. Tank Destroyer Armed with Missiles (INF)
TDM............. Tartaric Dimalonate (STED)
TDM............. Task Description Memo (MCD)
TDM............. Technical Division Manager
TDM............. Technology Development Mission [*NASA*] (SSD)
TDM............. Telecommunications Data-Link Monitor (CET)
TDM............. Teledifusao de Macau [*Radio and television broadcasting company*] [*Macau*] (FEA)
TDM............. Telemetric Data Monitor
TDM............. Template Descriptor Memory
TDM............. Ternary Delta Modulation
TDM............. Tertiary Dodecyl Mercaplan (OA)
TDM............. Test Data Memorandum (AAG)
TDM............. Test Development Manager [*Military*] (CAAL)
TDM............. Text and Date Messaging (HGAA)
TDM............. Therapeutic Drug Monitoring
TDM............. Thermal Development Model
TDM............. Thermal Diffusion Method
TDM............. Thermodynamic Molding
TDM............. Time Division Multiplex [*Electronics*]
TDM............. Time Division Multiplexing [*Telecommunications*]
TDM............. Time-Division Multiplexor [*Computer science*] (DOM)
TDM............. Time Driven Monitor (MHDI)
TDM............. Time Duration Modulation (DEN)
TDM............. Tire Degradation Monitor (MCD)
TDM............. Tool Design Manual (MCD)
TDM............. Torpedo Detection Modification [*SONAR*]
TDM............. Total Dissolvable Manganese [*Chemistry*]
TDM............. Tracking Data Message (SSD)
TDM............. Transportation Demand Management [*MOCD*] (TAG)
TDM............. Trehalose Dimycolate [*Biochemistry*]
TDM............. Trouble Detection and Monitoring
TDM............. True Dipole Moment [*Geodesy*]
TDM............. Tunnel-Diode Mixer
TDMA............ Tape Direct Memory Access
TDMA............ Tape Direct Memory Address (NITA)
TDMA............ Time Distributed Multiple Access (IAA)
TDMA............ Time-Division [*or Time-Domain*] Multiple Access [*Computer control system*]
TDMA............ Trophy Dealers and Manufacturers Association (EA)
TDMAC.......... Tridodecylmethylammonium Chloride [*Organic chemistry*]
TDMC........... Technical Data Management Center [*Department of Energy*] [*Information service or system Defunct*] (IID)
TDMD .... Time-Division Multiplex Device [*Radio*]
TDME .... Test, Diagnostic, and Measurement Equipment (MCD)
TDMG .... Telegraph and Data Message Generator (MCD)
TDMIC .... Training Division of Meridian International Center (EA)
TDMM .... International Union of Tool, Die, and Mold Makers
TDMO .... Technical Data Management Office [*Navy*]
TDMP .... Technical Data Management Program [*Navy*]
TDMP .... Technology Development Mission Polar [*Canada*] (SSD)
TDMR .... Technical Division Memo Report [*Army World War II*]
TDMRA .... Texas Delaine-Merino Record Association [*Later, TDSA*] (EA)
TDMS........... Telegraph Distortion Measuring System
TDMS........... Telegraphic Distortion Measuring Set (IAA)
TDMS........... Telemetry Data Monitor Set
TDMS........... Thermal Desorption Mass Spectroscopy
TDMS........... Time-Division Multiplex System [*Radio*] (MCD)
TDMS........... Time-Shared/Data Management System
TDMS........... Toxicology Data Management System [*Department of Health and Human Services*] (GFGA)
TDMS........... Transmission Distortion Measuring Set
TDMTB......... Tables of Distribution Mobilization Troop Basis [*Army*] (AABC)
TDM-VDMA... Time-Division Multiplex - Variable Destination Multiple Access [*Telecommunications*] (TEL)
TDMWG .... Technology Development Missions Working Group [*NASA*] (SSD)
TDN............. Target Doppler Nullifier [*RADAR*]
TDN............. Total Digestible Nutrients
TDN............. Travel as Directed Is Necessary in the Military Service (MUGU)
TDN............. Trimethyldihydronapthalene [*Organic chemistry*]
T-DNA.......... Transfer-Deoxyribonucleic Acid
TDNCA......... Texas Date Nail Collectors Association (EA)
TDNN........... Time Delay Neural Network [*Computer science*]
TDNS........... Total Data Network System (TEL)
TDNS........... Training Device Needs Statement [*Army*]
TDNT .... Theological Dictionary of the New Testament [*A publication*] (BJA)
TDO .... Task Direction Order [*Military*]
TDO .... Technical Development Objective
TDO .... Technical Direction Order
TDO .... Technical Directives Ordnance (NG)

TDO	Technical Divisions Office [*Jet Propulsion Laboratory, NASA*]
TDO	Telegraph Delivery Order
TDO	Time Delay Opening
TDO	Toledo, WA [*Location identifier FAA*] (FAAL)
TDO	Tornado
TDO	Training Development Office [*Army*]
TDO	Training Development Officer [*British*]
TDO	Transistor Dip Oscillator (IAA)
TDO	Transporte Aereco Dominicano [*Dominican Republic*] [*ICAO designator*] (FAAC)
TDO	Treasury Department Order [*A publication*] (DLA)
TDO	Tuesday Downtown Operators and Observers [*An association*] (EA)
TDOA	Time Delay of Arrival (MCD)
TDOA	Time Deposit, Open Account [*Banking*]
TDOA	Time Difference of Arrrival
TDOA/DD	Time Difference of Arrival and Differential Doppler (MCD)
TDOA/DME	Time Difference of Arrival / Distance Measuring Equipment (PDAA)
TDOC	Technical Document (DNAB)
TDOL	Tetradecanol [*Organic chemistry*]
TDOP	Time Dilution of Precision
TDOP	Truck Design Optimization Project [*Railroads*]
TDOS	Tape Disk Operating System [*Computer science*]
TDOT	Thorndike Dimensions of Temperament [*Psychology*]
TDP	Tactical Data Processor (DOMA)
TDP	Tag Distribution Protocol [*Computer science*]
TDP	Tajik Democratic Party (BUAC)
TDP	Tank Development Program [*Military*]
TDP	Target Data Processor (NVT)
TDP	Target Director Post [*RADAR*] [*Military*]
TDP	Technical Data Package [*Military*]
TDP	Technical Development Plan
TDP	Technical Documentation for Provisioning [*Military*] (AFIT)
TDP	Teledata Processing
TDP	Telefonica del Peru SA [*NYSE symbol*] (SAG)
TDP	Telegu Desam Party [*India*] [*Political party*]
TDP	Teluga Desam Party [*India*] (BUAC)
TDP	Temperature and Dew Point (KSC)
TDP	Temperature Density Plotter
TDP	Temporary Detention of Pay
TDP	Terminal Defense Program [*Military*]
TDP	Test Design Plan [*Army*]
TDP	Thermal Death-Point
TDP	Thermistor Detector Package
TDP	Thiamine Diphosphate [*Also, DPT, TPP*] [*Biochemistry*]
TDP	Thiodiphenol [*Organic chemistry*]
TDP	Thoracic Duct Pressure [*Medicine*] (MAE)
TDP	Thymidine Diphosphate [*Biochemistry*]
TDP	Toluene Disproportionation Process [*Organic chemistry*]
TdP	Torsade de Pointes [*Fringe of Pointed Tips*] [*Found on electrocardiograms*] [*Cardiology*] (DAVI)
TDP	Total Development Plan
TDP	Touchdown Protection [*Military*] (MCD)
TDP	Tracking and Display Processor (CAAL)
TDP	Tracking Data Processor
TDP	Trade and Development Program [*US International Development Cooperation Agency*]
TDP	Traffic Data Processing
TDP	Traffic Demand Predictor [*Aviation*]
TDP	Trainee Discharge Program [*Army*]
TDP	Transit Development Program [*TRB*] (TAG)
TDP	Trim and Drain Pump [*Navy*] (CAAL)
TDP	Tryptophan-Deaminase-Positive [*Microorganism*] (DB)
TDP	Turkish Democratic Party [*Bulgaria*] [*Political party*] (BUAC)
TDPA	Textile Data Processing Association [*Later, ATMI*] (EA)
TDPA	Thiodipropionic Acid [*Organic chemistry*]
TDPAC	Time Differential Perturbed Angular Correlation [*Physics*]
TDPB	Tactical Display Plotting Board
TDPD	Dominica/Melville Hall [*Dominica*] [*ICAO location identifier*] (ICLI)
TDPD	Technical Data Package Depository [*Army*]
TDPF	Tail Damping Power Factor [*Aviation*]
TDPF	Target Data Planning File (SAA)
TDPFO	Temporary Duty Pending Further Orders [*Military*]
TDPI	Tasmanian Department of Primary Industry [*State*] (EERA)
TDPI	Two-Dimensional Probabilistic Image (PDAA)
TDPJ	Truck Discharge Point Jet (NATG)
TDPL	Technical Data Package List [*Military*] (AABC)
TDPL	Top-Down Parsing Language
TDPM	Time-Domain Prony Method (IAA)
TDPM	Truck Discharge Point Mogas (NATG)
TDPMP	Technical Data Package Management Plan [*Army*]
TDPOB	Thrift Depositor Protection Oversight Board (BARN)
TDPP	Traffic Data Processing Program (MCD)
TDPR	Roseau [*Dominica*] [*ICAO location identifier*] (ICLI)
TDPRha	Thymidine Diphosphorhamnose [*Biochemistry*]
TDPS	Tracking Data Processor System (MCD)
TDPSA	Association for Totally Dependent Persons of South Australia
TDPSK	Time Differential Phase-Shift Keying
TDPU	Telemetry Data Processing Unit (CAAL)
TDQP	Trimethyldihydroquinoline Polymer [*Organic chemistry*]
TDR	Canair Cargo [*Canada ICAO designator*] (FAAC)
TDR	Short Tour Return Date [*Military*]
TDR	Tail Damping Ratio [*Aviation*]
TDR	Talos Discrepancy Report (MCD)
TDR	Tape Data Register
TDR	Target Detection and Recognition (MCD)

TDR	Target Discrimination RADAR (IEEE)
TDR	TDR: The Drama Review [*A publication*] (BRI)
TDR	Teacher Demonstration Rating (OA)
TDR	Teardown Deficiency Report
TDR	Technical Data Relay (IEEE)
TDR	Technical Data Report
TDR	Technical Data Requests
TDR	Technical Deficiency Report
TDR	Technical Design Review (NASA)
TDR	Technical Development Requirement
TDR	Technical Directive Records (NG)
TDR	Technical Documentary Report
TDR	Temperature-Dependent Resistor (BYTE)
TDR	Temperature Depth Recorder
TDR	Temporarily Disconnected at Subscriber's Request [*Telecommunications*] (TEL)
TDR	Tender [*Navy*] (NVT)
TDR	Terminal Digit Requested [*Telecommunications*] (TEL)
TDR	Test Data Recorder
TDR	Test Data Report (AAG)
TDR	Test Deficiency Report [*Nuclear energy*] (NRCH)
TD/R	Test Disable/Reset (AAG)
TDR	Test Discount Rate
TDR	Test Discrepancy Report (MCD)
TDR	Threat Detection RADAR [*Military*] (CAAL)
TdR	Thymidine [*Genetics*] (DAVI)
TDR	Time Delay Receiver (NITA)
TDR	Time Delay Relay
TDR	Time Domain Reflectometer (NITA)
TDR	Time Domain Reflectometry [*or Reflectometer*]
TDR	Todoroki [*Japan*] [*Seismograph station code, US Geological Survey Closed*] (SEIS)
TDR	Tone Dial Receiver
TDR	Tool Design Request (KSC)
TDR	Torque-Differential Receiver (MUGU)
TDR	Total Defect Rate
TDR	Track Data Request (CAAL)
TDR	Tracking and Data Relay [*NASA*]
TDR	Traffic Data Record (DA)
TDR	Training Device Requirement [*Army*] (AABC)
TDR	Transactional Document Recorder (NITA)
TDR	Transferable Development Rights [*Community planning*]
TDR	Transfer of Development Rights (COE)
TDR	Transistorized Digital Readout
TDR	Transmit Data Register [*Computer science*] (MDG)
TDR	Transnational Data and Communicative Report [*A publication*] (TSSD)
TDR	Transportation Discrepancy Report [*MTMC*] (TAG)
TDR	Trap Designator Register
TDR	Treasury Deposit Receipt
TDR	Triplet-Doublet Resonance [*Physics*]
TDR	Tropical Disease Research [*WHO*]
TDR	Tudor Corp. Ltd. [*Toronto Stock Exchange symbol*]
TDR	Turndown Ratio
TdR-³H	Tritiated Thymidine [*Genetics*] (DAVI)
TDRC	Total Diet Research Center [*Public Health Service*] (GRD)
TDRE	Tracking and Data Relay Experiment [*Telecommunications*] (TEL)
TDRF	Target Doppler Reference Frequency
TDRI	Tropical Development and Research Institute [*Research center British*] (IRC)
TDRL	Temporary Disability Retired List [*Military*]
T/DRLY	Time Delay Relay
TDRM	Time-Domain Reflectometry Microcomputer
TDRP	TearDrop Golf Co. [*NASDAQ symbol*] (SAG)
TDRR	Test Data Recording and Retrieval (NASA)
TDRRB	Technical Data Requirement Review Board
TDRRC	Training Device Requirements Review Committee [*Army*]
TDRS	Technical Data Requirements Sheet
TDRS	Telemetering Data Recording Set (CAAL)
TDRS	Telemetry Downlist Receiving Site (NASA)
TDRS	Text Data Retrieval System (NITA)
TDRS	Tracking and Data Relay Satellite [*NASA*]
TDRS	Traffic Data Recording System [*Bell System*]
TDRS	Transnational Data Reporting Service, Inc. [*Springfield, VA*] [*Telecommunications service*] (TSSD)
TDRS	Travelers, Defect Route Sheet (DNAB)
TDRSS	Tracking and Data Relay Satellite Services [*or System*] [*NASA*]
TDRSS	Tracking and Data Relay Satellite System [*Instrument*] (EERA)
TDRTC	Tank Destroyer Replacement Training Center
TDS	Tactical Data System
TDS	Tactical Deployment Support
TDS	Tactical Display System (CAAL)
TDS	Tactical Drone Squadron
TDS	Tape Data Selector
TDS	Tape Decal System
TDS	Target Data Sheet (MCD)
TDS	Target Designation System [*Navy*]
TDS	Tasmanian Deaf Society [*Australia*]
TDS	Teacher Demand and Shortage Survey [*Department of Education*] (GFGA)
TDS	Team Development Survey [*Test*] (TMMY)
TDS	Technical Database Services, Inc. [*Information service or system*] (IID)
TDS	Technical Data Specialist
TDS	Technical Data System (KSC)

TDS..............	Technical Description Sheet
TDS..............	Technical Directive System (MCD)
TDS..............	Technology Delivery System (NUCP)
TDS..............	Technology Demonstration Satellite [NASA] (NASA)
TDS..............	Teleflora Delivery Service (EA)
TDS..............	Telemetry Decommutation System
TDS..............	Telephone & Data Sys [AMEX symbol] (TTSB)
TDS..............	Telephone & Data Systems, Inc. [AMEX symbol] (SPSG)
TDS..............	Teleprocessing Design Center [Army] (PDAA)
TDS..............	Temperature-Depth-Salinity [Oceanography]
TDS..............	Temperature-Determined Sex [Laboratory science] (DAVI)
TDS..............	Temporary Duty Station [Air Force] (AFM)
TDS..............	Ter in Die Sumendum [To Be Taken Three Times a Day] [Pharmacy]
TDS..............	Tertiary Data Set [Computer science] (OA)
TDS..............	Test Data Sheet (KSC)
TDS..............	Test Data Specification (IAA)
TDS..............	Test Data System (NASA)
TDS..............	Thermal Degradation Sample [Apollo]
TDS..............	Thermal Desorption Spectroscopy
TDS..............	Third Dimension Society of Great Britain (BUAC)
TDS..............	Time Delay Switch
TDS..............	Time, Distance, Speed
TDS..............	Time Distribution System (MCD)
TDS..............	Time-Division Switching [Telecommunications]
TDS..............	Time-Domain Spectroscopy (IEEE)
TDS..............	Tool Data Sheet (MCD)
TDS..............	Tool Design Service (MCD)
TDS..............	Tool Design Study (MCD)
TDS..............	Torpedo Deflection Sight
TDS..............	Torpedo Destruction System
TDS..............	Total Dissolved Solids
TDS..............	Track Data Simulator
TDS..............	Track Data Storage
TDS..............	Tracking and Data System [NASA]
TDS..............	Training Depot Station [British military] (DMA)
TDS..............	Training Developments Study
TDS..............	Training Directors Seminar [LIMRA]
TDS..............	Transaction Distribution System
TDS..............	Transaction Driven System [Honeywell, Inc.]
TDS..............	Transistor Display and Data-Handling System [Computer science] (MDG)
TDS......:......	Translation and Docking Simulator [Navy] (KSC)
TDS..............	Transportation Data Sampler [BTS] (TAG)
TDS..............	Trap Designator Set
TDS..............	Trash Disposal System
TDS..............	Traverse des Sioux Library System, Mankato MN [OCLC symbol] (OCLC)
TDS..............	Tuned LASER Differential Spectrometry (IAA)
TDS..............	Tunnel Destruct System
TDSA	Technical Data Status Accounting (MCD)
TDSA	Technical Directive Status Accounting
TDSA	Telegraph and Data Signals Analyzer (MCD)
TDSA	Texas Delaine Sheep Association (EA)
TDSA	TRADEVMAN [Training Devices Man], Seaman Apprentice [Navy rating]
TDSC	3-D Systems Corp. [NASDAQ symbol] (TTSB)
TDSC	Three D Systems [NASDAQ symbol] (SAG)
TDSC	Training Device Support Center [Army]
TDSCC	Tidbinbilla Deep Space Communications Complex
TDSDT	Tactical Data System Development Testbed
TDSF...........	Tasmanian Department of Sea Fisheries [Australia]
TDSF...........	Technical Data Support Facility
TDSIC	Theatre/Drama, and Speech Information Center (IID)
TDSMO	Tactical Data Systems Management Office [Fort Leavenworth] [Army] (MCD)
TDSN	TRADEVMAN [Training Devices Man], Seaman [Navy rating]
TDSO	Training Device Supply Office [Navy] (DNAB)
TDSP	Technical Data Support Package [Navy]
TDSP	Top Down Structured Programming (MHDB)
TDSQB	Time Delay Squib [Navy]
TDSS	Telemetry Data Signal Simulator (MCD)
TDSS	Time-Dependent Stokes Shift [Physical chemistry]
TDSS	Time Dividing Spectrum Stabilization [Electronics] (OA)
TDSS	Turret Drive Subsystem (DWSG)
TDSSC	Tone Dial Switching System Control (IAA)
TDST...........	Track Data Storage (MSA)
TDSTP	Trainer Digital Self-Test Program
TDT.............	Tactical Data Terminal (MCD)
TDT.............	Tank Driver Trainer [Army]
TDT.............	Target Designation Transmitter
TDT.............	Target Docking Trainer [NASA] (KSC)
TDT.............	Task Dispatch Table [Computer science] (OA)
TDT.............	Tavil-Dara [Former USSR Seismograph station code, US Geological Survey Closed] (SEIS)
TDT.............	TCW/DW Term Trust 2000 [NYSE symbol] (SPSG)
TDT.............	Tentative Drainage Tomorrow [Surgery] (DAVI)
TDT.............	Terminal Death Time (OA)
TDT.............	Terminal Deoxynucleotidyl Transferase [An enzyme]
TDT.............	Terminal Deoxytransferase [An enzyme] (DAVI)
TDT.............	Terrestrial Dynamic Time (WGA)
TDT.............	Test Direction Team
TDT.............	Test Dwell Time
TDT.............	Thermal Death Time [Bacteriological testing]
TDT.............	Thiodiethanethiol [Organic chemistry]
TDT.............	This Day Tonight (ADA)

TDT.............	Tidioute, PA [Location identifier FAA] (FAAL)
TDT.............	Tone Decay Test [Audiometry]
TDT.............	Toronto Dance Theatre
TDT.............	Total Delay Time
TDT.............	Total Downtime
TDT.............	Tower Disconnect Technician (SAA)
TDT.............	Translation and Docking Trainer
TDT.............	Transmission Disequilibrium Test [Genetics]
TDT.............	Transonic Dynamic Tunnel [NASA]
TDT.............	Tumor Doubling Time [Cytology]
TDT.............	Tunnel-Diode Transducer
TDT.............	Turret Director Trainer [British military] (DMA)
TDTA	Templin Darley Test of Articulation [Speech and language therapy] (DAVI)
TDT and CU...	Target Designation Transmitter and Control Unit
TD/TDNA......	Tardive Dyskinesia/Tardive Dystonia National Association (EA)
TDT/FC........	Tank Destroyer Tactical and Firing Center
TDTG	True Date-Time Group [Military]
TDTL	Tunnel-Diode Transistor Logic
TDTL	Tunnel Diode Tunnel Logic (NITA)
TDTO	Transmission and Drive Train Oil
TDTOX	Tetradichloroxylene (COE)
TDTS	Tactical Data Transfer System (NATG)
TDTTEABL....	Tax Detectable to the Extent Allowed by Law
TDU	Tactical Deception Unit (NVT)
TDU	Tactical Display Unit (NVT)
TDU	Talos Defense Unit (SAA)
TDU	Target Detection Unit
TDU	Teamsters for a Democratic Union (EA)
TDU	Threat Display Unit (MCD)
TDU	Time Display Unit (NASA)
TDU	Tondu [British depot code]
TDU	Torpedo Development Unit [Ministry of Technology] [British]
TDU	Towed Unit [Aerial Target] (CAAL)
TDU	Tracking Display Unit
TDU	Trash Disposal Unit (DNAB)
TDU	Traverse Displacement Unit (DNAB)
TDU	Trigger Delay Unit
TDU	Tropendienstunfaehig [Unfit for service in tropics] [German military - World War II]
TDUM	Tape Dump and Utility Monitor [Computer science]
TDUP	Technical Data Usage Program
TDUR	Therapeutic Drug Utilization Review [Insurance] (WYGK)
TDV	Technology Development Vehicle (IEEE)
TDV	Terminal Delivered Vehicle [Army]
TDV	Test Data Van (NASA)
TDV	Test Data Variation
TDV	Touchdown Velocity [Aviation]
TDV	Tumbleweed Diagnostic Vehicle
TDVA	37th Division Veterans Association (EA)
TDW	Amarillo, TX [Location identifier FAA] (FAAL)
TDW	Tidewater, Inc. [NYSE symbol] (SPSG)
TDW	Tons Deadweight (DS)
TDW	Trunk Destination Words (CET)
TDW	Turbo Debugger for Windows [Computer science] (PCM)
TDWB	Touch-Down Weight-Bearing [Orthopedics and rehabilitation] (DAVI)
TDWG	Taxonomic Databases Working Group for Plant Sciences (EERA)
TDWO	Test and Development Work Order
TDWR	Terminal Doppler Weather RADAR (DWSG)
TDWT	Transonic Dynamic Wind Tunnel [NASA] (KSC)
TDWU	Transport and Dock Workers' Union [India]
TDX	Thermal Demand Transmitter (MSA)
TDX	Time-Division Exchange
TDX	Torque-Differential Transmitter (MUGU)
TDX	Tracking Dog Excellent
TDX	Transportation Data Xchange, Inc. (IID)
TDX	Tridex Corp. [AMEX symbol] (SPSG)
TDX	Wrangler Aviation, Inc. [FAA designator] (FAAC)
TDXT	ThreeDX Technologies, Inc. [NASDAQ symbol] (SAG)
TDY	Air Today, Inc. [ICAO designator] (FAAC)
TDY	Teledyne, Inc. [NYSE symbol] (SPSG)
TDY	Temporary Duty
TDY	Trading Bay, AK [Location identifier FAA] (FAAL)
TDYPrE	Teledyne Inc. Sr'E' Pfd [NYSE symbol] (TTSB)
TDZ	Thioridazine [Tranquilizer]
TDZ	Thymus-Dependent Zone [Hematology] (MAE)
TDZ	Toledo, OH [Location identifier FAA] (FAAL)
TDZ	Torpedo Danger Zone (NVT)
TDZ	Touchdown [Aviation] (FAAC)
TDZ	Trade Development Zone (ADA)
TDZ	Transcontinental Dislocation Zone [Geology]
TDZ	Tridel Enterprises, Inc. [Toronto Stock Exchange symbol]
TDZA	Trade Development Zone Authority [Northern Territory, Australia]
TDZ/CL........	Touchdown Zone/Centerline [Aviation] (DNAB)
TDZE	Touchdown Zone Elevation [Aviation] (DA)
TDZL	Touchdown Zone Light System [Aviation] (FAAC)
TE	Electron Temperature [Plasma physics] (OA)
TE	[The] Engelettes [An association Defunct] (EA)
T-e	Erythrocyte Tri-Iodothyronine [Endocrinology] (DAVI)
TE	Light Temporarily Extinguished [Navigation]
TE	Ling-Temco-Vought [LTV] [ICAO aircraft manufacturer identifier] (ICAO)
TE	Table of Equipment [Army]
T/E	Tactical Emergency [Army]

TE	Tageseinfluesse [*Weather factors, a gunnery term*] [*German military - World War II*]
TE	Tail End (AAEL)
TE	Talmudic Encyclopedia [*A publication*] (BJA)
TE	Tamper Evident
TE	Tangent Elevation (MSA)
TE	Tape Error [*Computer science*] (IAA)
TE	Task Element
TE	Tatin Experimental [*British military*] (DMA)
TE	Tax-Equivalent (EBF)
TE	Taxiway Edge Lighting [*Aviation*] (DA)
TE	Teacher of Electrotherapy [*British*]
TE	Technical Engineer
TE	Technical Evaluation [*Army*]
TE	Technical Exchange
TE	Technician [*Communications*] [*Navy rating*]
TE	Technological Engineer [*A publication*]
TE	TECO Energy [*NYSE symbol*] (TTSB)
TE	TECO Energy, Inc. [*NYSE symbol*] (SPSG)
TE	Telecom Eireann [*Dublin, Ireland*] [*Telecommunications service*] (TSSD)
TE	Telecommunications Engineering (WDAA)
TE	Tele-Engineering Corp. [*Telecommunications service*] (TSSD)
TE	Telegram
TE	Telegraph Editor [*Journalism*] (WDMC)
TE	Teleman [*Navy rating British*]
TE	Telemetry Event [*Telecommunications*] (IAA)
TE	Telephone Equipment Room [*NFPA pre-fire planning symbol*] (NFPA)
TE	Teller of the Exchequer [*British*] (ROG)
Te	Tellurium [*Chemical element*]
TE	Temperature Element [*Nuclear energy*] (NRCH)
TE	Temporary Employee [*Business term*] (MHDB)
TE	Tenants by the Entirety [*Legal term*]
TE	Tennis Elbow [*Medicine*] (DMAA)
TE	Tension Equalizer [*Electrical*] Wave
TE	Terminal [*Computer science*] (IAA)
TE	Terminal Equipment
TE	Terminal Exchange (MCD)
TE	Test and Engineering (MCD)
TE	Test Ear [*Otorhinolaryngology*] (DAVI)
TE	Test Equipment
TE	Test Exception [*Nuclear energy*] (NRCH)
TE	Test Explicit
Te	Tetanus [*Medicine*] (WGA)
TE	Tetracycline [*Antibiotic compound*]
TE	Text Editor [*Computer science*]
TE	Theatre in Education (EA)
TE	Theistic Evolutionist
TE	Theological Educator [*A publication*]
TE	Theological Examination
TE	Thermactor Emission [*Automotive engineering*]
TE	Thermal Efficiency
TE	Thermal Element (KSC)
TE	Thermal Expansion Load [*Nuclear energy*] (NRCH)
TE	Thermoelectric
TE	Thioesterase [*An enzyme*]
TE	Threat Evaluation (NVT)
TE	Threshold Element (IAA)
TE	Threshold Energy [*Medicine*] (MAE)
TE	Threshold Exceeded
TE	Thromboembolic [*Medicine*]
TE	Throughput Efficiency (CAAL)
TE	Thunder Engines Corp. [*Vancouver Stock Exchange symbol*]
TE	Thymus Epithelial [*Cell*] [*Immunology*] (DAVI)
TE	Tight End [*Football*]
Te	Tigre (BJA)
TE	Time Earliest/Expected (NASA)
TE	Time Electronics (GFGA)
TE	Time Equipment (IAA)
TE	Time Error in Psychophysical Judgments [*Psychology*]
TE	Time Estimation (DAVI)
T/E	Time Expired (ADA)
TE	Time to Echo [*Medicine*]
TE	Timing Electronics (KSC)
TE	Tissue-Equivalent [*Medicine*] (MAE)
TE	Tocopherol Equivalent [*Nutrition*]
TE	Toluene-Ethanol [*Scintillation solvent*]
TE	Tonsillectomy [*Medicine*] (DAVI)
TE	Tonsils Excised [*Medicine*] (DAVI)
TE	Tooth Extracted (MAE)
TE	Top Eliminator [*Automobile racing*] (DICI)
TE	Topographical Engineer
TE	Tornisterempfaenger [*Pack-type portable receiver*] [*German military - World War II*]
TE	Total Earnings (MHDB)
TE	Total Estrogen [*Medicine*] (MAE)
TE	Total Expenditure
TE	Totally Embedded (DAVI)
TE	Totally Enclosed (MSA)
TE	Toxoplasma Encephalitis [*Neurology*] (DAVI)
TE	Trace Elements [*Chemistry*] (DAVI)
TE	Tracheary Element [*Botany*]
TE	Tracheoesophageal [*Also, TOE*] [*Medicine*]
TE	Tracking Enhancement (MCD)
TE	Traction Engine [*British*]
TE	Trade Expenses [*Business term*]
TE	Trading Expert
TE	Trailing Edge [*Aviation*]
TE	Training and Evaluation (OICC)
TE	Training Equipment
TE	Training Establishment [*British military*] (DMA)
TE	Trajectory Engineer
TE	Transearth (SAA)
TE	Transequatorial [*Scatter*]
TE	Transient Eddy
TE	Transient Event [*Nuclear energy*] (NRCH)
TE	Transistor Equivalent [*Electronics*] (IAA)
TE	Transitional Engineering (MCD)
TE	Transmission Error [*Automotive engineering*]
TE	Transportation Engineer Magazine [*A publication*] (EAAP)
TE	Transport Empty
T/E	Transporter-Erector [*NASA*] (KSC)
TE	Transposable Element [*Genetics*]
TE	Transverse Electric [*or Electrostatic*] [*Wave propagation mode*]
TE	Transverse Electrostatic (IAA)
TE	Treadmill Exercise (DAVI)
TE	Trial and Error
TE	Triple Expansion (DS)
TE	Trunk Equalizer [*Telecommunications*] (OA)
TE	Tuning Eye
TE	Turbine Electric Drive
TE	Turbine Engine (WDAA)
TE	Twin Engine
TE2	Type Equipment (MCD)
TE2	That's Entertainment, Part 2 [*Initialism is shortened form of movie title*]
TEA	Targeted Export Assistance Program [*Later, MAP*] [*Department of Agriculture*]
TEA	Task Equipment Analysis
TEA	T Early Alpha [*Genetics*]
TEA	Technical Engineers Association (EA)
TEA	Technical Exchange Agreement
TEA	Tegra Enterprises, Inc. [*Vancouver Stock Exchange symbol*]
TEA	Tela [*Honduras*] [*Airport symbol*] (AD)
TEA	Templeton Emerging Market Appreciation Fund [*NYSE symbol*] (SAG)
TEA	Templeton Energ Mkts Apprec [*NYSE symbol*] (TTSB)
TEA	Temporary Employment Assistance
TEA	Tensile Energy Absorption [*Physics*]
TEA	Test and Evaluation Agency
TEA	Test Engineer's Assistant [*Computer-aided design tool*]
TEA	Test Equipment Accessory (MCD)
TEA	Test Equipment Analysis
TEA	Tetraethylammonium [*Organic chemistry*]
TEA	Textile Educators' Association [*Australia*]
TEA	Textile Export Association of the US (EA)
TEA	Thai Exiles Association (CINC)
TEA	Theatre Education Association (NTPA)
TEA	Theatre Equipment Association (EA)
TEA	The Easy Animator [*Computer software*]
TEA	Thermal Energy Analysis [*or Analyzer*]
TEA	Thiazoylethylamine [*Organic chemistry*]
TEA	Thromboendarterectomy [*Medicine*] (DMAA)
TEA	Tiselius Electrophoresis Apparatus
TEA	Titanic Enthusiasts of America [*Later, THS*] (EA)
TEA	Torque Equilibrium Attitude (SSD)
TEA	Total Elbow Arthroplasty [*Medicine*] (DMAA)
TEA	Total Endarterectomy [*Cardiology*] (DAVI)
TEA	Trade Expansion Act [*1962*]
TEA2	Training Effectiveness Analysis
TEA	Trans European Airways [*Belgium ICAO designator*] (FAAC)
TEA	Transferred Electron Amplifier
TEA	Transportability Engineering Analysis [*Army*]
TEA	Transversely Excited Atmospheric [*LASER*] (RDA)
TEA	Treasury Enforcement Agent
TEA	Triethanolamine [*Organic chemistry*]
TEA	Triethylaluminum [*Organic chemistry*]
TEA	Triethylamine [*Organic chemistry*]
TEA	Triethylammonium [*Organic chemistry*]
TEA	Tunnel-Emission Amplifier (IEEE)
TEAA	Triethylammonium Acetate [*Organic chemistry*]
TEAAC	Trade Expansion Act Advisory Committee [*Terminated, 1975*] (EGAO)
TEAB	Tetraethylammonium Bromide [*Organic chemistry*]
TEAC	Technical Education Advisory Council (BUAC)
TEAC	Test and Evaluation Advisory Council [*Military*] (CAAL)
TEAC	Tetraethylammonium Chloride [*Organic chemistry*]
TEAC	Texas Eastern Athletic Conference (PSS)
TEAC	Tokyo Electro Acoustical Co. [*Acronym is now name of electronics company and brand name of its products*]
TEAC	Transition Education Advisory Committee (AIE)
TEAC	Turbine Engine Analysis Check (AABC)
TEACH	[*The*] Equity and Choice Act
TEACH	Teacher
TEACH	Teacher Equity and Choice Act [*Proposed*]
TEACH	Teaching Each Other about Conquering Handicaps (EA)
TEACH	Training and Education Activities Clearing House [*Military*]
TEACHCERT	Teaching Certificate
Teach Mus	Teaching Music [*A publication*] (BRI)
TEAD	Tooele Army Depot [*Utah*] (AABC)

TEADDA...... Teledyne Electrically-Alterable Digital Differential Analyzer (IAA)

TE/AE........ Tigers East/Alpines East (EA)

TEAE......... Triethylaminoethyl [*Organic chemistry*]

TEA-ER....... Traffic Executives Association, Eastern Railroads [*Later, ERA*]

TEAF.......... Tetraethyl-Ammonium Fluoride [*Organic chemistry*]

TEAF.......... Total Environmental Action Foundation [*Defunct*] (EA)

TEAF.......... Triethylammonium Formate [*Organic chemistry*]

TEAHA....... Trans-East African Highway Authority (EA)

TEAHAT...... Thrombolysis Early in Acute Heart Attack Trial [*Cardiology study*]

TEAL.......... Tactics, Equipment, and Logistics Conference [*between US, Great Britain, Australia, and Canada*] [*Developed "duck" designations for Mallard and Gander military communications systems*]

TEAL.......... Tasman Empire Airways Ltd. [*Australia*] (ADA)

TEAL.......... Teeside Automated Library (NITA)

TEAL.......... Transversely Excited Atmospheric LASER (RDA)

TEAL.......... TriTeal Corp. [*NASDAQ symbol*] (SAG)

TEA laser.... Transversely Excited Atmospheric-Pressure LASER (MED)

TEALS........ Triethanolamine Lauryl Sulfate [*Organic chemistry*]

TEAM........ [*The*] European-Atlantic Movement [*British*]

TEAM........ [*The*] Evangelical Alliance Mission (EA)

TEAM........ National TechTeam, Inc. [*NASDAQ symbol*] (NQ)

TEAM........ Natl TechTeam Inc. [*NASDAQ symbol*] (TTSB)

TEAM........ Teacher Education and Mathematics Project (EDAC)

TEAM........ Teacher Education and Media [*Project*]

Team......... Team, Inc. [*Associated Press*] (SAG)

TEAM........ Teamster Economic Action Mobilization

TEAM........ Tech-Base Enhancement for Autonomous Machines [*Military*] (RDA)

TEAM........ Technical Engineer-Architect Management (MCD)

TEAM........ Technical Engineering and Maintenance

TEAM........ Technique for Evaluation and Analysis of Maintainability

TEAM........ Techniques for Effective Alcohol Management [*NHTSA*] (TAG)

TEAM........ Technology Evaluation and Acquisition Method

TEAM........ Teleterminals Expandable Added Memory

TEAM........ Tellington-Jones Equine Awareness Movement

TEAM........ Terminology Evaluation and Acquisition Method

TEAM........ Test and Evaluation of Air Mobility

TEAM........ Test, Evaluation, Analysis, and Modeling [*Army*] (RDA)

TEAM........ The Environmental Assessment Management (BCP)

TEAM........ Together Everyone Achieves More

TEAM........ Top European Advertising Media

TEAM........ Torpedo Evasive Maneuvering (MCD)

TEAM........ Total Environment Analysis and Management (EERA)

TEAM........ Total Exposure Assessment Methodology [*or Monitoring*] [*Environmental chemistry*]

TEAM........ Training and Education in Adoption Methods [*Conference sponsored by the North American Council on Adoptable Children*]

TEAM........ Training/Employment of Automotive Mechanics [*Project*]

TEAM........ Training Equipment and Maintenance [*Aviation*] (DA)

TEAM........ Training in Expanded Auxiliary Management

TEAM........ Trend Evaluation and Monitoring [*Congressional Clearinghouse on the Future*] (EA)

TEAM........ Trimmed Element Analysis Method [*Computer modeling*]

TEAM........ Truck Expense Analysis and Management [*Computer science*]

TEAM........ Truth, Esteem, Attitude, and Motivation [*Name of actor Chuck Norris' anti-gang project*]

TEAM........ Tube Earphone and Microphone (DNAB)

TEAM A....... Theological Education Association of Mid-America, Library Section [*Library network*]

TEAMA....... Top End Aboriginal Music Association [*Australia*]

TEAME....... Teacher Educators and Advisers in Media Education (AIE)

TEAMMATE... Total Electronic Advanced Microprocessing Maneuvers and Tactics Equipment [*A game*]

TeamRn...... Team Rental Group [*Associated Press*] (SAG)

TEAMS........ Technical Evaluation and Acquisition Management Support [*Air Force*]

TEAMS........ Test Evaluation and Monitoring System

TEAMS........ Tests of Engineering Aptitude, Mathematics, and Science

TEAMS........ Texas Educational Assessment of Minimum Skills

TEAMS........ Trend and Error Analysis Methodology System (MCD)

TEAM-UP .... Test, Evaluation, Analysis, and Management Uniformity Plan [*or Procedure*] [*Army*]

TE & I........ Technology Evaluation and Integration (MCD)

TE & R........ Tactical Engagement and Range [*Army*]

TEAP.......... Tetraethylammonium Perchlorate [*Organic chemistry*]

TEAP.......... Trajectory Error Analysis Program [*NASA*]

TEAP.......... Transversely Excited Atmospheric Pressure

TEAP.......... Triethylammonium Phosphate [*Organic chemistry*]

TEAPA........ Triethanolamine Phosphoric Acid [*Organic chemistry*]

TEAR.......... [*The*] Evangelical Alliance Relief [*of The TEAR Fund*] (EA)

TEAR.......... Time, Elevation, Azimuth, Range (MCD)

TEARR........ Times, Elevations, Azimuths, Ranges, and Range Rates [*Aerospace*]

TEARS .... [*The*] Exeter Abstract Reference System [*Exeter University*] [*Information service or system*] (IID)

TEARS .... Traffic Engineering for Automatic Route Selection (PDAA)

TEAS .... Technical and Engineering Acquisition Support [*Air Force*]

TEAS .... Test and Evaluation, Aircraft Survivability

TEAS .... Threat Evaluation and Action Selection [*Civilian defense program*]

TEAS .... Time Elapsed After Study (MHDI)

TEASE........ Tracking Errors and Simulation Evaluation [*RADAR*]

TEASER....... Tunable Electron Amplifier for Stimulated Emission of Radiation (MCD)

TEASOL....... Teaching of English to Adult Speakers of Other Languages [*Australia*]

teasp .... Teaspoonful

TEAT .... Obras de Teatro Estrenadas en Espana [*Ministerio de Cultura*] [*Spain Information service or system*] (CRD)

TEA-TOW ..... Training Effectiveness Analysis - Tube-Launched Optically Tracked Wire-Guided (MCD)

TEAV........... Totalisator Employees' Association of Victoria [*Australia*]

TEAWC........ Totally-Enclosed Air Water-Cooled Reactor [*Nuclear energy*] (IAA)

TEB .... Tape Error Block [*Computer science*] (IAA)

TEB .... Tax-Exempt Bond [*Investment term*]

TEB .... Teterboro [*New Jersey*] [*Airport symbol*] (AD)

TEB .... Teterboro, NJ [*Location identifier FAA*] (FAAL)

TEB .... Textile Economics Bureau

TEB .... Tone Encoded Burst

TEB .... Transcutaneous Endomyocardial Biopsy [*Cardiology*] (CPH)

TEB .... Transient Electric Birefringence [*Physics*]

TEB .... Triethylbenzene [*Organic chemistry*]

TEB .... Triethylborane [*Organic chemistry*]

TEB .... Tris-Ethylenediaminetetra-Acetate Borate [*Organic chemistry*] (MAH)

TEB .... Tropical Experiment Board [*of World Meteorological Organization and International Council on Scientific Unions*]

TEBA .... Tutmonda Esperantista Biblioteka Asocio [*International Association for Esperanto in Libraries - IAEL*] (EAIO)

TEBAC........ Triethylbenylammonium Chloride [*Organic chemistry*]

TEBBS........ The Ethics Bulletin Board System (AAGC)

TEBDA........ Truck Equipment and Body Distributor Association [*Later, NTEA*] (EA)

TeBG.......... Testosterone Binding Globulin [*Endocrinology*] (AAMN)

TeBG.......... Testosterone-Estradiol Binding Globulin [*Endocrinology*]

TEBG.......... Testosterone-Estradiol-Binding Globulin (STED)

TEBOL........ Terminal Business-Oriented Language

TEBPP........ Theoretical and Experimental Beam-Plasma Physics

TEBUTATE.... Tertiary Butyl Acetate [*USAN*] [*Organic chemistry*]

TEC .... Blacksburg, VA [*Location identifier FAA*] (FAAL)

TEC .... Commercial Intertech [*NYSE symbol*] (SAG)

TEC .... [*The*] Electrification Council (EA)

TEC .... [*The*] Elongated Collectors [*An association*] (EA)

TEC .... [*The*] Entertainment Channel [*Pay-television network*] [*Obsolete*]

TEC .... [*The*] Executive President's Council [*New Deal*]

TEC .... Tactical Electromagnetic Coordinator [*IEEE*]

TEC .... Tactical Exercise Controller [*Marine Corps*] (MCD)

TEC .... Target Engagement Console

TEC .... Target Entry Console

TEC .... Tarif Exterieur Commun [*Common External Tariff*] [*for EEC countries*]

TEC .... Tasmanian Environment Centre [*State*] (EERA)

TEC .... Teacher Education Center (EDAC)

TEC .... Tea Cyprus Ltd. [*ICAO designator*] (FAAC)

TEC .... Technical

TEC .... Technical Education Center

TEC .... Technical Escort Center [*Army*] (RDA)

TEC .... Technical Evaluation Committee [*Environmental Protection Agency*] (GFGA)

TEC .... Technician Education Council [*British*] (DI)

Tec........... Technischord [*Record label*]

TEC .... Technological Excellence Commission

TEC .... Technology for Energy Corporation (NRCH)

TEC .... Tele-Engineering Corp. [*Framingham, MA*] [*Telecommunications*] (TSSD)

TEC .... Telemetry and Command

TEC .... Telephone Engineering Center [*Telecommunications*] (TEL)

TEC .... Temporary Engineering Change (AAG)

TEC .... Temporary Extended Compensation [*Labor*]

TEC .... Ternary Eutectic Chloride [*Fire extinguishing agent*]

TEC .... Test and Evaluation Committee [*DoD*] (RDA)

TEC .... Test Equipment Center [*NASA*] (NASA)

TEC .... Test Equipment Committee (AAG)

TEC .... Test Evaluation and Control (IAA)

TEC .... Test of Ecology Comprehension (EDAC)

TEC .... Thermal End Cover

TEC .... Thermal Expansion Coefficient

TEC .... Thermal Unit End Cover (MCD)

TEC .... Thermionic Energy Converter (RDA)

TEC .... Thermoelectric Cooler (IAA)

TEC .... Thermo Electron Corp. (EFIS)

TEC .... Thymic Epithelial Cell [*Cytology*]

TEC .... Tlemcen [*Algeria*] [*Seismograph station code, US Geological Survey*] (SEIS)

TEC .... Tokyo Electronics Corp.

TEC .... Ton Equivalent of Coal

TEC .... Topographic Engineering Center [*Ft. Belvoir, VA*] [*Army*] (RDA)

TEC .... TOS [*TIROS Operational Satellite*] Test Evaluation Center [*Goddard Space Flight Center*] (NOAA)

TEC .... Total Electron Content (MCD)

TEC .... Total Environment Centre (EERA)

TEC .... Total Eosinophil Count [*Hematology*]

TEC .... Total Estimated Cost

TEC .... Total Exchange Capacity (DB)

TEC .... Tower en Route Control [*Aviation*] (FAAC)

TEC .... Track Entry Console (MCD)

TEC .... Tract Evaluation Computer (NATG)

TEC .... Training and Enterprise Council [*British*]

TEC .... Training Evaluation and Control

TEC .... Training Exercise Coordinator [*Military*] (NVT)

TEC .... Training Extension Course [*Army*]

TEC .... Transearth Coast [*AEC*]

TEC .... Transient Early Curvature [*Orthopedics*]

TEC	Transient Erythroblastopenia of Childhood [*Hematology*]
TEC	Transitional Executive Council [*Implemented in 1993 to work with the Cabinet and ensure fair political campaigning*] [*South Africa*] (ECON)
TEC	Transmission Electronic Control [*Bradley Fighting Vehicle*] [*Army*] (DWSG)
TEC	Tripartite Engineering Committee [*Allied German Occupation Forces*]
TEC	Triple Erasure Correction
TEC	Tropical Experiment Council [*of World Meteorological Organization and International Council on Scientific Unions*]
TEC	Truck Electrical Center [*Volvo White Truck Corp.*]
TEC	Turtle Excluder Device [*Fishing*]
TEC	Type Equipment Code (MCD)
TECA	Tartan Educational and Cultural Association (EA)
TECA	Technetium Albumin Study [*Radiology*] (DAVI)
TECA	Technical Evaluation and Countermeasures Assignment
TECA	Temporary Emergency Court of Appeals
TECA	Totally Enclosed - Closed-Air Circuit
TECA	Tower en Route Control Area [*Aviation*] (FAAC)
TECAD	Technical Advisory [*Military*] (CAAL)
TECADS	Techniques to Counter Air Defense Suppression (MCD)
TECC	Technology Education for Children Council (EA)
TECC	Texas Educational Computer Courseware Database [*Texas Education Computer Cooperative*] [*Information service or system Defunct*] (CRD)
TECC	Texas Education Computer Cooperative [*Houston*] [*Information service or system*] (IID)
TECCE	Tactical Exploitation Collection and Coordination Element (MCD)
TECCS	Tactical Engagement Close Combat System [*Army*]
TECD	Tech Data Corp. [*Clearwater, FL*] [*NASDAQ symbol*] (NQ)
TECD	Training Equipment Change Directives [*Navy*]
TECDA	Thai Environmental and Community Development Association (EERA)
TECDOC	Technical Documentation [*DoD*]
TECE	Teleprinter Error Correction Equipment
TECEPT	Training Equipment Cost Effectiveness Prediction Techniques [*Navy*]
TECG	Test and Evaluation Coordinating Group [*Military*] (CAAL)
TECH	Teach Each Customer How [*Tire repair training seminar*] [*Technical Rubber Co.*]
TECH	Techne Corp. [*NASDAQ symbol*] (SAG)
TECH	Technical (AAG)
tech	Technical (STED)
Tech	Technical (TBD)
tech	Technical College (WDAA)
TECH	Technician
TECH	Technique
tech	Technique (STED)
Tech	Technological (AL)
TECH	Technological Education Clearinghouse
TECH	Technologist
Tech	Technology (AL)
tech	Technology (DD)
TECH	Technology (AAG)
TECH	Texas Instruments, Canon, Hewlett-Packard [*Joint Venture*]
TECH	Toxic, Explosive, Corrosive, Hazardous Cargo [*Shipping*] (DS)
TECHAD	Technical Advisor [*Navy*]
Tech Adj	Technical Adjutant [*British military*] (DMA)
TECHAUTHIND	Technical Paper / Author Cross-Index System (DNAB)
TECHAV	Technical Availability [*Navy*] (NVT)
Tech(CEI)	Technician (Council of Engineering Institutions) [*British*] (DI)
TechCh	Technical Chemicals & Products Co. [*Associated Press*] (SAG)
TechChm	Technical Chemicals & Products [*Associated Press*] (SAG)
TechClne	Techniclone International Corp. [*Associated Press*] (SAG)
TECHCON	Technical Control (COE)
TechData	Tech Data Corp. [*Associated Press*] (SAG)
TECHDATA	Technical Data [*DoD*]
TECHDOC	Technical Documentation (COE)
Teche	Teche Holding Co. [*Associated Press*] (SAG)
Tech Ed	Technical Editor (DGA)
TechEl	Tech Electro Industries, Inc. [*Associated Press*] (SAG)
TECHEVAL	Technical Evaluation [*Navy*] (NG)
TECH EX	Technical Exchange (MHDI)
TechFrce	Tech Force Corp. [*Associated Press*] (SAG)
TechGeol	Technical Associate of the Geological Society [*British*] (DBQ)
TECHGL	Technological
Tech Inf Bull	Technical Information Bulletin. National Information Service on Drug Abuse [*A publication*]
TECHINFO	Technical Information [*DoD*]
TECHINT	Technical Intelligence [*Spy satellites, etc.*]
Techknit	TechKnits, Inc. [*Associated Press*] (SAG)
TECHL	Technical
TECHLGY	Technology
TECHMAN	Technical Manual (DNAB)
TECH MEMO	Technical Memorandum (MHDB)
TechMIWPC	Technician Member of the Institute of Water Pollution Control [*British*] (DI)
TECHMOD	Technology Modernization (AAGC)
TECHMOD	Technology Modernization Program [*DoD*]
TECHN	Technical (EY)
TECHN	Technician
TECHN	Technology
Techn Dict	Crabb's Technological Dictionary [*A publication*] (DLA)
Techne	Techne Corp. [*Associated Press*] (SAG)
Technign	Technigen Corp. [*Associated Press*] (SAG)
Technitrl	Technitrol, Inc. [*Associated Press*] (SAG)

TECHNOL	Technologic
Technols	Technologies
TECHNO-NET	Asia Network for Industrial Technology Information and Extension [*Singapore*] (BUAC)
Technop	Technopaegnion [*of Ausonius*] [*Classical studies*] (OCD)
TECH-NOSET-ASIA	Asian Network for Industrial Technology Information and Extension (BUAC)
TECHNOTE	Technical Note [*or Notice*] (DNAB)
TECHNQ	Technique
TECHOPEVAL	Technical Operational Evaluation
TECHREP	Technical Representative [*Military*]
TECH REPT	Technical Report (MHDI)
Tech Rev	Technische Revue (MEC)
TechRMS	Technological Qualification in Microscopy, Royal Microscopical Society [*British*] (DBQ)
TECHS	Technical School [*Air Force*]
TECHSAT	Technology Satellite (MCD)
TechSol	Technology Solutions Co. [*Associated Press*] (SAG)
TECHSPECS	Technical Specifications (IAA)
TechSvc	Technology Service Group, Inc. [*Associated Press*] (SAG)
TECHSVS	Technical Services [*Army*]
TECHTAF	Technical Training Air Force
TECHTNG	Technical Training (NVT)
TECHTNGSq	Technical Training Squadron [*Air Force*]
TECHTRA	Air Technical Training [*Navy*]
TECHWARE	Technology for Water Resources [*Belgium*] (BUAC)
TechWeldI	Technician of the Welding Institute [*British*] (DBQ)
TECL	Test Equipment Configuration Log [*NASA*] (KSC)
TECL	Transmission-Engine Communication Link [*Automotive engineering*]
TECM	Test Equipment Commodity Manager
TECMA	Technical Ceramics Manufacturers Association (EA)
TECMOD	Technology Modernization (MCD)
TECN	Technalysis Corp. [*NASDAQ symbol*] (NQ)
TEC-NACS	Teachers Educational Council - National Association Cosmetology Schools
TECNET	Technologies Network [*Database*] [*EC*] (ECED)
Tecnmtx	Tecnomatix Technologies Ltd. [*Associated Press*] (SAG)
TecnolM	Tecnol Medical Products, Inc. [*Associated Press*] (SAG)
TECO	Tanzania Extract Co. (BUAC)
TECO	Technical Co-Operation Committee [*OECD*] (DS)
TECO	TECO Energy, Inc. [*Associated Press*] (SAG)
TECO	Terra Cotta [*Pronounced "tee-ko"*] [*Type of American art pottery*]
TECO	Texas Ecologists, Inc. (EFIS)
TECO	Text Editor and Corrector [*Computer science*] (MHDI)
TECO	Tooling Expenditure Control Order (MCD)
TECO	Trinity Engineering Co. [*Huxley, IA*] [*Telecommunications service*] (TSSD)
TECO	Turbine Engine Checkout
TECOM	Test and Evaluation Command [*Aberdeen Proving Ground, MD*] [*Army*]
TECOMAP	Technical Conference of the Observation and Measurement of Atmospheric Pollution [*Helsinki, 1973*]
TecOpS	Tech/Ops Sevcon, Inc. [*Associated Press*] (SAG)
TecOpsSv	Tech-Ops Sevcon, Inc. [*Associated Press*] (OAQ)
TECP	Tetrachloropropane (LDT)
TECP	Training Equipment Checkout Procedure
TECR	Technical Reason [*Aviation*]
TECR	Technical Requirement (AABC)
Tec R	Technology Review [*A publication*] (BRI)
TECR	Test Equipment Change Requirement (NATG)
TECRAS	Technical Reconnaissance and Surveillance (MCD)
TECS	Technical Editing and Composition System [*Computer science*] (DGA)
TECS	Television Confirming Sensor (MCD)
TECS	Text Editing and Composition System [*Computer science*] (DGA)
TECS	Total Energy Control System
TECS	Total Environmental Control System [*Army*] (RDA)
TECS	Treasury Enforcement Communications System [*Customs Service*]
TECSTAR	Technical Missions, Structures and Career Development [*Military*]
TECTRA	Technology Transfer Data Bank [*California State University*] [*Sacramento*] [*Information service or system*] (IID)
TECU	Tecumseh Products Co. [*NASDAQ symbol*] (NQ)
TECU	Thermoelectric Environmental Control Unit
TECU	Transportation Employees' Canadian Union
TECUA	Tecumseh Products CI'A' [*NASDAQ symbol*] (TTSB)
TECUB	Tecumseh Products CI'B' [*NASDAQ symbol*] (TTSB)
Tecum	Tecumseh Products Co. [*Associated Press*] (SAG)
TECV	Test of Energy Concepts and Values (EDAC)
TECV	Traumatic Epiphyseal Coxa Vara [*Medicine*] (DMAA)
TED	Electrical Distributor [*A publication*] (EAAP)
TED	International Association for Training and Education in Distribution
TED	Tasks of Emotional Development (STED)
TED	Tasks of Emotional Development Test [*Psychology*]
TED	Tax-Exempt Dividend (MHDW)
TED	Teacher Education Division [*Council for Exceptional Children*]
TED	Technology, Entertainment and Design [*Conference*]
TED	Teddy Air AS [*Norway ICAO designator*] (FAAC)
Ted	Teddy Boy (ODBW)
TeD	Te Deum [*Music*]
TeD	Telefunken-Decca [*Video disk system*]
TED	Teleprinter Error Detector (IAA)
TED	Television Disc (NITA)
TED	Tenders Electronic Daily [*Office for Official Publications of the European Communities*] [*Database Luxembourg*]
TED	Terminal Editor (ADA)

TED	Test and Evaluation Division [*National Weather Service*]
TED	Test Engineering Division [*Navy*]
TED	Test Engineering Documentation (MCD)
TED	Test, Evaluation, and Development (MUGU)
TED	Text Editor [*Computer science*] (MHDI)
TED	Thermal Emission Detector (EDCT)
TED	Thermionic Emission Detector [*For gas chromatography*]
TED	Thermoelectric Device
TED	Thisted [*Denmark*] [*Airport symbol*] (OAG)
TED	Thomas Edmund Dewey [*Republican candidate for President, 1948*]
TED	Threshold Erythema Dose [*Medicine*]
TED	Threshold Extension Demodulator
TED	Thromboembolic Disease [*Medicine*]
TED	Toledo Edison Co. [*AMEX symbol*] (SAG)
TED	Toledo Edison Co. [*NYSE symbol*] (SPSG)
TED	Total Energy Detector
TED	Trace Element Doping
TED	Tracheo Esophageal Dysraphism (STED)
TED	Tracking Error Detector (MCD)
TED	Trailing Edge Down [*Aviation*] (MCD)
TED	Training Equipment Development [*Military*]
TED	Traitement Electronique des Donnees [*Electronic Data Processing - EDP*] [*French*]
TED	Transfer Effective Date [*Military*] (AFM)
TED	Transferred Electron Device [*Air Force*]
TED	Transient Enhanced Diffusion (AAEL)
TED	Translation Error Detector (DIT)
TED	Transmission Electron Diffraction (MCD)
TED	Trawl Efficiency Device [*Marine science*] (OSRA)
TED	Tris-Ethylenediaminetetraacetate Dithiothreitol (STED)
TED	Triteal Enterprise Desktop [*Computer science*] (IGQR)
TED	Troop Exercise Director (CINC)
TED	True Economic Depreciation
TED	Trunk Encryption Device [*Telecommunications*] (TEL)
TED	Turbine Electric Drive
TED	Turbine Engine Diagnosis [*Army*]
TED	Turbine Engine Division [*Air Force*]
TED	Turtle Excluder Device [*Marine science*] (OSRA)
TED	Turtle Exclusion Device [*Tool attached to shrimp boats in the Gulf of Mexico which allows the endangered Kemp's ridley turtle to escape the shrimp nets*] [*Facetious translations: "Trawler Extinction Device," "Trawling Efficiency Device"*]
TEDA	Theatre Equipment Dealers Association [*Later, TEA*] (EA)
TEDA	Triethylenediamine [*Organic chemistry*]
TEDAR	Telemetered Data Reduction (AAG)
TEDC	Technical Education Center
TEDC	Tellurium Diethyldithiocarbamate [*Organic chemistry*]
TEDCO	Thames Estuary Development Co. (BUAC)
TEDDS	Tactical Environmental Dissemination and Display System (MCD)
TEDE	Temperature-Enhanced Displacement Effect
TEDES	Telemetry Data Evaluation System
TEDIS	Trade Data Interchange System [*Telecommunications*] (OSI)
TEDIS	Trade Electronic Data Interchange System (BUAC)
TEDL	Transferred-Electron-Device Logic (MSA)
TEDMA	Triethylene Dimethacrylate [*Organic chemistry*]
TEDMX	Templeton Developing Markets [*Mutual fund ticker symbol*] (SG)
TEDP	Tetraethyl Dithionopyrophosphate [*Organic chemistry*]
TEDPAS	Technical Data Package Automated System
TEDPrA	Toledo Edison 8.32% Pfd [*AMEX symbol*] (TTSB)
TEDPrC	Toledo Edison 7.76% Pfd [*AMEX symbol*] (TTSB)
TEDPrD	Toledo Edison 10% Pfd [*AMEX symbol*] (TTSB)
TEDPrE	Toledo Ed 8.84%cm Pfd [*NYSE symbol*] (TTSB)
TEDPrF	Toledo Edison $2.365 Pfd [*NYSE symbol*] (TTSB)
TEDPrK	Toledo Edison Adj A Pfd [*NYSE symbol*] (TTSB)
TEDPrL	Toledo Edison Adj Rt B Pfd [*NYSE symbol*] (TTSB)
TEDS	Tactical Expendable Drone System (MCD)
TEDS	Target Effluent Detection System (MCD)
TEDS	Teleteach Expanded Delivery System [*US Air Force*] [*Wright-Patterson AFB, OH*] [*Telecommunications*] (TSSD)
TEDS	Tenders Electronic Dialling System (WDAA)
TEDS	Thromboembolic Disease Stockings [*Cardiology*] (DAVI)
TEDS	Thromboembolus Deterrant Stocking (MEDA)
TEDS	Turbine-Electric Drive Submarine (DNAB)
TEDS	Twin Exchangeable Disc Storage (NITA)
TEDSCO	Test Equipment Documentation Scheduling Committee
TEE	[*The*] Entrepreneurial Economy [*Corporation for Enterprise Development*] [*A publication*]
TEE	National Golf Properties [*NYSE symbol*] (SPSG)
TEE	Natl Golf Properties [*NYSE symbol*] (TTSB)
TEE	Tape Editing Equipment
TEE	Tbessa [*Algeria*] [*Airport symbol*] (OAG)
TEE	Teeples Ranch [*Montana*] [*Seismograph station code, US Geological Survey Closed*] (SEIS)
TEE	Teeshin Resources Ltd. [*Vancouver Stock Exchange symbol*]
TEE	Telecommunications Engineering Establishment [*British*]
TEE	Terminal Effects and Experimentation (MCD)
TEE	Terminal Eocene Event [*Palaeontology*]
TEE	Test Equipment Engineering (AAG)
TEE	Text Entry and Edit (DGA)
TEE	Theological Education by Extension [*Church of England*]
TEE	Thermal Effect of Exercise (MEDA)
TEE	Torpedo Experimental Establishment [*British*]
TEE	Total Effective Exposure [*Advertising*]
TEE	Training Effectiveness Evaluation
TEE	Transesophageal Echocardiography

TEE	Trans-Europ-Express [*Continental high-speed train*]
TEE	Triaxial Earth Ellipsoid
TEE	Tried Everything Else [*Medicine*] (WDAA)
TEE	Tubular Extendible Element (PDAA)
TEE	Tyee [*Alaska*] [*Airport symbol*] (AD)
TEE	Tyrosine Ethyl Ester [*Organic chemistry*] (MAE)
TEEAR	Test Equipment Error Analysis Report (IAA)
TEEC	Transactions Editorial Executive Committee (ACII)
TEECG	Tactical Exercise Evaluation Control Group [*Marine Corps*] (DOMA)
TeeCm	Tee Comm Electronics, Inc. [*Associated Press*] (SAG)
TeeCom	Tee Com Electronics, Inc. [*Associated Press*] (SAG)
TEED	Training, Enterprise, and Education Directorate (BUAC)
TEEF	Tax-Exempt Equity Fund
Teekay	Teekay Shipping Corp. [*Associated Press*] (SAG)
TEEL	Temporary Expedient Equipment List [*Army*] (AABC)
TEEM	Techno-Economic-Environmental Model (EERA)
TEEM	Technology through Electricity, Electronics, and Microelectronics (AIE)
TEEM	Test for Examining Expressive Morphology [*Educational test*]
TEEM	Trans-Europ-Express-Marchandises [*Continental high-speed train*]
TEENS TAP	Teens Teaching AIDS Prevention [*An association*] (EA)
TEES	Texas Engineering Experiment Station [*Texas A & M University*] [*Research center*]
TEES	Thermochemical Environmental Energy System [*Service mark*] [*Battelle Development Corp.*]
TEESS	Tank Engine Exhaust Smoke System (MCD)
TEEZI	Threat Evaluation Equipment Zone of Interior (SAA)
TEF	[*The*] Eagle Foundation [*Defunct*] (EA)
TEF	[*The*] Environmental Fund [*Later, PEB*] (EA)
TEF	Tear Efficiency Factor [*Textiles*]
Tef	Tefillin (BJA)
TEF	Telefonica de Espana ADS [*NYSE symbol*] (TTSB)
TEF	Telefonica de Espana SA [*NYSE symbol*] (SPSG)
TEF	Telfer [*Australia Airport symbol*] (OAG)
TEF	Temperance Education Foundation [*Defunct*] (EA)
TEF	Test and Evaluation Facility [*Nuclear energy*] (NUCP)
TEF	Test and Evaluation Flight [*Military*]
TEF	Tetralogy of Fallot [*Neonatology*] (DAVI)
TEF	Textile Employers Federation (BUAC)
TEF	Thermal Effect of Food (MEDA)
TEF	Thermatic Effect of Food [*Medicine*] (WDAA)
TEF	Thyrotroph Embryonic Factor [*Genetics*]
TEF	Tilted Electric Field (PDAA)
TEF	Total Effective Fare (PDAA)
TEF	Total Energy Feasibility (IAA)
TEF	Total Environment Facility (SAA)
TEF	Toxic Equivalency Factor [*Environmental Protection Agency*]
TEF	Tracheoesophageal Fistula [*Medicine*]
TEF	Transfer on End of File (SAA)
TEF	Transverse Electric Field
TEF	Trunk Extension-Flexion [*Medicine*] (DMAA)
TEF	Tunable Etalon Filter
TEF	Turkey Embryo Fibroblast [*Biochemistry*]
TEFA	Total Essential Fatty Acid [*of foodstuffs*]
TEFA	Total Esterified Fatty Acid
TEFA	Tube-Excited X-Ray Fluorescence Analyzer
TEFAP	Temporary Emergency Food Assistance Program [*Department of Agriculture*]
TEFC	Totally Enclosed - Fan Cooled
TEFC	Totally-Enclosed Force-Cooled Reactor [*Nuclear energy*] (IAA)
TEFL	Teaching English as a Foreign Language
TEFLON	Tetrafluoroethylene Resin [*Du Pont*]
TEFORS	Technological Forecasting and Simulation for Program Selection (MCD)
TEFP	Transportability Engineering Focal Point
TEFRA	Tax Equity and Fiscal Responsibility Act (AAGC)
TEFRA	Tax Equity and Fiscal Responsibility Act of 1982
TEFS	Transmural Electrical Field Stimulation [*Medicine*] (DMAA)
TEG	Tactical Employment Guide [*Military*] (CAAL)
TEG	Technical Exchange Group (AAEL)
Teg	Tegula [*Entomology*]
TEG	Templar Mining [*Vancouver Stock Exchange symbol*]
TEG	Tenkodogo [*Upper Volta*] [*Airport symbol*] (AD)
TEG	Test Element Group
TEG	Tetraethylene Glycol [*Organic chemistry*]
TEG	Thermoelectric Generator
TEG	Thromboelastogram [*or Thromboelastograph*] [*Medicine*]
TEG	Top Edge Gilt [*Bookbinding*]
teg	Top-Edge Gilt [*Bookbinding*] (WDMC)
TEG	Training and Education Group (NITA)
TEG	Triethylene Glycol [*Organic chemistry*]
TEG	Triethyl Gallium [*Organic chemistry*]
Tegal	Tegal Corp. [*Associated Press*] (SAG)
TEGAS	Test Generation and Simulation
TEGAS	Time Generation and Simulation [*Telecommunications*] (TEL)
TEGD	Technical Enforcement Guidance Document [*Environmental Protection Agency*]
TEGDME	Tetraethylene Glycol Dimethyl Ether [*Organic chemistry*]
TEGDN	Triethylene Glycol Dinitrate [*An explosive*]
TEGFET	Two-Dimensional Electron Gas Field-Effect Transistor (AAEL)
TEGG	Thermogrip Electric Glue Gun
TEGI	Train-Elevated Guideway Interaction (PDAA)
TEGMA	Terminal Elevator Grain Merchants Association (EA)
TEGMA	Triethylene Glycol Dimethacrylate [*Organic chemistry*] (MCD)
TEGO	Taylor's Encyclopedia of Government Officials [*A publication*]

TEGOX	Templeton Global Opportunities [*Mutual fund ticker symbol*] (SG)
TEGWAR	[*The*] Exciting Game Without Any Rules [*Card game*]
TEH	Blare Lake, AK [*Location identifier FAA*] (FAAL)
Teh	Tehillim (BJA)
TEH	Tehran [*Iran*] [*Seismograph station code, US Geological Survey*] (SEIS)
TEH	Tehua [*Race of maize*]
TEH	Tempelhof Airways, Inc. [*Germany ICAO designator*] (FAAC)
TEH	Twin-Engined Helicopter (MCD)
TEHOS	Tetrakis(ethylhexoxy)silane [*Organic chemistry*]
TEHP	Thermoelectric Heat Pump (MCD)
TEI	[*The*] Entrepreneurship Institute (EA)
TEI	Societa' Tea Italia [*Italy ICAO designator*] (FAAC)
TEI	Tax Executives Institute (EA)
TEI	Technical Education Institute (AIE)
TEI	Technical Engineering Item (MCD)
TEI	Telecommunications Engineering, Inc. [*Dallas, TX*] (TSSD)
TEI	Templeton Emerging Markets Income Fund [*NYSE symbol*] (SPSG)
TEI	Templeton Emerg Mkts Income [*NYSE symbol*] (TTSB)
TEI	Temporary Engineering Instruction [*Navy*] (NG)
TEI	Text Encoding Initiative [*Computer science*]
TEI	Thorne Ecological Institute (EA)
TEI	Time Error Indicated
TEI	Trait Evaluation Index [*Psychology*]
TEI	Transearth Injection [*AEC*]
TEI	Transfer on Error Indication
TEI	Trucking Employers, Inc. [*Later, TMI*]
TEIB	Triethyleneiminobenzoquinone [*Organic chemistry*] (MAE)
TEIC	Tissue Equivalent Ionization Chamber
TEIGN	Teignmouth [*Urban district in England*]
TEIGNBR	Teignbridge [*England*]
Teikyo Marycrest U	Teikyo Marycrest University (GAGS)
TEIM	Travel Economic Impact Model [*Department of Commerce*]
TEIP	Tax-Exempt Investor Program [*Investment term*]
TEIRDC	Tamil Eelam International Research and Documentation Centre [*Canada*]
TEIS	Telecom Eireann Information Systems (BUAC)
TEIS	Training Equipment Item Specification (MCD)
TEISS	[*The*] Enhanced Integrated Soldier System [*Army*]
Teiss	Teissler's Court of Appeal, Parish of Orleans, Reports [*1903-17*] [*A publication*] (DLA)
Teissler	Teissler's Court of Appeal, Parish of Orleans, Reports [*1903-17*] [*A publication*] (DLA)
TEJ	Emmanuel School of Religion, Johnson City, TN [*OCLC symbol*] (OCLC)
TEJ	Tejas Gas Corp. [*NYSE symbol*] (SPSG)
TEJ	Transportes Aeros Ejecutivos SA de CV [*Mexico ICAO designator*] (FAAC)
TEJ	Transverse Expansion Joint [*Technical drawings*]
TEJA	Tutmonda Esperantista Jurnalista Asocio [*World Association of Esperanto Journalists - WAEJ*] (EAIO)
TEJAC	Trade Effluent Joint Advisory Committee [*British*] (DCTA)
Tejas	Tejas Gas Corp. [*Associated Press*] (SAG)
TejasGas	Tejas Gas Corp. [*Associated Press*] (SAG)
TejasGs	Tejas Gas Corp. [*Associated Press*] (SAG)
TejasPw	Tejas Power [*Associated Press*] (SAG)
TejnR	Tejon Ranch Co. [*Associated Press*] (SAG)
TEJO	Tutmonda Esperantista Junulara Organizo [*World Organization of Young Esperantists*] (EAIO)
TEJPr	Tejas Gas Cp 9.96% Dep Pfd [*NYSE symbol*] (TTSB)
TEJPrA	Tejas Gas 5.25% Cv Dep Pfd [*NYSE symbol*] (TTSB)
TEK	Teck Corp. [*Toronto Stock Exchange symbol Vancouver Stock Exchange symbol*]
TEK	Teekin [*Tonga*] [*Seismograph station code, US Geological Survey*] (SEIS)
TEK	Tektronix, Inc. [*NYSE symbol*] (SPSG)
TEK	Test Equipment Kit
TEK	Truppenentgiftungskompanie [*Personnel decontamination company*] [*German military - World War II*]
TEK	Tunnel Exploration Kit [*Army*] (VNW)
TEK A	Teck Corp Cl'A' [*TS symbol*] (TTSB)
TEKE	Tau Kappa Epsilon [*Fraternity*] (EA)
Tekelec	Tekelec, Inc. [*Associated Press*] (SAG)
TEKES	Technology Development Centre [*Finland*] (BUAC)
TEKSIF	Turkiye Tekstil ve Orme Sanayii Iscileri Sendikalari Federasyonu [*National Federation of Textile Unions*] [*Turkey*]
Tektrnx	Tektronix, Inc. [*Associated Press*] (SAG)
TEL	Task Execution Language
TEL	Taxpayers Education Lobby (EA)
TEL	TCC Industries [*NYSE symbol*] (TTSB)
TEL	TCC Industries, Inc. [*Formerly, Telecom Corp.*] [*NYSE symbol*] (SAG)
TEL	Telegram
tel	Telegram (WDMC)
tel	Telegraph (WDMC)
TEL	Telegraph
TEL	Telegraphic (NTCM)
TEL	Telemetry (KSC)
TEL	Telephone (AAG)
Tel	Telephone (TBD)
TEL	Telephone Group (IAA)
TEL	Telephone Station (IAA)
TEL	Telephonic (NTCM)
TEL	Telephony (NTCM)
TEL	Telescope (AAG)

Tel	Telescopium [*Constellation*]
TEL	Teletype (NTCM)
TEL	Teletypewriter [*Telecommunications*] (NOAA)
TEL	Television (IAA)
TEL	Telford Aviation, Inc. [*ICAO designator*] (FAAC)
TEL	Tell City, IN [*Location identifier FAA*] (FAAL)
tel	Telugu [*MARC language code Library of Congress*] (LCCP)
TEL	Terex Equipment Ltd.
TEL	Test Log
TEL	Test of Economic Literacy [*Educational test*]
TEL	Tests for Everyday Living [*Educational test*]
TEL	Tetraethyllead [*Organic chemistry*]
TEL	Thalner Electronic Laboratories, Inc. [*Ann Arbor, MI*] (TSSD)
TEL	Thomas Edward Lawrence [*Lawrence of Arabia*] [*British archaeologist, soldier, and writer, 1888-1935*]
TEL	Tokyo Electron Ltd. (IAA)
TEL	Total Energy Loss (IAA)
TEL	Training Equipment List
TEL	Transporter-Erector-Launcher [*Air Force*]
TELACS	Tunnel Explorer, Locator and Communications System [*Army*] (VNW)
Tel Add	Telegraphic Address (DS)
Telan	Telenoticiosa Americana [*Press agency*] [*Argentina*]
TELAR	Transporter-Erector-Launcher and RADAR (MCD)
TelArg	Telefonica de Argentina SA [*Associated Press*] (SAG)
TELATEL	Telephone and Telegraph (IAA)
TELATS	Tactical Electronic Locating and Targeting System (MCD)
TELAU	Teleautograph [*ICAO designator*] (FAAC)
Tel Aviv Univ Stud L	Tel Aviv University Studies in Law [*Tel-Aviv, Israel*] [*A publication*] (DLA)
Tel-Aviv U Stud L	Tel-Aviv University Studies in Law [*Tel-Aviv, Israel*] [*A publication*] (DLA)
TELB	Telephone Booth
TelBrasl	Telecommunicacoes Brasilerias SA Telebras [*Associated Press*] (SAG)
TELC	Telco Systems [*NASDAQ symbol*] (TTSB)
TELC	Telco Systems, Inc. [*NASDAQ symbol*] (NQ)
TelC	Tele-Communications Class A [*Associated Press*] (SAG)
TELC	Teleglobe Canada
TelC	Telegraph Communications [*Commercial firm Associated Press*] (SAG)
TELCAM	Telecommunication Equipment Low-Cost Acquisition Method [*Navy*]
TelC Int	Tele-Communications International, Inc. [*Associated Press*] (SAG)
TelCm	Tel-Communications [*Associated Press*] (SAG)
TelcNZ	Telecom Corp. of New Zealand [*Associated Press*] (SAG)
TELCO	Tata Engineering & Locomotive Co. [*India*]
Telco	Telco Systems, Inc. [*Associated Press*] (SAG)
TELCO	Telephone Central Office
TELCO	Telephone Communications (IAA)
TELCO	Telephone Company [*ICAO designator*] (FAAC)
telco	Telephone Company (IGQR)
TELCO	Telephone Operating Co. [*Also, TELOP*]
TELCO	The East London Community Organisation [*England*] (WDAA)
TELCOM	Telecommunications (NASA)
TELCOM	Telemetry & Communications Division (ACII)
TELCON	Telephone Conference [*or Conversation*] (AAG)
TELCOS	Telephone Companies
TelCSm	TelCom Semiconductor, Inc. [*Associated Press*] (SAG)
TelCTV	Tel-Com Wireless Cable TV Corp. [*Associated Press*] (SAG)
TELD	Teledate Equipment [*Military*]
TELD	Test of Early Language Development
TELD	Transferred Electron Logic Device (IAA)
TELDEC	Telefunken-Decca [*Video disk system*] (IAA)
TelDta	Telephone & Data Systems, Inc. [*Associated Press*] (SAG)
Teldy	Teledyne, Inc. [*Associated Press*] (SAG)
Teldyn	Teledyne, Inc. [*Associated Press*] (SAG)
TELE	Tech Electro Industries [*NASDAQ symbol*] (TTSB)
TELE	Tech Electro Industries, Inc. [*NASDAQ symbol*] (SAG)
TELE	Telegram
TELE	Telegraph
tele	Telemetry [*Cardiology*] (DAVI)
TELE	Telephone
TELE	Telephoto (NTCM)
Tele	Telescopium [*Constellation*]
TELE	Television (ADA)
TELE	Trilanguage Education Learning Environment Program [*New York City*] (EDAC)
Telebit	Telebit Corp. [*Associated Press*] (SAG)
TELEC	Telecommunication
TELEC	Teleglobe Canada
TELEC	Thermoelectronic LASER Energy Converter
TELECAMRA	Television Camera (MDG)
TELECAR	Telemetry Carrier Acquisition and Recovery (MCD)
TELECAST	Television Broadcasting (CET)
TELECC	Telecommunication
Telech	Telechips Corp. [*Associated Press*] (SAG)
Telechps	Telechips Corp. [*Associated Press*] (SAG)
TELECOM	Telecommunications (AFM)
TeleCom	Tele-Communications Class A [*Associated Press*] (SAG)
telecommun	Telecommunications (DD)
TELECOMS	Telecommunications Authority of Singapore (TSSD)
TELECON	Telephone [*or Teletype*] Conference [*or Conversation*] (AFM)
TELECON	Teletypewriter Conference (IAA)
TELECONV	Telephone Conversation
TELEDAC	Telemetric Data Converter
TeleDan	Tele Danmark Co. [*Associated Press*] (SAG)

TELEDAQ	Television Data Acquisition System (MCD)
TELEDIS.......	Teletypewriter Distribution (NATG)
TELEDOC	Telecommunications Documentation (NITA)
Teledta	Teledata Communications [*Associated Press*] (SAG)
Telef	Telefonica de Espana SA [*Associated Press*] (SAG)
TELEFAC	Telecommunications Facility
TELEFAC	Television Facsimile (NTCM)
TelefEsp	Telefonica de Espana SA [*Associated Press*] (SAG)
Teleflex	Teleflex, Inc. [*Associated Press*] (SAG)
TELEFLORA..	Telegraph Florists Delivery Service
TelefMex	Telefonos de Mexico [*Associated Press*] (SAG)
TELEG	Telegram
TELEG	Telegraph
TelegCm	Telegraph Communications [*Commercial firm Associated Press*] (SAG)
Telegen	Telegen Corp. [*Associated Press*] (SAG)
TELEMAN....	Telephone Management System
Telem Ant....	Telemetry Antenna
TELEMUX......	Telegraph Multiplexer (MHDB)
TELENET......	Cooperative Extension Service Telephone Network [*University of Illinois at Champaign-Urbana*] [*Telecommunications service*] (TSSD)
TELENET......	TELENET Communications Corp. [*GTE*] (TEL)
TELENGR	Telephone Engineer [*Telecommunications*] (IAA)
Telepad	Telepad Corp. [*Associated Press*] (SAG)
TELEPAK	Telemetering Package
Telepanel	Telepanel Systems, Inc. [*Associated Press*] (SAG)
TELEPH........	Telephone
TeleprtC........	Teleport Communications Group, Inc. [*Associated Press*] (SAG)
TELEPUTER...	Television and Computer (EECA)
TELER	Telecommunications Requirements (MCD)
TELERAN	Television and RADAR Navigation System (MUGU)
TELESAT	Telecommunications Satellite
Telescan	Telescan, Inc. [*Associated Press*] (SAG)
Telescription...	Television Transcription (NTCM)
TELESIM	Teletypewriter Simulator
Telesoft	Telesoft Corp. [*Associated Press*] (SAG)
TeleSpec	TeleSpectrum Worldwide, Inc. [*Associated Press*] (SAG)
TELESUN	Telecommunications Software User's Network [*Telesun Corp.*] [*Englewood, OH*] (TSSD)
Teletch	Teletouch Communications, Inc. [*Associated Press*] (SAG)
TELETECH....	National Telecommunications & Technology Fund, Inc. [*New York, NY*] (TSSD)
TeleTech	TeleTech Holdings, Inc. [*Associated Press*] (SAG)
Teletek	Teletek, Inc. [*Associated Press*] (SAG)
Teletouch ...	Teletouch Communications, Inc. [*Associated Press*] (SAG)
TELETYPE ...	Teletypewriter [*Telecommunications*]
TELEU	Tech Electro Industries Unit [*NASDAQ symbol*] (TTSB)
Televerket ...	National Swedish Telecommunications Administration [*Stockholm*] [*Information service or system*] (IID)
TELEW	Tech Electro Industries Wrrt [*NASDAQ symbol*] (TTSB)
TeleWest	TeleWest Communications PLC [*Associated Press*] (SAG)
TELEX	Automatic Teletypewriter Exchange Service [*of Western Union*]
TELEX	Telegraph Exchange [*Telecommunications*] (IAA)
TELEX	Teleprinter Exchange [*Telecommunications*] (IAA)
TELEX	Teleprocessing Executive [*Telecommunications*] (IAA)
TELEX	Teletype Exchange (NITA)
TelexChil	Telex Chile SA [*Associated Press*] (SAG)
TELF	Tamil Eelam Liberation Front [*Sri Lanka*] [*Political party*] (PPW)
TELFAD........	Telephone Executive Leader for a Day [*New England Telephone Co. program for high school students*]
TELG	Telegram
TELG	Telegraph
TELG	Telegraph Communications [*NASDAQ symbol*] (SAG)
TELGF	Telegraph Communic Ltd [*NASDAQ symbol*] (TTSB)
TELID	Teletypewriter Identification (NOAA)
TELINT	Telemetry Intelligence
TELIS	Test Equipment Logistics Information Source [*Army*]
TELISA........	Thermometric Enzyme-Linked Immunosorbent Assay [*Analytical biochemistry*]
TELIST	Telegraphist (DSUE)
TELL	[*The*] Excellent Lodge Leader [*Freemasonry*]
TELL	Teacher-Aiding Electronic Learning Link (PDAA)
TELL	Teletouch Communications, Inc. [*NASDAQ symbol*] (SAG)
Tellabs	Tellabs Co. [*Associated Press*] (SAG)
Tellurn	Tellurian, Inc. [*Associated Press*] (SAG)
Tellus	Tellus Industries, Inc. [*Associated Press*] (SAG)
TELLW	Teletouch Communicns Wrrt'A' [*NASDAQ symbol*] (TTSB)
TELM	Telegram (ROG)
TelMd	TelMed, Inc. [*Associated Press*] (SAG)
TelMed	TelMed, Inc. [*Associated Press*] (SAG)
TelMex	Telefonos de Mexico SA [*Associated Press*]
TELMKTG....	Telemarketing
Telmn	Telemundo Group, Inc. [*Associated Press*] (SAG)
TELMTR........	Telemotor
Telmun	Telemundo Group, Inc. [*Associated Press*] (SAG)
TELN	Telephone (IAA)
TELNET........	Georgia Telecommunications Network [*Georgia Hospital Association*] [*Atlanta, GA*] [*Telecommunications*] (TSSD)
TELNET........	Telecommunication Network (OSI)
TELNO	Telephone Number (IAA)
TELO	Tamil Eelam Liberation Organization [*Sri Lanka*] [*Political party*]
TELO	Tel Offshore Trust [*NASDAQ symbol*] (NQ)
Tel Off	Telegraph Office
TEL Off	TEL Offshore Trust [*Associated Press*] (SAG)

TELOP..........	Telephone Operating Co. [*Also, TELCO*]
TELOP..........	Television Optical (NTCM)
TELOPS........	Telemetry Online Processing System [*Computer science*]
TELOZ..........	TEL Offshore Tr UBI [*NASDAQ symbol*] (TTSB)
TELPAK........	Telephone Package
TelPeru........	Telefonica del Peru SA [*Associated Press*] (SAG)
TELR	Telor Ophthalmic Pharm [*NASDAQ symbol*] (TTSB)
TELR	Telor Ophthalmic Pharmaceuticals [*NASDAQ symbol*] (SAG)
TelrOph........	Telor Ophthalmic Pharmaceuticals [*Commercial firm Associated Press*] (SAG)
TELRY..........	Telegraph Reply (FAAC)
TELS	TEL Electronics, Inc. [*American Fork, UT*] [*NASDAQ symbol*] (NQ)
TELS	TELS Corp. [*Associated Press*] (SAG)
TELS	TELS Corp. [*NASDAQ symbol*] (SAG)
TELS	Test of Early Learning Skills [*Child development test*]
TELS	The English Language Skills Profile [*Gordfrey Thomson Unit Edinburgh University*] (TES)
TELS	Turbine Engine Loads Simulator
TELSAM........	Telephone Service Attitude Measurement [*Telephone interviews*] [*AT & T*]
TELSAR........	Tracking and Evolution of Solar Active Regions [*Marine science*] (OSRA)
TELSAT	Television Satellite (NTCM)
TelSave	Tel-Save Holdings, Inc. [*Associated Press*] (SAG)
Telscape	Telscape International, Inc. [*Associated Press*] (SAG)
TELSCAR	Transmit Electronically Location Shippers' Car Advice Reports
TELSCOM	Telemetry-Surveillance-Communications
TELSCPD	Telescoped
Telscpe	Telscape International, Inc. [*Associated Press*] (SAG)
TELSIM	Teletypewriter Simulation [*or Simulator*]
TELSTATS	Telemetry Station System [*Telecommunications*] (IAA)
TELSUN	Television Series for United Nations [*A foundation formed to produce, and telecast on a commercial basis, dramatized descriptions of UN activities*]
TEL SUR	Telephone Survey (MUGU)
TEL-SYS	Telephone System
TELT	Teltronics, Inc. [*NASDAQ symbol*] (NQ)
TELTA	Tethered Lighter-than-Air (KSC)
TELTAP	Telephone Tape (IAA)
TELTIPS........	Technical Effort Locator and Technical Interest Profile System [*Army*] (PDAA)
TELTRAC	Telemetry Tracking [*Telecommunications*] (IAA)
Teltrnd..........	Teltrend, Inc. [*Associated Press*] (SAG)
Teltron..........	Teltronics, Inc. [*Associated Press*] (SAG)
TELU	Total-Tel USA Communic [*NASDAQ symbol*] (TTSB)
TELU	Total Tel USA Communications [*NASDAQ symbol*] (SAG)
Telular..........	Telular Corp. [*Associated Press*] (SAG)
TELUQ	Tele-Universite [*University of Quebec*] [*Telecommunications service*] (TSSD)
TELUQ	Tele-Universite (University of Quebec) [*Quebec, PQ*] [*Telecommunications*] (TSSD)
TELUS..........	Telemetric Universal Sensor
TELV..........	TeleVideo Systems [*NASDAQ symbol*] (TTSB)
TELV	TeleVideo Systems, Inc. [*NASDAQ symbol*] (NQ)
Telvid	Tele Video Systems, Inc. [*Associated Press*] (SAG)
Telxon..........	Telxon Corp. [*Associated Press*] (SAG)
TEM	Memphis University School, Hyde Library, Memphis, TN [*OCLC symbol*] (OCLC)
TEM	Officers for Temporary Service [*Navy British*] (ROG)
TEM	Roswell Park Memorial Institute [*Research code symbol*]
TEM	Target Engagement Message (NVT)
TEM	Target Evaluation Maintenance (MCD)
TEM	Technical Error Message [*Aviation*]
TEM	TELEX Extended Memory (IAA)
TEM	Temiskaming & Northern Ontario Railway [*AAR code*]
tem	Temne [*MARC language code Library of Congress*] (LCCP)
TEM	Temora [*Australia Airport symbol*] (OAG)
TEM	Temperature (DEN)
TEM	Tempered (DEN)
Tem	[*The*] Templar [*1788-79*] [*London*] [*A publication*] (DLA)
TEM	Template (DEN)
TEM	Tempo [*Music*]
Tem	Tempo [*Record label*] [*Germany*]
Tem	Tempore [*In the Time Of*] [*Latin*] (DLA)
TEM	Temuco [*Chile*] [*Seismograph station code, US Geological Survey Closed*] (SEIS)
TeM	Tennessee Microfilms, Nashville, TN [*Library symbol Library of Congress*] (LCLS)
TEM	Terramar Resources Corp. [*Toronto Stock Exchange symbol Vancouver Stock Exchange symbol*]
TEM	Terrestrial Ecosystem Model [*for climate effects*]
TEM	Texas Episodic Model [*Environmental Protection Agency*] (GFGA)
TEM	Text Excursion Module (IAA)
TEM	Thermal Expansion Molding (MCD)
TEM	Thermoelectric Module
TEM	Tomato Extract Medium (OA)
TEM	Torpedo Evasive Maneuvering [*Navy*]
TEM	Trans-European North-South Motorway Project [*Switzerland*] (BUAC)
TEM	Transmission Electron Micrograph
TEM	Transmission Electron Microscope [*or Microscopy*]
TEM	Transmission Engineering Memorandum (IAA)
TEM	Transverse Electromagnetic [*Wave*] [*Radio*]
TEM	Transverse Electromagnetic Mode [*Telecommunications*] (IAA)
TEM	Transverse Exitation Mode (NITA)
TEM	Triethylenemelamine [*Organic chemistry*]

tem	Triethylene Melamine [*An arizidine mutagen*] [*Genetics*] (DOG)
TEM	Typical Egg Mass
TEMA	Tank Equipment Manufacturers Association (NUCP)
TEMA	Telecommunication Engineering and Manufacturing Association [*British*] (IAA)
TEMA	Test and Evaluation Management Agency [*Army*] (RDA)
TEMA	Test Macro [*Computer science*] (IAA)
TEMA	Test of Early Mathematics Ability
TEMA	Towing Equipment Manufacturers Association (NTPA)
TEMA	Trace Elements in Man and Animals [*An international symposium*]
TEMA	Training, Education and Mutual Assistance [*Marine science*] (OSRA)
TEMA	Training, Education, and Mutual Assistance in the Marine Sciences [*IOC working committee*] (MSC)
TEMA	Tubular Exchanger Manufacturers Association (EA)
TEMAC	Temporary Active Duty
TEMAC	Turbine Engine Monitoring and Control [*ASMAP Electronics Ltd.*] [*Software package*] (NCC)
TEMACDIFOT...	Temporary Active Duty in a Flying Status Involving Operational or Training Flights [*Navy*]
TEMACDIFOTINS...	Temporary Active Duty under Instruction in a Flying Status Involving Operationalor Training Flights [*Navy*]
TEMACDU	Temporary Active Duty [*Navy*]
TEMACINS	Temporary Active Duty under Instruction [*Navy*]
TEMADD	Temporary Additional Duty [*Navy*]
TEMADDCON...	Temporary Additional Duty in Connection with [*Specified activity*] [*Navy*]
TEMADDINS...	Temporary Additional Duty under Instruction [*Navy*]
TEMAF	Templeton Emerging Market Appreciation Fund [*Associated Press*] (SAG)
TEMANS	Tactical Effectiveness of Minefields in the Antiarmor Weapons System (PDAA)
TEMARS	Transportation Environmental Measurement and Recording System (MCD)
TEMAS	"Tell-Me-A-Story" Thematic Appreciation Test (EDAC)
TEMAW	Tactical Effectiveness of Minefields in Antiarmor Warfare Systems [*Army*] (INF)
TEMAWS	Tactical Effectiveness of Minefields in Antiarmor Warfare Systems [*Army*]
TEMC	Test and Evaluation Management Course (MCD)
TEM-CAS	Temporary-Casuality Pay Record [*Navy*] (DNAB)
TEMCON	Temporary Duty Connection [*Navy*] (DNAB)
TEMD	TelMed, Inc. [*NASDAQ symbol*] (SAG)
TEMDIFOT ...	Temporary Duty in a Flying Status Involving Operational or Training Flights [*Navy*]
TEMDIFOTINS...	Temporary Duty under Instruction in a Flying Status Involving Operational or Training Flights [*Navy*]
TEMDIFPRO...	Temporary Duty in a Flying Status Involving Proficiency Flying [*Navy*] (DNAB)
TEMDU	Temporary Duty [*Navy*]
TEMDUCON...	Temporary Duty in Connection With [*Specified activity*] [*Navy*]
TEMDU DIS...	Temporary Duty Pending Disciplinary Action [*Navy*] (DNAB)
TEMDU FFA...	Temporary Duty for Further Assignment [*Navy*] (DNAB)
TEMDU FFT...	Temporary Duty for Further Transfer [*Navy*] (DNAB)
TEMDUINS...	Temporary Duty under Instruction [*Navy*]
TEMDU PAT...	Temporary Duty as a Patient [*Navy*] (DNAB)
TEMDU PSI...	Temporary Duty - Programmed Student Input [*Navy*] (DNAB)
TEMDU SEP...	Temporary Duty Pending Separation [*Navy*] (DNAB)
TEMDW	TelMed Inc. Wrrt [*NASDAQ symbol*] (TTSB)
TEMEC	Translational Electromagnetic Environment Chamber (MCD)
TEMED	Tetramethylethylenediamine [*Also, TMED, TMEDA*] [*Organic chemistry*]
TEMEX	Templeton Foreign [*Mutual fund ticker symbol*] (SG)
TEMFI	Templeton Emerging Market Fund, Inc. [*Associated Press*] (SAG)
TEMFLY	Temporary Duty Involving Flying [*Navy*]
TEMFLYINS...	Temporary Duty Involving Flying under Instruction [*Navy*]
TEM-GEN	Temporary-General [*Navy*] (DNAB)
TEMGX	Templeton Smaller Cos. Growth [*Mutual fund ticker symbol*] (SG)
TEMIC	Telecommunications Executive Management Institute of Canada (TSSD)
TEMIC	Telefunken Microelectronik
TEMIF	Templeton Emerging Markets Income Fund [*Associated Press*] (SAG)
TEMINS	Temporary Duty under Instruction [*Navy*]
TEMIS	TRADOC [*Training and Doctrine Command*] Engineer Management Information System [*Army*]
TEMMA	Transmission Electron Microscopy and Microprobe Analysis (PDAA)
TEMMF	Tax-Exempt Money Market Fund [*Investment term*]
TEMO	Test and Evaluation Management Office [*Army*] (RDA)
TEMOD	Terminal Environment Module [*Computer science*] (MHDB)
TEMOD	Test Equipment Modernization [*Army*] (RDA)
TEMOD	Test, Measurement, and Diagnostic Equipment Modernization [*Military*] (RDA)
temp	Distemper (VRA)
TEMP	Electrical Resistance Temperature (MCD)
TEMP	[*The*] Expanded Memory Print Program (SAA)
TEMP	Tachyelectromagnetic Pulse
TEMP	Taxation Employment Number [*Canada*]
TEMP	Technique for Econometric Modeling Program (BUR)
temp	[*Egg*] Tempera (VRA)
TEMP	Temperance (ADA)
TEMP	Temperate Zone
TEMP	Temperature (AAG)
temp	Temperature (WA)
Temp	Temperature (DB)
TEMP	Tempered (AAG)

Temp	[*The*] Tempest [*Shakespearean work*] (BARN)
TEMP	Template (AAG)
TEMP	Template Environmental Management Plan (BCP)
TEMP	Tempo [*Music*]
TEMP	Temporal
TEMP	Temporary
Temp	Temporary Employee (WA)
Temp	Temporary Light [*Navigation signal*]
TEMP	Temporary Worker
temp	Tempore [*In the Time Of*] [*Latin*] (GPO)
TEMP	Test and Evaluation Management Plan [*Army*]
TEMP	Test Evaluation Master Plan (MCD)
TEMP	Texas Educational Microwave Project
TEMP	Thermal Energy Management Process (MCD)
T(EMP)	Time to Emplacement [*Military*]
TEMP	Total Energy Management Professionals [*Defunct*] (EA)
TEMP	Triethoxymethoxy Propanes [*Organic chemistry*]
Temp & M...	Temple and Mew's English Crown Cases [*1848-51*] [*A publication*] (DLA)
TEMPATT	Temporarily Attached [*Navy*] (DNAB)
TEMPB	Temporary Dummy Symbol B [*NASDAQ symbol*] (SAG)
Temp Ctf...	Temporary Certificate (MHDW)
TEMPDETD...	Temporary Detached Duty [*Navy*] (DNAB)
TEMP DEXT...	Tempus Dextra [*Right Temple*] [*Medicine*]
Temp Emer Ct App...	Temporary Emergency Court of Appeals [*United States*] (DLA)
TEMPER	Technological, Economic, Military, and Political Evaluation Routine [*Computer-based simulation model*]
TEMPER	Tent, Extendable, Modular, Personnel [*DoD*]
TEMPEST	Transient Electromagnetic Pulse Emanation Standard (MCD)
Temp Geo II...	Cases in Chancery Tempore George II [*England*] [*A publication*] (DLA)
TempGu	Templeton Global Utilities, Inc. [*Associated Press*] (SAG)
TEMPISTORS...	Temperature Compensating Resistors (NATG)
TEMPL	Template [*Engineering*]
Temple & M...	Temple and Mew's English Crown Cases [*A publication*] (DLA)
Temple & M (Eng)...	Temple and Mew's English Crown Cases [*A publication*] (DLA)
Temple U....	Temple University (GAGS)
TempII	Temple-Inland, Inc. [*Associated Press*] (SAG)
TEMPO	Tactical Electromagnetic Project Office [*Military*] (CAAL)
TEMPO	Technical Electronic Management Planning Organization
TEMPO	Technical Military Planning Operation (AAG)
TEMPO	Technique for Extreme Point Optimization (BUR)
TEMPO	Temporary (AAG)
TEMPO	Tetramethylpiperidinol N-oxyl [*Organic chemistry*]
TEMPO	Time and Effort Measurement through Periodic Observation (MCD)
TEMPO	Total Evaluation of Management and Production Output
TEMPOS	Timed Environment Multipartitioned Operating System
TEMP PRIM	Tempo Primo [*Original Tempo*] [*Music*]
TEMPRO	Template-Assisted Intelligence Report Fusion Process
TEMPROX	Temporary Duty Will Cover Approximately [*Navy*]
TEMPS	Transportable Electromagnetic Pulse Simulator (RDA)
TEMPSAL	Temperature-Salinity Data [*Oceanography*] (MCD)
TEMP SINIST...	Tempori Sinistro [*To the Left Temple*] [*Pharmacy*] (ADA)
TempSymbB...	Temporary Dummy Symbol B [*Associated Press*] (SAG)
Temp Univ LQ...	Temple University. Law Quarterly [*A publication*] (DLA)
TEMPUS	Trans-European Mobility Scheme for Unversity Students [*EC*] (ECED)
Temp Wood...	Manitoba Reports Tempore Wood [*Canada*] [*A publication*] (DLA)
TEMPY	Temporary
TEM-RET	Temporary Pay Record for a Retired Member [*Called to Active Duty*] [*Navy*] (DNAB)
TEMS	Teacher Examiner Mark Sheet (AIE)
TEMS	Technical Engineering Management Support [*Air Force*]
TEMS	Test Equipment Maintenance Set
TEMS	Thermal Elastic Model Study
TEMS	Tornado Electronic Messaging System [*Computer science*]
TEMS	Toyota Electronically Modulated Suspension [*Automotive engineering*]
TEMS	Transport Environment Monitoring System [*NASA*] (MCD)
TEMS	Turbine Engine Monitoring System
TEMSE	Technical and Managerial Support Environment (DOMA)
TEMSEPRAD...	Temporary Duty Connection, Separation Processing. Upon Completion and When Directed Detach; Proceed Home for Release from Active Duty in Accordance with Instructions [*Navy*]
TEMSS	Total Emergency Medical Services System
Temtex	Temtex Industries, Inc. [*Associated Press*] (SAG)
TEMWAIT	Temporary Duty Awaiting [*Specified event*] [*Navy*]
TEM wave...	Transverse Electromagnetic Wave [*Electronics*] (MED)
TEMWX	Templeton World [*Mutual fund ticker symbol*] (SG)
TEN	Canarias [*Formerly, Tenerife*] [*Spain*] [*Geomagnetic observatory code*]
Ten	Littleton's Tenures [*A publication*] (DSA)
TEN	Tee-Comm Electronics, Inc. [*Toronto Stock Exchange symbol*]
ten	Tenacious [*Quality of the bottom*] [*Nautical charts*]
TEN	Tenant (WDAA)
TEN	Tenerife [*Canary Islands*] [*Seismograph station code, US Geological Survey*] (SEIS)
TEN	Tenneco Inc. [*NYSE symbol*] (SAG)
TEN	Tennessee (ROG)
TEN	Tennessee Airways, Inc. [*ICAO designator*] (FAAC)
Ten	Tennessee Reports [*A publication*] (ILCA)
TEN	Tennis
TEN	Tenor

ten	Tenor (WDAA)
TEN	Tenuto [Held, Sustained] [Music]
TEN	The Entertainment Network (NITA)
TEN	Total Enteral Nutrition
TEN	Total Entertainment Network [Online gaming service]
TEN	Total Excreted [or Excretory] Nitrogen
TEN	Toxic Epidermal Necrolysis [Medicine]
TEN	Trainee Enrolled Nurse
TEN	Trans-European Network [European Union] (ECON)
tenac	Tenaculum [Medicine] (MAE)
Tenakh	Torah, Veni'im, Ketubim (BJA)
Ten App	Tennessee Appeals Reports [A publication] (DLA)
TENCAP	Tactical Exploitation of National Capabilities Program (COE)
TENCAP	Tactical Exploitation of National Space Capabilities
Ten Cas	Shannon's Tennessee Cases [A publication] (DLA)
Ten Cas	Thompson's Unreported Tennessee Cases [A publication] (DLA)
TEN COM	Tenants in Common (MHDB)
Tencor	Tencor Instruments, Inc. [Associated Press] (SAG)
TENCY	Tenancy (ROG)
TEND	Trend (FAAC)
TENDR	Tendring [England]
TENEMT	Tenement (ROG)
Tenera	Tenera Ltd. [Associated Press] (SAG)
TENES	Teaching English to the Non-English Speaking
TENET	[The] Texas Education Network [A data communications network] (TNIG)
TenetHlt	Tenet Healthcare Corp. [Associated Press] (SAG)
TENG	Technical Engineers Association
TEng	Technician Engineer [British] (DBQ)
TEngAMIN	Technician Engineer of the Institution of Metallurgists [British] (DBQ)
TENN	Tennessee (AAG)
Tenn	Tennessee (ODBW)
TENN	Tennessee Railway Co. [AAR code]
Tenn	Tennessee Supreme Court Reports [A publication] (DLA)
Tenn	Tennyson (BARN)
Tenn Admin Comp	Official Compilation of the Rules and Regulations of the State of Tennessee [A publication] (DLA)
Tenn Admin Reg	Tennessee Administrative Register [A publication] (DLA)
Tennant	Tennant Co. [Associated Press] (SAG)
Tenn App	Tennessee Appeals Reports [A publication] (DLA)
Tenn App	Tennessee Appellate Bulletin [A publication] (DLA)
Tenn App	Tennessee Civil Appeals Reports [A publication] (DLA)
Tenn App Bull	Tennessee Appellate Bulletin [A publication] (DLA)
Tenn Appeals	Tennessee Appeals Reports [A publication] (DLA)
Tenn App R	Tennessee Appeals Reports [A publication] (DLA)
Tenn Cas	Shannon's Unreported Tennessee Cases [1847-1894] [A publication] (DLA)
Tenn Cas (Shannon)	Thompson's Unreported Tennessee Cases [1847-69] [A publication] (DLA)
Tenn CCA	Tennessee Court of Civil Appeals (DLA)
Tenn CCA (Higgins)	Higgins' Tennessee Court of Civil Appeals Reports [A publication] (DLA)
Tenn Ch	Cooper's Tennessee Chancery Reports [A publication] (DLA)
Tenn Ch A	Tennessee Chancery Appeals [A publication] (DLA)
Tenn Chancery	Tennessee Chancery Reports (Cooper) [A publication] (DLA)
Tenn Chancery App	Tennessee Chancery Appeals Reports (Wright) [A publication] (DLA)
Tenn Ch App	Tennessee Chancery Appeals (Wright) [A publication] (DLA)
Tenn Ch App Dec	Tennessee Chancery Appeals Decisions [1895-1907] [A publication] (DLA)
Tenn Ch Ap Reps	Wright's Tennessee Chancery Appeals Reports [A publication] (DLA)
Tenn Ch R	Tennessee Chancery Reports (Cooper) [A publication] (DLA)
Tenn Civ A	Tennessee Civil Appeals [A publication] (DLA)
Tenn Civ App	Tennessee Civil Appeals [A publication] (DLA)
Tennco	Tenneco, Inc. [Formerly, Tennessee Gas Transmission Co.] [Associated Press] (SAG)
Tenn Code Ann	Tennessee Code, Annotated [A publication] (DLA)
Tenn Cr App	Tennessee Criminal Appeals [A publication] (DLA)
Tenn Crim App	Tennessee Criminal Appeals Reports [A publication] (DLA)
Tennessee R	Tennessee Reports [A publication] (DLA)
Tennessee Rep	Tennessee Reports [A publication] (DLA)
Tenn Jur	Tennessee Jurisprudence [A publication] (DLA)
Tenn Juris	Tennessee Jurisprudence [A publication] (DLA)
Tenn Law	Tennessee Lawyer [A publication] (DLA)
Tenn Leg Rep	Tennessee Legal Reporter [A publication] (DLA)
Tenn Priv Acts	Private Acts of the State of Tennessee [A publication] (DLA)
Tenn Pub Acts	Public Acts of the State of Tennessee [A publication] (DLA)
Tenn R	Tennessee Reports [A publication] (DLA)
Tenn Rep	Tennessee Reports [A publication] (DLA)
Tenn St U	Tennessee State University (GAGS)
Tenn Tech U	Tennessee Technological University (GAGS)
TENN-TOM	Tennessee-Tombigbee [Proposed waterway]
TENOC	Ten-Year Oceanographic Program [Navy]
TENOR	Tennessee Open Records [An association]
TENPrB	Tenneco $7.40 cm Pfd [NYSE symbol] (TTSB)
TENR	Technically Enhanced Naturally Radioactive (NRCH)
TENRAP	Technically Enhanced Naturally Radioactive Product (NRCH)
TENS	Tensile
TENS	Tension (AAG)
TENS	Training Element Need Statement
TENS	Transcutaneous Electrical Nerve Stimulation [Also, TES, TNS] [A method of pain control] [Medicine]
TENSEGRITY	Tensional Integrity [Construction principle named by Buckminster Fuller]
TENT	Tenant (ROG)
TENT	Tenement (ROG)
TENT	Tentative (AAG)
TENV	Totally Enclosed - Nonventilated
TENWF	Tee Comm Electronics, Inc. [NASDAQ symbol] (SAG)
TENX	Tee Comm Electronics, Inc. [NASDAQ symbol] (SAG)
TENXF	Tee-Comm Electronics [NASDAQ symbol] (TTSB)
TEO	Teal Industry Ltd. [Vancouver Stock Exchange symbol]
TEO	Technical Electronic Office [Data General Corp.]
TEO	Tel Argentina-France Tel'B'ADS [NYSE symbol] (TTSB)
TEO	Telecom Argentina Stet France Telecom SA [NYSE symbol] (SAG)
TEO	Telephone Equipment Order [Telecommunications] (TEL)
TEO	Teoloyucan [Mexico] [Geomagnetic observatory code]
TEO	Terapo [Papua New Guinea] [Airport symbol] (OAG)
TEO	Terato Resources Ltd. [Toronto Stock Exchange symbol]
TEO	Test Equipment Operator
TEO	Third World Education Outreach (EA)
TEO	To Expiry Only (AIA)
TEO	Total Extractable Organic [Analytical chemistry]
TEO	Transferred Electron Oscillator
TEO	Transmittal Engineering Order
TEOA	Test and Evaluation Objectives Annex (MCD)
TEOA	Triethanolamine [Organic chemistry]
TEOF	Triethyl Orthoformate [Organic chemistry]
TEOM	Tapered Element Oscillating Microbalance
TEOM	Transformer Environment Overcurrent Monitor (IEEE)
TEORS	Transient Electro-Optic Raman Scattering [Physics]
TEOS	Tetraethoxysilane [Organic radical]
TEOS	Tetraethyl Orthosilicate [Organic chemistry] (NASA)
TEOS	Tillotson Equation of State [Physical chemistry]
TEOSS	Tactical Emitter Operational Support System (MCD)
TEOTA	[The] Eyes of the Army (AAG)
TEOTWAWKI	The End of the World as We Know It
TEP	Table Editing Process
TEP	Tactical ELINT Processor (MCD)
TEP	Tape Edit Processor [Computer science]
TEP	Tau Epsilon Phi [Fraternity]
TEP	Technical Education Program (OICC)
TEP	Technical Evaluation Panel [In various federal government agencies] (NASA)
TEP	Temperature Extreme Pressure (DNAB)
TEP	Temporary Entry Permit
TEP	Tepecintle [Race of maize]
TEP	Teptep [Papua New Guinea] [Airport symbol] (OAG)
TEP	Terminal Error Program
TEP	Territory Enterprises Proprietary
TEP	Test and Evaluation Plan [Military] (CAAL)
TEP	Test Executive Processor (NITA)
TEP	Tetraethoxypropane [Organic chemistry]
TEP	Tetraethyl Pyrophosphate [Insecticide] [Pharmacology] (IAA)
TEP	Thermal Enzyme Probe
TEP	Thermoelectric Power [Thermodynamics]
TEP	Thromboendophlebectomy [Medicine] (MAE)
TEP	Token Economy Program [Psychiatry]
TEP	Tons Equivalent of Petroleum [Fuel measure]
TEP	Torpedo Ejection Pump (DNAB)
TEP	Total Extractable Protein [Food technology]
TEP	Toxicant Extraction Procedure
TEP	Trace Element Pattern (KSC)
TEP	Tracheo-Esophageal Puncture [Medicine]
TEP	Training Equipment Plan
TEP	Trans Equatorial Propagation
TEP	Transmitter Experiment Package
TEP	Transparent Electrophotographic (NITA)
TEP	Transparent Electrophotography [Proposed archival storage medium]
TEP	Transportable Equation Program (DNAB)
TEP	Triethylphosphate (LDT)
TEP	Triethyl-Phosphine [Organic chemistry]
TEP	Tubal Ectopic Pregnancy (STED)
TEP	Tube Evaluation Program
TEP	Tucson Electric Power Co. [NYSE symbol] (SPSG)
TEP	Tucson Ele Power(New) [NYSE symbol] (TTSB)
TEP	Turbine Extreme Pressure (MCD)
TEP	Turkiye Emekci Partisi [Workers' Party of Turkey] [Political party] (PPW)
TEP	Tyrone Energy Park (NRCH)
TEPA	Roswell Park Memorial Institute [Research code symbol]
TEPA	Tetraethylenepentamine [Organic chemistry]
TEPA	Triethylenephosphoramide [Also, APO] [Organic chemistry]
TEPAC	Tube Engineering Panel Advisory Council [Defunct] (EA)
TEPC	Test and Evaluation Planning Committee [Military] (CAAL)
TEPC	Tissue Equivalent Proportional Counter (PDAA)
Tepco	Teppco Partners Ltd. [Associated Press] (SAG)
TEPCO	Tokyo Electric Power Co. (ECON)
TEPD	Trademark Examining Procedure Directives [A publication]
TEPE	Target Engagement Proficiency Exercise [Military]
TEPE	Time-Sharing Event Performance Evaluator (CIST)
TEPG	Test Evaluation Planning Group (MCD)
TEPG	Thermionic Electrical Power Generator (IEEE)
TEPG	Triethylphosphine Gold (STED)
TEPH	Thromboembolic Pulmonary Hypertension [Medicine] (CPH)
TEPI	Technical Equipment Planning Information
TEPI	Terminal Endpoint Identifier (TNIG)
TEPI	Terminal Phase Intercept
TEPI	Training Equipment Planning Information [Military] (AFM)

TEPI	Triadal Equated Personality Inventory [*Psychology*]
TEPIAC	Thermophysical and Electronic Properties Information Analysis Center [*Later, HTMIAC*] [*Purdue University*]
TEPIC	Tris(epoxypropyl)isocyanurate [*Organic chemistry*]
tepid	Tepidarium (VRA)
TEPID	Tepidus [*Lukewarm*] [*Pharmacy*] (ROG)
TEPIGEN	Television Picture Generator (MCD)
TEPL	Test of English Proficiency Level [*G. Rathmell*] (TES)
TEPLX	Templeton Growth [*Mutual fund ticker symbol*] (SG)
TEPOS	Test Program Operating System
TEPP	Tetraethyl Pyrophosphate [*Insecticide*] [*Pharmacology*]
TEPP	Triethylenepyrophosphate (DB)
TEPP	Turbine Engine Power Plant (DWSG)
TEPPS	Technique for Establishing Personnel Performance Standards [*Navy*]
TEPR	Tomahawk Experimental Reaction [*Navy*]
TEPR	Training Equipment Progress Report
TEPrB	Toledo Edison 4 1/4% Pfd [*AMEX symbol*] (TTSB)
TEPRSSC	Technical Electronic Product Radiation Safety Standards Committee (MCD)
TEPS	National Commission on Teacher Education and Professional Standards [*Defunct*]
TEPSA	Trans European Policy Studies Association (EA)
TEQ	Total Engagement Quality [*Computer science*]
TEQ	Toxicity Equivalent
TEQ	Trian Equities Ltd. [*Vancouver Stock Exchange symbol*]
TEQ	Twenty-Foot Equivalent [*Shipping*]
TEQU	Test Equivocal, Possible Low Titer [*Laboratory science*] (DAVI)
TER	Australian Territory (EERA)
TER	Tape Error Recovery [*Routine*] [*Computer science*] (ECII)
TER	Tardeable Emmission Rights (EERA)
TER	Tau Epsilon Rho [*Fraternity*]
TER	Technical Evaluation Report [*Nuclear energy*] (NRCH)
TER	Telecommunications Electronic Reviews [*A publication*]
TERI	Teleprinter Retransmitting [*Telecommunications*] (IAA)
TER	Teradyne, Inc. [*NYSE symbol*] (SPSG)
TER	Tera Mines Ltd. [*Toronto Stock Exchange symbol*]
TER	Terceira [*Azores*] [*Airport symbol*] (OAG)
TER	Tere [*Rub*] [*Pharmacy*]
Ter	Terence [*Second century BC*] [*Classical studies*] (OCD)
ter	Tereno [*MARC language code Library of Congress*] (LCCP)
TER	Terrace
Ter	Terrace (TBD)
ter	Terracotta (VRA)
TER	Terra Mines Ltd. [*Toronto Stock Exchange symbol Vancouver Stock Exchange symbol*]
TER	Terranova [*Guatemala*] [*Seismograph station code, US Geological Survey*] (SEIS)
TER	Terrazzo
TER	Territorial Airlines, Inc. [*ICAO designator*] (FAAC)
TER	Territory
Ter	Terry's Delaware Reports [*A publication*] (DLA)
TER	Tertiary (KSC)
Ter	Terumot (BJA)
TER	Test Effectiveness Ratio [*Computer science*]
TFR	Test Equipment Readiness [*NASA*] (NASA)
TER	Test Evaluation Report [*NASA*] (KSC)
TER	Thermal Enhancement Ratio
TE-R	Thermostable E-Rosetting [*Cells*] [*Medicine*]
TER	Threefold (DAVI)
TER	Three Times [*Pharmacy*] (DAVI)
TER	Time and Event Recorder
TER	Time Estimating Relationship (NASA)
TER	Total Elbow Replacement (STED)
TER	Total Endoplasmic Reticulum [*Cytology*]
TER	Total Energy Ratio [*Mechanical engineering*]
TER	Total Expense Ratio [*Finance*]
TER	Total External Reflection
TE/R	Trailing Edge Radius (MSA)
TER	Training Equipment Requirements Plan
TER	Transcapillary Escape Rate
TER	Transcapillary Escape Route [*Medicine*] (DAVI)
TER	Transepithelial Electrical Resistance [*Cytology*]
TER	Transfer Effectiveness Ratio
TER	Transmission Engineering Recommendation [*Telecommunications*] (IAA)
TER	Transmission Equivalent Resistance (IEEE)
TER	Travel Expense Report (SAA)
TER	Triple Ejection [*or Ejector*] Rack (NVT)
TER	True Height Above Aerodrome Level [*Aviation*] (AIA)
TERA	Tax Equity and Responsibility Act of 1982 (WYGK)
TERA	Temporary Early Retirement Authority (DOMA)
TERA	Tera Computer [*NASDAQ symbol*] (TTSB)
TERA	Tera Computer Co. [*NASDAQ symbol*] (SAG)
TERA	Terminal Effects Research and Analysis Group [*New Mexico Institute of Mining and Technology*] [*Research center*] (RCD)
TERA	Test of Early Reading Ability
TERA	#The Early Retirement Authority
TERA	Tradable Emission Reduction Assessments [*Environmental Protection Agency*]
tera-	Trillion 10^{12} (IDOE)
TERA	TSCA [*Toxic Substances Control Act*] Experimental Release Application [*Environmental Protection Agency*]
TERAC	Tactical Electromagnetic Readiness Advisory Council (MCD)
TeraCo	Tera Computer Co. [*Associated Press*] (SAG)
TERAG	Transportable Electronic Receiving Antenna Group (DWSG)
TERAS	Tactical Energy Requirements and Supply System (MCD)
TERAT	Teratology (ROG)
TERAW	Tera Computer Wrrt [*NASDAQ symbol*] (TTSB)
Terb	Terbutaline (STED)
TERB	Terrazzo Base
TERC	Technical Education Research Centers, Inc. [*Cambridge, MA*] [*Research center*]
TERC	Tertiary Education Research Centre [*British*] (AIE)
TERC	Total Environmental Remediation Contracts (AAGC)
TERC	Total Environmental Restoration Contract (COE)
TERC	Total Environmental Restoration Contracts (BCP)
TERCO	Telephone Rationalization by Computer (PDAA)
TERCOM	Terrain Comparison [*Military*] (MUSM)
TERCOM	Terrain Contour Mapping (MCD)
TERCOM	Terrain Contour Matching [*Navigation system*] [*Air Force*]
TERCOM	Terrain Correlation Method
TERD	Turbine Electric Reduction Drive
Terdyn	Terradyne, Inc. [*Associated Press*] (SAG)
TEREBINTH	Terebinthinae Oleum [*Oil of Turpentine*] [*Pharmacology*] (ROG)
TEREC	Tactical Electromagnetic Reconnaissance [*Air Force*] (IAA)
TEREC	Tactical Electronic Reconnaissance [*Aircraft*]
TERENA	Trans-European Research and Education Networking Association [*Formed from merger of Reseaux Associes pour le Recherche Europeenne and European Academic and Research Network*] [*Internet*]
Terent	Terentius Clemens [*Flourished, 2nd century*] [*Authority cited in pre-1607 legal work*] (DSA)
TERENVSVC	Terrestrial Environmental Services [*Army*] (AABC)
Terex	Terex Corp. [*Associated Press*] (SAG)
TERF	Trudeau Early Retirement Fund [*Established 1982 by Canadians who hoped t·hat the money would persuade their prime minister to retire from office*] [*Defunct*]
TERG	Training Equipment Requirements Guide (KSC)
TERI	Table of Equipment Ready Issue [*Navy*] (ANA)
TERI	Tata Energy Research Institute [*New Delhi, India*] (ECON)
TERI	Torpedo Effective Range Indicator
TERL	Test Engineer Readiness List [*NASA*] (NASA)
TERL	Test Equipment Readiness List [*NASA*] (NASA)
Terleu	Tertiary Leucine (BABM)
TERLS	Thumba Equatorial Launching Station [*Indian rocket station*]
TERM	Tank Extended Range Munition [*Army*]
TERM	Temporary Equipment Recovery Mission (CINC)
TERM	Terminal (AAG)
Term	Terminal (EBF)
TERM	Terminate (AFM)
TERM	Termination (ECII)
TERM	Terminology
TERM	Termite (ADA)
Term	Term Reports [*North Carolina*] [1816-18] [*A publication*] (DLA)
Term	Term Reports, English King's Bench (Durnford and East's Reports) [*A publication*] (DLA)
Termes de la Ley	Terms of the Common Laws and Statutes Expounded and Explained by John Rastell [1685] [*A publication*] (DLA)
TFRMIA	Association Internationale de Terminologie [*International Association of Terminology*] [*Quebec, PQ*] (EAIO)
TERMINACTRAORD	Directed to Request Termination of Inactive Duty Training Orders [*Navy*]
TERMINON	Termination (ROG)
TERMINOQ	Banque de Terminologie de Quebec [*Terminology Bank of Quebec*] [*French Language Board*] [*Information service or system*]
TERMN	Termination
Term NC	Taylor's North Carolina Term Reports [*A publication*] (DLA)
TERMNET	International Network for Terminology [*INFOTERM*] [*Vienna, Austria*]
TERM PWR	Terminator Power [*Computer science*]
Term R	Term Reports, English King's Bench (Durnford and East's Reports) [*A publication*] (DLA)
Term Rep	Term Reports, English King's Bench (Durnford and East's Reports) [*England*] [*A publication*] (DLA)
Term Rep (NC)	Taylor's North Carolina Term Reports [4 *North Carolina*] [*A publication*] (DLA)
TERMS	Terminal Management System [*Military*] (AABC)
TERMTRAN	Terminal Translator (KSC)
TERN	Terminal and Enroute Navigation (PDAA)
TERN	Transnational European Rural Network [*Belgium*] (EAIO)
TERO	Tribal Employment Rights Office
TERP	Terminal Equipment Replacement Program [*Electronic communications system*] [*Department of State*]
TERP	Terminal Instrument Procedure [*Aviation*]
TERP	Terrain Elevation Retrieval Program (IEEE)
TERP	Turbine Engine Reliability Program (PDAA)
TERPACIS	Trust Territory of the Pacific Islands
TERPE	Tactical Electronic Reconnaissance Processing and Evaluation [*Air Force*] (MCD)
TERPES	Tactical Electronic Reconnaissance Processing and Evaluation System (MCD)
TERPROM	Terrain Profile Matching [*British*]
TERPS	Tactical Electronic Reconnaissance Processing (and Evaluation) System [*Navy*] (MCD)
TERPS	Terminal Enquiry/Response Programming System [*British*]
TERPS	Terminal Instrument Procedures [*Military*]
TERPS	Terminal Planning System [*Military*]
TERR	Terrace
terr.	Terrace (VRA)
Terr.	Terrace (DD)
TERR	Terraza

Terr............	Terrell's Reports [38-71 Texas] [A publication] (DLA)
TERR...........	Territory (AFM)
Terr............	Terrorist [Slang term used by whites in Zimbabwe to refer to a black nationalist guerrilla]
Terra...........	Terra Industries, Inc. [Associated Press] (SAG)
TERRA.........	Terrain Evaluation and Retrieval for Road Alignment (IAA)
TERRA.........	Terricide-Escape by Rethinking, Research, Action [An association]
TERRACE.....	Terrace [Commonly used] (OPSA)
Terrace.......	Terrace Holdings, Inc. [Associated Press] (SAG)
Terr & Wal...	Terrell and Walker's Reports [38-51 Texas] [A publication] (DLA)
Terr & Walk...	Terrell and Walker's Reports [38-51 Texas] [A publication] (DLA)
TerraNit......	Terra Nitrogen Co. Ltd. [Formerly, Agricultural Minerals Ltd.] [Associated Press] (SAG)
TERRAP.......	TERRAP [Territorial Apprehensiveness] Programs [Commercial firm] (EA)
TERREL.......	Terrain Elevation (SAA)
TERRES.......	Territorial Residents
TERRESTAR...	Terrestrial Application of Solar Technology and Research (MCD)
TERRHICO ...	Territorial Rhine Coordination [NATO] (NATG)
TERRIT.......	Territory
Terr L	Territories Law [Northwest Territories] [A publication] (DLA)
Terr L (Can)...	Territories Law Reports [1885-1907] [Canada] [A publication] (DLA)
Terr LR.......	Territories Law Reports [1885-1907] [Canada] [A publication] (DLA)
TerrNov......	Terra Nova Bermuda Holdings Ltd. [Associated Press] (SAG)
Terrorilla	Terrorism and Guerrilla Warfare [Israel]
TERS...........	Tactical Electronic Reconnaissance System (IEEE)
TERS...........	Tactical Event Reporting System (DOMA)
TerS...........	Terra Santa [Jerusalem] (BJA)
TER SIM	Tere Simul [Rub Together] [Latin] (ADA)
TERSS	Tasmanian Earth Resources Satellite Station [Commonwealth] [State] (EERA)
TERSSE.......	Total Earth Resources System for the Shuttle Era [NASA]
TERT...........	Telomerase Reverse Transcriptase [An enzyme]
tert.............	Tertiary [Also, t] [Chemistry]
TERT...........	Tertiary [Period, era, or system] [Geology]
TERT...........	Tertius [Third] [Latin]
Tert.............	Tertullian [160-240AD] [Classical studies] (OCD)
TERT...........	Tracking/Erosion Resistance Tester
TERTM........	Thermal Expansion Resin Transfer Molding
TERTSD	Tertiary Sand [Agronomy]
Tertul..........	Tertullianus [Flourished, 2nd-3rd century] [Authority cited in pre-1607 legal work] (DSA)
Teruv..........	Teruvenkatachariar's Railway Cases [India] [A publication] (DLA)
TES.............	[The] Engineers School (MCD)
TES.............	[The] Executive Speaker (IID)
TES.............	Tableaux Entrees-Sorties [Database] [EC] (ECED)
TES.............	Tactical Environment Simulator [Navy] (MCD)
TES.............	Tactical Environment System [Navy]
TES.............	Target Engagement Simulator [Military] (MCD)
TES.............	Team Effectiveness Survey [Test]
TeS.............	Technical Editing Services [British]
TES.............	Technical Enforcement Support [Environmental Protection Agency] (GFGA)
TES.............	Technical Engagement Simulation
TES.............	Technical Enquiry Service [British] (DCTA)
TES.............	Technical Environmental Systems, Inc. (EFIS)
TES.............	Telemetry Evaluation Station
TES.............	Temporary Employment Subsidy [British] (DCTA)
TES.............	Terminal Emulation Server [Computer science] (CIST)
TES.............	Terminal Encounter System
TeS.............	Terre Sainte (BJA)
TES.............	Territorial Experiment Stations Division [of ARS, Department of Agriculture]
TES.............	Tessenei [Ethiopia] [Airport symbol] (AD)
tes.............	Tessera (VRA)
TES.............	Test and Evaluation Squadron
TES.............	Test and Evaluation Support
TES.............	Test Squadron [Air Force]
TES.............	Tetraethylsulfamide [Organic chemistry]
TES.............	Text Editing System
TES.............	Theatre Education Society (EA)
TES.............	Therapeutic Electrical Stimulation
TES.............	Thermal Emission Spectrometer
TES.............	Thermal Energy Storage
TES.............	Thermoset Elastomer Styrene Plastic [Materials science]
TES.............	Thin Elastic Shell
TES.............	Thymic Epithelial Supernatant [Endocrinology]
TES.............	Tidal Electric Station
TES.............	Time Encoded Speech [Telecommunications] (TEL)
TES.............	Times Educational Supplement [A publication] (BRI)
TES.............	Training Equipment Summary (MCD)
TES.............	Transcutaneous Electrical Stimulation [Also, TENS, TNS] [A method of pain control] [Medicine]
TES.............	Transmural Electrical Stimulation
TES.............	Transportable Earth Station [British]
TES.............	Transportes Aereos de El Salvador SA de CV [ICAO designator] (FAAC)
TES.............	Transthoracic Endoscopic Sympathectomy
TES.............	Treatment of Emergent Symptom [Medicine] (MEDA)
TES.............	Triethylsilyl [Organic chemistry]
TES.............	Tris(hydroxymethyl)methylaminoethanesulfonic Acid [A buffer]
TES.............	Tropospheric Emission Sensor
TES.............	Tungsten Electron Snatcher
TES.............	Twelve English Statesmen [A publication]
TES.............	Two Electron Satellite (AAEL)

TESA..........	Television and Electronics Service Association
TESAC........	Temperature-Salinity-Currents [Oceanography] (IID)
TESAR........	Tactical Endurance Synthetic Aperture RADAR [Army] (RDA)
TESAT........	Teaching Sample Table (PDAA)
TESC..........	[The] Evergreen State College [Olympia, WA]
TESC..........	Tescorp, Inc. [NASDAQ symbol] (SAG)
TESCO........	Truck Equipment Sales Co. (EFIS)
TESCP........	Tescorp 10% 1990 Cv Pfd [NASDAQ symbol] (TTSB)
Tescp.........	Tescorp, Inc. [Associated Press] (SAG)
Tescrp........	Tescorp, Inc. [Associated Press] (SAG)
TESE..........	Tactical Exercise Simulator and Evaluator (NVT)
TESEM........	Television Esmeraldena Compania de Economia Mixta [Ecuador] (EY)
TE(S)FC......	Totally-Enclosed (Separately) Fan-Cooled [Reactor] (DEN)
TESG..........	Target Echo Signature Generator [SONAR]
TESH..........	Technical Shop (NASA)
TESH..........	Test Shop
TESI...........	Tangram Enterprise Solutions, Inc. [NASDAQ symbol] (SAG)
TESI...........	Teaching Events Stress Inventory (EDAC)
TESI...........	Transfer of Electrostatic Images [Electrophotography]
TESICO	Threshold Electron Secondary Ion Coincidence [Spectroscopy]
TESL..........	Teaching English as a Second Language
TESLA........	Technical Standards for Library Automation (AL)
TESLAC.......	Testolactone [Antineoplastic drug]
TESM.........	Triethylstannylmaleate [Organic chemistry]
Tesma........	Tesma International, Inc. [Associated Press] (SAG)
TESMA........	Theatre Equipment and Supply Manufacturers Association [Later, TEA] (EA)
TESOL........	Teachers of English to Speakers of Other Languages (EA)
Tesor.........	Tesoro Petroleum Corp. [Associated Press] (SAG)
Tesoro	Tesoro Petroleum Corp. [Associated Press] (SAG)
TESPA........	Triethylenethiophosphoramide [Antineoplastic drug] (DAVI)
TESR..........	Tactical Environment Satellite Readout (MCD)
TESR..........	Test Equipment Status Report
TESR..........	Time of Sunrise
TESRP	Test and Evaluation Support Resource Plan (MCD)
TESS..........	[The] Educational Software Selector [Database] (AEE)
TESS..........	Tactical and Environmental Support System [Military] (CAAL)
TESS..........	Tactical Electromagnetic Systems Study (IEEE)
TESS..........	Tactical Engagement Simulation System [Developed by Sandia National Laboratories for the Defense Nuclear Agency]
TESS..........	Technical Engineering and Spacelift Services [Air Force] (AAGC)
TESS..........	Temporary Employment Subsidy Scheme [Department of Employment] [British]
TESS..........	TESSCO Technologies [NASDAQ symbol] (TTSB)
TESS..........	TESSCO Technologies, Inc. [NASDAQ symbol] (SAG)
TESS..........	The Expert System Shell (NITA)
TESS..........	Time of Sunset
TESS..........	Times Educational Supplement Scotland (AIE)
TESS..........	Top Electronic Security Systems [Commercial firm British]
TESS..........	Total Energy Systems Service (IAA)
TESS..........	Total Engineering Support System (HGAA)
TESS..........	TRW Environmental Safety Systems, Inc. (GAAI)
TESSA........	Tax-Exempt Special Savings Account [British]
Tessa.........	Tax Exempt Special Savings Account [British] (ODBW)
TESSA........	Total Energy Suppression Shield Array [Nuclear structure]
TESSAC.......	Tactical Electromagnetic Systems Study Action Council [Navy] (ANA)
TESSAR	Test Event Sequencing, Simulating, and Recording System (PDAA)
TESSCO.......	TESSCO Technologies, Inc. [Associated Press] (SAG)
TEST..........	Tanner Eclectic Stuttering Therapy Program
TEST..........	Teen-Age Employment Skills Training, Inc.
TEST..........	Testament
Test...........	Testamentary [Legal term] (DLA)
TEST..........	Testator (ADA)
TEST..........	Testatrix (WDAA)
TEST..........	Testimonial (ADA)
TEST..........	Testing
TEST..........	Thesaurus of Engineering and Scientific Terms [A publication]
TEST..........	Track Evaluation System [Canadian National Railways]
TEST..........	Transamerica Electronic Scoring Technique [Credit risk evaluation]
TEST..........	Tubal Embryo Stage Transfer
TEST..........	Two Element Synthesis Telescope (ADA)
TestAbr.......	Testament of Abraham [Pseudepigrapha] (BJA)
TestAsh.......	Testament of Asher [Pseudepigrapha] (BJA)
TestBen.......	Testament of Benjamin [Pseudepigrapha] (BJA)
testco.........	Terra Sancta Tourist Co. Ltd. [Jordan]
TESTCOMDNA...	Test Command Defense Nuclear Agency [Military] (AABC)
TESTFAC......	Test Facility
TESTG.........	Test Group [Military]
TESTICLES...	Teamwork, Enthusiasm, Stamina, Tenacity, Initiative, Courage, Loyalty, Excellence, and a Sense of Humor [Military slang] (VNW)
TestIss........	Testament of Issachar [Pseudepigrapha] (BJA)
TestJos	Testament of Joseph [Pseudepigrapha] (BJA)
TestJud.......	Testament of Judah [Pseudepigrapha] (BJA)
TestLevi.......	Testament of Levi [Pseudepigrapha] (BJA)
TestNaph	Testament of Naphtali [Pseudepigrapha] (BJA)
TESTO........	Testigo [Witness] [Latin] (ADA)
TESTOR.......	Testator (ROG)
TESTOS.......	Testosterone [Endocrinology] (DAVI)
TESTRAN	Test Translator [Computer science]
TestReub.....	Testament of Reuben [Pseudepigrapha] (BJA)
TESTRIX......	Testatrix (ROG)
TESTS.........	Technical-Engineering-Science Training for Secretaries
TESTS.........	Test Squadron (MCD)

TestSim	Testament of Simeon [*Pseudepigrapha*] (BJA)
TESTT	Testament
TESTW	Test Wing [*Military*]
TestXII	Testaments of the Twelve Patriarchs [*Pseudepigrapha*] (BJA)
TESTY	Testamentary (ROG)
TestZeb	Testament of Zebulun [*Pseudepigrapha*] (BJA)
TESV	Tephrosia Symptomless Virus [*Plant pathology*]
TESY	Terminal Editing System [*Computer science*] (PDAA)
TET	East Tennessee State University, Johnson City, TN [*OCLC symbol*] (OCLC)
TET	Teacher Effectiveness Training [*A course of study*]
TET	Teacher of Electrotherapy [*British*]
TET	Technical Evaluation Team (MCD)
TET	Technical Evaluation Test (MCD)
TET	Telescope and Electron Telescope
TET	Test Equipment Team (AAG)
TET	Test Equipment Tool (AAG)
TET	Test Evaluation Team [*NASA*] (KSC)
Tet	Tetanus [*Medicine*]
TET	Tete [*Mozambique*] [*Airport symbol*] (OAG)
TET	Tete [*Mozambique*] [*Seismograph station code, US Geological Survey*] (SEIS)
TET	Tetrachloride [*Chemistry*] (AAG)
Tet	Tetracycline [*Antibiotic compound*]
TET	Tetrahedron (FAAC)
Tet	Tetralogy [*Medicine*]
TET	Tetralogy of Fallot [*Neonatology*] (DAVI)
TET	Tetrode [*Electronics*]
TET	Thermionic Emission Technique
TET	Thermometric Enthalpy Titration [*Analytical chemistry*]
TET	Tipton Environmental Technology, Inc. (EFIS)
TET	Titanium Elevon Track
TET	Total Elapsed Time (KSC)
TET	Trailing Edge Tracking [*Aviation*] (LAIN)
TET	Transistor Evaluation Test
TET	Transportable Electronic Tower (MCD)
TET	Traveling-Wave Tube (IAA)
TET	Treadmill Exercise Test [*Physiology*] (CPH)
TET	Troop Evaluation Tests [*Army*]
TET	Tubal Embryo Stage Transfer [*Alternative to traditional in-vitro fertilization (IVF)*] [*Also, TEST*] (PAZ)
TET	Turbine Entry Temperature [*Aviation*]
TET	Turbo-Electric Tanker
TETA	Test Equipment Technical Adviser
TETA	Test-Estrin Time(d) Action [*Pharmacology*] (DAVI)
TETA	Travelers Emergency Transportation Association [*Sought to pool transportation of salesmen traveling similar routes*] [*World War II*]
TETA	Triethylenetetramine [*Organic chemistry*]
TETAM	Tactical Effectiveness Testing of Antitank Missiles [*DoD*]
TETB	Tetbury [*England*]
TETC	Teroson Europe Technical Centre [*Research center Germany*]
TETCYC	Tetracycline [*An Antibiotic*] [*Pharmacology*] (DAVI)
TETD	Tetraethylthiuram Disulfide [*Also, TTD*] [*Organic chemistry*]
TETEP	Test for Entrance into Teacher Education Programs [*Achievement test*]
TETF	Terminal Equipment Test Facility [*Army*] (RDA)
TETFLEYNE	Tetrafluorethylene [*Organic chemistry*]
TETM	Tetraethylthiuram Monosulfide [*Organic chemistry*]
TETM	Thermal Effects Tests Model
TETOC	Council for Technical Education and Training for Overseas Countries [*British*]
TETR	Test and Training Satellite [*Also, TATS, TTS*] [*NASA*]
TETR	Tetragonal
TETRA	Terminal Tracking Telescope
TETRA	Terminal Trajectory Telescope (IAA)
tetra	Tetraploid [*Genetics*]
Tetra	Tetra Technologies, Inc. [*Associated Press*] (SAG)
TETRAC	Tension Truss Antenna Concept
TETRAC	Tetraiodothyroacetic Acid [*Organic chemistry*] (MAH)
TetraTc	Tetra Tech, Inc. [*Associated Press*] (SAG)
TETROON	Tethered Meteorological Balloon (IAA)
TETROON	Tetrahedral Balloon [*Meteorology*]
TETSS	Test and Evaluation Technical Support Services [*Army*]
TET TOX	Tetanus Toxin (WDAA)
Tet Tox	Tetanus Toxoid [*Medicine*] (CPH)
TEtWH	Woods Memorial Hospital, Etowah, TN [*Library symbol*] [*Library of Congress*] (LCLS)
TEU	Te Anau [*New Zealand*] [*Airport symbol*] (OAG)
TEU	Technical Edit Unit [*Navy*] (DNAB)
TEU	Technical Escort Unit [*Army*] (AABC)
TeU	Tekst en Uitleg (BJA)
TEU	Telemetry Equipment Unit
TEU	Temple University, Philadelphia, PA [*OCLC symbol*] (OCLC)
TEU	Test of Economic Understanding
TEU	Tetraethyl Urea [*Organic chemistry*]
TEU	Trailing Edge Up
TEU	Transducer Excitation Unit
TEU	Tropical Experimental Unit [*British military*] (DMA)
TEU	Turret Electronics Unit [*Military*] (RDA)
TEU	Twenty-Foot Container Equivalent Unit [*MARAD*] (TAG)
TEU	Twenty-Foot Equivalent Unit [*Used to compare capacity of containerships*]
TEUC	TADS [*Target Acquisition Designation Sight*] Electronics Unit Card [*Army*]
TEUC	Temporary Extended Unemployment Compensation [*Labor*]
TEUN	Trust for Education on the United Nations (EA)
TEUT	Teuton
TEV	Tadpole Edema Virus [*Medicine*] (DMAA)
TEV	Talipes Equinovarus [*Anatomy*]
T Ev	Taylor on Evidence [*12th ed.*] [*1931*] [*A publication*] (DLA)
TEV	Terminal Equipment Vehicle [*British military*] (DMA)
TeV	Tetra-Electron Volt
TEV	Thermoelectric Voltage
TEV	Thermostatic Expansion Valve [*Refrigeration*]
TEV	Time Expanded Video
TEV	Tobacco Etch Virus
TEV	Today's English Version [*of the Bible*]
TEV	Tomato Etch Virus
TEV	Total Economic Value
TEV	Total Evaporative Emissions [*Automotive engineering*]
TEV	T-Platform Electric Van [*Chrysler*] [*Automotive engineering*]
TeV	Trillion Electron Volts
TEV	Turbo-Electric Vessel
TEV	Victoria College, Victoria, TX [*OCLC symbol*] (OCLC)
Teva	Teva Pharmaceutical Industries Ltd. [*Associated Press*] (SAG)
TEVA	Tutmonda Esperantista Vegetara Asocio [*World Esperantist Vegetarian Association - WEVA*] (EAIO)
TEVAL	Target Engagement Evaluation [*Military*]
TEVI	Teva Pharmaceutical Industries Ltd. [*NASDAQ symbol*] (NQ)
TEVIY	Teva Pharm Indus ADR [*NASDAQ symbol*] (TTSB)
TEVROC	Tailored Exhaust Velocity Rocket
TEVROK	Tailored Exhaust Velocity Rocket
TEW	Tactical Early Warning
TEW	Tactical Electronic Warfare [*Aircraft*] (NATG)
TEW	Total Equivalent Weight
TE/W	Tractive Effort to Weight Ratio (MCD)
TEW	Transort of Equatorial Waters [*Project*] [*Marine science*] (OSRA)
TEWA	Target Evaluation and Weapon Assignment (MCD)
TEWA	Threat Evaluation and Weapons Assignment (NVT)
TE wave	Transverse Eletric Wave [*Electronics*] (MED)
TEWC	Totally-Enclosed Water-Cooled [*Reactor*] (DEN)
TEWDS	Tactical Electronic Warfare Deception System (MCD)
TEWG	Tactical Electronic Warfare Group [*Military*]
TEWG	Test and Evaluation Work Group [*Military*] (CAAL)
TEWG	Transitional Environmental Working Group (EERA)
TEWGp	Tactical Electronic Warfare Group [*Air Force*] (AFM)
TEWI	Total Environmental Warming Impact
TEWI	Total Equivalent Warming Impact [*Greenhouse gases*]
TEWK	Tewkesbury [*Municipal borough in England*]
TEWL	Test of Early Written Language Edition (TMMY)
TEWL	Transepidermal Water Loss [*Physiology*]
TEWR	Thrust to Earth Weight Ratio (IAA)
TEWS	Tactical Effectiveness of Weapons Systems [*Army*] (AABC)
TEWS	Tactical Electronic Warfare Set
TEWS	Tactical Electronic Warfare Squadron [*Air Force*]
TEWS	Tactical Electronic Warfare Support (MCD)
TEWS	Tactical Electronic Warfare System (DOMA)
TEWS	Threat Evaluation and Weapon Selection [*Military*] (CAAL)
TEWSq	Tactical Electronic Warfare Squadron [*Air Force*]
TEWT	Tactical Exercise without Troops
TEWTS	Tactical Electronic Warfare Training Squadron
TEX	Automatic Teleprinter Exchange Service [*of Western Union Corp.*]
TEX	Catex Compagnie [*France ICAO designator*] (FAAC)
TEX	Tau Epsilon Xi [*Text Formatter*] [*Computer science*]
TEX	Teleprinter Exchange Service [*Telecommunications*] (IAA)
TEX	Teletype Exchange
TEX	TELEX
TEX	Temperature Excess (PDAA)
TEX	Terex Corp. [*NYSE symbol*] (SPSG)
tex	Tex [*Formerly, den*] [*Linear density*] [*SI unit*]
Tex	Texan (WDAA)
Tex	Texas (ODBW)
TEX	Texas (AAG)
Tex	Texas Supreme Court Reports [*A publication*] (DLA)
TEX	Textile (AABC)
TEX	Transaction Exception Code [*Military*] (AFIT)
TEX	Tumbling Explorer [*Aerospace*]
TEX	University of Texas at Tyler, Tyler, TX [*OCLC symbol*] (OCLC)
Tex A&I U	Texas A&I University (GAGS)
Tex A&M U	Texas Agricultural and Mechanical University (GAGS)
Tex A Civ	White and Wilson's [*or Willson's*] Civil Cases, Texas Court of Appeals [*A publication*] (DLA)
Tex A Civ Cas	White and Wilson's [*or Willson's*] Civil Cases, Texas Court of Appeals [*A publication*] (DLA)
Tex A Civ Cas (Wilson)	Texas Court of Appeal Civil Cases (Wilson) [*or Willson*] [*A publication*] (DLA)
Texaco	Texaco, Inc. [*Associated Press*] (SAG)
TEXACO	Texas Co.
TEXACO	Texas Petroleum Co. (EFIS)
Tex Admin Code	Texas Administrative Code [*A publication*] (DLA)
Tex App	Texas Civil Appeals Cases [*A publication*] (DLA)
Tex App	Texas Court of Appeals Reports (Criminal Cases) [*A publication*] (DLA)
Tex App Civ Cas (Wilson)	White and Wilson's [*or Willson's*] Civil Cases, Texas Court of Appeals [*A publication*] (DLA)
TexarkF	Texarkana First Financial Corp. [*Associated Press*] (SAG)
TEXAS	Tactical Exchange Automation System (MCD)
Texas Civ	Texas Civil Appeals Reports [*A publication*] (DLA)
Texas Civ App	Texas Civil Appeals Reports [*A publication*] (DLA)
Texas Cr App	Texas Court of Appeals Reports [*A publication*] (DLA)

Texas Crim... Texas Criminal Reports [*A publication*] (DLA)
Texas Crim App... Texas Criminal Appeals Reports [*A publication*] (DLA)
Texas Crim Rep... Texas Criminal Reports [*A publication*] (DLA)
Texas Cr Rep... Texas Criminal Reports [*A publication*] (DLA)
Texas Ct App... Texas Court of Appeals Reports [*A publication*] (DLA)
Texas Ct App Civ Cas... Texas Civil Cases [*A publication*] (DLA)
Texas Ct of App... Texas Court of Appeals Reports [*A publication*] (DLA)
Texas Ct Rep... Texas Court Reporter [*1900-1908*] [*A publication*] (DLA)
Texas Dig.... Texas Digest [*A publication*] (DLA)
Texas R...... Texas Reports [*A publication*] (DLA)
Texas Rep .. Texas Reports [*A publication*] (DLA)
TexBi........ Texas Biotechnology Corp. [*Associated Press*] (SAG)
TexBiotch........ Texas Biotechnology Corp. [*Associated Press*] (SAG)
Tex Bus Corp Act Ann... Texas Business Corporation Act, Annotated
[*A publication*] (DLA)
TEXC........... Texas Central Railroad Co. [*AAR code*]
Tex Christ U... Texas Christian University (GAGS)
Tex Civ App... Texas Civil Appeals Reports [*A publication*] (DLA)
Tex Civ Cas... Texas Court of Appeals Decisions, Civil Cases (White and Wilson)
[*or Willson*] [*1876-92*] [*A publication*] (DLA)
Tex Civ Rep... Texas Civil Appeals Reports [*A publication*] (DLA)
Tex Code Ann... Texas Codes, Annotated [*A publication*] (DLA)
Tex Code Crim Proc Ann... Texas Code of Criminal Procedure, Annotated
[*A publication*] (DLA)
TEXCOM...... Test and Experimentation Command [*TRADOC*] [*Fort Hood, TX*]
Tex Cr.......... Texas Criminal [*A publication*] (DLA)
Tex Cr App... Texas Criminal Appeals Reports [*A publication*] (DLA)
Tex Crim... Texas Criminal Reports [*A publication*] (DLA)
Tex Crim Rep... Texas Criminal Reports [*A publication*] (DLA)
Tex Cr R...... Texas Criminal Appeals Reports [*A publication*] (DLA)
Tex Cr Rpts... Texas Criminal Reports [*A publication*] (DLA)
Tex Ct App... Texas Court of Appeals Reports [*A publication*] (DLA)
Tex Ct App Civ... Texas Civil Cases [*A publication*] (DLA)
Tex Ct App Dec Civ... Texas Civil Cases [*A publication*] (DLA)
Tex Ct App R... Texas Court of Appeals Reports [*A publication*] (DLA)
Tex Ct Rep... Texas Court Reporter [*A publication*] (DLA)
TEXDEALAM... Textile Dealers Association of America (EA)
Tex Dec....... Texas Decisions [*A publication*] (DLA)
Tex Dig Op Att'y Gen... Digest of Opinions of the Attorney General of Texas
[*A publication*] (DLA)
Tex Elec Code Ann... Texas Election Code, Annotated [*A publication*] (DLA)
Texfi........... Texfi Industries, Inc. [*Associated Press*] (SAG)
TEXFI........... Textured Fibres (EFIS)
Tex Gen Laws... General and Special Laws of the State of Texas [*A publication*]
(DLA)
TEXGRP....... Texas Group [*Navy*] (DNAB)
TEXIN........... Texas Intersection Air Quality Model [*Environmental Protection
Agency*] (GFGA)
TexInd .... Texas Industries, Inc. [*Associated Press*] (SAG)
Tex Ins Code Ann... Texas Insurance Code, Annotated [*A publication*] (DLA)
TexInst......... Texas Instruments, Inc. [*Associated Press*] (SAG)
Tex Jur....... Texas Jurisprudence [*A publication*] (DLA)
Tex Jur 2d... Texas Jurisprudence [*2nd ed.*] [*A publication*] (DLA)
Tex Law...... Texas Lawman [*A publication*] (DLA)
Tex Law & Leg... Texas Law and Legislation [*A publication*] (DLA)
TexLex........ Texas Lexicon [*Slang*]
Tex LJ .... Texas Law Journal [*A publication*] (DLA)
Tex L Rep... Texas Law Reporter [*1882-84*] [*A publication*] (DLA)
TexMer....... Texas Meridian Resources Ltd. [*Associated Press*] (SAG)
TexMex....... Texas and Mexico [*Refers to fashion, food, language, or lifestyle that
has characteristics of these two regions*]
TEX MEX...... Texas Mexican Railway Co.
Texo............ Texoil, Inc. [*Associated Press*] (SAG)
Texoil .... Texoil, Inc. [*Associated Press*] (SAG)
TEXP.......... Time Exposure [*Photography*]
TEXP.......... Titan Exploration, Inc. [*NASDAQ symbol*] (SAG)
TEXPLOT...... Texas Instruments Plotter (NITA)
TEXPROCIL... [*The*] Cotton Textiles Export Promotion Council of India (ECON)
TexRegl .... Texas Regional Bancshares, Inc. [*Associated Press*] (SAG)
Tex Rev Civ Stat Ann (Vernon)... Texas Revised Civil Statutes, Annotated (Vernon)
[*A publication*] (DLA)
TEXS........... Tactical Explosive System [*Military*] (RDA)
TEXS........... Texas Star Resources Corp. [*NASDAQ symbol*] (SAG)
Tex S .... Texas Supreme Court Reports, Supplement [*A publication*] (DLA)
Tex S Ct ..... Texas Supreme Court Reporter [*A publication*] (DLA)
Tex Sess Law Serv... Texas Session Law Service (Vernon) [*A publication*] (DLA)
TEXSF........ Texas Star Resources [*NASDAQ symbol*] (TTSB)
TEXSIM/B... TEGAS Extended Simulator Behavioral (NITA)
TEXSIS........ Texas Student Information System (EDAC)
Tex So Intra L Rev... Texas Southern Intramural Law Review [*A publication*] (DLA)
Tex So U ... Texas Southern University (GAGS)
TexStar........ Texas Star Resources Corp. [*Associated Press*] (SAG)
Tex Stat Ann... Texas Statutes, Annotated [*A publication*] (DLA)
Tex Supp ... Texas Supplement [*A publication*] (DLA)
Tex Suppl ... Texas Supplement [*A publication*] (DLA)
TEXT .... Texas Experimental TOKAMAK [*Atomic physics*]
TEXT .... Textile
text .... Texture (VRA)
TEXT .... Trans-European Exchange and Transfer Consortium (AIE)
Tex Tax-Gen Ann... Texas Tax-General, Annotated [*A publication*] (DLA)
Tex Tech U... Texas Tech University (GAGS)
TEXTINDY .. Textile Industry (IAA)
TEXTIR........ Text Indexing and Retrieval [*Computer science*]
TEXTLINE..... Text Online (NITA)

TEXTOR .... TOKAMAK [*Toroidal Kamera Magnetic*] Experiment for Technical
Oriented Research [*Oak Ridge National Laboratory*]
Textr .... Textron, Inc. [*Associated Press*] (SAG)
TEXT REC .... Textus Receptus [*The Received Text*] [*Latin*]
Textron .... Textron, Inc. [*Associated Press*] (SAG)
Tex Unrep Cas... Posey's Unreported Cases [*Texas*] [*A publication*] (DLA)
TexUtil......... Texas Utilities Co. [*Associated Press*] (SAG)
Tex Woman's U... Texas Woman's University (GAGS)
TEY .... Tax Equivalent Yield (EBF)
TEY .... Thingeyri [*Iceland*] [*Airport symbol*] (OAG)
TEY .... Total Electron Yield [*Spectroscopy*]
TEZ .... Tezpur [*India*] [*Airport symbol*] (OAG)
TEZG .... Tribological Experiments in Zero Gravity
TF............... [*The*] FORUM [*Foundation of Research for Understanding Man*] (EA)
TF............... French Southern Territories [*Internet country code*]
TF............... Iceland [*International civil aircraft marking*] (ODBW)
TF............... Tabulating Form (AAG)
TF............... Tactical Fighter (AFM)
TF............... Tactile Fremitus [*Medicine*]
TF............... Taeria Foundation (EA)
Tf............... Tafel (BJA)
TF............... Tail-Flick Reflex (DB)
TF............... Talker Function [*Telecommunications*] (IAA)
TF............... Tallulah Falls Railway Co. [*AAR code*]
TF............... Tank Farm (NATG)
TF............... Tape Feed
TF............... Target File (MCD)
TF............... Task Force
TF............... Tax Foundation (EA)
TF............... Tax Free (WDAA)
TF............... Tayu Fellowship (EA)
TF............... Teaching Fellow
TF............... Tear Fund [*An association*] (EA)
TF............... Teased Fibers [*Neurology*]
TF............... Technical File (MCD)
TF............... Technological Forecasting
TF............... Telegram for Delivery by Telephone
TF............... Telegraph Form (ROG)
TF............... Telephone (NATG)
TF............... Temperature Factor
TF............... Temporary Fix (AAG)
TF............... Terminal Forecast
TF............... Terminal Frame (NATG)
TF............... Terrain-Following [*Helicopter*]
TF............... Territorial Force [*Military British*]
TF............... Test Facility [*NASA*] (NASA)
TF............... Test Fixture (KSC)
TF............... Test Flight [*Air Force*]
TF............... Test Frame [*Telecommunications*] (TEL)
TF............... Test to Failure (SAA)
TF............... Tetralogy of Fallot [*Cardiology*]
TF............... Text-Fiche
TF............... THEOS [*They Help Each Other Spiritually*] Foundation (EA)
TF............... Thermionic Field (IAA)
TF............... Thin-Film
TF............... Thoreau Fellowship (EA)
TF............... Thread Forming (MSA)
TF............... Threshold Factor (OA)
TF............... Threshold Function (IAA)
TF............... Thymidine Factor [*Endocrinology*]
TF............... Thymol Flocculation [*Clinical chemistry*]
TF............... Thymus Factor (DB)
TF............... Tibet Fund (EA)
TF............... Tile Floor [*Technical drawings*]
TF............... Till Forbidden [*i.e., repeat until forbidden to do so*] [*Advertising*]
Tf............... Till Forbidden (EBF)
TF............... Time Factor (CAAL)
TF............... Time Frame
TF............... Time Frequency (IAA)
T/F............. Time of Fail (MSA)
T/F............. Time of Fall (SAA)
TF............... Time of Flight [*Ballistics*]
TF............... Time to Function
TF............... Tissue-Damaging Factor [*Medicine*] (MAE)
TF............... Tissue Factor [*Clinical chemistry*]
TF............... To Fill
TF............... To Follow
TF............... Tolkien Fellowships [*Defunct*] (EA)
TF............... Tolstoy Foundation (EA)
TF............... Tool Fabrication (SAA)
TF............... Tool Foundation [*See also ST*] [*Amsterdam, Netherlands*] (EAIO)
TF............... Toroidal Field (MCD)
TF............... Torpedo Fighter Aircraft [*Navy*]
TF............... Total Float (IAA)
TF............... Total Flow (MAE)
TF............... Total Flowers [*Plant pathology*]
TF............... Total Forfeiture [*of all pay and allowances*] [*Army*] (AABC)
TF............... Toward Freedom (EA)
TF............... Toxicology Forum (EA)
TF............... Tracheal Fistula [*Otorhinolaryngology*] (DAVI)
TF............... Tracking Filter
TF............... Trailfinders [*Travel agency*] [*British*]
TF............... Trainer Fighter
TF............... Training Film [*Military*]
TF............... Training Flight [*British military*] (DMA)

TF	TransAfrica Forum (EA)
TF	Transcription Factor [Genetics]
TF	Transfer (IAA)
TF	Transfer Factor [Immunochemistry]
TF	Transfer Fee [Banking]
TF	Transfer Function (AAG)
T/F	Transfer of Function [Military] (AFM)
TF	Transferrin [Also, T, TRF] [Biochemistry]
Tf	Transferrin (DB)
TF	Transformation Frequency (DB)
TF	Transformers [JETDS nomenclature] [Military] (CET)
TF	Transform Fault [Geology]
TF	Transfrontal (AAMN)
TF	Transmit Filter (MHDB)
TF	Transmitter Frequency
TF	Transportation Factor (MCD)
TF	Transportes Aereos Regionais (TAR) SA [Brazil ICAO designator] (ICDA)
TF	Transversal Filter (IAA)
TF	Trap Flag [Computer memory language] (PCM)
TF	Travail Force [Penal Servitude] [French]
TF	Travellers Fare [Train catering service] [British]
TF	Trench Feet [or Fever]
TF	Trench Fighter [British military] (DMA)
TF	Trichloroethylene Finishing
TF	Triple Frequency
TF	Triple Fronted [Classified advertising] (ADA)
TF	Tritium Fluoride
TF	Tropical Fresh Water [Vessel load line mark]
T/F	True/False (CDAI)
Tf	Trufocus [Lamp base type] (NTCM)
TF	Trunk Frame [Telecommunications] (TEL)
TF	Trust Fund
TF	Tube Feeding [Medicine] (DMAA)
TF	Tuberculin Filtrate [Medicine]
TF	Tubular Fluid [Medicine] (MAE)
TF	Tuning Fork (AAMN)
TF	Turbofan [Engine]
TF	Twins Foundation (EA)
TF	Type of Flight (SAA)
TF	Type of Foundation [IRS]
TF	Veeneal [ICAO designator] (AD)
TF1	Channel One [French television station]
TFA	[The] Ferroalloys Association (EA)
TFA	Municipal Income Trust [Formerly, Allstate Municipal Income Trust] [NYSE symbol] (SPSG)
TFA	Tackett Family Association (EA)
TFA	Take Five Australia [An association]
TFA	Target Factor Analysis [Statistical technique]
TFA	Task Force A
TFA	Task Force Alpha [DoD]
TFA	Tasmanian Floricultural Association [Australia]
TFA	Tax Free America (FA)
TFA	Teach for America
TFA	Teaching-Family Association (NTPA)
TFA	Technology Forecasting and Assessment (IAA)
TFA	TELEX File Adapter (IAA)
TFA	Tenant Farmers' Association [British] (DBA)
TFA	Tennessee Forestry Association (WPI)
TFA	Test Form Analyzer (CIST)
TFA	Texas Forestry Association (WPI)
TFA	Textile Finishers Association (DBA)
TFA	Tie Fabrics Association [Defunct] (EA)
TFA	Timing Filter Analyzer
TFA	Top Farmers of America Association [Defunct] (EA)
TFA	Total Fatty Acids
TFA	Total Fibrinolytic Activity (DB)
TFA	Transaction Flow Auditing (ADA)
TFA	Trans Fatty Acids
TFA	Transfer Function Analyzer
TFA	Trans-Florida Airlines, Inc. [ICAO designator] (FAAC)
TFA	Transistor Feedback Amplifier
TFA	Transmit Frame Acquisition [Telecommunications] (LAIN)
TFA	Transverse Fascicular Area [Neuroanatomy]
TFA	Transverse Film Attenuator
TFA	Tree-Based Floorplanning Algorithm (AAEL)
TFA	Triathlon Federation of Australia
TFA	Trifluoroacetic [or Trifluoroacetyl] Acid [Organic chemistry]
TFA	Trifluoroacetic Anhydride [Organic chemistry]
TFA	Trifluoroacetyl [Organic chemistry]
TFA	Tube Failure Alarm
TFA	Two-Way Finite Automata
TFA	United States Trout Farmers Association
TFAA	Track and Field Athletes of America
TFAA	Trifluoroacetic Anhydride [Organic chemistry]
TFAA	Trout Farmers' Association of Australia
TFAD	Thin-Film Active Device (IAA)
TFAG	Tropical Forest Action Group (EA)
TFAI	Territoire Francaise des Afars et des Issas [French Territory of the Afars and Issas]
TFAI	Trifluoroacetylimidazole [Organic chemistry]
TFAIP	Task Force on Alternatives in Print (EA)
TF & T	Theatre, Film, and Television Biographies Master Index [A publication]
TFANP	Task Force Against Nuclear Pollution (EA)

TFAP	Trifluoroacetylprolyl Chloride (BARN)
TFAP	Tropical Forestry Action Plan [World Bank, UN, and other groups]
TFAR	Tentative Findings and Recommendations
TFA/USA	Track and Field Association of the United States of America (EA)
TFAW	Tasmania Fellowship of Australia Writers [Australia]
TFB	Municipal Income Trust [Formerly, Allstate Municipal Income Trust] [NYSE symbol] (SPSG)
TFB	Municipal Income Trust II [NYSE symbol] (TTSB)
TFB	Technology for Business (NITA)
TFB	Testing Facilities Branch [Social Security Administration]
TFB	Thai Farmers' Bank
TFB	Thin-Film Barrier
TFB	Towed Flexible Barge (PDAA)
TFB	Trifascicular Block [Medicine] (AAMN)
TFBA	Textile Fibers and By-Products Association [Charlotte, NC]
TFBC	Timber Frame Business Council (NTPA)
TFBP	Transferrin Binding Protein [Biochemistry]
TFBPA	Textile Fibers and By-Products Association (EA)
TFBR	Technical Feedback Report (DNAB)
TFC	[The] Felician College [Chicago, IL]
TFC	[The] Freedom Council [Defunct] (EA)
TFC	Municipal Income Trust [Formerly, Allstate Municipal Income Trust] [NYSE symbol] (SPSG)
TFC	Municipal Income Trust III [NYSE symbol] (TTSB)
TFC	Tactical Fire Control (MCD)
TFC	Tactical Flag Commander (MCD)
TFC	Tactical Flight Control
TFC	Tactical Fusion Center (MCD)
TFC	Tank Fire Control
TFC	Tantalum Foil Capacitor
TFC	Task Force Commander [Navy] (DNAB)
TFC	Tasmanian Forestry Commission [State] (EERA)
TFC	Terminal Flight Control (NATG)
TFC	Territorial Fund Campaign [Red Cross]
TFC	Thin-Film Capacitor
TFC	Thin-Film Cell
TFC	Thin-Film Circuit
TFC	Time from Cutoff [NASA] (NASA)
TFC	Time of First Call [Navy]
TFC	Toccoa Falls College [Georgia]
TFC	Top Flight Club [Northwest Airlines' club for frequent flyers] (EA)
TFC	Torpedo Fire Control
TFC	Total Fault Coverage (AAEL)
TFC	Total Final Cost [Business term]
TFC	Total Fixed Cost
TFC	Total Flow Control [Automotive engineering]
TFC	Total Fuel Consumption (KSC)
TFC	Traffic
TFC	Traffic Control (NG)
TFC	Transfer Function Computer
TFC	Transfer Function, Cumulative
TFC	Transferrin, Common Form [or Siderophilin] (DAVI)
TFC	Transistorized Frequency Converter
TFC	Transmission Fault Control [Telecommunications] (TEL)
TFC	Transparent Ferroelectric Ceramics [Physics]
TFC	Transportation Facilitation Center [Department of Transportation]
TFC	Transport for Christ International (EA)
TFC	Trifluoromethyldichlorocarbanilide [Organic chemistry]
TFC	Trigonometric Function Computer
TFC	Trilon Financial Corp. [Toronto Stock Exchange symbol Vancouver Stock Exchange symbol]
TFC	Trustees for Conservation [Defunct] (EA)
TFC	Turret Fire Control
TFC	United States Overseas Tax Fairness Committee (EA)
TFC	US-Japan Trade Facilitation Committee (IMH)
TFCA	Thin-Film Cell Array
TF-CAS	Time Frequency Collision Avoidance System
TFCB	Thanks for Coming By [Exxon slogan]
TFCC	Tactical Flag Command Center [Navy]
TFCC	Tank Fire Combat Computer
TFCC	Task Force Command Center [Navy] (DOMA)
TFCC	Triangular Fibrocartilage Complex [Anatomy]
TFCCS	Tactical Flag Command Center System [Navy]
TFCE	TFC Enterprises [NASDAQ symbol] (TTSB)
TFCE	TFC Enterprises, Inc. [NASDAQ symbol] (SAG)
TFC Ent	TFC Enterprises, Inc. [Associated Press] (SAG)
TFCF	Twenty-First Century Foundation (EA)
TFCG	Thin-Film Crystal Growth
TFCG	Tropical Forestry Contact Group [Australia]
TFCHS	Tasmanian Federation of Cooperative Housing Societies [Australia]
TFCM	Three Factor Contribution Method [Insurance]
TFCNN	Task Force Commander, North Norway [NATO] (NATG)
TFCO	Tufco Technologies [NASDAQ symbol] (SAG)
TFCOS	Task Force on Children Out of School (EA)
TFCP	Technical Facility Change Procedure (AAG)
TFCS	Tank Fire Control System
TFCS	Task Force for Child Survival (EA)
TFCS	Torpedo Fire Control System
TFCS	Treasury Financial Communication System [Department of the Treasury]
TFCS	Triplex Flight Control System [or Subsystem] [NASA] (NASA)
TFCSD	Task Force for Child Survival and Development [An association] (EA)
TFCSD	Total Federal Commissioned Service to Date [Military]
TFCU	Transportable Field Calibration Unit

TFCX............ TOKAMAK [*Toroidal Kamera Magnetic*] Fusion Core Experiment [*Plasma physics*]
TFCYC......... Terry Fox Canadian Youth Centre
TFD.............. Tactical Fighter Dispenser (MCD)
TFD.............. Target-to-Film Distance [*X-Ray machine*] [*Navy*]
TFD.............. Television Feasibility Demonstration [*NASA*] (KSC)
TFD.............. Terrain-Following Display
TFD.............. Test Flow Diagram (MCD)
TFD.............. Thin-Film Diode Descriptor Electronics
TFD.............. Thin-Film Distillation
TFD.............. Time Frequency Digitizer (MCD)
TF/D............ Time-Frequency Dissemination (IEEE)
TFD.............. Total Frequency Deviation (AAG)
TFD.............. Transcription Factor Database (EERA)
TFd.............. Transfer Factor, Dialyzable (STED)
TFD.............. Tube Flood and Drain
TFD.............. Tube Form Die (MCD)
TFDA............ Textile Fabric Distributors Association [*Later, TDA*] (EA)
TFDD............ Text File Device Driver [*Computer science*] (PCM)
TFDM............ Tactical Fighter Defense Munitions [*Air Force*]
TFDM............ Tactical Fighter Dispensing Munition (AFM)
TFDM............ Technical Feasibility Demonstration Model
TFDOP......... Total Field Detection only Processor (CAAL)
TFDRL......... Trustees of the Franklin Delano Roosevelt Library [*Abolished, 1958*] [*Library is now operated by the General Services Administration*]
TFDS............ Tactical Ferret Display System
TFDS............ Tactical Fighter Display Systems [*Air Force*]
TFDS............ Tactical Flag Data System (NG)
TFDS............ Troms Fylkes Dampskipsselskap [*Shipping line*] [*Norway*]
TFDTB......... Tactical Fighter Dispenser Test Bed
TFDU .... Thin Film Deposition Unit
TFE.............. Orlando, FL [*Location identifier FAA*] (FAAL)
TFE.............. Polytetrafluoroethylene (DAVI)
TFE.............. Tactical Field Exchange [*Air Force*] (DOMA)
TFE.............. Targets for Excellence
TFE.............. Television Film Exhibit (NTCM)
TFE.............. Terminal Flight Evaluation
TFE.............. Terrain-Following Evaluator
TFE.............. Tetrafluoroethylene [*Organic chemistry*]
TFE.............. Thermal Field Emission (IAA)
TFE.............. Thermionic Fuel Element [*Nuclear energy*]
TFE.............. Thin-Film Electrode [*Electrochemistry*]
TFE.............. Time from Event [*NASA*] (KSC)
TFE.............. Total Fly-By Energy
TFE.............. Trainer Flight Equipment (MCD)
TFE.............. Transform Fault Effect [*Geology*]
TFE.............. Transportation Feasibility Estimator
TFE.............. Trifluoroethanol [*Organic chemistry*]
TFE.............. Turbofan Engine
TFE.............. Two-Flow Electronic [*Automotive engineering*]
TFE.............. Two-Fraction Fast Exchange [*Biophysics*]
TFECB......... Task Force on Emphysema and Chronic Bronchitis [*Public Health Service and National Lung Association*] (EA)
TFECS......... Theater Force Evaluation by Combat Simulation (MCD)
TFED............ Thin Film Electroluminescent Display (AAEL)
TFEDRA...... Task Force for European Digital Road-mapping Association
TFEDSA....... Tetrafluoroethanedisulfonic Acid [*Organic chemistry*]
TFEF............ Triangle Fraternity Education Fund
TFEL............ Thin-Film Electroluminescence
TFEO............ Tetrafluoroethylene-Epoxide [*Organic chemistry*]
TFEO............ Tetrafluoroethylene Oxide [*Organic chemistry*]
TFER............ Transfer
TFET............ Thin-layer Field-Effect Transistor (IAA)
TFEV............ Timed Forced Expiratory Volume [*Laboratory science*] (DAVI)
TFEWJ......... Task Force on Equality of Women in Judaism [*Defunct*] (EA)
TFEWR......... Through-Focus Exit Wave Reconstruction [*Electron microscopy*]
TFF .... Fletcher School of Law and Diplomacy, Tufts University, Medford, MA [*OCLC symbol*] (OCLC)
TFF .... Tactical Fighter Force (ADA)
TFF .... Tangential Flow Filtration
TFF .... Tefe [*Brazil*] [*Airport symbol*] (OAG)
TFF .... Terrain-Following Flight
TFF .... The Friendship Force [*An association*] (EA)
TFF .... Thermoplastic Covered Fixture Wire Flexible Stranding (IAA)
TFF .... Thin-Film FET [*Field-Effect Transistor*] (IAA)
TFF .... Time of Free Fall [*NASA*] (KSC)
TFF .... Toggle Flip-Flop [*Computer science*] (IAA)
TFF .... Total Feedwater Flow
TFF .... Transverse Flow Fan
TFF .... Tropical Forest Foundation (EA)
TFF .... Tube-Fed Food [*Medicine*] (DMAA)
TFF .... Tuning Fork Filter
TFF .... Turbine Flow Function
TFFA............ Desirade/Grande-Anse, Guadeloupe [*French Antilles*] [*ICAO location identifier*] (ICLI)
TFFASF....... Temporaries Food for All Seasons Foundation (EA)
TFFB............ Basse-Terre/Baillif [*French Antilles*] [*ICAO location identifier*] (ICLI)
TFFC............ [*The*] Fixx Fan Club (EA)
TFFC............ Saint-Francois [*French Antilles*] [*ICAO location identifier*] (ICLI)
TFFC............ Task Force on Families in Crisis (EA)
TFFD............ Fort-De-France, Martinique [*French Antilles*] [*ICAO location identifier*] (ICLI)
TFFE............ Terrain-Following Flight Evaluator
Tf-Fe............ Transferrin-Bound Iron [*Biochemistry*] (MAE)
TFFET .... Thin-Film Field-Effect Transistor (IAA)

TFFF .... Fort-De-France/Le Lamentin, Martinique [*French Antilles*] [*ICAO location identifier*] (ICLI)
TFFG............ Saint-Martin/Grand'Case, Guadeloupe [*French Antilles*] [*ICAO location identifier*] (ICLI)
TF Fincl .... TF Financial Corp. [*Associated Press*] (SAG)
TFFIS........... Tasmanian Forests and Forest Industry Strategy [*Australia*]
TFFJ............ Saint-Barthelemy [*French Antilles*] [*ICAO location identifier*] (ICLI)
TFFLU.......... Trimmers, Firemen, and Foundry Labourers Union [*British*]
TFFM............ Grand-Bourg/Marie-Galante [*French Antilles*] [*ICAO location identifier*] (ICLI)
TFFR............ Pointe-A-Pitre/Le Raizet, Guadeloupe [*French Antilles*] [*ICAO location identifier*] (ICLI)
TFFR............ Task Force Final Report [*DoD*]
TFFS .... Les Saintes/Terre-De-Haut [*French Antilles*] [*ICAO location identifier*] (ICLI)
TFFS .... Thermoform, Fill, and Seal [*Pharmaceutical packaging*]
TFFT .... Truly Fast Fourier Transform (PDAA)
TFG.............. [*The*] Fashion Group (EA)
TFG.............. [*The*] Futures Group [*Commercial firm*] (EA)
TFG.............. Tactical Fighter Group [*Air Force*]
TFG.............. Tentative Fiscal Guidance (MCD)
TFG.............. Tentative Force Guidance (NG)
TFG.............. Terminal Facilities Guide [*DoD*]
TFG.............. Test File Generator [*Computer science*]
TFG.............. Textile Foremen's Guild
TFG.............. Thermo Fibergen, Inc. [*AMEX symbol*] (SAG)
TFG.............. Thrust Floated Gyroscope (PDAA)
TFG.............. Transmit Format Generator
TFG.............. Typefounding (ADA)
TFGA............ Tasmanian Field and Game Association [*Australia*]
TFGM........... Tank-Fired Guided Missile (MCD)
TFGM........... Tentative Fiscal Guidance Memorandum [*Military*] (AFIT)
TFGNA .... Timber Framers Guild of North America (NTPA)
TFGP............ Tactical Fighter Group [*Air Force*]
TFH.............. Temporal Fourier Hologram (PDAA)
TFH.............. Thai Flying Helicopter Service Co. Ltd. [*Thailand*] [*ICAO designator*] (FAAC)
TFH.............. Thick-Film Hybrid
TFH.............. Touch for Health Foundation (EA)
TFH.............. Transfer Function Hazard
TFH.............. Transfinancial Holdings [*AMEX symbol*] [*Formerly, Anuhco, Inc.*] (SG)
TFH.............. Transit Financial Holdings, Inc. [*Toronto Stock Exchange symbol*]
TFH.............. Tufts University, Health Sciences Library, Boston, MA [*OCLC symbol*] (OCLC)
TFHC............ Thick-Film Hybrid Circuit (IAA)
TFHRC .... Turner-Fairbank Highway Research Center [*FHWA*] (TAG)
TFI .... Deutsches Teppich-Forschungsinstitut [*German Carpet Research Institute - GCRI*] (EAIO)
TFI .... [*The*] Fertilizer Institute (EA)
TFI .... Table Fashion Institute (EA)
TFI .... Tastee Freez International (EFIS)
TFI .... Taurus Footwear, Inc. [*Toronto Stock Exchange symbol*]
TFI .... Tax Foundation, Inc.
TFI .... Tax-Free Investment [*Finance*]
TFI .... TCI Communications Financing I [*NYSE symbol*] (SAG)
TFI .... TCI Communications Financing II [*NYSE symbol*] (SAG)
TFI .... Textile Foundation, Inc.
TFI .... Theatre for Ideas [*Defunct*] (EA)
TFI .... Thick Film Ignition [*System*] [*Ford Motor Co.*] [*Automotive engineering*]
TFI .... Thick-Film Integrated [*Electronics*]
TFI .... Time from Ignition [*Apollo*] [*NASA*]
TFI .... Total Fluorescence Intensity [*Physics*]
tfi .... Travel for Industry [*Commercial firm*] [*British*]
TFI .... Tropical Forest Initiative (EERA)
TFI .... True Fibrous Involution [*Medicine*]
TFI .... Tufi [*Papua New Guinea*] [*Airport symbol*] (OAG)
TFIB............. Thin-Film Interface Barrier
TFIC............. Tasmanian Fishing Industry Council [*Australia*]
TFIC............. Thin-Film Integrated Circuit (IAA)
TFIFO........... Transmit First-In First-Out [*Computer science*]
TFI-I............ Thin-Film Ignition [*Automotive engineering*]
TFIM............ Tool Fabrication Instruction Manual (MCD)
TFIO............. Thin Film Integrated Optics (PDAA)
TFIPr........... TCI Commun Fin 1 8.72%'TOPrS' [*NYSE symbol*] (TTSB)
TFIS............. Thai Aquatic Sciences and Fisheries Information System [*Marine science*] (OSRA)
TFIS............. Theft from Interstate Shipment [*FBI standardized term*]
TFITC........... Tasmanian Fishing Industry Training Council [*Australia*]
TFITC........... Tasmanian Food Industry Training Council [*Australia*]
TFITC........... Tasmanian Forest Industries Training Council [*Australia*]
TFITC........... Tasmanian Furniture Industry Training Council [*Australia*]
TFL.............. Tail-Flick Latency
TFL.............. Taiwan Federation of Labor [*Nationalist China*]
TFL.............. Tanganyika Federation of Labor
TFL.............. Tasmanian Football League [*Australia*]
TFL.............. Tayflight Ltd. [*British ICAO designator*] (FAAC)
TFL.............. Technology for Learning [*Los Angeles County Office of Education Initiative*]
TFL.............. Telemetry Format Load (MCD)
TFL.............. Tensor Fascia Lata [*Anatomy*]
TFL.............. Through Flow Line
TFL.............. Time from Launch [*NASA*]
TFL.............. Time to Failure Location

TFL	Training for Life [Young Men's Christian Association] [British]
TFL	Transformerless (IAA)
TFL	Transient Fault Locator
TFL	Trees for Life [An association] (EA)
TFLA	Texas Foreign Language Association (EDAC)
TFLAC	Fellowship of Reconciliation Task Force on Latin America and Caribbean (EA)
TFLAC	Task Force on Latin America and the Caribbean (EA)
TFLC	Tulane Factors of Liberalism-Conservatism [Psychology]
TFLWA	Torchbearers for Legacy in Western Australia
TFM	Tactical Flight Management (MCD)
TFM	Tape File Management
TFM	Teaching Family Model [Psychology]
TFM	Telefomin [Papua New Guinea] [Airport symbol] (OAG)
TFM	Tentative Final Monograph [Food and Drug Administration]
TFM	Terminal Forecast Manual
TFM	Testicular Feminization [Endocrinology]
TFM	Testicular Feminization Mutation [Medicine] (DB)
Tfm	Testicular Feminization Syndrome (STED)
TFM	TFTR [Tokamak Fusion Test Reactor] Flexibility Modification
TFM	Thin-Film Microelectronics
TFM	Time Quantized Frequency Modulation [Telecommunications] (IAA)
TFM	Tool Fabrication Manual (MCD)
TFM	Toronto International Furniture Market [Canada] (ITD)
TFM	Total Fluid Movement (STED)
TFM	Total Forest Management (WPI)
TFM	Traffic Flow Management [FAA] (TAG)
TFM	Transmission Electron Microscopy (STED)
TFM	Transmit Frame Memory
TFM	Transmitter Frequency Multiplier
TFM	Transportation Financial Management [Army]
TFM	Transverse Field Modulator
TFM	Trifluoromethylnitrophenol [Organic chemistry]
TFM	Turbine Flow Meter (KSC)
TFM	Two-Fluid Manometer
TFMA	Technical Facility Modification Authorization (AAG)
TFMBA	Tasmanian Fine Merino Breeders' Association [Australia]
TFME	Thin-Film Mercury Electrode [Electrochemistry]
TFMG	Tank Force Management Group [Army]
TFMMS	Total Force Manpower Management System [Navy] (GFGA)
TFMO	Tank Forces Management Office [Army]
TFMP	Test Facility Master Plan [DoD] (RDA)
TFMPP	Trifluoromethyl(phenyl)piperazine [Organic chemistry]
TFMRA	Top Fuel Motorcycle Riders Association (EA)
TFMRC	Thermo-Fluid Mechanics Research Centre [University of Sussex] [British] (CB)
TFMS	Tactical Frequency Management System (MCD)
TFMS	Text and File Management System
TFMS	Traffic Facilities Management System [Australia]
TFMS	Trunk and Facilities Maintenance System [Telecommunications] (TEL)
TFMSA	Trifluoromethanesulfonic Acid [Organic chemistry]
TFN	Till Further Notice
TFN	Total Fecal Nitrogen
TFN	Total Fixed Nitrogen [Chemistry]
TFN	Total Fruit Number [Botany]
TFN	Totally Functional Neutrophil (STED)
TFN	Track File Number (CAAL)
TFN	Transferrin (STED)
TFNA	Tennis Foundation of North America [Later, ATF] (EA)
TFNC	Tasmanian Field Naturalists' Club [Australia]
TFNG	Thirty-Five New Guys [Group of new astronauts] [NASA]
TFNR	Taper-Faced Napier Ring [Automobile engines]
TFNS	Territorial Force Nursing Service
TFO	Telemedicine for Ontario [Toronto, ON] [Telecommunications] (TSSD)
TFO	Tiffany Resources, Inc. [Vancouver Stock Exchange symbol]
TFO	Tonto Forest Array [Arizona] [Seismograph station code, US Geological Survey Closed] (SEIS)
TFO	Transactions for Others [Military]
TFO	Triplex-Forming Oligonucleotide [Biochemistry]
TFO	Tuning Fork Oscillator
TFOA	Things Falling Off Aircraft (MCD)
TFOCA	Tactical Fiber Optic Cable Assembly [Army]
TFOE	Task Force on the Environment [American Library Association]
TFOF	Taxi Fleet Operators' Federation [British] (BI)
TFOL	Tape File Octal Load
TFON	Telefonos de Mexico SA de CV [NASDAQ symbol] (NQ)
TFONY	Telefonos de Mexico'A'ADR [NASDAQ symbol] (TTSB)
TFOPS	Task Force Operations [Navy] (NVT)
T (for) D	Termination for Default (MCD)
TFORMR	Transformer
TFOS	Total Federal Officer Service [Military] (AABC)
TFOTB	[The] Friends of Tom Baker (EA)
TFOUT	Thin-Film Oxygen Uptake Test
TFOV	Total Field of View (MCD)
TFP	American Society for the Defense of Tradition, Family and Property (EA)
TFP	[The] Feminist Press (EA)
TFP	[The] Friends Program (EA)
TFP	[The] Fund for Peace [An association] (EA)
TFP	Teachers for Peace (EAIO)
TFP	Teachers Freedom Party (EA)
TFP	Temporary Forfeiture of Pay
TFP	Test Facility Program [NASA] (KSC)

TFP	Therapeutic Feeding Program
TFP	Total Factor Productivity [Economics]
TFP	Total Finish Positions [Horse racing]
TFP	Total Force Policy [DoD]
TFP	Trans-Fiberoptic-Photographic [Electron microscopy]
TFP	Transportability Focal Point [Army] (MCD)
TFP	Travaux. Faculte de Philosophie et Lettres. Universite Catholique de Louvain [A publication] (BJA)
TFP	Trees on Farms Program (EERA)
TFP	Treponemal False Positive (STED)
TFP	Trifluoperazine [Also, Trifluoroperazine] [Organic chemistry]
TFP	Trifluoroperazine [Also, Trifluoperazine] [Organic chemistry]
TF/P	Tubular Fluid Plasma [Medicine] (MAE)
TF/P	Tubule Fluid-to-Plasma [Ratio] [Medicine] (DAVI)
TFPA	Tall Fashion Promotions of Australia
TFPA	Tubular Finishers and Processors Association [Defunct] (EA)
TFPC	Thin-Film Photovoltaic Cell
TFPCA	Thin-Film Photovoltaic Cell Array
TFPCTS	Thin-Film Personal Communications and Telemetry System (MCD)
TFPECTS	Thin-Film Personal Communications and Telemetry System (MCD)
TFPG	Task Force Planning Group [DoD]
TFPI	Tissue Factor Pathway Inhibitor [Biochemistry]
TFPIA	Textile Fiber Products Identification Act [1960]
(TF/P)In	Tubule Fluid-to-Plasma Insulin Ratio [Medicine] (DAVI)
TFPL	Task Force Pro Libra Ltd. (IID)
TFPL	Texas Forest Products Laboratory
TFPL	Training Film Production Laboratory [Military]
TFR	Pueblo, CO [Location identifier FAA] (FAAL)
TFR	Taft's Foundation Reporter [A publication]
TFR	Tape-to-File Recorder
TFR	Tarbes [France] [Airport symbol] (AD)
TFR	Teknikvetenskapliga FoskningsRadet [Swedish Research Council for Engineering Sciences]
TFR	Television Film Recorder
TFR	Temporary Flight Restrictions (COE)
TFR	Terrain-Following RADAR
TFR	Territorial Force Reserve [British]
TFR	Test Failure Report (CAAL)
TFR	Theoretical Final Route [Telecommunications] (TEL)
TFR	Thin-Film Resist
TFR	TOKAMAK [Toroidal Kamera Magnetic] at Fontenay-aux-Roses
T/FR	Top of Frame (AAG)
TFR	Torus Fontenay AWY-Roses
TFR	Total Fertility Rate [Medicine]
TFR	Total Final Reports
TFR	Total Flow Resistance (STED)
TFR	Total Follicular Response (OA)
TFR	Trafalgar Resources, Inc. [Vancouver Stock Exchange symbol]
TFR	Trainer Facilities Report [Army]
TFR	Transaction Formatting Routines
TFR	Trans European Airways SA [France ICAO designator] (FAAC)
TFR	Transfer
TFR	Transfer Function Response
TfR	Transferrin Receptor [Immunology]
TFR	Traveler/Failure Report [Deep Space Instrumentation Facility, NASA]
TFR	Trouble and Failure Report [NASA]
TFR	Tubular Flow Reactor
TFR	Tunable Frequency Range
TFRC	TechForce Corp. [NASDAQ symbol] (SAG)
TFR/CAR	Trouble and Failure Report/Corrective Action Report
TFRCD	Traffic Received (FAAC)
TFRD	Test Facilities Requirements Document
TFS	Tactical Fighter Squadron [Air Force]
TFS	Tape File Supervisor
TFS	Tasmanian Fire Service [Australia]
TFS	Tax Free Shopping
TFS	Tbilisi [Former USSR Geomagnetic observatory code]
TFS	Teacher Follow-Up Survey [Department of Education] (GFGA)
TFS	Telemetry Format Selection (NASA)
TFS	Tenerife-Reina Sofia [Canary Islands] [Airport symbol] (OAG)
TFS	Tennessee Folklore Society (EA)
TFS	Terrain-Following System
TFS	Testicular Feminization Syndrome [Endocrinology]
TFS	Thomson Financial Services [The Thomson Corp.] [Publishing]
TFS	Three-Five Systems [NYSE symbol] (TTSB)
TFS	Three Five Systems Co. [NYSE symbol] (SAG)
TFS	Thrombus-Free Surface [Hematology]
TFS	Time and Frequency Standard
TFS	Tin-Free Steel
TFS	Torpedo Firing System (DNAB)
TFS	Traffic Flow Security [Telecommunications] (TEL)
TFS	Traffic Forecasting System [Telecommunications] (TEL)
TFS	Transaction Forwarding System [Computer science]
TFS	Transport Ferry Service [English Channel]
TFS	Transverse Feed System
TFS	Trim Fuel System (MCD)
TFS	Trunk Forecasting System [Telecommunications] (TEL)
TFS	Tube-Fed Saline (DB)
TFS	Tuliptree Flower Spiroplasma [Plant pathology]
TFS	Tunable Frequency Source
TFS	Turbine First Stage [Nuclear energy] (NRCH)
TFS	Turbine Flow Sensor
TFS	Type Finish Specification (MCD)
TFSA	304th Fighter Squadron Association (EA)
TFSA	Thin-Film Spreading Agent [For enhanced oil recovery]

TFSC .... Turkish Federated State of Cyprus
TFS-CT........ Tin-Free Steel Chromium-Type (PDAA)
TFSF .... Time to First System Failure (MHDI)
TFSK .... Time Frequency Shift Keying [Computer science] (IAA)
TFSO .... Tonto Forest Seismological Observatory [Arizona]
TFSP .... Task Force on Service to the Public [Canada]
TFSQ .... Tactical Fighter Squadron [Air Force]
TFSR .... Tools for Self Reliance [British] (EAIO)
TFSS .... Technical Facilities Subsystem [Space Flight Operations Facility, NASA]
TFSUSS ...... Task Force on Scientific Uses of the Space Station [NASA]
TFT .... Tabular Firing Table [Military] (AABC)
TFT .... Tangential Flow Torch [For plasma generation]
TFT .... Technical Feasibility Testing [Army]
TFT .... Temporary Facility Tool (SAA)
TFT .... Temporary Full-Time (GFGA)
TFT .... Termo Fibertek, Inc. [AMEX symbol] (SPSG)
TFT .... Thermal Fatigue Test
TFT .... Thermo Fibertek [AMEX symbol] (TTSB)
TFT .... Thin-Film Field-Effect Transistor
TFT .... Thin-Film Technique
TFT .... Thin-Film Technology
TFT .... Thin-Film Transducer
TFT .... Thin-Film Transistor
TFT .... Threshold Failure Temperatures
TFT .... Thrombus Formation Time (DB)
TFT .... Thyroid Function Test [Endocrinology] (DAVI)
TFT .... Tight Filum Terminale [Medicine] (DMAA)
TFT .... Tight Fingertip [Medicine]
TFT .... Time-to-Frequency Transformation [Electronics] (OA)
TFT .... Tit for Tat [Slang]
TFT .... Transfer Factor Test [Medicine] (DAVI)
TFT .... Trifluorothymidine [Pharmacology]
TFT .... Triple Thin Film [Electronics]
TFT .... Two-Fingered Terror [Keyboarding technique]
TFT³ .... Trillion Cubic Feet (WDAA)
TF/TA.......... Terrain Following/Terrain Avoidance (MCD)
TFTAS.......... Tactical Fighter Training Aggressor Squadron [Air Force]
TFTASq........ Tactical Fighter Training Aggressor Squadron [Air Force]
TFTB .... Taping for the Blind (EA)
TFTC .... Thin-Film Thermocouple (IAA)
TFTE .... Temporary Full-Time Equivalent (GFGA)
TFTG .... Tactical Fighter Training Group [Military]
TF/TG.......... Task Force/Task Group
TFTNGSq...... Tactical Fighter Training Squadron [Air Force]
TFTP .... Task Force on Teaching as a Profession [Defunct] (EA)
TFTP .... Television Facility Test Position [Telecommunications] (TEL)
TFTP .... Trivial File Transfer Protocol (BYTE)
TFTR .... TOKAMAK [Toroidal Kamera Magnetic] Fusion Test Reactor [Princeton, NJ]
TFTR .... Toroidal Fusion Test Reactor [Nuclear energy] (MCD)
TFTS .... Tactical Fighter Training Squadron [Air Force] (MCD)
TFTS .... TOW [Tube-Launched, Optically Tracked, Wire-Guided (Weapon)] Field Test Set (MCD)
TFT screen... Thin Film Transistor Screen
TFTT .... TOW [Tube-launched, Optically-tracked, Wire-guided] Field Tactical Trainer [Army] (INF)
TFTU .... Tanzania Federation of Free Trade Unions
TFTW .... Tactical Fighter Training Wing [Air Force] (MCD)
TFU .... Tactical Forecast Unit
TFU .... Telecommunications Flying Unit [British]
TFU .... Test Facility Utilization [NASA] (NASA)
TFU .... Theoretical First Unit [Economics]
TFU .... Time and Frequency Unit (ECII)
TFU .... Tool Follow Up
TFUC .... Theoretical First Unit Cost
TFUI .... Touch-and-Feel User Interface
TFV .... Tangential Force Variation [Automotive tire testing]
TFV .... Twin Falls Victory [Tracking ship] [NASA]
TFVA .... Training Film and Video Association (NITA)
TFVC .... Traffic Flow Visualization and Control [FHWA] (TAG)
TFW .... Tactical Fighter Wing [Air Force]
TFW .... Tethered Free-Floating Worker
TFW .... Thermoplastic Fan Wheel
TFW .... Tokyo Financial Wire [COMLINE International Corp.] [Japan Information service or system] (CRD)
TFW .... Tropical Fresh Water
TFW .... Tufts University, Medford, MA [OCLC symbol] (OCLC)
TFW .... Turbulent Far Wake
TFWC .... Tactical Fighter Weapons Center [Air Force] (AFM)
TFWCRG ...... Tactical Fighter Weapons Center Range Group [Military]
TFWG .... Tactical Fighter Wing [Air Force]
TFWRR .... Task Force on Women's Rights and Responsibilities [National Council on Family Relations] (EA)
TFWS .... Tactical Fighter Weapon School [Air Force] (MCD)
TFWS .... Task Force on Women in Sports [of NOW] (EA)
Tfwy .... Trafficway (TBD)
TFX .... Tactical Fighter Experimental [Air Force]
TFX .... Teleflex, Inc. [NYSE symbol] (SAG)
TFX .... Thymic Factor X [Endocrinology]
TFX .... Toxic Effect (AAEL)
TFX .... Tri-Service Fighter, Experimental (MCD)
TFXA .... Time-Focused Crystal Analyzer [Spectrometer]
TFX-N .... Tactical Fighter Experimental - Navy
TFX-O .... Tactical Fighter Experimental - Offensive

TFX-R .... Tactical Fighter Experimental - Reconnaissance
TFY .... Tarfaya [Morocco] [Airport symbol] (AD)
TFY .... Target Fiscal Year (MCD)
TFY .... Tayside Aviation Ltd. [British ICAO designator] (FAAC)
TFYAA .... Task Force on Youth Allowance Administration [Australia]
TFYAP .... Tobacco Free Young America Project (EA)
TFYQA .... Think for Yourself and Question Authority [Term coined by Dr. Timothy Leary]
TFZ .... Tail Fuze (MSA)
TFZ .... Traffic Zone (FAAC)
TFZ .... Trifluroperazine [Tranquilizer]
TFZ .... Tropospheric Frontal Zone
Tg .... Generation Time (DAVI)
Tg .... Glass Transition
TG .... Positioning Devices [JETDS nomenclature] [Military] (CET)
TG .... Tail Gear
TG .... Tangent [Mathematics] (IAA)
TG .... Tangent Group (EA)
TG .... Tape Gauge
TG .... Target Gate (CAAL)
TG .... Task Group [Military]
TG .... Task Guidance
TG .... Tasmanian Greens [Australia Political party]
TG .... Technology Gap
TG .... Telecom Gold (NITA)
TG .... Telegram
TG .... Telegraph
TG .... Teleilaet Ghassul (BJA)
TG .... Temporary Gentleman [British slang term for officer for duration of the war] [World War I]
TG .... Tendon Graft [Orthopedics] (DAVI)
tg .... Teragram (MEC)
TG .... Terminal Guidance
TG .... Terminator Group
TG .... Testamentsgesetz [Law on Wills] [German] (ILCA)
TG .... Test Group
TG .... Test Guaranteed
TGAS .... Testosterone Glucuronide [Medicine] (MAE)
TG .... Tetraglycine (DAVI)
TG .... Tetrapyrrole Group [British] (EAIO)
TG .... Text Change [Computer science] (PCM)
TG .... Thai Airways [ICAO designator] (AD)
TG .... Thapsigargin [Organic chemistry]
TG .... Theatre Guild (EA)
TG .... Thermal Gravimetry (EDCT)
TG .... Thermogravimetry
TG .... Thioglucose [Biochemistry]
TG .... Thioglycolate [Biochemistry]
TG .... Thioguanine [Also, T] [Antineoplastic drug]
TG .... Third Generation (EA)
TG .... Thoracic Ganglion [Neuroanatomy]
TG .... Thromboglobulin [Clinical chemistry]
TG .... Thyroglobulin [Also, Thg] [Endocrinology]
TG .... Timing Gage (IAA)
TG .... Timing Gate (AAG)
TG .... Tinted Glass
TG .... Tithing [Church of England]
tg .... Togo [MARC country of publication code Library of Congress] (LCCP)
TG .... Togo [ANSI two-letter standard code] (CNC)
TG .... Tollgate [Maps and charts]
TG .... Top Grille (OA)
TG .... Torpedo Group
TG .... Torque Generator (IAA)
TG .... Total Graph (OA)
TG .... Toxic Goiter [Medicine] (MAE)
TG .... Track Geometry [In TG-01, an Austrian built subway inspection car]
TG .... Tracking and Guidance
TG .... Traders Group Ltd. [Toronto Stock Exchange symbol Vancouver Stock Exchange symbol]
TG .... Traffic Guidance [Aviation]
TG .... Training Group (WDAA)
TG .... Transfer Gate (IAA)
T-G .... Transformational-Generative [Linguistics]
TG .... Transformational Grammar
TG .... Transgenic [Genetics]
TG .... Transglutaminase [An enzyme]
TG .... Transgranular [Metallurgy]
TG .... Translators' Guild (WDAA)
TG .... Transmissible Gastroenteritis [Virus]
TG .... Transmission Group (IAA)
TG .... Treated Group [Medicine] (DB)
TG .... Tredegar Indus [NYSE symbol] (TTSB)
TG .... Tredegar Industries, Inc. [NYSE symbol] (SPSG)
TG .... Tribune de St. Gervais [A publication]
TG .... Trigeminal Ganglion [Neuroanatomy]
TG .... Trigger (IAA)
TG .... Trigger Generator
TG .... Triglyceride [Biochemistry]
TG .... Tropical Gulf [American air mass]
TG .... Tumor Growth [Medicine] (DB)
TG .... Tuned Grid (KSC)
TG .... Turbine Generator (NRCH)
TG .... Turbogenerator
TG .... Tying Goals [Sports]

TG	Type Genus
TGA	Antibody Thyroglobulin [*Immunology*]
TGA	[*The*] Generation After [*An association*] (EA)
TGA	[*The*] Glutamate Association - United States (EA)
TGA	Taurocholate-Gelatin Agar [*Microbiology*]
T/GA	Temperature Gauge [*Automotive engineering*]
TGA	Therapeutic Goods Administration [*Australia*]
TGA	Thermal Gas Analysis (AAEL)
TGA	Thermal Gravimetric Analysis (AAEL)
TGA	Thermogravimetric [*or Thermogravimetry*] Analysis [*Instrumentation*]
TGA	Thioglycolic Acid [*Organic chemistry*]
TGA	Togo Airlines [*ICAO designator*] (FAAC)
TGA	Toilet Goods Association [*Later, CTFA*] (EA)
TGA	Tolmetin Glycine Amide [*Biochemistry*]
TGA	Total Glycoalkaloids [*Analytical biochemistry*]
TGA	Touristische Gemeinschaft der Alpenlander [*Alpine Tourist Commission - ATC*] [*Zurich, Switzerland*] (EAIO)
TGA	Trace Gas Analysis
TGA	Trans Global Airlines [*FAA*] (TAG)
TGA	Transient Global Amnesia [*Medicine*]
TGA	Transposition of Great Arteries [*Cardiology*]
TGA	Treasury General Account [*Department of the Treasury*]
TGA	Triglycollamic Acid [*Organic chemistry*]
TGA	Tropical Growers' Association (EAIO)
TGA	Tumor Glycoprotein Assay [*Medicine*] (DMAA)
TGAb	Thyroglobulin Antibody
TGAC	Table Grape Advisory Committee [*Western Australia*]
TGAC	Technical Grade Active Constituent (EERA)
TGAC	Therapeutic Goods Advertising Code [*Australia*]
TGAI	Todd Giddings and Associates, Inc. (EFIS)
TGAL	Tegal Corp. [*NASDAQ symbol*] (SAG)
TGAL	Teledyne Geotech Alexandria Laboratories
T-GAM	Training - Guided Air Missile (MUGU)
TGAOTU	[*The*] Great Architect of the Universe [*Freemasonry*]
TGAQ	Treasury of Great American Quotations [*A publication*]
TGAR	Total Graft Area Rejected [*Medicine*] (MAE)
TGARQ	Telegraphic Approval Requested (NOAA)
TGAS	TACAN [*Tactical Air Navigation*] Guidance Augmentation System [*Military*] (CAAL)
TGAS	Trace Gas Acquisition System
Tgase	Transglutaminase (DB)
TGAT	Task Group on Assessment and Testing [*British*] (DET)
TG-ATS	Theatre Guild-American Theatre Society (EA)
TGaV	Volunteer State Community College, Learning Resources Center, Gallatin, TN [*Library symbol Library of Congress*] (LCLS)
TGB	Temporary Guidebase [*Oil*] (DICI)
TGB	Tongued, Grooved, and Beaded [*Lumber*]
TGB	Torpedo Gunboat (ROG)
TGB	Triple A and Gvt Ser'97(New) [*AMEX symbol*] (TTSB)
TGB	Triple A Government Series 1997, Inc. [*AMEX symbol*] (SAG)
TGB	Turbine Generator Building [*Nuclear energy*] (NRCH)
TGB	Twist-Grain-Boundary [*Liquid crystal science*]
TGBL	Through Government Bill of Lading [*Military*] (AABC)
TGBR	Trans-Global Resources NL [*NASDAQ symbol*] (NQ)
TGBRY	Trans-Global Resource NL ADR [*NASDAQ symbol*] (TTSB)
TGC	[*The*] Grantsmanship Center (EA)
TGC	Tasmanian Gaming Commission [*Australia*]
TGC	Tasmanian Golf Council [*Australia*]
TGC	Teleglobe Canada
TGC	Terminator Group Controller (IAA)
TGC	TG Aviation Ltd. [*British ICAO designator*] (FAAC)
TGC	Theater Ground Command [*Military*]
TGC	Therapeutic Goods Committee [*Australia*]
TGC	Thermocouple Gauge Control
TGC	Throttle Governor Control
TGC	Time Gain Compensation [*Radiology*] (DAVI)
TGC	Time Gain Control (IAA)
TGC	Tomato Genetics Cooperative (EA)
TGC	Total Gas-Phase Carbon [*Environmental chemistry*]
TGC	Tougaloo College, Tougaloo, MS [*OCLC symbol*] (OCLC)
TGC	Transfer Gear Case (MCD)
TGC	Transmit Gain Control (MSA)
TGC	Travel Group Charter [*Airline fare*]
TGC	Trenton, TN [*Location identifier FAA*] (FAAL)
TGCA	Texas Gun Collectors Association
TGCA	Tobacco Growers' Council of Australia
TGCA	Transportable Ground Control Approach (IAA)
TGCA	Transportable Group Control Approach (NG)
TGCI	TGC Industries [*NASDAQ symbol*] (TTSB)
TGCI	TGC Industries, Inc. [*NASDAQ symbol*] (SAG)
TGC In	TGC Industries, Inc. [*Associated Press*] (SAG)
TGC Ind	TGC Industries, Inc. [*Associated Press*] (SAG)
TGC Inds	TGC Industries, Inc. [*Associated Press*] (SAG)
TGCR	Tactical Generic Cable Replacement
TGCS	Transportable Ground Communications Station
TGD	Task Group Delta (MCD)
TGD	Technical Guidance Directions
TGD	Titograd [*Former Yugoslavia*] [*Airport symbol*] (OAG)
TGD	Trajectory and Guidance Data
TGDDM	Tetraglycidyl(diaminodiphenyl)methane [*Organic chemistry*]
TGE	Tokyo International Financial Futures Exchange [*Japan*] (NUMA)
TGE	Trabajos Aereos SA [*Spain ICAO designator*] (FAAC)
TGE	Transmissible Gastroenteritis [*Virus*]
TGE	Traverse Gravimeter Experiment (KSC)
TGE	Trialkoxyglyceryl Ether [*Organic chemistry*]

TGE	Tryptone Glucose Extract [*Cell growth medium*]
TGE	Tuskegee, AL [*Location identifier FAA*] (FAAL)
TGEB	Tasmanian Grain Elevators Board [*Australia*]
TGEEP	Terminal Guidance Environmental Effects Program (MCD)
TGEN	Targeted Genetics [*NASDAQ symbol*] (TTSB)
TGEN	Targeted Genetics Corp. [*NASDAQ symbol*] (SAG)
TGEP	Turbine Generator Emergency Power [*Nuclear energy*] (NRCH)
TGET	Target Ground Elapsed Time
TGET	Target Therapeutics [*NASDAQ symbol*] (TTSB)
TGET	Target Therapeutics, Inc. [*NASDAQ symbol*] (SAG)
TGEV	Transmissible Gastroenteritis Virus [*Virology*]
TGF	Aerotaxis del Golfo, SA de CV [*Mexico*] [*FAA designator*] (FAAC)
TGF	Emerging Tigers Fund [*NYSE symbol*] (SAG)
TGF	Therapeutic Gain Factor [*Medicine*]
TGF	Through Group Filter [*Telecommunications*] (TEL)
TGF	Top Groove Fill [*Lubricating oil test*]
TGF	Tragicorum Graecorum Fragmenta [*A publication*] (OCD)
TGF	Training Guarantee Fund [*Australia*]
TGF	Transforming Growth Factor
TGF	Transonic Gasdynamics Facility [*Air Force*]
TGF	Treasury Guard Force
TGF	Triglycine Fluoberyllate [*Ferroelectrics*]
TGF	Tubuloglomerular Feedback (DB)
TGF	Tumor Growth Factor [*Oncology*]
TGFA	Tasmanian Game Fishing Association [*Australia*]
TGF-A	Transforming Growth Factor - Alpha
TGFA	Triglyceride Fatty Acid [*Biochemistry*]
TGFC	Tammy Graham Fan Club (EA)
TGFC	Terri Gibbs Fan Club (EA)
TGFM	Tasmanian Guild of Furniture Manufacturers [*Australia*]
TGG	Kuala Trengganu [*Malaysia*] [*Airport symbol*] (OAG)
TGG	Templeton Global Government Income Trust [*NYSE symbol*] (CTT)
TGG	Templeton Global Gvts [*NYSE symbol*] (TTSB)
TGG	Temporary Geographic Grid
TGG	Third Generation Gyro (MCD)
TGG	Turkey Gamma G [*Immunology*]
TGGE	Temperature-Gradient Gel Electrophoresis [*Analytical biochemistry*]
TGH	Tongoa [*Vanuatu*] [*Airport symbol*] (OAG)
TGH	Tripler General Hospital [*Army*] (GFGA)
TGI	Tactics Guide Issued (CAAL)
TGI	Taghi Ghambar [*Iran*] [*Seismograph station code, US Geological Survey*] (SEIS)
TGI	Tangier, VA [*Location identifier FAA*] (FAAL)
TGI	Target Group Index [*British Market Research Bureau Ltd.*] [*Information service or system*]
TGI	Target Intensifier
TGI	Telco Group, Inc. [*Telecommunications service*] (TSSD)
TGI	Textbuch zur Geschichte Israels [*A publication*] (BJA)
TGI	Tingo Maria [*Peru*] [*Airport symbol*] (OAG)
TGI	Tournament Golf International
TGIA	Toy and Giftware Importers Association [*British*] (DBA)
TGIC	Tobacco Growers' Information Committee (EA)
TGIC	Triad Guaranty [*NASDAQ symbol*] (TTSB)
TGIC	Triad Guaranty, Inc. [*NASDAQ symbol*] (SAG)
TGIC	Triglycidyl Isocyanurate [*Organic chemistry*]
TGID	Transmission Group Identifier [*Telecommunications*] (MHDI)
TGID	Trunk Group Identification [*Telecommunications*] (TEL)
TGIF	Tactical Ground Intercept Facility [*Air Force*] (DOMA)
TGIF	Terminal Guidance Indirect Fire (MCD)
TGIF	Thank God It's Friday [*Meaning work-week is nearly over*]
TGIF	Toe Goes in First [*As is "You're so dumb you have TGIF on your shoes"*]
TGIF	Transportable Ground Intercept Facility
TGIF	Tumor-Growth Inhibitory Factor [*Medicine*] (DB)
TGIF-OTMWDUM	Thank God It's Friday - Only Two More Work Days Until Monday [*Pentagon saying*]
TGIS	Thank God It's Summer
TGIS	Thomas Group [*NASDAQ symbol*] (TTSB)
TGIS	Thomas Group, Inc. [*NASDAQ symbol*] (SAG)
TGJ	Tiga [*Loyalty Islands*] [*Airport symbol*] (OAG)
TGL+	[*The*] Graphics Link Plus [*Printer software*] [*TerraVision*] (PCM)
TGL	Tagula [*Papua New Guinea*] [*Airport symbol*] (OAG)
TGL	Tangent Oil & Gas [*Vancouver Stock Exchange symbol*]
TGL	Task Group Leader
TGL	Temperature Gradient Lamp [*Spectroscopy*]
TGL	Thin Glass Laminate
TGL	Toggle (AAG)
TGL	Touch and Go Landings [*Aviation*]
TGL	Trans-Atlantic Airlines Ltd. [*Gambia*] [*ICAO designator*] (FAAC)
TGL	Treasury Gold License (MCD)
TGL	Triangular Guide Line
TGL	Triglyceride [*Biochemistry*] (MAE)
TGL	Triglyceride Lipase [*Clinical chemistry*]
TGL	Triglycerides [*Clinical chemistry*]
TGL	Triton Group Ltd. [*AMEX symbol*] (SPSG)
TGLC	Total Gate Leakage Current
TGLE	Transglobe Energy Corp. [*NASDAQ symbol*] (SAG)
TGLEF	Transglobe Energy [*NASDAQ symbol*] (TTSB)
TGLM	Task Group Lung Model [*ICRP*]
TG-LORAN	Traffic-Guidance Long-Range Aid to Navigation (DEN)
TGLS	Tongueless
TGLVQ	Terminal Guidance for Lunar Vehicles [*Aerospace*] (AAG)
TGL.WS	Triton Group Ltd Wrrt [*AMEX symbol*] (TTSB)
TGM	Tactical Generic Multiplex
TGM	Task Group Manager (CAAL)

TGM............	Telegram (ROG)
TGM............	Tirgu Mures [Romania] [Airport symbol] (OAG)
TGM............	Torpedo Gunner's Mate [Obsolete Navy British]
TGM............	Total Gaseous Mercury [Environmental chemistry]
TGM............	Training Guided Missile [Air Force]
TGM............	Transportability Guidance Manual
TGM............	Trunk Group Multiplexer [Telecommunications] (TEL)
TGM............	Turbine Generator Management
TGMA..........	Tone Generator and Master Alarm (KSC)
TGMD	Test of Gross Motor Development [Sensorimotor skills test]
TG-MS.........	Thermogravimetry - Mass Spectrometry
TGMTS.........	Tank Gunnery and Missile Tracking System
TGMV..........	Tomato Golden Mosaic Virus
TGN............	Anchorage, AK [Location identifier FAA] (FAAL)
TGN............	Tarragona [Spain] [Airport symbol] (AD)
TGN	Tournigan Mining Explorations Ltd. [Vancouver Stock Exchange symbol]
TGN	Trans Golgi Network [Cytology]
TGN............	Trigeminal Neuralgia [Medicine]
TGN............	Trigen Energy [NYSE symbol] (TTSB)
TGN............	Trigen Energy Corp. [NYSE symbol] (SAG)
TGN............	Trunk Group Number [Telecommunications] (TEL)
TGNMO........	Total Gaseous Non-Methane Organic [Environmental chemistry]
TGNR..........	Tactics Guide Not Required (CAAL)
TGNSW........	Teachers' Guild of New South Wales [Australia]
TGNU..........	Transitional Government of National Unity [South Africa]
TGO............	Canada-Transport Canada [ICAO designator] (FAAC)
TGO............	Time to Go [Apollo] [NASA]
TGO............	Togo [ANSI three-letter standard code] (CNC)
TGO............	Tongliao [China] [Airport symbol] (OAG)
TGO............	Total Gross Output (GNE)
TGO............	Tuned Grid Oscillator
TGOPS.........	Task Group Operations [Navy] (NVT)
TG or UA	Temperance, Grog, or Underage [British military]
TGOWG........	Teleoperator Ground Operations Working Group [NASA] (NASA)
TGP............	[The] Giraffe Project [An association] (EA)
TGP............	Technigen Platinum Corp. [Vancouver Stock Exchange symbol]
TGP............	Theft of Government Property [FBI standardized term]
TGP............	Timothy Grass Pollen [Immunology]
TGP............	Tobacco Glycoprotein [Biochemistry]
TGP............	Tone Generator Panel
TGP............	Turbulence-Generating Pot [Automotive engineering]
TGPA	Technigen Corp. [NASDAQ symbol] (SAG)
TGPAF	Technigen Corp. [NASDAQ symbol] (TTSB)
TGPG..........	St. Georges [Grenada] [ICAO location identifier] (ICLI)
TGPO..........	Tasmanian Government Printing Office [Australia]
TGPSG........	Tactical Global Positioning System Guidance (MCD)
TGPWU........	Transport, General and Port Workers' Union [Aden]
TGPY	Point Saline [Grenada] [ICAO location identifier] (ICLI)
TGR............	Tenderness, Guarding, Rigidity [On abdominal examination] [Medicine] (DAVI)
TGR	Things Gone Right [Measure of automobile customer satisfaction]
TGR	Touggourt [Algeria] [Airport symbol] (OAG)
TGRBX........	Mgn. Stanley D. Witter Pacific Growth Cl.B [Mutual fund ticker symbol] (SG)
TGRLSS	Two-Gas Regenerative Lift Support System
TGrT...........	Tusculum College, Greeneville, TN [Library symbol Library of Congress] (LCLS)
TGS............	[The] Galactic Society (EA)
TGS............	Gulf States Utilities Co., Beaumont, TX [OCLC symbol] (OCLC)
TGS............	Target Generating System
TGS............	Taxiing Guidance System [Aviation]
TGS............	Telemetry Ground Station
TGS............	Telemetry Ground System (NASA)
TGS............	Telemetry Guidance System [From computer game "Hacker II"]
TGS............	Template Graphics Software
TGS............	Terminal Guidance Sensor [or System]
TGS............	Thermogravimetric [or Thermogravimetry] System [Instrumentation]
TGS............	Ticket-Granting Server
TGS............	Tide Gauge System
TGS............	Tincture of Green Soap [Medicine] (DMAA)
TGS............	Top Gear Switch [Automotive engineering]
TGS............	Traite de Grammaire Syriaque [A publication] (BJA)
TGS............	Transcontinental Geophysical Survey (NOAA)
TGS............	Transfer Generator System (IAA)
TGS............	Translator Generator System (IEEE)
TGS............	Transportable Ground Station
TGS............	Transportadora De Gas ADS [NYSE symbol] (TTSB)
TGS............	Transportadora de Gas Del Sur SA [NYSE symbol] (SAG)
TGS............	Trichlorogalactosucrose [Medicine] (WDAA)
TGS............	Triglycine Sulfate [Ferroelectrics]
TGS............	True Ground Speed
TGS............	Turbine Generator System [Nuclear energy] (NRCH)
TGS............	Turkish General Staff (NATG)
TGS............	Turret Gun System [Army]
TGS............	Tuxtla Gutierrez [Mexico] [Airport symbol] (AD)
TGSE..........	Tactical Ground Support Equipment
TGSE..........	Telemetry Ground Support Equipment [NASA] (KSC)
TGSF..........	Test Group Support Facility
TGSI...........	Concept Tech Group [NASDAQ symbol] (SAG)
TGSI...........	Trans Global Services, Inc. [NASDAQ symbol] (SAG)
TGSI...........	Trans Global Svcs [NASDAQ symbol] (TTSB)
TGSIFC.......	T. G. Sheppard International Fan Club (EA)
TGSIW........	Trans Global Svcs Wrrt [NASDAQ symbol] (TTSB)
TGSM..........	Terminally Guided Submissile (MCD)
TGSM..........	Terminally Guided Submunitions (MCD)
TGSR..........	Triglyceride Secretion Rate [Physiology]
TGSS..........	Terminal Guidance Sensor System
TGSS..........	Transmission Gear Selection Switch [Automotive engineering]
TGSS..........	Turbine Gland Sealing System [Nuclear energy] (NRCH)
TGSSA........	Transactions. Geological Society of South Africa [A publication]
TGSS/UGS ...	Tactical Ground Sensor System/Unattended Ground Sensor (MCD)
TGT............	AB Nyge Aero [Sweden] [FAA designator] (FAAC)
TGT............	Tail Gate
TGT............	Tanga [Tanzania] [Airport symbol] (OAG)
TGT............	Target (AAG)
TGT............	Teams-Games-Tournaments [Education] (AEE)
TGT............	Thermocouple Gauge Tube
TGT............	Thromboplastin Generation Test [Hematology]
TGT............	Thromboplastin Generation Time [Hematology] (MAE)
TGT............	Ticket-Granting Ticket [Computer science]
TGT............	Tissue Glucose Threshold [Medicine] (BARN)
TGT............	TOW [Tube-launched, Optically Tracked, Wire-Guided (weapon)] Gunnery Trainer [Army] (INF)
TGT............	Transformational Grammar Tester (IAA)
TGT............	True Ground Track (MCD)
TGT............	Turbine Gas Temperature (NATG)
TGTBT........	Too Good to be True [Internet language] [Computer science]
TGTM..........	Transportability Guidance Technical Manual
TGTP..........	Tuned Grid Tuned Plate [Electronic plate] (IAA)
TGTU..........	Tail-Gas Treating Unit [Petroleum engineering]
TGU............	Technical Guidance Unit (NVT)
TGU............	Tegucigalpa [Honduras] [Airport symbol] (OAG)
TGU............	Templeton Global Utilities, Inc. [AMEX symbol] (SPSG)
TGU............	Triglycidylurazol [Antineoplastic drug]
TGU............	Tri Gold Industry [Vancouver Stock Exchange symbol]
TGURG........	Telegraphic Authority Requested (NOAA)
TGV............	Targovishte [Bulgaria] [Airport symbol] (OAG)
TGV............	Thomson Gold Co. [Vancouver Stock Exchange symbol]
TGV............	Thoracic Gas Volume [Medicine] (AAMN)
TGV............	Tobacco Growers of Victoria [Australia]
TGV............	Train a Grande Vitesse [High-speed train]
TGV............	Transposition of the Great Vessels [Cardiology]
TGV............	Turbine Governor Valve [Nuclear energy] (NRCH)
TGV............	Two Gentlemen of Verona [Shakespearean work]
TGVI...........	TGV Software, Inc. [NASDAQ symbol] (SAG)
TGV Sft.......	TGV Software, Inc. [Associated Press] (SAG)
TGW............	Terminally Guided Warhead [or Weapon]
TGW............	Things Gone Wrong [Measure of automobile customer satisfaction]
TGW............	Tropospheric Gravity Wave [Planetary science]
TGWU..........	Transport and General Workers' Union [British]
TGX............	Taguatinga [Brazil] [Airport symbol] (AD)
TGX............	Theragenics Corp. [NYSE symbol]
TGX............	Tube-Generated X-Ray
TGY............	Punta Gorda [British Honduras] [Airport symbol] (AD)
TGY............	Tryptone Glucose Yeast [Cell growth medium] (MAE)
TGYA	Tryptone Glucose Yeast Agar [Cell growth medium] [Medicine] (DMAA)
TGZ............	Tuxtla Gutierrez [Mexico] [Airport symbol] (OAG)
TGZM..........	Temperature-Gradient Zone-Melting [Chemistry]
TGZMP........	Temperature-Gradient Zone-Melting Process [Chemistry] (IAA)
Th..............	C. H. Boehringer Sohn, Ingelheim [Germany] [Research code symbol]
TH.............	Harriman Public Library, Harriman, TN [Library symbol Library of Congress] (LCLS)
TH.............	Hot Leg Temperature [Nuclear energy] (NRCH)
TH.............	Reports of the Witwatersrand High Court [Transvaal, South Africa] [A publication] (DLA)
T-H............	Taft-Hartley [Act]
TH.............	Tally Ho [Air Force]
TH.............	Tape-Handler [Computer science] (IAA)
TH.............	Tax Haven (MHDW)
Th.............	T-Cell, Helper Type [Immunology]
TH.............	Teacher of Hydrotherapy [British]
TH.............	Teaching Hospital [British]
TH.............	Technische Hochschule [Technical College] [German]
TH.............	Telegraph (IAA)
TH.............	Telegraph Apparatus [JETDS nomenclature] [Military] (CET)
TH.............	Tell Halaf (BJA)
TH.............	Temporary Hold
TH.............	Terraced Heterostructure (NITA)
TH.............	Terrain Height (MCD)
TH.............	Territory of Hawaii [to 1959]
TH.............	Test Header (Fire Pump) [NFPA pre-fire planning symbol] (NFPA)
TH.............	Tetrahydrocortisol (MAE)
TH.............	Thai Airways [ICAO designator] (AD)
TH.............	Thailand [IYRU nationality code] [ANSI two-letter standard code] (CNC)
th.............	Thailand [MARC country of publication code Library of Congress] (LCCP)
TH.............	Tharsis Region [A filamentary mark on Mars]
TH.............	Theatre (ROG)
TH.............	Their Highnesses (ADA)
Th.............	T-Helper [Immunology]
Th.............	Thenar [Anatomy]
th.............	Thenardite [CIPW classification] [Geology]
Th.............	Theodotion (BJA)
Th.............	Theogonia [of Hesiod] [Classical studies] (OCD)
TH.............	Theology
TH.............	Theophylline [Pharmacology] (DAVI)

TH	Theraplix [France] [Research code symbol]
TH	Therapy [Medicine] (DHSM)
TH	Thermal
T/H	Thermal and Hydraulic [Nuclear energy] (NRCH)
TH	Thermoid (SAA)
Th	Thessalonians [New Testament book] (BJA)
TH	Thick [Automotive engineering]
Th	Thin [Philately]
Th	Thionine [Organic chemistry]
Th	Thiopental [An anesthetic]
Th	Thomas de Piperata [Flourished, 1268-72] [Authority cited in pre-1607 legal work] (DSA)
th	Thoracic [Anatomy] (MAE)
TH	Thoracic Surgery [Medicine]
Th	Thorax [Anatomy] (DAVI)
Th	Thorium [Chemical element]
TH	Thoroughbred (WGA)
TH	Thorvald Hansen [Steamship] (MHDW)
TH	Threat
TH	Threshold (WGA)
TH	Thrill [Cardiology] (DAVI)
TH	Through-Hole [Computer science]
TH	Thunder
TH	Thursday
TH	Thyrohyoid [Medicine] (MAE)
TH	Thyroid Hormone [Thyroxine] [Endocrinology]
TH	Thyssen Henschel
TH	Titan Holdings [NYSE symbol] (TTSB)
TH	Titan Holdings, Inc. [NYSE symbol] (SAG)
TH	Toilet-Paper Holder
TH	Toluene-Hyamine [Scintillation solvent]
TH	Tommy Hilfiger [Fashion designer]
TH	Total Hysterectomy [Medicine]
TH	Town Hall (ROG)
TH	Townhouse
TH	Toy and Hobby Retailer [A publication]
TH	Tracing-Hold
TH	Tracking Head (IAA)
TH	Trailer Height [Automotive engineering]
T-H	Transhydro (AABC)
TH	Transient Hyperphosphatasemia [Medicine]
TH	Transmission Header [Computer science] (IBMDP)
TH	Transponder-Hopping
T/H	Transportation and Handling [Army]
TH	Trinity House [British] (BARN)
TH	True Heading
TH	Trust House [British]
TH	Two Hands
TH	Tyrosine Hydroxylase [An enzyme]
TH	Tzivos Hashem (EA)
TH₂0	Free Water Reabsorption (DAVI)
TH₂0	Titrated Water (DAVI)
ThĀ	Associate in Theology (ADA)
THA	Taft-Hartley Act [1947]
THA	Tasmanian Hockey Association [Australia]
T-HA	Terminal High Altitude
THA	Tetrahydroaminoacridine [Pharmacology]
tha	Thai [MARC language code Library of Congress] (LCCP)
THA	Thai Airways International Ltd. [Thailand] [ICAO designator] (FAAC)
THA	Thailand [ANSI three-letter standard code] (CNC)
THA	Thames Ontario Library Service Board [UTLAS symbol]
ThA	Thoracic Aorta [Medicine]
THA	Thorcheron Hunter Association [Defunct] (EA)
THA	Time Warner Financing Trust PERCS [NYSE symbol] (SAG)
THA	Time Warner Fin Tr'PERCS' [NYSE symbol] (TTSB)
THA	Total Hip Arthroplasty [Orthopedics]
THA	Total Hydrocarbon Analyzer
THA	Total Hydroxyapatite [Clinical chemistry] (MAE)
THA	Tower Hill School, Wilmington, DE [OCLC symbol] (OCLC)
THA	Transient Hemispheric Attack [Medicine] (DAVI)
THA	Transvaal Horse Artillery [British military] (DMA)
THA	Treasury Historical Association (EA)
THA	Treponema Hemagglutination [Test] [Medicine] (DB)
THA	Tullahoma [Tennessee] [Airport symbol] (AD)
THA	Tullahoma, TN [Location identifier FAA] (FAAL)
THA	Turk Haberler Ajansi [Press agency] [Turkey]
THAA	Total Haloacetic Acid [Environmental chemistry]
THAA	Tourist House Association of America (EA)
THAAD	Theater High-Altitude Area Defense [Military]
THAB	Tetrahexylammonium Benzoate [Organic chemistry]
THABTS	Thereabouts [Legal term British]
Thac Cr Cas	Thacher's Criminal Cases [1823-42] [Massachusetts] [A publication] (DLA)
Thach Cr	Thacher's Criminal Cases [Massachusetts] [A publication] (DLA)
Thacher Cr	Thacher's Criminal Cases [Massachusetts] [A publication] (DLA)
Thacher Cr Cas	Thacher's Criminal Cases [Massachusetts] [A publication] (DLA)
Thacher Crim Cas (Mass)	Thacher's Criminal Cases [Massachusetts] [A publication] (DLA)
Thack	Thackeray Corp. [Associated Press] (SAG)
THAE	Transcatheter Hepatic Artery Embolization [Medicine]
THAF	Tree House Animal Foundation (EA)
THAI	Thai Airways International
Thai	Thai Fund [Associated Press] (SAG)
Thai	Thailand
ThaiCF	Thai Capital Fund, Inc. [Associated Press] (SAG)

Thail	Thailand
THAJ	Tasmania House of Assembly - Journals [A publication]
THAL	Thalamus (DB)
Thal	Thalassemia [Medicine]
THAM	2-Amino-2-(Hydroxymethyl)-1,3-Propanediol (DAVI)
THAM	Tris(hydroxymethyl)aminomethane [Also, TRIS] [Biochemical analysis]
THAMA	Toxic and Hazardous Materials Agency [Army] (RDA)
THAN	Transient Hyperammonemia of Newborn [Neonatology] (DAVI)
TH & B	[The] Toronto, Hamilton & Buffalo Railway Co. [Nickname: To Hell and Back]
TH & C	Terpin Hydrate and Codeine [Medicine]
Th & C	Thompson and Cook's New York Supreme Court Reports [1873-75] [A publication] (DLA)
TH & P	Terre Haute & Peoria Railroad [Nickname: Take Hold and Push]
THANSW	Teacher Housing Authority of New South Wales [Australia]
THAP	Tactical High-Altitude Penetration [MCD]
THAQ	Tetrahydroanthraquinone [Organic chemistry]
THARIES	Total Hip Articular Replacement with Internal Eccentric Shells [Orthopedics]
THaroL	Lincoln Memorial University, Harrogate, TN [Library symbol Library of Congress] (LCLS)
THART	Theodore Army Terminal
THAS	Tumbleweed High-Altitude Samples (MUGU)
ThAT	Theologie des Alten Testaments [A publication] (BJA)
THAT	Twenty-Four-Hour Automatic Teller [Trademark for self-service banking display panel]
THav	Trousdale County Public Library, Hartsville, TN [Library symbol] [Library of Congress] (LCLS)
THAWS	Tactical Homing and Warning System
Thayer	Thayer's Reports [18 Oregon] [A publication] (DLA)
Thayer Prelim Treatise Ev	Thayer's Preliminary Treatise on Evidence [A publication] (DLA)
THB	Thaba Tseka [Lesotho] [Airport symbol] (OAG)
Th B	Theologiae Baccalaureas [Bachelor of Theology]
ThB	Theologische Buecherei. Neudrucke und Berichte aus dem 20 Jahrhundert [Munich] [A publication] (BJA)
THB	Third-Harmonic Band
THB	[The] Toronto, Hamilton & Buffalo Railway Co. [AAR code]
THBC	Troy Hill Bancorp [NASDAQ symbol] (TTSB)
THBC	Troy Hill Bancorp, Inc. [NASDAQ symbol] (SAG)
THBF	Total Hepatic Blood Flow
THBF	Traditional Hi-Bye Function [Army]
THBI	Thyroid Hormone Binding Inhibitor [Clinical chemistry]
ThBNL	National Library, Bangkok, Thailand [Library symbol Library of Congress] (LCLS)
THBP	Tetrahydrobenzopyrene [Organic chemistry]
Th Br	Thesaurus Brevium [2 eds.] [1661, 1687] [A publication] (DLA)
THBR	Thoroughbred Half-Bred Registry (EA)
THBR	Thyroid Hormone Binding Ratio [Clinical chemistry]
THBY	Thereby
Th C	Candidate of Theology
THC	Houston Community College System, Learning Resource Center, Houston, TX [OCLC symbol] (OCLC)
THC	Target Homing Correlator
THC	Tar Heel Aviation, Inc. [ICAO designator] (FAAC)
THC	Tchien [Liberia] [Airport symbol] (OAG)
THC	Tenet Healthcare [NYSE symbol] (TTSB)
THC	Tenet Healthcare Corp. [NYSE symbol] (SAG)
THC	Tetrahydrocannabinol [Active principle of marijuana]
THC	Tetrahydrocortisol
THC	THC Homecare, Inc. [Associated Press] (SAG)
THC	Thermal Converter (MSA)
THC	Thermohaline Circulation [Oceanography]
THC	Thiocarbanidin [Pharmacology]
THC	Third-Harmonic Distortion [Physics] (IAA)
THC	Throttled Homogeneous Combustion
THC	Thrust Hand Controller [NASA] (KSC)
THC	Total Hydrocarbon
THC	Total Hydrocarbons (AAEL)
THC	Transhepatic Cholangiogram [Medicine]
THC	Translation Hand Controller [NASA]
THC	Transplantable Hepatocellular Carcinoma [Medicine] (DB)
THC	Trident Health Care, Inc. [Toronto Stock Exchange symbol]
THC	Troissier-Hanot-Chauffard [Syndrome] [Medicine] (DB)
THC	True Heading Computer (DNAB)
THC	Tube Humidity Control
T-HCA	Trans-Hydroxycrotonic Acid [Organic chemistry]
THCA	Trihydroxycholestanoic Acid [Biochemistry]
THCA	Trihydroxycoprostanic Acid [Biochemistry]
Th Ca Const Law	Thomas' Leading Cases in Constitutional Law [A publication] (DLA)
ThCar	Thermo Cardiosystems, Inc. [Associated Press] (SAG)
Th CC	Thacher's Criminal Cases [1823-42] [Massachusetts] [A publication] (DLA)
THCC	Tube Heating and Cooling Control
Th C Const Law	Thomas' Leading Cases on Constitutional Law [A publication] (DLA)
THC-CRC	Tetrahydrocannabinol Cross-Reacting-Cannabinoid [Active principle of marijuana] (PDAA)
THCF	Thompson-Huston Co. of France
THC Hm	THC Homecare, Inc. [Associated Press] (SAG)
THCI	THC Homecare, Inc. [NASDAQ symbol] (SAG)
THCN	Tetrahydrocorynantheine [Biochemistry]
THCOL	Thorn Color [Botany]

THCS	Temperature of Hot-Channel Sodium [*Nuclear energy*] (NRCH)
TH-CULT	Throat Culture [*Medicine*] (DAVI)
THCUR	Thorn Curvature [*Botany*]
tHcy	Total Homocysteine [*Clinical chemistry*]
THD	611 897 Alberta Ltd. [*Canada*] [*FAA designator*] (FAAC)
ThD	Doctor of Thinkology [*Honorary degree awarded the scarecrow by the wizard in 1939 film "The Wizard of Oz"*]
Thd	Ribothymidine [*Also, T*] [*A nucleoside*]
THD	Testicular Hypothermia Device [*Medicine*]
Th D	Theologiae Doctor [*Doctor of Theology*]
THD	Third Canadian General Investment Trust Ltd. [*Toronto Stock Exchange symbol*]
THD	Third-Harmonic Distortion [*Physics*] (IAA)
THD	Thread (AAG)
THD	Thunderhead [*Meterology*] (FAAC)
THD	Total Harmonic Distortion [*Electronics*]
THD	Tube Heat Dissipator
THD	University of Houston, Downtown College, Houston, TX [*OCLC symbol*] (OCLC)
THDA	Telluraheptadecanoic Acid [*Organic chemistry*]
THDA	Thermal Hydrodealkylation [*Petroleum technology*]
THDA	Toluene Hydrodealkylation [*Organic chemistry*]
THDC	Technical Handbook Distribution Code (MCD)
THDG	True Heading (GAVI)
THDI	Thread Die
ThDip	Diploma in Theology (ADA)
THDNK	Threaded Neck
THDO	3D0 Company [*NASDAQ symbol*] (TTSB)
THDO	Three Do Co. [*NASDAQ symbol*] (SAG)
THDOC	Tetrahydrodeoxycorticosterone [*Biochemistry*]
ThDP	Thiamine Diphosphate [*Biochemistry*]
THDPC	Threadpiece
THDr	Doctor of Theology
THDR	Thunder [*Meteorology*] (FAAC)
THDS	Thermal Helium Desorption Spectrometry (MCD)
THDS	Time Homogenous Data Set (MCD)
THE	T & H Resources Ltd. [*Toronto Stock Exchange symbol*]
THE	Tape-Handling Equipment
THE	Technical Help to Exporters [*British Standards Institution*]
THE	Teresina [*Brazil*] [*Airport symbol*] (OAG)
THE	Tetrahydrocortisone [*Endocrinology*]
ThE	Theologische Existenz Heute [*Munich*] [*A publication*] (BJA)
THE	Thomas Hewett Edward Cat [*In TV series "T.H.E. Cat"*]
THE	Tonic Hind Limb Extension (BABM)
THE	Total Height Expansion
THE	Transhepatic Embolization [*Medicine*]
THE	Transportable Helicopter Enclosure (RDA)
THE	Tropical Hypereosinophilia [*Medicine*] (DMAA)
THE	Tube Heat Exchanger
THEA	Theatrical
THEAT	Theatrical
Theat J	Theatre Journal [*A publication*] (BRI)
Theb	Thebais [*of Statius*] [*Classical studies*] (OCD)
THEBES	[*The*] Electronic Banking Economics Society [*New York, NY*] (EA)
THECC	Truck and Heavy Equipment Claims Council (EA)
THEED	Tetrahydroxyethylethylenediamine [*Organic chemistry*]
THEED	Transmission High-Energy Electron Diffraction (AAEL)
THEIC	Tris(hydroxyethyl)isocyanurate [*Organic chemistry*]
THEL	Tactical High Energy Laser [*Military project developed jointly by the United States and Israel*]
Thel	Theloall's Le Digest des Briefs [*2 eds.*] [*1579, 1687*] [*A publication*] (DLA)
THELEP	Chemotherapy of Leprosy Program [*World Health Organization*] (BABM)
Them	American Themis [*A publication*] (DLA)
Them	La Themis [*A publication*] (DLA)
Them	Themistocles [*of Plutarch*] [*Classical studies*] (OCD)
THEN	Those Hags Encourage Neuterism [*Organization opposed to NOW (National Organization for Women)*]
THenF	Freed-Hardeman College, Loden-Daniel Library, Henderson, TN [*Library symbol*] [*Library of Congress*] (LCLS)
Theo	Theological (AL)
Theo	Theology (AL)
THEO	Theology
THEO	Theophylline [*Pharmacology*]
THEO	Theoretical
Theo Am A...	Theobald's Act for the Amendment of the Law [*A publication*] (DLA)
Theobald	Theobald on Wills [*11 eds.*] [*1876-1954*] [*A publication*] (DLA)
Theoc..........	Theocritus [*Third century BC*] [*Classical studies*] (OCD)
Theod	Theodotion (BJA)
Theog	Theogonia [*of Hesiod*] [*Classical studies*] (OCD)
THEOL	Theological
TheolArb	Theologische Arbeiten [*A publication*] (BJA)
TheolM	Master of Theology
THEOLOG....	Theology Student (DSUE)
Theol St	Theological Studies [*A publication*] (BRI)
Theom L......	Theomonistic Licensee
Theoph	Theophilus [*Sixth century*] [*Early Christian bishop*] (BARN)
Theoph	Theophrastus [*Third Century BC*] [*Classical studies*] (BARN)
Theophil	Theophilus [*Flourished, 6th century*] [*Authority cited in pre-1607 legal work*] (DSA)
Theophr	Theophrastus [*Third century BC*] [*Classical studies*] (OCD)
Theopomp ...	Theopompus Historicus [*Fourth century BC*] [*Classical studies*] (OCD)
Theo Pr & S...	Theobald's Principal and Surety [*1832*] [*A publication*] (DLA)
Theo Pres Pr...	Theory of Presumptive Proof [*A publication*] (DLA)
THEOR.........	Theorem (ROG)
THEOR.........	Theoretical (AAG)
THEOS	Theosophy
theos	Theosophy (WDAA)
THEOS	They Help Each Other Spiritually [*Motto of THEOS Foundation*]
THEOS R......	Theosophical Review [*A publication*] (ROG)
Theo Wills...	Theobald on Wills [*13th ed.*] [*1971*] [*A publication*] (DLA)
THEP	TOGA [*Tropical Ocean and Global Atmosphere*] Heat Exchange Program [*Marine science*] (OSRA)
THEP	Topical Hazard Evaluation Program [*Toxicology*] [*Military*] (RDA)
THer...........	Ladies Hermitage Association, Hermitage, TN [*Library symbol Library of Congress*] (LCLS)
THER	Therapeutic
THER	Therapeutic [*Range*] [*Laboratory science*] (DAVI)
THER	Therapy (DAVI)
ther...........	Therapy (STED)
Ther...........	Theriaca [*of Nicander*] [*Classical studies*] (OCD)
ther...........	Thermometer (STED)
THER	Thermometer (DAVI)
THERAP	Therapeutic
therap	Therapy (STED)
therapeut.....	Therapeutic [*Medicine*] (WDAA)
TheraTx	TheraTx, Inc. [*Associated Press*] (SAG)
TherD	Therapeutic Discovery Corp. [*Associated Press*] (SAG)
TherDiscA....	Therapeutic Discovery Corp. [*Associated Press*] (SAG)
THERE	[*The*] Heterogeneous Environment for Remote Execution [*Computer science*]
TherEl	Thermo Electron Corp. [*Associated Press*] (SAG)
The Rep.......	[*The*] Reporter, Phi Alpha Delta [*A publication*] (DLA)
The Rep.......	[*The*] Reports, Coke's English King's Bench [*A publication*] (DLA)
ther ex........	Therapeutic Exercise (STED)
Ther Ex.......	Therapeutic Exercise [*Physical therapy*] (DAVI)
THERM	Thermal (DEN)
THERM	Thermometer (AAG)
therm.........	Thermometer (STED)
THERM	Thermostat (DEN)
THERMA	Transfer of Heat Reduced Magnetically
Thermat	Thermatrix, Inc. [*Associated Press*] (SAG)
Thermed	Thermedics, Inc. [*Associated Press*] (SAG)
THERMISTOR...	Thermal Resistor
THERMO	Thermal and Hydrodynamic Experiment Research Module in Orbit (MCD)
THERMO	Thermodynamic Property Values Database [*Chemical Information Systems, Inc.*] [*Information service or system*] (CRD)
THERMO	Thermostat (AAG)
thermochem...	Thermochemistry (BARN)
THERMODYN...	Thermodynamics (AAG)
THerP	[*The*] Papers of Andrew Jackson, Hermitage, TN [*Library symbol Library of Congress*] (LCLS)
THERP	Technique for Human Error Rate Prediction
TherRe.........	Thermo Remediation [*Associated Press*] (SAG)
THES	Theses of Economics and Business in Finland [*Helsinki School of Economics Library*] [*Information service or system*] (CRD)
Thes............	Theseus [*of Plutarch*] [*Classical studies*] (OCD)
THES	Thesis (ADA)
Thes............	Thessalonians [*New Testament book*]
THES	Times Higher Education Supplement (AIE)
THESIS	[*The*] Honeywell Engineering Status Information System (SAA)
THESLA.........	Tennessee Health Science Library Association [*Library network*]
Thesm.........	Thesmophoriazusae [*of Aristophanes*] [*Classical studies*] (OCD)
Thess..........	Thessalonians [*New Testament book*]
Thess..........	Thessaly [*District of both ancient and modern Greece*] (BARN)
THETA.........	[*The*] Handicapped and Elderly Travelers Association [*Defunct*] (EA)
THETA.........	Teenage Health Education Teaching Assistants [*National Foundation for the Prevention of Oral Disease*]
THETA.........	Tunneling Hot-Electron Transfer Amplifier [*Semiconductor technology*]
THEUS	Theoretical Earth Utilization System (PDAA)
ThExNF	Theologische Existenz Heute. Neue Folge [*A publication*] (BJA)
THF............	Freelance Research Service, Houston, TX [*OCLC symbol*] (OCLC)
THF............	Target Height Finding (MCD)
THF............	Tetrahydrocortisol [*Endocrinology*] (DAVI)
THF............	Tetrahydro F [*Also, called tetrahydrocortisone*] [*Endocrinology*] (DAVI)
THF............	Tetrahydrofluorenone [*Organic chemistry*]
THF............	Tetrahydrofolate [*Biochemistry*]
THF............	Tetrahydrofolic [*Biochemistry*]
THF............	Tetrahydrofolic Acid [*Also, THFA*] [*Organic chemistry*]
THF............	Tetrahydrofuran [*Organic chemistry*]
THF............	The Healthcare Forum (EA)
THF............	The Heritage Foundation (EA)
THF............	Thermal Hysteresis Factor
THF............	Thymic Humoral Factor [*Endocrinology*]
THF............	Thymic Hypocalcemic Factor [*Biochemistry*]
THF............	Tian Hua Fen [*Chinese herbal medicine*]
THF............	Tremendously High Frequency [*Telecommunications*] (TEL)
THF............	Trust Houses Forte Ltd. [*Hotel empire*]
THFA..........	Tetrahydrofolic Acid [*Biochemistry*]
THFA..........	Tetrahydrofurfuryl Alcohol [*Organic chemistry*]
THFA..........	Thermal Hartree-Fock Approximation (PDAA)
THFA..........	Three-Conductor, Heat and Flame Resistant, Armor Cable
THFC..........	Troy Hess Fan Club (EA)
THFF..........	First Financial Corp. [*NASDAQ symbol*] (SAG)
THFF..........	First Finl Corp. Ind [*NASDAQ symbol*] (TTSB)

THFM..........	Therefrom [Legal term British]
THFOR........	Therefor [Legal term British] (ROG)
THFR..........	Three-Conductor, Heat and Flame Resistant, Radio Cable
THFROM......	Therefrom [Legal term British] (ROG)
THG	Biloela [Australia Airport symbol]
THG	Thangool [Queensland] [Airport symbol] (AD)
THG	Third-Harmonic Generation [Physics]
THG	Thomson, GA [Location identifier FAA] (FAAL)
THG	Thurston Aviation Ltd. [British ICAO designator] (FAAC)
Thg	Thyroglobulin [Also, TG] [Endocrinology]
THGA	Thread Gauge
THGA	Trihydroxyglutamic Acid [Organic chemistry]
THGA	Trihydroxyglutaric Acid [Organic chemistry]
THGAS	Tasmanian Hospitality Group Apprenticeship Scheme [Australia]
TH GAZ	Therapeutic Gazette [Philadelphia] [A publication] (ROG)
THGG	Transportable Horizontal Gravity Gradiometer
THH	Telangectasia Hereditaria Hemorrhagica [Medicine] (DB)
THH	Telangiectasia Hereditaria Haemorrhagica (STED)
THHF	Tetrahydrohomofolate [Organic chemistry]
ThHK	Theologischer Hand-Kommentar zum Neuen Testament [A publication] (BJA)
THHN	Thermoplastic, Heat-Resistant, High-Temperature, Nylon-Jacketed [Electric cable]
THHP	Target Health Hazard Program [Occupational Safety and Health Administration]
THI	Telehop, Inc. [Fresno, CA] [Telecommunications] (TSSD)
THI	Temperature-Humidity Index
THi	Tennessee Historical Society, Nashville, TN [Library symbol Library of Congress] (LCLS)
THI	Terre Haute [Indiana] [Seismograph station code, US Geological Survey] (SEIS)
THI	Texas Heart Institute [University of Texas] [Research center] (RCD)
THI	Theodor Herzl Institute (EA)
THI	Thermo Instrument Sys [AMEX symbol] (TTSB)
THI	Thermo Instrument Systems, Inc. [AMEX symbol] (SPSG)
THI	Thios Resources, Inc. [Vancouver Stock Exchange symbol]
THI	Time Handed In [Navy]
THI	Total Height Index (OA)
THI	Transient Hypogammaglobinemia of Infancy [Immunology] (DAVI)
THI	Travelers Health Institute [Later, ITHI]
THI	Trihydroxyindol [Organic chemistry]
THI	Trihydroxyindole (STED)
Thia	Theologia [Theology] [Latin] (BARN)
THIA	Thiamylal [An anesthetic] (DAVI)
THIEF	[The] Human-Initiated Equipment Failures
THIlfgr	Tommy Hilfiger Sportwear, Inc. [Associated Press] (SAG)
THIMX	Thornburg Intermed. Muni Cl.A [Mutual fund ticker symbol] (SG)
THINGS	Totally Hilarious Incredibly Neat Games of Skill [Milton-Bradley product]
ThinkNw	Think New Ideas, Inc. [Associated Press] (SAG)
THIO	Thioglycolato (OTCD)
THIO	Thiopental [An anesthetic]
Thiokl	Thiokol Corp. [Associated Press] (SAG)
Thio-T	Triethylenethiophosphoramide [Also, ThioTepa, TSPA] [Antineoplastic drug] (DAVI)
THioTEPA	Triethylenethiophosphoramide [Also, TSPA] [Antineoplastic drug]
THIP	Tetrahydroisooxazolopyridineol [Organic chemistry]
THIQ	Tetrahydraisoquinolon (DAVI)
THIR	Temperature-Humidity Infrared Radiometer
THIR	Third Financial [NASDAQ symbol] (TTSB)
THIR	Third Financial Corp. [NASDAQ symbol] (SAG)
TH-IR	Tyrosine Hydroxylase-Immunoreactivity [Physiology]
THIRA	Thorium High-Temperature Reactor Association
THIS	[The] Hospitality and Information Service [For diplomatic residents and families in Washington, DC]
THIS	Terrace Holdings [NASDAQ symbol] (TTSB)
THIS	Terrace Holdings, Inc. [NASDAQ symbol] (SAG)
THIS	Tobacco and Health Information Services (NITA)
THISW	Terrace Holdings Wrrt [NASDAQ symbol] (TTSB)
THJ	Laurel, MS [Location identifier FAA] (FAAL)
THJ	Theodore [Queensland] [Airport symbol] (AD)
THJ	Thermal Joining
THK	Taiheiyo Hoso Kyokai [Pacific Broadcasting Association] [Japan] (EAIO)
THK	Thackeray Corp. [NYSE symbol] (SPSG)
THK	Thakhek [Laos] [Airport symbol] (AD)
THK	Thick [or Thickness] (AAG)
THKF	Thick Film (MSA)
THKNS	Thickness
THKR	Thicker (MSA)
ThkTools......	Thinking Tools, Inc. [Associated Press] (SAG)
THL	Air Thanet [British ICAO designator] (FAAC)
Th L	Licentiate in Theology
THL	Tachilek [Myanmar] [Airport symbol] (OAG)
THL	Tally-Ho Explorations Ltd. [Vancouver Stock Exchange symbol]
THL	Terminal Home Leave (WDAA)
'tHL	'T Heiling Land [Nijmegen] [A publication] (BJA)
THL	Thermoluminescence [Also, TL]
THL	Thule [Denmark] [Geomagnetic observatory code]
THL	Transhybrid Loss [Telecommunications] (TEL)
THL	Tuned Hybrid Lattice
THL	University of Houston, Law Library, Main, Houston, TX [OCLC symbol] (OCLC)
ThlBer........	Theologischer Literaturbericht [A publication] (BJA)
THLD	Threshold
THLEN	Thorn Length [Botany]
THLR	Thaler [Numismatics]
THLRA	Taft-Hartley Labor Relations Act (OICC)
THLS	Turret Head Limit Switch
ThM	Master of Theology (GAGS)
THM	Tapia House Movement [Trinidad and Tobago] [Political party] (PPW)
Th M	Theologiae Magister [Master of Theology]
THM	Therm (MSA)
THM	Thermwood Corp. [AMEX symbol] (SPSG)
THM	Thompson Falls, MT [Location identifier FAA] (FAAL)
THM	Thomson Newspapers Ltd. [Toronto Stock Exchange symbol]
THM	Total Heme Mass [Medicine] (MAE)
THM	Traveling Heater Method
THM	Trihalomethane [Organic chemistry]
THM	TRIS, HEPES, Mannitol [A buffer]
THM	Trotting Horse Museum (EA)
THM	Turbo Hydramatic [Automotive engineering]
THM	University of Tennessee at Martin, Martin, TN [OCLC symbol] (OCLC)
THMA	Trailer Hitch Manufacturers Association (EA)
ThmBet........	Thomas & Betts Corp. [Associated Press] (SAG)
ThmFib........	Thermo Fibertek, Inc. [Associated Press] (SAG)
THMFP........	Trihalomethane Formation Potential [Environmental chemistry]
THMF-TS-TGSE...	Teachers Have More Fun - They Should - They Get Stewed Enough [Slogan] [Bowdlerized version]
ThmoCrd......	Thermo Cardiosystems, Inc. [Associated Press] (SAG)
Thmolse	Thermolase Corp. [Associated Press] (SAG)
ThmoM	Thermo-Mizer Environmental Corp. [Associated Press] (SAG)
ThmoMz......	Thermo-Mizer Environmental Corp. [Associated Press] (SAG)
ThmoOp......	Thermo Opportunity Fund, Inc. [Associated Press] (SAG)
THMOV	Thistle Mottle Virus [Plant pathology]
THMP	Tetrahydromethanopterin [Biochemistry]
THMP	Thermal Industries [NASDAQ symbol] (TTSB)
THMP	Thermal Industries, Inc. [NASDAQ symbol] (NQ)
ThmPBE	Thompson PBE, Inc. [Associated Press] (SAG)
Thmqst	Thermoquest Corp. [Associated Press] (SAG)
THMS	Thermistor [Electronics]
Thmsn	Thomson CSF SA [Associated Press] (SAG)
THMT	Tactical High-Mobility Terminal (DOMA)
THMTG	Target Holding Mechanism, Tank Gunnery
THMZ	Thermo-Mizer Environmental [NASDAQ symbol] (TTSB)
THMZ	Thermo-Mizer Environmental Corp. [NASDAQ symbol] (SAG)
THMZ	Three Hundred Mile Zone
THMZW	Thermo-Mizer Env Wrrt [NASDAQ symbol] (TTSB)
THN	Athens Air [Greece] [ICAO designator] (FAAC)
THN	Thermo Remediation [AMEX symbol] (SPSG)
THN	ThermoRetec Corp. [Formerly, Thermo Remediation] [AMEX symbol]
THN	Thin (FAAC)
THN	Trihydroxynaphthalene [Organic chemistry]
THN	Trollhattan [Sweden] [Airport symbol] (OAG)
THNG	Thing
THNK	Think New Ideas, Inc. [NASDAQ symbol] (SAG)
THNR	Thinner [Freight]
THNR T........	Thinner Than [Freight]
THNYX	Thornburg Intermed. N.Y. Muni Cl.A [Mutual fund ticker symbol] (SG)
THO	Thogoto Virus [Virology]
Tho	Thomas Aquinas [Deceased, 1274] [Authority cited in pre-1607 legal work] (DSA)
Tho	Thomas de Piperata [Flourished, 1268-72] [Authority cited in pre-1607 legal work] (DSA)
Tho	Thomas Mieres [Flourished, 1429-39] [Authority cited in pre-1607 legal work] (DSA)
THO	Thomsonite [A zeolite]
THO	Thorco Resources, Inc. [Toronto Stock Exchange symbol]
THO	Thor Industries [NYSE symbol] (TTSB)
THO	Thor Industries, Inc. [NYSE symbol] (SPSG)
THO	Thorshofn [Iceland] [Airport symbol] (OAG)
THO	Though
THO	Thursdays Only [British railroad term]
THO	Titrated Water [Laboratory science] (DAVI)
THO	Tonto Hills Observatory [Arizona] [Seismograph station code, US Geological Survey Closed] (SEIS)
THO	Trans-Hudson Orogen [Geology]
THO	Tritium-Labeled Water [Laboratory Science] (DAVI)
ThO$_2$	Thorium Dioxide (DAVI)
Tho de For...	Thomas de Formaginis [Flourished, 1331-38] [Authority cited in pre-1607 legal work] (DSA)
Tho de Lya...	Thomas de Elya [Authority cited in pre-1607 legal work] (DSA)
THOF	Thereof
THOF	Triple Conductor, Heat, Oil, and Flame Resistant (IAA)
Tho For........	Thomas de Formaginis [Flourished, 1331-38] [Authority cited in pre-1607 legal work] (DSA)
Tho Form....	Thomas de Formaginis [Flourished, 1331-38] (DSA)
Tho Foroli....	Thomas Foroliviensis [Authority cited in pre-1607 legal work] (DSA)
Tho Grama...	Thomas Grammaticus [Flourished, 16th century] [Authority cited in pre-1607 legal work] (DSA)
THOLD	Threshold (NASA)
Thom	Thomas' Reports [1 Wyoming] [A publication] (DLA)
THOM	Thompson PBE [NASDAQ symbol] (TTSB)
THOM	Thompson PBE, Inc. [NASDAQ symbol] (SAG)
Thom	Thomson's Nova Scotia Reports [A publication] (DLA)
THOMAM	Trihydroxymethylaminomethane (DB)
Thom & Fr...	Thomas and Franklin's Chancery Reports [1 Maryland] [A publication] (DLA)

Thomas....... Thomas' Reports [*1 Wyoming*] [*A publication*] (DLA)
ThomasG...... Thomas Group, Inc. [*Associated Press*] (SAG)
Thomas Mortg... Thomas on Mortgages [*A publication*] (DLA)
Thomas Negl... Thomas on Negligence [*A publication*] (DLA)
Thom B & N.. Thomson on Bills and Notes [*A publication*] (DLA)
Thom BBS ... Thompson. Benefit Building Societies [*A publication*] (ILCA)
Thom Bills... Thomson on Bills and Notes [*A publication*] (DLA)
Thom Camp... Thomas Campegius [*Deceased, 1564*] [*Authority cited in pre-1607 legal work*] (DSA)
THOMCAT.... Thomas Register Catalog File [*A publication*]
Thom Co Lit.. Thomas' Edition of Coke upon Littleton [*A publication*] (DLA)
Thom Co Litt.. Thomas' Edition of Coke upon Littleton [*A publication*] (DLA)
Thom Const L... Thomas' Leading Cases on Constitutional Law [*A publication*] (DLA)
Thom Cooley Law... Thomas M. Cooley Law School (GAGS)
Thom Dec.... Thomson's Nova Scotia Reports [*1834-52*] [*A publication*] (DLA)
ThomIn....... Thomas Industries, Inc. [*Associated Press*] (SAG)
THOMIS....... Total Hospital Operating and Medical Information System
Thom Jefferson U... Thomas Jefferson University (GAGS)
Thom LC...... Thomas' Leading Cases on Constitutional Law [*A publication*] (DLA)
ThomMA...... Thomaston Mills Class B [*Associated Press*] (SAG)
ThomMB...... Thomaston Mills Class B [*Associated Press*] (SAG)
Thom Mort.... Thomas on Mortgages [*A publication*] (DLA)
Thom N Sc... Thomson's Nova Scotia Reports [*1834-51, 1856-59*] [*Canada*] [*A publication*] (DLA)
THOMOTROL... Thyratron Motor Control [*Electronics*] (IAA)
Thomp & C... Thompson and Cook's New York Supreme Court Reports [*A publication*] (DLA)
Thomp & Cook... Thompson and Cook's New York Supreme Court Reports [*A publication*] (DLA)
Thomp & M Jur... Thompson and Merriam on Juries [*A publication*] (DLA)
Thomp & St... Thompson and Steger's Code [*Tennessee*] [*A publication*] (DLA)
Thomp & St Code... Thompson and Steger's Code [*Tennessee*] [*A publication*] (DLA)
Thomp Cal... Thompson's Reports [*39, 40 California*] [*A publication*] (DLA)
Thomp Car... Thompson on Carriers [*A publication*] (DLA)
Thomp Cas... Thompson's Cases [*Tennessee*] [*A publication*] (DLA)
Thomp Ch Jur... Thompson on Charging the Jury [*A publication*] (DLA)
Thomp Cit... Thompson's Ohio Citations [*A publication*] (DLA)
Thomp Corp... Thompson's Commentaries on Law of Private Corporations [*A publication*] (DLA)
Thomp Dig... Thompson's Digest of Laws [*Florida*] [*A publication*] (DLA)
Thomp Ent... Thompson's Entries [*A publication*] (DLA)
Thomp Farm... Thompson's Law of the Farm [*A publication*] (DLA)
Thomp H & Ex... Thompson on Homesteads and Exemptions [*A publication*] (DLA)
Thomp High... Thompson on the Law of Highways [*A publication*] (DLA)
Thomp Liab Off... Thompson on Liability of Officers of Corporations [*A publication*] (DLA)
Thomp Liab St... Thompson on Liability of Stockholders [*A publication*] (DLA)
Thomp Liab Stockh... Thompson on Liability of Stockholders [*A publication*] (DLA)
Thomp NB Cas... Thompson's National Bank Cases [*A publication*] (DLA)
Thomp Neg... Thompson's Cases on Negligence [*A publication*] (DLA)
Thomp Pat... Thompson on Patent Laws of All Countries [*13th ed.*] [*1905*] [*A publication*] (DLA)
Thomp Prov Rem... Thompson's Provisional Remedies [*A publication*] (DLA)
Thomps Cas... Thompson's Tennessee Cases [*A publication*] (DLA)
Thompson... Thompson's Reports [*39, 40 California*] [*A publication*] (DLA)
Thompson & C... Thompson and Cook's New York Supreme Court Reports [*A publication*] (DLA)
Thompson's Fla Dig... Thompson's Digest of Laws [*Florida*] [*A publication*] (DLA)
Thompson Unrep (PA)... Thompson's Unreported Cases (Pennsylvania) [*A publication*] (DLA)
Thomp Tenn Cas... Thompson's Unreported Tennessee Cases [*A publication*] (DLA)
Thomp Trials... Thompson on Trials [*A publication*] (DLA)
Thom Rep.... Thomson's Nova Scotia Reports [*A publication*] (DLA)
Thom Sc Acts... Thomson's Scotch Acts [*A publication*] (DLA)
Thom Sel Dec... Thomson's Nova Scotia Select Decisions [*A publication*] (DLA)
Thoms Jud Fac... Thoms' Judicial Factors [*A publication*] (DLA)
Thom St Sum... Thomas' Leading Statutes Summarized [*A publication*] (DLA)
Thom Un Jur... Thomas' Universal Jurisprudence [*2nd ed.*] [*1829*] [*A publication*] (DLA)
THON.......... Thereon [*Legal term British*]
Tho Parpal... Thomas Parpalea [*Flourished, 16th century*] [*Authority cited in pre-1607 legal work*] (DSA)
THOPS........ Tape-Handling Operational System [*Computer science*] (IEEE)
THOR.......... Tandy [*Corp.*] High-Performance Optical Recording System [*Dye-polymer technology*] (PCM)
THOR.......... Tape-Handling Optional Routines [*Honeywell, Inc.*]
THOR.......... Thesaurus-Oriented Retrieval [*Information service or system*]
THOR.......... Thoracentesis [*Fluid*] [*Medicine*] (DAVI)
THOR.......... Thoratec Labs Corp. [*NASDAQ symbol*] (SAG)
Thor.......... Thorax [*Anatomy*] (DAVI)
Thor.......... Thorington's Reports [*107 Alabama*] [*A publication*] (DLA)
THOR.......... Thought Organizer [*Computer program produced by Fastware, Inc.*]
THOR.......... Trace Hierarchy of Requirements [*Science Applications International Corp.*]
THOR.......... Transistorized High-Speed Operations Recorder
THOR.......... Tsing Hua Open-Pool Reactor [*Formosa*]
THORAC..... Thoraci [*To the Throat*] [*Pharmacy*]
THORAD ..... Thor-Agena D [*Rocket*] [*NASA*]
THORAD ..... Transistorized High-Speed Operations Recorder Advanced (IAA)
Thoratc....... Thoratec Labs Corp. [*Associated Press*] (SAG)
Thor Bank.... Thorborn on Bankers' Law [*A publication*] (DLA)
THOREX...... Thorium Extraction (GAAI)

ThorInd........ Thor Industries, Inc. [*Associated Press*] (SAG)
ThornG........ Thornton's Notes of Ecclesiastical and Maritime Cases [*1841-50*] [*A publication*] (DLA)
THORNB ..... Thornbury [*England*]
Thornbg....... Thornburg Mortgage Asset Corp. [*Associated Press*] (SAG)
Thorn Conv... Thornton's Conveyancing [*A publication*] (DLA)
Thornt & Bl Bldg & Loan Ass'ns... Thornton and Blackledge's Law Relating to Building and Loan Associations [*A publication*] (DLA)
Thornton Gifts... Thornton on Gifts and Advancements [*A publication*] (DLA)
Thoro.......... Thoroughfare [*Maps and charts*]
THORP........ Thermal Oxide Reprocessing Plant [*Nuclear energy*]
Thorpe .... Thorpe's Annual Reports [*52 Louisiana*] [*A publication*] (DLA)
Thorpe Anc L... Thorpe's Ancient Laws of England [*A publication*] (DLA)
THORS........ Thermal-Hydraulic Out-of-Reactor Safety Facility [*Department of Energy*]
Thos Co Lit... Thomas' Edition of Coke upon Littleton [*A publication*] (DLA)
THOT .... Thought
THOT .... Transportation Horoscope of Trade Goods (PDAA)
THOU .... Thousand (AFM)
THOUS....... Thousand (NASA)
THP........... [*The*] Hunger Project (EA)
THP........... Take-Home Pay (MHDB)
THP........... Terminal Handling Processor
THP........... Terminal Holding Power [*Advertising*] (IIA)
THP........... Tetrahydropalmatine [*Organic chemistry*]
THP........... Tetrahydropapaveroline [*Biochemistry*]
thp........... Tetrahydropyranyl [*Organic chemistry*]
THP........... Tetrakis(hydroxymethyl)phosphonium [*Organic chemistry*]
THP........... Thermal Hysteresis Proteins [*Biochemistry*]
THP........... Thermopolis, WY [*Location identifier FAA*] (FAAL)
THP........... Thermo Power [*AMEX symbol*] (TTSB)
THP........... Thermo Power Corp. [*Formerly, Tecogen, Inc.*] [*AMEX symbol*] (SPSG)
THP........... Thousands Position (IAA)
THP........... Through Hole Probe
THP........... Through the Hole Plating [*Electronics*] (EECA)
THP........... Thrust Horsepower [*Jet engines*]
THP........... Total Hydroxyproline [*Clinical chemistry*] (MAE)
THP........... Transmitter Holding Register (MHDB)
THP........... Trihexphenidyl Hydrochloride [*An anti-cholinergic*] (DAVI)
THP........... Trihydroxypropane [*Organic chemistry*]
THP........... (Trimethylhydrazinium) Propionate [*Biochemistry*]
THP........... Tris(hydroxymethyl)phosphine [*Organic chemistry*]
THPA .... Tetrahydrophthalic Anhydride [*Organic chemistry*]
THPA .... Tetrahydropteric Acid [*Organic chemistry*] (MAE)
THPC .... Tetrakis(hydroxymethyl)phosphonium Chloride [*Flame retardant*]
Th PC.......... Thick Paper Copy (DGA)
THPDX........ Tetrahydropyranyldoxorubicin [*Antineoplastic drug*]
THPF.......... Total Hepatic Plasma Flow [*Physiology*]
THPFB .... Treated Hard-Pressed Fiberboard [*Technical drawings*]
THPI .... Tetrahydrophthalimide [*Organic chemistry*]
THPO .... Tris(hydroxymethyl)phosphine Oxide [*Organic chemistry*]
ThPract........ Theologie en Practijk [*Rotterdam*] [*A publication*] (BJA)
ThPrM........ Theologisch-Praktische Monatsschrift [*A publication*] (BJA)
THPS .... Tetrakis(hydroxymethyl)phosphonium Sulfate [*Flame retardant*] [*Organic chemistry*]
THQ........... Telecommunications Headquarters (NITA)
THQ........... Tetrahydroxyquinone [*Chemical indicator*]
THQ........... Theater Headquarters [*Military*]
Th Q........... Theologische Quartalschrift [*A publication*] (ODCC)
THQ........... THQ, Inc. [*Associated Press*] (SAG)
THQ........... Troop Headquarters
THR .... Target Heart Rate [*Exercise*] (INF)
THR .... Tehran [*Iran*] [*Airport symbol*] (OAG)
THR .... Their (ROG)
THR .... Their Royal Highnesses [*British*] (ROG)
THR .... There (ROG)
THR .... Three Rivers Financial Corp. [*AMEX symbol*] (SAG)
THR .... Three Rivers Finl [*AMEX symbol*] (TTSB)
Thr .... Threni (BJA)
Thr .... Threonine [*Also, T*] [*An amino acid*]
thr .... Threonine [*An amino acid*] (DOG)
THR .... Threshold
Thr .... Threshold Lights [*Aviation*] (DA)
THR .... Through (ADA)
THR .... Throughput
THR .... Throughput Rate
THR .... Thrust (AAG)
THR .... Total Heat Rejection (IAA)
THR .... Total Hip Replacement [*Medicine*]
THR .... Total Hydrocarbon Reforming [*Hydrogen production*]
THR .... Transhepatic Resistance (DB)
THR .... Transmittal Header Record [*Computer science*]
THR .... Transmitter Holding Register
THR .... Turbine Heat Rate (DNAB)
THRABTS...... Thereabouts [*Legal term British*] (ROG)
THRAPP...... Tasmanian Historical Research Association. Papers and Proceedings [*A publication*]
THRAR....... Thereafter [*Legal term British*] (ROG)
THRAT .... Thereat [*Legal term British*] (ROG)
THRB .... Theodore Roosevelt Birthplace National Historic Site
THR-CT....... Thrombin Control [*Hematology*] (DAVI)
THRD......... TF Financial [*NASDAQ symbol*] (TTSB)
THRD......... TF Financial Corp. [*NASDAQ symbol*] (SAG)
THRD......... Thread

thrd............	Thread (VRA)
ThrD............	Three D Departments, Inc. [Associated Press] (SAG)
ThrdFn.........	Third Financial Corp. [Associated Press] (SAG)
THREAD......	Three-Dimensional Reconstruction and Display (MHDB)
THREATCON...	Terrorist Threat Condition (COE)
ThreeFS........	Three Five Systems Co. [Associated Press] (SAG)
THRES........	Threshold (IAA)
THRF	Thyrotrophic Hormone-Releasing Factor [Endocrinology]
ThrFibr........	Thermo Fibergen, Inc. [Associated Press] (SAG)
THRFT........	Thrift
THRFTR	Thereafter (FAAC)
THRFTY	Thrifty
Thrgen.........	Theragenics Corp. [Associated Press] (SAG)
Thr Hist Tr...	Thrupp's Historical Law Tracts [A publication] (DLA)
THR HOLD...	Throttle Hold (GAVI)
THRIC.........	Treasure Hunter Research and Information Center (EA)
THRILLO......	Transfer to Higher Rated Job in Lieu of Layoff (MCD)
THRIN.........	Therein
THRINAR	Thereinafter [Legal term British] (ROG)
THRINBEFE...	Thereinbefore [Legal term British] (ROG)
Thring J St Com...	Thring on Joint Stock Companies [5th ed.] [1889] [A publication] (DLA)
Thring LD	Thring on the Land Drainage Act [1862] [A publication] (DLA)
ThrInst.........	Thermo Instrument Systems, Inc. [Associated Press] (SAG)
THRIP.........	Thriplow [England]
THRIVE........	Tower Hamlets Reading Initiative via Exploration [British] (AIE)
THRM..........	Thermal (AAG)
Thrmady.......	Thermadyne Holdings Corp. [Associated Press] (SAG)
ThrmBio.......	Thermo Bioanalysis Corp. [Associated Press] (SAG)
ThrmIn.........	Thermal Industries, Inc. [Associated Press] (SAG)
Thrmogn.......	Thermogenesis Corp. [Associated Press] (SAG)
Thrmolse	Thermolase Corp. [Associated Press] (SAG)
Thrmotx.......	Thermotrex Corp. [Associated Press] (SAG)
ThrmP.........	Thermo Process Systems, Inc. [Associated Press] (SAG)
ThrmPw.......	Thermo Power Corp. [Associated Press] (SAG)
ThrmRe........	Thermo Remediation [Associated Press] (SAG)
THRMST	Thermostat
THRMSTC ...	Thermostatic (MSA)
ThrmTch	Thermo Tech Technologies [Associated Press] (SAG)
ThrmTer......	Thermo Terratech [Associated Press] (SAG)
Thrmtx........	Thermotrex Corp. [Associated Press] (SAG)
Thrmwd.......	Thermwood Corp. [Associated Press] (SAG)
ThrnAV........	Thorn Apple Valley, Inc. [Associated Press] (SAG)
THRO	Theodore Roosevelt National Memorial Park
THRO	Through
THRO	Throw the Hypocritical Rascals Out [An association]
ThroBL........	Through Bill of Lading [Shipping]
THROE.........	Tesseral Harmonic Resonance of Orbital Elements (PDAA)
THROF.........	Thereof
THROM........	Thrombosis (AAMN)
THROMB..	Thrombin Timo Tritium [Hematology] (DAVI)
thromb........	Thrombosis (CPH)
thrombo........	Thrombophlebitis [Medicine] (DAVI)
thrombo........	Thrombosis [Medicine] (BARN)
THRON........	Thereon [Legal term British] (ROG)
Throop Pub Off...	Throop's Treatise on Public Officers [A publication] (DLA)
ThrOptk........	Thermo Optek Corp. [Associated Press] (SAG)
THROT.........	Throttle (AAG)
THROUGHWAY...	Throughway [Commonly used] (OPSA)
THROUT.......	Thereout [Legal term British] (ROG)
THRP	Therapist
THRPST.......	Therapist
THRPY	Therapy
ThrRvF.........	Three Rivers Financial Corp. [Associated Press] (SAG)
ThrSent........	Thermo Sentron, Inc. [Associated Press] (SAG)
THRSHL......	Thrust Shell
ThrSpec.......	ThermoSpectra Corp. [Associated Press] (SAG)
ThrSpect	Thermo Spectra Corp. [Associated Press] (SAG)
THRSUM......	Threat Summary Message (MCD)
THRT	TheraTech, Inc. [NASDAQ symbol] (SAG)
THRT	Threat [or Threatening] [FBI standardized term]
THRT	Throat
ThrTch	TheraTech, Inc. [Associated Press] (SAG)
THRU	Through (AAG)
THRU	Toxic Hazards Research Unit [NASA] (KSC)
thruout........	Throughout (REAL)
THRUPON ...	Thereupon [Legal term British] (ROG)
THRUSH	Technological Hierarchy for the Removal of Undesirables and the Subjugation of Humanity [Fictitious organization in "The Man from UNCLE" television series]
Thrust	Thrustmaster, Inc. [Associated Press] (SAG)
THRUST.......	Tsunami Hazard Reduction Using Systems Technology [Marine science] (OSRA)
THRUST.......	Tsunami Hazard Reduction Using System Technology (USDC)
THRUT.......	Throughout (FAAC)
Thr Verb Agr...	Throop on the Validity of Verbal Agreements [A publication] (DLA)
ThrVolt........	Thermo Voltek Corp. [Associated Press] (SAG)
THRWY	Thruway
THRX	Theragenics Corp. [NASDAQ symbol] (NQ)
thry............	Theory (VRA)
THS............	[The] Hydrographic Society [Dagenham, Essex, England] (EAIO)
THS............	St. Thomas, PA [Location identifier FAA] (FAAL)
THS............	Tactical Hybrid Switch (LAIN)
THS............	Target Homing System
THS............	Technical High School (ADA)

THS............	Tenement House Smell [British] (ROG)
THS............	Territorial Highway System [FHWA] (TAG)
THS............	Tetrahydro-11-Deoxycortisol
THS............	Tetrahydro-Compound S [Organic chemistry] (MAE)
THS............	Textile History Society [Defunct] (EA)
THS............	Theatre Historical Society (EA)
THS............	Theatre History Studies [A publication] (BRI)
THS............	ThermoSpectra Corp. [AMEX symbol] (SAG)
THS............	Thermostat Switch
THS............	Thomas Hardy Society (EAIO)
THS............	Three-Stage Least Squares [Econometrics]
ThS............	Thymidylate Synthase [Also, TS] [An enzyme]
THS............	Titanic Historical Society (EA)
THS............	Tourist Hospitality Service [British]
THS............	Transmission Hydraulic Switch [Automotive engineering]
THS............	Transparent Hull Submersible [Navy]
THS............	Transports Aeros Hispanos SA [Spain ICAO designator] (FAAC)
THS............	Trimmable Horizontal Stabilizer [Aviation]
THS............	Tube Heating Supply
THSA	Thomas Hardy Society of America [Defunct] (EA)
THSA	Traveling Hat Salesmen's Association [Defunct] (EA)
THSAM	Topographie Historique de la Syrie Antique et Medievale [A publication] (BJA)
THSC	Totipotent Hematopoietic Stem Cell [Hematology] (MAE)
THSD	Thousand (FAAC)
THSG	Transactions. Historical Society of Ghana [A publication]
THSP	Temporary-Help Supplier Personnel
THSP	Thermal Spray [Also, TS] [Coating technology]
ThSzemle ...	Theologiai Szemle [Budapest] [A publication] (BJA)
THT	Papeete [Orstom] [Society Islands] [Seismograph station code, US Geological Survey] (SEIS)
THT	Teacher of Hydrotherapy [British]
THT	Terrence Higgins Trust [British] (WDAA)
THT	Tetrahydrothiophene [Organic chemistry]
Tht	Theaetetus [of Plato] [Classical studies] (OCD)
THT	Through Hole Technology (AAEL)
THT	Thrust Resources, Inc. [Vancouver Stock Exchange symbol]
THT	THT, Inc. [Associated Press] (SAG)
THT	Token-Holding Time [Computer science]
THT	Total Homing Time
THT	Turk Hava Tasimaciligi [Turkish Air Transport] [ICAO designator] (FAAC)
THT	Two Hole Transition (AAEL)
THTA	Thread Tap
THTD	Too Hard to Do (CAAL)
THTF	Thermal Hydraulic Test Facility [Nuclear energy] (NRCH)
THTH	Too Hot to Handle
THTMS	Tetramethylthiuram Monosulfide [Also, TMTD] [Organic chemistry]
THTN	Threaten (FAAC)
THTO	Thereto
THTO	Threading Tool (AAG)
THTR	Theater (AFM)
thtr	Theatre (VRA)
THTR	Thorium High-Temperature Reactor [Nuclear energy]
THTRA	Thorium High Temperature Reactor Association (IAA)
THTX	TheraTx, Inc. [NASDAQ symbol] (SAG)
THU	Tetrhydrouridine [Biochemistry]
THU	Thule [Greenland] [Seismograph station code, US Geological Survey Closed] (SEIS)
THU	Thunder Airlines Ltd. [Canada] [FAA designator] (FAAC)
THU	Thunder Explorations [Vancouver Stock Exchange symbol]
THU	Thursday (AFM)
THU	Truck Hub Unit [Suspension] [Automotive engineering]
Thuc	De Thucydide [of Dionysius Halicarnassensis] [Classical studies] (OCD)
THUC	Thucydides [Greek historian, c. 460-400BC] [Classical studies] (ROG)
THUD	Thorium, Uranium, Deuterium
THUDD	Thermal Uplink Data Display [Computer science]
THUG	Thyroid Uptake Gradient (DB)
THUMB	Tiny Humans Underground Military Bureau [Government organization in TV cartoon series "Tom of T.H.U.M.B."]
THUMS	Texaco, Humble, Union, Mobil, and Shell [Petroleum companies]
Thur	Thursday (WGA)
THURIS	[The] Human Role in Space [Study] (SSD)
Thur Mar L Rev...	Thurgood Marshall Law Review [A publication] (DLA)
THURS	Thursday
Thurs	Thursday (ODBW)
THURST	Thurstable [England]
THUT	Thyroid Hormone Uptake Test [Clinical chemistry]
THV	Terminal Homing Vehicle
THV	Thoracic Vertebra [Medicine]
THV	Tool Handling Vehicle (MCD)
THV	Total Heart Volume [Physiology]
THV	York, PA [Location identifier FAA] (FAAL)
THW	Tag Heuer International SA [NYSE symbol] (SAG)
ThW	Theologisches Woerterbuch zum Neuen Testament [A publication] (BJA)
THW	Therewith [Legal term British] (ROG)
THW	Thermoplastic, Heat-Resistant, Wet-Location [Electric cable]
Thw	Thwartship (DS)
THW	Torsion Head Wattmeter
ThWAT	Theologisches Woerterbuch zum Alten Testament [A publication] (BJA)

ThWB .... Theologisches Woerterbuch zum Neuen Testament [*A publication*] (BJA)
ThWBNT ...... Theologisches Woerterbuch zum Neuen Testament [*A publication*] (BJA)
THWD .... Thought He was Dead (WDAA)
THWITH ...... Therewith [*Legal term British*] (ROG)
THWM .... Trinity High-Water Mark
THWN .... Thermoplastic, Heat-Resistant, Wet-Location, Nylon-Jacketed [*Electric cable*]
ThWNT .... Theologisches Woerterbuch zum Neuen Testament [*A publication*] (BJA)
THWR .... Thrower
THWT .... Throwout [*Mechanical engineering*]
Thwy .... Thruway (BARN)
THX .... Houston Exploration Co. (The) [*NYSE symbol*] (SAG)
THX .... Thor Explorations [*Vancouver Stock Exchange symbol*]
THX .... Three Rivers, TX [*Location identifier FAA*] (FAAL)
Thx .... Thromboxane (DB)
THX .... Thyroxine [*Also, T4, Ty*] [*An amino acid Endocrinology*]
THX .... Tomlinson-Holman Cross-Over [*Motion picture theater sound system*]
THX .... Total Hypophysectomy [*Medicine*]
THY .... Thylungra [*Queensland*] [*Airport symbol*] (AD)
thy .... Thymectomy (STED)
Thy .... Thymine [*Also, T*] [*Biochemistry*]
THY .... Thymocyte [*Clinical chemistry*]
thy .... Thymus (STED)
thy .... Thyratron (IDOE)
THY .... Thyratron [*Electronics*] (IAA)
THY .... Transitional Hospitals Corp. [*NYSE symbol*] (SAG)
THY .... Turk Hava Yollari [*Turkish Airlines*] [*ICAO designator*] (FAAC)
THY .... Turk Hava Yollari AO [*Turkish Airlines, Inc.*]
THYB .... Tai Hei Yo Bashi [*Bridge over the Great Ocean*] (EA)
THYMOTRO... Thyratron Motor Control [*Electronics*] (MCD)
THYMOTROL... Thyratron Motor Control [*Electronics*]
Thym Turb ... Thymol Turbidity [*Clinical chemistry*] (CPH)
THYP .... Total Hydroxyproline [*Clinical chemistry*]
THYR .... Thyristor [*Electronics*]
THZ .... Tahoua [*Niger*] [*Airport symbol*] (OAG)
THz .... Terahertz
TI .... Table Indicator [*Computer science*]
TI .... Tamarind Institute (EA)
TI .... Tamiment Institute (EA)
TI .... Tape Indicator [*Computer science*] (IAA)
TI .... Tape Inverter
TI .... Target Identification
TI .... Target Indicator
TI .... Target Intelligence (MCD)
TI .... Tariff Item
TI .... Taxable Income
TI .... Teardown Inspection
ti .... Technical Indexes Ltd. [*Information service or system*] (IID)
TI .... Technical Information (CINC)
TI .... Technical Inspection [*Military*]
TI .... Technical Institute
TI .... Technical Instruction [*or Instructor*]
TI .... Technical Integration [*NASA*] (NASA)
TI .... Technical Intelligence [*Military*]
TI .... Technical Interchange (KSC)
TI .... Technology Incubator
TI .... Technology Insertion [*Military*] (RDA)
TI .... Technoogy Innovation (IAA)
TI .... Tehrik-i-Istiqlal [*Solidarity Party*] [*See also TIP Pakistan*] [*Political party*] (FEA)
TI .... Telecom Italia SpA Ord ADS [*NYSE symbol*] [*Formerly, Societa Fin Tel Ord ADS*] (SG)
TI .... Telecommunication Industry
TI .... Teleos Institute (EA)
TI .... Television Intercity [*FCC*] (NTCM)
TI .... Temperature Indicator
ti .... Temperature of Injectate
TI .... Temporal Integration (STED)
TI .... Temporary Instruction [*Nuclear energy*] (NRCH)
TI .... Temporary Intermittent (GNE)
TI .... Teresian Institute (EA)
TI .... Terminal Ileum [*Gastroenterology*] (DAVI)
TI .... Terminal Interface
TI .... Terminal Island [*San Pedro*] [*Navy base*]
TI .... Termination Instruction
TI .... Terminator Interrupt [*Computer science*] (IAA)
TI .... Terrestrial Interference (WDMC)
TI .... Test Implicit
TI .... Test Index (CAAL)
TI .... Test Instruction (MCD)
TI .... Test Instrumentation
TI .... Texas Instruments (NITA)
TI .... Texas Instruments, Inc.
TI .... Texas International (GAVI)
TI .... Texas International Airlines [*ICAO designator*] (AD)
TI .... Textile Industry (WDAA)
TI .... Textile Institute [*Manchester, England*] (EAIO)
TI .... Thalassemia Intermedia [*Hematology*]
TI .... Therapeutic Index [*Medicine*] (DMAA)
TI .... Thermal Imaging [*Criminology*] (LAIN)
TI .... Thermoforming Institute (NTPA)
TI .... Think Ink [*An association*] (EA)

TI .... Thoracic Index [*Medicine*] (MAE)
TI .... Thread Institute [*Defunct*] (EA)
TI .... Threat Identification (COE)
TI .... Threshold of Intelligibility (STED)
TI .... Thymidine-Labeling Index [*Biochemical analysis*]
TI .... Thymus Independent [*Cells*] [*Hematology*]
TI .... Thyroxin Iodine (STED)
TI .... Tie In (MCD)
TI .... Tiferet Israel (BJA)
TI .... Timaeus [*of Plato*] [*Classical studies*] (OCD)
TI .... Time Index
TI .... Time Information (STED)
TI .... Time Interval (IEEE)
TI .... Time-to-Intercept
TI .... Tippers International (EA)
TI .... Tissue Invasiveness [*Medicine*] (DB)
TI .... Titanium [*Chemical element*]
TI .... Title [*Online database field identifier*] [*Computer science*]
TI .... Title Information [*Publishing*]
TI .... TI Travel International, Inc. [*Vancouver Stock Exchange symbol*]
TI .... Titus [*New Testament book*]
TI .... Toastmasters International (EA)
TI .... Tobacco Institute (EA)
TI .... Together, Inc. (EA)
TI .... Together International/Anti-Soviet Research Center [*Defunct*] (EA)
TI .... Tonic Immobility [*Neurophysiology*]
TI .... Topical Irritation [*Medicine*] (LDT)
TI .... Torpedo Instructor [*British military*] (DMA)
T/I .... Torque/Inertia
TI .... Total Immersion [*Language study*]
TI .... Total Inventory (DOMA)
TI .... Total Iron (STED)
TI .... Tourismo Internazionale [*International Touring*] [*Italian*]
T/I .... TPFDD Interface
TI .... Track Identity
TI .... Track Initiator
TI .... Trade and Industry Index [*Information Access Corp.*] [*Information service or system*] (IID)
TI .... Trade International (BARN)
TI .... Traditional Instruction
TI .... Traffic Identification
TI .... Training Instructor
TI .... Training Integrator [*or Integration*] (MCD)
TI .... Trajectory Integration (CAAL)
TI .... Transaction Interpretation (MCD)
TI .... Transfer Impedance (IEEE)
TI .... Transfrigoroute International (EA)
TI .... Transillumination
TI .... Translational Inhibition (STED)
TI .... Translational Inhibitor (DB)
TI .... Transmission Identification (NG)
TI .... Transportation Institute [*Camp Springs, MD*] (EA)
TI .... Transport Index [*Nuclear energy*] (NUCP)
TI .... Transverse Inlet [*Medicine*] (MAE)
TI .... Treasure Island [*San Francisco Bay*] [*Navy base*]
TI .... Treasury Instruction (ADA)
TI .... Trial Installation (MCD)
TI .... Tricuspid Incompetence [*Cardiology*] (MAE)
TI .... Tricuspid Insufficiency [*Cardiology*]
TI .... Troop Information
TI .... Trunk Index (STED)
TI .... Trusteeship Institute (EA)
TI .... Trypsin Inhibitor [*Food technology*]
TI .... Tube Investments Ltd. [*British*]
TI .... Tumor-inducing [*Plasmids*] [*Plant cytology*]
TI .... Tumor Inducing [*Medicine*] (STED)
TI .... Tungsten Institute [*Defunct*] (EA)
TI .... Tuning Indicator (DEN)
TI .... Tuning Inductance (IAA)
ti .... Tunisia [*MARC country of publication code Library of Congress*] (LCCP)
TI .... Turing Institute [*British*] (IRUK)
TI .... Turismo Internazionale [*Automobile model designation*]
TI .... Type Item [*Military*]
TIA .... [*The*] International Alliance, an Association of Executive and Professional Women [*Baltimore, MD*] (EA)
TIA .... [*The*] Internet Adapter [*Intermind Corp.*]
TIA .... Tactical Identification and Acquisition [*Navy*] (NG)
TIA .... Taian [*Republic of China*] [*Seismograph station code, US Geological Survey*] (SEIS)
TIA .... Task Item Authorization (MCD)
TIA .... Taxation Institute of Australia (EERA)
TIA .... Tax Institute of America [*Later, NTA-TIA*] (EA)
TIA .... Teacher Investigator Awards
TIA .... Telecommunications Industry Association (EA)
TIA .... Temperature Indicating Alarm [*Engineering*]
TIA .... Temporary Incapacity Allowance
TIA .... Tennis Industry Association (NTPA)
TIA .... Test Interface Assembly
TIA .... Test of Inference Ability In Reading Comprehension [*Phillips and Patterson*] (TES)
TIA .... Thallium Acetate
TIA .... Thanks in Advance [*Internet language*] [*Computer science*]
TIA .... Thin-Layer Immunoassay [*Analytical biochemistry*]
TIA .... Tiaprofenic Acid

TIA	Tilapia International Association (EAIO)
TIA	Tirana [Albania] [Airport symbol] (OAG)
TIA	Tortilla Industry Association (EA)
TIA	Total Inactive Aerospace Vehicle [or Aircraft] Authorization
TIA	Traffic Improvement Association
TIA	Transient Ischemic Attack [Medicine]
TIA	Transimpedance Amplifier [Instrumentation]
TIA	Trans International Airlines [ICAO designator] (FAAC)
TIA	Transportation in America [BTS] (TAG)
TIA	Transportation Intelligence Agency (AAG)
TIA	Transportation Intermediaries Association (NTPA)
TIA	Travel Industry Association of America (EA)
TIA	Treaties and Other International Acts
TIA	Trend Impact Analysis [The Futures Group, Inc.] [Information service or system] (IID)
TIA	Trends, Indicators, and Analyses [on the Southeast Asia war] [Classified Air Force document]
TIA	Tri-Basin Resources Ltd. [Vancouver Stock Exchange symbol]
TIA	Tricot Institute of America [Defunct] (EA)
TIA	Trouser Institute of America [Absorbed by NOSA] (EA)
TIA	Trypsin Inhibitor Activity [Food technology]
TIA	Tumor-Induced Angiogenesis [Immunology]
TIA	Turbidimetric Immunoassay [Immunology]
TIA	Typographers International Association (EA)
TIAA	Task Identification and Analysis (MCD)
TIAA	Teachers Insurance and Annuity Association [New York, NY] (EA)
TIAA	Texas Intercollegiate Athletic Association (PSS)
TIAA	Timber Importers Association of America
TIAA	Travel Industry Association of America
TIAA-CREF	Teachers Insurance and Annuity Association-College Retirement Equities Fund (AEE)
TIAC	Technical Information Advisory Committee [AEC]
TIAC	Technical Information Analysis Centers
TIAC	Texas Instruments Automatic Computer
TIAC	Tourism Industry Association of Canada
TIAC	Travel [later, Tourism] Industry Association of Canada
TIACS	TEWS [Tactical Electronic Warfare System] Intermediate Age Commercial System
TIAFT	[The] International Association of Forensic Toxicologists [Newmarket, Suffolk, England] (EAIO)
TI Agree	Treaties and Other International Agreements of the United States of America [A publication] (DLA)
TIAH	Totally Implantable Artificial Heart
TIA-IR	Transient Ischemic Attack-Incomplete Recovery [Cardiology] (DAVI)
TIALD	Thermal Imaging, Airborne LASER Designator [Royal Air Force] [British]
TIAM	Terminal Interactive Access Method [Computer science] (IAA)
TI & A	Task Identification and Analysis
TI & E	Troop Information and Education
TIAP	Theater Intelligence Architecture Program (DOMA)
TIARA	Tactical Intelligence and Related Activity
TIARA	Target Illumination and Recovery Aid
TIARA	Telephone Installation and Requisition Application (MCD)
TIARA	There Is a Radical Alternative [Parliamentary slang] [British] (DI)
TIAS	Target Identification and Acquisition System
TIAS	Team Integrated Avionic System (MHDI)
TIAS	True Indicated Airspeed (GAVI)
TIAVSC	[The] International Assets Valuation Standards Committee [of the American Institute of Real Estate Appraisers] [British] (EAIO)
TIAX	Trans International Airlines [Air carrier designation symbol]
TIB	Tasmanian Imperial Bushmen [British military] (DMA)
TIB	Tax Interpretation Bulletins [Canada] (IID)
TIB	Technical Information Base (MCD)
TIB	Technical Information Branch [US Public Health Service] [Information service or system] (IID)
TIB	Technical Information Bulletin [Cincinnati, OH] (AAG)
TIB	Technical Information Bureau [British]
TIB	Technical Intelligence Branch [National Coal Board] (PDAA)
TIB	Technische Informationsbibliothek [Technical Information Library] [Germany]
TIB	Temporary Importation Bond (MCD)
TIB	This I Believe Test [Education]
Tib	Tiberius [of Suetonius] [Classical studies] (OCD)
Tib	Tibet (VRA)
tib	Tibetan [MARC language code Library of Congress] (LCCP)
Tib	Tibia [Anatomy] (DAVI)
tib	Tibia [Medicine] (STED)
tib	Tibialis [Muscle] (DAVI)
Tib	Tibullus [First century BC] [Classical studies] (OCD)
TIB	Total Ischemic Burden (DB)
TIB	Tourist Information Board (WDAA)
TIB	Toxicology Information Brief [Environmental] (GNE)
TIB	Training Improvement Board [Military] (CAAL)
TIB	Treasury Indexed Bond (ADA)
TIB	Triisopropylbenzene [Also, TIPB] [Organic chemistry]
TIB	Trimmed in Bunkers [Shipping] (DS)
TIB	Tuck in Back [Sit up straight] [Slang British] (DI)
TIB	Tumor Immunology Bank [Medicine] (STED)
TIB	Twin I-Beam [Ford Motor Co.] [Truck front suspension]
TIBA	Traffic Information Broadcast by Aircraft (DA)
TIBA	Triiodobenzoic Acid [Plant growth regulator]
TIBA	Triisobutylaluminum [Organic chemistry]
TIBA	Triisobutylamine [Organic chemistry]
TIBAL	Triisobutylaluminum (EDCT)
TIBALD	Tibaldstone [England]

TIB and FIB	Tibia and Fibula (DSUE)
TIBC	Total Iron-Binding Capacity [Hematology]
TIBL	Thermal Internal Boundary Layer (GFGA)
TIBO	Tetrahydroimidazobenzodiazepin [Antiviral]
TIBOE	Transmitting Information by Optical Electronics (KSC)
TIBS	Tactical Information Broadcast System [Air Force] (DOMA)
TIBS	Through Ice Bathymetry System (EERA)
TIBTPG	Texas Instruments Bourdon Tube Pressure Gauge
tic	Diverticulum [Gastroenterology] (DAVI)
TIC	[The] Interchurch Center (EA)
TIC	Tactical Information Coordinator (DOMA)
TIC	Tactical Intelligence Concepts (MCD)
TIC	Tactical Intercom Systems (MCD)
TIC	Taken into Consideration
TIC	Tantalum Integrated Circuit [Electronics] (PDAA)
TIC	Tantalum Producers International Study Center [Later, Tantalum-Niobium International Study Center] (EAIO)
TIC	Tape Identification Card
TIC	Tape Intersystem Connection [Computer science]
TIC	Targeted Industry Categories (AAGC)
TIC	Target Integration Center (MCD)
TIC	Target Intercept Computer [Military]
TIC	Tax Information Circular [Canada] (IID)
TIC	Teacher in Charge (ADA)
TIC	Teacher Information Center (EA)
TIC	Technical Information Capability
TIC	Technical Information Center [Department of Energy]
TIC	Technical Information Coordinator [Environmental Protection Agency] (GFGA)
TIC	Technical Institute Council (EA)
TIC	Technical Instructors Course [Air Force] (AFM)
TIC	Technical Intelligence Center [Navy]
TIC	Technical Interface Concepts (RDA)
TIC	Technicon Integrator/Calculator
TIC	Technology and Innovation Council [Information Industry Association]
TIC	Technology Innovation Center [University of Iowa] [Research center] (RCD)
TIC	Telecommunications Information Center [George Washington University] [Information service or system] (IID)
TIC	Telemetry Instruction Conference (KSC)
TIC	Telemetry Instrumentation Controller
TIC	Temperature Indicator Controller
TIC	Tenancy in Common (MHDB)
TIC	Tentatively Identified Compounds (GNE)
TIC	Terminal Identification Code
TIC	Texas Instruments Co.
TIC	Thai Information Center (EA)
TIC	Thermal Image Camera (PDAA)
TIC	Thermionic Integrated Circuit [Electronics]
TIC	Thermostatic Ignition Control [Automotive engineering]
TIC	Time Interval Counter
TIC	Tinak [Marshall Islands] [Airport symbol] (OAG)
TIC	Token Ring Interface Coupler (PCM)
TIC	Tool Issue Center [Military] (AFIT)
TIC	Total Inorganic Carbon [Chemistry]
TIC	Total Installed Cost [Engineering]
TIC	Total Ion Chromatography
TIC	Total Ion Current [Spectroscopy]
TIC	Total Item Change (NASA)
TIC	Toumodi [Ivory Coast] [Seismograph station code, US Geological Survey] (SEIS)
TIC	Tourist Information Council (WDAA)
TIC	Trade Information Committee [Department of State] (EA)
TIC	Transaction Identification Code [Military] (AFIT)
TIC	Transducer Information Center (MCD)
TIC	Transfer-In Channel (CMD)
TIC	Transport Industries Committee [Trades Union Congress] [British] (DCTA)
TIC	Transvaal Indian Congress [South Africa] (PD)
TIC	Travel Information Center [An association] (EA)
TIC	Troops-in-Contact
TIC	True Interest Cost [Finance]
TIC	Trypsin Inhibitory Capacity [Biochemistry]
TIC	Tuned Integrated Circuit
TICA	[The] International Cat Association (EA)
TICA	Tactical Intercom Assembly [Ground Communications Facility, NASA]
TICA	Technical Information Center Administration [Conference]
TICA	Thermal Insulation Contractors' Association [British] (BI)
TICA	Timpanogos Cave National Monument
TICACE	Technical Intelligence Center Allied Command Europe [NATO] (NATG)
TICAF	[The] Industrial College of the Armed Forces [Later, UND]
TICAS	Taxonometric Intra-Cellular Analytic System (OA)
TICC	Technical Industrial Cooperation Contract
TICC	Technical Intelligence Coordination Center [NATO] (NATG)
TICCIH	[The] International Committee for the Conservation of the Industrial Heritage (EA)
TICCIT	Time-Shared Interactive Computer-Controlled Information Television [System] [Mitre Corp. Brigham Young University 1971]
TICE	Time Integral Cost Effectiveness
TICER	Temporary International Council for Educational Reconstruction (DLA)
TICF	Transient Installation Confinement Facility [Military] (AABC)
Tichb Tr	Report of the Tichborne Trial [London] [A publication] (DLA)
TICKS	Two Incomes, Kids [Lifestyle classification]

Ticktmst.......	Ticketmaster Group, Inc. [*Associated Press*] (SAG)	TIDS............	Tower Integrated Display System [*FAA*] (TAG)
TICLER.........	Technical Input Checklist/Evaluation Report (MCD)	TIDUP.........	Technical Information Directive Update Panel
TICM............	Test Interface and Control Module (MCD)	Tidwtr..........	Tidewater, Inc. [*Associated Press*] (SAG)
TICM............	Thermal Imaging Common Modules	TIDY...........	Teletypewriter Integrated Display (NVT)
TICM............	Trust Investment Committee Memorandum [*A publication*] (DLA)	TIDY...........	Track Identity
TICO............	Technical Information Contact Officer [*Navy*] (DNAB)	TIE	[*The*] Information Exchange (EA)
TICO............	Transactions. International Congress of Orientalists [*A publication*] (BJA)	TIE	[*The*] Information Exchange on Young Adult Chronic Patients (EA)
TICODS........	Time Compression Display System (NVT)	TIE	[*The*] Institute of Ecology [*Defunct*]
TICOM	Texas Institute for Computational Mechanics [*University of Texas at Austin*] [*Research center*] (RCD)	TIE	[*The*] Issue Exchange (EA)
TICOS	Truncated Icosahedra [*Crystallography*]	TIE	Target Identification Equipment (MCD)
TICP...........	Theater Inventory Control Point [*Military*] (AABC)	TIE	Team Initiated Enterprise
TICP...........	Travaux. Institut Catholique de Paris [*A publication*] (BJA)	TIE	Technical Idea Exchange (MCD)
TICR...........	Transmit Interrupt Control Register [*Computer science*] (CIST)	TIE	Technical Independent Evaluator [*Army*]
TICS	Teacher Interactive Computer System (IEEE)	TIE	Technical Information Exchange [*National Bureau of Standards*]
TICS	Telecommunication Information Control System	TIE	Technical Integration and Evaluation [*Apollo*] [*NASA*]
TICS	Timing and Injection Rate Control System [*Diesel engines*]	TIE	Technology Information Exchange (IID)
TICS	Turret Interaction Crew Simulator (MCD)	TIE	Telescopes in Education
TICT...........	Tactical Intelligence Collection Team [*Military*] (AFM)	TIE	Temporary/Intermittent Employee
TICT...........	Twisted Intramolecular Charge Transfer [*Biochemistry*]	TIE	Terminal Interface Equipment
TICTAC........	Time Compression Tactical Communications	TIE	Texas Information Exchange
TIC-TOC.......	Telecommunications Information Centre-Telecommunications Office for Consumers (NITA)	TIE	Texas Israel Exchange [*A trade and research venture*]
TICU...........	Trauma Intensive Care Unit [*Medicine*]	TIE	Threshold Ignition Energy (MCD)
TICUS	Tidal and Current Survey (NOAA)	TIE	TIE Communications, Inc. [*AMEX symbol*] (SPSG)
TICUS	Tidal Current Survey System [*National Oceanic and Atmospheric Administration*]	TIE	Tientsin [*Republic of China*] [*Seismograph station code, US Geological Survey*] (SEIS)
TICWAN.......	Trailerable Intracoastal Waterway Aids to Navigation [*Boat*]	TIE	Time Interval Error [*Telecommunications*] (TEL)
TID.............	Tactical Information Display	TIE	Tippi [*Ethiopia*] [*Airport symbol*] (OAG)
TID.............	Tactical Intrusion Detectors (MCD)	TIE	Titanium Metals [*NYSE symbol*]
TID.............	Target Identification Device [*Military*] (CAAL)	TIE	Toxicity Identification Evaluation
TID.............	Task Initiation Date (WDAA)	TIE	Toyota Industrial Equipment
TID.............	Tax Installment Deduction	TIE	Training ICON Environment
TID.............	Technical Information Division [*Romar Consultants, Inc.*] [*Information service or system*] (IID)	TIE	Training Instrumentation Evaluation (MCD)
TID.............	Technology Information Division [*Department of Energy, Mines, and Resources*] (IID)	TIE	Transient Ischemic Episode [*Medicine*]
TID.............	Ter in Die [*Three Times a Day*] [*Pharmacy*]	TIE	Transnationals Information Exchange
TID.............	Test Identify (CAAL)	TIE	Travel Industry for the Environment
TID.............	Thermal Identification Device	TIEA...........	Tax Information Exchange Agreement (ECON)
TID.............	Thermal Imaging Devices (MCD)	TIED............	Troop Information and Education Division
TID.............	Thermionic Ionization Detector [*Instrumentation*]	Tiedeman Real Prop...	Tiedeman on Real Property [*A publication*] (DLA)
TID.............	Thread Identifier [*Computer science*]	Tied Lim Police Power...	Tiedeman's Treatise on the Limitations of Police Power in the United States [*A publication*] (DLA)
TID.............	Ticket Information Data	Tied Mun Corp...	Tiedeman's Treatise on Municipal Corporations [*A publication*] (DLA)
TID.............	Time Interval Distribution	TIEG...........	Teen International Entomology Group [*Later, YES*] (EA)
TID.............	Titrated Initial Dose (AAMN)	TIE-IN	Technology Information Exchange-Innovation Network [*Ohio State Department of Development*] [*Information service or system*] (IID)
TID.............	Total Integrated Dose [*Nuclear energy*] (NRCH)	TIEO...........	Toyota Industrial Engine Operations [*Torrance, CA*]
TID.............	Total Ion Detector (OA)	TIER...........	Tierce [*Unit of measurement*] (ROG)
TID.............	Touch Information Display	TIERS...........	Title I Evaluation and Reporting System [*Department of Education*]
TID.............	Touch Input Device [*Computer science*] (IAA)	TIES	[*The*] Interactive Encyclopedia System [*University of Maryland research project*] (PCM)
TID.............	Traitement Integre des Donnees [*Integrated Data Processing - IDP*] [*French*]	TIES	Tactical Information Exchange System [*Navy United Nations*] (MCD)
TID.............	Traveling Ionospheric Disturbance	TIES	Technological Information Exchange System [*UNIDO*] [*United Nations*]
TID.............	Trifluoromethyl(iodophenyl)deazirine [*Biochemistry*]	TIES	Textbook Information and Exchange Service [*Regional clearinghouses for used textbooks*]
TID.............	Turn-In Document [*DoD*]	TIES	Theater Information and Engagement System [*Military*] (MCD)
TID.............	Type Issue/Defuel Codes (AAGC)	TIES	The International English School (AIE)
TIDA...........	30th Infantry Division Association (EA)	TIES	Time-Independent Escape Sequence [*Computer science*] (CDE)
TIDA...........	Tuberoinfundibular Dopaminergic System [*Medicine*] (DMAA)	TIES	Torpedo Installation and Exercise System [*Military*] (DWSG)
TIDAR.........	Texas Instruments Digital Analog Readout	TIES	Total Information for Educational Systems [*Saint Paul, MN*] (BUR)
TIDAR.........	Time Delay Array RADAR	TIES	Total Integrated Engineering System
Tidd...........	Tidd's Costs [*A publication*] (DLA)	TIES	Translators' and Interpreters' Educational Society (EA)
Tidd...........	Tidd's Practice [*A publication*] (DLA)	TIES	Transmission and Information Exchange System
TIDDAC........	Time in Deadband Digital Attitude Control	TIEYACP	[*The*] Information Exchange on Young Adult Chronic Patients (EA)
Tidd App......	Appendix to Tidd's Practice [*A publication*] (DLA)	TIF	[*The*] International Foundation (EA)
Tidd Co.......	Tidd's Costs [*A publication*] (DLA)	TIF	Tagged Image File [*Computer science*] (PCM)
Tidd Pr	Tidd's Practice [*A publication*] (DLA)	TIF	Tagged Image File [*Image format*] (AAEL)
Tidd Prac.....	Tidd's Practice [*A publication*] (DLA)	TIF	Taif [*Saudi Arabia*] [*Airport symbol*] (OAG)
Tidd's Pract...	Tidd's Practice [*A publication*] (DLA)	TIF	Tape Inventory File (IEEE)
TIDE...........	Tactical International Data Exchange (NG)	TIF	Target Intelligence File (CINC)
TIDE...........	Technical Intelligence Data Extraction (MCD)	TIF	Task Initiation Force [*Nuclear energy*] (NRCH)
TIDE...........	Tide West Oil [*NASDAQ symbol*] (TTSB)	TIF	Task Initiation Form [*Nuclear energy*] (NRCH)
TIDE...........	Tide West Oil Co. [*NASDAQ symbol*] (NQ)	TIF	Tax Increment Financing
TIDE...........	Timer Demodulator	TIF	Taxpayer Information File [*IRS*]
TIDE...........	Transponder Interrogation and Decoding Equipment [*Telecommunications*] (IAA)	TIF	Technical Information File
TIDE...........	Travel Industry and Disabled Exchange (EA)	TIF	Telecommunication Interference Filter [*Computer science*]
TideMrk.......	TideMark Bancorp [*Associated Press*] (SAG)	TIF	Telecoms Infotech Forum [*Hong Kong*] (DDC)
TideR..........	Tidelands Royalty [*Associated Press*] (SAG)	TIF	Telephone Influence Factor
TideR..........	Tidelands Royalty Class B [*Associated Press*] (SAG)	TIF	Telephone Interference Factor (DEN)
TIDES..........	Time-Division Electronics Switching System (KSC)	TIF	Terminal Independent Format
TideWst.......	Tide West Oil Co. [*Associated Press*] (SAG)	TIF	Testicular Interstitial Fluid [*Physiology*]
TIDF...........	Trunk Intermediate Distribution Frame [*Telecommunications*] (TEL)	TIF	Text Interchange Format [*Telecommunications*] (OSI)
TIDG	TAPER Isolated Dynamic Gain (IAA)	TIF	Thin Iron Film
TIDL...........	Test Instrumentation Data Link	TIF	Tiffany & Co. [*NYSE symbol*] (SPSG)
TIDMA.........	Tape Interface Direct Memory Access	TIF	Tiflis [*Tbilisi*] [*Former USSR Seismograph station code, US Geological Survey*] (SEIS)
TIDOC	Technical Information Documentation Center [*Advisory Group for Aerospace Research and Development*] (NATG)	TIF	Tilapia International Foundation (EA)
TIDOS	Table and Item Documentation System	TIF	Tomato Intercellular Fluid
TIDP..........	Technical Interface Design Plans	TIF	Transfer if Indicators Off (SAA)
TIDP-TE	Technical Interface Design Plan - Test Edition (RDA)	TIF	Transport International par Fer [*International Transport of Goods by Railway*] [*French*]
TIDR	Tool Investigation and Disposition Report (SAA)	TIF	Treaties in Force [*A publication*] (DLA)
TIDS...........	Tactical Information Distribution Systems [*Army*] (RDA)	TIF	True Involute Form
TIDS...........	Talker Idle State [*Telecommunications*] (IAA)	TIF	Tumor-Inducing Factor [*Oncology*]
TIDS...........	Technical Information Distribution Service [*Publisher*]		

TIF	Tumor-Infiltrating Lymphocyte [*Immunotherapy*]
TIF	Tumor Inhibitory Factor [*Oncology*]
TIFA	Tourist Information Facts and Abstracts [*Economic Documentation and Information Ltd.*] [*Ringmer Near Lewes, East Sussex, England*] [*Information service or system*] (IID)
TIFA	Trucks Involved in Fatal Accidents [*NHTSA*] (TAG)
Tif & Bul Tr...	Tiffany and Bullard on Trusts and Trustees [*A publication*] (DLA)
Tif & Sm Pr...	Tiffany and Smith's New York Practice [*A publication*] (DLA)
Tifany	Tiffany & Co. [*Associated Press*] (SAG)
TIFET	Thin-Layer Field Effect Transistor (IAA)
TIFF	[*The*] Integrated FORSTAT [*Force Status and Identity Reporting System*] File
TIFF	Tagged Image File Format [*Computer science*]
tiff	Tagged Image File Format [*Computer science*]
TIFF	Tag Image File Format [*Computer science*]
Tiff	Tiffany's Reports [*28-39 New York Court of Appeals*] [*A publication*] (DLA)
TIFF	Tokyo International Film Festival [*Japan*]
Tiffany	Tiffany's Reports [*28-39 New York Court of Appeals*] [*A publication*] (DLA)
Tiffany Landl & T...	Tiffany on Landlord and Tenant [*A publication*] (DLA)
Tiffany Landlord & Ten...	Tiffany on Landlord and Tenant [*A publication*] (DLA)
Tiffany Real Prop...	Tiffany on Real Property [*A publication*] (DLA)
TIFFE	Tokyo International Financial Futures Exchange [*Japan*] (NUMA)
Tif Gov	Tiffany on Government and Constitutional Law [*A publication*] (DLA)
TIFO	Technical Inspection Field Office, Office of the Inspector General
TIFR	Tata Institute for Fundamental Research [*British*]
TIFR	Total Improved Frequency Response
TIFR	Total Investment for Return (MHDW)
TIFS	Total In-Flight Simulation [*or Simulator*] [*Air Force*]
TIG	[*The*] Inspector General [*Army*]
TIG	Tactical Intelligence Group [*Military*]
TIG	Target Image Generator
TIG	Taxicab Industry Group (EA)
TIG	Telegram Identification Group [*Telecommunications*] (TEL)
TIG	Teletype Input Generator
TIG	Tetanus Immune Globulin [*Immunology*]
TIG	TIG Holdings [*NYSE symbol*] (TTSB)
TIG	TIG Holdings, Inc. [*NYSE symbol*] (SPSG)
tig	Tigre [*MARC language code Library of Congress*] (LCCP)
TIG	Tigris Minerals [*Vancouver Stock Exchange symbol*]
TIG	Time in Grade [*Air Force*]
TIG	Time of Ignition
TIG	Transamerica Insurance (EFIS)
TIG	Transearth Injection Geometry (SAA)
TIG	Tungsten-Inert-Gas
TIGA	TI [*Texas Instruments, Inc.*] Graphics Architecture [*Computer science*]
TIGA	Transport Issues Group Australia (EERA)
TIGCX	DW TCW/DW Income & Growth Cl.C [*Mutual fund ticker symbol*] (QG)
TIGEM	Telethon Institute of Genetics and Medicine [*Italy*]
TIGER	Terrestrial Initiative in Global Environmental Research [*UK government research program*]
TIGER	Terrorist Intelligence Gathering Evaluation and Review [*British*]
TIGER	Topologically Integrated Geographic Encoding and Referencing [*Bureau of the Census*]
TIGER	Topologically Integrated Geographic Encoding Referencing
TIGER	Total Information Gathering and Executive Reporting [*International Computers Ltd.*]
TIGER	Traitement Integral des Galaxies par l'Etude de leurs Raies [*An integral field spectrograph*]
TIGER	Traveling Industrial Gaseous Emission Research [*Vehicle*] [*Exxon Corp.*]
TIGER	Treasury Investment Growth Receipt (MHDW)
TIGFFO	Teenage, Infants, and Girls' Fashion Fair Organisation [*British*] (BI)
TIG(H)	Tetanus Immune Globulin (Human) [*Immunology*]
TIGHAR	[*The*] International Group for Historic Aircraft Recovery [*Wilmington, DE*]
TIG Hd	TIG Holdings, Inc. [*Associated Press*] (SAG)
TIGN	Time of Ignition
TIGOR	Time Interval Gage of Relays [*Telecommunications*] (IAA)
TIGR	[*The*] Institute of Genomic Research
TIGR	Tiger Direct [*NASDAQ symbol*] [*BLOC Development*] (SG)
TIGR	Topographically Integrated Geographic Referencing[*and Coding System*] [*Electronic map used for political demography*]
TIGR	Transmission Integrated Rotor
TIGR	Treasury Investment Growth Receipts [*Merrill Lynch & Co.*] [*Finance*]
TIGR	Turbine-Integrated Geared Rotor
Ti Gracch	Tiberius Gracchus [*of Plutarch*] [*Classical studies*] (OCD)
TIGRIS	Televised Images of Gaseous Region in Interplanetary Space
TIGR/NIST	The Institute for Genomic Research National Institute of Standards and Technology (HGEN)
TIGRs	Treasury Investment Growth Receipt (EBF)
TIGS	Terminal Independent Graphics System
TIGT	Turbine Inlet Gas Temperature [*Aviation*]
TIH	Technical Information Handbook
TIH	Their Imperial Highnesses
TIH	Tikehau [*French Polynesia*] [*Airport symbol*] (OAG)
TIH	Time in Hold (SAA)
TIH	Time Interval Histogram (DB)
TIH	Toromont Industries Ltd. [*Toronto Stock Exchange symbol*]
TIH	Total Installed Horsepower
TIH	Trinity International Holdings [*British*]
TIH	Trunk Interface Handler
TIHB	Target Intelligence Handbook (MCD)
TIHBSS	[*The*] I Hate Barney Secret Society (EA)
TIHP	Total Installed Horsepower
TII	European Association for the Transfer of Technologies, Innovation, and Industrial Information [*Information service or system*] (IID)
TII	[*The*] Independent Institute [*An association*] (EA)
TII	Table and Item Inventory (SAA)
TII	Talos Integration Investigation
TII	Texas Instruments, Inc.
TII	Texas Instruments, Incorporated, IS & S Library, Dallas, TX [*OCLC symbol*] (OCLC)
TII	Thomas Indus [*NYSE symbol*] (TTSB)
TII	Thomas Industries, Inc. [*NYSE symbol*] (SPSG)
TII	Tiffin, OH [*Location identifier FAA*] (FAAL)
TII	TII Industries, Inc. [*Associated Press*] (SAG)
TII	Tooling Inspection Instrumentation (NASA)
TII	Total Inactive Aerospace Vehicle [*or Aircraft*] Inventory
TII	Tourismo Internationale Injection [*International Touring-fuel Injection*] [*Italian*]
TII	Trusteeship Institute, Inc. (EA)
TII	Turn Indicator Interference
TIIAL	[*The*] International Institute of Applied Linguistics
TIIAP	Telecommunications and Information Infrastructure Assistance Program [*Department of Commerce*]
TIIC	Technical Industrial Intelligence Committee [*US Military Government, Germany*]
TIID	Technical Industrial Intelligence Division [*Allied Board set up to send experts into Germany to ferret out Germany's war-developed scientific secrets*] [*Post-World War II*]
TIIF	Tactical Imagery Interpretation Facility [*Military*]
TIII	TII Indus [*NASDAQ symbol*] (TTSB)
TIII	TII Industries, Inc. [*NASDAQ symbol*] (SAG)
TII Inds	TII Industries, Inc. [*Associated Press*] (SAG)
TIIP	Terrain-Intelligence Integration Prototype [*Army*] (RDA)
TIIPS	Technically Improved Interference Prediction System (IEEE)
TIJ	Tijuana [*Mexico*] [*Airport symbol*] (AD)
TIJI	Tribune Internationale des Jeunes Interpretes [*International Rostrum of Young Performers - IRP*] (EAIO)
TIK	Oklahoma City, OK [*Location identifier FAA*] (FAAL)
TIK	Target Indicator Kit
TIK	Thermal Imagery Kit (DWSG)
TIK	Tiara Enterprises Ltd. [*Vancouver Stock Exchange symbol*]
tik	Ticking (VRA)
TIK	Tiksi [*Former USSR Seismograph station code, US Geological Survey*] (SEIS)
TIK	Tixie [*Former USSR Geomagnetic observatory code*]
TIKP	Turkiye Isci Koylu Partisi [*Worker-Peasant Party of Turkey*] [*Political party*] (PD)
TIL	Tajikistan International Airlines [*FAA designator*] (FAAC)
TIL	Technical Indexes Ltd. (NITA)
TIL	Technical Information and Library Services [*Ministry of Technology*] [*British*]
TIL	Temperature Indicating Label
TIL	Temporary Instructor Lieutenant [*Navy British*]
TIL	Tire Inflation Label [*Automotive engineering*]
TIL	Tree Island Industries Ltd. [*Toronto Stock Exchange symbol Vancouver Stock Exchange symbol*]
T-i-L	Truth-in-Lending Act [*1968*]
TIL	Tumor Infiltrating Lymphocyte [*Oncology*]
TIL	Tumor Infiltration Factor [*Medicine*] (WDAA)
TILA	Telemail International Licensees' Association (TSSD)
TILA	Truth-in-Lending Act [*1968*]
Til & Sh Pr...	Tillinghast and Shearman's New York Practice [*A publication*] (DLA)
TILCAR	Tactical Infantry Load Carrier Amphibious Remote [*Military*] (PDAA)
TILF	Tactical Integrity Loss Factor
TILL	Total Initial Lamp Lumens
Till & Yates App...	Tillinghast and Yates on Appeals [*A publication*] (DLA)
Tillman	Tillman's Reports [*68, 69, 71, 73, 75 Alabama*] [*A publication*] (DLA)
TILLO	Transfer in Lieu of Layoff (MCD)
TILMC	Timber Industry Labor-Management Committee (WPI)
TILMC	Tobacco Industry Labor/Management Committee (EA)
TILO	Technical Industrial Liaison Office
Til Prec	Tillinghast's Precedents [*A publication*] (DLA)
TILRA	Tribal Indian Land Rights Association (EA)
TILS	Tactical Instrument Landing System
TILS	Technical Information & Liaison Service [*Information service or system*] (IID)
TILSRA	Truth in-Lending Simplification and Reform Act [*1980*]
Tils St L	Tilsley on Stamp Laws [*3rd ed.*] [*1871*] [*A publication*] (DLA)
TILT	Taxpayer Inquiry Lookup Table [*IRS*]
TILT	Texas Instruments Language Translator [*Computer science*] (IAA)
TILT	Transmission Intercept and Landing Terminated (MCD)
TIM	Star Asia [*Philippines*] [*FAA designator*] (FAAC)
TIM	Table Input to Memory
TIM	Tactical Instrumental Missile (MCD)
TIM	Tangential Inlet Manifold
TIM	Target Intelligence Material (MCD)
TIM	Technical Information Manager [*Environmental Protection Agency*] (GFGA)
TIM	Technical Information Manual
TIM	Technical Information on Microfilm [*British*] (DIT)
TIM	Technical Interchange Meeting (NASA)
TIMS	TEFLON Insulation Material
TIM	Tembagapura [*Indonesia*] [*Airport symbol*] (OAG)
TIM	Temperature Independent Material (IAA)

TIM	Temperature Indicator Monitor
TIM	Terminal Interface Monitor (IAA)
TIM	Test Instrumented Missile [*Army*]
TIM	Test Interface Module (CAAL)
TIM	Test Item Malfunction (MCD)
TIM	Texas Instruments, Inc., Central Library Services, Dallas, TX [*OCLC symbol*] (OCLC)
TIM	Thailand Independence Movement [*Communist-directed activity outside Thailand*] [*Merged with TPF*]
TIM	Thermoplastic Injection Molding (EDCT)
TIM	Ticket Issue Machines
TIM	Time Indicator (IAA)
TIM	Time Indicator, Miniature (MUGU)
TIM	Time Initiator Monitor (SAA)
TIM	Time in Mode (EG)
TIM	Time Interval Measurement
TIM	Time Interval Meter
TIM	Time Interval Monitor (NASA)
Tim	Timely [*Record label*]
TIM	Time Meter (AAG)
TIM	Timisoara [*Romania*] [*Seismograph station code, US Geological Survey*] (SEIS)
TIM	Timminco Ltd. [*Toronto Stock Exchange symbol*]
Tim	Timoleon [*of Plutarch*] [*Classical studies*] (OCD)
Tim	Timon of Athens [*Shakespearean work*]
Tim	Timothy [*New Testament book*]
TIM	Titanium Mesh [*Medicine*]
TIM	Token/Net Interface Module [*Telecommunications*] (TSSD)
TIM	Topic Indexing Matrix
TIM	Total Information Management (NITA)
TIM	Total Ion Scanning Mode [*Spectroscopy*]
TIM	Track Imitation (MSA)
TIM	Tracking Information Memorandum
TIM	Tracking Instruction Manual
TIM	Tracking Instrument Mount (MUGU)
TIM	Track Initiator Monitor (CAAL)
TIM	Transient Intermodulation [*Distortion*]
TIM	Transistor Information Microfile
TIM	Transthoracic Intracardiac Monitoring [*Medicine*] (DMAA)
TIM	Trends in Microbiology [*A publication*]
TIM	Trigger Inverter Module
TIM	Triose Phosphate Isomerase [*An enzyme*]
TIMA	Technical Illustrators Management Association [*Later, IG*]
TIMA	Truth in Mileage Act of 1986
TIMADS	Timber Management Decision System (PDAA)
TIMAR	Near-Term Improvement in Materiel Asset Reporting [*Military*] (AABC)
TIMARC	Time Multiplexed Analogue Radio Control (PDAA)
TIMASS	Time Interval Miss Distance Acoustical Scoring System (MCD)
TIMATION	Time Location System [*Navy*]
TIMB	Timballes [*Kettle drum*]
TIMB	Timber (ADA)
TimbCo	Timberland Co. [*Associated Press*] (SAG)
TimbLdg	Timber Lodge Steakhouse, Inc. [*Associated Press*] (SAG)
TimbSf	Timberline Software Corp. [*Associated Press*] (SAG)
TIMC	Tumor-Induced Cytatocity [*Medicine*] (DAVI)
TIM/DL	Trunk Interface Module for Data Links [*Telecommunications*]
TIME	Technique for Information Management and Employment
TIME	Technology, Immediate-Diagnosis, Mammography Effective Treatment
TIME	Terminal Instruction (System) for Managed Education
TIME	Tsunami Inundation Modeling Exchange Project [*Marine science*] (OSRA)
Time A	Time Australia [*A publication*] (APTA)
Timeline	Timeline, Inc. [*Associated Press*] (SAG)
TimeIn	Timeline, Inc. [*Associated Press*] (SAG)
Times L (Eng)	Times Law Reports [*England*] [*A publication*] (DLA)
Times LR	Times Law Reports [*England*] [*A publication*] (DLA)
Times LR	Times Law Reports [*Ceylon*] [*A publication*] (DLA)
Times L Rep	Times Law Reports [*England*] [*A publication*] (DLA)
Times L Rep	Times Law Reports [*Ceylon*] [*A publication*] (DLA)
TimeWa	Time Warner, Inc. [*Associated Press*] (SAG)
TimeWarn	Time Warner, Inc. Holding Co. [*Associated Press*] (SAG)
TIMI	Technical Information Maintenance Instruction
TIMI	Thrombolysis in Myocardial Infarction (Study) [*Medicine*]
TIMIG	Time in Grade [*Army*]
TIMINT	Time Interval (AABC)
TIMIX	[*The*] International Microcomputer Information Exchange (EA)
TIMIX	Texas Instruments Minicomputer Information Exchange (IAA)
TiMixE	TI-MIX [*Texas Instruments Mini/Microcomputer Information Exchange*] Europe (EA)
Timken	[*The*] Timken Co. [*Associated Press*] (SAG)
TIMM	The Intelligent Machine Model (NITA)
TIMM	Thermionic Integrated Micromodule
TimM	Times Mirror Co. [*Associated Press*] (SAG)
TimM01	Times Mirror Co. [*Associated Press*] (SAG)
TimMir	Times Mirror Co. [*Associated Press*] (SAG)
TIMMS	Total Integrated Manpower Management System
TIMNET	Time Share International Data Communications Network [*Telecommunications*] (IAA)
TIMOT	Track, Initiation, Monitoring Overlap Technician (SAA)
TIMP	Tavistock Institute of Medical Psychology [*British*]
TIMP	Texas Instructional Media Project [*Education*]
TIMP	Timpani [*Kettle drum*]
timp	Timpani (WDAA)

TIMP	Tissue Inhibitor of Metalloproteinases [*Biochemistry*]
TIMS	[*The*] Institute of Management Sciences [*Providence, RI*] (EA)
TIMS	[*The*] International Molinological Society (EA)
TIMS	Tactical Incapacitating Munitions System (MCD)
TIMS	Technical Information Management System
TIMS	Technology Integration of Missile Subsystems (MCD)
TIMS	Telecommunications Instruction Module System (IAA)
TIMS	Telephone Information and Management Systems (ADA)
TIMS	Test Interactive Management System
TIMS	Text Information and Management System [*Computer science*]
TIMS	Thaad Information Management System
TIMS	Theoretical Indicative Margin System (NUMA)
TIMS	Thermal Infrared Mapping Spectrometer (SSD)
TIMS	Thermal Infrared Multispectral Scanner [*Airborne instrument for geological applications*]
TIMS	Thermal Ionization Mass Spectrometry
TIMS	Total Ion Measurement Source
TIMS	Traffic and Incident Management System
TIMS	Transmission Impairment Measuring Set [*Telecommunications*] (TEL)
TIMS	Transmission Impairment Measuring System (IAA)
TIMS	Trust for Investments in Mortgages (MHDW)
TIMSA	Thermal Insulation Manufacturers and Suppliers Association (DBA)
TIMSS	Third International Mathematics and Science Study [*Education research*]
TIMT	Titanium Metals Corp. [*NASDAQ symbol*] (SAG)
TIM/TOM	Table Input to Memory/Table Output from Memory (NITA)
TIN	Taino Tours [*Dominican Republic*] [*ICAO designator*] (FAAC)
TIN	Taro Industries Ltd. [*Toronto Stock Exchange symbol*]
TIN	Task Implementation Notice
TIN	Taxpayer Identification Number [*IRS*]
TIN	Temperature Independent [*Ferrite computer memory core*]
TIN	Temple-Inland [*NYSE symbol*] (TTSB)
TIN	Temple-Inland, Inc. [*NYSE symbol*] (SPSG)
TIN	Temporary Identification Number [*Military*]
TIN	Temporary Instruction Notice
TIN	Ter in Nocte [*Three Times a Night*] [*Pharmacy*]
TIN	Tindouf [*Algeria*] [*Airport symbol*] (OAG)
TIN	Tinemaha [*California*] [*Seismograph station code, US Geological Survey*] (SEIS)
TIN	Tooling Impound Notice
TIN	Transaction Identification Number (AFM)
TIN	Transmission Identification Number [*Automotive engineering*]
TIN	Triangulated Irregular Network (EERA)
TIN	Tubulointerstitial Nephritis [*Nephrology*]
T/In	Turn In (DGA)
TINA	[*The*] Integrated Nozzle Assembly (MCD)
TINA	There Is No Alternative [*Nickname given to British Prime Minister Margaret Thatcher because she so often uses this phrase to defend her government's economic policies*]
TINA	Truth in Negotiations Act
TINA-C	Telecommunications Information Networking Architecture Consortium (DDC)
TINALEA	This Is Not a Legally Enforceable Agreement [*Legal term*] (NUCP)
tinc	Tinctura [*tincture*] [*Latin*] [*Pharmacology*] (DAVI)
TINC	Tincture (ADA)
TINCT	Tinctura [*Tincture*] [*Pharmacy*]
TINDECO	Tin Decorating Co.
TINDX	Texas Instruments Index Access Method
TINE	There Is No Excuse (ECON)
TI-NET	Transparent Intelligent Network
TINET	Travel Industry Network, Inc. [*Winter Springs, FL*] [*Telecommunications*] (TSSD)
TINFO	Tieteellisen Informoinnin Neuvosto [*Finnish Council for Scientific Information and Research Libraries*] (EAIO)
TIN/FS	Taxpayer Identification Number/File Source [*IRS*]
Tink	Two Incomes, No Kids [*Lifestyle classification*]
TINKER	Timber Information Keyword Retrieval [*Timber Research and Development Association*] [*Information service or system*] (IID)
TINNER	Tea and Dinner [*Slang British*] (DSUE)
TINO	There Is No Opposition [*Parliamentary slang*] [*British*] (DI)
TINOP	Transponder Inoperative [*Aviation*] (FAAC)
TINPOT	There Is No Possible Other Tactic [*Parliamentary slang*] [*British*] (DI)
TINR	Target Identification Navigation RADAR
TINS	Tax Identification Number System [*IRS*]
TINS	Thermal Imaging Navigation Set [*Hughes Aircraft Co.*] [*Navy*] (ECON)
TINS	Trains Inertial Navigation System (IAA)
Tinsley	Tinsley Labs, Inc. [*Associated Press*] (SAG)
TINSTAAFL	There Is No Such Thing as a Free Lunch [*Principle of economics indicating that one cannot get something for nothing*] [*See also TANSTAAFL*]
TINSY	Treasure Island Naval Shipyard [*San Francisco Bay*]
TINT	Target Intercept Timer (MCD)
TINT	Teletype Interpreter (PDAA)
TINTA	Tele-Communications International, Inc. [*NASDAQ symbol*] (SAG)
TINTA	Tele-Communications Intl [*NASDAQ symbol*] (TTSB)
TINTM	Triisononyl Trimellitate [*Organic chemistry*]
TINTS	Tactical Intelligence Transfer System
TINTS	Turret Integrated Night Thermal Sight
Tinw	Tinwald's Reports, Scotch Court of Session [*A publication*] (DLA)
TIO	Target Indication Officer [*Navy*]
TIO	Target Information Officer [*Marine Corps*] (DOMA)
TIO	Target Insertion Orbit [*NASA*] (NAKS)
TIO	Technical Information Office
TIO	Technology Innovation Office [*Environmental Protection Agency*]

TIO............... Technology Integration Office [*Army*] (RDA)
TIO............... Television Information Office [*Defunct*] (EA)
TIO............... Terminal Input/Output (NITA)
TIO............... Test Input/Output [*Computer science*]
TIO............... Time Interval Optimization (IEEE)
TIO............... Tiouine [*Morocco*] [*Seismograph station code, US Geological Survey*] (SEIS)
TIO............... Transistorized Image Orthicon
TIO............... Transistorized Image Orthicon Camera (IAA)
TIO............... Troop Information Officer
TIO............... Trust Investment Officer [*Banking*] (TBD)
TIOC............ Terminal Input/Output Controller (NITA)
TIOC............ Terminal Input/Output Coordinator [*Computer science*] (IBMDP)
TIOC............ Triumph International Owners Club (EA)
TIOF............ [*The*] International Osprey Foundation (EA)
TIOH............ [*The*] Institute of Heraldry [*Military*]
TIOL............ Texas Instruments Cassette Operating Language (IAA)
TIOLR .... Texas Instruments Online Reporting System [*Computer science*]
TIOM........... Telegraph Input-Output Multiplexer [*Telecommunications*] (OA)
TIOM........... Terminal Input/Output Module [*Computer science*]
TIOS............ Tactical Integrated Ocean Surveillance [*Military*] (CAAL)
TIOT............ Task Input/Output Table [*Computer science*] (BUR)
TIOTM......... Triisooctyl Trimellitate [*Organic chemistry*]
TIOWQ .... Terminal Input/Output Wait Queue [*Computer science*]
TIP............... C & M Aviation, Inc. [*ICAO designator*] (FAAC)
TIP............... [*The*] Information Partnership [*Information service or system*] (IID)
TIP............... [*The*] Information Place [*Information service or system*] (IID)
TIP............... TACAMO [*Take Charge and Move Out*] Improvement Program
TIP............... Tactical Implementation Time
TIP............... Tactical Improvement Program [*Military*]
TIP............... Tactile Information Presentation [*Biotechnology*]
TIP............... TAO [*Tropical Atmosphere-Ocean*] Implementation Panel [*Marine science*] (OSRA)
TIP............... Target Identification Point (NATG)
TIP............... Target Impact Point
TIP............... Target Industries Program [*Occupational Safety and Health Administration*]
TIP............... Target Input Panel
TIP............... Target Intelligence Package (MCD)
TIP............... Task Initiation and Prediction
TIP............... Tax-Based Incomes Policy
TIP............... Taxpayer Information Processing [*IRS*]
TIP............... Teachers Instructional Plan
TIP............... Technical Improvement Program
TIP............... Technical Information Package [*Environmental Protection Agency*] (AEPA)
TIP............... Technical Information Panel [*Terminated, 1971*] [*AEC*]
TIP............... Technical Information Pilot [*A publication Obsolete*]
TIP............... Technical Information Pool
TIP............... Technical Information Processing (IEEE)
TIP............... Technical Information Program
TIP............... Technical Information Project [*MIT*]
TIP............... Technical Integration Panel [*NASA*] (SSD)
TIP............... Technology in Production (IAA)
TIP............... Technology Internship Program [*Oak Ridge National Laboratory*]
TIP............... Tehrik-i-Istiqlal [*Solidarity Party*] [*See also TI Pakistan*] [*Political party*] (FEA)
TIP............... Telefiche Image Processor (NITA)
TIP............... TELENET Interface Processor
TIP............... Telephone Information Processing (MCD)
TIP............... Teletype Input Processing
TIP............... Temperature-Independent Paramagnetism
TIP............... Terminal Impact Prediction
TIP............... Terminal Interface Package [*Computer science*]
TIP............... Terminal Interface [*Message*] Processor [*Computer science DoD*]
TIP............... Terminal Interface Program (NITA)
TIP............... Thermal Inactivation Point [*Medicine*] (DMAA)
TIP............... Threshold by Identification of Pictures (DAVI)
TIP............... Thrust Inlet Pressure (MCD)
TIP............... Tiburon Petroleum [*Vancouver Stock Exchange symbol*]
TIP............... Tilt Isolation Platform
TIP............... Times of Increased Probability [*Earthquake prediction*]
Tip............... Tipperary [*County in Ireland*] (WGA)
TIP............... TIROS [*Television and Infrared Observation Satellite*] Information Processor [*Telecommunications*]
TIP............... To Insure Promptness
TIP............... Tool Inventors Program [*Automobile tool design*]
TIP............... Total Information Processing (BUR)
TIP............... Total Isomerization Process [*Petroleum refining*]
TIP............... Toxic Integration Program [*Environmental Protection Agency*]
TIP............... Toxicology Information Program [*National Library of Medicine*] [*Bethesda, MD*]
TIP............... Tracking Impact Prediction [*of satellites*]
TIP............... Track Initiation and Prediction [*RADAR*]
TIP............... Training Implementation Plan [*Military*]
TIP............... Transaction Interface Package [*Sperry UNIVAC*] [*Computer science*]
TIP............... Transaction Interface Processor
TIP............... Transient [*or Traveling or Traversing*] In-Core Probe [*Nuclear energy*] (NRCH)
TIP............... Transient Ischemic Paroxysm (DB)
TIP............... Trans-Israel Pipeline
TIP............... Transit Improvement Program [*Satellite*] (MCD)
TIP............... Translation Inhibitory Protein
TIP............... Transponder Interrogator Processor
TIP............... Transportation Improvement Program

TIP............... Transport Individuel Publique [*Also known as PROCOTIP*] [*French auto cooperative*]
TIP............... Traveling in Core Probe (IAA)
TIP............... Traverisng In-Core Probe
TIP............... Tripoli [*Libya*] [*Airport symbol*] (OAG)
TIP............... Troop Information Program
TIP............... Tumor-Inducing Principle [*Plant cytology*]
TIP............... Tumor Inhibitory Principle [*Oncology*]
TIP............... Tumor Insularis Pancreatis [*Medicine*] (DB)
TIP............... Turbine Inlet Pressure (MSA)
TIP............... Turbine Integral Propellant (MCD)
TIP............... Turn In a Pusher [*Organization combating drug traffic*]
TIPA............. Triisopropanolamine [*Organic chemistry*]
TIPACS .... Texas Instruments Planning and Control System
TIPAT........... Technical Information on Patents [*Swiss Intellectual Property Office*] [*Bern*] [*Information service or system*] (IID)
TIPB............. Triisopropylbenzene [*Also, TIB*] [*Organic chemistry*]
TIPC............. Texas Instruments Pressure Controller
TIPCC.......... TI [*Texas Instruments*] Programmable Calculator Club (EA)
TIPE............. Transponder, Interrogator, Pinger, and Echo Sounder
TIPEM.......... Toolkit for Interoperable Privacy-Enhanced Messaging [*RSA Data Security, Inc.*]
TIPG............. Thomson Information/Publishing Group [*The Thomson Corp.*]
TIPI.............. Tactical Information Processing and Interpretation [*Military*] (AFM)
TIPI.............. Transportable Automated Intelligence Processing and Interpretation System (MCD)
TIPIC........... Turkish Investment Promotion and Information Center [*Subdivision of the Union of Chambers of Commerce, Industry, and Commodity Exchanges of Turkey*]
TIPIF........... Instant Publisher [*NASDAQ symbol*] (TTSB)
TIPIF........... [*The*] Instant Publisher, Inc. [*NASDAQ symbol*] (SAG)
TIPISPO ...... Tactical Intelligence Processing and Interpretation System Program Office [*Air Force*] (PDAA)
TIPIT........... TDRSS [*Tracking and Data Relay Satellite System*] Interface Prepocessor Into TELOPS [*Telemetry Online Processing System*]
TIPITEF........ Tactical Information Processing and Interpretation Total Environment Facility (MCD)
TIPL............. Tactical Imagery Processing Laboratory [*Army*] (MCD)
TIPL............. Tactical Information Processing Laboratory [*Army*] (MCD)
TIPL............. Teach Information Processing Language
TIPMG .... [*The*] International Project Management Group, Inc. [*Glyndon, MD*] [*Telecommunications*] (TSSD)
TIPP............. Target Intelligence Production Program
TIPP............. Technology and Information Policy Program [*Syracuse University*] [*Research center*] (RCD)
TIPP............. Time Phasing Program [*NASA*] (KSC)
TIPP............. Tipperary [*County in Ireland*]
Tippery .... Tipperary Corp. [*Associated Press*] (SAG)
TIPPP.......... Tidewater Interagency Pollution Prevention Program (BCP)
TIPPS.......... Tetraiodophenolphthalein Sodium [*Pharmacology*]
TIPPS.......... Total In-House Publication Production System (MCD)
TIPPS.......... Trans-Ionospheric Pulse Pairs
TIPR............ Tactical Inertial Performance Requirements
TIPR............ Tactics Inspection Procedures Report
TIPRE.......... Tactical Inertial Performance Requirements (MCD)
TIPRO .... Texas Independent Producers and Royalty Owners Association (EA)
TIPS............. Intrahepatic Portosystemic Shunt [*Medicine*]
TIPS............. [*The*] Italia Philatelic Society (EA)
TIPS............. Tactical Imagery Processing Set
TIPS............. Tactical Information about Perilous Situations [*New York City Fire Department program*]
TIPS............. Tactical Information Processing System [*Military*] (CAAL)
TIPS............. Teaching Improvement Project System [*University of Kentucky*] [*Research center*] (RCD)
TIPS............. Teaching Individual Protective Strategies and Teaching Individual Positive Solutions [*In association name TIPS Program*] (EA)
TIPS............. Teaching Information Processing System
TIPS............. Technical Information and Product Service
TIPS............. Technical Information for Product Safety [*Consumer Product Safety Commission*] (IID)
TIPS............. Technical Information Periodicals Service [*General Electric Co.*]
TIPS............. Technical Information Processing System [*Rockwell International Corp.*] [*Downey, CA*] (AFM)
TIPS............. Technical Interest Profiles (SAA)
TIPS............. Techniques in Product Selection [*National Association of Manufacturers*]
TIPS............. Telemetry Impact Prediction System [*Air Force*]
TIPS............. Telemetry Integrated Processing System [*Air Force*]
TIPS............. Terminal Information Processing [*Aviation*] (FAAC)
TIPS............. Test Information Processing System [*Air Force*]
TIPS............. Test of Integrated Process Skills (EDAC)
TIPS............. Textile Industry Product Safety [*A publication*]
TIPS............. Text Information Processing System
TIPS............. The Internet Product Site
TIPS............. Thermally Induced Phase Separation [*Chemistry*]
TIPS............. Thousands of Instructions Per Second (NITA)
Tips............. Tiny Income, Parents Supporting [*Lifestyle classification*]
TIPS............. Total Information Processing System [*Veterans Administration*]
TIPS............. Total Integrated Pneumatic System (MCD)
TIPS............. Transistorized Inverter Power Supply
TIPS............. Transjugular Intrahepatic Portosystemic Shunt
TIPS............. Transportation Induced Pollution Surveillance [*Marine science*] (MSC)
TIPS............. Treasury's Inflation Protection Securities
TIPS............. Trends in Pharmacological Sciences [*A publication*]
TIPS............. Triisopropysilyl [*Organic chemistry*]

TIPS	Truevision Image Processing Software [AT & T]
TIPS	Tunable Infrared Photomission Sensor
TIPSY	Task Input Parameter Synthesizer
TIP/TAP	Target Input Panel and Target Assign Panel
TIPTOP	Tape Input - Tape Output [Honeywell, Inc.] [Computer science]
TIP TOP	Tax Information Plan and Total Owed Purchase Accounting
TIQ	Paris, TN [Location identifier FAA] (FAAL)
TIQ	Task Input Queue [Computer science] (IBMDP)
TIQ	Tetrahydroisoquinoline [Biochemistry]
TIQ	Tinian [Mariana Islands] [Airport symbol] (OAG)
TI/QC	Technical Inspection/Quality Control (MCD)
TIQRC	Toxicology Information Query Response Center [National Library of Medicine]
TIR	Antair, SA de CV [Mexico] [FAA designator] (FAAC)
TIR	China Tire Holdings Ltd. [NYSE symbol] (SPSG)
TIR	Target Illuminating RADAR [Air Force]
TIR	Target Indication Room [Navy]
TIR	Target Industries [Industry segments which have been selected by the US Department of Commerce for special trade promotion emphasis]
TIR	Target Instruction Register
TIR	Technical Information Release
TIR	Technical Information Report (IEEE)
TIR	Technical Intelligence Report
TIR	Telecommunications Industry Research [British] (ECON)
TIR	Temperature Indicator Recorder (ECII)
TIR	Terminal Imaging RADAR [Military] (RDA)
TIR	Terminal Innervation Ratio [Psychiatry]
TIR	Test Incidence and Reporting System
TIR	Test Incident Report (IAA)
TIR	Thermal Infrared (PDAA)
tir	Tigrina [MARC language code Library of Congress] (LCCP)
TIR	Time in Rate
TIR	Tirana [Albania] [Seismograph station code, US Geological Survey] (SEIS)
TIR	Tiree Island [Scotland] [Airport symbol] (AD)
TIR	Tirupati [India] [Airport symbol] (OAG)
TIR	Tolerance in Radius
TIR	Tooling Investigation Report
TIR	Total Image Readout
TIR	Total Immunoreaction [Immunochemistry]
TIR	Total Immunoreactive [Medicine] (STED)
TIR	Total Indicated Runout
TIR	Total Indicator Reading
TIR	Total Internal Reflecting
TIR	Total Item Record (MCD)
TIR	Transaction Item Report [Navy] (NG)
TIR	Transmission Infrared [Spectroscopy]
TIR	Transport International Routier [International Transport of Goods by Road] [French]
TIR	True Indicated Radius (IAA)
TIRA	Thrift Industry Recovery Act [1987]
TIRA	Thrift Institutions Restructuring Act [1982]
TIRACS	Telecommanded Inertially Referenced Attitude Control System (MCD)
TIRAS	Technical Information Retrieval and Analysis System (CAAL)
TIRB	Transportation Insurance Rating Bureau [Later, AAIS] (EA)
TIRC	Temperature Indicator Recorder Controller (ECII)
TIRC	Tobacco Industry Research Committee (EA)
TIRC	Toxicology Information Research Center [Department of Energy] [Oak Ridge National Laboratory Oak Ridge, TN]
TIRC	Toxicology Information Response Center [Information service or system] (IID)
TIRC	TRADOC [Training and Doctrine Command] Instrumentation Review Committee [Army]
TIRC	Transimpedence Receiver Circuit
TIRC	T Tauri Infrared Companion [Object believed to be first planet sighted that is not in our solar system]
TIRE	EC02, Inc. [NASDAQ symbol] (SAG)
TIRE	Eco 2 Inc. [NASDAQ symbol] (TTSB)
TIRE	Tank Infrared Elbow [Night vision device] [Army] (RDA)
TIRE	Tires as Imaginative Recreation Equipment
TIREC	TIROS [Television and Infrared Observation Satellite] Ice Reconnaissance [NASA]
TIREM	Terrain Integration Rough Earth Model
TIRES	Transient Infrared Emission Spectroscopy
TIRES	Transportation Interface and Reporting System [GSA] (TAG)
TIREW	Eco 2 Inc. Wrrt'A' [NASDAQ symbol] (TTSB)
TIRF	Total Internal Reflection Fluorescence
TIRF	Traffic Injury Research Foundation of Canada [Research center] (RCD)
TIRFM	Total Internal Reflectiona Fluorescence Microscopy
TIR-FPL	Total Internal Reflection Face-Pumped LASER
TIRH	Theoretical Indoor Relative Humidity
TIRIS	Texas Instruments Registration and Identification System [Texas Instruments, Inc.] [Automobile anti-theft protection]
TIRIS	Traversing Infrared Inspection System
TIRKS	Trunks Integrated Record Keeping System [Bell System]
TIRL	Telmatique International Research Laboratories (TELE)
TIRM	Transparent Infrared Material
TIRMMS	Technical Information Reports for Music-Media Specialists [Music Library Association publication series]
TIROD	Test Instruction Record of Discussion (MCD)
TIROS	Television and Infrared Observation Satellite [NASA]
TIROS	Television Infrared Observational Satellite [Marine science] (OSRA)
TIROS	Topographical Infrared Operations Satellite (NASA)

TIROS-M	Television and Infrared Observation Satellite - Meteorological [NASA] (DNAB)
TIROS-N	Television Infrared-Observation Satellite NOAA [National Oceanographic and Atmospheric Administration] [Navy] (ANA)
TIRP	Textile Information Retrieval Program (NITA)
TIRP	Total Internal Reflection Prism
TIRPC	Transport-Independendt Remote Procedure Call [Computer science]
TIRPF	Total Integrated Radial Peaking Factor (IEEE)
TIRR	[The] Institute for Rehabilitation and Research [Houston, TX]
TIRR	Tactics Inspection Results Report
TIRR	Texas Institute of Rehabilitation and Research (BABM)
TIRR	Trainer Installation Requirements Report
TIRS	Tactical Information Recording System [Military] (CAAL)
TIRS	Target Index Reference System [Army] (DOMA)
TIRS	Terrain Index Reference System [Army] (INF)
TIRS	Thermal Infrared Scanner (RDA)
TIR/SLIT	Transaction Item Reporting / Serial Lot Item Tracking [Navy] (DNAB)
TIRT	Tidelands Royalty Trust "B" [NASDAQ symbol] (NQ)
TIRT	Total Internal Reflection Technique
TIRTZ	Tidelands Rlty Tr B SBI [NASDAQ symbol] (TTSB)
TIRU	Service du Traitement Industriel des Residus Urbains [France]
TIRU	Trade Information Research Unit [ITC] [United Nations] (DUND)
TIS	[The] Infantry School [Army]
TIS	Tactical Intelligence Squadron (MCD)
TIS	Tactical Interdiction System
TIS	Taft Information System [Provides information on private foundations] (IID)
TIS	Target Identification Software [Military] (CAAL)
TIS	Target Information Sheet [Air Force]
TIS	Target Information System
TIS	Tate Integrated Systems
TIS	Technical Information Section [Navy]
TIS	Technical Information Series (IAA)
TIS	Technical Information Service [American Institute of Aeronautics and Astronautics] (IID)
TIS	Technical Information Service [Caribbean Industrial Research Institute] [Trinidad and Tobago]
TIS	Technical Information Services [Acurex Corp.] (IID)
TIS	Technical Information Staff [Environmental Protection Agency] (GFGA)
TIS	Technical Information Systems [Department of Agriculture]
TIS	Technical Interface Specification (NATG)
TIS	Technical Research Centre of Finland, Espoo, Finland [OCLC symbol] (OCLC)
TIS	Technology, Information, and Society
TIS	Technology Information System [Lawrence Livermore National Laboratory] [University of California] (IID)
TIS	Telemetry Input System
TIS	Telephone Information Services [Commercial firm] [British]
TIS	Temperature Indicating Switch
TIS	Terminal Interface Subsystem [Telecommunications] (TEL)
TIS	Termination Inventory Schedule (SAA)
TIS	Tern Island Station (SAA)
TIS	Terrain Information System
TIS	Tesis [Russian Federation] [ICAO designator] (FAAC)
TIS	Test Information Sheet (MCD)
TIS	Test Instrumentation System
TIS	Test Interface Subsystem (NASA)
TIS	Test Interface Summary (MCD)
TIS	Test Item Simulator [Fort Huachuca, AZ] [United States Army Electronic Proving Ground] (GRD)
TIS	Tetracycline-Induced Steatosis [Medicine]
TIS	Tetrahydroisoquinoline Sulfonamide [A drug]
TIS	Theater Intelligence Section [Navy]
TIS	The Information System (NITA)
TIS	Thermal Imaging Scanner
TIS	Thermal Imaging Sight [Artillery] [Army] (INF)
TIS	Thermal Insulation System
TIS	Thursday Island [Australia Airport symbol] (OAG)
TIS	Timber Industry Strategy [Victoria, Australia]
TIS	Time in Service [Military] (DOMA)
TIS	Time Resources Corp. [Vancouver Stock Exchange symbol]
TIS	TIS Mortgage Investment Co. [NYSE symbol] (CTT)
TIS	TIS Mortgage Investors Co. [Associated Press] (SAG)
TIS	TIS Mtge Investment [NYSE symbol] (TTSB)
TIS	Tissue (ADA)
tis	Tissue (VRA)
TIS	Tobacco Inspection Service [Philippines]
TIS	Tool Induced Shift (AAEL)
TIS	Total Information System [Computer science]
TIS	Tracking and Injection Station
TIS	Tracking Instrumentation Subsystem (MCD)
TIS	Track Initiation Supervisor (SAA)
TIS	Trade Information Service [ESCAP] [United Nations] (DUND)
TIS	Trading Information System [AutEx Systems] [Information service or system] (CRD)
TIS	Traffic Information System
TIS	Transaction Information Systems
TIS	Transdermal Infusion System (STED)
TIS	Transit Injection Station (IAA)
TIS	Transponder Interrogation SONAR
TIS	Travelers Information Service [Oracle Corp.] [Information service or system] (IID)
TIS	Travel Information Service (EA)
TIS	Travel to Interview Scheme (AIE)

TIS...............	Triskaidekaphobia Illuminatus Society (EA)
TIS...............	Trusted Information Systems [Commercial firm]
TIS...............	Trypsin-Insoluble Segment [Cytochemistry]
TIS...............	Tumor in Situ [Oncology]
TIS...............	Two-Impinging-Stream Reactor [Chemical engineering]
TISA............	Technical Information Support Activities [Army]
TISA............	Technique for Interactive Systems Analysis (NVT)
TISA............	Top Image Systems Ltd. [NASDAQ symbol] (SAG)
TISA............	Troop Issue Subsistence Activity [Military] (AABC)
TISA............	Troop Issue Support Agency (MCD)
TISAB..........	Total Ionic Strength Adjustment Buffer (PDAA)
TISAL..........	Tactical Instrument Steep Approach and Landing System (MCD)
TISAP..........	Technical Information Support Activities Project [Army] (DIT)
TISAP..........	Totalized Interface Subroutine and Post Processor [Computer science] (BUR)
TISC............	Technology Integration Steering Committee [Army] (RDA)
TISC............	Textile Industry Support Campaign [British] (DBA)
TISC............	Timed Induction with Supercharge [Automotive engineering]
TISC............	Tire Industry Safety Council (EA)
TISC............	Treasury Inter-Services Committee [British military] (DMA)
TISCA..........	Technical Information System for Carrier Aviation [Navy] (MCD)
TISCO..........	Tata Iron and Steel Co. (ECON)
TISE............	Take It Somewhere Else [The Solid Waste Syndrome] (GNE)
TISE............	Technical Information Service (IAA)
TISE............	Technical Information Service Extension (SAA)
TISEA..........	Tasmanian Institute of Senior Educational Administrators [Australia]
TISEO..........	Target Identification System, Electro-Optical [Air Force]
TISHX..........	Flag Investors Communications Cl.A [Mutual fund ticker symbol] (SG)
TISK............	Thailand Informations und Solidaritaetskomitee [Germany]
TISL............	Telecommunications and Information Systems Laboratory [University of Kansas] [Research center] (RCD)
TISL............	Thomson Information Services Ltd. [The Thomson Corp.] [Publishing]
TISN............	Todai International Science Network
TISO............	Threat Integrated Staff Officer [Army]
TISO............	TRADOC [Training and Doctrine Command] Integration Staff Officer [Army]
TISO............	Troop Issue Subsistence Officer [Military] (AABC)
TISP............	Technical Information Support Personnel [Department of Labor]
TISP............	Thickness-Insensitive Solar Paint [Coating technology]
TISP............	Total Immunoreactive Serum Pepsinogen (STED)
TISPOC........	Trent Institute for the Study of Popular Culture [Trent University] [Canada Research center] (RCD)
TISq............	Tactical Intelligence Squadron [Air Force]
TIS-RET	Thermal Imaging System - Reticle
TISS............	Tactical Intermediate Support System [Military] (MCD)
TISS............	Therapeutic Intervention Scoring System (MEDA)
TISS............	Thermal Imaging Sensor System
TISS............	Trans-Ionospheric Sensing System (DWOO)
TISS............	Troop Issue Support System [Army]
TISSG..........	Travel Industry Systems Standards Group [British]
TIST............	St. Thomas/Harry S. Truman [Virgin Islands] [ICAO location identifier] (ICLI)
TISTHR........	Tool Inspection Small Tools Historical Record (MCD)
TISU............	Trade Information Supply Unit [ITC] [United Nations] (DUND)
TISWAS	Today is Saturday-Wear a Smile (WDAA)
TISX............	St. Croix/Alexander Hamilton [Virgin Islands] [ICAO location identifier] (ICLI)
TISX............	Trusted Information Systems, Inc. [NASDAQ symbol] (SAG)
Tit..............	Divus Titus [of Suetonius] [Classical studies] (OCD)
TIT..............	Technician-in-Training (ADA)
TIT..............	Technology in Training [DoD]
TIT..............	Terminal Interface Table (MCD)
TIT..............	Ternary Digit (IAA)
TIT..............	Test Item Taker
TIT..............	Thermal Inactivation Time
TIT..............	Thermoisolation Technique
Tit..............	Titan [Record label]
Tit..............	Tithe (ILCA)
TIT..............	Title [Bibliography]
TIT..............	Titular (WDAA)
Tit..............	Titus [New Testament book]
Tit..............	Titus Andronicus [Shakespearean work]
TIT..............	Total Indication Time (MCD)
TIT..............	Total Insertion Time
TIT..............	Treponema Immobilization Test [Clinical chemistry]
TIT..............	Triiodothyronine [Endocrinology] (MAE)
TIT..............	Trouble Indicator Trunk [Telecommunications] (IAA)
TIT..............	Turbine Inlet Temperature
TIT..............	Turbine Interstage Temperature
TIT..............	Tustin Institute of Technology [California]
Tit A............	Titus Andronicus [Shakespearean work] (BARN)
TitalPh.........	Tital Pharmaceuticals, Inc. [Associated Press] (SAG)
TITAN..........	Teamster's International Terminal and Accounting Network (IAA)
TitanCp........	Titan Corp. [Associated Press] (SAG)
TitanEx	Titan Exploration, Inc. [Associated Press] (SAG)
TitanHld	Titan Holdings, Inc. [Associated Press] (SAG)
TitanMet	Titanium Metals Corp. [Associated Press] (SAG)
TitanW........	Titan Wheel International [Associated Press] (SAG)
TITC............	Toxic Substances Control Act Interagency Testing Committee [Environmental Protection Agency] (GFGA)
TITC............	Traction-Immune Track Circuits [Railway signals system] [British]
TITE............	Technologies and Innovations in Training Equipment
TITE............	TEWS [Tactical Electronic Warfare System] Intermediate Test Equipment [Military]
TITE............	Tijuana & Tecate Railway Co. [Later, TTR] [AAR code]
TITF............	Test Item Transmittal Form (IAA)
TITh............	Triiodothyronine [Also, T$_3$] [Endocrinology]
TITL............	Title
TitleWve	Title Wave Stores, Inc. [Associated Press] (SAG)
TITO............	Troops In, Troops Out
TITOS..........	Telivision Infrared Orbital Satellite [Instrument] (EERA)
TITPG..........	Taft Institute for Two-Party Government [Later, TTI] (EA)
titr..............	Titrate [Analytical chemistry]
TITTI............	Texas Instruments Transistor Transistor Logic (IAA)
TI/TTR..........	Target Illumination/Target Tracking RADAR (MCD)
TITUS..........	Textile Information Treatment Users' Service [French Textile Institute] [Bibliographic database] [Information service or system] (IID)
TIU..............	Tape Identification Unit
TIU..............	Target Indication Unit [Navy]
TIU..............	Technical Information Unit [Environmental Protection Agency] (AEPA)
TIU..............	Telecommunications International Union [Defunct] (EA)
TIU..............	Telephone Interface Unit [Telecommunications]
TIU..............	Terminal Interface Unit [Bell System]
TIU..............	Timaru [New Zealand] [Airport symbol] (OAG)
TIU..............	Time Isolation Unit
TIU..............	Toxicologically Insignificant Usage
TIU..............	Trigger Inverter Unit
TIU..............	Trustworthy Interface Unit [Telecommunications] (OSI)
TIU..............	Trypsin Inhibitory Unit [Food analysis]
TIUC............	Textile Information Users Council (EA)
TI UCL..........	Texas Instruments Universal Command Language (NITA)
TIUP............	Term Intrauterine Pregnancy (STED)
TIUS............	Truck Inventory and Use Survey [BTS] (TAG)
TIUV............	Total Intrauterine Volume [Gynecology]
TIV..............	Target Intensifier Vidicon
TIV..............	Thermactor Idle Vacuum [Automotive engineering]
TIV..............	Time in View
TIV..............	Tipula Iridescent Virus [Medicine] (DB)
TIV..............	Tivat [Former Yugoslavia] [Airport symbol] (OAG)
TIV..............	Tiverton [Municipal borough in England]
TIV..............	Tiverton Petroleums Ltd. [Toronto Stock Exchange symbol]
TIV..............	Tivoli Music Hall [London] (DSUE)
TIV..............	Total Indicator Variation (IAA)
TIVC............	Thoracic Inferior Vena Cava [Medicine] (MAE)
TIVICON........	Texas Instruments Vidicon (IAA)
Tivoli	Tivoli Industries, Inc. [Associated Press] (SAG)
TivoliSy	Tivoli Systems, Inc. [Associated Press] (SAG)
TIVS............	Thermally Initiated Venting System (MCD)
TIVS............	Tivoli Systems, Inc. [NASDAQ symbol] (SAG)
TIW..............	Tacoma [Washington] [Airport symbol] (AD)
TIW..............	Tacoma, WA [Location identifier FAA] (FAAL)
TIW..............	Tactical Intelligence Wing [Military]
TIW..............	Tamarind Institute Workshop [Graphic arts school] [New Mexico]
TIW..............	TEFLON-Insulated Wire
tiw	Three Times a Week [Pharmacology]
TIW..............	Today's Insurance Woman [National Association of Insurance Women (International)] [A publication]
TIW..............	Twice a Week [Pharmacy] (DAVI)
TIWE............	Tropical Instability Wave Experiment [Marine science] (OSRA)
TIWG	Terrorism Incident Working Group [Bureau of Diplomatic Security] [Department of State] (EGAO)
TIWG	Test Integration Working Group [Military] (GFGA)
tiwk............	Tree Times a Week [Medicine] (STED)
TIWP............	Toxicology Information Working Party (PDAA)
TIWSS	Theater Integrated Warfare Scenarios Study
TIX..............	Titusville [Florida] [Airport symbol] (AD)
TIX..............	Titusville, FL [Location identifier FAA] (FAAL)
TIX..............	Transfer on Index [Telecommunications] (IAA)
TIX..............	Triax Airlines Ltd. [Nigeria] [ICAO designator] (FAAC)
TIXA............	Thioxanthone [Organic chemistry]
TIXI............	Turret Integrated Xenon Illuminator
TIY..............	Tidjikja [Mauritania] [Airport symbol] (OAG)
TIY..............	Tir Systems Ltd. [Vancouver Stock Exchange symbol]
TIZ..............	Tari [Papua New Guinea] [Airport symbol] (OAG)
TIZ..............	Traffic Information Zone (DA)
TIZZY..........	Tinny and Buzzing [Sounds]
TJ	Cameroon [Aircraft nationality and registration mark] (FAAC)
TJ	East Germany [License plate code assigned to foreign diplomats in the US]
TJ	Oceanair [ICAO designator] (AD)
TJ	Tait's Justice of the Peace [A publication] (DLA)
TJ	Tajikistan [Internet country code]
TJ	Talk Jockey [Radio]
TJ	Talmud Jerushalmi (BJA)
TJ	Targum Jonathan (BJA)
TJ	Technical Journal (MCD)
TJ	Telephone Jack (DEN)
TJ	Temperature Junction (MCD)
TJ	Tendon Jerk [Neurology] (DAVI)
TJ	Terajoule [SI unit of energy]
TJ	Test Jack (DEN)
TJ	Thermal Junction (KSC)
TJ	Thomas Jefferson [US president, 1743-1826]
TJ	Tight Junction (STED)
TJ	Tijuana [Mexico]
TJ	Tomato Juice
TJ	Tommy John [Baseball pitcher]

TJ .... Trajectory (AABC)
TJ .... Trans-Jordan (BJA)
TJ .... Triceps Jerk
TJ .... Troell-Junet [Syndrome] [Genetics] (DAVI)
TJ .... Trunk Junctor [Telecommunications] (IAA)
TJ .... Turbojet
TJA .... Table Jellies Association (DBA)
TJA .... Tarija [Bolivia] [Airport symbol] (OAG)
TJA .... Trial Judge Advocate [Army]
TJA .... Turbojet Aircraft
TJaC .... Jackson State Community College, Jackson, TN [Library symbol] [Library of Congress] (LCLS)
TJADC .... Theater Joint Air Defense Command [Military] (AABC)
TJAETDS ..... Turbine and Jet Aircraft Engine Type Designation System
TJAG .... [The] Judge Advocate General [Army]
TJAGC .... [The] Judge Advocate General's Corps [Army]
TJaGH .... Jackson-Madison County General Hospital, Learning Center, Jackson, TN [Library symbol Library of Congress] (LCLS)
TJAGSA ...... [The] Judge Advocate General's School, Army
TJaL .... Lane College, Jackson, TN [Library symbol Library of Congress] (LCLS)
TJaLam .... Lambuth College, Jackson, TN [Library symbol Library of Congress] (LCLS)
TJaLaw .... Tennessee State Law Library, Jackson, TN [Library symbol Library of Congress] (LCLS)
TJAS .... Tom Jones Appreciation Society (EAIO)
TJaU .... Union University, Jackson, TN [Library symbol Library of Congress] (LCLS)
TJB .... Tijuana Brass [Musical group]
TJB .... Tilting Journal Bearing
TJB .... Time-Sharing Job Control Block [Computer science] (IBMDP)
TJB .... Trench Junction Box
TJBQ .... Aguadilla/Borinquen [Puerto Rico] [ICAO location identifier] (ICLI)
TJC .... [The] Jockey Club (EA)
TJC .... Targeted Jobs Credit [Tax credit]
TJC .... Temple Junior College [Texas]
TJC .... Thomas Jefferson Center (EA)
TJC .... Thornton Junior College [Illinois]
TJC .... Tower Jettison Command (SAA)
TJC .... Trajectory Chart
TJC .... Trinidad [Colorado] [Seismograph station code, US Geological Survey] (SEIS)
TJC .... Tyler Junior College [Texas]
TJC .... Vanderbilt University Library, Nashville, TN [OCLC symbol] (OCLC)
TJCCAA ...... Tennessee Junior and Community College Athletic Association (PSS)
TJCDR .... Temporary Joint Committee on Deficit Reduction
TJCG .... Vieques/Camp Garcia Airstrip [Puerto Rico] [ICAO location identifier] (ICLI)
TJCI .... Paramark Enterprises, Inc. [NASDAQ symbol] (SAG)
TJCI .... T.J. Cinnamons [NASDAQ symbol] (TTSB)
TJCI .... TJ Cinnamons, Inc. [NASDAQ symbol] (SAG)
TJ Cinn .... TJ Cinnamons, Inc. [Associated Press] (SAG)
TJCIW .... T J Cinnamons Wrrt'A' [NASDAQ symbol] (TTSB)
TJCIZ .... T J Cinnamons Wrrt'B' [NASDAQ symbol] (TTSB)
TJ Cn .... TJ Cinnamons, Inc. [Associated Press] (SAG)
TJCO .... T J International [NASDAQ symbol] (TTSB)
TJCO .... TJ International, Inc. [NASDAQ symbol] (NQ)
TJCP .... Culebra [Puerto Rico] [ICAO location identifier] (ICLI)
TJD .... Trajectory Diagram
TJDP .... Targeted Jobs Demonstration Program (EDAC)
TJE .... Trojan Energy Corp. [Vancouver Stock Exchange symbol]
TJE .... Turbojet Engine
TJEDS .... Trainer Jet Exhaust Decontamination System
TJefC .... Carson-Newman College, Jefferson City, TN [Library symbol Library of Congress] (LCLS)
TJETS .... Thomas Jefferson Equal Tax Society (EA)
TJF .... Test Jack Field [Telecommunications] (IAA)
TJF .... Time-to-Jitter Flag
TJFA .... Fajardo [Puerto Rico] [ICAO location identifier] (ICLI)
TJFC .... [The] Johnsons Fan Club (EA)
TJFC .... Tex Jones Fan Club [Defunct] (EA)
TJFC .... Tom Jones Fan Club (EA)
TJFC .... Tomy Jennings Fan Club (EA)
TJFF .... Ramey [Puerto Rico] [ICAO location identifier] (ICLI)
TJFF .... Trans-Jordan Frontier Force [British military] (DMA)
TJFS .... T. J.'s [Tom Jones'] Fans of Soul (EA)
TJG .... Tom Jones Gadabouts (EA)
TJG .... Travel Journalists Guild (EA)
TJGTOI .... [The] Judge GTO International (EA)
TJI .... Tex Johnston, Inc.
TJI .... Trujillo [Honduras] [Airport symbol] (AD)
TJI .... Trus-Joist I-Beam
TJID .... Terminal Job Identification (BUR)
TJIG .... San Juan/Isla Grande [Puerto Rico] [ICAO location identifier] (ICLI)
TJ Intl .... TJ International, Inc. [Associated Press] (SAG)
TJISRF .... Thomas Jefferson Institute for the Study of Religious Freedom (EA)
TJK .... Tajikair [Tajikistan] [ICAO designator] (FAAC)
TJM .... Tower Jettison Motor
TJM .... Vanderbilt Medical Center, Nashville, TN [OCLC symbol] (OCLC)
TJMZ .... Mayaguez [Puerto Rico] [ICAO location identifier] (ICLI)
TJN .... Twin Jet Nebulizer [Pharmacology] (DAVI)
TJNR .... Roosevelt Roads Naval Air Station [Puerto Rico] [ICAO location identifier] (ICLI)
T Jo .... T. Jones' English King's Bench Reports [84 English Reprint] [A publication] (DLA)

TJOC .... Theater Joint Operations Center [Military]
TJoE .... Emmanuel School of Religion, Johnson City, TN [Library symbol Library of Congress] (LCLS)
TJoMC .... Johnson City Medical Center Hospital, Learning Resources Center, Johnson City, TN [Library symbol Library of Congress] (LCLS)
T Jones .... T. Jones' English King's Bench Reports [84 English Reprint] [A publication] (DLA)
T Jones (Eng)... T. Jones' English King's Bench Reports [84 English Reprint] [A publication] (DLA)
TJoS .... East Tennessee State University, Johnson City, TN [Library symbol Library of Congress] (LCLS)
TJoS-M .... East Tennessee State University, Medical Library, Johnson City, TN [Library symbol Library of Congress] (LCLS)
TJoV .... United States Veterans Administration Center, Johnson City, TN [Library symbol Library of Congress] (LCLS)
TJP .... Tactical Jamming Pod [Military] (CAAL)
TJP .... Turbojet Propulsion
TJPOI .... Twisted Jute Packing and Oakum Institute [Defunct] (EA)
TJPS .... Ponce/Mercedita [Puerto Rico] [ICAO location identifier] (ICLI)
TJQ .... Tanjung Pandan [Indonesia] [Airport symbol] (OAG)
TJQ .... Treasury of Jewish Quotations [A publication]
TJR .... Tactical Jammer [Military] (CAAL)
TJR .... Tajee Resources Ltd. [Vancouver Stock Exchange symbol]
TJR .... Total Joint Replacement [Orthopedics] (DAVI)
TJR .... Trunk and Junction Routing [Telecommunications] (TEL)
TJRC .... Thomas Jefferson Research Center [Later, TJC] (EA)
TJS .... Tactical Jamming System
TJS .... Target Jamming System
TJS .... Tenajon Resources Corp. [Formerly, Tenajon Silver] [Vancouver Stock Exchange symbol]
TJS .... Terminal Jamming System
TJS .... Transverse Junction Stripe (MCD)
TJSF .... Temperature Jump-Stopped Flow [Spectroscopy]
TJSJ .... San Juan/Puerto Rico International [Puerto Rico] [ICAO location identifier] (ICLI)
TJ Sys .... TJ Systems Corp. [Associated Press] (SAG)
TJT .... Tactical Jamming Transmitter [Navy]
TJT .... TJT, Inc. [Associated Press] (SAG)
TJT .... Tough Jeans Territory [Sears, Roebuck & Co. advertising slogan]
TJT .... Tri-Junction Transistor (IAA)
TJTA .... Taylor-Johnson Temperament Analysis [Psychology]
TJTC .... Targeted Jobs Tax Credits [Federal program]
TJTCC .... Targeted Jobs Tax Credit Coalition (EA)
TJTTFC .... Tom Jones "Tom Terrific" Fan Club (EA)
Tju .... Tjuringa: an Australasian Benedictine Review [A publication] (APTA)
TJVQ .... Vieques [Puerto Rico] [ICAO location identifier] (ICLI)
TJW .... North Haven, ME [Location identifier FAA] (FAAL)
TJX .... T.J. Maxx Stores (EFIS)
TJX .... TJX Companies [NYSE symbol] (SPSG)
TJX .... TJX Companies [Associated Press] (SAG)
TJXPrC .... TJX Co's $3.125 cm Cv'C'Pfd [NYSE symbol] (TTSB)
TJY .... Tulsa, OK [Location identifier FAA] (FAAL)
TJZS .... San Juan [Puerto Rico] [ICAO location identifier] (ICLI)
Tk .... Milli Kutuphane [National Library], Ankara, Turkey [Library symbol Library of Congress] (LCLS)
TK .... Taegu [South Korea] (ECON)
TK .... Talent-Keyhole [Satellite photography] [Military] (LAIN)
TK .... Tank (AAG)
TK .... Tanker
Tk .... T-Cell, Killer Type [Immunology]
TK .... Teekay Shipping [NYSE symbol] (TTSB)
TK .... Teekay Shipping Corp. [NYSE symbol] (SAG)
TK .... Thick (ROG)
TK .... Through Knee [Medicine]
TK .... Thymidine Kinase [An enzyme]
TK .... Tokelau Islands [ANSI two-letter standard code] (CNC)
TK .... Tokodynamometer [Obstetrics] (DAVI)
TK .... To Kum [i.e., To Come] [Publishing]
TK .... Tool Kits [JETDS nomenclature] [Military] (CET)
TK .... Torath Kohanim (BJA)
TK .... Track
TK .... Transducer Kit (MCD)
TK .... Transketolase [An enzyme]
TK .... Truck (AAG)
TK .... Trunk (IAA)
TK .... Trunk Equipment [Telecommunications] (TEL)
TK .... Turkey [IYRU nationality code]
TK .... Turk Hava Yollari [ICAO designator] (AD)
TK .... Turkish Airlines [Airline flight code] (ODBW)
TK .... Turner-Kieser [Syndrome] [Medicine] (DB)
TK .... Tuskegee R. R. [AAR code]
TK .... Tyrosine Kinase Domain [Genetics]
TKA .... Air Troika [Russian Federation] [ICAO designator] (FAAC)
TKA .... Talkeetna, AK [Location identifier FAA] (FAAL)
TKA .... Tanaka [New Britain] [Seismograph station code, US Geological Survey] (SEIS)
TKA .... Terminator Kit Assembly [Robot]
TKA .... Thermokinetic Analysis
TKA .... Throttle Kicker Actuator [Automotive engineering]
TKA .... Total Knee Arthroplasty [Medicine]
TKA .... Toy Knights of America (EA)
TKA .... Transketolase Activity [Medicine] (MAE)
TKAM .... Knoxville Academy of Medicine, Knoxville, TN [Library symbol Library of Congress] (LCLS)
TKB .... Kingsville, TX [Location identifier FAA] (FAAL)

TKB	Task Builder [*Computer science*] (MHDI)
TKBD	Tackboard [*Technical drawings*]
TKBN	Tank Battalion [*Marine Corps*]
TKC	Thiokol Corp. [*NYSE symbol*] (SPSG)
TKC	Tiko [*Cameroon*] [*Airport symbol*] (AD)
TKCS	Knoxville City School, Knoxville, TN [*Library symbol Library of Congress*] (LCLS)
TKD	Takada [*Japan*] [*Seismograph station code, US Geological Survey*] (SEIS)
TKD	Takoradi [*Ghana*] [*Airport symbol*] (AD)
TKD	Thymidine Kinase Deficiency [*Medicine*] (DMAA)
TKD	Tokodynamometer
TKD	Top Kit Drawing
TKDE	Tetrakis(dimethylamino)ethylene [*Organic chemistry*]
TkDtyr	Tank Destroyer [*Military*]
TKE	Tau Kappa Epsilon [*Fraternity*] [*Later, TEKE*]
TKE	Tenakee [*Alaska*] [*Airport symbol*] (OAG)
TKE	Tenakee Springs, AK [*Location identifier FAA*] (FAAL)
TKE	Total Kinetic Energy
TKE	Track Angle Error
TKE	Trek Airways [*South Africa ICAO designator*] (FAAC)
TKE	Turbulent Kinetic Energy
TKEBH	East Tennessee Baptist Hospital, Knoxville, TN [*Library symbol Library of Congress*] (LCLS)
TKECH	East Tennessee Children's Hospital, Pediatric Library, Knoxville, TN [*Library symbol*] [*Library of Congress*] (LCLS)
TKETHi	East Tennessee Historical Society, Knoxville, TN [*Library symbol Library of Congress*] (LCLS)
TKF	Turkish Investment Fund [*NYSE symbol*] (SPSG)
TKFGRS	Test of Kindergarten First Grade Readiness Skills [*K. Codding*] (TES)
TKFSM	Fort Sanders Regional Medical Center, Knoxville, TN [*Library symbol Library of Congress*] (LCLS)
TKG	Bandar Lampung [*Indonesia*] [*Airport symbol*] (OAG)
TKG	Capsule Technology Group, Inc. [*Toronto Stock Exchange symbol*]
TKG	Tanking (AAG)
TKG	Telukbetung [*Sumatra, Indonesia*] [*Airport symbol*] (AD)
TKG	Tokodynagraph
TKG	Tongkang [*Ship's rigging*] (ROG)
TKGA	[*The*] Knitting Guild of America (EA)
TKGS	Church of Jesus Christ of Latter-Day Saints, Genealogical Society Library, Knoxville Branch, Knoxville, TN [*Library symbol Library of Congress*] (LCLS)
TKH	Thick [*Aviation*] (DA)
TKH	Tikhaya Bay [*Later, HIS*] [*Former USSR Geomagnetic observatory code*]
TKi	Kingsport Public Library, Kingsport, TN [*Library symbol Library of Congress*] (LCLS)
TKI	McKinney, TX [*Location identifier FAA*] (FAAL)
TKI	Trial Kit Installation (CAAL)
TKI	Turks Islands [*West Indies*] [*Airport symbol*] (AD)
TKIBU	Transmission-Keying Indicator Buffer (DNAB)
TKIF	Training Name and Address Key Index File [*IRS*]
TKiH	Holston Valley Community Hospital, Health Science Library, Kingsport, TN [*Library symbol Library of Congress*] (LCLS)
TKImJ	Johnson Bible College, Knoxville, TN [*Library symbol Library of Congress*] (LCLS)
TKIO	[*The*] Tokio Marine & Fire Insurance Co. Ltd. [*NASDAQ symbol*] (NQ)
TKIOY	[*The*] Tokio Marine & Fire Insurance Co. (MHDW)
TKIOY	Tokio Marine/Fire ADR [*NASDAQ symbol*] (TTSB)
TKJ	Tok, AK [*Location identifier FAA*] (FAAL)
TKK	Token Kenkyu Kai [*Defunct*] (EA)
TKK	Toyo Kogyo Co. [*Auto manufacturer*]
TKK	Truk [*Caroline Islands*] [*Airport symbol*] (OAG)
TKKTFSLB	[*The*] Kandy-Kolored Tangerine-Flake Streamline Baby [*Title of book by Tom Wolfe*]
TKL	Knoxville-Knox County Public Library, Knoxville, TN [*OCLC symbol*] (OCLC)
TKL	Public Library of Knoxville and Knox County, Knoxville, TN [*Library symbol Library of Congress*] (LCLS)
TKL	Tackle [*Mechanical engineering*]
TKL	Tak [*Thailand*] [*Airport symbol*] (AD)
TKL	Taku Lodge, AK [*Location identifier FAA*] (FAAL)
TKL	Tanker Oil & Gas [*Vancouver Stock Exchange symbol*]
TKL	Tokelau Islands [*ANSI three-letter standard code*] (CNC)
TKLaw	Tennessee State Law Library, Knoxville, TN [*Library symbol Library of Congress*] (LCLS)
TKLC	TEKELEC [*Calabasas, CA*] [*NASDAQ symbol*] (NQ)
TKLI	Tachykinin-Like Immunoreactivity [*Laboratory science*] (DAVI)
TKLMI	Lakeshore Mental Health Institute, Staff Library, Knoxville, TN [*Library symbol Library of Congress*] (LCLS)
TKM	Merrill Lynch & Co. [*NYSE symbol*] (SAG)
TKM	Takamatsu [*Japan*] [*Seismograph station code, US Geological Survey*] (SEIS)
TKM	TRIS, Potassium Chloride, Magnesium Chloride [*A buffer*]
TKMT	Municipal Technical Advisory Service, Knoxville, TN [*Library symbol*] [*Library of Congress*] (LCLS)
TKN	Tek-Net International Ltd. (Canada) [*Vancouver Stock Exchange symbol*]
TKN	Thermotrex Corp. [*AMEX symbol*] (SPSG)
TKN	Tokuno Shima [*Japan*] [*Airport symbol*] (OAG)
TKN	Total Kjeldahl Nitrogen [*Organic analysis*]
TKN	University of Tennessee, Knoxville, TN [*OCLC symbol*] (OCLC)
TKNO	To Keep Needle Open [*Pharmacology*] (DAVI)
TKO	Mankato, KS [*Location identifier FAA*] (FAAL)
TKO	Taseko Mines Ltd. [*Vancouver Stock Exchange symbol*]
TKO	Technical Knockout [*Boxing*]
TKO	Technische Kontrollorganisation
TKO	To Keep Open [*Medicine*]
TKO	Trunk Offer [*Telecommunications*] (TEL)
TKO	Trunk Offering (NITA)
TKOC	Taseko Mines Ltd. [*NASDAQ symbol*] (SAG)
TKOCF	Taseko Mines [*NASDAQ symbol*] (TTSB)
TKOF	Takeoff [*Aviation*]
TKOS	Tokos Medical Corp. [*NASDAQ symbol*] (SAG)
TKP	[*The*] Knapp Press [*Book publisher*]
TKP	Takapoto Island [*French Polynesia*] [*Airport symbol*] (OAG)
TKP	Thermokeratoplasty [*Medicine*] (CPH)
TKP	Theta Kappa Phi [*Fraternity*]
TKP	Ton-Kilometer Performed
TKP	Toplumcu Kurtulus Partisi [*Communal Liberation Party*] [*Cyprus*] [*Political party*] (EY)
TKP	Trans Korea Pipeline
TKP	Turkiye Komunist Partisi
TKPH	Park West Hospital, Knoxville, TN [*Library symbol Library of Congress*] (LCLS)
TKPK	Basseterre/Golden Rock [*St. Kitts Island*] [*ICAO location identifier*] (ICLI)
TKP-ML	People's Revolutionary Union - Marxist-Leninist [*Turkey*] (PD)
TKPN	Charlestown/Newcastle [*Nevis Island*] [*ICAO location identifier*] (ICLI)
TKPP	Tetrapotassium Pyrophosphate [*Organic chemistry*] (DICI)
TKPS	Tuvalu and Kiribati Philatelic Society (EA)
TKPT	Pellissippi Stat Technical Community College, Knoxville, TN [*Library symbol*] [*Library of Congress*] (LCLS)
TKQ	Kigoma [*Tanzania*] [*Airport symbol*] (OAG)
TKR	Canadian Interagency Forest Fire Centre [*ICAO designator*] (FAAC)
TKR	Tanker (AAG)
TKR	Terrestrial Kilometric Radiation [*Physics*]
TKR	Thakurgaon [*Bangladesh*] [*Airport symbol*] (AD)
TKR	[*The*] Timken Co. [*Formerly, TDX*] [*NYSE symbol*] (SPSG)
TKR	Total Knee Replacement [*Medicine*]
tkr	Turkmen Soviet Socialist Republic [*MARC country of publication code Library of Congress*] (LCCP)
TKS	Knoxville City School, Knoxville, TN [*OCLC symbol*] (OCLC)
TKS	Tackstrip [*Technical drawings*]
TKS	Tamavack Resources, Inc. [*Vancouver Stock Exchange symbol*]
TKS	Thanks (ADA)
TKS	Throttle Kicker Solenoid [*Automotive engineering*]
TKS	Tokushima [*Japan*] [*Seismograph station code, US Geological Survey*] (SEIS)
TKS	Tokushima [*Japan*] [*Airport symbol*] (OAG)
TKS	Tokyo Kikai Seisakusho [*Japan*]
TKS	Tomkins PLC [*NYSE symbol*] (SAG)
TKS	Tomkins plc ADS [*NYSE symbol*] (TTSB)
TK-SC	Tennessee State Supreme Court Law Library, Knoxville, TN [*Library symbol Library of Congress Obsolete*] (LCLS)
TKSMC	Saint Mary's Medical Center, Medical Library, Knoxville, TN [*Library symbol Library of Congress*] (LCLS)
TKSMC-N	Saint Mary's Medical Center, Nursing School Library, Knoxville, TN [*Library symbol Library of Congress*] (LCLS)
TK SUP	Track Supervisor (CAAL)
TKT	Tashkent [*Former USSR Geomagnetic observatory code*]
TKT	Ticker Tape Resources Ltd. [*Vancouver Stock Exchange symbol*]
TKT	Ticket
TKT	Transkaryotic Therapies, Inc.
TKTF	Tanker Task Force
TKTM	Ticketmaster Group, Inc. [*NASDAQ symbol*] (SAG)
TKTN	Task Termination Notice [*Computer science*] (MHDB)
TKTRANSR	Tank Transporter [*Military*] (AABC)
TKTS	Thermodynamic Kelvin Temperature Scale
TKTU	Thymidine Kinase (Activity) Transforming Unit [*Biochemistry*]
TKTVA	Tennessee Valley Authority, Knoxville, TN [*Library symbol Library of Congress*] (LCLS)
TKTX	Transkaryotic Therapies, Inc. [*NASDAQ symbol*] (SAG)
TKU	Takayasuyama [*Japan*] [*Seismograph station code, US Geological Survey*] (SEIS)
TKU	Turku [*Finland*] [*Airport symbol*] (OAG)
TKV	Tatakoto [*French Polynesia*] [*Airport symbol*] (OAG)
TKW	Thermal Kilowatts
TKWC	Whittle Communications Corp., Knoxville, TN [*Library symbol*] [*Library of Congress*] (LCLS)
TKX	Kennett, MO [*Location identifier FAA*] (FAAL)
TKY	Takayama [*Japan*] [*Seismograph station code, US Geological Survey*] (SEIS)
TKY	Turkey Creek [*Western Australia*] [*Airport symbol*] (AD)
TL	Central African Republic [*International civil aircraft marking*] (ODBW)
TL	Empresas Telex-Chile [*NYSE symbol*] (TTSB)
Tl	Lateral Touch Neuron [*of a leech*]
TL	Reports of the Witwatersrand High Court [*Transvaal, South Africa*] [*A publication*] (DLA)
TL	Skyport [*Airport symbol*]
TL	Tackline [*British naval signaling*]
T/L	Tactical Landing
TL	Tail Lamp [*Automotive engineering*]
TL	Tail-Lift [*of trucks and vans*] (DCTA)
T/L	Talk/Listen (NASA)
TL	Tank Lease (ADA)
TL	Tape Library (BUR)
TL	Target Language
TL	Target Loss (OA)

TL	Task Leader (NRCH)
T/L	Task List (KSC)
TL	Taxilane [FAA] (TAG)
TL	Team Leader (AABC)
TL	Technical Letter
TL	Technical Library
TL	Technical Limit
TL	Telegraphist-Lieutenant [Navy British]
TL	Telex Chile SA [NYSE symbol] (SAG)
TL	Temporal Lobe (DB)
T-L	Tennessee State Law Library, Nashville, TN [Library symbol Library of Congress] (LCLS)
TL	Terminal Limen
TL	Terminology Library [Computer science] (IAA)
TL	Terra Lliure [Free Land] [Spanish terrorist group]
TL	Test Laboratory (AFM)
TL	Test Link
TL	Test Load
TL	Test Log (IEEE)
TL	Testolactone [Biochemistry]
TL	Texas League [Baseball]
Tl	Thallium [Chemical element]
TL	Therapeutic Level [Medicine]
TL	Thermal Liquefaction [Chemical engineering]
TL	Thermoluminescence [Also, THL]
TL	Thoreau Lyceum (EA)
TL	Throws Left-Handed [Baseball]
TL	Thrust Level (NASA)
TL	Thrust Line
TL	Thymic Lymphoma [Medicine]
T-L	Thymus-Dependent Lymphocyte [Hematology] (DAVI)
TL	Thymus-Derived Lymphocyte [Hematology]
TL	Thymus Leukemia [Hematology]
TL	Ticket of Leave (ADA)
TL	Tie Line [Communication channel]
TL	Time Lapse (MAE)
TL	Time Latest (NASA)
TL	Time Lengths
T-L	Time-Life Books [Publisher]
TL	Time Limit
TL	Time Line
TL	Timeline (NAKS)
T/L	Time Loan [Banking]
T/L	Time/Loss Analysis (COE)
TL	Time of Landing
TL	Time to Launch [Navy] (CAAL)
TL	Title List
tl	Tokelau Islands [MARC country of publication code Library of Congress] (LCCP)
TL	Ton Load
TL	Tool Life
TL	Tool List
TL	Tools [JETDS nomenclature] [Military] (CET)
TL	Torpedo Lieutenant [Navy British]
TL	Torus Longitudinalis [Anatomy]
TL	Total
TL	Total Body Length [Of Crustacea]
TL	Total Length
TL	Total Lipids [Clinical chemistry]
TL	Total Load [Engineering]
TL	Total Loss [Insurance]
tl	Total Loss [Insurance] (ODBW)
TL	Total Luminescence [Spectroscopy]
TL	Tower of London
TL	Tracker Lock [NASA] (KSC)
TL	Trade-Last
TL	Trade List (IIA)
tl	Trade List (ODBW)
TL	Trading Limit
TL	Trailer Length [Specifications] [Automotive engineering]
T/L	Training Literature
TL	Transaction Language
TL	Transaction Listing (AFM)
TL	Transfer Line [Manufacturing]
TL	Transformation Line [Telecommunications] (IAA)
T/L	Transformer Load (NASA)
TL	Transforming Lens
TL	Transient Load (MCD)
TL	Transistor Logic (IAA)
TL	Transition Level (DA)
TL	Translocation Defect [Medicine]
TL	Trans Mediterranean [ICAO designator] (AD)
TL	Transmission Level [or Line]
TL	Transmission Line [Telecommunications] (IAA)
TL	Transmission Loss [Telecommunications] (IAA)
TL	Transmittal Letter (AAG)
TL	Transmitter Location
T/L	Transporter/Launcher [NASA] (KSC)
T/L	Transporter/Loader (MCD)
T/L	TraveLodge International, Inc. (EFIS)
TL	Trial
TL	Triboluminescence [Atomic physics]
TL	Triple-Layer [Pharmacy]
TL	Triple Lindy [Dance step]
TL	Truckload [24,000 pounds or more]
TL	Truck Lock [Nuclear energy] (NRCH)
TL	Trunk Load [Telecommunications] (IAA)
TL	Tubal Ligation [Medicine]
TL	Turkish Lira (BJA)
TL	Turntable Ladder
TL	Twin Lens [Photography] (DGA)
TL2	Taxonomic Literature, edition 2 [Index] (EERA)
TL50	Median Tolerance Limit (GNE)
TLA	Talker Listener Adapter (NITA)
TLA	Tatlar Resources Ltd. [Vancouver Stock Exchange symbol]
TLA	TELEX Line Adapter (IAA)
TLA	Teller [Alaska] [Airport symbol] (OAG)
TLA	Teller, AK [Location identifier FAA] (FAAL)
TLA	Temporary Lodging Allowance [Military]
TLA	Terminal Low Altitude
TLA	Textile Labor Association [India]
TLA	Theatre Library Association (EA)
TLA	Thin-Layer Activation [Engine wear testing]
TLA	Thin Line Array (MUSM)
TLA	Three-Letter Acronym [Computer hacker terminology] (NHD)
TLA	Throttle Lever Angle (MCD)
TLA	Time Line Analysis
TLA	Toy Libraries Association [British]
TLA	Transaction Log Analysis
TLa	Transition Layer
TLA	Translift Airways Ltd. [British ICAO designator] (FAAC)
TLA	Translumbar Aortogram [Medicine]
TLA	Transluminal Angioplasty [Cardiology] (DAVI)
TLA	Transmission Line Adapter [or Assembly]
TLA	Transportation Lawyers Association (EA)
TLA	Travel and Living Allowance [Military] (AABC)
TLA	Trunk Line Association
TLAA	T-Lymphocyte-Associated Antigen [Hematology] (DAVI)
TLAB	Tellabs, Inc. [NASDAQ symbol] (NQ)
TLAB	Translation Lookaside Buffer [Computer science] (CMD)
TLABX	DW TCW/DW Latin America Growth Cl.B [Mutual fund ticker symbol] (SG)
TLAC	Test Listening Accuracy in Children [Educational test]
TLAC	Top Loading Air Cleaner (MCD)
TLACV	Track-Laying Air-Cushion Vehicle
TLAM	Tomahawk Land Attack Missile (MCD)
TLAM/C	Tomahawk Land Attack Missile/Conventional [Navy] (ANA)
TLAM-N	Tomahawk Land Attack Missile - Nuclear (MCD)
T-LAR	That Looks about Right [Aviation]
TLAS	Tactical Logical and Air Simulation
TLAT	TOW [Tube-Launched, Optically Tracked, Wire-Guided (Weapon)] Light Antitank Battalion (MCD)
T Lawyr	Tax Lawyer [A publication] (ILCA)
TLAY	Tule Lake Aster Yellows [Plant pathology]
TLB	Table Lookaside Buffer [Computer science] (MHDB)
TLB	Talbots, Inc. [NYSE symbol] (SPSG)
TLB	Temporary Lighted Buoy [Maps and charts]
TLB	Texas-Louisiana Freight Bureau, St. Louis MO [STAC]
TLB	The Living Bank [An association] (EA)
TLB	Time-Life Books
TLB	Tortola [British Virgin Islands] [Airport symbol] (AD)
TLB	Tractor/Loader/Backhoe
TLB	Trailer Launch Bridge (DWSG)
TLB	Translation Lookaside Buffer [Computer science] (BUR)
TLBAA	Texas Longhorn Breeders Association of America (EA)
TL/BBC	Tax Limitation/Balanced Budget Coalition [Defunct] (EA)
TLBID	TLB [Translation - Lookaside - Buffers] Identifier
TLBR	Tactical LASER Beam Recorder (MCD)
TLC	Caribbean Express, Inc. [ICAO designator] (FAAC)
TLC	[The] Learning Channel [Cable-television system]
TLC	Lee College, Cleveland, TN [OCLC symbol] (OCLC)
TLC	Maximum Recoil Pressure [Medicine] (DAVI)
TLC	Tactical Leadership Course [Army] (INF)
TLC	Tangent Latitude Computer
TLC	Tank Landing Craft [Army British]
TLC	Task Level Controller
TLC	Teachable Language Comprehender (PDAA)
TLC	Teaching, Learning and Curriculum Model (EDAC)
TLC	Technology Life Cycle (NITA)
TLC	Telecommand (NASA)
TLC	Tele-Link, Inc. [Miami, FL] [Telecommunications service] (TSSD)
TLC	Teletype, Line Printer, Card Reader Controller (NOAA)
TLC	Television Licensing Center [Defunct] (EA)
TLC	Temperature Level Control (IAA)
TLC	Tender Loving Care
TLC	Test of Language Competence [Educational test]
TLC	Texaco Lubricants Co. [Automotive industry supplier]
TLC	Texas Lutheran College
TLC	Textile Laundry Council (EA)
TLC	The Learning Co.
TLC	The Library Corp.
TLC	Thermochromic Liquid Crystal
TLC	Thin-Layer Chromatography [Analytical chemistry]
TLC	Tillicum Industry [Vancouver Stock Exchange symbol]
TLC	Time-Lapse Cinematography
TLC	Time Line Controller
TLC	T-Lymphocyte Clones [Immunology]
TLC	Tom's Love Connection (EA)
TLC	Total L-Chain Concentration
TLC	Total Library Computerization

TLC	Total Light Chain Concentration [*Immunology*] (DAVI)
TLC	Total Load Control (MCD)
TLC	Total Lung Capacity [*Physiology*]
TLC	Total Lung Compliance [*Medicine*]
TLC	Total Lymphocyte Count [*Clinical chemistry*]
TLC	Touch and Learn Computer
TLC	Touch Logic Controlled [*Electronics*]
TLC	Traditional Life Cycle (PDAA)
TLC	Traffic Load Control (COE)
TLC	Transferable Loan Certificate
TLC	Transient Late Curvature [*Orthopedics*]
TLC	Translunar Coast [*Aerospace*]
TLC	Transmit Level Control (PDAA)
TLC	Tri-County Library Council, Inc. [*Library network*]
TLC	Trilateral Commission [*International study group*]
TLC	Troubles/Requests Logging and Coordination [*Staff*] [*Computer science*]
TLC	Type and Learn Concept [*Minolta Corp. office system*]
TLCA	Tangent Latitude Computer Amplifier
TLCACT	Trades and Labour Council of the Australian Capital Territory
TLC BOL/MXFree...	Trade Agreement Between the Republic of Bolivia and the United States of Mexico
TLCC	Thin-Line Communications Connectivity
TLC(C)	Trades and Labour Congress of Canada [*1883-1956*]
TLCC	Training Launch Control Center (IAA)
TLC CA/CHIFree...	Trade Agreement Between the Republic of Chile and Canada
TLCCP	Total Life Cycle Competition Plan [*Army*]
TLC CR/MXFree...	Trade Agreement Between the Republic of Costa Rica and the United States of Mexico
TLCCS	Total Life Cycle Competition Strategy [*Army*]
TLCE	Transmission Line Conditioning Equipment (MCD)
TLCF	Tactical Link Control Facility [*Military*] (CAAL)
TLCF	Teleconference (COE)
TLCI	Tea Leaf Club International (EA)
TLC/IR	Thin-Layer Chromatography/Infrared [*Analytical chemistry*]
TLCK	Tosyllysine Chloromethyl Ketone [*Biochemistry*]
T-LCL	T-Cell Lymphosarcoma Cell Leukemia [*Oncology*]
TlCl	Thallium Chloride [*A radioactive isotope*] (DAVI)
TLCM	TelCom Semiconductor, Inc. [*NASDAQ symbol*] (SAG)
TLCM	TelCom Seminconductor [*NASDAQ symbol*] (TTSB)
TlcmArg	Telecom Argentina Stet France Telecom SA [*Associated Press*] (SAG)
TLCPC	Trunk Line-Central Passenger Committee
TLCQ	Trades and Labour Council of Queensland [*Australia*]
TLCSC	Top Level Computer Software Component
TLCT	Total Life Cycle Time
TL-CTR	Trunk Line-Central Territory Railroad Tariff Bureau
TLCV	Tobacco Leaf Curl Virus [*Plant pathology*]
TLCWA	Trades and Labour Council of Western Australia
TLD	Technical Logistics Data [*Army*] (AABC)
TLD	Tele Danmark A/S ADS [*NYSE symbol*] (TTSB)
TLD	Tele Danmark Co. [*NYSE symbol*] (SAG)
TLD	Telephone Line Doubler (IAA)
TLD	Thermoluminescent Device
TLD	Thermoluminescent Dosimeter [*or Dosimetry*]
TLD	Thoracic Lymph Duct [*Medicine*] (MAE)
TLD	Tiled [*Classified advertising*] (ADA)
tld	Tooled (BARN)
TLD	Top-Level Demonstration [*Military*] (INF)
TLD	Top-Level Domain [*Internet Name*]
TLD	Traffic Loading Device (CAAL)
TLD	Tumor Lethal Dose [*Medicine*] (MAE)
T/LD₁₀₀	Minimum Dose Causing Malformation or Death of 100 Percent of Fetuses [*Radiation therapy*] (DAVI)
TLDB	Transportation Legislative Data Base [*Battelle Memorial Institute*] [*Department of Energy Information service or system*] (IID)
TLDC	Taiwan Land Development Corp.
TLDC	Teledata Communications [*NASDAQ symbol*] (SAG)
TLDCF	Teledata Communication [*NASDAQ symbol*] (TTSB)
TLDF	Thomas Legal Defense Fund (EA)
TLDI	Technical Logistics Data and Information [*Army*] (AABC)
TLDIP	Technical Logistics Data Information Program
TLDP	Technical Logistics Data Program [*Navy*] (DNAB)
TLE	Air Toulouse [*France ICAO designator*] (FAAC)
TLE	[*The*] Learning Exchange [*Defunct*] (EA)
TLE	Target Location Error [*Military*] (AABC)
TLE	Technical Liaison Engineer
TLE	Temperature-Limited Emission
TLE	Template Language Extension [*Computer science*]
TLE	Temporal Lobe Epilepsy [*Medicine*]
TLE	Temporary Living Expenses
TLE	Temporary Lodging Entitlement (DOMA)
TLE	Temporary Lodging Expense [*DoD*]
TLE	Test Laboratory Engineer (IAA)
TLE	Theoretical Line of Escape (WDAA)
TLE	Thin-Layer Electrophoresis [*Analytical chemistry*]
TLE	Thin Leading Edge
TLE	Time-Life Education
TLE	Tool Loading Elevator (AAEL)
TLE	Total Erickson Resources Ltd. [*Toronto Stock Exchange symbol Vancouver Stock Exchange symbol*]
TLE	Total Lipid Extract [*Biochemistry*]
TLE	Toward Liberal Education [*In book title*]
TLE	Tower Lighting Equipment
TLE	Tracking Light Electronics (KSC)

TLE	Traffic Law Enforcement
TLE	Transferline Heat Exchanger [*Chemical engineering*]
TLE	Treaty Limited Equipment (DOMA)
TLE	Tulear [*Madagascar*] [*Airport symbol*] (OAG)
TLebC	Cumberland College of Tennessee, Lebanon, TN [*Library symbol Library of Congress*] (LCLS)
TLEICS	Treasury Law Enforcement Information and Communications System
T-lens	Therapeutic Contact Lens [*Opthalomology*] (DAVI)
Tlepd	Telepad Corp. [*Associated Press*] (SAG)
TLET	Transitional Low-Emission Truck
TLEV	Transitional Low-Emission Vehicle
TLF	Leather Factory [*AMEX symbol*] (TTSB)
TLF	Leather Factory, Inc. [*AMEX symbol*] (SPSG)
TLF	Temporary Loading Facilities (MCD)
TLF	Temporary Lodging Facility
TLF	Terminal Launch Facility
TLF	Thrust Required for Level Flight [*Aviation*] (MCD)
TLF	Time Line Form
TLF	Trunk Link Frame [*Telecommunications*] (TEL)
TLF	Trypanosome Lytic Factor [*Biochemistry*]
TLF	Two-Level Fluctuation [*Physics*]
TLFB	Texas-Louisiana Freight Bureau
TLFC	Terri LaVelle Fan Club (EA)
TLFC	Traci Lords Fan Club [*Defunct*] (EA)
TLFE	Tasmanian Licensed Fruit Exporters [*Australia*]
TLFN	Tunison Laboratory of Fish Nutrition [*Cortland, NY*] [*Department of the Interior*] (GRD)
TLG	Consolidated Thompson-Lundmark Gold Mines Ltd. [*Toronto Stock Exchange symbol*]
TLG	Tail Landing Gear
TLG	Talgar [*Also, AAB*] [*Alma-Ata*] [*Former USSR Seismograph station code, US Geological Survey*] (SEIS)
TLG	Telegram (IAA)
TLG	Telegraph (AAG)
TLG	Tentative Logistics Guidance (MCD)
TLG	Thin-Layer Gel [*Filtration*] [*Analytical chemistry*]
TLG	Tilting
TLG	Timing Level Generator (IAA)
TLG	Tres Lagoas [*Brazil*] [*Airport symbol*] (AD)
TLGB	Tube-Launched Guided Projectiles (MCD)
TLGD	Tollgrade Communications [*NASDAQ symbol*] (TTSB)
TLGN	Telegen Corp. [*NASDAQ symbol*] (SAG)
TLGZ	Telegraph Communications [*NASDAQ symbol*] (SAG)
TLGZF	Telegraph Communications Wrrt [*NASDAQ symbol*] (TTSB)
TLH	Tallahassee [*Florida*] [*Airport symbol*] (OAG)
TLH	Tulloch Resources [*Vancouver Stock Exchange symbol*]
TLHS	Thin Line Handling System (DWSG)
TLI	Tank Level Indicator (DNAB)
TLI	Telephone Line Interface (IEEE)
TLI	Term Life Insurance
TLI	Theoretical Lethality Index (MCD)
TLI	Thymidine-Labeling Index [*Oncology*]
TLI	Time-Life International
tli	Tlingit [*MARC language code Library of Congress*] (LCCP)
TLI	T-Logic, Inc. [*Information service or system*] (IID)
TLI	Tolitoli [*Indonesia*] [*Airport symbol*] (OAG)
TLI	Total Lymphoid Irradiation
TLI	Transferable Loan Instrument (MHDW)
TLI	Translunar Injection [*Aerospace*]
TLI	Transport Layer Interface [*Application program interface*] (TNIG)
TLI	Triangle Resources, Inc. [*Vancouver Stock Exchange symbol*]
TLI	Trinidad Light Infantry [*British military*] (DMA)
TLI	True Life Institute (EA)
TLIB	Tape Library [*National Center for Atmospheric Research*]
TLIB	Transportation Library [*National Academy of Sciences*] [*Information service or system*] (IID)
TLIC	Transport Holdings 'A' [*NASDAQ symbol*] (TTSB)
TLIC	Transport Holdings, Inc. [*NASDAQ symbol*] (SAG)
TLIEF	Thin-Layer Isoelectric Focusing [*Analytical chemistry*]
TLII	Trans Leasing International, Inc. [*Northbrook, IL*] [*NASDAQ symbol*] (NQ)
TLII	Trans Leasing Intl. [*NASDAQ symbol*] (TTSB)
TLIR	Time-Limited Impulse Response [*Telecommunications*] (IAA)
TLJ	Laredo Junior College, Laredo, TX [*OCLC symbol*] (OCLC)
TLJ	Tatalina [*Alaska*] [*Airport symbol*] (OAG)
TLJ	Tatalina, AK [*Location identifier FAA*] (FAAL)
TLJ	Travancore Law Journal [*India*] [*A publication*] (DLA)
TLJP	Thermal Liquid Junction Potential (PDAA)
TLK	Indonesian Telekomunikas [*NYSE symbol*] (SAG)
TLK	New York, NY [*Location identifier FAA*] (FAAL)
TLK	P.T. Telekomunikasi ADS [*NYSE symbol*] (TTSB)
TLK	Talkeetna Mountains [*Alaska*] [*Seismograph station code, US Geological Survey*] (SEIS)
TLK	Talking [*Telecommunications*] (TEL)
TLK	Test Link (IEEE)
TLK	University of Tennessee, Law Library, Knoxville, TN [*OCLC symbol*] (OCLC)
TLL	Tallinn [*Former USSR Airport symbol*] (OAG)
TLL	Tank Lighter
T-LL	T-Cell Lymphoblastic Lymphoma [*Oncology*]
TLL	Teachers' Labour League [*British*] (AIE)
TLL	Television LASER Link
TLL	Tender Load List
TLL	Threshold Lactose Load [*Clinical chemistry*]

TLL	Tololo Astronomical Observatory [*Chile*] [*Seismograph station code, US Geological Survey*] (SEIS)
TLL	Tom's Look of Love (EA)
TLL	Transporter, Loader, Launcher
TLLD	Total Load
TLLE	Twin Linear Loop Exciter (IAA)
TLLM	Temperature and Liquid Level Monitor [*Nuclear energy*] (NRCH)
TLLS	Tellus Industries, Inc. [*Sacramento, CA*] [*NASDAQ symbol*] (NQ)
TLLTD	Tre Lateral Load Transfer Distribution
TLLW	Tank Lighter (Medium Tank-Well Type)
TLM	Median Tolerance Limit (GNE)
TLM	Tape-Laying Machine (AAEL)
TLM	Technical Liaison Memo
TLM	Telemeter [*or Telemetry*] (AAG)
TLM	Thin Lipid Membrane (OA)
TLM	Tilimsen [*Algeria*] [*Airport symbol*] (OAG)
TLM	Toledo-Lucas County Public Library, Toledo, OH [*OCLC symbol*] (OCLC)
TLM	Tolmezzo [*Italy*] [*Seismograph station code, US Geological Survey*] (SEIS)
TLM	Transformer Load Management (IAA)
TLM	Transmission Line Method [*Photovoltaic energy systems*]
TLM	Transmitted Light Microscope
TLM	Trillium Telephone Systems, Inc. [*Toronto Stock Exchange symbol*]
TLM	Tube-Launched Missile (MCD)
TLMA	Tag and Label Manufacturers Association (DGA)
TLMA	Trial Lawyers Marketing Association (EA)
TLMA	Tunnel Lining Manufacturers Association [*British*] (DBA)
TLMB	Telemetry Data Buffer
TLMB	Tobacco Leaf Marketing Board [*Australia*]
TLMCTLPNL	Telemetry Control Panel (IAA)
TLMD	Telemundo Group 'A' [*NASDAQ symbol*] (TTSB)
TLMD	Telemundo Group, Inc. [*NASDAQ symbol*] (SAG)
TLMDW	Telemundo Group Wrrt [*NASDAQ symbol*] (TTSB)
TLMG	Telemetering (AAG)
TLMI	Tag and Label Manufacturers Institute (EA)
TLMIX	Hibernia La. Munic. Income [*Mutual fund ticker symbol*] (SG)
TLMO	Truncated Localized Molecular Orbital (DB)
TLMP	Tongass Land Management Plan (WPI)
TLMS	Tape Library Management System
TLMY	Telemetry (MSA)
TLN	Talang [*Sumatra*] [*Seismograph station code, US Geological Survey Closed*] (SEIS)
TLN	Tasmanian Law Newsletter [*A publication*]
TLN	Thermolysin [*An enzyme*]
TLN	Title plus Last Name
TLN	Torque-Limiting Nut
TLN	Toulon/Hyeres [*France*] [*Airport symbol*] (OAG)
TLN	Transmittal Locator Number [*Computer science*]
TLN	Trunk Line Network
TLO	Eagle Canyon Airlines, Inc. [*FAA designator*] (FAAC)
TLO	[*The*] Last One [*A microcomputer program manufactured by DJ-AI*]
TLO	[*The*] Lifestyles Organization (EA)
TLO	Technical Liaison Office [*Military*]
TLO	Terminal Learning Objective
TLO	Tol [*Papua New Guinea*] [*Airport symbol*] (OAG)
TLO	Toledo [*Spain*] [*Seismograph station code, US Geological Survey*] (SEIS)
TLO	Total Loss Only
tlo	Total Loss Only [*Insurance*] (ODBW)
TLO	Tracking Local Oscillator
TLO	Training Liaison Officer [*Ministry of Agriculture, Fisheries, and Food*] [*British*]
TLOBS	Tailored List of Base Spares [*Military*] (AFIT)
TLOF	Touchdown Lift-Off Surface [*OST*] (TAG)
TLOS	Tailored List of Spares [*Military*] (AFIT)
TLOS	Troop List for Operations and Supply
TLO(S)	Turbine Lube Oil (System) [*Nuclear energy*] (NRCH)
TLOST	Turbine Lube Oil Storage Tank [*Nuclear energy*] (NRCH)
TLP	Tabular List of Parts (AAG)
TLP	Tactical Leadership Program [*Military*]
T/LP	Tail Lamp [*Automotive engineering*]
TLP	Talpa [*New Mexico*] [*Airport symbol*] (AD)
TLP	Tapered Link Pin
TLP	Target Letter Position [*Psychology*]
TLP	Telegraph Line Pair (BUR)
TLP	Telephone Line Patch
TLP	Tension-Leg Platform [*Oil exploration*]
TLP	Term Lease Plan (IAA)
TLP	Term-Limit Pricing [*Agreement*] [*Price Commission*]
TLP	Therapeutic Learning Program [*Psychology*]
TLP	Threshold Learning Process (IEEE)
TLP	Top Load Pad (NRCH)
TLP	Top Load Plane [*Nuclear energy*] (NRCH)
TLP	Torpedo Landplane [*Navy*]
TLP	Total Language Processor [*Computer science*] (IEEE)
TLP	Total Liquid Product [*Chemical engineering*]
TLP	Total Loss of Pay [*Court-martial sentence*] [*Military*]
TLP	Transient Lunar Phenomena
TLP	Transmission Level Point [*Telecommunications*]
TLP	Tribal Liaison Program [*Bureau of the Census*] (GFGA)
TLP	Troop-Leading Procedure [*Military*] (INF)
TLP	Trouble Location Problem (AAG)
TLP	Truck Loading Point (NATG)
tlp	Tulip (VRA)
TLP	Tulip Air [*Netherlands ICAO designator*] (FAAC)
TLP&SC	Transportation Loss Claim and Security Council of the American Trucking Associations (NTPA)
TLPC	Castries/Vigie [*St. Lucia*] [*ICAO location identifier*] (ICLI)
TLPC	Tailpiece
TLPJ	Trial Lawyers for Public Justice (EA)
TLPL	Vieux-Fort/Hewanorra International [*St. Lucia*] [*ICAO location identifier*] (ICLI)
TLPR	Terrestrial Low-Power Reactor
TLPWD	Tory Legacy Plus World Depression [*British*] (DI)
TLQ	Temporary Lodging Quarters [*Military*] (DNAB)
TLQ	Tender Load Quantities (DNAB)
TLQ	Total Living Quotient (MAE)
TLR	Northern Airlines [*British ICAO designator*] (FAAC)
TLR	Tailor
TLR	Talgarno [*Western Australia*] [*Airport symbol*] (AD)
TLR	Tally Resources [*Vancouver Stock Exchange symbol*]
TLR	Tanganyika Law Reports [*1921-52*] [*A publication*] (DLA)
TLR	Tanzania Gazette Law Reports [*A publication*] (DLA)
TLR	Tape Loop Recorder
TLR	Teller
Tlr	Teller [*Banking*] (TBD)
TLR	Tiler [*Freemasonry*]
TLR	Tiller (MSA)
TLR	Times Law Reports [*1884-1952*] [*England*] [*A publication*] (DLA)
TLR	Toll Line Release
TLR	Tool Liaison Request (AAG)
TLR	Top Level Requirements [*Navy*]
TLR	Topped Long Resid [*Petroleum technology*]
TLR	Trailer (AAG)
TLR	Travancore Law Reports [*India*] [*A publication*] (DLA)
TLR	Triangulation-Listening-Ranging [*SONAR*]
TLR	Tulare, CA [*Location identifier FAA*] (FAAL)
TLR	Twin Lens Reflex [*Camera*] (MCD)
TLRB	Textile Labor Relations Board [*Terminated, 1937; functions absorbed by US Conciliation Service, Department of Labor*]
TLRC	Canadian Association of Toy Libraries and Parent Resource Centers (EAIO)
TLRC	Technology and Livelihood Resource Center [*Philippines*] [*Information service or system*] (IID)
TLRG	Tailoring
TLRG	Target List Review Group (CINC)
TLRMTD	Trailer Mounted
TLRN	Tellurian, Inc. [*NASDAQ symbol*] (SAG)
TLRNC	Tolerance (FAAC)
TLRP	Trace Last Reference Position (IAA)
TLRP	Track Last Reference Position
TLR (R)	Tanganyika Law Reports (Revised) [*1921-52*] [*A publication*] (DLA)
TLR/S	Total Logistic Readiness/Sustainability Analysis [*Military*]
TLRS	Tramway and Light Railway Society [*British*] (BI)
TLRS	Transportable LASER Ranging Station [*for measurement of earth movement*]
TLRV	Tracked Levitated Research Vehicle
TLS	Laredo State University, Laredo, TX [*OCLC symbol*] (OCLC)
TLS	Tactical Landing System
TLS	Talasea [*New Britain*] [*Seismograph station code, US Geological Survey*] (SEIS)
TLS	Tank LASER Sight (MCD)
TLS	Tape Librarian System
TLS	Target Level of Safety (DA)
TLS	Target Location System
TLS	Teaching and Learning Support (AIE)
TLS	Technical Library Service (IID)
TLS	Tekniska Litteratursallskapet (NITA)
TLS	Telecommunication Liaison Staff (IEEE)
TLS	Telemetry Listing Submodule
TLS	Telepanel Systems [*Toronto Stock Exchange symbol*] (SPSG)
TLS	Telescope (KSC)
TLS	Terminal Landing System (KSC)
TLS	Territorial Long Service Medal [*Military British*]
TLS	Testing the Limits for Sex [*Psychology*]
TLS	Test Line Signal (IAA)
TLS	Theater Level Scenario [*Military*]
TLS	Thin Liquid Stillage [*Fermentation byproduct*]
TLS	Thoracolumbosacral [*Drain*] [*Surgery*] (DAVI)
TLS	Throttle Lever Setting (KSC)
TLS	Tifton Loamy Soil [*Agronomy*]
TLS	Time-Limited Signal
TLS	Time Line Sheet [*NASA*]
TLS	Time Literary Supplement [*A publication*] (WDAA)
TLS	Times Literary Supplement [*A publication*] (BRI)
TLS	TLC Air, Inc. [*ICAO designator*] (FAAC)
TLS	Top Left Side (MCD)
TLS	Top Level Specification [*Military*] (CAAL)
TLS	Total Library System [*OCLC*]
TLS	Total Logic Solution
TLS	Total Luminescence Spectroscopy
TLS	Toulouse [*France*] [*Airport symbol*] (OAG)
TLS	Training Launch Station (MCD)
TLS	Transcation Layer Security [*Computer science*] (IGQR)
TLS	Translocated in Liposarcoma [*Genetics*]
TLS	Transparent LAN [*Local Area Network*] Service (TNIG)
TLS	Tulsa [*Diocesan abbreviation*] [*Oklahoma*] (TOCD)
TLS	Two-Level System [*Physics*]
TLS	Typed Letter Signed

TLSA............	Torso Limb Suit Assembly (MCD)
TLSA............	Transparent Line Sharing Adapter
TLSC............	Target Logistics Support Costs
TLSCP..........	Telescope (MSA)
TLSD............	Torque-Limiting Screwdriver
TLSER..........	Theoretical Linear Solvation Energy Relationship [*Physical chemistry*]
TLSFT..........	Tailshaft
TLSG............	Turret Lathe Stop Gauge
TLSGT..........	Tactical Landing System Guidance Techniques (MCD)
TLSI.............	Telepanel Systems, Inc. [*NASDAQ symbol*] (SAG)
TLSIF...........	Telepanel Systems [*NASDAQ symbol*] (TTSB)
TLSO............	Thoracolumbosacral Orthosis [*Medicine*]
TLSP............	TeleSpectrum Worldwide, Inc. [*NASDAQ symbol*] (SAG)
TLSP............	Transponder Location by Surface Positioning [*RADAR*]
TLSS............	Tactical Life Support System [*G-suit developed by Boeing Co.*]
TLSS............	Technical Library Services Section
TLT	LeTourneau College, Longview, TX [*OCLC symbol*] (OCLC)
TLT	Telecommunications Translator (IAA)
TLT	Teleprinter Load Tables (KSC)
TLT	Telstar Resource Corp. [*Vancouver Stock Exchange symbol*]
TLT	Terminal List Table (IAA)
TLT	Toilet
TLT	Transportable Link Terminal [*AMC*]
TLT	Travancore Law Times [*India*] [*A publication*] (DLA)
TLT	Tryptophan Load Test (DB)
TLT	Tuluksak [*Alaska*] [*Airport symbol*] (OAG)
TLT	Tuluksak, AK [*Location identifier FAA*] (FAAL)
TLT	Turtle Airways Ltd. [*Fiji*] [*ICAO designator*] (FAAC)
TLTA............	Thin Line Towed Array [*Navy*] (CAAL)
TLTA............	Two-Loop Test Apparatus [*Nuclear energy*] (NRCH)
TLTB............	Trunk Line Tariff Bureau
TLTK............	Teletek, Inc. [*NASDAQ symbol*] (NQ)
TLTK............	Tool Truck
TLTM	Third Level Thermal Margin [*Nuclear energy*] (NRCH)
TLTN............	Teltrend, Inc. [*NASDAQ symbol*] (SAG)
TL to TL.......	Tangent Line to Tangent Line [*Engineering*]
TLTP............	Teaching and Learning Technology Programme [*British*] (TELE)
TLTP............	Teletype (IAA)
TLTP............	Too Long to Print (FAAC)
TLTP............	Trunk Line Test Panel [*Telecommunications*] (TEL)
TLTR............	Translator (AFM)
TLTS............	Tracking Loop Test Set
TLTV............	Total Loan-to-Value [*Real estate*] (EMRF)
TLTYP..........	Teletype
TLU.............	Table Look Up [*Computer science*]
TLU.............	Teaching-Learning Unit (AEE)
TLU.............	Terminal Logic Unit [*Telecommunications*] (TEL)
TLU.............	Threshold Logic Unit
TLU.............	Tight Little Unit [*Ski-bum slang*]
TLU.............	Time of Last Update
TLU.............	Tolu [*Colombia*] [*Airport symbol*] (OAG)
TLU.............	Transportable LASER Unit
TLU.............	Tropical Livestock Unit [*Ratio of livestock to humans*]
TLV.............	Talemon Investments Ltd. [*Vancouver Stock Exchange symbol*]
TLV.............	Target Launch Vehicle [*NASA*]
TLV.............	Tel Aviv-Yafo [*Israel*] [*Airport symbol*] (OAG)
TLV.............	Television (IAA)
TLV.............	Test Launch Vehicle (MCD)
TLV.............	Threshold Limit Value [*Industrial hygiene*]
TLV.............	Total Lung Volume [*Physiology*]
TLV.............	Track Levitated Vehicle [*Department of Transportation*]
TLv.............	Transition Level
TLV.............	Transporter - Loader Vehicle [*NASA*] (NASA)
TLV.............	Two-Lung Ventilation [*Medicine*]
TLV.............	Type Length and Value (TNIG)
TLV-C..........	Threshold Limit Value - Ceiling [*Industrial hygiene*] (PDAA)
TLV-STEL.....	Threshold Limit Value - Short Term Exposure Limit [*Industrial hygiene*] (PDAA)
TLV-TWA......	Threshold Limit Value - Time-Weighted Average [*Industrial hygiene*] (PDAA)
TLV/TWA......	Threshold Limit Value/Time-Weighted Average (AAEL)
TLW.............	[*The*] Lighted Way [*An association*] (EA)
TLW.............	Talasea [*New Britain, New Guinea*] [*Airport symbol*] (AD)
TLW.............	Test Load Wire
TLW.............	Torpedo Lieutenant's Writer [*British military*] (DMA)
TLW.............	Total Lung Water [*Medicine*] (DMAA)
TLWD..........	Tailwind [*Aviation*] (FAAC)
TLWM..........	Trinity Low-Water Mark
TLWS...........	Terrier Land Weapon System
TLX.............	TELEX [*Automated Teletypewriter Exchange Service*] [*Western Union Corp.*]
TLX.............	Thin-Layer Explosive (MCD)
TLX.............	Transfer-Line Exchanger [*Manufacturing technology*]
TLX.............	Trans-Lux [*AMEX symbol*] (TTSB)
TLX.............	Trans-Lux Corp. [*AMEX symbol*] (SPSG)
TLX.............	Tri-Line Expressways Ltd. [*Toronto Stock Exchange symbol*]
TLX.............	Trophoblast/Lymphocyte Cross-Reactive (Antigens) [*Immunochemistry*]
TLXA............	Toolex-Alpha [*NASDAQ symbol*] (SAG)
TLXAF..........	Toolex-Alpha N.V. [*NASDAQ symbol*] (TTSB)
TLXAF..........	Toolex International NV [*NASDAQ symbol*] [*Formerly, Toolex-Alpha NV*]
TLXN...........	Telxon Corp. [*NASDAQ symbol*] (NQ)
TLY	Tally
tlymn...........	Tallyman

TLZ	Target Launch Zone
TLZ	Theologische Literaturzeitung [*A publication*] (ODCC)
TLZ	Thermolase Corp. [*AMEX symbol*] (SAG)
TLZ	Titanium-Lead-Zinc
TLZ	Transfer on Less than Zero
TM	Assessment and Evaluation [*Educational Resources Information Center (ERIC) Clearinghouse*] [*The Catholic University of America*] (PAZ)
TM	Institute of Travel Management [*British*] (DBA)
TM	[*The*] Maccabees [*Southfield, MI*] (EA)
Tm	Maximal Renal Tubular Excretory Capacity [*Medicine*] (DAVI)
TM	Memphis-Shelby County Public Library and Information Center, Memphis, TN [*Library symbol Library of Congress*] (LCLS)
TM	National Income Tax Magazine [*A publication*] (DLA)
TM	Table Maintenance (NASA)
TM	Tactical Manager [*Military*] (CAAL)
TM	Tactical Missile [*Air Force*]
TM	Tactical Monitor
TM	Tailor-Made (DSUE)
TM	Take-Off Mass (SAA)
TM	Talking Machine
TM	Tangent Mechanism
TM	Tape Mark [*Computer science*] (BUR)
TM	Tape Module (DEN)
TM	Target Mechanism (MCD)
TM	Task Memory [*Computer science*] (IAA)
TM	Taurine Mustard [*Antineoplastic drug*]
TM	Tax Magazine [*A publication*] (DLA)
TM	Tax Management [*A publication*] (DLA)
TM	Tax Memo [*A publication*] (DLA)
TM	Tax Module [*IRS*]
TM	T-Cell Marker [*Biochemistry*]
TM	Team (AABC)
TM	Team Manager
TM	Team Member
TM	Technical Management (AAGC)
TM	Technical Manager
TM	Technical Manual
TM	Technical Memorandum
TM	Technical Minutes
TM	Technical Monograph
TM	Tectorial Membrane [*of the cochlea*] [*Ear anatomy*]
TM	Telegramme Multiple [*Telegram with Multiple Addresses*] [*French*] (ROG)
TM	Tele-Metropole, Inc. [*Toronto Stock Exchange symbol*]
TM	Telemetry
TM	Telephone Museum (EA)
TM	Temperature, Mean
TM	Temperature Meter
TM	Temperature Monitor (NRCH)
TM	Temple Magazine [*A publication*] (ROG)
TM	Temple of Man (EA)
TM	Temporomandibular [*Anatomy*]
TM	Tenu'at Ha-Moshavim (BJA)
TM	Terminal Multiplexer [*Computer science*] (IAA)
TM	Test Manual
TM	Test Mode
TM	Test Model [*NASA*]
TM	Texas Mexican Railway Co. [*AAR code*]
TM	Thalassemia Major [*Hematology*]
TM	Thames Measurement [*Formula for rating yachts*] [*British*]
TM	Thayer-Martin Medium [*Medicine*] (DMAA)
TM	Their Majesties
TM	Thematic Mapper [*Satellite technology*]
TM	Thermal Mapper
TM	Third Market [*Securities*]
TM	Third Mortgage (MHDW)
Tm	Thulium [*Chemical element*]
TM	Tight Money (MHDW)
TM	Time (FAAC)
TM	Time Management (MCD)
TM	Time, Mission
TM	Time Modulation
TM	Time Monitor
TM	Time Motion Technique
TM	Times Mirror Co. (EFIS)
T-M.............	Time-to-Market (AAEL)
TM	Timing of Movements [*Physiology*]
Tm	Timothy [*New Testament book*]
TM	Titanium Chloride [*Inorganic chemistry*]
TM	Toastmaster, Inc. [*NYSE symbol*] (SPSG)
TM	Tobramycin [*An antibiotic*]
TM	Tolerant Majority [*An association Defunct*] (EA)
TM	Tone Modulation
TM	Ton-Miles
TM	Tons per Minute
TM	Top Man
TM	Top Management
TM	Torpedoman's Mate [*Navy rating*]
T/M.............	Torque Meter (NG)
TM	Torque Motor
TM	Tour du Monde [*World Tour*] [*French*] ('JA)
TM	Town Major [*British military*] (DMA)
TM	Trabecular Meshwork (DAVI)
TM	Traceability Member (NAKS)

TM .... Track Monitor (CAAL)
TM .... Tractor Monoplane
TM .... Trademark
TM .... Trade Mission
TM .... Traffic Manager [*or Management*]
TM .... Traffic Model (NASA)
TM .... Trager's Medium [*Chemically defined culture medium*]
TM .... Trained Man [*British military*] (DMA)
TM .... Training Manual [*Military*]
TM .... Training Memorandum (DAS)
TM .... Training Missions [*Air Force*]
TM .... Trainmaster [*Railroading*]
TM .... Transaction Manager [*Computer science*]
TM .... Transaction Mode (IAA)
TM .... Transcendental Meditation
TM .... Transfer Memorandum
TM .... "Transitional" Mucosa [*Oncology*]
TM .... Transition Management
TM .... Transition Metal (MCD)
TM .... Translator Code Magnet (IAA)
TM .... Transmediastinal (DB)
TM .... Transmedullary [*Anatomy*]
TM .... Transmembrane Domain [*Genetics*]
TM .... Transmembrane Substitution Mutants [*Genetics*]
TM .... Transmetatarsal [*Anatomy*]
TM .... Transmission Matrix (IEEE)
TM .... Transmittal Memorandum (MCD)
Tm .... Transport Maximum [*Physiology*] (DAVI)
TM .... Transport Mechanism [*Physiology*]
TM .... Transport Medium [*Laboratory science*] (DAVI)
TM .... Transport Messenger [*Laboratory science*] (DAVI)
TM .... Transport Module (AAEL)
TM .... Transverse Magnetic
TM .... Travelwriter Marketletter [*Information service or system*] (IID)
TM .... Trench Mortar
TM .... Trial Modification (SAA)
TM .... Trombone, Muted
TM .... Tropical Maritime
TM .... Tropical Medicine
TM .... Tropomyosin [*Biochemistry*]
TM .... True Mean
TM .... True Motion [*RADAR*] (DEN)
TM .... Truncation Mutant
TM .... Trunk Mark [*Telecommunications*] (IAA)
TM .... Tuberal Magnocellular [*Nuclei, neuroanatomy*]
TM .... Tunicamycin [*Biochemistry*]
TM .... Tuning Meter (DEN)
TM .... Turing Machine [*Mathematical model*] [*Computer science*]
TM .... Turkmenistan [*Internet country code*]
TM .... Twisting Moment
TM .... Tympanic Membrane [*Anatomy*]
TM .... Type Metal [*Printing*] (DGA)
TM1 .... Torpedoman's Mate, First Class [*Navy rating*]
T/M² .... Metric Tons per Square Meter
TM2 .... Torpedoman's Mate, Second Class [*Navy rating*]
T/M³ .... Metric Tons per Cubic Meter
TM3 .... Torpedoman's Mate, Third Class [*Navy rating*]
TMA .... Memphis Academy of Arts, Memphis, TN [*Library symbol Library of Congress*] (LCLS)
TMA .... Memphis State University, Memphis, TN [*OCLC symbol*] (OCLC)
TMA .... [*The*] Mosquito Association (EA)
TMA .... Taiwan Maintenance Agency [*Military*] (AABC)
TMA .... Target Motion Analyzer
TMA .... Technical Manual Management Agent
TMA .... Telecommunications Management Association (NITA)
TMA .... Telecommunications Managers Association [*Orpington, England*] (TSSD)
TMA .... TeleManagement Associates [*Telecommunications service*] (TSSD)
TMA .... Telemarketing Managers Association (NTPA)
TMA .... Telemetry Manufacturers' Association (IAA)
TMA .... Telephone Management and Accounting (HGAA)
TMA .... Temperature Monitoring Apparatus
TMA .... Tennis Manufacturers Association [*Later, ATF*] (EA)
TMA .... Terminal Maneuvering Area [*Aviation*]
TMA .... Tetramethylammonium [*Organic chemistry*]
TMA .... Theatre Managers' Association [*Australia*]
TMA .... Theatrical Management Association [*British*] (DBA)
TMA .... Theatrical Mutual Association (EA)
TMA .... Thermal Analytical, Inc. (EFIS)
TMA .... Thermomagnetic Analysis [*Analytical chemistry*]
TMA .... Thermomechanical Analysis [*or Analyzer*]
TMA .... Thienylmalonic Acid [*Organic chemistry*]
TMA .... Thiomalic Acid [*Organic chemistry*]
TMA .... Thomas More Association (EA)
TMA .... Thornburg Mortgage Asset [*NYSE symbol*] (TTSB)
TMA .... Thornburg Mortgage Asset Corp. [*NYSE symbol*] (SPSG)
TMA .... Thrombotic Microangiopathy [*Nephrology*]
TMA .... Thyroid Microsomal Antibody [*Immunology*]
TMA .... Tifton, GA [*Location identifier FAA*] (FAAL)
TMA .... Tile Manufacturers Association (EA)
TMA .... Time-Modulated Antenna
TMA .... Tobacco Mechanics' Association [*A union*] [*British*] (DCTA)
TMA .... Tobacco Merchants Association of United States (EA)
TMA .... Toiletry Merchandising Association [*Later, NASM*] (EA)
TMA .... Tooling and Manufacturing Association (EA)

TMA .... Toronto Musicians Association [*Canada*] (WWLA)
TMA .... Torpedo Main Assembly
TMA .... Total Maintenance Actions (MCD)
TMA .... Total Market Coverage [*Advertising*] (NTCM)
TMA .... Total Materiel Assets [*Military*]
TMA .... Toy Manufacturers of America (EA)
TMA .... Toyota Manufacturing Australia Ltd.
TMA .... Trace Metals Analyzer
TMA .... Traffic Management Advisor [*FAA*] (TAG)
TMA .... Traffic Management Agency (CINC)
TMA .... Trailer Manufacturers Association [*Later, NAMPS*] (EA)
TMA .... Trainee Mobility Assistance [*Australia*]
TMA .... Training Media Association (EA)
TMA .... Transistor Magnetic-Pulse Amplifier
TMA .... Translater Mixer Amplifier (DWSG)
TMA .... Trans Mediterranean Airlines [*Lebanon*] [*ICAO designator*] (FAAC)
TMA .... Trans-Mediterranean Airways (BJA)
TMA .... Transmetatarsal Amputation [*Medicine*]
TMA .... Transportation Management Area (PA)
TMA .... Transportation Management Association
TMA .... Transport Museum Association (EA)
TMA .... Travelling and Meal Allowance
TMA .... Treasury Management Association
TMA .... Treestand Manufacturers Association
TMA .... Trimac Ltd. [*Toronto Stock Exchange symbol*]
TMA .... Trimellitic Acid [*Organic chemistry*]
TMA .... Trimellitic Anhydride [*Chemistry*]
TMA .... Trimethoxyamphetamine [*Organic chemistry*] (MAE)
TMA .... Trimethoxyphenyl Aminopropane [*Organic chemistry*] (MAE)
TMA .... Trimethyladenine [*Biochemistry*]
TMA .... Trimethylaluminum [*Organic chemistry*]
TMA .... Trimethylamine [*Organic chemistry*]
TMA .... Trimethylammonium [*Organic chemistry*]
TMA .... Truck Manufacturers (NTPA)
TMA .... Truck Manufacturers Association
TMA .... Truck Master Association [*Auto enthusiast organization*]
TMA .... Turnaround Management Association (NTPA)
TMAA .... Tractor and Machinery Association of Australia
TMAA .... Trimethylamine Alane [*Organic chemistry*]
TMaab .... Thyroid Microsomal Autoantibody [*Immunology*]
TMAB .... Telecommunications Managers Association - Belgium
TMAB .... Temporary Missile Assembly Building (AAG)
TMAB .... Tetramethylammonium Borohydride [*Organic chemistry*]
TMA BITS .... TMA [*Tobacco Merchants Association*] Bibliographic Index to the Tobacco Scene [*Database*]
TMAC .... Agrico Chemical Co., Memphis, TN [*Library symbol Library of Congress*] (LCLS)
TMAC .... Telecommunication Management and Control [*AT & T*]
TMAC .... Temperature-Modulated Air Cleaner [*Automotive engineering*]
T-MAC .... Test of Minimal Articulation Competence [*Speech evaluation test*]
TMAC .... Time-Division Multiplexed Analogue Components (NITA)
TMAC .... Treasury Multi-User Acquisition Contract (AAGC)
TMAC .... Trimellitic Anhydride Chloride [*Organic chemistry*]
TMACA .... Telecommunications Managers Association of the Capital Area (TSSD)
TMACS .... Tone Multiplex Apollo Command System [*NASA*] (KSC)
TMACS .... Training Management Control System [*Army*] (INF)
TM/ACS .... True-Motion, Anti-Collision System (PDAA)
TMAD .... Tank Main Armament Development (MCD)
TMAD .... Target Marker Air Droppable (MCD)
TMAD .... Target Marker and Dispenser (MCD)
TMadH .... Nashville Memorial Hospital, Madison, TN [*Library symbol Library of Congress*] (LCLS)
TMadM .... Madison Academy, Madison College, TN [*Library symbol Library of Congress*] (LCLS)
TMADWG .... Tank Main Armament Development Working Group [*Army*]
TMAE .... Tetrakis(dimethylamino)ethylene [*Organic chemistry*]
TMAG .... Tasmanian Museum and Art Gallery [*Australia*]
TMAG .... Travel More Advantageous to the Government (AAG)
TMAH .... Tetramethylammonium Hydroxide [*Organic chemistry*]
TMAI .... Tetramethylammonium Iodide [*Organic chemistry*]
TMAIC .... Trimethallyl Isocyanurate [*Organic chemistry*]
TMAM .... Training and Doctrine Command Mission Area Manager [*Army*]
TMAMA .... Textile Machinery and Accessory Manufacturers Association [*British*] (BI)
TMAN .... Todays Man, Inc. [*NASDAQ symbol*] (SAG)
TM & B .... Tunnels, Mines, and Booby Trap School [*Army*] (VNW)
TM & DE .... Test, Measuring, and Diagnostic Equipment [*Later, TMDE*] [*Army*] (AABC)
TMANQ .... Today's Man [*NASDAQ symbol*] (TTSB)
TMAO .... Trimethylamine Oxide [*Organic chemistry*]
TMAO .... Troop Movement Action Officer
TMAO .... Troop Movement Assignment Order
TMAP .... Tactical Multipurpose Automated Platform [*Military*]
TMAP .... Teleoperated Mobile Antiarmor Platform [*Army*] (INF)
TMAP .... Temporary Mortgage Assistance Payments Program [*HUD*]
TMAP .... Thermal Modeling and Analysis Project [*Marine science*] (OSRA)
TMAR .... Trico Marine Services, Inc. [*NASDAQ symbol*] (SAG)
TMAR .... Trico Marine Svcs [*NASDAQ symbol*] (TTSB)
TMARS .... Technical Manual Audit and Requirement Reporting System (MCD)
TMaryB .... Blount Memorial Hospital, Medical Library, Maryville, TN [*Library symbol Library of Congress*] (LCLS)
TMaryC .... Maryville College, Maryville, TN [*Library symbol Library of Congress*] (LCLS)
TMAS .... Tank Main Armament Systems (RDA)

TMAS............	Taylor Manifest Anxiety State [Psychology]
TMAS............	Technical and Management Advisory Service [ADPA] (MCD)
TMASA..........	Timber Merchants' Association of South Australia
TMaU............	University of Tennessee at Martin, Martin, TN [Library symbol Library of Congress] (LCLS)
TMAV............	Timber Merchants' Association of Victoria [Australia]
TMAX............	Maximum Time [Telecommunications] (TEL)
T-MAX	Temperature Maximum (DAVI)
T$_{max}$	Time of Maximum Concentration [Laboratory science] (DAVI)
TMAY............	Tell Me About Yourself [Interviewing technique]
TMB..............	David W. Taylor Model Basin [Also, DATMOBAS, DTMB] [Later, DTNSRDC, NSRDC]
TMB.............	Miami, FL [Location identifier FAA] (FAAL)
TMB.............	Tambrands, Inc. [NYSE symbol] (SPSG)
TMB.............	Task Maintenance Burden
TMB.............	Taylor Model Basin [Navy]
TMB.............	Tetramethylbenzene [Organic chemistry]
TMB.............	Tetramethylbenzidine [Organic chemistry]
TMB.............	Textes Mathematiques Babyloniens [A publication] (BJA)
TMB.............	Thimble
TMB.............	Thrimethylborate (AAEL)
TMB.............	Tide-Measuring Buoy
TMB.............	Time Maintenance Began [Military] (AFIT)
TMB.............	Too Many Birthdays (MEDA)
TMB.............	Transient Monocular Blindness [Medicine]
TMB.............	Transportation Management Bulletin [NASA] (NASA)
TMB.............	Trench Mortar Battery [British military] (DMA)
TMB.............	Trimethoxyboroxine [Organic chemistry]
TMB.............	Trimethylbenzene [Organic chemistry]
tmb.............	Trombone (WDAA)
TMB.............	Tumble (MSA)
TMB.............	University of Texas, Medical Branch Library, Galveston, TX [OCLC symbol] (OCLC)
TMBA...........	Brooks Art Gallery, Memphis, TN [Library symbol Library of Congress] (LCLS)
TMBA...........	Tetramethylene-bis-Acetamide [Biochemistry]
TMBA...........	Trimethylbenzaldehyde [Organic chemistry]
TMBA...........	Trimethylbenzanthracene [Carcinogen]
TMBAC.........	Trimethylbenzylammonium Chloride [Also, BTM] [Organic chemistry]
TM/BAC........	True-Motion, Basic Collision Avoidance (PDAA)
TMBC..........	Buckeye Cellulose Corp., Technical Division Library, Memphis, TN [Library symbol Library of Congress] (LCLS)
TMBD..........	Tetramethylbutanediamine [Also, TMBDA]
TMBDA........	Tetramethylbutanediamine [Organic chemistry]
TMBDB	Thermal Margin beyond Design Basis [Nuclear energy] (NRCH)
TMBGIC	They Might Be Giants Information Club (EA)
TMBH..........	Baptist Memorial Hospital, Memphis, TN [Library symbol Library of Congress] (LCLS)
TMBH-N.......	Baptist Memorial Hospital, School of Nursing, Memphis, TN [Library symbol Library of Congress] (LOL3)
TMBL..........	Buckman Laboratories, Inc., Memphis, TN [Library symbol Library of Congress] (LCLS)
TMBL..........	Tacoma Municipal Belt Line Railway [AAR code]
TMBO..........	Team Management by Objectives [Management technique] (ADA)
TMBP..........	(Tetramethylbutyl)phenol [Organic chemistry]
TMBR..........	Brown [Tom], Inc. [NASDAQ symbol] (SAG)
TMBR..........	Timber (AAG)
TMBR..........	Tom Brown [NASDAQ symbol] (TTSB)
TMBR Sh	TMBR Sharp Drilling, Inc. [Associated Press] (SAG)
TMBS..........	Timberline Software [NASDAQ symbol] (TTSB)
TMBS..........	Timberline Software Corp. [NASDAQ symbol] (NQ)
TMBS..........	Torque Motor Beam Steerer (MCD)
TMBU..........	Table Maintenance Block Update (NASA)
TM Bull.......	Trade Mark Bulletin, New Series [A publication] (DLA)
TMC............	Chief Torpedoman's Mate [Navy rating]
TMC............	Houston Academy of Medicine for Texas Medical Center, Houston, TX [OCLC symbol] (OCLC)
TMC............	Mailbox Club International (EA)
TMC............	[The] Maintenance Council of the American Trucking Associations (EA)
TMC............	[The] Mouse Club (EA)
TMC............	[The] Movie Channel [Cable-television system]
TMC............	Table Mountain [California] [Seismograph station code, US Geological Survey Closed] (SEIS)
TMC............	Tactical Medical Center
T/MC...........	Talker per Megacycle (SAA)
TMC............	Tambolaka [Indonesia] [Airport symbol] (OAG)
TMC............	Tape Management Catalog
TMC............	Target Market Coverage [Advertising] (BARN)
TMC............	Tarmac Plc [British ICAO designator] (FAAC)
TMC............	Telamarketing Communications, Inc. [Louisville, KY] [Telecommunications] (TSSD)
TMC............	Telecommunications Management College (NITA)
TMC............	Telecommunications Management Corp. [Needham Heights, MA] (TSSD)
TMC............	Telecommunications Marketing Corp. [Bay Shore, NY] (TSSD)
TMC............	TeleMonteCarlo [Private television operation] [Italy]
TMC............	Telephone Manufacturing Company (IAA)
TMC............	Temporary Minor Change (MCD)
TMC............	Terminal Control (DA)
TMC............	Terramycin Capsule [Antibacterial, trademark of Pfizer, Inc.]
TMC............	Terrestrial Microcosm Chamber [For environmental studies]
TMC............	Test, Monitor, and Control [Aviation]
TMC............	Test Monitoring Center [ASTM] [Engineering standards]
TMC............	Test Monitoring Console (NASA)
TMC.............	The Maintenance Council
TMC.............	#The Military Coalition
TMC.............	Thermal Micrometeoroid Cover (MCD)
TMC.............	Thick Molding Compound [Plastics technology]
TM-C...........	Thomas Micro-Catalogs
TMC.............	Three-Mode Control (AAG)
TMC.............	Threshold Management Center [Environmental Protection Agency] (GFGA)
TMC.............	Thrust Magnitude Control (KSC)
TMC.............	Thrust Management Computer (GAVI)
TMC.............	Times Mirror 'A' [NYSE symbol] (TTSB)
TMC.............	Times Mirror Co. [NYSE symbol] (SAG)
TMC.............	Titan Missile Contractor (AAG)
TMC.............	Tool Management Culture
TMC.............	Total Manufacturing Cost (MHDB)
TMC.............	Total Market Coverage [Advertising]
TMC.............	Tourism Ministers Council (EERA)
TMC.............	Toyota Motor Corp.
TMC.............	Traffic Management Center [Highway operations]
TMC.............	Traffic Management Channel [Navigation and driver information systems]
TMC.............	Traffic Message Channel [FHWA] (TAG)
TMC.............	Transmedia Enterprises, Inc. [Vancouver Stock Exchange symbol]
TMC.............	Transmission Maintenance Center [Telecommunications] (TEL)
TMC.............	Transmural Colitis [Crohn's disease] (CPH)
TMC.............	Transportation Management Center
TMC.............	Transportation Materiel Command [AMC - Mobility]
TMC.............	Transport Module Controller (AAEL)
TMC.............	Transport Movement Control [Military] (AFM)
TMC.............	Travel Management Center [General Services Administration] (GFGA)
TMC.............	Triamcinolone [Synthetic steroidal drug]
TMC.............	Trimethylcyclohexanol [Organic chemistry]
TMC.............	Trinity Ministries Center (EA)
TMC.............	Triple Molecular Collision
TMC.............	Tube Moisture Control
TMC.............	Type Maintenance Code (MCD)
TMCA...........	Thrust Management Control Analysis
TMCA...........	Titanium Metals Corp. of America
TMCA...........	Toxic Materials Control Activity [General Motors Corp.]
TMCA...........	Trimethyl Colchicinic Acid [Organic chemistry] (MAE)
TMCA...........	Truth Missionaries Chapter of Positive Accord (EA)
TMCBC........	Christian Brothers College, Memphis, TN [Library symbol Library of Congress] (LCLS)
TMCC...........	Chapman Chemical Co., Memphis, TN [Library symbol Library of Congress] (LCLS)
TMCC...........	Theater Movement Control Center [Military] (AABC)
TMCC...........	Time-Multiplexer Communications Channels
TMCC...........	Traffic Management Computer Complex [FAA] (TAG)
TMCDI..........	Trimethylcyclododecatriene [Organic chemistry]
TM Cent.......	TM Century, Inc. [Associated Press] (SAG)
TMCF...........	Campbell Foundation, Memphis, TN [Library symbol Library of Congress] (LCLS)
TMCF...........	Toastmasters and Masters of Ceremonies Federation [British] (BI)
TMCH...........	City of Memphis Hospital, Memphis, TN [Library symbol Library of Congress] (LCLS)
TM CHG......	Technical Manual Change Number [Army]
TMCI...........	Telemetering Control Indicator
TMCI...........	TM Century [NASDAQ symbol] (NQ)
TMCIEI.........	TMCI Electronics, Inc. [Associated Press] (SAG)
TMCIOB.......	Technician Member of the Chartered Institute of Building [British] (DI)
TMckB	Bethel College, McKenzie, TN [Library symbol Library of Congress]
TMckB-C	Cumberland Presbyterian Theological Seminary, Bethel College, McKenzie, TN [Library symbol Library of Congress] (LCLS)
TMCL...........	Target Map Coordinate Locator [Military]
TMCM..........	Master Chief Torpedoman's Mate [Navy rating]
TMCM..........	Tooling Machine Control Medium (MCD)
TMCN..........	Technical Management Requirements Document Change Notice (MCD)
TMCOMP	Telemetry Computation
TMCOT........	Tetramethylcyclooctatetraene [Organic chemistry]
TMCP..........	Technical Manual Control Panel (IAA)
TMCP..........	Thermal Mechanical Controlled Processing (PDAA)
TMCP..........	Trimethylcyclopentanone [Organic chemistry]
TMCPrP	Times Mirror cm Sr'B'Pfd [NYSE symbol] (TTSB)
TMCR..........	Technical Manual Change Request [or Requirement]
TMCR..........	Technical Manual Contract Requirement
TMCRL........	Tailored Master Cross Reference List [Military] (AABC)
TMCS..........	Memphis City Schools Professional Library, Memphis, TN [Library symbol Library of Congress] (LCLS)
TMCS..........	Senior Chief Torpedoman's Mate [Navy rating]
TMCS..........	Tactical Maintenance Control System
TMCS..........	Toshiba Minicomputer Complex System
TMCS..........	Trimethylchlorosilane [Organic chemistry]
TMCXD........	Transverse Magnetic Circular X-Ray Dichroism [Physics]
TMD............	Meharry Medical College, Nashville, TN [OCLC symbol] (OCLC)
TMD............	Tactical Metrology Device (DWSG)
TMD............	Tactical Missile Defense [Army] (DOMA)
TMD............	Tactical Mission Data [Military] (AFM)
TMD............	Tactical Munitions Dispenser (MCD)
TMD............	Tagged Material Detector (DWSG)
TMD............	Technical Manual Designation
TMD............	Telemedia, Inc. [Toronto Stock Exchange symbol]

TMD............ Telemetered Data (AAG)
TMD............ Temperature of Maximum Density
TMD............ Tensor Meson Dominance [*Physics*] (OA)
TMD............ Test & Measurement Division (ACII)
TMD............ Tetramethyldioxetane [*Organic chemistry*]
TMD............ Text Matter Depth [*Typography*] (DGA)
TMD............ Theater Missile Defense
TMD............ Theoretical Maximum Density
TMD............ Thermedics, Inc. [*AMEX symbol*] (SPSG)
TMD............ Timbedra [*Mauritania*] [*Airport symbol*] (AD)
TMD............ Timed (MSA)
TMD............ Toluene-Methanol-Dioxane [*Scintillation solvent*]
TMD............ Total Mean Downtime [*Computer science*] (IAA)
TMD............ Toxicology and Microbiology Division [*Cincinnati, OH*] [*Environmental Protection Agency*] (GRD)
TMD............ Training Media Database [*Access Innovations, Inc.*] [*Information service or system*] (CRD)
TMD............ Transient Mass Distribution Code [*Nuclear energy*] (NRCH)
TMD............ Transmed Airlines [*Egypt*] [*ICAO designator*] (FAAC)
TMD............ Transmembrane Domain [*Genetics*]
TMD............ Trimethylhexamethylene Diamine [*Organic chemistry*]
TMDA........... Tetramethyldiamine (DB)
TMDA........... Training Media Distributors Association [*Later, TMA*] (EA)
TMDAG .... This Mode of Transportation has been Determined to be More Advantageous to the Government
TMDC........... Technical Manual Data Cards [*DoD*] (MCD)
TMDC........... Transportation Movement Document Control (MCD)
TMDE........... Test Management and Diagnostic Equipment [*Army*]
TMDE........... Test, Measuring [*or Measurement*], and Diagnostic Equipment [*Formerly, TM & DE*] [*Army*] (AABC)
TMDESE....... Test, Measurement, and Diagnostic Equipment Support Equipment [*Army*]
TMDESG ...... Test, Management, and Diagnostic Equipment Support Group [*Army*] (MCD)
TMDI........... Tactical Missile Defense Initiative (DOMA)
TMDI........... Theater Missile Defense Initiative [*Army*] (DOMA)
TMDI........... Theoretical Maximum Daily Intake [*Toxicology*]
TMDI........... Transponder Miss Distance Indicator
TMDI........... Trimethylhexamethylene Diisocyanate [*Organic chemistry*]
TMDI........... United States Defense Industrial Plant Equipment Center, Memphis, TN [*Library symbol Library of Congress*] (LCLS)
TMDL........... Technical Manual Data List [*DoD*]
TMDL........... Total Maximum Daily Load [*Environmental Protection Agency*]
TMDO .... Training Management Development Office [*Army*]
TMDP........... Technetium Methylene Diphosphonate [*Organic chemistry*]
TMDR .... Technical Manual Data Record [*DoD*] (MCD)
TMDS........... Test, Measurement, and Diagnostic Systems [*Army*] (RDA)
TMDS........... Tetramethyldisilazane [*Organic chemistry*]
TMDS........... Transition Minimized Differential Signaling
TMDS........... Trilineage Myelodysplasia Syndrome [*Medicine*]
TMDT........... Total Mean Downtime
TMDT........... Trace Metals Detection Technique
TMDT........... Trimethyldodecatetraene [*Organic chemistry*]
TME .... Eastwood Hospital, Memphis, TN [*Library symbol Library of Congress*] (LCLS)
TME .... [*The*] Main Event [*A publication*]
TME .... Tame [*Colombia*] [*Airport symbol*] (OAG)
TME .... Teacher of Medical Electricity [*British*]
TME .... Temperature Measuring Equipment (IAA)
TME .... Termex Resources, Inc. [*Vancouver Stock Exchange symbol*]
TME .... Test and Measurement Equipment (MCD)
TME .... Test Maintenance Equipment [*Computer science*]
TME .... Test Marketing Exemption [*Environmental Protection Agency*]
TME .... Tetramethylethylene [*Organic chemistry*]
TME .... Theatre Mask Ensemble
TME .... Thermal Electron Corp. (EFIS)
TME .... Thermal Marrow Expansion [*Roentgenology*]
TME .... Thermal/Mechanical Enzyme [*Fermentation*]
TME .... Thrust Monopropellant Engine
TME .... Times Mirror 4.25%'PEPS'2001 [*NYSE symbol*] (TTSB)
TME .... Times Mirror Co. [*NYSE symbol*] (SAG)
TME .... Tivoli Management Environment
TME .... TME Resources, Inc. [*Vancouver Stock Exchange symbol*]
TME .... Torpedoman's Mate, Electrical [*Navy rating*]
TME .... Total Market Estimate (ADA)
TME .... Total Metabolizable Energy [*Nutrition*]
TME .... Transmissible Mink Encephalopathy
TME .... Transmural Enteritis [*Medicine*]
TME .... Transverse-Mounted Engine
TME .... Trimethylolethane [*Organic chemistry*]
TME .... True Metabolizable Energy
TMEA .... Typewriter Manufacturers Export Association [*Defunct*]
TMEC........... TRADOC [*Training and Doctrine Command*] Materiel Evaluation Committee [*Army*]
TmEco .... Thermo Ecotek Corp. [*Associated Press*] (SAG)
TMECO........ Time of Main Engine Cutoff [*Aerospace*] (MCD)
TMED .... Tetramethylethylenediamine [*Also, TEMED, TMEDA*] [*Organic chemistry*]
TMED .... Trimedyne, Inc. [*NASDAQ symbol*] (NQ)
TMEDA........ Tetramethylethylenediamine [*Also, TEMED, TMED*] [*Organic chemistry*]
TMEDA........ Trimethylenediamine [*Organic chemistry*]
TME/FH....... Total Maintenance Effort per Flight Hour [*Navy*] (NG)
TMEI .... TMCI Electronics [*NASDAQ symbol*] (TTSB)
TMEI .... TMCI Electronics, Inc. [*NASDAQ symbol*] (SAG)

TMEIW......... TMCI Electronics Wrrt [*NASDAQ symbol*] (TTSB)
TMEL .... Tender Master Equipment List
TMEL .... Trimethylethyllead [*Organic chemistry*]
TMEMC........ Test and Measurement Equipment for Maintenance Calibration
TM-ENG ...... Technical Manual - Engineering [*Marine Corps*]
TMEP.......... Trademark Manual of Examining Procedure [*A publication*] (DLA)
TMeP.......... Trimethylpsoralen [*Photochemotherapeutic compound*]
TMEPS........ Transverse-Mounted Engine Propulsion System
TMER.......... Technical Manual Evaluation Record (MCD)
TMES.......... Tactical Missile Electrical Simulator [*Obsolete*]
TMESS........ Telemessage (DS)
TMET.......... Treadmill Exercise Test [*Medicine*] (DMAA)
TMETN........ Trimethylolethane Trinitrate [*Organic chemistry*]
TMEV.......... Theiler's Murine Encephalitis Virus
TMF........... Technical Transmitter Holding Fixture
TMF........... Technical Transmitter Holding Future (MCD)
TMF........... Telemetry Module Facility
TMF........... Test Mode Fail [*Apollo*] [*NASA*]
TMF........... Thermo Opportunity Fund, Inc. [*AMEX symbol*] (SAG)
TMF........... Third Moment of Frequency (PDAA)
TMF........... Thrust Management Function (GAVI)
TMF........... Time Marker Frequency
TMF........... Time Multiplication Factor [*Offshore racing*]
TMF........... Transaction Monitoring Facility [*Tandem Computers*]
TMF........... Transfer Mold Forming (MCD)
TMF........... Transformed Mink Fibroblast [*Cell line*] [*Laboratory science*] (DAVI)
TMF........... Transmission Monitoring Facility (NITA)
TMF........... Transporter Maintenance Facility [*NASA*] (NASA)
TMF........... Trunk Maintenance Files [*Telecommunications*] (TEL)
TMFC.......... Ted McGinley Fan Club (EA)
TMFGC........ Technical Manual Functional Group Code
TMFL-......... Time of Flight (MSA)
TMG........... Goodwyn Institute, Memphis, TN [*Library symbol Library of Congress*] (LCLS)
TMG........... Tactical Missile Group [*Air Force*]
TMG........... Tactical Multinet Gateway [*Computer science Military*] (RDA)
TMG........... Tape Manufacturers Group [*British*] (DBA)
TMG........... Tetramethylguanidine [*Organic chemistry*]
TMG........... Thermal Meteoroid [*or Micrometeoroid*] Garment [*NASA*] (KSC)
TMG........... Thermomagnetometry [*Analytical chemistry*]
TMG........... Thermometeroid Garnet (IAA)
TMG........... Thiomethylgalactoside [*Organic chemistry*]
TMG........... Time Mark Generator
TMG........... Timing
TMG........... Tomanggong [*Malaysia*] [*Airport symbol*] (OAG)
TMG........... Track Made Good [*Aviation*]
TMG........... Traffic Monitoring Guide [*FHWA*] (TAG)
TMG........... TransMontaigne, Inc. [*Formerly, TransMontaigne Oil*] [*AMEX symbol*]
TMG........... Transmontaigne Oil Co. [*AMEX symbol*] (SAG)
TMG........... Trimethylgallium [*Organic chemistry*]
TMG........... Trimethylguanosine [*Biochemistry*]
TMG........... Tubular Maximum Reabsorption Rate for Glucose [*of Kidney*] [*Nephrology*] (DAVI)
TMGA.......... Tetramethyleneglutaric Acid [*Organic chemistry*]
TMGC.......... W. R. Grace & Co., Agricultural Chemicals Group, Memphis, TN [*Library symbol Library of Congress*] (LCLS)
TMGD.......... Timing Devices (MSA)
TMGE.......... Thermomagnetic-Galvanic Effect
TMGFC........ [*The*] Mel Gibson Fan Club [*Defunct*] (EA)
TMGG.......... Goldsmith Civic Garden Center, Memphis, TN [*Library symbol Library of Congress*] (LCLS)
TMGRS .... Trace Material Generation Rate Simulator
TMGS.......... Church of Jesus Christ of Latter-Day Saints, Genealogical Society Library, Memphis Branch, Memphis, TN [*Library symbol Library of Congress*] (LCLS)
TMGS.......... Terrestrial Magnetic Guidance System [*Aerospace*] (AAG)
TMGS.......... Transportable Mobile Ground Station (MCD)
TMH........... Harding Graduate School of Religion, Memphis, TN [*Library symbol Library of Congress*] (LCLS)
TMH........... Tanahmerah [*Indonesia*] [*Airport symbol*] (OAG)
TMH........... Tasmania Museum and Art Gallery, Tasmania [*State*] (EERA)
TMH........... Texte und Materialien der Frau Professor Hilprecht Collection of Babylonian Antiquities im Eigentum der Universitaet Jena (BJA)
TMH........... Tomahawk Resources [*Vancouver Stock Exchange symbol*]
TMH........... Tons per Man-Hour
TMH........... Trainable Mentally Handicapped
TMH........... Trimethylhexane [*Organic chemistry*]
TMH........... Trolley-Mounted Hoist (NRCH)
TMHA.......... Memphis Housing Authority, Memphis, TN [*Library symbol Library of Congress*] (LCLS)
TMHA.......... [*The*] Military Housing Association
TMHB.......... Harland Bartholomew & Associates, Memphis, TN [*Library symbol Library of Congress*] (LCLS)
TMHC.......... Transcultural Mental Health Centre [*Australia*]
TMHF.......... Transit Missile Hold Facility [*Military*] (IAA)
TMHI.......... Holiday Inns of America, Memphis, TN [*Library symbol Library of Congress*] (LCLS)
TMHI-U........ Holiday Inn University, Olive Branch, MS [*Library symbol Library of Congress*] (LCLS)
TMHL.......... Triplet Metastable Helium Level
TMHR .... Tandem Mirror Hybrid Reactor (PDAA)
TMI........... International Harvester Co., Memphis, TN [*Library symbol Library of Congress*] (LCLS)
TMI........... [*The*] Media Institute (EA)

TMI	Midwestern State University, George Moffett Library, Wichita Falls, TX [*OCLC symbol*] (OCLC)
TMI	[*The*] Monroe Institute (EA)
TMI	[*The*] Mortgage Index, Inc. [*Remote Computing Corp.*] [*Information service or system*] (IID)
TMI	Taylor Mountain [*Idaho*] [*Seismograph station code, US Geological Survey*] (SEIS)
TMI	Team, Inc. [*AMEX symbol*] (SPSG)
TMI	Technical Management Items (NASA)
TMI	Technical Manual Index [*Navy*]
TMI	Teen Missions International (EA)
TMI	Telecommunications Management, Inc. [*Oakbrook, IL*] [*Telecommunications*] (TSSD)
TmI	Telematica, Inc. [*Telecommunications service*] (TSSD)
TMI	Telemeter Magnetics, Inc. (IAA)
TMI	Texas Microelectronics, Inc. (IAA)
TMI	Thornicroft's Mounted Infantry [*Military British*] (ROG)
TMI	Threatened Myocardial Infarction [*Cardiology*] (MEDA)
TMI	Three Mile Island [*Pennsylvania*] [*Site of nuclear reactor accident, 1979*]
TMI	Time Air Corp. [*Toronto Stock Exchange symbol*]
TMI	Time Manager International [*Commercial firm British*]
TMI	Tolyl(mono)isocyanate [*Organic chemistry*]
TMI	Tool Manufacturing Instruction (AAG)
TMI	Tracking Merit Interception
TMI	Transfer on Minus (SAA)
TMI	Trans-Mars Injection [*Aerospace*]
TMI	Transmural Myocardial Infarction [*Cardiology*]
TMI	Travel Managers International (EA)
TMI	Trimethylindium [*Organic chemistry*]
TMI	Trucking Management, Inc. (EA)
TMI	Tumlingtar [*Nepal*] [*Airport symbol*] (OAG)
TMI	Tune-Up Manufacturers Institute (EA)
TMI	Tuning Meter Indicator (IAA)
TMIA	Tasmanian Music Industry Association [*Australia*]
TMIA	Three Mile Island Alert (EA)
TMIAC	Tasmanian Meat Industry Advisory Council [*Australia*]
TMIC	Test Management Information System
TMIC	Thomas Marketing Information Center [*Thomas Publishing Co.*] [*Information service or system*] (IID)
TMIC	Toxic Materials Information Center [*Oak Ridge National Laboratory*] (IID)
TMICP	Topographic Map Inventory Control Point [*Army*] (AABC)
TMIF	Tumor-Cell Migratory Inhibition Factor [*Immunology*]
TMIFC	Tom Mix International Fan Club (EA)
TMIG	Time in Grade [*Navy*]
TMIL	Traffic Management Information Letter [*MTMC*] (TAG)
TMiIM	Milligan College, Milligan College, TN [*Library symbol Library of Congress*] (LCLS)
TMIMGTechE..	Technician Member of the Institution of Mechanical and General Technician Engineers [*British*] (DI)
TMIMIS	Technical Manual Integrated Management Information Systems [*DoD*]
TMIN	Minimum Time [*Telecommunications*] (TEL)
TMIN	Tokyo Metropolitan Institute for Neuroscience [*Japan*]
TMiNA	United States Naval Air Station Library, Millington, TN [*Library symbol Library of Congress*] (LCLS)
TMINDCD	Technical Manual Indenture Code [*Army*]
TMiNH	United States Naval Hospital, Millington, TN [*Library symbol Library of Congress*] (LCLS)
TMINS	Technical Manual Identification Numbering System (MCD)
TMINS	Three Mile Island Nuclear Station (NRCH)
TMIP	Training Management Instruction Packet
TMIP	Travel Model Improvement Program [*BTS*] (TAG)
TMIS	Tank Management Information System (MCD)
TMIS	Technical and Management Information System (SSD)
TMIS	Technical Medical Information System (DAVI)
TMIS	Technical Meetings Information Service
TMIS	Technician Maintenance Information System (MHDB)
TMIS	Television Management Information System (IAA)
TMIS	Television Measurement [*or Metering*] Information System (OA)
TMIS	Theater Medical Information System (DOMA)
TMIS	Total Management Information System
TMIS	Transmission Impairment Measuring Set [*Telecommunications*] (IAA)
TMIU	Teletype Modulator Interface Units (MCD)
TMJ	Temporomandibular Joint [*Anatomy*]
TMJ	Temporomandibular Joint [*Dentistry*] (DAVI)
TMJ	Temporomandibular Joint Disorder [*Medicine*]
TMJS	Temporomandibular Joint Syndrome [*Medicine*]
TMK	Kimberly-Clark Corp., Memphis, TN [*Library symbol Library of Congress*] (LCLS)
TMK	Timiskaming [*Quebec*] [*Seismograph station code, US Geological Survey Closed*] (SEIS)
TMK	Tiravita Munnerrat Kalam
TMK	Tomahawk Airways, Inc. [*ICAO designator*] (FAAC)
TMK	Tomsk [*Former USSR Geomagnetic observatory code*]
TMK	To My Knowledge [*Computer science*] (DOM)
TMK	Tonnage Mark [*Found on each side of the ship aft*] (DS)
TMK	Torchmark Corp. [*NYSE symbol*] (SPSG)
TMK	Transistor Mounting Kit
TMK	Trumark Resource Corp. [*Vancouver Stock Exchange symbol*]
TmkCa	Torchmark Capital LLC, Inc. [*Associated Press*] (SAG)
Tmk Plc	Tomkins Ltd. [*Associated Press*] (SAG)
Tmk plc	Tomkins PLC [*Associated Press*] (SAG)
TMKPR	Timekeeper (WGA)

TMKPrM	Torchmark Capital 'MIPS' [*NYSE symbol*] (TTSB)
TML	Lakeside Hospital, Memphis, TN [*Library symbol Library of Congress*] (LCLS)
TML	Tamale [*Ghana*] [*Airport symbol*] (OAG)
TML	Tandem Matching Loss [*Telecommunications*] (TEL)
TML	Technical Manual List (MCD)
TML	Television Microwave Link [*FAA*] (TAG)
TML	Terminal (AABC)
TML	Terrestrial Microwave Link
TML	Tetramethyl Lead (MCD)
TML	Texas Tech University, School of Medicine at Lubbock, Library of the Health Science, Lubbock, TX [*OCLC symbol*] (OCLC)
TML	Thermomechanical Loading
TML	Three-Mile Limit
TML	Titanium Metallurgical Laboratory (MCD)
TML	Total Mass Loss (AAEL)
TML	Traffic Management Laboratory [*FHWA*] (TAG)
TML	Transmanche-Link [*Eurotunnel*] (ECON)
TML	Transportable Moisture Limit [*Shipping*] (DS)
TML	Two Mixed Layer (IAA)
TMLBC	Le Bonheur Children's Medical Center, Health Sciences Library, Memphis, TN [*Library symbol Library of Congress*] (LCLS)
TMLE	Transient-Mode Liquid Epitaxy
TMLG	Memphis Light, Gas, and Water Division Library, Memphis, TN [*Library symbol Library of Congress*] (LCLS)
TMLJ	Thurgood Marshall Law Journal [*A publication*] (DLA)
TMLN	Timeline, Inc. [*NASDAQ symbol*] (SAG)
TMLO	LeMoyne-Owen College, Memphis, TN [*Library symbol Library of Congress*] (LCLS)
TM/LP	Thermal Margin/Low Pressure [*Nuclear energy*] (NRCH)
TML Rev	Thurgood Marshall Law Review [*A publication*] (DLA)
TMM	Memphis State University, Memphis, TN [*Library symbol Library of Congress*] (LCLS)
TMM	Tamatave [*Madagascar*] [*Airport symbol*] (OAG)
TMM	Tank Master Mechanic (MCD)
TMM	Tax Management Memorandum [*Bureau of National Affairs*] [*A publication*] (DLA)
TMM	Technologico De Monterrey [*Mexico*] [*Seismograph station code, US Geological Survey*] (SEIS)
TMM	TELEX Main Memories [*Telecommunications*] (IAA)
TMM	Test Message Monitor
TMM	Thermal Mathematical Model
TMM	Times Mirror Magazines [*A publication*]
TMM	Too Many Metaphors [*Used in correcting manuscripts, etc.*]
TMM	Traffic Management Corp. Airlines [*FAA designator*] (FAAC)
TMM	Transition Metal-Metalloid [*Physical chemistry*]
TMM	Transportacion Maritima ADS [*NYSE symbol*] (TTSB)
TMM	Transportacion Maritima Mexicana [*NYSE symbol*] (SPSG)
TMM	Trehalose Monomycolate [*Biochemistry*]
TMM	Trimethylenemethane [*Organic chemistry*]
TMM	Trimethylolmelamine [*Organic chemistry*]
TMM A	Transp't'n Marit Part Ctfs ADS [*NYSE symbol*] (TTSB)
TMMAB	Mid-America Baptist Theological Seminary, Memphis, TN [*Library symbol Library of Congress*] (LCLS)
TMM-B	Memphis State University, Bureau of Business Research Library, Memphis, TN [*Library symbol Library of Congress*] (LCLS)
TMMB	Truck Mixer Manufacturers Bureau (EA)
TMMBC	Mid-South Bible College, Memphis, TN [*Library symbol Library of Congress*] (LCLS)
TMMC	Tetramethylammonium Manganese Chloride [*Organic chemistry*]
TMMC	Theater Materiel Management Center [*Military*] (AABC)
TMMD	Tactical Moving Map Display (MCD)
TMM-E	Memphis State University, Engineering Library, Memphis, TN [*Library symbol Library of Congress*] (LCLS)
TMME	Toyota Motor Marketing and Engineering [*Automotive industry, corporate subsidiary*]
TMMEE	Memphis Eye and Ear Hospital, Memphis, TN [*Library symbol Library of Congress*] (LCLS)
TMMexA	Transportacion Maritima Mexicana [*Associated Press*] (SAG)
TMMG	Teacher of Massage and Medical Gymnastics [*British*]
TMMH	Methodist Hospital, Stratton Medical Library, Memphis, TN [*Library symbol Library of Congress*] (LCLS)
TMMH-P	Methodist Hospital, Pathology Library, Memphis, TN [*Library symbol Library of Congress*] (LCLS)
TMMIS	Technical Manual Management Information System [*Navy*] (DNAB)
TMM-L	Memphis State University, School of Law, Memphis, TN [*Library symbol Library of Congress*] (LCLS)
TMMM	Textes et Monuments Figures Relatifs aux Mysteres de Mithra [*A publication*] (BJA)
TMMM	Tomahawk Multi-Mission Missile (DOMA)
TMMNA	Toyota Motor Manufacturing of North America
TMMP	Technical Manual Management Program [*Navy*] (NVT)
TMMPS	Tris(methoxy)mercaptopropylsilane [*Organic chemistry*]
TMMS	Tactical Missile Maintenance Squadron [*Air Force*]
TMM-SH	Memphis State University, Speech and Hearing Center, Memphis, TN [*Library symbol Library of Congress*] (LCLS)
TMMT	Technical Manual Management Team [*DoD*]
TMN	Charlotte Amalie, St. Thomas, VI [*Location identifier FAA*] (FAAL)
TMN	Memphis and Shelby County Public Library and Information Center, Memphis, TN [*OCLC symbol*] (OCLC)
TMN	National Cotton Council of America, Memphis, TN [*Library symbol Library of Congress*] (LCLS)
TMN	Tamana [*Kiribati*] [*Airport symbol*] (OAG)
TMN	Tax Matters Newsletter [*Australia A publication*]
TMN	Technical and Management Note (IEEE)

TMN............	Telecommunications Management Network (MCD)
TMN............	Timber Mountain [*Nevada*] [*Seismograph station code, US Geological Survey*] (SEIS)
TMN............	Tjumenaviatrans [*Russian Federation*] [*ICAO designator*] (FAAC)
TMN............	Transmedia Network [*NYSE symbol*] (TTSB)
TMN............	Transmedia Network, Inc. [*NYSE symbol*] (SAG)
TMN............	Transmission (AFM)
TMN............	Trigeminal Mesencephalic Nucleus [*Neuroanatomy*]
TMN............	True Mach Number
TMNA............	Transmedia Asia Pacific [*NASDAQ symbol*] (TTSB)
TMNA............	Transmedia Asia Pacific, Inc. [*NASDAQ symbol*] (SAG)
TMNE............	Transmedia Europe, Inc. [*NASDAQ symbol*] (SAG)
TMNT............	Teen-Age Mutant Ninja Turtles [*Name of comic book and cartoon characters and line of toys by Playmates Toys*]
TMO............	Table Mountain Observatory [*Marine science*] (OSRA)
TMO............	Targets Management Office [*MIRCOM*] (RDA)
TMO............	Technology Management Office [*Army*]
TMO............	Telegraph Money Order
TMO............	Test Manufacturing Order (NASA)
TMO............	Thermo Electron [*NYSE symbol*] (TTSB)
TMO............	Thermo Electron Corp. [*NYSE symbol*] (SPSG)
TMO............	Thermomagnetic Optical Disk
TMO............	Thermomagneto-Optic (MCD)
TMO............	Time Out
TMO............	Tooling Manufacturing Outline
TMO............	Tool Manufacturing Order [*NASA*] (NASA)
TMO............	Total Materiel Objective [*Military*]
TMO............	Traffic Management Office [*or Officer*] [*Air Force*] (AFM)
TMO............	Transition Metal Oxide (MCD)
TMO............	Transportation Management Office (COE)
TMO............	Transportation Management Officer (AAGC)
TMO............	Transportation Movements Office [*or Officer*] [*Military*]
TMO............	Treminco Resources Ltd. [*Toronto Stock Exchange symbol Vancouver Stock Exchange symbol*]
TMO............	Trimethylamine N-Oxide [*Organic chemistry*]
TMO............	Tumeremo [*Venezuela*] [*Airport symbol*] (OAG)
TMOB............	Trade Marks Opposition Board [*Information service or system*] (IID)
TM(od)............	[*The*] Masons (of detroit) [*Rock music group*]
TMOD............	TMDE [*Test, Measuring, and Diagnostic Equipment*] Modernization [*Army*] (RDA)
TMOE............	Trimethoxyethane [*Organic chemistry*]
TMOF............	Trypsin-Modulating Oostatic Factor [*Biochemistry*]
T-MOP............	Methotrexate, 6-Thioguanine, Oncovin, Prednisone [*Antineoplastic drug regimen*] (DAVI)
TMOP............	Trimethylolpropane [*Organic chemistry*]
TMOPS............	TRADOC [*Training and Doctrine Command*] Mobilization and Operations Planning System [*Military*]
TMOR............	Technical Manual Ordtask Requirement (MCD)
TMorM............	Morristown College, Morristown, TN [*Library symbol Library of Congress*] (LCLS)
TMorNR............	Nolichucky Regional Library Center, Morristown, TN [*Library symbol Library of Congress*] (LCLS)
TMorW............	Walters State Community College, Learning Resources Center, Morristown, TN [*Library symbol*] [*Library of Congress*] (LCLS)
TMOS............	Telecommunications Management and Operations Support (CIST)
TMOS............	Tetramethoxysilane [*Organic chemistry*]
TMOS............	Thermosetting (MSA)
T-MOS............	Trench-Metal Oxide Silicon [*Transistor*]
TMOS............	Two Main Orbiting Spacecraft (SAA)
TMOT............	Target [*or Total*] Maximum Operating Time
TMOTFSM............	[*The*] Master of the Free School, Margate [*Pseudonym used by Zachariah Cozens*]
TMP............	East Timor [*ISO three-letter standard code*] (CNC)
TMP............	[*The*] Madison Project (EA)
TMP............	[*The*] Management Processor (MCD)
TMP............	Tampere [*Finland*] [*Airport symbol*] (OAG)
TMP............	Target Materials Program [*DoD*]
TMP............	Technical Manual Parts [*Army*] (AABC)
TMP............	Technical Manual Plan [*DoD*]
TMP............	Telecommunications Management Program (COE)
TMP............	Telecommunications Modernization Project (AAGC)
TMP............	Teleprinter Message Pool
TMP............	Temazepam [*Tranquilizer*]
TMP............	Temperature (BUR)
Tmp............	[*The*] Tempest [*Shakespearean work*]
tmp............	Temporary (BARN)
TMP............	Terminal Monitor Program [*Computer science*] (BUR)
TMP............	Terminal Panel (NASA)
TMP............	Ternary Mobile Phase [*Physical chemistry*]
TMP............	Terrain Mortar Positioning [*Military*] (INF)
TMP............	Test Maintenance Panel [*Computer science*]
TMP............	Test Management Protocol [*Telecommunications*] (OSI)
TMP............	Test Market Plan [*Advertising*] (NTCM)
TMP............	Test Market Profile [*Advertising*] (NTCM)
TMP............	Test Methods and Procedures
TMP............	Tetramesitylporphyrin [*Organic chemistry*]
TMP............	Tetramethoxypropane [*Organic chemistry*]
TMP............	Tetramethylpiperidine [*Organic chemistry*]
TMP............	Thallium Myocardial Perfusion [*Test*] [*Cardiology*] (DAVI)
TMP............	Theodolite Measuring Point (MUGU)
TMP............	Thermal Mass Penalty (KSC)
TMP............	Thermal Modeling Program
TMP............	Thermo Magnetic Printing (HGAA)
TMP............	Thermomechanical Processing
TMP............	Thermo Mechanical Pulp (EERA)

TMP............	Thermomechanical Pulps
TMP............	Thermomicrophotometry
TMP............	Thiamine Monophosphate (DB)
TMP............	Thymidine Monophosphate [*Biochemistry*]
TMP............	Thymine Ribonucleoside-5-Phosphate [*Genetics*] (DAVI)
TMP............	Thymocyte Mitogenic Protein [*Immunology*]
TMP............	Thymolphthalein Monophosphate [*Biochemistry*]
TMP............	Time Management Processor (NASA)
TMP............	Times Mirror Press
TMP............	Top Management Program
TMP............	Total Material Package [*Military*] (DNAB)
TMP............	Total Milk Proteinate [*Trademark of New Zealand Milk Products, Inc.*]
TMP............	Traditional Medical Practice
TMP............	Transistor Mounting Pad
TMP............	Transitional Manpower Program [*Navy*] (DNAB)
TMP............	Transmembrane Potential [*Biochemistry*]
TMP............	Transmembrane Pressure [*Biomedicine*]
TMP............	Transmembrane Protein [*Biochemistry*]
TMP............	Trans Mountain Pipe Line Co. Ltd. [*Toronto Stock Exchange symbol Vancouver Stock Exchange symbol*]
TMP............	Transportable Measurement Package (MCD)
TMP............	Transportation Motor Pool [*Military*] (AABC)
TMP............	Transversely Magnetized Plasma
TMP............	Trimetaphosphate [*Organic chemistry*]
TMP............	Trimethoprim [*Also, T*] [*Antibacterial compound*]
TMP............	Trimethylolpropane [*Organic chemistry*]
TMP............	Trimethylpentane [*Organic chemistry*]
TMP............	Trimethyl Phosphate [*Organic chemistry*]
TMP............	Trimethylphosphine [*Organic chemistry*]
TMP............	Trimethylpsoralen [*Photochemotherapeutic compound*] (AAMN)
TMP............	Tropical Medicine and Parasitology [*U.S. National Institutes of Health*]
TMPA............	Traffic Management Program Alert [*Aviation*] (FAAC)
TMPA............	Transocean Marine Paint Association [*Netherlands*] (EAIO)
TMPA............	Trimethylphosphoramide [*Organic chemistry*]
Tmpah............	Tubular Maximum for Para-Aminohippuric Acid [*Biochemistry*] (MAE)
TMPC............	Memphis Planning Commission, Memphis, TN [*Library symbol Library of Congress*] (LCLS)
TMPC............	Theater Mission Planning Center (AAGC)
TmpChin............	Templeton China World Fund [*Associated Press*] (SAG)
TMPD............	Tempered (MSA)
TMPD............	Tetramethyl-para-phenylenediamine [*Analytical chemistry*]
TMPD............	Trimethylpentanediol [*Organic chemistry*]
TMPDF............	Trade Marks, Patents, and Designs Federation [*British*] (DBA)
TmpDrgn............	Templeton Dragon Fund [*Associated Press*] (SAG)
TMPDS............	Temporomandibular Pain and Dysfunction Syndrome [*Medicine*] (DMAA)
TMPEP............	Timber Management Policy Reform Program (GNE)
TMPG............	Ton-Miles per Gallon [*Automotive fuel*]
TmpGlb............	Templeton Global Income Fund [*Associated Press*] (SAG)
TMPH............	Ton-Mile Per Hour [*Heavy tires*] (DICI)
TMPI............	Plough, Inc., Memphis, TN [*Library symbol Library of Congress*] (LCLS)
TMPI............	Target Material Production Instruction [*Air Force*]
TMPL............	Temple
tmpl............	Temple (VRA)
TMPN............	Tetramethylpiperidinol N-oxyl [*Organic chemistry*]
TMPO............	Total Materiel Procurement Objective [*Military*]
TMPO............	Traffic Management and Proceedings Office [*CONUS*] (MCD)
TMPRG............	Tempering
TMPRLY............	Temporarily (MDG)
TMPROC............	Telemetry Processing
TmpRus............	Templeton Russia Fund [*Associated Press*] (SAG)
TmpRuss............	Templeton Russia Fund [*Associated Press*] (SAG)
TMPRY............	Temporary (AFM)
TMPS............	Temperature Monitoring Power Supply
TMPS............	Test Maintenance Panel Subassembly [*Computer science*]
TMPS............	Theater Mission Planning System [*Military*] (CAAL)
TMPS............	Tracking Modifier Power Supply
TMPS............	Trans-Mississippi Philatelic Society (EA)
TMP/SMX............	Trimethoprim-Sulfamethoxazole [*Antibacterial*] [*Antineoplastic drug*]
TMP-SMX............	Trimethoprim-Sulfamethoxazole [*Medicine*] (TAD)
TMP-SMZ............	Trimethoprim-Sulfamethoxazole [*Antineoplastic drug*] (MEDA)
TMP-SMZ-DS............	Trimethoprim-Sulfamethoxazole-Double-Strength [*Antineoplastic drug*] (MEDA)
TMPSS............	Trailer-Mounted Power Support System (DWSG)
TMPT............	Tactical Marine Petroleum Terminal (MCD)
TMPTA............	Trimethylolpropane Triacrylate [*Organic chemistry*]
TMPTMA............	Trimethylolpropane Trimethacrylate [*Organic chemistry*]
TMPV............	Torque Motor Pilot Valve (NASA)
TmpViet............	Templeton Vietnam Opportunities Fund [*Associated Press*] (SAG)
TMPW............	TMP Worldwide, Inc. [*NASDAQ symbol*] (SAG)
TMP Wr............	TMP Worldwide, Inc. [*Associated Press*] (SAG)
TMPZ............	Tetramethylpyrazine [*Biochemistry*]
TMQ............	Tambao [*Upper Volta*] [*Airport symbol*] (AD)
TMQ............	Thames Air Services & Charter Ltd. [*Nigeria*] [*ICAO designator*] (FAAC)
TMQ............	Thermoquest Corp. [*AMEX symbol*] (SAG)
TMQAP............	Technical Manual Quality Assurance Plan [*Navy*] (DNAB)
TMR............	Meridian Resource [*NYSE symbol*] [*Formerly, Texas Meridian Resources*] (SG)
TMR............	Tactical Microwave Radio
TMR............	Tactical Missile Receiver
TMR............	Tamanrasset [*Algeria*] [*Airport symbol*] (OAG)
TMR............	Tandem Mirror Reactor (MCD)

TMR............	Technical Memorandum Report
TMR............	Technology Management Review [*Military*] (AFIT)
TMR............	Telecommunications Marketing Resource Ltd. [*Telecommunications service*] (TSSD)
TMR............	Teledyne Materials Research (IAA)
TMR............	Telemanagement Resources, Inc. [*Charlotte, NC*] [*Telecommunications*] (TSSD)
TMR............	Temo Resources Ltd. [*Vancouver Stock Exchange symbol*]
TMR............	Terrestrial Myriametric Radiation [*Physics*]
TMR............	Test Malfunction Report
TMR............	Tetramethylrhodamine [*Fluorescent dye*]
TMR............	Texas Meridian Resources [*AMEX symbol*] (TTSB)
TMR............	Texas Meridian Resources Ltd. [*AMEX symbol*] (SPSG)
TMR............	Thermistor Micropower Resistor
TMR............	Timberline Air [*Canada*] [*FAA designator*] (FAAC)
TMR............	Timber Management Research [*Department of Agriculture*] (GRD)
TMR............	Time Meter Reading
TMR............	Timer (AAG)
TMR............	Tissue Maximal Ratio (STED)
TMR............	Tomakomai [*Japan*] [*Seismograph station code, US Geological Survey*] (SEIS)
TMR............	Topical Magnetic Resonance [*Medical diagnostic technique*]
TMR............	Total Materiel Requirement [*Military*] (AABC)
TMR............	Total Metal Removed
TMR............	Total Mission Recorder [*Navy*]
TMR............	Trainable Mentally Retarded
TMR............	Transmembrane Receptors [*Biochemistry*]
TMR............	Transportation Movements Release [*Military*] (AABC)
TMR............	Transvaal Mounted Rifles [*British military*] (DMA)
Tmr............	Trimmer [*British military*] (DMA)
TMR............	Triple Modular Redundancy [*Computer science*]
TMR............	True Money Rate [*Finance*]
TMR............	True Motion RADAR (IAA)
TMRA..........	Technical and Miscellanous Revenue Act (MHDB)
TMRAO........	Table Mountain Radio Astronomy Observatory
TMRBM.......	Transportable Medium-Range Ballistic Missile
TMRC..........	Technical Maintenance Repair Center (MCD)
TMRC..........	Theoretical Maximum Residue Contribution [*to acceptable daily intake*] [*Environmental Protection Agency*]
TMRD	Technical Management Requirements Document
TMRD	Transportation Movement Requirements Data (MCD)
TM Rec	Trade Mark Record [*United States*] [*A publication*] (DLA)
TM/RF.........	Telemetry/Radio Frequency
TMRI...........	RAMCON, Inc., Environmental Engineering Library, Memphis, TN [*Library symbol Library of Congress*] (LCLS)
TMRI...........	Tetramethylrhodamine Isothiocyanate [*Analytical biochemistry*]
TMRK..........	Canadian Trade Marks [*Canada Systems Group*] [*Information service or system*] (IID)
TMRK..........	Trimark Holdings [*NASDAQ symbol*] (TTSB)
TMRK..........	Trimark Holdings, Inc. [*NASDAQ symbol*] (SPSG)
TMRM..........	Tetramethylrhodamine-Maleimide [*Organic chemistry*]
TMRP..........	Technology Mobilization and Reemployment Program [*Department of Labor*]
TMRP..........	Tropical Meteorology Research Programme [*Marine science*] (OSRA)
TMR Prac	Trademark Rules of Practice [*A publication*] (DLA)
TMRS..........	Traffic Measuring and Recording System [*Telecommunications*] (TEL)
TmRSV	Tomato Ringspot Virus
TMRVDP......	Terminal-Modified RADAR Video Data Processor [*Noise control*]
TMS	[*The*] Magnolia Society (EA)
TMS	[*The*] Manufacturing System [*Burroughs Machines Ltd.*] [*Software package*] (NCC)
TMS	[*The*] Masonry Society (EA)
TMS	[*The*] Metallurgy Society [*Formerly, MS*] (IAA)
TMS	Minerals, Metals, and Materials Society (EA)
TMS	Sao Tome Island [*Sao Tome Islands*] [*Airport symbol*] (OAG)
TMS	Siena College, Memphis, TN [*Library symbol Library of Congress*] (LCLS)
TMS	Southern Missionary College, Collegedale, TN [*OCLC symbol*] (OCLC)
TMS	Tactical Missile Squadron [*Air Force*]
TMS	Tape Management Software [*Computer science*] (IAA)
TMS	Tape Management System (MCD)
TMS	Target Marking System
TMS	Target Materials Squadron (MCD)
TMS	Technisonic [*Record label*]
TMS	Technological Market Segmentation
TMS	Telecommunications Message Switcher
TMS	Telegraphy with Manual Switching [*Telecommunications*] (IAA)
TMS	Telemeter Transmitter (IAA)
TMS	Telemetry Modulation System
TMS	Telemetry Multiplex System
TMS	Teleoperator Maneuvering System (MCD)
TMS	Telephone Management System (HGAA)
TMS	Telex Management Systems (NITA)
TMS	Temperature Management Station
TMS	Temperature Measurement Society
TMS	Temporomandibular Syndrome [*Medicine*]
TMS	Temsco Helicopters, Inc. [*ICAO designator*] (FAAC)
TMS	Tesla Memorial Society (EA)
TMS	Test and Monitoring Station
TMS	Test Monitor System
TMS	Tetramethoxysilane [*Organic chemistry*]
TMS	Tetramethylsilane [*Organic chemistry*]
TMS	Textile Market Studies [*British*]

TMS	Text Message System (MCD)
TMS	Thallium Myocardial Scintigraphy [*Cardiology*]
TMS	Thematic Mapper Simulator [*for aerial photography*]
TMS	Thermal Management System [*Dell Computer Corp.*] (PCM)
TMS	Thermal Maneuvering System (SSD)
TMS	Thermomechanical System [*Instrumentation*]
TMS	Thread Mate System [*Dentistry*]
TMS	Thrust Measuring System
TMS	Tight Model Series (MCD)
TMS	Time and Motion Study (NG)
TMS	Time Multiplexed Switching [*Telecommunications*]
TMS	Time-Shared Monitor System [*Computer science*] (IEEE)
TMS	Times Square Energy Resource Ltd. [*Vancouver Stock Exchange symbol*]
TMS	Tissu Musculaire Specifique [*France*] [*Medicine*]
TMS	Tomisaki [*Mera*] [*Japan*] [*Seismograph station code, US Geological Survey*] [*Closed*] (SEIS)
TMS	Top Management Simulation [*Game*]
TMS	TOW [*Tube-Launched, Optically Tracked, Wire-Guided (Weapon)*] Missile System (RDA)
TMS	Toyota Motor Sales, Inc.
TMS	Track Monitor Supervisor (IAA)
TMS	Trademark Section, Official Gazette [*Federal government*]
TMS	Trademark Society (EA)
TMS	Traffic Management System [*FAA*] (TAG)
TMS	Traffic Measurement System
TMS	Traffic Monitoring System [*FHWA*] (TAG)
TM/S	Trained in Minesweeping [*British military*] (DMA)
TMS	Trainee Management System (MCD)
TMS	Training Material Support
TMS	Training Media Services
TMS	[*The*] Tramway Museum Society [*British*] (DCTA)
TMS	Transaction Management System (BUR)
TMS	Transcranial Magnetic Stimulation [*Proposed therapy for depression*]
TMS	Transmatic Money Service
TMS	Transmission Measuring Set [*Bell Laboratories*]
TMS	Transportation Management School [*Navy*]
TMS	Transport Management Survey (MCD)
TMS	Trascranial Magnetic Stimulation [*Medicine*]
TMS	Treasury Management Services [*British*]
TMS	Treasury Market Securities (MHDW)
TMS	TriMas Corp. [*NYSE symbol*] (SPSG)
TMS	Trimethoprim and Sulfamethoxazole [*Antibacterials*] (DAVI)
TMS	Trimethylsilane (STED)
TMS	Trimethylsilyl [*Organic chemistry*]
TMS	Truth-Maintenance System [*Artificial intelligence*] (ECON)
TMS	Turbine Management Station
TMS	Turbulence Measuring System
TMS	Type, Model, and Series
TMSA..........	Technical Marketing Society of America (EA)
TMSA..........	Telecommunications Marketing/Sales Association [*Defunct*] (EA)
TMSA..........	Thomas More Society of America (EA)
TMSA..........	Trimethylsilyl Azide [*Organic chemistry*]
TMSAN........	Trimethylsilylacetonitrile [*Organic chemistry*]
TMSB..........	Memphis and Shelby County Bar Association, Memphis, TN [*Library symbol Library of Congress*] (LCLS)
TMSC..........	Southwestern at Memphis, Memphis, TN [*Library symbol Library of Congress*] (LCLS)
TMSC..........	Talcott Mountain Science Center for Student Involvement, Inc. [*Avon, CT*] [*Telecommunications service*] (TSSD)
TMSC..........	Texas Male Sterility Cytoplasm [*Agriculture*] (OA)
TMSCC........	Shelby County Court House, Memphis, TN [*Library symbol*] [*Library of Congress*] (LCLS)
TMSCH	Memphis and Shelby County Health Department, Memphis, TN [*Library symbol Library of Congress*] (LCLS)
TMSCJ........	Trade Movement Society of Carpenters and Joiners [*A union*] [*British*]
TMSCI........	Trimethylsilyl Chloride [*Organic chemistry*]
TMSCN	Trimethylsilylcyanide [*Organic chemistry*]
TMS-CPG.....	Trimethylsilylated Controlled-Pore Glass [*Packing for chromatography*]
TMSCS........	Memphis and Shelby County Safety Council, Memphis, TN [*Library symbol Library of Congress*] (LCLS)
TMSD..........	Total Military Service to Date
TMSD..........	Training Material Support Detachment [*Army*]
TMSDC	Thermomechanical Model Software Development Center [*Research center*] (RCD)
TMSDEA	Trimethylsilyldiethylamine [*Organic chemistry*]
TMSi...........	Trimethylsilyl (STED)
TMSI..........	Trimethylsilylimidazole (STED)
TMSIM........	(Trimethylsilyl)imidazole [*Also, TSIM*] [*Organic chemistry*]
TMSM..........	Shiloh Military Trail Library, Memphis, TN [*Library symbol Library of Congress*] (LCLS)
TMSM..........	Trimethylstannylmaleate [*Organic chemistry*]
TMSMC........	Semmes-Murphey Clinic, Memphis, TN [*Library symbol Library of Congress*] (LCLS)
TMSO..........	Southern College of Optometry, Memphis, TN [*Library symbol Library of Congress*] (LCLS)
TMSq..........	Tactical Missile Squadron [*Air Force*]
TMSR..........	Technical Manual Status Report (MCD)
TMSR..........	Thrustmaster, Inc. [*NASDAQ symbol*] (SAG)
TMSS..........	Shelby State Community College, Memphis, TN [*Library symbol Library of Congress*] (LCLS)
TMSS..........	Technical Manual Specifications and Standards [*Military*] (AFIT)
TMSS..........	Technical Munitions Safety Study [*Air Force*]

TMSS..........	Tecmar Music Synthesis System
TMSS..........	Towanda-Monroeton Shippers Lifeline, Inc. [*AAR code*]
TMSSR	Technical Manual Status and Schedule Report (MCD)
TMST	Thomaston Mills, Inc. [*NASDAQ symbol*] (NQ)
TMST	Treadmill Stress Test [*or Study*] [*Cardiology*] (DAVI)
TMSTA........	Thomaston Mills 'A' [*NASDAQ symbol*] (TTSB)
TMSTB........	Thomaston Mills 'B' [*NASDAQ symbol*] (TTSB)
TMStF..........	Saint Francis Hospital, Medical Library, Memphis, TN [*Library symbol Library of Congress*] (LCLS)
TMStJ..........	Saint Jude Children's Research Hospital, Memphis, TN [*Library symbol Library of Congress*] (LCLS)
TMStJo........	Saint Joseph Hospital, Memphis, TN [*Library symbol Library of Congress*] (LCLS)
TMSVCS	TOW [*Tube-Launched, Optically Tracked, Wire-Guided (Weapon)*] Missile Sight Video Camera System (MCD)
TMT	Tactical Marine Terminal (MCD)
TMT	Talcott Mountain [*Connecticut*] [*Seismograph station code, US Geological Survey Closed*] (SEIS)
TMT	Tarsometatarsal [*Joint*] [*Anatomy*] (DAVI)
TMT	TCW/DW Term Trust 2003 [*NYSE symbol*] (SPSG)
TMT	Temora [*New South Wales*] [*Airport symbol*] (AD)
TMT	Temperature (MDG)
TMT	Terminal Monitor Program [*Computer science*] (MDG)
TMT	Testing Methods and Techniques [*Telecommunications*] (TEL)
TMT	Tetramethylthiourea [*Also, TMTU*] [*Organic chemistry*]
TMT	Thermal Measurement Treatment
TMT	Thermomechanical Treatment
TMT	Thousand Metric Tons (IMH)
TMT	Tire Management Terminal [*Automotive engineering*]
TMT	Total Maintenance Time (MCD)
TMT	Total Mission Time
TMT	TOW [*Tube-Launched, Optically Tracked, Wire-Guided (Weapon)*] Missile Transporter (MCD)
TMT	Toxic Materials Transport [*Business Publishers, Inc.*] [*Information service or system*] (CRD)
TMT	Trail Making Test [*Psychiatry*] (DAVI)
TMT	Trans Midwest Airlines, Inc. [*ICAO designator*] (FAAC)
TMT	Transmit (FAAC)
TMT	Transonic Model Tunnel [*NASA*]
TMT	Transportation Motor Transport [*Military*] (AABC)
TMT	Treatment [*Medicine*]
TMT	Troy Mineral & Tech [*Vancouver Stock Exchange symbol*]
TMT	Turret Maintenance Trainer (MCD)
TMTC..........	Thru-Mode [*or Tri-Mode*] Tape Converter
TMTC..........	Too Many to Count [*Laboratory science*] (DAVI)
TMTD..........	Tetramethylthiuram Disulfide [*Also, THTMS, TMTDS*] [*Organic chemistry*]
TMTDS........	Tetramethylthiuram Disulfide [*Also, TMTD, THTMS*] [*Organic chemistry*]
TMTF	Tile, Marble, and Terrazzo Finishers and Shopmen International Union
TMTFSGCIU...	Tile, Marble, Terrazzo, Finishers, Shopworkers, and Granite Cutters International Union (NTPA)
TMTG..........	Tactical Missile Training Group [*Military*]
TMTI	State Technical Institute at Memphis, Memphis, TN [*Library symbol Library of Congress*] (LCLS)
TMTP	Tennessee Psychiatric Hospital and Institute, Memphis, TN [*Library symbol Library of Congress*] (LCLS)
TMTR..........	Thermistor (AAG)
TMTR..........	Transmitter
TMTS	Memphis Theological Seminary of the Cumberland Presbyterian Church, Memphis, TN [*Library symbol Library of Congress*] (LCLS)
TMTS	Tactical Missile Training Squadron [*Air Force*]
TMTSF........	Tetramethyltetraselenafulvene [*Organic chemistry*]
TMTU..........	Tetramethylthiourea [*Also, TMT*] [*Organic chemistry*]
TMTX..........	Temtex Indus [*NASDAQ symbol*] (TTSB)
TMTX..........	Temtex Industries, Inc. [*NASDAQ symbol*] (NQ)
TMU	Groton, CT [*Location identifier FAA*] (FAAL)
TMU	Tactical Mobile Unit [*Police*]
TMU	Temperature Measurement Unit (NASA)
TMU	Temuco [*Chile*] [*Seismograph station code, US Geological Survey*] (SEIS)
TMU	Test Maintenance Unit [*Computer science*]
TMU	Tetramethylurea [*Organic chemistry*]
TMU	Thermal-Mechanical Unit
TMU	Time Measurement Unit [*Industrial engineering*]
TMU	Time-Multiplexer Unit [*Telecommunications*] (IAA)
TMU	Traffic Management Unit [*FAA*] (TAG)
TMU	Transmission Message Unit
TMU	Turret Mock-Up (MCD)
TMU	Twin and Multiply (IAA)
TMUP..........	Union Planters National Bank, Memphis, TN [*Library symbol Library of Congress*] (LCLS)
TMurH	Highland Rim Regional Library Center, Murfreesboro, TN [*Library symbol Library of Congress*] (LCLS)
TMurS..........	Middle Tennessee State University, Murfreesboro, TN [*Library symbol Library of Congress*] (LCLS)
TMurS-M	Center for Popular Music, Middle Tennessee State University, Murfreesboro, TN [*Library symbol*] [*Library of Congress*] (LCLS)
TMUS..........	Temporarily Mounted User Set [*Computer science*] (ADA)
TMUS..........	Toy Manufacturers of the United States
TMUSAE	United States Army Engineers Library, Memphis, TN [*Library symbol Library of Congress*] (LCLS)
TMUSDC......	United States Department of Commerce, Memphis, TN [*Library symbol Library of Congress*] (LCLS)
TMUX..........	Transmultiplexer (LAIN)
TMV	Tactical Wheeled Vehicle
TMV	Tanker Motor Vessel [*Shipping*] (DS)
TMV	Telemetry Van
TMV	Texas A & M University, Medical Sciences Library, College Station, TX [*OCLC symbol*] (OCLC)
TMV	Tobacco Mosaic Virus
TMV	Torpedoman's Mate, Aviation [*Navy rating*]
TMV	Total Molecular Volume [*Chemistry*]
TMV	Triplicated Majority Voting (IAA)
TMV	True Mean Value
TMV	Turnip Mosaic Virus
TMV	United States Veterans Administration Hospital, Memphis, TN [*Library symbol Library of Congress*] (LCLS)
TMV-C	Turnip Mosaic Virus - Common
TMV-L	Turnip Mosaic Virus - Legume
TMVP..........	Tobacco Mosaic Virus Protein
TMVS..........	Times Mirror Videotex Services, Inc. [*Information service or system Inactive*] (IID)
TMW	Tactical Missile Wing [*Air Force*]
TMW	Tamworth [*Australia Airport symbol*] (OAG)
TMW	Thermal Megawatt [*Also, Mwt*]
TMW	Tomorrow [*Amateur radio shorthand*] (WDAA)
TMW	Toyota Motor Workers' Union
TMW	Transverse Magnetic Wave [*Radio*]
TMWC..........	Waring Cox Law Firm, Memphis, TN [*Library symbol*] [*Library of Congress*] (LCLS)
TMWR	Tax Management Weekly Report [*Bureau of National Affairs*] [*Information service or system*] (CRD)
TMWR	Technical Manual Work Request
TMWR	Technical Manual Work Requirement (MCD)
TMX	Tactical Missile Experimental (IAA)
TMX	Tamoxifen [*Antineoplastic drug*]
TMX	Tandem Mirror Experiment [*Atomic fusion*]
TMX	Telefonos de Mexico [*NYSE symbol*] (SAG)
TMX	Telefonos de Mexico 'L'ADS [*NYSE symbol*] (TTSB)
TMX	Telemeter Transmitter
TMX	Timimoun [*Algeria*] [*Airport symbol*] (AD)
TMX	Transportacion Aerea Mexicana [*Mexico ICAO designator*] (FAAC)
TMXDI..........	Tetramethylxylene Diisocyanate [*Organic chemistry*]
TMXDI..........	Trimethylxylene Diisocyanate [*Organic chemistry*]
TMXI..........	Thermatrix, Inc. [*NASDAQ symbol*] (SAG)
TMXO..........	Tactical Miniature Crystal Oscillator
TMXRT........	Three-Mirror X-Ray Telescope [*NASA*]
TMZ	Houston, TX [*Location identifier FAA*] (FAAL)
TMZ	Termez [*USSR*] [*Airport symbol*] (AD)
TN	Australian Airlines [*Airline flight code*] (ODBW)
Tn	Intraocular Tension [*Ophthalmology*] (DAVI)
TN	[*The*] Navigators (EA)
Tn	Normal Intraocular Pressure [*Ophthalmology*] (DAVI)
Tn	Normal Intraocular Tension [*Ophthalmology*] (DAVI)
TN	Public Library of Nashville and Davidson County, Nashville, TN [*Library symbol Library of Congress*] (LCLS)
TN	Stewardsman [*Nonrated enlisted man*] [*Navy*]
TN	Tagesarbeitsnormen [*Workday Standards*] [*German*]
T/N	Tar and Nicotine [*In cigarettes*]
TN	Tariff Number
TN	Tarragon Oil & Gas Ltd. [*Toronto Stock Exchange symbol*]
TN	Task Number [*Computer science*] (IAA)
TN	Taunton [*British depot code*]
TN	TDRSS [*Tracking and Data Relay Satellite System*] Network [*NASA*] (SSD)
TN	Team Nursing
TN	Technical Note
TN	Technology Needs (MCD)
TN	Telephone (NATG)
TN	Telephone Number
TN	Tell en-Nasbeh (BJA)
TN	Temperature Normal [*Medicine*]
TN	Temple Name (BJA)
TN	Tennessee [*Postal code*]
TN	Tennessee Reports [*A publication*] (DLA)
TN	Terminal Node
TN	Test Narrative (CAAL)
TN	Test Negative [*Clinical chemistry*]
TN	Test Number (AAG)
TN	Texas & Northern Railway Co. [*AAR code*]
TN	Thanks (IAA)
TN	Thermonuclear
TN	Tin
tn	Titanite [*CIPW classification*] [*Geology*]
TN	Ton
TN	Tonbridge [*Postcode*] (ODBW)
TN	Tone (MSA)
tn	Toned (VRA)
TN	Total Negative (MAE)
TN	Total Nitrogen [*Analytical chemistry*]
TN	Town
TN	Track Number
TN	Trade Name (DEN)
TN	Train (AAG)
TN	Trans-Australia Airlines [*ICAO designator*] (AD)
TN	Transferable Notice [*Business term*]

TN	Transfer on Negative
TN	Transfield (NSW) Pty. Ltd. [*Transavia Division*] [*Australia ICAO aircraft manufacturer identifier*] (ICAO)
TN	Translator's Note
TN	Transport
TN	Transportation
Tn	Transposon [*Genetics*] (DOG)
TN	Transverse Nerve [*Neuroanatomy*]
TN	Treasury Note (EBF)
TN	Triafol
TN	Trigeminal Nucleus (DB)
TN	Troponin [*Biochemistry*]
T/N	True Name
TN	True Negative [*Medicine*]
TN	True North
Tn	Tukulti-Ninurta (BJA)
TN	Tuning (IAA)
TN	Tuning Unit [*JETDS nomenclature*] [*Military*] (CET)
TN	Tunisia [*IYRU nationality code*] [*ANSI two-letter standard code*] (CNC)
TN	Twelfth Night [*Shakespearean work*]
TN	Twisted Nematic [*Telecommunications*] (TEL)
TN²	[*The*] News Is the News [*Television comedy program*]
TNA	Jinan [*China*] [*Airport symbol*] (OAG)
TNA	[*The*] National Archives [*of the United States*]
TNA	Office of Terrorism and Narcotics Analysis [*Bureau of Intelligence and Research*] [*Department of State*] [*Washington, DC*] (GRD)
TNA	Tanavco Airways Ltd. [*Tanzania*] [*ICAO designator*] (FAAC)
TNA	Tasmanian Netball Association [*Australia*]
TNA	Telecommunications Network Architects [*Telecommunications service*] (TSSD)
TNA	Telocator Network of America (EA)
TN A	Tennessee Appeals Reports [*A publication*] (DLA)
TNA	Terra Nova (Bermuda)Hldg [*NYSE symbol*] (TTSB)
TNA	Terra Nova Bermuda Holdings Ltd. [*NYSE symbol*] (SAG)
TNA	Tetranitroadamantane [*Explosive*] [*Organic chemistry*]
TNA	Tetranitroaniline [*Organic chemistry*]
TNA	The National Alliance of Professional and Executive Women's Networks [*Later, TIA*] (EA)
TNA	Thermal Neutron Activation [*FAA*]
TNA	Thermal Neutron Analysis [*For detection of explosives*]
TNA	Thermal Nuclear Analyzer
TNA	Thomas Nelson - Australia [*Publisher*]
Tna	Tigrinya (BJA)
TNA	Time of Nearest Approach
TNA	Tin City [*Alaska*] [*Seismograph station code, US Geological Survey*] (SEIS)
TNA	Total Nucleic Acid
TNA	Total Nutrient Admixtures [*Parenteral emulsions*]
TNA	Training Needs Analysis (AIE)
TNA	Transient Network Analyzer (IEEE)
TNA	Transistor Noise Analyzer (IAA)
TNA	Trigeminal Nouralgia Association (EA)
TNA	Trinitroaniline [*Organic chemistry*]
TNA	Tropicana Development Corp. [*Vancouver Stock Exchange symbol*]
TNA	Turn Altitude [*Aviation*] (FAAC)
TNAC	Aquinas Junior College, Nashville, TN [*Library symbol*] [*Library of Congress*] (LCLS)
TNAC	Turkish News Agency of Cyprus (EAIO)
TNAE	United States Army Engineer District, Nashville, Nashville, TN [*Library symbol Library of Congress*] (LCLS)
TNAF	Training Name and Address File [*IRS*]
TNAM	Theater Network Analysis Model [*Europe*] (MCD)
TNANG	Tennessee Air National Guard (MUSM)
TNAS	Tuberculosis Nursing Advisory Service (DAVI)
TNAUK	Talking Newspaper Association, United Kingdom
TNAZ	Trinitroazetidine [*An explosive*]
TNB	Tanabu [*Japan*] [*Seismograph station code, US Geological Survey Closed*] (SEIS)
TNB	Technical News Bulletin [*National Bureau of Standards*]
TNB	Technion News Bulletin [*Haifa*] [*A publication*] (BJA)
TNB	Thio(nitro)benzoic Acid [*Analytical biochemistry*]
TNB	Thomas & Betts [*NYSE symbol*] (TTSB)
TNB	Thomas & Betts Corp. [*NYSE symbol*] (SPSG)
TNB	Transnasal Butorphanol [*Analgesic*]
TNB	Trinitrobenzene [*Explosive*]
TNB	Tru-Cut Needle Biopsy [*Surgery*] (DAVI)
TNB	Turnbull Associates [*British ICAO designator*] (FAAC)
TNBA	Tri-Normal-Butylaluminum [*Organic chemistry*]
TNBA	Tri-normal-butylamine [*Organic chemistry*]
TNBe	Belmont College, Nashville, TN [*Library symbol Library of Congress*] (LCLS)
TNBH	Baptist Hospital, Medical Library, Nashville, TN [*Library symbol Library of Congress*] (LCLS)
TNBP	Tri-N-Butyl Phosphate [*Organic chemistry*] (AAMN)
TNBS	Trinitrobenzenesulfonic Acid [*Biochemistry*]
TNBT	American Baptist Theological Seminary, Nashville, TN [*Library symbol Library of Congress*] (LCLS)
TNBT	Tetranitro Blue Tetrazolium [*A dye*] [*Organic chemistry*]
TNBT	The Next Big Thing
TNC	Country Music Foundation Library and Media Center, Nashville, TN [*Library symbol Library of Congress*] (LCLS)
TNC	National Aviation Consultants Ltd. [*Canada ICAO designator*] (FAAC)
TNC	[*The*] National Crossbowmen (EA)
TNC	[*The*] Nature Conservancy (EA)

TNC	[*The*] Nerve Center (EA)
TNC	Tail Number Change [*Air Force*] (AFIT)
TNC	Tekniska Nomenklaturcentralen [*Swedish Center for Technical Terminology*] [*Information service or system*] (IID)
TNC	Terminal Network Controller
TNC	Terminal Node Controller [*Computer science*]
TNC	Texas Nuclear Corp. (KSC)
TNC	Theater Naval Commander
TNC	Theatres National Committee [*British*] (DBA)
TNC	Threaded-Neill-Concelman (DOM)
TNC	Threaded Nut Connector (IAA)
TNC	Threaded-Nut Coupling [*Electronics*] (EECA)
TNC	Thymic Nurse Cell [*Cytology*]
TNC	Tide Net Controller (NATG)
TNC	Tin City [*Alaska*] [*Airport symbol*] (OAG)
TNC	Tin City, AK [*Location identifier FAA*] (FAAL)
TNC	Too Numerous to Count
TNC	Total Nonstructural Carbohydrates
TNC	Total Numerical Control (IAA)
TNC	Town & Country CI'A' [*AMEX symbol*] (TTSB)
TNC	Town & Country Corp. [*AMEX symbol*] (SPSG)
TNC	Track Navigation Computer
TNC	Track No Conversion
TNC	Track Number Conversion (IAA)
TNC	Trade Negotiations Committee [*Australia*]
TNC	Trans-National Communications, Inc.
TNC	Transnational Corp.
TNC	Transnational Operation (EERA)
TNC	Transport Network Controller
TNC	Trevecca Nazarene College [*Tennessee*]
TNC	Trinitrocellulose [*Organic chemistry*]
TNC	Trionics Technology Ltd. [*Vancouver Stock Exchange symbol*]
TNC	Tripartite Naval Commission [*Allied German Occupation Forces*]
TnC	Troponin C [*Biochemistry*]
TNC	Turbid No Creamy Layer [*Laboratory science*] (DAVI)
TNC	Twisted Nematic Liquid [*Telecommunications*] (IAA)
TNCA	Oranjestad/Reina Beatrix, Aruba Island [*Netherlands Antilles*] [*ICAO location identifier*] (ICLI)
TNCA	Thionaphthenecarboxylic Acid [*Organic chemistry*]
TNCB	Kralendijk/Flamingo, Bonaire Island [*Netherlands Antilles*] [*ICAO location identifier*] (ICLI)
TNCC	Tripartite Nuclear Cross-Sections Committee [*British, Canadian, and US*]
TNCC	Willemstad/Hato, Curacao Island [*Netherlands Antilles*] [*ICAO location identifier*] (ICLI)
TNCD	Ten Nation Committee on Disarmament [*Defunct, 1960*]
TNCE	Oranjestad/F. D. Roosevelt, Sint Eustatius Island [*Netherlands Antilles*] [*ICAO location identifier*] (ICLI)
TNCF	Curacao [*Netherlands Antilles*] [*ICAO location identifier*] (ICLI)
TNCL	Tail Number Configuration List [*Navy*] (NG)
TNCM	Philipsburg/Prinses Juliana, Sint Maarten Island [*Netherlands Antilles*] [*ICAO location identifier*] (ICLI)
Tnco	Tenneco, Inc [*Formerly, Tennessee Gas Transmission Co.*] [*Associated Press*] (SAG)
TNCR	Tencor Instruments [*NASDAQ symbol*] (TTSB)
TNCR	Tencor Instruments, Inc. [*NASDAQ symbol*] (SAG)
TN Cr	Tennessee Criminal Appeals Reports [*A publication*] (DLA)
TNCS	Saba/Yrausquin [*Netherlands Antilles*] [*ICAO location identifier*] (ICLI)
TnCSI	Technician of the Construction Surveyor's Institute [*British*] (DBQ)
TNCSS	Temporary National Commission on Supplies and Shortages [*Initiated 1974*]
TNCV	Televisao Nacional de Cabo Verde [*National Television of Cape Verde*] (EY)
TNCX	Network Connection [*NASDAQ symbol*] (TTSB)
TNCX	Network Connection, Inc. [*NASDAQ symbol*] (SAG)
TNCXW	Network Connection Wrrt [*NASDAQ symbol*] (TTSB)
TND	Telecommunications Network for the Deaf
TND	Term Normal Delivery [*Obstetrics*] (MAE)
TND	Tim Donut Ltd. [*Canada ICAO designator*] (FAAC)
TND	Tinned
TND	Todwind Development Corp. [*Vancouver Stock Exchange symbol*]
TND	Trace Narcotics Detector
TND	Trade Names Database [*Information service or system*] (IID)
TND	Trade Names Dictionary [*Later, BTC*] [*A publication*]
TND	Traditional Neighborhood Development Ordinance
TND	Trinidad [*Cuba*] [*Airport symbol*] (AD)
TND	Turned (AAG)
TNDC	Disciples of Christ Historical Society, Nashville, TN [*Library symbol Library of Congress*] (LCLS)
TNDC	Thai National Documentation Center (IID)
TNDC	Thai National Documentation Centre (NITA)
TNDC	Trade Negotiations among Developing Countries (IMH)
TND:CI	Trade Names Dictionary: Company Index [*Later, CTB*] [*A publication*]
TNDCY	Tendency (FAAC)
TNDP	Tetranitrodiphenyl [*Organic chemistry*]
TNDS	Tactical Navigational Display System
TNDS	Total Network Data System [*Bell System*]
TNDV	Tobacco Necrotic Dwarf Virus [*Plant pathology*]
Tndycft	Tandycrafts, Inc. [*Associated Press*] (SAG)
TNDZR	Tenderizer
TNE	Tanegashima [*Japan*] [*Airport symbol*] (OAG)
TNE	Taxis Aereos del Noroeste SA de CV [*Mexico ICAO designator*] (FAAC)
TNE	Terra Nova Energy [*Vancouver Stock Exchange symbol*]
TNE	The New England (EFIS)

TNE	TRIS, Sodium Chloride, EDTA [*A buffer*]
TNEC	Temporary National Economic Committee [*Congressional committee which studied the American economic system*] [*World War II*]
TNEF	Trinitroethyl Formal [*An explosive*]
TNEL	Thomas Nelson (EFIS)
TNEL	Total Noise Exposure Level (DA)
TNEOC	Trinitroethyl Orthocarbonate [*An explosive*]
TNEOF	Trinitroethyl Orthoformate [*An explosive*]
TNEP	Total Noise Equivalent Power [*Electronics*] (EECA)
TNET	Terminal and Computer Network (MHDI)
TNetix	T-Netix, Inc. [*Associated Press*] (SAG)
TNF	Fisk University, Nashville, TN [*Library symbol Library of Congress*] (LCLS)
TNF	Tactical Nuclear Force (MCD)
TNF	Theater Nuclear Forces
TNF	Thin Nickel Film
TNF	Third Normal Form [*Databases*]
TNF	Timing Negative Film
TNF	Trainfire
TNF	Transfer on No Overflow
TNF	Trinitrofluorenone [*Organic chemistry*]
TNF	True North Film [*Vancouver Stock Exchange symbol*]
TNF	Tumor Necrosis Factor [*Immunology*] [*Antineoplastic drug*]
TNF	Tumor Neurosis Factor [*Biochemistry*]
TNF-A	Tumor Necrosis Factor-Alpha
TNFB	Free-Will Baptist Bible College, Nashville, TN [*Library symbol Library of Congress*] (LCLS)
TNFE	Twisted Nematic Field Effect [*Telecommunications*] (IAA)
TNFI	North Face, Inc. (The) [*NASDAQ symbol*] (SAG)
TNFR	Tumor Necrosis Factor Receptor [*Immunology*]
TNF/S	Theater Nuclear Forces Security [*DoD*]
TNFS	Theater Nuclear Forces Survivability (MCD)
TNFS3	Theater Nuclear Forces, Survivability, Security, and Safety (MCD)
TNFSS	Theater Nuclear Forces Survivability and Security (MCD)
TNG	G & B Aviation Ltd. [*British ICAO designator*] (FAAC)
TNG	[*The*] Newspaper Guild (EA)
TNG	Tanger [*Morocco*] [*Airport symbol*] (OAG)
TNG	Tangerang [*Java*] [*Seismograph station code, US Geological Survey*] (SEIS)
TNG	Tennessee Air National Guard (164th Airlift Group) [*FAA designator*] (FAAC)
TNG	The Next Generation
TNG	Tongue (MSA)
TNG	Touch N' Go [*Computer Interface*] [*Touch N' Go Systems, Inc*] (PCM)
TNG	Training (AAG)
TNG	Transdermal Nitroglycerine Patch [*Medicine*]
TNG	Trinitroglycerin [*Also, TNT*] (DAVI)
TNG	Tungco Resources Corp. [*Vancouver Stock Exchange symbol*]
TNGANCH	Training Anchorage [*Navy*] (NVT)
TNGE	Tonnage [*Shipping*]
TNGLIT	Training Literature [*Military*]
TNGS	Theory of Neuronal Group Selection [*Neurology*]
TngS	Training Subject
TNGSUP	Training Support [*Navy*] (NVT)
TNGSVCS	Training Services [*Navy*] (NVT)
TNGT	Tonight (FAAC)
TNH	Tampa-Hillsborough County Public Library, Tampa, FL [*OCLC symbol*] (OCLC)
TNH	Tax Notes Highlights [*Tax Analysts*] [*Information service or system*] (CRD)
TNH	Terra Nitrogen Co. Ltd.[*Formerly, Agricultural Minerals Ltd.*] [*NYSE symbol*] (SAG)
TNH	Terra Nitrogen L.P. [*NYSE symbol*] (TTSB)
TNH	Tienshul [*Republic of China*] [*Seismograph station code, US Geological Survey*] (SEIS)
TNH	Turn Height [*Aviation*] (FAAC)
TNH	Turnhouse Flying Club [*British*] [*FAA designator*] (FAAC)
TNHCA	Hospital Corp. of America, Research/Information Services, Nashville, TN [*Library symbol Library of Congress*] (LCLS)
TNHQ	Theater Navy Headquarters
TNI	[*The*] Network, Inc. [*An association*] (EA)
TNI	[*The*] Networking Institute [*Commercial firm*] (EA)
TNI	Peipeinimaru, TT [*Location identifier FAA*] (FAAL)
TNI	Thin Nickel Iron
TNI	Total Nodal Irradiation [*Oncology*]
TNI	Traffic Noise Index [*Department of Transportation*]
TNI	Transaction Network Svcs. [*NYSE symbol*]
TNI	Transcisco Indus [*AMEX symbol*] (TTSB)
TNI	Transcisco Industries [*AMEX symbol*] (SPSG)
TNI	Trans International Gold [*Vancouver Stock Exchange symbol*]
TNI	Transnational Institute [*Netherlands*]
TnI	Troponin I [*Biochemistry*]
TNIA	[*The*] Network Inc. of America [*Information service or system*] (IID)
TNIF	Thin Nickel Iron Film
TnIMBM	Technician of the Institute of Municipal Building Management [*British*] (DBQ)
TNIP	TDRSS/NASCOM [*Tracking and Data Relay Satellite System/NASA Communications Network*] Interface Panel (SSD)
TNIU	Trustworthy Network Interface Unit [*Telecommunications*] (OSI)
TNJ	Joint University Libraries, Nashville, TN [*Library symbol Library of Congress*] (LCLS)
TNJ	Tanjung Pinang [*Indonesia*] [*Airport symbol*] (OAG)
TNJ-L	Joint University Libraries, Vanderbilt School of Law, Nashville, TN [*Library symbol Library of Congress*] (LCLS)

TNJ-M	Joint University Libraries, Vanderbilt Medical Center, Nashville, TN [*Library symbol Library of Congress*] (LCLS)
TNJ-P	Joint University Libraries, George Peabody College for Teachers, Nashville, TN [*Library symbol Library of Congress*] (LCLS)
TNJ-R	Joint University Libraries, Vanderbilt School of Religion, Nashville, TN [*Library symbol Library of Congress*] (LCLS)
TNJ-S	Joint University Libraries, Scarritt College for Christian Workers, Nashville, TN [*Library symbol Library of Congress*] (LCLS)
TNK	Tank (AAG)
TNK	Tinkers Knob [*California*] [*Seismograph station code, US Geological Survey*] (SEIS)
TNK	Torah Nebi'im Ketubim [*Teaching, prophets, writing*] [*Pronounced Tanakh*] [*The Hebrew Bible*]
TNK	Tunkwa Copper Mining [*Vancouver Stock Exchange symbol*]
TNK	Tununak [*Alaska*] [*Airport symbol*] (OAG)
TNK	[*The*] Two Noble Kinsmen [*Shakespearean work*]
TNL	David Lipscomb College, Nashville, TN [*Library symbol Library of Congress*] (LCLS)
TNL	Technical Newsletter
TNL	Technitrol, Inc. [*AMEX symbol*] (SPSG)
TNL	Terminal Net Loss
TNL	Times Newspapers Ltd. [*British*]
TNL	Tunnel (MSA)
TnL	Tunnel Luminescence [*Physics*]
TNLCD	Twisted Nematic Liquid Crystal Display [*Telecommunications*] (IAA)
TNLDIO	Tunnel Diode [*Electronics*]
TNLR	Railroad Tunnel [*Board on Geographic Names*]
TNM	Meharry Medical College, Nashville, TN [*Library symbol Library of Congress*] (LCLS)
TNM	Nelson [*Thomas*], Inc. [*NYSE symbol*] (SAG)
TNM	Tashota-Nipigon Mines [*Vancouver Stock Exchange symbol*]
TNM	Telecommunications and Network Management
TNM	Tetranitromethane [*Organic chemistry*]
TNM	Texas-New Mexico Railway Co. [*AAR code*]
TNM	Thomas Nelson [*NYSE symbol*] (TTSB)
TNM	Thyroid Node Metastasis [*Medicine*] (STED)
TNM	Topical Nitrogen Mustard [*Dermatology*]
TNM	Transmission Network Manager [*IBM Corp.*] (CIST)
TNM	Tumor, Node, and Metastasis [*Criteria for staging*] [*Pathology*] (DAVI)
TNM	Tumor, Node, Metastases [*System*] [*Medicine*] (HCT)
TNM	Twisted Nematic Mode [*Telecommunications*] (IAA)
TNM.B	Thomas Nelson 'B' [*NYSE symbol*] (TTSB)
TNMCS	Total Not-Mission Capable, Supply [*Air Force*] (DOMA)
TNMH	Metro General Hospital, Nashville, TN [*Library symbol Library of Congress*] (LCLS)
TNMPH	Methodist Publishing House Library, Nashville, TN [*Library symbol Library of Congress*] (LCLS)
TNMR	Tritium Nuclear Magnetic Resonance [*Spectrometry*]
TNN	[*The*] Nashville Network [*Cable-television system*]
TNN	Nashville Public Library, Nashville, TN [*OCLC symbol*] (OCLC)
TNN	Tainan [*Taiwan*] [*Airport symbol*] (OAG)
TNN	Tanana [*Alaska*] [*Seismograph station code, US Geological Survey*] (SEIS)
TNN	Technology Transfer Network [*Environmental Protection Agency*] (AEPA)
TNN	The Nurturing Network (PAZ)
TNO	Nederlandse Centrale Organisatie voor Toegepast Natuurwetenschappelijk Onderzoek [*Netherlands Institute for Applied Scientific Research*]
TNO	Tamarindo [*Costa Rica*] [*Airport symbol*] (OAG)
TNO	Tenore Oil & Gas [*Vancouver Stock Exchange symbol*]
TNO	Texas & New Orleans R. R. [*AAR code*]
TNO	Torino [*Italy*] [*Seismograph station code, US Geological Survey*] (SEIS)
TNO	Transfer on No Overflow (SAA)
TNO	True North Communications, Inc. [*Formerly, Foote, Cone & Belding*] [*NYSE symbol*] (SAG)
TNO	True North Communicns [*NYSE symbol*] (TTSB)
TNOC	Threads No Couplings
TNOP	Total Network Operations Plan [*Telecommunications*] (TEL)
TNOR	Temiskaming & Northern Ontario Railway
TNOT	Total Not Operating Time
TNP	[*The*] National Party [*Grenada*] [*Political party*] (EY)
TNP	[*The*] New Party [*Australia Political party*]
TNP	Thailand National Police (CINC)
TNP	Theatre National Populaire [*France*]
TNP	TNP Enterprises [*NYSE symbol*] (TTSB)
TNP	TNP Enterprises, Inc. [*NYSE symbol*] (SPSG)
TNP	Tonopah [*Nevada*] [*Seismograph station code, US Geological Survey*] (SEIS)
TNP	Total Net Positive (STED)
TNP	Transkei National Party [*Political party*] (EY)
TNP	Trinitrophenol [*or Trinitrophenyl*] [*Organic chemistry*]
TNP	Trojan Nuclear Plant (NRCH)
TNP	Twentynine Palms [*California*] [*Airport symbol*] (OAG)
TNP	Twentynine Palms, CA [*Location identifier FAA*] (FAAL)
TNPA	Tri-Normal-Propylaluminum [*Organic chemistry*]
TNPA	Tri-normal-propylamine [*Organic chemistry*]
TNPC	Taiwan New PC [*Personal Computer*] Consortium [*Computer science*]
TNPF	Tidewater Nicaragua Project Foundation (EA)
TNPG	[*The*] Nuclear Power Group [*British*]
TNPH	Tennessee Department of Public Health, Nashville, TN [*Library symbol Library of Congress*] (LCLS)

TNPK	Turnpike
TNP-KLH	Trinitrophenyl Keyhole Limpet Hemocyanin [*Immunology*]
TNPM	Transient Neonatal Pustular Melanosis [*Medicine*] (MEDA)
TNPO	Terminal Navy Post Office (AFM)
TNPP	Planned Parenthood of Nashville, Nashville, TN [*Library symbol Library of Congress*] (LCLS)
TNPP	Tris(nonylphenyl) Phosphite [*Organic chemistry*]
TNPZOW	Towarzystwo Niesienia Pomocy Zydom Ofiarom Wojny [*A publication*] (BJA)
TNQ	Tongo [*Sierra Leone*] [*Airport symbol*] (AD)
TNR	Antananarivo [*Madagascar*] [*Airport symbol*] (OAG)
TNR	[*The*] New Repertory
TNR	Tanana Air Service [*ICAO designator*] (FAAC)
TNR	Tananarive [*Malagasy*] [*Airport symbol*] (AD)
TNR	Tanganyika Notes and Records [*A publication*]
TNR	Tenera, Inc. [*AMEX symbol*] (SAG)
TNR	Thinner
TNR	Titan Resources Ltd. [*Vancouver Stock Exchange symbol*]
TNR	Tone Not Relevant
TNR	Tonic Neck Reflex [*Physiology*]
TNR	Total Network Recall [*Systems Enhancement Corp.*] [*Computer science*] (PCM)
TNR	Trainer (AAG)
TNR	Transit Nuclear Radiation
TNR	Trinucleotide Repeat Sequence [*Genetics*]
TNR	True Negative Rate [*Medicine*] (DAVI)
TNRCC	Texas Natural Resource Conservation Commission
TNRCC	Texas Natural Resources Conservation Council (DOGT)
TNRDA	Transit Network Route Decision Aid [*FHWA*] (TAG)
TNRE	Transit Nuclear Radiation Effect
TNRIS	Texas Natural Resources Information System [*Austin*] [*Information service or system*] (IID)
TNRIS	Transportation Noise Research Information Service [*Department of Transportation*]
TNRY	Tannery
TNS	[*The*] Names Society (EA)
TNS	[*The*] National Switchboard [*Phoenix, AZ*] [*Telecommunications*] (TSSD)
TNS	[*The*] New Salesmanship [*Book by Steve Salerno*]
TNS	[*The*] Next Step [*Physics*]
TNS	Servicios Aereos do Vale Amazonico SA [*Brazil*] [*ICAO designator*] (FAAC)
TNS	Tactical Navigation System (DWSG)
TNS	Tank Nitrogen Supply (AAG)
TNS	Tanos Petroleum Corp. [*Vancouver Stock Exchange symbol*]
TNS	Taunus [*Federal Republic of Germany*] [*Seismograph station code, US Geological Survey*] (SEIS)
TNS	Telecommunications Network Services [*Data Resources*] [*Information service or system*] (CRD)
TNS	Tennessee State Library and Archives, Nashville, TN [*OCLC symbol*] (OCLC)
TNS	Thames Navigation Service [*British*] (DS)
TNS	Thermal Night Site
TNS	Thomas Nast Society (EA)
TNS	Times Network for Schools (NITA)
TNS	Toensberg [*Norway*] [*Airport symbol*] (AD)
TNS	Toluidinylnaphthalene Sulfonate [*Organic chemistry*]
TNS	Topical Numismatic Society (EA)
TNS	Toronto Normal School
TNS	Total Nuclear Score (STED)
TNS	Track Number Sorted Table (SAA)
TNS	Transaction Network Service [*AT & T*]
TNS	Transcutaneous Nerve Stimulation [*Also, TENS, TES*] [*A method of pain control*] [*Medicine*]
TNS	Transit Network Selection [*Computer science*] (DDC)
TNS	Triple Nine Society (EA)
TNS	Tumor Necrosis Serum (PDAA)
TNS	Tunable Noise Source
TNSA	[*The*] National Spiritual Alliance of the United States of America
TNSA	Technical Nuclear Safety (MCD)
TNSB	Southern Baptist Convention Historical Commission, Nashville, TN [*Library symbol Library of Congress*] (LCLS)
TNSB-S	Sunday School Board of the Southern Baptist Convention, Nashville, TN [*Library symbol*] [*Library of Congress*] (LCLS)
TNSDUNSPHI	[*The*] National Society to Discourage Use of the Name Smith for Purposes of Hypothetical Illustration
TNSI	[*A*] Text-Book of North-Semitic Inscriptions [*A publication*] (BJA)
TNSI	Transaction Network Services [*NASDAQ symbol*] (SAG)
TNSI	Transaction Network Svcs [*NASDAQ symbol*] (TTSB)
TNSL	Tensile
TNSL	Tinsley Laboratories, Inc. [*NASDAQ symbol*] (NQ)
TNSL	Tinsley Labs [*NASDAQ symbol*] (TTSB)
TNSN	Tension (MSA)
TNSP	Transportation (CINC)
TNSTI	Nashville State Technical Institute, Educational Resource Center, Nashville, TN [*Library symbol*] [*Library of Congress*] (LCLS)
TNStT	Saint Thomas Hospital, Health Sciences Library, Nashville, TN [*Library symbol Library of Congress*] (LCLS)
TNT	Miami, FL [*Location identifier FAA*] (FAAL)
TNT	[*The*] Next Trend
TNT	Target Network Television [*Cable television network*] (NTCM)
TNT	Tax Notes Today [*Database*] [*Tax Analysts*] [*Information service or system*] (CRD)
TNT	Teleconference Network of Texas [*University of Texas*] [*San Antonio*] [*Telecommunications*] (TSSD)
TNT	Test for the Necessity of Therapy [*Medicine*]
TNT	Theater Network Television (IAA)
tnt	Tint (VRA)
TNT	Tinto Gold Corp. [*Vancouver Stock Exchange symbol*]
TNT	Titles Now Troublesome [*School books*] [*American Library Association*]
TNT	TNT Tariff Agents, Inc., New York NY [*STAC*]
TNT	Tobramycin-Nafcillin-Ticarcillin [*Antibiotic combination*]
TNT	Toronto [*Ontario*] [*Seismograph station code, US Geological Survey Closed*] (SEIS)
TNT	Torque, Nip, and Tension [*Winding technology*]
TNT	Tramcinolone and Nystatin (STED)
TNT	Transient Nuclear Test
TNT	Transnational Terrorism (ADA)
TNT	Trans North Turbo Air Ltd. [*Canada ICAO designator*] (FAAC)
TNT	Transparent Network Transport [*Computer science*] (CDE)
TNT	Transportation News Ticker [*Knight-Ridder Business Information Services*] [*Information service or system*] (CRD)
TNT	Treasury Northern Territory [*Australia*]
TNT	Trim, Neat, and Terrific [*Slang*]
TNT	Trinitrotoluene [*Explosive*]
TnT	Troponin T [*Biochemistry*]
TNT	Tuned-Not-Tuned (IAA)
TNT	Turner Network Television [*Cable-television system*]
TNT	Twist and Turn [*Barbie doll collector term*]
TNTA	Textron Aero-Structures, Nashville, TN [*Library symbol*] [*Library of Congress*] (LCLS)
TNTBP	Trinitrotoluene and Black Powder (SAA)
TNTC	Too Numerous to Count [*Microbiology*]
TNTC	Tyndale New Testament Commentary [*A publication*] (BJA)
TNTDL	Tabulated Numerical Technical Data List
TNTDR	Thermonuclear TOKAMAK Demonstration Reactor [*Particle physics*]
TNTF	TNT Freightways Corp. [*NASDAQ symbol*] (SAG)
TNT Frt	TNT Freightways Corp. [*Associated Press*] (SAG)
TNTHA	Tennessee Hospital Association, Nashville, TN [*Library symbol Library of Congress*] (LCLS)
TNTN	Trevecca Nazarene College, Nashville, TN [*Library symbol Library of Congress*] (LCLS)
TNT-S	Test for The Necessity of Therapy for Seniors [*Medicine*]
TNTU	University of Tennessee, Nashville, TN [*Library symbol Library of Congress*] (LCLS)
TNTV	Tentative (AFM)
TNTX	T-Netix, Inc. [*NASDAQ symbol*] (SAG)
TNU	Newton, IA [*Location identifier FAA*] (FAAL)
tnu	Tennessee [*MARC country of publication code Library of Congress*] (LCCP)
TNU	Upper Room Devotional Library and Museum, Nashville, TN [*Library symbol Library of Congress*] (LCLS)
TNUK	Thomas Nelson - United Kingdom [*Publisher*]
TNUM	United Methodist Publishing House, Nashville, TN [*Library symbol Library of Congress*] (LCLS)
TNUSA	Ted Nugent United Sportsmen of America
TNV	Navasota, TX [*Location identifier FAA*] (FAAL)
TNV	Toonavia [*France ICAO designator*] (FAAC)
TNV	Tobacco Necrosis Virus
TNV	Total Net Value
TNV	Total Nonvolatile [*Chemistry*]
TNV	Trinova Corp. [*NYSE symbol*] (SPSG)
TNVAC	Tennessee Valley Athletic Conference (PSS)
TNVS	Thermal Night Vision System
TNW	Tactical Nuclear Warfare (MCD)
TNW	Tactical Nuclear Weapon
TNW	Talking Newspaper Week [*British*]
TNW	Theater Nuclear Weapon
TNW/CW	Tactical Nuclear Warfare/Chemical Warfare (MCD)
TN WP	Thermonuclear Weapon (WDAA)
TNWRRI	Tennessee Water Resources Research Center [*Knoxville, TN*] [*Department of the Interior*] (GRD)
TNX	Thanks [*Communications operator's procedural remark*]
TNX	Tonopah, NV [*Location identifier FAA*] (FAAL)
TNX	Transfer on No Index (SAA)
TNX	Trinitroxylene [*Organic chemistry*]
TNY	Trinity University, Library, San Antonio, TX [*OCLC symbol*] (OCLC)
TNYT	The New York Times Online (NITA)
TNYTI	[*The*] New York Times Index
TNZ	Rex Aviation (New Zealand) Ltd. [*ICAO designator*] (FAAC)
TNZ	Tarata [*New Zealand*] [*Seismograph station code, US Geological Survey*] (SEIS)
TNZ	Thermoneutral Zone
TNZ	Transfer on Nonzero
TNZ	Transfer on No Zero (IAA)
TNZ	Tranzonic Cos. [*AMEX symbol*] (SPSG)
TNZ.A	Tranzonic Cos 'A' [*AMEX symbol*] (TTSB)
TNZ.B	Tranzonic Cos Cl'B' [*AMEX symbol*] (TTSB)
TO	Alkan Air Ltd. [*ICAO designator*] (AD)
TO	Games Taken Out [*Baseball*]
TO	No Evidence of Primary Tumor [*Oncology*] (DAVI)
TO	Oak Ridge Public Library, Oak Ridge, TN [*Library symbol Library of Congress*] (LCLS)
TO	Old Tuberculin (STED)
TO	Original Tuberculin (STED)
TO	Table of Organization
TO	Tactical Observer
TO	Tactical Officer [*Military*] (RDA)
TO	Takeoff [*Aviation*]

T-0	Takeoff [*NASA*] (NAKS)
T/0	Take Over (MCD)
TO	Tandem Outlet
T/0	Target of Opportunity
TO	Target Organ [*Medicine*] (AAMN)
TO	Targum Onkelos (BJA)
TO	Task Order (MCD)
TO	TDRS [*Tracking and Data Relay Satellite*] Operations [*NASA*] (SSD)
TO	Technical Objective
TO	Technical Observer
TO	Technical Officer [*Military British*]
TO	Technical Order
TO	Tech/Ops Sevcon [*AMEX symbol*] (TTSB)
TO	Tech-Ops Sevcon, Inc. [*AMEX symbol*] (SAG)
TO	Telegraphic Order (WDAA)
TO	Telegraph Office
TO	Telemetry Oscillator (IAA)
TO	Telephone Office
TO	Telephone Order [*Medicine*]
TO	Tell el-Obed (BJA)
TO	Temperature, Oral [*Medicine*]
TO	Terminal Office [*Computer science*] (IAA)
TO	Test Operation (AAG)
TO	Test Outline (CAAL)
TO	Theater of Operations [*Military*]
TO	Theatre Ontario [*Canada*] (WWLA)
TO	Theiler's Original [*Strain of mouse encephalitis virus*]
TO	Thiazole Orange [*Organic chemistry*]
TO	Through Ownership [*Shipping*]
TO	Ticked Off [*Slang*]
T-0	Time of Launch [*NASA*] (KSC)
TO	Time Opening
TO	Time-Out
TO	Time Over (IAA)
TO	Tinctura Opii [*Tincture of Opium*]
TO	Tincture of Opium [*Pharmacology*] (DAVI)
TO	Tonga [*ANSI two-letter standard code*] (CNC)
to	Tonga [*MARC country of publication code Library of Congress*] (LCCP)
TO	Tonight Only [*Newspapers*] (DGA)
TO	Tonnage Opening (DS)
T/0	To Oblige (AIA)
TO	Tool Offset (IAA)
TO	Tool Order
TO	Tops Order (MCD)
TO	Toronto
To	Toronto Stock Exchange [*Canada*]
TO	Torpedo Officer [*Obsolete Navy British*]
TO	Total Obstruction (STED)
TO	Township
TO	Tracheo-Oesophageal [*Medicine*] (DAVI)
TO	Tracking Officer (IAA)
TO	Traded Options Market [*London Stock Exchange*]
TO	Traditional Orthography [*Writing system*]
TO	Traffic Officer
TO	Trained Operator [*British military*] (DMA)
TO	Transfer Order
TO	Transfer Out (STED)
TO	Transistor Outline [*Package*] (AAEL)
TO	Transmission Only [*Telecommunications*]
TO	Transmitter Oscillator
TO	Transportation Officer [*Military*]
TO	Transverse Optic
TO	Travel Order
TO	Treasury Obligation [*Finance*]
TO	Treasury Order [*British*] (ROG)
TO	Tricuspid Valve Opening [*Cardiology*]
TO	Troy Ounce
TO	Trust Officer [*Banking*] (TBD)
TO	Tryptophan Oxygenase [*Also, TP, TPO*] [*An enzyme*]
TO	Tuberculin Ober [*Supernatant portion*] [*Medicine*]
TO	Tuberculin Old [*or Original*] [*Also, OT*] [*Medicine*]
TO	Tubo-Ovarian [*Medicine*] (MAE)
TO	Tuesdays Only [*British railroad term*]
TO	Turned On (STED)
T/0	Turned Out [*for Examination*] [*Tea trade*] (ROG)
TO	Turn-Off
TO	Turnout (AAG)
TO	Turnover [*Number*] [*With reference to enzyme activity*]
TO	[*A*] Turn Over [*A prospective customer who cannot be sold by one clerk and is turned over to another*] [*Merchandising slang*]
TO	Tyler's Original [*Mice*] (DB)
TO	Type of Organization Code [*IRS*]
TO	Tyrosine Oxidase [*An enzyme*]
TOA	Table of Allowances
TOA	Table of Organization and Allowance
TOA	Take-Off Angle (AAEL)
TOA	Telecommunications Officers' Association [*Australia*]
TOA	Terms of Agreement [*Army*] (AABC)
TOA	Terre Ocean Atmosphere [*Marine science*] (OSRA)
TOA	Theatre Owners of America [*Later, NATO*] (EA)
TOA	Thermal Optical Analysis
TOA	Time of Arrival (AFM)
TOA	Time Out of Area (MCD)

TOA	Tolsona [*Alaska*] [*Seismograph station code, US Geological Survey*] (SEIS)
TOA	Top of the Atmosphere [*Meterology*]
TOA	Tornado Watch [*Telecommunications*] (OTD)
TOA	Torrance, CA [*Location identifier FAA*] (FAAL)
TOA	Total Obligational Authority [*Military*]
TOA	Toyota Owners Association (EA)
TOA	Trace Organic Analysis [*Environmental Protection Agency*] (GFGA)
TOA	Trade-Off Analysis [*Military*]
TOA	Transferred on Assembly (IAA)
TOA	Trans Oceanic Airways Ltd. [*British*]
TOA	Transportation Operating Agencies (AFM)
TOA	Transportation Operations Authority (MCD)
TOA	Trim on Assembly (MCD)
TOA	Tromsoe [*Norway*] [*Airport symbol*] (AD)
TOA	Truck Operation Analysis
TOA	Tubemakers of Australia Ltd. [*Commercial firm*]
TOA	Tubo-Ovarian Abscess [*Medicine*]
TOA	Type of Address (TNIG)
TOA	Type of Agent
TOAA	Total Overall Aerospace Vehicle [*or Aircraft*] Authorization
TOAA	Trawler Owners' Association of Australia
TOAC	Tool Accessory (AAG)
TOAD	Take Off and Die [*Surfers' slang for a very dangerous wave*]
TOAD	Terahertz Optical Asymmetric Demultiplexer [*Optical computing*]
TOAD	Tobyhanna Army Depot [*Pennsylvania*] (AABC)
TOAD	Towed Optical Assessment Device [*Marine science*] (MSC)
TOADS	Take Off and Die Syndrome
TOADS	Terminal-Oriented Administrative Data System
TOAI	Total Overall Aerospace Vehicle [*or Aircraft*] Inventory
TOAL	Test of Adolescent Language
TOAL	Total Ordnance Alteration Application List [*Navy*]
TOAMAC	[*The*] Optimum Army Materiel Command (RDA)
TO-AN	Tropical Ocean-Atmosphere Newsletter [*Now Tropical Ocean-Global Atmosphere Notes*] (USDC)
TO & E	Tables of Organization and Equipment [*Military*] (AAG)
TOAP	Test of Academic Performance (TMMY)
TOAP	Thioguanine, Oncovin [*Vincristine*], ara-C, Prednisone [*Antineoplastic drug regimen*]
Toastmst.	Toastmaster, Inc. [*Associated Press*] (SAG)
TOB	Tackling Offending Behavior (WDAA)
TOB	Takeoff Boost [*Aviation*]
TOB	Telemetry Output Buffer [*Computer science*]
TOB	Tender Option Bond [*Finance*]
TOB	Test One BIT [*Binary Digit*] (SAA)
TOB	Tobacco (ADA)
Tob	Tobacco Branch, Internal Revenue Bureau [*United States*] (DLA)
TOB	Tobias [*Old Testament book*] [*Douay version*]
TOB	Tobit [*Old Testament book*] [*Roman Catholic canon*] (ROG)
TOB	Toboggan
TOB	Tobramycin (DB)
TOB	Tobruk [*Libya*] [*Airport symbol*] (OAG)
TOB	Tow Bar (MCD)
TOB	Transistor Output Buffer (DNAB)
TOB	Tube over Bar [*Suspension*] (MCD)
TOB	Type of Blast
TOBA	Theater Owners Booking Association [*Vaudeville*] [*Facetious translation: Tough on Black Artists*]
TOBA	Thoroughbred Owners and Breeders Association (EA)
TOBA	Tough on Black Actors [*Facetious translation of acronym for Theater Owners Booking Association*]
TOBE	Test of Basic Experiences [*Child development test*]
TOBEC	Total Body Electrical Conductivity [*Medicine*] (WDAA)
Tobey	Tobey's Reports [*9, 10 Rhode Island*] [*A publication*] (DLA)
TOBI	Test of Basic Information [*Education*]
TOBI	Towed Ocean Bottom Instrument [*Oceanography*]
TOBI	Toxicity Bibliography [*MEDLARS*]
TOBP	Tobramycin Peak [*An antibiotic*] (DAVI)
TobRV	Tobacco Ring Spot Virus
TOBS	Telemetering Ocean Bottom Seismometer [*Marine science*] (MSC)
TOBT	Tobramycin, Trough [*An antibiotic*] (DAVI)
TOBWE	Tactical Observing Weather Element [*Air Force*]
TOC	AT&T Capital Corp. [*NYSE symbol*] (SAG)
TOC	[*The*] Operations Council of the American Trucking Associations (EA)
TOC	Table of Coincidences [*Telecommunications*] (TEL)
TOC	Table of Contents
TOC	Tactical Operations Center [*Military*]
TOC	Tagliabue Open Cup [*Analytical chemistry*]
TOC	Tag Open Cup [*Flash point test*]
TOC	Tanker Operational Circular
TOC	Task Order Contract
TOC	Task-Oriented Costing [*Telecommunications*] (TEL)
TOC	Tasmanian Olympic Council [*Australia*]
TOC	Technical Operating Center [*Telecommunications*] (TSSD)
TOC	Technical Order Compliance [*Military*]
TOC	Television Operating Center
TOC	Television Operators Caucus (EA)
TOC	Test of Cure [*Medicine*]
TOC	Test Operations Center [*NASA*] (NASA)
TOC	Test Operations Change [*NASA*] (NASA)
TOC	Tetradichlorozylene (GNE)
TOC	Theater of Operations Command [*Military*]
TOC	Thermo Optek Corp. [*AMEX symbol*] (SAG)
TOC	Thomson Corp. [*TS symbol*] (TTSB)

TOC	Tiers Ordre Carmelitaine [*Carmelite Third Order*] [*An association Italy*] (EAIO)
TOC	Timber Operators Council (EA)
TOC	Time of Correlation (MCD)
TOC	Time Optimal Control (MCD)
TOC	Time Out Circuit (MHDI)
TOC	Timing Operation Center
TOC	Tinctura Opii Camphorata [*Paregoric Elixir*] [*Pharmacy*] (ROG)
TOC	To Be Continued (FAAC)
TOC	Toccoa, GA [*Location identifier FAA*] (FAAL)
TOC	Tocklai [*India*] [*Seismograph station code, US Geological Survey*] (SEIS)
TOC	Tooling Order Change
TOC	Top of Climb [*Aviation*]
TOC	TOS [*TIROS Operational Satellite*] Operations Center (NOAA)
TOC	Total Operational Cost [*Engineering*]
TOC	Total Optical Color [*Photography*] (OA)
TOC	Total Organic Carbon
TOC	Total Organic Compound [*Organic chemistry*] (DAVI)
TOC	Total Oxidizable Carbon (AAEL)
TOC	Traditional Organized Crime
TOC	Traffic Order Change (SAA)
TOC	Trainer Operator Console (SAA)
TOC	Training Occupational Classification (AIE)
TOC	Transfer of Control
TOC	Transportation Operating Command [*MTMC*] (TAG)
TOC	Transportation Operations Center
TOC	Trap Oxidizer-Continuous [*Automotive engineering*]
TOC	Tubo-Ovarian Complex [*Anatomy*] (DAVI)
TOC	Turn-On Command (KSC)
TOCA	[*The*] Order of the Crown in America (EA)
TOCA	Turf and Ornamental Communicators Association (NTPA)
TOCAP	Terminal-Oriented Control Applications Program
TOCC	TDRSS [*Tracking and Data Relay Satellite System*] Operations Control Center [*NASA*]
TOCC	Technical and Operations Control Center [*INTELSAT*]
TOCC	Test Operations Control Center [*NASA*]
TOCC	Transfer of Control Card
TOC/CP	Tactical Operations Center/Command Post [*Military*]
TOCCWE	Tactical Operations Control Center Weather Element [*Air Force*]
TOCDF	Tooele Chemical Agent Disposal Facility [*Utah*]
TOC/ECP	Technical Order Compliance/Engineering Change Proposal [*Military*] (AFIT)
TOCED	Table of Contents Editor Processor [*Computer science*]
Toch	Tocharian [*Language group*] (BARN)
TOCI	Total Organic Chlorine [*Analytical chemistry*]
TOCM	Trust Officers Committee Minutes [*A publication*] (DLA)
TOCN	Technical Order Change Notice [*Air Force*] (MCD)
TOCOM	Tokyo Commodity Exchange for Industry [*Japan*] (ECON)
TOCP	Tri-ortho-cresyl Phosphate [*Organic chemistry*]
TOCR	Turn-Off Controlled Rectifier (PDAA)
TOCS	Technological Aides to Creative Thoughts (IAA)
TOCS	Terminal Operations Control System
TOCS	Terminal-Oriented Computer System
TOCS	Textile Operational Control System [*Computer science*]
TOCS	Tool Order Control System (MCD)
TOCS	Tropical Ocean Climate Study [*Marine science*] (OSRA)
TOCSY	Total Correlation Spectroscopy
TOCT	Teacher Occupational Competency Tests (TES)
TOCTTOU	Time of Check to Time of Use (MHDI)
TOCU	Tornado Operational Conversion Unit [*British military*] (DMA)
TOD	Target-Organ Damage [*Medicine*]
TOD	Technical Objective Directive [*or Document*] [*Air Force*] (MCD)
TOD	Technical Operations Department
TOD	Technical Order Dilemma (SAA)
TOD	Test Operations Directorate (RDA)
TOD	Theater-Oriented Depot [*Military*]
TOD	Theoretical Oxygen Demand [*Analytical biochemistry*]
TOD	Time of Day
TOD	Time of Delivery
TOD	Time of Departure (NVT)
TOD	Time of Despatch [*British*]
TOD	Tioman [*Malaysia*] [*Airport symbol*] (OAG)
TOD	Titanium Optimized Design [*Plate*] [*Orthopedics*] (DAVI)
TOD	Todd Shipyards [*NYSE symbol*] (TTSB)
TOD	Todd Shipyards Corp. [*NYSE symbol*] (SAG)
TOD	Top of Descent (GAVI)
TOD	Top of Duct (OA)
TOD	Total Oxygen Demand [*Analytical chemistry*]
TOD	Tourist-Oriented-Directional [*Traffic sign*]
TOD	Trade-Off Determination [*Military*] (AABC)
TOD	Transfer on Death [*Finance*]
TOD	Transit Oriented Design (PA)
TOD	Turnover Device
TODA	Takeoff Distance Available [*FAA*] (TAG)
TODA	Technical Order Distribution Activity
TODA	Third-Octave Digital Analyzer
TODARS	Terminal-Oriented Data Analysis and Retrieval System [*National Institute of Standards and Technology*]
TODAS	Towed Oceanographic Data Acquisition System (MSC)
TODAS	Typewriter-Oriented Documentation-Aid System
TodayM	Today's Man, Inc. [*Associated Press*] (SAG)
TodaysBc	Todays Bancorp, Inc. [*Associated Press*] (SAG)
TODC	Technical Order Distribution Code [*Air Force*]
TODC	Theater-Oriented Depot Complex [*Military*] (AABC)
TODD	[*The*] Todd-AO Corp. [*NASDAQ symbol*] (NQ)
TODDA	Todd-AO Corp.'A' [*NASDAQ symbol*] (TTSB)
TODD-AO	Todd-American Optical Co. [*Wide-screen system used by producer Michael Todd and the American Optical Co.*]
ToddAO	Todd AO Corp. [*Associated Press*] (SAG)
ToddShp	Todd Shipyards Corp. [*Associated Press*] (SAG)
TODE	Transcript of Data Extraction (DNAB)
To de For	Thomas de Formaginis [*Flourished, 1331-38*] [*Authority cited in pre-1607 legal work*] (DSA)
TODES	Transcript of Data Extraction System (MCD)
TODH	Todhunter International, Inc. [*NASDAQ symbol*] (SAG)
TODH	Todhunter Intl [*NASDAQ symbol*] (TTSB)
Todhuntr	Todhunter International, Inc. [*Associated Press*] (SAG)
TODN	Telephone Order Dispatch Notice
TODO	Technical Order Distribution Office [*or Officer*]
TODOS	Tools for Designing Office Information Systems (NITA)
TODR	Takeoff Distance Required [*Aviation*] (AIA)
TODS	Technical Oriented Disk System [*Computer science*] (ECII)
TODS	Test-Oriented Disk System (IEEE)
TODS	Transactions on Database Systems
TODT	Tool Detail (AAG)
TOE	Epidermatophyton
TOE	Table of Organization Equipment
TOE	Tables of Organization and Equipment [*Military*]
TOE	Talker Omission Error (MUGU)
TOE	Tape Overlap Emulator [*Computer science*] (IAA)
TOE	Term of Enlistment [*Military*]
TOE	Texas, Oklahoma & Eastern Railroad Co. [*AAR code*]
TOE	Theory of Everything [*Cosmology*]
toe	Theory of Everything
TOE	Thread One End (MSA)
TOE	Time of Entry (MCD)
TOE	Time of Event [*Military*] (CAAL)
TOE	Ton of Oil Equivalent [*Energy equivalent*]
TOE	Tons of Oil Equivalent
TOE	Tony, Oscar, Emmy [*Refers to actors who have won these three major awards, for stage, film, and television work, respectively*]
TOE	Top of Edge (AAG)
TOE	Total Operating Expense
TOE	Tozeur [*Tunisia*] [*Airport symbol*] (OAG)
TOE	Tracheoesophageal [*Also, TE*] [*Medicine*]
TOE	Trainborne Operational Equipment
TOE	Tryout Employment [*Job Training and Partnership Act*] (OICC)
TOE	United States Department of Energy, Office of Scientific and Technical Information, Oak Ridge, TN [*Library symbol*] [*Library of Congress*] (LCLS)
TOEFL	Teaching of English as a Foreign Language
TOEFL	Test of English as a Foreign Language
TOEIC	Test of English for International Communication
TOEL	Time Only Emitter Location System (MCD)
TOEMTB	Tables of Organization and Equipment Mobilization Troop Basis [*Army*] (AABC)
TO EPR	Takeoff Engine Pressure Ratio (GAVI)
TOES	[*The*] Other Economic Summit [*of North America*] (CROSS)
TOES	Telephone Order Entry System (AAGC)
TOES	Toxic Oil Epidemic Syndrome [*Medicine*] (DMAA)
TOES	Trade-Off Evaluation System
TOESD	Test of Early Socioemotional Development [*Child development test*]
TOES-NA	[*The*] Other Economic Summit of North America (EA)
TOET	Test of Elementary Training (WDAA)
TOEWG	Table of Organization and Equipment Working Group [*Army*]
TOF	Beverly, MA [*Location identifier FAA*] (FAAL)
TOF	[*The*] Obesity Foundation (EA)
TOF	Test Operations Facility [*NASA*] (MCD)
TOF	Tetralogy of Fallot [*Cardiology*]
TOF	Time of Filing
TOF	Time of Fire [*Military*] (CAAL)
TOF	Time of Flight
TOF	Tofutti Brands [*AMEX symbol*] (TTSB)
TOF	Tofutti Brands, Inc. [*AMEX symbol*] (SPSG)
TOF	Tone Off [*Telecommunications*] (TEL)
TOF	To Order From
TOF	Topcliffe FTU [*British ICAO designator*] (FAAC)
TOF	Top of File
TOF	Top of Form [*Computer science*]
TOF	Total Organ Failure [*Medicine*] (WDAA)
TOF	Tracheo-Esophageal Fistula [*Medicine*] (DAVI)
TOF	Transfer of Function (MCD)
TOF	Turnover Frequency [*Chemical engineering*]
TOFA	Tall Oil Fatty Acids [*Organic chemistry*]
T of A	Terms of Agreement (NATG)
TOFA	Time-of-Flight and Absorbance [*Physics*]
T of A	Transposition of Aorta [*Cardiology*] (MAE)
TOFABS	Time-of-Flight Aerosol Beam Spectrometry
TOFC	Tony Orlando Fan Club [*Defunct*] (EA)
T of C	Tournament of Champions
TOFC	Trailer on Flatcar [*Railroad*]
TOFCN	Technical Order Field Change Notice [*Air Force*] (MCD)
TOFD	Time of Flight Diffraction [*Nuclear energy*] (NUCP)
TOFD	Time of Flight Diffraction [*Ultrasonic imaging*]
TOFDC	Total Operational Flying Duty Credit [*Military*] (AABC)
TOFF	Tatham Offshore [*NASDAQ symbol*] (TTSB)
TOFF	Tatham Offshore, Inc. [*NASDAQ symbol*] (SAG)
TOFI	Time-of-Flight Isochronous Spectrometer

TOFL	Takeoff Field Length [Aviation]
TOFM	Tooling Form (AAG)
TOFMS	Time-of-Flight Mass Spectrometer
T of OPNS	Theater of Operations [Military]
To For	Thomas de Formaginis [Flourished, 1331-38] [Authority cited in pre-1607 legal work] (DSA)
TOFRAN	Tofranil [Also, called imipramine hydrochloride] [An antidepressant] [Geigy Pharmaceuticals] (DAVI)
TOFS	Time-of-Flight Spectrometer [or Spectroscopy]
TOFSARS	Time-of-Flight Scattering and Recoiling Spectrometry
TOFSIMS	Time-of-Flight Secondary Ion Mass Spectrometry
Tofutti	Tofutti Brands, Inc. [Associated Press] (SAG)
TOG	Takeoff Gross [Weight] [Aviation]
TOG	Target-Observer-Gun [Method] [Army]
TOG	Target Opportunity Generator (KSC)
TOG	Technical Operations Group [Air Force]
TOG	Temagami Oil & Gas Ltd. [Toronto Stock Exchange symbol]
TOG	Togane [Japan] [Seismograph station code, US Geological Survey Closed] (SEIS)
TOG	Together
TOG	Toggle
TOG	Togiak [Alaska] [Airport symbol] (OAG)
TOG	Togiak Village, AK [Location identifier FAA] (FAAL)
TOG	Top of Grade (MCD)
TOG	Toronto Game [Simulation game]
TOG	Total Canada Oil & Gas Ltd. [Later, Rigel Energy] [AMEX symbol] (SPSG)
TOG	Total Oil and Grease [Environmental science]
TOGA	Saratoga Beverage Group [NASDAQ symbol] (SAG)
TOGA	Saratoga Beverage Group 'A' [NASDAQ symbol] (TTSB)
TOGA	Take Off/Go Around (MCD)
TOGA	Tests of General Ability [Education] (AEBS)
TOGA	Tooling Gauge (AAG)
TOGA	Tropical Ocean-Global Atmosphere [Program] (USDC)
TOGA	Tropical Ocean Global Atmosphere Program (EERA)
TOGA	Tropical Oceans and Global Atmosphere Project [World Meteorological Organization]
TOGA COARE	TOGA [Tropical Ocean Global Atmosphere Program] Coupled Ocean-Atmosphere Response Experiment (EERA)
TOGA NEG	Tropical Ocean Global Atmosphere Program Numerical Experiment Group (EERA)
Tog Cand	Oratio in Senatu in Toga Candida [of Cicero] [Classical studies] (OCD)
TOGI	Trans-Oceanic Geophysical Investigations [Marine science] (MSC)
TOGLA	Tea Operators' and General Labourers' Association [A union] [British]
TOGMV	Tomato Golden Mosaic Virus [Plant pathology]
TOGO	Time to Go (SAA)
TOGR	Together (ROG)
TOGS	Thermal Observation and Gunnery Sights [British]
TOGS	Transmission-Operating Gear Switch [Automotive engineering]
TOGV	Transposition of the Great Vessels [Medicine] (DAVI)
TOGW	Takeoff Gross Weight [Aviation]
TOH	Natchitoches, LA [Location identifier FAA] (FAAL)
TOH	Oak Ridge Hospital, Oak Ridge, TN [Library symbol Library of Congress] (LCLS)
TOH	Tesero Oolite Horizon [Geology]
TOH	Time Overhead (NVT)
Toh	Tohoroth [or Toharoth] (BJA)
TOH	Transient Osteoporosis of Hip [Medicine] (DMAA)
TOH	Tyrosine Hydroxylase [An enzyme]
TOHILA	Title 1 Home Improvement Lenders Association (NTPA)
TOHM	Terohmmeter (IEEE)
Toho	Tohoroth [or Toharoth] (BJA)
TOHP	Takeoff Horsepower [Aviation]
TOHP	Trials of Hypertension Prevention [Medicine]
TOI	Tactical Operations Initiation
TOI	Target of Interest [Military] (CAAL)
TOI	Technical Operation Instruction (KSC)
TOI	Technical Operations, Inc. (MCD)
TOI	Term of Induction [Military]
TOI	Time of Intercept [Military] (CAAL)
TOI	Transfer Orbital Insertion [NASA]
TOI	Troy, AL [Location identifier FAA] (FAAL)
TOID	Technical Order Identification (MCD)
TOIL	Time Off in Lieu
TOIL	Toilet
TOJ	Telecommunications of Jamaica [Commercial firm] (ECON)
TOJ	Time on Jamming (IAA)
TOJ	Track on Jamming
TOJV	Track-on-Jam Valid [Military]
TOK	Thrust Okay [NASA] (KSC)
TOK	Tokheim Corp. [NYSE symbol] (SPSG)
TOK	Tokyo [Japan] [Seismograph station code, US Geological Survey] (SEIS)
TOK	Torokina [Papua New Guinea] [Airport symbol] (OAG)
TOKAMAK	Toroidal Kamera Magnetic [Thermonuclear-fusion system] [Acronym formed from the Russian]
Tokhem	Tokheim Corp. [Associated Press] (SAG)
TokioF	Tokio Marine & Fire Insurance Co. Ltd. [Associated Press] (SAG)
TokosMd	Tokos Medical Corp. [Associated Press] (SAG)
TOKTEN	Transfer of Know-How through Expatriate Nationals [British] (DI)
TOKTEN	Transfer of Know-How Through Expatriate Nationals [Council of Scientific and Industrial Research] [India]
TOL	Tailored Outfitting List (MCD)

TOL	Temporary Occupation License (EERA)
TOL	Test-Oriented Language [Computer science]
TOL	Ticket of Leave
TOL	Tol-Air Services, Inc. [ICAO designator] (FAAC)
TOL	Toledo [Spain] [Seismograph station code, US Geological Survey] (SEIS)
TOL	Toledo [Ohio] [Airport symbol] (OAG)
TOL	Tolerance (AAG)
tol	Tolerated (DAVI)
TOL	Toll Brothers [NYSE symbol] (TTSB)
TOL	Toll Brothers, Inc. [NYSE symbol] (SPSG)
TOL	Tower of London
TOL	Tree of Life [Internet phylogeny project originating from the University of Arizona, Tucson]
TOL	Trial of Labor [Gynecology]
TOL	Trucial Oman Levies [British military] (DMA)
TOL	University of Toledo, Toledo, OH [OCLC symbol] (OCLC)
TOLA	Takeoff and Landing Analysis [Air Force]
TOLA	Test of Oral and Limb Apraxia (TMMY)
TOLA	Theatre of Latin America [Defunct] (EA)
TOLAR	Terminal On-Line Availability Reporting
TOLCAT	Takeoff and Landing Clear Air Turbulence [Aviation]
TOLCAT	Takeoff and Landing Critical Atmosphere Turbulence [Aviation] (MCD)
TOLCCS	Trends in Online Computer Control Systems (PDAA)
TOLD	TELECOMS On-Line Data System [Telecommunications] (TEL)
TOLD	Test of Language Development [Education]
TolE	Toledo Edison Co. [Associated Press] (SAG)
TOLED	Transparent Organic Light-Emitting Device [Photonics]
TOLH	Test of Legible Handwriting (TES)
TOLIMAC	Total Library Management Concept (TELE)
TOLIP	Trajectory Optimization and Linearized Pitch [Computer program]
TOLL	Tollerford [England]
Tolland	Tolland Bank [Associated Press] (SAG)
TollBro	Toll Brothers, Inc. [Associated Press] (SAG)
Toller	Toller on Executors [A publication] (DLA)
Toll Ex	Toller on Executors [A publication] (ILCA)
TOLO	Time of Lockout (SAA)
TOLO	Tool and Operation Liaison Order (AAG)
TOLO	Tooling Layout (AAG)
TOLO	Type of Legal Organization
TOLP	Test for Oral Language Production [Educational test]
TOLR	Toll Restricted [Telecommunications] (TEL)
TOLR	Transmitting Objective Loudness Rating [of telephone connections] (IEEE)
TOLS	Times On-Line Services [Information service or system] (IID)
Tolst Div	Tolstoy on Divorce and Matrimonial Causes [A publication] (DLA)
TOLT	Test of Logical Thinking (EDAC)
TOLT	Towing Light (AAG)
TOLTE	Teleprocessing Online Test (NITA)
TOLTEP	Teleprocessing On-Line Test Executive Program [IBM Corp.]
TOLTS	Total On-Line Testing System [Honeywell, Inc.]
TOM	GMT [Greenwich Mean Time] of Orbital Midnight
TOM	[The] Old Man
TOM	Table of Organization and Management
TOM	Technical Operations Manager [Navy]
TOM	Teleprinter on Multiplex [Telecommunications] (IAA)
TOM	Terz'Ordine dei Minimi [Third Order of Minimi] [Italy] (EAIO)
TOM	Test Set, Overall Missile (IAA)
TOM	Texas College of Osteopathic Medicine, Fort Worth, TX [OCLC symbol] (OCLC)
TOM	Text on Microform [Information Access Co. - IAC] [Information service or system] (IID)
TOM	The Office Manager (NITA)
TOM	Third Order of Mary (EA)
TOM	Thompson-Lundmark Gold Mines Ltd. [Toronto Stock Exchange symbol]
TOM	Time of Maximum [Particle physics]
tom	Tomato (BARN)
TOM	Tombouctou [Mali] [Airport symbol] (OAG)
TOM	Tomie [Japan] [Seismograph station code, US Geological Survey Closed] (SEIS)
TOM	Tommy Hilfiger [NYSE symbol] (TTSB)
TOM	Tommy Hilfiger, Inc. [NYSE symbol] (SPSG)
Tom	Tomus [Volume] [Latin]
TOM	Toolmanager [Computer science] (IAA)
TOM	Topological Optimization Module [Computer science] (OA)
TOM	Toronto, Ottawa, Montreal [Derogatory reference to people in these cities; used by other Canadians who think people living in these cities "run things"]
TOM	Totem Capital Corp. [Vancouver Stock Exchange symbol]
TOM	Tracking Operation Memorandum [Obsolete]
TOM	Transistor Oscillator Multiplier (IAA)
TOM	Translator Octal Mnemonic
TOM	Transmitted Optical Microscopy
TOM	Transparent Office Manager [Computer science] (IAA)
TOM	Typical Ocean Model [Oceanography]
TOMA	Technical Order Management Agency [Military] (AFIT)
TOMA	Test of Mathematical Abilities
TOMA	Turn Off My Addiction [Proposed clinic]
TOMAC	Toroidal Magnetic Chamber (DI)
TOMAC	Trioctylmethylammonium Chloride [Organic chemistry]
TOMAL	Test of Memory and Learning (TMMY)
Tom & J Comp	Tomkins and Jenckens' Compendium of the Modern Roman Law [A publication] (DLA)

Tom & Lem Gai... Tomkins and Lemon's Translation of Gaius [*A publication*] (DLA)
TOMARA Texas Outlaw Midget Automobile Racing Association [*Car racing*]
TOMB Technical Organizational Memory Bank (RDA)
TOMCAT Telemetry On-Line Monitoring Compression and Transmission
TOMCAT Teleoperator for Operations, Maintenance, and Construction Using Advanced Technology
TOMCAT Theater of Operations Missile Continuous-Wave Antitank Weapon
TOMCIS Test of Multiple Corridor Identification System (IAA)
TOMH Regional Mental Health Center of Oak Ridge, Oak Ridge, TN [*Library symbol Library of Congress*] (LCLS)
TOMHS Treatment of Mild Hypertension Study
Tom Inst Tomkins' Institutes of Roman Law [*A publication*] (DLA)
TOMI-R Test of Motor Impairment Henderson Revision (TES)
Tomkins & J Mod Rom Law... Tomkins and Jencken's Compendium of the Modern Roman Law [*A publication*] (DLA)
Toml Tomlins' Election Cases [*1689-1795*] [*A publication*] (DLA)
Toml Cas Tomlins' Election Cases [*1689-1795*] [*A publication*] (DLA)
Toml Cr L Tomlin's Criminal Law [*A publication*] (DLA)
Tomlins Tomlins' Law Dictionary [*A publication*] (DLA)
Toml Law Dict... Tomlins' Law Dictionary [*A publication*] (DLA)
Toml LD Tomlins' Law Dictionary [*A publication*] (DLA)
Toml Supp Br... Tomlins' Supplement to Brown's Parliamentary Cases [*A publication*] (DLA)
TOMM Time-Oriented Metropolitan Model (MCD)
TOMMI Total Online Medical Material Integration [*Computer science*]
TOMMS Terminal Operations and Movements Management System (MCD)
TomNDV Tomato Necrotic Dwarf Virus
TOMO Tomogram [*Radiology*] (DAVI)
TOMO Tomography [*Radiology*] (DAVI)
TOMP Toxic Organic Management Plan [*Pollution prevention*]
Tompkn Tompkins County Trust [*Associated Press*] (SAG)
TOMR Tomorrow (ROG)
TomRSV Tomato Ringspot Virus
TomRSV-S Tomato Ringspot Virus - Seed Borne
TOMS Torus Oxygen Monitoring System (IEEE)
TOMS Total Ozone Mapping Spectrometer (MCD)
TOMS Total Ozone Mapping Spectrophotometer [*Marine science*] (OSRA)
TOMS Total Ozone Mapping System [*Meteorology*]
TOMS Total Ozone Measurement Scanner (SSD)
TOMS Transactions on Mathematical Software
TOMSI Transfer of Master Scheduled Item
TOMSS Theater of Operations Medical Support System [*Military*] (MCD)
TOMT Target Organizational Maintenance Trainer (MCD)
TOMUS [*The*] On-Line Multi-User System [*Carlyle Systems, Inc.*] [*Information service or system*] (IID)
TOMV Tomato Mosaic Virus [*Plant pathology*]
TON Aero Tonala [*Mexico ICAO designator*] (FAAC)
TON Taiwanese Oscilliation Network [*For solar observation*]
TON Talk Only (IAA)
TON Threshold Odor Number [*Water analysis*]
TON Tone On [*Telecommunications*] (TEL)
TON Tonga [*ANSI three-letter standard code*] (CNC)
TON Tongariro [*New Zealand*] [*Seismograph station code, US Geological Survey Closed*] (SEIS)
TON Tonic [*Permanently Strengthening*] [*Pharmacy*] (ROG)
TON Tonopah Resources, Inc. [*Vancouver Stock Exchange symbol*]
TON Top of the News [*A publication*]
TON Turnover Number
TON Tyrone, PA [*Location identifier FAA*] (FAAL)
TONAC Technical Order Notification and Completion System (AAG)
TONC Transient On-State Characteristics (PDAA)
TONE Touch Tone America [*NASDAQ symbol*] (TTSB)
TONE Touch Tone America, Inc. [*NASDAQ symbol*] (SAG)
TONEW Touch Tone America Wrrt [*NASDAQ symbol*] (TTSB)
tonf Ton-Force (WPI)
TON/FT² Tons per Square Foot
TONI Test of Nonverbal Intelligence
TONI-2 Test of Nonverbal Intelligence-2 (TES)
TONL Union Carbide Nuclear Co., Oak Ridge National Laboratories, Oak Ridge, TN [*Library symbol*] [*Library of Congress*] (LCLS)
TONLAR Tone-Operated Net Loss Adjuster Receiving
TONL-B Union Carbide Nuclear Co., Oak Ridge National Laboratories, Biology Library, OakRidge, TN [*Library symbol Library of Congress*] (LCLS)
TONL-G Union Carbide Nuclear Co., Oak Ridge National Laboratories, Gaseous Diffusi, Oak Ridge, TN [*Library symbol*] [*Library of Congress*] (LCLS)
TONL-T Union Carbide Nuclear Co., Oak Ridge National Laboratories, Thermal-Nuclear Library, Oak Ridge, TN [*Library symbol Library of Congress*] (LCLS)
TONL-Y Union Carbide Nuclear Co., Oak Ridge National Laboratories, Y-12 Technical Library, Oak Ridge, TN [*Library symbol Library of Congress*] (LCLS)
TONN Tonnage [*Shipping*]
TONOC Tonight (DAVI)
TONS Topical Numismatic Society (EA)
TONS Transportation Office Network System [*Department of Transportation*] (GFGA)
TONT Tonto National Monument
TOO Target of Opportunity [*Military*] (CAAL)
TOO Test Operations Order [*NASA*]
TOO Threshold of Odor (NASA)
TOO Time of Origin [*Communications*]

TOO Toolangi [*Australia Seismograph station code, US Geological Survey*] (SEIS)
TOO To Order Only [*Commerce*] (ODBW)
TOOL Teams of Our Lady [*See also END*] (EAIO)
TOOL Test-Oriented Operated Language [*Programming language*] [*Computer science*]
ToolAlph Toolex-Alpha [*Associated Press*] (SAG)
TOOL CD Tool Requirement Code [*Army*]
TOOLS Technology for Object-Oriented Linking and Sharing [*Computer science*]
TOOS Torque Overload Switch (NRCH)
TOOS Transaction-Oriented Operating System (IAA)
TOOTJFC [*The*] One and Only Tom Jones Fan Club (EA)
TootsRI Tootsie Roll Industries, Inc. [*Associated Press*] (SAG)
TOP Aero Top SRL Societa [*Italy ICAO designator*] (FAAC)
TOP [*The*] Olympic Programme (ECON)
TOP [*The*] Opportunity Prospector [*A publication*]
TOP [*The*] Option Process [*HUD*]
TOP Table of Output Products
TOP Tactical Operations Plot [*Military*] (CAAL)
TOP Targeted Outreach Program [*Department of Labor*]
TOP Target Occulting Processor (MCD)
TOP Tax-Offset Pension [*Account*]
TOP Teacher Organizing Project (EA)
TOP Technical and Office Protocol [*Data communications standards*]
TOP Technical, Office, and Professional Department [*UAW*]
TOP Technical Operating Procedure
TOP Temple Opportunity Program [*Temple University*] (EA)
TOP Temporal, Occipital Parietal (STED)
TOP Temporarily Out of Print
TOP Termination of Pregnancy (MAE)
TOP Terrestrial Observation Panel (EERA)
TOP Tertiary Operation
TOP Tertiary Orientation Program [*Australia*]
TOP Test and Operations Plan
TOP Test Operating Procedure
TOP Test Outline Plan [*Army*] (AABC)
TOP Thematic Organization Point [*Psychology*]
TOP Tissue Oncotic Pressure (STED)
TOP Tool Package (IAA)
TOP Top Air Havacilik Sanayi Ve Ticaret, AS [*Turkey*] [*FAA designator*] (FAAC)
TOP Topeka [*Kansas*] [*Airport symbol*] (OAG)
TOP Topeka, KS [*Location identifier FAA*] (FAAL)
Top Topic [*Record label*] [*Great Britain*]
Top Topica [*of Aristotle*] [*Classical studies*] (OCD)
top Topical
TOP Top of Potentiometer [*Electronics*] (IAA)
TOP Topographic
TOP Topoisomerase [*An enzyme*]
TOP Topology
TOP Topolovo [*Former USSR Seismograph station code, US Geological Survey*] (SEIS)
TOP Toponymic [*Anatomy*]
TOP Torque Oil Pressure [*Air Force*]
TOP Total Obscuring Power [*Smoke cloud*]
TOP Total Office Products Group [*Commercial firm British*]
TOP Trade Opportunities Program [*Departments of State and Commerce*]
TOP Training for Opportunities in Programming (IAA)
TOP Training Operation Plan [*Military*] (CAAL)
TOP Transient Overpower Accident [*Nuclear energy*]
TOP Transovarial Passage [*Virology*]
TOP Transverse Optical Pumping (MCD)
TOP Trap Oxidizer-Periodic [*Automotive engineering*]
TOP Trinity Occasional Papers [*A publication*]
TOP Turn Out Perfection [*US Air Force Southern Command's acronym for the Zero Defects Program*]
TOP Turn Over, Please [*Correspondence*] (ROG)
TOP Two-Axis Optical Pickoff (PDAA)
TOPA Test of Phonological Awareness (TMMY)
TOPA Tooling Pattern
TopAir Top Air Manufacturing, Inc. [*Associated Press*] (SAG)
T-OPAM Tentative OMA [*Operations and Maintenance Army*] Program Analysis Memorandum
TOPAR Total Pain Relief
TOPAZ Technique for the Optimum Placement of Activities in Zones (PDAA)
TOPCAP Total Objective Plan for Career Airmen Personnel [*Air Force*] (AFM)
TOPCAT Texas Onboard Program of Computer Assisted Training (NITA)
TOPCAT Trajectory Optimization Program for Comparing Advanced Technology (MCD)
TOPDIE Thermally Optimized Die
TOPES Telephone Office Planning and Engineering System [*Telecommunications*] (TEL)
TOPEX Ocean Topography Experiment [*Marine science*] (OSRA)
TOPEX Topographic Experiment [*Proposed oceanographic satellite*]
TOPEX Typhoon Operational Experiment [*Meteorology*]
TOPEX Typhoon Operation Experiment (EERA)
TOPF Transplant Organ Procurement Foundation (EA)
TOPG Topping (MSA)
TOPHAT Terrier Operation Proof High-Altitude Target (MUGU)
TOPI Three-Dimensional OPFOR [*Opposing Force*] Plastic Individual Target [*Army*] (INF)
TOPI Tons of Paper In [*Computer science*] (IAA)
TOPIC [*The*] Objective Personnel Inventory - Civilian [*Air Force*]

TOPIC	Teletext Output of Price Information by Computer [*London Stock Exchange*]
TOPIC	Time-Ordered Programmer Integrated Circuit [*NASA*]
TOPICS	Test of Performance in Computational Skills [*Educational test*]
TOPICS	Total On-Line Program and Information Control System [*Japan*]
TOPICS	Traffic Operations to Increase Capacity and Safety [*Department of Transportation*]
TopIm	Top Image Systems Ltd. [*Associated Press*] (SAG)
TopImge	Top Image Systems Ltd. [*Associated Press*] (SAG)
TOPIX	Tokyo Stock Price Index [*Japan*] (ECON)
TOPKAT	Toxicity Prediction by Komputer Assisted Technology
TOPL	Terminal-Operated Production Language (IAA)
TOPLAS	Transactions on Programming Languages and Systems (MCD)
TOPLINE	Total Officer Personnel Objective Structure for the Line Officer Force (DNAB)
TOPM..........	Takeoff Performance Monitor [*Aviation*] (DA)
TOPM..........	Top Air Manufacturing, Inc. [*NASDAQ symbol*] (NQ)
TOPM..........	Top Air Mfg [*NASDAQ symbol*] (TTSB)
TOPMIS	Total Officer Personnel Management [*Army*] (RDA)
TOPMS	Take off Performance Monitoring System
TOPNS	Theater of Operations [*Military*]
TOPO	Test Operations and Policy Office [*TECOM*] (RDA)
TOPO	Tons of Paper Out [*Computer science*] (IAA)
TOPO	Topography (AFM)
TOPO	Tri-n-Octyl Phosphine Oxide [*Organic chemistry*]
TOPO	Trioctylphosphine Oxide [*Organic chemistry*]
TOPOCOM....	Topographic Command [*Army*]
TOPOENGR...	Topographical Engineer
TOPOG	Topography
TOPO-MIBK..	Trioctylphosphorine Oxide/Methyl Isobutyl Keton [*Solvent mixture*]
TOPOPLT	Topographic Platoon (DNAB)
TOPP	[*The*] Organization of Plastics Processors [*Defunct*] (EA)
TOPP	Task Oriented Plant Practice (MHDI)
TOPP	Terminal-Operated Production Program (BUR)
TOPP	Threat Orientation Protection Posture [*Military equipment*]
TOPP	Topps Co. [*NASDAQ symbol*] (TTSB)
TOPP	[*The*] Topps Co., Inc. [*NASDAQ symbol*] (NQ)
TOPP	Training Outside Public Practice (PDAA)
TOPPER	Toy Press Publishers, Editors, and Reporters
Topps..........	Topps Co., Inc. [*Associated Press*] (SAG)
TOPR	Taiwan Open Pool Reactor
TOPR	Thermoplastic Optical Phase Recorder (IAA)
TOPREP	Total Objective Plan for Reserve Personnel [*Air Force*] (AFM)
Topro	Topro, Inc. [*Associated Press*] (SAG)
TOPrS	Trust Originated Preferred Securities [*Finance*]
TOPS	[*The*] Operational PERT System
TOPS	[*The*] Optimum Publishing System [*IBM Corp.*]
TOPS	Tactical Optical Projection System (NVT)
TOPS	Tailored Owner Protection System [*Automotive optional warranty*]
TOPS	Take Off Pounds Sensibly (EA)
TOPS	Technical Order Page Supplement [*Air Force*]
TOPS	Telemetry On-Line Processing System [*Computer science*]
T(OPS).........	Telephone Off-Premises Station [*Telecommunications*] (OTD)
TOPS	Telephone Order Personalities and Smiles [*Organization of chief telephone operators*]
TOPS	Telephone Order Processing System
TOPS	Telephone Order Purchasing System (MCD)
TOPS	Teleregister Omni Processing and Switching [*Computer science*]
TOPS	Teletype Optical Projection System (IEEE)
TOPS	Terminal-Oriented Planning System (MCD)
TOPS	Tested Overhead Projection Series [*Education*]
TOPS	Testing and Operating System
TOPS	Test of Problem Solving [*Intelligence test*]
TOPS	Test Operations Procedures [*Army*] (RDA)
TOPS	Theatre Organ Preservation Society [*British*]
TOPS	The Online Publishing System (NITA)
TOPS	Thermal Noise Optical Optimization Communication System [*NASA*]
TOPS	Thermodynamic Ocean Prediction System [*Navy*] (GFGA)
TOPS	Thermoelectric Outer Planet Spacecraft [*NASA*]
TOPS	Time-Sharing Operating System [*Computer science*]
TOPS	Top One Percent Society (EA)
TOPS	Tops Appliance City [*NASDAQ symbol*] (SAG)
TOPS	Total Ocean Profiling System [*Marine science*] (OSRA)
TOPS	Total Operations Processing System [*Computer science*]
TOPS	Total Organ Perfusion System
TOPS	Total Ozone Portable Spectroradiometer [*Measures ozone layer*] (ECON)
TOPS	Total Personnel Service
TOPS	Toward Other Planetary Systems [*NASA*]
TOPS	Traffic Operator Position System [*Telecommunications*] (TEL)
TOPS	Training Operations and Planning Station (MCD)
TOPS	Training Opportunities Schemes [*Department of Employment*] [*British*]
TOPS	Transcendental Network [*Centram Systems West, Inc.*] [*Berkeley, CA*] [*Telecommunications*] (TSSD)
TOPS	Transistorized Operational Phone System (MCD)
TOPS	Transparent Operating System [*Computer science*] (CDE)
TOPS	Transportation Operational Personal Property System [*Army*]
TOPS	Truck Ordering and Pricing System
TOPS	United States Travelers' Overseas Personalized Service [*Also known as USTOPS*]
TopsApl	Tops Appliance City [*Associated Press*] (SAG)
TOPSEC	Top Secret [*Security classification*]
TOPSEP	Targeting/Optimization for Solar Electric Propulsion [*NASA*]
TOPSI	Topside Sounder, Ionosphere [*NASA*]
TopSrce.......	Top Source, Inc. [*Associated Press*] (SAG)
TOPSTAR.....	[*The*] Officer Personnel System, The Army Reserve (AABC)
Top Stereochem...	Topics in Stereochemistry (MEC)
TOPSY	Test Operations Planning System
TOPSY	Thermally Operated Plasma System
TOPSY	Time-Sharing Operation of Product Structure Directory System (PDAA)
TOPTS	Test-Oriented Paper-Tape System [*Computer science*] (IEEE)
TOPV	Trivalent Oral Poliomyelitis Vaccine [*Medicine*]
TOPV	Trivalent Oral Polio Vaccine (STED)
TOQ	Tocopilla [*Chile*] [*Airport symbol*] (AD)
TOR	Tactical Operational Requirement [*Military*] (CAAL)
TOR	Tactical Operations Room [*Air Force*]
TOR	Tall Oil Rosin [*Organic chemistry*]
TOR	Technical Operating Report
TOR	Technical Operations Research (KSC)
TOR	Technical Override
TOR	Technical Oversight Representative
TOR	Technique of Operations Review [*Engineering*]
TOR	Telegraph on Radio [*Telecommunications*] (TEL)
TOR	Teleprinter on Radio [*Telecommunications*] (TSSD)
TOR	Teleprinter Over Radio (NITA)
TOR	Teletype on Radio [*Telecommunications*] (IAA)
TOR	Tentative Operational Requirement
TOR	Terms of Reference [*Army*] (AABC)
TOR	Test Operation Report (KSC)
TOR	Thermal Overload Relay (IAA)
tor	Third Order Regular of Saint Francis (TOCD)
TOR	Third Order Regular of St. Francis [*Roman Catholic men's religious order*]
TOR	Threshold of Regulation [*FDA*]
TOR	Time of Receipt [*Military*] (AABC)
TOR	Time of Reception [*Communications*]
TOR	Time on Risk [*Insurance*] (AIA)
TOR	Tool Order Release (SAA)
TOR	Top of Range (AAEL)
TOR	Torhsen Energy Corp. [*Vancouver Stock Exchange symbol*]
TOR	Torishima [*Japan*] [*Seismograph station code, US Geological Survey Closed*] (SEIS)
TOR	Tornado Warning [*Telecommunications*] (OTD)
TOR	Toronto (ROG)
TOR	Toronto Airways Ltd. [*Canada ICAO designator*] (FAAC)
Tor	Torpedo [*Army*]
TOR	Torque (AAG)
TOR	Torrance [*California*]
Tor	Torrid Zone (BARN)
TOR	Torrington, WY [*Location identifier FAA*] (FAAL)
TOR	Totalizing Relay
TOR	Tournament of Roses Association (EA)
TOR	Track-on-Repeater [*Military*]
TOR	Traffic on Request [*Aviation*] (FAAC)
TOR	Turn-On Rate (CAAL)
TORA	Take-Off Run Available [*FAA*] (TAG)
TORA	TRADOC [*Training and Doctrine Command*] Operations Research Activity [*Military*]
TORAC	Torpedo Acquisition
TORACCS	Tool Order-Reporting and Cost Control System (SAA)
TORAH........	Tough Orthodox Rabbis and Hassidim [*An association*]
TORC	Test of Reading Comprehension
TORC	Traffic Overload Reroute Control
TORCH	Tests of Reading Comprehension [*Australian Council for Educational Research Ltd.*] (TES)
TORCH	Toxoplasma, Other [*Viruses*], Rubella, Cytomegaloviruses, Herpes [*Virus*]
TORCH	Toxoplasmosis, Rubella, Cytomegalovirus, and Herpes Simplex (STED)
TorchEn	Torch Energy Royalty Trust [*Associated Press*] (SAG)
TORCHS.......	Toxoplasmosis, Other Viruses, Rubella, Cytomegalovirus, Herpes Virus, and Syphilis [*Titer*] (DAVI)
TOREADOR...	Torero-Matador [*Said to have been coined by Georges Bizet for opera "Carmen"*]
TORES	Toxicological Research (SAA)
TORF	Time of Retrofire [*NASA*] (KSC)
TORI	Trusting, Opening, Realizing, and Interdepending [*Discovery processes developed by J. Gibb*] (DHP)
torm............	Tormentor [*Theater*] (WDMC)
TORM	Torquemeter
TORNL........	Torsional
Toro	Toro Corp. [*Associated Press*] (SAG)
Toronto U Faculty L Rev...	Toronto University. Faculty Law Review [*Canada*] [*A publication*] (DLA)
TORP	Test of Orientation for Rehabilitation Patients [*Occupational therapy*]
TORP	Torpedo (AABC)
TORP	Total Ossicular Replacement Prosthesis
TORPCM......	Torpedo Countermeasures and Deception
TORPEX	Torpedo Exercise (NVT)
TORPRON	Torpedo Squadron
TORQ	Torquay [*England*]
TORQ	Torque [*Automotive engineering*]
TORQUE.....	Tests of Reasonable Quantitative Understanding of the Environment [*Education*]
TORQUE.....	Truck Operators Road Qualifying Exam [*National Highway Traffic Safety Administration*]
TORR	Takeoff Run Required [*Aviation*] (AIA)
TORR	Torricelli [*Unit of pressure*]

TORR..........	Torrington [England]
TorRoy.........	Toreador Royalty Corp. [Associated Press] (SAG)
TORS..........	Time-Ordered Reporting System (MCD)
TORS..........	Torsion [Automotive engineering]
TORS..........	Trade Opportunity Referral Service [Department of Agriculture] [Information service or system] (IID)
TORSEN......	Torque Sensing Differential [Audi] [Automotive engineering]
TORSV........	Tomato Ringspot Virus [Plant pathology]
TORT..........	Tactical Operational Readiness Trainer
tort...........	Tortoise (VRA)
TORT..........	Truck Operator Road Test [Part of TORQUE]
Tortel..........	Torotel, Inc. [Associated Press] (SAG)
TORTOS.......	Terminal Oriental Real-Time Operating System [Computer science] (IAA)
TOS...........	Tactical Offense Subsystem
TOS...........	Tactical Operation Simulator
TOS...........	Tactical Operations Squadron [Air Force]
TOS...........	Tactical Operations System [ADSAF]
TOS...........	Taken on Strength [British military] (DMA)
TOS...........	Taken Out of Service [Telecommunications] (TEL)
TOS...........	Taligent Object Services [Taligent, Inc.] [Computer science]
TOS...........	Tape Operating System [IBM Corp.] [Computer science]
TOS...........	Technical Operational Support
TOS...........	Technical Operations Squadron [Air Force]
TOS...........	Temporarily Out of Service (DEN)
TOS...........	Temporarily Out of Stock [Business term]
TOS...........	Tension of Oculus Sinister [Left eye] (STED)
TOS...........	Terminal-Oriented Software [Computer science] (IEEE)
TOS...........	Terminal-Oriented System [Computer science] (IEEE)
TOS...........	Term of Service [Military]
TOS...........	Test Operating System (MCD)
TOS...........	Thermally and Oxidatively Stable
TOS...........	Thoracic Outlet Syndrome [Medicine]
TOS...........	Time-on-Station [Military] (INF)
TOS...........	Time-On-Stream [Theory] [Engineering]
TOS...........	Time-Ordered System (MCD)
TOS...........	Time-Sharing Operating System [Computer science] (IAA)
TOS...........	TIROS [Television and Infrared Observation Satellite] Operational Satellite [NASA]
TOS...........	TIROS [Television Infrared Observational Satellite] Operational System [Marine science] (OSRA)
TOS...........	Top of Stack [Computer science]
TOS...........	Top of Steel [Flooring] (AAG)
TOS...........	Torque Overload Switch [Nuclear energy] (NRCH)
Tos...........	Tosafoth (BJA)
TOS...........	Tosco Corp. [NYSE symbol] (SPSG)
TOS...........	Tosco Corp., Los Angeles, CA [OCLC symbol] (OCLC)
Tos...........	Tosefta (BJA)
Tos...........	Tosyl [Also, Ts] [Organic chemistry]
TOS...........	Toxic Oil Syndrome [Medicine]
TOS...........	Traffic Orientation Scheme (DA)
TOS...........	Tramiel Operating System [Atari, Inc.]
TOS...........	Transfer Orbit Stage [Satellite booster]
TOS...........	Tromso [Norway] [Airport symbol] (OAG)
TOS...........	Tropical Air Services [Belize] [ICAO designator] (FAAC)
TOS...........	Trucial Oman Scouts [British military] (DMA)
TOS...........	Turkiye Ogretmenler Sendikasi
TOS...........	Type of Service (TNIG)
TOS...........	Type of Shipment
TOS2..........	Tactical Operations System Operable Segment (MCD)
TOSA..........	Takeoff Space Available [Aviation] (DA)
Tosaf..........	Tosafoth (BJA)
TOSAR........	Topological Representation of Synthetic and Analytical Relations of Concepts (PDAA)
TosArgOMe...	Tosylarginine Methyl Ester [Also, TAME] [Biochemistry]
TOSBAC......	Toshiba Scientific and Business Automatic Computer [Toshiba Corp.]
TOSC..........	Tactical Ocean Surveillance Coordinator [Military] (CAAL)
TOSC..........	Technical Outreach Service to Communities
TOSC..........	To Other Service Center [IRS]
TOSC..........	Touch-Operated Selector Control
TOSCA........	Test of Scholastic Abilities [Achievement test]
TOSCA........	Total On-Line Searching and Cataloging Activities [Information service or system]
TOSCA........	Toxic Substances Control Act [1976]
Tosco..........	Tosco Corp. [Associated Press] (SAG)
TOSCOM......	TOS [TIROS Operational Satellite] Communications System (NOAA)
TOSCW.......	Top of Stack Control Word [Computer science] (MHDI)
TOSD..........	Telephone Operations and Standards Division [Rural Electrification Administration] [Telecommunications] (TEL)
TOSD..........	Third Order of Saint Dominic [Rome, Italy] (EAIO)
TOSE..........	Tooling Samples
Tosef..........	Tosefta (BJA)
Toseph.......	Tosephta (BJA)
TOSF..........	Tertiary of Third Order of St. Francis [Later, SFO] [Roman Catholic religious order]
TOSF..........	Test of Oral Structures and Functions [Speech evaluation test]
TOSFQ........	Teacher Occupational Stress Factor Questionnaire (EDAC)
TOSI...........	Technical On-Site Inspection
TOSL..........	Terminal-Oriented Service Language
TOSMIC......	Toluenesulfonylmethyl Isocyanide [or Tosylmethylisocyanide] [Organic chemistry]
TOSMIC......	Tosylmethyl Isocyanide [Organic chemistry]
TOS/OITDS...	Tactical Operations System/Operations and Intelligence Tactical Data Systems [Military] (RDA)
TOSP..........	Top of Stack Pointer (MHDB)

TOSPDR.......	Technical Order System Publication Deficiency Report [Military] (AFIT)
TosPheCH₂Cl...	Tosylphenylalanine Chloromethyl Ketone [Biochemistry]
TOSR..........	Technical Order Status Report (MCD)
TOSR..........	Thermally and Oxidatively Stable Resin
TOSS..........	Tactical Operational Scoring System (MCD)
TOSS..........	Tactical Operations Support System (MCD)
TOSS..........	Technical Operations and Systems Support (AAGC)
TOSS..........	Television Ordnance Scoring System (MCD)
TOSS..........	Terminal-Oriented Support System
TOSS..........	Test Operation Support Segment
TOSS..........	Tethered Orbiting Satellite Simulator
TOSS..........	TIROS [Television and Infrared Observation Satellite] Operational Satellite System [NASA]
TOSS..........	Total Office Support System (HGAA)
TOS-S.........	Transfer Orbit Stage - Shortened Version [Space technology]
TOSS..........	Transient and/or Steady State [Nuclear energy] (NRCH)
TOSS..........	Turbine-Operated Suspension System [NASA]
TOSSA........	Transient or Steady-State Analysis [Computer science]
TOSSG........	TACS/TADS OED [Tactical Air Control System/Tactical Air Defense System Operational Effectiveness Demonstration] Special Study Group [Military]
TOST..........	Turbine Oil Stability Test [Lubricant testing] [Automotive engineering]
TOST..........	Turbine Oxidation Stability Test (OA)
Tosyl..........	Tolylsulfonyl [Organic chemistry]
TOT...........	Denver, CO [Location identifier FAA] (FAAL)
T/OT..........	Table of Organization (Tentative)
TOT...........	Takeoff Trim [Aviation] (MCD)
TOT...........	Task Oriented Training (MCD)
TOT...........	Telephone Organization of Thailand (NITA)
TOT...........	Terms of Trade
TOT...........	Texaco Overseas Tankerships
TOT...........	Texas Opera Theatre
TOT...........	Theatrum Orbis Terrarum [Dutch firm]
TOT...........	Time of Takeoff [Air Force] (AFIT)
TOT...........	Time of Transmission [Communications]
TOT...........	Time of Travel (MCD)
TOT...........	Time on Tape [Military]
TOT...........	Time on Target [Artillery support]
TOT...........	Time on Track
TOT...........	Time over Target [Air support]
TOT...........	Tincture of Time [Medical slang for treatment of problems that are better left alone]
TOT...........	Tip-of-Tongue Phenomenon [Medicine]
tot...........	To Derive a Total (IDOE)
TOT...........	Toe-Out-in-Turns [Automotive engineering]
TOT...........	Total (AAG)
tot...........	Total (WDMC)
TOT...........	TOTAL 'B' ADS [NYSE symbol] (TTSB)
TOT...........	Total Corp. [NYSE symbol] (SAG)
TOT...........	Total Operating Time [Medicine] (STED)
TOT...........	Total Outage Time (IAA)
TOT...........	TOTAVIA Aviation Information Services [Canada] [FAA designator] (FAAC)
TOT...........	Totem Industries [Vancouver Stock Exchange symbol]
Tot...........	Tothill's English Chancery Reports [A publication] (DLA)
Tot...........	Tothill's Transactions in Chancery [21 English Reprint] [A publication] (DLA)
TOT...........	Totnes [Municipal borough in England]
TOT...........	Tottori [Japan] [Seismograph station code, US Geological Survey] (SEIS)
TOT...........	Tourist Organization of Thailand (DS)
TOT...........	Trade-Off and Technology
TOT...........	Transfer of Technology [Telecommunications] (TEL)
TOT...........	Transfer-of-Training
TOT...........	Transmission Oil Temperature [Automotive engineering]
TOT...........	Transovarial Transmission [Virology]
TOT...........	Transportation Office Will Furnish the Necessary Transportation [Military]
TOT...........	Trioctyltin [Organic chemistry]
TOT...........	Tris-ortho-thymotide [Organic chemistry]
TOT...........	Turbine Outlet Temperature (NG)
TOT...........	Turn-On Time
TOT...........	Type of Transport [Shipping] (DS)
TOTAL........	Teacher Organized Training for the Acquisition of Language (EDAC)
Total..........	Total [Associated Press] (SAG)
TOTAL-C.....	Total Cholesterol [Medicine] (STED)
TotalRs.......	Total Research Corp. [Associated Press] (SAG)
TotCont.......	Total Containment Co. [Associated Press] (SAG)
TOTE..........	Autotote Corp. [NASDAQ symbol] (NQ)
TOTE..........	Teleprocessing On-Line Test Executive [Computer science] (IBMDP)
TOTE..........	Test-Operator-Test-Exit [Unit] [Psychology]
TOTE..........	Time Out to Enjoy (EA)
TOTE..........	Transportable Operations Tactical Equipment (NITA)
TOTEM........	Theater Operations and Tactical Evaluation Model
TOTEM........	Tomahawk Test Missile (MCD)
TOTES........	Time-Ordered Techniques Experiment System
TOTFORF.....	Total Forfeiture [of all pay and allowances] [Army] (AABC)
Toth..........	Tothill's English Chancery Reports [A publication] (DLA)
Toth..........	Tothill's Transactions in Chancery [21 English Reprint] [A publication] (DSA)
Tothill (Eng)..	Tothill's English Chancery Reports [A publication] (DLA)
Tothill (Eng)..	Tothill's Transactions in Chancery [21 English Reprint] [A publication] (DLA)
TOTJ..........	Training on the Job

TOTL............	Test Operating Time Log
TOTL.........	Total Research [*NASDAQ symbol*] (TTSB)
TOTL..........	Total Research Corp. [*NASDAQ symbol*] (NQ)
TOTLN	Totalization (ECII)
TotlPet........	Total Petroleum (North America) Ltd. [*Associated Press*] (SAG)
TotlSys	Total System Services, Inc. [*Associated Press*] (SAG)
TotlTel........	Total Tel USA Communications [*Associated Press*] (SAG)
TOTLZ.........	Totalize
TOTM.........	Trioctyl Trimellitate [*Chemistry*]
TOTO	Tongue of the Ocean [*Area of the Bahama Islands*] [*Navy*]
TOTO	Totable Tornado Observatory [*National Oceanic and Atmospheric Administration*]
TOTP.........	Tooling Template
TOTP...........	Top of the Pops [*Television program*] [*British*]
TOTP.........	Triorthotolylphosphate [*Organic chemistry*]
TOTPAR......	Total Pain Relief [*Medicine*]
tot prot	Total Protein (MAE)
TOTR	Test Observation and Training Room [*Military*] (CAAL)
TOTRAD	Tape Output Test Rack Autonetics Diode
TotRenl.......	Total Renal Care Holdings, Inc. [*Associated Press*] (SAG)
TOTS...........	Total Operating Traffic System [*Bell System*]
TOTS...........	Tower Operator Training System [*Air traffic control*]
TOTS...........	Turn Off Television Saturday [*of Action for Children's Television organization*]
TottaAc	Totta & Acores Financing Ltd. [*Associated Press*] (SAG)
TOU	Neah Bay, WA [*Location identifier FAA*] (FAAL)
TOU	Oak Ridge Associated Universities, Oak Ridge, TN [*Library symbol Library of Congress*] (LCLS)
TOU	Time of Use [*Utility rates*]
TOU	Touho [*New Caledonia*] [*Airport symbol*] (OAG)
Tou	Toulon [*France*] (BARN)
TOU	Touraine [*South Vietnam*] [*Airport symbol*] (AD)
TOU	Trace Operate Unit
Touch	Sheppard's Touchstone [*A publication*] (DLA)
TouchSt	TouchStone Software Corp. [*Associated Press*] (SAG)
Toull	Toullier's Droit Civil Francais [*A publication*] (DLA)
TOUR	Coach USA [*NASDAQ symbol*] (TTSB)
TOUR	Tourist Class Passengers [*British*]
Tourg Dig ...	Tourgee's North Carolina Digest [*A publication*] (DLA)
TOURN........	Tournament
Touro C	Touro College (GAGS)
TOURS........	Tourist Observation and Underwater Research Submarine (PDAA)
TOUS.........	Test on Understanding Science
TOUS.........	Transmission Oscillator Ultrasonic Spectrometer
TouTne	Touch Tone America, Inc. [*Associated Press*] (SAG)
TouTone	Touch Tone America, Inc. [*Associated Press*] (SAG)
TOV............	El Indio, TX [*Location identifier FAA*] (FAAL)
TOV............	El Tocuyo [*Venezuela*] [*Seismograph station code, US Geological Survey*] (SEIS)
TOV............	Telemetering Oscillator Voltage
TOV............	Thrombosed Oral Varix (DB)
TOV............	Time out of View
TOV............	Tooele Valley Railway Co. [*AAR code*]
TOV............	Transfer on Overflow (IAA)
TOVA	[*The*] Other Victims of Alcoholism (EA)
TOVA	Test of Variables of Attention (TMMY)
TOVALOP....	Tanker Owners Voluntary Agreement on Liability for Oil Pollution
TOVC	Top of Overcast [*Meteorology*] (FAAC)
TOVD	Transistor-Operated Voltage Divider
TOVR	Turnover (NVT)
TOVS	TIROS [*Television and Infrared Observation Satellite*] Operational VerticalSounder [*NASA*]
TOW...........	Cooperstown, ND [*Location identifier FAA*] (FAAL)
TOW...........	Takeoff Weight [*Aviation*]
TOWM.........	Tank and Orbiter Weight [*NASA*] (MCD)
TOW...........	Target on Wire [*British military*] (DMA)
TOW...........	Time of Wait [*Vehicle location systems*]
TOW...........	Time of Week (SSD)
TOW...........	Tororo [*Uganda*] [*Airport symbol*] (AD)
TOW...........	Towards (ROG)
TOW...........	Tower Air, Inc. [*ICAO designator*] (FAAC)
TOW...........	Towing
TOW...........	Tube-Launched, Optically Tracked, Wire-Guided [*Weapon*]
TOWA	Terrain and Obstacle Warning and Avoidance
TOW CAP....	TOW [*Tube-Launched, Optically Tracked, Wire-Guided (Weapon)*] Cover Artillery Protection
towd............	Toward (VRA)
TOWE..........	Test of Written Expression (TMMY)
TOWER........	Testing Orientation and Work Evaluation for Rehabilitation
TowerS........	Tower Semiconductor Ltd. [*Associated Press*] (SAG)
TO WHD	Two Wheeled [*Freight*]
TOWK	Test of Word Knowledge (TMMY)
TOWL..........	Test of Written Language
TOWL..........	Test of Written Language-2 [*Hammill and Larsen*] (TES)
Towle Const...	Towle's Analysis of the United States Constitution [*A publication*] (DLA)
Town Co	Townshend's Code [*A publication*] (DLA)
Town Com Law...	Townsend on Commercial Law [*A publication*] (DLA)
TownCty......	Town & Country Jewelry Corp. [*Associated Press*] (SAG)
town ha	Town Hall (VRA)
Town Jud.....	Townsend's Judgment [*A publication*] (DLA)
Town Pl.......	Townshend's Pleading [*A publication*] (DLA)
Town Pr.......	Townshend's Practice [*A publication*] (DLA)
Town Pr Pl...	Townshend's Precedents of Pleading [*A publication*] (DLA)
Townsh Pl ...	Townshend's Pleading [*A publication*] (DLA)

Townsh Sland & L...	Townshend on Slander and Libel [*A publication*] (DLA)
Town Sl & Lib...	Townshend on Slander and Libel [*A publication*] (DLA)
Town St Tr...	Townsend's Modern State Trials [*1850*] [*A publication*] (DLA)
Town Sum Proc...	Townshend's Summary Landlord and Tenant Process [*A publication*] (DLA)
TOWPROS ...	TOW [*Tube-Launched, Optically Tracked, Wire-Guided (Weapon)*] Protective Shelters (MCD)
TOWR	Tower Air [*NASDAQ symbol*] (TTSB)
TOWR	Tower Air, Inc. [*NASDAQ symbol*] (SAG)
TowrAir.......	Tower Air, Inc. [*Associated Press*] (SAG)
TowrTch......	Tower Tech, Inc. [*Associated Press*] (SAG)
Towson St U...	Towson State University (GAGS)
TOWT..........	Take Off Weight (IAA)
TOWV	Stratosphere Corp. [*NASDAQ symbol*] (SAG)
TOX............	Tetradichloroxylene (COE)
TOX............	Time of Expiration (MHDB)
TOX............	Tocantina [*Goias, Brazil*] [*Airport symbol*] (AD)
TOX............	Total Organic Halide (ACII)
TOX............	Total Oxidants
tox	Toxemia (BARN)
tox	Toxic (CPH)
Tox.............	Toxicity (DB)
TOX............	Toxicology
tox	Toxicology [*Medicine*] (WDAA)
tox	Toxin (CPH)
TOXBACK......	Toxicology Information Backup (NITA)
TOXBACK......	TOXLINE Back-File
TOXBIB	Toxicity Bibliography [*MEDLARS*]
TOXGR.........	Toxic Granulation-Differential [*Laboratory science*] (DAVI)
TOXI...........	Toxic Granulation [*Laboratory science*] (DAVI)
TOXICOL	Toxicology
toxicol	Toxicology [*Medicine*] (WDAA)
TOXICON......	Toxicology Information Conversational On-Line Network [*National Library of Medicine*] [*Later, TOXLINE*]
TOXLINE	Toxicology Information On-Line [*National Library of Medicine*] [*Bethesda, MD Bibliographic database*]
TOXLIST	Toxic Regulatory Listings [*American Petroleum Institute*] [*Information service or system*] (CRD)
TOXNET	Toxicology Data Network [*National Library of Medicine*] [*Information service or system*] (IID)
TOXO	Toxoplasmosis [*Medicine*]
TOXREP.......	Toxic Incident Report
TOXREPT	Toxic Incident Report (MUGU)
TOXT...........	Toxteth (ROG)
TOXTIPS	Toxicology Testing in Progress (NITA)
TOY............	Toyama [*Japan*] [*Seismograph station code, US Geological Survey*] (SEIS)
TOY............	Toyota Canada, Inc. [*ICAO designator*] (FAAC)
TOY............	Toys R Us [*NYSE symbol*] (TTSB)
TOY............	Toys R Us, Inc. [*NYSE symbol*] (SPSG)
TOY............	Troy, IL [*Location identifier FAA*] (FAAL)
Toy Biz	Toy Biz, Inc. [*Associated Press*] (SAG)
TOYDV	Tomato Yellow Dwarf Virus [*Plant pathology*]
TOYH	THQ, Inc. [*NASDAQ symbol*] (SAG)
TOYM..........	Ten Outstanding Young Men of America [*Jaycees' program*]
TOYMV	Tomato Yellow Mosaic Virus [*Plant pathology*]
TOYO	Toyota Motor Corp. [*NASDAQ symbol*] (NQ)
Toyota	Toyota Motor Co. [*Associated Press*] (SAG)
TOYOY	Toyota Motor Corp. ADR [*NASDAQ symbol*] (TTSB)
ToyRU.........	Toys R Us, Inc. [*Associated Press*] (SAG)
TOZ............	Harvard University, Tozzer Library, Cambridge, MA [*OCLC symbol*] (OCLC)
TOZ............	Touba [*Ivory Coast*] [*Airport symbol*] (OAG)
TOZ............	Towarzystwo Ochrony Zdrowia [*A publication*] (BJA)
TP..............	East Timor [*ISO two-letter standard code*] (CNC)
tp	Mean Transit Time [*Radiology*] (DAVI)
TP..............	Palestinian Talmud (BJA)
TP..............	[*The*] Prosperos (EA)
T-P.............	Tabloncillo Perla [*Race of maize*]
TP..............	Tail-Pinch Stress
TP..............	Tangible Property [*Business*] (MHDW)
TP..............	Tank Parliament [*British*]
TP..............	Tank Piercing [*Ammunition*] [*Military*]
TP..............	Tank Pressure (DS)
TP..............	Tape (BUR)
tp	Tape (WDMC)
TP..............	Target Point
TP..............	Target Polynucleotide (DB)
TP..............	Target Population
TP..............	Target Practice [*Military*]
TP..............	Task Processor [*Telecommunications*] (TSSD)
TP..............	Tasmanian Police [*Australia*]
TP..............	Taxpayer
TP..............	Tax Planning [*A publication*] (DLA)
TP..............	Teaching Practice
TP..............	Technical Pamphlet
TP..............	Technical Paper
TP..............	Technical Performance (MCD)
TP..............	Technical Problem
TP..............	Technical Professional
TP..............	Technical Proposal
TP..............	Technical Publication
TP..............	Technographic Publication
TP..............	Technology Parameter
TP..............	Technophility Index [*Mining technology*]

TP	Telecommunications Processor [*FAA*] (TAG)
TP	Telemetry Processor
TP	Telephone (CET)
TP	Teleprensa [*Press agency*] [*Colombia*]
TP	Teleprinter
TP	Teleprocessing [*Computer science*] (MCD)
TP	Television Pickup [*FCC*] (NTCM)
TP	Temperature and Pressure [*Temporoparietal*] [*Anatomy*] (DAVI)
T + P	Temperature and Pulse [*Medicine*]
TP	Temperature Probe (AAG)
T/P	Temperature to Precipitation Ratio [*Botany*]
TP	Tempo Primo [*Original Tempo*] [*Music*]
TP	Temporary Patient [*British*]
TP	Tempore Paschale [*At Easter Time*] [*Latin*]
TP	Tensile Properties (MCD)
TP	Tentative Pamphlet
TP	Terminal Phalanx [*Anatomy*]
TP	Terminal Point (NATG)
TP	Terminal Pole [*Telecommunications*] (TEL)
TP	Terminal Portability [*Telecommunications*] (DOM)
TP	Terminal Processor
TP	Terminal Protocol (MHDI)
TP	Term Pass (AAG)
TP	Terrestrial Plants
TP	Territorial Party [*Northern Marianas*] (PPW)
TP	Terza Posizione [*Third Position*] [*Italy*]
TP	Testosterone Propionate [*Endocrinology*]
T/P	Test Panel (AAG)
TP	Test Plan
TP	Test Point
TP	Test Port (KSC)
TP	Test Position
TP	Test Positive [*Clinical chemistry*]
TP	Test Pressure [*Nuclear energy*] (NRCH)
TP	Test Procedure (NATG)
TP	Test Process
TP	Test Program
TP	[*The*] Texas & Pacific Railway Co. [*Absorbed into Missouri Pacific System*] [*AAR code*]
TP	Text Processing (NITA)
TP	Text Processor
TP	Thermoplastic [*Also, T*] [*Plastics technology*]
TP	Thermosphere Probe
TP	Thiamphenicol [*Antimicrobial compound*]
TP	Thiopental [*An anesthetic*]
TP	Third Party [*Insurance*] (ODBW)
TP	Thomas Power [*"Tay Pay"*] O'Connor [*Irish journalist and politician, 1848-1929*]
TP	Thomson Press (India) Ltd. [*Publisher*]
TP	Threshold Potential (MAE)
TP	Thrombocytopenic Purpura [*Medicine*]
TP	Thrombophlebitis [*Medicine*]
TP	Throttle Positioner [*Automotive engineering*]
TP	Throttle Potentiometer [*Automotive engineering*]
TP	Thymic Polypeptide [*Endocrinology*]
TP	Thymidine Phosphorylase [*An enzyme*]
TP	Thymolphthalein [*Organic chemistry*]
TP	Thymopentin [*Biochemistry*]
TP	Thymopoietin
TP	Thymus Protein
TP	Tibialis Posterior [*Anatomy*]
TP	Tie Plate [*Technical drawings*]
TP	Tie Point
TP	Timber Products Inspection (WPI)
T-P	Timbre Poste [*Postage Stamp*] [*French*]
TP	Time Pulse
tp	Time-to-Peak Tension (DAVI)
TP	Time to Perigee (MCD)
TP	Timing Point (AFM)
TP	Timpano [*Music*]
TP	Tin Plate
TP	Tinted Printing [*Paper*] (DGA)
TP	Tire Pressure [*Automotive engineering*]
TP	Title Page [*Bibliography*]
tp	Title Page (WDMC)
TP	Toilet Paper [*To be "TP'd" is to have your yard covertly decorated with unrolled toilet paper*] [*Slang*]
TP	Toll Point [*Telecommunications*] (TEL)
TP	Toll Prefix [*Telecommunications*] (TEL)
TP	Toothpick
TP	Top
TP	To Pay (ADA)
TP	Top Priority
TP	Torpedo Part of Beam (MSA)
TP	Totally Positive
TP	Total Particulate Matter [*BTS*] (TAG)
TP	Total Parts
TP	Total Phenolic Levels [*Chemistry*]
TP	Total Phosphorus [*Analytical chemistry*]
TP	Total Points
TP	Total Positives [*Medicine*] (DMAA)
TP	Total Power
TP	Total Pressure
TP	Total Production [*or Product*] [*Ecology*]
TP	Total Protein
TP	Touchdowns Passing [*Football*]
TP	Tower Proof [*Gunpowder*] (DICI)
TP	Township
TP	Toxic Pregnancy [*Gynecology*]
TP	Tracking Program (MUGU)
TP	Trade Protection Service [*or Society*] [*British*]
TP	Traffic Post
TP	Trailer Point [*MTMC*] (TAG)
TP	Training Period [*Military*] (AFM)
TP	Training Plan (NASA)
TP	Training, Practicing [*Ammunition*]
TP	Train Printer [*Computer science*] (IAA)
TP	Transaction Processing [*Computer science*]
TP	Transaction Program [*Computer science*] (BYTE)
TP	Transaction Provider (WDMC)
TP	Transannular Patch [*Cardiology*]
TP	Transfer on Positive
TP	Transforming Principle [*Bacteriology*]
TP	Transition Period (NASA)
TP	Transition Plans (MCD)
TP	Translucent Paper (ADA)
TP	Transnational Prospectives [*A publication*]
TP	Transplant
TP	Transportation Priority [*Military*] (AFM)
TP	Transporter (DCTA)
TP	Transport Pack
TP	Transport Pilot
TP	Transport Protein [*Superseded by SC, Secretory Component*] [*Immunology*]
TP	Transport Protocol [*Computer science*]
TP	Transvaal Province [*Republic of South Africa*]
TP	Transvaal Supreme Court Reports [*South Africa*] [*A publication*] (DLA)
TP	Transverse Process [*Neurosurgery*] (DAVI)
TP	Travaux Forces a Perpetuite [*Penal Servitude for Life*] [*French*]
TP	Travaux Publics [*Public Works*] [*French*]
TP	Travers Pensions [*Formerly, Naval Knights of Windsor*] [*Military British*] (ROG)
TP	Treaty Port
TP	TreePeople (EA)
TP	Tree Project (EA)
TP	Treponema Pallidum [*A spirochete*] [*Clinical chemistry*]
TP	Trial Preparation (LAIN)
TP	Trigger Point [*Medicine*] (DMAA)
TP	Trigger Pulse [*Telecommunications*] (IAA)
TP	Trigonal Prism [*Medicine*] (DB)
TP	Trigonometrischer Punkt [*Triangulation Point*] [*German military - World War II*]
TP	Triphosphate (MAE)
TP	Triple Play [*Baseball*]
TP	Triple Pole [*Switch*]
TP	Troop
TP	Troop Program [*Military*] (AABC)
TP	Tropical Pacific [*American air mass*]
TP	Troubleshooting Procedure [*DoD*]
TP	True Position
TP	True Positive [*Medicine*]
TP	True Profile [*Technical drawings*]
TP	Trumpet
TP	Tryptophan [*An amino acid*] (MAE)
TP	Tryptophan Pyrrolase [*Also, TPO*] [*An enzyme*]
TP	Tube Precipitin [*Laboratory science*] (DAVI)
TP	Tuberculin Precipitation [*Medicine*]
TP	Tuned Plate (DEN)
TP	Turboprop (AAG)
TP	Turbopump (AAG)
TP	Turning Point
TP	Tyndale Paper [*A publication*] (APTA)
TP	Type (NASA)
TPA	Austin Peay State University, Clarksville, TN [*OCLC symbol*] (OCLC)
TPA	Taildragger Pilots Association (EA)
TPA	Tala Pozo [*Argentina*] [*Seismograph station code, US Geological Survey Closed*] (SEIS)
TPA	Tallgrass Prairie Alliance (EA)
TPA	Tampa/St. Petersburg/Clearwater [*Florida*] [*Airport symbol*]
TPA	Tannic Acid, Phosphomolybdic Acid, Amido Acid Black [*A staining technique*]
TPA	Tantalum Producers Association [*Defunct*] (EA)
TPA	Tape Pulse Amplifier
TPA	Target Position Analyzer [*Military*] (CAAL)
TPA	Target Presentation Area [*Army*] (RDA)
TPA	Tariff Programs and Appraisals [*Canada Customs*]
TPA	TASS [*Towed Array SONAR System*] Probability Area (NVT)
TPA	Technical Performance Audit
TPA	Technical Practice Aid (ADA)
TPA	Technical Publications Agent (MCD)
TPA	Technical Publications Announcement
TPA	Telemetry Power Amplifier
TPA	Telepanel, Inc. [*Vancouver Stock Exchange symbol*]
TPA	Telephone Pioneers of America (EA)
TPA	Temperature-Programmed Analysis
TPA	Tennis Professionals Association [*Canada*]
TPa	Terapascal [*Pressure unit*]
TPA	Terephthalic Acid [*Also, TA*] [*Organic chemistry*]
TPA	Test Plans and Analysis

TPA	Test Point Access (IAA)
TPA	Test Preparation Area [NASA] (KSC)
TPA	Test Project Agreement (NG)
TPA	Tetradecanoylphorbolacetate [Also, PMA, PTA] [Organic chemistry]
TPA	Tetrapropylammonium [Chemical radical]
TPA	Texture Profile Analysis [Food technology]
TPA	Thermal Polarization Analysis (DB)
TPA	Thermal Polyaspartate [Organic chemistry]
TPA	Thermoparticulate Analysis (DB)
TPA	Theta Phi Alpha [Sorority]
TPA	Third Party Administrator
TPA	Timber Producers Association of Michigan and Wisconsin (EA)
TPA	Time-Phased Allocation (MCD)
TPA	Tissue Plasminogen Activator [Anticlotting agent]
tPA	Tissue Plasminogen Activator [Medicine] (WDAA)
TPA	Tissue Polypeptide Antigen [Immunochemistry]
t-PA	Tissue-Type Plasminogen Activator (STED)
TPA	Toll Pulse Accepter [Telecommunications] (TEL)
TPA	Tons per Annum (ADA)
TPA	Top Pumparound [Chemical engineering]
TPA	Total Parenteral Alimentation [Medicine] (DMAA)
TPA	Total Phobic Anxiety (STED)
TPA	Tournament Players Association (EA)
TPA	Track Production Area [Air Force]
TPA	Trading Partner Agreement (AAGC)
TPA	Traffic Pattern Altitude [Aviation]
TPA	Training Problem Analysis (MCD)
TPA	Transfer of Pay Account [Military]
TPA	Transient Program Area
TPA	Transistor Power Amplifier (LAIN)
TPA	Transmission Products Association [Defunct] (EA)
TPA	Trans-Pacific Airlines Ltd.
TPA	Transportation Payment Act of 1972 (AAGC)
TPA	Transportes Aereos Mercantiles Panamericanos [Colombia] [ICAO designator] (FAAC)
TPA	Travel by Personal Auto Authorized [Military]
TPA	Travelers Protective Association of America [St. Louis, MO] (EA)
TPA	Travel Professionals Association (EA)
TPA	Treponema Pallidum Agglutination [Medicine] (DAVI)
TPA	Trim Power Assembly
TPA	Tri-Party Agreement (DOGT)
TPA	Triphenylamine [Organic chemistry]
TPA	Tripropylamine [Organic chemistry]
TPA	Truck Performance Analysis
TPA	Tube and Pipe Association, International (NTPA)
TPA	Tumor Polypeptide Antigen [Oncology] (DAVI)
TPA	Tunable Parametric Amplifier
TPA	Turboprop Aircraft
TPA	Turbopump Assembly (KSC)
TPA	Tutmonda Parolspuro-Asocio [Universal Association for Speech Tracing - UAST] (EAIO)
TPA	Two-Photon Absorption (PDAA)
TPA	Type of Professional Activity
TPAA	Timber Preservers' Association of Australia
TPAA	Travelers Protective Association of America (EA)
TPAC	TCI Pacific Communications [NASDAQ symbol] (SAG)
TPAC	Technology Policy and Assessment Center [Georgia Institute of Technology] [Research center] (RCD)
TPAC	Telescope Precision Angle Counter
TP-AD	Technical Publications - Administration [Naval Facilities Engineering Command Publications]
TPAD	Telepad Corp. [NASDAQ symbol] (SAG)
TPAD	Teleprocessing Analysis and Design Program [Computer science] (IAA)
TPAD	Trunnion Pin Attachment Device [NASA]
TPADA	TelePad Corp. 'A' [NASDAQ symbol] (TTSB)
TPADL	TelePad Corp. Wrrt 'D' [NASDAQ symbol] (TTSB)
TPADM	TelePad Corp. Wrrt'C' [NASDAQ symbol] (TTSB)
TPADU	TelePad Corp. Unit [NASDAQ symbol] (TTSB)
TPADW	TelePad Corp. Wrrt'A' [NASDAQ symbol] (TTSB)
TPADZ	TelePad Corp. Wrrt'B' [NASDAQ symbol] (TTSB)
TP-AGB	Thermally Pulsing, Asymptotic Giant Branch [Astronomy]
TPAI	Teacher Performance Assessment Instruments (EDAC)
TPAL	Term Infants, Premature Infants, Abortions, Living Children [Obstetric History] (STED)
TPAM	Teleprocessing Access Method
TPAM	Three-Phase Aquatic Microcosms [Technique for study of waters]
TP & C	Thermal Protection and Control (NASA)
TP & N	Triple Pole and Neutral [Switch]
TP & P	Time, Place, and Person
TP & W	Toledo, Peoria & Western Railroad Co.
TPAOH	Tetrapropylammonium Hydroxide [Organic chemistry]
TPAP	Time-Phased-Action Plan [DoD]
TPAP	Transaction Processing Applications Program (MHDI)
TPAPOABITCOS	[The] Precentor and Prebendary of Alton Borealis in the Church of Sarum [Pseudonym used by Arthur Ashley Sykes]
TPAR	Tactical Penetration Aids Rocket
TPARR	TRADOC Program Analysis and Resource Review [Military] (MCD)
TP-ASE	Transaction Processing Application Service Element [Telecommunications] (OSI)
TPAT	Test Point Algorithm Technique (MCD)
TPB	Nebraska Library Commission, Lincoln, NE [OCLC symbol] (OCLC)
TPB	Tape Playback BIT [Binary Digit] [Computer science]
TPB	Tarnished Plant Bug [Entomology]
TPB	Tetraphenylbutadiene [Organic chemistry]

TPB	Tetraphenylbutane [Organic chemistry]
TPB	Triphenylbenzene [Organic chemistry]
TpB	Trypan Blue [Biological stain]
TPB	Tryptone Phosphate Broth
TPB	Twinwire Pulp Board (DGA)
TPBA	Transdisciplinary Play-Based Assessment [Test] (TMMY)
T(PBEIST)	Transport - Planning Board European Inland Surface Transport (NATG)
TPBF	Total Pulmonary Blood Flow [Physiology]
TPBI	Third Party Bodily Injury [Insurance] (AIA)
TPBK	Tape Block
T(PBOS)	Transport - Planning Board Ocean Shipping (NATG)
TPBS	Tetrapropylenbenzenesulfonate [Organic chemistry]
TPBS	Three-Phase Radionuclide Bone Scanning [Radiology] (DAVI)
TPBT	Technical Papers for the Bible Translator [A publication] (BJA)
TPBV	Two-Point Boundary Value (PDAA)
TPBVP	Two-Point Boundary Value Problem
TPC	Air Caledonie [France ICAO designator] (FAAC)
TPC	Nebraska Library Commission, Lincoln, NE [OCLC symbol] (OCLC)
TPC	Tactical Pilotage Chart
TPC	Tangential Period Correction
TPC	Technical Performance Criteria (SSD)
TPC	Technical Prime Contractor
TPC	Technical Progress Committee [British] (DCTA)
TPC	Technical Protein Colloid
TPC	Technology Partnerships Canada [Science and technology strategy]
TPC	Tejas Power Corp. [AMEX symbol] (SPSG)
TPC	Telecommunications Planning Committee [Civil Defense]
TPC	Telecommunications Program and Control (IAA)
TPC	Telemetry Preprocessing Computer (MCD)
TPC	Telephone Pickup Coil
TPC	Telescoping Plugged Catheter (STED)
TPC	Telopeptide-Poor Collagen (DB)
TPC	Temporary Procedure Change [Environmental science] (COE)
TPC	Territorial Production Complex [Russian]
TPC	Test Point Controller
TPC	Texas Petroleum Corp. [Vancouver Stock Exchange symbol]
TPC	Thermafor Pyrolytic Cracking [A chemical process developed by Surface Combustion]
TPC	Thermally Protected Composite
TPC	Thick Paper Copy (DGA)
TPC	Third Party Traffic [Radio]
TPC	Thromboplastic Plasma Component [Factor VIII] [Also, AHF, AHG, PTF Hematology]
TPC	Thymolphthalein complexone [Analytical reagent]
TPC	Timber Promotion Council [Victoria, Australia]
TPC	Time Polarity Control
TPC	Time Projection Chamber [High-energy physics]
TPC	Time-to-Pulse-Height Converter (STED)
TPC	Tire Performance Criteria [General Motors Corp.]
TPC	Tons per Centimeter (DCTA)
TPC	Topical Pulmonary Chemotherapy [Medicine]
TPC	Topographic Center [Defense Mapping Agency]
TPC	Total Package Contract
TPC	Total Patient Care [Nursing] (DAVI)
TPC	Total Plasma Catecholamines [Hematology] (DMAA)
TPC	Total Plasma Cholesterol [Clinical chemistry]
TPC	Total Print Control [Computer science] (IAA)
TPC	Total Program Costs (KSC)
TPC	Total Project Cost (DOMA)
TPC	Total Protein Concentration
TPC	Tournament Players Championship
TPC	TPC Corp. [AMEX symbol] [Formerly, Tejas Power Corp.] (SG)
TPC	Trade Policy Committee [Advisory to President] [Abolished, 1963]
TPC	Trade Practices Commission (EERA)
TPC	Training Plans Conference
TPC	Transaction Processing Performance Council (EA)
TPC	Transistor Photo Control
TPC	Trans-Pacific Freight Conference of Japan/Korea Agent, San Francisco CA [STAC]
TPC	Transport Plane Commander
TPC	Transvascular Protein Clearance [Medicine]
TPC	Travaux Publics Canada [Public Works Canada - PWC]
TPC	Travel by Privately-Owned Conveyance Permitted for Convenience [Military] (AFM)
TPC	Treated Paper Copier [Reprography]
TPC	Treatment Planning Conference [Medicine] (STED)
TPC	Treponema Pallidum Complement [Clinical chemistry] (MAE)
TPC	Tricalcium Phosphate Ceramic [Inorganic chemistry]
TPC	Triple Paper-Covered [Wire insulation] (DEN)
TPC	Triple-Product Convolver [Acousto-optic technology] (RDA)
TPC	True Partition Coefficient (DB)
TPC	Turbopump Control
TPC	Turns per Centimeter [Yarn]
TPC	Twentynine Palms [California] [Seismograph station code, US Geological Survey] (SEIS)
TPC	Twisted-Pair Cable
TPCA	Test Procedure Change Authorization (NATG)
TPCB	[The] Personal Computer Book
TPCC	Third-Party Call Control [Telecommunications] (DDC)
TPCC	Trade Promotion Coordinating Committee [Department of Commerce] (EGAO)
TPCCOA	Telephone Provincial Clerical and Contract Officers' Association [A union] [British]
TPCD	Tetraphenylcyclopentadienone [Organic chemistry]

TPCF............	Treponema Pallidum Complement Fixation [*Clinical chemistry*]
TPCK............	Tosylaminophenylethyl Chloromethyl Ketone [*Organic chemistry*]
TPCK............	Tosyl Phenylalanine Chloromethyl Ketone [*Biochemistry*]
TPCN	Task Plan Change Notice (MCD)
TPCO	Teleprinter Coordinator
TPCOMP	Tape Compare [*Computer science*] (IAA)
TPCP	Trainer Power Control Panel
TPCP............	Treponema Pallidum Cryolysis Complement Fixation [*Test for Syphilis*] (DAVI)
TPCR	Task Plan Change Request (MCD)
TPCRP	Tool and Production Change Planning Record (SAA)
TPCS............	Torquay Pottery Collectors' Society (EA)
TPCSDS-T....	Target Practice Cone Stabilized Discarding Sabot with Tracer [*Army*] (DOMA)
TPCU	Test Power Control Unit (IAA)
TPCU	Thermal Preconditioning Unit
TPCV	Total Packed Cell Volume [*Hematology*] (DMAA)
TPCV............	Turbine Power Control Valve
TPD	Five Associated University Libraries, Rochester, NY [*OCLC symbol*] (OCLC)
TPD	South African Law Reports, Transvaal Provincial Division [*South Africa*] [*A publication*] (DLA)
T/PD............	Table of Personnel Distribution (NATG)
TPD	TAFE (Technical and Further Education) and People with Disabilities [*Australia*]
TPD..............	Tape Playback Discriminator
TPD..............	Tapped (MSA)
TPD..............	Technical Programs Division [*Environmental Protection Agency*] (GFGA)
TPD..............	Technical Publications Documentation [*Army*]
TPD..............	Temperature-Programmed Desorption [*Catalysis*]
TPD..............	Temporary Partial Disablement [*Insurance*] (AIA)
TPD..............	Terminal Protective Device (MSA)
TPD..............	Terracamp Development [*Vancouver Stock Exchange symbol*]
TPD..............	Test Plasma Produced by Discharge (MCD)
TPD..............	Test Point Data
TPD..............	Test Procedure Deviation [*Nuclear energy*] (NRCH)
TPD..............	Test Procedure Drawing [*NASA*] (KSC)
TPD..............	Theophylline, Proxyphylline, and Dyphylline [*Antineoplastic drug regimen*]
TPD..............	Thermoplastic Photoconductor Device
TPD..............	Thiamine Propyl Disulfide (MAE)
TPD..............	Thrifty Payless Hldg'B' [*NYSE symbol*] (TTSB)
TPD..............	Time Pulse Distributor (MCD)
TPD..............	Toilet Paper Dispenser [*Technical drawings*]
TPD..............	Tons per Day
TPD..............	Torque Proportioning Differential [*Automotive engineering*]
TPD..............	Total Permanent Disability [*or Disablement*] [*Insurance*] (AIA)
TPD..............	Total Program Diagnostic [*Computer science*] (IAA)
TPD..............	Total Purity by Difference [*Gas analysis*]
TPD..............	Tournament Players Division of the Professional Golfers Association of America [*Later, TPA*]
TPD..............	Toxics and Pesticides Division [*Environmental Protection Agency*] (GFGA)
TPD..............	Training Programs Directorate [*Army*]
TPD..............	Transient Photodichroism [*Physics*]
TPD..............	Transpolar Drift
TPD..............	Trivial Problem Discriminator [*Computer science*] (IAA)
TPD..............	Tropical Pancreatic Diabetes [*Endocrinology*] (DAVI)
TPD..............	Tumor-Producing Dose [*Virology*]
TPDB............	Tape Deblock
TPDC............	Test Point Data Chart [*Military*]
TPDC............	Training and Performance Data Center [*Military*]
TPDDI..........	Twisted Pair Distributed Data Interface [*Computer science*] (CIST)
TPDE............	Temperature Programmed Decomposition (EDCT)
Tpd I............	Tipped In (DGA)
TPDLRI........	Textile Printers and Dyers Labor Relations Institute (EA)
TPDRS	Time-Phased Downgrading and Reclassification System [*Military*] (DNAB)
TPDS	Tape Playback Discriminator System
TPDS	Test Procedures Development System (NASA)
TPDSA........	Totally and Permanently Disabled Soldiers' Association [*Australia*]
TPDSASR....	Tooling Project Data Sheet Assembly Sequence Record
TPDS-T	Target Practice Discarding Sabot-Tracer [*Projectile*] (MCD)
TPDT............	Tree-Walking Pushdown Transducer (MHDI)
TPDT............	Triple-Pole, Double-Throw [*Switch*]
TPDT............	True Position Dimensioning and Tolerancing (PDAA)
TPDU............	Transport Protocol Data Unit [*Telecommunications*] (OSI)
TPDUP..........	Tape Duplicate [*Computer science*] (IAA)
TPE	Five Associated University Libraries, Rochester, NY [*OCLC symbol*] (OCLC)
TPE	Tactical Performance Evaluation
TPE	Taipei [*Taiwan*] [*Airport symbol*] (OAG)
TPE	Task of Public Education Questionnaire (AEBS)
TPE	Teacher Performance Evaluation (EDAC)
TPE	Technology, People, Environment [*National Science Foundation project*]
TPE	Telomere Position Effect [*Genetics*]
TPE	Test Planning and Evaluation
TPE	Test Project Engineer (NASA)
TPE	Tetraphenylethylene [*Organic chemistry*]
TPE	Therapeutic Plasma Exchange [*Hematology*] (CPH)
TPE	Thermoplastic Elastomer [*Plastics technology*]
TPE	Threshold Photoelectron [*Spectroscopy*]
TPE	Total Potential Energy

TPE	Total Protective Environment [*Immunology*] (DAVI)
TPE	Total Publishing Environment [*Computer science*] (IAA)
TPE	T-Pulse Effectiveness [*Neurology*]
TPE	Transaction Processing Executive (MCD)
TPE	Transmission Parity Error [*Computer science*] (IAA)
TPE	Transport Planning and Economics [*British*]
TPE	Triple Crown Electronics, Inc. [*Toronto Stock Exchange symbol*]
TPE	Turbopropeller Engine
TPE	Twisted-Pair Ethernet [*Intel Corp.*]
TPE	Two-Photon Excitation [*Fluorescence spectrometry*]
TPE	Two Pion Exchange [*Nuclear physics*] (OA)
TPEA	Television Program Export Association (EA)
TPEA	Texas Produce Export Association (NTPA)
TPED	Trade and Professional Exhibits Directory [*Later, TSW*] [*A publication*]
T-PEES........	Triplane Elevated Evaluation System [*Army*] (RDA)
TPEG............	Producers Entertainment Group [*NASDAQ symbol*] (SAG)
TPEG............	Producers Entertainment Grp [*NASDAQ symbol*] (TTSB)
TPEGP..........	Producers Entmt 8.50% Cv'A'Pfd [*NASDAQ symbol*] (TTSB)
TPEM............	Tactical Peripherals Equipment Monitor [*Military*]
TPEN............	Tetrakis(pyridylmethyl)ethylenediamine [*Organic chemistry*]
TPEO............	Trunk Piston Engine Oil [*Automotive lubricants*]
TPER............	Total Primary Energy Requirement [*BTS*] (TAG)
TPES............	Threshold Photoelectron Spectroscopy [*Physics*]
TPESP..........	Technical Panel on the Earth Satellite Program
TPEY............	Tellurite-Polymyxin-Egg Yolk [*Agar*] [*Microbiology*]
TPF	[*The*] Pygmy Fund (EA)
TPF	Tactical Patrol Force [*Police*]
TPF	Tailored Probability Forecast
TPFI	Tampa, FL [*Location identifier FAA*] (FAAL)
TPF	Taxis Aereos del Pacifico, SA de CV [*Mexico*] [*FAA designator*] (FAAC)
TPF	Telemetry Processing Facility (MCD)
TPF	Temporary Program File [*Computer science*]
TPF	Terminal Phase Finalization [*or Finish*] [*NASA*] (KSC)
TPF	Terrestrial Planet Finder [*Proposed*]
TPF	Tetraphenylfuran [*Organic chemistry*]
TPF	Thai Patriotic Front [*Communist-directed activity outside Thailand*] [*Merged with TIM*]
TPF	Theoretical Point of Fog (MSA)
TPF	Thymus Permeability Factor
TPF	Time Prism Filter [*Telecommunications*] (TEL)
TPF	Toilet Preparations Federation [*British*] (BI)
TPF	Total Package Fielding [*Army*]
TPF	Total Peaking Factor [*Nuclear energy*] (NRCH)
TPF	Trainer Parts Fabrication (AAG)
TPF	Transaction Processing Facility (HGAA)
TPF	Transfer Phase Final (MCD)
TPF	Tri-Pacific Resources Ltd. [*Vancouver Stock Exchange symbol*]
TPF	Tube and Pipe Fabricators Association, International (EA)
TPF	Tug Processing Facility [*NASA*] (NASA)
TPF	Two-Phase Flow
TPF	Two Photon Fluorescence [*Electronics*] (OA)
TPF-A............	Total Package Fielding - Activation [*Military*]
TPFA............	Tube and Pipe Fabricators Association, International (EAIO)
TPF & C........	Towers, Perrin, Forster & Crosby [*Compensation and actuarial consulting company*]
TPFC............	[*The*] Platters Fan Club (EA)
TPFC............	Tasmanian Public Finance Corp. [*Australia Commercial firm*]
TPF-C............	Total Package Fielding-(Unit)Conversion [*Military*]
TPFDD..........	Time-Phased Force Deployment Data [*Military*] (AABC)
TPFDL..........	Time-Phased Force Deployment List [*Military*] (AFM)
TPFDL..........	Troop Program Field Deployment List [*Military*]
TPFI	Terminal Pin Fault Insertion
TPFN............	2-Spirited of the First Nations (AC)
TPFP............	Transkei People's Freedom Party [*South Africa*] [*Political party*] (PPW)
TPFR............	Time to Peak Filling Rate [*Cardiology*]
TPFW............	Thermoplastic Fan Wheel
TPFW............	Three-Phase Full Wave
TPG	Taiping [*China*] [*Airport symbol*] (AD)
TPG	Tapping
TPG	Technology Planning Guide [*Military*] (AFIT)
TPG	Telecommunication Program Generator
TPG	Telecom Publishing Group (IID)
TPG	Teletype Preamble Generator
TPG	Test Pattern Generation (AAEL)
TPG	Thermionic Power Generator
TPG	Timing Pulse Generator
TPG	TNT Post Group
TPG	Topping [*Meteorology*] (FAAC)
TPG	Total Pressure Gauge
TPG	Transmembrane Potential Gradient (DAVI)
TPG	Transmission Project Group (IAA)
TPG	Transplacental Gradient [*Obstetrics*] (MAE)
TPG	Transportes Aereos Pegaso SA de CV [*Mexico ICAO designator*] (FAAC)
TPG	Trinity Peninsula Group [*Geology*]
TPG	Triphenylguanidine [*Organic chemistry*]
TPG	Trypticase, Peptone, Glucose
TPGC	Tryptophan Peptone Glucose [*Broth*] [*Microbiology*] (DAVI)
TPGC	Temperature-Programmed Gas Chromatography
TpGGv..........	Templeton Global Governments Income Trust [*Associated Press*] (SAG)
TPGID	Tank Precision Gunnery in Bore Device [*Army*]

TPGS	[*The*] Pennsylvania German Society (EA)
TPGS	Tocopherol Polyethylene Glycol Succinate [*Organic chemistry*]
TPGY	Trypticose-Peptone-Glucose-Yeast Extract-Trypsin [*Medium*] [*Microbiology*] (DAVI)
TPH	Central Transport Rental Group Ltd. [*Formerly, Tiphook Ltd. ADS*] [*NYSE symbol*] (SAG)
TPH	Central Trans Rental Gp ADS [*NYSE symbol*] (TTSB)
TPH	Temperature Programmed Hydrogenation [*Chemical engineering*]
TPH	Theosophical Publishing House
TPH	Thromboembolic Pulmonary Hypertension [*Medicine*]
TPH	Through Plated Hole [*Printed circuit board feature*] (IAA)
TPH	Tonopah [*Nevada*] [*Airport symbol*] (AD)
TPH	Tonopah, NV [*Location identifier FAA*] (FAAL)
TPH	Tons per Hour
TPH	Total Petroleum Hydrocarbon [*Analytical chemistry*]
TPH	Total Possessed Hours (MCD)
TPH	Transplacental Hemorrhage [*Obstetrics*] (MAE)
TPH	Triphenyltin Hydroxide (COE)
TPH	Triumph Resources Corp. [*Vancouver Stock Exchange symbol*]
TPH	University of Texas, Health Science Center at Houston, School Public Health, Houston, TX [*OCLC symbol*] (OCLC)
TPHA	Treponema Pallidum Hemagglutination
TPHA	Truman Philatelic and Historical Association (EA)
TPHASAP	Telephone as Soon as Possible (NOAA)
TPHAT	Telephone at [*Followed by time*] (NOAA)
TPHAYC	Telephone at Your Convenience (NOAA)
TPHC	Time-to-Pulse Height Converter
TPhI	Turfan Pahlavi (BJA)
TPHO	Telephotograph
TPHR	Tons per Hour
TPHSG	Troop Housing [*Army*] (AABC)
TPHW	Three-Phase Half Wave
TPI	[*The*] Progress Interview
TPI	P.T. Tri Polyta Indonesia ADS [*NYSE symbol*] (TTSB)
TPI	Tape Phase Inverter
TPI	Tape-Position Indicator (DEN)
TPI	Tapini [*Papua New Guinea*] [*Airport symbol*] (OAG)
TPI	Target Position Indicator
TPI	Task Parameter Interpretation
TPI	Tax and Price Index
TPI	Taxpayer Inquiry [*IRS*]
TPI	Tax Planning Ideas [*A publication*] (DLA)
TPI	Teatro Popolare Italiano [*Italian theatrical troupe*]
TPI	Technical Proficiency Inspection [*Military*]
TPI	Technical Proposal Instructions [*Environmental science*] (COE)
TPI	Teeth per Inch [*of cog wheels*]
TPI	Tennessee Polytechnic Institute
TPI	Terminal Phase Ignition [*NASA*]
TPI	Terminal Phase Initiate [*NASA*] (KSC)
TPI	Terminal Phase Initiation [*NASA*] (NAKS)
TPI	Terminal Phase Insertion [*NASA*]
TPI	Test Program Instruction (MCD)
TPI	Test Program Interaction (MCD)
TPI	Text Preparation and Interchange [*Telecommunications*]
TPI	Thai Petro-chemical Industry
TPI	Thermal Protection Investigation
TPI	Thermoplastic Imide [*Plastics*]
TPI	Thermoplastic Polyimide
TPI	Thermo Process Systems, Inc. [*AMEX symbol*] (SPSG)
TPI	Threads per Inch
TPI	Time Perception Inventory [*Test*]
TPI	Timing Pulse Idler
TPI	Tire Pressure Indicating System (MCD)
TPI	Title, Page, and Index
TPI	Tons per Inch
TPI	Topair Ltd. [*Czechoslovakia*] [*ICAO designator*] (FAAC)
TPI	Total Positive Income [*IRS*]
TPI	Town Planning Institute [*Later, Royal Town Planning Institute*] [*British*] (ILCA)
TPI	Tracks per Inch [*Magnetic storage devices*] [*Computer science*]
TPI	TRADOC Procurement Instruction (MCD)
TPI	Training Place in Industry (AIE)
TPI	Training Plan Information (MCD)
TPI	Transmission Performance Index [*Telecommunications*] (TEL)
TPI	Treponema Immobilization Test [*Clinical chemistry*] (MAE)
TPI	Treponema Pallidum Immobilization [*or Immobilizing*] [*Clinical chemistry*]
TPI	Trim Position Indicator
TPI	Triosephosphate Isomerase [*An enzyme*]
TPI	Triphosphoinositide [*Biochemistry*]
TPI	Tropical Products Institute [*Overseas Development Administration*] [*British*] (DS)
TPI	Truss Plate Institute (EA)
TPhI	Tuned Port Fuel Injection
TPI	Turns per Inch
TPIA	Take Pride in America Program [*Forest Service*] (GFGA)
TPIA	Treponema Pallidum Immune Adherence [*Clinical chemistry*]
TPIB	Technical Panel for International Broadcast (NTCM)
TPIC	Thermophysical Properties Information Center [*Purdue University*] (PDAA)
TPIC	Town Planning Institute of Canada
TPID	Telecommunications Performance and Interface Document (MCD)
TPIE	TPI Enterprises [*NASDAQ symbol*] (TTSB)
TPIE	TPI Enterprises, Inc. [*NASDAQ symbol*] (NQ)
TPI En	TPI Enterprises, Inc. [*Associated Press*] (SAG)
TPIF	Thornton Pacific Investment Fund
TPIFY	Tri Polyta Indonesia [*NASDAQ symbol*] (SAG)
TPIM	Tool Process Instruction Manual (MCD)
TPIN	True Personal Identification Number [*Banking*]
TPINIT	Tape Initializer [*Computer science*] (IAA)
TPIS	Telecommunicatinos Products Information Retrieval and Simulation (MHDI)
TPIS	Tire Pressure Indicating System (MCD)
TPJ	Tangkuban-Prahu [*Java*] [*Seismograph station code, US Geological Survey Closed*] (SEIS)
TPK	Test of Practical Knowledge
TPK	Tropicair Cargo [*Burundi*] [*FAA designator*] (FAAC)
TPK	Tulare Free Public Library, Tulare, CA [*OCLC symbol*] (OCLC)
TPK	Turnpike
TPK	Turns per Knot [*Navy*] (CAAL)
TPKE	Turnpike (MCD)
Tpke	Turnpike (TBD)
TPKrR	Theologicka Priloha (Krestanske Revue) [*A publication*] (BJA)
TPL	Table Producing Language [*1971*] [*Computer science*] (IID)
TPL	Tabular Parts List
TPL	Target Position Location (MCD)
TPL	Teacher Programming Language [*Computer science*] (PDAA)
TPL	Technical Publications Library (MCD)
TPL	Technical Publications List [*Environmental science*] (COE)
TPL	Telecommunications Programming Language (IAA)
TPL	Temple [*Texas*] [*Airport symbol*] (OAG)
TPL	Temple, TX [*Location identifier FAA*] (FAAL)
TPL	Terminal per Line [*Telecommunications*]
TPL	Terminal Processing Language
TPL	Terminal Programming Language [*Computer science*] (IAA)
TPL	Test Parts List
TPL	Test Plan (CAAL)
TPL	Test Plan Log (MCD)
TPL	Test Point Logic
TPL	Texas Pacific Land Trust [*NYSE symbol*] (SPSG)
TPL	Texas Pac Ld Tr [*NYSE symbol*] (TTSB)
TPL	Text Processing Language [*Computer science*]
TPL	THERE Programming Language [*Computer science*]
TPL	Third Party Liability
TPL	Tocopilla [*Chile*] [*Seismograph station code, US Geological Survey*] (SEIS)
TPL	Toll Pole Line [*Telecommunications*] (TEL)
TPL	Tons Poids Lourd [*Deadweight Tons*] [*French*]
TPL	Topsail [*Ship's rigging*] (ROG)
TPL	Toronto Public Library [*UTLAS symbol*]
TPL	Total Peak Loss (IAA)
TPL	Track Path Length [*Army*] (RDA)
TPL	Traditional Products Line (MHDI)
TPL	Training Parts List (AAG)
TPL	Transfer on Plus (SAA)
TPL	Transient Protection Limit [*Environmental science*] (COE)
TPL	Transistorized Portable Laboratory
TPL	Trap Processing Line
TPL	Tripartite Leader [*Genetics*]
TPL	Triple (MSA)
TPL	Triumph Petroleums Ltd. [*Vancouver Stock Exchange symbol*]
TPL	Troop Program List [*Army*]
TPL	Tropicalized (MSA)
TPL	Trust for Public Land (EA)
TPL	Tunable Pulsed LASER
TPL	Turbopool Ltd. [*British ICAO designator*] (FAAC)
TPL	Turns per Layer
TPL	Twyford Plant Laboratories Ltd. [*British*] (IRUK)
TPL	Tyrosine Phenol Lyase (DB)
TPL-6	Titanium Proximal Loading-6-Inch Stem [*Total hip system*] [*Orthopedics*] (DAVI)
TPLA	[*The*] Product Liability Alliance (EA)
TPLA	Triphenyllead Acetate [*Organic chemistry*]
TPLA	Turkish People's Liberation Army (PD)
TPLAB	Tape Label [*Information*] [*Computer science*]
TPLAF	Thai People's Liberation Armed Forces [*Thailand*]
TPLC	Test Program Logic Computer (DWSG)
TPLD	Test Planning Liaison Drawing (AAG)
TPLF	Tigre People's Liberation Front [*Ethiopia*] [*Political party*] (PD)
T-PLL	T-Cell Prolymphocytic Leukemia [*Oncology*]
TPLP	Tobacco Products Liability Project (EA)
TPLP	Turkish People's Liberation Party [*Political party*] (PD)
TPLP/F	Turkish People's Liberation Party/Front
TPLS	Technology in Public Libraries Section [*Public Library Association*]
TPLS	Terminal Position Location System
TPLS	Texas Panhandle Library System [*Library network*]
TPLS	Tunable Pulsed LASER System
TPLSM	Two Photon Laser Scanning Microscope
TPLSM	Two-Photon Laser Scanning Microscopy
T/PLT	Tapping Plate [*Automotive engineering*]
TPLW	Triple Wall
TPM	Tanks Plus or Minus (EFIS)
TPM	Tape Preventive Maintenance
TPM	Tape Processing Machine
TPM	Technical Performance Management
TPM	Technical Performance Measurement (AAGC)
TPM	Technical Performance Measurement System [*NASA*]
TPM	Technical Performance Module (MCD)
TPM	Technical Project Manager (BCP)
TPM	Telemetry Processor Module

TPM	Teleprocessing Monitor
TPM	Temporary Pacemaker [*Cardiology*] (MEDA)
TPM	Tepoztlan [*Mexico*] [*Seismograph station code, US Geological Survey*] (SEIS)
TPM	Terminal Phase Maneuver [*Aerospace*] (MCD)
TPM	Terminal Phase Midcourse [*Aerospace*] (MCD)
TPM	Test Performance Management [*Army*]
TPM	Test Planning Manager [*NASA*] (KSC)
TPM	Theoretical Platers per Meter [*Chromatography*]
TPM	Thermal Power Monitor [*Nuclear energy*] (NRCH)
TPM	Thermal Protection Material
TPM	Third-Party Maintenance (BTTJ)
TPM	Thrombophlebitis Migrans (DB)
TPM	Timber Products Manufacturers (EA)
TPM	Title Page Mutilated
TPM	Tons per Minute
TPM	Tons per Month
TPM	Torpedo Prize Money [*British military*] (DMA)
TPM	Total Active Preventive Maintenance Time (MCD)
TPM	Total Downtime for Preventive Scheduled Maintenance [*Quality control*] (MCD)
TPM	Total Particulate Matter [*The "tar" of cigar and cigarette smoke*]
TPM	Total Passivation Module (CIST)
TPM	Total Passive Motion
TPM	Total Polar Material [*Analytical chemistry*]
TPM	Total Population Management [*Department of Agriculture*]
TPM	Total Preventative Maintenance [*Manufacturing*]
TPM	Total Productive Maintenance [*Japanese industrialization theory*]
TPM	Tours par Minute [*Revolutions per Minute*] [*French*]
TPM	TP Monitor [*Computer science*]
TPM	Transfer Phase Midcourse [*Aerospace*] (MCD)
TPM	Transfiguration Prison Ministries (EA)
TPM	Transmission and Processing Model
TPM	Trigger Pricing Mechanism
TPM	Triphenylmethane [*Class of organic dyes*] [*Organic chemistry*]
TPM	Triplate Module
TPM	Trophopathia Pedis Myelodysplastica (DB)
TPM	Tubular Products Manual [*A publication*] (EAAP)
TPM1	Terminal Phase Midcourse Number 1 [*NASA*] (NAKS)
TPM2	Terminal Phase Midcourse Number 2 [*NASA*] (NAKS)
TPMA	Thermodynamic Properties of Metals and Alloys (KSC)
TPMA	Timber Products Manufacturers Association [*Later, TPM*]
TP-MAU	Twisted-Pair Medium Attachment Unit (PCM)
TPMF	Tax Practitioner Master File [*IRS*]
TPMG	[*The*] Provost Marshal General [*Army*]
TPMI	Personnel Management [*NASDAQ symbol*] (TTSB)
TPMI	Personnel Management, Inc. [*NASDAQ symbol*] (SAG)
TP-MIC	Twisted-Pair Media Interface Connector (DDC)
TPMM	Teleprocessing Multiplexer Module
TPMM	Triphenylmethyl Methacrylate [*Organic chemistry*]
TP-MO	Technical Publications - Maintenance Operation [*Naval Facilities Engineering Command Publications*]
TP monitor	Teleprocessing Monitor [*Computer science*] (IGQR)
TP monitor	Transaction Processing Monitor [*Computer science*] (IGQR)
TPMP	Tendor Production Management Program
TPMP	Texas Pacific-Missouri Pacific Terminal [*Railroad of New Orleans*] [*AAR code*]
TPMR	Transfer of Program Management Responsibility
TPMR	Trunked Private Mobile Radio
TPMS	Transaction Processing Management System (NITA)
TPMV	Tomato (Peru) Mosaic Virus
TPN	Pan American University, Library, Edinburg, TX [*OCLC symbol*] (OCLC)
TPN	Sandoz Pharmaceuticals [*Research code symbol*]
TPN	Tapini [*Papua New Guinea*] [*Seismograph station code, US Geological Survey Closed*] (SEIS)
TPN	Tetrachlorophthalodinitrile [*Organic chemistry*]
TPN	Thalamic Projection Neurons [*Neurology*]
TPN	Total Parenteral Nutrition
TPN	Total Petroleum (North America) Ltd. [*AMEX symbol Toronto Stock Exchange symbol*] (SPSG)
TPN	Total Petrol'm NA [*AMEX symbol*] (TTSB)
TPN	Triphosphopyridine Nucleotide [*See NADP*] [*Biochemistry*]
TPN	Two-Position Nozzle (MCD)
TPND	Theft, Pilferage, and Nondelivery [*Insurance*]
TPNEG	Travel Will Be Performed at No Expense to the Government [*Military*]
TPNG	Territory of Papua and New Guinea
TPNG	Topping (AAG)
TPNH	Triphosphopyridine Nucleotide (Reduced) [*See NADPH*] [*Biochemistry*]
TPNL	Townsend Plan National Lobby (EA)
T/PNL	Trim Panel [*Automotive engineering*]
TPNS	Teleprocessing Network Simulator
TPNZ	Tappan Zee Fin'l [*NASDAQ symbol*] (TTSB)
TPNZ	Tappen Zee Financial, Inc. [*NASDAQ symbol*] (SAG)
TPO	Sandoz Pharmaceuticals [*Research code symbol*]
TPO	Tanalian Point, AK [*Location identifier FAA*] (FAAL)
TPO	Tank Pressurizing Orifice (KSC)
TPO	Technical Planning Office
TPO	Technical Programs Office (COE)
TPO	Technical Project Officer
TPO	Technology Planning Objectives (MCD)
TPO	Telecommunications Program Objective [*Army*] (AABC)
TPO	Temperature-Programmed Oxidation [*For surface analysis*]
Tpo	Tempo [*Record label*] [*Germany*]

TPO	Temporary Printing Officer (DGA)
TPO	Tentative Program Objectives [*Navy*]
TPO	Test of Perceptual Organization [*Neuropsychology test*]
TPO	Test Program Outline [*Military*]
TPO	Thermoplastic Olefinic [*Elastomer*]
TPO	Thermoplastic Polyolefin [*Materials science*]
TPO	Threshold Planning Quantity (ERG)
TPO	Thrombopoietin [*Hematology*]
TPO	Thyroid Peroxidase [*An enzyme*]
TPO	Track Production Officer [*NATO Air Defense Ground Environment*] (NATG)
TPO	Trade Promotion Organisation
TPO	Transmitter Power Output (NTCM)
TPO	Transportation Packaging Order (AFM)
TPO	Traveling Post Office
TPO	Tree Preservation Order [*Town planning*] [*British*]
TPO	Tryptophan Oxygenase [*Also, TO, TP*] [*An enzyme*]
TPO	Tryptophan Peroxidase [*An enzyme*] (AAMN)
TPO	Tuned Plate Oscillator
TPOA	Travel Ports Amer [*NASDAQ symbol*] (TTSB)
TPOA	Travel Ports of America, Inc. [*NASDAQ symbol*] (SAG)
TPOCP	Turbopump Oxidizer Cavity Purge (SAA)
TPOD	Test Plan of the Day
TPOH	[*The*] Pursuit of Happiness [*Rock music group*]
TPOM	Tentative Program Objectives Memorandum [*Military*] (CAAL)
TPOM	Tube Propagation d'Ondes Magnetron
T-POP	TOGA [*Tropical Ocean and Global Atmosphere*] Program on Prediction [*Marine science*] (OSRA)
TPOR	Thrombopoietin Receptor [*Hematology*]
TPorH	Highland Hospital, Portland, TN [*Library symbol Library of Congress*] (LCLS)
TPORT	Transport
T-POS	Target Position
TPOS	Track Position
TPP	Tarapoto [*Peru*] [*Airport symbol*] (OAG)
TPP	Teacher Participation Project (EDAC)
TPP	Technical Performance Parameter (MCD)
TPP	Technology Program Plan [*Military*] (AFIT)
TPP	Telephony Preprocessor [*Telecommunications*] (TEL)
TPP	Teletype Page Printer
TPP	Teppco Partners Ltd. [*NYSE symbol*] (SPSG)
TPP	Teppco Ptnrs L.P. [*NYSE symbol*] (TTSB)
TPP	Tertiary-Pentylphenol [*Organic chemistry*]
TPP	Test Point Pace (KSC)
TPP	Test Point Prelaunch Automatic Checkout Equipment [*NASA*] (IAA)
TPP	Test Program Plan (MCD)
TPP	Tetraphenylporphine [*Organic chemistry*]
TPP	Tetraphenylporphyrin [*Biochemistry*]
TPP	Textured Peanut Protein [*Food industry*]
TPP	Thermally Protected Plastic
TPP	Thermal Power Plant (CINC)
TPP	Thermal Protection Panel
TPP	Thiamine Pyrophosphate [*Also, DPT, TDP*] [*Biochemistry*]
TPP	Thomson Professional Publishing [*The Thomson Corp.*]
TPP	Toledo Progressive Party [*Belize*] [*Political party*] (PPW)
TPP	Tool and Production Planning (SAA)
TPP	Total Package Procurement [*Government contracting*]
TPP	Total Program Planning/Procurement
TPP	Trained Profile Panel [*Sensory testing*]
TPP	Training Program and Planning
TPP	Transducer Power Programmer
TPP	Transients, Patients, and Prisoners [*Military*]
TPP	Trans-Pluto Probe
TPP	Transport Policies and Programme [*British*] (DCTA)
TPP	Transuranium Processing Plant
TPP	Trinidad [*Pointe-A-Pierre*] [*Trinidad-Tobago*] [*Seismograph station code, US Geological Survey*] (SEIS)
TPP	Triphenylphosphine [*Organic chemistry*]
TPP	Triphenyl Phosphite [*Organic chemistry*]
TPP	Tripolyphosphate [*Food industry*]
TPP	Tri-Power Petroleum Corp. [*Toronto Stock Exchange symbol*]
TPP	True Path Party [*Turkey Political party*]
TPP	Two-Phase Principle
TPPC	Total Package Procurement Concept [*Government contracting*]
TPPC	Transaction Processing Performance Council (BTTJ)
TPPC	Trans-Pacific Passenger Conference [*Later, PCC*] (EA)
TPPCR	Tool and Production Planning Change Record (SAA)
TPPD	Technical Program Planning Division [*Air Force*] (MCD)
TPPD	Technical Program Planning Document [*Air Force*] (IAA)
TPPE	Thermoplastic Polyester [*Materials science*]
TPPE	Two-Photon Photoemission Spectroscopy
TPPEP	Turkey Point Performance Enforcement Program [*Nuclear energy*] (NRCH)
TPPG	Training Program and Planning Guidance
TPPGM	Tentative Planning and Programming Guidance Memorandum [*Navy*] (NVT)
TPPI	Trans-Pacific Petrochemical Indotama
TPPIS	Treasury Payroll/Personnel Information System
TP-PL	Technical Publications - Planning [*Naval Facilities Engineering Command Publications*]
TP-PMD	Twisted Pair-Physical Medium Dependent [*Telecommunications*] (CDE)
TPPN	Total Peripheral Parenteral Nutrition
TPPN	Trans-Pacific Profiler Network [*Marine science*] (OSRA)
TPPP	Third Party Prescription Program

TPPP............ Triple P [*NASDAQ symbol*] (SAG)
TPPPF.......... Triple P N.V. [*NASDAQ symbol*] (TTSB)
TPPR............ Tape-to-Printer [*Computer science*] (IAA)
TPPS............ Tape Post-Processing System
TPPS............ Tetraphenylporphinesulfonate [*Reagent*]
TPPTS.......... Triphenylphosphine Trisulphonate [*Organic chemistry*]
TP-PU .... Technical Publications - Public Utilities [*Naval Facilities Engineering Command Publications*]
TPQ............. AMIGOS [*Access Method for Indexed Data Generalized for Operating System*] Bibliographic Council, Dallas, TX [*OCLC symbol*] (OCLC)
TPQ............. Tepic [*Mexico*] [*Airport symbol*]
TPQ............. Threshold Planning Quantity [*Hazardous substances*]
TPQI............ Teacher-Pupil Question Inventory
TPR............. Air Transport Pyrenees [*France ICAO designator*] (FAAC)
TPR............. AMIGOS [*Access Method for Indexed Data Generalized for Operating System*] Bibliographic Council, Dallas, TX [*OCLC symbol*] (OCLC)
TPR............. Tamper-Protected Recording [*3M Co.*]
TPR............. Tape Programmed Row [*Data scanner*]
TPR............. Taper (MSA)
TPR............. Target Practice Round (SAA)
TPR............. Team Power Rating [*Hockey*]
TPR............. Technical Program Review
TPR............. Technical Progress Report
TPR............. Technical Proposal Requirement (MCD)
TPR............. Teleprinter (AAG)
TPR............. Telescopic Photographic Recorder
TPR............. Teletypewriter [*International telex abbreviation*] (WDMC)
TPR............. Temperature (DAVI)
TPR............. Temperature Profile Recorder (AAG)
TPR............. Temperature-Programmed Reaction [*Chemistry*]
TPR............. Temperature-Programmed Reduction [*For analysis of surfaces*]
TPR............. Temperature, Pulse, Respiration [*Medicine*]
TPR............. Temporary Price Reduction
TPR............. Termination of Parental Rights (PAZ)
TPR............. Terrain Profile Recorder
TPR............. Testosterone Production Rate [*Endocrinology*] (MAE)
TPR............. Test Performance Recorder
TPR............. Test Phase Report
TPR............. Test Problem Report [*NASA*] (NASA)
TPR............. Test Procedure Record (NATG)
TPR............. Test Program Report
TPR............. Tetratricopeptide Repeat [*Genetics*]
TPR............. Thermoplastic Recording
TPR............. Thermoplastic Rubber
TPR............. Third Party Reimbursement (HCT)
TPR............. Threepenny Review [*A publication*] (BRI)
TPR............. Tom Price [*Australia Airport symbol*]
TPR............. Tool Performance Report [*Navy*] (DNAB)
TPR............. Total Peripheral Resistance
TPR............. Total Pulmonary Resistance [*Cardiology*]
TPR............. T-Pulse Response [*Telecommunications*] (IAA)
TPR............. Trade Practices Reports [*Australia A publication*]
TPR............. Trained Personnel Requirements [*Air Force*]
TPR............. Transmitter Power Rating
TPR............. Transpro, Inc. [*NYSE symbol*] (SAG)
TPR............. Trapped Pressure Ratio [*Gas analysis*]
TPr............. Trooper
Tpr............. Trooper [*Military*] (WDAA)
TPR............. True Positive Rate [*Medicine*] (DMAA)
TPRA .... Tape-to-Random Access [*Computer science*] (IAA)
TPRA .... Target Practice Round, Aerobee (SAA)
TPRAM .... Triple-Port Random Access Memory [*Computer science*]
TPRC .... Thermophysical Properties Research Center [*DoD*]
TPRC .... Trade Policy Research Centre [*British*] (ECON)
TPRC .... Transition Program for Refugee Children [*Department of Education*] (GFGA)
TPRD .... Technology Planning and Research Division [*Central Electricity Generating Board*] [*British*] (IRUK)
TPRG .... Technology Performance Requirements Guideline
TPRI............ Teacher-Pupil Relationship Inventory
TPRI............ Time Problems Inventory [*Test*]
TPRI............ Total Peripheral Resistance Index
TPRI............ Training Priority Requirements Index
TPRL .... Thermophysical Properties Research Laboratory [*Purdue University*] [*Research center*] (RCD)
TPRO .... Topro, Inc. [*NASDAQ symbol*] (SAG)
TPROC .... Test Procedure Specification [*NASA*] (IAA)
TPROW .... Topro Inc. Wrrt [*NASDAQ symbol*] (TTSB)
TPRR .... Test Procedures and Results Report
TPRS .... Temperature-Programmed Reaction Spectroscopy
TPRS .... Temperature-Programmed Reaction System
TPRU .... Technical Processing and Reporting Unit (CAAL)
TPRU .... Tropical Pesticides Research Unit [*Later, Centre for Overseas Pest Research*] [*British*]
TPRV .... Transient Peak Reverse Voltage
TPS............. Bibliographic Center for Research, Denver, CO [*OCLC symbol*] (OCLC)
TPS............. [*The*] Planetary Society
TPS............. Tactical Paint Scheme (MCD)
TPS............. Tactical Probe System (SAA)
TPS............. Tandem Propeller Submarine
TPS............. Tangent Plane System (MUGU)
TPS............. Tank Pressure Sensing (AAG)

TPS............. Tape Plotting System
TPS............. Tape Processing System (CMD)
TPS............. Tape Programming System (NITA)
TPS............. Tape Punch Subassembly
TPS............. Task Parameter Synthesizer
TPS............. Technical Publishing Society [*Later, STC*]
TPS............. Technical Publishing Software [*Interleaf, Inc.*]
TPS............. Technology Policy Statement [*1982*] [*India*]
TPS............. Technopolymer Structure [*Engineering plastics*]
TPS............. Telecommunications Programming System
TPS............. Telemation Program Services
TPS............. Telemetry Processing System [*Space Flight Operations Facility, NASA*]
TPS............. Teleprocessing System [*Computer science*] (IAA)
TPS............. Television Program Standard
TPS............. Terminal Performance Specification
TPS............. Terminal Polling System
TPS............. Terminal Programming System [*Computer science*] (ECII)
TPS............. Terminals per Station [*Telecommunications*]
TPS............. Test Package Set (DOMA)
TPS............. Test Pilot School [*Navy*]
TPS............. Test Plotting System
TPS............. Test Point Selector
TPS............. Test Preparation Sheet [*NASA*] (AAG)
TPS............. Test Procedure Specification [*NASA*] (KSC)
TPS............. Test Program Set [*Aviation*] (MCD)
TPS............. Theater Production Service (AEBS)
TPS............. Thermally Processed Silver (NITA)
TPS............. Thermal Protection System [*or Subsystem*]
TPS............. Thermoplastic Storage
TPS............. Thomas Paine Society [*Nottingham, England*] (EAIO)
TPS............. Threat Platform Simulator [*Military*] (CAAL)
TPS............. Throttle Position Sensor [*Automotive engineering*]
TPS............. Thyristor Power Supply [*Electronics*] (IAA)
TPS............. Tiered Premium System [*Insurance*] (WYGK)
TPS............. Top Source, Inc. [*AMEX symbol*] (SPSG)
TPS............. Top Source Technol [*AMEX symbol*] (TTSB)
TPS............. Total Parameter Space [*Statistics*]
TPS............. Total Product Support
TPS............. Toughened Polystyrene (EDCT)
TPS............. Tough Plastic-Sheathed
TPS............. Toyota Production System [*Innovative lean-production manufacturing*] (ECON)
TPS............. Tracking Antenna Pedestal System (IAA)
TPS............. Track Processing Special (SAA)
TPS............. Tracks per Second (WGA)
TPS............. Trade Promotion Services Group [*British*]
TPS............. Trail Pilot Sensor
TPS............. Training Package System Planning (IAA)
TPS............. Tramp Power Supply
TPS............. Transaction Processing System [*Trademark of Software Consulting Service, Inc.*]
TPS............. Transactions per Second
TPS............. Transduodenal Pancreatic Sphincteroplasty
TPS............. Translunar Propulsion Stage [*Aerospace*] (AAG)
TPS............. Trans-Pacific Sections [*Marine science*] (OSRA)
TPS............. Transportation Protective Service [*MTMC*] (TAG)
TPS............. Trans Rampart Industry [*Vancouver Stock Exchange symbol*]
TPS............. Trapani [*Italy*] [*Airport symbol*] (OAG)
TPS............. Tree Pruning System
TPS............. Trigger-Price System [*Department of the Treasury*]
TPS............. Triphenylsulfonium Chloride [*Organic chemistry*]
TPS............. Troops [*Military British*]
TPS............. Trypsin (MAE)
TPS............. Tube Pin Straightener
TPS............. Tumor Polysaccharidal Substance [*Oncology*]
TPS............. Turkey Point Station [*Nuclear energy*] (NRCH)
TPS............. Turner Program Services [*Broadcasting*]
TPS............. Tuvalu Philatelic Society (EA)
TPS............. Twisted-Pair Shielded
TPSB............ Telemetry Processing System Buffer [*Space Flight Operations Facility, NASA*]
TPSC............ Test Planning and Status Checker [*Computer science*]
TPSC............ Trade Policy Staff Committee [*Federal interagency group*]
TPSE............ Thermal Protection Subsystem Evaluation (NASA)
TPSE............ Transaction Processing Service Element [*Telecommunications*]
TPSE............ (Tritylphenyl)sulfonylethanol [*Organic chemistry*]
TPSF............ Telephonie sans Fil [*Wireless Telephony*]
TPSF............ Terminal Profile Security File [*IRS*]
TPSFG .... Two-Post Signal Flow Graph (PDAA)
TPSI............ Texas Preschool Screening Inventory (EDAC)
TPSI............ Torque Pressure in Pounds per Square Inch
TPSIS .... Transportation Planning Support Information System [*TRB*] (TAG)
TPSL............ Tyoevaeen ja Pienviljelijaein Sosialidemokraattinen Liitto [*Social Democratic League of Workers and Smallholders*] [*Finland Political party*] (PPE)
TPSMP........ Test Program Set Management Plan
TPSN............ Transposition (AAG)
TPSN............ Troop Program Sequence Number [*Military*]
TPSO............ Triphenylstibine Oxide [*Organic chemistry*]
TPSP............ Tape Punch Subassembly Panel
TPSRS .... Terminal Primary and Secondary RADAR System (DA)
TPSS .... Thermal Protection System Selection
TPSS .... Trespass [*Legal shorthand*] (LWAP)
TPST .... Training and Personnel Systems Technology (MCD)

TPST............	Triple-Pole, Single-Throw [Switch]
TPST............	True Positive Stress Test [Medicine] (DMAA)
TPSTe..........	Triisopropylbenzenesulfonyl Tetrazolide [Organic chemistry]
TPSTHCP&TEIU...	Textile Processors, Service Trades, Health Care, Professional and Technical Employees International Union (NTPA)
TPSU............	Transaction Processing Service User [Telecommunications]
TPSY............	Task Parameter Synthesizer (SAA)
TPT..............	Bibliographic Center for Research, Denver, CO [OCLC symbol] (OCLC)
TPT..............	Tactical Petroleum Terminal
TPT..............	Tail Pipe Temperature (NG)
TPT..............	Tappet [Mechanical engineering]
TPT..............	Tappit Resources [Vancouver Stock Exchange symbol]
TPT..............	Target Practice [Ammunition] with Tracer
TPT..............	Tasmanian Peace Trust [Australia]
TPT..............	Telecommunication Products Plus Technology [Pennwell Publishing Co.] [Littleton, MA] (TSSD)
TPT..............	Teleprinter Planning Table
TPT..............	Temporary Part Time [Personnel] (MCD)
TPT..............	Test Pilot Training
TPT..............	Test Program Tape (MCD)
TPT..............	Tetraisopropyl Titanate [Organic chemistry]
TPT..............	Tetraphenyl Tetrazolium [Histochemical stain] (AAMN)
TPT..............	Third-Party Transaction [Business term]
TPT..............	Time Period Tape [Database] [Arbitron Ratings Co.] [Information service or system] (CRD)
TPT..............	Time Priority Table
TPT..............	Time to Peak Tension
TPT..............	Tiputa [Tuamotu Archipelago] [Seismograph station code, US Geological Survey] (SEIS)
TPT..............	Total Pressure Transducer
TPT..............	Total Prime Time (WDMC)
TPT..............	Total Protein Tuberculin [Medicine] (MAE)
TPT..............	Totul pentru Tara ["All for the Fatherland"] [Romania] [Political party] (PPE)
TPT..............	Toy Preference Test [Psychology] (AEBS)
TPT..............	Training Proficiency Test [Army] (INF)
TPT..............	Transonic Pressure Tunnel [NASA]
TPT..............	Transport
TPT..............	Trenton-Princeton Traction Co. [Absorbed into Consolidated Rail Corp.] [AAR code]
TPT..............	Triphenyltetrazolium Chloride (EDCT)
TPT..............	Troop Proficiency Trainer
TPT..............	Trumpet
tpt...............	Trumpet (WDAA)
TPT..............	Typhoid-Paratyphoid [Medicine]
TPTA............	Thiophosphoryl Triamide [Fertilizer technology]
TPTA............	Tin Triphenyl [or Triphenyltin] Acetate [Organic chemistry]
TPTB............	[The] Powers That Be [E-Mail discussion]
TPTC............	Teleprocessing Test Center (MHDI)
TPTC............	Temperature Pressure Test Chamber (IAA)
TPTC............	Triphenyltin Chloride [Organic chemistry]
TPTD............	Test Pilot Training Division
TPTD............	Transported
TPTE............	(Tritylphenyl)thioethanol [Organic chemistry]
TPTF............	Tributyl Phosphate Task Force (EA)
TPTG............	Terminal Program Testing Guide
TPTG............	Tuned Plate Tuned Grid [Electronic tube]
TPTH............	Triphenyltin Hydroxide [Organic chemistry]
TPTHS..........	Total Parathyroid Hormone Secretion [Endocrinology] (MAE)
TPTMS.........	Tropical Pacific Thermal Monitoring System [Marine science] (OSRA)
TPTN............	Toilet Partition [Technical drawings]
TPTOL..........	True Position Tolerance (MSA)
TPTP............	Tape-to-Tape [Computer science] (IAA)
TPTR............	Transporter
TPTR............	Trumpeter
TPTRL..........	Time-Phased Transportation Requirements List [Military] (AABC)
TPTS............	Two-Phase Thermosyphon [Heat exchanger]
TPTX............	Thyroid-Parathyroidectomy [Endocrinology] (DAVI)
TPTX............	Thyroparathyroidectomized [Medicine]
TPTZ............	Triphenyltetrazolium Chloride [Also, RT, TTC] [Chemical indicator]
TPTZ............	Tris(pyridyl)-s-triazine [Analytical chemistry]
TPU..............	Capitol Consortium Network, Washington, DC [OCLC symbol] (OCLC)
TPU..............	Tactical Patrol Unit [Military] (LAIN)
TPU..............	Tank and Pump Unit [Mechanized infantry battalion] (INF)
TPU..............	Tank Petroleum Unit [Army] (INF)
TPU..............	Tape Preparation Unit
TPU..............	Taputuquara [Brazil] [Airport symbol] (AD)
TPU..............	Tarn Pure Technology Corp. [Vancouver Stock Exchange symbol]
TPU..............	Task Processing Unit
TPU..............	Tax Payers United [Australia]
TPU..............	Telecommunications Processing Unit
TPU..............	Terminal Processing Unit [Computer science] (IAA)
TPU..............	Text Processing Utility [Computer science]
TPU..............	Thermal Processing Unit [AAEL]
TPU..............	Thermoplastic Urethane [or Polyurethane] [Plastics technology]
TPU..............	Threatened Plants Unit [EERA]
TPU..............	Time Processing Unit [Automotive engineering Electronics]
TPU..............	Transient Personnel Unit [Navy] (DNAB)
TPU..............	Transverse Propulsion Unit (PDAA)
TPU..............	Troop Program Unit [Army] (AABC)
TPU..............	Trunk Processing Unit [Bell System]
TPU..............	Turbo Pascal Unit [Borland International] [Computer science] (PCM)
TPUHC............	Turbopower Unit

TPUC............	Telephone Pickup Coil
TPUG............	Toronto PET Users Group [Canada]
TPuGH.........	Giles County Hospital, Pulaski, TN [Library symbol] [Library of Congress] (LCLS)
TP/UMF.......	Total Package/Unit Materiel Fielding [Army] (RDA)
TPUN............	Test Procedure Update Notice (NASA)
TPUR............	Transperineal Urethral Resection [Medicine] (DAVI)
TPUS............	Transportation and Public Utilities Service [Later, part of Transportation and Communication Service, GSA]
TPV..............	Capitol Consortium Network, Washington, DC [OCLC symbol] (OCLC)
TPV..............	Tetanus/Pertussis Vaccine [Medicine] (DB)
TPV..............	Thermophotovoltaic
TPV..............	Thermoplastic Vulcanizate [Plastics technology]
TPV..............	Time to Peak Flow Velocity [Cardiology]
TPV..............	Tonopah [Nevada] [Seismograph station code, US Geological Survey Closed] (SEIS)
TPV..............	Total Pore Volume [Geology]
TPV..............	Transverse Pallial Vein
TPV..............	Triple Polio Vaccine [Medicine]
TPVE............	Two Phase Vacuum Extraction [Engineering]
TPVM............	Teleprocessing Virtual Machine (MHDI)
TPVR............	Total Pulmonary Vascular Resistance (AAMN)
TPW..............	Target Planning Worksheet (DOMA)
TPW..............	Tenth-Power Width
TPW..............	Title Page Wanting
TPW..............	Toledo, Peoria & Western Railroad Co. [AAR code]
TPW..............	Tons per Week
TPW..............	True Polar Wandering [Geophysics]
TPW..............	Turbo Pascal for Windows [Computer science]
TPWAC.........	Territory Parks and Wildlife Advisory Council [Northern Territory, Australia]
TPWBH........	Tax Paid Wine Bottling House
TPWD...........	Texas Department of Parks & Wildlife Department
TPWG...........	Test Planning Working Group [Military]
TPWIC..........	Theater Prisoner of War Information Center
TPWU...........	Tanganyika Plantation Workers Union
TPWU...........	Tea Plantation Workers' Union [Kenya]
TPX..............	Total Pancreatectomy [Medicine]
TPX..............	Transponder (KSC)
TPX..............	Transportes Aereos de Xalapa, SA de CV [Mexico] [FAA designator] (FAAC)
tpx...............	Triplex [Paper] (DGA)
TPY..............	FEDLINK [Federal Library and Information Network], Washington, DC [OCLC symbol] (OCLC)
TPY..............	Tapestry (ADA)
TPY..............	Tipperary Corp. [AMEX symbol] (SAG)
TPY..............	Tocantinopolis [Brazil] [Airport symbol] (AD)
TPY..............	Tons per Year
TPY..............	Trans-Provincial Airlines Ltd. [Canada ICAO designator] (FAAC)
tpyt..............	Triptych (VRA)
TPZ..............	FEDLINK [Federal Library and Information Network], Washington, DC [OCLC symbol] (OCLC)
TPZ..............	Thioperazine [or Thioproperazine] [Tranquilizer]
TPZ..............	Transportes La Paz SA de CV [Mexico ICAO designator] (FAAC)
TQ.................	Las Vegas Airlines [ICAO designator] (AD)
TQ.................	[The] Questers (EA)
TQ.................	Tale Quale [Of Conditions on Arrival] [Latin]
TQ.................	Thought Quality [Psychology]
TQ.................	Three-Quarter Midget [Horse racing]
TQ.................	Three-Quarter Size [Car racing]
TQ.................	Tocopherolquinone [Vitamin E] [Biochemistry]
TQ.................	Torquay [Postcode] (ODBW)
TQ.................	Total Quality
Tq.................	Tourniquet [Medicine] (MAE)
TQ.................	Track Quality
TQ.................	Transition Quarter [Between fiscal years 1976 and 1977]
TQ.................	Turf Quality (OA)
TQ.................	Tyrolean Airways [Austria ICAO designator] (ICDA)
TQ2...............	Thirst Quencher
TQ-3.............	Tocotrienolquinone [Biochemistry]
TQA..............	Abilene, TX [Location identifier FAA] (FAAL)
TQA..............	ILLINET [Illinois Library Information Network], Springfield, IL [OCLC symbol] (OCLC)
TQA..............	Total Quality Assurance (OA)
TQB..............	ILLINET [Illinois Library Information Network], Springfield, IL [OCLC symbol] (OCLC)
TQC..............	Indiana Cooperative Library Services Authority, Indianapolis, IN [OCLC symbol] (OCLC)
TQC..............	Technical Quality Control [Telecommunications] (TEL)
TQC..............	Time, Quality, Cost
TQC..............	Tobacco Quota Committee [Australia]
TQC..............	Total Quality Control
TQCA............	Textile Quality Control Association (EA)
TQCM............	Thermoelectric Quartz Crystal Microbalance
TQD..............	Indiana Cooperative Library Services Authority, Indianapolis, IN [OCLC symbol] (OCLC)
TQD..............	Ter Quaterve in Die [Three or Four Times a Day] [Pharmacy]
TQD..............	Total Quality Design (RDA)
TQE..............	Michigan Library Consortium, Detroit, MI [OCLC symbol] (OCLC)
TQE..............	Technical Quality Evaluation [Polaris]
TQE..............	Tekamah, NE [Location identifier FAA] (FAAL)
TQE..............	Timer Queue Element
TQF..............	Michigan Library Consortium, Detroit, MI [OCLC symbol] (OCLC)
TQF..............	[The] Queen's Flight [British ICAO designator] (FAAC)

TQF	Threshold Quality Factor
TQG	MIDLNET [*Midwest Regional Library Network*], St. Louis, MO [*OCLC symbol*] (OCLC)
TQG	Tactical Quiet Generator (RDA)
TQH	MIDLNET [*Midwest Regional Library Network*], St. Louis, MO [*OCLC symbol*] (OCLC)
TQH	Tahlequah, OK [*Location identifier FAA*] (FAAL)
TQI	MINITEX [*Minnesota Interlibrary Teletype Exchange*], Minneapolis, MN [*OCLC symbol*] (OCLC)
TQI	Training Quality Index [*Military*] (CAAL)
TQJ	MINITEX [*Minnesota Interlibrary Teletype Exchange*], Minneapolis, MN [*OCLC symbol*] (OCLC)
TQK	NELINET [*New England Library Information Network*], Newton, MA [*OCLC symbol*] (OCLC)
TQL	NELINET [*New England Library Information Network*], Newton, MA [*OCLC symbol*] (OCLC)
TQL	Total Quality Leadership
TQLR	Tune-In, Question, Listen, Review Technique [*Education*] (EDAC)
TQM	OCLC [*Online Computer Library Center*] Western Services Center, Claremont, CA [*OCLC symbol*] (OCLC)
TQM	Total Quality Management
TQM	Transport Quartermaster
TQMG	[*The*] Quartermaster General [*Army*]
TQMRI	Total Quality Management Readiness Index [*Test*] (TMMY)
TQMS	Technical Quartermaster Sergeant
TQMS	Total Quality Management System (MCD)
TQMS	Triple Quadrupole Mass Spectrometer
TQMS	Troop Quartermaster-Sergeant [*British military*] (DMA)
TQN	OCLC [*Online Computer Library Center*] Western Services Center, Claremont, CA [*OCLC symbol*] (OCLC)
TQNT	TriQuint Semiconductor [*NASDAQ symbol*] (TTSB)
TQNT	Triquint Semiconductor, Inc. [*NASDAQ symbol*] (SAG)
TQO	OHIONET, Columbus, OH [*OCLC symbol*] (OCLC)
TQP	OHIONET, Columbus, OH [*OCLC symbol*] (OCLC)
TQP	Total Quality and Productivity
TQP	Transistor Qualification Program
TQPF	[*The*] Valley/Wall Blake [*Anguilla Island*] [*ICAO location identifier*] (ICLI)
TQPP	Total Quality Planning and Producibility (MCD)
TQQ	Pennsylvania Area Library Network, Philadelphia, PA [*OCLC symbol*] (OCLC)
TQQPRI	Tentative Qualitative Quantitative Personnel Requirements Information [*Army*]
TQR	Pennsylvania Area Library Network, Philadelphia, PA [*OCLC symbol*] (OCLC)
TQR	Saginaw, MI [*Location identifier FAA*] (FAAL)
TQR	Tenquille Resources Ltd. [*Vancouver Stock Exchange symbol*]
TQS	Pittsburgh Regional Library Center, Pittsburgh, PA [*OCLC symbol*] (OCLC)
TQS	Total Quality Service
TQS	Tres Esquinas [*Colombia*] [*Airport symbol*] (OAG)
TQT	Pittsburgh Regional Library Center, Pittsburgh, PA [*OCLC symbol*] (OCLC)
TQT	Transistor Qualification Test
TQTMT	TACJAM [*Tactical Communications Jamming System*] Quickfix, Trail Blazer Maintenance Trainer [*Army*]
TQTP	Transistor Qualification Test Program
TQTYREC	Total Quantity Recommended [*Army*]
TQU	Southeastern Library Network, Atlanta, GA [*OCLC symbol*] (OCLC)
TQV	Southeastern Library Network, Atlanta, GA [*OCLC symbol*] (OCLC)
TQV	St. Moritz [*Switzerland*] [*Airport symbol*] (AD)
TQW	Pittsburgh, PA [*Location identifier FAA*] (FAAL)
TQW	State University of New York, OCLC [*Online Computer Library Center*], Albany, NY [*OCLC symbol*] (OCLC)
TQX	State University of New York, OCLC [*Online Computer Library Center*], Albany, NY [*OCLC symbol*] (OCLC)
TQY	Tanquery Resources Ltd. [*Vancouver Stock Exchange symbol*]
TQY	Wisconsin Library Consortium, Madison, WI [*OCLC symbol*] (OCLC)
TQZ	Wisconsin Library Consortium, Madison, WI [*OCLC symbol*] (OCLC)
TR	Caines' Term Reports [*New York*] [*A publication*] (DLA)
TR	Compania de Aviacion Trans-Europa [*Spain ICAO designator*] (ICDA)
t$_r$	Recovery Time (IDOE)
TR	Right Triceps [*Anatomy*] (DAVI)
t$_r$	Rise Time (IDOE)
TR	Royal Air [*ICAO designator*] (AD)
TR	Stewardsman Recruit [*Navy*]
TR	Tactical RADAR [*Military*] (IAA)
TR	Tactical Reconnaissance (NATG)
TR	Talyllyn Railway [*Wales*]
TR	Tank Regiment (MCD)
TR	Tape Reader
TR	Tape Recorder
T/R	Tape Recorder (NAKS)
TR	Tape Register
TR	Tape Resident
TR	Tare (ROG)
TR	Target Recognition (AFM)
TR	Target Rifle (WDAA)
TR	Tariff Reform
TR	Task Register [*Computer science*] (BYTE)
TR	Taxa Referencial de Juros [*Brazil*] (ECON)
TR	Taxation Reports [*England*] [*A publication*] (DLA)
TR	Tax Rate
TR	Teaching and Research [*Medicine*]
TR	Teaching Resources (AEBS)

TR	Team Recorder [*Sports*]
TR	Tear [*Deltiology*]
TR	Technical Readiness
TR	Technical Regulation
TR	Technical Report
T/R	Technical Report (NAKS)
TR	Technical Reporter [*World Council of Credit Unions*] [*A publication*]
TR	Technical Report Program (NITA)
TR	Technical Representative
TR	Technical Requirement (MCD)
TR	Technical Review [*Nuclear energy*] (NRCH)
TR	Tekniska Rapporter (NITA)
TR	Telegraphe Restant [*Telegram to Be Called for at a Telegraph Office*] [*French*] (ROG)
TR	Telegraph Repeater [*Telecommunications*] (IAA)
TR	Telephone Rentals [*Commercial firm*]
TR	Tell-Rimah (BJA)
TR	Temperature Range
TR	Temperature Recorder
TR	Temperature, Rectal [*Medicine*]
TR	Temperature Rise (EDCT)
TR	Temporary Regulation (AAGC)
TR	Temporary Resident
TR	Tempore Regis [*In the Time of the King*] [*Latin*]
TR	Terbium [*Symbol is Tb*] [*Chemical element*] (ROG)
TR	Terminalischer Reiz [*Terminal Stimulus*] [*German Psychology*]
TR	Terminal Ready [*Computer science*]
TR	Terminal Rendezvous
TR	Terminal Repeat [*Genetics*]
TR	Term Reports [*Legal*] [*British*]
TR	Term Reports, English King's Bench [*Durnford and East's Reports*] [*England*] [*A publication*] (DLA)
TR	Terms of Reference
TR	Territorial Reserve [*British military*] (DMA)
TR	Testa Rossa [*Red engine cylinder head*] [*Ferrari automotive model designation*] [*Italian*]
TR	Test Regulation (MCD)
TR	Test Report
TR	Test Request
TR	Test-Retest
TR	Test Routine (AAG)
TR	Test Run
TR	Tetrazolium Reduction (MAE)
TR	Tetrode [*Electronics*] (IAA)
TR	Textus Receptus (BJA)
TR	Thalamic Radiation [*Neurology*]
TR	Theater Reserve [*Army*] (DOMA)
TR	Theatre Royal (ROG)
TR	Thematic Resource Nomination [*National Register of Historic Places*]
TR	Theodore [*Teddy*] Roosevelt [*US president, 1858-1919*]
TR	Therapeutic Radiology
TR	Thermal Resistance (IAA)
TR	Thioredoxin [*Also, TD, Trx*] [*Biochemistry*]
TR	Thioredoxin Reductase [*An enzyme*]
TR	Thio Rubber (EDCT)
TR	Threaded Rod
TR	Threat Reaction [*Military*] (CAAL)
TR	Throws Right-Handed [*Baseball*]
TR	Thrust Reverser (MCD)
TR	Thyroid Hormone Receptor [*Endocrinology*]
TR	Time Delay Relay [*Computer science*] (IAA)
TR	Timed-Release [*Pharmacy*]
T/R	Time of Rise (MSA)
TR	Time Rate [*Payment system*]
TR	Time Record (MCD)
TR	Time Release (MAE)
TR	Time Resolved [*Fluoroscopy*]
TR	Time Routine [*Computer science*] (IAA)
TR	Times Roman [*Typography*] (DGA)
TR	Time to Repetition [*Medicine*]
TR	Time to Retrofire
TR	Time-to-Retrograde [*NASA*] (KSC)
TR	Tinctura [*Tincture*] [*Pharmacy*]
TR	Tincture [*Pharmacy*] (DAVI)
TR	Tirailleur Regiments [*Military*]
TR	Tone Relevant
TR	Tons Registered [*Shipping*]
TR	Tool Resistant [*Rating for safes*]
TR	Toothed Ring [*Technical drawings*]
TR	Tootsie Roll Indus [*NYSE symbol*] (TTSB)
TR	Tootsie Roll Industries, Inc. [*NYSE symbol*] (SPSG)
TR	Topical Report [*Nuclear energy*] (NRCH)
TR	Topotactic Reaction [*Inorganic synthesis*]
TR	Top Register (OA)
TR	Toronto Stock Exchange [*Canada*]
TR	Torpedo Reconnaissance Aircraft [*Navy*]
TR	Torque Receiver (IAA)
TR	Torque Repeater (IAA)
TR	Torque Synchro Receiver (MUGU)
TR	Total Reaction (DA)
TR	Total Regulation
TR	Total Resistance (MAE)
TR	Total Response [*Medicine*] (MAE)
TR	Total Revenue
TR	Touchdowns Running [*Football*]

TR..............	Touche Remnant [*Investment firm*] [*British*]
TR..............	Towel Rack (MSA)
TR..............	Tower
TR..............	Trace
TR..............	Tracer
tr...............	Traces (VRA)
TR..............	Track
TR..............	Tracking RADAR
TR..............	Tract
tr...............	Traction [*Orthopedics*] (DAVI)
TR..............	Trade
TR..............	Trade Representative (MHDW)
TR..............	Traffic Route [*Telecommunications*] (TEL)
TR..............	Tragedy
TR..............	Trail [*Commonly used*] (OPSA)
Tr...............	Trail (AL)
TR..............	Trailer (AAG)
TR..............	Train (ADA)
TR..............	Trainee (WDAA)
TR..............	Trainer (AAG)
TR..............	Training (ROG)
TR..............	Training Regulations [*Military*]
TR..............	Training Requirements
TR..............	Tramway (ROG)
TR..............	Transaction
TR..............	Transaction Record
TR..............	Transbrasil [*ICAO designator*] (AD)
T/R.............	Transceiver
TR..............	Transcontinental Resources [*Vancouver Stock Exchange symbol*]
Tr...............	Transcript (DLA)
TR..............	Transducers [*JETDS nomenclature*] [*Military*] (CET)
TR..............	Transfer (DEN)
TR..............	Transferable Rouble [*International Bank for Economic Co-Operation*] (EY)
TR..............	Transfer Register
TR..............	Transfer Reset
TR..............	Transformation Ratio
TR..............	Transformer (DEN)
T-R.............	Transformer-Rectifier
T/R.............	Transformer Rectifier (NAKS)
TR..............	Transfusion Reaction [*Medicine*]
TR..............	Transfusion Receptors [*Oncology*]
TR..............	Transient Response (IEEE)
TR..............	Transilluminator [*Chromatography*]
TR..............	Transistor [*Electronics*] (EECA)
TR..............	Transitive
TR..............	Translate [*or Translation, or Translator*]
TR..............	Translation (IAA)
TR..............	Translation Register
tr...............	Translator
TR..............	Transmission Report [*Telecommunications*] (TEL)
T/R.............	Transmit and Receive (WDMC)
TR..............	Transmit-Receive (IDOE)
TR..............	Transmitter
TR..............	Transmitter Receiver (IAA)
T/R.............	Transmitter/Receiver (NAKS)
TR..............	Transom (MSA)
TR..............	Transponder RADAR (IAA)
TR..............	Transport
TR..............	Transportability Report [*Army*]
TR..............	Transportation [*or Travel*] Request [*Military*]
T/R.............	Transportation Request (NAKS)
TR..............	Transpose
tr...............	Transpose [*Proofreading*] (WDMC)
TR..............	Transverse (DEN)
TR..............	Travel and Relocation
T/R.............	Travel Request
TR..............	Travel Required [*Civil Service*]
TR..............	Trawler
TR..............	Tray (WGA)
TR..............	Tread (WGA)
TR..............	Treasurer
TR..............	Treasury Receipt
TR..............	Treatise (ROG)
TR..............	Treatment [*Medicine*] (AAMN)
TR..............	Treaty (ROG)
TR..............	Treble [*Knitting*]
TR..............	Treble [*Music*]
Tr...............	Treble (WDAA)
TR..............	Trees [*Ecology*]
TR..............	Tremor [*Medicine*] (AAMN)
TR..............	Trenton [*Diocesan abbreviation*] [*New Jersey*] (TOCD)
TR..............	Trial (ROG)
TR..............	Trial Report
TR..............	Tributary (ROG)
TR..............	Tricuspid Regurgitation [*Cardiology*]
TR..............	Trident Aircraft Ltd. [*Canada ICAO aircraft manufacturer identifier*] (ICAO)
TR..............	Trigonal [*Molecular geometry*]
Tr...............	Trill (WDAA)
TR..............	Trillo [*Trill*] [*Music*]
tr...............	Trinidad and Tobago [*MARC country of publication code Library of Congress*] (LCCP)
TR..............	Triple Reduction (DS)
TR..............	Triple Screw [*Shipping*] (DS)
TR..............	Trip Report
TR..............	Tristia [*of Ovid*] [*Classical studies*] (OCD)
Tr...............	Tristram's Consistory Judgments [*England*] [*A publication*] (DLA)
TR..............	Tritium Ratio [*Measure of tritium activity*] [*AEC*]
TR..............	Tritium Recovery [*Nuclear energy*] (NRCH)
Tr...............	Trityl [*Organic chemistry*]
TR..............	Triumph [*Automobile model*]
TR..............	Troop
TR..............	Trouble Report
TR..............	Trough (ADA)
TR..............	Troupe (ROG)
TR..............	Truck
TR..............	Trumpet
Tr...............	Trumpet (WDAA)
TR..............	Trunnion [*Pivot*]
TR..............	Truro [*Postcode*] (ODBW)
TR..............	Truss (MSA)
TR..............	Trust
Tr...............	Trust [*Banking*] (TBD)
TR..............	Trustee (AL)
TR..............	Trustee
T/R.............	Trust Receipt (EBF)
Tr...............	Trypsin (DB)
TR..............	Tubercular Rueckstand [*Medicine*]
TR..............	Tuberculin R [*Also called new tuberculin*] [*Infectious diseases*] (DAVI)
TR..............	Tuberculin Residue [*Medicine*]
TR..............	Tuberculin Rest [*Infectious diseases*] (DAVI)
TR..............	Tubular Reabsorption [*Medicine*] (MAE)
TR..............	Tunnel Rectifier
TR..............	Turbidity Reducing (AAMN)
TR..............	Turbine Rate (NVT)
TR..............	Turkey [*ANSI two-letter standard code*] (CNC)
TR..............	Turkish Reactor
TR..............	Turnaround Requirements (MCD)
T/R.............	Turnaround Requirements [*NASA*] (NAKS)
TR..............	Turning Radius [*Automotive engineering*]
TR..............	Turn Rule (WDMC)
TR8CCA.......	TR8 Car Club of America (EA)
Tra..............	Epistulae ad Traianum [*of Pliny the Younger*] [*Classical studies*] (OCD)
TRA.............	La Tuyere a Reverse Aval [*Concorde*]
TRA.............	[*The*] Razorback Award (IAA)
TRA.............	Tackle Representatives Association (EA)
TRA.............	Taiwan Relations Act [*1979*] (DOMA)
TRA.............	Tandem Rotary Activator
TRA.............	Tape Recorder Amplifier
TRA.............	Taramajima [*Japan*] [*Airport symbol*] (OAG)
TRA.............	Tasmanian Racing Authority [*Australia*]
TRA.............	Tasmanian Rifle Association [*Australia*]
TRA.............	Tax Reform Act [*1969, 1976, 1984, 1986*]
TRA.............	Tax Reform Australia
TRA.............	Technical Requirement Analysis (OA)
TRA.............	Technical Review and Analysis
TRA.............	Technical Review Authority [*Environmental science*] (COE)
TRA.............	Technical Risk Assessment (MCD)
TRA.............	Telecommunications Resellers Association (NTPA)
TRA.............	Temperature Recording Alarm [*Engineering*]
TRA.............	Temporary Rental Allowance
TRA.............	Temporary Reserved Airspace [*ICAO designator*] (FAAC)
TRA.............	Temporary Restricted Area [*Former USSR*] (NATG)
TRA.............	Terminal Repeat Array [*Genetics*]
TRA.............	Terra Industries [*NYSE symbol*] (TTSB)
TRA.............	Terra Industries, Inc. [*Formerly, Inspiration Resources Corp.*] [*NYSE symbol*] (SPSG)
TRA.............	Terrain-Related Accident [*Aviation*]
TRA.............	Test Reactor Area [*Environmental science*] (COE)
TRA.............	Test Requirement Analysis (CAAL)
TRA.............	Textile Refinishers Association (EA)
TRA.............	Theodore Roosevelt Association (EA)
TRA.............	Therapeutic Recreation Associate [*Rehabilitation*] (DAVI)
TRA.............	Thoroughbred Racing Associations (EA)
TRA.............	Thrace Requirements Analysis [*Military*]
TRA.............	Throttle Resolver Angle (MCD)
TRA.............	Thrust Reduction Altitude (GAVI)
TRA.............	Tinctura [*Tincture*] [*Pharmacy*] (ROG)
TRA.............	Tire and Rim Association (EA)
TRA.............	Total Renin Activity [*Medicine*] (DMAA)
TRA.............	Tournament of Roses Association [*Later, TOR*] (EA)
TRA.............	Tracan Oil & Gas [*Vancouver Stock Exchange symbol*]
TRA.............	Trade Readjustment Allowance [*or Assistance*]
TRA.............	Trade Recovery Act
TRA.............	Trade Relations Association (EA)
TRA.............	Training
TRA.............	Training Readjustment Allowance (OICC)
TRA.............	Training-Related Activity (WDAA)
TRA.............	Training Requirements Analysis [*NASA*] (NASA)
TRA.............	Transaldolase [*An enzyme*] (MAE)
TRA.............	Transavia Holland BV [*Netherlands ICAO designator*] (FAAC)
TRA.............	Transfer
tra..............	Transfer (STED)
TRA.............	Transportation Reform Alliance
TRA.............	Transracial Adoption
TRA.............	Travnik [*Yugoslavia*] [*Seismograph station code, US Geological Survey Closed*] (SEIS)

TrA	Triangulum Australe [*Constellation*]
TRA	Triaxial Recording Accelerometer
TRA	Tripoli Rocketry Association (EA)
TRA	Triumph Register of America (EA)
TRA	Tubular Reactor Assembly [*Nuclear energy*] (NRCH)
TRA	Tumor-Resistant Antigen [*Medicine*] (STED)
TRA	Turkish Reactor Assembly (SAA)
TRA	Turnaround Requirements Analysis [*NASA*] (NASA)
TRA	United States Army TRADOC, Institute for Military Assistance, Library, Fort Bragg, NC [*OCLC symbol*] (OCLC)
TRAA	Towing and Recovery Association of America (EA)
TRAAC	Transit Research and Attitude Control [*Navy satellite*]
TRAACS	Transit Research and Attitude Control Satellite [*Navy*] (IEEE)
TRAb	Thyrotrophin Receptor Antibody [*Medicine*] (STED)
trab	Trabeated (VRA)
TRAB	Triaminobenzene [*Organic chemistry*]
TRABOT	Terrier RADAR and Beacon Orientation Test (MUGU)
TRAC	DTIC [*Defense Technical Information Center*] Technical Awareness Circular [*Information service or system*] (CRD)
TRAC	Tactical Radar Correlator [*Army*] (DOMA)
TRAC	Tandem Razor and Cartridge [*Gillette Co.*]
TRAC	Target Research Analysis Center (CINC)
TRAC	Tax Reform Action Coalition (EA)
TRAC	Technical Reports Announcement Checklist
TRAC	Telecommunications Research and Action Center [*Washington, DC*] [*Information service or system Telecommunications*] (TSSD)
TRAC	Teleprocessing Recording for Analysis by the Customer
TRAC	Telescoping Rotor Aircraft Concept (MCD)
TRAC	Terrain Responsive Atmospheric Code [*Environmental science*] (COE)
TRAC	Test of Reading Affective Cues [*Psychology*]
TRAC	Texas Reconfigurable Array Computer
TRAC	Text Reckoning and Compiling [*Computer science*]
TRAC	Thermally Regenerative Alloy Cell
TRAC	The Russian-American Center (EA)
TRAC	Total Record Access Control (SAA)
TRAC	Total Recycling Advisory Committee [*Northern Territory, Australia*]
TRAC	Tracer (AABC)
trac	Tracery (VRA)
TRAC	Track Data Corp. [*NASDAQ symbol*] (SAG)
TRAC	Tracking and Communications [*Aviation*] (IAA)
TRAC	Tractor (AAG)
TRAC	Trade Reform Action Coalition [*Defunct*] (EA)
TRAC	TRADOC Analysis Command
TRAC	TRADOC [*Training and Doctrine Command*] Research and Analysis Center [*Army*]
TRAC	Train Regulation Advisory Control (PDAA)
TRAC	Transaction Reporting and Control System (MCD)
TRAC	Transient Radiation Analysis by Computer (KSC)
TRAC	Transient Reactor Analysis Code (NRCH)
TRAC	Transportation Account Code (AFM)
TRAC	Trials Recording and Analysis Console (PDAA)
TRACAB	Terminal RADAR Approach Control in Tower Cab [*Aviation*] (FAAC)
TRACAD	Training for [*US Military Academy*] Cadets (NVT)
TRACAL	Traffic Control and Landing [*Aviation*] (IAA)
TRACALS	Traffic Control and Landing System [*Aviation*] (IAA)
TRACALS	Traffic Control Approach and Landing System [*Aviation electronics*]
TRACAP	Transient Circuit Analysis Program [*Computer science*]
TRACC	Target Review and Adjustment for Continuous Control (MCD)
TRACDR	Tractor-Drawn
TRACE	Tactical Readiness and Checkout Equipment
TRACE	Tactical Resources and Combat Effectiveness Model (MCD)
TRACE	Tape-Controlled Reckoning and Checkout Equipment [*Component of automatic pilot*] [*Aviation*] (IAA)
TRACE	Tape-Controlled Recording Automatic Checkout Equipment [*Component of automatic pilot*] [*Aviation*]
TRACE	Task Reporting and Current Evaluation
TRACE	Taxiing and Routing of Aircraft Coordinating Equipment (MCD)
TRACE	Taxiway Routing and Coordination Equipment [*Aviation*]
TRACE	Technical Report Analysis, Condensation, Evaluation
TRACE	Teleprocessing Recording for Analysis by the Customer (IEEE)
TRACE	Test Equipment for Rapid Automatic Checkout and Evaluation [*Pan American Airways*]
TRACE	Time Repetitive Analog Contour Equipment (PDAA)
TRACE	Time-Shared Routines for Analysis, Classification, and Evaluation (DIT)
TRACE	Tolls Recording and Computing Equipment (IEEE)
TRACE	Toronto Region Aggregation of Computer Enthusiasts [*Canada*]
TRACE	Total Remote Access Center (MHDI)
TRACE	Total Resource Allocation Cost Estimating (RDA)
TRACE	Total Risk Assessing Cost Estimate [*Army*] (RDA)
TRACE	Trace [*Commonly used*] (OPSA)
TRACE	Trace Remote Atmospheric Chemical Evaluation [*National Center for Atmospheric Research*]
TRACE	Tracking and Communications, Extraterrestrial
TRACE	Track Retrieve and Account for Configuration of Equipment (MCD)
TRACE	Traffic Routing and Control Equipment (MCD)
TRACE	Training and Approaches to Careers Education [*Project*] (AIE)
TRACE	Trane Air Conditioning Economics [*The Trane Co.*]
TRACE	Transaction, Accounting, Control, and Endorsing (PDAA)
TRACE	Transaction Control and Encoding (IAA)
TRACE	Transistor Radio Automatic Circuit Evaluator
TRACE	Transition Region and Coronal Explorer [*Satellite*]
TRACE	Transportable Automated Control Environment
TRACE	Transport and Atmospheric Chemistry Near the Equator

Trace & M	Tracewell and Mitchell's United States Comptroller's Decisions [*A publication*] (DLA)
TRACEN	Training Center
TRACE-P	Total Risk Assessing Cost Estimate - Production [*Army*] (RDA)
TRACER	Technical Reporting of Automated Configuration Electrical Requirements
TRACER	Turnaround Time, Repair Survival Rate and Cost Evaluation Report [*Navy*] (DNAB)
TRACERS	Teleprocessed Record and Card Entry Reporting System (MCD)
TRACES	Technology in Retrospect and Critical Events in Science [*IITRI*]
TRACES	Trace [*Commonly used*] (OPSA)
TRACEX	Amphibious Tractor Exercise [*Navy*] (NVT)
Tracey Evidence	Tracey's Cases on Evidence [*A publication*] (DLA)
TRAC-F	TRADOC [*Training and Doctrine Command*] Analysis Command - Fort Leavenworth [*Kansas*] [*Army*]
TRACH	Trachea [*or Tracheotomy*] [*Medicine*]
trach	Trachea (STED)
trach	Tracheostomy (STED)
Trach	Tracheostomy [*Medicine*] (DAVI)
trach	Tracheotomy (STED)
Trach	Trachiniae [*of Sophocles*] [*Classical studies*] (OCD)
Trach Asp	Tracheal Aspiration (CPH)
TRACHY	Tracheotomy (DSUE)
TRACINFO	Tracer, Number as Indicated. Furnish Information Immediately or Advise
TRACIR	Tracking Air with Circularly Polarized Radar [*Marine science*] (OSRA)
TRACIRS	[*The*] Recording and Controlling of In-Transit Requisition System [*Army*]
TRACIS	Traffic Records Criminal Justice Information System (OICC)
TRACK	Timing Results and Competition Knowledge [*Auto racing*]
TRACK	Track [*Commonly used*] (OPSA)
TrackD	Track Data Corp. [*Associated Press*] (SAG)
TRACKEX	Tracking Exercise [*Navy*] (NVT)
TRAC-MTRY	TRADOC [*Training and Doctrine Command*] Analysis Command-Monterey [*California*] [*Army*] (GRD)
TRACOMD	Training Command [*Navy*] (DNAB)
TRACOMDLANT	Training Command, Atlantic Fleet [*Navy*]
TRACOMDPAC	Training Command, Pacific Fleet [*Navy*]
TRACOMDSUBPAC	Training Command, Submarines, Pacific Fleet [*Navy*]
TRACOMDWESTCOAST	Training Command, West Coast [*Navy*]
TRACOMP	Tracking Comparison
TRACON	Terminal RADAR Approach Control [*FAA*]
TRACON	Terminal RADAR Approach Control Facility [*Aviation*] (FAAC)
TRACON	Terminal RADAR Control (IAA)
TRACOPS	Trailerless Collective Protection System (DWSG)
Tracor	Tracor, Inc. [*Associated Press*] (SAG)
TracrP	Tracer Petroleum Corp. [*Associated Press*] (SAG)
TracrPt	Tracer Petroleum Corp. [*Associated Press*] (SAG)
TRACS	Teleprocessing Remote Access Control System (HGAA)
TRACS	Tool Record Accountability System [*NASA*] (NASA)
TRACS	Traffic Reporting and Control System (IAA)
TRACS	Transport and Road Abstracting and Cataloguing System (NITA)
TRACS	Travel Accounting Control System [*Citicorp Diners Club*]
TRACS	Triangulation Ranging and Crossfix System [*Military*] (CAAL)
TracSup	Tractor Supply Co. [*Associated Press*] (SAG)
tract	Traction
TRACT	Triggered Reconnection Adiabatically Compressed Torus (MCD)
TRACW	Track Data Corp. Wrrt [*NASDAQ symbol*] (TTSB)
TRAC-WSMR	TRADOC [*Training and Doctrine Command*] Analysis Command - White Sands Missile Range [*New Mexico*] [*Army*]
TRACY	Technical Reports Automated Cataloging - Yes [*National Oceanic and Atmospheric Administration*]
TRAD	Terminal RADAR [*Aviation*] (FAAC)
TRAD	Tradition
TRAD	Traductrice (IAA)
TRAD	Training Requirements Analysis Directorate [*Army*]
TRAD	Training Research and Development (IAA)
TRADA	Timber Research and Development Association [*Research center British*] (IRC)
TRADAC	Trajectory Determination and Acquisition Computation
TRADACOMS	Trading Data Communications (TELE)
TRADAD	Trace to Destination and Advise [*Military*]
TRADAR	Transaction Data Recorder (DNAB)
TRADAT	Transit Data Transmission System (SAA)
TrADAT	(Triazolyl-Azo) diaminotoluene [*Organic chemistry*]
TRADCOM	Transportation Corps Research and Development Command [*Army*]
TRADE	Tracking RADAR Angle Deception Equipment (NG)
TRADE	Trading
TRADE	Training Devices (RDA)
TRADE	Training Devices and Equipment
TRADEC	Training Device Computer (DNAB)
Trade Cas	Trade Cases [*Commerce Clearing House*] [*A publication*] (DLA)
Trademark Bull	Bulletin. United States Trademark Association Series [*A publication*] (DLA)
Trademark Bull (NS)	Trademark Bulletin. United States Trademark Association (New Series) [*New York*] [*A publication*] (DLA)
TRADER	Training Devices Requirements Office [*TRADOC*] (MCD)
TRADER	Transient Radiation Effects Recorder (MCD)
Trade Reg Rep	Trade Regulation Reporter [*Commerce Clearing House*] [*A publication*] (DLA)
Trade Reg Rev	Trade Regulation Review [*A publication*] (DLA)
TRADES	Technology Requirement and Definition Study
TRADES	TRADOC Data Evaluation Study (MCD)
TRADET	Training Detachment [*Navy*]
TRADEVCO	Trading & Development Bank Ltd. [*Liberia*]

Tra Devel Aust... Training and Development in Australia [*A publication*]
TRADEVMAN... Training Devices Man [*Navy rating*]
TRADEX...... Target Resolution and Discrimination Experiment [*ARPA*]
TRADEX...... Tracking RADAR Experiment (IAA)
TRADEX...... Trade Data Element Exchange
TRADIC...... Transistor Digital Computer
TRADIC...... Transistorized Airborne Digital Computer [*Air Force*]
TRADIC...... Transistorized Digital Computer [*Air Force*] (IAA)
TRADIS...... Tape Repeating Automatic Data Integration System
TRADIS...... Tropical Resources for Agricultural Development Information System [*Overseas Development Natural Resources Institute*] [*British Information service or system*] (IID)
TRADO...... Transporte Aereo Dominicano [*Dominican Republic*] [*ICAO designator*] (FAAC)
TRADOC...... Training and Doctrine Command [*Army*]
TRADOC-R... Training and Doctrine Command Regulation [*Army*]
TRADR...... Tactical Radio Analysis, Division Restructuring [*Army*]
TRADSTAT... World Trade Statistics Database [*Data-Star*] [*British Information service or system*] (IID)
Trad Un Dig... Trades Union Digest [*A publication*]
TRAE...... Transport Airlift Estimator [*Air Force*]
TRAEX...... Training and Experience [*Military*] (AFM)
TRAF...... Traffic
TRAF...... Tumor Neurosis Factor Receptor-Associated Factor [*Biochemistry*]
TRAFAC...... Training Facility [*Navy*] (DNAB)
TRAFCO...... Television, Radio and Film Communications [*of the Methodist Church*]
TRAFF...... Traffic (ROG)
Traff Cas..... Railway, Canal, and Road Traffic Cases [*A publication*] (DLA)
TRAFFIC...... Trade Records Analysis of Flora and Fauna in Commerce [*An association*]
TRAFFIC...... Transaction Routing and Form Formatting in COBOL [*Common Business-Oriented Language*] [*Computer science*] (MHDI)
TRAFFICWAY... Trafficway [*Commonly used*] (OPSA)
TRAFO...... Transformer (IAA)
TRAFOLPERS... Transfer Following Enlisted Personnel
TRAG...... Traffic Responsive Advance Green [*Control strategy*]
TRAG...... Tragedy
Trag...... Tragoedopodagra [*of Lucian*] [*Classical studies*] (OCD)
TRAI...... Tackle Representatives Association International [*Later, TSSAA*] (EA)
TRAIF...... Torso Restraint Assembly with Integrated Flotation
TRAIL...... Trail [*Commonly used*] (OPSA)
TRAILS...... Trail [*Commonly used*] (OPSA)
TRAIN...... Telerail Automated Information Network [*Association of American Railroads*]
TRAIN...... To Restore American Independence Now [*An association*]
TRAIN...... Tourist Railway Association, Inc. (EA)
train...... Training
TRAIN...... Training
TRAINBASEFOR... Training Base Force, Pacific Fleet [*Navy*]
TRAINCON... Training Conference (MCD)
TRAINDIV... Training Division [*Canadian Navy*]
TRAINLANT... Training Atlantic Fleet [*Navy*]
TRAINMAN... Training Management [*Navy*] (DNAB)
TRAINPACHQ... Training Group Pacific Headquarters [*Canadian Navy*]
TRAINRON... Training Squadron [*Later, SERRON*] [*Navy*]
TRA INT'L... Tackle Representatives Association International [*Later, TSSAA*] (EA)
TRAIS...... Transportation Research Activities Information Service [*Department of Transportation*]
TRAJ...... Timed Repetitive Ankle Jerk (STED)
TRAJ...... Trajectory (AAG)
TRAJ/PS...... Trajectory/Parametric Study (SAA)
TRAK...... Canterbury Park Holdings [*NASDAQ symbol*] (SAG)
TRAK...... Canterbury Pk Hldg Corp. [*NASDAQ symbol*] (TTSB)
TRAK...... Track [*Postal Service standard*] (OPSA)
TrakAu...... Trak-Auto Corp. [*Associated Press*] (SAG)
TRAK TROL... Trackless Trolley [*Freight*]
TRAKW...... Canterbury Pk Hldg Wrrt [*NASDAQ symbol*] (TTSB)
TRALA...... Truck Renting and Leasing Association (EA)
TRALANT...... Fleet Training Command, Atlantic [*Navy*]
TRALINET... TRADOC Library Information Network (MCD)
TRAM...... Target Recognition Attack Multisensor [*DoD*]
TRAM...... Tensioned Replacement Alongside Method (MCD)
TRAM...... Test Reliability and Maintainability (CIST)
TRAM...... Test Reliability and Maintenance Program [*Navy*] (NVT)
TRAM...... Tethered Rover for Atmospheric Measurement [*Ozone measurement*]
TRAM...... Tracking RADAR Automatic Monitoring (AFM)
TRAM...... Tractor, Rubber-Tired, Articulated, Multipurpose (DOMA)
TRAM...... Training Readiness Analysis Monitor (MCD)
TRAM...... Translocating Chain Associating Membrane [*Biochemistry*]
TRAM...... Transputer Module [*Computer science*]
TRAM...... Transverse Rectus Abdominis Myocutaneous [*Breast reconstruction*] (DAVI)
TRAM...... Treatment Rating Assessment Matrix [*Medicine*] (MAE)
TRAM...... Treatment Response Assessment Method [*Medicine*] (MAE)
TRAMAR...... Tropical Rain Mapping Radar [*Instrument*] (EERA)
TRAMEA...... TRADOC [*Training and Doctrine Command*] Management Engineering Activity [*Military*]
TRAMID...... Training for [*US Naval Academy/Naval Reserve Officers Training Corps*] Midshipmen (NVT)
TRAMIS...... TRADOC [*Training and Doctrine Command*] Management Information System [*Army*]

TRAMIT...... Especialidades Farmaceuticas en Tramite de Registro [*Ministerio de Sanidad y Consumo*] [*Spain Information service or system*] (CRD)
TRAMMS...... Transportation Automated Material Movements System [*Army*] (PDAA)
TRAMOD...... Training Requirements Analysis Model (MCD)
TRAMP...... Target Radiation Measurement Program (IAA)
TRAMP...... Temperature Regulation and Monitor Panel
TRAMP...... Test Retrieval and Memory Print [*Computer science*]
TRAMP...... Time-Shared Relational Associative Memory Program [*Computer science*] (IEEE)
TRAMPCO...... Thioguanine, Rubidomycin [*Daunorubicin*], ara-C, Methotrexate, Prednisolone, Cyclophosphamide, Oncovin [*Vincristine*] [*Antineoplastic drug regimen*]
TRAMPCOL... Thioguanine, Rubidomycin [*Daunorubicin*], ara-C, Methotrexate, Prednisolone, Cyclophosphamide, Oncovin , L-Asparaginase [*Vincristine*] [*Antineoplastic drug regimen*]
TRAMPL...... TRADOC Master Priority List (MCD)
TRAMPS...... Temperature Regulator and Missile Power Supply
TRAMPS...... Text Information Retrieval and Management Program System [*Computer science*] (IAA)
TRAMPS...... Traffic Measure and Path Search [*Telecommunications*] (TEL)
TRAMPS...... Transportation Movement Planing System (SAA)
TRAMS...... Traffic Routing and Management System (NITA)
TRAN...... Tax Revenue Anticipation Note [*Finance*]
TRAN...... Transaction
TRAN...... Transformer
TRAN...... Transfusion (STED)
TRAN...... Transient (AABC)
TRAN...... Transit
Tran...... Transit (TBD)
TRAN...... Transmit
TRAN...... Transport
TRANC...... Transient Center [*Marine Corps*]
TRAND...... Tone Reproduction and Neutral Determination [*Chart*] [*Printing technology*]
Tr & Cr...... Troilus and Cressida [*Shakespearean work*] (BARN)
TR & DL...... Tung Research and Development League [*Defunct*] (EA)
T/R & G...... Transmit, Receive, and Guard (MSA)
Tr & H Pr... Troubat and Haly's Pennsylvania Practice [*A publication*] (DLA)
Tr & H Prec Ind... Train and Heard's Precedents of Indictment [*A publication*] (DLA)
TRANDIR...... Translation Director (IEEE)
Tr & TT...... Trial and Tort Trends [*A publication*] (DLA)
TRANET...... Tracking [*or Transit*] Network [*Navy*]
TRANET...... Transnational Network for Appropriate/Alternative Technologies
TRANEX...... Transaction Executive (IAA)
TranIn...... Trans-Industries, Inc. [*Associated Press*] (SAG)
TranInc...... Transamerica Income Shares, Inc. [*Associated Press*] (SAG)
TRAN-PRO... Transaction Processing [*Computer science*]
Tranq...... De Tranquillitate Animi [*of Seneca the Younger*] [*Classical studies*] (OCD)
tranq...... Tranquilize(r) [*Pharmacology*] (DAVI)
TRANQ...... Tranquillo [*Quietly*] [*Music*] (ROG)
TRANS...... Telemetry Redundancy Analyzer System
TRANS...... Transaction
Trans...... Transaction [*Banking*] (TBD)
TRANS...... Transcript (ADA)
TRANS...... Transfer (AAG)
trans...... Transfer (ODBW)
trans...... Transference (STED)
TRANS...... Transformer (AFM)
trans...... Transformer (IDOE)
TRANS...... Transient (AFIT)
TRANS...... Transistor (ADA)
trans...... Transit (ODBW)
TRANS...... Transition (ROG)
TRANS...... Transitive
TRANS...... Transitory
trans...... Translated (WA)
TRANS...... Translation
trans...... Translation (WDAA)
Trans...... Translator (DLA)
TRANS...... Transmission
trans...... Transmit (IDOE)
TRANS...... Transmittance (AAG)
trans...... Transmitter (IDOE)
TRANS...... Transparency (VRA)
TRANS...... Transparent (MSA)
TRANS...... Transport [*or Transportation*] (AAG)
trans...... Transportation (DD)
TRANS...... Transpose [*Proofreading*]
TRANS...... Transverse
trans...... Transverse (IDOE)
TRANSA...... Transaction (MSA)
TRANSAC...... Transistorized Automatic Computer
TransAct...... TransAct Technologies Inc. [*Associated Press*] (SAG)
TRANSAIEE... Transactions of the American Association of Electrical Engineers (IAA)
TRANSALT...... Transition Altitude [*Aviation*] (DA)
Trans & Proc Roy Soc SA... Transactions and Proceedings. Royal Society of South Australia [*A publication*]
Trans & Proc Roy Soc Vic... Transactions and Proceedings. Royal Society of Victoria [*Australia A publication*]
Trans & Wit... Transvaal and Witswatersrand Reports [*A publication*] (DLA)

Trans Ap...... Transcript Appeals [New York] [1867-68] [A publication] (DLA)
Trans App...... Transcript Appeals [New York] [A publication] (DLA)
Trans Appeal R... New York Transcript Appeals Reports [A publication] (DLA)
Trans Aust Med Congress... Transactions. Australian Medical Congress [A publication]
TRANSC....... Transcribe (IAA)
TRANSC....... Transcription (IAA)
Transc A..... Transcript Appeals [New York] [A publication] (DLA)
TRANSCAD... Transportation Computer Assisted Design [MTMC] (TAG)
TRANSCAER... Transportation Community Awareness and Emergency Response
TRANSCEIVER... Transmitter-Receiver (NATG)
Transcis...... Transcisco Industries [Associated Press] (SAG)
Transcm...... Transcom International Ltd. [Associated Press] (SAG)
Transcnd...... Tanscend Services, Inc. [Associated Press] (SAG)
Transcnd...... Transcend Services, Inc. [Associated Press] (SAG)
TRANSCOM... Transportable Communications
TRANSCOM... Transportation Command [Army]
TRANSCOM... Transportation Operations Coordinating Committee [FHWA] (TAG)
TRANSCOM... United States Transportation Command [MTMC] (TAG)
TRANSCON... Transcontinental (MCD)
Transcor...... Transcor Waste Services, Inc. [Associated Press] (SAG)
TRANSCR .... Transcribed
transcr........ Transcription (WDAA)
Transcr A..... Transcript Appeals [New York] [A publication] (DLA)
TRANSCRON... Transcription (ROG)
Trans D........ Transverse Diameter [Anatomy] (CPH)
trans D........ Transverse Diameter (STED)
TRANSDEC... SONAR Transducer Test and Evaluation Center, Naval Electronics Laboratory [San Diego, CA] [Navy]
TRANSDEF... Transducer Evaluation Facility
TRANS/DEP... Transportation of Dependents [Navy] (DNAB)
TRANSDIV... Transport Division [Navy]
TRANSDOC... Transport Documentation (NITA)
TRANSEC... Transmission Security [Communications]
TRANSED..... Transition Education
transf.......... Transfer (VRA)
transf........... Transferred (WDAA)
TRANSF....... Transferred
TRANSF....... Transformer (AAG)
TRANSFAX... Facsimile Transmission [Telecommunications]
TRANSFD.... Transferred (ROG)
TRANSFDESENGR... Transformer Design Engineer (IAA)
TRANSFER... Transportation Simulation for Estimating Requirements (DNAB)
TRANSFIG.... Transfiguration
TRANSFLTNG... Transitional Flight Training (NVT)
TRANSFOR... Translator for Structured FORTRAN [Formula translation] [Computer science] (MHDI)
TRANSFORM... Trade-Off Analysis - Systems/Force Mix Analysis [Military]
TRANSFRMR... Transformer
TRANSGRPPHIBFOR... Transportation Group Amphibious Forces [Navy]
TRANSGRPSOPAC... Transport Group, South Pacific Force [Navy]
TransH......... Trnasport Holdings, Inc. [Associated Press] (SAG)
TransHab..... Transportation Habitat
TransHosp ... Transitional Hospitals Corp. [Associated Press] (SAG)
Trans ILA..... Transactions. International Law Association [1873-1924] [A publication] (DLA)
TRANSIM..... Transit Simplified Receiver [Satellite navigation system]
TRANSIM..... Transportation Simulator (DNAB)
Trans Instn Eng Aust... Transactions. Institution of Engineers of Australia [A publication]
TRANSIS...... Transportation Safety Information System [Department of Transportation] (IID)
TRANSISTOR... Transfer Resistor
TRANSITEX... Transit Exercise (NVT)
transl.......... Translate (WDAA)
TRANSL....... Translation (AAG)
Transl......... Translation (TBD)
transl......... Translucent (VRA)
TRANSLANG... Translator Language [Computer science]
TRANSLANT... Transit Atlantic [By ship or aircraft] (DOMA)
TRANSLANT... Transports, Atlantic Fleet [Navy]
TRANSLANTEX... Transatlantic Training Exercise (MCD)
Translat....... Translation (BJA)
TRANSLEV ... Transition Level (DA)
TRANSLIT.... Transliteration
TRANSLOC... Trade-Off Analysis Systems/Force Mix (MCD)
TRANSLOC... Transportable LORAN-C (MCD)
TranslRev... Translation Review [A publication] (BRI)
TranslRevS... Translation Review Supplement [A publication] (BRI)
Transm....... Transamerica Corp. [Associated Press] (SAG)
TRANSM...... Transmission (AFM)
Transm........ Transmission (TBD)
transm........ Transmission (STED)
transm........ Transmitted (STED)
TRANSMAN... Enlisted Transfer Manual [Military]
TRANSMGTSCOL... Transportation Management School [Navy] (DNAB)
TRANSMO.... Transportation Model [Military]
TRANSMON... Transmission (ROG)
TRANSMONUNIT... Transient Monitoring Unit (DNAB)
TRANSMTG... Transmitting
TRANSMUX... Transmission Multiplexer (NITA)
Transn........ Transition [A publication]
Transnatl ... Transnational (DLA)
Transnat'l Rep... Transnational Reporter [A publication] (DLA)
Transocn...... Transocean Offshore, Inc. [Associated Press] (SAG)

TRANSP...... Transparency (AAG)
TRANSP...... Transportation
transp......... Transportation (VRA)
TRANSPAC... North Pacific Ocean Monitoring for Climate Research [Japan-USA] [Marine science] (OSRA)
TRANSPAC... Thermal Structure Monitoring Program in the Pacific [Marine science] (MSC)
TRANSPAC... Transpacific
TRANSPACMAG... Trans-Pacific Magnetic Anomaly Study [National Oceanic and Atmospheric Administration] (NOAA)
TRANSPHIBLANT... Transports, Amphibious Force, Atlantic Fleet [Navy]
TRANSPHIBPAC... Transports, Amphibious Force, Pacific Fleet [Navy]
Trans Phil Inst Vic... Transactions. Philosophical Institute of Victoria [Australia A publication]
Trans Phil Soc NSW... Transactions. Philosophical Society of New South Wales [Australia A publication]
TRANSPIRE... Transpiration-Cooled Stacked Platelet Injection (MCD)
transpl........ Transplant
transpl .... Transplantation (STED)
TRANSPLAN... Transaction Network Service Planning Model [Telecommunications] (TEL)
TRANSPONDER... Transmitter/Responder [Telecommunications] (EECA)
transputer.... Transistor Computer
Trans Qld Phil Soc... Transactions. Queensland Philosophical Society [Australia A publication]
TRANSRA .... Transistorized RADAR (IAA)
TRANSRON... Transport Squadron [Navy]
Trans Roy Soc NSW... Transactions. Royal Society of New South Wales [Australia A publication]
Trans Roy Soc SA... Transactions. Royal Society of South Australia [A publication]
TransSBA..... Transactions. Society of Biblical Archaeology [London] [A publication] (BJA)
Trans Sect... Transverse Section [Medicine] (AAMN)
trans sect .... Transverse Section (STED)
transsex...... Transsexual (DAVI)
TransSys..... Transition Systems, Inc. [Associated Press] (SAG)
Transtl .... Transitional (DLA)
TranstxGs.... Transtexas Gas Corp. [Associated Press] (SAG)
TRANSV...... Transvaal [South Africa] (ROG)
TRANSV...... Transverse (AAG)
TRAO .... Trade Remedy Assistance Office (AAGC)
TRAP .... Tactical Recovery of Aircraft and Personnel
TRAP .... Tandem Recursive Algorithm Process (HGAA)
TRAP .... Tank, Racks, Adapters, Pylons [Military]
TRAP .... Tape Recorder Action Plan [Committee] [NASA/Air Force]
TRAP .... Tartrate Resistant Acid Phosphatase [An enzyme]
TRAP .... Telepresent Rapid Aiming Platform [Remotely operated rifle]
TRAP .... Telomere Repeat Amplification Protocol [Analytical biochemistry]
TRAP .... Telomeric Repeat Amplification Protocol [Analytical biochemistry]
TRAP .... Terminal Radiation Airborne Program [Air Force]
TRAP .... Tetra-N-Propylammonium Perruthenate [Organic chemistry]
TRAP .... Thioguanine, Rubidomycin [Daunorubicin], Cytosine arabinoside , Prednisone [ara-C] [Antineoplastic drug regimen]
TRAP .... Thrombin Receptor Activating Peptide [Biochemistry]
TRAP .... Thrombospondin-Related Anonymous Protein [Biochemistry]
TRAP .... Time Response Approximation
TRAP .... Tracker Analysis Program (MCD)
TRAP .... Transmission Reliability Analysis Program
trap............ Trapezius [Muscle] [Anatomy] (DAVI)
TRAP .... Trapezoid (MSA)
trap............ Trapping (VRA)
TRAP .... Treasury Relief Aid Project
TRAP .... Tyrosine-Rich Amelogenin Polypeptide [Biochemistry of dental enamel]
TRAPAC...... Fleet Training Command, Pacific [Navy]
TRAPATT.... Trapped Plasma Avalanche Transit Time [Bell Laboratories] (IAA)
TRAPATT.... Trapped Plasma Avalanche Triggered Transit [Bell Laboratories]
TRAPCON ... Transportable RADAR Approach Control [Army]
TRAPP .... Training and Retention as Permanent Party [Army] (AABC)
Tr App .... Transcript Appeals [New York] [1867-68] [A publication] (DLA)
TRAPS .... Tactical Rapid Access Processing System (KSC)
TRAPS .... Training Requirements and Planning Subsystem [Military]
TRAPS .... Transportable Reliable Acoustic Path SONAR (MCD)
TRAPS .... Troop Reaction and Posture Sequence (MCD)
TRAPV .... Trap on Overflow BIT [Binary Digit] Set [Computer science]
TRAQS .... Trans Tasman Recognition Arrangement for Qualifications and Skills [Australia]
TRAR .... Total Radiation Absolute Radiometer [NASA]
TRARON ...... Training Squadron
TRAS .... Tax Return Avoidance Syndrome
TRAS .... Training Requirements Analysis System [Army]
TRASANA..... TRADOC [Training and Doctrine Command] Systems Analysis Activity [White Sands Missile Range, NM] [Army]
TRASANA..... TRADOC [Training and Doctrine Command] Systems Analysis Agency [Army]
TRASER....... Transformer LASER (IAA)
TRASH........ Trash Remover and Satellite Hauler [Proposed device to remove orbiting space debris]
TRASH........ Tsunami Research Advisory System of Hawaii
TRASOP....... Tax Reduction Act Stock Ownership Plan
TRASSO....... TRADOC Systems Staff Officer [or Office] [Army]
TRASTA....... Training Station [Navy]
TRAT.......... Torpedo Readiness Assistance Team
TRAT.......... Trade Aptitude Test [Vocational guidance test]
TRAT.......... Triacetylhexahydrotriazine [Organic chemistry]

TRATE.........	Trace Test and Evaluation
TRATEL.......	Tracking through Telemetry [Air Force]
Tratt...........	Trattenuto [Music]
TRAU	Tanganyika Railway African Union
trau...........	Trauma (DAVI)
trau...........	Traumatic (DAVI)
TrAu...........	Triangulum Australe [Constellation]
TRAV	Intrav, Inc. [NASDAQ symbol] (SAG)
TRAV	Television, Radio, and Audio-Visuals of the Presbyterian Church in the United States (NTCM)
TRAV	Training Availability [Navy] (NVT)
TRAV	Travancore [India] (ROG)
Trav............	Travel-Holiday [A publication] (BRI)
TRAV	Travels [or Traveler]
TRAV	Traverse (AABC)
TravAet.......	Travelers Aetna Property Casualty Corp. [Associated Press] (SAG)
Trav & Tw L of N...	Travers and Twiss on Law of Nations [A publication] (DLA)
TravBt.........	Travis Boats & Motors, Inc. [Associated Press] (SAG)
TRAVC	Travail Canada [Labour Canada - LC]
TRAVCHAR...	Cost Travel Chargeable
Trav-Cochin...	Indian Law Reports, Kerala Series [A publication] (DLA)
TRAVEL.......	Transportable Vertical Erectable Launcher
Travel	[The] Travelers Group, Inc. [Associated Press] (SAG)
Travelrs	[The] Travelers Corp. [Associated Press] (SAG)
Travelrs	Travelers Group, Inc. [Associated Press] (SAG)
TRAVINFO....	Travel Information
TRAVIS	Traffic Retrieval Analysis Validation and Information System [Telecommunications] (TEL)
TRAVIS	Travel Industry School (AIE)
Travl	[The] Travelers Corp. [Associated Press] (SAG)
Trav LJ	Travancore Law Journal [India] [A publication] (DLA)
Trav LR........	Travancore Law Reports [India] [A publication] (DLA)
Trav LT........	Travancore Law Times [India] [A publication] (DLA)
TRAVNEC.....	Subject Travel Was Necessary at This Time and Time Consumed in Administrative Channels Prevented Written Orders Being Issued
TravPC........	Travelers Corp. P & C Capital I [Associated Press] (SAG)
TravPrt........	Travel Ports of America, Inc. [Associated Press] (SAG)
TRAWL	Tape Read and Write Library
TRAX	Three-Axis (IAA)
TRAXS	Total Reflection Angle X-Ray Spectroscopy
Tray Lat Max...	Trayner's Latin Maxims and Phrases, Etc. [A publication] (DLA)
Tray Leg Max...	Trayner's Latin Maxims and Phrases [A publication] (ILCA)
TRB.............	Tactical Review Board [Military] (CAAL)
TRB.............	Tapered Roller Bearing
TRB.............	Tax Review Board [Canada]
TRB.............	Technical Reference Branch [Department of Transportation] (IID)
TRB.............	Technical Review Board [NASA] (KSC)
TRB.............	Test Requirement Bulletins [NASA] (KSC)
TRB.............	Test Review Board [NASA] (NASA)
TRR.............	Tom Robinson Band
TRB.............	Topical Reference Books [A publication]
TRB.............	Torpedo Recovery Boat
TRR.............	Toyota Roflex Burn [Automotive engineering]
TRB.............	Trabaccolo [Small coasting vessel of the Adriatic] (DS)
TRB.............	Trans Air Bretagne [France ICAO designator] (FAAC)
TRB.............	Transit Research Board (COE)
TRB.............	Transportation Research Board (EA)
TRB.............	Trapped Radiation Belt
TRB.............	Treble
TRB.............	[The] Tribune Co. [NYSE symbol] (SPSG)
Trb.............	Tribunus [Tribune] [Latin]
TRB.............	Trombone [Music]
TRB.............	Troop Basis (MUGU)
TRB.............	Turbo [Colombia] [Airport symbol] (OAG)
TRB.............	United States Army TRADOC, Engineering School Library and Learning Resource Center, Fort Belvoir, VA [OCLC symbol] (OCLC)
TRBC	Triangle Bancorp [NASDAQ symbol] (SAG)
TRBF	Total Renal Blood Flow [Medicine]
TRBL...........	Trouble (FAAC)
TRBL...........	Troubleshooting (NASA)
TRBN..........	Trombone [Music]
trbn............	Trombone (WDAA)
TRBO	Turbochef, Inc. [NASDAQ symbol] (SAG)
TRBP	Trainable Retractable Bow Propeller
TRBR	Transportation Branch [Navy] (DNAB)
TRBS	Texas Regional Banc'A' [NASDAQ symbol] (TTSB)
TRBS	Texas Regional Bancshares, Inc. [NASDAQ symbol] (SAG)
TRBU	Treasury Bulletin
TRC.............	[The] Radiochemical Centre [British]
TRC.............	[The] Ranchero Club (EA)
TRC.............	[The] Revitalization Corps (EA)
TRC.............	Tandemly Repeated Core [Genetics]
TRC.............	Tanned Red Cell [Clinical chemistry]
TRC.............	Tape Reader Calibrator
TRC.............	Tape Reader Control
TRC.............	Tape Record Coordinator [Computer science]
TRC.............	Tape Relay Center (NATG)
TRC.............	Tasmanian Rowing Council [Australia]
TRC.............	Tasmanian Rural Counselling [Australia]
TRC.............	Taste Receptor Cell [Biochemistry]
TrC.............	Tayloreed Corporation, Rochester, NY [Library symbol Library of Congress] (LCLS)
TRC.............	Taylor Ranch [California] [Seismograph station code, US Geological Survey] (SEIS)

TRC.............	Technical Repair Center [Air Force] (AFIT)
TRC.............	Technical Research Center (MCD)
TRC.............	Technical Resources Center [Syracuse University] [Research center]
TRC.............	Technical Review Committee [International Atomic Energy Agency] (NRCH)
TRC.............	Technical Review Committee [Environmental Protection Agency] (GFGA)
TRC.............	Technical Review Criteria (ERG)
TRC.............	Technology Reports Centre [British]
TRC.............	Technology Resource Center [Information service or system Phillipines] (IID)
TRC.............	Tejon Ranch [AMEX symbol] (TTSB)
TRC.............	Tejon Ranch Co. [AMEX symbol] (SPSG)
TRC.............	Telecommunications Research Center [University of Louisville] [Research center] (RCD)
TRC.............	Telemetry and Remote Control (IEEE)
TRC.............	Telephone Relay Coupler (HGAA)
TRC.............	Temperature Recording Controller
TRC.............	Teryl Resources Corp. [Vancouver Stock Exchange symbol]
TRC.............	Test of Relational Concepts [Edmonston and Thane] (TES)
TRC.............	Test Readiness Certificate (AAG)
TRC.............	Textile Research Council [British]
TRC.............	Thames Rowing Club [British] (DI)
TRC.............	Therapeutic Referral Center (DAVI)
TRC.............	Therapeutic Residential Center (DAVI)
TRC.............	Thermal Regenerative Cracking [Hydrocarbon pyrolysis process]
TRC.............	Thermodynamics Research Center [College Station, TX] [Department of Commerce] (GRD)
TRC.............	Thoroughbred Racing Communications [An association] (EA)
TRC.............	Thrombosis Research Center [Temple University] [Research center] (RCD)
TRC.............	Tierce [Unit of measurement]
TRC.............	Time Ratio Control (IAA)
TRC.............	Tithe Rent-Charge
TRC.............	Tobacco Research Council [British] (BI)
TRC.............	Token Ring Controller
TRC.............	Toplc [Record label] [Great Britain]
TRC.............	Toroidal Propellant Container
TRC.............	Torreon [Mexico] [Airport symbol] (OAG)
TRC.............	Total Recordable Cases [Environmental science] (COE)
TRC.............	Total Relevant Cost
TRC.............	Total Renin Concentration [Laboratory science] (DAVI)
TRC.............	Total Residual Chlorine [Environmental chemistry]
TRC.............	Total-Response Chromatogram
TRC.............	Total Ridge Count [Anthropology]
TRC.............	Tough Rubber-Sheathed Cable
TRC.............	Toyon Research Corp.
TRC.............	Tracking, RADAR-Input, and Correlation
TRC.............	Trade Relations Council of the United States (EA)
TRC.............	Traffic Count and Listing [Aviation] (DA)
TRC.............	Traffic Records Committee (EA)
TRC.............	Training Readiness Condition
TRC.............	Trans Air Charter, Inc. [ICAO designator] (FAAO)
TRC.............	Transcaribbean (MCD)
TRC.............	Transmission Release Code (DNAB)
TRC.............	Transmit (NITA)
TRC.............	Transmit/Receive Control Unit
TRC.............	Transmitter Circuit (IAA)
TRC.............	Transportation Research Center [Ohio]
TRC.............	Transportation Research Command [Army] (IAA)
TRC.............	Transverse Redundancy Check [Computer science] (IBMDP)
TRC.............	Travelers Research Center [Oceanography]
TRC.............	TRC, Companies [Associated Press] (SAG)
trc.............	Treble Crochet
TRC.............	Triumph Roadster Club (EA)
TRC.............	Trona Railway Co. [AAR code]
TRC.............	Truth & Reconciliation Committee (WDAA)
TRC.............	Type Requisition Code [Military]
TRC.............	United States Army TRADOC, Fort Leavenworth Post Library, Commander, General Staff, Fort Leavenworth, KS [OCLC symbol] (OCLC)
TRCA	Tricycle Racing Club of America
TRC-AS	Transmit/Receive Control Unit-Asynchronous Start/Stop
TRCC	T-Carrier Restoration Control Center [Bell System]
TRCC	Theodore Roosevelt Centennial Commission [Government agency] [Terminated, 1959]
TRCC	Tripartite Research Coordination Committee (SAA)
TRCCC	Tracking RADAR Central Control Console [BMEWS]
TRCD	Tricord Systems [NASDAQ symbol] (TTSB)
TRCD	Tricord Systems, Inc. [NASDAQ symbol] (SAG)
TrCda	TransCanada Pipeline Ltd. [Associated Press] (SAG)
TRCE..........	Tactical Radio Communications Equipment
TRCE..........	Terrace [Classified advertising] (ADA)
TRCE..........	Thermionic Reactor Critical Experiment [NASA]
TRCE..........	Trace
TRCF	Transcription-Repair Coupling Factor [Genetics]
TRCH	Tanned Red Cell Hemagglutination [Immunology] (MAE)
Tr Ch	Transactions of the High Court of Chancery (Tothill's Reports) [A publication] (DLA)
TRCHI	Tanned Red Cell Hemagglutination Inhibition Test [Immunology]
TRCHII	Tanned Red Cell Hemagglutination Inhibition Immunoasay [Immunology] (PDAA)
Trchmrk	Torchmark Corp. [Associated Press] (SAG)
TRCI...........	Technology Research [NASDAQ symbol] (TTSB)

TRCI............	Technology Research Corp. [*Clearwater, FL*] [*NASDAQ symbol*] (NQ)
TRCK	Truck
TRCKNG......	Trucking
TRCO	Technical Representative of the Contracting Officer (MCD)
TRCO	Transportation Research Command [*Army*] (KSC)
Tr Co	Trust Company (MHDB)
TRCONS......	Theater Rate Consolidation Data File [*Military*]
Tr Consist J...	Tristram's Consistory Judgments [*1872-90*] [*England*] [*A publication*] (DLA)
TRCP	Tape Recorder Control Panel (MCD)
TRCR	Tracer (MSA)
TRCR	Tractor
TRCR	Trail Riders of the Canadian Rockies (EA)
TRCR	Transcend Services [*NASDAQ symbol*] (TTSB)
TRCR	Transcend Services, Inc. [*NASDAQ symbol*] (SAG)
Tr-Cro	Trichromatic (DGA)
TRCS	Tactical Radio Communications System
TRCS	Techniques for Determining RADAR Cross Section [*Air Force*]
TRCS	Traffic Reporting and Control System (NITA)
TRC-SC	Transmit/Receive Control Unit-Synchronous Character
TRC-SF	Transmit/Receive Control Unit-Synchronous Framing
TRCTR	Tractor
TRCV	Total Red Cell Volume [*Immunology*] (DAVI)
TRCV	Tri-color Visual Approach Slope Indicator [*Aviation*] (FAAC)
TRCVR	Transceiver (CET)
TRCVR	Transceiver Transmitter Receiver (IAA)
TRCW	Transcor Waste Services [*NASDAQ symbol*] (TTSB)
TRCW	Transcor Waste Services, Inc. [*NASDAQ symbol*] (SAG)
TRD	Registry of Tissue Reactions to Drugs [*Later, DETP*] (EA)
TRD	Target-Recognizing Domain [*Genetics*]
TRD	Taxa Referencial Diaria [*Brazil*] (ECON)
TRD	Technical Requirements Document
TRD	Technical Resource Document
TRD	Technical Review Document (GNE)
TRD	Test Requirements Document [*NASA*] (AAG)
TRD	Texas Red-Conjugated Dextran [*Analytical biochemistry*]
TRD	Thermo-Reactive Deposition [*Metal treating*]
TRD	Thread (AAG)
TRD	Three-Axis Rotational Control-Direct (SAA)
TRD	Tongue-Retaining Device [*Medicine*]
TRD	Toyota Racing Development [*Toyota Motor Corp.*]
TRD	Traction Retinal Detachment [*Ophthalmology*] (DAVI)
TRD	Trade
Trd	Trade (BARN)
TRD	Transferred (ROG)
TRD	Trans Island Air [*Barbados*] [*ICAO designator*] (FAAC)
TRD	Transit Routing Domain (TNIG)
TRD	Transmission Ratio Distortion [*Genetics*]
TRD	Trapped Radiation Detector
TRD	Tread
Trd	Trinidad (BARN)
TRD	Trivandrum [*India*] [*Seismograph station code, US Geological Survey*] (SEIS)
TRD	Trondheim [*Norway*] [*Airport symbol*] (OAG)
TRD	Trouble Reporting Desk [*NASA*] (KSC)
TRD	Troudor Resources, Inc. [*Vancouver Stock Exchange symbol*]
TRD	Try Repeating Dose [*Medicine*]
TRD	Turbine Reduction Drive
TRD	United States Army TRADOC, Fort Dix Post Library, Fort Dix, NJ [*OCLC symbol*] (OCLC)
TRDAC	Timber Research and Development Advisory Council [*Australia*]
TRDC	Tobacco Research and Development Council [*Australia*]
TRDC	Transport Research and Development Command [*Army*] (MCD)
TRDCR........	Tandem-Rocket Dual-Combustion Ramjet (MCD)
TRDE	Transparent Rotating Disk Electrode [*Electrochemistry*]
TRDET	Trouble Detection (IAA)
TRDFX	Capstone: Growth Fund [*Mutual fund ticker symbol*] (SG)
TRDG	Trading (DCTA)
Trdg	Trading (TBD)
TRDI	Trim Die (AAG)
TRDJSDOPII...	[*The*] Reverend Doctor Jonathan Swift, Dean of Patrick's in Ireland [*Pseudonym used by Jonathan Swift*]
TRDL	Tactical Reconnaissance Data Link (MCD)
TRDM	Tactical Reconnaissance Data Marking
TRDMRK......	Trademark
TRDO	Treasury Regional Disbursing Office (AAGC)
TRDR	Test Readiness Design Review
TrDrpG........	Tear Drop Golf Co. [*Associated Press*] (SAG)
TrDrpGf.......	TearDrop Golf Co. [*Associated Press*] (SAG)
TRDS	Towards (ROG)
TRDSMAN....	Tradesman
TRDT	Trident Intl [*NASDAQ symbol*] (TTSB)
TRDT	Trim and Drill Template (MCD)
TRDT	Triple Rotating Directional Transmission [*Military*] (CAAL)
TRDTO	Tracking RADAR Data Takeoff
TRDx	Texas Red-Labeled Dextran [*Analytical biochemistry*]
TRDX	Tridex Corp. [*NASDAQ symbol*] (SAG)
TRE	Tactical Readiness Evaluation [*Submarines*] (DOMA)
TRE	Tactical Receive Element (DOMA)
TRE	Tactical Receive Equipment (DOMA)
TRE	Tax-Response Element [*Genetics*]
TRE	Telecommunications Research Establishment [*British military*] (DMA)
TRE	Temperature-Resistant Element (DNAB)
TRE	Tempore Regis Edwardi [*In the Time of King Edward*] [*Latin*] (DLA)
TRE	Terratech Resources, Inc. [*Toronto Stock Exchange symbol*]
TRE	Theologische Realenzyklopaedie [*A publication*]
TRE	Thymic Reticuloepithelial (DB)
TRE	Thyroid Hormone Response Element [*Endocrinology*]
TRE	Thyroid-Responsive Element [*Genetics*]
TRE	Tidal Regenerator Engine
TRE	Timing Read Error
TRE	Tiree Island [*Scotland*] [*Airport symbol*] (OAG)
TRE	Total Rare Earths (NRCH)
TRE	Total Resource Effectiveness Index [*Environmental Protection Agency*]
TRE	Toxicity Reduction Evaluation
TRE	Training Equipment (KSC)
TRE	Training Readiness Evaluation (MCD)
TRE	Training-Related Expenses [*Work Incentive Program*]
TRE	Trans-Eastern Airlines Ltd. [*Kenya*] [*ICAO designator*] (FAAC)
TRE	Transient Radiation Effects
TRE	Transmit Reference Equivalent (NITA)
TRE	Treasury
TRE	Tremont Corp. [*NYSE symbol*] (SPSG)
TRE	Trente [*Italy*] [*Seismograph station code, US Geological Survey Closed*] (SEIS)
TRE	Trent University [*UTLAS symbol*]
TRE	True Radiation Emittance
TRE	Turbidity Removal Evaporator [*Environmental science*] (COE)
TRE	Type Rating Examiner [*Aviation*] (DA)
TRE	United States Army TRADOC, Fort Eustis Post Library and Translation School Library, Fort Eustis, VA [*OCLC symbol*] (OCLC)
TREA	[*The*] Retired Enlisted Association (EA)
TREA	Triethanolamine [*Medicine*] (DMAA)
TREA & A ...	[*The*] Real Estate Appraiser and Analyst [*Society of Real Estate Appraisers*] [*A publication*]
Tread	Treadway's South Carolina Constitutional Reports [*A publication*] (DLA)
Tread	Treadway's South Carolina Law Reports [*1812-16*] [*A publication*] (DLA)
TREAD	Troop Recognition and Detection (MCD)
Treadco	Treadco, Inc. [*Associated Press*] (SAG)
Tread Const...	Treadway's South Carolina Constitutional Reports [*A publication*] (DLA)
Treadway Const (SC)...	Treadway's South Carolina Constitutional Reports [*A publication*] (DLA)
TREAS	Treasure
TREAS	Treasurer (EY)
treas	Treasurer (DD)
Treas	Treasurer (TBD)
Treas	Treasury (EBF)
TREAS	Treasury (ROG)
treas	Treasury (VRA)
Treas Dec	Treasury Decisions under Customs and Other Laws [*United States*] [*A publication*] (DLA)
Treas Dec Int Rev...	Treasury Decisions under Internal Revenue Laws [*A publication*] (DLA)
TREAS DEPT...	Department of the Treasury
Treas Dept Cir...	Treasury Department Circular [*A publication*] (DLA)
Treas Regs...	United States Treasury Regulations [*A publication*] (DLA)
TREASURE...	Timber, Recreation, Enviroment, Aesthetics for a Sustained, Usable, Resource (WPI)
TREAT........	Transient Radiation Effects Automated Tabulation
TREAT........	Transient Reactor Test Facility
TREAT........	Treatment (AAG)
TrEAT..........	Trial for Early Alcohol Treatment
TREAT........	Trouble Report Evaluation and Analysis Tool (MCD)
Treat Tro	Treatise on Trover and Conversion [*A publication*] (DLA)
TREB..........	Treble (ROG)
TREC..........	Text Retrieval Conference [*Sponsored by National Institute of Standards and Technology*]
TREC..........	Total Rosette-Forming Cell [*Medicine*] (DMAA)
TREC..........	Tracking RADAR Electronic Component (AFM)
TREC..........	Transistor Radiation Effects Compilation [*Program*] (MCD)
TRECOM......	Transportation Research and Engineering Command (MUGU)
TRECOM......	Transportation Research Command [*Fort Eustis, VA*] [*Army*]
TRED	TDA [*Taxpayer Delinquent Account*] Report Edit Data [*IRS*]
TRED	Technology-Based Regional Economic Development
TRED	Transmitting and Receiving Equipment Development (MCD)
TRED	Treadco, Inc. [*NASDAQ symbol*] (SPSG)
Tred	Tredgold's Cape Colony Reports [*A publication*] (DLA)
TREDA	Tumen River Economic Development Area [*Northeast Asia*]
TREDAT	Tree Crops Database
Tredgar.......	Tredegar Industries [*Associated Press*] (SAG)
Tredgar.......	Tredegar Industries, Inc. [*Associated Press*] (SAG)
TREDS	TRADOC Educational Data System
TREDS-NRI...	TRADOC [*Training and Doctrine Command*] Educational Data System - Nonresident Instruction [*Army*]
TREE	Doubletree Corp. [*NASDAQ symbol*] (SPSG)
TREE	Teacher Recruitment for Educational Excellence (EDAC)
TREE	Transient Radiation Effects on Electronics [*Military*]
TREE	Tropical Rainforest Ecology Experiment [*Marine science*] (OSRA)
TREE	Trustee
TREE/BEE TEST...	Tree/Bee Test of Auditory Discrimination [*Janet B. Fudala*] (TES)
TREELS........	Time-Resolved Electron Energy-Loss Spectroscopy
TREES.........	Time-Resolved Europium Excitation Spectroscopy
TREES.........	Transient Radiation Effects on Electronic Systems [*Air Force*] (MCD)
TREESHIP	Trusteeship [*Legal shorthand*] (LWAP)

TREESS........	Tactical Reflected and Emitted Energy Suppression System
TREF............	Temperature Rising Elution Fractionation [*Analytical chemistry*]
Trehern.........	British and Colonial Prize Cases [*A publication*] (DLA)
TREK...........	Touring Riders Emergency Kare [*An association*]
TREKZINE	Trek Magazine [*Generic term for a publication of interest to fans of the television program "Star Trek"*]
TREM...........	Tape Reader Emulator Module
TREM...........	TRADOC Research Center [*Monterey, CA*] [*Army*] (GRD)
Trem............	Tremaine's Pleas of the Crown [*England*] [*A publication*] (DLA)
trem.............	Tremolo [*Tremulous*] [*Music*] (WGA)
TREM...........	Tropical Rainfall Explorer Mission (MCD)
Tremnt.........	Tremont Corp. [*Associated Press*] (SAG)
TREMORS...	Tsunami Risk Evaluation through Seismic Moment from Real-Time System [*Marine science*] (OSRA)
Trem PC	Tremaine's Pleas of the Crown [*England*] [*A publication*] (DLA)
tren............	Trendelenburg [*Position*] [*Surgery*] (DAVI)
TREN	Trenwick Group [*NASDAQ symbol*] (TTSB)
TREN	Trenwick Group, Inc. [*NASDAQ symbol*] (NQ)
tren.............	Tris(aminoethyl)amine [*Organic chemistry*]
TREND........	Trade-Offs for Lifting Reentry Vehicle Evaluation and Nominal Design
Trend	Trendelenburg (MEDA)
TREND........	Tropical Environmental Data
TrendL........	Trend-Lines, Inc. [*Associated Press*] (SAG)
TR (Eng)......	Term Reports [*99-101 English Reprint*] [*A publication*] (DLA)
TRENS........	Transcutaneous Random Electrical Nerve Stimulator [*Medicine*]
Trenton St C...	Trenton State College (GAGS)
TrentS.........	Trenton Savings Bank [*Associated Press*] (SAG)
Trep............	Treponema [*Microbiology*]
Tr Eq..........	Fonblanque's Treatise of Equity [*A publication*] (DLA)
TRER	Transient Radiation Effect on Radiation (SAA)
TRES...........	Tayside Rehabilitation Engineering Services [*British*] (IRUK)
TRES...........	Terminal Replacement and Enquiry System (NITA)
TRES...........	Terminal Retrieval and Enquiry Services [*Department of Employment*] [*British*]
TRES...........	Thermally Regenerative Electrochemical System [*Power source*]
TRES...........	Time-Resolved Emission Spectra
TRES...........	Treasurer
TRES...........	Tree Source Industries [*Formerly, WTD Industries*] [*NASDAQ symbol*]
TRES...........	TresCom International [*NASDAQ symbol*] (TTSB)
TRES...........	TresCom International, Inc. [*NASDAQ symbol*] (SAG)
TRES...........	Trestle (WGA)
TresCom.......	TresCom International, Inc. [*Associated Press*] (SAG)
TRESI..........	Target Resolution Extraction of Statistical Invariances
TRESNET	Trent Interlibrary Loan and Communication Network [*Canada Information service or system*] (IID)
TRESNET	Trent Resource Sharing Network [*Ontario Library Service Trent*] [*Richmond Hill, ON*] [*Telecommunications*] (TSSD)
TREVI..........	Terrorisme, Radicalisme, Extremisme, Violence Internationale [*International anti-terrorist group*] [*Belgium*]
Trev Tax Suc...	Trevor's Taxes on Succession [*4th ed.*] [*1881*] [*A publication*] (DLA)
TREX...........	Transnational Re'A' [*NASDAQ symbol*] (TTSB)
TREX...........	Transnational Re Corp. [*NASDAQ symbol*] (SAG)
Trex............	Tyrannosaurus Rex [*A dinosaur*]
TrexMed	Trex Medical Corp. [*Associated Press*] (SAG)
TRF.............	Air Transafrik Ltd. [*Ghana*] [*ICAO designator*] (FAAC)
TRF.............	Tank Range-Finder
TRF.............	Tariff
TRF.............	T-Cell Replacing Factor [*Biochemistry*]
TRF.............	Teacher Rating Form (EDAC)
TRF.............	Technical Reference File
TRF.............	Technical Replacement Factor
TRF.............	Tele-Radio Systems Ltd. [*Toronto Stock Exchange symbol*]
TRF.............	Telomeric Repeat-Binding Factor [*Genetics*]
TRF.............	Templeton Russia Fund [*NYSE symbol*] (SAG)
TRF.............	Temporary Release Failure (WDAA)
TRF.............	Terminal Renal Failure [*Medicine*]
TRF.............	Terminal Restriction Fragment [*Cytology*]
TRF.............	Terminal Restriction Fragment [*Genetics*]
TRF.............	Terrestrial Radio Frequency
TRF.............	Test Tube and Ring-Shaped Forms [*AIDS cytology*]
TRF.............	Thermal Radiation at Microwave Frequencies
TRF.............	Thymus Cell Replacing Factor [*Immunology*]
TRF.............	Thymus-Dependent Cell-Replacing Factor [*Hematology*] (DAVI)
TRF.............	Thyrotrophin-Releasing Factor [*Later, TRH*] [*Endocrinology*]
TRF.............	Tissue Respiratory Factors [*Medicine*]
TRF.............	Tragicorum Romanorum Fragmenta [*A publication*] (OCD)
TRF.............	Transducer Repair Facility
TRF.............	Transfer (AABC)
Trf..............	Transfer (EBF)
TRF.............	Transferrin [*Also, T, TF*] [*Biochemistry*]
TRF.............	Transition Reflection Formalism (AAEL)
TRF.............	Transportation Research Forum (EA)
TRF.............	Transportation Research Foundation
TRF.............	Tropical Forest Program (EERA)
TRF.............	Tuna Research Foundation (EA)
TRF.............	Tuned Radio Frequency
trf..............	Tuned Radio Frequency (IDOE)
TRF.............	Turf Research Foundation [*Defunct*] (EA)
TRF.............	United States Army TRADOC, Fort McClellan, Fort McClellan, AL [*OCLC symbol*] (OCLC)
TRFA...........	Triple Revolving Fund Account (AABC)
TRFAD	Thomas Roderick Fraser and Andrew Dewar [*Pseudonym*]
TRFB...........	Tariff Board [*Canada*]

TRFC...........	Tanya Roberts Fan Club (EA)
TRFC...........	Tex Ritter Fan Club (EA)
TRFC...........	Total Rosette-Forming Cell [*Laboratory science*] (DAVI)
TRFC...........	Traffic (MSA)
TRFC...........	Tristan Rogers Fan Club [*Defunct*] (EA)
TRFCA	Tea Research Foundation (Central Africa) [*Malawi*] (EAIO)
TRFCS	Temperature Rate Flight Control System
TRFD...........	Tramford International Ltd. [*NASDAQ symbol*] (SAG)
Trfd............	Transferred [*Army*]
TRFI............	Trans Financial [*NASDAQ symbol*] (TTSB)
TRFI............	Trans Financial Bancorp, Inc. [*Bowling Green, KY*] [*NASDAQ symbol*] (NQ)
TR/FLRES ...	Transferred to Fleet Reserve (DNAB)
TR Fnc.........	TR Financial Corp. [*Associated Press*] (SAG)
TRFO...........	Time Resolved Fluorescence Spectroscopy
TRFS...........	Trace Fuselage Station (MCD)
TRFW..........	Tramford International Ltd. [*NASDAQ symbol*] (SAG)
TRFY...........	Trafficway [*Postal Service standard*] (OPSA)
TRG.............	Atlantic Island Air [*Iceland*] [*ICAO designator*] (FAAC)
TRG.............	[*The*] Record Group [*Funded by N. V. Philips*]
TRG.............	Tactical Reconnaissance Group
TRG.............	Tauranga [*New Zealand*] [*Airport symbol*] (OAG)
TRG.............	T-Cell Rearranging Gene [*Genetics*]
TRG.............	Technical Research Group, Inc. (MCD)
TRG.............	Technical Review Group
TRG.............	Telecommunications Research Group [*Culver City, CA*] [*Telecommunications*] (TSSD)
TRG.............	Tertiary Research Group [*British*]
TRG.............	Tory Reform Group [*British*] (DBA)
TRG.............	Track-Rich Grains [*s*] [*Cosmic-ray path in meteorites*]
TRG.............	Trailing (AAG)
TRG.............	Training
trg..............	Triangle (BARN)
TRG.............	Trilogy Resource Corp. [*Toronto Stock Exchange symbol*]
TRG.............	Triton Research Group (EA)
TRG.............	Trudeau, R. G., Bloomfield Hills MI [*STAC*]
TRG.............	Tuned Rotor Gyro (MCD)
TRG.............	United States Army TRADOC, Fort Benning Post and Infantry School Library, Fort Benning, GA [*OCLC symbol*] (OCLC)
TrGasSur	Transportadora de Gas Del Sur SA [*Associated Press*] (SAG)
TRGB...........	Tail Rotor Gearbox [*Aviation*] (DA)
TRGC...........	Theta Rho Girls' Club (EA)
Trge............	Triangle (WDAA)
TrgGpRM	Training Group, Royal Marines [*British*]
TRGH...........	Trough [*Freight*]
TRGI............	Trident Rowan Group [*NASDAQ symbol*] (SAG)
TRGI............	Triglycerides Incalculable [*Laboratory science*] (DAVI)
TRGL...........	Toreador Royalty [*NASDAQ symbol*] (TTSB)
TRGL...........	Toreador Royalty Corp. [*NASDAQ symbol*] (NQ)
TRGP...........	Tactical Reconnaissance Group [*Air Force*]
TRGP...........	Transit Group [*NASDAQ symbol*] [*Formerly, Geni Parcel Service*] (SG)
TRGT...........	Target (AAG)
TRH.............	Airmark Aviation, Inc. [*ICAO designator*] (FAAC)
TRH.............	Technical Reference Handbook
TRH.............	Test Requirements Handbook (MUGU)
TRH.............	Their Royal Highnesses
TRH.............	Thyroid-Stimulating Hormone Releasing Hormone (DB)
TRH.............	Thyrotrophin-Releasing Hormone [*Formerly, TRF*] [*Endocrinology*]
TRH.............	Transatlantic Holdings [*NYSE symbol*] (SPSG)
TRH.............	Truss Head [*Engineering*]
TRH.............	United States Army TRADOC, Fort Benjamin Harrison Library System, Fort Benjamin Harrison, IN [*OCLC symbol*] (OCLC)
TRHAZCON...	Training Hazardous Condition (MCD)
TRHD...........	Twin-Row High-Density [*Trees*] (DICI)
TRH-R..........	Thyrotrophin-Releasing Hormone Receptor [*Endocrinology*]
TRI.............	Bristol, TN [*Location identifier FAA*] (FAAL)
TRI.............	[*The*] Refractories Institute (EA)
TRI.............	Tactical Reconnaissance/Intelligence [*Air Force*] (AFM)
TRI.............	Technical Report Instruction (AAG)
TRI.............	Technical Research Institute [*Japan*]
TRI.............	Telecomputer Research, Inc. [*Bala Cynwyd, PA*] [*Information service or system Telecommunications*] (TSSD)
TRI.............	Telemanagement Resources International, Inc. (TSSD)
TRI.............	Test Requirement Identification (DNAB)
TRI.............	Tetrazolium Reduction Inhibition (MAE)
TRI.............	Textile Research Institute (EA)
TRI.............	Time-Reversal Invariance [*Physics*]
TRI.............	Tin Research Institute (EA)
TRI.............	Tire Retreading Institute (EA)
TRI.............	Tootsie Roll Industries, Inc. (EFIS)
TRI.............	Torsion Reaction Integrating
TRI.............	Total Response Index [*Psychology*]
TRI.............	Toxic Chemical Release Inventory [*National Library of Medicine*] [*Information service or system*] (CRD)
TRI.............	Toxic Release Inventory [*Environmental Protection Agency*]
TRI.............	Toxics Release Inventory [*Environmental Protection Agency*]
TRI.............	Transaction Routing Index
TRI.............	Translation Research Institute (EA)
TR-I	Translations Register - Index (MCD)
TRI.............	Transmission Interface Converter (IAA)
TRI.............	Transpacific Resources, Inc. [*Toronto Stock Exchange symbol*]
TRI.............	Transponder Receiver Isolation
TRI.............	Transportation Research Institute [*Oregon State University*] [*Research center*] (RCD)

TRI............ Transportation Research Institute [*Carnegie-Mellon University*]
TRI............ Triangle
Tri............. Triangulation
Tri............. Triangulum [*Constellation*]
TRI............ Triassic [*Period, era, or system*] [*Geology*]
TRI............ Trichloroethylene [*Anesthesiology*]
TRI............ Trichloroethylene [*A solvent*] [*Chemistry*] (DAVI)
TRI............ Tri-City Airport [*Tennessee*] [*Airport symbol*] (OAG)
TRI............ Triclinic [*Crystallography*] (IAA)
TRI............ Tri-College Library, Moorhead, MN [*OCLC symbol*] (OCLC)
TRI............ Tricycle (AAG)
TRI............ Trieste [*Grotta Gigante*] [*Italy*] [*Seismograph station code, US Geological Survey*] (SEIS)
TRI............ Trinet Corporate Realty Trust [*NYSE symbol*] (SPSG)
TRI............ Triode (AAG)
TRI............ TrNet Corporate Rlty Tr [*NYSE symbol*] (TTSB)
TRI............ Tropical Research Institute [*Smithsonian Institution*]
TRI............ Tropical Resources Institute [*Yale University*] [*Research center*] (RCD)
TRI............ Trucking Research Institute [*Research center*] (RCD)
TRI............ Tuboreticular Inclusions [*Hematology*]
TRI............ Tubuloreticular Inclusion [*Medicine*] (DAVI)
TRIA.......... Target Radiant Intensity, Aerobee (SAA)
TRIA.......... Telemetry Range Instrumentation Aircraft
TRIA.......... Temperature Removable Instrument Assembly [*Nuclear energy*] (NRCH)
TRIA.......... Tracking Range Instrumented Aircraft (PDAA)
TRIA.......... Triacontanol [*Plant growth regulator*]
Tria........... Triangulum [*Constellation*]
TRIAC .... Test Resources Improvement Advisory Council [*Military*]
TRIAC .... Triiodothyroacetic Acid [*Endocrinology*]
TRIAC .... Triode Alternating Current (IAA)
TRIAC .... Triode Alternating Current Semiconductor Switch
TRIAD .... Target Resolving Information Augmentation Device (MCD)
TriadGty...... Triad Guaranty, Inc. [*Associated Press*] (SAG)
TriadSy....... Triad Systems Corp. [*Associated Press*] (SAG)
TRIAL......... Technique to Retrieve Information from Abstracts of Literature [*Computer science*]
Trial Advoc Q... Trial Advocate Quarterly [*A publication*] (DLA)
Trial Law Forum... Trial Lawyers Forum [*A publication*] (DLA)
TrianBc....... Triangle Bancorp [*Associated Press*] (SAG)
Triarc........ Triarc Co. [*Associated Press*] (SAG)
TRIASS....... Triumph Adler Assembler (IAA)
TriathB....... Triathalon Broadcasting Co. [*Associated Press*] (SAG)
TRIB.......... Tire Retread Information Bureau (EA)
TRIB.......... Transfer Rate of Information BITs [*Binary Digits*] [*Dial telephone network American National Standards Institute*]
TRIB.......... Tribal
TRIB.......... Tribulation (DSUE)
Trib........... Tribunal
Trib........... Tribunale [*Ordinary Court of First Instance*] [*Italian*] (DLA)
TRIB.......... Tribunus [*Tribune*] [*Latin*] (OCD)
trib........... Tribus [*Tribe*] [*Latin*]
TRIB.......... Tributary
TRIB.......... Tribute (ADA)
TRIB.......... Trinity Biotech [*NASDAQ symbol*] (SAG)
Trib Bks...... Tribune Books [*A publication*] (BRI)
TRIBE........ Teaching and Research in Bicultural Education [*Indian organization in Maine*]
TriBeCa...... Triangle Below Canal Street [*Artists' colony in New York City*] [*See also NoHo, SoHo, SoSo*]
TriBeta....... Beta Beta Beta [*An association*] (NTPA)
Tri Bish....... Trial of the Seven Bishops [*A publication*] (DLA)
TRIB POT.... Tribunicia Potestas [*Latin*] (OCD)
Tribune....... [*The*] Tribune Co. [*Associated Press*] (SAG)
TRIBY .... Trinity Biotech plc ADS [*NASDAQ symbol*] (TTSB)
TRIC.......... Television and Radio Industry Club [*British*] (DBA)
TRIC.......... Trachoma-Inclusion Conjunctivitis [*Ophthalmology*]
TRIC.......... Tracking RADAR Input and Correlation (MSA)
TRIC.......... Transaction Identification Code [*Military*] (AFIT)
TRIC.......... Transition Radiation and Ionization Calorimeter (SSD)
TRIC.......... Transit Research Information Center [*Department of Transportation*] [*Washington, DC*] (GRD)
TRIC.......... Tri-Camera (IAA)
TRIC.......... Trichloroethylene [*A solvent*] [*Chemistry*] (DAVI)
TRIC.......... Tricks for Research in Cancer
TRIC.......... Triclinic [*Crystallography*]
TRIC.......... Tri County Bancorp [*NASDAQ symbol*] (SAG)
Tric........... Tricycle [*A publication*]
TRICAP ...... Triple Capability [*Army*]
TRICAP ...... Triple Capacity Division [*Army*] (VNW)
triCB .... Trichlorobiphenyl [*Chemistry*] (DAVI)
TRICC........ Tariff Rules of the Interstate Commerce Commission
TRICCSMA... Trident Command and Control Systems Maintenance Facility (DNAB)
TRICE........ Textile Care and Rental Industry Council for Education (AIE)
TRICE........ Transistorized Real-Time Incremental Computer
TRICE........ Transistorized Real-Time Incremental Computer Expandable (IAA)
TRICH .... Trichinosis [*Gastroenterology*] (DAVI)
Trich .... Trichomonas [*A protozoan*] [*Medicine*]
Trich .... Trichoptera [*Entomology*]
Tri-Chro...... Trichromatic (DGA)
Trich V........ Trichomonas Vaginitis [*A parasite*] (DAVI)
TRICI .... Trichinopoli Cigar (DSUE)
TRICINE...... Tris(hydroxymethyl)methylglycine [*Biochemical analysis*]
TRICL......... Triclinic

TriCn.......... Tri-Continental Corp. [*Associated Press*] (SAG)
TriCnty....... Tri County Bancorp [*Associated Press*] (SAG)
TRICO........ Tri- [*or Triple*] Coincidence Navigation (IAA)
TriCoBn...... Trico Bancshares [*Commercial firm Associated Press*] (SAG)
TricoMr....... Trico Marine Services, Inc. [*Associated Press*] (SAG)
TRICOMS..... Triad Computer Systems (DOMA)
TriCon........ Tri-Continental Corp. [*Associated Press*] (SAG)
Tricord........ Tricord Systems, Inc. [*Associated Press*] (SAG)
TRICS .... Threat Reactive Integrated Combat System
TRICS .... Trajectory Incremental Correction System (MCD)
TRID .... Track Identity
TRID .... Trident Microsystems [*NASDAQ symbol*] (SAG)
TRID .... Triduum [*Three Days*] [*Latin*] (ADA)
TRIDAC ...... Three-Dimensional Analog Computer [*British*] (MCD)
TRIDECC...... Three (TRI) Dimensional Error Correcting Code (NITA)
TRIDENT...... South Atlantic Cooperative Investigation Phase [*Marine science*] (MSC)
TridentR...... Trident Rowan Group [*Associated Press*] (SAG)
Tridex......... Tridex Corp. [*Associated Press*] (SAG)
TridMic....... Trident Microsystems, Inc. [*Associated Press*] (SAG)
TRIDO......... Table Ronde Internationale pour le Developpement de l'Orientation [*International Round Table for the Advancement of Counselling - IRTAC*] (EAIO)
TRIDOP....... Tridoppler
Tri E of Cov... Trial of the Earl of Coventry [*A publication*] (DLA)
TRI-FED...... Triathlon Federation/USA (EA)
TRIFED/USA... Triathlon Federation/USA [*Later, TRI-FED*] (EA)
TRIFLATE..... Trifluoromethanesulfonate [*Organic chemistry*]
TRIFLIC....... Trifluoromethanesulfonic [*Organic chemistry*]
triFMA .... Time-Resolved Immunofluorometric Assay [*Clinical chemistry*]
trifr........... Triforium (VRA)
TRIG .... Triangulation (AABC)
TRIG .... Trigger (AAG)
trig............ Triglycerides [*Clinical chemistry*]
TRIG .... Trigonal [*Crystallography*]
trig............ Trigonometric (IDOE)
trig............ Trigonometry (IDOE)
TRIG .... Trigonometry
TRIGA .... Training Reactor, Isotopes General Atomic [*Nuclear energy*]
TRIGA .... Traitement Industrial des Gadoues [*French company*]
TRIGAT .... Third Generation Antitank [*Army*]
TrigenE ...... Trigen Energy Corp. [*Associated Press*] (SAG)
TRIGLYME .... Triethylene Glycol Dimethyl Ether [*Organic chemistry*]
TRIGON....... Trigonometry (ROG)
TRIGS .... TR-1 [*Aircraft*] Ground Station [*Air Force*] (DOMA)
TRII........... Transcrypt International, Inc. [*NASDAQ symbol*] (SAG)
TRIL.......... Tailored Requirements Items List (MCD)
Tri-Lite .... Tri-Lite, Inc. [*Associated Press*] (SAG)
TRIM.......... Agreement on Trade-Related Investment Measures
TRIM.......... Tailored Reliable Integrated Modular
TRIM.......... Tailored Retrieval and Information Management
TRIM.......... Target Radiant Intensity Measurement (MCD)
TRIM.......... Targets, Receivers, Impacts, and Methods
TRIM.......... Task Related Instructional Methodology (PDAA)
TRIM.......... Tax Reform Immediately (EA)
TRIM.......... Tax Reform Information Materials
TRIM.......... Technical Requirements Identification Matrix (MCD)
TRIM.......... Technique for Report and Index Management [*No longer available*] [*Information service or system*] (IID)
TRIM.......... Technique for Responsive Inventory Management (MHDB)
TRIM.......... Tele-Research Item Movement, Inc. [*Commercial firm*] (WDMC)
TRIM.......... Test Rules for Inventory Management
TRIM.......... Thin Region Integral Method
TRIM.......... Throw Away/Repair Implications on Maintenance
TRIM.......... Timely Responsive Integrated Multiuse System (MCD)
TRIM.......... Trails, Roads, and Interdiction Missions [*or Multisensor*] Program [*Navy*]
TRIM.......... Training Relation and Instruction Mission [*Vietnam, France, United States*] [*Military*]
TRIM.......... Training Requirements and Information Management System [*Navy*]
TRIM.......... Transfer Income Model [*Department of Health and Human Services*] (GFGA)
TRIM.......... Transformation of Imagery [*Computer science NASA*]
TRIM.......... Transport of Ions in Matter (AAEL)
TRIM.......... Tri-Mask Process (IAA)
TRIM.......... Trimmer [*Mining engineering*]
TRI-M .... Tri-M Music Honor Society [*Modern Music Masters Society*] [*Acronym is based on former name,*] (EA)
trim arh....... Triumphal Arch (VRA)
Trimark....... Trimark Holdings, Inc. [*Associated Press*] (SAG)
Trimas........ TriMas Corp. [*Associated Press*] (SAG)
Trimble....... Trimble Navigation Ltd. [*Associated Press*] (SAG)
Trimed........ Trimedyne, Inc. [*Associated Press*] (SAG)
TRIMET....... Trimethylolethane [*Organic chemistry*]
TRIMIS .... Tri-Service Medical Information Systems [*Military*]
TRIMM........ Triple Missile Mount (MCD)
TRIMMS ...... Telecom Canada Remote Interface Monitoring and Management System
TRIMMS ...... Total Refinement and Integration of Maintenance Management Systems [*Army*]
TRIMS .... Trade-Related Investment Measures [*International finance*] (ECON)
TRIMS .... Training Requirements and Information Management System (MCD)
TRIMS .... Transportation Integrated Management System [*Air Force*]
TRIN .... Trading Index [*Short term*] (MHDW)
TRIN .... Trans International Airlines

Trin............	Trinidad
TRIN............	Trinity
Trin............	Trinity Term [British Legal term] (DLA)
TRINCO........	Trincomalee [Sri Lanka port city] (DSUE)
TriNet.........	Trinet Corporate Realty Trust [Associated Press] (SAG)
Trinidad LR...	Trinidad Law Reports [A publication] (DLA)
Trinitech......	Trinitech Systems, Inc. [Associated Press] (SAG)
Trinity C......	Trinity College (GAGS)
TrinityIn......	Trinity Industries, Inc. [Associated Press] (SAG)
Trinity U......	Trinity University (GAGS)
Trinova........	Trinova Corp. [Associated Press] (SAG)
Trint T	Trinity Term [British Legal term] (DLA)
TRIO............	Transplant Recipients International Organization (EA)
Trion...........	Trion, Inc. [Associated Press] (SAG)
TRIOS..........	Thermionic Reactor for Installed Oceanic Service (KSC)
TrioTch........	Trio-Tech International [Associated Press] (SAG)
TRIP............	Agreement on Trade-Related Aspects of Intellectual Property Rights
Trip.............	All India Reporter, Tripura [A publication] (DLA)
TRIP............	[The] Road Information Program (EA)
TRIP............	Tartar Reliability Improvement Plan [Military]
TRIP............	Technical Reports Indexing Project (KSC)
TRIP............	Terrier/Tartar Reliability Improvement Program (SAA)
TRIP............	Test Requirement Implementation Plan (CAAL)
TRIP............	Thunderstorm Research International Project [Meteorology]
TRIP............	Total Replenishment Inventory Program (PDAA)
TRIP............	Toxic Release Inventory Program (GNE)
TRIP............	Trade-Related Aspects of Intellectual Property Right
TRIP............	Trajectory Integration Program (PDAA)
TRIP............	Transformation and Identification Program [Commercial & Industrial Development Bureau] [Software package] (NCC)
TRIP............	Transformation-Induced Plasticity [Steel]
TRIP............	Translating Research into Practice
TRIP............	Transport Infrastructure Programme [EDF]
TRIP............	Triangle Pacific [NASDAQ symbol] (TTSB)
TRIP............	Triangle Pacific Corp. [NASDAQ symbol] (SAG)
TRIP............	Triplicate (AABC)
Trip.............	Tripoli
Trip.............	Tripolitania [Libya] (BJA)
TRIP............	Truck Routing Improvement Program (IAA)
TriPacf........	Triangle Pacific Corp. [Associated Press] (SAG)
TRIPER........	Trident Planned Equipment Replacement (DNAB)
Tri per P......	Trials per Pais [A publication] (DLA)
TRIPI..........	Tactical Reconnaissance Information Processing and Interpretation (SAA)
Tripl...........	Triplicate (WGA)
Triple-A.......	Adult Alternative Album [Radio stations]
TripleP........	Triple P [Associated Press] (SAG)
TripleS........	Triple S Plastics Co. [Associated Press] (SAG)
TRipLII........	Lauderdale County Hospital, Ripley, TN [Library symbol Library of Congress] (LCLS)
TRIPLTEE.....	True Temperature Tunnel [Acronym pronounced, "Triple T"]
TRIPOD........	Tactical Reconstruction Information Pod [Navy] (ANA)
TRIPOD........	Transit Injector Polaris Derived (AAG)
TRIPOLD.......	Transit Injector Polaris Derived
TriPolyta......	Tri Polyta Indonesia [Associated Press] (SAG)
Tripos.........	Tripos, Inc. [Associated Press] (SAG)
Tripp..........	Tripp's Reports [5, 6 Dakota] [A publication] (DLA)
TRIPQUIC	Toxic Release Inventory Quick Analysis Tool Kit [Environmental Protection Agency] (AEPA)
TRIPREC......	Triplet Recall [Neuropsychology test]
TRIPS	TALON Reporting and Information Processing System (NITA)
TRIPS	Trade-Related Intellectual Property (ECON)
TRIPS	Transformation-Induced Plasticity (Steel)
TRIPS	Transportation Intelligent Planning System [MTMC] (TAG)
TRIPS	Transportation Planning Suite [MVA Systematica] [Software package] (NCC)
TRIPS	Travel Information Processing System (NITA)
TRIPS	Triplets [Slang] (DSUE)
Triquint.......	Triquint Semiconductor, Inc. [Associated Press] (SAG)
TRIR...........	Time-Resolved Infrared [Spectroscopy]
TRIREFFAC...	Trident Refit Facility (DNAB)
TRIS...........	Target Radiant Spectral Intensity Measurements from a Spin-Stabilized Vehicle (SAA)
TRIS...........	Toxic Release Inventory System [Environmental Protection Agency]
TRIS...........	Tracking RADAR Instrumentation Ship (SAA)
TRIS...........	Transmit-Receive Image System (DNAB)
TRIS...........	Transportation Research Information Services [National Academy of Sciences] [Bibliographic database] [Washington, DC]
Tris	Tris(2,3-dibromopropyl)phosphate [Also, TDBP, TDBPP, Tris-BP] [Flame retardant, mutagen]
TRIS...........	Tris(hydroxymethyl)aminomethane [Also, THAM] [Biochemical analysis]
TrIs	Trito-Isaiah (BJA)
TRI-SACH	Tri-State Automated Clearing House Association (MHDB)
TRISAFE	Triple Redundancy Incorporating Self-Adaptive Failure Exclusion (MCD)
TRISAT	Target Recognition through Integral Spectrum Analysis Techniques (MCD)
Tris-BP	Tris(2,3-dibromopropyl)phosphate [Also, TDBP, TDBPP, Tris] [Flame retardant, mutagen]
TRISECT	Total Reconnaissance Intelligence System Evaluation and Comparison Technique (MCD)
Trism..........	Trism, Inc. [Associated Press] (SAG)
TRISM	Tri-State Motor Transit Co. (EFIS)
TRISNET	Transportation Research Information Services Network [Department of Transportation] [Library network]
Tris Pr Pr....	Tristram's Probate Practice [25th ed.] [1978] [A publication] (DLA)
TRISS	Tactical Reconnaissance Intelligence Support Squadron
Trist...........	Supplement to 4 Swabey and Tristram's Probate and Divorce Reports [England] [A publication] (DLA)
TRIST..........	Traveling Image Storage Tube (MCD)
Trist...........	Tristram's Consistory Judgments [England] [A publication] (DLA)
TRISTAN	Terridic Reactor Isotope Separator To Analze Nuclides [Brookhaven National Laboratory]
Tristar.........	Tristar Corp. [Associated Press] (SAG)
Tristram......	Tristram's Consistory Judgments [1872-90] [A publication] (DLA)
Tristram......	Tristram's Probate Practice [25th ed.] [1978] [A publication] (DLA)
Tristram......	Tristram's Supplement to 4 Swabey and Tristram [A publication] (DLA)
TRISYLL	Trisyllable (ROG)
TRIT............	Triiodothyronine [Endocrinology] (MAE)
TRIT............	Tritura [Triturate] [Pharmacy]
TRITAC	DIFAR Triangular Tactic (NVT)
TRITAC	Tri-Service Tactical Communications System [DoD]
TRITAC	Triservice Tactical Switch
TRITB	Tasmanian Retail Industry Training Board [Australia]
TRITB	Tasmanian Rural Industry Training Board [Australia]
TRITC	Tetramethyl Rhodamine Isothiocyanate [Organic chemistry]
TriTeal	TriTeal Corp. [Associated Press] (SAG)
TritEng........	Triton Energy Corp. [Associated Press] (SAG)
TRITET	Triode-Tetrode (IAA)
Triton..........	Triton Group Ltd. [Associated Press] (SAG)
TRITRAFAC...	Trident Training Facility (DNAB)
TRIUMF	Tri-University-Meson Facility [Nuclear research facility at the University of British Columbia]
TRIUN..........	Department of Trusteeship and Information from Non-Self-Governing Territories ofthe United Nations
TRI-US........	Toxic Release Inventory User Support [Environmental Protection Agency] (AEPA)
TRIW...........	Trinity Biotech [NASDAQ symbol] (SAG)
TRIWF	Trinity Biotech plc Wrrt'A' [NASDAQ symbol] (TTSB)
TRIX...........	Total Rate Imaging with X-Rays
TRIX...........	Transcom International Ltd. [NASDAQ symbol] (SAG)
TRIXIE	Transistor and Nixie Tube (IAA)
TRIZ...........	Trinity Biotech [NASDAQ symbol] (SAG)
TrizecH........	Trizec Hahn Corp. [Associated Press] (SAG)
TrizecHhn.....	Trizec Hahn Corp. [Associated Press] (SAG)
TRIZF	Trinity Biotech plc Wrrt'B' [NASDAQ symbol] (TTSB)
TRJ.............	AJT Air International [Russian Federation] [ICAO designator] (FAAC)
TRJ.............	Tarija [Bolivia] [Seismograph station code, US Geological Survey] (SEIS)
TRJ.............	Thermocouple Reference Junction
TRJ.............	Towards Racial Justice [British]
TRJ.............	United States Army TRADOC, Fort Jackson, Fort Jackson, SC [OCLC symbol] (OCLC)
Tr Judge J....	Trial Judges' Journal [A publication] (DLA)
TRK............	Air Truck [Spain ICAO designator] (FAAC)
TRK............	Roche Products Ltd. [Great Britain] [Research code symbol]
TRK............	Speedway Motorsports [NYSE symbol] (TTSB)
TRK............	Speedway Motorsports, Inc. [NYSE symbol] (SAG)
TRK............	Tank Range-Finder Kit
TRK............	Tarakan [Indonesia] [Airport symbol] (OAG)
TRK............	Track (AAG)
TRK............	Transketolase [An enzyme] (MAE)
TRK............	Truck (AAG)
TRK............	Truckee, CA [Location identifier FAA] (FAAL)
TRK............	Trunk (AAG)
TRK............	United States Army TRADOC, Fort Knox, Library Service Center, RSL Section, Fort Knox, KY [OCLC symbol] (OCLC)
TRKA	Trak Auto [NASDAQ symbol] (TTSB)
TRKA	Trak-Auto Corp. [NASDAQ symbol] (NQ)
TRKD..........	Tracked
TRKDR.........	Truck-Drawn
TRKG	Tracking (AAG)
TrKH	Die Transkriptionen des Hieronymus in Seinem Kommentarwerken [A publication] (BJA)
TRKHD........	Truck Head
TRKMTD	Truck-Mounted (AABC)
TRKR..........	Tracker
TRKS	Track [Commonly used] (OPSA)
TRKWHL.......	Trick Wheel
TRL............	Tariff Reform League [British] (ROG)
TRL............	Terrell, TX [Location identifier FAA] (FAAL)
TRL............	Test Readiness List [NASA] (NASA)
TRL............	Thermodynamics Research Laboratory [National Institute of Standards and Technology] (MCD)
TRL............	Time Recovery Loop [Navy Navigation Satellite System] (DNAB)
TRL............	Tool Room Lathe
TRL............	Total Renal Care Hldgs [NYSE symbol] (TTSB)
TRL............	Total Renal Care Holdings, Inc. [NYSE symbol] (SAG)
TRL............	Trading Law [British]
TRL............	Trail (MCD)
Trl.............	Trail (TBD)
TRL............	Training Research Laboratory [Army Research Institute for the Behavioral and Social Sciences] (RDA)
TRL............	Transistor Resistor Logic
trl.............	Translator [MARC relator code] [Library of Congress] (LCCP)
TrL.............	Transmitted Light [Microscopy]
TRL............	Transportation Research Laboratory

TRL.............	Transuranium Research Laboratory [*AEC*]
TRL.............	Trax Petroleums [*Vancouver Stock Exchange symbol*]
TRL.............	Trial (ROG)
TRL.............	Trillo [*Trill*] [*Music*] (ROG)
TRL.............	Trunk Register Link [*Telecommunications*] (TEL)
TRL.............	United States Department of Transportation, Library, Washington, DC [*OCLC symbol*] (OCLC)
TRLA............	Textile Rental and Laundry Association [*Australia*]
Trla.............	Triola [*Record label*] [*Finland*]
TRLA............	Truck Renting and Leasing Association (EA)
TRLA(NSW)...	Textile Rental and Laundry Association of New South Wales [*Australia*]
TRLA(Q)......	Textile Rental and Laundry Association (Queensland) [*Australia*]
TRLA(V).......	Textile Rental and Laundry Association (Victoria) [*Australia*]
TRLAWA	Textile Rental and Laundry Association of Western Australia
TRLB...........	Temporarily Replaced by Lighted Buoy Showing Same Characteristic [*Maps and charts*]
TRLFSW	Tactical Range Landing Force Support Weapon
TRLN	Triangle Research Library Network (COE)
TRLP...........	Transport Landplane [*Navy*]
TRLR	Trailer
Tr LR	Trinidad Law Reports [*A publication*] (DLA)
TRLS...........	Trail [*Commonly used*] (OPSA)
TRLSC	Time-Resolved Liquid Scintillation Counting [*Analytical procedure*]
TR-LSC	Time-Resolved Liquid Scintillation Counting [*Instrumentation*]
TRLU	TISEO RADAR Logic Unit [*Air Force*] (MCD)
TRLVL.........	Transition Level [*Aviation*] (FAAC)
TRLY...........	Trolley
TRM............	Task Response Module [*Office furniture*]
TRM............	Tay River Petroleum [*Vancouver Stock Exchange symbol*]
TRM............	TCW/DW Term Trust 2002 [*NYSE symbol*] (SPSG)
TRM............	Technical Reference Model [*Army*] (RDA)
TRM............	Terminal Response Monitor
TRM............	Test Request Message [*Computer science*]
TRM............	Test Requirements Manual
TRM............	Test Responsibility Matrix (MCD)
TRM............	Theater Rates Model [*Military*]
TRM............	Thermal, CA [*Location identifier FAA*] (FAAL)
TRM............	Thermal Remanent Magnetization [*Geophysics*] (IEEE)
TRM............	Thermal Resistance Measurement
TRM............	Thermoremanence
TRM............	Thermoremanent Magnetism [*or Magnetization*]
TRM............	Thickness Readout Module
TRM............	Thomason, Richland, and Martens [*Air-charter business*]
TrM.............	Three R Microfilm Service, Record Retention & Retrieval Corp., Lynbrook, NY [*Library symbol*] [*Library of Congress*] (LCLS)
TRM............	Time Ratio Modulation
TRM............	Time Release Mechanism [*Martin-Baker seat system*] [*Aviation*] (NG)
TRM............	Time-Reversal Mirrors [*For acoustic study*]
TRM............	Totally Reflective Mirror
TrM.............	Track Magnetic [*Aviation*] (DA)
TRM............	TRADOC Resources Management (MCD)
TRM............	TRADOC [*Training and Doctrine Command*] Review of Manpower
TRM............	Transports Aeriens Mediterraneens [*France ICAO designator*] (FAAC)
TRM............	Trial Run Model (SAA)
TRM............	Turner [*Maine*] [*Seismograph station code, US Geological Survey*] (SEIS)
TRM............	United States Army TRADOC, Fort Monroe Post Library and Headquarters Technical Library, Fort Monroe, VA [*OCLC symbol*] (OCLC)
TRMAP	Theater Rate Mapping Data File [*Military*]
TRMB..........	Trimble Navigation Ltd. [*NASDAQ symbol*] (SAG)
TRMC..........	Tetramethylrhodamino-Isothiocyanate [*Organic chemistry*] (MAH)
TRMC..........	Time-Resolved Microwave Conductivity [*Physical chemistry*]
TRMCpy	TRM Copy Centers Corp. [*Associated Press*] (SAG)
TRMD..........	Trimmed
TRME..........	Theater Readiness Monitoring Equipment (MCD)
TRMF..........	Test Report Management Forms (MCD)
TRMF..........	Theater Readiness Monitoring Facility [*Missile testing*]
TRMF..........	Theodore Roethke Memorial Foundation (EA)
Trmfrd	Tramford International Ltd. [*Associated Press*] (SAG)
TRMG..........	Tread Rubber and Tire Repair Materials Manufacturers Group (NTPA)
TRMG	Tread Rubber Manufacturers Group (EA)
TRMG	Trimming
TRMI..........	Tubular Rivet and Machine Institute (EA)
TRMK..........	Trustmark Corp. [*NASDAQ symbol*] (SPSG)
TRML..........	Target Reference Material List [*Air Force*]
TRML..........	Terminal (AFM)
TRML..........	Tropical Research Medical Laboratory [*Army*]
TRMM.........	TRM Copy Centers [*NASDAQ symbol*] (TTSB)
TRMM.........	TRM Copy Centers Corp. [*NASDAQ symbol*] (SPSG)
TRMM.........	Tropical Rainfall Measurement Mission [*NASA*] [*Marine science*] (OSRA)
TRMM.........	Tropical Rainfall Measuring Mission [*Proposed satellite*]
TrMMex	Transportacion Maritima Mexicana [*Associated Press*] (SAG)
TRMNL........	Terminal
TRMPS	Temperature Regualtor and Missile Power Supply (IAA)
TRMR	Trimmer [*Mining engineering*]
TRMS..........	Technical Requirements Management System
TRMS..........	Test Resource Management System [*TECOM*] (RDA)
TRMS..........	Time-Resolved Mass Spectrometry (DB)
TRMS..........	Transmission Resource Management System [*Australia*]
TRMS..........	True Root Mean Square [*Statistics*]
TRM-SMX	Trimethoprim-Sulfamethoxazole [*Medicine*] (DMAA)
TRMT..........	Termite
TRMT..........	Treatment (AFM)
TRN	OCLC [*Online Computer Library Center*] Training Symbol, Columbus, OH [*OCLC symbol*] (OCLC)
TR(N)...........	Registered Technologist (Nuclear) (DAVI)
TRN	Technical Research Note (IEEE)
TRN	Tectoreticular Neuron [*Neurology*]
TRN	Temporary Record Number
TRN	Teriton Resources Ltd. [*Vancouver Stock Exchange symbol*]
TRN	Theron Airways [*South Africa ICAO designator*] (FAAC)
TRN	Thomson Regional Newspapers [*The Thomson Corp.*] [*Publishing*]
trn.............	Threaded ReadNews [*Computer science*] (IGQR)
TRN	Three-Axis Rotational Control-Normal (SAA)
TRN	Track Reference Number (IAA)
TRN	Trade Name (MSA)
TRN	Trainee
TRN	Transfer (DEN)
TRN	Transformation Research Network [*Canada Research center*] (RCD)
TRN	Translation (IAA)
TRN	Transmit (BUR)
TRN	Trinidad [*Trinidad-Tobago*] [*Seismograph station code, US Geological Survey*] (SEIS)
TRN	Trinity Indus [*NYSE symbol*] (TTSB)
TRN	Trinity Industries, Inc. [*NYSE symbol*] (SPSG)
TRN	Trunnion (NASA)
TRN	Turin [*Italy*] [*Airport symbol*] (OAG)
tRNA	Ribonucleic Acid, Transfer [*Replaces sRNA*] [*Biochemistry, genetics*]
TRNA	Topolino Register of North America (EA)
tRNA	Transfer Ribonucleic Acid (CPH)
TrnAsia	Transmedia Asia Pacific, Inc. [*Associated Press*] (SAG)
TrnatH	Transatlantic Holdings [*Associated Press*] (SAG)
TrnB...........	Trinity Biotech [*Associated Press*] (SAG)
TrnBi..........	Trinity Biotech [*Associated Press*] (SAG)
TrnBio	Trinity Biotech [*Associated Press*] (SAG)
TRNBKL	Turnbuckle [*Aerospace*] (AAG)
TRNC..........	Turkish Republic of North Cyprus (BARN)
TRNCAP......	Training Capability [*Military*]
TRN CRD	Turn Coordination (MSA)
TRND	Trend-Lines'A'Inc. [*NASDAQ symbol*] (TTSB)
TRND	Trend-Lines, Inc. [*NASDAQ symbol*] (SAG)
TRND	Turned (MSA)
TrnDE..........	Transamerica Delaware Ltd. [*Associated Press*] (SAG)
TRNE	Trainee (AABC)
TRNFR	Transfer (KSC)
TRNG	Training
Trng...........	Training (TBD)
TRNGL	Triangle (MSA)
TrnGlb	Trans Global Services, Inc. [*Associated Press*] (SAG)
TrnGlbR	Trans-Global Resources NL [*Associated Press*] (SAG)
TRNGR	Turning Gear
TRNGRS	Training Readiness Squadron
TRNI	Trans-Industries, Inc. [*NASDAQ symbol*] (NQ)
TrnLsg	Trans Leasing International, Inc. [*Associated Press*] (SAG)
TrnmdEu......	Transmedia Europe, Inc. [*Associated Press*] (SAG)
Trnmedia	Transmedia Network, Inc. [*Associated Press*] (SAG)
TrnNtw	Transaction Network Services [*Associated Press*] (SAG)
TRNPK	Turnpike [*Commonly used*] (OPSA)
TRNPS	Transpose (MSA)
TRNR	Touche Remnant Natural Resources [*Investment fund*] [*British*]
TRNR	Trainer (AAG)
TrnReCp	Transnational Re Corp. [*Associated Press*] (SAG)
TRNS	Terrain-Referenced Navigation System [*Navy*]
TRNS	Transition (AABC)
TRNS	Transmation, Inc. [*NASDAQ symbol*] (NQ)
TrnsEn	Trans Energy, Inc. [*Associated Press*] (SAG)
TrnsFin	Trans Financial, Inc. [*Associated Press*] (SAG)
TRNSFR	Transfer
TrnsglbE	Transglobe Energy Corp. [*Associated Press*] (SAG)
TrnsGlbl	Trans Global Services, Inc. [*Associated Press*] (SAG)
Trnskry	Transkaryotic Therapies, Inc. [*Associated Press*] (SAG)
TrnsLx	Trans-Lux Corp. [*Associated Press*] (SAG)
Trnsm.........	Transamerica Corp. [*Associated Press*] (SAG)
Trnsmt	Transmation, Inc. [*Associated Press*] (SAG)
TRNSMT	Transmitter
TRNSN	Transition (MSA)
Trnsnt	TransNet Corp. [*Associated Press*] (SAG)
TRNSP	Transport [*or Transportation*] (AFM)
TrnspAm	Transport Corp. of America, Inc. [*Associated Press*] (SAG)
TRNSPF	Transportation Flight [*Military*]
TRNSPLF	Transportation Liaison Flight [*Military*]
TRNSPN......	Transportation (KSC)
TRNSPOPS...	Transportation Operations Squadron
TRNSPR	Transporter (KSC)
Trnspro	Transpro, Inc. [*Associated Press*] (SAG)
TRNSPRT.....	Transport
TRNSPRTN...	Transport
TRNSPS	Transportation Squadron
TrnsRty	Transcontinental Realty Investors [*Associated Press*] (SAG)
TrnsTec	TransTechnology Corp. [*Associated Press*] (SAG)
TrnsWst	TransAmerican Waste Industries, Inc. [*Associated Press*] (SAG)
TrnsWste	TransAmerican Waste Industries [*Associated Press*] (SAG)
TrnSwtc	TranSwitch Corp. [*Associated Press*] (SAG)
TrnSyA........	Transaction System Architects, Inc. [*Associated Press*] (SAG)
TRNT	TransNet [*NASDAQ symbol*] (TTSB)
TRNT	TransNet Corp. [*NASDAQ symbol*] (NQ)

TRNTBL	Turntable (MSA)
TRNTY	Trinity
Trnwck	Trenwick Group, Inc. [Associated Press] (SAG)
TrnWEnt	Trans World Entertainment Corp. [Associated Press] (SAG)
TR (NY)	Caines' Term Reports [New York] [A publication] (DLA)
Trnzn	Tranzonic Cos. [Associated Press] (SAG)
TRO	Air Molokai-Tropic Airlines [ICAO designator] (FAAC)
TRO	Taree [Australia Airport symbol] (OAG)
TRO	Tarron Industry [Vancouver Stock Exchange symbol]
TRO	Tax Reduction Option
TRO	Technical Records Office [or Officer] [British]
TRO	Technical Reviewing Office (AFM)
TRO	Temporary Restraining Order
TRO	Terminal Release Order [Military] (AFIT)
TRO	Test Requirements Outline
TRO	Traffic Regulation Order (WDAA)
TRO	Transportation Officer
TRO	Trip Reduction Ordinance [MOCD] (TAG)
Tro	Troades [of Euripides] [Classical studies] (OCD)
Tro	Troilus and Cressida [Shakespearean work]
TRO	Tromsoe [Norway] [Seismograph station code, US Geological Survey] (SEIS)
TRO	Tropical [Broadcasting antenna]
TRO	Truck Route Order [Army] (AABC)
TRO	United States Army TRADOC, Fort Sill Post Library, Fort Sill, OK [OCLC symbol] (OCLC)
TROA	[The] Retired Officers Association (EA)
TROA	Thoroughbred Racehorse Owners' Association [Australia]
TROC	Tritium Removal with Organic Compound [Nuclear energy]
TROC	Trocadero [London] (DSUE)
TROC	Trochiscus [Lozenge] [Pharmacy] (ROG)
TROC	Trouble Reporting Operations Center [Federal Telecommunications System] (GFGA)
TROCA	Tangible Reinforcement Operant Conditioning Audiometry
TROCH	Troche [Lozenge] [Pharmacy] (DAVI)
TROCH	Trochiscus [Lozenge] [Pharmacy]
TRODI	Touchdown Rate of Descent Indicator [Aviation]
TROF	Trough [Meteorology] (FAAC)
TROFF	Typesetting Run Off (DGA)
TROICA	Trans-Siberian Investigation of the Chemistry of the Atmosphere
TROL	Tapeless Rotorless On-Line Cryptographic Equipment (NATG)
Trol	Troland [Unit of light intensity at the retina]
TROLAMINE	Triethanolamine [USAN] [Organic chemistry]
TROLL	Time-Shared Reactive On-Line Laboratory [Computer science] (MHDI)
TRO Lrn	TRO Learning, Inc. [Associated Press] (SAG)
TROM	Trombone
TROMB	Tromba [Trumpet] [Music] (ROG)
TROMB	Trombone
TROMEX	Tropical Oceanographic and Meteorological Experiment [National Science Foundation]
TROMP	Testable Read Only Memory Programmed [Computer science] (DGA)
TROMP	Trompette [Trumpets] [Music]
TRON	[The] Real-Time Operating System Nucleus [Computer science] (PCM)
TRON	Trion, Inc. [NASDAQ symbol] (NQ)
TROO	Transponder On-Off
TROP	Tropical
Trop	Tropical Agriculture [A publication]
TROP	Tropopause [Meteorology] (FAAC)
TROPAG	Tropical Agriculture [Royal Tropical Institute] [Bibliographic database] [Netherlands]
TROPARC	Center for Tropical and Subtropical Architecture Planning and Construction [University of Florida] [Research center] (RCD)
TROP CAN	Tropic of Cancer (WDAA)
TROP CAP	Tropic of Capricorn (WDAA)
TROPEX	Tropical Experiment [Proposed by BOMEX]
Trop F H	Tropical Fish Hobbyist [A publication]
TROPH	Trophy
TROPIC HEAT	Tropical Pacific Upper Ocean Heat and Mass Budgets [USA] [Marine science] (OSRA)
TROPICS	Tour Operators Integrated Computer System [Airline ticket system]
TROPM	Tropical Man [Leiden] [A publication]
TROPMED	Regional Project for Tropical Medicine and Public Health [SEAMEO] [Thailand] [Research center] (IRC)
TropMed	Tropical Medicine (DAVI)
TROPO	Tropospheric
TROPRAN	Tropical Regional Analysis [National Weather Service]
TROS	Tape Resident Operating System [Computer science] (IEEE)
TROS	Time-Sharing Real-Time Operating System (IAA)
TROS	Transducer Read Only Storage (IAA)
TROS	Transformer Read Only Storage
TROSCOM	Troop Support Command [Formerly, MECOM] [St. Louis, MO] [Army]
TROT	Trail Riders of Today (EA)
TROTTS	Theater Realignment of Traffic Transportation Support (MCD)
Troub & H Prac	Troubat and Haly's Pennsylvania Practice [A publication] (DLA)
Troub Lim Partn	Troubat on Limited Partnership [A publication] (DLA)
TROV	Telepresence-Controlled Remotely-Operated Vehicle [NASA]
TROV	Tethered Remotely Operational Vehicle [Marine science] (MSC)
TROV	Turnip Rosette Virus [Plant pathology]
TROW	T.Rowe Price Assoc [NASDAQ symbol] (TTSB)
TROW	T. Rowe Price Associates, Inc. [Baltimore, MD] [NASDAQ symbol] (NQ)
Trow D & Cr	Trower's Debtor and Creditor [1860] [A publication] (DLA)

Trow Eq	Trower's Manual of the Prevalance of Equity [1876] [A publication] (DLA)
TroyHill	Troy Hill Bancorp, Inc. [Associated Press] (SAG)
Troy St U	Troy State University (GAGS)
Troy St U (Dorhan)	Troy State University at Dorhan (GAGS)
TRP	Maryland State Police [FAA designator] (FAAC)
TRP	Table of Replaceable Parts
TRP	Tamper Resistant Packaging [Food and Drug Administration]
TRP	Tangible Research Property [Business]
TRP	Target Rating Point [Television] (WDMC)
TRP	Target Reference Point (AABC)
TRP	Target Reporting Parameters (MCD)
TRP	Technical Report
TRP	Technical Requirements Package (MCD)
TRP	Technology Reinvestment Project [for converting military to civilian applications]
TRP	Television Remote Pickup
TRP	Terminal Rendezvous Phase
TRP	Threat Recognition Processor [Navy] (MCD)
TRP	Threat Recognizer Programmer
TRP	Thunderstorm Research Project [Environmental Science Services Administration]
TRP	Timber Rights Purchase
TRP	Time-Resolved Phosphorimetry [Analytical chemistry]
TRP	Time to Repair Part
TRP	Timing Release Pin
TRP	Total Refractory Period (MAE)
TRP	Trade Pattern (MSA)
TRP	Traffic Regulation Point [Military]
TRP	Trainable Retractable Propeller
TRP	Training Review Panel (CAAL)
TRP	TransCanada Pipeline Ltd. [NYSE symbol Toronto Stock Exchange symbol Vancouver Stock Exchange symbol] (SPSG)
TRP	TransCanada P.L. [NYSE symbol] (TTSB)
TrP	Transpatent [German] (DLA)
TRP	Tree Point, AK [Location identifier FAA] (FAAL)
TRP	Trichorhinophalangeal [Syndrome] (DAVI)
TRP	Tricommand Review Panel [Military] (AFIT)
TRP	Tripped
TRP	Troop (AFM)
TRP	Tropical (WGA)
TRP	Trujillo [Peru] [Seismograph station code, US Geological Survey] (SEIS)
Trp	Tryptophan [Also, W] [An amino acid]
trp	Tryptophan [An amino acid] (DOG)
TRP	Tubular Reabsorption [or Resorption] of Phosphate
TRPA	Tryptophan-Rich Prealbumin [Biochemistry]
TrpAG97	Triple A Government Series 1997, Inc. [Associated Press] (SAG)
TRPB	Thoroughbred Racing Protective Bureau (EA)
TRPC	Triple Phosphate (DAVI)
TRPCAR	Troop Carrier [Military] (CINC)
TRPCAR(M)	Troop Carrier (Medium) (CINC)
TRPCD	Tropical Continental [Meteorology] (FAAC)
TRPCD	Tropical Continental Air Mass [Meteorology] (FAAC)
TRPCL	Tropical [Meteorology] (FAAC)
TRPCSq	Troop Carrier Squadron [Air Force]
TRPF	Tax Resisters' Penalty Fund (EA)
TRPGDA	Tripropylene Glycol Diacrylate [Organic chemistry]
TRPH	Total Recoverable Petroleum Hydrocarbon
TRPI	Training Requirement Priority Index
TRPK	Turnpike [Commonly used] (OPSA)
TRPL	Terneplate [Materials]
TRPL	Triple
trpl	Triplicate (WDMC)
TRPLYR	Trapping Layer [Meteorology] (FAAC)
TRPM	Plymouth/Blackburne [Montserrat Island] [ICAO location identifier] (ICLI)
Trp-mRNA	Ribonucleic Acid, Messenger - Tryptophan Constitutive [Biochemistry, genetics]
TRPN	Transportation
TRPO	Track Reference Printout
TRPO	Trialkylphosphine Oxide [Organic chemistry]
TRPO	Truck and Recreation Products Office
TRPR	Trooper
TRPS	Temperature Regulating Power Supply
TRPS	Trichorhinophalangeal Syndrome (DAVI)
TRPS	Tripos, Inc. [NASDAQ symbol] (SAG)
TRPS	Troops
TRPSC	Triple Screw
TRPSK	Transmitted Reference Phase Shift Keying [Computer science] (IAA)
TRPT	Theoretical Renal Phosphorus Threshold [Medicine] (MAE)
TRPT	Time to Reach Peak Tension
TRQ	Tarauaca [Brazil] [Airport symbol] (AD)
TRQ	Task Ready Queue
TRQ	Torque (AAG)
TRQ	Total Requirements (AAG)
TRQ	United States Army TRADOC, Fort Ord, CDEC Library, Fort Ord, CA [OCLC symbol] (OCLC)
TRR	[The] Research Ranch [An association] (EA)
TRR	Tactical Range Recorder [Navy]
TRR	Tactical Reaction Reconnaissance
TRR	Taiwan Research Reactor
TRR	Take Real Result [Computer science] (IAA)
TRR	Tape Read Register
TRR	Target Ranging RADAR

TRR	Tarraleah [*Tasmania*] [*Seismograph station code, US Geological Survey*] (SEIS)
TRR	Teaching and Research Reactor
TRR	Technical Report Request
TRR	Technical Requirements Review (MCD)
TRR	Technical Risk Reduction [*Military*]
TRR	Test and Research Reactor [*Nuclear energy*] (NRCH)
TRR	Test Readiness Review [*NASA*] (NASA)
TRR	Tethered RADAR Reflector
TRR	Thailand Research Reactor
TRR	Theoretical Research Report
TRR	Thioredoxin Reductase [*An enzyme*]
TRR	Topical Report Request [*or Review*] [*Nuclear energy*] (NRCH)
TRR	Trade Regulation Reporter [*A publication*] (DLA)
TRR	Trade Regulation Rule (MHDW)
TRR	Trader Resource Corp. [*Toronto Stock Exchange symbol*]
TRR	Tramson Ltd. [*Sudan*] [*ICAO designator*] (FAAC)
TRR	Transfer Relay Rack (CAAL)
TRR	Transmitted-Reflected-Reflected [*Wave mechanics*]
TRR	TRC Cos. [*NYSE symbol*] (TTSB)
TRR	TRC Cos., Inc. [*NYSE symbol*] (SPSG)
TRR	Trincomalee [*Ceylon*] [*Airport symbol*] (AD)
TRR	Trouble Recorder (IAA)
TRR	True Rate of Return [*Finance*] (ADA)
TRR	United States Army TRADOC, Fort Rucker Post Library and Aviation School Library, Fort Rucker, AL [*OCLC symbol*] (OCLC)
TRRA	Terminal Railroad Association of St. Louis [*AAR code*]
TRRA	Tilt Rotor Research Aircraft
TRRA H & TS...	Terminal Railroad Association Historical and Technical Society (EA)
TRRAPS	Transportable Reliable Acoustic Path Sonobuoy (NVT)
TRRB	Test Readiness Review Board [*NASA*]
TRRC	Test Resources Review Committee [*DoD*]
TRRC	Textile Resource and Research Center (EA)
TRRF	[*The*] Refrigeration Research Foundation (EA)
TRRF	Training Review File [*IRS*]
TRRG	Tax Reform Research Group [*Defunct*] (EA)
TRRL	Tooling Rejection and Rework Laboratory
TRRL	Transport and Road Research Laboratory [*Departments of the Environment and Transport*] [*Information service or system*] (IID)
TRRN	Terrain (FAAC)
TRR of ST L...	Terminal Railroad Association of St. Louis
TRRR	Trilateral Range and Range Rate System
TRRT	Test Results Review Team [*Nuclear energy*] (NRCH)
TRRT	Tooling Rejection and Rework Tag
TRS	Tactical RADAR System
TRS	Tactical Radio Set
TRS	Tactical Reconnaissance Squadron [*Air Force*]
TRS	Tactical Reconnaissance System
TRS	Tandy Radio Shack (NITA)
TRS	Tape Recorder Subsystem
TRS	Target Range Servo
TRS	Technical Repair Standards
TRS	Technical Requirements Specification (MCD)
TRS	Technical Research Ship
TRS	Telecommunications Relay Service [*Hearing-impaired technology*]
TRS	Teleoperator Retrieval System [*NASA*]
TRS	Telephone Repeater Station (IAA)
TRS	Terrestrial Radio System
TRS	Testa Rossa Sport
TRS	Test Reference System
TRS	Test Requirement Specification (MCD)
TRS	Test Requirements Summary (MUGU)
TRS	Test Research Service [*Defunct*] (EA)
TRS	Test Research Station
TRS	Test Response Spectrum (IEEE)
TRS	Tetrahedral Research Satellite
TRS	Textes Religieux Sumeriens du Louvre [*A publication*] (BJA)
TRS	Text Retrieval Systems [*Computer science*]
TRS	Theatre Recording Society (EA)
TRS	Thermal Radiation Simulator
TRS	Thermal Reactor Safety [*Nuclear energy*] (NRCH)
TRS	Thermal Residue Stress (MCD)
TRS	Third Readiness State (AAG)
TRS	Threat Reaction System
TRS	Ticket Reservation Systems, Inc.
TRS	Time Reference System (MCD)
TRS	Time-Resolved Spectrometry
TRS	Time-Reversal Symmetry [*Solid state physics*]
TRS	Toll Room Switch [*Telecommunications*] (TEL)
TRS	Top Right Side (MCD)
TRS	Torry Research Station [*British*]
TRS	Total Reduced Sulfur [*Environmental chemistry*]
TRS	Total Reducing Sugars [*Food science*]
TRS	Tough Rubber-Sheathed [*Cable*] (DEN)
TRS	Traceability and Reporting System
TRS	Track and Store [*Computer science*] (IAA)
TRS	Trade Registration System [*British*] (NUMA)
TRS	Training Reservation System (MCD)
TRS	Transfer (ADA)
TRS	Transitional Support [*Telecommunications*] (OTD)
TRS	Transmission-Regulated Spark [*Automotive engineering*]
TRS	Transmit-Receive Switch (IAA)
TRS	Transmitter (IAA)
TRS	Transportable Relay Station
TRS	Transport International Aerien [*Belgium ICAO designator*] (FAAC)
TRS	Transpose (ROG)
trs	Transpose [*Printing*] (WA)
TRS	Transverse Rupture Strength [*Metallurgy*]
TRS	Traumatic Surgery [*Medical specialty*] (DHSM)
TRS	Travel Related Services Co., Inc.
TRS	Treasure Island Resources [*Vancouver Stock Exchange symbol*]
TRS	Tree-Ring Society (EA)
TRS	Trieste [*Italy*] [*Seismograph station code, US Geological Survey Closed*] (SEIS)
TRS	Trieste [*Italy*] [*Airport symbol*] (OAG)
TRS	Tropical Rainforest Society [*Australia*]
TRS	Tropical Revolving Storm [*Meteorology*]
TRS	Troubleshooting Record Sheet [*NASA*] (NASA)
TRS	Truss [*Shipping*]
TRS	Trustees
TRS	Tuberculosis Record System [*Medicine*] (DB)
TRS	Tuboreticular Structure [*Cytology*]
TRS	Tug Rotational System [*NASA*] (NASA)
TRS	Twin Ridge Substrate [*NITA*]
TRS	United States Department of Transportation, Transportation System Center, Cambridge, MA [*OCLC symbol*] (OCLC)
TRSA	Tax Reduction and Simplification Act of 1977
TRSA	Terminal RADAR Service Area [*Aviation*] (FAAC)
TRSA	Textile Rental Services Association of America (EA)
TRSA	Training System Requirements Analysis (DOMA)
TRSB	Time Reference Scanning Beam [*Aviation*]
TRSBG	Transcribing (MSA)
TRSBMLS	Time Reference Scanning Beam Microwave Landing System [*Aviation*] (OA)
TRSBR	Transcriber (MSA)
TR/SBS	Teleoperator Retrieval/Skylab Boost System [*Aerospace*] (MCD)
TRSC	Triad Systems [*NASDAQ symbol*] (TTSB)
TRSC	Triad Systems Corp. [*NASDAQ symbol*] (NQ)
TRSCB	Transcribe (MSA)
Trscrypt	Transcrypt International, Inc. [*Associated Press*] (SAG)
TRSD	Test Requirements/Specification Document [*NASA*] (MCD)
TRSD	Total Radiance Spectral Distribution
TRSD	Total Rated Service Date [*Air Force*] (AFM)
TRSD	Transferred
TRSD	Transposed
Tr Ser	Treaty Series [*A publication*] (DLA)
TRSF	Torque-Regulated Speed Follower
TRSG	Third Reich Study Group (EA)
TRSG	Track RADAR Simulation Group [*Military*] (CAAL)
TRSH	Trim Shell
TRSI	Test of Retail Sales Insight
TRSL	Toms River Signal Laboratory [*Army*] (MCD)
TRSM	Trism, Inc. [*NASDAQ symbol*] (SAG)
TRSN	Torsion (MSA)
TRSN	Transition (FAAC)
TRSOC	Trademark Society, Inc.
TRSP	Total Radiance Spectral Polarization
trsp	Transept (VRA)
TRSP	Transport Seaplane [*Navy*]
TRSq	Tactical Reconnaissance Squadron [*Air Force*] (AFM)
TRSR	Taxi and Runway Surveillance RADAR
TRSRY	Treasury
TRSS	Tactical Remote Sensor System (DWSG)
TRSS	Teleoperator and Robotic System Simulation (MCD)
TRSS	Triple Screw Ship
TRSSCOMM...	Technical Research Ship Special Communications [*System*] [*Pronounced "triss-com"*] [*Navy*]
TRSSGM	Tactical Range Surface-to-Surface Guided Missile
TRSSM	Tactical Range Ship-to-Shore Missile (IAA)
TRSSM	Tactical Range Surface-to-Surface Missile
TRST	Throttle Reset
TRST	Trust
TRST	Trustco Bank Corp. New York [*NASDAQ symbol*] (SAG)
TrstNY	Trustco Bank Corp. New York [*Associated Press*] (SAG)
TRSV	Tobacco Ring Spot Virus
TRSY	Treasury (AABC)
Trsy	Treasury (TBD)
TRT	San Antonio, TX [*Location identifier FAA*] (FAAL)
TRT	TACFIRE Remote Terminal (MCD)
TRT	Tanker Recovery Team [*Air Force*] (DOMA)
TRT	Technical Review Team [*Nuclear energy*] (NRCH)
TRT	Television Resource Teachers [*Canada*]
TRT	Telomerase Reverse Transcriptase [*Genetics*]
TRT	Tempo di Restituzione Termica [*Thermal Restitution Test*] [*Italian*] [*Medicine*]
TRT	TEREC [*Tactical Electronic Reconnaissance*] Remote Terminal (DWSG)
TRT	Testosterone Replacement Therapy [*Medicine*] (WDAA)
TRT	Text Retrieval Terminal [*Computer science*] (DGA)
TRT	Thermoradiotherapy [*Radiation therapy*] (DAVI)
TRT	Tiaret [*Algeria*] [*Airport symbol*] (AD)
TRT	Token Rotation Timer (CIST)
TRT	Torpedo Rocket Thrown
TRT	Total Relaxation Time [*Cardiology*]
TRT	Total Repair Time [*Automotive maintenance*]
TRT	Total Running Time [*Broadcasting*] (WDMC)
TrT	Track True [*Aviation*] (DA)
TRT	Trademark Registration Treaty
TRT	Traffic Route Testing [*Telecommunications*] (TEL)

TRT............. Trans Arabian Air Transport [*Sudan*] [*ICAO designator*] (FAAC)
TRT............. Translate and Test (IAA)
TRT............. Transonic Research Tunnel (MCD)
trt............... Treatment [*Medicine*]
TRT............. Treherbert [*Cardiff*] [*Welsh depot code*]
TRT............. Trent Regional Library System [*UTLAS symbol*]
TRT............. Tretes [*Java*] [*Seismograph station code, US Geological Survey*] (SEIS)
TRT............. Trim Template (MCD)
TRT............. Trinity Resources Ltd. [*Toronto Stock Exchange symbol*]
Trt.............. Trityl [*Biochemistry*]
TRT............. Tropical Radio Telegraph [*Telecommunications*] (IAA)
TRT............. Tuned Receiver Tuner
TRT............. Turkish Radio & Television Corp.
TRT............. Turn Round Time (NITA)
TRT............. Turret (AABC)
TRT............. Twisted Racetrack
TRT............. United States Army TRADOC, Fort Bliss, Fort Bliss, TX [*OCLC symbol*] (OCLC)
TrT₃............ Total Reverse Triiodothyronine
TRTA........... Tasmanian Registered Teachers' Association [*Australia*]
TRTA........... Traders' Road Transport Association [*British*] (BARN)
TRTAI.......... Radiance Technique Association International (EA)
TRTBX......... DW TCW/DW Total Return Cl.B [*Mutual fund ticker symbol*] (SG)
TRTC........... Tactical Record Traffic Center (MCD)
TRTC........... Trio-Tech International [*NASDAQ symbol*] (SAG)
TRTC........... Trio-Tech Intl [*NASDAQ symbol*] (TTSB)
TRTD........... Treated (MSA)
TR/TEA........ Transportability Report/Transportability Engineering Analysis [*Army*]
TRTF........... Tactical Reconnaissance Task Force (CINC)
TRTF........... Tactical Record Traffic Facsimile (MCD)
TRTF........... Tasking Requirements and Tasking File (MCD)
TRTG .... Tactical RADAR Threat Generator (MCD)
TRTG .... Treating
TRTITC........ Tasmanian Road Transport Industry Training Council [*Australia*]
TRTL........... Transistor-Resistor-Transistor Logic (IEEE)
TRTMNT ...... Treatment
TRTMT .... Treatment (MSA)
TRTP........... Toxicology Research and Testing Program [*National Institutes of Health*]
TRTS........... Tactical Reconnaissance Training Squadron
TRTS........... Tactical Record Traffic System (MCD)
TRTS........... Track RADAR Test Set (MCD)
TRTS........... Triple Redundant Timing Systems (MCD)
TRTT........... Tactical Record Traffic Terminal [*Army*] (MCD)
TRU............. Tape Restore Unit [*Computer science*] (CIST)
TRU............. Tasmanian Rugby Union [*Australia*]
TRU............. Taurus Resources [*Vancouver Stock Exchange symbol*]
TRU............. Test Replaceable Unit
TRU............. Thermal Receiver Unit [*Army*]
TRU............. Time Release Unit (MCD)
TRU............. Torch Energy Royalty Trust [*NYSE symbol*] (SPSG)
TRU............. Total Recycle Unit (OA)
TRU............. Transformer-Rectifier Unit (MCD)
TRU............. Transmit-Receive Unit
TRU............. Transportable Radio Unit [*Military*]
TRU............. Transuranic [*or Transuranium*] [*Chemistry*]
TRU............. Transuranic Nuclides (COE)
TRU............. Transuranium Processing Plant (NRCH)
TRU............. Triangle Airline (Uganda) Ltd. [*FAA designator*] (FAAC)
TRU............. Truancy [*FBI standardized term*]
TRU............. True (GAVI)
Tru............. Trueman's New Brunswick Equity Cases [*1876-93*] [*A publication*] (DLA)
TRU............. Trujillo [*Peru*] [*Airport symbol*] (OAG)
TRU .... Truk [*Caroline Islands*] [*Seismograph station code, US Geological Survey Closed*] (SEIS)
TRU .... Truncated Variant [*Genetics*]
TRU .... Trustee (WGA)
TRU .... Turbidimetry Unit (DB)
TRU .... Turbidity Reducing Unit (AAMN)
TRU .... United States Army TRADOC, Fort Hood, Fort Hood, TX [*OCLC symbol*] (OCLC)
TRU/ARPS ... Theater Reserve Unit/Army Readiness Package, South
TRUB .... Temporarily Replaced by Unlighted Buoy [*Maps and charts*]
TRUD .... Time Remaining until Dive [*Air Force*]
TRUE .... Teacher Resources for Urban Education (AEBS)
TRUE .... Training in Urban Environment [*Navy*] (DOMA)
True............ Trueman's New Brunswick Reports [*A publication*] (DLA)
Trueman Eq Cas... Trueman's New Brunswick Equity Cases [*A publication*] (DLA)
Truem Eq Cas... Trueman's New Brunswick Equity Cases [*A publication*] (DLA)
TrueNrth ...... True North Communications, Inc. [*Formerly, Foote, Cone & Belding*] [*Associated Press*] (SAG)
Truevision ... Truevision, Inc. [*Associated Press*] (SAG)
TRUEX .... Transuranium Extraction
TRUF .... Transferable Revolving Underwriting Facility [*Finance*] (ADA)
TRUFOS....... True Unidentified Flying Objects
TRUK .... Builders Transport [*NASDAQ symbol*] (TTSB)
TRUK .... Builders Transport, Inc. [*NASDAQ symbol*] (NQ)
trum .... Trumeau (VRA)
TRUMF......... Total Package Unit Material Fielding [*Army*]
TRUMP .... Target Radiation Ultraviolet Measurement Program (AAG)
TRUMP .... Technical Review Updated Manuals and Publications (MCD)
TRUMP .... Teller Register Unit Monitoring Program (IEEE)
TRUMP .... Threat Reaction Upgrade Modernization (MCD)

TRUMP .... Total Revision and Upgrading of Maintenance Procedures [*Marine Corps*]
TRUMP .... Transportable Understanding Mechanism Package [*Software system*] (IT)
TRUMP .... Tribal Class Update and Modernization Project [*Canadian Navy*]
Trump.......... Trump Hotels & Casino Resorts, Inc. [*Associated Press*] (SAG)
TRUN .... Trunnion [*Pivot*] (KSC)
TRUNANG .... Trunnion Angle (MCD)
Truppie........ Trucker with Upscale Living Quarters in His or Her Vehicle [*Lifestyle classification*]
Tru Railw Rep... Truman's American Railway Reports [*A publication*] (DLA)
TRURON ...... Truronensis [*Signature of the Bishop of Truro*] [*Latin*] (ROG)
TRUS .... Transrectal Ultrasonography [*Medicine*]
TRUS .... Transrectal Ultra Sounds [*Medicine*]
TRUST .... Tamper-Resistant Unattended Safeguard Technique (PDAA)
TRUST .... Television Relay Using Small Terminals (MCD)
TRUST .... Terminal Repeller Unconstrained Subenergy Tunneling [*An algorithm for global optimization*]
TRUST .... Toluidine Red Unheated Serum Test
TRUST .... Total Reevaluation Under SPRINT Thrust [*Army*]
TRUST .... Transportable Units and Self-Sufficient Teams (MCD)
TRUST .... Trieste United States Troops
Trust Co Mag... Trust Companies Magazine [*1904-38*] [*A publication*] (DLA)
TrustInf........ Trusted Information Systems, Inc. [*Associated Press*] (SAG)
Trust Lett...... Trust Letter. American Bankers Association [*A publication*] (ILCA)
TrUstmk....... Trustmark Corp. [*Associated Press*] (SAG)
TrustNJ........ Trust Co. of New Jersey [*Associated Press*] (SAG)
Trust Terr ..... Trust Territory Reports [*A publication*] (DLA)
TRUSX .... ISI Total Return U.S. Treas. [*Mutual fund ticker symbol*] (SG)
TRUT .... Time Remaining until Transition [*Air Force*]
TRUV .... Truevision, Inc. [*NASDAQ symbol*] (SAG)
TRUW .... Transuranic Waste (GAAI)
TRUX .... Deflecta-Shield Corp. [*NASDAQ symbol*] (TTSB)
TRV............. Tank Recovery Vehicle [*Army*] (AABC)
TRV............. Thrust Reduction Valve
TRV............. Timing Relay Valve
TRV............. Tobacco Rattle Virus
TRV............. Torpedo-Recovery Vessel [*Navy British*]
TRV............. Transavia (Pty) Ltd. [*South Africa ICAO designator*] (FAAC)
TRV............. Transient Recovery Voltage (IEEE)
TRV............. Traveler Group, Inc. Capital I [*NYSE symbol*] (SAG)
TRV............. Travelers Group [*NYSE symbol*] (TTSB)
TRV............. [*The*] Travelers, Inc. [*NYSE symbol*] (SAG)
TRV............. Traverse
TRV............. Treviso [*Italy*] [*Seismograph station code, US Geological Survey Closed*] (SEIS)
TRV............. Trivandrum [*India*] [*Airport symbol*] (OAG)
TRV............. Trove Resources [*Vancouver Stock Exchange symbol*]
TRV............. Tupaia Retrovirus [*Medicine*] (DB)
TRV............. United States Army TRADOC, Fort Lee Post, Logistic Center, Logistic, Quartermaster, Fort Lee, VA [*OCLC symbol*] (OCLC)
TRVA .... Thermally Released Volatile Aromatics [*i.e., odors*] [*Slang*]
TRVB .... Tables of Redemption Values for US Savings Bonds
TRVEH .... Tracked Vehicle (AABC)
TRVL .... Travel
TRVLG .... Traveling (MSA)
TRVLMT....... Travel Limit
TRVLR .... Traveler (MSA)
TRVM.......... Transistorized Voltmeter
TRVN .... Tavern
TrvPC......... Travelers Corp. P & C Capital II [*Associated Press*] (SAG)
TRVPrA .... Travelers Grp 8.125%'A'Dep Pfd [*NYSE symbol*] (TTSB)
TRVPrB .... TravelersGrp5.5%CV'B'Pfd [*NYSE symbol*] (TTSB)
TRVPrD .... Travelers Grp 9.25% Dep Pfd [*NYSE symbol*] (TTSB)
TRVS .... Travis Boats & Motors, Inc. [*NASDAQ symbol*] (SAG)
TRV/SRV...... Tower Restoral Vehicle and Surveillance Restoral Vehicle [*Air Force*] (DOMA)
trvtn............ Travertine (VRA)
TRVV .... Time Radius and Velocity Vector
TRV.WS....... Travelers Grp Wrrt [*NYSE symbol*] (TTSB)
TRW........... Tactical Reconnaissance Wing [*Air Force*] (MCD)
TRW........... Tarawa [*Kiribati*] [*Airport symbol*] (OAG)
TRW........... Trade Winds Resources [*Vancouver Stock Exchange symbol*]
TRW........... Trail Riders of the Wilderness [*Later, AFA*] (EA)
TRW........... Trans Western Airlines of Utah [*ICAO designator*] (FAAC)
TRW........... TRW, Inc. [*Formerly, Thompson Ramo Wooldridge, Inc.*] [*NYSE symbol*] (SPSG)
TRW........... United States Army TRADOC, Fort Leonard Wood Post Library, Fort Leonard Wood, MO [*OCLC symbol*] (OCLC)
TRWA .... Trackway
TRWC .... Threat Responsive Weapon Control [*Military*] (CAAL)
TRWG .... Tactical Reconnaissance Wing [*Air Force*]
TRW IND ..... TRW Information Networks Division [*TRW, Inc.*] [*Torrance, CA*] (TSSD)
TrwlBc........ Transworld Bancorp [*Associated Press*] (SAG)
TRWOV........ Transit Without Visa
TRWPrB ...... TRW Inc.,$4.40 Cv II Pref [*NYSE symbol*] (TTSB)
TRWPrD ...... TRW Inc.,$4.50 Cv II Pref [*NYSE symbol*] (TTSB)
TRWY .... Throughway [*Postal Service standard*] (OPSA)
TRX............. Air Terrex [*Czechoslovakia*] [*ICAO designator*] (FAAC)
Trx .... Thioredoxin [*Also, TD, TR*] [*Biochemistry*]
TRX............. Transaction
TRX............. Transceiver [*Amateur radio shorthand*] (WDAA)
TRX............. Transsexual (DAVI)
TRX............. Trenton, MO [*Location identifier FAA*] (FAAL)

TRX.............	Triplex
TRX.............	Tri-State Resources Ltd. [*Vancouver Stock Exchange symbol*]
TRX.............	Two-Region Physics Critical Experiment (NRCH)
TRX.............	United States Army TRADOC, Ordnance and Chemical School Library, Aberdeen Proving Ground, MD [*OCLC symbol*] (OCLC)
TRXAS........	Time Resolved X-Ray Absorption Spectroscopy
TRXRD.......	Time-Resolved X-Ray Diffraction
TRXRF.......	Total Reflection X-ray Fluorescence (MEC)
TRY.............	Teens for Retarded Youth [*Program in Fairfax County, Virginia*]
TRY.............	Toronto Railway
TRY.............	Tororo [*Uganda*] [*Airport symbol*] (OAG)
TRY.............	Treviso [*Italy*] [*Airport symbol*] (AD)
TRY.............	Triarc Co., Inc. [*Formerly, DWG Corp.*] [*NYSE symbol*] (SPSG)
TRY.............	Triarc Cos CI'A' [*NYSE symbol*] (TTSB)
TRY.............	Tri-Arc Energy Ltd. [*Vancouver Stock Exchange symbol*]
TRY.............	Tri Star Airlines, Inc. [*FAA designator*] (FAAC)
TRY.............	Troy [*New York*] [*Seismograph station code, US Geological Survey*] (SEIS)
TRY.............	Truly (ROG)
Try.............	Tryptophan [*An amino acid*] (MAE)
TRY.............	United States Army TRADOC, TRADOC System Analysis [*TRASANA*], White Sands Range, NM [*OCLC symbol*] (OCLC)
Trye Jus Filiz...	Trye's Jus Filizarii [*A publication*] (ILCA)
Tryp.............	Tryptophan (MEDA)
TRYPSN......	Trypsin [*An enzyme*] (DAVI)
TRZ.............	Prime Air, Inc. [*FAA designator*] (FAAC)
TRZ.............	Taradale [*New Zealand*] [*Seismograph station code, US Geological Survey*] (SEIS)
TRZ.............	Tartrozine (STED)
TRZ.............	Thioridazine [*Tranquilizer*]
TRZ.............	Tiruchirappalli [*India*] [*Airport symbol*] (OAG)
TRZ.............	Triazolam (STED)
TRZ.............	Trichinopoly [*India*] [*Airport symbol*] (AD)
TRZ.............	United States Army Intelligence Center and School Library, Fort Huachuca, AZ [*OCLC symbol*] (OCLC)
TRZO	Terrazzo [*Classified advertising*] (ADA)
TRZON.......	Three Ton Range and Azimuth Only (IAA)
TS.............	Cleveland [*Postcode*] (ODBW)
TS.............	Iraq [*Later, BZ*] [*License plate code assigned to foreign diplomats in the US*]
TS.............	Samoa Air [*ICAO designator*] (AD)
Ts.............	Skin Temperature [*Medicine*]
TS.............	[*The*] Steamboaters (EA)
TS.............	Taboo Search [*Optimization method*]
TS.............	Tab Set [*Typography*] (WDMC)
ts.............	Tab Set [*Typesetting*] (WDMC)
TS.............	Tailshaft Survey
TS.............	Tall Salicornia Zone [*Ecology*]
TS.............	Tamper Switch [*NFPA pre-fire planning symbol*] (NFPA)
TS.............	Tangent to Spiral
TS.............	Tank Scope (DNAB)
TS.............	Tank Steamer
TS.............	Taoist Sanctuary [*Later, DS*] (EA)
TS.............	Taper Shank [*Screw*]
TS.............	Taper Sided
TS.............	Tape Status [*Computer science*] (OA)
T/S.............	Target Seeker
TS.............	Target Strength
TS.............	Task Statement (MCD)
TS.............	Task-Switched [*Computer science*] (BYTE)
TS.............	Tasmanian Swimming Inc. [*Commercial firm Australia*]
TS.............	Tasto Solo [*Bass without Accompaniment*] [*Music*]
TS.............	Taxpayers' Society [*British*]
TS.............	Tax Shelter
TS.............	Tax Straddle (MHDW)
TS.............	Taylor-Schechter Collection. University Library [*Cambridge, England*] (BJA)
TS.............	Tay-Sachs [*Disease*] [*Medicine*] (DB)
TS.............	Teachers Section [*Library Education Division*] [*American Library Association*]
TS.............	Teacher Survey
TS.............	Team Supervisor (FAAC)
TS.............	Team Surtees [*Automobile manufacturer*]
ts.............	Teaspoon [*Measure*] (WGA)
TS.............	Technical School (ADA)
TS.............	Technical Secretariat (NATG)
TS.............	Technical Services Co.
TS.............	Technical Specification (MCD)
TS.............	Technical Support (NASA)
TS.............	Ted Smith Aircraft [*ICAO aircraft manufacturer identifier*] (ICAO)
TS.............	Telecommunications System
TS.............	Telegraph System (MSA)
TS.............	Telephone Set (IAA)
TS.............	Telephone Switchboard (LAIN)
TS.............	Television, Sound Channel
TS.............	Television Studio-Transmitter-Link [*FCC*] (NTCM)
TS.............	Telophase Society [*Commercial firm*] (EA)
T-S.............	Temperature-Salinity [*Oceanography*]
TS.............	Temperature Sensitive
TS.............	Temperature Sensitivity (STED)
TS.............	Temperature Switch
TS.............	Template Set-Up (MCD)
TS.............	Temporal Stem [*Brain anatomy*]
TS.............	Tenancy Service [*New South Wales, Australia*]
TS.............	Tennyson Society (EA)

TS.............	Tensile Strength
ts.............	Tensile Strength (IDOE)
TS.............	Tensile Stress
TS.............	Ten Silhouettes [*Psychological testing*]
T$_s$.............	Tension, Schiotz [*Opthalmology*] (DAVI)
TS.............	Tentative Specification
TS.............	Teratology Society (EA)
TS.............	Terminal [*or Greater*] Sensation
TS.............	Terminal Series (IAA)
TS.............	Terminal Service
TS.............	Terminal Station (IAA)
TS.............	Terminal Strip (DEN)
TS.............	Terminal Student (OICC)
TS.............	Terminating System (IAA)
TS.............	Terra Santa [*Jerusalem*] [*A publication*] (BJA)
TS.............	Test
TS.............	Test and Set [*Computer science*] (IAA)
TS.............	Test Items [*JETDS nomenclature*] [*Military*] (CET)
TS.............	Testosterone Sulfate (STED)
TS.............	Test Set (KSC)
TS.............	Test Site [*NASA*] (NASA)
TS.............	Test Solution [*of a chemical*] [*Medicine*]
TS.............	Test Specification (MSA)
T/S.............	Test Stand (AAG)
TS.............	Test Stand (NAKS)
TS.............	Test Station [*NASA*] (MCD)
TS.............	Test Stimulus
TS.............	Test Summary
TS.............	Test System
TS.............	Textes Sogdiens. Edites. Traduits et Commentes [*A publication*] (BJA)
TS.............	Texts and Studies [*Cambridge*] [*A publication*] (BJA)
TS.............	Text Setting [*Computer science*] (PCM)
TS.............	Theologische Studien [*Utrecht*] [*A publication*] (BJA)
TS.............	Theosophical Society
TS.............	Thermal Microscope Stage
TS.............	Thermal Spray [*Also, THSP*] [*Coating technology*]
TS.............	Thermal Stethoscope [*Medical instrumentation*]
TS.............	Thermal Synchrotron [*High-energy physics*]
TS.............	Thermosetting [*Plastics technology*]
T/S.............	Thermosonic (AAEL)
TS.............	Thermospray [*Also, TSP*] [*Ionization Physics*]
TS.............	Thermostable (STED)
TS.............	Thiosporin (STED)
T/S.............	Third Stage [*Aerospace*] (AAG)
TS.............	Thoracic Surgery [*Medicine*]
TS.............	Thoreau Society (EA)
TS.............	Threaded Stud
TS.............	Three-State [*Computer science*] (IAA)
TS.............	Three Stooges Club (EA)
TS.............	Thunderstorm [*Meteorology*] (FAAC)
TS.............	Thymidylate Synthase [*Also, ThS*] [*An enzyme*]
TS.............	Thymostimulin [*Endocrinology*]
T/S.............	Thyroid:Serum [*Radioiodide ratio*]
TS.............	Tibet Society (EA)
TS.............	Tide Surveyor [*British*] (ROG)
TS.............	Tidewater Southern Railway Co. [*AAR code*]
TS.............	Till Sale
TS.............	Tilt and Shift [*Camera lens*] (DICI)
TS.............	Time Scheduled (NASA)
TS.............	Time Service (IAA)
TS.............	Time Shack [*NAS operations desk*]
TS.............	Time-Sharing [*Computer science*]
TS.............	Time Slot [*Telecommunications*] (TEL)
TS.............	Time Switch (MSA)
TS.............	Timing Selector
TS.............	Timing System (MCD)
TS.............	Tinting Strength [*Dye chemistry*]
TS.............	Tippers [*Shipping*] (DCTA)
TS.............	Tip Speed
TS.............	Tissue Space (STED)
TS.............	Titan Society (EA)
TS.............	Titration System Software [*Metter Instruments*]
TS.............	Tocopherol Supplemented (STED)
TS.............	Today Show [*Television program*]
TS.............	Toe Sign (STED)
TS.............	Tolkien Society [*Hove, East Sussex, England*] (EAIO)
TS.............	Toll Switching [*Trunk*] [*Telecommunications*] (TEL)
TS.............	Tool Sharpness
TS.............	Tool Shed (IIA)
TS.............	Tool Steel
TS.............	Tool Storage
TS.............	Tool Strength (ADA)
TS.............	Too Short [*Symbol stamped in shoes which are not actually of the size marked*]
TS.............	Topic Statement (WGA)
TS.............	Top Secret
TS.............	Top Spare
TS.............	Torch Soldering
TS.............	Torpedo Station (MCD)
TS.............	Torque Synchro Transmitter (IAA)
TS.............	Torque Transmitter (IAA)
TS.............	Torstar Corp. [*Toronto Stock Exchange symbol*]
Ts.............	Tosyl [*Also, Tos*] [*Organic chemistry*]
TS.............	Totally Smutted [*Plant pathology*]

TS	Total Solids [*Medicine*]
TS	Tough Situation [*Bowdlerized version*]
TS	Tough Stuff
TS	Tourette Syndrome [*Neurology*]
TS	Touring Sedan [*As in Olds 98 TS*]
TS	Touring Sport [*Automobile model*]
TS	Tower Station
TS	Toxic Substance (MAE)
TS	Toxic Syndrome [*Medicine*] (STED)
TS	Traceability Serial (NAKS)
TS	Trachael Spiral [*Medicine*] (STED)
TS	Tracheal Sound [*Medicine*] (AAMN)
ts	Tracheosyringeal [*Neuroanatomy of birds*]
TS	Tracking Scope
TS	Tracking Supervisor (SAA)
TS	Tracking System (AAG)
TS	Track Store Unit (IAA)
TS	Trademark Society (EA)
TS	Trade Study (MCD)
TS	Traffic Superintendent [*British*] (DCTA)
TS	Trained Soldier [*British military*] (DMA)
TS	Training School (DAVI)
TS	Training Services (COE)
TS	Training Ship
TS	Training Squadron [*British military*] (DMA)
TS	Transaction Services (MCD)
TS	Transfer Set
TS	Transient Source
TS	Transient State (AAG)
TS	Transient Synovitis [*Medicine*]
TS	Transitional Sleep (STED)
TS	Transition State [*Physical chemistry*]
TS	Transit Storage
TS	Translation Service
TS	Translator Synthesizer (DWSG)
TS	Transmission Service [*Telecommunications*]
TS	Transmission Set
TS	Transmit [*or Transmitter*] (IAA)
TS	Transmittal Sheet [*Military*]
TS	Transmitted Shock
TS	Transmitter Station
TS	Transparent Substrate [*Materials science*]
TS	Transplantation Society (EA)
TS	Transport and Supply
TS	Transport Service (ROG)
TS	Transport Ship (ROG)
TS	Transsexual [*Medicine*]
T/S	Transtage [*Upper stage for Titan III C rocket*]
TS	Transvaal Supreme Court Reports [*South Africa*] [*A publication*] (DLA)
TS	Transversale Spyder [*Ferrari automotive model designation*]
TS	Transverse Section [*Medicine*]
TS	Transverse Sinus (DB)
TS	Transverse Staggering (IAA)
TS	Transverse System [*Cytology*]
TS	Transverse Tubular System (DAVI)
TS	Travelling Showmen [*Public-performance tariff class*] [*British*]
TS	Travel Supplement [*Publishing*]
TS	Treadmill Score [*Medicine*] (DMAA)
TS	Treasury Solicitor [*British*]
TS	Treasury Stock
TS	Treatment System [*Nuclear energy*] (NRCH)
TS	Treaty Series [*A publication*] (ILCA)
TS	Tree Sparrow [*Ornithology*]
TS	Tres Sage [*Wisest*] [*Presiding officer in the French rite Freemasonry*]
TS	Trichostasis Spinulosa (DB)
TS	Tricuspid Stenosis [*Cardiology*]
T/S	Trimethoprim Sulfamethoxazole
TS	Trinidad Sector [*World War II*]
TS	Triple Strength
TS	Tristate [*Electronics*] (IAA)
TS	Tropical Sprue [*Medicine*] (MAE)
TS	Troubleshoot (MCD)
ts	Trucial States [*United Arab Emirates*] [*MARC country of publication code Library of Congress*] (LCCP)
TS	Trumann Southern Railroad (IIA)
TS	Trust Secretary
TS	Trypticase Soy [*Plate*] [*Laboratory*] (DAVI)
Ts	T Suppressor [*Cell*] [*Immunology*]
TS	Tuberous Sclerosis [*Medicine*]
TS	Tube Sheet (MSA)
TS	Tub-Sized [*Paper*]
TS	Tubular [*Tracheal*] Sound
TS	Tumor Specific [*Medicine*]
TS	Tuning Stability
TS	Turbine Steamship (WDAA)
ts	Turboshaft Engine (IEEE)
TS	Turbosynchro Transmitter (IAA)
TS	Turner Society [*British*] (EAIO)
TS	Turner Syndrome [*Medicine*] (DMAA)
T/S	Turn-In Slip [*Military*]
TS	Turn per Second (IAA)
T-S	Turonian-Santonian [*Paleontology*]
TS	Tutto Solo [*All by Itself*] [*Music*]
TS	Twin Screw (ADA)
TS	Two-Stage Least Squares [*Statistics*]
TS	Tyneside Scottish [*British military*] (DMA)
TS	Type of Shift (IAA)
TS	Typescript
TS	Type-Specific [*Antibodies*] [*Microbiology*] (DAVI)
TS	Type Specification
TS	United States Treaty Series [*A publication*] (DLA)
TSA	Aloha Airlines, Inc. [*Air carrier designation symbol*]
TSA	[*The*] Securities Association [*British*]
TSA	Sports Authority [*NYSE symbol*] (TTSB)
TSA	[*The*] Sports Authority, Inc. [*NYSE symbol*] (SAG)
TSA	Tablettes Sumeriennes Archaiques [*A publication*] (BJA)
TSA	Taipei-Sung Shan [*Taiwan*] [*Airport symbol*] (OAG)
TSA	Tamworth Swine Association (EA)
TSA	Target Service Agent [*Computer science*]
TSA	Target Service Agents [*Computer science*] (PCM)
TSA	Target Signature Analysis
TSA	Target System Alternatives (MCD)
TSA	Targhee Sheep Association (EA)
TSA	Tariff Schedules of the United States, Annotated
TSA	Tasmanian Shippers' Association [*Australia*]
TSA	Tasmanian Soccer Association [*Australia*]
TSA	Taxiway Safety Area [*FAA*] (TAG)
TSA	Tax-Sheltered Annuity
TSA	Technical Safety Appraisal [*Environmental science*] (COE)
TSA	Technical Supplemental Allowance [*Military*]
TSA	Technical Support Activity [*Army*] (RDA)
TSA	Technical Support Agent (MCD)
TSA	Technical Support Alliance [*Computer science*] (PCM)
TSA	Technical Support Asset
TSA	Technical Surgical Assistance [*Medicine*] (MAE)
TSA	Technical Systems Audit [*Environmental science*] (COE)
TSA	Technology Student Association (EA)
TSA	Telegraph System Analyzer
TSA	Tele-Systems Associates, Inc. [*Bloomington, MN*] [*Telecommunications service*] (TSSD)
TSA	Temperature Swing Adsorption [*Chemical engineering*]
TSA	Temporary Substitution Approval
TSA	Test of Syntactic Abilities [*Speech and language therapy*] (DAVI)
TSA	Test Signal Analyser (NITA)
TSA	Test Site Activation [*NASA*] (KSC)
TSA	Test Start Approval [*NASA*] (NASA)
TSA	Test Support Agent (MCD)
TSA	Texas Shrimp Association (EA)
TSA	Textile Salesmen's Association [*Defunct*] (EA)
TSA	Textile Services Association [*British*] (DBA)
TSA	Theater Service Area (MCD)
TSA	Theater Storage Area [*Military*]
TSA	Theosophical Society in America (FA)
TSA	Theosophical Society in Australia
TSA	Thermal Swing Adsorption [*Chemical engineering*]
TSA	Time Series Analysis
TSA	Time-Shared Amplifier
TSA	Time Slot Access
TSA	Time Study Analysis
TSA	Tissue-Specific Antigens [*Immunology*] (DAVI)
TSA	Tolkien Society of America
TSA	Toluenesulfonic Acid [*Organic chemistry*]
TSA	Tom Skinner Associates (EA)
TSA	Total Molecular Surface Area
TSA	Total Scan Area (OA)
TSA	Total Shoulder Arthroplasty [*Orthopedics*] (DAVI)
TSA	Total Source Analysis, Inc. (EFIS)
TSA	Total Surface Area [*Chemistry*]
TSA	Total Survey Area (WDMC)
TSA	Total System Analyzer (IAA)
TSA	Tourette Syndrome Association (EA)
TSA	Tourism South Australia
TSA	Toxic Shock Antigen [*Immunology*] (DAVI)
TSA	Toy Safety Act (MHDB)
TSA	Track Subsystem Analyst (MUGU)
TSA	Track Supply Association
TSA	Training Services Agency [*Department of Employment*] [*British*]
TSA	Training Situation Analysis [*Navy*]
TSA	Training Support Agency [*Army*]
TSA	Transair France [*ICAO designator*] (FAAC)
TSA	Trans America Industries [*Vancouver Stock Exchange symbol*]
TSA	Transition State Analog
TSA	Transportation Service, Army
TSA	Transportation Standardization Agency [*DoD*]
TSA	Transportation Stores Assignment [*British*]
TSA	Tree Structured Attribute (IAA)
TSA	Tripoli Science Association (EA)
TSA	Troop Support Agency [*Army*] (AABC)
TSA	Troubleshooting Aid (MCD)
TSA	Trypticase Soy Agar [*Cell growth medium*]
TSA	Tsunami Watch [*Telecommunications*] (OTD)
TSA	Tuberous Sclerosis Association of Great Britain
TSA	Tube Support Assembly [*Nuclear energy*] (NRCH)
TSA	Tumor-Specific Antibody [*Immunology*] (DAVI)
TSA	Tumor-Specific Antigens [*Immunology*]
TSA	Tumor Surface Antigen (DB)
TSA	Turkish Studies Association (EA)
TSA	Twilight Sentinel Amplifier [*Automotive engineering*]
TSA	Two-Step Antenna

TSA............. Type-Specific Antibody [*Immunology*]
TSA............. University of Texas, Health Science Center at San Antonio, San Antonio, TX [*OCLC symbol*] (OCLC)
TSAA........... Tobacco Salesmen's Association of America (EA)
TSAA........... Tuberous Sclerosis Association of America [*Also known as American Tuberous Sclerosis Association and Asociacion de Esclerosis Tuberosa de America*] (EA)
TSaab.......... Thyroid-Stimulating Autoantibody [*Endocrinology*]
TSAB........... Theatre-Screen Advertising Bureau [*Defunct*]
TSAb........... Thyroid-Stimulating Antibodies [*Endocrinology*]
TSab........... Thyroid-Stimulating Antibody (DB)
TSABF......... Troop Support Agency Bagger Fund (MCD)
TSAC........... Target Signature Analysis Center (MCD)
TSAC........... Testing Accessories (AAG)
TSAC........... Time Slot Assignment Circuit [*Telecommunications*] (TEL)
TSAC........... Title, Subtitle, and Caption
TSAC........... Topographic Scientific Advisory Committee [*Terminated, 1973*] [*Army*] (EGAO)
TSAC........... Tracking System Analytical Calibration
TSAC........... Trade Standards Advisory Council [*Australia*]
TSAC........... TransSouth Athletic Conference (PSS)
TSAD........... Test System Analysis Directorate [*Army*] (MCD)
TSAD .... Trajectory-Sensitive Arming Device (SAA)
TSAD .... Tub-Sized Air-Dried [*Paper*] (DGA)
TSAE........... Training Support Activity - Europe (MCD)
TSAF........... Todos Santos Ambulance Fund [*An association*] (EA)
TSAF........... Transportation Service for the Army in the Field (MCD)
TSAF........... Typical System Acquisition Flow
TSAG .... Tracking System Analysis Group [*NASA*]
TSAG .... Trivalent Sodium Antimony Gluconate [*Pharmacology*]
TsAGI.......... Tsentralyni Aero-Gidrodinamichescky Institute [*Institute of Aeronautical Research*] [*Former USSR*]
TSAI............ Transaction Sys Architects 'A' [*NYSE symbol*] (TTSB)
TSAI............ Transaction Systems Architects, Inc. [*NASDAQ symbol*] (SAG)
TSAK........... Test Stand Adapter Kit
TSAK........... Training Support Activity - Korea (MCD)
TSAM........... [*The*] Skill Alignment Module [*Army*] (INF)
TSAM........... Time Series Analysis and Modeling [*Software*]
TSAM........... Training Surface-to-Air Missile
TSAM²......... Total System Acquistion Management Methodology [*Army*] (RDA)
TS & POP.... Testing and Popping (SAA)
TS&S.......... Transtechnology Systems & Services (EFIS)
TS & SCP .... Task, Schedule, and Status Control Plan (AAG)
TSANet........ Technical Support Alliance Network (DDC)
TSANZ .... Transplantation Society of Australia and New Zealand
TSAP.......... Time Series Analysis Package
TSAP.......... Toxic Shock-Associated Protein [*Biochemistry*] (DAVI)
TSAP.......... Transport Service Access Point [*Telecommunications*]
TSAPG .... Telecommunications Systems Architecture Planning Group (DNAB)
TSAP GOOS... Technical and Scientific Advisory Panel for GOOS (EERA)
TSAPI.......... Telephony Services Application Programming Interface [*Novell, Inc.*] (PCM)
TSAR .... Telemetry System Application Requirements
TSAR .... Throttleable Solid Augmented Rocket (MCD)
TSAR .... Timed Scanned Array RADAR
TSAR .... Time-Sharing Activity Report System [*Computer science*] (IAA)
TSAR .... Time Sows and Reaps [*Acronym used in name of Tsar Publishing Co.*]
TSAR .... TransAmerica Solar Auto Run [*In name of solar-powered car TSAR Phoenix*]
TSAR .... TRANSCOM [*Transportation Command*] Siting and Readiness [*Model*]
TSAR .... Transmission Security Analysis Report (AFM)
TSAR .... Transportation Statistics Annual Report [*BTS*] (TAG)
TSAR .... Tristar Corp. [*NASDAQ symbol*] (SAG)
TSARC......... Test Schedule and Review Committee [*Army*] (AABC)
TSARCOM.... Troop Support and Aviation Materiel Readiness Command [*Army*]
TSAS........... Tactile Situational Awareness System [*Aviation*]
TSAS........... Total Severity Assessment Score (DAVI)
TSAS........... Training Standards Advisory Service (AIE)
TSAT........... TCI Satellite Entertainment, Inc. [*NASDAQ symbol*] (SAG)
TSAT........... Tube-Slide Agglutination Test [*Clinical chemistry*]
TSATA......... TCI Satellite Entertainment
TSATLC........ Trans-Atlantic [*Aviation*] (FAAC)
TSAU........... Time Slot Access Unit [*Telecommunications*] (TEL)
TSAZ........... Target Seeker-Azimuth
TSAZ........... Target Selector Azimuth (IAA)
TSB............. [*The*] School Brigade [*Army*] (INF)
TSB............. Technical Service Bulletin
TSB............. Temporary Stowage Bag [*NASA*] (KSC)
TSB............. Terminal Status Block [*Computer science*] (IBMDP)
TSB............. Test Support Building
TSB............. Textiles Surveillance Body [*Textile trade agreement*]
TSB............. Thermally Stabilized Burner [*Engineering*]
TSB............. Thrust Section Blower (AAG)
TSB............. Total Serum Albumin (DB)
TSB............. Towed SONAR Body
TSB............. Toxic Substances Bulletin [*A publication*]
TSB............. Trade Show Bureau (EA)
TSB............. Transportation Services Branch [*Air Force*]
TSB............. Transports Aeriens du Benin [*ICAO designator*] (FAAC)
TSB............. Trustee Savings Bank [*British*]
TSB............. Trypticase Soy Broth [*Cell growth medium*]
TSB............. Tsumeb [*Namibia*] [*Airport symbol*] (OAG)
TSB............. Twin Sideband

TSB............. Typtone Soy Broth [*Cell growth medium*] (DAVI)
TSBA........... Teeswater Sheep Breeders Association [*British*] (DBA)
TSBA........... Transactions of the Society of Biblical Archaeology [*London*] [*A publication*] (BJA)
TSBARA ...... Tasmanian Small Bore and Air Rifle Association [*Australia*]
TSBB........... Transtracheal Selective Bronchial Brushing [*Medicine*] (AAMN)
TSB(CI)........ Trustee Savings Bank (Channel Islands) [*British*]
TSBD........... Tracking Servobridge Detector (MCD)
TSBFA......... Traditional Siamese Breeders and Fanciers Association (EA)
TSBP........... Time-Sharing Business Package [*Computer science*] (IAA)
TSBS........... Trenton Savings Bank [*NASDAQ symbol*] (SAG)
TSBY........... Tuscola & Saginaw Bay Railway Co., Inc. [*AAR code*]
TSC............. Air Transat [*Canada ICAO designator*] (FAAC)
TSC............. Passed a Territorial Army Course in Staff Duties [*British*]
TSC............. Stephan Co. [*AMEX symbol*] (SAG)
TSC............. Tactical Support Center
TSC............. Tanker Service Committee
TSC............. Tape Station Conversion (CET)
TSC............. Targeted Selection Criteria (GFGA)
TSC............. Target Selection Console (MCD)
TSC............. Tarleton State College [*Later, TSU*] [*Texas*]
TSC............. Technetium Sulfur Colloid [*Medicine*] (MAE)
TSC............. Technical Services Center, Memphis, Tenn (AAGC)
TSC............. Technical Subcommittee
TSC............. Technical Support Center [*Nuclear energy*] (NRCH)
TSC............. Techniscope Development [*Vancouver Stock Exchange symbol*]
TSC............. Telecommunications Systems Corp. (IAA)
TSC............. Teleconferencing Systems Canada Ltd. [*Etobicoke, ON*] [*Telecommunications service*] (TSSD)
TSC............. Teledyne Systems Corp.
TSC............. Telephone Software Connection, Inc.
TSC............. Television Scan Converter
TSC............. Terminal Sterilization Chamber
TSC-C.......... Terrestrial Science Center (MCD)
tsc............. Territorial Staff Course [*British military*] (DMA)
TSC............. Test Acquisition Module Self Check (CAAL)
TSC............. Test Score Category [*DoD*]
TSC............. Test Set Computer
TSC............. Test Set Connection
TSC............. Test Setup Complete [*NASA*] (NASA)
TSC............. Test Shipping Cask [*Nuclear energy*] (NRCH)
TSC............. Test Steering Committee [*Military*]
TSC............. Test Support Controller [*or Coordinator*] [*NASA*] (KSC)
TSC............. Texas Southmost College
TSC............. Thermally Stimulated Conductivity [*or Currents*]
TSC............. Thermally Stimulated Current [*Electronics*] (AAEL)
TSC............. Thermal Shape Control (SSD)
TSC............. Thermal Stress Crack [*Plastics*]
TSC............. Thermal Stress Cracking (EDCT)
TSC............. Thermal Surface Coating
TSC............. Thiosemicarbazide [*Organic chemistry*]
TSC............. Three-State Control [*Computer science*]
TSC............. Time-Sharing Control (NITA)
TSC............. Time-Sharing Control Task [*Computer science*] (BUR)
TSC............. Tonic Sol-Fa College [*London*]
TS-C........... Tooling Supplement to Contract (SAA)
TSC............. Top Secret Control (MCD)
TSC............. Totally Self-Checking
TSC............. Total Standing Crop (EES)
TSC............. Total System Control [*Architecture*]
TSC............. Total System Cost [*Aviation*]
TSC............. Towson State University, Towson, MD [*OCLC symbol*] (OCLC)
TSC(I)......... Toxic Substances Coordinator [*Environmental Protection Agency*] (GFGA)
TSC............. Tractor Supply Co. (EFIS)
TSC............. Training Support Center [*Army*] (MCD)
TSC............. Transfer System C (SAA)
TSC............. Transit Switching Center [*Telecommunications*] (TEL)
TSC............. Transmitter Start Code [*Bell System*]
TSC............. Transmitting Switch Control (IAA)
TSC............. Transportation Systems Center [*Department of Transportation*] [*Cambridge, MA*]
TSC............. TransSouth Conference (PSS)
TSC............. Transverse Spinal Sclerosis [*Medicine*] (DB)
TSC............. Treatment Services Control
TSC............. Tri-Service Support Center [*Military*] (MCD)
TSC............. Tristate Control [*Electronics*] (IAA)
TSC............. Troop Support Center [*Army*]
TSC............. Troop Support Command [*Formerly, MECOM*] [*Army*]
TSC............. Trouble-Shooting Checklist [*Test for academic institutions*]
TSC............. Tryptose-Sulfite Cyclosterone [*Agar*] [*Microbiology*] (DAVI)
TSC............. Tryptose-Sulphite Cyclosterone [*Agar*] (BABM)
TSC............. Tuberous Sclerosis Complex [*Medicine*]
TSC............. Tuscaloosa Oil & Gas [*Vancouver Stock Exchange symbol*]
TSC............. Two-Stage Command [*NASA*] (GFGA)
TSC............. Two Subcarrier (IAA)
TSCA........... Target Satellite Controlled Approach (MUGU)
TSCA........... Textile Supplies and Credit Association (EA)
TSCA........... TIGA Sailboard Class Association [*Defunct*] (EA)
TSCA........... Timing Single-Channel Analyzer
TSCA........... Tool Subcontract Authorization (AAG)
TSCA........... Top Secret Control Agency (MCD)
TSCA........... Toxic Substances Control Act [*1976*]
TSCA........... Traditional Small Craft Association (EA)
TSCAP .... Thermally Stimulated Capacitance [*Photovoltaic energy systems*]

TSCAPP .... Toxic Substances Control Act Plant and Production Data [*Chemical Information Systems, Inc.*] [*Information service or system*]
TSCATS........ Toxic Substances Control Act Test Submissions [*Database*] [*Environmental Protection Agency*]
TSCBC .... Tri-State College Bowling Conference (PSS)
TSCC........... Technology Solutions [*NASDAQ symbol*] (TTSB)
TSCC........... Technology Solutions Co. [*NASDAQ symbol*] (SPSG)
TSCC........... Telemetry Standards Coordination Committee
TSCC........... Test Support Control Center [*NASA*] (KSC)
TSCC........... Top Secret Control Channels [*Military*]
TSCC........... Toxic Substances Coordinating Committee [*Environmental Protection Agency*] (GFGA)
TSCD .... Test Specification and Criteria Document (MCD)
TSCD .... Tool Specification Control Drawing (MCD)
TSCDP .... Technical Service Career Development Program [*Military*]
TSCF .... Task Schedule Change Form [*Nuclear energy*] (NRCH)
TSCF .... Template Set-Up Check Fixture (MCD)
TSCF .... Top Secret Cover Folder (AAG)
TSCHLT........ Test Support Center High-Level Terminal (CAAL)
TSCIXS .... Tactical Support Center Information Exchange Subsystem
TSCLT .... Transportable Satellite Communications Link Terminal
TSCM .... Taylor Series Correction Method
TSCM .... Technical Surveillance Countermeasures [*Program*] [*Air Force*]
TSCM .... Temperature Scram Circuit Monitor [*Environmental science*] (COE)
TSCM .... Test Station Configuration Model (MCD)
TSCN .... Telescan, Inc. [*NASDAQ symbol*] (SAG)
TSCN .... Trainer Specification Change Notice (MCD)
TSCO .... Test Support Coordination Office [*NASA*] (MCD)
TSCO .... Test Support Coordinator (NASA)
TSCO .... Top Secret Control Officer [*Military*]
TSCO .... Tractor Supply [*NASDAQ symbol*] (SAG)
TSCO .... Tri-Service Contracting Officer (AAGC)
TSCOM .... TS Communications [*Springfield, IL*] [*Telecommunications*] (TSSD)
t-scope........ Tachistoscope (WDMC)
TSCP .... Tactical Satellite Communications Program (SAA)
TSCP .... Telscape International, Inc. [*NASDAQ symbol*] (SAG)
TSCP .... Top Secret Control Proceeding [*Navy*]
TSCP .... Training Simulator Control Panel [*NASA*] (MCD)
TSCPAM ...... Tentative Summary CPAM [*Military*] (CAAL)
TSCR .... Telecom Securitor Cellular Radio Ltd. [*British*]
TSCRA .... Texas and Southwestern Cattle Raisers Association (EA)
TSCRS .... Teacher's Self-Control Rating Scale
TSCS .... Tactical Satellite Communications System [*Air Force*] (CET)
TSCS .... Tactical Software Control Site [*Missile system evaluation*] (RDA)
TSCS .... Tennessee Self-Concept Scale [*Psychology*]
TSCS .... Top Secret Control Section [*Navy*]
TSCS .... Transportation System Capability Study [*MTMC*] (TAG)
TSCT .... Time-Sharing Control Task (NITA)
TSCT .... Transportable Satellite Communications Terminal
TSCV .... Transmission Spark Control Valve [*Automotive engineering*]
TSCVT......... TACSATCOM Single Channel Vehicular Terminal System (MCD)
TSCVT......... Thomas Self-Concept Values Test [*Psychology*]
TSCW.......... Top Secret Codeword (MOD)
TSD............. Tactical and Staff Duties [*British military*] (DMA)
TSD............. Tactical Situation Display
TSD............. TARAN [*Tactical Attack RADAR and Navigation*] System Data
TSD............. Target Skin Distance
TSD............. Tay-Sachs Disease [*Medicine*]
TSD............. Technical Support Division [*Environmental Protection Agency*] (GFGA)
TSD............. Technical Support Document
TSD............. Temperature-Dependent Sex Determination [*Reptile Embryology*]
TSD............. Temperature-Salinity-Density-Depth [*Oceanography*]
TSD............. Tertiary of the Order of St. Dominic [*Roman Catholic religious order*]
TSD............. Test Sequence Document (SAA)
TSD............. Test Start Date [*NASA*] (NASA)
TSD............. Theater Shipping Document [*Military*]
TSD............. Theory of Signal Detection
TSD............. Thermally Stimulated Depolarization [*Chemistry*]
TSD............. Thermionic Specific Detector [*Analytical instrumentation*]
TSD............. Third-Degree Stochastic Dominance [*Agricultural statistics*]
TSD............. Time-Span-of-Discretion (PDAA)
TSD............. Time-Speed-Distance [*Vehicle testing*]
TSD............. Time Synchronization Device
TSD............. Torque Screwdriver
TSD............. Total Spectral Density
TSD............. Total Squared Distance
TSD............. Touch Sensitive Digitizer [*Electronics*] (OA)
TSD............. Toured Sea Duty (DNAB)
TSD............. Track Situation Display
TSD............. Traffic Situation [*Status*] Display
TSD............. Transfer Summary Dictated [*Followed by date*] [*Medical records*] (DAVI)
TSD............. Transient Signal Detector
TSD............. Transportation Safeguards Division
TSD............. Transportation Stores Depot [*British military*] (DMA)
T/S/D......... Treatment, Storage, and Disposal (GAAI)
TSD............. Treatment, Storage and Disposal Facilities (AAGC)
TSD............. Treatment, Storage, or Disposal [*Hazardous waste management*]
TSD............. Triple-Sequence Diffusion
TSD............. Tubeless Steel Disc [*Wheel*] [*Automotive engineering*]
TSD............. United States Army TRADOC, Fort Devens, USAISD, Fort Devens, MA [*OCLC symbol*] (OCLC)
TSDA .... Tasmanian Soft Drink Association [*Australia*]
TSDA .... Television Service Dealers' Association (IAA)

TSDA .... Theory of Signal Detection Analysis
TSDA .... Thermal Single-Determinant Approximation (PDAA)
TSDB .... SCB [*Statistika Centralbyran*] Time Series Data Base [*Sweden Information service or system*] (CRD)
TSDC .... Tennessee State Data Center [*Tennessee State Planning Office*] [*Nashville*] [*Information service or system*] (IID)
TSDC .... Thermally Stimulated Discharge Current [*Voltage-induced polarization*]
TSDC .... TOGA [*Tropical Ocean and Global Atmosphere*] Subsurface Data Center [*Marine science*] (OSRA)
TSDD .... Temperature-Salinity-Density-Depth (IEEE)
TSDF........... Tactical Software Development Facility
TSDF........... Target System Data File
TSDF........... Torres Strait Defence Force [*Australia*]
TSDF........... Treatment, Storage, and Disposal Facility [*Hazardous waste*]
TSDG .... Toxic Substances Dialogue Group [*Environmental Protection Agency*] (GFGA)
TS-DHFR..... Thymidylate Synthetase Dihydrofolate Reductase [*Biochemistry*]
TSDI........... Tactical Situation Display Indicator
TSDK .... Torque Screwdriver Kit
TSDM.......... Time-Shared Data Management [*System*] [*Computer science*] (IEEE)
TS/DMS....... Time-Shared/Data Management System
TSDOS .... Time-Shared Disk Operating System [*Computer science*] (IEEE)
T/SDPS .... Tube/Sea Differential Pressure Subsystem
TSDR .... Treatment, Storage, Disposal, or Recycling [*Hazardous waste management*]
TSDS .... Technological Services Delivery System [*UNIDO*]
TSDS .... Two-Speed Destroyer Sweeper [*Military*]
TSDSM .... Test Site Data Source Matrix
TSDU .... Target System Data Update
TSDU .... Transport Service Data Unit [*Telecommunications*]
TS D/W....... Tons Deadweight (DS)
TSE .... Memphis, TN [*Location identifier FAA*] (FAAL)
TSE .... Tactical Support Element (AFM)
TSE .... Tactical Support Equipment [*Military*] (MCD)
TSE .... Taipei Stock Exchange [*Taiwan*]
TSE .... Target State Estimator (MCD)
TSE .... Target Support Element (MCD)
TSE .... Technical Support Effort
TSE .... Technical Support Equipment
TSE .... Telecommunications Systems Engineering (IAA)
TSE .... Telemetry Support Equipment (IAA)
TSE .... Tender Support Equipment
TSE .... Terminal Source Editor
TSE .... Testicular Self-Examination
TSE .... Test of Spoken English
TSE .... Test Scoring Equipment
TSE .... Test Set Electrical
TSE .... Test Support Equipment [*NASA*]
TSE .... Texas South-Eastern Railroad Co. [*AAR code*]
TSE .... Thorn Security and Electronics [*A division of Thorn EMI Corp.*] (ECON)
TSE .... Time Slice End [*Computer science*] (OA)
TSE .... Tokyo Stock Exchange [*Japan*]
TSE .... Toronto Stock Exchange [*Toronto, ON*]
TSE .... Total Shielding Effectiveness (IAA)
TSE .... Total Skin Examination [*Dermatology*] (DAVI)
TSE .... Total Subsystem Evaluation
TSE .... Track Security Element [*Military*] (INF)
TSE .... Transmile Air Service (M) Sdn, Bhd. [*Malaysia*] [*FAA designator*] (FAAC)
TSE .... Transmissible Spongiform Encephalothi [*Medicine*]
TSE .... Transmission Secondary Emission [*Physics*]
TSE .... Transportation Support Equipment (NASA)
TSE .... Trisodium Edetate [*Inorganic chemistry*] (MAE)
TSE .... Turboshaft Engine
TSE1 .... Tissue-Specific Extinguisher 1 [*Genetics*]
TSEA.......... Trade Show Exhibitors Association (NTPA)
TSEA.......... Training Subsystem Effectiveness Analysis
TSEB.......... Total Skin Electron Beam [*Medicine*] (DMAA)
TSEB.......... Twin Sideband (IAA)
TSEC.......... Taft Sanitary Engineering Center
TSEC.......... Telecommunications Security [*Army*] (AABC)
TSEC.......... Terminal Secondary RADAR Beacon [*Aviation*] (FAAC)
TSEC.......... Top Secret (MCD)
T-SECT........ Transverse Cross Section [*Medicine*] (CPH)
TSED.......... Training Simulators Engineering Department
TSEE........... Test Support Equipment Evaluation (MCD)
TSEE........... Thermally Stimulated Exoelectron Emission [*Dosimetry*]
TSEG.......... Tactical Satellite Communications Executive Steering Group
TSEG.......... Toronto Stock Exchange - Gold
TSEGX........ Hancock(J) Emerg. Growth Cl.B [*Mutual fund ticker symbol*] (SG)
TS-EI.......... Thermospray-Electron Ionization [*Chemistry*]
TSEI........... Toronto Stock Exchange - Industrials
TSEI........... Transportation Safety Equipment Institute (EA)
T/S-EL......... Target Selector-Elevation (SAA)
TSEL........... Tentative Safe Exposure Level [*Toxicology*]
TSEM.......... Toronto Stock Exchange - Mines
TSEM.......... Tower Semiconductor Ltd. [*NASDAQ symbol*] (SAG)
TSEM.......... Transmission Secondary Electron Multiplication [*Physics*] (IAA)
TSEM.......... Transmission Secondary Emission Multiplier [*Physics*]
TSEMf......... Tower Semiconductor [*NASDAQ symbol*] (TTSB)
Tseng.......... Tseng Labs, Inc. [*Associated Press*] (SAG)
TSEO........... Toronto Stock Exchange - Oils
TSEPP......... Telecom Small Enterprise Policy Panel [*Australia*]

TSEQ............ Time Sequenced [*NASA*] (KSC)
TSERR .... Type of Leaf Serration [*Botany*]
TSES........... Technical Simulation and Evaluation System
TSES .... Transportable Satellite Earth Station
TSESG .... Tactical Satellite Executive Steering Group
TSET .... Transmitter Signal Element Timing (IAA)
T-setting ...... Time-Exposure Setting [*Photography*] (WDMC)
TSewU .... University of the South, Sewanee, TN [*Library symbol Library of Congress*] (LCLS)
TSewU-T....... University of the South, School of Theology, Sewanee, TN [*Library symbol Library of Congress*] (LCLS)
TSEXEC........ Time-Shared Executive [*Computer science*] (IAA)
TSF .... Tab Sequence Format
TSF .... Tactical Strike Fighter (MCD)
TSF .... Tasmanian Soccer Federation [*Australia*]
TSF .... Telephone Service Fitting
TSF .... Ten-Statement FORTRAN [*Computer science*] (IEEE)
TSF .... Terminal Sterilization Facility
TSF .... Tetraselenofulvalene [*Organic chemistry*]
TSF .... Textured Soy Flour
TSF .... Thai Support Foundation (EA)
TSF .... Theological Students Fellowship [*Defunct*] (EA)
TSFZ .... Thermally Stable Fuel (MCD)
TSF .... Thermoplastic Structural Foam (MCD)
TSF .... Thin Solid Films (IEEE)
TSF .... Thrombopoietic Stimulating Factor [*Medicine*]
TSF .... Through Supergroup Filter (IAA)
TSF .... Tissue-Coding Factor [*Clinical chemistry*] (MAE)
TSF .... Tower Shielding Facility [*Nuclear energy*]
TSF .... Track Synthesis Frequency
TSF .... Transverse Shear Force
TSF .... Treasury Security Force [*Department of the Treasury*]
TSF .... Triceps Skinfold [*Medicine*]
TSF .... Truncation Safety Factor [*In biological systems*]
TSF .... T/SF Communications Corp. [*Associated Press*] (SAG)
TSF .... Two-Seater Fighter [*Air Force British*]
TSFA............ Two-Step Formal Advertising (MCD)
TSFC............ Tactical Support Functional Components (NVT)
TSFC............ Thrust Specific Fuel Consumption
TSFC............ Tom Sneva Fan Club (EA)
TSFC............ Twisted Sister Fan Club (EA)
TSFCER........ Technical System for Continued Emissions Reduction [*Environmental Protection Agency*]
TSFET.......... Theater Service Forces, European Theater [*World War II*]
TSFGA .... Tasmanian Stone Fruit Growers' Association [*Australia*]
TSFO........... Training Set, Fire Observation (MCD)
TSFO........... Training Set, Forward Observer [*Army*]
TSFO........... Transportation Support Field Office [*Federal disaster planning*]
TSFQ........... Tactical Simulator Forward Observer [*Military*]
TSFR............ Transfer (AFM)
Tsfr............. Transfer (TBD)
TSFS............ Trunk Servicing Forecasting System [*Telecommunications*] (TEL)
TSFSOILITU... [*The*] Search for Signs of Intelligent Life in the Universe [*Lily Tomlin one-woman show written by Jane Wagner*]
TSFSR .... Transcaucasian Soviet Federation Socialist Republic
TSFT .... Telesoft Corp. [*NASDAQ symbol*] (SAG)
TSFZ .... Traveling Solvent Floating Zone (AAEL)
TSG............. Sabre Group Holdings, Inc. (The) [*NYSE symbol*] (SAG)
TSG............. [*The*] Stelle Group (EA)
TSG............. [*The*] Surgeon General [*Army*]
TSG............. Tanacross, AK [*Location identifier FAA*] (FAAL)
TSG............. Technical Service Group (IAA)
TSG............. Technical Specialty Group [*AIAA*]
TSG............. Technical Steering Group (OICC)
TSG............. Technical Subgroup (NATG)
TSG............. Technology Support Group
TSG............. Telecommunications Strategy Group [*Australia*]
TSG............. Tempered Safety Glass [*Automotive engineering*]
TSG............. Territorial Support Group [*Scotland Yard*] [*British*]
TSG............. Test and Switching Gear [*NASA*] (KSC)
TSG............. Test Signal Generator
TSG............. Time Signal Generator
TSG............. Timeslot Generator [*Telecommunications*] (TEL)
TSG............. Timing Systems Group [*NASA*]
TSG............. Touraine-Solente-Gole [*Syndrome*] [*Medicine*] (DB)
TSG............. Tracking Signal Generator
TSG............. Transglobe Resources [*Vancouver Stock Exchange symbol*]
TSG............. Transport Supplement Grant [*British*]
TSG............. Transversely Adjusted Gap (IEEE)
TSG............. Travel Security Guide [*Control Risks Information Services - CRIS*] [*British Information service or system*] (IID)
TSG............. Triggered Spark Gap (IAA)
TSG............. Tri-Service Group [*NATO*]
TSG............. Troubleshooting Guide (MCD)
TSG............. Truebner's Simplified Grammars [*A publication*]
TSG............. Tumor-Specific Glycoprotein [*Biochemistry*] (DAVI)
TSG............. United States Army TRADOC, Fort Gordon, United States Army Signal School and Fort Gordon, Fort Gordon, GA [*OCLC symbol*] (OCLC)
TSGA .... Technical Service Guild of Australia
TSGA .... Three-Conductor, Shipboard, General Use, Armor Cable
TSGAD .... Tri-Service Group on Air Defense [*NATO*] (NATG)
TSGAS .... Time-Shared General Accounting System [*Computer science*] (MHDI)
TSGB .... Tensor Society of Great Britain

TSGBX .... DW TCW/DW Small Cap. Growth Cl.B [*Mutual fund ticker symbol*] (SG)
TSGCEE....... Tri-Service Group on Communications and Electronic Equipment [*NATO*] (NATG)
TSGF........... T-Suppressor-Cell Growth Factor [*Immunology*]
TSGI........... Technology Service Group, Inc. [*NASDAQ symbol*] (SAG)
TSGI........... Technology Service Grp [*NASDAQ symbol*] (TTSB)
TSGIW........ Technology Service Grp Wrrt [*NASDAQ symbol*] (TTSB)
TSGIX......... Hancock(J) Govt. Inc. Cl.B [*Mutual fund ticker symbol*] (SG)
TSGMS .... Test Set Guided Missile Set [*or System*]
TSGP .... Test Sequence Generator Program [*European Space Research and Technology Center*] (NASA)
TSGR .... Thunderstorm with Hail [*Meteorology*]
TSGS .... Thunderstorm with Small Hail [*Meteorology*] (FAAC)
TSGS .... Time Series Generation System
TSGT........... Technical Sergeant [*Military*]
TSGT........... Throgmorton Secured Growth Trust [*Commercial firm British*]
TSGT(C)....... Technical Sergeant (Commissary) [*Marine Corps*]
TSh............. Tanzanian Shilling [*Monetary unit*] (ODBW)
TSH............. Target Sleeve Housing (COE)
TSH............. Teche Holding [*AMEX symbol*] (TTSB)
TSH............. Teche Holding Co. [*AMEX symbol*] (SAG)
TSH............. Temperature Switch, High [*Nuclear energy*] (NRCH)
TSH............. Tendency to Seek Help Questionnaire (EDAC)
TSH............. Tensor Surface Harmonic [*Physics*]
TSH............. Their Serene Highnesses
TSH............. Thermodynamic Suppression Head
TSH............. Through-Surface Hardening [*Metallurgy*]
TSH............. Thyroid-Stimulating Hormone [*Thyrotrophin*] [*Also, TTH Endocrinology*]
TSH............. Toluenesulfonyl Hydrazide [*Organic chemistry*]
TSh............. Torah Shelemah [*A publication*] (BJA)
TSH............. Transfer Scheme Handbook (AIE)
TSH............. TSC Shannock Corp. [*Toronto Stock Exchange symbol Vancouver Stock Exchange symbol*]
TSH............. Tshikapa [*Zaire*] [*Airport symbol*] (OAG)
TSHC .... Two-Stage Hydrocracker [*Chemical engineering*]
TSHIRTS....... TSHIRTS: [*The*] Society Handling the Interchange of Remarkable T-Shirts [*Defunct*] (EA)
TSHR .... Thyrotropin-Stimmulating Hormone Receptor [*Endocrinology*]
TSH-RF........ Thyroid-Stimulating Hormone-Releasing Factor [*Endocrinology*] (MAE)
TSH-RH........ Thyroid-Stimulating Hormone-Releasing Factor [*Endocrinology*] (CPH)
TSHTX .... Hancock(J) High Yld. Tax Free Cl.B [*Mutual fund ticker symbol*] (SG)
TSHYX .... Hancock(J) High Yld. Bond Cl.B [*Mutual fund ticker symbol*] (SG)
TSI .... Target Signature Investigation
TSI .... Task Status Index [*Computer science*] (OA)
TSI............. Tax Shelter Insider [*Newsletter Management Corp.*] [*Defunct Information service or system*] (CRD)
TSI............. Tayson Systems, Inc. [*Telecommunications service*] (TSSD)
TSI............. Technical Standardization Inspection [*Military*]
TSI............. Technical Systems, Inc. (IAA)
TSI............. Telebase Systems, Inc. [*Information service or system*] (IID)
TSI............. Teleconferencing Systems International, Inc. [*Elk Grove Village, IL*] (TSSD)
TSI............. Teleguard System International [*Vancouver Stock Exchange symbol*]
TSI............. Television Services International [*British*]
TSI............. Tensile Safety Index [*Engineering design*]
TSI............. Test of Social Insight [*Psychology*]
TSI............. Tests of Social Intelligence [*Psychology*]
TSI............. Test Structure Input (NITA)
TSI............. Test Support Instructions [*NASA*] (KSC)
TSI............. Theological School Inventory [*Psychology*]
TSI............. Thermal Services, Inc. (EFIS)
TSI............. Threshold Signal-to-Interference Ratio (IEEE)
TSI............. Threshold Soot Index
TSI............. Thyroid-Stimulating Immunoglobulin [*Endocrinology*]
TSI............. Timber Stand Improvement (DICI)
TSI............. Time-Significant Item (MCD)
TSI............. Time Slot Input [*Telecommunications*] (IAA)
TSI............. Time Slot Interchange [*Telecommunications*] (TEL)
TSI............. Time Sterile Indicator
TSI............. Tons per Square Inch (MCD)
TSI............. Top Surface Imaging [*Microlithography*]
TSI............. Total Solar Irradiance [*Solar physics*]
TSI............. Total Sum Insured (AIA)
TSI............. Transistor Specialities, Inc. (IAA)
TSI............. Transmitting Subscriber Information [*Computer science*]
TSI............. Transmitting Subscriber's Identification (NITA)
TSI............. Transportation Safety Institute [*Department of Transportation*]
TSI............. Transport Studies and Inquiries [*British*]
TSI............. Trans-Service Inc., Bala-Cynwyd PA [*STAC*]
TSI............. Triad Systems Integration Corp.
TSI............. Trinitech Systems [*AMEX symbol*] (TTSB)
TSI............. Trinitech Systems, Inc. [*AMEX symbol*] (SPSG)
TSI............. Triple Sugar-Iron [*Agar*] [*Microbiology*]
TSI............. True Speed Indicator (IAA)
tsi............. Tsimshian [*MARC language code Library of Congress*] (LCCP)
TSI............. Turbo Sport Intercooler [*Automotive engineering*]
TSI............. Turkish Standards Institution
TSIA........... Tasmanian Sawmillers' Industrial Association
TSIA........... Trading Stamp Institute of America (EA)
TSIA........... Triple Sugar-Iron Agar [*Microbiology*]
TSIAB.......... Torres Strait Islander Advisory Board [*Australia*]

TSIAJ............	This Scherzo Is a Joke [*Used by American composer Charles Edward Ives*]
TSIC............	Time Slot Interchange Circuit [*Telecommunications*] (IAA)
TSID............	Track Sector Identification
TSIE............	Transformed Special Index of the External Standard [*Scintillation analysis*]
TSIFL..........	Trade Society of Iron Foundry Labourers [*A union*] [*British*]
TSIFT..........	Transportable Selected Ion Flow Tube [*Medicine*]
T/SIG..........	Turn Signal [*Automotive engineering*]
TSII............	TSI, Inc. [*NASDAQ symbol*] (NQ)
TSI Inc.......	TSI, Inc. [*Associated Press*] (SAG)
TSIL............	Time-Significant Item List (AAG)
TSIM............	Thinking Tools, Inc. [*NASDAQ symbol*] (SAG)
TSIM............	(Trimethylsilyl)imidazole [*Also, TMSIM*] [*Organic chemistry*]
TSIMA..........	Torres Strait Islander Media Association [*Australia*]
TSIMS..........	Telemetry Simulation Submodule
TSIN............	Total Soluble Inorganic Nitrogen [*Analytical chemistry*]
TS in A........	Theosophical Society in America (EA)
TSIO............	Time-Shared Input/Output [*Data processing*]
TSI-OH........	Tube Sheet Inlet and Outlet Head (MSA)
TSIP............	Tank [*Missile*] Sight Improvement Program [*Army*]
TSIP............	Technical Study Implementation Plan (SSD)
TSIR............	Total System Integration Responsibility
TSIS............	Total Specifications Information System
TSIT............	Technical Service Intelligence Team [*Military*]
TSIU............	Telephone System Interface Unit
TSIX............	Transition Systems [*NASDAQ symbol*] (TTSB)
TSIX............	Transition Systems, Inc. [*NASDAQ symbol*] (SAG)
TSJ............	Tsushima [*Japan*] [*Airport symbol*] (OAG)
TSJC............	Trinidad State Junior College [*Colorado*]
TSK............	Computer Task Group [*NYSE symbol*] (TTSB)
TSK............	Computer Task Group, Inc. [*NYSE symbol*] (SPSG)
TSK............	Fort Hamilton Post Library, Morale Support Activities, Brooklyn, NY [*OCLC symbol*] (OCLC)
TSK............	Task
TSK............	Time Shift Keying
TSK............	Torque Screwdriver Kit
TSK............	Tsukuba - Telemeter [*Japan*] [*Seismograph station code, US Geological Survey*] (SEIS)
TSKT............	Test Kit (AAG)
TSL............	Chicago, IL [*Location identifier FAA*] (FAAL)
TSL............	[*The*] Software Link, Inc. [*Software manufacturer*]
TSL............	Temporary Storage Location
TSL............	Test Set Logic
TSL............	Test Source Library
TSL............	Test Stand Level (AAG)
TSL............	Test Support List (CAAL)
TSL............	Texas Short Line Railway [*AAR code*]
TSL............	Thermally-Stimulated Luminescence (PDAA)
TSL............	Thin Shock Layer
TSL............	Three State Logic [*Computer science*] (IAA)
TSL............	Time Series Language (MHDB)
TSL............	Time Spent Listening (WDMC)
TSL............	Top of Slab [*Technical drawings*]
TSL............	Torsatron/Stellarator Laboratory [*University of Wisconsin - Madison*] [*Research center*] (RCD)
TSL............	Total Service Life [*Telecommunications*] (TEL)
TSL............	Total Signal Lines (IAA)
TSL............	Translator (IAA)
TSL............	Trans Siberian Landbridge (DS)
TSL............	Tree Searching Language [*Computer science*] (PDAA)
TSL............	Triservice LASER
TSL............	Tristate Logic [*Electronics*]
TSL............	Troop Safety Line
TSL............	Troubleshooting Loop
TSL............	Tsaile [*Navajo Community College*] [*Arizona*] [*Seismograph station code, US Geological Survey*] (SEIS)
TSL............	Two-Stage Liquefaction [*Chemical engineering*]
TSL............	Typesetting Lead (MSA)
TSL............	United States Army TRADOC, Defense Language Institute, Presidio of Monterey, CA [*OCLC symbol*] (OCLC)
TSLAET........	Technician of the Society of Licensed Aircraft Engineers and Technologists [*British*] (DBQ)
TSLC............	TOGA [*Tropical Ocean and Global Atmosphere*] Sea Level Center [*Marine science*] (OSRA)
TSLCC-E......	Total System Life Cycle Cost-Effectiveness
TSLCN........	Texas State Library Communication Network [*Library network*]
TSLD............	Troubleshooting Logic Diagram (NASA)
TSLI............	Time Since Last Inspection (MCD)
TSLS............	Toxic Shock-Like Syndrome [*Medicine*]
TSLS............	Triservice LASER Seeker [*DoD*]
TSLS............	Two-Stage Least Squares [*Statistics*]
TSM............	Methodist Theological School in Ohio, Delaware, OH [*OCLC symbol*] (OCLC)
TSM............	Tactical Survey Meter
TSM............	Tail Service Mast [*NASA*] (KSC)
TSM............	Tandem Scanning Microscope
TSM............	Target Signature Model
TSM............	Target-to-Surface-to-Missile Path
TSM............	Tentative Standard Method [*of analysis*]
TSM............	Terminal Support Module
TSM............	Test Site Manager [*Army*]
TSM............	Test Standards Module
TSM............	Test Support Manager [*NASA*] (KSC)
TSM............	Thermal Scale Model (MCD)

TSM............	Thermoplastic Solid Molding [*Materials science*]
TSM............	Thickness-Shear-Mode [*Instrumentation*]
TSM............	Time Scheduled Maintenance
TSM............	Time-Shared Monitor System [*Computer science*] (IEEE)
TSM............	Time-Sharing Multiplex [*Telecommunications*] (IAA)
TSM............	Time, Space, and Matter [*Princeton University course title*] (AEE)
TSM............	Ton Statute Mile (AAG)
TSM............	Total Scheduled Maintenance [*Army*]
TSM............	Total Suspended Matter [*Environmental science*]
TSM............	Total System Management Concept (MCD)
TSM............	Trade Study Management (NASA)
TSM............	TRADOC System Manager [*Army*]
TSM............	Training and Doctrine Command System Manager [*Army*] (MCD)
TSM............	Training Site Manager (MCD)
TSM............	Training System Manager (MCD)
TSM............	Transair Mali SA [*ICAO designator*] (FAAC)
TSM............	Transportability Summary Manual [*MTMC*] (TAG)
TSM............	Transportation Systems Management
TSM............	Troop Sergeant-Major [*British military*] (DMA)
TSM............	Trouble Shooting Manual (IAA)
TSM............	Type, Series, and Model (MCD)
TSM............	Type-Specific M (Protein) [*Immunology*]
TSMA............	Tinplate Stockholders' and Merchants' Association [*British*] (BI)
TSMAF..........	Tesma International, Inc. [*NASDAQ symbol*] (SAG)
TSMAF..........	Tesma Intl'A' [*NASDAQ symbol*] (TTSB)
TSMC............	Taiwan Semiconductor Manufacturing Co.
TSMC............	Technical Supply Management Code
TSMC............	Transportation Supply and Maintenance Command
TSMDA..........	Test-Section Melt-Down Accident [*Nuclear energy*] (NRCH)
TSMFM..........	Tunneling Stabilized Magnetic Force Microscopy [*Physics*]
TSMG............	Thompson Submachine Gun
TSMNO..........	Transmitting Capability Out of Service [*Aviation*] (FAAC)
TSMO............	TACSATCOM Management Office
TSMO............	TRADOC Systems Management Office [*Military*] (RDA)
TSMOK..........	Transmitting Capability Returned to Service [*Aviation*] (FAAC)
tsm publishing...	Technical, Scientific, and Medical Publishing (WDMC)
TSMR............	Thickness Shear-Mode Resonator [*Sensor for signal transduction*]
TSMS............	Time Series Modeling System (MHDB)
TSMS............	Tobacco Strippers Mutual Society [*A union*] [*British*]
TSMT............	Transmit
TSMT............	Trident SONAR Maintenance Trainer (DWSG)
TSMTR..........	Transmitter (DA)
TSMTS..........	Tri-State Motor Tariff Service
TSMU............	Time-Sharing Multiplex Unit [*Telecommunications*] (IAA)
ts mutation...	Temperature Sensitive Mutation [*Genetics*] (DOG)
TSN............	[*The*] Sierra Network [*Computer science*]
TSN............	[*The*] Sports Network [*Cable-television system*] [*Information service or system*] (IID)
TSN............	Tailshaft Renewed
TSN............	Tan Son Nhut [*Air base*] [*Vietnam*]
TSN............	Tape Serial Number [*Computer science*]
TSN............	Task Sequence Number (IAA)
TSN............	TooSyn International [*TS Symbol*] (TTSB)
TSN............	Tecsyn International, Inc. [*Toronto Stock Exchange symbol*]
TSN............	Temporary Sort Number [*Computer science*]
TSN............	Test Sequence Network (CAAL)
TSN............	Thymosin [*A thymus hormone*]
TSN............	Tianjin [*China*] [*Airport symbol*] (OAG)
TSN............	Tientsin [*China*] [*Airport symbol*] (AD)
TSN............	Time since New [*Navy*] (NG)
TSN............	Traffic Safety Now [*Defunct*] (EA)
TSN............	Trans-Air Services Ltd. [*Nigeria*] [*ICAO designator*] (FAAC)
TSN............	Trimethoprim, Sulfamethoxazole, Nystatin [*Medicine*]
TSN............	Tryptone Sulfite Neomycin (OA)
TSN............	Tryptophan Peptone Sulfide Neomycin [*Agar*] (MAE)
TSN............	Tsingtau [*Republic of China*] [*Seismograph station code, US Geological Survey*] (SEIS)
TSN............	United States Army TRADOC, Fort Wadsworth, Chaplains Center Library, Fort Wadsworth, NY [*OCLC symbol*] (OCLC)
TSNA............	Tobacco-Specific Nitrosamine [*Biochemistry*]
TSNC............	Time-Sharing and Multiplexing Numerical Control [*Telecommunications*] (IAA)
TSNG............	Tseng Labs [*NASDAQ symbol*] (TTSB)
TSNG............	Tseng Labs, Inc. [*Newtown, PA*] [*NASDAQ symbol*] (NQ)
TSNI............	(Toluenesulfonyl)nitroimidazole [*Organic chemistry*]
TSNT............	(Toluenesulfonyl)nitrotriazole [*Organic chemistry*]
TSNT............	Transient (FAAC)
TSO............	Carrollton, OH [*Location identifier FAA*] (FAAL)
TSo............	Fayette County Free Library, Somerville, TN [*Library symbol Library of Congress*] (LCLS)
TSO............	Isles Of Scilly-Tresco [*Airport symbol*] (OAG)
TSO............	Table Structure Overview [*NASA*]
TSO............	Tactical Surveillance Officer (MCD)
TSO............	Target Systems Office [*Army Materiel Command*] (RDA)
TSO............	Technical Service Order [*Aviation*] (DA)
TSO............	Technical Service Organization [*A generic term*]
TSO............	Technical Specification Order
TSO............	Technical Staff Officer
TSO............	Technical Standard Order [*FAA*]
TSO............	Technical Standing Order (KSC)
TSO............	Technical Support Organization [*AEC*]
TSO............	Telecommunications Service Order [*Telecommunications*] (TEL)
TSO............	Telephone Service Observation [*Telecommunications*] (TEL)
TSO............	Terminator Sensor Output
TSO............	Tesoro Petroleum [*NYSE symbol*] (TTSB)

TSO	Tesoro Petroleum Corp. [*NYSE symbol*] (SPSG)
TSO	Test Site Office [*NASA*]
TSO	Test Support Operations [*NASA*] (KSC)
TSO	The Stationery Office [*British*] (WDAA)
TSO	Thrust Section Observer (AAG)
TSO	Time-Sharing Option [*Computer science*]
TSO	Time Since Overhaul [*of engine, or other equipment*]
TSO	Time Slot Zero [*Telecommunications*] (IAA)
TSO	Toronto Symphony Orchestra (CDAI)
TSO	Town Suboffice
TSO	Trading Standards Officer (ODBW)
TSO	Training for Skill Ownership (AIE)
TSO	Transaero Airlines [*Former USSR ICAO designator*] (FAAC)
TSO	Transportation Supply Officer [*Military*]
TSO	Tulsa [*Oklahoma*] [*Seismograph station code, US Geological Survey Closed*] (SEIS)
TSOA	Technical Standard Order Authorization (MCD)
TSOA	Triumph Sports Owners Association (EA)
TSOC	Tape System Output Converter [*Computer science*] (IAA)
TSOC	Time-Sharing Operating Control System [*Computer science*] (IAA)
TSOC	Totally Synthetic Organic Chemical [*or Compound*] (GNE)
TSODB	Time Series Oriented Database
TSO/E	Time-Sharing Option Extensions (HGAA)
TSOET	Tests of Elementary Training [*Military British*]
TSOL	[*The*] Sound of London [*Record label*]
TSOL	True Sounds of Liberty [*Musical group*]
TSOP	[*The*] Sound of Philadelphia [*Song*]
TSOP	Tactical Standing Operating Procedure [*Army*]
TSOP	Technical Standard Operating Procedure [*NASA*] (KSC)
TSoP	Thin Small-Outline Package [*Computer science*]
TSoR	Tems of Reference (WDAA)
TSOR	Tentative Specific Operational Requirement [*Military*]
TSORT	Transmission System Optimum Relief Tool [*Telecommunications*] (TEL)
TSOS	Time-Sharing Operating System [*Computer science*] (IEEE)
TSOSC	Test Set Operational Signal Converter (AAG)
TSO/VTAM	Time-Sharing Option for the Virtual Telecommunications Access Method [*Computer science*] (MHDI)
TSP	[*The*] Sentencing Project (EA)
TSP	Tailspike Protein [*Biochemistry*]
TSP	Teaspoonful (GPO)
tsp	Teaspoonful (ODBW)
TSP	Technical Specification
TSP	Technical Support Package [*NASA*]
TSP	Tehachapi, CA [*Location identifier FAA*] (FAAL)
TSP	Telecommunications Service Priority [*Telecommunications*] (OTD)
TSP	Telemetry Simulation Program
TSP	Telephone Switching Planning (ADA)
TSP	Teleprocessing Services Program [*General Service Administration*]
TSP	Temperature-Sensitive Parameter (AAEL)
TSP	Temperature-Sensitive Period
TSP	Temporary Standard Practice [*or Procedure*] (AAG)
TSP	Terminal Simulator Panel [*IBM Corp.*] (CIST)
TSP	Terminal Support Processor [*Computer science*] (PDAA)
TSP	Test Site Position [*NASA*] (KSC)
TSP	Test Software Program [*NASA*] (NASA)
TSP	Test Status Panel (MCD)
TSP	Test Support Package
TSP	Test Support Plan [*Army*]
TSP	Test Support Position
TSP	Test Support Program
TSP	Tesuque Peak [*New Mexico*] [*Seismograph station code, US Geological Survey*] (SEIS)
TSP	Textured Soy Protein [*Food industry*]
TSP	Thermospray [*Also, TS*] [*Ionization Physics*]
TSP	Theta Sigma Phi [*Later, Women in Communications*]
TSP	Threat Support Package [*DoD*]
TSP	Threat Support Plan (MCD)
TSP	Thrift Savings Plan [*Office of Personnel Management*] (GFGA)
TSP	Thrombospondin [*or Thrombin-Sensitive Protein*] [*Hematology*]
TSP	Throttle Solenoid Positioner [*Automotive engineering*]
TSP	Thyroid-Stimulating Hormone of the Prepituitary Gland [*Endocrinology*]
TSP	Time and Space Processing (MCD)
TSP	Time Series Processor [*Computer science*] (CIST)
TSP	Time Series Processor Software [*Bureau of the Census*] (GFGA)
TSP	Time-Share Peripherals [*Computer science*] (IAA)
TSP	Time Sorting Program
TSP	Titanium Sublimation Pump (OA)
TSP	Toronto Sun Publishing Corp. [*Toronto Stock Exchange symbol*]
TSP	Torpedo Seaplane [*Navy*]
TSP	Torpedo Setting Panel [*Military*] (CAAL)
TSP	Total Serum Protein [*Medicine*]
TSP	Total Suspended Particulates
TSP	Total Systems Performance [*MODCOMP*]
TSP	Tracking Signal Processor (LAIN)
TSP	Traffic Service Position [*Telephone*]
TSP	Transponder
TSP	Transshipment Point (AFM)
TSP	Traveling Salesman Problem [*Mathematics*]
TSP	Traveling Scholar Program (EA)
TSP	Trial Shot Point
TSP	Tribal Sovereignty Program [*Later, SGFID*] (EA)
TSP	Trimethylsilyl Propionate [*Organic chemistry*]
TSP	Triple-Super Phosphates

TSP	Triservice Program [*Military*]
TSP	Trisodium Phosphate [*Inorganic chemistry*]
TSP	Tropical Spastic Paraparesis [*Neurology*]
TSP	Tube Support Plate [*Nuclear energy*] (NRCH)
TSP	Twisted Shielded Pairs [*Cables*] (NASA)
TSP	United States Army TRADOC, Carlisle Barracks, Carlisle Barracks, PA [*OCLC symbol*] (OCLC)
TSPA	Triethylenethiophosphoramide [*Also, THioTEPA*] [*Antineoplastic drug*]
TSPAC	Trans-Pacific (FAAC)
TSPAK	Time Series Package [*Bell System*]
TSPAP	Total Serum Prostatic Acid Phosphatase [*Medicine*] (MAE)
TSPC	Thermal Sciences and Propulsion Center [*Purdue University*] [*Research center*] (RCD)
TSPC	Toxic Substances Priority Committee [*Terminated, 1984*] [*Environmental Protection Agency*] (EGAO)
TSPC	Tropical Stored Products Centre [*Tropical Products Institute*] [*Overseas Development Administration*] [*British*] (DS)
TSPE	Thunderstorm with Ice Pellets [*ICAO*] (FAAC)
TSPEC	Test Specification (MSA)
TSPED	Trade Shows and Professional Exhibits Directory [*Formerly, TPED*] [*Later, TSW*] [*A publication*]
TSPI	Time-Space-Position-Information (MCD)
TSPIRS	Timber Sales Program Information Reporting System [*Department of the Interior*]
TSPL	Telephone Systems Programming Language [*Computer science*] (MHDB)
TSPLIB	Traveling Salesman Problem Library [*Electronic mail*]
TSPM	Total Suspended Particulate Matter
TSpMH	South Pittsburg Municipal Hospital, South Pittsburg, TN [*Library symbol Library of Congress*] (LCLS)
tspn	Teaspoon [*Measure*] (WGA)
TSPO	Threat Simulator Project Office [*Army Intelligence Agency*] (RDA)
TSPP	Tanker Safety and Pollution Prevention
TSPP	Technetium Stannous Pyrophosphate [*Radiochemistry*]
TSPP	Tetrasodium Pyrophosphate [*Inorganic chemistry*]
TSPP	Training System Procurement Package
TSPR	Total Systems Performance Reliability [*or Responsibility*] (MCD)
TSPR	Training System Program Requirements (MCD)
TSPRT	Truncated Sequential Probability Ratio Test (PDAA)
TSPRTR	Truncated Sequential Probability Ratio Test for Reliability (PDAA)
TSPS	Time-Sharing Programming System [*Computer science*] (IEEE)
TSPS	Traffic Service Position System [*Telecommunications*]
TSPSCAP	Traffic Service Position System Real-Time Capacity Program [*Telecommunications*] (TEL)
TSPT	Transport (WGA)
TSPZ	Torres Strait Protected Zone [*Commonwealth*] (EERA)
TSP-Z	Trisodium Phosphate - Zephiran [*Clinical chemistry*]
TSPZA	Torres Strait Protected Zone Authority [*Australia*]
TSQ	Technical Services Quarterly [*A publication*]
TSQ	Time and Super Quick
TSQ	Trade Specialty Qualification (MCD)
TSQ	Triple Stage Quadrupole [*Instrumentation*]
TSQAP	Tasmanian Shellfish Quality Assurance Program (EERA)
TSR	Tactical SONAR Range (NVT)
TSR	Tactical Strike and Reconnaissance
TSR	Tactical Studies Rules [*In corporation name TSR, Inc.*]
TSR	Technically Specified Natural Rubber
TSR	Technically Specified Rubber (EDCT)
TSR	Technical Sales Representative
TSR	Technical Services Report [*A publication*] (EAAP)
TSR	Technical Services Representative (MCD)
TSR	Technical Status Review [*NASA*] (NASA)
TSR	Technical Study Report
TSR	Technical Summary Report
TSR	Technical Support Review (SSD)
TSR	Telecommunications Service Request (CET)
TSR	Telemarketing Sales Representative
TSR	Telemarketing Service Representative (WDMC)
TSR	Telephone Sales Representative (WDMC)
TSR	Telephone Support Request
TSR	TeleService Resources
TSR	Temporary Storage Register
TSR	Tensile Strength Retention [*Textile technology*]
TSR	Terminate and Stay Resident [*Computer science*]
TSR	Testosterone Sterilized Rat
TSR	Test Schedule Request
TSR	Test Status Report [*NASA*] (NASA)
TSR	Test Summary Report (IAA)
TSR	Test Support Requirements (KSC)
TSR	Thermally Stable Resin
TSR	Thermal Shock Rig [*Nuclear energy*] (NRCH)
TSR	Thermal Stress Relief [*Mechanical engineering*]
TSR	Thermochemical Sulfate Reduction [*Chemistry*]
TSR	Thermo Sentron [*AMEX symbol*] (TTSB)
TSR	Thermo Sentron, Inc. [*AMEX symbol*] (SAG)
TSR	Thyroid Hormone Secretion Rate (OA)
TSR	Thyroid-to-Serum Ratio [*Medicine*] (MAE)
TSR	Tile-Shingle Roof [*Technical drawings*]
TSR	Time Sharing Resources, Inc. [*Information service or system*] (IID)
TSR	Time Status Register
TSR	Time to Sustained Respirations [*Obstetrics*]
TSR	Timisoara [*Romania*] [*Airport symbol*] (OAG)
TSR	Tokyo Shoko Research Ltd. [*Database producer*] [*Japan*]
TSR	Torpedo-Spotter Reconnaissance [*Obsolete Military British*]
TSR	Total Shoulder Replacement [*Medicine*]

TSR............	Total Solar Radiation [*Botany*]
TSR............	Total Stress Range [*Nuclear energy*] (NUCP)
TSR............	Total System Responsibility
TSR............	Towed SONAR Response
TSR............	Tower Shielding Reactor [*Nuclear energy*]
TSR............	Trade Study Report
TSR............	Training Support Requirements [*Military*]
TSR............	Transistor Saturable Reactor
TSR............	Transportable Surveillance RADAR (MCD)
TSR............	Trans Service Airlift [*Zaire*] [*ICAO designator*] (FAAC)
TSR............	Trans-Siberian Railway
TSR............	Traveling Stock Reserve
TSR............	Tri-Star Resources [*Vancouver Stock Exchange symbol*]
TSR............	TSR, Inc. [*Associated Press*] (SAG)
TSR............	Tsuruga [*Japan*] [*Seismograph station code, US Geological Survey*] (SEIS)
TSR............	Turbine Shaft Rate [*Military*] (CAAL)
TSR............	Turnover Summary Report [*Military*]
TSR............	United States Army TRADOC, Redstone Arsenal, USAMMCS [*United States Army Missile and Munitions Center School*] Technical Library, Redstone Arsenal, AL [*OCLC symbol*] (OCLC)
TSRA	Thunderstorm with Rain [*ICAO*] (FAAC)
TSRA	Torres Strait Regional Authority [*Australia*]
TSRA	Total System Requirements Analysis (NASA)
TSRA	Training Support Requirements Analysis (MCD)
TSRB	Teachers and Schools Registration Board [*Australia*]
TSRB	Top Salaries Review Board [*British*]
TSRC	Theta-Sensitive Regulatory Cell [*Hypothetical*] [*Hematology*]
TSRC	Transmitter-Receiver (IAA)
TSRC	Transportation Systems Review Committee [*MTMC*] (TAG)
TSRC	Tubular and Split Rivet Council [*Later, TRMI*] (EA)
TSRE	Tropospheric Scatter Radio Equipment (AAG)
TSRG	Trans Energy [*NASDAQ symbol*] (TTSB)
TSRG	Trans Energy, Inc. [*NASDAQ symbol*] (SAG)
TSRI	Technical Skill Reenlistment Incentive
TSRI	TSR, Inc. [*Hauppauge, NY*] [*NASDAQ symbol*] (NQ)
TSRL	[*The*] Special Relief League [*Defunct*] (EA)
TSRL	Total Support Requirements List
TSRLM	Tandem Scanning Reflected Light Microscopy
TSRMP	Training System Resource Management Plan [*Army*]
TSRO	Two-Stage Reverse Osmosis [*Chemical engineering*]
TSRP	Technical Support Real Property
TSRP	Toll Service Results Plan [*Bell System*]
TSR PEIS	Tritium Supply and Recycling Programmatic Environmental Impact Statement
TSRS	Training Site Requirements Study [*DoD*]
TSRT...........	Teacher Situation Reaction Test
TSRTAMAA...	Tactical Surveillance, Reconnaissance, and Target Acquisition Mission Area Analysis (MCD)
TSR/TST	The Skills Required /The Skills Trained [*Test*] [*John Alden Associates*] (TE3)
TSRU	Tuberculosis Surveillance Research Unit [*Netherlands*] (EAIO)
TSRV	Torpedo Ship Ranging Vessel [*Canadian Navy*]
TSRV	Transport Systems Research Facility (GAVI)
TSRV	Transport Systems Research Vehicle
TSS............	New York [*New York*] E. 34th Street [*Airport symbol*] (OAG)
TSS............	[*The*] Safety Society (EA)
TSS............	St. Andrews School, St. Andrews, TN [*Library symbol Library of Congress*] (LCLS)
TSS............	[*The*] Super Show (ITD)
TSS............	TACFIRE Software Specialist (MCD)
TSS............	Tactical Shelter System (DOMA)
TSS............	Tactical Strike System
TSS............	Tactical Surveillance Sonobuoy (MCD)
TSS............	Tangential Signal Sensitivity
TSS............	Tank Surveillance Service [*Military Traffic Management Command*]
TSS............	Tape Search System
TSS............	Tape Storage System
TSS............	Target Selection Standard [*Military*] (INF)
TSS............	Target Selector Switch
TSS............	Target Sensing Switch
TSS............	Task-State Segment [*Operating system data structure*] [*Computer science*]
TSS............	Teacher Stress Scale (EDAC)
TSS............	Tebessa [*Algeria*] [*Airport symbol*] (AD)
TSS............	Technical Sales Seminars [*Department of Commerce*]
TSS............	Technical School Squadron [*Army*]
TSS............	Technical Services Staff [*Environmental Protection Agency*] (GFGA)
TSS............	Technical Specification Sheet
TSS............	Technical Staff Surveillance [*Military*] (IAA)
TSS............	Technical Support Services
TSS............	Technical Support Staff [*Environmental Protection Agency*] (GFGA)
TSS............	Telecommunications Security System (MCD)
TSS............	Telecommunications Service System (NITA)
TSS............	Telecommunication Switching System
TS/S...........	Telemeter Set/Synthesized (DWSG)
TSS............	Teletype Switching System [*or Subsystem*]
TSS............	Temporary Storage Site [*DoD*]
TSS............	Tensile Shear Specimen [*Plastics technology*]
TSS............	Terminal Security System [*Computer science*]
TSS............	Terminal Send Side
TSS............	Terminal Support Subsystems (NITA)
TSS............	Terminal Support System
TSS............	Test Set Simulator
TSS............	Tethered Satellite System (MCD)
TSS............	Threatened Species Strategy (EERA)
TSS............	Thrust Stand System
TSS............	Time-Shared Supervisory System (IAA)
TSS............	Time-Shared System (NITA)
TSS............	Time-Sharing System [*Computer science*]
TSS............	Toll Switching System [*Telecommunications*] (TEL)
TSS............	Topographic Support System [*Army*] (RDA)
TSS............	Toroidal Space Station
TSS............	Toroidal Support Submarine
TSS............	Total Ship Survivability (DOMA)
TSS............	Total Soluble Sulfur [*Analytical chemistry*]
TSS............	Total Subscriber Satisfaction [*HBO (Home Box Office) rating system*]
TSS............	Total Sum of Squares
TSS............	Total Suspended Solids [*Environmental chemistry*]
TSS............	Total Systems Services, Inc. [*NYSE symbol*] (SPSG)
TSS............	Total System Svcs [*NYSE symbol*] (TTSB)
TSS............	TOW [*Tube-Launched, Optically Tracked, Wire-Guided (Weapon)*] Subsystem [*Army*]
TSS............	Toxic Shock Syndrome [*Medicine*]
TSS............	Track Store Switch (IAA)
TSS............	Track Suspension System [*MTMC*] (TAG)
TSS............	Tradeoff Study Suggestion (SSD)
TSS............	Trade Support System (MHDW)
TSS............	Traffic Separation Scheme
TSS............	Traffic Surveillance System [*Traffic management*]
TSS............	Trainer System Software
TSS............	Training Services [*Job Training and Partnership Act*] (OICC)
TSS............	Training Subsystem (MCD)
TSS............	Training Support Service [*ILO*] [*United Nations*] (DUND)
TSS............	Train Supervisory System (IAA)
TSS............	Transcription Start Signal (DB)
TSS............	Transistor Servo Simulator
TSS............	Transition State Spectroscopy [*Physics*]
TSS............	Transmission Surveillance System [*Bell System*]
TSS............	Transparent Semiconductor Shutter
TSS............	Transverse Spinal Sclerosis [*Orthopedics*] (DAVI)
TSS............	Treatment System Support
TSS............	Trend-Set Industry [*Vancouver Stock Exchange symbol*]
TSS............	Tropical Sea Airlines [*Thailand*] [*ICAO designator*] (FAAC)
TSS............	Tropical Splenomegaly Syndrome [*Medicine*] (MAE)
TSS............	Tropospheric Scatter System
TSS............	Trunk Servicing System [*Bell System*]
TSS............	Tsurugisan [*Anabuki*] [*Japan*] [*Seismograph station code, US Geological Survey*] (SEIS)
TSS............	Tug Structural Support [*NASA*] (NASA)
TSS............	Turbine Steam Ship
TSS............	Turbine Supersonic Speed (ERG)
TSS............	Turner's Syndrome Society of the US (EA)
TSS............	Tutor Support Scheme [*Australia*]
TSS............	Twin Screw Steamer [*Nautical*]
TSS............	Typescripts [*Typography*] (WDAA)
TSS............	Typographic Support System (MCD)
TSS............	United States Army TRADOC, Fort Story, Fort Story, VA [*OCLC symbol*] (OCLC)
TSSA...........	Tackle and Shooting Sports Agents Association (EA)
TSSA...........	Telecommunications Sales Superintendents' Association [*A union*] [*British*]
TSSA...........	Telemetry Subcarrier Spectrum Analyzer
TSSA...........	Test Scorer and Statistical Analyzer [*Computer science*]
TSSA...........	Test Site Support Activity [*NASA*]
TSSA...........	Thunderstorm with Sandstorm [*Meteorology*]
TSSA...........	Trade Show Services Association [*Defunct*] (EA)
TSSA...........	Transport Salaried Staff's Association [*A union*] [*British*] (DCTA)
TSSA...........	Trench Shoring and Shielding Association (NTPA)
TSSA...........	Tumor-Specific Surface Antigen [*Immunology*]
TSSAA	Tackle and Shooting Sports Agents Association (EA)
TSSAM	Tri-Service Standoff Attack Missile [*Military*]
TSS & TP.....	Test Suite Structure and Test Purpose [*Telecommunications*]
TSSB...........	Tapping Students' Science Beliefs: A Resource for Teaching and Learning [*Test*] (TMMY)
TSSB...........	Two-Step Sealed Bidding (AAGC)
TSSC...........	Target Selection and Seeking Console
TSSC...........	Target System Service Charge (NG)
TSSC...........	Toxic Substances Strategy Committee [*Nuclear energy*] (NRCH)
TSS-C	Transmission Surveillance System - Cable [*Telecommunications*] (TEL)
TSSCC	Toy Stores Steiff Collectors Club (EA)
TSSCS	Tactical Synchronous Satellite Communication System
TSSD	Torsional Simple Shear Device [*Nuclear energy*] (NUCP)
TSSD	Typesetting System for Scientific Document [*Computer science*] (PDAA)
TSSDT	Thrust Subsystem Design Team [*NASA*]
TSSE...........	Tactical Security Support Equipment [*Military*]
tsse............	Terrasse (DD)
TSSE...........	Toxic Shock Syndrome Exotoxin
T/SSI	Technology/Scientific Services, Inc.
TSSIC	Tool and Stainless Steel Industry Committee (EA)
TSSLS	Titan Standardized Space Launch System (SAA)
TSSM..........	Thruster Subsystem Module [*NASA*]
TSSM..........	Total Ship Simulation Model
TSSMCP	Time-Sharing System Message Control Program (NITA)
TSSMS	Time Sharing Services Management System (GFGA)
TSSN	Thunderstorm with Snow [*Meteorology*] (FAAC)
TSSNM	Technologist Section of the Society of Nuclear Medicine (EA)
TSSOP	Thin Shrink Small Outline Package (AAEL)

TSSP............	Tactical Satellite Signal Processor (RDA)
TSSP............	Thickness-Sensitive Solar Paint [Coating technology]
TSSP............	Two Stripper in Series Permeater [Chemical engineering]
TS/SPAR......	Time Sharing System Performance Activity Recorder (PDAA)
TSSPS.........	Tsentralniya Suvet na Profesionalnite Suyuzi [Central Council of Trade Unions] [Bulgaria]
TSSR............	Theater Stock Status Report [Military]
TSSS............	Trainer Software Support System [Military]
TSSS............	Triple S Plastics [NASDAQ symbol] (SAG)
TSSSP.........	Tennessee Study of State Science Policy [National Science Foundation] (EA)
TSSST.........	Time-Space-Space-Space-Time [Telecommunications] (TEL)
TSSST.........	Threat Simulation System Terminal [Military]
TSSST.........	Toxic Shock Syndrome Toxin [Medicine]
TSSU...........	Test Signal Switching Unit (MCD)
TSSU...........	Theater Sterile Supply Unit [Surgery] (DAVI)
TSSW..........	TouchStone Software [NASDAQ symbol] (TTSB)
TSSW..........	TouchStone Software Corp. [NASDAQ symbol] (SAG)
TST.............	Media Logic, Inc. [AMEX symbol] (SPSG)
TST.............	[The] Science Teacher [A publication]
TST.............	Tail Stop and Turning [Automotive engineering]
TST.............	Tail Suspension Test (DB)
TST.............	Technical and Scholastic Test [Vocational guidance test]
TST.............	Telemetry Simulation Terminal
TST.............	Television Signal Tracer (DEN)
TST.............	Temperature Sensing Transducer
TST.............	Temporal Scaling Test (DB)
TST.............	Test (AAG)
TST.............	Test Support Table
TSt..............	Texts and Studies [A publication] (BJA)
TST.............	Thermistor Sterilization Test
TST.............	Threshold Setting Tracer
TST.............	Time-Shared Terminal [Computer science] (IAA)
TST.............	Time-Sharing Terminals, Inc.
TST.............	Time-Space-Time [Digital switching] [Telecommunications] (TEL)
TST.............	Titmus Stereocuity Test [Medicine] (DAVI)
TST.............	Torres Strait Treaty (EERA)
TST.............	Total Story Time [Broadcasting] (WDMC)
TST.............	Total Surface Tested
TST.............	Toxic Shock Toxin [Biochemistry]
TST.............	Trang [Thailand] [Airport symbol] (OAG)
TST.............	Transaction Step Task
TST.............	Transition State Theory [Physical chemistry]
TST.............	Transmission Scheme Translator (MCD)
TST.............	Transmission System Test (MCD)
TST.............	Treadmill Stress Testing [Physiology]
TST.............	Treatment Selection Team (DOGT)
TST.............	Triceps Skinfold Thickness [Medicine]
TST.............	Trilogy Screening Technique
TST.............	Troubleshooting Time (SAA)
TST.............	Truncated Sequential Test (PDAA)
TST.............	Trust
TST.............	Tuberculin Skin Test [Medicine] (PDAA)
TST.............	Tumor Skin Test [Medicine] (MAE)
TST.............	Twenty Statements Test
TST.............	Two-Station Training
TST.............	United States Army TRALINET, Systems Center, ATPL-AOT, Fort Monroe, VA [OCLC symbol] (OCLC)
TSTA...........	Tailored Ship Training Availability [Navy] (DOMA)
TSTA...........	Technology Security Technical Assessment [DoD]
TSTA...........	Toxoplasmin Skin Test Antigen (STED)
TSTA...........	Transmission, Signaling, and Test Access
TSTA...........	Tritium Systems Test Assembly (MCD)
TSTA...........	Tumor-Specific Tissue Antigen [Immunology] (DAVI)
TSTA...........	Tumor-Specific Transplantation Antigen [Immunology]
TSTC...........	Target Selection and Tracking Console
TSTD...........	Total Ship Test Director [Navy] (CAAL)
TSTE...........	Training System Test and Evaluation (MCD)
TSTEE.........	Trustee
TSTEQ.........	Test Equipment
TSTF...........	Two-Step,Two-Frequency
TSTFA.........	Tasmania Sashimi Tuna Fisherman's Association (EERA)
TSTFLT........	Test Set Fault (AAG)
TSTG...........	Testing (MSA)
TSTI...........	TST Impreso, Inc. [NASDAQ symbol] (SAG)
TSTI...........	TST/Impresso [NASDAQ symbol] (TTSB)
TSTICT........	Test Incoming Trunk [Telecommunications] (IAA)
TSTImp........	TST Impreso, Inc. [Associated Press] (SAG)
TStL & KC ...	Toledo, St. Louis & Kansas City Railroad
TSTM..........	Thunderstorm [Meteorology] (FAAC)
TSTN..........	Triple Supertwist Nematic [Video technology] (PCM)
TSTNG........	Testing
TSTO..........	Testing Tool (AAG)
TSTO..........	Test Site Tool Order [NASA] (AAG)
TSTO..........	Two-Stage-to-Orbit [Aerospace technology] (PS)
TSTP..........	Talking Screen Textwriting Program (EDAC)
TSTP..........	Test of Selected Topics in Physics
TSTP..........	Thermistor Sterilization Test Program
TSTP..........	Total Ship Test Program [Navy] (CAAL)
TSTP..........	Traffic Safety Training Program
TSTPAC.......	Transmission and Signaling Test Plan and Analysis Concept [Telecommunications] (TEL)
TSTP/AFS	Total Ship Test Program/Active Fleet Surface Ships [Navy] (CAAL)
TSTPI..........	Tapered Steel Transmission Pole Institute [Defunct] (EA)
TSTP/SP	Total Ship Test Program/Ship Production [Navy] (CAAL)

TSTR............	Tester (MSA)
TSTR............	Transistor (AAG)
TSTRZ..........	Transistorized (MSA)
TSTS............	Tail Section Test Stand (AAG)
TSTS............	Thermal Sight Test Set [Army]
TSTS............	Third Stage Test Set [Aerospace] (MCD)
TSTS............	Thrust Structure Test Stand (AAG)
TSTS............	Tomahawk System Test Set
TSTS............	Tracking System Test Set (AAG)
TSTS............	Tracking System Test Stand (IAA)
TSTWCS	Temporary Short-Time Working Compensation Scheme (AIE)
TSU.............	Contract Air Cargo, Inc. [FAA designator] (FAAC)
TSU.............	Tabiteuea South [Kiribati] [Airport symbol] (OAG)
TSU.............	Tandem Signal Unit [Telecommunications] (TEL)
TSU.............	Tape Search Unit (CET)
TSU.............	Tariff Selection Unit (OA)
TSU.............	Tarleton State University [Formerly, TSC] [Texas]
TSU.............	Task-Specific Utility
TSU.............	Technical Service Unit
TSU.............	Technical Support Unit (IAA)
TSU.............	Telecommunications Study Unit [American Topical Association] [Defunct] (EA)
TSU.............	Telephone Signal Unit [Telecommunications] (TEL)
TSU.............	Telescope Sight Unit (MCD)
TSU.............	Tennessee State University, Nashville, TN [Library symbol Library of Congress OCLC symbol] (LCLS)
TSU.............	Terminating Signal Unit [Electronics] (ECII)
TSU.............	Test Signal Unit [Telecommunications] (TEL)
TSU.............	Texas Southern University
TSU.............	Thermal Systems Unit (KSC)
TSU.............	This Side Up
TSU.............	Time Standard Unit
TSU.............	Transfer Switch Unit (AAG)
TSU.............	Transportation System Utilization Program [Department of Energy]
TSU.............	Trans-Species Unlimited [Later, ARM] (EA)
TSU.............	Triple Sugar-Urea Base [Agar] [Microbiology]
TSU.............	Trunk Switching Unit (NITA)
TSU.............	Tsu [Japan] [Seismograph station code, US Geological Survey] (SEIS)
TSU.............	Tsumeb [South-West Africa] [Geomagnetic observatory code]
TSU.............	Tulsa-Sapulpa Union Railway Co. [AAR code]
TSU.............	Twin and Subtract (SAA)
TSUP	Trunk Supervisor [Telecommunications] (IAA)
TSUR	Tectonic Surface Uplift Rate [Biology]
TSUS	Tariff Schedules of the United States [Later, HTSUS]
TSUS	Territorial Seas of the United States (COE)
TSUSA	Tariff Schedules of the United States, Annotated
TSV.............	Terminal Stage Vehicle
TSV.............	Thermal Sensitive Vote [Automotive interior comfort survey]
TSV.............	Thru-Sight Video [Army training device] (INF)
TSV.............	Tobacco Streak Virus
TSV.............	Total Stomach Volume [Medicine] (STED)
TSV.............	Townsville [Australia Airport symbol] (OAG)
TSV.............	Tropair Airservices [British ICAO designator] (FAAC)
TSV.............	Turbine Stop Valve [Nuclear energy] (NRCH)
TSV.............	Turnkey Systems Vendor [Computer science] (MHDI)
TSV.............	Twin Springs [Nevada] [Seismograph station code, US Geological Survey Closed] (SEIS)
TSVP	Tournez s'il Vous Plait [Please Turn Over] [See also PTO] [French]
TSVR	Total Systemic Vascular Resistance
TSVS	Time-Sharing - Virtual System [Computer science] (MCD)
TSW............	Southwestern Baptist Theological Seminary, Fort Worth, TX [OCLC symbol] (OCLC)
TSW............	Task Status Word (NITA)
TSW............	Technical Scope of Work
TSW............	Telesoftware (NITA)
TSW............	Temperature Switch (MSA)
TSW............	Test Software (MCD)
TSW............	Test Switch
TSW............	The Searchers Workbench (NITA)
TSW............	Time Switch [Telecommunications] (TEL)
TSW............	Trade Shows Worldwide [Formerly, TSPED] [A publication]
TSW............	Trans European Airways [Switzerland ICAO designator] (FAAC)
TSW............	Transfer Switch
TSW............	Transmitting Slide Wire
TSW............	Trau, Schau, Wem [Trust, but Be Careful Whom] [Motto of Christian I, Elector of Saxony (1560-91)] [German]
TSW............	Tropical Summer Winter [Vessel load line mark]
TSW............	Tsunami Warning [Telecommunications] (OTD)
tsw.............	Tswana [MARC language code Library of Congress] (LCCP)
TSW............	T Switch Cell [Immunology]
TSW............	Turbine-Building Service Water [Nuclear energy] (NRCH)
TSWE..........	Test of Standard Written English
TSWG..........	Training Support Working Group [Army]
TSWL..........	Tulsa Studies in Women's Literature [A publication] (BRI)
TSWTT.........	Test Switch Thrust Termination
TSWV..........	Tomato Spotted Wilt Virus
TSX.............	Telephone Satellite, Experimental
TSX.............	Time-Sharing Execution [Computer science] (IAA)
TSX.............	Time-Sharing Executive [Modular Computer Systems] [Computer science]
TSX.............	Time-Sharing Executive System [Computer science] (IAA)
TSX.............	Transfer and Set Index (SAA)
TSX.............	True Seed Exchange [Later, SSE] (EA)
TSX-4..........	Touring Sport Extra-4WD [In automotive name Ghia Vignale TSX-4]

TSX Cp	TSX Corp. [*Associated Press*] (SAG)
TSXX	TSX Corp. [*NASDAQ symbol*] (SAG)
TSY	Tech-Sym [*NYSE symbol*] (TTSB)
TSY	Tech-Sym Corp. [*NYSE symbol*] (SPSG)
TSY	Trypticase Soy Yeast [*Cell growth medium*] (MAE)
TT	Caroline Islands (VRA)
TT	Chad [*International civil aircraft marking*] (ODBW)
TT	Marshall Islands (VRA)
TT	Royal West [*ICAO designator*] (AD)
TT	Tablet Triturate [*Pharmacy*]
TT	Tactical Training [*Followed by location*] [*Military*]
TT	Tactile Tension [*Ophthalmology*]
TT	Tail-to-Tail [*Polymer structure*]
TT	Talar Tilt [*Angle of ankle joint*]
TT	Talith and Tefillin (BJA)
TT	Talking Task (STED)
TT	Talmud Torah (BJA)
TT	Tanganyika Territory
TT	Tank Technology (WDAA)
TT	Tank Top (DS)
TT	Tank Truck [*Freight*]
TT	Tantato Resources, Inc. [*Vancouver Stock Exchange symbol*]
TT	Target Towing Aircraft [*Navy*]
TT	Teacher Training
TT	Technical Team
TT	Technical Test
TT	Technical Training (OICC)
TT	Technical Translation [*A publication Obsolete*]
TT	Technology Transfer (DS)
TT	Teetotaler [*Slang*]
TT	Telecommunications Technician [*British military*] (DMA)
TT	Telegraphic Transfer [*of funds*] [*Banking*]
TT	Telephone Therapy (DHP)
TT	Teletype
TT	Teletypewriter [*Telecommunications*]
TT	Teletypewriter and Facsimile Apparatus [*JETDS nomenclature*] [*Military*] (CET)
TT	Teller Terminal (MHDW)
TT	Tell Taanach (BJA)
TT	Tempelurkunden aus Tello [*A publication*] (BJA)
TT	Temperature Transmitter [*Nuclear energy*] (NRCH)
TT	Temporarily Transferred [*Telecommunications*] (TEL)
TT	Tendon Transfer [*Surgery*]
T/T	Terminal Timing (KSC)
TT	Terminal Timing [*NASA*] (NAKS)
TT	Terminal Transferase (STED)
tt	Terminus Technicus (BJA)
TT	Terms of Trade (MHDW)
TT	Testamentary Trust [*Legal term*]
TT	Test Temperature [*Nuclear energy*] (NRCH)
TT	Test Terminator (IAA)
TT	Test [*or Testing*] Time (IAA)
TT	Test Tube (IAA)
TT	Tetanus Toxoid [*Medicine*]
TT	Tetrathionate [*Nutrient broth*] [*Microbiology*]
TT	Tetrazol (MAE)
TT	Texas Tower (SAA)
TT	Text Telephone [*Hearing-impaired technology*] [*See also TDD*]
TT	Text Typewriter (PAZ)
TT	Theology Today [*A publication*] (BRI)
TT	Thermally Tuned (IAA)
TT	Thermal-Tow
TT	Thermomagnetic Treatment (IAA)
TT	Thermometric Titrimetry
TT	Thermostat Switch (IAA)
TT	Think Time [*Computer order entry*]
TT	Thomas Thorpe [*Publisher of a 1609 edition of Shakespeare's sonnets*]
TT	Thrombin Time [*Hematology*]
TT	Thrust Termination
TT	Thymol Turbidity [*Clinical chemistry*]
TT	Tibial Torsion [*Orthopedics*] (DAVI)
TT	Tibial Tubercle [*Anatomy*]
TT	Tibial Tuberosity (STED)
TT	Ticarcillin and Tobramycin [*Antibacterial mixture*]
TT	Tidningarnas Telegrambyra [*Press agency*] [*Sweden*]
TT	Tight Torso [*Women's fashions*]
TT	Tile Threshold (MSA)
TT	Tilt Table [*Orthopedics*] (DAVI)
TT	Tilt Trailers (DCTA)
TT	Timetable (DS)
T/T	Timing and Telemetry
TT	Tine Test (STED)
TT	Title Terms (NITA)
Tt	Titus [*New Testament book*] (BJA)
TT	Tobacco Tax Ruling Term (DLA)
TT	Tobramycin-Ticarcillin [*Antibiotic combination*]
TT	Token Test (EDAC)
TT	[*The*] Toledo Terminal Railroad Co. [*AAR code*]
TT	Tolytriazole [*Organic chemistry*]
TT	Tooling Tag (SAA)
TT	Tooling Template (MCD)
TT	Tooth Treatment [*Dentistry*] (DAVI)
TT	Topical Time [*A publication*]
TT	Top-to-Top (IAA)

TT	Torpedo Tube
TT	Total Run Time [*Robotic assay*]
TT	Total Task Chaining [*Psychology*]
TT	Total Temperature (MCD)
TT	Total Thyroxin (STED)
TT	Total Thyroxine [*Endocrinology*]
TT	Total Time (MSA)
TT	Totus Tuus [*All Yours*] [*Latin*]
TT	Touch-Tone [*Telecommunications*] (IAA)
TT	Touring Twin Carburetor [*Automobile model*]
TT	Tourism Tasmania [*Australia*]
TT	Tourist Trophy [*Motorcycle racing*] [*British*]
TT	Townsend Thoreson [*Company running English Channel ferries*]
TT	Tow Truck
T/T	Trace of/Trace of Referring to findings of traces of different substances on tests (DAVI)
TT	Tracking Technician (SAA)
TT	Tracking Telescope
TT	Traffic Tester [*Telecommunications*] (TEL)
TT	Training Text
TT	Transaction Terminal (BUR)
TT	Transferred to (STED)
TT	Transfer Trip [*Telecommunications*] (IAA)
TT	Transformation Toughened (MCD)
TT	Transient Tachypnea [*Medicine*] (DMAA)
TT	Transit Time [*of blood through heart and lungs*]
TT	Transmitting Tract [*Botany*]
TT	Transmitting Typewriter [*Telecommunications*] (IAA)
TT	Transonic Tunnel [*NASA*]
TT	Transport Trust [*British*] [*An association*] (DBA)
TT	TransTechnology [*NYSE symbol*] (TTSB)
TT	TransTechnology Corp. [*NYSE symbol*] (SPSG)
TT	Trans-Texas Airways
TT	Transthoracic [*Medicine*]
TT	Transtracheal [*Medicine*] (DAVI)
TT	Travel and Tourism Program [*Association of Independent Colleges and Schools specialization code*]
T/T	Travel/Tourism
TT	Trees for Tomorrow (EA)
TT	Tree Test [*Psychology*]
TT	Tree Tops
TT	Tributary Team [*Military*]
TT	Tricycle and Tail Skid [*Aerospace*] (AAG)
T/T	Trienoic/Tetraenoic [*Ratio of unsaturated chemicals*]
TT	Trigesimo-Secundo [*Book from 10 to 12-1/2 centimeters in height*] [*Bibliography*]
TT	Trinidad and Tobago [*ANSI two-letter standard code*] (CNC)
TT	Trinity Term
TT	Triple Thermoplastic (SAA)
TT	Troop Test
TT	Trunk Test [*Telecommunications*] (IAA)
TT	Trust Termination
TT	Trust Territories
TT	Trust Territory of the Pacific Islands [*Postal code*]
tt	Trust Territory of the Pacific Islands [*MARC country of publication code Library of Congress*] (LCCP)
TT	Tuberculin Tested [*Milk*]
TT	Tube Thoracostomy (STED)
TT	Tufted Titmouse [*Ornithology*]
TT	Tumor Thrombus (STED)
TT	Turbine Tanker
TT	Turbine Trip (IEEE)
TT	Turnover Time (STED)
TT	Turntable (ADA)
TT	Turret Trainer [*British military*] (DMA)
TT	Twitch Tension [*Neurology*] (DAVI)
TT	Tyne and Tees [*50th Northumbrian Division*] [*British military*] (DMA)
TT	Tyrosine Transaminase (STED)
TT$_3$	Total Triiodothyronine [*Endocrinology*]
TT4	Total Thyroxine [*Endocrinology*]
TTA	Tan Tan [*Morocco*] [*Airport symbol*] (OAG)
TTA	Tasmanian Touch Association [*Australia*]
TTA	Tatalina [*Alaska*] [*Seismograph station code, US Geological Survey*] (SEIS)
TTA	Teacher Training Agency [*British*] (DET)
TTA	Telecommunications and Telephone Association [*Arlington, VA*] [*Telecommunications service*] (TSSD)
TTA	Telecommunication Traffic Association [*British*] (BI)
TTA	Television Technicians' Association (IAA)
TTA	Test Target Array (AFM)
TTA	Theatre Television Authority (EA)
TTA	Theatrical Traders Association Ltd. [*British*] (BI)
TTA	Thenoyltrifluoroacetone [*Also, TTB*] [*Organic chemistry*]
TTA	Thermomechanical Test Area [*NASA*] (NASA)
TTA	Throughput Time Average [*Compression algorithm*] (MCD)
TTA	Throughput Transmitted Algorithm
TTA	Thrust Termination Assembly
TTA	Tilt Table Angle [*Vehicle rollover*] [*Automotive safety*]
TTA	Time to Apogee [*Aerospace*] (MCD)
TTA	Tolyltriazole [*Organic chemistry*]
TTA	Toronto Theatre Alliance [*Canada*] (WWLA)
TTA	Total Tangible Assets [*Business term*] (ADA)
TTA	Total Titratable Acidity [*Analytical chemistry*]
TTA	Total Toe Arthroplasty [*Medicine*] (DMAA)
TTA	Tourism Training Australia

TTA............ Trade and Tourism Alliance [Defunct] (EA)
TTA............ Traffic Trunk Administration [Telecommunications] (TEL)
TTA............ Trainer Training Assistance [Australia]
TTA............ Transformation Toughened Alumina (MCD)
TTA............ Transit Time Accelerometer
TTA............ Transporte e Trabalho Aero [Mozambique] [ICAO designator] (FAAC)
TTA............ Trans-Texas Airways
TTA............ Transtracheal Aspiration [Medicine]
TTA............ Travel and Tourism Association (EA)
TTA............ Travel Time Authorized
TTA............ Triplet-Triplet Annihilation [Spectroscopy]
TTA............ Tritolylamine [Organic chemistry]
TTA............ Turbine-Alternator Assembly (MCD)
TTAB........ Tasmanian Totalisator Agency Board [Australia]
TTAB........ Tetradecyltrimethylammonium Bromide [Organic chemistry]
TTAB........ Trademark Trial and Appeal Board [of Patent Office]
TTAC........ Tracking, Telemetry, and Command [AEC] (IAA)
TTAD........ Temporary Tour of Active Duty [Military]
TTADB .... Tactical Terrain Analysis Database [Army]
TTAF........ Technical Training Air Force
TT&C........ Telemetry, Tracking, and Commanding (COE)
TT&C........ Tracking, Telemetry, and Command (CIST)
TT&C........ Tracking Telemetry and Control (NAKS)
TT & E........ Technical Test and Evaluation
TT & L........ Treasury Tax and Loan Account [Banking]
TT&Ls........ Treasury and Loan Accounts (EBF)
TT & P........ Training, Transient and Patient
TTAP........ Telemetry Technical Analysis Position (MCD)
TTAP........ Tiger Team Assessment Program (COE)
TTAT........ TACFIRE Training Assistance Team (MCD)
TTAT........ Torpedo Tube Acceptance Trials [Navy] (NG)
TTAW........ Table Tennis Association of Wales (DBA)
TTAWA........ Typewriter Trade and Allied Workers' Association [A union] [British]
TTB............ Tanker, Transport, Bomber [Requirements] [Air Force]
TTB............ Target Triggered Burst
TTB............ Tatuoca [Brazil] [Geomagnetic observatory code]
TTB............ Technical Test Battery [Aptitude test]
TTB............ Teletypewriter Buffer (CET)
TTB............ Test Two Bits (IAA)
TTB............ Tetragonal Tungsten Bronze
TTB............ Time to Blackout
TTB............ Toll Testboard [Telecommunications] (TEL)
TTB............ Trifluoro(thienyl)butanedione [Also, TTA] [Organic chemistry]
TTB............ Twin Traction-Beam [Ford Motor Co.] [Truck four-wheel drive front suspension]
TTB............ Typing Test for Business
TTBASIC ...... Tattletale Beginner's All-Purpose Symbolic Instruction Code [Computer science]
TTBB............ First Tenor, Second Tenor, First Bass, and Second Bass [in all-male choral groups]
TTBL............ Task Table (MHDB)
TTBOY .... To the Best of You [An association] (EA)
TTBS............ Timber Trades' Benevolent Society [British] (BI)
TTBT............ Threshold Test Ban Treaty [1974]
TTBWR ...... Twisted Tape Boiling Water Reactor (IEEE)
TTC............ Tactical Telephone Central [Telecommunications] (IAA)
TTC............ Taltal [Chile] [Airport symbol] (AD)
TTC............ Tape to Card
TTC............ Tape Transport Cassette
TTC............ Target Track Central
TTC............ Target Tracking Console (MCD)
TTC............ Tatung [Republic of China] [Seismograph station code, US Geological Survey] (SEIS)
TTC............ Teacher Training College
TTC............ Technical Training Center [Air Force]
TTC............ Technical Training Command [Army Air Forces] [World War II]
TTC............ Technology Training Corporation (AAGC)
TTC............ Telecommunications Techniques Corp.
TTC............ Telecommunication Training Centre [Fiji] [Telecommunications]
TTC............ Telemetry, Tracking, and Command (NASA)
TTC............ Telemetry Traffic Control (SSD)
TTC............ Telephone Terminal Cables (KSC)
TTC............ Telephone Toll Call (IAA)
TTC............ Teletype Center [Telecommunications] (IAA)
TTC............ Teletype Message Converter [Telecommunications] (IAA)
TTC............ Teletypewriter Center [Military]
TTC............ Television Training Centre Ltd. [British] (CB)
TTC............ Temperature Test Chamber
TTC............ Tender to Contract Policy [Export Credits Guarantee Department] [British]
TTC............ Terminating Toll Center (DEN)
TTC............ Test Transfer Cask [Nuclear energy] (NRCH)
TTC............ Tetrazoliumchloride (EDCT)
TTC............ Textile Technology Centre (AC)
TTC............ [The] Thomson Corp.
TTC............ Tight Tape Contact
TTC............ Time to Circularize Orbit (MCD)
TTC............ Time to Control
TTC............ Tin Telluride Crystal
TTC............ Tobacco Tax Council (EA)
TTC............ Tobramycin, Ticarcillin, and Cephalothin
TTC............ Toro Co. [NYSE symbol] (TTSB)
TTC............ Toro Corp. [NYSE symbol] (SPSG)
TTC............ Toronto Transit Commission [Canada] (BARN)
TTC............ Tow Target Cable

TTC............ Tracking, Telemetry, and Command
TTC............ Tracking, Telemetry, and Control [NASA] (NASA)
TTC............ Training Technology Centers [Army]
TTC............ Transient Temperature Control
TTC............ Translation Thrust Control
TTC............ Translunar Trajectory Characteristics [AEC] (IAA)
TTC............ Transportation Test Center [Department of Transportation] [Pueblo, CO] (GRD)
TTC............ Travel for Tomorrow Council (EA)
TTC............ Travelmaster Travel Club [Defunct] (EA)
TTC............ Treasure Trove Club (EA)
TTC............ Triphenyltetrazolium Chloride [Also, RT, TPTZ] [Chemical indicator]
TTC............ Tropic Test Center [Army] (MCD)
TTC............ Tube Temperature Control
TTC............ Tubulinyl Tyrosine Carboxypeptidase
TTC............ Tunnel Thermal Control (NASA)
TTCA............ Thiothiazolidinecarboxylic Acid [Organic chemistry]
T/TCA........ Thrust/Translation Control Assembly [NASA] (KSC)
TTCA............ Thrust Translation Controller Assembly [NASA] (NAKS)
TTCA............ Tibetan Terrier Club of America (EA)
TTCA............ T-Ten Class Association (EA)
TTC & M...... Telemetry, Tracking, Command, and Monitoring
TTCC............ [The] Technical Cooperation Committee [Army] (AABC)
TTCC............ Tomahawk Tactical Commanders Course (DOMA)
TTCE............ Tooth-to-Tooth Composite Error
TTCE............ Transportation Terminal Command Europe [MTMC] (TAG)
TTC/FES...... Tender to Contract and Forward Exchange Supplement [Export Credits Guarantee Department] [British] (DS)
TTCI............ Transient Temperature Control Instrument
TTC-L........ Toyota Total Clean-Lean [Automotive engineering]
TTCMSC...... Tonga and Tin Can Mail Study Circle (EA)
TTCN............ Tree and Tabular Combined Notation [Telecommunications] (OSI)
TTCP............ Scarborough/Crown Point, Tobago [Trinidad and Tobago] [ICAO location identifier] (ICLI)
TTCP............ [The] Technical Cooperation Program [US, UK, Canada, Australia] [Research]
TTCP............ Transmitting Typewriter with Card Punch (IAA)
TTCP............ Tripartite Technical Cooperation Program [Military] (NG)
TTCQF........ Technology Transfer Component Qualification Facility (SSD)
TTCS............ Tank Turret Camouflage System [Army]
TTCS............ Target Tracking and Control System (MCD)
TTCS............ Toy Train Collectors Society (EA)
TTCS............ Truck Transportable Communications Station
TTCT............ Torrance Tests of Creative Thinking [Educational test]
TTCU............ Teletypewriter Control Unit (AABC)
TTCV............ Tracking, Telemetry, Command, and Voice [Aerospace]
TTD............ Palm Island [Windward Islands, West Indies] [Airport symbol] (AD)
TTD............ Tactical Terrain Data [Army]
TTD............ Tank Training Devices (MCD)
TTD............ Teachers Training Diploma
TTD............ Technical Test Director
TTD............ Technical Training Detachment
TTD............ Temporary Text Delay
TTD............ Temporary Total Disablement [Insurance] (AIA)
TTD............ Temporary Travel Document (NATG)
TTD............ Tetraethylthiuram Disulfide [Also, TETD] [Organic chemistry]
TTD............ Thermal Time Distribution [Chemical engineering]
TTD............ Things to Do
TTD............ [The] Third Degree [A publication] (EAAP)
TTD............ Tissue Tolerance Dose (MAE)
TTD............ Totals to Date (MCD)
TTD............ Total Time to Doctorate
TTD............ Transponder Transmitter Detector
TTD............ Transportation Technical Data [Army]
TTD............ Triazolo-Thiadiazine [Organic chemistry]
TTD............ Trichothiodystrophy [Medicine]
TTD............ Trondhjemite-Tonalite-Dacite [Geology]
TTD............ Troutdale, OR [Location identifier FAA] (FAAL)
TTDF............ Tariff and Trade Data Files (NITA)
TTDI............ Teacher Training in Developing Institutions
TTD keyterm index... Textile Technology Digest Keyterm Index (NITA)
TTDL............ Terminal Transparent Delay Language (NITA)
TTDL............ Terminal Transparent Display Language [Computer science] (MHDI)
TTDR............ Tracking Telemetry Data Receiver (AAG)
TTDT............ Tactical Test Data Translator (MUGU)
TTE............ Autotote Corp. CI'A' [AMEX symbol] (TTSB)
TTE............ Task Training Exercise
TTE............ Technical Training Engineer
TTE............ Technical [or Tactical] Training Equipment (MCD)
TTE............ Telephone Terminal Equipment
TTE............ Temporary Test Equipment (AAG)
TTE............ Tentative Tables of Equipment
TTE............ Ternate [Indonesia] [Airport symbol] (OAG)
TTE............ Thermal Transfer Equipment (IAA)
TTE............ Thermal Transient Equipment [Nuclear energy] (NRCH)
TTE............ Time-Tagged Event [Remote sensing]
TTE............ Time to End
TTE............ Time to Event [NASA] (KSC)
TTE............ Tool and Test Equipment [DoD]
TTE............ Total Tax Expenditures [Economics]
TTE............ Total Transportation Expenditure [Department of Transportation]
TTE............ Trailer Test Equipment (AAG)
TTE............ Trigon Tech, Inc. [Vancouver Stock Exchange symbol]
TTE............ Two-dimensional Transthoracic

TTEB	Transfert de la Technologie de l'Energie dans les Batiments [*Buildings Energy Technology Transfer Program*] [*Canada*]
TTEC	TeleTech Holdings, Inc. [*NASDAQ symbol*] (SAG)
TTEC	Teletypewriter Technician
TTEE	Trustee
TTeF	Tetratellurafulvalene [*Organic chemistry*]
TTEGDA	Tetraethylene Glycol Diacrylate [*Organic chemistry*]
TTEL	Tool and Test Equipment List [*NASA*] (NASA)
TTELF	Tadiran Telecomm [*NASDAQ symbol*] (TTSB)
TTEM	Tooling Test Equipment Team (AAG)
T-TEN	Toyota Technical Education Network
TTEP	Tactical Torpedo Evaluation Program [*Navy*]
TTEP	Training and Training Equipment (MCD)
TTET	Turbine Transport Evaluation Team [*FAA*] (MUGU)
TTF	Tactical Task Force (AFM)
TTF	Tactical Training Flight [*Military*]
TTF	Tanker Task Force (AFM)
TTF	Target Towing Flight [*British military*] (DMA)
TTF	Test to Failure (NATG)
TTF	Tetrathiofulvalene [*Organic chemistry*]
TTF	Thai Fund [*NYSE symbol*] (SPSG)
TTF	Thoriated-Tungsten Filament (SAA)
TTF	Thyroid Transcription Factor [*Genetics*]
TTF	Timber Trades Federation (DAS)
TTF	Time to Failure
TTF	Time to Fire [*Military*] (CAAL)
TTF	Tone Telegraph Filter
TTF	Training Task Force
TTF	Transcription Termination Factor [*Genetics*]
TTF	Transient Time Flowmeter [*Nuclear energy*] (NRCH)
TTF	Transistor Test Fixture
TTF	Trend Type Forecast (ADA)
TTF	TrueType Font [*Computer science*] (CDE)
TTF	Two/Ten Foundation (EA)
TTFA	Target Transformation Factor Analysis [*Environmental Protection Agency*] (GFGA)
TTFA	Thallium Trifluoroacetate [*Organic chemistry*]
TTFA	Training Technology Field Activity [*Army*]
TTF & T	Technology Transfer, Fabrication, and Test (RDA)
TTFB	Tetrachlorotrifluoromethylbenzimidazole [*Organic chemistry*]
TTFC	Tactical and Technical Fire Control (MCD)
TTFC	Tanya Tucker Fan Club (EA)
TTFD	Thiamine Tetrahydrofurfuryl Disulfide [*Pharmacology*]
TTFE	Transportation Terminal Command Far East [*MTMC*] (TAG)
TTFF	Time to First Fix [*Quality control*]
TTF file	TrueType Font File [*Computer science*] (IGQR)
TTFN	Ta Ta for Now
TTFT	Tetra(trifluoromethyl)thiophene [*Organic chemistry*]
TTF-TCNQ	Tetrathiafulvene-Tetracyanoquinodimethane [*Organic chemistry*]
TTFTT	Terminal Tax Filing Time Trauma
TTFW	Too Taoky for Words [*Slang*]
TTG	General Trustco of Canada [*Toronto Stock Exchange symbol*]
TTG	Gibson General Hospital, Trenton, TN [*Library symbol Library of Congress*] (LCLS)
TTG	Tactical Training Group [*Military*]
TTG	Tactical Transport Group [*Military*]
TTG	Tartagal [*Argentina*] [*Airport symbol*] (AD)
TTG	Technical Translation Group (IEEE)
TTG	Tellurite, Taurocholate, and Gelatin [*Microbiology*] (DMAA)
TTG	Test Target Generator
TTG	Time to Go [*Air Force*]
TTG	Titograd [*Yugoslavia*] [*Seismograph station code, US Geological Survey*] (SEIS)
TTG	Tobacco Tax Guide [*Internal Revenue Service*]
TTG	Tonalite-Trondhjemite-Granodiorite [*Geology*]
TTG	Travel with Troops Going
TTG	Trondhjemite-Tonalite-Granodiorite [*Geology*]
TTGA	Tellurite-Taurocholate-Gelatin Agar [*Microbiology*]
TTGAC	Travel and Tourism Government Affairs Council (EA)
TTGD	Time-to-Go Dial
TTGR	Time-to-Go Rating [*Air Force*] (IAA)
TTH	Thyrotrophic Hormone [*Also, TSH*] [*Endocrinology*]
TTH	Title Tech, Inc. [*Vancouver Stock Exchange symbol*]
TTH	Tritiated Thymidine (MAE)
TTHA	Triethylenetetraminehexaacetic Acid [*Organic chemistry*]
TTHE	Thermal Transient Histogram Equivalent [*Nuclear energy*] (NRCH)
TTHFA	Twisted-Pair, Telephone, Heat and Flame Resistant, Armored [*Wire technology*] (IAA)
TTHFC	Tom T. Hall Fan Club [*Defunct*] (EA)
TTHM	Total Trihalomethane [*Analytical chemistry*]
TTI	Robert A. Taft Institute of Government (EA)
TTI	Tactical Target Illustration (AFM)
TTI	[*The*] Teachers, Inc. (EA)
TTI	Technology Transfer Institute [*Santa Monica, CA*] [*Telecommunications*] (TSSD)
TTI	Teletype Input (IAA)
TTI	Teletype Test Instruction (KSC)
TTI	Tension Time Index (AAMN)
TTI	Texas Transportation Institute [*Texas A & M University*] [*Research center*]
TTI	Thoracic Trauma Index [*Automotive safety research*]
TTI	TIE/Telecommunications Canada Ltd. [*Toronto Stock Exchange symbol*]
TTI	Time-Temperature Index
TTI	Time Temperature Indicator (IEEE)

TTI	Time Template Indicator
TTI	Time to Intercept [*Missiles*] (NG)
TTI	Training-Testing Intervals
TTI	Transmitter Terminal Identification (CIST)
TTI	TransTest, Inc. (EFIS)
TTI	Transthoracic Impedance [*Medicine*]
TTI	Traveling Ticket Inspector (DCTA)
TTI	Travel Trends International [*Commercial firm British*]
TTI	True Total Ion
TTI	Tuck Tummy In [*Slang*]
TTI	Turner Teleport, Inc. [*Atlanta, GA*] [*Telecommunications service*] (TSSD)
TTI	Tyco Toys [*NYSE symbol*] (TTSB)
TTI	Tyco Toys, Inc. [*NYSE symbol*] (SPSG)
TTIA	Timber Trade Industrial Association [*Australia*]
TTIA	Tube Temperature Indication and Alarm
TTIB	Tension-Time Index per Beat [*Neurology*] (DAVI)
TTIC	Test Technology Information Center (MCD)
TTIC	Tropical Timber Information Center [*College of Environmental Science and Forestry at Syracuse*] [*Research center*] (RCD)
TTIF	Training Taxpayer Information File [*IRS*]
TTIG	Training Task Indentification Guide
TTII	Therapeutic Technologies (EFIS)
TT/IOTE	Technical Testing/Initial Operator Test and Evaluation [*Army*]
TTIPS	Ticker Tape Information Processing System [*Online stock information service*]
TTIS	Traveling Trickle Irrigation System
TTITS	Thrust Termination Initiator Test Set
TTIU	Trustworthy Terminal Interface Unit [*Telecommunications*] (OSI)
TTJ	Thermo Technology International [*Vancouver Stock Exchange symbol*]
TTJ	Tottori [*Japan*] [*Airport symbol*] (OAG)
TTK	Terminate Task Key
TTK	Tie Trunk [*Telecommunications*]
TTK	Tokyo Tsushin Kogyo [*Tokyo Telecommunications Engineering Co.*]
TTK	Two-Tone Keying
TTL	Tatalina [*Alaska*] [*Seismograph station code, US Geological Survey Closed*] (SEIS)
TTL	Teletype Telling
TTL	Texas Tech University, School of Law Library, Lubbock, TX [*OCLC symbol*] (OCLC)
TTL	Theological Translation Library [*A publication*]
TTL	Thomson T-Line [*Commercial firm British*]
TTL	Through the Lens [*Trademark of Spiratone, Inc.*]
TTL	Time-to-Live (TNIG)
TTL	Title [*Online database field identifier*] [*Computer science*]
TTL	Torotel, Inc. [*AMEX symbol*] (SPSG)
TTL	Torrent Resources Ltd. [*Vancouver Stock Exchange symbol*]
TTL	To Take Leave
TTL	Total
TTL	Total Time to Launch [*NASA*] (KSC)
TTL	TRADOC Troop List (MCD)
TTL	Trail Termination Line (MCD)
TTL	Training and Test Lung [*Simulator*] [*Medicine*] (DAVI)
TTL	Transistor-Transistor Logic [*Also, T²L*]
TTL	Transit-Time LIDAR (MCD)
TTL	Tribal Trust Land [*Zimbabwe*]
TTL	Tribothermoluminescence
TTL	Tubulinyl Tyrosine Ligase
TTL	Turtle Island [*Fiji*] [*Airport symbol*] (OAG)
TTL	Twin Trapezoidal Links [*Mazda*] [*Automotive engineering*]
TTLC	Themes and Topics of Literature Criticism [*A publication*]
TTLC	Total Threshold Limit Concentration [*Environmental chemistry*]
TTLM	Through-the-Lens Light Metering (MCD)
TTLR	Tanganyika Territory Law Reports [*1921-47*] [*A publication*] (DLA)
TTLS	Team Training Launch Station (AAG)
TTLS	Transistor-Transistor Logic Schottky (CIST)
TtlWrld	Total World Telecommunications, Inc. [*Associated Press*] (SAG)
TTM	Tablon de Tamara [*Colombia*] [*Airport symbol*] (AD)
TTM	Tactical Target Materials
TTM	Tactical Telemetry
TTM	Temperature Test Model
T/TM	Test and Training Monitor (AAG)
TTM	Thermal Test Model
TTM	Torpedo Tube Missile (MCD)
TTM	Total Time Management [*Industrial engineering*]
TTM	Transit Time Modulation (DEN)
TTM	Turtle Mountains [*California*] [*Seismograph station code, US Geological Survey*] (SEIS)
TTM	Two-Tone Modulation
TTMA	TRACON Traffic Management Advisor [*FAA*] (TAG)
TTMA	Truck Trailer Manufacturers Association (EA)
TTMA	Tufted Textile Manufacturers Association [*Later, CRI*] (EA)
TTMAD	Testing-Teaching Module of Auditory Discrimination [*Child development test*]
TTMC	Tactical Target Materials Catalogue (MCD)
T/TMC	Traffic/Traffic Management and Control [*British*]
TTMCFC	Theater-Type Mobilization Corps Force Capabilities [*Military*]
TTMCFO	Theater-Type Mobilization Corps Force Objective [*Military*]
TTMF	Touch-Tone Multifrequency (CET)
TTML	Transistor-Transistor Micrologic (IAA)
TTMM	Tergotrochanteral Muscle Motoneuron [*Zoology*]
TTMM	True Tape Motion Memory
TTMP	Tactical Targets Materials Program (AFM)
TTMP	Transit Time Magnetic Pumping

TTMS	Telephoto Transmission Measuring Set
TTMT	Tower Tech [NASDAQ symbol] (TTSB)
TTMT	Tower Tech, Inc. [NASDAQ symbol] (SAG)
TTN	Highland Express [British ICAO designator] (FAAC)
TTN	Taitung [Taito] [Republic of China] [Seismograph station code, US Geological Survey] (SEIS)
TTN	Technology Transfer Network [Michigan State Department of Commerce] [Lansing, MI] [Information service or system] (IID)
TT/N	Test Tone to Noise Ratio [Telecommunications] (TEL)
TTN	[The] Titan Corp. [NYSE symbol] (SPSG)
TTN	Transient Tachypnea of Newborn [Gynecology]
TTN	Trenton [New Jersey] [Airport symbol] (OAG)
TTN	Trenton, NJ [Location identifier FAA] (FAAL)
TTN	Trevecca Nazarene College, Nashville, TN [OCLC symbol] (OCLC)
TTN	Triton Canada Resources Ltd. [Toronto Stock Exchange symbol]
TTN	Tumor Site, T-Stage, N-Stage [Oncology]
TTNA	Trinidad and Tobago National Alliance [Political party] (PPW)
TTNB	Transient Tachypnea of the Newborn [Medicine] (MEDA)
TTNF	Two/Ten National Foundation [Later, TTF] (EA)
TTNG	Tightening (MSA)
TTNN	(Tetrahydrotetramethylnaphthyl) Naphthoic Acid [Antineoplastic drug]
TTNN	[The] True Nature Network (EA)
TTNP	Tactical Telephone Numbering Plan (MCD)
TTNP	Titan Pharmaceuticals [NASDAQ symbol] (TTSB)
TTNP	Titan Pharmaceuticals, Inc. [NASDAQ symbol] (SAG)
TTNPB	((Tetrahydrotetramethylnaphthalenyl)propenyl)benzoic Acid [Antineoplastic drug]
TTNPr	Titan Corp., $1.cm Cv Pfd [NYSE symbol] (TTSB)
TTNPU	Titan Pharmaceuticals Unit [NASDAQ symbol] (TTSB)
TTNS	The Times Network for Schools (NITA)
TTNS	TOW [Tube-Launched, Optically Tracked, Wire-Guided (Weapon)] Thermal NightSight [Night vision device] [Army] (RDA)
TTNV	Tomato Top Necrosis Virus [Plant pathology]
TTO	Tactical Technology Office [Arlington, VA] [DoD] (GRD)
TTO	Tactical Training Officer [Army]
TTO	Telecommunications Technical Officer [British]
TTO	Teletype Output [Telecommunications] (IAA)
TTO	Ten-to-Twelve-Year Oscillation [Meteorology]
TTO	Terminal Training Objective [Army] (INF)
TTO	To Take Out [Medicine]
TTO	Total Toxic Organics [Environmental chemistry]
TTO	Traffic Trunk Order [Telecommunications] (TEL)
TTO	Trailing-Throttle Oversteer [Automobile driving]
TTO	Transit Tracers in the Ocean [Oceanography]
TTO	Transmitter Turn-Off
TTO	Travel and Transportation Order
TTO	Trinidad and Tobago [ANSI three-letter standard code] (CNC)
TTO	Truck Technical Operations [Automobile manufacturer corporate structure]
TTOE	Tentative Tables of Organization and Equipment [Army]
TTOMT	Tank Turret Organizational Maintenance Trainer [Army]
TTOS	Toy Train Operating Society (EA)
TT/OTE	Technical Testing/Operational Testing Evaluation [Army]
TTP	Tabular [or Tabulator] Tape Processor [Computer science] (IAA)
TTP	Tactical Targeting Program (AFM)
TTP	Tactics, Techniques, and Procedures
TTP	Tape-to-Print
TTP	Temporary Transmission Permit [Australia]
TTP	Test Transfer Port [Nuclear energy] (GFGA)
TTP	Tetilla Peak [New Mexico] [Seismograph station code, US Geological Survey] (SEIS)
TTP	Thermal-Transfer Printing
TTP	Thermistor Test Program
TTP	Thrombotic Thrombocytopenic Purpura [Medicine]
TTP	Thymidine Triphosphate [Biochemistry]
TTP	Time-to-Peak [tension] [Neurology] (DAVI)
TTP	Time to Perigee (MCD)
TTP	Total Taxable Pay
TTP	Total Temperature Probe (MCD)
TTP	Trailer Transfer Point
TTP	Trainer Test Procedure [Army]
TTP	Transverse Thrust Propeller
TTP	Tricapped Trigonal Prism [Physical chemistry]
TTP	Trick-Taking Potential [Statistics]
TTP	Tristetraprolin [Biochemistry]
TTP	Turn toward Peace [Later, WWWC] [An association] (EA)
TTP	Tu-Tahl Petroleum, Inc. [Vancouver Stock Exchange symbol]
TTPA	Triethylenethiophosphoramide [Antineoplastic drug] (MAE)
TTP & S	Trainees, Transients, Patients, and Students Program [Military]
TTPB	Tasmanian Timber Promotion Board [Australia]
TTPC	Titanium Toroidal Propellant Container
TTPC	Tripartite Technical Procedures Committee (SAA)
TTPE	Total Taxable Pay Earned
TTPES	Torpedo Tube Pump Ejection System [Navy] (CAAL)
TTPFC	Terry and the Pirates Fan Club (EA)
TTPG	(Thenoylthio)propionylglycine [Biochemistry]
TTPH	Team Trainer, Pearl Harbor
TTP-HUS	Thrombotic Thrombocytopenic Purpura-Hemolytic Uremic Syndrome [STED]
TTPI	Trust Territory of the Pacific Islands
TTPO	Theater Targets Product Office [Army] (RDA)
TTPP	Port-Of-Spain/Piarco, Trinidad [Trinidad and Tobago] [ICAO location identifier] (ICLI)
TTPR	Trainer Test Procedures and Results [Army]
TTPRR	Trainer Test Procedures and Results Report [DoD]

TTPS	Port-Of-Spain/Port-Of-Spain, Trinidad [Trinidad and Tobago] [ICAO location identifier] (ICLI)
TTQ	Murphy, NC [Location identifier FAA] (FAAL)
TTQ	Tourism Training Queensland [Australia]
TTQ	Tryptophan Tryptophylquinone [Biochemistry]
TTQAP	Teletherapy Treatment Quality Assurance Program [Nuclear energy] (NRCH)
TTR	2002 Target Term Trust [NYSE symbol] (TTSB)
TTR	Table Top Rotaprint (DGA)
TTR	Tab-Tronic Recorder (DIT)
TTR	Tactical Technical Requirements (RDA)
TTR	Tall Timbers [An association] (EA)
TTR	Tana Toraja [Indonesia] [Airport symbol] (OAG)
TTR	Tape-Reading Tripping Relay
TTR	Tape Reading Typing Relay (IAA)
TTR	Target Tracking Receiver [Military] (CAAL)
TTR	Target Track [or Tracking] RADAR [Air Force]
TTR	Tarl Town Reports [New South Wales] [A publication] (DLA)
TTR	Tatra Air [Slovakia] [ICAO designator] (FAAC)
TTR	Teletype Translator [Telecommunications] (IAA)
TTR	Teletypewriter Translator (CET)
TTR	Terminal Radiation Airborne Program Translator [Air Force] (IAA)
TTR	Thermal Test Reactor [Nuclear energy] (AAG)
TTR	Thermal Timing Relay
TTR	Thermal Transpiration Ratio
TTR	Thermotolerance Ratio [Roentgenology]
TTR	Tijuana & Tecate Railway Co. [AAR code]
TTR	Timed Token Rotation (CIST)
TTR	Time-Temperature Recorder
TTR	Time to Repair [Military] (CAAL)
TTR	Tonopah Test Range
TTR	Toshiba Training Reactor [Japan] (NRCH)
TTR	Total Tank Requirement
TTR	Touch-Tone Receiver [Telecommunications] (IAA)
TTR	Transient Thermal Radiation
TTR	Transistor Telegraph Relay [Telecommunications] (IAA)
TTR	Transmission Test Rack (NITA)
TTR	Transthoracic Resistance (STED)
TTR	Transthyretin [Biochemistry]
TTR	Travel with Troops Returning
TTR	Triceps Tendon Reflex (STED)
TTR	Triplet-Triplet Resonance [Physics]
TTR	Trunk Test Rack (NITA)
TTR	Trust Territory Reports of Pacific Island [A publication] (DLA)
TTR	Two Thousand Two Target Term Trust, Inc. [NYSE symbol] (SAG)
TTR	Type-Token Ratio [Education of the hearing-impaired]
TTRA	TETRA Technologies [NASDAQ symbol] (TTSB)
TTRA	Tetra Technologies, Inc. [NASDAQ symbol] (SAG)
TTRA	Tongass [National Forest] Timber Reform Act
TTRA	Travel and Tourism Research Association (EA)
TTRB	Timken Tapered Roller Bearing
TTRC	Transistorized Thyratron Ring Counter
TTRDC	Tourism and Travel Research Development Council [Australia]
TTRE	Task Training Remedial Exercise [Army]
TTRI	Thermo Tech Technologies [NASDAQ symbol] (SAG)
TTRI	Time-Temperature Recorder and Integrator (MCD)
TTRIF	Thermo Tech Technologies Inc. [NASDAQ symbol] (TTSB)
TTRR	Technical Test Readiness Review [Army]
TTRR	Tracor, Inc. [NASDAQ symbol] (SAG)
TTRRW	Tracor Inc.Wrrt'A' [NASDAQ symbol] (TTSB)
TTRSA	Twisted Telephone Radio, Shielded, Armored
TTRT	Target Token Rotation Time [Computer science]
TTS	TACFIRE Training System (MCD)
TTS	Tactical Test Set (MCD)
TTS	Tactical Training Squadron
TTS	Tank Thermal Site
TTS	Target Trajectory Sensor
TTS	Tarleton State University, Dick Smith Library, Stephenville, TX [OCLC symbol] (OCLC)
TTS	Tarsal Tunnel Syndrome [Medicine] (STED)
TTS	TASD (Transporti Aerei Speciali) [Italy ICAO designator] (FAAC)
TTS	Technical Training Squadron (MCD)
TTS	Telecommunications Terminal Systems
TTS	Telecom Technology Showcase [British]
TTS	Telemetry Transmission System
TTS	Tele-Tech Services [McAfee, NJ] [Information service or system Telecommunications] (TSSD)
TTS	Teletypesetter
TTS	Teletypesetting (NITA)
TTS	Teletypesetting Code (NITA)
TTS	Teletypewriter System
TTS	Temperature Test Set
TTS	Temporary Threshold Shift
TTS	Terminal Testing Section [Social Security Administration]
TTS	Terrain Trend System (NITA)
TTS	Test and Training Satellite [Also, TATS, TETR] [NASA]
TTS	Text-to-Speech [Computer science]
TTS	Thanks to Scandinavia (EA)
TTS	[The] Theban Tombs Series [London] [A publication] (BJA)
TTS	Thermal Transfer Standard
TTS	Thermo-Time Switch [Electronics]
TTS	Thomas Tallis Society [British]
TTS	Three-State Transceiver [Computer science] (IAA)
TTS	Through the Skin (DAVI)
TTS	Thule Tracking Station (MCD)

TTS	Thurstone Temperament Schedule [*Psychology*]
TTS	Time to Station (DA)
TTS	Tintina Mines Ltd. [*Toronto Stock Exchange symbol*]
TTS	Tissue Type Specific [*Antigen*]
TTS	Total Technical Services, Inc. (EFIS)
TTS	Total Tectonic Subsidence
TTS	Touring Twin Carburetor Sport [*Automobile model*]
TTS	Tracker Test Set [*Dragon*] (MCD)
TTS	[*The*] Training School at Vineland [*An association*] (EA)
TTS	Transaction Terminal System (NITA)
TTS	Transaction Tracking System (PCM)
TTS	Transdermal Therapeutic System [*Medicine*]
TTS	Transducer Tubing System
TTS	Transistor-Transistor Logic Schottky Barrier (IEEE)
TTS	Transmission Temperature Switch [*Automotive engineering*]
TTS	Transmission Test Set (IEEE)
TTS	Transponder Test Set
TTS	Transportable Telemetry Set
TTS	Transport Ticket Society [*British*] (DBA)
TTS	Triple Transit Suppression (IAA)
TT's	Tripoli Trots [*Term used by entertainers in World War II*]
TTS	True to Scale
TTS	Tsaratanana [*Madagascar*] [*Airport symbol*] (OAG)
TTS	T Tauri Stars [*Astronomy*]
TTS	Tuesday, Thursday, Saturday (BARN)
TTSA	Tactical Traffic and System Analysis (MCD)
TTSA	Tandem Truck Safety Act [*1984*] (GFGA)
TTSA	Tank Turret Safety Adapter [*Army*]
TTSA	Transition Training Squadron, Atlantic [*Navy*]
TTSD	Technical Test Support Divisions [*Army*] (RDA)
TTSD	Telephone Tracking System Directory (MCD)
TTSF	Test and Timesharing Facility [*Social Security Administration*]
TTSF	Time to Subsequent Fix [*Quality control*]
TTSF	Tongass [*National Forest*] Timber Supply Fund [*Department of the Interior*]
TTSG	Twinless Twins Support Group (EA)
TTSL	Total Time Spent Listening [*Radio*] (WDMC)
TTSM	Theater Transition and Sustainment Model
TTSOA	Telecommunications Traffic and Supervisory Officers' Association [*Australia*]
TTSP	Training Test Support Package [*Army*]
TTSP	Transition Training Squadron, Pacific [*Navy*]
TTSPN	Two Terminal Series Parallel Networks
TTSR	Temporary Threshold Shift Reduction (SAA)
TTSS	[*The*] Trumpeter Swan Society (EA)
TTSt	Trierer Theologische Studien [*Trier*] [*A publication*] (BJA)
TTSU	Tracker Test Set Supplemental Unit (MCD)
TTSW	Tractor Truck, Six Wheel [*Automotive engineering*]
TTT	Tactical Training Team [*Military*] (CAAL)
TTT	Taitung [*Taiwan*] [*Airport symbol*] (OAG)
TTT	Tallulah, LA [*Location Identifier FAA*] (FAAL)
TTT	Tatiko-Tekhnicheskye-Trebovaniya [*Tactical Technical Requirement*] [*for military materiel*] [*Former USSR*] (RDA)
TTT	Template Tracing Technique (DA)
TTT	Tetrathiotetracene [*Organic chemistry*]
TTT	Texas College, Tyler, TX [*OCLC symbol*] (OCLC)
TTT	Thermo Terratech [*AMEX symbol*] (TTSB)
TTT	Thymol Turbidity Test [*Clinical chemistry*]
TTT	Time Temperature Transformation
TTT	Time, Temperature, Turbulence [*Fuel technology*]
TTT	Time to Target (AAG)
TTT	Time to Turn [*Ship or aircraft*]
TTT	Tolbutamide Tolerance Test [*Clinical chemistry*]
TTT	Total Twitch Time (STED)
TTT	Training of Teacher Trainers
TTT	Transamerican Trailer Transport
TTT	Trilateral Tracking Technique
TTT	Trinidad & Tobago Television Co.
TTT	True Temperature Tunnel
TTT	Tyne Tees Television [*British*] (DI)
TTTA	Teletypewriter Terminal Assembly
TTTA	Timber Trade Training Association [*British*] (DBA)
TTTA	Tobacco Trade Travellers' Association [*British*] (BI)
TTTA	Training Technology Transfer Act of 1984 (WYGK)
TTTAP	Territorial Teacher Training Assistance Program [*Department of Education*] (GFGA)
TTTE	Tri-National Tornado Training Establishment [*British military*] (DMA)
TTTL	Transistor-to-Transistor-to-Transistor Logic (HGAA)
TTTN	Tandem Tie Trunk Network (PDAA)
TTTP	Transmitting Typewriter with Tape Punch (IAA)
TTTS	Tanker-Transport Trailer System (MCD)
TTTS	Tanker Transport Training System [*Air Force*]
TTTT	Tartar-Talos-Terrier-Typhon [*Military*] (DNAB)
TTTT	Test Tube Turbidity Test [*Laboratory science*] (DAVI)
TTTV	Tyne Tees TeleVision (WDAA)
TTU	Tantalus Resources Ltd. [*Vancouver Stock Exchange symbol*]
TTU	Target Transfer Unit (MCD)
TTU	Tartu [*Dorpat, Jurjeio*] [*Former USSR Seismograph station code, US Geological Survey Closed*] (SEIS)
TTU	Tennessee Technical University, Cookville, TN [*OCLC symbol*] (OCLC)
TTU	Terminal Timing Unit [*NASA*] (KSC)
TTU	Terminal Transportation Unit [*Military*] (GFGA)
TTU	Tetuan [*Morocco*] [*Airport symbol*] (OAG)
TTU	Texas Technological University (PDAA)
TTU	Through-Transmission Ultrasound [*Materials testing*] (RDA)
TTU	Thrust Termination Unit (MSA)
TTU	Timing Terminal Unit (NASA)
TTU	Tracer Test Unit (IAA)
TTU	Transportable Treatment Unit
TTU	Transportation Terminal Unit [*Army*]
TTUC	Tasmanian Trades Union Council [*Australia*]
TTuGS	Church of Jesus Christ of Latter-Day Saints, Genealogical Society Library, Tennessee South District Branch, Tullahoma, TN [*Library symbol Library of Congress*] (LCLS)
TTUL	Talk to U Later [*Internet language*] [*Computer science*]
TTUSA	Trireme Trust USA [*An association*] (EA)
TTUTD	Tetanus Toxoid Up-to-Date (STED)
TTV	Cabletel Communications [*AMEX symbol*] (TTSB)
TTV	Cabletel Communications Corp. [*AMEX symbol*] (SAG)
TTV	Taiwan Television Enterprise (EY)
TTV	Teletape Video
TTV	Tenth Thickness Value [*Nuclear energy*] (NRCH)
TTV	Termination, Test, and Verification (NASA)
TTV	Territorial Petroleum [*Vancouver Stock Exchange symbol*]
TTV	Thermal Test Vehicle
TTV	Total Thickness Variation (AAEL)
TTV	Tow Test Vehicle [*Aerospace*]
TTV	Tracheal Transport Velocity (STED)
TTV	Transfusion Transmitted Virus [*Medicine*] (STED)
TTVM	Thermal Transfer Voltmeter
TTVP	Temporary Transvenous Pacemaker [*Cardiology*] (DAVI)
TTVP	Trentiner Tiroler Volkspartei [*Trentino Tirol People's Party*] [*Italy Political party*] (PPE)
TTVW	Total Towed Vehicle Weight [*Automotive engineering*]
TTW	Tactical Training Wing [*Air Force*]
TTW	Teletypewriter [*Telecommunications*]
TTW	Total Temperature and Weight
TTWA	Travel to Work Area (AIE)
TTWB	Touch-Toe Weight-Bearing (STED)
TTWB	Turbine Trip with Bypass [*Nuclear energy*] (NRCH)
TTWL	Twin Tandem Wheel Loading [*Aviation*]
TTWS	Terminal Threat Warning System
TTX	Air Team, AS [*Norway*] [*FAA designator*] (FAAC)
TTX	Den Sivile Flyskole [*Norway ICAO designator*] (FAAC)
TTX	Teletex [*Telecommunications*]
TTX	Tetrodotoxin [*A poison*] [*Biochemistry*]
TTX	Thiothixene [*Tranquilizer*]
TTX	Tultex Corp. [*NYSE symbol*] (SPSG)
TTX	Tut Enterprises, Inc. [*Toronto Stock Exchange symbol*]
TTXAU	Teletex Access Unit [*Telecommunications*] (OSI)
TTXG	TransTexas Gas [*NASDAQ symbol*] (TTSB)
TTXG	Transtexas Gas Corp. [*NASDAQ symbol*] (SAG)
TTY	Teletype (CAAL)
TTY	Teletypewriter [*Telecommunications*]
TTY	Teletypewriter Equipment (IAA)
TTY	TELEX-Type [*Terminal*]
TTY	Torque-to-Yield [*Automotive engineering*]
TTYA	Teletypewriter Assembly
TTYC	TTY Controller (NITA)
TTYD	Tele-Typewriters for the Deaf [*An association*]
TTYL	Talk to You Later [*Internet language*] [*Computer science*]
TTYP	Tintype (VRA)
TTYPP	Teletype Point-To-Point Online Communications Driver (NITA)
TTYQ/RSS	Teletypewriter Query-Reply Subsystem (CET)
TTZ	Tactical-Technical Assignment [*Army*] (RDA)
TTZ	Titizima [*Bonin Islands*] [*Seismograph station code, US Geological Survey Closed*] (SEIS)
TTZ	Tornquist-Teisseyre Zone [*Geology*]
TTZ	Transformation Toughened Zirconia [*Metallurgy*]
TTZ	Treats, Inc. [*Toronto Stock Exchange symbol*]
TTZP	Piarco, Trinidad [*Trinidad and Tobago*] [*ICAO location identifier*] (ICLI)
TU	Societe Tunisienne de l'Air [*Tunisia*] [*ICAO designator*]
TU	Take-Up (IAA)
TU	Tanking Unit (AAG)
TU	Tanners' Union [*British*]
TU	Tape Unit
TU	Task Unit [*Military*]
TU	Taxicrinic Unit [*Computer science*]
TU	Technical Service Unit [*Military*]
TU	Technical Utilization (NAKS)
TU	Technische Universitat [*Technical University*] [*German*]
TU	Technology Utilization
TU	Temporary Unit (BCP)
TU	Tenebrio Unit [*Endocrinology*]
TU	Terminal Unit
TU	Testo Unico [*Consolidated Statutes*] [*Italian*] (ILCA)
TU	Test Unit
TU	Texas Utilities Co. (EFIS)
TU	Thank You [*Communications operator's procedural remark*]
TU	Thermal Unit
TU	Thiouracil [*Biochemistry*] (MAE)
TU	Thulium [*Symbol is Tm*] [*Chemical element*] (ROG)
TU	Time-of-Update
TU	Timing Unit
TU	Todd Unit [*Medicine*] (MAE)
TU	Torah Umesorah - National Society for Hebrew Day Schools [*Defunct*] (EA)
TU	Toxic Unit [*Medicine*]

TU..............	Trade Union
TU..............	Traffic Unit
TU..............	Training Unit [*Army*]
TU..............	Transfer Unconditionally
TU..............	Transfer Unit (AAG)
TU..............	Transmission Unit [*Telecommunications*]
TU..............	Transport Unit (MCD)
TU..............	Transuranium [*Chemistry*]
TU..............	Tritium Unit [*Nuclear energy*]
TU..............	Trophic Unit [*Analytical biochemistry*]
TU..............	Trout Unlimited (EA)
TU..............	Tuba
TU..............	Tube
Tu..............	Tubercle [*Anatomy*] [*Medicine*]
TU..............	Tuberculin Unit
TU..............	Tudor (ROG)
TU..............	Tuesday
TU..............	Tugboatmen's Union [*British*]
TU..............	Tuition
TU..............	Tulane University [*New Orleans, LA*]
TU..............	Tulsa University [*Oklahoma*] (PDAA)
TU..............	Tuning Unit [*JETDS nomenclature*] [*Military*] (IAA)
TU..............	Tunis Airline (DS)
TU..............	Tupolev [*Former USSR ICAO aircraft manufacturer identifier*] (ICAO)
TU..............	Turbidity Unit
TU..............	Turkey [*NATO*]
tu	Turkey [*MARC country of publication code Library of Congress*] (LCCP)
TU..............	Type Unique [*French standard troop train, World War I*]
TU..............	University of Tennessee, Knoxville, TN [*Library symbol Library of Congress*] (LCLS)
TUA	Syndicat International des Travailleurs Unis de l'Automobile, de l'Aerospatiale,et de l'Outillage Agricole d'Amerique [*International Union, United Automobile, Aerospace, and Agricultural Implement Workers of America - UAW*] [*Canada*]
TUA..............	Teichuronic Acid [*Biochemistry*]
TUA..............	Telecommunications Users' Association (TSSD)
TUA..............	Telephone Users Association (EA)
TUA..............	Test Unit Adapter [*Aviation*]
TuA..............	Texte und Arbeiten [*Beuron*] [*A publication*] (BJA)
TUA..............	Time Use Analysis [*Test*]
TUA..............	Tuai [*New Zealand*] [*Seismograph station code, US Geological Survey*] (SEIS)
TUA..............	Tulcan [*Ecuador*] [*Airport symbol*] (OAG)
TUA..............	Turkmenistan [*ICAO designator*] (FAAC)
TUAC	Trade Union Advisory Committee [*British*] (DAS)
TUAC	Union Internationale des Travailleurs Unis de l'Alimentation et du Commerce [*United Food and Commercial Workers Union*] [*Canada*]
TUAC OECD...	Trade Union Advisory Committee to the Organization for Economic Cooperation and Development [*Paris, France*] (EAIO)
TuAF..............	Turkish Air Force
T/U/Ag..........	Trustee under Agreement [*Legal term*] (DLA)
TUAL..............	Tentative Unit Allowance List [*Air Force*] (AFM)
Tu & Rus.....	Turner and Russell's English Chancery Reports [*1822-24*] [*A publication*] (DLA)
TUANZ..........	Telecommunications Users Association of New Zealand (DDC)
TUAR	Turning Arbor
TUB..............	Temporary Unlighted Buoy [*Maps and charts*]
TUB..............	Troop Unit Basis [*Military*]
TUB..............	Tubarao [*Brazil*] [*Airport symbol*] (AD)
tub	Tubing (VRA)
TUB..............	Tubing (AAG)
TUB..............	Tubingen [*Federal Republic of Germany*] [*Seismograph station code, US Geological Survey*] (SEIS)
TUB..............	Tubouterine [*Junction*] [*Gynecology*] (DAVI)
TUB..............	Tubuai Island [*Austral Islands*] [*Airport symbol*] (OAG)
TUB..............	Tubular [*Automotive engineering*]
tub	Tubular (VRA)
TUB..............	[*The*] Unborn Book [*A publication*]
TUBA	Tubists Universal Brotherhood Association (EA)
Tubbys..........	Tubby's, Inc. [*Associated Press*] (SAG)
TUBCS	Trade Union Badge Collectors Society [*British*] (DBA)
TUBE..............	Terminating Unfair Broadcasting Excesses [*Student legal action organization*] (EA)
TUBE..............	Trans-Urban Bicentennial Exposition
tuberc	Tuberculosis [*Medicine*]
TUBITAK	Scientific and Technical Research Council of Turkey [*Ankara*] [*Information service or system*] (IID)
TUBLR	Tubular [*Freight*]
TubMex........	Tubos De Acero De Mexico [*Associated Press*] (SAG)
TUBO	Tuboscope Vetco International [*NASDAQ symbol*] (SAG)
TUBO	Tuboscope Vetco Intl [*NASDAQ symbol*] (TTSB)
TUBS	Tubular Tires [*Cyclist term*] [*British*] (DSUE)
Tubscp..........	Tuboscope Vetco International Corp. [*Associated Press*] (SAG)
TUBY	Tubby's, Inc. [*NASDAQ symbol*] (SAG)
TUC..............	Teaching Usefulness Classification [*of a hospital patient*]
TUC..............	Technology Utilization Center
TUC..............	Telecommunications Users Coalition (EA)
TUC..............	Teleordering Users' Council [*British*]
TUC..............	Temporary Unemployment Compensation [*Labor*]
TUC..............	Terminal Usage Charge [*Computer science*] (HGAA)
TUC..............	Time of Useful Consciousness [*Medicine*]
TUC..............	Tracer Resources [*Vancouver Stock Exchange symbol*]
TUC..............	Trades Union Congress [*British*]
TUC..............	Trade [*or Trades*] Union Council
TUC..............	Transportation, Utilities, Communications
Tuc..............	Tucana [*Constellation*]
TUC..............	Tucker Properties [*NYSE symbol*] (SPSG)
TUC..............	Tucson [*Arizona*] [*Seismograph station code, US Geological Survey*] (SEIS)
TUC..............	Tucuman [*Argentina*] [*Airport symbol*] (OAG)
TUC..............	Type Unit Code (CINC)
TUC..............	University of Tennessee at Chattanooga, Chattanooga, TN [*OCLC symbol*] (OCLC)
TUCA	Tilt-Up Concrete Association (EA)
TUCA	Transient Undercooling Accident [*Nuclear energy*]
TUCA	Turning Cam [*Tool*] (AAG)
TUCC	Transport Users' Consultative Council [*British*] (ILCA)
TUCC	Triangle Universities Computation Center [*Durham, NC*]
TUCE	Test of Understanding of College Economics
TUCHA	Type Unit Characteristics
Tu Civ LF....	Tulane Civil Law Forum [*A publication*] (DLA)
Tuck..............	Tucker and Clephane's Reports [*21 District of Columbia*] [*1892-93*] [*A publication*] (DLA)
TUCK	Tucker Drilling [*NASDAQ symbol*] (TTSB)
TUCK	Tucker Drilling Co., Inc. [*NASDAQ symbol*] (NQ)
Tuck..............	Tucker's New York Surrogate's Court Reports [*A publication*] (DLA)
Tuck..............	Tucker's Reports [*District of Columbia*] [*A publication*] (DLA)
Tuck..............	Tucker's Reports [*156-175 Massachusetts*] [*A publication*] (DLA)
Tuck..............	Tucker's Select Cases [*Newfoundland*] [*A publication*] (DLA)
Tuck & C	Tucker and Clephane's Reports [*21 District of Columbia*] [*A publication*] (DLA)
Tuck & Cl	Tucker and Clephane's Reports [*21 District of Columbia*] [*1892-93*] [*A publication*] (DLA)
Tuck Bl Com...	Tucker's Blackstone's Commentaries [*A publication*] (DLA)
Tuck Dist of Col...	Tucker's District of Columbia Appeals [*A publication*] (DLA)
TuckDr..........	Tucker Drilling Co., Inc. [*Associated Press*] (SAG)
Tucker..........	Tucker's New York Surrogate's Court Reports [*A publication*] (DLA)
TuckerPr......	Tucker Properties [*Associated Press*] (SAG)
Tucker's Blackstone...	Tucker's Blackstone's Commentaries [*A publication*] (DLA)
Tuck Lect.....	Tucker's Lectures [*A publication*] (DLA)
Tuck Pl	Tucker's Pleadings [*A publication*] (DLA)
Tuck Sel Cas...	Tucker's Select Cases [*1817-28*] [*Newfoundland*] [*A publication*] (DLA)
Tuck Sur.....	Tucker's Surrogate Reports, City of New York [*A publication*] (DLA)
Tuck Surr.....	Tucker's Surrogate Reports, City of New York [*A publication*] (DLA)
TUCN	Trades Union Congress of Nigeria
Tucn..............	Tucana [*Constellation*]
TUCOPS........	[*The*] Universal Coterie of Pipe Smokers (EA)
TUCOSP........	Tehran Union Catalogue of Scientific Periodicals [*A publication*]
TUCR	Troop Unit Change Request
TUCSA	Trade Union Council of South Africa
TucsEP..........	Tucson Electric Power Co. [*Associated Press*] (SAG)
TUD	Tambacounda [*Senegal*] [*Airport symbol*] (OAG)
TUD	Technology Utilization Division [*NASA*] (IEEE)
TUD	Total Underground Distribution (IAA)
TUD	Total Urethral Discharge [*Medicine*]
TUD	Tugold Resources, Inc. [*Vancouver Stock Exchange symbol*]
TUDAT	Tunnel-Diode Arithmetic Tester (IAA)
TUDC	Tauroursodeoxycholate [*Biochemistry*]
TUDC	Trade Unionists' Defence Committee [*Australia*]
TUDCA	Tauroursodeoxycholic Acid [*Biochemistry*]
Tud Cas Merc Law...	Tudor's Leading Cases on Mercantile Law [*3 eds.*] [*1860-84*] [*A publication*] (DLA)
Tud Cas RP...	Tudor's Leading Cases on Real Property [*4 eds.*] [*1856-98*] [*A publication*] (DLA)
Tud Char Tr...	Tudor's Charitable Trusts [*2nd ed.*] [*1871*] [*A publication*] (DLA)
Tud Char Trusts...	Tudor's Charitable Trusts [*2nd ed.*] [*1871*] [*A publication*] (DLA)
Tudor Lead Cas Real Prop...	Tudor's Leading Cases on Real Property [*A publication*] (DLA)
Tudor's LCML...	Tudor's Leading Cases on Mercantile Law [*A publication*] (DLA)
Tudor's LCRP...	Tudor's Leading Cases on Real Property [*A publication*] (DLA)
TUDRIP........	Tube Plate Drilling Program [*Kongsberg Vaapenfabrikk*] [*Software package*] (NCC)
TUDS	Tunnel Detection System (MCD)
TUE..............	Texas Utilities Electric Co. [*NYSE symbol*] (SPSG)
TUE..............	Tolerance of Unrealistic Experience [*Psychometrics*]
TUE..............	Trainer Unique Equipment [*Navy*]
TUE..............	TU Electric Capital I [*NYSE symbol*] (SAG)
TUE..............	TU Electric Capital II [*NYSE symbol*] (SAG)
TUE..............	TU Electric Capital III [*NYSE symbol*] (SAG)
TUE..............	Tuesday (AFM)
Tue..............	Tuesday (ODBW)
TUE..............	Tupile [*Panama*] [*Airport symbol*] (OAG)
TUE..............	University of Tokyo (EDUCATSS) [*UTLAS symbol*]
TUEL	Trade Union Educational League
TUEPr	Texas Util Elec Dep Pfd [*NYSE symbol*] (TTSB)
TUEPrA	Texas Util Elec'A'Dep Pfd [*NYSE symbol*] (TTSB)
TUEPrB	Texas Util Elec'B'Dep Pfd [*NYSE symbol*] (TTSB)
TUEPrM	TU Electric Cap 1 8.25%'TOPrS' [*NYSE symbol*] (TTSB)
TUEPrN	TU Electric Cap II 9.00%'TOPrS' [*NYSE symbol*] (TTSB)
TUEPrO	TU Elec Cap II 8.00%'QUIPS' [*NYSE symbol*] (TTSB)
TUES........	Tuesday (EY)
Tues........	Tuesday (ODBW)
TUES........	Tuesday Morning [*NASDAQ symbol*] (TTSB)
TUES........	Tuesday Morning Corp. [*NASDAQ symbol*] (NQ)
TuesM........	Tuesday Morning Corp. [*Associated Press*] (SAG)
TUF........	Tactical Undercover Function [*Chicago police operation*]
TUF........	Thermal Utilization Factor (MCD)

TUF.............	Time of Useful Function [*Computer science*] (MHDB)
TUF.............	Totally User Friendly
TUF.............	Tours [*France*] [*Airport symbol*] (OAG)
TUF.............	Trade Union Federation [*British*] (EY)
TUF.............	Transmitter Underflow
TUFA...........	Total Unsaturated Fatty Acid [*of foodstuffs*]
TUFA...........	Trans Unsaturated Fatty Acids
TUFCDF.......	Thorium-Uranium Fuel Cycle Development Facility [*Nuclear energy*]
Tufco..........	Tufco Technologies [*Associated Press*] (SAG)
TUFEC........	Thailand-UNESCO Fundamental Education Centre
TUFF-TUG....	Tape Update of Formatted Files-Format Table Tape Updater and Generator [*Computer science*]
TUFI...........	This Umbrella Folds Itself [*Trademark for type of umbrella*]
TUFL...........	Trade Unionists for Labour [*British*]
TU-FM	University of Tennessee Center for the Health Sciences/Memphis Department of Family Medicine, Memphis, TN [*Library symbol Library of Congress*] (LCLS)
TUFMIS.......	Tactical Unit Financial Management Information System
Tufts U........	Tufts University (GAGS)
TUFX...........	Turning Fixture
TUG	British Columbia Trade Union Group [*Canada*] (CROSS)
TUG	Maritrans, Inc. [*NYSE symbol*] (SPSG)
TUG	Tape Unit Group [*Telecommunications*] (TEL)
TUG	Telecommunications Users Group [*Montclair, NJ*] [*Telecommunications service*] (TSSD)
TUG	Teleram Users Group (EA)
TUG	Tire Uniformity Grading [*Automotive engineering*]
TUG	Total Urinary Gonadotropin [*Clinical chemistry*]
TUG	Touch and Go Ltd. [*Former USSR*] [*FAA designator*] (FAAC)
TUG	Towed Universal Glider
TUG	TRANSAC [*Transistorized Automatic Computer*] Users Group
TUG	Transistorized Automatic Computer Users' Group (IAA)
TUG	Transtex Universal Gateway [*Computer science*]
Tug	Tugrik [*Monetary unit*] [*Mongolia*] (BARN)
TUG	Tuguegarao [*Philippines*] [*Airport symbol*] (OAG)
TUG	Tunable Ultraviolet Generation
TUGV	Tactical Unmanned Ground Vehicle [*Army*] (PS)
TUH	Tullahoma, TN [*Location identifier FAA*] (FAAL)
TU-H	University of Tennessee Center for the Health Sciences/Knoxville, Preston Medical Library, Knoxville, TN [*Library symbol Library of Congress*] (LCLS)
TUHTKP	Time Urgent Hard Target Kill Potential (MCD)
TUI..............	Green Bay, WI [*Location identifier FAA*] (FAAL)
TUI..............	Text User Interface [*Computer science*]
TUI..............	Tool Usage Instructions (MCD)
TUI..............	Trade Union Immunities [*British*]
TUI..............	Trade Union International
TUI..............	Trade Unions International of Transport Workers (EAIO)
TUI..............	Trypsin Units Inhibited [*Food technology*]
TUI..............	Tuition (DSUE)
TUI..............	Tuninter [*Tunisia*] [*ICAO designator*] (FAAC)
TUI..............	Turaif [*Saudi Arabia*] [*Airport symbol*] (OAG)
TUIAFPW	Trade Unions International of Agriculture, Forestry, and Plantation Workers [*See also UISTAFP*] [*Prague, Czechoslovakia*] (EAIO)
TUIC...........	Trade Unions Industrial Council [*Australia*]
TUIFU	[*The*] Ultimate in Foul Ups [*Military slang*] [*Bowdlerized version*]
TUIMWE	Trade Unions International of Miners and Workers in Energy [*See also UISMTE*] (EAIO)
TUIP...........	Transurethral Incision of the Prostate [*Medicine*]
TUIPAE	Trade Unions International of Public and Allied Employees [*Berlin, Federal Republic of Germany*] (EAIO)
TUIR	Time until in Range
TUIREC	Trade Union International Research and Education Group [*England*] (EAIO)
TUITW	Trade Unions International of Transport Workers (EAIO)
TUIWC	Trade Unions International of Workers in Commerce [*Prague, Czechoslovakia*] (EAIO)
TUJ.............	Tubouterine Junction [*Anatomy*]
TUJ.............	Tum [*Ethiopia*] [*Airport symbol*] (OAG)
TUK.............	Nantucket, MA [*Location identifier FAA*] (FAAL)
TUK.............	TEA (UK) Ltd. [*British ICAO designator*] (FAAC)
TUK.............	Tuckahoe Financial Corp. [*Toronto Stock Exchange symbol*]
TUK.............	Turbat [*Pakistan*] [*Airport symbol*] (OAG)
tuk.............	Turkmen [*MARC language code Library of Congress*] (LCCP)
TUL.............	Aero Toluca Internacional, SA de CV [*Mexico*] [*FAA designator*] (FAAC)
TuL.............	Tod und Leben nach der Vorstellungen der Babylonier [*A publication*] (BJA)
TUL.............	Tula Peak, New Mexico [*Spaceflight Tracking and Data Network*] [*NASA*]
TUL.............	Tulsa [*Oklahoma*] [*Airport symbol*] (OAG)
TUL.............	Tulsa [*Oklahoma*] [*Seismograph station code, US Geological Survey*] (SEIS)
TUL.............	Tulsa City-County Library System, Tulsa, OK [*OCLC symbol*] (OCLC)
TU-L............	University of Tennessee, Law Library, Knoxville, TN [*Library symbol Library of Congress*] (LCLS)
TULACS	Tactical Unit Location and Communication System (MCD)
Tulane U.......	Tulane University (GAGS)
TULAR	Tularemia [*An infectious, plague-like disease*] (DAVI)
TULC...........	Trade Union Leadership Council (EA)
TULCC	Triangle University Library Cooperative Committee [*Library network*]
Tul Civ LF	Tulane Civil Law Forum [*A publication*] (DLA)
TULE...........	Transistorized Universal Logic Elements
TULF...........	Tamil United Liberation Front [*Sri Lanka*] (PD)

TULIP..........	Transurethral Ultrasound - Guided LASER-Induced Prostatectomy [*Medicine*]
TULIPS	Telemetered Ultrasonic Liquid Interface Plotting System (PDAA)
TULRA	Trade Union and Labour Relations Act [*1974 and 1976*] [*British*] (DCTA)
TULS...........	TRON [*The Real-Time Operating System Nucleus*] Universal Language System [*Computer science*]
TU-LS	University of Tennessee, Graduate School of Library and Information Sciences, Knoxville, TN [*Library symbol*] [*Library of Congress*] (LCLS)
Tultex	Tultex Corp. [*Associated Press*] (SAG)
TUM...........	Aeriantur-M Airlines [*Moldova*] [*FAA designator*] (FAAC)
TUM...........	Technical University in Munich [*Germany*]
TUM...........	Terminal User's Manual
TuM	Texte und Materialien der Frau Professor Hilprecht Collection of Babylonian Antiquities im Eigentum der Univerisitaet Jena [*A publication*] (BJA)
TuM	Torah Umesorah - National Society for Hebrew Day Schools
TUM...........	Total Unscheduled Maintenance Time
TUM...........	Trades Union Movement
TUM...........	Training User's Manual [*A publication*] [*Environmental science*] (COE)
TUM...........	Tumut [*Australia Airport symbol*] (OAG)
TUM...........	Tumwater [*Washington*] [*Seismograph station code, US Geological Survey*] (SEIS)
TUM...........	Tuning Unit Member (IEEE)
TUM...........	University of Tennessee, Center for the Health Sciences, Memphis, TN [*OCLC symbol*] (OCLC)
TU-M	University of Tennessee Medical Units, Memphis, TN [*Library symbol Library of Congress*] (LCLS)
TUM...........	[*The*] Unsatisfied Man [*A publication*]
TUMA..........	Tumacacori National Monument
TU-MDC......	University of Tennessee, Downtown Memphis Center, Memphis, TN [*Library symbol Library of Congress*] (LCLS)
TUME.........	[*The*] Ultimate Musical Experience [*Rock music group*]
TU-MS	University of Tennessee Center for the Health Sciences Library, Stollerman Library, Memphis, TN [*Library symbol Library of Congress*] (LCLS)
TuMV	Turnip Mosaic Virus
TUN	Air Tungaru [*British ICAO designator*] (FAAC)
TUN	Flint, MI [*Location identifier FAA*] (FAAL)
TUN	Technical University of Nova Scotia [*UTLAS symbol*]
TUN	Tennessee State University, Downtown Campus, Nashville, TN [*OCLC symbol*] (OCLC)
TUN	Transfer Unconditionally
TUN	Tuning (AAG)
TUN	Tunis [*Tunisia*] [*Seismograph station code, US Geological Survey Closed*] (SEIS)
TUN	Tunis [*Tunisia*] [*Airport symbol*] (OAG)
TUN	Tunisia [*ANSI three letter standard code*] (CNC)
Tun	Tunisia (VRA)
TUN	Turner Energy & Resources [*Vancouver Stock Exchange symbol*]
TUNA	Tunable Attribute Display Subsystem (CAAL)
TUNE	DMX, Inc. [*NASDAQ symbol*] (SAG)
TUNEL	Tunnel [*Commonly used*] (OPSA)
TUNG	Tungsten (AAG)
TUNICAT......	Tunicatae [*Coated*] [*Pharmacy*]
TUNISAIR	Societe Tunisienne de l'Air [*Airline*] [*Tunisia*]
TUNL	Triangle Universities Nuclear Laboratory [*Research center*] (RCD)
TUNL	Tunnel
TUNLS	Tunnel [*Commonly used*] (OPSA)
TUNNEL.......	Tunnel [*Commonly used*] (OPSA)
TUNNELS	Tunnel [*Commonly used*] (OPSA)
TUNNET	Tunnel Transit Time (IAA)
TUNNL	Tunnel [*Commonly used*] (OPSA)
TUO	Taupo [*New Zealand*] [*Airport symbol*] (OAG)
TUO	Technology Utilization Office [*NASA*]
TUO	Teuton Resources Corp. [*Vancouver Stock Exchange symbol*]
TUO	Tucson Observatory [*Arizona*] [*Seismograph station code, US Geological Survey*] (SEIS)
TUOC	Tactical Unit Operations Center (AFM)
TUP............	Technology Utilization Program [*Defunct*]
TUP............	Telephony [*or Telephone*] User Part [*Telecommunications*] (TEL)
TUP............	Temple University Press
TUP............	Torres United Party [*Australia Political party*]
TUP............	Tovarystvo Ukrainskykh Progresystiv [*Ukrainian Progressive Association*] [*Russian Political party*] (PPE)
TUP............	Trickle Up Program (EA)
TUP............	Tupelo [*Mississippi*] [*Airport symbol*] (OAG)
TUP............	Tupik [*Former USSR Seismograph station code, US Geological Survey*] (SEIS)
TUP............	Tupperware Corp. [*NYSE symbol*] (TTSB)
TUP............	Twin Unit Pack [*for vehicles*]
Tup App.......	Tupper's Appeal Reports [*Ontario*] [*A publication*] (DLA)
TUPC	Transfer Underwater Pressure Chamber (DNAB)
TUPC	T. U. P. Charlton's Georgia Reports [*A publication*] (DLA)
T U P Charlt...	T. U. P. Charlton's Georgia Reports [*A publication*] (DLA)
TUPE..........	Tanganyika Union of Public Employees
TUPE..........	Tupelo National Battlefield
TUPJ...........	Roadtown/Beef Island [*Virgin Islands*] [*ICAO location identifier*] (ICLI)
TUPONA.......	[*The*] United Provinces of North America [*See also EFISGA*] [*Suggested early name for Canada*]
Tupp	Tupper's Appeal Reports [*Ontario*] [*A publication*] (DLA)
Tupp	Tupper's Upper Canada Practice Reports [*A publication*] (DLA)
Tupp App......	Tupper's Appeal Reports [*Ontario*] [*A publication*] (DLA)

Tupper......... Tupper's Appeal Reports [*Ontario*] [*A publication*] (DLA)
Tupper......... Tupper's Upper Canada Practice Reports [*A publication*] (DLA)
TUPS .... Technical User Performance Specifications [*US Independent Telephone Association*] [*Telecommunications*] (TEL)
TUPW .... Virgin Gorda [*Virgin Islands*] [*ICAO location identifier*] (ICLI)
TUQ .... Tougan [*Upper Volta*] [*Airport symbol*] (AD)
TUR .... Aerotur SA [*Mexico ICAO designator*] (FAAC)
TUR .... American Turners [*An association*]
TUR .... Temporary Unattached Register [*Employment*] [*British*]
TUR .... Total Unemployment Rate
TUR .... Toxics Use Reduction [*Environmental science*]
TUR .... Toxic Use Reduction [*Manufacturing*]
TUR ,.......... Traffic Usage Recorder [*Telecommunications*]
TUR .... Transurethral Resection [*of prostate gland*]
TUR .... Tucurui [*Brazil*] [*Airport symbol*] (OAG)
TUR .... Turbat [*Former USSR Seismograph station code, US Geological Survey Closed*] (SEIS)
TUR .... Turbine
TUR .... Turkey [*ANSI three-letter standard code*] (CNC)
tur.............. Turkish [*MARC language code Library of Congress*] (LCCP)
TUR .... Turner Corp. [*AMEX symbol*] (SPSG)
Tur.............. Turner's Reports [*35-48 Arkansas*] [*A publication*] (DLA)
Tur.............. Turner's Reports [*99-101 Kentucky*] [*A publication*] (DLA)
Tur.............. Turner's Select Pleas of the Forest [*Selden Society Publication, Vol. 13*] [*A publication*] (DLA)
TUR .... Turret (MSA)
Tur & R ...... Turner and Russell's English Chancery Reports [*37 English Reprint*] [*1822-24*] [*A publication*] (DLA)
Tur & Ru .... Turner and Russell's English Chancery Reports [*37 English Reprint*] [*1822-24*] [*A publication*] (DLA)
Tur & Rus.... Turner and Russell's English Chancery Reports [*37 English Reprint*] [*1822-24*] [*A publication*] (DLA)
TURB .... Transurethral Resection of the Bladder [*Medicine*] (AAMN)
TURB .... Turbidity (AAMN)
TURB .... Turbinate [*Medicine*] (DAVI)
TURB .... Turbine (AAG)
TURB .... Turbulence
TURBC .... Turbulence (FAAC)
TURBN .... Transurethral Resection of Bladder Neck [*Medicine*] (DAVI)
TURBO......... Turbocharger [*Automotive engineering*]
TURBOALT... Turboalternator (AAG)
TURBOCAT... Turbine-Powered Catapult
Turbochf ...... Turbochef, Inc. [*Associated Press*] (SAG)
TURBOGEN... Turbogenerator (AAG)
TURBOPROP... Turbine Propelled (WDAA)
TURBT .... Transurethral Resection of Bladder Tumor [*Medicine*] (MAH)
TURBT .... Turbulent [*NWS*] (FAAC)
TURC .... Trades Union Research Centre (AIE)
TURCO......... Turnaround Control [*Navy*]
TURF .... Thorium-Uranium Recycle Facility [*Oak Ridge National Laboratory*]
TURI .... Toxics Use Reduction Institute [*University of Massachusetts, Lowell*] [*Research center*] (RCD)
TURK .... Turkey
Turk .... Turkey (VRA)
Turkest .... Turkestan
TurkmSSR... Turkmen Soviet Socialist Republic
Turksh .... Turkish Investment Fund [*Associated Press*] (SAG)
TURN .... Toward Utility Rate Normalization
Turn............ Turner's Reports [*35-48 Arkansas*] [*A publication*] (DLA)
Turn............ Turner's Reports [*99-101 Kentucky*] [*A publication*] (DLA)
Turn............ Turner's Select Pleas of the Forest [*Selden Society Publication, Vol. 13*] [*A publication*] (DLA)
Turn & P...... Turner and Phillips' English Chancery Reports [*A publication*] (DLA)
Turn & Ph... Turner and Phillips' English Chancery Reports [*A publication*] (DLA)
Turn & R ..... Turner and Russell's English Chancery Reports [*37 English Reprint*] [*A publication*] (DLA)
Turn & R (Eng)... Turner and Russell's English Chancery Reports [*37 English Reprint*] [*A publication*] (DLA)
Turn & Rus... Turner and Russell's English Chancery Reports [*37 English Reprint*] [*A publication*] (DLA)
Turn & Russ... Turner and Russell's English Chancery Reports [*37 English Reprint*] [*A publication*] (DLA)
Turn Anglo Sax... Turner's History of the Anglo Saxon [*A publication*] (DLA)
TurnB.......... Turner Broadcasting System, Inc. [*Associated Press*] (SAG)
TURNBKLE... Turnbuckle [*s*] [*Freight*]
Turn Ch Pr... Turner's Practice of the Court of Chancery [*4th ed.*] [*1821*] [*A publication*] (DLA)
Turn Cop...... Turner on Copyright in Designs [*1849*] [*A publication*] (DLA)
Turn Pat...... Turner on Patents [*1851*] [*A publication*] (DLA)
TURNPIKE... Turnpike [*Commonly used*] (OPSA)
TURNPK...... Turnpike [*Commonly used*] (OPSA)
Turn Pr....... Turnbull's Practice [*New York*] [*A publication*] (DLA)
Turn Qui Tit... Turner on Quieting Titles [*A publication*] (DLA)
TurnrC .... Turner Corp. [*Associated Press*] (SAG)
TURP .... Transurethral Resection of the Prostate [*Medicine*]
turp............ Turpentine [*Chemistry*] (DAVI)
TURPS .... Terrestrial Unattended Reactor Power System
turq............ Turqoise (VRA)
TURQ .... Turquoise (ROG)
TURS .... Terminal Usage Reporting System [*Computer science*]
TURV .... Transurethral Resection of Valves [*Urology*] (DAVI)
TUS............ Tailored Upper Stage (MCD)
TUS............ Treasurer of the United States (AFM)
TUS............ Tucson [*Arizona*] [*Airport symbol*] (OAG)
TUS............ Tugboat Underwriting Syndicate [*Defunct*] (EA)

TUS............. Tuscarora [*New York*] [*Seismograph station code, US Geological Survey Closed*] (SEIS)
TUS............. Tushaun Resources, Inc. [*Vancouver Stock Exchange symbol*]
TUS............. Tuskegee Institute, Tuskegee, AL [*OCLC symbol*] (OCLC)
TUS............. Tussis [*Cough*] [*Pharmacy*]
TUSA .... Third United States Army [*Terminated, 1973*]
TUSA .... Trekville USA (EA)
TUSAB .... [*The*] United States Army Band (AABC)
TUSAC .... [*The*] United States Army Chorus (AABC)
TUSAFG .... [*The*] United States Air Force Group, American Mission for Aid to Turkey
TUSC .... Technology Use Studies Center [*Southeastern State College*]
TUSC .... Tuscarora, Inc. [*NASDAQ symbol*] (NQ)
Tusc .... Tusculanae Disputationes [*of Cicero*] [*Classical studies*] (OCD)
TuscIn......... Tuscarora, Inc. [*Associated Press*] (SAG)
TU-SI .... University of Tennessee, Space Institute Library, Tullahoma, TN [*Library symbol Library of Congress*] (LCLS)
TUSIDBAD ... Tomb of the Unknown Soldier Identification Badge [*Military decoration*] (GFGA)
Tuskegee U... Tuskegee University (GAGS)
TUSLOG........ Turkish-United States Logistic Group
TUSLOG....... [*The*] United States Logistics Group [*Military*] (AABC)
TUSLOGDET... Turkish-United States Logistics Group Detachment (DNAB)
tuss............ Tussis [*Cough*] [*Latin*] (CPH)
TUSSI .... Temple University Short Syntax Inventory [*Educational test*]
TUSSIL......... Tussilago [*Coltsfoot*] [*Pharmacology*] (ROG)
TUSS MOL... Tussi Molesta [*When the Cough Is Troublesome*] [*Pharmacy*]
TUSS URG... Tussi Urgente [*When the Cough Is Troublesome*] [*Pharmacy*]
TUST .... Texarkana Union Station Trust [*AAR code*]
TUT .... GB Air Academy Ltd. [*British ICAO designator*] (FAAC)
TUT .... Tafuna, AS [*Location identifier FAA*] (FAAL)
TUT .... Tenants' Union of Tasmania [*Australia*]
TUT .... Transistor under Test (IEEE)
TUT .... Travailleurs Unis des Transports [*United Transportation Union - UTU*] [*Canada*]
TUT .... Travailleurs Unis du Telegraphe [*United Telegraph Workers - UTW*] [*Canada*]
TUT .... Tube Template (MCD)
TUT .... Tube under Test (MSA)
TUT .... Tucson - Telemeter [*Arizona*] [*Seismograph station code, US Geological Survey Closed*] (SEIS)
tut............. Turko-Tataric [*MARC language code Library of Congress*] (LCCP)
TUT .... Twente University of Technology (NITA)
TUT .... University of Saint Thomas, Houston, TX [*OCLC symbol*] (OCLC)
TUTase .... Terminal Uridylyl Transferase [*An enzyme*]
TUTR .... TRO Learning [*NASDAQ symbol*] (TTSB)
TUTR .... TRO Learning, Inc. [*NASDAQ symbol*] (SAG)
TUT's .... Totally Unified Theories [*Cosmology*]
TUTS .... True Ultimate Tensile Strength (MCD)
TUTT........... Tropical Upper Tropospheric Trough [*Meteorology*]
Tutt & C...... Tuttle and Carpenter's Reports [*52 California*] [*A publication*] (DLA)
Tutt & Carp... Tuttle and Carpenter's Reports [*52 California*] [*A publication*] (DLA)
Tuttle......... Tuttle and Carpenter's Reports [*52 California*] [*A publication*] (DLA)
Tuttle & Carpenter... Tuttle and Carpenter's Reports [*52 California*] [*A publication*] (DLA)
TUU .... Compania Aerea de Servicios Tur Air [*Spain ICAO designator*] (FAAC)
TUU .... Huntington, WV [*Location identifier FAA*] (FAAL)
TUU .... Tabuk [*Saudi Arabia*] [*Airport symbol*] (OAG)
TUU .... Transitional Ultraspherical-Ultraspherical Filter (PDAA)
TUUL .... Trade Union Unity League
TUUL .... Transurethral Ultrasonic Uterolithotripsy [*Urology*]
TUV............ Tactical Unmanned Vehicle [*Military*] (INF)
TUV............ Technischer Ueberwachungs-Verein [*Technical Watch-Over Association*] [*European product safety organization*] (CDE)
TUV............ Tucupita [*Venezuela*] [*Airport symbol*] (OAG)
TUV............ Turavia [*Poland ICAO designator*] (FAAC)
TUV............ Tuvalu [*ANSI three-letter standard code*] (CNC)
TUVX .... Tulip Virus X [*Plant pathology*]
TUW............ Trustee under Will [*Legal term*] (DLA)
TUW............ Tubala [*Panama*] [*Airport symbol*] (OAG)
TUWAH .... Trade Union Women of African Heritage (EA)
TUWC .... Tactical Utilization Working Committee [*Navy*] (MCD)
TUWR .... Turning Wrench [*Tool*] (AAG)
TUX............ Tuxedo (DSUE)
TUX............ Tuxpan [*Mexico*] [*Airport symbol*] (AD)
TUX............ Tuxpeno [*Race of maize*]
TUY............ Empresa Aerotuy [*Venezuela*] [*ICAO designator*] (FAAC)
TUY............ Tulum [*Mexico*] [*Airport symbol Obsolete*] (OAG)
TUZI .... Tuzigoot National Monument
TV .... Grupo Televisa S.A. [*NYSE symbol*] (SPSG)
TV .... Grupo Televisa S.A.GDS [*NYSE symbol*] (TTSB)
TV .... Haiti Trans Air [*ICAO designator*] (AD)
TV .... Taff Vale Railway [*Wales*]
TV .... Talipes Varus [*Orthopedics*] (DAVI)
T/V .... Tank Vessel (COE)
TV .... Target Valve (MCD)
T/V .... Target Vehicle [*Air Force*] (AAG)
TV .... Target Velocity
TV .... Target Vulnerability (MCD)
TV .... Telefunken Variable Microgroove [*Record label*] [*Germany*]
TV .... Television
TV .... Television, Vision Channel
T/V .... Temperature-to-Voltage (IDOE)
TV .... Terminal Velocity [*Navy*]

TV	Test Vehicle
TV	Test Voltage (IAA)
TV	Tetrazolium Violet [*Also, TZV*]
TV	Thames Valley [*England*]
TV	Thermal Vacuum
T/V	Thermal Vacuum (NAKS)
TV	Threshold Value (NITA)
TV	Throttle Valve
TV	Thrust Vector [*Aerospace*] (NASA)
TV	Thyroid Vein [*Medicine*] (PDAA)
TV	Tidal Volume [*Amount of air that moves in and out of lungs under given conditions*] [*Physiology*]
TV	Time Variation of Gain
TV	Title Verso [*Publishing*] (WDMC)
TV	Total Value
TV	Total Volume
TV	Transamerica [*ICAO designator*] (AD)
TV	Transfer and Void (MCD)
TV	Transfer Varnish (DGA)
TV	Transfer Vector
TV	Transfer Voucher (AFM)
TV	Transport Vehicle [*Military*]
TV	Transvenous (DAVI)
TV	Transversion [*Molecular biology*]
TV	Transvestite [*Medicine*]
TV	Travel Voucher (GFGA)
TV	Traverse (IEEE)
TV	Trial Visit (AAMN)
TV	Trichomonas vaginalis [*A protozoan*] [*Medicine*]
TV	Trichomonas Vaginitis [*A parasitic infection*] (DAVI)
TV	Tricuspid Valve [*Anatomy*]
TV	Trinidad Volunteers [*British military*] (DMA)
TV	Trip Valve [*Railroad term*]
TV	Truncal Vagotomy [*Medicine*] (DMAA)
TV	Tuberculin Volutin [*Medicine*] (MAE)
TV	Tube Tester [*JETDS nomenclature*] [*Military*] (CET)
TV	Tube Voltmeter (IAA)
TV	Tunica Vaginalis [*Anatomy*]
TV	Turbo Vision [*Borland International*] [*Computer science*] (PCM)
TV	Tuvalu [*ANSI two-letter standard code*] (CNC)
Tv	Ventral Touch Neurons [*of a leech*]
TV	[*The*] Voluntaryists (EA)
TV5	Television Francophone par Satellite [*France*] (EAIO)
TVA	369th Veterans' Association (EA)
TVA	Morafenobe [*Madagascar*] [*Airport symbol*] (OAG)
TVA	Target Value Analysis [*Army*] (ADDR)
TVA	Taxe a la Valeur Ajoutee [*Value-Added Tax*] [*French Business term*]
TVA	Tax on Value Added [*European manufacturing tax*]
TvA	Television Associates Network [*Canada*]
TVA	Television Australia Ltd.
TVA	Temporary Variance Authority [*or Authorization*] [*NASA*] (AAG)
TVA	Temporary Volume Allowance
TVA	Temporary Voluntary Allowance
TVA	Tennessee Valley Authority [*Also, an information service or system*]
TVA	Tennessee Valley Authority [*NYSE symbol*] (SAG)
TVA	Tennessee Valley Authority, Technical Library, Knoxville, TN [*OCLC symbol*] (OCLC)
TVA	Tenn Val Auth 8.00%'QUIDS' [*NYSE symbol*] (TTSB)
TVA	Textile Veterans Association (EA)
TVA	Thrust Vector Actuator
TVA	Thrust Vector Alignment [*Aerospace*] (MCD)
TVA	Time Variant Automation (IAA)
TVA	Torah Va'Avodah (BJA)
TVA	Trans America Airlines, Inc. [*ICAO designator*] (FAAC)
TVA	Tuned Vertical Array (CAAL)
TVA 45	Tennessee Valley Authority [*Associated Press*] (SAG)
TVA 46	Tennessee Valley Authority [*Associated Press*] (SAG)
TVAA	Tennessee Valley Authority Act of 1933 (COE)
TVAC	Tennessee-Virginia Athletic Conference (PSS)
TVAC	Thrust Vector Activation Control [*Aerospace*]
TVAC	Time-Varying Adaptive Correlation
TVAHVF	Textile Veterans Association Hospitalized Veterans Fund [*Defunct*] (EA)
TVAR	Television Advertisers' Report [*A publication*] (DOAD)
TVAR	Test Variance (NASA)
TV-ARBS	Television Angle Rate Bombing System (MCD)
TVAT	Television Air Trainer
TVB	Cabool, MO [*Location identifier FAA*] (FAAL)
TVB	Television Broadcasts [*Hong Kong television company*] (ECON)
TVB	Television Bureau of Advertising (DOAD)
TVB	Tennessee Valley Authority [*NYSE symbol*] (SAG)
TVB	Tenn Val Auth 7.50%'QUIDS' [*NYSE symbol*] (TTSB)
TVB	Total Volatile Bases [*Chemistry*]
TVB	Treu und Bestaendig [*Faithful and Steadfast*] [*Motto of Johann Georg, Margrave of Brandenburg (1577-1624)*] [*German*]
TVBN	Total Volatile Basic Nitrogen [*Food analysis*]
TVBS	Television Broadcast Satellite [*NASA*]
TVC	Technical Value Committee (BARN)
TVC	Televideo Consultants, Inc. [*Evanston, IL*] [*Telecommunications*] (TSSD)
TVC	Television Camera (MHDB)
TVC	Temperature Valve Control
TVC	Thermal Vacuum Chamber (NASA)
TVC	Thermal Voltage Converter
TVC	Thoracic Vena Cava [*Medicine*]

TVC	Throttle Valve Control
TVC	Thrust Vector Control [*Aerospace*]
TVC	Thrust Vertical Control (MUSM)
TVC	Tientsin Volunteer Corps [*British military*] (DMA)
TVC	Timed Vital Capacity
TVC	Time-Varying Coefficient
TVC	Torsional Vibration Characteristics
TVC	Total Annual Variable Cost
TVC	Total Variable Cost Curve [*Economics*]
TVC	Total Variable Costs
TVC	Total Viable Cells [*Microbiology*]
TVC	Total Vital Capacity [*Medicine*] (DAVI)
TVC	Total Volume Capacity [*Physiology*]
TVC	Transvaginal Cone [*Medicine*] (MAE)
TVC	Traverse City [*Michigan*] [*Airport symbol*] (OAG)
TVC	Triple Voiding Cystogram [*Medicine*]
TVC	True Vocal Cord (MEDA)
TVCA	Thrust Vector Control Actuator [*Aerospace*] (NASA)
TVCA	Thrust Vector Control Assembly [*Aerospace*]
TVCA	Total Vegetative Control Agents [*Agriculture*]
TVCAM	Television Camera and Control Equipment
TVCD	Thrust Vector Control Driver [*Aerospace*] (NASA)
TVC/JIC	Thrust Vector Control/Jet Interaction Control
TVCL	Toxic Victims Compensation Legislation
TVCS	Television Communications Subsystem
TVCS	Thrust Vector Control System [*Aerospace*] (KSC)
TVCS	Tyler Vocational Card Sort [*Guidance*]
TVD	Teatr Voennykh Deistvii [*Theater of Military Operations*] [*Former USSR*]
TVD	Television Display (MCD)
TVD	Thermal Voltaic Detection [*Analytical chemistry*]
TVD	Total Virus Defense [*Computer Security System*]
TVD	Total Virus Defense [*McAfee*] [*Computer science*]
TVD	Toxic Vapor Detector
TVD	Toxic Vapor Disposal [*NASA*] (KSC)
TVD	Transmissable Virus Dementia [*Psychiatry*]
TVD	Triple-Vessel Disease [*Cardiology*] (DAVI)
TVD	True Vertical Depth [*Diamonds*]
TVD	Tuned Viscoelastic Damper
TVDALV	Triple Vessel Disease with Abnormal Left Ventricle [*Cardiology*]
TVDC	Test Volts, Direct Current
TVDC	Tidewater Virginia Development Council
TVDP	Terminal Vector Display Unit
TVDR	Tag Vector Display Register
TVDS	Toxic Vapor Detection System (SAA)
TVDT	Tumor Volume Doubling Time [*Cytology*]
TVDY	Television Deflection Yoke
TVE	Technology Validation Experiment (SDI)
TVE	Television Espanola [*Television network*] [*Spain*]
TVE	Test Vehicle Engine (AAG)
TVE	Thermal Vacuum Environment
TVE	Total Vertical Error [*Aviation*] (DA)
TVE	Town and Village Enterprise (EERA)
TVE	Township and Village Enterprise [*People's Republic of China*] (ECON)
TVE	Tricuspid Valve Echophonocardiogram [*Cardiology*]
TVED	Tuned Viscoelastic Damper
TVEI	Technical and Vocational Education Initiative [*Manpower Services Commission*] [*British*]
TVEI(P)	Technical and Vocational Education Initiative: Pilot (AIE)
TVEL	Target Velocity
TVEL	Track Velocity
TVER	Tumor Virus Epidemiology Repository [*National Institutes of Health*]
TVERS	Television Evaluation and Renewal Standards [*Student legal action organization*]
TVEXPIS	Television Experiment Interconnecting Station [*NASA*] (NASA)
TVF	Tactile Vocal Fremitus [*Medicine*]
TVF	Tape Velocity Fluctuation
TVF	Taylor Vortex Flow [*Fluid mechanics*]
TVF	Templeton Vietnam Opport Fd [*NYSE symbol*] (TTSB)
TVF	Templeton Vietnam Opportunities Fund [*NYSE symbol*] (SAG)
TVF	Thief River Falls [*Minnesota*] [*Airport symbol*] (OAG)
TVF	Total Variable Factor Curve [*Economics*]
TVFA	Total Volatile Fatty Acid [*of foodstuffs*]
TV Flme	TV Filme, Inc. [*Associated Press*] (SAG)
TVFN	Television Food Network
TVFS	Tactical Vehicle Fleet Simulation (MCD)
TVFT	Television Flyback Transformer
TVG	Tavares & Gulf R. R. [*AAR code*]
TVG	Television Games Network
TVG	Television Video Generator
TVG	Temperature-Voltage-Gases (DNAB)
TVG	Test Vector Generator
TVG	Threshold Voltage Generator
TVG	Time Variation of Gain
TVG	Triggered Vacuum Gap
TVG	TVG Technologies [*Associated Press*] (SAG)
TVGDHS	Television Ground Data Handling System [*NASA*]
TVGEN	TV Guide Entertainment Network
TVGLF	TVG Technologies [*NASDAQ symbol*] (SAG)
TVGLF	T V G Technologies Wrrt'C' [*NASDAQ symbol*] (TTSB)
TVG Tch	TVG Technologies [*Associated Press*] (SAG)
TVGTF	TVG Technologies [*NASDAQ symbol*] (SAG)
TVGUF	TVG Technologies [*NASDAQ symbol*] (SAG)
TVGWF	TVG Technologies [*NASDAQ symbol*] (SAG)

TVGWF.........	T V G Technologies Wrrt'A' [*NASDAQ symbol*] (TTSB)
TVGZF..........	TVG Technologies [*NASDAQ symbol*] (SAG)
TVGZF..........	T V G Technologies Wrrt'B' [*NASDAQ symbol*] (TTSB)
TVH.............	Total Vaginal Hysterectomy [*Gynecology*]
TVH.............	Transvaginal Hysterectomy [*Gynecology*] (DAVI)
TVH.............	Turkey Virus Hepatitis [*Medicine*] (DMAA)
TVHH	Television Household [*Ratings*] (NTCM)
TVI.............	Television Interface (ECII)
TVI.............	Television Interference [*Communications*]
TVI.............	Temperament and Values Inventory [*Interpersonal skills and attitudes test*]
TVI.............	Temperature-Viscosity Index (DAVI)
TVI.............	Thomasville, GA [*Location identifier FAA*] (FAAL)
TVI.............	Total Vision, Inc. [*Houston, TX*] (TSSD)
TVI.............	Trade Valuers Institute [*British*] (DBA)
TVI.............	Transcript/Video Index [*A publication*]
TVI.............	Transient Voltage Indicator
TVI.............	Turbo Vapor Injector
TVI.............	Tutored Videotape Instruction
TVIC............	Television Input Converter
TVIC............	Television Interference Committee
TVID...........	Television Frame Identification Data [*NASA*]
TVID...........	Television Sight Unit Identification (MCD)
TVIG...........	Television and Inertial Guidance
TVIS...........	Television Information Storage (IAA)
TVIS...........	Time Video Information Services, Inc. (IID)
T-VIS	Toyota's Variable Induction System [*Automotive engineering*]
TVIS...........	Tropical Vegetable Information Service [*Asian Vegetable Research and Development Center*] [*Information service or system*] (IID)
TVIS...........	Turbine Vibration Indication System (NG)
TVIST..........	Television Information Storage Tube
TVJ	Tavaj Transportes Aereos Regulares, SA [*Brazil*] [*FAA designator*] (FAAC)
TVJ	Thomas Jefferson University, Philadelphia, PA [*OCLC symbol*] (OCLC)
TV/JI	Thrust Vector/Jet Interaction
TVK	Target Value Kills (MCD)
TVK	Toimihenkilo - ja Virkamiesjarjestojen Keskusliitto [*Confederation of Intellectual and Government Workers*] [*Finland*]
TVKMF........	Theodore Von Karman Memorial Foundation (EA)
TVL	Aviata [*Former USSR*] [*FAA designator*] (FAAC)
TVL	Lake Tahoe [*California*] [*Airport symbol*] (OAG)
TVL	Television Listener (IDOE)
TVL	Television Listening (IDOE)
TVL	Tenth Value Layer
TVL	Thermo Voltek [*AMEX symbol*] (TTSB)
TVL	Thermo Voltek Corp. [*AMEX symbol*] (SAG)
TVL	Time Variation of Loss (IAA)
TVL	Townsville [*Australia Seismograph station code, US Geological Survey Closed*] (SEIS)
TVL	Transmit [*or Transmitting*] Variolosser (IAA)
Tvl	Transvaal [*South Africa*]
TVL	Transverse Vertical Longitudinal
TVL	Travel (AABC)
TVLADVP	Travel Advance Payment [*TDY*]
TVLALWADV...	Travel Allowance Advance [*in PCS*]
TVLALWS	Travel Allowance on Separation [*Army*]
TVLF..........	Transportable Very-Low-Frequency [*Transmitter*]
TVLI...........	Tivoli Indus Inc. [*NASDAQ symbol*] (TTSB)
TVLI...........	Tivoli Industries, Inc. [*NASDAQ symbol*] (SAG)
TVLIW.........	Tivoli Inds Wrrt'A' [*NASDAQ symbol*] (TTSB)
TVLIZ..........	Tivoli Inds Wrrt'B' [*NASDAQ symbol*] (TTSB)
TVLRO	Television Licensing and Records Office [*Post Office*] [*British*]
TVM	Tachometer Voltmeter
TVM	Target Via Missile [*Aviation*]
TVM	Tavria-Mak [*Ukraine*] [*FAA designator*] (FAAC)
TVM	Techno Venture Management [*Germany*]
TVM	Television Malta
TVM	Television Monitor [*Video only*]
TVM	Television Movie (WDAA)
TVM	Thrust Vectoring Motor [*Aerospace*] (MUGU)
TVM	TOW [*Tube-Launched, Optically Tracked, Wire-Guided (Weapon)*] Visual Module [*Army*]
TVM	Track-Via-Missile
TVM	Trailer Van Mount
TVM	Transistorized Voltmeter
TVM	TRV Minerals Corp. [*Vancouver Stock Exchange symbol*]
TVMAP........	Track-via-Missile Analog Processor [*Military*]
TVMS..........	Test of Visual-Motor Skills [*Sensorimotor skills test*]
TVMV..........	Tobacco Vein Mottling Virus
TVN	Target Velocity, North
TVN	Television News, Inc.
TVN	Televisora Nacional [*Television network*] [*Venezuela*]
TVN	Test Verification Network [*NASA*] (NASA)
TVN	Total Volatile Nitrogen [*Analytical chemistry*]
TVN	Transcolombiana de Aviacion SA [*Colombia*] [*ICAO designator*] (FAAC)
TVO	Ditta Transavio di I. Ballerio [*Italy ICAO designator*] (FAAC)
TVO	Taravao [*Society Islands*] [*Seismograph station code, US Geological Survey*] (SEIS)
TVO	Throttle Valve Opening [*Automotive engineering*]
TVO	Total Value of Ownership
TVO	Tractor Vaporizing Oil [*Automotive engineering*]
TVO	Transistor Volt-Ohmmeter (IDOE)
TVOC	Television Operations Center [*NASA*] (KSC)

TVOM..........	Transistorized Volt Ohm Milliammeter (IAA)
TVOM..........	Transistor Volt-Ohmmeter (IDOE)
TVOP..........	Television Observation Post (CET)
TVOR..........	Terminal Very High Frequency Omnirange (IAA)
TVOR..........	Terminal VHF [*Very-High Frequency*] Omnidirectional Range
TVOR..........	Terminal Visual Omnirange
TVOR..........	Translational Vestibulo-Ocular Reflex [*Ophthalmology*]
TVP...........	Tamil Vimukhti Peramena [*Sri Lanka*] [*Political party*] (PPW)
TVP...........	Test Verification Program [*NASA*] (NASA)
TVP...........	Textured Vegetable Protein [*Trademark of Archer Daniels Midland Co. for soybean product*]
TVP...........	Thermo-Photo-Voltaic
TVP...........	Time Variable Parameter (IAA)
TVP...........	Transvenous Pacemaker [*Cardiology*] (DAVI)
TVP...........	Transvesical Prostatectomy [*Urology*] (DAVI)
TVP...........	Tricuspid Valve Prolapse [*Cardiology*]
TVP...........	True Vapor Pressure
TVP...........	Victoria Public Library, Victoria, TX [*OCLC symbol*] (OCLC)
TVPC..........	TOW [*Tube-Launched, Optically Tracked, Wire-Guided (Weapon)*] Vehicle PowerConditioner (MCD)
TVPPA.........	Tennessee Valley Public Power Association (EA)
TVPS..........	Test of Visual-Perceptual Skills
TV Q	Television Quarterly [*A publication*] (BRI)
TVQ...........	Top Visual Quality
TVR...........	Tadcaster Volunteer Rifles [*British military*] (DMA)
TVR...........	Tag Vector Response (NITA)
TVR...........	Tavrey, Aircompany [*Ukraine*] [*FAA designator*] (FAAC)
TVR...........	Television Rating
TVR...........	Television Recording (WDMC)
TVR...........	Temperature Variation of Resistance [*Electricity*]
TVR...........	Tennessee Valley Region
TVR...........	Thermal Vapor Recompressors [*For evaporators*]
TVR...........	Time Variable Reflectivity (MCD)
TVR...........	Tonic Vibration Reflex [*or Response*] [*Medicine*]
TVR...........	Total Vascular Resistance [*Medicine*] (DMAA)
TVR...........	Trajectory Velocity RADAR (MCD)
TVR...........	Trevor (Wilkinson) [*Sports car named for its designer*] [*British*]
TVR...........	Tricuspid Valve Replacement [*Cardiology*]
TVRB..........	Tactical Vehicle Review Board [*Army*] (AABC)
TVRCC........	TVR Car Club [*Later, TVRCCNA*] (EA)
TVRE..........	Transportable Vehicle Refuelling Equipment (PDAA)
TVRI..........	Televisi Republik Indonesia [*Indonesian television network*] (FEA)
TVRM..........	Television Receiver/Monitor
TVRN..........	Tavern
TVRO..........	Television Receive Only [*Telecommunications*]
TVRP..........	Television Reading Program
TVRS..........	Television and Radio Suppression [*Electronics*]
TVRS..........	Television Video Recording System (MCD)
TVS...........	Tactical Vocoder System
TVS...........	Telemetry Video Spectrum
TVS...........	Telephone Video System [*NEC America, Inc.*] [*Wood Dale, IL*] [*Telecommunications*] (TSSD)
TVS...........	Television Subsystem [*Spacecraft*]
TVS...........	Thermal [*or Thermostatic*] Vacuum Switch [*Automotive engineering*]
TVS...........	Thrust Vector System [*Aerospace*]
TVS...........	Tornado Vortex Signature [*Marine science*] (OSRA)
TVS...........	Total Volatile Solids [*Analytical chemistry*]
TVS...........	Toxic Vapor Suit [*NASA*] (NASA)
TVS...........	Transient Voltage Suppressor
TVS...........	Triangular Voltage Sweep [*Electronics*] (AAEL)
TVS...........	Tube-Vehicle System (MCD)
TVS...........	Volunteer State Community College, Gallatin, TN [*OCLC symbol*] (OCLC)
TVSA..........	Thrust Vector Control Servoamplifier [*NASA*] (NAKS)
TVSA..........	Thrust Vector Position Servo Amplifier [*Aerospace*]
TV-SAT	Satellite Television [*Germany*]
TVSC..........	Television Videotape Satellite Communications [*Group W Productions*] [*Pittsburgh, PA*] (TSSD)
TVSD	Time-Varying Spectral Display
TVSG	Television Signal Generator
TVSM..........	Television System Monitor
TVSM..........	Time-Varying Sequential Measuring [*Device*]
TVSM..........	Time-Varying Signal Measurement (IAA)
TVSO..........	Television Space Observatory
TVSP..........	Tactical Vehicle Special Program [*Army*] (RDA)
TV SPOTTS...	Tuneful Viewer's Society for the Preservation of Television Theme Songs
TVSS..........	Tactile Vision Substitution System (PDAA)
TVSS..........	Television and Video Switching Subsystem (MCD)
TVSS..........	Television Systems Section
TVSS..........	Transient Voltage Surge Suppression
TVSSIS........	Television Subsystem Interconnecting Station [*NASA*] (NASA)
TVSU..........	Television Sight Unit
TVSV..........	Kingstown/Arnos Vale [*St. Vincent*] [*ICAO location identifier*] (ICLI)
TVSV..........	Thermostatic Vacuum Switching Valve [*Automotive engineering*]
TVSYS.........	Television System (IAA)
TVT...........	Target Verification Test [*Military*] (CAAL)
TVT...........	Television of Thailand (FEA)
TVT...........	Television Terminal (CMD)
TVT...........	Television Trainer/Tapes (MCD)
TVT...........	Television Typewriter
TVT...........	Thermal Vacuum Test
TVT...........	Tiverton, OH [*Location identifier FAA*] (FAAL)
TVT...........	Traffic Volume Trends [*BTS*] (TAG)
TVT...........	Transaviation, SA [*Spain*] [*FAA designator*] (FAAC)

TVT	Transmissible Veneral Tumour [*Medicine*] (DB)
TVT	Tunica Vaginalis Testis [*Anatomy*]
TVTA	Thermal Vacuum Test Article (NASA)
TV TR	Television Tower [*Mast*]
TVTV	Thermostatic Vacuum Transmitting Valve [*Automotive engineering*]
TVTV	Top Value Television [*Group of 26 young people who photographed the 1972 Democratic convention and presented it on TV*]
TVU	Taveuni [*Fiji*] [*Airport symbol*] (OAG)
TVU	Total Volume Urine [*in 24 hours*]
TVV	Thermal Vacuum Valve [*Automotive engineering*]
TVV	Thermal Vent Valve [*Automotive engineering*]
TVV	Transmissible Venereal Virus [*Infectious diseases*] (DAVI)
TVW	Tag Vector Word (NITA)
TVW	Total Ventricular Weight [*Cardiology*]
TVW	Towed Vehicle Weight [*Automotive engineering*]
TVWB	Thames Valley Water [*British*] (WDAA)
TVX	Target Vehicle Experimental [*Air Force*]
TVX	Tulip Virus X
TVX	TVX Gold [*NYSE symbol*] (TTSB)
TVX	TVX Gold, Inc. [*NYSE symbol*] (SAG)
TVX	TVX Mining Corp. [*Formerly, Treasure Valley Explorations Ltd.*] [*Toronto Stock Exchange symbol*]
TVX Gld	TVX Gold, Inc. [*Associated Press*] (SAG)
TVY	Tavoy [*Myanmar*] [*Airport symbol*] (OAG)
TVZ	Taupo Volcanic Zone [*Geology*]
TW	20th Century Indus [*NYSE symbol*] (TTSB)
TW	Tactical Warning (MCD)
TW	Tail Warning [*RADAR*] (NATG)
TW	Tailwater
TW	Tail Wind
TW	Taiwan [*ANSI two-letter standard code*] (CNC)
TW	Tankwagon
TW	Tapes and Recording Wires [*JETDS nomenclature*] [*Military*] (CET)
TW	Tap Water [*Medicine*]
TW	Taxiway [*Aviation*]
TW	Teamwork (MSA)
TW	Technical Win [*Boxing*] (DICI)
TW	Technical Works [*Air Force*] (MCD)
TW	Temperature Well (MSA)
TW	Tempered Water
TW	Temporary Warrant
TW	Terawatt
TW	Test Weight
TW	Textil-Wirtschaft [*Textile Industry*] [*Deutscher Fachverlag GmbH*] [*Information service or system*] (IID)
TW	Text Word(s) (NITA)
TW	Thermal Wire (KSC)
TW	Thermit Welding
TW	Thermoplastic Wire
TW	Thibierge-Weissenbach (DB)
T-W	Three Wheeler [*Type of motorcycle*]
T/W	Thrust-to-Weight
TW	Thumbwheel (MCD)
TW	Tight Wrapped (MSA)
TW	Tile Wainscot [*Technical drawings*]
TW	Time Word
TW	Top of Wall [*Technical drawings*]
TW	Torpedo Water
TW	Total Body Water
TW	Total Weight
TW	Total Woman [*Title of a 1973 book by Marabel Morgan and of TV seminars based on this book*]
TW	Total Work
TW	Trail Watcher (CINC)
TW	Transit Working [*Telecommunications*] (TEL)
TW	Trans World Airlines, Inc. [*ICAO designator*]
TW	Traveling Wave
TW	Travel Warrant
TW	Travel Writer [*A publication*] (EAAP)
TW	Tropical Worsted Uniform [*Army*] (VNW)
TW	Trow [*Ship's rigging*] (ROG)
TW	True Watt (MSA)
TW	Trustee under Will [*Legal term*] (DLA)
TW	Tru-Wall Group Ltd. [*Toronto Stock Exchange symbol*]
TW	Twaddell [*Specific gravity scale*] [*Physics*]
TW	Twentieth Century Industries [*NYSE symbol*] (SPSG)
TW	Twickenham [*Postcode*] (ODBW)
TW	Twin (IAA)
TW	Twin Screw (DS)
TW	Twisted (IAA)
TW	Twister (AAG)
TW	Typewriter (AAG)
TW3	That Was The Week That Was [*Also, TWTWTW*] [*Television program of English origin*]
TWA	Tap Water Agar [*Microbiology*]
TWA	Textile Waste Association [*Later, Textile Fibers and By-Products Association*] (EA)
TWA	Thames Water Authority [*British*]
TWA	Time Weighted Average [*Data sampling*]
TWA	Tooling Work Authorization
TWA	Toy Wholesalers Association of America (EA)
TWA	Trailing Wire Antenna [*on aircraft*]
TWA	Transaction Work Area
TWA	Transcontinental & Western Airlines [*Later, Trans World Airlines, Inc.*]
TWA	Trans World Airlines [*Associated Press*] (SAG)
TWA	Trans World Airlines, Inc. [*Humorously interpreted as "Try Walking Across" and "Teeny Weeny Airlines"*] [*AMEX symbol*] (SPSG)
TWA	Trans World Airlines, Inc. [*ICAO designator*] (FAAC)
TWA	Traveling-Wave Amplifier
TWA	Trelew [*Argentina*] [*Geomagnetic observatory code*]
TWA	Two-Way Alternate (IAA)
TWA	Typewriter Adapter (MHDB)
TWA	[*The*] Waferboard Association [*Later, SBA*] (EA)
TWA	[*The*] Woman Activist (EA)
TW/AA	Tactical Warning/Attack Assessment
TWAB	Textile Work Assignment Boards [*Terminated, 1935*]
TWAC	Tactical Weather Analysis Center (MCD)
TWAC	Time-Weighted Average Concentration [*Toxicology*]
TW/AD	Test Wing/Armament Division (MUSM)
Twad	Twaddell [*Physics*]
TWADL	Two-Way Air Data Link [*Tactical Air Command*]
TWAE	Time-Weighted Average Exposure [*Toxicology*]
TWAES	Tactical Warfare Analysis and Evaluation System (MCD)
TWAH	This Week at Headquarters [*Military publication*] (DNAB)
TWAIN	Technology Without an Interesting Name [*Programming interface*] [*Computer science*] (IGQR)
TWALNDG	Turnaway Landing [*Navy*] (NVT)
TWAP	Thin Wire Analysis Program [*Air Force*]
TWAPA	Teens with a Positive Attitude
TWAR	Taiwan Acute Respiratory Disease [*Pneumonia-causing chlamydia strain named after the ailment that results from it*]
TWAS	Third World Academy of Sciences [*Trieste, Italy*] (EAIO)
TW/ASD	Test Wing/Aeronautical Systems Division (MUSM)
TWASPIT	Therapeutic Work Aid Station for Physically Inactive Thinkers (MCD)
TWAT	Traveling-Wave Amplifier Tube
TWA.WS	Trans World Airlines Wrrt [*AMEX symbol*] (TTSB)
TWB	Toowoomba [*Australia Airport symbol*] (OAG)
TWB	Total Water Burden [*Environmental science*]
TWB	Towed Vehicle Brake
TWB	Traveling-Wave Beam [*LASER*]
TWB	Twin with Bath [*Tourist accommodations*] (WDAA)
TWB	Typewriter Buffer
TWB	Wayland Baptist College, Plainview, TX [*OCLC symbol*] (OCLC)
TWBA	Tasmanian Wool Brokers' Association [*Australia*]
TWBC	Total White Blood Cells [*Medicine*]
TWBC	Transworld Bancorp [*NASDAQ symbol*] (NQ)
TWBFA	Treeing Walker Breeders and Fanciers Association (EA)
TWBNT	Theologisches Woerterbuch zum Neuen Testament [*A publication*] (BJA)
TWBS	Traditional Wooden Boat Society [*Defunct*] (EA)
TWC	Express Airlines II, Inc. [*ICAO designator*] (FAAC)
TWC	Suao [*Republic of China*] [*Seismograph station code, US Geological Survey*] (SEIS)
TWC	Teletype Service Without Voice Communication [*Telecommunications*] (IAA)
TWC	Tennessee Wesleyan College
TWC	Texas Wesleyan College
TWC	Texas Wesleyan College, Fort Worth, TX [*OCLC symbol*] (OCLC)
TWC	Texas Western College [*Later, UTEP*]
TWC	Theater Weather Central [*Military*]
TWC	Three-Way Catalyst [*Vehicle exhaust control*]
TWC	Total Water Current (COE)
TWC	Total Wear Coefficient [*Materials science*]
TWC	Truncated Whitworth Coarse [*Thread*] (MSA)
TWC	[*The*] Weather Channel [*Cable TV programming service*]
TWCA	T. W. Cape and Associates [*Atlanta, GA*] [*Telecommunications service*] (TSSD)
TWCap	Time Warner Capital I [*Associated Press*] (SAG)
TWCF	Third World Conference Foundation (EA)
TWCF	Third World Conference Fund
TWCGX	Amer. Century Growth Fund [*Mutual fund ticker symbol*] (SG)
TWCIX	Amer. Century Select Fund [*Mutual fund ticker symbol*] (SG)
TWCRT	Traveling-Wave Cathode-Ray Tube (IEEE)
TWCS	Test of Work Competency and Stability [*Psychology*]
TWCS	Through-Water Communications System [*Navy*] (CAAL)
TWCS	Tomahawk Weapon Control System (DOMA)
TWCUX	Amer. Century Ultra Fund [*Mutual fund ticker symbol*] (SG)
TWD	Hualien [*Republic of China*] [*Seismograph station code, US Geological Survey*] (SEIS)
TWD	Tactical Weapons Delivery
TWD	Tail Wags Dog [*Airspace effects*]
TWD	Thermal Warning Device (MCD)
TWD	Torpedo Wire Dispenser
TWD	Total White and Differential Count [*Hematology*]
TWD	Touch Wire Display (PDAA)
TWD	Toward
TWD	Tween Deck [*on a ship*] (DS)
TWD	Twisted Double Shielded (MCD)
TWDC	Tyne and Wear Development Corp. [*British*] (ECON)
TWDD	Two-Way/Delay Dial [*Telecommunications*] (TEL)
TWDM	Two-Way Data Messaging
TWDR	Terminal Weather Doppler Radar [*FAA*] (TAG)
TWDS	Tactical Water Distribution System (MCD)
TWE	Tap Water Enema [*Medicine*]
TWE	TD Waterhouse Group [*NYSE symbol*]
TWE	Test of Written English [*Educational test*]
TWE	Textile Waste Exchange [*Later, Textile Fibers and By-Products Association*]
TWE	Thumb Wheel Encoder
TWE	Time Warner Entertainment (ECON)

TWE .... Transwede [*Sweden ICAO designator*] (FAAC)
TWE .... Trans-Western Exploration, Inc. [*Toronto Stock Exchange symbol*]
TWE .... Trans World Entertainment [*Movie production*]
TWE .... [*The*] Washington Establishment
TWEA .... Trading with the Enemy Act
TWEB .... Transcribed Weather Broadcast
TWEC .... Time-Warner Entertainment Co. (WDAA)
Tweener ...... Between Two Outfielders [*Baseball*] [*Also, a lifestyle classification*]
Twel N .... Twelfth Night [*Shakespearean work*] (BARN)
TWEP .... Terminate with Extreme Prejudice [*To kill*] [*Counterintelligence*]
TWER .... Tower Automotive [*NASDAQ symbol*] (TTSB)
TWER .... Tower Automotive, Inc. [*NASDAQ symbol*] (SAG)
TWERL .... Tropical Wind, Energy Conversion, and Reference Level [*National Science Foundation*]
TWERLE .... Tropical Wind, Energy Conversion, and Reference Level Experiment [*National Science Foundation*]
TWETC .... Tapwater Enema Till Clear [*Pharmacology*] (DAVI)
TWF .... Test of Word Finding (TES)
TWF .... Third World Forum [*Cairo, Egypt*] (EAIO)
TWF .... Third World Foundation [*British*] (EAIO)
TWF .... Transuranic Waste Facility [*Environmental science*] (COE)
TWF .... Transylvanian World Federation (EAIO)
TWF .... Trasco Wind-Force [*Vancouver Stock Exchange symbol*]
TWF .... Truncated Whitworth Fine [*Thread*] (MSA)
TWF .... Twin Falls [*Idaho*] [*Airport symbol*] (OAG)
TWF .... Yuli [*Republic of China*] [*Seismograph station code, US Geological Survey Closed*] (SEIS)
TWF1 .... Yuli [*Republic of China*] [*Seismograph station code, US Geological Survey*] (SEIS)
TWFC .... Tom Wopat Fan Club (EA)
TW Fin .... Time Warner Financing Trust PERCS [*Associated Press*] (SAG)
TWG .... Taitung [*Republic of China*] [*Seismograph station code, US Geological Survey*] (SEIS)
TWG .... Technical Working Group [*of the Conference on the Discontinuance of Nuclear Weapon Tests*]
TWG .... Telemetry Working Group
TWG .... Television Writer's Guild (NTCM)
TWG .... Test Working Group [*in various federal government agencies*] (KSC)
TWG .... Transfer Working Group (MCD)
TWG .... Transition Work Group
TWG .... Transport Working Group [*Australia*]
TWG .... Trans Wings AS [*Norway ICAO designator*] (FAAC)
TW Gam ...... Trans World Gaming Corp. [*Associated Press*] (SAG)
TWGC .... Treatment of War Gas Casualties (MCD)
TWGSS .... Tank Weapons Gunnery Simulation System (MCD)
TWH .... Catalina Island [*California*] [*Airport symbol Obsolete*] (OAG)
TWH .... Houston Baptist University, Houston, TX [*OCLC symbol*] (OCLC)
TWh .... Terawatt Hour (ADA)
TWH .... Toronto Western Hospital [*UTLAS symbol*]
TWHA .... Western Tasmanian Wilderness National Parks World Heritage Area (EERA)
TWHBEA ...... Tennessee Walking Horse Breeders' and Exhibitors' Association (EA)
TWHBEAA .... Tennessee Walking Horse Breeders' and Exhibitors' Association of America [*Later, TWHBEA*] (EA)
TWHD .... Tons per Workable Hatch per Day [*Shipping*]
TWHF .... Technoserve's World Harvest Fund (EA)
TWHH .... Transworld Home HealthCare, Inc. [*NASDAQ symbol*] (SAG)
TWHH .... Transworld Home Hlthcare [*NASDAQ symbol*] (TTSB)
TWHHW .... Transworld Home Hlthcr Wrrt [*NASDAQ symbol*] (TTSB)
TWHL .... Tail Wheel [*Aviation*]
TWHO .... [*The*] White House Office
TWHTA .... Tennessee Walking Horse Trainers' Association [*Later, Walking Horse Trainers Association*]
TW(I) .... Tail Warning (Indicator) [*RADAR*] (DEN)
TWI .... Threat Warning Information [*Air Force*]
TWI .... Titan Wheel International Co. [*NYSE symbol*] (SAG)
TWI .... Titan Wheel Intl [*NYSE symbol*] (TTSB)
TWI .... Toxic Waste Incinerator
TWI .... Trade-Weighted Index (ADA)
TWI .... Training with Industry Program [*Army*] (RDA)
twi .... Twi [*MARC language code Library of Congress*] (LCCP)
TWI .... Twilight (FAAC)
TWI .... [*The*] Way International [*An association*] (EA)
TWI .... [*The*] Welding Institute [*Information service or system*] (IID)
TWI .... Wichita, KS [*Location identifier FAA*] (FAAL)
TWI .... [*The*] Women's Institute (EA)
TWIB .... This Week in Baseball [*Television program*]
TWIC .... Theater Watch Intelligence Condition (NATG)
TWID .... Two-Way/Immediate Dial [*Telecommunications*] (TEL)
TWIDS .... Threat Warning Information Display System (MCD)
TWIF .... Tug-of-War International Federation [*Zevenhuizen, Netherlands*] (EAIO)
TWIFC .... Tammy Wynette International Fan Club (EA)
TWIFT .... Toronto Women in Film and Theatre [*Canada*] (WWLA)
TWIG .... Tandem Wing in Sound Effect (MCD)
TWIMC .... To Whom It May Concern
TWIN .... Test Ware Instrument (PDAA)
TWIN .... Third World Information Network [*British*] (EAIO)
TWIN .... Together Women in Neighborhoods
TWIN .... Twin City Bancorp [*NASDAQ symbol*] (TTSB)
TWIN .... Twin City Bancorp, Inc. [*NASDAQ symbol*] (SAG)
TWI-N .... Twi-Night [*or Twilight-Night*] [*Doubleheader in baseball*]
TwinCtyB ..... Twin City Bancorp, Inc. [*Associated Press*] (SAG)
TwinDs .... Twin Disc, Inc. [*Associated Press*] (SAG)
TWIP .... Twentieth of a Point [*Computer science*] (CDE)

TWIRP .... [*The*] Woman Is Requested to Pay [*Some claim that this acronym, originally a designation for certain school dances, evolved into a slang term denoting any male unable to afford a date*]
TWIS .... Technically Workable Ideal System [*Industrial engineering*]
TWIS .... Technical Writing Improvement Society
TWIsM .... This World Is Mine [*Record label*]
TWITAS .... Third World Institute of Theatre Arts Studies
TWITW .... [*The*] Wind in the Willows [*Book by Kenneth Grahame*]
TWIU .... Tobacco Workers International Union [*Later, BCTWIU*] (EA)
TWIX .... Teletypewriter Message
TWIZN .... Twilight Zone [*Aviation*]
TWJ .... Tack Welded Joint
TWK .... Hsinying [*Republic of China*] [*Seismograph station code, US Geological Survey*] (SEIS)
TWK .... Tool Welders Kit
TWK .... Too Well Known
TWK .... Traveling-Wave Klystron
TWK .... Typewriter Keyboard
TWL .... Leased Teletypewriter Service
TWL .... Telex World Letter [*MCI International, Inc.*] [*Rye Brook, NY*] (TSSD)
TWL .... Top Water Level
TWL .... Total Weight Loss (MCD)
TWL .... Tradewinds Aviation Ltd. [*Canada ICAO designator*] (FAAC)
TWL .... Transepidermal Water Loss [*Physiology*] (MAE)
TWL .... Transition to Working Life [*Project*] (AIE)
TWL .... Traveling-Wave LASER
TWL .... Tuberculosis Welfare League [*Defunct*] (EA)
TWL .... Twin Lakes [*California*] [*Seismograph station code, US Geological Survey*] (SEIS)
TWL .... Twin Wheel Loading [*Aviation*]
TWLA .... Turkish Women's League of America (EA)
TWLC .... Two Way Logic Circuit (PDAA)
TwldH .... Transworld Home HealthCare, Inc. [*Associated Press*] (SAG)
TwldHH .... Transworld Home HealthCare, Inc. [*Associated Press*] (SAG)
TWLT .... Twilight
TWM .... Kaohsiung [*Republic of China*] [*Seismograph station code, US Geological Survey Closed*] (SEIS)
TWM .... Tape Wrapping Machine
TWM .... Traveling-Wave Magnetron (IAA)
TWM .... Traveling-Wave MASER
TWM .... Two-Way Mirror
TWM1 .... Kaohsiung [*Republic of China*] [*Seismograph station code, US Geological Survey*] (SEIS)
TW-MAE-W... Third World Movement Against the Exploitation of Women [*Quezon City, Philippines*] (EAIO)
TWMAS .... Tobacco Workers' Mutual Assistance Society [*A union*] [*British*]
TWMBK .... Traveling-Wave Multiple-Beam Klystron (MSA)
TWMC .... Transport, Wages, Maintenance, and Care
TWMC .... Trans World Entertainment [*NASDAQ symbol*] (TTSB)
TWMC .... Trans World Entertainment Corp. [*NASDAQ symbol*] (NQ)
TWMD .... Toxics and Waste Management Division [*Environmental Protection Agency*] (GFGA)
TWMIP .... Third World Moving Images Project (EA)
TWMP .... Track Width Mine Plow (MCD)
TWMR .... Tungsten Water Moderated Reactor (KSC)
TWN .... Taiwan [*ANSI three-letter standard code*] (CNC)
TWN .... Taiwan Fund [*NYSE symbol*] (TTSB)
TWN .... Taiwan Fund, Inc. [*NYSE symbol*] (SPSG)
TWN .... Third World Network (EERA)
TWN .... Town (MCD)
TWN .... Twin Eagles Resources, Inc. [*Vancouver Stock Exchange symbol*]
TWN .... Twin Peaks [*California*] [*Seismograph station code, US Geological Survey*] (SEIS)
TWNA .... Truck Writers of North America [*An association*] (EA)
Tw Nat P .... Twiss. Law of Nations in Time of Peace [*2nd ed.*] [*1884*] [*A publication*] (DLA)
Tw Nat W .... Twiss. Law of Nations in Time of War [*2nd ed.*] [*1875*] [*A publication*] (DLA)
TwnCtry ...... Town & Country Trust [*Associated Press*] (SAG)
TWNE .... Towne
TWNG .... Towing
TWNHSE .... Townhouse [*Classified advertising*]
TWNP .... Tape-Wound Nylon Phenolic (SAA)
TWNS .... Trans World News Service (NTCM)
TWNT .... Theologisches Woerterbuch zum Neuen Testament [*A publication*] (BJA)
TWO .... Meishan [*Republic of China*] [*Seismograph station code, US Geological Survey*] (SEIS)
TWO .... Neoucom Processing Center, Rootstown, OH [*OCLC symbol*] (OCLC)
TWO .... Ontario, CA [*Location identifier FAA*] (FAAL)
TWO .... This Week Only (ADA)
TWO .... Tooling Work Order (MCD)
TWO .... Travelling-Wave Oscillator
TWO .... Twente Airlines [*Netherlands*] [*FAA designator*] (FAAC)
TWOATAF ..... Second Allied Tactical Air Force Central Europe
TWOC .... Taken Without Owner's Consent
TWODEPEP... Two Dimensional Elliptic, Parabolic and Eigenvalue Problems (MHDI)
TWODS .... [*The*] World of Dark Shadows (EA)
Two Gent .... Two Gentlemen of Verona [*Shakesperean work*] (BARN)
TWOM .... The Well Oiled Machine (NITA)
TWOM .... Traveling-Wave Optical MASER
TWOS .... Total Warrant Officer System [*Army*]
TWOS .... Tropical Wind Observing Ships [*Marine science*] (MSC)
TW/OT .... Travel without Troops

TWOV	Transit-without-Visa
TWP	Tactical Work Program
TWP	Task Work Package (KSC)
TWP	Technological War Plan
TWP	Territory Wildlife Park [Northern Territory, Australia]
TWP	Torwood [Australia Airport symbol Obsolete] (OAG)
TWP	Total Wave Pressure
TWP	Township
Twp	Township (DD)
twp	Township (REAL)
TWP	Traveling-Wave Phototube
TWP	Trawler Petroleum Explorations Ltd. [Vancouver Stock Exchange symbol]
TWP	Trial Work Period [Social Security Administration] (OICC)
TWP	Tropical Western Pacific [Marine science] (OSRA)
TWP	True Whig Party [Liberia] (AF)
TWP	Twisted Wire Pair
TWPA	Traveling-Wave Parametric Amplifier
TWPB	Total Work Package Budget (MCD)
TWPL	Teletypewriter, Private Line
TWPL	Total Weighted Pollutant Load (ERG)
TWPLA	Turkish Workers' and Peasants' Liberation Army
TWPP	Truncated Whitworth, British Standard Pipe (Parallel) [Thread]
TWPS	Traveling-Wave Phase Sifter
TWQ	Tungshih [Republic of China] [Seismograph station code, US Geological Survey] (SEIS)
TWQM	Tailwater Quality Numerical Model [Army Corps of Engineers]
TWR	Tactical Weather RADAR
TWR	Tape Write Register
TWR	Test Work Release (MCD)
TWR	Theater War Reserves [Army]
TWR	Third World Resources [A publication] (BRI)
TWR	Threat Warning RADAR
TWR	Threat Warning Receiver
TWR	Tom Walkinshaw Racing [Auto racing]
TWR	Tool Wear Rate
TWR	Torpedo Weapons Receiver
TWR	Total Wrist Replacement [Medicine]
TWR	Tower (AAG)
twr	Tower (VRA)
TWR	Towet
TWR	TransWorld Radio (EA)
TWR	Trans World Radio Pacific [Guam] (FEA)
TWR	Traveling-Wave Resonator
TWR	Twin Richfield Oils Ltd. [Toronto Stock Exchange symbol]
TWRA	Transpacific Westbound Rate Agreement (DS)
TwrAuto	Tower Automotive, Inc. [Associated Press] (SAG)
TWRG	Towering [Meteorology] (FAAC)
TWRI	Texas Water Resources Institute [Texas A & M University] [Department of the Interior Research center] (RCD)
TWRL	Taylor Woodrow Research Laboratories [Research center British] (IRUK)
TWRL	Two-Way Radio Link (LAIN)
TWRS	Towers
TWRSX	Hibernia Capital Apprec. [Mutual fund ticker symbol] (SG)
TWS	Southwestern at Memphis, Memphis, TN [OCLC symbol] (OCLC)
TWS	Tactical Warning System (AAG)
TWS	Tactical Weapon System (NG)
TWS	Tactical Weather Station [Military]
TWS	Tail Warning Set [or System] [Aerospace] (MCD)
TWS	Tartar Weapons System
TWS	Tasmanian Wilderness Society (EERA)
TWS	Teletypewriter Exchange Service
TWS	Terrier Weapons System
TWS	Test of Written Spelling [Education]
TWS	Texas World Speedway [Auto racing]
TWS	Thermal Weapon Sight [Army] (INF)
TWS	Thermal Wire Stripper
TWS	Thomas Wolfe Society (EA)
TWS	Timed Wire Service (WDAA)
TWS	Track-while-Scan [Communications]
TWS	Translator Writing System [Computer science] (IAA)
TWS	Trans West African Airlines Ltd. [Gambia] [ICAO designator] (FAAC)
TWS	Truncated Whitworth Special [Thread] (MSA)
TWS	Tsunami Warning System [National Oceanic and Atmospheric Administration]
TWS	Twin-Wheel Stripper
TWS	Two-Way Simultaneous (IAA)
TWS	[The] Wilderness Society (EERA)
TWS	[The] Wildlife Society (EA)
TWS-2	Test of Written Spelling-2 [Larsen and Hammill] (TES)
TWSB	Twin Sideband
TWSb/6	Antimony Sodium Dimercaptosuccinate [Stibocaptate] (BABM)
TWSBA	Tasmanian Wool Selling Brokers' Association [Australia]
TWSC	Twin Screw
TWSEAS	Tactical Warfare Simulation, Evaluation, and Analysis System [Marine Corps] (MCD)
TWSO	Tactical Weapon Systems Operation
TWSP	Tactical Warfare Simulation Program
TWSR	Track-while-Scan RADAR
TWSRO	Track-while-Scan on Receive Only (NG)
TWSRS	Track-while-Scan RADAR Simulator
TWSST	Time without Symptoms of Disease and Systemic Treatment [Medicine] (CDI)
TWST	TeleWest Communications Ltd. [NASDAQ symbol] (SAG)
TWST	Torus Water Storage Tank (IEEE)
TWSTY	TeleWest PLC ADS [NASDAQ symbol] [Formerly, TeleWest Communications ADS] (SG)
TWT	Sturgis, KY [Location identifier FAA] (FAAL)
TWT	Tawi-Tawi [Philippines] [Airport symbol] (OAG)
TWT	Time Wire Transmission (IAA)
TWT	Torpedo Water Tube
TWT	Toy World Test [Psychology]
TWT	Transonic Wind Tunnel [NASA] (AAG)
TWT	Traveling-Wave Tube [Radio]
TWT	Travel with Troops
TWT	Trisonic Wind Tunnel (NAKS)
TWT	Tritiated Waste Treatment [Subsystem] (MCD)
TWT	Tri-West Resources Ltd. [Vancouver Stock Exchange symbol]
TWT	Two-Way Time [Seismology]
TWT	Two-Way-Traffic-in-Ideas Conference [of Labor Party] [British]
TWT	West Texas State University, Canyon, TX [OCLC symbol] (OCLC)
TWT	[The] Write Thing [An association] (EA)
TWTA	Traveling-Wave Tube Amplifier [Radio]
TWTC	Taipei World Trade Center
TWTDS	Treatment Works Treating Domestic Sewage [Environmental Protection Agency]
TWTI	Total World Telecommunications, Inc. [NASDAQ symbol] (SAG)
TWTIX	Amer. Century Intermed.-Term Tax Free [Mutual fund ticker symbol] (SG)
TWTLX	Amer. Century Long-Term Tax Free [Mutual fund ticker symbol] (SG)
TWTSF	Transuranic Waste Treatment and Storage Facility [Environmental science] (COE)
TWTT	Two-Way Travel Time [Seismology]
TWTWTW	That Was The Week That Was [Also, TW3] [Television program of English origin]
TWU	Tactical Weapons Unit [British military] (DMA)
TWU	Tata Workers' Union [India]
TWU	Tawau [Malaysia] [Airport symbol] (OAG)
TWU	Technical Writing Unit [NASA]
TWU	Telecommunications Workers Union [Canada]
TWU	Texas Woman's University
TWU	Theatre Writers' Union [British] (DBA)
TWU	Tigri-Worji Union [Ethiopia]
TWU	Tobacco Workers' Union [British] (DCTA)
TWU	Trace Watch Unit (IAA)
TWU	Transport Workers' Union [British]
TWU	Transport Workers Union of America (EA)
TWU	University of the South, Sewanee, TN [OCLC symbol] (OCLC)
TWUA	Textile Workers Union of America [Later, ACTWU]
TWUA	Transport Workers' Union of Australia
TWUC	The Writers Union of Canada [Canada] (WWLA)
TWUD	Tactical Weapons Unit Diagnostics
TWUSX	Amer. Century Short Term Govt. [Mutual fund ticker symbol] (SG)
TWV	Tactical Wheeled Vehicle (DOMA)
TWV	Three-Way Valve [Hydraulics]
TWV	Two-Wire Vertical [Grape culture]
TWVMP	Tactical Wheeled Vehicle Modernization Program [Army]
TWVRP	Tactical Wheeled Vehicles Remanufacture Program [Army] (RDA)
TWW	Independent Television for Wales and the West of England
TWW	Trans Air Welwitchia [Angola] [FAA designator] (FAAC)
TWWD	Tapwater Wet Dressing [Surgery] (DAVI)
TWWHA	Tasmanian Wilderness World Heritage Area
TWWP	Third World Women's Project [Defunct] (EA)
TWWS	Two-Way/Wink Start [Telecommunications] (TEL)
TWWT	Tilting Wind-Water Tunnel [Environmental technology]
TWX	Telegraphic Message (MSA)
TWX	Teletype Wire Transmission (NAKS)
TWX	Teletypewriter Exchange Service [Western Union] [Term also used generically for teletypewriter message]
TWX	Teletypewriter Wire Transmission
TWX	Time Warner Capital I [NYSE symbol] (SAG)
TWX	Time Warner, Inc. [NYSE symbol] (SPSG)
TWX	Time Wire Transmission
TWXIL	TWX Interlibrary Loan Network [Library network]
TWXPrT	Time War Cp 1 8.78% Pfd Tr Sec [NYSE symbol] (TTSB)
TWY	Taxiway [Aviation] (AAG)
TWY	Twenty (ADA)
TWYL	Taxiway-Link [Aviation]
TWZ	Neifu [Republic of China] [Seismograph station code, US Geological Survey] (SEIS)
TWZO	Trade Wind Zone Oceanography
TX	Nondramatic Literary Works [US Copyright Office class]
TX	Tax
Tx	Taxes (EBF)
TX	Taxonomic Descriptor (NITA)
TX	Telephone Exchange (NITA)
TX	TELEX
TX	Terminal Executive [Computer science] (MHDB)
TX	Terminating Toll Operator [Telecommunications] (TEL)
TX	Tested Extra (MCD)
TX	Texaco, Inc. [NYSE symbol] (SPSG)
TX	Texas [Postal code]
TX	Texas Reports [A publication] (DLA)
Tx	Texas State Library and Historical Commission, Austin, TX [Library symbol Library of Congress] (LCLS)
TX	Text Editor
Tx	Therapy [Medicine]
TX	Thromboxane [Also, T, TA, Tx] [Biochemistry]
Tx	Thyroidectomy [Medicine]

TX .... Thyroidectomy [*Medicine*] (DB)
TX .... Time to Equipment Reset [*Computer science*] (MDG)
TX .... Toilet Exhaust (OA)
TX .... Torque Transmitter
TX .... Traction [*Medicine*]
TX .... Transformer
Tx .... Transfusion [*Medicine*] (CPH)
TX .... Translation Hand Controller X-Axis Direction (MCD)
TX .... Transmission [*Amateur radio shorthand*] (WDAA)
Tx .... Transmit (CIST)
TX .... Transmit (NITA)
TX .... Transmitter
TX .... Transparency [*Photography*] (WDMC)
Tx .... Transplant [*or Transplantation*] [*Medicine*]
TX .... Transportes Aereos Nacionales [*ICAO designator*] (AD)
TX .... Treatment
TX .... Treble Cash Ruling [*Business term*]
TXA .... Task Extension Area [*Computer science*] (IAA)
TXA .... Terminal Exchange Area [*Computer science*] (MHDB)
TXA .... Texair Charter, Inc. [*ICAO designator*] (FAAC)
TXA .... Texas A & M University, College Station, TX [*OCLC symbol*] (OCLC)
TXA .... Texeira [*Portugal*] [*Airport symbol*] (AD)
TXA .... Thromboxane A [*Also, TA, TxA*] [*Biochemistry*]
TxAb .... Abilene Public Library, Abilene, TX [*Library symbol Library of Congress*] (LCLS)
TxAbC .... Abilene Christian University, Abilene, TX [*Library symbol Library of Congress*] (LCLS)
TxAbH .... Hardin-Simmons University, Abilene, TX [*Library symbol Library of Congress*] (LCLS)
TxAbM .... McMurry College, Abilene, TX [*Library symbol Library of Congress*] (LCLS)
TxAdTC .... Trinity Christian Academy, Addison, TX [*Library symbol*] [*Library of Congress*] (LCLS)
TxAl .... Stella Hill Memorial Library, Alto, TX [*Library symbol Library of Congress*] (LCLS)
TxAlpS .... Sul Ross State University, Alpine, TX [*Library symbol Library of Congress*] (LCLS)
TxAlvC .... Alvin Junior College, Alvin, TX [*Library symbol Library of Congress*] (LCLS)
TxAm .... Amarillo Public Library, Amarillo, TX [*Library symbol Library of Congress*] (LCLS)
TxAmC .... Amarillo College, Amarillo, TX [*Library symbol Library of Congress*] (LCLS)
TxAmM .... Mason & Hanger-Silas Mason Co., Inc., Pantex Plant Library, Amarillo, TX [*Library symbol Library of Congress*] (LCLS)
TxAmSP ...... Southwestern Public Service Co., Amarillo, TX [*Library symbol Library of Congress*] (LCLS)
TxAmV .... United States Veterans Administration Hospital, Amarillo, TX [*Library symbol Library of Congress*] (LCLS)
TxAng .... Brazoria County Library, Angleton, TX [*Library symbol Library of Congress*] (LCLS)
TXANG .... Texas Air National Guard (MUSM)
TxArB .... Arlington Baptist Junior College, Arlington, TX [*Library symbol Library of Congress*] (LCLS)
TxAr-G .... Arlington Public Library, Genealogy Department, Arlington, TX [*Library symbol Library of Congress*] (LCLS)
TxArJ .... Jet Research Center, Inc., Arlington, TX [*Library symbol Library of Congress*] (LCLS)
TxArU .... University of Texas at Arlington, Arlington, TX [*Library symbol Library of Congress*] (LCLS)
TxAtH .... Henderson County Junior College, Athens, TX [*Library symbol Library of Congress*] (LCLS)
TxAu .... Austin Public Library, Austin, TX [*Library symbol Library of Congress*] (LCLS)
TxAuA .... Charles E. Stevens American Atheist Library and Archives, Inc., Austin, TX [*Library symbol Library of Congress*] (LCLS)
TxAu-AT ...... Austin Public Library, Austin-Travis County Collection, Austin, TX [*Library symbol Library of Congress*] (LCLS)
TxAuC .... Concordia Lutheran College, Austin, TX [*Library symbol Library of Congress*] (LCLS)
TxAuCC .... Austin Community College, Austin, TX [*Library symbol Library of Congress*] (LCLS)
TxAuCH .... Church Historical Society, Austin, TX [*Library symbol Library of Congress*] (LCLS)
TxAuDR .... Daughters of the Republic of Texas Museum, Austin, TX [*Library symbol Library of Congress*] (LCLS)
TxAuE .... Episcopal Theological Seminary of the Southwest, Austin, TX [*Library symbol Library of Congress*] (LCLS)
TxAuEd .... Texas Education Agency, Austin, TX [*Library symbol Library of Congress*] (LCLS)
TxAuGS .... Church of Jesus Christ of Latter-Day Saints, Genealogical Society Library, Austin Branch, Austin, TX [*Library symbol Library of Congress*] (LCLS)
TxAuHi .... Texas State Department of Highways and Public Transportation, Materials and Tests Research Library, Austin, TX [*Library symbol Library of Congress*] (LCLS)
TxAuHT .... Huston-Tillotson College, Austin, TX [*Library symbol Library of Congress*] (LCLS)
TxAuL .... Legislative Library Board, Legislative Reference Library, Austin, TX [*Library symbol Library of Congress*] (LCLS)
TxAuLBJ ...... Lyndon B. Johnson School of Public Affairs, Lyndon Baines Johnson Library, Austin, TX [*Library symbol Library of Congress*] (LCLS)
TxAuM .... Texas Medical Association, Austin, TX [*Library symbol Library of Congress*] (LCLS)

TxAuMH ...... Texas Department of Mental Health and Mental Retardation, Austin, TX [*Library symbol Library of Congress*] (LCLS)
TxAuP .... Austin Presbyterian Theological Seminary, Austin, TX [*Library symbol Library of Congress*] (LCLS)
TxAuPW .... Texas Department of Parks and Wildlife, Austin, TX [*Library symbol Library of Congress*] (LCLS)
TxAuR .... Radian Corp., Austin, TX [*Library symbol Library of Congress*] (LCLS)
TxAuSE .... Saint Edward's University, Austin, TX [*Library symbol Library of Congress*] (LCLS)
TxAuSHos ... Austin State Hospital, Austin, TX [*Library symbol Library of Congress*] (LCLS)
TxAuT .... Tracor, Inc., Technical Library, Austin, TX [*Library symbol Library of Congress*] (LCLS)
TxAuTI .... Texas Instruments, Inc., Austin Site Library, Austin, TX [*Library symbol*] [*Library of Congress*] (LCLS)
TxAuTL .... Travis County Law Library, Austin, TX [*Library symbol*] [*Library of Congress*] (LCLS)
TxAuW .... Texas Water Development Board, Austin, TX [*Library symbol Library of Congress*] (LCLS)
TXB .... Abilene Public Library, Abilene, TX [*OCLC symbol*] (OCLC)
TXB .... Bell Helicopter, Textron Canada [*FAA designator*] (FAAC)
TXB .... Texas Biotechnology [*AMEX symbol*] (TTSB)
TXB .... Texas Biotechnology Corp. [*AMEX symbol*] (SAG)
TXB .... Thromboxane B [*Also, TB, TxB*] [*Biochemistry*]
TxBea .... Tyrrell Public Library, Beaumont, TX [*Library symbol Library of Congress*] (LCLS)
TxBeaAM .... Beaumont Art Museum, Beaumont, TX [*Library symbol Library of Congress*] (LCLS)
TxBeaE .... Beaumont Enterprise & Journal, Beaumont, TX [*Library symbol Library of Congress*] (LCLS)
TxBeaG .... Gulf States Utilities Co., Beaumont, TX [*Library symbol Library of Congress*] (LCLS)
TxBeaL .... Lamar University, Beaumont, TX [*Library symbol Library of Congress*] (LCLS)
TxBeaMC .... Mobil Chemical Co., Research and Development Laboratory, Beaumont, TX [*Library symbol Library of Congress*] (LCLS)
TxBeaSE ...... Saint Elizabeth Hospital, Health Science Library, Beaumont, TX [*Library symbol Library of Congress*] (LCLS)
TxBee .... Bee County Public Library, Beeville, TX [*Library symbol Library of Congress*] (LCLS)
TxBeeC .... Bee County College, Beeville, TX [*Library symbol Library of Congress*] (LCLS)
TxBelM .... Mary Hardin-Baylor College, Belton, TX [*Library symbol Library of Congress*] (LCLS)
TxBHi .... Brownsville Historical Association, Brownsville, TX [*Library symbol Library of Congress*] (LCLS)
TxBl .... Bellaire City Library, Bellaire, TX [*Library symbol Library of Congress*] (LCLS)
TXBL .... Taxable
TxBIT .... Texaco, Inc., Bellaire, TX [*Library symbol Library of Congress*] (LCLS)
TxBor .... Hutchinson County Library, Borger, TX [*Library symbol Library of Congress*] (LCLS)
TxBorF .... Frank Phillips College, Borger, TX [*Library symbol Library of Congress*] (LCLS)
Tx-BPH .... Texas Regional Library, Division for the Blind and Physically Handicapped, Austin, TX [*Library symbol Library of Congress*] (LCLS)
TxBrd .... Brownwood Public Library, Brownwood, TX [*Library symbol Library of Congress*] (LCLS)
TxBrdH .... Howard Payne College, Brownwood, TX [*Library symbol Library of Congress*] (LCLS)
TxBreB .... Blinn College, Brenham, TX [*Library symbol Library of Congress*] (LCLS)
TxBry .... Bryan Public Library, Bryan, TX [*Library symbol Library of Congress*] (LCLS)
TxBryA .... Allen Academy, Bryan, TX [*Library symbol Library of Congress*] (LCLS)
TxBs .... Howard County Library, Big Spring, TX [*Library symbol Library of Congress*] (LCLS)
TxBS .... Texas Southmost College, Brownsville, TX [*Library symbol Library of Congress*] (LCLS)
TxBsaA .... Ambassador College, Big Sandy, TX [*Library symbol Library of Congress*] (LCLS)
TxBsC .... Howard County Library, Big Spring, TX [*Library symbol*] [*Library of Congress*] (LCLS)
TxBsH .... Howard County Junior College, Big Spring, TX [*Library symbol Library of Congress*] (LCLS)
TxBsV .... United States Veterans Administration Hospital, Big Spring, TX [*Library symbol Library of Congress*] (LCLS)
TxBUC .... Union Carbide Corp., Chemicals and Plastics Library, Brownsville, TX [*Library symbol Library of Congress*] (LCLS)
TXB.WS ...... Texas Biotechnology Wrrt [*AMEX symbol*] (TTSB)
TxBy .... Sterling Municipal Library, Baytown, TX [*Library symbol Library of Congress*] (LCLS)
TxByH .... Humble Oil & Refining Co., Technical Library, Baytown, TX [*Library symbol Library of Congress*] (LCLS)
TxByH-E ...... Humble Oil & Refining Co., Engineering Division Library, Baytown, TX [*Library symbol Library of Congress*] (LCLS)
TxByL .... Lee College, Baytown, TX [*Library symbol Library of Congress*] (LCLS)
TXC .... Abilene Christian University, Abilene, TX [*OCLC symbol*] (OCLC)
TXC .... Texaco Capital LLC [*NYSE symbol*] (SPSG)
TXC .... Thurman, CO [*Location identifier FAA*] (FAAL)

TXC............. Transaviaexport [*Belarus*] [*ICAO designator*] (FAAC)

TxCap .... Texaco Capital [*Associated Press*] (SAG)

TxCarP......... Panola College, Carthage, TX [*Library symbol Library of Congress*] (LCLS)

TxCaW .... West Texas State University, Canyon, TX [*Library symbol Library of Congress*] (LCLS)

TxCc............. La Retama Public Library, Corpus Cristi, TX [*Library symbol Library of Congress*] (LCLS)

TXCC........... TranSwitch Corp. [*NASDAQ symbol*] (SAG)

TxCcD .... Del Mar College, Corpus Christi, TX [*Library symbol Library of Congress*] (LCLS)

TxCcG .... United States Geological Survey, Office of Marine Geology, Corpus Cristi, TX [*Library symbol*] [*Library of Congress*] (LCLS)

TxCcGS........ Church of Jesus Christ of Latter-Day Saints, Genealogical Society Library, Corpus Christi Branch, Corpus Christi, TX [*Library symbol Library of Congress*] (LCLS)

TxCcMST ...... Art Museum of South Texas, Corpus Christi, TX [*Library symbol Library of Congress*] (LCLS)

TxCcNHi....... Nueces County Historical Society, La Retama Public Library, Corpus Christi, TX [*Library symbol Library of Congress*] (LCLS)

TxCcT.......... Texas A & I University at Corpus Christi, Corpus Christi, TX [*Library symbol Library of Congress*] (LCLS)

TxCcU .... University of Corpus Christi, Corpus Christi, TX [*Library symbol Library of Congress Obsolete*] (LCLS)

TX-CEL........ Throughput X-Cellerator [*Celeritas Technologies*] [*Cellular data transmission*] (PCM)

TxCeN .... Northwood Institute of Texas, Cedar Hill, TX [*Library symbol Library of Congress*] (LCLS)

TX Ci .... Texas Civil Appeals Reports [*A publication*] (DLA)

TxCiC .... Cisco Junior College, Cisco, TX [*Library symbol Library of Congress*] (LCLS)

TxClaC......... Clarendon College, Clarendon, TX [*Library symbol Library of Congress*] (LCLS)

TxClcU .... University of Houston at Clear Lake City, Houston, TX [*Library symbol Library of Congress*] (LCLS)

TxCle .... Cleburne Public Library, Cleburne, TX [*Library symbol Library of Congress*] (LCLS)

TxCli .... Nellie Pederson Civic Library, Clifton, TX [*Library symbol Library of Congress*] (LCLS)

TxClv .... Cleveland Public [*Charles O. Austin Memorial*] Library, Cleveland, TX [*Library symbol Library of Congress*] (LCLS)

TxClwC .... Celanese Corp., Clarkwood, TX [*Library symbol Library of Congress*] (LCLS)

TxCM .... Texas A & M University, College Station, TX [*Library symbol Library of Congress*] (LCLS)

TxCM-M....... Texas A & M University, Medical Sciences Library, College Station, TX [*Library symbol Library of Congress*] (LCLS)

TXCO .... [*The*] Exploration Co. [*NASDAQ symbol*] (NQ)

TxComf........ Comfort Public Library, Comfort, TX [*Library symbol Library of Congress*] (LCLS)

TxComS ...... East Texas State University, Commerce, TX [*Library symbol Library of Congress*] (LCLS)

TxComS-M... East Texas State University, Museum, Commerce, TX [*Library symbol Library of Congress*] (LCLS)

TxCoN .... Navarro Junior College, Corsicana, TX [*Library symbol Library of Congress*] (LCLS)

TxConM ...... Montgomery County Memorial Library, Conroe, TX [*Library symbol Library of Congress*] (LCLS)

TXCPrA .... Texaco Capital LLC 'MIPS' [*NYSE symbol*] (TTSB)

TXCPrB .... Texaco Cap LLC'B'Adj MIPS [*NYSE symbol*] (TTSB)

TxCr............. Crockett Public Library, Crockett, TX [*Library symbol Library of Congress*] (LCLS)

TX Cr........... Texas Criminal Appeals Reports [*A publication*] (DLA)

TxCrMA........ Mary Allen Junior College, Crockett, TX [*Library symbol Library of Congress*] (LCLS)

TxCvS .... ARCO Chemical Co., Channelview, TX [*Library symbol Library of Congress*] (LCLS)

TxCvT.......... Texas Butadine & Chemical Corp., Channelview, TX [*Library symbol Library of Congress*] (LCLS)

TXD............. McMurry College, Abilene, TX [*OCLC symbol*] (OCLC)

TXD............. Telephone Exchange (Digital) [*Telecommunications*] (TEL)

TXD............. Transmit Data [*Computer science*]

TxDa .... Dallas Public Library, Dallas, TX [*Library symbol Library of Congress*] (LCLS)

TxDaABC...... AMIGOS [*Access Method for Indexed Data Generalized for Operating System*] Bibliographic Council, Dallas, TX [*Library symbol Library of Congress*] (LCLS)

TxDaAC........ Anderson, Clayton & Co., Foods Division Technical Library, Dallas, TX [*Library symbol Library of Congress*] (LCLS)

TxDaAR-G..... Atlantic Richfield Co., Geoscience Library, Dallas, TX [*Library symbol Library of Congress*] (LCLS)

TxDaAR-R.... Atlantic Richfield Co., R and D Library, Dallas, TX [*Library symbol Library of Congress*] (LCLS)

TxDaAR-T .... Atlantic Richfield Co., Technical Library, Dallas, TX [*Library symbol Library of Congress*] (LCLS)

TxDaB.......... Dallas Baptist College, Dallas, TX [*Library symbol Library of Congress*] (LCLS)

TxDaBC........ Bishop College, Dallas, TX [*Library symbol Library of Congress*] (LCLS)

TxDaBM....... Burgess-Manning Co., Dallas, TX [*Library symbol Library of Congress*] (LCLS)

TxDaBU........ Baylor University in Dallas, Dallas, TX [*Library symbol Library of Congress*] (LCLS)

TxDaCB........ Criswell Bible College, Dallas, TX [*Library symbol*] [*Library of Congress*] (LCLS)

TxDaCC....... Christian College of the Southwest, Dallas, TX [*Library symbol Library of Congress*] (LCLS)

TxDaCCD ..... Callier Center for Communication Disorders, Dallas, TX [*Library symbol Library of Congress*] (LCLS)

TxDaCiA....... Court of Civil Appeals, Dallas, TX [*Library symbol Library of Congress*] (LCLS)

TxDaCL........ Core Laboratories, Inc., Dallas, TX [*Library symbol Library of Congress*] (LCLS)

TxDaCR....... Collins Radio Co., Dallas, TX [*Library symbol Library of Congress*] (LCLS)

TxDaCS........ Dallas County Community College System, Dallas, TX [*Library symbol Library of Congress*] (LCLS)

TxDaDC....... Dallas Christian College, Dallas, TX [*Library symbol Library of Congress*] (LCLS)

TxDaDF....... DeGoyler Foundation, Dallas, TX [*Library symbol Library of Congress*] (LCLS)

TxDaDL....... Dallas County Law Library, Dallas, TX [*Library symbol Library of Congress*] (LCLS)

TxDaDM....... DeGoyler and MacNaughton Library, Dallas, TX [*Library symbol Library of Congress*] (LCLS)

TxDaE .... El Centro College, Dallas, TX [*Library symbol Library of Congress*] (LCLS)

TxDaET .... East Texas State University, Metroplex Center, Dallas, TX [*Library symbol Library of Congress*] (LCLS)

TxDaFR....... Federal Reserve Bank of Dallas, Dallas, TX [*Library symbol Library of Congress*] (LCLS)

TxDaGI........ Geological Information Library of Dallas, Dallas, TX [*Library symbol*] [*Library of Congress*] (LCLS)

TxDaGS....... Church of Jesus Christ of Latter-Day Saints, Genealogical Society Library, Dallas Branch, Dallas, TX [*Library symbol Library of Congress*] (LCLS)

TxDah .... Dallam County Free Library, Dalhart, TX [*Library symbol*] [*Library of Congress*] (LCLS)

TxDaHi........ Dallas Historical Society, Dallas, TX [*Library symbol Library of Congress*] (LCLS)

TxDaI .... Informart Resources Center, Dallas, TX [*Library symbol*] [*Library of Congress*] (LCLS)

TxDaJS .... Johnson and Swanson, Law Library, Dallas, TX [*Library symbol Library of Congress*] (LCLS)

TxDaL .... Lone Star Gas Co., Dallas, TX [*Library symbol Library of Congress*] (LCLS)

TxDaM.......... Southern Methodist University, Dallas, TX [*Library symbol Library of Congress*] (LCLS)

TxDaM-B...... Southern Methodist University, Business Information Center, Dallas, TX [*Library symbol*] [*Library of Congress*] (LCLS)

TxDaME .... Mobil Exploration & Producing Services, Inc., Dallas, TX [*Library symbol Library of Congress*] (LCLS)

TxDaMF .... Dallas Museum of Fine Arts, Dallas, TX [*Library symbol Library of Congress*] (LCLS)

TxDaM L...... Southern Methodist University, Law Library, Dallas, TX [*Library symbol Library of Congress*] (LCLS)

TxDaMN....... Dallas Morning News, Dallas, TX [*Library symbol*] [*Library of Congress*] (LCLS)

TxDaM-P...... Southern Methodist University, Perkins School of Theology, Dallas, TX [*Library symbol Library of Congress*] (LCLS)

TxDaM-SE.... Southern Methodist University, Science/Engineering Library, Dallas, TX [*Library symbol Library of Congress*] (LCLS)

TxDaMV....... Mountain View College, Dallas, TX [*Library symbol Library of Congress*] (LCLS)

TxDaP.......... Dallas Power & Light Co., Dallas, TX [*Library symbol Library of Congress*] (LCLS)

TxDaPCC...... Parker College of Chiropractic, Dallas, TX [*Library symbol*] [*Library of Congress*] (LCLS)

TxDaPO........ Placid Oil Co. Exploration Library, Dallas, TX [*Library symbol Library of Congress*] (LCLS)

TxDaPP........ Planned Parenthood of Northeast Texas, Dallas, TX [*Library symbol Library of Congress*] (LCLS)

TxDaR.......... Richland College, Dallas, TX [*Library symbol Library of Congress*] (LCLS)

TxDaRI........ Rockwell International, Collins Radio Group, Technical Information Center, Dallas, TX [*Library symbol Library of Congress*] (LCLS)

TxDaS .... University of Texas, Health Science Center at Dallas, Dallas, TX [*Library symbol Library of Congress*] (LCLS)

TxDaSM........ Mobil Research & Development Corp., Dallas, TX [*Library symbol Library of Congress*] (LCLS)

TxDaSSC...... Super Conducting Super Collider Liability Library, Dallas, TX [*Library symbol*] [*Library of Congress*] (LCLS)

TxDaTI-A...... Texas Instruments, Inc., Apparatus Division Library, Dallas, TX [*Library symbol Library of Congress*] (LCLS)

TxDaTI-C...... Texas Instruments, Inc., Central Research and Engineering Library, Dallas, TX [*Library symbol Library of Congress*] (LCLS)

TxDaTI-F...... Texas Instruments, Inc., Forest Lane Technical Library, Dallas, TX [*Library symbol*] [*Library of Congress*] (LCLS)

TxDaTI-IS .... Texas Instruments, Inc., IS & S Library, Dallas, TX [*Library symbol Library of Congress*] (LCLS)

TxDaTI-N...... Texas Instruments, Inc., North Building Library, Dallas, TX [*Library symbol*] [*Library of Congress*] (LCLS)

TxDaTI-R...... Texas Instruments, Inc., Research Building Library, Dallas, TX [*Library symbol*] [*Library of Congress*] (LCLS)

TxDaTI-S...... Texas Instruments, Inc., Semiconductor Division, Dallas, TX [*Library symbol Library of Congress*] (LCLS)

TxDaTI-SS ... Texas Instruments, Inc., Science Services Division, Dallas, TX [*Library symbol Library of Congress*] (LCLS)

TxDaTS........ Dallas Theological Seminary and Graduate School, Dallas, TX [*Library symbol Library of Congress*] (LCLS)

TxDaU.......... University of Dallas, Irving, TX [*Library symbol Library of Congress*] (LCLS)

TxDaUSAF ... United States Army and Air Force Exchange Service, Dallas, TX [*Library symbol Library of Congress*] (LCLS)

TxDaUSFD ... United States Food and Drug Administration, Dallas, TX [*Library symbol Library of Congress*] (LCLS)

TxDaVA....... United States Veterans Administration Hospital, Dallas, TX [*Library symbol Library of Congress*] (LCLS)

TXDE.......... Toluene-Xylene-Dioxane-Ethanol [*Scintillation solvent*]

TxDeni........ Denison Public Library, Denison, TX [*Library symbol Library of Congress*] (LCLS)

TxDeniG....... Grayson County College, Denison, TX [*Library symbol Library of Congress*] (LCLS)

TxDib.......... T. L. L. Temple Memorial Library, Diboll, TX [*Library symbol Library of Congress*] (LCLS)

TxDN........... North Texas State University, Denton, TX [*Library symbol Library of Congress*] (LCLS)

TxDN-Hi....... North Texas State University, State Historical Collection, Denton, TX [*Library symbol Library of Congress*] (LCLS)

TxDpS.......... Shell Oil Co., Deer Park, TX [*Library symbol Library of Congress*] (LCLS)

TxDpSC........ Shell Chemical Co., Deer Park, TX [*Library symbol Library of Congress*] (LCLS)

TXDRMY ...... Taxidermy

TXDS .... TI Diskette Operating System (NITA)

TxDunv .... Duncanville Public Library, Duncanville, TX [*Library symbol Library of Congress*] (LCLS)

TxDW.......... Texas Woman's University, Denton, TX [*Library symbol Library of Congress*] (LCLS)

TXE .... El Paso Community College, El Paso, TX [*OCLC symbol*] (OCLC)

TxE............. El Paso Public Library, El Paso, TX [*Library symbol Library of Congress*] (LCLS)

TXE .... Telephone Exchange (Electronics) [*Telecommunications*] (IEEE)

TXE .... Telephone Exchange (Equipment) [*Telecommunications*]

TxEC .... El Paso Community College, El Paso, TX [*Library symbol Library of Congress*] (LCLS)

TxEdP .... Pan American University, Edinburg, TX [*Library symbol Library of Congress*] (LCLS)

TxEGS.......... Church of Jesus Christ of Latter-Day Saints, Genealogical Society Library, El Paso Branch, El Paso, TX [*Library symbol Library of Congress*] (LCLS)

TxEHD.......... Hotel-Dieu Medical-Nursing Educational Media Center, El Paso, TX [*Library symbol Library of Congress*] (LCLS)

TxENG.......... El Paso Natural Gas Co., Technical Information Center, El Paso, TX [*Library symbol Library of Congress*] (LCLS)

TxEU .... University of Texas at El Paso, El Paso, TX [*Library symbol Library of Congress*] (LCLS)

TxEWB .... United States Army, William Beaumont General Hospital, Medical and Technical Library, El Paso, TX [*Library symbol Library of Congress*] (LCLS)

TXF .... Corpus Christi State University, Corpus Christi, TX [*OCLC symbol*] (OCLC)

TxF............. Fort Worth Public Library, Fort Worth, TX [*Library symbol Library of Congress*] (LCLS)

TXF .... Tax Exchange Format [*Computer science*] (PCM)

TXF .... Texfi Indus [*NYSE symbol*] (TTSB)

TXF .... Texfi Industries, Inc. [*NYSE symbol*] (SPSG)

TxFACM .... Amon Carter Museum of Western Art, Fort Worth, TX [*Library symbol Library of Congress*] (LCLS)

TxFAl .... Alcon Laboratories, Inc., Fort Worth, TX [*Library symbol Library of Congress*] (LCLS)

TxFbAD .... United States Army, Air Defense School, Fort Bliss, TX [*Library symbol Library of Congress*] (LCLS)

TxFBH .... Bell Helicopter Co., Fort Worth, TX [*Library symbol Library of Congress*] (LCLS)

TxFCB .... Carter & Burgess, Inc., Fort Worth, TX [*Library symbol Library of Congress*] (LCLS)

TxFCC .... Fort Worth Christian College, Fort Worth, TX [*Library symbol Library of Congress*] (LCLS)

TxFCO .... Texas College of Osteopathic Medicine, Fort Worth, TX [*Library symbol Library of Congress*] (LCLS)

TxFF............ Fort Worth Art Museum, Fort Worth, TX [*Library symbol Library of Congress*] (LCLS)

TxFFAA .... United States Federal Aviation Administration, Fort Worth, TX [*Library symbol Library of Congress*] (LCLS)

TxFG .... General Dynamics/Convair Aerospace Division, Fort Worth, TX [*Library symbol Library of Congress*] (LCLS)

TxFGS .... Church of Jesus Christ of Latter-Day Saints, Genealogical Society Library, Fort Worth Branch, North Richland Hills, Fort Worth, TX [*Library symbol Library of Congress*] (LCLS)

TxFhH .... Darnell Army Hospital, Medical Library, Fort Hood, TX [*Library symbol Library of Congress*] (LCLS)

TxFJPS .... John Peter Smith Hospital, Fort Worth, TX [*Library symbol Library of Congress*] (LCLS)

TxFK .... Kimbell Art Museum, Fort Worth, TX [*Library symbol Library of Congress*] (LCLS)

TxFM .... Fort Worth Museum of Science and History, Fort Worth, TX [*Library symbol Library of Congress*] (LCLS)

TxFNA.......... United States National Archives and Record Center, Fort Worth, TX [*Library symbol Library of Congress*] (LCLS)

TxFNIMH...... National Institute of Mental Health, Clinical Research Center Medical Library, Fort Worth, TX [*Library symbol Library of Congress*] (LCLS)

TxFrB .... Brazosport Junior College, Freeport, TX [*Library symbol Library of Congress*] (LCLS)

TxFrD............ Dow Chemical Co., Texas Division, Freeport, TX [*Library symbol Library of Congress*] (LCLS)

TxFS .... Southwestern Baptist Theological Seminary, Fort Worth, TX [*Library symbol Library of Congress*] (LCLS)

TxFshBH ...... Brooke General Hospital, Medical Library, Fort Sam Houston, TX [*Library symbol Library of Congress*] (LCLS)

TxFshM........ Medical Field Service School, Fort Sam Houston, TX [*Library symbol Library of Congress*] (LCLS)

TxFSJ........... Saint Joseph Hospital, Medical and Nursing Library, Fort Worth, TX [*Library symbol Library of Congress*] (LCLS)

TxFT............ Tarrant County Junior College, Fort Worth, TX [*Library symbol Library of Congress*] (LCLS)

TxFTC .... Texas Christian University, Fort Worth, TX [*Library symbol Library of Congress*] (LCLS)

TxFTE.......... Texas Electric Service Co., Fort Worth, TX [*Library symbol Library of Congress*] (LCLS)

TxFTM .... Terrell's Laboratories Medical Library, Fort Worth, TX [*Library symbol Library of Congress*] (LCLS)

TxFT-NE....... Tarrant County Junior College, Northeast Campus, Hurst, TX [*Library symbol Library of Congress*] (LCLS)

TxFT-S .... Tarrant County Junior College, South Campus, Fort Worth, TX [*Library symbol Library of Congress*] (LCLS)

TxFTW .... Texas Wesleyan College, Fort Worth, TX [*Library symbol Library of Congress*] (LCLS)

TXG............. Austin Public Library, Austin, TX [*OCLC symbol*] (OCLC)

TXG............. Taichung [*Formosa*] [*Airport symbol*] (AD)

TXG............. Transco Energy Corp. (EFIS)

TxGA............ United States Army, Army Engineering District, Office of Administrative Services, Galveston, TX [*Library symbol Library of Congress*] (LCLS)

TxGaiC.......... Cooke County Junior College, Gainsville, TX [*Library symbol Library of Congress*] (LCLS)

TxGar........... Nicholson Memorial Library, Garland, TX [*Library symbol Library of Congress*] (LCLS)

TxGarA.......... Amber University, Garland, TX [*Library symbol*] [*Library of Congress*] (LCLS)

TxGarD .... Dresser Industries, Inc., Garland, TX [*Library symbol Library of Congress*] (LCLS)

TxGarV......... Varo, Inc., Texas Division, Garland, TX [*Library symbol Library of Congress*] (LCLS)

TxGat........... Gatesville Public Library, Gatesville, TX [*Library symbol Library of Congress*] (LCLS)

TxGC........... Galveston Community College, Galveston, TX [*Library symbol Library of Congress*] (LCLS)

TxGeoS.......... Southwestern University, Georgetown, TX [*Library symbol Library of Congress*] (LCLS)

TxGilGS .... Church of Jesus Christ of Latter-Day Saints, Genealogical Society Library, Longview Branch, Gilmer, TX [*Library symbol Library of Congress*] (LCLS)

TxGML......... Texas A & M University, Moody College of Marine Sciences and Maritime Resources, Galveston, TX [*Library symbol Library of Congress*] (LCLS)

TxGoS........... Spanish Texas Microfilm Center, Goliad, TX [*Library symbol Library of Congress*] (LCLS)

TxGR........... Rosenberg Library, Galveston, TX [*Library symbol Library of Congress*] (LCLS)

TxGrp........... Grand Prairie Memorial Library, Grand Prairie, TX [*Library symbol Library of Congress*] (LCLS)

TxGUSFW .... United States National Marine Fisheries Service, Biological Laboratory, Galveston, TX [*Library symbol Library of Congress*] (LCLS)

TxH............. Houston Public Library, Houston, TX [*Library symbol Library of Congress*] (LCLS)

TXH............. Transfer on Index High

TXH............. University of Houston, Houston, TX [*OCLC symbol*] (OCLC)

TxHAE........... Atkinson Elementary School, Houston, TX [*Library symbol*] [*Library of Congress*] (LCLS)

TxHaJ .... Jarvis Christian College, Hawkins, TX [*Library symbol Library of Congress*] (LCLS)

TxHAM......... Houston Academy of Medicine for Texas Medical Center, Houston, TX [*Library symbol Library of Congress*] (LCLS)

TxHAS.......... Aramco Services Co., Corporate Information Center, Houston, TX [*Library symbol*] [*Library of Congress*] (LCLS)

TxHAWD ...... Arnold, White & Durkee, Houston, TX [*Library symbol Library of Congress*] (LCLS)

TxHBa........... National Lead Industries, Inc., Baroid Division, Houston, TX [*Library symbol Library of Congress*] (LCLS)

TxHBB.......... Baker, Botts, Shepherd & Coates, Houston, TX [*Library symbol Library of Congress*] (LCLS)

TxHBC........... Houston Baptist University, Houston, TX [*Library symbol Library of Congress*] (LCLS)

TxHBE.......... Burnett Elementary School, Houston, TX [*Library symbol*] [*Library of Congress*] (LCLS)

TxHBec......... Bechtel Group, Inc., Technical Library, Houston, TX [*Library symbol Library of Congress*] (LCLS)

TxHBhl......... Beverly Hills Intermediate School, Houston, TX [*Library symbol*] [*Library of Congress*] (LCLS)

TxHBJ .... Bernard Johnson, Inc., Houston, TX [*Library symbol*] [*Library of Congress*] (LCLS)

TxHBR .... Brown & Root, Inc., Technical Library, Houston, TX [*Library symbol Library of Congress*] (LCLS)

TxHC............ Houston Community College System, Houston, TX [*Library symbol Library of Congress*] (LCLS)

TxHCC........... Continental Carbon Co., Houston, TX [*Library symbol Library of Congress*] (LCLS)

TxHCC-L ...... Conoco, Inc., Law Library, Houston, TX [*Library symbol*] [*Library of Congress*] (LCLS)

TxHCC-N ...... Conoco, Inc., North American Exploration Headquarters, Houston, TX [*Library symbol*] [*Library of Congress*] (LCLS)

TxHCCo .... Compaq Computer Corp., Component Engineering Library, Houston, TX [*Library symbol*] [*Library of Congress*] (LCLS)

TxHCG .... Columbia Gulf Transmission Co., Houston, TX [*Library symbol Library of Congress*] (LCLS)

TxHCI .... Cameron Iron Works, Inc., Houston, TX [*Library symbol Library of Congress*] (LCLS)

TxHCS .... Community Welfare Planning Association, Social Research Library, Houston, TX [*Library symbol Library of Congress*] (LCLS)

TxHDC .... Dow Chemical Co., E and CS Information Center, Houston, TX [*Library symbol Library of Congress*] (LCLS)

TxHDE .... Dresser Industries, Inc., Lane-Wells Co., Houston, TX [*Library symbol Library of Congress*] (LCLS)

TxHDH .... Dobie High School, Houston, TX [*Library symbol*] [*Library of Congress*] (LCLS)

TxHDom .... Dominican College, Houston, TX [*Library symbol Library of Congress*] (LCLS)

TxHe .... Edwards Public Library, Henrietta, TX [*Library symbol Library of Congress*] (LCLS)

TxHE .... United States Air Force, Base Library, Ellington AFB, Houston, TX [*Library symbol Library of Congress*] (LCLS)

TxHebO .... Our Lady of Guadalupe Parish Library, Hebbronville, TX [*Library symbol Library of Congress*] (LCLS)

TxHeE .... Edwards Public Library, Henrietta, TX [*Library symbol*] [*Library of Congress*] (LCLS)

TxHE-NA ...... United States Air Force, National Aerospace Education Library, Ellington AFB, Houston, TX [*Library symbol Library of Congress*] (LCLS)

TxHF .... Captain Theodore C. Freeman Memorial Library, Houston, TX [*Library symbol Library of Congress*] (LCLS)

TxHFE .... Fluor Engineers & Constructors, Fluor Houston Library, Houston, TX [*Library symbol Library of Congress*] (LCLS)

TxHFO .... Fluor Ocean Services, Engineering Library, Houston, TX [*Library symbol Library of Congress*] (LCLS)

TxHFR .... Freelance Research Service, Houston, TX [*Library symbol Library of Congress*] (LCLS)

TxHFrE .... Freeman Elementary School, Houston, TX [*Library symbol*] [*Library of Congress*] (LCLS)

TxHFzE .... Frazier Elementary School, Houston, TX [*Library symbol*] [*Library of Congress*] (LCLS)

TxHG .... Gulf Coast Bible College, Houston, TX [*Library symbol Library of Congress*] (LCLS)

TxHGE .... Genoa Elementary School, Houston, TX [*Library symbol*] [*Library of Congress*] (LCLS)

TxHGfE .... Garfield Elementary School, Houston, TX [*Library symbol*] [*Library of Congress*] (LCLS)

TxHGO .... Gulf Oil Co.-US, Central Reference Library, Houston, TX [*Library symbol Library of Congress*] (LCLS)

TxHGP .... Gulf Publishing Co., Houston, TX [*Library symbol Library of Congress*] (LCLS)

TxHGS .... Church of Jesus Christ of Latter-Day Saints, Genealogical Society Library, Houston Branch, Houston, TX [*Library symbol Library of Congress*] (LCLS)

TxHGS-E ...... Church of Jesus Christ of Latter-Day Saints, Genealogical Society Library, Houston East Branch, Houston, TX [*Library symbol Library of Congress*] (LCLS)

TxHH .... Black, Syvalls & Bryson, Inc., HOMCO Division, Houston, TX [*Library symbol Library of Congress*] (LCLS)

TxHHC .... Houston Chronicle, Houston, TX [*Library symbol Library of Congress*] (LCLS)

TxHHG .... Houston-Galveston Area Council Library, Houston, TX [*Library symbol Library of Congress*] (LCLS)

TxHHH .... Herman Hospital, Houston, TX [*Library symbol Library of Congress*] (LCLS)

TxHHL .... Houston Lighting & Power Co., Houston, TX [*Library symbol Library of Congress*] (LCLS)

TxHHO .... Humble Oil & Refining Co., General Services Library, Houston, TX [*Library symbol Library of Congress*] (LCLS)

TxHHO-E ...... Humble Oil & Refining Co., Marketing Research Library, Houston, TX [*Library symbol Library of Congress*] (LCLS)

TxHHOM ...... Houston Oil and Mineral Corp., Corporate Library, Houston, TX [*Library symbol Library of Congress*] (LCLS)

TxHHP .... Houston Post, Houston, TX [*Library symbol Library of Congress*] (LCLS)

TxHHT .... Hughes Tool Co., Houston, TX [*Library symbol Library of Congress*] (LCLS)

TxHI .... International Business Machines Corporation, Corporation Library, Houston, TX [*Library symbol Library of Congress*] (LCLS)

TXHI .... THT, Inc. [*Formerly, Texas Hitech, Inc.*] [*NASDAQ symbol*] (NQ)

TxHiC .... Hill Junior College, Hillsboro, TX [*Library symbol Library of Congress*] (LCLS)

TxHIR .... Institute of Religion, Texas Medical Center, Houston, TX [*Library symbol Library of Congress*] (LCLS)

TxHJE .... Jessup Elementary School, Houston, TX [*Library symbol*] [*Library of Congress*] (LCLS)

TxHLD .... City of Houston Legal Department, Houston, TX [*Library symbol Library of Congress*] (LCLS)

TxHLJ .... Memorial Baptist Hospital, Lillie Jolly School of Nursing, Houston, TX [*Library symbol Library of Congress*] (LCLS)

TxHLS .... Lunar Science Institute, Houston, TX [*Library symbol Library of Congress*] (LCLS)

TxHLT .... Layne Texas Co., Houston, TX [*Library symbol Library of Congress*] (LCLS)

TxHM .... Museum of Fine Arts, Houston, TX [*Library symbol Library of Congress*] (LCLS)

TxHMa .... Magcobar Corp., Houston, TX [*Library symbol Library of Congress*] (LCLS)

TxHMC .... Houston Academy of Medicine, Houston, TX [*Library symbol Library of Congress*] (LCLS)

TxHMc .... McClelland Engineers, Inc., Houston, TX [*Library symbol Library of Congress*] (LCLS)

TxHMcE .... McCelland Engineers, Inc., Houston, TX [*Library symbol*] [*Library of Congress*] (LCLS)

TxHME .... Meador Elementary School, Houston, TX [*Library symbol*] [*Library of Congress*] (LCLS)

TxHMM .... Milwhite Co., Houston, TX [*Library symbol Library of Congress*] (LCLS)

TxHMoE .... Moore Elementary School, Houston, TX [*Library symbol*] [*Library of Congress*] (LCLS)

TxHMon .... Monsanto Co., Houston, TX [*Library symbol Library of Congress*] (LCLS)

TxHN .... National Association of Corrosion Engineers, Houston, TX [*Library symbol Library of Congress*] (LCLS)

TxHNASA .... National Aeronautics and Space Administration, Manned Spacecraft Center, Technical Library, Houston, TX [*Library symbol Library of Congress*] (LCLS)

TxHNH .... North Harris County College, Houston, TX [*Library symbol Library of Congress*] (LCLS)

TxHP .... Texas Research Institute of Mental Sciences, Houston, TX [*Library symbol Library of Congress*] (LCLS)

TxHPC .... Pace Co., Houston, TX [*Library symbol Library of Congress*] (LCLS)

TxHPen .... Pennzoil Exploration Library, Houston, TX [*Library symbol Library of Congress*] (LCLS)

TxHPH .... Port of Houston World Trade Center, Houston, TX [*Library symbol Library of Congress*] (LCLS)

TxHPI .... Prudential Insurance Co. of America, Houston, TX [*Library symbol Library of Congress*] (LCLS)

TxHPT .... Petro-Tex Chemical Corp., Research Library, Houston, TX [*Library symbol Library of Congress*] (LCLS)

TxHR .... Rice University, Houston, TX [*Library symbol Library of Congress*] (LCLS)

TxHRa .... Raymond International, Inc., Houston, TX [*Library symbol Library of Congress*] (LCLS)

TxHRH .... Roy M. Huffington, Inc., Library, Houston, TX [*Library symbol Library of Congress*] (LCLS)

TxHRI .... Houston Research Institute, Houston, TX [*Library symbol Library of Congress*] (LCLS)

TxHSB .... Southern Bible College, Houston, TX [*Library symbol Library of Congress*] (LCLS)

TxHSD .... Shell Development Co., Bellaire Research Center, Houston, TX [*Library symbol Library of Congress*] (LCLS)

TxHSDW ...... Shell Oil Development Co., Westhollow Research Center Library, Houston, TX [*Library symbol Library of Congress*] (LCLS)

TxHSE .... Stuchbery Elementary School, Houston, TX [*Library symbol*] [*Library of Congress*] (LCLS)

TxHSJM .... San Jacinto Museum of History Association, Deer Park, TX [*Library symbol Library of Congress*] (LCLS)

TxHSOC ...... Standard Oil Co. of Texas, Houston, TX [*Library symbol Library of Congress*] (LCLS)

TxHSOF .... Shell Oil Co., Information and Library Services Library, Houston, TX [*Library symbol Library of Congress*] (LCLS)

TxHSOIC ...... Shell Oil Co., Information and Computing Services Center Library, Houston, TX [*Library symbol Library of Congress*] (LCLS)

TxHSP .... Shell Pipe Line Corp., R and D Library, Houston, TX [*Library symbol Library of Congress Obsolete*] (LCLS)

TxHSR .... Southwestern Research Institute, Houston, TX [*Library symbol Library of Congress*] (LCLS)

TxHST .... University of Saint Thomas, Houston, TX [*Library symbol Library of Congress*] (LCLS)

TxHSTC .... South Texas Junior College, Houston, TX [*Library symbol Library of Congress*] (LCLS)

TxHSTL .... South Texas College of Law, Houston, TX [*Library symbol Library of Congress*] (LCLS)

TxHSU .... Superior Oil Exploration Library, Houston, TX [*Library symbol Library of Congress*] (LCLS)

TxHSW .... Schlumberger Well Services, Houston, TX [*Library symbol Library of Congress*] (LCLS)

TxHSWE ...... Shell Western E & P Inc., Woodcreek Library, Houston, TX [*Library symbol*] [*Library of Congress*] (LCLS)

TxHTC .... Transcontinental Gas Pipe Line Corp., Houston, TX [*Library symbol Library of Congress*] (LCLS)

TxHTE .... Texas Eastern Transmission Corp., Houston, TX [*Library symbol Library of Congress*] (LCLS)

TxHTen .... Tennessee Gas Transmission Co., Houston, TX [*Library symbol Library of Congress*] (LCLS)

TxHTexG ...... Texas Gas Exploration Co., Houston, TX [*Library symbol Library of Congress*] (LCLS)

TxHTexO ...... Texasgulf Oil & Gas Co., Houston, TX [*Library symbol Library of Congress*] (LCLS)

TxHTG .... Trunkline Gas Co., Houston, TX [*Library symbol Library of Congress*] (LCLS)

TxHTGP .... Tennessee Gas Pipeline Co., Houston, TX [*Library symbol Library of Congress*] (LCLS)

TxHTGS .... Texas Gulf Sulphur Co., Inc., Houston, TX [*Library symbol Library of Congress*] (LCLS)

TxHTI .... Texas Instruments, Inc., Houston, TX [*Library symbol Library of Congress*] (LCLS)

TxHTide .... Getty Oil Co., Houston, TX [*Library symbol Library of Congress*]

TxHTide(Res)... Getty Oil Co., Exploration and Production Research Library, Houston, TX [*Library symbol Library of Congress*] (LCLS)

TxHTI-I .... Texas Instruments, Inc., Industrial Products Division, Houston, TX [*Library symbol Library of Congress*] (LCLS)

TxHTM .... Texas Manufacturers Association, Houston, TX [*Library symbol Library of Congress*] (LCLS)

TxHTO .... Tenneco Oil Co., Exploration Research Library, Houston, TX [*Library symbol Library of Congress*] (LCLS)

TxHTRW ...... TRW Systems Group, Houston, TX [*Library symbol Library of Congress*] (LCLS)

TxHTSU .... Texas Southern University, Houston, TX [*Library symbol Library of Congress*] (LCLS)

TxHTSU-L .... Texas Southern University, Law Library, Houston, TX [*Library symbol*] [*Library of Congress*] (LCLS)

TxHTu .... Turner, Collie & Braden, Inc., Houston, TX [*Library symbol Library of Congress*] (LCLS)

TxHU .... University of Houston, Houston, TX [*Library symbol Library of Congress*] (LCLS)

TxHUC .... Union Carbide Corp., Houston, TX [*Library symbol Library of Congress*] (LCLS)

TxHU-D .... University of Houston, Downtown College, Houston, TX [*Library symbol Library of Congress*] (LCLS)

TxHU-L .... University of Houston, Law School, Houston, TX [*Library symbol Library of Congress*] (LCLS)

TxHurT .... Tarrant County Junior College District, Hurst, TX [*Library symbol Library of Congress*] (LCLS)

TxHUSC ...... United States Department of Commerce, Houston Field Office Library, Houston, TX [*Library symbol Library of Congress*] (LCLS)

TxHuT .... Sam Houston State University, Huntsville, TX [*Library symbol Library of Congress*] (LCLS)

TxHUTP .... Union Texas Petroleum Co., Houston, TX [*Library symbol Library of Congress*] (LCLS)

TxHVA .... United States Veterans Administration Hospital, Houston, TX [*Library symbol Library of Congress*] (LCLS)

TxHVE .... Vinson, Elkins, Searls, Connally & Smith, Law Library, Houston, TX [*Library symbol Library of Congress*] (LCLS)

TxHW .... Welex Division, Haliburton Co., Houston, TX [*Library symbol Library of Congress*] (LCLS)

TxHWB .... World Book Encyclopaedia Science Service, Inc., Houston, TX [*Library symbol Library of Congress*] (LCLS)

TxHWG .... Western Geophysical Co., Houston, TX [*Library symbol Library of Congress*] (LCLS)

TxHWH .... Westbury Senior High School, Houston, TX [*Library symbol Library of Congress*] (LCLS)

TxHWN .... Western Natural Gas Co., Houston, TX [*Library symbol Library of Congress*] (LCLS)

TXI .... Aereotaxis SA de CV [*Mexico ICAO designator*] (FAAC)

TXI .... Southwest Texas State University, San Marcos, TX [*OCLC symbol*] (OCLC)

TXI .... Texas Indus [*NYSE symbol*] (TTSB)

TXI .... Texas Industries, Inc. [*NYSE symbol*] (SPSG)

TXI .... Texas International Airlines, Inc. [*Air carrier designation symbol*]

TXI .... Torex Minerals Ltd. [*Vancouver Stock Exchange symbol*]

TXI .... Transfer with Index Incremented

TxIr .... Irving Municipal Library, Irving, TX [*Library symbol Library of Congress*] (LCLS)

TxIrG .... GTE Service Corp., Library, Irving, TX [*Library symbol*] [*Library of Congress*] (LCLS)

TxIrS .... Irving Independent School District, Irving, TX [*Library symbol Library of Congress*] (LCLS)

TXJ .... University of Texas at San Antonio, San Antonio, TX [*OCLC symbol*] (OCLC)

TxJaB .... Baptist Missionary Association Theological Seminary, Jacksonville, TX [*Library symbol Library of Congress*] (LCLS)

TxJaC .... Jacksonville College, Jacksonville, TX [*Library symbol Library of Congress*] (LCLS)

TxJaL .... Lon Morris College, Jacksonville, TX [*Library symbol Library of Congress*] (LCLS)

TxJoTI .... Texas Instruments, Inc., Johnson City Technical Library, Johnson City, TX [*Library symbol*] [*Library of Congress*] (LCLS)

TXK .... Stephen F. Austin University, Nacogdoches, TX [*OCLC symbol*] (OCLC)

TXK .... Telephone Exchange (Crossbar) [*Telecommunications*] (TEL)

TXK .... Texarkana [*Arkansas*] [*Airport symbol*] (OAG)

TxKeeS .... Southwestern Union College, Keene, TX [*Library symbol Library of Congress*] (LCLS)

TxKerS .... Schreiner Institute, Kerrville, TX [*Library symbol Library of Congress*] (LCLS)

TXKF .... Bermuda Naval Air Station [*Bermuda*] [*ICAO location identifier*] (ICLI)

TxKiC .... Central Texas College, Killeen, TX [*Library symbol Library of Congress*] (LCLS)

TxKilC .... Kilgore College, Kilgore, TX [*Library symbol Library of Congress*] (LCLS)

TxKT .... Texas A & I University, Kingsville, TX [*Library symbol Library of Congress*] (LCLS)

TXL .... Aereo Taxi de Leon SA de CV [*Mexico ICAO designator*] (FAAC)

TXL .... Berlin [*Germany Airport symbol*] (OAG)

TxL .... Lubbock City-County Libraries, Lubbock, TX [*Library symbol Library of Congress*] (LCLS)

TXL .... Transfer on Index Low (IAA)

TxLaH .... United States Air Force, Base Library, Lackland Air Force Base, TX [*Library symbol Library of Congress*] (LCLS)

TxLaM .... United States Air Force, Wilford Hall Medical Center, Lackland AFB, TX [*Library symbol Library of Congress*] (LCLS)

TxLapU .... Upjohn Co., Polymer Chemicals Division Library, La Porte, TX [*Library symbol Library of Congress*] (LCLS)

TxLar .... Laredo Public Library, Laredo, TX [*Library symbol Library of Congress*] (LCLS)

TxLarC .... Laredo Junior College, Laredo, TX [*Library symbol Library of Congress*] (LCLS)

TxLarU .... Laredo State University, Laredo, TX [*Library symbol Library of Congress*] (LCLS)

TxLC .... Lubbock Christian College, Lubbock, TX [*Library symbol Library of Congress*] (LCLS)

TxLcD .... Soil and Water Conservation Districts Foundation, Davis Conservation Library, League City, TX [*Library symbol Library of Congress*] (LCLS)

TxLeaHS ...... Leander High School, Leander, TX [*Library symbol*] [*Library of Congress*] (LCLS)

TxLeS .... South Plains College, Levelland, TX [*Library symbol Library of Congress*] (LCLS)

TXLI .... Texoil, Inc. [*NASDAQ symbol*] (SAG)

TxLib .... Liberty City Library, Liberty, TX [*Library symbol Library of Congress*] (LCLS)

TxLivP .... Polk County Enterprise, Livingston, TX [*Library symbol Library of Congress*] (LCLS)

TXLIW .... Texoil Inc. Wrrt'A' [*NASDAQ symbol*] (TTSB)

TXLIZ .... Texoil Inc. Wrrt'B' [*NASDAQ symbol*] (TTSB)

TX LJ .... Texas Law Journal [*A publication*] (DLA)

TxLjB .... Brazosport College, Lake Jackson, TX [*Library symbol Library of Congress*] (LCLS)

TxLMH .... Methodist Hospital, Lubbock, TX [*Library symbol Library of Congress*] (LCLS)

TxLoL .... LeTourneau College, Longview, TX [*Library symbol Library of Congress*] (LCLS)

TxLT .... Texas Tech University, Lubbock, TX [*Library symbol Library of Congress*] (LCLS)

TxLTM .... Texas Tech University, School of Medicine at Lubbock, Lubbock, TX [*Library symbol Library of Congress*] (LCLS)

TxLTM-E ...... Texas Tech University, Regional Academic Health Center, El Paso, TX [*Library symbol*] [*Library of Congress*] (LCLS)

TxLT-SW ...... Texas Tech University, Southwest Collection, Lubbock, TX [*Library symbol*] [*Library of Congress*] (LCLS)

TxLufA .... Angelina College, Lufkin, TX [*Library symbol Library of Congress*] (LCLS)

TxLufFS .... Texas Forest Service, Forest Products Laboratory Library, Lufkin, TX [*Library symbol Library of Congress*] (LCLS)

TxLufK .... Kurth Memorial Library, Lufkin, TX [*Library symbol Library of Congress*] (LCLS)

TxLvTI .... Texas Instruments, Inc., Lewisville Technical Library, Lewisville, TX [*Library symbol*] [*Library of Congress*] (LCLS)

TXM .... Middle Tennessee State University, Murfreesboro, TN [*OCLC symbol*] (OCLC)

TXM .... Tank Exchange Model

TXM .... Taxi Aereo de Mexico [*ICAO designator*] (FAAC)

TXM .... Teminabuan [*West Irian, Indonesia*] [*Airport symbol*] (AD)

Tx-M .... Texas State Medical Library, Austin, TX [*Library symbol Library of Congress*] (LCLS)

TXM .... Trex Medical Corp. [*AMEX symbol*] (SAG)

TXM .... Trimel Corp. [*Toronto Stock Exchange symbol*]

TxMaEB .... East Texas Baptist University, Marshall, TX [*Library symbol*] [*Library of Congress*] (LCLS)

TxMaIC .... ICI America, Inc., Darco Experimental Laboratory Library, Marshall, TX [*Library symbol Library of Congress*] (LCLS)

TxMaW .... Wiley College, Marshall, TX [*Library symbol Library of Congress*] (LCLS)

TxMCa .... McAllen Memorial Library, McAllen, TX [*Library symbol Library of Congress*] (LCLS)

TxMcaH .... Hidelgo County Library System, McAllen, TX [*Library symbol Library of Congress*] (LCLS)

TxMcgR .... North American Rockwell Corp., Solid Rocket Division, McGregor, TX [*Library symbol Library of Congress*] (LCLS)

TxMck .... McKinney Memorial Public Library, McKinney, TX [*Library symbol Library of Congress*] (LCLS)

TxMckC .... Collin County Community College District, McKinney, TX [*Library symbol*] [*Library of Congress*] (LCLS)

TxMckTI .... Texas Instruments, Inc., McKinney Technical Library, McKinney, TX [*Library symbol*] [*Library of Congress*] (LCLS)

TxMe .... Mesquite Public Library, Mesquite, TX [*Library symbol Library of Congress*] (LCLS)

TxMeE .... Eastfield College, Mesquite, TX [*Library symbol Library of Congress*] (LCLS)

TxMM .... Midland County Public Library, Midland, TX [*Library symbol Library of Congress*] (LCLS)

TxMtpN .... Northeast Texas Community College, Mount Pleasant, TX [*Library symbol*] [*Library of Congress*] (LCLS)

TXN .... Houston Public Library, Houston, TX [*OCLC symbol*] (OCLC)

TXN .... Taxation

TXN .... Texas Instruments [*NYSE symbol*] (TTSB)

TXN .... Texas Instruments, Inc. [*NYSE symbol*] (SPSG)

TXN .... Texas National Airlines [*ICAO designator*] (FAAC)

TXN .... Texas Northern Oil & Gas [*Vancouver Stock Exchange symbol*]

TXN .... Texas Satellite Network [*Telecommunications service*] (TSSD)

Txn. .... Transplant (STED)

TXN .... Tunxi [*China*] [*Airport symbol*] (OAG)

TxNacS .... Stephen F. Austin State University, Nacogdoches, TX [*Library symbol Library of Congress*] (LCLS)

TXO .... Texico, NM [*Location identifier FAA*] (FAAL)

TXO .... University of Texas of the Permian Basin, Odessa, TX [*OCLC symbol*] (OCLC)

TxOC .... Odessa College, Odessa, TX [*Library symbol Library of Congress*] (LCLS)

TxOE .... Ector County Public Library, Odessa, TX [*Library symbol Library of Congress*] (LCLS)

TxOEP .... El Paso Products Co., Odessa, TX [*Library symbol Library of Congress*] (LCLS)

TxOGS .... Church of Jesus Christ of Latter-Day Saints, Genealogical Society Library, Odessa Stake Branch, Odessa, TX [*Library symbol Library of Congress*] (LCLS)

TxOr .... Orange Public Library, Orange, TX [*Library symbol Library of Congress*] (LCLS)

TXOrD .... E. I. Du Pont de Nemours & Co., Sabine River Works, Orange, TX [*Library symbol Library of Congress*] (LCLS)

TxOrL .... Lamar University-Orange, Orange, TX [*Library symbol*] [*Library of Congress*] (LCLS)

TXP .... El Paso Public Library, El Paso, TX [*OCLC symbol*] (OCLC)

TXP .... Linea Aerea Taxpa Ltda. [*Chile*] [*ICAO designator*] (FAAC)

TxP .... Pasadena Public Library, Pasadena, TX [*Library symbol Library of Congress*] (LCLS)

TXP .... Taxpayer [*Legal shorthand*] (LWAP)

TxPac .... Texas Pacific Land Trust [*Associated Press*] (SAG)

TxPaIMS ...... Institute of Marine Science, University of Texas, Port Aransas, TX [*Library symbol Library of Congress*] (LCLS)

TxParC .... Paris Junior College, Paris, TX [*Library symbol Library of Congress*] (LCLS)

TxPBE .... Bailey Elementary School, Pasadena, TX [*Library symbol*] [*Library of Congress*] (LCLS)

TxPC .... Champion Papers, Inc., Pasadena, TX [*Library symbol Library of Congress*] (LCLS)

TxPCS .... Challenger School, Pasadena, TX [*Library symbol*] [*Library of Congress*] (LCLS)

TxPE .... Ethyl Corp., Pasadena, TX [*Library symbol Library of Congress*] (LCLS)

TxPFE .... Fisher Elementary School, Pasadena, TX [*Library symbol*] [*Library of Congress*] (LCLS)

TxPGaE .... Golden Acres Elementary School, Pasadena, TX [*Library symbol*] [*Library of Congress*] (LCLS)

TxPGE .... Gardens Elementary School, Pasadena, TX [*Library symbol*] [*Library of Congress*] (LCLS)

TxPISD .... Pasadena Independent School District, Pasadena, TX [*Library symbol*] [*Library of Congress*] (LCLS)

TxPISD-P ..... Pasadena Independent School District, Professional Library, Pasadena, TX [*Library symbol*] [*Library of Congress*] (LCLS)

TxPJE .... Jensen Elementary School, Pasadena, TX [*Library symbol*] [*Library of Congress*] (LCLS)

TxPJI .... Jackson Intermediate School, Pasadena, TX [*Library symbol*] [*Library of Congress*] (LCLS)

TxPKE .... Kruse Elementary School, Pasadena, TX [*Library symbol*] [*Library of Congress*] (LCLS)

TxPlao .... Plano Public Library, Plano, TX [*Library symbol Library of Congress*] (LCLS)

TxPlW .... Wayland Baptist College, Plainview, TX [*Library symbol Library of Congress*] (LCLS)

TxPME .... McMasters Elementary School, Pasadena, TX [*Library symbol*] [*Library of Congress*] (LCLS)

TxPMI .... Miller Intermediate School, Pasadena, TX [*Library symbol*] [*Library of Congress*] (LCLS)

TxPnT .... Texas-United States Chemical Co., Process Engineering Section, R and D Library, Port Neches, TX [*Library symbol Library of Congress*] (LCLS)

TxPo .... Gates Memorial Library, Port Arthur, TX [*Library symbol Library of Congress*] (LCLS)

TxPPE .... Parks Elementary School, Pasadena, TX [*Library symbol*] [*Library of Congress*] (LCLS)

TxPPH .... Pasadena High School, Pasadena, TX [*Library symbol*] [*Library of Congress*] (LCLS)

TxPPoE .... Pomeroy Elementary School, Pasadena, TX [*Library symbol*] [*Library of Congress*] (LCLS)

TxPPvI .... Park View Intermediate School, Pasadena, TX [*Library symbol*] [*Library of Congress*] (LCLS)

TxPQI .... Queens Intermediate School, Pasadena, TX [*Library symbol*] [*Library of Congress*] (LCLS)

TxPRbE .... Red Bluff Elementary School, Pasadena, TX [*Library symbol*] [*Library of Congress*] (LCLS)

TXPRD .... Tax Period

TxPRE .... Richey Elementary School, Pasadena, TX [*Library symbol*] [*Library of Congress*] (LCLS)

TxPRH .... Sam Rayburn High School, Pasadena, TX [*Library symbol*] [*Library of Congress*] (LCLS)

TxPS .... San Jacinto College, Pasadena, TX [*Library symbol Library of Congress*] (LCLS)

TxPSE .... Mae Smythe Elementary School, Pasadena, TX [*Library symbol*] [*Library of Congress*] (LCLS)

TxPSI .... Southmore Elementary School, Pasadena, TX [*Library symbol*] [*Library of Congress*] (LCLS)

TxPSjI .... San Jacinto Intermediate School, Pasadena, TX [*Library symbol*] [*Library of Congress*] (LCLS)

TxPSpE .... Sparks Elementary School, Pasadena, TX [*Library symbol*] [*Library of Congress*] (LCLS)

TxPSSE .... South Shaver Elementary School, Pasadena, TX [*Library symbol*] [*Library of Congress*] (LCLS)

TxPT .... Tenneco Chemicals, Inc., Pasadena, TX [*Library symbol Library of Congress*] (LCLS)

TxPTC .... Texas Chiropractic College, Pasadena, TX [*Library symbol*] [*Library of Congress*] (LCLS)

TxPTE .... Teague Elementary School, Pasadena, TX [*Library symbol*] [*Library of Congress*] (LCLS)

TxPvC .... Prairie View Agricultural and Mechanical College, Prairie View, TX [*Library symbol Library of Congress*] (LCLS)

TxPWE .... Williams Elementary School, Pasadena, TX [*Library symbol*] [*Library of Congress*] (LCLS)

TxPYE .... Young Elementary School, Pasadena, TX [*Library symbol*] [*Library of Congress*] (LCLS)

TXPYR .... Taxpayer

TXQ .... University of Texas, Austin, Law Library, Austin, TX [*OCLC symbol*] (OCLC)

TXR .... Lamar University, Beaumont, TX [*OCLC symbol*] (OCLC)

TXR .... Susitna Valley, AK [*Location identifier FAA*] (FAAL)

TXR .... Tanbar [*Queensland*] [*Airport symbol*] (AD)

TXR .... Tank Exchange Ratio (MCD)

TXR .... Taxirey SA de CV [*Mexico ICAO designator*] (FAAC)

TXR .... Triex Resources Ltd. [*Vancouver Stock Exchange symbol*]

TxRaC .... Ranger Junior College, Ranger, TX [*Library symbol Library of Congress*] (LCLS)

TXRC .... Texas Export [*AAR code*]

TxReTR .... Texas Research Foundation, Renner, TX [*Library symbol Library of Congress*] (LCLS)

TXRF .... Total-Reflection X-Ray Fluorescence [*Analytical chemistry*]

TXRF .... Total X-Ray Fluorescence (AAEL)

TxRi .... Richardson Public Library, Richardson, TX [*Library symbol Library of Congress*] (LCLS)

TxRiA .... Anderson Clayton Foods [*of Anderson, Clayton & Co.*], Richardson, TX [*Library symbol Library of Congress*] (LCLS)

TxRic .... Fort Bend County Library System, George Memorial Library, Richmond, TX [*Library symbol*] [*Library of Congress*] (LCLS)

TxRiS .... Sun Oil Co., Richardson, TX [*Library symbol Library of Congress*] (LCLS)

TxRr .... Round Rock Public Library, Round Rock, TX [*Library symbol*] [*Library of Congress*] (LCLS)

TXRX .... Transmitter-Receiver

TXS .... Hardin-Simmons University, Abilene, TX [*OCLC symbol*] (OCLC)

TXS .... Taxpayer Service [*IRS*]

TXS .... Telephone Exchange (Strowger) [*Telecommunications*] (TEL)

TXS .... Texas Airlines, Inc. [*ICAO designator*] (FAAC)

TXS .... Texas Star Resources Corp. [*Vancouver Stock Exchange symbol*]

TxSa .... San Antonio Public Library, San Antonio, TX [*Library symbol Library of Congress*] (LCLS)

TxSaBAM .... United States Air Force, School of Aerospace Medicine, Brooks Air Force Base, San Antonio, TX [*Library symbol Library of Congress*] (LCLS)

TxSaBHR .... United States Air Force, Human Resources Laboratory Library, Brooks Air Force Base, San Antonio, TX [*Library symbol Library of Congress*] (LCLS)

TxSaBM ...... Bexar County Medical Library Association, San Antonio, TX [*Library symbol Library of Congress*] (LCLS)

TxSaC .... San Antonio College, San Antonio, TX [*Library symbol Library of Congress*] (LCLS)

TxSaGH .... Robert B. Green Memorial Hospital, San Antonio, TX [*Library symbol Library of Congress*] (LCLS)

TxSaGS .... Church of Jesus Christ of Latter-Day Saints, Genealogical Society Library, San Antonio Branch, San Antonio, TX [*Library symbol Library of Congress*] (LCLS)

TxSaI .... Incarnate Word College, San Antonio, TX [*Library symbol Library of Congress*] (LCLS)

TxSaI .... Tom Green County Library, San Angelo, TX [*Library symbol Library of Congress*] (LCLS)

TxSaIA .... Angelo State University, San Angelo, TX [*Library symbol Library of Congress*] (LCLS)

TxSaO .... Our Lady of the Lake College, San Antonio, TX [*Library symbol Library of Congress*] (LCLS)

TxSaOC .... Oblate College of the Southwest, San Antonio, TX [*Library symbol Library of Congress*] (LCLS)

TxSaPA .... Palo Alto College, San Antonio, TX [*Library symbol*] [*Library of Congress*] (LCLS)

TxSaSFRE .... Southwest Foundation for Research and Education, San Antonio, TX [*Library symbol Library of Congress*] (LCLS)

TxSaSM ...... Saint Mary's University, San Antonio, TX [*Library symbol Library of Congress*] (LCLS)

TxSaSM-L .... Saint Mary's University, Law Library, San Antonio, TX [*Library symbol Library of Congress*] (LCLS)

TxSaSP .... St. Philip's College, San Antonio, TX [*Library symbol Library of Congress*] (LCLS)

TxSaSR .... Southwest Research Institute, San Antonio, TX [*Library symbol Library of Congress*] (LCLS)

TxSaStJ .... Saint John's Seminary, San Antonio, TX [*Library symbol Library of Congress*] (LCLS)

TxSaT .... Trinity University, San Antonio, TX [*Library symbol Library of Congress*] (LCLS)

TxSaT-W ...... Trinity University, Whitsett Library Museum, San Antonio, TX [*Library symbol Library of Congress*] (LCLS)

TxSaU .... University of Texas at San Antonio, San Antonio, TX [*Library symbol Library of Congress*] (LCLS)

TxSaUS .... United Services Automobile Association, San Antonio, TX [*Library symbol Library of Congress*] (LCLS)

TxSaV .... United States Veterans Administration Hospital, San Antonio, TX [*Library symbol Library of Congress*] (LCLS)

Tx-SC .... Texas State Law Library, Austin, TX [*Library symbol Library of Congress*] (LCLS)

TxSeTL .... Texas Lutheran College, Seguin, TX [*Library symbol Library of Congress*] (LCLS)

TxSh .... Sherman Public Library, Sherman, TX [*Library symbol*] [*Library of Congress*] (LCLS)

TxShA .... Austin College, Sherman, TX [*Library symbol Library of Congress*] (LCLS)

TxShoHH...... South Houston High School, South Houston, TX [*Library symbol*] [*Library of Congress*] (LCLS)

TxShoHI .... South Houston Intermediate School, South Houston, TX [*Library symbol*] [*Library of Congress*] (LCLS)

TxShoPE ...... Pearl Hall Elementary School, South Houston, TX [*Library symbol*] [*Library of Congress*] (LCLS)

TxShoSE ...... L.F. Smith Elementary School, South Houston, TX [*Library symbol*] [*Library of Congress*] (LCLS)

TxShoShE ... South Houston Elementary School, South Houston, TX [*Library symbol*] [*Library of Congress*] (LCLS)

TxShpM .... United States Air Force, Regional Hospital, Medical Library, Sheppard AFB, TX [*Library symbol Library of Congress*] (LCLS)

TxShTI .... Texas Instruments, Inc., Sherman Technical Library, Sherman, TX [*Library symbol*] [*Library of Congress*] (LCLS)

TxSiW .... Rob and Bessie Welder Wildlife Foundation, Sinton, TX [*Library symbol Library of Congress*] (LCLS)

TxSjM .... San Jacinto Museum of History Association, San Jacinto Monument, TX [*Library symbol Library of Congress*] (LCLS)

TxSmS .... Southwest Texas State University, San Marcos, TX [*Library symbol Library of Congress*] (LCLS)

TxSn .... Scurry County Library, Snyder, TX [*Library symbol Library of Congress*] (LCLS)

TxSvT .... Tarleton State University, Stephenville, TX [*Library symbol Library of Congress*] (LCLS)

TxSw .... Sweetwater City-County Library, Sweetwater, TX [*Library symbol Library of Congress*] (LCLS)

TXT .... Group One, Inc. [*FAA designator*] (FAAC)

TXT .... Texas Southern University, Houston, TX [*OCLC symbol*] (OCLC)

TXT .... Text

txt .... Text or ASCII File [*Computer science*]

TXT .... Textron, Inc. [*NYSE symbol*] (SPSG)

TxTA .... American Oil Co. [*Later, Amoco Oil Co.*], Texas City, TX [*Library symbol Library of Congress*] (LCLS)

TxTCM .... College of the Mainland, Texas City, TX [*Library symbol Library of Congress*] (LCLS)

TxTe .... Texarkana Public Library, Texarkana, TX [*Library symbol Library of Congress*] (LCLS)

TxTeC .... Texarkana College, Texarkana, TX [*Library symbol Library of Congress*] (LCLS)

TxTeET........ East Texas State University, Texarkana, TX [*Library symbol of Congress*] (LCLS)

TxTehW .... Westminster College, Tehuacana, TX [*Library symbol Library of Congress*] (LCLS)

TxTemC .... Temple Junior College, Temple, TX [*Library symbol Library of Congress*] (LCLS)

TxTemH .... Scott and White Memorial Hospital, Temple, TX [*Library symbol Library of Congress*] (LCLS)

TxTerS .... Southwestern Christian College, Terrell, TX [*Library symbol Library of Congress*] (LCLS)

TxTeS .... East Texas State University at Texarkana, Texarkana, TX [*Library symbol Library of Congress*] (LCLS)

txtl .... Textile (VRA)

TXTL .... Textile

TXTLE .... Textile

TxTM .... Text Maintenance [*Computer science*] (MHDB)

TxTMC .... Monsanto Co., Texas City, TX [*Library symbol Library of Congress*] (LCLS)

TXTPrA .... Textron, $2.08 Cv A Pfd [*NYSE symbol*] (TTSB)

TXTPrB .... Textron, $1.40 Cv B Pfd [*NYSE symbol*] (TTSB)

TXTPrT .... Textron Cap 1 7.92% Tr Sec [*NYSE symbol*] (TTSB)

TxTUC .... Union Carbide Corp., Chemicals and Plastics Division, Texas City, TX [*Library symbol Library of Congress*] (LCLS)

TxTy .... Tyler Carnegie Public Library, Tyler, TX [*Library symbol Library of Congress*] (LCLS)

TxTyB .... Butler College, Tyler, TX [*Library symbol Library of Congress*] (LCLS)

TxTyC .... Texas Eastern University, Tyler, TX [*Library symbol Library of Congress*] (LCLS)

TxTyT .... Texas College, Tyler, TX [*Library symbol Library of Congress*] (LCLS)

TxTyU .... University of Texas at Tyler, Tyler, TX [*Library symbol*] [*Library of Congress*] (LCLS)

TXU .... Tabou [*Ivory Coast*] [*Airport symbol*] (OAG)

txu .... Texas [*MARC country of publication code Library of Congress*] (LCCP)

TXU .... Texas Utilities [*NYSE symbol*] (TTSB)

TXU .... Texas Utilities Co. [*NYSE symbol*] (SPSG)

TXU .... Texoro Resources Ltd. [*Vancouver Stock Exchange symbol*]

TXU .... University of Texas at El Paso, El Paso, TX [*OCLC symbol*] (OCLC)

TxU .... University of Texas, Austin, TX [*Library symbol Library of Congress*] (LCLS)

TxU-A .... University of Texas, M. D. Anderson Hospital and Tumor Institute, Houston, TX [*Library symbol Library of Congress*] (LCLS)

TxU-B .... University of Texas, Business Administration and Economics Library, Austin, TX [*Library symbol Library of Congress*] (LCLS)

TxU-D .... University of Texas, School of Dentistry, Houston, TX [*Library symbol Library of Congress*] (LCLS)

TxU-Da .... University of Texas at Dallas, Richardson, TX [*Library symbol Library of Congress*] (LCLS)

TxU-GP .... University of Texas, Austin, Institute of Geo-Physics, Austin, TX [*Library symbol*] [*Library of Congress*] (LCLS)

TxU-Hu .... Humanities Research Center, University of Texas, Austin, TX [*Library symbol Library of Congress*] (LCLS)

TxU-J .... University of Texas, Lyndon Baines Johnson Presidential Library, Austin, TX [*Library symbol Library of Congress*] (LCLS)

TxU-L........... University of Texas, Law Library, Austin, TX [*Library symbol Library of Congress*] (LCLS)

TxU-LS .... University of Texas at Austin, Graduate School of Library and Information Science, Austin, TX [*Library symbol*] [*Library of Congress*] (LCLS)

TxU-M .... University of Texas, Medical School, Galveston, TX [*Library symbol Library of Congress*] (LCLS)

TxU-O .... University of Texas of the Permian Basin, Odessa, TX [*Library symbol Library of Congress*] (LCLS)

TxU-PH .... University of Texas, School of Public Health, Houston, TX [*Library symbol Library of Congress*] (LCLS)

TxU-STM...... University of Texas Medical School at San Antonio, San Antonio, TX [*Library symbol Library of Congress*] (LCLS)

TxUtEl.......... Texas Utilities Electric [*Associated Press*] (SAG)

TxUtEl.......... TU Electric Capital I [*Associated Press*] (SAG)

TxUtEl.......... TU Electric Capital II [*Associated Press*] (SAG)

TxUtEl.......... TU Electric Capital III [*Associated Press*] (SAG)

TxUvS .... Southwest Texas Junior College, Uvalde, TX [*Library symbol Library of Congress*] (LCLS)

TXV .... Fairfield, CA [*Location identifier FAA*] (FAAL)

TXV .... Puerto Vallarta Taxi Aereo, SA de CV [*Mexico*] [*FAA designator*] (FAAC)

TXV .... Throttling Expansion Valve [*Automotive air conditioning*]

TXV .... University of Houston, Victoria Center, Victoria, TX [*OCLC symbol*] (OCLC)

TxVeC .... Vernon Regional Junior College, Vernon, TX [*Library symbol Library of Congress*] (LCLS)

TxVi .... Victoria Public Library, Victoria, TX [*Library symbol Library of Congress*] (LCLS)

TxViC .... Victoria College, Victoria, TX [*Library symbol Library of Congress*] (LCLS)

TxVidGS .... Church of Jesus Christ of Latter-Day Saints, Genealogical Society Library, Beaumont Branch, Vidor, TX [*Library symbol Library of Congress*] (LCLS)

TxViHU .... University of Houston, Victoria Center, Victoria, TX [*Library symbol Library of Congress*] (LCLS)

TxW .... Waco-McLennan County Library, Waco, TX [*Library symbol Library of Congress*] (LCLS)

TxWaS .... Southwestern Assemblies of God College, Waxahachie, TX [*Library symbol Library of Congress*] (LCLS)

TxWB .... Baylor University, Waco, TX [*Library symbol Library of Congress*] (LCLS)

TxWB-B........ Baylor University, Armstrong Browning Library, Waco, TX [*Library symbol Library of Congress*] (LCLS)

TxWB-L........ Baylor University, Law School Library, Waco, TX [*Library symbol Library of Congress*] (LCLS)

TxWB-Mus ... Baylor University, Museum Collection, Waco, TX [*Library symbol Library of Congress*] (LCLS)

TxWB-N .... Baylor University School of Nursing, Dallas, TX [*Library symbol*] [*Library of Congress*] (LCLS)

TxWeaC .... Weatherford College, Weatherford, TX [*Library symbol Library of Congress*] (LCLS)

TxWeiM .... Weimar Mercury, Weimar, TX [*Library symbol Library of Congress*] (LCLS)

TxWFM .... Masonic Grand Lodge of Texas, Waco, TX [*Library symbol Library of Congress*] (LCLS)

TxWhaC .... Wharton County Junior College, Wharton, TX [*Library symbol Library of Congress*] (LCLS)

TxWhaW ...... Wharton County Library, Wharton, TX [*Library symbol Library of Congress*] (LCLS)

TxWic .... Kemp Public Library, Wichita Falls, TX [*Library symbol Library of Congress*] (LCLS)

TxWicM .... Midwestern State University, Wichita Falls, TX [*Library symbol Library of Congress*] (LCLS)

TxWM .... McClennan Community College, Waco, TX [*Library symbol Library of Congress*] (LCLS)

TxWPQ......... Paul Quinn College, Waco, TX [*Library symbol Library of Congress*] (LCLS)

TxWV .... United States Veterans Administration Hospital, Waco, TX [*Library symbol Library of Congress*] (LCLS)

TXX .... Southwestern University, Georgetown, TX [*OCLC symbol*] (OCLC)

TY .... Air Caledonie [*ICAO designator*] (AD)

TY .... Benin [*Aircraft nationality and registration mark*] (FAAC)

TY .... Talmud Yerushalmi (BJA)

TY .... Target Year

TY .... Tax Year

TY .... Tebul [*or Tevul*] Yom (BJA)

TY .... Teletypewriter [*Telecommunications*] (IAA)

Ty .... Temporary

TY .... Territorial Yeomanry [*British military*] (DMA)

TY .... Territory

TY .... Thank You

Ty .... Thyroxine [*Also, T4, Thx*] [*An amino acid Endocrinology*]

TY .... Total Yield (AABC)

TY .... Translation Hand Controller Y-Axis Direction (MCD)

TY	Transposon Yeast [*Genetics*]
TY	Tri-Continental [*NYSE symbol*] (TTSB)
TY	Tri-Continental Corp. [*NYSE symbol*] (SPSG)
TY	Truly
Ty	Tyndale New Testament Commentaries [*A publication*] (BJA)
TY	Type
Ty	Type (STED)
Ty	Typhoid (STED)
TY	Typhoid Fever (DSUE)
Ty	Tyrosine (STED)
TYA	Tygas Resources Corp. [*Vancouver Stock Exchange symbol*]
TYA	Yalova [*Turkey*] [*Airport symbol*] (AD)
TYAA	Textured Yarn Association of America (EA)
TYB	Tibooburra [*New South Wales*] [*Airport symbol*] (AD)
TYC	Thames Yacht Club [*Later, RTYC*] [*British*] (DI)
TYC	Toby Creek Resources Ltd. [*Vancouver Stock Exchange symbol*]
TYC	Trinity College, Hartford, CT [*OCLC symbol*] (OCLC)
TYC	Two-Year[-*Old*] Course [*Horse racing*]
TYC	Tyco International [*NYSE symbol*] (SPSG)
TYC	Tylerdale Connecting [*AAR code*]
T-YCDT	Ten-Year Chinese Dong Tang [*Turmoil*] Cycle [*Reference to the Kuomintang's defeat in 1946-48, Mao's Great Leap Forward in 1956, the Cultural Revolution in 1966, the Gang of Four's fall in 1976*] [*Term coined by William Safire*]
TYCO	Tylenol [*McNeil Consumer Products Co.*] (DAVI)
TYCO	Tylenol and Codeine [*Pharmacy*]
TYCO	Tylenol With Codeine (STED)
TycoInt	Tyco International [*Associated Press*] (SAG)
TYCOM	Type Commander
TYCOMSLANT	Type Commands, Atlantic (DNAB)
TYCOMSPAC	Type Commands, Pacific (DNAB)
TycoT	Tyco Toys [*Associated Press*] (SAG)
TycoToy	Tyco Toys, Inc. [*Associated Press*] (SAG)
TYD	Temporary Duty (MCD)
tyd	Type Designer [*MARC relator code*] [*Library of Congress*] (LCCP)
TYDAC	Typical Digital Automatic Computer
TYDE	Type Designators (MSA)
TYDV	Tobacco Yellow Dwarf Virus [*Plant pathology*]
TYE	Tyee Airways Ltd. [*Canada ICAO designator*] (FAAC)
TYE	Tye Explorations, Inc. [*Vancouver Stock Exchange symbol*]
TYE	Tyonek, AK [*Location identifier FAA*] (FAAL)
TYF	Panama City, FL [*Location identifier FAA*] (FAAL)
TYF	Tung Yeun Feng [*Republic of China*] [*Seismograph station code, US Geological Survey*] (SEIS)
TYFC	Tysons Financial [*NASDAQ symbol*] (TTSB)
TYFSOK	Thank You for Shopping Our K-Mart [*or Kresge's*] [*Slogan of K-Mart Corp.*]
TYG	Temple Youth Group [*Local groups of National Federation of Temple Youth, sometimes called TYG-ers, pronounced "tigers"*]
TYG	Trypticase, Yeast-Extract, Glucose [*Cell growth medium*]
tyg	Typographer [*MARC relator code*] [*Library of Congress*] (LCCP)
TYGN	Tylan General [*NASDAQ symbol*] (TTSB)
TYGN	Tylan General, Inc. [*NASDAQ symbol*] (SAG)
TYH	Tihany [*Hungary*] [*Geomagnetic observatory code*]
TYI	Rocky Mount, NC [*Location identifier FAA*] (FAAL)
TYJ	Tyrolean Jet Service [*Austria ICAO designator*] (FAAC)
TYK	Toyooka [*Japan*] [*Seismograph station code, US Geological Survey*] (SEIS)
TYL	Talara [*Peru*] [*Airport symbol*] (OAG)
TYL	TANU [*Tanganyika African National Union*] Youth League [*Tanganyika*]
tyl	Tylenol [*McNeil Consumer Products Co.*] (DAVI)
TYL	Tyler [*Diocesan abbreviation*] [*Texas*] (TOCD)
TYL	Tyler Corp. [*NYSE symbol*] (SPSG)
Tyl	Tyler's Vermont Supreme Court Reports [*1800-03*] [*A publication*] (DLA)
Tyl	Tyloma [*Also called a callus*] [*Orthopedics*] (DAVI)
TylanG	Tylan General, Inc. [*Associated Press*] (SAG)
Tyl Boun	Tyler on Boundaries, Fences, Etc. [*A publication*] (DLA)
TYLC	Tomato Yellow Leaf Curl [*Plant pathology*]
TYLCV	Tomato Yellow Leaf Curl Virus
Tyl Eccl L	Tyler's American Ecclesiastical Law [*A publication*] (DLA)
Tyl Eject	Tyler on Ejectment and Adverse Enjoyment [*A publication*] (DLA)
Tyler	Tyler Corp. [*Associated Press*] (SAG)
Tyler	Tyler's Vermont Reports [*1800-03*] [*A publication*] (DLA)
Tyler Ej	Tyler on Ejectment and Adverse Enjoyment [*A publication*] (DLA)
Tyler Steph Pl	Tyler's Edition of Stephen on Principles of Pleading [*A publication*] (DLA)
Tyl Fix	Tyler on Fixtures [*A publication*] (DLA)
Tyl Inf	Tyler on Infancy and Coverture [*A publication*] (DLA)
Tyl Part	Tyler on Partnership [*A publication*] (DLA)
Tyl St Pl	Tyler's Edition of Stephen on the Principles of Pleading [*A publication*] (DLA)
Tyl Us	Tyler on Usury, Pawns, and Loans [*A publication*] (DLA)
TYM	Tyumen Airlines [*Russian Federation*] [*ICAO designator*] (FAAC)
TYME-GRAM	Tymnet Telegram (NITA)
TYMNET	Timeshare, Inc. Network [*Telecommunications*] (TEL)
Tymp	Tympanic (STED)
Tymp	Tympanicity [*Referring to auscultation of the chest*] [*Medicine*] (DAVI)
tymp	Tympanium (VRA)
Tymp	Tympanium (STED)
TYMP	Tympanogram (STED)
Tymp	Tympanostomy (STED)
tymp	Tympanostomy [*Otorhinolaryngology*] (DAVI)
tymp	Tympany

Tymp Mem	Tympanic Membrane [*Anatomy*] (CPH)
tymp memb	Tympanic Membrane [*Otorhinolaryngology*] (DAVI)
TYMV	Turnip Yellow Mosaic Virus
TYN	Taiyuan [*China*] [*Airport symbol*] (OAG)
TYN	Taiyuan [*China*] [*Seismograph station code, US Geological Survey*] (SEIS)
TYN	Taywin Resources Ltd. [*Vancouver Stock Exchange symbol*]
TyndHB	Tyndale House Bulletin [*Cambridge*] [*A publication*] (BJA)
Tyng	Tyng's Reports [*2-17 Massachusetts*] [*A publication*] (DLA)
TYO	Tokyo [*Japan*] [*Airport symbol*] (OAG)
TYO	Two-Year-Old [*Horse racing*] (ROG)
TYOG	Take Your Own Gadgets
TYP	Transitional Year Program [*Brandeis University*] (EA)
TY-P	Trial Y-Plane
TYP	Type Aircraft (FAAC)
Typ	Typed (BJA)
TYP	Typical (AAG)
typ	Typical (STED)
TYP	Typography [*or Typographer*] (AAG)
TYP	[*The*] Youth Project (EA)
typ cons	Typus Conservandus [*Conserved Type*] [*Latin*]
TYPER	Typographical Error (AAG)
TYP-H	Typhoid H [*Infectious diseases*] (DAVI)
TYPH	Typhoon
TYPL	Type-Plate
TYPNO	Teletypewriter Communications out of Service (FAAC)
Typo	Typographed [*Philately*]
TYPO	Typographical
TYPO	Typographical Error (NTCM)
TYPOE	Ten Year Plan for Ocean Exploration [*National Council on Marine Resources and Engineering Development*] (MSC)
TYPOG	Typographer [*or Typography*]
typogr	Typography (VRA)
TYPOK	Teletypewriter Communications Returned to Service (FAAC)
TYPOUT	Typewriter Output
TYPr	Tri-Continental, $2.50 Pfd [*NYSE symbol*] (TTSB)
TYPSG	Typesetting
TYPSTG	Typesetting (MSA)
TYPW	Typewriter (ADA)
typw	Typewritten (WDAA)
TYPWRT	Typewriter
TYPWRTR	Typewriter
TYQ	Indianapolis, IN [*Location identifier FAA*] (FAAL)
TYR	Tyler [*Texas*] [*Airport symbol*] (OAG)
TYR	Tyramine (STED)
TYR	Tyrode (STED)
TYR	Tyrolean Airways [*Austria ICAO designator*] (FAAC)
TYR	Tyrone [*County in Ireland*] (ROG)
Tyr	Tyrone County [*Ireland*] (BARN)
Iyr	Tyrosine [*Also, Y*] [*An amino acid*]
tyr	Tyrosine [*An amino acid*] (DOG)
Tyr	Tyrwhitt and Granger's English Exchequer Reports [*1830-35*] [*A publication*] (DLA)
Tyr & Cr	Tyrwhitt and Granger's English Exchequer Reports [*1830-35*] [*A publication*] (DLA)
Tyrex	Tyrex Oil Co. [*Associated Press*] (SAG)
TyRIA	Thyroid Radioisotope Assay (BABM)
Tyrol	Tyrolean [*or Tirolean*] [*Reference to a state in western Austria*] [*Reference to an alpine region that is divided between Austria and Italy*] (BARN)
TyrRS	Tyrosyl-tRNA [*Transfer Ribonucleic Acid*] Synthetase
Tyr Trig	Tyranni Triginta [*of Scriptores Historiae Augustae*] [*Classical studies*] (OCD)
Tyrw	Tyrwhitt and Granger's English Exchequer Reports [*1830-35*] [*A publication*] (DLA)
Tyrw & G	Tyrwhitt and Granger's English Exchequer Reports [*1835-36*] [*A publication*] (DLA)
Tyrw & G (Eng)	Tyrwhitt and Granger's English Exchequer Reports [*1835-36*] [*A publication*] (DLA)
TYRX	Tyrex Oil [*NASDAQ symbol*] (TTSB)
TYRX	Tyrex Oil Co. [*NASDAQ symbol*] (NQ)
TYS	Knoxville [*Tennessee*] [*Airport symbol*] (OAG)
TYS	McGhee Tyson Airport [*FAA*] (TAG)
TYS	Tensile Yield Strength
TYS	Tyler Resources, Inc. [*Toronto Stock Exchange symbol*]
TYS	Tyseley [*British depot code*]
TYS	Tyson Valley [*Missouri*] [*Seismograph station code, US Geological Survey*] (SEIS)
TYSD	Total Years Service Date
TYSN	Tyson Foods, Inc. [*NASDAQ symbol*] (NQ)
TYSNA	Tyson Foods Cl'A' [*NASDAQ symbol*] (TTSB)
Tyson	Tyson Foods, Inc. [*Associated Press*] (SAG)
TYSP	Tibetan Youth Sponsorship Programs (EA)
TYT	Nantucket, MA [*Location identifier FAA*] (FAAL)
TYT	Type Training [*Navy*] (NVT)
TYTIPT	Type Training in Port [*Navy*] (NVT)
Tytler Mil Law	Tytler on Military Law and Courts-Martial [*A publication*] (DLA)
Tyt Mil L	Tytler on Military Law and Courts-Martial [*3rd ed.*] [*1812*] [*A publication*] (DLA)
TYTV	Tomato Yellow Top Virus
TYU	Tyuratam [*Satellite launch complex*] [*Former USSR*]
TYV	Little Rock, AR [*Location identifier FAA*] (FAAL)
TYV	Turnip Yellows Virus [*Plant pathology*]
TYVM	Thank You Very Much
TYW	Taiwan Equity Fd [*NYSE symbol*] (TTSB)

TYW.............. Taiwan Equity Fund, Inc. [*NYSE symbol*]   (SAG)
TYX.............. Tylox Resources Corp. [*Vancouver Stock Exchange symbol*]
TYY.............. Abilene, TX [*Location identifier FAA*]   (FAAL)
TYZ.............. Taylor [*Arizona*] [*Airport symbol Obsolete*]   (OAG)
TZ................ American Trans Air [*ICAO designator*]   (AD)
TZ................ Der Treue Zionswaechter [*Altona*] [*A publication*]   (BJA)
TZ................ Mali [*International civil aircraft marking*]   (ODBW)
TZ................ Tactical Zone [*Military*]   (AABC)
tz................ Tanzania [*MARC country of publication code Library of Congress*] (LCCP)
TZ................ Tanzania [*Internet country code*]
TZ................ Terrazo [*Technical drawings*]
TZ................ Tidal Zone
TZ................ Time Zero
TZ................ Transition Zone [*in plant growth*] [*Botany*]
TZ................ Translation Hand Controller Z-Axis Direction   (NASA)
TZ................ Transmitter Zone [*Telecommunications*]   (TEL)
TZ................ Transportation Zone [*Department of Transportation*]
TZ................ Treatment Zone   (GNE)
TZ................ Trennzahl Values [*For carrier gas flow rates*] [*Chromatography*]
TZ................ Tropical Zodiac
TZ................ Tuberculin Zymoplastiche [*Medicine*]   (MAE)
TZ................ Tubolare Zagato [*Automotive model designation*] [*Alfa-Romeo*]
TZ................ [*The*] Twilight Zone [*Television program created by Rod Serling*]
TZ................ Twilight-Zoner [*Undecided voter*] [*Political slang*]
TZ................ United Republic of Tanzania [*ANSI two-letter standard code*]   (CNC)
TZA.............. United Republic of Tanzania [*ANSI three-letter standard code*]   (CNC)
TZC.............. Tetrazolium Chloride Agar [*Biological stain*]
TZC.............. Trizec Corp. Ltd. [*Toronto Stock Exchange symbol*]

TZC.WS .... Trizec Corp. Ltd'A'Wrrt [*NYSE symbol*]   (TTSB)
TZD.............. Thiazolidinedione [*Biochemistry*]
TZD.............. True Zenith Distance [*Navigation*]
TZE.............. Topaz Exploration Ltd. [*Vancouver Stock Exchange symbol*]
TZE.............. Transfer on Zero
TZG.............. Thermofit Zap Gun
TZG.............. Waha Leaf [*British Honduras*] [*Airport symbol*]   (AD)
TZH.............. Trizec Hahn Corp. [*NYSE symbol*]   (SAG)
TZJ.............. Tubular Zippered Jacket
TZK.............. Tajikistan [*ICAO designator*]   (FAAC)
TZM.............. Titanium-Zirconium-Molybdenum [*Alloy*]
TZN.............. South Andros [*Bahamas*] [*Airport symbol*]   (OAG)
TZN.............. Tchaikazan Enterprises, Inc. [*Vancouver Stock Exchange symbol*]
Tzn.............. Total Estrogens After Zinc and Hydrochloric Acid [*Zn-HCl Treatment*] [*Laboratory*]   (DAVI)
TZO.............. Temporary Zoning Ordinance   (PA)
TZO.............. Thorne-Zytkow Object [*Astronomy*]
TZP.............. Temperate Zone Phase
TZP.............. Time Zero Pulse
TZP.............. Triazolopyridazine [*Potential antianxiety drug*]
TZR.............. Tanzania-Zambia Railway   (PDAA)
TZR.............. Torrez Resources Ltd. [*Vancouver Stock Exchange symbol*]
TZS.............. Technologie Zentrum Steyr [*Steyr Technology Center*] [*German*]
TZT.............. Triazinate [*Antineoplastic drug*]   (CDI)
TZTh.............. Tuebinger Zeitschrift fuer Theologie [*A publication*]   (BJA)
TZV.............. Tetrazolium Violet [*Also, TV*]
TZX.............. Trabzon [*Turkey*] [*Airport symbol*]   (OAG)
TZY.............. Warsaw, IN [*Location identifier FAA*]   (FAAL)
TZZ.............. Tabubil [*Papua New Guinea*] [*Seismograph station code, US Geological Survey*]   (SEIS)

U

By Acronym

U	Asymmetrical [Chemistry] (BARN)
U/	At the Umbilicus [Obstetrics] (DAVI)
U	Audio and Power Connectors [JETDS nomenclature] [Military] (CET)
u-----	Australasia [MARC geographic area code Library of Congress] (LCCP)
U	Benzon [Denmark] [Research code symbol]
U	Eased Up [Horse racing]
U	Eaton Laboratories, Inc. [Research code symbol]
U	Electric Tension [Symbol] [IUPAC]
u	Group Velocity [Symbol] (DEN)
U	Heat Transfer Coefficient (BARN)
U	Internal Energy [Symbol] [Thermodynamics]
U	International Unit [of enzyme activity] (DAVI)
U	Intrinsic Energy [Symbol] [Physics]
U	Mann-Whitney Rank Sum Statistic (STED)
u	Micro (IDOE)
u	Micron (DAVI)
U	Potential Difference [in Volts] (DMAA)
U	Quartermon Versor [Symbol of a function] [Mathematics] (ROG)
U	Shape Descriptor [U-turn, for example. The shape resembles the letter for which it is named]
U	Thermal Transmittance per Unit of Area [Heat transmission symbol]
U	Uafhaengige Parti [Independent Party] [Denmark Political party] (PPE)
U	Ubiquinone [Coenzyme Q] [Also, CoQ, Q, UQ] [Biochemistry]
u	Uebersetzen [Translate] [German]
U	Ugly Sky [Navigation]
U	Ugly Threatening Weather [Meteorology]
U	Ugutio [Huguccio] [Deceased, 1210] [Authority cited in pre-1607 legal work] (DSA)
U	Uhr [Clock] [German]
U	Ullage (AAG)
U	Ulna (STED)
U	Ultra High Frequency [Also, UHF] (DOAD)
U	Ultralente Insulin [Pharmacology] (DAVI)
U	Ultraphon & Supraphon [Record label] [Former Czechoslovakia]
U	Umpire [Baseball]
U	Unbalanced
U	Unburned [Ecology]
U	Uncertain (STED)
U	Uncirculated
U	Unclassified
U	Uncle [Phonetic alphabet] [Royal Navy World War I Pre-World War II] [World War II] (DSUE)
U	Uncle
U	Uncommon Species
U	Und [And] [German]
U	Undefined (IAA)
u	Undelete [Computer science] [Telecommunications]
U	Under
U	Underfloor (NASA)
u	Underfloor (NAKS)
U	Underwater [Missile launch environment symbol]
U	Unemployed Parent [Aid to Families with Dependent Children] (OICC)
U	Unemployment
U	Unerupted (MAE)
U	Unified
U	Unified Atomic Mass [Physics] (WDAA)
U	Unified Atomic Mass Unit [Nuclear energy] (IAA)
u	Unified Atomic Mass Unit (IDOE)
U	Uniform [Phonetic alphabet] [International] (DSUE)
U	Uniformly Labeled [Also, UL] [Compound, with radioisotope]
U	Union [or Unionist]
U	Union Association [Major league in baseball, 1884]
U	Unionist (WDAA)
U	Unionist Party [Northern Ireland] [Political party]
U	Union of Sets (IDOE)
U	Unit
U	United
U	United States Air Group [NYSE symbol] (SAG)
U	Unit of Measure (IAA)
U	Universal
U	Universal Set (IDOE)
U	Universal/Unrestricted [Film certificate] [British]
U	Universe (MHDB)
U	University
U	Unknown
U	Unlicensed (DA)
U	Unlimited Time [Broadcasting term]
U	Unnumbered Acknowledge [or Acknowledgement] [Telecommunications] (IAA)
U	Unoccupied
u	Unpaved Surface [Aviation] (DA)
U	Unpleasant
U	Unseated Rider [Horse racing]
U	Unsubscribe [Computer science] [Telecommunications]
U	Unsymmetrical
U	Unter [Among] [German]
U	Until (DA)
U	Untreated [Medicine]
U	Unwatched [With reference to a light] [Maps and charts]
U	Up [or Upper]
U	Update [Computer science]
U	Upjohn Co. [Research code symbol]
U	Upper (ROG)
U	Upper Bow [Music] (ROG)
U	Upper-Class Speech ["Non-U" designates the opposite]
U	Upper School [British]
u	Up (quark) [Atomic physics]
U	Upstage (WDMC)
U	Uracil [Biochemistry] (MAE)
U	Uranium [Chemical element]
U	Urban [District Council] [British]
U	Urban Association [Baseball]
U	Urethra (STED)
U	Urgent
U	Uridine [One-letter symbol; see Urd]
U	Uridylic Acid (STED)
U	Uridylic Acid [Biochemistry] (DB)
U	Urinal (ROG)
U	Urinary Concentration [Medicine] (STED)
U	Urinate [or Urine] [Medicine]
U	Urine (DAVI)
U	Urological Surgery [Medical specialty] (DHSM)
U	Urologist (DAVI)
U	Urology (DAVI)
U	Urschrift [Original, as of a document] [German military]
U	Uruguay [IYRU nationality code]
U	USAIR Group [NYSE symbol] (SPSG)
U	Use
U	Utah
U	Utah Reports [A publication] (DLA)
U	Utah State Library, Salt Lake City, UT [Library symbol Library of Congress] (LCLS)
U	Utendus [To Be Used] [Pharmacy]
U	Utility [Designation for all US military aircraft]
U	UTVA Aircraft Factory [Former Yugoslavia] [ICAO aircraft manufacturer identifier] (ICAO)
U	Uvula (STED)
U	U-Wave [on electrocardiogram] [Cardiology] (DAVI)
u	Velocity [Symbol]
U	You [Amateur radio shorthand] (WDAA)
U/1	One Finger Breadth below the Umbilicus [Obstetrics] (DAVI)
U²	Unclassified, Unlimited [DoD]
U/3	Upper Third [Referring to long bones] [Medicine] (DAVI)
U3A	University of the Third Age [British] (DET)
U24H	Twenty-Four-Hour Urine [Urology] (DAVI)
U-233	Uranium-233
U-234	Uranium-234
U-235	Uranium-235
U-236	Uranium-236
U-238	Uranium-238
UA	Ukrainian Soviet Socialist Republic [ISO two-letter standard code] (CNC)
UA	Ultra-Audible
UA	Umbilical Artery [Anatomy]
UA	Unable to Approve Arrival for the Time Specified [Aviation] (FAAC)
UA	Unaggregated (MAE)
UA	Unanesthetized [Physiology]
UA	Unassigned [Telecommunications] (IAA)
UA	Unauthorized Absence (MUGU)

UA...............	Unavailable
UA...............	Unbleached Arnold [*Paper*] (DGA)
UA...............	Unburned plus Ash [*Ecology*]
UA...............	Uncertain About (DAVI)
UA...............	Und Andere [*And Others*] [*German*]
UA...............	Under Age [*i.e., entitled neither to a daily rum ration nor money instead*] [*See also G, T*] [*Obsolete*] [*Navy*] [*British*]
U/A.............	Under Agreement [*Legal term*] (DLA)
UA...............	Understanding Aging (EA)
UA...............	Underwater Actuator
UA...............	Underwater Association for Scientific Research [*Margate, Kent, England*] [*Defunct*] (EAIO)
U/A.............	Underwriting Account [*Insurance*]
U/a.............	Underwriting Account (EBF)
UA...............	Unidad Alavesa [*Spain Political party*] (EY)
UA...............	Uniform Allowance [*Military*]
UA...............	Unionamerica Hldgs ADS [*NYSE symbol*] (TTSB)
UA...............	Unionamerica Holdings PLC [*NYSE symbol*] (SAG)
UA...............	Union Association [*Major league in baseball, 1884*]
UA...............	Union des Artistes [*Union of Artists*] [*Canada*]
UA...............	Unit Assets [*Army*]
UA...............	United (GAVI)
UA...............	United Air Lines, Inc. [*ICAO designator*]
ua...............	United Arab Republic [*Egypt*] [*MARC country of publication code Library of Congress*] (LCCP)
UA...............	United Artists Communications, Inc.
UA...............	United Association of Journeymen and Apprentices of the Plumbing and Pipe Fitting Industry of the United States and Canada (OICC)
UA...............	United Society of Artists [*British*] (BI)
UA...............	Unit First Appearance (SAA)
U/A.............	Unit of Account [*European Monetary Agreement*] (EY)
U$_a$...........	Unit of Activity (IDOE)
U/A.............	Units per Application (DNAB)
UA...............	University of Akron [*Ohio*] (PDAA)
UA...............	University of Alaska [*Anchorage, AK*]
UA...............	University of Arizona [*Tucson, AZ*]
UA...............	University of Auckland [*New Zealand*]
UA...............	Unnumbered Acknowledge [*or Acknowledgment*] [*Telecommunications*] (IEEE)
UA...............	Unstable Angina [*Medicine*]
UA...............	Until Advised (DA)
UA...............	Upper Arm
UA...............	Uranyl Ammonium Phosphate [*Inorganic chemistry*] (SAA)
UA...............	Urban Area (NTCM)
UA...............	Urbanized Area (OICC)
UA...............	Uric Acid
UA...............	Urinalysis [*Medicine*] (KSC)
UA...............	Urinary Basement Membrane Antigen [*Immunology*] (DAVI)
UA...............	Urine Aliquot (DB)
UA...............	Urniary Aldosterone [*Medicine*] (DB)
UA...............	Urocanic Acid [*Organic chemistry*] (AAMN)
UA...............	Urostomy Association [*British*] (DBA)
UA...............	User Agency
UA...............	User Agent [*Telecommunications*] (PCM)
UA...............	User Area [*Information storage*]
UA...............	Usque Ad [*As Far As*] [*Latin*] (ADA)
UA...............	Uterine Aspiration [*Medicine*]
UAA.............	Uas-One [*British ICAO designator*] (FAAC)
UAA.............	Undergarment Accessories Association (EA)
UAA.............	Uniform Adoption Act [*Proposed state law*]
UAA.............	Union des Avocats Arabes [*Arab Lawyers Union - ALU*] (EAIO)
UAA.............	United Action for Animals (EA)
UAA.............	United African Appeal (EA)
UAA.............	United American and Australasian Film Productions
UAA.............	United Arab Airlines
UAA.............	University Athletic Association (EA)
UAA.............	University Aviation Association (EA)
UAA.............	University of Alaska, Anchorage
UAA.............	Upper Advisory Area [*Aviation*] (DA)
UAA.............	Uracil Adenine Adenine [*Genetics*]
UAA.............	Urban Affairs Association (EA)
UAA.............	User Action Analyzer
UAA.............	Utility Arborist Association (EA)
UAAA	Alma-Ata [*Former USSR ICAO location identifier*] (ICLI)
UAAF	United Action Armed Forces [*A publication*]
UAAN	Uzunagach [*Former USSR ICAO location identifier*] (ICLI)
UAAPU........	Under Armor Auxiliary Power Unit [*US Army tanks*] (RDA)
UAAR	United Activists for Animal Rights (EA)
UAAS	Ukrainian Academy of Arts and Sciences in the US (EA)
UAAS	Union Africaine des Artistes de Spectacle [*Union of African Performing Artists - UAPA*] (EAIO)
UAAUSA........	Ukrainian Artists Association in USA (EA)
UAB	Underwriters Adjustment Bureau
UAB	Unemployment Assistance Board
UAB	University Appointments Board [*British*] (DAS)
UAB	University of Alabama in Birmingham
UAB	University of Alberta Biotron [*University of Alberta*] [*Research center*] (RCD)
UAB	Until Advised By (FAAC)
UABS	Union of American Biological Societies (BARN)
u-ac--..........	Ashmore and Cartier Islands [*MARC geographic area code Library of Congress*] (LCCP)
UAC	Umbilical Artery Catheter [*Neonatology*] (DAVI)
UAC	Underwriters Adjusting Company
UAC	Unified Arab Command (BJA)

UAC	Uniform Annual Cost
UAC	Uninterrupted Automatic Control
UAC	Union Army of Commemoration
UAC	United African Co.
UAC	United Air Charters [*Zimbabwe*] [*ICAO designator*] (FAAC)
UAC	United Aircraft Corp. [*Later, United Technologies Corp.*]
UAC	United American Croats
UAC	United Association of Coremakers [*A union*] [*British*]
UAC	Universal Airline Codes
UAC	Universal Area Code [*Bureau of Census*]
UAC	Universities Advisory Council
UAC	University Analytical Center [*University of Arizona*] [*Research center*] (RCD)
UAC	University of Alberta, Faculty of Library Science, Edmonton, AL, Canada [*OCLC symbol*] (OCLC)
UAC	Unusual Appearing Child [*Medicine*]
UAC	Upper Air Control (IAA)
UAC	Upper Area Control Center [*Aviation*]
UAC	Uracil Adenine Cytosine [*A triplet of bases coding for the amino acid, tyrosine*] (EES)
UAC	Uric Acid (DAVI)
UA/C	Uric Acid-Creatinine Ratio [*Physiology*] (MAH)
UAC	User Advisory Committee [*Environmental Protection Agency*] (GFGA)
UAC	Utah Administrative Code [*A publication*] (AAGC)
UAC	Utility Airplane Company [*Army*] (VNW)
UAC	Utility Airplane Council [*Defunct*] (EA)
UAC	Utility Assemble Communication Pool (IAA)
UAC	Utility Assemble Compool
UACA	Union Acceptance'A' [*NASDAQ symbol*] (TTSB)
UACA	Union Acceptance Corp. Class A [*NASDAQ symbol*] (SAG)
UACA	United American Contractors Association (EA)
UACANT.......	Union of Australian College Academics Northern Territory
UACASA......	Union of Australian College Academics South Australia
UACC	Universal Autograph Collectors Club (EA)
UACC	Upper Area Control Center [*Aviation*]
UACCDD	University Affiliated Cincinnati Center for Developmental Disorders [*University of Cincinnati*] [*Research center*] (RCD)
UACCI.........	United Association of Christian Counselors International (EA)
UACES	University Association for Contemporary European Studies [*British*]
UACL	United Aircraft of Canada Ltd.
UACMC.......	Union Arabe de Ciment et des Materiaux de Construction [*Arab Union for Cement and Building Materials - AUCBM*] (EAIO)
UACN	Unified Automated Communication Network
UACN	University of Alaska Computer Network [*Research center*] (RCD)
UACNPM.....	United American and Captive Nations Patriotic Movement (EA)
UACRL	United Aircraft Corp. Research Laboratory (KSC)
UACSC	United Aircraft Corporate Systems Center (KSC)
UACTA	United Against Cruelty to Animals [*British*] (DI)
UACTE	Universal Automatic Control and Test Equipment
UAD	Salinas, CA [*Location identifier FAA*] (FAAL)
UAD	Underwater Acoustic Decoupler
UAD	Undetermined Aerodynamic Disturbance (MCD)
UAD	Unit Assembly Drawing
UAD	Univex SRL [*Italy ICAO designator*] (FAAC)
UAD	Upper Advisory Route [*Aviation*] (DA)
UAD	Upper-Airway Disease (DAVI)
UAD	User Attribute Definition [*Computer science*] (IAA)
UADA	United Abalone Divers' Association [*Australia*]
UADBU.......	Unattended Automatic Dial Back Up [*Telecommunications*]
UADC	Universal Air Data Computer
UADP	Uniform Automated [*or Automatic*] Data Processing
UADPS........	Uniform Automated [*or Automatic*] Data Processing System
UADPS-ICP...	Uniform Automated [*or Automatic*] Data Processing System for Inventory Control Points [*Navy*]
UADPS/INAS...	Uniform Automated [*or Automatic*] Data Processing System/ Industrial Naval Air Station
UADPS-SP...	Uniform Automated [*or Automatic*] Data Processing System for Stock Points [*Navy*]
UADS	User Attribute Data Set [*Computer science*] (MDG)
UADV	University of Alberta Devonian Botanic Garden [*Canada*]
UADW	Universal Alliance of Diamond Workers [*See also AUOD*] [*Antwerp, Belgium*] (EAIO)
UAE.............	Unilateral Absence of Excretion [*Medicine*]
UAE.............	Uninterruptible Application Error [*Computer science*] (CDE)
UAE.............	United Arab Emirates [*ICAO designator*] (FAAC)
UAE.............	Unrecoverable Application Error [*Computer science*] (PCM)
UAE.............	User Agent Entity [*Telecommunications*] (OSI)
UAEDE........	Union des Associations Europeennes des Distributeurs d'Eau [*Union of European Associations of Water Suppliers*] [*Belgium*] (EAIO)
UAEE..........	Union des Associations Europeennes d'Etudiants [*Union of European Student Associations*]
UAEL..........	United Association of Equipment Leasing (NTPA)
UAEM..........	Union of Associations of European Meat Meal Producers [*See also UAPEFV*] [*Later, Eurpoean Renderers Association - EURA*] (EAIO)
UAEM..........	University Association for Emergency Medicine
UAES	Utah Agricultural Experiment Station [*Utah State University*] [*Research center*] (RCD)
UAF.............	Uganda Air Force (PDAA)
UAF.............	Ultimate Asbestos Fibril
UAF.............	Unit Authorization File
UAF.............	United Arab Emirates Air Force [*ICAO designator*] (FAAC)
UAF.............	Universal Active Filter (IAA)
UAF.............	University-Affiliated Facility
UAF.............	University of Alaska, Fairbanks

UAF............. Upper Atmospheric Facilities Program [*Washington, DC National Science Foundation*] (GRD)
UAFA .... Union of Arab Football Associations (EAIO)
UAFC .... Universal Air Freight Corp.
UAFF........... Frunze [*Former USSR ICAO location identifier*] (ICLI)
UAFMMEEC.. Union of Associations of Fish Meal Manufacturers in the EEC (EAIO)
UAF-MR...... University-Affiliated Facility for the Mentally Retarded
UAFRA......... Uniform Aircraft Financial Responsibility Act [*National Conference of Commissioners on Uniform State Laws*]
UAFSC .... Utilization Air Force Specialty Code
UAFS/T .... Universal Aircraft Flight Simulator/Trainer
UAFUR........ Urgent Amplified Failure of Unsatisfactory Report
UAG .... Uas-Two [*British ICAO designator*] (FAAC)
UAG .... Underwater Acoustic Group [*British*]
UAG .... Union of Anarchist Groups [*British*]
UAG .... United Auto Group [*NYSE symbol*] (SAG)
UAG .... Untersuchungen zur Altorientalischen Geschichte [*H. Winckler*] [*A publication*] (BJA)
UAG .... Upper Atmosphere Geophysics (KSC)
UAG .... Uracil Adenine Guanine [*Genetics*]
UAG .... User Advisory Group (RDA)
UAGA .... Uniform Anatomical Gift Act [*For organ donation*]
UAGSA........ University of Adelaide General Staff Association [*Australia*]
UAH .... Ua Huka [*Marquesas Islands*] [*Airport symbol*] (OAG)
UAH .... Union of Arab Historians (EA)
UAH .... United Amer Healthcare [*NYSE symbol*] (TTSB)
UAH .... United American Healthcare Corp. [*NYSE symbol*] (SPSG)
UAH .... University of Alabama in Huntsville
UAHC .... Union of American Hebrew Congregations (EA)
UAHRI......... University of Alabama in Huntsville Research Institute
UAHS .... Ulster Architectural Heritage Society
UAI............. Uni Air SA [*France ICAO designator*] (FAAC)
UAI............. Union Academique Internationale [*International Academic Union - IAU*] (EAIO)
UAI............. Union Astronomique Internationale [*International Astronomical Union - IAU*]
UAI............. Union des Associations Internationales [*Union of International Associations - UIA*] (EAIO)
UAI............. Universal Azimuth Indicator
UAI............. Urban Affairs Institute (EA)
UAI............. Uterine Activity Interval [*Obstetrics*]
UAICC .... Underwater Acoustic Interference Coordinating Committee [*Military*]
UAIDE .... Users of Automatic Information Display Equipment (EA)
UAII .... Chimkent [*Former USSR ICAO location identifier*] (ICLI)
UAIM .... United Andean Indian Mission [*Superseded by Ecuador Concerns Committee*]
UAIMS .... United Aircraft Information Management System
UAirSp........ United Air Specialists, Inc. [*Associated Press*] (SAG)
UAJ............. Uas-Three [*British ICAO designator*] (FAAC)
UAJ............. Union of Arab Jurists [*Baghdad, Iraq*] (EAIO)
UAJAPPFI .... United Association of Journeymen and Apprentices of the Plumbing and Pipe Fitting Industry of the U.S. and Canada (BARN)
UAJG .... Union d'Action des Jeunes de Guinee [*Guinean Union of Youth Action*]
UAK .... Kiev Aviation Plant [*Ukraine*] [*FAA designator*] (FAAC)
UAK .... Narssarssuaq [*Greenland*] [*Airport symbol*] (OAG)
U Akron ...... University of Akron (GAGS)
UAL............. UAL Corp. [*NYSE symbol*] (SPSG)
UAL............. Ukrainian American League (EA)
UAL............. Ultrasound-Assisted Lipoplasty [*Medicine*]
UAL............. Umbilical Artery Line [*Neonatology*] (DAVI)
UAL............. Unit Allowance List (SAA)
UAL............. Unit Area Loading (AAG)
UAL............. Unit Authorization List
UAL............. Unite, Action, Liberation [*Guadeloupe*] [*Political party*] (EY)
UAL............. Unite Arithmetique et Logique [*Arithmetic and Logic Unit - ALU*] [*French*]
UAL............. United Air Lines, Inc. [*ICAO designator*] (FAAC)
UAL............. Universal Airline Codes (MCD)
UAL............. Universal Assembly Language (IAA)
UAL............. University Associates, Ltd. (EFIS)
UAL............. Upper Acceptance Limit
UAL............. Urea-Ammonia Liquor
UAL............. User Adaptive Language
UAL............. User Agent Layer [*Telecommunications*] (OSI)
U Ala .... University of Alabama (GAGS)
U Ala (Birm)... University of Alabama at Birmingham (GAGS)
U Ala (Huntsville)... University of Alabama at Huntsville (GAGS)
U Alaska ...... University of Alaska (GAGS)
UALE........... Universala Artista Ligo de Esperantistoj [*Universal Artist League of Esperantists*] (EAIO)
UALI........... Unit Authorization List Item
UALI........... Universal Automatic LASER Interferometer (DNAB)
UALPrB .... UAL Corp. 12.25% Dep'B'Pfd [*NYSE symbol*] (TTSB)
UAM............ Ultrasonically Assisted Machining [*Manufacturing term*]
UAM............ Und Anderes Mehr [*And So Forth*] [*German*]
UAM............ Underwater-to-Air Missile [*Air Force*]
UAM............ Union Africaine et Malgache [*African and Malagasy Union*] [*Later, Common Afro-Malagasy Organization*]
UAM............ United American Mechanics (EA)
UAM............ United Asset Management Corp. [*NYSE symbol*] (SPSG)
UAM............ United Asset Mgmt [*NYSE symbol*] (TTSB)
UAM............ United States Medical Intelligence and Information Agency, Frederick, MD [*OCLC symbol*] (OCLC)
UAM............ Universidad Autonoma Metropolitana [*Mexico*] (CROSS)

UAM............ Unnormalized Aid Magnitude (SAA)
UAM............ Urban Airshed Model [*Environmental Protection Agency*] (GFGA)
UAMA .... United Arab Muslim Association [*Australia*]
UAMBD........ Union Africaine de Management de Banques pour le Developpement [*African Union of Development Bank Management*] [*Benin*] (EAIO)
UAMBD........ Union Africaine et Mauricienne de Banques pour le Developpement [*African and Mauritian Union of Banks for Development*] [*Benin*] (AF)
UAMC .... Utility Assemble Master Communication (IAA)
UAMC .... Utility Assemble Master Compool
UAMCMDS... Uniform Ambulatory Medical Case Minimum Data Set [*Department of Health and Human Services*] (GFGA)
UAMCT .... Union of Automobile, Motorcycle, and Cycle Technology
UAMH .... University of Alberta Microfungus Collection and Herbarium [*Canada*]
UAMR .... Union Association of Manufacturers' Representatives (EA)
UAMS .... Ukrainian Academy of Medical Sciences (EA)
UAMS .... Upper Atmosphere Mass Spectrometer
UAN .... Aviaton [*Ukraine*] [*FAA designator*] (FAAC)
UAN .... Unidentified Atmospheric Noise (DNAB)
UAN .... Unified Automatic Network [*Telecommunications*] (OA)
UAN .... United Animal Nations (EAIO)
UAN .... Urea-Ammonium Nitrate [*Fertilizer*]
UAN .... Uric Acid Nitrogen
UANAS .... Urea-Ammonium Nitrate Ammonium Sulfate [*Fertilizer*]
UANC .... United African National Congress
UANC .... United African National Council [*Zimbabwe*] [*Political party*] (PPW)
U & C .... Urethral and Cervical [*Medicine*]
U & C .... Usual and Customary
U & L .... Upper and Lower (MSA)
U & LC .... Uppercase and Lowercase [*i.e., capital and small letters*] [*Typography*]
U & M .... Utilization/Reutilization and Marketing [*DoD*]
U & O .... Use and Occupancy [*Real estate*]
U & P .... Uttering and Publishing [*Legal term*]
U & S .... Unified and Specified [*or Strategic*] Command (MCD)
UANM .... United African Nationalist Movement (EA)
UANM .... Universal African Nationalist Movement (EA)
UAO .... Unconventional Aerial Object
UAO .... Und Andere Orte [*And Elsewhere*] [*German*]
UAO .... Unexplained Aerial Object
UAO .... Unilateral Administrative Order
UAO .... Upper-Air Observation (SAA)
UAO .... Upper Airway Obstruction [*Medicine*] (DMAA)
UAOD .... United Ancient Order of Druids [*Freemasonry*] (ROG)
UAOO.......... Kzyl-Orda [*Former USSR ICAO location identifier*] (ICLI)
UAP .... UAP, Inc. [*Toronto Stock Exchange symbol*]
UAP .... Ua Pou [*Marquesas Islands*] [*Airport symbol*] (OAG)
UAP .... Ukraine Airtrack [*FAA designator*] (FAAC)
UAP .... Ulnar Anconeal Process
UAP .... Unabhaengige Arbeiterpartei [*Independent Labor Party*] [*Germany Political party*] (PPE)
UAP .... Unidentified Atmospheric Phenomena
UAP .... Union Africaine de Physique [*African Union of Physics - AUP*] (EAIO)
UAP .... Union of American Physicians [*Later, UAPD*] (EA)
UAP .... Unite Australia Party [*Political party*]
UAP .... United Aircraft Products, Inc. (EFIS)
UAP .... United Amateur Press (EA)
UAP .... United Australia Party [*Political party*]
UAP .... Universal Availability of Publications [*International Federation of Library Associations*]
UAP .... University-Affiliated Program
UAP .... Unmanned Airborne Position (MCD)
UAP .... Upper Air Project
UAP .... Upper Arlington Public Library, Upper Arlington, OH [*OCLC symbol*] (OCLC)
UAP .... Upper Atmosphere Phenomena (IAA)
UAP .... Urea-Ammonium Phosphate [*Organic chemistry*]
UAP .... User Area Profile
UAP .... Utility Amphibian Plane [*Navy*]
UAPA .... Union of African Performing Artists [*See also UAAS*] (EAIO)
UAPA .... United Amateur Press Association [*Later, UAP*] (EA)
UAPA .... United American Progress Association (EA)
UAPD .... Union of American Physicians and Dentists (EA)
UAPDU .... User Agent Protocol Data Unit [*Telecommunications*] (OSI)
UAPEFV ...... Union des Associations des Producteurs Europeens de Farine de Viande [*Union of Associations of European Meat Meal Producers UAEM*] [*Later, European Renderers Association - EURA*] (EAIO)
UAPPA .... Union of Air Pollution Prevention Associations (EAIO)
UAPRE......... University Association for Professional Radio Education [*Broadcast Education Association*] (NTCM)
UAPSP .... Utility Acid Precipitation Study Program [*Environmental science*] (COE)
UAPT .... United Association for the Protection of Trade [*British*]
UAQ .... San Juan [*Argentina*] [*Airport symbol*] (OAG)
UAQI .... Uniform Air Quality Index [*Environmental Protection Agency*] (GFGA)
UAR .... Underwater Acoustic Resistance
UAR .... Underwater Angle Receptacle
UAR .... Uni Air [*France ICAO designator*] (FAAC)
UAR .... Uniform Airman Record
UAR .... Unit Address Register
UAR .... United Arab Republic [*Egypt and Syria*] [*Obsolete*]
UAR .... Upper Air Route
UAR .... Upper Atmosphere Research
UAR .... Use as Required (MSA)

UARBC......... United Arab Republic Broadcasting Corp. (IAA)
UARC........... University Affiliated Research Centers (AAGC)
UARC........... Upper Atmospheric Research Collaboratory
UARCEE....... Union des Associations des Riziers de la CEE [*Union of Rice Associations of the EEC*] (ECED)
UARCO........ UARCO, Inc. [*Formerly, United Autographic Register Co.*]
UARDS........ Unexplained Acute Respiratory Distress Syndrome
UAREP........ Universities Associated for Research and Education in Pathology (EA)
UARG........... Utility Air Regulatory Group [*Environmental Protection Agency*] (GFGA)
UARI........... University of Alabama Research Institute (KSC)
U Ariz......... [*The*] University of Arizona (GAGS)
U Ark.......... University of Arkansas (GAGS)
UARL.......... United Aircraft Research Laboratories
UARP.......... Upper Atmospheric Research Program [*NASA*] [*Marine science*] (OSRA)
UARR.......... Uralsk [*Former USSR ICAO location identifier*] (ICLI)
UARRSI....... Universal Aerial Refueling Receptacle Slipaway Installation (MCD)
UARS.......... Underwater Acoustic Receiving System [*Navy*] (MCD)
UARS.......... Unmanned Aerial Reconnaissance System (DOMA)
UARS.......... Unmanned Arctic Research Submersible
UARS.......... Upper Atmosphere Research Satellite (MCD)
UART.......... Universal Asynchronous Receiver/Transmitter
U Arts........ University of the Arts (GAGS)
UARV.......... Unmanned Air Reconnaissance Vehicle (DOMA)
UARZ.......... University of Arizona (PDAA)
UARZ/COM... University of Arizona College of Medicine [*Tucson*]
UAS........... Uas-Four [*British ICAO designator*] (FAAC)
UAS........... Ulster Archaeological Society
UAS........... Uniform Accounting System (OICC)
UAS........... Union of African States
UAS........... Unit Approval System [*for approval of aircraft materials, parts, and appliances*] [*FAA*]
UAS........... Unit Assets by State [*Army*]
UAS........... United Arab States
UAS........... University Air Squadrons
UAS........... Unmanned Aerial [*or Aerospace*] Surveillance
UAS........... Unusual Aerial Sighting (ADA)
UAS........... Upper Air Space (WDAA)
UAS........... Upper Atmospheric Sounder
UAS........... Upstream Activating Sequence [*Genetics*]
UAS........... Upstream Activation Site [*Genetics*]
UAS........... Urea-Ammonium Sulfate [*Fertilizer*]
UAS........... Urgent Action Service International [*British Library*]
UASANSW ... University Academic Staff Association of New South Wales [*Australia*]
UASB.......... Upflow Anaerobic Sludge Blanket (EERA)
UASE.......... Union of Arab Stock Exchanges
UASI.......... United Air Specialists [*NASDAQ symbol*] (TTSB)
UASI.......... United Air Specialists, Inc. [*NASDAQ symbol*] (SAG)
UASL.......... User Agent Sublayer [*Telecommunications*] (OSI)
UASS.......... Unmanned Aerial Surveillance System (MCD)
UASSS........ Underwater Acoustic Sound Source System
UAST.......... Universal Association for Speech Tracing [*See also TPA*] (EAIO)
u-at--......... Australia [*MARC geographic area code Library of Congress*] (LCCP)
UAT........... Ultraviolet Acquisition Technique
UAT........... Unaligned Address Transfer [*Computer science*] (CIST)
UAT........... Under Armor Tow (MCD)
UAT........... Underway Acceptance Trials (MCD)
UAT........... Uniform Asymptotic Theory (IAA)
UAT........... Union Aeromaritime de Transport [*Privately-owned French airline*]
UAT........... Universal Air Transport [*British*] [*FAA designator*] (FAAC)
UAT........... Until Advised by the Tower [*Aviation*] (FAAC)
UAT........... Up as Tolerated [*Medicine*] (DAVI)
UAT........... Urban Arts Theatre (EA)
UAT........... User Acceptance Test (MCD)
UAT........... User Accounting Table [*Computer science*] (CIST)
UATA.......... Aralsk [*Former USSR ICAO location identifier*] (ICLI)
UATC.......... United Artists Theatre Circuit, Inc.
UATE.......... Universal Automatic Test Equipment
UATI.......... Union de Asociaciones Tecnicas Internacionales [*Union of International Engineering Organizations - UIEO*] [*Spanish*] (ASF)
UATI.......... Union des Associations Techniques Internationales [*Union of International Technical Associations - UITA*] (EAIO)
u-at-ne....... New South Wales [*MARC geographic area code Library of Congress*] (LCCP)
u-at-no....... Northern Territory [*Australia MARC geographic area code Library of Congress*] (LCCP)
UATP.......... Universal Air Travel Plan [*Commercial airlines credit system*]
u-at-qn....... Queensland [*MARC geographic area code Library of Congress*] (LCCP)
UATR.......... Chelkar [*Former USSR ICAO location identifier*] (ICLI)
u-at-sa....... South Australia [*MARC geographic area code Library of Congress*] (LCCP)
UATT.......... Aktyubinsk [*Former USSR ICAO location identifier*] (ICLI)
u-at-tm....... Tasmania [*MARC geographic area code Library of Congress*] (LCCP)
UATV.......... United Australian Television
u-at-vi....... Victoria [*MARC geographic area code Library of Congress*] (LCCP)
u-at-we....... Western Australia [*MARC geographic area code Library of Congress*] (LCCP)
UAU........... Underwater-to-Air-to-Underwater (IAA)
UAU........... Universities Athletics Union [*British*]
UAU........... Uracil Adenine Uracil [*A triplet of bases coding for the amino acid, tyrosine*] (EES)

UAU........... Uterine Activity Unit [*Medicine*] (DMAA)
UAUM......... Underwater-to-Air-to-Underwater Missile [*Air Force*]
UAUOC....... United American Ukrainian Organizations Committee (EA)
UAUOS........ United Association of Used Oil Services (NTPA)
UA/USA....... UNESCO Association/USA (EA)
UAuto......... Universal Automotive Industries, Inc. [*Associated Press*] (SAG)
UAV........... Ukrainian American Veterans (EA)
UAV........... Uninhabited Air Vehicle (WDAA)
UAV........... United Aviation Ltd. [*New Zealand*] [*ICAO designator*] (FAAC)
UAV........... University of the Andes [*Merida*] [*Venezuela*] [*Seismograph station code, US Geological Survey*] (SEIS)
UAV........... Unmanned Aerial [*or Air*] Vehicle (RDA)
UAVC.......... Univentricular Atrioventricular Connection [*Cardiology*] (DAVI)
UAV-CR...... Unmanned Aerial Vehicle-Close Range [*Military*]
UAV-SR...... Unmanned Aerial Vehicle - Short Range (DWSG)
UAW........... International Union, United Automobile, Aerospace, and Agricultural Implement Workers of America [*Also known as United Auto Workers*] (EA)
UAWB......... Universal Air Waybill [*Shipping*] (DS)
UAW-CAP... United Auto Workers Community Action Program (EA)
UAWFA....... United Auto Workers, Family Auxiliary (EA)
UAWIU........ United Allied Workers International Union (EA)
UAWNO....... Union of Australian Women National Office
UAW-V-CAP... United Auto Workers Voluntary Community Action Program
UAX........... Unit Automatic Exchange
UAZ........... East Hartford, CT [*Location identifier FAA*] (FAAL)
UAZ-EES..... University of Arizona-Engineering Experiment Station (PDAA)
UB............. Burma Airways Corp. [*Myanmar*] [*ICAO designator*] (ICDA)
UB............. Southall [*Postcode*] (ODBW)
Ub............. Ubertus de Bobio [*Flourished, 1214-37*] [*Authority cited in pre-1607 legal work*] (DSA)
UB............. Ultimobranchial [*Bodies*] [*Medicine*]
UB............. Ultimobrancial Body (STED)
UB............. Umno Baru [*New Umno*] [*Malaysia*] [*Political party*]
UB............. Unaccompanied Baggage (MCD)
UB............. Underwater Battery [*Navy*]
UB............. Undistributed Budget (MCD)
UB............. Unemployment Benefits [*Unemployment insurance*] (OICC)
UB............. Unicbank [*Unique Bank*] [*Hungary*]
UB............. Uniform Billing
UB............. UnionBanCal Corp. [*NYSE symbol*]
UB............. Union Bank [*British*] (ROG)
UB............. Unit Bond (SAA)
UB............. United Benefice
UB............. United Biscuits [*Commercial firm*] [*British*]
UB............. United Brands Co. (MHDW)
UB............. United Brethren in Christ
UB............. United Brotherhood [*Also written VC for secrecy*] [*Fenianism*] (ROG)
UB............. Unna's Boot (MEDA)
UB............. Unpaid Balance [*Business term*] (MHDB)
UB............. Upper Bench [*Legal*] [*British*] (ROG)
UB............. Upper Bound
UB............. Upper Brace (MCD)
UB............. Urea Briquettes [*Agronomy*]
UB............. Urinary Bladder (STED)
UB............. Usage Block (MSA)
UB............. User Board (MHDB)
UB............. Utica-Bend (SAA)
UB............. Utility Bridge (NASA)
UB1........... University of Connecticut, Stamford Branch, Stamford, CT [*OCLC symbol*] (OCLC)
UB2........... University of Connecticut, Hartford Branch, West Hartford, CT [*OCLC symbol*] (OCLC)
UB3........... University of Connecticut, Southeastern Branch, Groton, CT [*OCLC symbol*] (OCLC)
UB4........... University of Connecticut, MBA Library, Hartford, CT [*OCLC symbol*] (OCLC)
UB-92........ Uniform Billing Code of 1992
UBA........... Myanmar Airways [*ICAO designator*] (FAAC)
UBA........... Uberaba [*Brazil*] [*Airport symbol*] (OAG)
UBA........... Ulan Bator [*Mongolia*] [*Geomagnetic observatory code*]
UBA........... Ulusal Basin Ajansi [*News agency*] [*Turkey*] (MENA)
UBA........... Unblocking Acknowledge [*Telecommunications*] (TEL)
UBA........... Undenatured Bacterial Antigen
UBA........... Underwater Breathing Apparatus [*Navy*] (CAAL)
UBA........... Union of Burma Airways
UBA........... United Baltic Appeal (EA)
UBA........... United Bank for Africa Ltd.
UBA........... United Breweries of America (EA)
UBA........... Universal Ballet Academy [*Washington, DC*]
UBA........... Universal Beer Agar [*Brewery bacteria culture medium*]
UBAEC........ Union of Burma Atomic Energy Centre
UBAF.......... Union des Banques Arabes et Francaises [*Union of Arab and French Banks*] [*France*]
Ubal.......... Ubaldus [*Authority cited in pre-1607 legal work*] (DSA)
U Balt........ University of Baltimore (GAGS)
UBAN.......... Usbancorp, Inc. [*NASDAQ symbol*] (SAG)
UBARI......... Union of Burma Applied Research Institute
UBAT.......... Ultrasonic Bioassay Tank [*Aerospace*]
UBATS........ Ultrasonic Bioassay Tank System [*Aerospace*]
UBB........... Union Bank of Bavaria
UBB........... Union of Burma Bank (DS)
UBB........... United Braford Breeders (NTPA)
UBB........... Universal Building Block
UBBA.......... United Boys' Brigades of America [*Later, BGBA*] (EA)

UBBAWA United Beef Breeders' Association of Western Australia
UBBC Unsaturated (Vitamin) B_{12} Binding Capacity
Ub Bo Ubertus de Bobio [*Flourished, 1214-37*] (DSA)
UBBR University Bureaus of Business Research
UBC Ubiquitin-Conjugating [*Protein*]
UBC Unburned Carbon [*Fuel technology*]
UBC Undeb Bedyddwyr Cymru [*Baptist Union of Wales*] (EAIO)
UBC Uniform Broadband Channel [*Telecommunications*]
UBC Uniform Building Code (NRCH)
UBC United Black Christians (EA)
UBC United Bowhunters of Connecticut
UBC United Brotherhood of Carpenters and Joiners of America (EA)
UBC United Business Communications, Inc. [*Atlanta, GA*] [*Telecommunications*] (TSSD)
UBC Universal Bibliographic Control
UBC Universal Block Channel
UBC Universal Book Code (NITA)
UBC Universal Buffer Controller
UBC University of British Columbia [*Vancouver, BC*]
UBC University of British Columbia Library [*UTLAS symbol*]
UBC Unsaturated Binding Capacity (STED)
UBC Used Beverage Can
UBCA United Black Church Appeal (EA)
UBCD UnionBancorp, Inc. [*NASDAQ symbol*] (SAG)
UBcGS Church of Jesus Christ of Latter-Day Saints, Genealogical Society Library, Brigham City South Branch, Brigham City, UT [*Library symbol Library of Congress*] (LCLS)
UBCHEA United Board for Christian Higher Education in Asia (EA)
UBcI National Indian Training Center, Brigham City, UT [*Library symbol Library of Congress*] (LCLS)
UBCIM Universal Bibliographic Control and International MARC [*IFLA Core Program*]
UBCIO University of British Columbia Institute of Oceanography [*Canada*] (MSC)
UBCJ United Brotherhood of Carpenters and Joiners of America
UBCL Union of Black Clergy and Laity of the Episcopal Church [*Later, UBE*] (EA)
UBCLN University of British Columbia. Legal News [*A publication*] (DLA)
UBC Notes University of British Columbia. Legal Notes [*A publication*] (DLA)
UBCP United Bancorp Ohio [*NASDAQ symbol*] (SAG)
UBcT Thiokol Chemical Corp., Utah Division, Brigham City, UT [*Library symbol Library of Congress*] (LCLS)
UBCW United Brick and Clay Workers of America [*Later, ABCWIU*] (EA)
UBD Bureau of Land Management, Billings, MT [*OCLC symbol*] (OCLC)
UBD Union for Liberation and Democracy [*Suriname*] [*Political party*] (EY)
UBD Universal Business Directory for the Pacific Islands [*A publication*]
UBD Universiti Brunei Darussalam
UBD User Brain Damage [*Computer hacker terminology*] (NHD)
UBD Utility Binary Dump [*Computer science*]
UBDA Uniform Brain Death Act [*National Conference of Commissioners on Uniform State Laws*]
UBDC Urban Bikeway Design Collaborative (EA)
UBDd You Be Darned [*Bowdlerized version*] (DSUE)
Ub de Bo Ubertus de Bobio [*Flourished, 1214-37*] [*Authority cited in pre-1607 legal work*] (DSA)
UBDI Underwater Battery Director Indicator
UBDMA United Better Dress Manufacturers Association (EA)
UBE Union Bouddhique d'Europe [*Buddhist Union of Europe - BUE*] (EAIO)
UBE Union of Black Episcopalians [*Defunct*] (EA)
UBE Universal Bus Exercisor (NASA)
UBE Unsolicited Bulk Electronic Mail [*Computer science*] (IGQR)
UBEA United Business Education Association [*Later, NBEA*]
UBEC Union of Banana Exporting Countries (BUAC)
UBeGS Church of Jesus Christ of Latter-Day Saints, Genealogical Society Library, Beaver Branch, Beaver, UT [*Library symbol Library of Congress*] (LCLS)
UBF Underground Baggage Facility [*Aviation*] (DA)
UBF Union Bank of Finland
UBF Universal Boss Fitting
UBF Universal Buddhist Fellowship (EA)
UBF Unknown Black Female (DAVI)
UBF Upstream Binding Factor [*Genetics*]
UBF Uterine Blood Flow [*Medicine*] (MAE)
UBFA United Black Fund of America (EA)
UBFC Underwater Battery Fire Control [*Navy*]
UBFCS Underwater Battery Fire Control System [*Navy*]
UBG Limon [*Honduras*] [*Airport symbol*] (AD)
UBG Newberg, OR [*Location identifier FAA*] (FAAL)
UBG Ultimobranchial Glands [*Endocrinology*]
UBG Underground Building [*National Security Agency*]
UBG Urobilinogen [*Medicine*] (MAE)
UBHC Unburned Hydrocarbon [*Also, UHC*] [*Fuel technology*]
UBHR User Block Handling Routine [*Computer science*] (IBMDP)
UBI Buin [*Papua New Guinea*] [*Airport symbol*] (OAG)
UBI Ultraviolet Blood Irradiation
UBI Understanding British Industry [*An association*] (ODBW)
UBI Unibus Interface (IAA)
UBI Universal Battlefield Identification
UBI Unrelated Business Income (DICI)
UBIC Universal Bus Interface Controller (NASA)
UBIP Ubiquitous Immunopoietic Polypeptide [*Immunochemistry*]
UBIT Unrelated Business Income Tax
UBITA Upper Bound of Information Translation Amount (MHDI)
UBITRON Undulating Beam Interaction Electron Tube
UBJ Ube [*Japan*] [*Airport symbol*] (OAG)
UBJ Upper Ball Joint Suspension [*Automotive engineering*]
UBK Port Augusta [*South Australia*] [*Airport symbol*] (AD)
UBK Unbleached Kraft [*Pulp and paper processing*]
UBK U.S. Banknote (EFIS)
UBKA Ulster Bee Keepers' Association (BUAC)
UBKA Universitaetsbibliothek Karlsruhe [*Karlsruhe University Library*] [*Information retrieval*]
UBL Unbleached (MSA)
UBL Unblocking [*Telecommunications*] (TEL)
UBL Undifferentiated B-Cell Lymphoma [*Medicine*]
UBL Unit Basic Load [*Army*]
UBL United Beverages [*Vancouver Stock Exchange symbol*]
UBLA Uniform Bill of Lading Act [*Legal shorthand*] (LWAP)
UBLDP Union Belge et Luxembourgeoise de Droit Penal [*Belgian and Luxembourg Association of Penal Law*] (EAIO)
UBLSLJ University of Botswana, Lesotho, and Swaziland Law Journal [*A publication*] (DLA)
UBLU United Building Labourers' Union [*British*]
UBM Ultrasonic Bonding Machine
UBM Under-Bump Metallurgy (AAEL)
UBM Unit Bill of Material (MHDW)
UBM University of Bridgeport, Bridgeport, CT [*OCLC symbol*] (OCLC)
UBM Unknown Black Male (DAVI)
UBMT United Financial [*NASDAQ symbol*] (TTSB)
UBMT United Savings Bank FA [*Great Falls, MT*] [*NASDAQ symbol*] (NQ)
UBMTA Uniform Biological Material Transfer Agreement [*National Institutes of Health*]
UBN United Business Network [*United Business Communications, Inc.*] [*Atlanta, GA*] [*Telecommunications*] [*Defunct*] (TSSD)
UBN United States Bank Note [*Printer of U.S. postage stamps*] (BARN)
UBN Universal Broadband Network [*Telecommunications*]
UBNK Union Bank [*NASDAQ symbol*] (SPSG)
UBNKZ UnionBanCal 8.375% Dep 'A' Pfd [*NASDAQ symbol*] (TTSB)
UBNY United Bank Corp. of New York (EFIS)
UBO Uinta Basin Array [*Utah*] [*Seismograph station code, US Geological Survey Closed*] (SEIS)
UBO Uinta Basin Observatory
UBO Undetermined Brain Opacities [*Magnetic Resonance Imaging*] (CPH)
UBO Unemployment Benefit Office [*British*]
UBO Unidentified Bright Object
UBOA United Bus Owners of America (EA)
UBOD Ultimate Biological Oxygen Demand (COE)
U-BOOT Unterseeboot [*Submarine*] [*German*]
UBOT Unfavorable Balance of Trade (MHDW)
UBP Ubon Ratchathani [*Thailand*] [*Airport symbol*] (OAG)
UBP Ulusal Birlik Partisi [*National Unity Party*] [*Turkish Cyprus*] [*Political party*] (EY)
UBP Underwater Battery Plot [*Antisubmarine warfare*]
UBP Unit Beat Policing
UBP United Bahamian Party [*Political party*] (PPW)
UBP United Bermuda Party [*Political party*] (PPW)
UBP Upward Bound Programs [*Department of Labor*]
UBP Ureteral Back Pressure [*Medicine*] (MAE)
UBP Urstadt Biddle Properties [*NYSE symbol*] [*Formerly, HRE Properties*]
UBPC Utility Bill Performance Calculation (AAGC)
U-BPH Utah State Library Commission, Division of the Blind and Physically Handicapped,Salt Lake City, UT [*Library symbol Library of Congress*] (LCLS)
UBPLOT Underwater Battery Plotting Room [*Navy*] (NVT)
UBPR Uniform Bank Performance Report [*Federal Financial Institutions Examination Council*]
UB Pr Upper Bench Precedents Tempore Car. I [*A publication*] (DLA)
UBPVLS Uniform Boiler and Pressure Vessel Laws Society (EA)
UBR Uniform Business Rate [*Taxation*] [*British*]
UBR United Bison Resources [*Vancouver Stock Exchange symbol*]
UBR University Boat Race [*Cambridge and Oxford*] [*British*] (BARN)
UBR University of British Columbia Retrospective Conversion [*UTLAS symbol*]
UBR Unspecified Bit Rate [*Computer science*] (IGQR)
UBR Upper Burma Rulings [*India*] [*A publication*] (DLA)
UBRD Usage Based Requirements Determination [*Army*] (DOMA)
UBRF Upper Branchial Filament
U Bridgeport University of Bridgeport (GAGS)
UBS Columbus [*Mississippi*] [*Airport symbol*] (AD)
UBS Columbus, MS [*Location identifier FAA*] (FAAL)
UBS Uniform Bearing Stress
UBS Union Bank of Switzerland
UBS Union Broadcasting System [*Fictitious broadcasting organization in film "Network"*]
UBS Unit Backspace Character [*Computer science*]
UBS Unit-Based Scheme (AIE)
UBS United Bible Societies [*Stuttgart, Federal Republic of Germany*] (EA)
UBS United Broadcasting System [*Network in TV series "America 2-Night"*]
UBS United States Biological Survey [*US Government*] (EERA)
UBS Universal Builders Supply Co.
UBS University of British Columbia, School of Librarianship, Vancouver, BC, Canada [*OCLC symbol*] (OCLC)
UBS U.S. Bioscience [*AMEX symbol*] (TTSB)
UBS US Bioscience, Inc. [*AMEX symbol*] (SPSG)
UBSA United Business Schools Association [*Later, AICS*] (EA)
UBSC Union Bankshares Ltd. [*NASDAQ symbol*] (SAG)
UBSD Union of Bosnian Social Democrats [*Political party*] (BUAC)
UBSH Union Bankshares [*NASDAQ symbol*] (TTSB)

UBSH	Union Bankshares Corp. [*NASDAQ symbol*] (SAG)
UBS	United Bankshares [*NASDAQ symbol*] (TTSB)
UBSI	United Bankshares, Inc. [*NASDAQ symbol*] (NQ)
UBSO	Uinta Basin Seismological Observatory
UBST	Unbonded Spool Type (DNAB)
UBS.WS	U.S. Bioscience Wrrt [*AMEX symbol*] (TTSB)
UBT	Ubatuba [*Brazil*] [*Airport symbol Obsolete*] (OAG)
UBT	Universal Boattail Thor [*NASA*]
UBT	Universal Book Tester [*Measures performance of binding*]
UB/TIB	Universitatsbibliothek Hannover und Technische Informationsbibliothek [*University Library of Hannover and Technical Information Library*] [*Information service or system*] (IID)
UBTM	United Bellows Tankage Module
UBV	Ultraviolet-Blue-Visual [*Photometric system*]
UBVR	Ultraviolet-Blue-Visible-Red [*Photometry*]
UBW	Kuparuk, AK [*Location identifier FAA*] (FAAL)
UBW	Unbewusste [*Unconscious Mind*] [*Psychology*]
UBW	University of Connecticut, Waterbury Branch, Waterbury, CT [*OCLC symbol*] (OCLC)
UBWPS	United Bargemen and Watermen's Protective Society [*A union*] [*British*]
UBWV	United Bankshares, Inc. [*Associated Press*] (SAG)
UBX	Cuba, MO [*Location identifier FAA*] (FAAL)
UBZ	Upper Border Zone [*Geology*]
UC	UC Television Network Corp. [*Associated Press*] (SAG)
UC	Ulcerative Colitis [*Medicine*]
UC	Uldall Catheter [*Medicine*] (MEDA)
UC	Ultimate Collider [*Particle accelerator*]
UC	Ultracentrifugal [*Biochemistry*] (MAE)
UC	Umbilical Cable [*or Connector*]
UC	Umbilical Cable Unit Cooler [*Aerospace*] (AAG)
UC	Umbilical Connector
UC	Umbilical Cord (DB)
UC	Unaccompanied Child [*Airline notation*]
UC	Una Corda [*With one string or with the soft pedal*] [*Music*]
UC	Unchanged (MAE)
UC	Uncirculated Coins [*Numismatics*]
UC	Unclassifiable [*Laboratory science*] (DAVI)
U/C	Unclassified
UC	Unclipping [*Medicine*]
UC	Uncut Edges [*Bookbinding*]
UC	Undeducted Contributions
U/C	Under Carriage (MCD)
UC	Under Charge
UC	Under Construction
U/C	Under Conversion (NATG)
U/C	Under Cover (ADA)
U/C	Under Current (NASA)
UC	Undercut [*Technical drawings*]
UC	Underfashion Club (EA)
UC	Underwater Communications (MCD)
UCAL	Undifferentiated Carcinoma [*Oncology*]
UC	Unemployment Compensation [*Public human service program*] (PHSD)
UC	Unfair Competition (MHDW)
UC	Unichannel
Uc	Uniform, Coarse-Grained [*Soil*]
UC	Union Caledonienne [*Caledonian Union*] [*Political party*] (PPW)
UC	Union Camerounaise [*Cameroonese Union*] [*Political party*]
UC	Union Constitutionelle [*Constitutional Union*] [*Morocco*] [*Political party*] (PPW)
UC	Unitarian Church [*Australia*]
UC	Unit Call [*Also known as CCS*] [*Telecommunications*]
UC	Unit Chairman
UC	Unit Clerk
UC	Unit Cooler
UC	Unit Cost
UC	Unit Count (AFIT)
UC	United Canada Insurance Co.
UC	United Christian Party [*Australia Political party*]
UC	United Companies Financial [*NYSE symbol*] (SAG)
uc	United States Miscellaneous Caribbean Islands [*MARC country of publication code Library of Congress*] (LCCP)
UC	Unity College [*London, England*]
UC	University College
UC	University Colleges [*Public-performance tariff class*] [*British*]
UC	University of California
UC	University of Chicago [*Illinois*] (PDAA)
UC	University of Cincinnati [*Ohio*]
UC	Unloader Coil (IAA)
UC	Unoperated Control
UC	Unsatisfactory Condition (NASA)
uc	Unsatisfactory Condition (NAKS)
UC	Untreated Controls [*Medicine*]
uc	Up Center (WDMC)
UC	Up Converter
UC	Uplink Command
UC	Upper Canada
UC	Uppercase [*Typography*] (ADA)
UC	Upper Characters (IAA)
UC	Upper Control (IAA)
UC	Upper Cylinder
UC	Upstage Centre (WDAA)
UC	Uranium Canada Ltd.
UC	Uranium Carbide [*Inorganic chemistry*] (OA)
UC	Urban Contemporary (WDMC)
UC	Urban Council [*British*] (BARN)
UC	Urbis Conditae [*From the Foundation of the City; that is, of Rome*] [*Latin*]
UC	Urea Clearance [*Clinical chemistry*]
UC	Urethral Catheterization [*Medicine*] (MAE)
UC	Urinary Catheter [*Medicine*]
U/C	Urine Culture [*Clinical chemistry*] (MAE)
UC	Usable Control
UC	Using Command
UC	Usual Health-Care [*Medicine*]
UC	Uterine Contraction [*Obstetrics*] (AAMN)
UC	Utility Car [*British*]
UC	Utility Cargo
UC	Utility Corridor
UC	Utilization Control
UC1	Underwater Control Rating 1st Class [*British military*] (DMA)
UC2	Underwater Control Rating 2nd Class [*British military*] (DMA)
UCA	Champlain Enterprises, Inc. [*ICAO designator*] (FAAC)
UCA	Rome-Utica [*New York*] [*Airport symbol*] (AD)
UCA	Uganda Cooperative Alliance (BUAC)
UCA	Ulster Chemists Association (BUAC)
UCA	Ulster Curers Association (BUAC)
UCA	Undefinitized Contractual Actions (DOMA)
UCA	Under Color Addition [*Printing technology*]
UCA	Uniform Chart of Accounts [*DoD*]
UCA	United Carters' Association [*A union*] [*British*]
UCA	United Chemists' Association Ltd. [*British*] (BI)
UCA	United Collision [*Vancouver Stock Exchange symbol*]
UCA	United Congressional Appeal (EA)
UCA	United Council on Alcohol and Other Drugs (BUAC)
UCA	United States Court of Appeals for the District of Columbia, Judges Library, Washington, DC [*OCLC symbol*] (OCLC)
UCA	Unitized Component Assembly [*Aerospace*]
UCA	Units Consistency Analyzer [*Computer science*]
UCA	Universal Calibration Adapter
UCA	Upper Control Area (NATG)
UCA	Uracil Cytosine Adenine [*A triplet of bases coding for the amino acid, serine*] (EES)
UCA	User Computed Address [*Computer science*] (HGAA)
UCA	Utah Code, Annotated [*A publication*] (DLA)
UCA	Utica [*New York*] [*Airport symbol*] (OAG)
UCA	Utility Communications Architecture [*Standardized computer program for utility companies*] (PS)
UCAA	Upstate Collegiate Athletic Association (PSS)
UCABEL	Union Catalogue of Art Books in Edinburgh Libraries (TELE)
UCACE	Universities Council for Adult and Continuing Education (BUAC)
UCACEP	United Council of Associations of Civil Employees of Pakistan
UCAE	United Carters' Association of England [*A union*]
UCAE	Universities Council for Adult Education [*British*]
UCAID	University Corp. for Advanced Internet Development
UCAL	Universal Cable Adapter (IAA)
U Cal (Berkeley)	University of California at Berkeley (GAGS)
U Cal (Davis)	University of California at Davis (GAGS)
U Cal (Irvine)	University of California at Irvine (GAGS)
U Cal (Riverside)	University of California at Riverside (GAGS)
U Cal (San Diego)	University of California at San Diego (GAGS)
U Cal (San Francisco)	University of California at San Francisco (GAGS)
U Cal (Santa Barbara)	University of California at Santa Barbara (GAGS)
U Cal (Santa Cruz)	University of California at Santa Cruz (GAGS)
UCAM	United Campuses to Prevent Nuclear War (EA)
UCAN	Union of Catholic Asian News [*Kwun Tong, Hong Kong*] (EAIO)
UCAN	Utilities Conservation Action Now [*Federal Energy Administration*]
UCAN	Utility Consumers Action Network
UC & P	Uniform Customs and Practice for Documentary Credits [*International Chamber of Commerce*] [*A publication*] (DS)
UCAP	United Coconut Association of the Philippines (BUAC)
UCapF	United Capital Funding Partnership LP [*Associated Press*] (SAG)
UC App	Upper Canada Appeal Reports [*A publication*] (DLA)
UC App (Can)	Upper Canada Appeal Reports [*A publication*] (DLA)
UC App Rep	Upper Canada Appeal Reports [*A publication*] (DLA)
UCar	UCar International [*Associated Press*] (SAG)
UCAR	Union Carbide Corp. (EFIS)
UCAR	United Carolina Bancsh [*NASDAQ symbol*] (TTSB)
UCAR	United Carolina Bancshares Corp. [*NASDAQ symbol*] (NQ)
UCAR	University Corp. for Atmospheric Research (EA)
UCAR	Utilities Cost Analysis Report
UCarb	Union Carbide Corp. [*Associated Press*] (SAG)
UCarBk	United Carolina Bancshares Corp. [*Associated Press*] (SAG)
UCARCIDE	Union Carbide Biocide [*Trademark*] [*Union Carbide Corp.*]
UCARS	Uniform Cost Accounting and Reporting System
UCAS	Uniform Cost Accounting Standards (MCD)
UCAS	Union of Central African States (EY)
UCAS	Universities and Colleges Admissions Service [*British*] (DET)
UCATA	Uniform Contribution Among Tortfeasors Act [*National Conference of Commissioners on Uniform State Laws*]
UCATT	Union of Construction, Allied Trades, and Technicians [*British*]
UCAV	Uninhabited Combat Air Vehicle
UCaV	Urinary Calcium Excretion [*Laboratory science*] (DAVI)
UCAVJ	Union Continentale Africaine des Villes Jumelees [*Continental African Union of Twin Cities*]
UCB	Canadian Union Catalogue of Books [*National Library of Canada*] [*Information service or system*] (IID)
UCB	UCB [*Belgium*] [*Research code symbol*]

UCB .... UCB Chemie [Germany] [Research code symbol]
UCB .... Uganda Commercial Bank (BUAC)
UCB .... Unconjugated Bilirubin
UCB .... Union Chimique Belge [Belgium]
UCB .... Unit Control Block (MCD)
UCB .... United California Bank [Los Angeles] (IIA)
UCB .... United Cambridge Mines [Vancouver Stock Exchange symbol]
UCB .... United Commercial Bank Ltd. [Bangladesh]
UCB .... Universal Character Buffer
UCB .... University College Buckingham [British] (AIE)
UCB .... University of California, Berkeley
UCB .... University of California, Berkeley School of Library and Information Science, Berkeley, CA [OCLC symbol] (OCLC)
ucb .... Unless Caused by [Insurance] (BARN)
UCBC .... Parti de l'Unite et de la Communaute Belgo-Congolaise [Political party]
UCBEU .... Uniao Cultural Brasil-Estados Unidos [Brazil-United States Cultural Union] [Brazil] (EAIO)
UCBLL .... Language Laboratory [Research center] (RCD)
UCBR .... Unconjugated Bilirubin (MAE)
UCBSA .... United Cricket Board of South Africa (BUAC)
UCBSRP .... University of California, Berkeley, Sulfur Recovery Process
UCBT .... Union pour le Commerce des Bois Tropicaux dans la CEE [Association for Trade in Tropical Woods in the EEC] (ECED)
UCBT .... Universal Circuit Board Tester
UCBTAB .... User Control Block Table [Computer science] (MHDI)
UCBWM .... United Church Board for World Ministries (EA)
UCC .... Computing Center [University of Rochester] [Research center] (RCD)
UCC .... Uccle [Belgium] [Seismograph station code, US Geological Survey] (SEIS)
UCC .... Ulster Countryside Committee [England] (BUAC)
UCC .... Ultra Clean Coal (ERG)
UCC .... Umbilical Checkout Cable
UCC .... Unadjusted Contractual Changes
UCC .... Unified Classification Code (NITA)
UCC .... Uniform Classification Committee [Later, NRFC] (EA)
UCC .... Uniform Code Council (EA)
UCC .... Uniform Commercial Code [National Conference of Commissioners on Uniform State Laws]
UCC .... Uniform Credit Code
UCC .... Union Camp [NYSE symbol] (TTSB)
UCC .... Union Camp Corp. [NYSE symbol] (SPSG)
UCC .... Union Carbide Canada Ltd. [Toronto Stock Exchange symbol]
UCC .... Union Carbide Corp. (KSC)
UCC .... United Cancer Council (EA)
UCC .... United Church of Christ
UCC .... United Computer Corporation (NITA)
UCC .... Universal Checkout Console (NASA)
UCC .... Universal Checkout Console (NAKS)
UCC .... Universal Copyright Convention
UCC .... University College, Cardiff [Wales]
UCC .... University College Computer [London, England] (DEN)
UCC .... University College, Cork [Ireland]
UCC .... University Computer Center [New Mexico State University] [Research center] (RCD)
UCC .... University Computer Center [University of Minnesota] [Research center] (RCD)
UCC .... University Computer Center [North Dakota State University] [Research center] (RCD)
UCC .... University Computer Center [San Diego State University] [Research center] (RCD)
UCC .... University Computer Center [Oklahoma State University] [Research center] (RCD)
UCC .... University Computing Co. [International computer bureau]
UCC .... University of Corpus Christi [Texas] [Closed, 1973]
UCC .... Upper Canada College
UCC .... Upper Control Center (NATG)
UCC .... Uracil Cytosine Cytosine [A triplet of bases coding for the amino acid, serine] (EES)
UCC .... Urgent Care Center [Medicine]
UCC .... Uruguay Collectors Club (EA)
UCC .... Utility Control Console
UCC .... Yucca Flat, NV [Location identifier FAA] (FAAL)
UCCA .... Ukrainian Congress Committee of America (EA)
UCCA .... Universities Central Council on Admission [British]
UCCATS .... Urban Combat Computer-Assisted Training System
UCCBRA .... University College Cardiff Bee Research Association (BUAC)
UCCC .... Computing Center [University of Cincinnati] [Research center] (RCD)
UCCC .... Ukrainian Civic Congress of the Crimea (BUAC)
UCCC .... Uniform Consumer Credit Code [National Conference of Commissioners on Uniform State Laws]
UCCC .... Unmarried-Catholics Correspondence Club (EA)
UCCCCWCS... United Church of Christ Coordinating Center for Women in Church and Society (EA)
UCCCRJ .... United Church of Christ Commission for Racial Justice (EA)
UCCE .... Union des Capitales de la Communaute Europeenne [Union of Capitals of the European Community]
UCCE .... Universal Craftsmen Council of Engineers (EA)
UCCE .... Utah Council for Computers in Education (EDAC)
UCC/EMC ..... Union Carbide and Carbon/Electric Metallurgical Co. (AAG)
UCCES .... Uniform Child Custody Evaluation System [Test] (TMMY)
UCCET .... Union of Chambers of Commerce, Industry, Maritime Commerce and Commodity Exchanges of Turkey (BUAC)
UCCF .... United Campus Christian Fellowship [Defunct]
UC Ch .... Upper Canada Chancery Reports [1849-82] [A publication] (DLA)

UC Cham ..... Upper Canada Chambers Reports [A publication] (DLA)
UC Chamb .... Upper Canada Chambers Reports [1846-52] [A publication] (DLA)
UC Cham (Can)... Upper Canada Chambers Reports [1846-52] [A publication] (DLA)
UC Chan ...... Upper Canada Chancery Reports [A publication] (DLA)
UC Ch (Can)... Upper Canada Chancery Reports [A publication] (DLA)
UC Ch Rep ... Upper Canada Chancery Reports [1849-82] [A publication] (DLA)
UCCIS .... USAREUR [United States Army, Europe] Command and Control Information System
UCCJA .... Uniform Child Custody Jurisdiction Act (EDAC)
UCC Law Letter... Uniform Commercial Code Law Letter [A publication] (DLA)
UCCL/GC...... United Church Coalition for Lesbian/Gay Concerns (EA)
UCC-ND....... Union Carbide Corp. - Nuclear Division (MCD)
UCCP .... Upper Canada Common Pleas Reports [A publication] (DLA)
UCCP (Can)... Upper Canada Common Pleas Reports [A publication] (DLA)
UCCPD......... Upper Canada Common Pleas Division Reports [Ontario] [A publication] (DLA)
UCCPL .... United Citizens Coastal Protection League (EA)
UCCR .... Upper Canada Court Records [Report of Ontario Bureau of Archives] [A publication] (DLA)
UCCRC........ University of Chicago Cancer Research Center [Research center] (RCD)
UCC Rep Serv... Uniform Commercial Code Reporting Service [A publication] (DLA)
UCCRL .... Union Carbide and Carbon Research Laboratories (AAG)
UCCRP........ Union College Character Research Project (EA)
UCCRS........ Underwater Coded Command Release System
UCCS .... Ultrasonic Chemical Cleaning System
UCCS .... United Cabinet and Chairmakers' Society [A union] [British]
UCCS .... Universal Camera Control System
UCCS .... University Classification and Compensation System
U-CD .... Companion Dog [Prefix]
UCD .... Unchanged Charge Distribution [Fission]
UCD .... Uniform Call Distribution [Telephone system]
UCD .... Union de Centro Democratico [Union of the Democratic Center] [Spain Political party] (PPE)
UCD .... United Canadian Shares Ltd. [Toronto Stock Exchange symbol]
UCD .... Universal Classification Decimal (ECII)
UCD .... University College, Dublin [Ireland]
UCD .... University of California, Davis
UCD .... Upper Critical Depth [Oceanography] (WDAA)
UCd .... Urine Cadmium Level
UCD .... Urine Collection Device [NASA] (MCD)
UCD .... Usual Childhood Diseases [Medicine]
UCD .... Utah Construction and Development Co., Inc. (AAGC)
UCDA.......... University and College Designers Association (EA)
UC Davis L Rev... University of California (Davis). Law Review [A publication] (DLA)
UCDC.......... Ulster Constitution Defence Committee [Northern Ireland]
UCDC.......... Uniado do Centro Democrata Cristao [Union of the Christian Democratic Center] [Portugal Political party] (PPE)
UCDCC........ Union Centro y Democratica Cristiana de Catalunya [Union of the Center and Christian Democrats of Catalonia] [Spain Political party] (PPE)
UCdE.......... Emery County Library, Castle Dale, UT [Library symbol Library of Congress] (LCLS)
UCDEC........ Union Chretienne Democrate d'Europe Centrale [Christian Democratic Union of Central Europe - CDUCE] (EAIO)
UCdH.......... Emery County High School, Castle Dale, UT [Library symbol Library of Congress] (LCLS)
UCDL .... Union Chretienne Democrate Libanaise [Lebanese Christian Democratic Union] [Political party] (PPW)
UCDMC .... University of California at Davis, Medical Center (DAVI)
UCDP.......... Ukrainian Christian Democratic Party [Political party] (BUAC)
UCDP.......... Uncorrected Data Processor
UCDP.......... Uncorrelated Data Processor (IAA)
UCDS .... Uniform Clinical Data Set
UCDS .... Unit Chemical Defense Study (MCD)
UCDWN....... Until Cleared Down [Aviation] (FAAC)
UCDWR....... University of California Division of War Research
U-CDX........ Companion Dog Excellent [Prefix]
UCE........... Union Canadienne des Etudiants
UCE........... Union Carbide Electronics (IAA)
UCE........... Unit Checkout Equipment
UCE........... Unit Control Error (IAA)
UCE........... Unit Correction Entry
UCE........... University of Central England
UCE........... Unsolicited Commercial Electronic Mail [Computer science] (IGQR)
UCE........... Unsolicited Commercial E-Mail [Computer science]
UCE........... Upstream Control Element [Genetics]
UCE........... Ural Commodity Exchange [Russian Federation] (EY)
UCEA .... Uniform Conservation Easement Act [National Conference of Commissioners on Uniform State Laws]
UCEA .... Uniform Criminal Extradition Act [National Conference of Commissioners on Uniform State Laws]
UCEA .... Union Chimique Elf-Aquitaine [France]
UCEA .... University Continuing Education Association (NTPA)
UCEA .... University Council for Educational Administration (EA)
UCEA .... Used Clothing Exporters Association of America (EA)
UCE & A ...... Upper Canada Error and Appeal Reports [1846-66] [A publication] (DLA)
UCEC .... Utility Commission Engineers Conference
UCeDe .... Union del Centro Democratico [Union of the Democratic Center] [Argentina Political party] (EY)

UCEMT.........	University Consortium in Educational Media and Technology [*Later, UCIDT*]
U Cent Ark...	University of Central Arkansas (GAGS)
U Cent Okla...	University of Central Oklahoma (GAGS)
UCEP..........	Upper Critical End Points [*Supercritical extraction*]
UCEPCEE	Union du Commerce des Engrais des Pays de la Communaute Economique Europeenne [*Union of the Fertilizer Trade of Countries of the EEC*] [*Hasselt, Belgium*] (EAIO)
UCER	Unit Cost Exception Report [*Army*]
UCER	University Center for Energy Research [*Oklahoma State University*] [*Research center*] (RCD)
UC Err & App...	Upper Canada Error and Appeal Reports [*1846-66*] [*A publication*] (DLA)
UC Err & App (Can)...	Upper Canada Error and Appeal Reports [*1846-66*] [*A publication*] (DLA)
UCES	University Center for Environmental Studies [*Virginia Polytechnic Institute and State University*] [*Research center*] (RCD)
UCET..........	Universities Council for the Education of Teachers (AIE)
U Ceylon LR...	University of Ceylon. Law Review [*A publication*] (DLA)
UCF.............	Ulster Cancer Foundation [*Northern Ireland*] (EAIO)
UCF.............	Uniform Contract Format
UCF.............	Union Circulation File [*Library science*] (TELE)
UCF.............	Union Culturelle Francais [*French Cultural Union*]
UCF.............	Unit Control File [*Air Force*]
UCF.............	United Cat Federation (EA)
UCF.............	United Cooperative Farmers, Inc.
UCF.............	United Counties Farmers Ltd. (BUAC)
UCF.............	Universal Conduction Fluctuations [*Electronics*] (AAEL)
UCF.............	University of Central Florida [*Orlando, FL*]
UCF.............	Utility Control Facility
UCFA	Uniform Comparative Fault Act [*National Conference of Commissioners on Uniform State Laws*]
UCFA	Union pour la Communaute Franco-Africaine [*Union for the Franco-African Community*] [*Niger*]
UCFAC	United Council of Filipino Associations in Canada
UCFC	United Community Funds and Councils of America [*Later, UWA*] (EA)
UCFC	United Companies Financial Corp. [*NASDAQ symbol*] (SAG)
UCFC	United Cos. Financial [*NASDAQ symbol*] (TTSB)
UCFCMHPH...	Union Centrafricaine de la Fraternite Chretienne des Malades et Handicapes (EAIO)
UCFCP	United Cos. Fin'l 6.75%'PRIDES' [*NASDAQ symbol*] (TTSB)
UCFE..........	Unemployment Compensation, Federal Employees
UCFM..........	United Christian Fellowship Ministry [*Australia*]
UCFML.........	Union des Communistes de France Marxiste-Leniniste [*Marxist-Leninist Union of Communists of France*] [*Political party*] (PPW)
UCFRU........	Utah Cooperative Fishery Research Unit [*Utah State University*] [*Research center*] (RCD)
UCG	Ultrasonic Cardiography [*Medicine*] (DMAA)
UCG	Ultrasound Cardiogram (IAA)
UCG	Underground Coal Gasification
UCG	Unidirectional Categorical Grammar
UCG	University College Galway [*Ireland*]
UCG	Uracil Cytosine Guanine [*A triplet of bases coding for the amino acid, serine*] (EES)
UCG	Urinary Chorionic Gonadotrophin [*Endocrinology*]
UCGA	University Center in Georgia, Inc. [*Library network*]
UCGF	Undergraduate Computer Graphics Facility [*Stevens Institute of Technology*] [*Research center*] (RCD)
UCGIS........	University Consortium for Geographic Information Science
UCH	University College Hospital [*British*] (DI)
UCH	University of Connecticut, Health Center Library, Farmington, CT [*OCLC symbol*] (OCLC)
UCHCIS.......	Urban Comprehensive Health Care Information System (PDAA)
UCHD..........	Usual Childhood Diseases [*Medicine*]
UCHF	Uncoupled Hartree-Fock [*Physical chemistry*]
UCHI	Usual Childhood Illnesses (DAVI)
U Chicago....	[*The*] University of Chicago (GAGS)
UCHILS.......	University of Chicago Law School (DLA)
UCHM..........	Uniroyal Chemical [*NASDAQ symbol*] (TTSB)
UCHM..........	Uniroyal Chemical Corp. [*NASDAQ symbol*] (SAG)
UCHS..........	Uniting Church Historical Society [*Australia*]
UCHSC........	University of Colorado Health Sciences Center [*Denver*]
UCI.............	Imperial Chemical Industries [*British*]
UCI.............	Ultrasonic Contact Impedance [*Factory automation*] (BTTJ)
UCI.............	Union Cycliste Internationale [*International Cycling Union*] [*Switzerland*] (EA)
UCI.............	Unit Construction Index
UCI.............	United Charity Institutions of Jerusalem (EA)
UCI.............	Universite Cooperative Internationale [*International Cooperative University*]
UCI.............	University of California at Irvine
UCI.............	Updated Coordinating Instructions (DOMA)
UCI.............	Urethral Catheter in [*Medicine*] (CPH)
UCI.............	Urinary Catheter In [*or Input*] [*Medicine*]
UCI.............	User Class Identifier (NITA)
UCI.............	User-Communication Interface [*Telecommunications*]
UCI.............	Usual Childhood Illnesses (DAVI)
UCI.............	Utility Card Input
UCI.............	Utility Communicators International (EA)
UCIA	UCI Medical Affiliates [*NASDAQ symbol*] (TTSB)
UCIA	UCI Medical Affiliates, Inc. [*NASDAQ symbol*] (SAG)
UCIA	Union Carbide Corp. (EFIS)
UCIB	USAFE Command Intelligence Brief (MCD)
UCIC	Universal Counter Integrated Circuit [*Telecommunications*] (CIST)
UCID	Independent Democratic Union of Cape Verde [*Political party*] (PD)
UCID	User Control Interface Device [*Army*]
UCIDT	University Consortium for Instructional Development and Technology (EA)
UCIIM	Unione Cattolica Italiana Insegnanti Medi
UCIL...........	Uranium Corp. of India (BUAC)
UCIMC	University of California at Irvine, Medical Center (DAVI)
UCIMed........	UCI Medical Affiliates, Inc. [*Associated Press*] (SAG)
UCIMHPLD...	Union of Catholic Institutions for the Mentally Handicapped and Persons with Learning Disabilities [*Germany*] (EAIO)
UCIMT	University Center for Instructional Media and Technology [*University of Connecticut*] [*Research center*] (RCD)
U Cincinnati...	University of Cincinnati (GAGS)
UCIP	Union Catholique Internationale de la Presse [*International Catholic Union of the Press*] (EAIO)
UCIR	University Center for International Rehabilitation [*Michigan State University*] [*Research center*] (RCD)
UCIS	Unemployment Compensation Interpretation Service (DLA)
UCIS	University Center for International Studies [*University of Pittsburgh*] [*Research center*] (IID)
UCIS	University Computing and Information Services [*Villanova University*] [*Research center*] (RCD)
UCIS	Uprange Computer Input System
UCISA	Universities and Colleges Information Systems Association (BUAC)
UCISS	Union Catholique Internationale de Service Social [*Catholic International Union for Social Service*] [*Brussels, Belgium*] (EAIO)
UCIT	United Cities Gas [*NASDAQ symbol*] (TTSB)
UCIT	United Cities Gas Co. [*NASDAQ symbol*] (NQ)
UCitGs	United Cities Gas Co. [*Associated Press*] (SAG)
UCITS	Undertakings for Collective Investment in Transferable Securities [*European Community*]
UCJ...........	Unsatisfied Claim and Judgment [*State driver insurance*]
UCJG	Alliance Universelle des Unions Chretiennes de Jeunes Gens [*World Alliance of Young Men's Christian Associations*]
UC Jur	Upper Canada Jurist [*A publication*] (DLA)
UC Jur (Can)...	Upper Canada Jurist [*A publication*] (DLA)
UCK	Union Culturelle Katangaise [*Katangan Cultural Union*]
UCK	Unit Check (ECII)
UCKB	Upper Canada King's Bench Reports, Old Series [*1831-44*] [*A publication*] (DLA)
UCKB (Can)...	Upper Canada King's Bench Reports, Old Series [*1831-44*] [*A publication*] (DLA)
UCL.............	Uganda Creameries Ltd. (BUAC)
UCL.............	Ulnar Collateral Ligament [*Anatomy*]
UCL.............	Unclamp (IAA)
UCL.............	Uncomfortable Loudness [*Sound level*] (DAVI)
UCL.............	Union Chemical Laboratories [*Taiwan*] (BUAC)
UCL.............	Universal Computers Ltd. (NITA)
UCL.............	Universal Consolidated Ltd. [*British*]
UCL.............	University College of London (KSC)
UCL.............	University of Calgary Library [*UTLAS symbol*]
UCL.............	University of Connecticut, Law Library, West Hartford, CT [*OCLC symbol*] (OCLC)
UCL.............	Unocal Corp. [*NYSE symbol*] (SPSG)
UCL.............	Update Control List
UCL.............	Upper Confidence Level [*Industrial engineering*] (IEEE)
UCL.............	Upper Confidence Limit [*Statistics*]
UCL.............	Upper Control Limit [*Nuclear energy*]
UCL.............	Upper Cylinder Lubricant [*Automotive engineering*] (WDAA)
UCL.............	Urea Clearance [*Test*] [*Medicine*]
UCL.............	User Control List [*Computer science*] (HGAA)
UCLA	University at the Corner of Lenox Avenue [*Nickname for "The Tree of Life," a Harlem bookstore*]
UCLA	University of California, Los Angeles [*Databank originator*]
UCLA-Alaska L Rev...	UCLA [*University of California, Los Angeles*]-Alaska Law Review [*A publication*] (DLA)
UCLA Intra L Rev...	UCLA [*University of California, Los Angeles*] Intramural Law Review [*A publication*] (DLA)
UCLA J Envt'l L & Pol'y...	UCLA [*University of California, Los Angeles*] Journal of Environmental Law and Policy [*A publication*] (DLA)
UCLA Law Rev...	University of California at Los Angeles. Law Review [*A publication*] (DLA)
UCLA L Rev...	University of California at Los Angeles. Law Review [*A publication*] (DLA)
UCLAN	User Cluster Language [*Computer science*] (MHDB)
UCLA Pac Basin LJ...	UCLA [*University of California at Los Angeles*] Pacific Basin Law Journal [*A publication*] (DLA)
UCLC	Utah College Library Council [*Library network*]
UCLEA	University and College Labor Education Association (EA)
UCLG	United Cement, Lime, Gypsum, and Allied Workers International Union [*Formerly, CLGW*] (EA)
UCLJ..........	University of California, La Jolla
UCLJ..........	Upper Canada Law Journal [*1855-1922*] [*A publication*] (DLA)
UCLJ (Can)...	Upper Canada Law Journal [*A publication*] (DLA)
UCLJ NS......	Upper Canada Law Journal, New Series [*A publication*] (DLA)
UCLJ NS (Can)...	Upper Canada Law Journal, New Series [*A publication*] (DLA)
UCLJ OS......	Canada Law Journal, Old Series [*A publication*] (DLA)
UCLLL........	University of California Lawrence Livermore Laboratory (AAGC)
UCLM	Unity of Czech Ladies and Men [*Later, CSA*] (EA)
UCLMS	University College London Medical School [*England*] (BUAC)
UCLP..........	Unilateral Cleft of Lip and Palate [*Medicine*] (DMAA)
UCLR..........	University of Ceylon. Law Review [*A publication*] (DLA)
UCLRL	University of California Lawrence Radiation Laboratory
UCLS	Underwater Crash Locator System (MCD)

UCLT .... Until Cleared to Land by the Tower [*Aviation*] (FAAC)

UCLU .... University and College Lecturers' Union [*British*] (DET)

UCM .... Can You Come and See Me

UCM .... Unicom Corp. [*Formerly, Commonwealth Edison*] [*NYSE symbol*] (SAG)

UCM .... Union des Croyants Malagaches [*Malagasy Christian Union*]

UCM .... Union of Catholic Mothers [*British*] (DI)

UCM .... Unit Control Module [*Computer science*] (ECII)

UCM .... Universal Cable Module (PCM)

UCM .... Universal Christian Movement (EA)

UCM .... Universal Church of the Master (IIA)

UCM .... Universal Communications Monitor

UCM .... University Christian Movement [*Formerly, NSCF*] [*Defunct*]

UCM .... Unresolved Complex Mixture

UCM .... User Command [*Computer science*] (PCM)

UCM .... User Communications Manager [*Audio-video*] (NTCM)

UCMAA .... University of Calcutta Medical Association of America

UCMAE .... United Carters' and Motormen's Association of England [*A union*]

UCMJ .... Uniform Code of Military Justice

UCML .... Unit Committed Munitions List

UCMP .... UniComp, Inc. [*NASDAQ symbol*] (NQ)

UCMS .... Unit Capability Measurement System (AFM)

UCMS .... United Christian Missionary Society (EA)

UCMSU .... United Chain Makers' and Strikers' Union [*British*]

UCMT .... Unglazed Ceramic Mosaic Tile [*Technical drawings*]

UCN .... Buchanan [*Liberia*] [*Airport symbol*] (AD)

UCN .... Ultracold Neutron

UCN .... Unemployment Compensation News [*James E. Frick, Inc.*] [*Information service or system*] (CRD)

UCN .... Uniform Control Number (NASA)

UCN .... Union Civica Nacional [*National Civic Union*] [*Dominican Republic*] [*Political party*] (PPW)

UCN .... Union del Centro Nacional [*Union of the National Center*] [*Guatemala*] [*Political party*]

UCN .... Urocortin [*Neurochemistry*]

UCNC .... Union Carbide Nuclear Corp.

UCNI .... Unclassified Controlled Nuclear Information [*Department of Energy*]

UCNI .... Unified Communications Navigation Identification

UCNS .... Universities Committee for Non-Teaching Staff [*British*]

UCNS .... Universities Council for Non-Academic Staff (BUAC)

UCNSW .... Unitarian Church of New South Wales [*Australia*]

UCNT .... Undifferentiated Carcinoma of Nasopharyngeal Type [*Oncology*]

UCNV .... University College of Northern Victoria [*Australia*]

UCNW .... University College of North Wales

UCNY .... Underfashion Club of New York [*Formerly, CBWC*] (EA)

UCO .... Union Corp. [*NYSE symbol*] (SPSG)

UCO .... United Commercial Bank [*India*] (EY)

UCO .... Universal Code [*Used for giving transport aircraft meteorological information in wartime*] (NATG)

UCO .... Universal Communications Object (PCM)

UCO .... Universal Weather Landing Code

UCO .... Urethral Catheter Out [*Medicine*] (MAE)

UCO .... Urinary Catheter Out [*or Output*] [*Medicine*]

UCO .... Utility Compiler

UCOD .... University Clearing Office for Developing Countries

UCODE .... Universal Inversion Code

UCOFT .... Unit Combat Fire Trainer [*Army*]

U-COFT .... Unit Conduct of Fire Trainer [*Army*]

UCOL .... Union des Colons du Katanga [*Settlers' Union of Katanga*]

U Colo .... University of Colorado (GAGS)

UCOM .... Unified Command [*DoD*]

UCOM .... Union Catalog of Medical Monographs and Multimedia [*Medical Library Center of New York*] [*No longer available online*] [*Information service or system*] (CRD)

UCOM .... United Currency Options Market [*Philadelphia Stock Exchange*] (ECON)

UCON .... Utility Control

UCONN .... University of Connecticut

UCOP .... Unit Cost of Production (MHDW)

UCOPOM .... Union Europeenne du Commerce de Gros des Pommes de Terre [*European Union of the Wholesale Potato Trade*] [*Common Market*]

UCOR .... Uranium Enrichment Corp. [*South Africa*] (BUAC)

UCOR .... UroCor, Inc. [*NASDAQ symbol*] (SAG)

UCORC .... University of California/Operations Research Center

UCOS .... Upper Canada King's Bench Reports, Old Series [*1831-44*] [*A publication*] (DLA)

UCOS .... Uprange Computer Output System

UCOSDDEEC ... Union of Cafe Owners and Soft Drink Dealers of the European Economic Community [*Paris, France*] (EAIO)

UCosF .... United Companies Financial [*Associated Press*] (SAG)

UCOSL .... University of Colorado School of Law (DLA)

UCOT .... Upper Critical Ordering Transition [*Polymer physics*]

UCount .... United Counties Trust Co. [*Associated Press*] (SAG)

UCOWR .... Universities Council on Water Resources (EA)

UCP .... New Castle, PA [*Location identifier FAA*] (FAAL)

UCP .... Ubiquitous Crystallization Process [*Photovoltaic energy systems*]

UCP .... Uncoupling Protein [*Biochemistry*]

UCP .... Unified Command Plan [*Military*] (AFM)

UCP .... Uniform Customs and Practice for Documentary Credits [*International Chamber of Congress*] [*A publication*]

UCP .... Uniform Customs Practices (AAGC)

UCP .... Uninterruptable Computer Power

UCP .... Union Catalogue Profile [*Library science*] (TELE)

UCP .... Union Comorienne pour le Progres [*Comorian Union for Progress*] (PD)

UCP .... Union of Coffee Planters [*Madagascar*] (EAIO)

UCP .... Unit Construction Practice (IAA)

UCP .... Unit Construction Principle (IAA)

UCP .... United Cerebral Palsy (DAVI)

UCP .... United Christian Party [*Australia Political party*] (ADA)

UCP .... United Country Party [*Australia Political party*]

UCP .... Universal Commercial Paper [*Investment term*]

UCP .... University of Connecticut, Health Center Library, Processing Center, Farmington,CT [*OCLC symbol*] (OCLC)

UCP .... Update Control Process [*Telecommunications*] (TEL)

UCP .... Urethral Closure Pressure [*Medicine*] (STED)

UCP .... Urinary Coproporphyrin [*Urology*]

UCP .... Urinary C-Peptide [*Urology*]

UCP .... Utilities Conservation Program [*Navy*] (NG)

UCP .... Utility Control Program

UCPA .... United Cerebral Palsy Associations (EA)

UCPA .... University Counseling and Placement Association (AEBS)

UCPC .... University of Connecticut Paleobotanical Collection

UCPE .... Unit of Comparative Plant Ecology [*Natural Environment Research Council*] [*British*] (IRUK)

UCPF .... United Church Peace Fellowship [*Defunct*] (EA)

UCPN .... Union des Chefs et des Populations du Nord [*Union of Chiefs and Peoples of the North*] [*Togo*]

UCPN .... United Communist Party of Nepal [*Political party*] (EY)

UCPP .... Urban Crime Prevention Program [*Federal government*]

UCPP .... Urethral Closure Pressure Profile [*Medicine*] (STED)

UCPR .... Upper Canada Practice Reports [*A publication*] (DLA)

UC Pract ...... Upper Canada Practice Reports [*1850-1900*] [*A publication*] (DLA)

UC Pr (Can) ... Upper Canada Practice Reports [*A publication*] (DLA)

UCPREF .... United Cerebral Palsy Research and Educational Foundation (EA)

UC Pr R .... Upper Canada Practice Reports [*A publication*] (DLA)

UCPT .... Urinary Coproporphyrin Test [*Urology*]

UCPTE .... Union pour la Coordination de la Production et du Transport de l'Electricite [*Union for the Coordination of the Production and Transport of Electric Power - UCPTE*] (EAIO)

UCPU .... Universal Central Processor Unit [*Computer hardware*]

UCPU .... Urine Collection and Pretreatment Unit (NASA)

UCQ .... University of Central Queensland [*Australia*]

UCQB .... Upper Canada Queen's Bench Reports [*A publication*] (DLA)

UC QB OS .... Upper Canada Queen's Bench Reports, Old Series [*A publication*] (DLA)

UC QB OS (Can) ... Upper Canada Queen's Bench Reports, Old Series [*A publication*] (DLA)

UCR .... Committee on Uniform Crime Records (EA)

UCR .... UCar International [*NYSE symbol*] (SAG)

UCR .... Unconditioned Reflex [*or Response*] [*Psychometrics*]

UCR .... Under-Color Removal [*Printing technology*]

UCR .... Uniform Crime Reports [*FBI*]

UCR .... Union Centriste et Radicale [*France Political party*] (EY)

UCR .... Union Civica Radical [*Radical Civic Union*] [*Argentina*] (PD)

UCR .... Unit Cancer Risk [*Environmental science*] (COE)

UCR .... Unit Card Reader

UCR .... Unit Cost Report [*Military*] (RDA)

UCR .... University of California, Riverside (IID)

UCR .... Unsatisfactory Condition Report [*NASA*]

UCR .... Upper Canada Reports [*A publication*] (DLA)

UCR .... Upper Circulating Reflux [*Chemical engineering*]

UCR .... Upstream Control Region [*Biochemistry*]

UCR .... User Control Routine (MCD)

UCR .... Usual, Customary, and Reasonable (DAVI)

UCR .... Usual, Customary, and Reasonable Charges [*Medicine*]

UCR .... Utah Coal Route [*AAR code*]

UCRA .... Universal Child Restraint Anchorage

UCRAO .... University of Calgary, Rothney Astrophysical Observatory [*Canada*] (IRC)

UCRB .... Upper Circulating Reflux Bottom Section [*Chemical engineering*]

UCRC .... Underground Construction Research Council

UCRC .... Union Canadienne des Religieuses Contemplatives

UCRC .... United Civil Rights Committee

UCRE .... Urine Creatinine (STED)

UC Rep .... Upper Canada Reports [*A publication*] (DLA)

UCRG .... Union des Clubs pour le Renouveau de la Gauche [*Union of Clubs for the Renovation of the Left*] [*France Political party*] (PPE)

UCRI .... Union Carbide Research Institute (KSC)

UCRI .... Union Civica Radical Intransigente [*Left-wing radical political party*] [*Argentina*]

U-CRIS .... Utah Computer Retrieval Information Service [*Utah State Office of Education*] (OLDSS)

UCRL .... University of California Radiation Laboratory (MCD)

UCRL .... University of California Research Laboratory (KSC)

UCRP .... Ukrainian Conservative Republican Party [*Political party*] (BUAC)

UCRP .... Uniform Crime Reporting Program [*FBI*]

UCRP .... Union Civica Radical del Pueblo [*Moderate radical political party*] [*Argentina*]

UCRP .... Universal Control Reference Plasma (STED)

UCR/PACE .... Usual, Customary, and Reasonable/Performance and Cost Efficiency [*Medicine*] (MEDA)

UCRS .... Urban and Rural Commuter Service [*MOCD*] (TAG)

UCRT .... Upper Circulating Reflux Top Section [*Chemical engineering*]

UCS .... Canadian Union Catalogue of Serials [*National Library of Canada*] [*Information service or system*] (IID)

UCS .... Southern Utah State College, Cedar City, UT [*Library symbol Library of Congress*] (LCLS)

UCS	Unbalanced Current Sensing (MCD)
UCS	Unclosed Contract Status [Military] (AFIT)
UCS	Unconditioned Stimulus [Psychometrics]
UCS	Unconfined Compressive Strength [Rock mechanics]
UCS	Unconscious [Medicine]
Ucs	Unconscious (STED)
UCS	Uncontrolled Stimulus (HGAA)
UCS	Underwater Cable System
UCS	Underwater Communications System
UCS	Underwater Conservation Society [British] (DI)
UCS	Unican Security Systems Ltd. [Toronto Stock Exchange symbol]
UCS	Uniform Chromaticity Scale [Illuminant]
UCS	Uniform Communications System
UCS	Union de Campesinos Salvadorcenos [Peasant Union] [El Salvador]
UCS	Union of Catholic Students [British] (AEBS)
UCS	Union of Concerned Scientists (EA)
UCS	Unit Cost of Sales
UCS	Unit-Count System
UCS	United Carriers Systems, Inc. [ICAO designator] (FAAC)
UCS	United Community Services
UCS	United Computing Systems, Inc.
UCS	United Concerned Students (EA)
UCS	United States Army Corps of Engineers, Sacramento, Sacramento, CA [OCLC symbol] (OCLC)
UCS	Unit of Coastal Sedimentation [NERC] [British]
UCS	Universal Call Sequence
UCS	Universal Camera Site (KSC)
UCS	Universal Card Scanner [Computer science] (DIT)
UCS	Universal Cargo Sling
UCS	Universal Character Set [Computer science]
UCS	Universal Classification System
UCS	Universal Clothing System [Software package] (NCC)
UCS	Universal Command System (KSC)
UCS	Universal Communications Subsystem (NITA)
UCS	Universal Component System [Computer science] (PCM)
UCS	Universal Connector Strip
UCS	Universal Control System (NASA)
ucs	Universal Control System (NAKS)
UCS	University College School [British] (BI)
UCS	University Computer Services [Ball State University] [Research center] (RCD)
UCS	University Computing Services [University of Southern California] [Research center] (RCD)
UCS	University Computing Services [State University of New York at Buffalo] [Research center] (RCD)
UCS	Urine Collection System [NASA] (KSC)
UCS	User Control Store
UCS	Utilities Control System [NASA] (KSC)
UCS	Utility Consulting Services [Petroleum Information Corp.] [Information service or system] (IID)
UCSA	Ukrainian Canadian Servicemen's Association
UCSA	Uniform Conditional Sales Act [Legal shorthand] (LWAP)
UCSA	Uniform Controlled Substances Act [National Conference of Commissioners on Uniform State Laws]
UCSA	Union des Confederations Sportives Africaines [Association of African Sports Confederations - AASC] [Yaounde, Cameroon] (EAIO)
UCSA	United Chian Societies of America [Later, CSA] (EA)
UCSB	Universal Character Set Buffer [Computer science] (MHDB)
UCSB	University of California, Santa Barbara
UCSBS	Ukrainian Catholic Soyuz of Brotherhoods and Sisterhoods (EA)
UCSC	University City Science Center [Research center] (RCD)
UCSC	University of California, Santa Cruz
UCSD	Universal Communications Switching Device
UCSD	University of California, San Diego
UCSD-p	University of California at San Diego-p (NITA)
UC-SDRL	University of Cincinnati Structural Dynamics Research Laboratory
UCSEL	University of California Structural Engineering Laboratory (KSC)
UCSF	University of California, San Francisco
UCSJ	Union of Councils for Soviet Jews (EA)
UCSL	Unilever Computer Services Ltd. (NITA)
UCSL	Union Congolaise des Syndicats Libres [Congolese Union of Free Syndicates] [Leopoldville]
UCSM	Utility Control Strategy Model [Developed at Carnegie Mellon University for acid rain analysis]
UCSMP	University of Chicago School Mathematics Project (AEE)
UCSR	Ukrainian Center for Social Research (EA)
UCSR	Unionist Committee for Social Reform [British]
UCSS	Universal Communications Switching System (MCD)
UC/SSL	University of California/Space Sciences Laboratory (KSC)
UCST	Upper Critical-Solution-Temperature
UCSTR	Universal Code Synchronous Transmitter Receiver
UCSU	United Carters' and Storemen's Union [British]
UCSUR	University Center for Social and Urban Research [University of Pittsburgh] [Research center] (RCD)
UCSUS	Ukrainian Catholic Students of the United States [Defunct] (EA)
UCSW	University College of South Wales (WDAA)
UCT	Order of United Commercial Travelers of America [Columbus, OH] (EA)
UCT	Ultrasonic Computed Tomography [For examining interiors of solids]
UCT	Unchanged Conventional Treatment [Medicine]
UCT	Underwater Construction Team [Navy] (NVT)
UCT	Union Carbide Canada Equipment Trust Units [Toronto Stock Exchange symbol]
UCT	Unite Centrale de Traitement [Central Processing Unit - CPU] [French]

UCT	Units Compatibility Test
UCT	Universal Coordinated Time
UCT	University of Cape Town [South Africa]
UCT	University of Connecticut [Storrs] [Seismograph station code, US Geological Survey] (SEIS)
UCT	Urine Culture Tube [Clinical chemistry]
UCTA	United Commercial Travellers Association of Great Britain and Ireland, Inc. (BI)
UCTA	University and College Theatre Association (EA)
UCTA	Urine Collection/Transfer Assembly [Apollo] [NASA]
UCTC	Union Camerounaise des Travailleurs Croyants [Cameroonese Union of Believing Workers]
UCTC	United Counties Trust Co. [NASDAQ symbol] (SAG)
UCTD	Unclassifiable Connective Tissue Disease [Medicine] (DMAA)
UCTF	Union Culturelle et Technique de Langue Francaise [French-Language Cultural and Technical Union] [Paris, France] (EA)
UCTGA	United Commercial Travellers' Guild of Australia
UCTL	Up Control [Aerospace] (AAG)
UCTLIG	Universities and Colleges Teaching, Learning, and Information Group [Universities and Colleges Information Systems Association] (AIE)
UCTLV	United Committee for the Taxation of Land Values (BUAC)
UCTN	UC Television Network Corp. [NASDAQ symbol] (SAG)
UCTPA	United Coppersmiths Trade Protection Association [A union] [British]
UCTS	United Chairmakers' Trade Society [A union] [British]
UCTS	United Church Training School
UC TVNet	UC Television Network Corp. [Associated Press] (SAG)
UCU	University of California Union List, Berkeley, CA [OCLC symbol] (OCLC)
UCU	Uracil Cytosine Uracil [A triplet of bases coding for the amino acid, serine] (EES)
UCU	Urinary Care Unit [Medicine] (STED)
UCU	UtiliCorp United [NYSE symbol] (TTSB)
UCU	Utilicorp United, Inc. [NYSE symbol Toronto Stock Exchange symbol] (SPSG)
UCUE	Udmurt Commodity Universal Exchange [Russian Federation] (EY)
UCUPrA	UtiliCorp United $2.05 Pref [NYSE symbol] (TTSB)
UCUPrC	UtiliCorp Capital 8.875%'MIPS' [NYSE symbol] (TTSB)
UCV	Ulcus Cruris Varicosum (DB)
UCV	Uncontrolled Variable
UCV	Unimproved Capital Value [Business term] (ADA)
UCV	United Confederate Veterans
UCW	Union of Communications Workers [British] (ECON)
UCW	Unit Control Word [Computer science] (BUR)
UCW	United Church Women of the National Council of Churches (EA)
UCW	University College of Wales
UCW	University of Connecticut, Storrs, CT [OCLC symbol] (OCLC)
UCWA	United Construction Workers Association (OICC)
UCWE	Underwater Countermeasures and Weapons Establishment [British]
UCWR	Universities Council on Water Resources (MCD)
UCWR	Upon Completion Thereof Will Return To [Air Force]
UCWRE	Underwater Countermeasures and Weapons Research Establishment [British militar y] (DMA)
UCX	Unemployment Compensation, Ex-Servicemen
UCX	Urine Culture [Urology] (DAVI)
UCX	Utility Jet Transport [Air Force]
UCY	Union City, TN [Location identifier FAA] (FAAL)
UCY	United Calvinist Youth (EA)
UCY	United Caribbean Youth
UCYM	United Christian Youth Movement [Defunct] (EA)
UD	Georgian Bay [ICAO designator] (AD)
UD	Iloyd Your Trans-Australian Airline [ICAO designator] (AD)
UD	Ud Dictum [As directed] [Pharmacy] (DAVI)
UD	Ulcerative Dermatitis [Dermatology] (DAVI)
UD	Ulcerogenic Dose [Medicine] (DB)
UD	Ulnar Deviation [Medicine]
UD	Ultimate Dependability [Automotive designation]
UD	Ultra-Low Dispersion (CIST)
UD	Unable to Approve Departure for the Time Specified [Aviation] (FAAC)
UD	Unavoidable Delay
UD	Undated
U/D	Under Deck (ADA)
UD	Under Direct Vision (DAVI)
UD	Underdrive [Automotive engineering]
UD	Underground Distribution (MSA)
UD	Underwater Demolition [Navy] (NVT)
UD	Undesirable Discharge [Military]
UD	Undetected Defect
UD	Undifferentiated (BJA)
UD	Undiluted
UD	Unidentifiable (BJA)
UD	Unidirectional
UD	Uniflow Diesel [Nissan-designed engine]
UD	Union Democratique [New Caledonia] [Political party] (EY)
UD	Unit Designation
UD	Unit Diary
UD	Unit Director
UD	Unit Dose [Medicine]
UD	Unit Dose Package [Pharmacy] (DAVI)
UD	Unity-and-Diversity World Council (EA)
UD	Universal Dipole (DEN)
UD	University of Denver [Colorado]
UD	Unlawful Detainer [Legal term for an eviction proceeding]

UD	Unplanned Derating [*Electronics*] (IEEE)
UD	Update [*Computer science*] (NASA)
U/D	Update (NAKS)
U/D	Up/Down (KSC)
UD	Upper Deck [*Naval*]
UD	Urban District
UD	Urban Education [*Educational Resources Information Center (ERIC) Clearinghouse*] [*Columbia University*] (PAZ)
UD	Urethral Discharge [*Medicine*]
UD	Uridine Diphosphate [*Biochemistry*] (AAMN)
UD	Uroporphyrinogen Decarboxylase [*Also, UDase*] [*An enzyme*]
UD	Usable Depth (MCD)
UD	Usage Data
UD	Ut Dictum [*As Directed*] [*Latin*]
UD	Utility Dog [*Dog show term*]
UDA	Pusdiklat Perhubungan Udara/PLP [*Indonesia*] [*ICAO designator*] (FAAC)
UDA	Ulster Defence Association
UDA	Ultrasonic Detergent Action
UDA	Union for Democratic Action
UDA	United Democratic Alliance [*European political movement*] (ECON)
UDA	United States Department of the Interior, Alaska Resources, Anchorage, AK [*OCLC symbol*] (OCLC)
UDA	Universal Detective Association [*Defunct*] (EA)
UDA	Urban Development Agency [*British*]
UDA	Urtica Dioica Agglutinin [*Biochemistry*]
UDAA	Unlawfully Driving Away Auto
UDAC	User Digital Analog Controller
UDACE	Unit for the Development of Adult and Continuing Education (BUAC)
UDACS	Underwater Detection and Classification System (IAA)
UDAG	Urban Development Action Grant [*HUD*]
Udal	Udal's Fiji Law Reports [*A publication*] (DLA)
UDAL	United Distillers (Australia) Ltd. [*Commercial firm*]
U Dallas	University of Dallas (GAGS)
UDAM	Universal Digital Avionics Module (MCD)
UDAP	Unit for the Development of Alternative Products (BUAC)
UDAP	Universal Digital Autopilot
UDAR	Universal Digital Adaptive Recognizer (IEEE)
UDAS	Unified Direct Access Standards (IAA)
UDAS	Unified Direct Access System (BUR)
UDAS	Universal Data Acquisition System
UDAS	Universal Database Access Service [*Telecommunications*] (TSSD)
UDase	Uroporphyrinogen Decarboxylase [*Also, UD*] [*An enzyme*]
UDATS	Underwater Damage Assessment Television System (DNAB)
U Dayton	University of Dayton (GAGS)
UDB	Unified Data Base
UDB	Union Democratique Bretonne - Unvaniezh Demokratel Breizh [*Breton Democratic Union*] [*France Political party*] (PPW)
UDB	Universal Data Base (IAA)
UDB	Unliquidated Dollar Balances (AAGC)
UDB	Up-Data Buffer [*Computer science*]
UDB	Update Buffer (NAKS)
UDC	National Park Service, National Capital Region, Washington, DC [*OCLC symbol*] (OCLC)
UDC	Uganda Development Corp. (BUAC)
UDC	Ultrasonic Doppler Cardioscope [*Heartbeat monitor*]
UDC	Underdeveloped Countries
UDC	Underwater Decompression Computer [*Navy*] (CAAL)
UDC	Uniao Democratica de Cabo Verde [*Democratic Union of Cape Verde*]
UDC	Unidirectional Composite (MCD)
UDC	Unidirectional Current (IAA)
UDC	Union Delegates Committee [*Air carrier designation symbol*]
UDC	Union Democratica Cristiana [*Christian Democratic Union*] [*Bolivia*] [*Political party*] (PPW)
UDC	Union Democratique Centrafricaine [*Central African Democratic Union*] [*Political party*] (PPW)
UDC	Union Democratique du Cameroun [*Political party*] (EY)
UDC	Union Democratique du Centre [*Democratic Union of the Center*] [*Switzerland Political party*] (PPE)
UDC	Union du Centre [*Mayotte*] [*Political party*] (EY)
UDC	Union for Democratic Communications (EA)
UDC	Union of Democratic Control [*British*]
UDC	Union of the Democratic Centre [*Sahara*] [*Political party*] (PPW)
UDC	Union pour la Democratie Congolaise [*Political party*] (EY)
UDC	Unit Deployment of Containers (MCD)
UDC	Unit Descriptor Code (COE)
UDC	United Daughters of the Confederacy (EA)
UDC	United Developers Council (NTPA)
UDC	Unity-and-Diversity Council [*Later, UD*] (EA)
UDC	Universal Decimal Classification [*Online database field identifier*]
UDC	Universal Decimal Code (IAA)
UDC	Universal Digital Control
UDC	Universal Disk Controller [*Central Point Software*]
UDC	University of the District of Columbia
UDC	Up-Down Counter
UDC	Upper Dead Center
UDC	Urban Development Committee [*New South Wales, Australia*]
UDC	Urban Development Corp. [*New York State agency*]
UDC	Urban District Council [*British*]
UDC	Ursodeoxycholate [*Biochemistry*]
UDC	Ursodeoxycholic Acid
UDC	User Designation Codes [*Navy*] (NG)
UDC	User Dissemination Circuit [*Air Force Weather Center*]
UDC	Usual Diseases of Childhood [*Medicine*]
UDCA	Undesirable Discharge, Trial by Civil Authorities [*Navy*]
UDCA	Union pour la Defense des Commercants et des Artisans [*Union for the Defense of Traders and Artisans*] [*France Political party*] (PPE)
UDCA	Ursodeoxycholic Acid [*Pharmacology*]
UDCA	US Deaf Cycling Association (EA)
UD-CCM	University of Delaware Center for Composite Materials (RDA)
UDCCS	Uniform Data Classification Code Structure [*Navy*] (NG)
UDCD	Unit Data and Control Diagram (IAA)
UDCI	United Dental Care [*NASDAQ symbol*] (TTSB)
UDCI	United Dental Care, Inc. [*NASDAQ symbol*] (SAG)
UDCPA	Unfair and Deceptive Credit Practices Act (EBF)
UDCS	United Data Collection System
UDCV	Uniao Democratica de Cabo Verde [*Democratic Union of Cape Verde*]
UDD	Bermuda Dunes, CA [*Location identifier FAA*] (FAAL)
UDD	Bureau of Land Management, Denver, Denver, CO [*OCLC symbol*] (OCLC)
UDD	Cuddapan [*Queensland*] [*Airport symbol*] (AD)
UDD	Uddeholm [*Sweden*] [*Seismograph station code, US Geological Survey*] (SEIS)
UDD	Ulster Diploma in Dairying
UDD	Union Democratique Dahomeenne [*Benin*] [*Political party*]
UDD	Union for Democracy and Development [*Gabon*] (BUAC)
UDD	Union pour la Democratie et le Developpement [*Mali*] [*Political party*] (EY)
UDD	Union pour la Democratie et le Developpement Mayumba [*Gabon*] [*Political party*] (EY)
UDDA	Uniform Determination of Death Act [*National Conference of Commissioners on Uniform State Laws*]
UDDE	Undesirable Discharge, Desertion without Trial [*Navy*]
UDDF	Up and Down Drafts [*NWS*] (FAAC)
UDDIA	Union Democratique pour la Defense des Interets Africains [*Democratic Union to Defend African Interests*]
UDDL	Ultrasonic Dispersive Delay Line
UDDS	Union para la Democracia y el Desarrollo Social [*Equatorial Guinea*] [*Political party*] (EY)
UDDS	Urban Dynamometer Driving Schedule [*EPA engine test*]
UDE	Underwater Detection Establishment [*British*] (MCD)
UDE	Undetermined Etiology
UDE	Union Douaniere Equatoriale [*Equatorial Customs Union*]
UDE	United States Fish and Wildlife Service, Region 2, Albuquerque, NM [*OCLC symbol*] (OCLC)
UDE	Universal Data Entry
UDE	Universal Data Exchange [*Computer science*] (PCM)
UDE	University Department of Education (AIE)
UDEAC	Union Douaniere et Economique de l'Afrique Centrale [*Central African Customs and Economic Union*] (EAIO)
UDEAO	Union Douaniere des Etats de l'Afrique et l'Ouest [*Customs Union of West African States*] [*Later, CEAO*]
UDEC	Unitized Digital Electronic Calculator (MCD)
UDECMA-KMPT	Parti Democratique Chretien Malgache [*Malagasy Christian Democratic Party*] [*Political party*] (PPW)
UDECO	Umm Al-Dalkh Development Co. [*Abu Dhabi*] (BUAC)
UDEFEC	Union Democratique des Femmes Camerounaises [*Cameroonese Democratic Women's Union*]
U de J	Ursulines of Jesus [*Roman Catholic women's religious order*]
U Del	University of Delaware (GAGS)
UDENAMO ...	Uniao Democratica Nacional de Mocambique [*Mozambican National Democratic Union*] [*Later, FRELIMO*] [*Political party*]
U Denver	University of Denver (GAGS)
UDET	Universal Digital Element Tester (MCD)
UDETA	Unsymmetric Diethyltrianine (MCD)
U Det L Rev..	University of Detroit. Law Review [*A publication*] (DLA)
UDETO	Union Democratique Togolaise [*Togolese Democratic Union*]
U Detroit......	University of Detroit Mercy (GAGS)
UDF	Boise Interagency Fire Center, Boise, ID [*OCLC symbol*] (OCLC)
UDF	Federation Guadeloupeenne de l'Union pour la Democratie Francaise [*Guadeloupe Federation of the Union for French Democracy*] [*Political party*] (PPW)
UDF	Ulster Defence Force
UDF	Unducted Fan [*Type of prop engine developed by General Electric Co.*]
UDF	Union Defence Force [*British*]
UDF	Union Democrata Foral [*Spain Political party*] (EY)
UDF	Union of Democratic Forces [*Mauritania*] [*Political party*] (EY)
UDF	Union of Democratic Forces [*Bulgaria*] [*Political party*]
UDF	Union pour la Democratie Francaise [*Union for French Democracy*] [*France Political party*] (PPW)
UDF	Union pour la Democratie Francaise [*Union for French Democracy*] [*Wallis and Futuna Islands*] [*Political party*] (EY)
UDF	Union pour la Democratie Francaise [*Union for French Democracy*] [*Mayotte*] [*Political party*] (EY)
UDF	Union pour la Democratie Francaise [*Union for French Democracy*] [*New Caledonia*] [*Political party*] (PPW)
UDF	Union pour la Democratie Francaise [*Union for French Democracy*] [*Reunion*] [*Political party*] (PPW)
UDF	Union pour la Democratie Francaise [*Union for French Democracy*] [*French Guiana*] [*Political party*] (PPW)
UDF	Uniroyal, Dunlop, and Firestone [*Facetious translation of South African political party, United Democratic Front, which suppsedly executed dissenters with burning tires*]
UDF	Unit Derating Factor [*Electronics*] (IEEE)
UDF	Unit Development Folder (CIST)
UDF	Unit Dining Facilities

UDF	United Democratic Front [*South Africa*] [*Political party*] (PPW)
UDF	United Democratic Front [*India*] [*Political party*] (PPW)
UDF	Universal Disk Format (PCM)
UDF	Upside-Down Flipper
UDF	User Danger Factor (CIST)
UDF	User-Defined Function [*Computer science*] (PCM)
UDF	Utility and Data Flow (NASA)
UDFAA	Upholstery and Decorative Fabrics Association of America [*Defunct*] (EA)
UDFAM	User-Defined File Access Method [*Computer science*] (IT)
UDFE	Undesirable Discharge, Fraudulent Enlistment [*Navy*]
UDFFC	Unity-Displacement-Factor Frequency Changer (DICI)
UDFMA	Upholstery and Drapery Fabric Manufacturers Association [*Later, UFMA*]
UDFP	Union Democratique des Forces du Progres [*Benin*] [*Political party*] (EY)
UDFT	Union Democratique des Femmes Tunisiennes [*Democratic Union of Tunisian Women*]
UDG	National Fisheries Center, Kearneysville, WV [*OCLC symbol*] (OCLC)
UDG	Unit Derated Generation [*Electronics*] (IEEE)
UD(G)	United Distillers (Guiness) [*Commercial firm*]
UDG	Uracil DNA [*Deoxyribonucleic acid*]
UDG	Uracil DNA Glycosylase [*An enzyme*]
UDH	National Park Service, Harpers Ferry Center, Harpers Ferry, WV [*OCLC symbol*] (OCLC)
UDH	Universal Die Holder
UDH	Unplanned Derated Hours [*Electronics*] (IEEE)
UDHR	Universal Declaration of Human Rights
UDHS	Unit Demand History Summary [*Military*] (AABC)
UDI	Uberlandia [*Brazil*] [*Airport symbol*] (OAG)
UDI	Udine [*Italy*] [*Seismograph station code, US Geological Survey*] (SEIS)
UDI	Unilateral Declaration of Independence [*of Southern Rhodesia*]
UDI	Union Democratica Independiente [*Independent Democratic Union*] [*Chile*] [*Political party*] (PPW)
UDI	Union Democratique des Independants [*Democratic Union of Independents*] [*France Political party*] (PPE)
UDI	Unique Data Item (MCD)
UDI	United Dominion Indus [*NYSE symbol*] (TTSB)
UDI	United Dominion Industries Ltd. [*NYSE symbol*] (SPSG)
UDI	United States Department of the Interior, Natural Resources Library, Washington,DC [*OCLC symbol*] (OCLC)
UDI	Universal Digital Instrument (IAA)
UDI	Urban Development Institute [*Australia*]
UDI	Utility Data Institute [*Information service or system*] (IID)
UDIA	United Dairy Industry Association (EA)
UDICON	Universal Digital Communications Network [*Computer science*] (PDAA)
UDID	Unique Data Item Description (MCD)
UDIL	University Directors of Industrial Liaison (PDAA)
U-Dink	Upper Class - Double [*or Dual*] Income, No Kids [*Lifestyle classification*]
UDIR	USAREUR Daily Intelligence Report (MCD)
UDIRL	University of Durham Industrial Research Laboratories [*British*]
UDIT	Union pour la Defense des Interets du Tchad [*Union for the Defense of Chadian Interests*]
UDITPA	Uniform Division of Income for Tax Purposes Act
UDITS	Universal Digital Test Set
UDJ	Northern Prairie Wildlife Research Center, Jamestown, ND [*OCLC symbol*] (OCLC)
UDJM	Union Democratique de la Jeunesse Marocaine [*Democratic Union of Moroccan Youth*]
UDJV	Union Democratique de la Jeunesse Voltaique [*Voltaic Democratic Youth Union*]
UDK	United States Fish and Wildlife Service, Alaska Area Office, Anchorage, AK [*OCLC symbol*] (OCLC)
UDK	Upper Deck
UDK	User Defined Key [*Computer science*] (HGAA)
UDL	Bureau of Land Management, Boise District Office, Boise, ID [*OCLC symbol*] (OCLC)
UDL	Ultrasonic Delay Line
UDL	Underwater Data Link (MCD)
UDL	Uniform Data Language
UDL	Uniform Data Link
UDL	Unit Designation List (DOMA)
UDL	Unit Detail Listings [*Air Force*]
UDL(G)	Unit Document Listing (MCD)
UDL	Universal Development Laboratory [*Computer debugger*] [*Orion Instruments*]
UDL	Up-Data Link [*Computer science*]
UDL	Urine Disposal Lock (DNAB)
UDLP	United Defense Limited Partnership (RDA)
UDLP	United Democratic Labour Party [*Trinidad and Tobago*] [*Political party*] (PPW)
UDLP	United Dominica Labour Party [*Political party*] (PPW)
UDM	National Mine Health and Safety Academy, Beckley, WV [*OCLC symbol*] (OCLC)
UDM	Unassigned Direct Material [*Navy*] (DNAB)
UDM	Unidimensional Drafting Manual
UDM	Union Democratique Mauritanienne [*Mauritanian Democratic Union*] [*Political party*] (PD)
UDM	Union of Democratic Mineworkers [*British*]
UDM	Universal Drafting Machine Corp.
UDM	Upright Drilling Machine
UDMA	United Dance Merchants of America (EA)

UDMH	Unsymmetrical Dimethylhydrazine [*Rocket fuel base, convulsant poison*]
UDMH/H	Unsymmetrical Dimethylhydrazine Hydrazine Blend (NASA)
UDMU	Universal Decoder Memory Unit (DNAB)
UDN	Dnieproavia [*Ukraine*] [*FAA designator*] (FAAC)
UDN	National Park Service, National Register Division, Washington, DC [*OCLC symbol*] (OCLC)
UDN	Ulcerative Dermal Necrosis [*Medicine*]
UDN	Underwater Doppler Navigation
UDN	Uniao Democratica Nacional [*National Democratic Union*] [*Brazil*]
UDN	Union Democrata Nacional [*National Democratic Union*] [*El Salvador*] [*Political party*] (PPW)
UDN	Union Democratica Nicaraguense [*Nicaraguan Democratic Union*] [*Political party*] (PD)
UDO	Undetermined Origin [*Medicine*] (AAMN)
UDO	United Display Organization [*Switzerland*] (BUAC)
UDO	United States Fish and Wildlife Service, Billings, MT [*OCLC symbol*] (OCLC)
UDOFT	Universal Digital Operational Flight Trainer [*Navy*]
UDOFTT	Universal Digital Operational Flight Trainer Tool [*Navy*] (IAA)
UDom	United Dominion Realty Trust [*Associated Press*] (SAG)
UDomIn	United Dominion Industries Ltd. [*Associated Press*] (SAG)
UDomR	United Dominion Realty Trust, Inc. [*Associated Press*] (SAG)
UDOP	UHF [*Ultrahigh Frequency*] Doppler System
UDOP	Ultrahigh Doppler (NASA)
UDP	National Park Service, Denver, Denver, CO [*OCLC symbol*] (OCLC)
UDP	Ulster Diploma in Poultry Husbandry
UDP	Undecyl Dodecyl Phthalate
UDP	Uniao Democratica Popular [*Popular Democratic Unity*] [*Portugal*] [*Political party*]
UDP	Unidad Democratica Popular [*Popular Democratic Unity*] [*Peru*] [*Political party*] (PPW)
UDP	Unidad Democratica Popular [*Popular Democratic Unity*] [*Bolivia*] [*Political party*]
UDP	Unification du Droit Prive
UDP	Uniform Datagram Protocol [*Telecommunications*] (OSI)
UDP	Uniform Delivered Price [*Business term*] (MHDB)
UDP	Union pour la Democratie Populaire [*Union for People's Democracy*] [*Senegal*] [*Political party*] (PPW)
UDP	Unitary Development Plan (EERA)
UDP	United Data Processing (BUR)
UDP	United Democratic Party [*Belize*] [*Political party*] (PD)
UDP	United Democratic Party [*Basotho*] [*Political party*] (PPW)
UDP	Universal Datagram Protocol [*Computer science*] (PCM)
UDP	Urban Development Program [*University of Western Ontario*] [*Canada*] (IRC)
UDP	Uridine Diphosphate [*Biochemistry*]
UDP	User Datagram Protocol (BYTE)
UDPAG	Uridine(diphospho)acetylglucosamine [*Biochemistry*]
UDPB	Union des Democrates et Patriotes Burkinabe [*Burkino Faso*] [*Political party*] (EY)
UDPC	UNIVAC Data Processing Center (HGAA)
UDPG	Uridine Diphosphate Glucose [*Biochemistry*]
UDPGA	Uridine Diphosphate Glucuronic Acid [*Biochemistry*]
UDPgal	Uridine Diphosphate Galactose [*Biochemistry*] (MAH)
UDPGDH	Uridinediphosphoglucose Dehydrogenase [*An enzyme*]
UDPglu	Uridine Diphosphate Glucose [*Biochemistry*] (DAVI)
UDPGT	Uridine Diphosphate Glucuronosyltransferase [*An enzyme Biochemistry*]
UDPIA	Uniform Disclaimer of Property Interests Act [*National Conference of Commissioners on Uniform State Laws*]
UDP/IP	User Datagram Protocol/Internet Protocol [*Computer science*]
UDPK	United Democratic Party of Kurdistan [*Political party*] (BJA)
UDPL	United Dated Parts List [*Configuration listing*] (MCD)
UDPM	Ugandan Democratic Peoples Movement [*Political party*] (BUAC)
UDPM	Union Democratique du Peuple Malien [*Mali People's Democratic Union*] [*Political party*] (PPW)
UDPPDU	Unit Data Presentation Protocol Data Unit [*Telecommunications*] (OSI)
UDPS	Union pour la Democratie et le Progres Social [*Democratic Union of Social Progress*] [*Zaire*] [*Political party*]
UDPS	Union pour le Developpement et le Progres Social [*The Congo*] [*Political party*] (EY)
UDPT	Union Democratique des Populations Togolaises [*Democratic Union of Togolese People*]
UDQ	Bureau of Land Management, Library, New Orleans, New Orleans, LA [*OCLC symbol*] (OCLC)
UDR	Democratic Rural Union [*Brazil*]
UDR	Udaipur [*India*] [*Airport symbol*] (OAG)
UDR	Ulster Defence Regiment [*Military unit*] [*British*]
UDR	Undersampling Ratio
UDR	Union for Democratic Reforms [*Ukraine*] (BUAC)
UDR	Union pour la Defense de la Republique [*Union for the Defense of the Republic*] [*France Political party*] (PPE)
UDR	Union pour la Democratie Francaise [*Union for French Democracy*] [*Martinique*] [*Political party*] (PPW)
UDR	United Dominion Realty Trust, Inc. [*NYSE symbol*] (SPSG)
UDR	United Dominion Rlty Tr [*NYSE symbol*] (TTSB)
UDR	United States Department of the Interior, Bureau of Reclamation, Denver, CO [*OCLC symbol*] (OCLC)
UDR	Universal Digital Readout
UDR	Universal Document Reader (BUR)
UDR	Urgent Data Request [*GIDEP*]
UDR	Usage Data Report
UDR	Utility Data Reduction

UDRA............	Uniform Divorce Recognition Act [*National Conference of Commissioners on Uniform State Laws*]
UDRA............	United Drag Racers Association (EA)
UDRC............	Utility Data Reduction Control (IAA)
UDRC............	Utility Data Retrieval Control
UDRE............	User Differential Range Error [*Navigation systems*]
UDRI............	University of Dayton Research Institute [*Ohio*]
UDRN............	Union pour la Democratie et la Reconstruction Nationale [*Benin*] [*Political party*] (EY)
UDRO............	Utility Data Reduction Output (IAA)
UDRO............	Utility Data Retrieval Output
UDRP............	Uridine Diribose Phosphate [*Biochemistry*]
UDRPrA.......	Utd Dominion Rlty 9.25% 'A' Pfd [*NYSE symbol*] (TTSB)
UDRPS..........	Ultrasonic Data Recording and Processing System (NRCH)
UDRS............	Union Democratique pour le Renouveau Social [*Benin*] [*Political party*] (EY)
UDRS............	Universal Driver Rating System [*Harness racing*]
UDRT/RAD...	Union Democratique pour le Respect du Travail - Respect voor Arbeid en Democratie [*Democratic Union for the Respect of Labor*] [*Belgium Political party*] (PPW)
U/DRV..........	Underdrive [*Automotive engineering*]
UDS	Office of Surface Mining Reclamation and Enforcement, Region V, Denver, CO [*OCLC symbol*] (OCLC)
UDS	Ultra-Doppler Sonography [*Radiology*] (DAVI)
UDS	Ultramar Diamond Shamrock Corp. [*NYSE symbol*] (SAG)
UDS	Ultraviolet Detector System
UDS	Ultronic Data Systems (IAA)
UDS	Undeliverables [*Fundraising*]
UDS	Undeliverables [*Canadian*] [*Postal term*] (NFD)
UDS	Unified Data System [*Computer science*]
UDS	Union Democratique Senegalaise [*Senegalese Democratic Union*]
UDS	Union pour la Democratie et la Solidarite Nationale [*Benin*] [*Political party*] (EY)
UDS	Uniscope Display System (NITA)
UDS	Unit Data System [*Military*]
UDS	United Detection Systems, Inc. (EFIS)
UDS	Universal Data Set (CMD)
UDS	Universal Data System [*Army*]
UDS	Universal Data Systems [*Hardware manufacturer*]
UDS	Universal Digital Switch (MCD)
UDS	Universal Distributed System [*UNIVAC*]
UDS	Universal Documentation System [*NASA*]
UDS	Unscheduled DNA Synthesis [*Genetics*]
UDS	Urban Data Service [*International City Management Association*] (IID)
UDS	Urban Decision Systems, Inc. [*Information service or system*] (IID)
UDS	Urine Drug Screen [*Medicine*]
UDS	Utility Data Systems [*Information service or system*] (IID)
UDS	Utilization and Disposal Service [*Functions transferred to Property Management and Disposal Service*] [*General Services Administration*]
UDSG...........	Union Democratique et Sociale Gabonaise [*Gabonese Democratic and Social Union*]
UDSJ	Union for Democracy and Social Justice [*Djibouti*]
UDSL...........	Union of Scientific Leisure Clubs [*France*] (EAIO)
UDSM	Union Departemental de Syndicats du Mungo [*Departmental Union of the Trade Unions of Mungo*] [*Cameroon*]
UDSM	Union des Democrates Sociaux de Madagascar [*Union of Social Democrats of Madagascar*]
UDSR...........	Union Democratique et Socialiste de la Resistance [*Democratic and Socialist Union of the Resistance*] [*France Political party*] (PPE)
UDSR...........	United Duroc Swine Registry (EA)
UDSSP.........	Upper Delaware Segment Special Provisions [*Environmental science*] (COE)
UDT	Underdeck Tonnage
UDT	Underwater Demolition Team [*Navy*]
UDT	Unidirectional Transducer (IAA)
UDT	Union Dominions Trust [*Commercial firm*]
UDT	Union of Democratic Thais in the US (EA)
UDT	United Detector Technology
UDT	United Dominions Trust (BUAC)
UDT	United States Fish and Wildlife Service, Science Reference Library, Twin Cities,MN [*OCLC symbol*] (OCLC)
UDT	United Tire & Rubber Co. Ltd. [*Toronto Stock Exchange symbol*]
UDT	Universal Dataflow and Telecommunication [*IFLA Core Program*]
UDT	Universal Data Transcriber [*Navy*]
UDT	Universal Documents Transfer [*Computer science*] (ECII)
UDT	Universal Document Transport [*Computer science*] (OA)
UDT	Upgraded Data Terminal (MCD)
UDT	User Display Terminal
UDT	Utility Dog Title with a Tracking Dog Title
UDT	Utility Dog Tracker [*Degree of obedience training*]
UDTC...........	User-Dependent-Type Code
UDTD...........	Updated (MSA)
UDTDET.......	Underwater Demolition Team Detachment [*Navy*] (NVT)
UDT/EOD......	Underwater Demolition Team/Explosive Ordnance Proposal [*Navy*] (MCD)
UDTI	Universal Digital Transducer Indicator
UDTPHIBSPAC...	Underwater Demolition Teams, Amphibious Forces, Pacific Fleet [*Navy*]
UDTS	Universal Data Transfer Service [*ITT World Communications, Inc.*] [*Secaucus, NJ*] [*Telecommunications*] (TSSD)
UDTS	Universal Data Transmission System [*For international access*]
UDTUNIA......	Uniform Disclaimer of Transfers under Nontestamentary Instruments Act [*National Conference of Commissioners on Uniform State Laws*]
UDTV	Ultra-High Definition Television (DOM)
UDTX	Utility Dog and Tracking Excellent [*Degree of obedience training*]
UDTX	Utility Dog Title with a Tracking Dog Excellent Title
UDU	National Maritime Museum, San Francisco, CA [*OCLC symbol*] (OCLC)
UDU	Unabhaengige Demokratische Union [*Independent Democratic Union*] [*Austria Political party*] (PPE)
UDU	Underwater Demolition Unit
UDU	Union Democratique Unioniste [*Tunisia*] [*Political party*] (EY)
UDUAL........	Union de Universidades de America Latina [*Union of Latin American Universities*] [*Mexico*]
U Dubuque...	University of Dubuque (GAGS)
UDucGS	Church of Jesus Christ of Latter-Day Saints, Genealogical Society Library, Duchesne Branch, Stake Center, Duchesne, UT [*Library symbol Library of Congress*] (LCLS)
UDUF	Undesirable Discharge, Unfitness [*Navy*]
UDUPA........	Uniform Distribution of Unclaimed Property Act [*National Conference of Commissioners on Uniform State Laws*]
UDV	Union Democratique Voltaique [*Voltaic Democratic Union*] [*Banned, 1974*]
UD-Ve	Union Democratique pour la Cinquieme Republique [*Democratic Union for the Fifth Republic*] [*France Political party*] (PPE)
UDVST	Utility Dog Title with a Variable Surface Tracking Title
UDW	Ultradeep Water
UDW	Western Energy and Land Use Team, Fort Collins, CO [*OCLC symbol*] (OCLC)
UDX	Office of Surface Mining Reclamation and Enforcement, Washington, DC [*OCLC symbol*] (OCLC)
UDX	Utility Dog Excellent [*Dog show term*] [*Canada*]
UDY	USGS [*United States Geological Survey*] Water Resources Division, New York District, Albany, NY [*OCLC symbol*] (OCLC)
UDZ	United States Department of the Interior, Western Archeological Center, Tucson, AZ [*OCLC symbol*] (OCLC)
UE	Air La [*ICAO designator*] (AD)
UE	Ultrasonic Engineering (MCD)
UE	Uncertain Etiology Upper Esophagus [*Medicine*] (DAVI)
U/E	Unedged (DAC)
UE	Unemployment (GFGA)
UE	Unexpired (ADA)
UE	United Air [*ICAO designator*] (AD)
UE	United Electrical, Radio, and Machine Workers of America (EA)
UE	United Electrical, Radio, and Machine Workers of Canada [*See also OUE*]
UE	United Electrodynamics (AAG)
UE	United Empire [*Canada*]
UE	Unit Entry
UE	Unit Equipment [*as authorized to an Air Force unit*]
UE	Unit Establishment
UE	Unit Exception (CMD)
UE	Unit Exhausted [*Military*] (GFGA)
UE	Unity of Empire [*Award*] [*British*]
UE	University Entrance (WDAA)
UE	University Extension
UE	Until Exhausted
UE	Update and Ephemeria (MUGU)
UE	Upper Entrance [*Theater*]
UE	Upper Epidermis [*Botany*]
UE	Upper Esophagus [*Medicine*] (DMAA)
UE	Upper Extremity [*Medicine*]
U/E	Upper Extremity (STED)
UE	Urinary Energy [*Nutrition*]
UE	User Element [*Telecommunications*] (OSI)
UE	User Equipment
UE	Uterine Epithelium [*Medicine*]
UE	Utility Expenditure (MHDW)
UEA.............	Graphic Arts Union Employers of America (EA)
UEA.............	Ulex europeus Agglutinin [*Immunology*]
UEA.............	Unattended Equipment Area
UEA.............	Union Europeenne de l'Ameublement [*European Furniture Manufacturers Federation*] (EAIO)
UEA.............	Union Europeenne des Aveugles [*European Blind Union - EBU*] (EAIO)
UEA.............	Union of European Abattoirs [*Belgium*] (EAIO)
UEA.............	United Egg Association (EA)
UEA.............	United Epilepsy Association [*Later, EFA*] (EA)
UEA.............	Universala Esperanto Asocio [*Universal Esperanto Association*] (EAIO)
UEA.............	University of East Anglia [*England*]
UEA.............	University of East Asia [*Macao*] (BUAC)
UEA.............	Upper Extremity Arterial (STED)
UEA.............	Uranium Enrichment Associates [*Bechtel Corp., Union Carbide Corp., Westinghouse Electric Corp.*]
UEAC	Union of Central African States
UEAC	United European American Club
UEAC	Unit Equipment Aircraft
UEAES	Union Europeenne des Alcools, Eaux de Vie et Spiritueux [*European Union of Alcohol, Brandies and Spirits*] [*EC*] (ECED)
UEAI	Ulex Europaeus Agglutinin I
UEAI	Union Europeenne des Arabisants et des Islamisants [*European Union of Arab and Islamic Studies - EUAIS*] [*Spain*] (EAIO)
UE&C	United Engineers & Constructors, Inc. (EFIS)

UEAPME ...... Union Europeenne de l'Artisanat et des Petites et Moyennes Entreprises [*European Association of Craft, Small and Medium-Sized Enterprises*] [*EC*] (ECED)

U East LJ.... University of the East. Law Journal [*Manila, Philippines*] [*A publication*] (DLA)

UEAtc........... Union Europeenne pour l'Agrement Technique dans la Construction [*European Union of Agrement*] (EAIO)

UEAWG .... Urban Export Advisory Working Group [*Australia*]

UEAWS .... Union of European Associations of Water Suppliers [*Belgium*] (EAIO)

Ueb............. Uebereinkommen [*Agreement*] [*German*] (ILCA)

UEB............. Ultrasonic Epoxy Bonder

UEB............. Unexploded Bomb

UEB............. Union Economique BENELUX

UEB............. Union of Evangelical Baptists (EAIO)

UEB............. Upper Equipment Bay [*NASA*] (KSC)

UEBC........... Union Espanola Benefica de California (EA)

UEC............. Union des Etudiants Communistes [*France*]

UEC............. Union Electric Co.

UEC............. Union Europeenne de la Carrosserie [*European Union of Coachbuilders - EUC*] [*Belgium*]

UEC............. Union Europeenne des Experts Comptables Economiques et Financiers [*European Union of Public Accountants*]

UEC............. United Engineering Center

UEC............. Unit Endurance Chamber (MCD)

UEC............. Unmanned Equipment Cabinet

UEC............. Upper Epidermal Cell [*Botany*]

UEC............. Urban Elderly Coalition (EA)

UEC............. Urban Environment Conference (EA)

UEC............. USS Engineers & Consultants, Inc. [*Information service or system*] (IID)

UECA .... Underground Engineering Contractors Association [*Later, ECA*] (EA)

UECA .... Union Europeenne du Commerce Ambulant [*European Union of Door-to-Door Trade*] [*EC*] (ECED)

UECB........... Union Europeenne des Commerces du Betail

UECBV .... Union Europeenne du Commerce du Betail et de la Viande [*European Livestock and Meat Trading Union*] (EAIO)

UECL........... Ultra Electronics Components Ltd. (IAA)

UECL........... Union Europeenne des Constructeurs de Logements [*European Union of Independent Building Contractors*]

UECS .... Unified Electronic Computer System [*Air Force*]

UECU .... Union for Experimenting Colleges and Universities [*Later, UI*] (EA)

UECWA .... Underwater Explorers' Club of Western Australia

UED .... Air LA, Inc. [*ICAO designator*] (FAAC)

UED .... Ultrafast Electron Diffraction [*Physics*]

UED .... Ultrasonic Echo Detection (PDAA)

UED .... United Electro Dynamics (IAA)

UED .... Uranian Electrostatic Discharge [*Planetary science*]

UEDC .... Union Europeenne Democrate Chretienne [*European Christian Democratic Union*]

UEDS .... Uniao de Esquerda para a Democracia Socialista [*Left Union for Social Democracy*] [*Portugal Political party*] (PPE)

UEE .... Queenstown [*Australia Airport symbol*] (OAG)

UEE .... Unit Essential Equipment [*Military*] (NATG)

UEEA........... Union Europeenne des Exploitants d'Abbatoirs [*European Abbattoirs Union*] [*EC*] (ECED)

UEEB........... Union des Exploitations Electriques en Belgique

U/EECM....... Unattended/Expendable Electronic Countermeasure

UEEJ........... Union Europeenne des Etudiants Juifs [*European Union of Jewish Students - EUJS*] (EA)

UEF............. Uniform Electric Field

UEF............. Union Europaeischer Forstberufsverbaende [*Union of European Foresters*] [*Teningen-Heimbach, Federal Republic of Germany*] (EAIO)

UEF............. Union Europeenne des Federalistes

UEF............. Union Europeenne Feminine [*European Union of Women*]

UEF............. Union of European Foresters (BUAC)

UEF............. Upper End Fitting [*Nuclear energy*] (NRCH)

UEFA........... Union of European Football Associations [*Switzerland*] (EAIO)

UEFJA .... Uniform Enforcement of Foreign Judgments Act [*National Conference of Commissioners on Uniform State Laws*]

UEFJM .... Union of European Fashion Jewellery Manufacturers [*Italy*] (EAIO)

UEFS .... United Enginemen's Friendly Society [*A union*] [*British*]

UEFTU .... Union of European Foresters Trade Unions (BUAC)

UEG .... Unifocal Eosinophilic Granuloma (STED)

UEGO .... Universal Exhaust Gas Oxygen Sensor [*Fuel systems*] [*Automotive engineering*]

UEHB .... Uniform Effective Health Benefits

UEI.............. Union Energy [*Toronto Stock Exchange symbol*] (SPSG)

UEI.............. Union of Educational Institutions [*British*]

UEIC............ United East India Co.

UEIC............ Universal Electronics, Inc. [*NASDAQ symbol*] (SAG)

UEIC............ Univl Electronics [*NASDAQ symbol*] (TTSB)

UEIL............ Union Europeenne des Independants en Lubrifiants [*European Union of Independent Lubricant Manufacturers*] [*EC*] (ECED)

UEIS............ United Engineering Information System

UEITP.......... Union Europeenne des Industries de Transformation de Pomme de Terre [*European Union of the Potato Processing Industries*]

UEJ............. Unattended Expendable Jammer (MCD)

UEJDC .... Union Europeenne des Jeunes Democrates-Chretiens [*European Union of Young Christian Democrats*]

UEK............. Elmira, NY [*Location identifier FAA*] (FAAL)

UEL............. Quelimane [*Mozambique*] [*Airport symbol*] (OAG)

UEL............. Ultra Electronics Ltd. (IAA)

UEL............. Underwater Environmental Laboratory [*General Electric Co.*]

UEL............. United Empire Loyalist

UeL............. University of East London (ECON)

UEL............. UNIX Europe Ltd. (NITA)

UEL............. Upper Earnings Limit (PDAA)

UEL............. Upper Electrical Limit [*Nuclear energy*] (NRCH)

UEL............. Upper Explosive Limit

UEL............. Usage Exception List (MCD)

UE Law J ..... University of the East. Law Journal [*Manila, Philippines*] [*A publication*] (DLA)

UELF........... Union des Editeurs de Langue Francaise (EAIO)

UELL........... Chulman [*Former USSR ICAO location identifier*] (ICLI)

UELV........... Ultralite Expendable Launch Vehicle [*NASA*]

UEM............ Union Electrica Madrilena [*Spain*]

UEM............ Union Europeenne de Malacologie [*European Malacological Union*]

UEM............ Union Evangelique Mondiale [*World Evangelical Fellowship*]

UEM............ United Engineers Malaysia

UEM............ United Engineers (Malaysia) Berhad (ECON)

UEM............ Unite Electromagnetique [*Electromagnetic Unit*]

UEM............ Universal Electron Microscope

UEM............ University Extension Manuals [*A publication*]

UEMC.......... Unidentified Endosteal Marrow Cell [*Hematology*]

UEMN .... Union des Ecrivains du Monde Noir [*World Union of Black Writers - WUBW*] (EAIO)

UEMO .... Europaische Vereinigung der Allgemeinartze [*European Union of General Practitioners*] [*Denmark*] (EAIO)

UEMO .... Union Europeenne des Medecins Omnipraticiens [*European Union of General Practitioners*] (EA)

UEMS........... Unione Europea di Medicina Sociale [*European Union of Social Medicine - EUSM*] (EAIO)

UEMS........... Union Europeenne des Medecins Specialistes [*European Society of Medical Specialists*] [*Belgium*] (SLS)

UEMTA........ European Union for the Prevention of Cruelty to Animals (EAIO)

UEN .... Unisave Energy Ltd. [*Vancouver Stock Exchange symbol*]

UENCPB ...... Union Europeenne des Negociants en Cuirs et Peaux Bruts [*European Association of Traders in Leather and Raw Hides*] [*EC*] (ECED)

UENDC .... Union Europeenne des Negociants Detaillants en Combustibles [*European Union of Merchant Dealers in Combustibles*] [*Switzerland*]

UEO .... Kume Jima [*Japan*] [*Airport symbol*] (OAG)

UEO .... Union de l'Europe Occidentale [*Western European Union - WEU*] (EAIO)

UEO .... Union of Electrical Operatives [*British*]

UEO .... Unit Emplaning Officer [*Military British*]

UEOA .... Union des Etudiants Ouest Africains [*Union of West African Students*]

UEP............. Underwater Electric Potential

UEP............. Unequal Error Protection (IEEE)

UEP............. Uniform External Pressure

UEP............. Union Electric [*NYSE symbol*] (TTSB)

UEP............. Union Electric Co. [*NYSE symbol*] (SPSG)

UEP............. Union Europeenne de Pedopsychiatres [*European Union for Child Psychiatry*]

UEP............. Union of European Phoniatricians (BUAC)

UEP............. United Egg Producers (EA)

UEP............. Unit Evolutionary Period

UEP............. Unplanned Event Pickup [*NASA*] (KSC)

UEP............. Unusual End of Program [*Computer science*]

UEPC........... Union Europeenne des Promoteurs Constructeurs [*European Union of Developers and House Builders*] [*Belgium*] (EAIO)

UEPG........... United European Power Grid (IAA)

UEPH........... Unaccompanied Enlisted Personnel Housing [*Navy*] (DNAB)

UEPM.......... Urban and Environmental Planning and Management (COE)

UEPMD .... Union Europeenne des Practiciens en Medecine Dentaire [*European Union of Dental Medicine Practitioners*] (EAIO)

UEPPrA .... Union Electric, $3.50 Pfd [*NYSE symbol*] (TTSB)

UEPPrC .... Union Electric, $4.00 Pfd [*NYSE symbol*] (TTSB)

UEPPrD .... Union Electric, $4.50 Pfd [*NYSE symbol*] (TTSB)

UEPPrE .... Union Electric, $4.56 Pfd [*NYSE symbol*] (TTSB)

UEPPrG .... Union Electric, $6.40 Pfd [*NYSE symbol*] (TTSB)

UEPPrI .... Union Electric, $7.44 Pfd [*NYSE symbol*] (TTSB)

UEPR........... Unsatisfactory Equipment Performance Report [*Military*] (AABC)

UEPS .... Union Europeenne de la Presse Sportive [*European Sports Press Union*] (EAIO)

UEPS .... Union Europeenne des Pharmacies Sociales [*European Union of the Social Pharmacies*] [*EC*] (ECED)

UEPS .... United Elvis Presley Society (EAIO)

UER .... Unaided Equalization Reference (STED)

UER .... Union Europeenne de Radiodiffusion [*European Broadcasting Union - EBU*] (EAIO)

UER .... Unique Equipment Register (NASA)

UER .... Unite d'Enseignement et de Recherche [*Units of Teaching and Research*] [*University of Paris*]

UER .... Unit Equipment Report [*Marine Corps*] (DOMA)

UER .... Uniunea Evreilor Romani (BJA)

UER .... University Entrance Requirement [*British*] (DI)

UER .... Unplanned Event Record [*NASA*] (KSC)

UER .... Unsatisfactory Equipment Report

UER .... Ust-Elegest [*Former USSR Seismograph station code, US Geological Survey*] (SEIS)

UERA .... Umbilical Ejection Relay Assembly (AAG)

UERA .... Uniform Extradition and Rendition Act [*National Conference of Commissioners on Uniform State Laws*]

UERD .... Underwater Explosives Research Division [*Navy*]

UERDC......... Underwater Explosion Research and Development Center [*Navy*] (CAAL)

UERE .... Ultrasonic Echo Ranging Equipment
UERE .... User Equivalent Range Error
UERG .... Universitywide Energy Research Group [*University of California*] [*Research center*] (RCD)
UERL .... Underwater Explosives Research Laboratory
UERL .... Unplanned Event Record Log [*NASA*] (KSC)
UERMWA.... United Electrical, Radio, and Machine Workers of America
UERN .... Utilities Emergency Radio Network (IAA)
UERP .... Unione Europea di Relazioni Pubbliche [*European Union of Public Relations - International Service Organization - EURPISO*] (EAIO)
UERPIC........ Underground Excavation and Rock Properties Information Center (NITA)
UERPS .... Uniform Excess Reporting Procedures [*DoD*]
UERS .... Unusual Event Recording System [*Jet transport*]
UERT .... Union Explosivos-Rio Tinto [*Spain*]
UERT .... Universal Engineer Tractor, Rubber-Tired [*Army*]
UES............. Snow College, Ephraim, UT [*Library symbol Library of Congress*] (LCLS)
UES............. Unified Energy System [*Russia*]
UES............. Uniform Emission Standard (DCTA)
UES............. United Engineering Societies (IAA)
UES............. United Engineering Steels [*Commercial firm British*]
UES............. Universal Environmental Shelter (KSC)
UES............. University Extension Series [*A publication*]
UES............. Upper Esophageal Sphincter [*Anatomy*]
UES............. Upstream Expression Sequence [*Genetics*]
UES............. Waukesha, WI [*Location identifier FAA*] (FAAL)
UESA .... Ukrainian Engineers' Society of America (EA)
UESD .... Uniao da Esquerda Socialista Democratica [*Union of the Socialist and Democratic Left*] [*Portugal Political party*] (PPW)
UESEG .... United Earth Sciences Exploration Group [*British*]
UESK .... Unit Emergency Supply Kit
UESK .... Unit Essential Spares Kit [*Military*] (AFM)
UESP .... Upper Esophageal Sphincter Pressure (STED)
UESRG........ United Earth Sciences Research Group [*British*] (NUCP)
UEST........... Institute of Urban and Environmental Studies [*Brock University*] [*Canada Research center*] (RCD)
UET............. Quetta [*Pakistan*] [*Airport symbol*] (OAG)
UET............. Unattended Earth Terminal
UET............. Underground Explosion Test (IAA)
UET............. United Engineering Trustees (EA)
UET............. Unit Equipment Table [*Military*]
UET............. Universal Emulating Terminal
UET............. Universal Engineer Tractor [*Later, BEST*] [*Army*]
UET............. Universal Expenditure Tax [*British*] (DI)
UET............. Urban Environment Trust (BUAC)
UET............. Ur Excavations: Texts [*London*] [*A publication*] (BJA)
UETA.......... Universal Engineer Tractor, Armored [*Army*]
UETP........... University-Enterprise Training Partnership [*European Community*] (AIE)
UETRT .... Universal Engineer Tractor, Rubber-Tired [*Army*]
UCTO.......... Universal Emulating Terminal System [*Computer science*] (MHDB)
U Evansville... University of Evansville (GAGS)
UEVP .... Union Europeenne des Veterinaires Practiciens [*European Union of Practising Veterinary Surgeons*] (EAIO)
UEW............ United Electrical, Radio, and Machine Workers of America [*Also, UERMWA*] (NTCM)
UEW............ United Electrical Workers
UEWR .... Upgraded Early Warning RADAR [*Military*]
UEWS .... Ultimate Elastic Wall Stress [*Mechanical engineering*]
UEX............ Underexposed [*Photography*]
UEX............ Unit Exception (ECII)
UEX............ Ur Excavations [*A publication*] (BJA)
u/ext........... Upper Extremity [*Orthopedics*] (DAVI)
UF.............. Sydaero [*ICAO designator*] (AD)
UF.............. Ullrich-Feichtiger [*Syndrome*] [*Medicine*] (DB)
UF.............. Ultrafilter [*or Ultrafiltration*]
UF.............. Ultrafiltrable (STED)
UF.............. Ultrafiltration (EDCT)
UF.............. Ultrafine
UF.............. Ultrasonic Frequency (MSA)
UF.............. Unavailability Factor [*Electronics*] (IEEE)
UF.............. Uncertainty Factor [*Toxicology*]
UF.............. Under Frequency (DNAB)
UF.............. Underground Feeder
UF.............. Unemployed Father (OICC)
UF.............. Unflexed (STED)
UF.............. Uni Air International [*France ICAO designator*] (ICDA)
UF.............. Unified Forces [*Military*]
UF.............. Union de Fribourg: Institut International des Sciences Sociales et Politiques [*Union de Fribourg: International Institute of Social and Political Sciences*] [*Fribourg/Pensier, Switzerland*] (EAIO)
UF.............. United Focus [*Later, Omni Learning Institute*] (EA)
UF.............. United Force [*Guyana*] (PD)
UF.............. United Foundation
UF.............. United Front [*Sri Lanka*] [*Political party*] (FEA)
UF.............. United States Facilities [*NYSE symbol*] (SAG)
UF.............. Uniterra Foundation (EA)
UF.............. Unit of Fire [*Military*] (MUGU)
UF.............. Universal Feeder [*Medicine*] (DMAA)
UF.............. Universities Funding Council [*British*]
UF.............. University of Florida [*Gainesville*]
UF.............. Unknown Factor
UF.............. Unofficial Funds [*British*]

UF.............. Until Finished (STED)
UF.............. Uplink Frequency
UF.............. Upper Air Fallout [*Civil Defense*]
UF.............. Urea Formaldehyde
UF.............. Used For
UF.............. Used Fuel [*Nuclear energy*] (NUCP)
UF.............. Utility File
UF.............. Utilization Factor
UF_4.......... Uranium Tetrafluoride (COE)
UF_6.......... Uranium Hexafluoride (COE)
UF6.......... Uranium Hexafluoride
UFA............. State Flight Academy of Ukraine [*FAA designator*] (FAAC)
UFA............. Ukrainian Fraternal Association (EA)
UFA............. Unesterified Fatty Acid [*Biochemistry*]
UFA............. Unfinished Furniture Association (NTPA)
UFA............. Uniformed Firefighters Association
UFA............. Uniform Firearms Act
UFA............. Union des Femmes d'Algerie [*Union of Algerian Women*]
UFA............. Union of Flight Attendants (EA)
UFA............. United Families of America (EA)
UFA............. United Fathers of America (EA)
UFA............. University Film Association [*Later, UFVA*] (EA)
UFA............. Universum-Film Aktien-Gesellschaft [*German motion picture company*]
UFA............. Unsaturated Fatty Acid [*Organic chemistry*]
UFA............. Until Further Advised
UFA............. Upholstery Fillings Association (BUAC)
UFA............. Usable Floor Area [*Classified advertising*] (ADA)
UFA............. Use Frequency Analysis
UFAA.......... United Food Animal Association [*Defunct*] (EA)
UFAC.......... Unlawful Flight to Avoid Custody
UFAC.......... Upholstered Furniture Action Council (EA)
UFAED .... Unit Forecast Authorization Equipment Data (AFM)
UFAM.......... Universal File Access Method
UFAP.......... Ultrafine Ammonium Perchlorate (MCD)
UFAP.......... Union Francaise des Annuaires Professionels [*French Union for Professional Yearbooks*] [*Trappes*] [*Information service or system*] (IID)
UFAP .... Universal-Fine Ammonium Perchlorate [*Organic chemistry*] (MCD)
UFAP.......... Unlawful Flight to Avoid Prosecution
UFAS.......... Unified Flight Analysis System [*NASA*]
UFAS.......... Uniform Federal Accessibility Standards [*Department of Housing and Urban Development*] (GFGA)
UFAT.......... Unlawful Flight to Avoid Testimony
UFAW.......... Universities Federation for Animal Welfare [*British*]
UFAWU........ United Fishermen and Allied Workers' Union [*Canada*]
UFB............. Unfit for Broadcast (WDMC)
UFBS.......... Union des Francais de Bon Sens [*Union of Frenchmen of Good Sense*] [*Political party*] (PPW)
UFBS.......... United Friendly Boilermakers' Society [*A union*] [*British*]
UFC............. Unidirectional Fiber Composite (EDCT)
UFC............. Unidirectional Filamentary Composite
UFC............. Unified Fire Control (MCD)
UFC............. Uniform Freight Classification
UFC............. Union des Facteurs du Canada [*Letter Carriers' Union of Canada - LCUC*]
UFC............. United Fire & Casualty (EFIS)
UFC............. United Flight Classification
UFC............. United Flowers-by-Wire Canada
UFC............. United Free Church [*Scotland*]
UFC............. United Fruit Co. [*Railroad*] (MHDW)
UFC............. Unit Funded Costs (MCD)
UFC............. Universal Flight Computer
UFC............. Universal Foods Corp. [*NYSE symbol*] (SPSG)
UFC............. Universal Frequency Counter
UFC.......... Universities Funding Council [*British*] (ECON)
UFC............. Univl Foods [*NYSE symbol*] (TTSB)
UFC............. Urinary Free Cortisol
UFCA.......... Uniform Fraudulent Conveyance Act [*National Conference of Commissioners on Uniform State Laws*]
UFCA .... United Film Carriers Association [*Defunct*] (EA)
UFCA .... Urethane Foam Contractors Association [*Defunct*] (EA)
UFCC.......... Underwater Fire Control Computer [*Navy*] (CAAL)
UFCC .... Uniform Freight Classification Committee
UFCE.......... Union Federaliste des Communautes Ethniques Europeennes [*Federal Union of European Nationalities*]
UFCG .... Underwater Fire Control Group
UFCP .... Up-Front Control Panel (MCD)
UFCS .... UF-6 Chemical Feed Station [*Nuclear energy*] (NRCH)
UFCS .... Underwater Fire Control System
UFCS .... United Fellowship for Christian Service [*Later, BMMFI*] (EA)
UFCS .... United Fire & Casualty [*NASDAQ symbol*] (TTSB)
UFCS .... United Fire & Casualty Co. of Iowa [*NASDAQ symbol*] (NQ)
UFCS .... United Free Church of Scotland (DI)
UFCS .... Universal Fire Control System
UFCS .... Up-Front Control Set (MCD)
UFCT.......... United Federation of College Teachers [*AFL-CIO*]
UFCW .... United Food and Commercial Workers International Union (EA)
UFCWIU...... United Food and Commercial Workers International Union (EA)
UFD............. Davis County Library, Farmington, UT [*Library symbol Library of Congress*] (LCLS)
UFD .... Ultrafast Detection
UFD .... Ultrasonic Flow Detector (DB)
UFD .... Union des Forces Democratiques [*Union of Democratic Forces*] [*France Political party*] (PPE)

UFD .... Union des Forces Democratiques [*Union of Democratic Forces*] [*Mali*] [*Political party*] (EY)
UFD .... United Foods, Inc. [*AMEX symbol*] (SPSG)
UFD .... Unit Functional Diagram (IAA)
UFD .... Universal Firing Device [*Military*] (AABC)
UFD .... User File Directory (NASA)
UFD.A .... United Foods CI'A' [*AMEX symbol*] (TTSB)
UFD.B .... United Foods Cv CI'B' [*AMEX symbol*] (TTSB)
UFDC .... Union des Femmes Democratiques du Canada
UFDC .... Union des Forces Democratiques du Cameroun [*Union of Democratic Forces of Cameron*] [*Political party*] (EY)
UFDC .... United Federation of Doll Clubs (EA)
UFDC .... Universal Flight Director Computer
UFE .... Uniform Food Encoding (STED)
UFE .... Union des Feculeries de Pommes de Terre de la CE [*EC*] (ECED)
UFE .... Union des Francais a l'Etranger [*Union of French Citizens Abroad*] [*Political party*] (PPW)
UFE .... Union des Groupements Professionnels de l'Industrie de le Feculerie de Pommes deTerre [*Union of Professional Groups of the Potato Starch Industry*]
UFE .... Union of the Finance-Personnel in Europe [*EC*] (ECED)
UFE .... Universal Field Element (MCD)
UFedS .... United Federal Savings Bank [*Associated Press*] (SAG)
UFEM .... Ultrafem, Inc. [*NASDAQ symbol*] (SAG)
UFEMAT .... Federation Europeenne des Associations Nationales des Negociants en Materiaux deConstruction [*European Association of National Builders Merchants Associations*] (EAIO)
UFEMTO ...... Union des Femmes du Togo [*Togolese Women's Union*]
UFER .... Mouvement International pour l'Union Fraternelle entre les Races et les Peuples [*International Movement for Fraternal Union among Races and Peoples*]
UFERI .... Union des Federalistes et Republicains Independants [*Zaire*] [*Political party*] (EY)
UFESA .... United Fire Equipment Service Association (EA)
UFESAS .... Universal Fair and Exhibition Service (BUAC)
UFET .... Unipolar Field-Effect Transistor (IAA)
UFF .... Ufficiale [*Official, Officer*] (EY)
UFF .... U-Landshjaelp fra Folk til Folk [*Development Aid From People to People*] [*Denmark*] (EAIO)
UFF .... Ulster Freedom Fighters
UFF .... Ulster Furniture Federation (BUAC)
UFF .... Union et Fraternite Francaise [*French Union and Fraternity*] [*Political party*] (PPE)
UFF .... United Freedom Front [*Defunct*] (EA)
UF-F .... Universal Flip-Flop [*Computer science*]
UFF .... University Film Foundation (EA)
UFFCS .... IEEE Ultrasonics, Ferroelectrics, and Frequency Control Society (EA)
UFFI .... Urea-Formaldehyde Foam Insulation
UFFVA .... United Fresh Fruit and Vegetable Association (EA)
UFGCC .... Ultrafine Ground Calcium Carbonate [*Inorganic chemistry*]
UFH .... Ultra-Light Field Howitzer [*British*]
UFH .... Upper Facial Height [*Medicine*]
UFi .... Fillmore City Library, Fillmore, UT [*Library symbol Library of Congress*] (LCLS)
UFI .... Unifi, Inc. [*NYSE symbol*] (SPSG)
UFI .... Union des Foires Internationales [*Union of International Fairs*] (EAIO)
UFI .... Unit Fault Isolation (MCD)
UFI .... Universal Fermi Interaction
UFI .... Upstream Failure Indication (NITA)
UFI .... Usage Frequency Indicator
UFI .... User Friendly Interface
UFIB .... Union Federazioni Italiane Bocce [*Italian lawn bowling, or boccie, organization*]
UFIDA .... Union Financiere Internationale pour le Developpement de l'Afrique [*International Financial Union for the Development of Africa*]
UFIPTE .... Union Franco-Iberique pour la Coordination de la Production et du Transport de l'Electricite [*Franco-Iberian Union for Coordinating the Production and Transmission of Electricity*] (EAIO)
UFireC .... United Fire & Casualty Co. of Iowa [*Associated Press*] (SAG)
UFIRS .... Uniform Fire Incident Reporting System [*National Fire Protection Association*]
UFIRS .... Universal Far Infrared Sensor (MCD)
UFIS .... User-Friendly Information Society (TELE)
UFJC .... United Fund for Jewish Culture [*Defunct*] (EA)
UFL .... Underfull Employment [*Economics*]
UFL .... Upper Flammable Limit
U Fla .... University of Florida (GAGS)
UFLC .... Union Internationale des Femmes Liberales Chretiennes [*International Union of Liberal Christian Women*]
UFM .... Uganda Freedom Movement (PD)
UFM .... Union Fleuve de Mano [*Mano River Union - MRU*] (EAIO)
UFM .... United Financial Management Ltd. [*Toronto Stock Exchange symbol*]
UFM .... Universal Field Multiplexer [*Computer science*] (ECII)
UFM .... University for Man [*Manhattan, KS*]
UFM .... Unnormalized Floating Multiply (SAA)
UFM .... Upper Figure of Merit
UFM .... User to File Manager
UFMA .... United Fur Manufacturers Association (EA)
UFMA .... Upholstered Furniture Manufacturers Association (EA)
UFMA .... Upholstery Fabric Manufacturers Association [*Defunct*] (EA)
UFMCC .... Universal Fellowship of Metropolitan Community Churches (EA)
UFMG .... Universal Manufacturing [*NASDAQ symbol*] (SAG)
UFMG .... Univl Mfg [*NASDAQ symbol*] (TTSB)
UFMOP .... Unintentional Frequency Modulation on Pulse (MCD)
UFMT .... Urban Federation for Music Therapists [*Later, AAMT*] (EA)

UFN .... UniCare Financial (EFIS)
UFN .... Union Franco-Nigerienne [*French-Nigerian Union*]
UFN .... Until Further Notice
UFNSHD ...... Unfinished
UFO .... Ultralight Flight Organization (EA)
UFO .... Unflagged Order [*Laboratory science*] (DAVI)
UFO .... Unidentified Flying Object [*"Flying saucers"*] [*Facetious translation: "Undue Fuss Over"*]
UFO .... Unidentified Foreign Object [*Medicine*] (DAVI)
UFO .... Uniform Field Organization [*DoD*]
UFO .... United 510 Owners (EA)
UFO .... Unit Families Officer [*Military British*]
UFO .... Universal Fiber Optic (MCD)
UFO .... Unlimited Freak-Out [*Slang*] (DSUE)
UFO .... Unwanted Falling Objects (MCD)
UFO .... User Files On-Line [*Computer science*] (MHDI)
UFO .... User Friendly Operating System [*UFO Systems, Inc.*]
UFO .... Users Files on Line (IAA)
UFOA .... Union des Femmes de l'Ouest Africain [*West African Women's Union*]
UFOCAT .... UFO [*Unidentified Flying Object*] Catalog [*Center for Unidentified Flying Object Studies*]
UFOD .... Union Francaise des Organismes de Documentation (NITA)
UFOIN .... UFO Investigators Network [*British*]
UFOIRC .... Unidentified Flying Object Information Retrieval Center, Inc. (EA)
UFood .... United Foods, Inc. [*Associated Press*] (SAG)
UFOP .... Ultrafast-Opening Parachute (NG)
UFORA .... Unidentified Flying Objects Research Association (BUAC)
UFORDAT .... Umweltforschungsdatenbank [*Data Bank for Environmental Research Projects*] [*Deutsches Umweltbundesamt*] [*Germany*] [*Information service or system*] (CRD)
U format ...... Unknown Format (NITA)
UFORQ .... Unidentified Flying Object Research Queensland [*Australia*]
UFOS .... Unacceptable Face of Socialism (DSUE)
UFOs .... United Flying Octogenarians (EA)
UFP .... Ultrafine Powder [*Materials processing*]
UFP .... Under Frequency Protector (MCD)
UFP .... Unemployed Full Pay [*Military British*]
UFP .... Union Frontier Police [*European Economic Community*] (ECON)
UFP .... United Federal Party [*Northern Rhodesia*]
UFP .... United Federation of Planets (EA)
UFP .... United Federation of Police Officers (NTPA)
UFP .... Universal Folded Plate [*Structural system*] (RDA)
UFP .... Utility Facilities Program [*Computer science*] (IBMDP)
UFPA .... University Film Producers Association [*Later, UFVA*] (EA)
UFPC .... United Federation of Postal Clerks [*Formerly, NFPOC*] [*Later, APWU*] (EA)
UFPDP .... Union des Forces Populaires pour la Democratie et le Progres [*Niger*] [*Political party*] (EY)
UFPI .... Universal Forest Products [*NASDAQ symbol*] (SAG)
UFPI .... Univl Forest Products [*NASDAQ symbol*] (TTSB)
UFP-ICP .... Ultrafine Particle Inductively Coupled Plasma [*Spectrometry*]
UFPO .... Underground Facilities Protective Organization (EA)
UFPS .... Uniform Federal Procurement System (AAGC)
UFPT .... UFP Technologies [*Commercial firm NASDAQ symbol*] (SAG)
UFPT .... Ultra Fine Pitch Technology (AAEL)
UFP Tch ...... UFP Technologies [*Commercial firm Associated Press*] (SAG)
UFR .... UF-6 Recovery Room [*Nuclear energy*] (NRCH)
UFR .... Ultrafiltration Rate [*Biomedicine*]
UFR .... Under Frequency Relay
UFR .... Unfinanced Requirement [*Army*]
UFR .... United Africa Airline (Liberia), Inc. [*ICAO designator*] (FAAC)
UFR .... Urine Flow Rate
UFRC .... Ulster Federation of Rambling Clubs (BUAC)
UFRCC .... Uniform Federal Regional Council City
UFRM .... United Federal Savings & Loan of Rocky Mount [*NASDAQ symbol*] (NQ)
UFRM .... United Fed Svgs Bk Rocky Mt NC [*NASDAQ symbol*] (TTSB)
UFRWO .... United Federation of Russian Workers' Organizations of USA and Canada (EA)
UFS .... UFS, Inc. [*ICAO designator*] (FAAC)
UFS .... Ulster Folklife Society (EA)
UFS .... Ultimate Factor of Safety
UFS .... Under Frequency Sensing (MCD)
UFS .... United Farmers and Stockowners (EERA)
UFS .... United Features Syndicate [*Commercial firm*]
UFS .... United Feeder Service [*ICAO designator*] (FAAC)
UFS .... Universal Financial System (MHDW)
UFS .... Unnormalized Floating Subtract
UFS .... U.S. Foodservice [*NYSE symbol*] [*Formerly, JP Foodservice*]
UFSA .... Ukrainian Free Society of America (EA)
UFSAR .... Updated Final Safety Analysis Report [*Environmental science*] (COE)
UFSD .... Union Free School District (BARN)
uFSH .... Urinary Follicle-Stimulating Hormone [*Medicine*] (DMAA)
UFSI-IWA ..... Universities Field Staff International - Institute of World Affairs (EA)
UFSJ .... Unitarian Fellowship for Social Justice
UFSS .... Unified Flexible Spacecraft Simulation
UFSS .... Unmanned Free Swimming Submersibles (DNAB)
UFSSA .... United Farmers and Stockowners of South Australia
UFST .... United Federation of Canadian Star Trekkers
UFT .... Ultrasonic Frequency Transformer [*or Translator*]
UFT .... United Federation of Teachers [*New York*]
UFT .... United Fly Tyers (EA)
UFTA .... Uniform Fraudulent Transfer Act [*National Conference of Commissioners on Uniform State Laws*]

UFTA............	United Farmers Trading Agency (BUAC)
UFTAA	Universal Federation of Travel Agents' Associations [*International Federation of Travel Agencies and Universal Organization of Travel Agents' Associations*] [*Formed by a merger of Australia*] (EAIO)
UFTIW	Union of Forestry and Timber Industry Workers [*Bulgaria*] (BUAC)
UFTR	University of Florida Teaching Reactor
UFTS............	United Furnishing Trades Society [*A union*] [*British*]
UFU	Ulster Farmers' Union (BUAC)
UFU	United Fascist Union (EA)
UFU	United Fishermen Union [*British*]
UFU	Utility Flight Unit [*Navy*]
UFUA	United Firefighters Union of Australia
UFUSA........	United Firefighters Union of South Australia
UFUWA........	United Firefighters Union of Western Australia
UFV..............	Unsymmetrical Free Vibration
UFVA	University Film and Video Association (EA)
UFVF...........	University Film and Video Foundation (EA)
UFW	United Farm Workers of America (EA)
UFW	United Furniture Workers of America (EA)
UFW	Urban Fighting Weapon (MCD)
UFWA	United Farm Workers of America
UFWA	United Furniture Workers of America
UFWDA........	United Four-Wheel Drive Associations (EA)
UFWOC........	United Farm Workers Organizing Committee [*Later, UFW*]
UFWU	United Farm Workers Union
UFX..............	Uniflex, Inc. [*AMEX symbol*] (SAG)
UG	Norfolk Island Airlines [*Australia ICAO designator*] (ICDA)
UG	Radio Frequency Connectors [*JETDS nomenclature*] [*Military*] (CET)
UG	Uganda [*ANSI two-letter standard code*] (CNC)
ug	Uganda [*MARC country of publication code Library of Congress*] (LCCP)
Ug	Ugric [*Finno-Ugric Linguistic Family*] (BARN)
Ug	Ugutio [*Huguccio*] [*Deceased, 1210*] [*Authority cited in pre-1607 legal work*] (DSA)
UG	Uncertain Glory: Folklore and the American Revolution [*A publication*]
UG	Undergarment
UG	Undergoing (DNAB)
UG	Undergraduate
UG	Underground [*Technical drawings*]
Ug	Uniform, Fine-Grained [*Soil*]
UG	Union Guide (IAA)
UG	United Guardian, Inc. [*AMEX symbol*] (SAG)
UG	Unite Guyanaise [*Guyanese Unity*] [*Political party*] (PPW)
UG	Universal Generalization [*Rule of quantification*] [*Logic*]
UG	Universal Government
UG	Upgrading Training [*Job Training and Partnership Act*] (OICC)
UG	Urban Gorillas (EA)
UG	Urogastrone (DB)
UG	Urogenital [*Medicine*]
UG	User Group [*Computer science*]
UG	US-North Africa (Gibraltar) Convoy [*World War II*]
UG	Uteroglobin [*Physiology*]
UG	Utility Gateway
UGA	Uganda [*ANSI three-letter standard code*] (CNC)
UGA	Uganda Airlines Corp. [*ICAO designator*] (FAAC)
uga	Ugaritic [*MARC language code Library of Congress*] (LCCP)
UGA	Ugashik [*Alaska*] [*Airport symbol*] (OAG)
UGA	Ugashik, AK [*Location identifier FAA*] (FAAL)
UGA	Under General Anesthesia (DAVI)
UGA	Underwriters Grain Association (EA)
UGA	United Golfers' Association (EA)
UGA	Unity Gain Amplifier
UGA	University of Georgia (PDAA)
UGA	Unscreened Granulated Aluminate [*Inorganic chemistry*]
UGA	Uracil Guanine Adenine [*Genetics*]
UGAA	Untersuchungen zur Geschichte und Altertumskunde Aegyptens [*K. Sethe*] [*A publication*] (BJA)
UGAL	Union des Groupements d'Achat Cooperatifs de Detaillants de l'Europe [*Association of Cooperative Retailer-Owned Wholesalers of Europe - ACROWE*] (EAIO)
UGAN..........	Uganda
Ugan	Uganda (VRA)
Uganda Leg Focus...	Uganda Legal Focus [*A publication*] (DLA)
Uganda LF...	Uganda Law Focus [*A publication*] (DLA)
Uganda LR...	Uganda Protectorate Law Reports [*1904-51*] [*A publication*] (DLA)
UGAQ	United Graziers' Association of Queensland [*Australia*]
UGAQUE	United Graziers' Association of Queensland Union of Employees [*Australia*]
UGB	Pilot Point, AK [*Location identifier FAA*] (FAAL)
UGB	Union de Guerreros Blancos [*White Warriors' Union*] [*El Salvador*] [*Political party*] (PD)
UGB	Union Giovantu Benadir [*Benadir Youth Union*] [*Somalia*]
UGB	United Gulf Bank [*Middle East*]
UGB	Unity Gain Bandwidth
UGB	Upper Guard Band
UGB	Urban Growth Boundary
UGBW..........	Unity Gain Bandwidth
UGC	Ukrainian Gold Cross (EA)
UGC	Ultrasonic Grating Constant
UGC	United Gold Corp. [*Vancouver Stock Exchange symbol*]
UGC	United Nations Food and Agriculture Organization Intergovernmental Committee [*World Food Program*]
UGC	Unity Gain Crossover
UGC	Universal Guided Column

UGC	University Grants Commission [*India*]
UGC	University Grants Committee [*British*]
UGC	Uracil Guanine Cytosine [*A triplet of bases coding for the amino acid, cysteine*] (EES)
UGC	Urgench [*Former USSR Airport symbol*] (OAG)
UGCA...........	Union of German Cultural Associations [*Czech Republic*] (BUAC)
UGCAA	Union Generale des Cooperatives Agricoles d'Approvisionnement
UGCW..........	United Glass and Ceramic Workers of America (BUAC)
UGCW..........	United Glass and Ceramic Workers of North America
UGD	United Greenwood [*Vancouver Stock Exchange symbol*]
UGDP..........	University Group Diabetes Program [*Study group involving 12 medical schools*] [*Defunct*]
UGE	Undergraduate Engineering Program [*Air Force*]
UGEAO	Union Generale des Etudiants d'Afrique Occidentale [*General Union of West African Students*]
UGEC	Union Generale des Etudiants Congolais [*General Union of Congolese Students*]
UGEE	Yerevan/Zvartnots [*Former USSR ICAO location identifier*] (ICLI)
UGEED	Union Generale des Etudiants et Eleves Dahomeens
U Gefl AWG...	Um Gefaellige Antwort Wird Gebeten [*The Favor of an Answer Is Requested*] [*Correspondence*] [*German*]
UGEG	Union Generale des Etudiants Guineens [*General Union of Guinean Students*]
UGEM	Union Generale des Etudiants du Maroc [*General Union of Moroccan Students*]
UGEMA........	Union Generale des Etudiants Musulmans d'Algerie [*General Union of Moslem Students of Algeria*]
U Georgia	[*The*] University of Georgia (GAGS)
UGESP.........	Uniform Guidelines on Employee Selection Procedures [*Equal Employment Opportunity Commission*] (GFGA)
UGET	Union Generale des Etudiants Tunisiens [*General Union of Tunisian Students*]
UGF	Unidentified Growth Factor
UGF	United Givers Fund
UGF	Unserviceable Generation Factor [*Military*]
UGF	US-North Africa (Gibraltar) Convoy-Fast [*World War II*]
UGFNAB	Ultrasound-Guided Fine-Needle Aspiration Biopsy [*Medicine*]
UGG	Ugland Air AS [*Norway ICAO designator*] (FAAC)
UGG	Uracil Guanine Guanine [*A triplet of bases coding for the amino acid, tryptophan*] (EES)
UGGG..........	Tbilisi/Novoalexeyevka [*Former USSR ICAO location identifier*] (ICLI)
UGGI	Union Geodesique et Geophysique Internationale [*International Union of Geodesy and Geophysics*]
UGGSC........	Uggscombe [*England*]
UGH	Unstable-Type Glycated Hemoglobin [*Medicine*] (DB)
UGH	Uveitis, Glaucoma, and Hyphema Plus Vitreous Hemorrhage [*Syndrome*] [*Ophthalmology*] (DAVI)
UGH	Uveitis-Glaucoma-Hyphemia [*Ophthalmology*]
UGHA..........	United in Group Harmony Association (EA)
UGHP..........	Undergraduate Helicopter Pilot Training [*Army*]
UGI	Uganik [*Alaska*] [*Airport symbol*] (OAG)
UGI	UGI Corp. [*Formerly, United Gas Improvement Co.*] [*NYSE symbol*] (SPSG)
UGI	Union Geographique Internationale [*International Geographical Union*]
UGI	Upper Gastrointestinal [*Medicine*]
UGIB	Upper Gastrointestinal Bleeding [*Medicine*]
UGIH	Upper Gastrointestinal Tract Hemorrhage [*Medicine*]
UGIS	Upper Gastrointestinal Series [*Medicine*] (DAVI)
UgJ	Uganda Journal [*A publication*]
UGJA	United Galician Jews of America [*Defunct*] (EA)
UGL	Inter-Island Air, Inc. [*ICAO designator*] (FAAC)
UGL	Uglegorsk [*Former USSR Seismograph station code, US Geological Survey*] (SEIS)
UGL	Utility General
UGLAS	Uniform General Ledger Accounting Structure (NVT)
UGLC	University of Glasgow Language Centre (BUAC)
UGLE	United Grand Lodge of England [*Masonry*]
UGLE	Universal Graphics Language Executive (MCD)
Ug LF...........	Uganda Law Focus [*A publication*] (DLA)
UGLI	Universal Gate for Logic Implementation [*Computer science*] (MCD)
UGLIAC........	United Gas Laboratories Internally Programmed Automatic Computer
UGLJ	University of Ghana. Law Journal [*A publication*]
UGLNSW.......	United Grand Lodge [*Masons*] of New South Wales [*Australia*]
Ug LR...........	Uganda Law Reports [*Africa*] [*A publication*] (DLA)
UGLRC	Upper Great Lakes Regional Commission [*Department of Commerce*]
UGLY	Ugly Duckling Corp. [*NASDAQ symbol*] (SAG)
UglyDck.......	Ugly Duckling Corp. [*Associated Press*] (SAG)
UgM	Ugaritic Manual [*A publication*] (BJA)
UG/M	Umdrehungen je Minute [*Revolutions per Minute*] [*German*]
UGM	Underwater Guided Missile [*DoD*] (MCD)
UGM	Urogenital Mesenchyme [*Medicine*]
UGMA..........	Uniform Gifts to Minors Act [*National Conference of Commissioners on Uniform State Laws*]
UGME	Undergraduate Medical Education (HCT)
UGML	Universal Guided Missile Launcher [*Navy*] (MCD)
UGMM	Mukhrani [*Former USSR ICAO location identifier*] (ICLI)
UGN	Waukegan, IL [*Location identifier FAA*] (FAAL)
UGNCO	Unit Gas Noncommissioned Officer [*Army World War II*]
UGND	Underground (AABC)
UGNE	Unigene Laboratories [*NASDAQ symbol*] (TTSB)
UGNE	Unigene Laboratories, Inc. [*NASDAQ symbol*] (NQ)
UGNEZ.........	Unigene Labs Wrrt'B' [*NASDAQ symbol*] (TTSB)
UGO	Uige [*Angola*] [*Airport symbol Obsolete*] (OAG)
UGO	Unigesco, Inc. [*Toronto Stock Exchange symbol*]

UGO .... Unit Gas Offices [Army World War II]
UGO .... Unmanned Geophysical Observatory [National Science Foundation]
UGOC .... United Greek Orthodox Charities [Defunct] (EA)
UGOT .... Urine Glutamic-Oxaloacetic Transaminase [An enzyme]
UGP .... Union des Gaullistes de Progres [Union of Progressive Gaullists] [France Political party] (PPE)
UGP .... United Global Petroleum, Inc. [Vancouver Stock Exchange symbol]
UGPA .... Undergraduate Grade-Point Average [Higher education]
UGPCC .... Uniform Grocery Product Code Council [Later, UPCC] (EA)
UGPP .... Uridine Diphosphoglucose Pyrophosphorylase [An enzyme]
Ug Pr LR ..... Uganda Protectorate Law Reports [Africa] [A publication] (DLA)
UGR .... Ultrasonic Grain Refinement
UGR .... United Gunn Resources [Vancouver Stock Exchange symbol]
UGR .... Universal Graphic Recorder [Raytheon Co.]
UGrdn .... United-Guardian, Inc. [Associated Press] (SAG)
UGRE .... Undergraduate Record Examination [Education]
UGRR .... Underground Railroad [A smuggling system] [Criminal slang]
UGS .... Unattended Ground Sensors
UGS .... Uniaxial Gyrostabilizer
UGS .... Union de la Gauche Socialiste
UGS .... Union des Guineens au Senegal [Union of Guineans in Senegal] [Political party] (PD)
UGS .... Union Graduate School [Yellow Springs, Ohio]
UGS .... United Grounders' Society [A union] [British]
UGS .... Upper Group Stop [Nuclear energy] (NRCH)
UGS .... Upper Guide Structure [Nuclear energy] (NRCH)
UGS .... Urogenital Sinus [Anatomy]
UGS .... Urogenital System [Medicine]
UGS .... US-North Africa (Gibraltar) Convoy-Slow [World War II]
UGSA .... Uniform Grain Storage Agreement (AAGC)
UGSA .... Union Generale des Syndicats Algeriens [General Federation of Algerian Trade Unions]
UGSCAP ...... Union of German Social-Cultural Associations in Poland (BUAC)
UGSP .... United Galaxy Sanitation Patrol [In TV series "Quark"]
UGSS .... Sukhumi [Former USSR ICAO location identifier] (ICLI)
UGSS .... Union of Girls' Schools for Social Service [British] (BI)
UGSS .... Union of Local and Non Local General Service Staff [Food and Agriculture Organisation of the United Nations] (BUAC)
UgT .... Ugaritic Textbook [A publication] (BJA)
UGT .... Underground Test (MCD)
UGT .... Union General de Trabajadores de Espana [General Union of Spanish Workers] [In exile]
UGT .... United Bible Societies' Greek New Testament [A publication] (BJA)
UGT .... Upgraded Third-Generation Enroute Software Program [Computer science] (MCD)
UGT .... Upgrade Training [Military] (AFM)
UGT .... Urgent
UGT .... Urogenital Tract [Medicine]
UGT .... User Group Table [Computer science] (MHDB)
UGTA .... Union Generale des Travailleurs Algeriens [General Union of Algerian Workers]
UGTAN .... Union Generale des Travailleurs d'Afrique Noire [General Union of Workers of Black Africa]
UGTC .... Union Generale des Travailleurs Centrafricains [General Union of Central African Workers]
UGTC .... Union Generale des Travailleurs du Cameroun [General Union of Workers of Cameroon]
UGTCI .... Union Generale des Travailleurs de la Cote D'Ivoire [General Union of Workers of the Ivory Coast]
UGTD .... Uniform Geometrical Theory of Diffraction (MCD)
UGTD .... Union Generale des Travailleurs du Dahomey [General Union of Workers of Dahomey]
UGTK .... Union Generale des Travailleurs du Kamerun [General Union of Workers of the Cameroon]
UGTM .... Union Generale des Travailleurs de Mauritanie [General Union of Workers of Mauritania]
UGTM .... Union Generale des Travailleurs du Maroc [General Union of Workers of Morocco]
UGTS .... Union Generale des Travailleurs du Senegal [General Union of Workers of Senegal]
UGTT .... Union Generale de Travailleurs Tunisiens [General Federation of Tunisian Workers]
UGU .... Uracil Guanine Uracil [A triplet of bases coding for the amino acid, cysteine] (EES)
UGV .... Unmanned Ground Vehicle [Military robotics]
UGV/SJPO .... Unmannned Ground Vehicles/Systems Joint Project Office [Army] (RDA)
UGW .... United Garment Workers of America (EA)
UGWU .... United General Workers' Union [Belize] (BUAC)
UH .... Air-Cushion Vehicle built by Universal Hovercraft [US] [Usually used in combination with numerals]
UH .... Austin Airways [ICAO designator] (AD)
UH .... Ugaritic Handbook [C. H. Gordon] [A publication] (BJA)
UH .... Unavailable Hours [Electronics] (IEEE)
UH .... Underhatch
uH .... Unfractionated Heparin [Anticoagulant]
UH .... Union of Hungarians [Czech Republic] (BUAC)
UH .... United Humanitarians (EA)
UH .... Unit Head
UH .... Unit Heater [Technical drawings]
UH .... Unit Hydrograph
UH .... University of Hawaii [Honolulu, HI]
UH .... Upper Half
UH .... Upper Hemispherical (MCD)
UH .... U.S. Home [NYSE symbol] (TTSB)

UH .... US Home Corp. [NYSE symbol] (SPSG)
UH .... Utah [Obsolete] (ROG)
UH .... Utility Helicopter [Military] (AABC)
UHA .... Ukrains'ka Halyts'ka Armiia
UHA .... Ultrahigh Altitude
UHA .... Unable Higher Altitude [Aviation] (FAAC)
UHA .... Unexpected Home Attack [Medicine]
UHA .... Union House of Assembly [South Africa] (DAS)
UHA .... United Homeowners' Association (EA)
UHA .... Universitets- och Hogskoleambetet [National Board of Universities and Colleges] [Ministry of Education and Cultural Affairs] [Information service or system] [Sweden] (IID)
UHA .... Upper Half Assembly
UHAA .... United Horological Association of America [Later, AWI]
UHAB .... Urban Homesteading Assistance Board (EA)
UHAC .... United Hellenic American Congress (EA)
UHAL .... AMERCO [NASDAQ symbol] (SAG)
U Hartford ... University of Hartford (GAGS)
U Hawaii ..... University of Hawaii (GAGS)
UHB .... Ultra High Bypass [Aviation] (DA)
UHB .... Urban Haute Bourgeoisie (WDAA)
UHBI .... Upper Hemibody Irradiation [Radiation Therapy] (DAVI)
UHB-LED..... Ultra-High Brightness Light-Emitting Diode (AAEL)
UHBP .... Ekimcham [Former USSR ICAO location identifier] (ICLI)
UHC .... Ultimate Holding Company
UHC .... Unburned Hydrocarbon [Also, UBHC] [Fuel technology]
UHC .... Unburned Hydrocarbons
UHC .... Under Honorable Conditions [Military]
UHC .... Unit Hardware Cost (MCD)
UHC .... University Hospital Consortium
UHC .... University of Houston at Clear Lake City, Houston, TX [OCLC symbol] (OCLC)
UHCC .... University of Houston Coastal Center [Research center] (RCD)
UHCMWIU ... United Hatters, Cap, and Millinery Workers International Union
UHCO .... Universal American Financial Corp. [NASDAQ symbol] (SAG)
UHCO .... Universal Holding Corp. [NASDAQ symbol] (NQ)
UHCO .... Univl Holding Corp. [NASDAQ symbol] (TTSB)
UHCOW .... Universal Hldg Wrrt [NASDAQ symbol] (TTSB)
UHCP .... United Heritage Corp. [NASDAQ symbol] (NQ)
UHCS .... Ultrahigh Capacity Storage
UHD .... Unstable Hemoglobin Disease [Hematology] (DAVI)
UHDDS .... Uniform Hospital Discharge Data Set [National Center for Health Statistics]
UHDODT ..... Unable Higher Due Opposite Direction Traffic [Aviation] (FAAC)
UHDSDT ..... Unable Higher Due Same Direction Traffic [Aviation] (FAAC)
UHDT .... Unable Higher Due Traffic [Aviation] (FAAC)
UHDY .... Union of Hungarian Democratic Youth [Romania] [Political party] (BUAC)
UHE .... Uherske Hradiste [Former Czechoslovakia] [Airport symbol Obsolete] (OAG)
UHE .... Ultimate Hour Estimate (MCD)
UHE .... Ultrahigh Efficiency [Arc lamp]
UHE .... Ultrahigh Energy
UHE .... Usual Home Elsewhere [Bureau of the Census] (GFGA)
U Health Sc (Chicago)... University of Health Science Chicago Medicine School (GAGS)
UHECL .... Ultra-High-Speed Emitter Coupled Logic (CIST)
UHECR .... Ultra-High-Energy Cosmic Ray
UHF .... Ulster Historical Foundation (EA)
UHF .... Ultrahigh-Frequency [Electricity of radio waves]
UHF .... Uniform Heat Flux [Engineering]
UHF .... United Health Foundations [Defunct]
UHF .... Unrestricted Hartree-Fock [Wave-Function]
UHFDF .... Ultrahigh-Frequency Direction Finder
UHFF .... Ultrahigh-Frequency Filter
UHFG .... Ultrahigh-Frequency Generator
UHF/HF .... Ultrahigh-Frequency/High-Frequency (MCD)
UHFJ .... Ultrahigh-Frequency Jammer
UHFO .... Ultrahigh-Frequency Oscillator
UHFR .... Ultrahigh-Frequency Receiver
UHFRU .... Ultrahigh Frequency Radio Unit (MCD)
UHFS .... Unsteady Heat Flux Sensor
UHG .... Urban History Group [Defunct] (EA)
UHHH .... Khabarovsk/Novy [Former USSR ICAO location identifier] (ICLI)
UHHO .... Troitskoye [Former USSR ICAO location identifier] (ICLI)
UHI .... Upper Head Injection [Nuclear energy] (NRCH)
UHi .... Utah State Historical Society, Salt Lake City, UT [Library symbol Library of Congress] (LCLS)
UHJA .... United Hungarian Jews of America (EA)
UHK .... University of Hard Knocks [West Virginia] ["University" founded by Jim Comstock and based on the expression "school of hard knocks"]
UHL .... Unge Hoyres Landsforbund [Norway Political party] (EAIO)
UHL .... Universal Hypertrichosis Lanuginosa [Medicine] (MAE)
UHL .... User Header Label (CMD)
UHLCADS .... Ultra-High-Level Container Airdrop System [Military] (MCD)
UHLD .... Unholding Corp. [NASDAQ symbol] (TTSB)
UHLD .... Uni Holding Corp. [NASDAQ symbol] (SAG)
UHLI .... United Home Life Insurance Co. [Greenwood, IN] [NASDAQ symbol] (NQ)
UHlthCr....... United Healthcare Corp. [Associated Press] (SAG)
UHLVFD ...... Ultra High Luminance Vacuum Fluorescent Display [Automotive engineering]
UHM .... Universal Host Machine [Computer science] (MHDI)
UHML .... Lavrentiya [Former USSR ICAO location identifier] (ICLI)

UHMPE	Ultra-High Molecular Weight Polyethylene (EDCT)
UHMR	Beringovsky [Former USSR ICAO location identifier] (ICLI)
UHMS	Ultrasonic Helmet Mounted Sight [Army] (MCD)
UHMS	Undersea and Hyperbaric Medical Society (EA)
UHMW	Ultrahigh Molecular Weight
UHMW-PE	Ultrahigh Molecular Weight Polyethylene [Organic chemistry]
UHMWPE	Ultra High Molecular Weight Polythylene
UHN	Uranyl Hexahydrate Nitrate (GFGA)
UHOS	Universal Hospital Services [NASDAQ symbol] (SAG)
UHOS	Univl Hospital Svcs [NASDAQ symbol] (TTSB)
U Houston	University of Houston (GAGS)
UHP	Ugaritic-Hebrew Philology [Rome] [M. Dahood] [A publication] (BJA)
UHP	Ultra-High Performance [in UHP Imposer, a product of Opti-Copy, Inc.]
UHP	Ultra High Performance [Automotive engineering]
UHP	Ultra-High Porosity [Materials science]
UHP	Ultrahigh Power
UHP	Ultra-High Pressure [Water cutting tools]
UHP	Ultrahigh Purity
UHP	Undergraduate Helicopter Pilot Training [Army]
UHP	United Air Service [Nigeria] [ICAO designator] (FAAC)
UHPFB	University of Hawaii Press
UHPFB	Untreated Hard Pressed Fiberboard
UHPMIS	Urban Homesteading Program Management Information System [Department of Housing and Urban Development] (GFGA)
UHPr	U.S. Home Cv Pfd [NYSE symbol] (TTSB)
UHPS	Underground Hydro-Pumped Storage [Room]
UHPT	Undergraduate Helicopter Pilot Training (MCD)
UHR	Ultra High Reduction (NITA)
UHR	Ultrahigh Resistance
uhr	Ultrahigh Resistance (IDOE)
UHR	Ultrahigh Resolution
UHR	Underlying Heart Rhythm [Medicine] (DMAA)
UHR	United Hearne Resources Ltd. [Vancouver Stock Exchange symbol]
UHR	Upper Hybrid Resonance [Spectroscopy]
UHRA	Uganda Human Rights Activists (BUAC)
UHRA	United Hunts Racing Association [Later, NSHA]
UHRC	Ulcerohemorrhagic Rectocolitis [Medicine] (DB)
UHR-ESCA	Ultrahigh-Resolution Electron Spectrometer for Chemical Analysis
UHRF	Ultra High Resolution Facsimile (NITA)
UHrtg	United Heritage Corp. [Associated Press] (SAG)
UHS	Ultimate Heat Sink [Nuclear energy] (NRCH)
UHS	Ultrahigh Speed
UHS	Ulyanovsk Higher Civil Aviation School [Former USSR] [FAA designator] (FAAC)
UHS	Unitarian Historical Society [Later, UUHS] (EA)
UHS	United HIAS Service (EA)
UHS	Unit Handling System
UHS	Universal Health Services, Inc. [NYSE symbol] (NQ)
UHS	Universalist Historical Society [Later, UUHS] (EA)
UHS	University of Health Sciences - Chicago Medical School
UHS	Univl Health Svs Cl'B' [NYSE symbol] (TTSB)
UHSA	United Halsinglan Society of America [Defunct] (EA)
UHSC	University Health Services Clinic (DAVI)
UHS-CMS	University of Health Sciences - Chicago Medical School
UHSG	Unemployment and Health Study Group (BUAC)
UHT	Ultraheat Tested [Milk] (CDAI)
UHT	Ultraheat Treated
UHT	Ultrahigh Temperature
UHT	Ultrasonic Hardness Tester
UHT	Umbilical Handling Technician [Computer science] (IAA)
UHT	Underheat
UHT	United Hebrew Trades of the State of New York (EA)
UHT	Unit Horizontal Tail
UHT	Universal Hand Tool
UHT	Universal Health Realty Income Trust [NYSE symbol] (SPSG)
UHT	Universal Horizontal Tail [Aviation] (NG)
UHT	Univl Health Realty [NYSE symbol] (TTSB)
UHTPB	Unsaturated Hydroxyl-Terminated Polybutadiene [Organic chemistry]
UHTREX	Ultrahigh-Temperature Reactor Experiment [Nuclear energy]
UHTS	Universal Heights [NASDAQ symbol] (TTSB)
UHTS	Universal Heights, Inc. [NASDAQ symbol] (SAG)
UHTSW	Universal Heights Wrrt [NASDAQ symbol] (TTSB)
UHTV	Unmanned Hypersonic Test Vehicle (MCD)
UHV	Ultrahigh Vacuum
UHV	Ultrahigh Voltage
UHV	Under Hatch Valve
UHVA	United Hellenic Voters of America (EA)
UHVC	Ultrahigh Vacuum Chamber
UHV/CVD	Ultrahigh Vacuum Chemical Vapor Deposition [Coating technology] [Semiconductor technology]
UHVI	Ultra High Viscosity Index
UHVS	Ultrahigh Vacuum System
UH.WS	U.S. Home Wrrt [NYSE symbol] (TTSB)
UI	Flugfelag Nordurlands [Northlands Air] [ICAO designator] (AD)
UI	International Union of Graphic Reproduction Industries (BUAC)
UI	Ulcer Index (STED)
UI	Ultrasonic Industry (WDAA)
UI	Underground Injection [of wastes]
U/I	Under Instructions (ADA)
UI	Understanding Industry (AIE)
UI	Underwear Institute [Later, NKMA] (EA)
UI	Undifferentiated Infiltrating [Tumor] [Oncology]
UI	Unearned Income (MHDW)
UI	Unemployment Insurance

UI	Unexplained Infertility
U/I	Unidentified
UI	Union Institute (EA)
UI	Union Interparlementaire [Inter-Parliamentary Union] (EAIO)
UI	Union-Intersection [Statistics]
UI	Unique Indentifier [Computer science]
UI	United Inches
UI	United Inns (EFIS)
ui	United Kingdom Miscellaneous Islands [MARC country of publication code Library of Congress] (LCCP)
UI	Unit of Issue (KSC)
UI	Universal Instantiation [Rule of quantification] [Logic]
UI	Universal-International Studios (IIA)
UI	Unix International [Computer science] (PCM)
UI	Unnumbered Information [Telecommunications] (OSI)
UI	Unreported Income [IRS]
UI	Unsigned Integer [Computer science]
UI	Uranium Institute [British] (EAIO)
UI	Urban Initiatives (EA)
UI	Urban Institute (EA)
UI	Ureteral-Intestinal [Medicine] (DAVI)
UI	Urinary Incontinence (STED)
UI	Urinary Infection [Medicine]
UI	Uroporphyrin Isomerase [An enzyme] (AAMN)
UI	USE, Inc. [Acronym is now organization's official name] (EA)
UI	User Interface
UI	Ut Infra [As Below] [Latin]
UIA	Argentine Industrial Union (BUAC)
UIA	Uganda Investment Authority
UIA	Ukrainian Institute of America (EA)
UIA	Ultrasonic Industry Association (EA)
UIA	Unemployment Insurance Act [Canada]
UIA	Union Internationale Contre l'Alcoolisme
UIA	Union Internationale des Architectes [International Union of Architects] (EAIO)
UIA	Union Internationale des Avocats [International Union of Lawyers]
UIA	Union Internationale des Syndicats des Industries Alimentaires
UIA	Union of International Associations [See also UAI] [Brussels, Belgium] (EAIO)
UIA	United Inventors Association
UIA	United Israel Appeal [Australia]
UIA	Unit Identifier Applications (MCD)
UIA	Universidad Iberoamericana, Mexico, DF, Mexico [OCLC symbol] (OCLC)
UIA	Uranium Institute of America (EA)
UIA	Urban Impact Analysis (EG)
UIA	Usable Inside Area (MCD)
UIAA	Chita/Kadala [Former USSR ICAO location identifier] (ICLI)
UIAA	Union Internationale des Associations d'Alpinisme [International Union of Alpine Associations] [Switzerland]
UIAA	Union Internationale des Associations d'Annonceurs [International Union of Advertisers Associations]
UIAA	Union Internationale des Assureurs Aeronautiques
UIACM	Union Internationale des Automobile-Clubs Medicaux [International Union of Associations of Doctor-Motorists]
UIAL	United Italian American League (EA)
UIALC	United Italian American Labor Council (EA)
UIAMS	Union Internationale d'Action Morale et Sociale [International Union for Moral and Social Action]
UIAPME	Union Internationale de l'Artisanat et des Petites et Moyennes Entreprises [International Association of Crafts and Small and Medium-Sized Enterprises]
UIAPPA	Union Internationale des Associations de Prevention de la Pollution Atmospherique [International Union of Air Pollution Prevention Associations] (EAIO)
UIARVEP	Unione Italiana Agenti Rappresentati Viaggiatori e Piazzisti [Italian Union of Agents and Travelers]
UIAS	Unified Information Access System [California State University]
UIASPPA	Uniform Individual Accident and Sickness Policy Provisions Act [National Association of Insurance Commissioners]
UIAT	Union Internationale des Syndicats des Industries de l'Alimentation et des Tabacs
UIATF	United Indians of All Tribes Foundation (EA)
UIATU	Union of Independent Albanian Trade Unions (BUAC)
UIB	Quibdo [Colombia] [Airport symbol] (OAG)
UIB	Unidentified Infrared Band [Astrophysics]
UIB	Unione Italiana Bancari [Italian Union of Bank Employees]
UIB	Union Internationale des Maitres Boulangers [International Union of Master Bakers]
UIB	United Independent Broadcasters (NTCM)
UIBB	Bratsk [Former USSR ICAO location identifier] (ICLI)
UIBC	Unbound Iron-Binding Capacity (STED)
UIBC	Unsaturated Iron-Binding Capacity [Clinical chemistry]
UIBG	Union Internationale de Banque en Guinee (EY)
UIBPIP	United International Bureau for the Protection of Intellectual Property [Superseded by WIPO]
UIBWM	Trade Unions International of Workers of Building, Wood, and Building Materials Industries
UIC	U Interface Circuit (NITA)
UIC	Ultraviolet Image Converter
UIC	Underground Injection Control [Environmental Protection Agency]
UIC	Unemployment Insurance Code (OICC)
UIC	Unemployment Insurance Commission [Canada]
UIC	Unidad de Izquierda Comunista [Unity of the Communist Left] [Mexico Political party] (PPW)

UIC............... Unified Information Council [*Israel*] (BUAC)
UIC............... Union Internationale de Cristallographie [*International Union of Crystallography*] (EAIO)
UIC............... Union Internationale des Chemins de Fer [*International Union of Railways*] (EAIO)
UIC............... Union of Independent Companies [*British*] (DBA)
UIC............... Union of International Conventions
UIC............... United Industrial [*NYSE symbol*] (TTSB)
UIC............... United Industrial Corp. [*NYSE symbol*] (SPSG)
UIC............... United Insulator Co. (IAA)
UIC............... Unit Identification Code [*Army*] (AABC)
UIC............... University of Illinois
UIC............... Upper Information Center [*Aviation*]
UIC............... Urban Information Center [*Milwaukee Urban Observatory*] [*Ceased operations*] [*Information service or system*] (IID)
UIC............... Urea Inclusion Compound [*Chemistry*]
UIC............... Urinary Immune Complex
UIC............... User Identification Code
UICA .... Union Internationale des Constructeurs d'Ascenseurs [*International Union of Elevator Constructors - IUEC*]
UICA .... Union of Independent Colleges of Art (EA)
UICANY......... United Irish Counties Association of New York (EA)
UICB .... Union Internationale des Centres du Batiment [*International Union of Building Centers*] [*British*]
UICBP .... Uganda Institutional Capacity Building Project
UICC .... Union Internationale Contre le Cancer [*International Union Against Cancer*] [*Switzerland*]
UICC .... University of Illinois at Chicago Circle
UIC CR.......... Union of Towns and Communities of the Czech Republic (BUAC)
UICGF .... Union Internationale du Commerce en Gros de la Fleur [*International Union for the Wholesale Flower Trade*]
UICI .... UICI [*NASDAQ symbol*] [*Formerly, United Insurance*] (SG)
UICI .... UICI [*Associated Press*] (SAG)
UICI .... United Insurance [*NASDAQ symbol*] (TTSB)
UICI .... United Insurance Companies, Inc. [*NASDAQ symbol*] (NQ)
UICIO .... Unit Identification Code Information Officer [*Military*] (AABC)
UICM .... Union Internationale Catholique des Classes Moyennes [*International Catholic Union of the Middle Classes*]
UICM .... University of Illinois College of Medicine (HGEN)
UICN .... Union Mondiale Pour la Nature (EERA)
UICNR .... Union Internationale pour la Conservation de la Nature et de ses Resources [*International Union for Conservation of Nature and Natural Resources*] [*Switzerland*] (EAIO)
UICO .... UNICO, Inc. Delaware [*NASDAQ symbol*] (NQ)
UICO .... Unico Inc. Oklahoma [*NASDAQ symbol*] (TTSB)
UICP .... Uniform Inventory Control Point
UICP .... Uniform Inventory Control Points System [*Military*]
UICP .... Union Internationale de la Couverture et Plomberie (EA)
UICPA .... Union Internationale de Chimie Pure et Appliquee [*International Union of Pure and Applied Chemistry*]
UICR .... Union Internationale des Chauffeurs Routiers [*International Union of Lorry Drivers - IULD*] (EAIO)
UICSM .... University of Illinois Committee on School Mathematics
UICT............. Union Internationale Contre la Tuberculose [*International Union Against Tuberculosis - IUAT*] (EAIO)
UICTMR .... Union Internationale Contre la Tuberculose et les Maladies Respiratoires [*International Union Against Tuberculosis and Lung Disease - IUATLD*] (EAIO)
UICWA .... United Infants' and Children's Wear Association (EA)
UID .... Selected Decisions by Umpire for Northern Ireland, Respecting Claims to Benefit [*A publication*] (DLA)
UID .... Unemployment Insurance Department
UID .... Universal Identifier (IAA)
UID .... Uno In Die [*Once daily*] [*Pharmacy*] (DAVI)
UID .... Usable Inside Depth (MCD)
UID .... User Identification (AAEL)
UIDA .... Union Internationale des Organisations de Detaillants de la Branche Alimentaire [*International Federation of Grocers' Associations*]
UIDA............ United Indian Development Association (EA)
UIDAC.......... Unione Italiana Dipendenti Aziende Commerciali ed Affini [*Italian Union of Commerical and Allied Workers*]
U Idaho....... University of Idaho (GAGS)
UIDL .... Unique Identification Listing [*Computer science*] (IGQR)
UIE............. Institute for Education [*UNESCO*] (BUAC)
UIE............. UNESCO Institute for Education
UIE............. Union Internationale d'Editeurs [*International Publishers Association - IPA*] (EAIO)
UIE............. Union Internationale d'Electrothermie [*International Union for Electroheat*] (EAIO)
UIE............. Union Internationale des Editeurs [*International Union of Publishers*] (NTCM)
UIE............. Union Internationale des Etudiants [*International Union of Students - IUS*] (EAIO)
UIEA............. Union Internationale des Etudiants en Architecture [*International Union of Students in Architecture*]
UIEC............. Union Internationale de l'Exploitation Cinematographique [*International Union of Cinematographic Exhibitors*] (EAIO)
UIECS .... Union of International and European Civil Servants
UIEIS .... Union Internationale pour l'Etude des Insectes Sociaux [*International Union for the Study of Social Insects - IUSSI*] [*Netherlands*]
UIEO .... Union of International Engineering Organizations
UIEP .... Union Internationale des Entrepreneurs de Peinture
UIES............. Union Internationale d'Education pour la Sante [*International Union of Health Education - IUHE*] [*Paris, France*] (EAIO)

UIES............. Union Internationale d'Etudes Sociales [*International Union for Social Studies*]
UIEV............. Universal Imagery Exploitation Viewer (DNAB)
UIF............. Ultraviolet Interference Filter
UIF............. Undegraded Insulin Factor [*Medicine*] (MAE)
UIF............. Unfavorable Information File [*Military*]
Uif............. Unified (EBF)
Uif............. Uniform (EBF)
UIF............. Union Internationale de Ferrecarriles [*International Union of Railways*]
UIF............. Universal Intermolecular Force
UIF............. Unserviceable Items File
UIF............. USLIFE Income Fund [*NYSE symbol*] (TTSB)
UIF............. USLIFE Income Fund, Inc. [*NYSE symbol*] (SPSG)
UIFA............. Union Internationale des Femmes Architectes [*International Union of Women Architects - IUWA*] (EAIO)
UIFI............. Union Internationale des Fabricants d'Impermeables
UIFL............. Union Internationale des Federations de Detaillants en Produits Laitiers
uig............... Uigur [*MARC language code Library of Congress*] (LCCP)
UIG............. Uniform Inspection Guideline
UIG............. Uniglobe International Energy Corp. [*Vancouver Stock Exchange symbol*]
UIG............. User Instruction Group
UIGDC.......... Unione Internazionale des Giovani Democratici Cristiana [*International Union of Young Christian Democrats*]
UIGSE .... Union Internationale des Guides et Scouts d'Europe [*International Union of European Guides and Scouts - IUEGS*] [*Chateau Landon, France*] (EAIO)
UIH .... Qui Nhon [*South Vietnam*] [*Airport symbol*] (AD)
UIH .... University of Iowa Hospitals (DAVI)
UIH .... Urban and Industrial Health (KSC)
UIHE............. Union Internationale de l'Humanisme et de l'Ethique
UIHI............. United International Holdings, Inc. [*NASDAQ symbol*] (SAG)
UIHIA .... United Intl Hldgs'A' [*NASDAQ symbol*] (TTSB)
UIHMSU....... Union Internationale d'Hygiene et de Medecine Scolaires et Universitaires [*International Union of School and University Health and Medicine - IUSUHM*] [*Brussels, Belgium*] (EAIO)
UIHPS .... Union Internationale d'Histoire et de Philosophie des Sciences
UII............. Unified Industries, Inc.
UII............. Universal Identification Interface [*Allen-Bradley Co.*]
UII............. Utila Island [*Honduras*] [*Airport symbol Obsolete*] (OAG)
UIIDE .... Union Internationale des Infirmieres Diplomees d'Etat [*International Union of Registered Nurses*] [*France*] (EAIO)
UIIG .... Union Internationale de l'Industrie du Gaz [*International Gas Union - IGU*] [*Paris, France*] (EAIO)
UIII............. Irkutsk [*Former USSR ICAO location identifier*] (ICLI)
UIII............. Urban Information Interpreters, Inc. (IID)
UIIO............. Ust-Ordynsky [*Former USSR ICAO location identifier*] (ICLI)
UIJA............. Union Internationale des Journalistes Agricoles [*International Union of Agricultural Journalists*]
UIJC............. Universities and Industry Joint Committee (BUAC)
UIJDC .... Union Internationale de Jeunesse Democrate Chretienne [*International Union of Young Christian Democrats*]
UIJPLF......... Union Internationale des Journalistes et de la Presse de Langue Francaise [*International Union of French-Language Journalists and Press - IUFLJP*] (EAIO)
UIJS............. Union Internationale de la Jeunesse Socialiste [*International Union of Socialist Youth*]
UIKB............. Bodaybo [*Former USSR ICAO location identifier*] (ICLI)
UIKK............. Kirensk [*Former USSR ICAO location identifier*] (ICLI)
UIKW .... Vitim [*Former USSR ICAO location identifier*] (ICLI)
UIL............. Quillayute, WA [*Location identifier FAA*] (FAAL)
UIL............. Unione Italiana del Lavoro [*Italian Union of Labor*]
UIL............. United Capital Funding Partnership LP [*NYSE symbol*] (SAG)
UIL............. United Illuminating [*NYSE symbol*] (TTSB)
UIL............. United Illuminating Co. [*NYSE symbol*] (SPSG)
UIL............. UNIVAC Interactive Language [*Computer science*] (IEEE)
UIL............. University of Iowa, School of Library Science, Iowa City, IA [*OCLC symbol*] (OCLC)
UIL............. User Interface Language (SSD)
UILA............. Unione Italiana Lavoratori Assicurazioni [*Italian Union of Insurance Workers*]
UILAM .... Unione Italiana Lavoratori Albergo e Mensa [*Italian Union of Hotel and Restaurant Workers*]
UILE............. Union Internationale pour la Liberte d'Enseignement [*International Union for the Liberty of Education*]
UIL-GAS....... Unione Italiana Lavoratori Aziende Gas [*Italian Union of Gas Workers*]
UILI............. Union Internationale des Laboratoires Independents [*International Union of Independent Laboratories*] [*Elstree, Hertfordshire, England*] (EAIO)
U III .... University of Illinois (GAGS)
U III (Chicago)... University of Illinois at Chicago (GAGS)
U III LB......... University of Illinois. Law Bulletin [*A publication*] (DLA)
U III L Bull.... University of Illinois. Law Bulletin [*A publication*] (DLA)
UIllum.......... United Illuminating Co. [*Associated Press*] (SAG)
UILPrA......... Utd Cap Fd LP.9.625% CapSec'A' [*NYSE symbol*] (TTSB)
UILU .... University of Illinois, Urbana
UIM............. Quitman, TX [*Location identifier FAA*] (FAAL)
UIM............. Ufficio Informazioni Militare [*Office of Military Information*] [*Italian*]
UIM............. Ultra-Intelligent Machine
UIM............. Ultrasonic Interferometer Manometer [*Instrumentation*]
UIM............. Union Internationale des Magistrats [*International Association of Judges - IAJ*] (EAIO)

UIM.............. Union Internationale des Metis [*International Union of Individuals of Mixed Parentage*]
UIM.............. Union Internationale Monarchiste [*Weinsberg, Federal Republic of Germany*] (EAIO)
UIM.............. Union Internationale Motonautique [*Union of International Motorboating*] (EAIO)
UIM.............. Union of International Motorboating (EA)
UIMAS .... Ultrasound in Medicine - Australia Society
UIMC .... Union Internationale des Services Medicaux des Chemins de Fer [*International Union of Railway Medical Services*]
UIMI............. United Indian Missions, International (EA)
UIMJ........... Union Internationale des Maisons de Jeunesse [*Service de la FIJC*]
UIMP........... Union Internationale pour le Protection de la Moralite Publique [*International Union for the Protection of Public Morale*] [*France*]
UIMS .... User Interface Management System [*Computer science*]
UIMVT .... Union Internationale Contre les Maladies Veneriennes et les Treponematoses [*International Union Against the Venereal Diseases and the Treponematoses - IUVDT*]
UIN .... Quincy [*Illinois*] [*Airport symbol*] (OAG)
UIN .... Universal Internet Number
U Indianapolis... University of Indianapolis (GAGS)
UINF........... Union Internationale de la Navigation Fluviale [*International Union for Inland Navigation - IUIN*] (EAIO)
UINL .... Union Internationale du Notariat Latin [*International Union of Latin Notaries*]
UINN........... Nizhneudinsk [*Former USSR ICAO location identifier*] (ICLI)
UINP .... Unit of Insect Neurophysiology and Pharmacology [*University of Cambridge*] [*British*] (IRUK)
UIO .... Quito [*Ecuador*] [*Airport symbol*] (OAG)
UIO .... Union Internationale des Orientalistes [*International Union of Orientalists*]
UIO .... United Infertility Organization (EA)
UIO .... Units in Operation [*Business term*]
UIO .... Universal Input-Output [*Computer science*] (ECII)
UIO .... Utility Iterative Operation
UIOC .... Universal Input/Output Controller (NITA)
UIOD .... User Input/Output Devices [*Computer science*] (RDA)
UIOF .... Union Internationale des Organismes Familiaux [*International Union of Family Organizations - IUFO*] [*France*]
UIOGD .... Ut in Omnibus Glorificetur Deus [*That God May Be Glorified in All Things*] [*Latin*]
UIOOT .... Union Internationale des Organismes Officiels de Tourisme [*International Union of Official Travel Organizations*]
UIOVD.......... Union Internationale des Ouvriers du Vetement pour Dames [*International Ladies' Garment Workers' Union - ILGW*]
U Iowa......... [*The*] University of Iowa (GAGS)
U Iowa L Rev... University of Iowa. Law Review [*A publication*] (DLA)
UIP.............. Quimper [*France*] [*Airport symbol*] (OAG)
UIP.............. Unallowable Items Program [*IRS*]
UIP.............. Unfair Industrial Practice
UIP.............. Unione Italiana Pescatori [*Italian Union of Fishermen*]
UIP.............. Union Internationale d'Associations de Proprietaires de Wagons Particuliers [*International Union of Private Railway Truck Owners' Associations*] (EAIO)
UIP.............. Union Internationale de Patinage [*International Skating Union - ISU*] [*Davos-Platz, Switzerland*] (EAIO)
UIP.............. Union Internationale de Physique Pure et Appliquee [*International Union of Pure and Applied Physics*]
UIP.............. Union Internationale des Publicitaires
UIP.............. Union Interparlementaire
UIP.............. United Ireland Party
UIP.............. University of Illinois Press
UIP.............. Unusual Interstitial Pneumonitis (STED)
UIP.............. Usable in Place (MCD)
UIP.............. Usual Interstitial Pneumonia [*Medicine*]
UIP.............. Usual Interstitial Pneumonitis (STED)
UIPA .... United Indian Planners Association [*Defunct*] (EA)
UIPC .... Underground Injection Practices Council (EA)
UIPC .... Union Internationale de la Press Catholique [*International Union of the Catholic Press*] [*France*]
UIPC .... Union Internationale de la Presse Catholique [*International Catholic Press Union*]
UIPCG .... Union Internationale de la Patisserie, Confiserie, Glacerie [*International Union of Bakers and Confectioners*]
UIPD .... Ulrich's International Periodicals Directory [*A publication*]
UIPE............. Union Internationale de Protection de l'Enfance [*International Union for Child Welfare - IUCW*] [*Geneva, Switzerland*] [*Defunct*] (EA)
UIPFB .... Union Internationale de la Propriete Fonciere Batie [*International Union of Landed Property Owners*]
UIPI .... Union Internacional de Proteccion a la Infancia [*International Union for Child Welfare*]
UIPI .... Union Internationale de la Propriete Immobiliere [*International Union of Property Owners*] [*Paris, France*] (EAIO)
UIPM .... Union Internationale de la Presse Medicale [*International Union of the Medical Press*]
UIPMB .... Union Internationale de Pentathlon Moderne et Biathlon [*International Union for Modern Pentathlon and Biathlon*] (EAIO)
UIPN .... Union Internationale pour la Protection de la Nature [*International Union for the Protection of Nature - IUPN*] [*Later, IUCN*]
UIPPA .... Union Internationale de Physique Pure et Appliquee [*International Union of Pure and Applied Physics*]
UIPPI .... Union Internationale pour la Protection de la Propriete Industrielle [*International Union for the Protection of Industrial Property*]
UIPRE .... Union Internationale de la Presse Radiotechnique et Electronique [*Freiburg, Federal Republic of Germany*] (EAIO)

UIPVT .... Union Internationale Contre le Peril Venerien et la Treponematose [*International Union Against the Venereal Diseases and the Treponematoses*]
UIQ .... Upper Inner Quadrant [*Anatomy*]
UIR .... Quirindi [*Australia Airport symbol Obsolete*] (OAG)
UIR .... Unidentified Infrared Band [*Spectroscopy*]
UIR .... Union Internationale de Radiodiffusion [*International Broadcasting Union*] [*Also, IBU*] (NTCM)
UIR .... Union Internationale des Radioecologistes [*International Union of Radioecologists - IUR*] (EAIO)
UIR .... Union Internationale des Rembourreurs de l'Amerique du Nord [*Upholsterers' International Union of North America - UIU*] [*Canada*]
UIR .... Unitary Irreducible Representation
UIR .... United International Research, Inc.
UIR .... Unit Initial Range (MCD)
UIR .... University-Industry Research Program [*University of Wisconsin-Madison*] [*Information service or system*] (IID)
UIR .... Upper Information Region (NATG)
UIR .... Urban Intelligence Reports (CINC)
UIR .... User Instruction Register
UIR .... User Interface Requirement
UIRC .... Universal Interline Reservations Code
UIRD .... Union Internationale de la Resistance et de la Deportation [*International Union of Resistance and Deportee Movements*]
UIRR .... University-Industry Research Relationship
UIRV .... Universal Infrared Viewer (PDAA)
UIS .... Ulster-Irish Society (EA)
UIS .... Uncertain Inference System [*Logic*]
UIS .... Unemployment Insurance Service [*Department of Labor*]
UIS .... Union Internationale de Secours [*International Relief Union*]
UIS .... Union Internationale de Speleologie [*International Union of Speleology - IUS*] (EAIO)
UIS .... Union Internationale des Syndicats des Travailleurs des Transports [*Trade Unions International of Transport Workers*] (EAIO)
UIS .... Unisys Corp. [*NYSE symbol*] (SPSG)
UIS .... United Information Services, Inc. (IID)
UIS .... United Inventors and Scientists (IAA)
UIS .... Unit Identification System
UIS .... Universal Isolation Switch
UIS .... Unlimited Intermediate Storage [*Industrial engineering*]
UIS .... Upper Information Service (DA)
UIS .... Upper Internals Structure [*Nuclear energy*] (NRCH)
UIS .... Urban Information System (EERA)
UIS .... Utilization Information Service (STED)
UISA .... United Inventors and Scientists of America (EA)
UISAE .... Union Internationale des Sciences Anthropologiques et Ethnologiques [*International Union of Anthropological and Ethnological Sciences - IUAES*] (EAIO)
UISB .... Union Internationale des Sciences Biologiques [*International Union of Biological Sciences*]
UISC .... Unreported Interstate Shipment of Cigarettes
UISDC.......... Unemployment Insurance Service Design Center [*Department of Labor*]
UISE .... Union Internationale de Secours aux Enfants
UISG .... Union Internationale des Superieures Majeures [*International Union of Superiors General*] [*Rome, Italy*] (EAIO)
UISIF .... Union Internationale des Societies d'Ingenieurs Forestiers [*International Union of Societies of Foresters - IUSF*] [*Ottawa, ON*] (EAIO)
UISJM.......... Upper Internals Structure Jacking Mechanism [*Nuclear energy*] (NRCH)
UISM .... Union Internationale des Syndicats des Mineurs [*Miners' Trade Unions International*]
UISMM .... Union Internationale des Syndicats des Industries Metallurgiques et Mecaniques
UISMTE........ Union Internationale des Syndicats des Mineurs et des Travailleurs de l'Energie [*Trade Unions International of Miners and Workers in Energy - TUIMWE*] (EAIO)
UISN .... Union Internationale des Sciences de la Nutrition [*International Union of Nutritional Sciences - IUNS*] [*Wageningen, Netherlands*] (EA)
UISP .... Union Internationale des Societes de la Paix [*International Union of Peace Societies*]
UISP .... Union Internationale des Syndicats de Police [*International Union of Police Syndicates*] (EAIO)
UISPI .... Urethane Institute, Society of the Plastics Industry (EA)
UISPP .... Union Internationale des Sciences Prehistoriques et Protohistoriques [*International Union of Prehistoric and Protohistoric Sciences*]
UISPrA......... Unisys $3.75cm Cv A Pfd [*NYSE symbol*] (TTSB)
UISPTT .... Union Internationale Sportive des Postes, des Telephones, et des Telecommunications [*International Sports Union of Post, Telephone, and Telecommunications Services - ISUPTTS*] [*Switzerland*]
UISTABP...... Union Internacional de Sindicatos de Trabajadores de la Agricultura, de los Bosques, y de las Plantaciones [*Trade Unions International of Agricultural, Forestry, and Plantation Workers*]
UISTAF .... Union Internationale des Syndicats des Travailleurs Agricoles et Forestiers et des Organisations des Paysans Travailleurs
UISTAFP ...... Union Internationale des Syndicats des Travailleurs de l'Agriculture, des Forets, et des Plantations [*Trade Unions International of Agriculture, Forestry, and Plantation Workers - TUIAFPW*] [*Prague, Czechoslovakia*] (EAIO)
UISTAV .... Union Internationale pour la Science, la Technique, et les Applications du Vide [*International Union for Vacuum Science, Technique, and Applications - IUVSTA*] (EAIO)

UISTC .... Union Internationale des Syndicats des Travailleurs du Commerce [*Trade Unions International of Workers in Commerce*]

UISTICPS..... Union Internationale des Syndicats des Travailleurs des Industries Chimiques du Petrole et Similaires

UIS Transport... Union Internationale des Syndicats des Travailleurs des Transports [*Trade Unions International of Transport Workers*] [*Hungary*] (EAIO)

UIT.............. Jaluit [*Marshall Islands*] [*Airport symbol*] (OAG)

UIT.............. Ultraviolet Imaging Telescope

UIT.............. Union des Independants de Tananarive [*Union of Independents of Tananarive*]

UIT.............. Union Internationale des Telecommunications [*International Telecommunication Union*] [*French United Nations*] (DUND)

UIT.............. Union Internationale des Typographes [*International Typographical Union - ITU*]

UIT.............. Union Internationale de Tir [*International Shooting Union*] [*See also IS*] [*Germany*] (EAIO)

UIT.............. Unit Impulse Train

UIT.............. Unit Investment Trusts [*Standard and Poor's Corp.*] [*Information service or system*]

UIT.............. Utility Interim Tape (SAA)

UITA.......... Union Internationale des Travailleurs de l'Alimentation et des Branches Connexes [*International Union of Food and Allied Workers Associations*]

UITA.......... Union of International Technical Associations [*See also UATI*] [*ICSU*] [*Paris, France*] (EAIO)

UITAM .... Union Internationale de Mecanique Theorique et Appliquee [*International Union of Theoretical and Applied Mechanics*]

UITBB .... Union Internationale des Syndicats des Travailleurs du Batiment, du Bois, et desMateriaux de Construction [*Trade Unions International of Workers of the Building, Wood, and Building Materials Industries*]

UITCA .... International Union of Co-operative and Associated Tourism (EAIO)

Uitg............. Uitgave [*Edition*] [*Netherlands*] (ILCA)

UITP.......... Union Internationale des Transports Publics [*International Union of Public Transport*] (EAIO)

UIU.............. Universal Interactive Unit [*Telecommunications*]

UIU.............. University of Illinois, Urbana, IL [*OCLC symbol*] (OCLC)

UIU.............. Upholsterers' International Union of North America [*USWA*] [*Absorbed by*]

UIU.............. Upper Iowa University [*Fayette*]

UIUC .... University of Illinois, Urbana-Champaign

UIUH .... Khorinsk [*Former USSR ICAO location identifier*] (ICLI)

UIUSD......... Union Internationale Universitaire Socialiste et Democratique [*International Union of Social Democratic Teachers*]

UIUU .... Ulan-Ude/Mukhino [*Former USSR ICAO location identifier*] (ICLI)

UIV.............. Union Internationale des Villes et Pouvoirs Locaux [*International Union of Local Authorities*]

UIW............. United Iron Workers

UIW............. Usable Inside Width (MCD)

UIWU .... United Israel World Union (EA)

UIWV .... United Indian War Veterans, USA (EA)

UIZ.............. Utica, MI [*Location identifier FAA*] (FAAL)

UJ................ Air Sedona [*ICAO designator*] (AD)

UJ................ Union Jack

UJ................ Union Joint (MSA)

UJ................ Unique Jargon

UJ................ Uyoku Jiten [*A publication*]

UJA.............. United Jewish Appeal (EA)

UJAFJP .... United Jewish Appeal - Federation of Jewish Philanthropies of New York (EA)

UJASU .... Universal Jet Air Start Unit (DWSG)

UJB.............. UJB Financial Corp. [*Formerly, United Jersey Banks*] [*NYSE symbol*] (SPSG)

UJB.............. Umbilical Junction Box

UJB Fn......... UJB Financial Corp. [*Formerly, United Jersey Banks*] [*Associated Press*] (SAG)

UJC.............. Union de la Jeunesse Congolaise [*Congolese Youth Union*]

UJC.............. Union Jack Club [*British military*] (DMA)

UJC.............. Union Junior College [*New Jersey*]

UJC.............. Universal Japanese Coupe [*Automotive engineering*]

UJC.............. Universal Japanese Custom [*Motorcycle design*]

UJC.............. Urbana Junior College [*Ohio*]

UJC.............. Urgency Justification Code [*Military*] (AFIT)

UJCC(M-L)... Union de la Jeunesse Communiste du Canada (Marxiste-Leniniste)

UJCD........... Union de la Jeunesse de la Cote d'Ivoire [*Ivory Coast Youth Union*]

UJCL........... Universal Job Control Language

UJCML......... Union des Jeunesses Communistes Marxistes-Leninistes [*Union of Young Marxist-Leninist Communists*] [*France Political party*] (PPE)

UJD............. Ultriusque Juris Doctor [*Doctor of Either Law; i.e., Canon Law or Civil Law*] [*Latin*]

UJDG .... Union de la Jeunesse Democratique Gabonaise [*Union of Democratic Youth of Gabon*]

UJDK .... Union de la Jeunesse Democratique du Kongo [*Union of Democratic Youth of the Congo*]

UJE............. Universal Jewish Encyclopedia [*New York*] [*1939-1943*] [*A publication*] (BJA)

UJEKO .... Union de la Jeunesse Congolaise [*Congolese Youth Union*]

UJF............. Unsatisfied Judgment Fund [*Insurance*]

UJH............. International Union of Journeymen Horseshoers of the United States and Canada

UJJ .... Ujjain [*India*] [*Geomagnetic observatory code*]

UJL.............. Uninet Japan Ltd. [*Telecommunications*]

UJNR .... United States-Japan Cooperative Program on Natural Resources

U/JNT.......... Universal Joint [*Automotive engineering*]

UJS.............. Universal Jamming System

UJSP........... United States-Japan Science Program (MSC)

UJT............. Ultrasonic Journal Tester

UJT............. Unijunction Transistor

UJTL............ Universal Joint Task List

UJTO........... Unijunction Transistor Oscillator (IAA)

UJTS............ United Jewish Teachers Seminary [*Montreal*] [*A publication*] (BJA)

UJW............ Union of Jewish Women [*Zimbabwe*] (EAIO)

UJWF........... United Jewish Welfare Fund (IIA)

Uk............... British Library, London, United Kingdom [*Library symbol Library of Congress*] (LCLS)

UK............... Pfizer Ltd. [*Great Britain*] [*Research code symbol*]

'Uk.............. 'Ukzin (BJA)

UK............... Unabkoemmlich [*Indispensable, irreplaceable*] [*German military - World War II*]

UK............... Union Carbide [*NYSE symbol*] (TTSB)

UK............... Union Carbide Corp. [*Wall Street slang name: "Ukelele"*] [*NYSE symbol*] (SPSG)

UK............... Union Katangaise [*Katanga Union*]

UK............... Unit Check

uk .... United Kingdom [*MARC country of publication code Library of Congress*] (LCCP)

UK............... United Kingdom

UK............... University of Kansas [*Lawrence, KS*]

UK............... Unknown

UK............... Urinary Kallikrein [*Medicine*] (DMAA)

UK............... Urokinase [*An enzyme*]

UKA............. Air UK Ltd. [*British ICAO designator*] (FAAC)

UKA............. Ulster King-at-Arms

UKA............. United Kingdom Alliance

UKAACREG... United Kingdom Airways and Communication Region (IAA)

UkAc .... Accrington Public Library, Accrington, United Kingdom [*Library symbol Library of Congress*] (LCLS)

UKAC .... United Kingdom Automatic Control Council (ACII)

UKAC .... United Kingdom Automation Council [*London, England*]

UKADGE....... United Kingdom Air Defense Ground Environment

UKADR......... United Kingdom NATO Air Defense Region (NATG)

UKAEA......... United Kingdom Atomic Energy Authority [*London, England*] [*Databank originator and operator*] [*Research center*]

UKAEL .... United Kingdom Association for European Law [*British*]

UKAFFP .... United Kingdom Association of Frozen Food Producers (DBA)

UKaGS .... Church of Jesus Christ of Latter-Day Saints, Genealogical Society Library, KanabBranch, Stake Center, Kanab, UT [*Library symbol Library of Congress*] (LCLS)

UKAIRCCIS... United Kingdom Air Forces Command, Control, and Information System

UKAMBY...... United Kingdom Association of Manufacturers of Bakers Yeast (DBA)

U Kans........ University of Kansas (GAGS)

U Kans Med Ctr... University of Kansas Medicine Center (GAGS)

UKAPC........ United Kingdom Agricultural Production Committee

UKAPE........ United Kingdom Association of Professional Engineers [*A union*]

UKAPTD....... United Kingdom Alliance of Professional Teachers of Dancing (DBA)

UKARC........ United Kingdom Agricultural Research Council

UKASE........ University of Kansas Automated Serials

UKASS........ United Kingdom Amalgamated Society of Shipwrights [*A union*]

UKASS........ United Kingdom Association of Suggestion Schemes (DBA)

UKASTA....... United Kingdom Agricultural Supply Trade Association (DS)

UkAul.......... Ashton-Under-Lyne Public Library, Ashton-Under-Lyne, United Kingdom [*Library symbol Library of Congress*] (LCLS)

UKAWG....... United Kingdom Asian Women's Conference [*British*]

UKAWPCM... United Kingdom Association of Wood Packing Case Makers [*A union*]

UkB............. Birmingham Public Libraries, Birmingham, United Kingdom [*Library symbol Library of Congress*] (LCLS)

UKB .... United Kingdom Base [*World War II*]

UKB .... Universal Keyboard [*Computer science*] (AABC)

UKB .... Unvaniezh Kevredel Breizh [*Federalist Union of Brittany - FUB*] [*France*] (EAIO)

UKBB .... Kiev/Borispol [*Former USSR ICAO location identifier*] (ICLI)

UKBC .... United Kingdom Bomber Command (NATG)

UKBelQU...... Queen's University of Belfast, Belfast, United Kingdom [*Library symbol Library of Congress*] (LCLS)

UKBG .... United Kingdom Bartenders' Guild (BI)

UKBHU........ United Kingdom Band of Hope Union (EAIO)

UkBl............ Blackpool Central Library, Blackpool, United Kingdom [*Library symbol Library of Congress*] (LCLS)

UkBlG .... Blackpool Gazette & Herald Ltd., Blackpool, United Kingdom [*Library symbol Library of Congress*] (LCLS)

UkBoN .... Bolton Evening News, Bolton, United Kingdom [*Library symbol Library of Congress*] (LCLS)

UkBot.......... Burton-On-Trent Public Library, Burton-On-Trent, United Kingdom [*Library symbol Library of Congress*] (LCLS)

UkBP........... Birmingham Post & Mail Ltd., Birmingham, United Kingdom [*Library symbol Library of Congress*] (LCLS)

UkBrP.......... Bristol Evening Post, Bristol, United Kingdom [*Library symbol Library of Congress*] (LCLS)

UKBS .... United Kingdom Base Section [*World War II*]

UKBSA........ United Kingdom Board Sailing Association (DBA)

UkBU .... Birmingham University, Birmingham, United Kingdom [*Library symbol Library of Congress*] (LCLS)

UKC .... Air Ukraine Cargo [*FAA designator*] (FAAC)

UKC .... Ukrainian Gold Cross (EA)

UKC .... United Kennel Club (EA)

UKC .... Unit Kind Code [*Military*] (AFIT)

UKC	University of Kansas City [*Later, University of Missouri at Kansas City*]
UKCA	United Kingdom Coffee Association Ltd. (BI)
UKCC	United Kingdom Central Council [*for Nursing, Midwifery, and Health Visiting*]
UKCC	United Kingdom Commercial Corp.
UKCCD	United Kingdom Council for Computing Development (NITA)
UkCh	Chelmsford Library, Chelmsford, United Kingdom [*Library symbol Library of Congress*] (LCLS)
UKCHH	United Kingdom or Continent (Havre to Hamburg) (ROG)
UKCICC	United Kingdom Commanders-in-Chiefs' Committee
UKCIS	United Kingdom Chemical Information Service [*University of Nottingham*] [*Nottingham, England Information broker, databank originator, and host*]
UKCMET	United Kingdom Council for Music Education and Training (EAIO)
UkCoE	Essex County Newspapers Ltd., Colchester, United Kingdom [*Library symbol Library of Congress*] (LCLS)
UK/Cont (BH)...	United Kingdom or Continent (Bordeaux-Hamburg) [*Shipping*] (DS)
UK/Cont (GH)...	United Kingdom or Continent (Gibraltar-Hamburg) [*Shipping*] (DS)
UK/Cont (HH)...	United Kingdom or Continent (Havre-Hamburg) [*Shipping*] (DS)
UKCOSA	United Kingdom Council for Overseas Student Affairs (DS)
UkCoU	University of Essex, Wivenhoe Park, Colchester, England [*Library symbol*] [*Library of Congress*] (LCLS)
UkCov	Coventry Corp., Coventry, United Kingdom [*Library symbol Library of Congress*] (LCLS)
UkCr	Croydon Library, Croydon, United Kingdom [*Library symbol Library of Congress*] (LCLS)
UKCR	United Kingdom Communication Region [*Air Force*] (MCD)
UkCrA	Croydon Advertiser, Croydon, United Kingdom [*Library symbol Library of Congress*] (LCLS)
UkCraT	Cranfield Institute of Technology, Cranfield, Bedfordshire, United Kingdom [*Library symbol Library of Congress*] (LCLS)
UkCrC	Coulsdon Library, Croydon, United Kingdom [*Library symbol Library of Congress*] (LCLS)
UkCrP	Purley Library, Croydon, United Kingdom [*Library symbol Library of Congress*] (LCLS)
UKCS	United Kingdom Continental Shelf
UKCSB	United Kingdom Combat Support Boat
UKCSMA	United Kingdom Cutlery and Silverware Manufacturers Association (BI)
UKCTA	United Kingdom Commercial Travellers Association (DI)
UKCTRAIN	UK Catalogue Training (NITA)
UkCU	Cambridge University, Cambridge, United Kingdom [*Library symbol Library of Congress*] (LCLS)
UkCU-P	University of Cambridge, Scott Polar Research Institute, Cambridge, England [*Library symbol*] [*Library of Congress*] (LCLS)
UkCwN	North Wales Weekly News, Conway, United Kingdom [*Library symbol Library of Congress*] (LCLS)
Uk-D	British Library, Development and Systems Office, London, England [*Library symbol*] [*Library of Congress*] (LCLS)
UKD	Unusual Killing Device [*Counterintelligence*]
UKDA	United Kingdom Dairy Association (DBA)
UkDo	Doncaster Public Library, Doncaster, United Kingdom [*Library symbol Library of Congress*] (LCLS)
UKDRC	United Kingdom Dutch Rabbit Club (BI)
UkDw	Dewsbury Central Library, Dewsbury, United Kingdom [*Library symbol Library of Congress*] (LCLS)
UkE	Edinburgh Public Library, Edinburgh, United Kingdom [*Library symbol Library of Congress*] (LCLS)
UKE	Ukelele (DSUE)
UKE	Uke Resources [*Vancouver Stock Exchange symbol*]
UKEA	United Kingdom Energy Authority (DI)
UkEc	Eccles Public Library, Central Library, Eccles, United Kingdom [*Library symbol Library of Congress*] (LCLS)
UKELA	United Kingdom Environmental Law Association (DBA)
UKEMS	United Kingdom Environmental Mutagen Society (EAIO)
UkENL	National Library of Scotland, Edinburgh, United Kingdom [*Library symbol Library of Congress*] (LCLS)
UkEPh	Pharmaceutical Society of Great Britain, Scottish Department, Edinburgh, United Kingdom [*Library symbol Library of Congress*] (LCLS)
UkERCP	Royal College of Physicians, Edinburgh, United Kingdom [*Library symbol Library of Congress*] (LCLS)
UkERCS	Royal College of Surgeons, Edinburgh, United Kingdom [*Library symbol Library of Congress*] (LCLS)
UKERNA	United Kingdom Education and Research Networking Association (AIE)
UkES	Scottish Central Library, Edinburgh, United Kingdom [*Library symbol Library of Congress*] (LCLS)
UkEU	University of Edinburgh, Edinburgh, United Kingdom [*Library symbol Library of Congress*] (LCLS)
UKF	United Karate Federation (EA)
UKFA	United Kingdom Fellmongers Association (BI)
UKFBPW	United Kingdom Federation of Business and Professional Women (DI)
UKFC	United Kingdom Fortifications Club (DBA)
UKFF	Simferopol [*Former USSR ICAO location identifier*] (ICLI)
UKFO	United Kingdom for Orders [*Shipping*]
UKFR	United Kingdom Feline Register [*An association*] (DBA)
UkGM	Mitchell Library, Glasgow, United Kingdom [*Library symbol Library of Congress*] (LCLS)
UkGO	George Outram & Co. Ltd., Glasgow, United Kingdom [*Library symbol Library of Congress*] (LCLS)
UkGP	Royal Faculty of Procurators in Glasgow, Glasgow, United Kingdom [*Library symbol Library of Congress*] (LCLS)
UKGPA	United Kingdom Glycerine Producers' Association (BI)
UkGU	University of Glasgow, Glasgow, United Kingdom [*Library symbol Library of Congress*] (LCLS)
UkGUS	University of Strathclyde, Andersonian Library, Glasgow, Scotland [*Library symbol*] [*Library of Congress*] (LCLS)
UKH	Ukhta Airenterprise [*Former USSR*] [*FAA designator*] (FAAC)
UKH	United Keno Hill Mines Ltd. [*Toronto Stock Exchange symbol*]
UkHA	Atomic Energy Research Establishment, Didcot, Oxfordshire, United Kingdom [*Library symbol Library of Congress*] (LCLS)
UKHAD	United Kingdom and Havre, Antwerp, and Dunkirk [*Shipping*] (DS)
UkHe	Heywood Public Library, Heywood, Lancashire, United Kingdom [*Library symbol Library of Congress*] (LCLS)
UKHE	Petrovskoye [*Former USSR ICAO location identifier*] (ICLI)
UKHEF	United Kingdom Home Economics Federation [*British*]
UKHH	United Kingdom and Havre-Hamburg [*Shipping*] (DS)
UKHT	United Kingdom Housing Trust
UkHu	Huddersfield Public Libraries, Huddersfield, United Kingdom [*Library symbol Library of Congress*] (LCLS)
UKI	Ukiah [*California*] [*Seismograph station code, US Geological Survey*] (SEIS)
UKI	Ukiah [*California*] [*Airport symbol*] (AD)
UKI	Ukiah, CA [*Location identifier FAA*] (FAAL)
UKIAS	United Kingdom Immigrants Advisory Service
UKIBEK	United Kingdom Insurance Brokers European Committee
UKIC	United Kingdom Internet Consortium
UKII	Kishinev [*Former USSR ICAO location identifier*] (ICLI)
UKing	United Kingdom Fund [*Associated Press*] (SAG)
UKIP	United Kingdom Import Plan
UKIP	United Kingdom Independence Party [*British*] [*Political party*]
UKIPA	United Kingdom and Ireland Particleboard Association (EAIO)
UKIRT	United Kingdom Infrared Telescope
UKISC	United Kingdom Industrial Space Committee (DBA)
UKITO	United Kingdom Information Technology Organization
UKJATFOR ...	United Kingdom Joint Airborne Task Force [*British military*] (DMA)
UKJGA	United Kingdom Jute Goods Association Ltd. (BI)
UkK	Keighley Central Library, Keighley, United Kingdom [*Library symbol Library of Congress*] (LCLS)
UKK	Urho Kekkonen [*President of Finland*]
UkKi	Kilmarnock Public Library, Central Library, Dick Institute, Kilmarnock, United Kingdom [*Library symbol Library of Congress*] (LCLS)
UKKK	Kiev/Zhulyany [*Former USSR ICAO location identifier*] (ICLI)
UKKS	Semyenovka [*Former USSR ICAO location identifier*] (ICLI)
UkKuK	Knapp, Drewett & Sons Ltd., Kingston-Upon-Thames, United Kingdom [*Library symbol Library of Congress*] (LCLS)
UKL	Ukraine Airalliance [*FAA designator*] (FAAC)
UKL	Utashik Lake [*Alaska*] [*Seismograph station code, US Geological Survey*] (SEIS)
UkLA	Associated Newspapers Ltd., London, United Kingdom [*Library symbol Library of Congress*] (LCLS)
UkLB	Beaverbrook Newspapers Ltd., London, United Kingdom [*Library symbol Library of Congress*] (LCLS)
UkLBOA	British Optical Association, London, United Kingdom [*Library symbol Library of Congress*] (LCLS)
UkLC	Chemical Society, London, United Kingdom [*Library symbol Library of Congress*] (LCLS)
UkLCS	Institute of Commonwealth Studies, London, United Kingdom [*Library symbol Library of Congress*] (LCLS)
UKLDS	UK Library Database System (NITA)
UkLe	Leeds City Library, Leeds, United Kingdom [*Library symbol Library of Congress*] (LCLS)
UKLF	United Kingdom Land Forces [*Military*]
UkLG	Guildhall Library, Aldermanbury, London, United Kingdom [*Library symbol Library of Congress*] (LCLS)
UkLH	Hampstead Public Libraries, Central Library, London, United Kingdom [*Library symbol Library of Congress*] (LCLS)
UkLHu	A. J. Hurley Ltd., London, United Kingdom [*Library symbol Library of Congress*] (LCLS)
UkLi	Liverpool Public Libraries, Liverpool, United Kingdom [*Library symbol Library of Congress*] (LCLS)
UkLin	City of Lincoln Public Library, Lincoln, United Kingdom [*Library symbol Library of Congress*] (LCLS)
UkLIO	India Office Library and Records, Foreign and Commonwealth Office, London, United Kingdom [*Library symbol Library of Congress*] (LCLS)
UkLIP	IPC Newspapers Ltd., London, United Kingdom [*Library symbol Library of Congress*] (LCLS)
UkLiP	Liverpool Daily Post & Echo Ltd., Liverpool, United Kingdom [*Library symbol Library of Congress*] (LCLS)
UkLiPE	Liverpool Daily Post and Echo, Ltd., Liverpool, United Kingdom [*Library symbol*] [*Library of Congress*] (LCLS)
UkLiU	University of Liverpool, Liverpool, United Kingdom [*Library symbol Library of Congress*] (LCLS)
UkLJ	Jews' College, London, United Kingdom [*Library symbol Library of Congress*] (LCLS)
UKLL	Lvov [*Former USSR ICAO location identifier*] (ICLI)
UkLLA	Library Association, London, United Kingdom [*Library symbol Library of Congress*] (LCLS)
UkLLT	Lambeth Public Libraries, Tate Central Library, London, United Kingdom [*Library symbol Library of Congress*] (LCLS)
UkLMS	Morning Star Co-Operative Society, London, United Kingdom [*Library symbol Library of Congress*] (LCLS)
UkLNAL	National Art Library, Victoria and Albert Museum, London, United Kingdom [*Library symbol*] [*Library of Congress*] (LCLS)
UkLNw	North West London Press Ltd., London, United Kingdom [*Library symbol Library of Congress*] (LCLS)

UkLPh .... Pharmaceutical Society of Great Britain, London, United Kingdom [*Library symbol Library of Congress*] (LCLS)

UkLPo .... H. Pordes, Publisher and Bookseller, London, United Kingdom [*Library symbol Library of Congress*] (LCLS)

UkLPR .... Public Record Office, London, United Kingdom [*Library symbol Library of Congress*] (LCLS)

UkLQ .... Friends Reference Library, London, United Kingdom [*Library symbol Library of Congress*] (LCLS)

UKLR .... University of Kansas. Law Review [*A publication*] (DLA)

UkLRCP .... Royal College of Physicians, London, United Kingdom [*Library symbol Library of Congress*] (LCLS)

UkLRCS .... Royal College of Surgeons of England, London, United Kingdom [*Library symbol Library of Congress*] (LCLS)

UkLRSM ...... Royal Society of Medicine, London, United Kingdom [*Library symbol Library of Congress*] (LCLS)

UkLS .... Science Museum, London, United Kingdom [*Library symbol Library of Congress*] (LCLS)

UkLTh .... Thomasons Ltd., London, United Kingdom [*Library symbol Library of Congress*] (LCLS)

UkLU .... University of London, London, United Kingdom [*Library symbol Library of Congress*] (LCLS)

UkLuH .... Home Counties Newspapers Ltd., Luton, United Kingdom [*Library symbol Library of Congress*] (LCLS)

UkLU-K .... University of London, Kings College, London, United Kingdom [*Library symbol Library of Congress*] (LCLS)

UkLW .... Wellcome Historical Medical Library, London, United Kingdom [*Library symbol Library of Congress*] (LCLS)

UkLWa .... Wandsworth Borough News Co. Ltd., London, United Kingdom [*Library symbol Library of Congress*] (LCLS)

UKM .... UK MARC [*United Kingdom Machine-Readable Cataloging*] [*Source file*] [*UTLAS symbol*]

UKM .... United Kingdom Fund [*NYSE symbol*] (SPSG)

UKM .... Urea Kinetic Modeling [*Dialysis*] (CPH)

UkMa .... Manchester Public Libraries, Central Library, Manchester, United Kingdom [*Library symbol Library of Congress*] (LCLS)

UkMaG .... Guardian Newspapers Ltd., Manchester, United Kingdom [*Library symbol Library of Congress*] (LCLS)

UKMANZRA... United Kingdom Manufacturers and New Zealand Representatives Association (BI)

UK MARC ..... UK [*British Library*] Machine Readable Catalogue [*Bibliographic database*]

UKMC .... University of Kentucky Medical Center [*Lexington, KY*]

UKMCA .... United Kingdom Module Constructors Association (DBA)

UkMe .... Public Libraries, Central Library, Merthyr-Tydfil, United Kingdom [*Library symbol Library of Congress*] (LCLS)

UKMF .... United Kingdom Mobile Force

UKMF(A) ..... United Kingdom Mobile Force (Air) [*British military*] (DMA)

UKMF(L) ..... United Kingdom Mobile Force (Land) [*British military*] (DMA)

UkMg .... Margate Public Library, Margate, United Kingdom [*Library symbol Library of Congress*] (LCLS)

UKML .... United Knitwear Manufacturers League (EA)

UKMO .... United Kingdom Meteorological Office [*Marine science*] (OSRA)

UKMOSS ...... United Kingdom Ministry of Supply Staff

UKMRC .... United Kingdom Medical Research Council

UKN .... Unknown (KSC)

UKN .... Waukon, IA [*Location identifier FAA*] (FAAL)

UKNCIAWPRC... International Water Quality Association [*British*] (EAIO)

UKNCIAWPRC... United Kingdom National Committee of the International Association on Water Pollution Research and Control (EAIO)

UkNcU .... University of Newcastle upon Tyne, Newcastle upon Tyne, United Kingdom [*Library symbol*] [*Library of Congress*] (LCLS)

UK/NL .... United Kingdom/Netherlands (MCD)

UKNND .... United Kingdom National Nutrient Databank [*Ministry of Agriculture and Royal Society of Chemistry*]

UkNr .... Norwich Public Libraries, Norwich, United Kingdom [*Library symbol Library of Congress*] (LCLS)

UKNR .... University of Kansas Nuclear Reactor

UkNrE .... Eastern Counties Newspapers Ltd., Norwich, United Kingdom [*Library symbol Library of Congress*] (LCLS)

UKNSDC ...... United Kingdom National Serials Data Centre [*Information service or system*] (IID)

UKO .... Unverhofft Kommt Oft [*The Unexpected Often Happens*] [*Motto of Franz, Duke of Pomerania (1577-1620)*]

UKOA .... United Kingdom Offshore Operators' Association

UKOBA .... United Kingdom Outboard Boating Association (BI)

UkoIn .... United Kingdom Office for Library Networking

UKOLN .... United Kingdom Office of Library and Information Networking

UKOLUG ...... United Kingdom On-Line User Group [*Information service or system*] (IID)

UKOO .... Odessa/Tsentralny [*Former USSR ICAO location identifier*] (ICLI)

UKOOA .... United Kingdom Offshore Operators' Association (DS)

UKOP .... United Kingdom Official Publications [*Information service or system*] (IID)

UK OSCA ..... United Kingdom Optical Sensors Collaborative Association (ACII)

UkOxU .... Oxford University, Bodleian Library, Oxford, United Kingdom [*Library symbol Library of Congress*] (LCLS)

UkOxU-AS .... Oxford University, All Souls College, Oxford, United Kingdom [*Library symbol Library of Congress*] (LCLS)

UkOxU-N ...... Oxford University, Nuffield College, Oxford, United Kingdom [*Library symbol Library of Congress*] (LCLS)

UkOxU-Rh .... Oxford University, Bodleian Library, Rhodes House, Oxford, United Kingdom [*Library symbol Library of Congress*] (LCLS)

UKP .... UK Home Office [*British ICAO designator*] (FAAC)

UKPA .... United Kingdom Patternmakers' Association [*A union*]

UKPA .... United Kingdom Pilots Association (DS)

UKPCA .... United Kingdom Postal Clerks' Association [*A union*]

UkPe .... Sandeman Public Library, Perth, United Kingdom [*Library symbol Library of Congress*] (LCLS)

UKPI .... United Kingdom Provident Institute [*Commercial firm*]

UKPIA .... United Kingdom Petroleum Industry Association

UKPMA .... United Kingdom Preserves Manufacturers Association (DBA)

UKPO .... United Kingdom Post Office [*Telecommunications*] (TEL)

UKPPD .... United Kingdom Paper and Packaging Directory [*A publication*]

UkPS .... Portsmouth & Sunderland Newspapers Ltd., Portsmouth, Hants, United Kingdom [*Library symbol Library of Congress*] (LCLS)

UKPTF .... United Kingdom Provision Trade Federation (DBA)

UKR .... Air Ukraine [*ICAO designator*] (FAAC)

UKR .... Mukeiras [*South Arabia*] [*Airport symbol*] (AD)

UKR .... Ukraine

ukr .... Ukrainian [*MARC language code Library of Congress*] (LCCP)

UKR .... Ukrainian Soviet Socialist Republic [*ISO three-letter standard code*] (CNC)

UKR .... UK Retrospective (NITA)

UKR .... United Kingdom Atomic Energy Authority Office at Risley (IAA)

UKR .... Uranian Kilometric Radiation [*Planetary science*]

UKRA .... United Kingdom Reading Association [*British*]

UKRA .... United Kingdom Renderers Association (DBA)

UKREP .... United Kingdom Permanent Representative [*EEC*] (DS)

UkRiH .... Richmond Herald Ltd., Richmond, Surrey, United Kingdom [*Library symbol Library of Congress*] (LCLS)

UKRK .... Ukrains'ka Kooperativna Rada Kanadi

UkRoS .... G. & A. N. Scott Ltd., Rochdale, United Kingdom [*Library symbol Library of Congress*] (LCLS)

UkrSSR .... Ukranian Soviet Socialist Republic

UKS .... United Kingdom Subsatellite

UKSA .... United Kingdom Settlers' Association [*Australia*]

UKSA .... United Kingdom Shipmakers' Association [*A union*]

UKSASS .... United Kingdom Society of Amalgamated Smiths and Strikers [*A union*]

UKSATA .... United Kingdom-South Africa Trade Association

UKSC .... United Kingdom Society of Coachmakers [*A union*]

UKSCC .... United Kingdom Spoon Collectors Club (DBA)

UKSG .... United Kingdom Serials Group

UkSh .... Sheffield City Libraries, Central Library, Sheffield, United Kingdom [*Library symbol Library of Congress*] (LCLS)

UkShU .... University of Sheffield, Sheffield, United Kingdom [*Library symbol Library of Congress*] (LCLS)

UKSIA .... United Kingdom Sugar Industry Association (DBA)

UKSIM .... United Kingdom Society of Information Management (DBA)

UkSIO .... Slough Observer Ltd., Slough, United Kingdom [*Library symbol Library of Congress*] (LCLS)

UKSMA .... United Kingdom Sugar Merchants' Association (BI)

UKSPA .... United Kingdom Science Park Association (DBA)

UkSsB .... John H. Burrows & Sons Ltd., Southend-On-Sea, United Kingdom [*Library symbol Library of Congress*] (LCLS)

UKST .... United Kingdom Schmidt Telescope

UkSta .... Stamford Public Library and Museum, Stamford, United Kingdom [*Library symbol Library of Congress*] (LCLS)

UKSTC .... United Kingdom Strike Command (NATG)

UKSTU .... United Kingdom Schmidt Telescope Unit

UkSw .... Swansea Public Library, Swansea, United Kingdom [*Library symbol Library of Congress*] (LCLS)

UKT .... Quakertown, PA [*Location identifier FAA*] (FAAL)

UKT .... United Kingdom Tariff (DS)

UKTA .... United Kingdom Tea Association (DBA)

UKTA .... United Kingdom Trade Agency

UKTD .... United Kingdom Treasury Delegation

UKTM .... UK [*United Kingdom*] Trade Marks [*The Patent Office*] [*British Information service or system*] (IID)

UKTOTC .... United Kingdom Tariff and Overseas Trade Classification (DS)

UKTS .... United Kingdom Transplant Service (WDAA)

UKTS .... United Kingdom Treaty Series [*A publication*]

UKTTSMA ..... United Kingdom Timber Trade Shipowners Mutual Association Ltd. (DS)

UKU .... Nuku [*Papua New Guinea*] [*Airport symbol*] (OAG)

UKU .... Ukraine-Aviatrans [*FAA designator*] (FAAC)

UKUSA .... United Kingdom-United States Agreement [*Intelligence*] [*1947*]

U$_K$V .... Potassium-Excretion Rate [*Medicine*] (DAVI)

UKV .... Underground Keybox Vault (NATG)

UKW .... LVOV Airlines [*Ukraine*] [*FAA designator*] (FAAC)

UKW .... Ultrakurzwelle [*Ultrashort wave*] [*German*]

UkWC-A .... Windsor Castle, Royal Archives, Windsor, Berkshire, United Kingdom [*Library symbol*] [*Library of Congress*] (LCLS)

UkWE .... Eton College, Windsor, Berks, United Kingdom [*Library symbol Library of Congress*] (LCLS)

UKWE .... Ultrakurzwellenempfaenger [*Very-High-Frequency Receiver*] [*German*]

UkWg .... County Borough of Wigan Public Libraries, Central Library, Wigan, United Kingdom [*Library symbol Library of Congress*] (LCLS)

UKWGF .... United Kingdom Wool Growers Federation (DBA)

UKWGL .... United Kingdom Working Group on Landmines (WDAA)

UKWMO ...... United Kingdom Warning and Monitoring Organization (MUSM)

UkWoE .... Express & Star Ltd., Wolverhampton, United Kingdom [*Library symbol Library of Congress*] (LCLS)

UkWr .... Wrexham Public Library, Wrexham, United Kingdom [*Library symbol Library of Congress*] (LCLS)

UKY .... United Kingdom Energy [*Vancouver Stock Exchange symbol*]

UKY .... University of Kentucky (PDAA)

U Ky .... University of Kentucky (GAGS)

'Ukz .... 'Ukzin (BJA)

UL............... Air Lanka [*ICAO designator*] (AD)
UL............... Lansa, SRL [*Honduras*] [*ICAO designator*] (ICDA)
UL............... Ugaritic Literature [*C. H. Gordon*] [*A publication*] (BJA)
UI............... Uldericus de Bamberg [*Flourished, 12th century*] [*Authority cited in pre-1607 legal work*] (DSA)
UL............... Ulitsa [*Street*] (EY)
UL............... Ultralinear
UL............... Ultralow
UL............... Unauthorized Launch
UL............... Uncontrolled (index) Language (NITA)
UL............... Underlay
U/L............... Underlever [*Rifles*] (DICI)
UL............... Underload (NASA)
UL............... Underwriters Laboratories (EA)
UL............... Underwriters Laboratories, Inc.
UL............... Undifferentiated Lymphoma [*Medicine*] (MAE)
UL............... Uniformly Labeled [*Compound, with radioisotope*] [*Also, U*]
UL............... Unilever ADR [*NYSE symbol*] (TTSB)
UL............... Unilever Ltd. [*NYSE symbol*] (SPSG)
UL............... Unionist Liberal [*British*] (ROG)
UL............... Union Liberal [*Liberal Union*] [*Spain Political party*] (PPW)
UL............... Union List
UL............... United Left [*Peru*] [*Political party*]
U/l............... United per Liter (DAVI)
U/L............... Unit Linked
UL............... Unit Load
UL............... Universala Ligo [*Defunct*] (EA)
UL............... Universal League (EAIO)
UL............... Universal Life [*Insurance*]
UL............... University Library (WDAA)
u/l............... Unlimited [*Water depth*]
UL............... Unterlafette [*Bottom carriage*] [*German military - World War II*]
UL............... Up Left [*The rear left portion of a stage*] [*A stage direction*]
UL............... Up Link [*Computer science*]
U/L............... Uplink (NAKS)
UL............... Upper Laterals [*Botany*]
UL............... Upper Left [*S-band antenna*] (NASA)
UL............... Upper Leg
UL............... Upper Level [*Nuclear energy*] (NRCH)
UL............... Upper Limb [*Upper edge of sun, moon, etc.*] [*Navigation*]
UL............... Upper Limit
UL............... Upper List (NITA)
UL............... Upper Lobe [*Anatomy*]
UL............... Upstage Left (WDAA)
UL............... Urban League (MCD)
UL............... Usage List (MSA)
UL............... Useful Life (SAA)
UL............... User Language [*Computer science*] (DIT)
UL............... Utility Lead [*Telecommunications*] (TEL)
ULA............... San Julian [*Argentina*] [*Airport symbol*] (OAG)
ULA............... Ulamona Field Station [*New Britain*] [*Seismograph station code, US Geological Survey*] (SEIS)
ULA............... Uncommitted Logic Array [*Semiconductor technology*]
ULA............... Uniform Laws, Annotated [*A publication*] (DLA)
ULA............... Universal Logic Array [*Computer science*] (IAA)
ULA............... Upper Layer Architecture [*Telecommunications*] (OSI)
ULA............... Utah State University, Logan, UT [*Library symbol Library of Congress*] (LCLS)
ULA............... Zuliana de Aviacion [*Venezuela*] [*ICAO designator*] (FAAC)
ULAA............ Ukrainian Library Association of America (EA)
ULAA............ United Latin Americans of America (EA)
ULAB............ Unilab Corp. [*NASDAQ symbol*] (NQ)
ULAC............ Union Latinoamericana de Ciegos [*Latin American Blind Union - LABU*] [*Montevideo, Uruguay*] (EAIO)
ULAE............ Universal Limited Art Editions
ULAEY......... Union of Latin American Ecumenical Youth (EA)
ULAIDS........ Universal Locator Airborne Integrated Data System (MCD)
ULAJE.......... Union Latino-Americaine des Jeunesses Evangeliques [*Union of Latin American Evangelical Youth*]
ULAJE.......... Union Latinoamericana de Juventudes Ecumenicas [*Union of Latin American Ecumenical Youth - ULAEY*] (EAIO)
ULAK............ Kotlas [*Former USSR ICAO location identifier*] (ICLI)
ULANG......... User Language [*Computer science*]
ULAP........... Universitywide Library Automation Program (NITA)
ULAPC......... Union Latino-Americaine de la Presse Catholique
ULAS........... University of Louisville Archaeological Survey [*Research center*] (RCD)
ULASM....... Undersea Multichannel Large-Scale Scattering Meter [*NASA*] (MCD)
ULAST......... Union Latino Americana de Sociedades de Tisiologia [*Latin American Union of Societies of Phthisiology*]
U La Verne... University of La Verne (GAGS)
ULB............... Underwater Locator Beacon (MCD)
ULB............... Universal Logic Block (IEEE)
ULB............... University of Bradford
ULB............... Unlighted Buoy [*USCG*] (TAG)
ULBA............ Universal Love and Brotherhood Association [*Kyoto, Japan*] (EAIO)
ULBI............ ULtralife Batteries [*NASDAQ symbol*] (TTSB)
ULBI............ Ultralife Batteries, Inc. [*NASDAQ symbol*] (SAG)
ULBM.......... Underlay Battle Manager
ULBW.......... Ultralow Birth Weight [*Medicine*] (DMAA)
ULC............... Cache County Public Library, Logan, UT [*Library symbol Library of Congress*] (LCLS)
ULC............... Philippines Civil Liberties Union (PD)
ULC............... Ultra-Low Carbon [*Metallurgical engineering*]
ULC............... Underwriters' Laboratories of Canada

ULC............... Uniform Loop Clock
ULC............... Union de la Lutte Communiste [*Burkina Faso*] [*Political party*] (EY)
ULC............... Union Library Catalogue
ULC............... Unitary Launch Concept [*or Control*] (AAG)
ULC............... United Labor Congress [*Nigeria*]
ULC............... Unit Ledger Card [*Computer science*]
ULC............... Unit Level Code (AFM)
ULC............... Unit Level Computers [*Army*]
ULC............... Universal Life Church
ULC............... Universal Load Cell
ULC............... Universal Logic Circuit
ULC............... Unsafe Lane Change (WDAA)
ULC............... Upper and Lower Case (NITA)
ULC............... Upper Left Center [*The rear left center portion of a stage*] [*A stage direction*]
ULC............... Urban Libraries Council (EA)
ULC............... Utah State Library, Salt Lake City, UT [*OCLC symbol*] (OCLC)
ULCA............ Ukrainian Life Cooperative Association [*Defunct*] (EA)
ULCA............ Uncommitted Logic Array [*Semiconductor technology*] (EECA)
ULCA............ United Lutheran Church of America (WDAA)
ULCANS...... Ultralight Camouflage Aviation Net System [*Military*] (MUSM)
ULCANS...... Ultralightweight Camouflage Net System [*Army*]
ULCC........... Ulster Loyalist Central Coordinating Committee [*Ireland*]
ULCC........... Ultralarge Crude Carrier [*Oil tanker*]
ULCC........... Ultralow-Cement Castable [*Ceramics*]
ULCC........... University of London Computer Centre (NITA)
ULCE........... Unified Life Cycle Engineering (MCD)
ULCER........ Underwater Launch Control Energy Requirements
ULCER........ Underwater Launch Current and Energy Recorder
ULCHi......... Cache Valley Historical Society, Logan, UT [*Library symbol Library of Congress*] (LCLS)
ULCJ........... University Law College. Journal. Rajputana University [*India*] [*A publication*] (DLA)
ULCM.......... United Lutheran Church Men [*Defunct*] (EA)
ULCP........... University Laboratory Cooperative Program
ULCRA........ Urban Land (Ceiling and Regulation) Act [*India*] (ECON)
ULCS........... Uniform Lightness and Chromaticity Scale (PDAA)
ULCS........... Unit Level Circuit Switch (CAAL)
ULCS........... Unit Level Computer Logistics System [*Army*]
ULD............. Ultralow Distortion [*Electronics*] (ECII)
ULD............. Ultrasonic Leak Detector
ULD............. Ultrasonic Light Diffraction
ULD............. Union pour la Liberte et le Developpement [*Benin*] [*Political party*] (EY)
ULD............. United Liberal Democrats [*South Korea*]
ULD............. Unit Load Demand [*Nuclear energy*] (NRCH)
ULD............. Unit Load Device [*Shipping containers*]
ULD............. Unit Logic Device
ULD............. Universal Language Description [*Computer science*] (IAA)
ULD............. Upper Level Deck [*Cargo containers*]
ULD............. Upper-Limb Disorder [*Medicine*] (ECON)
ULDB.......... Ultra-Light Displacement Boat (PS)
ULDEST...... Ultimate Destination [*Army*] (AABC)
ULDF.......... United Left Democratic Front [*India*] [*Political party*] (PPW)
ULDMI........ Ultraprecise LASER Distance Measuring Instrument
ULDP.......... Ulster Loyalist Democratic Party [*Northern Ireland*] [*Political party*] (PPW)
ULDS.......... Union Liberale-Democratique Suisse [*Liberal Democratic Union of Switzerland*] [*Political party*] (PPE)
ULDT.......... Unable Lower Due Traffic [*Aviation*] (FAAC)
ULE............. Leisure International Airways Ltd. [*British ICAO designator*] (FAAC)
ULE............. Sule [*Papua New Guinea*] [*Airport symbol*] (OAG)
ULE............. Ultralow Expansion [*Trademark, Corning Glass Works*]
ULE............. Unit Location Equipment (MCD)
ULEA........... University Labor Education Association [*Later, UCLEA*]
ULEAC........ University of London and East Anglia Consortium [*British*] (AIE)
ULEB.......... Ultra-Low Emissions Bus [*Automotive engineering*]
ULECA........ Ultralow Energy Charge Analyzer [*Instrumentation*]
ULEE.......... Ultra-Low Emissions Engine [*Automotive engineering*]
ULES........... University of Lancaster Engineering Services [*Research center British*] (IRUK)
ULET........... Ultra-Low Emissions Truck [*Automotive engineering*]
ULETE........ Ultra-Low Emissions Truck Engine
ULEV.......... Ultra-Low-Emission Vehicle
ULew.......... Lewiston Public Library, Lewiston, UT [*Library symbol Library of Congress*] (LCLS)
ULEWAT...... Ultralow-Energy Wide-Angle Telescope
ULF............. Ultralow Frequency
ULF............. United Labour Front [*Trinidad and Tobago*] (PD)
ULF............. United Left Front [*Nepal*] [*Political party*] (EY)
ULF............. United Leukodystrophy Foundation (EA)
ULF............. University Labour Federation [*British*]
ULF............. Upper Limiting Frequency (ADA)
ULF............. Urban Land Foundation (EA)
ULFA........... United Liberation Front of Assam [*India*] [*Political party*] (ECON)
ULFJ........... Ultralow-Frequency Jammer
ULFO.......... Ultralow-Frequency Oscillator
ULG............. Upholstery Leather Group [*Later, AG*] (EA)
ULGCS........ United Lesbian and Gay Christian Scientists (EA)
ULGE.......... Utility, Lawn, and Garden Engines
ULGS........... Church of Jesus Christ of Latter-Day Saints, Genealogical Society Library, CacheBranch, Logan, UT [*Library symbol Library of Congress*] (LCLS)
ULGX.......... Urologix, Inc. [*NASDAQ symbol*] (SAG)
ULI............... ULI - the Urban Land Institute (EA)

ULI .... Ultra-Low Interstitial (PDAA)
ULI .... Underwriters Laboratories, Inc. [*Also, UL*]
ULI .... Uniono por la Linguo Internaciona Ido [*International Language Union*] (EA)
ULI .... Union pour la Langue Internationale Ido [*Union for the International Language Ido*]
ULI .... Universal Logic Implementer
ULI .... Unsigned Long Integer [*Computer science*]
ULI .... [*The*] Urban Land Institute [*An association*] (EAAP)
ULI .... Urban Law Institute of Antioch School of Law [*Defunct*] (EA)
ULIA .... Unattached List, Indian Army
ULIB .... Utility Library [*National Center for Atmospheric Research*]
ULICP .... Universal Log Interpretation Computer Program (PDAA)
ULIDAT .... Umweltliteraturedatenbank [*Data Bank for Environmental Literature*] [*Deutsches Umweltbundesamt*] [*Germany*] [*Information service or system*] (CRD)
ULIMO .... United Liberation Movement [*Liberia*] [*Political party*] (ECON)
ULIRG .... Ultraluminous Infrared Galaxy
ULIS .... Uniform Law on the International Sale of Goods
ULISC .... University Library and Information Services Committee [*Committee of Vice Chancellors and Principals*] [*British*] (AIE)
ULISYS .... Universal Library System (NITA)
ULJ .... Bedford, MA [*Location identifier FAA*] (FAAL)
ULL .... Savoonga, AK [*Location identifier FAA*] (FAAL)
ULL .... Ullage [*NASA*] (KSC)
ULL .... Uncomfortable Loudness Level (DAVI)
ULL .... Unitarian Laymen's League
ULL .... United States Department of Labor, Washington, DC [*OCLC symbol*] (OCLC)
ULL .... Unit Local Loading (AAG)
ULL .... University of London Library
ULL .... Upper Lip Length [*Medicine*]
ULLA .... Ultra-Low-Level Air-Drop [*British military*] (DMA)
ULLC .... Unit Level Learning Center
ULLDPE .... Ultra Linear Low-Density Polyethylene [*Plastics technology*]
ULLL .... Leningrad/Pulkovo [*Former USSR ICAO location identifier*] (ICLI)
UL-LL .... Upper-Limit, Lower-Limit (SAA)
UL-LLC .... Upper-Limit, Lower-Limit Comparator (SAA)
ULLNG .... Ultra-Large Liquified Natural Gas Carrier (PDAA)
ULLS .... Ultrasonic Liquid Level Sensor
ULLS .... Unit Level Logistics System [*Army*]
ULLV .... Unmanned Lunar Logistics Vehicle [*OMSF*]
ULM .... Meiji University, Maruzen Co. Ltd. [*UTLAS symbol*]
ULM .... Mine Safety and Health Administration, Denver, Denver, CO [*OCLC symbol*] (OCLC)
ULM .... New Ulm [*Minnesota*] [*Airport symbol Obsolete*] (OAG)
ULM .... Ultramar Capital Corp. [*Toronto Stock Exchange symbol*]
ULM .... Ultrasonic Light Modulator
ULM .... Undersea [*or Underwater*] Long-Range Missile [*Navy*]
ULM .... Universal Line Multiplexer
ULM .... Universal Logic Module
ULMA .... University Laboratory Managers Association [*Later, ALMA*] (EA)
ULMA .... Upper Level Management Advisor (IAA)
Ulm L Rec ... Ulman's Law Record [*New York*] [*A publication*] (DLA)
ULMS .... Undersea [*or Underwater*] Long-Range Missile System [*Redesignated "Trident"*] [*Navy*]
ULMS .... Union List of Montana Serials [*Library network*]
ULMS .... Unit Level Message Switch
ULN .... Ulan Bator [*Mongolia*] [*Airport symbol*] (OAG)
ULN .... United Lincoln Resources, Inc. [*Vancouver Stock Exchange symbol*]
ULN .... Unit Line Number (DOMA)
ULN .... University of Lowell, North Campus, Lowell, MA [*OCLC symbol*] (OCLC)
ULN .... Unlaunchable (IAA)
ULN .... Upper Limits of Normal [*Medicine*]
ULO .... Occupational Safety and Health Administration, Technical Data Center, Washington, DC [*OCLC symbol*] (OCLC)
ULO .... Unilateral Ovariectomy [*Gynecology*]
ULO .... United Labour Organization [*Burma*]
ULO .... Unmanned Launch Operations [*NASA*] (KSC)
ULO .... Unmanned Lunar Orbiter [*NASA*] (MCD)
ULO .... Unrestricted Line Officer [*Navy*] (DNAB)
ULOL .... Velikiye Luki [*Former USSR ICAO location identifier*] (ICLI)
ULOR .... Upward Light Output Ratio (PDAA)
ULOS .... Unliquidated Obligations (MCD)
ULOSSOM ... Union List of Selected Serials of Michigan [*Wayne State University Libraries*] [*Ceased*] [*Information service or system*] (IID)
ULOTC .... University of London Officer Training Corps [*British military*] (DMA)
U Louisville... University of Louisville (GAGS)
ULOW .... Unmanned Launch Operations - Western Test Range [*NASA*] (KSC)
ULP .... Quilpie [*Australia Airport symbol*] (OAG)
ULP .... Ulster Petroleums Ltd. [*Toronto Stock Exchange symbol*]
ULP .... Ultra-Lightweight Panel (PDAA)
ULP .... Ultra Long Play
ULP .... Ultralow Chamber Pressure (MCD)
ULP .... Unfair Labor Practice [*Department of Labor*]
ULP .... Unfair Labor Practices (WYGK)
ULP .... Uniform Latex Particles
ULP .... Universal Logic Primitive (PDAA)
ULP .... University of London Press (DGA)
ULP .... Unleaded Petrol [*British*] (ADA)
ULP .... Upper Layer Protocol [*Telecommunications*] (OSI)
ULP .... Utilitaire Logique Processor [*Programming language*] [*Computer science French*]
ULP .... Utility Landplane [*Navy*]

ULPA .... Ultra-Low Particulate Air (AAEL)
ULPA .... Uniform Limited Partnership Act [*National Conference of Commissioners on Uniform State Laws*]
ULPA .... Uniform Partnership Act (EBF)
ULPA .... United Lightning Protection Association (EA)
ULPR .... Ultralow-Pressure Rocket
ULQ .... Tulua [*Colombia*] [*Airport symbol*] (OAG)
ULQ .... Upper Left Quadrant (AAMN)
ULR .... Uganda Law Reports [*A publication*] (DLA)
ULR .... Uganda Protectorate Law Reports [*1904-51*] [*A publication*] (DLA)
ULR .... Ultralinear Rectifier
ULR .... Ultra Long Range (DA)
ULR .... Ultramar Corp. [*NYSE symbol*] (SPSG)
ULR .... Underwater Locator Beacon
ULR .... Uniform Law Review [*A publication*] (DLA)
ULR .... Union Labor Report [*Bureau of National Affairs*] [*Information service or system*] (CRD)
ULR .... Union Law Review [*South Africa*] [*A publication*] (DLA)
ULR .... United Liberty Resources Ltd. [*Vancouver Stock Exchange symbol*]
ULR .... University Law Review [*United States*] [*A publication*] (DLA)
ULR .... Utilities Law Reporter [*A publication*] (DLA)
ULRA .... United Lithuanian Relief Fund of America (EA)
ULRF .... Urban Land Research Foundation
ULRGW .... Ultra-Long Range Guided Weapon (IAA)
ULRSA .... Union and League of Romanian Societies of America (EA)
ULS .... Carroll Air Service, Inc. [*ICAO designator*] (FAAC)
ULS .... ULS Capital Corp. [*Toronto Stock Exchange symbol*]
ULS .... Ultimatist Life Society (EA)
ULS .... Ultraviolet Light Stabilizer
ULS .... Ulysses, KS [*Location identifier FAA*]
ULS .... Union List Subsystem [*Library science*] (TELE)
ULS .... United Leukodystrophy Foundation (EA)
ULS .... United Limited Sprints [*Auto racing*]
ULS .... United Lutheran Society (EA)
ULS .... Unit Level Switchboard (MCD)
ULS .... University Libraries Section [*Association of College and Research Libraries*]
ULS .... University of Lowell, South Campus, Lowell, MA [*OCLC symbol*] (OCLC)
ULS .... Unsecured Loan Stock (DCTA)
ULS .... Upward-Looking SONAR
ULSA .... Ultralow Sidelobe Antenna [*Air Force*] (MCD)
ULSCS .... University of London Shared Cataloguing System (NITA)
ULSI .... Ultralarge-Scale Integration [*of circuits*] [*Semiconductor technology*]
ULSIA .... Uniform Land Security Interest Act [*National Conference of Commissioners on Uniform State Laws*]
ULSP .... Unified Legal Services Program
ULSS .... Underwater LASER Surveying System (MCD)
ULSSSHCL... Union List of Serials in the Social Sciences and Humanities Held by Canadian Libraries [*National Library of Canada*] [*Information service or system*] (CRD)
ULSTD .... Union Label and Service Trades Department (of AFL-CIO) [*American Federation of Labor and Congress of Industrial Organizations*] (EA)
ULSV .... Unmanned Launch Space Vehicles [*NASA*] (KSC)
ULT .... Ultimate (AAG)
ULT .... Ultime [*Lastly*] [*Pharmacy*]
ult .... Ultimo [*In the Month Preceding the Present*] [*Latin*] (WGA)
ULT .... Ultrahigh Temperature (MAE)
ULT .... UltrAir, Inc. [*ICAO designator*] (FAAC)
ULT .... Ultralow Tar [*Cigarettes*] [*Tobacco industry*]
ULT .... Ultralow Temperature
ULT .... Ultramarine [*Philately*] (ROG)
ULT .... Ultramar Ltd. [*Toronto Stock Exchange symbol*]
ULT .... Uniform Low-Frequency Technique
ULT .... Unione per la Lotta alla Tubercolosi [*Union of Anti-Tuberculosis Association Workers*] [*Italy*]
ULT .... United Lodge of Theosophists (EA)
ULT .... Universal Learning Technology
ULT .... Universal Life Trust [*An association*] (EA)
ULT .... Upper Layer Thickness [*Of ocean waters*] [*Oceanography*]
ULTA .... Uniform Land Transactions Act [*National Conference of Commissioners on Uniform State Laws*]
ULTC .... Urban Library Trustees Council [*Later, ULC*] (EA)
ULTD .... Ultradata Corp. [*NASDAQ symbol*] (TTSB)
ULTE .... Ultimate Electronics [*Commercial firm NASDAQ symbol*] (SAG)
UltElct......... Ultimate Electronics [*Commercial firm Associated Press*] (SAG)
ULTI .... Ultralow-Temperature Isotropic [*Carbon*]
ULTK .... Ultrak, Inc. [*NASDAQ symbol*] (NQ)
ULTO .... Ultimo [*In the Month Preceding the Present*] [*Latin*]
UltPac......... Ultra Pac, Inc. [*Associated Press*] (SAG)
ult praes ..... Ultimum Praescriptum [*Last Prescribed*] [*Latin*] [*Pharmacy*] (DAVI)
ULT PRAESCR... Ultimo Praescriptus [*The Last Ordered*] [*Pharmacy*] (ROG)
ULTR .... UltraData Systems [*NASDAQ symbol*] (TTSB)
ULTR .... UltraData Systems, Inc. [*NASDAQ symbol*] (SAG)
ULTRA .... Ultramarine [*Philately*] (ROG)
ULTRA .... United Laser Toner Recyclers Association (NTPA)
ULTRACOM... Ultraviolet Communications
UltraD......... UltraData Systems, Inc. [*Associated Press*] (SAG)
UltraDt........ UltraData Systems, Inc. [*Associated Press*] (SAG)
Ultrafem...... Ultrafem, Inc. [*Associated Press*] (SAG)
ULTRAJ........ Ultrajectum [*Utrecht*] [*Imprint*] [*Latin*] (ROG)
Ultrak.......... Ultrak, Inc. [*Associated Press*] (SAG)
Ultralife .... Ultralife Batteries, Inc. [*Associated Press*] (SAG)
UltramDS...... Ultramar Diamond Shamrock Corp. [*Associated Press*] (SAG)

Ultramr........	Ultramar Capital Corp. [Associated Press] (SAG)
UltraStp......	Ultratech Stepper, Inc. [Associated Press] (SAG)
ULTRA-X.....	Universal Language for Typographic Reproduction Applications
Ultrdta........	Ultradata Corp. [Associated Press] (SAG)
ULTRW.......	Ultradata Sys Wrrt'A' [NASDAQ symbol] (TTSB)
ULTSIGN.....	Ultimate Assignment
ULTT...........	Tallin [Former USSR ICAO location identifier] (ICLI)
ULU............	Gulu [Uganda] [Airport symbol] (OAG)
ULV............	Ultralow Volume
ULVA..........	USS [United States Ship] Liberty Veterans Association (EA)
ULVZ..........	Ultra Low Velocity Zone [Seismology]
ULW...........	Unsafe Landing Warning
ULWA.........	Union of Latin Writers and Artists [Paris, France] (EAIO)
ULWB	Belozyorsk [Former USSR ICAO location identifier] (ICLI)
ULWC.........	Ultra-Lightweight Coated [Paper]
ULWT..........	Totma [Former USSR ICAO location identifier] (ICLI)
ULWW.........	Vologda [Former USSR ICAO location identifier] (ICLI)
ULY............	Ulyanovsk [Former USSR Airport symbol] (OAG)
ULZP..........	United Labor Zionist Party [Later, LZA] (EA)
UM.............	Air Zimbabwe [ICAO designator] (AD)
um.............	Micron (DAVI)
UM.............	Ouguiya [Monetary unit] (ODBW)
UM.............	Salt Lake County Library System, Midvale, UT [Library symbol Library of Congress] (LCLS)
UM.............	Ugaritic Manual [C. H. Gordon] [A publication] (BJA)
UM.............	Umbilical Mast [NASA] (KSC)
UM.............	Umot Me'uhadot [United Nations] [Hebrew]
UM.............	Unaccompanied Minor [Airline passenger]
UM.............	Under-Mentioned [i.e., mentioned later in a document]
UM.............	Underwater Mechanic
Um.............	Uniform, Medium-Grained [Soil]
UM.............	Uninsured Motorists [Insurance]
UM.............	Unio Mallorquina [Majorcan Union] [Political party] (PPW)
UM.............	Unione Maniferro [Somalia]
UM.............	Union Movement Party [British]
UM.............	Unitas Malacologica [An association Netherlands] (EAIO)
UM.............	United Medical (EFIS)
UM.............	United States Minor Outlying Islands [ANSI two-letter standard code] (CNC)
UM.............	Unit of Measure (MCD)
U/M............	Unit of Measure (NAKS)
UM.............	Universal Machine Gun (MCD)
UM.............	Universal Measuring Microscope
UM.............	Universal Monitor (MCD)
UM.............	University of Manitoba [Canada]
UM.............	University of Massachusetts [Amherst, MA]
UM.............	University of Miami [Florida]
UM.............	University of Miami, Florida [USA] [Marine science] (OSRA)
UM.............	University of Missouri Press
U/M............	Unmanned (NASA)
UM.............	Unmarried
UM.............	Unpopular Magnetic Fields
UM.............	Unpriced Material
UM.............	Unscheduled Maintenance
U/M............	Unscheduled Maintenance (NAKS)
UM.............	Upper Magazine [Typography]
UM.............	Upper Motor [Neurons] [Medicine]
UM.............	Uracil Mustard [Antineoplastic drug] (AAMN)
UM.............	Uromodulin
UM.............	Useful Method
UM.............	Use of Materials Bulletin [Department of Housing and Urban Development] [A publication] (GFGA)
UM.............	User Manual (MCD)
UM.............	Utilization Management (WYGK)
UMA...........	Lineas Aereas del Humaya, SA de CV [Mexico] [FAA designator] (FAAC)
UMA...........	Ultrasonic Manufacturers Association [Later, UIA] (EA)
UMA...........	Unified Memory Architecture [Computer science] (PCM)
UMA...........	Uniform - Memory - Access [Computer science]
UMA...........	Union de Mujeres Americanas [United Women of the Americas]
UMA...........	Union Mathematique Africaine [African Mathematical Union - AMU] (EA)
UMA...........	Union Medicale Arabe [Arab Medical Union] (EAIO)
UMA...........	Union Membership Agreement (DCTA)
UMA...........	Union Mondiale des Aveugles [World Blind Union - WBU] (EA)
UMA...........	United Maritime Administration
UMA...........	United Maritime Authority
UMA...........	United Methodist Association of Health and Welfare Ministries (EA)
UMA...........	United Motorcoach Association (NTPA)
UMA...........	Unit Mobilization Augmentation [Army] (DOMA)
UMA...........	Universal Measurement Assembly (MCD)
UMA...........	Universal Measuring Amplifier (KSC)
UMA...........	University of Mid-America [Consortium of six midwestern universities]
UMA...........	Unmanned Aircraft [Aviation]
UMA...........	Unscheduled Maintenance Action [Military] (AABC)
UMA...........	Upper Memory Area [Computer science]
UMA...........	Urinary Muramidase Activity [Medicine] (DMAA)
UMa...........	Ursa Major [Constellation]
UMAA.........	United Martial Arts Association (EA)
UMAA.........	University of Melbourne Alumni Association [Australia]
UMAB	University of Maryland at Baltimore
UMAC	UMI [University Microfilms International] Article Clearinghouse [Information service or system] (IID)
UMAC	Upper Midwest Athletic Conference (PSS)
UMACHA.....	Upper Midwest Automated Clearing House Association (MHDW)
UMAD.........	Umatilla Army Depot [Oregon] (AABC)
UMAH.........	Union Mondiale d'Avancee Humaine [World Union for Human Progress]
U Maine	University of Maine (GAGS)
U Maine L Rev...	University of Maine. Law Review [A publication] (DLA)
U Maine (Portland-Gorham)...	University of Maine at Portland-Gorham (GAGS)
UMaj...........	Ursa Major [Constellation]
UMan.........	Manti City Library, Manti, UT [Library symbol Library of Congress] (LCLS)
UMANA.......	Ukrainian Medical Association of North America (EA)
UMAP	United Methodist Associations of Preschools
UMAP	University of Michigan Assembly Program
UMARK.......	Unit Maintenance Aircraft Recovery Kit (MCD)
U Mary L Forum...	University of Maryland Law Forum [A publication] (DLA)
UMASS.......	University of Massachusetts [Amherst, MA]
U Mass	University of Massachusetts (GAGS)
UMASS.......	Unlimited Machine Access from Scattered Sites [Computer science]
U Mass (Boston)...	University of Massachusetts Boston (GAGS)
U Mass (Dartmouth)...	University of Massachusetts Dartmouth (GAGS)
U Mass (Lowell)...	University of Massachusetts Lowell (GAGS)
Umax.........	Maximum Solute Concentration [Chemistry] (DAVI)
Umax	Urinary Osmolality Maximum [Physiology] (MAH)
UMB..........	Ultramicrobacteria
Umb..........	Umbelliferyl [Biochemistry]
UMB..........	Umberatana [Australia Seismograph station code, US Geological Survey] (SEIS)
UMB..........	Umberto's Pasta Enterprises, Inc. [Vancouver Stock Exchange symbol]
UMB..........	Umbilical (MCD)
umb..........	Umbundu [MARC language code Library of Congress] (LCCP)
UMB..........	Umnak, AK [Location identifier FAA] (FAAL)
UMB..........	Union Medicale Balkanique [Balkan Medical Union] (EAIO)
UMB..........	Union Mondiale de Billard [World Billiards Union - WBU] [Switzerland]
UMB..........	United Merchant Bar [Commercial firm British]
UMB..........	Universal Masonic Brotherhood (EA)
UMB..........	Universal Missile Building (MCD)
UMB..........	Upper Memory Block [Computer science] (PCM)
UMBA........	United Mortgage Bankers of America [Philadelphia, PA] (EA)
UM-BBD......	University of Minesota Biocatalysis/Biodegradation Database
UMBC........	Umbilical Cord [Aerospace engineering]
UMBC........	United Malayan Banking Corp.
UMBC........	University of Maryland, Baltimore County
UMBF........	UMB Financial [NASDAQ symbol] (TTSB)
UMBF........	UMB Financial Corp. [NASDAQ symbol] (SAG)
UMB Fn	UMB Financial Corp. [Associated Press] (SAG)
UMBI.........	University of Maryland Biotechnology Institute
UMBL........	Umbilical (AAG)
Umbr.........	Umbrian [Language, culture, etc.]
UMBR........	Unclad-Metal Breeder Reactor
UMBR........	Universal Multiple Bomb Rack (NG)
UMBS........	University of Michigan Biological Station [Research center] (RCD)
UMBSM	University Marine Biological Station, Millport [UK] [Marine science] (OSRA)
UMB V	Umbilical Vein [Anatomy]
umb ven	Umbilical Vein [Anatomy] (DAVI)
UMC..........	Ukrainian Museum of Canada [UTLAS symbol]
UMC..........	Underwater Manifold Centre [Shell Oil Co.] [British]
UMC..........	Unibus Microchannel
UMC..........	Unidimensional Chromatography (DB)
UMC..........	Unidirectional Molding Compound (MCD)
UMC..........	Unified Management Corp. Database [Information service or system] (CRD)
UMC..........	Uniform Mechanical Code (COE)
UMC..........	Uniform Motion Coupling
UMC..........	Uniform Moving Charge
UMC..........	Uninsured Motorists Coverage [Insurance]
UMC..........	Union du Moyen-Congo [Union of the Middle Congo]
UMC..........	United Maritime Council
UMC..........	United Meridian Corp. [NYSE symbol] (SPSG)
UMC..........	United Methodist Church
UMC..........	United Microelectronics Corp. (NITA)
UMC..........	United Mining Corp. [Vancouver Stock Exchange symbol]
UMC..........	United Motor Courts
UMC..........	Unit Mail Clerk
UMC..........	Unit Mobility Center [Military] (AFIT)
UMC..........	Universal Match Corp.
UmC..........	Universal Microfilming Corporation, Salt Lake City, UT [Library symbol Library of Congress Obsolete] (LCLS)
UMC..........	University of Maryland, College Park, MD [OCLC symbol] (OCLC)
UMC..........	Unspecified Minor Construction Program [Navy] (DNAB)
UMCA........	Ultra Marathon Cycling Association (EA)
UMCA........	United Mining Councils of America (EA)
UMCA........	Universities Mission to Central Africa [Later, USPG] [British]
UMCA........	Uraba, Medellin & Central Airways, Inc.
UMCathA.....	Young Men's Catholic Association (BARN)
UMCC	United Maritime Consultative Committee
UMCEES	University of Maryland Center for Environmental and Estuarine Studies
UMCI	United Medicorp (EFIS)
UMCOM.......	United Methodist Communications [Information service or system] (IID)
UMCOR.......	United Methodist Committee on Relief (EA)
UMCP	Unit Maintenance Collection Point [Army] (INF)
UMCP	University of Maryland, College Park

UM/CR .... Unsatisfactory Material/Condition Report (MCD)
UMCS .... Unattended Multipoint Communications Station (MHDI)
UMD .... Ultrasonic Material Dispersion
UMD .... Union de Mouvements Democratiques [*Djibouti*] [*Political party*] (EY)
UMD .... Unitized Microwave Devices
UMD .... Unit Manning Document [*DoD*]
UMD .... Unit Movement Data [*Military*]
UMD .... University of Maryland [*College Park, MD*]
U Md .... University of Maryland (GAGS)
UMD .... University of Medicine and Dentistry of New Jersey
umd .... Unmarried (WDAA)
UMDA .... Umatilla Depot Activity [*Army*]
UMDA .... Uniform Marriage and Divorce Act [*National Conference of Commissioners on Uniform State Laws*]
UMDA .... United Micronesia Development Association
U Md (Baltimore)... University of Maryland, Baltimore (GAGS)
UMDC .... Union Mondiale Democrate Chretienne [*Christian Democratic World Union*]
UMDK .... United Movement for Democracy in Korea [*Later, UMDUK*] (EA)
U Md LF ...... University of Maryland Law Forum [*A publication*] (DLA)
UMDNJ .... University of Medicine and Dentistry of New Jersey [*Newark*]
UMDS .... United Medical and Dental Schools [*University of London*] [*England*] (HGEN)
UMDUK .... United Movement for Democracy and Unification in Korea [*Defunct*] (EA)
UME .... Ultramicroelectrode [*Electrochemical microscopy*]
UME .... Umea [*Sweden*] [*Airport symbol*] (OAG)
UME .... Underground Mine Engineer
UME .... Uniform Manufacturers Exchange (EA)
UME .... United Ministries in Education [*Later, HEMT/UMHE*] (EA)
UME .... Unit Mission Equipment (AAG)
UME .... Unit Mobility Equipment
UME .... Unit Monthly Equipment (MSA)
UmE .... University Music Editions, New York, NY [*Library symbol Library of Congress*] (LCLS)
UME .... University of Maryland, Eastern Shore, Princess Anne, MD [*OCLC symbol*] (OCLC)
UME .... Unpredictable Main Event
UME .... Urethane Mixing Equipment
UME .... User Network Interface Management Entity [*Computer science*] (DDC)
UMEA .... Universala Medicina Esperanto Asocio [*Universal Medical Esperanto Association*] (EAIO)
UMEB .... United Maritime Executive Board
UMEC .... Union Mondiale des Enseignants Catholiques [*World Union of Catholic Teachers*] [*Rome, Italy*]
UMED .... Unimed, Inc. [*NASDAQ symbol*] (NQ)
UMED .... Unimed Pharmaceuticals [*NASDAQ symbol*] (TTSB)
U Med Dent NJ... University of Medicine and Dentistry of New Jersey (GAGS)
UMEJ .... Union Mondiale des Etudiants Juifs [*World Union of Jewish Students - WUJS*] (EAIO)
UMEMPA ..... Union of Middle Eastern and Mediterranean Pediatric Societies [*Greece*] (EAIO)
UMEMPS ..... Union of Middle Eastern and Mediterranean Pediatric Societies [*See also USPMOM*] [*Athens, Greece*] (EAIO)
UMER .... Ultrasonically-Modulated Electron Resonance (PDAA)
UMeridn ..... United Meridian Corp. [*Associated Press*] (SAG)
UMES .... United Mechanical Engineers' Society [*A union*] [*British*]
UMES .... University of Maryland, Eastern Shore
UmF .... National Cash Register Co., New York, NY [*Library symbol Library of Congress*] (LCLS)
UMF .... Ultramicrofiche
UMF .... Uniform Magnetic Field
UMF .... Unit Media Facilitator
UMF .... University of Maine at Farmington, Farmington, ME [*OCLC symbol*] (OCLC)
UMF .... User Message Format
UMF .... Users Master File (IAA)
UMFA .... United Mineworker's Federation of Australia (EERA)
UMFC .... United Methodist Free Churches
UMFCBMA ... United Male and Female Cardboard Box Makers' Association [*A union*] [*British*]
UMFDC .... Union Mundial de Mujeres Democrata Cristianas [*World Union of Christian Democratic Women*] [*Venezuela Political party*] (EAIO)
UMFP .... Unit Materiel Fielding Point [*Army*] (RDA)
Umfrev Off Cor... Umfreville's Office of Coroner [*A publication*] (DLA)
UMFS .... United Mutual Fund Selector [*United Business Service Co.*]
UMG .... Universal Machine Gun (MCD)
UMG .... Universal Mercator Grid (NVT)
UMG .... US West [*NYSE symbol*] (SAG)
UMG .... US West Media Group [*NYSE symbol*] (TTSB)
U$_{Mg}$V ...... Magnesium Excretion [*Medicine*] (DAVI)
UMH .... United Mobile Homes [*AMEX symbol*] (TTSB)
UMH .... United Mobile Homes, Inc. [*AMEX symbol*] (SAG)
UMHE .... United Ministries in Higher Education [*Later, HEMT/UMHE*] (EA)
UMHK .... Union Miniere du Haut Katanga [*Mining Company of Upper Katanga*]
UMHP .... Union Mondiale des Societes d'Histoire Pharmaceutique [*World Organization of Societies of Pharmaceutical History*]
UMI .... Udruzena Metalna Industrija [*Belgrade, Yugoslavia*]
UMI .... Ukrainian Music Institute in America
UMI .... Ultra Microfiche (EECA)
UMI .... Underway Material Inspection [*Navy*] (NVT)
UMI .... Union de Melillenses Independientes [*Spanish North Africa*] [*Political party*] (MENA)

UMI .... Union Mathematique Internationale [*International Mathematical Union - IMU*] (EAIO)
UMI .... Union Mundial pro Interlingua (EA)
UMI .... United Methodist Information [*Database*] [*United Methodist Communications*] [*Information service or system*] (CRD)
UMI .... United States Minor Outlying Islands [*ANSI three-letter standard code*] (CNC)
UMI .... Unit Movement Identifier [*Army*] (AABC)
UMI .... University Microfilms, Inc. (WDMC)
UMI .... University Microfilms International [*Database producer*] (IID)
UMi .... Ursa Minor [*Constellation*]
U Miami (Fla)... University of Miami (Florida) (GAGS)
UMIB .... Urgent Marine Information Broadcast (COE)
U Mich .... [*The*] University of Michigan (GAGS)
UMICH .... University of Michigan [*Ann Arbor, MI*]
UMIFA .... Uniform Management of Institutional Funds Act [*National Conference of Commissioners on Uniform State Laws*]
UMII .... Vitebsk [*Former USSR ICAO location identifier*] (ICLI)
UMin .... Ursa Minor [*Constellation*]
UMINF .... United Movement of Iranian National Forces [*Defunct*] (EA)
U Minn .... University of Minnesota (GAGS)
UMIP .... Uniform Material Issue Priority [*Navy*]
UMIPS .... Uniform Material Issue Priority System [*Navy*] (NG)
UMIS .... Urban Management Information System
U Miss .... [*The*] University of Mississippi (GAGS)
U Miss (Med Cent)... University of Mississippi Medicine Center (GAGS)
UMIST .... University of Manchester Institute of Science and Technology [*Databank or iginator and research institute*] [*British*]
UMIX .... User-Manufacturer Information Exchange
UMJL .... Union Mondiale pour un Judaisme Liberal
UMK .... Umanak [*Greenland*] [*Airport symbol*] (AD)
UMK .... University of Missouri at Kansas City, Kansas City, MO [*OCLC symbol*] (OCLC)
UMKC .... University of Missouri at Kansas City
UML .... Universal Mission Load [*Military*] (AABC)
UML .... University of Missouri, Columbia School of Library and Information Science, Co lumbia, MO [*OCLC symbol*] (OCLC)
UMLC .... Institute of Estate Planning, University of Miami Law Center (DLA)
UMLC .... Universal Multiline Controller
UMLC .... University of Miami Law Center (DLA)
UMLER .... Uniform Machine Language Equipment Register [*RSPA*] (TAG)
UMLER .... Universal Machine Language Equipment Register [*Association of American Railroads*] [*Information service or system*] (CRD)
UMM .... Summit, AK [*Location identifier FAA*] (FAAL)
UMM .... Union Mondiale du Mapam [*World Union of Mapam - WUM*] (EAIO)
UMM .... United Merchants & Manufacturers, Inc. [*NYSE symbol*] (SPSG)
UMM .... Universal Measuring Machine
UMM .... University of Manitoba Medical Library [*UTLAS symbol*]
UM-MaP .... University of Maryland Mathematics Project
UMMC .... University of Michigan Medical Center (BABM)
UMMH .... Unscheduled Maintenance Manhours (MCD)
UMMIPS .... Uniform Materiel Movement and Issue Priority System [*Military*] (AFM)
UMMIPS .... Uniform Military Material Issue Priority System (DNAB)
UMMIS .... Uniform Material Movement and Issue Priority System [*Navy*] (ANA)
UMML .... Unione Medicale Mediterranea Latina [*Latin Mediterranean Medical Union - LMMU*] [*Mantua, Italy*] (EAIO)
UMML .... University of Miami Marine Laboratory [*Florida*]
UMMM .... Minsk/Loshitsa [*Former USSR ICAO location identifier*] (ICLI)
UMMMIPS ..... Uniform Military Material Movement and Issue Priority System (DNAB)
UMMS .... Unit Maintenance Management System
UMMZ .... University of Michigan Museum of Zoology
UMN .... Monett, MO [*Location identifier FAA*] (FAAL)
UMN .... Union des Musiciens Nordiques [*Nordic Musicians' Union - NMU*] (EAIO)
UMN .... Union pour la Majorite Nouvelle [*Union for the New Majority*] [*France Political party*] (PPE)
UMN .... Unsatisfactory Material Notice (MSA)
UMN .... Upper Motor Neuron [*Medicine*]
UMN .... Urban Ministry Network [*Melbourne, Victoria, Australia*]
UMNB .... Upper Motor Neurogenic Bladder [*Neurology*] (DAVI)
UMNCF .... United Merchant Navy Christian Fellowship [*British*]
UMNL .... Upper Motor Neuron Lesion [*Neurology*]
UMNO .... United Malays National Organization [*Malaysia*] [*Political party*]
UMO .... Umbertino's Restaurant [*Vancouver Stock Exchange symbol*]
UMO .... Unconventional Military Operations (MCD)
UMO .... Unit Movement Officer [*Army*] (INF)
UMO .... University of Maine, Orono
UMO .... Unmanned Orbital [*NASA*] (NASA)
umo .... Unmanned Orbital (NAKS)
UMobH .... United Mobile Homes, Inc. [*Associated Press*] (SAG)
U MO B Law Ser... University of Missouri. Bulletin. Law Series [*A publication*] (DLA)
U MO Bull L Ser... University of Missouri. Bulletin. Law Series [*A publication*] (DLA)
UMOC .... Ugly Man on Campus [*Contest*]
U Mo (Columbia)... University of Missouri at Columbia (GAGS)
UMOES .... Universal Masonic Order of the Eastern Star (EA)
UMOFC .... Union Mondiale des Organisations Feminines Catholiques [*World Union of Catholic Women's Organizations - WUCWO*] [*Canada*]
U Mo (KC) .... University of Missouri at Kansas City (GAGS)
UMOL .... Unmanned Orbital Laboratory
U MO L Bull ... University of Missouri. Law Bulletin [*A publication*] (DLA)
U Mont .... University of Montana (GAGS)

U Montevallo... University of Montevallo (GAGS)

U Mo (Rolla)... University of Missouri at Rolla (GAGS)

UMOS......... U-Grooved Metal Oxide Semiconductors (MCD)

UMOSBESL... Union Mondiale des Organisations Syndicales sur Base Economique et Sociale Liberale [*World Union of Liberal Trade Union Organizations*]

UMOSEA...... Union Mondiale pour la Sauvegarde de l'Enfance et de l'Adolescence [*World Union for the Safeguard of Youth*]

UMOST........ U-Groove Power Metal-Oxide Semiconductor Field Effect Transistor (IAA)

U Mo (St Louis)... University of Missouri at St. Louis (GAGS)

UMP............ Umpire (DSUE)

UMP............ Uniformly Most Powerful Test [*Statistics*]

UMP............ Uninflated Movement Party [*Australia Political party*] (ADA)

UMP............ Union of Moderate Parties [*Vanuatu*] [*Political party*] (PPW)

UMP............ Universal Military Pod (VNW)

UMP............ Upper Mantle Project [*Marine science*] (OSRA)

UMP............ Upper Merion & Plymouth Railroad Co. [*AAR code*]

UMP............ Upward Mobility Program

UMP............ Uracil Monophosphate [*Biochemistry*] (AAMN)

UMP............ Uridine Monophosphate [*Biochemistry*]

UMPAR........ Unit Mobilization Personnel Assignment Report [*Navy*] (DNAB)

UMPG......... University of Maine at Portland/Gorham

UMpGS........ Church of Jesus Christ of Latter-Day Saints, Genealogical Society Library, MountPleasant Branch, Stake Center, Mount Pleasant, UT [*Library symbol Library of Congress*] (LCLS)

UMPK......... Uridine Monophosphate Kinase (STED)

UMPLIS....... Informations- und Dokumentationssystem Umwelt [*Environmental Information and Documentation System*] [*Berlin*] [*Information retrieval*]

UMPR......... Uniform Military Personnel Record (AFM)

UMPS......... Union Mondiale des Pioniers de Stockholm [*World Union of Stockholm Pioneers*] (EAIO)

UMPT.......... Ultrahigh-Frequency Multi-Platform Transceiver [*Navy*] (MCD)

UMpW........ Wasatch Academy, Mount Pleasant, UT [*Library symbol Library of Congress*] (LCLS)

UMR........... Ultraviolet Mitogenic Radiation

UMR........... Unimar Indonesian Participating Units [*AMEX symbol*] (SPSG)

UMR........... Unimar Indonesian Ptc Units [*AMEX symbol*] (TTSB)

UMR........... Unipolar Magnetic Regions

UMR........... Unit Mail Room [*Air Force*] (AFM)

UMR........... Unit Manning Report [*Army*] (ADDR)

UMR........... University of Missouri at Rolla

UMR........... University of Missouri at Rolla, Library, Rolla, MO [*OCLC symbol*] (OCLC)

UMR........... Unsatisfactory Material Report [*Military*] (AABC)

UMR........... Upper Maximum Range

UMR........... Usual Marketing Requirement [*Business term*]

UMR........... Woomera [*Australia Airport symbol*] (OAG)

UMRAL........ University of Minnesota Rosemont Aeronautical Laboratories (SAA)

UMRB......... Upper Mississippi River Basin

UMRCC....... Upper Mississippi River Conservation Committee (EA)

UMREL........ Upper Midwest Regional Educational Laboratory, Inc.

UMREMP..... Upper Mississippi River Environmental Management Program [*Federal government*]

UMRG......... Ergli [*Former USSR ICAO location identifier*] (ICLI)

UMRL......... Union Mondiale des Romains Libres [*World Union of Free Romanians - WUFR*] [*Creteil, France*] (EAIO)

UMRR......... Riga/Spilve [*Former USSR ICAO location identifier*] (ICLI)

UMRR......... University of Missouri Research Reactor

UMRW........ Ventspils [*Former USSR ICAO location identifier*] (ICLI)

UMS........... Ultrasonic Motion Sensor (MCD)

UMS........... Unattended Machinery Spaces (DS)

UMS........... Undersea Medical Society, Inc.

UMS........... Unfederated Malay States

UMS........... United Missionary Society

UMS........... Unit Manning System [*Army*] (RDA)

UMS........... Unity Management System [*Bytex Corp.*]

UMS........... Universal Maintenance Standards

UMS........... Universal Memory System [*Intel Corp.*]

UMS........... Universal Military Service

UMS........... Universal MODEM [*Modulate/Demodulate*] System (DWSG)

UMS........... Universal Multiprogramming System [*Computer science*] (MHDB)

UMS........... University of Missouri at St. Louis, St. Louis, MO [*OCLC symbol*] (OCLC)

UMS........... Unmanned Multifunction Satellite

UMS........... Upstream Modulation Sequence [*Genetics*]

UMS........... Urethral Manipulation Syndrome [*Urology*] (DAVI)

UMS........... Utilities Management Services (ACII)

UMSA......... United States Marine Safety Association (EA)

UMSA......... Utah-Manhattan-Sundt & Associates (AAG)

UMSDC....... Unscheduled Maintenance Sample Data Collection (MCD)

UMSE......... Unconditional Mean Square Error [*Statistics*]

UMSE......... Unit Maintenance Support Equipment [*Army*]

UMSE......... Unmanned Surveillance Equipment

UMSN......... Union Mondiale de Ski Nautique [*World Water Ski Union - WWSU*] [*Montreaux, Switzerland*] (EAIO)

UMSP......... Universal Microscope Spectro-Photometer

UMSP......... User Maintenance Support Plan (MCD)

UMSPA....... Uniform Metric System Procedure Act [*National Conference of Commissioners on Uniform State Laws*]

UMSR......... Universal Movement for Scientific Responsibility [*See also MURS*] (EAIO)

UMSSS....... UDAM [*Universal Digital Avionics Module*] Microprocessor Software Support System (MCD)

UMS/VS...... Universal Multiprogramming System/Virtual Storage (NITA)

UMT........... Ultrasonic Material Testing

UMT........... Umiat, AK [*Location identifier FAA*] (FAAL)

UMT........... Union Marocaine du Travail [*Moroccan Labor Union*]

UMT........... Unit Ministry Team [*Military*] (INF)

UMT........... Unit of Medical Time [*Each 4-hour period after 40-hour work week*] [*British*]

UMT........... Universal Microwave Trainer

UMT........... Universal Military Training [*Participants known as Umtees*] [*Post World War II*] [*Army*]

UMT........... Uranium Mill Tailings (GAAI)

UMTA......... Urban Mass Transportation Act [*1964*]

UMTA......... Urban Mass Transportation Administration [*Department of Transportation*]

UMTD......... Using Mails to Defraud

UMTE......... Unmanned Threat Emitter (DWSG)

UMTR......... Universal Movement Theater Repertory [*Defunct*]

UMTR......... University of Maryland Teaching Reactor (NRCH)

UMTRA....... Uranium Mill Tailings Remedial Action (COE)

UMTRAP..... Uranium Mill Trailings Remedial Action Program [*Department of Energy*]

UMTRCA..... Uranium Mill Tailings Radiation Control Act (GFGA)

UMTRI........ University of Michigan Transportation Research Institute [*Research center*] (RCD)

UMTRIS...... Urban Mass Transportation Research Information Service [*National Academy of Sciences*] [*Database*] (IID)

UMTS......... Universal Military Training Service [*or System*] (GPO)

UMTS......... Universal Mobile Telecommunications Services

UMTS......... Universal Mobile Telecommunications System (TELE)

UMTSA....... Universal Military Training and Service Act

UMu........... Murray Public Library, Murray, UT [*Library symbol Library of Congress*] (LCLS)

UMU........... Umuarama [*Brazil*] [*Airport symbol*] (AD)

UMU........... Uplink Multiplexer Unit (MCD)

UMUC......... University of Maryland University College

UMUS......... Unbleached Muslin

UMVF......... Union Mondiale des Voix Francaises [*World Union of French-Speakers - WUFS*] (EAIO)

UMVF......... Unmanned Vertical Flight [*NASA*] (NASA)

UMVS......... United Methodist Voluntary Services

UMVUE...... Uniformly Minimum Variance Unbiased Estimator (PDAA)

UMW......... Mumbwa [*Zambia*] [*Airport symbol*] (AD)

UMW......... Ultramicrowaves

UMW......... United Mine Workers [*Also, UMWA*] (CDAI)

UMW......... Upper Midwest

UMWA........ International Union, United Mine Workers of America [*Also known as UMW*] (EA)

UMWA........ United Machine Workers' Association [*A union*] [*British*]

UMWSF...... United Methodist Women in Switzerland and in France (EAIO)

UMWW...... Vilnius [*Former USSR ICAO location identifier*] (ICLI)

UN........... East Coast Airlines [*ICAO designator*] (AD)

UN........... Nephi Public Library, Nephi, UT [*Library symbol Library of Congress*] (LCLS)

UN........... Ulnar Nerve [*Anatomy*] (DAVI)

UN........... Unassigned [*Telecommunications*] (TEL)

UN........... Under-Nourished (STED)

UN........... Underworld Nobility [*Used by Walter Winchell to refer to mobsters in television series "The Untouchables"*]

UN........... UNESCO Statistical Yearbook [*A publication*]

UN........... Unico National (EA)

UN........... Unified (AAG)

UN........... Unilateral Neglect [*Neurology*] (DAVI)

UN........... Unilever NV [*NYSE symbol*] (SPSG)

UN........... Union (MSA)

UN........... Union Flag [*Navy British*]

UN........... Union Nacional [*National Union*] [*Spain Political party*] (PPE)

UN........... Union Nationale [*National Union*] [*Canada Political party*]

UN........... Unit (AAG)

UN........... United

UN........... United Nations (EA)

UN........... University

UN........... Unknown [*Telecommunications*] (TEL)

UN........... Untreated [*Medicine*]

UN........... Urea-Nitrogen [*Medicine*]

UN........... Urinary Nitrogen [*Medicine*] (DAVI)

U-N11........ Unlicensed National Information Infrastructure (PCM)

UNA......... Ukrainian National Association (EA)

UNA......... Unable [*ICAO designator*] (FAAC)

UNA......... Unalaska [*Alaska*] [*Seismograph station code, US Geological Survey Closed*] (SEIS)

UNA......... Unattended Answering Accessory (MHDB)

UNA......... Underwear-Negligee Associates (EA)

UNA......... Unione Nazionale dell'Avicoltura [*Aviculture Union*] [*Italy*] (EY)

UNA......... United Nations Association

UNA......... United Native Americans (EA)

UNA......... United States Naval Academy, Annapolis, MD [*OCLC symbol*] (OCLC)

UNA......... Universair [*Spain ICAO designator*] (FAAC)

UNA......... Universal Network Architecture [*Telecommunications*]

UNA......... Universal Night Answering [*Telecommunications*] (TEL)

UNA......... Universitats-Netz Austria [*Austrian University Network*] (TNIG)

UNA......... Urinary Nitrogen Appearance (DAVI)

UNa......... Urine Sodium [*Nephrology*] (DAVI)

UNA......... Use No Abbreviations (DNAB)

UNAAA....... Ukrainian National Aid Association of America (EA)

UNAAF......... Unified Action Armed Forces [*Military*]
UNAB........... Unabridged (ADA)
UNABOM..... University/Airline Bomber [*FBI investigation*]
UNABR........ Unabridged
UNAC........... United Nations Africa Council
UNAC........... United Nations Appeal for Children
UNAC........... United Nations Association in Canada (EAIO)
UNAC........... United Nations Association of the Congo (EAIO)
UNACC........ Unaccompanied
unacc.......... Unaccompanied (WDAA)
UNACC........ United Nations Administrative Committee and Coordination (WDAA)
UNACOM..... Universal Army Communication System
UNACX........ United Accumalative Cl.A [*Mutual fund ticker symbol*] (SG)
UNADA........ United Nations Atomic Development Authority (NUCP)
UNADE........ Union Nacional Democratica [*National Democratic Union*] [*Ecuador*] [*Political party*] (PPW)
UNADS........ UNIVAC Automated Documentation System [*Computer science*]
UNAEC......... United Nations Atomic Energy Commission [*Superseded by Disarmament Commission, 1952*]
UNAECC...... United Nations Atomic Energy Control Commission
UNAF.......... Universities National Antiwar Fund
UNAFEI....... United Nations Asia and Far East Institute for the Prevention of Crime and Treatment of Offenders
UNAFPA...... Union des Associations des Fabricants de Pates Alimentaires de la Communaute Economique Europeenne [*Union of Organizations of Manufacturers of Pasta Products in the European Economic Community*]
UNA-H .... United Nations Association of Hungary (EAIO)
UNAH.......... Universidad Nacional Autonoma, Tegucigalpa [*Honduras*]
UNAIDS........ Joint United Nations Programme on Acquired Immune Deficiency Syndrome (ECON)
UNAIS......... United Nations Association International Service [*British*]
UNAKI.......... Union des Colons Agricoles du Kivu [*Union of Agricultural Settlers of Kivu*] [*Congo - Leopoldville*]
UNALC........ User Network Access Link Control
UNALOT...... Unallotted (AABC)
UNALTD...... Unaltered (ROG)
UNAM........ Unico American [*NASDAQ symbol*] (TTSB)
UNAM........ Unico American Corp. [*NASDAQ symbol*] (NQ)
UNAM........ Universidad Nacional Autonoma de Mexico (CROSS)
UNAMACE.... Universal Automatic Map Compilation Equipment
UNAMAP...... Users Network for Applied Modeling of Air Pollution [*Set of computer simulation models being developed by Battelle for EPA*]
UNA-MEX.... United Nations Association of Mexico (EAIO)
UNAMI........ Uniao Nacional Africana de Mocambique Independente [*Mozambique*] [*Political party*]
UNAMIC....... United Nations Advance Mission in Cambodia (ECON)
UNAMIR...... United Nations Assistance Mission in Rwanda
UNAN.......... Unanimous
UNANSD...... Unanswered (ROG)
UNAP.......... Unable to Approve [*ICAO designator*] (FAAC)
UNAP.......... Union Nationale Progressite [*National Progressive Union*] [*Burundi*]
UNAP.......... United Nations Association of Poland (EAIO)
UNAPEC...... United Nations Action Program for Economic Cooperation
UNAPEI....... Union Nationale des Associations de Parents et Amis de Personnes Handicapees Mentales [*Formerly, Union Nationale des Associations de Parents d'Enfants Inadeptes*] [*France*] (EAIO)
Unapix........ Unapix Entertainment, Inc. [*Associated Press*] (SAG)
UNAPOC...... United National Association of Post Office Craftsmen [*Later, APWU*]
UNAPPD...... Unappointed (ROG)
UNAR.......... Association for the United Nations in Russia (EAIO)
UNAR.......... Unable to Approve Altitude Requested [*Aviation*] (FAAC)
UNAR.......... Union Nationale Ruandaise [*Ruanda National Union*]
UNARU .... Union Nationale Africaine du Ruanda-Urundi [*African National Union of Ruanda-Urundi*]
UNAS .... Ukrainian National Academy of Sciences
UNAS .... United Nations Association of Sweden (EAIO)
UNASABEC... Union Nationale des Syndicats Agricoles Forestiers, des Bois, de l'Elevage, et de la Peche du Cameroun [*National Union of Farmers, Fishermen, Forest Guards, and Timber Workers of Cameroon*]
UNASGD ..... Unassigned (AABC)
UNASGN ..... Unassigned [*Navy*] (NVT)
UNASL .... United Nations Association of Sri Lanka (EAIO)
UNASSAD .... Union Nationale des Associations de Soins et Service a Domicile [*Also, National Organisation for Home Care*] [*France*] (EAIO)
UNASSD ...... Unassembled
UNAT .... Union Nationale des Agriculteurs Tunisiens [*National Union of Tunisian Farmers*]
UNAT .... United Nations Administrative Tribunal (EY)
UNAT .... United Nations Association of Turkey (EAIO)
UNATAC....... Union d'Assistance Technique pour l'Automobile et la Circulation Routiere [*Union of Technical Assistance for Motor Vehicle and Road Traffic*] [*Geneva, Switzerland*] (EAIO)
UNATNDD .... Unattended [*Aviation*] (FAAC)
UNATRACAM... Union des Associations Traditionelles du Cameroun [*Union of Traditional Associations of Cameroon*]
UNATRACO... Union des Syndicats des Travailleurs du Congo [*National Union of Workers of the Congo*]
UNATT .... Unattached (ROG)
UNATT .... Unattended (ADA)
UNATTRIB.... Unattributed
unattrib...... Unattributed (WDAA)
UNA-UK .... United Nations Association of Great Britain and Northern Ireland (EAIO)

UNAUS......... United Nations Association of the United States of America (AEBS)
UNA-USA .... United Nations Association of the United States of America (EA)
Unauth........ Unauthorized (DLA)
UNAUTHD .... Unauthorized (AABC)
U$_{Na}$V........ Sodium Excretion [*Rate*] [*Medicine*] (DAVI)
U$_{Na}$V........ Urine Sodium [*Medicine*] (DAVI)
U$_{Na}$V........ Urine Sodium Excretion [*Medicine*] (DAVI)
UNAVBL....... Unavailable (FAAC)
UNAVCO...... University NAVSTAR Consortium
UNAVEM...... United Nations Angola Verification Mission
UNAVIC....... United Nations Audiovisual Information Center
UNB .... Fredericton [*New Brunswick*] [*Seismograph station code, US Geological Survey*] (SEIS)
UNB .... Kanab, UT [*Location identifier FAA*] (FAAL)
UNB .... Unbound (ROG)
unb .... Unbound (WDMC)
UNB .... Unexploded Booklet [*Philately*]
UNB .... United Nations Beacon
UNB .... Universal Navigation Beacon
UNB .... University of New Brunswick [*Canada*]
UNB .... University of New Brunswick Library [*UTLAS symbol*]
UNBAL........ Unbalanced [*Telecommunications*] (TEL)
UnBanCal ...... UnionBanCal Corp. [*Associated Press*] (SAG)
UNBB .... Barnaul [*Former USSR ICAO location identifier*] (ICLI)
UNBC.......... UnionBanCal Corp. [*NASDAQ symbol*] [*Formerly, Union Bank*] (SG)
UnBCal .... UnionBanCal Corp. [*Associated Press*] (SAG)
UnBCh........ United Board Chaplain [*British military*]
UNBCL........ University of Nebraska College of Law [*Lincoln, NE*] (DLA)
UNBD.......... Unbound (WDAA)
Unbd.......... Unbound (WDMC)
Un Bd Ch .... United Board Chaplain [*British military*] (DMA)
UNBIS......... United Nations Bibliographic Information System [*United Nations Headquarters*] (IID)
UNBJ .... United National Bancorp [*NASDAQ symbol*] (NQ)
UNBJ .... United Natl Bancorp [*NASDAQ symbol*] (TTSB)
UnBkCp....... Union Bankshares Corp. [*Associated Press*] (SAG)
unbld .... Unbleached [*Paper*] (DGA)
UNBLK........ Unblanking (MSA)
UNBLSJ ...... University of New Brunswick. Law School. Journal [*A publication*] (DLA)
UNBNJ .... United National Bancorp [*Associated Press*] (SAG)
UnBnk........ Union Bank [*Associated Press*] (SAG)
UnBnOH...... United Bancorp Ohio [*Associated Press*] (SAG)
UNBRO .... United Nations Border Relief Operation
UNBSA....... United Nations Bureau of Social Affairs
UNBTAO...... United Nations Bureau of Technical Assistance Operations
UNC .... Uncertain (ADA)
UNC .... UNC, Inc. [*Formerly, United Nuclear Corporation*] [*NYSE symbol*] (SPSG)
UNC .... Uncirculated [*Numismatics*]
UNC .... Unclassified (KSC)
UNC .... Uncle (DSUE)
UNC .... Unconditional (IAA)
UNC .... Undercurrent (IAA)
UNC .... Unguia [*Colombia*] [*Airport symbol*] (AD)
UNC .... Unified Coarse [*Thread*]
UNC .... Unified National Coarse Thread (IAA)
UNC .... Union Nationale Camerounaise [*Cameroon National Union*]
UNC .... Union Nouvelle Caledonienne [*New Caledonia*] [*Political party*] (FEA)
UNC .... United Corporations Ltd. [*Toronto Stock Exchange symbol*]
UNC .... United Meridian [*NYSE symbol*] (TTSB)
UNC .... United National Convention [*Ghana*] [*Political party*] (PPW)
UNC .... United Nations Command
UNC .... United Network Co. [*TV broadcasting network*]
UNC .... United New Conservationists (EA)
UNC .... United Nuclear Corp. (EFIS)
UNC .... Universal Naming Convention [*Computer science*] (PCM)
UNC .... Universal Navigation Computer
UNC .... University of North Carolina [*Chapel Hill, NC*]
UNC .... University of North Carolina at Chapel Hill (HGEN)
UNC .... University of Northern Colorado [*Formerly, Colorado State College*] [*Greeley*]
UNC .... Uranyl Nitrate Concentrate [*Nuclear energy*]
UNCA......... United Nations Correspondents Association (EA)
UNCA......... United Neighborhood Centers of America (EA)
UNCAA........ United Nations Centre Against Apartheid (EA)
UNCACK...... United Nations Civil Assistance Command, Korea
UNCAFE...... United Nations Commission for Asia and the Far East
UNCAH....... Union Nacional de Campesinas Autenticos de Honduras [*National Union of Authentic Peasants of Honduras*] (PD)
UnCap........ United Capital Corp. [*Associated Press*] (SAG)
UNCAST...... United Nations Conference on Applications of Science and Technology [*1963*]
UNCASTD .... United Nations Advisory Committee on the Application of Science and Technology to Development (ASF)
UNCAT .... Uncatalogued (ADA)
UNCB.......... Uncle B Bakery, Inc. [*NASDAQ symbol*] (SAG)
UNCB.......... Uncle B's Bakery [*NASDAQ symbol*] (TTSB)
UNCC.......... Unable to Contact Company Radio [*Aviation*] (FAAC)
UNCC.......... Union Nationale des Cheminots du Cameroun [*National Union of Railway Workers of Cameroon*]
UNCC.......... United Nations Cartographic Commission (BARN)
UNCC.......... United Nations Compensation Commission (ECON)
UNCC.......... University of North Carolina at Charlotte
UNC-CH ...... University of North Carolina at Chapel Hill

UNCCP.........	United Nations Conciliation Commission for Palestine
UNCDF.........	United Nations Capital Development Fund
UNCDRP......	Universal Card Read-In Program (IAA)
UNCE..........	Novokuznetsk [Former USSR ICAO location identifier] (ICLI)
UNCE..........	United Nations Commission for Europe
UNCED.......	United Nations Conference on Environment and Development
UNCED.......	United Nations Convention on Biological Diversity [Rio de Janeiro, 1992] (EES)
UNCERT......	Uncertainty [Standard deviation] [Computer science]
UN/CETDG ...	United Nations Committee of Experts on the Transport of Dangerous Goods
UNCF.........	United Negro College Fund (EA)
UNCG.........	Uncage
UNCG.........	University of North Carolina, Greensboro
UNCHBP......	Center for Housing, Building, and Planning [United Nations]
UNCHE.......	United Nations Conference on the Human Environment (MSC)
UNCHR.......	United Nations Centre for Human Rights [Switzerland] (EAIO)
UNCHR.......	United Nations Commission on Human Rights
UNCHR.......	United Nations High Commissioner for Refugees (DLA)
UNCHS........	United Nations Center for Human Settlement [Kenya] [Research center] (IRC)
UNCI.........	United Nations Committee on Information (EA)
UNCID........	Uniform Rules of Conduct for Interchange of Trade Data by Teletransmission [ICC Publishing Co.] [A publication]
UNCInc	UNC, Inc. [Formerly, United Nuclear Corp.] [Associated Press] (SAG)
UNCIO.........	United Nations Conference on International Organization [San Francisco, 1945]
UNCIP........	United Nations Commission for India and Pakistan
UNCIR........	Uncirculated (WDAA)
UNCIRC.......	Uncircumcising Information Resources Center [National Support Group]
UNCITRAL....	United Nations Commission on International Trade Law (PDAA)
UNCIVPOL ...	United Nations Civilian Police [Peace-keeping force in Cyprus]
UNCIWC......	United Nations Commission for Investigation of War Criminals
UNCL.........	Kolpashevo [Former USSR ICAO location identifier] (ICLI)
UNCL.........	Unified Numerical Control Language (IAA)
UNCLAS......	Unclassified (AABC)
unclass.......	Unclassified (BARN)
UNCLE........	United Network Command for Law and Enforcement [Fictitious intelligence organization in various television series]
UncleB.......	Uncle B Bakery, Inc. [Associated Press] (SAG)
UNCLOS.......	United Nations Conference on the Law of the Sea
UNCLOS.......	United Nations Convention on the Law of the Sea (EFRA)
UNCLP........	Unclamp
UNCM.........	User Network Control Machine
UNCMAC......	United Nations Command Military Armistice Commission
UNCMD.......	United Nations Command
UnCmp.......	Union Camp Corp. [Associated Press] (SAG)
UNCMX.......	United Income [Mutual fund ticker symbol] (SG)
UNCN........	United Nations Censorship Network
UNCOD.......	United Nations Conference on Desertification
UNCOK.......	United Nations Committee on Korea
UNCOL........	Universal Computer Oriented Language [Programming language] [Computer science]
UN Comm Int'l Trade LYB...	United Nations Commission on International Trade Law. Yearbook [A publication] (DLA)
uncomp.......	Uncompensated (MEDA)
uncomp.......	Uncomplicated
uncon.........	Unconscious
UNCON	Uncontainerable Goods [Shipping] (DS)
uncond.......	Unconditioned
UNCONDL....	Unconditional (ROG)
UNCOND REF...	Unconditioned Reflex [Psychometrics] (AAMN)
UNCONFD....	Unconfirmed (ROG)
Uncons.......	Unconsolidated (TBD)
Unconsol Laws...	Unconsolidated Laws [A publication] (DLA)
UNCONSTAL...	Unconstitutional [Legal shorthand] (LWAP)
UNCOPUOS...	United Nations Committee on the Peaceful Uses of Outer Space
UNCOR.......	Uncorrected (WGA)
uncor	Uncorrected (STED)
uncorr........	Uncorrected
Uncov........	Uncover
UNCP.........	United Nations Conference of Plenipotentiaries
UNCR.........	United Nations Command (Rear)
UNCRD.......	United Nations Center for Regional Development
UNCRD.......	United Nations Centre for Regional Development (EERA)
UNCRO.......	United Nations Confidence Restoration Operation (ECON)
Uncro........	United Nations Confidence Restoration Operation in Croatia
unCS.........	Unconditioned Stimulus [Psychometrics] (AAMN)
UnCS	Uncorrected Stimulus [Neurology] (DAVI)
UNCSAT.......	United Nations Conference on Science and Technology (BARN)
UNCSD.......	United Nations Center for Science and Technology for Development (USDC)
UNCSF.......	United Nations Command Security Force [Military] (INF)
UNCSTD......	United Nations Center for Science and Technology for Development [Later, CSTD] (EAIO)
UNCSTD......	United Nations Centre for Science and Technology for Development (EA)
UNCSTD......	United Nations Conference on Science and Technology Education for Development (AIE)
UNCT.......	Unctus [Smeared] [Pharmacy]
UNCT	Uncut (ROG)
UNCTAD.......	United Nations Conference on Trade and Development
UNCTAD TDB...	United Nations Conference on Trade and Development, Trade and Development Board
UNCTC.........	United Nations Centre on Transnational Corporations (ECON)
UNCTD........	Uncoated
UNCTLD.......	Uncontrolled (DA)
UNCURK......	United Nations Commission for the Unification and Rehabilitation of Korea
UNCW........	Novy Vasyugan [Former USSR ICAO location identifier] (ICLI)
UND..........	Kunduz [Afghanistan] [Airport symbol Obsolete] (OAG)
UND..........	Undecaprenol [Organic chemistry]
UND..........	Under (AAG)
und	Undetermined [MARC language code Library of Congress] (LCCP)
Und...........	Undivided (DLA)
UND..........	Union Nacional Democratica [El Salvador] [Political party] (EY)
UND..........	Union Nationale et Democratique [National Democratic Union] [Monaco] [Political party] (PPW)
UND..........	Union Nigerienne Democratique [Political party] (EY)
UND..........	Unit Derating [Electronics] (IEEE)
UND..........	University of National Defense [Formerly, Industrial College of the Armed Forces and National War College]
UND..........	University of North Dakota, Grand Forks, ND [OCLC symbol] (OCLC)
UND..........	University of Notre Dame [Indiana] (KSC)
UND..........	UNUM Corp. [NYSE symbol] (SAG)
UND..........	UNUM Corp. 8.80% 'MIDS' [NYSE symbol] (TTSB)
UND..........	Urgency of Need Designator [Military] (AFM)
UND..........	User Need Date (KSC)
UNDA.........	International Catholic Association for Radio, Television and Audiovisuals [Belgium] (EAIO)
UNDA.........	Uniform Narcotic Drug Act [National Conference of Commissioners on Uniform State Laws]
Und Art Cop...	Underwood on Art Copyright [A publication] (DLA)
UNDAT.......	United Nations Development Advisory Team
UNDBK.......	Undivided Back [Deltiology]
UNDC........	Undercurrent
UNDC........	Union Nationale pour la Democratie aux Comoros [Political party] (EY)
UNDC........	United Nations Disarmament Commission [Also, DC, DC(UN)]
UNDCC.......	United Nations Development Cooperation Cycle
Und Ch Pr...	Underhill's Chancery Procedure [1881] [A publication] (DLA)
Und Conv....	Underhill on New Conveyancing [1925] [A publication] (DLA)
UNDD........	Union Nationale pour la Democratie et le Developpement [Madagascar] [Political party] (EY)
UNDEAC......	Central African Customs and Economic Union (EBF)
UNDED.......	Undereducated
UNDEF.......	Undefined
UNDELORDCAN...	Undelivered Orders Cancelled [Military]
UnDentC.....	United Dental Care, Inc. [Associated Press] (SAG)
UNDERC	University of North Dakota Energy Research Center [Grand Forks, ND] [Department of Energy] (GRD)
Underhill Ev...	Underhill on Evidence [A publication] (DLA)
Under Nat....	Underwater Naturalist [A publication] (BRI)
UNDERPASS...	Underpass [Commonly used] (OPSA)
UNDERSD....	Undersigned (ROG)
UNDERSECNAV...	Under Secretary of the Navy
UNDERSTG...	Understanding (ROG)
UNDERTG...	Undertaking (ROG)
Underw Nat...	Underwater Naturalist [A publication]
UNDERWRTNG...	Underwriting
UNDERWRTR...	Underwriter
UNDET.......	Undetermined
UNDETD......	Undetermined (WGA)
UNDETM......	Undetermined (AABC)
undet ori.....	Undetermined Origin [Medicine] (DAVI)
Undet Orig...	Undetermined Origin [Medicine] (CPH)
UNDEX.......	Underwater Explosion [Navy]
UNDEX........	UN Documents Index (NITA)
UNDEX........	United Nations Index [A publication]
UNDF........	Underfrequency
UNDG.........	Undergoing (AABC)
UNDG.........	Unidigital, Inc. [NASDAQ symbol] (SAG)
undglz.......	Underglaze (VRA)
UNDGRAD.....	Undergraduate
UNDGRD.....	Underground
UNDH........	Unit Derated Hours [Electronics] (IEEE)
UNDHR	United Nations Declaration of Human Rights (BJA)
UNDI	United Nations Document Index
UNDIS........	United Nations Documentation Information System (NITA)
Un Dk	Under Deck Tank [on a ship] (DS)
UNDK........	Undock [NASA] (KSC)
UNDLD........	Undelivered (FAAC)
UNDLD........	Underload
UNDO.........	Ukrainian National Democratic Organization
UNDO.........	Union for National Draft Opposition
UNDOF........	United Nations Disengagement Observer Force [Damascus, Syria]
UNDP........	Union Nationale pour la Democratie et le Progres [Cameroon] [Political party] (EY)
UNDP........	Union Nationale pour la Democratie et le Progres [Benin] [Political party] (EY)
UNDP........	Union Nationale pour la Democratie et le Progres [The Congo] [Political party] (EY)
UNDP........	Union Nationals Democracy Party [Myanmar] [Political party] (EY)
UNDP........	United Nations Development Program [Marine science] (OSRA)
UNDP.........	United Nations Development Programme (EA)
UNDP.........	University of Notre Dame Press
Und Part......	Underhill on Partnership [10th ed.] [1975] [A publication] (DLA)

UNDRC	United Nations Disaster Relief Coordination
UNDRO	United Nations Disaster Relief Office (EAIO)
UNDRO	United Nations Disaster Relief Organization (EERA)
undsgd	Undersigned (BARN)
UND SHER...	Under Sheriff (DLA)
UnDsp	Universal Display Corp. [Associated Press] (SAG)
UNDTCD	United Nations Department of Technical Cooperation for Development [United Nations] (GNE)
UNDTKR	Undertaker (WGA)
Und Torts.....	Underhill on Torts [A publication] (DLA)
Und Tr	Underhill on Trusts and Trustees [A publication] (DLA)
UNDV............	Undervoltage
Undvd	Undivided (TBD)
UNDW..........	Underwater (KSC)
UNDWC.......	Ultrasonically Nebulized Distilled Water Challenge
UNDWR	Underwear
UNE	Qacha's Nek [Lesotho] [Airport symbol] (OAG)
UNE	Underground Nuclear Explosion
UnE...............	Union Electric Co. [Associated Press] (SAG)
UNE	United Nations European Headquarters [Geneva, Switzerland]
UNE	Universal Nonlinear Element
UNE	University of New England [State] (EERA)
UNE	University of North Dakota, Law Library, Grand Forks, ND [OCLC symbol] (OCLC)
Une..............	Unnilennium [Chemistry] (MEC)
Une..............	Unnilnonium (AAEL)
UNE	Unst [Shetland Islands, Scotland] [Airport symbol] (AD)
UNE	Urinary Norepinephrine [Medicine] (DB)
UNE-A..........	University of New England - Armidale [Australia]
UNEASICO ...	Union des Etudiants et Anciens des Instituts Sociaux de Congo [Congolese Union of Students and Former Students of Social Institutes]
UN/EAT	United Nations Electoral Assistance Team
U Neb	University of Nebraska (GAGS)
UNEBIF	Union des Fabricants de Bijouterie Fantaisie [Union of European Fashion Jewelry Manufacturers] [Italy] (EAIO)
U Neb (Kearney)...	University of Nebraska at Kearney (GAGS)
U Neb (Omaha)...	University of Nebraska at Omaha (GAGS)
UNEC	Union Nationale des Etudiants Camerounais [National Union of Cameroonese Students]
UNEC	United Nations Education Conference
UNECA.........	United Nations Economic Commission for Africa (EA)
UNECE	United Nations Economic Commission for Europe
UNE-CHC	University of New England - Coffs Harbour Campus [Australia]
UNECLA	United Nations Economic Commission for Latin America (BARN)
UNECO.........	Union Economique du Congo [Economic Union of the Congo] [Usumbura]
UNECOLAIT...	Union Europeenne du Commerce Laitier [European Milk Trade Union] [Common Market]
UNECOSOC...	United Nations Economic and Social Council. Official Record [A publication] (DLA)
UNECTES	Union Europeenne des Conseillers Techniques et Scientifiques [European Union of Technical and Scientific Advisers] [EC] (ECED)
UNEDA.........	United Nations Economic Development Administration
UN/EDIFACT...	United Nations Rules for Electronic Data Interchange for Administration, Commerce, and Transport
UNEEG.........	Union Nationale des Eleves et Etudiants de la Guadeloupe [National Union of Pupils and Students of Guadeloupe] (PD)
UNEEM	Union Nationale des Eleves et Etudiants du Mali [National Union of Pupils and Students of Mali] (PD)
UNEF	Unified Extra Fine [Thread]
UNEF	Unified National Extra Fine Thread (IAA)
UNEF	United Nations Emergency Force [to separate hostile forces of Israel and Egypt]
UNEF	United Nations Emergency Force in the Middle East
UNEF	United Nations Environment Fund
UNEGA.........	Union Europeenne des Fondeurs et Fabricants de Corps Gras Animaux [European Union of Animal Fat Producers] (EA)
UnEl.............	Union Electric Co. [Associated Press] (SAG)
UnElec.........	Union Electric Co. [Associated Press] (SAG)
UNEM	Union Nationale des Etudiants du Maroc [National Union of Moroccan Students] (PD)
Unempl Ins Rep...	Unemployment Insurance Reports [Commerce Clearing House] [A publication] (DLA)
Unempl Ins Rep (CCH)...	Unemployment Insurance Reports (Commerce Clearing House) [A publication] (DLA)
UNEO	United Nations Emergency Operation (PDAA)
UNEP	United Nations Energy Planning [A publication]
UNEP	United Nations Environment Program [Marine science] (OSRA)
UNEP	United Nations Environment Programme [Kenya] [Database originator] (EAIO)
UNEP	University of New England Press [Australia] (ADA)
UNEPCOM....	United Nations Commission of the USSR (EERA)
UNEP GC	United Nations Environment Program Governing Council
UNEP/IRS	United Nations Environment Programme/International Referral System
UNEPNET-LAC...	UNEP [United Nations Environment Program] Network for Latin America and the Carribean (EERA)
UNEPPA.......	United Nations Environment Programme Participation Act of 1973
UNEPTA.......	United Nations Expanded Program of Technical Assistance
UNERG.........	United Nations Conference on New and Renewable Sources of Energy [1981]
UNESCAP.....	United Nations Economic and Social Commission for Asia and the Pacific

UNESCO......	United Nations Educational, Scientific, and Cultural Organization [Databa se originator and operator] [France Research center]
UNESCO......	United Nations International Children's Emergency Fund (EBF)
UNESCOR	United Nations Economic and Social Council Official Record [A publication] (DLA)
UNESDA......	Union of EEC Soft Drinks Associations (EAIO)
UNESEM......	Union Europeenne des Sources d'Eaux Minerales du Marche Commun [European Union of Natural Mineral Water Sources of the Common Market] (EAIO)
UNESOB......	United Nations Economic and Social Office in Beirut
UNETAS......	United Nations Emergency Technical Aid Service
UNETPSA......	United Nations Educational and Training Program for Southern Africa
UNEV..........	Unevaluated (MCD)
unev...........	Uneven [Quality of the bottom] [Nautical charts]
U Nev	University of Nevada at Reno (GAGS)
U Nev (Las Vegas)...	University of Nevada at Las Vegas (GAGS)
U Newark L Rev...	University of Newark. Law Review [A publication] (DLA)
U New Haven...	University of New Haven (GAGS)
UNEWY........	United News & Media ADR [NASDAQ symbol] (TTSB)
UNEWY........	United News & Media PLC [NASDAQ symbol] (SAG)
UNEWY........	United Newspapers Public Ltd. Co. (MHDW)
UNEX	Unexecuted
UNEXPL.......	Unexplained
UNEXPL.......	Unexploded
UNEXPL.......	Unexplored
UNEXSO......	Underwater Explorers Society (EA)
UNF	Unfinished [Technical drawings]
UNF	Unfused (KSC)
UNF	Unified Fine [Thread]
UNF	Unified National Fine (IAA)
UNF	Unifirst Corp. [NYSE symbol] (SPSG)
UNF	Union Flight [ICAO designator] (FAAC)
UNF	Union Freight R. R. [AAR code]
UNF	United National Front [Lebanon] (BJA)
UNF	Universal National Fine (MCD)
UNF	University of North Dakota, Medical Library, Grand Forks, ND [OCLC symbol] (OCLC)
UNFA	Union Nationale des Femmes Algeriennes [Algeria] [Political party] (EY)
UNFAO.........	United Nations Food and Agriculture Organization
UNFAV.........	Unfavorable
UNFB	United Nations Film Board
UNFC	United Nations Food Conference (BARN)
UNFCCC.......	United Nations Framework Convention on Climate Change
UNFDAC.......	United Nations Fund for Drug Abuse Control
UNFI	Unfinished
UNFI	Unifi, Inc. (MHDW)
UNFI	United Natural Foods, Inc. [NASDAQ symbol] (SAG)
UNFICYP.......	United Nations Forces in Cyprus (DMA)
UNFICYP.......	United Nations Peacekeeping Force in Cyprus
UNFIN..........	Unfinished
UNFN	United Nations Fund for Namibia (EERA)
UNFO	Unidentified Nonflying Objects
UNFP	Union Nationale des Forces Populaires [National Union of Popular Forces] [Political party Morocco]
UNFP	United National Federal Party [Zimbabwe] [Political party] (PPW)
UNFPA.........	United Nations Fund for Population Activities
UNFR...........	Uniforce Services [NASDAQ symbol] (TTSB)
UNFR...........	Uniforce Services, Inc. [NASDAQ symbol] (SAG)
UNFR...........	Uniforce Temporary Personnel, Inc. [New Hyde Park, NY] [NASDAQ symbol] (NQ)
UNFRM........	Uniform
UNFSSTD....	United Nations Financing System for Science and Technology for Development (EY)
UNFSTD.......	United Nations Fund for Science and Technology Development (EERA)
UNFT	Union Nationale des Femmes de Tunisie [National Union of Tunisian Women]
UNFTP	Unified Navy Field Test Program (MCD)
UNFURNOTE...	Until Further Notice [Military]
UNFY	Unify Corp. [NASDAQ symbol] (SAG)
UNG	Airung AEP [Ukraine] [FAA designator] (FAAC)
UNG	Kiunga [Papua New Guinea] [Airport symbol] (OAG)
UNG	Ungava [Canada]
UNG	Unguentum [Ointment] [Pharmacy]
UNGA..........	United Nations General Assembly (MCD)
UNGAOR	United Nations General Assembly Official Record [A publication] (DLA)
UNGEGN	United Nations Group of Experts on Geographical Names
unglz...........	Unglazed (VRA)
UNGOMAP ...	United Nations Good Offices Mission in Afghanistan and Pakistan [Later, OSGAP]
UNGT...........	Unguentum [Ointment] [Pharmacy]
UN-GTDI	United Nations Guidelines for Trade Data Interchange
UNH.............	Unihost Corp. [Toronto Stock Exchange symbol] [Formerly, Journey's End] (SG)
UNH.............	United Healthcare [NYSE symbol] (TTSB)
UNH.............	United Healthcare Corp. [Minnetonka, MN] [NYSE symbol] (NQ)
UNH.............	United Homes, Inc. [Vancouver Stock Exchange symbol]
UNH.............	University of New Hampshire (PDAA)
U NH............	University of New Hampshire (GAGS)
Unh.............	Unnilhexium [Chemistry] (MEC)
UNH.............	Uranyl Nitrate Hexahydrate [Inorganic chemistry]
U_{NH4+}	Urinary Ammonium (DAVI)
UNHC..........	Unison HealthCare [NASDAQ symbol] (TTSB)

UNHC............ Unison HealthCare Corp. [*NASDAQ symbol*] (SAG)
UNHC............ United Nations High Commission (BJA)
UNHCC.......... University of New Haven Computer Center [*Research center*] (RCD)
UNHCR .... United Nations High Commission [*or Commissioner*] for Refugees
UnHd .... Universal Holdings [*Associated Press*] (SAG)
UNHIX.......... United High, Inc. [*Mutual fund ticker symbol*] (SG)
UNHNOCY.... United Nations Headquarters Nongovernmental Organizations Committee on Youth (EA)
UNHQ............ United Nations Headquarters (DLA)
UNHRC .... United Nations Human Rights Commission (BJA)
UNHRD .... Unheard (FAAC)
UNI .... Athens/Albany, OH [*Location identifier FAA*] (FAAL)
UNI .... Community Express Airlines Ltd. [*BRT*] [*FAA designator*] (FAAC)
uni-............. One (IDOE)
uni-............. Single (IDOE)
UNI .... Undistributed Net Income [*Banking*]
UNI .... Uniao da Vitoria [*Brazil*] [*Airport symbol*] (AD)
Uni............. Unicorn [*Record label*]
UNI .... Unicorp Canada Corp. [*Toronto Stock Exchange symbol*]
UNI .... Uniform (DSUE)
UNI .... Uni-Marts, Inc. [*AMEX symbol*] (SPSG)
UNI .... Union Island [*Windward Islands*] [*Airport symbol*] (OAG)
UNI .... Union Nationale des Independents [*National Union of Independents*] [*Monaco*] (PPE)
UNI .... Union Nationale pour l'Independence [*National Union for Independence*] [*Djibouti*] (PPW)
UNI .... Unite Australia Party [*Australia Political party*]
UNI .... United News of India Ltd. [*News agency*] (FEA)
UNI .... United States International Airways
UNI .... Unity Railways Co. [*AAR code*]
UNI .... University (ADA)
UNI .... University of Northern Iowa [*Cedar Falls, IA*] (OICC)
UNI .... User Network Interface [*Computer science*]
UNIA .... Universal Negro Improvement Association [*Organization led by Marcus Aurelius Garvey*]
UNIA & ACLW... Universal Negro Improvement Association and African Communities League of the World (EA)
UNIACT........ Unisex Edition of the American College Testing Program Interest Inventory (EDAC)
UNIADUSEC... Union Internationale des Associations de Diplomes Universitaires en Sciences Economiques et Commerciales
UNIATEC...... Union Internationale des Associations Techniques Cinematographiques [*International Union of Technical Cinematograph Associations - IUTCA*] (EAIO)
UNIB .... University Bancorp, Inc. [*NASDAQ symbol*] (SAG)
UNIBANK ..... United City Bank [*Indonesia*] (EY)
UNIBI........... Unipolar Bipolar (IAA)
UNIBID......... UNISIST International Centre for Bibliographic Descriptions [*UNESCO*] [*Information service or system*] (IID)
UNIBORS ..... UNIVAC [*Universal Automatic Computer*] Bill of Material Processor Random System [*Computer science*] (IAA)
UNIBOSS ..... UNIVAC [*Universal Automatic Computer*] Bill of Material Processor Sequential System [*Computer science*] (IAA)
UNIBUS........ Universal Bus [*Digital Equipment Corp.*]
UNIC .... Union Internationale des Cinemas [*International Union of Cinemas*] (EAIO)
UNIC .... United International Club, Inc.
UNIC .... United Nations Information Centre
UNICA.......... Asociacion de Universidades del Caribe [*Association of Caribbean Universities and Research Institutes*] (EA)
UNICA.......... Union Internationale du Cinema Non Professionnel [*International Union of Amateur Cinema*] (EAIO)
UNICAP......... Universidade Catolica de Pernambuco [*Brazil*]
UNICCAP...... Universal Cable Circuit Analysis Program [*Bell System*]
UNICE .... Union des Industries de la Communaute Europeenne [*Union of Industries of the European Community*] [*Belgium*]
UNICE .... Union of Industrial and Employers' Confederations of Europe (EAIO)
UNICEF .... United Nations Children's Fund [*United Nations International Children's E mergency Fund*] [*Acronym is based on former name,*] (EA)
UNICEF-NZ... New Zealand National Committee for UNICEF (EAIO)
UNICHAL...... Union Internationale des Distributeurs de Chaleur [*International Union of Heat Distributors*] (EAIO)
UNICIS......... Unit Concept Indexing System
UNICLO........ United Nations Information Center and Liaison Office (PDAA)
UNICLO........ United Nations Information Centre and Liaison Office (PDAA)
UniCmp........ UniComp, Inc. [*Associated Press*] (SAG)
UNICO.......... Union pour les Interets du Peuple Congolais [*Union for the Interests of the Congolese People*]
UNICO.......... Universal Cooperatives (EA)
UnicoA......... Unico American Corp. [*Associated Press*] (SAG)
Unico Cp....... Unico Corp. [*Associated Press*] (SAG)
UNICOCYM... Union Internationale du Commerce et de la Reparation du Cycle et du Motocycle [*International Union of Cycle and Motocycle Trade and Repair*] [*Germany*]
UNICODE...... Unique Injector Concepts Development (MCD)
UNICOH .... Unidensity Coherent Light Recording (IAA)
UNICOL........ Union des Colons de la Province Orientale [*Union of Settlers in Orientale Province*]
UNICOL........ Universal Computer-Oriented Language (IAA)
UNICOM........ Underwater Integration Communication
Unicom......... Unicom Corp. [*Formerly, Commonwealth Edison*] [*Associated Press*] (SAG)
UNICOM....... Unidad Informativa Computable [*Computerized Information Unit*] [*Mexico Information service or system*] (IID)

UNICOM....... Unified Communications [*Radio station*]
UNICOM....... Universal Components [*Construction*]
UNICOM....... Universal Integrated Communication System [*Military*]
UNICOMP ..... Universal Compiler (IEEE)
UNICON .... Unidensity Coherent Light Recording (IEEE)
UNICOR .... Federal Prison Industries (AAGC)
UNICORN..... Unilateral Arms Control
UNICRIM..... Uniform Crime Reporting System (PDAA)
UNICYP....... United Nations International Force, Cyprus
unid .... Unidentified (VRA)
UNID .... Unidentified (DAVI)
UNIDA........... United Nations International Development Association (WDAA)
UNIDAHO..... Union des Independants du Dahomey [*Independents Union of Dahomey*]
UniDE.......... Unico, Inc. Delaware [*Associated Press*] (SAG)
UNIDENT..... Unidentified
UNIDF......... United Nations Industrial Development Fund
Unidig.......... Unidigital, Inc. [*Associated Press*] (SAG)
UNIDIR .... United Nations Institute for Disarmament Research [*Research center Switzerland*] (IRC)
UNIDO .... United Nations Industrial Development Organization [*Austria Also, an information service or system*] (IID)
UNIDROIT.... Institut International pour l'Unification du Droit Prive [*International Institute for the Unification of Private Law*] (EAIO)
Unidroit Yb... International Institute for the Unification of Private Law. Yearbook [*Rome, Italy*] [*A publication*] (DLA)
UNIEF .... USEUCOM [*United States European Command*] Nuclear Interface Element Fastbreak (MCD)
UNIENET...... United Nations International Emergency Network [*Marine science*] (OSRA)
UNIEP .... Union Internationale des Entrepreneurs de Peinture [*International Union of Master Painters - IUMP*] (EAIO)
Unif............ Unified (DLA)
UNIF .... Uniform (AFM)
UNIF .... Uniformity
UNIFAC....... Universal Functional Activity Coefficient [*Chemical engineering*]
UNIFAD....... United Nations Fund for Agricultural Development (WDAA)
UNIFC .... United Nations International Finance Cooperative (WDAA)
UNIFE .... Union des Industries Ferroviaires Europeennes [*Union of European Railway Industries*] (EA)
UNIFEM ...... United Nations Development Fund for Women (EA)
UNIFET .... Unipolar Field-Effect Transistor
Unifi............ Unifi, Inc. [*Associated Press*] (SAG)
Unific LYB ... Unification of Law Yearbook [*A publication*] (DLA)
Unificyp....... United Nations Peacekeeping Force in Cyprus [*1964*]
UNIFIL .... United Nations Interim Force in Lebanon
UniFirst....... Unifirst Corp. [*Associated Press*] (SAG)
Unif L Conf.. Proceedings, Uniform Law Conference of Canada [*A publication*] (DLA)
Unif L Conf Can... Uniform Law Conference of Canada [*A publication*] (DLA)
Uniflex......... Uniflex, Inc. [*Associated Press*] (SAG)
UNIFOM....... United Front of Political Movements [*Sierra Leone*] [*Political party*] (EY)
UNIFOR....... Unified Forces [*Military*]
UNIFORCE ... United Defense Force [*Established by the Brussels Treaty*] (NATG)
Uniform City Ct Act... Uniform City Court Act [*A publication*] (DLA)
Uniform Dist Ct Act... Uniform District Court Act [*A publication*] (DLA)
Uniform L Rev... Uniform Law Review [*A publication*] (DLA)
Unifrce........ Uniforce Services, Inc. [*Associated Press*] (SAG)
Unifrce........ Uniforce Temporary Personnel, Inc. [*Associated Press*] (SAG)
UNI-FREDI... Universal Flight Range and Endurance Data Indicator
Unif Sys Citation... Uniform System of Citation [*Legal term*] (DLA)
UnifyCp........ Unify Corp. [*Associated Press*] (SAG)
UNIGABON... Union Interprofessionnelle du Gabon [*Inter-Trade Union of Gabon*]
Unigen......... Unigene Labs, Inc. [*Associated Press*] (SAG)
Unign.......... Unigene Labs, Inc. [*Associated Press*] (SAG)
UNIH .... United Healthcare Corp. (MHDW)
UNIHEDD..... Universal Head-Down Display [*Computer science*] (PDAA)
UNIHI......... University of Hawaii [*Honolulu, HI*] (NOAA)
UniHoldg..... UniHolding Corp. [*Associated Press*] (SAG)
UNII .... Unit Instruments [*NASDAQ symbol*] (TTSB)
UNII .... Unit Instruments, Inc. [*California*] [*NASDAQ symbol*] (SAG)
UNII .... Yeniseysk [*Former USSR ICAO location identifier*] (ICLI)
UNIIMOG..... United Nations Iran-Iraq Military Observer Group
UNIKOM....... United Nations Iraq/Kuwait Observer Mission
unil .... Unilateral (DAVI)
Unilab......... Unilab Corp. [*Associated Press*] (SAG)
Unilab......... United Laboratories Inc. [*Philippines*]
UNILAC....... Universal Linear Accelerator
unilat.......... Unilateral
Unilevr........ Unilever Ltd. [*Associated Press*] (SAG)
UNIMA........ Unione Nazionale Imprese di Meccanizzazione Agricola [*Agricultural Mechanization Enterprises Union*] [*Italy*] (EY)
UNIMA........ Union Internationale de Grands Magasins [*International Union of Department Stores*]
UNIMA........ Union Internationale de la Marionnette [*International Puppeteers Union*] [*France*]
Unimar........ Unimar Co. [*Associated Press*] (SAG)
UNIMARC ... Universal Machine Readable Cataloging (ADA)
Unimark...... [*The*] Unimark Group [*Associated Press*] (SAG)
UNIMA-USA... American Center of the Union Internationale de la Marionette (EA)
Unimed........ Unimed, Inc. [*Associated Press*] (SAG)
UNIMERC..... Universal Numeric Coding System [*Distilling industry*]
UNIMOD ..... Unified Modular Plant [*Nuclear energy*]
UniMrt........ Uni-Marts, Inc. [*Associated Press*] (SAG)

UNINETT......	[*The*] University Network (TNIG)
Un Ins Co	Unemployment Insurance Code [*A publication*] (DLA)
UNIO.........	United Nations Information Organization
UNIONA........	Union [*Commonly used*] (OPSA)
UnionA........	Union Acceptance Corp. Class A [*Associated Press*] (SAG)
Unionam.......	Unionamerica Holdings PLC [*Associated Press*] (SAG)
UnionBc.......	UnionBancorp, Inc. [*Associated Press*] (SAG)
UnionBsh......	Union Bankshares Ltd. [*Associated Press*] (SAG)
UnionC........	Union Corp. [*Associated Press*] (SAG)
Union C (Ky)...	Union College (Kentucky) (GAGS)
Union C (NY)...	Union College (New York) (GAGS)
UNION FLEURS...	Union Internationale du Commerce de Gros en Fleurs [*International Union of the Wholesale Flower Trade*]
Union Pac LDB...	Union Pacific Law Department. Bulletin [*A publication*] (DLA)
UNIONS.......	Unions [*Commonly used*] (OPSA)
UNIP..........	United National Independence Party [*Nigeria*] [*Political party*]
UNIP..........	United National Independence Party [*Trinidad and Tobago*] [*Political party*] (PPW)
UNIP..........	United National Independence Party [*Zambia*] [*Political party*] (PD)
UNIPAC........	Unified Prediction and Analysis Code (MCD)
UNIPAC........	United Pump and Controls, Inc. (EFIS)
UNIPAC........	Unit Packaging
UNIPAC........	Universal Payload Accommodation Capsule
UNIPAL........	Universities Educational Fund for Palestinian Refugees [*British*]
UNIPEDE......	Union Internationale de Producteurs et Distributeurs d'Energie Electrique [*International Union of Producers and Distributors of Electrical Energy*] [*France*]
Uniphase	Uniphase Corp. [*Associated Press*] (SAG)
UNIPOCONGO...	Union des Populations Rurales du Congo [*Union of Rural People of the Congo*]
UNIPOL........	Universal Problem-Oriented Language [*Computer science*] (MCD)
UNIPOL........	Universal Procedure-Oriented Language
UNIPON	United Nations India-Pakistan Observer Mission (BARN)
UNIPRO	Unite et Progres du Burundi [*Unity and Progress of Burundi*]
UNIPRO	Universal Processor [*Computer science*]
UNIPZ.........	United National Independence Party of Zambia
uniq	Unique (VRA)
UniqMbl.......	Unique Mobility, Inc. [*Associated Press*] (SAG)
UNIQUAC......	Universal Quasichemical [*Chemical engineering*]
UNIQUE.......	Uniform Inquiry Update and Edit (MHDI)
UNIQUE.......	Uniform Inquiry Update Element
UNIR..........	Unemployment Insurance Review [*A publication*]
UNIR..........	Union de Izquierda Revolucionaria [*Union of the Revolutionary Left*] [*Peru*] [*Political party*] (PPW)
UNIR..........	Union Nationale pour l'Initiative et la Responsabilite [*National Union for Initiative and Responsibility*] [*France Political party*] (PPW)
UNIR..........	United Restaurants [*NASDAQ symbol*] (SAG)
UNIRAC.......	Union Involved Racketeering [*FBI undercover investigation*]
UNIRAR	Universal Radio Relay
UniroyC.......	Uniroyal Chemical Corp. [*Associated Press*] (SAG)
UNIRW.......	United Restaurants Wrrt'A' [*NASDAQ symbol*] (TTSB)
UNIRZ.......	United Restaurants Wrrt'B' [*NASDAQ symbol*] (TTSB)
UNIS	Ukrainian National Information Service (EA)
UNIS	Underwater Television and Inspection System
UNIS	Unison
UNIS	United Nations Information Service
UNIS	United Nations International School
UNISA........	University of South Africa
UniSA	University of South Australia
UNISAMS......	Universal Naval Integrated Surface-to-Air Missile System (DOMA)
UNISAP........	UNIVAC Share Assembly Program [*Sperry UNIVAC*] [*Computer science*] (IEEE)
UNISCAMTA...	Union Territoriale des Syndicats de Cadres, Agents de Maitrise, Techniciens, et Assimiles du Senegal [*Territorial Union of Leaders, Supervising Personnel, and Related Workers of Senegal*]
UNISCAN	United Kingdom and Scandinavia (NATG)
UNISCO........	Union des Interets Sociaux Congolais [*Congolese Union of Social Interests*]
UNISIST.......	United Nations Information System in Science and Technology (NITA)
UNISIST.......	United Nations Ingergovernmental System of Information in Science and Technology [*UNESCO*] [*Zagreb, Yugoslavia*]
UNISOM.......	United Nations Force in Somalia [*Military*] (INF)
UNISOMI......	Universal Symphony Orchestra and Music Institute (AEBS)
Unison........	Unison Software, Inc. [*Associated Press*] (SAG)
UnisonH.......	Unison HealthCare Corp. [*Associated Press*] (SAG)
UNISOR.......	University Isotope Separator at Oak Ridge
UNISPACE....	United Nations Conference on the Exploration and Peaceful Uses of Outer Space
UNISPEC......	Universal Spectroscopy [*Trademark*] [*Kevex Corp.*]
Unisrce.......	Unisource Worldwide, Inc. [*Associated Press*] (SAG)
UNISTAR......	UNIVAC Storage and Retrieval System [*Sperry UNIVAC*] [*Computer science*]
UNISTAR......	User Network for Information Storage, Transfer Acquisition, and Retrieval (MCD)
UNISTAT......	University Science Statistics Project [*Information service or system*] (IID)
UNISTOCK	Union Professionnelle des Stockeurs de Cereales dans la CEE [*Organization of Cereal Storage Firms in the European Economic Community*]
UNISWEP......	Unified Switching Equipment Practice (MCD)
Unisy	Unisys Corp. [*Associated Press*] (SAG)
Unisys	Unisys Corp. [*Associated Press*] (SAG)
UNIT	Ultimate Network of Intelligent Tire Technology

UNIT	Unitarian
Unit	Unit Corp. [*Associated Press*] (SAG)
UNIT	United Nations Information for Teachers [*Information service or system*] (AEBS)
UNIT	Unitrin, Inc. [*NASDAQ symbol*] (SAG)
UNIT	Universal Numerical Interchange Terminal
UNITA	Uniao Nacional para a Independencia Total de Angola [*National Union for the Complete Independence of Angola*] (AF)
UNITA	Union for the Total Liberation of Angola
UNITAF........	Unified Task Force (COE)
UNITAR.......	United Nations Institute for Training and Research [*New York*] [*ICSU*] [*Research center*]
UNITAS.......	United International Antisubmarine Warfare
UnitC.........	Unit Corp. [*Associated Press*] (SAG)
UNITE........	Union of Needletrade Industrial and Textile Employees (NTPA)
UNITE........	User Network Interface to Everything [*A discussion list on the Internet*] (TNIG)
Unitech.......	Unitech Industries, Inc. [*Associated Press*] (SAG)
UNITEL........	Universal Teleservice [*Satellite information service*]
UNITEL........	University Information Technology Corp. [*MIT-Harvard*]
UnitelV	Unitel Video, Inc. [*Associated Press*] (SAG)
UNITIL	UNITIL Corp. [*Associated Press*] (SAG)
UnitInd........	United Industrial Corp. [*Associated Press*] (SAG)
Unit Inst	Unit Instruments, Inc. (California) [*Associated Press*] (SAG)
UNITNG.......	Unit Training (NVT)
Unitog.........	Unitog Co. [*Associated Press*] (SAG)
UNITOPOS ...	Unit to Which Ordered Will Operate in an Overseas Area a Contemplated ContinuousPeriod of One Year or More [*Military*]
UNITOR.......	United Nations International TOKAMAK Reactor [*Proposed experimental fusion power plant*]
UNITRAC.......	Universal Trajector Compiler (IEEE)
Unitrde.......	Unitrode Corp. [*Associated Press*] (SAG)
UNITREP......	Unit Status and Identity Report [*DoD*]
Unitrin........	Unitrin, Inc. [*Associated Press*] (SAG)
UNITU........	United Nations International Telecommunication Union (WDAA)
UNITY........	United National Indian Tribal Year (DICI)
UNITY........	United National Indian Tribal Youth
UNIUM........	Union Nationale des Intellectuels et Universitaires Malgaches [*National Union of Intellectuals and University People of Madagascar*]
UNIV	Universal (AFM)
univ	Universal (WDAA)
UNIV	Universal International, Inc. [*NASDAQ symbol*] (SPSG)
UNIV	Universalist
Univ	Universalist (WDAA)
Univ	University (WDAA)
UNIV	University
univ	University (VRA)
UNIV	Univl International [*NASDAQ symbol*] (TTSB)
UNIVAC.......	Universal Automatic Computer [*Remington Rand Corp.*] [*Early computer*]
Univar.........	Univar Corp. [*Formerly, VWR United Corp.*] [*Associated Press*] (SAG)
UNIVAR.......	Universal Valve Action Recorder
UnivAuto......	Universal Automotive Industries, Inc. [*Associated Press*] (SAG)
Univax........	Univax Biologies, Inc. [*Associated Press*] (SAG)
UnivBcp.......	University Bancorp, Inc. [*Associated Press*] (SAG)
UniVBE	Universal VESA [*Video Electronics Standards Association*] Bios Extension (CDE)
Univ Bkmn...	University Bookman [*A publication*] (BRI)
Univ California Los Angeles L Rev...	University of California at Los Angeles. Law Review [*Los Angeles, California*] [*A publication*] (DLA)
Univ D	Doctor of the University
UNIVER.......	Universal Inverter and Register (MCD)
UNIVERSE....	Universities Expanded Ring and Satellite Experiment (NITA)
UnivFor.......	Universal Forest Products [*Commercial firm Associated Press*] (SAG)
Univ L Coll J...	University Law College. Journal. Rajputana University [*India*] [*A publication*] (DLA)
Univ LR	University Law Review [*A publication*] (DLA)
Univ L Rev...	University Law Review [*A publication*] (DLA)
Univ NSW Law J...	University of New South Wales. Law Journal [*A publication*]
Univ of Calif Davis L Rev...	University of California at Davis. Law Review [*Davis, California*] [*A publication*] (DLA)
Univ of Ghana LJ...	University of Ghana. Law Journal [*London, England*] [*A publication*] (DLA)
Univ of Manila L Gaz...	University of Manila. Law Gazette [*Manila, Philippines*] [*A publication*] (DLA)
Univ of Richmond L Not...	University of Richmond. Law Notes [*Richmond, Virginia*] [*A publication*] (DLA)
Univ of San Fernando Valley L Rev...	University of San Fernando Valley. Law Review [*Sepulveda, California*] [*A publication*] (DLA)
Univ of Tas LR...	University of Tasmania Law Review [*Australia A publication*]
Univ of Tulsa LJ...	University of Tulsa. Law Journal [*Tulsa, Oklahoma*] [*A publication*] (DLA)
UNIVRSL......	Universal
Univ S Inst of Crim Proceeding...	University of Sydney. Institute of Criminology. Proceedings [*Australia A publication*]
Univ Stud Hist Econ...	University Studies in History and Economics [*A publication*]
Univ Stud W Aust Hist...	University Studies in Western Australian History [*A publication*]
Univ Tas News...	University of Tasmania. News [*A publication*]
UNJA	Union Nationale de la Jeunesse Algerienne [*Algeria*] [*Political party*] (EY)
UNJBS	United Nations Joint Board of Strategy
UNJC	Unified National J Series Coarse [*Thread*]

UNJEF......... Unified National J Series Extra Fine [*Thread*]
UNJF.......... Unified National J Series Fine [*Thread*]
UNJS .... Unified National J Series Special [*Thread*]
UNJSPF .... United Nations Joint Staff Pension Fund (ECON)
UN Juridical YB... United Nations Juridical Year Book [*A publication*] (DLA)
UN Jur YB ... United Nations Juridical Year Book [*A publication*] (DLA)
UNK .... Unalakleet [*Alaska*] [*Airport symbol*] (OAG)
UNK .... Unknown (AFM)
unk........... Unknown (VRA)
UNK .... Unofficial (DAVI)
Unk .... Unqualified [*Marine Corps*] (MUSM)
UNKA .... Abakan [*Former USSR ICAO location identifier*] (ICLI)
UNKI .... Vanavara [*Former USSR ICAO location identifier*] (ICLI)
UNKK .... Krasnoyarsk [*Former USSR ICAO location identifier*] (ICLI)
UNKN .... Unknown
UNKO .... Sovetsky Rudnik [*Former USSR ICAO location identifier*] (ICLI)
UNKRA .... United Nations Korean Reconstruction Agency
UNKT .... Podkamennaya Tunguska [*Former USSR ICAO location identifier*] (ICLI)
UNK UNK .... Unknown Unknowns [*Design engineering*]
UNKW .... Baykit [*Former USSR ICAO location identifier*] (ICLI)
UNKWN....... Unknown
UNL .... United Leader Resources, Inc. [*Vancouver Stock Exchange symbol*]
UNL .... University of Nebraska - Lincoln
UNL .... University of New Brunswick Law Library [*UTLAS symbol*]
UNL .... Unleaded Fuel [*Automotive engineering*]
UNL .... Unlimited
UNL .... Unlisten (IAA)
UNL .... Unloading
UNLA .... Uganda National Liberation Army [*Political party*] (AF)
UNLCH........ Unlatch (MCD)
UNLD .... Unload (IAA)
UNLF .... Ugandan National Liberation Front [*Political party*] (PD)
UNLGTD....... Unlighted (FAAC)
UNLIM .... Unlimited
UNLIQ........ Unliquidated
UNLIS .... United National Life Insurance Society (EA)
UNLK .... Unlock
UNLKG .... Unlocking
UNLL .... United Nations League of Lawyers
UnINV .... Unilever NV [*Associated Press*] (SAG)
UNLOS........ United Nations Law of the Sea [*Conference*]
UNLR .... United Nations Law Reports [*A publication*] (DLA)
UNLTD .... Unlighted (DNAB)
UNLTD .... Unlimited
UNLV .... University of Nevada, Las Vegas
UNM .... National University of Mexico [*Mexico*] [*Seismograph station code, US Geological Survey Closed*] (SEIS)
UNM .... Unified Miniature
UNM .... United National Movement [*Saint Christopher and Nevis*] [*Political party*] (EY)
UNM .... United Nations Medal [*Military decoration*]
UnM .... University Microfilms International, Ann Arbor, MI [*Library symbol Library of Congress*] (LCLS)
UNM .... University of Nebraska, Medical Center, Omaha, NE [*OCLC symbol*] (OCLC)
UNM .... University of New Mexico (PDAA)
UNM .... Unmarried
UNM .... UNUM Corp. [*NYSE symbol*] (SPSG)
UNMA .... Unified Network Management Architecture [*Computer science*]
UNMAC .... United Nations Mixed Armistice Commission
UNMBX .... United Munic. Bond [*Mutual fund ticker symbol*] (SG)
UNMC .... United Nations Mediterranean Command (BJA)
UNMC .... United Nations Mediterranean Commission
UNMC .... University of Nebraska Medical Center [*Omaha, NB*]
UNMCB........ Unscheduled Not Mission Capable Both [*Maintenance and supply*] (MCD)
UNMCM .... Unscheduled Not Mission Capable Maintenance (MCD)
UNMD .... Unmanned (KSC)
UNMEM .... United Nations Middle East Mission (EY)
U NMex ...... [*The*] University of New Mexico (GAGS)
UNMG .... [*The*] Unimark Group [*NASDAQ symbol*] (SAG)
Unmibh....... United Nations Mission in Bosnia and Herzegovina [*1995*]
Unmih........ United Nations Mission in Haiti [*1993*]
UNMIH .... United Nations Mission in Haiti (ECON)
UNMKD .... Unmarked
UnM-L .... University Microfilms Ltd., Penn, Buckinghamshire, United Kingdom [*Library symbol Library of Congress*] (LCLS)
UNMO .... United Malays National Organisation [*Malaysia*] [*Political party*] (ECON)
UNMOGIP .... United Nations Military Observer Group for India and Pakistan (AABC)
Unmogip...... United Nations Military Observer Group in India and Pakistan [*1949*]
UNMON........ Unable to Monitor (FAAC)
Unmop........ United Nations Mission of Observers in Prevlaka [*Croatia, 1996*]
UNMO's....... United Nations Military Observers (BJA)
UNMSC....... United Nations Military Staff Committee (AABC)
UNMT .... United Nations Multilateral Treaties [*A publication*] (DLA)
UNMTD .... Unmounted
UNN .... University of Nizhny Novgorod [*Russia*]
UNNE .... Universidad Nacional del Nordeste [*Argentina*]
UNNECY ...... Unnecessary (ROG)
UNNEFO ...... United Nations of the New Emerging Forces [*Indonesia*]
UNNN......... Novosibirsk/Tolmachevo [*Former USSR ICAO location identifier*] (ICLI)

UNO .... Unicorn Resources [*Vancouver Stock Exchange symbol*]
UNO .... Unified Nimbus Observatory (MCD)
UNO .... Union Nacional de la Oposicion [*National Opposition Union*] [*Nicaragua*]
UNO .... Union Nacional Odriista [*Peruvian political party*]
UNO .... Union Nacional Opositora [*Electoral alliance*] [*Nicaragua*] (EY)
UNO .... United Nations Observer Corps (BJA)
UNO .... United Nations Organization [*ICSU*]
UNO .... United Nicaraguan Opposition
UNO .... Unit Number (COE)
UNO .... University of Nebraska at Omaha
UNO .... University of New Orleans [*Louisiana*]
Uno .... Unniloctium [*Chemistry*] (MEC)
Uno .... Unniloctium (AAEL)
UNO .... Uno Restaurant Corp. [*NYSE symbol*] (TTSB)
UNO .... Uno Restaurants, Inc. [*NYSE symbol*] (SAG)
UNO .... Utility Night Observer
U No Ala..... University of North Alabama (GAGS)
UNOASD...... United Nations Outer Space Affairs Division (EERA)
UNOBSD ..... Unobserved (ROG)
UNOC .... Union Nationale des Ouvriers Congolais [*National Union of Congolese Workers*]
UNOC .... United Nations Operation in the Congo
UNOCA .... United Nations Office Coordinating Humanitarian and Economic Aid to Afghanistan (ECON)
Unocal .... Unocal Corp. [*Associated Press*] (SAG)
UNO-CARA-PEN... Union Internationale pour la Cooperation Culturelle [*International Union for Cultural Co-operation*]
U No Car (Chapel Hill)... [*The*] University of North Carolina at Chapel Hill (GAGS)
U No Car (Greensboro)... [*The*] University of North Carolina at Greensboro (GAGS)
UNOCHA ...... United Nations Office for the Coordination of Humanitarian Assistance to Afghanistan (ECON)
U No Colo.... University of Northern Colorado (GAGS)
U No Dak..... University of North Dakota (GAGS)
UNODIR ...... Unless Otherwise Directed
UNOEOA ...... United Nations Office for Emergency Operations in Africa [*Defunct*] (EA)
Unof.......... Unofficial Reports [*A publication*] (DLA)
unoff......... Unofficial (CPH)
UNOFFL....... Unofficial (FAAC)
Un of Gh LJ... University of Ghana. Law Journal [*A publication*] (DLA)
U No Fla...... University of North Florida (GAGS)
UNOG .... United Nations Organization - Geneva
UNOGIL....... United Nations Observer Group in Lebanon
UNOINDC ..... Unless Otherwise Indicated
U No Iowa.... University of Northern Iowa (GAGS)
UNOLS........ University National Oceanographic Laboratory System [*National Science Foundation*]
Unomig....... United Nations Observer Mission in Georgia [*1993*]
UNON......... Unless Otherwise Noted (COE)
UNOO......... United Nations Oceanographic Organization
UNOP......... Unopened (ADA)
UNOP......... Unopposed
UNOPAR ..... Universal Operator Performance Analyzer and Recorder
UNOPS........ [*The*] United Nations Office for Project Services (ECON)
UNORDCAN... Unexecuted Portion of Orders Cancelled
UNOREQ ...... Unless Otherwise Requested (NVT)
U N Orleans... University of New Orleans (GAGS)
U N Orleans (Med Cent)... University of New Orleans Medicine Center (GAGS)
UnoRst........ Uno Restaurant Corp. [*Associated Press*] (SAG)
UNOS......... United Network for Organ Sharing [*Database*] (EA)
UNOSOM ..... United Nations Operation in Somalia (INF)
U No Tex..... University of North Texas (GAGS)
U Notre Dame... University of Notre Dame (GAGS)
UNP .... Uluru [*Ayers Rock - Mount Olga*] National Park (EERA)
UNP .... Unification National Party [*South Korea Political party*] (EY)
UNP .... Union Nacional Paraguaya [*Paraguayan political party*]
UNP .... Union Pacific [*NYSE symbol*] (TTSB)
UNP .... Union Pacific Corp. [*NYSE symbol*] (SPSG)
UNP .... Union Pacific Corp. (EFIS)
UNP .... United National Party [*Sri Lanka*] [*Political party*] (PPW)
UNP .... United Nations Philatelists (EA)
UNP .... United Northern Petroleum Corp. [*Vancouver Stock Exchange symbol*]
UNP .... University of Nebraska Press (DGA)
Unp .... Unnilpentium [*Chemical element*] (CDAI)
UNP .... Unpaged
UNP .... Unpostable [*Computer science*]
UNPA .... Unione Nazionale Protezione Antiaere [*Italy*]
UNPA .... United Nations Participation Act of 1945
UNPA .... United Nations Postal Administration
UN-PAAERD... United Nations Programme of Action for African Economic Recovery and Development [*1986-1990*]
UnPac........ Union Pacific Corp. [*Associated Press*] (SAG)
UNPAC........ Union Pacific Railroad Co.
UNPAD .... Universitas Negeri Padjadjaran [*Indonesia*]
UNPC .... United Nations Palestine Commission
UNPCC .... United Nations Palestine Conciliation Commission (BJA)
UNPD .... Unpaid (AABC)
UNPD-MSTR... Unpaid Master
UNPERF....... Unperformed [*Music*]
unperf........ Unperformed (WDAA)
UNPERFD ..... Unperformed (ROG)
UNPH .... Uniphase Corp. [*NASDAQ symbol*] (SAG)
UNPIK .... United Nations Partisan Infantry Korea

UNPKD......... Unpacked (IAA)
UNPO........... Unrepresented Nations and Peoples Organization
UNPOC........ United Nations Peace Observation Commission
Unpredep..... United Nations Preventive Deployment Force [*Macedonia*]
UNPROFOR... United Nations Protection Force [*Former Yugoslavia*] (ECON)
UNPROFOR... United Nations Protection Force in the Former Yugoslavia
UNPROFOR... United Nations Protective Forces
UnProp .... Union Property Investors, Inc. [*Associated Press*] (SAG)
UNPS........... Unified Network Planning Study
UNPS........... United Nations Philatelic Society [*Defunct*] (EA)
UNPS........... Universal Power Supply
UNPUB........ Unpublished
Unpub........... Unpublished (AAGC)
UNPUBD...... Unpublished
Unpx........... Unapix Entertainment, Inc. [*Associated Press*] (SAG)
UNQ........... Providence, RI [*Location identifier FAA*] (FAAL)
UNQ :.......... Unique
UNQ............. Unique Resources Ltd. [*Vancouver Stock Exchange symbol*]
Unq............. Unnilquadium [*Chemical element*] (CDAI)
UNQTE........ Unquote
UNQUAL ..... Unqualified (AABC)
unr............. Ukrainian Soviet Socialist Republic [*MARC country of publication code Library of Congress*] (LCCP)
UNR............. Ukrains'ka Natsional'na Rada
UNR............. Uniao Nacional Republicana [*National Republican Union*] [*Portugal Political party*] (PPE)
UNR............. Unicorp Resources Ltd. [*Toronto Stock Exchange symbol*]
UNR............. UNR Industries, Inc. [*Associated Press*] (SAG)
UNRAU .... Unified Numeric Representation Arithmetic Unit (PDAA)
UNRC.......... Unico Inc. [*NASDAQ symbol*] (TTSB)
UNRC.......... Unico, Inc. New Mexico [*NASDAQ symbol*] (SAG)
UNRCCFE.... United Nations Regional Cartographic Conferences on Asia and the Far East
UNRDBL ..... Unreadable (FAAC)
UNREF........ United Nations Refugee Fund
UNREF........ Unreformed (ROG)
UNREL........ Unreliable
UNRELBL.... Unreliable (FAAC)
UNREP........ Underway Replenishment [*Military*]
Unrep Cr C... Bombay Unreported Criminal Cases [*1862-98*] [*India*] [*A publication*] (DLA)
Unrep NY Est TC... Unreported New York Estate Tax Cases [*Prentice-Hall, Inc.*] [*A publication*] (DLA)
Unrep Wills Cas... Unreported Wills Cases [*Prentice-Hall, Inc.*] [*A publication*] (DLA)
UN Res........ United Nations Resolutions [*A publication*] (DLA)
UNRF........... Uganda National Rescue Front (PD)
UNRFNRE .... United Nations Revolving Fund for Natural Resources Exploration (EERA)
UNRGLTD ... Unregulated
UNRHCE ...... United Nations Regional Housing Center for ESCAP [*Economic and Social Commission for Asia and the Pacific*] [*India*] (EAIO)
UNRI........... UNR Industries [*NASDAQ symbol*] (TTSB)
UNRI........... UNR Industries, Inc. [*NASDAQ symbol*] (NQ)
UNRIAA........ United Nations Reports of International Arbitral Awards [*A publication*] (DLA)
UNRIPS........ United Nations Regional Institute for Population Studies [*Legon, Ghana*] (EAIO)
UNRISD .... United Nations Research Institute for Social Development (EA)
UNROD .... United Nations Relief Operation in Dacca
UNRPR .... United Nations Relief for Palestine Refugees
UNRRA .... United Nations Relief and Rehabilitation Administration [*"United Nations" derives from the wartime alliance of this name, not from any affiliation with the postwar international organization*]
UNRRC .... United Nations Relief and Rehabilitation Conference
UNRS........... Union pour la Nouvelle Republique Senegalaise [*Union for the New Senegalese Republic*] [*Political party*]
UNRSTD ...... Unrestricted (FAAC)
UNRTD........ United Nations Resources and Transport Division
UNRTDG ..... United Nations Recommendations on the Transport of Dangerous Goods
UNRWA....... United Nations Relief and Works Agency for Palestine Refugees in the Near East [*Austria*] (PD)
UNRWA....... United Nations Relief Works Agency (EERA)
UNRWAPR... United Nations Relief and Works Agency for Palestine Refugees in the Near East [*Austria*] (DLA)
UNRWAPRNE... United Nations Relief and Works Agency for Palestine Refugees in the Near East [*Pronounced: "Unwrap me"*] [*Austria*]
UnrylT........ Uniroyal Technology Corp. [*Associated Press*] (SAG)
UnrylTc........ Uniroyal Technology Corp. [*Associated Press*] (SAG)
UNS .... Umnak, AK [*Location identifier FAA*] (FAAL)
UnS............. Unconditioned Stimulus [*Psychometrics*] (AAMN)
UNS .... Unified Numbering Systems [*for metals*] (MCD)
UNS .... Unified Special [*Thread*]
UNS .... Unions [*Postal Service standard*] (OPSA)
UNS .... United News Shops [*British*]
UNS .... Universal News Service [*British*]
UNS .... Universal Night Sight
Uns .... Unnilseptium [*Chemistry*] (MEC)
uns............. Unsatisfactory (MAE)
uns............. Unstable (IDOE)
uns............. Unsymmetrical (IDOE)
UNS .... Unsymmetrical
UNSAC........ United Nations Scientific Advisory Committee [*ICSU*]
UNSAT........ Unsatisfactory (AABC)

unsat........... Unsaturated [*Chemistry*]
UNSATFY.... Unsatisfactory
UNSBL........ Unseasonable [*NWS*] (FAAC)
UNSC.......... United Nations Security Council
UNSC.......... United Nations Social Commission
UNSCC........ United Nations Standards Co-Ordinating Committee
UNSCC........ University of Nevada System Computing Center [*Research center*] (RCD)
UNSCCUR ... United Nations Scientific Conference on the Conservation and Utilization of Resources
UNSCEAR .... United Nations Scientific Committee on Effects of Atomic Radiation (EERA)
UNSCEAR .... United Nations Scientific Committee on the Effects of Atomic Radiation
UNSCOB ..... United Nations Special Committee on the Balkans [*Greece*]
UNSCOP ..... United Nations Special Committee on Palestine
UNSD.......... Unsweetened (ROG)
UNSDD........ United Nations Social Development Division
UNSDRI........ United Nations Social Defense Research Institute [*UN/Italy*]
UNSECNAV.. Under Secretary of the Navy
UNSERV....... Unserviceable (IAA)
UNSF .... United Nations Special Fund
UNSFH........ United Nations Security Forces, Hollandia (AABC)
UNSG.......... United Nations Secretary General
UNSGD........ Unsigned (WGA)
UNSIS......... United Nations Statistical Information System (DUND)
UNSKED ...... Unscheduled (FAAC)
UnSlf .... Universal Self Care, Inc. [*Associated Press*] (SAG)
UNSM......... United Nations Service Medal [*Military decoration*]
UNSN......... Unison Software [*NASDAQ symbol*] (TTSB)
UNSN......... Unison Software, Inc. [*NASDAQ symbol*] (SAG)
UNSO......... United Nations Statistical Office (EERA)
UNSO......... United Nations Sudano-Sahelian Office
UNSP......... Union Nationale pour la Solidarite et le Progres [*Benin*] [*Political party*] (EY)
UNSPDPM ... United Nations Subcommission on the Prevention of Discrimination and the Protection of Minorities [*Geneva, Switzerland*] (EAIO)
UNSR......... United Nations Space Registry (BARN)
UNSS .... United Nations Sales Section [*for UN documents*]
UNSSOD ..... United Nations Special Session on Disarmament (PDAA)
UNST .... Union Nordique pour la Sante et le Travail [*Nordic Union for Health and Work*] (EAIO)
UNSTAC ..... United Nations Science and Technology Advisory Committee (AIE)
UNSTBL....... Unstable
UNSTD......... Union Nationale des Syndicats des Travailleurs du Dahomey [*National Federation of Workers' Unions of Dahomey*]
UNSTDY....... Unsteady
UNSTHV....... Union Nationale des Syndicats des Travailleurs de la Haute Volta [*National Federation of Workers' Unions of the Upper Volta*]
UNSU.......... United Nations Staff Union (EA)
UNSU.......... United Nations Study Unit [*Philatelic organization*] (EA)
UNSUB........ Unknown Subject [*FBI*] [*Acronym also used as title of television series*]
UNSUPPR .... Unsuppressed (MSA)
UNSVC........ Unserviceable (AABC)
UNSVC-RT-R... Unserviceable Return Rate
UNSVM....... United Nations Service Medal
UNSW......... Union Switch & Signal [*NASDAQ symbol*] (TTSB)
UNSW......... Union Switch & Signal, Inc. [*NASDAQ symbol*] (SAG)
UNSW......... University of New South Wales [*State*] (EERA)
UNSW......... University of New South Wales Australia
UNSWIL....... University of New South Wales Institute of Languages [*Australia*]
UnSwtch ...... Union Switch & Signal, Inc. [*Associated Press*] (SAG)
UNSX......... Unisex
UNSYM....... Unsymmetrical
unsz c .... Unsized Canvas (VRA)
UNT .... Undergraduate Navigator Training [*Air Force*] (AFM)
UNT .... Underground Nuclear Test
UNT .... Unit Corp. [*NYSE symbol*] (SPSG)
UNT .... United Tariff Bureau, Inc., New York NY [*STAC*]
UNT .... Unst [*Scotland*] [*Airport symbol*] (OAG)
unt .... Untitled (VRA)
UNTA .... Union Nationale des Travailleurs Angolais [*National Union of Angolan Workers*]
UNTA .... United Nations Technical Assistance
UNTA .... United Nations Technical Assistance Program (EBF)
UNTAA........ United Nations Technical Assistance Administration
UNTAC........ United Nations Transitional Authority in Cambodia (ECON)
UNTAF........ United Nations Technical Assistance Fellowship
UNTAG........ United Nations Transition Assistance Group
UNTAM........ United Nations Technical Assistance Mission (BARN)
UNTC.......... Union Nationale des Travailleurs Congolais [*National Union of Congolese Workers*]
UNTC.......... United Nations Trusteeship Council (BARN)
UNTCI.......... Union Nationale des Travailleurs de Cote d'Ivoire [*National Union of Ivory Coast Workers*]
UNTCOK....... United Nations Temporary Committee on Korea
UNTCOR....... United Nations Trusteeship Council Official Record [*A publication*] (DLA)
UNTD.......... First United Bancshares, Inc. [*El Dorado, AR*] [*NASDAQ symbol*] (NQ)
UNTD.......... First United Bancshrs [*NASDAQ symbol*] (TTSB)
UNTD.......... United
UNTD.......... University Naval Training Division [*Canada*]
UNTDED....... United Nations Data Elements Directory [*A publication*]

UntdNat	United Natural Foods, Inc. [*Associated Press*] (SAG)
UNTE	Unit Corp. [*NASDAQ symbol*] (NQ)
UNTEA	United Nations Temporary Executive Authority [*Supervised transfer of Netherlands New Guinea to Indonesia*]
UnTech	United Technologies Corp. [*Associated Press*] (SAG)
UnTelev	United Television, Inc. [*Associated Press*] (SAG)
untemp	Untempered (VRA)
UNTEW	Unit Corp. Wrrt [*NASDAQ symbol*] (TTSB)
UnTex	Union Texas Petroleum [*Associated Press*] (SAG)
UNTFDPP	United Nations Trust Fund for Development Planning and Projections
UNTFSD	United Nations Trust Fund for Social Development
UNTG	United Nations Theatre Group (EA)
UNTHD	Unthreaded
UNTIS	United Nations Treaty Information System (DUND)
UNTM	Union Nationale des Travailleurs du Mali [*National Union of Malian Workers*]
UNTN	Union Nationale des Travailleurs Nigeriens [*National Union of Nigerian Workers*]
Un Trav Dec	Unreported Travancore Decisions [*A publication*] (DLA)
UNTS	Undergraduate Navigator Training System [*Air Force*]
UNTS	Unilateral Nevoid Telangiectasia [*Medicine*] (DMAA)
UNTS	Union Nationale des Travailleurs du Senegal [*National Union of Workers of Senegal*]
UNTS	United Nations Treaty Series [*Project*] [*University of Washington*]
UNTSFA	United Nations Trust Fund for Southern Africa (EERA)
UNTSO	United Nations Truce Supervision Organization
UNTT	Union Nationale des Travailleurs du Togo [*National Union of Togolese Workers*]
UNTT	United Nations Trust Territory
UNTW	Untwist
UNU	Juneau, WI [*Location identifier FAA*] (FAAL)
UNU	United Nations University [*Tokyo*]
UNU	United Nations University [*Marine science*] (OSRA)
UNU	Universidad de las Naciones Unidas [*United Nations University*] [*Spanish*] (DUND)
UNU	Universite des Nations Unies [*United Nations University*] [*French*] (DUND)
UNUIIST	United Nations University International Institute for Software
UNU/INTECH	United Nations University/Institute of New Technologies
UNUM	UNUM Corp. [*Associated Press*] (SAG)
UNUM25	UNUM Corp. [*Associated Press*] (SAG)
UNUMO	Universal Underwater Mobile [*Robot*]
UNUSBL	Unusable
UNUSL	Unusual (ROG)
UNU/WIDER	United Nations University / World Institute for Development Economics Research (DUND)
UNV	State College, PA [*Location identifier FAA*] (FAAL)
UNV	United Nations Volunteers (EAIO)
UNV	Unitel Video [*AMEX symbol*] (TTSB)
UNV	Unitel Video, Inc. [*AMFX symbol*] (SPSG)
UnvAm	Universal American Financial Corp. [*Associated Press*] (SAG)
UnvAmr	Universal American Financial Corp. [*Associated Press*] (SAG)
UnvDisp	Universal Display Corp. [*Associated Press*] (SAG)
UnvElc	Universal Electronics, Inc. [*Associated Press*] (SAG)
Unverd	Unverified
UnvFd	Universal Foods Corp. [*Associated Press*] (SAG)
UNVGX	United Vanguard Cl.A [*Mutual fund ticker symbol*] (SG)
UnvHgt	Universal Heights, Inc. [*Associated Press*] (SAG)
UnvHld	Universal Holdings [*Associated Press*] (SAG)
UnvHlt	Universal Health Services, Inc. [*Associated Press*] (SAG)
UnvHR	Universal Health Realty Income Trust [*Associated Press*] (SAG)
UnvHsp	Universal Hospital Services, Inc. [*Associated Press*] (SAG)
UnvHt	Universal Heights, Inc. [*Associated Press*] (SAG)
UnvInt	Universal International, Inc. [*Associated Press*] (SAG)
UnvMfg	Universal Manufacturing Co. [*Associated Press*] (SAG)
UnvSc	Universal Security Instruments, Inc. [*Associated Press*] (SAG)
UnvSec	Universal Security Instruments, Inc. [*Associated Press*] (SAG)
UnvSeis	Universal Seismic Associates [*Associated Press*] (SAG)
UnvSelf	Universal Self Care, Inc. [*Associated Press*] (SAG)
UnvslCp	Universal Corp. [*Associated Press*] (SAG)
UnvsOut	Universal Outdoor Holdings, Inc. [*Associated Press*] (SAG)
UnvStain	Universal Stainless & Alloy Products [*Associated Press*] (SAG)
UnvStdM	Universal Standard Medical Labs, Inc. [*Associated Press*] (SAG)
UNVX	Univax Biologics [*NASDAQ symbol*] (SAG)
UNWCC	Unions' Nation-Wide Coordinating Council for Oil and Allied Industries [*Defunct*] (EA)
UNWCC	United Nations War Crimes Commission [*"United Nations" derives from the wartime alliance of this name, not from any affiliation with the postwar international organization*]
UNWG	United Nations Women's Guild (EA)
UNWLA	Ukrainian National Women's League of America (EA)
UNWMG	Utility Nuclear Waste Management Group (EA)
UnwmK	Unwatermarked [*Philately*]
UNWMKD	Unwatermarked (WGA)
UNWR	Unwritten (ROG)
UNWRAP	United We Resist Additional Packaging [*Student legal action organization*]
UNX	Underground Nuclear Explosion
UNX	Univex Mining Corp. [*Vancouver Stock Exchange symbol*]
UNY	San Antonio, TX [*Location identifier FAA*] (FAAL)
UNY	United Nations of Yoga [*Stockholm, Sweden*] (EAIO)
UNY	University of New York (ROG)
UNYB	United Nations Year Book [*A publication*] (DLA)
UNYFA	Ukrainian National Youth Federation of America [*Later, Ukrainian Youth Association of America*] (EA)

UNYOM	United Nations Yemen Observation Mission
u-nz--	New Zealand [*MARC geographic area code Library of Congress*] (LCCP)
UNZ	Unzendake [*Japan*] [*Seismograph station code, US Geological Survey*] (SEIS)
UO	Direct Air [*ICAO designator*] (AD)
UO	Undelivered Orders [*Army*] (AABC)
U/O	Under Observation (DAVI)
UO	Und Oefters [*And Often*] [*German*]
UO	Union Office (ROG)
UO	Union Railroad of Oregon [*AAR code*]
UO	Unit Operator (NRCH)
UO	University of Oxford (ROG)
UO	Ureteral Orifice [*Anatomy*] (MAE)
UO	Urinary Output [*Medicine*]
U/O	Used On (MSA)
UO	Weber County Library, Ogden, UT [*Library symbol Library of Congress*] (LCLS)
UO2	Uranium Dioxide
UOA	Unattached Officers' Association [*A union*] [*British*]
UOA	United Ostomy Association (EA)
UOA	University of Arizona [*Seismograph station code, US Geological Survey Closed*] (SEIS)
UOA	Used on Assembly
UOA	Use of Other Automobiles [*Insurance*]
UOAQ	Unit Owners' Association of Queensland [*Australia*]
UOBTPS	United Operative Bricklayers' Trade Protection Society [*A union*] [*British*]
UOC	Ultimate Operating Capability
UOC	Ultimate Operational Configuration (AAG)
UOC	Unequilibrated Ordinary Chondrites
UOC	Unilens Optical [*Vancouver Stock Exchange symbol*]
UOC	Union de l'Ouest Cameroun [*Union of West Cameroon*]
UOC	United Orpington Club (EA)
UOC	Unit of Choice
UOC	Universal Output Computer
UOC	Unusual Occurrence Control
UOC	Uranium Ore Concentrate
UOC	Useable on Code (MCD)
UOCA	United Orpington Club of America [*Later, UOC*] (EA)
UOCB	Uncrossed Olivocochlear Bundle [*Otology*]
UOCMWD	Union of Operative Card Makers and Wire Drawers [*British*]
UOCO	Union Oil Co.
UOD	Ultimate Oxygen Demand [*Water conservation*] (WDAA)
UODDL	User-Oriented Data Display Language [*Computer science*]
UODG	Underwater Ordnance Development Group
UODO	United Oromo Democratic Organisation [*Ethiopia*]
UOE	Unit of Error (MCD)
u/o/e	Unopened Edges [*Bookbinding*] (DGA)
UOEF	Union de Obreros Estivadores de Filipinos [*Union of Longshoremen of the Philippines*]
UOF	Unplanned Outage Factor [*Electronics*] (IEEE)
UOF	Unusual Order Form (MHDI)
U of A	University of Alaska [*Anchorage, AK*]
U of A	University of Arkansas [*Fayetteville, AR*]
U of D	University of Detroit [*Michigan*]
U of D	University of Dublin [*Ireland*]
U of I	University of Illinois [*Urbana, IL*]
U of I	University of Iowa [*Iowa City, IA*] (OICC)
U of Kansas L Rev	University of Kansas. Law Review [*A publication*] (DLA)
U of M	University of Michigan [*Ann Arbor, MI*]
U of MLB	University of Missouri. Law Bulletin [*A publication*] (DLA)
U of Omaha Bull	Night Law School Bulletin. University of Omaha [*A publication*] (DLA)
UOFS	United States Forest Service, Intermountain Range and Experiment Station Library, Ogden, UT [*Library symbol Library of Congress*] (LCLS)
U of So	University of the South (GAGS)
U of T	University of Toronto [*Ontario*]
U of T School of LR	School of Law. Review. Toronto University [*Canada*] [*A publication*] (DLA)
U of W	University of Washington [*Seattle, WA*]
U of W	University of Windsor [*Ontario*]
UOG	Unit of Grading (MHDW)
UOGC	United Order of the Golden Cross [*Defunct*] (EA)
UOGF	Uranium Off-Gas Filter [*Nuclear energy*] (NRCH)
UOGS	Church of Jesus Christ of Latter-Day Saints, Genealogical Society Library, OgdenBranch, Ogden, UT [*Library symbol Library of Congress*] (LCLS)
UOH	Unplanned Outage Hours [*Electronics*] (IEEE)
UOHC	Under Other than Honorable Conditions [*Discharge*] [*Military*]
UOI	Unit of Instruction
UOI	University of Illinois [*Record label*]
UOI	User On-Line Interaction [*Computer science*]
UOIW	United Optical and Instrument Workers of America
UOJC	Union of Orthodox Jewish Congregations of America (EA)
UOJCA	Union of Orthodox Jewish Congregations of America (EA)
UOK	University of Oklahoma [*Record label*]
U Okla	[*The*] University of Oklahoma (GAGS)
UOL	Underwater Object Locator
UOL	Utility Octal Load
UOL	Utility-Oriented Language (MCD)
UOLP	UOL Publishing, Inc. [*NASDAQ symbol*] (SAG)
UOL Pub	UOL Publishing, Inc. [*Associated Press*] (SAG)
UOLS	Underwater Object Location and Search Operations [*Navy*] (NVT)

UOMA.......... Used Oil Management Association (NTPA)
UOMCA........ United Orthodox Ministers and Cantors Association of America and Canada (EA)
UOME.......... Union des Opposants Malgaches Exterieurs [*Madagascar*] [*Political party*] (EY)
UOMGCU..... United Operative Masons' and Granite Cutters' Union [*British*]
UOMS.......... Union des Originaires de Mauritanie du Sud [*Union of Natives of South Mauritania*]
UOMS.......... Unmanned Orbital Multifunction Satellite
UON............ Muong Sai [*Laos*] [*Airport symbol*] (AD)
UON............ Unless Otherwise Noted (OA)
UON............ Urgency of Need (MCD)
UOO............ Unavailable, On Order [*Business term*] (NTCM)
UOO............ Undelivered Orders Outstanding [*Military*] (AFM)
UOO............ Upravleniye Osobykh Otdelov [*Armed Forces Counterintelligence-Directorate*] [*Former USSR*] (LAIN)
UOP............ Understanding of the Problem (MCD)
UOP............ Unit of Production (MHDW)
UOP............ Unit Operating Procedure (NRCH)
UOP............ University of the Pacific [*Stockton, CA*]
UOP............ Urine Output [*Physiology*]
UOP............ User Operations Panel (SSD)
UOPA.......... Uranium Ore Processing Association
UOPDP........ Union Ouvriere et Paysanne pour la Democratie Proletarienne [*Peasant and Worker Union for Proletarian Democracy*] [*France Political party*] (PPE)
UOPH.......... Unaccompanied Officer Personnel Housing [*Navy*]
UOPLF......... United Oromo People's Liberation Front [*Ethiopia*] [*Political party*] (EY)
UOQ............ Upper Outer Quadrant [*Anatomy*]
UOr............. Orem City Library, Orem, UT [*Library symbol Library of Congress*] (LCLS)
UOR............ Uniform Officer Record
UOR............ Unplanned Outage Rate [*Electronics*] (IEEE)
UOR............ Unusual Occurrence Report (NUCP)
UOR............ Urgent Operation Requirement
UORC.......... Used Oil Recycling Coalition [*Automotive lubricants*]
U Ore.......... University of Oregon (GAGS)
UORS.......... Unusual Occurence Report (IAA)
UORS.......... Unusual Occurrence Reporting System [*Environmental science*] (COE)
UOrUC........ Utah Valley Community College, Orem, UT [*Library symbol*] [*Library of Congress*] (LCLS)
UORUSC...... Union of Orthodox Rabbis of the US and Canada (EA)
UOS............ Sewanee, TN [*Location identifier FAA*] (FAAL)
UOS............ Ultraviolet Ozone Spectrometer (MCD)
UOS............ Undelivered Orders Schedule [*Army*]
UOS............ Underwater Ordnance Station [*Navy*]
UOS............ United Order of Smiths [*A union*] [*British*]
UOS............ University of the South [*Record label*]
UOS............ Unless Otherwise Specified (MSA)
UOS............ Unmanned Orbital Satellite
UOS............ User Operations Support (SSD)
UOSAT........ University of Surrey Satellite
UOSG.......... User Operations Support Group (SSD)
UOSM.......... Urinary Osmolarity [*Medicine*]
UOT............ Uncontrollable Overtime
UOT............ Union, SC [*Location identifier FAA*] (FAAL)
UOT............ Unit of Trading
UOT............ Upper Outer Tube
UOTASP...... United Order of the Total Abstaining Sons of the Phoenix (ROG)
UOTC.......... University Officers Training Corps [*British military*] (DMA)
UOTHC........ Under Other than Honorable Conditions [*Discharge*] [*Military*]
UOTS.......... United Order True Sisters (EA)
UOUT.......... Universal Outdoor Holdings, Inc. [*NASDAQ symbol*] (SAG)
UOV............ Union Ouvriere du Viet-Nam [*Vietnam Labor Union*] [*South Vietnam*]
UOV............ Unit of Value (MHDW)
UOV............ Units of Variance
UOW............ Weber State College, Ogden, UT [*Library symbol Library of Congress*] (LCLS)
UOX............ Oxford, MS [*Location identifier FAA*] (FAAL)
UOX............ University [*Mississippi*] [*Airport symbol*] (OAG)
UOZ............ Upper Outer Zone [*Also called upper outer quadrant*] [*Anatomy*] (DAVI)
UP................ Bahamas Air [*ICAO designator*] (AD)
UP................ Lab. UPSA [*France*] [*Research code symbol*]
UP................ Oregon Short Line R. R. [*of Union Pacific Railroad Co.*] [*AAR code*]
UP................ Oregon-Washington R. R. & Navigation [*of Union Pacific Railroad Co.*] [*AAR code*]
UP................ Provo Public Library, Provo, UT [*Library symbol Library of Congress*] (LCLS)
UP................ Ulster Parliament (DAS)
UP................ Ultra Presse [*Press agency*] [*Colombia*]
UP................ Umbilical Pin
UP................ Uncertainty Principle [*Quantum mechanics*]
UP................ Uncertified Patient [*British*]
UP................ Uncovered Position (MHDW)
UP................ Undergraduate Program [*Subject area tests*]
UP................ Under-Proof [*Of spirituous liquors*] [*Distilling*]
UP................ Under Provisions Of [*Military*]
UP................ Unearned Premium [*Insurance*]
UP................ Unemployed Parent [*Department of Health and Human Services*]
UP................ Unified Programme [*Education*] (AIE)
UP................ Union del Pueblo [*Union of the People*] [*Mexico*] (PD)
UP................ Union Pacific Corp.

UP................ Union Patriotica [*Patriotic Union*] [*Colombia*] [*Political party*]
UP................ Union Patriotica [*Patriotic Union*] [*Spain Political party*] (PPE)
UP................ Union Popular [*Popular Union*] [*Uruguay*] (PD)
UP................ Uniprocessor
UP................ United Party [*Papua New Guinea*] [*Political party*] (PPW)
UP................ United Party [*Gambia*] [*Political party*] (PPW)
UP................ United Presbyterian
UP................ United Press [*Merged with International News Service to form UPI*]
UP................ United Provinces [*India*]
up................ United States Miscellaneous Pacific Islands [*MARC country of publication code Library of Congress*] (LCCP)
UP................ Unit Pack
UP................ Unit Price
UP................ Units Position (IAA)
UP................ Unity Party [*Sierra Leone*] [*Political party*] (EY)
UP................ Unity Party [*Liberia*] [*Political party*] (EY)
UP................ Universal Processor [*TRW, Inc.-Motorola, Inc.*] [*Computer science*]
UP................ University of the Philippines
UP................ University Partnership [*Australia*]
UP................ University Presses [*General term applied to presses of various universities*]
UP................ Unknown Precipitation [*ICAO*] (FAAC)
UP................ Unpostable [*Computer science*]
UP................ Unrealized Profit
UP................ Unrealized Profits (MHDW)
UP................ Unrotated Projectile [*Rocket*]
UP................ Unsaturated Polyester (EDCT)
UP................ Unsaturated Thermoset Polyester [*Organic chemistry*]
UP................ Unsolicited Proposal (MCD)
UP................ Unstained Pollen [*Botany*]
UP................ Update [*Online database field identifier*] [*Computer science*]
UP................ Upper (ADA)
UP................ Upper Peninsula [*Michigan*]
UP................ Upper Proof (ROG)
UP................ Upright Posture (MAE)
UP................ Upset Price [*Business term*] (MHDB)
UP................ Urban Planner (COE)
UP................ Urea Phosphate (OA)
UP................ Ureteropelvic [*Anatomy*]
UP................ Uridine Phosphorylase [*An enzyme*]
U/P.............. Urine-Plasma Ratio [*Clinical chemistry*]
UP................ Uroporphyrin [*Biochemistry*]
UP................ Urticaria Pigmentosa [*Dermatology*]
UP................ User Program (MCD)
UP................ Uteropedvic [*Gynecology*] (DAVI)
UP................ Utility Path (IEEE)
UP................ Utility Program (MCD)
UP................ Utilizable Protein [*Biochemistry*] (DICI)
UPA............ Air Foyle Ltd. [*British ICAO designator*] (FAAC)
UPA............ Ukrains'ka Povstans'ka Armila
UPA............ Ultimate Players Association (EA)
UPA............ Uncooled Parametric Amplifier
UPA............ Uniao das Populacoes de Angola [*Angolan People's Union*] [*Later, NFLA*]
UPA............ Uniform Partnership Act
UPA............ Union of Poles in America (EA)
UPA............ Union Panamericana [*Pan-American Union*] [*Washington, DC*]
UPA............ Union Postale Arabe [*Arab Postal Union*]
UPA............ Unique Product Advantage [*Advertising*]
UPA............ Unitary Pole Approximation
UPA............ United Patternmakers Association
UPA............ United Power Association (IAA)
UPA............ United Producers of America [*Motion picture company*]
UPA............ Units per Assembly [*Business term*] (MHDB)
UPA............ University Photographers Association of America
UPA............ University Press of America
UPA............ University Publications of America [*Database producer*] (IID)
UPA............ Unpressurized Aerosol [*Therapy*] [*Pharmacology*] (DAVI)
UPA............ Unwed Parents Anonymous (EA)
UPA............ Upala [*Costa Rica*] [*Airport symbol*] (AD)
UPA............ Urban Programme Authority [*Education*] (AIE)
UPA............ Urokinase Plasminogen Activator [*An enzyme*]
UPAA.......... University Photographers Association of America (EA)
UPAC.......... Ultra Pac [*NASDAQ symbol*] (TTSB)
UPAC.......... Ultra Pac, Inc. [*NASDAQ symbol*] (SAG)
UPAC.......... Unemployed and Poverty Action Council (EA)
UPAC.......... Unificacion y Progreso [*Unification and Progress*] [*Mexico Political party*] (PPW)
UPAC.......... Union Pacific Corp. (EFIS)
UPAC.......... United Parents of Absconded Children [*Defunct*] (EA)
U Pac.......... University of the Pacific (GAGS)
UPacRs....... Union Pacific Resources Group, Inc. [*Associated Press*] (SAG)
UPACS........ Universal Performance Assessment and Control System
UPADI......... Union Pan-Americana de Asociaciones de Igenieros [*Pan American Federation of Engineering Societies*] [*Uruguay*] (EAIO)
up ad lib..... Up Ad Libitum [*Ambulatory*] [*Patient may walk*] (DAVI)
UPAE.......... Union Postal de las Americas y Espana [*Postal Union of the Americas and Spain - PUAS*] (EAIO)
UPAEP........ Union Postal de las Americas, Espana, y Portugal [*Postal Union of the Americas, Spain, and Portugal*] [*Uruguay*] (EAIO)
UPAJ.......... Union Panafricaine des Journalistes
UPAM.......... United People's Association of Matabeleland [*Zimbabwe*] [*Political party*] (PPW)
UP & S....... Uniform Printing and Supply
UP & T....... Unit Personnel and Tonnage Table [*Military*]

UPANSW...... United Protestant Association of New South Wales [*Australia*]
UPAO.......... University Professors for Academic Order (EA)
UPAP.......... Union Pan Africaine des Postes [*Pan African Postal Union - PAPU*] (EAIO)
UPAP.......... Urban Planning Assistance Program
UPAPH........ United Patients Association for Pulmonary Hypertension (EA)
UPAR.......... Urokeinase Plasminogen Activator [*Biochemistry*]
UPAR.......... Urokinase-Type Plasminogen Activator Receptor [*Biochemistry*]
U-PARC....... University of Pittsburgh Applied Research Center [*Research center*] (RCD)
UPARR........ Urban Park and Recreation Recovery
UPAS .... Underpass [*Postal Service standard*] (OPSA)
UPAS .... Uniform Performance Assessment System [*Education*]
UPAT .... Union Panafricaine des Telecommunications [*Pan African Telecommunications Union - PATU*] (EAIO)
UPB .... Air Goyle Charter Ltd. [*British*] [*FAA designator*] (FAAC)
UPB .... Brigham Young University, Provo, UT [*Library symbol Library of Congress*] (LCLS)
UPB .... Union Patriotica Bonairiana [*Bonaire Patriotic Union*] [*Netherlands Antilles*] [*Political party*] (PPW)
UPB .... United Press of Bangladesh
UPB .... Universal Patents Bureau [*British*] (ROG)
UPB .... Upper Bound
UP/BA .... Unitary Payroll Benefit Accounting (MCD)
Up Ben Pr.... Upper Bench Precedents Tempore Car. I [*England*] [*A publication*] (DLA)
Up Ben Pre... Upper Bench Precedents Tempore Car. I [*A publication*] (DLA)
UPB-L......... Brigham Young University, J. Reuben Clark Law Library, Provo, UT [*Library symbol Library of Congress*] (LCLS)
UPC .... Air Foyle Airways Ltd. [*British*] [*FAA designator*] (FAAC)
UPC .... Pennsylvania State University, Commonwealth Campuses, University Park, PA [*OCLC symbol*] (OCLC)
UPC .... Uganda People's Congress [*Suspended*]
UPC .... Underwater Pipe Cutter
UPC .... UNESCO Publications Center (WDAA)
UPC .... Uniform Plumbing Code (DAC)
UPC .... Uniform Practice Code
UPC .... Uniform Probate Code
UPC .... Union del Pueblo Canario [*Union of the Canarian People*] [*Spain Political party*] (PPE)
UPC .... Union des Populations Camerounaises [*Union of Cameroonian Peoples*] (PD)
UPC .... Unione di u Populu Corsu [*Union of the Corsican People*] [*France Political party*] (PPE)
UPC .... Union of the Corsican People [*France*]
UPC .... Union Planters (EFIS)
UPC .... Union Planters [*NYSE symbol*] (TTSB)
UPC .... Union Planters Corp. [*NYSE symbol*] (CTT)
UPC .... Union pour le Progres Comorien [*Union for Comorian Progress*] [*Political party*] (PPW)
UPC ..,,...... Union Progressiste Congolaise [*Congolese Progressive Union*]
UPC .... United Pentecostal Church [*Australia*]
UPC .... United Poultry Concerns [*An association*] (EA)
UPC .... United Power Co. [*British*]
UPC .... United Presbyterian Church
UPC .... Unit of Packed Cells
UPC .... Unit of Processing Capacity
UPC .... Unit Processing Code (AFM)
UPC .... Unit Production Cost
UPC .... Universal Peripheral Control (CIST)
UPC .... Universal Peripheral Controller
UPC .... Universal Postal Congress (IAA)
UPC .... Universal Product Code [*Inventory control*]
UPC .... Unpostable Code [*Computer science*]
UPC .... Usage Parameter Control [*Computer science*] (DDC)
UPCA .... Uniform Planned Community Act [*National Conference of Commissioners on Uniform State Laws*]
UPCC .... Uniform Product Code Council [*Formerly, UGPCC*] (EA)
UPC-E......... Universal Product Code-Europe (NITA)
UPCHUK ..... University Program for the Comprehensive Handling and Utilization of Knowledge [*Humorous*]
UPCI .... Union pour Construire l'Independence [*New Caledonia*] [*Political party*] (EY)
UPCO......... Union Progressiste Congolaise [*Congolese Progressive Union*]
UPCON....... Upgraded Constellation (MCD)
upconv........ Up Converter (IDOE)
UPCP .... Union Planters [*NASDAQ symbol*] (SAG)
UPCPO....... Union Planters 8% Cv'E'Pfd [*NASDAQ symbol*] (TTSB)
UPCS .... United Pastrycooks' and Confectioners' Society [*British*] (BI)
UPCS .... Universal Philatelic Cover Society
UPD .... Air Foyle Charter Airways Ltd. [*British*] [*FAA designator*] (FAAC)
UPD .... Underpotential Deposition [*Electrochemistry*]
UPD .... Union des Patriotes Democratiques [*Haiti*] [*Political party*] (EY)
UPD .... United Port District (WDAA)
UPD .... Unit Power Density [*Lighting*]
UPD .... Universally Programmable Digitizer Update (IAA)
UPD .... Unpaid (ADA)
UPD .... Update
UPD .... Urban Planning Directorate [*British*]
UPDA........ United Plastics Distributors Association [*Later, NAPD*] (EA)
UPDATE...... Universal Prefabricated Depot Automatic Test Equipment (DNAB)
UPDATE...... Unlimited Potential Data through Automation Technology in Education (IEEE)

UPDEA........ Union des Producteurs, Transporteurs, et Distributeurs d'Energie Electrique d'Afrique [*Union of Producers, Conveyors, and Distributors of Electric Power in Africa - UPDEA*] (EAIO)
UPDFT .... Updraft (MSA)
UPDMA........ United Popular Dress Manufacturers Association [*Later, LACA*] (EA)
UPDP.......... Union des Patriotes Democrates et Progressistes [*Niger*] [*Political party*] (EY)
UPDRS........ Unified Parkinson's Disease Rating Scale
UPDT .... Update [*National Weather Service*] (FAAC)
UPE........... Union de Patriotas Espanoles [*Union of Patriots*] [*Spanish*]
UPE........... Union Panafricaine des Etudiants [*All Africa Students Union - AASU*] (EAIO)
UPE........... Unitary Pole Expansion
UPE........... Unit Proficiency Exercise
UPE........... Unsaturated Polyethylene [*Organic chemistry*]
UPE........... Upstream Promoter Element [*Genetics*]
UPEB .... Union de Paises Exportadores de Banano [*Union of Banana-Exporting Countries - UBEC*] (EAIO)
UPEBR........ Uncured Propellant End Burning Rocket (MCD)
UPECO........ Union Progressiste Congolaise [*Congolese Progressive Union*]
UPEI........... Union Petroliere Europeenne Independante [*Independent European Petroleum Union*] (EAIO)
UPEI........... University of Prince Edward Island [*Canada*]
UPEN .... Upper Peninsula Energy [*NASDAQ symbol*] (TTSB)
UPEN .... Upper Peninsula Energy Corp. [*NASDAQ symbol*] (NQ)
UPenE........ Upper Peninsula Energy Corp. [*Associated Press*] (SAG)
U Penn....... University of Pennsylvania (GAGS)
UPEP .... Undergraduate Preparation of Educational Personnel [*Office of Education*]
UPEP .... Urine Protein Electrophoresis [*Biochemistry*] (DAVI)
UPEPI......... Union of European Practitioners in Industrial Property [*EC*] (ECED)
UPEQUA....... Union Progressiste de l'Equateur [*Progressive Union of Equateur Province*] [*Congo - Leopoldville*]
UPES .... Ultraviolet Photoelectron Spectroscopy
UPET .... United Petroleum [*NASDAQ symbol*] (TTSB)
UPET .... United Petroleum Corp. [*NASDAQ symbol*] (SAG)
UPET .... Urokinase Pulmonary Embolism Trial
UPEU .... Uganda Public Employees' Union
UPF .... Uganda Popular Front [*Political party*] (PD)
UPF .... Ultrapherical Polynomial Filter (IAA)
UPF .... Union pour la France [*France Political party*]
UPF .... United Parkinson Foundation (EA)
UPF .... United Patriotic Front [*Defunct*] (EA)
UPF .... United People's Front [*Nepal*] [*Political party*] (EY)
UPF .... United People's Front [*Singapore*] [*Political party*] (PPW)
UPF .... Universal Proximal Femur [*Prosthesis*] [*Orthopedics*] (DAVI)
UPF .... Unofficial Personnel Folder
UPFAW .... United Packinghouse Food and Allied Workers [*Later, UFCWIU*] (EA)
UPFD .... United Pesticide Formulators and Distributors Association (EA)
UPFD .... United Product Formulators and Distributors Association (NTPA)
UPFDA........ United Pesticide Formulators and Distributors Association
UPFF .... Universal Proutist Farmers Federation (EA)
UPFM .... Union Progressive des Femmes Marocaines [*Progressive Union of Moroccan Women*]
UPG .... Ujung Pandang [*Indonesia*] [*Airport symbol*] (OAG)
UPG .... Union des Populations de Guinee [*Guinea People's Union*] (PD)
UPG .... Union du Peuple Gabonais [*Political party*] (EY)
UPG .... Union Progressiste Guineenne [*Guinean Progressive Union*]
UPG .... United Pacific Gold [*Vancouver Stock Exchange symbol*]
UPG .... United Parents under God (EA)
UPG .... Unpaying Guest [*In a rooming or boarding house*]
UPG .... Upgrade [*Computer science*]
UPG .... Uroporphyrinogen [*Biochemistry*] (MAE)
UPGMA........ Unweighted Pair-Group Method with Arithmetic Means [*Phylogenetic analysis*]
UPGRADE .... University of Pittsburgh Generalized Recording and Dissemination Experiment
UPGRADE .... User-Prompted Graphic Data Evaluation [*US Council on Environmental Quality*]
UPGS .... Church of Jesus Christ of Latter-Day Saints, Genealogical Society Library, Utah Valley Branch, Provo, UT [*Library symbol Library of Congress*] (LCLS)
UPGS .... Unione Progressista della Gioventu Somala [*Progressive Union of Somali Youth*]
UPGWA........ International Union, United Plant Guard Workers of America (EA)
UPH .... Unaccompanied Personnel Housing [*Military*]
UPH .... Underground Pumped Hydro [*Energy storage*]
UPH .... Union of Platers Helpers [*British*]
UPH .... Union Patriotique Haitienne [*Haitian Patriotic Union*] (EA)
UPH .... Units per Hours (AAEL)
UPHA .... United Professional Horsemen's Association (EA)
UPHC .... United Party of Haitian Communists
UPHCI........ Undistributed Personal Holding Company Income
UPHD .... Uphold [*Law*] (ROG)
UPHD .... Upholstered
UPHEWA...... United Presbyterian Health, Education, and Welfare Association [*Later, PHEWA*] (EA)
UPHG .... Upholstering
UPHLR........ Upholsterer
UPHLSTG.... Upholstering (WGA)
UPHLSTRNG.. Upholstering
UPHLSTRY... Upholstery
UPHOL........ Upholstery (WGA)
uphol .... Upholstry (VRA)

UPHPISEC....	Union for the Protection of the Human Person by International, Social, and Economic Cooperation [*Defunct*] (EA)
UPHSTR.......	Upholster
UPI.............	Fayetteville/Fort Bragg, NC [*Location identifier FAA*] (FAAL)
UPI.............	United Press International (EA)
UPI.............	Universal Personal Identifier (NITA)
UPI.............	Universal Presentation Interface [*Uniface Corp.*]
UPI.............	Upper Plenum Injection [*Nuclear energy*] (NRCH)
UPI.............	Uteroplacental Insufficiency [*Medicine*]
UPI.............	Uteroplacental Ischemia [*Obstetrics*] (DAVI)
UPIA	Underwater Photography Instruction Association [*Defunct*] (EA)
UPIA	Uniform Principal and Income Act [*National Conference of Commissioners on Uniform State Laws*]
UPIA	United Press International Audio (NTCM)
UPIC	Union Property Investors, Inc. [*NASDAQ symbol*] (SAG)
UPIC	Universal Personal Identification Code (MHDI)
UPICV	Uniao dos Povos das Ilhas do Cabo Verde [*Union of the Peoples of the Cape Verde Islands*]
UPICV-R	Uniao do Povo para Independencia de Cabo Verde-Ressusitacao [*Cape Verde*] [*Political party*] (EY)
UPIF...........	Universal Proutist Intellectual Federation (EA)
UPIGO.........	Union Professionnelle Internationale des Gynecologues et Obstetriciens [*International Union of Professional Gynecologists and Obstetricians*]
UPIINS.........	Uniform Procurement Instrument Identification Numbering System (MCD)
UPIN	United Press International News-Features (NTCM)
UPIN	United Press International Newspictures
UPIN	Universal Physician Identification Number
UPIR	Uniform Photographic Interpretation Report [*Military*] (AFM)
UPIRN	United Press International Radio Network (NTCM)
UPITN	United Press International Television News (NTCM)
U Pitt	University of Pittsburgh (GAGS)
UPIU	United Paperworkers International Union (EA)
UPJ.............	Underwater Pump Jet
UPJ.............	Ureteropelvic Junction [*Anatomy*]
UPJ.............	Uteropelvic Junction [*Anatomy*] (DAVI)
UPK	Uninvolved Psoriatic Keratinocyte (DB)
UPK	United Park City Mines Co. [*NYSE symbol*] (SPSG)
UPK	United Park City Mns [*NYSE symbol*] (TTSB)
UPK	Unpopped Kernel [*Popcorn*]
UPK	Upkeep Period [*Navy*] (NVT)
UPkMn........	United Park City Mines Co. [*Associated Press*] (SAG)
UPL............	Unidentified Process Loss
UPL............	Uniform Plumbing Code (COE)
UPL............	Union Populaire Locale [*Wallis and Futuna Islands*] [*Political party*] (FEA)
UPL............	Unit Personnel List [*Army*]
UPL............	Universal Programming Language [*Computer science*] (BUR)
UPL............	Universal Publications, London [*British*]
UPL............	Unusual Position of Limbs (DAVI)
UPL............	Upala [*Costa Rica*] [*Airport symbol Obsolete*] (OAG)
UPL............	Uplink
UPL............	Uranium Product Loadout [*Nuclear energy*] (NRCH)
UPL............	User Programming Language [*Burroughs Corp.*] [*Computer science*] (IEEE)
UPLAC	Union des Producteurs de Levure-Aliment de la CEE [*Union of Dried Yeast Producers of the Common Market*]
UPLC	Unauthorized Practice of Law Committee [*Appointed by Texas Supreme Court*]
UPLD	Upland [*Plateau, highland*] [*Board on Geographic Names*]
UPLF...........	Universal Payload Fairing [*NASA*] (KSC)
UPLF...........	Universal Proutist Labour Federation (EA)
UPLG	Union Populaire pour la Liberation de la Guadeloupe [*Popular Union for the Liberation of Guadeloupe*] (PD)
UPLI...........	United Poets Laureate International (EA)
UPLK	Uplink (NASA)
UPLM.........	Uplink Logic Module
UPInt	Union Planters Corp. [*Associated Press*] (SAG)
UPIntr	Union Planters [*Associated Press*] (SAG)
UPLR	Uganda Protectorate Law Reports [*1904-51*] [*A publication*] (DLA)
UPLR	United Provinces Law Reports [*India*] [*A publication*] (DLA)
UPLR	Unplanned Loss Report [*Navy*] (DNAB)
UPLT	United Provinces Law Times [*India*] [*A publication*] (DLA)
UPLV	Upper Leg Vein [*Anatomy*]
Up Lvl.........	Upper Level (TBD)
UPM............	Pennsylvania State University, University Park, PA [*OCLC symbol*] (OCLC)
UPM............	Uganda Patriotic Movement (PD)
UPM............	Ultrapure Metal
UPM............	Umdrehung per Minuten [*Revolutions per Minute*] [*German*]
UPM............	Union del Pueblo de Melilla [*Spanish North Africa*] [*Political party*] (MENA)
UPM............	Union du Peuple Malgache [*Malagasy People's Union*]
UPM............	Unione Politica Maltese [*Maltese Political Union*] [*Political party*] (PPE)
UPM............	Union Pontificale Missionnaire [*Pontifical Missionary Union - PMU*] [*Later, PMUPR*]
UPM............	Union Progressiste Mauritanienne [*Mauritanian Progressive Union*]
UPM............	Union Progressiste Melanesienne [*New Caledonia*] [*Political party*] (FEA)
UPM............	United People's Movement [*Antigua*] [*Political party*] (PPW)
UPM............	United People's Movement [*St. Vincent*] [*Political party*] (PPW)
UPM............	Unit Production Manager [*Filmmaking*]
UPM............	Universal Permissive Module [*Nuclear energy*] (IEEE)
UPM............	Unreached Peoples Mission (EA)
UPM............	UPM-Kymmene Corp. ADS [*NYSE symbol*]
UPMC	University of Pittsburgh Medical Center
UPMC	Urban Planning Ministers Conference (EERA)
UPMI	Union Progressiste Melanesienne [*Progressive Melanesian Union*] [*New Caledonia*] [*Political party*] (PPW)
UPMR	Unit Personnel Management Roster
UPMS	Under PM Services [*Computer science*] (PCM)
UPN	Union del Pueblo Navarrese [*Union of the Navarrese People*] [*Spain Political party*] (PPW)
UPN	Unique Patient Number (STED)
UPN	Unique Project Number (SSD)
UPN	United Paramount Network [*Television*]
UPN	United Party of Nigeria
UPN	Uruapan [*Mexico*] [*Airport symbol*] (OAG)
UPNCA	United Pants and Novelties Contractors Association [*Defunct*] (EA)
UPNE	University Press of New England
UPNI	Unionist Party of Northern Ireland [*Political party*] (PPW)
UP (Noth) ...	Ueberlieferungsgeschichte des Pentateuch (M. Noth) [*A publication*] (BJA)
UPNS	Ukrainian Philatelic and Numismatic Society (EA)
UPO	Undistorted Power Output
UPO	Unidentified Paleontological Object
UPO	Unit Personnel Office [*or Officer*] [*Military*]
UPO	Unstable Periodic Orbit
UPONF.........	United Political Organization National Front [*Yeman*] (BARN)
UPOR	Usual Place of Residence (MAE)
U Portland ...	University of Portland (GAGS)
UPORVC	Upper Peninsula Off Road Vehicle Committee [*Michigan*]
UPOS	Utility Program Operating System (IEEE)
UPOV	International Union for the Protection of New Varieties of Plants (EERA)
UPOV	Union Internationale pour la Protection des Obtentions Vegetales [*International Union for the Protection of New Varieties of Plants*] (EAIO)
UPP	Hawi, HI [*Location identifier FAA*] (FAAL)
UPP	Ultraprecision Parachute (NG)
UPP	Undeducted Purchase Price
UPP	UNESCO Publications and Periodicals
UPP	Union del Pueblo Patriotico [*Ecuador*] [*Political party*] (EY)
UPP	Unionist Progressive Party [*Egypt*] [*Political party*]
UPP	United Papermakers and Paperworkers [*Later, UPIU*] (EA)
UPP	United Peasants' Party [*Poland Political party*] (PD)
UPP	United People's Party [*Sierra Leone*] [*Political party*]
UPP	United People's Party [*Grenada*] [*Political party*] (PPW)
UPP	United Press of Pakistan
UPP	United Progressive Party [*Zambia*] [*Political party*]
UPP	United Progressive Party [*Trinidad and Tobago*] [*Political party*] (PPW)
UPP	Universal Plug and Play [*Software*]
UPP	Universal Procedure Pointer [*Computer science*]
UPP	Universal PROM Programmer
UPP	Universal Proximal Femoral Prosthesis [*Orthopedics*] (DAVI)
UPP	University of Pennsylvania Press (DGA)
UPP	University of Pittsburgh Press (DGA)
UPP	Upolu Point [*Hawaii*] [*Airport symbol*] (OAG)
UPP	Uppsala [*Sweden*] [*Seismograph station code, US Geological Survey*] (SEIS)
UPP	Urea (Prilled) in Paper Packets [*Agronomy*]
UPP	Urethral Pressure Profile [*Urology*] (DAVI)
UPP	Urethral Pressure Profilometry (STED)
UPP	User Parameter Processing (NASA)
UPP	Utility Print Punch
UPP	Uvulopalatopharyngoplasty [*Otorhinolaryngology*] (DAVI)
UPP	Uvulopalatoplasty [*Otorhinolaryngology*] (DAVI)
UPPA	United People's Party of Arunachal [*India*] [*Political party*] (PPW)
UPPC	Universal Pin Pack Connector
UPPE	Ultraviolet Photometric and Polarimetric Explorer
UPPF	United Presbyterian Peace Fellowship (EA)
UPPI	Union des Pilotes Professionels Internationaux [*International Professio nal Drivers Union*] [*French*]
UPPN	Union Postale des Pays du Nord [*Nordic Postal Union - NPU*] (EAIO)
UPPN	United People's Party of Nigeria
UPPOE........	University of Pittsburgh Production Organization Exercise [*Simulation game*]
UPPP	Uvulo-Palato-Pharyngoplasty [*Surgical procedure*] [*Initials are derived from the name of the problem the procedure cures*]
UPPR	Uniform Limited Partnership Act (EBF)
UPPR	Upper
UPPRA........	Upright Peripheral Plasma Renin Activity (STED)
UPPS	Ultimate Plant Protection System [*Nuclear energy*] (NRCH)
UPPS	Unified Pilot Publication System [*American Chemical Society*]
UPR	Ultraportable RADAR (MCD)
UPR	Ultrasonic Parametric Resonance (IEEE)
UPR	Ultraviolet Proton Radiation
UPR	Unearned Premiums Reserve [*Finance*]
UPR	Uniform Parole Reports [*Law Enforcement Assistance Administration*]
UPR	Union des Populations Rurales [*Union of Rural People*] [*Lomela-Kasai*]
UPR	Union Pacific Resources Group [*NYSE symbol*] (TTSB)
UPR	Union Pacific Resources Group, Inc. [*NYSE symbol*] (SAG)
UPR	University of Puerto Rico [*Mayaguez, PR*]
UPR	Unsaturated Polyester Resin [*Organic chemistry*]
UPR	Upper (AAG)
UPR	Uranium Production Reactor [*Nuclear energy*]

UPR .... Urethral Profile at Rest [*Medicine*]
UPR .... Utility, Plant, and Reissue [*Patent applications*]
UPrB .... USAir Grp $4.375 Cv Dep Pfd [*NYSE symbol*] (TTSB)
UPRC .... Uranium Policy Review Committee [*Australia*]
UPrE .... College of Eastern Utah, Price, UT [*Library symbol Library of Congress*] (LCLS)
UPREAL .... Unit Property Record and Equipment Authorization List
UPREC .... Upon Receipt
UPREL .... Unit Property Record and Equipment List
UPRG .... Unit Personnel Records Group [*Air Force*] (AFM)
UPRGp .... Unit Personnel Records Group [*Air Force*] (AFM)
UPrGS .... Church of Jesus Christ of Latter-Day Saints, Genealogical Society Library, PriceBranch, Price, UT [*Library symbol Library of Congress*] (LCLS)
UPRI .... Uteroplacental Respiratory Insufficiency [*Gynecology*]
UPRICO .... University of Puerto Rico [*Mayaguez, PR*]
UPROCO ...... Union Progressiste du Congo [*Progressive Union of the Congo*] [*Niangara*]
UPRONA ...... Union pour le Progres National [*Union for National Progress*] [*Burundi*] [*Political party*] (PPW)
UPRP .... Union des Paysans Ruraux et Progressistes [*Union of Rural and Progressive Farmers*] [*Congo-Kasai*]
UPRR .... Union Pacific Railroad Co.
UPS .... Ultraviolet Photoelectron Spectroscopy (EDCT)
UPS .... Ultraviolet Photoemission Spectroscopy
UPS .... Uncontested Physical Searches [*CIA term for break-ins*]
UPS .... Underground Press Syndicate [*Later, APS*] (EA)
UPS .... Under Provisions of Section [*Military*]
UPS .... Underwater Photographic Society (EA)
UPS .... Uniform Procurement System
UPS .... Uninterruptable Power Source (DAVI)
UPS .... Uninterruptable Power Supply (EERA)
UPS .... Uninterruptible AC [*Alternating Current*] Electric Power System (IAA)
UPS .... Uninterruptible Power Supply [*or System*]
UPS .... Union Progressiste Senegalaise [*Senegalese Progressive Union*] [*Political party*] (AF)
UPS .... United Parcel Service
UPS .... United Parcel Service Co. [*ICAO designator*] (FAAC)
UPS .... United Peregrine Society (EA)
UpS .... United Plant Savers [*An association*]
UPS .... Unit Personnel Section [*Military*]
UPS .... Unit Price Standards (MCD)
UPS .... Unit Proficiency System (AAG)
UPS .... Universal Plotting Sheet
UPS .... Universal Polar Stereographic Grid
UPS .... Universal Press Syndicate Co.
UPS .... Universal Processing System
UPS .... Universities and Public Schools Battalions [*Military units*] [*World War I*] [*British*]
UPS .... Upper Sideband [*Telecommunications*] (EECA)
UPS .... Upright Perigee Stage [*Aerospace*] (MCD)
UPS .... Urethral Profile under Stress [*Medicine*]
UPS .... Uroporphyrinogen Synthase (STED)
UPS .... Uterine Progesterone System [*Contraceptive device*]
UPSA .... Ukrainian Political Science Association in the United States (EA)
UPSA .... Ukrainian Professional Society of America (EA)
UPSA .... Uniform Program Salary Administration (MCD)
UPSA .... Upper Peninsula Sportsmen's Alliance
UPSD .... Union pour le Progres Social et le Democratie [*The Congo*] [*Political party*] (EY)
UPSF .... Universal Proutist Student Federation (EA)
Upsher-S ..... Upsher-Smith [*Commercial firm*] (DAVI)
UPSI .... User Program Sense Indicator
UPSI .... User Program Switch Indicator [*Computer science*]
UPSIS .... United States Political Science Information Service [*University of Pittsburgh*] (IID)
UPSLP .... Upslope [*NWS*] (FAAC)
UPSN .... University Peace Studies Network (EA)
UPSNET .... United Postal Service Network [*National mobile data network*] [*Proposed*] (ECON)
UPSR .... Unit Proficiency System Requirements (AAG)
UPSS .... Ukrainska Partiia Samostiinykiv-Sotsiialistiv [*Ukrainian Party of Socialist-Independentists*] [*Russian Political party*] (PPE)
UPSS .... United Postal Stationery Society (EA)
UPSSL .... University of Puget Sound School of Law (DLA)
Ups Sto .... Upshur's Review of Story on the Constitution [*A publication*] (DLA)
UPSTAGE ..... Upper-Stage Guidance Experiment
UPSTARS ..... Universal Propulsion Stabilization, Retardation, and Separation [*Air Force*]
UPSTART ..... Universal Parachute Support Tactical and Research Target (NG)
UPSTEP .... Undergraduated Pre-Service Teacher Education Program [*National Science Foundation*] (EA)
UPSTRM ..... Upstream [*Meteorology*] (FAAC)
UPT .... Undergraduate Pilot Training [*Air Force*]
UPT .... Universal Patents (EFIS)
UPT .... Upgrade Pilot Training
UPT .... Urgent Postal Telegram
UPT .... Urine Pregnancy Test [*Gynecology*] (DAVI)
UPT .... User Process Table
UPT .... US Platinum [*Vancouver Stock Exchange symbol*]
UPTA .... Uniform Perpetuation of Testimony Act [*National Conference of Commissioners on Uniform State Laws*]
UPTA .... United Parent-Teachers Association of Jewish Schools (EA)
UPTAS .... Utility Practical Transport Aircraft System [*Army*]

UPTC .... Union Panafricaine des Travailleurs Croyants [*Pan-African Union of Believing Workers*]
UPTD .... Unit Pulmonary Toxicity Dose [*Deep-sea diving*]
UPTE .... Ultra-Precision Test Equipment (PDAA)
UPTF .... Upper Plenum Test Facility [*Nuclear energy*] (NRCH)
UPT-H .... Undergraduate Pilot Training - Helicopter [*Air Force*]
UPTLM .... Up-Link Telemetry [*NASA*] (NASA)
Upt Mar W... Upton on Maritime Warfare and Prize [*A publication*] (DLA)
UPTP .... Universal Package Test Panel
UPTS .... Undergraduate Pilot Training System (IAA)
UPTT .... Unit Personnel and Tonnage Table [*Military*] (AABC)
Upt Tr Mar... Upton on Trade-Marks [*A publication*] (DLA)
UPU .... Union Postale Universelle [*Universal Postal Union*] [*Switzerland Also, an information service or system*] (IID)
UPU .... Universal Postal Union [*United Nations*] (MENA)
UPUC .... Unauthorized Publication or Use of Communications
UPUC .... Universal Postal Union Collectors (EA)
UPUC .... Universal Postal Union Convention
U Puerto Rico... University of Puerto Rico (GAGS)
U Puerto Rico, Mayaguez... University of Puerto Rico, Mayaguez (GAGS)
U Puget Sound... University of Puget Sound (GAGS)
UPUP .... Ulster Popular Unionist Party [*Northern Ireland*] [*Political party*] (PPW)
UPUP .... Ulster Progressive Unionist Party [*Northern Ireland*] [*Political party*] (PPW)
UPUP .... United Payors and United Providers, Inc. [*NASDAQ symbol*] (SAG)
UPUS .... United Public Utility Systems
UPUSA .... UPU [*Universal Postal Union*] Staff Association (EAIO)
U$_p$V .... Phosphate Excretion Rate [*Laboratory Science*] (DAVI)
UPV .... Unfired Pressure Vessel
UPV .... Universal Pre-Vent, Inc. [*Vancouver Stock Exchange symbol*]
UPV .... Upernavik [*Greenland*] [*Airport symbol*] (AD)
UPVC .... Unfired Pressure Vessel Code (AAG)
UPVC .... Unplasticized Polyvinyl Chloride
uPVC .... Unplasticized Polyvinyl Chloride (EDCT)
UPW .... Ultrapure Water (AAEL)
UPW .... Union of Post Office Workers [*British*] (DCTA)
UPW .... United Port Workers' Union [*Ceylon*]
UPW .... United Presbyterian Women (EA)
UPW .... United Public Workers of America
UPWA .... Union of Palestinian Women's Association in North America (EA)
UPWA .... Union of Polish Women in America (EA)
UPWA .... United Packinghouse Workers of America [*Later, UFCWIU*]
UPWA .... United Polish Women of America (EA)
UPWARD ..... Understanding Personal and Racial Dignity [*Navy program*]
UPWCA .... United Pest and Weed Control Association [*Australia*]
UPWD .... Upward (MSA)
UPWF .... Ukrainian Patriarchal World Federation (EA)
UPWP .... Unified Planning Work Program
UPWT .... Unitary Plan Wind Tunnel (KSC)
UPX .... Unapix Entertainment [*AMEX symbol*] (TTSB)
UPX .... Unapix Entertainment, Inc. [*AMEX symbol*] (SAG)
UPX.WS.B ... Unapix Enter Cl'B'Wrrt [*AMEX symbol*] (TTSB)
UPY .... Union of People's Youth [*Bulgaria*]
UPYF .... Universal Proutist Youth Federation (EA)
UPz .... Urkunden der Ptolemaerzeit [*U. Wilcken*] [*A publication*] (BJA)
UQ .... Fronte dell'Uomo Qualunque; Uomo Qualunque [*Common Man Front*] [*Italy Political party*] (PPE)
UQ .... Suburban Airlines [*ICAO designator*] (AD)
UQ .... Ubiquinone [*Also, CoQ, Q, U*] [*Biochemistry*]
UQ .... Ultraquick [*Flashing*] Light [*Navigation signal*]
UQ .... United African Airline [*Libya*] [*ICAO designator*] (ICDA)
UQ .... University of Queensland [*State*] (EERA)
UQ .... Upper Quadrant [*Anatomy*]
UQ .... Upper Quadrile
UQAC .... Universite du Quebec a Chicoutimi [*Canada*]
UQAH .... Universite du Quebec a Hull [*Canada*]
UQAM .... Universite du Quebec a Montreal [*Canada*]
UQAR .... Universite du Quebec a Rimouski [*Canada*]
UQB .... Universite de Quebec [*UTLAS symbol*]
UQC .... Underwater Telephone [*Navy*] (CAAL)
UQCP .... Uniform Quality Control Program
UQE .... Queen [*Alaska*] [*Airport symbol Obsolete*] (OAG)
UQGS .... Uniform Quality Grading System [*Tires*]
UQL .... Unacceptable Quality Level
UQM .... Unique Mobility [*AMEX symbol*] (TTSB)
UQM .... Unique Mobility, Inc. [*AMEX symbol*] (SAG)
UQOT .... Unquote (FAAC)
UQP .... Universities and the Quest for Peace [*An association*]
UQP .... University of Queensland Press [*Australia*]
UQS .... Nuiqsut Village, AK [*Location identifier FAA*] (FAAL)
Uqs .... 'Uqsin (BJA)
UQT .... User Queue Table
UQY .... Kansas City, MO [*Location identifier FAA*] (FAAL)
UR .... British International Helicopters [*ICAO designator*] (AD)
UR .... Empire Airlines [*ICAO designator*] (AD)
UR .... Lab. J. Uriach & Cia. SA [*Spain*] [*Research code symbol*]
UR .... Lloyd's Universal Register of Shipping [*British*] (ROG)
UR .... Red Carpet Airlines, Inc. [*ICAO designator*] (ICDA)
UR .... Uganda Rifles [*British military*] (DMA)
UR .... Ukraine [*International civil aircraft marking*] (ODBW)
UR .... Ullage Rocket (KSC)
UR .... Ultrared (IAA)
UR .... Unattended Repeater [*Telecommunications*] (OA)
UR .... Unconditioned Reflex [*Neurology*] (DAVI)

UR .... Unconditioned Response [*Psychometrics*]
U/R .... Underrange (IEEE)
UR .... Underreporter [*IRS*]
UR .... Under Review (MHDB)
UR .... Under the Rule [*Business term*]
UR .... Undulator Radiation [*High-energy physics*]
UR .... Unfinanced Requirement [*Army*] (AABC)
UR .... Unfractionated Reservoir [*Geology*]
UR .... Unfunded Requirement [*Military*] (AFIT)
UR .... Uniao Republicana [*Republican Union*] [*Portugal Political party*] (PPE)
UR .... Unidentified Remittance [*IRS*]
UR .... Uniform Regulations
UR .... Unitatis Redintegratio [*Decree on Ecumenism*] [*Vatican II document*]
UR .... Unit Real (IAA)
UR .... Unit Record [*Computer science*]
UR .... Unit Register
UR .... University of Rochester [*New York*] (KSC)
UR .... University Relations
UR .... Unprogrammed Requirements (MCD)
UR .... Unrelated (AAMN)
UR .... Unreleasable (MCD)
UR .... Unreliable
UR .... Unsatisfactory Report
UR .... Upper Rail
UR .... Upper Respiratory [*Medicine*]
UR .... Upper Right (MCD)
U/R .... Up Range [*NASA*] (KSC)
UR .... Up Right [*The rear right portion of a stage*] [*A stage direction*]
UR .... Uranium (ROG)
UR .... Urban Rat [*Virus*]
Ur .... Urdu [*Language*] (BARN)
UR .... Urgent Requirement (MCD)
UR .... Urinal (MSA)
UR .... Urine
UR .... Urology
Ur .... Uruguay
UR .... User Requirements [*Nuclear energy*] (NRCH)
ur .... USSR [*Union of Soviet Socialist Republics*] [*MARC country of publication code Library of Congress*] (LCCP)
UR .... Utility Room (MSA)
UR .... Utilization Review [*Preferred provider organization*] [*Medicine*]
UR .... Uti Rogas [*Be It as You Desire*] [*Used by Romans to express assent to a proposition*] [*Latin*]
UR .... Your [*Amateur radio shorthand*] (WDAA)
URA .... Ugana Revenue Authority
URA .... Uniformly Redundant Array
URA .... United Red Army [*Japan*] (PD)
URA .... United Republicans of America
URA .... Universities Research Association (EA)
URA .... Upper Respiratory Allergy [*Medicine*]
Ura .... Uracil [*Biochemistry*]
URA .... Urakawa [*Japan*] [*Seismograph station code, US Geological Survey*] (SEIS)
URA .... Uralinteravia [*Russian Federation*] [*ICAO designator*] (FAAC)
Ura .... Urania [*Record label*] [*USA, Europe, etc.*]
URA .... Uranium Recycle Acid [*Nuclear energy*] (NRCH)
URA .... Urban Redevelopment Authority
URA .... Urban Renewal Administration [*of HHFA*] [*Terminated*]
URA .... Urine Receptacle Assembly [*NASA*] (MCD)
URA .... User Range Accuracy (SSD)
URA .... User Requirements Analysis
URA .... Utilization Review Agency [*Insurance*]
URAC .... Union des Republiques de l'Afrique Centrale [*Union of Central African Republics*]
URAC .... Utilization Review Accreditation Commission
URACTY .... Your Activity
URAD .... Unit for Research on Addictive Drugs [*University of Aberdeen*] [*British*] (IRUK)
URAEP .... University of Rochester Atomic Energy Project
URAF .... Unidentified Remittance Amount File [*IRS*]
URAI .... Universities Research Association, Inc.
URAM .... Association of Concern for Ultimate Reality & Meaning (AC)
URAM .... Unrelated Adult Man
Uran .... Uranus [*Astronomy*] (BARN)
ur anal .... Urine Analysis [*or Urinalysis*] [*Urology*] (DAVI)
UR & M .... Urinalysis-Routine and Microscopic [*Urology*] (DAVI)
UranRes .... Uranium Resources, Inc. [*Associated Press*] (SAG)
URAPA .... Uniform Rendition of Accused Persons Act [*National Conference of Commissioners on Uniform State Laws*]
URARPAA .... Uniform Relocation Assistance and Real Property Acquisition Act [*1970*] (OICC)
URARPAPA... Uniform Relocation Assistance and Real Property Acquisition Policies Act of 1970
URARRED .... US Army Readiness Command (MCD)
URAS .... Union des Republicains d'Action Sociale [*Union of Republicans of Social Action*] [*France Political party*] (PPE)
URAUZ .... You Are Authorized (FAAC)
URAW .... Unrelated Adult Woman
URB .... Union Regionale de Bamileke [*Regional Union of Bamileke*] [*Cameroon*]
URB .... Unridable Bicycle
URB .... Urban
URB .... Urbana College, Urbana, OH [*OCLC symbol*] (OCLC)
URB .... Urbanization

URB .... Urban Shopping Centers [*NYSE symbol*] (SPSG)
URB .... Urubupunga [*Brazil*] [*Airport symbol*] (OAG)
Urb Aff Rep... Urban Affairs Reporter [*Commerce Clearing House*] [*A publication*] (DLA)
URBAMET .... Urbanisme, Amenagement, Equipments, et Transports [*Reseau URBAMET*] [*France Information service or system*] (CRD)
Urban Ed ..... Urban Education [*A publication*] (BRI)
URBANICOM... Association Internationale Urbanisme et Commerce [*International Association for Town Planning and Distribution*] (EAIO)
URBANK ...... Urban Development Bank
Urban Law Ann... Urban Law Annual [*A publication*] (ILCA)
Urban LJ ...... University of Detroit. Journal of Urban Law [*A publication*] (DLA)
Urban L Rev... Urban Law Review [*A publication*] (DLA)
URBC .... Uninfected Red Blood Cells [*Hematology*]
URBCOM ...... [*The*] Urban Communications Game
URBED .... Urban and Economic Development Ltd. (AIE)
Urb For .... Urban Forests [*A publication*]
URBK .... Union Rheinische Braunkohlen Kraftstoff [*West Germany*]
Urblaw .... Urban Law and Policy [*A publication*] (ILCA)
URBM .... Ultimate Range Ballistic Missile [*Air Force*]
URBN .... Urban Outfitters, Inc. [*NASDAQ symbol*] (SAG)
URBN .... Urban Outfitters [*NASDAQ symbol*] (TTSB)
UrbnOut .... Urban Outfitters, Inc. [*Associated Press*] (SAG)
UrbnShp .... Urban Shopping Centers [*Associated Press*] (SAG)
URBOE .... Ultimatist Religious Bodies on Earth (EA)
URBPOP ...... Urban Population File (MCD)
URC .... Uganda Railways Corp. (DCTA)
URC .... Ultrasonic Resin Cleaner [*Nuclear energy*] (NRCH)
URC .... Undersea Research Corp.
URC .... Uniform Resistance Capacitance [*Electronics*] (IAA)
URC .... Uniform Resource Characteristic [*Computer science*] (EERA)
URC .... Uniform Resource Citations [*Computer science*]
URC .... Uniform Rules for Collections
URC .... Union de Rassemblement et du Centre [*France Political party*] (ECON)
URC .... Union des Republicains du Cameroun [*Political party*] (EY)
URC .... Union du Rassemblement du Centre [*Mayotte*] [*Political party*] (EY)
URC .... United Racing Club [*Auto racing*]
URC .... United Ratepayers' Campaign [*British*] (BI)
URC .... United Reform Church [*Australia*]
URC .... United Reform Church in England and Wales
URC .... Unit Record Card
URC .... Unit Record Control
URC .... University Research Centre [*British*]
URC .... Upper Rib Cage [*Anatomy*]
URC .... Upper Right Center (WGA)
URC .... Ursuline College Library, Pepper Pike, OH [*OCLC symbol*] (OCLC)
URC .... Urumqi [*China*] [*Airport symbol*] (OAG)
URC .... Utility Radio Communication
URC .... Utility Regulatory Commission (COE)
URC .... Utilization Review Committee [*Medical records*] (DAVI)
URC A .... Uric Acid [*Laboratory science*] (DAVI)
URCC .... University of Rochester Cancer Center [*Research center*] (RCD)
URCE .... Union Restaurants Collectifs Europeens [*European Catering Association*] [*Germany*] (EAIO)
URCF .... Unidentified Remittance Control File [*IRS*]
URCG .... Uniform Rules for Contract Guarantees
URCLK .... Universal Receiver Clock
URCO .... Union des Ressortissants du Congo pour la Defense et la Promotion du Congo [*Union of Congolese for the Defense and Promotion of the Congo*]
URCOT .... Urban Research Centre on Office Technology [*Australia*]
URCRM .... Urals Research Center for Radiation Medicine [*Russia*]
URCS .... Uniform Railroad Cost System [*BTS*] (TAG)
URCS .... Uniform Ration Cost System (MCD)
URC SP .... Uric Acid-Urine Spot [*test*] [*Laboratory science*] (DAVI)
URD .... New York, NY [*Location identifier FAA*] (FAAL)
URD .... Underground Residential Distribution [*Cable*]
URD .... Underground Rural Distribution (IAA)
URD .... Unilateral Renal Disease [*Medicine*] (DB)
URD .... Union Republicana Democratica [*Democratic Republican Union*] [*Puerto Rico, Venezuela*]
URD .... Unit Reference Designation [*Army*]
URD .... Upper Respiratory Disease [*Medicine*]
urd .... Urdu [*MARC language code Library of Congress*] (LCCP)
Urd .... Uridine [*Also, U*] [*A nucleoside*]
URD .... User Requirements Document (MCD)
URDA .... Uniform Retirement Date Act [*National Conference of Commissioners on Uniform State Laws*]
URDA .... Urban Resources Development Agency (OICC)
URDB .... User Requirements Database (COE)
URDIS .... Your Dispatch [*Military*]
URDP .... Ukrains'ka Revoliutsiino-Demokratychna Partiia
URDS .... Unexplained Respiratory Distress Syndrome [*Medicine*]
URDS .... Unknown Respiratory Stress Syndrome [*Medicine*]
URDS .... User Requirements Data Base (MHDB)
URDU .... Urban Regional Development Unit (EERA)
URE .... Undergraduate Record Examination [*Education*]
URE .... Unintentional Radiation Exploitation (AFM)
URE .... User Range Error
UREA .... Urea Nitrogen [*Laboratory science*] (DAVI)
UREBA .... Union Revolutionnaire des Banques [*Burkina Faso*] (EY)
URED .... Unable to Read [*Laboratory science*] (DAVI)
U Redlands... University of Redlands (GAGS)

UREHE	Union for Research and Experimentation in Higher Education [*Later, UECU*]
UREKA	Unlimited Resources Ensure Keen Answers
UREP	Unit Representative [*Military*] (INF)
UREP	University Research Expeditions Programs
URES	University Residence Environment Scale [*Student attitudes test*]
URESA	Uniform Reciprocal Enforcement of Support Act
U-REST	Universal Range, Endurance, Speed, and Time (NG)
ureth	Urethra [*Anatomy*]
Urethane	Urethane Technologies, Inc. [*Associated Press*] (SAG)
URF	Relaxin [*Medicine*] (DAVI)
URF	Ukrainian Research Foundation [*Defunct*] (EA)
URF	Unassigned Reading Frame [*Genetics*]
URF	Unidentified Reading Frame [*Genetics*]
URF	Unidentified Remittance File [*IRS*]
URF	Union des Services Routiers des Chemins de Fer Europeens [*Union of European Railways Road Services*]
URF	United Religious Front [*Israel*] (BJA)
URF	United Republican Fund
URF	Urfa [*Turkey*] [*Airport symbol*] (AD)
URF	Uterine-Relaxing Factor [*Endocrinology*]
URFDA-NYC	United Retail Fish Dealers Association of New York City (EA)
UR-FST	Urine - Fasting [*Urology*] (DAVI)
URG	Air Urga [*Ukraine*] [*FAA designator*] (FAAC)
URG	Underway Replenishment Group [*Military*]
URG	United Rayore Gas [*Vancouver Stock Exchange symbol*]
URG	Unit Review Group [*Nuclear energy*] (NRCH)
URG	Universal Radio Group
URG	Urban Regeneration Grant [*British*]
URG	Urgent (AFM)
URG	Urheberrechtsgesetz [*German Copyright Act*] (DLA)
URG	Uruguaiana [*Brazil*] [*Airport symbol*] (OAG)
URGENT	Universal Relevance Group Enterprise in a National Theater [*Theater workshop*]
URGI	United Retail Group [*NASDAQ symbol*] (TTSB)
URGI	United Retail Group, Inc. [*NASDAQ symbol*] (SAG)
URGNSW	Underwater Research Group of New South Wales [*Australia*]
URGR	Underway Replenishment Group [*Military*]
URHB	Urban Renewal Handbook
U Rhode Island	University of Rhode Island (GAGS)
UR#HR	Urine - Number of Hours/Glucose Tolerance [*The symbol is replaced with the correct numeral*] [*Endocrinology*] (DAVI)
URi	Richmond City Library, Richmond, UT [*Library symbol Library of Congress*] (LCLS)
URI	Unexpected Real Incapacitation (DNAB)
URI	Uniform Resource Identifier [*Computer science*] (EERA)
URI	Unintentional RADAR Interference (IAA)
URI	Union Research Institute, Kowloon, Hong Kong [*Library symbol Library of Congress*] (LCLS)
URI	United Research, Inc.
URI	Universite Radiophonique Internationale [*International University of the Air*] (NTCM)
URI	University of Rhode Island
URI	University of Rhode Island, Kingston (USDC)
URI	University Research Initiative [*DoD*] (RDA)
URI	Unpublished Research Information [*Conducted by National Science Foundation*]
uri	Unrelated (DAVI)
URI	Upper Respiratory Infection [*Medicine*]
URI	Upper-Respiratory-Tract Infection [*Medicine*] (DAVI)
URI	Uranium Resources, Inc. [*Vancouver Stock Exchange symbol*]
URI	Uribe [*Colombia*] [*Airport symbol Obsolete*] (OAG)
URI	Utility Read-In Program (IAA)
URIA	Universal Real-Time Information and Administration
URICA	Universal Real-Time Information Control and Administration (MCD)
URICA	University of Rhode Island Computer Access [*University of Rhode Island Library*] (OLDSS)
URICA	Using Reading in Creative Activities
U Rich LN	University of Richmond. Law Notes [*A publication*] (DLA)
U Richmond	University of Richmond (GAGS)
URifGS	Church of Jesus Christ of Latter-Day Saints, Genealogical Society Library, Richfield Branch, Richfield, UT [*Library symbol Library of Congress*] (LCLS)
URII	Ukrainian Research and Information Institute [*Defunct*] (EA)
URiL	Richmond City Library, Richmond, UT [*Library symbol*] [*Library of Congress*] (LCLS)
URIMA	University Risk and Insurance Managers Association [*Later, URMIA*] (EA)
URIN	Random Urine [*Urology*] (DAVI)
URINT	Unintentional Radiation Intelligence (MCD)
URIPS	Undersea Radioisotope Power Supply
URIR	Unified Radioactive Isodromic Regulator
URIS	Urban and Regional Information System
URISA	American Urban and Regional Information Systems Association (EERA)
URISA	Urban and Regional Informations Systems Association
URISA	Urban and Regional Information Systems Association (EA)
URIX	Uranium Resources [*NASDAQ symbol*] (TTSB)
URIX	Uranium Resources, Inc. [*NASDAQ symbol*] (NQ)
URIZR	Your Recommendation is Requested (FAAC)
URJA	United Roumanian Jews of America (EA)
Urk	Urkunde [*Document, Deed, Instrument*] [*German*] (ILCA)
Urk	Urkunden des Aegyptischen Altertums [*G. Steindorff*] [*Leipzig*] [*A publication*] (BJA)
URKK	Krasnodar [*Former USSR ICAO location identifier*] (ICLI)

URL	Uniform Resource Locator [*Telecommunications*]
URL	Universal Reference Locator
URL	Universal [*or Uniform*] Resource Locator [*Computer science*]
URL	University of Regina Library [*UTLAS symbol*]
URL	Unrequited Love [*Slang*]
URL	Unrestricted Line Officer [*Navy*]
URL	Upper Reference Limit [*Analytical chemistry*]
URL	Uralavialy [*Russian Federation*] [*ICAO designator*] (FAAC)
URL	User Requirements Language [*Computer science*]
URLA	Uniform Reciprocal Licensing Act [*State law*] [*Insurance*]
Url Cl	Urling's Legal Guide for the Clergy [*A publication*] (DLA)
Url For Pat	Urling on Foreign Patents [*A publication*] (DLA)
Url Trust	Urling on the Office of a Trustee [*A publication*] (DLA)
URM	Uncle Remus Museum (EA)
URM	Uniform Reflectivity Mirror (PDAA)
URM	University Reform Movement [*in Latin America*]
URM	Unlimited Register Machine
URM	Urban Renewal Manual
URM	Uriman [*Venezuela*] [*Airport symbol*] (OAG)
URMD	Uromed Corp. [*NASDAQ symbol*] (SAG)
URMIA	University Risk Management and Insurance Association [*Madison, WI*] (EA)
URMIS	Uniform Retail Meat Identity Standard [*Pronounced "er-miss"*]
URMK	Kislovodsk [*Former USSR ICAO location identifier*] (ICLI)
UR M-L	Uniao Revolucionaria, Marxista-Leninista [*Marxist-Leninist Revolutionary Union*] [*Portugal Political party*] (PPE)
URMM	Mineralnye Vody [*Former USSR ICAO location identifier*] (ICLI)
URMS	Universal Reproducing Matrix System (PDAA)
URN	Covington/Cincinnati, OH [*Location identifier FAA*] (FAAL)
URN	Turan Air [*Azerbaijan*] [*FAA designator*] (FAAC)
URN	Ultrahigh Radio Navigation (NATG)
URN	Uniform Random Numerator [*Computer science*]
URN	Uniform Resource Name [*Computer science*] (EERA)
URN	Uniform Resource Names [*Computer science*]
URN	Union pour la Reconciliation Nationale [*Haiti*] [*Political party*] (EY)
URN	Unique Record Number [*Computer science*] (ADA)
URN	Unique Reference Number [*Customs*] (DS)
URN	Urine (NASA)
URNF	Unidentified Remittance Name File [*IRS*]
URNG	Unidad Revolucionaria Nacional Guatemalteca [*Guatemalan National Revolutionary Unity*] [*Political party*] (PD)
URNM	Uranium
URO	United Restitution Organization
URO	United Rink Operators [*Defunct*] (EA)
URO	UROHEALTH Systems'A'(New) [*AMEX symbol*] (TTSB)
URO	UROHEALTH Systems, Inc. [*AMEX symbol*] (SAG)
URO	Urology
URO	Uroporphyrin [*Biochemistry*]
URO	Uroporphyrinogen [*Biochemistry*]
URO	User Readout (MCD)
URO	Ustredni Rada Odboru [*Central Council of Trade Unions*] [*Czechoslovakia*]
URO-2H	Urobilinogen-2 Hour [*Gastroenterology*] (DAVI)
UROBA	United Russian Orthodox Brotherhood of America (EA)
UROBIL	Urobilinogen [*Medicine*] (DAVI)
UROC	United Railroad Operating Crafts [*Defunct*]
U Rochester	University of Rochester (GAGS)
UroCor	UroCor, Inc. [*Associated Press*] (SAG)
UROEA	UNESCO Regional Office for Education in Asia and Oceania [*Thailand*] (DLA)
uro-gen	Urogenital [*Medicine*] (CPH)
UROGEN	Uroporphyrinogen [*Biochemistry*]
Urohlt	UROHEALTH Systems, Inc. [*Associated Press*] (SAG)
Urohlth	UROHEALTH Systems, Inc. [*Associated Press*] (SAG)
UROL	Urology
UROLA	UNEP [*United Nations Environmental Programme*] Regional Office for Latin America (EAIO)
Urologix	Urologix, Inc. [*Associated Press*] (SAG)
Uromed	Uromed Corp. [*Associated Press*] (SAG)
UROP	Undergraduate Research Opportunities Program [*Pronounced "your-op"*] [*Massachusetts Institute of Technology*]
UROQ	UroQuest Medical Corp. [*NASDAQ symbol*] (SAG)
UroQst	UroQuest Medical Corp. [*Associated Press*] (SAG)
UROS	Uroporphyrinogen I Synthase [*An enzyme*]
URP	Undergraduate Research Participation [*National Science Foundation project*] [*Defunct*] (EA)
URP	Underreporter Program [*IRS*]
URP	Union Republicaine du Peuple [*Benin*] [*Political party*] (EY)
URP	Unique Radiolytic Product [*Food technology*]
URP	United Reef Petroleums Ltd. [*Toronto Stock Exchange symbol*]
URP	Unit Record Processor
URP	University of Rochester, Department of Physics
URP	Unmanned Recovery Platform [*Navy*] (NVT)
URP	Upper-Stage Reusable Payload
URP	Urban Renewal Project [*HUD*] (OICC)
URPC	User Level Remote Procedure Call [*Computer science*]
URPE	Union des Resistants pour une Europe Unie [*Union of Resistance Veterans for a United Europe*]
URPE	Union for Radical Political Economics (EA)
URPE	Union Revolucionaria Popular Ecuatoriana [*Ecuadorean Popular Revolutionary Union*] [*Political party*] (PPW)
URPG	President's Urban and Regional Policy Group [*Terminated, 1978*] (EGAO)
URPIS	Urban and Regional Planning Information Systems (EERA)
URPL	Urban and Regional Planning (PA)

URPP	Undergraduate Research Participation Program [*Formerly, URP*] (EA)
URQ	Unsatisfactory Report Questionnaire
URQ	Upper Right Quadrant [*Medicine*]
UR/QA	Utilization Review/Quality Assurance
URR	Ultra-Rapid Reader [*Computer science*]
URR	Ultrareliable RADAR (MCD)
URR	Unconstrained Requirements Report [*Army*]
URR	Union Railroad Co. [*Pittsburgh, PA*] [*AAR code*]
URR	United Redford Resources, Inc. [*Vancouver Stock Exchange symbol*]
URR	Unit Readiness Report [*Army*] (AABC)
URR	Universities Research Reactor [*British*]
URR	Upstream Regulatory Region [*Genetics*]
URRP	Urea Reduction Ratio
URR	Urrao [*Colombia*] [*Airport symbol*] (OAG)
URR	Utilization Research Report
URRC	Urological Rehabilitation and Research Center [*University of Alabama in Birmingham*] [*Research center*] (RCD)
URRM	Morozovsk [*Former USSR ICAO location identifier*] (ICLI)
URRR	Rostov-Na-Donu [*Former USSR ICAO location identifier*] (ICLI)
URS	Ugurusu [*Japan*] [*Seismograph station code, US Geological Survey*] (SEIS)
URS	Ultrasonic Renal Scanning [*Nephrology*] (DAVI)
URS	Unate Ringe Sum [*Logic expression*] (IEEE)
Urs	Underwriters [*Insurance*]
URS	UNESCO Relations Staff
URS	Uniformly Reflexive Structure (IAA)
URS	Uniform Reporting System
URS	Union of Railway Signalmen [*British*]
URS	United Research Service (MCD)
URS	Unit Readiness System
URS	Unit Reference Sheet [*Military*] (AABC)
URS	Universal Reference System
URS	Universal Regulating System
URS	University Research Support [*Department of Energy*]
URS	Unmanned Repeater Station [*Telecommunications*] (OA)
URS	Update Report System (TEL)
URS	Urban Resource Systems (EA)
URS	URS Corp. [*NYSE symbol*] (SPSG)
URS	Ursinus College, Collegeville, PA [*OCLC symbol*] (OCLC)
URS	User Readout Simulator [*Army*]
URS	Utilization Reporting System (MCD)
URSA	United Russia Societies Association [*London*]
URSA	Unit Replacement System Analysis [*Military*]
URSA	Universal Resource Sharing Application [*Interlibrary software*]
URSA	Urban and Rural Systems Associates
URSI	Union Radio Scientifique Internationale [*International Union of Radio Science*] [*Also, ISRU*] [*Belgium*]
URSIES	Ultravariable Resolution Single Interferometer Echelle Scanner (PDAA)
URSNSC	Union Regionale des Syndicats du Nyong-et-Sanaga
URSO	Ursodeoxycholic Acid (STED)
URSP	Universal RADAR Signal Processor
URSS	Sochi [*Former USSR ICAO location identifier*] (ICLI)
URSS	Union des Republiques Socialistes Sovietiques [*Union of Socialist Soviet Republics; USSR*]
URSTM	Unite de Recherche et de Service en Technologie Minerale de l'Abitibi-Temiscamingue [*University of Quebec at Abitibi-Temiscamingue*] [*Canada Research center*] (RCD)
URSW	Union Regionale des Syndicats du Wouri [*Regional Union of Wouri Unions*]
URT	Surat Thani [*Thailand*] [*Airport symbol*] (OAG)
URT	Unit Recruit Training [*Army*] (AABC)
URT	Universal RADAR Tracker
URT	University Research and Training [*Programs*]
URT	Upper Respiratory Tract [*Medicine*]
URT	Upright (MSA)
Urt	Urteil [*Judgment, Decision*] [*German*] (ILCA)
URT	Utility Radio Transmitter
URTA	University Resident Theatre Association (EA)
URTH	Unreasonable Risk to Health [*Drinking water standards*] [*Environmental Protection Agency*]
URTI	Universite Radiophonique et Televisuelle Internationale [*International Radio-Television University*]
URTI	Upper Respiratory Tract Infection [*Medicine*]
URTIA	Uniform Rights of the Terminally Ill Act [*National Conference of Commissioners on Uniform State Laws*]
UR-TIM	Urine-Time [*Urology*] (DAVI)
URTNA	Union des Radio-Televisions Nationales Africaines [*African National Radio-Television Union*] (AF)
URTRO	Unloaded Radial Tire Run-Out
URTU	United Road Transport Union [*British*] (DCTA)
URTWAE	United Road Transport Workers' Association of England [*A union*]
URU	Uruguay
Uru	Uruguay (VRA)
URUC	UNCTAD [*United Nations Conference on Trade and Development*] Reference UnitCatalogue [*Information service or system*] (DUND)
URV	Undersea Research Vehicle [*or Vessel*]
URV	Uraiavia [*Former USSR*] [*FAA designator*] (FAAC)
URVD	Unilateral Renovascular Disease [*Nephrology*] (DAVI)
UR VOL	Urine Volume [*Urology*] (DAVI)
URW	Ultrasonic Ring Welder
URW	United Racquetsports for Women (EA)
URW	United Rubber, Cork, Linoleum, and Plastic Workers of America (EA)
URW	Ural [*Former USSR*] [*FAA designator*] (FAAC)

URWA	United Railroad Workers of America
URWC	Urinal Water Closet (MSA)
URWRO	Unloaded Radial Wheel Run-Out
URY	Century Aviation, SA de CV [*Mexico*] [*FAA designator*] (FAAC)
URY	Gurayat [*Saudi Arabia*] [*Airport symbol*] (OAG)
URY	Union Railway of Memphis [*AAR code*]
URY	Uruguay [*ANSI three-letter standard code*] (CNC)
URZ	Uroozgan [*Afghanistan*] [*Airport symbol Obsolete*] (OAG)
US	Luminosity (WDMC)
US	Ubi Supra [*In the Place Mentioned Above*] [*Latin*]
US	Ultrasonic (AAMN)
US	Ultrasonic Spectroscopy
US	Ultrasonography (DAVI)
US	Ultrasound
U/S	Unassorted (ROG)
US	Uncle Sam
US	Unconditional Selection
US	Unconditional Stop (IAA)
US	Unconditional Surrender
US	Unconditioned Stimulus [*Psychometrics*]
US	Underlying Stock [*Finance*]
US	Under Secretary
U/S	Underside
US	Undersize (AAG)
US	Underspeed (MSA)
US	Underwater-to-Surface (IAA)
US	Underwriters' Special Request
US	Undistorted Signal (IAA)
US	Uniform System
US	Union Settlement Association (EA)
US	Unitary Symmetry (MCD)
US	United Serpents (EA)
US	United Service
US	United Sisters [*Defunct*] (EA)
US	United States [*ANSI two-letter standard code*]
us	United States [*MARC country of publication code Library of Congress*] (LCCP)
US	United States
US	United States Reports [*A publication*] (NTCM)
US	United States Supreme Court Reports [*A publication*] (AAGC)
US	Unites States of America [*IYRU nationality code*] (IYR)
US	Unit Secretary (MEDA)
US	Unit Separator [*Control character*] [*Computer science*]
US	Universal Service [*News agency*]
US	Unknown Significance
US	Unlike-Sexed
US	Unregistered Stock [*Finance*]
US	Unserviceable
U/S	Unsorted
US	Update State [*Online database field identifier*]
US	Upper Segment (STED)
us	Upper Stage (NAKS)
US	Upper Stage (MCD)
US	Uprighting Subsystem [*NASA*] (KSC)
US	Up Stage [*Away from audience*] [*A stage direction*]
US	Upstream (NTCM)
US	USair Express [*ICAO designator*] (AD)
US	US Ammunition Co. [*Vancouver Stock Exchange symbol*]
US	Useless
US	User Segment (SSD)
US	Usher Syndrome (STED)
US	US Supreme Court Reports (GPO)
US	Uterine Stroma
US	Utility Satellite (IAA)
us	Ut Supra [*As Above*] [*Latin*] (WGA)
US 1 Inds	US One Industries, Inc. [*Formerly, Transcom, Inc.*] [*Associated Press*] (SAG)
US3	Unit Self-Sufficiency System (MCD)
USA	INFO-DOC [*ACCORD*] [*UTLAS symbol*]
USA	Liberty ALL-STAR Eqty [*NYSE symbol*] (TTSB)
USA	Liberty All-Star Equity [*NYSE symbol*] (SPSG)
USA	Ukiyo-E Society of America (EA)
USA	Ullage Simulation Assembly (MCD)
USA	Ultrasonic Agitation
USA	Ultrastable Arc Lamp
USA	Ultraviolet Spectral Analysis
USA	Underwater Society of America (EA)
USA	Underwriters Service Association
USA	Unicycling Society of America [*Later, USA, Inc.*] (EA)
USA	Uniform Sales Act [*Legal shorthand*] (LWAP)
USA	Union of South Africa
USA	Union Syndicale de l'Agriculture [*Union of Agricultural Workers*] [*Morocco*]
USA	United Savers Association (EA)
USA	United Scenic Artists (EA)
USA	United Secularists of America (EA)
USA	United Seniors Association, Inc.
USA	United Shareholders Association (EA)
USA	United Shareowners of America [*Defunct*] (EA)
USA	United Shoppers Association
USA	United Sidecar Association [*Later, USCA*] (EA)
USA	United Soccer Association [*Later, NASL*]
USA	United Socialist Alliance [*Sri Lanka*] [*Political party*]
USA	United Spoilers of America [*Later, MERCPAC*] (EA)
USA	United Sprint Association (EA)

USA .... United States [ANSI three-letter standard code]
USA .... United States Army
USA .... United States Attorney (EPA)
USA .... United States Automobile Association, San Antonio, TX [OCLC symbol] (OCLC)
USA .... United States of ACORN [Publication of the Association of Community Organizations for Reform Now]
USA .... United States of America
USA .... United Steelworkers of America
USA .... United Stockcar Alliance [Auto racing]
USA .... United Student Aid Funds (EA)
USA .... United Students for America [Defunct] (EA)
USA .... United Support of Artists [In USA for Africa, the chorus of American pop stars who recorded "We Are the World" to benefit famine victims in Africa]
USA .... United Synagogue of America (EA)
USA .... Unit Services Assistant [Administration] (DAVI)
USA .... Unity for Safe Airtravel [Program of Air Line Pilots Association]
USA .... Universal Subject Access [Librarianship]
USA .... Unix Systems Association [Defunct] (EA)
USA .... Unsegmented Storage Analyzer [Instrumentation]
USA .... Urban Sanitary Authority [British]
USA .... US Air [ICAO designator] (FAAC)
USA .... Utility Shareholders Association (EA)
USAA .... United Specialty Agents Alliance [Also known as USA Alliance] (EA)
USAA .... United States Academy of Arms [Defunct] (EA)
USAA .... United States Arbitration Act [A publication] (DLA)
USAA .... United States Armor Association (EA)
USAA .... United States Athletes Association (EA)
USAA .... US Albacore Association (EA)
USAA .... US Armbrust Association (EA)
USAA .... US Armor Association (EA)
USAAA .... United States Army Audit Agency
USAAA .... US Amputee Athletic Association (EA)
USAAAVS .... United States Army Agency for Aviation Safety [Formerly, USABAAR] (AABC)
USAAAWR .... United States Army Audit Agency, Washington Region
USAAB .... United States Army Aviation Board
USAABELCTBD... United States Army Airborne and Electronics Board [Later, USAAESWBD]
USA/ABF .... USA Amateur Boxing Federation (EA)
USAABMDA... United States Army Advanced Ballistic Missile Defense Agency (AABC)
USAABMU .... United States Army Aircraft Base Maintenance Unit (AABC)
USAABNAELCTBD... United States Army Airborne and Electronics Board (IAA)
USAABNSOTBD... United States Army Airborne and Special Operations Test Board (GFGA)
USAAC .... United States Army Administration Center [Obsolete] (AABC)
USAAC .... United States Army Air Corps
USAAC .... United States Army Aviation Center [Fort Rucker]
USAACDA .... United States Army Aviation Combat Developments Agency [CDC]
USAACEBD... United States Army Airborne Communications and Electronics Board
USAACS .... United States Army Armor Center and School
USAADASCH... United States Army Air Defense Artillery School
USAADAT .... United States Army Alcohol and Drug Abuse Team Training (MCD)
USAADB .... United States Army Air Defense Board
USAADCEN... United States Army Air Defense Center
USAADCENFB... United States Army Air Defense Center and Fort Bliss (AABC)
USAADCS .... United States Army Air Defense Center and School
USAADEA .... United States Army Air Defense Engineering Agency [Formerly, USASADEA] [AEC]
USAADMAC... United States Army Aeronautical Depot Maintenance Center
USAADS .... United States Army Air Defense School (AABC)
USAADTA .... United States Army Aircraft Development Test Activity
USAADTC .... United States Army Armor and Desert Training Center
USAADVCOM... United States Army Advance Command
USAAEFA .... United States Army Aviation Engineering Flight Activity [Edwards Air Force Base, CA]
USAAESWBD... United States Army Airborne, Electronics, and Special Warfare Board (AABC)
USAAF .... United States Army Air Forces
USAAFIME .... United States Army Air Forces in the Middle East
USAAFINO .... United States Army Aviation Flight Information and Nav-Aids Office (AABC)
USAAFIO .... United States Army Aviation Flight Information Office
USAAFO .... United States Army Avionics Field Office [Formerly, USASAFO]
USAAFUK .... United States Army Air Forces in the United Kingdom
USAAGAR .... United States Army Advisor Group O - Army Reserve (AABC)
USAAGCDA .... United States Army Adjutant General Combat Developments Agency (SAA)
USAAGDPSC... United States Army Adjutant General Data Processing Service Center (AABC)
USAAGNG .... United States Army Advisory Group (National Guard) (AABC)
USAAGPC .... United States Army Adjutant General Publications Center
USAAGS .... United States Army Adjutant General's School (AABC)
USAALS .... United States Army Aviation Logistics School (INF)
USAAMA .... United States Army Advent Management Agency (MUGU)
USAAMC .... United States Army Aeromedical Center
USAAMC .... United States Army Artillery and Missile Center
USAAMCCOM... United States Army Armament, Munitions, and Chemical Command
USAAML .... United States Army Aviation Materiel Laboratories
USAAMRDC... United States Army Air Mobility Research and Development Center
USAAMRDL... United States Army Air Mobility Research and Development Laboratory [Also, AMR& DL, USAAMR & DL]

USAAMS .... United States Army Artillery and Missile School [Later, Field Artillery School]
USAAPDT .... United States Army Aviation Precision Demonstration Team (AABC)
USAAPSA .... United States Army Ammunition Procurement and Supply Agency
USAARC .... United States Antiaircraft Replacement Center
USAARCOM .... United States Army Armament Command
USAARDC .... United States Army Aberdeen Research and Development Center
USAARDEC... United States Army Armament Research Development and Engineering Center
USAARENBD... United States Army Armor and Engineer Board (AABC)
USAARL .... United States Army Aeromedical Research Laboratory [Ft. Rucker, AL] (AABC)
USAARMA .... United States Assistant Army Attache
USAARMBD... United States Army Armor Board
USAARMC .... United States Army Armor Center [Fort Knox, KY]
USAARMHRU... United States Army Armor Human Research Unit [Fort Knox, KY] (AABC)
USAARMS .... United States Army Armor School
USAARTYBD... United States Army Artillery Board
USAARTYCDA... United States Army Artillery Combat Developments (SAA)
USAARU .... United States Army Aeromedical Research Unit
USAAS .... United States Army Air Services [World War II]
USAAS .... United States Army Armor Signals (IAA)
USAASC .... United States Army Air Service Command
USAASCFBH... United States Army Administrative School Center and Fort Benjamin Harrison (AABC)
USAASD .... United States Army Aeronautical Services Detachment
USAASD-E .... United States Army Aeronautical Services Detachment, Europe (AABC)
USAASD-LA... United States Army Aeronautical Services Detachment, Latin America (AABC)
USAASD-PAC... United States Army Aeronautical Services Detachment, Pacific (AABC)
USAASL .... United States Army Atmospheric Sciences Laboratory (RDA)
USAASO .... United States Army Aeronautical Services Office (AABC)
USAASTA .... United States Army Aviation Systems Test Activity [Also, AASTA]
USAATBD .... United States Army Arctic Test Board
USAATC .... United States Army Arctic Test Center
USAATCO .... United States Army Air Traffic Coordinating Officer
USAATMS .... United States Army Air Traffic Management System
USAAVA .... United States Army Audio-Visual Agency (AABC)
USAAVCOM... United States Army Aviation Materiel Command (AABC)
USAAVLABS... United States Army Aviation Materiel Laboratories (AABC)
USAAVNBD... United States Army Aviation Board
USAAVNC .... United States Army Aviation Center [CONARC]
USAAVNDTA... US Army Aviation Development Test Activity [Fort Rucker, AL] (GRD)
USAAVNHRU... United States Army Aviation Human Research Unit [Ft. Rucker, AL] (AABC)
USAAVNS .... United States Army Aviation School [CONARC]
USAAVNSC... United States Army Aviation Systems Command
USAAVNTA .... United States Army Aviation Test Activity (AABC)
USAAVNTBD... United States Army Aviation Test Board
USAAVRADCOM... United States Army Aviation Research and Development Command
USAAVS .... United States Agency for Aviation Safety (MCD)
USAAVSCOM... United States Army Aviation Systems Command [Obsolete] (AABC)
USAB .... United States Activities Board (IAA)
USAB .... United States Air Base (AAG)
USAB .... United States Army, Berlin (AABC)
USAB .... USABancShares'A' [NASDAQ symbol] (TTSB)
USAB .... USABancshares, Inc. [NASDAQ symbol] (SAG)
USAB .... US Activities Board [IEEE]
USAB .... US Animal Bank (EA)
USABA .... US Association for Blind Athletes (EA)
USABAAR .... United States Army Board for Aviation Accident Research [Later, USAAAVS]
USABC .... United States Advanced Battery Consortium
USABD .... United States Army Air Defense Artillery Board
USABDA .... United States Amateur Ballroom Dancers Association (EA)
USABESRL .... United States Behavioral Science Research Laboratory [Obsolete] (IEEE)
USABF .... United States Amateur Baseball Federation
USA-BIAC .... USA - Business and Industry Advisory Committee to the OECD [Organization for Economic Cooperation and Development] (EA)
USABIOLABS... United States Army Biological Laboratories (AABC)
USABnc .... USABancshares, Inc. [Associated Press] (SAG)
USABRDL .... United States Army Biomedical Research and Development Laboratory [Fort Detrick, MD]
USABRL .... United States Army Ballistic Research Laboratories (AABC)
USABVAPAC... United States Army Broadcasting and Visual Activities, Pacific
USAC .... Union des Syndicats Autonomes Camerounais [Federation of Cameroonese Autonomous Unions]
USAC .... United States Activities Committee (IAA)
USAC .... United States Air Corps
USAC .... United States Alpine Club [Defunct]
USAC .... United States Apparel Council [Defunct] (EA)
USAC .... United States Archery Congress [Defunct] (EA)
USAC .... United States Army Corps (AABC)
USAC .... United States Auto Club (EA)
USAC .... United States of America Confederation [Later, USAC/RS] (EA)
USAC .... Universal Seismic Associates [NASDAQ symbol] (SAG)
USAC .... Univl Seismic Assoc [NASDAQ symbol] (TTSB)
USAC .... Urban Information Systems Inter-Agency Committee [HUD Terminated] (EGAO)

USAC .... US Aquaculture Council [Defunct] (EA)

USAC .... User Services Advisory Committee [NERComP]

USAC .... Utah State Agricultural College

USACA .... United States Advanced Ceramics Association

USACA .... United States Allied Commission Austria

USACA .... United States Army Civil Affairs [World War II]

USACA .... United States Army Communications Agency

USACA .... US A-Division Catamaran Association (EA)

USACAA .... United States Army Concepts Analysis Agency (AABC)

USACAC .... United States Army Combined Arms Center (AABC)

USACAC ...... United States Army Continental Army Command [CONARC] [Superseded by FORSCOM]

USACACDA ... United States Army Civil Affairs Combat Developments Agency (SAA)

USACAE .... United States Army Contracting Agency, Europe (AAGC)

USACAF .... United States Army Construction Agency, France

USACAG .... United States Army Combined Arms Group (SAA)

USACAK .... United States Army Construction Agency, Korea

US-ACAN ..... United States Advisory Committee on Antarctic Names [1947-]

USACAP ...... United States Army Chemical Activity, Pacific (DOMA)

USACARA .... United States Army Civilian Appellate Review Agency (GFGA)

USACARMSCDA... United States Army Combined Arms Combat Developments Agency

USACAS .... United States Army Civil Affairs School

USACATB ..... United States Army Combat Arms Training Board (AABC)

USACBRWOC... United States Army Chemical, Biological, and Radiological Weapons Orientation Course (AABC)

USACBRWOCAAB... United States Army Chemical, Biological, and Radiological Weapons Orientation Course Academic Advisory Board (AABC)

USACC .... United States Army Communications Command (AABC)

USACC .... USA Convertible Club [Defunct] (EA)

USACC .... US-Arab Chamber of Commerce [Defunct] (EA)

USACC-A ...... United States Army Communications Command - Alaska (AABC)

USACCA .... United States Army Congressional Correspondence Agency (AABC)

USACC-AMC... United States Army Communications Command - Army Materiel Command (AABC)

USACC COMMAGCY-HSC... United States Army Communications Command Communications Agency - Health Services Command (AABC)

USACC COMMAGCY-MTMC... United States Army Communications Command Communications Agency - Military Traffic Management Command (AABC)

USACC COMMAGCY-USACIDC... United States Army Communications Command Communications Agency - United States Army Criminal Investigation Command (AABC)

USACC COMMAGCY-USAINTC... United States Army Communications Command Communications Agency - United States Army Intelligence Center

USACC-CONUS... United States Army Communications Command - Continental United States (AABC)

USACCE .... United States Army Contracting Command, Europe (AAGC)

USACC-EUR... United States Army Communications Command - Europe (AABC)

USACC-FORCES... United States Army Communications Command - Forces (AABC)

USACCIA ...... United States Army Chemical Corps Intelligence Agency

USACCL .... United States Army Coating and Chemical Laboratory (AABC)

USACCO .... United States Army Commercial Communications Office

USACC-PAC... United States Army Communications Command - Pacific (AABC)

USACC-R/FMD... United States Army Communications Command Radio and Frequency Management Division

USACCSA ...... United States Army Command and Control Support Agency

USACC-SAFCA... United States Army Communications Command Safeguard Communications Agency

USACCSD .... United States Army Command and Control Support Detachment (AABC)

USACC SIG GP (AD)... United States Army Communications Command Signal Group (AD)

USACC-SO ... United States Army Communications Command - South (AABC)

USACC-T ...... United States Army Communications Command - Thailand (AABC)

USACCTC .... United States Army Chemical Corps Technical Committee

USACC-TRADOC... United States Army Communications Command - Training and Doctrine Command (AABC)

USACD .... Arms Control and Disarmament Agency (AAGC)

USACDA .... United States Arms Control and Disarmament Agency

USACDA .... United States Army Catalog Data Agency (AABC)

USACDC .... United States Army Combat Developments Command

USACDCADA... United States Army Combat Developments Command Air Defense Agency [Fort Bliss, TX] (AABC)

USACDCAGA... United States Army Combat Developments Command Adjutant General Agency

USACDCARMA... United States Army Combat Developments Command Armor Agency [Fort Knox, KY] (AABC)

USACDCARTYA... United States Army Combat Developments Command Artillery Agency (AABC)

USACDCAVNA... United States Army Combat Developments Command Aviation Agency [Fort Rucker, AL] (AABC)

USACDCCA... United States Army Combat Developments Command Combined Arms Agency [Fort Leavenworth, KS]

USACDCCAA... United States Army Combat Developments Command Civil Affairs Agency [Fort Gordon, GA] (AABC)

USACDCCAG... United States Army Combat Developments Command Combat Army Group [Fort Le avenworth, KS] [Obsolete] (AABC)

USACDCCARMSA... United States Army Combat Developments Command Combat Arms Agency

USACDCCBRA... United States Army Combat Developments Command Chemical-Biological-Radiological Agency [Fort McClellan, AL] (AABC)

USACDCCEA... United States Army Combat Developments Command Communications-Electronics Agency [Fort Monmouth, NJ] (AABC)

USACDCCHA... United States Army Combat Developments Command Chaplain Agency [Fort Lee, VA] (AABC)

USACDCCOMSG... United States Army Combat Developments Command Combat Systems Group (AABC)

USACDCCONFG... United States Army Combat Developments Command Concept and Force Design Group (AABC)

USACDCCSG... United States Army Combat Developments Command Combat Support Group [Fort Belvoir, VA] [Obsolete] (AABC)

USACDCCSSG... United States Army Combat Developments Command Combat Service Support Group [Fort Lee, VA] [Obsolete] (AABC)

USACDCDPFO... United States Army Combat Developments Command Data Processing Field Office (AABC)

USACDCEA... United States Army Combat Developments Command Engineer Agency [Later, USACDCENA] [Fort Belvoir, VA]. (AABC)

USACDCEC... United States Army Combat Developments Command Experimentation Center [or Command] [Fort Ord, CA]

USACDCENA... United States Army Combat Developments Command Engineer Agency [Formerly, USACDCEA] (AABC)

USACDCFAA... United States Army Combat Developments Command Field Artillery Agency [Fort Sill, OK] (AABC)

USACDCFINA... United States Army Combat Developments Command Finance Agency (AABC)

USACDCIA ... United States Army Combat Developments Command Infantry Agency [Later, USACDCINA] [Fort Benning, GA] (AABC)

USACDCIAS... United States Army Combat Developments Command Institute of Advanced Studies [Carlisle Barracks, PA] [Obsolete] (AABC)

USACDCICAS... United States Army Combat Developments Command Institute of Combined Arms and Support [Fort Leavenworth, KS] [Obsolete] (AABC)

USACDCIDDFO... United States Army Combat Developments Command Internal Defense and Development Field Office (AABC)

USACDCILC... United States Army Combat Developments Command Institute of Land Combat [Alexandria, VA] [Obsolete] (AABC)

USACDCINA... United States Army Combat Developments Command Infantry Agency [Formerly, USACDCIA] (AABC)

USACDCINCSG... United States Army Combat Developments Command Intelligence and Control Systems Group (AABC)

USACDCINS... United States Army Combat Developments Command Institute of Nuclear Studies [Fort Bliss, TX] [Obsolete] (AABC)

USACDCINTA... United States Army Combat Developments Command Intelligence Agency [Fort Holabird, MD] (MCD)

USACDCISA... United States Army Combat Developments Command Institute of Systems Analysis [Fort Belvoir, VA] [Obsolete] (AABC)

USACDCISS... United States Army Combat Developments Command Institute of Special Studies [Fort Belvoir, VA] [Obsolete] (AABC)

USACDCISSO... United States Army Combat Developments Command Institute of Strategic and Stability Operations [Obsolete] (AABC)

USACDCJAA... United States Army Combat Developments Command Judge Advocate Agency [Charlottesville, VA] (AABC)

USACDCMA... United States Army Combat Developments Command Maintenance Agency [Aberdeen Proving Ground, MD] (AABC)

USACDCMPA... United States Combat Developments Command Military Police Agency [Fort Gordon, GA] (AABC)

USACDCMSA... United States Army Combat Developments Command Medical Service Agency [Fort Sam Houston, TX] (AABC)

USACDCNG... United States Army Combat Developments Command Nuclear Group [Fort Bliss, TX]

USACDCNUA... United States Army Combat Developments Command Nuclear Agency (AABC)

USACDCOA... United States Army Combat Developments Command Ordnance Agency [Aberdeen Proving Ground, MD]

USACDCPALSG... United States Army Combat Developments Command Personnel and Logistics Systems Group (AABC)

USACDCPASA... United States Army Combat Developments Command Personnel and Administrative Services Agency [Fort Benjamin Harrison, IN] (AABC)

USACDCQA... United States Army Combat Developments Command Quartermaster Agency [Fort Lee, VA]

USACDCSA... United States Army Combat Developments Command Supply Agency [Later, USACDCSUA] [Fort Lee, VA] (AABC)

USACDCSAG... United States Army Combat Developments Command Systems Analysis Group [Fort Belvoir, VA] (AABC)

USACDCSOA... United States Army Combat Developments Command Special Operations Agency (AABC)

USACDCSSI... United States Army Combat Developments Command Strategic Studies Institute (AABC)

USACDCSUA... United States Army Combat Developments Command Supply Agency [Formerly, USACDCSA] (AABC)

USACDCSWA... United States Army Combat Developments Command Special Warfare Agency [Fort Bragg, NC] (AABC)

USACDCSWCAG... United States Army Combat Developments Command Special Warfare and Civil AffairsGroup [Fort Belvoir, VA]

USACDCSWG... United States Army Combat Developments Command Special Warfare Group

USACDCTA... United States Army Combat Developments Command Transportation Agency [Fort Eustis, VA] (AABC)

USACDEC..... United States Army Combat Developments Experimentation Command (GFGA)

USACE .... United States Army Corps of Engineers [Merged with General Equipment Command]

USACEBD..... United States Army Airborne Communications and Electronics Board (AABC)

USACECDA...   United States Army Communications-Electronics Combat Developments Agency [*Fort Huachuca, AZ*]

USACECOM...   United States Army Communications and Electronics Command

USACEEIA....   United States Army Communications-Electronics Engineering Installation Agency [*Fort Huachuca, AZ*] (AABC)

USACEEIA-PAC...   United States Army Communications-Electronics Engineering Installation Agency-Pacific (RDA)

USACEEIA-WH...   United States Army Communications-Electronics Engineering Installation Agency - Western Hemisphere (AABC)

USACEIBN....   United States Army Communications-Electronics Installation Battalion (AABC)

USACENCDCSA...   United States Army Corps of Engineers National Civil Defense Computer Support Agency (AABC)

USACERCOM...   United States Army Communications and Electronics Material and Readiness Command

USACERL.....   US Army Construction Engineering Research Laboratory (RDA)

USACESSEC...   United States Army Computer Systems Support and Evaluation Command

USACFSC.....   United States Army Community and Family Support (AAGC)

USACFSC.....   United States Army Community and Family Support Center (DOMA)

USACGSC....   United States Army Command and General Staff College

USACHB......   United States Army Chaplain Board

USACHS......   United States Army Chaplain School

USACI........   United States Advisory Commission on Information

USACIC........   United States Army Criminal Investigation Command (BARN)

USACICD......   United States Army Criminal Investigation Command [*Formerly, USACIDA*] (AABC)

USACIDA......   United States Army Criminal Investigation Division Agency [*Later, USACICD*] (AABC)

USACIECA....   United States Advisory Commission on International Educational and Cultural Affairs

USACII........   United States of America Standard Code for Information Interchange (NOAA)

USACIL.......   United States Army Criminal Investigation Laboratory (AABC)

USACIR........   United States Army Criminal Investigation Repository

USACISO......   United States Army Counterinsurgency Support Office, Okinawa [*Obsolete*] (AABC)

USACIU........   United States Army Command Information Unit (AABC)

USACJE........   United Synagogue of America Commission on Jewish Education (EA)

USACM........   US Association for Computational Mechanics (EA)

USACMA......   United States Army Club Management Agency (AABC)

USACMLC....   United States Army Chemical Center [*Later, United States Army Ordnance and Chemical Center and School*]

USACMLCB...   United States Army Chemical Corps Board

USACMLCS...   United States Army Chemical Center and School [*Later, United States Army Ordnance and Chemical Center and School*] (AABC)

USACMLCSCH...   United States Army Chemical Corps School

USACMLRDL...   United States Army Chemical Research and Development Laboratories

USACMLS....   United States Army Chemical School (AABC)

USACMR......   United States Army Court of Military Review (AABC)

USACMS.....   United States Army Command Management School

USACOJE.....   United Synagogue of America Commission on Jewish Education (EA)

USACOM......   United States Atlantic Command [*DoD*]

USACOMISA...   United States Army Communications Management Information Systems Activity

USACOMZEUR...   United States Army Communications Zone, Europe

USACOR ......   US Association for the Club of Rome (EA)

USACORADCOM...   United States Army Communications Research and Development Command

USACPEB.....   United States Army Central Physical Evaluation Board (AABC)

USACRAPAC...   United States Army Command Reconnaissance Activities, Pacific Command

USACRC......   United States Army Crime Records Center (AABC)

USACRF.......   United States Army Counterintelligence Records Facility (MCD)

USACRREL....   United States Army Cold Regions Research and Engineering Laboratory (AABC)

USAC/RS......   United States Amateur Confederation of Roller Skating (EA)

USACRTC.....   United States Army Cold Regions Test Center (INF)

USACS.......   United States Army Combat Surveillance Agency (AAG)

USACS........   United States Army Courier Service (AABC)

USACSA......   United States Army Combat Surveillance Agency

USACSA.......   United States Army Communications Systems Agency (AABC)

USACSA.......   United States Army Contracting Support Agency (AAGC)

USACSC......   United States Army Computer Systems Command [*Fort Belvoir, VA*]

USACSG......   United States Army CINPAC Support Group

USACSLA.....   United States Army Communications Security Logistics Agency (AABC)

USACSR......   United States Air Corps Specialist Reserve

USACSS......   United States Army Chief of Support Services

USACSS.......   United States Army Combat Surveillance School (AABC)

USACSSAA...   United States Army Computer Systems Selection and Acquisition Agency (AABC)

USACSSC.....   United States Army Computer Systems Support and Evaluation Command (IEEE)

USACSSEA...   United States Army Computer Systems Support and Evaluation Agency (AABC)

USACSSEC...   United States Army Computer Systems Support and Evaluation Command

USACSTA.....   United States Army Combat Systems Test Activity [*Aberdeen Proving Ground, MD*]

USACSTA.....   United States Army Courier Station (AABC)

USACSTATC...   United States Army Combat Surveillance and Target Acquisition Training Command

USACT.........   United States Accident Containment Team [*Government agency in 1985 movie "Warning Sign"*]

USACTA.......   US Army Central TMDE [*Test, Measurement, and Diagnostic Equipment*] Activity (RDA)

USACTC......   United States Army Clothing and Textile Center

USACTMC....   United States Army Clothing and Textile Materiel Center

USACWL.....   United States Army Chemical Warfare Laboratory

USaD..........   Deseret Medical, Inc., Sandy, UT [*Library symbol*] [*Library of Congress*] (LCLS)

USAD........   United States Army Dispensary (AABC)

USAD.........   USA Detergents [*NASDAQ symbol*] (TTSB)

USAD..........   USA Detergents, Inc. [*NASDAQ symbol*] (SAG)

USADA.......   United States Amateur Dancers Association (EA)

USADAC.....   United States Army Davison Aviation Command (GFGA)

USADACS....   United States Army Defense Ammunition Center and School (AABC)

USADAOA....   United States Army Drug and Alcohol Operations Agency

USADATCOM...   United States Army Data Support Command

USADC........   United States Army Data Support Command

USADC.......   United States Army Dental Clinic

USADCJ......   United States Army Depot Command, Japan (AABC)

USADEG......   United States Army Dependents' Education Group (AABC)

USADESCOM...   United States Army Depot Support Command

USA Det.....   USA Detergents, Inc. [*Associated Press*] (SAG)

USADIP........   United States Army Deserter Information Point (AABC)

USADJ........   United States Army Depot, Japan (AABC)

USADOFL.....   United States Army Diamond Ordnance Fuze Laboratory [*Later, HDL*]

USADOG......   USA Defenders of Greyhounds [*An association*] (EA)

USADP........   Uniform Shipboard Automatic Data Processing

USADPC.....   United States Army Data Processing Center

USADPS.....   Uniform Automatic Data Processing System [*Navy*]

USADRB.....   United States Army Discharge Review Board (AABC)

USADSC......   United States Army Data Services and Administrative Systems Command

USA Dt.......   USA Detergents, Inc. [*Associated Press*] (SAG)

USADTC......   United States Army Armor and Desert Training Center (AABC)

USAE.........   United States Army Engineer

USAEAGSC...   United States Army, Europe, Adjutant General Support Center (AABC)

USAEARA.....   United States Army Equipment Authorization Review Activity (AABC)

USAEARC.....   United States Army Equipment Authorizations Review Center (AABC)

USAEB ....   United States Army Engineer Board

USAEC ....   United States Army Electronics Command [*Obsolete*]

USAEC ....   United States Army Environmental Center (RDA)

USAEC ....   United States Atomic Energy Commission

USAECA......   United States Army Electronics Command Computation Agency [*Obsolete*] (AABC)

USAECAV.....   United States Army Engineer Construction Agency, Vietnam

USAECBDE...   United States Army Engineer Center Brigade (AABC)

USAECDA.....   United States Army Engineer Combat Developments Agency (SAA)

USAECFB.....   United States Army Engineer Center and Fort Belvoir (AABC)

USAECOM....   United States Army Electronics Command [*Obsolete*]

USAECR......   United States Army Engineer Center Regiment (AABC)

USAECV(P)...   United States Army Engineer Command, Vietnam (Provisional)

USAED.......   United States Army Engineer District

USAEDE.......   United States Army Engineer Division, Europe (AABC)

USAEDH......   United States Army Engineer Division, Huntsville (AABC)

USAEDLMV...   United States Army Engineer Division, Lower Mississippi Valley (AABC)

USAEDM......   United States Army Engineer Division, Mediterranean (AABC)

USAEDMR....   United States Army Engineer Division, Missouri River (AABC)

USAEDNA...   United States Army Engineer Division, North Atlantic (AABC)

USAEDNC ...   United States Army Engineer Division, North Central (AABC)

USAEDNE....   United States Army Engineer Division, New England (AABC)

USAEDNP ...   United States Army Engineer Division, North Pacific (AABC)

USAEDOR....   United States Army Engineer Division, Ohio River (AABC)

USAEDPO ...   United States Army Engineer Division, Pacific Ocean (AABC)

USAEDS......   US Atomic Energy Detection System (DOMA)

USAEDSA.....   United States Army Engineer Division, South Atlantic (AABC)

USAEDSP.....   United States Army Engineer Division, South Pacific (AABC)

USAEDSW....   United States Army Engineer Division, Southwestern (AABC)

USAEE.......   United States Association for Energy Economics (NTPA)

USAEEA ......   United States Army Enlistment Eligibility Activity (AABC)

USAEFMA ....   United States Army Electronics Command Financial Management Agency [*Obsolete*] (AABC)

USAEGD......   United States Army Engineer, Gulf District

USAEGIMRADA...   US Army Engineer, Geodesy, Intelligence, and Mapping Research and Development Agency (NOAA)

USAEHA......   United States Army Environmental Hygiene Agency [*Aberdeen Proving Ground, MD*] (AABC)

USAEHL .....   United States Army Environmental Health Laboratory

USAEIGHT...   Eighth United States Army (CINC)

USAEIS ......   United States Army Electronic Intelligence and Security (AABC)

USAEL ....   United States Army Electronics Laboratories (IAA)

USAELCTPG...   United States Army Electronic Proving Ground (IAA)

USAELRO.....   United States Army Electronics Logistics Research Office

USAELRU.....   United States Army Electronics Research Unit

USAEMA ......   United States Army Electronics Materiel Agency [*Formerly, USASSA*]

USAEMAFHPO...   United States Army Electronics Materiel Agency, Fort Huachuca Procurement Office

USAEMAFMPO...   United States Army Electronics Materiel Agency, Fort Monmouth Procurement Office

USAEMAPICO...   United States Army Electronics Materiel Agency, Plant Inventory Control Office
USAEMAWPO...   United States Army Electronics Materiel Agency, Washington Procurement Office
USAEMC ......   United States Army Engineer Maintenance Center   (SAA)
USAEMCA ....   United States Army Engineer Mathematical Computation Agency (AABC)
USAEMSA ....   United States Army Electronics Materiel Support Agency [*Formerly, USASMSA*]
USAENGCOMEUR...   United States Army Engineer Command, Europe   (AABC)
USAENPG ....   United States Army Engineer Power Group   (RDA)
USAENPG-ED...   United States Army Engineer Power Group Engineering Division [*Fort Belvoir, VA*]
USAEPA ....   United States Army Electronics Command Patent Agency [*Obsolete*]   (AABC)
USAEPG ....   United States Army Electronic Proving Ground [*Fort Huachuca, AZ*]
USAEPMARA...   United States Army, Europe, Personnel Management and Replacement Activity   (AABC)
USAEPOC .....   United States Army Engineer Procurement Office, Chicago
USAERA ....   United States Army Electronics Command Logistics Research Agency [*Obsolete*]   (AABC)
USAERADCOM...   United States Army Electronics Research and Development Command   (RDA)
USAERDA ....   United States Army Electronic Research and Development Agency
USAERDAW...   United States Army Electronics Research and Development Activity, White Sands [*New Mexico*]   (AABC)
USAERDL .....   United States Army Electronics Research and Development Laboratory [*Formerly, USASRDL*]   (MCD)
USAERDL .....   United States Army Engineer Research and Development Laboratories   (IAA)
USAEREC .....   United States Army Enlisted Records and Evaluation Center   (MCD)
USAERG ......   United States Army Engineer Reactor Group   (AABC)
USAERLO .....   United States Army Electronics Regional Labor Office
USAES ....   United States Army Engineer School
USAES ....   United States Association of Evening Students   (EA)
USAESC ......   United States Army Electronics Support Command   (AABC)
USAESC ......   United States Army Engineer Studies Center [*Fort Belvoir, VA*]
USAESEIA ...   United States Army Electronic Systems Engineering Installation Agency   (GFGA)
USAET & DL (ECOM)...   United States Army Electronics Technology and Devices Laboratory (Electronics Command)   (AABC)
USAETL ....   United States Army Engineer Topographic Laboratories [*Fort Belvoir, VA*]
USAEU ....   United States Army Exhibit Unit   (AABC)
USAEUR ....   United States Army, Europe   (MCD)
USAEWES ....   United States Army Engineer Waterways Experiment Station
USAF ....   Under Secretary of the Air Force   (AAGC)
USAF ....   United States Aikido Federation   (EA)
USAF ....   United States Air Force [*Washington, DC*]
USAF ....   United States Army Forces
USAF ....   United Student Aid Fund
USAF ....   United Students of America Foundation [*Defunct*]   (EA)
USAF ....   USA Foundation   (EA)
USAF ....   US Aquaculture Federation   (EA)
USAFA ....   United States Air Force Academy [*Colorado*]
USAFA ....   USA Finn Association   (EA)
USAFA ....   USA for Africa [*An association*]   (EA)
USAFA ....   US-Albania Friendship Association   (EA)
USAFABD ....   United States Army Field Artillery Board [*Fort Sill, OK*]   (AABC)
USAFAC ......   United States Army Finance and Accounting Center   (AABC)
USAFACFS ..   United States Army Field Artillery Center and Fort Sill   (AABC)
USAFACP .....   United States Air Force Ammunition Control Point
USAFACS ....   United States Air Force Air Crew School
USAFACS ....   United States Army Field Artillery Center and School
USAFADS .....   United States Air Force Air Demonstration Squadron
USAFADWC..   United States Air Force Air Defense Weapons Center   (MCD)
USAFAG ......   United States Air Force Auditor General
USAFAGOS...   United States Air Force's Air-Ground Operations School
USAFALCENT...   United States Air Force Airlift Center
USAFAP ......   United States Air Force Art Program
USAFAPC ....   United States Air Force Airframe Production Contract
USAFAPS ....   United States Air Force Air Police School
USAFAS ......   United States Army Field Artillery School [*Fort Sill, OK*]   (AABC)
USAFAS/MSL...   United States Army Field Artillery School Morris Swett Technical Library Division [*Fort Sill, OK*]
USAFAVLO...   United States Air Force Audiovisual Liaison Office
USAFB ....   United States Army Field Band   (AABC)
USAFBI ....   United States Army Forces in the British Isles
USAFBMD ...   United States Air Force Ballistic Missile Division
USAFBMS ...   United States Air Force Basic Military School
USAFBS ......   United States Air Force Bandsman School   (AFM)
USAFBS ......   United States Air Force Bombardment School
USAFCBI .....   United States Forces, China, Burma, India [*World War II*]
USAFCBIT ...   United States Forces, China, Burma, India Theater [*World War II*]
USAFCC ......   United States Army Forces in Central Canada [*World War II*]
USAFCED ....   United States Air Force Communications Electronics Doctrine   (IAA)
USAF CMR..   United States Air Force Court of Military Review   (AFM)
USAFCO ......   United States Air Force, Southern Command   (MCD)
USAF CPT ..   United States Air Force Cockpit Procedures Trainer
USAFCRL ....   United States Air Force Cambridge Research Laboratories
USAFD ....   United States Air Force Dictionary [*A publication*]
USAFE ....   United States Air Force in Europe
USAFEC ......   United States Army Forces in Eastern Canada [*World War II*]
USAFECI .....   United States Air Force Extension Course Institute
USAF/EDA....   Society of United States Air Force Flight Surgeons   (EA)

USAFEHL .....   United States Air Force Environmental Health Laboratory
USAFEISC ....   United States Air Forces in Europe Inspection and Safety Center
USAFEL ....   United States Air Force Epidemiological Laboratory   (AFM)
USAFEPC .....   United States Air Forces in Europe Personnel Center
USAFESA ....   United States Army Facilities Engineering Support Agency   (AABC)
USAFESA-ED...   United States Army Facilities Engineering Support Agency Engineering Division
USAFESA-RT...   United States Army Facilities Engineering Support Agency Research and TechnologyDivision
USAFESA-RTD...   United States Army Facilities Engineering Support Agency Research and TechnologyDivision
USAFESA-T...   United States Army Facilities Engineering Support Agency Technology Support Division [*Fort Belvoir, VA*]
USAFESA-TS...   United States Army Facilities Engineering Support Agency - Technology Support Division
USAFESA-TSD...   United States Army Facilities Engineering Support Agency - Technology Support Division
USAFE-T .....   United States Air Forces in Europe - Turkey
USAFETAC ...   United States Air Force Environmental Technical Applications Center [*Scott Air Force Base, IL*]   (AFM)
USAFETC .....   United States Air Force Environmental Technical Application Center [*Scott Air Force Base, IL*]
USAFETO ....   United States Army Forces, European Theater of Operations [*World War II*]
USAFETPS ...   United States Air Force Experimental Test Pilot School
USAFEURPCR...   United States Air Force European Postal and Courier Region (AFM)
USAFEUSA...   United States Army Forces (Korea), Eighth United States Army
USAFF ....   USA Film Festival   (EA)
USAFFACG...   United States Air Force Field Activity Group
USAFFACS ...   United States Air Force Field Activity Squadron
USAFFE ....   United States Army Forces, Far East [*World War II*]
USAFFGS ....   United States Air Force Flexible Gunnery School
USAFFSR ....   United States Air Force Flight Safety Research
USAFH ....   United States Air Force Hospital
USAFHA ......   USA Field Hockey Association   (EA)
USAFHD ......   United States Air Force Historical Division
USAFHG ......   United States Air Force Honor Guard
USAFHRC ....   United States Air Force Historical Research Center
USAFI ....   United States Armed Forces Institute
USAFIA ....   United States Army Forces in Australia
USAFIC ....   United States Association of Firearm Instructors and Coaches   (EA)
USAFICA .....   United States Army Forces in Central Africa [*World War II*]
USAFICPA ...   United States Army Forces in Central Pacific Area
USAFIFC .....   United States Air Force Instrument Flight Center   (AFM)
USAFIGED...   United States Armed Forces Institute Test of General Educational Development   (AEBS)
USAFIK ....   United States Army Forces in Korea
USAFIL ....   United States Army Forces in Liberia [*World War II*]
USAFIME .....   United States Armed Forces in Middle East
USAFINCISCOM...   United States Army Finance and Comptroller Information Systems Command   (AABC)
USAFINTEL...   United States Air Force Intelligence Publication
USAFINZ .....   United States Army Forces in New Zealand
USAFIP(NL)...   United States Army Forces in the Philippines (Northern Luzon) [*World War II*]
USAFISA .....   US Army Force Integration Staff Agency   (RDA)
USAFISPA ...   United States Army Forces in the South Pacific Area
USAFIT ....   United States Air Force Institute of Technology
USAFIWS ....   United States Air Force Interceptor Weapons School
USAFLANT ...   United States Air Forces, Atlantic   (AABC)
USAFM ....   United States Air Force Manual [*A publication*]   (AAGC)
USAFMC ......   United States Association of Former Members of Congress   (EA)
USAFMD ......   United States Army Frequency Management Directorate   (MCD)
USAFMEPCR...   United States Air Force Mideast Postal and Courier Region   (AFM)
USAFMEPCS...   United States Air Force Mideast Postal and Courier Service   (AFM)
USAFMIDPAC...   United States Army Forces, Middle Pacific [*See AFMIDPAC*] [*World War II*]
USAFMPC ....   United States Air Force Military Personnel Center
USAFMTC ....   United States Air Force Marksmanship Training Center
USAFMTO ....   United States Army Forces, Mediterranean Theater of Operations [*World War II*]
USAF/NRD ...   United States Air Force, National Range Division
USAFNS ......   United States Air Force Navigation School
USAFO ....   United States Army Field Office   (RDA)
USAFOB ......   USA Federation of Bocce   (EA)
USAFOCA ....   United States Army Field Operating Cost Agency   (AABC)
USAFOCS ....   United States Air Force Officer Candidate School
USAFOEHL...   United States Air Force Occupational and Environmental Health Laboratory [*Brooks Air Force Base, TX*]
USAFOF ......   United States Army Flight Operations Facility   (AABC)
USAFOMC...   US Air Force Occupational Measurement Center [*Randolph Air Force Base, TX*]   (GRD)
USAFOSR ....   United States Air Force Office of Scientific Research
USAFP ....   Uniformed Services Academy of Family Physicians   (EA)
USAFPAC ....   United States Air Forces, Pacific
USAFPACPCR...   United States Air Force Pacific Postal and Courier Region
USAFPCS ....   United States Air Force Postal and Courier Service
USAFPCS Eur-Me Rgn...   United States Air Force Postal and Courier Service, Europe-Mideast Region   (AFM)
USAFPCS LA Rgn...   United States Air Force Postal and Courier Service, Latin American Region   (AFM)
USAFPCS Pac Rgn...   United States Air Force Postal and Courier Service, Pacific Region   (AFM)

USAFPCS US Rgn... United States Air Force Postal and Courier Service, United States Region (AFM)
USAFPDC..... United States Air Force Personnel Development Center
USAFPEB ..... United States Air Force Physical Evaluation Board (AFM)
USAFPLREP... United States Air Force Plant Representative Office
USAFPOA..... United States Army Forces, Pacific Ocean Areas [World War II]
USAFPRO .... United States Air Force Plant Representative Office
USAFPS .... United States Air Force Pilot School
USAFR .... Union of South Africa
USAFR .... United States Air Force Representative (AFM)
USAFR .... United States Air Force Reserve
USAFRD....... United States Air Force Recruiting Detachment
USAFRED..... United States Air Force Forces, Readiness Command
USAFRG...... United States Air Force Recruiting Group
USAFRHL..... United States Air Force Radiological Health Laboratory
USAFRO....... United States Air Force Recruiting Office
USAFROTC... United States Air Force Reserve Officer Training Corps
USAFRR....... United States Air Force Resident Representative (MCD)
USAFRS .... United States Air Force Recruiting Service
USAFRSQ .... United States Air Force Recruiting Squadron
USAFS .... United States Army Finance School (AABC)
USAFSA...... United States Army Forces in South America
USAFSA...... United States Army Forces, South Atlantic [World War II]
USAFSAAS... United States Air Force School of Applied Aerospace Sciences (AFM)
USAFSACS... United States Air Force School of Applied Cryptologic Sciences (AFM)
USAFSAG..... United States Air Force Special Activities Group
USAFSAM .... United States Air Force School of Aerospace Medicine
USAFSAM/ED... Society of United States Air Force Flight Surgeons (EA)
USAFSAS..... United States Air Force Special Activities Squadron
USAFSAWC... United States Air Force Special Air Warfare Center (AFM)
USAFSBSS... United States Air Force Standard Base Supply System
USAFSC .... United States Army Food Service Center (AABC)
USAFSCHCS... United States Air Force School of Health Care Science
USAFSE .... United States Air Force Supervisory Examination (AFM)
USAFSG....... United States Army Field Support Group
USAFSNCOA... US Air Force Senior Noncommissioned Officer Academy (DOMA)
USAFSO....... United States Air Force Southern Air Division
USAFSO....... United States Air Forces Southern Command (AABC)
USAFSOC..... United States Air Force Special Operations Center (AFM)
USAFSOF..... United States Air Force Special Operations Force (AFM)
USAFSOS..... United States Air Force Special Operations School (AFM)
USAFSPA..... United States Air Force Security Policy Academy
USAFSRA..... United States Air Force Special Reporting Agency
USAFSS .... United States Air Force Security Service [Later, AFESC]
USAFSTC ..... United States Air Force Special Treatment Center (AFM)
USAFSTC ..... United States Army Foreign Science and Technology Center (AABC)
USAFSTRIKE... United States Air Forces Strike Command (AABC)
USAFTAC..... United States Air Force Technical Applications Center (MCD)
USAFTALC .. United States Air Force Tactical Airlift Center (AFM)
USAFTARC... United States Air Force Tactical Air Reconnaissance Center (AFM)
USAFTAWC... United States Air Force Tactical Air Warfare Center (AFM)
USAF TESTPLTSCH... United States Air Force Test Pilot School
USAFTFWC... United States Air Force Tactical Fighter Weapons Center (AFM)
USAFTMCP... United States Air Force Tactical Missile Control Point
USAFTPS ..... United States Air Force Test Pilot School (MCD)
USAFTS .... United States Air Force Technical School
USAFTTS ...... United States Air Force Technical Training School
USA FUNDS... United States Aid Funds [An association] (PAZ)
USAF-USPCR... United States Air Force - United States Postal Courier Region (AFM)
USAFWPLO... United States Air Force Water Port Logistics Office
USAFWPO... United States Air Force Water Port Liaison Office [or Officer] (AFM)
USAG........... Underwater Sound Advisory Group [Navy]
USAG........... United States Army Garrison (AABC)
USAG........... United States Army in Greece
USAGA........ United States of America Goju Association (DICI)
USAGEM...... US Atlantic and Gulf Ports/Eastern Mediterranean and North African Freight Conference [New York, NY] (EA)
USAGETA..... United States Army General Equipment Test Activity (AABC)
USAGF........ United States Army Ground Forces (MUGU)
USAGG........ United States Army Group, American Mission for Aid to Greece
USAG-HI...... United States Army Garrison-Hawaii
USAGIMRADA... United States Army Geodesy Intelligence and Mapping Research and Development Agency (AABC)
USAGMPA.... United States Army General Materiel and Petroleum Activity
USAGMPC.... United States Army General Materiel and Parts Center (AABC)
USAGPC...... United States Adjutant General Publications Center
USAGSC...... United States Army General Supplies Commodity Center
USAH.......... United States Army Hospital
USAH.......... USA Harvest [An association] (EA)
USAHA........ United States Animal Health Association (EA)
USAHAC...... United States Army Headquarters Area Command
USAHC....... United States Army Health Clinic (AABC)
USAHEL...... United States Army Human Engineering Laboratories (AABC)
USAHI......... United States Army History Institute (PDAA)
USAHOME... United States Army Homes [Prefabricated houses, shipped overseas]
USAHPSA... US Army Health Professional Support Agency (DOMA)
USAHS........ United States Army Hospital Ship
USAHSC...... United States Army Health Service Command
USAHSDSA... United States Army Health Services Data Systems Agency (AABC)
USAHTN...... United States Army Hometown News Center (AABC)
USAI .... US-Asia Institute (EA)
USAIA .... United States Army Institute of Administration (AABC)

USAIA......... United States Army Intelligence Agency (GFGA)
USAIAS....... United States Army Institute of Advanced Studies (SAA)
USAIB .... United States Army Infantry Board
USAIC .... United States Army Infantry Center [Fort Benning, GA]
USAIC .... United States Army Intelligence Center (IAA)
USAIC .... United States Army Intelligence Command
USAICA....... United States Army Interagency Communications Agency (AABC)
USAICS .... United States Army Intelligence Center and School [Fort Huachuca, AZ] (AABC)
USAID .... United States Agency for International Development [Also, AID]
USAIDR....... United States Army Institute of Dental Research (AABC)
USAID/REDSO/WCA... [The] US Agency for International Development's Regional Economic Development Services Office for West and Central Africa (ECON)
USAIDSC..... United States Army Information and Data Systems Command
USAIDSCOM... United States Army Information and Data Systems Command (AABC)
USAID/W..... United States Agency for International Development, Washington (PDAA)
USAIG........ United States Aircraft Insurance Group
USAIGC....... United States Association of Independent Gymnastic Clubs (EA)
USAIIA .... United States Army Imagery Interpretation Agency (AABC)
USAIIC .... United States Army Imagery Interpretation Center (AABC)
USAILC .... United States Army International Logistics Center
USAILCOM... United States Army International Logistics Command (AABC)
USAILG....... United States Army International Logistics Group (AABC)
USAIMA...... United States Army Institute for Military Assistance [Fort Bragg, NC] (AABC)
USAIMC...... United States Army Inventory Management Center (AABC)
USAIMS ...... United States Army Institute for Military Systems (AABC)
USAIN .... United States Agricultural Information Network
USA Inc ...... Unicycling Society of America, Inc. (EA)
USAINFHRU... United States Army Infantry Human Research Unit [Ft. Benning, GA] (AABC)
USAINSB..... United States Army Intelligence Security Board
USAINSBD ... United States Army Intelligence and Security Board (MCD)
USAINSCOM... United States Army Intelligence and Security Command
USAINTA..... United States Army Intelligence Agency (AABC)
USAINTB..... United States Army Intelligence Board
USAINTC..... United States Army Intelligence Center
USAINTCA... United States Army Intelligence Corps Agency
USAINTCDA... United States Army Intelligence Combat Developments (SAA)
USAINTELMDA... United States Army Intelligence Materiel Developments Agency (AABC)
USAINTS..... United States Army Intelligence School
USAIPSG..... United States Army Industrial and Personnel Security Group
USAIRA....... United States Air Attache
USAIRC....... United States Army Ionizing Radiation Center
UsairG....... United States Air Group [Associated Press] (SAG)
UsairG .... USAir Group, Inc. [Associated Press] (SAG)
USAIRLO..... United States Air Liaison Officer (CINC)
USAIRMILCOMUN... United States Air Force Representative, UN Military Staff Committee
USAIRO....... United States Army Inventory Research Office [Philadelphia, PA]
USAIRR....... United States Army Investigative Records Repository (AABC)
USAIS .... United States Army Infantry School
USAISC....... Information Systems Command [Army] (AAGC)
USAISC....... United States Army Information Systems Command [Fort Huachuca, AZ]
USAISC-5th Sig Cmd... United States Army Information Systems Command - 5th Signal Command (GFGA)
USAISC-7th Sig Cmd... United States Army Information Systems Command - 7th Signal Command (GFGA)
USAISC-A .... United States Army Information Systems Command - Alaska (GFGA)
USAISC-AMC... United States Army Information Systems Command - Army Materiel Command (GFGA)
USAISC-FORSCOM... United States Army Information Systems Command - Forces Command (GFGA)
USAISC-HSC... United States Army Information Systems Command - Health Services Command (GFGA)
USAISC-INSCOM... United States Army Information Systems Command - Intelligence and Security Command (GFGA)
USAISC-MTMC... United States Army Information Systems Command - Military Traffic Management Command (GFGA)
USAISC-SO... United States Army Information Systems Command - South (GFGA)
USAISC-TRADOC... United States Army Information Systems Command - Training and Doctrine Command (GFGA)
USAISC-WESTCOM... United States Army Information Systems Command - Western Command (GFGA)
USAISD....... United States Army Intelligence School, Fort Devens (GFGA)
USAISESA.... United States Army Information Systems Engineering Support Activity [Fort Huachuca, AZ]
USAISMA..... United States Army Information Systems Management Activity (GFGA)
USAISR....... United States Army Institute of Surgical Research [Ft. Sam Houston, TX] (AABC)
USAISSAA.... United States Army Information Systems Selection and Acquisition Activity (GFGA)
USAISSSC.... United States Army Information Systems Software Support Command (GFGA)
USA-ITA...... United States Association of Importers of Textiles and Apparel (EA)
USAITAC...... United States Army Intelligence and Threat Analysis Center (AABC)
USAITAD...... United States Army Intelligence Threat Analysis Detachment
USAITAG...... United States Army Intelligence Threat Analysis Group
USAITC .... United States Army Intelligence Training Center

USAITFG ...... United States Army Intelligence Threats and Forecasts Group (AABC)
USAJAPA ..... United States Amateur Jai Alai Players Association (EA)
USAJFKCENMA ... United States Army John Fitzgerald Kennedy Center for Military Assistance (AABC)
USAJFKCENSPWAR ... United States Army John Fitzgerald Kennedy Center for Special Warfare [*Airborne*] (AABC)
USAJFKSWCS ... US Army John F. Kennedy Special Warfare Center and School (RDA)
USAJHGSOWA ... United States Army Joint Household Goods Shipping Office of the Armed Forces
USAJPG ...... United States Army Jefferson Proving Ground (PDAA)
USAJSC .... United States Army Joint Support Command (AABC)
USAK .... USA Truck [*NASDAQ symbol*] (SAG)
USAKA .... US Army Kwajalein Atoll (DOMA)
USAKF .... USA Karate Federation (EA)
USA-KKA ...... USA-Korean Karate Association (EA)
USAKORSCOM ... United States Army Korea Support Command (AABC)
US AI .... US Alcohol Testing of America, Inc. [*Associated Press*] (SAG)
USALA .... United States Amateur Lacrosse Association
USALAPA ..... United States Army Los Angeles Procurement Agency (AABC)
USALC .... United States Army Logistics Center
US AIc .... US Alcohol Testing of America, Inc. [*Associated Press*] (SAG)
USALCA .... United States Army Logistic Control Activity (AABC)
USALCJ .... United States Army Logistics Center, Japan (AABC)
USALDC .... United States Army Logistics Data Center
USALDJ .... United States Army Logistics Depot, Japan
USALDRHRU ... United States Army Leadership Human Research Unit [*Presidio of Monterey, CA*] (AABC)
USALDSRA ..... United States Army Logistics Doctrine, Systems and Readiness Agency [*New Cumberland Army Depot, Harrisburg, PA*] (AABC)
USALEA .... United States Army Logistics Evaluation Agency (AABC)
USALGPM ..... United States Army Liaison Group, Project Michigan
USALMC .... United States Army Logistics Management Center [*Fort Lee, VA*]
USALOGC ...... United States Army Logistics Center (AABC)
USALOGCTR ... United States Army Logistics Center
USALS .... United States Army Language School
USALSA .... United States Army Legal Services Agency (AABC)
USALWL ...... United States Army Limited War Laboratory (AABC)
USAM .... Unified Space Applications Mission (MCD)
USAM .... Uniformly-Sampled-Autoregressive Moving Average (PDAA)
USAM .... Union des Syndicats Autonomes de Madagascar [*Federation of Malagasy Autonomous Unions*]
USAM .... Unique Sequential Access Method
USAM .... United States Army Mothers Organization, National (EA)
USAM .... United States Automated Mail Service [*Telecommunications*] (TSSD)
USAM .... US Attorney's Manual [*A publication*] (DLA)
USAMAA .... United States Army Memorial Affairs Agency (AABC)
USAM & TTC ... United States Army Mechanical and Technical Training Center [*Also called MECHTECH*]
USAMANRRDC ... United States Army Manpower Resources Research and Development Center (AABC)
USAMAPLA ... United States Army Military Assistance Program Logistics Agency
USAMAPS .... United States Army Military Academy Preparatory School
USAMARDA ... US Army Manpower Requirements and Documentation Agency
USAMB .... United States Army Maintenance Board (AABC)
USAMBRDL ... United States Army Medical Bioengineering Research and Development Laboratory [*Fort Detrick, MD*] [*Later, USABRDL*] (AABC)
USAMBRL ..... United States Army Medical Biomechanical Research Laboratory [*Walter Reed Army Medical Center*] (AABC)
USAMC .... United States Army Materiel Command [*Alexandria, VA*]
USAMC .... United States Army Medical Corps
USAMC .... United States Army Missile Command [*Obsolete*]
USAMC .... United States Army Mobility Command [*Later, Troop Support Command*]
USAMC .... United States Army Munitions Command [*Later, Armaments Command*]
USAMCALMSA ... United States Army Materiel Command Automated Logistics Management Systems Agency (AABC)
USAMCC ...... United States Army Metrology and Calibration Center (AABC)
USAMCFG .... United States Army Medical Center, Fort Gordon (AABC)
USAMCFO .... United States Army Materiel Command Field Office (RDA)
USAMCFSA ... United States Army Materiel Command Field Safety Agency (AABC)
USAMCI & SA ... United States Army Materiel Command Installations and Service Agency (AABC)
USAMC-IRO ... United States Army Materiel Command Inventory Research Office
USAMC-ITC ... United States Army Materiel Command Intern Training Center
USAMCLDC ... United States Army Materiel Command Logistics Data Center
USAMCLSSA ... United States Army Materiel Command Logistic Systems Support Agency (AABC)
USAMCSFO ... United States Army Materiel Command Surety Field Office
USAMD .... United States Army Missile Detachment (AABC)
USAMDAR ... United States Army Medical Depot Activity, Ryukyu Islands (AABC)
USAMDPC ... United States Army Maintenance Data Processing Center
USAMDW ..... United States Army Military District of Washington (BARN)
USAMEAF .... United States Army Middle East Air Forces [*World War II*]
USAMEC ...... United States Army Mobility Equipment Command [*Obsolete*]
USAMECOM ... United States Army Mobility Equipment Command [*Obsolete*] (AABC)
USAMEDCOMEUR ... United States Army Medical Command, Europe (AABC)
USAMEDDBD ... United States Army Medical Department Board (RDA)
USAMEDLAB ... United States Army Medical Laboratory
USAMEDS .... United States Army Medical Service
USAMEDSVS ... United States Army Medical Service Veterinary School (AABC)

USAMEDTC ... United States Army Medical Training Center [*Ft. Sam Houston, TX*] (AABC)
USAMEERU ... United States Army Medical Environmental Engineering Research Unit
USAMEOS .... United States Army Medical Equipment and Optical School (AABC)
USAMERCC ... United States Army Middle East Regional Communications Command
USAMERDC ... United States Army Mobility Equipment Research and Development Center (AABC)
USAMERDL ... United States Army Medical Equipment Research and Development Laboratory (AABC)
USAMETA ..... United States Army Management Engineering Training Activity [*Rock Island, IL*] (AABC)
USAMFSS .... United States Army Medical Field Service School (AABC)
USAMGIK ..... United States Army Military Government in Korea
USAMHRC .... United States Army Military History Research Collection (AABC)
USAMICOM ... United States Army Missile Command [*Obsolete*] (AABC)
USAMIDA ..... United States Army Major Item Data Agency (AABC)
USAMIIA ...... United States Army Medical Intelligence and Information Agency (AABC)
USAML .... United States Army Medical Laboratory (AABC)
USAMMA ..... United States Army Medical Materiel Agency (AABC)
USAMMAE ... United States Army Materiel Management Agency, Europe
USAMMAPAC ... United States Army Medical Materiel Agency, Pacific (AABC)
USAMMC ..... United States Army Maintenance Management Center (AABC)
USAMMCE ... US Army Medical Material Center-Europe (DOMA)
USAMMCS ... United States Army Missile and Munitions Center School (AABC)
USAMMCSA ... US Army Medical Material Center-Saudi Arabia (DOMA)
USA-MMDA ... US Army Medical Materiel Development Activity (RDA)
USAMMT ..... United States Army Military Mail Terminal
USAMN ...... United States Army Mothers, National [*Defunct*] (EA)
USAMOAMA ... United States Army Medical Optical and Maintenance Activity
USAMOCOM ... United States Army Mobility Command [*Later, Troop Support Command*]
USAMOMA ... United States Army Medical Optical and Maintenance Agency (AABC)
USAMP .... United States Army Maintenance Plant
USAMP .... United States Army Mine Planter
USAMP .... United Stets Automotive Materials Partnership
USAMP & CS/TCTFM ... United States Army Military Police and Chemical Schools/ Training Center and FortMcClellan
USAMPHIBFOR ... United States Amphibious Forces (AABC)
USAMPS ...... United States Army Military Police School (AABC)
USAMPTAO ... United States Army Military Personnel and Transportation Assistance Office (AABC)
USAMRAA ... United States Army Medical Research Acquisition Agency
USAMRDALC ... US Army Medical Research, Development, Acquisition, and Logistics Command (RDA)
USAMRDC ... United States Army Medical Research and Development Command [*Fort Detrick, MD*]
USAMRICD ... United States Army Medical Research Institute for Chemical Defense [*Aberdeen Proving Ground, MD*] (RDA)
USAMRIID ... United States Army Medical Research Institute of Infectious Diseases [*Fort Detrick, MD*] (AABC)
USAMRL ..... United States Army Medical Research Laboratory [*Fort Knox, KY*] (AABC)
USAMRMC ... US Army Medical Research and Materiel Command (RDA)
USAMRN ..... United States Army Medical Research and Nutrition (MCD)
USAMRNL ... United States Army Medical Research and Nutrition Laboratory [*Denver, CO*] (AABC)
USAMRSA ... United States Army Material Readiness Support Activity
USAMRU ..... United States Army Medical Research Unit [*Malaysia, Panama*] (AABC)
USAMRU-E ... United States Army Medical Research Unit - Europe (INF)
USAMS ...... United States Army Management School
USAMSAA ... United States Army Materiel Systems Analysis Agency
USAMSMADHS ... United States Army Medical Service Meat and Dairy Hygiene School
USAMSSA .... United States Army Management Systems Support Agency
USAMTU ..... United States Army Marksmanship Training Unit
USAMU ...... United States Army Marksmanship Unit [*Fort Benning, GA*]
USAMU ...... United States Army Medical Unit [*Frederick, MD*]
USAMUCOM ... United States Army Munitions Command [*Later, Armaments Command*]
USAMUFD ... United States Army Medical Unit, Fort Detrick [*Maryland*] (AABC)
USAMV ...... United States Association of Museum Volunteers [*Later, AAMV*] (EA)
USAN .... United States Adopted Name
USANA .... United States Army Nuclear Agency (AABC)
USANA .... USANA, Inc. [*Associated Press*] (SAG)
USANAFBA ... United States Army, Navy, and Air Force Bandsmen's Association [*Defunct*]
USANAVEUR ... United States Navy, Europe
USANC .... United States Army Nurse Corps
USANCA ..... US Army Nuclear and Chemical Agency (RDA)
USANCG ..... United States Army Nuclear Cratering Group (AABC)
USANCSG .... United States Army Nuclear and Chemical Surety Group [*Formerly, USANWSG*] (AABC)
US&FCS ...... United States and Foreign Commercial Service (AAGC)
US & FCS .... US and Foreign Commercial Service [*Department of Commerce*] (CROSS)
U San Diego ... University of San Diego (GAGS)
USANDL ...... United States Army Nuclear Defense Laboratory (AABC)
USANF .... United States Auxiliary Naval Force
U San Fernando Valley L Rev ... University of San Fernando Valley. Law Review [*A publication*] (DLA)

U San Fernando VL Rev... University of San Fernando Valley. Law Review [*A publication*] (DLA)
U San Fran... University of San Francisco (GAGS)
USANG......... United States Army National Guard
USanGS....... Church of Jesus Christ of Latter-Day Saints, Genealogical Society Library, Santaquin Stake Branch, Santaquin, UT [*Library symbol Library of Congress*] (LCLS)
USANIBC...... United States Army Northern Ireland Base Command [*World War II*]
USANIF...... United States Army Northern Ireland Force [*World War II*]
USA-NLABS... United States Army Natick Laboratories
USANP......... United South African National Party
U Santa Clara... University of Santa Clara (GAGS)
USANWCG .. United States Army Nuclear Weapon Coordination Group
USANWSG .. United States Army Nuclear Weapon Surety Group [*Later, USANCSG*]
USANWTC... United States Army Northern Warfare Training Center (AABC)
USAOAC...... United States Army Ordnance Ammunition Command [*Merged with Munitions Command, which later became Armaments Command*]
USAOC & S.. United States Army Ordnance Center and School [*Later, United States Army Ordnance and Chemical Center and School*] (AABC)
USAOCBRL... United States Army Ordnance Corps Ballistic Research Laboratory
USAOCCCL... United States Army Ordnance Corps Coating and Chemical Laboratory
USAOCCS .... United States Army Ordnance-Chemical Center and School
USAOCDPS... United States Army Ordnance Corps Development and Proof Services
USAOD......... United States Army Ordnance District
USAOEC...... United States Army Officer Evaluation Center
USAOGMS ... United States Army Ordnance Guided Missile School
USAOMC...... United States Army Ordnance Missile Command [*Later, Missile Command*]
USAOMMCS... United States Army Ordnance Missile and Munitions Center and School
USAOMSA.... United States Army Ordnance Missile Support Agency (AAG)
USAORDCORPS... United States Army Ordnance Corps
USAORDMMCS... United States Army Ordnance Munitions and Missile Center and School
USAORP ...... United States Army Oversea Research Program
USAORRF .... United States Army Ordnance Rocket Research Facility
USAOSA...... United States Army Overseas Supply Agency (CINC)
USAOSANO... United States Army Overseas Supply Agency, New Orleans
USAOSANY... United States Army Overseas Supply Agency, New York
USAOSASF... United States Army Overseas Supply Agency, San Francisco
USAOSREPLSTA... United States Army Oversea Replacement Station
USAOSWAC... United States Army Ordnance Special Weapons-Ammunition Command
USAOTEA..... United States Army Operational Test and Evaluation Agency
USAOWC...... United States Army Ordnance Weapons Command [*Merged with Missile Command*]
USAP .... United States Antarctic Program [*National Science Foundation*]
US Ap ...... United States Appeals Reports [*A publication*] (DLA)
USAP .... Universal Stainless & Alloy Products [*NASDAQ symbol*] (SAG)
USAP .... Univl Stainless/Alloy Prods [*NASDAQ symbol*] (TTSB)
USAP .... USA Petites [*An association*] (EA)
USAPA...... United States Army Photographic Agency [*Obsolete*]
USAPACDA... United States Army Personnel and Administration Combat Developments Activity (AABC)
USAPAE...... United States Army Procurement Agency, Europe (AABC)
USAPATACE... United States Army Publications and Training Aids Center, Europe
USAPAV...... United States Army Procurement Agency, Vietnam
USAPC...... United States Army Petroleum Center
USAPC...... United States Army Pictorial Center
USAPCC...... United States Army Personnel Coordination Center
USAPDA...... United States Army Physical Disability Agency
USAPDC...... United States Army Property Disposal Center [*Merged with Defense Logistics Services Center*]
USAPDCE..... United States Army Petroleum Distribution Command, Europe (AABC)
USAPDSC ... United States Army Personnel Data Support Center (AABC)
USAPDSK ... United States Army Petroleum Distribution System, Korea (AABC)
USAPEB...... United States Army Physical Evaluation Board (AABC)
USAPEQUA... United States Army Productions Equipment Agency
USAPERSCEN... United States Army Personnel Center
USAPFS...... United States Army Physical Fitness School [*Army*] (INF)
USAPG...... United States Army Participation Group (AABC)
USAPHC...... United States Army Primary Helicopter Center (AABC)
USAPHS...... United States Army Primary Helicopter School
USAPIA...... United States Army Personnel Information Activity (AABC)
USAPIC...... United States Army Photointerpretation Center
USAPO...... United States Army Antarctic Projects Office
USAPO...... USA Plowing Organization (EA)
USAPOP...... United States Army Port Operations, Pusan (AABC)
US App ...... United States Appeals Reports [*A publication*] (DLA)
USAPPA...... United States Army Publications and Printing Agency
USAPPC...... US Army Publications and Printing Command (DOMA)
USAPRC...... United States Army Physical Review Council (AABC)
USAPRDC ... United States Army Polar Research and Development Center
USAPRO...... United States Army Personnel Research Office
USAPSG...... United States Army Personnel Security Group (AABC)
USAPT .... United States Army Parachute Team
USAPWA...... United Stone and Allied Products Workers of America [*Later, USWA*] (EA)
USAQMC...... United States Army Quartermaster Corps [*Merged with Supply and Maintenance Command*]

USAQMCDA... United States Army Quartermaster Combat Developments Agency (SAA)
USAQMCENFL... United States Army Quartermaster Center and Fort Lee (AABC)
USAQMCS.... United States Army Quartermaster Center and School
USAQMS.... United States Army Quartermaster School
USAQMTC.... United States Army Quartermaster Training Command
USAR .... Uniform Systems of Accounts and Reports for Certified Air Carriers [*Civil Aeronautics Board*]
USAR .... United States Aeronautical Reserve
USAR .... United States Army Reserve
USARA...... United States Air Racing Association [*Formerly, PRPA*] (EA)
USARA...... US Army Ranger Association (EA)
USARACS ... United States Army Alaska Communications Center
USARADABD... United States Army Air Defense Artillery Board [*Fort Bliss, TX*]
USARADBD... United States Army Air Defense Board
USARADCOM... United States Army Air Defense Command
USARADSCH... United States Army Air Defense School
USARADSCH... United States Army Research and Development School (AAG)
USARAE...... United States Army Reserve Affairs, Europe (AABC)
USARAK...... United States Army Alaska
USARAL...... United States Army, Alaska
USARB...... United States Army Retraining Brigade (AABC)
USARBCO ... United States Army Base Command, Okinawa (AABC)
USARC...... United States Army Reserve Center (AABC)
USARCARIB... United States Army, Caribbean
USARCC...... US Association of Roller Canary Culturists (EA)
USA-RCEC ... USA-Republic of China Economic Council (EA)
USARCEN... United States Army Records Center
USARCENT... United States Army Forces, Central Command
USARCPC... United States Army Reserve Components Personnel Center (AABC)
USARCS...... United States Army Claims Service (AABC)
USARCSWIS... United States Army Claims Service Worldwide Information System (GFGA)
USARctBad... United States Army Recruiter Badge [*Military decoration*] (AABC)
USARDA...... United States Army Regional Dental Activity (AABC)
USARDAISA... United States Army Research, Development, and Acquisition Information Systems Agency (AABC)
USARDL...... United States Army Research and Development Laboratories
USARDORAG... United States Army Research and Development Operational Research Advisory Group (AABC)
USARDSG-GE... United States Army Research, Development, and Standardization Group - Germany (RDA)
USARDSG-UK... US Army Research, Development, and Standardization Group - United Kingdom (RDA)
USAREC...... United States Army Recruiting Command (AABC)
USARECSTA... United States Army Reception Station
USARENBD... United States Army Armor and Engineer Board (RDA)
USAREPG ... United States Army Electronic Proving Ground
USAREREC... United States Army Enlisted Records and Evaluation Center
USARET-RSGSTA... United States Army Returnee - Reassignment Station
USAREUR .... United States Army, Europe
USAREURAGLO... United States Army, Europe, Adjutant General Liaison Office (AABC)
USAREURCSTC... United States Army, Europe, Combat Support Training Center (AABC)
USAREURORDCOM... United States Army European Ordnance Command
USARF...... United States Army Reserve Forces
USARFA...... United States of America Rugby Fives Association (EA)
USARFANT... United States Army Forces, Antilles
USARFEO...... United States Army Frequency Engineering Office (MCD)
USARFT...... United States Army Forces, Taiwan
USARFU...... United States of America Rugby Football Union (EA)
USARHAW... United States Army, Hawaii
USARIA...... United States Army Rock Island Arsenal
USARIBSS... United States Army Research Institute for the Behavioral and Social Sciences (AABC)
USARIEM...... United States Army Research Institute of Environmental Medicine [*Natick, MA*] (AABC)
USARIOS ..... Association of Maritime Transport Users in the Central American Isthmus [*Guatemala*] (EAIO)
USARIS...... United States Army Information School [*Fort Slocum, New Rochelle, NY*]
USARJ .... United States Army, Japan
USARK...... United States Army, Korea (MCD)
USARLANT... United States Army Forces, Atlantic (AABC)
USARLT...... United States Army Reserve Losses Tally
USARMA...... United States Army Attache
USARMCOM... United States Army Armament Command
USARMIS... United States Army Mission
USARMLO... United States Army Liaison Officer
USARMY... Uncle Sam Ain't Released Me Yet
USARNG...... United States Army National Guard
USARO...... United States Army Research Office
USA-ROCEC... USA-Republic of China Economic Council [*Crystal Lake, IL*] (EA)
USAROD...... United States Army Research Office (Durham)
USAROTC ... United States Army Reserve Officer Training Corps
USAROTCR... United States Army Reserve Officers' Training Corps Region (AABC)
USARP...... United States Army Research Program (IAA)
USARP...... US Antarctic Research Program (EA)
USARPA...... United States Army Publications Agency (GFGA)
USARPA...... United States Army Radio Propagation Agency (AABC)
USARPAC... United States Army, Pacific
USARPACINTS... United States Army Pacific Intelligence School (AABC)
USARPERCEN... United States Army Reserve Personnel Center
USARR...... United States Army Readiness Regions (AABC)

USARRACL... United States Army Reserve Report Activity Control List
USARRADCOM... United States Army Armament Research and Development Command (RDA)
USARRED .... United States Army Forces, Readiness Command
USARS......... US Army Regimental System (INF)
USARS......... User Selected and Required Schedule (SAA)
USARSA....... United States Amateur Roller Skating Association [Later, USAC/RS] (EA)
USARSA....... United States Army School of the Americas [Fort Benning, AR] (INF)
USARSCV..... United States Army Support Command, Vietnam [Obsolete]
USARSG ..... United States Army Standardization Group
USARSO ..... United States Army Forces, Southern Command
USARSO-PR... United States Army Forces, Southern Command - Puerto Rico (AABC)
USARSOUTHCOM... United States Army Forces, Southern Command
USARSPACE... United States Army Space Command
USARSSO .... United States Army Safeguard Systems Office
USARSTRIKE... United States Army Forces Strike Command (AABC)
USARSUPTHAI.. United States Army Support, Thailand (AABC)
USART......... Universal Synchronous/Asynchronous Receiver and Transmitter [Computer science]
USARTL...... United States Army Research and Technical Labs (MCD)
USARTLS..... United States Army Reserve Troop List by State
USARUCU .... United States Army Reserve Unit Commander Unit
USARV........ United States Army, Vehicle (SAA)
USARV........ United States Army Vietnam [Obsolete]
USARV/MACV... United States Army, Vietnam / Military Assistance Command, Vietnam (VNW)
USARYIS...... United States Army, Ryukyu Islands
USAS .... United States Air Service
USAS .... United States Airspace System (NOAA)
USAS .... United States Antarctic Service [1939-41] [Navy]
USAS .... United States of America Standard (IEEE)
USAS .... United Students Against Sweatshops [An association]
USAS .... UNIVAC Standard Airline System (HGAA)
USAS .... US Aquatic Sports (EA)
USASA........ United States Army Security Agency
USASA........ Universities Staff Association of South Australia
USASAALA... United States Army Security Assistance Agency, Latin America (AABC)
USASAC...... United States Army Security Assistance Center
USASAC...... US Army Security Affairs Command (RDA)
USASACDA... United States Army Security Agency Combat Development Activity (AABC)
USASACDSA... United States Army Security Agency Command Data Systems Activity (AABC)
USASADEA... United States Army Signal Air Defense Engineering Agency [Later, USAADEA]
USASAE...... United States Army Security Agency, Europe (AABC)
USASAFLOG... United States Army Safeguard Logistics Command
USASAFO..... United States Army Signal Avionics Field Office [Later, USAAFO]
USASAFS..... United States Army Security Agency Field Station
USASAFSCOM... United States Army Safeguard System Command (AABC)
USASAGV .... US Army Security Agency Group, Vietnam (VNW)
USASAM...... United State Army School of Aviation Medicine (PDAA)
USASAPAC... United States Army Security Agency, Pacific (AABC)
USASASA.... United States Army Security Agency Systems Activity (AABC)
USASASA.... United States Army Small Arms Systems Agency
USASASSA... United States Army Security Agency Signal Security Activity (AABC)
USASATC & S... United States Army Security Agency Training Center and School (AABC)
USASATCOMA... United States Army Satellite Communications Agency (AABC)
USASATEC... United States Army Security Agency Test and Evaluation Center (AABC)
USASATSA... United States Army Signal Aviation Test Support Activity
USASC........ United States Army Safety Center
USASC........ United States Army Signal Corps [Merged with Communications and Electronics Command]
USASC........ United States Army Subsistence Center
USASC........ United States Army Support Center
USASCA...... United States Army Safeguard Communications Agency (RDA)
USASCA...... United States Army Satellite Communications Agency (IAA)
USASCAF..... United States Army Service Center for the Armed Forces (AABC)
USASC & FG... United States Army Signal Center and Fort Gordon (AABC)
USASCC...... United States Army Strategic Communications Command
USASCH...... United States Army Support Command, Hawaii (AABC)
USASCHEUR... United States Army School, Europe [Obsolete] (AABC)
USASCII...... United States of America Standard Code for Information Interchange
USASCOCR... United States of America Standard Character Set for Optical Character Recognition [Computer science]
USASCR...... United States Army Support Center, Richmond (AABC)
USASCS...... United States Army Signal Center and School
USASCS...... United States Army Signal Corps School (IAA)
USASCSA..... United States Army Signal Communications Security Agency
USASCSOCR... United States of America Standard Character Set for Optical Character Recognition [Computer science]
USASCSOCR... United States of America Standard Character Set for Optical Characters (IAA)
USASCV...... United States Army Support Command, Vietnam [Obsolete]
USASD........ United States Army Student Detachment (AABC)
USASDC...... United States Army Strategic Defense Command
USASEA...... United States Army Signal Engineering Agency
USASEL...... United States Army Signal Engineering Laboratory (IAA)
USASESA..... United States Army Signal Equipment Support Agency (MCD)
USASESS..... United States Army Southeastern Signal School (AABC)

USASETAF... United States Army Southern European Task Force
USASEUR.... United States Army School, Europe [Obsolete]
USASEXC.... United States Armed Services Exploitation Center (AABC)
USASF........ United States Army Special Forces (CINC)
USASFG...... United States Army Special Forces Group
USASFGV..... United States Army Special Forces Group, Vietnam
USASFV..... United States Army Special Forces, Vietnam [Obsolete]
USASG........ US Army Support Group (DOMA)
USASG(Aus)... United States Army Standardization Group (Australia)
USASG(Ca)... United States Army Standardization Group (Canada) (AABC)
USASG(UK)... United States Army Standardization Group (United Kingdom) (AABC)
USASGV..... United States Army Support Group, Vietnam [Obsolete]
USASI........ United States of America Standards Institute [Formerly, ASA] [Later, ANSI]
USASIGC..... United States Army Signal Corps [Merged with Communications and Electronics Command]
USASIGENGLAB... United States Army Signal Engineering Laboratory (IAA)
USASIGRSCHUNIT... United States Army Signal Research Unit (IAA)
USASIGS..... United States Army Signal School (AABC)
USASIGTC... United States Army Signal Training Center (IAA)
USASII........ United States of America Standard Code for Information Interchange (IAA)
USASIMSA... United States Army Signal Materiel Support Agency [Later, USAEMSA]
USASIS....... United States Army Strategic Intelligence School
USASLE...... Uniform Securities Agent State Law Examination [Investment term]
USASMA..... United States Army Sergeant Major Academy (AABC)
USASMC..... United States Army Supply and Maintenance Command
USASMC...... US Army Sergeants Major Course (INF)
USASMCOM... United States Army Supply and Maintenance Command (MUGU)
USASMSA.... United States Army Signal Materiel Support Agency [Later, USAEMSA]
USASMSA.... United States Army Signal Missile Support Agency (IAA)
USASMSG.... United States Army Signal Missile Support Group
USASOC..... US Army Special Operations Command (INF)
USASOPAC... United States Army Support Office, Pacific (AABC)
USASOS...... United States Army Services of Supply
USASPSAE... United States Army Special Services Agency, Europe (AABC)
USASPTAP... United States Army Support Activity, Philadelphia (AABC)
USASPTC.... United States Army Support Center (AABC)
USASPTCC... United States Army Support Command, Chicago
USASPTCM... United States Army Support Center, Memphis (AABC)
USASPTCP... United States Army Support Center, Philadelphia (AABC)
USASPTCR... United States Army Support Center, Richmond (AABC)
USASRDL .... United States Army Signal Research and Development Laboratory [Later, USAERDL]
USASRU ...... United States Army Surgical Research Unit (AABC)
USASSA....... United States Army Signal Supply Agency [Later, USAEC]
USASSAFMPO... United States Army Signal Supply Agency, Fort Monmouth Procurement Office
USASSAMRO... United States Army Signal Supply Agency, Midwestern Regional Office
USASSAUSAEPGPO... United States Army Signal Supply Agency, United States Army Electronic Proving Ground Procurement Office
USASSAWPO... United States Army Signal Supply Agency, Washington Procurement Office
USASSAWRO... United States Army Signal Supply Agency, Western Regional Office
USASSC....... United States Army Signal School and Center
USASSC & FBH... United States Army Soldier Support Center and Fort Benjamin Harrison (AABC)
USASSD...... United States Army Special Security Detachment
USASSDC .... United States Army Space and Strategic Defense Command
USASSG...... United States Army Special Security Group (AABC)
USASTAF.... United States Army Southern European Task Force
USASTAF.... United States Army Strategic Air Forces in the Pacific
USASTC..... United States Army Signal Training Center [Fort Gordon, GA]
USASTCEN... United States Army Signal Training Center (IAA)
USASTCFM... United States Army Signal Training Command and Fort Monmouth
USASTRATCOM... United States Army Strategic Communications Command [Later, USACC] (AABC)
USASTRATCOM-A... United States Army Strategic Communications Command - Alaska (AABC)
USASTRATCOM-CONUS... United States Army Strategic Communications Command - Continental United States (AABC)
USASTRATCOM-EUR... United States Army Strategic Communications Command - Europe (AABC)
USASTRATCOM-PAC... United States Army Strategic Communications Command - Pacific (AABC)
USASTRATCOM-SIGGP-T... United States Army Strategic Communications Command Signal Group - Thailand (AABC)
USASTRATCOM-SO... United States Army Strategic Communications Command - South (AABC)
USASTRATCOM-V... United States Army Strategic Communications Command - Vietnam [Obsolete] (AABC)
USASUPCOM-CRB... United States Army Support Command - Cam Ranh Bay [Obsolete] (AABC)
USASUPCOM-QN... United States Army Support Command - Qui Nhon [Obsolete] (AABC)
USASUPCOM-SGN... United States Army Support Command - Saigon [Obsolete] (AABC)
USASWCDA... United States Army Special Warfare Combat Developments Agency (SAA)
USASWL...... United States Army Signals Warfare Laboratory
USASWS....... United States Army Special Warfare School

USAT .... United States Army Transport
USATA .... United States Army Test, Measurement Diagnostic Equipment Activity
USATAC .... United States Army Terrain Analysis Center (MCD)
USATAC .... United States Army Training Center, Engineer [*Fort Leonard Wood, MO*]
USATACOM... United States Army Tank-Automotive Command [*Obsolete*]
USATAFO ...... United States Army Transportation Aviation Field Office
USATALS ..... United States Army Transportation and Aviation Logistics Schools (GFGA)
USATATSA... United States Army Transportation Aircraft Test and Support Activity
USATA(WH)... United States Army Transportation Agency (White House) (AABC)
USATB .... United States Army Training Board
USATC .... United States Air Target Chart
USATC .... United States Army Topographic Command
USATC .... United States Army Training Center
USATC .... United States Army Transportation Center and School
USATC .... United States Assault Training Center [*World War II*]
USATCA .... United States Army Terminal Command, Atlantic
USATCAD ...... United States Army Training Center, Air Defense
USATCARMOR... United States Army Training Center, Armor [*Fort Knox, KY*]
USATCBASIC... United States Army Training Center, Basic
USATCD .... United States Army Training Center, Air Defense
USATCEFLW... United States Army Training Center, Engineer, Fort Leonard Wood [*Missouri*] (AABC)
USATCENGR... United States Army Training Center, Engineer
USATCEUR... United States Army Terminal Command, Europe (AABC)
USATC FA.... United States Army Training Center, Field Artillery [*Fort Sill, OK*] (AABC)
USATCFE ..... United States Army Transportation Center and Fort Eustis (AABC)
USATCFLW... United States Army Training Center and Fort Leonard Wood (AABC)
USATCG .... United States Army Terminal Command, Gulf (AABC)
USATCINF.... United States Army Training Center, Infantry
USATCO .... Universal Satellite Corp. [*New York, NY*] [*Telecommunications*] (TSSD)
USATCO .... US Air Traffic Controllers Organization [*Defunct*] (EA)
USATCP .... United States Army Terminal Command, Pacific
USATCRTSA... United States Army Transportation Corps Road Test Support Activity
USATCS .... United States Army Transportation Center and School
USATDA .... United States Army Training Device Agency
USATDC .... United States Army Training and Doctrine Command (BARN)
USATDGL.... United States Army Terminal Detachment, Great Lakes (AABC)
USATEA .... United States Army Transportation Engineering Agency (AABC)
USATEC .... United States Army Test and Evaluation Command [*Obsolete*]
USATECOM... United States Army Test and Evaluation Command [*Obsolete*]
USATHAMA... United States Army Toxic and Hazardous Materials Agency (RDA)
USATHMC.... U.S. Army Toxic and Hazardous Materials Center (COE)
USATIA .... United States Army Transportation Intelligence Agency
USATL .... United States Army Technical Library (DIT)
USATLA .... USA Toy Library Association (EA)
USATMACE... United States Army Traffic Management Agency, Central Europe (AABC)
USATMC ...... United States Army Transportation Materiel Command
USATMC ...... United States Army Troop Medical Clinic (AABC)
USATOPOCOM... United States Army Topographic Command (AABC)
USATOWA.... United States Amateur Tug of War Association (EA)
USATRADOC... United States Army Training and Doctrine Command
USATRASANA... United States Army TRADOC Systems Analysis Activity (AABC)
USATRC .... United States Army Transportation Research Command
USATRECOM... United States Army Transportation Research and Engineering Command
USATREOG... United States Army Transportation Environmental Operations Group (AABC)
USATRFSTA... United States Army Transfer Station
USA Trk .... USA Truck Co. [*Associated Press*] (SAG)
USATRML.... United States Army Tropical Research Medical Laboratory
USATROSCOM... United States Army Troop Support Command
USATS .... U.S. Air Traffic Service Corporation [*FAA*] (TAG)
USATSA .... United States Army Technical Support Activity (AABC)
USATSA .... US Army Troop Support Agency (DOMA)
USATSARCOM... United States Army Troop Support and Aviation Materiel Readiness Command [*St. Louis, MO*]
USATSC .... United States Army Terrestrial Sciences Center (AABC)
USATSC .... United States Army Training Support Center
USATSCH.... United States Army Transportation School
USATSG .... United States Army, the Surgeon General
USATSG .... United States Army TMDE [*Test, Measurement, and Diagnostic Equipment*] Support Group
USATT .... Union des Syndicats Autonomes des Travailleurs Tchadiens [*Federation of Autonomous Workers Unions of Chad*]
USATTAY ..... United States Army Transportation Test Activity, Yuma [*Arizona*] (AABC)
USATTB .... United States Army Transportation Terminal, Brooklyn
USATTC .... United States Army Transportation Training Command
USATTC .... United States Army Tropic Test Center (AABC)
USATTCA ..... United States Army Transportation Terminal Command, Atlantic
USATTCARC... United States Army Transportation Terminal Command, Arctic
USATTCG ..... United States Army Transportation Terminal Command, Gulf
USATTCP ..... United States Army Transportation Terminal Command, Pacific
USATTU .... United States Army Transportation Terminal Unit (AABC)
USATUC .... United States Army Terminal Unit, Canaveral (AABC)
US Av .... United States Aviation Reports [*A publication*] (DLA)
USAVA .... USA Victory Alliance (EA)
USAVC .... United States Army Vehicle Club [*British*] (DBA)
USAVETS ..... United States Army Veterinary School
US Aviation Rep... United States Aviation Reports [*A publication*] (DLA)
US Avi Rep... United States Aviation Reports [*A publication*] (DLA)
US Av R .... United States Aviation Reports [*A publication*] (DLA)
USAW .... Underwater Security Advance Warnings [*Navy*]
USAWC .... United States Army War College
USAWC .... United States Army Weapons Command [*Later, Armaments Command*]
USAWECOM... United States Army Weapons Command [*Later, Armaments Command*] (AABC)
USAWES ...... United States Army Waterways Experiment Station (AABC)
USAWF .... United States Amateur Wrestling Foundation (EA)
USAWOA ...... United States Army Warrant Officers Association (EA)
USA Wste .... USA Waste Services, Inc. [*Associated Press*] (SAG)
USB .... Unified S-Band (MCD)
USB .... United Society of Brushmakers [*A union*] [*British*]
USB .... United Soybean Board (NTPA)
USB .... United States Bases [*British World War II*]
USB .... United States Biochemical Corp. [*Chemistry*] (DAVI)
USB .... Unit Selection Board (WDAA)
USB .... Universal Serial Bus [*Computer science*] (CDE)
USB .... Universal Serials and Book Exchange, Inc. [*ACCORD*] [*UTLAS symbol*]
USB .... Upflow Sludge Blanket [*Reactor, wastewater treatment*]
USB .... Upper Sideband
USB .... Upper Sternal Border [*Anatomy*] (DAVI)
USB .... Upper Surface Blown [*Jet flap*] [*Aviation*]
USB .... US Bass [*An association Defunct*] (EA)
USBA .... Union Syndicale des Bases Americaines [*Union of American Base Workers*] [*Morocco*]
USBA .... United States Badminton Association (EA)
USBA .... United States Bartenders Association (EA)
USBA .... United States Boardsailing Association (EA)
USBA .... United States Brewers Association [*Defunct*] (EA)
USBA .... US Base Association (EA)
USBA .... US Biathlon Association (EA)
USBA .... US Boomerang Association (EA)
USBATU .... United States - Brazil Aviation Training Unit
USBBC .... United States Beef Breeds Council (EA)
USBBS .... United States Bureau of Biological Survey [*Terminated, 1940; later, Fish and Wildlife Service*]
USBBY .... US Board on Books for Young People (EA)
USBC .... United States Banknote Corp. (EFIS)
USBC .... United States Bureau of the Census (OICC)
USBC .... Universal Standard Book Code (PDAA)
USBC .... US Bancorp [*NASDAQ symbol*] (NQ)
USBCA .... United States Braille Chess Association (EA)
USBCC .... United States Border Collie Club (EA)
USBCJ .... US Business Committee on Jamaica [*Defunct*] (EA)
USBCODE ..... Unipolar Straight Binary Code (IAA)
US BcOR...... United States Bancorp [*Associated Press*] (SAG)
USBCP .... U.S. Bancorp 8.125%'A'Pfd [*NASDAQ symbol*] (TTSB)
USBCSEE..... United States Business Council for Southeastern Europe (NTPA)
USBE .... Unified S-Band Equipment
USBE .... United States Book Exchange (SAA)
USBE .... Universal Serials and Book Exchange, Inc. [*Acronym now used as official name of association*] (EA)
USBEP .... United States Bureau of Engraving and Printing
USBER .... United States Mission, Berlin
USBF .... United States Baseball Federation (EA)
USBF .... United States Bocce Federation (EA)
USBF .... United States Brewers Foundation [*Later, USBA*]
USBF .... United States Bureau of Fisheries [*Terminated*]
USBF .... US Bobsled and Skeleton Federation (EA)
USBFA .... US Bass Fishing Association [*Later, USB*] (EA)
USBFDC ...... United States Bureau of Foreign and Domestic Commerce
USBG .... United States Bartenders Guild [*Later, USBA*] (EA)
USBG .... United States Botanic Garden
USBG .... US Bridge Corp. [*NASDAQ symbol*] (SAG)
USBGA .... United States Blind Golfer's Association (EA)
USBGN .... United States Bureau on Geographical Names [*Terminated, 1947; later, Board on Geographical Names*]
USBI .... United Space Booster, Inc. (NAKS)
USBIA .... United States Bowling Instructors Association (EA)
USBIA .... United States Bureau of Insular Affairs
USBIC .... United States Business and Industrial Council [*Washington, DC*] (EA)
US Bio .... United States Bioscience, Inc. [*Associated Press*] (SAG)
US Biosci..... US Bioscience, Inc. [*Associated Press*] (SAG)
USBISS .... United Society of Boilermakers and Iron and Steel Shipbuilders [*A union*] [*British*]
USBJA .... United States Barrel Jumping Association (EA)
USBL .... United States Basketball League
USBL .... United States Bureau of Lighthouses
USBLM .... United States Bureau of Land Management [*Department of the Interior*]
USBLS .... United States Bureau of Labor Statistics
USBM .... United States Bureau of Mines [*Department of the Interior*]
USBMG .... United States Berlin Mission in Germany
USBN .... United Sec Bancorp (WA) [*NASDAQ symbol*] (TTSB)
USBN .... United Security Bancorp (Washington) [*NASDAQ symbol*] (SAG)
US Bn .... United States Bancorp [*Associated Press*] (SAG)
USBN .... United States Bureau of Navigation
USBNP .... United States Bureau of Navy Personnel [*Terminated*]
USBP .... United States Border Patrol [*Department of the Treasury*]

USBPA.........	United States Bicycle Polo Association (EA)
USBPa.........	USbancorp, Inc. [*Associated Press*] (SAG)
USBPr.........	United States Bureau of Public Roads
USBR...........	United States Bureau of Reclamation [*Department of the Interior*] [*See also BOR*]
USBR...........	U.S. Bridge of N.Y. [*NASDAQ symbol*] (TTSB)
USBR...........	US Bridge on New York [*NASDAQ symbol*] (SAG)
USBrdge......	US Bridge Corp. [*Associated Press*] (SAG)
USBrdgNY...	US Bridge on New York [*Associated Press*] (SAG)
US Brg........	US Bridge on New York [*Associated Press*] (SAG)
USBRO.........	United States Base Requirements Overseas [*Military*] (AABC)
USBRW........	US Bridge of NY Wrrt [*NASDAQ symbol*] (TTSB)
USBS	Unified S-Band System [*Radio*]
USBS	United States Bureau of Standards
USBSA........	United States Beet Sugar Association (EA)
USBSA........	United States Boardsailing Association (EA)
USBSF........	US Bobsled and Skeleton Federation (EA)
USBSSW......	United Society of Boilermakers, Shipbuilders, and Structural Workers [*A union*] [*British*]
USBT	Upper Surface Blowing Technique [*Aviation*] (DA)
USBTA	United States Board of Tax Appeals [*Later, the Tax Court of the United States*]
USBTC	University-Small Business Technology Consortium [*Defunct*] (EA)
USBTC	US Battery Trade Council
USBUC	Upper Sideband Upconverter (IAA)
USBWA........	United States Basketball Writers Association (EA)
USC	Ultrasonic Storage Cell
USC	Under Secretaries Committee
USC	Under Separate Cover
USC	Unified Soil Classification (GNE)
USC	Union of Sephardic Congregations (EA)
USC	Union Sociale Camerounaise [*Cameroonese Social Union*]
USC	Unitarian Service Committee [*Later, UUSC*] [*Post-World War II*]
USC	United Satellite Communications [*Cable TV programming service*]
USC	United Service Club [*Charter jet service to Europe for servicemen and dependents*]
USC	United Sisters of Charity (EA)
USC	United Somali Congress [*Political party*] (EY)
USC	United States Canada [*Automobile content legislation*]
USC	United States Catalog [*A bibliographic publication*]
USC	United States Citizen
USC	United States Code [*Legal term*]
USC	United States Components (IAA)
USC	United States Congress
USC	United States Customs
USC	United States Custom Service, Washington, DC [*OCLC symbol*] (OCLC)
USC	United States of Colombia
USC	United Strasser Club
USC	United Survival Clubs (EA)
USC	Universal Specimen Chamber
USC	University of Santa Clara [*California*]
USC	University of South Carolina [*Columbia, SC*]
USC	University of Southern California [*Los Angeles*] [*Seismograph station code, US Geological Survey*] (SEIS)
USC	University Scholarships of Canada
USC	University Statistics Center [*New Mexico State University*] [*Research center*] (RCD)
USC	Up Stage Center [*Away from audience*] [*A stage direction*]
USC	U.S. Can [*NYSE symbol*] (TTSB)
USC	US Can Corp. [*NYSE symbol*] (SAG)
USC	US Check Airlines [*ICAO designator*] (FAAC)
USC	User Service Center (MCD)
USC	User Support Center (MCD)
USCA	Under Secretary for Civil Aviation
USCA	Uniformed Services Contingency Act
USCA	United Sidecar Association (EA)
USCA	United States Canoe Association (EA)
USCA	United States Canola Association (NTPA)
USCA	United States Code Annotated [*Law*] [*Based on official USC*]
USCA	United States Contract Awards (NITA)
USCA	United States Copper Association [*Later, American Bureau of Metal Statistics*] (EA)
USCA	United States Courts of Appeals
USCA	United States Croquet Association (EA)
USCA	United States Curling Association (EA)
USCA	US Canola Association (EA)
USCAA	United States Corporate Athletics Association (EA)
USCA App....	United States Code, Annotated, Appendix [*A publication*] (DLA)
USCAB........	United States Congressional Advisory Board (EA)
USCAC........	United States Continental Army Command [*Superseded by FORSCOM*]
USCAF	United States Competitive Aerobics Federation
USCAGS......	United States Coast and Geodetic Survey (IAA)
USCAL	University of Southern California, Aeronautical Laboratory (MCD)
US Cal Sch L Tax Inst...	University of Southern California School of Law Tax Institute (DLA)
USCAM	United States Civil Aviation Mission (AFM)
US Can	US Can Corp. [*Associated Press*] (SAG)
USC & G......	United States Coast and Geodetic Survey [*Later, National Ocean Survey*] (MUGU)
USCANS.......	Unified S-Band Communication and Navigation System [*NASA*]
USCANW......	US Committee Against Nuclear War [*Defunct*] (EA)
USCAP	United States and Canadian Academy of Pathology (NTPA)

USCAPP.......	Advanced Professional Programs, University of Southern California Law Center (DLA)
USC App	United States Code Appendix [*A publication*] (DLA)
USCAR........	United States Civil Administration, Ryukyu Islands
USCAR........	United States Council for Automotive Research [*General Motors, Ford, and Chrysler*] (ECON)
USCB	United Saudi Commercial Bank
USCB	United States Customs Bonded
USCBC........	US-China Business Council (EA)
USCBRA......	United States CB Radio Association (EA)
USCC	Union des Syndicats Croyants du Cameroun [*Federation of Cameroonese Believers' Unions*]
USCC	United Society of Cork Cutters [*A union*] [*British*]
USCC	United States Calorimetry Conference
USCC	United States Camaro Club (EA)
USCC	United States Capacitor Corp. (IAA)
USCC	United States Catholic Conference (EA)
USCC	United States Cellular Corp. [*Park Ridge, IL*] [*Telecommunications*] (TSSD)
USCC	United States Central Command [*Military*] (MUSM)
USCC	United States Chamber of Commerce
USCC	United States Circuit Court
USCC	United States Citizens' Congress [*Defunct*]
USCC	United States Claims Court (AAGC)
USCC	United States Commerical Co. [*World War II*]
USCC	United States Cotton Commission
USCC	United States Court of Claims [*Abolished, 1982*]
USCC	United States Criminal Code
USCC	United States Criminal Court
USCC	United States Customs Court [*Later, United States Court of International Trade*]
USCC	United Student Christian Council in United States
USCC	US Cancellation Club (EA)
USCCA........	United States Circuit Court of Appeals
USCCA........	United States Circuit Court of Appeals Reports [*A publication*] (DLA)
USCCAN......	United States Code Congressional and Administrative News [*A publication*]
USCCCA	United States Cross Country Coaches Association (EA)
USCCEC	United States Committee for Care of European Children [*Post-World War II*]
USCCHO	United States Conference of City Health Officers (EA)
USCCHSO	United States Conference of City Human Service Officials (EA)
USCCPA	United States Court of Customs and Patent Appeals [*Abolished, 1982*]
USCCSA.......	US Corporate Council on South Africa (EA)
USCDC........	United States Civil Defense Council (EA)
USCEA	United States Cigarette Export Association (NTPA)
USCEA	US Council for Energy Awareness (EA)
USCEC	University of Southern California, Engineering Center (MCD)
USCEF	US-China Education Foundation (EA)
USCEFI	United Social, Cultural, and Educational Foundation of India
USCEI	United States - China Educational Institute (EA)
US Cell	US Cellular Corp. [*Associated Press*] (SAG)
USCE/NPD ...	United States Army, Corps of Engineers, North Pacific Division (NOAA)
USCENTAF...	United States Central Command - Air Forces
USCENTCOM...	United States Central Command
US Cert Den...	Certiorari Denied by United States Supreme Court [*Legal term*] (DLA)
US Cert Dis...	Certiorari Dismissed by United States Supreme Court [*Legal term*] (DLA)
USCESS.......	US Cultural Exchange and Sports Society (EA)
USCF	United States Chess Federation (EA)
USCF	United States Churchill Foundation [*Later, WCF*]
USCF	United States Cycling Federation (EA)
USCG..........	United States Coast Guard
USCG..........	United States Consul General
USCG..........	United States Government Guaranteed (EBF)
USCGA........	United States Coast Guard Academy [*New London, CT*]
USCGA........	United States Coast Guard Auxiliary
USCGAD......	United States Coast Guard Air Detachment
USC-GARP ...	United States Committee for the Global Atmospheric Research Program [*Defunct*] (EA)
USCGAS.......	United States Coast Guard Air Station
USCGASB.....	United States Coast Guard Aircraft and Supply Base
USCGAUX ...	United States Coast Guard Auxiliary (EA)
USCGB........	United States Coast Guard Base
USCG-B........	United States Coast Guard Office of Boating Safety
USCGB........	Uphill Ski Club of Great Britain (EAIO)
USCGC........	United States Coast Guard Cutter
USCG-C........	United States Coast Guard Office of Chief of Staff
USCGD........	United States Coast Guard Depot
USCG-E........	United States Coast Guard Naval Engineering Division
USCG-M.......	United States Coast Guard Office of Merchant Marine Safety
USCG-MFSRS...	United States Coast Guard Marine Fire and Safety Research Staff [*Groton, CT*]
USCG-N	United States Coast Guard Office of Navigation
USC Gov't Rev...	University of South Carolina. Governmental Review [*A publication*] (DLA)
USCGR........	United States Coast Guard Reserve
USCGRC	United States Coast Guard Receiving Center
USCGR(T)....	United States Coast Guard, Reserve (Temporary)
USCGR(W)...	United States Coast Guard, Reserve (Women)
USCGS........	United States Coast and Geodetic Survey [*Later, National Ocean Survey*]

USCGSCF..... United States Coast Guard Shore Communication Facilities
USCGTS........ United States Coast Guard Training Station
USCH.......... University of South Carolina Herbarium
USCh .... US-China Industrial Exchange, Inc. [Associated Press] (SAG)
US ChInd ..... US-China Industrial Exchange, Inc. [Associated Press] (SAG)
USCHRB ...... US Council for Human Rights in the Balkans (EA)
USCHS .... United States Capitol Historical Society (EA)
USCHS........ US Catholic Historical Society (EA)
USCI .... United Satellite Communications Inc.
USCI .... United States Catheter Instrument [Commercial firm] (DAVI)
USCI .... United Synagogue of Conservative Judaism (EA)
USCI .... Universal Self Care [NASDAQ symbol] (TTSB)
USCI .... Universal Self Care, Inc. [NASDAQ symbol] (SAG)
USCI .... USCI, Inc. [Associated Press] (SAG)
USCIA .... United States Customs Inspectors' Association Port of New York
              (EA)
USCIAA .... United States Committee of the International Association of Art (EA)
USCIB .... United States Communications Intelligence Board [Later, National
              Security Agency]
USCIB .... United States Council for International Business (EA)
USCIB .... United States Council on International Banking (EA)
USCIB/IC...... United States Communications Intelligence Board Intelligence
              Committee [Obsolete]
USCICC .... United States Council of the International Chamber of Commerce
              [Later, USCIB] (EA)
USCICSW..... United States Committee of the International Council on Social
              Welfare (EA)
USCID......... US Committee on Irrigation and Drainage (EA)
USCIDFC...... US Committee on Irrigation, Drainage, and Flood Control [Later,
              USCID] (EA)
USCIGW....... Union of Salt, Chemical, and Industrial General Workers [British] (BI)
USCIIC .... United States Civilian Internee Information Center [Army] (AABC)
USCIIC(Br)... United States Civilian Internee Information Center (Branch) [Army]
              (AABC)
USCINCAFRED... United States Commander-in-Chief, Air Force Forces, Readiness
              Command
USCINCARRED... United States Commander-in-Chief, Army Forces, Readiness
              Command
USCINCCENT... Commander-in-Chief, United States Central Command
USCINCEUR... United States Commander-in-Chief, Europe
USCINCLANT... Commander-in-Chief, United States Atlantic Command
USCINCMEAFSA... United States Commander-in-Chief Middle East, Africa South of
              the Sahara, and Southern Asia (GFGA)
USCINCPAC... Commander-in-Chief, United States Pacific Command
USCINCRED... United States Commander-in-Chief, Readiness Command
USCINCREDCOM... Commander-in-Chief, US Readiness Command (MCD)
USCINCSO ... United States Commander-in-Chief, Southern Command (AFM)
USCINCSOC... United States Commander in Chief, Special Operations Command
              (DOMA)
USCINCSOCOM... United States Commander in Chief, Special Operations
              Command (DOMA)
USCINCSOUTH... United States Commander-in-Chief, Southern Command
USCINCSPACE... United States Commander in Chief, Space Command (DOMA)
USCINCTRANSCOM... United States Commander in Chief, Transportation
              Command (DOMA)
USCINSTRAT... United States Commander in Chief, Strategic Command (DOMA)
US Cir Ct Rep DC... Hayward and Hazelton's United States Circuit Court Reports
              [District of Columbia] [A publication] (DLA)
USCISCO...... United States Counterinsurgency Support Office
USCIW .... Universal Self Care Wrrt'A' [NASDAQ symbol] (TTSB)
USCIZ .... Universal Self Care Wrrt'B' [NASDAQ symbol] (TTSB)
USCJ.......... United Society of Carpenters and Joiners [A union] [British]
USCJ.......... United Synagogue of Conservative Judaism (NTPA)
USCJE......... United Synagogue Commission on Jewish Education [Later,
              USACJE] (EA)
USCL .... United Society for Christian Literature [British]
USCL .... United States Coalition for Life (EA)
USCLA .... United States Club Lacrosse Association (EA)
USCLASS..... US Classifications (NITA)
USCLHO...... United States Conference of Local Health Officers (EA)
USCM .... United States Conference of Mayors (EA)
USCM .... Unit Simulated Combat Mission (AAG)
USCM .... USCI, Inc. [NASDAQ symbol] (SAG)
USCMA .... United States Catholic Mission Association (EA)
USCMA .... United States Cheese Makers Association (EA)
USCMA .... United States Court of Military Appeals
USCMA .... United States Crutch Manufacturers Association (EA)
USCMA Adv Op... United States Court of Military Appeals, Advance Opinions
              [A publication] (DLA)
USCMC .... United States Catholic Mission Council (EA)
USCMH....... United States Commission of Maritime History (MSC)
USCMI .... United States Commission on Mathematical Instruction
USCo .... Underwriters Salvage Company
USCO .... United States Committee for the Oceans (EA)
USCO .... US Commercial Office [Department of Commerce, Department of
              State] (IMH)
USCOA........ Uniformed Services Contingency Option Act
USCOB........ United States Commander, Berlin
US Code Cong & Ad News... United States Code Congressional and Administrative
              News [A publication] (DLA)
USCOLD...... United States Committee on Large Dams of the International
              Commission on Large Dams (EA)
USCOMEAST... United States Commander, Eastern Atlantic (MCD)
USCOMEASTLANT... United States Commander, Naval Forces, Eastern Atlantic
              (NATG)

US Comp St... United States Compiled Statutes [A publication] (DLA)
USCOMSUBGRUEASTLANT... United States Commander, Submarines Group,
              Eastern Atlantic (NATG)
USCONARC... United States Continental Army Command [Superseded by
              FORSCOM]
US Cond Rep... Peters' Condensed United States Reports [A publication] (DLA)
US Const ..... United States Constitution [A publication] (DLA)
USCP .... United States Capitol Police
USCP .... University of South Carolina Press (DGA)
USCP .... University of Southern California Press (DGA)
USCPAA...... United States Cerebral Palsy Athletic Association (EA)
USCPFA...... US-China Peoples Friendship Association (EA)
USCPSHHM... United States Committee to Promote Studies of the History of the
              Habsburg Monarchy [Later, SAHH] (EA)
USCR .... United States Committee for Refugees (EA)
USCR .... US Census Report [Database] [Business Publishers, Inc.]
              [Information service or system] (CRD)
USCRA........ United States Citizens' Rights Association (EA)
USCRA........ United States Court Reporters Association (NTPA)
U Scranton... University of Scranton (GAGS)
USCS .... United States Coast Survey
USCS .... United States Code Service [A publication] (DLA)
USCS .... United States Commercial Standard
USCS .... United States Conciliation Service [Functions transferred to Federal
              Mediation and Conciliation Service, 1947]
USCS .... United States Customary System [System of units used in the US]
USCS .... United States Customs Service (MCD)
USCS .... Universal Ship Cancellation Society (EA)
USCS .... Urine Sampling and Collection System [NASA]
USCS .... US Commercial Service [International Trade Administration]
USCS .... USCS International, Inc. [NASDAQ symbol] (SAG)
USCSA .... U.S. Collegiate Skiing Association (PSS)
USCSB .... United States Communications Security Board
USCSC .... United States Chefs Ski Club (EA)
USCSC .... United States Civil Service Commission [Later, MSPB]
USCSC .... United States Collegiate Sports Council (EA)
USCSC .... United States Cuban Sugar Council [Defunct] (EA)
USCSCV...... US Committee for Scientific Cooperation with Vietnam (EA)
USCSE .... United States Civil Service Examination
USC-SFI....... United States Committee-Sports for Israel (EA)
USCS Int...... USCS International, Inc. [Associated Press] (SAG)
USCSRA....... United States Cane Sugar Refiners' Association (EA)
USCSSB....... United States Cap Screw Service Bureau [Later, Cap Screw and
              Special Threaded Products Bureau] (EA)
usc sUPP..... United States Code Supplement (BARN)
USCT .... Union des Syndicats Confederes du Togo [Federation of
              Confederated Unions of Togo]
USCT .... United States Colored Troops [Civil War]
USCTA .... United States Combined Training Association (EA)
US Ct Cl ...... United States Court of Claims (DLA)
USCTI .... United States Cutting Tool Institute (NTPA)
US-CUES.... US Campaign for the University of El Salvador (EA)
USCUN .... United States Committee for the United Nations [Later, UNA-USA]
USCV .... Union Scientifique Continentale de Verre [European Union for the
              Scientific Study of Glass - EUSSG] (EAIO)
USCWC .... United States Chemical Warfare Committee
USCWCC ...... United States Conference for the World Council of Churches (EA)
USCWF....... US Council for World Freedom (EA)
USC-WHO.... United States Committee for the World Health Organization (EA)
USD .... Ultimate Strength Design (IEEE)
USD .... Ultrasonic Separation Detector
USD .... Under Seas Defense Exposition (ITD)
USD .... Under Secretary of Defense [DoD] (RDA)
USD .... Unexplained Standard Deviation [Statistics]
USD .... Uniao Social Democratico [Social Democratic Union] [Portugal
              Political party] (PPE)
USD .... Unified School District
USD .... Union des Sociaux-Democrates [Burkina Faso] [Political party] (EY)
USD .... Union Social-Democrate [Social Democratic Union] [The Ivory Coast]
              [Political party] (EY)
USD .... Union Sociale Democratique [Cameroon] [Political party] (EY)
USD .... United Society of Drillers [A union] [British]
USD .... United States Dispensatory [Pharmacology]
USD .... United States Diving, Inc. (EA)
USD .... United States Dollars
USD .... United States Drone (SAA)
USD .... Universal Standard Data
USD .... University of San Diego
USD .... University of South Dakota, Vermillion, SD [OCLC symbol] (OCLC)
USD .... University Science Development [National Science Foundation]
USD .... Uranium Series Dating
USD .... Urban Sanitary District [British]
USD .... User-Supplied Data
USD(A) .... Under Secretary of Defense for Acquisition [DoD] (RDA)
USDA .... Uniform Simultaneous Death Act [National Conference of
              Commissioners on Uniform State Laws]
USDA .... United Square Dancers of America (EA)
USDA.......... United States Department of Agriculture [Washington, DC] [Database
              originator]
USDA.......... United States Disarmament Administration [Transferred to US Arms
              Control and Disarmament Agency, 1961]
USDA .... United States Duffers' Association [Defunct] (EA)
USDA .... US Darting Association (EA)
USDA.......... US Disc Sports Association (EA)
USD(A&T).... Under Secretary of Defense (Acquisition and Technology) (BCP)

USDA-APHIS-PP/Q... United States Department of Agriculture, Animal and Plant Health Inspection Service, Plant Protection and Quarantine Programs (PDAA)
USDA-ARS... United States Department of Agriculture, Agricultural Research Service
USDA/CRIS... USDA Current Research Information System (NITA)
USDA-FS...... United States Department of Agriculture - Forest Service (PDAA)
USDA-FSVP... USDA-Forest Service Volunteers Program (EA)
USDAO...... United States Defense Attache Office [*or Officer*] (AABC)
USDA RDD... USDA [*United States Department of Agriculture*] Regional Document Delivery [*Library network*]
USDA-REA... United States Department of Agriculture - Rural Electrification Administration (PDAA)
USDASL...... USDA [*United States Department of Agriculture*] Sedimentation Laboratory [*Research center*] (RCD)
USDATA...... United States Data Corp. (NITA)
USData....... USData Corp. [*Associated Press*] (SAG)
USDAW...... Union of Ship Distributive and Allied Workers [*British*] (DCTA)
Usdaw......... Union of Shop, Distributive, and Allied Workers [*British*] (ODBW)
USDB........ United States Disciplinary Barracks [*Military*]
USDC......... Underwater Search, Detection, Classification (AAG)
USDC......... United States Defense Committee (EA)
USDC......... United States Department of Commerce
USDC......... United States Display Consortium (PCM)
USDC......... United States District Court
USDC......... United States District of Columbia (DLA)
USDC......... USData Corp. [*NASDAQ symbol*] (SAG)
USDCFO...... United States Defense Communication Field Office (NATG)
USDC Haw... United States District Court, District of Hawaii (DLA)
USDC Haw... United States District Court, District of Hawaii, Reports [*A publication*] (DLA)
USDC Hawaii... United States District Court, District of Hawaii (DLA)
USDC Hawaii... United States District Court, District of Hawaii, Reports [*A publication*] (DLA)
USDD......... United States Department of Defense
USDE......... United States Department of Education
USDE......... United States Department of Energy (MCD)
USDEL....... United States Delegate (NOAA)
USDELIADB... United States Delegation, Inter-American Defense Board (AABC)
USDeliv....... US Delivery Systems, Inc. [*Associated Press*] (SAG)
US Dept Int... United States Department of the Interior (DLA)
US des AL... Union Syndicale des Artistes Lyriques [*French*] (ROG)
USDESEA...... United States Dependent Schools, European Area [*Army*]
USDF......... United States Dressage Federation (EA)
USDFRC...... US Dairy Forage Research Center [*Research center*] (RCD)
USDGA...... United States Durum Growers Association (EA)
USDH......... United States Direct Hire [*Military*]
USDHE & W... United States Department of Health, Education, and Welfare
USDHUD...... United States Department of Housing and Urban Development
USDI......... United States Department of the Interior
USDia......... US Diagnostics Co. [*Associated Press*] (SAG)
US Diag....... US Diagnostics Co. [*Associated Press*] (SAG)
US Dig....... United States Digest [*A publication*] (DLA)
USDISBad.... United States Distinguished International Shooter Badge [*Military decoration*] (AABC)
U S Dist Ct... United States District Court (BARN)
US Dist Ct Haw... United States District Court District of Hawaii (DLA)
USDJ......... United States Department of Justice
USDJ......... United States District Judge
USDL......... United States Department of Labor
USDL......... U.S. Diagnostic Labs [*NASDAQ symbol*] (TTSB)
USDL......... US Diagnostics [*NASDAQ symbol*] (SAG)
USDLGI...... United States Defense Liaison Group, Indonesia [*Army*] (AABC)
USDNDR...... US Decade for Natural Disaster Reduction [*1990's*]
USDO......... United States Disbursing Officer
USDOC....... United States Department of Commerce
USDOCO...... United States Documents Officer (AFM)
USDOCOLANDSOUTHEAST... United States Document Office, Allied Land Forces, Southeastern Europe (AABC)
USDOD....... United States Department of Defense
USDOE......... United States Department of Energy [*Also, an information service or system*]
USDOI......... United States Department of the Interior (MCD)
USDOT....... United States Department of Transportation (MCD)
USD(P)........ Undersecretary of Defense for Policy (MCD)
USDP........ University of San Diego Press (DGA)
USDP........ University of South Dakota Press (DGA)
USDR........ United States Divorce Reform [*Defunct*] (EA)
USDRE........ Office of the Under Secretary of Defense for Research and Engineering
USDRO........ US Defense Representative Office (DOMA)
USDRP........ Unia Socjaldemokratyczna Rzeczypospolitej Polskiej [*Social Democratic Union of the Republic of Poland*] [*Political party*]
USDS........ United States Department of State
USDS........ US Disc Sports Association (EA)
USDSA........ United States Deaf Skiers Association (EA)
USDSEA...... United States Dependent Schools, European Area [*Army*] (AABC)
USDT........ United States Department of the Treasury
USDT........ United States Department of Transportation
USDTA........ United States Dental Tennis Association (EA)
USDTP........ Ukrainska Sotsial Demokraticheskaia Truda Partiia [*Ukrainian Social Democratic Labor Party*] [*Russian Political party*] (PPE)
USDW........ Underground Sources of Drinking Water
USE......... Encyclopedia of United States Reports [*A publication*] (DLA)
USE.......... Underground Service Entrance

USE......... Undersea Scientific Expedition
USE......... Understanding Science in the Environment [*Australia*]
USE......... Unified S-Band Equipment
USE......... United States Economic Problems [*British World War II*]
USE......... United States Embassy
USE......... United States Envelope Co.
USE......... Unit Support Equipment
USE......... UNIVAC Scientific Exchange [*Later, UI, USE, Inc.*]
USE......... Universal Automatic Computer Scientific Exchange (IAA)
USE......... University of South Dakota, Law Library, Vermillion, SD [*OCLC symbol*] (OCLC)
USE......... University of Southern Europe [*Monaco*] (ECON)
USE......... University Space Experiments
USE......... Unmanned Surveillance Equipment
USE......... US English [*An association*] (EA)
USE......... User Support Environment (SSD)
USE......... Utilized Starch Equivalent (BARN)
USE......... Wauseon, OH [*Location identifier FAA*] (FAAL)
USEA........ Undersea (AABC)
USEA........ United States Energy Association (NTPA)
USEASA...... United States Eastern Amateur Ski Association [*Later, ESA*]
USEC........ United State Enrichment Corporation
USEC........ United States Endurance Cup [*Car racing*]
USEC........ United States Enrichment Corporation (DOGT)
USEC........ United States Mission to European Communities [*Department of State*]
USEC........ United System of Electronic Computers (IEEE)
USEC........ Universal Security Instruments, Inc. [*NASDAQ symbol*] (NQ)
USEC........ Univl Security Instr [*NASDAQ symbol*] (TTSB)
USecBc...... United Security Bancorp (Washington) [*Associated Press*] (SAG)
USECC...... United States Employees' Compensation Commission [*Functions transferred to Federal Security Agency, 1946*]
USECOM...... United States Army Electronics Command [*Obsolete*]
USECOM...... United States Economic Mission [*Foreign aid*] (VNW)
USecWar.... Under Secretary of War [*Obsolete*]
USED......... Underwater Sound Explosive Devices Branch [*Naval Weapons Station*] [*Yorktown, VA*]
USEE........ United States Exploring Expedition [*1838-42*] [*Navy*]
USEEM...... United States Establishment and Enterprise Microdata Base [*Brookings Institution*]
USEES........ United States Naval Engineering Experiment Station [*Annapolis, MD*]
USEFP........ United States Educational Foundation in Pakistan
USEG........ U.S. Energy [*NASDAQ symbol*] (TTSB)
USEG........ US Energy Corp. [*NASDAQ symbol*] (NQ)
USEI........ United States Society of Esperanto Instructors [*Later, AATE*]
USEJ........ United States Society for Esperantists Youth (EA)
USELMCENTO... United States Element Central Treaty Organization (AFM)
USEM........ United States Egg Marketers (EA)
USEMA...... [*The*] United States Electronic Mail Association
USEMB...... United States Embassy (MCD)
USEME...... Undergraduate Science Engineering and Mathematics Education [*National Science Foundation*] (EGAO)
USEMS........ United Steam Engine Makers' Society [*A union*] [*British*]
Usenet....... Usenix Network [*Computer science*] (IGQR)
USENET...... User Network (SSD)
US Enr....... United States Energy Corp. [*Associated Press*] (SAG)
US EnvS...... US Environmental Solutions, Inc. [*Associated Press*] (SAG)
USEO........ United States Employment Opportunities
USEO........ United States Engineer Office
USEORD...... Use Order [*Navy*] (NVT)
USEP........ United States Escapee Program
USEPA........ United States Environmental Protection Agency
US EPA........ United States Environmental Protection Agency
US EPA........ U.S. Environmental Protection Agency
US Eq Dig... United States Equity Digest [*A publication*] (DLA)
USER........ Ultra-Small Electronics Research [*DoD*]
USER........ Unique-to-Site Equipment Review (SAA)
USER........ User System Evaluator [*Computer science*] (MHDB)
USER........ User Systems Ergonomics Research [*Computer science*]
USERC........ US Environment and Resources Council [*Defunct*] (EA)
USERDA...... United States Energy Research and Development Administration [*Superseded by Department of Energy, 1977*]
USERIA...... Ultrasensitive Enzymatic Radioimmunoassay [*Clinical chemistry*]
USERID...... User Identification [*Computer science*]
USER INC.... Urban Scientific and Educational Research, Inc. [*Defunct*] (EA)
USERP........ United Scientists for Environmental Responsibility and Protection (EERA)
USERRA...... Uniformed Services Employment and Re-employment Rights Act [*Military*]
USERS........ Uniform Socio-Economic Reporting System [*Financial reporting system for voluntary health and welfare organizations*]
USES........ United States Employment Service [*Department of Labor*]
US ES........ US Energy Systems, Inc. [*Associated Press*] (SAG)
USES........ U.S. Environmental Solutions [*NASDAQ symbol*] (TTSB)
USES........ US Environmental Solutions, Inc. [*NASDAQ symbol*] (SAG)
USESF........ United States Exchange Stabilization Fund
US-ESRIC.... US-El Salvador Research and Information Center (EA)
USESSA...... United States Environmental Science Services Administration (AABC)
US ESys...... US Energy Systems, Inc. [*Associated Press*] (SAG)
USET........ United South and Eastern Tribes (EA)
USET........ United States Equestrian Team (EA)
USEU........ United States Mission to the European Union
USEUCOM...... United States European Command
USEUCOM.... United States European Communications (SAA)
USExpInc...... United States Exploration, Inc. [*Associated Press*] (SAG)

USEY	US Energy Systems, Inc. [*NASDAQ symbol*] (SAG)
USF	Lommen Health Science Library, University of South Dakota, Vermillion, SD [*OCLC symbol*] (OCLC)
USF	Und So Fort [*And So Forth*] [*German*]
USF	Uniaxial Stress Field
USF	United Scleroderma Foundation (EA)
USF	United Socialist Front [*Thailand*] [*Political party*] (PD)
USF	United Somali Front [*Political party*] (EY)
USF	United States Filter Corp. [*NYSE symbol*] (SAG)
USF	United States Fleet
USF	United States Forces (CINC)
USF	University of San Francisco [*California*]
USF	Upstream Stimualtory Factor [*Genetics*]
USF	U.S. Facilities Corp. (EFIS)
USF	U.S. Filter [*NYSE symbol*] (TTSB)
USF	US Filter Corp. [*NYSE symbol*] (SPSG)
USFA	United Sports Fans of America (EA)
USFA	United States Fencing Association (EA)
USFA	United States Fire Administration [*Federal Emergency Management Agency*] (GFGA)
USFA	United States Forces in Austria
USFA	United States Fuel Administration [*Terminated*]
USFA	US Farmers Association (EA)
US Facil	United States Facilities [*Associated Press*] (SAG)
US Facl	United States Facilities Corp. [*Associated Press*] (SAG)
USFADTC	United States Fleet Air Defense Training Center
USFAIRWINGMED	United States Fleet Air Wing, Mediterranean (NATG)
USF & G	United States Fidelity & Guaranty Co.
USFARS	United States Federation of Amateur Roller Skaters [*Later, USAC-RS*] (EA)
USFBI	United States Forces, British Isles [*World War II*]
USFC	United States Foil Co.
USFC	USFreightways [*NASDAQ symbol*] [*Formerly, TNT Freightways*] (SG)
USFC	USFreightways Corp. [*NASDAQ symbol*] (SAG)
USFCA	United States Fencing Coaches Association (EA)
USFCC	United States Fire Companies Conference [*Defunct*] (EA)
USFCC	US Federation for Culture Collections (EA)
USFCF	USF Constellation Foundation (EA)
USFCT	United States Forces, China Theater
USFET	United States Forces, European Theater [*American headquarters for occupation of Germany after SHAEF was dissolved*] [*World War II*]
USFF	United States Flag Foundation (EA)
USFFL	United States Flag Football League (EA)
USFG	USF & G Corp. [*Associated Press*] (SAG)
USFGC	US Feed Grains Council (EA)
USFGP	USF & G Pacholder Fund, Inc. [*Associated Press*] (SAG)
USFHA	USA Field Hockey Association (EA)
USFHP	Uniformed Services Family Health Plan [*DoD*]
USFI	Unione Sindacale Ferrovieri Italiani [*National Union of Italian Railway Workers*]
USFIA	United States Forces in Australia
US Filter	United States Filter Corp. [*Associated Press*] (SAG)
USFIP	United States Forces in the Philippines
USFIS	United States Foundation for International Scouting (EA)
USFISC	United States Foreign Intelligence Surveillance Court
USFIT	User Standards Forum for Information Technology (NITA)
USFJ	United States Forces, Japan (CINC)
USFK	United States Forces, Korea
USFL	US Football League [*Defunct*] (EA)
USFMG	United States Fastener Manufacturing Group [*Defunct*] (EA)
USFMG	United States Foreign Medical Graduate (DHSM)
USFMIA	United States Fishmeal Importers Association [*Defunct*] (EA)
USFOA	United States Forces, Occupation Austria [*World War II*]
USFOR	United States Forces
USFORAZ	United States Forces in Azores
USFORSCOM	US Forces Command [*Specified*] (DOMA)
USFP	Union Socialiste des Forces Populaires [*Socialist Union of Popular Forces*] [*Morocco*] [*Political party*] (PPW)
USFP	United States Federation of Pelota (EA)
USFP	United States Forces, Police
USFPS	United States Forces, Police Squadron
USFR	United States Fleet Reserve
US Frch	US Franchise Systems, Inc. [*Associated Press*] (SAG)
USFreight	USFreightways Corp. [*Associated Press*] (SAG)
USFS	United Society of Fitters and Smiths [*A union*] [*British*]
USFS	United States Foreign Service [*Department of State*]
USFS	United States Forest Service
USFS	United States Frequency Standard
USFS	US Flywheel Systems [*Research center*] (ECON)
USFS	US Franchise Systems, Inc. [*NASDAQ symbol*] (SAG)
USFSA	United States Figure Skating Association (EA)
USFSPA	Uniformed Services Former Spouse Protection Act [*Military*]
USFSS	United States Fleet SONAR School
USFSS	US Federation of Scholars and Scientists (EA)
USFTA	United States Floor Tennis Association [*Defunct*] (EA)
USFTL	US Flag and Touch Football League (EA)
USFU	Unglazed Structural Facing Units [*Technical drawings*]
USFV	United States Forces, Vietnam
USFVL Rev	University of San Fernando Valley. Law Review [*A publication*] (DLA)
USFWS	United States Fish and Wildlife Service [*Department of the Interior*]
USG	Ultrasonic Space Grating
USG	Ultrasonography
USG	Ultrasound Echography [*Medicine*] (DB)
USG	Ulysses Simpson Grant [*US general and president, 1822-1885*]

USG	Underwater Systems Group [*Range Commanders Council*] [*White Sands Missile Range, NM*]
USG	Undoped Silicate Glass (AAEL)
USG	Union of Superiors General (EA)
USG	United States Gallon (IAA)
USG	United States Gauge
USG	United States Government
USG	United States Gypsum Co. (EFIS)
USG	User Support Group (NITA)
USG	USG Corp. [*NYSE symbol*] (SPSG)
USG	US Grant Mining [*Vancouver Stock Exchange symbol*]
USGA	Ulysses S. Grant Association (EA)
USGA	United States Golf Association (EA)
USGA	US Green Alliance (EA)
USGAL	United States Gallon (IAA)
USGBX	Mgn. Stanley D. Witter U.S. Govt. Secs Cl.B [*Mutual fund ticker symbol*] (SG)
USGC	US Geodynamics Committee (EA)
USGCA	US Government Contract Awards (NITA)
USGCC/A	United States Group Control Council/Austria [*World War II*]
USGCC/G	United States Group Control Council/Germany [*World War II*]
USGCLR	United States-German Committee on Learning and Remembrance [*Defunct*] (EA)
USGCM	United States Government Correspondence Manual
USGCRP	United States Global Change Research Program (BARN)
USGF	United States Gymnastics Federation (EA)
USGIC	United States Global-Positioning-Satellite Industry Council
USGIPU	United States Group of the Inter-Parliamentary Union (EA)
USGL	United States Gold Corp. [*NASDAQ symbol*] (SAG)
USGL	U.S. Gold Corp. [*NASDAQ symbol*] (TTSB)
USGLI	United States Government Life Insurance
USGlobal	US Global Investors, Inc. [*Associated Press*] (SAG)
USGLW	Union of Saddlers and General Leather Workers [*British*]
USGM	United States Government Manual [*A publication*] (OICC)
US Gold	United States Gold Corp. [*Associated Press*] (SAG)
USGP	United States Grand Prix [*Auto racing*]
USGPM	United States Government Purchasing Mission [*World War II*]
USGPO	United States Government Printing Office
USGR	United States Government Report (IEEE)
USGRA	United States Government Report Announcements (IID)
USGRDR	United States Government Research and Development Reports [*Later, GRA*]
USGRDR-I	United States Government Research and Development Reports Index [*Later, GRI*]
USGRR	United States Government Research Reports [*National Bureau of Standards publication*]
USGS	United States Geological Survey [*Reston, VA*] [*Databank originator*]
USGS	U. S. Geological Survey
USGSA	United States Grain Standards Act (GFGA)
USGSA	United States Grass Ski Association (EA)
USGSA	United States Gymnastic Safety Association
USGSC	United States Global Strategy Council (EA)
USGSG	United States Government Standard Gage (IAA)
USGSS	United States Government Survey System (COE)
USGW	Underwater-to-Surface Guided Weapon (MCD)
USG.WS	USG Corp. Wrrt [*NYSE symbol*] (TTSB)
U SH	Shilling [*Monetary unit in Uganda*]
USH	United Scientific Holdings [*Defense equipment manufacturer*] [*British*]
USH	Universal Sleeve Housing (COE)
USH	Ushuaia [*Argentina*] [*Airport symbol*] (OAG)
USH	USLIFE Corp. [*NYSE symbol*] (SPSG)
USHA	United States Handball Association (EA)
USHA	United States Housing Authority [*Functions transferred to Public Housing Commissioner, 1947*]
USHB	Uniformed Services Health Benefits
USHBP	Uniformed Services Health Benefits Program
USHC	United States Housing Corp. [*Terminated, 1952*]
USHC	U.S. Healthcare [*NASDAQ symbol*] (TTSB)
USHC	US Healthcare, Inc. [*NASDAQ symbol*] (NQ)
USHCA	US Horse Cavalry Association (EA)
USHCC	US Hispanic Chamber of Commerce (EA)
USHDA	United States Highland Dancing Association (EA)
USHDI	United States Historical Documents Institute
USHE	Upstream Heat Exchanger (AAG)
USHG	United States Home Guard
USHG	U.S. Home & Garden [*NASDAQ symbol*] (TTSB)
USHG	US Home & Garden, Inc. [*NASDAQ symbol*] (SAG)
US HG	US Home & Garden, Inc. [*Associated Press*] (SAG)
USHGA	United States Hop Growers Association
USHGA	US Hang Gliding Association (EA)
USHGW	US Home & Garden Wrrt'A' [*NASDAQ symbol*] (TTSB)
USHH	Khanty-Mansiysk [*Former USSR ICAO location identifier*] (ICLI)
USHIGEO	United States National Committee for the History of Geology (EA)
USHL	United States Hockey League
USHL	United States Hydrograph Laboratory
USHL	United States Hygienic Laboratory
US Hlth	United States Healthcare, Inc. [*Associated Press*] (SAG)
USHm	US Home Corp. [*Associated Press*] (SAG)
USHMAC	United States Health Manpower Advisory Council
USHMC	US Holocaust Memorial Council
USHmcr	US HomeCare Corp. [*Associated Press*] (SAG)
USHme	US Home Corp. [*Associated Press*] (SAG)
USHmGrd	US Home & Garden, Inc. [*Associated Press*] (SAG)
USHO	United States Hydrographic Office [*Later, Naval Oceanographic Office*]

USHO.......... U.S. HomeCare [*NASDAQ symbol*] (TTSB)
USHO.......... US HomeCare Corp. [*NASDAQ symbol*] (SPSG)
USHP.......... United States Helium Plant [*Amarillo, TX*]
USHP.......... U-Ship Inc. [*NASDAQ symbol*] (TTSB)
USHRA........ United States Hot Rod Association [*Auto racing*]
USHSLA...... US Hide, Skin, and Leather Association (EA)
USHTA........ United States Handicap Tennis Association (EA)
USHWA....... United States Harness Writers' Association (EA)
USHWC....... US Helsinki Watch Committee (EA)
USI.............. Mabaruma [*Guyana*] [*Airport symbol*] (OAG)
USI.............. Ultrasonic System [*Vancouver Stock Exchange symbol*]
USI.............. Ultraviolet Spectroheliographic Instrument
USI.............. Union of Students in Ireland (AIE)
USI.............. United Schools International [*New Delhi, India*] (EAIO)
USI.............. United Service Institution (BARN)
USI.............. United Sons of Israel (EA)
USI.............. United States Industries, Inc. [*NYSE symbol*] (SAG)
USI.............. United States Industry
USI.............. United States Information Agency, Washington, DC [*OCLC symbol*] (OCLC)
USI.............. United States of Indonesia (BARN)
USI.............. Universal Software Interface [*MRI Systems Corp.*]
USI.............. University Systems, Inc. (AAGC)
USI.............. Unlawful Sexual Intercourse
USI.............. Unresolved Safety Issue [*Nuclear energy*] (NRCH)
USI.............. Unsigned Short Integer [*Computer science*]
USI.............. Update Software Identity (MCD)
usi.............. Update Software Identity (NAKS)
USI.............. Uranium Supply - Import Model [*Department of Energy*] (GFGA)
USI.............. Urinary Stress Incontinence [*Urology*] (DAVI)
USI.............. User Software Integration Subsystem [*Space Flight Operations Facility, NASA*]
USI.............. User System Interface (NITA)
USI.............. US, Inc. (EA)
USI.............. US Industries [*Subsidiary of the Hanson Group*] [*British*] (ECON)
USIA.......... United States Information Agency [*Formerly called BECA, it later became known as ICA or USICA, then again as USIA*]
USIA.......... US Inspection Agency (DOMA)
USIAC........ United States Inter-American Council [*Later, COA*] (EA)
USIAEA....... United States Mission to the International Atomic Energy Agency
USIAPR....... United States Information Agency Procurement [*A publication*] (AAGC)
USIB.......... United States Intelligence Board [*Later, NFIB*] [*National Security Council*]
USIBA........ United States International Book Association (NTCM)
USIC.......... Undersea Instrument Chamber [*Marine science*] (MSC)
USIC.......... Union Sportive Interuniversitaire Canadienne
USIC.......... United States Industrial Council (EA)
USIC.......... United States Information Center [*Department of State*] (MCD)
USIC.......... User-Specific Integrated Circuit [*Electronics*] (AAEL)
USIC.......... US Industrial Coalition [*For finding commercial use of nuclear technology*]
USICA........ United States International Communication Agency [*Also, ICA*] [*Formerly called BECA and USIA, it later became known again as USIA*]
USICC........ United States Industrial Chemical Co. (KSC)
USICC Rep... United States Interstate Commerce Commission Reports [*A publication*] (DLA)
USICCVR...... United States Interstate Commerce Commission Valuation Reports [*A publication*] (DLA)
US ICDBL.... US Branch of the International Committee for the Defense of the Breton Language (EA)
USICF........ Union Sportive Interuniversitaire Canadienne Feminine
USICID........ United States National Committee, International Commission on Irrigation and Drainage
US/ICID....... US Committee on Irrigation and Drainage [*Formerly, USCIDFC*] (EA)
US/ICOMOS.. United States Committee of the International Council on Monuments and Sites (EA)
USIDF........ United States Icelandic Defense Forces (MCD)
USIFA........ US International Fireball Association (EA)
USIHR........ US Institute of Human Rights (EA)
USIITA........ United States Indian International Travel Agency, Inc.
USILA........ United States Intercollegiate Lacrosse Association (EA)
USIMC....... United States International Marketing Center [*American Embassy, London*] (CB)
USIMCA...... United States International Moth Class Association (EA)
USINCC....... United States International Narcotics Control Commission
US Inds....... United States Industries, Inc. [*Associated Press*] (SAG)
USINOA....... US Immigration and Naturalization Officers' Association (EA)
USINS........ United States Immigration and Naturalization Service (BARN)
USINT........ United States Interests Section [*Foreign Service*]
USIO.......... Unidentified Submerged Illuminated Object (DNAB)
USIO.......... United States Industrial Outlook [*A publication*]
USIO.......... United States Institute of Oceanography (DNAB)
USIO.......... Unlimited Sequential Input/Output
USIP.......... United Solomon Islands Party (PPW)
USIP.......... University of Stockholm Institute of Physics
USIP.......... US Institute of Peace (EA)
USIPC........ Uniformed Services Identification and Privilege Card (AFM)
USIPU........ United States Inter-Parliamentary Union (EA)
USIRB........ United States Internal Revenue Bonded
USIS.......... Ultraviolet Stratospheric Imaging Spectrometer (MCD)
USIS.......... United States Information Service [*Name used abroad for USIA offices*]
USISA........ United States International Sailing Association (EA)

USISA........ United States International Skating Association
USISCA....... US Islands 17 Class Association [*Defunct*] (EA)
USISL........ United States Information Service Library (DIT)
USISSA....... United States International Speed Skating Association (EA)
US-ISY....... US International Space Year Association (EA)
USIT.......... Unit Share Investment Trust
USITA........ United States Independent Telephone Association (EA)
USITA........ United States International Tempest Association (EA)
USITC........ United States International Trade Commission
USITC Pub... United States International Trade Commission. Publication [*A publication*] (DLA)
USITE........ United States International Transportation Exposition (PDAA)
USITO........ United States Industrial & Trade Outlook [*A publication*]
USITT........ United States Institute for Theatre Technology (EA)
USITT........ USITT: The American Association of Design and Production Professionals in the Performing Arts (NTPA)
USIU.......... United States International University [*San Diego, CA*]
USJ.......... Uniformed Services Journal [*A publication*]
USJ.......... United States Jaycees (EA)
USJ.......... United States Judo (EA)
USJ.......... US Jet, Inc. [*ICAO designator*] (FAAC)
USJA.......... United States Judo Association (EA)
USJAC........ US-Japan Culture Center (EA)
US JAYCEE... United States Junior Chamber of Commerce [*Later, United States Jaycees*] (EA)
USJB.......... Union Saint-Jean-Baptiste (EA)
USJBC........ US-Japan Business Council (EA)
USJCA........ United States Joint Communication Agency (NATG)
USJCB........ Unites States Joint Communication Board (IAA)
USJCC........ United States Junior Chamber of Commerce [*Later, United States Jaycees*] (EA)
USJCC........ US-Japan Culture Center (EA)
USJCIRPTE... United States-Japan Committee on Industry Related Policies and Their Trade Effects [*Acronym pronounced "use-jay-krip-tee"*]
USJCS........ United States Joint Chiefs of Staff (NATG)
US-JCSC...... United States-Japan Committee on Scientific Cooperation [*Department of State*]
USJF.......... United States Judo Federation (EA)
USJF.......... United States Justice Foundation (EA)
USJNRP...... United States/Japan Natural Resources Panel
USJPRS....... United States Joint Publications Research Service
US-JTC....... United States-Japan Trade Council (EA)
USJTF........ United States Joint Task Force (AABC)
US Jur........ United States Jurist [*A publication*] (DLA)
USJUWTF... United States Joint Unconventional Warfare Task Force (AABC)
USK.......... Ultrasonic Kit
USK.......... United States Forces, Korea
USKA.......... United States Kart Association [*Defunct*] (EA)
USKBA........ United Strictly Kosher Butchers Association
USKBTC...... United States Kerry Blue Terrier Club (EA)
USKEC........ US-Korea Economic Council [*Later, KS*] (EA)
USKF.......... United States Korfball Federation (EA)
USKOREA.... United States Forces Korea
USKOS........ US-Korea Society [*Later, KS*] (EA)
USI.............. Salt Lake City Public Library, Salt Lake City, UT [*Library symbol Library of Congress*] (LCLS)
USL.......... Underwater Sound Laboratory [*New London, CT*] [*Navy*]
USL.......... Unemployed Supernumerary List [*Military British*]
USL.......... Unique Suppliers List
USL.......... United Satellites Ltd. [*London, England*] [*Telecommunications*] (TSSD)
USL.......... United Soccer League (EA)
USL.......... United States Laws (DLA)
USL.......... United States Legation
USL.......... Unit Spares List
USL.......... Universal Sign Language (EERA)
USL.......... Unix Systems Laboratory [*Computer science*]
USL.......... Upper Specified Limit
USL.......... Upper Square Law Limit (IAA)
USL.......... Up Stage Left [*Away from audience*] [*A stage direction*]
USL.......... Useless Loop [*Australia Airport symbol*] (OAG)
USL.......... US Long Distance [*Vancouver Stock Exchange symbol*]
USL.......... Usual (ROG)
USLA.......... United States Committee for Justice to Latin American Political Prisoners [*Defunct*] (EA)
USLA.......... United States Lifesaving Association (EA)
USLA.......... United States Luge Association (EA)
USL & H...... United States Longshoremen and Harborworkers Act
USLANT...... United States Atlantic Subarea [*NATO*]
USLANTCOM... US Atlantic Command [*Unified*] (DOMA)
US Law Ed... United States Supreme Court Reports, Lawyers' Edition [*A publication*] (DLA)
US Law Int... United States Law Intelligencer and Review [*Providence and Philadelphia*] [*A publication*] (DLA)
US Law Jour... United States Law Journal [*A publication*] (DLA)
US Law Mag... United States Law Magazine [*A publication*] (DLA)
USLC.......... Church of Jesus Christ of Latter-Day Saints, Historian's Office, Salt Lake City,UT [*Library symbol Library of Congress*] (LCLS)
USLC.......... United States Locals Collectors (EA)
USLCA........ United States Lacrosse Coaches' Association (EA)
USLCMBA... US Letter Carriers Mutual Benefit Association [*Washington, DC*] (EA)
USLD.......... Daughters of Utah Pioneers Museum Library, Salt Lake City, UT [*Library symbol Library of Congress*] (LCLS)
USLD.......... Ultrasonic Link Detector

USLD	Union des Syndicats Libres du Dahomey [*Federation of Free Unions of Dahomey*]
USLD	United States Long Distance [*NASDAQ symbol*] (SAG)
USLD	USLD Communications [*NASDAQ symbol*] [*Formerly, US Long Distance*] (SG)
USLD	US Long Distance [*NASDAQ symbol*] (SAG)
USLDMA	United States Lanolin and Derivative Manufacturers Association [*Defunct*] (EA)
USLE	Universal Soil Loss Equation [*Agricultural engineering*]
USL Ed	Lawyers' Edition, United States Supreme Court Reports [*A publication*] (DLA)
USL Ed 2d	Lawyers' Edition, United States Supreme Court Reports, Second Series [*A publication*] (DLA)
UslfeF	USLIFE Income Fund, Inc. [*Associated Press*] (SAG)
USIGS	Church of Jesus Christ of Latter-Day Saints, Genealogical Society Library, Salt Lake City, UT [*Library symbol Library of Congress*] (LCLS)
USLH	University of Southwestern Louisiana Herbarium
USLHS	United States Lighthouse Society (EA)
USLI	Ultra Large Scale Integration (NTCM)
USLIFE	USLIFE Corp. [*Associated Press*] (SAG)
USLime	United States Lime & Minerals Co. [*Associated Press*] (SAG)
USLJ	United States Law Journal [*New Haven and New York*] [*A publication*] (DLA)
USIL	Latter-Day Saints Museum, Salt Lake City, UT [*Library symbol Library of Congress*] (LCLS)
USLM	US Lime & Minerals [*NASDAQ symbol*] (SPSG)
USL Mag	US States Law Magazine [*A publication*] (DLA)
USLMRA	United States Lawn Mower Racing Association
USLO	United States Liaison Office [*or Officer*]
USLO	University Students for Law and Order
USLOK	US Liaison Office-Kuwait (DOMA)
US Long	US Long Distance [*Associated Press*] (SAG)
US LongD	United States Long Distance [*Associated Press*] (SAG)
USIOr	Oregon Short Line Law Department, Salt Lake City, UT [*Library symbol Library of Congress Obsolete*] (LCLS)
USLO SACA	United States Liaison Officer to Supreme Allied Commander, Atlantic (MUGU)
USLOT	US Liaison Office-Tunisia (DOMA)
USIP	Pioneer Memorial Museum, Salt Lake City, UT [*Library symbol Library of Congress*] (LCLS)
USLP	United States Labor Party
USLS	United States Lake Survey [*Marine science*] (MSC)
USLS	United States Lighthouse Society (EA)
USLSA	United States League of Savings Associations [*Later, USLSI*]
USLSA	United States Livestock Sanitary Association [*Later, United States Animal Health Association*] (EA)
USLSI	United States League of Savings Institutions [*Chicago, IL*] (EA)
USLSO	United States Logistics Support Office (AFM)
USISIM	College of Saint Mary of the Wasatch, Salt Lake City, UT [*Library symbol Library of Congress Obsolete*] (LCLS)
USIT	Utah Technical College at Salt Lake, Salt Lake City, UT [*Library symbol Library of Congress*] (LCLS)
USLTA	Uniform Simplification of Land Transfers Act (DICI)
USLTA	United States Lawn Tennis Association [*Later, USTA*] (EA)
USLTC	United States Lakeland Terrier Club (EA)
USLW	United States Law Week [*Bureau of National Affairs*] [*A publication*] (DLA)
USIW	Westminster College, Salt Lake City, UT [*Library symbol Library of Congress*] (LCLS)
USM	Underwater-to-Surface Missile [*Air Force*]
USM	Uniform Staffing Methodologies [*DoD*]
USM	United Securities Market [*British*] (CDAI)
USM	United States Mail
USM	United States Marine
USM	United States Mint
USM	United States Minutemen [*Defunct*] (EA)
USM	United States Representative to the Military Committee Memorandum [*NATO*]
USM	University of Southern Mississippi
USM	Unlisted Securities Market [*London Stock Exchange*]
USM	Unsaponifiable Matter [*Organic analytical chemistry*]
USM	Unscheduled Maintenance
USM	U.S. Cellular [*AMEX symbol*] (TTSB)
USM	US Cellular Corp. [*AMEX symbol*] (SPSG)
UsM	US Microfilm Corp., Jacksonville, FL [*Library symbol Library of Congress*] (LCLS)
USMA	Underfeed Stoker Makers' Association [*British*] (BI)
USMA	United States Maritime Administration
USMA	United States Military Academy [*West Point, NY*]
USMA	United States Military Attache
USMA	United States Monopoly Association (EA)
USMA	United Street Machine Association (EA)
USMA	US Maritime Academy (DOMA)
USMA	US Metric Association (EA)
USMA	US Military Academy (DOMA)
USMAC	United States Marine Air Corps
USMAC	United States Military Assistance Command
USMACSV	United States Military Assistance Command, South Vietnam [*Obsolete*]
USMACTHAI	United States Military Assistance Command, Thailand [*Obsolete*] (AFM)
USMACV	United States Military Assistance Command, Vietnam [*Obsolete*]
USMA/ESGS	United States Military Academy Department of Earth, Space, and Graphic Sciences [*West Point, NY*]
USMAG	United States Military Advisory Group
USMAPS	United States Military Academy Preparatory School
USMAPU	United States Military Academy Preparatory Unit
USMARC	Advisory Committee for the US Meat Animal Research Center [*Terminated, 1977*] (EGAO)
USMATS	United States Military Air Transport Service [*Later, Military Airlift Command*]
USMB	United States Marine Barracks
USMB	United States Metric Board [*Terminated*]
USMBHA	US-Mexico Border Health Association (EA)
USMBP	US-Mexico Border Program (EA)
USMC	United States Marine Corps
USMC	United States Maritime Commission [*Functions transferred to Department of Commerce, 1950*]
USMCA	United States Men's Curling Association [*Later, USCA*] (EA)
USMCA	US Mariner Class Association (EA)
USMCA	US Mirror Class Association (EA)
USMCAM	United States Military Community Activity, Mannheim
USMCAS	United States Marine Corps Air Station
USMCB	United States Marine Corps Base (MCD)
USMCC	United States Mint - Carson City (ROG)
USMCCCA	US Marine Corps Combat Correspondents Association (EA)
USMCDIA	United States Marine Corps Drill Instructors Association (EA)
USMCEB	United States Military Communications Electronics Board (NVT)
USMCMG	US Mine Countermeasures Group (DOMA)
USMCOC	United States-Mexico Chamber of Commerce [*See also CCMEU*] (EA)
USMCP	United States Military Construction Program (CINC)
USMCR	United States Marine Corps Reserve
USMCR(AF)	United States Marine Corps Reserve (Aviation Fleet)
USMCR(AO)	United States Marine Corps Reserve (Aviation, Organized)
USMCR(AV)	United States Marine Corps Reserve (Aviation, Volunteer)
USMCR(F)	United States Marine Corps Reserve (Fleet)
USMCR(LS)	United States Marine Corps Reserve (Limited Service)
USMCR(NAV)	United States Marine Corps Reserve (Naval Aviators)
USMCR(NAVO)	United States Marine Corps Reserve (Graduate Aviation Cadets, Volunteer)
USMCR(NAVT)	United States Marine Corps Reserve (Aviation Specialist Transport Pilot, Volunteer)
USMCR(O)	United States Marine Corps Reserve (Organized)
USMCRTC	United States Marine Corps Reserve Training Center
USMCR(V)	United States Marine Corps Reserve (Volunteer)
USMCR(VS)	United States Marine Corps Reserve (Volunteer Specialists)
USMCR(W)	United States Marine Corps Reserve (Women)
USMCSS	United States Marine Corps Selective Service Selectee
USMCSSV	United States Marine Corps Selective Service Volunteer
USMC(W)	United States Marine Corps (Women)
USMCWR	United States Marine Corps Women's Reserve
USMD	U.S. Medical Products [*NASDAQ symbol*] (TTSR)
USMECBL	United States Mission to the European Communities in Belgium and Luxembourg
USMEF	United States Meat Export Federation (EA)
USMEMILCOMUN	United States Members, United Nations Military Staff Committee
USMEOUN	United States Mission to the European Office of the United Nations
USMEPC	United States Military Enlistment Processing Command
USMEPCOM	United States Military Entrance Processing Command
USMES	Unified Science and Mathematics for Elementary Schools [*National Science Foundation*]
USMF	United States Sports Massage Federation (EA)
USMG	United States Medical Graduate
USMH	United States Marine Hospital
USMHS	United States Marine Hospital Service
USMI	Universal Software Market Identifier [*Technique Learning*] [*Information service or system*] (IID)
USMIAEAA	United States Mission to the International Atomic Energy Agency in Austria
USMICC	United States Military Information Control Committee (AFM)
USMID	Ultrasensitive Microwave Infrared Detector
USMILADREP	United States Military Advisor's Representative (CINC)
USMILADREPSMPO	United States Military Advisor's Representative, Southeast Asia Treaty Organization, Military Planning Office (CINC)
USMILATTACHE	United States Military Attache
USMILCOMUN	United States Delegation, United Nations Military Staff Committee
USMILGP	United States Military Group (COE)
USMILLIAS	United States Military Liaison Office
USMILREP	United States Military Representative (COE)
USMILTAG	United States Military Technical Advisory Group (AFM)
USMITT	United States Masters International Track Team [*Defunct*] (EA)
USML	United States Microgravity Laboratory [*NASA*]
USML	Universal Standard Medical Labs [*NASDAQ symbol*] (SAG)
USML	Univl Standard Medl Labs [*NASDAQ symbol*] (TTSB)
USML	US Munitions List (DOMA)
USMLM	United States Military Liaison Mission (MCD)
USML Mag	United States Monthly Law Magazine [*A publication*] (DLA)
USMLMCINCGSFG	United States Military Liaison Mission to Commander-in-Chief, Group Soviet Forces, Germany (AABC)
USMLO	United States Military Liaison Office
USMLS	United States Museum Librarian Society (EA)
USMM	Union Socialiste des Musulmans Mauritaniens [*Socialist Union of Mauritanian Moslems*]
USMM	United States Merchant Marine
USMMA	United States Merchant Marine Academy [*Kings Point, NY*]
USMMCC	United States Merchant Marine Cadet Corps
USMMVETS WW2	US Merchant Marine Veterans of World War II (EA)

USMNAM..... United States Military North African Mission [*World War II*]
USMO .... United States Marshals Office
US Month Law Mag... United States Monthly Law Magazine [*A publication*] (DLA)
USMP .... United States Mallard Project [*Army*]
USMP .... United States Microgravity Payload [*NASA*]
USMP .... US Microgravity Payload [*NASA*]
USMPA .... United States Modern Pentathlon Association (EA)
USMPBA ..... United States Modern Pentathlon and Biathlon Association [*Later, USMPA*] (EA)
USMPTC ...... United States Modern Pentathlon Training Center [*Military*] (AABC)
USMS .... Unattended Sensor Monitoring System
USMS .... United States Maritime Service
USMS .... United States Marshall Service [*Department of Justice*]
USMS .... United States Masters Swimming (EA)
USMS .... United States Mint - San Francisco (ROG)
USMSA .... United States Marine Safety Association (EA)
USMSA .... United States Military Sports Association
USMSGS ..... United States Maritime Service Graduate Station
USMSMI ..... United States Military Supply Mission to India (AFM)
USMSOS ..... United States Maritime Service Officers School
USMSR .... United States Military Specification Requirements (MCD)
USMSSB ..... United States Machine Screw Service Bureau [*Defunct*] (EA)
USMSTS ..... United States Maritime Service Training School
USMSTS ..... United States Maritime Service Training Ship
USMSTS ..... United States Maritime Service Training Station
USMT .... United States Military Transport
USMTF .... United States Message Text Format (COE)
USMTF .... United States Message Text Formating
USMTM .... United States Military Training Mission (MCD)
USMTMSA .. United States Military Training Mission to Saudi Arabia
USMWR ...... United States Mission Weekly Report [*Military*]
USMWW ..... United Society of Mechanical Wood Workers [*A union*] [*British*]
USMX .... USMX, Inc. [*Formerly, US Minerals & Explorations Co.*] [*NASDAQ symbol*] (NQ)
USN .... Ultrasonic Nebulizer
USN .... Under Secretary of the Navy
USN .... Union des Scolaires Nigeriens [*Union of Nigerian Scholars*]
USN .... United States Adopted Name (LDT)
USN .... United States Industries, Inc. [*NYSE symbol*] (SAG)
USN .... United States Navy
USNA .... United States National Army
USNA .... United States Naval Academy [*Annapolis, MD*]
USNA .... United States Naval Aircraft
USNA .... United States Naval Attache (GFGA)
USNA .... USANA, Inc [*NASDAQ symbol*] (SAG)
USNAAA...... United States Naval Academy Alumni Association
USNAAA...... United States Naval Academy Athletic Association
USNA ANNA... United States Naval Academy, Annapolis [*Maryland*]
USNAAS...... United States Naval Auxiliary Air Station
USNAB........ United States Naval Advanced Base [*World War II*]
USNAB........ United States Naval Amphibious Base
USNAC .... United States Naval Administrative Command
USNAC .... United States Naval Air Corps
USNAC .... United States of America National Committee of the International Dairy Federation (EA)
USNACC...... United States Naval Member of the Allied Control Commission [*Germany*]
USNADC ...... United States Naval Air Development Center
USNA-EPRD... United States Naval Academy Energy-Environment Study Group and Development Team
USNA-EW ... United States Naval Academy Division of Engineering and Weapons
USNAF........ United States Naval Avionics Facility
USNAG........ United States Navy Astronautics Group (SAA)
USNAHALO... United States NATO Hawk Liaison Office [*Missiles*] (NATG)
USNAMTC.... United States Naval Air Missile Test Center
USN & USMCRC... United States Navy and United States Marine Corps Reserve Center (DNAB)
USNARS ...... United States National Archives and Records Service (DIT)
USNAS .... United States Naval Air Service
USNAS........ United States Naval Air Station
USNATC...... United States Naval Air Training Center
USNATO ...... United States Mission to the North Atlantic Treaty Organization [*Department of State*] (NATG)
USNATRA .... United States Naval Training
US Naval ..... United States Naval Postgraduate School (GAGS)
USNAVCENT... US Naval Forces, [*US*] Central Command (DOMA)
USNAVEUR... United States Naval Forces Europe (MCD)
USNAVFORCONAD... United States Naval Forces, Continental Air Defense Command (DNAB)
USNAVMILCOMUN... United States Navy Representative, Military Staff Committee, United Nations (DNAB)
USNAVPRO.... United States Navy Plan Representative Office
USNAVREGDENCEN... United States Naval Regional Dental Center (DNAB)
USNAVREGMEDCEN... United States Naval Regional Medical Center (DNAB)
USNAVSO .... United States Navy Forces Southern Command (AFM)
USNAVSOUTHC... United States Navy Southern Command
USNAVSOUTHCOM... United States Navy Southern Command
USNAVSUPACT... United States Naval Supply Activity (CINC)
USNAVWEASERV... United States Naval Weather Service
USNAVYMILCOMUN... United States Naval Representative, United Nations Military Staff Committee
USNB .... United States Naval Base (MUGU)
USNBS .... United States National Bureau of Standards (IAA)
USNC .... United States National Commission for UNESCO [*of the Department of State*]

USNC .... United States National Committee [*IEC*]
USNCB .... United States National Central Bureau
USNCB .... United States Naval Construction Battalion [*SEABEES*] [*BUDOCKS; later, FEC, NFEC*]
USNCBS ...... US National Committee for Byzantine Studies (EA)
USNC/CIE .... US National Committee of the Commission Internationale de l'Eclairage [*International Commission on Illumination*] (EA)
USNC/DNDR... United States National Committee for the Decade for Natural Disaster Reduction
USNCEL ...... United States Naval Civil Engineering Laboratory [*Port Hueneme, CA*] (SAA)
USNCEREL... United States Naval Civil Engineering Research and Evaluation Laboratory
USNCFID...... United States National Committee for Federation Internationale de Documentation
USNC/IBP ... United States National Committee for the International Biological Program [*Defunct*] (EA)
USNCIEC...... United States National Committee of the International Electrotechnical Commission
USNC-IGY .... United States National Committee for the International Geophysical Year
USNCIPS...... United States National Committee of the International Peat Society (EA)
USNCPNM ... United States National Committee for the Preservation of Nubian Monuments [*Defunct*] (EA)
USNCSCOR... US National Committee for the Scientific Committee on Oceanic Research (EA)
USNCSM & FE... United States National Council on Soil Mechanics and Foundation Engineering
USNC-STR ... United States National Committee for Solar-Terrestrial Research (MCD)
USNC/TAM... US National Committee on Theoretical and Applied Mechanics (EA)
USNC/UPSI... United States National Committee/International Union of Radio Science (MCD)
USNC-URSI... United States National Committee for the Union Radio Scientifique Internationale [*International Union of Radio Science*] (EA)
USNCWEC.... United States National Committee of the World Energy Conference (EA)
USNCWFD ... US National Committee for World Food Day (EA)
USNDC........ United States Nuclear Data Committee [*Nuclear Regulatory Commission*]
USNDD........ United States Naval Drydocks
USNEDS....... United States Navy Experimental Diving Station
USNEES .... United States Naval Engineering Experiment Station [*Annapolis, MD*] (SAA)
USNEL .... United States Naval Electronics Laboratory
USNELM ...... United States Naval Forces, Eastern Atlantic and Mediterranean (MCD)
USNFCLC .... US National Federation of Christian Life Communities (EA)
USNFEC....... US National Fruit Export Council [*Defunct*] (EA)
USNFP .... US Nicaragua Friendship Project (EA)
USNFPN....... US Nuclear Free Pacific Network (EA)
USNFR .... United States Naval Fleet Reserve
USNG .... United States National Guard
USNH .... United States Naval Hospital
USNH .... United States, North of Cape Hatteras [*Shipping*]
USNHO .... United States Navy Hydrographic Office [*Later, NOO*] (NATG)
USNI .... United States Naval Institute (EA)
USN-I .... United States Regular Navy - Inductee
USN-I-CB ... United States Regular Navy - Inductee - Construction Battalion
USNID .... United States National Institute of Dance (EA)
USN(I)(SA)... United States Navy (Inductee) (Special Assignment)
USNL .... United States Navy League
USNLO .... United States Naval Liaison Officer
USNM .... United States National Museum [*Smithsonian Institution*]
USNMATOEROF... United States Mission to the North Atlantic Treaty Organization and European Regional Organizations in France
USNMDL ...... United States Navy Mine Defense Laboratory (MUGU)
USNMF .... United States Naval Missile Facility
USNMF .... United States Navy Memorial Foundation (EA)
USNMPS....... United States Naval Motion Picture Service (DNAB)
USNMR .... United States National Military Representative
USNMRC...... United States Naval Manpower Center (DNAB)
USNMSC...... United States Navy Medical Service Corps
USNMTC...... United States Naval Missile Test Center [*Point Mugu, CA*] (AAG)
USNO .... United Sabah National Organization [*Malaysia*] [*Political party*] (PPW)
USNO .... United States Naval Observatory
USNOA .... United States Norton Owners' Association (EA)
USNOADS .... United States Naval Observatory Automated Data Service [*Database*] [*Information service or system*] (CRD)
USNOBSY .... United States Naval Observatory Operating Bases System
USNOBSYSUBSTA... United States Naval Observatory, Time Service Sub-Station (DNAB)
USNODC ...... United States National Oceanographic Data Center [*Marine science*] (OSRA)
USNOO .... United States Naval Oceanographic Office [*Marine science*] (MSC)
US (Noth) .... Ueberlieferungsgeschichtliche Studien (M. Noth) [*A publication*] (BJA)
USNO-TS ..... United States Naval Observatory Time Service Division [*Washington, DC*]
USNOTS....... United States Naval Ordnance Test Station
USNOWSP .. United States Naval Ocean-Wide Survey Program (NOAA)
USNP .... United States Naval Prison
USNP .... United States Newspaper Program [*National Foundation on the Arts and the Humanities*] [*Information service or system*] (IID)

USNPACMISTESCEN...	US Navy Pacific Missile Test Center
USNPG.........	United States Naval Proving Ground
USNPGS	United States Naval Postgraduate School (MUGU)
USNPS........	United States National Parks Service [USA] (EERA)
USNPS........	United States Naval Postgraduate School
USNR..........	United States Naval Reserve
USNR..........	United States Navy Regulations
USN-R	United States Navy - Retired (DNAB)
USNR..........	U.S. Natural Resources, Inc. (EFIS)
USNR & SL...	United States Navy Radio and Sound Laboratory [San Diego, CA]
USNRB.........	United States Naval Repair Base
USNRC........	United States National Research Council [Toxicology]
USNRC........	United States Nuclear Regulatory Commission (NRCH)
USNRDL	United States Naval Radiological Defense Laboratory
USNRDL	United States Navy Research and Development Laboratory
USN(Ret)	United States Navy (Retired)
USNRF........	United States Naval Reserve Force
USNRL........	United States Naval Research Laboratory
USNRM......	United States Merchant Marine Reserve
USNRM1......	United States Merchant Marine Reserve Seagoing
USNRM2......	United States Merchant Marine Reserve Coastal Defense
USNRO	United States Organized Naval Reserve
USNRO1	United States Organized Naval Reserve Seagoing
USNRO2	United States Organized Naval Reserve Aviation
USN-ROTC...	United States Navy - Reserve Officers Training Corps
USNRP.........	United States National Reference Preparation [Centers for Disease Control]
USNR-R	United States Naval Reserve - Retired (DNAB)
USNR-S	United States Naval Reserve - Standby (DNAB)
USNRS........	United States Navy Recruiting Station
USNRSV	United States Naval Reserve, Selective Volunteer
USNRTC......	United States Naval Reserve Training Center
USNRV........	United States Naval Reserve, Volunteer
USNR(W)....	United States Naval Reserve (Women's Reserve)
USNS	United States National Committee on Standardization
USNS	United States Naval Ship [Civilian manned]
USNS	United States Naval Station
USNS	United States Navy Ship (NAKS)
USNS	United States NOTAM [Notice to Airmen] System [Aviation] (FAAC)
USNS	Universal Stabilized Night Sight
USNSA........	United States National Student Association [Later, USSA]
USNSC........	United States Naval Safety Code
USNSCF	United States Naval Shore Communication Facilities
USNSISSMFE...	US National Society for the International Society of Soil Mechanics and Foundation Engineering (EA)
USNSMC.......	United States Naval Submarine Medical Center
USNSMSES...	United States Navy Ship Missile System Engineering Station
USNSO........	United States Navy Southern Command
USNSPO	United States Navy Special Projects Office (DNAB)
USNSPS	United States National Stockpile Purchase Specification [for metals]
USN-SV.......	United States Regular Navy Selective Volunteer
USNTC	United States Naval Training Center
USNTDC.......	United States Naval Training Device Center
USNTI.........	United States Navy Travel Instructions
USNTPS	United States Naval Test Pilot School
USNTS	United States Naval Training School
USNUSL......	United States Navy Undersea Laboratory (IAA)
USNUSL......	United States Navy Underwater Sound Laboratory [BUSHIPS; later, ESC, NESC]
USNWC	United States Naval War College
USNZC	United States-New Zealand Council (EA)
USO	Udaipur Solar Observatory [India]
USO	Ultra Stable Oscillator [Instrumentation]
USO	Under Secretary of the Navy's Office
USO	Unidentified Submarine Object
USO	Unidentified Superconducting Object (ECON)
USO	Unilateral Salpingo-Oophorectomy [Gynecology] (MAE)
USO	United Service Organizations, Inc. (EA)
USO	United Siscoe Mines, Inc. [Toronto Stock Exchange symbol]
USO	United States Outfitters
USO	United States Overseas [Facetious translation of United Services Organization] (VNW)
USO	Unit Security Officer (AAG)
USO	Universal Service Order [Bell System] (TEL)
USO	Unmanned Seismological Observatory
USO	US 1 Indus [NYSE symbol] (TTSB)
USO	US Office - UTLAS Corp. [UTLAS symbol]
USO	US One Industries, Inc. [Formerly, Transcom, Inc.] [NYSE symbol] (SAG)
USOA..........	Uniform System of Accounts [Telecommunications] (TEL)
USOA..........	United States Olympic Association [Later, USOC]
USOA..........	United States Othello Association (EA)
USOA..........	United States Overseas Airlines
U So Ala......	University of South Alabama (GAGS)
USOAS.........	United States Mission to the Organization of American States [Department of State]
USO-ASPCC...	USO [United Service Organizations]-All Service Postal Chess Club [Later, ASPCC] (EA)
USOC	Uniform Service Order Code [Bell System] (TEL)
USOC	United States Olympic Committee (EA)
USOC	Universal Service Ordering Code [Telecommunications] (OTD)
USOCA........	United States Office of Consumer Affairs
USOCA........	US 1 Class Association
USOCA........	US Out of Central America [Defunct] (EA)
U So Cal......	University of Southern California (GAGS)

U So Cal Tax Inst...	University of Southern California Tax Institute (DLA)
U So Car......	University of South Carolina (GAGS)
USOCDC	US Overseas Cooperative Development Committee (EA)
USO-CLAT.....	US Relations Office of CLAT [Central Latinoamericana de Trabajadores] (EA)
USODA........	United States Organization for Disabled Athletes (EA)
U So Dak.....	University of South Dakota (GAGS)
USOE	United States Office of Education [Later, USDE]
USOECD......	United States Mission to the Organization for Economic Cooperation and Development [Department of State]
USOF..........	United States Orienteering Federation (EA)
USOFA.......	Under Secretary of the Army
US of A.......	Under Secretary of the Army
US of AF....	Under Secretary of the Air Force
USOFAF......	Under Secretary of the Air Force
US OfcP.......	US Office Products Co. [Associated Press] (SAG)
U So Fla	University of South Florida (GAGS)
US of S.......	Under Secretary of State
USOID........	United States Oversea Internal Defense [Army] (AABC)
USOLTA......	Uniform Simplification of Land Transfers Act [National Conference of Commissioners on Uniform State Laws]
USOM	United States Operations Mission [Military]
U So Maine...	University of Southern Maine (GAGS)
USOMC.......	United States Ordnance Missile Command
U So Miss ...	University of Southern Mississippi (GAGS)
USONIA.......	United States of North America [Name of a cooperative community in Pleasantville, NY designed by Frank Lloyd Wright]
USONR	United States Office of Naval Research
USOO	United States Oceanographic Office (PDAA)
USOP	Ultra Small Outline Package (AAEL)
USOP	United States of Poetry
USOPA........	United States Ordnance Producers Association [Inactive] (EA)
USOppS	US Opportunity Search, Inc. [Associated Press] (SAG)
USOR.........	US Order, Inc. [NASDAQ symbol] (SAG)
US Ord.......	US Order, Inc. [Associated Press] (SAG)
USOS	U.S. Opportunity Search [NASDAQ symbol] (TTSB)
USOS	US Opportunity Search, Inc. [NASDAQ symbol] (SAG)
USOSP........	United States Ocean Survey Plan (NOAA)
U Southwestern La...	[The] University of Southwestern Louisiana (GAGS)
USOVA........	United States Outdoor Volleyball Association (EA)
USp.............	Springville City Library, Springville, UT [Library symbol Library of Congress] (LCLS)
USP............	Ultrasensitive Position (AFM)
USP............	Underwater Sound Projection
USP............	Uniform Specification Program (AAG)
USP............	Unique Selling Point
USP............	Unique Selling Proposition [Advertising]
USP............	Unique Selling Proposition [Finance]
USP............	United Socialist Party [South Korea Political party] (PPW)
USP............	United Somali Party
USP............	United States Patent
USP............	United States Penitentiary
USP............	United States Pharmacopeia [Following name of a substance, signifies substance meets standards set by USP]
USP............	United States Pharmacopeial Convention [Database producer] (EA)
USP............	United States Postal Service Library, Washington, DC [OCLC symbol] (OCLC)
USP............	United States Property
USP............	Unit Stream Power [Hydrology]
USP............	Unit Support Plan (MCD)
USP............	Universal Signal Processor
USP............	Universal Systems Patching [Mod-Tap System, Inc.]
USP............	Unsuppressed Selling Price
USP............	Upper Sequential Permissive [Nuclear energy] (NRCH)
USP............	Upper Solution Point
USP............	Urban Studies Project
USP............	Usage Sensitive Pricing [Telecommunications]
USP............	US Precious Metals, Inc. [Toronto Stock Exchange symbol Vancouver Stock Exchange symbol]
USP............	Utility Seaplane [Navy, Coast Guard]
USP............	Utility Storage Print (SAA)
USP............	Utility Summary Program
USP70........	US Patents 70 (NITA)
USP77	US Patents 77 (NITA)
USPA..........	Uniformed Services Pay Act
USPA..........	Uniform Single Publication Act [National Conference of Commissioners on Uniform State Laws]
USPA.........	United States Parachute Association (EA)
USPA...	United States Passport Agency [Department of State]
USPA.........	United States Pilots Association (EA)
USPA.........	United States Polo Association (EA)
USPA.........	United States Potters' Association (EA)
USPA.........	US Patents (NITA)
USPA.........	US Patents Alert [Derwent, Inc.] [Database]
USPA.........	US Psychotronics Association (EA)
USPAACC.....	United States PanAsian American Chamber of Commerce (EAIO)
USPACFIT...	United States Pacific States [Military] (MUSM)
USPACOM....	United States Pacific Command [Military]
USPAK........	US-Pakistan Economic Council (EA)
USP&FO......	United States Property and Fiscal Officer (AAGC)
USPAP........	Uniform Standards for Professional Appraisal Practice
US Pat Q.....	United States Patent Quarterly [A publication] (DLA)
US Pat Quar...	United States Patent Quarterly [A publication] (DLA)
US Pat Quart...	United States Patent Quarterly [A publication] (DLA)
US Pawn......	United States Pawn, Inc. [Associated Press] (SAG)

USPC .... Union des Syndicats Professionels du Cameroun [*Federation of Professional Trade Unions of Cameroon*]
USPC .... United States Parole Commission [*Formerly, United States Parole Board*]
USPC .... United States Peace Corps (EA)
USPC .... United States Pharmacopoeial Convention
USPC .... United States Pony Clubs (EA)
USPC .... United States Privacy Council (EA)
USPC .... United States Procurement Committee
USPC .... United States Purchasing Commission
USPC .... US Peace Council (EA)
USPCA .... United States Police Canine Association (EA)
USPCC .... Utility and Support Programming Control Committee (SAA)
USPCF .... US Professional Cycling Federation [*Later, USPRO*] (EA)
USPCI .... U.S. Pollution Control, Inc. (EFIS)
USPCS .... US Philatelic Classics Society (EA)
USPCU .... US Postal Chess Union (EA)
USPD .... Unabhaengige Sozialdemokratische Partei Deutschlands [*Independent Social Democratic Party of Germany*] [*Political party*] (PPE)
USPD .... US Publicity Director [*A publication*]
USPDCA ...... United States Professional Diving Coaches Association (EA)
USPDI .... United States Pharmacopeia Dispensing Information
USPDI .... United States Professional Development Institute
USPDO .... United States Property and Disbursing Officer
USPE .... United States Purchasing Exchange
USPE .... Unsatisfactory Specimen [*Laboratory science*] (DAVI)
USPEC .... United States Paper Exporters Council [*Defunct*] (EA)
USPEPA ...... United States Poultry and Egg Producers Association (EA)
USPET .... Urokinase Streptokinase Pulmonary Embolism Trial (STED)
USPF .... US Powerlifting Federation (EA)
USPFO .... United States Property and Fiscal Officer [*Military*]
US/PFUN..... United States People for the United Nations [*Defunct*] (EA)
USPG .... Uniform System of Accounts Prescribed for Natural Gas Companies
USPG .... United Society for the Propagation of the Gospel [*Society for the Propaga tion of the Gospel in Foreign Parts and UMCA*] [*Formed by a merger of*] (EAIO)
USpGS .... Church of Jesus Christ of Latter-Day Saints, Genealogical Society Library, Springville Branch, Springville, UT [*Library symbol Library of Congress*] (LCLS)
USPh .... United States Pharmacopoeia
USPH .... U.S. Physical Therapy [*NASDAQ symbol*] (TTSB)
USPH .... US Physical Therapy, Inc. [*NASDAQ symbol*] (SAG)
USPHS .... United States Postal History Society [*Defunct*] (EA)
USPHS .... United States Public Health Service
USPHSR ...... United States Public Health Service Reserve
USPHT .... United States Precision Helicopter Team
USPhys .... US Physical Therapy, Inc. [*Associated Press*] (SAG)
USPI .... Unione Stampa Periodica Italiana [*Press association*] (EY)
USPIN .... United States Pacific Issues Network [*Defunct*] (EA)
USPIRG .... US Public Interest Research Group (EA)
USPL .... Uniform System of Accounts, Public Utilities, and Licensees [*Federal Power Commission*]
USPL .... Unpriced Spare Parts List
USPLS .... United States Public-Land Surveys
USPLTA ...... United States Professional Lawn Tennis Association [*Later, USPTA*] (EA)
USPM .... United Society of Pattern Makers [*A union*] [*British*]
USPMF .... US Patent Model Foundation (EA)
USPMOM .... Union des Societes de Pediatrie du Moyen-Orient et de la Mediterranee [*Union of Middle Eastern and Mediterranean Pediatric Societies - UMEMPS*] [*Athens, Greece*] (EAIO)
USPN .... United States Pawn, Inc. [*NASDAQ symbol*] (SAG)
USPN .... U.S. Pawn [*NASDAQ symbol*] (TTSB)
USPN .... US Pawn, Inc. [*NASDAQ symbol*] (NQ)
USPO .... United Sabah People's Organization [*Pertubuhan Rakyat Sabah Bersatu*] [*Malaysia*] [*Political party*] (PPW)
USPO .... United States Patent Office [*Department of Commerce*]
USPO .... United States Post Office [*Later, United States Postal Service*]
USPP .... United States Pacifist Party [*Political party*] (EA)
USPP .... United States Park Police [*Department of the Interior*]
USPP .... University Science Policy Planning [*Program*] [*National Science Foundation*]
USPPA .... United States Pulp Producers Association [*Later, API*] (EA)
USPPI .... United States Producer Price Index [*Database*] [*Department of Labor*] [*Information service or system*] (CRD)
USPPS .... US Possessions Philatelic Society (EA)
USPQ .... United States Patents Quarterly
USPRI .... USP Real Estate Investment Trust SBI [*Associated Press*] (SAG)
USPRO .... US Professional Cycling Federation (EA)
USPS .... United States Postal Service
USPS .... United States Power Squadrons (EA)
USPSA .... US Practical Shooting Association (EA)
USPSDA ...... United States Private Security and Detective Association (EA)
USPSF .... United States Pigeon Shooting Federation [*Defunct*] (EA)
USPT .... United Societies of Physiotherapists (EA)
USPTA .... United States Physical Therapy Association (EA)
USPTA .... United States Pony Trotting Association [*Defunct*] (EA)
USPTA .... United States Professional Tennis Association (EA)
USPTA .... US Paddle Tennis Association (EA)
USPTO .... United States Patent and Trademark Office
USPTR .... United States Professional Tennis Registry (EA)
USPTS .... USP Real Estate Investment Trust SBI [*NASDAQ symbol*] (SPSG)
USPTS .... USP Real Est Inv Tr SBI [*NASDAQ symbol*] (TTSB)
USPWIC .... United States Prisoner of War Information Center [*Army*] (AABC)

USPWIC(Br)... United States Prisoner of War Information Center (Branch) [*Army*] (AABC)
USQ .... Squeezed Files [*Computer science*] (MHDI)
USQMC .... United States Quartermaster Corps
USR .... Ukrainska Partiia Sotsialistov Revolyutsionerov [*Ukrainian Socialist Revolutionary Party*] [*Russian Political party*] (PPE)
USR .... Ultrasonic Radiation
USR .... Under Speed Relay (MCD)
USR .... Unheated Serum Reagin (Test) [*Clinical chemistry*] (AAMN)
USR .... United States [*Supreme Court*] Reports
USR .... United States Reserves
USR .... Unit Site Representative [*Army*]
USR .... Unit Status Report [*Army*]
USR .... Universal Series Regulator (IAA)
USR .... Unsatisfactory Service Report (CIST)
USR .... Up Stage Right [*Away from audience*] [*A stage direction*]
USR .... User Service Request
USR .... User Service Routine [*Digital Equipment Corp.*]
USR .... User Status Reporting (MCD)
USR .... Usher of the Scarlet Rod (ROG)
USR .... US Shoe Corp. [*NYSE symbol*] (SPSG)
USRA .... United Sportsman Racers Association [*Defunct*] (EA)
USRA .... United States Racquetball Association (EA)
USRA .... United States Railway Association [*In 1974, superseded United States Railroad Administration, which had been absorbed by the Department of Transportation in 1939*] [*Terminated in 1987*]
USRA .... United States Revolver Association (EA)
USRA .... United States Rowing Association (EA)
USRA .... United Street Rod Association [*Defunct*] (EA)
USRA .... Universities Space Research Association (EA)
USRA .... University Space Physics Association
USRAC .... US Repeating Arms Company
USRAD........ United States Fleet Shore Radio Station
USR-Borotbists... Ukrainska Partiia Sotsialistov Revolyutsionerov-Borotbists [*Ukrainian Socialist Revolutionary Party-Fighters*] [*Russian Political party*] (PPE)
USRCMM ..... US Region of Congregation of Mariannhill Missionaries [*Later, CMM*] (EA)
USRCPAC .... United States Reserve Components and Personnel Administration Center
USRCS .... United States Revenue Cutter Service
USRCSI........ United States Red Cedar Shingle Industry
USRD .... Underwater Sound Reference Detachment [*Orlando, FL*] [*Navy*]
US-RDA .... Union Soudanaise - Rassemblement Democratique Africain [*Mali*] [*Political party*] (EY)
USRDA........ US Recommended Daily Allowance [*Nutrition*]
USRD/NRL.... Underwater Sound Reference Division, Naval Research Laboratory
USRE .... US Facilities Corp. [*Costa Mesa, CA*] [*NASDAQ symbol*] (NQ)
USREC .... United States Environment and Resources Council [*Marine science*] (MSC)
USREDA....... United States Rice Export Development Association [*Later, RCMD*]
USREDCOM... United States Readiness Command
US Reg .... United States Register [*Philadelphia*] [*A publication*] (DLA)
US Reh Den... Rehearing Denied by United States Supreme Court [*Legal term*] (DLA)
US Reh Dis... Rehearing Dismissed by United States Supreme Court [*Legal term*] (DLA)
US Rep........ United States Reports [*A publication*] (DLA)
US Rep (L Ed)... United States Supreme Court Reports, Lawyers' Edition [*A publication*] (DLA)
USREPMC.... United States Representative to the Military Committee [*NATO*]
USREPMILCOMLO... United States Representative to the Military Committee Liaison Office [*NATO*]
USREPMILCOMUN... United States Representative, Military Staff Committee, United Nations
USREPOF..... United States Navy Reporting Office [*or Officer*]
US Rest .... US Restaurant Properties Ltd. [*Formerly, Burger King Investors*] [*Associated Press*] (SAG)
US Rev St.... United States Revised Statutes [*A publication*] (DLA)
USRFP......... US Requests for Proposals [*Washington Representative Service*] [*Information service or system Defunct*] (CRD)
USRL .... Laryak [*Former USSR ICAO location identifier*] (ICLI)
USRL .... Underwater Sound Reference Laboratory [*Navy*]
USRM .... United States Revenue Marine
USRN .... Nizhnevartovsk [*Former USSR ICAO location identifier*] (ICLI)
USRNMC....... United States Representative to NATO Military Committee (AABC)
USRO .... Ultrasmall Structures Research Office [*University of Michigan*] [*Research center*] (RCD)
USRO .... United States Mission to NATO and European Regional Organizations
USRO .... United States Navy Routing Office
US Robt....... United States Robotics, Inc. [*Associated Press*] (SAG)
USRP .... United States Refugee Program
USRPA........ United States Racing Pigeon Association [*Defunct*] (EA)
USRPHC ...... US Real Property Holding Co.
USRR .... Surgut [*Former USSR ICAO location identifier*] (ICLI)
USRRC........ United States Road Racing Championship
USRR Lab Bd Dec... Decisions of the United States Railroad Labor Board [*A publication*] (DLA)
USRS .... United States Reclamation Service
USRS .... United States Revised Statutes
USRS .... United States Robotics Society (CSR)
USRS .... United States Rocket Society (EA)
USRS .... Squeezed Rowing Society (EA)
USRSA .... United States Racquet Stringers Association (EA)

USRSG......... United States Representative, Standing Group [*Military*] (AABC)
USRT.......... Universal Synchronous Receiver/Transmitter
USRTA......... United States Recreational Tennis Association (EA)
USRV.......... US SerVis [*NASDAQ symbol*] (TTSB)
USRV.......... US SerVis, Inc. [*NASDAQ symbol*] (SAG)
USRX.......... United States Robotics Corp. [*NASDAQ symbol*] (SAG)
USRX.......... U.S. Robotics [*NASDAQ symbol*] (TTSB)
USRX.......... US Robotics, Inc. [*NASDAQ symbol*] (SPSG)
USS .... Shuttle, Inc. [*ICAO designator*] (FAAC)
USS .... Ultrasound Scanning
USS .... Ultraviolet Scanning Spectrometer
USS .... Underwater Sound Source
USS .... Unified S-Band System [*Radio*]
USS .... Union Syndicale Suisse [*Swiss Federation of Trade Unions*]
USS .... Unique Signal Switch
USS .... United Scholarship Service [*Later, NCAIAE, NCAIE*]
USS .... United Seamen's Service (EA)
USS .... United States Naval Vessel
USS .... United States Sellers [*Standard threads*] (DEN)
USS .... United States Senate
USS .... United States Ship
uss........... United States Ship (NAKS)
uss........... United States Standard (NAKS)
USS .... United States Standard
USS .... United States Steamer
USS .... United States Surgical Corp. [*NYSE symbol*] (SPSG)
USS .... United States Swimming, Inc. (EA)
USS .... United Swedish Societies (EA)
USS .... Universal Scheduling System (IAA)
USS .... Universities Superannuation Scheme
USS .... Unsmoked Sheets (PDAA)
USS .... Uptake Signal Sequence [*Genetics*]
USS .... USAF [*United States Air Force*] Security Service
USS .... Usage Sensitive Service [*Telecommunications*]
USS .... USAREUR [*United States Army, Europe*] Support System
USS .... User Services Support (SSD)
USS .... User Support System (MCD)
USS .... US Steel Canada, Inc. [*Toronto Stock Exchange symbol*]
USS .... US Steel Corp. [*Also, USSC*] [*Later, USX Corp.*]
USS .... U.S. Surgical [*NYSE symbol*] (TTSB)
USS .... Utility Support Structure (MCD)
uss........... Utility Support Structure (NAKS)
USSA .... Underground Security Storage Association [*Defunct*]
USSA .... Uniaxial Split-Sphere Apparatus [*Mineralogy*]
USSA .... Union Suisse des Syndicats Autonomes [*Swiss Association of Autonomous Unions*]
USSA .... United Saw Service Association (EA)
USSA .... United States Salvage Association [*Defunct*] (EA)
USSA .... United States Security Authority [*for NATO affairs*]
USSA .... United States Ski Association (EA)
USSA .... United States Snowshoe Association (EA)
USSA .... United States Space Administration (IAA)
USSA .... United States Sports Academy (EA)
USSA .... United States Standard Atmosphere (KSC)
USSA .... United States Student Association (EA)
USSA .... United States Swimming Association (EA)
USSA .... United Sugar Samplers' Association [*Defunct*]
USSA .... US Sidewinder Association (EA)
USSA .... US Soling Association (EA)
USSAC .... United States Army Ambulance Service Association [*Defunct*] (EA)
USSAC .... United States Security Authority for CENTO Affairs (AABC)
USSAF .... United States Strategic Air Force [*Later, Strategic Air Command*]
USSAF .... US Sports Acrobatic Federation (EA)
USSAFE .... United States Strategic Air Forces in Europe
USSAG .... United States Support Activities Group [*Military*]
USSAG/7AF... United States Support Activities / Seventh Air Force [*Vietnam*] (VNW)
USSAH .... United States Soldiers' and Airmen's Home (AABC)
USSALDP ..... U.S.-South Africa Leadership Development Program (EA)
USSALEP ..... US-South Africa Leader Exchange Program (EA)
USSAN .... United States Security Authority, NATO
USSAS .... United States Security Authority for SEATO Affairs (AABC)
USSatB .... United States Satellite Broadcasting Co. [*Associated Press*] (SAG)
USSB .... United States Satellite Broadcasting Co., Inc. [*Minneapolis, MN*] [*Telecommunications*] (TSSD)
USSB .... United States Savings Bond (WDAA)
USSB .... United States Shipping Board [*Terminated, 1933*]
USSB .... United States Shipping Board Decisions [*A publication*] (DLA)
USSB .... U.S. Satellite Broadcasting 'A' [*NASDAQ symbol*] (TTSB)
USSBA .... United States Seniors Bowling Association [*Later, Seniors Division of the American Bowling Congress*] (EA)
USSBB .... United States Shipping Board Bureau Decisions [*A publication*] (DLA)
USSBD .... United States Savings Bonds Division [*Department of the Treasury*]
USSBF .... United States Skibob Federation (EA)
USSBIA .... United States Stone and Bead Importers Association (EA)
USSBL .... United States Stickball League (EA)
USSBS .... United States Strategic Bombing Survey [*Disbanded, 1946*]
USSC .... United States Sentencing Commission
USSC .... United States Servas Committee (EA)
USSC .... United States Strike Command [*Military combined Tactical Air Command and Strategic Army Command Force*]
USSC .... United States Supreme Court
USSC .... Upper-Sideband, Suppressed-Carrier (IDOE)
USSC .... US Steel Corp. [*Also, USS*] [*Later, USX Corp.*] (MCD)
USSC .... US Systems Corp. (EA)

USSCA .... US Ski Coaches Association (EA)
US-SCAN ..... United States Special Committee on Antarctic Names [*1943-47*]
USSC Rep.... United States Supreme Court Reports [*A publication*] (DLA)
USSCS .... United States Soil Conservation Service (BARN)
USSCT .... United States Supreme Court
USSDP .... Uniformed Services Savings Deposits Program (AABC)
USSE .... Severouralsk [*Former USSR ICAO location identifier*] (ICLI)
USSE .... Ultrasonic Soldering Equipment
USSEA .... United States Scientific Export Association
USSEA .... United States Society for Education through Art (EA)
USSEA .... United States Space Education Association (EA)
USSECMILCOMUN... [*The*] Secretary, United States Delegation United Nations Military Staff Committee
USSEF .... United States Ski Educational Foundation (EA)
USSEI .... United States Society of Esperanto Instructors [*Later, AATE*] (AEBS)
USSerVis .... US SerVis, Inc. [*Associated Press*] (SAG)
USSES .... US Sheep Experiment Station [*University of Idaho*] [*Research center*] (RCD)
USSF ....:.... Ulster Special Service Force [*British military*] (DMA)
USSF .... United States Soccer Federation (EA)
USSF .... United States Softball Federation
USSF .... United States Space Foundation (EA)
USSF .... United States Special Forces
USSF .... United States Steel Foundation
USSF .... United States Surfing Federation (EA)
USSF .... United States Swimming Foundation (EA)
USSFA .... United States Soccer Football Association [*Later, USSF*] (EA)
USSFFA .... United Soft Serve and Fast Food Association [*Later, NSSFFA*] (EA)
USSF LRRP... United States Special Forces Long Range Reconnaisance Patrol (VNW)
USSF(P)...... United States Special Forces (Provisional) (CINC)
USSFR .... US Scottish Fiddling Revival (EA)
USSG .... United States Standard Gauge
USSGA .... United States Seniors Golf Association [*Defunct*] (EA)
USSGREP ..... United States Standing Group Representative [*NATO*]
USSH .... United States Soldiers' Home
USSHN .... Usher Syndrome Self-Help Network (EA)
USSI .... Ivdel [*Former USSR ICAO location identifier*] (ICLI)
USSI .... Ultrasonic Soldering Iron
USSI .... United States Strategic Institute (EA)
USSI .... USS Interphase (EA)
USSIA .... United States Shellac Importers Association (EA)
USSIAFCM.... USS Intrepid Association of Former Crew Members (EA)
USSID .... United States Signal Intelligence Directive (AABC)
US-SIOP ..... United States Single Integrated Operational Plan (NATG)
USSIS .... United States Signals Intellignce System (MCD)
USSLL .... United States Savings and Loan League [*Later, USLSI*] (EA)
USSMA .... US Spanish Merchants Association (EA)
U33NBA ...... USS [*United States Ship*] Natoma Bay Association (EA)
USSOA .... USS [*United States Ship*] Oklahoma Association (EA)
USSOC .... United States Special Operations Command [*DoD*]
USSOCOM ... United States Special Operations Command [*DoD*]
USSOUTHCOM... United States Southern Command [*Air Force*]
USSP .... Unsuppressed Selling Price
USSP .... User Systems Support Plan
USSPA .... Uniformed Services Special Pay Act (DNAB)
USSPA .... United States Student Press Association [*Superseded by CPS*]
USSPACECOM... United States Space Command
USSPC .... US Student Pugwash Committee (EA)
USSPEI .... Union des Syndicats des Services Publics Europeens et Internationaux [*European and International Public Services Union*] [*Later, EUROFEDOP*] (EAIO)
USSPG .... United States Senate Press Photographers Gallery (EA)
USSPG .... US Sweetener Producers Group [*Later, ASA*] (EA)
USSPL .... United Ship Scrapers' Protection League [*A union*] [*British*]
USSPPG .... United States Senate Press Photographers Gallery (EA)
USSPrA .... U.S. Surgical $2.20 Dep'DECS' [*NYSE symbol*] (TTSB)
USSR .... State Music Trust [*Record label*] [*Former USSR*]
USSR .... Uninterrupted Sustained Silent Reading
USSR .... Union of Soviet Socialist Republics [*See also SSSR, CCCP*]
USSRA .... United States Squash Racquets Association (EA)
USSRCFT..... USSR State Committee for Foreign Tourism [*Defunct*] (EAIO)
US Srg....... United States Surgical Co. [*Associated Press*] (SAG)
USSRM .... State Music Trust [*78 RPM*] [*Record label*] [*Former USSR*]
USSRN .... Under Secretary of State for the Royal Navy [*British*]
USSS .,....... Sverdlovsk [*Former USSR ICAO location identifier*] (ICLI)
USSS .... Undersea Surveillance System (MCD)
USSS .... United States Secret Service [*Department of the Treasury*]
USSS .... United States Signals Intelligence System (MCD)
USSS .... United States Steamship
USSS .... Unmanned Sensing Satellite System
USSSA .... United States Slo-Pitch Softball Association (EA)
USSSA .... United States Snowshoe Association (EA)
USSSI .... United Stamp Society for Shut-Ins (EA)
USSSI .... United States Satellite Systems, Inc. [*Defunct*] (TSSD)
USSSI .... United States Synchronized Swimming, Inc. (EA)
USSSMA...... US Shake and Shingle Manufacturers Association (EA)
USSSO .... United States Sending Satellite Office [*Navy*]
USSST .... United States Sellers Standard Thread
USSS/UD .... United States Secret Service Uniformed Division
USSTAF .... United States Strategic Air Force [*Later, Strategic Air Command*]
USSTAFE..... United States Strategic Tactical Air Force, Europe
US Stat....... United States Statutes at Large [*A publication*] (DLA)
US St at L ... United States Statutes at Large [*A publication*] (DLA)

USSTRICOM... United States Strike Command [*Military combined Tactical Air Command and Strategic Army Command Force*]
USSTS .... US Student Travel Service (EA)
US St Tr ...... United States State Trials [*Wharton*] [*A publication*] (DLA)
US Sup Ct... United States Supreme Court Reporter [*A publication*] (DLA)
US Sup Ct (L Ed)... United States Supreme Court Reports, Lawyers' Edition [*A publication*] (DLA)
US Sup Ct R... United States Supreme Court Reporter [*A publication*] (DLA)
US Sup Ct Rep... United States Supreme Court Reporter [*A publication*] (DLA)
US Sup Ct Reps... Supreme Court Reporter [*A publication*] (DLA)
US Surg .... United States Surgical Corp. [*Associated Press*] (SAG)
USSWA .... United States Ski Writers Association [*Later, NASJA*] (EA)
UST .... Ultrasonic Test
UST .... Ultrasonic Transducer [*Crystal*] [*Used in measuring human cardiac output*]
UST .... Unblocked Serial Telemetry (MCD)
UST .... Underground Storage Tank [*Environmental Protection Agency*]
UST .... Undersea Technology
UST .... Uniform Specification Tree
UST .... Union Senegalaise du Travail [*Senegalese Labor Union*]
UST .... Union Socialiste Tchadienne [*Chadian Socialist Union*]
UST .... United States Testing Co., Inc. (NASA)
UST .... United States Time
UST .... United States Tobacco Co. (EFIS)
UST .... United States Treaties and Other International Agreements [*A publication*] (DLA)
UST .... Unit Security Technician
UST .... Universal Servicing Tool (NASA)
UST .... Universal Standard Time
UST .... Universal Subscriber Terminal (DNAB)
UST .... University of Saint Thomas [*Texas*]
UST .... User Symbol Table [*Computer science*] (MHDB)
UST .... Ustilago [*A fungus*]
UST .... UST, Inc. [*Formerly, US Tobacco*] [*NYSE symbol*] (SPSG)
UST .... Ustus [*Burnt*] [*Pharmacy*]
USTA .... Union des Syndicats des Travailleurs Algeriens [*Federation of Unions of Algerian Workers*]
USTA .... United States Telephone Association (EA)
USTA .... United States Tennis Association, Inc. (EA)
USTA .... United States Trademark Association (EA)
USTA .... United States Trotting Association (EA)
USTA .... United States Twirling Association (EA)
USTA .... Unlisted Securities Trading Act [*1936*]
USTA .... US Tornado Association (EA)
USTA .... US Triathlon Association [*Later, TRI-FED*] (EA)
USTA .... US Trivia Association [*Defunct*] (EA)
USTAF .... United States/Thai Forces
USTAG .... United States Technical Advisory Group (IAA)
USTA/NJTL .. USTA [*United States Tennis Association*] National Junior Tennis League (EA)
UStatn .... United Stationers, Inc. [*Associated Press*] (SAG)
US Tax Cas... United States Tax Cases [*Commerce Clearing House*] [*A publication*] (DLA)
USTB .... United States Travel Bureau
USTB .... UST Corp. [*NASDAQ symbol*] (NQ)
USTBF .... United States Tenpin Bowling Federation (EA)
USTC .... Union Syndicale de Travail Centrafricaine [*Union of Central African Workers*] (EY)
USTC .... United States International Trade Commission (EBF)
USTC .... United States Tariff Commission [*Later, ITC*]
USTC .... United States Tax Cases [*Commerce Clearing House*] [*A publication*] (DLA)
USTC .... United States Testing Co., Inc.
USTC .... United States Tourist Council (EA)
USTC .... United States Transportation Commission [*Proposed commission to consolidate CAB, ICC, and FMC*]
USTC .... Universal Systems Technologies Corp.
USTC .... University of Science and Technology of China
USTC .... US-Tibet Committee (EA)
USTC .... US Trade Center [*Mexico*] (IMH)
USTC .... U.S. Trust [*NASDAQ symbol*] (TTSB)
USTC .... US Trust Corp. [*NASDAQ symbol*] (NQ)
USTCA .... United States Track Coaches Association [*Later, TFA/USA*]
USTC & TBA... US Tennis Court and Track Builders Association (EA)
UST Cp .... UST Corp. [*Associated Press*] (SAG)
USTD .... Union des Syndicats des Travailleurs du Dahomey [*Federation of Workers' Unions of Dahomey*]
USTD .... United States Treasury Department
USTD .... United States Treaty Development [*A publication*] (DLA)
USTDA .... United States Truck Drivers Association
USTDC .... United States Forces, Taiwan Defense Command (CINC)
USTDC .... US Travel Data Center (EA)
US Tech .... United States Technologies, Inc. [*Associated Press*] (SAG)
UStel .... UStel Co. [*Associated Press*] (SAG)
US TEL .... US Telephone, Inc. [*Dallas, TX*] [*Telecommunications*] (TSSD)
USTES .... United States Training and Employment Service [*Abolished, 1971*] [*Department of Labor*]
USTEX .... USAA Tax Exempt Long Term Fund [*Mutual fund ticker symbol*] (SG)
USTF .... Uniformed Services Treatment Facility [*DoD*]
USTF .... United States Tuna Foundation (EA)
USTFA .... United States Trout Farmers Association (EA)
USTFF .... United States Track and Field Federation [*Later, TFA/USA*]
USTFFA .... United States Touch and Flag Football Association (EA)

USTG .... Union Syndicale des Travailleurs de Guinee [*Guinean Federation of Workers*]
UStgD .... Dixie College, St. George, UT [*Library symbol Library of Congress*] (LCLS)
UStgGS .... Church of Jesus Christ of Latter-Day Saints, Genealogical Society Library, St. George Branch, St. George, UT [*Library symbol Library of Congress*] (LCLS)
UStgW .... Washington County Library, St. George, UT [*Library symbol Library of Congress*] (LCLS)
USTHF .... US Team Handball Federation (EA)
USTIIC .... United States Technical Industrial Intelligence Committee (MCD)
USTL .... UStel [*NASDAQ symbol*] (SAG)
USTL .... UStel Inc. [*NASDAQ symbol*] (TTSB)
USTMA .... United States Trademark Association (BARN)
USTOA .... United States Tour Operators Association (EA)
USTOL .... Ultrashort Takeoff and Landing [*Aviation*] (MCD)
USTOPS ...... United States Travelers' Overseas Personalized Service [*Also known as TOPS*]
USTR .... United States Trade Representative [*Formerly, SRTN*] [*Executive Office of the President*]
USTR .... United Stationers [*NASDAQ symbol*] (TTSB)
USTR .... United Stationers, Inc. [*NASDAQ symbol*] (NQ)
USTRA .... United States Touring Riders Association [*Defunct*] (EA)
US Tran .... United States Transportation Systems, Inc. [*Associated Press*] (SAG)
USTRANSCOM... United States Transportation Command
USTRC .... United States Transportation Research Command [*Army*]
US Treas Dept... United States Treasury Department (DLA)
US Treas Reg... United States Treasury Regulations [*A publication*] (DLA)
US Treaty Ser... United States Treaty Series [*A publication*] (DLA)
US Trn .... United States Transportation Systems, Inc. [*Associated Press*] (SAG)
US Trst .... US Trust Corp. [*Associated Press*] (SAG)
USTS .... Ultrahigh Frequency Satellite Terminal System (MCD)
USTS .... Union Syndicale des Travailleurs du Soudan [*Federation of Sudanese Workers*] [*Mali*]
USTS .... United States Time Standard [*National Institute of Standards and Technology*]
USTS .... United States Transmission Systems, Inc. [*Secaucus, NJ*] (TSSD)
USTS .... United States Travel Service [*Replaced by United States Travel and Tourism Administration*] [*Department of Commerce*]
USTS .... U.S. Transportation Sys [*NASDAQ symbol*] (TTSB)
USTS .... US Transportation Systems, Inc. [*NASDAQ symbol*] (SAG)
USTSA .... United States Trade Secrets Act (AAGC)
USTSA .... US Targhee Sheep Association (EA)
USTSA .... US Telecommunications Suppliers Association [*Later, TIA*] (EA)
USTTA .... United States Table Tennis Association (EA)
USTTA .... United States Travel and Tourism Administration [*Formerly, US Travel Service*] [*Department of Commerce*]
U St Thomas... University of St. Thomas (GAGS)
USTTI .... US Telecommunications Training Institute [*Washington, DC*] [*Telecommunications*] (TSSD)
USTU .... Ultrasonic Test Unit
USTU .... US Taekwondo Union (EA)
USTU .... US Taxpayers Union (EA)
USTV .... Universal Subscription Television
USTV .... Unmanned Supersonic Test Vehicle (MCD)
USTVA .... United States Tennessee Valley Authority
USTW .... Sovetsky [*Former USSR ICAO location identifier*] (ICLI)
USTWA .... US Tennis Writers Association (EA)
USTZD .... Unsensitized
USU .... Ultimate Sampling Unit (GFGA)
USU .... Unbundled Stock Unit [*Investment term Obsolete*]
USU .... Uniformed Services University of the Health Sciences Library, Bethesda, MD [*OCLC symbol*] (OCLC)
USU .... United Stevedores' Union [*British*]
USU .... Usually
USU .... Utah State University (PDAA)
USUA .... United States Ultralight Association (EA)
USUARIOI ... Association of Maritime Transport Users in the Central American Isthmus [*Guatemala, Guatemala*] (EAIO)
USUB .... Unglazed Structural Unit Base [*Technical drawings*]
USUCA .... United Steel Workers' Union of Central Africa [*Rhodesia and Nyasaland*]
USUCVD ...... Unsterile Uncontrolled Vaginal Delivery (STED)
USUHS .... Uniformed Services University of the Health Sciences [*Bethesda, MD*] [*DoD*] (EGAO)
US/UK .... United States/United Kingdom
USUN .... United States United Nations Delegation (CINC)
USUNEP .... United States Committee for the United Nations Environment Program (EA)
USURP .... Usurpandus [*To Be Used*] [*Pharmacy*]
USUSA .... United Societies of the United States of America [*McKeesport, PA*] (EA)
USV .... United States Volunteers [*Civil War*]
USV .... Unmanned Strike Vehicle
USV .... U-Save Foods Ltd. [*Vancouver Stock Exchange symbol*]
USV .... U.S. Restaurant Properties [*NASDAQ symbol*] (TTSB)
USV .... US Restaurant Properties Ltd. [*Formerly, Burger King Investors*] [*NYSE symbol*] (SAG)
USVA .... United States Volleyball Association (BARN)
USVAAD ...... United States Veteran's Administration Administrator's Decisions [*A publication*] (DLA)
USVAC .... United States Veterans' Assistance Center (OICC)
USVAd .... United Services Advisors, Inc. [*Associated Press*] (SAG)
USVB .... United States Veterans Bureau
USVBA .... United States Volleyball Association (EA)

USVBA.........	US Venetian Blind Association (EA)
USVBDD	United States Veterans Bureau Director's Decisions [*A publication*] (DLA)
USvBk..........	United Savings Bank FA [*Associated Press*] (SAG)
USVH..........	United States Veterans Hospital
USVIP..........	Uniformed Services Voluntary Insurance Program
USVMD........	Urine Specimen Volume Measuring Device
USVMS........	Urine Sample Volume Measurement System (MCD)
USVMS........	Urine Specimen Volume Measuring System [*Medicine*] (STED)
USVRU........	Ultra-Stable Voltage Reference Unit (PDAA)
USVS	United Services Advisors, Inc. [*San Antonio, TX*] [*NASDAQ symbol*] (NQ)
USVSP........	United Svcs Advisor(Pfd) [*NASDAQ symbol*] (TTSB)
USVT	Universal Stray Voltage Tester
USW	Ultrashort Wave
USW	Ultrasonic Welding
USW	Undersea Warfare
USW	Under Secretary of War [*Obsolete*]
USW	United Steelworkers [*Trade union*] [*British*]
USW	US West Communications Group [*NYSE symbol*] [*Formerly, US West, Inc.*] (SG)
USW	U S WEST Communic Grp [*NYSE symbol*] (TTSB)
USW	US West, Inc. [*NYSE symbol*] (SPSG)
USW	US Wheat Associates (EA)
USWA..........	American Association for Study of the United States in World Affairs (EA)
USWA..........	United Shoe Workers of America [*Later, ACTWU*] (EA)
USWA..........	United States Wayfarer Association (EA)
USWA..........	United Steelworkers of America [*Also known as USW*] (EA)
USWA..........	United We Stand America
USWAB........	United States Warehouse Act Bonded
USWACC......	United States Women's Army Corps Center
USWACS......	United States Women's Army Corps School
USWAP........	United South West Africa Party [*Namibia*] [*Political party*]
USWAP........	United Steel Workers' Association of the Philippines
US Wats......	US Wats, Inc. [*Associated Press*] (SAG)
USWB..........	United States Weather Bureau [*Later, National Weather Service*]
USWBC........	United States War Ballot Commission [*World War II*]
USWC..........	US Wireless Corp. [*NASDAQ symbol*] (SAG)
USWCA........	United States Women's Curling Association (EA)
USWDIV......	Undersea Warfare Division [*Navy*] (DNAB)
USWest.......	US West [*Associated Press*] (SAG)
USWF..........	United States Weightlifting Federation (EA)
USWF..........	United States Wrestling Federation (EA)
USWFA........	United States Water Fitness Association (EA)
USWGA........	United States Wholesale Grocers' Association [*Later, NAWGA*] (EA)
USWI..........	United States West Indies
USWI..........	US WATS [*NASDAQ symbol*] (TTSB)
USWI..........	US Wats, Inc. [*NASDAQ symbol*] (SAG)
USWISOMWAGMOHOTM...	United Single Women in Search of Men Who Aren't Gay, Married, or Hung-Up on Their Mothers [*Fictitious association*]
USWISRA	U.S. Women's Intercollegiate Squash-Racquet Association (PSS)
USWLA	United States Women's Lacrosse Association (EA)
USWM	US West [*Associated Press*] (SAG)
USWMS........	Uniform State Waterway Marking System (DICI)
USWP..........	Ultrashort Wave Propagation Panel (IAA)
USWP..........	United States Water Polo (EA)
USWPrA.......	U.S.West Fin 7.96%'TOPrS' [*NYSE symbol*] (TTSB)
US WreCp....	US Wireless Corp. [*Associated Press*] (SAG)
USWSRA......	United States Women's Squash Racquets Association (EA)
USWSSB......	United States Wood Screw Service Bureau [*Defunct*] (EA)
USWst.........	US West, Inc. [*Associated Press*] (SAG)
USWTCA......	United States Women's Track Coaches Association (EA)
USWV........	United Spanish War Veterans
USX	Ultrasoft X-Ray
USX	US Express [*ICAO designator*] (FAAC)
USX	US Steel Corp. [*Formerly, USS, USSC*]
USX	USX-Marathon Group [*Associated Press*] (SAG)
USX Ca	USX Capital LLC [*Associated Press*] (SAG)
USXDel.......	USX Delhi Group [*Associated Press*] (SAG)
USXFS........	Ultrasoft X-Ray Fluorescence [*Spectroscopy*]
USXMar.......	USX-Marathon Group [*Associated Press*] (SAG)
USXP	United States Exploration, Inc. [*NASDAQ symbol*] (SAG)
USXP	U.S. Exploration [*NASDAQ symbol*] (TTSB)
US Xprss	US Xpress Enterprises, Inc. [*Associated Press*] (SAG)
USXRS........	Ultrasoft X-Ray Spectroscopy
USXUSS......	USX US Steel Group [*Formerly, US Steel Corp.*] [*Associated Press*] (SAG)
USXX	U.S. Technologies [*NASDAQ symbol*] (TTSB)
USXX	US Technologies, Inc. [*NASDAQ symbol*] (NQ)
USY	United Synagogue Youth
USY	US Pay-Tel, Inc. [*Vancouver Stock Exchange symbol*]
USYC..........	United States Youth Council [*Defunct*] (EA)
USYEC........	US Yugoslav Economic Council (EA)
USYRU........	US Yacht Racing Union (EA)
USYSA........	United States Youth Soccer Association (EA)
USZI	United States Zone of the Interior
UT..............	Conference Internationale pour l'Unite Technique des Chemins de Fer
UT..............	Tooele Public Library, Tooele, UT [*Library symbol Library of Congress*] (LCLS)
UT..............	Ullrich-Turner [*Syndrome*] [*Medicine*] (DB)
UT..............	Ultrasonic Test
UT..............	Ultrathin

UT..............	Umbilical Tower [*Aerospace*]
UT..............	Unauthorised Taking [*Legal term*] (WDAA)
uT..............	Unbound Testosterone (STED)
UT..............	Unbound Testosterone [*Endocrinology*] (DMAA)
UT..............	Uncontrolled Term [*Online database field identifier*]
UT..............	Under the Tongue [*Pharmacy*]
U/T..............	Under Training [*British military*] (DMA)
U/T..............	Under Trust [*Legal term*] (DLA)
UT..............	Underway Trials [*Shipbuilding*]
UT..............	Unemployed Time [*Military British*]
UT..............	Unexpired Term [*Real estate*] [*British*] (ROG)
UT..............	Union Terminal Railway Co. [*AAR code*]
UT..............	Union Territory [*India*] (BARN)
UT..............	Unit (MCD)
UT..............	Unitech (IAA)
UT..............	United Technologies Corp.
UT..............	United Territory
UT..............	United Together [*An association Defunct*] (EA)
UT..............	United TransNet [*NYSE symbol*] (TTSB)
UT..............	Units Tens (IAA)
UT..............	Unit Tester (NASA)
UT..............	Unit Trust (ILCA)
UT..............	Universal Time [*Astronomy*]
UT..............	Universal Torpedo (MCD)
UT..............	Universal Trainer
UT..............	Universal Tube (IAA)
UT..............	Universal Turret (MCD)
UT..............	University of Tasmania [*State*] (EERA)
UT..............	University of Tennessee
UT..............	University of Texas
UT..............	University of Toronto [*Ontario*]
UT..............	University of Tulsa [*Oklahoma*]
UT..............	Unna-Thost [*Syndrome*] [*Medicine*] (DB)
UT..............	Unrelated (Children Raised) Together [*Medicine*] (STED)
UT..............	Unspecified Temperature
UT..............	Untested
U/T..............	Untrained
UT..............	Untreated [*Medicine*] (DAVI)
UT..............	Upper Torso
UT..............	Upper Tractor (ECII)
UT..............	Up Through [*Parapsychology*]
UT..............	Up Time
UT..............	Urinary Tract [*Medicine*]
UT..............	Urticaria (DB)
UT..............	User's Terminal (MCD)
UT..............	User Test
UT..............	Using Television (WDMC)
Ut..............	Utah (ODBW)
UT..............	Utah [*Postal code*]
U T..............	Utah Reports [*A publication*] (DLA)
UT..............	Utah Territory [*Prior to statehood*]
UT..............	Utendum [*To Be Used*] [*Pharmacy*] (ROG)
UT..............	Uterus [*Anatomy*] (DAVI)
ut..............	Uterus (STED)
UT..............	Utilitiesman [*Navy rating*]
UT..............	Utility (BUR)
UT..............	Utility Boat
UT..............	Utility Player
UT1..............	Utilitiesman, First Class [*Navy rating*]
UT2..............	Utilitiesman, Second Class [*Navy rating*]
UT3..............	Utilitiesman, Third Class [*Navy rating*]
UTA..............	Ultrasonic Thermal Action
UTA..............	Umtali [*Zimbabwe*] [*Airport symbol*] (AD)
UTA..............	Union des Transports Aeriens [*France ICAO designator*] (FAAC)
UTA..............	Union de Transports Aeriens [*Air Transport Union*] [*Private airline*] [*France*] (EY)
UTA..............	United Technologies Automotive
UTA..............	United Typothetae of America [*Later, Printing Industries of America*]
UTA..............	Unit Training Assembly [*Military*] (AABC)
UTA..............	Unit Trust Association [*British*]
UTA..............	University of Tasmania Association [*Australia*]
UTA..............	University of Texas at Arlington
UTA..............	Upper Terminal Area (NATG)
UTA..............	Upper Testing Area (IAA)
UTA..............	Urban Transportation Administration [*HUD*]
U$_{TA}$..............	Urinary Titratable Acidity [*Laboratory science*] (DAVI)
UTA..............	Used Truck Association (NTPA)
UTA..............	User Transfer Address
UTAC	Union Tunisienne de l'Artisanat et du Commerce [*Tunisian Union of Artisans and Merchants*]
UTACV	Urban Tracked Air-Cushion Vehicle [*Transit*] [*Department of Transportation*]
UTAD	Utah Army Depot (AABC)
UTAEC	University of Tennessee, Atomic Energy Commission (SAA)
UTAH	Utah Railway Co. [*AAR code*]
Utah	Utah Supreme Court Reports [*A publication*] (DLA)
Utah 2d......	Utah Reports, Second Series [*A publication*] (DLA)
Utah Admin Bull...	State of Utah Bulletin [*A publication*] (DLA)
Utah Admin Code...	Utah Administrative Code [*A publication*] (AAGC)
Utah Admin R...	Administrative Rules of Utah [*A publication*] (DLA)
Utah Code Ann...	Utah Code, Annotated [*A publication*] (DLA)
Utah IC Bull...	Utah Industrial Commission. Bulletin [*A publication*] (DLA)
UtahMed......	Utah Medical, Inc. [*Associated Press*] (SAG)
Utah PUC......	Utah Public Utilities Commission Report [*A publication*] (DLA)
Utah R.........	Utah Reports [*A publication*] (DLA)

Utah St U.....	Utah State University (GAGS)
UTAL............	Upper Transition Altitude (SAA)
UT & E.........	User Test and Evaluation [*Army*] (DOMA)
UT & GS......	Uplink Text and Graphics System (NASA)
UTANG........	Utah Air National Guard (MUSM)
UTAP...........	Unified Transportation Assistance Program [*Proposed*]
UTAP...........	Urban Transportation Assistance Program [*Canada*]
UTARS.........	Utility Aircraft Requirements Study [*Army*] (DOMA)
UTAS...........	Underwater Target-Activated Sensor (MCD)
UTASN........	University of Texas at Austin School of Nursing
UT/AT..........	Underway Trial/Acceptance Trial [*Navy*] (NVT)
UTATA	Uniform Testamentary Additions to Trusts Act [*National Conference of Commissioners on Uniform State Laws*]
UTB.............	Muttaburra [*Australia Airport symbol*] (OAG)
UTB.............	Uni Taschenbuecher GmbH [*German publishers cooperative*]
UTB.............	United Tariff Bureau
UTB.............	University of Toronto Library, Brieflisted Records [*UTLAS symbol*]
UTB.............	Utilitiesman, Boilerman [*Navy rating*]
UTBG...........	Unbound Testosterone-Binding Globulin [*Immunology*] (DAVI)
UTBG...........	Unbound Thyroxine Binding Globulin [*Endocrinology*] (AAMN)
UTBU...........	Unhealthy to be Unpleasant [*Theatrical play*] (IIA)
UTC.............	Coordinated Universal Time (USDC)
UTC.............	Uncle Tom's Cabin [*Title of book by Harriet Beecher Stowe*]
UTC.............	Under the Counter (WDAA)
UTC.............	Underwater Training Centre [*British*]
UTC.............	United Canso Oil & Gas Ltd. [*Toronto Stock Exchange symbol*]
UTC.............	United States Tax Court, Library, Washington, DC [*OCLC symbol*] (OCLC)
UTC.............	United Technologies Corp. [*Information service or system*] (IID)
UTC.............	United Technology Center (IAA)
UTC.............	United Telephone Cables (IAA)
UTC.............	United Transformer Corp. (IAA)
UTC.............	United Trust & Credit [*Finance group*] [*British*]
UTC.............	Unit Test Cases (NASA)
UTC.............	Unit Time Coding
UTC.............	Unit Total Cost
UTC.............	Unit Training Center [*Military*]
UTC.............	Unit Type Code (AFM)
UTC.............	Universal Test Console (KSC)
UTC.............	Universal Time Code
UTC.............	Universal Time Coordinated [*The universal time emitted by coordinated radio stations*]
UTC.............	Universal Time Corrected (MCD)
UTC.............	University of Tennessee at Chattanooga
UTC.............	University Teachers Certificate
UTC.............	University Training Corps [*British*]
UTC.............	Urban Technology Conference
UTC.............	Urban Training Center
UTC.............	Utilitiesman, Chief [*Navy rating*]
UTC.............	Utilities Telecommunications Council (EA)
UTC.............	Utilities, Transportation, Communication
UTC.............	Utility Tape Copy (SAA)
UTCA...........	Constructionman Apprentice, Utilitiesman, Striker [*Navy rating*]
UTCAA	Uncle Tom Cobley and All [*Refers to everyone*] [*Slang British*] (DSUE)
UTCC	University of Tennessee at Knoxville Computer Center [*Research center*] (RCD)
UT-CEM	University of Texas-Center for Electromechanics
UTCI............	Uniroyal Technology [*NASDAQ symbol*] (TTSB)
UTCI............	Uniroyal Technology Corp. [*NASDAQ symbol*] (SAG)
UTCIW........	Uniroyal Technology Wrrt [*NASDAQ symbol*] (TTSB)
UTCL...........	Union des Travailleurs Communistes Libertaires [*Union of Libertarian Communist Workers*] [*France Political party*] (PPW)
UTCLK........	Universal Transmitter Clock
UTCM..........	Utilitiesman, Master Chlef [*Navy rating*]
UTCN	Constructionman, Utilitiesman, Striker [*Navy rating*]
UTCPTT.......	Union Internationale des Organismes Touristiques et Culturels des Postes et des Telecommunications [*International Union of Tourist and Cultural Associations in the Postal and Telecommunications Services*]
UTCS	Urasenke Tea Ceremony Society (EA)
UTCS	Urban Traffic Control System
UTCS	Utilitiesman, Senior Chief [*Navy rating*]
UTCT...........	Undermanned Tank Crew Test [*Military*] (MCD)
UTD	Undetermined
UTD	Uniform Theory of Diffraction (IAA)
UTD	United
Utd..............	United (TBD)
UTD	United Air [*South Africa ICAO designator*] (FAAC)
UTD	Universal Transfer Device
UTD	University of Texas at Dallas (MCD)
UTD	Up to Date (MAE)
UTD	Uranium-Thorium Dating
UTD	User Terminal and Display Subsystem [*Space Flight Operations Facility, NASA*]
UtdAHlt.......	United American Healthcare Corp. [*Associated Press*] (SAG)
UtdAuto.......	United Auto Group [*Associated Press*] (SAG)
UTDC	Urban Transportation Development Corp. [*Canada*]
UtdCosF.......	United Companies Financial [*Associated Press*] (SAG)
UTDD	Dushanbe [*Former USSR ICAO location identifier*] (ICLI)
UTDF	Universal Tracking Data Format (SSD)
UtdHmL	United Home Life Insurance Co. [*Associated Press*] (SAG)
UT DICT.......	Ut Dictum [*As Directed*] [*Latin*]
UtdIns..........	United Insurance Co., Inc. [*Associated Press*] (SAG)
UtdIntH	United Inernational Holding, Inc. [*Associated Press*] (SAG)

UTDL...........	United Leisure Corp. [*NASDAQ symbol*] (SAG)
UtdLeisr.......	United Leisure Corp. [*Associated Press*] (SAG)
UTDLW........	United Leisure Wrrt'A' [*NASDAQ symbol*] (TTSB)
UtdMM........	United Merchants & Manufacturers, Inc. [*Associated Press*] (SAG)
UtdNews......	United News & Media PLC [*Associated Press*] (SAG)
UTDO..........	Oktyabrsky [*Former USSR ICAO location identifier*] (ICLI)
UtdPay........	United Payors and United Providers, Inc. [*Associated Press*] (SAG)
UtdPetr	United Petroleum Corp. [*Associated Press*] (SAG)
UtdPetrol.....	United Petroleum Corp. [*Associated Press*] (SAG)
UtdR	United Restaurants, Inc. [*Associated Press*] (SAG)
UtdRest........	United Restaurants, Inc. [*Associated Press*] (SAG)
UtdTst	United Trust, Inc. [*Associated Press*] (SAG)
UtdVideo......	United Video Satellite [*Associated Press*] (SAG)
UtdVs..........	United Vision Group [*Associated Press*] (SAG)
UtdWis........	United Wisconsin Services, Inc. [*Associated Press*] (SAG)
UtdWste.......	United Waste Systems [*Associated Press*] (SAG)
UTE.............	Chandler, AZ [*Location identifier FAA*] (FAAL)
UTE.............	Underwater Tracking Equipment (MCD)
UTE.............	Union Technique de l'Electricite [*France*]
UTE.............	Universal Test Equipment
UTE.............	Utilization of Theoretical Energy
UTEA...........	Unit Training Effectiveness Analysis [*Army*]
UTEC...........	Universal Test Equipment Compiler (KSC)
UTEC...........	Urethane Technologies [*NASDAQ symbol*] (TTSB)
UTEC...........	Urethane Technologies, Inc. [*NASDAQ symbol*] (SAG)
UTEC...........	Utah University Engineering College
UTED	Dzhizak [*Former USSR ICAO location identifier*] (ICLI)
UTEELRAD ..	Utilization of Enemy Electromagnetic Radiation (MSA)
UTEK..........	Ultratech Stepper [*NASDAQ symbol*] (TTSB)
UTEK..........	Ultratech Stepper, Inc. [*NASDAQ symbol*] (SAG)
UTEND	Utendus [*To Be Used*] [*Pharmacy*]
utend mor sol...	Utendus More Solito [*To be Used in the Usual Manner*] [*Latin Pharmacy*] (MAE)
U Tenn	University of Tennessee (GAGS)
U Tenn (Chattanooga)...	University of Tennessee at Chattanooga (GAGS)
U Tenn (Martin)...	University of Tennessee at Martin (GAGS)
U Tenn (Memphis)...	University of Tennessee at Memphis (GAGS)
U Tenn (Oak Ridge)...	University of Tennessee at Oak Ridge (GAGS)
UTEP	University of Texas at El Paso
UTES...........	Unit Training Equipment Site [*Military*] (AABC)
UTET...........	Unione Tipografico-Editrice Torinese [*Publisher*] [*Italy*]
U Tex (Arlington)...	[*The*] University of Texas at Arlington (GAGS)
U Tex (Austin)...	[*The*] University of Texas at Austin (GAGS)
U Tex (Dallas)...	[*The*] University of Texas at Dallas (GAGS)
U Tex (El Paso)...	[*The*] University of Texas at El Paso (GAGS)
U Tex Health Sci Ctr (Houston)...	University of Texas Health Science Center at Houston (GAGS)
U Tex Health Sci Ctr (San Antonio)...	University of Texas Health Science Center at San Antonio (GAGS)
U Tex Med Br (Galveston)...	University of Texas Medicine Branch at Galveston (GAGS)
U Tex Pan Amer...	University of Texas Pan American (GAGS)
U Tex Perm Basin...	University of Texas at Permian Basin (GAGS)
UTF.............	Underwater Tank Facility
UTF.............	Underwater Test Facility [*GE*]
UTF.............	UNDEX [*Underwater Explosion*] Test Facility [*Navy*] (RDA)
UTF.............	Unit Test Folder [*Military*]
UTF.............	Unsuccessful Tenderers Fees
UTF.............	Usual Throat Flora [*Medicine*] (DAVI)
UTF.............	Valparaiso [*Chile*] [*Seismograph station code, US Geological Survey*] (SEIS)
UTFO	Untouchable Force Organization [*Rap recording group*]
UTG	United Tasmania Group [*Political party Australia*]
UTG	University of Toronto Library, Government Documents [*UTLAS symbol*]
UTGA	United Tobacco Growers Association [*Defunct*] (EA)
UTGT	Under Thirty Group for Transit [*Defunct*] (EA)
UTH	Udon Thani [*Thailand*] [*Airport symbol*] (OAG)
UTH	Union Texas Petroleum [*NYSE symbol*] (TTSB)
UTH	Union Texas Petroleum Holdings, Inc. [*NYSE symbol*] (SPSG)
UT-H	University of Tasmania - Hobart [*Australia*]
UTH	Upper Turret Half
UTHE	Union des Associations des Etablissements Thermaux de la CE [*Union of Associations of Thermal Baths Establishments in the EC*] (ECED)
UTHSCSA....	University of Texas Health Science Center at San Antonio
UTI.............	International Universal Time [*Telecommunications*] (TEL)
UTI.............	Undistributed Taxable Income
UTI.............	Union Telegraphique Internationale (MSC)
UTI.............	United Transport International [*Bennett's Transport*] [*British*]
UTI.............	Universal Text Interchange [*Computer science*] (PCM)
UTI.............	Universal Trident Industries Ltd. [*Vancouver Stock Exchange symbol*]
UTI.............	Urinary Tract Infection [*Medicine*]
UTI.............	Urinary Trypsin Inhibitor [*Medicine*] (DB)
UTI.............	User Test Instrumentation [*Army*]
UTI.............	UTI Energy [*AMEX symbol*] (TTSB)
UTI.............	UTI Energy Corp. [*AMEX symbol*] (SPSG)
UTI.............	Uttaradit [*Thailand*] [*Airport symbol*] (AD)
UTIA	University of Toronto, Institute of Aerophysics (MCD)
UTIAS	University of Toronto, Institute for Aerospace Studies [*Research center*] (MCD)
UTIC...........	USAREUR Tactical Intelligence Center (MCD)
UTICI	Union Technique des Ingenieurs Conseils [*French*]
UTICS	University of Texas Institute for Computer Science (NITA)
UTI Eng......	UTI Energy Corp. [*Associated Press*] (SAG)

UT-IG	University of Texas at Austin Institute for Geophysics [*Research center*] (RCD)
UTII	Unitech Industries, Inc. [*NASDAQ symbol*] (SAG)
UTIL	Utility [*or Utilization*] (AFM)
UtilC	Utilicorp United, Inc. [*Associated Press*] (SAG)
UTILCO	Utilicorp United, Inc. (EFIS)
UtiliCo	Utilicorp United, Inc. [*Associated Press*] (SAG)
UTILIDOR	Utility Corridor (SAA)
Util L Rep	Utilities Law Reporter [*Commerce Clearing House*] [*A publication*] (DLA)
UTILN	Utilitarian (AAG)
Util Sect Newl	Utility Section Newsletter [*A publication*] (DLA)
Utilx	Utilx Corp. [*Associated Press*] (SAG)
UTIN	United Trust [*NASDAQ symbol*] (TTSB)
UTIN	United Trust, Inc. [*NASDAQ symbol*] (SAG)
UT INF	Ut Infra [*As Below*] [*Latin*] (ADA)
UTIPS	Upgraded Tactical Information Processing System [*Computer science*]
UTIRS	United Tiberias Institutions Relief Society (EA)
UTJ	Union for Traditional Judaism (EA)
UTJ	Uterotubal Junction [*Medicine*]
UTK	University of Tennessee, at Knoxville
UTK	Uranium Tetrafluoride in Kiln [*Nuclear energy*] (NUCP)
UTK	Utirik [*Marshall Islands*] [*Airport symbol*] (OAG)
UTK/PSL	University of Tennessee at Knoxville Plasma Science Laboratory
UTL	Uganda Telecom Ltd.
UTL	Ultratrace-Level [*Analytical chemistry*]
UTL	UNITIL Corp. [*AMEX symbol*] (SPSG)
UTL	Unit Transmission Loss
UTL	Unit Transmittal Letter [*Army*]
UTL	UnivEd Technologies Ltd. [*British*] (IRUK)
UTL	Universal Transporter Loader (MCD)
UT-L	University of Tasmania - Launceston [*Australia*]
UTL	University of Toledo, College of Law, Toledo, OH [*OCLC symbol*] (OCLC)
UTL	University of Toronto Library [*UTLAS symbol*]
UTL	Up Telecommunications Switch
UTL	User Trailer Label (CMD)
UTL	Utila Island [*Honduras*] [*Airport symbol*] (AD)
UTLAS	UTLAS International Canada [*Formerly, University of Toronto Library Automation System*] [*Library network*]
UTLB	Unified Translation Lookaside Buffer [*Computer science*] (PCM)
UTLBX	Mgn. Stanley D. Witter Utilities Cl.B [*Mutual fund ticker symbol*] (SG)
UTLC	University of Tennessee College of Law (DLA)
UtlCC	Utilicorp Capital LP [*Associated Press*] (SAG)
UTLD	Utah Test of Language Development [*Education*]
UTLD-3	Utah Test of Language Development-3 [*Merlin J. Mecham*] (TES)
UTLM	Up Telemetry (MCD)
UTLR	University of Tasmania Law Review [*Australia A publication*]
UTLTY	Utility
UTLX	UTILX Corp. [*NASDAQ symbol*] (SPSG)
UTLY	Utility (BUR)
UTLZTN	Utilization
UTM	Union des Travailleurs de Mauritanie [*Union of Workers of Mauritania*]
UTM	Union des Travailleurs de Mayotte [*Comoros*] (PD)
UTM	Universal Testing Machine
UTM	Universal Test Message
UTM	Universal Transverse Mercator [*Cartography*]
UTM	Universal Transverse Mercator Map Projection (EERA)
UTM	Universal Turing Machine [*Mathematical model*] [*Computer science*] (BYTE)
UTM	University of Tennessee at Martin
UTM	Unsafe to Monitor (ACII)
UTMA	Uniform Transfers to Minors Act [*National Conference of Commissioners on Uniform State Laws*]
UTMA	United Tank Makers' Association [*A union*] [*British*]
UTMAWTU	United Turners', Machinists', and Athletic Woodworkers' Trade Union [*British*]
UTMB	University of Texas Medical Branch [*Galveston*]
UTMC	United Technologies Microelectronics Center (NITA)
UTMCI	Union des Travailleurs de la Moyenne Cote d'Ivoire [*Union of Middle Ivory Coast Workers*]
UTMC/K	University of Tennessee Medical Center/Knoxville
UTMD	Utah Medical, Inc. [*NASDAQ symbol*] (NQ)
UTMD	Utah Medical Products [*NASDAQ symbol*] (TTSB)
UTMDAH	University of Texas, M. D. Anderson Hospital
UT/MI	Underway Trials and Material Inspection (MCD)
UTML	Utility Motor Launch
UTMS	Urban Transportation Modeling System [*TRB*] (TAG)
UTN	University of Tennessee at Nashville
UTN	Upington [*South Africa*] [*Airport symbol*] (OAG)
UTN	Urban Telephone Network (OA)
UTN	Utensil (MSA)
Utne R	Utne Reader [*A publication*] (BRI)
UTNOTREQ	Utilization of Government Facilities Not Required as It Is Considered Such Utilization Would Adversely Affect Performance of Assigned Temporary Duty
UTNRS	Underwater Terrain Navigation and Reconnaissance Simulator (MCD)
utnsl	Utensil (VRA)
UTO	Indian Mountain, AK [*Location identifier FAA*] (FAAL)
UTO	United Telephone Organizations
UTO	United Towns Organisation [*See also FMVJ*] [*Paris, France*] (EAIO)
UTO	Upper Tibial Osteotomy [*Medicine*] (DMAA)
UTO	Utopia Creek [*Alaska*] [*Airport symbol*] (OAG)

UTOA	United Truck Owners of America (EA)
UTOA	United TVRO [*Television Receive Only*] Owners Association [*Defunct*] (EA)
UTOC	United Technologies Online Catalog [*United Technologies Corp.*] [*Information service or system*] (IID)
UTOCO	Utah Oil Co.
UTOG	Unitog [*NASDAQ symbol*] (TTSB)
UTOG	Unitog Co. [*NASDAQ symbol*] (NQ)
UTOL	Universal Translator Oriented Language
UTOLCL	University of Toledo College of Law (DLA)
U Toledo	[*The*] University of Toledo (GAGS)
U Toledo Intra LR	University of Toledo. Intramural Law Review [*A publication*] (DLA)
UTOP	Utopian (WDAA)
UTOPIA	Universal Terminalized Online Printing and Investigative Aid [*Bancroft-Parkman, Inc.*] [*Information service or system*]
U Tor L Rev	University of Toronto. School of Law. Review [*A publication*] (DLA)
U Toronto Sch L Rev	University of Toronto. School of Law. Review [*A publication*] (DLA)
UTP	Unified Test Plan
UTP	United Teaching Profession (MCD)
UTP	United Trade Press (Holdings) Ltd. [*Commercial firm British*]
UTP	Unit Territory Plan
UTP	Unit Test Plan
UTP	Universal Tape Processor
UTP	Universal Test Point (CAAL)
UTP	Unlisted Trading Privileges
UTP	Unshielded Twisted-Pair [*Computer science*] (PCM)
UTP	Upper Thames Patrol [*British military*] (DMA)
UTP	Upper Trip Point
UTP	Upper Turning Point
UTP	Urban Transportation Planning [*Department of Transportation*] (GFGA)
UTP	Uridine Triphosphatase [*An enzyme*]
UTP	Uridine Triphosphate [*Biochemistry*]
UTP	User Test Program [*Army*]
UTP	Utapao [*Thailand*] [*Airport symbol Obsolete*] (OAG)
UTP	Utility Tape Processor
UTPA	Uniform Trustees' Powers Act [*National Conference of Commissioners on Uniform State Laws*]
UTPase	Uridine Triphosphatase [*An enzyme*]
UTPE	United Trekkers of Planet Earth [*An association*] (EA)
UTPL	Urban Transportation Planning Laboratory [*University of Pennsylvania*] [*Research center*] (RCD)
UTPMS	Unit Trust Portfolio Management Service [*Investment term British*]
UTPP	Urban Transportation Planning Package [*Bureau of the Census*] (GFGA)
UTPS	UMTA [*Urban Mass Transit Administration*] Transportation Planning System
UTP3	Urban Transport Planning System [*Australia*]
UTQ	Hinesville, GA [*Location identifier FAA*] (FAAL)
UTQFP	Ultra-Thin Quad Flat-Pack (AAEL)
UTQG	Uniform Tire Quality Grade
UTQGS	Uniform Tire Quality Grading Standards [*Department of Transportation*] (GFGA)
UTR	Underwater Tracking Range
UTR	Union Transportation [*AAR code*]
UTR	Unitrode Corp. [*NYSE symbol*] (SPSG)
UTR	Universal Torah Registry (EA)
UTR	Universal Training Reactor [*Nuclear energy*] (GFGA)
UTR	University of Toronto, Thomas Fisher Rare Book Library [*UTLAS symbol*]
UTR	University Training Reactor
UTR	Unprogrammed Transfer Register
UTR	Untranslated Region [*Genetics*]
UTR	Up Time Ratio
UTR	Urticarial Transfusion Reaction [*Medicine*]
utra	Uniform Trust Receipts Act [*Legal shorthand*] (LWAP)
UTRA	Upper Torso Restraint Assembly
UTRANSRON	Utility Transport Squadron (DNAB)
UTRAO	Radio Astronomy Observatory [*University of Texas at Austin*] [*Research center*] (RCD)
UTRC	United Techniques Research Center [*Navy*] (DNAB)
UTRC	United Technologies Research Centre
UTREP	University of Tennessee Rehabilitation Engineering Program
UtRetail	United Retail Group, Inc. [*Associated Press*] (SAG)
UTRF	Update Training File [*IRS*]
UTRIP	Universal Triangulation Program (IAA)
UTROAA	Units to Round Out the Active Army
UTRON	Utility Squadron [*Navy*]
UTRONFWDAREA	Utility Squadron, Forward Area [*Navy*]
UTRP	Underwater Tactical Range, Pacific
UTRR	University of Teheran Research Reactor
UTRTD	Untreated
UTRWW	Unitrode Corp. [*NASDAQ symbol*] (SAG)
UTRWW	Unitrode Corp. Wrrt [*NASDAQ symbol*] (TTSB)
UTS	Huntsville, TX [*Location identifier FAA*] (FAAL)
UTS	Ullrich-Turner Syndrome [*Genetics*]
UTS	Ultimate Tensile Strength [*or Stress*]
UTS	Ultra-Thin Silicon (AAEL)
UTS	Umbilical Test Set
UTS	Underwater Telephone System
UTS	Unified Transfer System [*Computer to translate Russian to English*]
UTS	Union des Travailleurs du Senegal [*Senegalese Workers Union*]
UTS	Union Theological Seminary

UTS............. United Tanners' Society [*A union*] [*British*]
UTS............. United Theological Seminary, Dayton, OH [*OCLC symbol*] (OCLC)
UTS............. United Tri-Star Resources Ltd. [*Toronto Stock Exchange symbol*]
UTS............. Unit Training Standard
UTS............. Unit Trouble Shooting
UTS............. Universal Terminal System [*Sperry UNIVAC*] [*Computer science*]
UTS............. Universal Test Station
UTS............. Universal Thrust Stand
UTS............. Universal Time Sharing [*Computer science*] (IEEE)
UTS............. Universal Timesharing System (NITA)
UTS............. Universal Time Standards (NG)
UTS............. Universal Treatment Standard [*Environmental protection agency*]
UTS............. University of Technology, Sydney [*Australia*] (ECON)
UTS............. University Tutorial Series [*A publication*]
UTS............. Unmanned Teleoperator Spacecraft (MCD)
UTS............. Update Transaction System (TEL)
UTS............. Urine-Transfer System [*Apollo*] [*NASA*]
UTS............. Utility Interim Table Simulation (SAA)
UTS............. Utility Tactical Support (SAA)
UTS............. Utsunomiya [*Japan*] [*Seismograph station code, US Geological Survey*] (SEIS)
UTSA .... Uniform and Textile Service Association (NTPA)
UTSCC .... University of Texas System Cancer Center [*Houston, TX*] [*Research center*]
UTSE........... United Transport Service Employees [*Later, BRAC*] (EA)
UTS-FO .... Union Territoriale des Syndicats - Force Ouvrieres [*Territorial Federation of Trade Unions - Workers' Force*] [*French Somaliland*]
UTSI........... University of Tennessee Space Institute
UTSL........... University of Texas School of Law (DLA)
UTSL........... Use the Source, Luke [*Computer hacker terminology, used to parody commands to Luke Skywalker in the movie "Star Wars"*] (NHD)
UTSM........... Tamdy-Bulak [*Former USSR ICAO location identifier*] (ICLI)
UTS-M......... Universal Timesharing System for Mainframes (HGAA)
UTSMS .... University of Texas Southwestern Medical School
UTSN .... Used Truck Sales Network (EA)
UTSS .... Samarkand [*Former USSR ICAO location identifier*] (ICLI)
UTSS .... Universal Threat System for Simulators
UTS-S .... Universal Timesharing System for Superminis (HGAA)
UTST........... Termez [*Former USSR ICAO location identifier*] (ICLI)
UT SUP .... Ut Supra [*As Above*] [*Latin*]
UT SUPR ..... Ut Supra [*As Above*] [*Latin*]
UTSV .... Union Theological Seminary in Virginia
UTS/VS .... Universal Timesharing System/Virtual Storage (NITA)
UTT............. Umtata [*South Africa*] [*Airport symbol*] (OAG)
UTT............. Unattenuated (AAEL)
UTT............. Utility Tactical Transport (MCD)
UTT............. UT Technologies [*Vancouver Stock Exchange symbol*]
UTT............. Uttering [*FBI standardized term*]
UTTA........... United Thoroughbred Trainers of America (EA)
UTTAS .... Utility Tactical Transport Aircraft System [*Helicopter*] [*Military*]
UTT Avn ..... Utility Tactical Transport Aviation Company [*US Army helicopters*] (VNW)
UTTC........... Universal Tape-to-Tape Converter
UTTCO .... Utility Tactical Transport Company [*US Army helicopters*] (VNW)
UTTL........... Uttlesford [*England*]
UTTO .... Universal Tractor Transmission Oil [*Lubricants*]
UTTR .... Utah Test and Training Range [*Air Force*]
UTTS .... Union Territoriale du Senegal des Travailleurs [*Senegalese Workers Union*]
UTTS .... Universal Target Tracking Station (MCD)
UTTT........... Tashkent/Yuzhny [*Former USSR ICAO location identifier*] (ICLI)
UTU............. Ulster Teacher's Union [*Ireland*] (AIE)
UTU............. Ultrasonic Test Unit
UTU............. Underway Training Unit
UTU............. United Transportation Union (EA)
UTU............. Ustupo [*Panama*] [*Airport symbol*] (OAG)
utu............. Utah [*MARC country of publication code Library of Congress*] (LCCP)
UTUC .... Uganda Trades' Union Congress
UTUC .... United Trades Union Congress [*India*]
U Tulsa........ [*The*] University of Tulsa (GAGS)
UTV............. Ulster Television [*Ireland*] (DI)
UTV............. Uncompensated Temperature Variation (TEL)
UTV............. Underwater Television
UTV............. Universal Test Vehicle [*Military*]
UTVI........... United Television, Inc. [*NASDAQ symbol*] (NQ)
UTVI........... United Televison [*NASDAQ symbol*] (TTSB)
UTW............. Queenstown [*South Africa*] [*Airport symbol*] (AD)
UTW............. Ultrathin Window [*Spectroscopy*]
UTW............. Under the Wing [*Aircraft*]
UTW............. Union of Textile Workers [*British*] (EAIO)
UTW............. United Telegraph Workers [*Later, C/UBC*] (EA)
UTW............. Utilitiesman, Water and Sanitation [*Navy rating*]
UTWA .... United Textile Workers of America (EA)
UTWG .... Utility Wing [*Navy*] (MUGU)
UTWING........ Utility Wing [*Navy*]
UTWINGSERVLANT... Utility Wing, Service Force, Atlantic [*Navy*]
UTWINGSERVPAC... Utility Wing, Service Force, Pacific [*Navy*]
UTX............. Jupiter, FL [*Location identifier FAA*] (FAAL)
UTX,............ United Technologies [*NYSE symbol*] (TTSB)
UTX............. United Technologies Corp. [*NYSE symbol*] (SPSG)
UTZ............. Ultrasound [*Radiology*] (DAVI)
UU .... Reunion Air [*ICAO designator*] (AD)
UU .... Uglies Unlimited (EA)
UU .... Ulster Unionist [*British*] (WDAA)

UU .... Ulster Unionist Party
UU .... Ultimate User [*Nuclear energy*]
UU .... Unemployment Unit [*An association British*]
UU .... Unicorns Unanimous [*An association*] (EA)
UU .... Union University [*Tennessee*]
UU .... University of Utah, Salt Lake City, UT [*Library symbol Library of Congress*] (LCLS)
UU .... Urine Urobilin [*Clinical chemistry*] (DAVI)
UU .... Urine Urobilinogen [*Clinical chemistry*]
UU .... User Unit (MCD)
UUA .... Southern Utah State College, Cedar City, UT [*OCLC symbol*] (OCLC)
UUA .... Unitarian Universalist Society for Alcohol and Drug Education
UUA .... UNIVAC Users Association [*Later, AUUA*]
UUA .... Universal Automatic Computer Users' Association (IAA)
UUA .... Uracil Uracil Adenine [*A triplet of bases coding for the amino acid, leucine*] (EES)
UUABCWG ... Unitarian Universalist Association Black Concerns Working Group (EA)
UUAC .... United Unionist Action Council [*Northern Ireland*]
UUARC .... United Ukrainian American Relief Committee (EA)
UUA/WO ..... Unitarian Universalist Association of Congregations-Washington Office (EA)
UUA/WOSC... Unitarian Universalist Association-Washington Office for Social Concern [*Later, UUA/WOSJ*] (EA)
UUA/WOSJ... Unitarian Universalist Association of Congregations-Washington Office for SocialJustice (EA)
UUB .... Brigham Young University, School of Library and Information Science, Provo, UT [*OCLC symbol*] (OCLC)
UUB .... UUB Financial [*Associated Press*] (SAG)
UUBCWG ...... Unitarian Universalist Black Concerns Working Group (EA)
UUBP .... Bryansk [*Former USSR ICAO location identifier*] (ICLI)
UUC .... Salt Lake County Library System, Salt Lake City, UT [*OCLC symbol*] (OCLC)
UUC .... Ulster University College (ACII)
UUC .... United University Club [*British*]
UUC .... Uracil Uracil Cytosine [*A triplet of bases coding for the amino acid, phenylalanine*] (EES)
UUCA .... United Underwear Contractors Association [*Defunct*] (EA)
UUCD .... USA-USSR Citizens' Dialogue [*Defunct*] (EA)
UUCF .... Unitarian Universalist Christian Fellowship (EA)
UUCP .... Unix-to-Unix Call Procedure [*Telecommunications*] (OSI)
UUCP .... Unix-to-Unix Copy Program [*Computer science*]
UUCP .... UNIX-to-UNIX Copy Protocol (TNIG)
UUD .... Logan Public Library, Logan, UT [*OCLC symbol*] (OCLC)
U-UD........... Utility Dog [*Prefix*]
UUE .... University of Utah, Eccles Health Science Library, Salt Lake City, UT [*OCLC symbol*] (OCLC)
UUE .... Use until Exhausted
UUEE .... Moskva/Sheremetyevo [*Former USSR ICAO location identifier*] (ICLI)
UUEM .... Kalini/Migalovo [*Former USSR ICAO location identifier*] (ICLI)
UUEncode.... Binary to Text Encoding [*Computer science*]
UUEW .... United Unions for Employees and Workers [*Lebanon*]
UUFSJ .... Unitarian Universalist Fellowship for Social Justice (EA)
UUG .... Uracil Uracil Guanine [*A triplet of bases coding for the amino acid, leucine*] (EES)
UUGS........... Unitarian and Universalist Genealogical Society [*Defunct*] (EA)
UUHS .... Unitarian Universalist Historical Society (EA)
UUID .... Universally Unique Identifier [*Computer science*]
UUIP .... Uppsala University Institute of Physics [*Sweden*]
UUK .... Kuparuk, AK [*Location identifier FAA*] (FAAL)
UU-L .... University of Utah, Law Library, Salt Lake City, UT [*Library symbol Library of Congress*] (LCLS)
UULGC......... Unitarian Universalist Lesbian Gay Caucus (EA)
UUM .... Underwater-to-Underwater Missile [*Air Force*]
UU-M .... University of Utah, Library of Medical Sciences, Salt Lake City, UT [*Library symbol Library of Congress*] (LCLS)
UUM .... University of Utah, Salt Lake City, UT [*OCLC symbol*] (OCLC)
UUMA .... Unitarian Universalist Ministers Association (EA)
UUMN .... Unitarian Universalist Musicians' Network (EA)
UUMP .... Unification of Units of Measurement Panel [*ICAO*] (DA)
UUMPS .... Unitarian Universalist Ministers' Partners Society (EA)
UUN .... Urinary Urea Nitrogen [*Clinical medicine*]
UUnet .... UUnet Technologies, Inc. [*Associated Press*] (SAG)
UUNT .... UUNET Technologies [*NASDAQ symbol*] (TTSB)
UUNT .... UUnet Technologies, Inc. [*NASDAQ symbol*] (SAG)
UUO .... Unimplemented User Operation [*Computer science*] (EECA)
UUO .... Weber State College, Ogden, UT [*OCLC symbol*] (OCLC)
UUOO.......... Voronezh [*Former USSR ICAO location identifier*] (ICLI)
UUP .... Salt Lake City Public Library, Salt Lake City, UT [*OCLC symbol*] (OCLC)
UUP .... Uaupes [*Brazil*] [*Airport symbol*] (AD)
UUP .... Ulster Unionist Party [*British Political party*]
UUP .... Ulster Unionist Party [*Northern Ireland*] [*Political party*]
UUP .... United Unionists Party [*Northern Ireland*]
UUP .... Urine Uroporphyrin [*Medicine*] (MAE)
UUPP .... Unused Undeducted Purchase Price
UUR .... Under Usual Reserves
UURWAW ...... United Union of Roofers, Waterproofers, and Allied Workers (EA)
UUS .... User-to-User Signaling [*Telecommunications*] (DOM)
UUS .... Utah State University, Logan, UT [*OCLC symbol*] (OCLC)
UUSAE......... Unitarian Universalist Society for Alcohol Education [*Later, UUA*] (EA)
UUSC .... Unitarian Universalist Service Committee (EA)
UUSS .... University of Utah Seismograph Stations [*Research center*] (RCD)
UUT .... Unit under Test

U Utah .... University of Utah (GAGS)
UUTI .... Uncomplicated Urinary Tract Infection [Medicine]
UUU .... Manumu [Papua New Guinea] [Airport symbol] (OAG)
UUU .... Uracil Uracil Uracil [A triplet of bases coding for the amino acid, phenylalanine] (EES)
UUUC .... United Ulster Unionist Coalition [Northern Ireland]
UUUM .... Moskva [Former USSR ICAO location identifier] (ICLI)
UUUM .... United Ulster Unionist Movement [Northern Ireland]
UUUP .... United Ulster Unionist Party [Northern Ireland] [Political party] (PPW)
UUUU .... Moskva [Former USSR ICAO location identifier] (ICLI)
UUUU .... Unidentified [Marketing surveys] (NTCM)
UUUU .... Unwilling, Led by the Unqualified, Doing the Unnecessary, for the Ungrateful [Military slogan] (VNW)
UUV .... Unmanned Undersea Vehicle [Military robotics]
UUV .... Untethered Underwater Vehicle (DOMA)
UUW .... Westminster College, Salt Lake City, UT [OCLC symbol] (OCLC)
UUWF .... Unitarian Universalist Women's Federation (EA)
UUWW .... Moskva/Vnukovo [Former USSR ICAO location identifier] (ICLI)
UUYEP .... US-USSR Youth Exchange Program (EA)
UUYT .... Ust-Kulom [Former USSR ICAO location identifier] (ICLI)
UUYY .... Syktyvkar [Former USSR ICAO location identifier] (ICLI)
UUZ .... Utah State Library, Processing Center, Salt Lake City, UT [OCLC symbol] (OCLC)
UV .... Air Kangaroo Island [Airline code] [Australia]
UV .... Ultra Vans (EA)
UV .... Ultraviolet [Electromagnetic spectrum range]
uv .... Ultraviolet (VRA)
UV .... Ultravisible
UV .... Umbilical Vein [Medicine]
UV .... Unabhaengige Volkspartei [Independent People's Party] [Political party Germany] (EAIO)
UV .... Unadilla Valley Railroad (IIA)
UV .... Under Voltage
uv .... Under Voltage (NAKS)
UV .... Underwater Vehicle
UV .... Union Valdotaine [Valdotaine Union] [Italy Political party] (EAIO)
UV .... Union Valenciana [Spain Political party] (EY)
UV .... Universal Airways [ICAO designator] (AD)
uv .... Upper Volta [MARC country of publication code Library of Congress] (LCCP)
Uv .... Uppsala Virus [Medicine] (MAE)
UV .... Ureterovesical [Urology] (DAVI)
UV .... Urethrovesical [Urology] (DAVI)
UV .... Urinary Volume [Physiology]
UV .... Uterine Vein [Anatomy]
UV .... Uterine Volume
UV .... Utility Value [Psychology]
UVA .... Ultraviolet Absorption
IIVA .... Ultraviolet A (l ight)
UVA .... Ultraviolet Light, Long Wave
UVA .... Universal Airways, Inc. [ICAO designator] (FAAC)
UvA .... Universiteit van Amsterdam
UVA .... University of Virginia
UVA .... Ureterovesical Angle [Urology] (DAVI)
UVA .... Urethrovesical Angle [Urology] (DAVI)
UVA .... Uvalde, TX [Location identifier FAA] (FAAL)
UVAL .... Ultraviolet Argon LASER
UVAN .... Ukrainian Academy of Arts and Sciences of Canada
UVAR .... University of Virginia Reactor
UVAS .... Ultraviolet Astronomical Satellite (PDAA)
UVAS .... Unmanned Vehicle for Aerial Surveillance (MCD)
UVASER ...... Ultraviolet Amplification by Stimulated Emission of Radiation
UVASERS .... Ultraviolet Amplification by Stimulated Emission of Radiation System
UVB .... Ultraviolet B [or Ultraviolet light, midrange sunbeam, spectrum] [Dermatology] (DAVI)
UV-B .... Ultraviolet Band
UV-B .... Ultraviolet-Biological (USDC)
UVB .... Ultraviolet B (Light)
UVB .... Ultraviolet Light, Midrange Sunbeam Spectrum [Ultraviolet B] [Dermatology] (DAVI)
UVBF .... Umbilical Vein Blood Flow
UVC .... Pennsylvania State University, Capitol Campus, Middletown, PA [OCLC symbol] (OCLC)
UVC .... Ullucus Virus C [Plant pathology]
UVC .... Ultrahigh Vacuum Chamber
UVC .... Ultraviolet Communications System
UVC .... Ultraviolet Light Cured
UVC .... Umbilical Venous Catheter [Medicine] (MEDA)
UVC .... Uniform Vehicle Code
UVCA .... Uniform Vehicle Code Annotated
UVCB .... Under-Voltage Circuit-Breaker [Electronics] (EECA)
UVCB .... Unknown or Variable Composition, Complex Reaction Products, and Biological Materials [Chemical Abstracts Services]
UVCE .... Unconfined Vapor Cloud Explosion
UVCS .... Ultraviolet Coronagraph Spectrometer [Solar Physics]
UVD .... Ultrasonic Vapor Degresser
UVD .... Ultraviolet Detector
UVD .... Undervoltage Device
UVD .... Unintegrated Viral DNA [Deoxyribonucleic Acid] [Pathology]
UVD .... Upper Vas Deferens [Anatomy]
UVDB .... Union des Verts pour le Developpement du Burkina [Burkina Faso] [Political party] (EY)
UVDC .... Urban Vehicle Design Competition
UVDIAL .... Ultraviolet Differential Absorption LIDAR [Light Detection and Ranging] (PDAA)

UVD-SV .... Upper Vas Deferens-Seminal Vesicle Complex [Anatomy]
UVE .... Ouvea [Loyalty Islands] [Airport symbol] (OAG)
UVED .... Under-Vehicle Explosive Device (WDAA)
UVEPROM .... Ultra-Violet Erasable Programmable Read Only Memory
UV-EPROMS ... Ultraviolet-Erasable Programmable Read-Only Memories [Computer science]
UVEROM ...... Ultraviolet Eraseable Read Only Memory (PDAA)
UVF .... St. Lucia [West Indies] Hewanorra Airport [Airport symbol] (OAG)
UVF .... Ulster Volunteer Force
UVF .... Ultraviolet Filter
UVF .... Ultraviolet Floodlight (AAG)
UVF .... Underground Validation Facility [Nuclear energy] (NUCP)
UVF .... Unmanned Vertical Flight [NASA] (NASA)
UVFLT .... Ultraviolet Floodlight
UVFO .... Ultraviolet Fiber Optics
UVG .... UV [Ultraviolet] Spectrometry Group [British]
UVGS .... Church of Jesus Christ of Latter-Day Saints, Genealogical Society Library, Uintah Basin Branch, Vernal, UT [Library symbol Library of Congress] (LCLS)
UVH .... Univentricular Heart [Cardiology]
UVHFDS ...... Ultraviolet Hydrogen Fire Detection System (DNAB)
UVI .... Ultraviolet Irradiation
UVI .... Uvira [Zaire] [Seismograph station code, US Geological Survey Closed] (SEIS)
UVIC .... University of Victoria [British Columbia]
UVICON ...... Ultraviolet Image Converter (WGA)
UVIL .... Ultraviolet Inspection Light
UVIL .... Ultraviolet Ion LASER
UVIRSG ...... Ultraviolet Infrared Scene Generator
UVJ .... Ureterovesical Junction [Anatomy] (MAE)
UVL .... New Valley [Egypt] [Airport symbol] (OAG)
UVL .... Ultraviolet Lamp
UVL .... Ultraviolet LASER
UVL .... Ultraviolet Light
UVL .... Umbilical Venous Line (STED)
UVL .... Universal [Former USSR] [FAA designator] (FAAC)
UVLI .... Ustav Vedeckych Lekarskych Informaci [Institute for Medical Information] [Former Czechoslovakia Database operator] [Information service or system] (IID)
UVLS .... Ultraviolet Light Stabilizer
UVM .... Ultraviolet Meter
UVM .... Universal Vendor Marking (WGA)
UVM .... Universitas Viridis Montis [University of the Green Mountains; i.e., University of Vermont]
UVM .... University of Vermont (PDAA)
UVM .... University of Vermont, Burlington (USDC)
UVMC .... United Voluntary Motor Corps (EA)
UVN .... Unionville [Nevada] [Seismograph station code, US Geological Survey Closed] (SEIS)
UVNO .... Ultraviolet Nitric-Oxide Experiment
UVO .... Uvol [Papua New Guinea] [Airport symbol] (OAG)
UVOH .... Union of Voluntary Organisations for the Handicapped [British] (DBA)
UVP .... Ultrahigh Vacuum Pump
UVP .... Ultrasound Vibration Potential [Determination of electrokinetic potential]
UVP .... Ultraviolet Photometry
UVP .... Under-Voltage Protection [Electronics] (EECA)
UVP .... Unified Vocational Preparation [Manpower Services Commission] [British]
UVPES .... Ultraviolet Photoelectron Spectroscopy
UVPJU .... Uganda Vernacular, Primary and Junior Secondary Teachers' Union
UVPROM ...... Ultraviolet Programmable Read Only Memory
UVPS .... Ultrahigh Vacuum Pumping Station
UV-PSdA ...... Unione Valdostana-Partito Sardo d'Azione [Italy] [Political party] (ECED)
UVR .... Uitenhage Volunteer Rifles [British military] (DMA)
UV-R .... Ultraviolet-Biological [Marine science] (OSRA)
UVR .... Ultraviolet Radiation
UVR .... Ultraviolet Radiometer (MCD)
UVR .... Ultraviolet Receiver
UVR .... Ultraviolet Resistant
UVR .... Ultraviolet Rocket
UVR .... Under Voltage Relay
UVR .... University of Virginia Reactor
UVR .... User Visible Resources
UVROM .... Ultraviolet Read Only Memory (IAA)
UVRR .... Ultraviolet Resonance Raman [Spectroscopy]
UVS .... Ultraviolet Spectrometer
UVS .... Under Voltage Sensing (MCD)
UVS .... Uninterruptable Voltage Source [Electric power supply]
UVS .... United Voluntary Services (EA)
UVS .... Universal Versaplot Software (IAA)
UVS .... Unmanned Vehicle System
UVSC .... Ultraviolet Solar Constant
UVSC .... Uranium Ventilation Scrubber Cell [Nuclear energy] (NRCH)
UVSG .... Ultra Violet Spectrometry Group [British] (DBA)
UVSG .... United Video Satellite [NASDAQ symbol] (SAG)
UVSGA .... United Video Satellite Gp'A' [NASDAQ symbol] (TTSB)
UVSL .... Universal Automotive Inds [NASDAQ symbol] (TTSB)
UVSL .... Universal Automotive Inds, Inc. [NASDAQ symbol] (SAG)
UVSLW .... Universal Auto Ind Wrrt [NASDAQ symbol] (TTSB)
UVSP .... Ultraviolet Spectral Photometer
UVT .... Ultraviolet Transmission
UVT .... Ultraviolet Tube
UVT .... Universal Voltage Tester

U Vt	University of Vermont (GAGS)
UVT	Usable Vector Table
UVTEI	Ustredi Vedeckych, Technickych, a Ekonomickych Informaci [*Former Czechoslovakia*] [*Information service or system*] (IID)
UVV	Universal Corp. [*NYSE symbol*] (SPSG)
UVV	Univl Corp. [*NYSE symbol*] (TTSB)
UV-VIS	Ultraviolet/Visible [*Spectroscopy*]
UVVO	United Vietnam Veterans Organization (EA)
UVX	Univar Corp. [*Formerly, VWR United Corp.*] [*NYSE symbol*] (SPSG)
UW	Air Rwanda [*Rwanda*] [*ICAO designator*] (ICDA)
UW	Perimeter Airlines [*ICAO designator*] (AD)
UW	Ultimate Weapon (AAG)
UW	Ultrasonic Wave
UW	Unburned, Warmed [*Ecology*]
UW	Unconventional Warfare [*Army*]
UW	Underwater
UW	Underwater Weapons [*British*]
U/W	Underway (NVT)
U/W	Under Will [*Legal term*] (DLA)
U/W	Underwriter [*Insurance*]
U/w	Underwriters (EBF)
UW	Unilateral Weakness (STED)
UW	Unique Word (IAA)
UW	United Way (OICC)
UW	United Weldors International Union
UW	University of Washington [*Seattle, WA*]
UW	University of Wisconsin [*Madison, WI*] (MCD)
UW	Unladen Weight (BARN)
UW	Untere Winkelgruppe [*Angles up to 45*] [*German military - World War II*]
UW	Uppity Women [*An association*] (EA)
UW	Upset Welding
UW	Upwind [*Aviation*] (FAAC)
UW	Urbach-Wiethe [*Syndrome*] [*Medicine*] (DB)
UW	Usable Width (MCD)
UW	USA Waste Service [*NYSE symbol*] (TTSB)
UW	USA Waste Services, Inc. [*NYSE symbol*] (SPSG)
U/W	Used With
UW	Utility Water (AAG)
UWA	Ukrainian Workingmen's Association [*Later, UFA*] (EA)
UWA	United Way of America (EA)
UWA	United Weighers Association (EA)
UWA	United Women of the Americas (EA)
UWA	United World Atheists (EA)
UWA	University of Western Australia [*State*] (EERA)
UWA	Unsuccessful Work Attempt (DHP)
UWA	User Working Area
UWA	Uwajima [*Japan*] [*Seismograph station code, US Geological Survey*] (SEIS)
UWA	Ware, MA [*Location identifier FAA*] (FAAL)
UWAC	Ukrainian Women's Association of Canada
UWAGE	Union Women's Alliance to Gain Equality [*Defunct*] (EA)
UWAL	Underwater Wide-Angle Lens
UWAL	University of Washington Aeronautical Laboratory (MCD)
UWARC	United Whiteruthenian [*Byelorussian*] American Relief Committee (EA)
UWARS	Universal Water-Activated Release System (DWSG)
U Wash	University of Washington (GAGS)
U Wash L Rev	University of Washington. Law Review [*A publication*] (DLA)
UWASIS	United Way of America Services Identification System
UWAT	User Written Application Test [*Computer science*]
UWATS	Universal Weapons Assembly Test Standard (MCD)
UWATU	Underway Training Unit
UWAVM	Underwater Antivehicle Mine (MCD)
UWAVWA	Union of West African Voluntary Workcamps Associations [*Ghana*] (EAIO)
UWAYTUNORVA	Underway Training Unit, Norfolk, Virginia (DNAB)
UWB	Ultra-Wide Band
U/WB	Unit of Whole Blood (STED)
UWB	Universal White Brotherhood [*An association France*] (EAIO)
UWBBR	University of Wisconsin - Madison Bureau of Business Research [*Research center*] (RCD)
UWBS	Uniform Work Breakdown Structure
UWC	Ulster Workers' Council
UWC	Underwater Communications [*Navy*] (CAAL)
UWC	Universal Water Charts [*Air Force*]
UWC	Universal Winding Co. (MCD)
UWC	University of the Western Cape [*South Africa*]
UWC	Widener College, Chester, PA [*OCLC symbol*] (OCLC)
UWCCCM	Union of Watch, Clock, and Clock Case Makers [*British*]
UWCE	Underwater Weapons and Countermeasures Establishment (BARN)
UWCS	Underwater Weapons Control System
UWCSEA	United World College of South East Asia [*Singapore*] (ECON)
UWCSS	Universal Weapon Control Stabilization System
UWD	Underwater Weapons Department [*British military*] (DMA)
UWDD	Undersea Warfare Development Division [*Navy*] (MCD)
UWE	University Women of Europe (EA)
UWE	Uwekahuna [*Hawaii*] [*Seismograph station code, US Geological Survey*] (SEIS)
UWEAMA	Under Water Equipment & Apparel Manufacturers' Association (BUAC)
UWERT	United World Education and Research Trust (EAIO)
UWESO	Uganda Women's Effort to Save Orphans (BUAC)
UWF	United World Federalists [*Later, World Federalists Association*] (EA)
UWF	University of West Florida [*Pensacola*]

UWF	Unknown White Female (DAVI)
UWFC	Underwater Fire Control [*Navy*] (CAAL)
UWFCS	Underwater Fire Control System
UWFPC	Union Wallisienne et Futunienne pour la Caledonie [*Wallisian and Futunian Union for Caledonia*] [*Political party*] (PPW)
UWG	Gesetz Gegen den Unlauteren Wettbewerb [*Law Against Unfair Competition*] [*German*] (DLA)
UWG	Ukraine Working Group (NTPA)
UWGB	University of Wisconsin at Green Bay
UWH	Underwater Habitat
UWH	Underwater Welding Habitat [*Deep-sea diving*]
UWHAT	Understanding without Heavy Acronym Training (AIE)
UW-HF	Upset Welding-High Frequency
UWH/WCS	Universal World Harmony/World Council of Service (BUAC)
UWI	Dalton, GA [*Location identifier FAA*] (FAAL)
UWI	United Way International (EA)
UWI	United Westburne Industries Ltd. [*Toronto Stock Exchange symbol*]
UWI	University of the West Indies [*Jamaica*]
UW-I	Upset Welding-Induction
UWICED	University of the West Indies Centre for Environment and Development [*Barbados*]
U Windsor L Rev	University of Windsor. Law Review [*A publication*] (DLA)
UWIS	University of Wisconsin (PDAA)
U Wis	University of Wisconsin (GAGS)
U Wis (Eau Claire)	University of Wisconsin at Eau Claire (GAGS)
U Wis (La Crosse)	University of Wisconsin at La Crosse (GAGS)
U Wis (Milwaukee)	University of Wisconsin at Milwaukee (GAGS)
U Wis (Oshkosh)	University of Wisconsin at Oshkosh (GAGS)
U Wis (Platteville)	University of Wisconsin at Platteville (GAGS)
U Wis (River Falls)	University of Wisconsin at River Falls (GAGS)
U Wis (Stevens Point)	University of Wisconsin at Stevens Point (GAGS)
U Wis (Stout)	University of Wisconsin at Stout (GAGS)
U Wis (Superior)	University of Wisconsin at Superior (GAGS)
UWIST	University of Wales Institute of Science and Technology [*British*]
U Wis (Whitewater)	University of Wisconsin at Whitewater (GAGS)
UWKD	Kazan [*Former USSR ICAO location identifier*] (ICLI)
UWL	New Castle, IN [*Location identifier FAA*] (FAAL)
UWL	Underwater Launch
UWL	University of Winnipeg Library [*UTLAS symbol*]
UWL	Unstirred Water Layer (DB)
UWL	Utowana Lake [*New York*] [*Seismograph station code, US Geological Survey*] (SEIS)
UWLA Rev	University of West Los Angeles. School of Law. Law Review [*A publication*] (DLA)
UWM	Uniform Wave Motion
UWM	United World Mission (EA)
UWM	University of Wisconsin at Milwaukee [*Seismograph station code, US Geological Survey*] (SEIS)
UWM	Unknown White Male (DAVI)
UWM	Unwed Mother (STED)
UWMA	United Women's Muslim Association [*Kenya*] (BUAC)
UWMAK	University of Wisconsin TOKAMAK
UWMAS	United Wallpaper Merchants Association of Scotland (BUAC)
UWNDS	Upper Winds [*Meteorology*] (FAAC)
UWNE	Brotherhood of Utility Workers of New England (EA)
UWNR	University of Wisconsin - Madison Nuclear Reactor Laboratory [*Research center*] (RCD)
UWO	University of Western Ontario (MCD)
UWO	University of Western Ontario Library [*UTLAS symbol*]
UWO	University of Western Ontario, School of Library and Information Science, Lond on, ON, Canada [*OCLC symbol*] (OCLC)
UWOA	Unclassified without Attachment
UWOA	Unconventional Warfare Operations Area [*Army*] (AABC)
UWORDTECH	Underwater Ordnance Technician [*Navy*] (DNAB)
UWP	Dominica United Workers' Party [*Political party*] (EY)
UWP	United Workers' Party [*St. Lucia*] [*Political party*] (PPW)
UWP	United Workers' Party [*Guyana*] [*Political party*] (EY)
UWP	United Workers' Party [*Hungary Political party*] (PPW)
UWP	Up with People (EA)
UWPC	United World Press Cooperative [*Later, The Peoples Media Cooperative*] (EA)
UWPP	Penza [*Former USSR ICAO location identifier*] (ICLI)
UWR	Underwater Range (MUGU)
U/Wr	Underwriter [*Insurance*] (DLA)
UWR	Unexpected Wildlife Refuge (EA)
UWR	United Water Res [*NYSE symbol*] (TTSB)
UWR	United Water Resources [*Associated Press*] (SAG)
UWR	United Water Resources, Inc. [*NYSE symbol*] (SPSG)
UWRA	Uniform Warehouse Receipts Act (LWAP)
UWRA	Urban Water Research Association (EERA)
UWRC	Urban Wildlife Research Center (EA)
UW-RF	University of Wisconsin-River Falls
UWRR	University of Wyoming Research Reactor
UWS	Undersea Weapon System
UWS	University of Western Sydney [*State*] (EERA)
UWS	Unmanned Weather Station
UWS	User Work Station (NASA)
uws	User Work Station (NAKS)
UWSAMBS	United Women's Societies of the Adoration of the Most Blessed Sacrament [*Later, NUWSAMBS*] (EA)
UWSDDMS	Underwater Weapons System Design Disclosure Management Systems (KSC)
UWSEC	Underwater Weapons Systems Engineering Center [*Navy*] (DNAB)
UWS-M	University of Western Sydney - Macarthur [*Australia*]
UWS-N	University of Western Sydney - Nepean [*Australia*]

UWSRD........	Underwater Weapons Systems Reliability Data (KSC)
UWST..........	United Waste Systems [*NASDAQ symbol*] (SAG)
UWT............	Underwater Telephone
UWT............	Uniform Wave Train
UWT............	Union of Tanzania Women (BUAC)
UWT............	Union of Women Teachers [*British*] (DI)
UWT............	United World Education and Research Trust [*British*] (EAIO)
UWT............	Unit Weight (MSA)
UWT............	Urban Wildlife Trust (BUAC)
UWTM.........	Underwater Team (MSA)
UWTR.........	Underwater (AABC)
UWTR.........	University of Washington Training Reactor
UWU............	Los Angeles, CA [*Location identifier FAA*] (FAAL)
UWU............	Utility Workers Union of America
UWUA..........	Utility Workers Union of America (EA)
UWUSA.......	United Workers' Union of South Africa (BUAC)
UWW...........	Unisource Worldwide, Inc. [*NYSE symbol*] (SAG)
UWW...........	University without Walls [*Twenty-one-university consortium*]
UWWR........	Unpublished Scholarly Writings on World Religions (BJA)
UWWW........	Kuybyshev/Kurumoch [*Former USSR ICAO location identifier*] (ICLI)
UWY............	Upper Airway [*Aviation*] (DA)
U Wyo........	University of Wyoming (GAGS)
UWZ............	United Wisconsin Services, Inc. [*NYSE symbol*] (SAG)
UWZ............	United Wisconsin Svcs [*NYSE symbol*] (TTSB)
UX..............	Air Illinois [*ICAO designator*] (AD)
UX..............	Unexploded (BARN)
UX..............	Uranium X [*Proactinium*] (STED)
ux..............	Uxor [*Wife*] [*Latin*] (WGA)
UXAA..........	Unexploded Antiaircraft [*Shell*]
UXAPB........	Unexploded Antipersonnel Bomb
UXB............	Unexploded Bomb
UXGB..........	Unexploded Gas Bomb
UXIB............	Unexploded Incendiary Bomb
UXL.............	Laidlaw One 5.75% Ex Nts 2000 [*NYSE symbol*] (TTSB)
UXL.............	Laidlaw One, Inc. [*NYSE symbol*] (SAG)
UXM...........	Universal Extension Mechanism (KSC)
UXO............	Unexploded Ordnance
UXOI...........	Unexploded Ordnance Incident
UXPLD........	Unexploded Bomb (SAA)
UXPM..........	Unexploded Parachuted Mine
UXS.............	Unexploded Shell [*British military*] (DMA)
UXTGM........	Unexploded Type G Mine
UXW............	South Bend, IN [*Location identifier FAA*] (FAAL)
UY...............	Cameroon Airlines [*ICAO designator*] (AD)
UY...............	Unit Years [*Electronics*] (IEEE)
UY...............	Universal Youth
UY...............	Uruguay [*ANSI two-letter standard code*] (CNC)
uy...............	Uruguay [*MARC country of publication code Library of Congress*] (LCCP)
UYA............	University Year for ACTION [*Refers to federal program, ACTION, which is not an acronym*]
UYA............	Yute Air Alaska, Inc. [*ICAO designator*] (FAAC)
UYC............	Cameroon Airlines [*ICAO designator*] (FAAC)
UYC............	Uxbridge Yeomanry Cavalry [*British military*] (DMA)
UYF............	London, OH [*Location identifier FAA*] (FAAL)
UYL.............	Nyala [*Sudan*] [*Airport symbol*] (OAG)
UYLNA.........	Ukrainian Youth League of North America [*Defunct*] (EA)
UYN............	Yulin [*China*] [*Airport symbol*] (OAG)
UYVDRA......	Upper Yarra Valley and Dandenong Regional Authority [*of Victoria*] [*State*] (EERA)
UZ...............	Air Resorts Airlines [*ICAO designator*] (AD)
UZ...............	Nefertiti [*ICAO designator*] (AD)
UZ...............	Uhrzuender [*Clockwork fuze*] [*German military - World War II*]
UZ...............	Upper Zone [*Geology*]
Uz...............	Uzbek (BARN)
UZ...............	Uzbekistan [*Internet country code*]
UZA............	Urbanized Area [*APTA*] [*FHWA*] (TAG)
U Zambia LB...	University of Zambia. Law Bulletin [*A publication*] (DLA)
uzb.............	Uzbek [*MARC language code Library of Congress*] (LCCP)
UZB............	Uzbekistan Havo Jullary [*Uzbekistan Airways*] [*ICAO designator*] (FAAC)
UZH............	Uzhgorod [*Unuar*] [*Former USSR Seismograph station code, US Geological Survey*] (SEIS)
UZK............	Indianapolis, IN [*Location identifier FAA*] (FAAL)
UZM............	Unsaturated Zone Monitoring [*Environmental Protection Agency*] (ERG)
UZM............	Uoologisk Museum
uzr.............	Uzbek Soviet Socialist Republic [*MARC country of publication code Library of Congress*] (LCCP)
UZRA..........	United Zionist Revisionists of America [*Later, Herut - USA*] (EA)
UZU............	Curuzu Cuatia [*Argentina*] [*Airport symbol*] (OAG)
UZW............	Und Zwar [*That Is*] [*German*]

V

By Acronym

V	Abstracted Valuation Decisions [*A publication*] (DLA)
V	Base Value (IDOE)
V	Chest [*Anatomy*] (DAVI)
V	Coefficient of Variation [*Statistics*] (BARN)
V	Dead Space [*Medicine*] (DAVI)
V	Deflection of the Vertical
V	Digestum Vetus [*A publication*] (DSA)
V	Electric Potential [*Symbol*] [*IUPAC*]
V	Electromotive Force [*Symbol*] [*See also E, EMF Electrochemistry*] (DEN)
V	Five [*Roman numeral*]
V	Five Dollars [*Slang*]
V	Five-Year Sentence [*Criminal slang*]
V	Fixed-Wing Aircraft [*Navy symbol*]
V	Frequency [*Spectroscopy*]
V	Gas Volume [*in Gas Phase*] (DAVI)
V	Gas Volume per Unit Time [*Medicine*] (DAVI)
V	High Frequency (WDMC)
V	Minute Volume [*Laboratory science*] (DAVI)
v	Mixed Venous Blood [*Medicine*] (DAVI)
V	Potential (IDOE)
V	Potential Difference [*Symbol*]
V	Potential Energy [*Symbol*] [*IUPAC*]
V	Promotional Fare [*Also, K, L, Q*] [*Airline fare code*]
V	Quinque [*Five*] [*Latin*]
V	Ranger-Parachutist [*Army skill qualification identifier*] (INF)
V	Reluctivity (IDOE)
V	[*A*] Safe [*Criminal slang*]
V	Sanol Arzneimittel Dr. Schwarz [*Germany*] [*Research code symbol*]
V	Shape Descriptor [*V-sign, for example. The shape resembles the letter for which it is named.*]
v	Specific Volume [*Symbol*] [*IUPAC*]
V	Staff Transport [*When V is the first of two letters in a military aircraft designation*]
V	Swiss Volksbank [*Bank*]
V	Unusual Visibility
V	V3 London Gun [*British military*] (DMA)
V	Vacated [*Same case vacated*] [*Used in Shepard's Citations*] [*Legal term*] (DLA)
V	Vaccella [*Flourished, 12th century*] [*Authority cited in pre-1607 legal work*] (DSA)
V	Vaccinated [*Medicine*]
V	Vacuole
V	Vacuum (AAG)
V	Vacuum Tube (IAA)
V	Vagabond
V	Vagina [*Anatomy*] (DAVI)
V	Vale (ROG)
V	Valine [*One-letter symbol; see Val*]
V	Valley (ROG)
V	Value
V	Valve
V	Van
V	Vanadium [*Chemical element*]
V	Van Container [*Shipping*] (DS)
V	Vancouver Stock Exchange [*Canada*]
V	Vapor
V	Variable
V	Variable Region [*Immunochemistry*]
V	Variant [*Genetics*]
V	Variation
V	Variety Theatres and Shows [*Public-performance tariff class*] [*British*]
V	Varnish (AAG)
V	Varnish-Treated [*Insulation*] (MSA)
V	Varsity
V	Vascular Tissue [*Botany*]
V	Vatican City
V	Vector [*Mathematics*]
V	Vector (IDOE)
V	Veen, Publishers [*Holland*]
V	Vehicles (MCD)
V	Vein
V	Vel [*Or*] [*Pharmacy*]
V	Velocity
V	Velocity (IDOE)
V	Vendor (AAG)

V	Venerable
V	Venereology [*Medical Officer designation*] [*British*]
V	Venezuela [*IYRU nationality code*] (IYR)
V	Venous [*Medicine*]
v	Venous in the Blood Phase [*Medicine*] (DAVI)
V	Venstre [*Liberal Party*] [*Norway Political party*] (PPE)
V	Venstre (Liberale Parti) [*Liberal Party*] [*Denmark Political party*] (PPE)
V	Vent
V	Ventilation [*Medicine*] (DAVI)
V	Ventilator
V	Ventral
v	Ventral (WDAA)
V	Ventur [*Quality of carburetor barrel*] [*Automotive engineering*]
V	Venturi [*Automotive engineering*]
V	Venue
V	Verapamil [*A coronary vasodilator*]
V	Verb
V	Verb (WDMC)
V	Verbal
V	Verbalize [*or Verbalization*] (DAVI)
V	Verbatim [*FAR clauses*] (AAGC)
V	Verdict [*Legal shorthand*] (LWAP)
V	Verfassung [*Constitution*] [*German*] (ILCA)
V	Verfuegung [*Order, Decree*] [*German*] (ILCA)
V	Vergeltung [*Retaliation*] [*German*]
V	Vermessung [*Survey*] [*German military*]
V	Vermiculite
V	Vermont Reports [*A publication*] (DLA)
V	Verordnung [*Decree, Regulation, Ordinance*] [*German*] (ILCA)
V	Verse
v	Verse (WDMC)
V	Versicle
V	Versiculo [*In Such a Way*] [*Latin*] (ROG)
V	Version
V	Version (WDAA)
V	Verso [*Left-hand page*] [*Latin*]
V	Verso (WDMC)
V	Versus [*Against*]
v	Versus [*Against*] (WA)
V	Vert [*Heraldry*]
V	Verte [*or Vertatur*] [*Turn Over*] [*Latin*]
V	Vertex
V	Vertical [*RADAR*]
v	Vertical (WDMC)
V	Vertical in Line [*Aircraft engine*]
V	Verticillium Wilt [*Plant pathology*]
V	Very
v	Very (WDMC)
V	Very High Frequency [*Also, VHF*] (DOAD)
V	Vespers
V	Veto (OICC)
V	Via [*By Way Of*] [*Latin*] (ADA)
V	Vibrio [*Microbiology*]
V	Vic [*Phonetic alphabet*] [*Pre-World War II*] (DSUE)
V	Vicar [*or Vicarage*]
V	Vice [*In a position or title*]
v	Vicinal [*Also, vic*] [*Chemistry*]
V	Victor [*Phonetic alphabet*] [*International*] [*World War II*] (DSUE)
V	Victoria [*State*] (EERA)
V	Victory [*As in "the V campaign" in Europe, during World War II*]
V	Victualling [*British military*] (DMA)
v	Vide [*See*] [*Latin*] (WGA)
V	Video (SAA)
V	Video (VRA)
V	Viel [*Coarse*] [*Latin*] (DAVI)
v	View [*Computer science*] [*Telecommunications*]
V	Village
V	Vinblastine [*See VBL*]
V	Vincentius Hispanus [*Deceased, 1248*] [*Authority cited in pre-1607 legal work*] (DSA)
V	Vincristine [*Also, LCR, O, V, VC, VCR*] [*Antineoplastic drug*]
V	Vinegar [*Phonetic alphabet*] [*Royal Navy World War I*] (DSUE)
V	Vinyl
V	Violet
V	Violin [*Music*]

V	Virgin
V	Virginia Reports [*A publication*] (DLA)
V	Viridian, Inc. [*Toronto Stock Exchange symbol*] [*Formerly, Sherritt, Inc.*] (SG)
V	Virtual (HGAA)
V	Virulent
V	Virus
V	Viscosity
V	Viscosity, Kinematic [*Symbol*]
V	Viscount [*or Viscountess*]
V	Vise Break Distance [*Stress test for steel*]
V	Visibility
V	Vision
V	Visit
V	Visiting Practice Only [*Chiropody*] [*British*]
V	Visitor (DAVI)
V	Visual
V	Visual Acuity [*Also, VA*] [*Ophthalmology*]
V	Visual Capacity (AAMN)
V	Visual Magnitude [*When followed by a two-digit number*]
v	Vitamin (MAE)
V	Vivra, Inc. [*NYSE symbol*] (SPSG)
V	Vixisti [*You Lived*] [*Latin*]
V	Vixit [*He Lived*] [*Latin*]
V	VMS Hotel (SPSG)
V	Vocative
V	Voce [*Voice*] [*Latin*]
V	Voice
v	Voice (WDMC)
V	Voice Data [*NASA*]
V	Void [*Decision or finding held invalid for reasons given*] [*Used in Shepard's Citations*] [*Legal term*] (DLA)
V	Volcano (ROG)
V	Volt [*Symbol*] [*SI unit of electric potential difference*]
V	Voltage
v	Voltage (IDOE)
V	Voltare [*Turn Over*] [*Latin*] (ROG)
V	Volti [*Turn Over*] [*Music*]
V	Voltmeter
V	Volts
V	Volume [*Bibliography*]
V	Volume [*Symbol*] [*IUPAC*]
v	Volume (WDMC)
V	Voluntary Aided School [*British*]
V	Volunteer [*US Naval Reserve*]
V	Vomiting [*Medicine*]
V	Von [*Of, From*] [*German*]
V	VOR [*Very-High-Frequency Omnidirectional Range*] Federal Airway [*Followed by identification*]
V	Vous [*You*] [*French*] (ROG)
V	Vowel
v	Vowel (WDMC)
V	VTOL [*Vertical Takeoff and Landing*] [*or STOL - Short Takeoff and Landing when V is the second or only letter in a military aircraft designation*]
V	Vulgate [*Latin translation of the Bible*] [*A publication*] (BJA)
V	Wrong Verb Form [*Used in correcting manuscripts, etc.*]
V₁	Fifth Cranial Nerve, Opththalmic Division (DAVI)
V₁	Takeoff Decision Speed [*Aviation*]
V-1	Vergeltungswaffe 1 [*Pilotless flying bomb employed by the Germans*] [*World War II*]
v1of	Lift-Off Speed [*Aviation code*] (AIA)
V1S	Vee One Side (DAC)
V2	Antigua [*International civil aircraft marking*] (ODBW)
V₂	Fifth Cranial Nerve, Maxillary Division (DAVI)
V₂	Takeoff Safety Speed [*Aviation*]
V-2	Vergeltungswaffe 2 [*Rocket bomb employed by the Germans during World War II*] [*Translation: Vengeance Weapon*]
V2S	V-Groove on Two Sides [*Lumber*]
V3	Belize [*International civil aircraft marking*] (ODBW)
V₃	Fifth Cranial Nerve, Mandibular Division (DAVI)
V3	Takeoff Speed Over Screen [*Aviation code*] (AIA)
V4	Steady Initial Climb Speed [*Aviation code*] (AIA)
V4	St. Kitts and Nevis [*Aircraft nationality and registration mark*] (FAAC)
V8	Brunei Darussalam [*Aircraft nationality and registration mark*] (FAAC)
Vₐ	Alveolar Gas Volume [*Medicine*] (DAVI)
VA	Alveolar Ventilation
Vₐ	Alveolar Ventilation per Minute [*Medicine*] (DAVI)
VA	Alveolar Volume [*Clinical chemistry*] (AAMN)
VA	Attack Squadron [*Symbol*] (MCD)
VA	Avian Aircraft Ltd. [*Canada ICAO aircraft manufacturer identifier*] (ICAO)
VA	Department of Veterans Affairs [*Pre-1989, Veterans Administration*] (AAGC)
VA	Gilmer's Virginia Reports [*A publication*] (DLA)
VA	University of Virginia, Charlottesville, VA [*OCLC symbol*] (OCLC)
Va	Vacarius [*Flourished, 1144-70*] [*Authority cited in pre-1607 legal work*] (DSA)
Va	Vaccella [*Flourished, 12th century*] [*Authority cited in pre-1607 legal work*] (DSA)
VA	Vacuum Aspiration [*Medicine*]
VA	Valentine (WGA)
Va	Valid [*Decision or finding held valid for reasons given*] [*Used in Shepard's Citations*] [*Legal term*] (DLA)
VA	Valium Anonymous (EA)

VA	Valmet Corp. ADS [*NYSE symbol*] (TTSB)
VA	Valproic Acid [*Anticonvulsant compound*]
VA	Value (ECII)
VA	Value Added (ADA)
VA	Value Analysis
Va	Vanadium [*Chemical*] (EERA)
VA	Vancouver Stock Exchange [*Canada*]
VA	Variable Annuity
Va	Variance (WGA)
va	Variety (DAVI)
VA	Variometer (IAA)
VA	Vatican City [*ANSI two-letter standard code*] (CNC)
VA	Vehicle Analyst (MCD)
VA	Vehicular Accident [*British police*]
VA	Velocity Aid
VA	Velocity at Apogee (MCD)
VA	Venezolana Internacional de Aviacion Sociedad Anonima (VIASA) [*Venezuela ICAO designator*] (ICDA)
VA	Venoarterial [*Cardiology*] (DAVI)
VA	Ventral Area [*Anatomy*]
VA	Ventricular Aneurysm [*Cardiology*]
VA	Ventricular Arrhythmia [*Cardiology*]
VA	Ventriculoatrial [*Cardiology*] (WGA)
VA	Verb Active
VA	Verbal Adjective
VA	VERLORT [*Very-Long-Range Tracking*] Azimuth [*NASA*]
VA	Vermiculite Association (EA)
VA	Verpflegungsausgabestelle [*Rations distributing point*] [*German military - World War II*]
VA	Vertebral Artery [*Anatomy*]
VA	Vertical Amplifier (IAA)
VA	Vesicular-Arbuscular [*Mycorrhiza*] [*Botany*]
VA	Veterans Administration (TDOB)
VA	Veterans Adminstration (EBF)
VA	[*Department of*] Veterans Affairs
V-A	Vibroacoustic (NASA)
V-A	Vibro-Acoustic (NAKS)
VA	Vibroacoustic Test (NASA)
VA	Vicar Apostolic
VA	Vice Admiral [*Also, VADM, VADML*]
VA	Vickers-Armstrong Gun
V-A	Vickers-Armstrong Ltd.
VA	Victims Anonymous (EA)
VA	Victor Airways [*Aviation*] (FAAC)
VA	Victoria and Albert Order [*British*]
VA	Victualling Allowance [*British military*] (DMA)
VA	Video Amplifier
V/A	Video/Analog (NASA)
V/A	Video/Audio [*Telecommunications*]
VA	Vincent's Angina [*Medicine*]
VA	Vinyl Acetate [*Organic chemistry*] (WDAA)
VA	Viola [*Music*]
va	viola (WDAA)
V-A	Viper-Arrow (SAA)
VA	Viral Antigen [*Medicine*] (DMAA)
VA	Virginia [*Postal code*]
Va	Virginia Reports [*A publication*] (AAGC)
VA	Virginia Supreme Court Reports [*A publication*] (DLA)
VA	Virtual Address
VA	Virus-Antibody [*Immunology*]
VA	Visual Acuity [*Also, V*] [*Ophthalmology*]
VA	VisualAge
VA	Visual Aid
VA	Visual Arts [*US Copyright Office class*]
VA	Visual Training Aid Specialist [*Navy*]
VA	Vita Apollonii [*of Philostratus*] [*Classical studies*] (OCD)
VA	Vital Area (NRCH)
VA	Vixit Annos [*Lived a Certain Number of Years*] [*Latin*] (WDAA)
VA	Voice Actuation (MCD)
VA	Voice of America
VA	Volcanic Ash [*ICAO*] (FAAC)
VA	Voltage Amplifier (IAA)
VA	Voltaire Alternative
VA	Voltammeter (IAA)
VA	Volt-Ampere (IDOE)
V/A	Volts per Ampere (IDOE)
VA	Voluntary Aid (ADA)
VA	Voluntary Associate (WDAA)
VA	Volunteer Artillery [*Military British*] (ROG)
VA	Volunteers in Asia [*An association*] (BUAC)
VA	Vorausabteilung [*Advance detachment*] [*German military - World War II*]
VA	Vorderasien (BJA)
VA	Vote America (EA)
VA	Votre Altesse [*Your Highness*] [*French*]
V/A	Voucher Attached [*Banking*]
VA	Voyage Alliance [*Later, IVA*] (EA)
VA	Vulnerability Assessment
VA	Vulnerable Area (NATG)
VAA	Vaasa [*Finland*] [*Airport symbol*] (OAG)
VAA	Variable Attenuator Amplified
VAA	Vegetarian Association of America [*Defunct*] (EA)
VAA	Vehicle Assembly Area [*NASA*] (NAKS)
VAA	Venda Airways [*South Africa ICAO designator*] (FAAC)
VAA	Venezuelan American Association of the United States (EA)

VAA............	Verticilliuum albo-atrium [*A fungus*]
VAA............	Viatical Association of America (NTPA)
VAA............	Victorian Apiarists' Association [*Australia*]
VAA............	Victorian Athletics Association [*Australia*]
VAA............	Vietnamese American Association
VAA............	Viewpoint Adapter Assembly (NASA)
VAA............	Voice Access Arrangement
VAAC	Vanadyl Acetylacetonate [*Organic chemistry*]
VAAC	Vectored Thrust Aircraft [*Aviation*] (DA)
VA Acts........	Acts of the General Assembly, Commonwealth of Virginia [*A publication*] (DLA)
VAAH	Ahmadabad [*India*] [*ICAO location identifier*] (ICLI)
VAAJ	Veterinary Association for Arbitration and Jurisprudence (BUAC)
VAAK	Akola [*India*] [*ICAO location identifier*] (ICLI)
VAAL...........	Vaal Reefs Exploration [*NASDAQ symbol*] (NQ)
VaalRf	Vaal Reefs Exploration & Mining Co. Ltd. [*Associated Press*] (SAG)
VAALY	Vaal Reefs Ex&Mng ADR [*NASDAQ symbol*] (TTSB)
VAAM..........	Voice Actuated Address Mechanism (PDAA)
VA & I	Verb Active and Intransitive (ROG)
VAAP	Volunteer Army Ammunition Plant (AABC)
VA App	Virginia Appeals [*A publication*] (DLA)
VAAR	Veterans Administration Acquisition Regulation [*A publication*] (AAGC)
VAAR	Vinyl Alcohol Acetate Resin [*NASA*] (KSC)
VAAS	Vermont Academy of Arts and Sciences
VAAT...........	Vibration and Acoustic Testing (IAA)
VAAT...........	Victorian Animal Aid Trust [*Australia*]
VAAU	Aurangabad [*India*] [*ICAO location identifier*] (ICLI)
VAAUS	Venezuelan American Association of the United States (EA)
VAB............	Value Added Bank [*Electronic commerce*]
VAB............	Van Allen Belts
VAB............	Variable Action Button (NVT)
VAB............	Vehicle Assembly Building [*NASA*] (AFM)
VAB............	Vertical Assembly Building [*NASA*]
VAB............	Vertical Axis Bearing
VAB............	Victorian Artificial Breeders [*Australia*]
VAB............	Victorian Association of Bakers [*Australia*]
VAB............	Vinblastine, Actinomycin D, Bleomycin [*Antineoplastic drug regimen*]
VAB............	Vincristine/Actinomycin D/Bleomycin (DB)
VAB............	Voice Answer Back
VAB............	Voluntary Agencies Bureau (BUAC)
VAB............	Vorderasiatische Bibliothek [*H. Winckler and A. Jeremias*] [*Leipzig*] [*A publication*] (BJA)
VABA	Value Added by Advertising
VA Bar News...	Virginia Bar News [*A publication*] (DLA)
VABB	Bombay [*India*] [*ICAO location identifier*] (ICLI)
VABCA	Department of Veterans Affairs Board of Contract Appeals (AAGC)
VABCD	Vinblastine, Adriamycin, Bleomycin, CCNU [*Lomustine*], Dacarbazine [*Antineoplastic drug regimen*]
VaBch	Virginia Beach Federal Financial Corp. [*Associated Press*] (SAG)
VABD	Van Allen Belt Dosimeter
VABF..........	Bombay [*India*] [*ICAO location identifier*] (ICLI)
VABF..........	Variety Artistes' Benevolent Fund [*British*] (ROG)
VABF..........	Virginia Beach Federal Financial Corp. [*NASDAQ symbol*] (SAG)
VABF..........	Virginia Beach Fed Finl [*NASDAQ symbol*] (TTSB)
VABI..........	Bilaspur [*India*] [*ICAO location identifier*] (ICLI)
VAB-I	Vinblastine, Actinomycin D [*Dactinomycin*], Bleomycin [*Antineoplastic drug regimen*]
VAB-II	Vinblastine, Actinomycin D [*Dactinomycin*], Bleomycin, Cisplatin [*Antineoplastic drug regimen*]
VAB-III	Vinblastine, Actinomycin D [*Dactinomycin*], Bleomycin, Cisplatin, Chlorambucil, Cyclophosphamide [*Antineoplastic drug regimen*]
VAB-IV	Vinblastine, Actinomycin D [*Dactinomycin*] Bleomycin, Cisplatin, Cyclophosphamide, Chlorambucil, and Adriamycin [*Antineoplastic drug regimen*] (DAVI)
VABJ...........	Bhuj [*India*] [*ICAO location identifier*] (ICLI)
VABM..........	Belgaum [*India*] [*ICAO location identifier*] (ICLI)
VABM..........	Value Added by Manufacturer [*Business term*] (MHDW)
VABM..........	Vertical Angle Bench Mark
VABO	Baroda/Vadodara [*India*] [*ICAO location identifier*] (ICLI)
VABP	Bhopal [*India*] [*ICAO location identifier*] (ICLI)
VABPF	Vice Admiral British Pacific Fleet
VABR	Vehicle Assembly Building Repeater [*NASA*] (KSC)
VABS	Value Added Backbone Server (AEPA)
VABS	Vineland Adaptive Behavior Scale [*Psychology*] (EDAC)
VABV	Bhaunagar [*India*] [*ICAO location identifier*] (ICLI)
VAB-V	Vinblastine, Actinomycin D [*Dactinomycin*], Bloeomycin, Cisplatin, and Cyclophosphamide [*Antineoplastic drug regimen*] (DAVI)
VAC............	AC [*Alternating Current*] Voltage (ACII)
VAC............	Alternating Current Volts
VAC............	Fifth Amphibious Corps
VAC............	Vacancy [*Real estate*] (ADA)
VAC............	Vacant (AFM)
VAC............	Vacate
VAC............	Vacation
vac............	Vacation (ODBW)
VAC............	Vacationair, Inc. [*Canada ICAO designator*] (FAAC)
Vac	Vaccella [*Flourished, 12th century*] [*Authority cited in pre-1607 legal work*] (DSA)
VAC............	Vaccination [*or Vaccine*] [*Medicine*]
VAC............	Vacuolar Apical Compartment [*Cytology*]
VAC............	Vacuum (AABC)
vac............	Vacuum (IDOE)
vac............	Vacuum Cleaner (WDAA)
VAC............	Value-Added Carrier [*Telecommunications*]

VAC............	Variable Air Capacitor
VAC............	Variance at Completion (MCD)
VAC............	Vascular Anticoagulant [*Medicine*] (DB)
VAC............	Vector Analog Computer
VAC............	Vehicle Assembly and Checkout [*NASA*] (NASA)
VAC............	Ventriculoarterial Connections [*Cardiology*] (DAVI)
VAC............	Ventriculoatrial Conduction [*Cardiology*] (DAVI)
VAC............	Verified Audit Circulation [*Newspaper auditing firm*] [*Advertising*]
VAC............	Verified Audit Circulation Corp. (NTCM)
VAC............	Vertical Air Current
VAC............	Veterans Administration Center
VAC............	Veterans Affairs Canada [*See also AACC*]
VAC............	Vice-Admiralty Court [*British*]
VAC............	Victor Analog Computer [*Computer science*]
VAC............	Victorian Arts Council [*Australia*]
VAC............	Video Amplifier Chain
VAC............	Vidicon Alignment Coil
VAC............	Vincristine, Actinomycin D, Cyclophosphamide [*Antineoplastic drug regimen*]
VAC............	Vincristine, Adriamycin, Cyclophosphamide [*Also, VACY*] [*Antineoplastic drug regimen*]
VAC............	Virus Capsid Antigen (DB)
VAC............	Visual Aid Console
VAC............	Visual Approach Chart [*Aviation*] (FAAC)
VAC............	Vital Area Center (CAAL)
VAC............	Voltage-Alternating Current (NITA)
VAC............	Volt-Ampere Characteristics [*Microwave emission*]
Vac	Volts AC (IDOE)
V_{ac}	Volts AC (IDOE)
vac............	Volts AC (IDOE)
VAC............	Volts Alternating Current
VAC............	Voluntary Action Center
VAC............	Volunteer Adviser Corps (EA)
VACA	Victorian Amateur Canoe Association [*Australia*]
VACAA	Victorian Autistic Childrens and Adults' Association [*Australia*]
VACAB	Veterans Administration Contract Appeals Board
VACAPES	Virginia Capes [*Navy*] (CAAL)
VACAR	Vincristine, Adriamycin, Cyclophosphamide, and Actinomycin D [*Dactinomycin*] (DAVI)
VA Cas........	Virginia Cases (Brockenbrough and Holmes) [*A publication*] (DLA)
VA Cas........	Virginia Criminal Cases [*3-4 Virginia*] [*1789-1826*] [*A publication*] (DLA)
VACB	Virginia Association of Community Bankers (TBD)
Vacc...........	Vaccella [*Flourished, 12th century*] [*Authority cited in pre-1607 legal work*] (DSA)
vacc...........	Vaccinate
VACC	Value-Added Common Carrier [*Telecommunications*]
VAcC	Visual Acuity with Spectacle Correction
VACCA	Victorian Aboriginal Child Care Agency [*Australia*]
VACCAD	Veterans Administration Construction Contract Appeals Board (AAGC)
VACCI	Vaccine [*Medicine*]
VAcCL.........	Visual Acuity with Contact Lens Correction
VACD	Voluntary Association for Community Development [*Canada*] (BUAC)
VAC DIST.....	Vacuum Distilled (WDAA)
VacDry........	Vacu-Dry Co. [*Associated Press*] (SAG)
VACE..........	Verification and Checkout Equipment
VACF..........	Vietnamese-American Children's Fund [*Defunct*] (EA)
VACG	Vocational Assessment and Curriculum Guide [*Test*] (TMMY)
VACHA	Virginias Automated Clearing House Association
VA Ch Dec....	Wythe's Virginia Chancery Reports [*1788-99*] [*A publication*] (DLA)
VA Cir.........	Virginia Circuit Court Opinions [*A publication*] (DLA)
VACM.........	Vector Averaging Current Meter [*Marine science*] (MSC)
VACM.........	Vincristine, Adriamycin, Cyclophosphamide, Methotrexate [*Antineoplastic drug regimen*]
VA Col Dec...	Virginia Colonial Decisions (Randolph and Barrandall) [*A publication*] (DLA)
Va Commonwealth U...	Virginia Commonwealth University (GAGS)
VACR	Variable Amplitude Correction Rack [*Telecommunications*] (OA)
VACR	Visual Aircraft Recognition (MCD)
VACRPD.......	Victorian Advisory Council on Recreation for People with Disabilities [*Australia*]
VACRS	Vocational Assistance Commission for Retired Servicemen (CINC)
VACS	Virtual Accounting Collecting System (MHDB)
VACSA	Victorian Aboriginal Community Services Association [*Australia*]
VACSAT	Vaccine Satellite Program (MCD)
VACSSS	Veterans Affairs Cooperative Study of Systemic Sepsis
VACT..........	Alternating Current Test Volts (MSA)
VACTERL	Vertebral, Anal, Cardiac, Tracheosophageal, Renal, and Limb [*Defects*]
VACTL........	Vertical Assembly Component Test Laboratory
VACU.........	Virtual Access Control Unit
VACURG	Veterans Administration Cooperative Urological Research Group
VACVVD.......	Vacuum and Vent Control Valve Distributor [*Automotive engineering*]
VACVVT	Vacuum and Vent Control Valve Thermactor [*Automotive engineering*]
VACW	Alternating Current Working Volts (MSA)
VACY	Vincristine, Adriamycin, Cyclophosphamide [*Also, VAC*] [*Antineoplastic drug regimen*]
VAD	Vacuum Arc Degassing [*Metal technology*]
VAD	Val d'Or Explorations [*Vancouver Stock Exchange symbol*]
VAD	Valdosta, GA [*Location identifier FAA*] (FAAL)
VAD	Value Added and Data [*Communications network*]
VAD	Value-Added Dealer [*Business term*]
VAD	Value-Added Distributor

VAD	Value-Added Driver [*Computer science*] (PCM)
VAD	Vandenberg Addendum Document [*Air Force*] (NASA)
VAD	Vapor Axial Deposition [*Optical fiber technology*]
VAD	Vascular Access Device [*Cardiology*] (DAVI)
VAD	Velocity-Azimuth Display
VAD	Venous Access Device [*Cardiology*] (DAVI)
VAD	Ventricle-Assist Device [*Cardiology*]
VAD	Ventricular Assist Device (STED)
VAD	Vereinigte Arbeitnehmerpartei Deutschland [*United Employees' Party of Germany*] [*Political party*] (PPW)
VAD	Vertebral or Vascular Defects, Anorectal Malformation, Cardiac Anomaly, Tracheoesophageal Fistula, Renal Anomaly, Limb Anomaly [*Syndrome*] (DAVI)
VAD	Vertical Axial Deposition [*Sumitomo*] (AAEL)
VAD	Veterans' Affairs Decisions, Appealed Pension and Civil Service Retirement Cases [*United States*] [*A publication*] (DLA)
VAD	Veterans Against Drugs
VAD	Vincristine, Adriamycin, Decadron [*Antineoplastic drug*] (CDI)
VAD	Vincristine, Adriamycin, Dexamethasone [*Antineoplastic drug regimen*] (MEDA)
VAD	Virus-Adjusting Diluent (STED)
VAD	Vitamin A Deficiency [*Medicine*] (DMAA)
VAD	Voltmeter Analog-to-Digital Converter
VAD	Voluntary Aid Detachment [*British World War I nursing unit*]
VAD	Vought Aeronautics Division [*Ling-Temco-Vought*]
VAD	Vulcan Air Defense (MCD)
VADA	Versatile Automatic Data Exchange
VADA	Victorian Abalone Divers' Association [*Australia*]
VADA	Vincristine, Adriamycin, Cyclophosphamide, Actinomycin D [*Dactinomycin*] [*Antineoplastic drug regimen*] (DAVI)
VADAC	Voice Analyzer Data Converter
VADBX	Mgn. Stanley D. Witter Val. Added Mkt. Equity [*Mutual fund ticker symbol*] (SG)
VADC	Victorian Association for Deserted Children [*Australia*]
VADC	Video Analog to Digital Converter
VADC	Voice Analyzer and Data Converter (MCD)
VADE	Vandenberg Automatic Data Equipment [*Air Force*]
VADE	Vandenberg Automatic Data Evaluation [*Air Force*]
VADE	Versatile Automatic Data Exchange (MCD)
VADE	Victorian Association for Drama in Education [*Australia*]
VADE	Voice Analog to Digital Encoder
VA Dec	Virginia Decisions [*A publication*] (DLA)
VADER	Vacuum Arc Double-Electrode Remelting [*Metallurgy*]
VADF	Vietnamese Air Defense Force (MCD)
VADG	Victorian Antique Dealers' Group [*Australia*]
VADIC	Vincristine, Adriamycin, DIC [*Dacarbazine*] [*Antineoplastic drug regimen*]
VADIS	Voice and Data Integrated System [*Telecommunications*] (TEL)
VADM	Vice Admiral [*Also, VA, VADML*]
VADM	Virtual Axial Dipole Moment [*Geophysics*]
VADMS	Voice-Analog-Digital Manual Switch (MCD)
VADN	Victorian Association of Day Nurseries [*Australia*]
VADR	Vincristine, Adriamycin Doxorubicin, and Cyclophosphamide (STED)
VADRC	Vincristine, Adriamycin, Cyclophosphamide [*Antineoplastic drug regimen*] (DAVI)
VADS	Value Added and Data Services
VADS	Velocity-Aligned Doppler Spectroscopy
VADS	Vendor Automated Data System (MCD)
VADS	Verdix ADA Development System (NITA)
VADS	Veterans Assistance Discharge System (MCD)
VADS	Visual-Aural Digit Span Test [*Educational test*]
VADS	Vulcan Air Defense Systems (MCD)
VAE	Ciudad de Valles [*Mexico*] [*Airport symbol*] (AD)
VAE	Vinta Exploration Ltd. [*Vancouver Stock Exchange symbol*]
VAE	Vinyl Acetate - Ethylene [*Organic chemistry*]
VAE	Votre Altesse Electorale [*Your Electoral Highness*] [*French*]
VAEC	Variety and Allied Entertainments Council [*British*] (BI)
VAeff	Effective Alveolar Ventilation [*Medicine*] (DAVI)
VAEITB	Victorian Arts and Entertainment Industry Training Board [*Australia*]
VAEP	Variable, Attributes, Error Propagation (IEEE)
VaEP	Virginia Electric & Power Co. [*Associated Press*] (SAG)
VAER	Visual Auditory Evoked Response (STED)
VAERS	Vaccine Adverse Event Reporting System [*Food and Drug Administration*]
VAES	Voice-Activated Encoding System
VAEVC	Vinyl Acetate - Ethylene - Vinyl Chloride [*Organic chemistry*]
VAF	Valence [*France*] [*Airport symbol*] (OAG)
VAF	Vane Airflow Meter [*Automotive engineering*]
VAF	Variety Artistes' Federation [*British*] (BI)
VAF	Vendor Approval Form
VAF	Vernacular Architecture Forum (EA)
VAF	Vietnamese Air Force (MCD)
VAF	Viral Antibody-Free [*Environment*]
VAF	Volume Air Flow [*Automotive engineering*]
VAF	Voluntary Application Fill (DNAB)
VAF	Vote America Foundation (EA)
VAFA	Victorian Amateur Football Association [*Australia*]
VAFAC	Vincristine, Amethopterin [*Methotrexate*], Fluorouracil, Adriamycin, Cyclophosphamide [*Antineoplastic drug regimen*]
VAFB	Vandenberg Air Force Base [*California*]
VAFC	VESA [*Video Electronics Standards Association*] Advanced Feature Connector
VAFD	Valley Federal Savings Bank [*NASDAQ symbol*] (NQ)
VAFD	Valley Fed Svgs Bk Sheffield [*NASDAQ symbol*] (TTSB)
VAFF	Variable Aperture Far Field
VAFI	Victorian Association of Forest Industries [*Australia*]
VAFL	Victorian Amateur Football League [*Australia*]
VaFst	Virginia First Financial Corp. [*Associated Press*] (SAG)
VaFstSvg	Virginia First Financial Corp. [*Associated Press*] (SAG)
VAFTAD	Volcanic Ash Forecast Transport and Dispersion [*Model*] [*Marine science*] (OSRA)
VAG	Vagabond (DSUE)
VAG	Vagar [*Faeroe Islands*] [*Airport symbol*] (AD)
vag.	Vagina (STED)
Vag	Vagina (STED)
VAG	Vaginal [*Medicine*]
VAG	Vaginitis [*Medicine*]
VAG	Vagrancy [*FBI standardized term*]
vag.	Vagrant (WDAA)
VAG	Vananda Gold [*Vancouver Stock Exchange symbol*]
VAG	Vancouver Art Gallery [*Canada*]
VAG	Varginha [*Brazil*] [*Airport symbol*] (OAG)
VAG	Vernacular Architecture Group [*British*]
VAG	Vertex Adjacency Graph (MHDI)
VAG	Volkswagen Audi Group
VAGA	Visual Artists and Galleries Association (EA)
Vag Hyst	Vaginal Hysterectomy [*Gynecology*] (CPH)
VAGO	Goa [*India*] [*ICAO location identifier*] (ICLI)
VAGP	Victorian Academy for General Practice [*Australia*]
VAH	Heavy Attack Squadron [*Symbol*] (MCD)
VAH	Vaihoa [*Tuamotu Archipelago*] [*Seismograph station code, US Geological Survey*] (SEIS)
VAH	Vertical Array Hydrophone
VAH	Veterans Administration Hospital [*Later, VAMC*]
VAH	Virilizing Adrenal Hyperplasia [*Medicine*]
VAH	Vitiated Air Heater
VAHPA	Victorian Allied Health Professionals Association [*Australia*]
VAHR	Veterans Administration Hospital Representative [*Red Cross*]
VAHS	Virus-Associated Hemophagocytic Syndrome [*Medicine*]
VAHT	Vertical Axis Hydropower Turbine
VAHUDIA	Veterans Affairs, Housing and Urban Development, and Independent Agencies Appropriations Act of 1990 (COE)
VAI	Vanimo [*Papua New Guinea*] [*Airport symbol*] (OAG)
VAI	Vassar Attitude Inventory [*Education*]
VAI	Ventilation Air Intake [*Hovercraft*]
VAI	Video Arts International, Inc.
VAI	Video-Assisted Instruction
VAI	Visual Alignment Indicators [*Tire maintenance*]
VAI	Vocational Awards International [*British*]
VAI	Volleyball Association of Ireland (EAIO)
VAI	Voluntary Action Indicated [*FDA*]
VAI	Vorticity Area Index [*Meteorology*]
VA IC Ops	Virginia Industrial Commission Opinions [*A publication*] (DLA)
VAID	Indore [*India*] [*ICAO location identifier*] (ICLI)
VAIN	Vaginal Intraepithelial Neoplasia [*Medicine*] (DAVI)
VAIO	Video Audio Integrated Operation [*Computer science*]
VAIR	Virginia Association for Institutional Research (EDAC)
Vaizey	Vaizey's Law of Settlements [*1887*] [*A publication*] (DLA)
VAJ	Vajont [*Belluno*] [*Italy*] [*Seismograph station code, US Geological Survey*] (SEIS)
VAJB	Jabalpur [*India*] [*ICAO location identifier*] (ICLI)
VAJJ	Bombay/Juhu [*India*] [*ICAO location identifier*] (ICLI)
VAJM	Jamnagar [*India*] [*ICAO location identifier*] (ICLI)
VAK	Aerial Refueling Squadron [*Navy symbol*] (DNAB)
VAK	Chevak [*Alaska*] [*Airport symbol*] (OAG)
VAK	Vak-Rosat [*Former USSR*] [*FAA designator*] (FAAC)
VAK	Vertical Access Kit (NASA)
VAK	Vertical Assembly Kit (NASA)
VAKD	Khandwa [*India*] [*ICAO location identifier*] (ICLI)
VAKE	Kandla [*India*] [*ICAO location identifier*] (ICLI)
VAKP	Kolhapur [*India*] [*ICAO location identifier*] (ICLI)
VAKS	Keshod [*India*] [*ICAO location identifier*] (ICLI)
VAKT	Visual-Auditory-Kinesthetic-Tactile
VAKUME	Visual Audio Kinetic Unit Multiples and Environments (PDAA)
VAL	Light Attack Aircraft [*Symbol*] (MCD)
VAL	Plattsburgh, NY [*Location identifier FAA*] (FAAL)
VAL	University of Virginia, Law Library, Charlottesville, VA [*OCLC symbol*] (OCLC)
Val	Valcausus [*Gualcosius*] [*Flourished, 11th-12th century*] [*Authority cited in pre-1607 legal work*] (DSA)
VAL	Valentia [*Ireland*] [*Seismograph station code, US Geological Survey*] (SEIS)
val	Valentine (BARN)
VAL	Valid [*or Validation*] (KSC)
Val	Valine [*Also, V*] [*An amino acid*]
val	Valine [*An amino acid*] (DOG)
Val	Valium [*A tranquilizer*] [*Roche Laboratories*] (DAVI)
VAL	Valley (MSA)
Val	Valley Girl [*Lifestyle classification*]
VAL	Valspar Corp. [*NYSE symbol*] (SPSG)
VAL	Valuation
VAL	Value
val	Value (IDOE)
VAL	Value Investment Corp. [*Toronto Stock Exchange symbol*]
VAL	Value-Oriented Algorithmic Language [*Computer science*] (PDAA)
VAL	Valve
VAL	Variable Angle Launcher
VAL	Vehicle Authorization List [*Military*] (AFM)
VAL	Vertical Assault Lift
VAL	Vicarm Arm Language

VAL............. Victorian Athletic League [Australia]
VAL............. Vieques Air Link [Caribbean airline]
VAL............. Visual Approach and Landing Chart [Aviation]
VAL............. Vortex Arc LASER
VAL............. Voyageur Airways Ltd. [Canada ICAO designator] (FAAC)
VAL............. Vulnerability Assessment Laboratory [White Sands Missile Range, NM] [Military] (RDA)
Valassis....... Valassis Communications [Associated Press] (SAG)
VA Law J...... Virginia Law Journal [Richmond] [A publication] (DLA)
VALB........... Veterans of the Abraham Lincoln Brigade (EA)
VALCO......... Volta Aluminum Co. Ltd.
Val Com ...... Valen's Commentaries [A publication] (DLA)
VALD........... Valued (ROG)
VALDEFD...... Value Defined (MHDW)
VA L Dig...... Virginia Law Digest [A publication] (DLA)
VALDN......... Validation
Valdosta St C... Valdosta State College (GAGS)
VALE........... [The] Valley Railroad Co. [AAR code]
VALE........... Valley Systems [NASDAQ symbol] (TTSB)
VALE........... Valley Systems, Inc. [NASDAQ symbol] (SAG)
VALE........... Visual Acuity, Left Eye [Ophthalmology] (MAE)
VALE........... Vocational Assessment of Lost Earnings (DHP)
Valero......... Valero Energy Corp. [Associated Press] (SAG)
ValFrg......... Valley Forge Corp. [Associated Press] (SAG)
VALH.......... Value Holdings [NASDAQ symbol] (SAG)
Valhi........... Valhi, Inc. [Associated Press] (SAG)
ValHldg........ Value Holdings [Associated Press] (SAG)
ValHlth........ Value Health, Inc. [Associated Press] (SAG)
VALI........... Validate (AABC)
VALID......... Validation (NASA)
VALIPR........ Validation In-Process Review [DoD]
VA L LJ....... Virginia Law Journal [A publication] (DLA)
VALL.......... Vortex Arc LASER Light
Vallen......... Vallen Corp. [Associated Press] (SAG)
VALLEY........ Valley [Commonly used] (OPSA)
VALLEYS....... Valleys [Commonly used] (OPSA)
ValliCor....... ValliCorp Holdings, Inc. [Associated Press] (SAG)
ValLn.......... Value Line, Inc. [Associated Press] (SAG)
VALLY......... Valley [Commonly used] (OPSA)
VallyRs........ Valley Resources, Inc. [Associated Press] (SAG)
VALM.......... Valmont Indus [NASDAQ symbol] (TTSB)
VALM.......... Valmont Industries, Inc. [NASDAQ symbol] (NQ)
Valmnt........ Valmont Industries, Inc. [Associated Press] (SAG)
VALN.......... Vallen Corp. [NASDAQ symbol] (NQ)
VALN .... Valuation
VALNET........ Veterans Administration Library Network [Veterans Administration Washington, DC]
VALOR........ Veterans Administration Libraries Online Resources
VALOR........ Veterans Affairs Learning Opportunities Residency Program
VAlP........... Vortex Arc LASER Pump
Valparaiso U... Valparaiso University (GAGS)
VALPO......... Valparaiso (DSUE)
VALRA........ Variable-Area Light-Reflecting Assembly [Invented by T. C. Howard of Synergetics, Inc.]
VA L Reg...... Virginia Law Register [A publication] (DLA)
VA L Reg NS... Virginia Law Register, New Series [A publication] (DLA)
Val Rep .... Valuation Reports, Interstate Commerce Commission [A publication] (DLA)
Val Rep ICC... Valuation Reports, Interstate Commerce Commission [A publication] (DLA)
Vals .... Valium [A tranquilizer] [Roche Laboratories] (DAVI)
VALS........... Value and Lifestyle [Classifications] [Marketing]
VALS........... Values and Lifestyles Program (WDMC)
VALS........... Victorian Aboriginal Legal Service [Australia]
VALSAS .... Variable Length Word Symbolic Assembly System (IEEE)
Valspar........ Valspar Corp. [Associated Press] (SAG)
VALT........... VTOL [Vertical Takeoff and Landing] Approach and Landing Technology [Program]
ValTech .... Valence Technology, Inc. [Associated Press] (SAG)
VALT(S)....... Vulnerability and Lethality Test (System) (MCD)
VALU.......... Value Line [NASDAQ symbol] (TTSB)
VALU .... Value Line, Inc. [NASDAQ symbol] (NQ)
VALUE .... Validated Aircraft Logistics Utilization Evaluation [Navy]
VALUE .... Visible Achievement Liberates Unemployment [DoD project for disadvantaged youth]
ValueCty....... Value City Department Stores [Associated Press] (SAG)
ValueLn....... Value Line, Inc. [Associated Press] (SAG)
ValuePr....... Value Property Trust [Associated Press] (SAG)
ValuJet .... ValuJet Airlines, Inc. [Associated Press] (SAG)
VALUON....... Valuation
ValVis......... ValueVision International, Inc. [Associated Press] (SAG)
VA L Wk Dicta Comp... Virginia Law Weekly Dicta Compilation [A publication] (DLA)
VALY.......... Vallicorp Holdings [NASDAQ symbol] (TTSB)
VALY.......... Vallicorp Holdings, Inc. [NASDAQ symbol] (NQ)
ValySy .... Valley Systems, Inc. [Associated Press] (SAG)
VAM........... Ameravia [Uruguay] [FAA designator] (FAAC)
VAM........... Medium Attack Aircraft [Navy symbol] (NVT)
VAM........... University of Virginia, C. Moore Health Sciences Library, Charlottesville, VA [OCLC symbol] (OCLC)
VAM........... Vacuum-Assisted Molding [Automotive technology]
VAM........... Value Added Manufacture [Program]
VAM........... Value Added Market (MHDB)
VAM........... Value Aluminizing Machine

VAM............. Vamos [Greece] [Seismograph station code, US Geological Survey] (SEIS)
VAM............. Vector Airborne Magnetometer (IEEE)
VAM............. Vehiculos Automotores Mexicanos [Commercial firm]
VAM............. Vending and Affixing Machine
VAM............. Vesicular Arbuscular Mycorrhizae [Botany]
VAM............. Veterans Administration Matters [FBI standardized term]
VAM............. Vibration and Acoustic Monitoring [Environmental science] (COE)
VAM............. Vinyl Acetate Monomer [Organic chemistry]
VAM............. Virtual Access Method
VAM............. Vista Mines, Inc. [Toronto Stock Exchange symbol]
VAM............. Visual Approach Monitor [Aviation]
VAM............. Vogel's Approximation Method
VAM............. Voltammeter
VAM............. VP-16-213 [Etoposide], Adriamycin, Methotrexate [Antineoplastic drug regimen]
VAMA......... Vinyl Acetate Maleic Acid (DICI)
VAMAS .... Versailles Project on Advanced Materials and Standards
VAMC......... Veterans Administration Medical Center [Formerly, VAH]
VAMC......... Visual Approach Monitor Chart (PDAA)
VAMCO........ Village & Marketing Corp. [Jamaica]
VAMD......... Virginia & Maryland Railroad [AAR code]
VAME......... Victorian Association for Multicultural Education [Australia]
VAMFO....... Variable Angle Monochromatic Fringe Observation [Film thickness determination]
VAMH .... Voluntary Association for Mental Health (BUAC)
VAMHN .... Victorian Aboriginal Mental Health Network [Australia]
VAMIA .... Victorian Abattoir and Meat Inspection Authority [Australia]
VAMIS .... Versatile Automated Maintenance Information System (MCD)
VAMIS .... Virginia Medical Information System [Library network]
VAMOS .... Verified Additional Military Occupational Specialty
VAMOSC ...... Visibility and Management of Operating and Support Costs [Army]
VAMP......... Value Analysis of Management Practices (MCD)
vamp .... Vampire (BARN)
VAMP......... Vandenberg Atlas Modification Program [Air Force] (MCD)
VAMP......... Variable [or Visual] Anamorphic Motion Picture [Training device to provide realistic environment during simulated flight training] (MCD)
VAMP......... Vector Arithmetic Multiprocessor [Computer science] (IEEE)
VAMP......... Vesicle-Associated Membrane Protein [Biochemistry]
VAMP......... Vietnam Ammunition Program (AFM)
VAMP......... Vincristine, Actinomycin, Methotrexate, Prednisone [Antineoplastic drug regimen]
VAMP......... Vincristine Amethopterin [Antitumor agent]
VAMP......... Vincristine, Amethopterin [Methotrexate], Mercaptopurine, Prednisone [Antineoplastic drug regimen]
VAMP......... Visual-Acoustic-Magnetic Pressure (IEEE)
VAMP......... Visual-Acoustic-Magnetic Program [NOO]
VAMP......... Visual Anamorphic Motion Picture (AIA)
VAMP......... Visual Approach for Management Planning (WDAA)
VAMP......... Volume, Area, and Mass Properties (PDAA)
VAMP......... Voluntary Association of Master Pumpers [Nineteenth Century]
VAMP......... Vulnerability Assessment Modeling Program [Air Force]
VAMR......... Vernon's Annotated Missouri Rule [A publication] (DLA)
VAMS......... Vernon's Annotated Missouri Statutes [A publication] (DLA)
VAMS......... Victor Airspeed Measuring System (MCD)
VAMS......... Visual Analog Mood Scale
VAMSI........ Visual Approach Multiple Slope Indicator [Aviation]
VAMT......... Vertical Assault Medium Transport (MCD)
van............. Advantage [Tennis] (BARN)
VAN........... Northern Virginia Community College, Springfield, VA [OCLC symbol] (OCLC)
VAN........... Value Added Network [Computer science Telecommunications]
VAN........... Van [Turkey] [Airport symbol] (OAG)
VAN........... Vance, SC [Location identifier FAA] (FAAL)
VAN........... Vandeno [Race of maize]
Van........... Vanguard [Record label]
VAN........... Vanguard Tracking Station [NASA] (NASA)
VAN........... Vanier College [UTLAS symbol]
VAN........... Vanilla (WDAA)
VAN........... Vannovskaya [Former USSR Seismograph station code, US Geological Survey] (SEIS)
VAN........... Vanwin Resources Corp. [Vancouver Stock Exchange symbol]
VAN........... Variable Area Nozzle
VAN........... Varotsos Alexopoulos Nomicos [Authors of a technique for predicting earthquakes]
VAN........... Vehicle Area Network [Automotive engineering]
VAN........... Voluntary Arts Network (BUAC)
VAN........... Vorlaeufige Arbeitsnormen
VANA......... Vector-Automated Network Analyzer [Computer science] (CIST)
VANAC........ Veterans Affairs National Acquisition Center (AAGC)
VANC......... Vancouver [Canada] (WDAA)
Vand......... De Bello Vandalico [of Procopius] [Classical studies] (OCD)
VAND .... Nanded [India] [ICAO location identifier] (ICLI)
VAND .... Vacuum-Air-Nitrogen Distribution
VAND .... Van Den Bergh [Liver function test]
VAND .... Van Diemens Co. [NASDAQ symbol] (SAG)
V and A .... Valuable and Attractive [A marking used by RAF on such supplies as watches and cameras] [British]
V & A .... Victoria and Albert Museum [London, England]
V & B......... Vesey and Beames' English Chancery Reports [35 English Reprint] [A publication] (DLA)
V & DA .... Video and Data Acquisition (MCD)
V & DA .... Video and Data Processing Assembly (NASA)
V & E......... Vinethene and Ether

Vanderbilt LR...   Vanderbilt Law Review [*A publication*] (DLA)
Vanderbilt U...   Vanderbilt University (GAGS)
Vander L......   Vanderlinden's Laws of Holland [*A publication*] (DLA)
Vanderstr....   Vanderstraaten's Reports [*1869-71*] [*Ceylon*] [*A publication*] (DLA)
Vanderstraaten...   Vanderstraaten's Decisions in Appeal, Supreme Court [*1869-71*] [*Sri L.*] [*A publication*] (DLA)
V & ET........   Verification and Evaluation Tests (MCD)
V & H.........   Vertical and Horizontal [*Telecommunications*] (TSSD)
V & IA ......   Victorian and Interstate Airways [*Australia*]
V & MM......   Vandalism and Malicious Mischief [*Insurance*]
V & P.........   Vagotomy and Pyloroplasty [*Medicine*]
V & P.........   Vendor and Purchaser [*Sales*] (ROG)
V & S.........   Vernon and Scriven's Irish King's Bench Reports [*1786-88*] [*A publication*] (DLA)
V & T.........   Vodka and Tonic
V & T.........   Volume and Tension [*of pulse*]
VAND UNIV Q...   Vanderbilt University Quarterly [*Tennessee*] [*A publication*] (ROG)
V & V.........   Verification and Validation [*Computer science*]
V&V...........   Visions & Values (WDAA)
VAN EYCK...   Visual Arts Network for the Exchange of Cultural Knowledge (TELE)
VANFIS.......   Visible and Near-Visible Frequency Intercept System [*Navy*]
VANFISH......   Victorian Adoption Network for Information and Self Help [*Australia*]
Van Fleet Coll Attack...   Van Fleet on Collateral Attack [*A publication*] (DLA)
VangAir.......   Vanguard Airlines, Inc. [*Associated Press*] (SAG)
VANGI.........   Variable-Area Nozzle by Gas Injection (SAA)
VANHC........   Veterans Administration Nursing Home Care Program (GFGA)
Van Hey Eq...   Van Heythuysen's Equity Draftsman [*2nd ed.*] [*1828*] [*A publication*] (DLA)
Van Hey Mar Ev...   Van Heythuysen on Maritime Evidence [*A publication*] (DLA)
Van Hey Rud...   Van Heythuysen's Rudiments of English Law [*A publication*] (DLA)
VANHP.........   Virginia Natural Heritage Program [*Virginia State Department of Conservation and Historic Resources*] [*Information service or system*] (IID)
VANIS ....   Volume Analysis Information System Software
Van K.........   Van Koughnet's Reports [*15-21 Upper Canada Common Pleas*] [*1864-71*] [*A publication*] (DLA)
Van K & H...   Upper Canada Common Pleas Reports [*1864-71*] [*A publication*] (DLA)
Van L.........   Vander Linden's Practice [*Cape Colony*] [*A publication*] (DLA)
Van N ....   Van Ness' Prize Cases, United States District Court, District of New York [*A publication*] (DLA)
VAN N.........   Van Norden Magazine [*New York*] [*A publication*] (ROG)
Van Ness Prize Cas...   Van Ness' Prize Cases, United States District Court, District of New York [*A publication*] (DLA)
VANP ....   Nagpur [*India*] [*ICAO location identifier*] (ICLI)
van pt ....   Vanishing Point (VRA)
VANR ....   Nasik Road [*India*] [*ICAO location identifier*] (ICLI)
VANS ....   Value Added Network Service [*Computer science Telecommunications*]
VANS ....   Vans, Inc. [*NASDAQ symbol*] (SPSG)
VANS ....   Vehicle Austere Night Sight [*Army*] (MCD)
Van Sant Ch J...   Van Santvoord's Lives of the Chief Justices of the United States [*A publication*] (DLA)
Van Sant Eq Pr...   Van Santvoord's Equity Practice [*A publication*] (DLA)
Van Sant Pl...   Van Santvoord's Pleadings [*A publication*] (DLA)
Van Sant Prec...   Van Santvoord's Precedents [*A publication*] (DLA)
VANT ....   Vibration and Noise Tester (SAA)
Vantive ....   Vantive Corp. [*Associated Press*] (SAG)
VANUSL.......   Vanderbilt University School of Law (DLA)
VANWACE....   Vulnerability Analysis of Nuclear Weapons in Allied Command, Europe [*Army*] (AABC)
VAO ....   Veterans Administration Office
VAO ....   Voting Assistance Officer
VAOKN.........   Visual Acuity by Optokinetic Nystagmus
VAOR ....   VHF [*Very-High-Frequency*] Aural Omnirange
VAOT ....   Victorian Association of Occupational Therapists [*Australia*]
VAP ....   Photographic Squadron (Heavy) [*Navy symbol*] (NVT)
VAP.............   Vaginal Acid Phosphatase [*An enzyme*]
VAP.............   Valence-Alternation Pair [*Solid-state physics*]
VAP.............   Value-Added Process [*Computer science*] (PCM)
VAP.............   Van Kam Am Cap Adv PA Mun [*NYSE symbol*] (TTSB)
VAP.............   Van Kampen Merritt Advantage Pennsylvania Municipal Income Trust [*NYSE symbol*] (SPSG)
VAP.............   Vapor (NAKS)
VAP.............   Vaporization [*or Vaporizer*] (KSC)
vap.............   Vaporization (MEC)
VAP.............   Variant Angina Pectoris [*Cardiology*] (DAVI)
VAP.............   Vascular Adhesion Protein [*Biochemistry*]
VAP.............   Vehicle Antenna Position [*NASA*]
VAP.............   Velocity Analysis Program
VAP.............   Ventilator-Associated Pneumonia [*Medicine*]
VAP.............   Versatile Automatic Test Equipment Assembly Program [*Computer science*] (IAA)
VAP.............   Vertical Axis Pivots
VAP.............   Veteran Air Pilots
VAP.............   Vibrationally Adiabatic Potential [*Chemical physics*]
VAP.............   Video/Audio Participative [*Education*] (OA)
VAP.............   Videotex Access Point [*Computer science*] (IT)
VAP.............   Vinblastine, Actinomycin D [*Dactinomycin*], Platinol [*Cisplatin*] [*Antineoplastic drug regimen*]
VAP.............   Vincristine, Adriamycin, Prednisone [*Antineoplastic drug regimen*]
VAP.............   Vincristine, Adriamycin, Procarbazine [*Antineoplastic drug regimen*]
VAP.............   Viral Attachment Protein [*Biochemistry*]
VAP.............   Voluntary Assistance Program
VAP.............   Voting Age Population

VAP.............   Vulnerability Assessment Procedure (AAGC)
VAPA...........   Video Alliance for the Performing Arts (EA)
VAPC..........   Vector Adaptive Predictive Coding [*Telecommunications*]
VAPC..........   Veterans Administration Prosthetics Center [*Later, VAREC*]
VAP-Cyclo...   Vincristine, Adriamycin, Prednisolone, Cyclophosphamide [*Antineoplastic drug regimen*]
VAPH..........   Visual Acuity with Pin Hole
VAPI...........   Visual Approach Path Indicator [*Aviation*]
VAP-II.........   Vinblastine, Actinomycin D [*Dactinomycin*] Cisplatin (DAVI)
VAPLA........   Victorian Amateur Power Lifting Association [*Australia*]
VAPO ....   Pune [*India*] [*ICAO location identifier*] (ICLI)
VAPO ....   Vaporizing Oil
Va Poly Inst...   Virginia Polytechnic Institute and State University (GAGS)
VAPOX ....   Vapor Deposit Oxide (IAA)
VAPP ....   Vaccine-Associated Paralytic Poliomyelitis [*Medicine*]
VAPPRF.......   Vapor Proof (IAA)
VAPR ....   Porbandar [*India*] [*ICAO location identifier*] (ICLI)
VAPR ....   Veterans Administration Procurement [*or Purchase*] Regulations
VAPS ....   Virtual Avionics Prototyping System [*Virtual Prototypes, Inc.*]
VAPS ....   Volume, Article [*or Chapter*], Paragraph, Sentence [*Numbers*] [*Indexing*]
VAPS ....   V/STOL Approach System (MCD)
VAPSS ....   Victorian Association of Principals of Secondary Schools [*Australia*]
VaPw ....   Virginia Power Capital Trust I [*Associated Press*] (SAG)
VAQ ....   Tactical Electronic Warfare Squadron [*Navy symbol*] (DNAB)
VA/Q ....   Ventilation-Perfusion [*Ratio*] [*Radiology*] (DAVI)
VAQ ....   Visiting Airmen's Quarters [*Air Force*]
VAQ ....   Visual Air Quality
Va/Qc..........   Ventilation/Perfusion Quotient [*Medicine*] (MAE)
VAR ....   Corps of Volunteers Artillery Regiment [*British military*] (DMA)
VA R ....   Gilmer's Virginia Reports [*A publication*] (DLA)
VAR ....   Reactive Volt-Ampere
VAR ....   Vacuum Arc Remelting [*Steel alloy*]
VAR ....   Valet Air Services [*FAA designator*] (FAAC)
VAR ....   Validation Analysis Report [*Social Security Administration*]
VAR ....   Valley Air Services, Inc. [*ICAO designator*] (FAAC)
VAR ....   Value-Added Remarketer [*or Reseller or Retailer*] [*Business term*]
VAR ....   Value-Added Reseller
VAR ....   Value-at-Risk
VAR ....   Varanasi [*India*] [*Seismograph station code, US Geological Survey*] (SEIS)
VAR ....   Variable (AFM)
var ....   Variable (WDAA)
Var ....   Variable (EBF)
Var ....   Variae [*of Cassiodorus*] [*Classical studies*] (OCD)
var,...........   Varian (WDAA)
VAR ....   Varian Associates [*NYSE symbol*] (SPSG)
VAR ....   Variance Analysis Report (MCD)
VAR ....   Variant [*Numismatics*]
VAR ....   Variation
var ....   Variation (WDAA)
VAR ....   Variegated
var ....   Varietas [*Variety*] [*Biology*]
VAR ....   Variety
var ....   Variety (WDAA)
VAR ....   Variometer (WGA)
VAR ....   Various
var ....   Various (WDAA)
Var ....   Various (EBF)
VAR ....   Varistor [*Telecommunications*] (IAA)
VAR ....   Varitech Resources [*Vancouver Stock Exchange symbol*]
VAR ....   Varna [*Bulgaria*] [*Airport symbol*] (OAG)
VAR ....   Varnish [*Technical drawings*]
var ....   Varnish (VRA)
Var ....   Varsity [*Record label*]
VAR ....   Varying (IAA)
VAR ....   Vector Autoregressive Model [*Mathematics*]
VAR ....   Velocity Acceleration Relationship
VAR ....   Vendor Approval Request (AAG)
VAR ....   Verification Analysis Report (NASA)
VAR ....   Vertical Acceleration Ramp
VAR ....   Vertical Air Rocket (NATG)
VAR ....   Veterans Administration Regulations
VAR ....   Victorian Administrative Reports [*Australia A publication*]
VAR ....   Video-Audio Range [*Radio*]
VAR ....   Vintage Austin Register [*Ashover, Derbyshire, England*] (EAIO)
VAR ....   Virginia Register of Regulations [*A publication*] (AAGC)
VAR ....   Visual-Aural Range [*Radio*]
VAR ....   Voltage Adjusting Rheostat
VAR ....   Voltage Ampere Reactance [*AC electric motors*]
VAR ....   Voltage in Acceptable Range (MCD)
VAR ....   Volt-Ampere Reactive
VAR ....   Voluntary Auto Restraints [*Import quotas on automobiles*]
VAR ....   Volunteer Air Reserve [*Air Force*]
VAR ....   Votre Altesse Royale [*Your Royal Highness*] [*French*]
VAR ....   Vrij Anti-Revolutionaire Partij [*Free Anti-Revolutionary Party*] [*Netherlands Political party*] (PPE)
VARA..........   Vereiniging van Arbeiders Radio Amateurs
VARACTOR...   Variable Reactor [*Electronics*] (EECA)
VARAD........   Varying Radiation (IEEE)
VA R Ann.....   Virginia Reports, Annotated [*A publication*] (DLA)
VARBLK.......   Variable Block [*Computer science*]
VARC..........   Variable Axis Rotor Control System [*Telecommunications*] (TEL)
VARC ....   Virginia Associated Research Campus [*Later, Continuous Electron Beam Accelerator Facility*] [*Research center*] (RCD)

VARCAP.......	Variable Capacitor (IAA)
Varco...........	Varco International, Inc. [Associated Press] (SAG)
Var Cond	Variable Condenser [Radio]
vard	Varied [Quality of the bottom] [Nautical charts]
VAR DIAL.....	Various Dialects (WDAA)
VARE	Victorian Association for Religious Education [Australia]
VARE	Visual Acuity, Right Eye [Ophthalmology] (MAE)
VAREC	Veterans Administration Rehabilitation Engineering Center [Formerly, VAPC]
VAR ED & TR...	Various Editions and Translations (WDAA)
Va Reg Regs...	Virginia Register of Regulations [A publication] (AAGC)
VA Rep Anno...	Virginia Reports, Annotated [A publication] (DLA)
VARES	Vega Aircraft RADAR Enhancing System [FAA]
VARG..........	Ratnagiri [India] [ICAO location identifier] (ICLI)
VARGUS	Variable Generator of Unfamiliar Stimuli [Computer program]
VARH	Volt-Ampere Reactive Hour (IAA)
VARHM	Var-Hour Meter [Electricity]
VARI	Vacuum-Assisted Resin Infusion (RDA)
VARI	Vacuum-Assisted Resin Injection
vari	Various (VRA)
VARI	Varityper
VARIA	Variamento [In a Varied Style] [Music] (ROG)
VARIAC	Variable Capacitor (IAA)
Varian	Varian Associates [Associated Press] (SAG)
VARICAP.....	Variable Capacitor
VARICC........	Victorian Asbestos Removal Industry Consultative Committee [Australia]
Variflex.......	Variflex, Inc. [Associated Press] (SAG)
Vari-L Co	Vari-L Co. [Associated Press] (SAG)
VARIMU	Variable Mu Tube [Electronics] (IAA)
VARION	Variation (ROG)
VARISTOR ...	Variable Resistor
VARITRAN ...	Variable-Voltage Transformer (IEEE)
Varitrn	Varitronic Systems, Inc. [Associated Press] (SAG)
Varity	Varity Corp. [Associated Press] (SAG)
VARK	Rajkot [India] [ICAO location identifier] (ICLI)
VARL	Vari-L Co. [NASDAQ symbol] (SAG)
VARL	Vari-L Company [NASDAQ symbol] (TTSB)
VAR LECT ...	Varia Lectio [Variant Reading] [Latin] (ROG)
Varlen.........	Varlen Corp. [Associated Press] (SAG)
VARM	Varmeter [Engineering]
VARN	Variation (FAAC)
VARN..........	Varnish
var nov	Varietas Nova [New Variety] [Biology]
VARO	Veterans Administration Regional Office (AFM)
VARP	Raipur [India] [ICAO location identifier] (ICLI)
VARP	Vietnam Asset Reconciliation Procedure [Military] (AABC)
VARPC.........	Veterans Administration Records Processing Center
VARR	Variable Range Reflector (IEEE)
VARR	Visual-Aural Radio Range (MSA)
VARs...........	Value-Added Remarketers (NITA)
VARS	Variable Attribute Raster Scan System (NITA)
VARS	Various (ROG)
VARS	Varsity Spirit [NASDAQ symbol] (TTSB)
VARS	Varsity Spirit Corp. [NASDAQ symbol] (SAG)
VARS	Vertical Azimuth Reference System (NATG)
VARS	Visual Aerial Reconnaissance and Surveillance [Military] (VNW)
VARS	Visual Artists Rights Society (BUAC)
VARS	Vocational Adaptation Rating Scales [Test]
VARSITY	University [British] (ROG)
VarSprt	Varsity Spirit Corp. [Associated Press] (SAG)
VART	Volunteer Air Reserve Training [Air Force]
VARTU	Volunteer Air Reserve Training Unit [Air Force]
VARUNB	Variable Unblocked (MHDB)
VAR/VAD......	Value-Added Reseller / Value-Added Dealer (BTTJ)
VARVS	Variable Acuity Remote Viewing System (MCD)
VAS.............	Aviatrans [Former USSR ICAO designator] (FAAC)
VAS.............	Sivas [Turkey] [Airport symbol] (OAG)
VAS.............	Validation System (SSD)
VAS.............	Value-Added Service [Telecommunications] (TEL)
VAS.............	Value-Added Service [Medical benefits]
VAS.............	Value-Added Statement (ADA)
VAS.............	Variable Angle Scatterometer (MCD)
VAS.............	Vascular [Cardiology] (DAVI)
vas..............	Vas Deferens [Urology] (DAVI)
vas..............	Vasectomy (STED)
VAS.............	Vasectomy (WDAA)
VAS.............	Vasectomy Advancement Society of Great Britain (BUAC)
VAS.............	Vassijaure [Sweden] [Seismograph station code, US Geological Survey Closed] (SEIS)
VAS.............	Vector Addition System
VAS.............	Venomological Artifact Society (EA)
VAS.............	Vesicle Attachment Sites [Neurology]
VAS.............	Veterinary Assistant Surgeon [British military] (DMA)
VAS.............	Vibration Analysis System
VAS.............	Victorian Agricultural Strategy [State] (EERA)
VAS.............	Videodisc Authoring System (NITA)
VAS.............	Virtual Acoustic Synthesis [Electronics] (PS)
VAS.............	Visible Atmospheric Sounder (MCD)
VAS.............	VISSR [Visible-Infrared Spin Scan Radiometer] Atmospheric Sounder [NASA]
VAS.............	Visual Analog [Pain] Scale
VAS.............	Visual Analysis System [Military]
VAS.............	Visual Attack System
VAS.............	Visual Audit Sheet (DNAB)
VAS.............	Visual Augmentation System
VAS.............	Vortex Advisory System [FAA]
VASA	Sihora [India] [ICAO location identifier] (ICLI)
VASA	Victorian Ambulance Services Association [Australia]
VASA	Viola d'Amore Society of America (EA)
VA SBA	Virginia State Bar Association, Reports [A publication] (DLA)
VASC	Vascular
vasc...........	Vascular (STED)
VASC	Verbal Auditory Screen for Children
VASC	Vision and Autonomous Systems Laboratory, Carnegie Mellon University [Research center] (RCD)
VAsC..........	Visual Acuity without Spectacle Correction [Unaided]
VASC	Visual-Auditory Screen Test for Children (DAVI)
VASCA	Electronic Valve and Semiconductor Manufacturers' Association (IAA)
VASCA	Vacation and Senior Citizens Association (EA)
VASCAR	Visual Average Speed Computer and Recorder [Speed trap]
VASCO	Value-Added Supply Chain Optimization [Automotive industry cost management]
VASD	Value-Added System Distributor (HGAA)
Vas Dis.......	Vascular Disease (CPH)
VASE..........	Variable Alternatively Spliced Exon [Genetics]
VASE..........	Variable Angle Spectroscopic Ellipsometer
VASE..........	Visualization Application Steering Environment [Computer science]
Vasenlisten...	Vasenlisten zur Griechischen Heldensage [A publication] (OCD)
VASG	Songadh [India] [ICAO location identifier] (ICLI)
VASI	Vertical Approach Slope Indicator
VASI	Visual Approach Slope Indicator [Aviation]
VASI	Volunteer Ambulance School of Instruction [Military British] (ROG)
VASIM	Voltage and Synchro Interface Module
vasio-Para ...	Veterans Administration Seating Interface Orthosis for Paraplegics (DAVI)
VASIS	Visual Approach Slope Indicator System [Aviation]
VASL	Sholapur [India] [ICAO location identifier] (ICLI)
VASO	Vasomedical, Inc. [NASDAQ symbol] (SAG)
VASODIL......	Vasodilatation [Physiology] (AAMN)
vasodil........	Vasodilation (STED)
VAS of GB ...	Vasectomy Advancement Society of Great Britain
VASOG	Veterans Administration Surgical Oncology Group
Vasomed	Vasomedical, Inc. [Associated Press] (SAG)
VASP	Value-Added Service Provider [Agreement] (IT)
VASP	Variable Automatic Synthesis Program [NASA]
VASP	Vasodilator-Stimulated Phosphoprotein [Physiology]
VASP	Viacao Aerea Sao Paulo SA [Airline] [Brazil]
VAS RAD	Vascular Radiology [Medicine] (DMAA)
VASRD.........	Veterans Administration Schedule for Rating Disabilities (AABC)
VASS	Van Allen Simplified Scoring [Tennis] (IIA)
VASS	Variable Angle Sample Spinning [Physics]
VASS	VAX Applicant Search System [Science Applications International Corp.]
VASS	Victorian Architectural Students' Society [Australia]
VASS	Visual Analysis Subsystem [Military]
VASS	Visually Activated Switch System (MCD)
Vassar C......	Vassar College (GAGS)
VASSEL.......	Validation of ASW [Antisubmarine Warfare] Subsystem Effectiveness Levels [Navy] (CAAL)
VASSS	Van Alen Simplified Scoring System [Tennis]
VAST	Vehicle Activity Status Transmission (PDAA)
VAST	Vehicle Automatic State Transmitter (PDAA)
VAST	Versatile Automatic Specification Tester
VAST	Versatile Avionics Ship Test (IAA)
VAST	Versatile Avionics Shop Test System (SAA)
VASTU	Versatile Avionics System Tester (GFGA)
VAST	Virtual Archival Storage Technology [Computer science]
VAST	Visual Audio Sensory Theater
Vastar.........	Vastar Resources, Inc. [Associated Press] (SAG)
VASTT	Versatile Aerial Simulation TOW [Tube-Launched, Optically Tracked, Wire-Guided (Weapon)] Target (MCD)
Va St U	Virginia State University (GAGS)
VASU	Surat [India] [ICAO location identifier] (ICLI)
vas vit	Vas Vitreum [A Glass Vessel] [Latin Pharmacy] (MAE)
VAS VITR....	Vas Vitreum [A Glass Vessel] [Pharmacy]
VAT.............	Vacuum Arc Thrustor Program (MCD)
VAT.............	Value-Added Tax
VAT.............	Vane Air Temperature [Automotive engineering]
VAT.............	Variable Antigen Type (DB)
VAT.............	Variable Area Turbine
VAT.............	Variable Autotransformer (IAA)
VAT.............	Variant Antigenic Type [Genetics, immunology]
VAT.............	Varity Corp. [NYSE symbol Toronto Stock Exchange symbol Vancouver Stock Exchange symbol] (SPSG)
VAT.............	Vatican
Vat.............	Vatican (VRA)
VAT.............	Vatican City [ANSI three-letter standard code] (CNC)
VAT.............	Vatomandry [Madagascar] [Airport symbol] (OAG)
VAT.............	Vatomandry [Malagasy] [Airport symbol] (AD)
VAT.............	Ventricular Activation Time [Cardiology]
VAT.............	Ventricular (Pacing), Atrial (Sensing), Triggered (Mode, Pacemaker) (STED)
VAT.............	Vernier Auto Track (IAA)
VAT.............	Vertically Anchored Tire
VAT.............	Veterinary Admissions Test (BARN)
VAT.............	Veterinary Aptitude Test
VAT.............	Vibration Acceptance Test
VAT.............	Vibroacoustic Test (NASA)

VAT............ Village Assistance [or Action] Team (DNAB)
VAT............ Vincristine, Cytosine Arabinoside, 6-Thioguanine, Daunomycin [Antineoplastic drug regimen] (DAVI)
VAT............ Vineyards Association of Tasmania [Australia]
VAT............ Vinyl Asbestos Tile [Technical drawings]
VAT............ Virtual Address Translation
VAT............ Virtual Address Translator (NITA)
VAT............ Visibility, Amount, Height of Cloud Top, Base [Weather] [DoD]
VAT............ Visual Acquisition Technique
VAT............ Visual Action Time
VAT............ Visual Apperception Test [Psychology]
VAT............ Vitro Assistance Team
VAT............ Vocational Apperception Test [Psychology]
VAT............ Voice-Activated Transcription [Machine] (DAVI)
VAT............ Voice-Activated Typewriter
VAT............ Voice Activation Technology (NITA)
VAT............ Voltage Amplifier Tube
VAT............ Volt-Ampere Tester
VAT............ Vulnerability Analysis Team (MCD)
VATA.......... Vertical Assembly and Test Area (SSD)
VATA.......... Vibroacoustic Test Article (NASA)
Va Tax Rev... Virginia Tax Review [A publication] (DLA)
VATB.......... Visibility, Amount of Clouds, Height of Cloud Top, Height of Cloud Base [Environmental science] (COE)
VatBA.......... Biblioteca Apostolica Vaticana, Vatican City, Vatican City [Library symbol Library of Congress] (LCLS)
VATD .... Vincristine, ara-C [Cytarabine], Thioguanine, Daunorubicin [Antineoplastic drug regimen]
VATE.......... Vandenberg Automatic Test Equipment [Air Force]
VATE.......... Versatile Automatic Test Equipment [Computers]
V-ATE......... Vertical Anisotropic Etch [Raytheon Co.]
VATE.......... Victorian Association for the Teaching of English [Australia] (BUAC)
VATER........ Vascular Tracheoesophageal-Limb-Reduction [Endocrinology]
VATER........ Vertebral, Anal, Tracheal, Esophageal, Renal
VATER .... Vertebral and/or Vascular Defects, Anorectal Malformation, Tracheoesophageal Fistula, Radial, Ray, or Renal Anomaly [Syndrome] [Medicine] (DAVI)
VATER .... Vertebral Defects, Imperforate Anus, Tracheoesophageal Fistula, Radial and RenalDysplasia [Syndrome] [Medicine] (DAVI)
VATERL....... Vertebral Defects, Imperforate Anus, Tracheoesophageal Fistula, Radial and RenalDysplasia, Limb Anomalies [Syndrome] [Medicine] (DAVI)
VATF.......... Vibration and Acoustic Test Facility (NASA)
VAtf........... Visual Acuity with Trial Frame
VATG.......... Vinyl Acetate Toxicology Group (NTPA)
VATH .... Vinblastine, Adriamycin, Thiotepa [Antineoplastic drug regimen]
VATH .... Vinblastine, Adriamycin, Thiotepa, Halotestin [Fluoxymesterone] [Antineoplastic drug regimen]
VATLIT........ Very Advanced Technology Light Twin (MCD)
VATLS......... Visual Airborne Target Locator System [Military]
VATOL .... Verical Altitude and Take-Off and Landing (PDAA)
VATP.......... Vector Adaptive Transform Processing [Computer science] (PCM)
VATR.......... Variable Aperture Target Recognition (MCD)
VATs........... Variable Antigen, Surface (STED)
VATS.......... Vehicle Acquisition and Tracking System (SAA)
VATS.......... Vehicle Anti-Theft System [General Motors Corp.]
VATS.......... Vehicle Automatic Test System
VATS.......... Vernon's Annotated Texas Statutes [A publication] (DLA)
VATS.......... Versatile Avionics Test [or Tester] Shop [NASA] (DNAB)
VATS.......... Vertical-Lift Airfield for Tactical Support (NVT)
VATS.......... Vibration Analysis Test Set (DWSG)
VATS.......... Video-Assisted Thoracoscopic Surgery
VATS.......... Video-Augmented Tracking System (MCD)
VATS/SNAP... Video-Augmented Tracking System/Single Seat Night Attack Program (MCD)
VAT STA ..... Vatican State (WDAA)
VATT.......... Vatican Advanced Technology Telescope [At Mount Graham, AZ]
Vatt........... Vattel's Law of Nations [A publication] (DLA)
Vattel......... Vattel's Law of Nations [A publication] (DLA)
Vattel Law Nat... Vattel's Law of Nations [A publication] (DLA)
VATTR......... Value Added Tax Tribunal Reports [A publication]
VA/TVTA ..... Vibroacoustic/Thermal/Vacuum Test Article (NASA)
VAU........... Vertical Accelerometer Unit
VAU .... Vertical Arithmetic Unit
vau........... Virginia [MARC country of publication code Library of Congress] (LCCP)
VAU .... Volume Accumulator Unit
VAU .... Volunteer Air Units
VAUB.......... Vehicle Authorization Utilization Board [Military]
VAUD.......... Vaudeville
Vaug.......... Vaughan's English Common Pleas Reports [124 English Reprint] [A publication] (DLA)
Vaugh........ Vaughan's English Common Pleas Reports [124 English Reprint] [A publication] (DLA)
Vaughan ...... Vaughan's English Common Pleas Reports [124 English Reprint] [A publication] (DLA)
Vaughan (Eng)... Vaughan's English Common Pleas Reports [124 English Reprint] [A publication] (DLA)
Vaughn .... Vaughn's, Inc. [Associated Press] (SAG)
VAUS .... Value Added Utilisation System (EERA)
VAUSSI....... Veteran's Association of the USS [United States Ship] Iowa (EA)
VAUX .... Vauxhall [Automobile] (DSUE)
Vaux .... Vaux's Recorder's Decisions [1841-45] [Philadelphia, PA] [A publication] (DLA)
V AUX......... Verb Auxiliary [Grammar] (WDAA)

Vaux (PA).... Vaux's Recorder's Decisions [1841-45] [Philadelphia, PA] [A publication] (DLA)
Vaux Rec Dec... Vaux's Recorder's Decisions [1841-45] [Philadelphia, PA] [A publication] (DLA)
VAV............ Variable Air Volume
VAV............ Vava'u [Tonga Island] [Airport symbol] (OAG)
VAV............ Vaxjo [Sweden] [Airport symbol] (AD)
VAV............ Visicalc Advanced Version (HGAA)
VAV............ VP-16-213 [Etoposide], Adriamycin, Vincristine [Antineoplastic drug regimen]
VAVP .... Variable Angle, Variable Pitch
VAVS.......... Veterans Administration Voluntary Service
VAW.......... Carrier Airborne Early Warning Squadron [Navy symbol] (NVT)
VAW.......... Vertical Arc Welder
VAWM......... Washim [India] [ICAO location identifier] (ICLI)
VAWP......... Voice-Activated Word Processor [Computer science]
VAWT......... Vertical Axis Wind Turbine [Power generator] [See also VAWTG]
VAWTG....... Vertical Axis Wind Turbine Generator [Also, VAWT]
VAX........... Alexandria Public Library, Alexandria, VA [OCLC symbol] (OCLC)
VAX........... Heavy Attack Aircraft, Experimental
VAX........... Vesta Airex [Czechoslovakia] [ICAO designator] (FAAC)
VAX........... Virtual Address Extension [Computer science]
VAXBI......... Virtual Address Extension Backplane Interconnect [Computer science] (CIST)
VAX-L......... Aircraft Attack, Experimental-Light [Navy]
VAXSIM .... Virtual Address Extension System Integrity Monitor [Computer science] (CIST)
VAX/VMS ..... Virtual Address Extension/Virtual Memory System [Computer science] (DOM)
VAY........... Valandovo [Yugoslavia] [Seismograph station code, US Geological Survey] (SEIS)
Vayr.......... Vayikra Rabba (BJA)
VAZ........... Voyageur Arizona Municipal Income Fund [AMEX symbol] (SPSG)
VAZ........... Voyageur Arizona Muni Income [AMEX symbol] (TTSB)
V$_B$........... Base Voltage (IDOE)
VB............ Birmingham European Airways [Airline flight code] (ODBW)
VB............ Bombing Plane [Navy symbol]
VB............ Dive Bomber Squadron [Navy symbol]
VB............ Vacancy Bit (IAA)
VB............ Valence Band (AAEL)
VB............ Valence Bond (DEN)
VB............ Valve Box
VB............ Van Buren [Catheter] [Surgery] (DAVI)
VB............ Vanity Bar [Classified advertising] (ADA)
VB............ Vapor Barrier [Boots] [Army] (INF)
VB............ Vascular Bundle [Botany]
VB............ Venous Blood [Medicine] (DMAA)
VB............ Ventrobasal Complex [Brain anatomy]
VB............ Verb
vb............ Verb (WDAA)
VB............ Verbal (WDAA)
VB............ Veronal Buffer (DB)
VB............ Vertebral-Basilar Arteries [Anatomy] (CPH)
VB............ Vertebral Body [Anatomy] (DAVI)
VB............ Vertical Beam [of light]
VB............ Vertical Bomb [Air Force]
VB............ Vertical Bridgman (AAEL)
VB............ Vertical Main Boiler [on a ship] (DS)
VB............ Veterinary Board [Tasmania, Australia]
VB............ Veterinary Bulletin [Database] [Commonwealth Bureau of Animal Health] [Information service or system] (CRD)
VB............ Viable Birth [Medicine]
VB............ Vibration (AAG)
VB............ Vibrator (IAA)
VB............ Vinblastine, Bleomycin [Antineoplastic drug regimen]
VB............ Vir Bonus [A Good Man] [Latin]
vb............ Virgin Islands, British [MARC country of publication code Library of Congress] (LCCP)
VB............ Virus Buffer [Medicine] (DB)
VB............ Visbreaker [Petroleum technology]
VB............ Visual Basic [Computer science] (PCM)
VB............ Vital Reaction [on Autopsy] [Pathology] (DAVI)
VB............ Viven and Bassiere [Rifle grenade]
VB............ Voelkischer Beobachter [A publication]
VB............ Voice Band [Telecommunications]
VB............ Voice Bank [Telecommunications] (TEL)
VB............ Voltage Board (IAA)
VB............ Voluntary Bankruptcy (MHDW)
VB............ Volunteer Battalion [Military]
VB............ Vorgeschobener Beobachter [Forward Observer] [German military]
VB............ Vulgate Bible
VB............ Westair Commuter Airlines [ICAO designator] (AD)
V-B1.......... Vitamin B$_1$ [Also called thiamine] (DAVI)
V-B6.......... Vitamin B$_6$ [Also called pyridoxine] (DAVI)
V-B12......... Vitamin B$_{12}$ [Also called Cyanocobolamine] (DAVI)
VBA........... Vagahova Ballet Academy [Russia]
VBA........... Variable Body Armor (INF)
VBA........... VB Anderson Co. [BTAC] (DAVI)
VBA........... Vegetarian Brotherhood of America [Defunct] (EA)
VBA........... Verbal Adjective (WDAA)
VBA........... Very Big Accelerator (PDAA)
VBA........... Veterans Benefits Administration [Department of Veterans Affairs]
VBA........... Vibrating Beam Accelerometer [Inertial sensor] (IEEE)
VBA........... Victorian Bar Association [Australia]

VBA.............. Vincristine, BCNU [*Carmustine*], Adriamycin [*Antineoplastic drug regimen*]

VBA.............. Visual Basic, Applications Edition [*Microsoft Corp.*] [*Computer macro language*] (PCM)

VBA.............. Visual Basic for Applications [*Microsoft Corp.*]

VBAA .... Vanilla Bean Association of America (EA)

VBAC .... Vaginal Birth After Caesarean [*Obstetrics*]

VBAI............ Vertebrobasilar Artery Insufficiency [*Medicine*]

VBAN .... Ann [*Myanmar*] [*ICAO location identifier*] (ICLI)

VBAN .... V Band Corp. [*NASDAQ symbol*] (NQ)

V Band......... V Band Corp. [*Associated Press*] (SAG)

VBAP .... Vincristine, BCNU [*Carmustine*], Adriamycin, Prednisone [*Antineoplastic drug regimen*]

VBAS .... Anisakan [*Myanmar*] [*ICAO location identifier*] (ICLI)

VBAS .... Von Braun Astronomical Society (EA)

VBAT........... Battery Voltage [*Automotive engineering*]

V$_{BB}$............ Base-Voltage Supply (IDOE)

vbb............. Volgens Bygaande Brief [*According to Accompanying Letter*] [*Correspondence*] [*Afrikaans*]

VBBA .... Vietnam-British Business Association (BUAC)

VBBM.......... Bhamo [*Myanmar*] [*ICAO location identifier*] (ICLI)

VBBP.......... Bokepyin [*Myanmar*] [*ICAO location identifier*] (ICLI)

VBBS .... Bassein [*Myanmar*] [*ICAO location identifier*] (ICLI)

VBC............. Bridgewater College, Bridgewater, VA [*OCLC symbol*] (OCLC)

VBC............. Variable Boost Control [*System*] [*Automotive engineering*]

VBC............. Velocity Bin Commanded

VBC............. Venetian Blind Council [*Formerly, VBI*]

VBC............. Versatile Base [*Bus*] Connector [*Electronics*] (BARN)

VBC............. Veterans Benefit Counselor [*Veterans Administration*] (GFGA)

VBC............. Victorian Bar Council [*Australia*]

VBC............. Vincristine, Bleomycin, Cisplatin [*Antineoplastic drug regimen*] (DAVI)

VBC............. Vinylbenzyl Chloride [*Organic chemistry*]

VBC............. Vocational Behavior Checklist (TES)

VBC............. Vogel-Bonner Citrate [*Growth medium*]

VBCI........... Coco Island [*Myanmar*] [*ICAO location identifier*] (ICLI)

VBCITC....... Victorian Building and Construction Industry Training Council [*Australia*]

VBD .... Vector-Borne Disease

VBD .... Veronal-Buffered Diluent

VBD .... Vertebrobasilar Dolichoectasia [*Medicine*]

VBD .... Vinblastine, Bleomycin, Diamminedichloroplatinum [*Cisplatin*] [*Antineoplastic drug regimen*]

VBD .... Voice Band Data (KSC)

VBDMA .... Vinylbenzyldimethylamine [*Organic chemistry*]

VBE............. Vernacular Black English (WGA)

VBE............. Vibrating Plate Extractor [*Chemical engineering*]

VBE............. Video BIOS [*Basic Input-Output System*] Extension [*Computer science*] (PCM)

VBE/AI .... VESA [*Video Electronics Standards Association*] BIOS Extension/Audio Interface [*Basic Input-Output System*] (PCM)

VBEFA......... Vehicle Builders Employees Federation of Australia

VBF............. Bomber-Fighter Squadron [*Navy symbol*]

VBF............. Bombing-Fighting Aircraft [*Navy symbol*]

VBF............. Variable Bandwidth Filter

VBF............. Vibrated Fluid Bed [*Chemical engineering*]

VBF............. Vibratory Bowl Feeder

VBF............. Vinegar Brewers Federation [*British*] (DBA)

VBG .... Lompoc, CA [*Location identifier FAA*] (FAAL)

VBG .... Vagotomy and Bilroth Gastroenterostomy [*Medicine*] (DB)

VBG .... Vein Aortocoronary Artery Bypass Graft [*Cardiology*] (AAMN)

VBG .... Vertical Banded Gastroplasty [*Medicine*] (MEDA)

VBGG.......... Gangaw [*Myanmar*] [*ICAO location identifier*] (ICLI)

VBGH.......... Volunteer Battalion Gordon Highlanders [*British military*] (DMA)

VBGQ .... Vacuum Brazed - Gas Quenched

VBGW .... Gwa [*Myanmar*] [*ICAO location identifier*] (ICLI)

VBHB .... Hmawbi [*Myanmar*] [*ICAO location identifier*] (ICLI)

VBHH .... Hebo [*Myanmar*] [*ICAO location identifier*] (ICLI)

VBHL .... Homalin [*Myanmar*] [*ICAO location identifier*] (ICLI)

VBHN .... Htilin [*Myanmar*] [*ICAO location identifier*] (ICLI)

VBI.............. Venetian Blind Institute [*Later, VBC*] (EA)

VBI.............. Vertebral-Basilar Insufficiency [*Medicine*] (CPH)

VBI.............. Vertical Blanking Intermission [*Telecommunications*] (OTD)

VBI.............. Vertical Blanking Interval [*Telecommunications*]

VBI.............. Video Bible Institute [*Defunct*] (EA)

VBI.............. Vital Bus Inverter [*Computer science*] (IEEE)

VBIDB......... Victorian Building Industries Disputes Board [*Australia*]

V-BIG.......... Ventricular Bigeminy [*Medicine*]

VBJ............. Vacuum Bell Jar

VBKG .... Kengtung [*Myanmar*] [*ICAO location identifier*] (ICLI)

VBKK .... Kutkai [*Myanmar*] [*ICAO location identifier*] (ICLI)

VBKM .... Kalemyo [*Myanmar*] [*ICAO location identifier*] (ICLI)

VBKP .... Kyaukpyu [*Myanmar*] [*ICAO location identifier*] (ICLI)

VBKU .... Kyauktu [*Myanmar*] [*ICAO location identifier*] (ICLI)

VBL............. BOCES [*Boards of Cooperative Educational Services*], Monroe 1, Penfield, NY [*OCLC symbol*] (OCLC)

VBL............. Vector Biology Laboratory [*University of Notre Dame*] [*Research center*] (RCD)

VBL............. Verbal

VBL............. Verordnungsblatt [*Official Gazette*] [*German*] (ILCA)

VBL............. Vertical-Blank [*Computer science*] (BYTE)

VBL............. Vinblastine [*Velban, Vincaleukoblastine*] [*Also, V, Ve, VLB*] [*Antineoplastic drug*]

VBL............. Voyager Biological Laboratory [*NASA*]

VBLK .... Loikaw [*Myanmar*] [*ICAO location identifier*] (ICLI)

VBLN .... Lonekin [*Myanmar*] [*ICAO location identifier*] (ICLI)

VBLO .... Langkho [*Myanmar*] [*ICAO location identifier*] (ICLI)

VBLS .... Lashio [*Myanmar*] [*ICAO location identifier*] (ICLI)

VBLS .... Voice-Based Learning System (EDAC)

V BLT......... Vee Built [*Ship classification term*] (DS)

VBLY .... Lanywa [*Myanmar*] [*ICAO location identifier*] (ICLI)

VBM .... BOCES [*Boards of Cooperative Educational Services*], Monroe 2, Orleans, Spencerport, NY [*OCLC symbol*] (OCLC)

VBM .... Valence Band Maximum [*Physics*]

VBM .... Valence Bond Maximum [*Physics*]

VBM .... Vincristine, Bleomycin, Methotrexate [*Antineoplastic drug regimen*]

VBMA .... Vacuum Bag Manufacturers Association [*Defunct*] (EA)

VBMAA .... Venetian Blind Manufacturers' Association of Australia

VBME .... Voice of the Broad Masses of Eritrea, Asmara

VBMH .... Mong-Hpayak [*Myanmar*] [*ICAO location identifier*] (ICLI)

VBMI .... Mongyai [*Myanmar*] [*ICAO location identifier*] (ICLI)

VBMK .... Myitkyina [*Myanmar*] [*ICAO location identifier*] (ICLI)

VBML .... Meiktila [*Myanmar*] [*ICAO location identifier*] (ICLI)

VBMM .... Moulmein [*Myanmar*] [*ICAO location identifier*] (ICLI)

VBMN .... Manaung [*Myanmar*] [*ICAO location identifier*] (ICLI)

VBMO .... Momeik [*Myanmar*] [*ICAO location identifier*] (ICLI)

VBMP .... Mong Pyin [*Myanmar*] [*ICAO location identifier*] (ICLI)

VBMR .... Ventilation Barrier Machine Room [*Nuclear energy*] (NRCH)

VBMS .... Mong-Hsat [*Myanmar*] [*ICAO location identifier*] (ICLI)

VBMS .... Victorian Business Migration Service [*Australia*]

VBMT .... Mong Tong [*Myanmar*] [*ICAO location identifier*] (ICLI)

VBMU .... Myauk U [*Myanmar*] [*ICAO location identifier*] (ICLI)

VBMW .... Magwe [*Myanmar*] [*ICAO location identifier*] (ICLI)

VBMWMO ... Vintage BMW [*Bavarian Motor Works*] Motorcycle Owners (EA)

VBN .... Verbal Noun

VBN .... Veterans Bedside Network (EA)

VBN .... Vrnjacka Banja [*Yugoslavia*] [*Airport symbol*] (AD)

VBNA .... Victorian Bush Nursing Association [*Australia*]

VBNC .... Viable but Not Culturable [*Microbiology*]

VBNJ .... Vista Bancorp [*NASDAQ symbol*] (SAG)

VBNK .... Village Bancorp [*NASDAQ symbol*] (SAG)

VBNM .... Naungmon [*Myanmar*] [*ICAO location identifier*] (ICLI)

VBNP .... Nampong [*Myanmar*] [*ICAO location identifier*] (ICLI)

VBNS .... Namsang [*Myanmar*] [*ICAO location identifier*] (ICLI)

vBNS .... Very High-Speed Backbone Network Service [*Computer science*] (IGQR)

vBNS .... Very High Speed Backbone Network System [*Computer science*]

VBNT .... Namtu [*Myanmar*] [*ICAO location identifier*] (ICLI)

VBNU .... Nyaung U [*Myanmar*] [*ICAO location identifier*] (ICLI)

VBO .... Oswego County BOCES [*Boards of Cooperative Educational Services*], Mexico, NY [*OCLC symbol*] (OCLC)

VBO .... Veterans Benefits Office

VBO .... Voltage Breakover (IAA)

VBOB .... Veterans of the Battle of the Bulge (EA)

V (Bomb)..... Vergeltungswaffe Bomb [*German "vengeance weapon"*]

VBOMP....... Virtual Base Organization and Maintenance Processor

VBOS .... Veronal-Buffered Oxalated Saline

VBot........... Verstreute Boghazkoei-Texte [*A. Goetze*] [*A publication*] (BJA)

VBP............. Vacuum Backing Pump

VBP............. Valid BIT [*Binary Digit*] Register [*Computer science*] (MHDB)

VBP............. Vinblastine, Bleomycin, and Platinol [*Antineoplastic drug regimen*] (MAE)

VBP............. Vinblastine, Bleomycin, Prednisone [*Antineoplastic drug*] (CDI)

VBP............. Virtual Block Processor

VBP............. Vortex Breakdown Position

VBPA .... Pa-An [*Myanmar*] [*ICAO location identifier*] (ICLI)

VBPB .... Phaungbyin [*Myanmar*] [*ICAO location identifier*] (ICLI)

VBPE .... Paletwa [*Myanmar*] [*ICAO location identifier*] (ICLI)

VBPF .... Variable Bandpass Filter

VBPG .... Pegu [*Myanmar*] [*ICAO location identifier*] (ICLI)

VBPI .... Pearl Island [*Myanmar*] [*ICAO location identifier*] (ICLI)

VBPK .... Pauk [*Myanmar*] [*ICAO location identifier*] (ICLI)

VBPL .... Pinlebu [*Myanmar*] [*ICAO location identifier*] (ICLI)

VBPP .... Papun [*Myanmar*] [*ICAO location identifier*] (ICLI)

VBPR .... Prome [*Myanmar*] [*ICAO location identifier*] (ICLI)

VBPT .... Putao [*Myanmar*] [*ICAO location identifier*] (ICLI)

VBPU .... Pakokku [*Myanmar*] [*ICAO location identifier*] (ICLI)

VBPW .... Palaw [*Myanmar*] [*ICAO location identifier*] (ICLI)

VBR .... Vacuum Bottoms Recycle [*Petroleum refining*]

VBR .... Valuation Board of Review [*Australia*]

VBR .... Variable BIT [*Binary Digit*] Rate [*Telecommunications*]

VBR .... Ventricle Brain Ratio [*Medicine*]

VBR .... Vinyl Bromide [*Organic chemistry*]

VBR .... Virginia Blue Ridge Railway [*AAR code*]

VBRA .... Sittwe [*Myanmar*] [*ICAO location identifier*] (ICLI)

VBRA .... Vehicle Builders and Repairers Association [*British*] (EAIO)

VBRK .... Vacation Break U.S.A. [*NASDAQ symbol*] (TTSB)

VBRK .... Vacation Break U.S.A., Inc. [*NASDAQ symbol*] (SAG)

VBRM .... Mandalay [*Myanmar*] [*ICAO location identifier*] (ICLI)

VBRN .... Mergui [*Myanmar*] [*ICAO location identifier*] (ICLI)

VBRR .... Rangoon/Mingaladon [*Myanmar*] [*ICAO location identifier*] (ICLI)

VBS .... Vacation Bible Schools (EA)

VBS .... Variable Ballast System

VBS .... Veronal-Buffered Saline

VBS .... Vertebral-Basilar System [*Medicine*] (CPH)

VBS .... Virtual Bragg Scattering [*Physics*]

VBS .... Vision Business Systems Ltd. (NITA)

VBSA .... Saw [*Myanmar*] [*ICAO location identifier*] (ICLI)

VBSA .... Value-Based Self-Assessment [*Model*] (AAGC)

VB Script .... Visual Basic Script [*Computer science*] (IGQR)

VBS:FBS ..... Veronal-Buffered Saline-Fetal Bovine Serum (MAE)

VBSK	Sinkaling Khamti [*Myanmar*] [*ICAO location identifier*] (ICLI)
VBSL	Salingyi [*Myanmar*] [*ICAO location identifier*] (ICLI)
VBSO	Sidoktaya [*Myanmar*] [*ICAO location identifier*] (ICLI)
VBSS	Visit, Board, Search, and Secure (DOMA)
VBST	Shante [*Myanmar*] [*ICAO location identifier*] (ICLI)
VBSW	Shinbweyang [*Myanmar*] [*ICAO location identifier*] (ICLI)
VBSY	Sandoway [*Myanmar*] [*ICAO location identifier*] (ICLI)
VBT	Bombing, Torpedo Plane [*Navy symbol*]
VBT	Valence-Bond Theory [*Physical chemistry*]
VBT	Variable Bandwidth Tuning
VBT	Vertebral Body Tenderness [*Medicine*] (DAVI)
VBT	Veterinary Board of Tasmania [*Australia*]
VBT	Videos for Business and Training [*A publication*]
VBTA	Vermont Business Teachers Association (EDAC)
VBTL	Tachilek [*Myanmar*] [*ICAO location identifier*] (ICLI)
VBTN	Tanai [*Myanmar*] [*ICAO location identifier*] (ICLI)
VBTV	Tavoy [*Myanmar*] [*ICAO location identifier*] (ICLI)
VBTY	Tanyang [*Myanmar*] [*ICAO location identifier*] (ICLI)
VBU	Vibrating Bag Unloader
VBULE	Vestibule [*Classified advertising*] (ADA)
VBUSA	Vacation Break U.S.A., Inc. [*Associated Press*] (SAG)
VBV	Vanuabalavu [*Fiji*] [*Airport symbol*] (OAG)
VBV	Veterinary Board of Victoria [*Australia*]
VBVP	Kawthaung [*Myanmar*] [*ICAO location identifier*] (ICLI)
VBW	Air Burkina [*Burkina Faso*] [*ICAO designator*] (FAAC)
VBW	Bridgewater, VA [*Location identifier FAA*] (FAAL)
VBW	Video Bandwidth
VBWR	Vallecitos Boiling Water Reactor
VBX	Visual Basic Extension [*Computer science*]
VBY	Visby [*Sweden*] [*Airport symbol*] (OAG)
VBYE	Ye [*Myanmar*] [*ICAO location identifier*] (ICLI)
VC	Acuity of Color Vision [*Ophthalmology*] (DAVI)
VC	British Aircraft Corp. Ltd. [*ICAO aircraft manufacturer identifier*] (ICAO)
VC	Capillary Volume [*Clinical chemistry*] (AAMN)
VC	Circular Velocity
V_c	Collector Voltage (IDOE)
VC	Color Vision [*Ophthalmology*]
VC	Composite Aircraft Squadron [*Navy symbol*]
VC	Creditreform Databank [*Verband der Vereine Creditreform eV*] [*Information service or system*] (IID)
VC	Cruise Speed [*Aviation*]
V_c	Pulmonary Capillary Blood Volume [*Cardiology*] (DAVI)
VC	St. Vincent and the Grenadines [*ANSI two-letter standard code*] (CNC)
VC	Vacuolated Cell
VC	Validity Check [*Data entry test program*] [*Computer science*] (IAA)
VC	Valuable Cargo
VC	Valuation Clause
VC	Vanadium Carbide (PDAA)
V_c	Vancouver Stock Exchange [*Canada*]
VC	Vaporizer Concentrate [*Nuclear energy*] (NRCH)
VC	Variable Capacitor (DEN)
VC	Variable Charge (DCTA)
VC	Variable Cost (AAGC)
VC	Varnished Cambric [*Insulation*]
VC	Vascular Catheterization (CPH)
VC	Vasoconstrictor [*Medicine*]
VC	Vatel Club (EA)
vc	Vatican City [*MARC country of publication code Library of Congress*] (LCCP)
VC	Vector Character (NASA)
vc	Vector Character (NAKS)
V/C	Vector Control (KSC)
V_c	Vecuronium [*A muscle relaxant*]
VC	Vegetative Capability [*Biology*]
VC	Vehicular Communications (MCD)
VC	Velocity Character (MCD)
VC	Velocity, Closing
VC	Velocity Compounded
VC	Velocity Counter (KSC)
vc	Velocity Counter (NAKS)
VC	Vena Cava [*Anatomy*]
VC	Vencor, Inc. [*NYSE symbol*] (SAG)
VC	Vendor Call (MCD)
VC	Vendor Code (MCD)
VC	Vendor Contact
VC	Venereal Case [*Medical slang*]
VC	Venice Committee (EA)
VC	Venous Capacitance [*Clinical chemistry*] (AAMN)
VC	Ventilated Containers [*Shipping*] (DCTA)
V/C	Ventilation/Circulation Ratio [*Medicine*] (MAE)
VC	Ventilatory Capacity [*Physiology*]
VC	Ventral Column (DB)
VC	Ventricular Complex [*Cardiology*]
VC	Ventricular Coupling [*Cardiology*]
VC	Venture Capital [*or Capitalist*] [*Finance*]
VC	VePesid, Carboplatin [*Antineoplastic drug*] (CDI)
VC	Verb-Consonant [*Education of the hearing-impaired*]
VC	Verbi Causa [*For Example*] [*Latin*]
VC	Verification Condition
VC	Vernair Flying Services [*British ICAO designator*] (ICDA)
VC	Vernal Conjunctivitis [*Ophthalmology*]
VC	Versatility Code
VC	Vertical Center (SAA)

VC	Vertical Circle (IAA)
VC	Vertical Curve
VC	Vertical Spacing (IAA)
VC	Veterinary Corps [*Military*]
VC	Vicar Choral
VC	Vice Chairman [*or Chairperson or Chairwoman*]
VC	Vice Chancellor
VC	Vice-Chancellor's Courts [*England*] (DLA)
VC	Vice Commodore [*Navy*] (NVT)
VC	Vice Consul
VC	Victoria Carriers [*Steamship*] (MHDB)
VC	Victoria Cross [*British*]
VC	Videocassette (DAVI)
VC	Video Channel [*Auckland, NZ*]
VC	Video Correlator
VC	Videodisc Controller
VC	Vietcong [*Vietnamese Communists*]
VC	Vigilance Committee
VCh	Vigiliae Christianae [*A publication*] (ODCC)
VC	Village of Childhelp (EA)
vc	Vincentian Congregation (TOCD)
VC	Vincentian Congregation (India) (TOCD)
VC	Vincristine [*Also, LCR, O, V, VCR*] [*Antineoplastic drug*] (AAMN)
VC	Vinyl Chloride [*Organic chemistry*]
VC	Vinyl Chloride Plastic (EDCT)
VC	Vinylidene Chloride (EDCT)
VC	Violoncello [*Music*]
VC	Vir Clarissimus [*A Most Illustrious Man*] [*Latin*]
VC	Virginia Central Railway [*AAR code*]
VC	Virtual Circuit [*Manager*] (TNIG)
VC	Virtual Classroom [*Educational teleconferencing*]
VC	Viscous Coupling [*Automotive engineering*]
VC	Viscous Criterion
VC	Visicalc (HGAA)
VC	Vision Controllor [*Printer technology*]
VC	Visiting Committee [*British*]
VC	Visual Capacity [*Acuity*]
VC	Visual Coincidence (SAA)
VC	Visual Communication (WDAA)
VC	Visual Cortex
VC	Visum Cultum [*Seen Cultivated*] [*Botany*] (ROG)
VC	Vital Capacity
VC	Vitamin Capsule [*Pharmacy*] (DAVI)
VC	Vitreous Carbon
VC	Vitrified Clay [*Technical drawings*]
VC	Vocal Cord
VC	Voice Ciphony (CET)
VC	Voice Circuit (SSD)
VC	Voice Coil
VC	Voice Coil of Speaker [*Computer hardware*] (IAA)
VC	Voltage Changer (IAA)
VC	Voltage Comparator [*or Compensator*] (DEN)
VC	Volt-Coulomb (DEN)
VC	Volume Control (DEN)
VC	Volume of Compartment [*Technical drawings*]
VC	Volume to Capacity Ratio (EDCT)
VC	Volumetric Control (WDAA)
VC	Voluntary Closing [*Prosthesis*] [*Medicine*]
VC	Volunteer Consultant [*Red Cross*]
VC	Volunteer Corps
VC	Voters for Choice [*Later, VFC*] (EA)
VC	Voyage Charter
VC	Vuelta de Correo [*Return Mail*] [*Spanish*]
VCA	Vacant Code Announcement (DNAB)
VCA	Valve Control Amplifier (MDG)
VCA	Vancomycin-Colistin-Anisomycin [*Growth-inhibiting mixture*] [*Microbiology*]
VCA	Vanished Children's Alliance (EA)
VCA	Vegetarian Catering Association [*British*] (BI)
VCA	Vehicle Certification Agency (BUAC)
VCA	Vehicle Checkout Area
VCA	Venture Clubs of the Americas (EA)
VCA	Vespa Club of America (EA)
VCA	Veteran Corps of Artillery, State of New York, Constituting the Military Society of the War of 1812 (EA)
VCA	Veterinary Companies of America (EFIS)
VCA	Victims of Crime Assistance Act
VCA	Victims of Crime Association [*Australia*]
VCA	Victorian Council of the Arts [*Australia*]
VCA	Video Capture Adapter (PCM)
VCA	Viewdata Corp. of America, Inc. [*Miami Beach, FL*] [*Telecommunications*] (TSSD)
VCA	Vinchina [*Argentina*] [*Seismograph station code, US Geological Survey*] (SEIS)
VCA	Vinylene Carbonate [*Organic chemistry*] (WDAA)
VCA	Viral Capsid Antibody [*Hematology*]
VCA	Viral Capsular Antigen [*Immunology*]
VCA	Virtual City Associates Ltd. [*London, England*] [*Telecommunications*] (TSSD)
VCA	Virtual Crystal Approximation (WDAA)
VCA	Viscosity Control Agent
VCA	Visual Course Adapter (MUGU)
VCA	Vitrified China Association [*Defunct*]
VCA	Voice Connecting Arrangement [*Telecommunications*] (TEL)
VCA	Voltage-Controlled Amplifier (NTCM)

VCA............	Voltage Control of Amplification
VCA............	Voltage-Current Adapter (IAA)
VCAA........	Veteran and Classic Aeroplane (BUAC)
VCAC.........	Victorian Consumer Affairs Committee [Australia]
VCAD.........	Vertical Contact Analog Display
VC Adm	Victoria Reports, Admiralty [A publication] (DLA)
VCAGX......	Vista Capital Growth [Mutual fund ticker symbol] (SG)
VCAI..........	Veterinary Centers of America [NASDAQ symbol] (SAG)
VCAI..........	Veterinary Ctrs of Amer [NASDAQ symbol] (TTSB)
VCAM.........	Vascular Cell Adhesion Molecule [Cytology]
VCAM.........	Vincam Group [NASDAQ symbol] (TTSB)
VCAM.........	Volunteer Committees of Art Museums (EA)
VCAMCUS....	Volunteer Committees of Art Museums of Canada and the United States (EA)
VC&GCA	Victoria Cross and George Cross Association (BUAC)
VC & GCAssn...	Victoria Cross and George Cross Association [British] (DBA)
VCAP.........	Vehicle Charging and Potential Experiment (NASA)
VCAP	Vincristine, Cyclophosphamide, Adriamycin, Prednisone [Antineoplastic drug regimen]
VCAP-I........	VP-16[Etoposide], Cyclophosphamide, Adriamycin, Platinol [Antineoplastic drug regimen] (DAVI)
V-CAP III....	VP-16-213 [Etoposide], Cyclophosphamide, Adriamycin, Platinol [Cisplatin] [Antineoplastic drug regimen]
VCAR	Vector Aeromotive [NASDAQ symbol] (TTSB)
VCAR	Vector Aeromotive Corp. [NASDAQ symbol] (NQ)
VCARE	Veterans Council for American Rights and Equality (EA)
VCARL	Vector Aeromotive Wrrt [NASDAQ symbol] (TTSB)
VCARW	Vector Aeromotive Wrrt [NASDAQ symbol] (TTSB)
VCAS	Vice-Chief of the Air Staff [British]
VCAS	Victorian Children's Aid Society [Australia]
VCASS	Visually Coupled Airborne Systems Simulator (IEEE)
VCAT	Veterinary College Admission Test (PGP)
VCB............	CBNU Learning Resources Center, Virginia Beach, VA [OCLC symbol] (OCLC)
VCB............	Construction Battalion [USNR classification]
VCB............	Vertical Location of the Center of Buoyancy
VCB............	Visual Control Board
VCBA.........	Variable Control Block Area [Computer science]
VCBFE........	Vauxhall College of Building and Further Education [London, England]
VCBI..........	Colombo/Katunayake [Sri Lanka] [ICAO location identifier] (ICLI)
V$_{CC}$...........	Collector-Voltage Supply (IDOE)
VCC...........	Vancouver Community College Library [UTLAS symbol]
VCC...........	Variable Ceramic Capacitor
VCC...........	Variable Characteristic Car (ADA)
VCC...........	Variable Command Count (MCD)
VCC...........	Variable Cycle Controller (IAA)
VCC...........	Vasoconstrictor Center [Physiology]
VCC...........	Vehicle Crew Chief [NASA] (KSC)
VCC...........	Verification Code Counter (MCD)
vcc...........	Verification Code Counter (NAKS)
VCC...........	Vermilion Community College, Ely, MN [OCLC symbol] (OCLC)
VCC...........	Versatile Corp. [Toronto Stock Exchange symbol]
VCC...........	Vertical Centering Control
VCC...........	Vertical Channel Computer (SAA)
VCC...........	Veteran Car Club of Great Britain (BI)
VCC...........	Vice-Chancellor's Courts (DLA)
VCC...........	Video Coaxial Connector
VCC...........	Video Compact Cassette [Video recorder] [Philips]
VCC...........	Vietcong Captured
VCC...........	Viet Cong Suspect Confirmed (VNW)
VCC...........	Virginia Community College System
VCC...........	Virtual Channel Connection [Computer science] (DDC)
VCC...........	Virtual Conference Center (PCM)
VCC...........	Viscous-Damped Converter Clutch [Automotive engineering]
VCC...........	Visual Communications Congress
VCC...........	Vogelback Computing Center [Northwestern University] [Research center] (RCD)
VCC...........	Voice Control Center [NASA] (KSC)
VCC...........	Voice-Controlled Carrier [Telecommunications] (IAA)
VCC...........	Voltage Coefficient of Capacitance
VCC...........	Voltage-Controlled Capacitor
VCC...........	Voltage-Controlled Clock (IAA)
VCC...........	Voluntary Census Committee (EA)
VCC...........	Volunteer Cadet Corps [British]
VCC...........	Volunteer Capital [NYSE symbol] (TTSB)
VCC...........	Volunteer Capital Corp. [NYSE symbol] (SPSG)
VCC...........	Volvo Concept Car [Automotive engineering]
VCC...........	Vuilleumier Cycle Cooler
VCCA	Anuradhapura [Sri Lanka] [ICAO location identifier] (ICLI)
VCCA	Victorian Credit Cooperative Association [Australia]
VCCA	Vintage Chevrolet Club of America (EA)
VCCB	Batticaloa [Sri Lanka] [ICAO location identifier] (ICLI)
VCCC	Colombo/Ratmalana [Sri Lanka] [ICAO location identifier] (ICLI)
VCCC	Vintage and Classic Car Club [Australia]
VCCC	Vuilleumier Cycle Cryogenic Cooler
VCCCM	Victorian Centre for the Conservation of Cultural Material [Australia]
VCCE	Victorian Council of Christian Education [Australia]
VCCFT........	Victorian Council for Children's Films and Television [Australia]
VCCG	Galoya/Amparai [Sri Lanka] [ICAO location identifier] (ICLI)
VCCI...........	Victorian Chamber of Commerce and Industry [Australia]
VCCJ..........	Jaffna/Kankesanturai [Sri Lanka] [ICAO location identifier] (ICLI)
VCCO	Voltage-Controlled Crystal Oscillator (IAA)
VCCR	Victorian Cervical Cytology Registry [Australia]
VCCR	Vienna Convention on Consular Relations (EERA)
VCCS	Video and Cable Communications Section of the ALA (NITA)
VCCS	Visually Coupled Control System (MCD)
VCCS	Voltage-Controlled Current Source [Electronics]
VCCT.........	Trincomalee/China Bay [Sri Lanka] [ICAO location identifier] (ICLI)
VCCUS.......	Venezuelan Chamber of Commerce of the United States
VCCW........	Wirawila [Sri Lanka] [ICAO location identifier] (ICLI)
VCD...........	Value City Department Stores [NYSE symbol] (SPSG)
VCD...........	Value City Dept Stores [NYSE symbol] (TTSB)
VCD...........	Vapor Compression Distillation
VCD...........	Variable-Capacitance Diode
VCD...........	Variable Center Distance [Computer science] (OA)
VCD...........	Verification Control Document (NASA)
VCD...........	Vernier Engine Cutoff [Aerospace]
VCD...........	Vibrational Circular Dichroism [Spectrometry]
VCD...........	Victoria Diego Resource Corp. [Vancouver Stock Exchange symbol]
VCD...........	Victoria River Downs [Australia Airport symbol]
VCD...........	Visiting Card (BJA)
VCD...........	Voltage Crossing Detector
VCDP.........	Victorian Council of Deaf People [Australia]
VCDRO.......	Voltage-Controlled Dielectric Resonator Oscillator (CIST)
VCDS	Vapor Compression Distillation Subsystem (NASA)
VCDS	Vice-Chief of Defence Staff [British]
VCDS(P & L)...	Vice Chief of Defence Staff Personnel and Logistics [British] (RDA)
VCE............	Vagina, Ectocervix, and Endocervix [Medicine] (DMAA)
VCE............	Vapor Cloud Explosion
VCE............	Vapor Compression Evaporation
VCE............	Variable Cycle Engine (MCD)
VCE............	Vehicle Condition Evaluation (MCD)
V$_{CE}$...........	Velocity of Contractile Element (DAVI)
VCE............	Venice [Italy] [Airport symbol] (OAG)
VCE............	Vertical Centrifugal
VCE............	Vice
VCE............	Vinyl Chloride Ethylene [Organic chemistry]
VCE............	Vinyl Chloride-Ethylene Copolymer (EDCT)
VCE............	Virtual Coulomb Excitation (PDAA)
VCE............	Voice (NASA)
VCEA.........	Victorian Congress of Employer Associations [Australia]
VCEL.........	Vanguard Cellular Systems, Inc. [NASDAQ symbol] (NQ)
VCELA.......	Vanguard Cellular Sys [NASDAQ symbol] (TTSB)
VCEMA.......	Vinyl Chloride Ethylene Methyl Acrylate [Organic chemistry]
VcePw	Voice Powered Tech International, Inc. [Associated Press] (SAG)
VC Eq........	Victoria Reports, Equity [A publication] (DLA)
VCEVA.......	Vinyl Chloride-Ethylene-Vinylacetate Copolymer (EDCT)
VCF...........	Vaginal Contraceptive Film [Medicine] (BARN)
VCF...........	Vapor Chamber Fin
VCF...........	Vapor Crystal Facility [Material processing center] (SSD)
VCF...........	Variable Crystal Filter (DEN)
Vcf...........	Velocity of Circumferential Fiber Shortening [Cardiology]
VCF...........	Venture Capital Fund [Finance]
VCF...........	Verified Circulation Figure [Advertising]
VCF...........	Victor Fly [Italy ICAO designator] (FAAC)
VCF...........	Victorian Cycling Federation [Australia]
VCF...........	Vietnam-Canada Foundation
VCF...........	Vincristine, Cyclophosphamide, Fluorouracil [Antineoplastic drug regimen]
VCF...........	Visual Comfort Factor
VCF...........	Voltage-Controlled Filter
VCF...........	Voltage-Controlled Frequency (IEEE)
VCF...........	Voyageur CO Ins Muni Income [AMEX symbol] (TTSB)
VCF...........	Voyageur Colorado Insured Municipal Income Fund [AMEX symbol] (SPSG)
VCF&L	[Department of] Conservation, Forests and Lands of Victoria [State] (EERA)
VCFC.........	Vik Chandler Fan Club (EA)
VCFGH.......	Victorian Council on Fitness and General Health [Australia]
VCFL.........	Victorian Country Football League [Australia]
VCFUSA.....	Vietnamese Catholic Federation in the USA (EA)
VCG	Calcutta Volunteer Guards [British military] (DMA)
VCG	Vapor Crystal Growth [Materials processing]
VCG	Vectorcardiogram [Medicine]
VCG	Vehicle Control Group
VCG	Verification Condition Generator
VCG	Vertical Line Through Center of Gravity (IAA)
VCG	Vertical Location of the Center of Gravity
VCG	Vice-Consul General [British] (ROG)
VCG	Video Command Generator (MCD)
VCG	Voltage-Controlled Generator
VCGEN.......	Verification Condition Generator (MHDB)
VCGS	Vapor Crystal Growth System [Materials processing]
VCGS	Vice Chief of the General Staff [in the field] [Military British] (RDA)
VCGS	Victorian Clinical Genetics Services [Australia]
VCH	Veterinary Convalescent Hospital
VCH	Vichadero [Uruguay] [Airport symbol Obsolete] (OAG)
VCH	Victoria County History [Classical studies] (OCD)
VCH	Video Concert Hall
VCH	Vinylcyclohexene [Organic chemistry]
VCHO	Vicar Choral
VCHP	Variable Conductance Heat Pipe
v-chr.........	Vice-Chair of the Board (DD)
VCI............	Valassis Communcations [NYSE symbol] (TTSB)
VCI............	Valassis Communications, Inc. [NYSE symbol] (SPSG)
VCI............	Variety Clubs International (EA)
VCI............	Vegetation Condition Index [for detecting and tracking droughts] [National Oceanic and Atmospheric Administration]
VCI............	Vehicle Cone Index [Engineering] (OA)

VCI	Velocity Change Indicator (NASA)
vci	Velocity Change Indicator (NAKS)
VCI	Vibration Control Index
VCI	Videtics International Corp. [Vancouver Stock Exchange symbol]
VCI	Vietcong Infrastructure
VCI	Virtual Channel Identifier [Computer science] (DDC)
VCI	Virtual Circuit Identifier [Computer science]
VCI	Visual Comfort Index
VCI	Volatile Corrosion Inhibitor [See also VPI] [Metallurgy]
VCID	Very Close in Defense
VCIGS	Vice-Chief of the Imperial General Staff [British]
VCIM	Varnished Cambric Insulation Material
VCINS	Vietcong Infrastructure Neutralization System
VCIP	Veterans Cost-of-Instruction Program [Higher Education Act]
VCIR	Visual Communication and Image Representation [Computer science]
VCIS	Voluntary Cooperative Information System [American Public Welfare Association] (EGAO)
V-CITE	Vertical-Cargo Integration Test Equipment [NASA] (MCD)
VCJCS	Vice Chairman, Joint Chiefs of Staff (DOMA)
VCJD	Variant of Creutzfeldt-Jakob Disease [Medicine]
VC-K	Eli Lilly & Co. [Research code symbol] [Canada]
VCK	Video Camera Kit
VCK	Vietcong Killed
VC KIA(BC)	Vietcong Killed in Action (Body Count)
VC KIA(POSS)	Vietcong Killed in Action (Possible)
VCKV	Vacuum Control Check Valve [Automotive engineering]
VCL	Vehicle Checkout Laboratory
VCL	Vertical Center Line
VCL	Violincello [Music]
VCL	Virtual Channel Link [Computer science] (DDC)
VCL	Visual Component Library [Computer science]
VCL	Voice Communications Laboratory
VCL	Voluntary College Letter [British]
VCLE	Versicle
VCLF	Vertical Cask-Lifting Fixture [Nuclear energy] (NRCH)
VCLK	Video Clock [Computer science]
VCLLO	Violoncello [Music]
VCLO	Voltage-Controlled Local Oscillator
VCM	Vacuum (AAG)
VCM	Vacuum Condensible Material [Astronomy] (OA)
VCM	Vehicle Condition Monitor [Automotive engineering]
VCM	Vehicle Control Module [Automotive engineering]
VCM	Ventilation Control Module [NASA]
VCM	Veracruz [Mexico] [Seismograph station code, US Geological Survey] (SEIS)
VCM	Vertical Current Meter
VCM	Vertical Cutter Motion
VCM	Vibrating Coil Magnetometer
VCM	Vibration Conditioning Monitoring (ACII)
VCM	Victoria College of Music [London] (ROG)
VCM	Victorian Chamber of Mines [Australia]
VCM	Viking Continuation Mission [NASA]
VCM	Vinyl Chloride Monomer [Organic chemistry]
VCM	Virtual Circuit [Call] Manager (TNIG)
VCM	Visual Countermeasure
VCM	Volatile Combustible Material
VCM	Volatile Condensable Material
vcm	Volatile Condensable Material (NAKS)
VCM	Voltage-Controlled Multivibrator
VCM	Voorhees College, Denmark, SC [OCLC symbol] (OCLC)
VCMA	Vacuum Cleaner Manufacturers Association (EA)
VCMA	Vinyl Chloride Methyl Acrylate [Organic chemistry]
VCMA	Vinyl Chloride-Methyl Acrylate Copolymer (EDCT)
VCmax	Maximum Viscous Response [Medicine]
VCMMA	Vinyl Chloride-Methylmethacrylate Copolymer (EDCT)
VCMP	Vincristine, Cyclophosphamide, Melphalan, Prednisone [Antineoplastic drug regimen]
VCMR	Victorian Council for the Mentally Retarded [Australia]
VCMS	Vehicle Cost Management System (NITA)
VCN	Avcon, Aviation Consulting Ltd. [Switzerland] [FAA designator] (FAAC)
VCN	Christopher Newport College, Newport News, VA [OCLC symbol] (OCLC)
VCN	Millville, NJ [Location identifier FAA] (FAAL)
VCN	New Communist Party of the Netherlands [Political party] (BUAC)
VCN	Vancomycin-Colistin-Nystatin [Growth-inhibiting mixture] [Microbiology]
VCN	Vancomycin Hydrochloride, Colistimethate Sodium, Nystatin, [Medium] [Microbiology] (DAVI)
VCN	Vendor Contract Notice
VCN	Verification Completion Notice (NASA)
VCN	Vibrio cholerae Neuraminidase [An enzyme]
VCN	Vinyl Cyanide [Organic chemistry]
VCN	Visual Communications Network, Inc. [Cambridge, MA]
VCN	Vulcan Resources [Vancouver Stock Exchange symbol]
VCNA	VTAM Communications Network Application (NITA)
VCNB	Ventura Cnty Natl Bancorp [NASDAQ symbol] (TTSB)
VCNB	Ventura County National Bancorp [NASDAQ symbol] (SAG)
VCNC	Voltage-Controlled Negative Capacitance (IAA)
VCNM	Vice Chief of Naval Material Command
VCNO	Vice Chief of Naval Operations
VCNR	Voltage-Controlled Negative Resistance (IAA)
VCNS	Vice-Chief of the Naval Staff [British]
VCNTY	Vicinity (AFM)
VC/NVA	Vietcong/North Vietnamese Army
VCO	Aviacion Colombiana Ltd. [Colombia] [ICAO designator] (FAAC)
V_{co}	Carbon Monoxide [Endogenous production] [Medicine] (DAVI)
VCO	Glendale, AZ [Location identifier FAA] (FAAL)
VCO	Variable Crystal Oscillator (IAA)
VCO	Variable Cycle Operation
VCO	Vehicle Control Officer [Air Force] (AFM)
VCO	Verbal Concrete Object
VCO	Verbit & Co., Consultants to Management [Bala Cynwyd, PA] [Telecommunications] (TSSD)
VCO	Vertical Control Operator [Military]
VCO	Viceroy's Commissioned Officer [British military] (DMA)
VCO	Victorian College of Optometry [Australia]
VCO	Vina Concha y Toro ADS [NYSE symbol] (TTSB)
VCO	Vina Concha y Toro SA [NYSE symbol] (SAG)
VCO	Voice Carry-Over [Hearing-impaired technolgoy]
VCO	Voice Coder [Telecommunications] (IAA)
VCO	Voice Controlled Oscillator [Telecommunications] (TEL)
VCO	Voltage-Controlled Oscillator
vco	Voltage Controlled Oscillator (NAKS)
VCO	Voluntary Conservation Organisation (EERA)
VCO	Volunteer Conservation Officers
VCO_2	Carbon Dioxide Production [Medicine] (DAVI)
VCOA	Vinyl Chloride-Octyl Acrylate (EDCT)
VCOA	Volkswagen Convertible Owners of America [Defunct] (EA)
VCoA	Volvo Club of America (EA)
VCOAD	Voluntary Committee on Overseas Aid and Development (BUAC)
VCOD	Vertical Carrier Onboard Delivery
VC of A	Vizsla Club of America (EA)
VCOFGWBS	Vietnamese Cross of Gallantry with Bronze Star [Military decoration] (AABC)
VCOFGWGS	Vietnamese Cross of Gallantry with Gold Star [Military decoration] (AABC)
VCOFGWP	Vietnamese Cross of Gallantry with Palm [Military decoration] (AABC)
VCOFGWSS	Vietnamese Cross of Gallantry with Silver Star [Military decoration] (AABC)
VC of S	Vice Chief of Staff
VC of SA	Vice Chief of Staff, Army [Later, VCSA] (AABC)
VCOI	Veterans Cost-of-Instruction
VCOM	VitalCom Inc. [NASDAQ symbol] (TTSB)
V Conv R	Victorian Conveyancing Cases [Australia A publication]
VCOP	Variable Control Oil Pressure (MSA)
VCOS	Vehicle Control and Operating System [Army]
VCOS	Vice-Chiefs of Staff [British]
VCOS	Visible Caching Operating System [AT & T]
VCOT	Virtual Community of Tomorrow [Internet resource] [Computer science]
VCOV	Volunteer Consultant for Office of Volunteers [Red Cross]
VCP	Sao Paulo [Brazil] Viracopos Airport [Airport symbol] (OAG)
VCP	Vacuum Condensing Point (IAA)
vcp	Vacuumm Condensing Point (EDCT)
VCP	Valosin-Containing Protein [Biochemistry]
VCP	Vandenberg Contract Report (NAKS)
VCP	Variable Cam Phaser [Automotive engineering]
VCP	Variable Cam Phasing [Automotive engineering]
VCP	Vector Collecting Program [Electronics design] (IAA)
VCP	Vector Correction Program (SAA)
VCP	Vehicle Check Point [Military]
VCP	Vehicle Collecting Point
VCP	Velocity Control Programmer
VCP	VERDAN [Versatile Differential Analyzer] Checkout Panel
VCP	Veterinary Collecting Post [British military] (DMA)
VCP	Veterinary Creolin-Pearson
VCP	Victorian Centre for Photography [Australia]
VCP	Video Cassette Player
VCP	Vincristine, Cyclophosphamide, Prednisone [Antineoplastic drug regimen]
VCP	Virtual Channel Processor [Computer science]
VCP	Virtual Communication Path [Computer science] (IAA)
VCP	Virtual Control Panel (NITA)
VCP	Virtual Control Processor [Computer science] (IAA)
VCP	Virtual Counterpoise Procedure [Physical chemistry]
VCP	Virus Cancer Program [National Cancer Institute]
VCP	Visual Comfort Probability (IAA)
VCP	Vitrified Clay Pipe (COE)
VCP	Voice Communication Panel
VCP	Voltage-Controlled Potentiometer (CIST)
VCP	Voluntary Cooperation Program [World Meteorological Organization] [United Nations]
VCP	Votorantim Celulose e Papel [Brazil]
VCP-1	[Cisplatin] VP-16[Etoposide], Cycophosamide, Platinol [Cisplatin] [Antineoplastic drug regimen] (DAVI)
VCPA	Victorian Country Press Association [Australia]
VCPA	Vintage & Classic Power Craft Association (BUAC)
VCPA	Virginia-Carolina Peanut Association (EA)
VCPA	Virginia Crab Packers Association [Defunct] (EA)
VCPI	Virtual Control Program Interface [Computer science] (PCM)
VCPLA	Veterinary College of the People's Liberation Army of China (BUAC)
VCPM	Video-Enhanced Contrast Polarization Microscopy
VCPOR	Vanguardia Comunista del Partido Obrero Revolucionario [Bolivia] [Political party] (PPW)
VCPP	Virginia-Carolina Peanut Promotions [An association] (EA)
VCPS	Velocity Control Propulsion Subsystem [NASA]
VCPS	Video Copyright Protection Society [British]
VC PW	Vietcong Prisoner of War

VCR	Aviacor [*Former USSR*] [*FAA designator*] (FAAC)
VCR	Go-Video [*AMEX symbol*] (TTSB)
VCR	Go-Video, Inc. [*AMEX symbol*] (SPSG)
VCR	Vacuum Contact Relay
VCR	Valclair Resources Ltd. [*Vancouver Stock Exchange symbol*]
VCR	Valuation by Components Rule (ADA)
Vcr	Vancouver [*Canada*] (BARN)
VCR	Variable Compression Ratio
VCR	Vasoconstrictive [*Physiology*]
VCR	Vertical Crater Retreat [*Mining technology*]
VCR	Video Cartridge Recorder (IAA)
VCR	Video Cassette Recorder
VCR	Vincristine [*Also, LCR, O, V, VC*] [*Antineoplastic drug*]
VCR	Visual Control Room
VCR	Viva Cristo Rey [*Long Live Christ the King*] [*Spanish*]
VCR	Vocal Character Recognition
VCR	Voltage Coefficient of Resistance
VCR	Voltage Control Resistor (IAA)
VCR	Volume-Concentration Ratio (DB)
VCR	Voluntary Content Rating System [*Solid Oak software*] [*Computer science*] (PCM)
VCRA	Veterans Cycle Racing Association [*British*] (DBA)
VCRAS	Office of Vice Chancellor for Research and Advanced Study [*University of Alaska*] [*Research center*] (RCD)
VCRC	Vector Control Research Centre [*India*]
VCRC	Voice Circuit Reconfiguration Confirmation (SSD)
VC Rep	Vice-Chancellor's Reports [*English, Canadian*] [*A publication*] (DLA)
VCRI	Verification Cross Reference Index
VCRO	Validity Check and Readout (NITA)
VCRT	Variable Contrast Resolution Test [*Optics*]
VCR.WS	Go-Video Wrrts [*AMEX symbol*] (TTSB)
VCS	Cruiser-Scouting Aircraft Squadron [*Navy symbol*]
VCS	Vacuum Actuated Control Switch (IAA)
VCS	Vacuum Control Switch
VCS	Validation Control System
VCS	Vane Control System (MCD)
VCS	Vapor Coating System
VCS	Vapor Cooling System
VCS	Variable Correlation Synchronization
VCS	Vasoconstrictor Substance [*Physiology*]
VCS	Vehicular Communications System
VCS	Velocity Cutoff System (KSC)
VCS	Vent Collection System [*Engineering*]
VCS	Ventilation Control System [*NASA*] (KSC)
VCS	Ventricular Conduction System [*Cardiology*] (CPH)
VCS	Verbal Communication Scales [*Educational testing*]
VCS	Verification Control Sheet (NASA)
vcs	Verification Control Sheet (NAKS)
VCS	Vernier Control System
VCS	Version Control System [*Computer science*]
VCS	Veterans Canteen Service [*Veterans Administration*]
VCS	Veterinary Cancer Society (EA)
VCS	Vice Chief of Staff
VCS	Victorian Computer Society (IAA)
VCS	Video Cassette System
VCS	Video Clutter Suppression (CAAL)
VCS	Video Communications System
VCS	Video Compression Sampler [*Computer science*]
VCS	Video Computer System [*Atari, Inc.*]
VCS	Video Contrast Seeker
VCS	Vietcong Suspect
VCS	View Control System (HGAA)
VCS	Viking Change Status [*NASA*]
VCS	Virginia & Carolina Southern R. R. [*AAR code*]
VCS	Visual Call Sign [*Communications*]
VCS	Visual Channel Selection [*Computer science*]
VCS	Visually Coupled System (IEEE)
VCS	Vocabulary Comprehension Scale [*Educational test*]
VC's	Vocal Chords [*Musical slang*]
VCS	Voice Command System [*Ground Communications Facility, NASA*]
vcs	Voice Command System (NAKS)
VCS	Voice Communication System
VCS	Voice Control Switch [*NASA*]
VCS	Voltage Calibration Set
VCS	Voltage-Current-Sequence (MCD)
VCS	Voluntary and Christian Service (BUAC)
VCSA	Vice Chief of Staff, Army [*Formerly, VC of SA*]
VCSA	Victorian Catholic Schools Association [*Australia*]
VCSA	Victorian Council for Sustainable Agriculture [*Australia*]
VCSA	Vintage and Classic Sailing Association [*British*] (DBA)
VCSA	Viral Cell Surface Antigen [*Medicine*] (DMAA)
VC/SAF	Vice Chief of Staff, Air Force
VCSCT	Vacuum Control Switch - Cold Temperature [*Automotive engineering*]
VCSDI	Vacuum Control Switch - Deceleration Idle [*Automotive engineering*]
VCSEA	Victorian Community Services Employers' Association [*Australia*]
VCSEL	Vertical-Cavity Surface Emitting LASER
VCSF	Ventricular Cerebrospinal Fluid [*Medicine*] (STED)
VCSFO	Veterans Canteen Service Field Office [*Veterans Administration*]
VCSI	Voice Control Systems [*NASDAQ symbol*] (TTSB)
VCSL	Voice Call Signs List
VCSO	Vice Chief of Staff [*Army*] (AAGC)
VCSP	Voice Call Signs Plan
VCSR	Voltage-Controlled Shift Register
VCSS	Value Creation Study Society (CINC)
VCSS	Victorian Council of Social Service [*Australia*]

VCSS	Voice Communications Security System
VCT	St. Vincent and the Grenadines [*ANSI three-letter standard code*] (CNC)
VCT	Variable Cycle Technology
VCT	Venous Clotting Time [*Clinical chemistry*]
VCT	Victims of Crime Trust [*British*] (WDAA)
VCT	Victor (WGA)
VCT	Victoria [*Texas*] [*Airport symbol*] (OAG)
VCT	Victorian Conservation Trust [*Australia*]
VCT	Video Contrast Tracker (PDAA)
VCT	Vidicon Camera Tube
VCT	Vintage Carriages Trust [*British*] (DBA)
VCT	Vinyl Composition Tile
VCT	Viscount Air Services, Inc. [*ICAO designator*] (FAAC)
VCT	Vitrified Clay Tile [*Technical drawings*]
VCT	Voice Code Translation (BUR)
VCT	Voltage Clock Trigger (IAA)
VCT	Voltage-Controlled Transfer (IAA)
VCT	Voltage-Controlled Twist [*Of liquid crystals*]
VCT	Voltage Control Transfer
VCT	Voltage Curve Tracer
VCT	Volume Control Tank [*Nuclear energy*] (NRCH)
VctA	Vector Aeromotive Corp. [*Associated Press*] (SAG)
VCTA	Victorian Commercial Teachers Association [*Australia*] (BUAC)
VCTA	Victorian Commercial Travellers' Association [*Australia*]
VctAer.........	Vector Aeromotive Corp. [*Associated Press*] (SAG)
VctAr..........	Vector Aeromotive Corp. [*Associated Press*] (SAG)
VCTCA	Virtual Channel to Channel Adapter
VCTD	Vendor Contract Technical Data
VCTR	Vector (NASA)
VCTR	VECTRA Technologies [*NASDAQ symbol*] (SPSG)
VCTRY	Victory
VCTS	Vacuum Control Temperature Switch [*Automotive engineering*]
VCTS	Variable Cockpit Training System (MCD)
VCTV	Viewer-Controlled Cable Television [*AT&T*] (CIST)
VCTV	Viewer Controlled Television (WDMC)
VCTY	Vicinity (NVT)
VCU	Variable Correction Unit (IAA)
VCU	Very Close-Up [*Cinematography*] (NTCM)
VCU	Video Combiner Unit (IAA)
VCU	Video Control Unit (MCD)
vcu	Video Control Unit (NAKS)
VCU	Videocystourethrography [*Medicine*]
VCU	Virginia Commonwealth University
VCU	Viscous Coupling Unit [*Automotive engineering*]
VCU	Voiding Cystourethrogram [*Medicine*]
VCU	Voltage Control Unit
VCUG	Vesicoureterogram [*Urology*]
VCUG	Voiding Cystourethrogram [*Medicine*]
VCV	Clinch Valley College of the University of Virginia, Wise, VA [*OCLC symbol*] (OCLC)
VCV	Vacuum Check Valve
VCV	Vacuum Control Valve [*Automotive engineering*]
VCV	Van Kam Am Cap CA Val Mun [*NYSE symbol*] (TTSD)
VCV	Van Kampen Merritt California Value Municipal Trust [*NYSE symbol*] (SPSG)
VCV	Variable Compression Vector (MHDI)
VCV	Vicia Cryptic Virus [*Plant pathology*]
VCV	Victorville, CA [*Location identifier FAA*] (FAAL)
VCV	Vietnam Combat Veterans (EA)
VCV	Vowel-Consonant-Vowel (STED)
VCVAC	Vinyl Chloride Vinyl Acetate [*Organic chemistry*]
VCVAC	Vinyl Chloride-Vinyl Acetate Copolymer (EDCT)
VCVDC	Vinyl Chloride Vinylidene Chloride [*Organic chemistry*]
VCVS	Vehicle Component Verification System [*Automotive engineering*]
VCVS	Voltage-Controlled Voltage Source
VCW	Victoria West [*South Africa*] [*Airport symbol*] (AD)
VCXO	Voltage-Controlled Crystal Oscillator
VCY	Valley City, ND [*Location identifier FAA*] (FAAL)
VCY	Ventura County Railway Co. [*Army*]
VCY	Vicinity [*Aviation*] (FAAC)
VCz	Vapor-Pressure-Controlled Czochralski (AAEL)
VCZ	Vinylcarbazole [*Organic chemistry*]
VD	Double Vibrations [*Cycles*]
V_D	Drain Voltage (IDOE)
VD	Leo Pharm. Products [*Denmark*] [*Research code symbol*]
VD	Photographic Squadron [*Navy symbol*]
VD	RTZ Services Ltd. [*British ICAO designator*] (ICDA)
VD	Vacuum Distillation (PDAA)
VD	Valuation Decisions [*A publication*] (DLA)
VD	Vandyke [*Graphics*]
VD	Vapor Density
vd	Various Date (WDAA)
vd	Various Dates (WDMC)
VD	Various Dates [*Bibliography*]
VD	Vascular Disease [*Cardiology*] (DAVI)
VD	Vasodilation [*Cardiology*] (DAVI)
VD	Vasodilator [*Cardiology*] (DAVI)
VD	Vault Door (AAG)
VD	Venereal Disease
VD	Ventilating Deadlight [*Technical drawings*]
VD	Ventricular Dilator [*Neuron*] [*Medicine*]
VD	Verbal Discrimination [*Psychology*]
VD	Verbum Domini [*Home*] [*A publication*] (BJA)
VD	Vertical Deviation (DAVI)

VD	Vertical Drive
VD	Vessel Disease [Medicine] (DB)
VD	Viceroy-Designate [British]
VD	Victoria Docks [British] (ROG)
VD	Victorian Decoration [British]
VD	Video Decoder
VD	Video Disk (BUR)
VD	Video Display (IAA)
VD	Violent Defectives [British]
VD	Viral Diarrhea [Medicine] (DMAA)
VD	Virtual Data
VD	Visiting Dignitary
V/D	Voice/Data (BUR)
VD	Void (AAG)
VD	Void [Urology] (DAVI)
VD	Voided [Medicine] (STED)
VD	Voltage Detector
VD	Voltage Drop (MSA)
Vd	Volume Dead Air Space (MAE)
VD	Volume Deleted [Finance]
VD	Volume Discount [Investment term]
VD	Volume of Distribution
VD	Volunteer Decoration [British]
V_DA	Alveolar Dead-space Volume [Medicine] (DAVI)
VDA	Valve Drive Amplifier
VDA	Valve Driver Assembly (NASA)
VDA	Variable Data Area (NASA)
VDA	Variable Depth ASDIC (NATG)
VDA	Vehicle Dynamics Area
VDA	Velocity Dealiasing Algorithm [Marine science] (OSRA)
VDA	Vendor Data Article
VDA	Venous Digital Angiogram [Cardiology] (DAVI)
V_DA	Ventilation of the Alveolar Dead-space [Medicine] (DAVI)
VDA	Verbal Delay Announcement (NITA)
VDA	Versatile Drone Autopilot (MCD)
VDA	Vertical Danger Angle [Navigation]
VDA	Victorian Docklands Authority [Australia]
VDA	Video Dimension Analysis [Sports medicine]
VDA	Video Distribution Amplifier
VDA	Viola d'Amore [Music]
VDA	Vision Distribution Amplifier (IAA)
VDA	Visual Data Analysis
VDA	Visual Discriminatory Acuity
VDA	Volga-Dnepr [Former USSR ICAO designator] (FAAC)
VDA	Volksbund fuer das Deutschtum im Ausland [NAZI Germany]
VDAC	Vaginal Delivery after Caesarean [Obstetrics]
VDAC	Vendor Data Article Control
VDAC	Video Display Controller (IAA)
VDAC	Voltage-Dependent, Anion-Selective Channels [In the membrane of a mitochondrion]
VDA/D	Video Display Adapter with Digital Enhancement [AT & T]
VDAM	Virtual Data Access Method (IEEE)
$V_D$an	Ventilation per Minute of the Anatomic Dead-space [Medicine] (DAVI)
$V_D$an	Volume of the Anatomic Dead-space [Medicine] (DAVI)
VDANL	Vehicle Dynamics Analysis [Computer simulation] [Automotive engineering]
VDAS	Vehicle Data and Acquisition System [Automotive engineering]
VDAS	Vibration Data Acquisition System (KSC)
VDAS	Video Data Acquisition System
VDAS	Voltage-Dependent, Anion-Selective [Proteins] [Biochemistry]
VDB	Brooklyn College, Brooklyn, NY [OCLC symbol] (OCLC)
VdB	Van Den Bergh [Liver function test]
VDB	Vector Data Buffer
VDB	Vehicle Data Bus [Automotive engineering]
VDB	Very Dear Brother [Freemasonry]
VDB	Victor D. Brenner [Designer's mark, when appearing on US coins]
VDB	Video Display Board
VDB	Vrijzinnige-Democratische Bond [Radical Democratic League] [Netherlands Political party] (PPE)
VDBG	Battambang [Cambodia] [ICAO location identifier] (ICLI)
VDBR	Volume of Distribution of Bilirubin [Medicine] (MAE)
VDBS	Vanguard Discount Brokerage Services [Finance]
VDC	DC [Direct Current] Voltage (ACII)
VDC	Vanadocene Dichloride [Antineoplastic drug]
VDC	Van Dorn (EFIS)
VDC	Variable Diode Circuit
VDC	Variable Displacement Compressor [Automotive engineering]
VDC	Vasodilator Center [Physiology]
VDC	VDC Communications [Formerly, VDC Corp.] [AMEX symbol]
VDC	VDC Corp. Ltd. [Associated Press] (SAG)
VDC	Vendor Data Control (MCD)
VDC	Ventilation Duct Chase [Nuclear energy] (NRCH)
VDC	Venture Development Corp. [Natick, MA] [Telecommunications] (TSSD)
VDC	Verbum Dei Community (TOCD)
VDC	Video Data Controller (NITA)
VDC	Video Display Controller [Computer science] (MHDI)
VDC	Video Display Corp. (EFIS)
VDC	Video-Documentary Clearinghouse (EA)
VDC	Vietnam Day Committee [Antiwar group] (VNW)
VDC	Vinylidene Dichloride (EDCT)
VDC	Vocational Development Checklist (EDAC)
VDC	Voltage-Direct Current (NITA)
VDC	Voltage Doubler Circuit
VDC	Voltage to Digital Converter

V_{dc}	Volts DC (IDOE)
V_{dc}	Volts DC (IDOE)
VDC	Volts Direct Current
VDC	Volunteer Defense Corps
VDC	Volunteer Development Corps (EA)
VDCC	Voltage-Dependent Calcium Channel [Neurobiology]
VDCE	[Department of] Conservation and Environment, Victoria [State] (EERA)
VDCE	Victorian Department of Conservation and Environment [Australia]
VDCLF	VDC Corp. [NASDAQ symbol] (TTSB)
VDCLF	VDC Corp. Ltd. [NASDAQ symbol] (SAG)
VDCP	Video Data Collection Program
VDCT	Direct-Current Test Volts
VDCT	Viaduct [Commonly used] (OPSA)
VDCU	Videograph Display Control Unit
VDCW	Direct-Current Working Volts
VDD	Verification Description Document (NASA)
VDD	Version Description Document (KSC)
VDD	Video Detector Diode
VDD	Virtual Display Driver [Computer science]
VDD	Visual Display Data
VDD	Voice Digital Display
VDDI	Voyager Data Detailed Index [NASA] (KSC)
VDDL	Virtual Data Description Language [Computer science] (MHDB)
VDDL	Voyager Data Distribution List [NASA] (KSC)
VDDP	Video Digital Data Processing
VDDR	Vitamin D-Dependent Rickets [Medicine]
VDDS	Voice/Document Delivery System [Computer science]
VDDS	Voyager Data Description Standards [NASA] (KSC)
VDE	Vacuum Deposition Equipment
VDE	Valverde [Canary Islands] [Airport symbol] (OAG)
VDE	Variable Displacement Engine
VDE	Variable Display Equipment
VDE	Verband Deutscher Elektrotechniker [Association of German Electrical Engineers] (EG)
VDE	Video Display Editor [Computer science] (CDE)
VDE	Visual Development Environment [Computer science] (PCM)
VDE	Voice Data Entry (NITA)
VDECS	Vehicle Detector and Cueing System
V DEF	Verb Defective [Grammer] (WDAA)
VDEF	Vie de France [NASDAQ symbol] (TTSB)
VDEF	Vie de France Corp. [McLean, VA] [NASDAQ symbol] (NQ)
VDEh	Verein Deutscher Eisenhuttenleute [German Iron and Steel Engineers Association] (IID)
VDEL	Variable Delivery
VDEL	Venereal Disease Experimental Laboratory
VDEM	Vasodepressor Material [Physiology] (MAE)
V DEP	Verb Deponent [Grammer] (WDAA)
VDEQ	Virginia Department of Environmental Quality (DOGT)
VDES	Voice Data Encoding System [Telecommunications] (IAA)
VDET	Voltage Detector (IEEE)
VDETS	Voice Data Entry Terminal System
VDEV	"V" Device [Military decoration] (AABC)
VDF	Ventricular Diastolic Fragmentation [Medicine] (DMAA)
VDF	Very-High-Frequency Direction-Finding
VDF	Vibration Damping Fastener
VDF	Video Frequency
VDF	Vinylidene Fluoride [Organic chemistry]
VDF	Voice Data Fax [Telecommunications]
VDF	Volunteer Defence Force [St. Christopher and Nevis] (BUAC)
VDFB	Victorian Dried Fruits Board [Australia]
VDFG	Variable Diode Function Generator
VDFM	Virtual Disk File Manager [Computer science] (CIST)
VDFP	Village Development Fund Project [Mali] (BUAC)
VDG	Royal Inniskilling Dragoon Guards [Military unit] [British]
VDG	Vehicle Data Guide
VDG	Venereal Disease Gonorrhea
VDG	Vertical and Direction Gyro
VDG	Vertical Display Generator (NG)
VDG	Video Data Generator (NITA)
VDG	Video Display Generator
vdg	Voiding (MAE)
VdgB	Vereinigung der Gegenseitigen Bauernhilfe [Mutual Farmers' Aid Society] [Germany]
VDGI	Vietnamese Government Information Department (VNW)
VdGS	Viola da Gamba Society [British] (DBA)
VDGS	Visual Docking Guidance System [Aviation] (DA)
VdGSA	Viola da Gamba Society of America (EA)
VDH	Valvular Disease of the Heart [Medicine]
VDH	Van Der Hout Associates Ltd. [Toronto Stock Exchange symbol]
VDH	Variable Length Divide or Halt (SAA)
VDH	Vickers Diamond Hardness (IAA)
VDI	Variable Duration Impulse (IAA)
VDI	Vat Dye Institute [Later, American Dye Manufacturers Institute] (EA)
VDI	Vegetation Drought Index [Agriculture] (WDAA)
VDI	Vendor Documentation Inventory (NASA)
VDI	Verein Deutscher Ingenieure [Society of German Engineers]
VDI	Vertical Direction Indicator (CAAL)
VDI	Vertical Display Indicator (NG)
VDI	Vidalia, GA [Location identifier FAA] (FAAL)
VDI	Video Data Interrogator (SAA)
VDI	Video Device Interface [Computer science] (PCM)
VDI	Video Display Input
VDI	Video Display Interface
VDI	Virtual Device Interface [Computer technology]

VDI	Visual Display Input
VDI	Visual Doppler Indicator (IAA)
VDI	Vocational Development Inventory (EDAC)
VDI	Voluntary Data Inquiry
VDICAPP	Verein Deutscher Ingenieure-Commission on Air Pollution Prevention (EAIO)
VDIEO	Vendor Data Information Engineering Order (MCD)
VDIF	Video Display Information File (PCM)
VDIFF	Visual Difference [Computer science] (NHD)
VDIG	Vertical Display Indicator Group
VDIKRL	Verein Deutscher Ingenieure-Kommission Reinhaltung der Luft [VDI - Commis sion on Air Pollution Prevention] (EAIO)
VDI-N	VDI-Nachrichten [VDI-Verlag GmbH] [Database]
V disc	Victory Disc [Music] (WDMC)
VDISK	Virtual Disk [Computer science]
VDJ	Variable-Diversity-Joining [Genetics]
VDK	Vicinal Diketone [Organic chemistry]
VDKC	Kompong Cham [Cambodia] [ICAO location identifier] (ICLI)
VDKH	Kompong Chnang [Cambodia] [ICAO location identifier] (ICLI)
VDKT	Kratie [Cambodia] [ICAO location identifier] (ICLI)
VDL	Van Diemen's Land [Former name of Tasmania]
VDL	Variable Delay Line
VDL	Vasodepressor Lipid [Physiology]
VDL	Ventilating Deadlight
VDL	VHF Digital Link [FAA] (TAG)
VDL	Video Data Link (NVT)
VDL	Vienna Definition Language [1960] [Computer science] (CSR)
VDL	Visual Detection Level (MAE)
VDL	Voice Direct Line
VDLF	Variable Depth Launch Facility (AAG)
VDLIB	Virtual Disk Library [Computer science] (MHDI)
VDM	Variable Direction Microphone
VDM	Varian Data Machines
VDM	Vasodepressor Material [Physiology]
VDM	Vector Dominance Model [Physics]
VDM	Vector Drawn Map
VDM	Vehicle Deadlined for Maintenance (AFM)
VDM	Verbi Dei Minister [Minister, or Preacher, of the Word of God] [Latin]
VDM	Vibration Damping Mount
VDM	Video Delta Modulation
VDM	Viedma [Argentina] [Airport symbol] (OAG)
VDM	Vienna Development Method [Computer science]
VDM	Virtual Device Metafile [Computer technology] (DGA)
VDM	Virtual Dipole Moment [Geodesy]
VDM	Virtual DOS [Disk Operating System] Machine [Computer science] (PCM)
VDM	Visual Display Module (EECA)
V$_{DM}$	Volume of Mechanical Dead Space [Medicine] (DAVI)
VDME	Vibrating Dropping Mercury Electrode [Electrochemistry]
VDMID	Victorian Department of Manufacturing and Industry Development [Australia]
VDMIE	Verbum Domini Manet in Eternum [The Word of the Lord Endureth Forever] [Latin]
VDMK	Democratic Community of Vojvodina Hungarians [Former Yugoslavia] [Political party]
VDMO	Vinyl (dimethyl) Oxazolinone [Organic chemistry]
VDMOS	Vertical Double Diffused Metal Oxide Semiconductor (MCD)
VDMS	Video Delta Modulation System
VDMS	Vocal Data Management System
VDMSC	Volunteer Durham Medical Staff Corps [British military] (DMA)
VDN	Varudeklarationsnamnden [Labeling system] [Sweden]
VDN	Vedron Ltd. [Toronto Stock Exchange symbol]
VdN	Voix des Notres [Record label] [France]
VDNCOA	Veterans Division of the Non-Commissioned Officers Association of the USA (EA)
VDNCS	Vapor-Deposited Noncrystalline Solid (PDAA)
VDNH	VD [Venereal Disease] National Hotline [Later, NSTDH] (EA)
VDNX	Videonics, Inc. [NASDAQ symbol] (SAG)
VDO	Red Air, SA [Belgium] [FAA designator] (FAAC)
VDO	Vadso [Norway] [Airport symbol] (AD)
VDO	Videotron Groupe Ltee. SV [Toronto Stock Exchange symbol]
VDOP	Vertical Dilution of Precision
VD/OS	Vacuum Distillation/Overflow Sampler [Nuclear energy] (NRCH)
VDOS	Vibrational Density of States [Physics]
VDP	Vacuum Diffusion Pump
VDP	Valle de la Pascua [Venezuela] [Airport symbol] (AD)
VDP	Van der Pauw (AAEL)
VDP	Variable Length Divide or Proceed (SAA)
VDP	Vehicle Deadlined for Parts
VDP	Vehicle Development Process [Automotive project management]
VDP	Venture Database Publisher [Computer science]
VDP	Verenigde Democratische Partijen [United Democratic Parties] [Surinam] [Political party] (PPW)
VDP	Vertical Data Processing
VDP	Vertical Dipole (MCD)
VDP	Vertical Director Pointer (SAA)
VDP	Vibration Diagnostic Program
VDP	Vibration-Dissociation Process
VDP	Video Datagram Protocol [Computer science]
VDP	Video Data Processor
VDP	Videodisc Player [RCA Corp.]
VDP	Video Display Processor [Computer science] (CIST)
VDP	Vinblastine, Dacabazine, Cisplatin (CDI)
VDP	Vincristine, Daunorubicin, Prednisone [Antineoplastic drug regimen]
VDP	Visual Descent Point [Aviation] (FAAC)

VDP	Volunteer Reservists in Drill Pay Status [Navy]
VDPA	Victorian Dairy Products Association [Australia]
VDPI	Vehicle Direction and Position Indicator
VDPI	Voyager Data Processing Instructions [NASA] (KSC)
VDPP	Phnom-Penh [Cambodia] [ICAO location identifier] (ICLI)
VDPS	Voice Data Processor System
VDPT	Pongtuk [Cambodia] [ICAO location identifier] (ICLI)
VDQ	Visual Display of Quality
VDQS	Vins Delimites de Qualite Superieure [Designation on French wine labels]
VDR	Validated Data Record
VDR	Variable Deposit Requirement [Business term] (ADA)
VDR	Variable Diameter Rotor
VDR	Vehicle Data Recorder
VDR	Vehicle Deselect Request [NASA] (KSC)
VDR	Vendor Data Request
VDR	Venous Diameter Ratio [Cancer detection]
VDR	Video Disc Recorder
VDR	Videodisk Recorder (WDMC)
VDR	Videotape Recorder (IAA)
VDR	Villa Dolores [Argentina] [Airport symbol] (AD)
VDR	Vitamin D Receptor [Genetics]
VDR	Voice & Data Resources, Inc. [Ashbury Park, NJ] [Information service or system Telecommunications] (TSSD)
VDR	Voice Digitization Rate
VDR	Voltage-Dependent Resistor (DEN)
VDR	Voyage Data Recorder
VDRA	Voice and Data Recording Auxiliary [NASA] (KSC)
V$_{DRB}$	Rebreathing Ventilation [Medicine] (DAVI)
VDRE	Vitamin D-Responsive Element [Biochemistry]
VDRG	Vendor Data Release Group (MCD)
V$_{drive}$	Drive Voltage (IDOE)
VDRL	Venereal Disease Research Laboratory
VDRR	Vitamin D-Resistant Rickets [Medicine] (DMAA)
VDRS	Vehicular Disc Reproduction System (DICI)
VDRS	Verdun Depression Rating Scale [Medicine] (MAE)
VDRT	Venereal Disease Reference Test [of Harris]
VDRY	Vacu-Dry Co. [NASDAQ symbol] (NQ)
VDS	Vadso [Norway] [Airport symbol] (OAG)
VDS	Van der Stratten [Auto racing team]
VDS	Vapor Deposited Silica [Optical fiber technology]
VDS	Vapor Detection System
VDS	Vapor Distribution System (AAEL)
VDS	Variable Depth SONAR
VDS	Variable Drop Size [Color printing]
VDS	Vasodilator Substance [Physiology]
VDS	Vehicle Description Summary [General Motors Corp.]
VDS	Vehicle Descriptor Section
VDS	Vehicle Dynamics Simulator [NASA] (NASA)
VDS	Vendor Data Service
VDS	Vendor Direct Shipment
VDS	Venereal Disease Syphilis
VDS	Vertical Display System [Navy]
VDS	Victorian Deaf Society [Australia]
VDS	Video Digitizer System (MCD)
VDS	Vindesine [Also, E] [Antineoplastic drug]
VDS	Viola d'Amore Society (EA)
VDS	Virtual DMA [Direct Memory Access] Service [Computer science] (PCM)
VDS	Visual Display System
VDS	Visual Docking Simulator
VDS	Voice Data Switch
VDS	Volatile Dissolved Solids (MCD)
VDS	Volunteer Development Scotland (AIE)
VDSA	Veut Dieu Saint Amour [Knights Templar] [Freemasonry]
VDSD	Visual Distress Signaling Device [Environmental science] (COE)
VDSL	Very High Bit-Rate Digital Subscriber Line (AAEL)
VDSM	Internationaler Verband der Stadt-, Sport-, und Mehrzweckhallen [International Federation of City, Sport, and Multi-Purpose Halls] (EAIO)
VDSQ	Video Data Sequence (NTCM)
VDSR	Siem-Reap [Cambodia] [ICAO location identifier] (ICLI)
VDSS	Variable Depth SONAR System
VDSS	Volume of Distribution at Steady State
VDST	Stung Treng [Cambodia] [ICAO location identifier] (ICLI)
VDSV	Sihanouk [Cambodia] [ICAO location identifier] (ICLI)
VDT	Van Doorne's Transmissie BV [Netherlands Automotive engineering]
VDT	Varactor Diode Test
VDT	Variable Data Table
VDT	Variable Deflection Thruster [Helicopter]
VDT	Variable Density Tunnel
VDT	Variable Depth Transducer [Navy] (NVT)
VDT	Variable Differential Transformer
VDT	Vayudoot [India] [ICAO designator] (FAAC)
VDT	Vehicle Data Table [NASA] (MCD)
VDT	Vertical Deflection Terminal (IAA)
VDT	Video Data Terminal [Computer science]
VDT	Video Dial Tone [Telecommunications service]
VDT	Video [or Visual] Display Terminal [Computer science]
VDT	Visual Display Terminal (EECA)
VDTA	Vacuum Dealers Trade Association (EA)
VDTS	Variable Display Training System
VDTS	Vehicle Data Transmission System
VDTT	Very Difficult to Test [Audiology]
VDU	Refugio, TX [Location identifier FAA] (FAAL)

VDU	Vacuum Distillation Unit [*Petroleum technology*]
VDU	Variable Delay Unit (IAA)
VdU	Verband der Unabhaengigen [*League of Independents*] [*Dissolved, 1956*] [*Austria*] (PPE)
VDU	Video [*or Visual*] Display Unit [*Computer science*]
VDU	Video Distribution Unit
VDU	Visual Display Unit (OA)
VDUAC	Victorian Drug Users' Advisory Committee [*Australia*]
VDUC	VAS [*VISSR Atmospheric Sounder*] Data Utilization Center (USDC)
VDUC	VDU Controller (NITA)
VDV	Vacuum Differential Valve [*Automotive engineering*]
VDV	Ventricular End-Diastolic Volume [*Medicine*] (MAE)
VDV	Vojski Drzavne Varnosti [*Yugoslavia*]
VDV	Vozdushno-Desantnye Voiska [*Airborne Troops*] [*An autonomous command*] [*Former USSR*]
VD-VF	Vacuum Distillation - Vapor Filtration
VDVS	Voeune Sai [*Cambodia*] [*ICAO location identifier*] (ICLI)
V$_D$V$_T$	Physiologic Dead Space in Percent of Tidal Volume [*Medicine*] (DAVI)
VDW	Venus Departure Window [*NASA*]
VDW	Very Deep Water
VDWE	Van der Waals Epitaxy [*Physics*]
VDX	Vandorex Energy [*Vancouver Stock Exchange symbol*]
VDZ	Valdez [*Alaska*] [*Airport symbol*] (OAG)
V$_E$	Airflow per Unit of Time [*Medicine*] (DAVI)
Ve	Biblioteca Nacional, Caracas, Venezuela [*Library symbol Library of Congress*] (LCLS)
V$_E$	Emitter Voltage (IDOE)
V$_E$	Environmental Variance (DAVI)
VE	Minute Ventilation [*Medicine*] (DAVI)
V$_E$	Respiratory Minute Volume [*Medicine*] (DAVI)
VE	Vaginal Epithelium [*Endocrinology*]
VE	Vaginal Examination [*Medicine*]
VE	Value Effectiveness
VE	Value Engineering [*Military*]
VE	Valve Engineer (WDAA)
VE	Varicose Eczema [*Medicine*]
VE	Vehicle Engineering [*Kennedy Space Center*] (NAKS)
VE	Vehicle Experimental (MCD)
Ve	Velban [*See VBL*]
VE	Velocity Equipment (MCD)
VE	Velocity, Equivalent
VE	Velocity Equivalent (NAKS)
VE	Velocity Error
ve	Venezuela [*MARC country of publication code Library of Congress*] (LCCP)
VE	Venezuela [*ANSI two-letter standard code*] (CNC)
VE	Venous Emptying [*Cardiology*] (DAVI)
VE	Ventilating Equipment (MSA)
VE	Ventilation [*Medicine*] (DAVI)
VE	Ventricular Escape [*Medicine*] (DB)
VE	Ventricular Extrasystole [*Cardiology*] (DAVI)
VE	Verbal Emotional (Stimuli) [*Psychology*]
V-E	VERLORT [*Very-Long-Range Tracking*] Elevation [*NASA*]
VE	Vernal Equinox
VE	Vernier Engine [*as a modifier*] (AAG)
VE	Vertex [*Obstetrics*] (DAVI)
VE	Vertical Exaggeration [*Geology*]
Ve	Vesey, Senior's, English Chancery Reports [*27, 28 English Reprint*] [*A publication*] (ILCA)
VE	Vesicular Exanthema [*Virus*]
VE	Veuve [*Widow*] [*French*] (ROG)
VE	Vibration Eliminator (OA)
VE	Victory in Europe [*as in VE-Day*]
VE	Vidatron Enterprise Ltd. [*Vancouver Stock Exchange symbol*]
VE	Viewing Essential (WDAA)
VE	Vinyl Ester
VE	Viral Encephalitis [*Neurology*] (DAVI)
VE	Virtual Environment [*Computer science*] (ECII)
VE	Visalia Electric Railroad Co. [*AAR code*]
VE	Visual Efficiency
VE	Visual Emissions [*Environmental Protection Agency*] (GFGA)
VE	Visual Examination (MEDA)
VE	Vitelline Envelope [*Fertilization*]
VE	Vocational Education (OICC)
VE	Vocational Expert (DHP)
VE	Voltage (IAA)
VE	Voltage Efficiency [*Electrochemistry*]
VE	Volume Ejection [*Medicine*]
V$_E$	Volume of Expired Gas [*Medicine*] (DAVI)
VE	Voluntary Effort [*A cost containment program established by AHA, AMA, and FAH*]
VE	Volunteer Examiners (OTD)
VE	Votre Eminence [*Your Eminence*] [*French*]
VEA	Value Engineering Audit
VEA	Value Engineers Association (BARN)
VEA	Variable Energy Absorber (MCD)
VEA	Vehicle Engineering Analysis
VEA	Veliger Escape Aperture
VEA	Ventricular Ectopic Activity [*Cardiology*] (MAE)
VEA	Ventricular Ectopic Arrhythmia [*Cardiology*] (AAMN)
VEA	Veterans Educational Assistance [*Act*]
VEA	Victorian Exporters' Association [*Australia*]
VEA	Viral Envelope Antigens [*Immunology*]
VEA	Virtual Effective Address (NITA)

VEA	Vocational Education Act [*1963*]
VEAD	Visually Evoked Afterdischarge (DB)
VEAG	Vereinigte Energiewerke AG (ECON)
VEAMCOP	Viking Error Analysis Monte Carlo Program [*Computer science*]
VEAN	Along [*India*] [*ICAO location identifier*] (ICLI)
VE & B	Vehicle Energy and Biotechnology (MCD)
Ve & B	Vesey and Beames' English Chancery Reports [*35 English Reprint*] [*A publication*] (DLA)
VEAP	Veterans Educational Assistance Program [*DoD*]
VEAT	Agartala [*India*] [*ICAO location identifier*] (ICLI)
VEAZ	Aizwal [*India*] [*ICAO location identifier*] (ICLI)
Veazey	Veazey's Reports [*36-44 Vermont*] [*A publication*] (DLA)
VEB	Variable Elevation Beam [*RADAR*]
VEB	Vehicle Equipment Bay (MCD)
VEB	Ventricular Ectopic Beats [*Cardiology*]
VEB	Venus Entry Body [*NASA*]
VEB	Vneshekonombank [*State Bank for Foreign Economic Affairs*] [*Former USSR*]
VEB	Vocational Education Board (OICC)
VEB	Volvo Engine Brake [*Volvo AB*] [*Diesel engines*]
VEBA	Calcutta (Behala) [*India*] [*ICAO location identifier*] (ICLI)
VEBA	Vereinigte Elektrizitaets und Bergwerks, AG [*Holding company*] [*Germany*]
VEBA	Voluntary Employee Benefit Association [*Type of trust established by a company, a union, or both to provide members with various insurance benefits*]
VEBC	Berachampa [*India*] [*ICAO location identifier*] (ICLI)
VEBD	Baghdogra [*India*] [*ICAO location identifier*] (ICLI)
VEBG	Balurghat [*India*] [*ICAO location identifier*] (ICLI)
VEBK	Bokaro [*India*] [*ICAO location identifier*] (ICLI)
VEBL	Barbil [*India*] [*ICAO location identifier*] (ICLI)
VEBR	Visual Evoked Brain Response
VEBS	Bhubaneswar [*India*] [*ICAO location identifier*] (ICLI)
VEBW	Vacuum Electron Beam Welder
VEC	Vacation Exchange Club (EA)
VEC	Valence Electron Concentration (PDAA)
VEC	Value Engineering Change
VEC	Variable Energy Cyclotron (IEEE)
VEC	Vector (KSC)
VEC	Vector Control (MUGU)
VEC	Venezolana Servicios Expresos de Carga Internacional CA [*Venezuela*] [*ICAO designator*] (FAAC)
VEC	Vertical Electrical Chase [*Nuclear energy*] (NRCH)
VEC	Vibration Exciter Control
VEC	Video-Enhanced Contrast Technique [*Microscopy*]
VEC	Visual Education Consultants, Inc. (AEBS)
VEC	Vocational Education Committee (ACII)
VEC	Voice Equivalent Channel (MCD)
VEC	Volunteer-Examiner Coordinator (OTD)
VeCAL	Archivo del Libertador, Caracas, Venezuela [*Library symbol Library of Congress*] (LCLS)
VECAS	Vertical Escape Collision Avoidance System [*Aviation*]
VECC	Calcutta [*India*] [*ICAO location identifier*] (ICLI)
VECC	Value Engineering Control Committee [*Military*]
VECC	Variable Energy Content Curves (NOAA)
VECF	Calcutta [*India*] [*ICAO location identifier*] (ICLI)
VECG	Vector Electrocardiogram [*Cardiology*] (DAVI)
VECHCC	Voluntary Effort to Contain Health Care Costs (EA)
VECI	Vehicle Emission Control Information [*Automotive engineering*]
VECI	Vehicular Equipment Complement Index (IEEE)
VECIB	Vehicle Engineering Change Implementation Board (NASA)
VECK	Chakulia [*India*] [*ICAO location identifier*] (ICLI)
VECM	Vocational Education Curriculum Materials Database [*University of California, Berkeley*] [*Information service or system*] (CRD)
VECO	Cooch-Behar [*India*] [*ICAO location identifier*] (ICLI)
VECO	Veeco Instruments [*NASDAQ symbol*] (TTSB)
VECO	Veeco Instruments, Inc. [*NASDAQ symbol*] (SAG)
VECO	Vernier Engine Cutoff [*Aerospace*]
VECOS	Vehicle Checkout Set
VECP	Value Engineering Change Proposal [*Military*]
VECP	Visually Evoked Cortical Potential [*Neurophysiology*]
VECR	Vendor Engineering Change Request [*DoD*]
VECS	Videotex Editing Communications System (NITA)
VECS	Vocational Education Curriculum Specialists (OICC)
Vect	De Vectigalibus [*of Xenophon*] [*Classical studies*] (OCD)
V-ECT	Ventricular Ectopy
VECTAC	Vectored Attack [*Navy*] (NVT)
VECTAR	Value, Expertise, Client, Time, Attorney, Result [*Lawyer evaluation method*]
VectBk	Vectra Banking [*Associated Press*] (SAG)
VectraTc	Vectra Technologies [*Commercial firm Associated Press*] (SAG)
VECX	Car Nicobar [*India*] [*ICAO location identifier*] (ICLI)
VED	Vacuum Energy Diverter
VED	Vacuum Erection Device [*Medicine*]
VED	Ventricular Ectopic Depolarization
VED	Viscoelastic Damper
VED	Vitral Exhaustion and Depression (DAVI)
VED	Volumetric Energy Density [*of fuels*]
VEDA	Vestibular Disorders Association (EA)
VEDAR	Visible Energy Detection and Ranging
V-E (Day)	Victory in Europe Day [*World War II*]
VEDB	Dhanbad [*India*] [*ICAO location identifier*] (ICLI)
VEDC	Vitreous Enamel Development Council [*British*] (DI)
VEDIC	Video-Enhanced Differential Interference Contrast [*Microscopy*]
VEDILIS	Vehicle Discharge Lighting System

VEDR	Value Engineering Design Review
VEDS	Vehicle Emergency Detection System [NASA] (KSC)
VEDS	Vocational Education Data System
V Ed S	Vocational Education Specialist (PGP)
VEDZ	Deparizo [India] [ICAO location identifier] (ICLI)
V$_{EE}$	Emitter-Voltage Supply (IDOE)
VEE	Vagina, Ectocervix, and Endocervix [Cytopathology]
VEE	Vendee [Legal shorthand] (LWAP)
VEE	Venetie [Alaska] [Airport symbol] (OAG)
VEE	Venezuelan Equine Encephalomyelitis [Virus]
VEEAP	Vocational Education Evaluation and Assessment Process [Pennsylvania] (EDAC)
VEEC	Victorian Environmental Education Council (EERA)
VEECO	Vacuum Electronics Engineering Co. (MCD)
VeecoInst	Veeco Instruments, Inc. [Associated Press] (SAG)
VEEDX	Vontobel Eastern European Debt [Mutual fund ticker symbol] (SG)
VEEEX	Vontobel Eastern European Equity [Mutual fund ticker symbol] (SG)
VEEG	Vector Electroencephalograph
VEEGA	Venus-Earth-Earth-Gravity-Assist [Spacecraft trajectory]
VEEI	Vehicle Electrical Engine Interface [NASA] (NASA)
VEEI	Vehicle Electronics Engineering Institute
VEEITC	Victorian Electrical and Electronic Industry Training Committee [Australia]
VEEP	Vice President
VEER	Variable Emergence Electronically Rotated (MCD)
VEESS	Vehicle Engine Exhaust Smoke System [Army] (RDA)
VEF	Variable Electronic Filter
VEF	Ventricular Ejection Fraction [Cardiology] (DAVI)
VEF	Victorian Education Foundation [Australia]
VEF	Viscoelastic Fiber
VEF	Viscoelastic Flow
VEF	Vision Educational Foundation (EA)
VEF	Visually Evoked Field [Neurophysiology]
VEFCA	Value Engineering Functional Cost Analysis
VEFCO	Vertical Function Checkout
VEFV	Voice-Excited Formant Vocoder (PDAA)
VEG	Maikwak [Guyana] [Airport symbol] (OAG)
VEG	Value Engineering Guideline
Veg	Vega [Record label] [France]
VEG	Vega Aircompany [Russian Federation] [ICAO designator] (FAAC)
VEG	Vegetable [or Vegetation] (KSC)
VEG	Vitreous Environmental Group
VEGA	Venera [Venus] and Gallei [Halley] [Russian spacecraft]
VEGANET	Vegetarian Awareness Network (EA)
VEGAS	Virtual-Egress Analysis and Simulation (ECON)
VEGEDINE	Association of Vegetarian Dietitians and Nutrition Educators (EA)
Veg Ex	Vegetable Exchange [Dietetics]
VEGF	Vascular Endothelial Growth Factor [Biochemistry]
VEGIL	Vehicle Equipment and Government-Furnished Infrared Locator
VECK	Gorakhpur [India] [ICAO location identifier] (ICLI)
VEGL	Value Engineering Guideline
veg pcht	Vegetable Parchment [Paper] (DGA)
VEGT	Gauhati [India] [ICAO location identifier] (ICLI)
VEGY	Gaya [India] [ICAO location identifier] (ICLI)
VEH	Emory and Henry College, Emory, VA [OCLC symbol] (OCLC)
V$_{EH}$	Extrahepatic Distribution [Gastroenterology] (DAVI)
VEH	Valence Effective Hamiltonian [Physical chemistry]
VEH	Vehicle (AFM)
VEH	Vehicular Cargo (COE)
VEH	Veterinary Evacuation Hospital
VEHCAR	Cargo Loaded on Vehicles [MTMC] (TAG)
VEHDYN	Vehicle Dynamics
vehic	Vehicle (DAVI)
VEHIC	Vehicle
vehic	Vehiculum [Vehicle] [Latin] (MAE)
VEHID	Vehicle Identification [NASA] (MCD)
VEHK	Hirakud [India] [ICAO location identifier] (ICLI)
VEI	Value Engineered Indicator (NG)
VEI	Value Engineering Incentive [Office of Federal Procurement Policy]
VEI	Vehicle End Item (NASA)
VEI	Visual Exposure Indicator [Advanced photo system]
VEI	Volcanic Explosivity Index [Measure of amounts of gas and ash that reach the atmosphere]
VEIM	Imphal [India] [ICAO location identifier] (ICLI)
VEIS	Vocational Education Information System
VEITA	Vietnam Era Veterans Inter-Tribal Association (EA)
VEIX	VAALCO Energy [NASDAQ symbol] (TTSB)
VEJ	Aero Ejecutivos CA [Venezuela] [ICAO designator] (FAAC)
VEJH	Jharsuguda [India] [ICAO location identifier] (ICLI)
VEJP	Jeypore [India] [ICAO location identifier] (ICLI)
VEJS	Jamshedpur [India] [ICAO location identifier] (ICLI)
VEJT	Jorhat [India] [ICAO location identifier] (ICLI)
VEK	Veterana Esperantista Klubo [Esperantist Club of Veterans - ECV] (EAIO)
VEKH	Katihar [India] [ICAO location identifier] (ICLI)
VEKJ	Keonjhar [India] [ICAO location identifier] (ICLI)
VEKM	Kamalpur [India] [ICAO location identifier] (ICLI)
VEKN	Konark [India] [ICAO location identifier] (ICLI)
VEKR	Kailashahar [India] [ICAO location identifier] (ICLI)
VEKU	Silchar/Kumbhirgram [India] [ICAO location identifier] (ICLI)
VEKW	Khowai [India] [ICAO location identifier] (ICLI)
VEL	Vehicle Emissions and Fuel Economy Laboratory [Texas A & M University] [Research center] (RCD)
VEL	Vehicular Electronics Laboratory
Vel	Vela [Constellation]

VEL	Vellum
VEL	Velocity (AFM)
vel	Velocity (IDOE)
vel	Velvet (VRA)
VEL	Verified Encoded Logging (NTCM)
VEL	Vernal [Utah] [Airport symbol] (OAG)
VEL	Virginia Electric & Power Co. [NYSE symbol] (SPSG)
VEL	Virginia Power Capital Trust I [NYSE symbol] (SAG)
VELARC	Vertical Ejection Launch Aero-Reaction Control (MCD)
VELC	Velcro Industries NV [NASDAQ symbol] (NQ)
VELCF	Velcro Indus NV [NASDAQ symbol] (TTSB)
VELCOR	Velocity Correction
Velcro	Velcro Industries NV [Associated Press] (SAG)
VELCRO	Velour and Crochet [Interlocking nylon tapes - one with tiny loops, the other with tiny hooks - invented as a reusable fastener by George de Mestral]
VELES	Vibrational Energy Loss Electron Spectroscopy
VELF	Velocity Filter (IEEE)
VELG	Velocity Gain (AAG)
Vell Pat	Velleius Paterculus [First century AD] [Classical studies] (OCD)
VELOC	Velocity
VELORT	Very Long Range Tracking [Radar] (NAKS)
VELPrE	Virginia El & Pwr $5 Pfd [NYSE symbol] (TTSB)
VELPrT	Va Pwr Cap Tr 1 8.05% Pfd [NYSE symbol] (TTSB)
VELR	Lilabari/North Lakhimpur [India] [ICAO location identifier] (ICLI)
vel sim	Vel Similis [Or Similar] [Latin] (WGA)
VEM	Eastern Mennonite College, Harrisonburg, VA [OCLC symbol] (OCLC)
VEM	Value Engineering Model (NG)
VEM	Vasoexcitor Material [Physiology]
VEM	Vector Element by Element Multiply (IAA)
VEM	Vendor Engineering Memorandum (MCD)
VEM	Versatile Exercise Mine [Navy British]
VEM	Vertical Extent of Mortality [Intertidal organisms]
VEM	Virtual Electrode Model (OA)
VEM	Voice E-Mail Messages [Computer science]
VEMASID	Vehicle Magnetic Signature Duplicator (MCD)
V$_{Emax}$	Maximum Flow Per Unit of Time [Respiratory] (DAVI)
VEMB	Victorian Egg Marketing Board [Australia]
VEMH	Malda [India] [ICAO location identifier] (ICLI)
VEMN	Mohanbari [India] [ICAO location identifier] (ICLI)
VEMP	Vincristine, Endoxan [Cyclophosphamide], 6-Mercaptopurine, Prednisone [Antineoplastic drug regimen] (DAVI)
VEMS	Vehicle and Equipment Maintenance System [Software]
VEMS	Vehicle Environment Management System [Automotive engineering]
VEMS	Versatile Exercise Mine System [Military] (PDAA)
VEMZ	Mazuffarpur [India] [ICAO location identifier] (ICLI)
VEN	Capital Aviation Services Ltd. [Canada ICAO designator] (FAAC)
VEN	Variable Exhaust Nozzle
Ven	Vendome [Record label] [France]
VEN	Veneer (WDAA)
VEN	Venerable
Ven	Venerable (WDAA)
VFN	Venereal (WDAA)
VEN	Venetian
VEN	Venezuela [ANSI three-letter standard code] (CNC)
VEN	Venice [Italy] [Seismograph station code, US Geological Survey Closed] (SEIS)
VEN	Venice [Diocesan abbreviation] [Florida] (TOCD)
VEN	Venite [95th Psalm]
VEN	Ventral (WDAA)
VEN	Ventricle (WDAA)
VEN	Venture Gold Corp. [Vancouver Stock Exchange symbol]
VEN	Venture Stores [NYSE symbol] (TTSB)
VEN	Venture Stores, Inc. [NYSE symbol] (SPSG)
VEN	Venus (WDAA)
Ven	Venus and Adonis [Shakespearean work]
VenAmCham	Venezuelan-American Chamber of Commerce and Industry (EA)
Ven & Ad	Venus and Adonis [Shakespearean poem] (BARN)
Vencor	Vencor, Inc. [Associated Press] (SAG)
VenCty	Ventura County National Bancorp [Associated Press] (SAG)
VEND	Vendor (KSC)
VEND	Venerated
VENDAC	Vendor Data Control
VENDOR FACTS	Vendor Field Analytical and Characterization Technologies System (AEPA)
VENet	Vegetarian Education Network (EA)
VENET	Venetian (ROG)
VEN EX	Venditione Exponas [Writ of Execution for Sheriff to Sell Goods] [Latin] (ROG)
VENEZ	Venezuela
Venez	Venezuela (VRA)
VEN FA	Venire Facias [Writ to Sheriff to Summon Jury] [Latin] (ROG)
VENG	Vengold, Inc. [NASDAQ symbol] (SAG)
VENGF	Vengold Inc. [NASDAQ symbol] (TTSB)
Vengold	Vengold, Inc. [Associated Press] (SAG)
VENP	Nawapara [India] [ICAO location identifier] (ICLI)
VENP	Vincristine, Endoxan [Cyclophosphamide], Natulan , Prednisone [Procarbazine] [Antineoplastic drug regimen]
VenPK	Venizelikon Phileleftheron Komma [Venizelist Liberal Party] [Greek Political party] (PPE)
VENPr	Venture Strs $3.25 Cv Dep Pfd [NYSE symbol] (TTSB)
VENR	Veneer
VENS	Versatile Exercise Mine System (DOMA)
VenSt	Venture Stores, Inc. [Associated Press] (SAG)

VENT...........	Ventilating
VENT...........	Ventilation (AFM)
VENT...........	Ventilator
VENT...........	Ventricular [Cardiology]
VENT...........	Ventriloquist
vent...........	Ventriloquist (WDMC)
Vent...........	Ventris' English Common Pleas Reports [86 English Reprint] [A publication] (DLA)
Vent...........	Ventris' English King's Bench Reports [A publication] (DLA)
VENT...........	Venturian Corp. [NASDAQ symbol] (NQ)
Vent (Eng)...	Ventris' English Common Pleas Reports [86 English Reprint] [A publication] (DLA)
Vent (Eng)...	Ventris' English King's Bench Reports [A publication] (DLA)
VENTEX......	Venting Experiment [Marine science] (OSRA)
VENT FIB ...	Ventricular Fibrillation [Also, VF, VFIB] [Cardiology] (AAMN)
ventr...........	Ventral
Ventr...........	Ventris' English Common Pleas Reports [86 English Reprint] [A publication] (DLA)
ventric	Ventricular
Ventricular Rhythm... Cardiology (DAVI)
Ventritx.......	Ventritex, Inc. [Associated Press] (SAG)
VentSt.........	Venture Stores, Inc. [Associated Press] (SAG)
Venture.......	Venture Seismic Ltd. [Associated Press] (SAG)
Venturn.......	Venturian Corp. [Associated Press] (SAG)
Venul..........	Venuleius Saturninus [Flourished, 2nd century] [Authority cited in pre-1607 legal work] (DSA)
VENUS........	Valuable and Effective Network Utility Services (BUR)
VENUS........	Variable and Efficient Network Utility Service (IAA)
VENUS........	Vertical Alignment Design by the Nodal-Tangent and Undulation System (PDAA)
VENUS........	Video-Enhanced User System [Video conferencing]
VENUS........	Vulcain Experimental Nuclear Study [Nuclear reactor] [Belgium]
VEO...........	Value Engineering Organization
VEO...........	Veronex Resources Ltd. [Vancouver Stock Exchange symbol]
VEO...........	Visual Emission Observation [Environmental Protection Agency] (GFGA)
VEO...........	Voluntary Environmental Organisation (EERA)
VEOP	Veterans Education Outreach Program [Department of Education] (GFGA)
VEOS	Versatile Electro-Optical System (MCD)
VEOXF	Veronex Resources Ltd. (MHDW)
VEP...........	Value Engineering Program
VEP...........	Value Engineering Proposal [Army] (RDA)
VEP...........	Vector Equilibrium Principle [Crystallography]
VEP...........	Vertical Extrusion Press
VEP...........	Veterans Education Project (EA)
VEP...........	Visual Evoked Potential [Electrophysiology]
VEP...........	Visually Evoked Potential [Neurophysiology]
VEP...........	Vocational Exploration Program [Office of Youth Programs]
VEP...........	Voter Education Project (EA)
VEPA..........	Vincristine, Endoxan [Cyclophosphamide], Prednisone, Adriamycin [Antineoplastic drug regimen]
VEPA..........	Vocational Education Planning Areas (OICC)
VEPB..........	Port Blair [India] [ICAO location identifier] (ICLI)
VEPC..........	Voice-Excited Predictive Coding (CIST)
VEPCO........	Virginia Electric & Power Co.
VEPG	Pasighat [India] [ICAO location identifier] (ICLI)
VEPG	Value Engineering Program Guideline
VEPH..........	Panagarh [India] [ICAO location identifier] (ICLI)
VEPIS.........	Vocational Education Program Information System
VEPL..........	Vendor Engineering Procurement Liaison (MCD)
VEPM..........	Value Engineering Program Manager [Military] (AABC)
VEPN..........	Phulbani [India] [ICAO location identifier] (ICLI)
VEPOL	Vehicular Planimetric Dead Reckoning Computer Operating Language
VEPP...........	Padampur [India] [ICAO location identifier] (ICLI)
VEPR...........	Value Engineering Program Requirement [Office of Federal Procurement Policy] (NG)
VEPT...........	Patna [India] [ICAO location identifier] (ICLI)
VEQ.............	Variation in Estimated Quantity (AAGC)
VEQ.............	Visiting Enlisted Quarters [Army] (AABC)
VEQ.............	Vuelos Ejecutivos de Quertaro, SA de CV [Mexico] [FAA designator] (FAAC)
VER...........	Boonville, MO [Location identifier FAA] (FAAL)
VER...........	Vacuum Enhanced Recovery [Computer science]
VER...........	Ventricular Escape Rhythm (STED)
VER...........	Venus, SA [Greece] [FAA designator] (FAAC)
VER...........	Veracruz [Mexico] [Airport symbol] (OAG)
VER...........	Verandah [Classified advertising] (ADA)
VER...........	Verapamil [A coronary vasodilator]
VER...........	Veratridine (STED)
VER...........	Vereda
VER...........	Verein [Association] [German]
Ver...........	Vereniging [Association] [Dutch] (ILCA)
VER...........	Verge (ROG)
VER...........	Verify (AFM)
Ver...........	Veritas [A publication]
VER...........	Vermifuge [Destroying Worms] [Pharmacy] (ROG)
VER...........	Vermilion (ROG)
VER...........	Vermillion Resources [Vancouver Stock Exchange symbol]
VER...........	Vermont (ROG)
Ver...........	Vermont Reports [A publication] (DLA)
VER...........	Vernier [Engine] (AAG)
VER...........	Verse
ver...........	Verse (WDAA)

ver...........	Version (WDAA)
VER...........	Version (ROG)
VER...........	Vert [Heraldry]
VER...........	Vertex (WGA)
VER...........	Vertical (KSC)
VER...........	Vertical Earth Rate
VER...........	Vertical Ejector Rack (MCD)
VER...........	Veterans Employment Representative [Department of Labor]
VER...........	Visual Evoked Response
VER...........	Voluntary Export Restraints
VERA	Ranuna [India] [ICAO location identifier] (ICLI)
VERA	Variable Eddington Radiation Approximation (MCD)
VERA	Veramark Technologies [NYSE symbol] [Formerly, MOSCOM Corp.]
VERA	Versatile Experimental Reactor Assembly (DEN)
VERA	Veterans' Employment and Readjustment Act of 1972
VERA	Vision Electric Recording Apparatus [BBC]
VERA	Voluntary Early Retirement Authority [DoD]
VERAS	Vehicule Experimental de Recherches Aerothermodynamique et Structurale [Glider] [France]
VERB	Verbatim (MSA)
VERB	Verbessert [Improved] [German]
verb	Verbum [Verb] [Latin]
VERB	Victor Electrowriter Remote Blackboard [Educational device of Victor Comptometer Corp.]
VERB	Visual Electronic Remote Blackboard (PDAA)
VERB ET LIT...	Verbatim et Literatim [Word for Word, An Exact Copy] [Latin] (ROG)
Verb Sap	Verbum Sapienti Sat Est [A Word to the Wise Is Sufficient] [Latin]
VERC	Ranchi [India] [ICAO location identifier] (ICLI)
VERC	Vacation Eligibility and Request Card [Military]
VERC	Vehicle Effectiveness Remaining Converter
Verc	Vervet [African green monkey] [Medicine] (DMAA)
VERDAN.....	Versatile Differential Analyzer
VERDAN.....	Vertical Digital Analyzer (IAA)
VERDIN......	Antijam MODEM [Modulate, Demodulate], Very-Low Frequency (CAAL)
VERDT	Verdict (ROG)
VERDUP......	Verify Duplication (DNAB)
VEREAD	Value Engineering Retrieval of Esoteric Administrative Data (PDAA)
VEREX	Verification Expert
verfx	Verifax (VRA)
VERG	Rayaguda [India] [ICAO location identifier] (ICLI)
Verg	Vergil [First century BC] [Classical studies] (OCD)
VERGL........	Vergleische [Compare] [German] (ROG)
Ver Hist	Verae Historiae [of Lucian] [Classical studies] (OCD)
VERI...........	Vineyard Environmental Research Institute [Research center] (RCD)
VERI...........	Visual-Empirical Region of Influence
VERIC	Vocational Education Resources Information Center
VERIF........	Verification (MSA)
Verifne........	Verifone, Inc. [Associated Press] (SAG)
Verilink.......	Verilink Corp. [Associated Press] (SAG)
VERIS	Vitamin E Research and Information Service (EA)
Veritas........	Veritas Music Entertainment, Inc. [Associated Press] (SAG)
VeritasSf......	Veritas Software Corp. [Associated Press] (SAG)
VeritCarit.....	Veritatem in Caritate. Orgaan van de Protestanse Theologische Faculteit te Brussel [A publication] (BJA)
VeritDGC.....	Veritas DGC, Inc. [Associated Press] (SAG)
Verity..........	Verity, Inc. [Associated Press] (SAG)
VERITY	Virtual and Electronic Resources for Information Skills Training for Young People (TELE)
VERK	Rourkela [India] [ICAO location identifier] (ICLI)
VERL	Raxaul [India] [ICAO location identifier] (ICLI)
VERL	Vitelline Envelope Receptor for Lysin [Fertilization]
VERLORT.....	Very-Long-Range Tracking [NASA]
VERLOT	Very-Long-Range Tracking [NASA] (DNAB)
VERM..........	Vermilion (ROG)
VERM..........	Vermont
Verm...........	Vermont Reports [A publication] (DLA)
Vermont R ...	Vermont Reports [A publication] (DLA)
Vermont Rep...	Vermont Reports [A publication] (DLA)
VermPu........	Vermont Pure Holdings [Commercial firm Associated Press] (SAG)
Vermt...........	Vermont Reports [A publication] (DLA)
VERN	Rangeilunda [India] [ICAO location identifier] (ICLI)
VERN	Vernacular (ADA)
VERN	Vernier [Engineering]
Vern...........	Vernon's English Chancery Reports [23 English Reprint] [A publication] (DLA)
Vern & S	Vernon and Scriven's Irish King's Bench Reports [1786-88] [A publication] (DLA)
Vern & Sc ...	Vernon and Scriven's Irish King's Bench Reports [1786-88] [A publication] (DLA)
Vern & Scr ...	Vernon and Scriven's Irish King's Bench Reports [1786-88] [A publication] (DLA)
Vern & Scriv...	Vernon and Scriven's Irish King's Bench Reports [1786-88] [A publication] (DLA)
Vern & S (Ir)...	Vernon and Scriven's Irish King's Bench Reports [1786-88] [A publication] (DLA)
VERNAV.......	Vertical Navigation System
Vern (Eng)...	Vernon's English Chancery Reports [23 English Reprint] [A publication] (DLA)
VERNITRAC...	Vernier Tracking by Automatic Correlation [Aerospace]
Vernitrn	Vernitron Corp. [Associated Press] (SAG)
Vernon's Ann CCP...	Vernon's Annotated Texas Code of Criminal Procedure [A publication] (DLA)

Vernon's Ann Civ St... Vernon's Annotated Texas Civil Statutes [*A publication*] (DLA)

Vernon's Ann PC... Vernon's Annotated Texas Penal Code [*A publication*] (DLA)

Vernt............ Vernitron Corp. [*Associated Press*] (SAG)

VERONICA ... Very Easy Rodent-Oriented Net-Wide Index of Computerized Archives

VERP .... Vertical Effective Radiated Power (MCD)

VERP .... Viragen Europe Ltd. [*NASDAQ symbol*] (SAG)

VERP .... Visitor Experience and Resource Protection [*Park tourism management*]

Verpl Cont ... Verplanck on Contracts [*A publication*] (DLA)

Verpl Ev...... Verplanck on Evidence [*A publication*] (DLA)

Verr............ In Verrem [*of Cicero*] [*Classical studies*] (OCD)

Ver Rep....... Vermont Reports [*A publication*] (DLA)

VERRP .... Voluntary Early Release and Retirement Program [*Army*]

VERS .... Versed Sine [*Engineering*] (KSC)

vers............ Versed Sine (IDOE)

VERS .... Versicherung [*Insurance*] [*German Business term*]

VERS .... Version (ROG)

Versa .... Versa Technologies, Inc. [*Associated Press*] (SAG)

VERSACOMM... Versatile Contour Measuring Machine (MCD)

Versar.......... Versar, Inc. [*Associated Press*] (SAG)

VERSE .... Voluntary Early Retirement Scheme (WDAA)

VERSO .... Reverso [*Left-Hand Page of Open Book*] (ROG)

VERST .... Versatile

VERT .... Venture Evaluation and Review Technique

Vert............. Vermont Reports [*A publication*] (DLA)

vert............. Vertebra (STED)

Vert............. Vertebra [*or Vertebral*] [*Anatomy*] (DAVI)

VERT .... Vertebrate

VERT .... Vertical (MCD)

vert............. Vertical (IDOE)

Vert............. Vertical Lights [*Navigation signal*]

VERT .... Vertical Polarization (AFM)

VERT .... Vertigo (WDAA)

VERT-2-EXP... Vertical Double-Expansion [*Engine*] (DNAB)

VERT-3-EXP... Vertical Triple-Expansion [*Engine*] (DNAB)

VERT-4-EXP... Vertical Quadruple-Expansion [*Engine*] (DNAB)

VERT-AM ..... Vocational Education Readiness Test in Auto Mechanics (TES)

VERTAR .... Versatile Test Analysis RADAR (MCD)

VERT-BW .... Vocational Education Readiness Test in Basic Wiring (TES)

VERTCL .... Vertical Clearance (DNAB)

VERTEB........ Vertebrate

VERTEX........ Vertical Transport and Exchange [*Oceanographic research program*]

VertexC........ Vertex Communications Corp. [*Associated Press*] (SAG)

VertexI......... Vertex Industries, Inc. [*Associated Press*] (SAG)

VERTIC .... Verification Technology Information Centre [*British*] (CB)

VERTICAM .... Vertical Camera (WDAA)

VERTIJET ..... Vertical Takeoff and Landing Jet [*Aircraft*]

VERTIS .... Vehicle, Road, and Traffic Intelligence Society

VERTOL .... Vertical Takeoff and Landing [*Also, VTOL*]

VERT-QF...... Vocational Education Readiness Test in Quantity Foods (TES)

VERTREP ..... Vertical Replenishment [*Navy*] (NVT)

VertxPh........ Vertex Pharmaceuticals, Inc. [*Associated Press*] (SAG)

VERU .... Rupsi [*India*] [*ICAO location identifier*] (ICLI)

veru .... Verumontanum [*Anatomy*] (DAVI)

VERVIS .... Vertical Visibility [*Aviation*] (DA)

VerwG.......... Verwaltungsgericht [*Administrative Court or Tribunal*] [*German*] (ILCA)

VES .... Vacuum Evaporator System

VES .... Vapor Extraction System [*Engineering*]

VES .... Variable Elasticity of Substitution [*Industrial production*]

VES .... Variable Explanation Sheet [*Army*]

VES .... Vector Element by Element Sum (IAA)

VES .... Vehicle Ecological System (AAG)

VES .... Vehicle Engagement Simulator (MCD)

VES .... Versailles, OH [*Location identifier FAA*] (FAAL)

Ves .... Vesey, Senior's, English Chancery Reports [*27, 28 English Reprint*] [*A publication*] (DLA)

VES .... Vesica [*Bladder*] [*Latin*] (ADA)

VES .... Vesicula [*Blister*] [*Latin*] (ADA)

VES .... Vesicular (AAMN)

VES .... Vespere [*In the Evening*] [*Latin*] (ADA)

VES .... Vessel (AABC)

ves............. Vessel (VRA)

VES .... Vestaur Securities [*NYSE symbol*] (TTSB)

VES .... Vestaur Securities, Inc. [*NYSE symbol*] (SPSG)

VES .... Vestry [*Ecclesiastical*] (WGA)

VES .... Veterans Employment Service [*Later, VETS*] [*of USES*]

VES .... Veterinary Evacuating Station [*British military*] (DMA)

VES .... Victorian Era Series [*A publication*]

VES .... Vieques Air Link, Inc. [*ICAO designator*] (FAAC)

VES .... Vision Enhancement System

VES .... Visual Effects Simulator (MCD)

VES .... Visual Efficiency Scale

VES .... Voluntary Euthanasia Society [*British*] (DBA)

VES .... Vulcan Engagement Simulator (MCD)

VESA.......... Video Electronics Standards Association

VESA.......... Video Electrononics Standards Association

Ves & B .... Vesey and Beames' English Chancery Reports [*35 English Reprint*] [*A publication*] (DLA)

Ves & Bea... Vesey and Beames' English Chancery Reports [*35 English Reprint*] [*A publication*] (DLA)

Ves & Beam... Vesey and Beames' English Chancery Reports [*35 English Reprint*] [*A publication*] (DLA)

Ves & B (Eng)... Vesey and Beames' English Chancery Reports [*35 English Reprint*] [*A publication*] (DLA)

VESAT......... Venus Environmental Satellite [*NASA, proposed*]

VESC......... Vehicle Equipment Safety Commission

VESCAD ...... Vehicle Electrical System Computer-Aided Design

VESCA(S)..... Vessels and Cargo

VESCF .... Variable Eletronegativity Self-Consistent Field [*Physics*]

VESDA .... Very Early Smoke Detection Alarm

VESE .... Value Engineering Staff Engineer

VESG .... Vocational Education Services Grant (OICC)

VESI........... Victor Educational Services Institute [*Educational division of Victor Comptometer Corp.*]

VESIAC .... Vela Seismic Information Analysis Center (SAA)

Vesic .... Vesicula [*Blister*] [*Latin*]

vesic........... Vesicular

VESID .... Vocational and Educational Services for Individuals with Disabilities

Ves Jr......... Vesey, Junior's, English Chancery Reports [*30-34 English Reprint*] [*A publication*] (DLA)

Ves Jr (Eng)... Vesey, Junior's, English Chancery Reports [*30-34 English Reprint*] [*A publication*] (DLA)

Ves Jr Suppl... Supplement to Vesey, Junior's, English Chancery Reports, by Hovenden [*34 English Reprint*] [*A publication*] (DLA)

Ves Jun .... Vesey, Junior's, English Chancery Reports [*30-34 English Reprint*] [*A publication*] (DLA)

Ves Jun Supp... Supplement to Vesey, Junior's, English Chancery Reports, by Hovenden [*34 English Reprint*] [*A publication*] (DLA)

Ves Jun Supp (Eng)... Supplement to Vesey, Junior's, English Chancery Reports, by Hovenden [*34 English Reprint*] [*A publication*] (DLA)

VESMC........ Vinyl Ester Sheet Molding Compound [*Plastics*]

VESO .... Vocalization of the Egyptian Syllabic Orthography [*W. F. Albright*] [*A publication*] (BJA)

VESP........... Value Engineering Supplier Program

Vesp .... Vespae [*Wasps*] [*of Aristophanes*] [*Classical studies*] (OCD)

VESP........... Vesper [*Evening*] [*Pharmacy*]

VESPER .... Vehicle Sizing and Performance (MCD)

VESR .... Vallecitos Experimental Superheat Reactor

VESR .... Value Engineering Study Request (MCD)

VESS........... Vehicle Exhaust Smoke System (MCD)

VESS........... Visual Environment Simulation System (MCD)

Ves Sen....... Vesey, Senior's, English Chancery Reports [*27, 28 English Reprint*] [*A publication*] (DLA)

Ves Sen Supp... Supplement to Vesey, Senior's, English Chancery Reports [*28 English Reprint*] [*A publication*] (DLA)

Ves Sr .... Vesey, Senior's, English Chancery Reports [*27, 28 English Reprint*] [*A publication*] (DLA)

Ves Sr (Eng)... Vesey, Senior's, English Chancery Reports [*27, 28 English Reprint*] [*A publication*] (DLA)

Ves Sr Supp... Supplement to Vesey, Senior's, English Chancery Reports [*28 English Reprint*] [*1747-56*] [*A publication*] (DLA)

Ves Sr Supp (Eng)... Supplement to Vesey, Senior's, English Chancery Reports [*28 English Reprint*] [*A publication*] (DLA)

Ves Supp ..... Supplement to Vesey, Junior's, English Chancery Reports, by Hovenden [*34 English Reprint*] [*1789-1817*] [*A publication*] (DLA)

VEST .... Vertical Earth Scanning Test (SAA)

VEST .... Vestibular [*Medicine*] (CPH)

VEST .... Vestibule (MSA)

VEST .... Vestro Natural Foods [*NASDAQ symbol*] (TTSB)

VEST .... Vestro Natural Foods, Inc. [*NASDAQ symbol*] (NQ)

VEST .... Vestry [*Ecclesiastical*] (ROG)

VEST .... Volunteer Engineers, Scientists, and Technicians [*An association*]

VESTA......... Vehicle Structure Analysis [*Automotive design*]

VestaIns ..... Vesta Insurance Group [*Associated Press*] (SAG)

Vestro......... Vestro Foods, Inc. [*Associated Press*] (SAG)

VestSe......... Vestaur Securities, Inc. [*Associated Press*] (SAG)

VES UR....... Vesica Urinaria [*Urinary Bladder*]

VESV.......... Vesicular Exanthema Swine Virus

VET .... Care Vet Pharmacy [*Vancouver Stock Exchange symbol*]

VET .... Value Engineering Training

VET .... Vehicle Elapsed Time (MCD)

VeT .... Ventilatory Threshold [*Cardiology*]

VET .... Verbal Test

VET .... Versatile Engine Tester

VET .... Vertical Test (SAA)

VET .... Vestigial Testes [*Anatomy*]

VET .... Vestigial Testis (STED)

Vet............. Veteran (STED)

Vet............. Veteran (AL)

VET .... Veteran (AFM)

VET .... Veterans Administration, Somerville, NJ [*OCLC symbol*] (OCLC)

VET .... Veterans Services [*Public human service program*] (PHSD)

Vet............. Veterinarian (STED)

VET .... Veterinary (AFM)

VET .... Vibrational Energy Transfer [*LASER*] (MCD)

v et............ Vide Etiam [*See Also*] [*Latin*] (MAE)

VET .... Video Editing Terminal [*Computer science*]

VET .... Vidicon Electron Tube

VET .... Visual Editing Terminal (NITA)

VET .... Voice Entry Terminal (NITA)

VET .... Voluntary Early Transition [*Military*]

VET ADMIN... Veterans Administration (WDAA)

VetAm......... Veterinary Centers of America, Inc. [*Associated Press*] (SAG)

VetCtAm...... Veterinary Centers of America, Inc. [*Associated Press*] (SAG)

VETDOC....... Veterinary Documentation (NITA)

VETDOC .... Veterinary Literature Documentation [*Derwent Publications Ltd.*] [*Bibliographic database London, England*]

VETF .... Vaccinia Early Transcription Factor [Genetics]
VETF .... Value Engineering Task Force
VETFR .... Veterans Transition Franchise Initiative Program
Vet Human Toxicology... Veterinary and Human Toxicology (MEC)
Vet Int .... Veteres Intrationes [A publication] (DLA)
VETJ .... Tezu [India] [ICAO location identifier] (ICLI)
VETK .... Tarakeshwar [India] [ICAO location identifier] (ICLI)
Vet MB .... Bachelor of Veterinary Medicine
Vet Med....... Veterinary Medicine (DAVI)
VETMIS....... Vehicle Technical Management Information System
VETMIS....... Vertical Technical Management Information System (MCD)
Vet Na B .... Old Natura Brevium [A publication] (DLA)
Vet N B....... Vetus Natura Brevium [A publication] (DSA)
Vet N Br ..... Old Natura Brevium [A publication] (ILCA)
VETP .... Vandenberg Engineering Test Program (SAA)
VETRN .... Veterinarian
VETRNRY.... Veterinary
VETRONICS... Vehicle Electronics [Program] [Army]
VETS .... Pet Practice [NASDAQ symbol] (TTSB)
VETS .... [The] Pet Practice, Inc. [NASDAQ symbol] (SAG)
VETS .... Tusra [India] [ICAO location identifier] (ICLI)
VETS .... Vehicle Electrical Test System (ADA)
VETS .... Venture Touring Society
VETS .... Vertical Engine Test Stand
VETS .... Veterans Adjustment Scale (MEDA)
VETS .... Veterans' Employment and Training Service [Department of Labor]
VetSci......... Veterinary Science
Vett Cens.... De Veterum Censura [of Dionysius Halicarnassensis] [Classical studies] (OCD)
VETX .... Vertex Industries [NASDAQ symbol] (TTSB)
VETX .... Vertex Industries, Inc. [Clifton, NJ] [NASDAQ symbol] (NQ)
VETY .... Vocabulary Etymology
VEU .... Very Extreme Ultraviolet (MCD)
VEUK .... Utkela [India] [ICAO location identifier] (ICLI)
VEUV .... Very Extreme Ultraviolet (MCD)
VEV .... Barakoma [Solomon Islands] [Airport symbol] (OAG)
VEV .... Vernier Engine Vibration [Aerospace]
VEV .... Vietnam Era Veterans (OICC)
VEV .... Vlaams Economisch Verbond
VEV .... Voice-Excited VOCODER
VEVA........... Vereingung der Europaischen Verbande des Automatenwirtschaft [Federation of European Coin-Machine Associations] (EAIO)
VEVERP ...... Vietnam Era Veteran Recruitment Program
VEVITA....... Vietnam Era Veterans Inter-Tribal Association (EA)
VEVRA .... Vietnam Era Veterans Readjustment and Assistance Act of 1974 (WYGK)
VEVZ........... Vishakhapatnam [India] [ICAO location identifier] (ICLI)
VEWAA ...... Vocational Evaluation and Work Adjustment Association (EA)
VEWS.......... Very Early Warning System
VEWU .... Vietnam Educational Workers' Union [North Vietnam]
VEX............. Tioga, ND [Location identifier FAA] (FAAL)
VEXP........... Virtual Machine Experience
VEY .... Vestmannaeyjar [Iceland] [Airport symbol] (OAG)
Vez............. Vezey's [or Vesey's] English Chancery Reports [A publication] (DLA)
VEZO........... Zero [India] [ICAO location identifier] (ICLI)
VF .... British Air Ferries [ICAO designator] (AD)
VF .... Fighter Plane [Navy symbol]
VF .... Fighter Squadron [Navy symbol]
VF .... Flaps-Down Speed [Aviation]
VF .... Golden West [ICAO designator] (AD)
VF .... Vache Follet [Mad Cow] [Deragatory term for French meat]
VF .... Vacuum Fluorescent [Graphic arts] (DGA)
VF .... Valley Forge [AMEX symbol] (TTSB)
VF .... Valley Forge Corp. [AMEX symbol] (SPSG)
VF .... Value Foundation (EA)
VF .... Vanity Fair [A publication] (WDMC)
VF .... Vanity Fair Mills, Inc. (EFIS)
VF .... Vaporizer Feed [Nuclear energy] (NRCH)
VF .... Variable Factor [Economics]
VF .... Variable Frequency [Electricity] (MSA)
VF .... Variant Frequency [Biology]
VF .... Vector Field
VF .... Velocity Failure
VF .... Ventral Funiculus [Anatomy]
VF .... Ventricular Fibrillation [Also, vent fib, VFIB] [Cardiology]
VF .... Ventricular Fluid [Cardiology] (MAE)
VF .... Ventricular Flutter [Cardiology] (AAMN)
VF .... Verification of Function
VF .... Vertical File
VF .... Vertical Flight (NASA)
VF .... Very Fair
VF .... Very Fine [Condition] [Antiquarian book trade, numismatics, etc.]
VF .... Very Fine Soil [Agronomy]
VF .... VFW [Vereinigte Flugtechnische Werke]-Fokker [Germany ICAO aircraft manufacturer identifier] (ICAO)
VF .... Viane Francaise [French Meat]
VF .... Vicarius Foraneus [Vicar-Forane] [Latin]
VF .... Video Frequency
VF .... View Factor
VF .... Viewfinder [Photography]
VF .... Villers Foundation [Later, Families USA Foundation] (EA)
VF .... Vinyl Fabric [Technical drawings]
VF .... Vinylferrocene [Organic chemistry]
VF .... Vinyl Fluoride (EDCT)

VF .... Virile Female Project [RJ Reynolds Tobacco Co. marketing strategy for proposed Dakota brand]
VF .... Virtual Floppy [Computer science] (PCM)
VF .... Viscosity Factor (IAA)
VF .... Vision Field [Ophthalmology] (DAVI)
VF .... Vision Foundation (EA)
VF .... Vision Frequency
VF .... Visiting Friends [An association] (EA)
VF .... Visual Field [Ophthalmology] (DAVI)
VF .... Vocal Fremitus
VF .... Voice Foundation (EA)
VF .... Voice Frequency [Communications]
VF .... Volcanic Front [Geology]
V/F .... Voltage to Frequency [Converter] [Computer science]
VF .... Volunteer Fireman
VF .... Vulcan Fiber (EDCT)
VF .... Vulcanized Fiber
VFA .... Vahey Family Association (EA)
VFA .... Variation Flow Analysis
VFA .... Victoria Falls [Zimbabwe] [Airport symbol] (OAG)
VFA .... Video Free America (EA)
VFA .... Video Frequency Amplifier
VFA .... Videotape Facilities Association (EA)
VFA .... Virginia Forestry Association (WPI)
VFA .... Visiting Forces Agreement [United States and Philippines]
VFA .... Visual Flight Attachment [Aviation] (RDA)
VFA .... Volatile Fatty Acid [Organic chemistry]
VFA .... Volunteer Fire Alarm (TEL)
VFAM .... Vincristine, 5-Fluorouracil, Adriamycin, Mitomycin C [Antineoplastic drug regimen] (DAVI)
VFAS........... Vertical Force Accounting System
VFAS/TL...... Vertical Force Accounting System/Troop List (MCD)
VFAT........... Virtual File Allocation Table [Computer science] (CDE)
VFAT........... Visual Functioning Assessment Tool [Educational test]
VF AW .... Fighter Squadron - All Weather [Navy symbol] (MCD)
VFAW .... Victorian Fellowship of Australian Writers [Australia]
VFAX .... Heavier-than-Air Fighter/Attack/Experimental [Aircraft]
V_{FB} .... Feedback Voltage (IDOE)
VFB .... Fighter Bombing Plane [Navy symbol]
VFB .... Vertical Format Buffer
VFB .... Visual Form Builder [Computer science] (PCM)
VFC .... Ferrum College, Ferrum, VA [OCLC symbol] (OCLC)
VFC .... Variable File Channel
VFC .... Variable Frequency Clock (IAA)
VFC .... Variable Frequency Control
VFC .... Variable Frequency Crystal (IAA)
VFC .... Vector Function Chainer (MHDB)
VFC .... Ventricular Function Curve [Cardiology] (AAMN)
VFC .... Vertical Format Control
VFC .... Vertical Forms Control (MHDB)
VFC .... Very Fine Cognac
VFC .... V Fan Club (EA)
VFC .... VF Corp. [NYSE symbol] (SPSG)
VFC .... Video Film Converter (OA)
VFC .... Video Frequency Carrier [or Channel] (CET)
VFC .... Virtual File Cabinet
VFC .... Visual Field Control [Aviation]
VFC .... Voice Frequency Carrier [or Channel]
VFC .... Volatile Flavor Compound
VFC .... Voltage to Frequency Converter
VFC .... Volunteer Field Consultant [Red Cross]
VFC .... Vortex Flow Control
VFC .... Voters for Choice/Friends of Family Planning (EA)
VFC/FFP...... Voters for Choice/Friends of Family Planning [Later, VFC] (EA)
VFCG .... Voice Frequency Telegraph [Telecommunications] (OSI)
VF Cp .... VF Corp. [Associated Press] (SAG)
VFCP.......... Voix des Femmes Canadiennes pour la Paix [Canadian Voice of Women for Peace] [See also VOW] [Canada] (EAIO)
VFCPC .... Victorian Federation of Catholic Parents' Clubs [Australia]
VFCS........... Vehicle Flight Control System
VFCT........... Voice Frequency Carrier [or Channel] Telegraph [or Teletype]
VFCTT......... Voice Frequency Carrier Teletype (MSA)
VFD............. Vacuum Fluorescent Display [Computer science]
VFD............. Value for Duty [Business term]
VFD............. Variable Frequency Drive [Instrumentation]
VFD............. Verified Free Distribution [British]
VFD............. Vocal Feedback Device [Aid for stutterers developed at the University of Pittsburgh by Dr. George Shames]
VFD............. Voltage Fault Detector [Electronics] (IAA)
VFD............. Volunteer Fire Department
VFDF........... Very Fast Death Factor
VFDF........... Victorian Football Development Foundation [Australia]
VFDM.......... Vsemirnaia Federatsiia Demokraticheskoi Molodezhi [World Federation of Democratic Youth]
VFDMIS ...... Vertical Force Development Management Information Systems
VFDR .... Variable-Flow Directed Rocket
VFE............. Vendor-Furnished Equipment (NASA)
VFEA .... Vacuum Freezing Ejector Absorption (PDAA)
VFEI .... Virtual Factory Equipment Interface (AAEL)
VFEQT........ Voice Frequency Equipment [Telecommunications] (IAA)
VFER .... Veterans Federal Employment Representative [Civil Service Commission]
VFET........... Vertical Field Effect Transistor (IAA)
VFF............. Valence Force Field
VFF............. Victorian Farmers Federation (EERA)

VFF............	Voice Frequency Filter
VFF............	Volunteer Firefighter
VFFC..........	Virginia First Financial [*NASDAQ symbol*] (TTSB)
VFFC..........	Virginia First Financial Corp. [*NASDAQ symbol*] (SAG)
VFFDR........	Variable Fuel Flow Ducted Rocket (MCD)
VFFIA.........	Victorian Farmers' Federation Industrial Association [*Australia*]
VFFT..........	Voice Frequency Facility Terminal [*Telecommunications*] (TEL)
VFG............	Valley Fig Growers (EA)
VFH............	Vacuum Film Handling
VFH............	Vertical Flow Horizontal
VFHS..........	Valley Forge Historical Society (EA)
VFHT..........	Vacuum Film Handling Technique
VFI............	Valve Fuel Injection [*Automotive engineering*]
VFI............	Verification Flight Instrumentation (NASA)
VFI............	Verifone, Inc. [*NYSE symbol*] (SAG)
VFI............	VF RADAR Intercept Officer (DNAB)
VFI............	Vinyl Fabrics Institute [*Later, Chemical Fabrics and Film Association*] (EA)
VFI............	Visual Field Information [*Aviation*]
VFI............	Vocational Foundation, Inc. (EA)
VFI............	Vocational Foundation, Inc. [*An association*] (EA)
VFI............	Volunteers for Israel (EA)
VFIB..........	Ventricular Fibrillation [*Also, vent fib, VF*] [*Cardiology*]
VFIIX.........	Vanguard FIS: GNMA [*Mutual fund ticker symbol*] (SG)
VFINX........	Vanguard Index Trust: 500 Ptfl. [*Mutual fund ticker symbol*] (SG)
VFIT..........	Visual Field(s) Intact [*Ophthalmology*] (DAVI)
VFITC.........	Victorian Fishing Industry Training Committee [*Australia*]
VFK...........	Variable Function Key [*Computer science*] (ECII)
VFL............	LeMoyne College, Syracuse, NY [*OCLC symbol*] (OCLC)
VFL............	Variable Field Length (MCD)
VFL............	Variable Focal Length
VFL............	Ventricular Filling Pressure [*Cardiology*] (DAVI)
VFL............	Ventricular Flutter [*Cardiology*] (DAVI)
VFL............	Victorian Football League [*Receives television coverage in the US through the Entertainment and Sports Programming Network*] [*Australia*]
VFL............	Voice Frequency Line [*Telecommunications*] (TEL)
VFL............	Voyageur FL Insured Muni Inc. [*AMEX symbol*] (TTSB)
VFL............	Voyageur Florida Insured Municipal Income Fund [*AMEX symbol*] (SPSG)
VFLA..........	Volume Folding and Limiting Amplifier
VFLC..........	Video Fluorometric Detection Liquid Chromatograph
VFLX..........	Variflex, Inc. [*NASDAQ symbol*] (SAG)
VF(M).........	Fighter Plane (Two-Engine) [*Navy symbol*]
VFM...........	Vacuum Forming Machine
VFM...........	Value for Money [*Accounting*]
VFM...........	Van Karn Am Cap FL Qual Mun [*NYSE symbol*] (TTSB)
VFM...........	Van Kampen Merritt Florida Quality Municipal [*NYSE symbol*] (SPSG)
VFM...........	Variable Frequency Monitor [*Sony Corp.*]
VFM...........	Vendor-Furnished Material (MOD)
VFM...........	Vertical Flight Maneuver
VFM...........	View Finder Monitor (NAKS)
VFM...........	Vinyl Fluoride Monomer (EDCT)
VFM...........	Volt Frequency Monitor (DNAB)
VFMED........	Variable Format Message Entry Device [*Computer science*] (MCD)
VF(N).........	Night Fighter Squadrons [*Navy symbol*]
VFN...........	Verticillium Wilt, Fusarium Wilt, Nematode Resistance [*Tomato culture*]
VFNP.........	Victorian Food and Nutrition Program [*Australia*]
VFO...........	Vandenberg Field Office [*Air Force*] (MCD)
VFO...........	Vaporized Fuel Oil [*Process*]
VFO...........	Variable Frequency Oscillator
VFO...........	Viking Flight Operations [*NASA*]
VFO...........	Voice Frequency Oscillator (NITA)
VFOAR........	Vandenberg Field Office of Aerospace Research [*Air Force*] (PDAA)
VFON.........	Volunteer Flight Officers Network
V-format.....	Variable Length File Format (NITA)
V for V.......	Volunteers for Vision [*Defunct*] (EA)
VFP...........	Fighter Squadron, Photo [*Navy symbol*] (MCD)
VFP...........	Vacuum Flash Pyrolysis
VFP...........	Vacuum Fore Pump
VFP...........	Variable-Factor Programming
VFP...........	Variance Frequency Processor (MCD)
VFP...........	Ventricular Filling Pressure [*Medicine*] (DB)
VFP...........	Ventricular Fluid Pressure [*Cardiology*] (MAE)
VFP...........	Vereenigde Feministiche Partij [*Belgium Political party*] (EY)
VFP...........	Veterans for Peace (EA)
VFP...........	Vitreous Fluorophotometry [*Ophthalmology*] (DAVI)
VFP...........	Volatile Fission Product [*Nuclear energy*] (NUCP)
VFP...........	Volunteers for Peace (EA)
VFP...........	Vsemirnaja Federacija Profsojuzov [*World Federation of Trade Unions*]
VFPC..........	Vertical Flight Performance Criteria
VFPR.........	Via Flight Planned Route [*Aviation*] (FAAC)
VFR...........	Vehicle Flight Readiness (KSC)
VFR...........	Vehicle Force Ratio (MCD)
VFR...........	Verein fuer Raumschiffahrt [*Society for Space Travel*] [*Germany*]
VFR...........	Visiting Friends and Relatives [*Airlines*]
VFR...........	Visual Flight Rules [*Aviation*]
VFR...........	Volunteer Field Representative [*Red Cross*]
VFRA..........	Volume Footwear Retailers of America [*Later, FDRA*]
VFRC..........	Valley Forge Research Center [*University of Pennsylvania*] [*Research center*] (RCD)
VFRCTS.......	Visual Flight Rules Control Tower Simulator [*Aviation*] (MCD)
VFS...........	Vapor Feed System
VFS...........	Variable Frequency Synthesizer [*Ariel Corp.*] [*Computer science*]
VFS...........	Ventilated Flight Suit
VFS...........	Video Frame Store (NITA)
VFS...........	Virtual File Server [*Telecommunications*] (OSI)
VFS...........	Virtual File Store [*Telecommunications*] (OSI)
VFS...........	Visual Flight Simulator
VFS...........	Voice from the Silence [*An association*] (EA)
VFS...........	Volume Fraction of Solids in a Slurry
VFSB..........	Verein der Freunde Schloss Blutenburg [*Association of Friends of Schloss Blutenburg-AFSB*] [*Germany*] (EAIO)
VFSC..........	Vermont Financial Services Corp. [*NASDAQ symbol*] (NQ)
VFSC..........	Vermont Fin'l Svcs [*NASDAQ symbol*] (TTSB)
VFSS..........	Variable Frequency Selection System [*Aviation*] (DA)
VFSS..........	Voice Frequency Signaling System
VFST..........	Victorian Foundation for Survivors of Torture [*Australia*]
VFSW.........	Variable Frequency Sine Wave
VFT...........	Vacuum Form Tool (MCD)
VFT...........	Vacuum Friction Test
VFT...........	Velocity False Target [*Military*] (CAAL)
VFT...........	Ventricular Fibrillation Threshold [*Cardiology*]
VFT...........	Verbal Fluency Test [*Speech and language therapy*] (DAVI)
VFT...........	Verification Flight Test (MCD)
VFT...........	Vertical Flight Test (MCD)
VFT...........	Very Fast Train (EERA)
VFT...........	Viking Flight Team [*NASA*]
VFT...........	Voice Frequency Telegraphy (NATG)
VFT...........	Voice Frequency Terminal
VFTG..........	Voice Frequency Telegraphy
VFTTA........	Visa for Travel to Australia (ADA)
VFU...........	Van Wert, OH [*Location identifier FAA*] (FAAL)
VFU...........	Vertical Format Unit (BUR)
VFU...........	Vocabulary File Utility
VFUNDW......	Voluntary Fund for the United Nations Decade for Women (EA)
VFV...........	Variable Fuel Vehicle [*General Motors Corp.*] [*Automotive engineering*]
VFV...........	Venus Flyby Vehicle [*NASA*]
VFVC..........	Vacuum Freezing, Vapor Compression [*Desalination*]
VFW...........	Variable/Fixed Wavelength [*Electronics*]
VFW...........	Verwaltungsamt fuer Wirtschaft [*Executive Committee for Economics*] [*Germany*]
VFW...........	Veterans of Foreign Wars of the USA (EA)
VFW...........	Veterans of Future Wars [*Facetious organization formed by Princeton students in 1930's*]
VFW...........	Video for Windows [*Microsoft Corp.*] (PCM)
VFX...........	Variable Frequency Mixer (IAA)
VFX...........	Vector Float-to-Fix (IAA)
VFY...........	Verify (AFM)
VG............	British Virgin Islands [*ANSI two-letter standard code*] (CNC)
VG............	British Virgin Islands [*Internet country code*]
VG............	City Flug [*ICAO designator*] (AD)
V$_g$..........	Generator Voltage (IDOE)
V$_G$..........	Genetic Variance (DAVI)
VG............	Grundriss der Vergleichenden Grammatik der Semitischen Sprachen [*A publication*] (BJA)
VG............	Light Transport Plane [*Single-engine*] [*Navy symbol*]
VG............	Validity Generalization Testing (OICC)
VG............	Varga Aircraft Corp. [*ICAO aircraft manufacturer identifier*] (ICAO)
VG............	Variable Geometry [*Refers to an aircraft that is capable of altering the sweep of the wings while in flight*] (NATG)
VG............	Vector Generator [*Computer graphics*]
VG............	Vein Graft [*Cardiology*] (DAVI)
VG............	Velocity Gravity
VG............	Ventricular Gallop [*Cardiology*]
VG............	Ventrogluteal [*Anatomy*] (DAVI)
VG............	Verbi Gratia [*For Example*] [*Latin*]
VG............	Vertical Grain
V-G...........	Vertical Gust (MCD)
VG............	Vertical Gyro (MCD)
VG............	Very Good [*Condition*] [*Antiquarian book trade, numismatics, etc.*]
VG............	Vibration Greatness
VG............	Vicarius Generalis [*Vicar-General*] [*Latin*]
VG............	Vice Grand [*Freemasonry*] (ROG)
VG............	Vinylguaiacol [*Biochemistry*]
VG............	Virgin (WDAA)
VG............	Viscosity Grade [*Automotive engineering*]
VG............	Vocational Guidance (ADA)
VG............	Voice Grade [*Telecommunications*] (TEL)
VG............	Volksgrenadier [*Title given to infantry divisions with distinguished combat records*] [*Germany*] [*World War II*]
VG............	Voltage Gain
VG............	Volunteer Guards [*British military*] (DMA)
VG............	Votre Grace [*Your Grace*] [*French*]
VG............	Votre Grandeur [*Your Highness*] [*French*]
Vg............	Vulgate [*Latin translation of the Bible*] (BJA)
VGA...........	Air Vegas Airlines, Inc. [*FAA designator*] (FAAC)
VGA...........	Vapor Generation Accessory [*Instrumentation*]
VGA...........	Variable Gain Amplifier
VGA...........	Variable Graphic Array (EDCT)
VGA...........	Vegetable Growers' Association [*Australia*]
VGA...........	Vertical Gyro Alignment
VGA...........	Very General Algorithm (KSC)
VGA...........	Victorian Green Alliance [*Political party Australia*]
VGA...........	Victorian Gymnastic Association [*Australia*]
VGA...........	Video Graphics Adapter [*Computer science*]

VGA	Video Graphics Array [Computer technology]
VGA	Vijayawada [India] [Airport symbol] (OAG)
VGAA	Vegetable Growers Association of America [Defunct] (EA)
VGAM	Vector Graphics Access Method
VG & VF	Vicar General and Vicar Foreign [British] (ROG)
VGAT	Visual General Aviation Trainer
VGAU	Victorian Government Advertising Unit [Australia]
VGB	British Virgin Islands [ANSI three-letter standard code] (CNC)
VGBD	Virtual Grain Boundary Dislocation
VGC	Variable Gas Capacitor
VGC	Velocity Gate Capture [Military] (CAAL)
VGC	Verdstone Gold Corp. [Vancouver Stock Exchange symbol]
VGC	Very Good Condition [Doll collecting]
vgc	Very Good Condition (ODBW)
VGC	Vesterheim Genealogical Center (EA)
VGC	Victorian Grants Commission [Australia]
VGC	Video Graphics Controller [Apple Computer, Inc.]
VGC	Vintage Glider Club of Great Britain (BUAC)
VGC	Viscosity Gravity Constant
VGCA	Voice Gate Circuit Adaptors [Computer science] (MCD)
VGCAC	Victorian Government China Advisory Committee [Australia]
VGCB	Cox's Bazar [Bangladesh] [ICAO location identifier] (ICLI)
VGCC	Victorian Government Computing Centre [Australia]
VGCC	Voltage-Gated Calcium Channel [Neurophysiology]
VGCF	Vapor-Phase-Grown Carbon Fiber
VGCH	Vent Gas Collection Header [Nuclear energy] (NRCH)
VGCL	Vietnam General Confederation of Labor
VGCM	Comilla [Bangladesh] [ICAO location identifier] (ICLI)
VGCO	Virginia Gas Co. [NASDAQ symbol] (SAG)
V_{GD}	Gate-Drain Voltage (IDOE)
VGD	Valentine Gold [Vancouver Stock Exchange symbol]
VGD	Valuer-General's Department [Australia]
VGD	Vanguard Airlines, Inc. [FAA designator] (FAAC)
VGDC	Victorian Geographic Data Committee [State] (EERA)
VGDIP	Very God-Damned Important Person
VGE	Air Service Vosges [France ICAO designator] (FAAC)
VGE	Valery Giscard d'Estaing [Former French President]
VGE	Video-Game Epilepsy [Neurology]
VGE	Visual Gross Error
VGEG	Chittagong [Bangladesh] [ICAO location identifier] (ICLI)
VGF	Escort Fighter Squadron [Navy symbol]
VGF	Vaccinia Growth Factor [Biochemistry]
VGF	Vertical Gradient Freeze [Crystal growing technique]
VGFR	Virus Growth Factor [Biochemistry]
VGFR	Dhaka [Bangladesh] [ICAO location identifier] (ICLI)
VGFTU	Vietnam General Federation of Trade Unions [North Vietnam]
VGG	Valhalla Gold Group [Vancouver Stock Exchange symbol]
VGG	Vertical Gravity Gradient [Geophysics]
VGG	Video Graphics Generator
VGH	Vancouver General Hospital
VGH	Velocity, Normal Gravity, and Height
VGH	Verlagsgruppe Georg von Holtzbrinck [Commercial firm Germany]
VGH	Very Good Health [Medicine]
VGH	Veterinary General Hospital
VGHN	Vaughn Communications [NASDAQ symbol] (TTSB)
VGHN	Vaughn's, Inc. [NASDAQ symbol] (NQ)
VGHQ	Dhaka [Bangladesh] [ICAO location identifier] (ICLI)
VGI	Variable Geometry Inlet
VGI	Veiling Glare Index [Vision research]
VGI	Vertical Gyro Indicator
VGIFUW	Virginia Gildersleeve International Fund for University Women (BUAC)
VGIMU	Velocity to Be Gained Related to IMU Orientation (MCD)
VGIN	Visible Genetics, Inc. [NASDAQ symbol] (SAG)
VGIS	Ishurdi [Bangladesh] [ICAO location identifier] (ICLI)
VGJR	Jessore [Bangladesh] [ICAO location identifier] (ICLI)
VGLI	Veterans Group Life Insurance
VGLIS	Video Guidance, Landing, and Imaging System [NASA]
V/GLLD	Vehicular/Ground LASER Locator Designator (MCD)
VGLM	Lalmonirhat [Bangladesh] [ICAO location identifier] (ICLI)
VGM	George Mason University, Fairfax, VA [OCLC symbol] (OCLC)
VGM	Van Kam Am Cap Inv Gr Mun [NYSE symbol] (TTSB)
VGM	Van Kampen Merritt Trust for Investment Grade Municipals [NYSE symbol] (SAG)
VGM	Variable Grating Mode (PDAA)
VGM	Ventriculogram [A roentgenogram]
VGM	VGM Capital Corp. [Formerly, Vestgron Mines Ltd.] [Toronto Stock Exchange symbol]
VGM	Vice Grand Master (BJA)
VGM	Villa Grajales [Mexico] [Seismograph station code, US Geological Survey Closed] (SEIS)
VGML	Vegetarian Meal [Airline notation]
VGMPU	Victorian Government Major Projects Unit [Australia]
VGMU	Vulcan Gunner Monitor Unit (MCD)
VGN	Variable Geometry Nozzle
VGN	Virginian Railway Co. [AAR code]
VGND	Ground Velocity (GAVI)
vgnt	Vignette (VRA)
VGO	Vacuum Gas Oil [Petroleum technology]
VGO	Vanderbilt Gold [PC symbol] (TTSB)
VGO	Vereinigte Gruenen Oesterreich [United Green Party of Austria] [Political party] (EY)
VGO	Vicar General's Office [British] (ROG)
VGO	Vickers Gas Operated [British military] (DMA)
VGO	Vigo [Spain] [Airport symbol] (OAG)

VGOR	Vandenberg Ground Operations Requirement [Air Force] (NASA)
VGOR	Vandenberg Ground Operations Requirement [NASA] (NAKS)
VGOR	Vehicle Ground Operation Requirements [NASA] (NASA)
VGP	Vehicle Ground Point [NASA] (NASA)
VGP	Viral Glycoprotein [Medicine] (DMAA)
VGP	Virtual Geomagnetic Pole [Geophysics]
VGPI	Visual Glide Path Indicator
VGPI	Visual Ground Position Indicator (NATG)
VGPL	Voice Grade Private Line [Telecommunications] (ITD)
VGPO	Velocity Gate Pulloff [Military] (CAAL)
VGPO	Victorian Government Printing Office [Australia]
VGR	Variable Gear Ratio [Automotive steering systems]
VGR	Variable Geometry Rotor
VGR	Vermont Government Register [A publication] (AAGC)
VGR	Video Graphics Recorder (EECA)
VGR	Vigoro Corp. [NYSE symbol] (SPSG)
VGR	Virgin Gorda [British Virgin Islands] [Airport symbol] (AD)
VgrdCell	Vanguard Cellular Systems, Inc. [Associated Press] (SAG)
VGRIX	Vista Growth & Income [Mutual fund ticker symbol] (SG)
VGRJ	Rajshahi [Bangladesh] [ICAO location identifier] (ICLI)
VGS	Escort-Scouting Squadron [Navy symbol]
V_{GS}	Gate-Source Voltage (IDOE)
VGS	Variable Geometry Structure
VGS	Variable-Grade Gravity Sewer
VGS	Vehicle Generating System
VGS	Velocity Gate Stealer [Military] (CAAL)
VGS	Video Guidance Sensor (AAEL)
VGS	Vings [Bulgaria] [ICAO designator] (FAAC)
VGS	Volunteer Gliding Schools [British]
VGSD	Saidpur [Bangladesh] [ICAO location identifier] (ICLI)
VGSG	Thakuragaon [Bangladesh] [ICAO location identifier] (ICLI)
VGSH	Shamshernagar [Bangladesh] [ICAO location identifier] (ICLI)
VGSI	Visual Glide Slope Indicator
VGSO	Victorian Government Solicitor's Office [Australia]
VGSY	Sylhet Osmani [Bangladesh] [ICAO location identifier] (ICLI)
VGT	Las Vegas [Nevada] North Terminal [Airport symbol] (OAG)
VGT	Las Vegas, NV [Location identifier FAA] (FAAL)
VGT	National Victoria & Grey Trustco Ltd. [Toronto Stock Exchange symbol]
VGT	Variable Geometry Turbocharger [Automotive engineering]
VGT	Vehicle Ground Test [NASA] (NASA)
VGT	Videographic Terminal
VGTE	Vulcan Gunner Tracking Evaluation (MCD)
VGTJ	Dhaka/Tejgaon [Bangladesh] [ICAO location identifier] (ICLI)
VGU	Des Moines, IA [Location identifier FAA] (FAAL)
VGU	Video Generation Unit (NITA)
VGV	Vacuum Gate Valve
VGVT	Vertical Ground Vibration Test (MCD)
VGW	Variable Geometry Wing [Aircraft]
VGWA	Variable Geometry Wing Aircraft (AAG)
VGWO	Velocity Gate Walkoff [Military] (CAAL)
VGX	Velocity to Be Gained [Body X-Axis] [NASA] (NASA)
VGY	Velocity to Be Gained [Body Y-Axis] [NASA] (NASA)
VGZ	Velocity to Be Gained [Body Z-Axis] [NASA] (NASA)
VGZ	Vista Gold Corp. [AMEX symbol] (SAG)
VGZR	Dhaka/Zia International [Bangladesh] [ICAO location identifier] (ICLI)
VH	Air Burkina [ICAO designator] (AD)
VH	Air Volta [ICAO designator] (AD)
VH	Ambulance Plane [Navy symbol]
Vh	Heater Voltage [Electronics] (OA)
V_H	Hepatic Distribution Volume [Gastroenterology] (DAVI)
VH	Rescue Squadrons [Navy symbol]
VH	Vacuum Housing
VH	Vaginal Hysterectomy [Gynecology]
VH	Value Health, Inc. [NYSE symbol] (SAG)
VH	Variable Heavy
VH	Varia Historia [of Aelianus] [Classical studies] (OCD)
V/H	Velocity/Height
VH	Venice Hospital [Venice, FL]
VH	Venous Hematocrit [Medicine] (MAE)
VH	Vent Hole [Technical drawings]
VH	Ventricular Hypertrophy [Cardiology] (DAVI)
VH	Vertical Hook (IAA)
VH	Very Hard (IAA)
VH	Very Heavy [Cosmic ray nuclei]
VH	Very High
VH	Veterans Hospital
VH	Vickers Hardness Number [Also, HV, VHN] (AAG)
VH	Viral Hepatitis [Medicine]
VH	Vir Honestus [A Worthy Man] [Latin]
VH	Virtual Hospital [University of Iowa] [Online database]
VH	Visually Handicapped [Ophthalmology] (DAVI)
VH	Vitreous Hemorrhage [Ophthalmology] (DAVI)
V/H	Vulnerability/Hardness [Refers to a weapon system's weakness and capabilities in withstanding adverse operating environments]
VH-1	Video Hits One [Cable-television system] [Companion to MTV]
VHA	Van Houten Associates [Information service or system] (IID)
VHA	Variable Housing Allowance (MCD)
VHA	Very High Accuracy (NITA)
VHA	Very High Achievement [Tertiary entrance]
VHA	Very High Altitude
VHA	Very High Aluminum [Rock composition]
VHA	Vision Homes Association (BUAC)
VHA	Voluntary Hospitals of America (EA)
VHAA	Very High Altitude Abort [NASA] (KSC)

VHAD	Vehicle Headlight Aiming Device [*Automotive engineering*]
VHAP	Volatile Hazardous Air Pollutant (EG)
VHB	Buffalo and Erie County Public Library, Buffalo, NY [*OCLC symbol*] (OCLC)
VHB	Very Heavy Bombardment [*Air Force*]
VHB	Very High Bond Tape [*3M Co.*]
VHb	Vitreoscilla Hemoglobin [*Genetics*]
VHBR	Very High Burning Rate (MCD)
VHBW	Very-High-Speed Black and White [*Photography*]
VHC	Hollins College, Hollins College, VA [*OCLC symbol*] (OCLC)
VHC	Saurimo [*Angola*] [*Airport symbol*] (OAG)
VHC	Ventech Healthcare Corp., Inc. [*Toronto Stock Exchange symbol*]
VHC	Vertical Hold Control
VHC	Very High Contrast [*Liquid crystal display*]
VHC	Very Highly Commended
VHCA	Veterans Health Care Act (AAGC)
VHCC	Very High Current Configuration [*Magnetic field*]
VHCH	Cheung Chau [*Hong Kong*] [*ICAO location identifier*] (ICLI)
VHD	Valvular Heart Disease
VHD	Ventricular Heart Disease [*Cardiology*] (DAVI)
VHD	Very High Density [*Computer science*] (CDE)
VHD	Video High Density [*Television*]
VHD	Viral Haemorrhagic Disease
VHD	Viral Hematodepressive Disease (MAE)
VHDL	Very-High Density Lipoprotein [*Biochemistry*]
VHDL	VHSIC [*Very-High-Speed Integrated Circuit*] Hardware Description Language [*Computer science*]
VHDV	Very High Dollar Value
VHE	Very-High Energy
VHE	Volatile Human Effluents
VHEMT	Voluntary Human Extinction Movement
VH Eq Dr	Van Heythuysen's Equity Draftsman [*2nd ed.*] [*1828*] [*A publication*] (DLA)
VHES	Vitro Hanford Engineering Service [*Nuclear energy*] (NUCP)
VHF	Vacuum Hydrogen Furnace
VHF	Very-High-Frequency [*Electronics*]
VHF	Visual Half-Field
VHF/AM	Very-High-Frequency, Amplitude Modulated (NASA)
VHFC	Van Halen Fan Club (EA)
VHF/DF	Very-High-Frequency Direction-Finding
VHFF	Very-High-Frequency Filter
VHF-FM	Very-High-Frequency, Frequency Modulated (NOAA)
VHFG	Very-High-Frequency Generator
VHFI	Very-High-Frequency Indeed [*Ultrahigh frequency*] [*British*]
VHFJ	Very-High-Frequency Jammer
VHFO	Very-High-Frequency Oscillator
VHFOR	Very-High-Frequency Omnirange (AFM)
VHFR	Very-High-Frequency Receiver
VHFRT	Very-High Frequency Radio Telephony (PDAA)
VHFS	Vint Hill Farms Station [*Army*]
VHFT	Very-High-Frequency Termination
VHHH	Hong Kong/International [*Hong Kong*] [*ICAO location identifier*] (ICLI)
VHHK	Hong Kong [*Hong Kong*] [*ICAO location identifier*] (ICLI)
VHI	Valhi, Inc. [*NYSE symbol*] (SPSG)
VHI	Vapro Hazard Index [*Environmental science*]
VHI	Vehicle Heading Indicator
VHI	Voluntary Health Insurance Board [*Ireland*] (BUAC)
VHIC	Vermont Health Care Information, Consortium
VHIP	Vehicle Hit Indicator, Pyrotechnic
VHIS	Vietnam Head Injury Study
VHKT	Kai Tak [*Hong Kong*] [*ICAO location identifier*] (ICLI)
VHL	Very High-Level Language [*Computer science*] (DDC)
VHL	Viceroy Homes Ltd. [*Toronto Stock Exchange symbol*]
VHL	Von Hippel-Lindau Disease
VHLFA	VHL Family Alliance (EA)
VHLH	Very Heavy Lift Helicopter
VHLL	Very-High-Level Language
VHM	Vibrating Head Magnetometer (IAA)
VHM	Virtual Hardware Monitor [*Computer science*] (IEEE)
VHM	Visitation Nuns [*Roman Catholic religious order*]
VHM	Vista Hermosa [*Mexico*] [*Seismograph station code, US Geological Survey Closed*] (SEIS)
VHMA	Veterinary Hospital Managers Association (NTPA)
VHMCP	Voluntary Home Mortgage Credit Program [*of HHFA*] [*Terminated*]
VHMWPE	Very-High Molecular Weight Polyethylene (PDAA)
VHN	Van Horn, TX [*Location identifier FAA*] (FAAL)
VHN	Vickers Hardness Number [*Also, HV, VH*]
VHO	Very High Output
VHO	Vila Coutinho [*Mozambique*] [*Airport symbol Obsolete*] (OAG)
VHO	Vista Hermosa [*Mexico*] [*Seismograph station code, US Geological Survey*] (SEIS)
VHO	Volatile Halogenated Organic [*Analytical chemistry*]
VHOC	Volatile Halogenated Organic Compound [*Environmental chemistry*]
VHOL	Very-High-Order Language
VHORG	Vertically and Horizontally Organized Grid (AAEL)
VHP	County of Henrico Public Library, Richmond, VA [*OCLC symbol*] (OCLC)
VHP	Variable Horsepower
VHP	Very High Performance
VHP	Very High Polarization [*Raw sugar grade*]
VHP	Very High Pressure
VHP	Very High Productivity (AAEL)
VHP	Viral Hepatitis Panel [*Hematology*] (DAVI)
VHP	Vooruitstrewende Hervormings Partij [*Progressive Reform Party*] [*Surinam*] [*Political party*] (PPW)

VHPA	Vietnam Helicopter Pilots Association (EA)
VHPCC	Very High Performance Computing and Communication (USDC)
VHPIC	Very-High Performance Integrated Circuit [*Electronics*] (PDAA)
VHR	Very-Highly Repeated [*Genetics*]
VHR	Very High Reduction (NITA)
VHR	Very High Resistance (IDOE)
VHR	Video-to-Hardcopy Recorder
VHRC	Victoria Harness Racing Club [*Australia*]
VHRR	Very High Resolution Radiometer [*NASA*]
VHRTG	Veterans' Hospital Radio and Television Guild (EA)
VHRVM	Very-High-Resistance Voltmeter (IDOE)
VHS	Hampden-Sydney College, Hampden-Sydney, VA [*OCLC symbol*] (OCLC)
VHS	Honorary Surgeon to the Viceroy of India
vHs	Van Hove Singularities [*Physics*]
VHS	Variable Hard Sphere (AAEL)
VHS	Versatile High Speed [*Copier*]
VHS	Vertical and Horizontal Spread [*Landfills*] (EG)
VHS	Vertical and Horizontal Spread Model [*Environmental science*] (COE)
VHS	Very High Speed [*Copier*]
VHS	Victorian House of Studies
VHS	Video Home System
VHS	Viral Hemorrhagic Septicemia [*Medicine*]
VHS	Virtual High School
VHS & RA	Veterans Health Services and Research Administration [*Department of Veterans Affairs*]
VHSB	Virtual Home Space Builder
VHS-C	Video Home System - Compact
VHSD	Very High Speed Data (LAIN)
VHSI	Very-High-Speed Integrated [*Electronics*]
VHSIC	Very-High-Speed Integrated Circuit [*Electronics*]
VHSK	Sek Kong [*Hong Kong*] [*ICAO location identifier*] (ICLI)
VHSOC	Very-High-Speed Optic Cable
VHST	Very-High-Speed Transit
VHT	Banyan Hotel Investment Fund [*Formerly, VMS Hotel Investment Fund*] [*AMEX symbol*] (SPSG)
VHT	Banyan Hotel Inv Fund [*AMEX symbol*] (TTSB)
VHT	Vehicle-Hours of Travel (COE)
VHT	Vehicle Hours Traveled [*MOCD*] (TAG)
VHT	Very High Temperature (COE)
VHT	Vignetted Halftone [*Graphic arts*] (DGA)
VHTR	Very-High-Temperature Reactor [*Nuclear energy*]
V/HUD	Vertical/Heads-Up Display [*Aviation*] (MCD)
VHUP	Veterinary Hospital of the University of Pennsylvania
VHV	Very-High Voltage (IAA)
VHVI	Very High Viscosity Index [*Petroleum oils*]
VHW	Verband Hannoverscher Warmblutzuchter [*Germany*] (EAIO)
VHWG	Vulnerability and Hardening Working Group
VHY	Vess, Henry, Kansas City MO [*STAC*]
VHY	Vichy [*France*] [*Airport symbol*] (AD)
V Hyst	Vaginal Hysterectomy [*Gynecology*] (DAVI)
VI	Congregation of the Incarnate Word and the Blessed Sacrament [*Roman Catholic women's religious order*]
VI	In Bankruptcy or Receivership [*Investment term*] (DFIT)
VI	Inertial Velocity
V_i	Input Voltage (IDOE)
V_I	Inspired Volume per Minute [*Medicine*] (DAVI)
VI	Internal Velocity (SSD)
VI	Six [*Roman numeral*] (DAVI)
VI	St. Croix Island (VRA)
VI	St. John Island (VRA)
VI	St. Thomas Island (VRA)
VI	Vaginal Irrigation [*Medicine*]
VI	Valley Industries (EFIS)
VI	Value Included Entry [*Business term*]
VI	Values Inventory [*Management test*]
VI	Vancouver Island
VI	Variable Intensity Light [*Aviation*] (DA)
VI	Variable Interval [*Reinforcement schedule*]
VI	Vasoinhibitory [*Medicine*]
VI	Vastus Intermedius [*Muscle*] (DAVI)
VI	Vector International (EA)
VI	Vegetation Index
VI	Velocity, Internal
VI	Vendor Item [*Sales*] (AAG)
VI	Vent Isolation [*Nuclear energy*] (NRCH)
VI	Verb Intransitive
VI	Vereniging Intercoop [*International Agricultural Society Intercoop*] [*Switzerland*] (EAIO)
VI	Vermiculite Institute [*Defunct*]
VI	Vertical Incidence (IAA)
VI	Vertical Interval [*Mapmaking*]
VI	Vested Interest [*Business term*] (MHDW)
VI	Veterinary Inspector (ADA)
VI	Vial
VI	Vibration Institute (EA)
VI	Victoria Institute [*British*] (DAS)
vi	Vide Infra [*See Below*] [*Latin*] (WGA)
VI	Video Integrator
VI	Vieques Airlink [*ICAO designator*] (AD)
Vi	Vincentius Hispanus [*Deceased, 1248*] [*Authority cited in pre-1607 legal work*] (DSA)
VI	Vinegar Institute (EA)
VI	Vinyl Institute (NTPA)
VI	Violet

Vi	Virginia State Library, Richmond, VA [*Library symbol Library of Congress*] (LCLS)
VI	Virgin Islands (IAA)
VI	Virgin Islands of the US [*ANSI two-letter standard code*] (CNC)
vi	Virgin Islands of the US [*IYRU nationality code*] [*MARC country of publication code Library of Congress*] (LCCP)
VI	Virgin Islands of the US [*Postal code*]
VI	Virgin Islands Reports [*A publication*] (DLA)
Vi	Virginium (MAE)
VI	Virgo Intacta [*Medicine*]
VI	Virtual Interface [*Computer science*]
Vi	Virulence [*Antigen*] [*Immunology*]
VI	Viscosity Improver [*Element in multigrade engine oil*]
VI	Viscosity Index
VI	Visibility Impairment [*Environmental Protection Agency*]
VI	Visual Identification
VI	Visual Impairment
VI	Visual Information
VI	Visual Inspection
VI	Visual Interface [*Computer science*] (NHD)
Vi	Vivianus Tuscus [*Flourished, 13th century*] [*Authority cited in pre-1607 legal work*] (DSA)
VI	Vocational Information (DHP)
VI	Volume Index [*Medicine*] (DHSM)
VI	Volume Indicator [*Radio equipment*]
VI	Volume Investigation [*Three-dimensional imaging technology developed at The Toronto Hospital in Canada*]
VI	Voluntary Indefinite [*Status*] [*Army*] (INF)
VI	Voluntary Interceptor [*World War II British*]
VI	Volunteers for Israel (EA)
VIA	Arlington County Department of Libraries, Arlington, VA [*OCLC symbol*] (OCLC)
VIA	Variable Income Annuity
VIA	Variety Initiatives for Disabled Access [*An association*] (BUAC)
VIA	Versatile Interface Adapter [*Telecommunications*] (IAA)
VIA	Viacom, Inc. [*AMEX symbol*] (SPSG)
VIA	Viacom Inc CI'A' [*AMEX symbol*] (TTSB)
VIA	Viaduct
VIA	VIASA, Venezolana International de Aviacion SA [*Venezuela*] [*ICAO designator*] (FAAC)
VIA	Victorian Importers' Association [*Australia*]
VIA	Video Image Analysis
VIA	Videotex Industry Association (EA)
VIA	Videotex Industry Association Ltd. (NITA)
VIA	Viral Interval Antigen [*Virology*]
VIA	Virus Inactivating Agency [*Medicine*]
VIA	Virus Infection Associated Antigen [*Immunology*]
VIA	Vision Institute of America [*Later, VSP*] (EA)
VIA	Visually Impaired Association (BARN)
VIA	Vocational Interests and Vocational Aptitudes [*Psychology*]
VIA	Voice Interactive Avionics [*Army*]
VIA	Voluntary Insurance Association [*Australia*]
VIA	Volunteers in Asia (EA)
VIA.B	Viacom Inc. CI'B' [*AMEX symbol*] (TTSB)
ViAb	Washington County Public Library, Abingdon, VA [*Library symbol Library of Congress*] (LCLS)
ViAbC	Virginia Highlands Community College, Abingdon, VA [*Library symbol*] [*Library of Congress*] (LCLS)
VIABLE	Vertical Installation Automated Baseline [*Army*]
ViAc	Eastern Shore Public Library, Accomac, VA [*Library symbol Library of Congress*] (LCLS)
Viac	Viacom, Inc. [*Associated Press*] (SAG)
VIAC	Vienna Allied Command [*British military*] (DMA)
ViacB	Viacom, Inc. [*Associated Press*] (SAG)
Viacom	Viacom, Inc. [*Associated Press*] (SAG)
VIADCT	Viaduct [*Commonly used*] (OPSA)
VIADUCT	Viaduct [*Commonly used*] (OPSA)
VIAFF	Vancouver International Amateur Film Festival [*Canada*]
VIAG	Agra [*India*] [*ICAO location identifier*] (ICLI)
VIAH	Aligarh [*India*] [*ICAO location identifier*] (ICLI)
ViAl	Alexandria Library, Alexandria, VA [*Library symbol Library of Congress*] (LCLS)
VIAL	Allahabad [*India*] [*ICAO location identifier*] (ICLI)
ViAIA	United States Army Material Command Headquarters, Technical Library, Alexandria, VA [*Library symbol Library of Congress*] (LCLS)
ViAlbS	Southside Virginia Community College, Christanna Campus, Alberta, VA [*Library symbol Library of Congress*] (LCLS)
ViAID	Defense Technical Information Center, Cameron Station, Alexandria, VA [*Library symbol Library of Congress*] (LCLS)
ViAIDL	Defense Logistics Agency, Cameron Station, Alexandria, VA [*Library symbol Library of Congress*] (LCLS)
ViAIP	Jacob Simpson Payton Library, Alexandria, VA [*Library symbol Library of Congress*] (LCLS)
ViAITh	Protestant Episcopal Theological Seminary in Virginia, Alexandria, VA [*Library symbol Library of Congress*] (LCLS)
ViAm	Amherst County Public Library, Amherst, VA [*Library symbol*] [*Library of Congress*] (LCLS)
ViAnGS	Church of Jesus Christ of Latter-Day Saints, Genealogical Society Library, Annandale Branch, Annandale, VA [*Library symbol Library of Congress*] (LCLS)
ViAnN	Northern Virginia Community College, Annandale, VA [*Library symbol Library of Congress*] (LCLS)
Viansa	Vicky and Sam [*Sebastiani*] [*Brand name of wines made by the Sebastianis*]

VIAP	Vanuatu Independent Alliance Party [*Political party*] (PPW)
VIAR	Amritsar [*India*] [*ICAO location identifier*] (ICLI)
ViAr	Arlington County Department of Libraries, Arlington, VA [*Library symbol Library of Congress*] (LCLS)
VIAR	Volcani Institute of Agricultural Research [*Israel*] (BUAC)
ViAr-A	Arlington County Department of Libraries, Aurora Hills Branch, Arlington, VA [*Library symbol Library of Congress*] (LCLS)
ViArAL	Center for Applied Linguistics, Arlington, VA [*Library symbol Library of Congress*] (LCLS)
VIARC	Victorian Immigration Advice and Rights Centre Inc. [*Australia Commercial firm*]
ViAr-Ch	Arlington County Department of Libraries, Cherrydale Branch, Arlington, VA [*Library symbol Library of Congress*] (LCLS)
ViAr-Cl	Arlington County Department of Libraries, Clarendon Branch, Arlington, VA [*Library symbol Library of Congress*] (LCLS)
ViAr-F	Arlington County Department of Libraries, Fairlington Branch, Arlington, VA [*Library symbol Library of Congress*] (LCLS)
ViAr-G	Arlington County Department of Libraries, Glencarlyn Branch, Arlington, VA [*Library symbol Library of Congress*] (LCLS)
ViArHD	United States Historical Documents Institute, Inc., Arlington, VA [*Library symbol Library of Congress*] (LCLS)
ViArM	Marymount College, Arlington, VA [*Library symbol Library of Congress*] (LCLS)
ViArNG	National Graduate University, Arlington, VA [*Library symbol Library of Congress*] (LCLS)
ViAr-W	Arlington County Department of Libraries, Westover Branch, Arlington, VA [*Library symbol Library of Congress*] (LCLS)
VIAS	Viasoft, Inc. [*NASDAQ symbol*] (SAG)
VIAS	Voice Interference Analysis Set [*or System*]
VIASA	Venezolana Internacional de Aviacion Sociedad Anonima [*Airline*] [*Venezuela*]
ViaSat	ViaSat, Inc. [*Associated Press*] (SAG)
ViAsM	Mobil Chemical Co., Industrial Chemicals Division, Ashland, VA [*Library symbol Library of Congress*] (LCLS)
Viasoft	Viasoft, Inc. [*Associated Press*] (SAG)
ViAsR	Randolph-Macon College, Ashland, VA [*Library symbol Library of Congress*] (LCLS)
Viatel	Viatel, Inc. [*Associated Press*] (SAG)
VIATLS	Visual Airborne Target Locator System [*Military*] (PDAA)
VIA WIS.E	Viacom Inc.'99 Wrrt [*AMEX symbol*] (TTSB)
VIA WS.C	Viacom Inc.'97 Wrrt [*AMEX symbol*] (TTSB)
VIB	Vanilla Information Bureau (EA)
VIB	Veal Infusion Broth [*Immunology*]
VIB	Vertical Integration Building [*NASA*]
VIB	Vibraphone [*Music*]
VIB	Vibrate (AAG)
VIB	Vibrator (IAA)
vib	Vibrator [*Printing*] (DGA)
VIB	Vitamin Information Bureau [*Defunct*] (EA)
VIB	Vocational Interest Blank [*Psychology*] (DAVI)
VIB	Volume Inside Bark [*Forestry*] (EES)
VIB	Volume Inside Bark
VIB	Volunteer Infantry Brigade [*British military*] (DMA)
VIBAC	Vehicle Ice-Breaking Air Cushion (PDAA)
VIBDX	Vontobel Intl. Bond [*Mutual fund ticker symbol*] (SG)
VIBG	Vibrating (AAG)
VIBGYOR	Violet, Indigo, Blue, Green, Yellow, Orange, Red [*Mnemonic for the colors of the spectrum*]
VIBH	Banihal [*India*] [*ICAO location identifier*] (ICLI)
VIBI	Virgini Immaculatae Bavaria Immaculata [*To the Immaculate Virgin Immaculate Bavaria*] [*Motto of the Order of St. George of Bavaria*] [*Latin*]
VIBK	Bikaner [*India*] [*ICAO location identifier*] (ICLI)
VIBL	Bakshi Ka Talab [*India*] [*ICAO location identifier*] (ICLI)
VIBL	Variable Intensity Back Lighting (NITA)
ViBlbV	Virginia Polytechnic Institute and State University, Blacksburg, VA [*Library symbol Library of Congress*] (LCLS)
ViBluC	Bluefield College, Bluefield, VA [*Library symbol Library of Congress*] (LCLS)
VIBN	Varanasi [*India*] [*ICAO location identifier*] (ICLI)
VIBN	Vibration (AAG)
VIBOR	Vienna Interbank Offered Rate [*Austria*] (NUMA)
Vi-BPH	Virginia State Library for the Visually and Physically Handicapped, Richmond, VA [*Library symbol Library of Congress*] (LCLS)
VIBR	Kulu/Bhuntar [*India*] [*ICAO location identifier*] (ICLI)
VIBR	Vibration
VIBRA	Vehicle Inelastic Bending Response Analysis [*Computer program*]
VIBRAM	Vitale Bramani [*Inventor of rubber soles for boots used in mountain climbing*]
ViBrC	Bridgewater College, Bridgewater, VA [*Library symbol Library of Congress*] (LCLS)
VIBRECON	Vibration-Recording Console (SAA)
VIBROT	Vibrational-Rotational [*Spectra*] [*Computer science*]
ViBS	Sullins College, Bristol, VA [*Library symbol Library of Congress*] (LCLS)
VIBS	Vocabulatory, Information, Block Design, Similarities [*Psychology*]
ViBsgM	Mountain Empire Community College, Big Stone Gap, VA [*Library symbol*] [*Library of Congress*] (LCLS)
VIBT	Bhatinda [*India*] [*ICAO location identifier*] (ICLI)
VIBT	Vibrator (IAA)
ViBV	Virginia Intermont College, Bristol, VA [*Library symbol Library of Congress*] (LCLS)
VIBW	Bhiwani [*India*] [*ICAO location identifier*] (ICLI)
VIBY	Bareilly [*India*] [*ICAO location identifier*] (ICLI)

ViC............	McIntire Public Library, Charlottesville, VA [*Library symbol Library of Congress*] (LCLS)
VIC............	University of Victoria Library [*UTLAS symbol*]
VIC............	Value Incentive Clause [*General Services Administration*]
VIC............	Values Inventory for Children [*Attitude test*]
VIC............	Van Kam Am Cap InvGr CA Mun [*NYSE symbol*] (TTSB)
VIC............	Van Kampen Merritt Investment Grade California Municipal [*NYSE symbol*] (SPSG)
VIC............	Vapor Injection Curing [*Plastics technology*]
VIC............	Variable Instruction Computer
VIC............	Varnish Insulating Compound
VIC............	Vasoinhibitory Center [*Physiology*]
VIC............	Vehicle for Initial Crawling [*Physical therapy*] (DAVI)
VIC............	Vehicle Identification Code (SSD)
VIC............	Vehicle Intercommunications System (MCD)
VIC............	Very Important Cargo [*Shipping*]
VIC............	Very Important Contributors [*Political*]
VIC............	Very Important Customer
VIC............	Veterinary Investigation Centre [*Ministry of Agriculture, Fisheries, and Food*] [*British*]
VIC............	Vicar [*or Vicarage*]
Vic............	Vicar (WDAA)
VIC............	Vicenza [*Italy*] [*Airport symbol*] (AD)
VIC............	Vices [*Times*] [*Pharmacy*]
vic............	Vicinal [*Also, v*] [*Chemistry*]
vic............	Vicinalis [*Neighboring*] [*Latin*]
VIC............	Vicinity (AABC)
Vic............	Victor [*Record label*]
vic............	Victoria [*Platen Press*] (DGA)
VIC............	Victoria [*British Columbia*] [*Seismograph station code, US Geological Survey*] (SEIS)
VIC............	Victoria [*Diocesan abbreviation*] [*Texas*] (TOCD)
VIC............	Video Image Correlation
VIC............	Video Interface Controller [*Computer science*]
VIC............	Vienna International Centre [*United Nations*]
VIC............	Viking Integrated Change [*NASA*]
VIC............	Virginia Intermont College
VIC............	Virginia State Library, Richmond, VA [*OCLC symbol*] (OCLC)
VIC............	Virgin Islands Code [*A publication*] (DLA)
VIC............	Virgin Islands Corp. [*Intended to promote VI economic development, dissolved 1966*] [*Department of the Interior*]
VIC............	Virtual Interaction Controller
VIC............	Visibility of Intransit Cargo [*Shipping*]
VIC............	Visitor Information Center [*Kennedy Space Center*]
VIC............	Visitor Information Centre [*Australian National Botanic Gardens*] (EFRA)
vic............	Visitors Information Center (NAKS)
VIC............	Visual Information Center [*Oldsmobile*] [*Automotive engineering*]
VIC............	Vortex in Cell [*Fluid Mechanics*]
VIC............	VSC Tech, Inc. [*Vancouver Stock Exchange symbol*]
VICA..........	Vision Industry Council of America (EA)
VICA..........	Vocational Industrial Clubs of America (EA)
Vic ACR......	Victorian Accident Compensation Reports [*Australia A publication*]
ViCAF.........	United States Army, Foreign Science and Technical Center, Charlottesville, VA [*Library symbol Library of Congress*] (LCLS)
ViCAHi........	Abermarle County Historical Society, Charlottesville, VA [*Library symbol Library of Congress*] (LCLS)
Vical..........	Vical, Inc. [*Associated Press*] (SAG)
VICAM.........	Virtual Integrated Communications Access Method [*Sperry UNIVAC*]
VICANA........	Vietnamese Cultural Association of North America (EA)
VIC and ALB..	Victoria and Albert Museum [*London*] (DSUE)
Vic Ap........	Vicar Apostolic (BARN)
VICAP........	Violent Criminal Apprehension Program [*Quantico, VA*] [*National Center for the Analysis of Violent Crime Department of Justice*]
VICAR.........	Video Image Communication and Retrieval
VIC C.........	Victoria Cross (DSUE)
VICC..........	Visual Information Control Console [*Telecommunications*] (IAA)
VICCC.........	Victorian Indo-Chinese Community Council [*Australia*]
VICCI.........	Voice-Initiated Cockpit Control and Integration [*Aviation*] (PDAA)
VICE..........	Vast Integrated Communications Environment [*Carnegie Mellon University*] [*Pittsburgh, PA*]
VICE..........	Vilnius Commodity Exchange [*Lithuania*] (EY)
VICE..........	Virus Instructional Code Emulator [*Computer science*]
VICES.........	Voice Internal Communications Equipment for Submarines (PDAA)
Vic Fam Alm..	Victorian Family Almanac [*A publication*]
VICG..........	Chandigarh [*India*] [*ICAO location identifier*] (ICLI)
VICGEN........	Vicar General's Office [*British*]
ViChe.........	Chesapeake Public Library, Chesapeake, VA [*Library symbol*] [*Library of Congress*] (LCLS)
ViCheC........	Tidewater Community College, Chesapeake, VA [*Library symbol*] [*Library of Congress*] (LCLS)
Vic His J.....	Victorian Historical Journal [*A publication*]
Vic Hist J....	Victorian Historical Journal [*A publication*]
ViChT.........	John Tyler Community College, Chester, VA [*Library symbol Library of Congress*] (LCLS)
VICI..........	Vantage Information Consultants, Inc. [*Information service or system*] (IID)
VICI..........	Velocity Indicating Coherent Integrator
VICI..........	Ventures in Community Improvement Demonstration Project (EDAC)
VICI..........	Video Console Indexing
VICI..........	Video Isolation Channel Identifier (MCD)
VICI..........	Voice Input Child Identicant [*Pronounced "Vicki"*] [*Young robot in television show "Small Wonder"*]
VICI..........	Voice Input Code Identifier (MCD)

Vic Inst Ed Res Bull...	Victorian Institute of Educational Research. Bulletin [*A publication*]
VICK..........	Vicksburg National Military Park
VICL..........	Vical, Inc. [*NASDAQ symbol*] (SAG)
VICL..........	Vienna International Centre Library [*Information service or system*] (IID)
ViCIR.........	Robbins Mills, Inc., Clarksville, VA [*Library symbol Library of Congress*] (LCLS)
VICO..........	Virginia International Co.
VICO..........	Volkswagen Insurance Co.
ViCoC.........	Castle Hill Museum, Cobham, VA [*Library symbol Library of Congress*] (LCLS)
VICOED........	Visual Communications Education
VICOM.........	Visual Communications Management
Vicon.........	Vicon Industries, Inc. [*Associated Press*] (SAG)
VICON.........	Visual Confirmation [*of voice takeoff clearing system*] [*Aviation*]
Vicor.........	Vicor Corp. [*Associated Press*] (SAG)
VICORE........	Visual Conceptual Reading
Vicorp........	Vicorp Restaurants, Inc. [*Associated Press*] (SAG)
VICORP........	Village Inn Restaurants (EFIS)
VICORP........	Virgin Island Corp. (BUAC)
ViCou.........	Walter Cecil Rawls Library and Museum, Courtland, VA [*Library symbol Library of Congress*] (LCLS)
ViCovI........	Industrial Rayon Corp., Covington, VA [*Library symbol Library of Congress*] (LCLS)
ViCovW........	West Virginia Pulp & Paper Co., Covington, VA [*Library symbol Library of Congress*] (LCLS)
ViCP..........	Piedmont Virginia Community College, Learning Resources Center, Charlottesville, VA [*Library symbol Library of Congress*] (LCLS)
VICP..........	[*National*] Vaccine Injury Compensation Program [*Established under the 1986 federal Childhood Vaccine Injury Act*] (PAZ)
VICP..........	VINES [*Virtual Networking Software*] Interprocess Communications Protocol [*Computer science*] (PCM)
VICP..........	Virtual Network System Internet Control Protocol [*Banyan Systems, Inc.*] [*Telecommunications*] (PCM)
VICPIC........	Victorian Prison Industries Commission [*Australia*]
VICR..........	Vicor Corp. [*NASDAQ symbol*] (TTSB)
VICRA.........	National Radio Astronomy Observatory, Charlottesville, VA [*Library symbol Library of Congress*] (LCLS)
VICS..........	Variable Inertia Charging System [*Mazda Motor Co.*] [*Automotive engineering*]
VICS..........	Vehicle Information and Communications System [*FHWA*] (TAG)
VICS..........	Vehicle Information and Control System [*Highway traffic management*]
VICS..........	Verbal Interaction Category System [*Student teacher test*]
VICS..........	Vocational Information through Computer Systems [*Philadelphia School District*] [*Pennsylvania*] [*Information service or system*] (IID)
VICS..........	Voluntary Interindustry Communication Standard [*Retail Apparel Industry*]
Vic's Res.....	Victoria's Resources [*A publication*]
ViCT..........	Institute of Textile Technology, Charlottesville, VA [*Library symbol Library of Congress*] (LCLS)
VICT..........	Victoria Bankshares, Inc. [*NASDAQ symbol*] (NQ)
VICTA.........	Valett Inventory of Critical Thinking Abilities [*Child development test*]
Vict Acts.....	Victoria Acts of Parliament [*A publication*] (DLA)
VictBn........	Victoria Bankshares, Inc. [*Associated Press*] (SAG)
Vict CS	Victorian Consolidated Statutes [*A publication*] (ILCA)
Vict L	Victorian Law Journal [*A publication*] (DLA)
Vict L (Austr)...	Victorian Reports (Law)(Australia) [*A publication*] (ILCA)
Vict R	Victorian Reports (Australian) [*A publication*] (DLA)
Victrm........	Victormaxx Technologies [*Associated Press*] (SAG)
Vict UL Rev...	Victoria University. Law Review [*A publication*] (DLA)
ViCVH.........	Virginia Highway Research Council, Charlottesville, VA [*Library symbol Library of Congress*] (LCLS)
VICX..........	Kanpur/Chakeri [*India*] [*ICAO location identifier*] (ICLI)
ViD...........	Danville Public Library, Danville, VA [*Library symbol Library of Congress*] (LCLS)
VID...........	Vaginal Intraepithelial Dysplasia [*Gynecology*] (DAVI)
VID...........	Variable Intermittent Duty (IAA)
VID...........	Vide [*or Videte*] [*See*] [*Latin*]
VID...........	Video (AAG)
VID...........	Video-Data [*Computer graphics*] (BYTE)
VID...........	Videodensitometry [*Laboratory science*] (DAVI)
VID...........	Video Image Display Assembly [*Space Flight Operations Facility, NASA*]
Vid...........	Vidian's Exact Pleader [*1684*] [*A publication*] (DLA)
VID...........	Vidin [*Bulgaria*] [*Airport symbol*] (OAG)
vid...........	Vidua [*Widow*] [*Latin*] (WGA)
VID...........	Vienna Institute for Development (EAIO)
VID...........	Virtual Image Display (MCD)
VID...........	Visual Identification (CAAL)
VID...........	Volunteers for International Development [*Later, Peaceworkers*] (EA)
ViDA	Averette College, Danville, VA [*Library symbol Library of Congress*] (LCLS)
VIDA	Ventricular Impulse Detector and Alarm [*Cardiology*]
VIDA	Victorian Institute for Dryland Agriculture [*Australia*] (BUAC)
VIDA	VidaMed, Inc. [*NASDAQ symbol*] (SAG)
VIDAC........	Virtual Data Acquisition and Control [*Computer science*] (HGAA)
VIDAC........	Visual Information Display and Control
VidaMd.......	VidaMed, Inc. [*Associated Press*] (SAG)
VIDAMP.......	Video Amplifier
VIDAP........	Vibration Data Accuracy Program
VIDAR........	Velocity Integration, Detection, and Ranging (NG)

VIDAS.........	Video Image Digitiser and Storage System [*Sirton Computer*] [*London, England*]
VIDAS.........	Vitek ImmunoDiagnostic Assay System
VIDAT.........	Visual Data Acquisition
ViDC...........	Danville Community College, Danville, VA [*Library symbol Library of Congress*] (LCLS)
VIDC...........	Vienna Institute for Development and Cooperation [*Austria*] (BUAC)
VIDC...........	Virgin Islands Department of Commerce (EA)
VIDD...........	Delhi/Safdarjung [*India*] [*ICAO location identifier*] (ICLI)
VIDD...........	Vehicle Intrusion Detection Device
VIDD...........	Vertical Interval Data Detector (NASA)
VidDsp........	Video Display Corp. [*Associated Press*] (SAG)
VIDE...........	Video Display [*NASDAQ symbol*] (TTSB)
VIDE...........	Video Display Corp. [*NASDAQ symbol*] (NQ)
VIDEA.........	Victoria International Development Association [*Canada*] (BUAC)
VIDEC........	Vibration Analysis and Detection Concept (DNAB)
VIDEC........	Video Digitally Enhanced Compression (PCM)
VIDEM........	Vietnam Demonstration [*FBI security file*]
VIDEO.........	Visual Data Entry On-Line [*Computer science*]
VIDEO.........	VORTEX Interactive Data Entry Operation (NITA)
VideoL........	Video Lottery Technologies, Inc. [*Associated Press*] (SAG)
VideoLab	VideoLabs, Inc. [*Associated Press*] (SAG)
VideoLan	VideoLan Technologies, Inc. [*Associated Press*] (SAG)
Videonics	Videonics, Inc. [*Associated Press*] (SAG)
VideoSen.....	Video Sentry Corp. [*Associated Press*] (SAG)
Videotr........	Videotron Holdings PLC [*Associated Press*] (SAG)
VideoU........	Video Updates, Inc. [*Associated Press*] (SAG)
VideoUpd....	Video Updates, Inc. [*Associated Press*] (SAG)
VIDF...........	Delhi [*India*] [*ICAO location identifier*] (ICLI)
VIDF...........	Vertical Side of Intermediate Distribution Frame [*Telecommunications*] (TEL)
VIDF...........	Video Frequency (IEEE)
VIDI...........	Visual Input Detection Instrumentation (MCD)
VIDIAC........	Video Input to Automatic Computer (NITA)
VIDIAC........	Visual Information Display and Control (DGA)
VIDICODER...	Video Interphone Communications System (SAA)
VidJuke.......	Video Jukebox Network, Inc. [*Associated Press*] (SAG)
VidLan........	VideoLan Technologies, Inc. [*Associated Press*] (SAG)
VIDN...........	Dehra Dun [*India*] [*ICAO location identifier*] (ICLI)
VIDO	Veterinary Infectious Disease Organization [*University of Saskatchewan*] [*Canada Research center*] (RCD)
VIDOC........	Video Documentary (NTCM)
VIDOC........	Visual Information Documentation [*Military*]
VIDP	Delhi/Indira Gandhi International [*India*] [*ICAO location identifier*] (ICLI)
VIDPI.........	Visually Impaired Data Processors International (EA)
VIDR...........	Dadri [*India*] [*ICAO location identifier*] (ICLI)
ViDR...........	Dan River Mills Co., Danville, VA [*Library symbol Library of Congress*] (LCLS)
VID-R..........	Visual Information Display and Retrieval System [*Computer science*] (PDAA)
ViDS	Stratford College, Danville, VA [*Library symbol Library of Congress*] (LCLS)
VIDS	Vehicle Integrated Defense System [*Military*]
VIDS	Vertical Instruments Display System (MCD)
VIDS	Virtual Image Display System
VIDS	Visual Information Display System (MCD)
VIDSEC.......	Video Systems Exposition and Conference (PDAA)
VidServ.......	VideoServer, Inc. [*Associated Press*] (SAG)
VIDS/MAF....	Visual Information Display System/Maintenance Action Form (NVT)
VIDT..........	Variable Inductance Displacement Transducer (PDAA)
VidU...........	Video Updates, Inc. [*Associated Press*] (SAG)
VIE............	Vacuum Insulated Evaporator (PDAA)
VIE............	Vampire Information Exchange (EA)
VIE............	Vibration Isolation Equipment (RDA)
VIE............	Victorian Institute of Engineers [*Australian*] (BUAC)
VIE............	Vienna [*Austria*] [*Airport symbol*] (OAG)
VIE............	Vienna [*Austria*] [*Seismograph station code, US Geological Survey*] (SEIS)
vie............	Vietnamese [*MARC language code Library of Congress*] (LCCP)
VIE............	Vigilance, Initiative, Excellence [*Aerospace Defense Command's acronym for the Zero Defects Program*]
VIE............	Villeneuve Resources [*Vancouver Stock Exchange symbol*]
VIE............	Virtual Information Environment [*Computer science*] (PCM)
VIE............	Visual Indicating Equipment [*Telecommunications*] (IAA)
VIE............	Voluntary Import Expansion [*International trade*] (ECON)
VIE............	Volunteers in Education
Vie deFr	Vie de France Corp. [*Associated Press*] (SAG)
VIEEW.........	Video Enhanced Evaluation of Weathering [*Automotive paint durability*]
ViEIM.........	Merck & Co., Inc., Stonewall Process Development Library, Elkton, VA [*Library symbol Library of Congress*] (LCLS)
ViEmoE.......	Emory and Henry College, Emory, VA [*Library symbol Library of Congress*] (LCLS)
ViEmP........	Greenville County Library, Emporia, VA [*Library symbol Library of Congress*] (LCLS)
VIEN...........	Vienna [*Austria*] (WDAA)
Vien...........	Viennola [*Record label*] [*Austria*]
VIEO..........	Vendor's Item Engineering Order
VIERS	Virgin Islands Ecological Research Station
VIESA.........	Vocational Interest, Experience, and Skill Assessment [*Vocational guidance test*]
VIEW..........	View [*Commonly used*] (OPSA)
VIEW..........	Viewlogic Systems [*NASDAQ symbol*] (TTSB)
VIEW..........	Viewlogic Systems, Inc. [*NASDAQ symbol*] (SPSG)

VIEW...........	Virtual Interface Environment Workstation
VIEW..........	Visible, Informative, Emotionally Appealing, Workable [*Package evaluation in marketing*]
VIEW..........	Visually Impaired Empowering Women [*New Zealand*] (BUAC)
VIEW..........	Vital Information for Education and Work (OICC)
VIEW..........	Vocational Information for Education and Work (AEBS)
ViewIg........	Viewlogic Systems, Inc. [*Associated Press*] (SAG)
VIEWS........	VAST/IMA [*Versatile Avionics System Tester/Intermediate Maintenance Activity*] Effectiveness by Workload Simulation
VIEWS........	Vibration Indicator Early Warning System (MCD)
VIEWS........	Views [*Commonly used*] (OPSA)
VIEWS........	Virtual Interactive Environment Workstation [*NASA*] (BYTE)
VIEWS........	Vocational Information and Evaluation Work Samples [*Vocational guidance test*]
ViewT.........	View Tech, Inc. [*Associated Press*] (SAG)
ViewTc........	View Tech, Inc. [*Associated Press*] (SAG)
ViF............	Fairfax County Public Library, Fairfax, VA [*Library symbol Library of Congress*] (LCLS)
VIF............	Vanier Institute of the Family [*Canada*]
VIF............	Variance Inflation Factor [*Statistics*]
VIF............	Vertical Infrared Fuze (CAAL)
VIF............	Video Information [*Winslow Associates*] [*No longer available*] [*Information service or system*] (IID)
VIF............	Virion Infectivity Factor [*Genetics*]
VIF............	Virus-Induced Interferon [*Cell biology*]
VIF............	Visual Image Formula [*of psychotherapist Joseph Bird's self-help theory*]
VIF............	Voice Interface Frame [*Telecommunications*] (IAA)
ViFarL........	Longwood College, Farmville, VA [*Library symbol Library of Congress*] (LCLS)
VIFB..........	Farrukhabad [*India*] [*ICAO location identifier*] (ICLI)
ViFbE	United States Army Engineer School, Fort Belvoir, VA [*Library symbol Library of Congress*] (LCLS)
ViFbEM.......	United States Army, Engineer Museum, Fort Belvoir, VA [*Library symbol Library of Congress*] (LCLS)
ViF-BPH......	Fairfax County Public Library, Services for the Blind and Physically Handicapped, Alexandria, VA [*Library symbol Library of Congress*] (LCLS)
VIFC..........	VTOL [*Vertical Takeoff and Landing*] Integrated Flight Control
VIFD..........	Faridkot [*India*] [*ICAO location identifier*] (ICLI)
ViFeAM.......	United States Army, Air Mobility Research and Development Laboratory, Fort Eustis, VA [*Library symbol Library of Congress*] (LCLS)
ViFeAT.......	United States Army Transportation School, Fort Eustis, VA [*Library symbol Library of Congress*] (LCLS)
ViFerF........	Ferrum College, Ferrum, VA [*Library symbol Library of Congress*] (LCLS)
VIFF..........	Vectoring in Forward Flight (MCD)
VIFF..........	Visualization and Image File Format [*Computer science*] (CIST)
ViFGM	George Mason College [*Later, George Mason University*], Fairfax, VA [*Library symbol Library of Congress*] (LCLS)
VIFI..........	Voyager Information Flow Instructions [*NASA*] (KSC)
VIFL..........	Food Technology Service, Inc. [*NASDAQ symbol*] (SAG)
ViFL..........	Food Technology Svc [*NASDAQ symbol*] (TTSB)
ViFIL..........	United States Army Logistics Management Center, Fort Lee, VA [*Library symbol Library of Congress*] (LCLS)
ViFlQ..........	Quartermaster Technical Library, Fort Lee, VA [*Library symbol Library of Congress*] (LCLS)
VIFM..........	Video-Intensified Fluorescence Microscopy
ViFmTD.......	United States Army, Training and Doctrine Command Library, Fort Monroe, VA [*Library symbol Library of Congress*] (LCLS)
ViFmTS.......	United States Army Tralinet Systems Center, Fort Monroe, VA [*Library symbol Library of Congress*] (LCLS)
ViFmUS.......	United States Army Field Forces Library, Fort Monroe, VA [*Library symbol Library of Congress*] (LCLS)
ViFmyA.......	United States Army, Fort Meyer Post Library, Fort Meyer, VA [*Library symbol Library of Congress*] (LCLS)
VIFPA..........	Virgin Islands Family Planning Association (BUAC)
ViFraC	Camp Manufacturing Co., Franklin, VA [*Library symbol Library of Congress*] (LCLS)
ViFraPC	Paul D. Camp Community College, Franklin, VA [*Library symbol Library of Congress*] (LCLS)
ViFre..........	Central Rappahannock Regional Library, Fredericksburg, VA [*Library symbol Library of Congress*] (LCLS)
ViFreJM.......	James Monroe Memorial Foundation, Fredericksburg, VA [*Library symbol Library of Congress*] (LCLS)
ViFreM........	Mary Washington College of the University of Virginia, Fredericksburg, VA [*Library symbol Library of Congress*] (LCLS)
ViFroA.........	American Viscose Co., Front Royal, VA [*Library symbol Library of Congress*] (LCLS)
VIFSC..........	VTOL [*Vertical Takeoff and Landing*] Integrated Flight System Control
ViFvW.........	Woodrow Wilson Rehabilitation Center, Fishersville, VA [*Library symbol*] [*Library of Congress*] (LCLS)
VIFZ..........	Ferojpur [*India*] [*ICAO location identifier*] (ICLI)
VIG............	Vaccinia Immune Globulin [*Medicine*]
VIG............	Van Kam Am Cap Inv Grade [*NYSE symbol*] (TTSB)
VIG............	Van Kampen Merritt Investment Grade Municipal [*NYSE symbol*] (SPSG)
VIG............	Video Image Generator
VIG............	Video Integrating Group
Vig............	Vigente [*In Force*] [*Italian*] (ILCA)
VIG............	Vigil (ROG)
VIG............	Vigilant Identification (MCD)
VIG............	Vignette (ADA)

VIG............	Vigoroso [With Vigor] [Music] (ROG)
vig.............	Vigorous (DAVI)
VIG............	Visible Gold, Inc. [Vancouver Stock Exchange symbol]
VIGB..........	Variable Inlet Guide Blades (MCD)
ViGcS.........	Scott County Library, Gate City, VA [Library symbol Library of Congress] (LCLS)
VIGIL.........	Vertical Indicating Gyro Internally Lighted (MCD)
Vigl...........	Viglius ab Ayta Zuichemus [Deceased, 1577] [Authority cited in pre-1607 legal work] (DSA)
VIGN.........	Guna [India] [ICAO location identifier] (ICLI)
VIGORN......	Vigorniensis [Signature of the Bishops of Worcester] [Latin] (ROG)
Vigoro.......	Vigoro Corp. [Associated Press] (SAG)
ViGpD........	Deepsea Ventures, Inc., Gloucester Point, VA [Library symbol Library of Congress] (LCLS)
ViGpM........	Virginia Institute of Marine Science, Gloucester Point, VA [Library symbol Library of Congress] (LCLS)
VIGR..........	Gwalior [India] [ICAO location identifier] (ICLI)
VIGS..........	Vertical Impact Guidance System [Army] (MCD)
VIGS..........	Video Disc Gunnery Simulator [Army] (INF)
VIGS..........	Video Interactive Gunnery System [Military] (INF)
VIGS..........	Virtual Induced Gap States (AAEL)
VIGS..........	Visual Glide Slope
VIH...........	Rolla/Vichy, MO [Location identifier FAA] (FAAL)
VIH...........	Velocity Impact Hardening
ViHa..........	Charles H. Taylor Memorial Library, Hampton, VA [Library symbol Library of Congress] (LCLS)
ViHal.........	Hampton Institute, Hampton, VA [Library symbol Library of Congress] (LCLS)
ViHal.........	Halifax County-South Boston Regional Library, Halifax, VA [Library symbol Library of Congress] (LCLS)
ViHaNASA...	National Aeronautics and Space Administration, Langley Research Center, Hampton, VA [Library symbol Library of Congress] (LCLS)
ViHar.........	Rockingham Public Library, Harrisonburg, VA [Library symbol Library of Congress] (LCLS)
ViHarEM......	Eastern Mennonite College, Harrisonburg, VA [Library symbol Library of Congress] (LCLS)
ViHarT.......	James Madison University, Harrisonburg, VA [Library symbol Library of Congress] (LCLS)
ViHaT.........	Thomas Nelson Community College, Hampton, VA [Library symbol Library of Congress] (LCLS)
ViHaV........	United States Veterans Administration Center, Medical Library, Hampton, VA [Library symbol Library of Congress] (LCLS)
ViHdsC.......	Hampden-Sydney College, Hampden-Sydney, VA [Library symbol Library of Congress] (LCLS)
ViHi..........	Virginia Historical Society, Richmond, VA [Library symbol Library of Congress] (LCLS)
ViHo..........	Hollins College, Hollins College, VA [Library symbol Library of Congress] (LCLS)
ViHop........	Appomattox Regional Library, Hopewell, VA [Library symbol Library of Congress] (LCLS)
ViHopA.......	Allied Corp., Hopewell, VA [Library symbol Library of Congress] (LCLS)
ViHopAT.....	American Tobacco Co., Department of Research and Development, Hopewell, VA [Library symbol Library of Congress] (LCLS)
ViHopHC.....	Hercules Powder Co. [Later, Hercules, Inc.], Cellulose Products Division, Hopewell, VA [Library symbol Library of Congress] (LCLS)
ViHopHV.....	Hercules Powder Co. [Later, Hercules, Inc.], Virginia Cellulose Division, Hopewell, VA [Library symbol Library of Congress] (LCLS)
VIHR..........	Hissar [India] [ICAO location identifier] (ICLI)
VII...........	Vacuum-Impregnated Inductor
VII...........	Vicon Indus [AMEX symbol] (TTSB)
VII...........	Vicon Industries, Inc. [AMEX symbol] (SPSG)
VII...........	Viscosity Index Improver [for motor oil]
VII...........	Vocational Interest Inventory [Vocational guidance test]
VIII-vwf.....	Von Willebrand's Factor VIII [Hematology] (DAVI)
VII-R.........	Vocational Interest Inventory-Revised [Test] (TMMY)
VIIS..........	Virgin Islands National Park
Viisage......	Viisage Technology, Inc. [Associated Press] (SAG)
VIJ...........	Vera Institute of Justice (EA)
VIJ...........	Virgin Gorda [British Virgin Islands] [Airport symbol] (OAG)
VIJN..........	Jhansi [India] [ICAO location identifier] (ICLI)
VIJO..........	Jodhpur [India] [ICAO location identifier] (ICLI)
VIJP..........	Jaipur [India] [ICAO location identifier] (ICLI)
VIJR..........	Jaiselmer [India] [ICAO location identifier] (ICLI)
VIJU..........	Jammu [India] [ICAO location identifier] (ICLI)
VIK...........	Kavik River, AK [Location identifier FAA] (FAAL)
VIK...........	Vik [Iceland] [Seismograph station code, US Geological Survey Closed] (SEIS)
VIK...........	Viking International Airlines [ICAO designator] (FAAC)
VIKA..........	Kanpur [India] [ICAO location identifier] (ICLI)
VIKA..........	Viking Air Lines
VIKD..........	Kud [India] [ICAO location identifier] (ICLI)
ViKeS.........	Southside Virginia Community College, John H. Daniel Campus, Keysville, VA [Library symbol Library of Congress] (LCLS)
Viking OP	Viking Office Products, Inc. [Associated Press] (SAG)
VIKJ..........	Khajuraho [India] [ICAO location identifier] (ICLI)
VIKO..........	Kota [India] [ICAO location identifier] (ICLI)
VIL...........	Avia Airlines [Ghana] [FAA designator] (FAAC)
VIL...........	Dakhla [Mauritania] [Airport symbol] (OAG)
ViL...........	Jones Memorial Library, Lynchburg, VA [Library symbol Library of Congress] (LCLS)
VIL...........	University of Victoria Law Library [UTLAS symbol]
VIL...........	Vendor Item List [Sales] (AAG)
VIL...........	Vertical Injection Logic [Computer science]
VIL...........	Vertically Integrated Liquid (USDC)
VIL...........	Very Important Ladies
VIL...........	Very Important Launch (MUGU)
VIL...........	Villa
VIL...........	Villa Cisneros [Spanish Sahara] [Airport symbol] (AD)
VIL...........	Village
VIL...........	Villa Mercy [Maryland] [Seismograph station code, US Geological Survey Closed] (SEIS)
Vi-L..........	Virginia State Law Library, Richmond, VA [Library symbol Library of Congress] (LCLS)
VIL...........	Vivisection Investigation League (EA)
VIL...........	VTI Industries, Inc. [Vancouver Stock Exchange symbol]
VilagBcp.....	Village Bancorp [Associated Press] (SAG)
ViLanAF......	United States Air Force, Langley Air Force Base Library, Langley AFB, VA [Library symbol Library of Congress] (LCLS)
Vil & Br......	Vilas and Bryant's Edition of the Wisconsin Reports [A publication] (DLA)
Vilas........	Vilas' Criminal Reports [1-5 New York] [A publication] (DLA)
ViLaw........	Brunswick-Greensville Regional Library, Lawrenceville, VA [Library symbol Library of Congress] (LCLS)
ViLawS.......	Saint Paul's College, Lawrenceville, VA [Library symbol Library of Congress] (LCLS)
ViLBW........	Babcock & Wilcox Co., Lynchburg, VA [Library symbol Library of Congress] (LCLS)
ViLC..........	Lynchburg College, Lynchburg, VA [Library symbol Library of Congress] (LCLS)
ViLCV.........	Central Virginia Community College, Lynchburg, VA [Library symbol Library of Congress] (LCLS)
VILD..........	Ludhaiha [India] [ICAO location identifier] (ICLI)
VILIB.........	Virtual Library Libraries (TELE)
VILIOR.......	Vladimir Ilyich Lenin, Initiator of the October Revolution [Given name popular in Russia after the Bolshevik Revolution]
VILK..........	Lucknow [India] [ICAO location identifier] (ICLI)
VILL..........	Village
Vill..........	Villandry Festival [Record label] [France]
VILLAG	Village [Commonly used] (OPSA)
VILLAGE	Village [Commonly used] (OPSA)
VILLAGES	Villages [Commonly used] (OPSA)
Villanova U..	Villanova University (GAGS)
ViLLB.........	Liberty Baptist College, Lynchburg, VA [Library symbol] [Library of Congress] (LCLS)
VILLE........	Ville [Commonly used] (OPSA)
VILLG........	Village [Commonly used] (OPSA)
VillGr........	Village Green Bookstore, Inc. [Associated Press] (SAG)
VillGrBk.....	Village Green Bookstore [Associated Press] (SAG)
VillGrBk.....	Village Green Bookstore, Inc. [Associated Press] (SAG)
VILLIAGE	Village [Commonly used] (OPSA)
ViLoGH.......	Gunston Hall Plantation Library, Lorton, VA [Library symbol Library of Congress] (LCLS)
VILP..........	Lalitpur [India] [ICAO location identifier] (ICLI)
VILP..........	Vector Impedance Locus Plotter
ViLRM	Randolph-Macon Woman's College, Lynchburg, VA [Library symbol Library of Congress] (LCLS)
VilSpM........	Village Super Market, Inc. [Associated Press] (SAG)
VILTCH	Verapamil, Imipramine, Lidocaine, Tamoxifen, Chlorpromazine, Haloperidol [Antineoplastic drug regimen]
ViLuV.........	Virginia Oak Tannery, Luray, VA [Library symbol Library of Congress] (LCLS)
ViLx..........	Botetourt-Rockbridge Regional Library, Lexington, VA [Library symbol Library of Congress] (LCLS)
ViLxV.........	Virginia Military Institute, Lexington, VA [Library symbol Library of Congress] (LCLS)
ViLxW........	Washington and Lee University, Lexington, VA [Library symbol Library of Congress] (LCLS)
ViLxW-L......	Washington and Lee University, Law Library, Lexington, VA [Library symbol Library of Congress] (LCLS)
VIM...........	Air-Via [Bulgaria] [ICAO designator] (FAAC)
VIM...........	Vacuum Induction Melting [Metallurgy]
VIM...........	Van Kam Am Cap Ins Muni [NYSE symbol] (TTSB)
VIM...........	Van Kampen Merritt Trust for Insured Municipals [NYSE symbol] (SAG)
VIM...........	Variable Intake Manifold
VIM...........	Vendor Independent Messaging [Computer science] (PCM)
VIM...........	Vendor Initial Measurement [Sales]
VIM...........	Ventral Intersegmental Muscles [Anatomy]
VIM...........	Vertical Improved Mail [Mail-delivery system for large buildings in which all tenants pick up their mail from lockboxes in a central mailroom]
VIM...........	Vibrational Microlamination (MCD)
VIM...........	Vibration Isolation Module
VIM...........	Video Intensified Microscopy
VIM...........	Vinyl Insulation Material
VIM...........	Vision Intensified Microscopy
VIM...........	Visitor Impact Management [Park tourism management]
VIM...........	Vocational Instructional Materials Section (EA)
VIM...........	Voice Input Module [Cascade Graphics Development Ltd.] [Software package] (NCC)
ViMan........	Ruffner-Carnegie Public Library, Manassas, VA [Library symbol Library of Congress Obsolete] (LCLS)
ViManCo......	Prince William County Public Library, Manassas, VA [Library symbol Library of Congress] (LCLS)
ViMarC	Marion Junior College, Marion, VA [Library symbol Library of Congress] (LCLS)

ViMat.......... Mathews Memorial Library, Mathews, VA [*Library symbol Library of Congress*] (LCLS)

ViMcC.......... Central Intelligence Agency, McLean, VA [*Library symbol Library of Congress*] (LCLS)

VIMCOS...... Vehicle for the Investigation of Maintenance Control System (PDAA)

ViMelE........ Eastern Shore Community College, Learning Resources Center, Melfa, VA [*Library symbol Library of Congress*] (LCLS)

VIMEX.......... Visit Mexico [*Airline fares*]

VIMG............ Moga [*India*] [*ICAO location identifier*] (ICLI)

VIMHEX...... Venezuela International Meteorological and Hydrological Experiment [*Colorado State University project*]

ViMidL.......... Lord Fairfax Community College, Learning Resources Center, Middletown, VA [*Library symbol Library of Congress*] (LCLS)

ViMiN.......... Notre Dame Institute, Middleburg, VA [*Library symbol Library of Congress*] (LCLS)

ViMiNS........ National Sporting Library, Inc., Middleburg, VA [*Library symbol Library of Congress*] (LCLS)

VIMIX.......... Variable Intake and Mixture [*Fuel systems*] [*Automotive engineering*]

V IMP.......... Verb Impersonal [*Grammar*] (WDAA)

VIMP............ Vertical Impulse

V IMPER...... Verb Imperative [*Grammar*] (WDAA)

Vimrx.......... VimRx Pharmaceuticals, Inc. [*Associated Press*] (SAG)

VIMS............ Mandasor [*India*] [*ICAO location identifier*] (ICLI)

VIMS............ Variable Integration Measurement System

VIMS............ Vehicle Integrated Management System

VIMS............ Verification Information Management System (DNAB)

VIMS............ Versatile Interior Multiplex System (PDAA)

VIMS............ Victorian Institute of Marine Science [*State*] (EERA)

VIMS............ Virginia Institute of Marine Science [*College of William and Mary*] [*Research center*]

VIMS............ Visible-Infrared Mapping Spectrometer [*Instrumentation*]

VIMS............ Visual Infrared Mapping Spectrometer

VIMSIS........ Victorian Institute of Marine Sciences Information System [*State*] (EERA)

VIMTPG........ Virtual Interactive Machine Test Program Generator

ViMtvL.......... Mount Vernon Ladies' Association of the Union, Mount Vernon, VA [*Library symbol Library of Congress*] (LCLS)

ViMv............ Blue Ridge Regional Library, Martinsville, VA [*Library symbol*] [*Library of Congress*] (LCLS)

VIMVAR...... Vacuum Induction Melt, Vacuum Arc Remelt

ViMvD.......... E. I. Du Pont de Nemours & Co., Martinsville, VA [*Library symbol Library of Congress*] (LCLS)

V$_{in}$.............. Input Voltage (IDOE)

VIN............... Miami, FL [*Location identifier FAA*] (FAAL)

ViN............... Norfolk Public Library, Norfolk, VA [*Library symbol Library of Congress*] (LCLS)

VIN............... Vaginal Intraepithelial Neoplasia [*Gynecology*] (DAVI)

VIN............... Vehicle Identification Number

VIN............... Vendor Identification Number [*Sales*] (MCD)

VIN............... Victorian Industrial Notes [*A publication*]

VIN............... Vinair-Helicopteros Ltda. [*Portugal ICAO designator*] (FAAC)

VIN............... Vinbarbital [*A hypnotic and sedative*] (DAVI)

Vin............... Vincentius Hispanus [*Deceased, 1248*] [*Authority cited in pre-1607 legal work*] (DSA)

VIN............... Vineyard [*California*] [*Seismograph station code, US Geological Survey Closed*] (SEIS)

VIN............... Vinum [*Wine*] [*Pharmacy*] (ROG)

VIN............... Vinyl [*Technical drawings*]

VIN............... Voltage Input (TEL)

Vin Abr........ Supplement to Viner's Abridgment of Law and Equity [*England*] [*A publication*] (DLA)

Vin Abr (Eng)... Viner's Abridgment of Law and Equity [*1741-53*] [*A publication*] (DLA)

VinaConc..... Vina Concha y Toro SA [*Associated Press*] (SAG)

VINACON-TROL... Vietnam National Export-Import Goods Control Co. (BUAC)

VINAFPA...... Vietnam Family Planning Association (BUAC)

ViNarC......... Celanese Corp., Narrows, VA [*Library symbol Library of Congress*] (LCLS)

ViNC............ Chrysler Art Museum, Jean Outland Chrysler Library, Norfolk, VA [*Library symbol Library of Congress*] (LCLS)

Vinc............. Vincentius Hispanus [*Deceased, 1248*] [*Authority cited in pre-1607 legal work*] (DSA)

Vinc Cr & Lib... Vincent on Criticism and Libel [*A publication*] (DLA)

Vinc Cr L..... Vincent's Manual of Criminal Law [*A publication*] (DLA)

Vincent de Franch... Vincentius de Franchis [*Deceased, 1601*] [*Authority cited in pre-1607 legal work*] (DSA)

Vin Comm ... Viner's Abridgment [*or Commentaries*] [*A publication*] (DLA)

VIND............ Vicarious Interpolations Not Desired

VIND............ Vindication (ROG)

ViNE............ Eastern Virginia Medical School, Norfolk, VA [*Library symbol Library of Congress*] (LCLS)

ViNe............ Newport News Public Library, Newport News, VA [*Library symbol Library of Congress*] (LCLS)

VINE............ Very Informal Newsletter (NITA)

ViNeA......... Southeastern Universities Research Association, CEBAF Library, Newport News, VA [*Library symbol*] [*Library of Congress*] (LCLS)

ViNeC......... Christopher Newport College, Newport News, VA [*Library symbol Library of Congress*] (LCLS)

ViNeM......... Mariners' Museum, Newport News, VA [*Library symbol Library of Congress*] (LCLS)

ViNeN.......... Newport News Shipbuilding & Dry Dock Co., Newport News, VA [*Library symbol Library of Congress*] (LCLS)

Viner Abr..... Viner's Abridgment of Law and Equity [*1741-53*] [*A publication*] (DLA)

VINES......... Virtual Networking Software [*Banyan Systems*]

VINES.......... Virtual Network System [*Computer science*] (CIST)

ViNeV.......... Virginia Associated Research Center, Newport News, VA [*Library symbol Library of Congress*] (LCLS)

ViNEVM........ Eastern Virginia Medical School, Norfolk, VA [*Library symbol*] [*Library of Congress*] (LCLS)

VINF............ Vista Information Solutions, Inc. [*NASDAQ symbol*] (SAG)

VINF............ VISTA Info Solutions [*NASDAQ symbol*] (TTSB)

VINFA.......... Volunteers in the National Forests Act [*1972*]

VINH............ Nuh [*India*] [*ICAO location identifier*] (ICLI)

VINI............. Viniculture (WDAA)

Vining.......... Vinings Investment Properties Trust [*Associated Press*] (SAG)

VINITI.......... Vsesoyuznyy Institut Nauchnoy i Tekhnicheskoy Informatsii [*All-Union Institute of Scientific and Technical Information*] [*Former USSR*]

VINL............ Naranaup [*India*] [*ICAO location identifier*] (ICLI)

Vinland........ Vinland Property Trust [*Associated Press*] (SAG)

ViNM........... Norfolk County Medical Society, Inc., Norfolk, VA [*Library symbol Library of Congress*] (LCLS)

ViNMoN...... Monsanto Chemical Co., Norfolk, VA [*Library symbol Library of Congress*] (LCLS)

Vinn ad Inst... Vinnius' Commentary on the Institutes of Justinian [*A publication*] (DLA)

ViNO............ Old Dominion University, Norfolk, VA [*Library symbol Library of Congress*] (LCLS)

ViNott.......... Nottoway County Library, Nottoway, VA [*Library symbol Library of Congress*] (LCLS)

Vin Palaeot... Vincentius Palaeotus [*Deceased, 1498*] [*Authority cited in pre-1607 legal work*] (DSA)

ViNR............ F. S. Royster Guano Co., Norfolk, VA [*Library symbol Library of Congress*] (LCLS)

ViNS............ Norfolk State College, Norfolk, VA [*Library symbol Library of Congress*] (LCLS)

VINS............ Velocity Inertia Navigation System

VINS............ Very Intense Neutron Source [*Nuclear science*] (OA)

ViNSC.......... United States Armed Forces Staff College, Norfolk, VA [*Library symbol Library of Congress*] (LCLS)

ViNSo.......... Sovran Bank Corp. Library, Norfolk, VA [*Library symbol*] [*Library of Congress*] (LCLS)

Vin Supp...... Supplement to Viner's Abridgment of Law and Equity [*A publication*] (DLA)

ViNT............ Norfolk Testing Laboratories, Norfolk, VA [*Library symbol Library of Congress*] (LCLS)

VINT............ Video Integrate (NVT)

VInt............. Vie Intellectuelle [*A publication*] (BJA)

VINT^2.......... Vehicle Integrated Intelligence [*Army*]

Vint Can Law... Vinton's American Canon Law [*A publication*] (DLA)

VintgPt......... Vintage Petroleum [*Associated Press*] (SAG)

ViNWe......... Virginia Wesleyan College, Norfolk, VA [*Library symbol Library of Congress*] (LCLS)

VIO.............. Avionic Ltd. [*Greece*] [*FAA designator*] (FAAC)

VIO.............. Verbal Intelligence Quotient (DAVI)

VIO.............. Very Important Object (DCTA)

VIO.............. Veterinary Investigation Officer [*Ministry of Agriculture, Fisheries, and Food*] [*British*]

VIO.............. Video Input/Output

VIO.............. Violet (AAG)

VIO.............. Violino [*Violin*] [*Music*] (ROG)

VIO.............. Vior Miniere d'Exploration Societe, Inc. [*Toronto Stock Exchange symbol*]

VIO.............. Virtual Input/Output [*Computer science*] (IBMDP)

VIO.............. Visual Intercept Officer [*Navy*]

VIOC............ Variable Input-Output Code

VIOL............ Viola [*Music*] (ROG)

viol.............. Violaceus [*Purple*] [*Latin*] (WGA)

VIOLE.......... Violone [*Double Bass*] [*Music*] (ROG)

VIOLENT...... Viewers Intent on Listing Violent Episodes on Nationwide Television [*Student legal action organization*]

VIOLO.......... Violino [*Violin*] [*Music*] (ROG)

VION............ Vion Pharmaceuticals [*NASDAQ symbol*] (TTSB)

Vion............. Vion Pharmaceuticals, Inc. [*Associated Press*] (SAG)

VION............ Vion Pharmaceuticals, Inc. [*NASDAQ symbol*] (SAG)

VionPh......... Vion Pharmaceuticals, Inc. [*Associated Press*] (SAG)

VIONU.......... Vion Pharmaceuticals Unit [*NASDAQ symbol*] (TTSB)

VIONW......... Vion Pharmaceuticals Wrrt'A' [*NASDAQ symbol*] (TTSB)

VIONZ.......... Vion Pharmaceuticals Wrrt'B' [*NASDAQ symbol*] (TTSB)

ViOr............. Orange County Public Library, Orange, VA [*Library symbol Library of Congress*] (LCLS)

VIP.............. Valuable-Items Policy [*Insurance*] (MHDI)

VIP.............. Value Improving Products

VIP.............. Value in Performance

VIP.............. Variable Incentive Pay [*Military*] (NVT)

VIP.............. Variable Individual Protection [*Insurance*]

VIP.............. Variable Inductance Pickup

VIP.............. Variable Information Processing [*Naval Ordnance Laboratory*] [*Information retrieval*]

VIP.............. Variable Input Phototypesetter

VIP.............. Variable Interest Plus [*Banking*]

VIP.............. Variation in Price (MHDB)

VIP.............. Vasoactive Inhibitory Principle [*Biochemistry*]

VIP.............. Vasoactive Intestinal Peptide [*or Polypeptide*] [*Biochemistry*]

VIP.............. Vasoinhibitory Peptide [*Medicine*] (MAE)

VIP.............. Vector Inner Product (IAA)

VIP.............. Vector Instruction Processor

VIP.............. Vehicle Inspection Program

VIP.............. Venous Impedance Plethysmography [*Medicine*] (DMAA)

VIPEVM........ Ventilated Improved Pit [*Latrine*]

VIP............. Ventral Intraparietal [*Brain anatomy*]
VIP............. Verification Integration Plan (SSD)
VIP............. Verifying Interpreting Punch (IAA)
VIP............. Verifying the Installation of Products [*Military*] (SAA)
VIP............. Vermont Information Processes, Inc. [*Information service or system*] (IID)
VIP............. Versatile Information Processor [*Computer science*]
VIP............. Very Important Passenger
VIP............. Very Important Patient (MAE)
VIP............. Very Important Person
VIP............. Very Important Poor
VIP............. Very Important Pregnancy [*In book title, "VIP Program"*]
VIP............. Vice President (AAG)
VIP............. Videodisc Innovation Project (NITA)
VIP............. Video Inertial Pointing [*System*] [*NASA*]
VIP............. Video Integrator and Processor
VIP............. Viewers in Profile [*A. C. Nielsen Co. reports for television industry*]
VIP............. Virgil Partch [*Cartoonist*]
VIP............. Virtual Image Processing [*Optics*]
VIP............. Virtual Instruction Package (IAA)
VIP............. Virtual Network System Internet Protocol [*Banyan Systems, Inc.*] [*Telecommunications*] (PCM)
VIP............. Viscosity-Index Improver [*for motor oil*]
VIP............. Visible Ink Press [*Publisher*]
VIP............. Vision Information Program (IID)
VIP............. Vision Inspection Processor (NITA)
VIP............. Visit-Investigate-Purchase [*Department of Commerce program*]
VIP............. Visitor Information Publications [*Defunct*] (EA)
VIP............. V-Isolation with Polysilicon Backfill (IAA)
VIP............. Visual Identification Point (AFM)
VIP............. Visual Image Processor (IAA)
VIP............. Visual Image Projection
VIP............. Visual Indicator Panel (IAA)
VIP............. Visual Information Processing
VIP............. Visual Information Processor (COE)
VIP............. Visual Information Projection
VIP............. Visual Input [*System*] [*AT & T*]
VIP............. Visual Interactive Programming [*Computer science*]
ViP............. Visual Programmer [*Computer science*] (PCM)
VIP............. Vital Initial of Pregnancy [*In vitro fertilization*] [*Obstetrics*] (DAVI)
VIP............. Vocational Information Profile [*Test*] [*National Computer Systems and the U.S. Employment Service*] (TES)
VIP............. Vocational Interest Profile (DHP)
VIP............. Vocational Interviewing and Placement (DNAB)
VIP............. Voice Information Processor
VIP............. Voice Integrated Presentations [*Telecommunications*] (RDA)
VIP............. Voice Intelligibility Processor [*Audio technology*] (ECON)
VIP............. Voltage Impulse Protection (IAA)
VIP............. Volume Inverse Pricing [*Business term*]
VIP............. Voluntary Interruption of Pregnancy [*Obstetrics*] (MAE)
VIP............. Volunteer Informant Program [*Navy*] (DNAB)
VIP............. Volunteers in Prevention, Probation, Prisons [*An association*] (EA)
VIP............. V-Shaped Isolation Regions Filled with Polycrystalline Silicon (IAA)
VIP............. Vulcanized Interlinked Polyethylene [*Union Carbide Corp.*]
VIP............. Vulcan Packaging, Inc. [*Toronto Stock Exchange symbol*]
VIP............. Vulnerability Impact (COE)
VIPA........... Volunteers in the Parks Act [*1969*]
VIPER.......... Verifiable Integrated Processor for Enhanced Reliability [*Computer science*] (BYTE)
VIPER.......... Video Processing and Electronic Reduction (IEEE)
VIPER.......... Visually Impaired Personal Electronic Reader (WDAA)
VIPERSCAN... Viper Rocket with Scanner (SAA)
ViPet.......... Petersburg Public Library, Petersburg, VA [*Library symbol Library of Congress*] (LCLS)
ViPetA........ Allied Chemical Corp., Fibers Division, Technical Center Library, Petersburg, VA [*Library symbol Library of Congress*] (LCLS)
ViPetS........ Virginia State College, Petersburg, VA [*Library symbol Library of Congress*] (LCLS)
VIPG.......... VIP Global Capital [*NASDAQ symbol*] (SAG)
VIP Glbl...... VIP Global Capital [*Associated Press*] (SAG)
VIPI........... Very Important Person Indeed
VIPI........... Vinings Investment Properties Trust [*NASDAQ symbol*] (SAG)
VIPI........... Volunteers in Probation, Inc. [*Later, VIP Division of National Council on Crime and Delinquency*] (EA)
VIPID......... Visual Information Processing Interface Device (MCD)
VIPIS......... Vinings Investment Property [*NASDAQ symbol*] [*Formerly, Mellon Mortgage Trust*] (SG)
VIPK.......... Pathankot [*India*] [*ICAO location identifier*] (ICLI)
VIPL.......... Patiala [*India*] [*ICAO location identifier*] (ICLI)
ViPo.......... Portsmouth Public Library, Portsmouth, VA [*Library symbol Library of Congress*] (LCLS)
ViPoN......... Norfolk Naval Hospital, Portsmouth, VA [*Library symbol Library of Congress*] (LCLS)
ViPoVC....... Virginia Chemicals, Inc., Portsmouth, VA [*Library symbol Library of Congress*] (LCLS)
ViPoVS....... Virginia Smelting Co., Portsmouth, VA [*Library symbol Library of Congress*] (LCLS)
VIPP.......... Variable Information Processing Package
VIPP.......... Venda Independent People's Party [*Political party*] (PPW)
ViPrA......... American Cyanamid Co., Pigments Division, Piney River, VA [*Library symbol Library of Congress*] (LCLS)
VIPRA......... Vest Individual Protective Reflective Adjustable [*System*] [*Military*] (INF)
VIPRE......... Visual Precision (WDAA)
VIPRE FIRE... Visual Precision Fire Control [*Navy*] (DNAB)

VIPS........... Variable Induction Port System [*Automotive engineering*]
VIPS........... Variable Item Processing System
VIPS........... Verbal Instruction Programmed System
VIPS........... Versatile Isotope Power System (MCD)
VIPS........... Veterans in Public Service Act
VIPS........... Video Image Processing System
VIPS........... Video Interactive Processing System
VIPS........... Voice Information Processing System [*UNISYS Corp.*] [*Blue Bell, PA*] [*Telecommunications service*] (TSSD)
VIPS........... Voice Interruption Priority System
VIPSC......... Vinings Invstmt Prop [*NASDAQ symbol*] (TTSB)
VIPT.......... Nainital (Pantnagar) [*India*] [*ICAO location identifier*] (ICLI)
VIPT.......... Vinland Property [*NASDAQ symbol*] (NQ)
VIPTI......... Visually Impaired Piano Tuners International (EA)
VIPTS......... Vinland Property Tr SBI [*NASDAQ symbol*] (TTSB)
ViPur......... Purcellville Library, Purcellville, VA [*Library symbol Library of Congress*] (LCLS)
VIQ........... Neillsville, WI [*Location identifier FAA*] (FAAL)
VIQ........... Verbal Intelligence Quotient (DB)
VIQ........... Violetvale [*Queensland*] [*Airport symbol*] (AD)
VIQG.......... Qazigund [*India*] [*ICAO location identifier*] (ICLI)
ViQM.......... United States Marine Corps Schools, Quantico, VA [*Library symbol Library of Congress*] (LCLS)
ViQM-E........ United States Marine Corps Schools, Educational Center, Quantico, VA [*Library symbol Library of Congress*] (LCLS)
VIR........... A. H. Robins Co., Richmond, VA [*OCLC symbol*] (OCLC)
VIR........... Point Barrow, AK [*Location identifier FAA*] (FAAL)
ViR........... Richmond Public Library, Richmond, VA [*Library symbol Library of Congress*] (LCLS)
VIR........... Si Vires Permittant [*If the Strength Will Bear It*] [*Pharmacy*] (ROG)
VIR........... Valve in Receiver (DICI)
VIR........... Variable Interest Rate
VIR........... Vendor Information Request [*Sales*]
VIR........... Vendor Item Release [*Sales*]
VIR........... Vertical Interval Reference [*Automatic color adjustment*] [*Television*]
VIR........... Victoria Imperatrix Regina [*Victoria Empress and Queen*] (ILCA)
VIR........... Victorian Industrial Reports [*A publication*]
VIR........... Virco Manufacturing Co. [*AMEX symbol*] (SPSG)
VIR........... Virco Mfg [*AMEX symbol*] (TTSB)
VIR........... Virgin Atlantic [*British ICAO designator*] (FAAC)
Vir........... Virginia Cases (Brockenbrough and Holmes) [*A publication*] (DLA)
VIR........... Virgin Islands of the US [*ANSI three-letter standard code*] (CNC)
Vir........... Virgin's Reports [*52-60 Maine*] [*A publication*] (DLA)
Vir........... Virgo [*Constellation*]
VIR........... Viridis [*Green*] [*Pharmacy*]
VIR........... Virology
VIR........... Virulent
VIR........... Visibility Impairment Research (COE)
VIR........... Visible [*or Visual*] and Infrared Radiometer [*NASA*]
VIR........... Vulcanized India Rubber
ViRa.......... Radford College, Radford, VA [*Library symbol Library of Congress*] (LCLS)
ViRA.......... Richmond Academy of Medicine, Richmond, VA [*Library symbol Library of Congress*] (LOLS)
VIRA.......... Vehicular Infrared Alarm (MCD)
VIRA.......... Venus International Reference Atmosphere [*Meteorology*]
VIRA.......... Video Review Award
Vira-A........ Vidarabine [*Also, ara-A*] [*Biochemistry*]
VIR AC........ Viral Antibody, Acute [*Immunology*] (DAVI)
ViRACL........ Associates Catalog Librarians, Richmond, VA [*Library symbol*] [*Library of Congress*] (LCLS)
VIRAD......... Virtual RADAR Defense [*Army*] (MCD)
Viragen....... Viragen, Inc. [*Associated Press*] (SAG)
ViRAM......... Richmond Academy of Medicine, Richmond, VA [*Library symbol*] [*Library of Congress*] (LCLS)
VIR & Regs... Virgin Islands Rules and Regulations [*A publication*] (DLA)
ViRaP......... Radford Public Library, Radford, VA [*Library symbol Library of Congress*] (LCLS)
ViRAV......... Atlantic Varnish & Paint Co., Richmond, VA [*Library symbol Library of Congress*] (LCLS)
VIRB.......... Raibarelli/Fursatganj [*India*] [*ICAO location identifier*] (ICLI)
ViRBG......... Lewis Ginter Botanical Gardens, Inc., Richmond, VA [*Library symbol*] [*Library of Congress*] (LCLS)
ViRBL......... Bryne Library Consulting, Richmond, VA [*Library symbol*] [*Library of Congress*] (LCLS)
ViRC.......... Museum of the Confederacy, Richmond, VA [*Library symbol Library of Congress*] (LCLS)
ViRCC......... [*The*] Computer Co., Richmond, VA [*Library symbol Library of Congress*] (LCLS)
ViRCCF........ Christian Children's Fund, Richmond, VA [*Library symbol*] [*Library of Congress*] (LCLS)
Virch PM..... Virchow on Post Mortem Examinations [*A publication*] (DLA)
Virco......... Virco Manufacturing Corp. [*Associated Press*] (SAG)
ViRCU......... Virginia Commonwealth University, Richmond, VA [*Library symbol Library of Congress*] (LCLS)
ViRCU-A....... Virginia Commonwealth University, Academic Division, Richmond, VA [*Library symbol Library of Congress*] (LCLS)
ViRCU-H....... Virginia Commonwealth University, Health Sciences Division, Richmond, VA [*Library symbol Library of Congress*] (LCLS)
ViReA......... American College of Radiology, Reston, VA [*Library symbol*] [*Library of Congress*] (LCLS)
ViREP......... Virginia Electric & Power Co., Richmond, VA [*Library symbol Library of Congress*] (LCLS)
ViREx......... Experiment, Inc., Richmond, VA [*Library symbol Library of Congress*] (LCLS)

ViRFR	Federal Reserve Bank of Richmond, Richmond, VA [*Library symbol Library of Congress*] (LCLS)
VIRG	Reengus [*India*] [*ICAO location identifier*] (ICLI)
ViRG	Richmond Guano Co., Richmond, VA [*Library symbol Library of Congress*] (LCLS)
VIRG	Virgin
Virg	Virgin's Reports [*52-60 Maine*] [*A publication*] (DLA)
Virg	Virgo [*Constellation*]
Virg Cas	Virginia Cases (Brockenbrough and Holmes) [*A publication*] (DLA)
VirgErp	Viragen Europe Ltd. [*Associated Press*] (SAG)
VirgGas	Virginia Gas Co. [*Associated Press*] (SAG)
VirgGs	Virginia Gas Co. [*Associated Press*] (SAG)
Virgin	Virgin's Reports [*52-60 Maine*] [*A publication*] (DLA)
Virg LJ	Virginia Law Journal [*Richmond*] [*A publication*] (DLA)
ViRGS	Church of Jesus Christ of Latter-Day Saints, Genealogical Society Library, Richmond Stake Branch, Richmond, VA [*Library symbol Library of Congress*] (LCLS)
ViRGS	VISSR [*Visible-Infrared Spin Scan Radiometer*] Image Registration and Gridding System (MCD)
ViRHC	Henrico County Public Library, Richmond, VA [*Library symbol Library of Congress*] (LCLS)
VIRI	Voice Vision of the Islamic (BUAC)
VIR IS	Virgin Islands (WDAA)
VIRIS	Visible/Infrared Intelligent Spectrometer
Vir LJ	Virginia Law Journal [*A publication*] (DLA)
VIRM	Variable-Interest-Rate Mortgage [*Real estate*]
ViRMu	Virginia Museum of Fine Arts, Richmond, VA [*Library symbol Library of Congress*] (LCLS)
VIRNS	Velocity Inertia RADAR Navigation System
ViRo	Roanoke Public Library, Roanoke, VA [*Library symbol Library of Congress*] (LCLS)
VIRO	Virogroup, Inc. [*NASDAQ symbol*] (SAG)
ViRoA	American Viscose Co., Roanoke, VA [*Library symbol Library of Congress*] (LCLS)
ViRoC	Roanoke County Public Library, Roanoke, VA [*Library symbol*] [*Library of Congress*] (LCLS)
ViroGp	Virogroup, Inc. [*Associated Press*] (SAG)
ViRoMH	Roanoke Memorial Hospital, Roanoke, VA [*Library symbol*] [*Library of Congress*] (LCLS)
ViRoNW	Norfolk & Western Railway Co., Roanoke, VA [*Library symbol Library of Congress*] (LCLS)
ViroPh	ViroPharma, Inc. [*Associated Press*] (SAG)
ViRoV	Virginia Western Community College, Brown Library, Roanoke, VA [*Library symbol Library of Congress*] (LCLS)
ViRPM	Philip Morris Research Center, Richmond, VA [*Library symbol Library of Congress*] (LCLS)
ViRPol	W. P. Poythress Co., Richmond, VA [*Library symbol Library of Congress*] (LCLS)
ViRR	Reynolds Metals Co., Richmond, VA [*Library symbol Library of Congress*] (LCLS)
VIRR	Visible [*or Visual*] and Infrared Radiometer [*NASA*]
ViRRC	J. Sargeant Reynolds Community College, Downtown Campus, Richmond, VA [*Library symbol Library of Congress*] (LCLS)
ViRR-E	Reynolds Metals Co., Executive Office Library, Richmond, VA [*Library symbol Library of Congress*] (LCLS)
ViRRob	A. H. Robins Co., Richmond, VA [*Library symbol Library of Congress*] (LCLS)
ViRR-P	Reynolds Metals Co., Packaging Research Division, Richmond, VA [*Library symbol Library of Congress*] (LCLS)
ViRR-T	Reynolds Metals Co., Technical Information Services Library, Richmond, VA [*Library symbol Library of Congress*] (LCLS)
VIRS	Vertical Interval Reference Signal [*Automatic color adjustment*] [*Television*] (IAA)
VIRS	Visual Technology Research Simulator (MCD)
ViRSBF	Southern Baptist Convention Foreign Mission Board, Richmond, VA [*Library symbol*] [*Library of Congress*] (LCLS)
ViRStM	Saint Mary's Hospital, Health Sciences Library, Richmond, VA [*Library symbol*] [*Library of Congress*] (LCLS)
Virt	De Virtutibus [*of Philo*] (BJA)
Virt	Virtually (ILCA)
ViRU	University of Richmond, Richmond, VA [*Library symbol Library of Congress*] (LCLS)
ViRUCA	United States Circuit Court of Appeals, Fourth Circuit, Richmond, VA [*Library symbol Library of Congress*] (LCLS)
VirusRes	Virus Research Institute, Inc. [*Associated Press*] (SAG)
ViRUT	Union Theological Seminary, Richmond, VA [*Library symbol Library of Congress*] (LCLS)
ViRUV	United Virginia Bankshares, Inc., Richmond, VA [*Library symbol Library of Congress*] (LCLS)
ViRV	United States Veterans Administration Hospital, Richmond, VA [*Library symbol Library of Congress*] (LCLS)
ViRVal	Valentine Museum, Richmond, VA [*Library symbol Library of Congress*] (LCLS)
ViRVB	Virginia Baptist Historical Society, University of Richmond, Richmond, VA [*Library symbol Library of Congress*] (LCLS)
ViRVI	Virginia Institute for Scientific Research, Richmond, VA [*Library symbol Library of Congress*] (LCLS)
ViRVM	Valentine Meat Juice Co., Richmond, VA [*Library symbol Library of Congress*] (LCLS)
ViRVU	Virginia Union University, Richmond, VA [*Library symbol Library of Congress*] (LCLS)
VIS	Jet Servisx SA de CV [*Mexico ICAO designator*] (FAAC)
VIS	Minority Vendor Information Service [*National Minority Supplier Development Council, Inc.*] (IID)
VIS	Site Visitation [*Environmental science*] (COE)
VIS	Vaginal Irrigation Smear [*Medicine*] (MAE)
VIS	Variable Induction System [*Automotive engineering*]
VIS	Variable Inflation System
VIS	Variance Index Score [*Statistics*]
VIS	Vector Instruction Set [*Computer science*]
VIS	Vegetarian Information Service (EA)
VIS	Vehicle Indicator Section
VIS	Vehicle Information System [*Automotive engineering*]
VIS	Vehicle Interface Subsystem [*Army*] (RDA)
VIS	Vehicular Intercommunications System
VIS	Verification Information System (NASA)
vis	Verification Information System (NAKS)
VIS	Veterinary Investigation Service [*Ministry of Agriculture, Fisheries, and Food*] [*British*]
VIS	Vibration Isolation System
VIS	Victim Impact Statement
VIS	Video Imaging System
VIS	Video Information System [*Tandy Corp.*] (DOM)
VIS	Videotex Information System [*Radio Shack*] [*Information service or system*] (IID)
VIS	Vietnamese Information Service
VIS	Virtual Information Storage (BUR)
VIS	Visalia [*California*] [*Airport symbol*] (OAG)
VIS	Viscosity
VIS	Viscount [*or Viscountess*]
VIS	Viscount Resources Ltd. [*Vancouver Stock Exchange symbol*]
VIS	Vishakhapatnam [*Andhra, Waltair*] [*India*] [*Seismograph station code, US Geological Survey*] (SEIS)
vis	Visibility (NAKS)
VIS	Visible [*or Visibility*] (AFM)
VIS	Vision (AAMN)
VIS	Visit [*or Visitor*]
Vis	Visiting (CMD)
VIS	Vista
VIS	Visual
vis	Visual (NAKS)
VIS	Visual Imagery System [*NASA*]
VIS	Visual Information Storage
VIS	Visual Information System
VIS	Visual Instruction Set [*Computer science*]
VIS	Visual Instrumentation Subsystem
VIS	Visual Spectrophotometry
VIS	VNR [*Van Nostrand Reinhold*] Information Services (IID)
VIS	Vocational Interest Schedule (DB)
VIS	Voice Information Service [*Telecommunications*]
VIS	Voice Interactive Subsystem (MCD)
VIS	Voice Intercom Subsystem (MCD)
VIS	Voltage Inverter Switch (IAA)
VIS	Volt Information Sciences, Inc. (EFIS)
VIS	Voters Information Service [*Provides congressional voting records*]
ViSa	Salem Public Library, Salem, VA [*Library symbol Library of Congress*] (LCLS)
VISA	Vancomycin Intermediate-Resistant Staphylococcus Aureas
VISA	Vancomycin Intermediate-Resistant Staphylococcus Aureas [*Infectious microbiology*]
VISA	Ventricular Inhibiting Synchronous with Atrium [*Cardiac pacemaker*] [*Trademark*]
VISA	Virginia Intercollegiate Soccer Association (PSS)
VISA	Vocational Interest and Sophistication Assessment [*Vocational guidance test*]
VISAM	Variable-Length Indexed Sequential Access Method [*Computer science*] (MHDB)
VISAM	Virtual Index Sequential Access Method (IAA)
VISAR	Velocity Interferometer System for any Reflector [*Instrumentation*]
ViSaRC	Roanoke College, Salem, VA [*Library symbol Library of Congress*] (LCLS)
ViSaV	United States Veterans Administration Hospital, Salem, VA [*Library symbol Library of Congress*] (LCLS)
VISB	Sikandrabad [*India*] [*ICAO location identifier*] (ICLI)
VISC	Video Disc
VISC	Video Instruction Set Computing (AAEL)
visc	Visceral
VISC	Viscosity (AAG)
visc	Viscosity (NAKS)
VISC	Viscount [*or Viscountess*]
ViSC	Visualization in Scientific Computing [*Computer science*] (EERA)
VISC	Vitreous Infusion Suction Cutter [*Ophthalmology*]
ViSCA	Video System Control Architecture [*Computer science*] (CDE)
VISCO	Visual Systems Corp.
VISCOM	Visual Communications
VIS-COM-UK...	Visual Communications Exhibition and Conference, United Kingdom (ITD)
VISCT	Viscount [*or Viscountess*]
VISDA	Visual Information System Development Association (MHDB)
VisEd	Visual Edge Systems, Inc. [*Associated Press*] (SAG)
VisEdge	Visual Edge Systems, Inc. [*Associated Press*] (SAG)
VISG	Viisage Technology, Inc. [*NASDAQ symbol*] (SAG)
VisGene	Visible Genetics, Inc. [*Associated Press*] (SAG)
Vishay	Vishay Intertechnology, Inc. [*Associated Press*] (SAG)
VISI	Volar Intercalated Segment Instability [*Orthopedics*]
VISIC	Visual Science Information Center (ECII)
VisiCalc	Visible Calculation [*Electronic spreadsheet program brand*]
VISID	Visual Identification (MSA)
Visigenic	Visigenic Software, Inc. [*Associated Press*] (SAG)
VisioCo	Visio Corp. [*Associated Press*] (SAG)

VISioN	Victorian Information Services Network [Australia]
Vision	Visioneer, Inc. [Associated Press] (SAG)
VISION	Visual Imaging Systems in Origination Network (DGA)
VISION	Volunteers in Service to India's Oppressed and Neglected (EA)
VisionSci	Vision Sciences, Inc. [Associated Press] (SAG)
VISIT	Project VISIT - Vehicle Internal Systems Investigative Team (EA)
VISIT	Visual Information Systems for Image Transformation [Air Force]
VISITS	Very Important Small Institution Travel Support
VISITT	Vendor Information System for Innovative Treatment Technology [Database] [Environmental Protection Agency]
VISL	Visual
VIS LAB	Visibility Laboratory [Research center] (RCD)
VISM	Simla [India] [ICAO location identifier] (ICLI)
VISMEM	Visual Memory Task [Neuropsychology test]
VISMOD	Visual Modifications [Program] [Army] (RDA)
VISMR	Viscometer [Engineering]
VISN	Sight Resource [NASDAQ symbol] (TTSB)
VISN	Sight Resources Corp. [NASDAQ symbol] (SAG)
VISN	Vision Interfaith Satellite Network
VIS/NIR	Visible and Near-Visible Infrared (MCD)
VISNZ	Sight Resource Wrrt [NASDAQ symbol] (TTSB)
VISP	Saharanpur/Sarsawa [India] [ICAO location identifier] (ICLI)
VISP	Vehicle Inspection by System Parameter [Automotive diagnostics]
VISPA	Virtual Storage Productivity Aid [Computer science] (MHDB)
VISPAC	Videotex Information Service Providers Association of Canada [Defunct] (IID)
ViSpN	National Technical Information Service, Springfield, VA [Library symbol Library of Congress] (LCLS)
VISQI	Visual Image Quality Indicator (PDAA)
VISR	Srinagar [India] [ICAO location identifier] (ICLI)
VISR	Virginia Institute for Scientific Research [University of Richmond] [Research center] (MCD)
VISSR	Visible-Infrared Spin Scan Radiometer [NASA]
VIST	Satna [India] [ICAO location identifier] (ICLI)
ViSt	Staunton Public Library, Staunton, VA [Library symbol Library of Congress] (LCLS)
VIST	Vista [Commonly used] (OPSA)
VIST	Vista 2000, Inc. [NASDAQ symbol] (SAG)
VISTA	Variable Interlace System for Television Applications
VISTA	Variable (Stability) In-Flight Simulator Test Aircraft
VISTA	Varied Intelligent System Target Acquisition
VISTA	Verbal Information Storage and Text Analysis [in FORTRAN computer language]
VISTA	Very Intelligent Surveillance and Target Acquisition [Army] (RDA)
VISTA	Videodisc Interpersonal Skills Training and Assessment (INF)
VISTA	Viewing Instantly Security Transactions Automatically [Wall Street]
VISTA	Vista [Commonly used] (OPSA)
VISTA	Visual Information for Satellite Telemetry Analysis
VISTA	Visually Impaired Secretarial/Transcribers Association [Indianapolis, IN] (EA)
VISTA	Visual Storage Administrator [Windows] [Computer science] (PCM)
VISTA	Visual Talking [Telecommunications] (IAA)
VISTA	Volunteers in Service to America (EA)
Vista2000	Vista 2000, Inc. [Associated Press] (SAG)
VISTAB	Vistaril [A central nervous system depressant] (DAVI)
VistaBcP	Bista Bancorp [Associated Press] (SAG)
VistaBcp	Vista Bancorp [Associated Press] (SAG)
VistaG	Vista Gold Corp. [Associated Press] (SAG)
VistaInf	Vista Information Solutions, Inc. [Associated Press] (SAG)
ViSte	Sterling Public Library, Sterling, VA [Library symbol Library of Congress] (LCLS)
VISTE	Vista 2000 Inc. [NASDAQ symbol] (TTSB)
ViStM	Mary Baldwin College, Staunton, VA [Library symbol Library of Congress] (LCLS)
VISTRAC	Visual Target Reconnaissance and Acquisition (MCD)
ViStrR	Robert E. Lee Memorial Association, Stratford Hall, Stratford, VA [Library symbol Library of Congress] (LCLS)
VISTTA	Visibility Impairment for Sulfur Transformation and Transport in the Atmosphere [Environmental Protection Agency] (GFGA)
VISTTA	Visibility Impairment from Sulfur Transformation and Transport in the Atmosphere [Environmental science] (COE)
VISUAL	Verbalize, Identify, Survey, Underline, Accept, and List [Method of problem solving developed by J. Kirby] (DHP)
VIS-UV	Visible Ultraviolet Spectrometer (MCD)
VIS/UV	Visual/Ultraviolet (SSD)
ViSwC	Sweet Briar College, Sweet Briar, VA [Library symbol Library of Congress] (LCLS)
VISWE	Vista 2000 Wrrt'A' [NASDAQ symbol] (TTSB)
VISX	VISX, Inc. [NASDAQ symbol] (SAG)
VIT	Roanoke, VA [Location identifier FAA] (FAAL)
VIT	Technical Research Centre of Finland
VIT	Van Kam Am Cap Interm [NYSE symbol] (TTSB)
VIT	Van Kampen Merritt Intermediate Term High Income Trust [NYSE symbol] (SPSG)
VIT	Variable Impedance Tube
VIT	Variable Inductive Transducer [Automotive engineering]
VIT	Variable Injection Timing [Diesel engines]
VIT	Vehicle Information Terminal
VIT	Venom Immunotherapy [Immunology] [Emergency medicine] (DAVI)
VIT	Vertical Interval Test [Automatic color adjustment] [Television] (IAA)
VIT	Vertically Integrated Team [Engineering]
VIT	Very Important Traveler
VIT	Very Intelligent Terminal (IAA)
VIT	Vibration Isolation Table
VIT	Victoria Resources [Vancouver Stock Exchange symbol]

VIT	Vineyard Telemeter [California] [Seismograph station code, US Geological Survey Closed] (SEIS)
VIT	Virginia International Terminals
Vit	Vita [of Josephus] [Classical studies] (OCD)
Vit	Vitae Parallelae [of Plutarch] [Classical studies] (OCD)
VIT	Vital
Vit	Vitamin
Vit	Vitamin (DB)
Vit	Vitellius [of Suetonius] [Classical studies] (OCD)
vit	Vitellus [Yolk] [Latin Pharmacy] (MAE)
VIT	Vitoria [Spain] [Airport symbol] (OAG)
VIT	Vitreous (AAG)
VIT	Voice Interactive Technology
VITA	Veterans Time Trial Association [Bicycling] (DICI)
VitA	Vitamin A [Used to indicate either dehydroretinol or retinol] (DAVI)
VITA	VMEbus International Trade Association (EA)
VITA	Volunteer Income Tax Assistance Program [Internal Revenue Service]
VITA	Volunteers for International Technical Assistance (IAA)
VITA	Volunteers in Technical Assistance (EA)
VitA₁	Vitamin A₁ [Also called retinol] (DAVI)
VitA₂	Vitamin A₂ [Also called dehydroretinal] (DAVI)
VITAE	Video Imaging Technique for Assessing Exposure [to pesticides]
VITAL	Variably Initialized Translator for Algorithmic Languages [Computer science]
VITAL	VAST [Versatile Avionics Shop Test] Interface Test Application Language
VITAL	Verification of Interceptor Tactics Logic (SAA)
VITAL	Virtual Image Takeoff and Landing [Simulator] (MCD)
VitalSgn	Vital Signs, Inc. [Associated Press] (SAG)
Vita Luc	Vita Lucani [of Suetonius] [Classical studies] (OCD)
VITAP	Viking Targeting Analysis Program [NASA]
VITAR	Veterinary Institute for Tropical and High Altitude Research [Peru] (BUAC)
VITAS	Visual Target Acquisition System [Navy] (MCD)
VITAS	Vocational Interest, Temperament, and Aptitude System [Aptitude test]
Vit Auct	Vitarum Auctio [of Lucian] [Classical studies] (OCD)
VitB	Vitamin B [A member of the vitamin B complex] (DAVI)
VitB₁	Vitamin B₁ [Also called thiamine] (DAVI)
VitB₂	Vitamin B₂ [Also called riboflavin] (DAVI)
VitB₃	Vitamin B₃ [Also called niacin and nicotinamide] (DAVI)
VitB₅	Vitamin B₅ [Also called calcium pantothenate and pantothenic acid] (DAVI)
VitB₆	Vitamin B₆ [Water-soluble substances including pyridoxine, pyridoxal, and pyridoxamine] (DAVI)
VitB₁₂	Vitamin B₁₂ [Also called cobalamin and cyanocobalamin] (DAVI)
VitB₁₂b	Vitamin B₁₂b [Also called hydroxycobalamin] (DAVI)
VitB_c	Vitamin B_c [Also called folic acid] (DAVI)
VITC	Vertical Internal Time Code [Electronic musical instruments]
VITC	Vertical Interval Time Code (NTCM)
VitC	Vitamin C [Also called ascorbic acid] (DAVI)
vit cap	Vital Capacity (MAE)
VitchAm	Vitech America, Inc. [Associated Press] (SAG)
VitD	Vitamin D [Also called calciferol a collective name for several fat-soluble compounds] (DAVI)
VitD₂	Vitamin D₂ [Also called ergocalciferol] (DAVI)
VitD₃	Vitamin D₃ [Also called cholecalciferol and natural vitamin D] (DAVI)
VitE	Vitamin E [Also called alpha-tocopherol] (DAVI)
VITEAC	Video Transmission Engineering Advisory Committee [Army] (PDAA)
VITEK	Life Technology (MCD)
Vitel	Vitellus [Yolk] [Pharmacy]
Vitesse	Vitesse Semiconductor Corp. [Associated Press] (SAG)
VITG	Vietnam Individual Training Group [Deactivated in December, 1972] [Military] (VNW)
VitG	Vitamin G [Also called riboflavin] (DAVI)
VitH	Vitamin H [Also called biotin] (DAVI)
VITIC	Viticulture
VITIS-VEA	VITIS-Viticulture and Enology Abstracts [International Food Information Service] [Information service or system] (IID)
VITK	Futurebiotics, Inc. [NASDAQ symbol] (SAG)
VitK	Vitamin K [A group of fat-soluble vitamins that promote clotting of the blood] (DAVI)
VitK₁	Vitamin K₁ [Also called phytonadione] (DAVI)
VitK₂	Vitamin K₂ [Also called menaquinone] (DAVI)
VITKW	Futurebiotics Inc. Wrrt [NASDAQ symbol] (TTSB)
VITL	Vital Signs, Inc. [NASDAQ symbol] (SAG)
VitL	Vitamin L [A factor necessary for lactation in rats] (DAVI)
VitL₁	Vitamin L₁ [A factor necessary for lactation in rats and found in beef-liver extract] (DAVI)
Vitlnk	Vitalink Pharmacy Services, Inc. [Associated Press] (SAG)
VitM	Vitamin M [Also called folic acid] (DAVI)
Vit Ov Sol	Vitello Ovi Solutus [Dissolved in the Yolk of an Egg] [Pharmacy]
VitPP	Vitamin PP [Also called nicotinamide and nicotinic acid] (DAVI)
vitr	Vitreous [Ophthalmology] [Latin] (DAVI)
VITR	Vitreum [Glass] [Latin] (ADA)
Vitr	Vitruvius [First century BC] [Classical studies] (OCD)
VITRAN	Vibration Transient Analysis (MCD)
VitranCo	Vitran Corp., Inc. [Associated Press] (SAG)
Vitro	Vitro, Sociedad Anonima [Associated Press] (SAG)
VITROLAIN	Vitreous Enamel Porcelain (IAA)
Vitronic	Vitronics Corp. [Associated Press] (SAG)
VITS	Vertical Interval Test Signal (IEEE)
vit stat	Vital Statistics (BARN)
VITT	Vehicle Integration Test Team [NASA] (MCD)

VitU	Vitamin U [*Also called antiulcer vitamin and cabagin vitamin*] (DAVI)
ViU	University of Virginia, Charlottesville, VA [*Library symbol Library of Congress*] (LCLS)
VIU	Vehicle in Use
VIU	Video Interface Unit (MCD)
viu	Video Interface Unit (NAKS)
VIU	Voice Intercommunications Unit
VIU	Voice Interface Unit [*Telecommunications*] (TEL)
VIUD	Udaipur [*India*] [*ICAO location identifier*] (ICLI)
ViU-ES	University of Virginia, School of General Studies, Eastern Shore Branch, WallopsIsland, VA [*Library symbol Library of Congress*] (LCLS)
ViU-H	University of Virginia Medical Center, Health Sciences Library, Charlottesville,VA [*Library symbol Library of Congress*] (LCLS)
ViU-L	University of Virginia, Law Library, Charlottesville, VA [*Library symbol Library of Congress*] (LCLS)
ViU-Mu	University of Virginia, Music Library, Charlottesville, VA [*Library symbol Library of Congress*] (LCLS)
VIURAM	Video Interface Unit Random Access Memory
ViU-ST	University of Virginia, Science/Technology Information Center, Charlottesville, VA [*Library symbol Library of Congress*] (LCLS)
VIV	Variable Inlet Vane [*Nuclear energy*] (NRCH)
VIV	Viajes Internacionales de Vacaciones SA [*Spain ICAO designator*] (FAAC)
VIV	Vivace [*Lively*] [*Music*]
VIV	Vivian, LA [*Location identifier FAA*] (FAAL)
VIV	Vivid-Inventive-Vital [*Spring fashions*]
VIV	Vivigani [*Papua New Guinea*] [*Airport symbol*] (OAG)
VIV	Vlaamse Ingenieurs-Vereiniging
VIVA	Viajes Internacionales de Vacaciones SA [*Spain ICAO designator*] (FAAC)
VIVA	Victory in Vietnam Association
VIVA	Virgin Islands Visitors Association
VIVA	Visually Impaired Veterans of America (EA)
VIVA	Voices in Vital America
ViVb	Department of Public Libraries and Information, City of Virginia Beach, Reference Department, Virginia Beach, VA [*Library symbol Library of Congress*] (LCLS)
ViVbC	CBN University, Virginia Beach, VA [*Library symbol*] [*Library of Congress*] (LCLS)
ViVbGS	Church of Jesus Christ of Latter-Day Saints, Genealogical Society Library, Norfolk Virginia Stake Branch, Virginia Beach, VA [*Library symbol Library of Congress*] (LCLS)
ViVbRE	Association for Research and Enlightenment, Virginia Beach, VA [*Library symbol Library of Congress*] (LCLS)
VIVED	Virtual Visual Environment Display [*Helmet equipped with liquid crystal display screens viewed through wide-angle lenses*] [*NASA*]
Vivi	Vivianus Tuscus [*Flourished, 13th century*] [*Authority cited in pre-1607 legal work*] (DSA)
VIVI	Vivisection [*Medicine*] (WDAA)
Vivia	Vivianus Tuscus [*Flourished, 13th century*] [*Authority cited in pre-1607 legal work*] (DSA)
VividTch	Vivid Technologies, Inc. [*Associated Press*] (SAG)
Vivra	Vivra, Inc. [*Associated Press*] (SAG)
Vivus	Vivus, Inc. [*Associated Press*] (SAG)
ViW	College of William and Mary, Williamsburg, VA [*Library symbol Library of Congress*] (LCLS)
ViWaR	Rappahannock Community College, North Campus, Warsaw, VA [*Library symbol Library of Congress*] (LCLS)
ViWarUS	United States Army, Post Library, Vint Hill Farms Station, Warrenton, VA [*Library symbol Library of Congress*] (LCLS)
ViWb	Waynesboro Public Library, Waynesboro, VA [*Library symbol Library of Congress*] (LCLS)
ViWbD	E. I. Du Pont de Nemours & Co., Benger Laboratory, Waynesboro, VA [*Library symbol Library of Congress*] (LCLS)
ViWbF	Fairfax Hall Junior College, Waynesboro, VA [*Library symbol Library of Congress*] (LCLS)
ViWC	Colonial Williamsburg, Inc., Williamsburg, VA [*Library symbol Library of Congress*] (LCLS)
ViWI	Institute of Early American History and Culture, Williamsburg, VA [*Library symbol Library of Congress*] (LCLS)
ViWiN	United States National Aeronautics and Space Administration, Technical Library, Wallops Island, VA [*Library symbol Library of Congress*] (LCLS)
ViWis	Lonesome Pine Regional Library, Wise, VA [*Library symbol*] [*Library of Congress*] (LCLS)
ViWisC	Clinch Valley College of the University of Virginia, Wise, VA [*Library symbol Library of Congress*] (LCLS)
ViW-L	College of William and Mary, Law School, Williamsburg, VA [*Library symbol Library of Congress*] (LCLS)
ViWn	Handley Library, Winchester, VA [*Library symbol Library of Congress*] (LCLS)
ViWnS	Shenandoah College and Conservatory of Music, Winchester, VA [*Library symbol Library of Congress*] (LCLS)
ViWR	Williamsburg Regional Library, Williamsburg, VA [*Library symbol*] [*Library of Congress*] (LCLS)
ViWSC	National Center for State Courts, Williamsburg, VA [*Library symbol*] [*Library of Congress*] (LCLS)
ViWyC	Wytheville Community College, Wytheville, VA [*Library symbol Library of Congress*] (LCLS)
VIX	Vitoria [*Brazil*] [*Airport symbol*] (OAG)
VIX	Vixit [*He Lived*] [*Latin*]
VIY	Nashville, TN [*Location identifier FAA*] (FAAL)
ViYNW	United States Naval Weapons Station, Yorktown, VA [*Library symbol Library of Congress*] (LCLS)
VIZ	Videlicet [*Namely*] [*Latin*]
Viz	Vizardinus [*Guizzardinus*] [*Deceased, 1222*] [*Authority cited in pre-1607 legal work*] (DSA)
VIZ	Vizianagram [*India*] [*Seismograph station code, US Geological Survey*] (SEIS)
VIZ	Vizmo [*Projection device*] (NTCM)
viz.	Vizmo (WDMC)
Vizar	Vizardinus [*Guizzardinus*] [*Deceased, 1222*] [*Authority cited in pre-1607 legal work*] (DSA)
viz-code	Visual Time Code (WDMC)
Viz Pr	Vizard's Practice of the Court in Banc [*A publication*] (DLA)
VJ	Trans-Colorado [*ICAO designator*] (AD)
VJ	Utility Plane [*Navy symbol*]
VJ	Vacuum-Jacketed (KSC)
VJ	Variable Joining [*Genetics*]
VJ	Ventriculojugular [*Medicine*]
VJ	Video Jockey [*Television version of disc jockey; originated on all-rock-music cable station MTV*]
VJ	Visiting Judges [*British*]
VJ	V-Joint [*Technical drawings*]
VJ	Vogel: Johnson Agar [*Microbiology*] (DAVI)
VJA	Adelphi University, Garden City, NY [*OCLC symbol*] (OCLC)
VJA	V-8 Juice Agar [*Microbiology*]
VJA	ValuJet Airlines, Inc. [*ICAO designator*] (FAAC)
VJB	Verdan Junction Box
VJB	Victorian Judgements Bulletin [*Australia A publication*]
VJB	Vila de Joao Belo [*Mozambique*] [*Airport symbol*] (AD)
VJC	Vallejo Junior College [*California*]
VJC	Vermont Junior College
VJC	Virginia Junior College [*Minnesota*] [*Later, Mesabi Community College*]
V-J (Day)	Victory over Japan [*Japanese surrender, World War II, 14 August 1945*]
VJET	ValuJet Airlines [*NASDAQ symbol*] (TTSB)
VJET	ValuJet Airlines, Inc. [*NASDAQ symbol*] (SAG)
VJH	Victorian Journal of History [*A publication*]
VJJ	Johnson & Johnson Dental Products Co., Science Information Center, East Windsor,NJ [*OCLC symbol*] (OCLC)
VJMC	Vintage Japanese Motorcycle Club (EA)
VJNRL	Virginia Journal of Natural Resources Law [*A publication*] (DLA)
VJSW	Voice Jamming Simulator, Weapons (SAA)
VJTA	Veterans' Job Training Act
VJV	Van Kam Am Cap NJ Val Mun [*AMEX symbol*] (TTSB)
VJV	Van Kampen Merritt New Jersey Value Municipal, Inc. [*AMEX symbol*] (SPSG)
VJWI	Velcro-Jumping while Intoxicated
VK	Air Tungaru [*ICAO designator*] (AD)
VK	Ventral Wall, Kidney [*Anatomy*]
VK	Verbundkatalog Maschinenlesbarer Katalogdaten Deutscher Bibliotheken [*Deutsches Bibliotheksinstitut*] [*Germany Information service or system*] (CRD)
VK	Vertical Keel
VK	Vervet [*African green monkey*] [*Medicine*] (DMAA)
VK	Vogt-Koyanagi [*Syndrome*] [*Medicine*] (DB)
VK	Volume Kill (WDAA)
VKA	Van Kam Am Cap Adv Muni [*NYSE symbol*] (TTSB)
VKA	Van Kampen Amer. Cap. Advantage Muni Income Trust [*NYSE symbol*] (SAG)
VKA	Van Kampen Merritt Advanced Municipal Income Trust [*NYSE symbol*] (SPSG)
VKA	Vienna-Kobenzl [*Austria*] [*Seismograph station code, US Geological Survey*] (SEIS)
VKA	Volatile Keying Assembly (AFM)
VKACBd	Van Kampen Amer. Cap. Bond Fund [*Associated Press*] (SAG)
VKACCV	Van Kampen Amer. Cap. Convertible Securities [*Associated Press*] (SAG)
VKACInc	Van Kampen Amer. Cap. Income Trust [*Associated Press*] (SAG)
VKAdM2	Van Kampen Amer. Cap. Advantage Muni. Income Trust I [*Associated Press*] (SAG)
VKAdPA	Van Kampen Amer. Cap. Advantage PA Muni. Income [*Associated Press*] (SAG)
VKAdvM	Van Kampen Amer. Cap. Advantage Muni. Income Trust [*Associated Press*] (SAG)
VKC	Canisius College, Buffalo, NY [*OCLC symbol*] (OCLC)
VKC	Van Kam Am Cap CA Muni [*AMEX symbol*] (TTSB)
VKC	Van Kampen Merritt California Municipal Trust [*AMEX symbol*] (CTT)
VKC	Vernal Keratoconjunctivitis [*Ophthalmology*] (DAVI)
VKCal	Van Kampen Merritt California Municipal Trust [*Associated Press*] (SAG)
VKCAQ	Van Kampen Merritt California Quality Municipal Trust [*Associated Press*] (SAG)
VKCAV	Van Kampen Merritt California Value Municipal Trust [*Associated Press*] (SAG)
VKE	Von Karman Equation
VKF	Von Karman Gas Dynamics Facility [*Arnold Air Force Base, TN*] [*Air Force*]
VKFLO	Van Kampen Merritt Florida Municipal Opportunity [*Associated Press*] (SAG)
VKFLQ	Van Kampen Merritt Florida Quality Municipal Trust [*Associated Press*] (SAG)
VKG	Premiair [*Norway*] [*FAA designator*] (FAAC)
VKG	Scanair Ltd. [*Denmark ICAO designator*] (FAAC)
VKG	Viking

VKH	Vogt-Koyanagi-Harada [Syndrome] [Ophthalmology]
VKI	Van Kam Cap Adv Mun II [AMEX symbol] (TTSB)
VKI	Van Kampen Merritt Advanced Muncipal Income Trust II [AMEX symbol] (SPSG)
VKI	Von Karman Institute (NATG)
VKIFD	Von Karman Institute for Fluid Dynamics [Belgium]
VKIGM	Van Kampen Merritt Investment Grade Municipal Trust [Associated Press] (SAG)
VkingOP	Viking Office Products [Associated Press] (SAG)
VKITH	Van Kampen Merritt Intermediate Term High Income Trust [Associated Press] (SAG)
VKL	Aerovekel SA [Mexico ICAO designator] (FAAC)
VKL	Van Kam Am Cap Sel Sec Mun [AMEX symbol] (TTSB)
VKL	Van Kampen Merritt Select Securities Municipal Trust [AMEX symbol] (SPSG)
VKLTH	Van Kampen Merritt Limited Term High Income Trust [Associated Press] (SAG)
VKM	Van Kampen Merritt (EFIS)
VKMAd	Van Kampen Merritt Advanced Municipal Income Trust [Associated Press] (SAG)
VKMAd2	Van Kampen Merritt Advantage Municipal Income Trust 2 [Associated Press] (SAG)
VKMAPA	Van Kampen Merritt Advantage Pennsylvania Municipal Income Trust [Associated Press] (SAG)
VKMAV	Van Kampen Merritt Massachusetts Value Municipal [Associated Press] (SAG)
VKMGX	Van Kampen U.S. Govt Cl.A [Mutual fund ticker symbol] (SG)
VKMHX	Van Kampen TF High Inc. Cl.A [Mutual fund ticker symbol] (SG)
VKMIT	Van Kampen Merritt Municipal Income Trust [Associated Press] (SAG)
VKMMO2	Van Kampen Merritt Municipal Opportunity Trust 2 [Associated Press] (SAG)
VKMMO	Van Kampen Merritt Municipal Opportunity Trust [Associated Press] (SAG)
VKMMT	Van Kampen Merritt Municipal Trust [Associated Press] (SAG)
VKMOT	Van Kampen Amer. Cap. Muni. Opportunity Trust [Associated Press] (SAG)
VKMOT2	Van Kampen Amer. Cap. Muni. Opportunity Trust 2 [Associated Press] (SAG)
VKMPX	Van Kampen Penn. TF Inc. Cl.A [Mutual fund ticker symbol] (SG)
VKMTFL	Van Kampen Merritt Trust for Investment Grade Florida [Associated Press] (SAG)
VKMTNJ	Van Kampen Merritt Trust for Investment Grade New Jersey [Associated Press] (SAG)
VKMTNY	Van Kampen Merritt Trust for Investment Grade New York [Associated Press] (SAG)
VKMTPA	Van Kampen Merritt Trust for Investment Grade Pennsylvania [Associated Press] (SAG)
VKMuTr	Van Kampen Amer. Cap. Muni. Trust [Associated Press] (SAG)
VKMVM	Van Kampen Merritt Value Municipal Income Trust [Associated Press] (SAG)
VKN	Barre-Montpelier, VT [Location identifier FAA] (FAAL)
VKNG	Viking Office Products [NASDAQ symbol] (SAG)
VKNJV	Van Kampen Merritt New Jersey Value Municipal Income [Associated Press] (SAG)
VKNYQ	Van Kampen Merritt New York Quality Municipal [Associated Press] (SAG)
VKNYV	Van Kampen Merritt New York Value Municipal Income Trust [Associated Press] (SAG)
VKO	Moscow Vnukovo Airport [Former USSR Airport symbol] (OAG)
VKO	Vnukovo Airlines [Former USSR] [FAA designator] (FAAC)
VKOHQ	Van Kampen Merritt Ohio Quality Municipal [Associated Press] (SAG)
VKOHV	Van Kampen Merritt Ohio Value Municipal Income Trust [Associated Press] (SAG)
VKPAQ	Van Kampen Merritt Pennsylvania Quality Municipal Trust [Associated Press] (SAG)
VKPAV	Van Kampen Merritt Pennsylvania Value Municipal Trust [Associated Press] (SAG)
VKQ	Van Kam Am Cap Mun Tr [NYSE symbol] (TTSB)
VKQ	Van Kampen Merritt Municipal Trust [NYSE symbol] (SPSG)
VKR	Video Kinescope Recording (PDAA)
VKS	Van Kam Am Cap Str Sec Mun [NYSE symbol] (TTSB)
VKS	Van Kampen Merritt Strategic Sector Municipal Trust [NYSE symbol] (SPSG)
VKS	Vicksburg [Mississippi] [Airport symbol] (AD)
VKS	Vicksburg, MS [Location identifier FAA] (FAAL)
VKSelS	Van Kampen Merritt Select [Associated Press] (SAG)
VKStrS	Van Kampen Merritt Strategic Sector Municipal Trust [Associated Press] (SAG)
VKT	Vane Kindergarten Test [Child development test]
VKT	Vehicle Kilometers Traveled (GFGA)
VKT	Vehicle Kit Test
VKT	Vilocity [Former USSR] [FAA designator] (FAAC)
VKTCA	Van Kampen Merritt Trust for Investment Grade California [Associated Press] (SAG)
VKTFL	Van Kampen Amer. Cap. Trust for Investment Grade FL [Associated Press] (SAG)
VKTIG	Van Kampen Merritt Trust for Investment Grade Municipals [Associated Press] (SAG)
VKTIM	Van Kampen Merritt Trust for Insured Municipals [Associated Press] (SAG)
VKTNJ	Van Kampen Amer. Cap. Trust for Investment Grade NJ [Associated Press] (SAG)
VKTNY	Van Kampen Amer. Cap. Trust for Investment Grade NY [Associated Press] (SAG)
VKTPA	Van Kampen Amer. Cap. Trust for Investment Grade PA [Associated Press] (SAG)
VKV	Van Kam Am Cap Value Muni [NYSE symbol] (TTSB)
VKV	Van Kampen Merritt Value Municipal Income Trust [NYSE symbol] (SPSG)
VKValMu	Van Kampen Amer. Cap. Value Muni. Income Trust [Associated Press] (SAG)
VL	Actual Volume of the Lung [Medicine] (DAVI)
VL	Mid-South Commuter Airlines [ICAO designator] (AD)
VL	Valmet OY [Finland ICAO aircraft manufacturer identifier] (ICAO)
VL	Value Leader [Automotive marketing]
VL	Value Line Investment Survey [Finance]
VL	Vandalia Line [Railroad]
V-L	Van Langenhoven [Rifle]
VL	Vapor Return Line
V/L	Vapor-to-Liquid
VL	Variable Length
VL	Variable Light [Immunology]
VL	Varia Lectio [Variant Reading] [Latin]
VL	Vario-Losser [Electronics]
VL	Vector Length (MHDB)
VL	Velar Lobe
VL	Velocity Limit
VL	Ventralis Lateralis [Brain anatomy]
VL	Ventrolateral [Anatomy]
VL	Vereinigte Linke [United Left] [Germany Political party] (PPW)
VL	Vereniging Lucht [Clean Air Society in the Netherlands-CLAN] (EAIO)
VL	Vertical Ladder [Technical drawings]
VL	Vertical Landing (MCD)
VL	Vestre Landsret [Western Court of Appeal] [Denmark] (ILCA)
VL	Vice Lieutenant [British]
VL	Videlicet [Namely] [Latin]
VL	Vide Locum [See the Place Indicated] [Latin]
VL	Video Lead Locator (AAEL)
VL	Video Logic (IEEE)
VL	View Loss
VL	Viking Lander [NASA]
VL	Ville
VL	Violation of Lawful [Order] [Military]
VL	Violin [Music] (ROG)
vl	Violin (WDAA)
VL	Visceral Leishmaniasis [Medicine]
VL	Vision, Left Eye
VL	Visual Laydown
VL	Voltage-Logic [Electronics] (IAA)
VL	Vraie Lumiere [True Light] [Freemasonry] [French] (ROG)
VL	Vulgar Latin [Language] (BARN)
VLA	Vachel Lindsay Association (EA)
VLA	Valhalla Energy Corp. [Vancouver Stock Exchange symbol]
VLA	Vandalia, IL [Location identifier FAA] (FAAL)
VLA	Vertical Landing Aid [Military] (CAAL)
VLA	Vertical Launch ASROC [Antisubmarine Rocket]
VLA	Vertical-Launched Antisubmarine Rocket (MCD)
VLA	Vertical Line Array
VLA	Very Large Airplane (PDAA)
VLA	Very Large Antenna [Telecommunications] (IAA)
VLA	Very Large Array [Radioscope]
VLA	Very Late Activation Antigen [Immunology]
VLA	Very Low Altitude
VLA	Veterans' Land Act [Canada]
VLA	Video Logarithmic Amplifier
VLA	Viola [Music]
vla	Viola (WDAA)
VLA	Virginia Library Association
VLA	Visual Landing Aid
VLA	Vladivostok [Russia] [Seismograph station code, US Geological Survey] (SEIS)
VLA	Voice of Liberty Association (EA)
VLA	Volga [Former USSR] [FAA designator] (FAAC)
VLA	Volume Limiting Amplifier
VLA	Voluntary Licensing Authority [Embryology] [British]
VLA	Volunteer Lawyers for the Arts (EA)
VLAB	VideoLabs, Inc. [NASDAQ symbol] (SAG)
VLAC	Vertical Lift Aircraft Council (EA)
VLAD	Vertical Line Array DIFAR (MCD)
VLAD	Vertical Line Array Directional
Vlad	Vladivostok [Russian port] (BARN)
VLADD	Visual Low-Angle Drogue Delivery (AFM)
VLAM	Variable Level Access Method [Computer science]
VLAM	Vlamertinghe [City in Flanders] [World War I] [Army] (DSUE)
VLAN	Banyan Strategic Realty Trust [NASDAQ symbol] (SAG)
VLAN	Virtual Local Area Network [Computer science] (DDC)
VLANS	Banyan Strategic Realty Tr [NASDAQ symbol] (TTSB)
VLAO	Vientiane [Laos] [ICAO location identifier] (ICLI)
VLAP	Attopeu [Laos] [ICAO location identifier] (ICLI)
VLAP	Vietnam Laboratory Assistance Program [Naval Oceanographic Office]
VLAPA	Vietnam Laboratory Assistance Program, Army (RDA)
VLAT	Very Large Array Telescope [NASA]
VLATME	Very-Lighweight Air Traffic Management Equipment (MCD)
VLB	Glider [Special] [Navy symbol]
VLB	Vacuum Lens Blank
VLB	Vertical Lift Bridge (BARN)

VLB .... Very Long Baseline
VLB .... Verzeichnis Lieferbarer Buecher [*List of Deliverable Books, i.e., books in print*] [*Germany*]
VLB .... VESA [*Video Electronics Standards Association*] Local Bus   (PCM)
VLB .... Vinblastine   (DB)
VLB .... Vincaleukoblastine [*Also, V, VBL, Ve*] [*Antineoplastic drug*]
VLB .... Visual LASER Beam
VLBA .... Very Long Baseline Array
VLBC .... Very Large Bulk-Cargo Carrier   (PDAA)
VLBI .... Very Long Baseline Interferometer [*or Interferometry*]
VLBI .... Viking Lander Biological Instrument [*NASA*]
VLBR .... Very Low Birth Rate
VLBTI .... Very Long-Burning Target Indicator [*British military*]   (DMA)
VLBW .... Very Low Birth Weight [*Medicine*]
VLC .... Valencia [*Spain*] [*Airport symbol*]   (OAG)
VLC .... Valley Line Co. [*Steamship*]   (MHDW)
VLC .... Variable-Length Coding [*Computer science*]
VLC .... Vehicle Launch Center [*Automotive industry project management*]
VLC .... Viking Lander Capsule [*NASA*]
VLC .... Violoncello [*Music*]
VLC .... Vital Load Center   (MSA)
VLCBX .... Very Large Computerized Branch Exchange [*Computer science*]   (MHDB)
VLCC .... Very Large Cargo [*or Crude*] Carrier [*Oil tanker*]
VLCD .... Very-Low-Calorie Diet
VLCD .... Very-Low-Cost Display   (IAA)
VLCE .... Visible LASER Communication Experiment
VLCF .... Vectored Lift Cannon Fighter [*Air Force*]   (MCD)
VLCF .... Victoria League for Commonwealth Fellowship [*British*]
VLCFA .... Very-Long-Chain Saturated Fatty Acid [*Organic chemistry*]
VLCFQ .... Victoria League for Commonwealth Fellowship in Queensland [*Australia*]
VLCFSA....... Victoria League for Commonwealth Fellowship in South Australia
VLCFV........ Victoria League for Commonwealth Fellowship in Victoria [*Australia*]
VLCHV........ Very-Low-Cost Harassment Vehicle   (MCD)
VLCR .... Variable Length Cavity Resonance
VLCS .... Voltage-Logic-Current-Switching [*Electronics*]
VLCTY .... Velocity [*NWS*]   (FAAC)
VLD .... Vacuum Leak Detector
VLD .... Valdez [*Alaska*] [*Seismograph station code, US Geological Survey Closed*]   (SEIS)
VLD .... Valdosta [*Georgia*] [*Airport symbol*]   (OAG)
VLD .... Vendor List of Drawings
VLD .... Very Low Density [*Biochemistry*]   (DAVI)
VLD .... Village and Local Development
VLD .... Visual Laydown Delivery [*AFM*]
VLD .... Vulnerability/Lethality Division [*Ballistic Research Laboratory*]   (RDA)
VLDB .... Very-Large Data Base   (ADA)
VLDBS .... Very-Large Data Base System
VLDF .... Very-Long Delay Fuze [*Military*]   (CAAL)
VLDL .... Very-Low-Density Lipoprotein [*Biochemistry*]
VLDLP .... Very-Low-Density Lipoprotein [*Biochemistry*]   (DAVI)
VLDP .... Vanguard for Liberation and Democracy Party [*Guyana*] [*Political party*]   (BUAC)
VLDP .... Volunteer Leadership Development Program [*Canada*]
VLDS .... Variable Length Distinguishing Sequence   (IAA)
VLDS .... Verbal Language Development Scale [*Speech and language therapy*]   (DAVI)
VLD-TG ...... Very-Low-Density Lipoprotein Triglyceride [*Biochemistry*]   (AAMN)
VLDTN .... Validation   (AAG)
VLE .... Landing-Gear-Extended Speed [*Aviation*]
VLE .... Valle, AZ [*Location identifier FAA*]   (FAAL)
VLE .... V & L Enterprises [*ACCORD*] [*UTLAS symbol*]
VLE .... Vapor-Liquid Equilibrium
VLE .... Vapour Levitation Epitaxy   (NITA)
VLE .... Violone [*Violins*] [*Music*]
vle .... Violone   (WDAA)
VLE .... Visible Light Emission
VLE .... Voice Line Expansion [*Telecommunications*]   (IAA)
VLEA .... Very Long Endurance Aircraft   (PDAA)
VLEACH ...... Vadoze Zone Leaching Model [*Environmental Protection Agency*]   (AEPA)
VLEASS....... Very Long Endurance Acoustic Submarine Simulator
VLED........... Visible Light-Emitting Diodes
VLF .... Valdresfly, AS [*Norway*] [*FAA designator*]   (FAAC)
VLF .... Variable Length Field
VLF .... Vectored Lift Fighter   (MCD)
VLF .... Vertical Laminar Flow   (AAEL)
VLF .... Vertical Launch Facility
VLF .... Very Low Flow
VLF .... Very-Low Fluence [*Physics*]
VLF .... Very-Low-Frequency [*Electronics*]
VLF .... Victoria Law Foundation [*Australia*]
VLFC .... Very Low Flow Constant [*Environmental science*]   (COE)
VLFD .... Very-Low-Frequency Direct [*Electronics*]   (IAA)
VLFD .... Via Low Frequency Direct [*Aviation*]   (FAAC)
VlFdAla....... Valley Federal Savings Bank [*Associated Press*]   (SAG)
VLFG .... Valley Forge Scientific [*NASDAQ symbol*]   (TTSB)
VLFG .... Valley Forge Scientific [*NASDAQ symbol*]   (NQ)
VLFJ .... Very-Low-Frequency Jammer [*Electronics*]
VLFR .... Very-Low-Frequency Receiver [*Electronics*]
VLFS .... Variable Low-Frequency Standard
VLFS .... Very Large Floating Structure [*Oceanography*]
VLG .... Maximum Landing Gear Operating Speed [*Aviation code*]   (AIA)
VLG .... Trans Air Valtologia [*Moldova*] [*ICAO designator*]   (FAAC)

VLG .... Valerie Gold Resources [*Vancouver Stock Exchange symbol*]
VLG .... Ventral Nucleus of the Lateral Geniculate Body [*Medicine*]   (DMAA)
VLG .... Vertical Load Gun
VLG .... Village   (MCD)
Vlg .... Village   (TBD)
VLG .... Villa Gesell [*Argentina*] [*Airport symbol*]   (OAG)
VLG .... Visible Light Generator
VLGE .... Village Super Market, Inc. [*NASDAQ symbol*]   (NQ)
VLGEA .... Village Super Market'A' [*NASDAQ symbol*]   (TTSB)
VLGM .... Vertical Loading Gun Mount   (MCD)
VLGS .... Villages [*Commonly used*]   (OPSA)
VLH .... Ventrolateral Nucleus of the Hypothalamus [*Neurology*]   (DAVI)
VLH .... Very Large Herbivores
VLH .... Very Lightly Hinged [*Philately*]
VLH .... Volatile Liquid Hydrocarbon
VLHS .... Bane Houei Say [*Laos*] [*ICAO location identifier*]   (ICLI)
VLI .... Port Vila [*Vanuata*] [*Airport symbol*]   (OAG)
VLI .... Variable Life Insurance
VLI .... Vasopressin-like Immunoreactivity [*Medicine*]   (DB)
VLI .... Very-Low Impedance   (IAA)
VLI .... Very-Low Inertia
VLI .... Video Load Impedance
VLIA .... Virus-Like Infectious Agent [*Medicine*]
VLIS .... Viking Lander Imaging System [*NASA*]
VLIS .... Viking Library System [*Library network*]
VLIW........... Very Long Instruction Word [*Computer architecture*] [*Multiflow Computer, Inc.*]
VLJ .... Val Joyeux [*France*] [*Later, CLF*] [*Geomagnetic observatory code*]
VLK .... Viqueque [*Timor*] [*Airport symbol*]   (AD)
VLKB .... Very Large Knowledge Base [*Computer science*]
VLKG .... Khong Island [*Laos*] [*ICAO location identifier*]   (ICLI)
VLKT .... Kene Thao [*Laos*] [*ICAO location identifier*]   (ICLI)
VLL .... Valladolid [*Spain*] [*Airport symbol*]   (OAG)
VLL .... Valley SAR Training Unit [*British ICAO designator*]   (FAAC)
VLL .... Very Low-Luminosity [*Astronomy*]
VLLB .... Luang Prabang [*Laos*] [*ICAO location identifier*]   (ICLI)
VLLC .... Very Long Linear Collider [*Proposed*] [*Former USSR*]
VLLD .... Vehicular LASER Locator Designator
VLLN .... Luong Nam Tha [*Laos*] [*ICAO location identifier*]   (ICLI)
VLLO .... Violoncello [*Music*]
VLLW .... Very Low-Level Waste   (BARN)
VLLY .... Valley [*Commonly used*]   (OPSA)
VLM .... Variable Length Multiply
vlm .... Vellum   (VRA)
VLM .... Virtual Loadable Module [*Computer science*]
VLM .... Visceral Larval Migrans [*Medicine*]
VLM .... Vlaamse Luchttransportmaatschappij NV [*Belgium ICAO designator*]   (FAAC)
VLM .... Vortex Lattice Method
VLMB .... Vertical Launch Modular Booster   (MCD)
VLMS .... Villa-Lobos Music Society   (EA)
VLMS .... Vintage Light Music Society [*British*]
VLMTRC ..... Volumetric
VLN .... Training Glider [*Navy symbol*]
VLN .... Valan Ltd. [*Moldova*] [*FAA designator*]   (FAAC)
VLN .... Valencia [*Venezuela*] [*Airport symbol*]   (OAG)
VLN .... Vanua-Lava [*Sola*] [*New Hebrides*] [*Seismograph station code, US Geological Survey*]   (SEIS)
VLN .... Variable Length   (IAA)
VLN .... Very Low Nitrogen [*Fuel technology*]
VLN .... Villebon Resources Ltd. [*Vancouver Stock Exchange symbol*]
VLN .... Violin [*Music*]
VLNC .... Valence Technology [*NASDAQ symbol*]   (TTSB)
VLNC .... Valence Technology, Inc. [*NASDAQ symbol*]   (SAG)
VLNT .... VideoLan Tech [*NASDAQ symbol*]   (TTSB)
VLNT.......... VideoLan Technologies, Inc. [*NASDAQ symbol*]   (SAG)
VLNT.......... Violent [*NWS*]   (FAAC)
VLNTW ...... Videolan Technologies Wrrt [*NASDAQ symbol*]   (TTSB)
VLO .... Maximum Landing Gear of Operating Speed   (GAVI)
VLO .... Maximum Speed to Extend or Retract Landing Gear [*Aviation code*]   (AIA)
VLO .... Valero Energy [*NYSE symbol*]   (TTSB)
VLO .... Valero Energy Corp. [*NYSE symbol*]   (SPSG)
VLO .... Vereniging van Luguaart Onderhoudbedrywe [*Association of Aviation Maintenance Organizations*]   (EAIO)
VLO .... Vertical Lockout
VLOF.......... Lift-off Speed   (GAVI)
VLOL .... Violating Local Option Law   (WGA)
VLON .... Verwaltungslexikon [*Administration Dictionary*] [*NOMOS Datapool*] [*Information service or system*]
VLOOC........ Very Large Ore-Oil Carrier   (PDAA)
VLOPr......... Valero Energy $3.125 Cv Pfd [*NYSE symbol*]   (TTSB)
VLOS .... Oudomsay [*Laos*] [*ICAO location identifier*]   (ICLI)
VLP .... Valparaiso [*Chile*] [*Seismograph station code, US Geological Survey*]   (SEIS)
VLP .... Valpar Resources [*Vancouver Stock Exchange symbol*]
VLP .... Value Property Trust [*NYSE symbol*]   (SAG)
VLP .... Vaporizing Liquid Plenum
VLP .... Vasopressin-Like Peptide [*Biochemistry*]
VLP .... Ventriculolumbar Perfusion [*Medicine*]   (MEDA)
VLP .... Vertical Landing Point   (AFM)
VLP .... Vertical Long Period
VLP .... Video Long Player [*Video disk system*] [*Philips/MCA*]
VLP .... Vincristine, L-Asparaginase, Prednisone [*Antineoplastic drug regimen*]

VLP............	Virus-Like Particle
VLP............	Volunteer Lawyers for the Poor [*An association*]
VLPD..........	Very Long-Period Displacement [*Volcanology*]
VLPE..........	Very Long Period Experiment [*Geophysics*]
VLPK..........	Paksane [*Laos*] [*ICAO location identifier*] (ICLI)
VLPO..........	Ventrolateral Preoptic
VLPP..........	Very Low Pressure Pyrolysis
VLPS..........	Pakse [*Laos*] [*ICAO location identifier*] (ICLI)
VLPS..........	Vandenberg Launch Processing System [*Aerospace*] (MCD)
VLPV..........	Phong Savanh [*Laos*] [*ICAO location identifier*] (ICLI)
VLR............	Randolph-Macon Woman's College, Lynchburg, VA [*OCLC symbol*] (OCLC)
VLR............	Transport Glider [*Navy symbol*]
VLR............	Valar Resources Ltd. [*Vancouver Stock Exchange symbol*]
VLR............	Vallenar [*Chile*] [*Airport symbol*] (AD)
VLR............	Variable Loan Rate [*Business term*]
VLR............	Vertical-Looking RADAR
VLR............	Very Long Range
VLR............	Very Low Range
VLR............	Very Low Resistance (IDOE)
VLR............	Violation of Law of Road [*Traffic offense charge*]
VLR............	Voice Logging Recorder (DWSG)
VLR............	Volare [*Russian Federation*] [*ICAO designator*] (FAAC)
VLR............	Voluntary Loss Rate [*of Air Force officers resigning before retirement*]
VLRP..........	Vitamin Laboratories of Roche Products [*Australia*] (BUAC)
VLRSN........	Violation of Lawful Regulation Issued by the Secretary of the Navy
VLS............	Vacuum Loading System
VLS............	Valesdir [*Vanuata*] [*Airport symbol*] (OAG)
VLS............	Valsamata [*Kephallenia*] [*Greece*] [*Seismograph station code, US Geological Survey*] (SEIS)
VLS............	Valstieciu Liaudininku Sajunga [*Peasant Populist Union*] [*Lithuania*] [*Political party*] (PPE)
VLS............	Vandenberg Launch and Landing Site [*NASA*] (NAKS)
VLS............	Vandenberg Launch Site [*Air Force*]
VLS............	Vapor-Liquid-Solid
VLS............	Vertical Launch System [*Military*]
VLS............	Vertical Liquid Spring
VLS............	Very Long Shot [*A photograph or motion picture sequence taken from a considerable distance*]
VLS............	Very Low Speed
VLS............	Viking Lander System [*NASA*] (KSC)
VLS............	Village Voice Literary Supplement [*A publication*] (BRI)
VLS............	Virtual Linkage System [*or Subsystem*]
VLS............	Visible Light Sensors (MCD)
VLS............	Visual Lunacy Society (EA)
VLS............	Volume Loadability Speed (IEEE)
VLS............	Vry Langs Skip [*Free Alongside Ship*] [*Afrikaans*]
VLSB..........	Sayaboury [*Laos*] [*ICAO location identifier*] (ICLI)
VLSB..........	Very Low Surface Brightness [*Optics*]
VLSD..........	Viscous Limited-Slip Differential
VLSI..........	Very-Large-Scale Integration [*of circuits*] [*Electronics*]
VLSI..........	VLSI Technologies [*Associated Press*] (SAG)
VLSI..........	VLSI Technology [*NASDAQ symbol*] (TTSB)
VLSI..........	VLSI Technology, Inc. [*NASDAQ symbol*] (NQ)
VLSIC........	Very-Large-Scale Integrated Circuit [*Electronics*]
VLSID........	Very Large Scale Integrated Device (SSD)
VLSIIC........	VLSI Implementation Centre [*Queen's University, Kingston*] [*Research center Canada*]
VLSIPS........	Very-Large-Scale Immobilized Polymer Synthesis [*Affymax Research Institute*] [*Organic chemistry*]
VLSK..........	Savannakhet [*Laos*] [*ICAO location identifier*] (ICLI)
VLSM..........	Vertical Launched Standard Missile (MCD)
VLSN..........	Sam Neua [*Laos*] [*ICAO location identifier*] (ICLI)
VLSTRACK..	Vapor-Liquid-Solid Tracking [*Model*] (USDC)
VLSV..........	Saravane [*Laos*] [*ICAO location identifier*] (ICLI)
VLSW..........	Vertical Launch SEAWOLF [*Military British*]
VLSW..........	Virtual Line Switch
VLT............	Van Kam Am Cap Hi Inc. [*NYSE symbol*] (TTSB)
VLT............	Van Kampen Merritt Limited Term High Income Trust [*NYSE symbol*] (SPSG)
vlt............	Vault (VRA)
VLT............	Vault
VLT............	Vault Explorations, Inc. [*Vancouver Stock Exchange symbol*]
VLT............	Vehicle Licensing and Traffic [*British*]
VLT............	Very Large Telescope [*Proposed*] [*European Southern Observatory*]
VLT............	Very Low Titanium [*Geology*]
VLT............	Video Layout Terminal [*Computer science*]
VLT............	Video Lottery Terminal (ECON)
VLT............	Visible Light Transmittance
VLT............	Volute
VLTA..........	Veterans' Lawn Tennis Association of Great Britain (BUAC)
VLTG..........	Voltage (AAG)
VLTK..........	Thakhek [*Laos*] [*ICAO location identifier*] (ICLI)
VLTP..........	Variable Length Text Processor (MHDI)
VLTS..........	Video Lottery Tech [*NASDAQ symbol*] (TTSB)
VLTS..........	Video Lottery Technologies, Inc. [*NASDAQ symbol*] (SPSG)
VLTSV........	Virusoid Lucerne Transient Streak Virus
VLTT..........	Vehicular Leger Toot Terrain [*Light All-Terrain Vehicle*] [*French*] (MCD)
VLU............	Vacuum Lifting Unit
VLU............	Vehicle Location Unit [*FTA*] (TAG)
VLU............	Video Logic Unit (MCD)
VLU............	Worldwide Value Fund [*NYSE symbol*] (SPSG)
VLV............	Valdivia [*Chile*] [*Seismograph station code, US Geological Survey*] (SEIS)
VLV............	Valera [*Venezuela*] [*Airport symbol*] (OAG)
VLV............	Valve (AAG)
VLV............	Vanguard Launch Vehicle (SAA)
VLV............	Velvet Exploration Co. Ltd. [*Vancouver Stock Exchange symbol*]
VLV............	Very-Low Volume
VLV............	Visna Lentivirus
VLV............	Voice of the Listener & Viewer (BUAC)
VLVA..........	Very-Large Low-Velocity Anomaly [*Seismology*]
v-LVN........	Ventral Lateral Ventricular Nerve [*Anatomy*]
VLVS..........	Voltage-Logic-Voltage-Switching [*Electronics*]
VLVT..........	Vientiane/Wattay [*Laos*] [*ICAO location identifier*] (ICLI)
VLW............	Village Level Workers [*India*]
VLW............	Washington and Lee University, Lexington, VA [*OCLC symbol*] (OCLC)
VLXG..........	Xieng Khouang [*Laos*] [*ICAO location identifier*] (ICLI)
VLXK..........	Xieng Khouang (Plaine Des Jarres) [*Laos*] [*ICAO location identifier*] (ICLI)
VLY............	Valley (MCD)
VLY............	Valley National Bancorp [*NYSE symbol*] (SPSG)
VLY............	Valley Natl Bancorp [*NYSE symbol*] (TTSB)
VLY............	Valley Oil & Gas [*Vancouver Stock Exchange symbol*]
VLY............	Volley (DA)
VlyBcp........	Valley National Bancorp [*Associated Press*] (SAG)
VlyFrg........	Valley Forge Scientific Corp. [*Associated Press*] (SAG)
VLYS..........	Valleys [*Postal Service standard*] (OPSA)
VLZ............	Valdez [*Alaska*] [*Seismograph station code, US Geological Survey*] (SEIS)
VM............	Heading to a Manual Termination (GAVI)
VM............	Ocean Airways [*ICAO designator*] (AD)
VM............	Validation Material [*Social Security Administration*]
VM............	Valles Marineris [*A filamentary mark on Mars*]
VM............	Value Management
VM............	Vane Meter [*Automotive engineering*]
VM............	Vasomotor [*Physiology*]
VM............	Vastus Medialis [*A muscle*]
VM............	Vector Message
VM............	Velocity Meter
VM............	Velocity Modulation
VM............	Ventilation Management
VM............	Ventricular Mass [*Medicine*] (DB)
VM............	Ventricular Muscle [*Cardiology*] (MAE)
VM............	Verner-Morrison [*Syndrome*] [*Medicine*] (DB)
VM............	Vertical Magnet
VM............	Vertical Meridian [*Optics, Eye anatomy*]
VM............	Verturi Mask [*Medicine*] (MEDA)
VM............	Vestibular Membrane [*Medicine*]
VM............	Victorian Museum [*State*] (EERA)
VM............	Victory Medal [*British*]
VM............	Vietminh (CINC)
vm............	Vietnam [*MARC country of publication code Library of Congress*] (LCCP)
VM............	Viomycin [*Antibiotic compound*] (AAMN)
VM............	Viral Myocarditis [*Medicine*]
VM............	Virgin and Martyr [*Church calendars*]
VM............	Vir Magnificus [*A Great Man*] [*Latin*]
VM............	Virtual Machine [*Computer science*]
VM............	Virtual Memory [*Computer science*] (MCD)
vm............	Virtual Memory (NAKS)
VM............	Virtual Multi-Access [*Computer science*] (IAA)
VM............	Viscosity Modifier [*Lubricants*]
VM............	V-Mail Specialists [*Navy*]
VM............	Voice Modulation
VM............	Volatile Matter
VM............	Volksmarine
VM............	Voltmeter
vm............	Voltmeter (NAKS)
V/m............	Volts per Meter [*Also, VPM*]
V/M............	Volts per Mil (DEN)
VM............	Vorigen Monats [*Of Last Month*] [*German*]
VM............	Votre Majeste [*Your Majesty*] [*French*]
VM............	Voyager Mars [*NASA*]
VM-26PP	VM-26 [*Teniposide*], Procarbazine, Prednisone [*Antineoplastic drug regimen*]
VMA............	Marine Attack Squadron [*Navy symbol*] (NVT)
VMA............	Monmouth Airlines, Inc. [*ICAO designator*] (FAAC)
VMA............	Valid Memory Address [*Computer science*]
VMA............	Valve Manufacturers Association of America (EA)
VMA............	Vanillylmandelic Acid [*Also, HMMA*] [*Biochemistry*]
VMA............	Vehicle Maintenance Area
VMA............	Virtual Machine Assist [*IBM Corp.*]
VMA............	Virtual Memory Allocation
VMA............	Visual Maneuverability Aids (MCD)
VMA............	Voices of Multicultural America [*A publication*]
VMA............	Voids in Mineral Aggregate (DICI)
VMA............	Volume Merchandising Allowance (DOAD)
VMAAI	Violin Makers Association of Arizona International (EA)
VMA(AW).....	Marine Attack Squadron (All-Weather) [*Navy symbol*] (NVT)
VMAD	Vincristine, Methotrexate, Adriamycin, Actinomycin D [*Antineoplastic drug regimen*]
VMAD	Virgin Mean Annual Discharge [*Of a river system*]
VMAI..........	Veterinary Medical Association of Ireland (BI)
v-mail.........	Video-Mall [*Computer science*] (IGQR)
VM & P.......	Varnish Makers' and Painters' Naphtha

VMAP............ Video Map Equipment
VMAPS.......... Virtual Memory Array Processing System
VMAQ........... Marine Tactical Electronic Warfare Squadron [Navy symbol] (DNAB)
Vmark........... Vmark Software, Inc. [Associated Press] (SAG)
VMAT............ Marine Attack Training Squadron [Navy symbol] (DNAB)
VMAT............ Veterinary Medicine Aptitude Test (GAGS)
VMAT(AW)... Marine All-Weather Attack Training Squadron [Navy symbol] (DNAB)
VMAVA .... Verdun-Meuse-Argonne Veterans Association (EA)
VMAX........... Maximum Velocity
VMAX........... Victormaxx Technologies [NASDAQ symbol] (SAG)
VMAXW........ Victormaxx Technologies Wrrt [NASDAQ symbol] (TTSB)
VMB............. Marine Medium and Heavy Patrol Bomber Squadron [Land-based and seaplane] [Navy symbol]
VMB............. Mary Baldwin College, Staunton, VA [OCLC symbol] (OCLC)
VMB............. Vermont Motor Rate Bureau Inc., Barre VT [STAC]
VMB............. Veterinary Medicines Board [Tasmania, Australia]
VMBA........... Victorian Medical Benevolent Association [Australia]
VMBC........... Vintage Motor Bike Club (EA)
VMBF........... Marine Fighter Bomber Squadron [Navy symbol]
VMBLOK....... Virtual Machine Control Block [Computer science] (IBMDP)
VMBR........... Visual Motor Behavior Rehearsal [Psychology]
VM/BSE....... Virtual Machine/Basic System Extension (NITA)
VMC............. James Madison University, Harrisonburg, VA [OCLC symbol] (OCLC)
VMC............. Minimum Control Speed with Critical Engine Out (GAVI)
VMC............. Variable Message Cycle
VMC............. Variable Mica Capacitor
VMC............. Vasomotor Center [Physiology]
VMC............. Vector Move Convert (IAA)
VMC............. Vehicle Maintenance Council (NTPA)
VMC............. Velocity Minimum Control (AAG)
VMC............. Veritable Master of Crewelwork
VMC............. Vermont Monitoring Cooperative (USDC)
VMC............. Vertical Machining Center [Automotive manufacturing]
VMC............. Vertical Motion Compensation (CAAL)
VMC............. VESA [Video Electronics Standards Association] Media Channel (PCM)
VMC............. Viet Montagnard Cong
VMC............. Villa Madonna College [Kentucky]
VMC............. Villa Maria College [Erie, PA]
VMC............. Ville Marie [Quebec] [Seismograph station code, US Geological Survey Closed] (SEIS)
VMC............. Virginia Medical College
VMC............. Visual Meteorological Conditions [Aviation]
VMC............. Vitramon Microwave Corp. (IAA)
VMC............. Void Metallic Composite
VMC............. VP-16 [Etoposide], Methotrexate, Citrovorum factor [Antineoplastic drug regimen] (DAVI)
VMC............. Vulcan Materials [NYSE symbol] (TTSB)
VMC............. Vulcan Materials Co. [NYSE symbol] (SPSG)
Vmca........... Minimum Control Speed in Air [Aviation code] (AIA)
VMCB........... Virtual Machine Control Block
VMCC........... Vintage Motor Cycle Club [British] (DBA)
VMCCA .... Veteran Motor Car Club of America (EA)
VMCCA .... Vintage Motor Car Club of America (BUAC)
VMCF........... Virtual Machine Communication Facility
Vmcg........... Minimum Control Speed on the Ground [Aviation code] (AIA)
VMCG........... Vector Magnetocardiogram [Medicine] (DMAA)
VMCJ........... Marine Composite Reconnaissance [Photo] Squadron [Navy symbol]
Vmcl .... Minimum Control Speed for the Landing Approach [Aviation code] (AIA)
VMCM........... Vector-Measuring Current Meter [Instrumentation]
VM/CMS ..... Virtual Machine/Conversational Monitor System [Computer science]
VMCP........... Vincristine, Melphalan, Cyclophosphamide, Prednisone [Antineoplastic drug regimen]
VMCR........... Volunteer Marine Corps Reserve
VMD............. Doctor of Veterinary Medicine
VMD............. Marine Photographic Squadron [Navy symbol]
VMD............. Vector Meson Dominance [Particle physics] (OA)
VMD............. Vertical Magnetic Dipole (IEEE)
VMD............. Vertical Main Distribution (IAA)
VMD............. Veterinary Medicines Directorate (BUAC)
VMD............. Virtual Manufacturing Device [Telecommunications] (OSI)
VMD............. Volume Median Diameter [Particle size]
VMDA .... Veterinary Manufacturers' and Distributors' Association [Australia]
VMDF........... Vertical Side of Main Distribution Frame [Telecommunications] (TEL)
VMDI............ Vector Miss Distance Indicator
VMDP .... Veterinary Medical Data Program [Association of Veterinary Medical Data Program Participants] [Information service or system] (IID)
vMDV........... Virulent Marek Disease Virus [Medicine] (DMAA)
VME............. Aviacion Comercial de America, SA de DV [Mexico] [FAA designator] (FAAC)
VME............. British Columbia Ministry of Education [UTLAS symbol]
VME............. Versa Micromodule Extension (AAEL)
VME............. Villa Mercedes [Argentina] [Airport symbol] (OAG)
VME............. Vinyl Methyl Ether [Organic chemistry]
VME............. Virtual Machine Environment [International Computers Ltd.]
VME............. Virtual-Memory Environment [Computer science] (EECA)
VME............. Virtual Memory Extended [Computer science] (CIST)
VME............. Volve Marine Engines
VME............. Volvo Mechanical Equipment [Auto industry supplier]
VME............. Volvo, Michigan, Euclid [In company name VME Americas, Inc.]
VMEC........... Vehicle Mounted Explosive Container (MCD)
VMEI............ Veritas Music Entertainment [NASDAQ symbol] (TTSB)
VMEI............ Veritas Music Entertainment, Inc. [NASDAQ symbol] (SAG)
VMEIW......... Veritas Music Entmt Wrrt [NASDAQ symbol] (TTSB)

VMF............. Marine Fighter Squadron [Navy symbol]
VMF............. Vacuum Melting Furnace
VMF............. Variable Message Formats (RDA)
VMF............. Vertical Maintenance Facility (NASA)
VMF............. Virtual Memory File [Computer science] (PCM)
VMFA........... Marine Fighter Attack Squadron [Navy symbol] (NVT)
VMFAT......... Marine Fighter Attack Training Squadron [Navy symbol]
VMF(AW)..... Marine Fighter Squadron (All-Weather) [Navy symbol] (NVT)
VMFI............ Voltage Monitor and Fault Indicating
VMF(N)........ Marine Night Fighter Squadron [Navy symbol]
VMFP........... Marine Tactical Reconnaissance Squadron [Navy symbol] (DNAB)
VMFPDET .... Marine Tactical Reconnaissance Squadron Detachment [Navy symbol] (DNAB)
VMG............. Banyan Mortgage Investment Fund [Formerly, VMS Mortgate Investment Fund] [NYSE symbol] (SPSG)
VMG............. Banyan Mortgage Inv Fund [NYSE symbol] (TTSB)
VMG............. Velocity Made Good [Boating]
Vmg............. Velocity Made Good (WGA)
VMG............. Vickers Machine Gun [British military] (DMA)
VMG............. Video Mapping Group
VMG............. Video Micrographics (NITA)
VMG............. Video Mixer Group
VMG............. Voluntary Movement Group (EAIO)
VMGR........... Marine Aerial Refueler/Transport Squadron [Navy symbol] (NVT)
VMGSE .... Vehicle Measuring Ground Support Equipment (KSC)
VMH............. Misericordia Hospital, Medical Library, Bronx, NY [OCLC symbol] (OCLC)
VMH............. Ventral Medial Hypothalamus [Anatomy]
VMH............. Victoria Medal of Honour
VMH............. Visual Maneuvering Height [Aviation] (DA)
VMHI............ Victorian Military History Institute [Defunct] (EA)
VMI............. Developmental Test of Visual-Motor Integration [Beery & Buktenica]
VMI............. Variable Moment of Inertia [Nuclear physics]
VMI............. Vendor-Managed Inventory [Electronic commerce]
VMI............. Vertical Markets Information Database [Amidon/Litman Associates] [Information service or system] (CRD)
VMI............. Vertical Motion Index (PCM)
VMI............. Vibration Measurement Integrator
VMI............. Videodisc-Mouse Interface
VMI............. Video Mosaic Imaging [Computer science]
VMI............. Virginia Military Institute, Lexington, VA [OCLC symbol] (OCLC)
VMI............. Vision Mundial Internacional (BUAC)
VMI............. Visual Maneuvering Indicator (MCD)
VMI............. [Developmental Test of] Visual-Motor Integration [Also, Beery-Buktenica Test] (PAZ)
VMI............. Voicemail International, Inc. [Cupertina, CA] [Telecommunications] (TSSD)
VMIA........... Vinyl Metal Industry Association [Defunct] (EA)
VMIAC .... Victorian Mental Illness Awareness Council [Australia]
VMIC........... Vermont Maple Industry Council (EA)
VMID .... Virtual Machine Identifier
VMIF............ Veterans' Mortgage Indemnity Fund [Department of Veterans Affairs]
VMII 1986.... Vertical Markets Information Index 1986 [Amidon/Litman Associates] [A publication]
V/mil........... Volts per Mil
VMIRL .... VMI [Virginia Military Institute] Research Laboratories [Research center] (RCD)
VMJ............. Marine Utility Squadron [Navy symbol]
VMJ............. Vertical Multijunction [Solar cell]
VMK............. Vita-Metall-Keramik [German dental material for crowns and bridgework]
VMKey .... Voice Master Key
VML............. Marine Glider Squadron [Navy symbol]
VML............. Mohawk Valley Library Association, Schenectady County Public Library, Schenect ady, NY [OCLC symbol] (OCLC)
VML............. Valley Migrant League (EA)
VML............. Victorian Music Library [Australia]
VML............. Virtual Memory Linking [Computer science]
VML............. Virtual Microsystems Ltd. (NITA)
VMLB........... Vertical Medium-Lead Burst [Neuron]
VMLH........... Ventromedial and Lateral Hypothalami [Neuroanatomy]
VMLI........... Veterans Mortgage Life Insurance
VMLS/MLA... Veterinary Medical Libraries Section/Medical Library Association (EA)
VMM........... Vacuum Melting Module
VMM........... Vegetarian Matchmakers (BUAC)
VMM........... Vehicle Maintenance Monitor [Automotive engineering]
VMM........... Vehicle Model Movement
VMM........... Vertical Milling Machine
VMM........... Video Map Module
VMM........... Virtual Machine Manager [Computer science] (PCM)
VMM........... Virtual Machine Monitor [Computer science] (IEEE)
VMM........... Virtual Memory Manager [Computer science] (BYTE)
VMM........... Volunteer Missionary Movement [London Colney, Hertfordshire, England] (EAIO)
VMM........... Volunteer Missionary Movement - U.S. Office (EA)
VMM........... Voyageur Minnesota Municipal Income Fund [AMEX symbol] (SPSG)
VMM........... Voyageur Minn Muni Income II [AMEX symbol] (TTSB)
VMMC........... Macau [Macau] [ICAO location identifier] (ICLI)
VMMC........... Veterans Memorial Medical Center
VMMPS........ Vehicle Management and Mission Planning System [NASA]
VMN............. Ventromedial Nucleus [Brain anatomy]
VMN............. Voyageur Minnesota Municipal Income Fund, Inc. [AMEX symbol] (SPSG)
VMN............. Voyageur Minn Muni Income [AMEX symbol] (TTSB)

VMNICM	Vaikunth Mehta National Institute of Cooperative Management [India] (BUAC)
VMO	Marine Observation Squadron [Navy symbol]
VMO	Maximum Operating Speed (MCD)
VMO	Van Kam Am Cap Muni Opp [NYSE symbol] (TTSB)
VMO	Van Kampen Merritt Municipal Opportunity Trust [NYSE symbol] (SPSG)
VMO	Vastus Medialis Obliquus [Muscle]
VMO	Velocity Max Operating (GAVI)
VMO	Velocity-Modulated Oscillator
VMO	Very Massive Object [Astronomy]
VMO	Visiting Medical Officer (ADA)
VMO(AS)	Marine Observation Squadron (Artillery Spotting) [Navy symbol]
VMOS	Vertical Metal-Oxide Semiconductor (IAA)
VMOS	V-Groove Metal-Oxide Semiconductor (MCD)
VMOS	Virtual Memory Operating System [Sperry UNIVAC] [Computer science] (IEEE)
VMOS	V-Type Metal Oxide Semiconductor (NITA)
VMOSFET	Vertical Metal-Oxide-Semiconductor Field-Effect Transistor (IDOE)
VMOW	Vice Minister of War (MCD)
VMP	Validation Master Plan [Pharmaceutical processing]
VMP	Value as Marine Policy [Insurance] (DS)
VMP	Variable Major Protein [Genetics]
VMP	Vegetation Management Program [of the Northern Territory] (EERA)
vMP	Ventral Midline Precursor [Neuroanatomy]
VMP	Vertically Moored Platform [Offshore drilling]
VMP	Visiting Medical Practitioner
VMPA	Vancouver Museums and Planetarium [Canada] (BUAC)
VMPA	Vancouver Museums and Planetarium Association [Canada]
VMPE	Virtual Memory Performance Enhancement [Computer science] (MHDI)
VMPP	Vincristine, Melphalan, Prednisone, Procarbazine [Antineoplastic drug regimen]
VM/Prolog	Virtual Machine/Programming in Logic [Computer science] (HGAA)
VMR	Marine Transport Squadron [Navy symbol]
VMR	Variance to Mean Rate
VMR	Vasomotor Rhinitis [Medicine]
VMR	Victoria Mounted Rifles [British military] (DMA)
VMR	Violation Monitor and Remover [Bell System]
VMR	Volumetric Mixing Ratio
VMRA	Volunteer Military Rejectee (DNAB)
VMRA	Victorian Medical Record Association [Australia]
VMRB	Vereinigte Metallwerke Ranshofen-Berndorf [AG]
VMRC	Virginia Mason Research Center [Virginia Mason Hospital and Mason Clinic] [Research center] (RCD)
VMRGX	Vanguard Morgan Growth [Mutual fund ticker symbol] (SG)
VMRI	Veterinary Medical Research Institute [Iowa State University] [Research center] (RCD)
VMRK	VMARK Software [NASDAQ symbol] (TTSB)
VMRK	Vmark Software, Inc. [NASDAQ symbol] (SAG)
VMRMDS	Vehicle-Mounted Road Mine Detector System
VMRO	Vnatresna Makedonska Revolucionerna Organizacija [Internal Macedonian Revolutionary Organization (Known popularly among English-speaking nations as the IMRO)] [Former Yugoslavia] [Political party] (PPE)
VMRO	Vutreshna Makidoniski Revoliutsionna Organizatsiia [Internal Macedonian Revolutionary Organization] [Bulgaria] [Political party] (PPE)
VMRO-DPMNE	Internal Macedonian Revolutionary Organization - Democratic Party for MacedonianNational Unity [Political party]
VMRO(U)	Vnatresna Makedonska Revolucionerna Organizacija (Udruzena) [Internal Macedonian Revolutionary Organization (United)] [Former Yugoslavia] [Political party] (PPE)
VMRR	Vendor Material Review Report [NASA] (KSC)
VMRS	Vehicle Maintenance Reporting Standard [American Trucking Association]
VMRS	Vessel Movement Reporting System
VMRX	VIMRx Pharmaceuticals [NASDAQ symbol] (TTSB)
VMRXZ	VIMRx Pharma Wrrt'B' [NASDAQ symbol] (TTSB)
VMS	Valve Monitoring System (IAA)
VMS	Valve Mounting System
VMS	Variable Magnetic Shunt [Electronics] (IAA)
VMS	Variable Mass System
VMS	Variable Memory System [Computer science] (IAA)
VMS	Variable Message Sign
VMS	Variable Message System
VMS	Vehicle Management System
VMS	Vehicle Monitoring System (RDA)
VMS	Vehicle Motion Sensor
VMS	Velocity Measurement System
vms	Velocity Measuring System (NAKS)
VMS	Vertical Market Structure (MHDB)
VMS	Vertical Motion Simulator [NASA]
VMS	Vibration Measuring System
VMS	Vicinity Map Series [Bureau of the Census] (GFGA)
VMS	Victorian Military Society (EAIO)
VMS	Videofile Microwave System
VMS	Video Modulation System
VMS	Video Movie System [For video recording tapes]
VMS	Viewfinder Metering System (KSC)
VMS	Virtual Memory Operating System [Computer science]
VMS	Visual Management System (EERA)
VMS	Visual Memory Scale [Educational test]
VMS	Visual Motion Simulator (MCD)
VMS	Voice Mall System [Telecommunications] (IAA)
VMS	Voice Messaging System [Telecommunications]
VMS	Volcanic-Associated Massive Sulphide [Geology]
VMS	Vortex Magnetic Separation [Ore processing]
VMSB	Marine Scout Bombing Squadron [Navy symbol]
VMSC	Vineland Measurement of Social Competence [Speech and language therapy] (DAVI)
VM/SE	Virtual Machine/System Extension (NITA)
VMSEA	Vehicle Monitoring System Electronics Assembly (RDA)
VMSFRJ	Variable-Mode Solid-Fueled Ramjet (MCD)
Vmsl	Minimum Speed in a Stall [Aviation code] (AIA)
Vmso	Minimum Speed in a Stall, Flaps Down [Aviation code] (AIA)
VM/SP	Virtual Machine/System Product [Operating system for large IBM mainframe computers]
VMSP	Volunteer Management Support Program [ACTION]
VMT	Validate Master Tape
VMT	Van Kam Am Cap Mun Inc. [NYSE symbol] (TTSB)
VMT	Van Kampen Merritt Municipal Income Trust [NYSE symbol] (CTT)
VMT	Variable Microcycle Timing
VMT	Variable Mu Tube [Electronics]
VMT	Vehicle-Miles Traveled
VMT	Vehicular Miles Traveled (WPI)
VMT	Velocity-Modulated Transistor [Solid-state physics]
VMT	Velocity-Modulated Tube
VMT	Very Many Thanks
VMT	Video Matrix Terminal
VMT	Virtual Memory Technique [Computer science] (MDG)
VMT	Virtual Method Table [Computer science] (PCM)
VMT	Voltage-Modulated Transmission [Electronics]
VMT	Von Mises Theory
VMT	Vowel Matching Test [Education] (EDAC)
VMTB	Marine Torpedo Bomber Squadron [Navy symbol]
VMTH	Veterinary Medical Teaching Hospital [University of California, Davis]
VMTOL	Very Many Takeoffs and Landings (MCD)
VMTP	Versatile Message Transaction Protocol [Computer science]
VMTSS	Virtual Machine Time-Sharing System [Computer science] (IEEE)
VMU	Baimuru [Papua New Guinea] [Airport symbol] (OAG)
Vmu	Minimum Unstick Speed [Aviation code] (AIA)
VMU	Variable Match Unit (IAA)
VMU	Vehicle Management Unit [Powertrain] [Automotive engineering]
VMU	Velocity Measuring Unit (MCD)
VMU	Voice Management Unit (DA)
VMV	Van Kam Am Cap MA Val Mun [AMEX symbol] (TTSB)
VMV	Van Kampen Merritt Massachusetts Value Municipal Trust [AMEX symbol] (SPSG)
VMV	Vincristine, Methotrexate, VP-16 [Etoposide] [Antineoplastic drug regimen] (DAVI)
VMV	Viola Mottle Virus
VMW	Mary Washington College, Fredericksburg, VA [OCLC symbol] (OCLC)
VMW	Vertically Modulated Well (AAEL)
VMW	Vierteljahrschrift fuer Musikwissenschaft [A publication]
VMWWI	Victory Medal World War I [British]
VMWWII	Victory Medal World War II [British]
VMX	Voice Message Exchange (CI3T)
VMY	York College of the City University of New York, Jamaica, NY [OCLC symbol] (OCLC)
VMZ	Ventrolateral Marginal Zone [Embryology]
VN	Hang Khong Vietnam [ICAO designator] (AD)
VN	Training Plane [Navy symbol]
VN	Vangold Resources, Inc. [Vancouver Stock Exchange symbol]
VN	(Vanillyl)nonanamide [Biochemistry]
VN	Van Ness' Prize Cases [United States] [A publication] (DLA)
VN	Vegetative Nucleus [Botany]
VN	Ventral Nerve [Neuroanatomy]
VN	Ventral Nozzle
VN	Verbal Noun
VN	Verb Neuter
VN	Verify Number If No Answer [Telecommunications] (TEL)
VN	Vietnam [ANSI two-letter standard code] (CNC)
vn	Vietnam, North [vm (Vietnam) used in records cataloged after January 1978] [MARC country of publication code Library of Congress] (LCCP)
VN	VietNow (EA)
VN	VietNow National [An association] (EA)
vn	Vinyl (VRA)
vn	Violin (WDAA)
VN	Violin [Music]
VN	Virus Neutralization
VN	Visiting Nurse
VN	Vladimir Nabokov [In book title, "VN: The Life and Art of Vladimir Nabokov"]
VN	Vocational Nurse
VN	Volatile Nitrogen (OA)
VN	Vomeronasal [Anatomy]
VN	Von Neumann [Procedure] [Statistics]
VN	Vulnerability Number
VNA	Air Viet-Nam
VNA	Mercy Hospital, Library, Watertown, NY [OCLC symbol] (OCLC)
VNA	Radio Hanoi [North Vietnam radio programming which targeted US troops in South Vietnam] (VNW)
VNA	Very Narrow Aisle Truck (PDAA)
VNA	Veterinary Nurses' Association [Australia]
VNA	Vienna, GA [Location identifier FAA] (FAAL)
VNA	Vietnamese National Army
VNA	Vietnam News Agency

VNA	Virtual Network Application [Computer science]
VNA	Visiting Nurse Association
VNA	Volatile Nitrosamine [Organic chemistry]
VNA	Warbelow's Air Ventures, Inc. [ICAO designator] (FAAC)
VNAA	Visiting Nurse Associations of America (EA)
VNAF	Republic of Vietnam Air Force (VNW)
VNAF	Vietnam Air Force
VNAF	Vietnam Armed Forces
VNAF I & M...	Vietnam Air Force Improvement and Modernization Program
VNAS	Vehicle Navigation Aid System
VNAV	Vertical Navigation Mode (IEEE)
V N B	Vetus Natura Brevium [A publication] (DSA)
VNB	Wadhams Hall Seminary College, Library, Ogdensburg, NY [OCLC symbol] (OCLC)
VNBG	Bajhang [Nepal] [ICAO location identifier] (ICLI)
VNBJ	Bhojpur [Nepal] [ICAO location identifier] (ICLI)
VNBL	Baglung [Nepal] [ICAO location identifier] (ICLI)
VNBP	Bharatpur [Nepal] [ICAO location identifier] (ICLI)
VNBR	Bajura [Nepal] [ICAO location identifier] (ICLI)
VNBT	Baitadi [Nepal] [ICAO location identifier] (ICLI)
VNBW	Bhairawa [Nepal] [ICAO location identifier] (ICLI)
VNC	North Country Reference and Research Resources Council, Union List of Serials, Canton, NY [OCLC symbol] (OCLC)
VNC	Variable Neutralizing Capacitor
VNC	Venice, FL [Location identifier FAA] (FAAL)
VNC	Ventral Nerve Cord [Neuroanatomy]
VNC	Victorian Naturalists' Club (EERA)
VNC	Video Network Computer [PCM]
VNC	Vietnamese Civilian (VNW)
VNC	VNC Video Network [Vancouver Stock Exchange symbol]
VNC	Voice Numerical Control
VNC	Votes National Committee (EA)
VNCCI	Volunteer - The National Center [Later, NVC] (EA)
VNCF	Vietnam-Canada Foundation
VNCG	Chandragarhi [Nepal] [ICAO location identifier] (ICLI)
VNCM	Vietnam Campaign Medal [Military decoration]
VNCS	Vietnam Christian Service [Defunct] (EA)
VND	Jefferson Community College, Library, Watertown, NY [OCLC symbol] (OCLC)
VND	Vanda [Antarctica] [Seismograph station code, US Geological Survey] (SEIS)
VNDG	Dang [Nepal] [ICAO location identifier] (ICLI)
VNDH	Dhangarhi [Nepal] [ICAO location identifier] (ICLI)
VNDNG	Vending
VNDP	Dolpa [Nepal] [ICAO location identifier] (ICLI)
VNDPT	Visual Numerical Discrimination Pre-Test [Medicine] (DMAA)
VNDR	Dhorpatan [Nepal] [ICAO location identifier] (ICLI)
VNDT	Doti [Nepal] [ICAO location identifier] (ICLI)
VNE	Ogdensburg Public Library, Ogdensburg, NY [OCLC symbol] (OCLC)
VNE	Velocity Never to Exceed
VNE	Verbal Nonemotional (Stimuli) [Psychology]
VNEPX	Vontobel Intl. Equity [Mutual fund ticker symbol] (SG)
VNESE	Vietnamese
VNET	Virtual Networks [Computer science] (HGAA)
VNETF	Vietnam Expediting Task Force [Military]
VNF	Paul Smiths College, Library, Paul Smiths, NY [OCLC symbol] (OCLC)
VNF	Vietnam Foundation (EA)
VNG	Ventral Surface, Nephridial Gland [Anatomy]
VNG	W. Alton Jones Cell Science Center Library, Lake Placid, NY [OCLC symbol] (OCLC)
VNGD	Vanguard Airlines [NASDAQ symbol] (TTSB)
VNGD	Vanguard Airlines, Inc. [NASDAQ symbol] (SAG)
VNGK	Gorkha [Nepal] [ICAO location identifier] (ICLI)
VNHP	Vermont Natural Heritage Program [Information service or system] (IID)
VNI	Violini [Violins] [Music]
VNIC	Voltage Negative Immittance Converter
VNIIMP	Vsesoiuznyi Nauchno-Issledovatel'skii Institut Miasnoi Promyshlennosti [All-Union Scientific Research Institute of the Meat Industry]
VNIR	Visible and Near Infrared (EERA)
VNIR	Visible and Near-Visible Infrared (MCD)
VNIS	Vehicle Navigation Information System [Automotive engineering]
VNJI	Jiri [Nepal] [ICAO location identifier] (ICLI)
VNJL	Jumla [Nepal] [ICAO location identifier] (ICLI)
VNJP	Janakpur [Nepal] [ICAO location identifier] (ICLI)
VNJS	Jomsom [Nepal] [ICAO location identifier] (ICLI)
VNKT	Kathmandu/International [Nepal] [ICAO location identifier] (ICLI)
VNL	Bogalusa, LA [Location identifier FAA] (FAAL)
VNL	Variable Neodymium LASER
VNL	Via Net Loss [Telecommunications]
VNLD	Lamidada [Nepal] [ICAO location identifier] (ICLI)
VNLF	Via Net Loss Factor (TEL)
VNLK	Lukla [Nepal] [ICAO location identifier] (ICLI)
VNLT	Langtang [Nepal] [ICAO location identifier] (ICLI)
VNM	Van Kam Am Cap NY Qual Mun [NYSE symbol] (TTSB)
VNM	Van Kampen Merritt New York Quality Municipal [NYSE symbol] (SPSG)
VNM	Vietnam [ANSI three-letter standard code] (CNC)
VNMA	Manang [Nepal] [ICAO location identifier] (ICLI)
VNMC	Vietnam Marine Corps
VNMG	Meghauli [Nepal] [ICAO location identifier] (ICLI)
VNMN	Mahendranagar [Nepal] [ICAO location identifier] (ICLI)

VNN	Eastern Virginia Medical Authority, Norfolk, VA [OCLC symbol] (OCLC)
VNN	Mount Vernon, IL [Location identifier FAA] (FAAL)
VNN	Vacant National Number [Telecommunications] (TEL)
VNN	Van Nuys Byzantine [Diocesan abbreviation] [California] (TOCD)
VNN	Vietnam Navy
VNNG	Nepalgung [Nepal] [ICAO location identifier] (ICLI)
VNO	Cruising Speed [Aviation code] (AIA)
VNO	Maximum Structural Cruising Speed (GAVI)
VNO	Value Not Obtained
VNO	Vilnius [Former USSR Airport symbol] (OAG)
VNO	Vital National Objective (AAG)
VNO	Vomeronasal Organ [Anatomy]
VNO	Vornado Realty Trust [NYSE symbol] (SPSG)
VNODC	Vietnamese National Oceanographic Data Center [Marine science] (OSRA)
VNP	Vehicle Network Protocol [Automotive engineering]
VNP	Venda National Party [Political party] (PPW)
VNP	Vietnam Nationalist Party [Political party] (VNW)
VNPA	Victorian National Parks Association [Australia]
VNPK	Pokhara [Nepal] [ICAO location identifier] (ICLI)
VNPL	Phaplu [Nepal] [ICAO location identifier] (ICLI)
VNQDD	Viet Nam Quoc Dan Dang [Political party] (VNW)
VNR	Van Nostrand Reinhold Co., Inc. [Publisher]
VNR	Vanrook [Queensland] [Airport symbol] (AD)
VNR	Variable Navigation Ratio
VNR	Veneer [Technical drawings]
vnr	Veneer (VRA)
VNR	Video News Release [A news release in the form of video tape]
VNR	Viennair Luftfahrt GmbH [Austria ICAO designator] (FAAC)
VNR	Vietnam Reactor
VNR	Vitronectin Receptor [Biochemistry]
VNR	Voltage-[Controlled Differential] Negative Resistance [Electronics] (BARN)
VNRB	Rajbiraj [Nepal] [ICAO location identifier] (ICLI)
VNRC	Vegetarian Nutritional Research Center (PDAA)
VNRK	Rukumkot (Chaurjhari) [Nepal] [ICAO location identifier] (ICLI)
VNRP	Rolpa [Nepal] [ICAO location identifier] (ICLI)
VNRS	Vietnamese National Railway System (CINC)
VNRT	Rumjatar [Nepal] [ICAO location identifier] (ICLI)
VNS	Norfolk State College, Norfolk, VA [OCLC symbol] (OCLC)
VNS	Vagus Nerve Stimulation [Physiology]
VNS	Varanasi [India] [Airport symbol] (OAG)
VNS	Vasomotor Nervous System [Physiology]
VNS	Vehicular Navigation System [Military]
VNS	Ventral Nervous System [Neuroanatomy]
VNS	Venus Air Services Ltd. [Ghana] [ICAO designator] (FAAC)
VNS	Very North Shore [Women's Wear Daily]
VNS	Vicarious Nucleophilic Substitution [Organic chemistry]
VNS	Villonodular Synovitis [Medicine] (DAVI)
VNS	Visiting Nurse Service
VNS	Vladimir Nabokov Society (EA)
VNS	Volumetric Neutron Source (COE)
VNS	Voter News Service
VNSB	Syanboche [Nepal] [ICAO location identifier] (ICLI)
VnSc	Florence Williams Public Library, Christiansted, St. Croix, VI [Library symbol Library of Congress] (LCLS)
VNSF	Vietnamese Special Forces (CINC)
VNSI	Simara [Nepal] [ICAO location identifier] (ICLI)
VNSK	Surkhet [Nepal] [ICAO location identifier] (ICLI)
VNSL	Variable Nozzle Slow Landing (MCD)
VNSM	Kathmandu [Nepal] [ICAO location identifier] (ICLI)
VNSP	Vacant Nozzle Shield Plug [Nuclear energy] (NRCH)
VNSR	Safebagar [Nepal] [ICAO location identifier] (ICLI)
VnSt	Saint Thomas Public Library, Charlotte Amalie, VI [Library symbol Library of Congress] (LCLS)
VNST	Simikot [Nepal] [ICAO location identifier] (ICLI)
VnStC	College of the Virgin Islands, St. Thomas, VI [Library symbol Library of Congress] (LCLS)
VNSWBAC	Victoria/New South Wales Border Anomalies Committee [Australia]
VNT	Compania Anonima Nacional Telefonos de Venezuela [NYSE symbol] (SAG)
VNT	Variable-Nozzle Turbocharger [Automotive engineering]
VNT	Ventora Resources Ltd. [Vancouver Stock Exchange symbol]
VNT	Virus Neutralization Test [Analytical biochemistry]
VNTJ	Taplejung [Nepal] [ICAO location identifier] (ICLI)
VNTP	Tikapur [Nepal] [ICAO location identifier] (ICLI)
VNTR	Tumlingtar [Nepal] [ICAO location identifier] (ICLI)
VNTR	Variable Number of Tandem Repeats
VNTR locus...	Variable Number of Tandem Repeats Locus [Genetics] (DOG)
VNTS	Vertical Nutrient-Solution Transport System [i.e., plant stem] [Slang]
VNTSC	Volpe National Transportation Systems Center (BARN)
VNTV	Vantive Corp. [NASDAQ symbol] (SAG)
VNTX	Ventritex, Inc. [NASDAQ symbol] (SPSG)
VNU	Verenigde Nederlandse Uitgeversbedrijven [Publishing group] [Netherlands]
VNV	Van Kam Am Cap NY Val Mun [NYSE symbol] (TTBS)
VNV	Van Kampen Merritt New York Value Municipal Income Trust [NYSE symbol] (SPSG)
VNV	Vlaamsch Nationaal Verbond [Flemish National League] [Dissolved] [Belgium] [Political party] (PPE)
VNVO	Verbal-Nonverbal Operation [Psychometrics]
VNVT	Biratnagar [Nepal] [ICAO location identifier] (ICLI)
VNW	Van Wert, OH [Location identifier FAA] (FAAL)
VNX	Oceanographic Development Squadron [Navy symbol] (DNAB)

VNX	Venexcargo (Transporte Aereo de Carga SA) [*Venezuela*] [*ICAO designator*] (FAAC)
VNX	Vilanculos [*Mozambique*] [*Airport symbol*] (AD)
VNXL	Vane Axial
VNY	Van Nuys, CA [*Location identifier FAA*] (FAAL)
VO............	Battleship Observation Squadron [*Navy symbol*]
VO............	De Verborum Obligationibus [*A publication*] (DLA)
Vo............	Initial Velocity
VO............	Observation Plane [*Navy symbol*]
V₀............	Output Voltage (IDOE)
VO............	[*The*] Seagram Co. Ltd. [*NYSE symbol Toronto Stock Exchange symbol Vancouver Stock Exchange symbol*]
VO............	Tyrolean Airways [*ICAO designator*] (AD)
VO............	Vacuum-Tube Oscillator (IAA)
VO............	Valuation Officer (WDAA)
VO............	Valve Oscillator (DEN)
VO............	Variable Oversight
VO............	Varying Order [*British*]
VO............	Vehicle Operations [*NASA*] (NASA)
VO............	Verbal Orders
VO............	Verbindungsoffizier [*Liaison Officer*] [*German military - World War II*]
VO............	Verb-Object [*Education of the hearing-impaired*]
VO............	Vernehmungsoffizier [*Interrogation Officer*] [*German military - World War II*]
VO............	Verpflegungsoffizier [*Mess Officer*] [*German military - World War II*]
VO............	Verso
VO............	Vertical Oculus
VO............	Vertical Output (IAA)
VO............	Very Old [*Wines and spirits*]
VO............	Veterinary Officer [*British*]
VO............	Victorian Order [*British*] (ROG)
VO............	Video Operator (NTCM)
VO............	Viking Orbiter [*NASA*]
VO............	Violation of [*Local*] Ordinance
Vo............	Violin (WDAA)
VO............	Violino [*Violin*] [*Music*] (ROG)
VO............	Virtual Office
VO............	Visa Office [*Department of State*]
VO............	Visiting Order (WDAA)
VO............	Vocal (AAG)
VO............	Voice (AAG)
VO............	Voice Over [*Commentary read over a program*] [*Television*]
VO............	Volatile Oil
VO............	Volcanic Origin (AAG)
VO............	Volt (ROG)
VO............	Volume
VO............	Voluntary Opening [*Prosthesis*] [*Medicine*]
VO............	Von Oben [*From the Top*] [*German*]
VO............	VOTEC, Servicos Aereos Regionais SA [*Brazil ICAO designator*] (ICDA)
VO............	Voucher (MCD)
VO₂............	Volume Oxygen Consumption [*Medicine*] (DAVI)
VOA	Vibrational Optical Activity [*Spectroscopy*]
VOA	Voice of America [*United States Information Agency*]
VOA	Volkswagen of America
VOA	Volt-Ohm-Ammeter (IDOE)
VOA	Volunteers of America (EA)
VOAEL	Vocationally Oriented Adult Education and Literacy Program [*Australia*]
VO-AG	Vocational Agriculture [*Education*]
VOAPA	Vultee Owners and Pilots Association (EA)
VOARS........	Velocity over Altitude Ratio Sensor (MCD)
VOB	Vacuum Optical Bench
VOB	Volume over Bark [*Forestry*]
VOB	Volume Over Bark [*Forestry*] (EES)
VOBANC........	Voice Band Compression (CET)
VOBG........	Bangalore [*India*] [*ICAO location identifier*] (ICLI)
VOBI	Bellary [*India*] [*ICAO location identifier*] (ICLI)
VOBL BZ	Verordnungsblatt fuer die Britische Zone [*Official Gazette of the Former British Zone of Occupation*] [*German*] (ILCA)
VOBR	Bidar [*India*] [*ICAO location identifier*] (ICLI)
VOBZ........	Vijayawada [*India*] [*ICAO location identifier*] (ICLI)
VOC	Certificate of Vocational Preparation (AIE)
VOC	Observation Spotter Squadron [*Navy symbol*]
VOC	Onondaga Community College, Syracuse, NY [*OCLC symbol*] (OCLC)
VOC	Variable Oil Capacitor
VOC	Variable Output Circuit (DEN)
VOC	Vehicle Observer Corps [*Road Haulage Association*] [*British*] (DCTA)
VOC	Vehicle Out of Commission [*Army*] (AFIT)
VOC	Verbal Orders of the Commander
VOC	Victorian Olympic Council [*Australia*]
VOC	Vincent Owners Club (EA)
VOC	Virago Owners Club (EA)
VOC	Vocabulary [*Linguistics*]
VOC	Vocal (ADA)
VOC	Vocational
Voc	Vocational (AL)
VOC	Vocative
VOC	Voice of Calvary [*An association*]
VOC	Voice of the Customer [*Business term*]
VOC	Voice-Operated Coder
VOC	Voice-Operated Control [*Telecommunications*] (IAA)
VOC	Voice-Operated Relay Circuit (IAA)
VOC	Voice Order Circuit (CET)

VOC	Volatile Organic Chemical
VOC	Volatile Organic Compound [*Environmental chemistry*]
VOC	Voltage-Operated Channel (DB)
VOC	Volunteer Officer Candidate [*Army*]
VOCA	Victims of Crime Act of 1984
VOCA	Victims of Crime Association [*Australia*]
VOCA	Visiting Orchestra Consultative Association [*British*] (DI)
VOCA	Voice Communications Assembly [*Ground Communications Facility, NASA*]
VOCA	Voice of China and Asia Missionary Society (EA)
VOCA	Voice Output Communications Aid
VOCA	Voltmeter Calibrator
VOCA	Volunteers in Overseas Cooperative Assistance (EA)
VOCA	VP-16 [*Etoposide*] Vincristine, Cyclophosphamide, Adriamycin [*Antineoplastic drug regimen*] (DAVI)
VOCAB	Vocabulary
VOCAL	Verification of On-Chip Chip Array Logic (NITA)
VOCAL	Vessel Ordnance Allowance List
VOCAL	Victims of Child Abuse Laws (EA)
VOCAL	Victims of Crime and Leniency (EA)
VOCAL	Vocabulary Language (MHDI)
VOCAL	Voluntary Organisations of Communication and Language (DBA)
VOCAP	, Cyclophosphamide, Adriamycin, Platinol [*Vincristine*] [*Cisplatin*] [*Antineoplastic drug regimen*]
VOCAT	Vocational
VOCAT	Vocative [*Grammar*] (ROG)
VOCB	Coimbatore [*India*] [*ICAO location identifier*] (ICLI)
VOCC	Cochin [*India*] [*ICAO location identifier*] (ICLI)
VOCCN	Van Ommeren [*AM symbol*] (TTSB)
VOCED	Vocational Education [*Database*] [*Australia*]
VOCG	Verbal Orders of Commanding General
VOCL	Calicut [*India*] [*ICAO location identifier*] (ICLI)
VOCLF	VocalTec Communications Ltd. [*NASDAQ symbol*] [*Formerly, Vocal Tec Ltd.*] (SG)
VOCLF	VocalTec Ltd [*NASDAQ symbol*] (TTSB)
VOCM	St. John's, NF [*AM radio station call letters*]
VOCM	Vehicle Out of Commission for Maintenance [*Military*]
VOCM-FM	St. John's, NF [*FM radio station call letters*]
VOCN	Vocation
VOCNA	Velocette Owners Club of North America (EA)
VOCNL	Vocational
VOCO	Verbal Orders of Commanding Officer
VOCODER	Voice Coder (NITA)
VOCOM	Voice Communications
VOCP	Cuddapah [*India*] [*ICAO location identifier*] (ICLI)
VOCP	Vehicle Out of Commission for Parts [*Military*]
VocRehab	Vocational Rehabilitation (OICC)
VOCS	Verbal Orders of the Chief of Staff
VOCSU	Voice-Operated Carrier Switching Unit (IAA)
VOC-TIES	Vocational Training Inventory and Exploration Survey [*Nancy Scott*] (TES)
VOCTOR	Void On Call to Operating Room (DAVI)
VOCX	Carnicobar [*India*] [*ICAO location identifier*] (ICLI)
VOD	Old Dominion University, Norfolk, VA [*OCLC symbol*] (OCLC)
VOD	Vacuum Oxygen Decarburization [*Stainless-steel processing*]
VOD	Vehicle On-Board Delivery
VOD	Velocity of Detonation (IEEE)
VOD	Veno-Occlusive Disease [*of the liver*]
VOD	Venous Occlusive Disease [*Medicine*] (DB)
VOD	Verification of Deposit [*Finance*] (EMRF)
VOD	Vertical On-Board Delivery [*Navy*] (NVT)
VOD	Via Omni Direct [*Aviation*] (FAAC)
VOD	Video on Demand (ECON)
VOD	Vision, Right Eye
VOD	Visio Oculus Dextra [*Vision, right eye*] [*Latin*] [*Ophthalmology*] (DAVI)
VOD	Vodafone Group [*NYSE symbol*] (SPSG)
VOD	Vodafone Group ADR [*NYSE symbol*] (TTSB)
VODACOM	Voice Data Communications
Vodafone	Vodafone Group [*Associated Press*] (SAG)
VODARO	Vertical Ozone Distribution from the Absorption and Radiation of Ozone (AAG)
VODAS	Voice-Operated Device Antising (CET)
VODAT	Voice-Operated Device for Automatic Transmission
Vodavi	Vodavi Technology [*Associated Press*] (SAG)
VODC	Viking Orbiter Design Change [*NASA*]
VODER	Voice Coder
VODER	Voice-Operated Demonstrator
VODG	Dundigul [*India*] [*ICAO location identifier*] (ICLI)
VODIS	Voice Operated Database in Inquiry System (NITA)
VODK	Donakonda [*India*] [*ICAO location identifier*] (ICLI)
VODK	[*The*] Voice of Democratic Kampuchea [*Radio station of the Red Khmers*] (PD)
VODP	Verbal Orders by Direction of the President
VODS	Video Operator Distress Syndrome (HGAA)
VOE	Venus Orbit Ejection [*NASA*] (MCD)
VOE	Verificationof Employement (EMRF)
VOE	Visual Order Error
VOE	Vocational Office Education [*NASA employment program*]
VOE	Voice of Ethiopia
VOEC	Vegetable Oil Export Corp. (EA)
VOECRN	Vietnamese Organization to Exterminate Communists and Restore the Nation (EA)
VOEE	Voice of Ethiopia External Service
VOEN	Voice of Ethiopia National Service

VOF............	Covington, GA [Location identifier FAA] (FAAL)
VOF............	Observation Fighter Squadron [Navy symbol]
VOF............	Van Kam Am Cap FL Mun Op [AMEX symbol] (TTSB)
VOF............	Van Kampen Merritt Florida Municipal Opportunity Fund [AMEX symbol] (SPSG)
VOF............	Variable Operating Frequency (NATG)
VOF............	Vennootschap Onder Firma [Limited Partnership] [Dutch] (ILCA)
VOF............	Victorian Overseas Foundation [Australia]
VOF............	Volatile Organic Fraction [Automotive exhaust emission testing]
VOF............	Volatile Organic Fractions
VOF............	Vsesoiuznoe Obshchestvo Filatelistov [or Fizioterapistov]
V of A.........	Volunteers of America (EA)
V of R.........	Vale of Rheidol Light Railway [Wales]
V of S.........	Veterans of Safety (EA)
VOG............	Airvolga [Former USSR] [FAA designator] (FAAC)
VOG............	Observation Plane Squadron [Navy symbol]
VOG............	Vanguard Operations Group
VOG............	Vectoroculogram
VOG............	Vessel Off-Gas [Nuclear energy] (NRCH)
Vog............	Vogue [Record label] [France]
VOG............	Volgograd [Former USSR Airport symbol] (OAG)
VOGAA........	Voice-Operated Gain-Adjusting Amplifier [NASA]
VOGAD........	Voice-Operated Gain-Adjusting Device [NASA]
VOGAD........	Voice Operated Gain Adjustment Device (NITA)
VOGB.........	Gulbarga [India] [ICAO location identifier] (ICLI)
VOGIN........	Nederlandse Vereniging van Gebruikers van Online Informatie-Systemen [Netherlands Association of Users of Online Information Systems] (EAIO)
VOGOV.......	Verbal Orders of the Governor
VOH...........	Vohemar [Madagascar] [Airport symbol] (OAG)
VOHAP.......	Volatile Organic Hazardous Air Pollutant [Environmental Protection Agency]
VOHCA.......	Veterans Omnibus Health Care Act of 1976
VOHY.........	Hyderabad [India] [ICAO location identifier] (ICLI)
VOI............	Vacation Ownership Interests
VOI............	Vehicle Ordnance Installation
VOI............	Video Output Impedance
VOI............	Vocational Opinion Index (OICC)
VOI............	Voinjama [Liberia] [Airport symbol] (OAG)
VOICE........	Victims of Incest Can Emerge (EA)
VOICE........	Vocabulary of Intelligence Concept Expressions
VOICE........	Vocal Output and Input-Controlled Environment
VOICE........	Voice of Informed Community Expression
VOICE........	Volunteer Oil Industry Communications Effort [Program] [Phillips Petroleum Co.]
VoiceC.......	Voice Control Systems [Associated Press] (SAG)
VOICECON ...	Voice Telephone Conference
Voice It.......	Voice It Woldwide, Inc. [Associated Press] (SAG)
VoicePw	Voice Powered Tech International, Inc. [Associated Press] (SAG)
VOICES	Victims of Institutionalised Cruelty, Exploitation and Supporters Inc. [Australia]
VOICES........	Voice-Operated Identification Computer Entry System (PDAA)
VOIR..........	Venus Orbiting and Imaging RADAR [NASA]
VOIS	Visual Observation Instrumentation Subsystem [Lunar space program]
VOIS	Visual Observation Integration Subsystem (AAG)
VOIS	Vocal Output for Industrial Systems (NITA)
VOIS	Voice-Operated Inspection System [Software]
VOISC........	Variable Orifice Idle Spark Control [Automotive engineering]
VOK	Camp Douglas, WI [Location identifier FAA] (FAAL)
VOK	Vry op Kaai [Free on Quay] [Afrikaans]
VOKM........	Khamampet [India] [ICAO location identifier] (ICLI)
VOKS	Vsesoiuznoe Obshchestvo Kul'turnoi Sviazi s Zagranitsei [All-Union Society for Cultural Relations with Foreign Countries] [Former USSR]
VOL............	Variable Orientation Launcher (AAG)
VOL............	Video on Line [Computer science] [Italy]
VoL............	Voice of the Listener [British] [An association] (DBA)
Vol............	Volans [Constellation]
VOL............	Volante [Lightly and Rapidly] [Music] (ROG)
Vol............	Volar [Anatomy] (WGA)
vol............	Volatile [Chemistry] (DAVI)
VOL............	Volatilis [Volatile] [Pharmacy]
Vol............	Volcanic [Quality of the bottom] [Nautical charts]
VOL............	Volcano [Maps and charts]
VOL............	Volos [Greece] [Airport symbol] (AD)
VOL............	Volume
vol............	Volume (VRA)
Vol............	Volume (TBD)
VOL............	Volume Label (IAA)
vol%..........	Volume Percent (DAVI)
VOL............	Voluntary [or Volunteer] (AFM)
vol............	Volunteer (WDAA)
vol............	Volvendus [To be rolled] [Latin] (DAVI)
VOL............	Volvo AB [Sweden ICAO designator] (FAAC)
VOLA..........	Volume, American Stock Exchange [Selection symbol]
vol adm	Voluntary Admission [Psychiatry] (DAVI)
VOLAG........	Voluntary Agency [Generic term for a charitable organization]
VOLAR........	Volunteer Army [Project, absorbed by MVA, 1972]
Vol Ash......	Volcanic Ash [Quality of the bottom] [Nautical charts]
volc...........	Volcanic (VRA)
VOLC.........	Volcanics [Lithology]
VOLC.........	Volcano
VOLCAL......	Volume Calculator (MHDI)
VOLCAS	Voice-Operated Loss Control and Suppressor

VOLCAT	Volume Catalog (IAA)
VolCC........	Volunteer Capital Corp. [Associated Press] (SAG)
VOLCOM.....	Value of Life Committee (EA)
VOLCUF.....	Voluntary Organisations' Liaison Council for Under-Fives [British] (DI)
VOLERE	Voluntary/Legal/Regulatory (IEEE)
VOLG	Victorian Office of Local Government [Australia]
VOLID	Volume Identifier (MHDI)
VOLIR	Volumetric Indicating RADAR
VOLKS.......	Volkswagen [Automobile] (DSUE)
VOLLIM......	Voltage Limiter (IAA)
VOLMET.....	Meteorological Information for Aircraft in Flight [ICAO] (FAAC)
Voln..........	Volans [Constellation]
VOLN.........	Volume, New York Stock Exchange [Selection symbol]
VOLNTRY....	Voluntary
Volr...........	Volunteer [British military] (DMA)
VOLRY	Voluntary
VOLS	Voluntary Overseas Libraries Service
VOLSCAN....	Volumetric Scanning RADAR
VOLSER.....	Volume/Serial
volt...........	Volatile [Chemistry] (DAVI)
VOLT..........	Volt Information Sciences, Inc. [NASDAQ symbol] (NQ)
VOLT..........	Volt Info Sciences [NASDAQ symbol] (TTSB)
VOLT..........	Volume, Toronto Stock Exchange [Selection symbol]
VOLTAN	Voltage Amperage Normalizer
VoltInf........	Volt Information Sciences, Inc. [Associated Press] (SAG)
VOLUM	Volumetric (WDAA)
VOLV	Volvendus [To Be Rolled] [Pharmacy] (ADA)
VOLV	Volvo AB [Sweden NASDAQ symbol]
VOLVAR......	Volume-Variety (PDAA)
VOLVEND....	Volvendus [To Be Rolled] [Pharmacy]
Volvo.........	Volvo AB [Associated Press] (SAG)
vol/vol	Volume per Volume [Ratio] (STED)
vol/vol	Volume Ratio [Volume per Volume] [Pharmacology] (DAVI)
VOLVY.......	Volvo AB 'B' ADR [NASDAQ symbol] (TTSB)
VOLWARE....	Volume-Weighted Averages of Realized Prices
VOLY	Voluntary (ROG)
VOM..........	Nux Vomica Strychnia [Strychnine-producing plant] [Pharmacy] (ROG)
VOM..........	Vinyl Chloride Monomer [Chemistry] (DAVI)
VOM..........	Voice of the Mediterranean [Broadcasting service jointly owned by Maltese and Libyan Governments] (EY)
VOM..........	Volcano Resources Corp. [Vancouver Stock Exchange symbol]
VOM..........	Volt-Ohm Meter
vom..........	Voltohmmeter (NAKS)
VOM..........	Volt-Ohm-Milliammeter
VOM..........	Volt-Ohm-Milliampere Meter [Electronics] (IAA)
VOM..........	Vomited (DAVI)
vom..........	Vomited (STED)
VOMA.........	Volt-Ohm-Milliampere [Electronics] (IAA)
VOMD	Madurai [India] [ICAO location identifier] (ICLI)
VOMD	VAFB [Vandenberg Air Force Base] Operations and Maintenance Documentation (NASA)
VOMF.........	Madras [India] [ICAO location identifier] (ICLI)
VOMG	Magadi [India] [ICAO location identifier] (ICLI)
VOMH	Mahad [India] [ICAO location identifier] (ICLI)
VOMI.........	Volksdeutsche Mittelstelle [NAZI Germany]
VOML.........	Mangalore [India] [ICAO location identifier] (ICLI)
VOMM	Madras [India] [ICAO location identifier] (ICLI)
VOM URG	Vomitione Urgente [The Vomiting Being Troublesome] [Pharmacy] (ROG)
VOMY	Mysore [India] [ICAO location identifier] (ICLI)
VON	Avon, CO [Location identifier FAA] (FAAL)
VON	Victorian Order of Nurses
VON	Voice on the Net [A consortium of internet users, vested interests, and software companies] (PCM)
VON	Vons Companies [NYSE symbol] (SPSG)
VON	Vons Cos. [NYSE symbol] (TTSB)
v-onc	Viral Oncogene (LDT)
Von H Const Hist...	Von Holst's Constitutional History of the United States [A publication] (DLA)
Von Ihr Str for L...	Von Ihring's Struggle for Law [A publication] (DLA)
VONJY	Elan Populaire pour l'Unite Nationale [Popular Impulse for National Unity] [Malagascar] [Political party] (PPW)
VONS	Committee for the Defense of Persons Unjustly Persecuted [Former Czechoslovakia] [Political party] (PD)
VONS	Nagarjunsagar [India] [ICAO location identifier] (ICLI)
Vons	Vons Companies [Associated Press] (SAG)
VOO	Ventricular Pacing, No Sensing, No Other Function [Pacemaker] [Cardiology] (MEDA)
VOofA	Vasa Order of America [Cranston, RI] (EA)
Voorh Code...	Voorhies' Code [New York] [A publication] (DLA)
Voorh Cr Jur...	Voorhies' Criminal Jurisprudence of Louisiana [A publication] (DLA)
Voorh St	Voorhies' Louisiana Revised Statutes [A publication] (DLA)
VOP	Valued as in Original Policy [Insurance]
VOP	Value of Production
VOP	Value Option Package [Automotive marketing]
VOP	Venous Occlusion Plethysmography [Medicine] (DMAA)
VOP	Vertical Ozone Profile
VOP	Very Old Pale [Designation on brandy labels]
VOP	Viral Oncology Program [National Cancer Institute]
VOP	Voice-over-Packet [Telecommunications]
VOPA	Verbal Order Purchase Agreement [Sales]
VOPAN........	Voice Pitch Analysis [Consumer Response Corp.]
VOPB	Port Blair [India] [ICAO location identifier] (ICLI)

VOPB .... Voice of the People of Burma [*Radio station of the Burma Communist Party*] (PD)
VOPNAV ...... Vice Chief of Naval Operations
VOPO .... Volkspolizei [*Also, VP*]
VOPP .... Veterinary Medicine, Optometry, Podiatry, and Pharmacy [*HEW program*]
VOPR .... Voice-Operated Relay
VOPT .... Voice of the People of Thailand [*Radio station of the Communist Party of Thailand*] (PD)
VOQ .... Van Kam Am Cap OH Qual Mun [*NYSE symbol*] (TTSB)
VOQ .... Van Kampen Merritt Ohio Quality Municipal [*NYSE symbol*] (SPSG)
VOQ .... Vehicle Owner's Questionnaire [*Auto safety research*]
VOQ .... Visiting Officers' Quarters [*Military*]
VOR .... Sunna Air Ltd. [*Iceland*] [*ICAO designator*] (FAAC)
VOR .... Vehicle Occupancy Rate [*MOCD*] (TAG)
VOR .... Vehicle off the Road [*British*]
VOR .... Vendor [*Legal shorthand*] (LWAP)
VOR .... Vertical Omnidirectional Radio
VOR .... Very-High-Frequency Omnidirectional Range
VOR .... Very High Frequency Omnidirectional Range Station (COE)
VOR .... Very-High-Frequency Omnirange (IDOE)
VOR .... Vestibulo-Ocular Reflex [*Neurology*]
VOR .... Visual Omnidirectional Range (DNAB)
VOR .... Visual Omnirange [*Directional Beacon*] [*Aviation*] (NG)
VOR .... Voice of Reason
VOR .... Voice of the Retarded [*An association*] (PAZ)
VOR .... Voice-Operated Relay
VORAD .... Vehicle On-board RADAR Accident Avoidance [*Automotive safety*]
VORAD .... Vehicular On-Board RADAR [*Automotive engineering*] (PS)
VOR/ATCS .... VHF [*Very-High-Frequency*] Omnidirectional Radio Beacon and Air Traffic Communications Station (SAA)
VORDAC ...... VHF [*Very-High-Frequency*] Omnidirectional Range and Distance Measuring Equipmentfor Average Coverage (IAA)
VORDAC ...... VHF [*Very-High-Frequency*] Omnidirectional Range/Distance-Measuring for AirCoverage
VORDME ...... VHF [*Very-High-Frequency*] Omnidirectional Range/Distance-Measuring Equipment (CET)
VOR/DMET ... VHF [*Very-High-Frequency*] Omnidirectional Range/Distance-Measuring Equipment Compatible with TACAN
VOR-FIX ...... Vestibuloocular Reflex with Fixation Light [*Ophthalmology*]
VORG .... Ramagundam [*India*] [*ICAO location identifier*] (ICLI)
VORG .... Victorian Ornithological Research Group (EERA)
VORLOC ...... VHF [*Very-High-Frequency*] Omnirange Localizer (CET)
VORM .... Ramnad [*India*] [*ICAO location identifier*] (ICLI)
VORM .... Vormittags [*In the Morning*] [*German*]
Vornado ...... Vornado Realty Trust, Inc. [*Associated Press*] (SAG)
VORR .... Raichur [*India*] [*ICAO location identifier*] (ICLI)
VORS .... Vestibulo-Ocular Reflex Suppression [*Ophthalmology*]
Vorsokr ...... Fragmente der Vorsokratiker [*A publication*] (OCD)
VORTAC ...... Combined VOR and TACAN Navigational Facility [*FAA*] (TAG)
VORTAC ...... Variable Omnirange Tactical (NASA)
VORTAC ...... VHF [*Very-High-Frequency*] Omnidirectional Range Collocated with TACAN [*Tactical Air Navigation System*] (IAA)
VORTAC ...... VHF [*Very High Frequency*] Omnidirectional Range Tactical Air Navigation (IAA)
VORTAC ...... VHF [*Very-High-Frequency*] Omnirange TACAN
VORTAL ...... Vertical Ommi-Range, Take-Off, Approach, and Landing System (PDAA)
VORTAN ...... Visual Omnirange/Tactical Air Navigation (MCD)
VORTEX ...... Varian Omnitaste Real Time Executive [*Computer science*] (IAA)
VORTEX ...... Venus Orbiter Radiometric Temperature Experiment [*NASA*]
VORTEX ...... Verification of the Origins of Rotation in Tornadoes Experiment
VORTEX ...... Versatile Omnitask Real-Time Executive (NITA)
VOR/VORTAC ... Very High Frequency Omnidirectional Radio Range [*FAA*] (TAG)
VORY .... Rajahmundry [*India*] [*ICAO location identifier*] (ICLI)
VOS .... Observation Scout Plane [*Navy symbol*]
VOS .... Vacuum Oven Sublimation [*Automotive exhaust emission testing*]
VOS .... Vehicle on Stand (MCD)
VOS .... Vehicle Origin Survey [*R. L. Polk & Co.*] [*Information service or system*] (IID)
VOS .... Vertical Obstacle SONAR (IAA)
VOS .... Vessel of Opportunity [*Marine science*] (OSRA)
VOS .... Veterans of Safety (EA)
VOS .... Veterinary Orthopaedic Society (NTPA)
VOS .... Virtual Operating System
VOS .... Visicoder Oscillograph System
VOS .... Vision, Left Eye
VOS .... Vision on Sound (IAA)
VOS .... Visio Oculus Sinister [*Vision Left Eye*] [*Latin*] [*Ophthalmology*] (DAVI)
VOS .... Vitello Ovi Solutus [*Dissolved in the Yolk of an Egg*] [*Pharmacy*] (ROG)
VOS .... Voice-Operated Switch [*or System*]
VOS .... Voluntary Observing Ship [*Marine science*] (OSRA)
VOS .... Voluntary Observing Ships [*Marine science*] (MSC)
VOS .... Volunteer Observing Ship [*Marine science*] (OSRA)
Vos .... Voskhod (BJA)
VOS .... Vostok [*Former USSR Geomagnetic observatory code*]
VOSA .... Variable Orifice Sound Attenuator [*System*] (DNAB)
VOSA .... Verbal Orders of the Secretary of the Army
VOSAF .... Verbal Orders of the Secretary of the Air Force
VOSC .... VAST [*Versatile Avionics Shop Test*] Operating System Code
VOSE .... Vacuum Operation of Spacecraft Equipment (IAA)
VOSH .... Volunteer Optometric Services to Humanity/International (EA)
VOSL .... Variable Operating and Safety Level (DNAB)
VO/SOT .... Voiceover/Sound on Tape [*Television*] (NTCM)

VOST .... Volatile Organic Sampling Train [*For air analysis*]
VOSW .... Very Old Scotch Whisky
VOT .... Valve Opening Time [*Nuclear energy*] (NRCH)
VOT .... Van Kam Am Cap Mun Opp II [*NYSE symbol*] (TTSB)
VOT .... Van Kampen Merritt Municipal Opportunity Trust 2 [*NYSE symbol*] (SPSG)
VOT .... Very Old Tawny [*Wines and spirits*]
VOT .... VHF [*Very-High-Frequency*] Omnitest
VOT .... Virtual Onsite Technology [*Telecommunications*]
VOT .... Visual Omnirange Test [*Aviation*] (IAA)
VOT .... Visual Organization Test (STED)
VOT .... Vocational Office Trainee
VOT .... Voice Onset Time
VOT .... Voice Output Terminal [*Computer science*] (WDMC)
VOT .... VOR [*Very-High-Frequency Omnidirectional Range*] Test Signal (CET)
vot .... Votic [*MARC language code Library of Congress*] (LCCP)
VOTA .... Vibration Open Test Assembly [*Nuclear energy*] (NRCH)
VOTACT ...... Validation of Theoretical Automatic Checkout Techniques (MCD)
VOTAG .... Verbal Orders of the Adjutant General
VOTC .... Volume Table of Contents [*Computer science*]
VOTCA .... Victims of Terrorism Compensation Act
VO-TECH ...... Vocational-Technical
VOTE/COPE ... Voice of Teachers for Education/Committee on Political Education of New York State United Teachers
VOTEM .... Voice-Operated Typewriter Employing Morse [*Telecommunications*] (IAA)
VOTERM ...... Voice Terminal (NITA)
VOTJ .... Tanjore [*India*] [*ICAO location identifier*] (ICLI)
VOTM .... Vacuum-Operated Throttle Modulator [*Automotive engineering*]
VOTP .... Tirupeti [*India*] [*ICAO location identifier*] (ICLI)
VOTR .... Tiruchchirappalli [*India*] [*ICAO location identifier*] (ICLI)
VOTS .... VAX OSI [*Virtual Address Extension Open Systems Interconnection*] TransportService (TNIG)
VOTV .... Trivandrum [*India*] [*ICAO location identifier*] (ICLI)
VOTX .... Tambaram [*India*] [*ICAO location identifier*] (ICLI)
VOU .... Visio Oculus Uterque [*Vision, Each Eye*] [*Ophthalmology*] [*Latin*] (MAE)
VOU .... Voucher (AFM)
VOU .... Vouglans [*France*] [*Seismograph station code, US Geological Survey*] (SEIS)
VOU DED .... Voucher Deduction [*Military*] (DNAB)
V$_{OUT}$ .... Output Voltage (IDOE)
VOV .... Van Kam Am Cap OH Val Mun [*AMEX symbol*] (TTSB)
VOV .... Van Kampen Merritt Ohio Value Municipal Trust [*AMEX symbol*] (SPSG)
VOV .... Very Old Version
VOV .... Video Output Voltage
VOV .... Voice of the Viewer (WDAA)
VOV .... Voice of Vietnam [*Propaganda broadcast aimed at US POWs*] (VNW)
VOVB .... Vikarabad [*India*] [*ICAO location identifier*] (ICLI)
VOVR .... Vellore [*India*] [*ICAO location identifier*] (ICLI)
VOW .... Canadian Voice of Women for Peace [*See also VFCP*]
VOW .... Voice of Women
VOW .... Voice Order Wire
VOWA .... Warangal [*India*] [*ICAO location identifier*] (ICLI)
VOWF .... Value-Operated Water Flash (DNAB)
VOWR .... St. John's, NF [*AM radio station call letters*]
VOX .... Audiovox CI'A' [*AMEX symbol*] (TTSB)
VOX .... Audiovox Corp. [*AMEX symbol*] (SAG)
VOX .... Voice Controlled Relay
VOX .... Voice-Operated Changeover
vox .... Voice-Operated Control (IDOE)
VOX .... Voice-Operated Keying [*Computer science*]
VOX .... Voice-Operated Transmission
vox .... Voice Operated Transmitter (NAKS)
VOX .... Voice Output Exchange
voxel .... Volume Element (MAE)
VOXEL .... Volume Pixel
Voxel .... Voxel Co. [*Associated Press*] (SAG)
VOXL .... Voxel [*NASDAQ symbol*] (SAG)
VOXLW .... Voxel Wrrt [*NASDAQ symbol*] (TTSB)
VOX POP .... Vox Populi [*Voice of the People*] [*Latin*]
VOXW .... Voxware, Inc. [*NASDAQ symbol*] (SAG)
Voxware ...... Voxware, Inc. [*Associated Press*] (SAG)
VOY .... Viceroy Resources Corp. [*Toronto Stock Exchange symbol Vancouver Stock Exchange symbol*]
VOY .... Voice-Operated Relay (IAA)
voy .... Voyage (DS)
VOYA .... Voice of Youth Advocates [*A publication*] (BRI)
VoyAZ .... Voyageur Arizona Municipal Income Fund [*Associated Press*] (SAG)
VoyCO .... Voyageur Colorado Insured Municipal Income Fund [*Associated Press*] (SAG)
VoyFla .... Voyageur Florida Insured Municipal Income [*Associated Press*] (SAG)
VoyMN .... Voyageur Minnesota Municipal Income Fund, Inc. [*Associated Press*] (SAG)
VoyMN2 ...... Voyageur Minnesota Municipal Income Fund 2, Inc. [*Associated Press*] (SAG)
VoyMN3 ...... Voyageur Minnesota Municipal Income Fund 3, Inc. [*Associated Press*] (SAG)
VoyMO .... Voyageur Missouri Municipal Income Fund [*Associated Press*] (SAG)
VP .... All India Reporter, Vindhya Pradesh [*1951-57*] [*A publication*] (DLA)
VP .... Patrol Plane [*Navy symbol*]

VP............	Patrol Squadron [*Navy symbol*]
V$_p$............	Pinchoff Voltage (IDOE)
V$_p$............	Plasma Volume [*Laboratory science*] (DAVI)
V$_p$............	Plate Volage (IDOE)
VP............	Shore Based [*Navy symbol*]
VP............	Vacant Property (ADA)
VP............	Vacuum Packaged
VP............	Vacuum Pickup
VP............	Vacuum Pump
VP............	Validation Parameter (DA)
VP............	Validation Plan [*Social Security Administration*]
VP............	Valve Pit (AAG)
VP............	Valve Positioner
VP............	Vanishing Point [*Term in art/drawing*]
VP............	Vanuaaku Pati [*New Hebrides*] [*Political party*] (PD)
VP............	Vanuatu Pati (PD)
VP............	Vapor Pressure
VP............	Variable Pitch [*as, an aircraft propeller*]
VP............	Variable Procedure (AAG)
VP............	Variable Property
VP............	Variant Pinocytic [*Cell*] [*Medicine*]
VP............	Variegate Porphyria [*Medicine*]
VP............	Variot-Pironneau [*Syndrome*] [*Medicine*] (DB)
VP............	Various Paging [*Bibliography*]
vp............	Various Places [*MARC country of publication code Library of Congress*] (LCCP)
VP............	Various Publishers [*Bibliography*]
VP............	Vasopressin [*Endocrinology*]
VP............	Vector Processor
VP............	Vegetable Parchment [*Paper*] (DGA)
VP............	Velocity of Propagation (IAA)
VP............	Velocity Pressure
VP............	Venereal Pamphlet [*Navy*]
VP............	Venipuncture [*Medicine*] (MAE)
VP............	Venous Pressure [*Medicine*]
VP............	Vent-Clearing Pressure [*Nuclear energy*] (NRCH)
V-P............	Ventilation-Perfusion Scintigraphy
VP............	Vent Pipe [*Technical drawings*]
VP............	Ventral Pioneer [*Neuron*]
VP............	Ventral Posterior [*Anatomy*]
VP............	Ventricular Premature [*beat*] [*Cardiology*] (DAVI)
V$_p$............	Ventricular Premature [*Medicine*] (DB)
VP............	Ventriculoperitoneal [*Medicine*]
VP............	Verb Passive
VP............	Verb Phrase
VP............	Verification Polarization (NASA)
VP............	Verification Program [*Branch*] [*Forecast Systems Laboratory*] (USDC)
VP............	Verifying Punch (CMD)
VP............	Verstell Propeller (MCD)
VP............	Vertex Processor
VP............	Vertical Planning (NG)
VP............	Vertical Polarization
VP............	Vest Pocket
VP............	Vice President
v-p............	Vice-President (DD)
VP............	Vice-Principal [*British*]
VP............	Videoplayer
VP............	Video Processor (NVT)
VP............	Vietnam Press
VP............	Viewpoint (NASA)
VP............	Vincristine and Prednisone [*Antineoplastic drug regimen*]
VP............	Vinylphenol [*Biochemistry*]
VP............	Vinylpyrrolidinone [*Organic chemistry*]
VP............	Viral Particle [*Medicine*]
VP............	Viral Protein [*Biochemistry, genetics*]
VP............	Virtual Control Program (NITA)
VP............	Virtual Machine Control Program [*Computer science*] (IAA)
VP............	Virtual Path [*Computer science*] (DDC)
VP............	Virtual Pitch [*Neurophysiology*]
VP............	Virtual Processor
VP............	Virus Protein (DB)
VP............	Visa Petition
VP............	Visitor's Passport [*British*]
VP............	Vivre et Penser [*A publication*] (BJA)
VP............	Voges-Proskauer [*Bacteriology*]
VP............	Void in Part [*Decision or finding held invalid in part for reasons given*] [*Used in Shepard's Citations*] [*Legal term*] (DLA)
VP............	Volkspartie [*People's Party*] [*Liechtenstein*] [*Political party*] (PPE)
VP............	Volkspolizei [*Also, VOPO*]
VP............	Volume-Pressure (MAE)
VP............	Voluntary Patient [*British*]
VP............	Vorposten [*Outpost*] [*German military*]
VP............	Vossa Paternidade [*Yours Paternally*] [*Portuguese*]
VP............	Voting Pool [*Said of disposition of stocks*]
VP............	Vulnerable Period [*Physiology*]
VP............	Vulnerable Point
VP............	Vulnerable Prisoner (WDAA)
VP-16-213 ...	Vepeside [*Etoposide*] [*Antineoplastic drug*]
VPA............	Silver Plains [*Queensland*] [*Airport symbol*] (AD)
VPA............	Valproic Acid [*Anticonvulsant compound*]
VPA............	Value Purchase Agreement (HGAA)
VPA............	Vascular Permeability Assay [*Clinical chemistry*]
VPA............	Vegetable Protein Association [*British*] (DBA)
VPA............	Vehicle Power Adapter
VPA............	Vibration Pickup Amplifier

VPA............	Victorian Psychologists' Association [*Australia*]
VPA............	Videotape Production Association (EA)
VPA............	Village Produce Association [*British*] (BI)
VPA............	Virginia Port Authority
VPA............	Virtual Population Analysis
VPA............	Visual Packaging Association [*Defunct*] (EA)
VPA............	Volatile Profile Analysis [*Food chemistry*]
VPA............	Volume Purchase Agreement [*Sales*]
VPA............	Vote Profile Analysis
VPAFA.........	Victorian Public Authorities Finance Agency [*Australia*]
VPAM.........	Verapamil [*Antineoplastic drug*] (CDI)
VPAM.........	Virtual Partitioned Access Method
VP and VLE...	Vapour Pressures and Vapour Liquid Equilibria (NITA)
VPAP.........	Voluntary Petroleum Allocation Program [*Presidential*]
VPATH	Vertical Path (GAVI)
VPB............	Medium and Heavy Patrol Bomber Squadron [*Land based and seaplane*] [*Navy symbol*]
VPB............	Patrol-Bombing Plane [*Navy symbol*]
VPB............	Vendors per Block [*Sales*]
VPB............	Ventricular Premature Beat [*Cardiology*]
VPB............	Vertical Plot Board [*Navy*]
VPB............	Veteran Air [*Ukraine*] [*FAA designator*] (FAAC)
VPB............	Vinblastine, Platinol [*Cisplatin*], Bleomycin [*Antineoplastic drug regimen*]
VPB............	Virtually-Pivoted Beam LASER (IAA)
VPBA	Varipolarization Beacon Antenna
VPBA	Virginia Poultry Breeders Association (EA)
VPBC	Virginia Poultry Breeders Club [*Later, VPBA*] (EA)
VPB(HL).......	Patrol Bomber, Four-Engine, Landplane [*Navy symbol*]
VPB(HS).......	Patrol Bomber, Four-Engine, Seaplane [*Navy symbol*]
VPB(ML).......	Patrol Bomber, Two-Engine, Landplane [*Navy symbol*]
VPB(MS)......	Patrol Bomber, Two-Engine, Seaplane [*Navy symbol*]
VPC............	La Vente par Correspondance [*Mail Order*] [*Business term French*]
VPC............	Vaccines for Children [*Medicine*]
VPC............	Vacuum Pump Chamber
VPC............	Vapor Permeation Curing [*Plastics technology*]
VPC............	Vapor-Phase Chromatography [*Medicine*] (DMAA)
VPC............	Variable Padder Capacitor
VPC............	Vehicle-Platform Center [*Ford Motor Co.*] (ECON)
VPC............	Vehicle Platform Center [*Automotive industry project management*]
VPC............	Ventricular Premature Contraction [*Cardiology*]
VPC............	Vertebrate Pests Committee (EERA)
VPC............	Vertical Path Computer (PDAA)
VPC............	Veterinary Products Committee [*British*]
VPC............	Victorian Psychological Council [*Australia*]
VPC............	Video Processor Control (MCD)
VPC............	Violence Policy Center (EA)
VPC............	Virginia Panel Corp. (IAA)
VPC............	Virtual Path Connection [*Computer science*] (DDC)
VPC............	Virtual Processor Complex [*Computer science*] (CDE)
VPC............	Virus-Producing Cell
VPC............	Visual Punch Card
VPC............	Voltage Phasing Control (DEN)
VPC............	Voltage to Pulse Converter
VPC............	Volume Packed Cells
VPC............	Volume Percent (MAE)
VPC............	Volume-Pulse-Charge
VPC............	Volunteer Program Consultant [*Red Cross*]
VPC............	Volunteers for Peaceful Change (EA)
VPC............	Vulval Precursor Cell [*Genetics*]
VPCA	Video Prelaunch Command Amplifier
VPCDS	Video Prelaunch Command Data System [*Air Force*]
VPCE..........	Vapor-Phase Catalytic Exchange (MCD)
VPCF..........	Vapor Pressure Correction Factor [*Nuclear energy*] (IAA)
VPCIS	Voice-Operated Computerized Identification System (PDAA)
VPCMF........	Vincristine, Prednisone, Cyclophosphamide, Methotrexate, Fluorouracil [*Antineoplastic drug regimen*]
VPCPr	Vincristine, Prednisone, Vinblastine, Chlorambucil, Procarbazine [*Antineoplastic drug regimen*]
VP/CSS	Virtual Program/Conversation Software System (NITA)
VPD	Vapor-Phase Deacidification [*of books and documents*]
VPD	Vapor Phase Decomposition (AAEL)
VPD	Vapor Phase Deposition [*Coating technology*]
VPD	Vapor Phase Desorption (AAEL)
VPD	Vapor Pressure Deficit [*Meteorology*]
VPD	Variable Power Drivetrain [*Automotive engineering*]
VPD	Variation per Day [*Navigation*]
VPD	Vehicle/Pedestrian Deviation [*FAA*] (TAG)
VPD	Vehicle Performance Data
VPD	Vehicle Propulsion Directorate [*Army and NASA joint operation*] (RDA)
VPD	Vehicles per Day [*Military*] (AFM)
VPD	Ventricular Premature Depolarization [*Cardiology*]
VPD	Vertically Polarized Dipole (MCD)
VPD	Vice President of Diversity
VPD	Victorian Parliamentary Debates [*A publication*]
VPD	Vierte Partei Deutschlands [*Fourth Party of Germany*] [*Political party*] (PPW)
VPD	Villa Park Dam [*California*] [*Seismograph station code, US Geological Survey*] (SEIS)
VPD	Visual Pattern Discrimination (PDAA)
VPDB	Vienna PeeDee Belemnite
VPDF	Vacuum Pump Discharge Filter
VPDS	Virtual Private Data Services [*Computer science*] (CIST)
VPE............	Vapor Growth Epitaxy [*Materials processing*] (IAA)

VPE	Vapor-Phase Epitaxy
VPE	Vapour Phase Epitaxy (AAEL)
VPE	Vehicle Positioning Equipment (MCD)
VPE	Video Processing Equipment
VPE	Visual Programming Environment
VPE	Vulcanized Polyethylene (IAA)
VPELA	Victorian Planning and Environmental Law Association [*Australia*]
VP-F	Falkland Islands [*International civil aircraft marking*] (ODBW)
VPF	Vacuum Pump Filter
VPF	Variable Parts Feeder
VPF	Variable Phase Filter
VPF	Vascular-Permeability Factor [*Medicine*]
VPF	Vector Processing Facility (NITA)
VPF	Vector Product Format
VPF	Vertical Processing Facility [*NASA*] (MCD)
VPF	Vibratory Pan Feeder
VPF	Victorian Police Force [*Australia*]
VPF	Victorian Protestant Federation [*Australia*]
VPF	Viscoplastic Flow
VPFAS	Vice President of the Faculty of Architects and Surveyors [*British*] (DBQ)
VPFG	Variable Phase Function Generator
VPG	Vallentine Peace Group [*Political party Australia*]
VPG	Variable-Rate Pulse Generator
VPG	Vehicle Product Group
VPG	Velopharyngeal Gap [*Medicine*] (DMAA)
VPGG	Valine-Proline-Glycine-Glycine [*Biochemistry*]
VPGS	Venous Pressure Gradient Support Stocking
VPGS	Vice-President of the Geological Society [*British*]
VPGVG	Valine-Proline-Glycine-Valine-Glycine [*Biochemistry*]
VPH	Variation per Hour [*Navigation*]
VPH	Vehicles per Hour [*Traffic*] (AFM)
V PH	Vertical Photography (WDAA)
VPH	Veterans of Pearl Harbor (EA)
VPH	Vickers Pyramid Hardness Number (PDAA)
VPH	Viewers Per Household [*Television ratings*] (DOAD)
VPH	Volkspolizeihelfer
VPHD	Vertical Payload Handling Device [*NASA*] (MCD)
VPHM	ViroPharma, Inc. [*NASDAQ symbol*] (SAG)
VPI	Vacuum Pressure Impregnation (IEEE)
VPI	Valve Position Indicator (KSC)
VPI	Vapor-Phase Inhibitor [*See also VCI*] [*Chemical technology*]
VPI	Vehicle Performance Index [*Automobile technology*]
VPI	Vehicle Personality Module [*Automotive engineering*]
VPI	Velopharyngeal Insufficiency [*Medicine*] (MEDA)
VPI	Vendor Parts Index [*Sales*]
VPI	Vertical Point of Intersection [*Transportation*]
VPI	Very Promotable Item (WDMC)
VPI	Vessel Patentcy Index [*Medicine*]
VPI	Veterinary Pet Insurance
VPI	Vintage Petroleum [*NYSE symbol*] (SPSG)
VPI	VIP Dynasty International Marketing Corp. [*Vancouver Stock Exchange symbol*]
VPI	Virginia Polytechnic Institute and State University [*Blacksburg*]
VPI	Virginia Polytechnic Institute and State University, Blacksburg, VA [*OCLC symbol*] (OCLC)
VPI	Virtual Path Identifier [*Computer science*] (DDC)
VPI	Vocational Preference Inventory [*Psychology*]
VPIC	Victorian Prison Industries Commission [*Australia*]
VPIR	Vapor-Phase Infrared (DB)
VPIT	Vice President of Information Technology
VPJT	Vertical Power Jump Test
VPK	Military Industrial Commission [*Soviet-Russian*] (DOMA)
VPK	Vehicle per Kilometer (AABC)
VPK	Verdi Peak [*California*] [*Seismograph station code, US Geological Survey*] (SEIS)
VPK	Vest Pocket Kodak [*Camera*]
VPK	Volts Peak (NSA)
VPK	Voyenno-promyshlennaya Komissiya [*Military Industrial Commission*] [*Former USSR*] (LAIN)
VPKA	Volkspolizeikreisamt
VP(L)	US Navy Patrol Squadron (Land) (CINC)
VPL	Variable Pulse LASER
VPL	Vendor Parts List (AAG)
VPL	Ventral Posterolateral [*Anatomy*]
VPL	Virginia Beach Public Library System, Virginia Beach, VA [*OCLC symbol*] (OCLC)
VPL	Virtual Path Link [*Computer science*] (DDC)
VPL	Virtual Private Line [*Computer science*] (CIST)
VPL	Visible Panty Line [*In reference to clothing*]
VPL	Voice-Programming Language [*Computer science*]
VPL	Volunteer Prison League [*Defunct*] (EA)
VPL	Vulcano Piano [*Lipari Islands*] [*Seismograph station code, US Geological Survey*] (SEIS)
VP-LA	Anguilla [*International civil aircraft marking*] (ODBW)
VPLCC	Vehicle Propellant Loading Control Center
VPLIC	Victorian Public Library and Information Cooperative [*Australia*]
VP-LMA	Montserrat [*International civil aircraft marking*] (ODBW)
VPLR	Vacuum Pack Life Raft (DWSG)
VPLS	Vice-President of the Linnaean Society [*British*]
VP-LV	Virgin Islands [*International civil aircraft marking*] (ODBW)
VPM	Vacuum Pumping Module
VPM	Variation per Minute [*Navigation*]
VPM	Vascular Permeability Mediator [*Hematology*]
VPM	Vehicle Project Manager [*NASA*] (NASA)

VPM	Vehicles per Mile
VPM	Velocity Preset Module (MCD)
VPM	Vendor Part Modification (AAG)
VPM	Ventroposteriomedial [*Medicine*] (DB)
VPM	Versatile Packaging Machine
VPM	Vertical Panel Mount
VPM	Vertical Polarization Mode
VPM	Vibrations per Minute
VPM	Voice-Processing Module [*Computer science*]
VPM	Voix du Peuple Murundi [*Voice of the Murundi People*]
VPM	Volts per Meter [*Also, V/m*]
VPM	Volts per Mil
VPM	Volts per Mile (IAA)
VPM	Volumes per Million [*Measure of gas contamination*]
VPMA	Vegetable Parchment Manufacturers Association [*Later, API*] (EA)
VPMOS	Verified Primary Military Occupational Specialty
VPMR	Vanguard Party of the Malagasy Revolution
VPMS	Virchow-Pirquet Medical Society (EA)
VPN	Vendor Parts Number
VPN	Vickers Pyramid Number [*Hardness test*]
VPN	Virtual Page Number
VPN	Virtual Private Network [*US Sprint Communications Co.*] [*Atlanta, GA*] (TSSD)
VPN	Vopnafjordur [*Iceland*] [*Airport symbol*] (OAG)
VPNL	Variable Pulse Neodymium LASER
VPO	Vanadium Phosphate [*Inorganic chemistry*]
VPO	Vanadium-Phosphorus Oxide [*Inorganic chemistry*]
VPO	Vapor-Phase Oxidation [*Chemical processing*]
VPO	Vapor Pressure Osmometer [*or Osmometry*] [*Analytical chemistry*]
VPO	Vegetation Protection Ordinance [*Brisbane*] (EERA)
VPO	Vienna Philharmonic Orchestra
VPO	Viking Project Office [*NASA*] (KSC)
VPOC	Variable Performance Optimizing Controller (IAA)
VPOF	Vacuum-Processed Oxide Free
VPOP	Vice Directorate for Production Office Procedure [*Defense Intelligence Agency*] (MCD)
VPP	Vacuum Pickup Pencil
VPP	Value Payable by Post
VPP	Variable Pitch Propeller
VPP	Variable Polarity Plasma [*Welding*]
VPP	Vector Parallel Processor [*Computer science*]
VPP	Vegetable Protein Products [*Food technology*]
VPP	Velocity per Performance
VPP	Velocity Prediction Program
VPP	Vertebrate Pest Program (EERA)
VPP	Vertical Pinpoint (AFM)
VPP	Vertical Pouch Packager
VPP	Very Public Person
VPP	Vested Pension Plan (MHDB)
VPP	Viral Poroine Pneumonia [*Veterinary medicine*]
VPP	Virtual Pivot Point [*Suspension*] [*Tandem bike*]
VPP	Viscous Plastic Processing [*Materials science and technology*]
VPP	Vocational Preparation Programme (AIE)
V P-P	Volt Peak-to-Peak (NASA)
VPP	Voluntary Projects Programme [*British*]
VPP	Voluntary Protection Program [*OSHA*]
VPP	Volunteer Political Party [*Northern Ireland*]
VPPB	Vendor Provisioning Parts Breakdown (AAG)
VPPD	Vice Presidential Protective Division [*US Secret Service*]
VPPN	Vampire Pen Pal Network [*Defunct*] (EA)
VPPPA	Voluntary Protection Programs Participants' Association
VPPS	Vehicle Parking Protection Services [*British*]
VPQ	Van Kam Am Cap PA Qual Mun [*NYSE symbol*] (TTSB)
VPQ	Van Kampen Merritt Pennsylvania Quality Municipal [*NYSE symbol*] (SPSG)
VPR	Vacuum Pipette Rig (PDAA)
VPR	Valveless Pulse Rocket
VPR	Vaporize
VPR	Variable Parameter Record [*Statistics*] (IAA)
VPR	Variable Parameter Regression [*Statistics*]
VPR	Ventricle Pressure Response [*Cardiology*]
VPR	Video Plankton Recorder [*Oceanography*]
VPR	Virtual PPI [*Plan-Position Indicator*] Reflectoscope [*RADAR*]
VPR	Virtual Processor Ratio [*Computer science*]
VPR	Vital Pacific Resources Ltd. [*Vancouver Stock Exchange symbol*]
VPR	Voice Position Report (DA)
VPR	Voluntary Price Reduction (AABC)
VPRBC	Volume of Packed Red Blood Cells [*Medicine*] (DB)
VPRC	Volume of Packed Red Cells [*Hematology*]
VPRES	Vice-President
VPRESSVB	Vice-Presidential Service Badge [*Military decoration*]
VPRF	Variable Pulse Repetition Frequency (IEEE)
VPRGS	Vice-President of the Royal Geographical Society [*British*]
VPRI	Plant Research Institute, Burnley [*Victoria*] [*State*] (EERA)
VPRI	Vice-President of the Royal Institute [*British*]
VPR-NMP	Virtual PPI [*Plan-Position Indicator*] Reflectoscope with Navigational Microfilm Projector [*RADAR*]
VPRON	US Navy Patrol Squadron (CINC)
VPRS	Vice-President of the Royal Society [*British*]
VPRT	Vector Pressure Ratio Transducer
VPS	Eglin Air Force Base [*Florida*] [*Airport symbol*] (AD)
VPS	Fort Walton Beach [*Florida*] [*Airport symbol*] (OAG)
VP(S)	US Navy Patrol Squadron (Sea-Based) (CINC)
VPS	Vacuum Pickup System
VPS	Vacuum Pipe Still [*Chemical engineering*]

VPS..............	Vacuum Pump System
VPS..............	Valparaiso, FL [*Location identifier FAA*] (FAAL)
VPS..............	Valvular Pulmonic Stenosis [*Cardiology*] (DAVI)
VPS..............	Vanguard Planning Summary [*Air Force*]
VPS..............	Vapor Phase Soldering (PDAA)
VPS..............	Variable Parameter System
VPS..............	Variable Power Supply (MCD)
VPS..............	Vatican Philatelic Society (EA)
VPS..............	Vectors Per Second (CDE)
VPS..............	Vehicle Power Supply [*Automotive engineering*]
VPS..............	Ventriculoperitoneal Shunt [*Neurology*] (DAVI)
VPS..............	Vernier Propulsion System [*Aerospace*]
VPS..............	Versatile Pacific Shipyards [*Shipbuilder*] [*Vancouver, Canada*]
VPS..............	Vibrations per Second
VPS..............	Vibrator Power Supply
VPS..............	Video-Pac Systems Ltd. [*Hollywood, CA*] [*Telecommunications service*] (TSSD)
VPS..............	Video Programme Service (NITA)
VPS..............	Viewers-per-Set [*Television ratings*] (WDMC)
VPS..............	Vinylpolysilane [*Organic chemistry*]
VPS..............	Virtual Programming System (NITA)
VPS..............	Visitor Program Service of Meridian House International (EA)
VPS..............	Visual Programs Systems
VPS..............	Voice Control Systems [*AMEX symbol*] (SAG)
VPS..............	Voice Processing System [*Computer science*] (IT)
VPS..............	Volcan Poas [*Costa Rica*] [*Seismograph station code, US Geological Survey*] (SEIS)
VPS..............	Voluntary Product Standard [*National Bureau of Standards*]
VPS..............	Voluntary Product Standards
VPSA	Vice-President of the Society of Antiquaries [*British*]
VPSAB	Victorian Post-Secondary Accreditation Board [*Australia*]
VPSB	Veterans Placement Service Board [*Post-World War II*]
VPSS	Vector Processing Subsystem
VPSSIHM	Volunteer Program of the Sisters, Servants of the Immaculate Heart of M ary (EA)
VPSS/VF	Vector Processing Subsystem/Vector Facility [*Computer science*] (HGAA)
VPSW	Virtual Program Status Word
VPT..............	Patrol Torpedo Plane [*Navy symbol*]
VPT..............	Ventral Posterior Thalamic [*Electrode for stimulation*]
VPT..............	Vibratron Pressure Transducer
VPT..............	Video Pulse Termination
VPT..............	Virtual Path Terminator [*Computer science*] (DDC)
VPT..............	Virtual Printer Technology [*Dataproducts Corp.*] (PCM)
VPT..............	Voice plus Telegraph [*Telecommunications*] (TEL)
VPT..............	Volume-Price Trend [*Finance*]
VPTAR	Variable Parameter Terrain-Avoidance RADAR
VPTI.............	Voice Powered Tech International [*NASDAQ symbol*] (SAG)
VPTI.............	Voice Powered Tech Intl [*NASDAQ symbol*] (TTSB)
VPTIW	Voice Powered Tech Intl Wrrt [*NASDAQ symbol*] (TTSB)
VPTR	Value Pointer (MHDI)
VPTRM	Viscous Partial Thermoremanent Magnetization [*Geophysics*]
VPU	Pace University Library, Union List of Serials, New York, NY [*OCLC symbol*] (OCLC)
VPU	Vacuum Penetration Unit
VPU	Vibrator Power Unit (MSA)
VPU	Vulnerable Prisoners' Unit (WDAA)
VPUA	Vibration Pickup Amplifier
VPUG	Ventura Publisher User's Group (EA)
VPUR	Vermont Pure Hldgs Ltd [*NASDAQ symbol*] (TTSB)
VPUR	Vermont Pure Holdings [*NASDAQ symbol*] (SAG)
VPV	Van Kam Am Cap PA Val Mun [*NYSE symbol*] (TTSB)
VPV	Van Kampen Merritt Pennsylvania Value Municipal Income Trust [*NYSE symbol*] (SPSG)
VPVCPr........	Vincristine, Prednisone, Vinblastine, Chlorambucil, Procarbazine [*Antineoplastic drug regimen*]
VPVH	Viewers-per-Viewing Household [*Television ratings*] (NTCM)
VPW.............	Variable Pulse Width [*Automotive engineering*]
VPW.............	Ventral Prostate Weight [*Medicine*]
VPW.............	Vertically Polarized Wave
VPX.............	Pineville, WV [*Location identifier FAA*] (FAAL)
VPY.............	Vila Pery [*Mozambique*] [*Airport symbol*] (AD)
VPY.............	Vinylpyridine [*Organic chemistry*]
VPZ.............	Valparaiso [*Indiana*] [*Airport symbol*] (OAG)
VPZ.............	Valparaiso, IN [*Location identifier FAA*] (FAAL)
VPZ.............	Virtual Processing Zero
VPZS...........	Vice-President of the Zoological Society [*British*]
VQ...............	Fleet Air Reconnaissance Squadron [*Navy symbol*] (CINC)
VQ...............	Oxley Airlines [*ICAO designator*] (AD)
VQ...............	Vector Quantizer [*Computer science*]
V/Q..............	Ventilation/Perfusion [*Quotient*] [*Medicine*]
VQ...............	Very Quick [*Flashing*] Light [*Navigation signal*]
VQ...............	Virtual Quantum
VQ...............	Voluntary Quit [*Unemployment insurance*] [*Bureau of Labor Statistics*] (OICC)
VQA	Al Sigl Center Library, Rochester, NY [*OCLC symbol*] (OCLC)
VQA	Vendor Quality Assurance
VQAR	Vendor Quality Assurance Representative [*Nuclear energy*] (NRCH)
VQB	Bausch & Lomb, Inc., Library, Rochester, NY [*OCLC symbol*] (OCLC)
VQB	Valuers' Qualification Board [*Victoria, Australia*]
VQB	Visual Query Builder [*Computer science*] (PCM)
VQC	Canandaigua Veterans Administration Medical Center Library, Canandaigua, NY [*OCLC symbol*] (OCLC)
VQC	Van Kam Am Cap CA Qual Mun [*NYSE symbol*] (TTSB)

VQC	Van Kampen Merritt California Quality Municipal Fund [*NYSE symbol*] (SAG)
VQC	Variable Quartz Capacitor
VQC	Vendor Quality Certification
VQD	Center for Governmental Research Library, Rochester, NY [*OCLC symbol*] (OCLC)
VQD	Vendor Quality Defect
VQE	Colgate-Rochester Divinity School, Library, Rochester, NY [*OCLC symbol*] (OCLC)
VQE	San Antonio, TX [*Location identifier FAA*] (FAAL)
VQF	Convalescent Hospital for Children, Library, Rochester, NY [*OCLC symbol*] (OCLC)
VQFP	Very Fine-Pitch Quad Flatpack (CIST)
VQG	Eastman Dental Center, Basil G. Bibby Library, Rochester, NY [*OCLC symbol*] (OCLC)
VQH	Eastman Kodak Co., KAD Library, Rochester, NY [*OCLC symbol*] (OCLC)
VQI	Eastman Kodak Co., Business Library, Rochester, NY [*OCLC symbol*] (OCLC)
VQJ	Eastman Kodak Co., Engineering Division, Library, Rochester, NY [*OCLC symbol*] (OCLC)
VQK	Eastman Kodak Co., Health and Safety Laboratory, Library, Rochester, NY [*OCLC symbol*] (OCLC)
V Qk Fl	Very-Quick Flashing Light
VQL	Eastman Kodak Co., Photographic Technology Library, Rochester, NY [*OCLC symbol*] (OCLC)
VQL	Variable Quantization Level [*Algorithm developed by Aydin Monitor Corp.*] [*Telecommunications*]
VQM	Detroit, MI [*Location identifier FAA*] (FAAL)
VQM	Eastman Kodak Co., Research Laboratories, Library, Rochester, NY [*OCLC symbol*] (OCLC)
VQMG	Vice-Quartermaster-General
VQN	General Railway Signal Co., Library, Rochester, NY [*OCLC symbol*] (OCLC)
VQO	Genesee Hospital, Stabins Health Science Library, Rochester, NY [*OCLC symbol*] (OCLC)
VQO	Provincetown, MA [*Location identifier FAA*] (FAAL)
VQP	Highland Hospital, Williams Health Science Library, Rochester, NY [*OCLC symbol*] (OCLC)
VQQ	Mixing Equipment Co., Library, Rochester, NY [*OCLC symbol*] (OCLC)
VQR	Virginia Quarterly Review [*A publication*] (BRI)
VQS	Isla De Vieques, PR [*Location identifier FAA*] (FAAL)
VQS	Mobil Chemical Co., Plastics Division, Research Library, Macedon, NY [*OCLC symbol*] (OCLC)
VQS	Valve Qualification Study
VQS	Vieques [*Puerto Rico*] [*Airport symbol*] (OAG)
VQS	Vieques [*Puerto Rico*] [*Seismograph station code, US Geological Survey Closed*] (SEIS)
VQT	Monroe Community College, L. V. Good Library, Rochester, NY [*OCLC symbol*] (OCLC)
VQ-T	Turks and Caicos Islands [*International civil aircraft marking*] (ODBW)
VQT	Viewers for Quality Television (EA)
VQU	Monroe Community Hospital, Medical-Nursing Library, Rochester, NY [*OCLC symbol*] (OCLC)
VQV	Monroe County Department of Health, Library, Rochester, NY [*OCLC symbol*] (OCLC)
VQV	Vacaville, CA [*Location identifier FAA*] (FAAL)
VQW	Monroe Development Center, Library, Rochester, NY [*OCLC symbol*] (OCLC)
VQX	Park Ridge Hospital, Medical Library, Rochester, NY [*OCLC symbol*] (OCLC)
VQY	Pennwalt Corp., Pharmaceutical Division, Library, Rochester, NY [*OCLC symbol*] (OCLC)
VQZ	R. T. French Co., Library, Rochester, NY [*OCLC symbol*] (OCLC)
VQZD	Vendor Quality Zero Defects
VR...............	Fleet Tactical Support [*Navy symbol*] (NVT)
VR...............	Heading to a Radial (GAVI)
VR...............	Relative Voltage
VR...............	Takeoff Rotation Velocity (GAVI)
VR...............	Transportes Aereos de Cabo Verde [*ICAO designator*] (AD)
VR...............	Transport Plane [*Multiengine*] [*Navy symbol*]
VR...............	Transport Squadron [*Navy symbol*]
VR...............	Vagabonds Removed [*Prison van nickname used during reign of VR, Victoria Regina*] [*British*] (DSUE)
VR...............	Vale of Rheidol Light Railway [*Wales*]
VR...............	Validation and Recovery
VR...............	Validation Report [*Army*]
VR...............	Valley Resources [*AMEX symbol*] (TTSB)
VR...............	Valley Resources, Inc. [*AMEX symbol*] (SPSG)
VR...............	Valtionrautatiet [*Finnish State Railways*]
VR...............	Valuation Reports, Interstate Commerce Commission [*A publication*] (DLA)
VR...............	Valve Replacement [*Cardiology*]
VR...............	Vanguardia Revolucionaria [*Revolutionary Vanguard*] [*Peru*] [*Political party*] (PPW)
VR...............	Variable Rate [*Reinforcement*] [*Medicine*] (DAVI)
VR...............	Variable Ratio [*Reinforcement*]
VR...............	Variable Reluctance
VR...............	Variable Resistance [*or Resistor*] (IAA)
VR...............	Variant Reading
VR...............	Variety Reduction (WDAA)
VR...............	Varnishing Resistant [*Ink*] (DGA)
VR...............	Vascular Resistance [*Medicine*] (MAE)
VR...............	Vehicle Recovery

VR............	Velocity, Relative (MCD)
VR............	Vendor Rating [Sales]
VR............	Venous Reflux [Medicine] (DMAA)
VR............	Venous Return [Medicine]
VR............	Ventilation Rate
VR............	Ventral Root [of a spinal nerve] [Anatomy]
VR............	Ventricular Rate [Cardiology]
VR............	Verbal Reprimand (DAVI)
VR............	Verb Reflexive
VR............	Verification Receiver
V-R............	VERLORT [Very-Long-Range Tracking] Range [NASA]
VR............	Vermont Reports [A publication] (DLA)
VR............	Vertical Redundancy [Telecommunications] (IAA)
VR............	Vertical Resistance
VR............	Vertical Retort
VR............	Vertical Rule (DGA)
VR............	Very High Speed Radial Tire [Automotive engineering]
VR............	Very Respectfully [Letter closing]
VR............	Vested Right
VR............	Veterinary and Remount Service [British military]
V-R............	Vibrational-Rotational [Chemical kinetics]
VR............	Vicar Rural
VR............	Victoria Regina [Queen Victoria]
VR............	Video Recorder (NASA)
VR............	Virginia Register of Regulations [A publication] (AAGC)
V R............	Virtual Equal Real [Computer science] (MHDI)
VR............	Virtual Equals Real [Computer science] (IAA)
VR............	Virtual Reality
VR............	Virtual-Reality Machine [Video technology] (ECON)
VR............	Virtual Route [Computer science]
VR............	Viscous Response [Medicine]
VR............	Vision, Right Eye
VR............	Visit Request (AAG)
VR............	Visor
VR............	Visual Reconnaissance
VR............	Visual Resources [A publication]
VR............	Visual Route (DA)
VR............	Vital Records [Genealogy]
VR............	Vital Records [Medical records] (DAVI)
VR............	Vocal Resonance
VR............	Vocational Rehabilitation
VR............	Vocational Rehabilitation Programs [Public human service program] (PHSD)
VR............	Voice of Reason [Later, Americans for Religious Liberty] (EA)
VR............	Voltage Reference (DEN)
VR............	Voltage Regulator
VR............	Voltage Relay
VR............	Voltage Repair
Vr............	Volume of Relaxation [Medicine] (DMAA)
VR............	Volume Reduction [Nuclear energy] (NRCH)
VR............	Voluntary Redundancy (WDAA)
VR............	Voluntary Returnees [Immigration Service]
VR............	Volunteer Regiment [British military] (DMA)
VR............	Volunteer Reserve (DJA)
VR............	Vox Reformata: Australasian Journal for Christian Scholarship [A publication] (APTA)
VR............	Voyage Repairs [Navy] (NVT)
Vr............	Vroom's Law Reports [30-85 New Jersey] [A publication] (DLA)
VR............	Vulcanized Rubber
VR............	Vulnerability Reduction [Military] (RDA)
VRA	Radford College, Radford, VA [OCLC symbol] (OCLC)
VRA	Rough-Air [or Turbulence] Speed [Aviation]
VRA	Value Received Analysis (MHDW)
VRA	Varadero [Cuba] [Airport symbol] (OAG)
VRA	Vertical Reference Attitude
VRA	Vertical Rising Aircraft
VRA	Veterans Readjustment Appointment
VRA	Veterans Readjustment Authority
VRA	[The] Victorian Railways of Australia (DCTA)
VRA	Victorian Rowing Association [Australia]
VRA	Viking RADAR Altimeter [NASA]
VRA	Vocational Rehabilitation Act [1973]
VRA	Vocational Rehabilitation Administration [Later, Social and Rehabilitation S ervice] [HEW]
VRA	Vocational Rehabilitation Association
VRA	Voltage Reference Amplifier
VRA	Voltage Regulator Alarm
VRA	Voluntary Restraint Arrangement [Import quotas]
VRA	Voluntary Restriction Agreement [Pact between the US and Japan on automotive imports]
VRA	Voting Rights Act [1965, 1970, 1975]
VRAD	Vertically Referenced Attitude Display
VRAH	Vertical Receiving Array Hydrophone
VRAM	Variable Random Access Memory [Computer science]
VRAM	Variable Rate Adaptive Multiplexing [Telecommunications] (TEL)
VRAM	Video Random Access Memory
VRAM	Virtual Random Access Memory [Computer science]
VRAMHP	Vancouver-Richmond Assoc. for Mentally Handicapped People
VR & C	Vocational Rehabilitation and Counseling Service [Veterans Administration]
VR & E	Vocational Rehabilitation and Education (MAE)
VRASS	Voice Recognition and Synthesis System [Aviation Navy]
VRB	Valve-Regulated Battery [Energy source]
VRB	Variable
VRB	Variable Reenlistment Bonus [Military] (AABC)
VRB	Vehicle Retaining Board
VRB	Vero Beach [Florida] [Airport symbol] (OAG)
VRB	Vero Beach, FL [Location identifier FAA] (FAAL)
VRB	VHF [Very-High-Frequency] Recovery Beacon [NASA] (KSC)
VRB	Violet Red Bile [Microorganism growth medium]
VRB	Visibility Reducing Particles [Environmental science] (COE)
VRB	Visual Report Builder [Computer science] (PCM)
VRB	Vocational Rehabilitation for the Blind [Public human service program] (PHSD)
VRB	Voice Rotating Beacon
VRB	Volunteer Reenlistment Bonus
VRBA	Veterans' Readjustment Benefits Act of 1966 (WYGK)
VRBA	Violet Red Bile Agar [Microorganism growth medium]
VRBC	Volume, Red Blood Cell [Hematology] (MAE)
VRBG	Viceroy's Bodyguard [British military] (DMA)
vrbl	Variable (BARN)
VRBM	Variable Range Ballistic Missile [DoD] (MCD)
VRBQ	Valuers' Registration Board of Queensland [Australia]
VRBT	Valuers' Registration Board of Tasmania [Australia]
VR-C	Cayman Islands [International civil aircraft marking] (ODBW)
VRC	Fleet Tactical Support Squadron Carrier [Navy symbol] (CINC)
VRC	Taxi Aereo de Veracruz [Mexico ICAO designator] (FAAC)
VRC	Valve Remanufacturers Council (EA)
VRC	Valve Repair Council (NTPA)
VRC	Vampire Research Center (EA)
VRC	Varco International, Inc. [NYSE symbol] (SPSG)
VRC	Varco Int'l [NYSE symbol] (TTSB)
VRC	Variable Reluctance Cartridge
VRC	Vehicle Reference Controller [Military]
VRC	Vehicle Research Corp.
VRC	Vehicle Roadside Communications
VRC	Vehicle-to-Roadside Communication [Traffic management]
VRC	Vertical Redundancy Check [Telecommunications] (BUR)
VRC	Vertical Ride Control (OA)
VRC	Vibrating Reed Capacitor
VRC	Victorian Relief Committee AT
VRC	Victoria Rifles of Canada (DMA)
VRC	Virac [Philippines] [Airport symbol] (OAG)
VRC	Virginia Commonwealth University, Richmond, VA [OCLC symbol] (OCLC)
VRC	Virtual Redundancy Check [Computer science]
VRC	Viscometer Recorder-Controller
VRC	Visible Record Computer (IAA)
VRC	Visual Record Computer
VRC	Voice Recognition Chip [Electronics] (EECA)
VRC	Voice Recognition Control (MCD)
VRC	Volunteer Rifle Corps [Military British] (ROG)
VRCA	Voice Recording Assembly [Ground Communications Facility, NASA]
VRCAMS	Vehicle-Road Compatibility Analysis and Modification System (RDA)
VRCCC	Vandenberg Range Communications Control Center [Air Force] (MCD)
VRCD	Variable-Rate Certificate of Deposit [Banking]
VRCI	Variable Resistive Components Institute (EA)
VRC-LRC	Vertical-Longitudinal Redundancy Check [Electronics] (ECII)
VRCM	Variable Relay Control Module [Cooling systems] [Automotive engineering]
VR CON	Viral Antibody, Convalescent [Immunology] (DAVI)
VRCR	Vertical Redundancy Check Register [Telecommunications] (IAA)
VRCS	Vector Reaction Control System (SSD)
VRCS	Vehicle to Roadside Communication System
VRCS	Vernier [Engine] Reaction Control System [Aerospace] (NASA)
VRCS	Veterinary and Remount Conducting Section [British military] (DMA)
VRCTR	Varactor (MSA)
VRD	Vacuum-Tube Relay Driver
VRD	Variable Ratio Divider (IAA)
VRD	Vehicle Reception Depot [British military] (DMA)
VRD	Victoria River District [Region] (EERA)
VRD	Virtual Resource Unit, Deferred
VRD	Voltage Regulating Diode
VRD	Volunteer Reserve Decoration [British]
VRDCA	Victoria River District Conservation Association (EERA)
VRDDO	Variable Retention of Diatomic Differential [Physics]
VRDO	Variable Rate Demand Obligation [Finance]
VRDS	Vacuum Residuum Desulfurization [Petroleum refining]
VRDU	Variable Range Delay Unit (PDAA)
VRDV	Vacuum Retard Delay Valve [Automotive engineering]
VRE	Vancomycin Resistant Enterococcus
VRE	Vibrating Reed Electrometer
VRE	Voltage Regulator-Exciter
VRE	Volume Review Exercise (DNAB)
VREF	Reference Velocity (GAVI)
VREF	Reference Voltage [Automotive engineering]
Vref	Reference Voltage (IDOE)
VREFI	Vanguard Real Estate Fund I [Associated Press] (SAG)
VREFII	Vanguard Real Estate Fund II [Associated Press] (SAG)
V REFL	Verb Reflexive [Grammar] (WDAA)
V/REG	Voltage Regulator [Automotive engineering]
VREL	Velocity, Relative (GFGA)
VRES	Vacuum Reservoir [Automotive engineering]
VRES	VICORP Restaurants [NASDAQ symbol] (TTSB)
VRES	VICORP Restaurants, Inc. [NASDAQ symbol] (NQ)
VREST	Vacuum Restrictor [Automotive engineering]
VR et I	Victoria Regina et Imperatrix [Victoria, Queen and Empress]
V Rev	Very Reverend
VRF	Aircraft Ferry Squadron [Navy]

VRF	Ferry Squadron [*Navy symbol*] (NVT)
VRF	Vascular Research Foundation
VRF	Versatile Repair Facility
VRF	Vertical Random Format (NITA)
VRF	Vertical Removal Fixture (NASA)
VRF	Vietnam Refugee Fund (EA)
VRF	Visual Receptive Field [*Neurobiology*]
VRF	Visual Recording Facility (MCD)
VRFI	Voice Reporting Fault Indicator
VRFWS	Vehicle Rapid-Fire Weapon System [*Army*]
VRFWSS	Vehicle Rapid-Fire Weapons System Successor (IEEE)
VRFY	Verify (MSA)
VR-G	Gibraltar [*International civil aircraft marking*] (ODBW)
V-RG	Vaccinia-Rabies Glycoprotein [*Medicine*]
VRG	Veering (WGA)
VRG	Vegetarian Resource Group (EA)
VRG	Vertical Reference Gyro (DA)
VRG	Viacao Aerea Rio-Grandense SA [*Brazil*] [*ICAO designator*] (FAAC)
VRG	Vibratory Rate Gyro (AAEL)
VRG	Visual Reference Gate [*Aviation*] (FAAC)
VRG	Vocationally Related Annual Goal
VRGC	Voucher Register and General Control [*Military*] (AABC)
VRGN	Gan [*Maldives*] [*ICAO location identifier*] (ICLI)
VRGN	Viragen, Inc. [*NASDAQ symbol*] (SAG)
VRH	Var-Hour Meter [*Electricity*]
VRH	Vertical Receiving Hydrophone
VR(HL)	Transport, Four-Engine, Landplane [*Navy symbol*]
VRHMU	Visor Rectical Helmet Mounted Unit [*Navy*] (MCD)
VR(HS)	Transport, Four-Engine, Seaplane [*Navy symbol*]
VRHU	Hanimaadhoo [*Maldives*] [*ICAO location identifier*] (ICLI)
VRI	Aerotaxi Villa Rica, SA de CV [*Mexico*] [*FAA designator*] (FAAC)
VRI	Varistor [*Telecommunications*] (TEL)
VRI	Varitech Investors Corp. [*Toronto Stock Exchange symbol*]
VRI	Vastar Resources [*NYSE symbol*] (TTSB)
VRI	Vastar Resources, Inc. [*NYSE symbol*] (SAG)
VRI	Vehicle Research Institute [*Society of Automotive Engineers*]
VRI	Verbal Response Inventory
VRI	Veterans Reopened Insurance
VRI	Victoria Regina et Imperatrix [*Victoria, Queen and Empress*]
VRI	Viral Respiratory Infection [*Medicine*]
VRI	Visual Rule Instrument Landing (AAG)
VRI	Vrincioaia [*Romania*] [*Seismograph station code, US Geological Survey*] (SEIS)
VRI	Vulcanized Rubber Installation
VRIFS	Vector Recurrent Iterated Function System [*Iterated Systems, Inc.*] [*Digital imaging*]
VRII	Virus Research Institute, Inc. [*NASDAQ symbol*] (SAG)
VRIL	Vendor Repairable Items List
VRIS	Varistor [*Electronics*]
VRIS	Vietnam Refugee and Information Services
VRISL	Vancouver Island [*NWS*] (FAAC)
VRIV	Vestibular Relay Neuron [*Neurology*]
VRK	Varkaus [*Finland*] [*Airport symbol*] (OAG)
VRK	Video Recorder Kit
VRK	Viral Respiratory Kit [*Medicine*]
VRKD	Kadhdhoo [*Maldives*] [*ICAO location identifier*] (ICLI)
VRL	Validation Reject Listing (MCD)
VRL	Vanterra Resources Ltd. [*Vancouver Stock Exchange symbol*]
VRL	Vertical Recovery Line [*NASA*] (NASA)
VRL	Vertical Reference Line [*Technical drawings*]
VRL	Veterinary Research Laboratory [*Montana State University*] [*Research center*]
VRL	Vibration Research Laboratory [*Stanford University*] (MCD)
VRL	Victorian Rugby League [*Australia*]
VRL	Vila Real [*Portugal*] [*Airport symbol*] (OAG)
VRL	Virus Reference Laboratory
VRL	Virus Reference Library (MAE)
VRL	Voar Ltd. [*Angola*] [*FAA designator*] (FAAC)
VRLK	Verilink Corp. [*NASDAQ symbol*] (SAG)
VRLN	Varlen Corp. [*NASDAQ symbol*] (NQ)
VRLRA	Victorian Rugby League Referees' Association [*Australia*]
VRLTRY	Vale of Rheidol Light Railway [*Wales*]
VRLY	Voltage Relay
VRM	Randolph-Macon College, Ashland, VA [*OCLC symbol*] (OCLC)
VRM	Van Riebeeck Medal [*British military*] (DMA)
VRM	Variable Range Marker [*RADAR technology*]
VRM	Variable-Rate Mortgage [*Real estate*]
VRM	Variable Reluctance Microphone
VRM	Vendor Receiving Memorandum [*Sales*]
VRM	Venus RADAR Mapper [*Planetary exploration*]
VRM	Vermiculite [*Technical drawings*]
VRM	Virtual Resource Manager [*Computer science*] (IAA)
VRM	Viscous Remanant Magnetization
VRM	Visible Record Machine (NITA)
VRM	Visual Response Management
VRM	Voice Recognition Module [*Computer science*]
VRM	Voltage Regulator Module
VRM	Volumetric Redox Measurement [*Analytical chemistry*]
VRMA	Vacation Rental Managers Association (NTPA)
VR(ML)	Transport, Two-Engine, Landplane [*Navy symbol*]
VRML	Virtual Reality Markup [*or Modeling*] Language [*Software program*]
VRML	Virtual Reality Modeling Language [*Computer science*]
VRMM	Male/International [*Maldives*] [*ICAO location identifier*] (ICLI)
VR(MS)	Transport, Two-Engine, Seaplane [*Navy symbol*]
VRMS	Voltage Root Mean Square

VRN	Vernier [*Engine*] (AAG)
VRN	Verona [*Italy*] [*Airport symbol*] (OAG)
VRN	Vessel Radiated Noise
VRN	Voronezhavia [*Former USSR*] [*FAA designator*] (FAAC)
VRNA	Viral Ribonucleic Acid [*Medicine*] (DMAA)
VRNF	Von Recklinghausen Neurofibromatosis [*Medicine*]
VRNR	Vernier [*Engine*] (NASA)
VRNT	Vernitron Corp. [*NASDAQ symbol*] (SAG)
VRNTP	Vernitron $1.20 Exch Pfd [*NASDAQ symbol*] (TTSB)
VRO	Aerovitro SA de CV [*Mexico ICAO designator*] (FAAC)
VRO	Roanoke College, Salem, VA [*OCLC symbol*] (OCLC)
VRO	Vanguard Real Estate Fund I [*AMEX symbol*] (SPSG)
VRO	Variable Ratio Oiling
VRO	Verified Record Output [*Computer science*]
VRO	Veterinary Research Officer [*British*]
VROC	Vertical Rate of Climb [*Aviation*]
VROM	Video ROM (NITA)
VROM	Vocabulary Read-Only Memory [*Computer science*]
VRONY	Videotron Hldgs Plc 'ADS' [*NASDAQ symbol*] (TTSB)
VRONY	Videotron Holdings PLC [*NASDAQ symbol*] (SAG)
VROOM	Vintage Racers of Old Motorcycles (EA)
Vroom	Vroom's Law Reports [*30-85 New Jersey*] [*A publication*] (DLA)
VROOMM	Virtual Real-Time Object-Oriented Memory Manager [*Computer science*]
Vroom (NJ)	Vroom's Law Reports [*30-85 New Jersey*] [*A publication*] (DLA)
VROT	Velocity, Rotation (MCD)
VROT	Victorian Rare or Threatened Plants [*State*] (EERA)
VRP	Richmond Public Library, Richmond, VA [*OCLC symbol*] (OCLC)
VRP	Vapor Reheat Process
VRP	Variable Reluctance Pickup
VRP	Vector-to-Raster Processor [*Computer graphics terminology*]
VRP	Vehicle Recycling Partnership [*Agreement involving General Motors Corp., Ford Motor Co., and Chrysler Corp.*]
VRP	Ventral Root Potential [*Neurophysiology*]
VRP	Very Reliable Product (AAMN)
VRP	Vestra Reverendissima Paternitas [*Your Very Reverend Paternity*] [*Latin*]
VRP	Virtual Rapid Prototyping (AAEL)
VRP	Visual Record Printer
VRP	Visual Reporting Point (DA)
VRP	Visual Reporting Post (MCD)
VRP	Visual Routine Processor [*Computer science*]
VR-PC	Vanguardia Revolucionaria - Proletario Comunista [*Revolutionary Vanguard - Proletarian Communist*] [*Peru*] [*Political party*] (PPW)
VRPF	Voltage-Regulated Plate Filament
VRPPS	Variable Rate Perpetual Preference Share [*Finance*]
VRPS	Vintage Radio and Phonograph Society (EA)
VRPS	Voltage-Regulated Power Supply
VRPSES	Vocational Rehabilitation Program (EDAC)
VRR	Rochester Regional Research Library Council, Rochester, NY [*OCLC symbol*] (OCLC)
VRR	Validity, Repeatability, and Reliability [*Examination*]
VRR	Valley Railroad
VRR	Ventral Root Reflex [*Medicine*] (DMAA)
VRR	Verification Readiness Review (NASA)
VRR	Veterans Reemployment Rights
VRR	Vibrating Reed Relay
VRR	Visual Radio Range
vrr	Visual Radio Range (IDOE)
VRR	Visual Rapid Reorder (MCD)
VRRC	Vehicle Radio Remote Control
VRRI	Vocational and Rehabilitation Research Institute [*University of Calgary*] [*Research center*] (RCD)
VRRTFL	Variable Reach Rough Terrain Forklift [*Military*]
VRS	Rochester 3R's Union List of Serials, Rochester, NY [*OCLC symbol*] (OCLC)
VRS	Vacuum Regulator Solenoid [*Automotive engineering*]
VRS	Vacuum Relief System [*Nuclear energy*] (NRCH)
VRS	Vehicle Registration System [*Army*]
VRS	Vehicular RADIAC [*Radioactivity Detection, Indication, and Computation*] System
VRS	Velocity Response Shape (CET)
VRS	Veterinary and Remount Service [*British military*] (DMA)
VRS	Vibration Reducing Stiffener [*Automotive engineering*]
VRS	Video Reception System
VRS	Video Relay System
VRS	Virtual Reality and Simulation
VRS	Visual Reference System
VRS	Visual Response System
VRS	Vocational Rating Scale (DHP)
VRS	Vocational Rehabilitation Services
VRS	Voice Recognition System
VRS	Voice Recording Subsystem
VRS	Voice Recording System (CIST)
VRS	Voice Recording System (NITA)
VRS	Voice Retrieval System (NITA)
VRS	Volatile Reducing Substance (OA)
VRS	Volume Reduction and Solidification [*Hazardous waste disposal*]
VRS	Volunteer Reserve Section
VRS	Vortex Rate Sensor
VRS	Voter Research & Surveys [*Commercial firm*]
VRSA	Versa Technologies [*NASDAQ symbol*] , (TTSB)
VRSA	Versa Technologies, Inc. [*NASDAQ symbol*] (NQ)
VRSA	Voice Reporting Signal Assembly
VRSI	Viral Response System (EFIS)

VRSP	Voltage Regulator Supervisory Panel (MCD)
VRSS	Voice Reporting Signal System
VRSY	Varitronic Systems, Inc. [NASDAQ symbol] (NQ)
VRT	Vacuum Rectifying Tube
VRT	Vanguard Real Estate Fd II [AMEX symbol] (TTSB)
VRT	Vanguard Real Estate Fund II [AMEX symbol] (SPSG)
VRT	Variable Reluctance Transducer
VRT	Vehicle Reaction Time
VRT	Vernon, TX [Location identifier FAA] (FAAL)
VRT	Vibration-Rotation-Tunneling [Spectroscopy]
VRT	Video Round Table [American Library Association]
VRT	Visual Reaction Time (MHDB)
VRT	Visual Recognition Threshold
VRT	Vocational Rehabilitation Therapist
VRT	Voltage Reduction Technology (PCM)
VRT	Voltage Reference Tube
VRT	Voltage Regulator Tube
VRT	Volume-Rendering Technique [Computer graphics] (BYTE)
VRT	Voluntary Reserve Training [British military] (DMA)
VRTC	Vehicle Research and Test Center [National Highway Traffic Safety Administration] (GRD)
V-RTIF	Vandenberg Real Time Interface (MCD)
VRTITC	Victorian Road Transport Industry Training Committee [Australia]
VRTL	Vertel Corp. [NASDAQ symbol]
VRT MOTN	Vertical Motion [NWS] (FAAC)
VRTS	VERITAS Software [NASDAQ symbol] (TTSB)
VRTS	Veritas Software Corp. [NASDAQ symbol] (SAG)
VRTX	Vertex Pharmaceuticals [NASDAQ symbol] (TTSB)
VRTX	Vertex Pharmaceuticals, Inc. [NASDAQ symbol] (SPSG)
VRTX	Virtual Real-Time Executive
VRTY	Variety
VRTY	Verity, Inc. [NASDAQ symbol] (SAG)
VRU	University of Richmond, Richmond, VA [OCLC symbol] (OCLC)
VRU	Vehicle Reference Unit
VRU	Velocity Reference Unit
VRU	Vertical Reference Unit (MCD)
VRU	Victorian Rugby Union [Australia]
VRU	Virtual Resource Unit (MCD)
VRU	Voice Read Out Unit [Telecommunications] (IAA)
VRU	Voice Recognition Unit
VRU	Voice Response Unit
VRU	Voltage Readout Unit
VRU	Vryburg [South Africa] [Airport symbol] (OAG)
VRV	Vacuum Regulator Valve [Automotive engineering]
VRV	Ventricular Residual Volume [Cardiology] (MAE)
VRV	Viper Retrovirus
VRV	Visual Range Visibility [Aviation] (MCD)
VRX	Vestor Exploration [Vancouver Stock Exchange symbol]
VRX	Virtual Resource Executive [Software] [NCR Corp.]
VRX-MP	VRX-Multiprocessor (NITA)
VRY	Fayetteville/Fort Bragg, NC [Location Identifier FAA] (FAAL)
VRY	Vaeroy [Norway] [Airport symbol] (OAG)
VRY	Very [Automotive advertising]
VRYG	Varying
VRZ	Aero Veracruz SA de CV [Mexico ICAO designator] (FAAO)
VRZ	Voronezh [USSR] [Airport symbol] (AD)
VS	Air Antisubmarine Squadron [Navy]
VS	Design Speed for Maximum Gust Intensity (GAVI)
VS	Search Plane [Navy symbol]
VS	Shore-Based Search Squadron [Navy symbol]
VS	Single Vibrations [Half cycles]
VS	Staging Velocity [NASA] (NASA)
VS	Vaccination Scar [Medicine]
VS	Vacuum Switch
VS	Vagal Stimulation [Medicine] (DAVI)
VS	Vaginal Stroma
VS	Valley & Siletz Railroad Co. [AAR code]
VS	Values Scale, Second Edition [Test] (TMMY)
VS	Vapor Seal [Technical drawings]
VS	Vapor Suppression [Nuclear energy] (NRCH)
VS	Variable Speed (IEEE)
VS	Variable Sweep (IEEE)
VS	Variance Score [Statistics]
VS	Vascular Strand [Botany]
VS	Vascular System (SAA)
VS	Vectoring Service
VS	Vector Scan [Digital imaging] (IAA)
VS	Vegan Society [Oxford, England] (EAIO)
VS	Vehicle Station [NASA] (KSC)
VS	Velocity Search (MCD)
VS	Velocity, Staging
vs	Velocity Staging [NASA] (NAKS)
Vs	Venae Sectio [Venesection] [Latin Medicine] (MAE)
V/S	Vendor Supplier [Sales] (MCD)
VS	Venerable Sage [Freemasonry] (ROG)
VS	Venesection [Medicine]
VS	Venstresocialisterne [Left Socialists Party] [Denmark Political party] (PPE)
VS	Ventilation System [NASA]
VS	Ventral Subiculum [Brain anatomy]
VS	Ventricular Septum [Cardiology] (DAVI)
VS	Vent Stack [Technical drawings]
VSS	Venture Capital/Special Situations [Business term]
VS	Verbal Scale
VS	Vergilian Society (EA)

VS	Vermont Statutes [A publication] (DLA)
VS	Vernacular Society (EA)
VS	Verse
VS	Versus [Against] [Latin]
vs	Versus [Against] (EBF)
VS	Vertically Selective [Cell] (DB)
VS	Vertical [Activity] Sensor [Physiology]
VS	Vertical Software [AI Software] [Computer science]
VS	Vertical Sounding [Telecommunications] (OA)
VS	Vertical Speed [Aviation]
VS	Vertical Spread (MHDB)
VS	Vertical Stereoscopic [Photograph]
VS	Vertical Stripes [Navigation markers]
VS	Vertical System [Government arrangement] (OICC)
VS	Very Small Inclusions [Diamond clarity grade]
VS	Very Soft (IAA)
VS	Very Soluble
VS	Very Special [Age of the Cognac]
VS	Very Strong [Spectral]
VS	Very Superior
VS	Very Susceptible [Plant pathology]
VS	Vesicular Sound [in auscultation of chest] [Medicine]
VS	Vesicular Stomatitis [Also, VSV] [Virus]
VS	Vestiarski Sisters (TOCD)
VS	Vestigial Sideband (NITA)
VS	Veterinary Surgeon
VS	Vibration Seconds
VS	Victorian Society (EA)
VS	Victorian Studies [A publication] (BRI)
VS	Video and Synchronization [Telecommunications] (IAA)
VS	Video Selection
VS	Vide Supra [See Above] [Latin]
vs	Vietnam, South [vm (Vietnam) used in records cataloged after January 1978] [MARC country of publication code Library of Congress] (LCCP)
VS	Vieux Style [Old Style] [French]
VS	Villas
VS	Villonodular Synovitis [Medicine] (MAE)
VS	Vinyl Sulfone [Organic chemistry]
VS	Violoncello Society (EA)
VS	Virgil Society (EA)
VS	Virgin Atlantic Airways [ICAO designator] (AD)
VS	Virtual Scheduling [Computer science] (DDC)
VS	Virtual Storage [Computer science]
VS	Virtual System
VS	Visceral Sinus
VS	Visible Supply
VS	Visual Signaling [Military]
VS	Visual Storage [Computer science]
VS	Visum Siccum [Seen in a Dried State] [Botany] (NOG)
VS	Vitae Sophistarum [of Philostratus] [Classical studies] (OCD)
VS	Vital Signs [Medicine]
VS	Vivisection
VS	Vocal Students Practice Aid Records [Record label]
VS	Vocal Synthesis
VS	Vogt-Spielmeyer [Syndrome] [Medicine] (DB)
VS	Voicespondence Club (EA)
VS	Voice Stress (LAIN)
VS	Voice Switching [Telecommunications] (IAA)
vs	Voids [Medicine] (MAE)
VS	Volatile Solids [Environmental science]
VS	Voltage Switching (IAA)
VS	Voltaire Society (EA)
VS	Volti Subito [Turn Over Quickly] [Music]
VS	Voltmeter Switch (MSA)
Vs	Volt-Seconds [Webers] (IDOE)
VS	Volumetric Solution
VS	Voluntary School (AIE)
VS	Voluntary Sterilization
VS	Voorschrift [Rule, Order] [Dutch] (ILCA)
VS	Voting Stock [Investment term] (MHDW)
VS	Votre Seigneurie [Your Lordship] [French]
VS	Vulcan Society (EA)
VS	Without Glasses [Ophthalmology] (DAVI)
VS1	Virtual Storage One [Computer science] (HGAA)
VSA	Vacuum Society of Australia
VSA	Vacuum Swing Adsorption [Chemical engineering]
VSA	Vancouver School of Art
VSA	Variable Speed Assembly [Mechanical powertrain]
VSA	Variable Stability Aircraft (NASA)
VSA	Variant-Specific Surface Antigen [Genetics, immunology]
VSA	Variation Simulation Analysis [Automotive engineering]
VSA	Vegetarian Society of Australia
VSA	Vehicle Security Association (EA)
VSA	Vehicle Service Agreement [Extended service contract]
VSA	Vehicle Service Assessment
VSA	Velocity Sensor Antenna
VSA	Verification Site Approval [NASA] (MCD)
VSA	Vermont Statutes, Annotated [A publication] (DLA)
VSA	Vernier Solo Accumulator [Aerospace] (AAG)
VSA	Vertical Sensor Assembly
VSA	Very Special Arts (EA)
VSA	Vibrating String Accelerometer
VSA	Victorian Society in America (EA)
VSA	Victualling Store Allowance [British military] (DMA)

VSA.............. Videocom Satellite Associates [Dedham, MA] [Telecommunications] (TSSD)
VSA.............. Videographic Systems of America, Inc. [Ceased operation] [Information service or system] (IID)
VSA.............. Villahermosa [Mexico] [Airport symbol] (OAG)
VSA.............. Vintage Sailplane Association (EA)
VSA.............. Violin Society of America (EA)
VSA.............. Viscoelastic Stress Analysis
VSA.............. Visitor Studies Association (NTPA)
VSA.............. Visual Skills Appraisal [Child development test]
VSA.............. Voice-Stress Analyzer (ECII)
VSA.............. Voltage-Sensitive Amplifier
Vs/A............ Volt-Seconds per Ampere [Henrys] (IDOE)
VSA/1800..... Volvo Sports America 1800 (EA)
vSAA.......... Very Severe Aplastic Anemia [Hematology]
V/SABAC...... Victoria/South Australia Border Anomalies Committee
V-SAC........ Vehicle Speed Activated Converter [Automotive engineering]
VSAD.......... Vacuum Spark Advance Disconnect [Auto air pollution control device]
V/SAF........ Vulnerability and Survivability of the Armed Forces (MCD)
VSAG.......... Viral Superantigen [Immunochemistry]
VSALS........ Vision Approach and Landing System [Aviation]
VSAM........ Variable, Spanned, and Undefined Mode (IAA)
VSAM........ Virtual Sequential Access Method
VSAM........ Virtual Storage Access Method [Computer science]
VSAM........ Virtual System Access Method
VS & A........ Veronis, Suhler & Associates, Inc. [Telecommunications service] (TSSD)
VS&PT........ Vehicle Summary and Priority Table (COE)
VSAT.......... Very Small Aperture Satellite Terminal [Telecommunications] (IGQR)
VSAT.......... Very Small Aperture Terminal [Telecommunications] (TSSD)
VSAT.......... ViaSat, Inc. [NASDAQ symbol] (SAG)
VSB.......... Scout-Bombing Plane [Navy symbol]
VSB.......... Sweet Briar College Library, Sweet Briar, VA [OCLC symbol] (OCLC)
VSB.......... Venae Sectio Brachii [Bleeding in the Arm] [Pharmacy] (ROG)
VSB.......... Vent and Supply Bay
VSB.......... Verbal Substantive (WDAA)
VSB.......... Vestigial Sideband [Radio]
VSB.......... Vickers Ltd. [British ICAO designator] (FAAC)
VSB.......... Video Source Book [A publication]
VSB.......... Visible (BARN)
VSB.......... Volunteer Services for the Blind [Later, ASB] (EA)
VSB-AM....... Vestigial Sideband - Amplitude Modulation
VSBF.......... Vestigial Sideband Filter
VSBL.......... Visible (MSA)
VSBNSW...... Veterinary Surgeons' Board of New South Wales [Australia]
VSBNT........ Veterinary Surgeons' Board of the Northern Territory [Australia]
VSBQ......... Veterinary Surgeons' Board of Queensland [Australia]
VSBS........ Very Small Business System
VSBS........ Voluntary Standards Bodies (IAA)
VSBSA........ Veterinary Surgeons' Board of South Australia
VSBY.......... Visibility (BARN)
VSBYDR...... Visibility Decreasing Rapidly [NWS] (FAAC)
VSBYIR........ Visibility Increasing Rapidly [NWS] (FAAC)
VSC.......... Aerovias Especiales de Carga Ltda. [Colombia] [ICAO designator] (FAAC)
VSC.......... Valdosta State College [Georgia]
VSC.......... Variable Speech Control [Device that permits distortion-free rapid playback of speech recorded on tape]
VSC.......... Variable Speed Chopper
VSC.......... Varnville [South Carolina] [Seismograph station code, US Geological Survey] (SEIS)
VSC.......... Vehicle Sectoring Code
VSC.......... Vehicle System Control
VSC.......... Vela Seismological Center [Alexandria, VA]
VSC.......... Vendor Shipping Configuration (AAG)
VSC.......... Ventral Spinal Cord [Anatomy]
VSC.......... Vermont State College
VSC.......... Vibration Safety Cutoff [NASA] (KSC)
VSC.......... Victorian Safety Council [Australia]
VSC.......... Vidicon Camera System (MCD)
V-S/C........ Viking Spacecraft [NASA]
VSC.......... Vincentian Sisters of Charity [Roman Catholic religious order]
VSC.......... Virginia State College [Petersburg]
VSC.......... Virginia State College, Petersburg, VA [OCLC symbol] (OCLC)
VSC.......... Virtual Subscriber Computer
VSC.......... VirusScan Configuration [Computer science]
VSC.......... Vocations for Social Change [Employment clearinghouse] [Defunct] (EA)
VSC.......... Volatile Sulfur Compound [Chemistry]
VSC.......... Voltage-Saturated Capacitor
VSC.......... Volunteer Staff Corps [British] (ROG)
VSCA.......... Vacation and Senior Citizens Association (EA)
VSCA.......... Vietnamese Senior Citizens Association (EA)
VSCAN........ Vendor Scan
VSCAN........ Visual Scan
VSCC.......... Vintage Sports Car Club [Australia]
VSCC.......... Vintage Sports Car Club [British] (DBA)
VSCC.......... Voltage-Sensitive Calcium Channel [Physiology]
VSCCA........ Vintage Sports Car Club of America (EA)
VSCCA........ Vintage Sports Car Club of Australia
VSCCSA...... Vintage Sports Car Club of South Australia
VSCDF........ Vatican's Sacred Congregation for the Doctrine of the Faith
VSCE.......... Variable Stream Control Engine [NASA] (MCD)
VSCF.......... Variable Speed Constant Frequency
VSCI.......... Vision-Sciences Inc. [NASDAQ symbol] (TTSD)

VSCNY........ Vedanta Society of the City of New York (EA)
VSCP.......... Vital Statistics Cooperative Program [Department of Health and Human Services] (GFGA)
VSCR.......... Virtual Storage Constraint Relief [IBM Corp.] (CIST)
VSCS.......... Voice Switch and Control System [FAA]
VSD.......... Valve Solenoid Driver
VSD.......... Variable Slope Delta
VSD.......... Variable Speed Drive
VSD.......... Vehicle Structures Directorate [Army and NASA joint operation] (RDA)
VSD.......... Vendor's Shipping Document
VSD.......... Ventral Septal Defect
VSD.......... Ventricular Septal Defect [Cardiology]
VSD.......... Versatile Signal Device
VSD.......... Vertical Situation Display
VSD.......... Video Subcarrier Detector
VSD.......... Village Self-Development
VSD.......... Virtually Safe Dose [Toxicology]
VSD.......... Virus Search and Destroy [Computer science]
VSD.......... Voter-Switch-Disagreement Detector (PDAA)
VSDA.......... Video Software Dealers Association (EA)
VSD/ADI...... Vertical Situation Display/Attitude Director Indicator (MCD)
VSDI.......... Voluntary Short-Term Disability Insurance
VSDM.......... Variable Scope Delta Modulation (NITA)
VSDM.......... Variable Slope Delta Modulation
VSDR.......... Vieteljahrsheft zur Statistik des Deutschen Reichs [Germany]
VSDT.......... Veterinary Surgeons' Disciplinary Tribunal [New South Wales, Australia]
VSE.......... Steam Explosion in Vessel [Nuclear energy] (NRCH)
VSE.......... Vancouver Stock Exchange [Canada]
VSE.......... Variable Stroke Engine
VSE.......... Vehicle Systems Engineer (SAA)
VSE.......... Vessel (Reactor) Steam Explosion [Nuclear energy] (IEEE)
VSE.......... Virtual Storage Extension [IBM Corp.] [Computer science]
VSE.......... VSE Corp. [Associated Press] (SAG)
VSE.......... Vuelos Asesorias y Representaciones SA de CV [Mexico ICAO designator] (FAAC)
VSE/AF...... Virtual Storage Exhibit/Advanced Function (NITA)
VSEC.......... VSE Corp. [NASDAQ symbol] (NQ)
VSEIF.......... Venture Seismic Ltd. [NASDAQ symbol] (SAG)
VSEL.......... Vertical Surface Emitting LASER
VSEL.......... Vickers Shipbuilding and Engineering Ltd. [British]
VSEN.......... Video Sentry [NASDAQ symbol] (TTSB)
VSEN.......... Video Sentry Corp. [NASDAQ symbol] (SAG)
VSEP.......... Very Superior Extra Pale [Designation on brandy labels] (WGA)
VSEPR........ Valence Shell Electron Pair Repulsion [Model for molecular structure]
VSERC........ Victorian Solar Energy Research Council [Australia]
VSES.......... Victoria State Emergency Service [Australia]
VSEW.......... Venture Seismic Ltd. [NASDAQ symbol] (SAG)
VSEWF........ Venture Seismic Ltd Wrrt [NASDAQ symbol] (TTSB)
VSF.......... Antisubmarine Fighter Squadron [Navy]
VSF.......... Springfield [Vermont] [Airport symbol] (OAG)
VSF.......... Springfield, VT [Location identifier FAA] (FAAL)
VSF.......... Vestigial Sideband Filter
VSF.......... VETRONICS [Vehicle Electronics] Simulation Facility [Army] (RDA)
VSF.......... Vitreous Silica Fabric
VSF.......... Voice Store and Forward [Voice messaging]
VSFC.......... Vince Smith Fan Club (EA)
VSFP.......... Venous Stop-Flow Pressure [Medicine]
VSFR.......... Vertical Seismic Floor Response (IEEE)
VSFR.......... Visibility Forecast (SAA)
VSFS.......... Voice Store and Forward Messaging System [Telecommunications] (IAA)
VSG.......... Variable Speed Gear (DEN)
VSG.......... Variable [or Variant] Surface Glycoprotein [Biochemistry]
VSG.......... Variant Surface Glycoprotein [Immunology]
VSG.......... Vernier Step Gauge [Aerospace]
VSG.......... Versatile Signal [or Symbol] Generator
VSG.......... Vertical Sweep Generator [Telecommunications] (OA)
VSG.......... Vibrating Structure Gyroscope
VSG.......... Video Symbology Generator
VSG.......... Viscous (USDC)
VSG.......... Viscous Semi-Geostrophic [Model] [Marine science] (OSRA)
VSG.......... Vulture Study Group [South Africa] (EAIO)
VSGN.......... Visigenic Software, Inc. [NASDAQ symbol] (SAG)
VSH.......... Village Self-Help
VSH.......... Vishay Intertechnolgy [NYSE symbol] (TTSB)
VSH.......... Vishay Intertechnology, Inc. [NYSE symbol] (SPSG)
VSH.......... Vishnu Resources [Vancouver Stock Exchange symbol]
VSHPS........ Vernier Solo Hydraulic Power System [Aerospace] (AAG)
VSI.......... College of Staten Island, St. George Campus Library, Staten Island, NY [OCLC symbol] (OCLC)
VSI.......... Stalling Speed in a Specified Flight Configuration (GAVI)
VSI.......... Valve Systems International (EFIS)
VSI.......... Variable Separation Incentive [DoD]
VSI.......... Velocity and Steering Indicator (MCD)
VSI.......... Vendor Shipping Instruction
VSI.......... Vertical Sideband [Radio frequency] [Telecommunications] (IAA)
VSI.......... Vertical Signal [or Situation] Indicator [Helicopters]
VSI.......... Vertical Speed Indicator [Aviation]
vsi.......... Vertical Speed Indicator (NAKS)
VSI.......... Very Seriously Ill [Army] (AABC)
VSI.......... Videoconferencing Systems, Inc. [Norcross, GA] [Telecommunications service] (TSSD)
VSI.......... Video Simulation Interface (NASA)

vsi	Video Simulation Interface (NAKS)
VSI	Video Sweep Integrator
VSI	Vinyl Siding Institute (EA)
VSI	Virtual Screen Interface [Computer science] (HGAA)
VSI	Virtual Socket Interface (AAEL)
VSI	Virtual Storage Interrupt (NITA)
VSI	Visual Simulator Interface (MHDI)
VSI	Visual Site Inspection (GNE)
VSI	Voluntary Separation Incentive [DoD]
VSI	Voluntary Service International [British] (EAIO)
VSI	Vuesenoria Ilustrisima [Your Illustrious Ladyship (or Lordship)] [Spanish]
VSIC	Veterinary Surgeon's Investigation Committee [New South Wales, Australia]
VSI Ent	VSI Enterprises [Associated Press] (SAG)
VSII	Very Serious III or Injured [Environmental science] (COE)
VS Ilma	Vossa Senhoria Ilustrissima [Your Illustrious Lordship] [Portuguese]
V/S IMMC	Virtual/Single Integrated Materiel Management Center [Army]
VSIN	VSI Enterprises [NASDAQ symbol] (SAG)
VSINC	Virus Subcommittee of the International Nomenclature Committee [Medicine] (DMAA)
VSIO	Visio Corp. [NASDAQ symbol] (SAG)
VSIP	Valence State Ionization Potentials [of atoms]
VSIP	Voluntary Separation Incentive Program [DoD]
VSIQ	Verbal Scale Intelligence Quotient (EDAC)
VSIS	V Channelled Substrate Inner Stripe (NITA)
VSJW	Vise Jaw [Tool] (AAG)
VSL	Special Libraries Cataloguing, Inc. [UTLAS symbol]
VSL	State Library of Victoria [State] (EERA)
VSL	Value of a Statistical Life [Mortality rating]
VSL	Valve Signal Light
VSL	Variable Safety Level
VSL	Variable Specification List
VSL	Ventilation Sampling Line (IEEE)
VSL	Vermont State Department of Libraries, Montpelier, VT [OCLC symbol] (OCLC)
VSL	Very Serious List [Hospital administration] (DAVI)
VSL	Victorian School of Languages [Australia]
VSL	Virtually Safe Level [Toxicology]
VSL	Virtual Shareware Library [Computer science] (DDC)
VSL	Viscous Shock Layer
VSL	Visual Software Library [Computer science]
VSL	Volume of the Sacred Law [Freemasonry]
VSL	VS Services Ltd. [Toronto Stock Exchange symbol]
VSLAN	Very Secure Local Area Network [Telecommunications] (CIST)
VSLE	Very Small Local Exchange [Telecommunications] (TEL)
VSLE	Voiceband Subscriber Loop Emulator [Telecom Analysis Systems, Inc.]
VSLF	Banyan Strategic Land Fd II [NASDAQ symbol] (TTSB)
VSLF	Banyan Strategic Land Fund [NASDAQ symbol] (SAG)
VSLF	Banyan Strategic Land Fund II [NASDAQ symbol] (SAG)
VSLI	Veterans Special Life Insurance [Veterans Administration]
VSLS	Very Slightly Soluble
VSM	Vascular Smooth Muscle [Anatomy]
VSM	Vehicle State Monitor
VSM	Vestigial Sideband Modulation
VSM	Vibrating Sample Magnetometer
VSM	Video Switching Matrix (KSC)
VSM	Vietnam Service Medal [Military decoration] (AFM)
VSM	Virtual Storage Manager (BUR)
VSM	Virtual Storage Memory [Computer science] (MCD)
VSM	Voice Switch Monitor (MCD)
VSM	Volcano System Monitor [Marine science] (OSRA)
VSMA	Vibrating Screen Manufacturers Association (EA)
VSMC	Vascular Smooth Muscle Cell [Cytology]
VSMF	Vendor Specification Microfilm File (DNAB)
VSMF	Visual Search Microfilm File [Trademark] [Computer science]
VSMF	Visual Search on Microfilm (NITA)
VSMOS	Verified Secondary Military Occupational Specialty
VSMOW	Vienna Standard Mean Ocean Water
VSMPC	Victorian School of Massage and Physical Culture [Australia]
VSMS	Video Switching Matrix System
VSMS	Vineland Social Maturity Scale [Psychology]
VSN	Scout-Training Plane [Navy symbol]
VSN	Video Switching Network (MCD)
VSN	Vision
VSN	Vision Airways Corp. [Canada ICAO designator] (FAAC)
VSN	Volume-Sequence-Number [Computer science]
VSN	Volume Serial Number [Computer science] (IAA)
VSNKh	Vysshego Soveta Narodnogo Khozyaystva [Supreme Council of National Economy] [Former USSR] (LAIN)
VSNL	Videsh Sanchar Nigam Ltd. [India] [Telecommunications service] (TSSD)
VSN(M)	Training Plane, 2-Engine [Navy symbol]
VSNP	Viking Society for Northern Research [British]
VSNR	Visioneer Inc. [NASDAQ symbol] (TTSB)
VSNS	Virgil C. Summer Nuclear Station (NRCH)
VSNY	Vegetarian Society of New York [Defunct] (EA)
VSO	Phuoc Long [Vietnam] [Airport symbol] (AD)
VSO	Scout Observation Plane [Navy symbol]
VSO	Stalling Speed in the Landing Configuration (GAVI)
VSO	Valdosta Southern Railroad [AAR code]
VSO	Verso (BJA)
VSO	Very Special Old
VSO	Very Stable Oscillator

VSO	Very Stable Oscillator (NAKS)
VSO	Very Superior Old [Designation on brandy labels]
VSO	Victualling Stores Officer [British military] (DMA)
VSO	Voltage-Sensitive Oscillator (IAA)
VSO	Voluntary Service Overseas [Military]
VSO	Voluntary Surgical Opinion [Health insurance] (GHCT)
VSOE	Venice Simplon Orient-Express [London-to-Venice train]
VSOIC	Very Small Outline Surface Mounted [Integrated Circuit] (AAEL)
VSOK	Vital Signs Normal [Medicine]
VSOK	Vital Signs Okay [on Physical Examination] (DAVI)
VSOM	Velocity Sensor, Oscillator, Multiplier (DNAB)
VSOP	Very Long Baseline Interferometry [Used in a space orbiting project]
VSOP	Very-Small-Outline Package (CIST)
VSOP	Very Superior Old Pale [Designation on brandy labels. Facetious French translation is "Versez sans Oublier Personne," or "Pour without Forgetting Anyone"]
VSOP	VLBI [Very Long Base-Line Interferometry] Space Observatory Program [Japan]
VSOP	VLBI [Very Long BaselineInterferometry] Space Observatory Programme
VSP	Variable Size Parameter [Thermodynamics]
VSP	Variable Soft Sphere (AAEL)
VSP	Vectored Slipstream Principle
VSP	Vehicle Scheduling Program [Computer science]
VSP	Vehicle Synthesis Program [Aerospace]
VSP	Vertical Seismic Profile [Geology]
VSP	Viacao Aerea Sao Paulo SA [Brazil] [ICAO designator] (FAAC)
VSP	Victorian Socialist Party [Australia Political party]
VSP	Video Signal Processor
VSP	Video System Processor [Telecommunications] (TSSD)
VSP	Vikki's Special People (EA)
VSP	Virtual Switching Point [Telecommunications] (TEL)
VSP	Vision Service Plan National [Defunct] (EA)
VSP	Visitor Services Project [National Park Service]
V SP	Visum Spontaneum [Seen Wild] [Botany] (ROG)
V SP	Visum Sporadicum [Seen Wild] [Botany] (ROG)
VSP	Voiture sans Permis [Car without license] [French]
VSP	Voltage-Stabilized Polyethylene (IAA)
VSPC	Virtual Storage Personal Computing [IBM Corp.] [Computer science]
VSPD	Variable Sensitivity Photodetector (AAEL)
V/SPD	Variable Speed
VSPEP	Vehicle Sizing and Performance Evaluation Program (MCD)
VSPFT	Vitalor Screening Pulmonary Function Test [Medicine] (DAVI)
VSPG	Vehicle Speed Pulse Generator [Automotive engineering]
VSPI	Visual Glide Path Indicator [Aviation] (FAAC)
VSPRITES	Virtual Sprites [Amiga computer hardware]
VSPS	Vernier Solo Power Supply [Aerospace] (AAG)
VSPX	Vehicle Scheduling Program Extended [Computer science]
VSQ	Very Special Quality
VSQC	Veterinary Specialists' Qualification Committee [Victoria, Australia]
VSQG	Very Small Quantity Generator [Environmental science]
VSR	Vacuum Short Resid [Petroleum technology]
VSR	Validation Summary Report
VSR	Vallecitos Experimental Superheat Reactor (NRCH)
VSR	Variable Length Shift Register [Computer science] (IAA)
VSR	Venous Stasis Retinopathy [Medicine] (MEDA)
VSR	Versar, Inc. [AMEX symbol] (SPSG)
VSR	Vertical Size Ratio [Ophthalmology]
VSR	Vertical Storage and Retrieval Systems
VSR	Very Short Range
vsr	Very Short Range (IDOE)
VSR	Very Short Run [Printing technology]
VSR	Very Special Reserve (ADA)
VSR	Vibration Sensitive Relay
VSR	Vietnam Supply Rate [Military] (MCD)
VSR	Vincit Sapientia Robur [Wisdom Overcomes Strength] [Motto of Johann Ernst, Duke of Saxony-Eisenach (1566-1638)] [Latin]
VSR	Visual Security Range (NATG)
VSR	Voltage-Sensing Relay
VSRADS	Very-Short-Range Air Defense Weapon System (MCD)
VSRADWS	Very-Short-Range Air Defense Weapon System (NATG)
VSRBM	Very-Short-Range Ballistic Missile
VSRC	Vehicle Safety Recall Campaign
VSRGSR	Very-Short-Range Ground Surveillance RADAR (MCD)
vsrs	Voussoirs (VRA)
VSS	Vampire Studies Society [Defunct] (EA)
VSS	Vapor Saver System [Automobile]
VSS	Vapor Suppression System [Nuclear energy] (IAA)
VSS	Variable Slit Set
VSS	Variable Soft Sphere (AAEL)
VSS	Variable SONAR System
VSS	Variable Stability System [Aviation]
VSS	Vascular Surgical Society [British]
VSS	Vassouras [Brazil] [Geomagnetic observatory code]
VSS	Vector Scoring System [Navy] (MCD)
VSS	Vehicle Speed Sensor [Automotive engineering]
VSS	Vehicle Stability System [Truck engineering]
VSS	Vehicle Surveillance System
VSS	Vehicle System Simulator
VSS	Velocity Sensor System
VSS	Vented Suppressive Shielding
VSS	Versions (ROG)
VSS	Vertical Sounding System
VSS	Vertical Spike Soderberg [Pot] [Aluminum processing]
VSS	Vertical Support Structure

VSS............	Vessel Support System (MCD)
VSS............	Victim Support Scheme [British] (DI)
VSS............	Victor Scoring System
VSS............	Video Satellite Systems Inc. (NITA)
VSS............	Video Select Switch (MCD)
VSS............	Video Signal Simulator (NATG)
VSS............	Video Storage System [or Subsystem]
VSS............	Video Supervisory Signal
VSS............	Viet Cong Security Service (VNW)
VSS............	Virgin Islands Seaplane Shuttle, Inc. [ICAO designator] (FAAC)
VSS............	Virtual Storage System [SEMIS]
VSS............	Visual Sensor Set
VSS............	Visual Systems Simulator [FAA]
VSS............	Vital Safety System [Environmental science] (COE)
VSS............	Vital Signs Stable [Medicine]
VSS............	Vocabulary Switching System [Computer science]
VSS............	Voice Signaling System
VSS............	VoiceStation System [Sydis, Inc.] [San Jose, CA] (TSSD)
VSS............	Voice Storage System [AT & T]
VSS............	Volatile Suspended Solids [Environmental science]
VSS............	Voltage-Sensing Switch
VSS............	Voltage to Substrate and Sources [Microelectronics]
VSS............	Voyager Spacecraft Subsystem [NASA]
VSS............	V/STOL Support Ship
VSSC...........	Vedanta Society of Southern California (EA)
VS-SC.........	Vestigial Sideband Suppressed Carrier (NITA)
VSSM..........	Video Scanner Switch Matrix
VSSP..........	Vendor Standard Settlement Program (AAG)
VSSSN........	Verification Status Social Security Number (AABC)
VST............	Banyan Short Term Income Trust [Formerly, VMS Short Term Income Trust] [AMEX symbol] (SPSG)
VST............	St. Thomas [Virgin Islands] [Seismograph station code, US Geological Survey] (SEIS)
VST............	Valve Seat (MSA)
VST............	Valve Setpoint Tolerance [Nuclear energy] (NRCH)
VST............	Vancouver School of Theology [University of British Columbia]
VST............	Vanstar Corp. [NYSE symbol] (TTSB)
VST............	Vanstates Resources Ltd. [Vancouver Stock Exchange symbol]
VST............	Variable Stability Trainer [Aviation]
VST............	Variable Surface Tracking
VST............	Vasteras [Sweden] [Airport symbol] (OAG)
VST............	Venom Skin Test [Immunology]
VST............	Very Small Truck (DICI)
VST............	Video Scroller Terminal [Computer science]
VST............	Video System Test
VST............	Visible Speech Translator (IAA)
VST............	Visit (NVT)
VST............	Vista [Commonly used] (OPSA)
VST............	Vocational Skills Training [Funds] [Job Corps]
VST............	Volume Sensitive Tariff [Telecommunications] (TEL)
VSTA..........	Virus-Serum-Toxin Act
VSTA..........	Vista [Commonly used] (OPSA)
VSTAG........	Vandenberg Shuttle Turnaround Analysis Group [NASA] (NASA)
VSTAR........	Variable Search and Track Air Defense RADAR
VSTBU........	Victorian State Building Trades Union [Australia]
VSTC..........	Vermont State Teachers College
VSTC..........	Very Short Time Constant (MCD)
VSTF..........	Very Short-Term Financing (MHDB)
vstib...........	Vestibule (VRA)
VSTM..........	Valve Stem (MSA)
vstmt	Vestment (VRA)
VSTNG........	Visiting
VSTO..........	Vertical/Short Takeoff [and Landing] (MCD)
V/STOL	Vertical/Short Takeoff and Landing [Aircraft]
VSTP..........	Visual Satellite Tracking Program
VSTPT........	Vulcan-Stinger Troop Proficiency Trainer [Army]
VSTR	Ventral Striatum [Neurology]
VSTR	Visitor
VSTR	Volt Second Transfer Ratio
VSTSP........	Visit Ship in Port [Navy] (NVT)
VSTT..........	Variable Speed Tactical Trainer [Air Force] (MCD)
VSTT..........	Variable Speed Training Target
VSUH..........	Virginia State University Herbarium
VSUK..........	Vegetarian Society of the United Kingdom (DBA)
VSULA........	Vaccination Scar Upper Left Arm [Medicine] (MAE)
v-supt	Vice-Superintendent (DD)
VSV............	Vacuum Switching Valve [Automotive engineering]
VSV............	Vesicular Stomatitis Virus [Also, VS]
VSVG	Vesicular Stomatitis Virus Glycoprotein [Biochemistry]
VSVR	VideoServer, Inc. [NASDAQ symbol] (SAG)
VSW............	Variable Sweep Wing
VSW............	Ventricular Stroke Work [Cardiology] (MAE)
VSW............	Vertrau Schau Wem [Trust, but Be Careful Whom] [Motto of Johann Georg, Duke of Wohlau (1552-92)] [German]
VSW............	Very Shallow Water (DOMA)
VSW............	Very Short Wave
VSW............	Visual Studies Workshop (EA)
VSW............	Vitrified Stoneware
VSW............	Voltage Standing Wave
VSWF	Voltage Standing-Wave Frequency (DNAB)
VSWR	Variable Standing Wave Ratio (MCD)
VSWR	Visual Standing Wave Ratio (NASA)
VSWR	Voltage Standing-Wave Ratio
VSX............	Navy Submarine Attack Airplane - Experimental (MCD)
VSYNC........	Vertical Synchronous [Computer science]

VSYNCH.......	Vertical Synchronization [Computer science] (IAA)
VT...............	Air-Cushion Vehicle built by Vosper Thorneycroft [England] [Usually used in combination with numerals]
VT...............	Air Polynesie [ICAO designator] (AD)
Vt...............	State of Vermont, Department of Libraries, Montpelier, VT [Library symbol Library of Congress] (LCLS)
VT...............	Target-on-Threshold Speed [Aviation]
Vt...............	Tidal Volume [Medicine] (DAVI)
V$_T$............	Tissue Volume [Laboratory science] (DAVI)
VT...............	Torpedo Plane [Navy symbol]
VT...............	Training Squadron [Navy symbol] (NVT)
VT...............	Vacuum Telegraphy [Telecommunications] (IAA)
VT...............	Vacuum Tube [Electronics]
vt...............	Vacuum Tube (IDOE)
VT...............	Vacuum Tuberculin [Medicine] (MAE)
VT...............	Validation Testing (MCD)
VT...............	Valitocin [Endocrinology]
VT...............	Vaportight (MSA)
VT...............	Variable Threshold (IAA)
VT...............	Variable Thrust
VT...............	Variable Time [Fuse] [Also known as a "proximity fuse"]
vt...............	Variable Time (IDOE)
VT...............	Variable Transformer
VT...............	Variable Transmission (ADA)
VT...............	Vascular Time
VT...............	Vasotocin
VT...............	Vat Petroleum [Vancouver Stock Exchange symbol]
VT...............	Vee-Twin [Automotive engineering]
VT...............	Vehicle Theft
VT...............	Vehicular Technology (MCD)
VT...............	Velocity, Target
V-T.............	Velocity Time (MUGU)
VT...............	Venous Thrombosis [Cardiology] (DAVI)
VT...............	Vent (NASA)
VT...............	Ventricular Tachycardia [Cardiology]
VT...............	Verb Transitive
VT...............	Verfuegungstruppen (BJA)
VT...............	Vermont [Postal code]
VT...............	Vermont Reports [A publication] (DLA)
Vt...............	Vermont Reports [A publication] (AAGC)
VT...............	Verotoxin [Biochemistry]
VT...............	Vertical Tab [Computer science] (DOM)
VT...............	Vertical Tabulate (NITA)
VT...............	Vertical Tabulation [or Tabulator] [Computer science]
VT...............	Vertical Tabulator (ECII)
VT...............	Vertical Tail
VT...............	Vesalius Trust (EA)
VT...............	Vetus Testamentum [Old Testament] [of the Bible] [Latin]
V-T.............	Vibrational-to-Translational [Energy transfer]
VT...............	Vibration Testing
VT...............	Victa Ltd. [Aviation Division] [Australia ICAO aircraft manufacturer identifier] (ICAO)
VT...............	Videotape
VT...............	Video Telemetry (CPH)
VT...............	Video Terminal
VT...............	Vinyl Tile [Technical drawings]
VT...............	Violet Tetrazolium (MAE)
VT...............	Virtual Terminal (BYTE)
VT...............	Viscous Traction [Automotive engineering] (PS)
VT...............	Viscous Transmission [Automotive engineering]
VT...............	Vision Test [Ophthalmology]
VT...............	Visual Telegraphy
VT...............	Visual Toss
VT...............	Vocational-Technical
VT...............	Voice Tube [Technical drawings]
VT...............	Volcano-Tectonic [Earthquake]
VT...............	Voltage Transformer (EECA)
VT...............	Voting Trust [Investment term]
VT2.............	Virtual Tourist 2
VTA............	Air Tahiti [France ICAO designator] (FAAC)
V$_T$A..........	Alveolar Tidal Volume [Medicine] (DAVI)
VTA............	Transport Aviation [Soviet-Russian] (DOMA)
VTA............	Vacuum-Tube Amplifier
VTA............	Variable Transfer Address
VTA............	Varnished Tube Association
VTA............	Vascular Targeting Agent [Medicine]
VTA............	Ventral Tegmental Area [Anatomy]
VTA............	Vertex Time of Arrival [FAA] (TAG)
VTA............	Vertical Tracking Angle [of a phonograph cartridge]
VTA............	Vesta Insurance Group [NYSE symbol] (SPSG)
VTA............	Victorian Temperance Alliance [Australia]
VTA............	Video Trade Association [British] (DBA)
VTA............	Virtual Terminal Agent [Computer science] (CIST)
VTA............	Vision Test Apparatus [Ophthalmology]
VTA............	Vocational Training Authority [Australian Capital Territory]
VTA............	Vodka Trade Association [British] (DBA)
VTAADS.......	Vertical the Army Authorization Document System
VTAB..........	Vertical Tabulation Character [Computer science]
VTAC..........	Victorian Transport Accident Commission [Australia]
VTAC..........	Video Timing and Control
V-TACH.......	Ventricular Tachycardia [Cardiology]
VT Admin Comp...	Vermont Administrative Procedure Compilation [A publication] (DLA)
VTAJX.........	Navy Trainer Advanced Jet - Experimental (MCD)
VTAM..........	Varian Telecommunication Access Method (IAA)

VTAM............	Virtual Telecommunications [or Teleprocessing] Access Method [IBM Corp.] [Computer science]
VTAM............	Virtual Terminal Access Method
VTAM............	VORTEX [Varian Omnitask Real-Time Executive] Telecommunications Access Method
VTAME..........	Virtual Telecommunications Access Method Entry
VTANG........	Vermont Air National Guard (MUSM)
V-TAS	Vericom Test Application System [Vericom Ltd.] [Software package] (NCC)
VTAS............	Visual Target Acquisition System [Navy]
VtB...............	Fletcher Free Library, Burlington, VT [Library symbol Library of Congress] (LCLS)
VTB...............	Torpedo-Bombing Plane [Navy symbol]
VTB...............	Vacuum Tower Bottoms [Petroleum chemistry]
VTB...............	Velocity Test Barrel
VtB...............	Verfahrenstechnische Berichte [Process Technology Reports] [A publication]
VtB...............	Verkehrswasserbaubibliothek [Bundesanstalt fuer Wasserbau] [Database]
VTB...............	Video Terminal Board [Computer science] (MHDB)
VTB...............	Vinyl T-Butylstyrene [Organic chemistry]
VTB...............	Visual Table Builder [Computer science] (PCM)
VTB...............	Vlaamsche Toeristenbond
VTB...............	Voltage Time to Breakdown (DEN)
VTB...............	Volunteer Talent Bank [American Association of Retired Persons]
VTBA............	Bangkok [Thailand] [ICAO location identifier] (ICLI)
VT BA	Vermont Bar Association Reports [A publication] (DLA)
VTBB............	Bangkok [Thailand] [ICAO location identifier] (ICLI)
VtBC.............	Champlain College, Burlington, VT [Library symbol Library of Congress] (LCLS)
VTBC............	Chanthaburi [Thailand] [ICAO location identifier] (ICLI)
VTBD............	Bangkok/International [Thailand] [ICAO location identifier] (ICLI)
VTBE............	Saraburi [Thailand] [ICAO location identifier] (ICLI)
VtBef............	Rockingham Free Public Library, Bellows Falls, VT [Library symbol Library of Congress] (LCLS)
VtBenn.........	Bennington Free Library, Bennington, VT [Library symbol Library of Congress] (LCLS)
VtBennC.......	Bennington College, Bennington, VT [Library symbol Library of Congress] (LCLS)
VtBennM......	Bennington Museum, Inc., Bennington, VT [Library symbol Library of Congress] (LCLS)
VtBennP.......	Putnam Memorial Hospital, Medical Library, Bennington, VT [Library symbol Library of Congress] (LCLS)
VTBF............	Chachoengsao/Phanom Sarakhan [Thailand] [ICAO location identifier] (ICLI)
VtBFB...........	Grand Lodge of Vermont, F & AM Library, Burlington, VT [Library symbol Library of Congress] (LCLS)
VTBG ....:..	Kanchanaburi [Thailand] [ICAO location identifier] (ICLI)
VTBH	Lop Buri/Sa Pran Nak [Thailand] [ICAO location identifier] (ICLI)
VTBI	Prachin Buri [Thailand] [ICAO location identifier] (ICLI)
VTBJ............	Phetchaburi/Tha Yang [Thailand] [ICAO location identifier] (ICLI)
VTBK............	Nakhon Pathom/Kamphaeng Saen [Thailand] [ICAO location identifier] (ICLI)
VTBL............	Lop Buri [Thailand] [ICAO location identifier] (ICLI)
VTBM............	Phetchaburi/Maruk [Thailand] [ICAO location identifier] (ICLI)
VTBN	Prachuap Khiri Khan/Pran Buri [Thailand] [ICAO location identifier] (ICLI)
VTBP............	Prachuap Khiri Khan [Thailand] [ICAO location identifier] (ICLI)
VTBR	Ratchaburi [Thailand] [ICAO location identifier] (ICLI)
VtBran	Brandon Free Public Library, Brandon, VT [Library symbol Library of Congress] (LCLS)
VTBR Case...	Victorian Taxation Board of Review Case [Australia A publication]
VtBrt	Brooks Memorial Library, Brattleboro, VT [Library symbol Library of Congress] (LCLS)
VtBrtS	School for International Training, Brattleboro, VT [Library symbol Library of Congress] (LCLS)
VTBS............	Chon Buri/Sattahip [Thailand] [ICAO location identifier] (ICLI)
VTBT............	Chon Buri/Bang Phra [Thailand] [ICAO location identifier] (ICLI)
VtBT.............	Trinity College, Burlington, VT [Library symbol Library of Congress] (LCLS)
VTBU............	Rayong/Utapao [Thailand] [ICAO location identifier] (ICLI)
VTBW...........	Prachin Buri/Watthana Nakhon [Thailand] [ICAO location identifier] (ICLI)
VTC.............	Vacuum Thermal Chamber (IAA)
VTC.............	Vandenberg Test Center [Air Force]
VTC.............	Variable Timing Control [Intake subsystem] [Automotive engineering]
VTC.............	Variable Trimmer Capacitor
VTC.............	Vehicular Traffic Control
VTC.............	Veractor Tuned Microwave Cavity
VTC.............	Vertical Trash Compactor (DWSG)
VTC.............	Viable Titanium Composite
VTC.............	Victorian Technology Centre [Australia]
VTC.............	Video Tape Center [Commercial firm British]
VTC.............	Video Teleconferencing
VTC.............	Vidicon Television Camera
VTC.............	Virtual Terminal Control [Computer science] (MHDB)
VTC.............	Viscosity Temperature Coefficient (IAA)
VTC.............	Visibility Transport Commission (COE)
VTC.............	Vitronics Corp. [AMEX symbol] (SPSG)
VTC.............	Vocational Training Course (WDAA)
VTC.............	Volunteer Training Corps [An organization for home defense] [World War I] [British]
VTC.............	Volvo Truck Corp.
VTC.............	Voting Trust Certificate [or Company] [Investment term]
VTC.............	Voting Trust Certificates (EBF)

VTCA............	Chiang Rai/Chiang Khong [Thailand] [ICAO location identifier] (ICLI)
VTCA............	Vernon's Texas Codes, Annotated [A publication] (DLA)
VTCA............	Vintage Thunderbird Club of America [Later, VTCI] (EA)
VtCasT.........	Castleton State College, Castleton, VT [Library symbol Library of Congress] (LCLS)
VTCB............	Chiang Rai/Ban Chiang Kham [Thailand] [ICAO location identifier] (ICLI)
VTCC............	Chiang Mai [Thailand] [ICAO location identifier] (ICLI)
VTCC............	Variable Temperature Compensation Capacitor
VTCC............	Video Terminal Cluster Controller [Computer science] (CIST)
VTCCHE	Tidewater Consortium, Librarians' Networking Committee [Library network]
VTCD............	Nan/Chiang Klang [Thailand] [ICAO location identifier] (ICLI)
VTCE............	Nan/Ban Pua [Thailand] [ICAO location identifier] (ICLI)
VTCE............	Vehicle Team Combat Exercise [Army] (INF)
VTCF............	Uttaradit (West) [Thailand] [ICAO location identifier] (ICLI)
VTCFITB.......	Victorian Textile, Clothing and Footwear Industry Training Board [Australia]
VTCH............	Mae Hong Son [Thailand] [ICAO location identifier] (ICLI)
VTCH............	Vitech America, Inc. [NASDAQ symbol] (SAG)
VTCI.............	Mae Hong Son/Pai [Thailand] [ICAO location identifier] (ICLI)
VTCI.............	Vintage Thunderbird Club International (EA)
VTCK............	Mae Hong Son/Khun Yuam [Thailand] [ICAO location identifier] (ICLI)
VTCL............	Lampang [Thailand] [ICAO location identifier] (ICLI)
VTCN............	Nan [Thailand] [ICAO location identifier] (ICLI)
VTCP............	Phrae [Thailand] [ICAO location identifier] (ICLI)
VTCR............	Chiang Rai [Thailand] [ICAO location identifier] (ICLI)
VTCS............	Mae Hong Son/Mae Sariang [Thailand] [ICAO location identifier] (ICLI)
VTCS............	Variable Thermal Control Surface
VTCS............	Vega Target Control System [Computer flight control of test vehicles]
VTCS............	Vehicular Traffic Control System (IEEE)
VTCS............	Video Telemetering Camera Systems (AAG)
VTCS............	Vinyltrichlorosilane (DB)
VTCT............	Vocational Training Charitable Trust [British]
VTD.............	Aircraft (Training) [Navy symbol]
VTD.............	Vacuum-Tube Detector (IAA)
VTD.............	Variable Time Delay
VTD.............	Variable Torque Distribution [Automotive engineering]
VTD.............	Vertical Tape Display (IAA)
VTD.............	Vision Testing Device [Ophthalmology]
VTDC............	Vacuum Tube Development Committee [Columbia University] (MCD)
VTDI............	Variable Threshold Digital Input
VTE.............	Variable Thrust Engine
VTE.............	Venous Thromboembolism [Medicine] (DAVI)
VTE.............	Vertical Tube Effects [Desalination]
VTE.............	Vertical Tube Evaporation [Desalination]
VTE.............	Vibration Test Equipment
VTE.............	Vicarious Trial and Error [Psychology]
VTE.............	Vientiane [Laos] [Airport symbol] (OAG)
VTE.............	Viscous Transonic Equation
VTE.............	Visual Task Evaluation [or Evaluator] (MHDI)
VTEC............	Verotoxin-Producing Escherichia Coli
VTEC-E........	Variable Valve-Timing and Lift Electronic Control System - Economy [Automotive technology]
V-TECS	Vocational Technical Education Consortium of States (OICC)
VTEK............	Vodavi Technology [NASDAQ symbol] (SAG)
VTEL............	Vtel Corp. [NASDAQ symbol] (SAG)
VTERL..........	Veterinary Toxicology and Entomology Research Laboratory [Department of Agriculture] [College Station, TX] (GRD)
VTERM.........	Variable Temperature Electrical Resistivity Measurement [Physics]
VTES............	Variable Thrust Engine System
VTES............	Vinyltriethoxysilane [Organic chemistry]
Vtesse	Viscomtesse [Vicountess] [French] (BARN)
V-test..........	Voluter Test [Radiology] (DAVI)
VTEX............	Vertex Communications Corp. [Kilgore, TX] [NASDAQ symbol] (NQ)
VTEX............	Vertex Communic'ns [NASDAQ symbol] (TTSB)
VTF.............	Vacuum Test Furnace
VTF.............	Van Kam Am Cap InvGr FL Mun [NYSE symbol] (TTSB)
VTF.............	Van Kampen Merritt Investment Grade Florida Municipal [NYSE symbol] (SPSG)
VTF.............	Variable Time, Fragmentation [Military] (CAAL)
VTF.............	Venezuelan Trust Fund [Inter-American Development Bank]
VTF.............	Vertical Test Facility [NASA]
VTF.............	Vertical Test Fixture
VTF.............	Vertical Test Flight (MCD)
VTF.............	Vertical Tracking Force [of a phonograph cartridge]
VTF.............	Videotex Terminal Facility (NITA)
VTF.............	Voltage Transfer Function
VTFE............	Vertical Tube Foam Evaporation [Chemical engineering]
VtFin............	Vermont Financial Services Corp. [Associated Press] (SAG)
VTFS............	Visual Technology Flight Simulator (MCD)
VTFT............	Value Task Force Team
VTG.............	Vantage [Washington] [Seismograph station code, US Geological Survey] (SEIS)
VTG.............	Vision Technology Group [Computer science]
VTG.............	Vitellogenin [Biochemistry]
VTG.............	Volume Thoracic Gas [Medicine]
VTG.............	Voting [Business term]
Vtg.............	Voting (EBF)
VThB............	Vocabulaire de Theologie Biblique [A publication] (BJA)
VtHi.............	Vermont Historical Society, Montpelier, VT [Library symbol Library of Congress] (LCLS)

VTI.............. Statens Vag- och Trafikinstitut [*Swedish Road and Traffic Research Institute*] [*Linkoping*] [*Information service or system*] (IID)
VTI.............. Valparaiso Technical Institute [*Indiana*]
VTI.............. Vermont Telecommunications, Inc. [*Winooski, VT*] [*Telecommunications*] (TSSD)
VTI.............. Vertical Technology Insertion [*Business term Army*] (RDA)
VTI.............. Video Terminal Interface
VTI.............. Vinton, IA [*Location identifier FAA*] (FAAL)
VTI.............. VLSI Technology Inc. (NITA)
VTI.............. Volume Thickness Index
VTI.............. Voluntary Termination Incentive [*Business term*]
VTIP............ Visual Target Identification Point (AFM)
VTIS............ Vessel Traffic Information System [*Boating*]
VTJ............. Johnson State College, Johnson, VT [*OCLC symbol*] (OCLC)
VTJ............. Van Kam Am Cap InvGr NJ Mun [*NYSE symbol*] (TTSB)
VTJ............. Van Kampen Merritt Investment Grade New Jersey Municipal [*NYSE symbol*] (SPSG)
VtJoT.......... Johnson State College, Johnson, VT [*Library symbol Library of Congress*] (LCLS)
VTK............ Vertical Track Distance (GAVI)
VTK............ Virally-Encoded Thymidine Kinase [*Medicine*]
VTL............ Vacuum-Tube Launcher
VTL............ Variable Threshold Logic
VTL............ Vertical Turret Lathe
VTL............ Video Tape Lecture
VTL............ Virtual Tape Library
VTL............ Vittel [*France*] [*Airport symbol*] (AD)
Vt Law....... Vermont Law School (GAGS)
VTLC.......... Virtual Terminal Line Controller [*Computer science*] (MHDB)
VTLK.......... Vitalink Pharmacy [*NASDAQ symbol*] (TTSB)
VTLK.......... Vitalink Pharmacy Services [*NASDAQ symbol*] (SAG)
VTLMB....... Victorian Tobacco Leaf Marketing Board [*Australia*]
Vt-LR......... Vermont Legislative Council, Montpelier, VT [*Library symbol Library of Congress*] (LCLS)
VTLS.......... Virginia Technical Library System [*Virginia Polytechnic Institute and State University Center for Library Automation*] [*Information service or system*]
VtLyL......... Lyndon State College, Lyndonville, VT [*Library symbol Library of Congress*] (LCLS)
VTM........... Vacuum-Tube Module
VTM........... Vehicles to the Mile [*Military*]
VTM........... Vehicle Test Meter [*TACOM*] [*Army*] (RDA)
VTM........... Verification Test Matrix
VTM........... Verification Traceability Matrix
VTM........... Versatile Tracking Mount (MCD)
VTM........... Vibration Test Module (MCD)
VTM........... Virtual Trade Mission
VTM........... Vocal Tract Model (MHDI)
VTM........... Voltage Tunable Magnetron
vtm............. Voltage-Tuned Magnetron (IDOE)
VTM........... Volume Tidal Mechanical (MAE)
VtMan........ Mark Skinner Public Library, Manchester, VT [*Library symbol Library of Congress*] (LCLS)
VtMarC ..... Marlboro College, Marlboro, VT [*Library symbol Library of Congress*] (LCLS)
VTMC........ Viable Titanium Matrix Composite
VtMiM....... Middlebury College, Middlebury, VT [*Library symbol Library of Congress*] (LCLS)
VtMiS........ Sheldon Art Museum, Middlebury, VT [*Library symbol Library of Congress*] (LCLS)
VTMO........ Voltage Tunable Microwave Oscillator
VtMor........ Morristown Centennial Library, Morrisville, VT [*Library symbol Library of Congress*] (LCLS)
VTMoV...... Velvet Tobacco Mottle Virus
VtMS......... Office of the Secretary of State, State Papers Division, Montpelier, VT [*Library symbol Library of Congress*] (LCLS)
VTMS......... Vehicle Thermal Management System
VTMS......... Vessel Traffic Management System (DS)
VTMS......... Vinyltrimethysilane [*Organic chemistry*]
VtMS-Ar..... Office of the Secretary of State, Vermont State Archives, Montpelier, VT [*Library symbol Library of Congress*] (LCLS)
VtN........... Brown Public Library, Northfield, VT [*Library symbol Library of Congress*] (LCLS)
VT(N)........ Night Torpedo Bomber Squadron [*Navy symbol*]
VTN........... Valentine, NE [*Location identifier FAA*] (FAAL)
VTN........... Van Kam Am Cap InvGr NY Mum [*NYSE symbol*] (TTSB)
VTN........... Van Kampen Merritt Investment Grade New York Municipal [*NYSE symbol*] (SPSG)
VTN........... Ventral Tegmental Nuclei [*Neuroanatomy*]
VTN........... Verification Test Network [*NASA*] (MCD)
VTN........... Video Tape Network [*Defunct*] (EA)
VTN........... Vitran Corp., Inc. [*Toronto Stock Exchange symbol*]
VTNA......... VTAM Telecommunications Network Architecture
VTNAF....... Vitran Corp. [*NASDAQ symbol*] (TTSB)
VTNAF....... Vitran Corp., Inc. [*NASDAQ symbol*] (SAG)
VTNF......... Variable Time Non-Fragmenting [*Military*] (CAAL)
Vtnm......... Vietnam (VRA)
VtNN.......... Norwich University, Northfield, VT [*Library symbol Library of Congress*] (LCLS)
VTNS......... Voltage Tunable Noise Source
VTO........... Vacuum-Tube Oscillator (IAA)
VTO........... Vertical Takeoff
VTO........... Viable Terrestrial Organism
VTO........... Visual Training Officer [*Navy*]
VTO........... Vitro, Sociedad Anonima ADS [*NYSE symbol*] (SPSG)

VTO........... Vocational Training Officer [*Navy*]
VTO........... Voltage Tunable Oscillator
VTOC......... Volume Table of Contents [*Computer science*]
VTOF......... Voltage-to-Frequency (IAA)
VTOGW..... Vertical Takeoff Gross Weight
VTOHL...... Vertical Takeoff and Horizontal Landing
VTOL........ Vertical Takeoff and Landing [*Also, VERTOL*] [*Acronym used for a type of aircraft*]
VTOVL....... Vertical Takeoff Vertical Landing
VTP........... Valid Target Presentation [*Military*] (CAAL)
VTP........... Value Truck Package
VTP........... Vandenberg Test Program [*Air Force*]
VTP........... Van Kam Am Cap InvGr PA Mun [*NYSE symbol*] (TTSB)
VTP........... Van Kampen Merritt Investment Grade Pennsylvania Municipal [*NYSE symbol*] (SPSG)
VTP........... Vehicle Test Plan [*NASA*] (NASA)
VTP........... Vendor Test Procedure
VTP........... Verification Test Plan [*or Program*] (NASA)
VTP........... Vertical Thermal Processor (AAEL)
vtp............ Videotape (VRA)
VTP........... VIEWDATA Terminal Program
VTP........... Virtual Terminal Protocol
VTP........... Visual Transmitter Power
VTP........... Voluntary Termination of Pregnancy [*Medicine*]
VTPA......... Vertical Turbine Pump Association [*Defunct*]
VTPA......... (Vinylthiazolidinylidene)phenylamine [*Organic chemistry*]
VTPH......... Prachuap Khiri Khan/Hua Hin [*Thailand*] [*ICAO location identifier*] (ICLI)
VTPI......... Nakhon Sawan/Takhli [*Thailand*] [*ICAO location identifier*] (ICLI)
VtPifi......... Free Library, Pittsfield, VT [*Library symbol Library of Congress*] (LCLS)
VTPL........ Pretchabun/Lom Sak [*Thailand*] [*ICAO location identifier*] (ICLI)
VtPlaG....... Goddard College, Plainfield, VT [*Library symbol Library of Congress*] (LCLS)
VTPM........ Tak/Mae Sot [*Thailand*] [*ICAO location identifier*] (ICLI)
VTPN........ Nakhon Sawan [*Thailand*] [*ICAO location identifier*] (ICLI)
VtPom........ Abbott Memorial Library, Pomfret, VT [*Library symbol Library of Congress*] (LCLS)
VtPouG ..... Green Mountain College, Poultney, VT [*Library symbol Library of Congress*] (LCLS)
VTPP......... Phitsanulok [*Thailand*] [*ICAO location identifier*] (ICLI)
Vt-PR......... Vermont Public Records Library, Montpelier, VT [*Library symbol Library of Congress*] (LCLS)
VTPR......... Vertical Temperature Profile [*or Profiling*] Radiometer
VTPS......... Phitsanulok/Sarit Sena [*Thailand*] [*ICAO location identifier*] (ICLI)
VTPS......... Vibration Test Plotting System
VTPT......... Tak [*Thailand*] [*ICAO location identifier*] (ICLI)
VTPU......... Uttaradit [*Thailand*] [*ICAO location identifier*] (ICLI)
VtPuW....... Windham College, Putney, VT [*Library symbol Library of Congress*] (LCLS)
VTPY......... Tak/Sam Ngao [*Thailand*] [*ICAO location identifier*] (ICLI)
VTR........... Air Ostravia Ltd. [*Czechoslovakia*] [*FAA designator*] (FAAC)
VTR........... McGrath, AK [*Location identifier FAA*] (FAAL)
VTR........... Value of Time Research [*British*]
VTR........... Variable Takeoff Rating (GAVI)
VTR........... Variable Tandem Repetition [*Genetics*]
VTR........... Vehicle-Tracked Retriever [*An armored recovery vehicle*] [*Army*] (VNW)
VTR........... Vehicle Tracking Receiver
VTR........... Vehicle Track Recovery [*Military*]
VTR........... Vendor Trouble Report
VTR........... Verification Test Report (NASA)
VTR........... Vermont Railway, Inc. [*AAR code*]
VT R........ Vermont Reports [*A publication*] (DLA)
VTR........... Vertical Radial (MSA)
VTR........... Vertical Test Range
VTR........... Veto Resources Ltd. [*Vancouver Stock Exchange symbol*]
VTR........... Videotape Recorder [*or Recording*]
VTR........... Video-Tape Recording (IDOE)
VTR........... Vintage Triumph Register (EA)
VTR........... Visibility Transport Region (COE)
VTR........... Vitkovice Air [*Czech Republic*] [*ICAO designator*] (FAAC)
VTR........... Voltage Transformation Ratio [*Physics*]
VTRA......... Vectra Banking [*NASDAQ symbol*] (SAG)
VTRAM...... Variable Topology Random Access Memory [*Computer science*] (PDAA)
VTRAN...... Vast Translator (KSC)
VTRAP...... Vectra Bkg 9.50%'A'Pfd [*NASDAQ symbol*] (TTSB)
VtRaStM.... Saint Mary's Seminary, Randolph, VT [*Library symbol Library of Congress*] (LCLS)
VTRB........ Variable Trim Reentry Body (MCD)
VT Rep...... Vermont Reports [*A publication*] (DLA)
VTRIX....... Vanguard: Trustees' Equity: Intl. Ptfl. [*Mutual fund ticker symbol*] (SG)
V/TRK...... Vertical Track (GAVI)
VtRoc....... Rochester Public Library, Rochester, VT [*Library symbol Library of Congress*] (LCLS)
VTRR........ Visual Target RADAR Ranging
VTRS........ Videotape Recording System
VTRS........ Videotape Response System
VTRS........ Visual Technology Research Simulator (CAAL)
VTRU........ Variable Threshold Recently Used (MHDI)
VTS........... IEEE Vehicular Technology Society (EA)
VTS........... Vacuum Thermal Stability Test (MCD)
VTS........... Vandenberg Tracking Station [*Air Force*]

VTS	Vanillin Thiosemicarbazone (IIA)
VTS	Variable Time Step
VTS	Variable Tracking Strategy (MCD)
VTS	Vehicle Test Specification
VTS	Vehicle Time Reproducer (SAA)
VTS	Vehicle Tracking System [Automotive engineering]
VTS	Venture Touring Society (EA)
VTS	Veritas DGC, Inc. [NYSE symbol] (SAG)
VTS	Versatile Training Systems (MCD)
VTS	Vertical Test Site [NASA] (MCD)
VTS	Vertical Test Stand [NASA] (KSC)
VTS	Vertical Test System (NASA)
VTS	Vertical Thrust Stand
VTS	Vertical Tube Storage [Environmental science] (COE)
VTS	Vessel Traffic Service [Harbor RADAR system] [Coast Guard]
VTS	Vibration Test Specification
VTS	Vibration Test System
VTS	Viewfinder Tracking System
VTS	Viewscan Text System (NITA)
VTS	Virginia Theological Seminary, Alexandria, VA [OCLC symbol] (OCLC)
VTS	Virtual Terminal Service (TNIG)
VTS	Virtual Terminal System [Computer science] (MHDB)
VTS	Visual Typing System (MCD)
VTS	Vitosha [Bulgaria] [Seismograph station code, US Geological Survey] (SEIS)
VTS	Vocational Training Scheme [British]
VTS	Vocational Training Service
VTS	Vote Tally System
VTS	Vulcan Training System (MCD)
VTSA	Satun [Thailand] [ICAO location identifier] (ICLI)
VTSB	Surat Thani [Thailand] [ICAO location identifier] (ICLI)
VTSC	Narathiwat [Thailand] [ICAO location identifier] (ICLI)
VTSD	Chumpon [Thailand] [ICAO location identifier] (ICLI)
VTSD	Variable-Temperature Stepwise Desorption [Chemical engineering]
VTSE	Vehicle Team Subcaliber Exercise [Army] (INF)
VTSH	Songkhla [Thailand] [ICAO location identifier] (ICLI)
VtShelM	Shelburne Museum, Inc., Research Library, Shelburne, VT [Library symbol Library of Congress] (LCLS)
VTsIK	Vserossiyskiy Tsentral'nyy Ispolnitel'nyy Komitet [All-Russian Central Executive Committee of the Congress of Soviets] [Former USSR] (LAIN)
VTSK	Pattani [Thailand] [ICAO location identifier] (ICLI)
VTS/MA	Virtual Terminal Session/Multiple Access [Computer science] (HGAA)
VTSN	Nakhon Si Thammarat [Thailand] [ICAO location identifier] (ICLI)
VTSO	Surat Thani/Don Nok [Thailand] [ICAO location identifier] (ICLI)
VTSP	Phuket [Thailand] [ICAO location identifier] (ICLI)
VTSPS	Vsesoyuznyy Tsentral'nyy Sovet Professional'nykh Soyuzov [All-Union Central Council of Trade Unions] [Former USSR]
VTSR	Ranong [Thailand] [ICAO location identifier] (ICLI)
VTSRS	Verdun Target Symptom Rating Scale (MAE)
VTSS	Songkhla/Hat Yai [Thailand] [ICAO location identifier] (ICLI)
VTSS	Vitesse Semiconductor [NASDAQ symbol] (TTSB)
VTSS	Vitesse Semiconductor Corp. [NASDAQ symbol] (SPSG)
VTST	Trang [Thailand] [ICAO location identifier] (IOLI)
VTST	Variational Transition State Theory [Physical chemistry]
VT Stat Ann	Vermont Statutes, Annotated [A publication] (DLA)
VtStjA	St. Johnsbury Atheneum, St. Johnsbury, VT [Library symbol Library of Congress] (LCLS)
VtStjF	Fairbanks Museum of Natural Science, St. Johnsbury, VT [Library symbol Library of Congress] (LCLS)
VTSU	Virtual Terminal Support [Computer science] (IAA)
Vt-SWRL	Vermont Department of Libraries, Southwest Regional Library, Rutland, VT [Library symbol Library of Congress] (LCLS)
VTSY	Ya La [Thailand] [ICAO location identifier] (ICLI)
VTT	Vacuum Thermal Testing
VTT	Vacuum-Tube Transmitter
VTT	Valtion Teknillinen Tutkimuskeskus [Technical Research Center of Finland] [Espoo] [Information service or system] (IID)
VTT	Variable Threshold Transistor
VTT	Vertolet Zhpa [Ukraine] [FAA designator] (FAAC)
VTT	Video Teletraining [Military] (INF)
VTTC	Video Tape Time-Code (NITA)
VTTeddy	Vermont Teddy Bear Co. [Associated Press] (SAG)
VTU	Las Tunas [Cuba] [Airport symbol] (OAG)
VTU	Oxnard, CA [Location identifier FAA] (FAAL)
VTU	University of Vermont, Bailey Library, Burlington, VT [OCLC symbol] (OCLC)
VtU	University of Vermont, Burlington, VT [Library symbol Library of Congress] (LCLS)
VTU	Vehicle Tracking Unit [Automated traffic management]
vtu	Vermont [MARC country of publication code Library of Congress] (LCCP)
VTU	Vibrating Tie Under-Cutter (PDAA)
V + TU	Voice plus Teleprinter Unit
VTU	Voluntary Testing Unit (WDAA)
VTU	Volunteer Reserve Training Unit [Coast Guard]
VTU	Volunteer Training Unit
VTUA	Kalasin/Ban Na Khu [Thailand] [ICAO location identifier] (ICLI)
VTUB	Bakhon Phanom/Mukdahan [Thailand] [ICAO location identifier] (ICLI)
VTUC	Chaiyaphum [Thailand] [ICAO location identifier] (ICLI)
VTUD	Udon Thani [Thailand] [ICAO location identifier] (ICLI)
VTUE	Sakon Nakhon/Nam Phung Dam (North) [Thailand] [ICAO location identifier] (ICLI)

VTUF	Sakon Nakhon/Nam Phung Dam (South) [Thailand] [ICAO location identifier] (ICLI)
VTUG	Chaiyaphum/Phu Khieo [Thailand] [ICAO location identifier] (ICLI)
VTUH	Nakhon Ratchasima/Pak Chong [Thailand] [ICAO location identifier] (ICLI)
VTUI	Sakon Nakhon/Bankhai [Thailand] [ICAO location identifier] (ICLI)
VTUK	Khon Kaen [Thailand] [ICAO location identifier] (ICLI)
VTUL	Loei [Thailand] [ICAO location identifier] (ICLI)
VTUM	Nongkhai [Thailand] [ICAO location identifier] (ICLI)
VtU-Med	University of Vermont, College of Medicine, Burlington, VT [Library symbol Library of Congress] (LCLS)
VTU(MMS)	Volunteer Training Unit (Merchant Marine Safety)
VTUN	Nakhon Ratchasima [Thailand] [ICAO location identifier] (ICLI)
VTUP	Nakhon Phanom [Thailand] [ICAO location identifier] (ICLI)
VTUR	Roi Et [Thailand] [ICAO location identifier] (ICLI)
VTUS	Sakon Nakhon [Thailand] [ICAO location identifier] (ICLI)
VTUT	Ubon Ratchathani/Loeng Nok Tha [Thailand] [ICAO location identifier] (ICLI)
VTUU	Ubon Ratchathani [Thailand] [ICAO location identifier] (ICLI)
VTUW	Nakhon Phanom (West) [Thailand] [ICAO location identifier] (ICLI)
VtU-W	University of Vermont and State Agricultural College, Wilbur Collection, Burlington, VT [Library symbol Library of Congress] (LCLS)
VTUZ	Khon Kaen/Nam Phung Dam [Thailand] [ICAO location identifier] (ICLI)
VTV	Vacuum Transmitting Valve [Automotive engineering]
VT(V)	Vacuum-Tube (Voltmeter) (DEN)
VTV	Value Television [Television program]
VTV	Verification Test Vehicle [Military] (CAAL)
VtVe	Bixby Memorial Free Library, Vergennes, VT [Library symbol Library of Congress] (LCLS)
VTVM	Vacuum-Tube Voltmeter
VTW	Variable Transmission Window
VTW	Victorian Tapestry Workshop [Australia]
VTW	Voters Telecomm Watch [An association] (EA)
VtWeo	Wilder Memorial Library, Weston, VT [Library symbol Library of Congress] (LCLS)
VtWinoS	Saint Michael's College, Winooski, VT [Library symbol Library of Congress] (LCLS)
VTX	Vacuum-Tube Transmitter
VTX	Ventex Energy [Vancouver Stock Exchange symbol]
VTX	Vertex
VTX	Videotex [Telecommunications]
VTX	Vortex (AAG)
VTX	VTX Electronics [AMEX symbol] (SPSG)
VTXTS	Navy Jet Trainer (MCD)
VTY	Vatovaky [Madagascar] [Seismograph station code, US Geological Survey] (SEIS)
VTZ	Vishakhapatnam [India] [Airport symbol] (OAG)
VTZ	Vitjaz [Russian Federation] [ICAO designator] (FAAC)
VU	Air Ivoire [ICAO designator] (AD)
VU	Utility Speed (GAVI)
VU	Utility Squadron [Navy symbol] (MCD)
VU	Validation Unit (AAG)
VU	Vanity Unit [Classified advertising] (ADA)
VU	Vanuatu [Internet country code]
VU	Varicose Ulcer [Medicine]
VU	Vaterlaendische Union [Patriotic Union] [Liechtenstein] [Political party] (PPE)
VU	Vehicle Unit (KSC)
vu	Vehicle Unit (NAKS)
vu	Vehicle Utility (NAKS)
VU	Vehicle Utility (MCD)
VU	Velvet Underground [Musical group]
VU	Very Urgent
VU	Voice Unit [Signal amplitude measurement]
VU	Volksunie [People's Union] [Belgium Political party]
VU	Volksunite [United People's Party] [Belgium] [Political party]
VU	Volume Unit [Signal amplitude measurement]
vu	Volume Unit (NAKS)
VU	Von Unten [From the Bottom] [German]
VUA	Valorous Unit Award [Military decoration]
VUA	Verbal Underachievers [Education]
VUA	Virtual Unit Address (BUR)
VUB	Variational Upper Bound
VUB	Vrije Universiteit Brussel [Free University of Brussels] [Belgium] [Information service or system] (IID)
VUCC	Computer Center [Vanderbilt University] [Research center] (RCD)
VUCDT	Ventilation Unit Condensate Drain Tank (IEEE)
VUCP	Vietnamese Union Catalog Project, University of Michigan, Ann Arbor, MI [Library symbol] [Library of Congress] (LCLS)
VUCS	Ventilation Umbilical Connector System
VUD	Vertical Unit Displacement [Military] (INF)
VUE	Upper Hudson Library Federation, Albany, NY [OCLC symbol] (OCLC)
VUE	Visible/Ultraviolet Experiment
VUE	Visual User Environment [Military]
VUEC	Variable Underwater Experimental Community (PDAA)
VU-EVA	Volksunie-Europese Vrije Alliante [Belgium] [Political party] (ECED)
VUF	Vertical Upward Force
VUHZ	Vyzkumny Ustav Hutnictvi Zeleza, Dobra [Dobra Iron and Steel Research Institute] [Information service or system] (IID)
VUI	Video User Interface [Computer science] (DOM)
VUL	Variable Universal Life [Insurance]

VUL	Vulcan [*Taviliu*] [*New Britain*] [*Seismograph station code, US Geological Survey*] (SEIS)
VUL	Vulcan International Corp. [*AMEX symbol*] (SPSG)
VUL	Vulcan Int'l Corp. [*AMEX symbol*] (TTSB)
VUL	Vulcanize (AAG)
VUL	Vulgar (WDAA)
Vul	Vulgate [*Version of the Bible*] (BARN)
VUL	Vulnerary [*Medicine to heal wounds*] (ROG)
Vul	Vulpecula [*Constellation*]
VULBS	Virginia Union List of Biomedical Serials [*Library network*]
VULC	Vanguard Unionist Loyalist Coalition [*Northern Ireland*] [*Political party*]
VULC	Vulcanize
VULC	Vulcanizing
VulcCp	Vulcan International Corp. [*Associated Press*] (SAG)
VulcM	Vulcan Materials Co. [*Associated Press*] (SAG)
VULCN	Vulcanization
VULG	Vulgar
VULG	Vulgate [*Version of the Bible*]
Vulg	Vulgate (ODCC)
Vulp	Vulpecula [*Constellation*]
VULREP	Vulnerability Report [*Navy*] (NVT)
VUMS	Veterans of Underage Military Service (EA)
VUMS	Vyzkumny Ustav pro Matematickych Stroju [*Research Institute for Mathematical Machines*] [*Czechoslovakia*]
VUN	Air Ivoire Societe [*Ivory Coast*] [*ICAO designator*] (FAAC)
VUN	Vunikawai [*Fiji*] [*Seismograph station code, US Geological Survey*] (SEIS)
VUNC	Voice of United Nations Command
VUP	Valledupar [*Colombia*] [*Airport symbol*] (OAG)
VUP	Vela Uniform Platform
VUPD	Video Updates, Inc. [*NASDAQ symbol*] (SAG)
VUPDA	Video Update [*NASDAQ symbol*] (TTSB)
VUPDW	Video Update Wrrt'A' [*NASDAQ symbol*] (TTSB)
VUPDZ	Video Update Wrrt'B' [*NASDAQ symbol*] (TTSB)
VUPJ	Victorian Union for Progressive Judaism [*Australia*]
VUPP	Vanguard Unionist Progressive Party [*Northern Ireland*] [*Political party*]
VUQ	Dayton, OH [*Location identifier FAA*] (FAAL)
VUR	Vesicoureteral Reflux [*Nephrology*]
VUR	Vesicoureteral Regurgitation [*Nephrology*] (MEDA)
VUS	Versatile Upper Stage [*NASA*]
VUSA	Value America [*NASDAQ symbol*]
VUSA	Visit USA [*Airline fare*]
VUSVX	Vontobel U.S. Value [*Mutual fund ticker symbol*] (SG)
VUT	Union Theological Seminary Library, Richmond, VA [*OCLC symbol*] (OCLC)
VUTK	View Tech, Inc. [*NASDAQ symbol*] (SAG)
VUTKW	View Tech Wrrt [*NASDAQ symbol*] (TTSB)
VUTS	Verification Unit Test Set (AFM)
VUU	Virginia Union University [*Richmond*]
VUU	Virginia Union University, Richmond, VA [*OCLC symbol*] (OCLC)
VUV	Vacuum Ultraviolet
VUV	Very Ultraviolet (SSD)
VUVM	Voluntary Universal Marking Program (IAA)
VUW	Eugene Isle, LA [*Location identifier FAA*] (FAAL)
VUW	Victoria University of Wellington [*New Zealand*]
VUZ	Birmingham, AL [*Location identifier FAA*] (FAAL)
VV	First and Second Violins [*Music*] (ROG)
VV	Semo Aviation [*ICAO designator*] (AD)
VV	Vaccinia Virus
VV	Vacuum Valve
V/V	Validation/Verification (CAAL)
VV	Valve Voltmeter (IAA)
VV	Vanguard Ventures [*Vancouver Stock Exchange symbol*]
VV	Variable Venturi [*Automotive engineering*]
VV	Varicose Vein (MAE)
VV	Veins [*Medicine*]
VV	Velocity Vector (AAG)
VV	Velocity-Volume
VV	Venae [*Veins*] [*Latin*] [*Anatomy*] (DAVI)
vv.	Venerabiles [*Venerables*] [*Latin*] (WGA)
VV	Venovenous [*Cardiology*] (DAVI)
VV	Vent Valve
vv.	Vent Valve (NAKS)
VV	Verbs (ADA)
VV	Verses
VV	Vertebral Vein [*Anatomy*]
V/V	Vertical Velocity
vv.	Vertical Velocity (NAKS)
VV	Vertical Visibility (DA)
VV	Vesicovaginal [*Gynecology*] (DAVI)
V-V	Vibrational-to-Vibrational [*Energy transfer*]
VV	Vibrio Vulnificus [*A microorganism*]
VV	Vice Versa
vv.	Vice Versa (ODBW)
VV	Victims for Victims [*Defunct*] (EA)
VV	Vietnam Veterans (OICC)
VV	Village Voice [*A publication*] (BRI)
VV	Violini [*Violins*] [*Music*]
VV	Viper Venom (MAE)
V V	Virtual Equal Virtual [*Computer science*] (MHDI)
VV	Visna Virus
VV	Vista Ventures [*Commercial firm*] [*British*]
VV	Visum Vivum [*Seen Alive*] [*Botany*] (ROG)
VV	Viva Voce [*Spoken Aloud*] [*Latin*] (ADA)
VV	Voices [*Music*]
VV	Volume (NTCM)
V/V	Volume of Solute per Volume of Solution [*Pharmacology*] (DAVI)
vv.	Volumes (ODBW)
V/V	Volume/Volume
VV	Vulva and Vagina [*Physiology*]
VVA	Evaluation & Sale of Assets Agency
VVA	Southern Adirondack Library System, Saratoga Springs, NY [*OCLC symbol*] (OCLC)
VVA	Variable Valve Actuation [*Automotive engineering*]
VVA	Venturi Vacuum Amplifier [*Automotive engineering*]
VVA	Vietnam Veterans of America (EA)
VVAA	Vietnam Veterans Association of Australia
VVAG	Vietnam Veterans Arts Group [*Later, CTVWA*] (EA)
VV & A	Verified, Validated, and Accredited (RDA)
VV & C	Verification, Validation, and Certification (MHDB)
VVAOVI	Vietnam Veterans Agent Orange Victims (EA)
VVAP	Mouvement Socialiste Occitan - Volem Viure al Pais [*Occitanian Socialist Movement*] [*France Political party*] (PPW)
VVAW	Vietnam Veterans Against the War (EA)
VVB	Baruch College, New York, NY [*OCLC symbol*] (OCLC)
VVB	Mahanoro [*Madagascar*] [*Airport symbol*] (OAG)
VVBAA	Venetian and Vertical Blind Association of America [*Defunct*]
VVBM	Buonmethuot/Chung Duc [*Viet Nam*] [*ICAO location identifier*] (ICLI)
VVC	Colgate University, Hamilton, NY [*OCLC symbol*] (OCLC)
VVC	Variable Vacuum Capacitor [*or Capacitance*]
VVC	Variable Valve Control [*Automotive*]
VVC	Variable Voltage Capacitor (IAA)
VVC	Vertical Velocity Console
VVC	Villavicencio [*Colombia*] [*Airport symbol*] (OAG)
VVC	Volcano Veterinary Center [*Rwanda*]
VVC	Voltage Variable Capacitor
VVCB	Caobang [*Viet Nam*] [*ICAO location identifier*] (ICLI)
VVCC	Victorian Vice-Chancellors' Committee [*Australia*]
VVCC	Viri Clarissimi [*Most Illustrious Men*] [*Latin*]
VVCD	Voltage Variable Capacitance Diode
VVCEC	Voice and Video Control and Editing Components (MCD)
VVCS	Conson [*Viet Nam*] [*ICAO location identifier*] (ICLI)
VVCS	Vernier Velocity Correction System [*Aerospace*] (KSC)
VVCT	Cantho [*Viet Nam*] [*ICAO location identifier*] (ICLI)
VVCUS	Veteran Vespa Club, US [*Defunct*] (EA)
VVD	Downstate Medical Center, SUNY [*State University of New York*], Brooklyn, NY [*OCLC symbol*] (OCLC)
VVD	Valid Verifiable Defense [*Stamped on dismissed traffic tickets*]
VVD	Valverde [*Canary Islands*] [*Seismograph station code, US Geological Survey*] (SEIS)
VVD	Volkspartij voor Vrijheid en Democratie [*People's Party for Freedom and Democracy*] [*Netherlands Political party*] (EAIO)
VVD	Voltage Variable Diode
VVDB	Dienbienphu [*Viet Nam*] [*ICAO location identifier*] (ICLI)
VVDL	Dalat/Lienkhuong [*Viet Nam*] [*ICAO location identifier*] (ICLI)
VVDN	Danang [*Viet Nam*] [*ICAO location identifier*] (ICLI)
VVDS	Video Verter Decision Storage
VVE	Erie Community College-North, Buffalo, NY [*OCLC symbol*] (OCLC)
VVE	Vertical Vertex Error (OA)
VVEJ	Venus-Venus-Earth-Jupiter [*Trajectory*]
VVF	New York Medical College, New York, NY [*OCLC symbol*] (OCLC)
VVF	Veseco Vaginal Fistula [*Medicine*]
VVFO	Vier/Viers Family Organization (EA)
VVFR	Vesicovaginal Fistula Repair [*Gynecology*] (DAVI)
VVG	Aerovilla Ltda. [*Columbia*] [*FAA designator*] (FAAC)
VVG	New York State Institute for Research in Mental Retardation, Staten Island, NY [*OCLC symbol*] (OCLC)
VVGF	Vincent Van Gogh Foundation (EA)
VVGL	Hanoi/Gialam [*Viet Nam*] [*ICAO location identifier*] (ICLI)
VVH	Daemen College, Buffalo, NY [*OCLC symbol*] (OCLC)
VVH	Very Very Heavy [*Cosmic ray nuclei*]
VVH	Veterans Vigil of Honor (EA)
V/VH	Viewers-per-Viewing Household [*Television ratings*] (NTCM)
VVHR	Vibration Velocity per Hour
VVI	Beth Israel Medical Center, New York, NY [*OCLC symbol*] (OCLC)
VVI	Ventricular Pacing, Ventricular Sensing, Inhibited Mode [*Pacemaker*] [*Cardiology*] (MEDA)
VVI	Vertical Velocity Indicator (MCD)
vvi.	Vertical Velocity Indicator (NAKS)
VVI	Viad Corp. [*NYSE symbol*] [*Formerly, Dial Corp.*] (SG)
VVI	Vice Viewers International (EA)
VVI	Vietnam Veterans, Inc. [*Defunct*] (EA)
VVI	Vietnam Veterans Institute [*Research center*] (RCD)
VVI	Vocational Values Inventory [*Guidance in education*]
VVI	Voltage Variation Indicator
VVIC	Vietnam Era Veterans in Congress (EA)
VVID	Vivid Technologies, Inc. [*NASDAQ symbol*] (SAG)
VVIP	Very, Very Important Person
VVIR	Voice and Vision of the Iranian Revolution [*Iranian television*]
VVIRA	Vietnam Veterans Institute for Research and Advocacy (EA)
VVITA	Vietnam Veterans Inter-Tribal Association (EA)
VVJ	John Jay College of Criminal Justice, New York, NY [*OCLC symbol*] (OCLC)
VVK	New York Academy of Medicine, New York, NY [*OCLC symbol*] (OCLC)
VVK	Van Vleck [*Quantum mechanics*]
VVK	Vastervik [*Sweden*] [*Airport symbol*] (OAG)
VVKP	Kep [*Viet Nam*] [*ICAO location identifier*] (ICLI)

VVL..............	Mount Sinai School of Medicine of the City University of New York, New York, NY [*OCLC symbol*] (OCLC)
VVLK........	Laokay [*Viet Nam*] [*ICAO location identifier*] (ICLI)
VV LL	Variae Lectiones [*Variant Readings*] [*Latin*]
VVLP........	Vietnam Veterans Leadership Program [*ACTION*]
VVM..........	Memorial Sloan-Kettering Cancer Center, New York, NY [*OCLC symbol*] (OCLC)
VVM..........	Valve Voltmeter (IAA)
VVM..........	Vector Voltmeter
VVM..........	Velocity Vector Measurement
VVM..........	Vietnam Veterans Memorial (VNW)
VVMC........	Voice and Video Monitoring Component (MCD)
vvMDV......	Very Virulent Marek Disease Virus [*Medicine*] (DMAA)
VVMF........	Vietnam Veterans Memorial Fund [*Defunct*] (EA)
VVMS........	Velocity Vector Measurement System
VVN..........	Niagara University, Niagara University, NY [*OCLC symbol*] (OCLC)
VVNB........	Hanoi/Noibai [*Viet Nam*] [*ICAO location identifier*] (ICLI)
VVNS........	Nasan [*Viet Nam*] [*ICAO location identifier*] (ICLI)
VVNT........	Nhatrang [*Viet Nam*] [*ICAO location identifier*] (ICLI)
VVnW........	Veterans of the Vietnam War (EA)
VVO..........	New York Medical College, Westchester Medical Center, Valhalla, NY [*OCLC symbol*] (OCLC)
VVO..........	Very Very Old [*Designation on brandy labels*]
VVO..........	Vladivostok [*USSR*] [*Airport symbol*] (AD)
VVOH........	Vacuum Valve Operating Handle
VVOR........	Visual-Vestibulo-Ocular Reflex [*Ophthalmology*] (DAVI)
VVP..........	Bard College, Annandale-On-Hudson, NY [*OCLC symbol*] (OCLC)
VVPB........	Hue/Phubai [*Viet Nam*] [*ICAO location identifier*] (ICLI)
VVPK........	Pleiku/Cu-Hanh [*Viet Nam*] [*ICAO location identifier*] (ICLI)
VVPP........	Variable Volume Piston Pump
VVPQ........	Phuquoc [*Viet Nam*] [*ICAO location identifier*] (ICLI)
VVQ..........	Roosevelt Hospital, Medical Library, New York, NY [*OCLC symbol*] (OCLC)
VVQ..........	Visualizer-Verbalizer Questionnaire (EDAC)
VVQN........	Quinhon [*Viet Nam*] [*ICAO location identifier*] (ICLI)
VVR..........	Rockland Community College, Suffern, NY [*OCLC symbol*] (OCLC)
VVR..........	Vancouver Ventures [*Vancouver Stock Exchange symbol*]
VVR..........	Variable Voltage Rectifier
VVR..........	Vehicle Vapor Recovery [*Automobile*]
VVR..........	Viewdata/Videotex Report [*Link Resources Corp.*] [*Information service or system*] (CRD)
VVRG........	Rachgia [*Viet Nam*] [*ICAO location identifier*] (ICLI)
VVRI.........	Veterinary Virus Research Institute [*New York State Veterinary College*]
VVRM........	Vortex Valve Rocket Motor (MCD)
VVRS........	Viscous Vortex Rate Sensor
VVS..........	Connellsville, PA [*Location identifier FAA*] (FAAL)
VVS..........	Sarah Lawrence College, Bronxville, NY [*OCLC symbol*] (OCLC)
VVS..........	Vein Ventures Ltd. [*Vancouver Stock Exchange symbol*]
VVS..........	Very Very Slightly Flawed [*Gems*]
VVS..........	Very, Very Small Inclusions [*Diamond clarity grade*]
VVS..........	Very Very Superior
VVS..........	Voenno-Vozdushnye Sily [*Army Air Forces*] [*Part of the MO*] [*Former USSR*]
VVS..........	Voice Verification System
VVSA........	Velocity Vector Sensor Assembly
VVSO........	Very, Very Superior Old [*Designation on brandy labels*]
VVSOP......	Very, Very Superior Old Pale [*Designation on brandy labels*]
VVSS........	Vertical Volute Spring Suspension [*Technical drawings*]
VVS-VMF....	Voenno-Vozdushnye Sily - Voenno-Morskogo Flota [*Naval Air Force*] [*Former USSR*]
VVT..........	Teachers College, Columbia University, New York, NY [*OCLC symbol*] (OCLC)
VVT..........	Variable Valve Timing [*Automotive*]
VVT..........	Velocity Variation Tube
VVT..........	Ventricular Pacing, Ventricular Sensing, Triggered Mode [*Pacemaker*] [*Cardiology*] (MEDA)
VVT..........	Venturi Vacuum Transducer [*Engineering*]
VVT..........	Visual-Verbal Test [*Psychology*]
VVTC........	Vendor-Vendee Technical Committee
VVTS........	Hochiminh/Tansonnhat [*Viet Nam*] [*ICAO location identifier*] (ICLI)
VVTV........	ValueVision International, Inc. [*NASDAQ symbol*] (SAG)
VVTV........	ValueVision Intl'A' [*NASDAQ symbol*] (TTSB)
VVU..........	New York University, Medical Center, New York, NY [*OCLC symbol*] (OCLC)
VVUS........	Vivus, Inc. [*NASDAQ symbol*] (SAG)
VVV..........	Intercontinental Airlines Ltd. [*Nigeria*] [*ICAO designator*] (FAAC)
VVV..........	Ortonville, MN [*Location identifier FAA*] (FAAL)
VVV..........	Test Signal [*Telegraphy*] (IDOE)
VVV..........	Utica College of Syracuse University, Utica, NY [*OCLC symbol*] (OCLC)
VVV..........	Vacuum Vent Valve [*Automotive engineering*]
VVVH........	Vinh [*Viet Nam*] [*ICAO location identifier*] (ICLI)
VVVT........	Vungtau [*Viet Nam*] [*ICAO location identifier*] (ICLI)
VV/VTSHED...	Variable Volume/Variable Temperature Sealed Housing for Evaporative Determination [*Automotive emissions testing*]
VVVV........	Hanoi [*Viet Nam*] [*ICAO location identifier*] (ICLI)
VVW..........	Westchester Library System, Yonkers, NY [*OCLC symbol*] (OCLC)
VVWCA......	Vintage Volkswagen Club of America (EA)
VV:WT........	Vaccinia Virus: Wild Type [*Virology*]
VVX..........	Nassau Community College, Garden City, NY [*OCLC symbol*] (OCLC)
VVY..........	St. Luke's Hospital, Bolling Medical Library, New York, NY [*OCLC symbol*] (OCLC)

VVZ..........	Medical Library Center of New York, New York, NY [*OCLC symbol*] (OCLC)
VW..........	Air Concept [*Germany ICAO aircraft manufacturer identifier*] (ICAO)
VW..........	Ama-Flyg [*ICAO designator*] (AD)
VW..........	Early Warning Squadron [*Symbol*] (MCD)
Vw..........	Maximum Winch Launching Speed [*Gliders*] (AIA)
VW..........	Very Weak [*Spectral*]
VW..........	Very Worshipful
VW..........	Vessel Wall
VW..........	View (MCD)
vw..........	View (VRA)
VW..........	Volkswagen [*German automobile*]
VW..........	Volts Working [*Electronics*] (ECII)
VW..........	Von Willebrand [*disease and Factor*] [*Hematology*] (DAVI)
VWA..........	Vacuum Window Assembly
VWA..........	Vendor Working Authority
VWA..........	Verband der Weiblichen Angestellten [*Association of Female Employees*] [*West Germany*]
VWA..........	Vintage Wireless Association [*British*]
VWA..........	Volkswagen of America (ECON)
VWA..........	Volume-Weighted Average [*Statistics*]
VWAC........	Victorian Wheat Advisory Committee [*Australia*]
VWAHX......	Vanguard High Yield Muni Bond [*Mutual fund ticker symbol*] (SG)
VWAM........	Very Wide Area Mine (RDA)
VWAM........	Vets with a Mission [*An association*] (EA)
VWB..........	Bronx Community College Library, Bronx, NY [*OCLC symbol*] (OCLC)
VWB..........	Visual Workbench [*Computer science*] (PCM)
VWC..........	Victorian Writers' Centre [*Australia*]
VWC..........	Villa Walsh College [*New Jersey*]
VWC..........	Virtual Worlds Consortium (BUAC)
VWC..........	Vulcan Wheeled Carrier
VWCA........	Volkswagen Club of America (EA)
VWCL........	Volkswagen Caminhoes Limitada [*Brazil*]
VWD..........	Vereinigte Wirtschaftsdienste [*Press agency*] [*West Germany*]
VWD..........	Video-West Distributors Ltd. [*Vancouver Stock Exchange symbol*]
VWD..........	Vinyl Window and Door Institute (EA)
vWD..........	Von Willebrand's Disease [*Medicine*]
VWDU........	Viewing Window Deicing Unit
VWE..........	Vanadium Wire Equilibration [*Nuclear energy*] (NRCH)
VWED........	Vanadium Wire Equilibration Device [*Nuclear energy*] (NRCH)
VWEHX......	Vanguard FIS: High Yield Corp. Ptfl. [*Mutual fund ticker symbol*] (SG)
VWELX......	Vanguard: Wellington Fund [*Mutual fund ticker symbol*] (SG)
VWESX......	Vanguard FIS: Long-Term Corp. [*Mutual fund ticker symbol*] (SG)
VWF..........	Vehicle Work Flow
VWF..........	Vibration-Induced White Finger [*Medicine*]
vWf..........	Von Willebrand factor [*Also, vWF, VWF*] [*Hematology*]
VWFC........	Very-Wide-Field Camera
VWG..........	Vibrating Wire Gauge (WDAA)
VWG..........	Vital Wheat Gluten [*Vegetable protein*]
VWGA........	Vinifera Wine Growers Association (EA)
VWH..........	Vale of White Horse [*Hounds*]
VWH..........	Vertical Weld Head
VWHA........	Vertical Weld Head Assembly
VWIA........	Victorian Wine Industry Association [*Australia*]
VWIGX......	Vanguard Intl. Growth Ptfl. [*Mutual fund ticker symbol*] (SG)
VWINX......	Vanguard: Wellesley Income [*Mutual fund ticker symbol*] (SG)
VWITX......	Vanguard Mun. Intermed [*Mutual fund ticker symbol*] (SG)
VWL..........	College of William and Mary, Law School, Williamsburg, VA [*OCLC symbol*] (OCLC)
VWL..........	Variable Word Length
VWLTX......	Vanguard Mun. Long Term [*Mutual fund ticker symbol*] (SG)
VWM..........	College of William and Mary, Williamsburg, VA [*OCLC symbol*] (OCLC)
VWM..........	Ventricular Wall Motion [*Cardiology*] (DAVI)
VWM..........	Volume-Weighted Mean [*Statistical technique*]
VWMP........	Vietnam Women's Memorial Project (EA)
VWNDX......	Vanguard: Windsor Fund [*Mutual fund ticker symbol*] (SG)
VWNFX......	Vanguard: Windsor II Fund [*Mutual fund ticker symbol*] (SG)
VWO..........	Valves Wide Open [*Nuclear energy*] (NRCH)
VWO..........	Woolsey, GA [*Location identifier FAA*] (FAAL)
VWOA........	Veteran Wireless Operators Association (EA)
VWOA........	Volkswagen of America
VWP..........	Variable Width Pulse
VWP..........	Vietnam Workers' Party [*Political party*] (PPW)
VWPI.........	Vacuum Wood Preservers Institute (EA)
VWQMN......	Victorian Water Quality Monitoring Network [*State*] (EERA)
VWR..........	North Country Reference and Research Resources Council, Canton, NY [*OCLC symbol*] (OCLC)
VWR..........	Van Waters & Rogers (EFIS)
VWR..........	Volkswirtschaftsrat [*Political Economy Bureau*] [*German*]
VWRF........	Victorian Wheat Research Foundation [*Australia*]
VWRRC......	Virginia Water Resources Research Center [*Virginia Polytechnic Institute and State University*] [*Research center*] (RCD)
VWRS........	Vibrating Wire Rate Sensor
VWRSci......	VWR Corp. [*Associated Press*] (SAG)
VWRX........	VWR Corp. [*Seattle, WA*] [*NASDAQ symbol*] (NQ)
VWRX........	VWR Scientific Products [*NASDAQ symbol*] [*Formerly, VWR Corp.*] (SG)
VWS..........	Valdez, AK [*Location identifier FAA*] (FAAL)
VWS..........	Variable Word Size
VWS..........	Ventilated Wet Suit (DNAB)
VWS..........	Views [*Postal Service standard*] (OPSA)
VWS..........	Virginia Woolf Society (EA)

VWS.............	Voice Warning System
vWS.............	Von Willebrand Syndrome [Medicine] (DMAA)
VWS.............	Vortex Wake System [Aviation] (DA)
VWSS	Vertical Wire Sky Screen (KSC)
VWSTX	Vanguard Mun. Short Term [Mutual fund ticker symbol] (SG)
VWSWCA.....	Volkswagen Split Window Club of America (EA)
VWT.............	Victorian Women's Trust [Australia]
VWTA...........	Vintage White Truck Association (EA)
VW-TCA.......	Volkswagen Toy Collectors of America [Defunct] (EA)
VWU.............	Chincoteague Island, VA [Location identifier FAA] (FAAL)
VWV.............	Waterville, OH [Location identifier FAA] (FAAL)
VWW............	Velocity of Wireless Waves
VWWI	Veterans of World War I of USA [Defunct] (EA)
VWY.............	Visway Transport, Inc. [Toronto Stock Exchange symbol]
VX.............	Aces [ICAO designator] (AD)
VX.............	Air Development Squadron [Navy]
VX.............	Experimental Squadron [Symbol] (MCD)
VX.............	Nerve Gas [US Chemical Corps symbol]
VX.............	Vanex Resources Ltd. [Vancouver Stock Exchange symbol]
VX.............	Vauxhall [Automobile] [British]
VX.............	Velocity along the X-Axis (NASA)
vx.............	Velocity Along the X-Axis (NAKS)
VX.............	Vertex [Medicine]
VX.............	Vivas, Care [May You Live, Dear One] [Latin]
VX.............	Voice
VX.............	Volume Unknown [Medicine]
VX-1.............	OPTEVFOR [Operational Test and Evaluation Force] Air Test and Evaluation Squadron One, Naval Air Station, Patuxent River, MD (CAAL)
VX-4.............	OPTEVFOR [Operational Test and Evaluation Force] Air Test and Evaluation Squadron Four, Naval Air Station, Pt. Mugu, CA (CAAL)
VX-5.............	OPTEVFOR [Operational Test and Evaluation Force] Air Test and Evaluation Squadron Five, Naval Weapons Center, China Lake, CA (CAAL)
VXA.............	Harlem Hospital Center, Health Sciences Library, New York, NY [OCLC symbol] (OCLC)
VXC.............	Lichinga [Mozambique] [Airport symbol] (OAG)
VXC.............	Vila Cabral [Mozambique] [Airport symbol] (AD)
VXD	New York University, College of Dentistry Library, New York, NY [OCLC symbol] (OCLC)
VxD.............	Virtual Device Driver [Computer science] (PCM)
VXE.............	Elmira College, Elmira, NY [OCLC symbol] (OCLC)
VXE.............	Sao Vicente [Cape Verde Islands] [Airport symbol] (OAG)
VXF.............	State University of New York, College of Environmental Science and Forestry, Syracuse, NY [OCLC symbol] (OCLC)
VXG	New York Botanical Garden Library, Bronx, NY [OCLC symbol] (OCLC)
VXH	Herkimer County Community College, Herkimer, NY [OCLC symbol] (OCLC)
VXI.............	Iona College, New Rochelle, NY [OCLC symbol] (OCLC)
VXJ.............	Jewish Theological Seminary of America, New York, NY [OCLC symbol] (OCLC)
VXL.............	Albany Medical College, Schaffer Library of Health Sciences, Albany, NY [OCLC symbol] (OCLC)
VXM.............	General Theological Seminary, St. Mark's Library, New York, NY [OCLC symbol] (OCLC)
VXN	New York State Department of Health, Albany, NY [OCLC symbol] (OCLC)
VXO.............	Houghton College, Houghton, NY [OCLC symbol] (OCLC)
VXO.............	Variable Crystal Oscillator
VXO.............	Vaxjo [Sweden] [Airport symbol] (OAG)
VXP.............	State University of New York, College of Optometry, New York, NY [OCLC symbol] (OCLC)
VXR.............	Rochester Museum and Science Center, Rochester, NY [OCLC symbol] (OCLC)
VXR.............	Ventrex Laboratories, Inc. (EFIS)
VXR.............	Vertex Resources Ltd. [Vancouver Stock Exchange symbol]
VXT.............	Tompkins-Cortland Community College, Dryden, NY [OCLC symbol] (OCLC)
VXU.............	Chautauqua-Cattaraugus Library System, Jamestown, NY [OCLC symbol] (OCLC)
VXV.............	Hudson Valley Community College, Troy, NY [OCLC symbol] (OCLC)
VXW.............	Vassar College, Poughkeepsie, NY [OCLC symbol] (OCLC)
VXX.............	Long Island University, C. W. Post Center, Greenvale, NY [OCLC symbol] (OCLC)
VXX.............	Venturex Resources [Vancouver Stock Exchange symbol]
VXY.............	Centro de Estudios Puertorriquenos, New York, NY [OCLC symbol] (OCLC)
VXZ.............	Dowling College, Oakdale, NY [OCLC symbol] (OCLC)
VY.............	Abelag Airways [Belgium ICAO designator] (ICDA)
VY.............	Coral Air [ICAO designator] (AD)
VY.............	Valley (ADA)
VY.............	Various Years [Bibliography]
vy.............	Various Years (WDMC)
VY.............	Velocity along the Y-Axis (NASA)
VY.............	Very (ROG)
VY.............	Victualling Yard [Obsolete Navy British] (ROG)
VYA.............	Molloy College, Rockville Centre, NY [OCLC symbol] (OCLC)
VYAN	Victorian Youth Advocacy Network [Australia]
VYB.............	St. Barnabas Medical Staff Library, Livingston, NJ [OCLC symbol] (OCLC)
VYB.............	Vivian, Younger & Bond Ltd.
VYB.............	Vyborg [Former USSR Seismograph station code, US Geological Survey Closed] (SEIS)

VYC.............	Cornell University, Medical College, New York, NY [OCLC symbol] (OCLC)
VYC.............	Yvic Airlines [Nigeria] [ICAO designator] (FAAC)
VYD.............	Capital District Library Council, Troy, NY [OCLC symbol] (OCLC)
VYD.............	Vryheid [South Africa] [Airport symbol] (OAG)
VYE.............	Manhattanville College, Purchase, NY [OCLC symbol] (OCLC)
VYF.............	Fordham University, Bronx, NY [OCLC symbol] (OCLC)
VYG.............	Finger Lakes Library System, Ithaca, NY [OCLC symbol] (OCLC)
VYGS.............	Vermont Yankee Generating Station [Nuclear energy] (NRCH)
VYI.............	Kahului, HI [Location identifier FAA] (FAAL)
VYJ.............	Martinsburg, WV [Location identifier FAA] (FAAL)
VYK.............	Christ the King Seminary, East Aurora, NY [OCLC symbol] (OCLC)
VYK.............	Colombia, SC [Location identifier FAA] (FAAL)
VYL.............	Lehman College, Bronx, NY [OCLC symbol] (OCLC)
VYL.............	Victorian Young Lawyers [Australia]
VYM.............	United States Merchant Marine Academy, Kings Point, NY [OCLC symbol] (OCLC)
VYM.............	Voyageur Minnesota Municipal Income [AMEX symbol] (SPSG)
VYM.............	Voyageur Minn Muni Income III [AMEX symbol] (TTSB)
VYN.............	Dallas-Fort Worth, TX [Location identifier FAA] (FAAL)
VYN.............	Union Theological Seminary, New York, NY [OCLC symbol] (OCLC)
VYNP.............	Vermont Yankee Nuclear Plant (NRCH)
VYNPS	Vermont Yankee Nuclear Power Station (NRCH)
VYQ.............	Upstate Medical Center, Syracuse, NY [OCLC symbol] (OCLC)
VYR.............	Rome Air Development Center, Griffiss AFB, NY [OCLC symbol] (OCLC)
VyrexCp........	Vyrex Corp. [Associated Press] (SAG)
VYRX.............	Vyrex Corp. [NASDAQ symbol] (TTSB)
VyrxCp........	Vyrex Corp. [Associated Press] (SAG)
VYRXU.........	Vyrex Corp. Unit [NASDAQ symbol] (TTSB)
VYRXW........	Vyrex Corp. Wrrt [NASDAQ symbol] (TTSB)
VYS.............	St. Bonaventure University, St. Bonaventure, NY [OCLC symbol] (OCLC)
VYS.............	Visceral Yolk Sac [Embryology]
VYT.............	Clarkson College of Technology, Potsdam, NY [OCLC symbol] (OCLC)
VYT.............	Valley FTU [British ICAO designator] (FAAC)
VYTL...........	Viatel, Inc. [NASDAQ symbol] (SAG)
VYWT...........	Volunteer Youth Worker Training (WDAA)
VZ.............	Aquatic Airlines [ICAO designator] (AD)
VZ.............	Sisters of Charity of St. Vincent de Paul (TOCD)
VZ.............	Varicella-Zoster [Also, VZV] [A virus]
V-Z.............	Varicella-Zoster [Antibody] [Immunology] (DAVI)
VZ.............	Velocity along the Z-Axis (NASA)
vz.............	Velocity Along the Z-Axis (NAKS)
VZ.............	Ventricular Zone [Anatomy]
VZ.............	Virtual Zero
Vz.............	Vizardinus [Guizzardinus] [Deceased, 1222] [Authority cited in pre-1607 legal work] (DSA)
Vz	Zener Voltage [Electronics] (OA)
Vzar.............	Vizardinus [Guizzardinus] [Deceased, 1222] [Authority cited in pre-1607 legal work] (DSA)
VZB.............	State University of New York at Stony Brook, Health Sciences Library, Stony Brook, NY [OCLC symbol] (OCLC)
VZC.............	Clinton-Essex-Franklin Library, Plattsburgh, NY [OCLC symbol] (OCLC)
VZD.............	Vendor Zero Defect
VZE.............	Mercy College, Dobbs Ferry, NY [OCLC symbol] (OCLC)
VZF.............	St. Francis College, Brooklyn, NY [OCLC symbol] (OCLC)
VZG.............	St. Joseph's College Library, Suffolk Campus, Patchogue, NY [OCLC symbol] (OCLC)
VZH.............	Hartwick College, Oneonta, NY [OCLC symbol] (OCLC)
VZI.............	Stony Brook Institute for Advanced Studies of World Religions, Stony Brook, NY [OCLC symbol] (OCLC)
VZIG.............	Varicella-Zoster Immune Globulin
VZJ.............	St. John Fisher College, Rochester, NY [OCLC symbol] (OCLC)
VZK.............	King's College, Briarcliff Manor, NY [OCLC symbol] (OCLC)
VZL.............	Pace University, Law Library, White Plains, NY [OCLC symbol] (OCLC)
VZL.............	Vinzolidine [Antineoplastic drug]
VZM.............	Margaret Woodbury Strong Museum, Rochester, NY [OCLC symbol] (OCLC)
VZM.............	Von Zeipel Method
VZN.............	College of New Rochelle, New Rochelle, NY [OCLC symbol] (OCLC)
VZO.............	Coatesville, PA [Location identifier FAA] (FAAL)
VZP.............	Pace University, New York, NY [OCLC symbol] (OCLC)
VZQ.............	Pratt Institute, Brooklyn, NY [OCLC symbol] (OCLC)
VZR.............	Roswell Park Memorial Institute, Buffalo, NY [OCLC symbol] (OCLC)
VZS.............	Skidmore College, Saratoga Springs, NY [OCLC symbol] (OCLC)
VZS.............	Valdez South [Alaska] [Seismograph station code, US Geological Survey] (SEIS)
VZT.............	St. Joseph's College, Brooklyn, NY [OCLC symbol] (OCLC)
VZU.............	Pace University, Pleasantville, Pleasantville, NY [OCLC symbol] (OCLC)
VZV.............	College of Mount Saint Vincent, New York, NY [OCLC symbol] (OCLC)
VZV.............	Herpes Varicella Zoster [Medicine] (TAD)
VZV.............	Varicella-Zoster Virus [Also, VZ]
VZW.............	College of White Plains, White Plains, NY [OCLC symbol] (OCLC)
VZW.............	Valdez West [Alaska] [Seismograph station code, US Geological Survey] (SEIS)
VZX.............	Western New York Library Resources Council, Buffalo, NY [OCLC symbol] (OCLC)
VZY.............	Montefiore Hospital, Bronx, NY [OCLC symbol] (OCLC)

VZZ.............. International Museum of Photography, Eastman House, Rochester,
NY [*OCLC symbol*] (OCLC)

W
By Acronym

W .... Acoustical Displacement (BARN)
W .... Angular Velocity (BARN)
W .... Climatic Data for the World [*A publication*]
W .... Coast Guard Ship [*When precedes vessel classification*] [*Navy symbol*]
W .... Dew [*Meteorology*] (BARN)
W .... Diameter of Driving-Wheel in Inches [*Railroad term*]
W .... Electrical Energy [*Symbol*] (DEN)
W .... Energy (IDOE)
w .... Flow Rate [*Heat transmission symbol*]
W .... Indefinite Ceiling [*Meteorology*] (BARN)
W .... Irradiance (BARN)
w .... Load per Unit of Length
W .... Mechanical Work of Breathing [*Medicine*] (DAVI)
W .... Mercredi [*French*] (ASC)
W .... Microwatt (IAA)
W .... Requires an Engineer [*Search and rescue symbol that can be stamped in sand or snow*]
W .... Total Load
w----- .... Tropics [*MARC geographic area code Library of Congress*] (LCCP)
W .... Tryptophan [*One-letter symbol; see Trp*]
W .... Tungsten [*Chemical element*] (DOG)
W .... Underwater [*JETDS nomenclature*]
W .... Waffle [*Used in correcting manuscripts, etc.*]
W .... Wages [*Economics*]
W .... Waist (ADA)
W .... Wait Time [*Computer science*]
W .... Wales
W .... Walk [*Baseball*]
W .... Wall
W .... Wallace Laboratories [*Research code symbol*]
W .... Waltz [*Music*]
W .... Wander AG [*Switzerland*] [*Research code symbol*]
W .... Wanderer Books [*Publisher's imprint*]
W .... Wanting
W .... War
W .... Warden
W .... Wardrobe (WDMC)
W .... Wardroom [*Aerospace*]
W .... Warehouse
W .... Warhead [*Nuclear*] (NG)
W .... Warm
W .... Warner-Lambert Pharmaceutical Co. [*Research code symbol*]
W .... Warning [*Railroad signal arm*] [*British*]
W .... Warning Area [*Followed by identification*]
W .... Warrant [*A document entitling holder to purchase a given issue of stock*] [*Investment term*]
W .... Washington Reports [*1890-1939*] [*A publication*] (DLA)
W .... Waste
W .... Watch Time
W .... Water
W .... Waterloo [*Army British*] (ROG)
W .... Watermeyer's Cape Of Good Hope Supreme Court Reports [*A publication*] (DLA)
W .... Water Point [*British Waterways Board sign*]
W .... Water Vapor Content
W .... Watt [*Symbol*] [*SI unit of power*] (GPO)
w .... Watt (WDMC)
W .... Wattle [*Ornithology*]
W .... Watt Meter (IAA)
W .... Watt's Pennsylvania Reports [*A publication*] (DLA)
W .... Waveguide (SAA)
W .... Wave Height Correction
W .... Weak [*Spectral*]
W+ .... Weakly Positive [*Laboratory science*] (DAVI)
W .... Weather
W .... Weather Aircraft Equipped with Meteorological Gear [*Designation for all US military aircraft*]
W .... Weather Review [*A publication*]
W .... Web
W .... Weber [*Hearing test*] (MAE)
W .... Weber Fraction [*Psychology*]
W .... Wednesday
W .... Week
w .... Week (WDMC)
W .... Weekend Travel [*Also, Z*] [*Airline fare code*]

W .... Weekly
W .... Weekly Dose [*Medicine*]
W .... Weeping [*Shrub*]
W .... Wehnelt [*A unit of roentgen ray hardness*] (AAMN)
W .... Weight
W .... Weight (WDMC)
W .... Weld (DAS)
W .... Welding Program [*Association of Independent Colleges and Schools specialization code*]
W .... Welsh [*or Welch*]
W .... Wendell's Reports [*1826-41*] [*New York*] [*A publication*] (DLA)
W .... Wenig Fine [*Latin*] (DAVI)
W .... Wesleyan
W .... West [*or Western*]
W .... Westcoast Energy, Inc. [*Toronto Stock Exchange symbol*]
W .... Westcoast Energy, Inc. [*Vancouver Stock Exchange symbol*]
W .... Westerhout [*Astronomy*]
W .... Western Airlines (MHDW)
W .... Westinghouse [*as in "Group W"*]
W .... West Point, NY [*Mint mark when appearing on US coins*]
W .... Westvaco Corp. [*NYSE symbol*] (SPSG)
W .... Wet
W .... Wet Dew
W .... Wheaton's Reports [*14-25 United States*] [*A publication*] (DLA)
W .... Wheeled [*Vehicles*] (NATG)
W .... Whip
W .... Whiskey [*Phonetic alphabet*] [*International*] (DSUE)
W .... White [*Light, buoy, beacon*]
W .... White (DAVI)
W .... White (VRA)
W .... White Cell [*Medicine*] (AAMN)
W .... White Return [*Round trip fare for specified period*] [*British*]
W .... Whole [*Response*] [*Medicine*]
W .... Whole Word Designator [*Computer science*]
W .... Whorls and Compounds [*Fingerprint description*]
W .... Wicked (DAS)
W .... Wicket
w .... Wicket (ODBW)
w .... Wide (ODBW)
W .... Wide
W .... Widow [*or Widower*]
W .... Widowed (DAVI)
W .... Width
W .... Width (WDMC)
W .... Wife
w .... wife (WDAA)
W .... Wilderness [*State*] (EERA)
W .... Will Advise [*Business term*]
W .... Wille [*Will Factor*] [*Psychology*]
w .... Will Factor [*Psychology*]
W .... William [*Phonetic alphabet*] [*Royal Navy World War I Pre-World War II*] [*World War II*] (DSUE)
W .... William (King of England) (DLA)
W .... Wilson's [*or Willson's*] Reports [*Texas Civil Cases, Court of Appeals*] [*A publication*] (DLA)
W .... Win [*Sports*]
W .... Winch (DS)
W .... Wind [*In reference to wind velocity*]
W .... Window (NASA)
W .... Windward [*Botany*]
W .... Winnipeg Stock Exchange [*Canada*]
W .... Wins [*Sports*]
W .... Winter [*Vessel load line mark*]
W .... Wire
W .... Wireless [*Communication*] (IAA)
W .... Wisconsin Reports [*A publication*] (DLA)
W .... Wisdom (WDAA)
W .... With
w .... With (WDMC)
w/ .... With (VRA)
W .... Withdrawal
W .... Within (WGA)
W .... Without Voice Facilities on Range or Radiobeacon Frequency
W .... Witwatersrand Local Division Reports [*South Africa*] [*A publication*] (DLA)
W .... Wolfram [*Tungsten*] [*Chemical element*]

W	Woman (ADA)
W	Women's Reserve, Unlimited Service [*USNR officer designation*]
W	Won [*Sports statistics*]
W	Won [*Monetary unit*] [*South Korea*]
W	Wood
W	Wooden [*Shipping*] (ROG)
W	Woodfree [*Paper*] (DGA)
W	Woody Plant [*Botany*]
W	Word
W	Word Fluency (DAVI)
W	Work [*or w*] [*Symbol IUPAC*]
W	Workmen's Compensation [*Insurance*]
W	World
w	WORLDSCALE [*Worldwide Tanker Nominal Freight Scale*] (DS)
W	Worshipful [*Freemasonry*]
W	Wright's Ohio Reports [*1831-34*] [*A publication*] (DLA)
W	Write
W	Writer Officer [*British military*]
W	Wrong
W	Wyoming Reports [*A publication*] (DLA)
W2	Second Statute of Westminster [*A publication*] (DSA)
W-2	Wage and Tax Statement [*IRS*]
W2	William II [*German emperor and king of Prussia, 1888-1918*] (DSUE)
W 2d	Washington State Reports, Second Series [*A publication*] (DLA)
W3	WinWhatWhere (PCM)
W3	World-Wide Web [*Information service*] [*European Organization for Nuclear Research*] (ECON)
W3C	World Wide Web Consortium [*Internet*]
W-4	Employee's Withholding Allowance Certificate [*IRS*]
W-4A	Wage Withholding Form [*Revised version*] [*IRS*]
W4D	Worth Four-Dot Test [*Ophthalmology*]
WA	Appleton Public Library, Appleton, WI [*Library symbol Library of Congress*] (LCLS)
WA	Independent Watchmen's Association
WA	Wadsworth Athneneum [*Hartford, CT*]
WA	Waferboard Association (WPI)
WA	Wage Record [*Social Security Administration*] (OICC)
WA	Wagner Act of 1935 (WYGK)
WA	Wainscot
WA	Waiters Association (NTPA)
WA	Waiver
WA	Walking Association (EA)
WA	Wallcoverings Associations (NTPA)
WA	War Aims [*British*]
WA	Warbirds of America [*Later, WB*] [*An association*] (EA)
WA	Warm Air
W/A	Warrant of Arrest
wa	Wash (VRA)
WA	Washer
WA	Washington [*State*] [*Postal code*]
Wa	Washington Reports [*A publication*] (DLA)
Wa	Washington State Library, Olympia, WA [*Library symbol Library of Congress*] (LCLS)
WA	Wassmer Aviation [*France ICAO aircraft manufacturer identifier*] (ICAO)
WA	Water Agar [*Microbiology*]
WA	Water Authority [*British*] (DCTA)
WA	Watertown Arsenal [*Massachusetts*] [*Army*]
Wa	Watts' Reports [*1890-1939*] [*A publication*] (DLA)
WA	Wave Analyzer (IAA)
WA	Waveform Analyzer
WA	Weapon Armourer [*British military*] (DMA)
WA	Weapons Analyst [*British military*] (DMA)
WA	Weapons Assignment (NVT)
WA	Weather Almanac [*A publication*]
WA	Weather Atlas of the United States [*A publication*]
WA	Wedge Action [*British military*] (DMA)
WA	Weekly Announcements
WA	Weighted Average [*Accounting*]
WA	Weizmann Israel Archives [*Rehovoth*] (BJA)
WA	Welfare Administration [*Became Social and Rehabilitation Service*] [*HEW*]
WA	Wellness Associates (EA)
Wa	Wellsiania [*An association*] (EA)
WA	West Africa
WA	Western Airlines, Inc. [*ICAO designator*]
WA	Western Allegheny Railroad (IIA)
WA	Western Approaches [*to Great Britain and Ireland*] [*Obsolete*]
WA	Western Area
WA	Western Australia [*State*] (EERA)
WA	[*The*] Western Railway of Alabama [*AAR code*]
WA	Westminster Abbey [*London*]
WA	When Awake
WA	While Awake (CPH)
WA	Widal-Abrani [*Syndrome*] [*Medicine*] (DB)
WA	Wide Angle [*Photography*]
WA	Wideband Amplifier
WA	Wilderness Act (BCP)
WA	Will Adjust (AABC)
wa	Will Advise (HGAA)
WA	Williams Act [*1968*]
WA	Willwriters Association (BUAC)
WA	Wing Attack [*Netball*]
WA	Wire Armored [*Cables*]
WA	Wire Assembly (MSA)
WA	Wire Association [*Later, WAI*]
WA	Wiskott-Aldrich [*Syndrome*] [*Medicine*] (DB)
WA	With Answers
WA	With Average [*Insurance*]
WA	Withholding Agent (DLA)
WA	Wohl Associates [*Bala Cynwyd, PA*] [*Telecommunications*] (TSSD)
WA	Woman's Auxiliary (DAVI)
WA	Women's Reserve, Aviation Nonflying Duties [*USNR officer designation*]
WA	Womenwealth Ambika [*An association British*] (EAIO)
WA	Woodfree Antique [*Paper*] (DGA)
WA	Woolknit Associates (EA)
WA	Woolwich Armstrong Gun
WA	Word Add
WA	Word After [*Message handling*]
WA	Work Assignment (MCD)
WA	Work Authorization (MCD)
WA	Workers Anonymous [*Mythical organization created by columnist Arthur Hoppe that helps hard working individuals*]
WA	Workmanship Assurance
WA	Worksafe Australia
WA	Workshop Assembly [*Torpedo*]
WA	World Bank Atlas [*Monetary conversion rate*] (ECON)
WA	Wright Aeronautical Corp. (KSC)
WA	Writing Ability
WA	Writing Academy (EA)
WA1	Wongan Hills [*Australia Seismograph station code, US Geological Survey*] (SEIS)
WA2	Wagin [*Australia Seismograph station code, US Geological Survey*] (SEIS)
Wa 2d	Washington State Reports, Second Series [*A publication*] (DLA)
WA3	Talbot Brook [*Australia Seismograph station code, US Geological Survey*] (SEIS)
WaA	Aberdeen Public Library, Aberdeen, WA [*Library symbol Library of Congress*] (LCLS)
WAA	Wabash Motor Freight Tariff Association, Springfield IL [*STAC*]
WAA	Wales [*Alaska*] [*Airport symbol*] (OAG)
WAA	Wales, AK [*Location identifier FAA*] (FAAL)
WAA	War Assets Administration [*For disposal of US surplus war property*] [*Post-World War II*]
WAA	Warden's Association of America [*Later, NAAWS*] (EA)
WAA	Waris [*Papua New Guinea*] [*Seismograph station code, US Geological Survey*] (SEIS)
WAA	Wartime Aircraft Activity (AFM)
Wa A	Washington Appellate Reports [*A publication*] (DLA)
WAA	Water-Augmented Air Jet
WAA	Water Authorities Association [*British*] (ECON)
WAA	Watermark Association of Artisans (EA)
WAA	Water Services Association (BUAC)
WAA	Welded Aluminum Alloy
WAA	West Australian Airways (ADA)
WAA	Western Amateur Astronomers (EA)
WAA	Western Association of Africanists (BUAC)
WAA	Western Awning Association [*Later, NPEA*] (EA)
WAA	Wide-Aperture Array (MCD)
WAA	Wide Area Adapter [*Computer science*] (IGQR)
WAA	Wien Air Alaska [*Air carrier designation symbol*]
WAA	Women's Action Alliance (EA)
WAA	Woolclassers' Association of Australia
WAA	Worked All America [*Amateur radio*] [*Contacted at least one station in all counties*] (IAA)
WAA	Worker Adjustment Assistance
WAA	World Aluminum Abstracts [*Aluminum Association*] [*Information service or system A publication*] (IID)
WAA	World Atlatl Association (EA)
WAA	Writing Assistants' Association [*A union*] [*British*]
WAAA	Ujung Pandang/Hasanuddin [*Indonesia*] [*ICAO location identifier*] (ICLI)
WAAA	Walleye Anglers Association of America [*Defunct*] (EA)
WAAA	Western Armenian Athletic Association (EA)
WAAA	Winston-Salem, NC [*AM radio station call letters*]
WAA(A)	Women's Action Alliance (Australia)
WAAA	Women's Amateur Athletic Association [*British*] (DBA)
WAAB	Bau Bau/Betoambari [*Indonesia*] [*ICAO location identifier*] (ICLI)
WAABI	National Women's Association of Allied Beverage Industries (EA)
WAABI	World Association of Alcohol Beverage Industries (NTPA)
WAAC	Valdosta, GA [*FM radio station call letters*]
WAAC	War Artists' Advisory Committee [*British military*] (DMA)
WAAC	West African Airways Corp.
WAAC	Western Association for Art Conservation (EA)
WAAC	Women's Army Auxiliary Corps [*Name later changed to WAC*] [*World War II*]
WAAC	Women's Art Association of Canada [*1887, Lyceum Club and Women's Art Association from 1930*] (NGC)
WAAC	Working Ampere Alternating Current (IAA)
WAAC	World Academy of Arts and Culture (EA)
WAACC	Western Australian Automobile Chamber of Commerce (BUAC)
WAACC's Motor Ind...	WAACC's [*Western Australian Automobile Chamber of Commerce*] Motor Industry [*A publication*]
WAACP	Western Atlantic Airlift Command Post [*Navy*] (DNAB)
WAACS	Western Airways and Air Communications Service (IAA)
WAAD	Tice, FL [*FM radio station call letters*]
WAAD	Westinghouse Air Arm Division
WAADA	Western Australian Alcohol and Drug Authority
WAADS	Washington Air Defense Sector [*ADC*]

WAAE........... World Association for Adult Education

WAAECG...... Western Australian Aboriginal Education Consultative Group

WAAE-FM... New Bern, NC [*FM radio station call letters*]　(RBYB)

WAAER........ World Association for the Advancement of Educational Research (BUAC)

WAAF........... Women's Auxiliary Air Force [*Functioned under direct command of RAF*] [*World War II British*]

WAAF........... Women's Auxilliary Australian Air Force　(WDAA)

WAAF........... Worcester, MA [*FM radio station call letters*]

WAAFB........ Walker Air Force Base　(AAG)

WAAG.......... Galesburg, IL [*FM radio station call letters*]

WaAG........... Grays Harbor College, Aberdeen, WA [*Library symbol Library of Congress*]　(LCLS)

WAAG.......... Malimpung [*Indonesia*] [*ICAO location identifier*]　(ICLI)

WAAG.......... Western Australian Art Gallery

WAAGA........ Western Australian Asparagus Growers' Association

WAAH.......... Houghton, MI [*FM radio station call letters*]

WAAI........... Hurlock, MD [*FM radio station call letters*]

WAAI........... Malili [*Indonesia*] [*ICAO location identifier*]　(ICLI)

WAAIC......... Women's Association of the African Independent Churches

WAAJ........... Mamuju/Tampa Padang [*Indonesia*] [*ICAO location identifier*]　(ICLI)

WAAJ........... Water-Augmented Air Jet

WAAJ-FM.... Benton, KY [*FM radio station call letters*]　(RBYB)

WAAK......... Dallas, NC [*AM radio station call letters*]

WAAL.......... Binghamton, NY [*FM radio station call letters*]

WAAL.......... Ponggaluku [*Indonesia*] [*ICAO location identifier*]　(ICLI)

WAALD........ West African Association of Agricultural Librarians and Documentalists　(BUAC)

WaAlVA....... United States Veterans Administration Hospital, American Lake, WA [*Library symbol Library of Congress*]　(LCLS)

WAAM......... Ann Arbor, MI [*AM radio station call letters*]

WAAM......... Masamba/Andi Jemma [*Indonesia*] [*ICAO location identifier*]　(ICLI)

WAAM......... Wide-Area Antiarmor Munitions [*Military*]　(MCD)

WAAMA....... Woman's Auxiliary to the American Medical Association [*Later, AMAA*]　(EA)

WAAMAC.... Weight, Alignment, and Mass Center Determination Equipment　(AAG)

WAAMH....... Western Australian Association for Mental Health

WAAMMS.... Women's Auxiliary of the American Merchant Marine [*World War II*]

WaAn.......... Anacortes Public Library, Anacortes, WA [*Library symbol Library of Congress*]　(LCLS)

WAAN.......... West African Archaeological Newsletter [*A publication*]

WAAN.......... Wide-Area AppleTalk Network [*Telecommunications*]

WAANG........ Washington Air National Guard　(MUSM)

WaAnH........ Island Hospital, Anacortes, WA [*Library symbol*] [*Library of Congress*]　(LCLS)

WAAO.......... Andalusia, AL [*FM radio station call letters*]

WAAOT........ Western Australian Association of Occupational Therapists

WAAP.......... Burlington, NC [*Television station call letters*]

WAAP.......... Kolaka/Pomalaa [*Indonesia*] [*ICAO location identifier*]　(ICLI)

WAAP.......... World Association for Animal Production [*Rome, Italy*]　(EAIO)

WAAPA........ Western Australian Academy of the Performing Arts

WAAPC........ Western Australian Apple and Pear Council

WAAPM....... Wide-Area Antipersonnel Mine [*Military*]

WAAPM-CBU... Wide Area Antipersonnel Munition Cluster Bomb Unit　(VNW)

WAAR.......... Raha/Sugi Manuru [*Indonesia*] [*ICAO location identifier*]　(ICLI)

WAAR.......... Wartime Aircraft Activity Reporting [*System*]

WaArl.......... Indian Ridge Treatment Center, Staff Library, Arlington, WA [*Library symbol Library of Congress*]　(LCLS)

WaArl-R...... Indian Ridge Treatment Center, Resident Library, Arlington, WA [*Library symbol Library of Congress*]　(LCLS)

WAAS.......... Soroako [*Indonesia*] [*ICAO location identifier*]　(ICLI)

WAAS.......... Warning and Attack Assessment　(MCD)

WAAS.......... Wide-Area Active Surveillance [*Military*]　(MCD)

WAAS.......... Wide-Area Augmentation System [*Navigation systems*]

WAAS.......... Women's Auxiliary Army Service [*British*]

WAAS.......... World Academy of Art and Science [*Solna, Sweden*]　(EA)

WAASC........ Women's Auxiliary Army Service Corps [*British*]

WAAT.......... Makale/Pongtiku [*Indonesia*] [*ICAO location identifier*]　(ICLI)

WAAT.......... Tiptonville, TN [*FM radio station call letters*]

WAATI......... West African Association of Theological Institutions　(BUAC)

WAATS........ Weights Analysis for Advanced Transportation Systems [*NASA*]

WaAu.......... Auburn Public Library, Auburn, WA [*Library symbol Library of Congress*]　(LCLS)

WAAU.......... Kendari/Wolter Monginsidi [*Indonesia*] [*ICAO location identifier*]　(ICLI)

WaAuG........ Green River Community College, Auburn, WA [*Library symbol Library of Congress*]　(LCLS)

WAAV.......... Leland, NC [*AM radio station call letters*]

WAAV-FM.... Leland, NC [*FM radio station call letters*]　(RBYB)

WAAVP........ World Association for the Advancement of Veterinary Parasitology [*Thessaloniki, Greece*]　(EAIO)

WAAW........ Williston, SC [*FM radio station call letters*]

WAAX.......... Gadsden, AL [*AM radio station call letters*]

WAAY.......... Huntsville, AL [*Television station call letters*]

WAAZ.......... Crestview, FL [*FM radio station call letters*]

WAAZ.......... Ujung Pandang [*Indonesia*] [*ICAO location identifier*]　(ICLI)

WAB........... Aero Industries, Inc. [*ICAO designator*]　(FAAC)

WAB........... Wabag [*Papua New Guinea*] [*Seismograph station code, US Geological Survey*]　(SEIS)

WAB........... Wabag [*New Guinea*] [*Airport symbol*]　(AD)

WAB........... Wabash Railroad System [*AAR oode Obsolete*]

WAB........... Waffenabwurfbehaelter [*Parachute Weapons Container*] [*German military - World War II*]

WAB........... Wage Adjustment Board [*World War II*]

WAB........... Wage Appeals Board [*Department of Labor*]

WAB........... Wales Advisory Body for Local Authority Higher Education　(BUAC)

WAB........... Water-Activated Battery

WAB........... Weapons Allocation Branch　(SAA)

WAB........... Western Actuarial Bureau [*Later, ISO*]　(EA)

WAB........... Western Aphasia Battery [*Neuropsychology test*]

WAB........... Westinghouse Air Brake [*NYSE symbol*]　(TTSB)

WAB........... Westinghouse Air Brake Co. [*NYSE symbol*]　(SAG)

WAB........... When Authorized By

WAB........... Wine Advisory Board [*Later, WAG*]　(EA)

WAB........... Work Allotment Board [*New Deal*]

WAB........... World Association for Buiatrics [*Hanover, Federal Republic of Germany*]　(EAIO)

WABA.......... Aguadilla, PR [*AM radio station call letters*]

WABA.......... Welsh Amateur Basketball Association　(BUAC)

WABA.......... Welsh Amateur Boxing Association [*British*]　(DBA)

WABA.......... West African Banks Association [*Sierra Leone*]　(BUAC)

WABA.......... Western Australian Bar Association

WABA.......... Women's American Basketball Association [*Defunct*]　(EA)

Waban.......... Waban, Inc. [*Associated Press*]　(SAG)

Wabash....... Wabash National Corp. [*Associated Press*]　(SAG)

WABASH VLY ALSA... Wabash Valley Area Library Services Authority [*Library network*]

WaBB........... Bellevue Community College, Bellevue, WA [*Library symbol Library of Congress*]　(LCLS)

WABB.......... Biak/Frans Kaisiepo [*Indonesia*] [*ICAO location identifier*]　(ICLI)

WABB.......... Mobile, AL [*AM radio station call letters*]

WABB-FM.... Mobile, AL [*FM radio station call letters*]

WaBC.......... City University Library Resource Center, Bellevue, WA [*Library symbol*] [*Library of Congress*]　(LCLS)

WABC.......... New York, NY [*AM radio station call letters*]

WABC.......... WestAmerica Bancorp [*NASDAQ symbol*]　(SAG)

WABC.......... Westamerica Bancorporation [*NASDAQ symbol*]　(TTSB)

WABC.......... Western Australian Ballet Company

WABC.......... Western Australian Bible College

WABCO........ Westinghouse Air Brake Co.

WABC-TV.... New York, NY [*Television station call letters*]

WABD.......... Fort Campbell, KY [*AM radio station call letters*]

WABD.......... Moanamani [*Indonesia*] [*ICAO location identifier*]　(ICLI)

WABE.......... Atlanta, GA [*FM radio station call letters*]

WaBe.......... Bellingham Public Library, Bellingham, WA [*Library symbol Library of Congress*]　(LCLS)

WABE.......... Western Association of Broadcast Engineers [*Canada*]

WaBeAG...... Office of Attorney General, State of Washington, Bellingham Regional Office, Bellingham, WA [*Library symbol*] [*Library of Congress*]　(LCLS)

WABEC........ Western Australian Business Education College

WaBeCo....... Whatcom County Public Library, Bellingham, WA [*Library symbol Library of Congress*]　(LCLS)

WaBeCoL.... Whatcom County Law Library, Bellingham, WA [*Library symbol*] [*Library of Congress*]　(LCLS)

WaBeSJ....... Saint Jooeph Hospital, Bellingham, WA [*Library symbol Library of Congress*]　(LCLS)

WaBeSL....... Saint Luke's Hospital, Bellingham, WA [*Library symbol Library of Congress*]　(LCLS)

WaBeW....... Western Washington State College [*Later, WWU*], Bellingham, WA [*Library symbol Library of Congress*]　(LCLS)

WABF.......... Fairhope, AL [*AM radio station call letters*]

WABF.......... Numfor/Jemburwo [*Indonesia*] [*ICAO location identifier*]　(ICLI)

WaBfM........ Mission Creek Youth Camp, Staff Library, Belfair, WA [*Library symbol Library of Congress*]　(LCLS)

WaBfM-R.... Mission Creek Youth Camp, Resident Library, Belfair, WA [*Library symbol Library of Congress*]　(LCLS)

WABG.......... Greenwood, MS [*AM radio station call letters*]

WABG.......... Waghete [*Indonesia*] [*ICAO location identifier*]　(ICLI)

WaBGS........ Church of Jesus Christ of Latter-Day Saints, Genealogical Society Library, Bellevue Branch, Bellevue, WA [*Library symbol Library of Congress*]　(LCLS)

WABG-TV.... Greenwood, MS [*Television station call letters*]

WABH.......... Bath, NY [*AM radio station call letters*]

WABI.......... Bangor, ME [*AM radio station call letters*]

WABI.......... Nabire [*Indonesia*] [*ICAO location identifier*]　(ICLI)

WABI.......... Western Australian Biographical Index [*A publication*]　(APTA)

WABI.......... Windows Application Binary Interactive [*Computer science*]

WABI-TV...... Bangor, ME [*Television station call letters*]

WABJ.......... Adrian, MI [*AM radio station call letters*]

WABK-FM.... Gardiner, ME

WABL.......... Amite, LA [*AM radio station call letters*]

WABL.......... Ilaga [*Indonesia*] [*ICAO location identifier*]　(ICLI)

WABLC........ Wilmington Area Biomedical Libraries [*Library network*]

WABM.......... Birmingham, AL [*Television station call letters*]

WABN.......... Abingdon, VA [*AM radio station call letters*]

WABN.......... Kokonau [*Indonesia*] [*ICAO location identifier*]　(ICLI)

WABN-FM.... Abingdon, VA [*FM radio station call letters*]

WABO.......... Serui/Sujarwo Condronegoro [*Indonesia*] [*ICAO location identifier*]　(ICLI)

WABO.......... Waynesboro, MS [*AM radio station call letters*]

WaBODP...... Orcale Data Publishing, Bellevue, WA [*Library symbol*] [*Library of Congress*]　(LCLS)

WABO-FM.... Waynesboro, MS [*FM radio station call letters*]

WaBOH........ Overlake Hospital, Medical Library, Bellevue, WA [*Library symbol Library of Congress*]　(LCLS)

WaBoIS....... Info-Search/NW, Bothell, WA [*Library symbol*] [*Library of Congress*]　(LCLS)

WaBP.......... Puget Sound Power and Light Co., Bellevue, WA [*Library symbol Library of Congress*]　(LCLS)

WABP.......... Timika/Tembagapura [*Indonesia*] [*ICAO location identifier*]　(ICLI)

Wa-BPH	Washington Regional Library for the Blind and Physically Handicapped, Seattle, WA [*Library symbol Library of Congress*] (LCLS)
WABQ	Cleveland, OH [*AM radio station call letters*]
WaBr	Kitsap Regional Library, Bremerton, WA [*Library symbol Library of Congress*] (LCLS)
WABR	Tifton, GA [*FM radio station call letters*]
WABR	West Asia Blocking Ridge [*Meteorology*]
WaBrH	Harrison Memorial Hospital, Bremerton, WA [*Library symbol Library of Congress*] (LCLS)
WaBrNP	United States Navy, Puget Sound Naval Shipyard, Engineering Library, Bremerton, WA [*Library symbol Library of Congress*] (LCLS)
WaBrNR	United States Navy, Naval Regional Medical Center, Bremerton, WA [*Library symbol Library of Congress*] (LCLS)
WaBrNS	United States Navy, Naval Submarine Base, Bangor Library, Bremerton, WA [*Library symbol Library of Congress*] (LCLS)
WaBrO	Olympic College, Bremerton, WA [*Library symbol Library of Congress*] (LCLS)
WaBrOC	Olympic Center, Bremerton, WA [*Library symbol Library of Congress*] (LCLS)
WABS	Arlington, VA [*AM radio station call letters*]
WaBS	Bellevue School District, Instructional Materials Center, Bellevue, WA [*Library symbol Library of Congress*] (LCLS)
WABSIH	Society for Italic Handwriting, Western American Branch [*Later, WASIH*] (EA)
WABT	Dundee, IL [*FM radio station call letters*]
WABT	Enarotali [*Indonesia*] [*ICAO location identifier*] (ICLI)
WABT	Western Aphasia Battery Test [*Speech and language therapy*] (DAVI)
WABTOC	When Authorized by the Oversea Commander [*Military*]
WABU	Biak/Manuhua [*Indonesia*] [*ICAO location identifier*] (ICLI)
WABU	Boston, MA [*Television station call letters*]
WaBucR	Rainier School, Staff Library, Buckley, WA [*Library symbol Library of Congress*] (LCLS)
WaBucR-R	Rainier School, Resident Library, Buckley, WA [*Library symbol Library of Congress*] (LCLS)
WABV-AM	Abbeville, SC [*AM radio station call letters*] (BROA)
WABW	Pelham, GA [*Television station call letters*]
WABW	Waren [*Indonesia*] [*ICAO location identifier*] (ICLI)
WABX-FM	Evansville, IN [*FM radio station call letters*] (BROA)
WABY	Albany, NY [*AM radio station call letters*]
WABY-FM	Ravena, NY [*FM radio station call letters*] (RBYB)
WABZ	Albemarle, NC [*FM radio station call letters*]
WABZ	Biak [*Indonesia*] [*ICAO location identifier*] (ICLI)
WAC	Waca [*Ethiopia*] [*Airport symbol*] (OAG)
WAC	Wage Analysis and Control (MHDB)
WAC	Wagner Computer (IAA)
WAC	Wake Analysis and Control (MCD)
WAC	War Assets Corp. [*Post-World War II*] [*Succeeded by War Assets Administration*]
WAC	Warnaco Group [*NYSE symbol*] (SPSG)
WAC	Warnaco Group'A' [*NYSE symbol*] (TTSB)
WAC	Washington Administrative Code [*A publication*] (AAGC)
WAC	Waste Acceptance Criteria (GAAI)
WAC	Water Allocation Council [*New Zealand*] (BUAC)
WAC	Water Appeals Commission [*Northern Ireland*] (BUAC)
WAC	Weak Affinity Chromatography [*Analytical chemistry*]
WAC	Weapon Arming Computer (MCD)
WAC	Weapons Assignment Console
WAC	Weber Aircraft Co.
WAC	Weighted Average Coupon [*Finance*]
WAC	Welsh Arts Council (EAIO)
WAC	West Africa Command [*World War II*]
WAC	West Africa Committee (EA)
WAC	Western Archeological Center [*Department of the Interior*] (GRD)
WAC	Western Athletic Conference (EA)
WAC	Western Australian Club
WAC	Wheat Advisory Committee (Western Australia)
WAC	Wide-Open Throttle Air-Conditioning Cut-Off Switch [*Automotive engineering*]
WAC	Wildlife Advisory Committee [*Tasmania, Australia*]
WAC	Willys Air Cooled [*Automotive engineering*]
WAC	Wolfe Angel Committee [*Defunct*] (EA)
WAC	Women's Advisory Committee [*Trades Union Congress*] [*British*] (DCTA)
WAC	Women's Advisory Committee of the British Standards Institution (BUAC)
WAC	Women's Aerobic Circuit [*Exercise regimen at some health spas*]
WAC	Women's Army Corps [*Formerly, WAAC*] [*Abolished, 1978*] (GPO)
WAC	Women's Auxiliary Corps [*British*] (DAS)
WAC	Work Accomplishment Code [*Military*] (AFIT)
WAC	Work Activities Center
WAC	Work Assessment Course (AIE)
WAC	Work Assignment Card (MCD)
WAC	Worked All Continents [*Contacted at least one station on all continents*] [*Amateur radio*]
WAC	Worked All Countries [*Contacted at least one station in all countries*] [*Amateur radio*] (IAA)
WAC	Working Alternating Current (DEN)
WAC	World Aeronautical Chart (FAAC)
WAC	World Affairs Center for the United States [*Later, FPA*]
WAC	World Air Network Co. Ltd. [*Japan ICAO designator*] (FAAC)
WAC	World Archeological Congress
WAC	World Area Code (MCD)
WAC	World Assistance Corps [*Paris, France*] (EAIO)
WAC	Wright Aeronautical Corp. (MCD)
WAC	Write Address Counter
WaCa	Camas Public Library, Camas, WA [*Library symbol*] [*Library of Congress*] (LCLS)
WACA	Walnut Canyon National Monument
WACA	West African Court of Appeal, Selected Judgments [*A publication*] (DLA)
WACA	Western Agricultural Chemicals Association (EA)
WACA	Winchester Arms Collectors Association (EA)
WACA	Women's Apparel Chains Associations [*Defunct*] (EA)
WACA	World Airlines Clubs Association [*Montreal, PQ*] (EAIO)
WACA	World Association of Center Associates (EA)
WACAAI	Women's Africa Committee of the African-American Institute (EA)
WACACT	West African Centre for Agricultural Credit Training [*Sierra Leone*] (BUAC)
WACAF	West and Central African Action Plan (BUAC)
WACAS	Wave and Current Advisory Service [*British*]
WACASC	West African Consolidated Administrative Service Center [*Foreign Service*]
WACB	Taylorsville, NC [*AM radio station call letters*]
WACB	Women's Army Classification Battery (AABC)
WACB	World Association for Christian Broadcasting (IAA)
WaCbC	Clallam Bay Correctional Center, Clallam Bay, WA [*Library symbol*] [*Library of Congress*] (LCLS)
WACC	Hialeah, FL [*AM radio station call letters*] (RBYB)
WACC	Warning and Caution Computer [*Aviation*] (MCD)
WACC	Washing Corrosion Control (MCD)
WACC	Waste Acceptance Criteria Committee [*Environmental science*] (COE)
WACC	Weighted Average Cost of Capital [*Accounting*] (ADA)
WACC	WestAmerica Corp. [*NASDAQ symbol*] (SAG)
WACC	World Africa Chamber of Commerce (EA)
WACC	World Association for Christian Communication
WACCC	Worldwide Air Cargo Commodity Classification (DS)
WACCI	Western Australian Chamber of Commerce and Industry
WACCM	World Association for Chinese Church Music (EAIO)
WACD-FM	Antigo, WI [*FM radio station call letters*] (BROA)
WACE	Chicopee, MA [*AM radio station call letters*]
WACE	Weakly Acidic Cation-Exchange Resin (DB)
WaCeC	Centralia College, Centralia, WA [*Library symbol Library of Congress*] (LCLS)
WaCeM	Maple Lane School, Staff Library, Centralia, WA [*Library symbol Library of Congress*] (LCLS)
WACEO	Western Australian Catholic Education Office
WaCeW	Weyerhaeuser Co., Forestry Research Center, Centralia, WA [*Library symbol Library of Congress*] (LCLS)
WACF	Paris, IL [*FM radio station call letters*]
WACG	Augusta, GA [*FM radio station call letters*]
WACH	Columbia, SC [*Television station call letters*]
WACH	Wedge Adjustable Cushioned Heel [*Orthopedics*]
WACH	West African Clearing House [*Sierra Leone*]
WACH	Worship Arts Clearing House (EA)
WACHA	Wisconsin Automated Clearing House Association
WaChehG	Green Hill School, Staff Library, Chehalis, WA [*Library symbol Library of Congress*] (LCLS)
WaChehHS	W.F. West High School, Chehalis, WA [*Library symbol*] [*Library of Congress*] (LCLS)
WaChehYS	Washington State Twin City Center for Youth Services, Chehalis, WA [*Library symbol Library of Congress*] (LCLS)
WaChenE	Eastern Washington State College, Cheney, WA [*Library symbol Library of Congress*] (LCLS)
Wachovia	Wachovia Corp. [*Associated Press*] (SAG)
WACI	Atlantic City, NJ [*Television station call letters*]
WACI	Western Approaches Convoy Instructions [*British military*] (DMA)
WACI	Women's Army Corps of India [*British military*] (DMA)
WACIID	Winter Advanced Course for Immunology and Infectious Diseases [*Japan International Friendship and Welfare Foundation*]
WACJ	Bowman, SC [*FM radio station call letters*]
WACK	Newark, NY [*AM radio station call letters*]
WACK	Wait and Acknowledge (IAA)
WACK	Wait before Transmitting Positive Acknowledgment
WackCor	Wackenhut Corrections Corp. [*Associated Press*] (SAG)
WackhA	Wackenhut Corp. [*Associated Press*] (SAG)
WackhB	Wackenhut Corp. [*Associated Press*] (SAG)
WaCl	Asotin County Library, Clarkston, WA [*Library symbol Library of Congress*] (LCLS)
WACL	Wacoal Corp. [*Japan NASDAQ symbol*]
WACL	Waycross, GA [*AM radio station call letters*]
WACL	Worcester Area Cooperating Libraries [*Worcester, MA*] [*Library network*]
WACL	World Anti-Communist League [*South Korea*] (EAIO)
WACLIM	Climate Data Service for West Africa [*Marine science*] (OSRA)
WaClvSC	Spruce Canyon Correctional Center, Staff Library, Colville, WA [*Library symbol Library of Congress*] (LCLS)
WaClvSC-R	Spruce Canyon Correctional Center, Resident Library, Colville, WA [*Library symbol Library of Congress*] (LCLS)
WACLY	Wacoal Corp. ADS [*NASDAQ symbol*] (TTSB)
WACM	Western Association of Circuit Manufacturers
WACM	West Springfield, MA [*AM radio station call letters*]
WACMR	West African Council for Medical Research (BUAC)
WACN	West African College of Nursing (BUAC)
WACN	Women Awareness Centre Nepal (BUAC)
WACO	Waco, TX [*AM radio station call letters*]
WACO	World Air Cargo Organisation (PDAA)
WACO	Written Advice of Contracting Officer [*Military*]

Wacoal	Wacoal Corp. ADR [*Associated Press*] (SAG)
WACO-FM	Waco, TX [*FM radio station call letters*]
WACOJ	World Affairs Council of Jerusalem [*Israel*] (BUAC)
WaCol	Whitman County Library, Colfax, WA [*Library symbol Library of Congress*] (LCLS)
WACOTA	Western Australian Council on the Ageing
WACP	West African College of Physicians (BUAC)
WACPAC	Whimsical Alternative Coalition Political Action Committee (EA)
WACQ	Tallassee, AL [*AM radio station call letters*]
WACQ	Tuskegee, AL [*FM radio station call letters*]
WACR	Columbus, MS [*AM radio station call letters*]
WACRA	World Association for Case Method Research and Application
WACRAL	World Association of Christian Radio Amateurs and Listeners [*Hull, England*] (EAIO)
WACRES	Women's Army Corps Reserve
WACR-FM	Columbus, MS [*FM radio station call letters*]
WACRI	West African Cocoa Research Institution
WACRRM	Western Australian Centre for Remote and Rural Medicine
WACS	Dawson, GA [*Television station call letters*]
WACS	Warning and Caution System [*Aviation*] (MCD)
WACS	Weather Analysis Computer System [*Accu-Weather, Inc.*]
WACS	West African College of Surgeons [*See also COAC*] [*Nigeria*] (EAIO)
Wacs	West Australian Coastal Shipping Commission (BUAC)
WACS	Whole Animal Cell Sorting
WACS	Wide Angle Collimated Display System [*Aviation*] (DA)
WACS	Wire Automated Check System (MCD)
WACS	Women Associated with Crossdressers Communication Network (EA)
WACS	Workshop Attitude Control System (MCD)
WACS	World Association of Cooks Societies (EA)
WACSC	Western Australian Coastal Shipping Commission
WACSEE	Western Australian Centre for Self Esteem Education
WACSM	Women's Army Corps Service Medal [*Military decoration*]
WACT	Tuscaloosa, AL [*AM radio station call letters*]
WACT-FM	Tuscaloosa, AL [*FM radio station call letters*]
WACU	West African Customs Union
WACU	Western Association of College and University Business Officers (AEBS)
WACV	Montgomery, AL [*AM radio station call letters*]
WACVA	Women's Army Corps Veterans Association (EA)
WACX	Leesburg, FL [*Television station call letters*]
WACY	Appleton, WI [*Television station call letters*] (RBYB)
WACY 2000	World Association for Celebrating the Year 2000 [*British*]
WAD	Andriamena [*Madagascar*] [*Airport symbol*] (OAG)
WAD	Waddy Lake Resources, Inc. [*Toronto Stock Exchange symbol Vancouver Stock Exchange symbol*]
WAD	Washington Aqueduct Division [*Army*]
WAD	Weapon Assignment Display [*Air Force*]
WAD	Weapons Alert Designator [*Army*] (ADDR)
WAD	Wide-Angle Optics Weapon Assignment Display [*DoD*]
WAD	Wide-Area Display (MCD)
WAD	William Addison Dwiggino [*American type designer and illustrator, 1880-1956*]
WAD	Work Adjustment Program [*Education*]
WAD	Work Authorization and Delegation
WAD	Work Authorization Document [*NASA*]
WAD	World Association of Detectives (EA)
WAD	World Wide Military Command Control System Automated Data Processing
WAD	Wright Aeronautical Division [*Curtiss-Wright Corp.*]
WAD	WWMCCS [*Worldwide Military Command and Control System*] Architecture Division
WADA	Shelby, NC [*AM radio station call letters*]
WADA	Wum Area Development Agency [*Cameroon*] (BUAC)
WADAAA	Washington District Army Audit Agency (MUGU)
WADB	Point Pleasant, NJ [*FM radio station call letters*]
WADB	West African Development Bank [*Togo*] (EA)
WADC	Parkersburg, WV [*AM radio station call letters*]
WADC	Western Air Defense Command
WADC	Wright Air Development Center [*Air Force*]
W ADD	With Added [*Freight*]
WADD	Wright Air Development Division [*Air Force*]
Wad Dig	Waddilove's Digest of Ecclesiastical Cases [*1849*] [*A publication*] (DLA)
WADE	Wadesboro, NC [*AM radio station call letters*]
WADE	World Association of Document Examiners (EA)
Wade Am Mining Law	Wade on American Mining Law [*A publication*] (DLA)
Wade Attachm	Wade on Attachment and Garnishment [*A publication*] (DLA)
WADEBR	Wadebridge [*England*]
Wade Min	Wade on American Mining Law [*A publication*] (DLA)
Wade Not	Wade on the Law of Notice [*A publication*] (DLA)
Wade Retro L	Wade on Retroactive Laws [*A publication*] (DLA)
WADEX	Words and Authors Index [*Computer-produced index*]
WADF	Western Air Defense Force
WADFFU	Women's Association for the Defense of Four Freedoms for Ukraine (EA)
WADGPS	Wide-Area Differential Global Positioning Satellite
WADH	Wadham College [*Oxford University*] (ROG)
WADI	Corinth, MS [*FM radio station call letters*]
WADILC	Western Australian Dairy Industry Liaison Committee
WADIS	West African Development Information System (BUAC)
WADJ	Somerset, PA [*AM radio station call letters*]
WADK	Newport, RI [*AM radio station call letters*]
WADL	Mount Clemens, MI [*Television station call letters*]
WADL	Windshear Air Data Loader [*Aviation*]
WADM	Decatur, IN [*AM radio station call letters*]

WADM	Wide-Area Defense Missile (MCD)
Wad Mar & Div	Waddilove on Marriage and Divorce [*1864*] [*A publication*] (DLA)
WADN	Concord, MA [*AM radio station call letters*]
WADO	New York, NY [*AM radio station call letters*]
WADP	World Association for Dynamic Psychiatry (EAIO)
WADQ	Westport, NY [*FM radio station call letters*]
WADR	Remsen, NY [*AM radio station call letters*]
WADR	Waste Acid Detoxification and Reclamation [*Environmental science*]
WADR	Weight Analysis Data Report
WADS	Ansonia, CT [*AM radio station call letters*]
WADS	Wide-Angle Display System
WADS	Wide-Area Data Service [*Data transmission service*]
WADSEP	Walking and Dredging Self-Elevating Platform (PDAA)
WAD/SO	Work Authorization Document/Shop Order (NASA)
WADT	Brandon, VT [*FM radio station call letters*]
WADTF	Western Atmospheric Deposition Task Force [*Environmental Protection Agency*] (GFGA)
WADU	Norco, LA [*AM radio station call letters*]
WADU	Reserve, LA [*FM radio station call letters*]
WADV	Lebanon, PA [*AM radio station call letters*]
WADVBS	World Association of Daily Vacation Bible Schools [*Later, VBS*] (EA)
WADW	Pickford, MI [*FM radio station call letters*]
WAE	Aoulef [*Algeria*] [*Airport symbol*] (AD)
WaE	Everett Public Library, Everett, WA [*Library symbol Library of Congress*] (LCLS)
WAE	Transportation Systems, Inc. [*FAA designator*] (FAAC)
WAE	Weapon Aiming Error
WAE	When [*or While*] Actually Employed [*Government short jobs*]
WAE	Wills and Administration of Estates [*Law*]
WAE	Worked All Europe [*Contacted at least one station in all European countries*] [*Amateur radio*] (IAA)
WAE	World Association of Estonians (BUAC)
WAEA	World Airline Entertainment Association
WaEawC	Canyon View Group Home, East Wenatchee, WA [*Library symbol Library of Congress*] (LCLS)
WaEawE	Eastmont High School, East Wenatchee, WA [*Library symbol*] [*Library of Congress*] (LCLS)
WAEB	Allentown, PA [*AM radio station call letters*]
WAEB-FM	Allentown, PA [*FM radio station call letters*]
WAEC	Atlanta, GA [*AM radio station call letters*]
WAEC	War Agricultural Executive Committee [*British*] (DAS)
Wa-Ec	Washington State Library, Ecology Department, Olympia, WA [*Library symbol Library of Congress*] (LCLS)
WAEC	West African Economic Community [*Ivory Coast, Mali, Mauritania, Niger, Senegal, Upper Volta*] (ASF)
WAEC	West African Examinations Council (BUAC)
WAEC	Western Australian Electoral Commission
WAEC	Wheel at Each Corner [*Automotive engineering*]
WAED	Harkers Island, NC [*FM radio station call letters*]
WAED	Westinghouse Aerospace Electrical Division
WaEdE	Edmonds Community College, Edmonds, WA [*Library symbol Library of Congress*] (LCLS)
WAEDM	World Association for Emergency and Disaster Medicine [*Bristol, England*] (EAIO)
WaEE	Everett Community College, Everett, WA [*Library symbol Library of Congress*] (LCLS)
WAEF	Bedford, NH [*FM radio station call letters*]
WAEG	Evans, GA [*FM radio station call letters*]
WaEG	Everett General Hospital, Medical Library, Everett, WA [*Library symbol Library of Congress*] (LCLS)
WaEGS	Church of Jesus Christ of Latter-Day Saints, Genealogical Society Library, Everett, Washington Stake Branch, Everett, WA [*Library symbol Library of Congress*] (LCLS)
WaEH	Health Information Network Services, Everett, WA [*Library symbol*] [*Library of Congress*] (LCLS)
WaEHP	Hewlett-Packard Co., Lake Stevens Instrument Division, Everett, WA [*Library symbol*] [*Library of Congress*] (LCLS)
WAEI	Wautoma, WI [*FM radio station call letters*]
WAEJ	Waynesboro, GA [*FM radio station call letters*]
WAEJ	World Association of Esperanto Journalists [*See also TEJA*] [*Cittadella, Italy*] (EAIO)
WaEJP	Washington State Office of Juvenile Parole Services, Everett, WA [*Library symbol Library of Congress*] (LCLS)
WaEI	Ellensburg Public Library, Ellensburg, WA [*Library symbol Library of Congress*] (LCLS)
WAEL	Maricao, PR [*FM radio station call letters*]
WAEL	Mayaguez, PR [*AM radio station call letters*]
WaEIC	Central Washington State College, Ellensburg, WA [*Library symbol Library of Congress*] (LCLS)
WAEMA	Western and English Manufacturers Association [*Denver, CO*] (EA)
WAEMB	Western Australian Egg Marketing Board
WaEn	Enumclaw Public Library, Enumclaw, WA [*Library symbol*] [*Library of Congress*] (LCLS)
WAEN	Women's Alternative Economics Network [*An association*] (CROSS)
WAEO	World Aerospace Education Organisation (BUAC)
WaEp	Ephrata Public Library, Ephrata, WA [*Library symbol Library of Congress*] (LCLS)
WAEP	World Association for Element Building and Prefabrication [*Hamburg, Federal Republic of Germany*] (EAIO)
WAEPA	War Agencies Employees Protective Association
WAEPA	Western Australian Environmental Protection Agency
WAEPA	Western Australian Environment Protection Authority (EERA)
WAEPA	Worldwide Assurance for Employees of Public Agencies [*Falls Church, VA*] (EA)

WaEPH .... Providence Hospital, Everett, WA [*Library symbol Library of Congress*] (LCLS)
WaEpS .... Sunrise Group Home, Ephrata, WA [*Library symbol Library of Congress*] (LCLS)
WAER .... Syracuse, NY [*FM radio station call letters*]
WAER .... World Association for Educational Research [*See also AMSE*] [*Ghent, Belgium*] (EAIO)
WAES .... Teutopolis, IL [*FM radio station call letters*]
WAES .... Workshop on Alternative Energy Strategies
WAEV .... Savannah, GA [*FM radio station call letters*]
WAEW .... Crossville, TN [*AM radio station call letters*]
WAEY .... Princeton, WV [*FM radio station call letters*]
WaEYS .... Washington State Center for Youth Services, Everett, WA [*Library symbol Library of Congress*] (LCLS)
WAEZ .... Elizabethton, TN [*FM radio station call letters*] (RBYB)
WAF .... Flamenco Airways, Inc. [*ICAO designator*] (FAAC)
WAF .... Wafer (AAG)
Wa-F .... Washington State Film Library, Olympia, WA [*Library symbol Library of Congress*] (LCLS)
WAF .... West African Forces [*British military*] (DMA)
WAF .... Width across Flats (MSA)
WAF .... Wiring Around Frame (MSA)
WAF .... With All Faults [*i.e., to be sold as is*]
waf .... With All Faults (WDMC)
WAF .... Woman Activist Fund (EA)
WAF .... Women against Fundamentalism [*An association*] (BUAC)
WAF .... Women in the Air Force
WAF .... Women's Aglow Fellowship (EA)
WAF .... Women's Auxiliary Force [*World War I*] [*Later, Victory Corps*] [*British*]
WAF .... Word Address Format
WAF .... World AIDS Foundation
WAF .... World Apostolate of Fatima [*The Blue Army*] (EAIO)
WAF .... Wound Angiogensis Factor [*Biochemistry*]
WAF .... Wrap-Around-Fin (PDAA)
WAFA .... Western Australian Farmers' Association
WAFA .... Western Australian Football Association
WAFA .... World Association of Flower Arrangers (BUAC)
WAFAC .... Western Australian Fruit Advisory Council
WAFAH .... West African Federation of Associations for the Advancement of Handicapped Persons [*See also FOAPH*] [*Bamako, Mali*] (EAIO)
WAFB .... Baton Rouge, LA [*Television station call letters*]
WAFB .... Warren Air Force Base [*Wyoming*] (AAG)
WAFB .... Whiteman Air Force Base (SAA)
WAFB .... Workers Aid for Bosnia [*An association*] (BUAC)
WAFBB .... Western Australian Fire Brigade Board
WAFC .... Clewiston, FL [*AM radio station call letters*]
WAFC .... Wendel Adkins Fan Club [*Defunct*] (EA)
WAFC .... West African Fisheries Commission
WAFC .... West African Fisheries Commissioner (BUAC)
WAFC .... Western Area Frequency Coordinator
WAFC .... Western Australian Football Commission
WAFC .... Workers' Autonomous Federation of China (BUAC)
WAFC .... World Area Forecast Center [*Aviation*] (FAAC)
WAFC-FM ...... Clewiston, FL [*FM radio station call letters*]
WAF/CP .... Women and Foundations/Corporate Philanthropy (EA)
WAFD .... Webster Springs, WV [*FM radio station call letters*]
WAFE .... Wives of the Armed Forces, Emeritus [*Defunct*] (EA)
WAFE .... Womens Aid Federation [*England*] (BUAC)
WAFF .... Huntsville, AL [*Television station call letters*]
WAFF .... Wartime Fuel Factors
WAFF .... West African Frontier Force
WAFF .... Western Australian Farmers Federation (EERA)
WAFF .... Wrap-Around Folding Fin (MCD)
WAFFLE .... Wide-Angle Fixed-Field Locating Equipment
WAFG .... Fort Lauderdale, FL [*FM radio station call letters*]
WAFI .... Unadilla, GA [*FM radio station call letters*]
WAFIC .... Western Australian Fishing Industry Council
WAFIC .... Western Australian Furniture Industry Council
WAFITC .... Western Australian Forest Industry Training Council
WAFJ .... Belvedere, SC [*FM radio station call letters*]
WAFL .... Milford, DE [*FM radio station call letters*]
WAFL .... Write Anywhere File Layout [*Network Appliance Corp.*] [*Computer science*]
W Af LR ...... West African Law Reports [*A publication*] (DLA)
WAFM .... Amory, MS [*FM radio station call letters*]
WaForC .... Clearwater Correctional Center, Staff Library, Forks, WA [*Library symbol Library of Congress*] (LCLS)
WaForC-R ..... Clearwater Correctional Center, Resident Library, Forks, WA [*Library symbol Library of Congress*] (LCLS)
WAFP .... Woody Allen's Fall Picture [*Designation reflecting the filmmaker's reluctance to provide information about his movies in advance of their commercial release*] [*See also WASP*]
WAFR .... Tupelo, MS [*FM radio station call letters*]
W AFR .... West Africa
WAFR .... Wrap-Around Fin Rocket (MCD)
W Afr App .... West African Court of Appeal Reports [*A publication*] (DLA)
WaFrh .... San Juan Island Public Library, Friday Harbor, WA [*Library symbol*] [*Library of Congress*] (LCLS)
WAFRI .... West African Fisheries Research Institute (BUAC)
WAFRU .... West African Fungicide Research Unit (BUAC)
WAFRY .... Western Australian Federation of Rural Youth
WAFS .... Atlanta, GA [*AM radio station call letters*]
WAFS .... Women's Air Force Services [*British military*] (DMA)

WAFS .... Women's Auxiliary Ferrying Squadron [*Part of Air Transport Command*] [*World War II*]
WAFS .... Women's Auxiliary Fire Service [*British World War II*]
WAFS .... World Area Forecast System [*Meteorology*]
WAFSRN .... West African Farming Systems Research Network [*Burkina Faso*] (BUAC)
WaFsWS .... Western State Hospital, Staff Library, Fort Steilacoom, WA [*Library symbol Library of Congress*] (LCLS)
WAFT .... Valdosta, GA [*FM radio station call letters*]
WAFT .... Wichita Auditory Fusion Test
WaFtl .... United States Army, Fort Lewis Library System, Grandstaff Library, Fort Lewis, WA [*Library symbol Library of Congress*] (LCLS)
WAFUNIF ...... World Association of Former United Nations Interns and Fellows (BUAC)
WAFV .... Wheeled Armoured Fighting Vehicle [*Military*]
WaFW .... Whatcom Community College, Ferndale, WA [*Library symbol Library of Congress*] (LCLS)
WAFWA .... Western Association of Fish and Wildlife Agencies (EA)
WaFwS .... Federal Way School District Central Library, Federal Way, WA [*Library symbol Library of Congress*] (LCLS)
WAFX .... Suffolk, VA [*FM radio station call letters*]
WAFY .... Middletown, MD [*FM radio station call letters*]
WAFZ .... Immokalee, FL [*AM radio station call letters*] (RBYB)
WAG .... The Gambia [*International civil aircraft marking*] (ODBW)
WAG .... Wagon (MSA)
WAG .... Walgreen Co. [*NYSE symbol*] (SPSG)
WAG .... Wanganui [*New Zealand*] [*Airport symbol*] (OAG)
WAG .... Warfare Analysis Group [*Navy*]
WAG .... Waste Area Grouping [*Environmental science*] (COE)
WAG .... Water-Alternating Gas [*Petroleum engineering*]
WAG .... Wellsville, Addison & Galeton Railroad Corp. [*AAR code*]
WAG .... Western Australian Green Party [*Political party*]
WAG .... Wiederaufbaugesellschaft fuer die Juedische Bevoelkerung der Bucovina [*A publication*] (BJA)
WAG .... Wild Aim Guess [*Bowdlerized version*]
WAG .... Wild-Assed-Guess Principle [*Military slang*] (VNW)
WAG .... Wild-Ass-Guess [*Aviation*]
WAG .... Wine Appreciation Guild (EA)
WAG .... Wireless Air Gunner [*British military*] (DMA)
WAG .... Women's Action Group [*Zimbabwe*] (BUAC)
WAG .... Worked All Goose (IAA)
WAG .... World Airline (Gambia) Ltd. [*ICAO designator*] (FAAC)
WAG .... World Area Grid (MCD)
WAG .... Writers' Action Group [*British*]
WAG .... WWMCCS [*Worldwide Military Command and Control System*] Action Group
WAGA .... Atlanta, GA [*Television station call letters*]
WAGA .... Welsh Amateur Gymnastic Association (DBA)
WaGal .... Intermediate School District 113, Instructional Materials Center, Galvin, WA [*Library symbol Library of Congress*] (LCLS)
WAGB .... Wildfowlers' Association of Great Britain
WAGBI .... Wildfowlers' Association of Great Britain and Ireland (BI)
WAGC .... Centre, AL [*AM radio station call letters*]
WaGc .... Grand Coulee Public Library, Grand Coulee, WA [*Library symbol Library of Congress*] (LCLS)
WAGC .... World Amateur Golf Council (EA)
WAGCOM ..... War Game Comparison (MCD)
WAGE .... Leesburg, VA [*AM radio station call letters*]
WAGE .... Union Women's Alliance to Gain Equality [*Defunct*] (EA)
Wage & Hour Rep... Wage and Hour Reporter [*Bureau of National Affairs*] [*A publication*] (DLA)
WAGF .... Dothan, AL [*AM radio station call letters*]
WAGFEI .... Women's Action Group on Excision and Infibulation [*British Defunct*] (EAIO)
WAGF-FM .... Dothan, AL [*FM radio station call letters*] (RBYB)
WAGG .... Birmingham, AL [*AM radio station call letters*]
WAGGGS ..... World Association of Girl Guides and Girl Scouts [*See also AMGE*] [*British*] (EAIO)
WAGH .... Fort Mitchell, AL [*FM radio station call letters*]
WaGhP .... Purdy Treatment Center for Women, Gig Harbor, WA [*Library symbol Library of Congress*] (LCLS)
WAGI .... Gaffney, SC [*FM radio station call letters*]
WAGL .... Lancaster, SC [*AM radio station call letters*]
WAGL .... Western Australian Gould League
WAGM .... Presque Isle, ME [*Television station call letters*]
WAGN .... Menominee, MI [*AM radio station call letters*]
Wagner C ..... Wagner College (GAGS)
WAGO-FM .... Snow Hill, NC [*FM radio station call letters*] (RBYB)
WAGP .... Beaufort, SC [*FM radio station call letters*]
WAGP .... Women's Access Grant Program [*Australia*]
WAGR .... Lexington, MS [*FM radio station call letters*]
WAGR .... Lumberton, NC [*AM radio station call letters*]
WAGR .... Wald, Arnold, Goldberg, Rushton [*Test*] [*Statistics*]
WAGR .... Western Australian Government Railways (PDAA)
WAGR .... Wilms Tumor, Aniridia, Genitourinary Abnormalities, and Mental Retardation [*Syndrome*] [*Medicine*]
WAGR .... Windscale Advanced Gas-Cooled Reactor
WAGRC .... Western Australian Government Railways Commission
WAGRO .... Warsaw Ghetto Resistance Organization (EA)
WAGS .... Bishopville, SC [*AM radio station call letters*]
WAGS .... Washington Area Girls Soccer League (TAG)
WAGS .... Weighted Agreement Scores
WAGS .... Wireless Air Gunners School [*British military*] (DMA)
WAGS .... Worldwide Atmospheric Gravity Wave Study [*Ionospheric physics*]
Wag St .... Wagner's Missouri Statutes [*A publication*] (DLA)

Wag Stat ..... Wagner's Missouri Statutes [*A publication*] (DLA)
WAGT ..... Augusta, GA [*Television station call letters*]
WAGUL ..... West Australian Group of University Librarians
WAGV ..... Harlan, KY [*Television station call letters*]
WAGX ..... Manchester, OH [*FM radio station call letters*]
WAGY ..... Forest City, NC [*AM radio station call letters*]
WAH ..... Wage and Hour Division [*Department of Labor*] (IAA)
WAH ..... Wahluke [*Washington*] [*Seismograph station code, US Geological Survey*] (SEIS)
WAH ..... WestAir Holding (EFIS)
WAH ..... Womack Army Hospital Medical Library, Fort Bragg, NC [*OCLC symbol*] (OCLC)
WAHA ..... Wide-Angle High Aperture (MCD)
WAHC ..... Circleville, OH [*FM radio station call letters*]
WAHC ..... West African Health Community (EA)
WAHC ..... Western Australian Heritage Committee
WAHC ..... World Airlines Hobby Club (EA)
WAHD ..... Wilson, NC [*FM radio station call letters*]
WAHERE ..... Western Australian Herbarium Plant Specimen Database [*State*] (EERA)
WAHH-AM ... Wilmington, NC [*AM radio station call letters*] (RBYB)
WaHi ..... Washington State Historical Society, Tacoma, WA [*Library symbol Library of Congress*] (LCLS)
WAHI-FM ..... Augusta, IL [*FM radio station call letters*] (RBYB)
WaHJ ..... Jefferson County Rural Library District, Hadlock, WA [*Library symbol*] [*Library of Congress*] (LCLS)
WAHL ..... Ocracoke, NC [*FM radio station call letters*] (RBYB)
WAHLC ..... World Association for Hebrew Language and Culture (EAIO)
Wahlco ..... Wahlco Environment Systems, Inc. [*Associated Press*] (SAG)
WAHLI ..... Indonesian Wildlife Forum [*Indonesia*] (EERA)
WAHO ..... World Arabian Horse Organization [*Windermere, England*] (EAIO)
WAHQ ..... Carolina, PR [*FM radio station call letters*]
WAHR ..... Huntsville, AL [*FM radio station call letters*]
WAHS ..... Auburn Hills, MI [*FM radio station call letters*]
WAHS ..... West African Health Secretariat (BUAC)
WAHS ..... World Airline Historical Society (EA)
WAHT-AM ..... Clemson, SC [*AM radio station call letters*] (BROA)
WAHV-FM ..... Owosso, MI [*FM radio station call letters*] (RBYB)
WAHVM ..... World Association for the History of Veterinary Medicine [*Hanover, Federal Republic of Germany*] (EAIO)
WAHY-FM ..... Midway, KY [*FM radio station call letters*] (BROA)
WAI ..... Antsohihy [*Madagascar*] [*Airport symbol*] (OAG)
WAI ..... Wairiri [*Glentunnel*] [*New Zealand*] [*Seismograph station code, US Geological Survey*] [*Closed*] (SEIS)
WAI ..... Walk Around Inspection
WAI ..... Water Absorption Index [*Analytical chemistry*]
WAI ..... Water Alcohol Injection (MCD)
WAI ..... Western Atlas [*NYSE symbol*] (TTSB)
WAI ..... Western Atlas, Inc. [*NYSE symbol*] (SAG)
WAI ..... Wire Association International (EA)
WAI ..... Work Adjustment Inventory [*Test*] (TMMY)
WAI ..... Worked All Italy [*Amateur radio*] (IAA)
WAI ..... Work in America Institute (EA)
WAIA ..... World Association of Introduction Agencies (BUAC)
WAIABS ..... Western Australian Institute of Applied Business Studies
WAIAL ..... Western Australian Institute of Applied Linguistics
WAIB ..... Tallahassee, FL [*FM radio station call letters*] (RBYB)
WAIB ..... Western Aerosol Information Bureau
WAIB ..... Western Association of Insurance Brokers
WAIC ..... Springfield, MA [*FM radio station call letters*]
WAIC ..... Western Australian Industrial Court
WAIC ..... Western Australian International College
WAICA ..... West African Insurance Companies Association [*Liberia*] (BUAC)
WAICA ..... Women's Auxiliary of the ICA [*International Chiropractors Association*] (EA)
WAID ..... Clarksdale, MS [*FM radio station call letters*]
WAID ..... Wage and Information Documents [*IRS*]
WAIF ..... World Adoption International Fund
WAIFOR ..... West African Institute for Oilpalm Research [*Nigeria*] (BUAC)
WAIH ..... Potsdam, NY [*FM radio station call letters*]
WAIHA ..... Warm Autoimmune Hemolytic Anemia [*Medicine*]
WAIIC ..... Western State Agriculture and Industrial Investment Co. [*Nigeria*] (BUAC)
WAII-FM ..... Hattiesburg, MI [*FM radio station call letters*] (RBYB)
WAIJ ..... Grantsville, MD [*FM radio station call letters*]
WAIK ..... Galesburg, IL [*AM radio station call letters*]
WAIL ..... Key West, FL [*FM radio station call letters*]
WAIM ..... Anderson, SC [*AM radio station call letters*]
WAIM ..... Wide-Angle Impedance Matching (PDAA)
WAIMH ..... World Association for Infant Mental Health (NTPA)
WAIN ..... Columbia, KY [*AM radio station call letters*]
WAIN ..... Wainwright Bank & Trust [*NYSE symbol*] (TTSB)
WAIN ..... Wainwright Bank & Trust Co. [*NASDAQ symbol*] (CTT)
WainBk ..... Wainwright Bank & Trust Co. [*Associated Press*] (SAG)
WAIN-FM ..... Columbia, KY [*FM radio station call letters*]
Wainoc ..... Wainoco Oil Corp. [*Associated Press*] (SAG)
WAIOP ..... Will Accept, If Offered, the Position [*Aviation*] (FAAC)
WAIP ..... Worked All Italian Provinces [*Amateur radio*] (IAA)
WAIP ..... World Association for Infant Psychiatry [*Later, WAIPAD*] (EA)
WAIPAD ..... World Association for Infant Psychiatry and Allied Disciplines (EA)
WAIPAD ..... World Association for Infant Psychiatry and Other Disciplines (BUAC)
WAIQ ..... Montgomery, AL [*Television station call letters*]
WAIR ..... Atlanta, MI [*FM radio station call letters*]
WAIS ..... Buchtel, OH [*AM radio station call letters*]
WAIS ..... Wechsler Adult Intelligence Scale [*Education*]
WAIS ..... West Antarctic Ice Sheet [*Geology*]
WAIS ..... Wide Area Information Server [*Computer science*]
WAIS ..... Wide Area Information Service [*or Server*] [*Telecommunications*]
WAISER ..... West African Institute for Social and Economic Research (BUAC)
WAIS-R ..... Wechsler Adult Intelligence Scale-Revised [*Test*]
WAIT ..... Crystal Lake, IL [*AM radio station call letters*]
WAIT ..... Weighted Average Inlet Temperature [*Chemical engineering*]
WAIT ..... Western Australia Institute of Technology (NITA)
Wait Act & Def ... Wait's Actions and Defences [*A publication*] (DLA)
Wait Co ..... Wait's New York Annotated Code [*A publication*] (DLA)
Wait Dig ..... Wait's New York Digest [*A publication*] (DLA)
WAITI ..... Western Australian Institute of Translators and Interpreters
Wait L & P ... Wait's Law and Practice in New York Justices' Courts [*A publication*] (DLA)
Wait Pr ..... Wait's New York Practice [*A publication*] (DLA)
WAITR ..... West African Institute for Trypanosomiasis Research (BUAC)
WAITRO ..... World Association of Industrial and Technological Research Organizations [*Arhus, Denmark*]
WAITS ..... Wide Area Information Transfer System [*Computer science*] (PCM)
Waits Prac ... Wait's New York Practice [*A publication*] (DLA)
Wait St Pap ... Wait's State Papers of the United States [*A publication*] (DLA)
Wait Tab Ca ... Wait's New York Table of Cases [*A publication*] (DLA)
WAIV ..... Spring Valley, IL [*FM radio station call letters*]
WAIZ ..... Seneca, IL [*FM radio station call letters*] (RBYB)
WAJ ..... Wajima [*Japan*] [*Seismograph station code, US Geological Survey*] (SEIS)
WAJ ..... Water-Augmented Jet
WAJ ..... World Association of Judges (EA)
WAJA ..... Arso [*Indonesia*] [*ICAO location identifier*] (ICLI)
WAJA ..... West African Journalists Association (BUAC)
WAJA ..... West African Journal of Archaeology [*A publication*]
WAJAL ..... West African Joint Agency Ltd. (BUAC)
WAJB ..... Bokondini [*Indonesia*] [*ICAO location identifier*] (ICLI)
WAJC-FM ..... Lima, OH [*FM radio station call letters*] (BROA)
WAJCSC ..... W. Alton Jones Cell Science Center, Inc. [*Research center*] (RCD)
WAJD ..... Gainesville, FL [*AM radio station call letters*]
WAJD ..... Wakde [*Indonesia*] [*ICAO location identifier*] (ICLI)
WAJE ..... New Albany, IN [*FM radio station call letters*] (RBYB)
WAJF ..... Decatur, AL [*AM radio station call letters*]
WAJI ..... Fort Wayne, IN [*FM radio station call letters*]
WAJI ..... Sarmi/Orai [*Indonesia*] [*ICAO location identifier*] (ICLI)
WAJJ ..... Jayapura/Sentani [*Indonesia*] [*ICAO location identifier*] (ICLI)
WAJK ..... Kiwirok [*Indonesia*] [*ICAO location identifier*] (ICLI)
WAJK ..... La Salle, IL [*FM radio station call letters*]
WAJL ..... Lereh [*Indonesia*] [*ICAO location identifier*] (ICLI)
WAJL ..... Pine Castle-Sky Lake, FL [*AM radio station call letters*]
WAJM ..... Mulia [*Indonesia*] [*ICAO location identifier*] (ICLI)
WAJO ..... Marion, AL [*AM radio station call letters*]
WAJO ..... Oksibil [*Indonesia*] [*ICAO location identifier*] (ICLI)
WAJQ ..... Alma, GA [*AM radio station call letters*]
WAJQ-FM ..... Alma, GA [*FM radio station call letters*]
WAJR ..... Morgantown, WV [*AM radio station call letters*]
WAJR ..... Waris [*Indonesia*] [*ICAO location identifier*] (ICLI)
WAJS ..... Senggeh [*Indonesia*] [*ICAO location identifier*] (ICLI)
WAJS ..... Tupelo, MS [*FM radio station call letters*] (RBYB)
WAJT ..... Mount Vernon, IL [*FM radio station call letters*] (RBYB)
WAJU ..... Ubrub [*Indonesia*] [*ICAO location identifier*] (ICLI)
WAJV ..... Brooksville, MS [*FM radio station call letters*] (RBYB)
WAJW ..... Chesterton, IN [*FM radio station call letters*] (RBYB)
WAJW ..... Wamena [*Indonesia*] [*ICAO location identifier*] (ICLI)
WAJY ..... New Ellenton, SC [*FM radio station call letters*]
WAJZ ..... Jayapura Sector [*Indonesia*] [*ICAO location identifier*] (ICLI)
WAK ..... Alaska Juneau Aeronautics, Inc. [*ICAO designator*] (FAAC)
WAK ..... Ankazoabo [*Madagascar*] [*Airport symbol*] (OAG)
WAK ..... Wackenhut Corp. [*NYSE symbol*] (SPSG)
WAK ..... Wackenhut Corp. Cl'A' [*NYSE symbol*] (TTSB)
WAK ..... Wait Acknowledge
wak ..... Wakashan [*MARC language code Library of Congress*] (LCCP)
WAK ..... Wakkanai [*Japan*] [*Seismograph station code, US Geological Survey*] (SEIS)
WAK ..... Water Analyzer Kit
WAK ..... Wearable Artificial Kidney
WAK ..... Write Access Key
WAKA ..... Akimuga [*Indonesia*] [*ICAO location identifier*] (ICLI)
WAKA ..... Selma, AL [*Television station call letters*]
WAK B ..... Wackenhut Corp. 'B' [*NYSE symbol*] (TTSB)
WAKB ..... Wrens, GA [*FM radio station call letters*]
WAKC ..... Akron, OH [*Television station call letters*]
WAKD ..... Mindiptana [*Indonesia*] [*ICAO location identifier*] (ICLI)
WAKD ..... Sheffield, AL [*FM radio station call letters*] (RBYB)
WAKE ..... Bade [*Indonesia*] [*ICAO location identifier*] (ICLI)
WAKE ..... Valparaiso, IN [*AM radio station call letters*]
Wake Forest Intra L Rev ... Wake Forest Intramural Law Review [*A publication*] (DLA)
Wake Forest U ... Wake Forest University (GAGS)
WaKeH ..... Kennewick General Hospital, Kennewick, WA [*Library symbol*] [*Library of Congress*] (LCLS)
WaKel ..... Kelso Public Library, Kelso, WA [*Library symbol Library of Congress*] (LCLS)
WaKeM ..... Mid-Columbia Regional Library, Kennewick, WA [*Library symbol Library of Congress*] (LCLS)
WaKenS ..... Saint Thomas Seminary, Kenmore, WA [*Library symbol Library of Congress*] (LCLS)
WAKG ..... Agats [*Indonesia*] [*ICAO location identifier*] (ICLI)
WAKG ..... Danville, VA [*FM radio station call letters*]

WAKH .... Abohoy [Indonesia] [ICAO location identifier] (ICLI)
WAKH .... McComb, MS [FM radio station call letters]
WAKI .... McMinnville, TN [AM radio station call letters]
WaKiE .... Evergreen General Hospital Library, Kirkland, WA [Library symbol] [Library of Congress] (LCLS)
WaKiN .... Northwest College, Kirkland, WA [Library symbol Library of Congress] (LCLS)
WAKJ .... DeFuniak Springs, FL [FM radio station call letters] (RBYB)
WAKK .... McComb, MS [AM radio station call letters]
WAKK .... Merauke/Mopah [Indonesia] [ICAO location identifier] (ICLI)
WAKL .... West Asia Kontena Line [Singapore] (BUAC)
WAKM .... Franklin, TN [AM radio station call letters]
WAKN .... Primapun [Indonesia] [ICAO location identifier] (ICLI)
WAKN .... Winter Harbor, ME [FM radio station call letters] (RBYB)
WAKO .... Lawrenceville, IL [AM radio station call letters]
WAKO .... Okaba [Indonesia] [ICAO location identifier] (ICLI)
WAKO-FM .... Lawrenceville, IL [FM radio station call letters]
WAKP .... Kepi [Indonesia] [ICAO location identifier] (ICLI)
WAKPAT ...... Walking Pattern (MHDI)
WAKQ .... Paris, TN [FM radio station call letters]
WAKR .... Akron, OH [AM radio station call letters]
WAKS .... Marysville, OH [FM radio station call letters]
WAKT .... Panama City Beach, FL [FM radio station call letters]
WAKT .... Tanah Merah [Indonesia] [ICAO location identifier] (ICLI)
WAKU .... Crawfordville, FL [FM radio station call letters]
WAKW .... Cincinnati, OH [FM radio station call letters]
WAKX .... Holland, MI [FM radio station call letters]
WAKY .... Greensburg, KY [AM radio station call letters]
WAKY-FM .... Springfield, KY [FM radio station call letters] (RBYB)
WAL .... Chincoteague, VA [Location identifier FAA] (FAAL)
WAL .... Lawrence University, Appleton, WI [Library symbol Library of Congress] (LCLS)
WAL .... Sierra Leone [International vehicle registration] (ODBW)
WAL .... Wahlco Environment Systems [NYSE symbol] (SPSG)
WAL .... Wahlco Enviro Systems [NYSE symbol] (TTSB)
wal .... Walamo [MARC language code Library of Congress] (LCCP)
Wal .... Waldorf [Record label]
WAL .... Wallace [Idaho] [Seismograph station code, US Geological Survey] (SEIS)
WAL .... Walloon (ROG)
WAL .... Walnut (WGA)
wal .... Walnut (VRA)
WAL .... Walsh College, Canton, OH [OCLC symbol] (OCLC)
WAL .... Warfare Analysis Laboratory [Johns Hopkins University/Applied Physics Laboratory] (DOMA)
Wa-L .... Washington State Law Library, Olympia, WA [Library symbol Library of Congress] (LCLS)
WAL .... Waterloo Resources, Inc. [Vancouver Stock Exchange symbol]
WAL .... Watertown Arsenal Laboratory [Massachusetts] [Army]
WAL .... We Are Lost [Army]
WAL .... Weather Almanac [A publication]
WAL .... Western Airlines, Inc. [Facetious translation: What an Airline]
WAL .... Western Allegheny Railroad Co. [AAR code]
WAL .... Western American Literature [A publication] (BRI)
WAL .... Western Artic Air Ltd. [Canada ICAO designator] (FAAC)
W-AL .... Westinghouse-Astronuclear Laboratories
WAL .... Wide-Angle Lens
WAL .... World Association of Lawyers (EA)
WAL .... Wright Aeronautical Laboratories (MCD)
WALA .... Mobile, AL [Television station call letters]
WALA .... West African Library Association (BUAC)
Walach .... Walachian [Romanian dialect] (BARN)
WALB .... Albany, GA [Television station call letters]
WALB .... Walbro Corp. [NASDAQ symbol] (NQ)
Walbro .... Walbro Corp. [Associated Press] (SAG)
Wal by L ...... Wallis' Irish Chancery Reports, by Lyne [A publication] (DLA)
WALC .... West African Lands Committee. Report [A publication] (ILCA)
WALC .... Worldwide Aviation Logistics Conference (RDA)
WALC-FM .... Jerseyville, IL [FM radio station call letters] (BROA)
Wal Ch .... Walker's Michigan Chancery Reports [A publication] (DLA)
WalCS .... Wallace Computer Services, Inc. [Associated Press] (SAG)
Wald .... Walden [Record label]
WALD .... Walterboro, SC [AM radio station call letters]
Waldn .... Walden Residential Properties [Associated Press] (SAG)
WaldnRP .... Walden Residential Properties [Associated Press] (SAG)
WALDO .... Wichita Automatic Linear Data Output
WALDO .... Winona Tri College University Library Network [Library network]
WALE .... Providence, RI [AM radio station call letters]
WALF .... Alfred, NY [FM radio station call letters]
Walf Cust.... Walford's Laws of the Customs [1846] [A publication] (DLA)
Walf Part.... Walford's Parties to Actions [1842] [A publication] (DLA)
Walf Railw.. Walford on Railways [2nd ed.] [1846] [A publication] (DLA)
WALG .... Albany, GA [AM radio station call letters]
Walgrn.......... Walgreen Co. [Associated Press] (SAG)
WALH .... Mountain City, GA [AM radio station call letters]
WALI-FM .... Walterboro, SC [FM radio station call letters] (RBYB)
WALIP .... Western Australian Land Information Program [State] (EERA)
WALIS .... Western Australian Land Information System [State] (EERA)
WALJ .... Gordon, GA [FM radio station call letters]
WALK .... Patchogue, NY [AM radio station call letters]
WALK .... Walk [Postal Service standard] (OPSA)
WALK .... Walker Interactive Sys [NASDAQ symbol] (TTSB)
WALK .... Walker Interactive Systems [NASDAQ symbol] (SAG)
Walk .... Walker's Michigan Chancery Reports [A publication] (DLA)
Walk .... Walker's Pennsylvania Reports [1855-85] [A publication] (DLA)

Walk .... Walker's Reports [22-25, 38-51, 72-88 Texas] [1-10 Civil Appeals Texas] [A publication] (DLA)
Walk .... Walker's Reports [1 Mississippi] [A publication] (DLA)
Walk .... Walker's Reports [96, 109 Alabama] [A publication] (DLA)
Walk Am Law... Walker's American Law [A publication] (DLA)
Walk Bank L... Walker's Banking Law [2nd ed.] [1885] [A publication] (DLA)
Walk Ch....... Walker's Michigan Chancery Reports [A publication] (DLA)
Walk Chanc Rep... Walker's Michigan Chancery Reports [A publication] (DLA)
Walk Ch Cas... Walker's Michigan Chancery Reports [A publication] (DLA)
Walk Ch Mich... Walker's Michigan Chancery Reports [A publication] (DLA)
Walk Com L... Walker's Theory of the Common Law [A publication] (DLA)
Walk Eq Pl... Walker's Equity Pleader's Assistant [A publication] (DLA)
Walker.......... Walker's Michigan Chancery Reports [A publication] (DLA)
Walker.......... Walker's Pennsylvania Reports [1855-85] [A publication] (DLA)
Walker.......... Walker's Reports [22-25, 38-51, 72-88 Texas] [1-10 Civil Appeals Texas] [A publication] (DLA)
Walker.......... Walker's Reports [96, 109 Alabama] [A publication] (DLA)
Walker.......... Walker's Reports [1 Mississippi] [A publication] (DLA)
Walker's Ch R... Walker's Michigan Chancery Reports [A publication] (DLA)
Walk Exec .. Walker and Elgood's Executors and Administrators [6th ed.] [1926] [A publication] (DLA)
WALK-FM .... Patchogue, NY [FM radio station call letters]
WalkInt .... Walker Interactive Systems, Inc. [Associated Press] (SAG)
Walk Int.... Walker's Introduction to American Law [A publication] (DLA)
Walk LA Dig... Walker's Louisiana Digest [A publication] (DLA)
Walk (Mic) Ch... Walker's Michigan Chancery Reports [A publication] (DLA)
Walk Mich... Walker's Michigan Chancery Reports [A publication] (DLA)
Walk Michig Rep... Walker's Michigan Chancery Reports [A publication] (DLA)
Walk Miss ... Walker's Reports [1 Mississippi] [A publication] (DLA)
Walk PA .... Walker's Pennsylvania Reports [1855-85] [A publication] (DLA)
Walk Pat.... Walker on Patents [A publication] (DLA)
WALKS .... Walks [Commonly used] (OPSA)
Walk Tex ..... Walker's Reports [22-25, 38-51, 72-88 Texas] [1-10 Civil Appeals Texas] [A publication] (DLA)
Walk Wills... Walker on Wills [A publication] (DLA)
WALL .... Middletown, NY [AM radio station call letters]
WALL .... Wall [Postal Service standard] (OPSA)
Wall .... Wallace's Nova Scotia Reports [A publication] (DLA)
Wall .... Wallace's Supreme Court Reports [68-90 United States] [1863-74] [A publication] (DLA)
Wall .... Wallace's United States Circuit Court Reports [A publication] (DLA)
Wall .... Wallace's United States Reports [1863-74] [A publication] (AAGC)
WALL .... Wallachian (ROG)
WALL .... Wall Data [NASDAQ symbol] (TTSB)
WALL .... Wall Data, Inc. [NASDAQ symbol] (SAG)
WALL .... Wallingford [Municipal borough in England]
Wall .... Wallis' Irish Chancery Reports [A publication] (DLA)
Wall .... Wallis' Philadelphia Reports [1855-85] [Pennsylvania] [A publication] (DLA)
WALL .... Walloon (ROG)
WALL .... Western Australian Law Libraries
Walla Walla C... Walla Walla College (GAGS)
Wall CC .... Wallace's United States Circuit Court Reports [A publication] (DLA)
WallData ..... Wall Data, Inc. [Associated Press] (SAG)
Wallis.......... Wallis' Irish Chancery Reports [A publication] (DLA)
Wallis by L... Wallis' Irish Chancery Reports, by Lyne [1776-91] [A publication] (DLA)
Wallis by Lyne... Wallis' Irish Chancery Reports, by Lyne [1766-91] [A publication] (DLA)
Wallis (Ir).... Wallis' Irish Chancery Reports [A publication] (DLA)
Wall Lyn...... Wallis' Irish Chancery Reports, by Lyne [1776-91] [A publication] (DLA)
Wall Pr........ Wallace's Principles of the Laws of Scotland [A publication] (DLA)
Wall Rep .... Wallace's Supreme Court Reports [68-90 United States] [A publication] (DLA)
Wall Rep .... Wallace's "The Reporters" [A publication] (DLA)
Wall SC .... Wallace's Supreme Court Reports [68-90 United States] [A publication] (DLA)
WallSDI ...... Wall Street Deli Co. [Associated Press] (SAG)
WALM.......... Albion, MI [AM radio station call letters]
WalMart ...... Wal-Mart Stores, Inc. [Associated Press] (SAG)
WALN .... Carrollton, AL [FM radio station call letters] (RBYB)
WalnutF...... Walnut Financial Services, Inc. [Associated Press] (SAG)
WALO .... Humacao, PR [AM radio station call letters]
WaLo .... Longview Public Library, Longview, WA [Library symbol Library of Congress] (LCLS)
WaLoGS .... Church of Jesus Christ of Latter-Day Saints, Genealogical Society Library, Longview Stake Branch, Longview, WA [Library symbol Library of Congress] (LCLS)
WaLoL .... Lower Columbia College, Longview, WA [Library symbol Library of Congress] (LCLS)
WaLop .... Lopez Island Library District, Lopez, WA [Library symbol] [Library of Congress] (LCLS)
WALOPT .... Weapons Allocation and Desired Ground-Zero Optimizer [Military]
WaLoSH .... St. John's Hospital, Longview, WA [Library symbol] [Library of Congress] (LCLS)
WALP.......... Weapons Assignment Linear Program
WALP.......... World Association of Law Professors (EA)
Wal Prin .... Wallace's Principles of the Laws of Scotland [A publication] (DLA)
Walp Rub .... Walpole's Rubric of Common Law [A publication] (DLA)
WALQ .... Poughkeepsie, NY [FM radio station call letters] (RBYB)
WALR .... Athens, GA [FM radio station call letters]
WALR .... Atlanta, GA [AM radio station call letters] (RBYB)
WALR .... West African Law Reports [Gambia, Ghana, and Sierra Leone] [A publication] (DLA)

WaLrC .... Cedar Creek Youth Camp, Littlerock, WA [*Library symbol Library of Congress*] (LCLS)
WALRC Bull... Western Australia Law Reform Commission. Bulletin [*A publication*]
WALRUS...... Water and Land Resources Use Simulation
WALRUS...... Water and Land Resource Utilization Simulation
WALS.......... Oglesby, IL [*FM radio station call letters*] (RBYB)
WALS.......... Walshire Assurance [*NASDAQ symbol*] (TTSB)
WALS.......... Walshire Assurance Co. [*NASDAQ symbol*] (NQ)
WALS.......... West African Linguistic Society (BUAC)
WALS.......... World Association of Law Students (EA)
Walsh .... Walsh's Irish Registry Cases [*A publication*] (DLA)
Walshr......... Walshire Assurance Co. [*Associated Press*] (SAG)
WALT.......... Meridian, MS [*AM radio station call letters*]
WALT.......... Warning Assessment Logic Terminal [*Air Force*]
WALT.......... West's Automatic Law Terminal
WALTA......... Western Australian Lawn Tennis Association
Walter .... Walter Industries, Inc. [*Associated Press*] (SAG)
Walter .... Walter's Reports [*14-16 New Mexico*] [*A publication*] (DLA)
Walter C .... Walter's Code [*A publication*] (DLA)
Walt H & W... Walton on Husband and Wife [*Scotland*] [*A publication*] (DLA)
Walt Lim ...... Walter's Statute of Limitations [*4th ed.*] [*A publication*] (DLA)
WALTSTOW... Walthamstow [*England*]
Wal US Rep... Wallace's United States Reports [*A publication*] (DLA)
WALV.......... Cleveland, TN [*FM radio station call letters*]
WALX.......... Selma, AL [*FM radio station call letters*]
WALY.......... Bellwood, PA [*FM radio station call letters*]
WALZ.......... Machias, ME [*AM radio station call letters*] (RBYB)
WALZ-AM .... Machias, ME [*AM radio station call letters*] (RBYB)
WALZ-FM .... Machias, ME
WAM........... Ambatondrazaka [*Madagascar*] [*Airport symbol*] (OAG)
WAM........... Appleton Memorial Hospital, Appleton, WI [*Library symbol Library of Congress*] (LCLS)
WAM........... Emirates News Agency [*United Arab Emirates*] (MENA)
WAM........... Waitress-Actress-Model [*Lifestyle classification*]
WAM........... Walleye Measurements Program
WAM........... Wambrook [*Australia Seismograph station code, US Geological Survey*] (SEIS)
WAM........... Warburton Minerals [*Vancouver Stock Exchange symbol*]
WAM........... Wave Model (USDC)
WAM........... Weapon Allocation Model
WAM........... Weight after Melt [*Metallurgy*]
WAM........... Weighted Average Maturity [*Finance*]
WAM........... Western Apparel Manufacturers Show (ITD)
WAM........... Western Associated Modelers (EA)
WAM........... Western Australian Mint
WAM........... Western Australian Museum
W AM .... White American Male (WDAA)
WAM........... Wide-Area Mine [*Military*] (MCD)
WAM........... Women in Advertising and Marketing (EA)
WAM........... Women's Action Movement
WAM........... Words a Minute
WAM........... Work Analysis and Measurement (WDAA)
WAM........... Working Association of Mothers [*British*] (DI)
WAM........... Worth Analysis Model (IEEE)
wam............ Writer of Accompanying Material [*MARC relator code*] [*Library of Congress*] (LCCP)
WAMA .... Galela/Gamarmalamo [*Indonesia*] [*ICAO location identifier*] (ICLI)
WAMA .... Tampa, FL [*AM radio station call letters*]
WAMA .... Watermarc Food Management Co. [*NASDAQ symbol*] (SAG)
WAMA .... Watermarc Food Mgmt [*NASDAQ symbol*] (TTSB)
WAMA .... Weight after Mars Arrival [*NASA*]
WAMACCR... Western Australian Ministerial Advisory Council on Community Relations
WAMAP .... Watermarc Food Mgmt 9% Cv Pfd [*NASDAQ symbol*] (TTSB)
WaMaS........ Sno-Isle Regional Library, Marysville, WA [*Library symbol Library of Congress*] (LCLS)
WAMAW ...... Watermarc Food Mgmt Wrrt'A' [*NASDAQ symbol*] (TTSB)
WAMB .... Donelson, TN [*AM radio station call letters*]
WAMB .... Kotamubagu/Mopait [*Indonesia*] [*ICAO location identifier*] (ICLI)
WAmBc........ WestAmerica Bancorp [*Associated Press*] (SAG)
WAMB-FM ... Donelson, TN [*FM radio station call letters*]
WAMC .... Albany, NY [*FM radio station call letters*]
WAMC .... Tentena [*Indonesia*] [*ICAO location identifier*] (ICLI)
WAMC .... Western Australian Meat Commission
WAMC .... Wide Area Mine Clearance [*Army*] (DOMA)
WaMcA........ McChord Air Force Base, Base Library, McChord Air Force Base, WA [*Library symbol*] [*Library of Congress*] (LCLS)
WAMCE........ Western Association of Minority Consulting Engineers (IAA)
WAMD .... Aberdeen, MD [*AM radio station call letters*]
WAMD .... Jailolo/Kuripasai [*Indonesia*] [*ICAO location identifier*] (ICLI)
WAMDEVIN... West African Management Development Institutions Network [*Nigeria*] (BUAC)
WAMDII .... Wide-Angle, Michelson-Doppler Imaging Interferometer (SSD)
WAME.......... Camden, SC [*AM radio station call letters*] (RBYB)
WaMeH........ Eastern State Hospital, Medical Lake, WA [*Library symbol Library of Congress*] (LCLS)
WaMeI......... Interlake School, Staff Library, Medical Lake, WA [*Library symbol Library of Congress*] (LCLS)
WaMeL......... Lakeland Village School, Medical Lake, WA [*Library symbol Library of Congress*] (LCLS)
WaMeP........ Pine Lodge Correctional Center, Staff Library, Medical Lake, WA [*Library symbol Library of Congress*] (LCLS)
WaMeP-R .... Pine Lodge Correctional Center, Resident Library, Medical Lake, WA [*Library symbol Library of Congress*] (LCLS)
WAMEX........ West African Monsoon Experiment [*Marine science*] (OSRA)
WAMF.......... Tallahassee, FL [*FM radio station call letters*]
WAMF.......... Welsh Amateur Music Federation (BUAC)
WAMFLEX.... Wave Momentum Flux Experiment [*National Science Foundation*]
WAMG .... Gorontalo/Jalaluddin [*Indonesia*] [*ICAO location identifier*] (ICLI)
WAMG .... Wauwatosa-Milwaukee, WI [*FM radio station call letters*] (RBYB)
WAMH .... Amherst, MA [*FM radio station call letters*]
WAMH .... Tahuna/Naha [*Indonesia*] [*ICAO location identifier*] (ICLI)
WAMI.......... Opp, AL [*AM radio station call letters*]
WAMI.......... Toli Toli/Lalos [*Indonesia*] [*ICAO location identifier*] (ICLI)
WAMI.......... Washington, Alaska, Montana, and Idaho [*Program for states without medical schools*]
WAMI.......... Wide-Angle Michelson Interferometer (PDAA)
WAMI.......... World Association for Medical Informatics (IAA)
WAMI-FM .... Opp, AL [*FM radio station call letters*]
WaMiH .... Highline Community College, Midway, WA [*Library symbol Library of Congress*] (LCLS)
WaMil.......... Milton Memorial Library, Milton, WA [*Library symbol*] [*Library of Congress*] (LCLS)
WAMIS .... Watershed Management Information System
WAMITAB .... Waste Management Industry Training and Advisory Board (BUAC)
WAMK .... Kao/Kuabang [*Indonesia*] [*ICAO location identifier*] (ICLI)
WAMK .... Kingston, NY [*FM radio station call letters*]
WAML.......... Laurel, MS [*AM radio station call letters*]
WaMl........... Moses Lake Public Library, Moses Lake, WA [*Library symbol Library of Congress*] (LCLS)
WAML.......... Palu/Mutiara [*Indonesia*] [*ICAO location identifier*] (ICLI)
WAML.......... Watertown Arsenal Medical Laboratory [*Massachusetts*] [*Army*]
WAML.......... Western Association of Map Libraries (EA)
WAML.......... Work Authorization Material List (DNAB)
WAML.......... Wright Aero Medical Laboratory [*Air Force*]
WAMLA........ West African Modern Language Literature Association (BUAC)
WaMlB......... Big Bend Community College, Moses Lake, WA [*Library symbol Library of Congress*] (LCLS)
WaMlGS ...... Church of Jesus Christ of Latter-Day Saints, Genealogical Society Library, MosesLake Branch, Moses Lake, WA [*Library symbol Library of Congress*] (LCLS)
WAMM......... Bridgewater, VA [*FM radio station call letters*]
WAMM......... Manado/Sam Ratulangi [*Indonesia*] [*ICAO location identifier*] (ICLI)
WAMM......... Women Against Military Madness (EA)
WAMM......... Woodstock, VA [*AM radio station call letters*]
WAMMC ...... Western Australian Meat Marketing Corp. [*Commercial firm*]
WAMN .... Green Valley, WV [*AM radio station call letters*]
WAMN .... Melangguane [*Indonesia*] [*ICAO location identifier*] (ICLI)
WAMO .... Pittsburgh, PA [*FM radio station call letters*]
WAMO-AM... Pittsburgh, PA [*AM radio station call letters*] (RBYB)
WAMOC .... Women's Auxiliary to the Military Order of the Cootie (EA)
WaMonR....... Washington State Reformatory, Monroe, WA [*Library symbol Library of Congress*] (LCLS)
WaMonT ...... Twin Rivers Correctional Center, Monroe, WA [*Library symbol Library of Congress*] (LCLS)
WAMOSCOPE... Wave-Modulated Oscilloscope
WAMP .... Jackson, TN [*FM radio station call letters*] (RBYB)
WAMP .... Poso/Kasigunou [*Indonesia*] [*ICAO location identifier*] (ICLI)
WAMP .... Wire Antenna Modeling Program (PDAA)
WAMPUM .... Wage and Manpower Process Utilizing Machine [*Bureau of Indian Affairs*]
WAMPUM .... Wartime Availability of Medical Personnel upon Mobilization
WAMQ .... Bada [*Indonesia*] [*ICAO location identifier*] (ICLI)
WAMQ .... Great Barrington, MA [*FM radio station call letters*]
WAMR .... Morotai/Pitu [*Indonesia*] [*ICAO location identifier*] (ICLI)
WAMR .... Venice, FL [*AM radio station call letters*]
WAMRAC ..... World Association of Methodist Radio Amateurs and Clubs
WAMR-FM ... Miami, FL [*FM radio station call letters*] (RBYB)
WAMRL .... Western Australian Marine Research Laboratory
WAMRU .... West African Maize Research Unit (BUAC)
WAMS .... Weapon Aiming and Mode Selector (MCD)
WAMS .... Wholesale Applications Management System (MHDB)
WAMS .... Women's Automotive Maintenance Staff
WAMS .... World Association of Military Surgeons (BUAC)
WAMS-AM ... Wilmington, DE [*AM radio station call letters*] (BROA)
WAMSTAS ... Wide-Area Mine Seismic Target Acquisition Sensor [*Military*] (MCD)
WAMT.......... Ternate/Babullah [*Indonesia*] [*ICAO location identifier*] (ICLI)
WAMT.......... Titusville, FL [*AM radio station call letters*]
WAMT.......... Women and Manual Trades [*British*] [*An association*] (DBA)
WaMtJF .... John Fluke Manufacturing Co., Mountlake Terrace, WA [*Library symbol Library of Congress*] (LCLS)
WAMTMC .... Western Area Military Traffic Management Command (DICI)
WAMTMTS... Western Area, Military Traffic Management and Terminal Service (AABC)
WaMtv......... Mount Vernon Public Library, Mount Vernon, WA [*Library symbol Library of Congress*] (LCLS)
WaMtvGS .... Church of Jesus Christ of Latter-Day Saints, Genealogical Society Library, MountVernon Branch, Mount Vernon, WA [*Library symbol Library of Congress*] (LCLS)
WaMtvH....... Skagit Valley Hospital, Mount Vernon, WA [*Library symbol*] [*Library of Congress*] (LCLS)
WaMtvS....... Skagit Valley College, Mount Vernon, WA [*Library symbol Library of Congress*] (LCLS)
WAMU .... Washington, DC [*FM radio station call letters*]
WAMU .... Washington Mutual [*NASDAQ symbol*] (TTSB)
WAMU .... Washington Mutual, Inc. [*NASDAQ symbol*] (NQ)
WAMU .... West African Monetary Union (BUAC)
WAMU .... Wuasa [*Indonesia*] [*ICAO location identifier*] (ICLI)
WAMUM ...... Washington Mutual 7.60% 'E' Pfd' [*NASDAQ symbol*] (TTSB)
WAMUN ...... Wash Mutual $6 Cv Per'D'Pfd [*NASDAQ symbol*] (TTSB)

WAMUO....... Washington Mutual $2.28'C'Pfd [NASDAQ symbol] (TTSB)
WA Mutl ...... Washington Mutual, Inc. [Associated Press] (SAG)
WAMV .... Amherst, VA [AM radio station call letters]
WAMW .... Luwuk/Bubung [Indonesia] [ICAO location identifier] (ICLI)
WAMW .... Washington, IN [AM radio station call letters]
WAMW-FM... Washington, IN [FM radio station call letters]
WAMX .... Saline, MI [AM radio station call letters]
WAMY .... Amory, MS [AM radio station call letters]
WAMY .... World Assembly of Muslim Youth [Riyadh, Saudi Arabia] (EAIO)
WAMZ .... Louisville, KY [FM radio station call letters]
WAMZ .... Menado Sector [Indonesia] [ICAO location identifier] (ICLI)
WAn .... Antigo Public Library, Antigo, WI [Library symbol Library of Congress] (LCLS)
WAN .... Wane Aviation Ltd. [Kenya] [FAA designator] (FAAC)
WAN .... Wanigan
WAN .... Wanliss Street [New Britain] [Seismograph station code, US Geological Survey] (SEIS)
WAN .... Waverley [Queensland] [Airport symbol] (AD)
WAN .... Western Air Navigation Ltd. [Australia]
WAN .... Wide Area Network [Telecommunications]
WAN .... Women's Aquatic Network (EA)
WAN .... Women's Royal Australian Naval Service [World War II] (DSUE)
WAN .... Work Authorization Number (NASA)
WANA .... Anniston, AL [AM radio station call letters]
WANA .... Woodworking Association of North America (EA)
WANAP .... Washington [DC] National Airport
WaNasY...... Naselle Youth Camp, Staff Library, Naselle, WA [Library symbol Library of Congress] (LCLS)
WaNasY-R... Naselle Youth Camp, Resident Library, Naselle, WA [Library symbol Library of Congress] (LCLS)
WANB .... Waynesburg, PA [AM radio station call letters]
WANB-FM.... Waynesburg, PA [FM radio station call letters]
WANC .... Ticonderoga, NY [FM radio station call letters]
WANC .... Western Australian Naturalists' Club (EERA)
WAND .... Decatur, IL [Television station call letters]
WAND .... Milestone Scientific, Inc. [NASDAQ symbol] (SAG)
WAND .... Waveform Analysis for Nondestructive Evaluation [Military computer software] (RDA)
WAND .... Westinghouse Alphanumeric Display (IAA)
WAND .... Women and Development Unit (EA)
WAND .... Women's Action for New Directions [An association]
WAND .... Women's Action for Nuclear Disarmament (EA)
W & ACT .... Wey and Arun Canal Trust [British] (DBA)
WANDAH ..... Writing-Aid and Author's Helper (EDAC)
W & B .... Walferstan and Bristowe's Election Cases [1859-65] [A publication] (DLA)
W&B .... Weight and Balance (NAKS)
W & B .... Works and Building Services [British military] (DMA)
W & B Dig... Walter and Bates' Ohio Digest [A publication] (DLA)
W & C .... Westmorland and Cumberland Yeomanry [British military] (DMA)
W & C .... Wilson and Courtenay's Scotch Appeal Cases [A publication] (DLA)
W & C .... Wire and Cable (NASA)
W & C Conv... Wolstenholme and Cherry's Conveyancing Statutes [13th ed.] [1972] [A publication] (DLA)
W & D .... Wolferstan and Dew's English Election Cases [1856-58] [A publication] (DLA)
W&E .... [CSIRO Division of] Wildlife and Ecology [Commonwealth] (EERA)
WAND EF.... WAND [Women's Action for Nuclear Disarmament] Education Fund (EA)
Wandell....... Wandell's New York Reports [A publication] (DLA)
W & F......... Water and Feed
W & F......... Work and Flop [Printing] (WDMC)
WandGlt ...... Wandel & Goltermann Technologies [Associated Press] (SAG)
W & H .... Wage and Hour Division [Department of Labor] (OICC)
W & I......... Weighing and Inspection
W&I............ World & I [A publication] (BRI)
W & IR .... Work and Inspection Record (SAA)
W & J......... Washington and Jefferson College [Pennsylvania] (IIA)
W&K........... Winzler & Kelly (EFIS)
W & L......... Washington and Lee University [Lexington, VA]
W & L......... Weapon and/or Launcher
W & L......... Welshpool & Llanfair Light Railway [Wales]
W & L......... Westcott & Laurance Line [Steamship] (MHDW)
W & L Dig... Wood and Long's Digest [Illinois] [A publication] (DLA)
W & LLR .... Welshpool & Llanfair Light Railway [Wales]
WandIst...... Wanderlust Interactive, Inc. [Associated Press] (SAG)
WandIust...... Wanderlust Interactive, Inc. [Associated Press] (SAG)
W & M......... War and Marine (DS)
W & M......... Washburn and Moen [Wire gauge]
W & M......... William and Mary [King and Queen of England] (ROG)
W & M......... Wilson & McLane, Inc. [Information service or system] (IID)
W & M......... Woodbury and Minot's United States Circuit Court Reports [3 vols.] [A publication] (DLA)
W & M GA... Washburn and Moen Gauge (MSA)
W&M Q....... William and Mary Quarterly [A publication] (BRI)
W & N .... Weidenfeld & Nicolson [Publisher]
W & N .... Wharton & Northern [Railroad] (MHDB)
W & O Wills... Wilgram and O'Hara on Wills [A publication] (DLA)
W & PH ...... Wage and Purchase Hire
W & R .... Welfare and Recreation [Navy]
W & S .... Watts and Sergeant's Pennsylvania Reports [1841-1845] [A publication] (DLA)
W & S .... Whiskey and Soda
W & S .... Wilson and Shaw's Scotch Appeal Cases, English House of Lords [A publication] (DLA)

W & S App... Wilson and Shaw's Scotch Appeal Cases, English House of Lords [A publication] (DLA)
W & StP...... Winona & St. Peter Railroad
W & T......... Work-and-Turn [Printing] (WDMC)
W & T......... Wrightsville & Tennille Railroad (IIA)
W & T Eq Ca... White and Tudor's Leading Cases in Equity [9 eds.] [1849-1928] [A publication] (DLA)
W & TLC...... White and Tudor's Leading Cases In Equity [9 eds.] [1849-1928] [A publication] (DLA)
W & W .... De Witt and Weeresinghe's Appeal Court Reports [Ceylon] [A publication] (DLA)
W & W .... Wahlstrom & Widstrand [Publisher] [Sweden]
W & W .... White and Wilson's [or Willson's] Civil Cases, Texas Court of Appeals [A publication] (DLA)
W & W .... Williams & Wilkins [Publishing company]
W & WCC .... White and Wilson's [or Willson's] Civil Cases, Texas Court of Appeals [A publication] (DLA)
W & W Civ Cases Court of Appeals... White and Wilson's [or Willson's] Civil Cases, Texas Court of Appeals [A publication] (DLA)
W & W Con Cases... White and Wilson's [or Willson's] Civil Cases, Texas Court of Appeals [A publication] (DLA)
W & W Con Rep... White and Wilson's [or Willson's] Civil Cases, Texas Court of Appeals [A publication] (DLA)
W & WT ...... Water and Waste Treatment
WANE .... Fort Wayne, IN [Television station call letters]
WaNe.......... Pend Oreille County Library District, Newport, WA [Library symbol Library of Congress] (LCLS)
WANG......... Wang Laboratories [NASDAQ symbol] (TTSB)
WANG......... Wang Laboratories, Inc. [NASDAQ symbol] (SAG)
WangL........ Wang Laboratories, Inc. [Associated Press] (SAG)
WangLab .... Wang Laboratories, Inc. [Associated Press] (SAG)
WANGW....... Wang Labs Wrrt [NASDAQ symbol] (TTSB)
WANI-AM..... Opelika, AL [AM radio station call letters] (BROA)
WANL .... Albany, GA [AM radio station call letters]
WANL .... Westinghouse-Astronuclear Laboratories
WANM .... Tallahassee, FL [AM radio station call letters]
WANN .... Annapolis, MD [AM radio station call letters]
WANO .... Pineville, KY [AM radio station call letters]
WANO .... World Association of Nuclear Operators (ECON)
WANOPC..... World Association of Nuclear Power Operators [France] (BUAC)
WANR .... Warren, OH [AM radio station call letters]
WANS .... Anderson, SC [AM radio station call letters]
WANST........ Wanstead [England]
WANT .... Lebanon, TN [FM radio station call letters]
WANT .... Wages and Not Tips [An association] (EA)
WANT .... Wantage [Urban district in England]
WANT .... Warrant Apprehension Narcotics Team [In US Marshal Service's "Operation WANT"]
WANTC .... Western Australian Nanny Training College
WANU-FM.... Lewistown, PA [FM radio station call letters] (RBYB)
WANX .... Holly Hill, FL [FM radio station call letters] (RBYB)
WANY .... Albany, KY [AM radio station call letters]
WANY-FM.... Albany, KY [FM radio station call letters]
WAO .... Outagamie County Hospital, Appleton, WI [Library symbol Library of Congress] (LCLS)
WaO............ Timberland Regional Library, Olympia, WA [Library symbol Library of Congress] (LCLS)
WAO .... Weapons Assignment Officer [Air Force] (AFM)
WAO .... Western Australian Opera
WAO .... Wet-Air Oxidation (PDAA)
WAO .... Women's Aid Organization [Malaysia] (BUAC)
WAO .... Women's American ORT (EA)
WAO .... World Association for Orphans and Abandoned Children (BUAC)
WAOA .... Melbourne, FL [FM radio station call letters]
WaOAP........ Washington State Office of Adult Probation and Parole, Olympia, WA [Library symbol Library of Congress] (LCLS)
WaOAr........ State of Washington Department of General Administration, Division of Archives and Records Management, Olympia, WA [Library symbol Library of Congress] (LCLS)
WaOB .... Washington State Department of Public Assistance, Ben Tidball Memorial Library, Olympia, WA [Library symbol Library of Congress] (LCLS)
WAOB .... World Agricultural Outlook Board [Department of Agriculture] (GFGA)
WAOC .... St. Augustine, FL [AM radio station call letters]
WAOC .... Western Australian Olympic Council
WaOCA........ Washington State Court of Appeals, Olympia, WA [Library symbol Library of Congress] (LCLS)
WaOE .... Evergreen State College, Olympia, WA [Library symbol Library of Congress] (LCLS)
WaOEd........ Washington State Department of Education, Olympia, WA [Library symbol Library of Congress] (LCLS)
WaOEng...... Washington State Energy Office, Olympia, WA [Library symbol Library of Congress] (LCLS)
WAOE-TV..... Peoria, IL [TV station call letters] (RBYB)
WAOF .... Mount Juliet, TN [FM radio station call letters] (RBYB)
WaOGS........ Church of Jesus Christ of Latter-Day Saints, Genealogical Society Library, Olympia Branch, Olympia, WA [Library symbol Library of Congress] (LCLS)
WAOH......... Outagamie County Health Center, Appleton, WI [Library symbol] [Library of Congress] (LCLS)
WAOHE........ Western Australian Office of Higher Education
WaOhNH...... United States Naval Hospital, Medical Library, Oak Harbor, WA [Library symbol] [Library of Congress] (LCLS)
WAOK .... Atlanta, GA [AM radio station call letters]
WAOL .... Ripley, OH [FM radio station call letters]

WaOLI .... State of Washington Department of Labor and Industries Libraries, Olympia, WA [*Library symbol Library of Congress*] (LCLS)

WaOLN .... Washington Library Network, Olympia, WA [*Library symbol Library of Congress*] (LCLS)

WAOM .... Morehead, KY [*Television station call letters*]

WaONR .... Washington State Department of Natural Resources, Division of Geology and Earth Resources, Olympia, WA [*Library symbol Library of Congress*]

WaOP .... Washington State Patrol, Olympia, WA [*Library symbol*] [*Library of Congress*] (LCLS)

WAOP .... Western Australian Opinion Polls

WaOPI .... Washington Superindentent of Public Instruction, Olympia, WA [*Library symbol*] [*Library of Congress*] (LCLS)

WAOQ-FM .... Brantley, AL [*FM radio station call letters*] (BROA)

WAOR .... Niles, MI [*FM radio station call letters*]

WaOrc .... Orcas Island Library, East Sound, WA [*Library symbol*] [*Library of Congress*] (LCLS)

WaOrtS .... Washington Soldiers' Home, Staff Library, Orting, WA [*Library symbol Library of Congress*] (LCLS)

WaOrtS-R .... Washington Soldiers' Home, Resident Library, Orting, WA [*Library symbol Library of Congress*] (LCLS)

WAOS .... Austell, GA [*AM radio station call letters*]

WAOS .... Welsh Agricultural Organisation Society (DBA)

WAOS .... Wide-Angle Optical System

WaOSM .... Saint Martin's College, Olympia, WA [*Library symbol Library of Congress*] (LCLS)

WaOSP .... Saint Peter's Hospital, Olympia, WA [*Library symbol Library of Congress*] (LCLS)

WaOSPS .... South Puget Sound Community College Library, Olympia, WA [*Library symbol*] [*Library of Congress*] (LCLS)

WAOT .... Kingstree, SC [*FM radio station call letters*] (RBYB)

WaOT .... Washington State Department of Transportation, Olympia, WA [*Library symbol Library of Congress*] (LCLS)

WaOTC .... Olympia Technical Community College, Olympia, WA [*Library symbol Library of Congress*] (LCLS)

WAOU .... Tawas City, MI [*FM radio station call letters*] (RBYB)

WaOUT .... Washington Utilities and Transportation Commission, Olympia, WA [*Library symbol*] [*Library of Congress*] (LCLS)

WAOV .... Vincennes, IN [*AM radio station call letters*]

WAOW .... Wausau, WI [*Television station call letters*]

WAOW .... Women Against the Ordination of Women [*Australia*]

WAOX .... Bryan, OH [*FM radio station call letters*] (RBYB)

WAOY .... Saucier, MS [*FM radio station call letters*] (RBYB)

WAOZ .... Cincinnati, OH [*AM radio station call letters*]

WAP .... Alto Palena [*Chile*] [*Airport symbol*] (AD)

WAP .... Institute of Paper Chemistry, Appleton, WI [*Library symbol Library of Congress*] (LCLS)

WAP .... Wandering Atrial Pacemaker [*Cardiology*]

WAP .... Wapentake [*Subdivision of some English shires*]

WAP .... Warner Audio Publishing

W Ap .... Washington Appellate Reports [*A publication*] (DLA)

WAP .... Waste Analysis Plan [*Environmental Protection Agency*] (GFGA)

WAP .... Wax Appearance Point [*Temperature at which waxy substances in fuel start to precipitate*]

WAP .... Weak Anthropic Principle [*Term coined by authors John Barrow and Frank Tipler in their book, "The Anthropic Cosmological Principle"*]

WAP .... Weatherization Assistance Program (GNE)

WAP .... Weekly Average Price

WAP .... Weight after Processing [*Metallurgy*]

WAP .... Whale Adoption Project (EA)

WAP .... Whey Acidic Protein

WAP .... White Anglo-Saxon Protestant (DAVI)

WAP .... Wide-Angle Panorama [*Photography*] [*NASA*]

WAP .... Wideband Acoustical Processor (CAAL)

WAP .... Wire Adhesion Promoter

WAP .... Wired Access Point [*Telecommunications*] (IGQR)

WAP .... Wireless Access Protocol [*Telecommunications*] (IGQR)

WAP .... Wireless Application Protocol [*Computer science*]

WAP .... Women Against Pornography (EA)

WAP .... Women's Action for Palestine [*An association*] (BUAC)

WAP .... Women's Action Program [*HEW*]

WAP .... Work Activity Program

WAP .... Work Analysis Program [*Computer science*] (BUR)

WAP .... Work Assignment Procedure

WAPA .... Amahai [*Indonesia*] [*ICAO location identifier*] (ICLI)

WaPa .... Pasco Public Library, Pasco, WA [*Library symbol Library of Congress*] (LCLS)

WAPA .... San Juan, PR [*AM radio station call letters*]

wapa .... Wall Paper (VRA)

WAPA .... Western Area Power Administration [*Department of Energy*]

WAPA .... White American Political Association (EA)

WaPaAp .... Washington State Office of Adult Probation and Parole, Pasco, WA [*Library symbol Library of Congress*] (LCLS)

WaPaC .... Columbia Basin College, Pasco, WA [*Library symbol Library of Congress*] (LCLS)

WaPaGS ...... Church of Jesus Christ of Latter-Day Saints, Genealogical Society Library, PascoBranch, Pasco, WA [*Library symbol Library of Congress*] (LCLS)

WAPALS ...... Workload and Productivity Analysis (MCD)

WAPA-TV .... San Juan, PR [*Television station call letters*]

WAPB .... Bula [*Indonesia*] [*ICAO location identifier*] (ICLI)

WAPB .... Murfreesboro, TN [*AM radio station call letters*] (RBYB)

WAPC .... Appleton Post Crescent, Appleton, WI [*Library symbol*] [*Library of Congress*] (LCLS)

WAPC .... Banda [*Indonesia*] [*ICAO location identifier*] (ICLI)

WAPC .... Women against Pit Closures [*An association*] (BUAC)

WAPC .... Women's Auxiliary Police Corps [*British World War II*]

WAPCB ...... West African Produce Control Board [*World War II*]

WAPC-FM .... Terre Haute, IN [*FM radio station call letters*] (RBYB)

WAPCOS ...... Water and Power Development Consultancy Services

WAPD .... Dobo [*Indonesia*] [*ICAO location identifier*] (ICLI)

WAPD .... Western Air Procurement District

WAPD .... Western Australian Parliamentary Debates [*A publication*]

WAPDA ...... Water and Power Development Authority (IAA)

WAPD-FM .... Campbellsville, KY [*FM radio station call letters*] (RBYB)

WAPE .... Jacksonville, FL [*FM radio station call letters*] (RBYB)

WAPE .... Mangole [*Indonesia*] [*ICAO location identifier*] (ICLI)

WAPE .... Windows Application Programming Environment [*Computer science*] (BTTJ)

WAPF .... McComb, MS [*AM radio station call letters*]

WAPF .... West African Pharmaceutical Federation [*Lagos, Nigeria*] (EAIO)

WAPG .... High-Endurance Coast Guard Cutter [*Later, WHEC*] (CINC)

WAPH .... Labuhu/Usman Sadik [*Indonesia*] [*ICAO location identifier*] (ICLI)

WaPH .... Pullman Memorial Hospital, Pullman, WA [*Library symbol*] [*Library of Congress*] (LCLS)

WAPI .... Birmingham, AL [*AM radio station call letters*]

WAPI .... Saumlaki [*Indonesia*] [*ICAO location identifier*] (ICLI)

WAPI .... World Aerial Photographic Index [*Meteorology*]

WAPJ-FM .... Torrington, CT [*FM radio station call letters*] (RBYB)

WAPL .... Appleton Public Library, Appleton, WI [*Library symbol*] [*Library of Congress*] (LCLS)

WAPL .... Appleton, WI [*FM radio station call letters*]

WAPL .... Langgur/Dumatubun [*Indonesia*] [*ICAO location identifier*] (ICLI)

WAPL .... Western Aerial Photography Laboratory [*Department of Agriculture*]

WaPIP .... Pacific Lutheran University, Parkland, WA [*Library symbol Library of Congress*] (LCLS)

WAPMA ...... Western Australian Potato Marketing Authority

WAPMC ...... West African Postgraduate Medical College [*Nigeria*] (BUAC)

WAPME ...... Writers and Artists for Peace in the Middle East (EA)

WAPN .... Holly Hill, FL [*FM radio station call letters*]

WAPN .... Sanana [*Indonesia*] [*ICAO location identifier*] (ICLI)

WAPO-FM .... Mount Vernon, IL [*FM radio station call letters*] (RBYB)

WaPoN ...... North Olympic Library System, Port Angeles, WA [*Library symbol Library of Congress*] (LCLS)

WaPoP .... Peninsula College, Port Angeles, WA [*Library symbol Library of Congress*] (LCLS)

WAPOR ...... World Association for Public Opinion Research (EA)

WAPP .... Ambon/Pattimura [*Indonesia*] [*ICAO location identifier*] (ICLI)

WAPP .... Berryville, VA [*FM radio station call letters*]

Wap Pr R .... Waples on Proceedings in Rem [*A publication*] (DLA)

WAPPS ...... Work Aptitude Profile and Practice Set [*Test*]

WAPQ .... Crestline, OH [*FM radio station call letters*]

WAPR .... Namlea [*Indonesia*] [*ICAO location identifier*] (ICLI)

WAPR .... World Association for Psychosocial Rehabilitation (EAIO)

WAPR .... World Association for Psychosocial Rehabilitation - US Branch (EA)

WAPR-FM .... Selma, AL [*FM radio station call letters*] (RBYB)

WAPRI .... World Association of Pulp and Papermaking Research Institute (BUAC)

WAPS .... Akron, OH [*FM radio station call letters*]

WAPS .... Selaru [*Indonesia*] [*ICAO location identifier*] (ICLI)

WaPS .... Washington State University, Pullman, WA [*Library symbol Library of Congress*] (LCLS)

WAPS .... Weighted Airman Promotion System [*Air Force*]

WAPS .... Women of the American Press Service [*Accredited American women war correspondents*] [*World War II*]

WAPS .... World Association of Pathology Societies

WA/PSF ...... Work Authorization/Program Status Factor

WaPS-V ...... Washington State University, Veterinary Medical Library, Pullman, WA [*Library symbol Library of Congress*] (LCLS)

WAPT .... Jackson, MS [*Television station call letters*]

WaPt .... Port Townsend Public Library, Port Townsend, WA [*Library symbol*] [*Library of Congress*] (LCLS)

WAPT .... Taliabu [*Indonesia*] [*ICAO location identifier*] (ICLI)

WAPT .... Weidels Auditory Processing Test [*Speech and language therapy*] (DAVI)

WAPT .... Wichita Auditory Processing Test [*Child development test*]

WAPT .... Wild Animal Propagation Trust [*Defunct*]

WAPT .... Work Area Pointer Table [*Computer science*]

WAPTT ...... World Association for Professional Training in Tourism (BUAC)

WAPU-FM .... Colfax, IL [*FM radio station call letters*] (RBYB)

WaPuS .... Washington State University, Western Washington Research and Extension Center, Puyallup, WA [*Library symbol Library of Congress*] (LCLS)

WAPV-FM .... North Myrtle Beach, SC [*FM radio station call letters*] (RBYB)

WAPX .... Clarksville, TN [*FM radio station call letters*]

WAPZ .... Ambon Sector [*Indonesia*] [*ICAO location identifier*] (ICLI)

WAPZ .... Wetumpka, AL [*AM radio station call letters*]

WAQ .... Antsalova [*Madagascar*] [*Airport symbol*] (OAG)

WAQB-FM .... Brighton, NY [*FM radio station call letters*] (RBYB)

WAQC-FM .... Brunswick, GA [*FM radio station call letters*] (RBYB)

WAQE .... Rice Lake, WI [*AM radio station call letters*]

WAQE-FM .... Rice Lake, WI [*FM radio station call letters*]

WAQF-TV .... Batavia, NY [*TV station call letters*] (RBYB)

WAQG-FM .... Ozark, AL [*FM radio station call letters*] (RBYB)

WaQGS .... Church of Jesus Christ of Latter-Day Saints, Genealogical Society Library, Quincy Branch, Quincy, WA [*Library symbol Library of Congress*] (LCLS)

WAQI .... Miami, FL [*AM radio station call letters*]

WAQJ-FM .... Crystal Falls, MI [*FM radio station call letters*] (BROA)

WAQL-FM... McComb, MS [*FM radio station call letters*] (BROA)
WAQM-FM... Cambridge Springs, PA [*FM radio station call letters*] (BROA)
WAQP......... Saginaw, MI [*Television station call letters*]
WAQU-FM.... Selma, AL [*FM radio station call letters*] (BROA)
WAQV-FM.... Crystal River, FL [*FM radio station call letters*] (BROA)
WAQX......... Manlius, NY [*FM radio station call letters*]
WAQY......... East Longmeadow, MA [*AM radio station call letters*]
WAQY......... Springfield, MA [*FM radio station call letters*]
WAQZ......... Milford, OH [*FM radio station call letters*]
WAR .... NZ Warbirds Association, Inc. [*New Zealand*] [*ICAO designator*] (FAAC)
WAR .... Warrant
WAR .... Warrenton Railroad Co. [*AAR code*]
WAR .... Warrior Industry Ltd. [*Vancouver Stock Exchange symbol*]
WAR .... Warsaw [*Poland*] [*Seismograph station code, US Geological Survey*] (SEIS)
WAR .... Warwickshire (ROG)
WAR .... Wassermann Antigen Reaction [*Test for syphilis*] [*Medicine*]
WAR .... Weapon Accuracy and Results [*Model*] (MCD)
WAR .... We Are Ridiculous [*Antiwar slogan*]
WAR .... West African Regiment [*Military unit*] [*British*]
WAR .... White Aryan Resistance (EA)
WAR .... Whiteruthenian American Relief (EA)
WAR .... With All Risks [*Insurance*]
WAR .... Women Against Rape [*An association*] (EA)
WAR .... Work Acquisition Routine
WAR .... Work Authorization Report [*or Request*] [*NASA*] (MCD)
WAR .... Workers against Racism [*An association*] (BUAC)
WAR .... World Administrative Radio Conference for Space Communication
WAR .... World Affairs Report [*Database*] [*California Institute of International Studies*] [*Information service or system*] (CRD)
WARA......... Attleboro, MA [*AM radio station call letters*]
War Adv Att... Warren's Adventures of an Attorney in Search of Practice [*A publication*] (DLA)
WARAMS.... Wartime Alignment of Reserve and Active Medical Systems
War Bell...... Ward on Belligerent and Neutral Powers [*A publication*] (DLA)
WARBICA.... West African Regional Branch of the International Council on Archives (BUAC)
WARC......... Meadville, PA [*FM radio station call letters*]
WARC......... Washington Archaeological Research Center [*Washington State University*] [*Research center*] (RCD)
WARC......... Wharton Applied Research Center [*University of Pennsylvania*] [*Research center*] (RCD)
WARC......... Women's Amateur Rowing Council (BUAC)
WARC......... World Administrative Radio Conference [*International Telecommunication Union*] (NTCM)
WARC......... World Alliance of Reformed Churches [*Alliance of the Reformed Churches th roughout the World Holding the Presbyterian System and International Congregational Council*] [*Formed by a merger of*] (EAIO)
WARCAD...... War Department - Civil Affairs Division [*Obsolete*]
WARCAT...... Workload and Resources Correlation Analysis Technique [*Army*]
WARC-BS .... World Administrative Radio Conference for Broadcast Satellite Service [*International Telecommunication Union*] (NTCM)
WARC-MAR... World Administrative Radio Conference for Maritime Mobile Telecommunications
WARCO....... War Correspondent (DSUE)
War Cr L...... Warren's Ohio Criminal Law [*A publication*] (DLA)
WARCS........ West African Regional Computer Society [*Nigeria*] (BUAC)
WARC-ST..... World Administrative Radio Conference for Space Telecommunications
WARD......... Pittston, PA [*AM radio station call letters*]
Ward........... Warden's State Reports [*2, 4 Ohio*] [*A publication*] (DLA)
WARD......... Wardship
WARDA....... West Africa Rice Development Association
Ward & Sm... Warden and Smith's State Reports [*3 Ohio*] [*A publication*] (DLA)
Warden....... Warden's State Reports [*2, 4 Ohio*] [*A publication*] (DLA)
Warden & Smith... Warden and Smith's State Reports [*3 Ohio*] [*A publication*] (DLA)
Warden's Law & Bk Bull... Warden's Weekly Law and Bank Bulletin [*Ohio*] [*A publication*] (DLA)
War Dept BCA... United States War Department, Decisions of Board of Contract Adjustment [*A publication*] (DLA)
Ward Just.... Ward's Justice of the Peace [*A publication*] (DLA)
Ward Leg..... Ward on Legacies [*A publication*] (DLA)
Ward Nat..... Ward's Law of Nations [*A publication*] (DLA)
WARDS....... Welfare of Animals Used for Research in Drugs and Therapy
WaRe.......... Renton Public Library, Renton, WA [*Library symbol Library of Congress*] (LCLS)
WARE .... Ware, MA [*AM radio station call letters*]
Ware........... Ware's United States District Court Reports [*A publication*] (DLA)
WaRedEM.... Eastside Medical Laboratory, Redmond, WA [*Library symbol*] [*Library of Congress*] (LCLS)
WaRedPC.... Physio-Control, Information Center, Redmond, WA [*Library symbol*] [*Library of Congress*] (LCLS)
WaRedSu.... Sundstand Data Control Corp., Sundstrand Corp., Redmond, WA [*Library symbol*] [*Library of Congress*] (LCLS)
WAREH .... Wareham [*Municipal borough in England*]
WARES .... Workload and Resources Evaluation System [*Navy*]
Ware's CC Rep... Ware's United States District Court Reports [*A publication*] (DLA)
Ware's Rep... Ware's United States District Court Reports [*A publication*] (DLA)
WaRetV .... Washington Veterans' Home, Medical Library, Retsil, WA [*Library symbol Library of Congress*] (LCLS)
WaRetV-R.... Washington Veterans' Home, Resident Library, Retsil, WA [*Library symbol Library of Congress*] (LCLS)

WaReVG ..... Valley General Hospital, Renton, WA [*Library symbol Library of Congress*] (LCLS)
WAREX .... Warrant Issued for Extradite
WARF .... Jasper, AL [*AM radio station call letters*]
WARF .... Warfare (AFM)
WARF .... Warfarin [*Pharmacology*] (DAVI)
WARF .... Wartime Active Replacement Factors (AABC)
WARF .... Wartime Replacement Factors [*DoD*]
WARF .... Weekly Audit Report File [*IRS*]
WARF .... Wide-Aperture Research Facility [*For hurricane detection*]
WARF .... Work Adjustment Rating Form (TES)
WARFS .... Water Resources Forecasting System [*Marine science*] (OSRA)
WARG .... Summit, IL [*FM radio station call letters*]
WARHD....... Warhead (AAG)
WARHUD..... Wide-Angle Raster Head-Up Display (MCD)
WARI .... Abbeville, AL [*AM radio station call letters*] (RBYB)
WaRi.......... Richland Public Library, Richland, WA [*Library symbol Library of Congress*] (LCLS)
WARI .... Western Australian Agricultural Research Institute [*State*] (EERA)
WARI .... Wheezing Associated with Respiratory Injections
WaRiAR....... Atlantic Richfield Hanford Co., Richland, WA [*Library symbol Library of Congress*] (LCLS)
WaRiB .... Battelle Memorial Institute, Pacific Northwest Laboratory, Richland, WA [*Library symbol Library of Congress*] (LCLS)
WaRiBN...... Battelle-Northwest Hospital, Life Science Library, Richland, WA [*Library symbol Library of Congress*] (LCLS)
WaRiGS...... Church of Jesus Christ of Latter-Day Saints, Genealogical Society Library, Richland Branch, Richland, WA [*Library symbol Library of Congress*] (LCLS)
WaRiHS...... Hanford School Library, Richland, WA [*Library symbol*] [*Library of Congress*] (LCLS)
WaRiJ......... Joint Center for Graduate Study, Richland, WA [*Library symbol*] [*Library of Congress*] (LCLS)
WaRiMC...... Mid-Columbia Mental Health Center, Richland, WA [*Library symbol Library of Congress*] (LCLS)
WArI-R........ Indian Ridge Treatment Center, Resident Library, Arlington, WA [*Library symbol Library of Congress*] (LCLS)
WARIS .... Water Resources Information System [*New South Wales*] [*State*] (EERA)
WARIS .... Western Arid Resource Information System [*Queensland*] [*State*] (EERA)
WaRit .... Ritzville Public Library, Ritzville, WA [*Library symbol Library of Congress*] (LCLS)
WARITC ...... Western Australian Retail Industry Training Council
WARK .... Hagerstown, MD [*AM radio station call letters*]
WARKS .... Warwickshire [*County in England*]
WARL .... Western Australian Rugby League
WARLA .... Wide-Aperture Radio Location Array
WARL-FM .... Marengo, IN [*FM radio station call letters*] (BROA)
WARLOCE.... Wartime Lines of Communication, Europe (AABC)
WARLOG...... Wartime Logistics (AABC)
War L St...... Warren's Law Studies [*A publication*] (DLA)
WARM .... Scranton, PA [*AM radio station call letters*]
WARM .... Warranty [*Cost Effectiveness*] Model
WARM .... Wartime Reserve Mode [*Military*]
WARM .... Weapons Assignment Research Model [*Military*]
WARM .... Wood and Solid Fuel Association of Retailers and Manufacturers (EA)
WARM .... York, PA [*FM radio station call letters*]
WARMAN .... Warsaw Metropolitan Area Network (TELE)
WARMAPS... Wartime Manpower Planning System
WARMEDY... Warm, Family Comedy [*Type of television show*]
WARMER ..... World Action for Recycled Material and Energy from Rubbish (EERA)
WARN .... Warning (NASA)
WARN .... Weather Amateur Radio Network (NOAA)
WARN .... Women of All Red Nations (EA)
WARN .... Worker Adjustment and Retraining Notification (AAGC)
WARN .... Worker Adjustment and Retraining Notification Act [*1988*]
WARN .... Worldwide Accelerated Response Network (BUAC)
WARNA .... Worker Adjustment and Retraining Notification Act [*1988*]
Warnaco ..... Warnaco Group, Inc. [*Associated Press*] (SAG)
WarnL......... Warner-Lambert Co. [*Associated Press*] (SAG)
WARNORD... Warning Order [*Military*] (INF)
Warntc........ Warrantech Corp. [*Associated Press*] (SAG)
WARO .... Naples, FL [*AM radio station call letters*]
WARO-FM.... Naples, FL [*FM radio station call letters*] (RBYB)
War Op .... Warwick's Opinions [*City Solicitor of Philadelphia, PA*] [*A publication*] (DLA)
WARP .... Warp 10 Technologies, Inc. [*NASDAQ symbol*] (SAG)
WARP .... Weather and Radar Processor [*FAA*] (TAG)
WARP .... Web Artists' Rights Protection
WARP .... Wind Amplified Rotor Platform
WARP .... Wind Amplifier Rotor Platform
WARP .... Worldwide Ammunition Reporting Program (NG)
WARP .... Worldwide AUTODIN [*Automatic Digital Information Network*] Restoral Plan (CET)
Warp10........ Warp 10 Technologies, Inc. [*Associated Press*] (SAG)
WARPAC...... Wartime Repair Parts Consumption (MCD)
WARPATH.... World Association to Remove Prejudice Against the Handicapped
WARPF .... Warp 10 Technologies [*NASDAQ symbol*] (TTSB)
War Prof Dut... Warren. Moral, Social, and Professional Duties of Attorneys and Solicitors [*2nd ed.*] [*1851*] [*A publication*] (DLA)
WARQ .... Columbia, SC [*FM radio station call letters*]
Warr .... Warrant [*A document entitling holder to purchase a given issue of stock*] [*Investment term*]

WARR.........	Warranty (MSA)
WARR.........	Warrenton, NC [*AM radio station call letters*] (RBYB)
WARR.........	Waste Acid Release Reduction [*Environmental science*]
WARRAMP...	Wartime Requirements for Ammunition, Materiel, and Personnel
WARRC.......	Western Aerospace Rescue and Recovery Center [*Air Force*]
WARRC.......	World Acaricide Resistance Reference Centre (BUAC)
Warren	Warren Bancorp, Inc. [*Associated Press*] (SAG)
Warren-T	Warren-Teed [*Commercial firm*] (DAVI)
WARRS.......	West African Rice Research Station (BUAC)
WARRT.......	Warrant (ROG)
WARRTD.....	Warranted (WGA)
Wars.........	[*The*] Jewish Wars [*of Josephus*] [*A publication*] (BJA)
WARS	Warfare Analysis and Research System [*Navy*]
WARS	Wide-Area Remote Sensors
WARS	Worldwide Ammunition Reporting System [*Military*]
WARSCAP....	Wartime Support Capability
WARSIC......	Water Resources Scientific Information Center [*US Geological Survey*] [*Reston, VA Database originator*] (IT)
WARSIM......	Warfighters' Simulation [*DoD*]
WARSL	War Reserve Stockage List (MCD)
WART	Weighted Average Remaining Term [*Finance*]
WART	Wenceslaus Anxiety Representation Taxonomy [*Satirical psychology term*]
WARTA	Western Australian Road Transport Association
Warth Code..	West Virginia Code [*1899*] [*A publication*] (DLA)
WARU.........	Peru, IN [*AM radio station call letters*]
WARU-FM...	Peru, IN [*FM radio station call letters*]
WARV	Warwick, RI [*AM radio station call letters*]
Warv Abst....	Warvelle on Abstracts of Title [*A publication*] (DLA)
Warv El RP...	Warvelle's Elements of Real Property [*A publication*] (DLA)
Warv V & P...	Warvelle's Vendors and Purchasers of Real Property [*A publication*] (DLA)
WARW	Bethesda, MD [*FM radio station call letters*]
WARW	Warwickshire [*County in England*]
WARWICKS..	Warwickshire [*County in England*]
Warwick's Op...	Warwick's Opinions [*City Solicitor of Philadelphia, PA*] [*A publication*] (DLA)
WARWS	Warwickshire [*County in England*]
WARX	Hagerstown, MD [*FM radio station call letters*]
WARY	Valhalla, NY [*FM radio station call letters*]
WaS............	Seattle Public Library, Seattle, WA [*Library symbol Library of Congress*] (LCLS)
WAs............	Vaughn Public Library, Ashland, WI [*Library symbol Library of Congress*] (LCLS)
WAS............	Wadley Southern Railway Co. [*AAR code Obsolete*]
WAS............	Wallops Station [*Later, WFC*] [*NASA*]
WAS............	Walsten Air Services [*Canada ICAO designator*] (FAAC)
WAS............	War at Sea (NVT)
WAS............	Ward Atmosphere Scale [*Psychology*]
WAS............	Ware Resources Ltd. [*Vancouver Stock Exchange symbol*]
WAS............	Warnor & Swasey Co., Solon, OH [*OCLC symbol*] (OCLC)
WAS............	Washington [*District of Columbia*] [*Airport symbol*] (OAG)
WAS............	Washington Academy of Sciences (BUAC)
WAS............	Washington Const. Grp [*NYSE symbol*] (TTSB)
WAS............	Washington Construction Group [*NYSE symbol*] [*Formerly, Kasler Holding*] (SG)
was............	Washo [*MARC language code Library of Congress*] (LCCP)
WAS............	Waste-Activated Sludge
WAS............	Waynesburg Southern [*AAR code*]
WAS............	Weapons Alert System [*NORAD*] (MCD)
WAS............	Weapons Application Study (SAA)
WAS............	Weekly Arrival Schedule [*Military*] (AFIT)
WAS............	Western Associated Schools [*Australia*]
WAS............	Wide Analysis Sheet
WAS............	Wide-Angle Sensor
WAS............	Wide Area Surveillance [*Military*]
WAS............	Wideband Antenna System
WAS............	Wiskott-Aldrich Syndrome [*Immunology*]
WAS............	Witwatersrand Agricultural Society [*South Africa*] (BUAC)
WAS............	Women's Addiction Service [*National Institute of Mental Health*]
WAS............	Work Adjustment Scale [*Test*] (TMMY)
WAS............	Worked All States [*Contacted at least one station in all states*] [*Amateur radio*]
WAS............	World Aquaculture Society (EA)
WAS............	World Archaeological Society (EA)
WAS............	World Around Songs (EA)
WAS............	World Artifex Society (EAIO)
WAS............	World Association for Sexology (EA)
WASA.........	Havre De Grace, MD [*AM radio station call letters*]
WaSA..........	Seattle Art Museum, Seattle, WA [*Library symbol Library of Congress*] (LCLS)
WASA	Wax Anti-Settling Additive [*Diesel fuel*]
WASA	Welsh Amateur Swimming Association (BUAC)
WASA	West African Science Association (BUAC)
WASA	West African Shippers Association [*British*] (DBA)
WASA	Western Australian Society of Arts
WASA	Women's All-Star Association (EA)
WaSAA	Catholic Archdiocese of Seattle, Archives, Seattle, WA [*Library symbol Library of Congress*] (LCLS)
WaSAB	Atomic Bomb Casualty Commission, Seattle, WA [*Library symbol Library of Congress*] (LCLS)
WASAC.......	Welsh Association of Sub Aqua Clubs (BUAC)
WASAC.......	Working Group of the Army Study Advisory Committee (AABC)
WaSAD	Alcohol and Drug Institute, Seattle, WA [*Library symbol*] [*Library of Congress*] (LCLS)

WASAG........	Washington Special Action Group [*National Security Council*]
WASAL........	Wisconsin Academy of Sciences, Arts, and Letters
WASAMA.....	Woman's Auxiliary to the Student American Medical Association (DAVI)
WASAR........	Wide Application System Adapter
WASAW.......	Western Australian Sewerage and Waste Quality Infrastructure Program [*State*] (EERA)
WASB	Brockport, NY [*AM radio station call letters*]
WaSB..........	Pacific Northwest Bibliographic Center, Seattle, WA [*Library symbol Library of Congress*] (LCLS)
WASB	Steenkol/Bintuni [*Indonesia*] [*ICAO location identifier*] (ICLI)
WaSBa........	Battelle Human Affairs Research Center, Seattle, WA [*Library symbol Library of Congress*] (LCLS)
WASB-FM	Brockport, NY [*FM radio station call letters*]
WaSBG........	Bogle & Gates, Law Library, Seattle, WA [*Library symbol*] [*Library of Congress*] (LCLS)
WaSBH........	Ballard Community Hospital Library, Seattle, WA [*Library symbol*] [*Library of Congress*] (LCLS)
WaSBo........	[*The*] Boeing Co., Commercial Airplane Group, Technical Libraries, Seattle, WA [*Library symbol Library of Congress*] (LCLS)
WaSBo-A	[*The*] Boeing Co., Aerospace Division, Technical Library, Kent, WA [*Library symbol Library of Congress*] (LCLS)
WaSBo-B	Boeing Co., Technical Libraries, Bellevue, WA [*Library symbol*] [*Library of Congress*] (LCLS)
WaSBo-K	Boeing Co., Technical Libraries, Kent, WA [*Library symbol*] [*Library of Congress*] (LCLS)
WaSC	Ransiki/Abresso [*Indonesia*] [*ICAO location identifier*] (ICLI)
WaSC	Seattle Central Community College, Seattle, WA [*Library symbol Library of Congress*] (LCLS)
WASC	Spartanburg, SC [*AM radio station call letters*]
WASC	West Africa Supply Centre [*World War II*]
WASC	Western Administrative Support Center [*Marine science*] (OSRA)
WASC	Western Association of Schools and Colleges (EA)
WASC	Western Australian Shippers' Council
WASC	White Anglo-Saxon Catholic
WASC	Williams Awareness Sentence Completion [*Personality development test*] [*Psychology*]
WASCAL	Wide-Angle Scanning Array Lens Antenna
WaSC-D.......	Seattle Central Community College, District Technical Services, Seattle, WA [*Library symbol*] [*Library of Congress*] (LCLS)
WASCL	Western Australian Society for Computers and the Law
WaSC-N.......	North Seattle Community College, Seattle, WA [*Library symbol Library of Congress*] (LCLS)
WaSCO	Children's Orthopedic Hospital and Medical Center, Seattle, WA [*Library symbol Library of Congress*] (LCLS)
WASCO	War Safety Council
WaSC-S.......	South Seattle Community College, Seattle, WA [*Library symbol Library of Congress*] (LCLS)
WaSC-Sh.....	Shoreline Community College, Seattle, WA [*Library symbol Library of Congress Obsolete*] (LCLS)
WASD	Wide-Angle Self-Destruct (MCD)
WASDA.......	Water and Sewer Distributors of America (NTPA)
WASE..........	Kebar [*Indonesia*] [*ICAO location identifier*] (ICLI)
WASE..........	Radcliff, KY [*FM radio station call letters*] (BDYD)
WASE..........	Saint Elizabeth Hospital, Appleton, WI [*Library symbol Library of Congress*] (LCLS)
WASEC.......	Warner Amex Satellite Entertainment Co. [*Cable television*]
WaSelY.......	Yakima Valley School, Selah, WA [*Library symbol Library of Congress*] (LCLS)
WaSEPA	United States Environmental Protection Agency, Region X Library, Seattle, WA [*Library symbol*] [*Library of Congress*] (LCLS)
WASES	Western Australian State Emergency Service
WASEX	War at Sea Exercise [*Navy*] (DOMA)
WASF..........	Fak Fak/Torea [*Indonesia*] [*ICAO location identifier*] (ICLI)
WaSF..........	Fircrest School, Staff Library, Seattle, WA [*Library symbol Library of Congress*] (LCLS)
WASF..........	Water Authorities Superannuation Fund [*British*]
WASF..........	Western Australian Sports Federation
WaSFC........	Firland Correctional Center, Staff Library, Seattle, WA [*Library symbol Library of Congress*] (LCLS)
WaSFC-R.....	Firland Correctional Center, Resident Library, Seattle, WA [*Library symbol Library of Congress*] (LCLS)
WASFL........	Western Australian State Football League
WaSFP........	Foster, Pepper & Shefelman, Law Library, Seattle, WA [*Library symbol*] [*Library of Congress*] (LCLS)
WaSF-R	Fircrest School, Resident Library, Seattle, WA [*Library symbol Library of Congress*] (LCLS)
WaSFRC	Federal Records Center, Seattle, WA [*Library symbol Library of Congress*] (LCLS)
WaSFSI.......	Forest Service Information Network Northwest, University of Washington Campus, Seattle, WA [*Library symbol*] [*Library of Congress*] (LCLS)
WASG	Atmore, AL [*AM radio station call letters*]
WaSG	Seattle Genealogical Society, Seattle, WA [*Library symbol Library of Congress*] (LCLS)
WaSGAO......	United States General Accounting Office, Seattle Regional Office, Seattle, WA [*Library symbol*] [*Library of Congress*] (LCLS)
WaSGen	Genetic Systems Corp., Seattle, WA [*Library symbol*] [*Library of Congress*] (LCLS)
WASGFC.....	Western Association of State Game and Fish Commissioners [*Later, Western Association of Fish and Wildlife Agencies*] (EA)
WaSGH........	Group Health Cooperative of Puget Sound, Medical Library, Seattle, WA [*Library symbol Library of Congress*] (LCLS)
WaSGH-H	Group Health Cooperative of Puget Sound, Kathleen Hill Library, Seattle, WA [*Library symbol*] [*Library of Congress*] (LCLS)

WaSGS .... Church of Jesus Christ of Latter-Day Saints, Genealogical Society Library, Seattle North Branch, Seattle, WA [*Library symbol Library of Congress*] (LCLS)

WaSGS .... Good Samaritan Hospital, Seattle, WA [*Library.symbol Library of Congress*] (LCLS)

WaSGSH ..... Good Samaritan Hospital, Seattle, WA [*Library symbol*] [*Library of Congress*] (LCLS)

WaSh .... Shelton Public Library, Shelton, WA [*Library symbol Library of Congress*] (LCLS)

WaSH .... Virginia Mason Hospital, Medical Library, Seattle, WA [*Library symbol Library of Congress*] (LCLS)

WASH .... Washer (AAG)

WASH .... Washington (AAG)

Wash .... Washington (ODBW)

WASH .... Washington, DC [*FM radio station call letters*]

Wash .... Washington Reports [*A publication*] (DLA)

Wash .... Washington's Reports [*1, 2 Virginia*] [*A publication*] (DLA)

Wash .... Washington's Reports [*16-23 Vermont*] [*A publication*] (DLA)

Wash .... Washington State Reports [*A publication*] (DLA)

Wash .... Washington's United States Circuit Court Reports [*A publication*] (DLA)

Wash .... Washington Territory Reports [*1854-88*] [*A publication*] (DLA)

WASH .... Washington Trust Bancorp [*NASDAQ symbol*] (TTSB)

WASH .... Washington Trust Bancorp, Inc. [*NASDAQ symbol*] (NQ)

WASH .... Water and Sanitation for Health Project [*Agency for International Development*]

WASH .... Women against Sexual Harassment [*An association*] (BUAC)

Wash 2d ..... Washington Reports, Second Series [*A publication*] (DLA)

Wash Admin Code... Washington Administrative Code [*A publication*] (DLA)

Wash Admin Reg... Washington State Register [*A publication*] (DLA)

Wash & Haz PEI... Washburton and Hazard's Reports [*Prince Edward Island, Canada*] [*A publication*] (DLA)

Wash & Lee U... Washington and Lee University (GAGS)

Wash App.... Washington Appellate Reports [*A publication*] (DLA)

Washb Easem... Washburn on Easements and Servitudes [*A publication*] (DLA)

Wash B News... Washington Bar News [*A publication*] (DLA)

Washb Real Prop... Washburn on Real Property [*A publication*] (DLA)

Washburn .... Washburn's Reports [*18-23 Vermont*] [*A publication*] (DLA)

Washburn U... Washburn University of Topeka (GAGS)

Wash C....... Washington College (GAGS)

WaShC........ Washington Correction Center, Staff Library, Shelton, WA [*Library symbol Library of Congress*] (LCLS)

WASHCAP... Washington Operations Capabilities System

Wash CC...... Washington's United States Circuit Court Reports [*A publication*] (DLA)

Wash CCR ... Washington's United States Circuit Court Reports [*A publication*] (DLA)

WaSHCH...... Highline Community Hospital Library, Seattle, WA [*Library symbol*] [*Library of Congress*] (LCLS)

Wash Co...... Washington County Reports [*Pennsylvania*] [*A publication*] (DLA)

Wash Co (PA)... Washington County Reports [*Pennsylvania*] [*A publication*] (DLA)

Wash Co R... Washington County Reports [*Pennsylvania*] [*A publication*] (DLA)

Wash Co Repr... Washington County Reports [*Pennsylvania*] [*A publication*] (DLA)

WaSHCR...... Fred Hutchinson Cancer Research Center, Seattle, WA [*Library symbol Library of Congress*] (LCLS)

WaShC-R..... Washington Correction Center, Resident Library, Shelton, WA [*Library symbol Library of Congress*] (LCLS)

Wash Cr L... Washburn on Criminal Law [*A publication*] (DLA)

Wash DC .... Washington, D.C. (VRA)

Wash Dec.... Washington Decisions [*A publication*] (DLA)

Wash Dig..... Washburn's Vermont Digest [*A publication*] (DLA)

Wash Ease... Washburn on Easements and Servitudes [*A publication*] (DLA)

WashEn .... Washington Energy Co. [*Associated Press*] (SAG)

WASHFAX... Washington Area Secure High-Speed Facsimile System (MUSM)

WashFed ..... Washington Federal, Inc. (Seattle) [*Associated Press*] (SAG)

Wash Fin Rep (BNA)... Washington Financial Reports (Bureau of National Affairs) [*A publication*] (DLA)

WashGs .... Washington Gas Light Co. [*Associated Press*] (SAG)

WashHm...... Washington Homes, Inc. [*Associated Press*] (SAG)

WaSHi .... Seattle Historical Society, Seattle, WA [*Library symbol Library of Congress*] (LCLS)

WaShIR .... ITT Rayonier, Inc., Olympic Research Center, Shelton, WA [*Library symbol Library of Congress*] (LCLS)

Wash Jur..... Washington Jurist [*A publication*] (DLA)

Wash Law Rep... Washington Law Reporter [*District of Columbia*] [*A publication*] (DLA)

Wash Legis Serv... Washington Legislative Service (West) [*A publication*] (DLA)

Wash LR (Dist Col)... Washington Law Reporter (District of Columbia) [*A publication*] (DLA)

Wash L Rep... Washington Law Reporter [*District of Columbia*] [*A publication*] (DLA)

Wash M....... Washington Monthly [*A publication*] (BRI)

WASHMIC... Washington Military Industrial Complex

WashNt........ Washington Natural Gas [*Associated Press*] (SAG)

WASHO....... Western Association of State Highway Officials

Wash PUR ... Washington Public Utility Commission Reports [*A publication*] (DLA)

Wash Rev Code... Revised Code of Washington [*A publication*] (DLA)

Wash Rev Code Ann... Washington Revised Code, Annotated [*A publication*] (DLA)

Wash RP ..... Washburn on Real Property [*A publication*] (DLA)

Wash SBA ... Washington State Bar Association. Proceedings [*A publication*] (DLA)

Wash St....... Washington State Reports [*A publication*] (DLA)

Wash St Reg... Washington State Register [*A publication*] (AAGC)

Wash St U ... Washington State University (GAGS)

WashSvg ..... Washington Savings Bank FSB (MD) [*Associated Press*] (SAG)

WASH T....... Washington Territory (ROG)

Wash T........ Washington Territory Opinions [*1854-64*] [*A publication*] (DLA)

Wash T........ Washington Territory Reports [*1854-88*] [*A publication*] (DLA)

WashTech.... Washington Alliance of Technology Workers

Wash Ter.... Washington Territory Opinions [*1854-64*] [*A publication*] (DLA)

Wash Ter.... Washington Territory Reports [*1854-88*] [*A publication*] (DLA)

Wash Ter NS... Allen's Washington Territory Reports, New Series [*A publication*] (DLA)

Wash Terr ... Washington Territory Opinions [*1854-64*] [*A publication*] (DLA)

Wash Terr ... Washington Territory Reports [*1854-88*] [*A publication*] (DLA)

WASHTO .... Western Association of State Highway and Traffic Officials

WashTrst..... Washington Trust Bancorp, Inc. [*Associated Press*] (SAG)

Wash Ty ..... Washington Territory Opinions [*1854-64*] [*A publication*] (DLA)

Wash Ty ..... Washington Territory Reports [*1854-88*] [*A publication*] (DLA)

Wash UJ Urb & Contemp L... Washington University. Journal of Urban and Contemporary Law [*A publication*] (DLA)

Wash UL Rev... Washington University. Law Review [*A publication*] (DLA)

Wash U (Mo)... Washington University (Missouri) (GAGS)

Wash VA..... Washington's Reports [*1, 2 Virginia*] [*A publication*] (DLA)

WashWtr..... Washington Water Power Co. [*Associated Press*] (SAG)

WASI .... Inanwatan [*Indonesia*] [*ICAO location identifier*] (ICLI)

WASI .... Whimbey Analytical Skills Inventory [*Educational test*]

WASIA .... Women's Armed Services Integration Act of 1948

WASID .... Water and Soil Investigation Department [*Pakistan*] (BUAC)

WaSIF........ International Fisheries Commission, Seattle, WA [*Library symbol Library of Congress*] (LCLS)

WASIH .... Western American Society for Italic Handwriting [*Formerly, WABSIH*] (EA)

WaSJB........ John Bastyr College of Naturopathic Medicine, Seattle, WA [*Library symbol*] [*Library of Congress*] (LCLS)

WASJ-FM ... Maynardville, TN [*FM radio station call letters*] (BROA)

WASK .... Kaimana (Utarom) [*Indonesia*] [*ICAO location identifier*] (ICLI)

WaSK .... King County Medical Society, Seattle, WA [*Library symbol Library of Congress*] (LCLS)

WASK .... Lafayette, IN [*AM radio station call letters*]

WaSKC .... King County Library System, Seattle, WA [*Library symbol Library of Congress*] (LCLS)

WASK-FM ... Battle Ground, IN [*FM radio station call letters*] (RBYB)

WaSKR .... Keller, Rohrback, Law Library, Seattle, WA [*Library symbol*] [*Library of Congress*] (LCLS)

WaSKTK ..... Karr, Tuttle, Koch, Campbell, Mawer, Morrow, & Sax, Seattle, WA [*Library symbol*] [*Library of Congress*] (LCLS)

WASL......... Dyersburg, TN [*FM radio station call letters*]

WAsL '........ Vaughn Public Library, Ashland, WI [*Library symbol*] [*Library of Congress*] (LCLS)

WaSLP........ Lane, Powell, Moss & Miller Library, Seattle, WA [*Library symbol*] [*Library of Congress*] (LCLS)

WAsM......... Memorial Medical Center, Health Sciences Library, Ashland, WI [*Library symbol Library of Congress*] (LCLS)

WASM .... Merdei [*Indonesia*] [*ICAO location identifier*] (ICLI)

WaSM .... Mountaineers, Inc., Seattle, WA [*Library symbol Library of Congress*] (LCLS)

WASM .... White Anglo-Saxon Male

WaSMA....... Moss Adams Information Center, Seattle, WA [*Library symbol*] [*Library of Congress*] (LCLS)

WASMAC ..... Western Australian Survey and Mapping Advisory Council [*State*] (EERA)

WASME....... World Assembly of Small and Medium Enterprises [*See also AMPME*] [*India*] (EAIO)

WaSMH .... Virginia Mason Hospital, Medical Library, Seattle, WA [*Library symbol*] [*Library of Congress*] (LCLS)

WaSMHI ...... Museum of History and Industry, Seattle, WA [*Library symbol*] [*Library of Congress*] (LCLS)

WaSMo....... Mountaineers, Inc., Seattle, WA [*Library symbol*] [*Library of Congress*] (LCLS)

WASN .... Campbell, OH [*AM radio station call letters*]

WAsN.......... Northland College, Ashland, WI [*Library symbol Library of Congress*] (LCLS)

WasN .... Washington National Corp. [*Associated Press*] (SAG)

WASN .... Western Australian School of Nursing

WASNA .... Western Apicultural Society of North America (EA)

WaSNH .... Northwest Hospital, Effie M. Storey Learning Center, Seattle, WA [*Library symbol Library of Congress*] (LCLS)

WaSNPS..... United States National Park Service, Pacific Northwest Region, Seattle, WA [*Library symbol*] [*Library of Congress*] (LCLS)

WaSnqE....... Echo Glen Children's Center, Staff Library, Snoqualmie, WA [*Library symbol Library of Congress*] (LCLS)

WaSnqE-R ... Echo Glen Children's Center, Resident Library, Snoqualmie, WA [*Library symbol Library of Congress*] (LCLS)

WASO .... Babo [*Indonesia*] [*ICAO location identifier*] (ICLI)

WASO .... Covington, LA [*AM radio station call letters*]

WASO .... Women's Association for Symphony Orchestras [*Later, AMSO*] (EA)

WASOG....... West African Society of Gastroenterology [*Ghana*] (BUAC)

WASOG....... World Association on Sarcoidosis and Other Granulomatous Disorders (EAIO)

WaSOnc....... Oncogen Library, Seattle, WA [*Library symbol*] [*Library of Congress*] (LCLS)

WASP .... Brownsville, PA [*AM radio station call letters*]

WASP .... MARINALG International, World Association of Seaweed Processors (EA)

WASP .... Oliver, PA [*FM radio station call letters*]

WaSp.......... Spokane Public Library, Spokane, WA [*Library symbol Library of Congress*] (LCLS)

WASP .... Wafer Scale Associative String Processor (NITA)

WASP .... Wafer Scale Systolic Processor (NITA)

WASP .... Wait-and-See Parsing [*Computer science*] (BYTE)

WASP .... War Air Service Program [*Department of Commerce*]

WASP .... Water and Steam Program [*NASA*]

WASP .... Water Quality Analysis Simulation Program [*Environmental Protection Agency*] (AEPA)

WASP .... Weather-Atmospheric Sounding Projectile [*Research rocket*]

WASP .... Weber Advanced Spatial Perception Test [*Vocational guidance test*]

WASP .... Weed-Activated Spray Process [*Agriculture*]

WASP .... Weightless Analysis Sounding Probe [*NASA*]

WASP .... West African Society for Pharmacology (BUAC)

WASP .... Westinghouse Advanced Systems Planning Group

WASP .... White Anglo-Saxon Protestant

Wasp .... White Anglo-Saxon Protestant (ODBW)

WASP .... White Appalachian Southern Protestant [*Chicago slang*]

WASP .... White Ashkenazi Sabra with Pull [*Israeli variation on White Anglo-Saxon Protestant*]

WASP .... Wide Antiarmor Minimissile (MCD)

WASP .... Wien Automatic Systems Planning [*Nuclear energy*] (NUCP)

WASP .... Williams Aerial Systems Platform [*One-man flying platform*]

WASP .... Wind-Assisted Ship Propulsion (DS)

WASP .... Window Atmosphere Sounding Projectile [*NASA*]

WASP .... Wiskott-Aldrich Syndrome Protein [*Biochemistry*]

WASP .... Women's Airforce Service Pilots [*World War II*]

WASP .... Woody Allen's Spring Picture [*Designation reflecting the filmmaker's reluctance to provide information about his movies in advance of their commercial release*] [*See also WAFP*]

WASP .... Work Activity Sampling Plan

WASP .... Workshop Analysis and Scheduling Programming

WASP .... Workstation Automatic Script Processor (NITA)

WASP .... World Association of Societies of Pathology - Anatomic and Clinical (EA)

WASP .... World Associations for Social Psychiatry (EA)

WASP .... Wrap-Around Simulation Program [*Military*] (CAAL)

WASP .... Wyoming Atomic Simulation Project

WASPA .... White Anglo-Saxon Protestant Ambulatory [*Extension of WASP; indicates the necessity of being able-bodied as an additional requirement for success*]

WaSPaM ...... Pacific Medical Center, Seattle, WA [*Library symbol*] [*Library of Congress*] (LCLS)

WaSPATH .... PATH [*Program for Appropriate Technology in Health*] Library, Seattle, WA [*Library symbol*] [*Library of Congress*] (LCLS)

WaSpBM ...... United States Bureau of Mines, Mining Research Center, Spokane, WA [*Library symbol Library of Congress*] (LCLS)

WaSpBMW... United States Bureau of Mines, Western Field Operations Center, Spokane, WA [*Library symbol Library of Congress*] (LCLS)

WaSPC .... Seattle Pacific College, Seattle, WA [*Library symbol Library of Congress*] (LCLS)

WaSpCN ...... Center for Nursing Education, Spokane, WA [*Library symbol Library of Congress*] (LCLS)

WaSpCo .... Spokane County Library, Spokane, WA [*Library symbol Library of Congress*] (LCLS)

WaSpD .... Deaconess Hospital, School of Nursing, Spokane, WA [*Library symbol Library of Congress*] (LCLS)

WaSPe .... Perkins, Coie, Stone, Olsen & Williams, Seattle, WA [*Library symbol Library of Congress*] (LCLS)

WaSpG .... Gonzaga University, Spokane, WA [*Library symbol Library of Congress*] (LCLS)

WaSpGL ...... Church of Jesus Christ of Latter-Day Saints, Genealogical Society Library, Spokane Branch, Spokane, WA [*Library symbol Library of Congress*] (LCLS)

WaSpG-L ..... Gonzaga University, Law Library, Spokane, WA [*Library symbol Library of Congress*] (LCLS)

WaSpGS ...... United States Geological Survey, Spokane, WA [*Library symbol Library of Congress*] (LCLS)

WaSpH .... Holy Family Hospital, Spokane, WA [*Library symbol Library of Congress*] (LCLS)

WaSPH .... United States Public Health Service Hospital, Medical Service Library, Seattle, WA [*Library symbol Library of Congress*] (LCLS)

WaSpHiE ..... Eastern Washington State Historical Society, Museum Library, Spokane, WA [*Library symbol Library of Congress*] (LCLS)

WaSpIn .... Intermediate School District 101, Professional Materials Library, Spokane, WA [*Library symbol Library of Congress*] (LCLS)

WaSpJ .... Jesuit Archives of the Province of Oregon, Spokane, WA [*Library symbol Library of Congress*] (LCLS)

WaSpJP .... Washington State Office of Juvenile Parole Services, Spokane, WA [*Library symbol Library of Congress*] (LCLS)

WaSpJS .... Jesuit Scholastic Library, Spokane, WA [*Library symbol Library of Congress*] (LCLS)

WaSPM .... Providence Hospital, Medical Library and Learning Resource Center, Seattle, WA [*Library symbol Library of Congress*] (LCLS)

WaSpM .... Spokane County Medical Library, Spokane, WA [*Library symbol Library of Congress*] (LCLS)

WASPM .... Wide Area Side Penetrator Mine [*Army*] (ADDR)

WaSpMF ...... Murphey Favre, Inc., Spokane, WA [*Library symbol Library of Congress*] (LCLS)

WaSpN .... Fort Wright College, Spokane, WA [*Library symbol Library of Congress*] (LCLS)

WASP-NN .... White Anglo-Saxon Protestant Native Born of Native Parents

WaSPoD .... Population Dynamics, Seattle, WA [*Library symbol Library of Congress*] (LCLS)

WaSpPS ...... Spokane Public Schools, Curriculum Library, Spokane, WA [*Library symbol Library of Congress*] (LCLS)

WaSPrM .... Providence Hospital, Medical Library and Learning Resource Center, Seattle, WA [*Library symbol*] [*Library of Congress*] (LCLS)

WASPRU...... West African Stored Products Research Unit

WaSPS .... Seattle Public Schools, Library Technical Service, Seattle, WA [*Library symbol Library of Congress*] (LCLS)

WaSpS........ Spokane Community College, Spokane, WA [*Library symbol Library of Congress*] (LCLS)

WASPS .... Women's Agricultural Security Production Service [*British military*] (DMA)

WASPS .... Women's Auxiliary Service Platoon

WaSpSC ...... Spokane Community College, Spokane, WA [*Library symbol*] [*Library of Congress*] (LCLS)

WaSpSF ...... Spokane Falls Community College, Spokane, WA [*Library symbol Library of Congress*] (LCLS)

WaSpSH ...... Sacred Heart Medical Center, Spokane, WA [*Library symbol Library of Congress*] (LCLS)

WaSpSL ...... Saint Luke's Hospital, Spokane, WA [*Library symbol Library of Congress*] (LCLS)

WaSpSL...... Spokane County Law Library, Spokane, WA [*Library symbol Library of Congress*] (LCLS)

WaSpStL..... Saint Luke's Hospital, Spokane, WA [*Library symbol*] [*Library of Congress*] (LCLS)

WaSpStM ... Saint Michael's Institute, Spokane, WA [*Library symbol Library of Congress*] (LCLS)

WaSPTS ...... Preston, Thorgrimson, Shidler, Gates & Ellis, Seattle, WA [*Library symbol*] [*Library of Congress*] (LCLS)

WaSpVA ...... United States Veterans Administration Hospital, Spokane, WA [*Library symbol Library of Congress*] (LCLS)

WaSpW........ Whitworth College, Spokane, WA [*Library symbol Library of Congress*] (LCLS)

WASPWWII... Women Airforce Service Pilots WWII (EA)

WaSpYS ...... Washington State Center for Youth Services, Spokane, WA [*Library symbol Library of Congress*] (LCLS)

WASQ-FM... Saltville, VA [*FM radio station call letters*] (BROA)

WASR .... Manokwari/Rendani [*Indonesia*] [*ICAO location identifier*] (ICLI)

WASR .... Wolfeboro, NH [*AM radio station call letters*]

WaSS........... Schick's Schadel Hospital, Medical Library, Seattle, WA [*Library symbol Library of Congress*] (LCLS)

WASS .... Sorong/Jefman [*Indonesia*] [*ICAO location identifier*] (ICLI)

Wass .... Wassermann [*Test for syphilis*]

WASS .... Wavefront Analysis of Spatial Sampling [*Aircraft landing approach*]

WASS .... Wide-Angle Sun Seekers (SAA)

WASS .... Wide-Area Active Surveillance System [*Military*] (MCD)

WaSSB .... Washington State Office for the Services for the Blind, Seattle, WA [*Library symbol Library of Congress*] (LCLS)

WaSSC .... Saint Cabrini Hospital Library, Seattle, WA [*Library symbol*] [*Library of Congress*] (LCLS)

WaSSGB ...... Schroeter, Goldmark & Bender, Seattle, WA [*Library symbol*] [*Library of Congress*] (LCLS)

WaSSh........ Shoreline Community College, Seattle, WA [*Library symbol Library of Congress*] (LCLS)

WaSSH .... Swedish Hospital Medical Center, Seattle, WA [*Library symbol Library of Congress*] (LCLS)

WaSSM .... Seattle Midwifery School, Seattle, WA [*Library symbol*] [*Library of Congress*] (LCLS)

WASSM .... WWMCCS [*Worldwide Military Command and Control System*] ADP System SecurityManager [*Automatic Data Processing*] (MCD)

WASSO .... WWMCCS [*Worldwide Military Command and Control System*] ADP System SecurityOfficer [*Automatic Data Processing*] (MCD)

WASSP .... Wallingford Storm Sewer Package [*Hydraulics Research*] [*Software package*] (NCC)

WASSP .... Wire Arc Seismic Section Profiler

WaSSRB ...... Stoel, Rives, Boly, Jones & Grey, Law Library, Seattle, WA [*Library symbol*] [*Library of Congress*] (LCLS)

WaSSW .... Shannon & Wilson, Inc., Seattle, WA [*Library symbol Library of Congress*] (LCLS)

WaSSwH...... Swedish Hospital Medical Center, Seattle, WA [*Library symbol*] [*Library of Congress*] (LCLS)

WAST........... Teminabuan [*Indonesia*] [*ICAO location identifier*] (ICLI)

WAST........... Western Alaska Standard Time (IAA)

WASTA .... Western Australian Science Teachers' Association

WASTAC ...... Western Australian Satellite Technology Applications Consortium [*State*] (EERA)

WASTE........ Wisdom, Acclaim, and Status through Expenditures [*Fictional government agency in book "Alice in Blunderland"*]

WASTE........ World Association for Solid Waste Transfer and Exchange

WaSteM....... McNeil Island Correction Center, Steilacoom, WA [*Library symbol Library of Congress*] (LCLS)

WasteMI ...... Waste Management International [*Associated Press*] (SAG)

WasteTc ...... Waste Technology Corp. [*Associated Press*] (SAG)

WASTN .... Wireless Auxiliary Station [*Telecommunications*] (IAA)

WASU .... Boone, NC [*FM radio station call letters*]

WaSU .... Seattle University, Seattle, WA [*Library symbol Library of Congress*] (LCLS)

WaSUN........ United Nursing Homes, Seattle, WA [*Library symbol Library of Congress*] (LCLS)

WASV .... Asheville, NC [*Television station call letters*]

WaSVA .... United States Veterans Administration Hospital, Seattle, WA [*Library symbol Library of Congress*] (LCLS)

WASW .... Wasior [*Indonesia*] [*ICAO location identifier*] (ICLI)

WASWC ...... World Association of Soil and Water Conservation (EA)

WaSWG ...... West Seattle General Hospital, Seattle, WA [*Library symbol Library of Congress*] (LCLS)

WaSwH........ United General Hospital, Medical Staff Library, Sedro Woolley, WA [*Library symbol*] [*Library of Congress*] (LCLS)

WaSWK .... Williams, Kastner, Gibbs, Law Library, Seattle, WA [*Library symbol*] [*Library of Congress*] (LCLS)

WaSwN........ Northern State Multi-Service Center, Sedro Woolley, WA [*Library symbol*] [*Library of Congress*] (LCLS)

WASY .... Western Australian School of Yoga

WASZ........... Ashland-Lineville, AL [*FM radio station call letters*]

WaT............. Tacoma Public Library, Tacoma, WA [*Library symbol Library of Congress*] (LCLS)

WAT............. University of Waterloo Library [*UTLAS symbol*]

WAT............. Water [*Automotive engineering*]

Wat............. Waterford [*Crystal glassware*] (BARN)

Wat............. Watermeyer's Cape Of Good Hope Supreme Court Reports [*1857*] [*South Africa*] [*A publication*] (DLA)

WAT............. Waters Corp. [*NYSE symbol*] (SAG)

WAT............. Watertown Free Public Library, Watertown, MA [*OCLC symbol*] (OCLC)

WAT............. Watheroo [*Australia Seismograph station code, US Geological Survey Closed*] (SEIS)

WAT............. Weapons Assignment Technician (AFM)

WAT............. Web Action Time (MCD)

WAT............. Weeks after Treatment

WAT............. Weight, Altitude, and Temperature (IEEE)

WAT............. Weight Average Temperature [*Chemical engineering*]

WAT............. Wet Anode Tantalum

WAT............. White Adipose Tissue [*Physiology*]

WAT............. Wide-Angle Tail [*Galactic radio source*]

WAT............. Wide Area Telecommunications Service (NITA)

WAT............. Wideband Adapter Transformer

WAT............. Wings Air Transport Co. [*Sudan*] [*ICAO designator*] (FAAC)

WAT............. Word Association Test [*Psychology*]

WATA........... Boone, NC [*AM radio station call letters*]

WATA........... Western Australian Temperance Alliance

WATA........... Wisconsin Automatic Test Apparatus

WATA........... World Association of Travel Agencies (EAIO)

WaTAC........ Allenmore Community Hospital, Tacoma, WA [*Library symbol Library of Congress*] (LCLS)

WATAC........ Women and the Australian Church

WaTAH........ United States Army [*Madigan*] General Hospital, Tacoma, WA [*Library symbol Library of Congress*] (LCLS)

WATAO .... Worldwide Agricultural Technical Assistance Organization (BUAC)

WATB.......... Decatur, GA [*AM radio station call letters*] (RBYB)

WATBOL ..... Waterloo COBOL [*Common Business-Oriented Language*] [*University of Waterloo*] [*Canada*]

WATBRU ..... West African Timber Borer Research Unit (BUAC)

WATC.......... Atlanta, GA [*Television station call letters*]

WATC.......... [*The*] Washington Terminal Co. [*AAR code*]

WATC.......... Western Australian Tourism Commission

WATC.......... Western Australian Tourist Centre

WATC.......... Western Australian Treasury Corp. [*Commercial firm*]

WATC.......... Wide-Area Traffic Control (PDAA)

WATCJ......... Women's Air Training Corps

WATC.......... Women's Ambulance and Transportation Corps

WaTCC........ Tacoma Community College, Tacoma, WA [*Library symbol Library of Congress*] (LCLS)

Wat CGH...... Watermeyer's Cape Of Good Hope Reports [*South Africa*] [*A publication*] (DLA)

WaTCH........ Mary Bridge Children's Health Center, Tacoma, WA [*Library symbol Library of Congress*] (LCLS)

WATCH........ Watchers Against Television Commercial Harrassment [*Student legal action organization*]

WATCH .... Watch Trust for Environmental Education (BUAC)

WATCh......... What About the Children (WDAA)

WATCH .... Women Acting Together for Change [*Nepal*] [*An association*] (BUAC)

WATCh......... Women & the Church (WDAA)

WATCH .... Working Group on the Assessment of Toxic Chemicals [*British*]

WATCH .... World Against Toys Causing Harm

WATCH .... World Assembly of Technical and Creative Humorists (BUAC)

WATCH .... Writers & Their Copyright Holders (WDAA)

WATCHCON... Watch Condition (DOMA)

WATCIM ...... Waterloo Centre for Integrated Manufacturing [*University of Waterloo*] [*Canada Research center*] (RCD)

WaTCJ........ Cascadia Juvenile Diagnostic Center, Tacoma, WA [*Library symbol Library of Congress*] (LCLS)

WATCON...... Waterloo Concordance (NITA)

Wat Con ...... Watkins on Conveyancing [*9th ed.*] [*1845*] [*A publication*] (DLA)

Wat Cop ...... Watkins on Copyholds [*6th ed.*] [*1829*] [*A publication*] (DLA)

Wat Cr Dig... Waterman's Criminal Digest [*United States*] [*A publication*] (DLA)

Wat Cr Proc... Waterman's Criminal Procedure [*A publication*] (DLA)

WaTD........... Doctors Hospital, Tacoma, WA [*Library symbol Library of Congress*] (LCLS)

WATD .... Marshfield, MA [*FM radio station call letters*]

WATDOC...... Water Resources Document Reference Centre [*Canadian Department of Fisheries and the Environment*] [*Database*] (IID)

WATDOC...... Water Resources Document Reference System (NITA)

WATE.......... Knoxville, TN [*Television station call letters*]

WATER .... Water Awareness Training Education and Recruitment

WATER .... Women's Alliance for Theology, Ethics, and Ritual (EA)

WATERF ...... Waterford [*County in Ireland*] (ROG)

WATERFD .... Waterford [*County in Ireland*]

Waterhse...... Waterhouse Investor Services, Inc. [*Associated Press*] (SAG)

WATERLIT ... Water Literature (NITA)

Watermeyer... Watermeyer's Cape Of Good Hope Reports [*South Africa*] [*A publication*] (DLA)

Watermrcc.... Watermarc Food Management Co. [*Associated Press*] (SAG)

WATF.......... Waterford Wedgwood Ltd. [*NASDAQ symbol*] (NQ)

WatfdW........ Waterford Wedgewood PLC ADR [*Associated Press*] (SAG)

WATFIV........ Waterloo FORTRAN [*Formula Translating System*] IV [*University of Waterloo*] [*Canada*] (HGAA)

WATFOR...... Waterloo FORTRAN [*University of Waterloo*] [*Canada*]

WaTFS........ Fort Steilacoom Community College, Tacoma, WA [*Library symbol Library of Congress*] (LCLS)

WATFY........ Waterford Glass Group PLC (MHDW)

WATFZ........ Waterford Wedgwood plcADs [*NASDAQ symbol*] (TTSB)

WaTG.......... Tacoma Branch Genealogical Library, Tacoma, WA [*Library symbol Library of Congress*] (LCLS)

WATG .... Trion, GA [*FM radio station call letters*]

WATG .... Wave-Activated Turbine Generator (PDAA)

WaTGC........ Griffin College, Tacoma, WA [*Library symbol*] [*Library of Congress*] (LCLS)

WaTGH........ Tacoma General Hospital, Pierce County Medical Library, Tacoma, WA [*Library symbol Library of Congress*] (LCLS)

WaTGS .... Church of Jesus Christ of Latter-Day Saints, Genealogical Society Library, Tacoma Branch, Tacoma, WA [*Library symbol Library of Congress*] (LCLS)

WATH .... Athens, OH [*AM radio station call letters*]

WATI .... Wisconsin Assisted Technology Initiative

WATI-FM ..... Vincennes, IN [*FM radio station call letters*] (BROA)

WATJ.......... Chardon, OH [*AM radio station call letters*]

WaTJP .... Washington State Office of Juvenile Parole Services, Tacoma, WA [*Library symbol Library of Congress*] (LCLS)

Wat Just...... Waterman's Justices' Manual [*A publication*] (DLA)

WATK.......... Antigo, WI [*AM radio station call letters*]

Watk Con .... Watkins on Conveyancing [*A publication*] (DLA)

Watk Conv .. Watkins on Conveyancing [*A publication*] (DLA)

Watk Cop.... Watkins on Copyholds [*A publication*] (DLA)

Watk Copyh.. Watkins on Copyholds [*A publication*] (DLA)

Watk Des..... Watkins on Descents [*A publication*] (DLA)

WatkJn........ Watkins-Johnson Co. [*Associated Press*] (SAG)

WATL.......... Atlanta, GA [*Television station call letters*]

WATLC........ Trades and Labour Council of Western Australia

WATLCC...... Western Australian Tripartite Labour Consultative Council

WaTLG........ Lakewood General Hospital and Convalescent Center, Tacoma, WA [*Library symbol Library of Congress*] (LCLS)

WATM......... Altoona, PA [*Television station call letters*]

WATN......... Watertown, NY [*AM radio station call letters*]

WaTO.......... Oakridge Group Home, Tacoma, WA [*Library symbol Library of Congress*] (LCLS)

WATO .... Oak Ridge, TN [*AM radio station call letters*]

WATOC........ World Association of Theoretically Oriented Chemists (BUAC)

WaToH........ Heritage College, Toppenish, WA [*Library symbol*] [*Library of Congress*] (LCLS)

WATOX........ Western Atlantic Ocean Experiment [*Marine science*] (OSRA)

WaToY........ Yakim Nation Library, Toppenish, WA [*Library symbol*] [*Library of Congress*] (LCLS)

WaTP.......... Pioneer Group Home, Tacoma, WA [*Library symbol Library of Congress*] (LCLS)

WaTPC........ Pierce County Library, Tacoma, WA [*Library symbol Library of Congress*] (LCLS)

WATP-FM .... Laurel, MS [*FM radio station call letters*] (BROA)

WaTPG .... Puget Sound General Hospital, Tacoma, WA [*Library symbol Library of Congress*] (LCLS)

WaTPL........ Pierce County Law Library, Tacoma, WA [*Library symbol*] [*Library of Congress*] (LCLS)

WATPL........ Wartime Traffic Priority List (NATG)

WaTPM........ Pierce County Medical Library, Tacoma, WA [*Library symbol Library of Congress*] (LCLS)

WaTPS........ Tacoma Public Schools, Professional and Curriculum Library, Tacoma, WA [*Library symbol Library of Congress*] (LCLS)

WATQ-FM .... Chetek, WI [*FM radio station call letters*] (BROA)

WATR .... Tetra Tech [*NASDAQ symbol*] (TTSB)

WATR .... Tetra Tech, Inc. [*NASDAQ symbol*] (SPSG)

WATR .... Water Attenuation by Tritium Relaxation [*Physics*]

WATR .... Waterbury, CT [*AM radio station call letters*]

WATR .... Waterville [*AAR code*]

WatrIn .... Waters Instruments, Inc. [*Associated Press*] (SAG)

WatrJ .... Water-Jel Technologies [*Associated Press*] (SAG)

WatrJel........ Water-Jel Technologies [*Associated Press*] (SAG)

Watrm .... Watermarc Food Management Co. [*Associated Press*] (SAG)

WatrPnt .... Water Point Systems [*Associated Press*] (SAG)

WatrsCp....... Waters Corp. [*Associated Press*] (SAG)

WATS.......... Sayre, PA [*AM radio station call letters*]

WATS.......... Survey of Motor Freight Transportation and Public Warehousing [*BTS*] (TAG)

WATS........... Watson Pharmaceuticals [*NASDAQ symbol*] (TTSB)

WATS........... Watson Pharmaceuticals, Inc. [*NASDAQ symbol*] (SAG)

WAT's........... Wide-Angle [*Galilean*] Telescopes

WATS........... Wide-Area Military Traffic Management and Terminal Service

WATS........... Wide-Area Telecommunications [*formerly, Telephone*] Service [*American Telephone & Telegraph Co. contract billing system*]

WATS........... Wide-Area Telephone Service [*Telecommunications*] (IAA)

WATS........... Wide Area Transmission Service [*or System*]

WATS........... Women's Auxiliary Territorial Service [*British military*] (DMA)

WATS........... Women's Auxiliary Training Service

Wats Arb ..... Watson on Arbitration [*A publication*] (DLA)

Watsc .... Watsco, Inc. [*Associated Press*] (SAG)

Wats Cler Law... Watson's Clergyman's Law [*A publication*] (DLA)

Watsco .... Watsco, Inc. [*Associated Press*] (SAG)

Wats Com Man... Watson's United States Commissioners' Manual [*A publication*] (DLA)

Wats Comp Eq... Watson's Compendium of Equity [*A publication*] (DLA)

Wats Const Hist... Watson's Constitutional History of Canada [*A publication*] (DLA)

Wat Set-Off... Waterman on Set-Off [*A publication*] (DLA)
WatsGen...... Watson General Corp. [*Associated Press*] (SAG)
WaTSJ......... Saint Joseph Hospital, Tacoma, WA [*Library symbol Library of Congress*] (LCLS)
Wats Med Jur... Watson's Medical Jurisprudence [*A publication*] (DLA)
WatsnPh...... Watson Pharmaceuticals, Inc. [*Associated Press*] (SAG)
Watson........ Watson's Compendium of Equity [*2 eds.*] [*1873, 1888*] [*A publication*] (DLA)
Watson Eq... Watson's Compendium of Equity [*A publication*] (DLA)
Wats Part.... Watson on Partnership [*2nd ed.*] [*1807*] [*A publication*] (DLA)
Wats Sher... Watson's Office and Duty of Sheriff [*2nd ed.*] [*1848*] [*A publication*] (DLA)
WATSTORE... National Water Data Storage and Retrieval System [*US Geological Survey*] [*Information service or system*] (CRD)
WATT.......... Cadillac, MI [*AM radio station call letters*]
WATTE......... West African Tropical Testing Establishment (BUAC)
WATTec....... Welding and Testing Technology Energy Conference [*Acronym is used as name of association*]
Wat Tres...... Waterman on the Law of Trespass [*A publication*] (DLA)
Watts........... Watts' Pennsylvania Reports [*1832-40*] [*A publication*] (DLA)
Watts........... Watts' Reports [*16-24 West Virginia*] [*A publication*] (DLA)
Watts & S.... Watts and Sergeant's Pennsylvania Reports [*1841-45*] [*A publication*] (DLA)
Watts & Serg... Watts and Sergeant's Pennsylvania Reports [*1841-45*] [*A publication*] (DLA)
Watts & S (PA)... Watts and Sergeant's Pennsylvania Reports [*1841-45*] [*A publication*] (DLA)
WattsInd...... Watts Industries [*Associated Press*] (SAG)
Watts (PA)... Watts' Pennsylvania Reports [*1832-40*] [*A publication*] (DLA)
WaTU........... University of Puget Sound, Tacoma, WA [*Library symbol Library of Congress*] (LCLS)
WATU.......... Western Approaches Tactical Unit [*Navy*]
WATV........... Birmingham, AL [*AM radio station call letters*]
WATW.......... Ashland, WI [*AM radio station call letters*]
WaTW........... Weyerhaeuser Co., Tacoma, WA [*Library symbol Library of Congress*] (LCLS)
WATW.......... Wood Awning Type Window
WaTWH....... Western State Hospital, Staff Library, Tacoma, WA [*Library symbol Library of Congress*] (LCLS)
WaTWH-R.... Western State Hospital, Resident Library, Tacoma, WA [*Library symbol Library of Congress*] (LCLS)
WaTW-T...... Weyerhaeuser Co., Technical Center, Tacoma, WA [*Library symbol Library of Congress*] (LCLS)
WATX........... Algood, TN [*AM radio station call letters*]
WATZ........... Alpena, MI [*AM radio station call letters*]
WATZ-FM.... Alpena, MI [*FM radio station call letters*]
WaU............. University of Washington, Seattle, WA [*Library symbol Library of Congress*] (LCLS)
wau.............. Washington [*MARC country of publication code Library of Congress*] (LCCP)
WAU............ Weapon Assignment Unit [*Military*] (CAAL)
WAU............ Women's Advisory Unit [*South Australia*]
WAUA-FM.... Petersburg, WV [*FM radio station call letters'*] (BROA)
WAUB.......... Auburn, NY [*AM radio station call letters*]
WAUC.......... Wauchula, FL [*AM radio station call letters*]
WAUD.......... Auburn, AL [*AM radio station call letters*]
WaU-D......... University of Washington, Drama Library, Seattle, WA [*Library symbol Library of Congress*] (LCLS)
WaU-EA....... University of Washington, East Asia Library, Seattle, WA [*Library symbol Library of Congress*] (LCLS)
WAUE-FM.... Beaver Dam, KY [*FM radio station call letters*] (BROA)
WaU-FE....... University of Washington, Far Eastern Library, Seattle, WA [*Library symbol Library of Congress Obsolete*] (LCLS)
WAUG.......... New Hope, NC [*AM radio station call letters*]
WaU-HS....... University of Washington, Health Sciences Library, Seattle, WA [*Library symbol Library of Congress*] (LCLS)
WAUI-FM..... Shelby, OH [*FM radio station call letters*] (BROA)
WAUK.......... Waukesha, WI [*AM radio station call letters*]
WaU-L......... University of Washington, Law Library, Seattle, WA [*Library symbol Library of Congress*] (LCLS)
WAUL-AM.... Brantley, AL [*AM radio station call letters*] (BROA)
WaU-MC...... University of Washington, Harborview Medical Center Library, Seattle, WA [*Library symbol Library of Congress*] (LCLS)
WAUM-FM... Duck Hill, MS [*FM radio station call letters*] (BROA)
WAUN.......... Kewaunee, WI [*FM radio station call letters*]
WAUO-FM.... Hohenwald, TN [*FM radio station call letters*] (BROA)
WAUP.......... Syracuse, NY [*Television station call letters*] (BROA)
WAUQ-FM.... Charles City, VA [*FM radio station call letters*] (BROA)
WAUR.......... Sandwich, IL [*AM radio station call letters*]
WAUS.......... Berrien Springs, MI [*FM radio station call letters*]
WAUS.......... World Association of Upper Silesians (EA)
WausauP..... Wausau Paper Mills [*Associated Press*] (SAG)
W Aust Hist Soc... Western Australian Historical Society. Journal [*A publication*]
W Austl R.... Western Australia Law Reports [*A publication*] (DLA)
W Aust Repr Acts... Reprinted Acts of Western Australia [*A publication*] (DLA)
WAUX.......... Lake Geneva, WI [*AM radio station call letters*] (RBYB)
WAUXCP...... West Auxiliary Airborne Command Post (MCD)
WaV............. Fort Vancouver Regional Library, Vancouver, WA [*Library symbol Library of Congress*] (LCLS)
WAV............ Waveform Audio [*Computer science*]
WAV............ West-Avin Oy [*Finland ICAO designator*] (FAAC)
wav.............. Windows Sound File [*Computer science*]
WAV............ Wirtschaftliche Aufbau Vereinigung [*Economic Reconstruction Union*] [*Germany Political party*] (PPE)
WAVA.......... Arlington, VA [*FM radio station call letters*]
WAVA.......... World Association of Veteran Athletes (EAIO)
WAVA.......... World Association of Veterinary Anatomists (EA)
WAVAW....... Women Against Violence Against Women (EA)
WAVB.......... Lajas, PR [*AM radio station call letters*]
WaVC........... Clark College, Vancouver, WA [*Library symbol Library of Congress*] (LCLS)
WAVC.......... Duluth, MN [*FM radio station call letters*]
WAVD.......... Decatur, AL [*AM radio station call letters*]
WAVE.......... Louisville, KY [*Television station call letters*]
WAVE.......... Water-Augmented Vehicle
WAVE.......... Weather Altimeter Voice Equipment
WAVE.......... Westinghouse Audio Visual Electronics (IAA)
WAVE.......... Women and Vocational Education [*Australia*]
WAVE.......... World Association of Veterinary Educators (BUAC)
Wavefrnt..... Wavefront Technologies, Inc. [*Associated Press*] (SAG)
WAVEGD..... Waveguide Standards (IAA)
Waver.......... Waverly Press, Inc. [*Associated Press*] (SAG)
WAVES........ Weight and Value Engineering System [*Computer science*]
WAVES........ Women Accepted for Volunteer Emergency Service [*US Navy Women's Reserve*] [*World War II and later*]
Waves.......... Women Accepted for Volunteer Emergency Service [*Military*] (WDAA)
WAVES........ Women Appointed Volunteer Emergency Services [*British World War II*]
WAVES........ Women's Audio Visual Education Scheme (BUAC)
WAVES........ Worker and Visitor Entrance System [*Secret Service*] (GFGA)
WaveSys..... Wave Systems Corp. [*Associated Press*] (SAG)
WaveTec..... Wave Technologies International, Inc. [*Associated Press*] (SAG)
Wavetech.... Wavetech, Inc. [*Associated Press*] (SAG)
WAVF.......... Hanahan, SC [*FM radio station call letters*]
WAVFH........ World Association of Veterinary Food-Hygienists [*See also AMVHA*] [*Berlin, Federal Republic of Germany*] (EAIO)
WAVG.......... Louisville, KY [*AM radio station call letters*]
WAVH.......... Bay Minette, AL [*FM radio station call letters*]
WaVHS........ United States Park Service, Fort Vancouver National Historical Site, Vancouver, WA [*Library symbol Library of Congress*] (LCLS)
WAVI........... Christiansted, VI [*FM radio station call letters*]
WAVJ........... Princeton, KY [*AM radio station call letters*]
WAVJ-FM.... Princeton, KY [*FM radio station call letters*] (RBYB)
WAVK.......... Marathon, FL [*FM radio station call letters*]
WAVL........... Apollo, PA [*AM radio station call letters*]
WAVLD........ World Association of Veterinary Laboratory Diagnosticians (EAIO)
WAVM.......... Maynard, MA [*FM radio station call letters*]
WaVMH....... Vancouver Memorial Hospital, Vancouver, WA [*Library symbol Library of Congress*] (LCLS)
WAVMI........ World Association of Veterinary Microbiologists, Immunologists, and Specialists in Infectious Diseases [*See also AMVMI*] [*Maisons-Alfort, France*] (EAIO)
WaVN.......... NERCO Minerals Co., Vancouver, WA [*Library symbol*] [*Library of Congress*] (LCLS)
WAVN.......... Southaven, MS [*AM radio station call letters*]
WAVO.......... Rock Hill, SC [*AM radio station call letters*]
WAVO.......... WavePhore, Inc. [*NASDAQ symbol*] (SAG)
WAVO.......... WAVO Corp. [*NASDAQ symbol*]
WAVP.......... Avon Park, FL [*AM radio station call letters*]
WAVP.......... Western Australian. Votes and Proceedings [*A publication*]
WAVP.......... World Association of Veterinary Pathologists (EAIO)
WAVPM....... Women Against Violence in Pornography and Media (EA)
WAVPPBT.... World Association of Veterinary Physiologists, Pharmacologists, Biochemists, and Toxicologists (BUAC)
WAVQ.......... Inglis, FL [*FM radio station call letters*]
WAVR.......... Waverly Inc. [*NASDAQ symbol*] (TTSB)
WAVR.......... Waverly, NY [*FM radio station call letters*]
WAVR.......... Waverly Press, Inc. [*NASDAQ symbol*] (NQ)
WAVS.......... Davie, FL [*AM radio station call letters*]
WAVS.......... Wide Angle Visual System (MCD)
WaVSB........ Washington State School for the Blind, Vancouver, WA [*Library symbol Library of Congress*] (LCLS)
WaVSD........ Washington State School for the Deaf, Vancouver, WA [*Library symbol Library of Congress*] (LCLS)
WAVSFDP.... World Association of Veterinary Specialists in Fish Diseases and Productions (BUAC)
WaVStJ........ Saint Joseph Community Hospital, Vancouver, WA [*Library symbol Library of Congress*] (LCLS)
WAVT........... Pottsville, PA [*FM radio station call letters*]
WAVT........... Wave Technologies Intl [*NASDAQ symbol*] (TTSB)
WAVT........... Wave Technologies Intl, Inc. [*NASDAQ symbol*] (SAG)
WAVU.......... Albertville, AL [*AM radio station call letters*]
WAVV.......... Marco, FL [*FM radio station call letters*]
WaVVA........ United States Veterans Administration Hospital, Vancouver, WA [*Library symbol Library of Congress*] (LCLS)
WAVW......... Vero Beach, FL [*FM radio station call letters*]
WAVX.......... Thomaston, ME [*FM radio station call letters*]
WAVX.......... Wave Systems'A' [*NASDAQ symbol*] (TTSB)
WAVX.......... Wave Systems Corp. [*NASDAQ symbol*] (SAG)
WAVY.......... Portsmouth, VA [*Television station call letters*]
WAVZ.......... New Haven, CT [*AM radio station call letters*]
WAW........... University of Washington, School of Librarianship, Seattle, WA [*OCLC symbol*] (OCLC)
WaW............ Walla Walla Public Library, Walla Walla, WA [*Library symbol Library of Congress*] (LCLS)
WAW........... Ward's Auto World [*A publication*]
WAW........... Warsaw [*Poland*] [*Airport symbol*] (OAG)
WAW........... Waynesburg & Washington Railroad Co. [*Absorbed into Consolidated Rail Corp.*] [*AAR code*]
WAW........... Wings Airways [*ICAO designator*] (FAAC)

WAW .... Write-After-Write [Computer science]
WAWA .... Water Authority of Western Australia
WAWA .... West African Women's Association (BUAC)
WAWA .... West Africa Wins Again [A reminder that visitors to this region must exercise caution if they wish to avoid bureaucratic harrassment and overcharging]
WAWA .... Woolens and Worsteds of America [Defunct] (EA)
WaWAE .... U.S. Army Corps of Engineers, Walla Walla District, Walla Walla, WA [Library symbol] [Library of Congress] (LCLS)
WaWaW ...... Weller Public Library, Waitsburg, WA [Library symbol] [Library of Congress] (LCLS)
WAWB .... Ashland, VA [Television station call letters]
WAWC .... Syracuse, IN [FM radio station call letters]
WaWC .... Walla Walla College, College Place, WA [Library symbol Library of Congress] (LCLS)
WAWC .... West Africa War Council [World War II]
WAWC .... Western Australian Week Council
WaWCL .... Walla Walla County Rural Library, Walla Walla, WA [Library symbol] [Library of Congress] (LCLS)
WAWD .... Fort Walton Beach, FL [Television station call letters]
WAWE .... World Association of Women Entrepreneurs (BUAC)
WAWE .... World Association of Women Executives (BUAC)
WaWeC .... Central Washington Hospital, Health Sciences Library, Wenatchee, WA [Library symbol Library of Congress] (LCLS)
WAWE-FM .. Mableton, GA [FM radio station call letters] (BROA)
WaWeN .... North Central Regional Library, Wenatche, WA [Library symbol Library of Congress] (LCLS)
WaWeW ...... Wenatchee Valley College, Wenatchee, WA [Library symbol Library of Congress] (LCLS)
WaWeYS ..... Washington State Center for Youth Services, Wenatchee, WA [Library symbol Library of Congress] (LCLS)
WAWF .... William Allen White Foundation (EA)
WAWF .... World Arm Wrestling Federation (EA)
WAWF .... World Association for World Federation [Netherlands]
WAWF-FM ... Kankakee, IL [FM radio station call letters] (BROA)
WAWG .... Where Are We Going
WAWH-FM .. Dublin, GA [FM radio station call letters] (BROA)
WAWHS ...... Walla Walla High School, Walla Walla, WA [Library symbol] [Library of Congress] (LCLS)
WAWI-FM .... Lawrenceburg, TN [FM radio station call letters] (BROA)
WaWiS .... Wilbur Public Schools System, Wilbur, WA [Library symbol Library of Congress] (LCLS)
WAWJ-FM ... Du Quoin, IL [FM radio station call letters] (BROA)
WAWK .... Kendallville, IN [AM radio station call letters]
WAWL .... Red Bank, TN [FM radio station call letters]
WAWM-FM... Marco, FL [FM radio station call letters] (BROA)
WAWN-FM... Franklin, PA [FM radio station call letters] (BROA)
WaWnvGH ... Woodenville Group Home, Woodenville, WA [Library symbol Library of Congress] (LCLS)
WaWP .... Washington State Penitentiary, Walla Walla, WA [Library symbol Library of Congress] (LCLS)
WAWR .... Workers Army of the Welsh Republic (BUAC)
WAWR-AM... Salisbury, MD [AM radio station call letters] (BROA)
WAWRC...... Western Australian Water Resources Council (EERA)
WAWS .... Jacksonville, FL [Television station call letters]
WAWSS ...... West African Weed Science Society (BUAC)
WAWT-AM ... Portsmouth, VA [AM radio station call letters] (BROA)
WAWV .... Sylacauga, AL [FM radio station call letters]
WaWV .... United States Veterans Administration Hospital, Walla Walla, WA [Library symbol Library of Congress] (LCLS)
WAWV .... World Association of Wildlife Veterinarians (BUAC)
WaWW .... Whitman College, Walla Walla, WA [Library symbol Library of Congress] (LCLS)
WaWWC ..... Walla Walla Community College, Walla Walla, WA [Library symbol Library of Congress] (LCLS)
WAWX-AM... Augusta, GA [AM radio station call letters] (BROA)
WAWY-AM... Madison, WI [AM radio station call letters] (BROA)
WAWZ .... Zarephath, NJ [FM radio station call letters]
WAX........... Waxman Indus [NYSE symbol] (TTSB)
WAX........... Waxman Industries, Inc. [NYSE symbol] (SPSG)
WAX........... Weak Anion Exchanger [Chemistry]
WAX........... Weapon Assignment and Target Extermination
WAXB-FM ... Patterson, NY [FM radio station call letters] (RBYB)
WAXD .... Wide-Angle X-Ray Diffraction
WAXE .... Vero Beach, FL [AM radio station call letters]
WAXG-FM... Mt. Sterling, KY [FM radio station call letters] (BROA)
WAXI .... Rockville, IN [FM radio station call letters]
WAXI .... Wistar Adult Xiphisternum [Chondrocyte] (DB)
WAXJ-FM ... Frederiksted, Virgin Islands [FM radio station call letters] (BROA)
WAXL-FM ... Santa Claus, IN [FM radio station call letters] (RBYB)
WAXM .... Big Stone Gap, VA [FM radio station call letters]
WAXM .... Waxman Industries, Inc. (MHDW)
Waxmn ...... Waxman Industries, Inc. [Associated Press] (SAG)
WAXN-TV ... Kannapolis, NC [TV station call letters] (RBYB)
WAXO .... Lewisburg, TN [AM radio station call letters]
WAXQ .... New York, NY [FM radio station call letters]
WAXR-FM... Geneseo, IL [FM radio station call letters] (BROA)
WAXS .... Oak Hill, WV [FM radio station call letters]
WAXS .... Wide-Angle X-Ray Scattering
WAXS .... World Access, Inc. [NASDAQ symbol] (SAG)
WAXT......... Alexandria, IN [FM radio station call letters]
WAXX......... Eau Claire, WI [FM radio station call letters]
WAXY .... South Miami, FL [AM radio station call letters]
WAXZ......... Georgetown, OH [FM radio station call letters]
WAY........... Way [Postal Service standard] (OPSA)

WAY........... Waynesburg [Pennsylvania] [Seismograph station code, US Geological Survey Closed] (SEIS)
WAY........... Waynesburg, PA [Location identifier FAA] (FAAL)
WAY........... Wayne State College, Wayne, NE [OCLC symbol] (OCLC)
WAY........... Worked All Yokosuka [Amateur radio] (IAA)
WAY........... World Assembly of Youth [Bronshoj, Denmark] (EAIO)
WaY .... Yakima Valley Regional Library, Yakima, WA [Library symbol Library of Congress] (LCLS)
WAYA .... Spring City, TN [FM radio station call letters]
WaYacL ...... Larch Mountain Correctional Center, Staff Library, Yacolt, WA [Library symbol Library of Congress] (LCLS)
WaYacL-R ... Larch Mountain Correctional Center, Resident Library, Yacolt, WA [Library symbol Library of Congress] (LCLS)
WAYB .... Graysville, TN [FM radio station call letters]
WAYB .... Waynesboro, VA [AM radio station call letters]
WAYC .... Bedford, PA [AM radio station call letters]
WAYC .... Welsh Association of Youth Clubs (BUAC)
WAYE .... Birmingham, AL [AM radio station call letters]
WAYF .... West Palm Beach, FL [FM radio station call letters]
WAYG .... Sarasota, FL [FM radio station call letters]
WaYG .... Yakim Valley Genelogical Society, Yakima, WA [Library symbol] [Library of Congress] (LCLS)
WaYGS .... Church of Jesus Christ of Latter-Day Saints, Genealogical Society Library, Yakima Branch, Yakima, WA [Library symbol Library of Congress] (LCLS)
WAYJ......... Fort Myers, FL [FM radio station call letters]
WaYJP .... Washington State Office of Juvenile Parole Services, Yakima, WA [Library symbol Library of Congress] (LCLS)
WAYK-FM ... Kalamazoo, MI [FM radio station call letters] (RBYB)
WAYL .... St. Augustine, FL [FM radio station call letters]
WAYM .... Columbia, TN [FM radio station call letters]
WaYM .... Yakima Valley Memorial Hospital, Yakima, WA [Library symbol Library of Congress] (LCLS)
WAYMCA .... World Alliance of Young Men's Christian Associations [Geneva, Switzerland] (EAIO)
WaYMHi ..... Yakima Valley Museum and Historical Association, Yakima, WA [Library symbol Library of Congress] (LCLS)
WAYN .... Rockingham, NC [AM radio station call letters]
WAYN .... Wayne Savings & Loan Co. [NASDAQ symbol] (SAG)
WAYN .... Wayne Svgs & Ln [NASDAQ symbol] (TTSB)
WayneB ...... Wayne Bancorp, Inc. [Associated Press] (SAG)
Wayne St C (Neb)... Wayne State College (Nebraska) (GAGS)
Wayne St U... Wayne State University (GAGS)
WayneSv ..... Wayne Savings & Loan Co. [Associated Press] (SAG)
WAYQ .... Daytona Beach, FL [Television station call letters]
WAYR .... Orange Park, FL [AM radio station call letters]
WAYS .... Macon, GA [FM radio station call letters]
WAYS .... Ways [Postal Service standard] (OPSA)
WaYSE .... Saint Elizabeth Hospital, Health Sciences Library, Yakima, WA [Library symbol Library of Congress] (LCLS)
WAYT......... Wabash, IN [AM radio station call letters]
WAYV .... Atlantic City, NJ [FM radio station call letters]
WAYX .... Waycross, GA [AM radio station call letters]
WAYX .... Chippewa Falls, WI [AM radio station call letters]
WaYY .... Yakima Valley College, Yakima, WA [Library symbol Library of Congress] (LCLS)
WaYYS .... Washington State Center for Youth Services, Yakima, WA [Library symbol Library of Congress] (LCLS)
WAYZ......... Waynesboro, PA [FM radio station call letters]
WAZ........... Worked All Zones [Contacted at least one station in all zones] [Amateur radio] (IAA)
WAZF......... Yazoo City, MS [AM radio station call letters]
WAZL......... Hazleton, PA [AM radio station call letters]
WAZR......... Woodstock, VA [FM radio station call letters]
WAZS......... Summerville, SC [AM radio station call letters]
WAZU .... Santa Claus, IN [FM radio station call letters] (RBYB)
WAZU-FM... Cincinnati, OH [FM radio station call letters] (RBYB)
WAZX......... Cleveland, GA [FM radio station call letters]
WAZX......... Smyrna, GA [AM radio station call letters]
WAZY......... Lafayette, IN [FM radio station call letters]
WAZZ......... Laurinburg, NC [FM radio station call letters]
W₈........... Base-Region Width (IDOE)
WB............ Wachovia Corp. [NYSE symbol] (SPSG)
WB............ Wage Board [Civil Service classification]
WB............ Wagon Box (MSA)
WB............ Wallboard
WB............ Wall Box (ROG)
WB............ Warbirds of America (EA)
WB............ Warehouse Book
WB............ Warner Brothers [Television network]
WB............ Washable Base (ADA)
WB............ Wash Basin
WB............ Wash Bucket
WB............ Waste Book (ROG)
WB............ Water Ballast [Shipping]
WB............ Water Board
W/B........... Water Boiler (KSC)
WB............ Waterboiler (NAKS)
WB............ Water Bottle
WB............ Water Box
WB............ Waterproof Breathable [Textile technology]
WB............ Wave-Band (ADA)
WB............ Waybill [Shipping]
WB............ Weak Base (AAEL)
WB............ Weatherboard (ADA)

WB..............	Weather Bomber [Air Force]
WB..............	Weather Bureau [Later, National Weather Service] (EA)
Wb..............	Weber [Symbol] [SI unit of magnetic flux]
WB..............	Wechsler-Bellevue [Psychological test]
WB..............	Wedge Biopsy [Medicine]
WB..............	Weekly Boarding
WB..............	Weekly Bulletin [Army] (AABC)
W/B..............	Weight and Balance
WB..............	Weight Bearing
WB..............	Welded Base (DAC)
wb..............	West Berlin [MARC country of publication code Library of Congress] (LCCP)
WB..............	Westbound
WB..............	Westbridge Computer Corp. [Toronto Stock Exchange symbol]
WB..............	Western Blot [Blood test]
WB..............	Westminster Biographies [A publication]
WB..............	Wet Bulb [Thermometer, of a psychrometer] [Meteorology]
WB..............	Whale Boat
WB..............	Wheelbarrow (MSA)
WB..............	Wheelbase
WB..............	White Bag Propellant [Army] (ADDR)
WB..............	White Balance [Television] (NTCM)
WB..............	Whole Blood
WB..............	Whole Body [Nuclear energy] (NRCH)
WB..............	Whole Body [Medicine]
WB..............	Whole Bow [Music] (ROG)
WB..............	Wideband [Radio transmission]
WB..............	Widebeam (NATG)
WB..............	Will Be (AABC)
WB..............	Willowbrook [Virus] (MAE)
WB..............	Wilson Blair [Agar] [Microbiology] (DAVI)
WB..............	Winchester Word Book [A publication]
WB..............	Wingback [Football]
WB..............	Winner's Bitch [Dog show term]
WB..............	Wirebar [Metal industry]
W/B..............	Wire Bonding (AAEL)
W/B..............	Wire Bundles (MCD)
WB..............	Woerterbuch der Aegyptischen Sprache [A publication] (BJA)
WB..............	Women's Bureau [Department of Labor]
WB..............	Wood Base [Technical drawings]
WB..............	Wood Burning [Fireplace] [Classified advertising]
WB..............	Wool Back [Knitting]
WB..............	Wool Bureau (EA)
WB..............	Word Before [Message handling]
WB..............	Workbench (AAG)
WB..............	Work Book
WB..............	World Bank (EERA)
WB..............	World Brotherhood
WB..............	Write-Back [Computer science] (PCM)
WB..............	Write Buffer
W/B..............	Writing on Back [Deltiology]
WB2	Warramunga Array [Australia Seismograph station code, US Geological Survey] (SEIS)
WB3..............	Warramunga Array [Australia Seismograph station code, US Geological Survey] (SEIS)
WBA..............	Washington Bay [Alaska] [Airport symbol] (AD)
WBA..............	Wax Bean Agglutinin [Biochemistry]
WBA..............	Weekly Benefit Amount [Unemployment insurance]
WBA..............	Weekly of Business Aviation [McGraw-Hill Information Services Co.] [Information service or system] (CRD)
WBA..............	Welsh Bowling Association (BUAC)
WBA..............	West Coast Air [Gambia] [ICAO designator] (FAAC)
WBA..............	Western Blot Assay [Analytical biochemistry]
WBA..............	Whole Body Activity (DAVI)
WBA..............	Wideband Amplifier
WBA..............	Wire Bundle Assembly (MCD)
WBA..............	Woman's Benefit Association [Later, NABA]
WBA..............	Works and Building, High Priority [British World War II]
WBA..............	World Bowling Association (BUAC)
WBA..............	World Boxing Association [Later, WBO] (EA)
WBA..............	World Buffalo Association Ltd. Agricultural Association (EA)
WBA..............	Worn by Astronaut [NASA] (KSC)
WBAA.........	West Lafayette, IN [AM radio station call letters]
WBAA-FM...	West Lafayette, IN [FM radio station call letters]
WBAB.........	Babylon, NY [FM radio station call letters]
WBAC.........	Cleveland, TN [AM radio station call letters]
WBAD.........	Leland, MS [FM radio station call letters]
WBAE.........	Wholesale Beer Association Executives of America (NTPA)
WBAEA.......	Wholesale Beer Association Executives of America (EA)
WBAF.........	Barnesville, GA [AM radio station call letters]
WBAG.........	Burlington-Graham, NC [AM radio station call letters]
WBAI.........	New York, NY [FM radio station call letters]
WBAI.........	Wesley Bull & Associates, Inc. [Seattle, WA] [Telecommunications] (TSSD)
WBAIS........	Walworth Barbour American International School in Israel (BJA)
WBAJ.........	Blythwood, SC [AM radio station call letters]
WBAK.........	Anduki/Seria [Brunei] [ICAO location identifier] (ICLI)
WBAK.........	Terre Haute, IN [Television station call letters]
WBAL.........	Baltimore, MD [AM radio station call letters]
WBAL-TV ...	Baltimore, MD [Television station call letters]
WBAM	Montgomery, AL [FM radio station call letters]
WBAMC	William Beaumont Army Medical Center (AABC)
WBAN	Rantoul, IL [AM radio station call letters]
WBAN	Weather Bureau, Air Force, Navy [Manuals] [Obsolete]
WBAN	West Coast Bancorp [NASDAQ symbol] (SAG)
WBANA........	Wild Blueberry Association of North America (EA)
WB & A	Washington, Baltimore & Annapolis Railroad [Nickname: Wobble, Bump, and Amble]
WBANK........	Bank of Canada Weekly Financial Statistics [I. P. Sharp Associates] [Information service or system] (CRD)
WBAP	Fort Worth, TX [AM radio station call letters]
WBAPTT......	Whole Blood Activated Partial Thromboplastin Time [Hematology] (DAVI)
WBAQ.........	Greenville, MS [FM radio station call letters]
WBAR.........	Bartow, FL [AM radio station call letters]
WBAR.........	Lake Luzerne, NY [FM radio station call letters]
WBAR.........	Wing Bar Lights [Aviation]
WBaraC	Circus World Museum, Baraboo, WI [Library symbol Library of Congress] (LCLS)
WBaraHi.....	Sauk County Historical Society, Baraboo, WI [Library symbol Library of Congress] (LCLS)
WBAS	Weather Bureau Airport Station [Obsolete]
WBAS	Woerterbuch der Aegyptischen Sprache [A publication] (BJA)
wbasayc	Write Back as Soon as You Can [Computer science]
WBasR........	Randall Consolidated School, Bassett, WI [Library symbol Library of Congress] (LCLS)
WBAT.........	Marion, IN [AM radio station call letters]
WBAT.........	Weight-Bearing as Tolerated [Orthopedics] (DAVI)
WBAT.........	Westport Bancorp [NASDAQ symbol] (TTSB)
WBAT.........	Westport Bancorp, Inc. [Westport, CT] [NASDAQ symbol] (NQ)
WBAT.........	Wideband Adapter Transformer
WBAT.........	World Bank Administrative Tribunal (BUAC)
WBAU.........	Garden City, NY [FM radio station call letters]
WBAV.........	Charlotte, NC [AM radio station call letters]
WBAV.........	Gastonia, NC [FM radio station call letters]
WBAW.........	Barnwell, SC [AM radio station call letters]
WBAW-FM...	Barnwell, SC [FM radio station call letters]
WBAWS.......	Weather, Briefing, Advisory, and Warning Service (AABC)
WBAX.........	Wilkes-Barre, PA [AM radio station call letters]
WBAY.........	Green Bay, WI [Television station call letters]
WBAZ.........	Southhold, NY [FM radio station call letters]
WBB..............	Beloit College, Beloit, WI [Library symbol Library of Congress] (LCLS)
WBB..............	Stebbins [Alaska] [Airport symbol] (OAG)
WBB..............	Stebbins, AK [Location identifier FAA] (FAAL)
WBB..............	Webb [Del E.] Corp. [NYSE symbol] (SPSG)
WBB..............	Wide Band Beam [Physics]
WBB..............	Woodfree Bank and Bond [Paper] (DGA)
WBB..............	World Bank Bond (MHDW)
WBBA.........	Pittsfield, IL [AM radio station call letters]
WBBA.........	Western Bird Banding Association (EA)
WBBA-FM...	Pittsfield, IL [FM radio station call letters]
WBBB.........	Burlington, NC [AM radio station call letters]
WBBC.........	Blackstone, VA [FM radio station call letters]
WBBCC	Wide Day Durnett Conservation Council (EERA)
WBBD-AM...	Wheeling, WV [AM radio station call letters] (RBYB)
WBBE-FM...	Gilford, FL [FM radio station call letters] (RBYB)
WBBF.........	Rochester, NY [AM radio station call letters]
WBBG.........	Youngstown, OH [FM radio station call letters]
WBBH.........	Fort Myers, FL [Television station call letters]
WBBJ.........	Jackson, TN [Television station call letters]
WBBK.........	Blakely, GA [AM radio station call letters]
WBBK-FM...	Blakely, GA [FM radio station call letters]
WBBL.........	Grand Rapids, MI [AM radio station call letters]
WBBM.........	Chicago, IL [AM radio station call letters]
WBBM-FM...	Chicago, IL [FM radio station call letters]
WBBM-TV ...	Chicago, IL [Television station call letters]
WBBN.........	Taylorsville, MS [FM radio station call letters]
WBBO-FM...	Ocean Acres, NJ [FM radio station call letters] (BROA)
WBBP.........	Memphis, TN [AM radio station call letters]
WBBQ.........	Augusta, GA [AM radio station call letters]
WBBQ-FM...	Augusta, GA [FM radio station call letters]
WBBR.........	New York, NY [AM radio station call letters]
WBBS	Fulton, NY [FM radio station call letters]
WBBT.........	Lyons, GA [AM radio station call letters]
WBBU.........	Baker, LA [FM radio station call letters]
WBBV.........	Vicksburg, MS [FM radio station call letters]
WBBW.........	Youngstown, OH [AM radio station call letters]
WBBX.........	Kingston, TN [AM radio station call letters]
WBBY.........	Cedar Bluff, VA [FM radio station call letters]
WBBZ.........	Ponca City, OK [AM radio station call letters]
WBC..............	Bath, ME [FM radio station call letters] (RBYB)
WBC..............	Warm-Blood Cardioplegia [Medicine]
WBC..............	Washington, DC [Location identifier FAA] (FAAL)
WBC..............	Water Binding Capacity [Also, WHC] [Food industry]
WBC..............	Wayland Baptist College [Texas]
WBC..............	Weather Bureau Central Office [Obsolete]
WBC..............	Weather Bureau Communications [Obsolete]
WBC..............	Weight and Balance Computer (GAVI)
WBC..............	Weight-Bearing with Crutches [Orthopedics] (DAVI)
WBC..............	Well Baby Clinic (STED)
WBC..............	Welsh Books Council
WBC..............	Westbridge Capital [NYSE symbol] (SAG)
WBC..............	Western Boundary Current [Marine science] (MSC)
WBC..............	Westinghouse Broadcasting Co.
WBC..............	Westpac Banking Corp. [Australia Commercial firm]
WBC..............	White Blood Cell [or Corpuscle] [Medicine]
WBC..............	White Blood Cell Count [Medicine]
WBC..............	Whole Blood Cell Count [Hematology] (DAVI)
WBC..............	Wideband Channel [Telecommunications]

WBC............ Wideband Coupler
WBC............ Wien Bridge Circuit [*Physics*]
WBC............ Wilkes-Barre Connecting Railroad [*AAR code*]
WBC............ Wilkes College Library, Wilkes-Barre, PA [*OCLC symbol*] (OCLC)
WBC............ Wire Bridge Circuit
WBC............ Women's Broadcasting Corp.
WBC............ Workers' Beer Co. (BUAC)
WBC............ World Book Congress
WBC............ World Boxing Council [*Information service or system*] (IID)
WBC............ World Business Council [*Washington, DC*] (EA)
WBC............ Wycliffe Bible Commentary [*A publication*] (BJA)
WBCA.......... Bay Minette, AL [*AM radio station call letters*]
WBCA.......... Welsh Black Cattle Association (EA)
WBCA.......... Welsh Black Cattle Society (DBA)
WBCA.......... Women's Basketball Coaches Association (EA)
WBCA.......... Wyandotte Bantam Club of America (EA)
WBCB.......... Levittown-Fairless Hills, PA [*AM radio station call letters*]
WBCC.......... Cocoa, FL [*Television station call letters*]
WBCC.......... White Blood Cell Count [*Hematology*] (DAVI)
WBCCI........ Wally Byam Caravan Club International (EA)
WBCD.......... Chattahoochee, FL [*FM radio station call letters*]
WBCD.......... White Blood Cell Differential [*Hematology*]
WBCE.......... Wickliffe, KY [*AM radio station call letters*]
WBCF.......... Florence, AL [*AM radio station call letters*]
WBCG.......... Murfreesboro, NC [*FM radio station call letters*]
WBCG.......... Water Bird Conservation Group [*Australia*]
WBCH.......... Hastings, MI [*AM radio station call letters*]
WBCH-FM...... Hastings, MI [*FM radio station call letters*]
WBC/HPF...... White Blood Cells per High Power Field [*Hematology*] (MAE)
WBC/hpf...... White Blood Cells per High Power Field (STED)
WBCI.......... WFS Bancorp [*NASDAQ symbol*] (TTSB)
WBCI.......... WFS Bancorp, Inc. [*NASDAQ symbol*] (SAG)
WBCI-FM...... Bath, ME [*FM radio station call letters*] (RBYB)
WBCJ-FM...... Spencerville, OH [*FM radio station call letters*] (RBYB)
WBCK.......... Battle Creek, MI [*AM radio station call letters*]
WBCL.......... Fort Wayne, IN [*FM radio station call letters*]
WBCM.......... Boyne City, MI [*FM radio station call letters*]
WBCN.......... Boston, MA [*FM radio station call letters*]
WBCO.......... Bucyrus, OH [*AM radio station call letters*]
WBCO.......... Wallace Barnes Co.
WBCO.......... Waveguide below Cutoff (IEEE)
WBCP.......... Urbana, IL [*AM radio station call letters*]
WBCR.......... Alcoa, TN [*AM radio station call letters*]
WBCR.......... Beloit, WI [*FM radio station call letters*]
WBCRR........ Wilkes-Barre Connecting Railroad (MHDB)
WBCS.......... Boston, MA [*FM radio station call letters*]
WBCS.......... Welsh Black Cattle Society (BUAC)
WBCS.......... Wideband Communications Subsystem
WBCSC........ Wide Band Cable Systems Committee (NITA)
WBCT.......... Grand Rapids, MI [*FM radio station call letters*]
WBCT.......... Whole-Blood Clotting Time [*Hematology*]
WBCT.......... Wideband Current Transformer
WBCU.......... Union, SC [*AM radio station call letters*]
WBCV.......... Bristol, TN [*AM radio station call letters*]
WBCV.......... Wideband Coherent Video (IEEE)
WBCW.......... Jeanette, PA [*AM radio station call letters*]
WBCX.......... Gainesville, GA [*FM radio station call letters*]
WBCY.......... Archbold, OH [*FM radio station call letters*]
WBD............ Befandriana [*Madagascar*] [*Airport symbol*] (OAG)
WBD............ Wallboard
WBD............ Ward's Business Directory [*A publication*]
WBD............ Washboard [*Musical instrument used in some jazz bands*]
WBD............ Watts Bar Dam [*TVA*]
WBD............ Webster's Biographical Dictionary [*A publication*]
WBD............ Wideband Data
WBD............ Wire Bound (IEEE)
WBD............ World Business Directory [*A publication*]
WBDA.......... Wideband Data Assembly [*Ground Communications Facility, NASA*]
WBDC.......... Huntingburg, IN [*FM radio station call letters*]
WBDC-TV...... Washington, DC [*Television station call letters*] (RBYB)
WBDDS........ Weapons Bay Door Drive Subsystem [*Military*]
WBDF.......... Wideband Dicke-Fix (CET)
WBDFX........ Wideband Dicke-Fix (MSA)
WBDG.......... Indianapolis, IN [*FM radio station call letters*]
WBDI.......... Wideband Data Interleaver (MCD)
WBDK.......... Algoma, WI [*FM radio station call letters*]
WBDL.......... Wideband Data Line [*or Link*]
WBDL-FM...... Reedsburg, WI [*FM radio station call letters*] (RBYB)
WBDN.......... Brandon, FL [*AM radio station call letters*]
WBDNA........ Women Band Directors National Association (EA)
WBDR-FM...... Cape Vincent, NY [*FM radio station call letters*] (BROA)
WBDS.......... Whole-Body Digital Scanner (STED)
WBdSJ........ Saint Joseph's Hospital, Beaver Dam, WI [*Library symbol Library of Congress*] (LCLS)
WBDX.......... Trenton, GA [*FM radio station call letters*]
WBDX.......... Wideband Data Switch
WBDY.......... Bluefield, VA [*FM radio station call letters*]
WBE............ Bealanana [*Madagascar*] [*Airport symbol*] (OAG)
WBE............ Waterloo County Board of Education, Professional Education Library [*UTLAS symbol*]
WBE............ West Bromwich [*England*] [*Seismograph station code, US Geological Survey Closed*] (SEIS)
WBE............ Whole-Body Extract [*Immunology*]
WBE............ Wideband Electronics
WBE............ Women's Business Enterprise
WBEA.......... Montauk, NY [*FM radio station call letters*]
WBEA.......... Western Business Education Association (AEBS)
WBEB.......... Philadelphia, PA [*FM radio station call letters*]
WBEC.......... Pittsfield, MA [*AM radio station call letters*]
WBEC-FM...... Pittsfield, MA [*FM radio station call letters*]
WBEE.......... Harvey, IL [*AM radio station call letters*]
WBEE.......... Rochester, NY [*FM radio station call letters*]
WB/EI.......... West Britain/East Ireland
WBEJ.......... Elizabethton, TN [*AM radio station call letters*]
WBEL.......... South Beloit, IL [*AM radio station call letters*]
WBelH.......... Holy Family Convent, Benet Lake, WI [*Library symbol Library of Congress*] (LCLS)
WBelSB........ Saint Benedict's Abbey, Benet Library, Benet Lake, WI [*Library symbol Library of Congress*] (LCLS)
WBEM.......... Web-Based Enterprise Management Initiative [*Computer science*]
WBEM.......... Windber, PA [*AM radio station call letters*]
WBEN.......... Buffalo, NY [*AM radio station call letters*]
WBEP.......... Workplace Basic Education Project [*Australia*]
WBer.......... Berlin Public Library, Berlin, WI [*Library symbol Library of Congress*] (LCLS)
WBER.......... Rochester, NY [*FM radio station call letters*]
WBES.......... Dunbar, WV [*FM radio station call letters*]
WBET.......... Brockton, MA [*AM radio station call letters*]
WBEU.......... Beaufort, SC [*AM radio station call letters*]
WBEV.......... Beaver Dam, WI [*AM radio station call letters*]
WBEX.......... Chillicothe, OH [*AM radio station call letters*]
WBEY.......... Crisfield, MD [*FM radio station call letters*] (RBYB)
WBEZ.......... Chicago, IL [*FM radio station call letters*]
WBF............ Whole Blood Folate [*Hematology*] (MAE)
WBF............ Wood Block Floor [*Technical drawings*]
WBF............ Wood-Burning Fireplace [*Classified advertising*] (WGA)
WBF............ Workmen's Benefit Fund of the USA [*Carle Place, NY*] (EA)
WBF............ World Batch Forum (ACII)
WBF............ World Bridge Federation
WBFA.......... Western Bohemian Fraternal Association [*Later, WFLA*] (EA)
WBFB-FM...... Belfast, ME [*FM radio station call letters*] (BROA)
WBFC.......... Kota Kinabalu [*Malaysia*] [*ICAO location identifier*] (ICLI)
WBFC.......... Stanton, KY [*AM radio station call letters*]
WBFC.......... West Bengal Financial Corp. [*India*] (BUAC)
WBFD.......... Bedford, PA [*AM radio station call letters*]
WBFF.......... Baltimore, MD [*Television station call letters*]
WBFF.......... World Bonsai Friendship Federation [*Japan*] (BUAC)
WBFH.......... Bloomfield Hills, MI [*FM radio station call letters*]
WBFI.......... McDaniels, KY [*FM radio station call letters*]
WBFI.......... Wild Bird Feeding Institute (EA)
WBFJ.......... Winston-Salem, NC [*AM radio station call letters*]
WBFJ-FM...... Winston-Salem, NC [*FM radio station call letters*]
WBFL.......... Bellows Falls, VT [*FM radio station call letters*]
WBFM.......... Wideband Frequency Modulation
WBFM-FM...... Sheboygan Falls, WI [*FM radio station call letters*] (RBYB)
WBFN.......... Quitman, MS [*AM radio station call letters*]
WBFO.......... Buffalo, NY [*FM radio station call letters*]
WBFP.......... Wood-Burning Fireplace [*Classified advertising*]
WBFR.......... Birmingham, AL [*FM radio station call letters*]
WBFS.......... Miami, FL [*Television station call letters*]
WBFX-TV...... Lexington, NC [*TV station call letters*] (RBYB)
WBG............ Webbing
WBG............ Wichabai [*Guyana*] [*Airport symbol*] (AD)
WBGA.......... Long Atip [*Malaysia*] [*ICAO location identifier*] (ICLI)
WBGA.......... Waycross, GA [*FM radio station call letters*]
WBGB.......... Bintulu [*Malaysia*] [*ICAO location identifier*] (ICLI)
WBGB.......... Mount Dora, FL [*AM radio station call letters*]
WBGC.......... Belaga [*Malaysia*] [*ICAO location identifier*] (ICLI)
WBGC.......... Chipley, FL [*AM radio station call letters*]
WBGD.......... Brick Township, NJ [*FM radio station call letters*]
WBGD.......... Long Semado [*Malaysia*] [*ICAO location identifier*] (ICLI)
WBGE.......... Long Geng [*Malaysia*] [*ICAO location identifier*] (ICLI)
WBGE.......... Peoria, IL [*FM radio station call letters*]
WBGF.......... Belle Glade, FL [*FM radio station call letters*]
WBGF.......... Wholesale Buyers' Gifts Fair [*British*] (ITD)
WBGG.......... Fort Lauderdale, FL [*FM radio station call letters*]
WBGG.......... Kuching [*Malaysia*] [*ICAO location identifier*] (ICLI)
WBGJ.......... Limbang [*Malaysia*] [*ICAO location identifier*] (ICLI)
WBGK.......... Mukah [*Malaysia*] [*ICAO location identifier*] (ICLI)
WBGL.......... Champaign, IL [*FM radio station call letters*]
WBGL.......... Long Akah [*Indonesia*] [*ICAO location identifier*] (ICLI)
WBGM.......... Marudi [*Indonesia*] [*ICAO location identifier*] (ICLI)
WBGM-FM...... New Berlin, PA [*FM radio station call letters*] (RBYB)
WBGN.......... Bowling Green, KY [*AM radio station call letters*]
WBGN.......... Sematan [*Indonesia*] [*ICAO location identifier*] (ICLI)
WBGO.......... Lio Matu [*Malaysia*] [*ICAO location identifier*] (ICLI)
WBGO.......... Newark, NJ [*FM radio station call letters*]
WBGP.......... Kapit [*Indonesia*] [*ICAO location identifier*] (ICLI)
WBGP.......... Waterborne Guard Post (NVT)
WBGQ.......... Bakelalan [*Malaysia*] [*ICAO location identifier*] (ICLI)
WBGR.......... Baltimore, MD [*AM radio station call letters*]
WBGR.......... Miri [*Indonesia*] [*ICAO location identifier*] (ICLI)
WBGS.......... Point Pleasant, WV [*AM radio station call letters*]
WBGS.......... Sibu [*Malaysia*] [*ICAO location identifier*] (ICLI)
WBGT.......... Staunton, VA [*FM radio station call letters*]
WBGT.......... Wet Bulb Globe Temperature
WBGT.......... Wet Bulb Globe Thermometer
WBGTI........ Wet Bulb Globe Temperature Index (RDA)
WBGU.......... Bowling Green, OH [*FM radio station call letters*]
WBGU-TV...... Bowling Green, OH [*Television station call letters*]

WBGV	Marlette, MI [*FM radio station call letters*]
WBGW	Fort Branch, IN [*FM radio station call letters*]
WBGW	Lawas [*Malaysia*] [*ICAO location identifier*] (ICLI)
WBGY	Simanggang [*Malaysia*] [*ICAO location identifier*] (ICLI)
WBGZ	Alton, IL [*AM radio station call letters*]
WBGZ	Bario [*Malaysia*] [*ICAO location identifier*] (ICLI)
WBH	Whole Blood Hematocrit [*Hematology*] (MAE)
WBH	Whole Body Hyperthermia [*Emergency medicine*] (DAVI)
WBHA	Hot Springs, VA [*FM radio station call letters*]
WBHB	Fitzgerald, GA [*AM radio station call letters*]
WBHC	Hampton, SC [*AM radio station call letters*]
WBHC-FM	Hampton, SC [*FM radio station call letters*]
WBHF	Cartersville, GA [*AM radio station call letters*]
WBHG	Meredith, NH [*FM radio station call letters*]
WBHI	Chicago, IL [*FM radio station call letters*]
WBHJ-FM	Tuscaloosa, AL [*FM radio station call letters*] (RBYB)
WBHK-FM	Warrior, AL [*FM radio station call letters*] (RBYB)
WBHL	Florence, AL [*FM radio station call letters*]
WBHM	Birmingham, AL [*FM radio station call letters*]
WBHN	Bryson City, NC [*AM radio station call letters*]
WBHO	Weather Bureau Hurricane Forecast Office [*Obsolete*]
WBHP	Huntsville, AL [*AM radio station call letters*]
WBHQ	Bloomfield, IN [*AM radio station call letters*]
WBHR	Jackson, MI [*FM radio station call letters*] (RBYB)
WBHS	Tampa, FL [*Television station call letters*]
WBHT	Mountain Top, PA [*FM radio station call letters*]
WBHV	State College, PA [*FM radio station call letters*]
WBHW-FM	Loogootee, IN [*FM radio station call letters*] (RBYB)
WBHX-FM	Tuckerton, NJ [*FM radio station call letters*] (BROA)
WBHY	Mobile, AL [*AM radio station call letters*]
WBHY-FM	Mobile, AL [*FM radio station call letters*]
WBI	Ward Behavior Inventory [*Psychology*]
WBI	Washington Beverage Insight [*Wells & Associates*] [*Information service or system*] (IID)
WBI	Web Browsing Intelligence
WB-I	Wechsler-Bellevue [*Test*] [*Psychiatry*] (DAVI)
WBI	Whiskey Butte [*Idaho*] [*Seismograph station code, US Geological Survey Closed*] (SEIS)
WBI	Will Be In (DAVI)
WBI	Will Be Issued
WBI	Wooden Box Institute [*Defunct*] (EA)
WBIB	Centreville, AL [*AM radio station call letters*]
WBIC	Royston, GA [*AM radio station call letters*]
WBIC	Weather and Battle-Induced Contaminant (PDAA)
WBIF	Wideband Intermediate Frequency (MCD)
WBIG	Aurora, IL [*AM radio station call letters*]
WBIG	Washington, DC [*FM radio station call letters*]
WBII	Washington Business Information, Inc. [*Information service or system*] (IID)
WBIL	Tuokegoo, AL [*AM radio station call letters*]
WBIL-FM	Tuskegee, AL [*FM radio station call letters*]
WBIM	Bridgewater, MA [*FM radio station call letters*]
WBIN	Benton, TN [*AM radio station call letters*]
WBIN-FM	Benton, TN [*FM radio station call letters*]
WBINVD	Write Back and Invalidate Data [*Cache*] [*Computer instruction*] (PCM)
WBIO	Philpot, KY [*FM radio station call letters*]
WBIP	Booneville, MS [*AM radio station call letters*]
WBIP	Whitaker's Books in Print [*J. Whitaker & Sons Ltd.*] [*Information service or system*] (IID)
WBIP-FM	Booneville, MS [*FM radio station call letters*]
WBIQ	Birmingham, AL [*Television station call letters*]
WBIR	Knoxville, TN [*Television station call letters*]
WBIS-TV	New York, NY [*TV station call letters*] (RBYB)
WBIT	Adel, GA [*AM radio station call letters*]
W-BIT	Wait-Bit (AAEL)
WBIT	Wechsler-Bellevue Intelligence Test [*Psychology*] (WDAA)
WBIT	World Bank of International Terms (BUAC)
WBIU	Denham Springs, LA [*AM radio station call letters*]
WBIV	Natick, MA [*AM radio station call letters*]
WBIW	Bedford, IN [*AM radio station call letters*]
WBIZ	Eau Claire, WI [*AM radio station call letters*]
WBIZ-FM	Eau Claire, WI [*FM radio station call letters*]
WBJB	Lincroft, NJ [*FM radio station call letters*]
WBJC	Baltimore, MD [*FM radio station call letters*]
WBJI	Blackduck, MN [*FM radio station call letters*]
WBJJ-FM	Jackson, LA [*FM radio station call letters*] (RBYB)
WBJW-FM	Albion, IL [*FM radio station call letters*] (RBYB)
WBJX	Racine, WI [*AM radio station call letters*]
WBK	Webb & Knapp (Canada) Ltd. [*Vancouver Stock Exchange symbol*]
WBK	Westpac Banking ADS [*NYSE symbol*] (SPSG)
WBKA	Semporna [*Malaysia*] [*ICAO location identifier*] (ICLI)
WBKB	Alpena, MI [*Television station call letters*]
WBKC	Painesville, OH [*AM radio station call letters*]
WBKC	Westbank Corp. [*NASDAQ symbol*] (SAG)
WBKD	Lahad Datu [*Malaysia*] [*ICAO location identifier*] (ICLI)
WBKE	North Manchester, IN [*FM radio station call letters*]
WBKG	Keningau [*Malaysia*] [*ICAO location identifier*] (ICLI)
WBKH	Hattiesburg, MS [*AM radio station call letters*]
WBKJ	Kosciusko, MS [*FM radio station call letters*]
WBKK	Amsterdam, NY [*FM radio station call letters*]
WBKK	Kota Kinabalu [*Malaysia*] [*ICAO location identifier*] (ICLI)
WBKL	Labuan [*Malaysia*] [*ICAO location identifier*] (ICLI)
WBKN	Brookhaven, MS [*FM radio station call letters*]
WBKO	Bowling Green, KY [*Television station call letters*]
WBKP	Pamol [*Malaysia*] [*ICAO location identifier*] (ICLI)
WBKP-TV	Calumet, MI [*TV station call letters*] (RBYB)
WBKR	Owensboro, KY [*FM radio station call letters*]
WBKR	Ranau [*Malaysia*] [*ICAO location identifier*] (ICLI)
WBKS	Sandakan [*Malaysia*] [*ICAO location identifier*] (ICLI)
WBKT	Kudat [*Malaysia*] [*ICAO location identifier*] (ICLI)
WBKV	West Bend, WI [*AM radio station call letters*]
WBKW	Tawau [*Malaysia*] [*ICAO location identifier*] (ICLI)
WBKY-FM	Portage, WI [*FM radio station call letters*] (RBYB)
WBKZ	Jefferson, GA [*AM radio station call letters*]
WBL	Weak Black Liquor [*Pulp and paper technology*]
WBL	Western Biological Laboratories
WBL	White Bluff [*Washington*] [*Seismograph station code, US Geological Survey*] (SEIS)
WBL	Wideband LASER
WBL	Wideband Limiting (IEEE)
WBL	Wissenschaftsgemeinschaft Blaue Liste
WBL	Women's Basketball League [*Defunct*] (EA)
WBL	Wood Blocking
WBL	Work Based Learning (AIE)
WBLA	Elizabethtown, NC [*AM radio station call letters*]
WBLB	Pulaski, VA [*AM radio station call letters*]
WBLC	Lenoir City, TN [*AM radio station call letters*]
WBLC	Water-Borne Logistics Craft
WBLD	Orchard Lake, MI [*FM radio station call letters*]
W Bld	Whole Blood (STED)
WBLE	Batesville, MS [*AM radio station call letters*]
WBLF	Bellefonte, PA [*AM radio station call letters*]
WBLG	Smiths Grove, KY [*FM radio station call letters*]
WBLI	Patchogue, NY [*FM radio station call letters*]
WBLJ	Dalton, GA [*AM radio station call letters*]
WBLK	Depew, NY [*FM radio station call letters*]
WBLL	Bellefontaine, OH [*AM radio station call letters*]
WBLM	Portland, ME [*FM radio station call letters*]
WBLMC	Worldwide Branch Locations of Multinational Companies [*A publication*]
WBLN	Murray, KY [*FM radio station call letters*]
WBLO	Weak Black Liquor Oxidation [*Pulp and paper technology*]
WBLQ	Block Island, RI [*FM radio station call letters*]
WBLR	Batesburg, SC [*AM radio station call letters*]
WBLS	New York, NY [*FM radio station call letters*]
WBLT	Bedford, VA [*AM radio station call letters*]
WBLU	Grand Rapids, MI [*FM radio station call letters*]
WBLV	Twin Lake, MI [*FM radio station call letters*]
WBLX	Fairhope, AL [*AM radio station call letters*]
WBLX	Mobile, AL [*FM radio station call letters*]
WBLY	Springfield, OH [*AM radio station call letters*]
WBLZ	Mt. Vernon, IN [*FM radio station call letters*]
WBM	Beloit Memorial Hospital, Beloit, WI [*Library symbol Library of Congress*] (LCLS)
WBM	Wapenamanda [*Papua New Guinea*] [*Airport symbol*] (OAG)
WB M	Weber Meter
WBM	Whole Boiled Milk (STED)
WBM	Wing Battle Manager [*Air Force*]
WBM	Woerterbuch der Mythologie [*A publication*] (BJA)
WBM	Women's Board of Missions
wb/m²	Weber per Square Meter [*Chemistry*] (DAVI)
WBMA	Western Building Material Association (EA)
WBMA	Whirlpool Bath Manufacturers Association [*Defunct*] (EA)
WBMA	Wirebound Box Manufacturers Association (EA)
WBMC	McMinnville, TN [*AM radio station call letters*]
WBMC	Weight before Mars Capture [*NASA*]
WBMCR	Wideband Multichannel Receiver
WBMD	Baltimore, MD [*AM radio station call letters*]
WBMG	Birmingham, AL [*Television station call letters*]
WBMG	Walter Bernard and Milton Glaser [*Founders of the magazine-design firm that bears their initials*]
WBMI	West Branch, MI [*FM radio station call letters*]
WBMI	Women's Board of Missions of the Interior
WBMJ	San Juan, PR [*AM radio station call letters*]
WBML	Macon, GA [*AM radio station call letters*]
WBMO	Weather Bureau Meteorological Observation Station [*Obsolete*]
WBMQ	Savannah, GA [*AM radio station call letters*]
WBMS	Wilmington, NC [*AM radio station call letters*]
WBMS	World Bureau of Metal Statistics [*British*] (EAIO)
WBMT	Boxford, MA [*FM radio station call letters*]
WBMV-FM	Mount Vernon, IL [*FM radio station call letters*] (BROA)
WBMW	Ledyard, CT [*FM radio station call letters*]
WBMX	Boston, MA [*FM radio station call letters*]
WbMyth	Woerterbuch der Mythologie [*A publication*] (BJA)
WBN	Waban, Inc. [*NYSE symbol*] (SPSG)
WBN	Well Behaved Net
WBN	Wellborn Nursery [*Neonatology*] (DAVI)
WBN	West by North
W Bn	White Beacon
WBN	Wide Band Noise (DAVI)
WBNA	Louisville, KY [*Television station call letters*]
WBNC	Conway, NH [*AM radio station call letters*]
WBNC-FM	Conway, NH [*FM radio station call letters*] (RBYB)
WBND	Westbound (FAAC)
W BNDR	With Binder [*Freight*]
WBNE	New Haven, CT [*Television station call letters*] (BROA)
WBNF	Marianna, FL [*FM radio station call letters*]
WBNG	Binghamton, NY [*Television station call letters*]
WBNH	Pekin, IL [*FM radio station call letters*]

WBNI .... Fort Wayne, IN [*FM radio station call letters*]
WBNJ .... Cape May Court House, NJ [*FM radio station call letters*]
WBNK .... Christianburg, VA [*FM radio station call letters*]
WBNL .... Boonville, IN [*AM radio station call letters*]
WBNL .... Wideband Noise Limiting
WBNL-FM ..... Boonville, IN [*FM radio station call letters*]
WBNM .... Gordon, GA [*AM radio station call letters*]
WBN-MMUMA... West Bengal Non-Ferrous Metal Merchants and Utensils Merchants Association [*India*] (BUAC)
WBNN .... Union City, IN [*FM radio station call letters*]
WBNO .... Bryan, OH [*FM radio station call letters*]
WBNP .... Watts Bar Nuclear Plant (NRCH)
WBNQ .... Bloomington, IL [*FM radio station call letters*]
WBNR .... Beacon, NY [*AM radio station call letters*]
WBNS .... Columbus, OH [*AM radio station call letters*]
WBNS .... Water Boiler Neutron Source Reactor [*Nuclear energy*]
WBNS-FM ..... Columbus, OH [*FM radio station call letters*]
WBNS-TV .... Columbus, OH [*Television station call letters*]
WBNT .... Oneida, TN [*FM radio station call letters*]
WBNU .... Charleston, SC [*Television station call letters*] (RBYB)
WBNV .... Barnesville, OH [*FM radio station call letters*]
WBNV .... Wideband Noise Voltage
WBNW .... Boston, MA [*AM radio station call letters*]
WB/NWRC ... Weather Bureau/National Weather Records Center [*Obsolete*] (KSC)
WBNX .... Akron, OH [*Television station call letters*]
WBNY .... Buffalo, NY [*FM radio station call letters*]
WBNZ .... Frankfort, MI [*FM radio station call letters*]
WBO .... Beroroha [*Madagascar*] [*Airport symbol*] (OAG)
WBO .... Weather Bureau Office [*Later, National Weather Service*]
WBO .... Western Buddhist Order [*British*] (EAIO)
WBO .... Wideband Oscilloscope
WBO .... Wideband Overlap
WBO .... Wien Bridge Oscillator [*Physics*]
W/BO .... With Blowout (MSA)
WBO .... World Boxing Organization (EA)
WBOB .... Galax, VA [*AM radio station call letters*]
WBOB .... Minneapolis, MN [*FM radio station call letters*]
WBOC .... Salisbury, MD [*Television station call letters*]
WBOD .... Waste Biochemical Oxygen Demand [*Oceanography*]
WBOG .... Tomah, WI [*FM radio station call letters*]
WBOK .... New Orleans, LA [*AM radio station call letters*]
WBOL .... Bolivar, TN [*AM radio station call letters*]
WBOM .... Danville, IL [*FM radio station call letters*] (RBYB)
WBOP .... Churchville, VA [*FM radio station call letters*]
WBOQ .... Gloucester, MA [*FM radio station call letters*]
WBOR .... Brunswick, ME [*FM radio station call letters*]
W/BOR .... White Border [*Deltiology*]
WBOS .... Brookline, MA [*FM radio station call letters*]
WBOW .... Terre Haute, IN [*AM radio station call letters*]
WBOX .... Bogalusa, LA [*AM radio station call letters*]
WBOX .... Varnado, LA [*FM radio station call letters*]
WBOY .... Clarksburg, WV [*Television station call letters*]
WBOZ .... San Juan, PR [*AM radio station call letters*] (RBYB)
WBOZ .... Woodbury, TN [*FM radio station call letters*]
WBP .... Wartime Basic Plan
WBP .... Water Bank Program [*Department of Agriculture*]
WBP .... Water Binding Potential [*of protein*]
WBP .... Weather- and Boil-Proof (IEEE)
WBP .... Women's Budget Program [*Australia*]
WBPA .... Elkhorn City, KY [*AM radio station call letters*]
WBPA .... Western Book Publishers Association (NTCM)
WBPAA .... Wine and Brandy Producers' Association of Australia
WBPASA ...... Wine and Brandy Producers' Association of South Australia
WBPB .... Wideband Patch Bay [*Telecommunications*] (IAA)
WBPC .... Water-Based Polishing Compound
WBPCASA.... Wine and Brandy Producers' Cooperative Association of South Australia
WBPF........... World Bicycle Polo Federation (EA)
WBPH........... Bethlehem, PA [*Television station call letters*]
WBPM .... Kingston, NY [*FM radio station call letters*]
WBPP .... Strasburg, VA [*FM radio station call letters*]
WBPR .... Westernbank Puerto Rico [*NASDAQ symbol*] (SAG)
WBPR .... Worcester, MA [*FM radio station call letters*]
WBPS .... Dedham, MA [*AM radio station call letters*] (RBYB)
WBPT........... Wet-Bulb Potential Temperature (PDAA)
WBPTT........ Whole Blood Partial Thromboplastin Time [*Hematology*]
WBPV .... Charlton, MA [*FM radio station call letters*]
WBPW......... Presque Isle, ME [*FM radio station call letters*]
WBPX .... Norwell, MA [*Television station call letters*] (BROA)
WBPZ........... Lock Haven, PA [*AM radio station call letters*]
WBQ .... Beaver [*Alaska*] [*Airport symbol*] (OAG)
WBQ .... Beaver, AK [*Location identifier FAA*] (FAAL)
WBQB .... Fredricksburg, VA [*FM radio station call letters*]
WBQN .... Barceloneta, PR [*AM radio station call letters*]
WBQQ .... Kennebunk, ME [*FM radio station call letters*]
WBR .... Water Boiler Reactor
WBR .... Weber
WBR .... Westbank Resources, Inc. [*Vancouver Stock Exchange symbol*]
WBR .... Wetboek van Burgerlijke Regtsvordering [*Code of Civil Procedure*] [*Dutch*] (ILCA)
WBR .... Whole Body Radiation
WBR .... Wideband Data Recorder
WBR .... Wideband Receiver
WBR .... Word Buffer Register (MSA)
WBR .... Workbench Rack (MCD)

WBRA .... Roanoke, VA [*Television station call letters*]
WBRA .... Wagon Building & Repairing Association (BUAC)
WBRB .... Mount Clemens, MI [*AM radio station call letters*]
WBRC .... Birmingham, AL [*Television station call letters*]
WBRC .... Walter Bagehot Research Council on National Sovereignty (EA)
WBRD .... Palmetto, FL [*AM radio station call letters*]
WBRD .... Wallboard
WBrE .... Elmbrook Memorial Hospital, Brookfield, WI [*Library symbol Library of Congress*] (LCLS)
WBRE .... Wilkes-Barre, PA [*Television station call letters*]
WBRF .... Galax, VA [*FM radio station call letters*]
WBRG .... Lynchburg, VA [*AM radio station call letters*]
W/BRG .... Wheel Bearing [*Automotive engineering*]
WBRH .... Baton Rouge, LA [*FM radio station call letters*]
WBRH .... Weather Bureau Regional Headquarters (FAAC)
WBRI .... Indianapolis, IN [*AM radio station call letters*]
WBrI .... International Foundation of Employee Benefit Plans, Information Center, Brookfield, WI [*Library symbol Library of Congress*] (LCLS)
WBRI .... Wheat and Barley Research Institute [*South Korea*] (BUAC)
WBRJ-FM ... Mount Sterling, IL [*FM radio station call letters*] (RBYB)
WBRK .... Pittsfield, MA [*AM radio station call letters*]
WBRM .... Marion, NC [*AM radio station call letters*]
WBRN .... Big Rapids, MI [*AM radio station call letters*]
WBRN-FM ... Big Rapids, MI [*FM radio station call letters*]
WBro .... Brodhead Memorial Public Library, Brodhead, WI [*Library symbol Library of Congress*] (LCLS)
WBRO .... Waynesboro, GA [*AM radio station call letters*]
WBRO .... Weather Bureau Regional Office [*Obsolete*]
W BRO .... Worshipful Brother [*Freemasonry*]
WBRQ .... Cidra, PR [*FM radio station call letters*]
WBRR .... Bradford, PA [*FM radio station call letters*]
WBRR .... Weather Bureau RADAR Remote [*Meteorology*]
WBRS .... Waltham, MA [*FM radio station call letters*]
WBRS .... Ward Behavior Rating Scale (DB)
WBRS .... Wideband Remote Switch (IEEE)
WBRS .... Wisconsin Behavior Rating Scale (TES)
WBRS .... Wrought Brass (MSA)
WBRT .... Bardstown, KY [*AM radio station call letters*]
WBRT .... Weather Bureau Radiotheolite [*Meteorology*]
WBRT .... Whole-Blood Recalcification Time [*Hematology*]
WBRU .... Providence, RI [*FM radio station call letters*]
WBRV .... Boonville, NY [*AM radio station call letters*]
WBRV-FM .... Boonville, NY [*FM radio station call letters*]
WBRW .... Bridgewater, NJ [*AM radio station call letters*]
WBRX .... Patton, PA [*FM radio station call letters*]
WBRY .... Woodbury, TN [*AM radio station call letters*]
WBRZ .... Baton Rouge, LA [*Television station call letters*]
WBS .... Wage Board Staff
WB-S .... Wage Board, Supervisor [*Civil Service classification*]
WBS .... Walking Beam Suspension (WDAA)
WBS .... Wallace Barnes Steel [*Wallace Barnes Co.*]
WBS .... Washington Bibliographic Service [*Information service or system*] (IID)
WBS .... Wassmann Biological Society (BUAC)
WBS .... Waterbody System (WPI)
WBS .... Waterloo County Board of Education [*UTLAS symbol*]
WBS .... WebChat Broadcasting Station
WBS .... Weight and Balance System (MCD)
WBS .... Wellington Botanical Society [*New Zealand*] (BUAC)
WBS .... Welsh Bibliographical Society [*British*]
WBS .... West by South
WBS .... Western Base Section [*England*] [*World War II*]
WBS .... Western Conservative Baptist Theological Seminary, Portland, OR [*OCLC symbol*] (OCLC)
WBS .... Whole Blood Serotonin [*Biochemistry*]
WBS .... Whole Body Scan [*Medicine*] (DMAA)
WBS .... Whole Body Shower
WBS .... Wideband System [*Ground Communications Facility, NASA*]
WBS .... Wide Body STOL [*Short Takeoff and Landing*] [*Aviation*] (IAA)
WBS .... Withdrawal Body Shakes [*Medicine*] (DMAA)
WBS .... Without Benefit of Salvage
WBS .... Women's Budget Statement [*Australia*]
WBS .... Work Breakdown Sheets [*Army*]
WBS .... Work Breakdown Structure [*Computer science*]
WBS .... World Bird Sanctuary (EA)
WBS .... World Broadcasting System (NTCM)
WBSA .... Boaz, AL [*AM radio station call letters*]
WBSA .... Weather Bureau Synoptic and Aviation Reporting Station [*Obsolete*]
WBSB .... Brunei/International [*Brunei*] [*ICAO location identifier*] (ICLI)
WBSB-FM ... Anderson, IN [*FM radio station call letters*] (RBYB)
WBSC .... Bennettsville, SC [*AM radio station call letters*]
WBSC .... Wideband Signal Conditioner (NASA)
WBSC .... Work Breakdown Structure Code (MCD)
WBSC .... World Buddhist Sangha Council [*China*] (BUAC)
WBSCB .... Work Breakdown Structure Control Board [*Army*] (AABC)
WbsCtyF ...... Webster City Federal Savings Bank [*Associated Press*] (SAG)
WBSD .... Burlington, WI [*FM radio station call letters*]
WBSEM .... Wire Bonder Specific Equipment Model [*Electronics*] (AAEL)
WBSF........... Melbourne, FL [*Television station call letters*]
WBSG .... Brunswick, GA [*Television station call letters*]
WBSH-FM ... Hagerstown, IN [*FM radio station call letters*] (RBYB)
WBSHP .... West Bengal Sexual Health Project
WBSI .... Western Behavioral Sciences Institute [*Defunct*] (EA)
WBSIGSTA... Weather Bureau Signal Station [*Obsolete*]

WBSJ-FM .... Portland, IN [*FM radio station call letters*] (RBYB)
WBSL.......... Bay St. Louis, MS [*AM radio station call letters*]
WBSL.......... Sheffield, MA [*FM radio station call letters*]
WBSL.......... Wide Beam Special LASER (MCD)
WBSM .... New Bedford, MA [*AM radio station call letters*]
WBSM .... Weber per Square Meter (IAA)
WBSN .... New Orleans, LA [*FM radio station call letters*]
WBSP .... Western Beet Sugar Producers [*Defunct*]
WBSQ-FM ... Bridgehampton, NY [*FM radio station call letters*] (BROA)
WBSR .... Pensacola, FL [*AM radio station call letters*]
WBSS .... Millville, NJ [*FM radio station call letters*]
WBST .... Muncie, IN [*FM radio station call letters*]
WBST .... Webster Financial [*NASDAQ symbol*] (TTSB)
WBST .... Webster Financial Corp. [*Waterbury, CT*] [*NASDAQ symbol*] (NQ)
WBST .... Wonderlic Basic Skills Test (TMMY)
WbstFn .... Webster Financial Corp. [*Associated Press*] (SAG)
WBSU .... Brockport, NY [*FM radio station call letters*]
WBSV .... Venice, FL [*Television station call letters*]
WBSW-FM ... Marion, IN [*FM radio station call letters*] (RBYB)
WBSX .... Ann Arbor, MI [*Television station call letters*]
WBSY .... Rose Hill, NC [*FM radio station call letters*]
WBSZ.......... Ashland, WI [*FM radio station call letters*]
WBT .... Charlotte, NC [*AM radio station call letters*]
WBT .... Wet Bulb Temperature
WBT .... Wichita Board of Trade [*Defunct*] (EA)
WBT .... Wideband Terminal (MCD)
WBT .... Wideband Transformer [*or Transmitter*]
WBT .... Windows-Based Terminal [*Computer science*]
WBT .... Women in Broadcast Technology (EA)
WBT .... Wycliffe Bible Translators (EA)
WBTA.......... Batavia, NY [*AM radio station call letters*]
WBTA.......... Wisconsin Board of Tax Appeals Decisions [*A publication*] (DLA)
WBTA-CCH Tax Reporter... Wisconsin Board of Tax Appeals Decisions (Commerce
            Clearing House) [*A publication*] (DLA)
WBTB.......... Beaufort, NC [*AM radio station call letters*]
WBTC.......... Uhrichsville, OH [*AM radio station call letters*]
WBTC.......... Waterways Bulk Transportation Council (EA)
WBTE.......... Weapon Battery Terminal Equipment [*Air Force*]
WBTE.......... Windsor, NC [*AM radio station call letters*]
WBTF.......... Attica, NY [*FM radio station call letters*]
WBTF.......... Wrightsville Beach Test Facility [*Department of the Interior*] (NOAA)
WBT-FM ..... Chester, SC [*FM radio station call letters*] (RBYB)
WBTG.......... Sheffield, AL [*AM radio station call letters*]
WBTG-FM .... Sheffield, AL [*FM radio station call letters*]
WBTH.......... Williamson, WV [*AM radio station call letters*]
WBTI........... Lexington, MI [*FM radio station call letters*]
WBTM.......... Danville, VA [*AM radio station call letters*]
WBTM HYDRO... Weather Bureau Technical Memorandum: Hydrology [*Office of
            Hydrology*] [*Washington, DC*] [*A publication*]
WBTN.......... Bennington, VT [*AM radio station call letters*]
WBTO .... Linton, IN [*AM radio station call letters*]
WBTQ.......... Buckhannon, WV [*FM radio station call letters*]
WBTR .... Carrollton, GA [*FM radio station call letters*]
WBTS .... Bridgeport, AL [*AM radio station call letters*]
WBTS.......... Waco, Beaumont, Trinity & Sabine Railway Co. [*AAR code*]
WBTS.......... Whereabouts [*Aviation*] (FAAC)
WBTS.......... Wideband Transmission System (KSC)
WBTT-FM ... Englewood, OH [*FM radio station call letters*] (RBYB)
WBTU .... Kendallville, IN [*FM radio station call letters*]
WBTV.......... Charlotte, NC [*Television station call letters*]
WBTV.......... Weather Briefing Television (AFM)
WBTW .... Florence, SC [*Television station call letters*]
WBTX.......... Broadway-Timberville, VA [*AM radio station call letters*]
WBTY.......... Homerville, GA [*AM radio station call letters*]
WBTZ-FM ... Plattsburgh, NY [*FM radio station call letters*] (RBYB)
WBU .... Boulder [*Colorado*] [*Airport symbol*] (OAG)
WBU .... Welsh Badminton Union (EAIO)
WBU .... Welsh Baseball Union (DBA)
WBU .... Wilberforce University, Wilberforce, OH [*OCLC symbol*] (OCLC)
WBU .... World Billiards Union (EAIO)
WBU .... World Blind Union (EA)
WBUB .... North Charleston, SC [*FM radio station call letters*]
WBUC.......... Buckhannon, WV [*AM radio station call letters*]
WBUC .... Western Boundary Undercurrent [*Atlantic Ocean*]
WBUC-FM ... Buckhannon, WV [*FM radio station call letters*]
WBUD.......... Trenton, NJ [*AM radio station call letters*]
WBUG.......... Amsterdam, NY [*AM radio station call letters*]
WBUG.......... Fort Plain, NY [*FM radio station call letters*]
WBUK .... Fort Shawnee, OH [*FM radio station call letters*]
WBUL.......... Shepherdsville, KY [*AM radio station call letters*]
WBUM-FM ... Baraga, MI [*FM radio station call letters*] (BROA)
WBUQ.......... Bloomsburg, PA [*FM radio station call letters*]
WBUR .... Boston, MA [*FM radio station call letters*]
WBur .... Burlington Public Library, Burlington, WI [*Library symbol Library of
            Congress*] (LCLS)
WBurSFC .... Saint Francis College, Burlington, WI [*Library symbol Library of
            Congress Obsolete*] (LCLS)
WBURY........ Westbury [*England*]
WBUS .... Kankakee, IL [*FM radio station call letters*]
WBUT .... Butler, PA [*AM radio station call letters*]
WBUX.......... Doylestown, PA [*AM radio station call letters*]
WBUY .... Holly Springs, MS [*Television station call letters*]
WBUZ.......... Delta, OH [*FM radio station call letters*]
WBV............ Wideband Voltage
WBVB .... Coal Grove, OH [*FM radio station call letters*]

WBVCO........ Wideband Voltage-Controlled Oscillator
WBVCXO...... Wideband Voltage-Controlled Crystal Oscillator
WBVD-FM ... Melbourne, FL [*FM radio station call letters*] (BROA)
WBVE-FM ... Beulah, MI [*FM radio station call letters*] (RBYB)
WBVI .... Fostoria, OH [*FM radio station call letters*]
WBVM .... Tampa, FL [*FM radio station call letters*]
WBVN .... Carrier Mills, IL [*FM radio station call letters*]
WBVP .... Beaver Falls, PA [*AM radio station call letters*]
WBVP .... Weeks Before Volume Production [*Automotive project management*]
WBVR .... Bowling Green, KY [*FM radio station call letters*]
WBVRC .... West Bromwich Volunteer Rifle Corps [*British military*] (DMA)
WBVTR .... Wideband Video Tape Recorder
WBW .... Wilkes-Barre, PA [*Location identifier FAA*] (FAAL)
WBW .... Wilson Butte [*Washington*] [*Seismograph station code, US Geological
            Survey*] (SEIS)
WBW .... World Bowling Writers (EA)
WBWB .... Bloomington, IN [*FM radio station call letters*]
WBWC .... Berea, OH [*FM radio station call letters*]
WBWI .... West Bend, WI [*FM radio station call letters*]
WBWL-AM ... Jacksonville, FL [*AM radio station call letters*] (BROA)
WBWN .... Le Roy, IL [*FM radio station call letters*]
WBWP .... Warner Brothers Worldwide Publishing [*Commercial firm*]
WBWT .... Wright Brothers Memorial Wind Tunnel [*Massachusetts Institute of
            Technology*] [*Research center*] (RCD)
WBWZ .... New Paltz, NY [*FM radio station call letters*]
WBX........... Wooden Box (MSA)
WBXB .... Edenton, NC [*FM radio station call letters*]
WBXE .... Baxter, TN [*FM radio station call letters*]
WBXL .... Baldwinsville, NY [*FM radio station call letters*]
WBXQ .... Cresson, PA [*FM radio station call letters*]
WBXR .... Hazel Green, AL [*AM radio station call letters*]
WBXX .... Battle Creek, MI [*FM radio station call letters*]
WBY........... Wimberly Resources [*Vancouver Stock Exchange symbol*]
WBYA .... Searsport, ME [*FM radio station call letters*]
WBYB-FM ... Leland, MI [*FM radio station call letters*] (BROA)
WBYE .... Calera, AL [*AM radio station call letters*]
WBYG .... Point Pleasant, WV [*FM radio station call letters*]
WBYN .... Boyertown, PA [*FM radio station call letters*]
WBYO .... Sellersville, PA [*FM radio station call letters*]
WBYP-FM ... Belzoni, MS [*FM radio station call letters*] (BROA)
WBYQ .... Baltimore, MD [*FM radio station call letters*]
WBYR .... Van Wert, OH [*FM radio station call letters*]
WBYS .... Canton, IL [*AM radio station call letters*]
WBYS-FM ... Canton, IL [*FM radio station call letters*]
WBYT .... Elkhart, IN [*FM radio station call letters*]
WBYU .... New Orleans, LA [*AM radio station call letters*]
WBYW .... Grand Rapids, MI [*FM radio station call letters*]
WBYY-FM ... Somersworth, NH [*FM radio station call letters*] (RBYB)
WBYZ .... Baxley, GA [*FM radio station call letters*]
WBZ............ Boston, MA [*AM radio station call letters*]
WBZ............ Wadati-Benioff Zone [*Geology*]
WBZ............ Works and Building, Low Priority [*British World War II*]
WBZA .... Glens Falls, NY [*AM radio station call letters*]
WBZB .... Selma, NC [*AM radio station call letters*]
WBZC.......... Pemberton, NJ [*FM radio station call letters*]
WBZE.......... Tallahassee, FL [*FM radio station call letters*]
WBZF-FM ... Marion, SC [*FM radio station call letters*] (BROA)
WBZI .... Xenia, OH [*AM radio station call letters*]
WBZK .... York, SC [*AM radio station call letters*]
WBZN .... Old Town, ME [*FM radio station call letters*]
WBZO .... Bay Shore, NY [*FM radio station call letters*]
WBZQ .... Greenville, NC [*AM radio station call letters*] (RBYB)
WBZR .... Destin, FL [*AM radio station call letters*]
WBZS.......... Alexandria, VA [*AM radio station call letters*] (RBYB)
WBZT .... West Palm Beach, FL [*AM radio station call letters*]
WBZ-TV ..... Boston, MA [*Television station call letters*]
WBZU .... Crewe, VA [*FM radio station call letters*] (RBYB)
WBZW .... Loudonville, OH [*FM radio station call letters*]
WBZX .... Columbus, OH [*FM radio station call letters*]
WBZY .... New Castle, PA [*AM radio station call letters*]
WBZZ.......... Pittsburgh, PA [*FM radio station call letters*]
W$_c$ .... Collector-Region Width (IDOE)
WC............ Cudahy Public Library, Cudahy, WI [*Library symbol Library of
            Congress*] (LCLS)
WC............ Wage Change
WC............ Wage Class (MHDI)
WC............ Wages Council [*British*] (DCTA)
W/C........... Waiver of Coinsurance [*Fire contract clause*]
WC............ Walkways Center [*Defunct*] (EA)
WC............ Walnut Council (EA)
WC............ War Cabinet [*World War II*]
WC............ War College
WC............ War Communications
WC............ Ward Clerk [*Medicine*]
WC............ Warning Computer [*Aviation*]
WC............ Watch Commanders
WC............ Watch Committee [*British*] (ILCA)
WC............ Water Chiller (DWSG)
WC............ Water Closet [*A toilet*] [*Slang*]
WC............ Water Cock (ROG)
wc............ Watercolor (VRA)
WC............ Water Column [*Mechanical engineering*]
WC............ Water Content
WC............ Water-Cooled (DEN)
WC............ Watered Capital (MHDW)

WC.............	Waterfront Center (EA)
WC.............	Waterways Commission [*Western Australia*]
W/C............	Watts per Candle [*Electricity*]
W/c............	Watts per Candle (IDOE)
W/C............	Wave Change
WC.............	WCN Investment [*Vancouver Stock Exchange symbol*]
WC.............	Weapon Carrier
WC.............	Weapons Command [*Later, Armaments Command*] [*Army*]
WC.............	Weapons Control [*or Controller*] (NVT)
WC.............	Weather Center [*Meteorology*] (DA)
WC.............	Weather Condition [*Nuclear energy*] (NRCH)
WC.............	Weber-Christian [*Syndrome*] [*Medicine*] (DB)
WC.............	We Care (EA)
W/C............	Week Commencing (ADA)
WC.............	Wesleyan Chapel (ROG)
WC.............	Westbeth Corp. (EA)
WC.............	West Central [*Refers especially to London postal district*]
WC.............	West Coast Airlines, Inc.
WC.............	Western Cedar [*Utility pole*] [*Telecommunications*] (TEL)
WC.............	Western Central
WC.............	Western Civilization
WC.............	Western Classification
WC.............	Western Command
WC.............	Westminster College [*London, England*]
WC.............	Westminster Commentaries [*Oxford*] [*A publication*] (BJA)
WC.............	Wet Chemical System [*NFPA pre-fire planning symbol*] (NFPA)
WC.............	Whale Center (EA)
WC.............	Wheel Center (MSA)
WC.............	Wheelchair
WC.............	White Cell [*Medicine*]
WC.............	White Cell Cast [*Hematology*] (MAE)
W/C............	White Clothing [*British military*] (DMA)
W/C............	White Collar [*Worker*] (DCTA)
WC.............	White Confederacy [*Defunct*] (EA)
WC.............	White Count [*Hematology*]
WC.............	Whole Complement (MAE)
WC.............	Whooping Cough [*Medicine*]
WC.............	Width Codes (AAG)
WC.............	Wien Air Alaska [*ICAO designator*] (AD)
WC.............	Wild Caught Animal [*Medicine*] (DMAA)
WC.............	Wildflower Club (BUAC)
WC.............	Will Call
WC.............	Wills Club (EA)
WC.............	Willys Club (EA)
WC.............	Wilshire Club [*Defunct*] (EA)
WC.............	Wind Current (COE)
WC.............	Wing Commander [*British military*]
WC.............	Wings Club (EA)
WC.............	Winston Cup
WC.............	Wire Chief [*Test clerk*] [*Telecommunications*] (TEL)
WC.............	Wireless Communication (IAA)
WC.............	With Corrections [*Publishing*]
WC.............	Without Charge
wc.............	Without Charge (ODBW)
WC.............	Woden's Coven [*Germany Defunct*] (EAIO)
W-C............	Women-Church: an Australian Journal of Feminist Studies in Religion [*A publication*] (APTA)
WC.............	Women in Communications (EA)
WC.............	Women's Centre [*India*] (BUAC)
WC.............	Women's College [*University of Sydney*] [*Australia*]
WC.............	Women's Reserve, Communications Duties [*USNR officer designation*]
WC.............	Wood Casing
WC.............	Wood Covers (DS)
WC.............	Woodfree Coated [*Paper*] (DGA)
WC.............	Woolwich College [*London, England*]
WC.............	Word Count [*Computer science*]
WC.............	Work Capacity (MAE)
WC.............	Work Card (AAG)
WC.............	Work Center (AFM)
WC.............	Work Circle (AAG)
WC.............	Work Control (AAG)
WC.............	Workers Compensation (WPI)
WC.............	Working Capital
WC.............	Working Circle [*Technical drawings*]
WC.............	Working Current (IAA)
WC.............	Workmen's Circle [*New York, NY*] (EA)
WC.............	Workmen's Compensation [*Department of Health and Human Services*]
WC.............	World Concern (EA)
WC.............	World Coordinate
WC.............	World's Classics [*A publication*]
WC.............	Write and Compute
WC.............	Written Component [*Qualification test*] [*Military*]
WCA............	Castro [*Chile*] [*Airport symbol*] (AD)
WCA............	Warm Cranking Amperes [*Battery*] [*Automotive engineering*]
WCA............	Warrant Claims Action [*Army*]
WCA............	Water Companies' Association [*British*]
WCA............	Waterproofing Contractors Association (NTPA)
WCA............	Weapon Control Area [*Military*] (CAAL)
WCA............	Weimaraner Club of America (EA)
WCA............	Wellness Councils of America (NTPA)
WCA............	West Coast Airlines, Inc.
WCA............	West Coast Airlines Ltd. [*Ghana*]
WCA............	West Coast of Africa (ROG)

WCA............	Western Coal Association [*Australia*]
WCA............	Western College Association (EA)
WCA............	Who Cares, Anyway
WCA............	Whole Core Accident [*Nuclear energy*] (NRCH)
WCA............	Wholesale Caterers' Alliance (BUAC)
WCA............	Wholesale Confectioners Alliance Ltd. [*British*] (BI)
WCA............	Wideband Cassegrain Antenna
WCA............	Wildlife Conservation Act (COE)
WCA............	Willys Club of America [*Later, WC*] (EA)
WCA............	Wind Correction Angle [*Aviation*] (DA)
WCA............	Windmill Class Association (EA)
WCA............	Wine Conference of America [*Defunct*] (EA)
WCA............	Winston S. Churchill Association [*Defunct*] (EA)
WCA............	Wireless Cable Association (TSSD)
WCA............	Wisco of Canada Ltd. [*Vancouver Stock Exchange symbol*]
WCA............	Women's Caucus for Art (EA)
WCA............	Women's Christian Association
WCA............	Women's Cricket Association [*British*]
WCA............	Wood Carver's Association [*British*] (DBA)
WCA............	Wool Council of Australia (BUAC)
WCA............	Working-Capital Account (MHDW)
WCA............	Workmen's Compensation Act
WCA............	World Calendar Association (BUAC)
WCA............	World Campus Afloat [*Cruise ship educational program*] (EA)
WCA............	World Christian Action [*Australia*]
WCA............	World Citizens Assembly [*Later, AWC*] (EA)
WCA............	World Communication Association (EA)
WCA............	Worst Case Analysis
WCAA..........	West Coast Athletic Association (WDAA)
WCAA..........	Window Coverings Association of America (EA)
WCAB..........	Rutherfordton, NC [*AM radio station call letters*]
WCAB..........	WorkCare Appeals Board [*Victoria, Australia*]
WCAB..........	Workers' Compensation Appeals Board
WCAB..........	Working Committee of the Aeronautical Board
WCAC..........	Western Christian Athletic Conference (PSS)
WCACA........	World Christian Anti-Communist Association [*Taiwan*] (BUAC)
WCACTC	West Coast Air Corps Training Center
WCAD..........	San Juan, PR [*FM radio station call letters*]
WCADL........	Weaker Community's Action for Development and Liberation [*India*] (BUAC)
WCAE..........	Nekoosa, WI [*AM radio station call letters*]
WCAF-FM	Carrabelle, FL [*FM radio station call letters*] (BROA)
WCAFS	Wideband Cassegrain Antenna Feed System
WCAHI	World Conference of Animal Health Industries [*Australia*]
WCAI	Water Conditioning Association International [*Later, WQA*] (EA)
WCAI	Wireless Cable Association International (NTPA)
WCAI	Wireless Cable Atlanta [*NASDAQ symbol*] (TTSB)
WCAI	Wireless Cable of Atlanta, Inc. [*NASDAQ symbol*] (SAG)
WCAK..........	Carlisle, KY [*FM radio station call letters*]
WCAL..........	Northfield, MN [*FM radio station call letters*]
WCAM	Camden, SC [*AM radio station call letters*]
WCAM	Wisconsin Center for Applied Microelectronics [*University of Wisconsin - Madison*] [*Research center*] (RCD)
WCAN	Canajoharie, NY [*FM radio station call letters*]
WCAN	Worldwide Crisis Alerting Network (MCD)
WC & EL......	Workers' Compensation and Employers' Liability [*Insurance*]
WC & Ins (Eng)...	Workmen's Compensation and Insurance Reports [*1912-33*] [*England*] [*A publication*] (DLA)
WC & Ins Rep...	Workmen's Compensation and Insurance Reports [*1912-33*] [*England*] [*A publication*] (DLA)
WC & IR	Workmen's Compensation and Insurance Reports [*1912-33*] [*England*] [*A publication*] (DLA)
WC & I Rep...	Workmen's Compensation and Insurance Reports [*1912-33*] [*A publication*] (DLA)
WCANSW.....	Workcover Authority of New South Wales [*Australia*]
WCAO	Baltimore, MD [*AM radio station call letters*]
WCAP	Lowell, MA [*AM radio station call letters*]
WCAP	Westinghouse Commercial Atomic Power
WCAP	Winfield Capital [*NASDAQ symbol*] (TTSB)
WCAP	Winfield Capital Corp. [*NASDAQ symbol*] (SAG)
WCAP	World Climate Applications Program [*WMO*] [*ICSU*]
WCAPW........	Winfield Capital Wrrt [*NASDAQ symbol*] (TTSB)
WCAR	Livonia, MI [*AM radio station call letters*]
WCAR	West Coast Formula Atlantic (Racing)
WCARRD	World Conference on Agrarian Reform and Rural Developments (BUAC)
WCARU........	Western Carolina University (PDAA)
WCASP	World Climate Applications and Services Program (EERA)
WCASS	World Conference of Ashkenazi and Sephardi Synagogues
WCAT..........	Athol, MA [*FM radio station call letters*]
WCAT..........	Orange-Athol, MA [*AM radio station call letters*]
WCAT..........	Weiss Comprehensive Articulation Test [*Education*]
WCAU..........	Philadelphia, PA [*Television station call letters*]
WCAV	Brockton, MA [*FM radio station call letters*]
WCAW.........	Charleston, WV [*AM radio station call letters*]
WCAX..........	Burlington, VT [*Television station call letters*]
WCAZ..........	Carthage, IL [*AM radio station call letters*]
WCAZ-FM	Carthage, IL [*FM radio station call letters*]
WCB............	War Communications Board [*World War II*]
WCB............	Warramunga Array [*Australia Seismograph station code, US Geological Survey*] (SEIS)
WCB............	Water Control Board
WCB............	Way Control Block
WCB............	Weekly Criminal Bulletin [*Canada Law Book, Inc.*] [*Information service or system*]

WCB............ Wellington County Board of Education [*UTLAS symbol*]
WCB............ West Africa Airlines Ltd. [*Ghana*] [*ICAO designator*] (FAAC)
WCB............ Will Call Back
WCB............ William C. Brown Publishers
WCB............ Workers' Compensation Board [*Australia*]
WCB............ Workmen's Compensation Board
WCB............ World Council for the Biosphere [*Switzerland*] (BUAC)
WCBA.......... Corning, NY [*AM radio station call letters*]
WCBA.......... Washington Chinese Business Association
WCBA.......... Women Cooperative Business Association [*Nigeria*] (BUAC)
WCBA-FM...... Corning, NY [*FM radio station call letters*]
WCBB.......... Augusta, ME [*Television station call letters*]
WCBC.......... Cumberland, MD [*AM radio station call letters*]
WCBC.......... Keyser, WV [*FM radio station call letters*]
WCBC.......... West Coast Bancorp (EFIS)
WCBC.......... World Candlepin Bowling Council
WCBD.......... Charleston, SC [*Television station call letters*]
WCBF-FM...... Clinton, KY [*FM radio station call letters*] (BROA)
WCBG.......... Chambersburg, PA [*AM radio station call letters*]
WCBH.......... Casey, IL [*FM radio station call letters*]
WCBI.......... Columbus, MS [*Television station call letters*]
WCBI.......... Westco Bancorp [*NASDAQ symbol*] (TTSB)
WCBI.......... Westco Bancorp, Inc. [*NASDAQ symbol*] (SAG)
WCB-ISEE...... World Council for the Biosphere-International Society for Environmental Education (BUAC)
WCBK.......... Martinsville, IN [*FM radio station call letters*]
WCBL.......... Benton, KY [*AM radio station call letters*]
WCBL.......... World Council of Blind Lions [*Later, ACBL*] (EA)
WCBL-FM...... Benton, KY [*FM radio station call letters*]
WCBM.......... Baltimore, MD [*AM radio station call letters*]
WCBN.......... Ann Arbor, MI [*FM radio station call letters*]
WCBO.......... West Coast Bancorp (Oregon) [*NASDAQ symbol*] (SAG)
WCBQ.......... Oxford, NC [*AM radio station call letters*]
WCBR.......... Arlington Heights, IL [*FM radio station call letters*]
WCBR.......... Richmond, KY [*AM radio station call letters*]
WCBS.......... New York, NY [*AM radio station call letters*]
WCBS.......... World Confederation of Billiards Sports [*Malaysia*] (EAIO)
WCBS-FM...... New York, NY [*FM radio station call letters*]
WCBS-TV...... New York, NY [*Television station call letters*]
WCBSU.......... West Coast Base Service Unit [*Navy*]
WCBT.......... Roanoke Rapids, NC [*AM radio station call letters*]
WCBU.......... Peoria, IL [*FM radio station call letters*]
WCBW.......... Columbia, IL [*FM radio station call letters*]
WCBX.......... Bassett, VA [*AM radio station call letters*]
WCBY.......... Cheboygan, MI [*AM radio station call letters*]
WCBZ.......... Williamston, NC [*FM radio station call letters*]
WCC............ Gerard P. Weeg Computing Center [*University of Iowa*] [*Research center*] (RCD)
WCC............ Sports Air Travel, Inc. [*ICAO designator*] (FAAC)
WCC............ Wales Craft Council (DBA)
WCC............ Wallace Communications Consultants [*Tampa, FL*] [*Telecommunications*] (TSSD)
WCC............ War Claims Commission [*Abolished, 1954*]
WCC............ War Cover Club (EA)
WCC............ War Crimes Commission (WDAA)
WCC............ Warfare Commanders Course (DOMA)
WCC............ Washington Computer Center (COE)
WCC............ Washington's United States Circuit Court Reports [*A publication*] (DLA)
WCC............ Waste Collection Containers
WCC............ Water-Cooled Copper
WCC............ Waters Computing Center [*Rose-Hulman Institute of Technology*] [*Research center*] (RCD)
WCC............ Watson Collectors Club (EA)
WCC............ Weapon Control Computer (MCD)
WCC............ Weapon Control Console [*Military*] (CAAL)
WCC............ Weapons Control Concept (MCD)
WCC............ Welsh Consumer Council [*British*] (ILCA)
WCC............ Westchester Community College [*Valhalla, NY*]
WCC............ Westchester Community College, Technical Services, Valhalla, NY [*OCLC symbol*] (OCLC)
WCC............ West Coast Conference (PSS)
WCC............ Western Canada Concept [*Political party*] (PPW)
WCC............ Western Carolina College [*Later, WCU*] [*North Carolina*]
WCC............ Westminster Choir College [*Princeton, NJ*]
WCC............ Whim Creek Consolidated [*Toronto Stock Exchange symbol*]
WCC............ White Cell Count [*Hematology*] (MAE)
WCC............ White Citizens' Council (WDAA)
WCC............ Whitney Communications Corp. [*New York, NY*]
WCC............ Widows Consultation Center [*Defunct*] (EA)
WCC............ Wildfire Coordinating Committee (EA)
WCC............ Wilson Cloud Chamber [*Physics*]
WCC............ Wingate Computer Center (HGAA)
WCC............ Women Church Convergence [*An association*] (EA)
WCC............ Women of the Church Coalition (EA)
WCC............ Women's Classical Caucus (EA)
WCC............ Women's College Coalition (EA)
WCC............ Women's Consultative Committee [*Ministry of Labour*] [*British World War II*]
WCC............ Women's Co-Ordination Council [*India*] (BUAC)
WCC............ Work Center Code
WCC............ Work Control Center (AAG)
WCC............ Workmen's Compensation Cases [*Legal*] [*British*]
WCC............ World Cheerleader Council (EA)
WCC............ World Climate Conference (BUAC)
WCC............ World Congress Centre [*Melbourne, Australia*]
WCC............ World Congress on Computing [*Trade show*]
WCC............ World Council of Christians [*Defunct*] (EA)
WCC............ World Council of Churches [*Geneva, Switzerland*]
WCC............ World Council of Clergy [*Defunct*] (EA)
WCC............ World Council of Clergyman (BUAC)
WCC............ World Crafts Council (EA)
WCC............ World Cultural Council (BUAC)
WCC............ World for Christ Crusade (EA)
WCC............ Worldwide Collectors Club [*Later, ISWSC*] (EA)
WCC............ Write Control Character [*Computer science*] (IAA)
WCCA.......... Shallotte, NC [*FM radio station call letters*]
WCCA.......... West Cameroon Cooperative Association (BUAC)
WCCA.......... West Coast Crossarm Association [*Defunct*]
WCCA.......... Whiteruthenian [*Byelorussian*] Congress Committee of America [*Later, Byelorussian Congress Committee of America*] (EA)
WCCA.......... Wholesale Cash and Carry Association (BUAC)
WCCA.......... Whooping Crane Conservation Association (EA)
WCCA.......... World Court Clubs Association [*Defunct*] (EA)
WCCA.......... Worst Case Circuit Analysis
WCCAC.......... Wyoming Community College Athletic Conference (PSS)
WCC&CRA...... World Championship Cutter and Chariot Racing Association (EA)
WCCB.......... Charlotte, NC [*Television station call letters*]
WCCC.......... Hartford, CT [*AM radio station call letters*]
WCCC.......... Warwick China Collectors Club [*Defunct*] (EA)
WCCC.......... Wayne County Community College [*Detroit, MI*]
WCCC.......... Wisconsin Clinical Cancer Center [*University of Wisconsin*] [*Research center*] (RCD)
WCCC.......... World Convention of Churches of Christ (EA)
WCCC-FM...... Hartford, CT [*FM radio station call letters*]
WCCD.......... Parma, OH [*AM radio station call letters*]
WCCDBP........ Weapon Control Computer Debug Program [*Military*]
WCCE.......... Buie's Creek, NC [*FM radio station call letters*]
WCCE.......... West Coast Commodity Exchange
WCCE.......... World Conference on Computers in Education
WCCE.......... World Council of Christian Education [*Later absorbed into Office of Education of World Council of Churches*]
WCCES.......... World Council of Comparative Education Societies (EA)
WCCESSA...... World Council of Christian Education and Sunday School Association [*Later, WCCE*] (EA)
WCCF.......... Punta Gorda, FL [*AM radio station call letters*]
WCCG.......... Hope Mills, NC [*FM radio station call letters*]
WCCH.......... Holyoke, MA [*FM radio station call letters*]
WCCI.......... Savanna, IL [*FM radio station call letters*]
WCCI.......... Western Country Clubs [*NASDAQ symbol*] (TTSB)
WCCI.......... Western Country Clubs, Inc. [*NASDAQ symbol*] (SAG)
WCCI.......... World Council for Curriculum and Instruction (EA)
WCCJ.......... Harrisburg, NC [*FM radio station call letters*] (RBYB)
WCCK.......... Calvert City, KY [*FM radio station call letters*]
WCCK.......... Weapons Control Check (NVT)
WCCL.......... New Orleans, LA [*Television station call letters*]
WCCL.......... Welsh Council for Civil Liberties (BUAC)
WCCLGF........ Welsh Consultative Council on Local Government Finance (BUAC)
WCCLS.......... Washington County Cooperative Library Services [*Library network*]
WCCM.......... Lawrence, MA [*AM radio station call letters*]
WCCMORS...... West Coast Classified Military Operations Research Symposium
WCCN.......... Neillsville, WI [*AM radio station call letters*]
WCCN.......... Wisconsin Coordinating Council on Nicaragua (EA)
WCCN-FM...... Neillsville, WI [*FM radio station call letters*]
WCC (NZ)...... Workers' Compensation Cases (New Zealand) [*A publication*] (DLA)
WCCO.......... Minneapolis, MN [*AM radio station call letters*]
WCCON.......... Whether Cleared Customs or Not [*Shipping*] (DS)
WCCO-TV...... Minneapolis, MN [*Television station call letters*]
WCCP.......... Clemson, SC [*AM radio station call letters*]
WCCP.......... Woodward-Clyde Consultants, Pasadena [*California*]
WCCP-FM...... Clemson, SC [*FM radio station call letters*]
WCCPPS........ Waste Channel and Containment Pressurization and Penetration System (IEEE)
WCCQ.......... Crest Hill, IL [*FM radio station call letters*]
WCCR.......... Clarion, PA [*FM radio station call letters*]
WCCR.......... Washington's United States Circuit Court Reports [*A publication*] (DLA)
WCCRS.......... Western Catholic Charismatic Renewal Services [*A publication*]
WCCS.......... Homer City, PA [*AM radio station call letters*]
WCCS.......... Window Contamination Control Number
WCCS.......... Wireless Crew Communications System (LAIN)
WCCS.......... World Chamber of Commerce Service (EA)
WCCSA.......... White Clay Creek Study Act of 1991 (COE)
WCCSIS.......... Westchester County Community Services Information System [*Westchester LibrarySystem*] [*Information service or system*] (IID)
WCCT.......... Harwich, MA [*FM radio station call letters*]
WCCU.......... Urbana, IL [*Television station call letters*]
WCCU.......... Wireless Crew Communication Unit [*NASA*] (NAKS)
WCC/US........ US Conference for the World Council of Churches (EA)
WCCV.......... Arecibo, PR [*Television station call letters*]
WCCV.......... Cartersville, GA [*FM radio station call letters*]
WCCW.......... Traverse City, MI [*AM radio station call letters*]
WCCW-FM...... Traverse City, MI [*FM radio station call letters*]
WCCX.......... Wackenhut Corrections Corp. [*NASDAQ symbol*] (SAG)
WCCX.......... Waukesha, WI [*FM radio station call letters*]
WCCY.......... Houghton, MI [*AM radio station call letters*]
WCCZ.......... Pinckneyville, IL [*FM radio station call letters*] (RBYB)
WCD............ Weapons Classification Defects [*Navy*] (NG)
WCD............ Weather Card Data (IAA)

WCD .... We Can Do [*An association*] (EA)
WCD .... Welsh Council for the Disabled (BUAC)
WCD .... Western Canadian Mining [*Vancouver Stock Exchange symbol*]
WCD .... Wet Chemical Oxidation [*Chemistry*]
WCD .... Work Center Description (AFM)
WCD .... Workshop for Cultural Democracy (EA)
WCD .... World Commission on Dams [*South Africa*]
WCD .... World Committee on Disability (EA)
WCD .... Worse Case Difference (IAA)
WCDA .... Vorheesville, NY [*FM radio station call letters*]
WCDA .... Women and Child Development Association [*India*] (BUAC)
WCDB .... Albany, NY [*FM radio station call letters*]
WCDB .... Wing Control During Boost
WCDB .... Work Control Data Base (NASA)
WCDC .... Adams, MA [*Television station call letters*]
WCDC .... West Coast [*Naval Publications*] Distribution Center
WC(DD)B .... Worker's Compensation (Dust Diseases) Board [*Australia*]
WCDE .... Elkins, WV [*FM radio station call letters*]
WCDF .... World Children's Day Foundation (EA)
WCDFMA .... Water Cooler and Drinking Fountain Manufacturers Association
WCDI .... World Council of Defense Investigators (NTPA)
WCDJ .... Truro, MA [*FM radio station call letters*]
WCDK .... Cadiz, OH [*FM radio station call letters*]
WCDL .... Carbondale, PA [*AM radio station call letters*]
WCDM .... Welsh Committee on Drug Misuse (BUAC)
W-CDMA .... Wideband Code Division Multiple Access
WCDMP .... World Climate and Data Monitoring Program [*Marine science*] (OSRA)
WCDMP .... World Climate Data and Monitoring Program (EERA)
WCDO .... Sidney, NY [*AM radio station call letters*]
WCDO .... War Consumable Distribution Objective (AFM)
WCDO-FM .... Sidney, NY [*FM radio station call letters*]
WCDP .... Widows', Children's, and Dependents' Pension [*British*]
WCDP .... World Climate Data Program [*WMO*] [*ICSU*]
WCDPC .... War Control Data Processing Center (IAA)
WCDQ .... Sanford, ME [*FM radio station call letters*]
WCDR .... Cedarville, OH [*FM radio station call letters*]
W/Cdr .... Wing Commander [*British military*]
WCDS .... Glasgow, KY [*AM radio station call letters*]
WCDS .... West Coast Naval Publications Distribution Center (DNAB)
WCDT .... Westminster Centre for Design and Technology [*British*] (AIE)
WCDT .... Winchester, TN [*AM radio station call letters*]
WCDV .... Covington, IN [*FM radio station call letters*]
WCDW-FM .... Conklin, NY [*FM radio station call letters*] (BROA)
WCDX .... Mechanicsville, VA [*FM radio station call letters*]
WCDZ .... Dresden, TN [*FM radio station call letters*]
WCE .... Weapon Control Equipment
WCE .... West Coast of England [*Shipping*]
WCE .... Western Corporate Enterprises, Inc. [*Toronto Stock Exchange symbol*]
WCE .... Wiener Canonical Expansion [*Mathematics*]
WCE .... World Christian Encyclopedia [*A publication*]
WCEB .... Corning, NY [*FM radio station call letters*]
WCEC .... West Coast Entertainment [*NASDAQ symbol*] (TTSB)
WCEC .... West Coast Entertainment Corp. [*NASDAQ symbol*] (SAG)
WCED .... Du Bois, PA [*AM radio station call letters*]
WCED .... World Commission on Environment and Development (EA)
WCEDM .... World Congress on Emergency & Disaster Medicine (WDAA)
WCEE .... Mount Vernon, IL [*Television station call letters*]
WCEE .... Women's Council on Energy and the Environment (EA)
WCEF .... Ripley, WV [*FM radio station call letters*]
WCEG .... Middleboro, MA [*AM radio station call letters*]
WCEH .... Hawkinsville, GA [*AM radio station call letters*]
WCEI .... Easton, MD [*AM radio station call letters*]
WCEI-FM .... Easton, MD [*FM radio station call letters*]
WCEL-FM .... Plattsburgh, NY [*FM radio station call letters*] (RBYB)
WCEM .... Cambridge, MD [*AM radio station call letters*]
WCEMA .... West Coast Electronic Manufacturers' Association [*Later, AEA*]
WCEM-FM .... Cambridge, MD [*FM radio station call letters*]
WCEN .... Mount Pleasant, MI [*AM radio station call letters*]
WCEN-FM .... Mount Pleasant, MI [*FM radio station call letters*]
WCER .... Canton, OH [*AM radio station call letters*]
WCER .... Wisconsin Center for Education Research [*Madison*]
WCES .... Wolfson Centre for Electrochemical Science [*British*] (CB)
WCES .... Women's Caucus of the Endocrine Society (EA)
WCES .... Wrens, GA [*Television station call letters*]
WCET .... Cincinnati, OH [*Television station call letters*]
WCET .... Weighted Common Examination Total (EDAC)
WCET .... World Council of Enterostomal Therapy Nurses (BUAC)
WCEU .... New Smyrna Beach, FL [*Television station call letters*]
WCEU .... World's Christian Endeavor Union (EA)
WCEV .... Cicero, IL [*AM radio station call letters*]
WCEZ .... Delaware, OH [*FM radio station call letters*]
WCf .... Chippewa Falls Public Library, Chippewa Falls, WI [*Library symbol Library of Congress*] (LCLS)
WCF .... Commmonwealth Weighlifting Federation (BUAC)
WCF .... Waste Calcination [*or Calcining*] Facility [*Nuclear energy*]
WCF .... Water Conditioning Foundation [*Later, WQA*] (EA)
WCF .... White Cathode Follower
WCF .... Winchester Center Fire [*Rifles*] (DICI)
WCF .... Winnipeg Commodity Exchange [*Canada*] (NUMA)
WCF .... Winston Churchill Foundation (EA)
WCF .... Women's Campaign Fund (EA)
WCF .... Workers' Christian Fellowship [*British*] (BI)
WCF .... Working Capital Fund
WCF .... Workload Control File
WCF .... World Congress of Faiths - The Inter-Faith Fellowship [*British*] (EAIO)
WCF .... World Congress of Flight
WCF .... World Curling Federation [*British*] (EAIO)
WCFA .... Wholesale Commission Florists of America [*Later, WF & FSA*]
WCFA .... Wildlife Conservation Fund of America (EA)
WCFB .... Daytona Beach, FL [*FM radio station call letters*]
WCFB .... Webster City Federal Savings Bank [*NASDAQ symbol*] (SAG)
WCFB .... Webster City Fed Svgs Bk [*NASDAQ symbol*] (TTSB)
WCFBA .... World Catholic Federation for the Biblical Apostolate [*Stuttgart, Federal Republic of Germany*] (EAIO)
WCFC .... Chicago, IL [*Television station call letters*]
WCFC .... Washington Capitals Fan Club (EA)
WCFE .... Plattsburgh, NY [*FM radio station call letters*]
WCFE-TV .... Plattsburgh, NY [*Television station call letters*]
WCFF .... Westinghouse Commercial Fuel Facility
WCFI .... Lajas, PR [*FM radio station call letters*]
WCFJ .... Chicago Heights, IL [*AM radio station call letters*]
WCFL .... Morris, IL [*FM radio station call letters*]
WCFN .... Springfield, IL [*Television station call letters*]
WCfNC .... Northern Wisconsin Colony and Training School, Chippewa Falls, WI [*Library symbol Library of Congress*] (LCLS)
WCFPR .... Washington Center of Foreign Policy Research (MCD)
WCFR .... Springfield, VT [*AM radio station call letters*]
WCFR .... Washington Citizens for Recycling (EA)
WCFR-FM .... Springfield, VT [*FM radio station call letters*]
WCFRU .... Washington Cooperative Fishery Research Unit [*University of Washington*] [*Research center*] (RCD)
WCfSJ .... Saint Joseph's Hospital, Chippewa Falls, WI [*Library symbol Library of Congress*] (LCLS)
WCFT .... Tuscaloosa, AL [*Television station call letters*]
WCFTB .... West Coast Freight Tariff Bureau
WCFU .... World Congress of Free Ukrainians (BUAC)
WCFW .... Chippewa Falls, WI [*FM radio station call letters*]
WCFX .... Clare, MI [*FM radio station call letters*]
WCFY .... Lafayette, IN [*AM radio station call letters*]
WCG .... War Crimes Group [*British*]
WCG .... Washington Calligraphers Guild (EA)
WCG .... Water-Cooled Garment
WCG .... Weapon Control Group [*Military*] (CAAL)
WCG .... West Coast Airlines Ltd. [*Ghana*] [*ICAO designator*] (FAAC)
WCG .... Willis Corroon Group ADS [*NYSE symbol*] (SPSG)
WCG .... Women of the Church of God (EA)
WCG .... Worldwide Church of God
WCGA .... Woodbine, GA [*AM radio station call letters*]
WCGA .... World Computer Graphics Association (EA)
WCGB .... Juana Diaz, PR [*AM radio station call letters*]
WCGC .... Belmont, NC [*AM radio station call letters*]
WCGL .... Jacksonville, FL [*AM radio station call letters*]
WCGLJO .... World Congress of Gay and Lesbian Jewish Organizations (EA)
WCGM .... Writable Character Generation Memory (NITA)
WCGM .... Writable Character Generation Module [*Computer science*] (BUR)
WCGO .... Chicago Heights, IL [*AM radio station call letters*]
WCGQ .... Columbus, GA [*FM radio station call letters*]
WCGR .... Canandaigua, NY [*AM radio station call letters*]
WCGR .... Waterloo Centre for Groundwater Research [*University of Waterloo*] [*Canada*] (IRC)
WCGS .... Western Collaborative Group Study [*University of California*] [*Psychology*]
WCGS .... Wolf Creek Generating Station [*Nuclear energy*] (NRCH)
WCGTC .... World Council for Gifted and Talented Children (EA)
WCGV .... Milwaukee, WI [*Television station call letters*]
WCGW .... Nicholasville, KY [*AM radio station call letters*]
WCGZ .... World Confederation of General Zionists [*Later, WCUZ*] (EA)
WCH .... Chaiten [*Chile*] [*Airport symbol*] (AD)
WCh .... Chippewa Falls Public Library, Chippewa Falls, WI [*Library symbol Library of Congress Obsolete*] (LCLS)
WCH .... Weekly Contact Hours
WCH .... West Coast Handling
WCH .... Wichita [*Diocesan abbreviation*] [*Kansas*] (TOCD)
WCH .... Working Class Hero (EA)
WCH .... World Congress of Herpetology (BUAC)
WCHA .... Chambersburg, PA [*AM radio station call letters*]
WCHA .... Western Collegiate Hockey Association (EA)
WCHA .... Wooden Canoe Heritage Association (EA)
WCHB .... Taylor, MI [*AM radio station call letters*]
WCHB-FM .... Detroit, MI [*FM radio station call letters*] (RBYB)
WCHC .... Worcester, MA [*FM radio station call letters*]
WCHE .... West Chester, PA [*AM radio station call letters*]
WCHEN .... Western Council on Higher Education for Nursing
W'CHESTER .... Winchester [*Borough in South England*] (ROG)
WCHF .... Wet Crude Handling Facilities [*Petroleum engineering*]
WCHG-FM .... Hot Springs, VA [*FM radio station call letters*] (BROA)
WCHI .... Chillicothe, OH [*AM radio station call letters*]
WCHI .... Women's Council for the Histadrut in Israel (EA)
WCHI .... Workingmens Cap Hldgs [*NASDAQ symbol*] (TTSB)
WCHI .... Workingmens Capital Holdings, Inc. [*NASDAQ symbol*] (SAG)
WCHJ .... Brookhaven, MS [*AM radio station call letters*]
WCHK .... Canton, GA [*AM radio station call letters*]
WCHL .... Chapel Hill, NC [*AM radio station call letters*]
WCHM .... Clarkesville, GA [*AM radio station call letters*]
WCHN .... Norwich, NY [*AM radio station call letters*]
WCHO .... Washington Court House, OH [*FM radio station call letters*]
WCHP .... Champlain, NY [*AM radio station call letters*]
WCHQ .... Camuy, PR [*AM radio station call letters*]

WCHQ-FM.... Camuy, PR [*FM radio station call letters*]
WCHR......... Trenton, NJ [*FM radio station call letters*]
WCHR......... Water Chiller
WCHR......... Worldwide Creme Horse Registry (EA)
WCHS......... Charleston, WV [*AM radio station call letters*]
WCHS-TV..... Charleston, WV [*Television station call letters*]
WCHT......... Escanaba, MI [*AM radio station call letters*]
WCHV......... Charlottesville, VA [*AM radio station call letters*]
WCHW........ Bay City, MI [*AM radio station call letters*]
WCHX......... Lewistown, PA [*FM radio station call letters*]
WCHY......... Savannah, GA [*AM radio station call letters*]
WCHY-FM.... Savannah, GA [*FM radio station call letters*]
WCHZ......... Harlem, GA [*FM radio station call letters*]
WCI........... Waiting Calls Indicator (NITA)
WCI........... Washington International College, Washington, DC [*OCLC symbol*]
              (OCLC)
WCI........... Weapon Control Index [*Military*] (CAAL)
WCI........... White Cast Iron
WCI........... White Consolidated Industries, Inc. (EFIS)
WCI........... Wildlife Conservation International (EA)
WCI........... Workshop Computer Interface
WCIA......... Champaign, IL [*Television station call letters*]
WCIA......... Watch & Clock Importers' Association (BUAC)
WCIA......... Welsh Centre for International Affairs [*British*] (CB)
WCIB......... Falmouth, MA [*FM radio station call letters*]
WCIC......... Pekin, IL [*FM radio station call letters*]
WCID......... Friendship, NY [*FM radio station call letters*]
WCIE......... Lakeland, FL [*FM radio station call letters*]
WCIE......... Spring Lake, NC [*AM radio station call letters*]
WCIE......... World Center for Islamic Education (EA)
WCIF......... Melbourne, FL [*FM radio station call letters*]
WCIH......... Elmira, NY [*FM radio station call letters*]
WCII.......... Spencer, NY [*FM radio station call letters*]
WCII.......... Winstar Communications [*NASDAQ symbol*] (SAG)
WCIK......... Bath, NY [*FM radio station call letters*]
WCIL......... Carbondale, IL [*AM radio station call letters*]
WCIL-FM .... Carbondale, IL [*FM radio station call letters*]
WCIN......... Cincinnati, OH [*AM radio station call letters*]
WC Ins Rep... Workmen's Compensation and Insurance Reports [*1912-33*]
              [*A publication*] (DLA)
WCIP......... Weapon Control Indicator Panel [*Military*] (CAAL)
WCIP......... World Climate Impacts Program [*WMO*] [*ICSU*]
WCIP......... World Climate Impact Studies Program [*Marine science*] (OSRA)
WCIP......... World Council of Indigenous Peoples [*Ottawa, ON*] (EAIO)
WCIQ......... Mount Cheaha State Park, AL [*Television station call letters*]
WCIR......... Beckley, WV [*FM radio station call letters*]
WCIRB....... Workers' Compensation Insurance Rating Bureau
WCIRP....... World Climate Impact Assessment and Response Strategies
              Program (EERA)
WCIS......... Morganton, NC [*AM radio station call letters*]
WCIS......... Wisconsin Career Information System [*Information service or system*]
WC-ISA...... Women's Commission of the Iranian Students Association (EA)
WCISP....... World Climate Impact Studies Program (EERA)
WCI Stl...... WCI Steel, Inc. [*Associated Press*] (SAG)
WCIT......... Lima, OH [*AM radio station call letters*]
WCIU......... Chicago, IL [*Television station call letters*]
WCIU......... Workshop Computer Interface Unit (MCD)
WCIV......... Charleston, SC [*Television station call letters*]
WCIW........ [*The*] World Community of Al-Islam in the West
WCIY......... Canandaigua, NY [*FM radio station call letters*]
WCIY......... Westmorland and Cumberland Imperial Yeomanry [*British military*]
              (DMA)
WCIZ......... Watertown, NY [*FM radio station call letters*]
WCJ.......... Caleta Josefina [*Chile*] [*Airport symbol*] (AD)
WCJA........ World Council of Jewish Archives (EAIO)
WCJB........ Gainesville, FL [*Television station call letters*]
WCJC........ Van Buren, IN [*FM radio station call letters*]
WCJC........ Webster City Junior College [*Iowa*]
WCJC........ Wharton County Junior College [*Texas*]
WCJCC...... World Confederation of Jewish Community Centers (EA)
WCJCS...... World Conference of Jewish Communal Service (EA)
WCJE........ World Council on Jewish Education
WCJM........ West Point, GA [*AM radio station call letters*]
WCJM-FM.... West Point, GA [*FM radio station call letters*]
WCJO........ Jackson, OH [*AM radio station call letters*]
WCJU........ Columbia, MS [*AM radio station call letters*]
WCJW........ Warsaw, NY [*AM radio station call letters*]
WCJX........ Five Points, FL [*FM radio station call letters*]
WCK......... Whiskey Creek Resources [*Vancouver Stock Exchange symbol*]
WCK......... Wilson Creek [*Kentucky*] [*Seismograph station code, US Geological
              Survey*] (SEIS)
WCKA........ Sutton, WV [*FM radio station call letters*]
WCKB .... Dunn, NC [*AM radio station call letters*]
WCKC........ Cadillac, MI [*FM radio station call letters*]
WCKD........ Madison, TN [*AM radio station call letters*] (RBYB)
WCKG........ Elmwood Park, IL [*FM radio station call letters*]
WckhB........ Wackenhut Corp. [*Associated Press*] (SAG)
WCKI......... Greer, SC [*AM radio station call letters*]
WCKJ-FM .... St. Johnsbury, VT [*FM radio station call letters*] (RBYB)
WCKL........ Catskill, NY [*AM radio station call letters*]
WCKM .... Lake George, NY [*FM radio station call letters*]
WCKM .... Saratoga Springs, NY [*AM radio station call letters*]
WCKN......... Surfside Beach-Garden City, SC [*AM radio station call letters*]
              (RBYB)
WCKO......... Norfolk, VA [*AM radio station call letters*] (RBYB)

WCKQ......... Campbellsville, KY [*FM radio station call letters*]
WCKR......... Hornell, NY [*FM radio station call letters*]
WCKS......... Fruithurst, AL [*FM radio station call letters*]
WCKT......... Lehigh Acres, FL [*FM radio station call letters*]
WCKW........ Garyville, LA [*AM radio station call letters*]
WCKW........ La Place, LA [*FM radio station call letters*]
WCKX......... London, OH [*FM radio station call letters*]
WCKY......... Cincinnati, OH [*AM radio station call letters*]
WCL.......... Washington College of Law, Washington, DC [*OCLC symbol*] (OCLC)
WCL.......... Water Coolant Line (MCD)
WCL.......... Water Coolant Loop (MCD)
WCL.......... WCI Canada Ltd. [*Toronto Stock Exchange symbol*]
WCL.......... Weekly Cost Ledger (MCD)
WCL.......... Wenckebach Cycle Length (DB)
WCL.......... Western Carolinas League [*Baseball*]
WCL.......... White Clip Level [*Video technology*]
WCL.......... White Cross League [*British*]
WCL.......... Whole Cell Lysate (DB)
WCL.......... Wholesale Commodity Line (GFGA)
WCL.......... Women for Caribbean Liberation (BUAC)
WCL.......... Word Connection List (DB)
WCL.......... Word Control Logic
WCL.......... World Confederation of Labour [*See also CMT*] [*Brussels, Belgium*]
              (EAIO)
WCL.......... Wright Center of Laboratories
WCLA........ Claxton, GA [*AM radio station call letters*]
WCLA........ Washington Contract Loggers Association (WPI)
WCLA........ West Coast Lumbermen's Association [*Later, WWPA*] (EA)
WCLA........ Workers' Compensation Legislation in Australia [*A publication*]
WCLA-FM .... Claxton, GA [*FM radio station call letters*]
WCL-ARS..... Agricultural Research Service Water Conservation Laboratory
              [*Tempe, AZ*]
WCLB-FM .... Fort Pierce, FL [*FM radio station call letters*] (RBYB)
WCLC........ Jamestown, TN [*AM radio station call letters*]
WCLC........ Watch Check List Completed [*Aviation*] (FAAC)
WCLC........ World Christian Life Community [*Italy*] (EAIO)
WCLC-FM .... Jamestown, TN [*FM radio station call letters*]
WCLCV....... White Clover Large Cryptic Virus [*Plant pathology*]
WCLD........ Cleveland, MS [*AM radio station call letters*]
WCLD........ Water-Cooled (AAG)
WCLD-AM.... Cleveland, MS [*AM radio station call letters*] (RBYB)
WCLD-FM.... Cleveland, MS [*FM radio station call letters*] (RBYB)
WCLE........ Calhoun, TN [*FM radio station call letters*]
WCLE........ Cleveland, TN [*AM radio station call letters*]
WCLF........ Clearwater, FL [*Television station call letters*]
WCLG........ Morgantown, WV [*AM radio station call letters*]
WCLG-FM .... Morgantown, WV [*FM radio station call letters*]
WCLH........ Wilkes-Barre, PA [*FM radio station call letters*]
WCLI......... Corning, NY [*AM radio station call letters*]
WCII......... Lakeshore Technical Institute, Educational Resource Center,
              Cleveland, WI [*Library symbol Library of Congress*] (LCLS)
WCLIB........ West Coast Lumber Inspection Bureau (EA)
WCLJ......... Bloomington, IN [*Television station call letters*]
WCLJ......... Workmen's Compensation Law Journal [*A publication*] (DLA)
WCLK........ Atlanta, GA [*FM radio station call letters*]
WCLL........ Wesson, MS [*FM radio station call letters*]
WCLL........ Western Collegiate Lacrosse League (PSS)
WCLM........ Highland Springs, VA [*AM radio station call letters*]
WCLMV....... White Clover Mosaic Virus [*Plant pathology*]
WCLN........ Clinton, NC [*AM radio station call letters*]
WCLN-FM .... Clinton, NC [*FM radio station call letters*]
WCLO........ Janesville, WI [*AM radio station call letters*]
WCLP........ Chatsworth, GA [*Television station call letters*]
WCLP........ Western Center on Law and Poverty (EA)
WCLP........ Women's Computer Literacy Project [*Commercial firm*] (EA)
WCLQ........ Wausau, WI [*FM radio station call letters*]
WCLR........ Piqua, OH [*FM radio station call letters*]
WCLR........ Wadsworth Center for Laboratories and Research (BUAC)
WCLR........ Workmen's Compensation Law Review [*A publication*] (DLA)
WCLS........ Oscoda, MI [*FM radio station call letters*]
WCLS........ Water Coolant Loop System (NAKS)
WCLT........ Newark, OH [*AM radio station call letters*]
WCLT-FM .... Newark, OH [*FM radio station call letters*]
WCLU........ Glasgow, KY [*AM radio station call letters*]
WCLV........ Cleveland, OH [*FM radio station call letters*]
WCLW........ Eden, NC [*AM radio station call letters*]
WCLX........ Mio, MI [*FM radio station call letters*]
WCLX........ Wisconsin Central Trans [*NASDAQ symbol*] (TTSB)
WCLX........ Wisconsin Central Transportation Corp. [*NASDAQ symbol*] (SPSG)
WCLY........ Raleigh, NC [*AM radio station call letters*]
WCLZ........ Brunswick, ME [*AM radio station call letters*]
WCLZ-FM .... Brunswick, ME [*FM radio station call letters*]
WCM......... Warland Creek [*Montana*] [*Seismograph station code, US Geological
              Survey Closed*] (SEIS)
WCM......... Water Control Module (KSC)
WCM......... Weapon Control Module (MCD)
WCM......... Welded Cordwood Module
WCM......... Wesleyan Calvinistic Methodists (ROG)
WCM......... Wesley Central Mission [*Australia*]
WCM......... Wheat Curl Mite [*Entomology*]
WCM......... Whole Cow's Milk
WCM......... Winchester City Museum [*British*]
WCM......... Winkelmann Countermeasures, Inc. [*Vancouver Stock Exchange
              symbol*]
WCM......... Wired-Core Matrix

WCM	Wired-Core Memory
WCM	Word Combine and Multiplexer
WCM	World-Class Manufacturing [*Management technique*]
WCM²	Writable Control Memory [*Computer science*] (BUR)
W/CM²	Watts per Square Centimeter (CET)
W/cm²	Watts per Square Centimeter (IDOE)
WCMA	Corinth, MS [*AM radio station call letters*]
WCMA	West Coast Mineral Association (EA)
WCMA	Window Coverings Manufacturers Association (NTPA)
WCMA	Wiping Cloth Manufacturers Association (BUAC)
WCMA	Wisconsin Cheese Makers' Association (EA)
WCMA	Wood Component Manufacturers Association (NTPA)
WCMA	Working Capital Management Account [*Merrill Lynch & Co.*]
WCMB	Harrisburg, PA [*AM radio station call letters*]
WCMC	Westchester County Medical Center
WCMC	Wildwood, NJ [*AM radio station call letters*]
WCMC	World Conservation Monitoring Centre [*Information service or system*] (IID)
WCMD	Advanced Certificate of the Welsh College of Music and Drama [*British*] (DBQ)
WCMD-FM	Barre, VT [*FM radio station call letters*] (RBYB)
WCME	Boothbay Harbor, ME [*FM radio station call letters*]
WCMF	Rochester, NY [*FM radio station call letters*]
WCMF	World Congress on Metal Finishing (PDAA)
WCMF-FM	Rochester, NY [*FM radio station call letters*]
WCMG	Marion, SC [*FM radio station call letters*]
WCMH	Columbus, OH [*Television station call letters*]
WCMI	Ashland, KY [*AM radio station call letters*]
WCMIA	West Coast Metal Importers Association (EA)
WCMJ	Cambridge, OH [*FM radio station call letters*]
WCMK	Bolton, VT [*FM radio station call letters*] (RBYB)
WCML	Alpena, MI [*FM radio station call letters*]
WCML	Women's Caucus for the Modern Languages (EA)
WCML-TV	Alpena, MI [*Television station call letters*]
WCMM	Gulliver, MI [*FM radio station call letters*]
WCMMF	World Congress of Man-Made Fibres (BUAC)
WCMN	Arecibo, PR [*AM radio station call letters*]
WCMN-FM	Arecibo, PR [*FM radio station call letters*]
WCMO	Marietta, OH [*FM radio station call letters*]
WCMP	Pine City, MN [*AM radio station call letters*]
WCMP-FM	Pine City, MN [*FM radio station call letters*]
WCMQ	Hialeah, FL [*FM radio station call letters*]
WCMQ	Miami Springs, FL [*AM radio station call letters*]
WCMR	Western Contract Management Region [*Air Force*]
WCMR	World Conference on Missionary Radio [*Later, ICB*] (NTCM)
WCMS	Norfolk, VA [*AM radio station call letters*]
WCMS-FM	Norfolk, VA [*FM radio station call letters*]
WCMT	Martin, TN [*AM radio station call letters*]
WCMT	Winston Churchill Memorial Trust (BUAC)
WCMT-FM	Martin, TN [*FM radio station call letters*]
WCMU	Mount Pleasant, MI [*FM radio station call letters*]
WCMU-TV	Mount Pleasant, MI [*Television station call letters*]
WCMV	Cadillac, MI [*Television station call letters*]
WCMV	White Clover Mosaic Virus
WCMV	Wild Cucumber Mosaic Virus [*Plant pathology*]
WCMW	Harbor Springs, MI [*FM radio station call letters*]
WCMW	Manistee, MI [*Television station call letters*]
WCMX	Leominster, MA [*AM radio station call letters*] (RBYB)
WCMY	Ottawa, IL [*AM radio station call letters*]
WCMZ	Sault Ste. Marie, MI [*FM radio station call letters*]
WCN	Walthard's Cell Nest [*Gynecology*] (AAMN)
WCN	Washoe City [*Nevada*] [*Seismograph station code, US Geological Survey*] (SEIS)
WCN	Wescan Energy Ltd. [*Vancouver Stock Exchange symbol*]
WCN	Women's Centre of Nigeria (BUAC)
WCN	Workload Control Number (MCD)
WCN	Worldway Corp. [*NYSE symbol*] [*Formerly, Carolina Freight Corp.*] (SG)
WCNA	Potts Camp, MS [*FM radio station call letters*] (RBYB)
WCNB	Connersville, IN [*AM radio station call letters*]
WCNC	Charlotte, NC [*Television station call letters*]
WCNC	Elizabeth City, NC [*AM radio station call letters*]
WCND	Shelbyville, KY [*AM radio station call letters*]
WCNDT	World Conference on Non-Destructive Testing (PDAA)
WCNG	Murphy, NC [*FM radio station call letters*]
WCNI	New London, CT [*FM radio station call letters*]
WCNJ	Hazlet, NJ [*FM radio station call letters*]
WCNK-FM	Key West, FL [*FM radio station call letters*] (BROA)
WCNL	Carlinville, IL [*FM radio station call letters*]
WCNN	North Atlanta, GA [*AM radio station call letters*]
WCNN	World Congress of Neural Networks
WCNO	Palm City, FL [*FM radio station call letters*]
WCNR	Bloomsburg, PA [*AM radio station call letters*]
WCNS	Latrobe, PA [*AM radio station call letters*]
WCNU	Crestview, FL [*AM radio station call letters*]
WCNW	Fairfield, OH [*AM radio station call letters*]
WCNX	Middletown, CT [*AM radio station call letters*]
WCNY	Syracuse, NY [*FM radio station call letters*]
WCNY-TV	Syracuse, NY [*Television station call letters*]
WCNZ	Sheboygan, WI [*AM radio station call letters*]
WCO	Columbia Helicopters, Inc. [*ICAO designator*] (FAAC)
WCO	Coolullah [*Australia*] [*Airport symbol*] (AD)
WCO	Walt Disney Co. (EFIS)
WCO	War Cabinet Office [*World War II*]
WCO	Warrant Communication Officer [*British military*] (DMA)
WCO	Waste Crankcase Oils
WCO	Weapons Control Officer
WCO	Weapons Control Order
WCO	Western Coordination Office [*Later, WOO*] [*NASA*]
WCO	Wet Chemical Oxidation [*Chemistry*]
WCOA	Pensacola, FL [*AM radio station call letters*]
W Coast Rep	West Coast Reporter [*A publication*] (DLA)
WCOAT	Wolfe Computer Operator Aptitude Test
WCOBL	Wolfe Programming Language Test: COBOL
WCOD	Hyannis, MA [*FM radio station call letters*]
WCOE	La Porte, IN [*FM radio station call letters*]
WCOF	St. Petersburg, FL [*FM radio station call letters*]
WCOF	Women's Catholic Order of Foresters [*Later, NCSF*] (EA)
WCOG-FM	Galeton, PA [*FM radio station call letters*] (BROA)
WCOH	Newnan, GA [*AM radio station call letters*]
WCOJ	Coatesville, PA [*AM radio station call letters*]
WCOK	Sparta, NC [*AM radio station call letters*]
WCOL	Columbus, OH [*AM radio station call letters*]
W (Colds)	Whole Colds [*Medicine*]
WCOL-FM	Columbus, OH [*FM radio station call letters*]
WCOM	Bayamon, PR [*FM radio station call letters*] (RBYB)
WCOM	MCI WorldCom [*Formerly, WorldCom, Inc.*] [*NASDAQ symbol*]
WCOM	WorldCom, Inc. [*NASDAQ symbol*] (SAG)
W Comm	Wing Commander [*British military*] (DMA)
WCOMMRGN	Western Communications Region [*Air Force*]
WCON	Cornelia, GA [*AM radio station call letters*]
WCON-FM	Cornelia, GA [*FM radio station call letters*]
WCOO	New Bern, NC [*AM radio station call letters*] (RBYB)
WCOP	Warner Robins, GA [*AM radio station call letters*]
WC Ops	Workmen's Compensation Opinions, United States Department of Commerce [*A publication*] (DLA)
WCOR	Lebanon, TN [*AM radio station call letters*]
WCOS	Columbia, SC [*AM radio station call letters*]
WCOS-FM	Columbia, SC [*FM radio station call letters*]
WCOT	Jamestown, NY [*FM radio station call letters*]
WCOT	Wall Coated Open Tubular [*Instrumentation*]
WCOTP	World Confederation of Organizations of the Teaching Profession [*Internat ional Federation of Secondary Teachers and IFTA*] [*Formed by a merger of*] (EAIO)
WCOU	Warsaw, NY [*FM radio station call letters*]
WCOU	Wheelwrights and Coachmakers Operatives' Union [*British*]
WCOV	Montgomery, AL [*Television station call letters*]
WCOW	Sparta, WI [*FM radio station call letters*]
WCOX	Camden, AL [*AM radio station call letters*]
WCOZ	St. Albans, WV [*AM radio station call letters*]
WCP	War Control Planners (EA)
WCP	Warner Insurance Services [*NYSE symbol*] (SPSG)
WCP	Waste Collector Pump (IEEE)
WCP	Wayne County Public Library, Wooster, OH [*OCLC symbol*] (OCLC)
WCP	Weapon Control Panel [*Aviation*]
WCP	Weapon Control Processor [*Military*] (CAAL)
WCP	Welder Control Panel
WCP	Western Canada Party [*Separatist political party*]
WCP	White Combination Potentiometer
WCP	Wing Chord Plane [*Aviation*]
WCP	Wing Command Post (MCD)
WCP	Work Control Plan (AAG)
WCP	World Climate Program [*WMO*] [*ICSU*]
WCP	World Community Projects (EA)
WCP	World Congress of Poets (EA)
WCP	World Council of Peace (NATG)
WCP	World Court Project (BUAC)
WCPA	Clearfield, PA [*AM radio station call letters*]
wc/pa	Watercolor on Paper (VRA)
WCPA	Western College Placement Association (AEBS)
WCPA	White Christians Patriots Association [*Canada*] (BUAC)
WCPA	World Centre for the Performing Arts
WCPA	World Constitution and Parliament Association (EA)
WCPAB	War Contracts Price Adjustment Board [*All functions dispersed, 1951*]
WCPB	Salisbury, MD [*Television station call letters*]
WCPC	Houston, MS [*AM radio station call letters*]
WCPD	Waterloo Centre for Process Development [*University of Waterloo*] [*Research center*] (RCD)
WCPE	Raleigh, NC [*FM radio station call letters*]
WCPH	Etowah, TN [*AM radio station call letters*]
WCPH	World Congress of Professional Hypnotists (EA)
WCPI	White Collar Productivity Improvement (MCD)
WCPK-AM	Chesapeake, VA [*AM radio station call letters*] (BROA)
WCPM	Cumberland, KY [*AM radio station call letters*]
WCPMEF	Willa Cather Pioneer Memorial and Educational Foundation (EA)
WCPN	Cleveland, OH [*FM radio station call letters*]
WCPO	Cincinnati, OH [*Television station call letters*]
WCPP	Women of Color Partnership Program (EA)
WCPQ	Havelock, NC [*AM radio station call letters*]
WCPR	Coamo, PR [*AM radio station call letters*]
WCPR	Weston, Clevedon & Portishead Railway [*British*]
WCPR-FM	Wiggins, MS [*FM radio station call letters*] (RBYB)
WCPS	Tarboro, NC [*AM radio station call letters*]
WCPS	Women's Caucus for Political Science (EA)
WCPS	World Confederation of Productivity Science (EAIO)
WCPSC	Western Conference of Public Services Commissioners
WCPT	World Confederation for Physical Therapy [*British*] (EA)
WCPV	Essex, NY [*FM radio station call letters*]
WCPX	Orlando, FL [*Television station call letters*]

WCPZ.......... Sandusky, OH [*FM radio station call letters*]
WCQA.......... Fredonia, NY [*FM radio station call letters*]
WCQL.......... Worst Cycle Quantity Level (PDAA)
WCQL.......... York Center, ME [*FM radio station call letters*]
WCQM.......... Park Falls, WI [*FM radio station call letters*]
WCQQ.......... Cedar Key, FL [*FM radio station call letters*] (RBYB)
WCQR.......... Fairlawn, VA [*AM radio station call letters*]
WCQR-FM.... Kingsport, TN [*FM radio station call letters*] (RBYB)
WCQS.......... Asheville, NC [*FM radio station call letters*]
WCR.......... Chandalar [*Alaska*] [*Airport symbol*] (OAG)
WCR.......... Chandalar Lake, AK [*Location identifier FAA*] (FAAL)
WCR.......... Walthard's Cell Rests [*Medicine*] (MEDA)
WCR.......... Warm Core Ring [*Oceanography*]
WCR.......... Water-Cooled Reactor
WCR.......... Water-Cooled Rod
WCR.......... Watercooler (AAG)
WCR.......... Waterloo and City Railway (ROG)
WCR.......... Welsh Community Resistance (BUAC)
WCR.......... Western Communications Region [*Air Force*] (MCD)
WCR.......... Willcrest Resources Ltd. [*Vancouver Stock Exchange symbol*]
WCR.......... Wire Contact Relay
WCR.......... Women's Council of Realtors [*of the National Association of Realtors*] (EA)
WCR.......... Word Control [*or Count*] Register
WCR.......... World Communication Report [*Database*] [*UNESCO*] (DUND)
WCRA.......... Effingham, IL [*AM radio station call letters*]
WCRA.......... Weather Control Research Association [*Later, Weather Modification Association*]
WCRA.......... Western College Reading Association (EA)
WCRA.......... Wet Crease Recovery Angle [*Textile technology*]
WCRA.......... Women's Cycle Racing Association (BUAC)
WCRB.......... Waltham, MA [*FM radio station call letters*]
WCRC.......... Effingham, IL [*FM radio station call letters*]
WCRC.......... Water Conditioning Research Council [*Later, WQRC*] (EA)
WCRC.......... Workers' Compensation and Rehabilitation Commission [*Western Australia*]
WCRD.......... War Consumables Requirements Document [*Military*] (AFIT)
WCRE.......... Cheraw, SC [*AM radio station call letters*]
WC Rep....... Workmen's Compensation Reports [*A publication*] (DLA)
WCRF.......... Cleveland, OH [*FM radio station call letters*]
WCRF.......... Weekly Collection Report File [*IRS*]
WCRF.......... World Cancer Research Fund
WCRH.......... Williamsport, MD [*FM radio station call letters*]
WCRJ.......... Jacksonville, FL [*AM radio station call letters*]
WCRK.......... Morristown, TN [*AM radio station call letters*]
WCRL.......... Oneonta, AL [*AM radio station call letters*]
WCRLA.......... Western College Reading and Learning Association (EA)
WCRM.......... Fort Myers, FL [*AM radio station call letters*]
WCRN.......... Worcester, MA [*AM radio station call letters*]
WCRO.......... Johnstown, PA [*AM radio station call letters*]
WCROS.......... White Crossover Vote [*Political science*]
WCRP.......... Guayama, PR [*FM radio station call letters*]
WCRP.......... World Climate Research Program (EERA)
WCRP.......... World Climate Research Programme [*WMO*] [*ICSU*]
WCRP.......... World Conference on Religion and Peace (EAIO)
WCRP/USA... World Conference on Religion and Peace, USA Section (EA)
WCRQ.......... Arab, AL [*FM radio station call letters*]
WCRR.......... Rural Retreat, VA [*AM radio station call letters*]
WCRRD.......... World Conference on Agrarian Reform and Rural Development (BUAC)
WCRS.......... Greenwood, SC [*AM radio station call letters*]
WC:RS.......... Women's Caucus: Religious Studies [*Defunct*] (EA)
WCRSI.......... Western Concrete Reinforcing Steel Institute [*Later, CRSI*] (EA)
WCRT.......... Terre Haute, IN [*FM radio station call letters*]
WCRV.......... Collierville, TN [*AM radio station call letters*]
WCRW.......... Chicago, IL [*AM radio station call letters*]
WCRX.......... Chicago, IL [*FM radio station call letters*]
WCRY.......... Fuquay-Varina, NC [*AM radio station call letters*]
WCRZ.......... Flint, MI [*FM radio station call letters*]
WCS.......... Wallace Computer Services, Inc. [*NYSE symbol*] (SPSG)
WCS.......... Wallace Computer Svc [*NYSE symbol*] (TTSB)
WCS.......... Wang Computer System
WCS.......... Waste Collection System [*NASA*] (MCD)
WCS.......... Waste Compaction Station [*Nuclear energy*] (NRCH)
WCS.......... Waste Control System (SSD)
WCS.......... Watercolor Spectrometer (PDAA)
WCS.......... Weak Calf Syndrome [*Veterinary medicine*]
WCS.......... Weapon Control Station [*Military*] (CAAL)
WCS.......... Weapon Control Status [*Military*] (INF)
WCS.......... Weapons Control Status
WCS.......... Weapons Control System
WCS.......... Wedgwood Collectors Society [*Defunct*] (EA)
WCS.......... Western Cover Society (EA)
WCS.......... Wildlife Conservation Society
WCS.......... Wilkie Collins Society [*British*] (DBA)
WCS.......... William Cobbett Society (EAIO)
WCS.......... Woman Citizen Series [*A publication*]
WCS.......... Work Control Station
WCS.......... Work Control Status
WCS.......... Work Control System (NASA)
WCS.......... Work Core Storage
WCS.......... World Congress on Superconductivity [*An association*]
WCS.......... World Conservation Strategy (GNE)
WCS.......... World Council of Conservative/Masorti Synagogues (EA)
WCS.......... World Council of Synagogues (EA)
WCS.......... Worm Community System [*Neurology database*]
WCS.......... Writable Control Storage [*Computer science*]
WCSA.......... Ripley, MS [*AM radio station call letters*]
WCSA.......... West Coast of South America
WCSB.......... Cleveland, OH [*FM radio station call letters*]
WCSB.......... Weapon Control Switchboard [*Military*] (CAAL)
WCSB(G)..... Weapon Control Switchboard (Gun)
WCSB(M)..... Weapon Control Switchboard (Missile)
WCSB(UB)... Weapon Control Switchboard (Underwater Battery)
WCSC.......... Charleston, SC [*Television station call letters*]
WCSC.......... Weapon Control System Console
WCSC.......... Weapons Control System Coordinator (NVT)
WCSC.......... West Coast Switching Center [*Jet Propulsion Laboratory, NASA*]
WCSC.......... World Correctional Service Center (EA)
WCSC.......... World Council of Service Clubs (BUAC)
WCSCV.......... White Clover Small Cryptic Virus [*Plant pathology*]
WCSD.......... Livingston, TN [*FM radio station call letters*]
WCSF.......... Joliet, IL [*FM radio station call letters*]
WCSFMA..... Wisconsin Cheese and Specialty Food Merchants Association (EA)
WCSG.......... Grand Rapids, MI [*FM radio station call letters*]
WCSG.......... WWMCCS [*Worldwide Military Command and Control System*] Council Support Group (MCD)
WCSH.......... Portland, ME [*Television station call letters*]
WCSI.......... Columbus, IN [*AM radio station call letters*]
WCSI.......... World Centre for Scientific Information
WCSICEC..... Working Committee of the Scientific Institutes for Crafts in the EEC Count ries [*Munich, Federal Republic of Germany*] (EAIO)
WCSJ.......... Morris, IL [*AM radio station call letters*]
WCSK.......... Kingsport, TN [*FM radio station call letters*]
WCSL.......... Cherryville, NC [*AM radio station call letters*]
WCSLEN...... Wide Character String Length [*Computer science*] (PCM)
WCSM.......... Celina, OH [*AM radio station call letters*]
WCSM.......... World Congress of Sports Medicine
WCSM.......... Worshipful Company of Spectacle Makers (BUAC)
WCSM-FM... Celina, OH [*FM radio station call letters*]
WCSMP....... World Climate System Monitoring Program [*Marine science*] (OSRA)
WCSN-FM... Orange Beach, AL [*FM radio station call letters*] (RBYB)
WCSO.......... Portland, ME [*FM radio station call letters*]
WCSP.......... Wisconsin Cheese and Sausage Promotions (EA)
WCSPA.......... West Coast Shrimp Producers Association (EA)
WCSR.......... Hillsdale, MI [*AM radio station call letters*]
WCSRC.......... Wild Canid Survival and Research Center - Wolf Sanctuary (EA)
WCSR-FM.... Hillsdale, MI [*FM radio station call letters*]
WCSS.......... Amsterdam, NY [*AM radio station call letters*]
WCSS.......... Weapons Control Subsystem (MCD)
WCSS.......... Weapons Control System Simulator
WCSS.......... West Coast Sound School [*Navy*]
WCST.......... Berkeley Springs, WV [*AM radio station call letters*]
WCST.......... Wescast Industries, Inc. [*NASDAQ symbol*] (SAG)
WCST.......... Wisconsin Card Sorting Test [*Neuropsychology test*]
WCstB.......... West Coast Bancorp (OR) [*Associated Press*] (SAG)
WCstEnt...... West Coast Entertainment Corp. [*Associated Press*] (SAG)
WCSTF.......... Wescast Industries'A' [*NASDAQ symbol*] (TTSB)
WCST-FM.... Berkeley Springs, WV [*FM radio station call letters*]
WCSU.......... Western Connecticut State University [*Danbury*]
WCSU.......... Wilberforce, OH [*FM radio station call letters*]
WCSUICA..... Women's Coalition to Stop US Intervention in Central America [*Later, WCSUICAC*] [*Defunct*] (EA)
WCSUICAC... Women's Coalition to Stop US Intervention in Central America and the Caribbean (EA)
WCSV.......... Crossville, TN [*AM radio station call letters*]
WCSV.......... Wheat Chlorotic Streak Virus [*Plant pathology*]
WCSW.......... Shell Lake, WI [*AM radio station call letters*]
WCSX.......... Birmingham, MI [*FM radio station call letters*]
WCSY.......... South Haven, MI [*AM radio station call letters*]
WCSY-FM.... South Haven, MI [*FM radio station call letters*]
WCSZ.......... Wildlife Conservation Society of Zambia (BUAC)
WCT.......... Trinity Memorial Hospital, Cudahy, WI [*Library symbol Library of Congress*] (LCLS)
WCT.......... War Crimes Tribunal [*Bertrand Russell*] [*Stockholm based pacifist organization founded during the Vietnam war*] (VNW)
WCT.......... Water-Cooled Tube [*Nuclear energy*] (IAA)
WCT.......... Waukesha County Institute, Pewaukee, WI [*OCLC symbol*] (OCLC)
WCT.......... West Coast Travel [*Information service or system*] (IID)
WCT.......... Westek Communications, Inc. [*Vancouver Stock Exchange symbol*]
WCT.......... Wetlands Conservation Team
WCT.......... Women Caring Trust [*An association*] (BUAC)
WCT.......... World Championship Tennis, Inc.
WCT.......... World Confederation of Teachers [*See also CSME*] [*Brussels, Belgium*] (EAIO)
WCT.......... Worthy Chief Templar
WCTA.......... Alamo, TN [*AM radio station call letters*]
WCTA.......... Western Coal Transportation Association (EA)
WCTA.......... Wholesale Confectionery and Tobacco Trade Alliance [*British*] (DBA)
WCTA.......... World Committee for Trade Action [*See also CMAP*] [*Brussels, Belgium*] (EAIO)
WCTB.......... Fairfield, ME [*FM radio station call letters*]
WCTB.......... West Country Tourist Board [*British*] (DCTA)
WCTB.......... Western Carriers Tariff Bureau
WCTC.......... New Brunswick, NJ [*AM radio station call letters*]
WCTD.......... Miami, FL [*Television station call letters*]
WCTD.......... World Congress of Teachers of Dancing (EA)
WCTE.......... Cookeville, TN [*Television station call letters*]
WCTEV.......... White Clover Temperate Virus [*Plant pathology*]
WCTF.......... Vernon, CT [*AM radio station call letters*]

WCTG .... Columbia, SC [*AM radio station call letters*]
WCTG .... Woodcutting (MSA)
WCTH .... Plantation Key, FL [*FM radio station call letters*]
WCTI .... New Bern, NC [*Television station call letters*]
WCTJ-AM .... Camp Lejeune, NC [*AM radio station call letters*] (RBYB)
WCTK .... New Bedford, MA [*AM radio station call letters*]
WCTL .... Union City, PA [*FM radio station call letters*]
WCTM .... Eaton, OH [*AM radio station call letters*]
WCTN .... Potomac-Cabin John, MD [*AM radio station call letters*]
WCTO-FM .... Easton, PA [*FM radio station call letters*] (BROA)
WCTP .... Wire Chief Test Panel [*Telecommunications*] (TEL)
WCTQ .... Venice, FL [*FM radio station call letters*]
WCTR .... Chestertown, MD [*AM radio station call letters*]
WCTR .... WCTU Railway Co. [*AAR code*]
WCTR .... World Conference on Transport Research (BUAC)
WCTS .... Maplewood, MN [*AM radio station call letters*]
WCTS .... Weapon Cost Test Site [*Military*] (CAAL)
WCTS .... Weapons Controller Training Squadron
W Ct SA ...... Union of South Africa Water Courts Decisions [*A publication*] (DLA)
WCTT .... Corbin, KY [*AM radio station call letters*]
WCTT .... Weapons Crew Training Test [*TCATA*] (RDA)
WCTTA .... Wholesale Confectionery and Tobacco Trade Alliance (BUAC)
WCTT-FM ...... Corbin, KY [*FM radio station call letters*]
WCTU .... National Woman's Christian Temperance Union (EA)
WCTU .... Tazewell, TN [*FM radio station call letters*]
WCTU .... Women's Christian Temperance Union (BUAC)
WCTU .... Women's Connubial Temperance Union [*Satirical*]
WCTV .... Thomasville, GA [*Television station call letters*]
WCTV .... Westcott Communications [*NASDAQ symbol*] (SPSG)
WCTW .... Catskill, NY [*FM radio station call letters*]
WCTY .... Norwich, CT [*FM radio station call letters*]
WCTZ .... Clarksville, TN [*AM radio station call letters*]
WCu .... Cumberland Public Library, Cumberland, WI [*Library symbol Library of Congress*] (LCLS)
WCU .... Water Cooler Unit (AAG)
WCU .... Weapons Control Unit (MCD)
WCU .... Welsh Chess Union (DBA)
WCU .... West Coast University [*Los Angeles, CA*]
WCU .... Western Carolina University [*Cullowhee, NC*]
WCU .... Western Catholic Union (EA)
WCU .... World Conservation Union (BUAC)
WCUB .... Two Rivers, WI [*AM radio station call letters*]
WCUC .... Clarion, PA [*FM radio station call letters*]
WCUE .... Cuyahoga Falls, OH [*AM radio station call letters*]
WCUG .... Cuthbert, GA [*AM radio station call letters*]
WCUH .... Western Carolina University Herbarium
WCUK .... West Coast of the United Kingdom
WCUL .... Culpeper, VA [*FM radio station call letters*]
WCUM .... Bridgeport, CT [*AM radio station call letters*]
WCUMBS ...... Western Canadian Universities Marine Biological Society
WCUNDDP ... World Committee for the United Nations Decade of Disabled Persons (EA)
WCUP .... L'Anse, MI [*FM radio station call letters*] (RBYB)
WCUS .... Waterborne Commerce of the United States [*DoD/COE*] (TAG)
WCUW .... Worcester, MA [*FM radio station call letters*]
WCUZ .... Grand Rapids, MI [*AM radio station call letters*]
WCUZ .... World Confederation of United Zionists (EA)
WCUZ-FM .... Grand Rapids, MI [*FM radio station call letters*]
WCV .... Wafer Check Valve
WCV .... Winant and Clayton Volunteers (EA)
WCV .... World Coalition against Vivisection (BUAC)
WCVA .... Culpeper, VA [*AM radio station call letters*]
WCVA .... Wales Council for Voluntary Action (DBA)
WCVB .... Boston, MA [*Television station call letters*]
WCVC .... Tallahassee, FL [*AM radio station call letters*]
WCVE .... Richmond, VA [*FM radio station call letters*]
WCVE-TV .... Richmond, VA [*Television station call letters*]
WCVF .... Fredonia, NY [*FM radio station call letters*]
WCVG .... Covington, KY [*AM radio station call letters*]
WCVH .... Flemington, NJ [*FM radio station call letters*]
WCVI .... Connellsville, PA [*AM radio station call letters*]
WCVJ .... Jefferson, OH [*FM radio station call letters*]
WCVK .... Bowling Green, KY [*FM radio station call letters*]
WCVL .... Crawfordsville, IN [*AM radio station call letters*]
WCVM .... Bronson, MI [*FM radio station call letters*]
WCVM .... Western College of Veterinary Medicine [*Canada*]
WCVN .... Covington, KY [*Television station call letters*]
WCVO .... Gahanna, OH [*FM radio station call letters*]
WCVP .... Murphy, NC [*AM radio station call letters*]
WCVP .... Robbinsville, NC [*FM radio station call letters*]
WCVQ .... Fort Campbell, KY [*FM radio station call letters*]
WCVR .... Randolph, VT [*AM radio station call letters*]
WCVS .... Virden, IL [*FM radio station call letters*]
WCVT .... Rossville, GA [*AM radio station call letters*]
WCVU .... Solana, FL [*FM radio station call letters*] (RBYB)
WCVV .... Belpre, OH [*FM radio station call letters*]
WCVW .... Richmond, VA [*Television station call letters*]
WCVY .... Coventry, RI [*FM radio station call letters*]
WCVZ .... Zanesville, OH [*FM radio station call letters*]
WCW .... Western College for Women [*Ohio*]
WCW .... Western College for Women, Oxford, OH [*Inactive*] [*OCLC symbol*] (OCLC)
WCW .... Wood Casement Window [*Technical drawings*]
WCW .... World Championship Wrestling
WCWA .... Toledo, OH [*AM radio station call letters*]

WCWB .... World Council for the Welfare of the Blind [*Later, WBU*] (EAIO)
WCWC .... Ripon, WI [*AM radio station call letters*]
WCWM .... Williamsburg, VA [*FM radio station call letters*]
WC/WO .... Working Committee on Weather Operations
WCWP .... Brookville, NY [*FM radio station call letters*]
WCWR .... Weil's Code of Wyoming Rules [*A publication*] (AAGC)
WCWS .... Wooster, OH [*FM radio station call letters*]
WCWT .... Centerville, OH [*FM radio station call letters*]
WCWV .... Summersville, WV [*FM radio station call letters*]
WCX .... Weak Cation Exchanger [*Chemistry*]
WCX .... Westmoreland Coal [*NYSE symbol*] (TTSB)
WCXJ .... Westmoreland Coal Co. [*NYSE symbol*] (SPSG)
WCXJ .... Braddock, PA [*AM radio station call letters*]
WCXL .... Kill Devil Hills, NC [*FM radio station call letters*]
WCXN .... Claremont, NC [*AM radio station call letters*]
WCXPrA .... Westmoreld Coal Cv Dep Ex Pfd [*NYSE symbol*] (TTSB)
WCXR .... Lewisburg, PA [*FM radio station call letters*] (RBYB)
WCXT .... Hart, MI [*FM radio station call letters*]
WCXU .... Caribou, ME [*FM radio station call letters*]
WCXX .... Madawaska, ME [*AM radio station call letters*]
WCY .... Viking Express, Inc. [*ICAO designator*] (FAAC)
WCY .... World Communications Year [*1983*]
WCYB .... Bristol, VA [*Television station call letters*]
WCYC .... Chicago, IL [*FM radio station call letters*]
WCYC .... Westmorland and Cumberland Yeomanry Cavalry [*British military*] (DMA)
WCYI .... Lewiston, ME [*FM radio station call letters*]
WCYJ .... Waynesburg, PA [*FM radio station call letters*]
WCYK .... Crozet, VA [*FM radio station call letters*]
WCYK-FM .... Crozet, VA [*FM radio station call letters*] (RBYB)
WCYMSC ...... World Council of Young Men's Service Clubs (BUAC)
WCYN .... Cynthiana, KY [*AM radio station call letters*]
WCYN-FM .... Cynthiana, KY [*FM radio station call letters*]
WCYO .... Irvine, KY [*FM radio station call letters*]
WCYT .... Lafayette Township, IN [*FM radio station call letters*]
WCYY .... Biddeford, ME [*FM radio station call letters*]
WCZI .... Washington, NC [*FM radio station call letters*]
WCZQ .... Monticello, IL [*FM radio station call letters*]
WCZR .... Charleston, WV [*AM radio station call letters*]
WCZT .... Avalon, NJ [*FM radio station call letters*]
WCZX .... Hyde Park, NY [*FM radio station call letters*]
WCZY .... Mount Pleasant, MI [*FM radio station call letters*]
WD .... Decisions Won [*Boxing*]
WD .... General Warranty Deed [*Real estate*]
Wd .... Seaweed [*Quality of the bottom*] [*Nautical charts*]
WD .... Two-Conductor Cables [*JETDS nomenclature*] [*Military*] (CET)
WD .... Wallerian Degeneration [*Medicine*]
WD .... Ward
wd .... Ward [*Medicine*] (WDAA)
WD .... Ward Air [*ICAO designator*] (AD)
WD .... War Damage
WD .... War Department [*Created, 1789; became Department of the Army, 1947*]
WD .... Warehouse Distributor
w/d .... Warm and Dry (MEDA)
WD .... Warranted
WD .... Washington Decisions [*A publication*] (DLA)
WD .... Waste Disposal [*Nuclear energy*] (NRCH)
WD .... Water Damage (ADA)
WD .... Water Department (WDAA)
WD .... Water Desurger
WD .... Water Division [*Environmental Protection Agency*] (GFGA)
WD .... Watt Demand Meter (MSA)
WD .... Waveform Digitizer [*Telecommunications*] (IAA)
WD .... Waveform Distortion [*Telecommunications*] (IAA)
WD .... Wavelength Dispersive [*Spectrometry*]
WD .... Weapon Description (MCD)
WD .... Weapon Director [*SAGE*]
WD .... Weapons Data [*Navy*]
WD .... Weather Division [*Air Force*] (MCD)
WD .... Web Depth
WD .... Weed (WDAA)
WD .... Weekdays (WDAA)
WD .... Well Deck
W-D .... Well-Developed [*Medicine*]
WD .... Well Differentiated [*Medicine*]
WD .... Well-Drained [*Soil*]
WD .... West Division (ROG)
WD .... Westminster Dragoons [*British military*] (DMA)
WD .... Wet Dressing
WD .... Wheel Drive [*Engineering*]
WD .... When Directed
WD .... When Discovered
WD .... When Distributed [*Stock exchange term*] (SPSG)
WD .... White Dwarf [*Galactic science*]
WD .... Whitney Damon Dextrose [*Agar*] (BABM)
WD .... Whole Depth
wd .... Wide (VRA)
WD .... Widow
WD .... Width (MSA)
wd .... Width (VRA)
W/D .... Width-to-Diameter [*Ratio*] (KSC)
WD .... Wife's Divorce (ROG)
WD .... Will Dated [*Genealogy*] (ROG)
WD .... Williams Domain [*Computer science*] (IAA)

WD............	Wilson Dam [*TVA*]
WD............	Wilson's Disease [*Medicine*]
WD............	Wind (MSA)
WD............	Wind Deflection [*Ballistics*]
WD............	Wind Direction
WD............	Window Detector
WD............	Window Dimension [*Technical drawings*]
WD............	Wing Defence [*Netball*]
WD............	Winner's Dog [*Dog show term*]
WD............	Wired Discrete (NASA)
WD............	Wiring Diagram (IAA)
WD............	With Dependents (MCD)
WD............	With Disease (MAE)
W/D............	Withdrawal (DLA)
WD............	Withdrawn (AFM)
WD............	Wood (AAG)
wd............	Wood (VRA)
WD............	Wood Door [*Technical drawings*]
WD............	Word
WD............	Word Display
WD............	Work [*or Working*] Day (AFM)
WD............	Work Description (MCD)
WD............	Work Directive (MCD)
WD............	Working Distance [*Microscopy*]
WD............	Working Draft (OSI)
WD............	Works Department
WD............	Would
WD............	Wound (AAMN)
WD............	Wrist Disarticulation [*Medicine*]
WD............	Write Data
WD............	Write Direct
WD............	Writer's Digest [*A publication*]
WD............	Writer's Directory [*A publication*]
WD............	Wrongful Death [*Legal shorthand*] (LWAP)
WD............	Wrongful Detention [*British*]
WD............	Wydmar Developmental Corp. [*Vancouver Stock Exchange symbol*]
WD (2d)......	Washington Decisions, Second Series [*A publication*] (DLA)
WD 40........	WD-40 Co. [*Associated Press*] (SAG)
WDA	Aram Public Library, Delavan, WI [*Library symbol Library of Congress*] (LCLS)
WDA	Wadi Ain [*South Arabia*] [*Airport symbol*] (AD)
WDA	Wallcovering Distributors Association (EA)
WDA	Wardair Canada Ltd. [*ICAO designator*] (FAAC)
WDA	Warehouse Distributors Association for Leisure and Mobile Products (EA)
WDA	Waste Disposal Authority [*British*]
WDA	Wave Data Analyzer [*Marine science*] (MSC)
WDA	Weapons Defended Area
WDA	Well Drillers' Association [*British*] (DBA)
WDA	Welsh Development Agency [*British*] (DE)
WDA	Western District Area [*Air Force*]
WDA	Wheel Drive Assembly
WDA	Wholesale Distributors Association (EA)
WDA	Wildlife Disease Association (EA)
WDA	Wilson's Disease Association (EA)
WDA	Withdrawal of Availability [*Military*] (AFM)
WDA	Women's Diocesan Association [*British*]
WDA	World Aquathemes Ltd. [*Vancouver Stock Exchange symbol*]
WDA	World Dance Alliance
WDA	World Development Action [*An association British*]
WDA	World Dredging Association (MSC)
WDA	Wrongful Death Act (LWAP)
WDAA	Wireless Dealers Association (NTPA)
WDAB	Travelers Rest, SC [*AM radio station call letters*]
WDAC	Lancaster, PA [*FM radio station call letters*]
WDAD	Indiana, PA [*AM radio station call letters*]
WDAE	Tampa, FL [*AM radio station call letters*]
WDAF	Kansas City, MO [*AM radio station call letters*]
WDAF	Western Desert Air Force
WDAF-TV	Kansas City, MO [*Television station call letters*]
WDAG	Word Driver and Gate [*Computer science*] (IAA)
WDAHAC.....	National Society Women Descendants of the Ancient and Honorable Artillery Company (EA)
WDAI	Pawley's Island, SC [*FM radio station call letters*]
WDAK	Columbus, GA [*AM radio station call letters*]
WDAL	Dalton, GA [*AM radio station call letters*] (RBYB)
WDALMP	Warehouse Distributors Association for Leisure and Mobile Products (EA)
WDAM	Laurel, MS [*Television station call letters*]
WDAN	Danville, IL [*AM radio station call letters*]
WDAO	Dayton, OH [*AM radio station call letters*]
WDAP	Huntingdon, TN [*AM radio station call letters*] (RBYB)
WDAP	World Dictionary of Awards and Prizes [*A publication*]
WDAQ	Danbury, CT [*FM radio station call letters*]
WDar	Darien Public Library, Darien, WI [*Library symbol Library of Congress*] (LCLS)
WDAR-FM....	Darlington, SC [*FM radio station call letters*]
WDAS	Philadelphia, PA [*AM radio station call letters*]
WDAS	Western Dance Appreciation Society [*British*] (DBA)
WDAS-FM....	Philadelphia, PA [*FM radio station call letters*]
WDAV	Davidson, NC [*FM radio station call letters*]
WDAY	Fargo, ND [*AM radio station call letters*]
WDAY-FM....	Fargo, ND [*FM radio station call letters*]
WDAY-TV....	Fargo, ND [*Television station call letters*]
WDAZ	Devils Lake, ND [*Television station call letters*]

WDB	Westminster Dictionary of the Bible [*A publication*] (BJA)
WDB	Wideband [*Radio*] (MCD)
WDB	Wide Deadband [*NASA*]
WDB	Wine Development Board (BUAC)
WDB	Winkelmann-Dibley Formula B [*Race car*]
WDB	With Due Bills [*Stocks*] (MHDW)
WDB	Word Driver BIT [*Binary Digit*] [*Computer science*] (MHDI)
WDB-1	Working Data Base (MHDI)
WDB-1	World Data Bank (NITA)
WDBA	Du Bois, PA [*FM radio station call letters*]
WDBB	Tuscaloosa, AL [*Television station call letters*]
WDBC	Escanaba, MI [*AM radio station call letters*]
WDBCA	War Department Board of Contract Appeals [*1942-50*] (AAGC)
WDBD	Jackson, MS [*Television station call letters*]
WDBF	Delray Beach, FL [*AM radio station call letters*]
WDBJ	Roanoke, VA [*Television station call letters*]
WDBK	Blackwood, NJ [*FM radio station call letters*]
WDBK	Wordbook (ROG)
WDBL	Springfield, TN [*AM radio station call letters*]
wdbl	Woodblock (VRA)
WDBL-FM	Springfield, TN [*FM radio station call letters*]
WDBM	East Lansing, MI [*FM radio station call letters*]
WDBN	Wrightsville, GA [*FM radio station call letters*]
WDBO	Orlando, FL [*AM radio station call letters*]
WDBOR.......	Wood Boring
WDBQ	Dubuque, IA [*AM radio station call letters*]
WDBR	Springfield, IL [*FM radio station call letters*]
WDBS-FM....	Bolingbroke, GA [*FM radio station call letters*] (RBYB)
WDBX-FM....	Carbondale, IL [*FM radio station call letters*] (RBYB)
WDC	War Damage Commission [*British*]
WDC	War Damage Corp. [*World War II*]
WDC	War Department Constabulary [*British military*] (DMA)
WDC	Washington [*Diocesan abbreviation*] [*District of Columbia*] (TOCD)
WDC	Washington Document Center
WDC	Waste Disposal Cask [*Nuclear energy*] (NRCH)
WDC	Waste Disposal Code
WDC	Water Data Center [*Department of Agriculture*] [*Information service or system*] (IID)
WDC	Weapon Delivery Computer (MCD)
WDC	Weapon Direction Computer [*Military*] (CAAL)
WDC	Western Defense Command [*Army*]
WDC	Western Digital [*NYSE symbol*] (TTSB)
WDC	Western Digital Corp. [*NYSE symbol*] (SPSG)
WDC	Westinghouse Defense Center
WDC	Whiskeytown Dam [*California*] [*Seismograph station code, US Geological Survey*] (SEIS)
WDC	Wideband Directional Coupler
WDC	Women's Distance Committee (EA)
WDC	Workers' Defence Committee [*Ghana*] [*Political party*] (PPW)
WDC	Workers' Defense Committee [*Poland*] (PD)
WDC	Working Direct Current (DEN)
WDC	World Darts Council (BUAC)
WDC	World Data Center [*National Academy of Sciences*] [*Data collection and exchange center*]
WDC	World Data Centre on Micro-Organisms (EERA)
WDC	World Data Centres (EERA)
WDC	World Data Centre Systems (BUAC)
WDC	World Development Corp.
WDC	World Disarmament Campaign (EAIO)
WDC	World Disarmament Conference (NATG)
WDC	World Druze Congress (EA)
WDC	Write Data Check (CMD)
WDCA	Washington, DC [*Television station call letters*]
WDC-A........	World Data Center A [*National Academy of Sciences*]
WDCA	World Diving Coaches Association (EA)
WDCB	Glen Ellyn, IL [*FM radio station call letters*]
WDC-B........	World Data Center B [*National Academy of Sciences*]
WDCC	Sanford, NC [*AM radio station call letters*]
WDCC	Well-Developed Collateral Circulation [*Medicine*] (DMAA)
WDC-C........	World Data Centre-C for Sunspot Index [*Belgium*] (BUAC)
WDCD	Albany, NY [*AM radio station call letters*] (RBYB)
WDCE	Richmond, VA [*FM radio station call letters*]
WDCF	Dade City, FL [*AM radio station call letters*]
WDCG	Durham, NC [*FM radio station call letters*]
WDCGG.......	World Data Center for Greenhouse Gases [*Marine science*] (OSRA)
WDCI	Bridgeport, WV [*FM radio station call letters*]
WDCL	Somerset, KY [*FM radio station call letters*]
WDCM	Cruz Bay, VI [*FM radio station call letters*]
WDCM	World Data Centre on Microorganisms (EERA)
WDCMC.......	War Department Classified Message Center [*Obsolete World War II*]
WDCN	Nashville, TN [*Television station call letters*]
WDCO	Cochran, GA [*Television station call letters*]
WDCO-TV	Cochran, GA [*Television station call letters*]
WDCP	Bad Axe, MI [*Television station call letters*] (BROA)
WDCQ	Pine Island Centre, FL [*AM radio station call letters*]
WDCR	Hanover, NH [*AM radio station call letters*]
WDCS	Cobleskill, NY [*AM radio station call letters*] (RBYB)
WDCS	Weapons Data Correlation System (MCD)
WDCS	Whale and Dolphin Conservation Society [*British*] (DBA)
WDCS	Wide-Band Digital Cross-Connect System [*Telecommunications*] (ITD)
WDCS	Women's Division of Christian Service [*of the Board of Missions, The Methodist Church*]
WDCS	Writable Diagnostic Control Store
WDCSA........	War Department Chief of Staff, US Army [*World War II*]

WDCSM	Walt Disney Comic Strip Maker [*Apple computer software*]
WDCT	Fairfax, VA [*AM radio station call letters*]
WDCT	Woodcut (ROG)
wdct	Woodcut (VRA)
WDCU	Washington, DC [*FM radio station call letters*]
WDCV	Carlisle, PA [*FM radio station call letters*]
WDCW	Syracuse, NY [*AM radio station call letters*]
WDCX	Buffalo, NY [*FM radio station call letters*]
WDCY	Douglasville, GA [*AM radio station call letters*]
WDCZ	Webster, NY [*FM radio station call letters*]
WDD	Wave Dynamics Division [*US Army Corps of Engineers*]
WDD	Western Development Division [*ARDC*]
WDD	Windows Distributed Desktop [*Software*] (IGQR)
WDD	Word Description Drawing (SAA)
WDDA	Wholesale Demand Deposit Accounting (DICI)
WDDA-FM	Elberton, GA [*FM radio station call letters*] (BROA)
WDDB	Wild Dog Destruction Board [*New South Wales, Australia*]
WDDC	Portage, WI [*FM radio station call letters*]
WDDC	Well Deck Debarkation Control [*Navy*] (CAAL)
WDDD	Johnston City, IL [*AM radio station call letters*]
WDDD	Marion, IL [*FM radio station call letters*]
WDDES	World Digital Database for Environmental Sciences [*Marine science*] (OSRA)
WDDES	World Digital Data for the Environmental Sciences (EERA)
WDDJ	Paducah, KY [*FM radio station call letters*]
WDDK	Greensboro, GA [*FM radio station call letters*]
WDDO	Macon, GA [*AM radio station call letters*]
WDDQ	Adel, GA [*FM radio station call letters*]
WDDT	Greenville, MS [*AM radio station call letters*]
WDDTY	What Doctors Don't Tell You (BUAC)
WDE	Weapons Directing Equipment (NVT)
WDE	Weapons Direction Evaluation (SAA)
wde	Wood-Engraver [*MARC relator code*] [*Library of Congress*] (LCCP)
WDEA	Ellsworth, ME [*AM radio station call letters*]
WDEB	Jamestown, TN [*AM radio station call letters*]
WDEB-FM	Jamestown, TN [*FM radio station call letters*]
WDEC	Americus, GA [*AM radio station call letters*]
WDEC-FM	Americus, GA [*FM radio station call letters*]
WDED	Wounded [*Military*]
WDEE	Reed City, MI [*AM radio station call letters*]
WDeep	Western Deep Levels Ltd. [*Associated Press*] (SAG)
WDEF	Chattanooga, TN [*AM radio station call letters*]
WDEF-FM	Chattanooga, TN [*FM radio station call letters*]
WDEF-TV	Chattanooga, TN [*Television station call letters*]
WDEH	Sweetwater, TN [*AM radio station call letters*]
WDEH-FM	Sweetwater, TN [*FM radio station call letters*]
WDEI	Wuhan Digital Engineering Institute (BUAC)
WDEK	De Kalb, IL [*FM radio station call letters*]
WDEL	Weapons Development Effectiveness Laboratory (MCD)
WDEL	Wilmington, DE [*AM radio station call letters*]
WDEMCO	Walt Disney Educational Media Co.
WDEN	Macon, GA [*AM radio station call letters*]
WDEN-FM	Macon, GA [*FM radio station call letters*]
WDEOAT	Wolfe Data Entry Operator Aptitude Test
WDEP	Western Deep Levels Ltd. [*NASDAQ symbol*] (NQ)
WDEPY	Western Deep Levels ADR [*NASDAQ symbol*] (TTSB)
WDEQ	De Graff, OH [*FM radio station call letters*]
WDER	Derry, NH [*AM radio station call letters*]
WDET	Detroit, MI [*FM radio station call letters*]
WDEV	Waterbury, VT [*AM radio station call letters*]
WDEV-FM	Warren, VT [*FM radio station call letters*]
WDEX	Monroe, NC [*AM radio station call letters*]
WDEZ	Wausau, WI [*FM radio station call letters*]
WDF	Wall Distribution Frame (MUGU)
WDF	Wave Digital Filter (PDAA)
WDF	Weapon Defense Facility (AAG)
WDF	Weather Data Facility
WDF	Western Desert Force [*World War II*]
WDF	Winkelmann-Dibley Ford [*Race car*]
WDF	Wood Door and Frame [*Technical drawings*]
WDF	Woodruff
WDF	World Darts Federation (EAIO)
WDF	World Draughts (Checkers) Federation [*See also FMJD*] [*Dordrecht, Netherlands*] (EAIO)
WDFB	Danville, KY [*FM radio station call letters*]
WDFB	Junction City, KY [*AM radio station call letters*]
WDFC	WD-40 Co. [*NASDAQ symbol*] (NQ)
WD/FE	Water Dispenser/Fire Extinguisher [*Apollo*] [*NASA*]
WDFF	Women's Division-Federated Farmers of New Zealand (BUAC)
WDFH	Ossining, NY [*FM radio station call letters*]
WDFL	Cross City, FL [*AM radio station call letters*]
WDFL-FM	Cross City, FL [*FM radio station call letters*]
WDFM	Defiance, OH [*FM radio station call letters*]
WDFM	Wright Dust Feed Mechanism (PDAA)
WDFN	Detroit, MI [*AM radio station call letters*]
WDFP	World Day for Peace (EA)
WDFSA	World Federation of Direct Selling Associations (BUAC)
WDFW	Washingtons [*State*] Department of Fish and Wildlife
WDFX	Cleveland, MS [*FM radio station call letters*]
WDFX-TV	Ozark, AL [*Television station call letters*] (RBYB)
WDG	Enid [*Oklahoma*] [*Airport symbol*] (OAG)
WDG	Enid, OK [*Location identifier FAA*] (FAAL)
WDG	Ministry of Agriculture Fisheries and Food [*British ICAO designator*] (FAAC)
WDG	Wallace Dam [*Georgia*] [*Seismograph station code, US Geological Survey*] (SEIS)
WDG	Weapons Display Generator (MCD)
WDG	Winding (MSA)
WDG	Wording (WGA)
WDG	World Diplomatic Guide [*A publication*]
WDGC	Downers Grove, IL [*FM radio station call letters*]
WDGE	Wakefield-Peacedale, RI [*FM radio station call letters*] (RBYB)
WDGF	War Department Ground Forces [*Obsolete*]
WDGF-FM	Middletown, RI [*FM radio station call letters*] (RBYB)
WDGG	Ashland, KY [*FM radio station call letters*] (RBYB)
WDGI	Wholesale Dry Goods Institute [*Later, NATAD*]
WDGL-FM	Baton Rouge, LA [*FM radio station call letters*] (BROA)
W Dgns	Westminster Dragoons [*British military*] (DMA)
WDGO	War Department General Order [*Obsolete*]
WDGR	Dahlonega, GA [*AM radio station call letters*]
WDGS	War Department General Staff [*Obsolete*]
WDG TBA	Wording to Be Agreed [*Insurance*] (AIA)
WDGY	St. Paul, MN [*AM radio station call letters*]
WDH	Watery Diarrhea, Hypokalemia [*Syndrome*] [*Medicine*]
WDH	Windhoek [*Namibia*] [*Airport symbol*] (OAG)
WDH	Winkelmann-Dibley Hillclimb [*Race car*]
WDH	Wiring Data Handbook
WDHA	Dover, NJ [*AM radio station call letters*]
WDHA	Watery Diarrhea, Hypokalemia, Achlorhydria [*Medicine*]
WDHCB	War Department Hardship Claims Board [*Obsolete*]
WDHC-FM	Berkeley Springs, WV [*FM radio station call letters*] (RBYB)
WDHD	Woodhead Indus [*NASDAQ symbol*] (TTSB)
WDHD	Woodhead Industries, Inc. [*NASDAQ symbol*] (NQ)
WDHH	Watery Diarrhea, Hypokalemia, Hypochlorhydria [*Syndrome*] [*Medicine*]
WDHHA	Watery Diarrhea, Hypochlorhydria, Hypokalemia, and Alkalosis [*Medicine*]
WDHI	Delhi, NY [*FM radio station call letters*]
WDHN	Dothan, AL [*Television station call letters*]
WDHR	Pikeville, KY [*FM radio station call letters*]
WDHS	Iron Mountain, MI [*Television station call letters*]
WDHS	Worldwide Dental Health Service (EA)
WDI	Wardair, Inc. [*Toronto Stock Exchange symbol*]
WDI	War Department Intelligence [*Obsolete*]
WDI	Warfarin Dose Index
WDI	Warhead Detection Indicator (AAG)
WDI	Weapon Data Index [*Navy*] (MCD)
WDI	Weapon Delivery Impairment (NVT)
WDI	Web Depth Index
WDI	Wind Direction Indicator [*ICAO*] (FAAC)
WDI	Wood and Iron [*Freight*]
WDIA	Memphis, TN [*AM radio station call letters*]
WDIC	Clinchco, VA [*AM radio station call letters*]
WDIC	Women's Development and Information Center [*Bolivia*] (BUAC)
WDICC	War Department Intelligence Collection Committee
WDIC-FM	Clinchco, VA [*FM radio station call letters*]
WDICPC	War Department Intelligence Collection Planning Committee
WDIF	Marion, OH [*FM radio station call letters*]
WDIF	Women's Democratic International Federation (NATG)
W Dig	New York Weekly Digest [*A publication*] (DLA)
WDIG	Steubenville, OH [*AM radio station call letters*]
WDigitl	Western Digital Corp. [*Associated Press*] (SAG)
WDIH	Salisbury, MD [*FM radio station call letters*]
WDIO	Duluth, MN [*Television station call letters*]
WDIP	Weapon Data Insert Panel (MCD)
WDIQ	Dozier, AL [*Television station call letters*]
WDIR	Wind Direction
WDIR	Working Directory (MHDI)
WDIRN	What Do I Read Next [*A publication*]
WDIS	Norfolk, MA [*AM radio station call letters*]
WDIV	Detroit, MI [*Television station call letters*]
WDIY	Allentown, PA [*FM radio station call letters*]
WDIZ	Orlando, FL [*FM radio station call letters*]
WdJ	Wissenschaft des Judentums [*A publication*] (BJA)
WDJB	Columbia City, IN [*FM radio station call letters*]
WDJC-AM	Birmingham, AL [*AM radio station call letters*] (RBYB)
WDJC-FM	Birmingham, AL [*FM radio station*] (RBYB)
WDJL	Huntsville, AL [*AM radio station call letters*]
WDJM	Framingham, MA [*AM radio station call letters*]
WDJR	Enterprise, AL [*FM radio station call letters*]
WDJS	Mount Olive, NC [*AM radio station call letters*]
WDJT	Milwaukee, WI [*Television station call letters*]
WDJW	Somers, CT [*FM radio station call letters*]
WDJX	Louisville, KY [*FM radio station call letters*]
WDJY	Trenton, FL [*FM radio station call letters*]
WDJZ	Bridgeport, CT [*AM radio station call letters*]
W Dk	Weather Deck [*of a ship*] (DS)
WDKA	Paducah, KY [*Television station call letters*]
WDKB	De Kalb, IL [*FM radio station call letters*]
WDKC	Covington, PA [*FM radio station call letters*]
WDKD	Kingstree, SC [*AM radio station call letters*]
WDKM	Adams, WI [*FM radio station call letters*]
WDKN	Dickson, TN [*AM radio station call letters*]
WDKR-FM	Maroa, IL [*FM radio station call letters*] (RBYB)
WDKX	Rochester, NY [*FM radio station call letters*]
WDKY	Danville, KY [*Television station call letters*]
WD KY	United States District Court for the Western District of Kentucky (DLA)
WDL	Wages Due Lesbians (BUAC)

WDL.............	Warren Library Association and County Division, Warren, PA [*OCLC symbol*] (OCLC)
WDL.............	Waveguide Directional Localizer
WDL.............	Weapon Data Link (MCD)
WDL.............	Weapons Density List (AABC)
WDL.............	Well-Differentiated Lymphocytic [*Lymphoma classification*]
WDL.............	Westdeutsche Luftwerbung [*Airline*] [*Germany*]
WDL.............	Western d'Eldona Resources Ltd. [*Toronto Stock Exchange symbol*]
WDL.............	Western Development Laboratories
WDL.............	White Defence League (BUAC)
WDL.............	Wien Displacement Law [*Physics*]
WDL.............	Wireless Data Link
WDL.............	Work Days Lost (COE)
WDL.............	Workers' Defense League (EA)
WD LA.........	United States District Court for the Western District of Louisiana (DLA)
WDLA	Walton, NY [*AM radio station call letters*]
WDLA-FM	Walton, NY [*FM radio station call letters*]
WDLB	Marshfield, WI [*AM radio station call letters*]
WDLC	Port Jervis, NY [*AM radio station call letters*]
WDLF	Old Fort, NC [*FM radio station call letters*]
WDLF...........	White-Dwarf Luminosity Function [*Galactic science*]
WDLI	Canton, OH [*Television station call letters*]
WDLJ	Indianola, MS [*AM radio station call letters*]
WDLK	Dadeville, AL [*AM radio station call letters*]
WDLL...........	Well-Differentiated Lymphatic [*or Lymphocytic*] Lymphoma [*Oncology*]
WDLM	East Moline, IL [*AM radio station call letters*]
WDLM-FM ...	East Moline, IL [*FM radio station call letters*]
WDLP	Panama City Beach, FL [*AM radio station call letters*]
WDLR	Delaware, OH [*AM radio station call letters*]
WDLR	Work Days Lost Restricted (COE)
WDLS	Dallas, PA [*FM radio station call letters*]
WDLT	Chickasaw, AL [*FM radio station call letters*]
WDLW-AM ...	Lorain, OH [*AM radio station call letters*] (BROA)
WDLX	Washington, NC [*FM radio station call letters*]
WDLY	Gatlinburg, TN [*FM radio station call letters*]
WDLY	Widely (FAAC)
WDM	Wavelength Division Multiplex [*or Multiplexing*] [*Telecommunications*]
WDM	Weapon Delivery Model (PDAA)
WDM	Weight after Departure from Mars [*NASA*]
WDM	Windows Driver Model [*Computer science*]
WDM	World Development Movement [*British*]
WDMA	Wholesale Druggists Merchandising Association (EA)
WDMB	War Department Manpower Board [*Obsolete*]
WDMCC	Walt Disney Memorial Cancer Institute
WDMCI	Walt Disney Memorial Cancer Institute
WDME-FM ...	Dover-Foxcroft, ME [*FM radio station call letters*]
WDMET.......	Wound Data Munitions Effectiveness Team (MCD)
WDMF	Weak Disordered Magnetic Field
WDMG	Douglas, GA [*AM radio station call letters*]
WDMG-FM...	Douglas, GA [*FM radio station call letters*]
WD Mich	United States District Court for the Western District of Michigan (DLA)
WDMJ..........	Marquette, MI [*AM radio station call letters*]
WDML	Wiring Diagram Maintenance List
WDML	Woodlawn, IL [*FM radio station call letters*]
WD MO.......	United States District Court for the Western District of Missouri (DLA)
WDMO	Weight before Departure from Mars Orbit [*NASA*]
WDMP	Dodgeville, WI [*AM radio station call letters*]
WDMP-FM ...	Dodgeville, WI [*FM radio station call letters*]
WDMS	Greenville, MS [*FM radio station call letters*]
WDMT	Eufaula, AL [*FM radio station call letters*]
WDMV	Pocomoke City, MD [*AM radio station call letters*]
WDMX	Vienna, WV [*FM radio station call letters*]
WDN	Walden Residential Prop [*NYSE symbol*] (TTSB)
WDN	Walden Residential Properties [*NYSE symbol*] (SAG)
WDN	Wooden
WDNA..........	Miami, FL [*FM radio station call letters*]
WDNC..........	Durham, NC [*AM radio station call letters*]
WDNC..........	United States District Court for the Western District of North Carolina (DLA)
WDNE	Elkins, WV [*AM radio station call letters*]
WDNE-FM ...	Elkins, WV [*FM radio station call letters*]
WDNG.........	Anniston, AL [*AM radio station call letters*]
WDNH.........	Honesdale, PA [*FM radio station call letters*]
WDNL	Danville, IL [*FM radio station call letters*]
WDNO	Laurel, DE [*FM radio station call letters*]
WDNOWRE...	Wooden Ware [*Freight*]
WDNR..........	Chester, PA [*FM radio station call letters*]
WDNR..........	Wisconsin Department of Natural Resources
WDNS	Bowling Green, KY [*FM radio station call letters*]
WDNT	Dayton, TN [*AM radio station call letters*]
WDNT-FM....	Dayton, TN [*FM radio station call letters*]
WDNX.........	Olive Hill, TN [*FM radio station call letters*]
WDNY.........	Dansville, NY [*AM radio station call letters*]
WDNY..........	United States District Court for the Western District of New York (DLA)
WDNY-FM...	Dansville, NY [*FM radio station call letters*]
WDO	Web Depth Order
WDO	Widespread Depression Orchestra
WDO	Window (MSA)
WDOC..........	Prestonsburg, KY [*AM radio station call letters*]
WDOD..........	Chattanooga, TN [*AM radio station call letters*]
WDOD-FM ...	Chattanooga, TN [*FM radio station call letters*]
WDOE	Dunkirk, NY [*AM radio station call letters*]
WDOE	Washington Department of Ecology
WDOG..........	Allendale, SC [*AM radio station call letters*]
WDOG-FM ..	Allendale, SC [*FM radio station call letters*]
WDOH..........	Delphos, OH [*FM radio station call letters*]
WDOK	Cleveland, OH [*FM radio station call letters*]
WD Okla	United States District Court for the Western District of Oklahoma (DLA)
WDOL..........	Englewood, OH [*FM radio station call letters*]
WDOM	Providence, RI [*FM radio station call letters*]
WDOP	Weighted Dilution of Precision
WDOPD.......	War Department, Operations Division, General Staff [*World War II*]
WDOR..........	Sturgeon Bay, WI [*AM radio station call letters*]
WDOR-FM ...	Sturgeon Bay, WI [*FM radio station call letters*]
WDOS	Oneonta, NY [*AM radio station call letters*]
WDOS	Wooton Desk Owners Society (EA)
WDOV..........	Dover, DE [*AM radio station call letters*]
WDOW........	Dowagiac, MI [*AM radio station call letters*]
WDOX..........	Wildwood Crest, NJ [*FM radio station call letters*]
WDOY	Fajardo, PR [*FM radio station call letters*]
WDOZ..........	Dearborn, MI [*AM radio station call letters*]
WDP	Weapons Direction Program
WDP	Wenner Difference Potentiometer
WDP	Women in Data Processing (EA)
WDP	Wood Panel (AAG)
WDP	Work Distribution Policy (AAG)
WD PA.........	United States District Court for the Western District of Pennsylvania (DLA)
WDPA	Wisconsin Dairy Products Association (EA)
WDPB	Seaford, DE [*Television station call letters*]
WDPC	Western Data Processing Center [*University of California, Los Angeles*]
WDPC-AM....	Dallas, GA [*AM radio station call letters*] (RBYB)
WDPG..........	Greenville, OH [*FM radio station call letters*]
WDPMG-ID..	War Department Provost Marshal General, Investigation Division [*Obsolete*]
WDPN..........	Alliance, OH [*AM radio station call letters*]
WDPR..........	Dayton, OH [*FM radio station call letters*]
WDPS	Dayton, OH [*FM radio station call letters*]
WDPT..........	Water-Drop-Penetration Time [*Agriculture*]
WDPX..........	Springfield, OH [*Television station call letters*] (BROA)
WDQN..........	Du Quoin, IL [*AM radio station call letters*]
WDQN-FM ...	Du Quoin, IL [*FM radio station call letters*]
WDR	Waddell & Reed Fin'l 'A' [*NYSE symbol*]
WDR	Warburg Dillon Read
WDR	Wardair International Ltd. [*Toronto Stock Exchange symbol Vancouver Stock Exchange symbol*]
Wdr.............	Wardmaster [*British military*] (DMA)
WDR	Westdeutscher Rundfunk [*Radio network*] [*West Germany*]
WDR	Wide Dynamic Range
WDR	Wider (WGA)
WDR	Winder, GA [*Location identifier FAA*] (FAAL)
WDR	Window Definition Record [*Computer science*]
WDR	Winged Russia [*Russian Federation*] [*ICAO designator*] (FAAC)
WDR	Withdrawal
WDR	Women's Drug Research Project (EA)
WDR	Write Drum
WDRB	Louisville, KY [*Television station call letters*]
WDRC	Hartford, CT [*AM radio station call letters*]
WDRC	Women's Defence Relief Corps [*World War I*] [*British*]
WDRC	World Data Referral Centre [*France*] (BUAC)
WDRC-FM ...	Hartford, CT [*FM radio station call letters*]
WDRE	Garden City, NY [*FM radio station call letters*]
WDRG..........	Danville, VA [*Television station call letters*]
WDRK	Callaway, FL [*FM radio station call letters*]
Wdr L	Wardmaster Lieutenant [*British military*] (DMA)
WDRM.........	Decatur, AL [*FM radio station call letters*]
WDROP.......	Water Distribution Register of Organic Pollutants [*National Institutes of Health*]
WDRP..........	Windsor, NC [*FM radio station call letters*]
WDRQ-FM ...	Detroit, MI [*FM radio station call letters*] (RBYB)
WDRR..........	Sanibel, FL [*FM radio station call letters*] (RBYB)
WDRSG.......	Workplace Deaths Relatives Support Group (BUAC)
Wdrst..........	Woodroast Systems, Inc. [*Associated Press*] (SAG)
WDRT..........	Water Detection Response Team [*DoD*]
WDRY..........	Coinmach Laundry Corp. [*NASDAQ symbol*] (SAG)
WDRZ..........	Etowah, TN [*FM radio station call letters*]
WDS	Four Winds Aviation Ltd. [*ICAO designator*] (FAAC)
WDS	Washington Document Service [*Information service or system*] (IID)
WD(S)..........	Waste Disposal (System) [*Nuclear energy*] (NRCH)
WDS	Watery Diarrhea Syndrome [*Medicine*] (DB)
WDS	Wavelenght-Dispersive Spectroscopy (AAEL)
WDS	Wavelength Dispersive Spectrometer
WDS	Wavelength Dispersive X-Ray Spectroscopy (EDCT)
WDS	Weapon Delivery System
WDS	Weapons Directing System [*Navy*]
WDS	Web Drug-Delivery System (DB)
WDS	Wet Dog Shakes Syndrome [*Medicine*] (DMAA)
WDS	Wire Data Service
WDS	Women's Design Service (BUAC)
WDS	Wood Dye Stain
WDS	Woodside [*California*] [*Seismograph station code, US Geological Survey*] (SEIS)
WDS	Woodward's Ltd. [*Toronto Stock Exchange symbol Vancouver Stock Exchange symbol*]

WDS .... Word Discrimination Score
WDS .... World Deist Society   (EA)
WDS .... Wounds
WDSC .... Dillon, SC [*AM radio station call letters*]
WDSD .... Dover, DE [*FM radio station call letters*]
WDSD .... Water Data Sources Directory [*US Geological Survey*] [*Information service or system*]   (CRD)
WDSD .... Wisconsin School for the Deaf, Delavan, WI [*Library symbol Library of Congress*]   (LCLS)
WDSE .... Duluth, MN [*Television station call letters*]
WDSI .... Chattanooga, TN [*Television station call letters*]
WDSK .... Cleveland, MS [*AM radio station call letters*]   (RBYB)
WDSL .... Mocksville, NC [*AM radio station call letters*]
WDSM .... Superior, WI [*AM radio station call letters*]
WDSN .... Reynoldsville, PA [*FM radio station call letters*]
WDSO .... Chesterton, IN [*FM radio station call letters*]
WDSP .... Arlington, NY [*FM radio station call letters*]
WDSPR .... Widespread
WDSPRD ..... Widespread   (FAAC)
WDSR .... Lake City, FL [*AM radio station call letters*]
WDSS .... War Department Special Staff [*Obsolete*]
WDSS .... Warning Decision Support System [*Marine science*]   (OSRA)
WDS SATSIM... Weapon Direction System Satellite Simulation [*Military*]   (CAAL)
WDST .... Woodstock, NY [*FM radio station call letters*]
WD STL ...... Wood or Steel [*Freight*]
WD STV ...... Wood Stove [*Freight*]
WDSU .... New Orleans, LA [*Television station call letters*]
WDSY .... Pittsburgh, PA [*AM radio station call letters*]
WDSY-FM .... Pittsburgh, PA [*FM radio station call letters*]   (RBYB)
WDT .... Warmth Detection Threshold
WDT .... Watch Dog Timer
WDT .... Wear Durability Trial
WDT .... Weight Data Transmitter   (IAA)
WDT .... Weight Distribution Table
WDT .... Width
WDT .... Wiedemann Developed Template   (MCD)
WDT .... World Cement Industries [*Vancouver Stock Exchange symbol*]
WDT .... Writers' Development Trust [*Canada*]   (EAIO)
WDTC .... Western Defense Tactical Command   (AAG)
WD Tenn .... United States District Court for the Western District of Tennessee   (DLA)
WD Tex....... United States District Court for the Western District of Texas   (DLA)
WDTF .... Wetting-Drying and Temperature Fluctuation [*Geochemistry*]
WDTL .... Cleveland, MS [*FM radio station call letters*]
WDTM .... Selmer, TN [*AM radio station call letters*]
WDTN .... Dayton, OH [*Television station call letters*]
WDTR .... Detroit, MI [*FM radio station call letters*]
WDTRS .... Westinghouse Development Test Requirement Specification   (IAA)
WDTU .... War Dog Training Unit [*British military*]   (DMA)
WDTV .... Weston, WV [*Television station call letters*]
WDu........... Durand Free Library, Durand, WI [*Library symbol Library of Congress*]   (LCLS)
WdU........... Wahlpartei der Unabhaengigen [*Electoral Party of Independents*] [*Austria Political party*]   (PPE)
WDU .... Water Data Unit   (DCTA)
WDU .... Weapons Director Unit   (MCD)
WDU .... Window Delcing Unit
WDU .... Wireless Development Unit
WDU .... Workers' Defence Union [*British*]
WDUB .... Granville, OH [*FM radio station call letters*]
WDUF .... Duffield, VA [*AM radio station call letters*]
WDUK .... Havana, IL [*FM radio station call letters*]
WDUN .... Gainesville, GA [*AM radio station call letters*]
WDUQ .... Pittsburgh, PA [*FM radio station call letters*]
WDUR .... Durham, NC [*AM radio station call letters*]
WDUV .... Bradenton, FL [*FM radio station call letters*]
WDUX .... Waupaca, WI [*AM radio station call letters*]
WDUX-FM.... Waupaca, WI [*FM radio station call letters*]
WDUZ .... Green Bay, WI [*AM radio station call letters*]
WDV .... War Department Vehicle [*Obsolete*]
WDV .... Water Dilution Volume [*Environmental chemistry*]   (FFDE)
WDV .... Western Diverging Volcanism [*Geology*]
WDV .... Wheat Dwarf Virus [*Plant pathology*]
WDV .... Winkelmann-Dibley Volkswagen [*Race car*]
WDV .... Worldwide Dollarvest Fund [*NYSE symbol*]   (SAG)
WDV .... Written Down Value [*Accounting*]
WDVA .... Danville, VA [*AM radio station call letters*]
WD VA .... United States District Court for the Western District of Virginia   (DLA)
WDVE .... Pittsburgh, PA [*FM radio station call letters*]
WDVI .... Dadeville, AL [*FM radio station call letters*]
WDVR .... Delaware Township, NJ [*FM radio station call letters*]
WDVX .... Clinton, TN [*FM radio station call letters*]
WDW .... Wholesale Dealer in Wines
WDW .... Window
WDW .... Wood and Wire [*Freight*]
WD Wash .... United States District Court for the Western District of Washington   (DLA)
WDWB .... Detroit, MI [*Television station call letters*]   (BROA)
WDWD-AM.... Atlanta, GA [*AM radio station call letters*]   (BROA)
WDWG .... Atmore, AL [*FM radio station call letters*]
WD Wis ...... United States District Court for the Western District of Wisconsin   (DLA)
wdwk .... Woodwork   (BARN)
WDWL .... Bayamon, PR [*Television station call letters*]
WDWN .... Auburn, NY [*FM radio station call letters*]

WDWN......... Well Developed - Well Nourished [*Medicine*]
WDWNBF..... Well-Developed Well-Nourished, Black Female   (DAVI)
WDWNBM.... Well-Developed, Well-Nourished, Black Male   (DAVI)
WDWNWF.... Well-Developed, Well-Nourished, White Female   (DAVI)
WDWNWM.. Well-Developed, Well-Nourished, White Male   (DAVI)
WDWRK ...... Woodwork [*Freight*]
WDWS .... Champaign, IL [*AM radio station call letters*]
WDWT .... Dwight, IL [*FM radio station call letters*]
WDWZ-AM.... Lanett, AL [*AM radio station call letters*]   (RBYB)
WDX .... Wavelenght-Dispersive X-Ray Spectroscopy   (AAEL)
WDX .... Wavelength Dispersive X-Ray [*Spectrometer*]
WDXA .... Wave-Length Dispersive X-Ray Analysis
WDXC .... Pound, VA [*FM radio station call letters*]
WDXD-FM.... Holly Hill, FL [*FM radio station call letters*]   (RBYB)
WDXE .... Lawrenceburg, TN [*AM radio station call letters*]
WDXE-FM.... Lawrenceburg, TN [*FM radio station call letters*]
WDXI .... Jackson, TN [*AM radio station call letters*]
WDXL .... Lexington, TN [*AM radio station call letters*]
WDXN .... Clarksville, TN [*AM radio station call letters*]
WDXO-FM.... Hazlehurst, MS [*FM radio station call letters*]   (BROA)
WDXR .... Golconda, IL [*FM radio station call letters*]
WDXR .... Paducah, KY [*AM radio station call letters*]
WDXRF .... Wavelength-Dispersive X-Ray Fluorescence
WDXRS .... Wavelength Dispersive X-Ray Spectrometry
WDXX .... Selma, AL [*FM radio station call letters*]
WDXY .... Sumter, SC [*AM radio station call letters*]
WDXZ .... Newberry, SC [*FM radio station call letters*]   (RBYB)
WDY .... Phoenix Airline Services, Inc. [*ICAO designator*]   (FAAC)
WDY .... Woody [*California*] [*Seismograph station code, US Geological Survey Closed*]   (SEIS)
WDY .... Wordy [*Used in correcting manuscripts, etc.*]
WDYL .... Chester, VA [*FM radio station call letters*]
WDYN .... Chattanooga, TN [*FM radio station call letters*]
WDYT .... What Do You Think
WDYTYCIWSS... Why Don't You Take Your Change In War Savings Stamps [*Cashier's sign*] [*World War II*]
WDZ .... Decatur, IL [*AM radio station call letters*]
WDZ .... Werner Dahnz Co. Ltd. [*Toronto Stock Exchange symbol*]
WDZE .... Carolina, PR [*Television station call letters*]
WDZL .... Miami, FL [*Television station call letters*]
WDZQ .... Decatur, IL [*FM radio station call letters*]
WDZR .... Mount Clemens, MI [*FM radio station call letters*]
WDZS .... Darlington, SC [*AM radio station call letters*]   (RBYB)
WDZZ .... Flint, MI [*FM radio station call letters*]
WE............. Eau Claire Public Library, Eau Claire, WI [*Library symbol Library of Congress*]   (LCLS)
W$_E$ .... Emitter-Region Width   (IDOE)
WE............. Morris Cerullo World Evangelism   (EA)
WE............. Staff Meteorologist [*AFSC*]
WE............. Votec [*ICAO designator*]   (AD)
WE............. Wage Earner [*Social Security Administration*]   (OICC)
WE............. War Establishment
WE............. Watch Error [*Navigation*]
WE............. Watchman-Examiner [*A publication*]   (BJA)
WE............. Water Equivalent   (MCD)
We............. Watt Electric
WE............. WDL Flugdienst GmbH [*Germany ICAO designator*]   (ICDA)
WE............. Weapons Electrical [*Navy British*]
WE............. Weapons Engineering [*Navy British*]
WE............. Weather Emergency
WE............. Webbing Equipment [*British military*]   (DMA)
We............. Weber Number [*IUPAC*]
WE............. Wednesday
WE............. Weekend   (ADA)
W/E........... Week Ending
WE............. Wescap Enterprises Ltd. [*Vancouver Stock Exchange symbol*]
WE............. Westcoast Energy [*NYSE symbol*]   (TTSB)
WE............. Westcoast Energy, Inc. [*NYSE symbol*]   (SPSG)
WE............. Western Electric Co.   (AAG)
WE............. Western Encephalitis [*Medicine*]   (MAE)
WE............. Western Encephalomyelitis [*Medicine*]   (MAE)
We............. Western Tithe Cases [*England*] [*A publication*]   (DLA)
We............. West's English Chancery Reports [*A publication*]   (DLA)
We............. West's Reports, English House of Lords [*A publication*]   (DLA)
WE............. White Edges   (ADA)
WE............. Whole Economy [*Department of Employment*] [*British*]
W/e........... Width-to-Length [*Ratio*]   (MDG)
WE............. Wing Elevon   (MCD)
WE............. With Equipment   (AABC)
WE............. Withholding Exemptions [*Army*]   (AABC)
WE............. Women and Employment [*An association*]   (EA)
WE............. Women Educators   (EA)
WE............. Women Employed [*Chicago, IL*]   (EA)
WE............. Women Entrepreneurs [*Defunct*]   (EA)
WE............. Women Exploited   (EA)
WE............. Women in Energy   (EA)
WE............. Women in Enterprise [*British*] [*An association*]   (DBA)
WE............. Women's Caucus of the Endocrine Society   (EA)
WE............. Women's Reserve, Engineering Duties [*USNR officer designation*]
WE............. Work Experience
WE............. World Ecologists Foundation [*Philippines*]   (EAIO)
WE............. World Education, Inc.
WE............. World Evangelism   (EA)
WE............. Write Enable [*Computer science*]   (IEEE)
W/E........... Writer/Editor   (MCD)

WEA............ Eastern Washington State College, Cheney, WA [*OCLC symbol*] (OCLC)
WEa............ East Troy Public Library, East Troy, WI [*Library symbol Library of Congress*] (LCLS)
WEA............ Royal West of England Academy
WEA............ Wall Effect Amplifier
WEA............ Warner-Eddison Associates, Inc. [*Information service or system*] (IID)
WEA............ Weak Equity Axiom
WEA............ Weather (AABC)
WEA............ Weatherford, TX [*Location identifier FAA*] (FAAL)
WEA............ Western Economic Association International (EA)
WEA............ Wilderness Education Association (EA)
WEA............ Women Employed Advocates (EA)
WEA............ Workers' Educational Association
WEA............ Workers Education Association (EERA)
WEAA........... Baltimore, MD [*FM radio station call letters*]
WEAAC........ Western European Airport Authorities Conference (MCD)
WEAAP........ Western European Association for Aviation Psychology (EA)
WEAB........... Adamsville, TN [*AM radio station call letters*]
WEAC........... Gaffney, SC [*AM radio station call letters*]
WEAC........... West European Advisory Committee [*Radio Free Europe*] (NTCM)
WEAC........... Winchester Engineering and Analytical Center [*Food and Drug Administration*] [*Winchester, MA*] (GRD)
WEACAP...... Weapon Capability (SAA)
WEADES...... Western Electric Air Defense Engineering Service (SAA)
WEADSC...... World Esperantist Association for Education, Science, and Culture [*Germany*] (EAIO)
WEAI........... Lynnville, IL [*FM radio station call letters*]
WEAI........... Western Economic Association International [*Later, WEA*] (EA)
WEAL........... Women's Equity Action League [*Defunct*] (EA)
WEAM........... Columbus, GA [*AM radio station call letters*]
WEA-N......... Westinghouse Engineers Association National [*Defunct*] (EA)
WEAN........... Women's Earth Action Network (BUAC)
WE & FA...... Welsh Engineers and Founders Association (DBA)
W/E & SP..... With Equipment and Spare Parts
WEANSW..... Workers' Educational Association of New South Wales [*Australia*]
WEAO........... Akron, OH [*Television station call letters*]
WEAP........... Women's Economic Agenda Project [*An association*]
WEAP........... World Environment Action Plan (EERA)
WEAPD........ Western Air Procurement District
WEAQ........... Eau Claire, WI [*AM radio station call letters*]
WEAR........... Pensacola, FL [*Television station call letters*]
WEARCON... Weather Observation and Forecasting Control System
WEARECONRON... Weather Reconnaissance Squadron [*Air Force*] (DNAB)
WEARESFAC... Weather Research Facility [*Navy*] (GFGA)
WEAS........... Savannah, GA [*AM radio station call letters*]
WEASA......... Workers' Educational Association of South Australia
WEASEL....... Weapon Selection (SAA)
WEASERVCOMM... Weather Service Command [*Navy*]
WEAS-FM.... Savannah, GA [*FM radio station call letters*]
WEAT........... Weathertight
WEAT........... West Palm Beach, FL [*AM radio station call letters*]
WEAT-FM.... West Palm Beach, FL [*FM radio station call letters*]
WEAU........... Eau Claire, WI [*Television station call letters*]
WEAV........... Plattsburgh, NY [*AM radio station call letters*]
WEAX........... Angola, IN [*FM radio station call letters*]
WEAX........... En Route Weather Forecast [*Navy*] (NVT)
WEAZ........... Union Park, FL [*FM radio station call letters*] (RBYB)
WEB............ Wagner Earth Bridge
WEB............ War Engineering Board
web............. Web (VRA)
WEB............ Webbing (AAG)
WEB............ Webco Industries [*AMEX symbol*] (TTSB)
WEB............ Webco Industries, Inc. [*AMEX symbol*] (SAG)
WEBA........... Allendale, SC [*Television station call letters*]
WEBA........... Women Exploited by Abortion (EA)
WEBA........... World Educational Broadcasting Assembly (BUAC)
WEBAstla..... World Equity Benchmark Shares [*Associated Press*] (SAG)
WEBAstr...... World Equity Benchmark Shares [*Associated Press*] (SAG)
WEBB........... Online System Svcs [*NASDAQ symbol*] (TTSB)
WEBB........... Waterville, ME [*FM radio station call letters*]
Webb........... Webb's Reports [*6-20 Kansas*] [*A publication*] (DLA)
Webb........... Webb's Reports [*11-20 Texas Civil Appeals*] [*A publication*] (DLA)
WEBB........... Writer's Electronic Bulletin Board [*Information service or system*] (IID)
Webb & D.... Webb and Duval's Reports [*1-3 Texas*] [*A publication*] (DLA)
Webb & Duval... Webb and Duval's Reports [*1-3 Texas*] [*A publication*] (DLA)
Webb Cr Dig... Webb's Digest of Texas Criminal Cases [*A publication*] (DLA)
WebbD......... Webb [*Del E.*] Corp. [*Associated Press*] (SAG)
WEB Bel....... World Equity Benchmark Shares [*Associated Press*] (SAG)
Webb Jud Act... Webb on the Judicature Act [*A publication*] (DLA)
Webb Pl & Pr... Webb's Kansas Pleading and Practice [*A publication*] (DLA)
Webb RR....... Webb's Railroad Laws of Maine [*A publication*] (DLA)
Webb Supr Ct Pr... Webb's English Supreme Court Practice [*A publication*] (DLA)
WEBBW........ Online System Svcs Wrrt [*NASDAQ symbol*] (TTSB)
WEBC........... Duluth, MN [*AM radio station call letters*]
WEBCan....... World Equity Benchmark Shares [*Associated Press*] (SAG)
Webcolnd.... Webco Industries, Inc. [*Associated Press*] (SAG)
WebDAV...... Web Distributed Authoring and Versioning (TELE)
WEBE........... Western European Basic Encyclopedia (MCD)
WEBE........... Westport, CT [*FM radio station call letters*]
WEBELOS.... We'll Be Loyal Scouts [*Boy Scout slogan*]
WEBFra........ World Equity Benchmark Shares [*Associated Press*] (SAG)
WEBG-AM.... Loretto, PA [*AM radio station call letters*] (RBYB)
WEBGer....... World Equity Benchmark Shares [*Associated Press*] (SAG)
WEB HK....... World Equity Benchmark Shares [*Associated Press*] (SAG)
WEB Ita....... World Equity Benchmark Shares [*Associated Press*] (SAG)
WEBJ........... Brewton, AL [*AM radio station call letters*]
WEB Jpn...... World Equity Benchmark Shares [*Associated Press*] (SAG)
WEBK........... Killington, VT [*FM radio station call letters*]
WEB Mal..... World Equity Benchmark Shares [*Associated Press*] (SAG)
WEB Mex..... World Equity Benchmark Shares [*Associated Press*] (SAG)
WEBN........... Cincinnati, OH [*FM radio station call letters*]
WEB Net...... World Equity Benchmark Shares [*Associated Press*] (SAG)
WEBO........... Owego, NY [*AM radio station call letters*]
Web Pat...... Webster's New Patent Law [*4th ed.*] [*1854*] [*A publication*] (DLA)
Web Pat Cas... Webster's Patent Cases [*1601-1855*] [*A publication*] (DLA)
Web PC........ Webster's Patent Cases [*1601-1855*] [*A publication*] (DLA)
WEBQ........... Eldorado, IL [*FM radio station call letters*]
WEBQ........... Harrisburg, IL [*AM radio station call letters*]
WEBR........... Washington, DC [*FM radio station call letters*] (RBYB)
WEBROCK.... Weather Buoy Rocket
WEBS........... Calhoun, GA [*AM radio station call letters*]
WEBS........... Weapons Effectiveness Buoy System
WEBS........... WebSecure, Inc. [*NASDAQ symbol*] (SAG)
Webs........... Webster's Patent Cases [*England*] [*A publication*] (DLA)
WEBS........... World Equity Benchmark Shares [*Investment term*]
WebSec....... WebSecure, Inc. [*Associated Press*] (SAG)
WEBSEC...... Western Beaufort Sea Ecological Cruise [*Coast Guard*]
WebSecr...... WebSecure, Inc. [*Associated Press*] (SAG)
WEB Sing.... World Equity Benchmark Shares [*Associated Press*] (SAG)
Webs Pat Cas... Webster's Patent Cases [*England*] [*A publication*] (DLA)
WEB Spn..... World Equity Benchmark Shares [*Associated Press*] (SAG)
Webst Dict... Webster's Dictionary [*A publication*] (DLA)
Webst Dict Unab... Webster's Unabridged Dictionary [*A publication*] (DLA)
Webster in Sen Doc... Webster in Senate Documents [*A publication*] (DLA)
Webster Pat Cas... Webster's Patent Cases [*1601-1855*] [*A publication*] (DLA)
Webster Pat Cas (Eng)... Webster's Patent Cases [*England*] [*A publication*] (DLA)
Webster U... Webster University (GAGS)
Webst Int Dict... Webster's International Dictionary [*A publication*] (DLA)
Webst New Int D... Webster's New International Dictionary [*A publication*] (DLA)
WEB Swd..... World Equity Benchmark Shares [*Associated Press*] (SAG)
WEB Swz..... World Equity Benchmark Shares [*Associated Press*] (SAG)
WEBT........... Valley, Al [*FM radio station call letters*] (RBYB)
Web Tr........ Trial of Professor Webster for Murder [*A publication*] (DLA)
WEB UK........ World Equity Benchmark Shares [*Associated Press*] (SAG)
WEBX........... Tuscola, IL [*FM radio station call letters*] (RBYB)
WEBY........... Milton, FL [*AM radio station call letters*]
WEBZ........... Mexico Beach, FL [*FM radio station call letters*]
WEC............ District One Technical Institute, Eau Claire, Eau Claire, WI [*OCLC symbol*] (OCLC)
WEC............ Eau Claire County Hospital, Eau Claire, WI [*Library symbol Library of Congress*] (LCLS)
WEC............ Universal Airlines, Inc. [*ICAO designator*] (FAAC)
WEC............ Wafer Environment Control (AAEL)
WEC............ Walking with Eyes Closed [*Equilibrium test*]
WEC............ Warhead Electrical Connector
WEC............ Water Export Control
WEC............ Weapon Engagement Console [*Military*] (CAAL)
WEC............ Weapon Engagement Controller [*Military*] (CAAL)
WEC............ Weekend College (DHP)
WEC............ Wescal Resources, Inc. [*Vancouver Stock Exchange symbol*]
WEC............ West European Container Liners [*Shipping*]
WEC............ Westinghouse Electric Corp.
WEC............ Wind Energy Conversion
WEC............ Wisconsin Energy Corp. [*NYSE symbol*] (SPSG)
WEC............ Women's Emergency Corps [*World War I*] [*British*]
WEC............ World Endurance Championship [*Auto racing*]
WEC............ World Energy Conference [*See also CME*] [*London, England*] (EAIO)
WEC............ World Energy Council
WEC............ World Engineering Conference (BUAC)
WEC............ World Environment Center (EA)
WEC............ World Environment Centre (EERA)
WEC............ Worldwide Evangelization Crusade (EA)
WECAF........ Western Central Atlantic Fisheries Commission [*Food and Agriculture Organization of the UN*]
WECAFC...... Western Central Atlantic Fisheries Commission [*Food and Agriculture Organization of the UN*] (EAIO)
WECB........... Seymour, WI [*FM radio station call letters*]
WECB........... Weapons Evaluation and Control Bureau [*USACDA*]
WECC........... St. Mary's, GA [*AM radio station call letters*]
WECC........... Western Collegiate Conference (PSS)
WECC........... Western European Calibration Cooperation (ACII)
WECC........... White English Celtic Catholic
WECC........... Wyoming Educational Computing Council (EDAC)
WECEN........ Weather Center [*Air Force*]
WECI........... Richmond, IN [*FM radio station call letters*]
WECI........... WEC International (EA)
WECI........... World Evangelisation Crusade International (BUAC)
WECK........... Cheektowaga, NY [*AM radio station call letters*]
WECL........... Elk Mound, WI [*FM radio station call letters*]
WECM........... Milton, FL [*AM radio station call letters*]
WECM........... Warranted Existing Class Maintained (DS)
WECN........... Naranjito, PR [*Television station call letters*]
WECO........... Wartburg, TN [*AM radio station call letters*]
WECO........... Western Electric Co. (MCD)
WECO........... Westinghouse Electric Corp.
WECO........... Worldwide Energy Corp. (EFIS)
WECO-FM.... Wartburg, TN [*FM radio station call letters*]
WECOM........ Weapons Command [*Later, Armaments Command*] [*Army*]

WECON........ Weather Controlled Messages (NVT)
WECPNL...... Weighted Equivalent Continuous Perceived Noise Level
WECQ .... Clyde, NY [*FM radio station call letters*]
WECR.......... Beech Mountain, NC [*FM radio station call letters*]
WECR-AM.... Newland, NC [*AM radio station call letters*] (RBYB)
WECS.......... Water-Glycol Evaporator Control System (SAA)
WECS.......... Willimantic, CT [*FM radio station call letters*]
WECS.......... Wind Energy Conversion System
WECST........ Waste Evaporator Condensate Storage Tank [*Nuclear energy*]
      (NRCH)
WECT.......... Wilmington, NC [*Television station call letters*]
WECT.......... World Encyclopaedia of Contemporary Theatre (BUAC)
WECU .... Peoria, IL [*FM radio station call letters*]
WECV.......... Chippewa Valley Museum, Eau Claire, WI [*Library symbol Library of Congress*] (LCLS)
WECW .... Elmira, NY [*FM radio station call letters*]
WECZ.......... Punxsutawney, PA [*AM radio station call letters*]
WED............ Walter Elias Disney [*These initials also identify the theme park division of Walt Disney Enterprises*]
WED............ War Emergency Dose (DEN)
WED............ Water Enforcement Division [*Environmental Protection Agency*] (EPA)
WED............ Weak Exchange Degeneracy [*Particle physics*] (OA)
WED............ Weapons Engineering Duty [*Navy*] (NG)
WED............ Wedau [*Papua New Guinea*] [*Airport symbol*] (OAG)
WED............ Wednesday (EY)
Wed............ Wednesday (ODBW)
WED............ West Delta Resources Ltd. [*Vancouver Stock Exchange symbol*]
WED............ Women's Enterprises Development [*Kenya*] (BUAC)
WED............ Work Force Effectiveness and Development Group [*Office of Personnel Management*] (GRD)
WED............ World Energy Development [*Gabon*] (BUAC)
WED............ World Environment Day
WEDA .... Western Dredging Association (EA)
WEDA .... Wholesale Egg Distributors' Association [*British*] (BI)
WEDA .... Wholesale Engineering Distributors Association (BUAC)
WEDA .... Women's Enterprise Development Agency [*Established in 1987*] [*British*]
WEDAC .... Westinghouse Digital Airborne Computer
WEDC.......... Chicago, IL [*AM radio station call letters*]
WEDC.......... Water, Engineering and Development Centre (BUAC)
WEDC.......... Wedco Technologies [*NASDAQ symbol*] (SAG)
Wedco .... Wedco Technologies [*Associated Press*] (SAG)
WEDCOM...... Weapon Effects on D-Region Communications [*Computer code*]
WEDD-FM.... Englewood, FL [*FM radio station call letters*] (RBYB)
WEDG.......... Buffalo, NY [*FM radio station call letters*] (RBYB)
WEDG.......... Women's Education Group (AIE)
WEDG.......... Wood Energy Development Group (BUAC)
Wedg & Hom... Wedgwood and Homan's Manual for Notaries and Bankers [*A publication*] (DLA)
WEDGE........ Waterless Electrical Data Generating Effortless
WEDGE........ Weapon Development Glide Entry
WEDGE........ Western Education Development Group [*University of British Columbia*] [*Canada Research center*]
Wedg Gov & Laws... Wedgwood on American Government and Laws [*A publication*] (DLA)
Wedgw Dict Eng Etymology... Wedgwood's Dictionary of English Etymology [*A publication*] (DLA)
WEDH .... Hartford, CT [*Television station call letters*]
WEDI .... Workgroup for Electronic Data Interchange (NTPA)
WEDJ........... Charlotte, NC [*FM radio station call letters*]
WEDM .... Indianapolis, IN [*FM radio station call letters*]
WEDN .... Norwich, CT [*Television station call letters*]
WEDNET ...... Women, Environment and Development Network [*Kenya*] (BUAC)
WEDO .... McKeesport, PA [*AM radio station call letters*]
WEDO .... Women's Environment and Development Organization
WEDR .... Miami, FL [*FM radio station call letters*]
WEDS .... Weapons Effect Display System [*AEC*]
Weds .... Wednesday (ODBW)
WEDSS .... Whole Earth Decision Support System (EERA)
WEDU .... Tampa, FL [*Television station call letters*]
WEDW .... Bridgeport, CT [*Television station call letters*]
WEDW .... Stamford, CT [*FM radio station call letters*]
WEDY .... New Haven, CT [*Television station call letters*]
WEE .... Western Equine Encephalitis [*Virus*] (DAVI)
WEE .... Western Equine Encephalomyelitis [*Virus*]
WEE .... Wind Erosion Equation (EERA)
WEE .... Work Experience Education (DNAB)
WEEA.......... Women's Educational Equity Act [*1974*]
WEEB.......... Southern Pines, NC [*AM radio station call letters*]
WEEC.......... Springfield, OH [*FM radio station call letters*]
WEECN .... Women's Educational Equity Communications Network [*Defunct*]
WEED.......... Rocky Mount, NC [*AM radio station call letters*]
WEEF.......... Highland Park, IL [*AM radio station call letters*]
WEEF.......... Western Electric Educational Fund
WEEI........... Boston, MA [*AM radio station call letters*]
WEEJ........... Port Charlotte, FL [*FM radio station call letters*]
WEEK.......... Peoria, IL [*Television station call letters*]
Week Cin LB... Weekly Cincinnati Law Bulletin [*A publication*] (DLA)
Week Dig..... New York Weekly Digest [*A publication*] (DLA)
Week Dig (NY)... New York Weekly Digest [*A publication*] (DLA)
Week Jur..... Weekly Jurist [*Bloomington, IL*] [*A publication*] (DLA)
Week Law & Bk Bull... Weekly Law and Bank Bulletin [*A publication*] (DLA)
Week Law Bull... Weekly Law Bulletin and Ohio Law Journal [*A publication*] (DLA)
Week Law Gaz... Weekly Law Gazette [*Ohio*] [*A publication*] (DLA)

Week L Gaz... Weekly Law Gazette [*Ohio*] [*A publication*] (DLA)
Week L Mag... Weekly Law Magazine [*1842-43*] [*A publication*] (DLA)
Week LR...... Weekly Law Reports [*A publication*] (DLA)
Week L Rec... Weekly Law Record [*A publication*] (DLA)
Week L Record... Weekly Law Record [*A publication*] (DLA)
Week LR (Eng)... Weekly Law Reports (England) [*A publication*] (DLA)
Week L Rev... Weekly Law Review [*San Francisco*] [*A publication*] (DLA)
Weekly Cin Law Bull... Cincinnati Weekly Law Bulletin [*A publication*] (DLA)
Weekly Law B... Weekly Law Bulletin [*Ohio*] [*A publication*] (DLA)
Weekly L Bull... Weekly Law Bulletin [*England*] [*A publication*] (DLA)
Weekly LR... Weekly Law Reports [*England*] [*A publication*] (DLA)
Weekly NC... Weekly Notes of Cases [*Pennsylvania*] [*A publication*] (DLA)
Week No...... Weekly Notes of Cases [*Pennsylvania*] [*A publication*] (DLA)
Week No...... Weekly Notes of Cases (Law Reports) [*England*] [*A publication*] (DLA)
Week No Cas... Weekly Notes of Cases [*Pennsylvania*] [*A publication*] (DLA)
Week No Cas... Weekly Notes of Cases (Law Reports) [*England*] [*A publication*] (DLA)
Week Notes Cas... Weekly Notes of Cases (Law Reports) [*England*] [*A publication*] (DLA)
Week R....... Weekly Reporter [*1853-1906*] [*A publication*] (DLA)
Week R (Eng)... Weekly Reporter (England) [*A publication*] (DLA)
Week Rep..... Weekly Reporter [*England*] [*A publication*] (DLA)
Week Reptr... Weekly Reporter [*London*] [*A publication*] (DLA)
Week Reptr... Weekly Reporter [*Bengal*] [*A publication*] (DLA)
Weeks .... Weeks Corp. [*Associated Press*] (SAG)
Weeks Att at Law... Weeks on Attorneys at Law [*A publication*] (DLA)
Weeks DA Inj... Weeks' Damnum Absque Injuria [*A publication*] (DLA)
Weeks Dep... Weeks on Depositions [*A publication*] (DLA)
Weeks Min... Weeks on Mines and Mineral Law [*A publication*] (DLA)
Weeks Min Leg... Weeks' Mining Legislation of Congress [*A publication*] (DLA)
Week Trans Rep... Weekly Transcript Reports [*New York*] [*A publication*] (DLA)
Week Trans Repts... Weekly Transcript Reports [*New York*] [*A publication*] (DLA)
WEEL.......... Shadyside, OH [*FM radio station call letters*]
WEEL.......... Workplace Environmental Exposure Level [*A guide series published by the AIHA - American Industrial Hygiene Association*] [*A publication*]
WEEM.......... Pendleton, IN [*FM radio station call letters*]
WEEN.......... Lafayette, TN [*AM radio station call letters*]
WEEP.......... Women's Educational Equity Program (EA)
WEEP.......... Work Experience on Employer's Premises [*Manpower Services Commission*] [*British*] (DI)
Weer........... Weerakoon's Appeal Court Reports [*Ceylon*] [*A publication*] (DLA)
WEER.......... Welfare Entered Employment Rate [*Job Training and Partnership Act*] (OICC)
WEERC........ Western Electric Engineering Research Center (IAA)
WEETAG ...... Women's Employment, Education, and Training Advisory Group (EERA)
WEEU.......... Reading, PA [*AM radio station call letters*]
WEEX-AM .... Easton, PA [*AM radio station call letters*] (RBYB)
WEEZ.......... Heidelberg, MS [*FM radio station call letters*]
WEF............ WAND [*Women's Action for Nuclear Disarmament*] Education Fund (EA)
WEF............ War Emergency Formula
WEF............ Waste Environmental Federation
WEF............ Water Emersion Facility
WEF............ Water Environment Federation (EAIO)
WEF............ With Effect From
wef............. With Effect From (WDAA)
WEF............ Women's Employment Federation [*British*] (BI)
WEF............ World Economic Forum (EAIO)
WEF............ World Education Fellowship (EA)
WEF............ World Evangelical Fellowship (EA)
WEF............ Write End of File (SAA)
WEFA.......... Wharton Econometric Forecasting Association [*FAA*] (TAG)
WEFAX........ Weather Facsimile (EERA)
WEFAX........ Weather Facsimile Experiment [*Environmental Science Services Administration*]
WEFC.......... Roanoke, VA [*Television station call letters*]
WEFC.......... Weather Facsimile [*Environmental Science Services Administration*] (IAA)
WEFC.......... Wells Financial [*NASDAQ symbol*] (TTSB)
WEFC.......... Wells Financial Corp. [*NASDAQ symbol*] (SAG)
WEFC.......... West European Fisheries Conference (BUAC)
WEFG.......... Whitehall, MI [*AM radio station call letters*]
WEFG-FM .... Whitehall, MI [*FM radio station call letters*]
WEFM.......... Michigan City, IN [*FM radio station call letters*]
WEFR.......... Erie, PA [*FM radio station call letters*]
WEFT.......... Champaign, IL [*FM radio station call letters*]
WEFT.......... Wings, Engines, Fuselage, Tail [*System for identifying aircraft*]
WEFX.......... Norwalk, CT [*FM radio station call letters*]
WEG............ Washington Energy [*NYSE symbol*] (TTSB)
WEG............ Washington Energy Co. [*NYSE symbol*] (SPSG)
WEG............ Weapons Evaluation Group [*Military*]
WEG............ Wind Energy Generator
WEGA.......... Vega Baja, PR [*AM radio station call letters*]
WEGC.......... Sasser, GA [*FM radio station call letters*] (RBYB)
WEGE.......... Crossville, TN [*FM radio station call letters*]
Wegenr........ Wegener Corp. [*Associated Press*] (SAG)
WEGG.......... Rose Hill, NC [*AM radio station call letters*]
WEGK-FM .... Starview, PA [*FM radio station call letters*] (RBYB)
WEGL.......... Auburn, AL [*FM radio station call letters*]
WEGM .... Hormigueros, PR [*FM radio station call letters*]
WEGO.......... Concord, NC [*AM radio station call letters*]
WEGP .... Presque Isle, ME [*AM radio station call letters*]

WEGQ	Lawrence, MA [*FM radio station call letters*]
WEGR	Memphis, TN [*FM radio station call letters*]
WEGS	Milton, FL [*FM radio station call letters*]
WEGS	Western European Geological Survey (EERA)
WEGW	Wheeling, WV [*FM radio station call letters*]
WEGX	Dillong, SC [*FM radio station call letters*]
WEGZ	Washburn, WI [*FM radio station call letters*]
WEH	Walter and Eliza Hall Institute of Medical Research [*Australia*]
WE-H	Weapons Employment Handbook [*DASA*] (MCD)
WEHA	Wills Eye Hospital Annual Conference (EA)
WEHC	Emory, VA [*FM radio station call letters*]
WEHH	Elmira Heights-Horseheads, NY [*AM radio station call letters*]
WEHM	East Hampton, NY [*FM radio station call letters*]
WEHO	Westwood Homestead Financial Corp. [*NASDAQ symbol*] (SAG)
WEHR	Shepherdsville, KY [*FM radio station call letters*]
WEHS	Aurora, IL [*Television station call letters*]
WEHT	Evansville, IN [*Television station call letters*]
WEI	Immanuel Lutheran College, Eau Claire, WI [*Library symbol Library of Congress*] (LCLS)
WEI	Weapon Effectiveness Index (MCD)
WEI	Weipa [*Australia Airport symbol*] (OAG)
WEI	Western European Institute for Wood Preservation (EAIO)
WEI	Women Employed Institute (EA)
WEI	Wood Energy Institute [*Later, WHA*] (EA)
WEI	Work Experience Instructor (OICC)
WEI	World Education (EA)
WEI	World Environment Institute
WEI	Wound Elastomeric Insulation (MCD)
WEIB	Northampton, MA [*FM radio station call letters*]
WEIC	Charleston, IL [*AM radio station call letters*]
WEICO	Westinghouse Electric International Co. (IAA)
Weight M & L	Weightman's Marriage and Legitimacy [*1871*] [*A publication*] (DLA)
Weight Med Leg Gaz	Weightman's Medico-Legal Gazette [*A publication*] (DLA)
WEI/IEO	Western European Institute for Wood Preservation/Institut de l'Europe Occidentale pour l'Impregnation du Bois (EAIO)
WEIL	Weil-Felix [*Test*] [*Laboratory science*] (DAVI)
WEIM	Fitchburg, MA [*AM radio station call letters*]
WeinRl	Weingarten Realty, Inc. [*Associated Press*] (SAG)
WEINX	AIM Weingarten Cl.A [*Mutual fund ticker symbol*] (SG)
WEIO	Eau Claire, WI [*AM radio station call letters*]
WEIQ	Mobile, AL [*Television station call letters*]
Weir	Weir's Criminal Rulings [*India*] [*A publication*] (DLA)
WEIR	Weirton, WV [*AM radio station call letters*]
Weirt	Weirton Steel Corp. [*Associated Press*] (SAG)
WEIS	Centre, AL [*AM radio station call letters*]
WEIS	World Event/Interaction Survey (DNAB)
WeisMk	Weis Markets, Inc. [*Associated Press*] (SAG)
Weitek	Weitek Corp. [*Associated Press*] (SAG)
WeitzrH	Weitzer Homebuilders, Inc. [*Associated Press*] (SAG)
WEIU	Charleston, IL [*FM radio station call letters*]
WEIU	Women's Educational and Industrial Union (EA)
WEIU-TV	Charleston, IL [*Television station call letters*]
WEI/WUV	Weapons Effectiveness Indices/Weighted Unit Values [*Military*]
WEJ	West Air Sweden AB [*ICAO designator*] (FAAC)
WEJC	Lexington, NC [*Television station call letters*]
WEJE	Churubusco, IN [*FM radio station call letters*] (RBYB)
WEJF	Palm Bay, FL [*FM radio station call letters*]
WEJL	Scranton, PA [*AM radio station call letters*]
WEJM	Chicago, IL [*AM radio station call letters*]
WEJM	Lansing, IL [*FM radio station call letters*]
WEJT	Shelbyville, IL [*FM radio station call letters*]
WEJY	Monroe, MI [*FM radio station call letters*]
WEJZ	Jacksonville, FL [*FM radio station call letters*]
WEK	Wewak [*Papua New Guinea*] [*Seismograph station code, US Geological Survey*] (SEIS)
WEKC	Williamsburg, KY [*AM radio station call letters*]
WEKG	Jackson, KY [*AM radio station call letters*]
WEKH	Hazard, KY [*FM radio station call letters*]
WEKL	Augusta, GA [*FM radio station call letters*]
WEKO	Cabo Rojo, PR [*AM radio station call letters*]
WEKR	Fayetteville, TN [*AM radio station call letters*]
WEKS	Zebulon, GA [*FM radio station call letters*]
WEKT	Elkton, KY [*AM radio station call letters*]
WEKU	Richmond, KY [*FM radio station call letters*]
WEKW	Keene, NH [*Television station call letters*]
WEKX	Jellico, TN [*FM radio station call letters*]
WEKY	Richmond, KY [*AM radio station call letters*]
WEKZ	Monroe, WI [*AM radio station call letters*]
WEKZ-FM	Monroe, WI [*FM radio station call letters*]
WEL	Luther Hospital, Eau Claire, WI [*Library symbol Library of Congress*] (LCLS)
WEI	Matheson Memorial Library, Elkhorn, WI [*Library symbol Library of Congress*] (LCLS)
WEL	Warren Explorations Ltd. [*Toronto Stock Exchange symbol*]
WEL	Weapons Effects Laboratory [*Army*] (RDA)
WEL	Weapons/Equipment List
WEL	Welfare
WEL	Welkom [*South Africa*] [*Airport symbol*] (OAG)
WEL	Wellcome Ltd. [*NYSE symbol*] (SPSG)
WEL	Wellesley College, Wellesley, MA [*OCLC symbol*] (OCLC)
WEL	Wellesley Hospital, Toronto [*UTLAS symbol*]
WEL	Wellington [*New Zealand*] [*Seismograph station code, US Geological Survey*] (SEIS)
wel	Welsh [*MARC language code Library of Congress*] (LCCP)
Wel	Welsh's Irish Registry Cases [*A publication*] (DLA)
WEL	Welt-Eis-Lehre [*Cosmic Ice Theory*] [*German*]
WEL	Women's Electoral Lobby [*Australia*] (BUAC)
WELA	East Liverpool, OH [*FM radio station call letters*]
WELAC	Western European Laboratory Accreditation Co-operation (ACII)
WELB	Elba, AL [*AM radio station call letters*]
WELC	Welch, WV [*AM radio station call letters*]
WELC	Welcome Home [*NASDAQ symbol*] (TTSB)
WELC	Welcome Home, Inc. [*NASDAQ symbol*] (SAG)
WELC	World Electrotechnical Congress (PDAA)
WELC-FM	Welch, WV [*FM radio station call letters*]
WEICL	Walworth County Law Library, Elkhorn, WI [*Library symbol Library of Congress*] (LCLS)
WELCO	Westinghouse Electric Company
WelcomH	Welcome Home, Inc. [*Associated Press*] (SAG)
WELD	Fisher, WV [*AM radio station call letters*]
WELD	Petersburg, WV [*FM radio station call letters*]
WELD	Welding
Weldtrn	Weldotron Corp. [*Associated Press*] (SAG)
WELE	Ormond Beach, FL [*AM radio station call letters*]
WELF	Dalton, GA [*Television station call letters*]
WelF	Wells Fargo & Co. [*Associated Press*] (SAG)
WELF	Woman's Education and Leadership Forum (EA)
Welfare L Bull	Welfare Law Bulletin [*A publication*] (DLA)
Welfare L News	Welfare Law News [*A publication*] (DLA)
Welf Eq	Welford's Equity Pleadings [*1842*] [*A publication*] (DLA)
Welf News	Welfare News [*A publication*]
WELG	Rogers City, MI [*FM radio station call letters*] (RBYB)
WelGrd	Wells-Gardner Electronics Corp. [*Associated Press*] (SAG)
WELH	Luther Hospital, Eau Claire, WI [*Library symbol*] [*Library of Congress*] (LCLS)
WELH	Providence, RI [*FM radio station call letters*]
WELI	New Haven, CT [*AM radio station call letters*]
WELK	Elkins, WV [*FM radio station call letters*]
WELL	Battle Creek, MI [*AM radio station call letters*]
WEIL	Lakeland Hospital, Elkhorn, WI [*Library symbol Library of Congress*] (LCLS)
WELL	Marshall, MI [*FM radio station call letters*]
WELL	Well [*Commonly used*] (OPSA)
WELL	Wellcare Management Group [*NASDAQ symbol*] (SAG)
Well	Wellington [*New Zealand*] (BARN)
WELL	Whole Earth Lectronic Link [*Telecommunications*]
WEILC	Lakeland Counseling Center, Elkhorn, WI [*Library symbol Library of Congress*] (LCLS)
Wellco	Wellco Enterprises, Inc. [*Associated Press*] (SAG)
Wellcome	Wellcome Ltd. [*Associated Press*] (SAG)
WELLE	WellCare Management Group [*NASDAQ symbol*] (TTSB)
WellHall	Wellington Hall Ltd. [*Associated Press*] (SAG)
Well High	Wellbeloved on Highways [*1829*] [*A publication*] (DLA)
WellMgt	Wellcare Management Group [*Associated Press*] (OAG)
Wellmn	Wellman, Inc. [*Associated Press*] (SAG)
WELLS	Wells [*Commonly used*] (OPSA)
WellsF	Wells Fargo & Co. [*Associated Press*] (SAG)
WellsFn	Wells Financial Corp. [*Associated Press*] (SAG)
Wells Inst Juries	Wells on Instruction to Juries and Bills of Exception [*A publication*]
Wells Jur	Wells on the Jurisdiction of Courts [*A publication*] (DLA)
Wells L & F	Well's Questions of Law and Facts [*A publication*] (DLA)
Wells Mar Wom	Wells on the Separate Property of Married Women [*A publication*] (DLA)
Wells Rep	Wells on Replevin [*A publication*] (DLA)
Wells Repl	Wells on Replevin [*A publication*] (DLA)
Wells' Res Ad	Wells' Res Adjudicata and Stare Decisis [*A publication*] (DLA)
Wellw Abr	Wellwood's Abridgment of Sea Laws [*A publication*] (DLA)
WELM	Elmira, NY [*AM radio station call letters*]
WELO	Tupelo, MS [*AM radio station call letters*]
WELP-AM	Easley, SC [*AM radio station call letters*] (BROA)
WelptHlt	Wellpoint Health Networks [*Associated Press*] (SAG)
WELR	Roanoke, AL [*AM radio station call letters*]
WELR-FM	Roanoke, AL [*FM radio station call letters*]
WELS	Kinston, NC [*AM radio station call letters*]
WELS	Wisconsin Evangelical Lutheran Synod
WELS	World-Wide Engineering Logistics Support [*Military*]
Welsb H & G	Welsby, Hurlstone, and Gordon's English Exchequer Reports [*1848-56*] [*A publication*] (DLA)
Welsb Hurl & G	Welsby, Hurlstone, and Gordon's English Exchequer Reports [*1848-56*] [*A publication*] (DLA)
Welsby H & G	Welsby, Hurlstone, and Gordon's English Exchequer Reports [*1848-56*] [*A publication*] (DLA)
Welsby H & G (Eng)	Welsby, Hurlstone, and Gordon's English Exchequer Reports [*1848-56*] [*A publication*] (DLA)
Welsf	Wellsford Residential Property [*Associated Press*] (SAG)
Welsfd	Wellsford Residential Property [*Associated Press*] (SAG)
Welsh	Welsh's Irish Case at Siligo [*1838*] [*A publication*] (DLA)
Welsh	Welsh's Irish Case of James Feighny [*1838*] [*A publication*] (DLA)
Welsh	Welsh's Irish Registry Cases [*A publication*] (DLA)
Welsh Reg Cas	Welsh's Irish Registry Cases [*A publication*] (DLA)
WELU	Aguadilla, PR [*Television station call letters*]
WELV	Ellenville, NY [*AM radio station call letters*]
WELW	Willoughby-Eastlake, OH [*AM radio station call letters*]
WELX	Callahan, FL [*AM radio station call letters*]
WELY	Ely, MN [*AM radio station call letters*]
WELY-FM	Ely, MN [*FM radio station call letters*]
WELZ	Belzoni, MS [*AM radio station call letters*]
WEM	War Eagle Mining Co. [*Vancouver Stock Exchange symbol*]

WEM............ Welfare of Enlisted Men [*Air Force*]
WEM............ Western European Metal Trades Employers Organization [*Cologne, Federal Republic of Germany*] (EA)
WeM........... Western Microfilm Ltd., Edmonton, AB, Canada [*Library symbol Library of Congress*] (LCLS)
WEM............ West Essex Militia [*British*]
WEM............ White European Male [*Lifestyle classification*] (ECON)
WEM............ Wireless and Electrical Mechanic [*British*] (DSUE)
WEM............ Workshops in Emergency Management [*RSPA*] (TAG)
WEM............ World's Epoch Makers [*A publication*]
WEM............ Woven Elastic Manufacturers Association [*Later, EFMCNTA*] (MSA)
WEMA........ Western Electronic Manufacturers Association [*Later, AEA*] (EA)
WEMA........ Winding Engine Manufacturers' Association [*British*] (BI)
WEMA........ Woven Elastic Manufacturers Association [*Later, EFMCNTA*] (EA)
WEMB........ Erwin, TN [*AM radio station call letters*]
WEMBA...... Weekend Executive Master of Business Administration (PGP)
WEMC........ Harrisonburg, VA [*FM radio station call letters*]
WEMD .... Western Electronics Maintenance Depot
WEMG .... Crete, IL [*FM radio station call letters*]
WEMG .... Knoxville, TN [*AM radio station call letters*]
WEMI.......... Appleton, WI [*FM radio station call letters*] (RBYB)
WEMJ.......... Laconia, NH [*AM radio station call letters*]
WEMM........ Huntington, WV [*FM radio station call letters*]
WEMOS .... International Women's Network on Pharmaceuticals [*Amsterdam, Netherlands*] (EAIO)
WEMP......... Milwaukee, WI [*AM radio station call letters*]
WEMR .... Tunkhannock, PA [*AM radio station call letters*]
WEMR .... Welding Equipment Maintenance and Repair [*UAW job classification*]
WEMR-FM ... Tunkhannock, PA [*FM radio station call letters*] (RBYB)
WEMSB....... Western European Military Supply Board [*NATO*] (NATG)
WEMT .... Greeneville, TN [*Television station call letters*]
WEMU .... Ypsilanti, MI [*FM radio station call letters*]
WEMX......... Ravena, NY [*FM radio station call letters*]
WEN............ Papa Westray [*Orkney Islands, Scotland*] [*Airport symbol*] (AD)
WEN............ The Women's Environmental Network (BUAC)
WEN............ Waive Exchange If Necessary
Wen............ Wendell's Reports [*New York*] [*A publication*] (DLA)
wen............. Wendic [*MARC language code Library of Congress*] (LCCP)
WEN............ Wendy's International, Inc. [*NYSE symbol*] (SPSG)
WEN............ Wendy's Intl [*NYSE symbol*] (TTSB)
WEN............ Wenkite [*A zeolite*]
WEN............ Wentworth Institute of Technology, Boston, MA [*OCLC symbol*] (OCLC)
WEN............ Wentworth Public Library [*UTLAS symbol*]
WEN............ Work and Economy Network in the European Churches (BUAC)
WEN............ World Environment News (BUAC)
WEN............ Worldmark Encyclopedia of the Nations [*A publication*]
WEN............ Write Enable [*Computer science*] (IAA)
WENA......... Yauco, PR [*AM radio station call letters*]
WenBr .... Wendt Bristol Health Service [*Associated Press*] (SAG)
WENC......... Whiteville, NC [*AM radio station call letters*]
W/ENCL...... With Enclosure (DNAB)
WEND......... Salisbury, NC [*FM radio station call letters*] (RBYB)
Wend.......... Wendell's Reports [*1826-41*] [*New York*] [*A publication*] (DLA)
WEND .... Wendover [*England*]
WENDB....... Water Enforcement National Data Base (GNE)
Wend Bl ..... Wendell's Blackstone [*A publication*] (DLA)
WENDCO.... Wendy's International, Inc. (EFIS)
Wendel....... Wendell's Reports [*New York*] [*A publication*] (DLA)
Wendell...... Wendell's Reports [*1826-41*] [*New York*] [*A publication*] (DLA)
Wendell Rep... Wendell's Reports [*New York*] [*A publication*] (DLA)
Wendell's Rep... Wendell's Reports [*New York*] [*A publication*] (DLA)
Wend (NY)... Wendell's Reports [*1826-41*] [*New York*] [*A publication*] (DLA)
Wend R ...... Wendell's Reports [*New York*] [*A publication*] (DLA)
Wend Rep ... Wendell's Reports [*New York*] [*A publication*] (DLA)
WENDS........ World Energy Data System [*Department of Energy*] [*Information service or system*] (IID)
Wendt......... Wendt's Reports of Cases [*Ceylon*] [*A publication*] (DLA)
WendtBr ...... Wendt Bristol Health Service [*Associated Press*] (SAG)
Wendt Mar Leg... Wendt's Maritime Legislation [*3rd ed.*] [*1888*] [*A publication*] (DLA)
Wendy .... Wendys International [*Associated Press*] (SAG)
Wendys........ Wendys International, Inc. [*Associated Press*] (SAG)
WENE......... Endicott, NY [*AM radio station call letters*]
WENELA ...... Witwatersrand Native Labour Association [*Nyasaland*]
WENG......... Englewood, FL [*AM radio station call letters*]
WENH......... Durham, NH [*Television station call letters*]
WENK .... Union City, TN [*AM radio station call letters*]
WENN......... Birmingham, AL [*FM radio station call letters*]
WENO......... Nashville, TN [*AM radio station call letters*]
WENOA....... Weekly Notice to Airmen [*FAA*]
WENR......... Englewood, TN [*AM radio station call letters*]
WENS .... Shelbyville, IN [*FM radio station call letters*]
WENS .... World Electroless Nickel Society [*Defunct*] (EA)
WENT......... Gloversville, NY [*AM radio station call letters*]
W Ent......... Winch's Book of Entries [*A publication*] (DLA)
WENU......... Hudson Falls, NY [*FM radio station call letters*]
WENY......... Elmira, NY [*AM radio station call letters*]
WENY-FM .... Elmira, NY [*FM radio station call letters*]
WENY-TV .... Elmira, NY [*Television station call letters*]
WENZ......... Cleveland, OH [*FM radio station call letters*]
Wenz .... Wenzell's Reports [*60 Minnesota*] [*A publication*] (DLA)
WEO........... War Economic Operation [*World War II*]
WEO........... Warehouse Economy Outlet [*A & P Co.*]
WEO........... Weaco Resources Ltd. [*Vancouver Stock Exchange symbol*]

WEO........... Weapons Engineer Officer [*British military*] (DMA)
WEO........... Western Europe and Others [*United Nations*]
WEO........... Where Economy Originates [*A & P Co. marketing slogan, now obsolete*]
WEO........... World Energy Outlook [*International Energy Agency*]
WEOA-AM .... Evansville, IN [*AM radio station call letters*] (BROA)
WEOG......... Western European and Others Group [*United Nations*]
WEOK......... Poughkeepsie, NY [*AM radio station call letters*]
WEOL......... Elyria, OH [*AM radio station call letters*]
WEOS .... Geneva, NY [*FM radio station call letters*]
WEOS .... Water Extraction of Orange Solids [*Citrus processing*]
WEOW......... Key West, FL [*FM radio station call letters*]
WEOW......... Weapons Engineer Officer's Writer [*British military*] (DMA)
WEOZ......... Saegertown, PA [*FM radio station call letters*]
WEP........... War and Emergency Plan [*DoD*]
WEP........... WatchGuard Event Processor
WEP........... Water Electrolysis Plenum
WEP........... Water Entry Point [*Navy*] (CAAL)
WEP........... Water-Extended Polyester
WEP........... Weak Equivalence Principle [*Gravity*]
WEP........... Weam [*Papua New Guinea*] [*Airport symbol*] (OAG)
WEP........... Weapon
WEP........... Weather Processor (MCD)
WEP........... Weekend Pass (DAVI)
WEP........... Whole Earth Party [*Australia*] (BUAC)
WEP........... Windfall Elimination Provision (GFGA)
WEP........... Windows Entertainment Pack [*Computer science*]
WEP........... Wisconsin Experiment Package [*NASA*] (MCD)
WEP........... Women's Equity Program [*Defunct*] (EA)
WEP........... Work Experience Program [*Department of Labor*]
WEP........... World Economic Prospects (NITA)
WEP........... World Employment Program [*of the International Labour Organization*] [*Geneva, Switzerland*] [*United Nations*]
WEP........... Writing, Editing, and Publishing
WEPA......... Eupora, MS [*AM radio station call letters*]
WEPA......... Welded Electronic Packaging Association
WEPC......... Belton, SC [*FM radio station call letters*]
WEPC......... Weapons and Equipment Policy Committee [*British*] (RDA)
WEPCO....... Western Desert Petroleum Company [*Egypt*] (BUAC)
WEPCOSE.... Weapon Control Systems Engineering [*Navy*] (NG)
WEPEX....... Weapons Exercise [*Navy*] (NVT)
WEPG......... South Pittsburg, TN [*AM radio station call letters*]
WE/PGM..... Write Enable/Program [*Computer science*]
WEPH......... Weapon Phenomenology (RDA)
WEP International... Women's Exchange Programme International (BUAC)
WEPM......... Martinsburg, WV [*AM radio station call letters*]
WEPOCS ..... Western Equatorial Pacific Ocean Circulation Study (USDC)
WEPOCS ..... Western Equatorial Pacific Ocean Climate Studies [*USA-Australia*] [*Marine science*] (OSRA)
WEPR......... Greenville, SC [*FM radio station call letters*]
WEPR......... Women Executives in Public Relations [*New York, NY*] (EA)
WEPREC..... West Pakistan Research and Evaluation Center
WEPS.......... Elgin, IL [*FM radio station call letters*]
WEPS.......... Weapons and Equipment Policy Statement [*Australia*]
WEPS.......... Weapons System [*Navy*]
WEPSO....... Naval Weapons Services Office [*Also known as NAVWPNSERVO, NWSO*]
WEPTA........ War Excess Profits Tax Act [*1917*]
WEPTAC ..... Weapons and Tactics Analysis Center [*Navy*] (MCD)
WEPTRAEX... Weapons Training Exercise (NVT)
WEPTU .... Weapons Reserve Training Units [*Navy*]
WEPU .... Weighted Elementary Pupil Unit [*Education*] (AEE)
WEPX......... Greenville, NC [*Television station call letters*] (BROA)
WEPZA........ World Export Processing Zones Association [*Flagstaff, AZ*] (EA)
WEQ........... Wind Erosion Equation
WEQQ-FM.... Pinetops, NC [*FM radio station call letters*] (BROA)
WEQR......... Goldsboro, NC [*FM radio station call letters*]
WEQX......... Manchester, VT [*FM radio station call letters*]
WER........... Water Electrolysis Rocket
WER........... Weight Estimating Relationship (KSC)
WER........... Werombi [*Australia Seismograph station code, US Geological Survey*] (SEIS)
WER........... Whole Earth Review [*A publication*] (BRI)
WER........... World Emergency Relief [*An association*] (EA)
WERA......... Plainfield, NJ [*AM radio station call letters*]
WERA......... Western Eastern Roadracers Association (EA)
WERA......... Western/English Retailers of America [*Defunct*] (EA)
WERA......... World Energy Research Authority
WERB......... Berlin, CT [*FM radio station call letters*]
WERC......... Birmingham, AL [*AM radio station call letters*]
WERC......... Warehousing Education and Research Council (EA)
WERC......... Waste Management Education and Research Consortium [*New Mexico State University*] [*Research center*] (RCD)
WERC .... Women's Education Resource Centre [*Women's Education Group*] [*British*] (CB)
WERC .... World Environment and Resources Council [*Louvain, Belgium*] (EAIO)
WERD......... East Point, GA [*AM radio station call letters*] (RBYB)
WERE......... Cleveland, OH [*AM radio station call letters*]
WERF......... Waste Experimental Reaction Facility [*Environmental science*] (COE)
WERG......... Erie, PA [*FM radio station call letters*]
WERH......... Hamilton, AL [*AM radio station call letters*]
WERH-FM .... Hamilton, AL [*FM radio station call letters*]
WERI .... Water and Energy Research Institute of the Western Pacific [*University of Guam*] [*Guam*] [*Research center*] (RCD)

WERI .... Westerly, RI [AM radio station call letters]
WERK .... Muncie, IN [AM radio station call letters]
WERK-FM .... Muncie, IN [FM radio station call letters]
WERL .... Eagle River, WI [AM radio station call letters]
WERL .... Water Engineering Research Laboratory [Cincinnati, OH] [Environmental Protection Agency] (GRD)
WERM .... World Encyclopedia of Recorded Music, 1925-55 [A publication]
WERN .... Madison, WI [FM radio station call letters]
WERN .... Werner Enterprises [NASDAQ symbol] (TTSB)
WERN .... Werner Enterprises, Inc. [Omaha, NE] [NASDAQ symbol] (NQ)
Werner .... Werner Enterprises, Inc. [Associated Press] (SAG)
WERO-FM .... Washington, NC [FM radio station call letters] (RBYB)
WERP .... Women's Economic Rights Project (EA)
WERPG .... Western European Regional Planning Group [NATO] (NATG)
WERQ .... Baltimore, MD [FM radio station call letters]
WERR .... Utuado, PR [FM radio station call letters]
WERS .... Boston, MA [FM radio station call letters]
WERS .... War Emergency Radio Service
WERS .... Weapons Effect Reporting Station [Civil defense]
WERS .... Wing Equipment Repair Squadron
WERSI .... Committee on Women's Employment and Related Social Issues (EA)
WERT .... Paulding, OH [FM radio station call letters]
WERT .... Van Wert, OH [AM radio station call letters]
WERT .... Women's Economic Round Table (EA)
WERTS .... Writers' Ever-Ready Textual Service [Rent-A-Script] [Satirical]
WERU .... Blue Hill, ME [FM radio station call letters]
WERX .... Edenton, NC [FM radio station call letters]
WERZ .... Exeter, NH [FM radio station call letters]
WES .... Sacred Heart Hospital, Eau Claire, WI [Library symbol Library of Congress] (LCLS)
WES .... Warhead Electrical System
WES .... Washington Ethical Society (EA)
WES .... Water Electrolysis System
WES .... Waterways Experiment Station [Army Corps of Engineers] [Vicksburg, MS]
WES .... Weapon Electrical System
WES .... Weapon Engineering Station (MCD)
WES .... Weapons Effects Systems (MCD)
WES .... Welding Engineering Society [Japan] (BUAC)
WES .... W. E. Schulz & Associates, Inc. [Telecommunications service] (TSSD)
WES .... Wesleyan [A publication]
WES .... West [or Western]
WES .... Westbury [British depot code]
WES .... Westcorp, Inc. [NYSE symbol] (SPSG)
WES .... Western Equestrian Soceity [British] (DBA)
WES .... Western Express Air Lines, Inc. [Canada] [FAA designator] (FAAC)
WES .... Westmills Carpets Ltd. [Toronto Stock Exchange symbol]
WES .... Weston [Massachusetts] [Seismograph station code, US Geological Survey] (SEIS)
WES .... Westport Public Library, Westport, CT [OCLC symbol] (OCLC)
WES .... Wind Electric System [Telecommunications] (TEL)
WES .... Wisdom of the East Series [A publication]
WES .... Women's Engineering Society (IAA)
WES .... Work Environment Scale [Test]
WES .... World Economic Summit
WES .... Worldmark Encyclopedia of the States [A publication]
WES .... World-Wide Education Service [Parents' National Educational Union] [British]
WES .... Writing Equipment Society [British] (DBA)
WESA .... Charleroi, PA [AM radio station call letters]
WESA .... White Sands National Monument [New Mexico]
WESA .... Wind Energy Society of America [Inactive]
WESA .... Wind Energy Systems Act of 1980
WESA-FM .... Charleroi, PA [FM radio station call letters]
Wes Aust ..... West Australian [A publication]
WESB .... Bradford, PA [AM radio station call letters]
Wesbanc ...... Wesbanco, Inc. [Associated Press] (SAG)
WESC .... Greenville, SC [AM radio station call letters]
WESC .... Weapon Engagement Simulation Component (MCD)
WESC .... Whole Earth Software Catalog [A publication]
WESC .... Wire-Explosion-Spray Coating (PDAA)
WESCAR ...... Western Carolines [Navy]
WESCARS ...... West Coast Amateur Radio Service (PDAA)
WESCARSUBAREA ... Western Carolines Subarea [Navy]
Wescast ...... Wescast Industries, Inc. [Associated Press] (SAG)
WESC-FM .... Greenville, SC [FM radio station call letters]
Wes CLJ ...... Westmoreland County Law Journal [A publication] (DLA)
WESCO .... Walnut Export Sales Co. (EA)
Wesco .... Wesco Financial Corp. [Associated Press] (SAG)
WESCO .... Westinghouse Corp.
WESCOBASESERVUNIT ... West Coast Base Service Unit [Navy]
WESCOM ...... Weapons System Cost Model
WESCOM ..... Western Command [Army] (AABC)
WESCON ...... Western Electronics Show and Convention [IEEE]
WESCOSOUNDSCOL ... West Coast Sound School [Navy]
W/ESDC ...... Weapons/Equipment System Designator Code
WESDET ...... Wing Engineer Squadron Detachment (DNAB)
WESDEX ...... Western Design Engineering Exposition (PDAA)
WESE .... Baldwyn, MS [FM radio station call letters]
WESE .... Wills Eye Society of Ex-Residents (EA)
WESED ...... Weapons System Evaluation Division [DoD]
WESEG ...... Weapons System Evaluation Group [DoD]
WESF .... Waste Encapsulation Storage Facility [Nuclear energy] (NRCH)
WESG .... Women Executives in State Government (EA)

WESH .... Daytona Beach, FL [Television station call letters]
WESIAC ...... Weapons Effectiveness Systems Industry Advisory Committee (MCD)
Weskett Ins... Weskett's Complete Digest of the Theory, Laws, and Practice of Insurance [A publication] (DLA)
Wesk Ins ..... Weskett's Complete Digest of the Theory, Laws, and Practice of Insurance [A publication] (DLA)
WESL .... East St. Louis, IL [AM radio station call letters]
Wesleyan U... Wesleyan University (GAGS)
WESM .... Princess Anne, MD [FM radio station call letters]
WESN .... Bloomington, IL [FM radio station call letters]
WESO .... Southbridge, MA [AM radio station call letters]
WESO .... Weapons Engineering Service Office [DoD]
WESOS .... Water-Extracted Soluble Orange Solids [Citrus processing]
WESP .... Dothan, AL [FM radio station call letters]
WESP .... War and Emergency Support Plan [DoD]
WESPAR ...... Weapon Evaluation System Photographic Analog Recorder (MCD)
WESPAY ...... Western Payments Alliance Automated Clearing (TBD)
WESPEX ...... War and Emergency Support Plan Exercise [DoD]
WESQ .... Rocky Mount, NC [FM radio station call letters]
WESR .... Onley-Onancock, VA [AM radio station call letters]
WESRAC ...... Western Research Application Center [University of Southern California]
WESREP ...... Weapon Engineering Station Representative (MCD)
Wes Res Law Jo... Western Reserve Law Journal [A publication] (DLA)
Wes Res Law Jrl... Western Reserve Law Journal [Ohio] [A publication] (DLA)
WESR-FM .... Onley-Onancock, VA [FM radio station call letters]
WESS .... East Stroudsburg, PA [FM radio station call letters]
WESS .... Weapons Effect Signature Simulator
WESS .... Weapons Engagement Scoring System
WESS .... Weapons System Status
WESS .... Western European Specialists Section [Association of College and Research Libraries]
WESSAS ...... Wisconsin Elementary and Secondary School Accounting System (EDAC)
WESSCO ...... Waste Equipment Sales & Service Co. (EFIS)
WESSEAFRON... Western Sea Frontier [Navy]
WEST .... Easton, PA [AM radio station call letters]
WEST .... Weapons Effectiveness Simulated Threat (MCD)
WEST .... Weapons Exhaust Study [Military] (MCD)
West .... Westbury's European Arbitration (Reilly) [A publication] (DLA)
West .... West Co., Inc. [Associated Press] (SAG)
WEST .... Western Earth Sciences Technologies [Research center] (RCD)
WEST .... Western Educational Society for Telecommunications [Defunct] (EA)
WEST .... Western Energy Supply and Transmission Associates [Utility antipollution group]
West .... Western's London Tithe Cases [England] [A publication] (DLA)
WEST .... Western Transportation Co. [Later, WTCO] [AAR code]
West .... Westminster [Record label]
West .... Westmoreland County Law Journal [Pennsylvania] [A publication] (DLA)
WEST .... West One Bancorp [NASDAQ symbol] (NQ)
West .... Weston's Reports [11-14 Vermont] [A publication] (DLA)
West .... West Publishing Co. (AAGC)
West .... West's English Chancery Reports [A publication] (DLA)
West .... West's Reports, English House of Lords [A publication] (DLA)
WEST .... Women's Enlistment Screening Test [Military]
WESTA .... White Sands Electromagnetic Pulse Systems Test Array [New Mexico] (RDA)
WestAB .... Westinghouse Air Brake Co. [Associated Press] (SAG)
WESTAF ...... Western Transport Air Force
WESTAR ...... Waterways Experiment Station Terrain Analyzer RADAR
WESTAR ..... West Star (NITA)
Westbank ...... Westbank Corp. [Associated Press] (SAG)
West Car U... Western Carolina University (GAGS)
West Ch ...... West's English Chancery Cases [25 English Reprint] [A publication] (DLA)
West Ch (Eng)... West's English Chancery Cases [25 English Reprint] [A publication] (DLA)
West Chester U Pa... West Chester University of Pennsylvania (GAGS)
West Chy ..... West's English Chancery Cases [25 English Reprint] [A publication] (DLA)
West Coast Rep... West Coast Reporter [A publication] (DLA)
WestcoB ...... Westco Bancorp, Inc. [Associated Press] (SAG)
WESTCOM ...... Western Command [Army]
West Com... Western's Commentaries on the Laws of England [A publication] (DLA)
WESTCOMMRGN... Western Communications Region [Air Force] (AFM)
West Conn St U... Western Connecticut State University (GAGS)
West Co Rep... West Coast Reporter [A publication] (DLA)
WestcotC ..... Westcott Communications Co. [Associated Press] (SAG)
Westcp .... Westcorp, Inc. [Associated Press] (SAG)
WESTDIVNAVFACENGCOM... Western Division, Naval Facilities Engineering Command (DNAB)
Westd Zeit... Westdeutsche Zeitschrift fuer Geschichte und Kunst [A publication] (OCD)
WESTE .... Weapons Effectiveness and System Test Environment [Air Force] (AFM)
WESTEC ...... Western Metal and Tool Exposition and Conference [American Society for Metals] (TSPED)
Westell .... Westell Technologies, Inc. [Associated Press] (SAG)
Westerfed .... Westerfed Financial Corp. [Associated Press] (SAG)
Western L Rev... Western Law Review [Canada] [A publication] (DLA)
Western Reserve LN... Western Reserve Law Notes [A publication] (DLA)
West Ext ...... West on Extents [1817] [A publication] (DLA)
WestFidl ...... Western Fidelity Funding, Inc. [Associated Press] (SAG)

Westfield St C...   Westfield State College   (GAGS)
WESTFORNET...   Western Forestry Information Network [*Forest service*] [*Library network*]
West Ga C...   West Georgia College   (GAGS)
West HL......   West's Reports, English House of Lords [*A publication*]   (DLA)
West II......   Second Statute of Westminster [*A publication*]   (DSA)
West Ill U...   Western Illinois University   (GAGS)
West J Med...   Western Journal of Medicine   (MEC)
West Jur...   Western Jurist [*Des Moines, Iowa*] [*A publication*]   (DLA)
West Ky U...   Western Kentucky University   (GAGS)
Westlake Int Private Law...   Westlake's Private International Law [*A publication*]   (DLA)
WESTLANT...   Western Atlantic Area
West Law M...   Western Law Monthly [*Ohio*] [*A publication*]   (DLA)
West Law Mo...   Western Law Monthly (Reprint) [*Ohio*] [*A publication*]   (DLA)
West Law Month...   Western Law Monthly [*Ohio*] [*A publication*]   (DLA)
West Law Rev...   Western Law Review [*Canada*] [*A publication*]   (DLA)
WestLB........   Westdeutsche Landesbank [*West German bank*]
Westl Confl...   Westlake's Conflict of Laws [*A publication*]   (DLA)
West Legal Obser...   Western Legal Observer [*A publication*]   (DLA)
West Leg Obs...   Western Legal Observer [*A publication*]   (DLA)
West L Gaz...   Western Law Gazette [*Cincinnati, OH*] [*A publication*]   (DLA)
West LM......   Western Law Monthly [*Ohio*] [*A publication*]   (DLA)
West L Mo...   Western Law Monthly [*Ohio*] [*A publication*]   (DLA)
West L Month...   Western Law Monthly [*Ohio*] [*A publication*]   (DLA)
Westl Priv Int Law...   Westlake's Private International Law [*A publication*]   (DLA)
West LR......   Western Law Reporter [*Canada*] [*A publication*]   (DLA)
West LR (Can)...   Western Law Reporter [*Canada*] [*A publication*]   (DLA)
West L Rev...   Western Law Review [*A publication*]   (DLA)
West LT......   Western Law Times [*Canada*] [*A publication*]   (DLA)
Westly........   Westerly [*A publication*]
Westm........   Westmeath [*County in Ireland*]   (WGA)
WESTM........   Westminster [*London*]
Westm........   Westmoreland County Law Journal [*Pennsylvania*] [*A publication*]   (DLA)
Westmark....   Westmark Group Holdings, Inc. [*Associated Press*]   (SAG)
WESTMD.....   Westmorland [*County in England*]
West Md C...   Western Maryland College   (GAGS)
Westm Hall Chron...   Westminster Hall Chronicle and Legal Examiner [*1835-36*] [*A publication*]   (DLA)
West Mich U...   Western Michigan University   (GAGS)
Westminster C...   Westminster College   (GAGS)
Westmk....   Westmark Group Holdings, Inc. [*Associated Press*]   (SAG)
Westm LJ....   Westmoreland County Law Journal [*A publication*]   (DLA)
Westmore Co LJ (PA)...   Westmoreland County Law Journal [*Pennsylvania*] [*A publication*]   (DLA)
Westmoreland...   Westmoreland County Law Journal [*Pennsylvania*] [*A publication*]   (DLA)
Westmoreland Co LJ...   Westmoreland County Law Journal [*Pennsylvania*] [*A publication*]   (DLA)
WESTN........   Western
WESTNAVELEX...   Naval Electronics Systems Command, Western Division, Mare Island, Vallejo, California
WESTNAVFACENGCOM...   Western Division, Naval Facilities Engineering Command
West NE C...   Western New England College   (GAGS)
West N Mex U...   Western New Mexico University   (GAGS)
WESTOMP......   Western Ocean Meeting Point
Weston........   Weston [*Roy F.*], Inc. [*Associated Press*]   (SAG)
Weston........   Weston's Reports [*11-14 Vermont*] [*A publication*]   (DLA)
WestOne......   West One Bancorp [*Associated Press*]   (SAG)
West Oregon St C...   Western Oregon State College   (GAGS)
WESTPAC....   IOC Sub-Commission for the Western Pacific   (BUAC)
WESTPAC....   Product Group for the Western Pacific   (EERA)
WESTPAC....   Western Pacific [*Military*]   (CINC)
WestPac......   Western Pacific Airlines, Inc. [*Associated Press*]   (SAG)
WESTPACBACOM...   Western Pacific Base Command [*Navy*]
WEST PACK...   Western Packaging Exposition   (TSPED)
WESTPACNORTH...   Western Pacific North [*Navy*]   (CINC)
WESTPACTRAMID...   Western Pacific Training Program for Midshipmen [*Navy*]   (DNAB)
West Pat...   West on Patents [*A publication*]   (DLA)
WESTPO......   Western Governors Policy Office
West Pr Int Law...   Westlake's Private International Law [*7th ed.*] [*1925*] [*A publication*]   (DLA)
West R........   Western Reporter [*A publication*]   (DLA)
WESTRAIL...   Western Australian Government Railways Commission
WESTRAX....   Western Tropical Atlantic Experiment   (USDC)
West Rep......   Western Reporter [*A publication*]   (DLA)
West Res Coll...   Western Reserve College
WESTS........   Women's Emergency Shelter and Training Scheme [*New South Wales, Australia*]
West School L Rev...   Western School Law Review [*A publication*]   (DLA)
WESTSEAFRON...   Western Sea Frontier [*Navy*]   (MUGU)
West's Op....   West's Opinions [*City Solicitor of Philadelphia, PA*] [*A publication*]   (DLA)
West's Symb....   West's Symboleographie [*Many eds.*] [*1590-1641*] [*A publication*]   (DLA)
WESTT........   Weapon System Tactical Tester
West Tex St U...   West Texas State University   (GAGS)
West T H.....   West's English Chancery Reports Tempore Hardwicke [*1736-39*] [*A publication*]   (DLA)
West T Hard...   West's English Chancery Reports Tempore Hardwicke [*1736-39*] [*A publication*]   (DLA)
West T Hardw...   West's English Chancery Reports Tempore Hardwicke [*1736-39*] [*A publication*]   (DLA)

West Ti Cas...   Western's London Tithe Cases [*1535-1822*] [*A publication*]   (DLA)
West Tithe Cas...   Western's London Tithe Cases [*England*] [*A publication*]   (DLA)
West Va...   West Virginia Reports [*A publication*]   (DLA)
WESTVACO...   West Virginia Pulp & Paper Co.   (EFIS)
West Va Col...   West Virginia Graduate College   (GAGS)
West Va L Rev...   Western Virginia Law Review [*A publication*]   (DLA)
West Va Rep...   West Virginia Reports [*A publication*]   (DLA)
West Va U...   West Virginia University   (GAGS)
Westvco...   Westvaco Corp. [*Associated Press*]   (SAG)
West Wash St U...   Western Washington State University   (GAGS)
West Week (Can)...   Western Weekly Notes (Canada) [*A publication*]   (DLA)
West Week N...   Western Weekly Notes [*Canada*] [*A publication*]   (DLA)
West Week N (Can)...   Western Weekly Notes (Canada) [*A publication*]   (DLA)
West Week NS...   Western Weekly, New Series [*Canada*] [*A publication*]   (DLA)
West Week Rep...   Western Weekly Reports [*Canada*] [*A publication*]   (DLA)
West Wkly...   Western Weekly Notes (Canada) [*A publication*]   (DLA)
WESU.........   Middletown, CT [*FM radio station call letters*]
WESV.........   Richton, MS [*FM radio station call letters*]
WESX.........   Salem, MA [*AM radio station call letters*]
WESY.........   Leland, MS [*AM radio station call letters*]
WESYP.........   Weapons System Plan [*Navy*]   (NG)
WET.........   Wagethe [*Indonesia*] [*Airport symbol*]   (OAG)
WET.........   Waste, Environment, and Technology [*Matrix*] [*Environmental Protection Agency*]
WET.........   Waste Extraction Test
WET.........   Water Exercise Technique [*In book title "The W.E.T. Workout"*]
WET.........   Weapons Effectiveness Testing
WET.........   Weighted Effective Temperature   (IAA)
WET.........   Western European Time   (IAA)
WET.........   Westfort Petroleums Ltd. [*Toronto Stock Exchange symbol*]
WET.........   Westinghouse Electronic Tubeless
WET.........   Wet Environment Trainer [*Navy*]
WET.........   Wettzell [*Federal Republic of Germany*] [*Seismograph station code, US Geological Survey*]   (SEIS)
WET.........   Whole Earth Telescope [*Global network of telescopes*]
WET.........   Whole Effluent Toxicity [*Environmental Protection Agency*]
WET.........   Work Experience and Training
WETA.........   War Estate Tax Act [*1917*]
WETA.........   Washington, DC [*FM radio station call letters*]
WETAC.........   Westinghouse Electronic Tubeless Analog Computer
WETAF.........   Weather Task Force
WETARFAC...   Work Element Timer and Recorder for Automatic Computing
WETA-TV ....   Washington, DC [*Television station call letters*]
WETB.........   Johnson City, TN [*AM radio station call letters*]
WETC.........   Wendell-Zebulon, NC [*AM radio station call letters*]
WETD.........   Alfred, NY [*FM radio station call letters*]
WETF.........   Weightless Environment Training Facility   (SSD)
WETH.........   Hagerstown, MD [*FM radio station call letters*]
WETH.........   Wetherley [*England*]
Weth.........   Wethey's Reports [*Canada*] [*A publication*]   (DLA)
Wethey........   Wethey's Reports, Upper Canada Queen's Bench [*A publication*]   (DLA)
Weth UC ......   Wethey's Reports, Upper Canada Queen's Bench [*A publication*]   (DLA)
WE TIP ....   We Turn in Pushers [*Organization combating drug traffic*]
WETK.........   Burlington, VT [*Television station call letters*]
WETL.........   South Bend, IN [*FM radio station call letters*]
WETM.........   Elmira, NY [*Television station call letters*]
WETM.........   Weather Team [*Air Force*]   (AFM)
WETN.........   Wheaton, IL [*FM radio station call letters*]
WETNETNG...   Wet-Net Training [*Navy*]   (NVT)
WETO.........   Western Environmental Technology Office   (ACII)
WETP.........   Work Experience Training Program   (OICC)
WETR-AM ....   Eden, NC [*AM radio station call letters*]   (RBYB)
WETS.........   Johnson City, TN [*FM radio station call letters*]
WETS.........   Weapon Effects Training Simulator   (MCD)
WETS.........   Week-End Training Site [*Military*]   (AABC)
WetSeal........   Wet Seal, Inc. [*Associated Press*]   (SAG)
WETSU ....   We-Eat-This-Stuff-Up [*Mobile guerrilla force coded password*] [*Bowdlerized version*]   (VNW)
WETT.........   Ocean City, MD [*AM radio station call letters*]
Wett.........   Wettstein's Novum Testamentum Graecum [*A publication*]   (BJA)
WETW-FM ...   Leonardtown, MD [*FM radio station call letters*]   (BROA)
WETZ.........   New Martinsville, WV [*AM radio station call letters*]
WETZ-FM.....   New Martinsville, WV [*FM radio station call letters*]   (RBYB)
WEU.........   University of Wisconsin-Eau Claire, Eau Claire, WI [*Library symbol Library of Congress*]   (LCLS)
WEU.........   Ward's Engine Update [*A publication*]
WEU.........   Western Economic Union   (DOMA)
WEU.........   Western European Union [*Also, WU*] [*See also UEO*]   (EAIO)
WEUC.........   Ponce, PR [*AM radio station call letters*]
WEUC-FM.....   Ponce, PR [*FM radio station call letters*]
WEUL.........   Kingsford, MI [*FM radio station call letters*]
WEUP.........   Huntsville, AL [*AM radio station call letters*]
WEUP.........   Minor Hill, TN [*FM radio station call letters*]
WEUX.........   Chippewa Falls, WI [*Television station call letters*]
WEV.........   Western European Vision
WEVA.........   Emporia, VA [*AM radio station call letters*]
WEVA.........   World Esperantist Vegetarian Association [*See also TEVA*] [*Dublin, Republic of Ireland*]   (EAIO)
WEVA-FM ....   Emporia, VA [*FM radio station call letters*]
WEVD.........   New York, NY [*AM radio station call letters*]
WEVE.........   Eveleth, MN [*AM radio station call letters*]
WEVE-FM .....   Eveleth, MN [*FM radio station call letters*]
WEVH.........   Hanover, NH [*FM radio station call letters*]

WEVL	Memphis, TN [*FM radio station call letters*]
WEVN	Keene, NH [*FM radio station call letters*]
WEVO	Concord, NH [*FM radio station call letters*]
WEVR	River Falls, WI [*AM radio station call letters*]
WEVR-FM	River Falls, WI [*FM radio station call letters*]
WEVS	Saugatuck, MI [*FM radio station call letters*]
WEVV	Evansville, IN [*Television station call letters*]
WEW	St. Louis, MO [*AM radio station call letters*]
WEW	Western Electronic Week
WEW	West Wind Aviation, Inc. [*Canada ICAO designator*] (FAAC)
WEW	Wewak [*Papua New Guinea*] [*Seismograph station code, US Geological Survey Closed*] (SEIS)
WEWAS	Water Equipment Wholesalers and Suppliers [*Formerly, WEWSA*]
WEWM	Pentwater, MI [*FM radio station call letters*] (RBYB)
WEWO	Laurinburg, NC [*AM radio station call letters*]
WEWS	Cleveland, OH [*Television station call letters*]
WEWSA	Water Equipment Wholesalers and Suppliers Association [*Later, WEWAS*] (EA)
WEX	Business Science Experts [*NOMOS Datapool*] [*Germany Information service or system*] (CRD)
WEX	Wexford [*County in Ireland*] (ROG)
WEX	Wine Exchange [*Computer network*]
WEX	Win-Eldrich Mines Ltd. [*Toronto Stock Exchange symbol*]
WEX	Wings Express, Inc. [*ICAO designator*] (FAAC)
WEXC	Greenville, PA [*FM radio station call letters*]
WEXC	Wolverine Exploration (EFIS)
WEXF	Wexford [*County in Ireland*] (ROG)
WEXFD	Wexford [*County in Ireland*]
WEXI	Huntington, IN [*FM radio station call letters*]
WEXITA	Women Executives International Tourism Association [*Defunct*] (EA)
WEXL	Royal Oak, MI [*AM radio station call letters*]
WEXS	Patillas, PR [*AM radio station call letters*]
WEXT	Wrist Extension [*Sports medicine*]
WEXT-FM	Sturtevant, WI [*FM radio station call letters*] (BROA)
WEXY	Wilton Manors, FL [*AM radio station call letters*]
WEY	West Yellowstone, MT [*Location identifier FAA*] (FAAL)
Weyco	Weyco Group, Inc. [*Associated Press*] (SAG)
WEYE	Surgoinsville, TN [*FM radio station call letters*]
Weyerh	Weyerhaeuser Co. [*Associated Press*] (SAG)
WEYI	Saginaw, MI [*Television station call letters*]
WEYM	Weymouth [*Municipal borough in England*]
WEYS	Key West, FL [*Television station call letters*]
WEYS	Weyco Group [*NASDAQ symbol*] (TTSB)
WEYS	Weyco Group, Inc. [*NASDAQ symbol*] (SAG)
WEYY	Talladega, AL [*FM radio station call letters*]
WEYZ	North East, PA [*AM radio station call letters*]
WEZ	Weapon Engagement Zone [*Army*] (ADDR)
WEZB	New Orleans, LA [*FM radio station call letters*]
WEZC	Hickory, NC [*FM radio station call letters*]
WEZE	Boston, MA [*AM radio station call letters*]
WEZF	Burlington, VT [*FM radio station call letters*]
WEZG	Jefferson City, TN [*FM radio station call letters*]
WEZI	New Market, VA [*FM radio station call letters*]
WEZJ	Williamsburg, KY [*AM radio station call letters*]
WEZJ-FM	Williamsburg, KY [*FM radio station call letters*]
WEZK	Knoxville, TN [*AM radio station call letters*]
WEZL	Charleston, SC [*FM radio station call letters*]
WEZN	Bridgeport, CT [*FM radio station call letters*]
WEZO	Farmer City, IL [*FM radio station call letters*] (RBYB)
WEZQ	Bangor, ME [*FM radio station call letters*]
WEZR	Brillion, WI [*FM radio station call letters*]
WEZS	Laconia, NH [*AM radio station call letters*]
WEZU	Witterungseinfluesse und Zeitunterschied [*Weather factors and time difference*] [*German military - World War II*]
WEZV	Brookston, IN [*FM radio station call letters*]
WEZW	Augusta, ME [*AM radio station call letters*] (RBYB)
WEZX	Scranton, PA [*FM radio station call letters*]
WEZY	Racine, WI [*FM radio station call letters*] (RBYB)
WEZZ	Clanton, AL [*FM radio station call letters*]
WF	Four-Conductor Cables [*JETDS nomenclature*] [*Military*] (CET)
WF	Wakefield [*Postcode*] (ODBW)
WF	Wake Forest University [*North Carolina*]
wf	Wallis and Futuna [*MARC country of publication code Library of Congress*] (LCCP)
WF	Wallis and Futuna [*ANSI two-letter standard code*] (CNC)
WF	Ward Foundation (EA)
WF	Wash Fountain (AAG)
WF	Water Filter
WF	Water Finish [*Paper*]
WF	Waterhouse-Fredericksen [*Syndrome*] [*Medicine*] (DB)
WF	Watershed Foundation (EA)
WF	Waveform [*Telecommunications*] (IAA)
WF	Wave Frequency [*Telecommunications*] (IAA)
W + F	Ways plus Filling [*Textile testing*]
WF	Weatherproof Faience [*Tile*] (DICI)
WF	Weighting Factor (EG)
WF	Weil-Felix Reaction [*Medicine*] (MAE)
WF	Welch Fusiliers [*British military*] (DMA)
WF	Weld Fixture
WF	Welfare Appointment Full Time [*Chiropody*] [*British*]
WF	Wells Fargo & Co. [*Associated Press*] (SAG)
WF	Western Front [*World War I*]
WF	Westfair Foods Ltd. [*Toronto Stock Exchange symbol*]
WF	West Feliciana Railroad (IIA)
WF	Wet Film [*Radiology*] (DAVI)
WF	White Falcon [*A publication*] (DNAB)
WF	White Fathers [*Roman Catholic men's religious order*]
WF	White Female
WF	White Fir [*Botany*]
WF	Wide Flange (DAC)
WF	Wideros Flyveselskap [*ICAO designator*] (AD)
WF	Wildfowl Foundation (EA)
WF	Wind Finding RADAR (IAA)
WF	Wind Force (WGA)
WF	Window-Frame
WF	Windstar Foundation (EA)
WF	Wingfold
WF	Wing Forward (WGA)
WF	Wire Foundation (EA)
WF	Wistar-Furth [*Rat strain*]
WF	Withdrawn Failing [*Education*] (WGA)
WF	Women's Firsts [*A publication*]
WF	Won on Foul [*Boxing*]
WF	Word Fluency [*Psychology*]
WF	Work Function [*Physics*]
W/F	Wow and Flutter
WF	Write Fault (MHDB)
WF	Write Forward
W/F	Writing on Face [*Deltiology*]
WF	Wrong Font [*Typesetting*] [*Proofreader's mark*]
wf	Wrong Font [*Publishing*] (WDAA)
WFA	Warfighter Associate [*Army*]
WFA	War Food Administration [*Determined military, civilian, and foreign requirements for human and animal food, and for food used industrially*] [*Terminated, 1945*] [*World War II*]
WFA	Wave Form Analyzer [*Instrumentation*]
WFA	Weatherford Family Association (EA)
WFA	Weight-for-Age (ADA)
WFA	Weightlifting Federation of Africa (EAIO)
WFA	Western Fairs Association (EA)
WFA	Western Falconry Association [*Defunct*] (EA)
WFA	White Fish Authority [*MAFF*] [*British*]
WFA	Wide-Frequency Antenna
WFA	Winemakers' Federation of Australia
WFA	Wire Fabricators Association [*Naperville, IL*] (EA)
WFA	Women's Football Association [*British*]
WFA	World Federalist Association
WFA	World Federation of Advertisers [*See also FMA*] [*Brussels, Belgium*] (EAIO)
WFA	World Footbag Association (EA)
WFA	World Friendship Association
WFAA	Dallas, TX [*Television station call letters*]
WFAA	World Federation of Americans Abroad [*France*] (EAIO)
WFAB	Ceiba, PR [*AM radio station call letters*]
WFAC	World Federal Authority Committee [*Dundas, ON*] (EAIO)
WFACT	Wildlife Foundation Australian Capital Territory
WFAD	Middlebury, VT [*AM radio station call letters*]
WFAE	Charlotte, NC [*FM radio station call letters*]
WFAFW	World Federation of Agriculture and Food Workers (EA)
WFaH	Hoard Historical Museum, Fort Atkinson, WI [*Library symbol Library of Congress*] (LCLS)
WFAI	Fayetteville, NC [*AM radio station call letters*]
WFALW	Weltbund Freiheitlicher Arbeitnehmerverbande auf Liberaler Wirtschaftsgrundlage [*World Union of Liberal Trade Union Organisations - WULTUO*] [*Zurich, Switzerland*] (EAIO)
WFAM	Augusta, GA [*AM radio station call letters*]
WFAN	New York, NY [*AM radio station call letters*]
WF & EQ	Wave Filters and Equalizers (MCD)
WF & FSA	Wholesale Florists and Florist Suppliers of America (EA)
WF & P	Wabash, Frisco, and Pacific Association (EA)
WF & S	Wichita Falls & Southern Railroad (IIA)
WFAOS	World Federation of Associations of YMCA Secretaries [*Nigeria*] (EAIO)
WFAOSB	World Food and Agricultural Outlook and Situation Board [*Department of Agriculture*]
WFAP	Women's Funding Assistance Project (EA)
WFAPS	World Federation of Associations of Pediatric Surgeons [*Barcelona, Spain*] (EAIO)
WFAR	Danbury, CT [*FM radio station call letters*]
WFAS	White Plains, NY [*AM radio station call letters*]
WFAS	Women's Financial Advisory Service [*Australia*]
WFAS-FM	White Plains, NY [*FM radio station call letters*]
WFAT	Portage, MI [*FM radio station call letters*]
WFAU	Gardiner, ME [*AM radio station call letters*]
WFAV	Fort Walton Beach, FL [*AM radio station call letters*]
WFAW	Fort Atkinson, WI [*AM radio station call letters*]
WFAW	World Federation of Agricultural Workers [*See also FMTA*] (EAIO)
WFAX	Falls Church, VA [*AM radio station call letters*]
WFAY	Fayetville, NC [*Television station call letters*]
WFAZ	Thomasville, NC [*FM radio station call letters*]
WFB	Waferboard Corp. Ltd. [*Toronto Stock Exchange symbol*]
WFB	Waterways Freight Bureau [*Defunct*] (EA)
WFB	Wide Flange Beam [*Metal industry*]
WFB	Works Fire Brigade (WDAA)
WFB	World Fellowship of Buddhists [*Bangkok, Tahiland*] (EAIO)
WFBA	Miami, FL [*AM radio station call letters*]
WFBB	Woodfree Bank and Bond [*Paper*] (DGA)
WFBBA	World Federation of Bergen-Belsen Associations (EA)
WFBC	Greenville, SC [*AM radio station call letters*]
WFBC-FM	Greenville, SC [*FM radio station call letters*]

WFBC-TV	Anderson, SC [*Television station call letters*] (RBYB)
WFBE	Flint, MI [*FM radio station call letters*]
WFBF	Buffalo, NY [*FM radio station call letters*]
WFBG	Altoona, PA [*AM radio station call letters*]
WFBI	Memphis, TN [*Television station call letters*]
WFBI	Wood Fiber Blanket Institute [*Defunct*]
WFBL	Baldwinsville, NY [*AM radio station call letters*]
WFBMA	Woven Fabric Belting Manufacturers Association (EA)
WFBQ	Indianapolis, IN [*FM radio station call letters*]
WFBR	Cambridge, MD [*FM radio station call letters*]
WFBSC	World Federation of Building Service Contractors (EA)
WFBTMA	World Federation of Baton Twirling and Majorette Associations (EA)
WFBY	World Fellowship of Buddhist Youth [*Bangkok, Thailand*] (EAIO)
WFBY-FM	Clarksburg, WV [*FM radio station call letters*] (RBYB)
WFBZ-FM	Trempealeau, WI [*FM radio station call letters*] (BROA)
WFC	Committee on the World Food Crisis [*Defunct*] (EA)
WFC	Paul McCartney Fan Club [*British*] (EAIO)
WFC	Wake Forest College [*Later, WFU*] [*North Carolina*]
WFC	Walleye Filter Changer
WFC	Wall Financial Co. [*Vancouver Stock Exchange symbol*]
WFC	Wall Financial Corp. [*Toronto Stock Exchange symbol*]
WFC	Wallops Flight Center [*Formerly, WS*] [*NASA*]
WFC	Wanted for Cash (MHDW)
WFC	War Finance Committee
WFC	Water Facts Consortium [*Defunct*] (EA)
WFC	Weld Flange Connection
WFC	Wells Fargo [*NYSE symbol*] (TTSB)
WFC	Wells Fargo & Co. [*NYSE symbol*] (SPSG)
WFC	Wesleyan Free Church
WFC	Western Football Conference
WFC	Western Forestry Center (EA)
WFC	West Florida Coast
WFC	Wheat Foods Council (EA)
WFC	Wide Field Camera
WFC	Wolf First Class [*A philanderer*] [*Slang*]
WFC	Women's Forage Corps [*World War I*] [*British*]
WFC	World Food Council [*United Nations*] (EAIO)
WFC	World Forestry Center (EA)
WFC	World Friendship Centre (EA)
WFC	World Fundraising Council (NFD)
WFC	Worldwide Fiero Club (EA)
WFCA	Ackerman, MS [*FM radio station call letters*]
WFCA	Western Forestry and Conservation Association (EA)
WFCA	World Floor Covering Association (NTPA)
WFCB	Chillicothe, OH [*FM radio station call letters*]
WFCC	Chatham, MA [*FM radio station call letters*]
WFCC	World Federation for Culture Collections (EAIO)
WFCE	World Federation of Czechoslovak Exile (EA)
WFCF	St. Augustine, FL [*FM radio station call letters*]
WFCG	Franklinton, LA [*AM radio station call letters*]
WFCH	Charleston, SC [*FM radio station call letters*]
WFCI	Franklin, IN [*FM radio station call letters*]
WFCJ	Miamisburg, OH [*FM radio station call letters*]
WFCL	Clintonville, WI [*AM radio station call letters*]
WFCLC	World Federation of Christian Life Communities [*See also FMCVC*] [*Rome, Italy*] (EAIO)
WFCM	Murfreesboro, TN [*FM radio station call letters*] (RBYB)
WFCMV	Wheeled Fuel-Consuming Motor Vehicle
WFCNLM	World Federation of the Cossack National Liberation Movement [*Later, WFCNLMC*] (EA)
WFCNLMC ...	World Federation of the Cossack National Liberation Movement of Cossackia (EA)
WFCO	Lancaster, OH [*FM radio station call letters*]
WFCO	Winton Financial [*NASDAQ symbol*] (TTSB)
WFCO	Winton Financial Corp. [*NASDAQ symbol*] (SAG)
WFCPrB	Wells Fargo Adj Rt B Pfd [*NYSE symbol*] (TTSB)
WFCPrC	Wells Fargo 9% 'C' Dep Pfd [*NYSE symbol*] (TTSB)
WFCPrD	Wells Fargo 8.875% Dep Pfd [*NYSE symbol*] (TTSB)
WFCPrF	Wells Fargo 9.875% Dep Pfd [*NYSE symbol*] (TTSB)
WFCPrG	Wells Fargo 9% Dep Pfd [*NYSE symbol*] (TTSB)
WFCR	Amherst, MA [*FM radio station call letters*]
WFCS	New Britain, CT [*FM radio station call letters*]
WFCS	World's Fair Collectors Society (EA)
WFCT	Bradenton, FL [*Television station call letters*]
WFCV	Fort Wayne, IN [*AM radio station call letters*]
WFCY	World Federation of Catholic Youth
WFCYWG	World Federation of Catholic Young Women and Girls [*Later, WFCY*]
WFD	Avro International Aerospace [*British*] [*FAA designator*] (FAAC)
WFD	Waveform Distortion [*Telecommunications*] (TEL)
WFD	Westfield Minerals Ltd. [*Toronto Stock Exchange symbol Vancouver Stock Exchange symbol*]
WFD	Women in Financial Development (NFD)
WFD	Woodford BAE [*British ICAO designator*] (FAAC)
WFD	Woods and Forests Department [*South Australia*]
WFD	Wool Forward [*Knitting*]
WFD	Work Function Difference [*Physics*] (IAA)
WFD	World Fax Directory [*Information service or system*] (IID)
WFD	World Federation of the Deaf [*Rome, Italy*]
WFD	World Food Day [*October 16*]
WFD	Worldwide Franchise Directory [*A publication*]
WFDA	Wholesale Floorcovering Distributors' Association [*British*] (BI)
WFDA	Wholesale Footwear Distributors' Association [*British*] (BI)
WFDA	World Fast-Draw Association (EA)
WFDD	Winston-Salem, NC [*FM radio station call letters*]
WFDF	Flint, MI [*AM radio station call letters*]

WFDF	World Flying Disc Federation (EAIO)
WFDFI	World Federation of Development Financing Institutions [*See also FEMIDE*] [*Madrid, Spain*] (EAIO)
WFDL	Lomira, WI [*FM radio station call letters*]
WFDR	Manchester, GA [*AM radio station call letters*]
WFDRHL	World Federation of Doctors Who Respect Human Life (United States Section) (EA)
WFDS	Warm Fog Dispenser System (MCD)
WFDS	Worthington Foods [*NASDAQ symbol*] (SAG)
WFDSA	World Federation of Direct Selling Associations [*Washington, DC*] (EA)
WFDSC	World Federation of Dark Shadows Clubs (EA)
WFDU	Teaneck, NJ [*FM radio station call letters*]
WFDW	World Federation of Democratic Women
WFDWRHL...	World Federation of Doctors Who Respect Human Life [*Ostend, Belgium*] (EAIO)
WFDY	World Federation of Democratic Youth [*See also FMJD*] [*Budapest, Hungary*] (EAIO)
WFe	Dwight T. Parker Public Library, Fennimore, WI [*Library symbol Library of Congress*] (LCLS)
WFE	Williams Flexion Exercises [*Orthopedics*] (DAVI)
WFE	Wiped Film Evaporation
WFE	With Food Element
WFE	World Federation of Europeans (By Birth or Descent) (EA)
WFEA	Manchester, NH [*AM radio station call letters*]
WFEA	World Federation of Educational Associations [*Later, WCOTP*] (EA)
WFEB	Sylacauga, AL [*AM radio station call letters*]
WFEB	Worcester Foundation for Experimental Biology
WFEN	Rockford, IL [*FM radio station call letters*]
WFEO	World Federation of Engineering Organizations [*Paris, France*]
WFES	Windshield Flight Environment Simulator (PDAA)
WFEWC	World Federation of Estonian Women's Clubs (EA)
WFEWCE	World Federation of Estonian Women's Clubs in Exile
WFEX	Western Fruit Express
WFEZ	Williston, FL [*FM radio station call letters*]
WFF	Wanderer Forum Foundation (EA)
WFF	Wavy Vortex Flow [*Fluid mechanics*]
WFF	Well-Formed Formula [*Logic*]
WFF	Western Frontier Force [*British military*] (DMA)
WFF	Whiting Field [*Milton*] [*Florida*] [*Seismograph station code, US Geological Survey*] [*Closed*] (SEIS)
WFF	William Faulkner Foundation [*Defunct*] (EA)
WFF	Wold Farm Foods [*Commercial firm British*]
WFF	World Friendship Federation
WFFA	Women's Fashion Fabrics Association [*Defunct*] (EA)
WFFC	Ferrum, VA [*FM radio station call letters*]
WFFC	Women in Flavor & Fragrance Commerce Inc.
WFFF	Columbia, MS [*AM radio station call letters*]
WFFF-FM	Columbia, MS [*FM radio station call letters*]
WFFF-TV	Burlington, VT [*Television station call letters*] (RBYB)
WFFG	Marathon, FL [*AM radio station call letters*]
WFFI	Western Fidelity Funding [*NASDAQ symbol*] (TTSB)
WFFI	Western Fidelity Funding, Inc. [*NASDAQ symbol*] (SAG)
WFFL	World Federation of Free Latvians (EA)
WFFM	Ashburn, GA [*FM radio station call letters*]
WFFM	World Federation of Friends of Museums [*See also FMAM*] [*Paris, France*] (EAIO)
WFFN	Cordova, AL [*FM radio station call letters*]
WFFT	Fort Wayne, IN [*Television station call letters*]
WFFTH	World Federation of Workers in Food, Tobacco, and Hotel Industries [*See also FMATH*] (EAIO)
WFFX	Tuscaloosa, AL [*FM radio station call letters*]
WFG	Water Fog
WFG	Waveform Function Generator
WFG	Waveform Generator
WFGA	Women's Farm and Garden Association [*British*] (BI)
WFGA-FM	Waycross, GA [*FM radio station call letters*] (RBYB)
WFGB	Kingston, NY [*FM radio station call letters*]
WFGC	Palm Beach, FL [*Television station call letters*]
WFGH	Fort Gay, WV [*FM radio station call letters*]
WFGI	State College, PA [*FM radio station call letters*]
WFGL	Fitchburg, MA [*AM radio station call letters*]
WFGM	Fairmont, WV [*FM radio station call letters*]
WFGN	Gaffney, SC [*AM radio station call letters*]
WFGO	Erie, PA [*FM radio station call letters*]
WFGR	Grand Rapids, MI [*FM radio station call letters*]
WFGW	Black Mountain, NC [*AM radio station call letters*]
WFGX	Fort Walton Beach, FL [*Television station call letters*]
WFGY	Altoona, PA [*FM radio station call letters*]
WFGZ	Lobelville, TN [*FM radio station call letters*]
WFH	World Federation of Hemophilia [*Montreal, PQ*] (EA)
WFHA	Windsor Family Historical Association (EA)
WFHA	World Federation of Hungarian Artists (EA)
WFHAAVSC...	World Federation of Health Agencies for the Advancement of Voluntary Surgical Contraception (EA)
WFHB	Bloomington, IN [*FM radio station call letters*]
WFHC	Henderson, TN [*FM radio station call letters*]
WFHE	Hickory, NC [*FM radio station call letters*]
WFHFF	World Federation of Hungarian Freedom Fighters (EA)
WFHJ	World Federation of Hungarian Jews (EA)
WFHK	Pell City, AL [*AM radio station call letters*]
WFHL	Decatur, IL [*Television station call letters*]
WFHN	Fairhaven, MA [*FM radio station call letters*]
WFHQ	Pennsuco, FL [*FM radio station call letters*]
WFHR	Wisconsin Rapids, WI [*AM radio station call letters*]

WFHSLPAC...	Water-Flooded Helical Screw Low-Pressure Air Compressor [*Navy*] (CAAL)
WFI.............	Fianarantsoa [*Madagascar*] [*Airport symbol*] (OAG)
WFI.............	Wait for It (DI)
WFI.............	Water for Injection [*Pharmacy*]
WFI.............	Westralian Forest Industries [*Australia Commercial firm*]
WFI.............	Wheat Flour Institute [*Miller's National Federation*] [*Absorbed by*] (EA)
WFI.............	Wishes and Fears Inventory [*Psychology*]
WFI.............	Wood Flooring Institute of America [*Later, WSFI*] (EA)
WFI.............	Wood Foundation Institute [*Defunct*] (EA)
WFI.............	World Federation of Investors (EAIO)
WFI.............	World Forest Institute (GNE)
WFI.............	Worldwide Friendship International (EA)
WFIA..........	Louisville, KY [*AM radio station call letters*]
WFIA..........	Wells Fargo Investment Advisors (ECON)
WFIA..........	Western Forest Industries Association (EA)
WFIC..........	Collinsville, VA [*AM radio station call letters*]
WFICM........	World Federation of International Music Competitions [*Switzerland*] (EAIO)
WFID..........	Rio Piedras, PR [*FM radio station call letters*]
WFIE..........	Evansville, IN [*Television station call letters*]
WFIF..........	Milford, CT [*AM radio station call letters*]
WFII-AM	Columbus, OH [*AM radio station call letters*] (BROA)
WFIL..........	Philadelphia, PA [*AM radio station call letters*] (RBYB)
WFIM..........	World Federation of Islamic Missions [*Karachi, Pakistan*] (EAIO)
WFIMC........	World Federation of International Music Competitions [*See also FMCIM*] (EAIO)
WFIN	Findlay, OH [*AM radio station call letters*]
WFIN	Women and Food Information Network [*Defunct*] (EA)
WFIP..........	Women's Financial Information Program [*American Association of Retired Persons*] (BARN)
WFIQ	Florence, AL [*Television station call letters*]
WFIR	Roanoke, VA [*AM radio station call letters*]
WFIS..........	Fountain Inn, SC [*AM radio station call letters*]
WFIS..........	World Federation of Iranian Students
WFIT..........	Melbourne, FL [*FM radio station call letters*]
WFIU..........	Bloomington, IN [*FM radio station call letters*]
WFIV..........	Kissimmee, FL [*AM radio station call letters*]
WFIV..........	White Light Fringe Image Velocimeter (PDAA)
WFIW..........	Fairfield, IL [*AM radio station call letters*]
WFIW-FM	Fairfield, IL [*FM radio station call letters*]
WFIX..........	Rogersville, AL [*FM radio station call letters*]
WFJA..........	Sanford, NC [*FM radio station call letters*]
WFJJ..........	World Federation of Jewish Journalists [*Tel Aviv, Israel*] (EAIO)
WFJY-AM	Portage, PA [*AM radio station call letters*] (BROA)
WFK..........	Frenchville [*Maine*] [*Airport symbol*] (OAG)
WFKJ..........	Cashtown, PA [*AM radio station call letters*]
WFKN	Franklin, KY [*AM radio station call letters*]
WFKS..........	Palatka, FL [*FM radio station call letters*]
WFKX..........	Henderson, TN [*FM radio station call letters*]
WFKY..........	Frankfort, KY [*AM radio station call letters*]
WFKZ..........	Plantation Key, FL [*FM radio station call letters*]
WFL..........	Windflower Mining Ltd. [*Vancouver Stock Exchange symbol*]
WFL..........	Within Functional Limits [*Physical therapy*] (DAVI)
WFL..........	Woman's Freedom League
WFL..........	Work Flow Language [*Computer science*] (BUR)
WFL..........	World Football League [*Dissolved, 1975*]
WFL..........	Worshipful [*Freemasonry*] (ROG)
WFL..........	Wredemann-Frang Law
WFLA..........	Tampa, FL [*AM radio station call letters*]
WFLA..........	Western Fraternal Life Association (EA)
WFLA-TV	Tampa, FL [*Television station call letters*]
WFLB..........	Fayetteville, NC [*AM radio station call letters*]
WFLC..........	Miami, FL [*FM radio station call letters*]
WFLD..........	Chicago, IL [*Television station call letters*]
WFLD..........	White Fine Lustre Double Weight [*Photographic paper*] (DGA)
WFLD..........	Work/Family Life Database [*Database*]
WFLE..........	Flemingsburg, KY [*AM radio station call letters*]
WFLE-FM....	Flemington, KY [*FM radio station call letters*]
WFLI..........	Cleveland, TN [*Television station call letters*]
WFLI..........	Lookout Mountain, TN [*AM radio station call letters*]
WFLK..........	Geneva, NY [*FM radio station call letters*]
WFLM..........	White City, FL [*FM radio station call letters*]
WFLN..........	Philadelphia, PA [*FM radio station call letters*]
WFLO..........	Farmville, VA [*AM radio station call letters*]
WFLO-FM	Farmville, VA [*FM radio station call letters*]
WFLP..........	Erie, PA [*AM radio station call letters*]
WFLQ..........	French Lick, IN [*FM radio station call letters*]
WFLR..........	Dundee, NY [*AM radio station call letters*]
WFLR-FM	Dundee, NY [*FM radio station call letters*]
WFLRY	World Federation of Liberal and Radical Youth [*Later, IFLRY*]
WFLS..........	Fredericksburg, VA [*AM radio station call letters*]
WFLS-FM	Fredericksburg, VA [*FM radio station call letters*]
WFLT..........	Flint, MI [*AM radio station call letters*]
WFLV-FM	Havana, FL [*FM radio station call letters*] (BROA)
WFLW..........	Monticello, KY [*AM radio station call letters*]
WFLX..........	West Palm Beach, FL [*Television station call letters*]
WFLY..........	Troy, NY [*FM radio station call letters*]
WFLZ..........	Tampa, FL [*FM radio station call letters*]
WFM.............	Water Flow Meter
WFM.............	Waveform Monitor
WFM.............	Waveguide Frequency Meter
WFM.............	Weatherproof Faience Mosaics (DICI)
WFM.............	Western Federation of Miners

WFM.............	Westford [*Massachusetts*] [*Seismograph station code, US Geological Survey*] (SEIS)
WfM.............	Wired for Management [*Computer science*] (IGQR)
WFM.............	World Federalist Movement [*Netherlands*] (EAIO)
WFMA..........	World Folk Music Association (EA)
WFMB..........	Springfield, IL [*AM radio station call letters*]
WFMB..........	World Federation of Merino Breeders [*Australia*]
WFMB-FM ...	Springfield, IL [*FM radio station call letters*]
WFMC..........	Goldsboro, NC [*AM radio station call letters*]
WFMC..........	Welding Filler Material Control [*Nuclear energy*] (NRCH)
WFMD..........	Frederick, MD [*AM radio station call letters*]
WFME..........	Newark, NJ [*FM radio station call letters*]
WFME..........	West Milford, NJ [*Television station call letters*]
WFME..........	World Federation for Medical Education (EA)
WFMF..........	Baton Rouge, LA [*FM radio station call letters*]
WFMG..........	Richmond, IN [*FM radio station call letters*]
WFMH..........	Cullman, AL [*AM radio station call letters*]
WFMH..........	World Federation for Mental Health (EA)
WFMH-FM ...	Cullman, AL [*FM radio station call letters*]
WFMI..........	Brookfield, WI [*FM radio station call letters*] (RBYB)
WFMI..........	Whole Foods Market [*NASDAQ symbol*] (TTSB)
WFMI..........	Whole Foods Market, Inc. [*NASDAQ symbol*] (SAG)
WFMJ..........	Youngstown, OH [*Television station call letters*]
WFMK..........	East Lansing, MI [*FM radio station call letters*]
WFML..........	Vincennes, IN [*FM radio station call letters*]
WFMLTA......	World Federation of Modern Language Teachers' Association (EA)
WFMN-FM ...	Flora, MS [*FM radio station call letters*] (BROA)
WFMO..........	Fairmont, NC [*AM radio station call letters*]
WFMPT........	Wet-Fluorescence Magnetic Particle Technique [*Corrosion crack detection*]
WFMQ..........	Lebanon, TN [*FM radio station call letters*]
WFMR..........	Menomonee Falls, WI [*FM radio station call letters*]
WFMS..........	Indianapolis, IN [*FM radio station call letters*]
WFMT..........	Chicago, IL [*FM radio station call letters*]
WFMU..........	East Orange, NJ [*FM radio station call letters*]
WFMU..........	Weather and Fixed Map Unit [*FAA*]
WFMV..........	South Congaree, SC [*FM radio station call letters*]
WFMW..........	Madisonville, KY [*AM radio station call letters*]
WFMW..........	World Federation of Methodist Women [*Seoul, Republic of Korea*] (EAIO)
WFMWNAA...	World Federation of Methodist Women, North America Area (EA)
WFMX..........	Statesville, NC [*FM radio station call letters*]
WFMY..........	Greensboro, NC [*Television station call letters*]
WFMZ..........	Allentown, PA [*FM radio station call letters*]
WFMZ-TV	Allentown, PA [*Television station call letters*]
WFN.............	Weapons and Facilities, Navy (NG)
WFN.............	Well-Formed Net
WFN.............	Westminster College, New Wilmington, PA [*OCLC symbol*] (OCLC)
WFN.............	Women's Fisheries Network (NTPA)
WFN.............	Women's Funding Network [*An association*] (EA)
WFN.............	World Federation of Neurology (EA)
WFNA..........	White Fuming Nitric Acid
WFNC..........	Fayetteville, NC [*AM radio station call letters*]
WFNM..........	Lancaster, PA [*FM radio station call letters*]
WFNMB........	World Federation of Nuclear Medicine and Biology (NUCP)
WFNMW	World Federation of Trade Unions of Non-Manual Workers [*See also FMTNM*] [*Antwerp, Belguim*] (EAIO)
WFNN..........	Villas, NJ [*FM radio station call letters*]
WFNO-AM....	Norco, LA [*AM radio station call letters*] (RBYB)
WFNP..........	Rosendale, NY [*FM radio station call letters*]
WFNQ..........	Forest City, NC [*FM radio station call letters*] (RBYB)
WFNR..........	Blacksburg, VA [*AM radio station call letters*]
WFNS..........	Plant City, FL [*AM radio station call letters*]
WFNS..........	Women's Forum on National Security [*Defunct*] (EA)
WFNS..........	World Federation of Neurosurgical Societies [*Nijmegen, Netherlands*] (EA)
WFNS	Writers Federation of Nova Scotia [*Canada*] (WWLA)
WFNT..........	Flint, MI [*AM radio station call letters*]
WFNW..........	Naugatuck, CT [*AM radio station call letters*]
WFNX..........	Lynn, MA [*FM radio station call letters*]
WFNZ..........	Charlotte, NC [*AM radio station call letters*] (RBYB)
WFO.............	Weather Forecast Office (USDC)
WFO.............	Weedman Family Organization (EA)
WFO.............	Western Fiordland Orthogneiss [*Geology*]
WFO.............	Wide Field Optics
WF/O	Wife Of [*Genealogy*]
WFO.............	Wilbur's, Inc. [*ICAO designator*] (FAAC)
WFOB..........	Fostoria, OH [*AM radio station call letters*]
WFOC..........	Western Field Operations Center [*Bureau of Mines*] [*Spokane, WA*] (GRD)
WFOF..........	Covington, IN [*FM radio station call letters*]
WFOF..........	Wide Field Optical Filter
WFOG	Suffolk, VA [*FM radio station call letters*]
WFOM..........	Marietta, GA [*AM radio station call letters*]
WFon...........	Fond Du Lac Public Library, Fond Du Lac, WI [*Library symbol Library of Congress*] (LCLS)
WFonM........	Marian College of Fond Du Lac, Fond Du Lac, WI [*Library symbol Library of Congress*] (LCLS)
WFonMM.......	Mercury Marine, Fond Du Lac, WI [*Library symbol Library of Congress*] (LCLS)
WFonSA.......	Saint Agnes Hospital, Fond Du Lac, WI [*Library symbol Library of Congress*] (LCLS)
WFont...........	Fontana Public Library, Fontana, WI [*Library symbol Library of Congress*] (LCLS)

WFonU......... University of Wisconsin-Fond Du Lac, Fond Du Lac, WI [*Library symbol Library of Congress*] (LCLS)
WFOR......... Hattiesburg, MS [*AM radio station call letters*]
WFOR-TV...... Miami, FL [*Television station call letters*] (RBYB)
WFOS......... Cheasapeake, VA [*FM radio station call letters*]
WFOT......... World Federation of Occupational Therapists [*London, ON*] (EAIO)
WFOV......... Wide Field of View
WFOW-FM.... Chatom, AL [*FM radio station call letters*] (RBYB)
WFOX......... Gainesville, GA [*FM radio station call letters*]
WFOY......... St. Augustine, FL [*AM radio station call letters*]
WFP.......... Warm Front Passage [*NWS*] (FAAC)
WFP.......... Water for People [*An association*] (EA)
WFP.......... Wearout Failure Period
WFP.......... Wideband Flexibility Point
WFP.......... Witness for Peace (EA)
WFP.......... World Federation of Parasitologists [*Bilthoven, Netherlands*] (EAIO)
WFP.......... World Food Programme [*Rome, Italy*] [*United Nations*]
WFP.......... World Food Programs (EERA)
WFP.......... Worldwide Fast for Peace [*An association Defunct*] (EA)
WFPA......... Fort Payne, AL [*AM radio station call letters*]
WFPA......... Washington Forest Protection Association (EA)
WFPA......... World Federation for the Protection of Animals [*Also known as FMPA, WTB*] [*Later, WSPA*]
WFPB-FM.... Falmouth, MA [*FM radio station call letters*] (RBYB)
WFPC......... Petersburg, IN [*FM radio station call letters*]
WFPC......... Wide Field/Planetary Camera
WFPFC....... Worldwide Fair Play for Frogs Committee (EA)
WFPG......... Atlantic City, NJ [*AM radio station call letters*]
WFPG-FM.... Atlantic City, NJ [*FM radio station call letters*]
WFPHA...... World Federation of Public Health Associations (EA)
WFPIS....... Whole Farm Plan Incentives Scheme [*of Victoria*] (EERA)
WFPK....... Louisville, KY [*FM radio station call letters*]
WFPL....... Louisville, KY [*FM radio station call letters*]
WFPLCA..... World Federation of Pipe Line Contractors Association (EA)
WFPMA..... World Federation of Personnel Management Associations [*Alexandria, VA*] (EA)
WFPMM...... World Federation of Proprietary Medicine Manufacturers
WFPP....... Whole Farm Planning Program [*of Tasmania*] (EERA)
WFPR....... Hammond, LA [*AM radio station call letters*]
WFPS....... Freeport, IL [*FM radio station call letters*]
WFPS....... Wild Flower Preservation Society (EA)
WFPT....... Frederick, MD [*Television station call letters*]
WFPT....... Welsh Figure Preference Test [*Psychology*]
WFPT....... World Federation for Physical Therapy
WFPX....... Fayetteville, NC [*Television station call letters*] (BROA)
WFQS....... Franklin, NC [*FM radio station call letters*]
WFQX....... Front Royal, VA [*FM radio station call letters*]
WFR........ MEMC Electronic Materials [*NYSE symbol*] (TTSB)
WFR........ MEMC Electronic Materials, Inc. [*NYSE symbol*] (SAG)
WFR........ Wafer (MSA)
WFR........ Weight Flow Rate (SAA)
WFR........ Weil-Felix Reaction [*Medicine*] (MAE)
WFR........ Wharf Resources Ltd. [*Toronto Stock Exchange symbol*]
WFR........ Wheal and Flare Reaction [*Immunology*]
WFR........ Wide-Finding RADAR (MCD)
WFR........ Worcestershire and Sherwood Foresters Regiment [*Military unit*] [*British*]
WFRA....... Franklin, PA [*AM radio station call letters*]
WFRA....... Wharf Resources Ltd. [*NASDAQ symbol*] (NQ)
WFRAF...... Wharf Resources Ltd [*NASDAQ symbol*] (TTSB)
WFRA-FM.... Franklin, PA [*FM radio station call letters*]
WFRB....... Frostburg, MD [*AM radio station call letters*]
WFRBC...... Washed, Filtered Red Blood Cells [*Hematology*]
WFRB-FM.... Frostburg, MD [*FM radio station call letters*]
WFRC....... Columbus, GA [*FM radio station call letters*]
WFRC....... Western Fisheries Research Committee [*Australia*]
WFRD....... Hanover, NH [*FM radio station call letters*]
WFRE....... Frederick, MD [*FM radio station call letters*]
WFRG....... Utica, NY [*FM radio station call letters*]
WFRH....... Kingston, NY [*FM radio station call letters*]
WFRJ....... Johnstown, PA [*FM radio station call letters*]
WFRL....... Freeport, IL [*AM radio station call letters*]
WFRM....... Coudersport, PA [*AM radio station call letters*]
WFRM-FM.... Coudersport, PA [*AM radio station call letters*]
WFRN....... Elkhart, IN [*AM radio station call letters*]
WFRN-FM.... Elkhart, IN [*FM radio station call letters*]
WFRO....... Fremont, OH [*AM radio station call letters*]
WFRO-FM.... Fremont, OH [*FM radio station call letters*]
WFRQ....... Waynesboro, TN [*FM radio station call letters*]
WFRR-FM.... Walton, IN [*FM radio station call letters*] (RBYB)
WFRS....... Smithtown, NY [*FM radio station call letters*]
WFRS....... World Federation of Rose Societies [*Hurlingham, Argentina*] (EAIO)
WFRV....... Green Bay, WI [*Television station call letters*]
WFRW....... Webster, NY [*FM radio station call letters*]
WFRX....... West Frankfort, IL [*AM radio station call letters*]
WFRX-FM.... West Frankfort, IL [*FM radio station call letters*]
WFRY-FM.... Watertown, NY [*FM radio station call letters*] (BROA)
WFS........ Waterhouse-Friderichsen Syndrome [*Medicine*]
WFS........ Weapon Fire Simulator (MCD)
WFS........ Welfare Food Service [*British*]
WFS........ Women for Sobriety (EA)
WFS........ Women in Fire Service (EA)
WFS........ Wood Furring Strips [*Technical drawings*]
WFS........ Work Function Surface
WFS........ World Fertility Survey [*Program*]

WFS........ World Food Security [*FAO program*] [*United Nations*]
WFS........ World Future Society (EA)
WFSA....... Wash Frock Salesmen's Association (EA)
WFSA....... Wilhelm Furtwangler Society of America (EA)
WFSA....... World Federation of Societies of Anaesthesiologists [*Bristol, England*] (EAIO)
WFSA....... World Forum on the Future of Sport Shooting Activities
WFSB....... 1st Washington Bancorp [*NASDAQ symbol*] (TTSB)
WFSB....... Hartford, CT [*Television station call letters*]
WFSB....... Washington Federal Savings Bank [*NASDAQ symbol*] (NQ)
WFS Bcp... WFS Bancorp, Inc. [*Associated Press*] (SAG)
WFSBP..... World Federation of the Societies of Biological Psychiatry (EA)
WFSC....... Franklin, NC [*AM radio station call letters*]
WFSE....... Edinboro, PA [*FM radio station call letters*]
WFSEC...... World Fellowship of Slavic Evangelical Christians (EA)
WFSF....... World Futures Studies Federation (EA)
WFS Fn.... WFS Financial, Inc. [*Associated Press*] (SAG)
WFS Fncl... WFS Financial, Inc. [*Associated Press*] (SAG)
WFSG....... Panama City, FL [*Television station call letters*]
WFSG....... Wilshire Financial Services Group, Inc. [*NASDAQ symbol*] (SAG)
WFSGI...... World Federation of the Sporting Goods Industry (EAIO)
WFSH....... Valparaiso-Niceville, FL [*AM radio station call letters*]
WFSI....... Annapolis, MD [*FM radio station call letters*]
WFSI....... WFS Financial [*NASDAQ symbol*] (TTSB)
WFSI....... WFS Financial, Inc. [*NASDAQ symbol*] (SAG)
WFSICCM... World Federation of Societies of Intensive and Critical Care Medicine (EAIO)
WFSJ-FM.... St. Augustine, FL [*FM radio station call letters*] (RBYB)
WFSK....... Nashville, TN [*FM radio station call letters*]
WFSL....... Washington Federal [*NASDAQ symbol*] (TTSB)
WFSL....... Washington Federal Savings & Loan Association of Seattle [*NASDAQ symbol*] (NQ)
WFSN-FM.... Port Charlotte, FL [*FM radio station call letters*] (RBYB)
WFSNSW... Wine and Food Society of New South Wales [*Australia*]
WFSO-FM.... Olivebridge, NY [*FM radio station call letters*] (RBYB)
WFSP....... Kingwood, WV [*AM radio station call letters*]
WFSP-FM.... Kingwood, WV [*FM radio station call letters*]
WFSQ....... Tallahassee, FL [*FM radio station call letters*]
WFSR....... Harlan, KY [*AM radio station call letters*]
WFSS....... Fayetteville, NC [*FM radio station call letters*]
WFSS....... Welsh Folk Song Society [*British*]
WFST....... Caribou, ME [*AM radio station call letters*]
WFSt....... Wehrmachtfuehrungsstab [*Armed Forces Operations Staff*] [*German military - World War II*]
WFSU....... Tallahassee, FL [*FM radio station call letters*]
WFSU-TV.... Tallahassee, FL [*Television station call letters*]
WFSW....... Panama City, FL [*FM radio station call letters*]
WFSW....... World Federation of Scientific Workers [*See also FMTS*] [*ICSU*] [*British*] (EAIO)
WFSY....... Panama City, FL [*FM radio station call letters*]
WFT........ Wafer Fabrication Template (AAEL)
WFT........ Warm Fluctuating Temperatures
WFT........ Weatherford International [*Formerly, EVI Weatherford Industries*] [*NYSE symbol*]
WFT........ West Fraser Timber Co. Ltd. [*Toronto Stock Exchange symbol Vancouver Stock Exchange symbol*]
WFT........ Wildfowl Trust [*British*]
WFTA....... Fulton, MS [*FM radio station call letters*]
WFTA....... Winograd Fourier Transform Algorithm (MCD)
WFTA....... World Federation of Taiwanese Associations (EA)
WFTC....... Minneapolis, MN [*Television station call letters*] (RBYB)
WFTC....... Western Flying Training Command [*AAFWFTC*]
WFTC....... Working Families Tax Credit
WFTD....... Marietta, GA [*AM radio station call letters*]
WFTD....... Women's Flying Training Detachment [*World War II*]
WFTE....... Salem, IN [*Television station call letters*]
WFTF....... Rutland, VT [*FM radio station call letters*]
WFTG....... London, KY [*AM radio station call letters*]
WFTH....... Richmond, VA [*AM radio station call letters*]
WFTI....... St. Petersburg, FL [*FM radio station call letters*]
WFTJW..... World Federation of Travel Journalists and Writers (EA)
WFTK....... Wake Forest, NC [*AM radio station call letters*]
WFTL....... Fort Lauderdale, FL [*AM radio station call letters*]
WFTM....... Maysville, KY [*AM radio station call letters*]
WFTM-FM.... Maysville, KY [*FM radio station call letters*]
WFTN....... Franklin, NH [*AM radio station call letters*]
WFTN-FM.... Franklin, NH [*FM radio station call letters*]
WFTO....... Fulton, MS [*AM radio station call letters*]
WFTP....... Weapons Fly-To Point [*Military*] (CAAL)
WFTR....... Front Royal, VA [*AM radio station call letters*]
WFTR-FM.... Front Royal, VA [*FM radio station call letters*]
WFTS....... Tampa, FL [*Television station call letters*]
WFTS....... Western Fish Toxicology Station [*Environmental Protection Agency*]
W FTTNGS... With Fittings [*Freight*]
WFTU....... World Federation of Trade Unions [*See also FSM*] [*Prague, Czechoslovakia*] (EAIO)
WFTUNMW... World Federation of Trade Unions of Non-Manual Workers [*Belgium*] (EY)
WFTV....... Orlando, FL [*Television station call letters*]
WFTVN...... Women's Film, Television, and Video Network (EAIO)
WFTW....... Fort Walton Beach, FL [*AM radio station call letters*]
WFTX....... Cape Coral, FL [*Television station call letters*]
WFTZ....... Manchester, TN [*FM radio station call letters*]
WFU........ Wake Forest University [*Winston-Salem, NC*]
WFU........ War Frauds Unit

WFUCA .... World Federation of UNESCO Clubs and Associations
WFUL .... West Florida Union List [*Library network*]
WFUM .... Flint, MI [*FM radio station call letters*]
WFUM-TV ...... Flint, MI [*Television station call letters*]
WFUN .... Ashtabula, OH [*AM radio station call letters*]
WFUN .... Bethalto, IL [*FM radio station call letters*]
WFUNA .... World Federation of United Nations Associations (EA)
WFUPA .... World Federation of Ukrainian Patriarchal Associations (EA)
WFUR .... Grand Rapids, MI [*AM radio station call letters*]
WFUR-FM ...... Grand Rapids, MI [*FM radio station call letters*]
WFUV .... New York, NY [*FM radio station call letters*]
WFUWO .... World Federation of Ukrainian Women's Organizations [*Toronto, ON*] (EA)
WFVA .... Fredericksburg, VA [*AM radio station call letters*]
WFVR .... Valdosta, GA [*AM radio station call letters*]
WFVT .... Rock Hill, SC [*Television station call letters*]
WFW .... Walden Forever Wild (EA)
WFW .... Windows for Workgroups [*Microsoft Corp.*]
WFW .... Word for Windows [*Computer science*]
WFWA .... Fort Wayne, IN [*Television station call letters*]
WFWC .... Walden Forever Wild Committee (EA)
WFWG .... Windows for Workgroups [*Microsoft Corp.*]
WFWI .... Fort Wayne, IN [*FM radio station call letters*]
WFWL .... Camden, TN [*AM radio station call letters*]
WFWM .... Frostburg, MD [*FM radio station call letters*]
WFXA .... Augusta, GA [*FM radio station call letters*]
WFXB-TV ...... Myrtle Beach, SC [*TV station call letters*] (RBYB)
WFXC .... Durham, NC [*FM radio station call letters*]
WFXD .... Marquette, MI [*FM radio station call letters*]
WFXE .... Columbus, GA [*FM radio station call letters*]
WFXF-FM ...... Chillicothe, IL [*FM radio station call letters*] (BROA)
WFXG .... Augusta, GA [*Television station call letters*]
WFXH .... Hilton Head Island, SC [*AM radio station call letters*] (RBYB)
WFXH-FM ...... Hilton Head Island, SC [*FM radio station call letters*]
WFXI .... Morehead City, NC [*Television station call letters*]
WFXK .... Tarboro, NC [*FM radio station call letters*]
WFXL .... Albany, GA [*Television station call letters*]
WFXM .... Forsyth, GA [*FM radio station call letters*]
WFXN .... Milton, WV [*FM radio station call letters*] (RBYB)
WFXO .... Iuka, MS [*FM radio station call letters*]
WFXP .... Erie, PA [*Television station call letters*] (RBYB)
WFXQ .... Chase City, VA [*FM radio station call letters*]
WFXR .... Roanoke, VA [*Television station call letters*]
WFXS .... Soddy-Daisy, TN [*FM radio station call letters*]
WFXT .... Boston, MA [*Television station call letters*]
WFXU .... Live Oak, FL [*Television station call letters*]
WFXV .... Utica, NY [*Television station call letters*]
WFXW .... Geneva, IL [*AM radio station call letters*]
WFXX .... South Williamsport, PA [*AM radio station call letters*]
WFXY .... Middlesboro, KY [*AM radio station call letters*]
WFXZ-TV ...... Jacksonville, NC [*TV station call letters*] (RBYB)
WFY .... World Federalist Youth [*Netherlands*]
WFYC .... Alma, MI [*AM radio station call letters*]
WFYI .... Indianapolis, IN [*FM radio station call letters*]
WFYI-TV ...... Indianapolis, IN [*Television station call letters*]
WFYN .... Rocky Mount, VA [*AM radio station call letters*]
WFY/NIO ...... World Federalist Youth - Youth Movement for a New International Order [*Amsterdam, Netherlands*] (EAIO)
WFYR .... Elmwood, IL [*FM radio station call letters*]
WFY-USA ...... World Federalist Youth - United States of America [*Later, Action for World Community: World Federalist Youth in the USA*] (EA)
WFYV .... Atlantic Beach, FL [*FM radio station call letters*]
WFYZ .... Ravenswood, WV [*FM radio station call letters*]
WFZ .... Weapons Free Zone
WFZ .... Wrapped Fracture Zone [*Geology*]
WG .... Grenada [*International vehicle registration*] (ODBW)
WG .... Riker Laboratories Ltd. [*Research code symbol*] [*British*]
WG .... Wage Garnishment (MHDB)
WG .... Wage Grade [*Federal employee job classification*]
WG .... Wartime Guidance [*Air Force*] (AFM)
WG .... Waste Gas [*Nuclear energy*] (NRCH)
WG .... Water Gauge
W/G .... Water Glycol (KSC)
WG .... Waveguide
WG .... Weather Group [*Air Force*]
WG .... Wedge (MSA)
WG .... Wegener's Granulomatosis [*Medicine*]
WG .... Weighing (ROG)
WG .... Weight Guaranteed
WG .... Welsh Guards [*Military unit*] [*British*]
WG .... West German
WG .... Wilcox & Gibbs (EFIS)
WG .... Window Guard (AAG)
WG .... Wine Gallon
WG .... Wing
Wg .... Wing (MUSM)
WG .... Wired Glass [*Technical drawings*]
WG .... Wire Gauge
WG .... With Grain
WG .... Women for Guatemala (EA)
WG .... Working Group
WG .... World Goodwill (EA)
WG .... Wright-Giemsa [*A stain*] [*Cytology*]
WG .... Write Gate (MHDB)
WG .... Writing [*Law*] (ROG)
WGA .... Wagga Wagga [*Australia Airport symbol*] (OAG)
WGA .... Waveguide Assembly
WGA .... Weekly Government Abstracts [*National Technical Information Service*]
WGA .... Weighted Guidelines Analysis [*Air Force*] (MCD)
WGA .... Wells-Gardner Electr [*AMEX symbol*] (TTSB)
WGA .... Wells-Gardner Electronics Corp. [*AMEX symbol*] (SPSG)
WGA .... Western Golf Association (EA)
WGA .... Western Growers Association (EA)
WGA .... Wharton Graduate Association
WGA .... Wheat Germ Agglutinin [*Biochemistry*]
WGA .... Wild Goose Association (EA)
WGA .... Women Grocers of America (EA)
WGA .... Working Group of Agriculture (EERA)
WGA .... Writers Guild of Alberta [*Canada*] (WWLA)
WGA .... Writers Guild of America, West (EA)
WGAA .... Cedartown, GA [*AM radio station call letters*]
WGAB .... Newburgh, IN [*AM radio station call letters*]
WGAC .... Augusta, GA [*AM radio station call letters*]
WGAD .... Gadsden, AL [*AM radio station call letters*]
WGAE .... Writers Guild of America, East (EA)
WGAE-US ...... World Government of the Age of Enlightenment - US (EA)
WGAF .... West Germany Air Force
WGAI .... Elizabeth City, NC [*AM radio station call letters*]
WGAI .... Working Group Agenda Item (SAA)
WGAJ .... Deerfield, MA [*FM radio station call letters*]
WGAL .... Lancaster, PA [*Television station call letters*]
WGAM .... Greenfield, MA [*AM radio station call letters*]
WGAM .... Working Group on Antarctic Meteorology [*Marine science*] (OSRA)
WGAN .... Portland, ME [*AM radio station call letters*]
WG & L .... Warren, Gorham & Lamont, Inc. [*Publisher*]
WGAO .... Franklin, MA [*FM radio station call letters*]
WGAO .... World Guide to Abbreviations of Organizations [*A publication*]
WGAP .... Maryville, TN [*AM radio station call letters*]
WGAP-FM ...... Maryville, TN [*FM radio station call letters*]
WGAR .... Cleveland, OH [*FM radio station call letters*]
WGARCR ...... Working Group against Racism in Children's Resources (AIE)
WGAS .... South Gastonia, NC [*AM radio station call letters*]
WGAS .... Wholesale Grocers' Association of Scotland (DBA)
WGAT .... Gate City, VA [*AM radio station call letters*]
WGAU .... Athens, GA [*AM radio station call letters*]
WGAW .... Gardner, MA [*AM radio station call letters*]
WGAW .... Writers Guild of America, West (EA)
WGAw .... Writers Guild of America, West (NTPA)
WGAY-FM ...... Washington, DC [*FM radio station call letters*] (RBYB)
WGAZ .... Goodman, WI [*FM radio station call letters*]
WGB .... Weltgewerkschaftsbund [*World Federation of Trade Unions*]
WGBA .... Green Bay, WI [*Television station call letters*]
WGBB .... Freeport, NY [*AM radio station call letters*]
WGBC .... Meridian, MS [*Television station call letters*]
WGBC .... Waveguide Operating below Cutoff (IEEE)
WGBD .... Attica, IN [*FM radio station call letters*]
WGBE-FM ...... Bryan, OH [*FM radio station call letters*] (RBYB)
WGBF .... Evansville, IN [*AM radio station call letters*] (RBYB)
WGBF .... Henderson, KY [*FM radio station call letters*]
WGBH .... Boston, MA [*FM radio station call letters*]
WGBH-TV ...... Boston, MA [*Television station call letters*]
WGBI .... Scranton, PA [*AM radio station call letters*]
WGBK-FM ...... Glenview, IL [*FM radio station call letters*] (BROA)
WGBM .... Mishicot, WI [*FM radio station call letters*]
WGBN .... New Kensington, PA [*AM radio station call letters*]
WGBO .... Joliet, IL [*Television station call letters*]
WGBQ .... Galesburg, IL [*FM radio station call letters*]
WGBR .... Goldsboro, NC [*AM radio station call letters*]
WGBS .... Philadelphia, PA [*Television station call letters*]
WGBV-FM ...... Glasgow, KY [*FM radio station call letters*] (BROA)
WGBW .... Green Bay, WI [*FM radio station call letters*]
WGBX .... Boston, MA [*Television station call letters*]
WGBY .... Springfield, MA [*Television station call letters*]
WGc .... Genoa City Public Library, Genoa City, WI [*Library symbol Library of Congress*] (LCLS)
WGC .... Waste Gas Compressor [*Nuclear energy*] (NRCH)
WGC .... Waveguide Shutter
WGC .... Western Gear Corp.
WGC .... Western Governors Conference
WGC .... West Georgia College [*Carollton*]
WGC .... Winslow Gold Corp. [*Vancouver Stock Exchange symbol*]
WGC .... World Games Council (EAIO)
WGC .... World Golf Championship
WGC .... World Gospel Crusades (EA)
WGC .... Worthy Grand Chaplain [*Freemasonry*]
WGC .... Worthy Grand Conductor [*Freemasonry*] (ROG)
WGCA .... Quincy, IL [*FM radio station call letters*]
WGCA .... Winegrape Growers' Council of Australia
WGCA .... Wisconsin Gift Cheese Association (EA)
WGCB .... Red Lion, PA [*AM radio station call letters*]
WGCB-FM ...... Red Lion, PA [*FM radio station call letters*]
WGCB-TV ...... Red Lion, PA [*Television station call letters*]
WGCC .... World Games Coordination Committee [*Karsruhe, Federal Republic of Germany*] (EAIO)
WGCCD .... Working Group on Climate Change Detection [*Marine science*] (OSRA)
WGCC-FM ...... Batavia, NY [*FM radio station call letters*]
WGCD-AM ...... Chester, SC [*AM radio station call letters*] (BROA)
WG/CDR ...... Wing Commander [*British military*] (NATG)

WGCDR........ Working Group for Community Development Reform [*Defunct*] (EA)
WGCF-FM.... Paducah, KY [*FM radio station call letters*] (RBYB)
WGCH.......... Greenwich, CT [*AM radio station call letters*]
WGCI.......... Chicago, IL [*AM radio station call letters*]
WGCI-FM..... Chicago, IL [*FM radio station call letters*]
WGCL.......... Bloomington, IN [*AM radio station call letters*]
WGCL.......... Window Glass Cutters League of America [*Later, GBBA*] (EA)
WGCM.......... Gulfport, MS [*AM radio station call letters*]
Wg Cmdr..... Wing Commander [*British military*] (DMA)
WGCM-FM.... Gulfport, MS [*FM radio station call letters*]
WGCO.......... Midway, GA [*FM radio station call letters*]
WGCQ.......... Immokalee, FL [*FM radio station call letters*] (RBYB)
WGCR.......... Brevard, NC [*AM radio station call letters*]
Wg Cr......... Wing Commander [*British military*] (DMA)
WGCS.......... Goshen, IN [*FM radio station call letters*]
WGCT.......... Ellettsville, IN [*FM radio station call letters*]
WGCTA........ Watson-Glaser Critical Thinking Appraisal (EDAC)
WGCU-TV.... Fort Myers, FL [*TV station call letters*] (RBYB)
WGCV.......... Petersburg, VA [*AM radio station call letters*]
WGCX.......... Fairhope, AL [*FM radio station call letters*]
WGCY.......... Gibson City, IL [*FM radio station call letters*]
WGD............ Windshield Guidance Display
WGD............ Working Group Director
WGD............ Working Group on Data (USDC)
WGD............ Worldwide Government Directory [*A publication*]
WGDA.......... Watermelon Growers and Distributors Association
WGDC.......... Waveguide Directional Coupler
WGDC.......... Working Group for Democracy in Chile (EA)
WGDE-FM.... Defiance, OH [*FM radio station call letters*] (BROA)
WGDHP........ Working Group on Domestic Hunger and Poverty (EA)
WGDL.......... Lares, PR [*AM radio station call letters*]
WGDL.......... Waveguide Delay Line
WGDN.......... Gladwin, MI [*AM radio station call letters*]
WGDN-FM.... Gladwin, MI [*FM radio station call letters*]
WGDR.......... Plainfield, VT [*FM radio station call letters*]
WGDS.......... Warm Gas Distribution System
WGDS.......... Waste Gas Disposal System [*Nuclear energy*] (NRCH)
WGDT.......... Waste Gas Decay Tank [*Nuclear energy*] (NRCH)
WGE............ Walgett [*Australia Airport symbol*] (OAG)
WGE............ World's Great Explorers [*A publication*]
WGEA.......... Geneva, AL [*AM radio station call letters*]
WGEE.......... Green Bay, WI [*AM radio station call letters*]
WGEE.......... Sturgeon Bay, WI [*FM radio station call letters*]
WGEEIA...... Western Ground Electronics Engineering Installation Agency (AAG)
WGEIO........ World Guide to Environmental Issues [*A publication*]
WGEL.......... Greenville, IL [*FM radio station call letters*]
WGEM.......... Quincy, IL [*AM radio station call letters*]
WGEM-FM.... Quincy, IL [*FM radio station call letters*]
WGEM-TV.... Quincy, IL [*Television station call letters*]
WGEN.......... Geneseo, IL [*AM radio station call letters*]
WGEN.......... Watson General Corp. [*NASDAQ symbol*] (SPSG)
WGEN-FM.... Geneseo, IL [*FM radio station call letters*]
WGER.......... Saginaw, MI [*FM radio station call letters*]
W GER........ West Germany (WDAA)
WGER.......... Working Group on Extraterrestrial Resources [*Defunct NASA*]
WGES.......... Oswego, NY [*FM radio station call letters*]
WGES.......... World's Greatest Environment Statement (EERA)
WGET.......... Gettysburg, PA [*AM radio station call letters*]
WGETS........ Wayne George Encoder Test Set
WGEV.......... Beaver Falls, PA [*FM radio station call letters*]
WGEZ.......... Beloit, WI [*AM radio station call letters*]
WGF............ Waveguide Filter
WGF............ Western Goals Foundation (EA)
WGF............ Women's Gas Federation [*British*] (BI)
WGF............ Wound Glass Fiber
WGFA.......... Watseka, IL [*AM radio station call letters*]
WGFA-FM.... Watseka, IL [*FM radio station call letters*]
WGFAR........ Wenner-Gren Foundation for Anthropological Research (EA)
WGFB.......... Plattsburgh, NY [*FM radio station call letters*]
WGFC.......... Floyd, VA [*AM radio station call letters*]
WGFD.......... Wyoming Game and Fish Department
WGFG.......... Branchville, SC [*FM radio station call letters*]
WGFL.......... High Springs, FL [*Television station call letters*]
WGFM.......... Cheboygan, MI [*FM radio station call letters*]
WGFN.......... Glen Arbor, MI [*FM radio station call letters*]
WGFP.......... Webster, MA [*AM radio station call letters*]
WGFR.......... Glens Falls, NY [*FM radio station call letters*]
WGFS.......... Covington, GA [*AM radio station call letters*]
WGFT.......... Youngstown, OH [*AM radio station call letters*]
WGFX.......... Gallatin, TN [*FM radio station call letters*]
WGG............ Warm Gas Generator
WGG............ Worthy Grand Guardian [*Freemasonry*]
WGG............ Worthy Grand Guide [*Freemasonry*]
WGGA.......... Gainesville, GA [*AM radio station call letters*]
WGGB.......... Springfield, MA [*Television station call letters*]
WGGB.......... Writers' Guild of Great Britain (DCTA)
WGGC.......... Glasgow, KY [*FM radio station call letters*]
WGGD.......... Melbourne, FL [*FM radio station call letters*]
WGGG.......... Gainesville, FL [*AM radio station call letters*]
WG-GGI...... Working Group on Geodesy and Geographic Information (EERA)
WGGH.......... Marion, IL [*AM radio station call letters*]
WGGI-FM..... Benton, PA [*FM radio station call letters*] (BROA)
WGGL.......... Houghton, MI [*FM radio station call letters*]
WGGM.......... Chester, VA [*AM radio station call letters*]
WGGN.......... Castalia, OH [*FM radio station call letters*]
WGGN.......... Sandusky, OH [*Television station call letters*]
WGGO.......... Salamanca, NY [*AM radio station call letters*]
WGGR.......... Greenwood, IN [*FM radio station call letters*]
WGGS.......... Greenville, SC [*Television station call letters*]
WGGT.......... Greensboro, NC [*Television station call letters*]
WGGY.......... Scranton, PA [*FM radio station call letters*]
WGGZ.......... Baton Rouge, LA [*FM radio station call letters*]
WGH............ Newport News, VA [*AM radio station call letters*]
WGH............ Warren Gamaliel Harding [*US president, 1865-1923*]
WGH............ Worthy Grand Herald [*Freemasonry*]
WGHB.......... Farmville, NC [*AM radio station call letters*]
WGHC.......... Clayton, GA [*AM radio station call letters*]
WGH-FM...... Newport News, VA [*FM radio station call letters*]
WGHI.......... Westmark Group Hldgs [*NASDAQ symbol*] (TTSB)
WGHI.......... Westmark Group Holdings, Inc. [*NASDAQ symbol*] (SAG)
WGHN.......... Grand Haven, MI [*AM radio station call letters*]
WGHN-FM.... Grand Haven, MI [*FM radio station call letters*]
WGHP.......... High Point, NC [*Television station call letters*]
WGHQ.......... Kingston, NY [*AM radio station call letters*]
WGHR.......... Marietta, GA [*FM radio station call letters*]
WGHT.......... Pompton Lakes, NJ [*AM radio station call letters*]
WGHT.......... Weight
WGI............ Waveguide Isolator
WGI............ Western Goldfields, Inc. [*Toronto Stock Exchange symbol*]
WGI............ Within-Grade Increase
WGI............ Word of God Institute [*Later, NIWG*] (EA)
WGI............ Work Glove Institute [*Later, WGMA*] (EA)
WGI............ World Geophysical Interval
WGI............ World Glacier Inventory (EERA)
WGIA.......... Blackshear, GA [*AM radio station call letters*]
WGIB.......... Birmingham, AL [*FM radio station call letters*]
WGIC.......... Wheat Gluten Industry Council (EA)
WGIC-FM..... Cookeville, TN [*FM radio station call letters*] (BROA)
WGIG.......... Brunswick, GA [*AM radio station call letters*]
WGII.......... Working Group on Internal Instrumentation [*NASA*]
WGIL.......... Galesburg, IL [*AM radio station call letters*]
WGINC........ Wine Grape Industry Negotiating Committee [*Victoria, Australia*]
WGIQ.......... Louisville, AL [*Television station call letters*]
WGIR.......... Manchester, NH [*AM radio station call letters*]
WGIR-FM..... Manchester, NH [*FM radio station call letters*]
WGIV-AM..... Charlotte, NC [*AM radio station call letters*] (BROA)
WGIX.......... Gouverneur, NY [*FM radio station call letters*]
WGJ............ Worm Gear Jack
WGJB.......... World's Greatest Jazz Band
WGK............ Wasser Gefahrdungsklasse [*Water hazard classification*] [*Germany*]
WGKA.......... Atlanta, GA [*AM radio station call letters*]
WGKC-FM.... Mahomet, IL [*FM radio station call letters*] (RBYB)
WGKI.......... Cadillac, MI [*Television station call letters*]
WGKP-FM.... Bensselaerville, NY [*FM radio station call letters*] (RBYB)
WGKR-FM.... Grand Gorge, NY [*FM radio station call letters*] (RBYB)
WGKS.......... Paris, KY [*FM radio station call letters*]
WGKU.......... Vanderbilt, MI [*Television station call letters*]
WGKX.......... Memphis, TN [*FM radio station call letters*]
WGKY.......... Wickliffe, KY [*FM radio station call letters*]
WGL............ Fort Wayne, IN [*AM radio station call letters*]
WGL............ Roanoke, IN [*FM radio station call letters*]
WGL............ Warangal [*India*] [*Seismograph station code, US Geological Survey*] (SEIS)
WGL............ Washington Gas Light Co. [*NYSE symbol*] (SPSG)
WGL............ Washington Gas Lt [*NYSE symbol*] (TTSB)
WGL............ Waveguide Load
WGL............ Weapons Guidance Laboratory
WGL............ Weighted Guidelines [*DoD*]
WGL............ Westar Group Ltd. [*Toronto Stock Exchange symbol Vancouver Stock Exchange symbol*]
WGL............ Western Guidance Laboratory [*Wright Air Development Center*] (MUGU)
WGL............ Westeuropaeische Gesellschaft fuer Luftfahrtpsychologie [*Western European Association for Aviation Psychology - WEAAP*] (EA)
WGL............ Wire Glass (AAG)
WGL............ Wire Grid Lens
WGL............ World Guide to Libraries [*A publication*]
WGL............ Wueste und Gelobtes Land [*A publication*] (BJA)
W GLAM...... West Glamorgan [*County in Wales*]
WGLB.......... Port Washington, WI [*AM radio station call letters*]
WGLB-FM.... Port Washington, WI [*FM radio station call letters*]
WGLC.......... Mendota, IL [*AM radio station call letters*]
WGLC-FM.... Mendota, IL [*FM radio station call letters*]
WGLD-FM.... Noblesville, IN [*FM radio station call letters*] (RBYB)
WGLE.......... Lima, OH [*FM radio station call letters*]
WGLF.......... Tallahassee, FL [*FM radio station call letters*]
WGLH.......... La Follette, TN [*AM radio station call letters*] (RBYB)
WGLI.......... Babylon, NY [*AM radio station call letters*]
WGLI.......... Warren, Gorham & Lamont, Inc. (DLA)
WGLL.......... Auburn, IN [*FM radio station call letters*] (RBYB)
WGLM.......... West Lafayette, IN [*FM radio station call letters*]
WGLO.......... Pekin, IL [*FM radio station call letters*]
WGLQ.......... Escanaba, MI [*FM radio station call letters*]
WGLR.......... Lancaster, WI [*AM radio station call letters*]
WGLR.......... Wissenschaftliche Gesellschaft fuer Luft- und Raumfahrt [*Scientific Association for Air and Space Travel*] [*German*]
WGLR-FM.... Lancaster, WI [*FM radio station call letters*]
WGLS.......... Glassboro, NJ [*FM radio station call letters*]
WGLS.......... Weighted Guidelines System (AAGC)
WGLT.......... Normal, IL [*FM radio station call letters*]

WGLU	Johnstown, PA [*FM radio station call letters*]
WGLV	Hartford, VT [*FM radio station call letters*]
WGLW	Welsh Grand Lodge of Wales [*Freemasonry*]
WGLX	Wisconsin Rapids, WI [*FM radio station call letters*]
WGLY	Waterbury, VT [*FM radio station call letters*]
WGLZ	West Liberty, WV [*FM radio station call letters*]
WGM	Waveguide Meter
WGM	Weighted Guidelines Method [*Navy*]
WGM	Wilmington [*California*] [*Airport symbol*] (AD)
WGM	World Gospel Mission (EA)
WGM	Worthy Grand Marshal [*or Master*] [*Freemasonry*]
WGMA	Spindale, NC [*AM radio station call letters*]
WGMA	Washington Gallery of Modern Art
WGMA	West Gulf Maritime Association (EA)
WGMA	Wet Ground Mica Association [*Defunct*] (EA)
WGMA	Work Glove Manufacturers Association (EA)
WGMA	Working Group on Multilateral Assistance [*Department of the Treasury*]
WGMB	Baton Rouge, LA [*Television station call letters*]
WGMC	Greece, NY [*FM radio station call letters*]
WGMC	West Germanic [*Language, etc.*]
WGMD	Rehoboth Beach, DE [*FM radio station call letters*]
WGME	Portland, ME [*Television station call letters*]
WGMF	Watkins Glen, NY [*AM radio station call letters*]
WGMG	Crawford, GA [*FM radio station call letters*]
WGMI	Bremen, GA [*AM radio station call letters*]
WGMK	Donalsonville, GA [*FM radio station call letters*]
WGML	Hinesville, GA [*AM radio station call letters*]
WGMM	Big Flats, NY [*FM radio station call letters*]
WGMO	Shell Lake, WI [*FM radio station call letters*]
WGMP	Philadelphia, PA [*AM radio station call letters*]
WGMR	Tyrone, PA [*FM radio station call letters*]
WGMS	Washington, DC [*FM radio station call letters*]
WGMS	Working Group on Marine Sediments [*Marine science*] (OSRA)
WGMS	World Glacier Monitoring Service [*of the International Union of Geodesy and Geophysics*] (EA)
WGMT	Lyndon, VT [*FM radio station call letters*]
WGMX	Marathon, FL [*FM radio station call letters*]
WGMY-AM	South Haven, MI [*AM radio station call letters*] (BROA)
WGMZ	Glencoe, AL [*Department of Commerce*]
WGN	Chicago, IL [*AM radio station call letters*]
WGN	Wagon
WGN	White Gaussian Noise [*Random interference caused by movement of electricity in line*] [*Telecommunications*] (IAA)
WGN	World's Greatest Newspaper [*Sometimes used in reference to Chicago Tribune*]
WGNA	Albany, NY [*AM radio station call letters*]
WGNA-FM	Albany, NY [*FM radio station call letters*]
WGNB	Zeeland, MI [*FM radio station call letters*]
WGNC	Gastonia, NC [*AM radio station call letters*]
WGNE	Panama City, FL [*AM radio station call letters*]
WGNE	Titusville, FL [*FM radio station call letters*]
WGNE	Working Group on Numerical Experimentation [*Marine science*] (OSRA)
WGNI	Wilmington, NC [*FM radio station call letters*]
WGNL	Greenwood, MS [*FM radio station call letters*]
WGNL	Waveguide Nitrogen Load
WGNM	Macon, GA [*Television station call letters*]
WGNN-FM	Fisher, IL [*FM radio station call letters*] (RBYB)
WGNO	New Orleans, LA [*Television station call letters*]
WGNP	Albany, GA [*FM radio station call letters*]
WGNR	Monee, IL [*FM radio station call letters*]
WGNR	Wegener Corp. [*NASDAQ symbol*] (NQ)
WGNRR	Women's Global Network on Reproductive Rights [*Formerly, International Contraception, Abortion, and Sterilisation Campaign*] (EA)
WGNS	Murfreesboro, TN [*AM radio station call letters*]
WGNT	Portsmouth, VA [*Television station call letters*]
WGN-TV	Chicago, IL [*Television station call letters*]
WGNU	Granite City, IL [*AM radio station call letters*]
WGNV	Milladore, WI [*FM radio station call letters*]
WGNX	Atlanta, GA [*Television station call letters*]
WGNY	Newburgh, NY [*AM radio station call letters*]
WGNY-FM	Newburgh, NY [*FM radio station call letters*]
WGNZ	Fairborn, OH [*AM radio station call letters*]
WGO	Wehrmacht Graeberoffizier [*Armed forces graves registration officer*] [*German military - World War II*]
Wg O	Wing Officer [*British military*] (DMA)
WGO	Winnebago Indus [*NYSE symbol*] (TTSB)
WGO	Winnebago Industries, Inc. [*NYSE symbol*] (SPSG)
WGOC	Blountville, TN [*AM radio station call letters*]
WGOC	World Government Organization Coalition (EAIO)
WGOCC	World Government Organization Coordinating Council [*Later, WGOC*] (EA)
WGOD	Charlotte Amalie, VI [*AM radio station call letters*]
WGOD-FM	Charlotte Amalie, VI [*FM radio station call letters*]
Wg Offr	Wing Officer [*British military*] (DMA)
WGOG	Walhalla, SC [*AM radio station call letters*]
WGOG-FM	Walhalla, SC [*FM radio station call letters*]
WGOH	Grayson, KY [*AM radio station call letters*]
WGOJ	Conneaut, OH [*FM radio station call letters*]
WGOK	Mobile, AL [*AM radio station call letters*]
WGOL	Lynchburg, VA [*FM radio station call letters*]
WGOM	Marion, IN [*AM radio station call letters*]
WGOR	Martinez, GA [*FM radio station call letters*]

WGOS	High Point, NC [*AM radio station call letters*]
WGOT	Merrimack, NH [*Television station call letters*]
WGOT	Williams Grove Old Timers [*An association*] (EA)
WGOV	Valdosta, GA [*AM radio station call letters*]
WGOW	Chattanooga, TN [*AM radio station call letters*]
WGOW-FM	Soddy-Daisy, TN [*FM radio station call letters*] (BROA)
WGOX	Inverness, FL [*Television station call letters*]
WGP	Waingapu [*Indonesia*] [*Airport symbol*] (OAG)
WGP	Wattle Grove Press
WGp	Weather Group [*Air Force*] (AFM)
WGP	Westgrowth Petroleums Ltd. [*Toronto Stock Exchange symbol*]
WGP	William Grand Prix Racing Ltd. [*Cayman Islands*] [*ICAO designator*] (FAAC)
WGP	Wire Grid Polarizer
WGPA	Bethlehem, PA [*AM radio station call letters*]
WGPC	Albany, GA [*AM radio station call letters*]
WGPC-FM	Albany, GA [*FM radio station call letters*]
WGPH	Vidalia, GA [*FM radio station call letters*]
WGPL-AM	Portsmouth, VA [*AM radio station call letters*] (RBYB)
WGPM-FM	Farmville, NC [*FM radio station call letters*] (RBYB)
WGPMS	Warehousing Gross Performance Measurement System (AFM)
WGPR	Detroit, MI [*FM radio station call letters*]
WGPR-TV	Detroit, MI [*Television station call letters*]
WGPT	Oakland, MD [*Television station call letters*]
WGPTDR	Danube Tourist Commission [*Formerly, Working Group for the Promotion of Tourism in the Danube Region*] [*Austria*] (EAIO)
WGPX	Burlington, NC [*Television station call letters*] (BROA)
WGQR	Elizabethtown, NC [*FM radio station call letters*]
WGr	Brown County Library, Green Bay, WI [*Library symbol Library of Congress*] (LCLS)
WGR	Buffalo, NY [*AM radio station call letters*]
WGR	War Guidance Requirements (AFM)
WGR	Water Graphite Reactor Experiment [*Nuclear energy*]
WGR	Westbridge Resources Ltd. [*Vancouver Stock Exchange symbol*]
WGR	Western Gas Resources [*NYSE symbol*] (SPSG)
WGR	Women in Government Relations (EA)
WGR	Working Group Report
WGRA	Cairo, GA [*AM radio station call letters*]
WGRA	Worksheet Global Recalculation Automatic [*Computer science*]
WGrB	Bellin Memorial Hospital, Green Bay, WI [*Library symbol Library of Congress*] (LCLS)
WGRB	Campbellsville, KY [*Television station call letters*]
WGrBC	Brown County Hospital, Green Bay, WI [*Library symbol Library of Congress*] (LCLS)
WGRC	Lewisburg, PA [*FM radio station call letters*]
WGRD	Grand Rapids, MI [*AM radio station call letters*]
WGRD	Working Group on Rural Development [*Department of Agriculture*] (EGAO)
WGRD-FM	Grand Rapids, MI [*FM radio station call letters*]
WGRE	Greencastle, IN [*FM radio station call letters*]
WGREPO	Western Governors Regional Energy Policy Office
WGRF	Buffalo, NY [*FM radio station call letters*]
WGRF	Working Group on Radiation Fluxes [*Marine science*] (OSRA)
WGRG	Owego, NY [*FM radio station call letters*]
WGRIDA	World GRID Association (EA)
WGRI-FM	Flint, MI [*FM radio station call letters*] (BROA)
WGRK	Greensburg, KY [*FM radio station call letters*]
WGRL	Indianapolis, IN [*FM radio station call letters*]
WGRM	Greenwood, MS [*AM radio station call letters*]
WGRM-FM	Greenwood, MS [*FM radio station call letters*]
WGRN	Greenville, IL [*FM radio station call letters*]
WGrN	Northeastern Wisconsin Technical Institute, Green Bay, WI [*Library symbol Library of Congress*] (LCLS)
WGrnbg	Greenburg [*William*] Jr. Desserts & Cafes, Inc. [*Associated Press*] (SAG)
WGrNM	Neville Public Museum, Green Bay, WI [*Library symbol Library of Congress*] (LCLS)
WGRO	Lake City, FL [*AM radio station call letters*]
WGRP	Greenville, PA [*AM radio station call letters*]
WGRPr	Western Gas Res $2.28 cm Pfd [*NYSE symbol*] (TTSB)
WGRPrA	Western Gas Res $2.625 Cv Pfd [*NYSE symbol*] (TTSB)
WGRQ	Colonial Beach, VA [*FM radio station call letters*]
WGRR	Hamilton, OH [*FM radio station call letters*]
WGRS	Guilford, CT [*FM radio station call letters*]
WGrSM	Saint Mary's Hospital, Green Bay, WI [*Library symbol Library of Congress*] (LCLS)
WGrSV	Saint Vincent Hospital, Green Bay, WI [*Library symbol Library of Congress*] (LCLS)
WGRT-FM	Port Huron, MI [*FM radio station call letters*] (RBYB)
WGrU	University of Wisconsin-Green Bay, Green Bay, WI [*Library symbol Library of Congress*] (LCLS)
WGRV	Greeneville, TN [*AM radio station call letters*]
WGrw	Greenwood Public Library, Greenwood, WI [*Library symbol*] [*Library of Congress*] (LCLS)
WGRW-FM	Anniston, AL [*FM radio station call letters*] (RBYB)
WGRX	Westminster, MD [*FM radio station call letters*]
WGRY	Grayling, MI [*AM radio station call letters*]
WGRY-FM	Grayling, MI [*FM radio station call letters*] (RBYB)
WGRZ	Buffalo, NY [*Television station call letters*]
WG(S)	Waste Gas (System) [*Nuclear energy*] (NRCH)
WGS	Waterford Generating Station [*Nuclear energy*] (NRCH)
WGS	Water Gas Shift [*Chemical reaction*]
WGS	Water Glycol Service Unit (MCD)
WGS	Waveguide Glide Slope
WGS	Weatherall Green Smith [*British*] (ECON)

WGS	Web Guide System
WGS	Work Group System [*Computer hardware*] (PCM)
WGS	World Geodetic System (MUGU)
WGS	World Government Sponsors
WGS	Worthy Grand Sentinel [*Freemasonry*]
WGS84	World Geodetic Spheroid 1984 (EERA)
WGSA	Working Group on Sustainable Agriculture [*Australia*]
WGSAT	Working Group on Satellites [*Marine science*] (OSRA)
WGSD	Mebane, NC [*AM radio station call letters*]
WGSC	War Gaming and Simulation Center [*National Defense University*]
WGSC	Wide Gap Spark Chamber [*Electronics*] (OA)
WGSE	Myrtle Beach, SC [*Television station call letters*]
WGSF	Bartlett, TN [*AM radio station call letters*] (RBYB)
WGSG	Mayo, FL [*FM radio station call letters*]
WGSI	Working Group on Sea Ice [*Marine science*] (OSRA)
WGSIM	Working Group on Satellite Ionospheric Measurements [*NASA*]
WGSJ	Worm Gear Screw Jack
WGSK	South Kent, CT [*FM radio station call letters*]
WGSL	Loves Park, IL [*FM radio station call letters*]
WGSM	Huntington, NY [*AM radio station call letters*]
WGSN	North Myrtle Beach, SC [*AM radio station call letters*]
WGSO	New Orleans, LA [*AM radio station call letters*]
WGSP	Charlotte, NC [*AM radio station call letters*]
WGSPR	Working Group for Space Physics Research
WGSQ	Cookeville, TN [*FM radio station call letters*]
WGSS-FM	Kingstree, SC [*FM radio station call letters*] (RBYB)
WGST	Atlanta, GA [*AM radio station call letters*]
WGST	Canton, GA [*FM radio station call letters*]
WGST	Waste Gas Storage Tank [*Nuclear energy*] (IEEE)
WGSU	Geneseo, NY [*FM radio station call letters*]
WGSV	Guntersville, AL [*AM radio station call letters*]
WGSY	Phenix City, AL [*FM radio station call letters*]
WGT	Water-Glycol Cooling Unit Technician (SAA)
WGT	Wayne General and Technical College, Orrville, OH [*Inactive*] [*OCLC symbol*] (OCLC)
WGT	Weapons Guidance and Tracking (SAA)
WGT	Weight [*Shipping*] (DS)
wgt	Weight (DAVI)
WGT	Wet Globe Temperature (PDAA)
WGTA	Summerville, GA [*AM radio station call letters*]
WGTA	Wisconsin General Test Apparatus [*Psychology*]
WGTC	New Carlisle, IN [*FM radio station call letters*]
WG-T-C	Waveguide-to-Coaxial [*Aerospace*] (AAG)
WGTC	Working Group on Tracking and Computation [*NASA*]
WGT/COMB..	Weighter/Combiner (MCD)
WGTD	Kenosha, WI [*FM radio station call letters*]
WGTE	Toledo, OH [*FM radio station call letters*]
WGTE-TV	Toledo, OH [*Television station call letters*]
WGTF	Dothan, AL [*FM radio station call letters*]
WGTH	Richlands, VA [*AM radio station call letters*] (RBYB)
WGTH-FM	Richlands, VA [*FM radio station call letters*]
WGTI	Wandel & Goltermann Tech [*NASDAQ symbol*] (TTSB)
WGTI	Wandel & Goltermann Technologies [*NASDAQ symbol*] (SAG)
WGTK	Middlebury, VT [*FM radio station call letters*]
WGTM	Wilson, NC [*AM radio station call letters*]
WGTN	Andrews, SC [*FM radio station call letters*]
WGTN	Georgetown, SC [*AM radio station call letters*]
WGTO	Cassopolis, MI [*AM radio station call letters*] (RBYB)
WGTQ	Sault Ste. Marie, MI [*Television station call letters*]
WGTR	Bucksport, SC [*FM radio station call letters*]
WGTS	Takoma Park, MD [*FM radio station call letters*]
WGTT	Alabaster, AL [*AM radio station call letters*]
WGTU	Traverse City, MI [*Television station call letters*]
WGTV	Athens, GA [*Television station call letters*]
WGTW	Burlington, NJ [*Television station call letters*]
WGTX-AM	Freeport, FL [*AM radio station call letters*] (RBYB)
WGTY	Gettysburg, PA [*FM radio station call letters*]
WGTZ	Eaton, OH [*FM radio station call letters*]
WGU	Western Governors University
WGU	Working Group on Untouchables (EA)
WGUC	Cincinnati, OH [*FM radio station call letters*]
WGUF	Marco, FL [*FM radio station call letters*]
WGUL	Dunedin, FL [*AM radio station call letters*]
WGUL-FM	Dade City, FL [*FM radio station call letters*] (RBYB)
WGUN	Atlanta, GA [*AM radio station call letters*]
WGUR-FM	Milledgeville, GA [*FM radio station call letters*] (BROA)
WGUS	North Augusta, SC [*AM radio station call letters*]
WGUSEASA..	Working Group of US Overseas Educational Advisers in South America [*Defunct*] (EA)
WGUY	Dexter, ME [*FM radio station call letters*]
WGVA	Geneva, NY [*AM radio station call letters*]
WGVE	Gary, IN [*FM radio station call letters*]
WGVK	Kalamazoo, MI [*Television station call letters*]
WGVL-AM	Greenville, SC [*AM radio station call letters*] (RBYB)
WGVM	Greenville, MS [*AM radio station call letters*]
WGVP	Valdosta, GA [*Television station call letters*]
WGVU	Allendale, MI [*FM radio station call letters*]
WGVU	Grand Rapids, MI [*Television station call letters*]
WGVU	Kentwood, MI [*AM radio station call letters*]
WGW	Wallila Gap [*Washington*] [*Seismograph station code, US Geological Survey*] (SEIS)
WGW	Waveguide Window
WGW	Wedgewood Resources [*Vancouver Stock Exchange symbol*]
WGW	Wheat Gluten World [*A publication*] (EAAP)
WGWC	Working Group on Waterborne Cryptosporidiosis [*Medicine*]

WGWC	Working Group on Weather Communications [*NATO*] (NATG)
WGWC	World Service Authority of the World Government of World Citizens (EAIO)
WGWD	Gretna, FL [*FM radio station call letters*]
WGWG	Boiling Springs, NC [*FM radio station call letters*]
WGWM-AM...	London, KY [*AM radio station call letters*] (RBYB)
WGWP	Working Group on Weather Plans [*NATO*] (NATG)
WGWR-FM...	Liberty, NY [*FM radio station call letters*] (BROA)
WGXA	Macon, GA [*Television station call letters*]
WGXL	Hanover, NH [*FM radio station call letters*]
WGXM	Dayton, OH [*FM radio station call letters*]
WGY	Schenectady, NY [*AM radio station call letters*]
WGYJ	Atmore, AL [*AM radio station call letters*]
WGYL	Vero Beach, FL [*FM radio station call letters*]
WGYM-AM...	Atlantic City, NJ [*AM radio station call letters*] (BROA)
WGYV	Greenville, AL [*AM radio station call letters*]
WGZB	Corydon, IN [*FM radio station call letters*]
WGZO-FM...	Parris Island, SC [*FM radio station call letters*] (BROA)
WGZR-FM...	Ridgeland, SC [*FM radio station call letters*] (BROA)
WGZS	Dothan, AL [*AM radio station call letters*]
WH.............	China Northwest Airlines [*ICAO designator*] (AD)
WH.............	Henry Wriothesley, Earl of Southampton; or Sir William Harvey; or William Hathaway; or William Herbert, Earl of Pembroke [*Possible identities of the W. H. to whom Shakespeare's sonnets were supposedly dedicated by publisher Thomas Thorpe in 1609*]
Wh.............	Interrogative [*Linguistics*]
WH.............	Southeastern Commuter Airlines [*ICAO designator*] (AD)
WH.............	Wage and Hour Cases [*Bureau of National Affairs*] [*A publication*] (DLA)
WH.............	Wainwright House (EA)
WH.............	Walking Hinge (KSC)
WH.............	Wall Hung [*Technical drawings*]
WH.............	Wall Hydrant [*NFPA pre-fire planning symbol*] (NFPA)
W-H............	Walsh-Healey Act [*Labor*]
WH.............	Warhead
W/H............	Warheading Building (NATG)
WH.............	Watchdog Title
WH.............	Water Heater
WH.............	Watt-Hour
WH.............	We Have, Ready with Called Party [*Telecommunications*] (TEL)
WH.............	Wehrmacht-Heer [*Marking on Army vehicles*] [*German military - World War II*]
WH.............	Well Healed [*Medicine*] (AAMN)
WH.............	Welsh Horse [*British military*] (DMA)
WH.............	Werding-Hoffman [*Syndrome*] [*Medicine*] (DB)
WH.............	Western Hemisphere
WH.............	Western Hemlock [*Utility pole*] [*Telecommunications*] (TEL)
WH.............	Wharf
Wh.............	Wharton's Pennsylvania Supreme Court Reports [*1835-41*] [*A publication*] (DLA)
Wh.............	Wheaton's International Law [*A publication*] (DLA)
Wh.............	Wheaton's Reports [*14-25 United States*] [*A publication*] (DLA)
Wh.............	Wheeler's New York Criminal Reports [*3 vols.*] [*A publication*] (DLA)
WH.............	Wheelhouse (MSA)
WH.............	Wheeling-Charleston [*Diocesan abbreviation*] [*West Virginia*] (TOCD)
WH.............	Where (AABC)
WH.............	Which
Wh.............	While (AIA)
WH.............	Whispered (ADA)
WH.............	White
WH.............	White [*Thoroughbred racing*]
wh.............	White (WDMC)
WH.............	White Hornet [*Immunology*]
WH.............	White House
WH.............	Whitman Co. [*NYSE symbol*] (SPSG)
WH.............	Whitman Corp. [*NYSE symbol*] (TTSB)
WH.............	Who
WH.............	Whole Homogenate (DB)
WH.............	Whore (DSUE)
WH.............	Wildwood House [*Publisher*] [*British*]
WH.............	William Heinemann [*Publisher*] [*British*]
WH.............	Wing Half (WDAA)
WH.............	Wings of Hope [*An association*] (EA)
WH.............	Withholding (AFM)
WH.............	Workable Hatch [*Shipping*] (DS)
WH.............	Work History (DHP)
WH.............	Work Hour (KSC)
WH.............	World Heritage (EERA)
WH.............	Wound Healing [*Medicine*] (DB)
WH2............	Whipple Mountains Number 2 [*California*] [*Seismograph station code, US Geological Survey*] (SEIS)
WH20..........	Flotation Healthcare Foundation (EA)
WHA	Madison, WI [*AM radio station call letters*]
WHA	Wadi Halfa [*Sudan*] [*Airport symbol*] (AD)
WHA	Wahaula [*Hawaii*] [*Seismograph station code, US Geological Survey*] (SEIS)
WHA	Walkaloosa Horse Association (EA)
WHA	Walsh-Healey Public Contracts Act (AAGC)
WHA	Washington Headquarters Association (EA)
WHA	Weld Head Assembly
WHA	Welsh Hockey Association (DBA)
WHA	Western Hardwood Association (EA)
WHA	Western History Association (EA)
WHA	Western Horsemen's Association [*British*] (DBA)
wha............	Whale (VRA)

WHA .... W. H. Allen [*Commercial firm British*]
WHA .... Women in Health Administration (NTPA)
WHA .... Women's Hockey Association [*Australia*]
WHA .... Wood Heating Alliance (EA)
WHA .... Work Health Authority [*Northern Territory, Australia*]
WHA .... Work Hours Act of 1962 (WYGK)
WHA .... World Heritage Area [*Commonwealth*] (EERA)
WHA .... World History Association (NTPA)
WHA .... World Hockey Association
WHA .... Wounded by Hostile Action
WHAA .... Madison, ME [*FM radio station call letters*]
WHAB .... Acton, MA [*FM radio station call letters*] (RBYB)
WHAB .... Westminster Historical Atlas to the Bible [*A publication*] (BJA)
WHAC .... Wolverine-Hoosier Athletic Conference (PSS)
WHAC .... World Hemophilia AIDS [*Acquired Immune Deficiency Syndrome*] Center (EA)
WHACK .... Warhead Attack Cruise Killer (MCD)
WHAD .... Delafield, WI [*FM radio station call letters*]
WHAD .... Worm Holes a Defect [*Wood industry*] (WPI)
WHAG .... Hagerstown, MD [*Television station call letters*]
WHAG .... Halfway, MD [*AM radio station call letters*]
WHAG .... Windows Help Authoring Guide [*Computer software*] [*Microsoft Corp.*] (PCM)
WHAI .... Bridgeport, CT [*Television station call letters*]
WHAI .... Greenfield, MA [*AM radio station call letters*]
WHAI .... Walter Hinchman Associates, Inc. [*Telecommunications Defunct*] (TSSD)
WHAI-FM ..... Greenfield, MA [*FM radio station call letters*]
WHAJ .... Bluefield, WV [*FM radio station call letters*]
WHAK .... Rogers City, MI [*AM radio station call letters*]
WHAL .... Shelbyville, TN [*AM radio station call letters*]
WHAL .... Wellington Hall Ltd. [*NASDAQ symbol*] (NQ)
WHAM .... Rochester, NY [*AM radio station call letters*]
WHAM .... Water Hammer
WHAM .... Water Hydrogen Ammonia Methane
WHAM .... Wayne Horizontal Acceleration Mechanism
WHAM .... Winning the Hearts and Minds [*of the people*] [*Vietnam pacification program*]
WHAM .... Wisconsin H-Alpha Mapper [*Astrophysics*]
WHAM .... Women, Heritage, and Museums [*British*] [*An association*] (DBA)
WHAM .... Women's Health Action and Mobilization (EA)
WHAM .... Work Handling and Maintenance [*Navy*] (NG)
WHAMM ...... Western Hemisphere Association of Meat Marketers (NTPA)
WHAN .... Wellness and Health Activation Networks (EA)
WH & G .... Welsby, Hurlstone, and Gordon's English Exchequer Reports [*1848-56*] [*A publication*] (DLA)
WH & HSA ... Welsh Hospitals and Health Services Association (DBA)
Wh & TLC .... White and Tudor's Leading Cases in Equity [*9 eds.*] [*1849-1928*] [*A publication*] (DLA)
Wh & Tud .... White and Tudor's Leading Cases in Equity [*9th ed.*] [*1928*] [*A publication*] (DLA)
WHAP .... Hopewell, VA [*AM radio station call letters*]
WHAP .... When [*or Where*] Applicable
WHAP .... Women's Health and Abortion Project (EA)
WHAR .... Clarksburg, WV [*AM radio station call letters*]
Whar .... Wharton's Pennsylvania Supreme Court Reports [*1835-41*] [*A publication*] (DLA)
WHAR .... Whereafter [*Legal*] [*British*] (ROG)
WHAR .... Wild Horses of America Registry (EA)
Whar Ag ...... Wharton on Agency [*A publication*] (DLA)
Whar Am Cr L... Wharton's American Criminal Law [*A publication*] (DLA)
Whar & St Med Jur... Wharton and Stille's Medical Jurisprudence [*A publication*] (DLA)
Whar Confl Law... Wharton's Conflict of Laws [*A publication*] (DLA)
Whar Con Law... Wharton's Conflict of Laws [*A publication*] (DLA)
Whar Conv... Wharton on Principles of Conveyancing [*1851*] [*A publication*] (DLA)
Whar Cr Ev... Wharton on Criminal Evidence [*A publication*] (DLA)
Whar Cri Pl... Wharton's Criminal Pleading and Practice [*A publication*] (DLA)
Whar Cr Law... Wharton's American Criminal Law [*A publication*] (DLA)
Whar Cr Pl... Wharton's Criminal Pleading and Practice [*A publication*] (DLA)
Whar Dig.... Wharton's Pennsylvania Digest [*A publication*] (DLA)
Whar Dom.... Wharton on the Law of Domicile [*A publication*] (DLA)
Whar Ev........ Wharton on Evidence in Civil Issues [*A publication*] (DLA)
Wharf........... Wharf Resources Ltd. [*Associated Press*] (SAG)
Wharfe......... Wharfedale [*Printing*] (DGA)
Whar Hom... Wharton's Law of Homicide [*A publication*] (DLA)
Whar Ind ..... Wharton's Precedents of Indictments and Pleas [*A publication*] (DLA)
Whar Innk.... Wharton on Innkeepers [*1876*] [*A publication*] (DLA)
Whar Law Dic... Wharton's Law Lexicon [*14th ed.*] [*1938*] [*A publication*] (DLA)
Whar Leg Max... Wharton's Legal Maxims [*3rd ed.*] [*1903*] [*A publication*] (DLA)
Whar Neg.... Wharton's Law of Negligence [*A publication*] (DLA)
Whar Prec Ind... Wharton's Precedents of Indictments and Pleas [*A publication*] (DLA)
Whar St Tr... Wharton's United States State Trials [*A publication*] (DLA)
Whart........... Legal Maxims with Observations by George Frederick Wharton [*A publication*] (DLA)
Whart........... Wharton's Pennsylvania Supreme Court Reports [*1835-41*] [*A publication*] (DLA)
Whart Ag..... Wharton on Agency [*A publication*] (DLA)
Whart Am Cr Law... Wharton's American Criminal Law [*A publication*] (DLA)
Whart & S Med Jur... Wharton and Stille's Medical Jurisprudence [*A publication*] (DLA)
Whart Confl Laws... Wharton's Conflict of Laws [*A publication*] (DLA)
Whart Cr Ev... Wharton on Criminal Evidence [*A publication*] (DLA)
Whart Crim Law... Wharton's American Criminal Law [*A publication*] (DLA)
Whart Cr Law... Wharton's American Criminal Law [*A publication*] (DLA)
Whart Cr Pl & Prac... Wharton's Criminal Pleading and Practice [*A publication*] (DLA)
Whart Ev...... Wharton on Evidence in Civil Issues [*A publication*] (DLA)
Whart Hom... Wharton's Law of Homicide [*A publication*] (DLA)
Whart Homicide... Wharton's Law of Homicide [*A publication*] (DLA)
Whart Law Dict... Wharton's Law Dictionary [*or Lexicon*] [*A publication*] (DLA)
Whart Law Lexicon... Wharton's Law Lexicon [*A publication*] (DLA)
Whart Lex.... Wharton's Law Lexicon [*A publication*] (DLA)
Whart Neg... Wharton on Negligence [*A publication*] (DLA)
Wharton....... Wharton's American Criminal Law [*A publication*] (DLA)
Wharton....... Wharton's Law Lexicon [*A publication*] (DLA)
Wharton....... Wharton's Pennsylvania Supreme Court Reports [*1835-41*] [*A publication*] (DLA)
Wharton Crim Evidence... Wharton's Criminal Evidence [*A publication*] (DLA)
Wharton Crim Proc... Wharton's Criminal Law and Procedure [*A publication*] (DLA)
Whart PA..... Wharton's Pennsylvania Supreme Court Reports [*1835-41*] [*A publication*] (DLA)
Whart State Tr... Wharton's United States State Trials [*A publication*] (DLA)
Whart St Tr... Wharton's United States State Trials [*A publication*] (DLA)
WHAS .... Louisville, KY [*AM radio station call letters*]
WHAS .... Whereas
WHAS .... Women's Health Advisory Service [*Australia*]
WHASA .... White House Army Signal Agency
WHAS-TV .... Louisville, KY [*Television station call letters*]
WHAT .... Philadelphia, PA [*AM radio station call letters*]
WHAT .... Wetland Habitat Alliance of Texas
WHAT .... What A World [*NASDAQ symbol*] (TTSB)
WHAT .... What A World, Inc. [*NASDAQ symbol*] (SAG)
WHAT .... What's Here and There [*Australia A publication*]
WHAT .... Windows Help Authoring Tools [*Computer software*] [*Microsoft Corp.*] (PCM)
WHAT .... Winds, Heights, and Temperatures
WhatA .... What A World, Inc. [*Associated Press*] (SAG)
WhatAW ...... What A World, Inc. [*Associated Press*] (SAG)
WHATSR ...... Whatsoever
WHA-TV ...... Madison, WI [*Television station call letters*]
WHATW .... What A World Wrrt [*NASDAQ symbol*] (TTSB)
WHAV .... Haverhill, MA [*AM radio station call letters*]
WHAV .... When Available (KSC)
WHAW .... Weston, WV [*AM radio station call letters*]
WHAY .... Whitley City, KY [*FM radio station call letters*]
WHAZ .... Troy, NY [*AM radio station call letters*]
WHB .... Kansas City, MO [*AM radio station call letters*]
WHB .... [*The*] Wandering Hand Brigade [*Men who are likely to take liberties with women*]
WHB .... Waste Heat Boiler [*Nuclear energy*] (CAAL)
WHB .... Weight-Bearing (DAVI)
WHB .... Wheel Bumpers [*Technical drawings*]
WhB .... Whole Blood [*Hematology*] (DAVI)
WHB .... Wire Harness Board (MCD)
WHBB .... Selma, AL [*AM radio station call letters*]
WHBC .... Canton, OH [*AM radio station call letters*]
WHBC-FM .... Canton, OH [*FM radio station call letters*]
WHBF .... Rock Island, IL [*Television station call letters*]
WHBFC .... Wayne Hann Band Fan Club (EA)
WHBG .... Harrisonburg, VA [*AM radio station call letters*]
WHBI .... Lake Worth, FL [*Television station call letters*]
WHBK .... Marshall, NC [*AM radio station call letters*]
WHBL .... Sheboygan, WI [*AM radio station call letters*]
WHBL .... World Home Bible League [*Later, BL*] (EA)
WHBM .... Park Falls, WI [*FM radio station call letters*]
WHBMA .... Wood Hat Block Manufacturers Association (EA)
WHBN .... Harrodsburg, KY [*AM radio station call letters*]
WHBN-FM .... Harrodsburg, KY [*FM radio station call letters*]
WHBQ .... Memphis, TN [*AM radio station call letters*]
WHBQ-TV .... Memphis, TN [*Television station call letters*]
WHBR .... Pensacola, FL [*Television station call letters*]
WHBS .... Eatonville, FL [*AM radio station call letters*]
WHBS .... Waste Heat Boiler Survey (DS)
WHBT .... Tallahassee, FL [*AM radio station call letters*]
WHBU .... Anderson, IN [*AM radio station call letters*]
WHBX .... Tallahassee, FL [*FM radio station call letters*]
WHBY .... Kimberly, WI [*AM radio station call letters*]
WHBY .... Whereby
WHBZ .... Port Royal, SC [*FM radio station call letters*] (RBYB)
WHC .... Wackenhut Corrections [*NYSE symbol*] (TTSB)
WHC .... Wage and Hour Cases [*A publication*] (AAGC)
WHC .... Wages for Housework Committee (EA)
WHC .... Washington Hospital Center, Washington, DC [*OCLC symbol*] (OCLC)
WHC .... Water Holding Capacity [*Also, WBC*] [*Food industry*]
WHC .... Watt-Hour Meter with Contact Device
WHC .... Westinghouse Hanford Co. (NRCH)
WHC .... Whitehorse [*Yukon Territory*] [*Seismograph station code, US Geological Survey*] (SEIS)
WHC .... White House Conference
WHC .... Winchester Capital [*Vancouver Stock Exchange symbol*]
WHC .... World Hereford Council (EAIO)
WHC .... World Heritage Committee [*See also CPM*] (EAIO)
WHCA .... War Hazards Compensation Act
WHCA .... White House Communications Agency (AABC)
WHCA .... White House Correspondents' Association (EA)
WHCA .... Women's Health Care Association [*Australia*]
WHCA .... World Hobie Class Association [*Later, IHCA*] (EA)

WH Cas .... Wage and Hour Cases [*Bureau of National Affairs*] [*A publication*] (DLA)
WHCB .... Bristol, TN [*FM radio station call letters*]
WHCC .... Waynesville, NC [*AM radio station call letters*]
WHCCY .... White House Conference on Children and Youth (EA)
WHCD-FM ..... Auburn, NY [*FM radio station call letters*] (BROA)
WHCDHP ...... Wainwright House Center for Development of Human Potential [*Later, WH*] (EA)
WHCDHR ..... Wainwright House Center for Development of Human Resources [*Later, WH*] (EA)
WHCE .... Highland Springs, VA [*FM radio station call letters*]
WHCF .... Bangor, ME [*FM radio station call letters*]
WHCF .... White House Conference on Families [*June 5-July 3, 1980*] (EGAO)
WHCG .... Metter, GA [*FM radio station call letters*]
WHcGS .... Church of Jesus Christ of Latter-Day Saints, Genealogical Society Library, Milwaukee Branch, Hales Corners, WI [*Library symbol Library of Congress*] (LCLS)
WHCH .... Munising, MI [*FM radio station call letters*]
wh ch........... Wheel Chair [*Medicine*] (DMAA)
wh ch........... White Child [*Medicine*] (DMAA)
WH Chron.... Westminster Hall Chronicle and Legal Examiner [*1835-36*] [*A publication*] (DLA)
WHCJ........... Savannah, GA [*FM radio station call letters*]
WHCL .... Clinton, NY [*FM radio station call letters*]
WHCLIS .... White House Conference on Library and Information Services [*Washington, DC, 1979*]
WHCLIST ..... White House Conference on Library and Information Services Taskforce
WHCM .... Parkersburg, WV [*FM radio station call letters*]
WHCN.......... Hartford, CT [*FM radio station call letters*]
WHCO.......... Sparta, IL [*AM radio station call letters*]
WHCOA........ White House Conference on Aging
WHCOLIS...... White House Conference on Library and Information Services
WHCP .... Portsmouth, OH [*Television station call letters*] (BROA)
WHCR .... New York, NY [*FM radio station call letters*]
Wh Cr Cas... Wheeler's New York Criminal Cases [*3 vols.*] [*A publication*] (DLA)
Wh Crim Cas... Wheeler's New York Criminal Cases [*A publication*] (DLA)
WHcS........... Sacred Heart School of Theology, Hales Corners, WI [*Library symbol Library of Congress*] (LCLS)
WHCS .... Well History Control System [*Later, Historical Well Data On-Line*] [*Petroleum Information Corp.*] [*Information service or system*] (IID)
WHCSA........ Welsh Health Common Services Authority
WHCT .... Hartford, CT [*Television station call letters*]
WHCU .... Ithaca, NY [*AM radio station call letters*]
WHCU .... Window Heat Control Unit
WHCY .... Blairstown, NJ [*FM radio station call letters*]
WHD .... Wage and Hour Division [*Department of Labor*]
WHD .... Warhead
WHD .... Western Hemisphere Defense
WHD .... Wheeler Dam [*TVA*]
WHD .... Wirlwind Resources Ltd. [*Vancouver Stock Exchange symbol*]
WHD .... Write Head Driver (SAA)
WHDB.......... Woods Hole Database, Inc. [*Information service or system*] (IID)
W-HDCS ...... Wyeth Laboratories - Human Diploid Cell Strain [*Rabies vaccine*]
WHDG.......... Rhinelander, WI [*FM radio station call letters*]
WHDH.......... Boston, MA [*Television station call letters*]
WHDL .... Olean, NY [*AM radio station call letters*]
WHDM......... McKenzie, TN [*AM radio station call letters*]
WHDM......... Watt-Hour Demand Meter
WHDQ.......... Claremont, NH [*FM radio station call letters*]
WHDS.......... Warhead Section [*Military*] (AABC)
WHE........... Water Hammer Eliminator
WHE........... Westland Helicopters Ltd. [*British ICAO designator*] (FAAC)
WHE........... Wheaton College, Norton, MA [*OCLC symbol*] (OCLC)
Wh e........... White Edges [*Bookbinding*] (DGA)
WHE........... Whole Human Embryo [*Type of cell line*]
Wheat.......... Wheaton's Reports [*14-25 United States*] [*A publication*] (DLA)
Wheat.......... Wheaton's United States Supreme Court Reports [*1816-27*] [*A publication*] (AAGC)
Wheat Cap... Wheaton on Maritime Captures and Prizes [*A publication*] (DLA)
Wheat El Int Law... Wheaton's Elements of International Law [*A publication*] (DLA)
WHEATH ...... Wheathampstead [*England*]
Wheat Hist Law Nat... Wheaton's History of the Law of Nations [*A publication*] (DLA)
Wheat Int Law... Wheaton's Elements of International Law [*7th ed.*] [*1944*] [*A publication*] (DLA)
Wheat Int Law... Wheaton's International Law [*A publication*] (DLA)
Wheat Law of Nat... Wheaton's History of the Law of Nations [*A publication*] (DLA)
Wheaton...... Wheaton's Reports [*14-25 United States*] [*A publication*] (DLA)
WHEB .... Portsmouth, NH [*FM radio station call letters*]
WHEC .... High-Endurance Coast Guard Cutter [*Formerly, WAPG*] (CINC)
WHEC .... Rochester, NY [*Television station call letters*]
WHEC .... Wildlife Habitat Enhancement Council (EA)
WHECON...... Wheel Control (MCD)
WHEE.......... Martinsville, VA [*AM radio station call letters*]
Wheel......... Wheeler's New York Criminal Cases [*A publication*] (DLA)
Wheel......... Wheelock's Reports [*32-37 Texas*] [*A publication*] (DLA)
Wheel Abr ... Wheeler's Abridgment of American Common Law Cases [*A publication*] (DLA)
Wheel Br Cas... Wheeling Bridge Case [*A publication*] (DLA)
Wheel Cr C... Wheeler's New York Criminal Cases [*A publication*] (DLA)
Wheel Cr Cas... Wheeler's New York Criminal Cases [*A publication*] (DLA)
Wheel Cr Ch... Wheeler's New York Criminal Cases [*A publication*] (DLA)

Wheel Cr Rec... Wheeler's New York Criminal Recorder [*1 Wheeler's Criminal Cases*] [*A publication*] (DLA)
Wheeler Abr... Wheeler's Abridgment [*A publication*] (DLA)
Wheeler Am Cr Law... Wheeler's Abridgment of American Common Law Cases [*A publication*] (DLA)
Wheeler CC... Wheeler's New York Criminal Cases [*A publication*] (DLA)
Wheeler Cr Cas... Wheeler's New York Criminal Cases [*A publication*] (DLA)
Wheeler Cr Cases... Wheeler's New York Criminal Cases [*A publication*] (DLA)
Wheeler Crim Cas... Wheeler's New York Criminal Cases [*A publication*] (DLA)
Wheeler's Cr Cases... Wheeler's New York Criminal Cases [*A publication*] (DLA)
Wheelock C... Wheelock College (GAGS)
Wheel Slav... Wheeler on Slavery [*A publication*] (DLA)
Wheel (Tex)... Wheelock's Reports [*32-37 Texas*] [*A publication*] (DLA)
WHEI .... Tiffin, OH [*FM radio station call letters*]
WHEI .... Women's Heathy Eating and Living [*Medicine*]
WHEL.......... Helen, GA [*FM radio station call letters*]
WHEM .... Eau Claire, WI [*FM radio station call letters*]
WHEN .... Syracuse, NY [*AM radio station call letters*]
WHENCESR... Whencesoever [*Legal*] [*British*] (ROG)
WHEN-FM.... Syracuse, NY [*FM radio station call letters*]
WHENR .... Whenever [*Legal*] [*British*] (ROG)
WHENSR...... Whensoever [*Legal*] [*British*] (ROG)
WHEO .... Stuart, VA [*AM radio station call letters*]
WHEP .... Foley, AL [*AM radio station call letters*]
WHEP .... Warhead Engagement Program [*Military*]
WHER .... Hattiesburg, MS [*FM radio station call letters*]
WHER .... Whether [*Legal*] [*British*] (ROG)
WHERER ...... Wherever [*Legal*] [*British*] (ROG)
WHERF .... Wood Heating Education and Research Foundation (EA)
WHES .... World Hunger Education Service (EA)
WHET .... Birnamwood, WI [*FM radio station call letters*]
WHETS .... Washington Higher Education Telecommunications System [*Washington State University*] [*Pullman*] [*Telecommunications service*] (TSSD)
WHEW-AM... Franklin, TN [*AM radio station call letters*] (RBYB)
WHF............. Waveguide Harmonic Filter
WHF............. Wharf
whf............... Wharf (WDAA)
Whf............. Wharfedale [*Printing*] (DGA)
WHF............. Women in Housing and Finance (EA)
WHF............. Women's Hall of Fame [*Later, NWHF*] (EA)
WHF............. World Heritage Fund [*UNESCO*]
WHFA.......... Western Hemisphere Friendship Association (EA)
WHFB.......... Benton Harbor, MI [*AM radio station call letters*]
WHFB-FM .... Benton Harbor, MI [*FM radio station call letters*]
WHFC .... Bel Air, MD [*FM radio station call letters*]
WHFD.......... Lawrenceville, VA [*FM radio station call letters*]
WHFE.......... Lakeland, GA [*FM radio station call letters*]
WHFG.......... Wharfage [*Shipping*]
WHFH .... Flossmoor, IL [*FM radio station call letters*]
WHFI .... Lindside, WV [*FM radio station call letters*]
WHFI .... Wholesome & Hearty Foods [*NASDAQ symbol*] (TTSB)
WHFI .... Wholesome & Hearty Foods, Inc. [*NASDAQ symbol*] (SAG)
WHFM .... Southampton, NY [*FM radio station call letters*]
WHFM .... Wherefrom [*Legal*] [*British*] (ROG)
WHFMS .... Woman's Home and Foreign Mission Society (EA)
WHFORE...... Wherefore [*Legal*] [*British*] (ROG)
WHFR .... Dearborn, MI [*FM radio station call letters*]
WHFR .... Wharfinger [*Shipping*] [*British*] (ROG)
WHFS .... Annapolis, MD [*FM radio station call letters*]
WHFT .... Miami, FL [*Television station call letters*]
WHFTB .... Waste Heat Fire Tube Boiler (DS)
WHFTBS ...... Waste Heat Fire Tube Boiler Survey (DS)
WHF-USA ... World Health Foundation, United States of America [*Defunct*] (EA)
WHFX .... Waycross, GA [*FM radio station call letters*]
WHGB.......... WHG Bancshares [*NASDAQ symbol*] (TTSB)
WHGB.......... WHG Bancshares Corp. [*NASDAQ symbol*] (SAG)
WHGBcs ...... WHG Bancshares Corp. [*Associated Press*] (SAG)
WHGC .... Bennington, VT [*FM radio station call letters*]
WHGDP........ World Hunger/Global Development Program [*Defunct*] (EA)
WHGE.......... Wharfage [*Shipping*]
WHGG.......... Roanoke Rapids, NC [*FM radio station call letters*]
WHGH.......... Thomasville, GA [*AM radio station call letters*]
WHGL.......... Canton, PA [*FM radio station call letters*]
WHGL.......... Troy, PA [*AM radio station call letters*]
WHGR.......... Houghton Lake, MI [*AM radio station call letters*]
WHGT.......... Waynesboro, PA [*AM radio station call letters*]
WHH........... Hartford Memorial Hospital, Hartford, WI [*Library symbol Library of Congress*] (LCLS)
WHH........... Werthamar-Helfand-Hohenberg Theory [*Solid state physics*]
WHH........... William Henry Harrison [*US president, 1773-1841*]
WHHA.......... White House Historical Association (EA)
WHHB.......... Holliston, MA [*FM radio station call letters*]
WHHH.......... Indianapolis, IN [*FM radio station call letters*]
WHHI .... Highland, WI [*FM radio station call letters*]
WHHK.......... Galva, IL [*FM radio station call letters*] (RBYB)
WHHL.......... Watanabe Hereditary Hyperlipidemic [*Rabbits*]
WHHM.......... Henderson, TN [*FM radio station call letters*]
WHHO.......... Hornell, NY [*AM radio station call letters*]
WHHS.......... Havertown, PA [*FM radio station call letters*]
WHHT .... Cave City, KY [*FM radio station call letters*]
WHHV.......... Hillsville, VA [*AM radio station call letters*]
WHHY.......... Montgomery, AL [*AM radio station call letters*]
WHHY-FM.... Montgomery, AL [*FM radio station call letters*]

WHi	State Historical Society of Wisconsin, Madison, WI [*Library symbol Library of Congress*] (LCLS)
WHI	Washington Homes [*NYSE symbol*] (TTSB)
WHI	Washington Homes, Inc. [*NYSE symbol*] (SPSG)
WHI	Wave Height Indicator [*Oceanography*]
WHI	Weekly Hospital Indemnity [*Insurance*]
WHI	Western Highway Institute (EA)
WHI	Whitney [*Hawaii*] [*Seismograph station code, US Geological Survey Closed*] (SEIS)
WHI	Wild Horse Industry [*Vancouver Stock Exchange symbol*]
WHI	Woman Health International [*Defunct*] (EA)
WHI	Women's Health Initiative [*National Institutes of Health*]
WHIA	Woolen Hosiery Institute of America [*Defunct*] (EA)
WHIC	Hardinsburg, KY [*AM radio station call letters*]
WHIC	Women's Health Information Centre [*British*] (CB)
WHID	Green Bay, WI [*FM radio station call letters*] (RBYB)
WHIDDA	Wideband High-Density Data Acquisition (MCD)
WHIE	Griffin, GA [*AM radio station call letters*]
WHIF	Palatka, FL [*FM radio station call letters*]
WHIG	Ward Howell International Group [*British*]
WHII	Women's Health in Industry [*Australia*]
WHIJ	Ocala, FL [*FM radio station call letters*]
WHIL	Mobile, AL [*FM radio station call letters*]
WHIM	West Warwick, RI [*AM radio station call letters*] (RBYB)
WHIM	Wet High-Intensity Magnet [*for mineral processing*]
WHIM	Women Happy in Minis [*Boise, Idaho, group opposing below-the-knee fashions introduced in 1970*]
WHIMS	Wet High Intensity Magnetic Separation (PDAA)
WHIN	Gallatin, TN [*AM radio station call letters*]
WHIN	Wherein [*Legal*] [*British*] (ROG)
WHIO	Dayton, OH [*AM radio station call letters*]
WHIO-TV	Dayton, OH [*Television station call letters*]
WHIP	Mooresville, NC [*AM radio station call letters*]
WHIP	Wafer Hybrid Interconnection Packaging (CIST)
WHIP	Walks plus Hits Divided by Innings Pitched [*Baseball*]
WHIP	Wideband High Intercept Probability
WHIPS	Widebeam High-Density Pulsed Source (MCD)
WHIQ	Huntsville, AL [*Television station call letters*]
WHIR	Danville, KY [*AM radio station call letters*]
WHIR-FM	Danville, KY [*FM radio station call letters*] (RBYB)
WHIS	Bluefield, WV [*AM radio station call letters*]
WHIS	Whiskeytown-Shasta-Trinity National Recreation Area
WHIS	Whistle [*Navigation*]
Whishaw	Whishaw's Law Dictionary [*A publication*] (DLA)
Whish LD	Whishaw's New Law Dictionary [*1829*] [*A publication*] (DLA)
WHISP	Woods Hole In-Situ Pump [*Marine biology*] [*Instrumentation*]
WHISPER	Windows Highly Intelligent Speech Recognition [*Computer science*]
WHIST	Worldwide Household Goods Information System for Traffic Management [*Army*] (AABC)
WHIT	Madison, WI [*AM radio station call letters*]
WHIT	Whittman-Hart Inc. [*NASDAQ symbol*] (TTSR)
Whitok Liens	Whitaker on Liens [*A publication*] (DLA)
WHITCH	Whitchurch [*England*]
White	White's Justiciary Court Reports [*3 vols.*] [*Scotland*] [*A publication*] (DLA)
White	White's Reports [*10-15 West Virginia*] [*A publication*] (DLA)
White	White's Reports [*31-44 Texas Appeals*] [*A publication*] (DLA)
White & Civ Cas Ct App	White and Willson's Civil Cases, Texas Court of Appeals [*A publication*] (DLA)
White & TL Cas	White and Tudor's Leading Cases in Equity [*A publication*] (DLA)
White & T Lead Cas Eq	White and Tudor's Leading Cases in Equity [*England*] [*A publication*] (DLA)
White & T Lead Cas in Eq (Eng)	White and Tudor's Leading Cases in Equity [*England*] [*A publication*] (DLA)
White & Tud LC	White and Tudor's Leading Cases in Equity [*9th ed.*] [*1928*] [*A publication*] (DLA)
White & Tudor	White and Tudor's Leading Cases in Equity [*A publication*] (DLA)
White & W	White and Willson's Reports, Civil Cases, Texas Court of Appeals [*A publication*] (DLA)
White & W Civ Cas Ct App	White and Wilson's [*or Willson's*] Civil Cases, Texas Court of Appeals [*A publication*] (DLA)
White & W Civil Cases Ct App	Texas Civil Cases [*A publication*] (DLA)
White & Willson	Texas Civil Cases [*A publication*] (DLA)
White & W (Tex)	White and Willson's Reports, Civil Cases, Texas Court of Appeals [*A publication*] (DLA)
White Char	Whiteford on Charities [*1878*] [*A publication*] (DLA)
White Coll	White's New Collection of the Laws, Etc., of Great Britain, France, and Spain [*A publication*] (DLA)
Whitehl	Whitehall Corp. [*Associated Press*] (SAG)
White LL	White's Land Law of California [*A publication*] (DLA)
White New Coll	White's New Collection of the Laws, Etc. of Great Britain, France, and Spain [*A publication*] (DLA)
Whit Eq Pr	Whitworth. Equity Precedents [*A publication*] (ILCA)
Whit Eq Pr	Whitworth's Equity Precedents [*A publication*] (DLA)
WhiteRvr	White River Corp. [*Associated Press*] (SAG)
White's Ann Pen Code	White's Annotated Penal Code [*Texas*] [*A publication*]
White's Rep	White's Reports [*31-44 Texas Appeals*] [*A publication*] (DLA)
White's Rep	White's Reports [*10-15 West Virginia*] [*A publication*] (DLA)
White Suppl	White on Supplement and Revivor [*A publication*] (DLA)
White W & M	Whiteley's Weights, Measures, and Weighing Machines [*1879*] [*A publication*] (DLA)
Whit Lien	Whitaker's Rights of Lien and Stoppage in Transitu [*1812*] [*A publication*] (DLA)
Whitm Adopt	Whitemore on Adoption of Children [*A publication*] (DLA)
Whitman Pat Cas (US)	Whitman's Patent Cases [*United States*] [*A publication*] (DLA)
Whitm BL	Whitmarsh's Bankrupt Law [*2nd ed.*] [*1817*] [*A publication*] (DLA)
WhitmE	Whitman Education Group [*Associated Press*] (SAG)
Whitm Lib Cas	Whitman's Massachusetts Libel Cases [*A publication*] (DLA)
WhitmM	Whitman Medical Corp. [*Associated Press*] (SAG)
Whitmn	Whitman Corp. [*Associated Press*] (SAG)
Whitm Pat Cas	Whitman's Patent Cases [*United States*] [*A publication*] (DLA)
Whitm Pat Law	Whitman's Patent Laws of All Countries [*A publication*] (DLA)
Whitm Pat Law Rev	Whitman's Patent Law Review [*Washington, DC*] [*A publication*] (DLA)
Whitney	Whitney's Land Laws [*Tennessee*] [*A publication*] (DLA)
WhitnyH	Whitney Holding Corp. [*Associated Press*] (SAG)
Whit Pat	Whitman's Patent Laws of All Countries [*A publication*] (DLA)
Whit Pat Cas	Whitman's Patent Cases [*United States*] [*A publication*] (DLA)
WHITS	Whitstone [*England*]
Whit Schol	Whitgift Scholar [*British*]
Whit St Tr	Whitaker's Rights of Lien and Stoppage in Transitu [*1812*] [*A publication*] (DLA)
Whitt	Whittlesey's Reports [*32-41 Missouri*] [*A publication*] (DLA)
Whittakr	Whittaker Corp. [*Associated Press*] (SAG)
Whittier C	Whittier College (GAGS)
WHITTL	Whittlesey [*Urban district in England*]
Whittlesey	Whittlesey's Reports [*32-41 Missouri*] [*A publication*] (DLA)
Whitworth C	Whitworth College (GAGS)
WHIY	Moulton, AL [*AM radio station call letters*]
WHIZ	Zanesville, OH [*AM radio station call letters*]
WHIZ-FM	Zanesville, OH [*FM radio station call letters*]
WHIZ-TV	Zanesville, OH [*Television station call letters*]
WHJB	Greensburg, PA [*AM radio station call letters*]
WHJC	Matewan, WV [*AM radio station call letters*]
WHJE	Carmel, IN [*FM radio station call letters*]
WHJJ	Providence, RI [*AM radio station call letters*]
WHJM	Knoxville, TN [*AM radio station call letters*]
WHJT	Clinton, MS [*FM radio station call letters*]
WHJY	Providence, RI [*FM radio station call letters*]
WHK	Cleveland, OH [*AM radio station call letters*]
WHK	Whakatane [*New Zealand*] [*Airport symbol*] (OAG)
WHKE	Kenosha, WI [*Television station call letters*]
WHKK-FM	Middletown, RI [*FM radio station call letters*] (BROA)
WHKL-FM	Crenshaw, MS [*FM radio station call letters*] (BROA)
WHKN	Millen, GA [*FM radio station call letters*]
WHKO	Dayton, OH [*FM radio station call letters*]
WHKP	Hendersonville, NC [*AM radio station call letters*]
WHKR	Rockledge, FL [*FM radio station call letters*]
WHKS	Port Allegany, PA [*FM radio station call letters*]
WHKW	Corydon, IN [*FM radio station call letters*]
WHKW	Louisville, KY [*AM radio station call letters*] (RBYB)
WHKX-FM	Bluefield, VA [*FM radio station call letters*] (BROA)
WHKY	Hickory, NC [*AM radio station call letters*]
WHKY-TV	Hickory, NC [*Television station call letters*]
WHKZ	Cayce, SC [*FM radio station call letters*]
WHL	Watt-Hour Meter with Loss Compensator (MSA)
WHL	Western Hockey League
WHL	Westland Helicopters Ltd. [*British*] (IRUK)
WHL	Wheel (AAG)
whl	Wholesale (MHDB)
WHL	Woodgate Air Services Ltd. [*Zambia*] [*FAA designator*] (FAAC)
WHL	World Heritage List [*UNESCO*]
WHL	World Heritage Listing
WHLA	La Crosse, WI [*FM radio station call letters*]
WHLA-TV	La Crosse, WI [*Television station call letters*]
WHLB	Virginia, MN [*AM radio station call letters*]
WHLC-FM	Highlands, NC [*FM radio station call letters*] (RBYB)
WHLD	Niagara Falls, NY [*AM radio station call letters*]
WHLD	Wheeled
WHLE	Byhalia, MS [*FM radio station call letters*]
WHLF	South Boston, VA [*AM radio station call letters*]
WHLG	Jensen Beach, FL [*FM radio station call letters*]
WHLI	Hempstead, NY [*AM radio station call letters*]
WHLJ-FM	Statenville, GA [*FM radio station call letters*] (BROA)
WHLM	Bloomsburg, PA [*FM radio station call letters*]
WHLN	Harlan, KY [*AM radio station call letters*]
WHLO	Akron, OH [*AM radio station call letters*]
WHLQ	Louisburg, NC [*FM radio station call letters*]
WHLS	Port Huron, MI [*AM radio station call letters*]
WHLS	Wheels [*Automotive advertising*]
WHLT	Hattiesburg, MS [*Television station call letters*]
WhlTech	Wheelabrator Technology [*Associated Press*] (SAG)
WHLV	Hattiesburg, MS [*AM radio station call letters*]
WHLX	Bethlehem, WV [*FM radio station call letters*]
WHLY	South Bend, IN [*AM radio station call letters*]
WHLZ	Manning, SC [*FM radio station call letters*]
WHM	Watt-Hour Meter
WHM	Weighmaster (WGA)
WHM	Wickham [*Australia Airport symbol*]
WHM	Wild Horse Parks [*Montana*] [*Seismograph station code, US Geological Survey Closed*] (SEIS)
WHMA	Anniston, AL [*AM radio station call letters*]
WHMA	Wiring Harness Manufacturers Association (NTPA)
WHMA	Women's Home Mission Association
WHMAA	Wool Hat Manufacturers Association of America (EA)
WHMA-FM	Anniston, AL [*FM radio station call letters*]

WH Man	Wage and Hour Reference Manual [*Bureau of National Affairs*] [*A publication*] (DLA)
WHMB	Indianapolis, IN [*Television station call letters*]
WHMC	Conway, SC [*FM radio station call letters*]
WHMC	Wilford Hall United States Air Force Medical Center [*Lackland Air Force Base, TX*] (GRD)
WHMC-TV	Conway, SC [*Television station call letters*]
WHMD	Hammond, LA [*FM radio station call letters*]
WHME	South Bend, IN [*FM radio station call letters*]
WHME-TV	South Bend, IN [*Television station call letters*]
WHMH	Sauk Rapids, MN [*FM radio station call letters*]
WHMI	Howell, MI [*AM radio station call letters*]
WHMI	Whitman Mission National Historic Site
WHMI-FM	Howell, MI [*FM radio station call letters*]
WHMIS	Wage and Hour Management Information System [*Department of Labor*] (GFGA)
WHMIS	Workplace Hazardous Materials Information System [*Canada*]
WHML	Wellcome Historical Medical Library [*Burroughs Wellcome Co.*] (DAVI)
WHMM	Washington, DC [*Television station call letters*]
WHMP	Northampton, MA [*AM radio station call letters*]
WHMP-FM ...	Northampton, MA [*FM radio station call letters*]
WHMQ	North Baltimore, OH [*FM radio station call letters*]
WHMS	Champaign, IL [*FM radio station call letters*]
WHMS	Well-Healed Midline Scar [*Surgery*] (DAVI)
WHMT	Humboldt, TN [*AM radio station call letters*]
WHMV & NSSA...	Woods Hole, Martha's Vineyard & Nantucket Steamship Authority (MHDB)
WHMX	Lincoln, ME [*FM radio station call letters*]
WHN	Wharton & Northern Railroad Co. [*Absorbed into Consolidated Rail Corp.*] [*AAR code*]
WHN	Whonnock Industries Ltd. [*Toronto Stock Exchange symbol Vancouver Stock Exchange symbol*]
WHN	Women's History Network (EA)
WHNC	Henderson, NC [*AM radio station call letters*]
WHND	Monroe, MI [*AM radio station call letters*]
WHND	Worm Holes No Defect [*Wood industry*] (WPI)
WHNN	Bay City, MI [*FM radio station call letters*]
WHNO	New Orleans, LA [*Television station call letters*]
WHNPA	White House News Photographers Association (EA)
WHNR	Cypress Gardens, FL [*AM radio station call letters*]
WHNR	Whenever [*Legal*] [*British*] (ROG)
WHNRC	Western Human Nutrition Research Center [*Department of Agriculture*] [*Research center*] (RCD)
WHNS	Asheville, NC [*Television station call letters*]
WHNS	Wartime Host Nation Support
WHNSIMS	Wartime Host Nation Support Information Management System (DOMA)
WHNSR	Whensoever [*Legal*] [*British*] (ROG)
WHNT	Huntsville, AL [*Television station call letters*]
WHNY	McComb, MS [*AM radio station call letters*]
WHNZ	Pinellas Park, FL [*AM radio station call letters*]
WHO	Des Moines, IA [*AM radio station call letters*]
WHO	War on Hunger Office [*Department of State*]
WHO	Waterhouse Investor Service [*NYSE symbol*] (SPSG)
WHO	Waterhouse Investor Svc [*NYSE symbol*] (TTSB)
WHO	Western Heraldry Organization (EA)
WHO	Westhill Resources [*Vancouver Stock Exchange symbol*]
WHO	[*The*] White House Office
WHO	World Health Organization [*The pronunciation "who" is not acceptable*] [*United Nations affiliate Databank originator*] [*Switzerland*]
WHO	World Housing Organization
WHO	Wrist-Hand Orthosis [*Medicine*]
WHOA	Montgomery, AL [*Television station call letters*]
WHOA	Walking Horse Owner's Association of America (EA)
WHOA	Why Have Overages Afterwards [*DoD*]
WHOA	Wild Horse Organized Assistance (EA)
WHOAA	Walking Horse Owner's Association of America (EA)
WHOB	Nashua, NH [*FM radio station call letters*]
WHOC	Philadelphia, MS [*AM radio station call letters*]
WHOD	Jackson, AL [*AM radio station call letters*]
WHOD-FM ...	Jackson, AL [*FM radio station call letters*]
WHO/EPR	World Health Organization/Panafrican Centre for Emergency Preparedness and Response [*United Nations*]
WHOER	Whoever [*Legal*] [*British*] (ROG)
WHOF	Whereof [*Legal*] [*British*] (ROG)
WHOF	Wildwood, FL [*AM radio station call letters*]
WHOG	Hobson City, AL [*AM radio station call letters*]
WHOG-FM ...	Ormond-by-the-Sea, FL [*FM radio station call letters*] (RBYB)
WHOI	Peoria, IL [*Television station call letters*]
WHOI	Woods Hole Oceanographic Institution [*Woods Hole, MA*] [*Research center*]
WHOIRP	World Health Organization International Reference Preparation (DAVI)
WHOK	Lancaster, OH [*FM radio station call letters*]
WHOL	Allentown, PA [*AM radio station call letters*]
WHOL	Wholesale (WGA)
WholeFd	Whole Foods Market, Inc. [*Associated Press*] (SAG)
WholHty.......	Wholesome & Hearty Foods [*Associated Press*] (SAG)
WHOLIS	World Health Organization Library Information System (IID)
WHOM	Mount Washington, NH [*FM radio station call letters*]
WHON	Centerville, IN [*AM radio station call letters*]
WHON	Whereon [*Legal*] [*British*] (ROG)
WHOO	Orlando, FL [*AM radio station call letters*]

WHOOPS	Washington Public Power Supply System (EBF)
WHOP	Hopkinsville, KY [*AM radio station call letters*]
WHOP-FM...	Hopkinsville, KY [*FM radio station call letters*]
WHOS	Decatur, AL [*AM radio station call letters*]
WHOSOR	Whosoever [*Legal*] [*British*] (ROG)
WHOT-FM...	Youngstown, OH [*FM radio station call letters*]
WHO-TV	Des Moines, IA [*Television station call letters*]
WHOU-FM...	Houlton, ME [*FM radio station call letters*]
Whous	Warehouse
WHOV	Hampton, VA [*FM radio station call letters*]
WHOW	Clinton, IL [*AM radio station call letters*]
WHOW-FM...	Clinton, IL [*FM radio station call letters*]
WHOY	Salinas, PR [*AM radio station call letters*]
WHOZ-AM...	Fairhope, AL [*AM radio station call letters*] (RBYB)
WHP	Harrisburg, PA [*AM radio station call letters*]
WHP	Los Angeles, CA [*Location identifier FAA*] (FAAL)
WHP	Water Horsepower
WHP	West Hartford Public Library, West Hartford, CT [*OCLC symbol*] (OCLC)
whp.........	Whirlpool (MAE)
WHP.........	White House Police [*Later, Executive Protective Service*]
WHP	WOCE [*World Ocean Circulation Experiment*] Hydrographic Experiment (USDC)
WHP	WOCE [*World Ocean Circulation Experiment*] Hydrographic Program [*Marine science*] (OSRA)
WHP	World Hydrocarbon Program (NITA)
WHPA	Hollidaysburg, PA [*FM radio station call letters*]
WHPA	Wellhead Protection Area [*Environmental science*] (COE)
WHPA	Wellhead Protection Area [*A publication*] (PA)
WHPA	Wellhead Protection Areas [*Environmental Protection Agency*] (AEPA)
WHPB	Belton, SC [*AM radio station call letters*]
WHPC	Garden City, NY [*FM radio station call letters*]
WHPC	Wage and Hour and Public Contracts Division [*Department of Labor*] [*Obsolete*]
WHPCA	Walsh-Healey Public Contracts Act [*1936*] [*Labor*]
WHPCD	Wage and Hour and Public Contracts Division [*Department of Labor*] [*Obsolete*]
WHPE	High Point, NC [*FM radio station call letters*]
WHPE	Windows Help Project Editor [*Microsoft Corp.*] (PCM)
WHPK	Chicago, IL [*FM radio station call letters*]
WHPL	West Lafayette, IN [*FM radio station call letters*]
whpl.........	Whirlpool
WHPN-TV ..	Janesville, WI [*Television station call letters*] (BROA)
WHPO	Hoopeston, IL [*FM radio station call letters*]
WHPO	White House Personnel Office [*Terminated, 1974*]
WHPO	WOCE [*World Ocean Circulation Experiment*] Hydrologic Program Office [*Marine science*] (OSRA)
WHPP	Waste Handling and Packaging Plant [*Department of Energy*] [*Oak Ridge National Laboratory*] (GAAI)
WHPR	Highland Park, MI [*FM radio station call letters*]
WHPT	Sarasota, FL [*FM radio station call letters*]
WHP-TV	Harrisburg, PA [*Television station call letters*]
WHPX	New London, CT [*Television station call letters*] (BROA)
WHPY	Clayton, NC [*AM radio station call letters*] (RBYB)
WHPZ-FM...	Bremen, IN [*FM radio station call letters*] (BROA)
WHQ	War Headquarters (NATG)
WHQ	Western Historical Quarterly [*A publication*] (BRI)
WHQL	Windows Hardware Quality Labs [*Computer science*]
WHQO	Skowhegan, ME [*FM radio station call letters*]
WHQQ	Charleston, IL [*FM radio station call letters*]
WHQR	Wilmington, NC [*FM radio station call letters*]
WHQT	Coral Gables, FL [*FM radio station call letters*]
WHQX-FM...	Cedar Bluff, VA [*FM radio station call letters*] (BROA)
WHR	Vail [*Colorado*] [*Airport symbol*] (OAG)
WHR	Wage and Hour Reporter [*Bureau of National Affairs*] [*A publication*] (DLA)
WHR	Waste Heat Removal
W-HR.........	Watt-Hour (AAG)
WHR	Western Hemisphere Reserve
WHR	Western Humanities Review [*A publication*] (BRI)
WHR	Whether
WHR	Whirlpool Corp. [*NYSE symbol*] (SPSG)
WHR	William H. Rorer [*Research code symbol*]
WHR	Women and Health Roundtable (EA)
WHR	Working Heart Rate [*Cardiology*]
WHRA	Welwyn Hall Research Association (PDAA)
WHRA	Western Historical Research Associates [*Defunct*] (EA)
WHRABTS...	Whereabouts [*Legal*] [*British*] (ROG)
WHRAS	Whereas [*Legal*] [*British*] (ROG)
WHRAT	Whereat [*Legal*] [*British*] (ROG)
WHRB	Cambridge, MA [*FM radio station call letters*]
WHRC	Norwell, MA [*Television station call letters*]
WHRC	Washington Home Rule Committee [*Later, SDDC*] (EA)
WHRC	White River [*NASDAQ symbol*] (TTSB)
WHRC	White River Corp. [*NASDAQ symbol*] (SAG)
WHRC	World Health Research Center
WHRD	Huntington, WV [*AM radio station call letters*]
WHRF	Bel Air, MD [*AM radio station call letters*]
WHRI	Women's Health Research Institute
WHRIN	Wherein
WHRK	Memphis, TN [*FM radio station call letters*]
WHRL	Albany, NY [*FM radio station call letters*]
Whrlpl	Whirlpool Corp. [*Associated Press*] (SAG)
WHRM	Watt-Hour Meter (IAA)

WHRM	Wausau, WI [*FM radio station call letters*]
WHR Man	Wage and Hour Reference Manual [*Bureau of National Affairs*] [*A publication*] (DLA)
WHRM-TV	Wausau, WI [*Television station call letters*]
WHRO	Hampton-Norfolk, VA [*Television station call letters*]
WHRO	Norfolk, VA [*FM radio station call letters*]
WHRR	Avon, NY [*FM radio station call letters*] (RBYB)
WHRR-FM	Dennysville, ME [*FM radio station call letters*] (RBYB)
WHRS-FM	Cookeville, TN [*FM radio station call letters*] (RBYB)
WHRT	World Heart Corp. [*NASDAQ symbol*] (SAG)
WHRU	Waste Heat Recovery Unit [*Chemical engineering*]
WHRV	Norfolk, VA [*FM radio station call letters*]
WHRW	Binghamton, NY [*FM radio station call letters*]
WHRY	Hurley, WI [*AM radio station call letters*]
WHRZ	Providence, KY [*FM radio station call letters*]
WHS	Warehouse (AABC)
whs	Warehouse (ODBW)
WHS	Washington Headquarters Service (EBF)
WHS	Washington Headquarters Services [*Military*]
WHS	Water Hydraulic Section
WHS	Wesleyan Historical Society [*British*]
WHS	Western Harvest Sea [*Vancouver Stock Exchange symbol*]
WHS	Whalsay [*Shetland Islands*] [*Airport symbol*] (OAG)
WHS	White Scale
WHS	William Hunter Society (EA)
WHS	Wolf-Hirschorn Syndrome [*Medicine*]
WHS	Women's Health Study
WHS	World Health Statistics Data Base [*World Health Organization*] [*Information service or system*] (IID)
WHS	Wound Healing Society
WHSA	Brule, WI [*FM radio station call letters*]
WHSB	Alpena, MI [*FM radio station call letters*]
WHSC	Hartsville, SC [*AM radio station call letters*]
WHSC	White House Science Council
WHSC-FM	Hartsville, SC [*FM radio station call letters*]
WHSCH	Whitworth Scholar [*British*]
WHSD	Hinsdale, IL [*FM radio station call letters*]
WHSD	W. H. Smith Distributors [*British*]
WHSE	Newark, NJ [*Television station call letters*]
WHSE	Warehouse (AAG)
W/HSE	Wheelhouse [*Automotive engineering*]
WHSG	Monroe, GA [*Television station call letters*]
WHSH	Marlborough, MA [*Television station call letters*]
WHSHS	Wilbur Hot Springs Health Sanctuary (EA)
WHSI	Smithtown, NY [*Television station call letters*]
WHSING	Warehousing
WHSL	East St. Louis, IL [*Television station call letters*]
WHSLE	Wholesale
whsle	Wholesale (WDAA)
WHSL-FM	High Point, NC [*FM radio station call letters*] (RBYB)
WHSLR	Wholesaler
WHSM	Hayward, WI [*AM radio station call letters*]
WHSMAN	Warehouseman [*Legal shorthand*] (LWAP)
WHSM-FM	Hayward, WI [*FM radio station call letters*]
WHSMN	Warehouseman (AABC)
WHSN	Bangor, ME [*FM radio station call letters*]
WHSNA	Welsh Harp Society of North America (EA)
WHSNG	Warehousing
WHSP	Vineland, NJ [*Television station call letters*]
WHSR	White House Situation Room (MCD)
WHSS	Hamilton, OH [*FM radio station call letters*]
WHSS	White House Signal Support
WHST	Tawas City, MI [*FM radio station call letters*]
WHSUPA	Wharton School, University of Pennsylvania (DLA)
WHSV	Harrisonburg, VA [*Television station call letters*]
WHSV	Weight-Hourly Space Velocity [*Fuel technology*]
WHSW	Baltimore, MD [*Television station call letters*]
WHSY	Hattiesburg, MS [*AM radio station call letters*]
WHT	Watt-Hour Demand Meter, Thermal Type (IEEE)
WHT	White (AAG)
WHT	Whitehall Corp. [*NYSE symbol*] (SPSG)
WHT	William Herschel Telescope
WHT	William Howard Taft [*US president, 1857-1930*]
WHT	Witholding Tax
WHT	Women's Health Trial [*Department of Health and Human Services*] (GFGA)
WHT	Wometco Home Theatre [*Subscription television service*]
WHTA	Fayetteville, GA [*FM radio station call letters*] (RBYB)
WHTA	Walking Horse Trainers Association (EA)
WHTB	Fall River, MA [*AM radio station call letters*]
WHTC	Holland, MI [*AM radio station call letters*]
WHTD	Three Lakes, WI [*FM radio station call letters*]
WHTE-FM	Valley Station, KY [*FM radio station call letters*] (RBYB)
WhtePne	White Pine Software, Inc. [*Associated Press*] (SAG)
Whtewg	Whitewing Labs, Inc. [*Associated Press*] (SAG)
Whtewng	Whitewing Labs, Inc. [*Associated Press*] (SAG)
WHTF	Starview, PA [*FM radio station call letters*]
WHTG	Eatontown, NJ [*AM radio station call letters*]
WHTG-FM	Eatontown, NJ [*FM radio station call letters*]
WHTH	Heath, OH [*AM radio station call letters*]
WHTJ	Charlottesville, VA [*Television station call letters*]
WHTK	Rochester, NY [*AM radio station call letters*]
WHTL	Whitehall, WI [*FM radio station call letters*]
WHTM	Harrisburg, PA [*Television station call letters*]
WHTM	Wisconsin Hydrologic Transport Model

WHTN	Murfreesboro, TN [*Television station call letters*]
WHTO	Muncy, PA [*FM radio station call letters*]
WHTO	Whereto [*Legal*] [*British*] (ROG)
WHTQ	Orlando, FL [*FM radio station call letters*]
WHTR-FM	Hudson Falls, NY [*FM radio station call letters*] (RBYB)
WHTS	Rock Island, IL [*FM radio station call letters*] (RBYB)
WHTS	Western Hemisphere Transmission System
WHTT	Buffalo, NY [*AM radio station call letters*]
WHTT-FM	Buffalo, NY [*FM radio station call letters*]
WHTZ	Newark, NJ [*FM radio station call letters*]
WHU	Well Head Unit
WHU	Wild Horse [*Utah*] [*Seismograph station code, US Geological Survey*] (SEIS)
WHUB	Cookeville, TN [*AM radio station call letters*]
WHUB-FM	Cookeville, TN [*FM radio station call letters*]
WHUC	Hudson, NY [*AM radio station call letters*]
WHud	Hudson Public Library, Hudson, WI [*Library symbol Library of Congress*] (LCLS)
WHUD	Peekskill, NY [*FM radio station call letters*]
WHudSO	Hudson Star-Observer, Hudson, WI [*Library symbol Library of Congress*] (LCLS)
WHUG	Jamestown, NY [*FM radio station call letters*]
WHUN	Huntingdon, PA [*AM radio station call letters*]
WHUR	Washington, DC [*FM radio station call letters*]
WHUS	Storrs, CT [*FM radio station call letters*]
WHUT	Anderson, IN [*AM radio station call letters*]
WHV	Woodchuck Hepatitis Virus
WHVE	Russell Springs, KY [*FM radio station call letters*] (RBYB)
WHVL	Hinesville, GA [*FM radio station call letters*] (RBYB)
WHVN	Charlotte, NC [*AM radio station call letters*]
WHVP	Hudson, NY [*FM radio station call letters*]
WHVP	Wedged Hepatic Venous Pressure
WHVR	Hanover, PA [*AM radio station call letters*]
WHVS	Wharves (WGA)
WHVT	Clyde, OH [*FM radio station call letters*]
WHVW	Hyde Park, NY [*AM radio station call letters*]
WHW	Women Helping Women (EA)
WHWC	Menomonie, WI [*FM radio station call letters*]
WHWC-TV	Menomonie, WI [*Television station call letters*]
WHWD-AM	Fort Wayne, IN [*AM radio station call letters*] (RBYB)
WHWE	Howe, IN [*FM radio station call letters*]
WHWH	Princeton, NJ [*AM radio station call letters*]
WHWK	Binghamton, NY [*FM radio station call letters*]
WHWL	Marquette, MI [*FM radio station call letters*]
WHWPNLA	World Health Workers for Peace and NonIntervention in Latin America (EAIO)
WHWT	Water and Hazardous Waste Team (GNE)
WHWTB	Waste Heat Water Tube Boiler (DS)
WHWTBS	Waste Heat Water Tube Boiler Survey (DS)
WHWTCA	West Highland White Terrier Club of America (EA)
WIIWTII	Wherewith [*Legal*] [*British*] (ROG)
WHX	Wheeling Pittsburgh Corp. [*Later, WHX Corp.*] [*NYSE symbol*] (SPSG)
WIIX	WHX Corp. [*NYSE symbol*] (TTSB)
WHX	WHX Corp. Holding Co. [*Associated Press*] (SAG)
WHX Cp	WHX Corp. Holding Co. [*Associated Press*] (SAG)
WHXPr	WHX Corp.'A'Cv Pfd [*NYSE symbol*] (TTSB)
WHXPrB	WHX Corp.'B'Cv Pfd [*NYSE symbol*] (TTSB)
WHXT	Citronelle, AL [*FM radio station call letters*]
WHY	Air Sorel Ltd. [*Canada ICAO designator*] (FAAC)
WHY	What Have You [*British*] (ADA)
WHY	World Hunger Year (EA)
WHYB	Menominee, MI [*FM radio station call letters*]
WHYC	Swanquarter, NC [*FM radio station call letters*]
WHYCOS	World Hydrological Cycle Observing System [*Marine science*] (OSRA)
WHYDFTFT	What Have You Done for the Fleet Today [*Navy*]
WHYFU	Why Have You Forsaken Us? [*Fundraising*]
WHYI	Fort Lauderdale, FL [*FM radio station call letters*]
WHYL	Carlisle, PA [*AM radio station call letters*]
WHYL-FM	Carlisle, PA [*FM radio station call letters*]
WHYM	Statesville, NC [*AM radio station call letters*]
WHYN	Springfield, MA [*AM radio station call letters*]
WHYN-FM	Springfield, MA [*FM radio station call letters*]
WHYS	Bluefield, VA [*AM radio station call letters*]
WHYT	Detroit, MI [*FM radio station call letters*]
WHYY	Philadelphia, PA [*FM radio station call letters*]
WHYY	Wilmington, DE [*Television station call letters*]
WHYZ	Sans Souci, SC [*AM radio station call letters*]
WHZR	Royal Center, IN [*FM radio station call letters*]
WHZT	Mahomet, IL [*FM radio station call letters*]
WHZZ	Lansing, MI [*FM radio station call letters*] (RBYB)
WI	Oak Harbor, Whidbey Island, WA [*Naval base*]
WI	Rottnest Airbus [*Airline code*] [*Australia*]
WI	Swift-Aire Lines [*ICAO designator*] (AD)
WI	Walk In (ADA)
WI	Wallops Island [*Off coast of Virginia*]
WI	Water Injection
WI	Water Inlet (DAC)
WI	Welding Institute [*Database originator and operator*] (EA)
WI	Westerners International (EA)
WI	West Indies [*Formerly, BWI*]
WI	Westminster Capital [*AMEX symbol*]
WI	Wexas International [*Commercial firm British*] (EAIO)
WI	When Issued [*Stock exchange term*] (SPSG)

WI ... White Information [*Banking*] [*British*]
WI ... Wilderness Inquiry [*An association*] (EA)
WI ... Wimpy International [*Commercial firm British*]
WI ... Windward Islands (WDAA)
WI ... Wine Institute (EA)
WI ... Winter [*Germany ICAO aircraft manufacturer identifier*] (ICAO)
WI ... Wire
wi ... Wire (VRA)
WI ... Wisconsin [*Postal code*]
WI ... Within
WI ... Women's Institute [*British*]
WI ... Women's Reserve, Intelligence Duties [*USNR officer designation*]
WI ... Word Intelligibility
WI ... World Impact (EA)
WI ... Worldwatch Institute (EA)
WI ... Wrought Iron
WIA ... Manitowoc Public Library, Manitowoc, WI [*OCLC symbol*] (OCLC)
WIA ... Waking Imagined Analgesia [*Medicine*]
WIA ... Watusi International Association (EA)
WIA ... Weather-Impacted Airspace (USDC)
WIA ... Weight Indicating Alarm [*Engineering*]
WIA ... Western Interpreters Association [*Later, NAI*] (EA)
WIA ... Wien-Auhof [*Austria*] [*Geomagnetic observatory code*]
WIA ... Windward Islands Airways International NV [*Netherlands ICAO designator*] (FAAC)
WIA ... Winward Islands Airways International [*Netherlands Antilles*] (EY)
WIA ... Women in Aerospace (EA)
WIA ... Women in Agribusiness [*An association*] (EA)
WIA ... Women in the Arts Foundation (EA)
WIA ... Wounded in Action [*Military*]
WIAA ... Interlochen, MI [*FM radio station call letters*]
WIAA ... Sabang [*Indonesia*] [*ICAO location identifier*] (ICLI)
WIAA ... Women's International Association of Aeronautics (IAA)
WIAB ... Banda Aceh/Maimun Saleh [*Indonesia*] [*ICAO location identifier*] (ICLI)
WIAC ... San Juan, PR [*AM radio station call letters*]
WIAC ... Women's Intercollegiate Athletic Conference (PSS)
WIAC ... Women's International Art Club
WIAC ... Women's International Art Club, London [*1899*] (NGC)
WIAC-FM ... San Juan, PR [*FM radio station call letters*]
WIACLALS ... West Indian Association for Commonwealth Literature and Language Studies [*Jamaica*] (EAIO)
WIACO ... World Insulation and Acoustic Congress Organization (EA)
WIAG ... Menggala/Astrakestra [*Indonesia*] [*ICAO location identifier*] (ICLI)
WIAI ... Danville, IL [*FM radio station call letters*]
WIAJ ... Semplak/Atang Senjaya [*Indonesia*] [*ICAO location identifier*] (ICLI)
WIAK ... Margahayu/Sulaiman [*Indonesia*] [*ICAO location identifier*] (ICLI)
WIAL ... Eau Claire, WI [*FM radio station call letters*]
WIAM ... Tasikmalaya/Cibeureum [*Indonesia*] [*ICAO location identifier*] (ICLI)
WIAM ... Williamston, NC [*AM radio station call letters*]
WIAN ... Ishpeming, MI [*AM radio station call letters*]
WI & CTF ... Welsh Industry and Commerce Trade Fair (ITD)
WIANG ... Wisconsin Air National Guard (MUSM)
WIAP ... Banyumas/Wirasaba [*Indonesia*] [*ICAO location identifier*] (ICLI)
WIAP ... Wartime Individual Augmentation Program [*Military*]
WIAP ... Westinghouse Industrial Atomic Power (MCD)
WIAR ... Leland, MI [*FM radio station call letters*]
WIAR ... Madiun/Iswahyudi [*Indonesia*] [*ICAO location identifier*] (ICLI)
WIAS ... Malang/Abdul Rachman Saleh [*Indonesia*] [*ICAO location identifier*] (ICLI)
WIAS ... West Indies Associated State
WIAS ... Whiteruthenian Institute of Arts and Science [*Later, BIAS*] (EA)
WIAT ... Wechsler Individual Achievement Test (TMMY)
WIB ... Lawrence University, Appleton, WI [*OCLC symbol*] (OCLC)
WIB ... Wallcovering Information Bureau (EA)
WIB ... Wartime Information Board [*World War II Canada*]
WIB ... Weather Information Branch [*Air Force*] (MCD)
WIB ... Western Independent Bankers (TBD)
WIB ... When Interrupt Block (NASA)
WIB ... When-Issued-Basis [*Business term*]
WIB ... Wine Information Bureau [*Australia*]
WIB ... Within-Batch (AAEL)
WIB ... Women's Information Bank (EA)
WIBA ... Madison, WI [*AM radio station call letters*]
WIBA ... Welsh Indoor Bowls Association (DBA)
WIBA-FM ... Madison, WI [*FM radio station call letters*]
WIBB ... Fort Valley, GA [*FM radio station call letters*]
WIBB ... Pekanbaru [*Indonesia*] [*ICAO location identifier*] (ICLI)
WIBC ... Indianapolis, IN [*AM radio station call letters*]
WIBC ... Women's International Bowling Congress (EA)
WIBC ... World Institute of Black Communications (EA)
WIBD ... Dumai/Pinangkampai [*Indonesia*] [*ICAO location identifier*] (ICLI)
WIBF ... Jenkintown, PA [*FM radio station call letters*]
WIBFD ... Will Be Forwarded (NOAA)
WIBG ... Ocean City, NJ [*AM radio station call letters*]
WIBI ... Carlinville, IL [*FM radio station call letters*]
WIBIS ... Will Be Issued (NOAA)
WIBM ... Jackson, MI [*FM radio station call letters*]
WIBN ... Earl Park, IN [*FM radio station call letters*]
WIBNI ... Wouldn't It Be Nice If [*Computer hacker terminology*] (NHD)
WIBP ... Semilinang/Peranap [*Indonesia*] [*ICAO location identifier*] (ICLI)
WIBR ... Baton Rouge, LA [*AM radio station call letters*]
WIBR ... Sipora/Rokot [*Indonesia*] [*ICAO location identifier*] (ICLI)
WIBS ... Bengkalis/Sungai Pakning [*Indonesia*] [*ICAO location identifier*] (ICLI)
WIBS ... Guayama, PR [*AM radio station call letters*]
WIBS ... Wool Industry Bureau of Statistics [*British*] (CB)
WIBT ... Tanjung Balai/Sungai Bati [*Indonesia*] [*ICAO location identifier*] (ICLI)
WIBU ... Poynette, WI [*AM radio station call letters*]
WIBV ... Belleville, IL [*AM radio station call letters*]
WIBW ... Topeka, KS [*AM radio station call letters*]
WIBW-FM ... Topeka, KS [*FM radio station call letters*]
WIBW-TV ... Topeka, KS [*Television station call letters*]
WIBX ... Utica, NY [*AM radio station call letters*]
WIBZ ... Wedgefield, SC [*FM radio station call letters*]
WIC ... Medical College of Wisconsin, Milwaukee, WI [*OCLC symbol*] (OCLC)
WIC ... War Insurance Corporation
WIC ... Warning Information Correlation (MCD)
WIC ... Washington Information Center (COE)
WIC ... Washington International Center (EA)
WIC ... Water Infiltration Course [*Army*]
WIC ... Wax Insulating Compound
WIC ... Wayfarer International Committee [*Axminster, Devonshire, England*] (EAIO)
WIC ... Weighted Ion Concentration [*Air pollution measure*]
WIC ... Welding Institute of Canada (EAIO)
WIC ... Welfare and Institutions Code (BARN)
WIC ... West India Committee [*British*] (EAIO)
WIC ... Wheat Industry Council (EA)
WIC ... Whitbread Investment Co. [*British*]
WIC ... Wick [*Scotland*] [*Airport symbol*] (OAG)
WIC ... WICOR, Inc. [*NYSE symbol*] (SPSG)
WIC ... WIC Western International Communications Ltd. [*Toronto Stock Exchange symbol Vancouver Stock Exchange symbol*]
WIC ... Wildlife Information Center (EA)
WIC ... Windsor Institute of Complementology [*Later, ICS*] (EA)
WIC ... Women in Cable (EA)
WIC ... Women in Communications
WIC ... Women in Crisis (EA)
WIC ... Women, Infants, and Children [*Supplemental food program*] [*Department of Agriculture*]
WIC ... Women's Interart Center (EA)
WIC ... Women's Issues Coordinator [*Australia*]
WIC ... Workplace Information Centre [*New South Wales, Australia*]
WIC ... Worksheet Inspection Card
WIC ... World Institute Council (EA)
WICA ... Judgments of the West Indian Court of Appeal [*A publication*] (DLA)
WICA ... While in Control Area [*Aviation*] (FAAC)
WICA ... Wind Cave National Park
WICA ... Witches International Craft Association (EA)
WICAT ... World Institute for Computer-Assisted Teaching (NITA)
WICB ... Ithaca, NY [*FM radio station call letters*]
WICB ... Washington Independent Community Bankers Association (TBD)
WICB ... Women in Cell Biology (EA)
WICBC ... World Invitation Club Basketball Championships [*British*]
WICBE ... World Information Centre for Bilingual Education [*See also CMIEB*] [*Paris, France*] (EAIO)
WICC ... Bridgeport, CT [*AM radio station call letters*]
WICC ... Wisconsin Collegiate Conference (PSS)
WICC ... Wisconsin Instructional Computing Consortium (EDAC)
WICC ... Women's Inter-Church Council of Canada
WICCA ... Women in Conscious Creative Action [*An association*] (EA)
WICD ... Champaign, IL [*Television station call letters*]
WICE ... World Industry Council for the Environment
WICEM ... World Industry Conference on Environmental Management
WICF ... Women's International Cultural Federation [*See also FICF*] (EAIO)
WICH ... Norwich, CT [*AM radio station call letters*]
WICHE ... Western Interstate Commission for Higher Education (GAGS)
Wichita St U ... Wichita State University (GAGS)
WichRO ... Wichita River Oil Corp. [*Associated Press*] (SAG)
WICI ... Sumter, SC [*FM radio station call letters*]
WICI ... Women in Communications, Inc. (EA)
WICK ... Scranton, PA [*AM radio station call letters*]
WICK ... Wicklow [*County in Ireland*] (ROG)
WICKF ... Wickford [*England*]
WICKL ... Wicklow [*County in Ireland*]
WickLu ... Wickes Lumber Co. [*Associated Press*] (SAG)
WICL ... Work Inspection Characteristics List
WICN ... Women in Chemistry Network [*Australia*]
WICN ... Worcester, MA [*FM radio station call letters*]
WICO ... Salisbury, MD [*AM radio station call letters*]
WICO ... W. I. Carr Sons & Co. Overseas [*Stockbroker*] [*Hong Kong*]
WICO-FM ... Salisbury, MD [*FM radio station call letters*]
WICOMATIC ... Wiring and Connective Device, Semiautomatic (DNAB)
WICOR ... WICOR, Inc. [*Associated Press*] (SAG)
WICR ... Indianapolis, IN [*FM radio station call letters*]
WICR ... Wilson's Creek Battlefield National Park
WICS ... Springfield, IL [*Television station call letters*]
WICS ... Westinghouse Integrated Compiling System (NITA)
WICS ... Women in Community Service (EA)
WICS ... Worldwide Intelligence Communications System (MCD)
WICT ... Grove City, PA [*FM radio station call letters*]
WICT ... Women in Cable and Telecommunications [*An association*] (NTPA)
WICU ... Erie, PA [*Television station call letters*]
WICY ... Malone, NY [*AM radio station call letters*]
WICZ ... Binghamton, NY [*Television station call letters*]
WICZ ... While in Control Zone [*Aviation*] (FAAC)
WID ... University of Wisconsin, Madison Library School, Madison, WI [*OCLC symbol*] (OCLC)
WID ... Weekly Intelligence Digest [*Military*] (CINC)

WID .... West India Dock
WID .... Widow [or Widower]
WID .... Width
WID .... Window Identifier [Computer science]
WID .... Wind River Resources [Vancouver Stock Exchange symbol]
WID .... With [Amateur radio shorthand] (WDAA)
WID .... Women in Design [An association] (NTPA)
WID .... Women in Development [Peace Corps]
WID .... Women in Development [Bureau of the Census] [A publication] (GFGA)
WID .... Women's Interest Division [Australia]
WID .... World Institute on Disability (EA)
WIDA .... Carolina, PR [AM radio station call letters]
WIDA-FM .... Carolina, PR [FM radio station call letters]
WIDB-AM .... Chicago, IL [AM radio station call letters] (BROA)
WIDE .... Biddeford, ME [AM radio station call letters]
WIDE .... Wide-Angle Infinity Display Equipment
WIDE .... WideCom Group [NASDAQ symbol] (SAG)
WIDE .... Wide-Field Infrared Explorer [Satellite]
WIDE .... Wiring Integration Design (IEEE)
WideC .... WideCom Group [Associated Press] (SAG)
WideCm ...... WideCom Group [Associated Press] (SAG)
WIDEF .... WideCom Group [NASDAQ symbol] (TTSB)
Widener U ... Widener University (GAGS)
WIDER .... World Institute for Development Economics Research [United Nations]
WIDETRACK... Wideband Transmission Relay Acoustic Communications (MCD)
WIDF .... Women's International Democratic Federation [See also FDIF] [Berlin, German Democratic Republic] (EAIO)
WIDG .... St. Ignace, MI [AM radio station call letters]
WIDI .... Women in Design International [Later, DI] (EA)
WIDJET .... Waterloo Interactive Direct Job Entry Terminal System [IBM Corp.]
WIDL .... Caro, MI [FM radio station call letters]
WIDOWAC .... Wing Design Optimization with Aerolastic Constraints [Computer program]
WIDP .... Guayama, PR [Television station call letters]
WIDR .... Kalamazoo, MI [FM radio station call letters]
WIDR .... Widower [Legal shorthand] (LWAP)
WIDS .... Russell Springs, KY [AM radio station call letters] (RBYB)
WIDS .... Waterborne Intrusion Detection System (MCD)
WIDU .... Fayetteville, NC [AM radio station call letters]
WIDU .... Wireless Intelligence and Development Unit [British military] (DMA)
WIDW .... WideCom Group [NASDAQ symbol] (SAG)
WIDWF .... WideCom Group Wrrt [NASDAQ symbol] (TTSB)
WIE............. University of Wisconsin-Superior, Jim Dan Hill Library, Superior, WI [OCLC symbol] (OCLC)
WIE............. Women in Education [Australia]
WIE............. Women in Engineering Centre (EAIO)
WIE............. Women in Entertainment [British]
WIE............. Women's Information Exchange (EA)
WIEB/WINB... Western Interstate Energy Board/Western Interstate Nuclear Board (EA)
WIEC........... World Institute of Ecology and Cancer [See also IMEC] (EAIO)
WIEL........... Elizabethtown, KY [AM radio station call letters]
Wien Stud ... Wiener Studien [A publication] (OCD)
WIEU........... Weekly Intelligence Estimate Update [Vietnam]
WIEZ........... Lewistown, PA [AM radio station call letters]
WIF............. Mid-Wisconsin Federated Library System, Fond Du Lac, WI [OCLC symbol] (OCLC)
WIF............. Water Immersion Facility [NASA] (KSC)
WIF............. Weapons Integration Facility (MCD)
WIF............. West India Fruit & Steamship [AAR code]
WIF............. West Indies Federation
WIF............. Wideroe's Flyveselskap AS [Norway ICAO designator] (FAAC)
WIF............. Wildfire Resources Ltd. [Vancouver Stock Exchange symbol]
WIF............. Wilt-Inducing Factor [Plant pathology]
WIF............. Women in Film (EA)
WIF............. Worldview International Foundation (EAIO)
WIFA........... Washington Institute of Foreign Affairs (EA)
WIFC........... Wausau, WI [FM radio station call letters]
WIFE........... Connersville, IN [AM radio station call letters]
WIFE........... Women Involved in Farm Economics (EA)
WIFE........... Women's Independent Film Exchange [Defunct] (EA)
WIFF........... Auburn, IN [AM radio station call letters]
WIFF........... Wang [Laboratories, Inc.] Image File Format [Computer science] (PCM)
WIFI........... Florence, NJ [AM radio station call letters]
WIFM........... Elkin, NC [AM radio station call letters] (RBYB)
WIFM-FM...... Elkin, NC [FM radio station call letters]
WIFN .... Marine City, MI [AM radio station call letters]
WIFNA......... White Inhibited Fuming Nitric Acid (SAA)
WIFO........... Jesup, GA [FM radio station call letters]
WIFP........... Women's Institute for Freedom of the Press (EA)
WIFR........... Freeport, IL [Television station call letters]
WIFS........... Work Injury Followback Survey [Bureau of Labor Statistics and National Center for Health Statistics] (GFGA)
WIFU .... Western Interprovincial Football Union [Canada]
WIFV........... Women in Film and Video [An association] (NTPA)
WIFX........... Jenkins, KY [FM radio station call letters]
WIG .... Washington Information Group, Ltd. [Research center] (TSSD)
WIG .... Wiggins Airways [ICAO designator] (FAAC)
Wig............. Wigram on Loills [A publication] (DLA)
WIG .... Wing in Ground
WIG .... Wisconsin State Library, Processing Center, Madison, WI [OCLC symbol] (OCLC)

WIG .... Wolfram Inert Gas (MCD)
WIG .... Women in Government [An association] (NTPA)
Wig Disc...... Wigram on Discovery [2nd ed.] [1840] [A publication] (DLA)
WIGE .... Wax-Impregnated Graphite Electrode
WIGE .... Wing-in-Ground Effect (PDAA)
Wig Ev .... Wigram on Extrinsic Evidence [A publication] (DLA)
WIGG .... Wiggins, MS [AM radio station call letters]
Wight......... Wightwick's English Exchequer Reports [145 English Reprint] [A publication] (DLA)
Wight El Cas... Wight's Scottish Election Cases [1784-96] [A publication] (DLA)
Wightw .... Wightwick's English Exchequer Reports [145 English Reprint] [A publication] (DLA)
Wightw (Eng)... Wightwick's English Exchequer Reports [145 English Reprint] [A publication] (DLA)
WIGL .... Orangeburg, SC [FM radio station call letters]
WIGM .... Medford, WI [AM radio station call letters]
Wigm Ev...... Wigmore on Evidence [A publication] (DLA)
WIGM-FM..... Medford, WI [FM radio station call letters]
WIGO .... What Is Going On [Humorous definition of science]
WIGORN ...... Wigorniensis [Signature of Bishop of Worcester] [British] (ROG)
WIGS .... Gouverneur, NY [AM radio station call letters]
Wig Wills .... Wigmore on Wills [A publication] (DLA)
WIGY .... Madison, ME [FM radio station call letters] (RBYB)
WIH .... State Historical Society of Wisconsin, Madison, WI [OCLC symbol] (OCLC)
WIH .... Work in Hand (ILCA)
WIHC.......... Newberry, MI [FM radio station call letters] (RBYB)
WIHN .... Normal, IL [FM radio station call letters]
WIHS .... Middletown, CT [FM radio station call letters]
WIHS .... Western Institute for Health Studies
WIHS .... Women's Interagency HIV [Human Immuno Deficiency Virus] Study [Medicine]
WII .... Beloit College Library, Beloit, WI [OCLC symbol] (OCLC)
WII .... Weatherford Enterra [NYSE symbol] (SAG)
WII .... Weatherford International (EFIS)
WIIA .... Tangerang/Budiarto [Indonesia] [ICAO location identifier] (ICLI)
WIIAD .... Winrock International Institute for Agricultural Development (EA)
WIIB........... Bandung/Husein Sastranegara [Indonesia] [ICAO location identifier] (ICLI)
WIIB........... Bloomington, IN [Television station call letters]
WIIC........... Cirebon/Panggung [Indonesia] [ICAO location identifier] (ICLI)
WIID .... Jakarta/Kemayoran [Indonesia] [ICAO location identifier] (ICLI)
WIIFM.......... What's In It For Me [Electronic mail language] [Computer science]
WIIFM.......... What's in It for Me? [Fundraising]
WIIG .... Jakarta/Pulau Panjang [Indonesia] [ICAO location identifier] (ICLI)
Wiig CRIL.... Wiig Criterion Referenced Inventory of Language [Test] (TMMY)
WIIH .... Jakarta/Halim Perdanakusuma [Indonesia] [ICAO location identifier] (ICLI)
WIII........... Cortland, NY [FM radio station call letters]
WIII........... Jakarta/Cengkareng [Indonesia] [ICAO location identifier] (ICLI)
WIIJ.......... Yogyakarta/Adi Sucipto [Indonesia] [ICAO location identifier] (ICLI)
WIIK.......... Kalijati [Indonesia] [ICAO location identifier] (ICLI)
WIIL.......... Cilacap/Tunggul Wulung [Indonesia] [ICAO location identifier] (ICLI)
WIIL.......... Kenosha, WI [FM radio station call letters]
WIIN .... Ridgeland, MS [AM radio station call letters] (RBYB)
WIIP.......... Jakarta/Pondok Cabe [Indonesia] [ICAO location identifier] (ICLI)
WIIP.......... Waters Intelligent Information Processor
WIIQ.......... Demopolis, AL [Television station call letters]
WIIR.......... Pelabuhan Ratu [Indonesia] [ICAO location identifier] (ICLI)
WIIR.......... Water-Insoluble Inorganic Residue (DICI)
WIIS.......... Key West, FL [FM radio station call letters]
WIIS.......... Semarang/Achmad Yani [Indonesia] [ICAO location identifier] (ICLI)
WIIS.......... Wang Integrated Image System
WIIS.......... Western Insurance Information Service
WIIS.......... Women in International Security (EA)
WIIT.......... Tanjung Karang/Branti [Indonesia] [ICAO location identifier] (ICLI)
WIIU.......... Worker's International Industrial Union
WIIW.......... Wiener Institut fuer Internationale Wirtschaftsvergleiche [Vienna Institute for Comparative Economic Studies] [Information service or system] (IID)
WIIWD .... What It Is We Do [Computer hacker terminology]
WIIX.......... Jakarta [Indonesia] [ICAO location identifier] (ICLI)
WIIZ.......... Blackville, SC [FM radio station call letters] (RBYB)
WIIZ.......... Jakarta [Indonesia] [ICAO location identifier] (ICLI)
WIJ .... Arrowhead Library System, Janesville Public Library, Janesville, WI [OCLC symbol] (OCLC)
WIJ .... Wit of the Jews [A publication]
WIJK.......... Evergreen, AL [AM radio station call letters]
WIJY.......... Hilton Head Island, SC [FM radio station call letters]
WIK........... Kenosha Public Library, Kenosha, WI [OCLC symbol] (OCLC)
WIK........... Waikato Aero Club, Inc. [New Zealand] [ICAO designator] (FAAC)
WIK........... Wien-Kobenzl [Austria] [Geomagnetic observatory code]
WIKB .... Batam/Hang Nadim [Indonesia] [ICAO location identifier] (ICLI)
WIKB .... Iron River, MI [AM radio station call letters]
WIKB-FM ..... Iron River, MI [FM radio station call letters]
WIKC.......... Bogalusa, LA [AM radio station call letters]
WIKD .... Petes Brewing Co. [NASDAQ symbol] (SAG)
WIKD .... Tanjung Pandan/Bulu Tumbang [Indonesia] [ICAO location identifier] (ICLI)
WIKE.......... Newport, VT [AM radio station call letters]
WIKI.......... Carrollton, KY [FM radio station call letters]
WIKK.......... Newton, IL [FM radio station call letters]
WIKK.......... Pangkal Pinang [Indonesia] [ICAO location identifier] (ICLI)
WIKN.......... Port Matilda, PA [FM radio station call letters]
WIKN .... Tanjung Pinang/Kijang [Indonesia] [ICAO location identifier] (ICLI)

WIKO .... Morehead, KY [*FM radio station call letters*]
WIKQ .... Greeneville, TN [*FM radio station call letters*]
WIKS .... New Bern, NC [*FM radio station call letters*]
WIKS .... Singkep/Dabo [*Indonesia*] [*ICAO location identifier*] (ICLI)
WIKS .... Wickes Lumber [*NASDAQ symbol*] (TTSB)
WIKS .... Wickes Lumber Co. [*NASDAQ symbol*] (SAG)
WIKX .... Punta Gorda, FL [*FM radio station call letters*]
WIKY .... Evansville, IN [*FM radio station call letters*]
WIKZ .... Chambersburg, PA [*FM radio station call letters*]
WIL .... Lakeland College, Sheboygan, WI [*OCLC symbol*] (OCLC)
WIL .... Nairobi-Wilson [*Kenya*] [*Airport symbol*] (OAG)
WIL .... St. Louis, MO [*FM radio station call letters*]
WIL .... Ward Indicator Light
WIL .... West Isle Air, Inc. [*FAA designator*] (FAAC)
WIL .... White Indicating Light [*or lamp*]
WIL .... Wilco Mining Co. Ltd. [*Toronto Stock Exchange symbol*]
WIL .... Wilkes [*Antarctica*] [*Seismograph station code, US Geological Survey Closed*] (SEIS)
WIL .... Wilmington [*Diocesan abbreviation*] [*Delaware*] (TOCD)
WIL .... Wilshire Technologies [*AMEX symbol*] (TTSB)
WIL .... Wilshire Technologies, Inc. [*AMEX symbol*] (SPSG)
WIL .... Windows Interface Language [*Computer science*] (PCM)
WIL .... Women in Leadership [*Project*]
WILA .... Danville, VA [*AM radio station call letters*]
Wilberforce... Wilberforce on Statute Law [*A publication*] (DLA)
Wilb Stat ..... Wilberforce on Construction and Operation of Statutes [*1881*] [*A publication*] (DLA)
WILC .... Laurel, MD [*AM radio station call letters*]
WILC .... West Central Illinois Library Cooperative [*Library network*]
Wilc Cond.... Wilcox's Condensed Ohio Reports (Reprint) [*1-7 Ohio*] [*A publication*] (DLA)
Wilc Cond Rep... Wilcox's Condensed Ohio Reports (Reprint) [*1-7 Ohio*] [*A publication*] (DLA)
Wilc Mun Corp... Wilcox on Municipal Corporations [*Ohio*] [*A publication*] (DLA)
WILCO .... Western Interstate Library Coordinating Organization
WILCO .... Will Comply [*Used after "Roger"*] [*Radio term*]
wilco .... Will Comply (ODBW)
WILCO .... Wiltshire Libraries in Cooperation (NITA)
Wilcox .... Wilcox's Lackawanna Reports [*Pennsylvania*] [*A publication*] (DLA)
Wilcox .... Wilcox's Reports [*10 Ohio*] [*A publication*] (DLA)
Wilcox Cond... Wilcox's Condensed Ohio Reports [*A publication*] (DLA)
WILD .... Boston, MA [*AM radio station call letters*]
WILD .... What I Like to Do [*Psychological testing*]
WILD .... Women's Independent Label Distribution Network (EA)
Wilde Conv... Wilde's Supplement to Barton's Conveyancing [*A publication*] (DLA)
Wilde Sup ... Wilde's Supplement to Barton's Conveyancing [*A publication*] (DLA)
Wildl A .... Wildlife in Australia [*A publication*]
Wildm Int L... Wildman's International Law [*A publication*] (ILCA)
Wildm Int Law... Wildman's International Law [*A publication*] (DLA)
Wildm Search... Wildman. Search, Capture, and Prize [*A publication*] (ILCA)
WildOats...... Wild Oats Markets, Inc. [*Associated Press*] (SAG)
WILE .... Byesville, OH [*FM radio station call letters*]
WILE .... Cambridge, OH [*AM radio station call letters*]
Wiley .... John Wiley & Sons [*Publisher*] (AAGC)
WileyJA .... Wiley [*John*] & Sons class A [*Associated Press*] (SAG)
WileyJB .... Wiley, John & Sons class A [*Associated Press*] (SAG)
WILF .... Williamsport, PA [*Television station call letters*]
WILI .... Willimantic, CT [*AM radio station call letters*]
WILI-FM ...... Willimantic, CT [*FM radio station call letters*]
WILJ .... West Indian Law Journal [*Jamaica*] [*A publication*] (DLA)
WILK .... Wilkes-Barre, PA [*AM radio station call letters*]
Wilk .... Wilkinson, Owen, Paterson, and Murray's New South Wales Reports [*1862-65*] [*A publication*] (DLA)
Wilk .... Wilkinson. Texas Court of Appeals and Civil Appeals [*A publication*] (DLA)
Wilk & Mur... Wilkinson, Owen, Paterson, and Murray's New South Wales Reports [*1862-65*] [*A publication*] (DLA)
Wilk & Ow... Wilkinson, Owen, Paterson, and Murray's New South Wales Reports [*1862-65*] [*A publication*] (DLA)
Wilk & Pat... Wilkinson, Owen, Paterson, and Murray's New South Wales Reports [*1862-65*] [*A publication*] (DLA)
Wilkes C...... Wilkes College (GAGS)
Wilk Funds... Wilkinson on Public Funds [*1839*] [*A publication*] (DLA)
Wilk Leg Ang Sax... Wilkins' Leges Anglo-Saxonicae Ecclesiasticae et Civiles [*A publication*] (DLA)
Wilk Lim...... Wilkinson. Limitation of Actions [*A publication*] (ILCA)
Wilk P & M... Wilkinson, Paterson, and Murray's New South Wales Reports [*1862-65*] [*A publication*] (DLA)
Wilk Prec..... Wilkinson on Precedents in Conveyancing [*4th ed.*] [*1890*] [*A publication*] (DLA)
Wilk Repl..... Wilkinson on Replevin [*1825*] [*A publication*] (DLA)
Wilk Sh....... Wilkinson's Office of Sheriff [*A publication*] (DLA)
Wilk Ship..... Wilkinson on Shipping [*1843*] [*A publication*] (DLA)
WILL .... Urbana, IL [*AM radio station call letters*]
Will .... Willes' English Common Pleas Reports [*125 English Reprint*] [*A publication*] (DLA)
Will .... William (King of England) (DLA)
Will .... Williams' Massachusetts Reports [*1 Massachusetts*] [*1804-05*] [*A publication*] (DLA)
Will .... Williams' Vermont Reports [*27-29 Vermont*] [*A publication*] (DLA)
Will .... Willson's Reports [*29-30 Texas Appeals*] [*1, 2, Texas Civil Appeals*] [*A publication*] (DLA)
WILL .... Women Legislator's Lobby
WILL .... Workshop In Library Leadership [*Canada*]
WILL .... Workshop Institute for Living-Learning (EA)

Will Abr....... Williams' Abridgment of Cases [*1798-1803*] [*A publication*] (DLA)
Willamette U... Willamette University (GAGS)
Willamt........ Willamette Industries, Inc. [*Associated Press*] (SAG)
Will Ann Reg... Williams' Annual Register [*New York*] [*A publication*] (DLA)
Will Auct ..... Williams' Auctions [*5th ed.*] [*1829*] [*A publication*] (DLA)
Will Bankt ... Williams' Law and Practice of Bankruptcy [*19th ed.*] [*1977*] [*A publication*] (DLA)
Will-Bund St Tr... Willis-Bund's Cases from State Trials [*A publication*] (DLA)
Willc Const... Willcock's The Office of Constable [*A publication*] (DLA)
Willc Med Pr... Willcock's Medical Profession [*1830*] [*A publication*] (DLA)
Willc Mun Corp... Willcock's Municipal Corp. [*A publication*] (ILCA)
Willcock Mun Corp... Willcock's Municipal Corp. [*A publication*] (DLA)
Will Com .... Williams on Rights of Common [*A publication*] (DLA)
Will Con Rep... Texas Civil Cases [*A publication*] (DLA)
WillCor .... Willis Corroon Ltd. [*Associated Press*] (SAG)
Will Cr L...... Willan's Criminal Law of Canada [*A publication*] (DLA)
Will Eq Jur... Willard's Equity Jurisprudence [*A publication*] (DLA)
Will Eq Pl... Willis on Equity Pleading [*1820*] [*A publication*] (DLA)
Willes.......... Willes' English Common Pleas Reports [*125 English Reprint*] [*A publication*] (DLA)
Willes (Eng)... Willes' English Common Pleas Reports [*125 English Reprint*] [*A publication*] (DLA)
Will Ex....... Williams on Executors [*15th ed.*] [*1970*] [*A publication*] (DLA)
WILL-FM ...... Urbana, IL [*FM radio station call letters*]
Williams..... Peere-Williams' English Chancery Reports [*A publication*] (DLA)
Williams..... [*The*] Williams Companies [*Associated Press*] (SAG)
Williams..... Williams' Reports [*1 Massachusetts*] [*A publication*] (DLA)
Williams..... Williams' Reports [*10-12 Utah*] [*A publication*] (DLA)
Williams..... Williams' Vermont Reports [*27-29 Vermont*] [*A publication*] (DLA)
Williams & B Adm Jur... Williams and Bruce's Admiralty Practice [*3 eds.*] [*1869-1902*] [*A publication*] (DLA)
Williams & Bruce Ad Pr... Williams and Bruce's Admiralty Practice [*3 eds.*] [*1869-1902*] [*A publication*] (DLA)
Williams B Pr... Williams' Bankruptcy Practice [*17 eds.*] [*1870-1958*] [*A publication*] (DLA)
Williams C... Williams College (GAGS)
Williams Common... Williams on Rights of Common [*A publication*] (DLA)
Williams Ex'rs... Williams on Executors [*A publication*] (DLA)
Williams Ex'rs R & T Ed... Williams on Executors, Randolph and Talcott Edition [*A publication*] (DLA)
Williams P... Peere-Williams' English Chancery Reports [*1695-1736*] [*A publication*] (DLA)
Williams Pers Prop... Williams on Personal Property [*A publication*] (DLA)
Williams Real Prop... Williams on Real Property [*A publication*] (DLA)
Williams Saund... Williams' Notes to Saunders' Reports [*A publication*] (DLA)
Williams Seis... Williams on Seisin [*A publication*] (DLA)
William W Story's Rept... William W. Story's United States Circuit Court Reports [*A publication*] (DLA)
Willis Eq...... Willis on Equity Pleading [*1820*] [*A publication*] (DLA)
Willis Int ..... Willis on Interrogatories [*A publication*] (DLA)
Williston...... Williston on Contracts [*A publication*] (DLA)
Williston...... Williston on Sales [*A publication*] (DLA)
Willis Trust... Willis on Trustees [*A publication*] (DLA)
Will Just...... Williams' Justice [*A publication*] (DLA)
Will LD....... Williams' Law Dictionary [*A publication*] (DLA)
Willm.......... Williams Companies [*Associated Press*] (SAG)
Willm25....... Williams Companies [*Associated Press*] (SAG)
Will Mass.... Williams' Reports [*1 Massachusetts*] [*A publication*] (DLA)
Will Mass Cit... Williams' Massachusetts Citations [*A publication*] (DLA)
Willms25..... Williams Companies [*Associated Press*] (SAG)
WillmVV ...... Willamette Valley Vineyards, Inc. [*Associated Press*] (SAG)
Willm W & D... Willmore, Wollaston, and Davison's English Queen's Bench Reports [*1837*] [*A publication*] (DLA)
Willm W & H... Willmore, Wollaston, and Hodges' English Queen's Bench Reports [*1838-39*] [*A publication*] (DLA)
Will P .... Peere-Williams' English Chancery Reports [*A publication*] (DLA)
Will Pet Ch... Williams' Petitions in Chancery [*1880*] [*A publication*] (DLA)
Will Real Ass... Williams' Real Assets [*1861*] [*A publication*] (DLA)
Will Real Est... Willard on Real Estate and Conveyancing [*A publication*] (DLA)
Will Real Pr... Williams on Real Property [*A publication*] (DLA)
Will Saund... Williams' Notes to Saunders' Reports [*A publication*] (DLA)
Wills Circ Ev... Wills on Circumstantial Evidence [*A publication*] (DLA)
Wills Cir Ev... Wills on Circumstantial Evidence [*A publication*] (DLA)
Will Seis ..... Williams on Seisin of the Freehold [*1878*] [*A publication*] (DLA)
Wills Est & Tr (P-H)... Wills, Estates, and Trusts (Prentice-Hall, Inc.) [*A publication*] (DLA)
Wills Est Tr... Wills, Estates, Trusts [*Prentice-Hall, Inc.*] [*A publication*] (DLA)
Will Sett...... Williams on the Settlement of Real Estates [*A publication*] (DLA)
Willson........ Willson's Reports, Civil Cases [*29-30 Texas Appeals*] [*1, 2 Texas Court of Appeals*] [*A publication*] (DLA)
Willson Civ Cas Ct App... White and Willson's Civil Cases, Texas Court of Appeals [*A publication*] (DLA)
Willson's CC... Texas Civil Cases [*A publication*] (DLA)
Willson Tex Cr Law... Willson's Revised Penal Code, Code of Criminal Procedure, and Penal Laws of Texas [*A publication*] (DLA)
Will St L...... Williams on the Study of the Law [*A publication*] (DLA)
WILL-TV ...... Urbana, IL [*TV station call letters*] (RBYB)
Will VT .... Williams' Vermont Reports [*27-29 Vermont*] [*A publication*] (DLA)
Will Woll & D... Willmore, Wollaston, and Davison's English Queen's Bench Reports [*1837*] [*A publication*] (DLA)
Will Woll & Dav... Willmore, Wollaston, and Davison's English Queen's Bench Reports [*1837*] [*A publication*] (DLA)
Will Woll & H... Willmore, Wollaston, and Hodges' English Queen's Bench Reports [*1838-39*] [*A publication*] (DLA)

Will Woll & Hodg... Willmore, Wollaston, and Hodges' English Queen's Bench Reports [*1838-39*] [*A publication*] (DLA)
WILM.......... Wilmington, DE [*AM radio station call letters*]
WILM.......... Wilmington Trust Co. [*NASDAQ symbol*] (NQ)
WILM.......... Wilmington Trust Corp. [*NASDAQ symbol*] (TTSB)
Wilm.......... Wilmot's Notes and Opinions, King's Bench [*97 English Reprint*] [*A publication*] (DLA)
Wilm Burg... Wilmot's Digest of the Law of Burglary [*A publication*] (DLA)
WilmCS...... Williams Coal Seam Royalty Trust [*Associated Press*] (SAG)
WilmCtr...... William Controls, Inc. [*Associated Press*] (SAG)
Wilm Judg... Wilmot's Notes and Opinions, King's Bench [*97 English Reprint*] [*A publication*] (DLA)
Wilm Mort... Wilmot on Mortgages [*A publication*] (DLA)
Wilm Op...... Wilmot's Notes and Opinions, King's Bench [*97 English Reprint*] [*A publication*] (DLA)
Wilmot's Notes... Wilmot's Notes and Opinions, King's Bench [*97 English Reprint*] [*A publication*] (DLA)
Wilmot's Notes (Eng)... Wilmot's Notes and Opinions, King's Bench [*97 English Reprint*] [*A publication*] (DLA)
WilmTr....... Wilmington Trust Corp. [*Associated Press*] (SAG)
Wilm W & D... Willmore, Wollaston, and Davison's English Queen's Bench Reports [*A publication*] (DLA)
WILN.......... Panama City, FL [*FM radio station call letters*]
WILO.......... Frankfort, IN [*AM radio station call letters*]
WILP-AM..... West Hazleton, PA [*AM radio station call letters*] (RBYB)
WILPF......... Women's International League for Peace and Freedom [*Switzerland*] (EAIO)
WILPF-US.... Women's International League for Peace and Freedom, US Section (EA)
WILQ......... Williamsport, PA [*FM radio station call letters*]
Wil Q.......... Wilson Quarterly [*A publication*] (BRI)
WILS.......... Lansing, MI [*AM radio station call letters*]
WILS.......... Wang Interactive Learning System [*Computer science*] (HGAA)
WILS.......... Western Illinois Library System [*Library network*]
Wils.......... Wilson's English Chancery Reports [*37 English Reprint*] [*A publication*] (DLA)
Wils.......... Wilson's English Common Pleas Reports, 3 [*95 English Reprint*] [*A publication*] (DLA)
Wils.......... Wilson's English King's Bench Reports [*95 English Reprint*] [*1742-74*] [*A publication*] (DLA)
WILS.......... Wisconsin Interlibrary Loan Service
Wils & Court... Wilson and Courtenay's Scotch Appeal Cases [*A publication*] (DLA)
Wils & S...... Wilson and Shaw's Scottish Appeal Cases [*1825-35*] [*A publication*] (DLA)
Wils & Sh.... Wilson and Shaw's Scottish Appeal Cases [*1825-35*] [*A publication*] (DLA)
Wils & S (Scot)... Wilson and Shaw's Scottish Appeal Cases [*1825-35*] [*A publication*] (DLA)
Wils Arb..... Wilson on Arbitrations [*A publication*] (DLA)
Wils Ch....... Wilson's English Chancery Reports [*37 English Reprint*] [*A publication*] (DLA)
Wils Ch (Eng)... Wilson's English Chancery Reports [*37 English Reprint*] [*A publication*] (DLA)
Wils CP....... Wilson's English Common Pleas [*A publication*] (DLA)
Wils (Eng)... Wilson's English Common Pleas Reports, 3 [*95 English Reprint*] [*A publication*] (DLA)
Wils Ent...... Wilson's Entries and Pleading [*3 Lord Raymond's King's Bench and Common PleasReports*] [*England*] [*A publication*] (DLA)
Wils Ex....... Wilson's English Exchequer Reports [*159 English Reprint*] [*1805-17*] [*A publication*] (DLA)
Wils Exch.... Wilson's English Exchequer Reports [*159 English Reprint*] [*A publication*] (DLA)
Wils Exch (Eng)... Wilson's English Exchequer Reports [*159 English Reprint*] [*A publication*] (DLA)
Wils Fines... Wilson on Fines and Recoveries [*A publication*] (DLA)
Wilshire...... Wilshire Financial Services Group, Inc. [*Associated Press*] (SAG)
WilshrO....... Wilshire Oil Co. of Texas [*Associated Press*] (SAG)
WilshTc...... Wilshire Technologies, Inc. [*Associated Press*] (SAG)
Wils Ind...... Wilson's Indiana Superior Court Reports [*A publication*] (DLA)
Wils Ind Gloss... Wilson's Glossary of Indian Terms [*A publication*] (DLA)
Wils Jud Acts... Wilson on the Judicature Acts, Etc. [*A publication*] (DLA)
Wils KB....... Sergeant Wilson's English King's Bench Reports [*1724-74*] [*A publication*] (DLA)
Wils Minn.... Wilson's Reports [*48-59 Minnesota*] [*A publication*] (DLA)
Wils Mod Eng Law... Wilson's History of Modern English Law [*A publication*] (DLA)
Wilson........ Wilson's English Chancery Reports [*37 English Reprint*] [*A publication*] (DLA)
Wilson........ Wilson's English King's Bench and Common Pleas Reports [*A publication*] (DLA)
Wilson........ Wilson's Exchequer in Equity Reports [*England*] [*A publication*] (DLA)
Wilson........ Wilson's Indiana Superior Court Reports [*A publication*] (DLA)
Wilson........ Wilson's Reports [*48-59 Minnesota*] [*A publication*] (DLA)
Wilson........ Wilson's Reports [*1-3 Oregon*] [*A publication*] (DLA)
Wilson & Shaw... Wilson and Shaw's Scottish Appeal Cases [*1825-35*] [*A publication*] (DLA)
Wilson's R... Wilson's Indiana Superior Court Reports [*A publication*] (DLA)
Wilson's Rev & Ann St... Wilson's Revised and Annotated Statutes [*Oklahoma*] [*A publication*] (DLA)
Wilson Super Ct (Ind)... Wilson's Indiana Superior Court Reports [*A publication*] (DLA)
Wils Oreg.... Wilson's Reports [*1-3 Oregon*] [*A publication*] (DLA)
Wils Parl L... Wilson's Parliamentary Law [*A publication*] (DLA)
Wils PC....... Wilson's English Privy Council Reports [*A publication*] (DLA)

Wils Super (Ind)... Wilson's Indiana Superior Court Reports [*A publication*] (DLA)
Wils Uses.... Wilson on Springing Uses [*A publication*] (DLA)
WILS/WLC... Wisconsin Interlibrary Loan Service - Wisconsin Library Consortium [*Library network*]
WILT-AM..... Mount Pocono, PA [*AM radio station call letters*] (RBYB)
WilTel......... Williams Telecommunications Co. [*Tulsa, OK*] [*Telecommunications service*] (TSSD)
WILTS......... Wiltshire [*County in England*]
Wilts.......... Wiltshire [*County in England*] (ODBW)
WILUCL...... Willamette University College of Law (DLA)
WILX.......... Onondaga, MI [*Television station call letters*]
WILY.......... Centralia, IL [*AM radio station call letters*]
WIM.......... Madison Public Library, Madison, WI [*OCLC symbol*] (OCLC)
WIM.......... Waksman Institute of Microbiology [*Rutgers University*] [*Research center*] (RCD)
WIM.......... Warm Ionized Medium [*Astrophysics*]
WIM.......... Washington, Idaho & Montana Railway Co. [*AAR code*]
WIM.......... Weigh in Motion
WIM.......... Women in Management [*Chicago, IL*] (EA)
WIM.......... Women in Medicine [*British*] [*An association*] (DBA)
WIM.......... Women in Mining National (EA)
WIMA......... Labuhan Bilik/Ajamu [*Indonesia*] [*ICAO location identifier*] (ICLI)
WIMA......... Lima, OH [*AM radio station call letters*]
WIMA......... Women's International Motorcycle Association (EA)
WIMA......... World International Medical Association (EA)
WIMA......... Writing Instrument Manufacturers Association (EA)
WIMB......... Gunung Sitoli/Binaka [*Indonesia*] [*ICAO location identifier*] (ICLI)
WIMB......... Wimborne Minster [*Urban district in England*]
WIMC......... Crawfordsville, IN [*FM radio station call letters*]
WIMC......... Whom It May Concern
WIME......... Padang Sidempuan/Aek Godang [*Indonesia*] [*ICAO location identifier*] (ICLI)
WIMEA....... Wiretap, Investigation Monitoring, and Eavesdrop Activities (MCD)
WIMEX....... Worldwide Military Command and Control System (MUSM)
WIMG......... Ewing, NJ [*AM radio station call letters*]
WIMG......... Padang/Tabing [*Indonesia*] [*ICAO location identifier*] (ICLI)
WIMG......... Women in Municipal Government (EA)
WIMI......... Ironwood, MI [*FM radio station call letters*]
WIMI......... Warburg Investment Management International
WIMI......... Watercraft Intensively Managed Items (AABC)
WIMIS........ Walk-In Management Information System [*Computer science*]
WIMK......... Iron Mountain, MI [*FM radio station call letters*]
WIMK......... Kisaran/Tanah Gambus [*Indonesia*] [*ICAO location identifier*] (ICLI)
WIML......... Kisaran/Aek Loba [*Indonesia*] [*ICAO location identifier*] (ICLI)
WIMM........ Medan/Polonia [*Indonesia*] [*ICAO location identifier*] (ICLI)
WIMM........ Weapons Integrated Materiel Manager [*Military*]
WIMN......... Stillwater, MN [*AM radio station call letters*]
WIMN......... Women in Mining National (EA)
WIMO........ Winder, GA [*AM radio station call letters*]
WIMP......... Prapat/Sibisa [*Indonesia*] [*ICAO location identifier*] (ICLI)
WIMP......... WARF [*Wartime Replacement Factors*] Intermediate Materiel Processor [*Military*]
WIMP......... Weakly Interacting Massive [*or Integrated Magnetic*] Particle [*Astrophysics*]
WIMP......... White, Imperialist, and Protestant [*British*]
WIMP......... Windows, Icons, Mice, and Pointer [*Computer science*] (OSI)
WIMP......... Windows, Icons, Mice, and Pucks [*Computer science*] (DGA)
WIMP......... windows, icons, mouse and pull-down menus [*computers*]
WIMP......... Windows/Icons/Mouse/Pull-Down-Menus [*Computer science*] (BYTE)
WIMP......... Windward Island Passages Monitoring Program (USDC)
WIMR......... Pematang Siantar/Gunung Pamela [*Indonesia*] [*ICAO location identifier*] (ICLI)
WIMS......... Michigan City, IN [*AM radio station call letters*]
WIMS......... Sibolga/Pinang Sori [*Indonesia*] [*ICAO location identifier*] (ICLI)
WIMS......... Wartime Instruction Manual for Merchant Ships [*For deck officers of the United States Merchant Marine; popularly known as the "Convoy Bible"*] [*World War II*]
WIMS......... Waveguide Impedance Measuring Set
WIMS......... Web Based Information Management System
WIMS......... Wholesale Inventory Management System (MHDB)
WIMS......... Winfrith Improved Multi-Group Scheme [*Nuclear energy*] (NUCP)
WIMS......... Works Information and Management System [*M & E White Consultants Ltd.*] [*Software package*] (NCC)
WIMS......... World Information Management System [*Air Force*] (GFGA)
WIMS......... Worldwide Integrated Management of Subsistence
WIMSA....... Webster Institute for Mathematics, Science, and Arts [*Webster College*]
WIMSA....... Women in Military Service for America Memorial Foundation
WIMT........ Lima, OH [*FM radio station call letters*]
WIMT......... Tebing Tingci/Pabatu [*Indonesia*] [*ICAO location identifier*] (ICLI)
WIMX-FM.... Gibsonburg, OH [*AM radio station call letters*] (BROA)
WIMZ......... Knoxville, TN [*FM radio station call letters*]
WIMZ......... Medan Sector [*Indonesia*] [*ICAO location identifier*] (ICLI)
WIN.......... INELEC Library Project, Menomonie, WI [*Inactive*] [*OCLC symbol*] (OCLC)
WIN.......... Irwin, Australia [*Spaceflight Tracking and Data Network*] [*NASA*]
WIN.......... Warfighter Information Network [*Army*]
WIN.......... Waste Information Network (COE)
WIN.......... Water-Insoluble Nitrogen [*Analytical chemistry*]
WIN.......... Weapon Index Number [*Military*] (CAAL)
WIN.......... Weapons Interception [*Military electronics*]
WIN.......... Well Information Network [*Database*]
WIN.......... Western Information Network
WIN.......... Whip Inflation Now [*Slogan of President Gerald R. Ford's anti-inflation program, 1974*] [*Program discontinued March, 1975*]

WIN .... White-Indian-Negro

Win .... Winch's English Common Pleas Reports [*124 English Reprint*] [*A publication*] (DLA)

WIN .... Windhoek [*Namibia*] [*Seismograph station code, US Geological Survey*] (SEIS)

WIN .... Window [*Technical drawings*]

WIN .... Windsor Board of Education [*UTLAS symbol*]

Win .... Winer's Unreported Opinions, New York Supreme Court [*A publication*] (DLA)

WIN .... Winlink (St. Lucia) Ltd. [*ICAO designator*] (FAAC)

WIN .... Winn-Dixie Stores [*NYSE symbol*] (TTSB)

WIN .... Winn-Dixie Stores, Inc. [*NYSE symbol*] (SPSG)

WIN .... Winona [*Diocesan abbreviation*] [*Minnesota*] (TOCD)

Win .... Winston's North Carolina Reports [*1863-64*] [*A publication*] (DLA)

WIN .... Winter

WIN .... Winthrop Laboratories [*Research code symbol*]

WIN .... Winton [*Australia Airport symbol*] (OAG)

WIN .... Wireless In-Building Network [*Motorola, Inc.*] [*Computer science*]

WIN .... Wollongong Integrated Network (HGAA)

WIN .... Women's International Network (EA)

WIN .... Work Incentive Program [*Later, ETSC*] (EA)

WIN .... Workshop in Nonviolence (EA)

WIN .... World Information Network [*Information service or system*] (IID)

WIN .... WWMCCS [*Worldwide Military Command and Control System*] Intercomputer Network [*DoD*]

W/IN² .... Watts per Square Inch

Win 95 .... Windows 95 [*Computer science*] (WDMC)

WINA .... Charlottesville, VA [*AM radio station call letters*]

WINA .... Webb Institute of Naval Architecture [*Glen Cove, NY*]

WINA .... Witton Network Analyzer

WINAP .... Women's Information Network for Asia and the Pacific [*ESCAP*] [*United Nations*] (DUND)

WINB .... Western Interstate Nuclear Board (NRCH)

WINBA .... World International Nail and Beauty Association (EA)

WINBAN .... Windward Islands' Banana Association

WINC .... Western Interstate Nuclear Compact [*Later, WIEB/WINB*]

WINC .... White Incumbent

WINC .... Winchester, VA [*AM radio station call letters*]

WINC .... Worldwide Integrated Communications [*Mohawk Data Sciences Corp.*] [*Parsippany, NJ*] [*Telecommunications*] (TSSD)

Win CE .... Windows Compact Edition [*Computer science*] (PCM)

WINC-FM ..... Winchester, VA [*FM radio station call letters*]

WINCH .... Winchcombe [*England*]

WINCH .... Winchester [*City in England*] (ROG)

Winch .... Winch's English Common Pleas Reports [*124 English Reprint*] [*A publication*] (DLA)

Winch (Eng)... Winch's English Common Pleas Reports [*124 English Reprint*] [*A publication*] (DLA)

WINCMD ...... [*A*] Windows Command [*Computer science*] (PCM)

WIND .... Chicago, IL [*AM radio station call letters*]

WIND .... Weather Information Network and Display

W IND .... West Indies (WDAA)

W Ind .... West Indies (VRA)

WIND .... Wind River Systems [*NASDAQ symbol*] (TTSB)

WIND .... Wind River Systems, Inc. [*NASDAQ symbol*] (SAG)

WIND .... Windsor [*Municipal borough in England*]

WIND .... Women in Distribution [*Commercial firm*]

WINDAV .... Wind Direction and Velocity Indicator [*Aviation*]

WINDEE .... Wind Tunnel Data Encoding and Evaluation [*System*] [*Boeing Co.*]

WIND I .... Windward Islands (WDAA)

WINDII .... Wind Imaging Interferometer

WinDix .... Winn-Dixie Stores, Inc. [*Associated Press*] (SAG)

WINDMG ...... Wind Magnitude (GAVI)

Windmr .... Windmere Corp. [*Associated Press*] (SAG)

WINDO .... Wide Information Network Data Online [*Government Printing Office*]

Windows NT... Windows New Technology [*Microsoft Corp.*] (IGQR)

WINDR .... Wind Direction (GAVI)

WindRivr ..... Wind River Systems, Inc. [*Associated Press*] (SAG)

WindRvr ..... Wind River Systems, Inc. [*Associated Press*] (SAG)

WINDS .... Weather Information Network and Display System [*NASA*]

Windsat .... Wind Satellite

WINE .... Brookfield, CT [*AM radio station call letters*]

WINE .... Canandaigua Wine Co., Inc. [*NASDAQ symbol*] (SAG)

WINE .... Warning and Indications in Europe (MCD)

WINE .... Webb Institute of Naval Engineering

WINEA .... Canandaigua Wine Cl'A' [*NASDAQ symbol*] (TTSB)

WINEB .... Canandaigua Wine Cl'B' [*NASDAQ symbol*] (TTSB)

Win Ent .... Winch's Book of Entries [*A publication*] (DLA)

Win Eq .... Winston's North Carolina Equity Reports [*A publication*] (DLA)

WINES .... World Integrated Nuclear Evaluation System [*Department of Energy*] (GFGA)

WINF .... Staunton, VA [*AM radio station call letters*]

WINF .... Winfrith [*England*]

Winfield .... Winfield Capital Corp. [*Associated Press*] (SAG)

Winfield Words & Phrases... Winfield's Adjudged Words and Phrases, with Notes [*A publication*] (DLA)

Winfld .... Winfield Capital Corp. [*Associated Press*] (SAG)

WINFORUM... Wireless Information Networks Forum (NTPA)

WING .... Dayton, OH [*AM radio station call letters*]

Wing .... Wingate's Maxims [*A publication*] (DLA)

WING-FM ..... Springfield, OH [*FM radio station call letters*] (RBYB)

Wing Max ..... Wingate's Maxims [*A publication*] (DLA)

WINGO .... Women's International Non-Government Organisation [*British*] (DI)

WINH-AM .... Winchester, KY [*AM radio station call letters*] (RBYB)

WinHEC .... Windows Hardware Engineering Conference

WINI .... Murphysboro, IL [*AM radio station call letters*]

WINJ .... Pulaski, TN [*FM radio station call letters*]

WINK .... Fort Myers, FL [*AM radio station call letters*]

WINK .... Warning in Korea (MCD)

WINK .... Winkleigh [*England*]

WINK-FM ..... Fort Myers, FL [*FM radio station call letters*]

WINKS .... Women in Numerous Kitchens [*World War II*]

WINK-TV ..... Fort Myers, FL [*Television station call letters*]

WINL .... Linden, AL [*FM radio station call letters*]

WinInd .... Winland Electronics, Inc. [*Associated Press*] (SAG)

WINM .... Angola, IN [*Television station call letters*]

WINN .... North Vernon, IN [*FM radio station call letters*]

Winn .... Winnipeg [*Canada*] (BARN)

WINN .... Winston Hotels [*NASDAQ symbol*] (TTSB)

WINN .... Winston Hotels, Inc. [*NASDAQ symbol*] (SAG)

Winnbg .... Winnebago Industries, Inc. [*Associated Press*] (SAG)

Winona St U... Winona State University (GAGS)

WINP .... Water Insoluble Nonstarchy Polysaccharide [*Food composition*]

WINQ .... Winchendon, MA [*FM radio station call letters*]

WINR .... Binghamton, NY [*AM radio station call letters*]

WINR .... Winthrop Resources [*NASDAQ symbol*] (TTSB)

WINR .... Winthrop Resources Corp. [*NASDAQ symbol*] (SAG)

WINRA .... Women in the National Rifle Association

WinrEnt .... Winners Entertainment [*Commercial firm Associated Press*] (SAG)

WINS .... New York, NY [*AM radio station call letters*]

WINS .... Warehouse Industry National Standards Guidelines (ACRL)

WINS .... Weapons and Integrated Navigation System (MCD)

WINS .... Wideband Information Network Services [*Computer science*]

WINS .... Windows - Internet Naming Service

WINS .... Winners Entertainment [*Commercial firm NASDAQ symbol*] (SAG)

WINS .... Winslow [*England*]

WINS .... Women in National Service [*Name given by Ladies' Home Journal to American housewives and their teen-age daughters, "the greatest reserve strength of America"*] [*World War II*]

WINS .... Women in Naval Service

WINS .... Women's Industrial and National Service Corps [*World War II British*]

WinsLoew ..... WinsLoew Furniture, Inc. [*Associated Press*] (SAG)

WINSNAMS... Wind Indicating Systems for Navigation Aircraft in Missile Support

Winsock .... Windows Sockets [*Internet*]

Winsock API... Windows Sockets Application Program Interface [*Computer science*] (IGQR)

Winst .... Winston's North Carolina Equity Reports [*A publication*] (DLA)

Winst .... Winston's North Carolina Law Reports [*A publication*] (DLA)

WINST .... Winstree [*England*]

WINSTAN ..... Wings, Nonstraight-Taper Analysis (MCD)

Winstar......... Winstar Communications [*Commercial firm Associated Press*] (SAG)

Winst Eq ...... Winston's North Carolina Equity Reports [*A publication*] (DLA)

Winst Eq (NC)... Winston's North Carolina Equity Reports [*A publication*] (DLA)

Winst L (NC)... Winston's North Carolina Law Reports [*A publication*] (DLA)

WinstonH..... Winston Hotels, Inc. [*Associated Press*] (SAG)

WinstRs......... Winston Resources Ltd. [*Associated Press*] (SAG)

WINT .... Crossville, TN [*Television station call letters*]

Wintel .... Windows Intel [*Computer science*] (IGQR)

Wintel .... Windows Intel [*Computer science*]

WINTEM .... Forecast Upper Wind and Temperature for Aviation [*ICAO*] (FAAC)

WinterSpt ... Winter Sports, Inc. [*Associated Press*] (SAG)

WINTEX .... Winter Exercise (MCD)

WinthpRs..... Winthrop Resources Corp. [*Associated Press*] (SAG)

Winthrop C... Winthrop College (GAGS)

Winton .... Winton Financial Corp. [*Associated Press*] (SAG)

Wint T .... [*The*] Winter's Tale [*Shakespearean work*] (BARN)

WINU .... Highland, IL [*AM radio station call letters*]

WINV .... Inverness, FL [*AM radio station call letters*]

WINW .... Canton, OH [*AM radio station call letters*]

WINX .... Rockville, MD [*AM radio station call letters*]

WINX-FM ..... Warrenton, VA [*FM radio station call letters*] (RBYB)

WINY .... Putnam, CT [*AM radio station call letters*]

WINZ .... Miami, FL [*AM radio station call letters*]

WIO .... Nashotah House, Nashotah, WI [*OCLC symbol*] (OCLC)

WIO .... Wilcannia [*Australia Airport symbol*] (OAG)

WIO .... Women's International ORT

WIOA .... San Juan, PR [*FM radio station call letters*]

WIOB .... Bengkayang [*Indonesia*] [*ICAO location identifier*] (ICLI)

WIOB .... Mayaguez, PR [*FM radio station call letters*]

WIOC .... Ponce, PR [*FM radio station call letters*]

WIOD .... Miami, FL [*AM radio station call letters*]

WIOG .... Bay City, MI [*FM radio station call letters*]

WIOG .... Nangapinoh [*Indonesia*] [*ICAO location identifier*] (ICLI)

WIOH .... Paloh/Liku [*Indonesia*] [*ICAO location identifier*] (ICLI)

WIOI .... New Boston, OH [*AM radio station call letters*]

WIOI .... Singkawang II [*Indonesia*] [*ICAO location identifier*] (ICLI)

WIOJ-AM ..... Jacksonville Beach, FL [*AM radio station call letters*] (BROA)

WIOK .... Falmouth, KY [*FM radio station call letters*]

WIOK .... Ketapang/Rahadi Usman [*Indonesia*] [*ICAO location identifier*] (ICLI)

WIOL-AM ..... Knoxville, TN [*AM radio station call letters*] (BROA)

WION .... Ionia, MI [*AM radio station call letters*]

WION .... Natuna/Ransi [*Indonesia*] [*ICAO location identifier*] (ICLI)

WIOO .... Carlisle, PA [*AM radio station call letters*]

WIOO .... Pontianak/Supadio [*Indonesia*] [*ICAO location identifier*] (ICLI)

WIOP .... Putusibau/Pangsuma [*Indonesia*] [*ICAO location identifier*] (ICLI)

WIOQ .... Philadelphia, PA [*FM radio station call letters*]

WIOS .... Sintang/Susilo [*Indonesia*] [*ICAO location identifier*] (ICLI)

WIOS .... Tawas City, MI [*AM radio station call letters*]

WIOT .... Toledo, OH [*FM radio station call letters*]

WIOU .... Kokomo, IN [*AM radio station call letters*]

WIOV	Ephrata, PA [*FM radio station call letters*]
WIOV	Reading, PA [*AM radio station call letters*]
WIOZ	Pinehurst, NC [*AM radio station call letters*]
WIOZ	Pontianak Sector [*Indonesia*] [*ICAO location identifier*] (ICLI)
WIOZ	Southern Pines, NC [*FM radio station call letters*]
WIP	Philadelphia, PA [*AM radio station call letters*]
WIP	Ripon College Library, Ripon, WI [*OCLC symbol*] (OCLC)
WIP	Wartime Intelligence Plan (NATG)
WIP	Weapon Indicator Panel [*Military*] (CAAL)
WIP	Weapons Installation Plan [*Navy*] (NG)
WIP	Women in Information Processing (EA)
WIP	Women in Prison (WDAA)
WIP	Women in Production (EA)
WIP	Women's Issues Plan [*Australia*]
WIP	Workgroup Indian Project [*Netherlands*]
WIP	Work Incentive Program [*Department of Health, Education, and Welfare; Department of Labor*] (DLA)
WIP	Working Group Indigenous Peoples [*Netherlands*] (EAIO)
WIP	Work in Place (AABC)
WIP	Work in Process
WIP	Work in Progress (AFM)
WIPA	Jambi/Sultan Taha [*Indonesia*] [*ICAO location identifier*] (ICLI)
WIPA	Pittsfield, IL [*FM radio station call letters*]
WIPACE	Wartime Intelligence Plan, Allied Command Europe (NATG)
WIPB	Muncie, IN [*Television station call letters*]
WIPC	Lake Wales, FL [*AM radio station call letters*]
WIPC	Rimbo Bujang [*Indonesia*] [*ICAO location identifier*] (ICLI)
WIPC	Wool Industry Policy Council [*Australia*]
WIPC	Writers in Prison Committee of International PEN [*British*] (EAIO)
WIPE	Tanjung Enim/Bangko [*Indonesia*] [*ICAO location identifier*] (ICLI)
WIPF	Kuala Tungkal [*Indonesia*] [*ICAO location identifier*] (ICLI)
WIPH	Sungai Penuh/Depati Parbo [*Indonesia*] [*ICAO location identifier*] (ICLI)
WIPHN	Women's International Public Health Network (EA)
WIPI	Bungo Tebo/Pasir Mayang [*Indonesia*] [*ICAO location identifier*] (ICLI)
WIPI	Easton, PA [*AM radio station call letters*]
WIPI	Word Intelligibility by Picture Identification [*Artificial intelligence*]
WIPIS	Who Is Publishing in Science [*An Institute for Scientific Information publication*] [*Trademark*]
WIPJ	Jambi/Dusun Aro [*Indonesia*] [*ICAO location identifier*] (ICLI)
WIPL	Bengkulu/Padang Kemiling [*Indonesia*] [*ICAO location identifier*] (ICLI)
WIPM	Mayaguez, PR [*Television station call letters*]
WIPM	West Indian People's Movement [*Netherlands Antilles*] [*Political party*] (EY)
WIPM	Work in Process Measurement (MCD)
WIPO	World Intellectual Property Organisation [*of United Nations*] (EERA)
WIPO	World Intellectual Property Organization [*Switzerland*] (IID)
WIPP	Palembang/Sultan Mahmud Badaruddin II [*Indonesia*] [*ICAO location identifier*] (ICLI)
WIPP	Waste Isolation Pilot Plant [*Department of Energy*]
WIPP	Work Isolation Pilot Project [*NASA*]
WIPPL	Women in Political and Public Life [*British*] (DI)
WIPQ	Pendoro [*Indonesia*] [*ICAO location identifier*] (ICLI)
WIPR	Rengat/Japura [*Indonesia*] [*ICAO location identifier*] (ICLI)
WIPR	San Juan, PR [*AM radio station call letters*]
WIPR-FM	San Juan, PR [*FM radio station call letters*]
WIPR-TV	San Juan, PR [*Television station call letters*]
WIPS	Ticonderoga, NY [*AM radio station call letters*]
WIPS	Washington Intelligence Data Processing System (SAA)
WIPS	Women in Production Service [*A voluntary, semimilitary organization of women employees, primarily at the E. I. du Pont de Nemours & Co., at Richmond, Va.*] [*World War II*]
WIPS	Word Image Processing System [*Datacopy Corp.*]
WIPTC	Women's International Professional Tennis Council (EA)
WIPU	Muko Muko [*Indonesia*] [*ICAO location identifier*] (ICLI)
WIPV	Keluang [*Indonesia*] [*ICAO location identifier*] (ICLI)
WIPX	Bridgeport, CT [*Television station call letters*] (BROA)
WIPY	Bentayan [*Indonesia*] [*ICAO location identifier*] (ICLI)
WIPZ	Palembang Sector [*Indonesia*] [*ICAO location identifier*] (ICLI)
WIQ	Appleton Public Library, Appleton, WI [*OCLC symbol*] (OCLC)
WIQB	Ann Arbor, MI [*FM radio station call letters*]
WIQH	Concord, MA [*FM radio station call letters*]
WIQO	Covington, VA [*FM radio station call letters*]
WIQQ	Leland, MS [*FM radio station call letters*]
WIQR	Prattville, AL [*AM radio station call letters*] (RBYB)
WIR	Racine Public Library, Racine, WI [*OCLC symbol*] (OCLC)
WIR	War Information Report [*British military*] (DMA)
WIR	Weapons Inspection Report [*Navy*] (NG)
WIR	Weekly Intelligence Review
WIR	Welfare in Review [*A publication*]
WIR	Western Investment Real Estate Trust SBI [*AMEX symbol*] (SPSG)
WIR	Western Inv RE Tr SBI [*AMEX symbol*] (TTSB)
WIR	West Indian Reports [*A publication*] (DLA)
WIR	West India Regiment
WIR	Wildrose Petroleum Ltd. [*Vancouver Stock Exchange symbol*]
WIR	Woman in Rock
WIR	Work Injury Reports [*Human Resources*] (WYGK)
WIR	Wuerttemberg Israelitische Religionsgemeinschaft [*A publication*] (BJA)
WIRA	Fort Pierce, FL [*AM radio station call letters*]
WIRA	Western Intercollegiate Rowing Association (PSS)
WIRA	Wool Industry Research Association [*British*] (DI)
WIRB	Melbourne, FL [*Television station call letters*]

WIRC	Hickory, NC [*AM radio station call letters*]
WIRC	Women's Information and Referral Centre [*Australia*]
WIRC	Women's International Resource Centre [*British*] (EAIO)
WIRD	Lake Placid, NY [*AM radio station call letters*]
WIRDS	Weather Information Remoting and Display System
WIRE	Encore Wire Corp. [*NASDAQ symbol*] (SAG)
WIRE	Lebanon, IN [*FM radio station call letters*]
WIRE	Waseca Inter-Library Resource Exchange [*Library network*]
WIRE	Weapons Interference Reduction Effort [*Navy*] (NG)
WIRE	Wisconsin Information Resources for Education (EDAC)
WIRE	Women's International Resource Exchange (EA)
Wireless	Wireless Cable of Atlanta, Inc. [*Associated Press*] (SAG)
Wirelesst	Wireless Telecom Group [*Formerly, Noise Com, Inc.*] [*Associated Press*] (SAG)
WirelssT	Wireless Telecom Group [*Associated Press*] (SAG)
WireOne	Wireless One, Inc. [*Associated Press*] (SAG)
WIRES	Women in Radio and Electrical Service [*World War II*]
WIRET	Western Investment Real Estate Trust [*Associated Press*] (SAG)
WIRF	Women's International Religious Fellowship (EA)
WIRG	Wiring
WIRGA	West Indian Royal Garrison Artillery [*British military*] (DMA)
WIRJ	Humboldt, TN [*AM radio station call letters*] (RBYB)
WIRK	West Palm Beach, FL [*FM radio station call letters*]
WIRL	Peoria, IL [*AM radio station call letters*]
WIRL	Wireless One [*NASDAQ symbol*] (TTSB)
WIRL	Wireless One, Inc. [*NASDAQ symbol*] (SAG)
WIRMIT	Women in RMIT [*Royal Melbourne Institute of Technology*] Group [*Australia*]
WIRN-FM	Buhl, MN [*FM radio station call letters*] (RBYB)
WIRO	Ironton, OH [*AM radio station call letters*]
WIRO	Wyoming Infrared Observatory
WIRP-FM	Pennsuco, FL [*FM radio station call letters*] (RBYB)
WIRQ	Rochester, NY [*FM radio station call letters*]
WIRR	Virginia-Hibbing, MN [*FM radio station call letters*]
WIRS	Wage Information Retrieval System [*IRS*]
WIRS	Watershed Information Resource System [*Environmental Protection Agency*] (AEPA)
WIRS	Workplace Industrial Relations Survey [*British*]
WIRS	Yauco, PR [*Television station call letters*]
WIRT	Hibbing, MN [*Television station call letters*]
WIRTSCH	Wirtschaft [*Economy, Industry*] [*German*]
WIRV	Irvine, KY [*AM radio station call letters*]
WIRX	St. Joseph, MI [*FM radio station call letters*]
WIRY	Plattsburgh, NY [*AM radio station call letters*]
WIS	Central [*Wisconsin*] [*Airport symbol*] (AD)
WIS	Columbia, SC [*Television station call letters*]
WIS	University of Wisconsin, Stevens Point, Stevens Point, WI [*OCLC symbol*] (OCLC)
WIS	Washington Inventory Service
WIS	Washington Irving Society [*Defunct*] (FA)
WIS	Water Induced Shift (AAEL)
WIS	Wave Information Study [*US Army Corps of Engineers*]
WIS	Weapon Interface Subsystem [*Army*]
WIS	Weather Information Service [*Air Force*] (MCD)
WIS	Wedgwood International Seminar (EA)
WIS	Winchester Diversified [*Vancouver Stock Exchange symbol*]
WIS	Wireless Interphone System (MCD)
WIS	Wisconsin (AAG)
Wis	Wisconsin (ODBW)
WIS	Wisconsin Power & Light Co. [*AMEX symbol*] (SAG)
Wis	Wisconsin Reports [*A publication*] (DLA)
Wis	Wisdom [*Old Testament book*]
WIS	Women in Sales Association (EA)
WIS	Women in Soccer (EA)
WIS	Women's Information Service (WDAA)
WIS	World Impact Services (EA)
WIS	Worldwide Information System [*Navy*]
WIS	Wright Investors' Service [*Information service or system*] (IID)
WIS	WWMCCS [*Worldwide Military Command and Control System*] Information Systems
Wis 2d	Wisconsin Reports, Second Series [*A publication*] (DLA)
WISA	Isabela, PR [*AM radio station call letters*]
WISA	West Indian Students Association (EA)
WISA	West Indies Sugar Association [*Later, SAC*]
WISA	Wholesale Interservices Support Agreement [*DoD*]
WISA	Wholesale Interservice Supply Agreement [*Military*] (NG)
WISA	Wire Industry Suppliers Association (NTPA)
WISA	Women's International Surfing Association (EA)
WISA	Wormald International Sensory Aids (NITA)
Wis Admin Code	Wisconsin Administrative Code [*A publication*] (DLA)
WISA Law Rep	Western Indian States Agency Law Reports [*A publication*] (DLA)
WISALR	Western Indian States Agency Law Reports [*A publication*] (DLA)
WISAP	Waste Isolation Safety Assessment Program
WISARD	Wideband System for Acquiring and Recording Data
Wisb	Laws of Wisby [*Maritime law*] [*A publication*] (DLA)
WiSB	Wisbech [*Municipal borough in England*]
WiSB	Women in Show Business (EA)
Wis BA Bull	Wisconsin State Bar Association. Bulletin [*A publication*] (DLA)
Wis Bar Bull	Wisconsin State Bar Association. Bulletin [*A publication*] (DLA)
WIS B BULL	Wisconsin Bar Bulletin [*A publication*] (LWAP)
Wis BTA	Wisconsin Board of Tax Appeals Reports [*A publication*] (DLA)
WISC	Madison, WI [*Television station call letters*]
WISC	Wang Information Services Corp. [*Telecommunications service*] (TSSD)
WISC	Wechsler Intelligence Scale for Children [*Education*]

WISC .... Wisconsin (AFM)
Wisc .... Wisconsin Reports [*A publication*] (DLA)
WISC .... Women's Information and Study Centre
WISC .... Writable Instruction Set Computer [*Term coined by Phil Koopman, Jr.*] (BYTE)
WiscCt .... Wisconsin Central Transportation Corp. [*Associated Press*] (SAG)
WiscEn .... Wisconsin Energy Corp. [*Associated Press*] (SAG)
WISCII .... Wang International Standard Code for Information Interchange [*Pronounced "whiskey"*] [*Canada*]
WISCNET ..... [*The*] Wisconsin Network [*Telecommunications service*] (TNIG)
WISCOM ...... Wisconsin Information Science and Communications Consortium [*University of Wisconsin - Madison*] [*Research center*] (RCD)
WISC-R .... Wechsler Intelligence Scale for Children - Revised [*Education*]
Wisc Stud BJ... Wisconsin Student Bar Journal [*A publication*] (DLA)
WISD .... Wisdom [*Old Testament book*]
Wisd of Sol... Wisdom of Solomon [*Old Testament book*]
WISE............ Asheville, NC [*AM radio station call letters*]
WISE............ Wang Intersystem Exchange
WISE............ Wardens in the South East (AIE)
WISE............ Warning Indicators System Europe (MCD)
WISE............ Weapon Installation System Engineering
WISE............ Welsh Initiative for Specialised Employment
WISE............ Wheaton Information System for Education (IAA)
WISE............ Whirlwind I SAGE [*Semi-Automatic Ground Equipment*] Evaluation (SAA)
WISE............ Whistle-Blowers Integrity in Science and Education [*An association*]
WISE............ Wholesalers Institutional Service Extension [*Division of National American Wholesale Grocers Association*]
WISE............ Wicat Interactive System for Education (NITA)
WISE............ Women in Space Earliest (SAA)
WISE............ Women into Science and Engineering [*1984 campaign sponsored by the Equal Opportunities Commission and the Engineering Council*] [*British*]
WISE............ Women's Information Service, Inc.
WISE............ Women's Issues, Status, and Education (EA)
WISE............ WordPerfect Information System Environment [*Computer science*]
WISE............ World Information Service on Energy (EA)
WISE............ World Information Synthesis and Encyclopaedia [*Project of American Association for the Advancement of Science and American Society for Information Science*]
WISE............ World Information Systems Exchange [*Defunct*] (EA)
WISE............ World-Wide Information Service [*Information service or system*] (IID)
WISER .... Western Information System for Energy Resources [*Dataline, Inc.*] [*Canada Information service or system*]
WiserO .... [*The*] Wiser Oil Co. [*Associated Press*] (SAG)
WISF............ Women in Sport Foundation [*Australia*]
WISH .... Indianapolis, IN [*Television station call letters*]
WISH .... Women in the Senate and House [*Political fund-raising group*]
WISH .... Women's Interview Study of Health
WISH .... World Institute for Scientific Humanism [*Defunct*] (EA)
WISHA .... Washington Industrial Safety and Health Act (NUCP)
WISI............ Warner Insurance Svcs [*NASDAQ symbol*] (TTSB)
WISI............ World Index of Space Imagery [*Meteorology*]
WISI............ World Information System in Informatics (NITA)
Wis IC .... Wisconsin Industrial Commission Workmen's Compensation Reports [*A publication*] (DLA)
Wis Int'l LJ... Wisconsin International Law Journal [*A publication*] (DLA)
WISJMPO .... Worldwide Military Command and Control Information Systems, Joint Program Office
WISK .... Americus, GA [*AM radio station call letters*]
WISK-FM ..... Americus, GA [*FM radio station call letters*]
WISL............ Shamokin, PA [*AM radio station call letters*]
WISL............ Western Intercollegiate Softball League (PSS)
WISL............ Westinghouse Information Systems Laboratory (IAA)
WISL............ Woven Integrated Structure Laminates [*Army*]
Wis Legis Serv... Wisconsin Legislative Service (West) [*A publication*] (DLA)
Wis Leg N ... Wisconsin Legal News [*Milwaukee*] [*A publication*] (DLA)
WISL-FM ..... Shamokin, PA [*FM radio station call letters*]
Wis LN .... Wisconsin Legal News [*Milwaukee*] [*A publication*] (DLA)
WISM........... Altoona, WI [*FM radio station call letters*]
WISN .... Milwaukee, WI [*AM radio station call letters*]
WISN-TV ..... Milwaukee, WI [*Television station call letters*]
WISO .... Ponce, PR [*AM radio station call letters*]
WISP .... Holmes Beach, FL [*FM radio station call letters*]
WISP .... Warning Improvement Study Plan (MCD)
WISP .... Wartime Information Security Program (MCD)
WISP .... Waves in Space Plasma (SSD)
WISP .... Weapon Iterface Subsystem Processor [*Military*] (INF)
WISP .... Weaponization of Increased Speed Projectiles (MCD)
WISP .... Wide-Range Imaging Spectrophotometer [*Naval Oceanographic Office*]
WISP .... Winter Icing and Storms Project [*Marine science*] (OSRA)
WisP............ Wisconsin Power & Light Co. [*Associated Press*] (SAG)
WISP .... Women in Scholarly Publishing (EA)
WISP .... Wyoming Infant Stimulation Program (EDAC)
WisPhrm....... Wisconsin Pharmacal Company, Inc. [*Associated Press*] (SAG)
WISPIT .... WISP [*Winter Icing and Storms Project*] Instrument Test [*Marine science*] (OSRA)
WISPr .... Wisc Pwr/Lt 4 1/2cm Pfd vtg [*AMEX symbol*] (TTSB)
Wis PSC ...... Wisconsin Public Service Commission Reports [*A publication*] (DLA)
Wis PSC Ops... Wisconsin Public Service Commission Opinions and Decisions [*A publication*] (DLA)
WISQ .... Whitewater, WI [*FM radio station call letters*]
WISR............ Butler, PA [*AM radio station call letters*]
Wis R .... Wisconsin Reports [*A publication*] (DLA)

Wis RC Ops... Wisconsin Railroad Commission Opinions and Decisions [*A publication*] (DLA)
Wis RCR...... Wisconsin Railroad Commission Reports [*A publication*] (DLA)
Wis Rep ...... Wisconsin Reports [*A publication*] (DLA)
WISS .... Berlin, WI [*AM radio station call letters*]
WISS .... Weapon Impact Scoring System [*Navy*] (MCD)
WISS .... Weekly Induction Scheduling System [*Navy*] (NG)
WISS .... Workstation-Independent Segment Storage [*Computer science*] (CIST)
WISS .... World Institute of Sephardic Studies (BJA)
WISSA .... Wholesale Interservice Supply Support Agreements [*Military*]
Wis SBA Bull... Wisconsin State Bar Association. Bulletin [*A publication*] (DLA)
WISS-FM ..... Berlin, WI [*FM radio station call letters*]
Wis Stat ...... Wisconsin Statutes [*A publication*] (DLA)
Wis Stat Ann (West)... West's Wisconsin Statutes, Annotated [*A publication*] (DLA)
WissUnNT... Wissenschaftliche Untersuchungen zum Neuen Testament [*Tuebingen*] [*A publication*] (BJA)
WIST .... Charlotte, NC [*AM radio station call letters*]
WIST........... Whitaker Index of Schizophrenic Thinking
Wis Tax App C... Wisconsin Tax Appeals Commission Reports [*A publication*] (DLA)
WIST-FM ..... Waxhaw, NC FM radio station call letters (RBYB)
WISU .... Federation of Westinghouse Independent Salaried Unions
WISU .... Terre Haute, IN [*FM radio station call letters*]
WISW .... Columbia, SC [*AM radio station call letters*] (RBYB)
WISWAVE.... Wave Information Studies Wave Model [*Computer science*]
WISZ........... Rockford, MI [*AM radio station call letters*] (RBYB)
WIT .... Washington Institute of Technology [*Washington, DC*]
WIT .... Whitbread Investment Trust [*British*]
WIT .... Wicat Interactive Terminal (NITA)
WIT .... Wier-in-Tube Sensor (PDAA)
WIT .... Winnebago International Travelers (EA)
WIT .... Wiring Interface Tester (MCD)
WIT .... Wisconsin Institute of Technology
WIT .... Witco Corp. [*NYSE symbol*] (SPSG)
WIT .... Witness (AABC)
WIT .... Wittenberg University, Springfield, OH [*OCLC symbol*] (OCLC)
WIT .... Wittering FTU [*British ICAO designator*] (FAAC)
WIT .... Witteveen [*Netherlands*] [*Seismograph station code, US Geological Survey*] (SEIS)
WIT .... Women in Telecommunications [*Defunct*] (EA)
WIT .... Women in Transition (EA)
WIT .... Workflow Innovation Toolkit (PCM)
WIT .... World Ice Theory [*Hans Horbiger*]
WIT .... Worst Injection Timing (PDAA)
WITA .... Knoxville, TN [*AM radio station call letters*]
WITA .... Tapak Tuan/Teuku Cut Ali [*Indonesia*] [*ICAO location identifier*] (ICLI)
WITA .... Women in the Army (MCD)
WITA .... Women in the Arts [*Defunct*] (EA)
WITA .... Women's International Tennis Association (EA)
WITAG .... West Indies Trade Advisory Group [*British Overseas Trade Board*] (DS)
WITAMIR .... Wisconsin Tandem Mirror
WITAN .... Wind-Time Analyzer
WITC........... Cazenovia, NY [*FM radio station call letters*]
WITC........... Meulaboh/Cut Nyak Dien [*Indonesia*] [*ICAO location identifier*] (ICLI)
WITCH .... Women Incensed over Traditional Coed Hoopla [*Feminist group*]
WITCH .... Women's Independent Cinema House [*British*]
WITCH .... Women's International Terrorist Conspiracy from Hell [*Feminist group*]
Witco .... Witco Corp. [*Associated Press*] (SAG)
WITF .... Harrisburg, PA [*FM radio station call letters*]
WITF .... What I Think and Feel (EDAC)
WITF .... Women's International Tennis Federation
WITF-TV ...... Harrisburg, PA [*Television station call letters*]
WITG .... Sinabang/Lasikin [*Indonesia*] [*ICAO location identifier*] (ICLI)
WITG .... Western International Trade Group [*Defunct*] (EA)
WITH .... Baltimore, MD [*AM radio station call letters*]
WITH .... Witheridge [*England*]
With Corp Cas... Withrow's American Corporation Cases [*A publication*] (DLA)
WITHDRL .... Withdrawal (ROG)
Withrow...... Withrow's American Corporation Cases [*A publication*] (DLA)
Withrow...... Withrow's Reports [*9-21 Iowa*] [*A publication*] (DLA)
WITHT .... Without (ROG)
WITI........... Milwaukee, WI [*Television station call letters*]
WITI........... Women in Technology International (NTPA)
WITIS.......... Weather Integration with Tactical Intelligence System (MCD)
WITK.......... Warner Robins, GA [*AM radio station call letters*] (RBYB)
Witkin Cal Summary... Witkin's Summary of California Law [*A publication*] (DLA)
WITL.......... Lansing, MI [*AM radio station call letters*]
WITL.......... Lhok Sukon [*Indonesia*] [*ICAO location identifier*] (ICLI)
WITL-FM...... Lansing, MI [*FM radio station call letters*]
WITM.......... Whok Seumawe/Malikus Saleh [*Indonesia*] [*ICAO location identifier*] (ICLI)
WITN.......... Washington, NC [*Television station call letters*]
WITNED ...... Witnessed
WITNESS .... Wire Installation Tester for Negating Errors by Sequencing and Standardization
WITNETH .... Witnesseth [*Legal*] [*British*] (ROG)
WITNS .... Witness [*Legal*] [*British*] (ROG)
WITR.......... Henrietta, NY [*FM radio station call letters*]
WITS.......... Sebring, FL [*AM radio station call letters*]
WITS.......... Seumayam [*Indonesia*] [*ICAO location identifier*] (ICLI)
WITS.......... Wang Integrated Technology Show [*British*]

WITS .... Washington Interagency Telecommunications System [*GSA*]
WITS .... Weather Information Telemetry System [*Air Force*] (CET)
WITS .... West Integrated Test Stand [*NASA*]
WITS .... Women in Technical Service [*World War II*]
WITS .... Work Item Tracking System [*Nuclear energy*] (NRCH)
WITS .... Worldwide Information and Trade System
WITS .... Worldwide Interactive Trading System [*Information service or system*] (IT)
WITSEC .... Witness Security Program [*US government program for protection of witnesses whose lives are endangered by their testimony*]
WITSS .... Witnesses [*Legal*] [*British*] (ROG)
WITT .... Banda Aceh/Blangbintang [*Indonesia*] [*ICAO location identifier*] (ICLI)
WITT .... Wittenborn [*Psychiatric rating scale*] (DMAA)
Witthaus & Becker's Med Jur... Witthaus and Becker's Medical Jurisprudence [*A publication*] (DLA)
WITTL .... Wittlesford [*England*]
WITV .... Charleston, SC [*Television station call letters*]
WITW .... We Interrupt This Week [*Television program*]
WITX .... Beaver Falls, PA [*FM radio station call letters*]
WITY .... Danville, IL [*AM radio station call letters*]
WITZ .... Jasper, IN [*AM radio station call letters*]
WITZ-FM .... Jasper, IN [*FM radio station call letters*]
WIU .... Warhead Interface Unit (MCD)
WIU .... Water Injection Unit
WIU .... Weather Intelligence Unit [*Army*] (MCD)
WIU .... Western Illinois University [*Macomb*]
WIU .... Western International University, Phoenix, AZ [*OCLC symbol*] (OCLC)
wiu .... Wisconsin [*MARC country of publication code Library of Congress*] (LCCP)
WIU .... Witu [*Papua New Guinea*] [*Airport symbol*] (OAG)
WIUAB .... Women's Inter-University Athletic Board [*British*] (BI)
WIUJ .... St. Thomas, VI [*FM radio station call letters*]
WIUM .... Macomb, IL [*FM radio station call letters*]
WIUP .... Indiana, PA [*FM radio station call letters*]
WIUS .... Macomb, IL [*FM radio station call letters*]
WIUV .... Castleton, VT [*FM radio station call letters*]
WIUW .... Warsaw, IL [*FM radio station call letters*] (RBYB)
Wiv .... [*The*] Merry Wives of Windsor [*Shakespearean work*]
WIV .... Waukesha Public Library, Waukesha, WI [*OCLC symbol*] (OCLC)
WIV .... WIC [*Women, Infants, and Children*] Income Verification Survey [*Food and Nutrition Service*] [*Department of Agriculture*] (GFGA)
WIVA .... Aguadilla, PR [*FM radio station call letters*]
WIVAB .... Women's Inter-Varsity Athletics Board [*British*] (DI)
WIVB .... Buffalo, NY [*Television station call letters*]
WIVH .... Christiansted, VI [*FM radio station call letters*]
WIVI .... Charlotte Amalie, VI [*FM radio station call letters*]
WiVik .... Windows Visual Keyboard [*Computer science*] (ECON)
WIVK .... Knoxville, TN [*AM radio station call letters*]
WIVK-FM .... Knoxville, TN [*FM radio station call letters*]
WIVR .... Eureka, IL [*FM radio station call letters*]
WIVV .... Vieques, PR [*AM radio station call letters*]
WIVY .... Jacksonville, FL [*FM radio station call letters*]
WIW .... Marathon County Public Library, Wausau, WI [*OCLC symbol*] (OCLC)
WIW .... Wer Informiert Woruber [*Who Advises about What*] [*Gesellschaft fuer Informationsmarkt-Forschung - GIF Detmold, Federal Republic of Germany*] [*Information service or system*] (IID)
WIW .... Who's Inventing What [*A publication*]
WIW .... Within Wafer (AAEL)
WIW .... WI Wheels International [*Vancouver Stock Exchange symbol*]
WIW .... Wooded Island [*Washington*] [*Seismograph station code, US Geological Survey*] (SEIS)
WIWC .... Kokomo, IN [*FM radio station call letters*]
WIWHA .... Western International Walking Horse Association (EA)
WIWNU .... Within Wafer Nonuniformity (AAEL)
WIWO .... Walk In, Walk Out (ADA)
WIWP .... World Institute for World Peace
WIWS .... Beckley, WV [*AM radio station call letters*]
WIX .... Steenbock Memorial Library, Madison, WI [*OCLC symbol*] (OCLC)
WIX .... Wait for Index (NASA)
WIX .... Whitman Education Group [*AMEX symbol*] [*Formerly, Whitman Medical*] (SG)
WIX .... Whitman Medical Corp. [*AMEX symbol*] (SAG)
WIX .... Windows Information Exchange [*Information service or system*] (IID)
WIX .... Winex Resources, Inc. [*Vancouver Stock Exchange symbol*]
WIXAMT .... Wixamtree [*England*]
WIXC .... Essexville, MI [*FM radio station call letters*]
WIXE .... Monroe, NC [*AM radio station call letters*]
WIXI .... Naples Park, FL [*FM radio station call letters*]
WIXK .... New Richmond, WI [*AM radio station call letters*]
WIXK-FM .... New Richmond, WI [*FM radio station call letters*]
WIXN .... Dixon, IL [*AM radio station call letters*]
WIXN-FM .... Dixon, IL [*FM radio station call letters*]
WIXO-FM .... Bartonville, IL [*FM radio station call letters*] (RBYB)
WIXQ .... Millersville, PA [*FM radio station call letters*]
WIXT .... Syracuse, NY [*Television station call letters*]
WIXV .... Savannah, GA [*FM radio station call letters*]
WIXX .... Green Bay, WI [*FM radio station call letters*]
WIXY .... Champaign, IL [*FM radio station call letters*]
WIXZ .... McKeesport, PA [*AM radio station call letters*]
WIY .... University of Wisconsin, Primate Research Center, Primate Library, Madison, WI [*OCLC symbol*] (OCLC)
WIYC .... Charlotte Amalie, VI [*FM radio station call letters*]
WIYD .... Palatka, FL [*AM radio station call letters*]
WIYN .... Deposit, NY [*FM radio station call letters*]
WIYY .... Baltimore, MD [*FM radio station call letters*]
WIZ .... Merlin Executive Aviation Group Ltd. [*British ICAO designator*] (FAAC)
WIZ .... Wiz Technology, Inc. [*AMEX symbol*] (SAG)
WIZA .... Savannah, GA [*AM radio station call letters*]
WIZA .... Workgroup for Indians in South America [*Netherlands*]
WIZB .... Abbeville, AL [*FM radio station call letters*] (RBYB)
WIZD .... Rudolph, WI [*FM radio station call letters*]
WIZE .... Springfield, OH [*AM radio station call letters*]
WIZ EC .... Wiz Technology [*ECM symbol*] (TTSB)
WIZF .... Erlanger, KY [*FM radio station call letters*]
WIZK .... Bay Springs, MS [*AM radio station call letters*]
WIZK-FM .... Bay Springs, MS [*FM radio station call letters*]
WIZM .... La Crosse, WI [*AM radio station call letters*]
WIZM-FM .... La Crosse, WI [*FM radio station call letters*]
WIZN .... Vergennes, VT [*FM radio station call letters*]
WIZO .... Franklin, TN [*AM radio station call letters*]
WIZO .... Women's International Zionist Organization [*Tel Aviv, Israel*] (EA)
WIZR .... Johnstown, NY [*AM radio station call letters*]
WIZS .... Henderson, NC [*AM radio station call letters*]
WIZT .... Wiztec Solutions Ltd. [*NASDAQ symbol*] (SAG)
WizTch .... Wiz Technology, Inc. [*Associated Press*] (SAG)
WiztecS .... Wiztec Solutions Ltd. [*Associated Press*] (SAG)
WIZTF .... Wiztec Solutions [*NASDAQ symbol*] (TTSB)
WIZY .... East Jordan, MI [*FM radio station call letters*]
WIZZ .... Streator, IL [*AM radio station call letters*]
WJ .... Joule [*Unit of work*] (ROG)
WJ .... Labrador Airways [*ICAO designator*] (AD)
WJ .... Torontair [*ICAO designator*] (AD)
WJ .... Wars of the Jews [*of Josephus*] [*A publication*] (BJA)
WJ .... Water Jacket (MSA)
WJ .... Watkins-Johnson [*NYSE symbol*] (TTSB)
WJ .... Watkins-Johnson Co. [*NYSE symbol*] (SPSG)
wj .... West Bank of the Jordan River [*MARC country of publication code Library of Congress*] (LCCP)
WJ .... Western Jurist [*United States*] [*A publication*] (DLA)
WJ .... Wood Jalousie
WJa .... Janesville Public Library, Janesville, WI [*Library symbol Library of Congress*] (LCLS)
WJA .... Women's Jewelry Association (EA)
WJA .... Woolen Jobbers Association (EA)
WJA .... World Jai-Alai (EFIS)
WJA .... World Jazz Association [*Defunct*] (EA)
WJA .... World Jurist Association (EAIO)
WJAA .... Austin, IN [*FM radio station call letters*]
WJaB .... Blackhawk Technical Institute, Janesville, WI [*Library symbol Library of Congress*] (LCLS)
WJAB .... Huntsville, AL [*FM radio station call letters*]
WJAC .... Johnstown, PA [*AM radio station call letters*]
WJAC-TV .... Johnstown, PA [*Television station call letters*]
WJAD .... Leesburg, GA [*FM radio station call letters*] (RBYB)
WJAE-AM .... Westbrook, ME [*AM radio station call letters*] (BROA)
WJAG .... Norfolk, NE [*AM radio station call letters*]
WJAK-AM .... Jackson, TN [*AM radio station call letters*] (RBYB)
WJAL .... Hagerstown, MD [*Television station call letters*]
WJaM .... Mercy Hospital, Janesville, WI [*Library symbol Library of Congress*] (LCLS)
WJAM .... Orrville, AL [*FM radio station call letters*]
WJAN .... Sunderland, VT [*FM radio station call letters*]
WJAQ .... Marianna, FL [*FM radio station call letters*]
WJAR .... Providence, RI [*Television station call letters*]
WJaRH .... Rock County Health Care Center, Janesville, WI [*Library symbol Library of Congress*] (LCLS)
WJAS .... Pittsburgh, PA [*AM radio station call letters*]
WJaSDHi .... Seventh Day Baptist Historical Society Library, Janesville, WI [*Library symbol*] [*Library of Congress*] (LCLS)
WJAT .... Swainsboro, GA [*AM radio station call letters*]
WJAT-FM .... Swainsboro, GA [*FM radio station call letters*]
WJAW .... McConnelsville, OH [*FM radio station call letters*]
WJAX .... Jacksonville, FL [*AM radio station call letters*]
WJAY .... Mullins, SC [*AM radio station call letters*]
WJAZ .... Summerdale, PA [*FM radio station call letters*]
WJB .... Wire Jig Board (MCD)
WJBB .... Haleyville, AL [*AM radio station call letters*]
WJBB-FM .... Haleyville, AL [*FM radio station call letters*]
WJBC .... Bloomington, IL [*AM radio station call letters*]
WJBC .... Winnipeg Jets Booster Club (EA)
WJBD .... Salem, IL [*AM radio station call letters*]
WJBD-FM .... Salem, IL [*FM radio station call letters*]
WJBF .... Augusta, GA [*Television station call letters*]
WJBI .... Batesville, MS [*AM radio station call letters*]
WJBK .... Detroit, MI [*Television station call letters*]
WJBL .... Ladysmith, WI [*FM radio station call letters*]
WJBM .... Jerseyville, IL [*AM radio station call letters*]
WJBO .... Baton Rouge, LA [*AM radio station call letters*]
WJBQ .... Fisher, WV [*FM radio station call letters*] (RBYB)
WJBR .... Wilmington, DE [*AM radio station call letters*]
WJBR-FM .... Wilmington, DE [*FM radio station call letters*]
WJBS .... Holly Hill, SC [*AM radio station call letters*]
WJBS .... West Jersey Bancshares [*NASDAQ symbol*] (TTSB)
WJBS .... West Jersey Bancshares, Inc. [*NASDAQ symbol*] (SAG)
WJBT .... Green Cove Springs, FL [*FM radio station call letters*]
WJBU .... William Jennings Bryan University [*Tennessee*]
WJBW .... Jupiter, FL [*FM radio station call letters*]
WJBX .... Fort Myers Beach, FL [*FM radio station call letters*]

WJBY	Rainbow City, AL [*AM radio station call letters*]
WJBZ	Seymour, TN [*FM radio station call letters*]
WJC	Washington and Jefferson College [*Pennsylvania*]
WJC	Washington Journalism Center (EA)
WJC	Western Journalism Center
WJC	William Jewell College [*Liberty, MO*]
WJC	Wood Junior College [*Mathison, MS*]
WJC	Worcester Junior College [*Massachusetts*]
WJC	World Jewish Congress, American Section (EA)
WJC	Worthington Junior College [*Minnesota*] [*Later, Worthington Community College*]
WJCAA	Wisconsin Junior College Athletic Association (PSS)
WJCAC	Western Junior College Athletic Conference (PSS)
WJCB	Norfolk, VA [*Television station call letters*]
WJCB	World Jersey Cattle Bureau [*Jersey, Channel Islands, England*]
WJCC	Western Joint Computer Conference
WJCC	Women's Joint Congressional Committee (EA)
WJCC-FM	Montgomery, AL [*FM radio station call letters*] (RBYB)
WJCD	Norfolk, VA [*FM radio station call letters*] (RBYB)
WJCE	Memphis, TN [*AM radio station call letters*]
WJCE	Russellville, KY [*FM radio station call letters*]
WJCH	Joliet, IL [*FM radio station call letters*]
WJCI-AM	Rantoul, IL [*AM radio station call letters*] (RBYB)
WJCK	Cedartown, GA [*FM radio station call letters*]
WJCL	Savannah, GA [*FM radio station call letters*]
WJCL-TV	Savannah, GA [*Television station call letters*]
WJCM	Sebring, FL [*AM radio station call letters*]
WJCO-FM	Harwichport, MA [*FM radio station call letters*] (RBYB)
WJCP-FM	Austin, IN [*FM radio station call letters*] (RBYB)
WJCR-FM	Upton, KY [*FM radio station call letters*] (RBYB)
WJCS-FM	Allentown, PA [*FM radio station call letters*] (RBYB)
WJCT	Jacksonville, FL [*FM radio station call letters*]
WJCT-TV	Jacksonville, FL [*Television station call letters*]
WJCU-FM	University Heights, OH [*FM radio station call letters*] (BROA)
WJCV	Jacksonville, NC [*AM radio station call letters*]
WJCW	Johnson City, TN [*AM radio station call letters*]
WJCX-FM	Pittsfield, ME [*FM radio station call letters*] (BROA)
WJD	Water Jet Drilling (PDAA)
WJD	Welded Joint Design
WJDA	Quincy, MA [*AM radio station call letters*]
WJDB	Thomasville, AL [*AM radio station call letters*]
WJDB-FM	Thomasville, AL [*FM radio station call letters*]
WJDF	Orange, MA [*FM radio station call letters*] (RBYB)
WJDJ	Burnside, KY [*FM radio station call letters*]
WJDK	Morris, IL [*FM radio station call letters*]
WJDM	Elizabeth, NJ [*AM radio station call letters*]
WJDQ	Meridian, MS [*FM radio station call letters*]
WJDR	Prentiss, MS [*FM radio station call letters*]
WJDS	Jackson, MS [*AM radio station call letters*]
WJDT	Rogersville, TN [*FM radio station call letters*]
WJDX	Jackson, MS [*FM radio station call letters*]
WJDY	Salisbury, MD [*AM radio station call letters*]
WJE	Willis, Joyce, McMinnville OR [*STAC*]
WJEB	Jacksonville, FL [*Television station call letters*]
WJEC	Vernon, AL [*FM radio station call letters*]
WJEC	Welsh Joint Education Committee [*British*]
WJED	Dogwood Lakes Estate, FL [*FM radio station call letters*]
WJEF	Lafayette, IN [*FM radio station call letters*]
WJEH	Gallipolis, OH [*AM radio station call letters*]
WJEJ	Hagerstown, MD [*AM radio station call letters*]
WJEK-FM	Seneca, IL [*FM radio station call letters*] (BROA)
WJEL	Indianapolis, IN [*FM radio station call letters*]
WJEM	Valdosta, GA [*AM radio station call letters*]
WJEN	Rutland, VT [*FM radio station call letters*]
WJEP	Ochlocknee, GA [*AM radio station call letters*]
WJEQ	Macomb, IL [*FM radio station call letters*]
WJER	Dover-New Philadelphia, OH [*AM radio station call letters*]
WJER	Dover, OH [*FM radio station call letters*]
WJersB	West Jersey Bancshares, Inc. [*Associated Press*] (SAG)
WJES	Johnston, SC [*AM radio station call letters*]
WJET	Erie, PA [*FM radio station call letters*]
WJET-TV	Erie, PA [*Television station call letters*]
WJEZ	Pontiac, IL [*FM radio station call letters*]
WJF	Lancaster, CA [*Location identifier FAA*] (FAAL)
WJF	Palmdale/Lancaster [*California*] Fox [*Airport symbol*] (OAG)
WJF	White Jewish Female [*Classified advertising*]
WJF	Widowed Jewish Female [*Classified advertising*]
WJFB	Lebanon, TN [*Television station call letters*]
WJFC	Jefferson City, TN [*AM radio station call letters*]
WJFC	Waylon Jennings Fan Club (EA)
WJFD	New Bedford, MA [*FM radio station call letters*]
WJFF	Jeffersonville, NY [*FM radio station call letters*]
WJFFC	Worldwide John Fogerty Fanclub (EAIO)
WJFI	Women's Jazz Festival [*Defunct*] (EA)
WJFJ	Women Judges' Fund for Justice (EA)
WJFK	Baltimore, MD [*AM radio station call letters*]
WJFK	Manassas, VA [*FM radio station call letters*]
WJFL	Tennille, GA [*FM radio station call letters*]
WJFM	Baton Rouge, LA [*FM radio station call letters*]
WJFP	Fort Pierce, FL [*FM radio station call letters*]
WJFR	Jacksonville, FL [*FM radio station call letters*]
WJFW	Rhinelander, WI [*Television station call letters*]
WJFX	New Haven, IN [*FM radio station call letters*]
WJGA	Jackson, GA [*FM radio station call letters*]
WJGF	Romney, WV [*FM radio station call letters*]
WJGG	Lexington-Fayette, KY [*FM radio station call letters*]
WJGO	World Jewish Genealogy Organization (EA)
WJGR	Jacksonville, FL [*AM radio station call letters*]
WJHB	Fair Bluff, NC [*AM radio station call letters*]
WJHD	Portsmouth, RI [*FM radio station call letters*]
WJHG	Panama City, FL [*Television station call letters*]
WJHL	Johnson City, TN [*Television station call letters*]
WJHM	Daytona Beach, FL [*FM radio station call letters*]
WJHO	Opelika, AL [*AM radio station call letters*]
WJHR	Flemington, NJ [*AM radio station call letters*]
WJHS	Columbia City, IN [*FM radio station call letters*]
WJHU	Baltimore, MD [*FM radio station call letters*]
WJIA	Guntersville, AL [*FM radio station call letters*] (RBYB)
WJIB	Cambridge, MA [*AM radio station call letters*]
WJIC	Salem, NJ [*AM radio station call letters*]
WJIE	Okolona, KY [*FM radio station call letters*]
WJIF	Opp, AL [*FM radio station call letters*]
WJIG	Tullahoma, TN [*AM radio station call letters*]
WJIK	Binghamton, NY [*FM radio station call letters*]
WJIL	Jacksonville, IL [*AM radio station call letters*]
WJIM	Lansing, MI [*AM radio station call letters*]
WJIM-FM	Lansing, MI [*FM radio station call letters*]
WJIR	Key West, FL [*FM radio station call letters*]
WJIS	Bradenton, FL [*FM radio station call letters*]
WJIT	Sabana, PR [*AM radio station call letters*]
WJIV	Cherry Valley, NY [*FM radio station call letters*]
WJIZ	Albany, GA [*FM radio station call letters*]
WJJA	Racine, WI [*Television station call letters*]
WJJB	Romney, WV [*FM radio station call letters*]
WJJC	Commerce, GA [*AM radio station call letters*]
WJJD	Chicago, IL [*AM radio station call letters*]
WJJF	Hope Valley, RI [*AM radio station call letters*]
WJJG	Elmhurst, IL [*AM radio station call letters*]
WJJH	Ashland, WI [*FM radio station call letters*]
WJJJ-FM	Pittsburgh, PA [*FM radio station call letters*] (RBYB)
WJJL	Niagara Falls, NY [*AM radio station call letters*]
WJJM	Lewisburg, TN [*AM radio station call letters*]
WJJM-FM	Lewisburg, TN [*FM radio station call letters*]
WJJN	Dothan, AL [*FM radio station call letters*]
WJJO	Watertown, WI [*FM radio station call letters*]
WJJQ	Tomahawk, WI [*AM radio station call letters*]
WJJQ-FM	Tomahawk, WI [*FM radio station call letters*]
WJJR	Rutland, VT [*FM radio station call letters*]
WJJS	Vinton, VA [*FM radio station call letters*]
WJJS-AM	Lynchburg, VA [*AM radio station call letters*] (BROA)
WJJT	Jellico, TN [*AM radio station call letters*]
WJJW	North Adams, MA [*FM radio station call letters*]
WJJX	Lynchburg, VA [*FM radio station call letters*]
WJJY	Brainerd, MN [*FM radio station call letters*]
WJJZ	Philadelphia, PA [*FM radio station call letters*]
WJKC	Christiansted, VI [*FM radio station call letters*]
WJKE	Stillwater, NY [*FM radio station call letters*]
WJKI	Woodruff, SC [*AM radio station call letters*]
WJKK	Vicksburg, MS [*FM radio station call letters*] (RBYB)
WJKL	Elgin, IL [*FM radio station call letters*]
WJKM	Hartsville, TN [*AM radio station call letters*]
WJKN	Jackson, MI [*AM radio station call letters*] (RBYB)
WJKS	Jacksonville, FL [*Television station call letters*]
WJKW-FM	Athens, OH [*FM radio station call letters*] (BROA)
WJKX	Ellisville, MS [*FM radio station call letters*]
WJKY	Jamestown, KY [*AM radio station call letters*]
WJLA	Washington, DC [*Television station call letters*]
WJLB	Detroit, MI [*FM radio station call letters*]
WJLC	South Boston, VA [*FM radio station call letters*]
WJLC	Wye Junction Latching Circulator
WJLCER	Women's Joint Legislative Committee for Equal Rights [*Defunct*] (EA)
WJLD	Fairfield, AL [*AM radio station call letters*]
WJLE	Smithville, TN [*AM radio station call letters*]
WJLE-FM	Smithville, TN [*FM radio station call letters*]
WJLF	Gainesville, FL [*FM radio station call letters*]
WJLH	Flagler Beach, FL [*FM radio station call letters*] (RBYB)
WJLK	Asbury Park, NJ [*AM radio station call letters*]
WJLK-FM	Asbury Park, NJ [*FM radio station call letters*]
WJLM	Salem, VA [*FM radio station call letters*]
WJLR	Austin, IN [*FM radio station call letters*]
WJLS	Beckley, WV [*AM radio station call letters*]
WJLS-FM	Beckley, WV [*FM radio station call letters*]
WJLT-AM	Natick, MA [*AM radio station call letters*] (BROA)
WJLU	New Smyrna Beach, FL [*FM radio station call letters*]
WJLW-FM	Allouez, WI [*FM radio station call letters*] (RBYB)
WJLY	Ramsey, IL [*FM radio station call letters*]
WJM	Waterjet Machining [*Factory automation*] (BTTJ)
WJM	Widowed Jewish Male [*Classified advertising*]
WJMA	Orange, VA [*AM radio station call letters*]
WJMA-FM	Orange, VA [*FM radio station call letters*]
WJMC	Rice Lake, WI [*AM radio station call letters*]
WJMC-FM	Rice Lake, WI [*FM radio station call letters*]
WJMD	Hazard, KY [*FM radio station call letters*]
WJMF	Smithfield, RI [*FM radio Edition*]
WJMG	Hattiesburg, MS [*FM radio station call letters*]
WJMH	Reidsville, NC [*FM radio station call letters*]
WJMI	Jackson, MS [*FM radio station call letters*]
WJMJ	Hartford, CT [*FM radio station call letters*]
WJMK	Chicago, IL [*FM radio station call letters*]

WJML	Petoskey, MI [*AM radio station call letters*]
WJMM	Versailles, KY [*FM radio station call letters*]
WJMN	Boston, MA [*FM radio station call letters*]
WJMN	Escanaba, MI [*Television station call letters*]
WJMO	Cleveland Heights, OH [*AM radio station call letters*]
WJMP	Kent, OH [*AM radio station call letters*]
WJMQ	Clintonville, WI [*FM radio station call letters*]
WJMR	Peshtigo, WI [*FM radio station call letters*]
WJMS	Ironwood, MI [*AM radio station call letters*]
WJMT	Merrill, WI [*AM radio station call letters*]
WJMU	Decatur, IL [*FM radio station call letters*]
WJMW	Bloomsburg, PA [*AM radio station call letters*]
WJMX	Cheraw, SC [*FM radio station call letters*]
WJMX	Florence, SC [*AM radio station call letters*]
WJMZ	Anderson, SC [*FM radio station call letters*]
WJNA-AM	Boynton Beach, FL [*AM radio station call letters*] (RBYB)
WJNC	Jacksonville, NC [*AM radio station call letters*]
WJNE-FM	Laurel, DE [*FM radio station call letters*] (BROA)
WJNF	Marianna, FL [*FM radio station call letters*]
WJNG-FM	Johnsonburg, PA [*FM radio station call letters*] (BROA)
WJNL-AM	Petoskey, MI [*AM radio station call letters*] (BROA)
WJNN	North Cape May, NJ [*FM radio station call letters*]
WJNO	West Palm Beach, FL [*AM radio station call letters*]
WJNR	Iron Mountain, MI [*FM radio station call letters*]
WJNS	Yazoo City, MS [*FM radio station call letters*]
WJNT	Pearl, MS [*AM radio station call letters*]
WJNW	Janesville, WI [*Television station call letters*]
WJNX	Fort Pierce, FL [*AM radio station call letters*]
WJNY	Watertown, NY [*FM radio station call letters*]
WJOB	Hammond, IN [*AM radio station call letters*]
WJOC	Chattanooga, TN [*AM radio station call letters*]
WJOD	Galena, IL [*FM radio station call letters*]
WJOI	Germantown, TN [*FM radio station call letters*]
WJOL	Joliet, IL [*AM radio station call letters*]
WJON	St. Cloud, MN [*AM radio station call letters*]
WJOR	St. Joseph, TN [*FM radio station call letters*]
WJOX	Birmingham, AL [*AM radio station call letters*]
WJOY	Burlington, VT [*AM radio station call letters*]
WJP	Water Jet Pump
WJPA	Washington, PA [*AM radio station call letters*]
WJPA-FM	Washington, PA [*FM radio station call letters*]
WJPB	Woodcock-Johnson Psychoeducational Battery [*Psychology*] (DAVI)
WJPD	Ishpeming, MI [*FM radio station call letters*]
WJPEB	Woodcock-Johnson Psychoeducational Battery [*Educational test*]
WJPF	Herrin, IL [*AM radio station call letters*]
WJPH	Monticello, FL [*FM radio station call letters*]
WJPL-FM	Farmington, IL [*FM radio station call letters*] (BROA)
WJPM	Florence, SC [*Television station call letters*]
WJPR	Lynchburg, VA [*Television station call letters*]
WJPS	Evansville, IN [*AM radio station call letters*]
WJPS	Newburgh, IN [*FM radio station call letters*]
WJPX	San Juan, Puerto Rico [*Television station call letters*] (BROA)
WJPY	Seaford, DE [*FM radio station call letters*]
WJPZ	Syracuse, NY [*FM radio station call letters*]
WJQI	Chesapeake, VA [*AM radio station call letters*]
WJQI	Virginia Beach, VA [*FM radio station call letters*]
WJQK	Zeeland, MI [*FM radio station call letters*]
WJQR	St. Augustine Beach, FL [*FM radio station call letters*] (RBYB)
WJQZ	Wellsville, NY [*FM radio station call letters*]
WJR	Detroit, MI [*AM radio station call letters*]
WJR	Wajir [*Kenya*] [*Airport symbol*] (OAG)
WJ-R	Woodcock-Johnson Psycho-Educational Battery-Revised (TES)
WJR	World Jewish Register [*A publication*] (BJA)
WJRA	Priceville, AL [*AM radio station call letters*]
WJRD	Russellville, AL [*AM radio station call letters*]
WJRE	Kewanee, IL [*FM radio station call letters*]
WJRH	Easton, PA [*FM radio station call letters*]
WJRI	Lenoir, NC [*AM radio station call letters*]
WJRM	Troy, NC [*AM radio station call letters*]
WJRO	Glen Burnie, MD [*AM radio station call letters*]
WJRQ	Saluda, SC [*FM radio station call letters*]
WJRR	Cocoa Beach, FL [*FM radio station call letters*]
WJRS	Jamestown, KY [*FM radio station call letters*]
WJRT	Flint, MI [*Television station call letters*]
WJRV	Loretto, PA [*AM radio station call letters*]
WJRZ	Manahawkin, NJ [*FM radio station call letters*]
WJRZ	Toms River, NJ [*AM radio station call letters*]
WJS	Wife's Judicial Separation [*Legal*] [*British*] (ROG)
WJSA	Jersey Shore, PA [*AM radio station call letters*]
WJSA-FM	Jersey Shore, PA [*FM radio station call letters*]
WJSB	Crestview, FL [*AM radio station call letters*]
WJSC	Johnson, VT [*FM radio station call letters*]
WJSE	Petersburg, NJ [*FM radio station call letters*]
WJSG	Hamlet, NC [*FM radio station call letters*]
WJSH	Terre Haute, IN [*AM radio station call letters*]
WJSK	Lumberton, NC [*FM radio station call letters*]
WJSL	Houghton, NY [*FM radio station call letters*]
WJSM	Martinsburg, PA [*AM radio station call letters*]
WJSM-FM	Martinsburg, PA [*FM radio station call letters*]
WJSN	Jackson, KY [*FM radio station call letters*]
WJSO	Pikeville, KY [*FM radio station call letters*]
WJSP	Columbus, GA [*Television station call letters*]
WJSP	Warm Springs, GA [*FM radio station call letters*]
WJSQ	Athens, TN [*FM radio station call letters*]
WJSR	Birmingham, AL [*FM radio station call letters*]
WJST	Fort Myers Villas, FL [*FM radio station call letters*] (RBYB)
WJSU	Anniston, AL [*Television station call letters*]
WJSU	Jackson, MS [*FM radio station call letters*]
WJSV	Morristown, NJ [*FM radio station call letters*]
WJSX-FM	Cape May, NJ [*FM radio station call letters*] (BROA)
WJSZ	Ashley, MI [*FM radio station call letters*]
WJT	World Journal Tribune [*Defunct New York City afternoon newspaper*]
WJTA	Kosciusko, MS [*FM radio station call letters*]
WJTA	Water Jet Technology Association (NTPA)
WJTB	North Ridgeville, OH [*AM radio station call letters*]
WJTC	Pensacola, FL [*Television station call letters*]
WJTD	McArthur, OH [*AM radio station call letters*]
WJTF	Panama City, FL [*FM radio station call letters*]
WJTG	Fort Valley, GA [*FM radio station call letters*]
WJTH	Calhoun, GA [*AM radio station call letters*]
WJTL	Lancaster, PA [*FM radio station call letters*]
WJTM	Frederick, MD [*FM radio station call letters*]
WJTN	Jamestown, NY [*AM radio station call letters*]
WJTO	Bath, ME [*AM radio station call letters*]
WJTP	Newland, NC [*AM radio station call letters*]
WJTT	Red Bank, TN [*FM radio station call letters*]
WJTV	Jackson, MS [*Television station call letters*]
WJTW	Joliet, IL [*FM radio station call letters*]
WJTY	Lancaster, WI [*FM radio station call letters*]
WJu	Juneau Public Library, Juneau, WI [*Library symbol Library of Congress*] (LCLS)
WJUB	Plymouth, WI [*AM radio station call letters*]
WJUC	Swanton, OH [*FM radio station call letters*] (RBYB)
WJUE	Battle Creek, MI [*Television station call letters*]
WJUF	Inverness, FL [*FM radio station call letters*] (RBYB)
WJUK	Mt, Pleasant, SC [*FM radio station call letters*]
WJUL	Lowell, MA [*FM radio station call letters*]
WJuMe	Dodge County Mental Health Center, Juneau, WI [*Library symbol Library of Congress*] (LCLS)
WJUN	Mexico, PA [*AM radio station call letters*]
WJUN-FM	Mexico, PA [*FM radio station call letters*]
WJUS	Fort Walton Beach, FL [*FM radio station call letters*]
WJUX	Monticello, NY [*FM radio station call letters*] (RBYB)
WJVL	Janesville, WI [*FM radio station call letters*]
WJVO	South Jacksonville, IL [*FM radio station call letters*]
WJVP-FM	Culebra, PR [*FM radio station call letters*] (RBYB)
WJVS	Cincinnati, OH [*FM radio station call letters*]
WJW	Cleveland, OH [*Television station call letters*]
WJWF	Columbus, MS [*AM radio station call letters*]
WJWJ	Beaufort, SC [*FM radio station call letters*]
WJWJ-TV	Beaufort, SC [*Television station call letters*]
WJWN	San Sebastian, PR [*Television station call letters*]
WJWR-AM	Newark, NJ [*AM radio station call letters*] (BROA)
WJWS	South Hill, VA [*AM radio station call letters*]
WJWV	Fort Gaines, GA [*FM radio station call letters*]
WJX	Wajax Ltd. [*Toronto Stock Exchange symbol*]
WJXA	Nashville, TN [*FM radio station call letters*]
WJXB	Knoxville, TN [*FM radio station call letters*]
WJXL	Jacksonville, AL [*AM radio station call letters*] (RBYB)
WJXN	Jackson, MS [*AM radio station call letters*]
WJXN	Utica, MS [*FM radio station call letters*]
WJXQ	Jackson, MI [*FM radio station call letters*]
WJXR	Macclenny, FL [*FM radio station call letters*]
WJXT	Jacksonville, FL [*Television station call letters*]
WJXX	Orange Park, FL [*Television station call letters*] (BROA)
WJXY	Conway, SC [*AM radio station call letters*]
WJXY-FM	Conway, SC [*FM radio station call letters*]
WJY	Westmoreland County Community College, Youngwood, PA [*OCLC symbol*] (OCLC)
WJYC	Delhi Hills, OH [*FM radio station call letters*]
WJYE	Buffalo, NY [*FM radio station call letters*]
WJYF	Nashville, GA [*FM radio station call letters*]
WJYJ	Fredericksburg, VA [*FM radio station call letters*]
WJYL	New Washington, IN [*FM radio station call letters*]
WJYM	Bowling Green, OH [*AM radio station call letters*]
WJYN-FM	Bethany Beach, DE [*FM radio station call letters*] (BROA)
WJYO	Fort Myers, FL [*FM radio station call letters*]
WJYP	South Charleston, WV [*AM radio station call letters*]
WJYR	Myrtle Beach, SC [*FM radio station call letters*]
WJYS	Hammond, IN [*Television station call letters*]
WJYY	Concord, NH [*FM radio station call letters*]
WJYZ	Albany, GA [*AM radio station call letters*]
WJZ	Baltimore, MD [*Television station call letters*]
WJZA	Columbus, OH [*FM radio station call letters*]
WJZB-FM	Houston, MS [*FM radio station call letters*] (RBYB)
WJZC-FM	Russellville, KY [*FM radio station call letters*] (BROA)
WJZD	Long Beach, MS [*FM radio station call letters*]
WJZE	Oak Harbor, OH [*FM radio station call letters*]
WJZF	La Grange, GA [*FM radio station call letters*]
WJZI-FM	Milwaukee, WI [*FM radio station call letters*] (RBYB)
WJZJ-FM	Glen Arbor, MI [*FM radio station call letters*] (BROA)
WJZK-FM	Charleston, SC [*FM radio station call letters*] (RBYB)
WJZM	Clarksville, TN [*AM radio station call letters*]
WJZR	Rochester, NY [*FM radio station call letters*]
WJZS	Orangeburg, SC [*AM radio station call letters*]
WJZT-FM	Midway, FL [*FM radio station call letters*] (RBYB)
WJZW	Woodbridge, VA [*FM radio station call letters*]
WJZY	Belmont, NC [*Television station call letters*]
WJZZ	Detroit, MI [*FM radio station call letters*]

wk .... Wake Island [*MARC country of publication code Library of Congress*] (LCCP)

WK .... Warburg-Keilin System [*Cytochrome-cytochrome oxidase system*] [*Named for Otto Warburg and D. Keilin*]

WK .... Warehouse Keeper [*British*] (ROG)

WK .... Waylands Korongo [*Tanzania*]

WK .... Weak (DAVI)

wk .... Week (WDMC)

WK .... Week (AFM)

WK .... Well-Known

WK .... Wernicke-Korsakoff [*Syndrome*] [*Medicine*]

WK .... Western Alaska [*Airlines*] (OAG)

WK .... Westkuestenflug [*ICAO designator*] (AD)

WK .... Wetboek van Koophandel [*Commercial Code*] [*Dutch*] (ILCA)

WK .... Wilson-Kimmelstiel [*Disease*] (MAE)

WK .... Wit Kommando [*White Commando*] [*South Africa*]

WK .... Work

Wk .... Work (AL)

WK .... Worksheet [*Data format*]

Wk .... Wreck [*Nautical charts*]

WKa .... Kaukauna Public Library, Kaukauna, WI [*Library symbol Library of Congress*] (LCLS)

WKA .... Waffenkarren [*Weapons Cart*] [*German military - World War II*]

WKA .... Wkay Resources [*Vancouver Stock Exchange symbol*]

WKAA .... Ocilla, GA [*FM radio station call letters*]

WKAB .... Berwick, PA [*FM radio station call letters*]

WKAC .... Athens, AL [*AM radio station call letters*]

WKACC .... Work Accomplishment Code [*Navy*] (NG)

WKAI .... Macomb, IL [*FM radio station call letters*]

WKAJ-FM .... Saratoga Springs, NY [*FM radio station call letters*] (RBYB)

WKAK .... Albany, GA [*FM radio station call letters*]

WKAL .... Kalkaska, MI [*AM radio station call letters*]

WKAM .... Goshen, IN [*AM radio station call letters*]

WKAN .... Kankakee, IL [*AM radio station call letters*]

WKAP .... Allentown, PA [*AM radio station call letters*] (RBYB)

WKAQ .... San Juan, PR [*AM radio station call letters*]

WKAQ-FM ... San Juan, PR [*FM radio station call letters*]

WKAQ-TV .... San Juan, PR [*Television station call letters*]

WKAR .... East Lansing, MI [*AM radio station call letters*]

WKAR-FM .... East Lansing, MI [*FM radio station call letters*]

WKAR-TV .... East Lansing, MI [*Television station call letters*]

WKAS .... Ashland, KY [*Television station call letters*]

WKAT .... North Miami, FL [*AM radio station call letters*]

Wk Aust ...... Weekend Australian [*A publication*]

WKAV .... Charlottesville, VA [*AM radio station call letters*]

WKAX .... Russellville, AL [*AM radio station call letters*]

WKAY .... Kannapolis, NC [*Television station call letters*]

WKAZ .... Miami, WV [*FM radio station call letters*]

WKB .... Warracknabeal [*Victoria, Australia*] [*Airport symbol*] (AD)

WKB .... Wentzel-Kramers-Brillouin Approximation [*Mathematics*]

WKBA .... Vinton, VA [*AM radio station call letters*]

WKBB .... West Point, MS [*FM radio station call letters*]

WKBC .... North Wilkesboro, NC [*AM radio station call letters*]

WKBC-FM .... North Wilkesboro, NC [*FM radio station call letters*]

WKBD .... Detroit, MI [*Television station call letters*]

WKBE .... Warrensburg, NY [*FM radio station call letters*]

WKBF .... Rock Island, IL [*AM radio station call letters*]

WKBG .... Martinez, GA [*FM radio station call letters*]

WKBH .... Holmen, WI [*AM radio station call letters*]

WKBH .... Trempealeau, WI [*FM radio station call letters*]

WKBI .... St. Mary, PA [*AM radio station call letters*]

WKBI-FM .... St. Mary, PA [*FM radio station call letters*]

WKBJ .... Milan, TN [*AM radio station call letters*]

WKBJ .... Wentzel-Kramers-Brillouin-Jeffreys [*Approximation or Method*] [*Physics*]

WKBK .... Keene, NH [*AM radio station call letters*]

WKBL .... Covington, TN [*AM radio station call letters*]

WKBL-FM .... Covington, TN [*FM radio station call letters*]

WKBM .... Coal City, IL [*FM radio station call letters*]

WKBN .... Youngstown, OH [*AM radio station call letters*]

WKBN-FM .... Youngstown, OH [*FM radio station call letters*]

WKBN-TV .... Youngstown, OH [*Television station call letters*]

WKBO .... Harrisburg, PA [*AM radio station call letters*]

WKBQ .... Jerseyville, IL [*FM radio station call letters*]

WKBQ .... St. Louis, MO [*AM radio station call letters*]

WKBR .... Manchester, NH [*AM radio station call letters*]

WKBS .... Altoona, PA [*Television station call letters*]

WKBT .... La Crosse, WI [*Television station call letters*]

WKBV .... Richmond, IN [*AM radio station call letters*]

WKBW .... Buffalo, NY [*Television station call letters*]

WKBX .... Kingsland, GA [*FM radio station call letters*]

WKBY .... Chatham, VA [*AM radio station call letters*]

WKBZ .... Muskegon, MI [*AM radio station call letters*]

WKBZ .... Whitehall, MI [*FM radio station call letters*]

WKC .... Walker Ridge [*California*] [*Seismograph station code, US Geological Survey*] (SEIS)

WKC .... Western Kenya Aircharters Co. Ltd. [*ICAO designator*] (FAAC)

WKC .... Westminster Kennel Club (EA)

WKCA .... Owingsville, KY [*FM radio station call letters*]

WKCB .... Hindman, KY [*AM radio station call letters*]

WKCB-FM .... Hindman, KY [*FM radio station call letters*]

WKCC .... Grayson, KY [*FM radio station call letters*]

WKCD .... Pawcatuck, CT [*FM radio station call letters*] (RBYB)

WKCE .... Maryville, TN [*AM radio station call letters*] (RBYB)

WKCF .... Clermont, FL [*Television station call letters*]

WKCG .... Augusta, ME [*FM radio station call letters*]

WKCH-FM .... Whitewater, WI [*FM radio station call letters*] (RBYB)

WKCI .... Hamden, CT [*FM radio station call letters*]

WKCJ .... Lewisburg, WV [*FM radio station call letters*]

WKCL .... Ladson, SC [*FM radio station call letters*]

WKCM .... Hawesville, KY [*AM radio station call letters*]

WKCM-FM .... Hawkesville, KY [*FM radio station call letters*]

WKCN .... Lumpkin, GA [*FM radio station call letters*]

WKCO .... Gambier, OH [*FM radio station call letters*]

WKCONSUPVR... Work Control Supervisor [*Air Force*]

WKCQ .... Saginaw, MI [*FM radio station call letters*]

WKCR .... New York, NY [*FM radio station call letters*]

WKCS .... Knoxville, TN [*FM radio station call letters*]

WKCT .... Bowling Green, KY [*AM radio station call letters*]

WKCU .... Corinth, MS [*AM radio station call letters*]

WKCV .... Kingsport, TN [*AM radio station call letters*]

WKCW .... Warrenton, VA [*AM radio station call letters*]

WKCX .... Rome, GA [*FM radio station call letters*]

WKCY .... Harrisonburg, VA [*AM radio station call letters*]

WKCY-FM .... Harrisonburg, VA [*FM radio station call letters*]

WKD .... Weekday

WKD .... Wilson-Kimmelstiel Disease [*Medicine*] (DMAA)

WKD .... Worked [*Amateur radio shorthand*] (WDAA)

WKDA .... Nashville, TN [*AM radio station call letters*]

WKDAY .... Weekday

WKDB .... Towson, MD [*AM radio station call letters*]

WKDD .... Akron, OH [*FM radio station call letters*]

WKDE .... Altavista, VA [*AM radio station call letters*]

WKDE-FM .... Altavista, VA [*FM radio station call letters*]

WKDF .... Nashville, TN [*FM radio station call letters*]

WKDI .... Denton, MD [*AM radio station call letters*]

WKDJ .... Clarksdale, MS [*FM radio station call letters*]

WKDK .... Newberry, SC [*AM radio station call letters*]

WKDL .... Silver Spring, MD [*AM radio station call letters*]

WKDM .... New York, NY [*AM radio station call letters*]

WKDN .... Camden, NJ [*FM radio station call letters*]

WKDO .... Liberty, KY [*AM radio station call letters*]

WKDO-FM .... Liberty, KY [*FM radio station call letters*]

WKDP .... Corbin, KY [*AM radio station call letters*]

WKDP-FM .... Corbin, KY [*FM radio station call letters*]

WKDQ .... Henderson, KY [*FM radio station call letters*]

WKDR .... Burlington, VT [*AM radio station call letters*]

WKDS .... Kalamazoo, MI [*FM radio station call letters*]

WKDU .... Philadelphia, PA [*FM radio station call letters*]

WKDV .... Manassas, VA [*AM radio station call letters*]

WKDW-AM .... Staunton, VA [*AM radio station call letters*] (RBYB)

WKDX .... Hamlet, NC [*AM radio station call letters*]

WKDZ .... Cadiz, KY [*AM radio station call letters*]

WKDZ-FM .... Cadiz, KY [*FM radio station call letters*]

WKE .... Wake [*Wake Island*] [*Seismograph station code, US Geological Survey Closed*] (SEIS)

WKEA .... Scottsboro, AL [*FM radio station call letters*]

WKEB-FM .... Medford, WI [*FM radio station call letters*] (BROA)

WKED .... Frankfort, KY [*AM radio station call letters*]

WKED-FM .... Frankfort, KY [*FM radio station call letters*]

WKEE .... Huntington, WV [*AM radio station call letters*]

WKEE-FM .... Huntington, WV [*FM radio station call letters*]

WKEF .... Dayton, OH [*Television station call letters*]

WKEI .... Kewanee, IL [*AM radio station call letters*]

WKEL .... Myrtle Beach, SC [*AM radio station call letters*]

WKEN .... Dover, DE [*AM radio station call letters*]

WKen .... Gilbert M. Simmons Public Library, Kenosha, WI [*Library symbol Library of Congress*] (LCLS)

WKenA .... Armitage Academy Library, Kenosha, WI [*Library symbol Library of Congress*] (LCLS)

WKenC .... Carthage College, Kenosha, WI [*Library symbol Library of Congress*] (LCLS)

WKEND .... Weekend

WKenG .... Gateway Technical Institute, Kenosha, WI [*Library symbol Library of Congress*] (LCLS)

WKenG-E .... Gateway Technical Institute, Elkhorn Campus, Elkhorn, WI [*Library symbol Library of Congress*] (LCLS)

WKenG-R .... Gateway Technical Institute, Racine Campus, Racine, WI [*Library symbol Library of Congress*] (LCLS)

WKenHi ...... Kenosha County Historical Association, Kenosha, WI [*Library symbol Library of Congress*] (LCLS)

WKenM .... Kenosha Memorial Hospital, Kenosha, WI [*Library symbol Library of Congress*] (LCLS)

WKenOS ...... Old Songs Library, Kenosha, WI [*Library symbol Library of Congress*] (LCLS)

WKenSC ...... St. Catherine's Hospital, Kenosha, WI [*Library symbol Library of Congress*] (LCLS)

WKenSD ...... Unified School District Number One, Media Center, Kenosha, WI [*Library symbol Library of Congress*] (LCLS)

WKenSD-B ... Unified School District Number One, Mary D. Bradford High School, Kenosha, WI [*Library symbol Library of Congress*] (LCLS)

WKenSD-R ... Unified School District Number One, Walter Reuther High School, Kenosha, WI [*Library symbol Library of Congress*] (LCLS)

WKenSD-T ... Unified School District Number One, Tremper High School, Kenosha, WI [*Library symbol Library of Congress*] (LCLS)

WKenU .... University of Wisconsin-Parkside, Kenosha, WI [*Library symbol Library of Congress*] (LCLS)

WKenU-A .... University of Wisconsin-Parkside, Archives and Art Research Center, Kenosha, WI [*Library symbol Library of Congress*] (LCLS)

WKEQ .... Burnside, KY [*AM radio station call letters*]

WKES........ St. Petersburg, FL [*FM radio station call letters*]
WKET........ Kettering, OH [*FM radio station call letters*]
WKEU........ Griffin, GA [*AM radio station call letters*]
WKEW........ Greensboro, NC [*AM radio station call letters*]
WKEX........ Blacksburg, VA [*AM radio station call letters*]
WKEY........ Covington, VA [*AM radio station call letters*]
WKEZ-AM.... Bluefield, WV [*AM radio station call letters*] (BROA)
WKF........ Well-Known Factor
WKFD........ Wickford, RI [*AM radio station call letters*] (RBYB)
WKFE........ Yauco, PR [*AM radio station call letters*]
WKFI........ Wilmington, OH [*AM radio station call letters*]
WKFL........ Bushnell, FL [*AM radio station call letters*]
WKFM........ Huron, OH [*FM radio station call letters*] (RBYB)
WKFR........ Battle Creek, MI [*FM radio station call letters*]
WKFT........ Fayetteville, NC [*Television station call letters*]
WKFX........ Kaukauna, WI [*FM radio station call letters*]
WKG........ Working (MSA)
WKGA........ Zion, IL [*AM radio station call letters*]
WKGB........ Bowling Green, KY [*Television station call letters*]
WKGB........ Susquehanna, PA [*FM radio station call letters*]
WKGC........ Panama City Beach, FL [*AM radio station call letters*]
WKGC........ Panama City, FL [*FM radio station call letters*]
WKGF........ Arcadia, FL [*AM radio station call letters*]
WKGF-FM.... Arcadia, FL [*FM radio station call letters*]
WKGG........ Cape Vincent, NY [*FM radio station call letters*]
WKGM........ Smithfield, VA [*AM radio station call letters*]
WKGN........ Knoxville, TN [*AM radio station call letters*]
WKGO........ Cumberland, MD [*FM radio station call letters*]
WKGP........ Workgroup Technology [*NASDAQ symbol*] (TTSB)
WKGQ........ Milledgeville, GA [*AM radio station call letters*]
WKGR........ Fort Pierce, FL [*FM radio station call letters*]
WKGT........ Century, FL [*FM radio station call letters*]
WKGV........ Working Voltage (IAA)
WKGX........ Lenoir, NC [*AM radio station call letters*]
WKHA........ Hazard, KY [*Television station call letters*]
WKHB-FM.... Hartford, KY [*FM radio station call letters*] (RBYB)
WKHC-FM.... Dahlonega, GA [*FM radio station call letters*] (RBYB)
WKHG........ Leitchfield, KY [*FM radio station call letters*]
WKHI........ Pocomoke City, MD [*FM radio station call letters*]
WKHJ........ Mountain Lake Park, MD [*FM radio station call letters*]
WKHK........ Colonial Heights, VA [*FM radio station call letters*]
WKHL........ Stamford, CT [*FM radio station call letters*]
WKHM........ Brooklyn, MI [*FM radio station call letters*]
WKHM........ Jackson, MI [*AM radio station call letters*]
WKHQ........ Charlevoix, MI [*FM radio station call letters*]
WKHR........ Bainbridge, OH [*FM radio station call letters*]
WKHS........ Worton, MD [*FM radio station call letters*]
WKHT........ Bishopville, SC [*FM radio station call letters*]
WKHW-FM... Pocomoke City, MD [*FM radio station call letters*] (RBYB)
WKHX........ Atlanta, GA [*AM radio station call letters*]
WKHX........ Marietta, GA [*FM radio station call letters*]
WKHY........ Lafayette, IN [*FM radio station call letters*]
WKi........ Kiel Public Library, Kiel, WI [*Library symbol Library of Congress*] (LCLS)
WKI........ Wankie [*Zimbabwe*] [*Airport symbol*] (AD)
WKIC........ Hazard, KY [*AM radio station call letters*]
WKID........ Vevay, IN [*FM radio station call letters*]
WKIG........ Glennville, GA [*AM radio station call letters*]
WKIG-FM.... Glennville, GA [*FM radio station call letters*]
WKII........ Port Charlotte, FL [*AM radio station call letters*] (RBYB)
WKIK........ La Plata, MD [*AM radio station call letters*] (RBYB)
WKIM........ Augusta, GA [*AM radio station call letters*]
WKIN........ Kingsport, TN [*AM radio station call letters*]
WKIO........ Urbana, IL [*FM radio station call letters*]
WKIP........ Poughkeepsie, NY [*AM radio station call letters*]
WKIQ........ Eustis, FL [*AM radio station call letters*]
WKIS........ Boca Raton, FL [*FM radio station call letters*]
WKIS........ Wilson Knight Interdiscipline Society (EA)
WKISF........ Wilson Knight Interdiscipline Society and Foundation (EA)
WKIT........ Brewer, ME [*FM radio station call letters*]
WKIX........ Raleigh, NC [*FM radio station call letters*]
WKIY........ West Kent Imperial Yeomanry [*British military*] (DMA)
WKIZ........ Key West, FL [*AM radio station call letters*]
WKJ........ Wakkanai [*Japan*] [*Airport symbol*] (OAG)
WKJA........ Belhaven, NC [*FM radio station call letters*]
WKJB........ Mayaguez, PR [*AM radio station call letters*]
WKJB-FM.... Mayaguez, PR [*FM radio station call letters*]
WKJC........ Tawas City, MI [*FM radio station call letters*]
WKJE........ Hertford, NC [*FM radio station call letters*]
WKJF........ Cadillac, MI [*AM radio station call letters*]
WKJF-FM.... Cadillac, MI [*FM radio station call letters*]
WKJG........ Fort Wayne, IN [*Television station call letters*]
WKJK........ Salem, IN [*FM radio station call letters*]
WKJL........ Clarksburg, WV [*FM radio station call letters*]
WKJN........ Hammond, LA [*FM radio station call letters*]
WKJQ........ Parsons, TN [*AM radio station call letters*]
WKJQ-FM.... Parsons, TN [*FM radio station call letters*]
WKJR........ Arcola, IL [*FM radio station call letters*] (RBYB)
WKJT........ Tryon, NC [*AM radio station call letters*]
WKJV........ Asheville, NC [*AM radio station call letters*]
WKJX........ Elizabeth City, NC [*FM radio station call letters*]
WKJY........ Hempstead, NY [*FM radio station call letters*]
WKJZ........ Hillman, MI [*FM radio station call letters*]
WKK........ Aleknagik [*Alaska*] [*Airport symbol*] (OAG)
WKK........ Aleknagik, AK [*Location identifier FAA*] (FAAL)
WKKB........ Key Colony Beach, FL [*FM radio station call letters*]
WKKC........ Chicago, IL [*FM radio station call letters*]
WKKD........ Aurora, IL [*AM radio station call letters*]
WKKD-FM.... Aurora, IL [*FM radio station call letters*]
WKKE........ St. Pauls, NC [*AM radio station call letters*]
WKKG........ Columbus, IN [*FM radio station call letters*]
WKKI........ Celina, OH [*FM radio station call letters*]
WKKJ........ Chillicothe, OH [*FM radio station call letters*]
WKKL........ West Barnstable, MA [*FM radio station call letters*]
WKKM........ Harrison, MI [*FM radio station call letters*]
WKKN........ Cordele, GA [*FM radio station call letters*]
WKKO........ Toledo, OH [*FM radio station call letters*]
WKKP........ McDonough, GA [*AM radio station call letters*]
WKKQ........ Nashwauk, MN [*AM radio station call letters*]
WKKR........ Auburn, AL [*FM radio station call letters*]
WKKS........ Vanceburg, KY [*AM radio station call letters*]
WKKS-FM.... Vanceburg, KY [*FM radio station call letters*]
WKKT-FM.... Statesville, NC [*FM radio station call letters*] (BROA)
WKKV........ Racine, WI [*FM radio station call letters*]
WKKW........ Clarksburg, WV [*FM radio station call letters*]
WKKX........ Granite City, IL [*FM radio station call letters*]
WKKY........ Geneva, OH [*FM radio station call letters*]
WKKZ........ Dublin, GA [*FM radio station call letters*]
WKL........ Waikoloa [*Hawaii*] [*Airport symbol*] (OAG)
WKLA........ Ludington, MI [*AM radio station call letters*]
WKLA-FM.... Ludington, MI [*FM radio station call letters*]
WKLB........ Manchester, KY [*AM radio station call letters*]
WKLB-FM.... Framingham, MA [*FM radio station call letters*] (RBYB)
WKLC........ St. Albans, WV [*FM radio station call letters*]
WKLD........ Oneonta, AL [*FM radio station call letters*]
WKLE........ Lexington, KY [*Television station call letters*]
WKLEERI.... W. K. Lypynsky East European Research Institute (EA)
WKLF........ Clanton, AL [*AM radio station call letters*]
WKLG........ Rock Harbor, FL [*FM radio station call letters*]
WKLH........ Milwaukee, WI [*FM radio station call letters*]
WKLI........ Albany, NY [*FM radio station call letters*]
WKLJ........ Sparta, WI [*AM radio station call letters*]
WKLK........ Cloquet, MN [*AM radio station call letters*]
WKLK-FM.... Cloquet, MN [*FM radio station call letters*]
WKLL........ Frankfort, NY [*FM radio station call letters*]
WKLM........ Millersburg, OH [*FM radio station call letters*]
WKLN........ St Augustine Beach, FL [*AM radio station call letters*]
WKLO........ Seymour, IN [*FM radio station call letters*] (RBYB)
WKLP........ Keyser, WV [*AM radio station call letters*]
WKLQ........ Holland, MI [*FM radio station call letters*]
WKLR........ Veedersburg, IN [*FM radio station call letters*] (RBYB)
WKLS........ Atlanta, GA [*FM radio station call letters*]
WKLT........ Kalkaska, MI [*FM radio station call letters*]
WKLV........ Blackstone, VA [*AM radio station call letters*]
WKLW........ Paintsville, KY [*AM radio station call letters*]
WKLW-FM... Paintsville, KY [*FM radio station call letters*]
WKLX........ Rochester, NY [*FM radio station call letters*]
WKLY........ Hartwell, GA [*AM radio station call letters*]
WKLY........ Weekly
Wkly Cin Law Bul... Weekly Cincinnati Law Bulletin [*Ohio*] [*A publication*] (DLA)
Wkly Dig...... New York Weekly Digest [*A publication*] (DLA)
Wkly Law Bul... Weekly Law Bulletin [*Ohio*] [*A publication*] (DLA)
Wkly Law Gaz... Weekly Law Gazette [*Ohio*] [*A publication*] (DLA)
Wkly L Bul... Weekly Law Bulletin [*Ohio*] [*A publication*] (DLA)
Wkly L Gaz... Weekly Law Gazette [*Ohio*] [*A publication*] (DLA)
Wkly NC...... Weekly Notes of Cases [*Pennsylvania*] [*A publication*] (DLA)
Wkly Notes Cas... Weekly Notes of Cases [*Pennsylvania*] [*A publication*] (DLA)
Wkly Notes Cas (PA)... Weekly Notes of Cases [*Pennsylvania*] [*A publication*] (DLA)
Wkly Rep..... Weekly Reporter [*London*] [*A publication*] (DLA)
WKLZ........ Petoskey, MI [*FM radio station call letters*]
WKM........ Hwange National Park [*Zimbabwe*] [*Airport symbol*] (OAG)
WKM........ State University of New York, Agricultural and Technical College, Cobleskill, Cobleskill, NY [*OCLC symbol*] (OCLC)
WKM........ Wankie Game Reserve [*Zimbabwe*] [*Airport symbol*] (AD)
WKMA........ Madisonville, KY [*Television station call letters*]
WKMB........ Stirling, NJ [*AM radio station call letters*]
WKMC........ Roaring Spring, PA [*AM radio station call letters*]
WKMG........ Newberry, SC [*AM radio station call letters*]
WKMI........ Kalamazoo, MI [*AM radio station call letters*]
WKMJ........ Louisville, KY [*Television station call letters*]
WKML........ Lumberton, NC [*FM radio station call letters*]
WKMM........ Kingwood, WV [*FM radio station call letters*]
WKMO........ Hodgenville, KY [*FM radio station call letters*]
WKMQ........ Winnebago, IL [*FM radio station call letters*]
WKMR........ Morehead, KY [*Television station call letters*]
WKMS........ Murray, KY [*FM radio station call letters*]
WKMT........ Kings Mountain, NC [*AM radio station call letters*]
WKMU........ Murray, KY [*Television station call letters*]
WKMX........ Enterprise, AL [*FM radio station call letters*]
WKMY........ Princeton, WV [*FM radio station call letters*]
WKMZ........ Martinsburg, WV [*FM radio station call letters*]
WKN........ Wakunai [*Papua New Guinea*] [*Airport symbol*] (OAG)
WKN........ Weaken
Wk N........ Weekly Notes of Cases [*Pennsylvania*] [*A publication*] (DLA)
WKNA........ Senatobia, MS [*FM radio station call letters*]
WKNB........ Clarendon, PA [*FM radio station call letters*] (RBYB)
WKNC........ Raleigh, NC [*FM radio station call letters*]
WKND........ Weekend
WKND........ Windsor, CT [*AM radio station call letters*]

WKNE .... Keene, NH [*AM radio station call letters*]
WKNE-FM .... Keene, NH [*FM radio station call letters*]
WKNG .... Tallapoosa, GA [*AM radio station call letters*]
WKNH .... Keene, NH [*FM radio station call letters*]
WKNI .... Lexington, AL [*AM radio station call letters*]
WKNJ .... Union Township, NJ [*FM radio station call letters*]
WKNK .... Edmonton, KY [*FM radio station call letters*] (RBYB)
WKNL .... Knoxville, TN [*AM radio station call letters*]
WKNL .... Walter Kidde Nuclear Laboratories, Inc. (MCD)
WKNN .... Pascagoula, MS [*FM radio station call letters*]
WKNO .... Memphis, TN [*FM radio station call letters*]
WKNO-TV .... Memphis, TN [*Television station call letters*]
WKNP .... Jackson, TN [*FM radio station call letters*]
WKNQ .... Dyersburg, TN [*FM radio station call letters*]
WKNR .... Cleveland, OH [*AM radio station call letters*]
WKNS .... Kinston, NC [*FM radio station call letters*] (RBYB)
WKNT .... Bowling Green, KY [*Television station call letters*]
WKNU .... Brewton, AL [*FM radio station call letters*]
WKNV .... Dublin, VA [*AM radio station call letters*]
WKNW .... Sault Ste. Marie, MI [*AM radio station call letters*]
WKNX .... Frankenmuth, MI [*AM radio station call letters*]
WKNY .... Kingston, NY [*AM radio station call letters*]
WKNZ .... Collins, MS [*FM radio station call letters*]
WKOA .... Lafayette, IN [*FM radio station call letters*]
WKOC .... Chesapeake, VA [*FM radio station call letters*] (RBYB)
WKOE .... Ocean City, NJ [*FM radio station call letters*]
WKOH .... Owensboro, KY [*Television station call letters*]
WKOI .... Richmond, IN [*Television station call letters*]
WKOK .... Northumberland, PA [*FM radio station call letters*]
WKOK .... Sunbury, PA [*AM radio station call letters*]
WKOL .... Plattsburgh, NY [*FM radio station call letters*] (RBYB)
WKOM .... Columbia, TN [*FM radio station call letters*]
WKON .... Owenton, KY [*Television station call letters*]
WKOO .... Jacksonville, NC [*FM radio station call letters*]
WKOP .... Binghamton, NY [*AM radio station call letters*]
WKOP .... Knoxville, TN [*Television station call letters*]
WKOR .... Columbus, MS [*FM radio station call letters*]
WKOR .... Starkville, MS [*AM radio station call letters*]
WKOS .... Kingsport, TN [*FM radio station call letters*]
WKOT .... Marseilles, IL [*FM radio station call letters*]
WKOV .... Wellston, OH [*FM radio station call letters*]
WKOW .... Madison, WI [*Television station call letters*]
WKOX .... Framingham, MA [*AM radio station call letters*]
WKOY .... Bluefield, WV [*AM radio station call letters*]
WKOZ .... Kosciusko, MS [*AM radio station call letters*]
WKP .... Wrotham Park [*Queensland*] [*Airport symbol*] (AD)
WKPA .... Lynchburg, VA [*AM radio station call letters*]
WKPB .... Henderson, KY [*FM radio station call letters*]
WKPC .... Louisville, KY [*Television station call letters*]
WKPD .... Paducah, KY [*Television station call letters*]
WKPE .... Orleans, MA [*AM radio station call letters*]
WKPE-FM .... Orleans, MA [*FM radio station call letters*]
WKPG .... Port Gibson, MS
WKPI .... Pikeville, KY [*Television station call letters*]
WKPK .... Gaylord, MI [*FM radio station call letters*]
WKPO-FM .... Evansville, WI [*FM radio station call letters*] (BROA)
WKPP .... Elizabethton, TN [*AM radio station call letters*] (RBYB)
WKPQ .... Hornell, NY [*FM radio station call letters*]
WKPR .... Kalamazoo, MI [*AM radio station call letters*]
WKPS .... State College, PA [*FM radio station call letters*] (RBYB)
WKPT .... Kingsport, TN [*AM radio station call letters*]
WKPT-TV .... Kingsport, TN [*Television station call letters*]
WKPV .... Ponce, PR [*Television station call letters*]
WKPW .... Knightstown, IN [*FM radio station call letters*]
WKPX .... Sunrise, FL [*FM radio station call letters*]
WKQB .... Southern Pines, NC [*FM radio station call letters*] (RBYB)
WKQDR ...... Work Queue Directory
WKQH .... Marathon, WI [*FM radio station call letters*] (RBYB)
WKQI .... Detroit, MI [*FM radio station call letters*]
WKQL .... Jacksonville, FL [*FM radio station call letters*]
WKQQ .... Lexington, KY [*FM radio station call letters*]
WKQS .... Gifford, FL [*FM radio station call letters*]
WKQT .... Newport, NC [*FM radio station call letters*]
WKQV .... Olyphant, PA [*FM radio station call letters*]
WKQV-AM ... Pittston, PA [*AM radio station call letters*] (RBYB)
WKQW .... Oil City, PA [*AM radio station call letters*]
WKQW-FM ... Oil City, PA [*FM radio station call letters*]
WKQX .... Chicago, IL [*FM radio station call letters*]
WKQZ .... Midland, MI [*FM radio station call letters*]
WKR .... Walker's Cay [*Bahamas*] [*Airport symbol*] (OAG)
WKR .... Whittaker Corp. [*NYSE symbol*] (SPSG)
wkr............. Wicker (VRA)
WKR .... Worker
WKR .... Work Ranch [*California*] [*Seismograph station code, US Geological Survey*] (SEIS)
WKR .... World Koala Research [*Australia*]
WKR .... Wrecker (AAG)
WKRA .... Holly Springs, MS [*AM radio station call letters*]
WKRA-FM .... Holly Springs, MS [*FM radio station call letters*]
WKRB .... Brooklyn, NY [*FM radio station call letters*]
WKRC-TV .... Cincinnati, OH [*Television station call letters*]
WKRE .... Exmore, VA [*FM radio station call letters*]
WKRF .... Tobyhanna, PA [*FM radio station call letters*] (RBYB)
WKRG .... Mobile, AL [*Television station call letters*]
WKRH-FM .... Minetto, NY [*FM radio station call letters*] (BROA)

WKRJ .... New Philadelphia, OH [*FM radio station call letters*]
WKRK .... Murphy, NC [*AM radio station call letters*]
WKRL .... North Syracuse, NY [*AM radio station call letters*]
WKRL-FM .... North Syracuse, NY [*FM radio station call letters*]
WKRM .... Columbia, TN [*AM radio station call letters*]
WKRN .... Nashville, TN [*Television station call letters*]
WKRO .... Cairo, IL [*AM radio station call letters*]
WKRO-FM .... Edgewater, FL [*FM radio station call letters*] (RBYB)
WKRP .... Charleston, WV [*Television station call letters*]
WKRP .... North Vernon, IN [*AM radio station call letters*]
WKRQ .... Cincinnati, OH [*FM radio station call letters*]
WKRR .... Asheboro, NC [*FM radio station call letters*]
WKRS .... Waukegan, IL [*AM radio station call letters*]
WKRT .... Cortland, NY [*AM radio station call letters*]
WKRU-AM ... Burnettown, SC [*AM radio station call letters*] (RBYB)
WKRV .... Vandalia, IL [*AM radio station call letters*]
WKRW .... Wooster, OH [*FM radio station call letters*]
WKRX .... Roxboro, NC [*FM radio station call letters*]
WKRY .... Key West, FL [*FM radio station call letters*]
WKRZ .... Wilkes-Barre, PA [*FM radio station call letters*]
WKS .... Weeks Corp. [*NYSE symbol*] (SAG)
WKS .... Wernicke-Korsakoff Syndrome [*Chemical dependence*] (DAVI)
WKS .... Works
WKS .... Worksheet File [*Computer science*]
WKS .... Workshop (AAG)
WKSA .... Isabela, PR [*FM radio station call letters*]
WKSA .... Wernicke-Korsakoff Syndrome Association [*Defunct*] (EA)
WKSB .... Williamsport, PA [*FM radio station call letters*]
WKSC .... Kershaw, SC [*AM radio station call letters*]
WKSC .... Western Kentucky State College [*Later, WKSU*]
WKSD-FM .... Paulding, OH [*FM radio station call letters*] (RBYB)
WKSE .... Niagara Falls, NY [*FM radio station call letters*]
WKSF .... Asheville, NC [*FM radio station call letters*]
WKSG .... Cedar Creek, FL [*FM radio station call letters*]
WKSH .... Sussex, WI [*AM radio station call letters*]
WKSI .... Greensboro, NC [*FM radio station call letters*]
WKSJ .... Mobile, AL [*FM radio station call letters*]
WKSJ .... Prichard, AL [*AM radio station call letters*]
WKSK .... West Jefferson, NC [*AM radio station call letters*]
WKSL .... Greencastle, PA [*FM radio station call letters*]
WKSM .... Fort Walton Beach, FL [*FM radio station call letters*]
WKSN .... Jamestown, NY [*AM radio station call letters*]
WKSO .... Orangeburg, SC [*FM radio station call letters*]
WKSO .... Somerset, KY [*Television station call letters*]
WKSP .... Workshop
WKSQ .... Ellsworth, ME [*FM radio station call letters*]
WKSR .... Pulaski, TN [*AM radio station call letters*]
WKSS .... Hartford, CT [*FM radio station call letters*]
WKST .... Ellwood City, PA [*FM radio station call letters*]
WKST .... New Castle, PA [*AM radio station call letters*]
WKSU .... Kent, OH [*FM radio station call letters*]
WKSU .... Western Kentucky State University [*Formerly, WKSC*]
WKSV-FM .... Thompson, OH [*FM radio station call letters*] (RBYB)
WKSW .... Urbana, OH [*FM radio station call letters*]
WKSX .... Johnston, SC [*FM radio station call letters*]
WKSY .... Marion, SC [*FM radio station call letters*]
WKSZ .... De Pere, WI [*FM radio station call letters*] (RBYB)
WKT .... Wicket
WKT .... Written Knowledge Test [*National Court Reporters Association*]
WKTA .... Evanston, IL [*AM radio station call letters*]
WKTC .... Goldsboro, NC [*FM radio station call letters*]
WKTE .... King, NC [*AM radio station call letters*]
WKTF .... Jackson, MS [*FM radio station call letters*]
WKTG .... Madisonville, KY [*FM radio station call letters*]
WKTI .... Milwaukee, WI [*FM radio station call letters*]
WKTJ .... Farmington, ME [*FM radio station call letters*]
WKTK .... Crystal River, FL [*FM radio station call letters*]
WKTL .... Struthers, OH [*FM radio station call letters*]
WKTM .... Soperton, GA [*FM radio station call letters*]
WKTN .... Kenton, OH [*FM radio station call letters*]
WKTO .... Samsula, FL [*FM radio station call letters*]
WKTP .... Jonesborough, TN [*AM radio station call letters*]
WKTQ .... South Paris, ME [*AM radio station call letters*]
WKTR .... Earlysville, VA [*AM radio station call letters*]
WKTS .... Marathon, FL [*FM radio station call letters*] (RBYB)
WKTT .... Cleveland, WI [*FM radio station call letters*]
WKTU .... Ocean City, NJ [*FM radio station call letters*]
WKTV .... Utica, NY [*Television station call letters*]
WKTX .... Cortland, OH [*AM radio station call letters*]
WKTY .... La Crosse, WI [*AM radio station call letters*]
WKTZ .... Jacksonville, FL [*FM radio station call letters*]
WKU .... Wakaura [*Wakayama Eri*] [*Japan*] [*Seismograph station code, US Geological Survey*] (SEIS)
WKU .... Western Kentucky University [*Formerly, WKSC*] [*Bowling Green*]
WKUB .... Blackshear, GA [*FM radio station call letters*]
WKUE .... Elizabethtown, KY [*FM radio station call letters*]
WKUL .... Cullman, AL [*FM radio station call letters*]
WKUN .... Monroe, GA [*AM radio station call letters*]
WKUZ .... Wabash, IN [*FM radio station call letters*]
WKVA .... Lewistown, PA [*AM radio station call letters*]
WKVE .... St. Marys, PA [*FM radio station call letters*]
WKVF .... West Kent Volunteer Force [*British military*] (DMA)
WKVG .... Jenkins, KY [*FM radio station call letters*]
WKVI .... Knox, IN [*AM radio station call letters*]
WKVI-FM ..... Knox, IN [*FM radio station call letters*]

WKVM	San Juan, PR [*AM radio station call letters*]
WKVN	Levittown, PR [*FM radio station call letters*]
WKVN	Quebradillas, PR [*AM radio station call letters*]
WKVQ	Eatonton, GA [*AM radio station call letters*]
WKVR	Huntingdon, PA [*FM radio station call letters*]
WKVS	Lenoir, NC [*FM radio station call letters*]
WKVT	Brattleboro, VT [*AM radio station call letters*]
WKVT-FM	Brattleboro, VT [*FM radio station call letters*]
WKVX	Wooster, OH [*AM radio station call letters*]
WKWC	Owensboro, KY [*FM radio station call letters*]
WKWF	Key West, FL [*AM radio station call letters*]
WKWI	Kilmarnock, VA [*FM radio station call letters*]
WKWK	Wheeling, WV [*AM radio station call letters*]
WKWK-FM	Wheeling, WV [*FM radio station call letters*]
WKWL	Florala, AL [*AM radio station call letters*]
WKWM	Kentwood, MI [*AM radio station call letters*]
WKWN	Trenton, GA [*AM radio station call letters*] (RBYB)
WKWQ	Batesburg, SC [*FM radio station call letters*]
WKWS	Charleston, WV [*FM radio station call letters*]
WKWT	Union City, TN [*FM radio station call letters*]
WKWX	Savannah, TN [*FM radio station call letters*]
WKWZ	Syosset, NY [*FM radio station call letters*]
WKXA	Findlay, OH [*FM radio station call letters*]
WKXB	Burgaw, NC [*FM radio station call letters*]
WKXC	Aiken, SC [*FM radio station call letters*]
WKXD	Monterey, TN [*FM radio station call letters*]
WKXE	White River Junction, VT [*FM radio station call letters*]
WKXF	Eminence, KY [*AM radio station call letters*]
WKXG	Greenwood, MS [*AM radio station call letters*]
WKXI	Jackson, MS [*AM radio station call letters*]
WKXI	Magee, MS [*FM radio station call letters*]
WKXJ	South Pittsburg, TN [*FM radio station call letters*]
WKXK-FM	Chicago, IL [*FM radio station call letters*] (RBYB)
WKXL	Concord, NH [*AM radio station call letters*]
WKXL-FM	Concord, NH [*FM radio station call letters*]
WKXM	Winfield, AL [*AM radio station call letters*]
WKXM-FM	Winfield, AL [*FM radio station call letters*]
WKXN	Greenville, AL [*FM radio station call letters*]
WKXO	Berea, KY [*AM radio station call letters*]
WKXO-FM	Berea, KY [*FM radio station call letters*]
WKXP	Benton, PA [*FM radio station call letters*]
WKXQ	Rushville, IL [*FM radio station call letters*]
WKXR	Asheboro, NC [*AM radio station call letters*]
WKXT	Knoxville, TN [*Television station call letters*]
WKXU-FM	Burlington, NC [*FM radio station call letters*] (BROA)
WKXV	Knoxville, TN [*AM radio station call letters*]
WKXW	Trenton, NJ [*FM radio station call letters*]
WKXX	Attala, AL [*FM radio station call letters*]
WKXY	Sarasota, FL [*AM radio station call letters*]
WKXZ	Norwich, NY [*FM radio station call letters*]
WKY	Oklahoma City, OK [*AM radio station call letters*]
WKY	Wakayama [*Japan*] [*Seismograph station code, US Geological Survey*] (SEIS)
WKY	Warwickshire Yeomanry [*British military*] (DMA)
WKY	West Kent Yeomanry [*British military*] (DMA)
WKY	Wistar-Kyoto [*Rat variety*]
WKYA-FM	Greenville, KY [*FM radio station call letters*] (RBYB)
WKYB	Hemingway, SC [*AM radio station call letters*]
WKYC	Cleveland, OH [*Television station call letters*]
WKYD	Andalusia, AL [*AM radio station call letters*]
WKYE	Johnstown, PA [*FM radio station call letters*]
WKYG	Parkersburg, WV [*AM radio station call letters*]
WKYI	Stamping Ground, KY [*FM radio station call letters*]
WKYK	Burnsville, NC [*AM radio station call letters*]
WKYL	Lawrenceburg, KY [*FM radio station call letters*]
WKYM	Monticello, KY [*FM radio station call letters*]
WKYN	Florence, KY [*AM radio station call letters*] (RBYB)
WKYO	Caro, MI [*AM radio station call letters*]
WKYQ	Paducah, KY [*FM radio station call letters*]
WKYR	Burkesville, KY [*AM radio station call letters*]
WKYR-FM	Burkesville, KY [*FM radio station call letters*]
WKYS	Washington, DC [*FM radio station call letters*]
WKYT	Lexington, KY [*Television station call letters*]
WKYU	Bowling Green, KY [*FM radio station call letters*]
WKYU-TV	Bowling Green, KY [*Television station call letters*]
WKYW	Frankfort, KY [*FM radio station call letters*]
WKYX	Paducah, KY [*AM radio station call letters*]
WKYY	Lancaster, KY [*AM radio station call letters*]
WKYZ	Gray, KY [*AM radio station call letters*]
WKZB-FM	Butler, AL [*FM radio station call letters*] (BROA)
WKZC	Scottville, MI [*FM radio station call letters*]
WKZD	Murrayville, GA [*AM radio station call letters*]
WKZE	Salisbury, CT [*FM radio station call letters*]
WKZE	Sharon, CT [*AM radio station call letters*]
WKZF	Bayboro, NC [*FM radio station call letters*]
WKZI	Casey, IL [*AM radio station call letters*]
WKZJ	Greenville, GA [*FM radio station call letters*]
WKZK	North Augusta, SC [*AM radio station call letters*]
WKZL	Winston-Salem, NC [*FM radio station call letters*]
WKZM	Sarasota, FL [*FM radio station call letters*]
WKZO	Kalamazoo, MI [*AM radio station call letters*]
WKZQ	Myrtle Beach, SC [*AM radio station call letters*]
WKZQ-FM	Myrtle Beach, SC [*FM radio station call letters*]
WKZR	Milledgeville, GA [*FM radio station call letters*]
WKZS	Auburn, ME [*FM radio station call letters*]

WKZT	Elizabethtown, KY [*Television station call letters*]
WKZT	Fulton, KY [*AM radio station call letters*]
WKZU	Ripley, MS [*FM radio station call letters*]
WKZV	Washington, PA [*AM radio station call letters*]
WKZW	Chillicothe, IL [*FM radio station call letters*] (RBYB)
WKZX	Cookeville, TN [*Television station call letters*]
WKZY	La Belle, FL [*FM radio station call letters*]
WKZZ	Douglas, GA [*FM radio station call letters*]
WL	Bursa Hava Yollari [*ICAO designator*] (AD)
WL	Wagons-Lits [*Railroad Sleeping or Pullman cars in Europe*] [*French*]
WL	Waiting List
WL	Wallenstein Laboratory [*Medium*] (BABM)
WL	Walther League (EA)
WL	War Legislation [*British World War II*]
WL	Warner-Lambert Pharmaceutical Co.
WL	Warning Letter [*Environmental science*] (COE)
WL	Warning Light (SAA)
WL	Water Line
WL	Waterload Test [*Clinical chemistry*]
WL	Wavelength [*Electronics*]
WL	Weapons Laboratory (MCD)
WL	Wehrmacht-Luftwaffe [*Marking on Air Force vehicles*] [*German military - World War II*]
WL	Well [*Postal Service standard*] (OPSA)
WL	Western Larch [*Utility pole*] [*Telecommunications*] (TEL)
WL	Western League [*Baseball*]
WL	Westland Helicopters Ltd. [*British ICAO aircraft manufacturer identifier*] (ICAO)
WL	West Longitude (SSD)
WL	Westminster Library [*A publication*]
WL	Wheeler Laboratories, Inc. (MCD)
WL	Wheel Locks
WL	White Laboratories, Inc. [*Research code symbol*]
WL	White Leghorn [*Poultry*]
WL	White Light (MSA)
WL	Wideband Limiter
WL	Width-to-Length [*Ratio*] (IAA)
WL	Wiener Library [*London*] (BJA)
WL	Wilmington Trust Corp. [*NYSE symbol*]
WL	Wind Load
WL	Wiring List
W-L	Wisconsin State Law Library [*Wisconsin State Library*], Madison, WI [*Library symbol Library of Congress*] (LCLS)
WL	With Restrictive Language (MCD)
WL	Women's Legion [*World War I*] [*British*]
WL	Women's Liberation (ADA)
WL	Women's Lobby [*Defunct*] (EA)
WL	Women's Reserve, Legal Specialist Duties [*USNR officer designation*]
WL	Wool
wl	Wool (VRA)
WL	Word in Life: Journal of Religious Education [*A publication*] (APTA)
WL	Word Length (IAA)
WL	Word Line
WL	Working Level
WL	Work Light
WL	Work Line (MSA)
WL	Workload (AABC)
WL	World List of Future International Meetings [*A publication*]
WL	Worldloppet (EA)
WL	World of Learning [*A publication*]
WL	Wyeth Laboratories [*Research code symbol*]
WL0	Water Line Zero (KSC)
WLA	Warner-Lambert [*NYSE symbol*] (TTSB)
WLA	Warner-Lambert Co. [*NYSE symbol*] (SPSG)
WLA	Washington Library Association
WLA	Wasteload Allocation [*Environmental science*] (FFDE)
WLA	Welsh Lacrosse Association (EAIO)
WLA	Wescosa Lumber Association [*Defunct*] (EA)
WLA	Western Lacrosse Association [*Canada*]
WLA	Western Literature Association (EA)
WLA	West London Aero Services Ltd. [*British ICAO designator*] (FAAC)
WLA	White Lung Association (EA)
WLA	Wire Line Adapter (MCD)
WLA	Wire Line Antenna
WLA	Wittsburg Lake [*Arkansas*] [*Seismograph station code, US Geological Survey Closed*] (SEIS)
WLA	Women's Land Army [*Part of the United States Crop Corps*] [*World War II*]
WLA	World Literary Academy (EAIO)
WLA	Written Language Assessment [*Grill and Kirwin*] (TES)
WLAB	Fort Wayne, IN [*FM radio station call letters*]
WLac	La Crosse Public Library, La Crosse, WI [*Library symbol Library of Congress*] (LCLS)
WLAC	Nashville, TN [*AM radio station call letters*]
WLAC	Watson Laboratories Air Materiel Command (SAA)
WLAC	Western Labour Arbitration Cases [*A publication*] (DLA)
WLAC-FM	Nashville, TN [*FM radio station call letters*]
WLacFW	United States Fish and Wildlife Service, Fish Control Laboratory, La Crosse, WI [*Library symbol Library of Congress*] (LCLS)
WLacL	La Crosse Lutheran Hospital, La Crosse, WI [*Library symbol Library of Congress*] (LCLS)
WLacSF	Saint Francis Hospital, La Crosse, WI [*Library symbol Library of Congress*] (LCLS)

WLacU......... University of Wisconsin-La Crosse, La Crosse, WI [*Library symbol Library of Congress*] (LCLS)
WLacVC...... Viterbo College, La Crosse, WI [*Library symbol Library of Congress*] (LCLS)
WLAD......... Danbury, CT [*AM radio station call letters*]
WLadM....... Mount Senario College, Ladysmith, WI [*Library symbol Library of Congress*] (LCLS)
WLAE......... New Orleans, LA [*Television station call letters*]
WLAF......... La Follette, TN [*AM radio station call letters*]
WLAF......... World League of American Football [*1991*]
WLAG .... La Grange, GA [*AM radio station call letters*]
WLag .... Lake Geneva Public Library, Lake Geneva, WI [*Library symbol Library of Congress*] (LCLS)
WLagB........ Badger Union High School District, Lake Geneva, WI [*Library symbol Library of Congress*] (LCLS)
WLagF .... Franciscan Education Center, Lake Geneva, WI [*Library symbol Library of Congress*] (LCLS)
WLagSD ...... Joint School District Number One, Lake Geneva, WI [*Library symbol Library of Congress*] (LCLS)
WLAJ......... Lansing, MI [*Television station call letters*]
WLAK......... Huntingdon, PA [*FM radio station call letters*]
WLAL-AM .... Cobleskill, NY [*AM radio station call letters*] (RBYB)
WLALW....... World Laboratory Animal Liberation Week
WLAM......... Gorham, ME [*AM radio station call letters*]
WLAM-FM ... North Windham, ME [*FM radio station call letters*] (RBYB)
WLAN .... Lancaster, PA [*AM radio station call letters*]
WLAN .... Wireless Local Area Network (AAEL)
WLAN-FM ... Lancaster, PA [*FM radio station call letters*]
WLANSW..... Women Lawyers' Association of New South Wales [*Australia*]
WLAP......... Lexington, KY [*AM radio station call letters*]
WLAQ .... Rome, GA [*AM radio station call letters*]
WLAR......... Athens, TN [*AM radio station call letters*]
WLAS......... Jacksonville, NC [*AM radio station call letters*]
WLAT......... Manchester, CT [*AM radio station call letters*]
WLAT......... Women Lawyers' Association of Tasmania [*Australia*]
WLA/TMDL... Wasteload Allocation / Total Maximum Daily Load [*Environmental Protection Agency*] (EPA)
WLAU .... Laurel, MS [*AM radio station call letters*]
WLAV......... Will Advise (FAAC)
WLAV-FM .... Grand Rapids, MI [*FM radio station call letters*]
WLAW......... Fairhaven, MA [*FM radio station call letters*]
W Law Bul... Weekly Law Bulletin [*Ohio*] [*A publication*] (DLA)
WLAX......... La Crosse, WI [*Television station call letters*]
WLAY......... Muscle Shoals, AL [*AM radio station call letters*]
WLAY-FM .... Muscle Shoals, AL [*FM radio station call letters*]
WLAZ-FM .... Clermont, FL [*FM radio station call letters*] (RBYB)
WLB........... National War Labor Board [*World War II*]
WLB........... Seagoing Buoy Tender [*Coast Guard*] (NVT)
WLB........... Wallboard (AAG)
WLB........... Weapons Logbook [*Military*] (AABC)
WLB........... Weekly Law Bulletin [*Ohio*] [*A publication*] (DLA)
WLB........... Westmoreland Coal [*AMEX symbol*]
W/L/B........ White Letter [*or Line*] Block [*Typography*] (DGA)
WLB........... Wilson Library Bulletin [*A publication*] (BRI)
WLBA......... Gainesville, GA [*AM radio station call letters*]
WLBB......... Carrollton, GA [*AM radio station call letters*]
WLBC......... Muncie, IN [*AM radio station call letters*]
WLBC-FM .... Muncie, IN [*FM radio station call letters*]
WLBE......... Leesburg, FL [*AM radio station call letters*]
WLBF......... Montgomery, AL [*FM radio station call letters*]
WLBG......... Laurens, SC [*AM radio station call letters*]
WLBH......... Mattoon, IL [*AM radio station call letters*]
WLBH-FM .... Mattoon, IL [*FM radio station call letters*]
WLBI......... Wafer-Level Burn-In (AAEL)
WLBI......... Warrior, AL [*FM radio station call letters*]
WLBJ......... Bowling Green, KY [*AM radio station call letters*]
WLBK......... De Kalb, IL [*AM radio station call letters*]
WLBL......... Auburndale, WI [*AM radio station call letters*]
WLBL-FM .... Wausau, WI [*FM radio station call letters*] (RBYB)
WLBM......... Wing-Level Bombing System (SAA)
WLBN......... Lebanon, KY [*AM radio station call letters*]
WLBQ......... Morgantown, KY [*AM radio station call letters*]
WLBR......... Lebanon, PA [*AM radio station call letters*]
WLBR......... Seagoing Buoy Tender Replacement Vessel [*USCG*] (TAG)
WLBT......... Jackson, MS [*Television station call letters*]
WL Bull ...... Weekly Law Bulletin [*Ohio*] [*A publication*] (DLA)
WL Bull (Ohio)... Weekly Law Bulletin [*Ohio*] [*A publication*] (DLA)
WLBW........ Fenwick Island, DE [*FM radio station call letters*]
WLBZ......... Bangor, ME [*Television station call letters*]
WLC........... Weapon-Launching Console (MCD)
WLC........... Weapons Laboratory Civil Engineering Division [*Kirtland Air Force Base, NM*]
WLC........... Wellco Enterprises [*AMEX symbol*] (TTSB)
WLC........... Wellco Enterprises, Inc. [*AMEX symbol*] (SPSG)
WLC........... Well Logging Cable
WLC........... West London College [*England*]
WLC........... White Light Coronagraph (KSC)
WLC........... Wildcat
WLC........... Wine Label Circle (EA)
WLC........... Wisconsin Library Consortium (NITA)
WLC........... World Literacy of Canada (EAIO)
WLCA......... Godfrey, IL [*FM radio station call letters*]
WLCAC....... Watts Labor Community Action Committee [*Los Angeles, CA*]
WLCB-TV .... Leesburg, FL [*TV radio station call letters*] (RBYB)
WLCC......... Luray, VA [*FM radio station call letters*]

WLCC......... Walker-Lybarger Construction Co. [*Colorado*]
WLCE......... White Light Coronagraph Experiment (KSC)
WLCH......... Lancaster, PA [*FM radio station call letters*]
WLCJ......... Women's League for Conservative Judaism (EA)
WLCK......... Scottsville, KY [*AM radio station call letters*]
WL(CL)........ War Legislation, Civil Liabilities [*British World War II*]
WLCM......... Charlotte, MI [*AM radio station call letters*]
WLCN......... Madisonville, KY [*Television station call letters*]
WLCQ......... Clarksville, VA [*FM radio station call letters*]
WLCS......... North Muskegon, MI [*FM radio station call letters*]
WLCS......... Workload and Cost Schedule [*Military*] (AABC)
WLCSS....... Weapon Launch Console Switching Section (MCD)
WLCT......... Lafayette, TN [*FM radio station call letters*]
WLCT......... Washington Legislative Council on Telecommunications (CIST)
WLCX......... Farmville, VA [*FM radio station call letters*]
WLCY......... Blairsville, PA [*FM radio station call letters*]
WLD........... South African Law Reports, Witwatersrand Local Division [*A publication*] (DLA)
WLD........... Warning Light Driver (IAA)
WLD........... Water and Land Division [*Environmental Protection Agency*] (GFGA)
WLD........... Weapon Loading Director (NVT)
WLD........... Welded (MSA)
wld........... Welded (VRA)
WLD........... Weldotron Corp. [*AMEX symbol*] (SPSG)
WLD........... Welsh Liberal Democrats [*Political party*] (EAIO)
WLD........... Werner Linear Dichroism (DB)
WLD........... West Longitude Date (AABC)
WLD........... Wilderness Airline (1975) Ltd. [*Canada ICAO designator*] (FAAC)
WLD........... Winfield/Arkansas City, KS [*Location identifier FAA*] (FAAL)
WLD........... Women Liberal Democrat [*British Political party*] (EAIO)
WLD........... World
WLD........... World Technology Industry [*Vancouver Stock Exchange symbol*]
WLDA .... Wholesale Leather Distributors Association [*British*] (BI)
WLDA .... World Airways [*NASDAQ symbol*] (TTSB)
WLDA .... World Airways, Inc. [*NASDAQ symbol*] (SAG)
WldAccep ... World Acceptance Corp. [*Associated Press*] (SAG)
WldAcp ...... World Acceptance Corp. [*Associated Press*] (SAG)
WldAir .... World Airways, Inc. [*Associated Press*] (SAG)
WLDC-FM ... Dwight, IL [*FM radio station call letters*] (BROA)
Wld Ch ...... World Champion (BARN)
WLDE......... Fort Wayne, IN [*FM radio station call letters*]
WLDF......... Women's Legal Defense Fund (EA)
WldFuel ..... World Fuel Services Corp. [*Associated Press*] (SAG)
WLDG .... Welding (IAA)
WLDJ......... Appomattox, VA [*FM radio station call letters*]
WLDLF .... Wildlife
WLDMT....... Weldment (MSA)
WLDN .... Walden Bancorp [*NASDAQ symbol*] (TTSB)
WLDND....... Wildland
WLDR......... Traverse City, MI [*FM radio station call letters*]
WLDR......... Welder (MSA)
WLDS......... Jacksonville, IL [*AM radio station call letters*]
WLDS......... Weldless
Wldtex .... Worldtex, Inc. [*Associated Press*] (SAG)
WldwDlr ..... Worldwide Dollarvest Fund [*Associated Press*] (SAG)
WLDX......... Fayette, AL [*AM radio station call letters*]
WLDY......... Ladysmith, WI [*AM radio station call letters*]
WLE........... Ward Lock Educational [*Publisher*] [*British*]
WLE........... Wellore Energy, Inc. [*Toronto Stock Exchange symbol*]
WLEA......... Hornell, NY [*AM radio station call letters*]
WLEC......... Sandusky, OH [*AM radio station call letters*]
WLED......... Littleton, NH [*Television station call letters*]
WLEE......... Richmond, VA [*FM radio station call letters*]
WLEE-FM.... Williamsburg, VA [*FM radio station call letters*] (RBYB)
WLEF......... Park Falls, WI [*Television station call letters*]
WLEM......... Emporium, PA [*AM radio station call letters*]
WLEN......... Adrian, MI [*FM radio station call letters*]
WLEO......... Ponce, PR [*AM radio station call letters*]
WLER......... Butler, PA [*FM radio station call letters*]
WLES......... Lawrenceville, VA [*AM radio station call letters*]
WLET......... Toccoa, GA [*AM radio station call letters*]
WLET......... Winland Electronics [*NASDAQ symbol*] (TTSB)
WLET......... Winland Electronics, Inc. [*NASDAQ symbol*] (SAG)
WLET-FM.... Toccoa, GA [*FM radio station call letters*]
WLEV......... Easton, PA [*FM radio station call letters*]
WLEW........ Bad Axe, MI [*AM radio station call letters*]
WLEW-FM... Bad Axe, MI [*FM radio station call letters*]
WLEX......... Lexington, KY [*Television station call letters*]
WLEY......... Cayey, PR [*AM radio station call letters*]
WLEZ......... Terre Haute, IN [*FM radio station call letters*]
WLF........... Walferdange [*Belgium*] [*Seismograph station code, US Geological Survey*] (SEIS)
WLF........... Wallis and Futuna [*ANSI three-letter standard code*] (CNC)
WLF........... Washington Legal Foundation (EA)
WLF........... Welfare (AABC)
WLF........... Whole Lithosphere Failure [*Geology*]
WLF........... Williams-Landel-Ferry [*Polymer physics*]
WLF........... Wolf River Resources [*Vancouver Stock Exchange symbol*]
WLF........... Women's Law Fund (EA)
WLF........... Women's Liberal Federation (WDAA)
WLF........... Word of Life Fellowship (EA)
WLF........... Workload Factor (AFM)
WLF........... World Law Fund (EA)
WLFA......... Asheville, NC [*FM radio station call letters*]
WLFA......... West Lancashire Field Artillery [*Military unit*] [*British*]

WLFA............	Wildlife Legislative Fund of America (EA)
WLFB............	Bluefield, WV [*Television station call letters*]
WLFB............	Wolfeboro Railroad Co., Inc. [*AAR code*]
WLFC............	Findlay, OH [*FM radio station call letters*]
WLFC............	Washington Library Film Circuit [*Library network*]
WLFD............	World League for Freedom and Democracy [*South Korea*] (EAIO)
WLFE............	St. Albans, VT [*FM radio station call letters*]
WLFG............	Grundy, VA [*Television station call letters*]
WLFH............	Little Falls, NY [*AM radio station call letters*]
WLFI.............	Lafayette, IN [*Television station call letters*]
WLFI.............	WinsLoew Furniture [*NASDAQ symbol*] (TTSB)
WLFI.............	WinsLoew Furniture, Inc. [*NASDAQ symbol*] (SAG)
WLFI.............	Winslow Furniture, Inc. [*NASDAQ symbol*] (SAG)
WLFJ.............	Greenville, SC [*FM radio station call letters*]
WLFL............	Raleigh, NC [*Television station call letters*]
WLFM............	Appleton, WI [*FM radio station call letters*]
WLFN............	La Crosse, WI [*AM radio station call letters*]
WLFPA.........	World League for the Protection of Animals
WLFR............	Pomona, NJ [*FM radio station call letters*]
WLFX............	Ocean Pines, MD [*FM radio station call letters*]
WLFX............	Welding Fixture (AAG)
WLG.............	Waldron Ledge [*Hawaii*] [*Seismograph station code, US Geological Survey*] (SEIS)
WLG.............	Washington Liaison Group (AFM)
WLG.............	Weekly Law Gazette [*Ohio*] [*A publication*] (ILCA)
WLG.............	Wellington [*New Zealand*] [*Airport symbol*] (OAG)
WLG.............	Work Learning Guide (AIE)
WL Gaz........	Weekly Law Gazette (Reprint) [*Ohio*] [*A publication*] (DLA)
WL Gaz (Ohio)...	Weekly Law Gazette (Ohio) [*A publication*] (DLA)
WLGC	Greenup, KY [*AM radio station call letters*]
WLGC-FM	Greenup, KY [*FM radio station call letters*] (RBYB)
WLGI	Hemingway, SC [*FM radio station call letters*]
WLGL	Riverside, PA [*FM radio station call letters*]
WLGM	Springfield, IL [*FM radio station call letters*] (RBYB)
WLGN	Logan, OH [*AM radio station call letters*]
WLGN-FM....	Logan, OH [*FM radio station call letters*]
WLGO	Lexington, SC [*AM radio station call letters*]
WLGP-FM....	Harkers Island, NC [*FM radio station call letters*] (RBYB)
WLGQ	Gaston, NC [*FM radio station call letters*]
WLGX	Carolina Beach, NC [*FM radio station call letters*]
WLH.............	Society for the Study of Women in Legal History (EA)
WLH.............	Walaha [*Vanuatu*] [*Airport symbol*] (OAG)
WLH.............	Wealth Resources Ltd. [*Vancouver Stock Exchange symbol*]
WLH.............	Wilhelmshaven [*Federal Republic of Germany*] [*Geomagnetic observatory code*]
WLHB	Women's League of Health and Beauty (EAIO)
WLHE..........	Water LASER Heat Exchange
WLHFP	Women's Labor History Film Project (EA)
WLHM.........	Logansport, IN [*FM radio station call letters*]
WLHN..........	Elwood, IN [*FM radio station call letters*]
WLHN..........	Wideband-Limiter-Heterodyne-Narrowband (PDAA)
WLHN..........	Wolohan Lumber [*NASDAQ symbol*] (TTSB)
WLHN..........	Wolohan Lumber Co. [*NASDAQ symbol*] (NQ)
WLHS	West Chester, OH [*FM radio station call letters*]
WLHT..........	Grand Rapids, MI [*FM radio station call letters*]
WLI.............	Inland Buoy Tender [*USCG*] (TAG)
WLI.............	Water Landing Impact (SAA)
WLI.............	Wellesley Island [*New York*] [*Seismograph station code, US Geological Survey Closed*] (SEIS)
WLI.............	Whole-Life Insurance (MHDB)
WLI.............	Wilderness Leadership International (EA)
WLI.............	Women's League for Israel (EA)
WLIB...........	New York, NY [*AM radio station call letters*]
WLIC...........	Construction Tender [*Coast Guard symbol*] (DNAB)
WLIC...........	Frostburg, MD [*FM radio station call letters*]
WLIC...........	Inland Construction Buoy Tender [*USCG*] (TAG)
WLIE...........	Bridgehampton, NY [*FM radio station call letters*]
WLIF...........	Baltimore, MD [*FM radio station call letters*]
WLIG	Riverhead, NY [*Television station call letters*]
WLIH	Whitneyville, PA [*FM radio station call letters*]
WLII...........	Caguas, PR [*Television station call letters*]
WLIJ...........	Shelbyville, TN [*AM radio station call letters*]
WLIK..........	Newport, TN [*AM radio station call letters*]
WLIL...........	Lenoir City, TN [*AM radio station call letters*]
WLIL-FM.....	Lenoir City, TN [*FM radio station call letters*]
WLIM..........	Patchogue, NY [*AM radio station call letters*]
WLIN..........	Gluckstadt, MS [*FM radio station call letters*]
WLIO..........	Lima, OH [*Television station call letters*]
WLIP..........	Kenosha, WI [*AM radio station call letters*]
WLIQ..........	Harriman, TN [*FM radio station call letters*]
WLIR	Spring Valley, NY [*AM radio station call letters*]
WLIS	Old Saybrook, CT [*AM radio station call letters*]
WLIT..........	Chicago, IL [*FM radio station call letters*]
WLIU..........	Lincoln University, PA [*FM radio station call letters*]
WLIV..........	Livingston, TN [*AM radio station call letters*]
WLIW..........	Garden City, NY [*Television station call letters*]
WLJ	Willamette Law Journal [*A publication*] (ILCA)
WLJA..........	Ellijay, GA [*AM radio station call letters*]
WLJA-FM.....	Ellijay, GA [*FM radio station call letters*]
WLJC..........	Beattyville, KY [*FM radio station call letters*]
WLJC-TV.....	Beattyville, KY [*Television station call letters*]
WLJE..........	Valparaiso, IN [*FM radio station call letters*]
WLJK..........	Aiken, SC [*FM radio station call letters*]
WLJL..........	Charlottesville, VA [*FM radio station call letters*]
WLJM-FM....	Lima, OH [*FM radio station call letters*] (RBYB)

WLJN...........	Elmwood Township, MI [*AM radio station call letters*]
WLJN...........	Traverse City, MI [*FM radio station call letters*]
WLJP...........	Monroe, NY [*FM radio station call letters*]
WLJQ...........	Colonial Heights, TN [*FM radio station call letters*]
WLJR...........	Birmingham, AL [*FM radio station call letters*]
WLJS...........	Jacksonville, AL [*FM radio station call letters*]
WLJT...........	Lexington, TN [*Television station call letters*]
WLJY...........	Marshfield, WI [*FM radio station call letters*]
WLJZ...........	Mackinaw City, MI [*FM radio station call letters*] (RBYB)
WLK............	Selawik [*Alaska*] [*Airport symbol*] (OAG)
WLK............	Selawik, AK [*Location identifier FAA*] (FAAL)
wlk............	Wales [*MARC country of publication code Library of Congress*] (LCCP)
WLK............	Walk
WLK............	Waterlink, Inc. [*NYSE symbol*]
WLK............	Westlake Industry [*Vancouver Stock Exchange symbol*]
WLK............	Wiest Lake [*California*] [*Seismograph station code, US Geological Survey*] (SEIS)
WLKA..........	Canandaigua, NY [*FM radio station call letters*]
WLKC..........	Henderson, NY [*FM radio station call letters*]
WLKE..........	Bar Harbor, ME [*FM radio station call letters*]
WLKF..........	Lakeland, FL [*AM radio station call letters*]
WLKG..........	Lake Geneva, WI [*FM radio station call letters*]
WLKI..........	Angola, IN [*FM radio station call letters*]
WLKK..........	Erie, PA [*AM radio station call letters*]
WLKL..........	Mattoon, IL [*FM radio station call letters*]
WLKM..........	Three Rivers, MI [*AM radio station call letters*]
WLKM-FM....	Three Rivers, MI [*FM radio station call letters*]
WLKQ..........	Buford, GA [*FM radio station call letters*]
WLKR..........	Norwalk, OH [*FM radio station call letters*]
WLKS..........	West Liberty, KY [*AM radio station call letters*]
WLKS-FM	West Liberty, KY [*FM radio station call letters*]
WLKT-FM	Lexington-Fayette, KY [*FM radio station call letters*] (RBYB)
WLKW..........	Providence, RI [*AM radio station call letters*]
wlkwy........	Walkway (VRA)
WLKWY.......	Walkway
WLKX..........	Forest Lake, MN [*FM radio station call letters*]
WLKY..........	Louisville, KY [*Television station call letters*]
WLKZ..........	Wolfeboro, NH [*FM radio station call letters*]
WLL............	Williamstown [*Massachusetts*] [*Seismograph station code, US Geological Survey Closed*] (SEIS)
WLLA..........	Kalamazoo, MI [*Television station call letters*]
WLLB-AM.....	Rumford, ME [*AM radio station call letters*] (BROA)
WLLC-FM	Charleston, SC [*FM radio station call letters*] (BROA)
WLLD..........	Upper Arlington, OH [*FM radio station call letters*]
WLLE..........	Raleigh, NC [*AM radio station call letters*]
WLLF..........	Mercer, PA [*FM radio station call letters*]
WLLG..........	Lowville, NY [*FM radio station call letters*]
WLLH..........	Lowell, MA [*AM radio station call letters*]
WLLI..........	Joliet, IL [*FM radio station call letters*]
WLLK..........	Somerset, KY [*FM radio station call letters*]
WLLL..........	Lynchburg, VA [*AM radio station call letters*]
WLLN..........	Lillington, NC [*AM radio station call letters*]
WLLR..........	East Moline, IL [*FM radio station call letters*]
WLLR..........	Moline, IL [*AM radio station call letters*]
WLLS..........	Hartford, KY [*AM radio station call letters*]
WLLS-FM	Hartford, KY [*FM radio station call letters*]
WLLT..........	Polo, IL [*FM radio station call letters*]
WLLV..........	Louisville, KY [*AM radio station call letters*]
WLLW-FM ...	Clyde, NY [*FM radio station call letters*] (RBYB)
WLLX..........	Lawrenceburg, TN [*FM radio station call letters*]
WLLY..........	Wilson, NC [*AM radio station call letters*]
WLLZ..........	Detroit, MI [*FM radio station call letters*]
WLM............	Coastal Buoy Tender [*Coast Guard symbol*] (DNAB)
WLM............	Warning Light Monitor
WLM............	Wellman, Inc. [*NYSE symbol*] (CTT)
WLM............	Western Law Monthly [*Cleveland, OH*] [*A publication*] (DLA)
WLM............	Western Lumber Manufacturers [*Later, Western Timber Association*] [*An association*] (EA)
WLM............	Willow Mountain [*Alaska*] [*Seismograph station code, US Geological Survey Closed*] (SEIS)
WLM............	Wire Line MODEMS
WLM............	Women's Liberation Movement (WDAA)
WLM............	Working Level Month [*Nuclear energy*]
WLMA..........	Greenwood, SC [*AM radio station call letters*]
WLMB..........	Toledo, OH [*Television station call letters*]
WLMC..........	Georgetown, SC [*AM radio station call letters*]
WLMD	Bushnell, IL [*FM radio station call letters*]
WLME..........	Cannelton, IN [*FM radio station call letters*]
WLMG..........	New Orleans, LA [*FM radio station call letters*]
WLMG..........	Welcome Laboratory for Molecular Genetics (HGEN)
WLMH..........	Morrow, OH [*FM radio station call letters*]
WLMI..........	Kane, PA [*FM radio station call letters*]
WLML..........	Montezuma, GA [*FM radio station call letters*]
WLMO..........	Worldwide Logistics Management Office [*Army*]
WLMP..........	Wholesale Logistics Modernization Program [*Army*]
WLMQ..........	Monterey, TN [*FM radio station call letters*] (RBYB)
WLMR..........	Chattanooga, TN [*AM radio station call letters*]
WLMR..........	Coastal Buoy Tender Replacement Vessel [*USCG*] (TAG)
WLMR..........	Wilmar Industries [*NASDAQ symbol*] (TTSB)
WLMS..........	Lecanto, FL [*FM radio station call letters*]
WLMT..........	Memphis, TN [*Television station call letters*]
WLMU..........	Harrogate, TN [*FM radio station call letters*]
WLMW..........	Manchester, NH [*FM radio station call letters*]
WLMX..........	Rossville, GA [*FM radio station call letters*]

WLN Washington Library Network [*Washington State Library*] [*Olympia, WA*] [*Library network*]
WLN Welcome North Mines [*Vancouver Stock Exchange symbol*]
WLN Wellington [*British depot code*]
WLN Western Library Network [*Formerly, Washington Library Network*] [*Olympia, WA*] [*Database*] [*Library of Congress*]
WLN Wiswesser Line Notation [*Chemical structure*]
WLNA Peekskill, NY [*AM radio station call letters*]
WLNB Ligonier, IN [*FM radio station call letters*]
WLNC Laurinburg, NC [*AM radio station call letters*]
WLNE New Bedford, MA [*Television station call letters*]
WLNG Sag Harbor, NY [*AM radio station call letters*]
WLNG-FM Sag Harbor, NY [*FM radio station call letters*]
WLNH Laconia, NH [*FM radio station call letters*]
WLNI Lynchburg, VA [*FM radio station call letters*]
WLNL Horseheads, NY [*AM radio station call letters*]
WLNO New Orleans, LA [*AM radio station call letters*] (RBYB)
WLNR Kinston, NC [*AM radio station call letters*] (RBYB)
WLNS Lansing, MI [*Television station call letters*]
WLNT Winchester, KY [*AM radio station call letters*]
WLNX Lincoln, IL [*FM radio station call letters*]
WLNY-TV Riverhead, NY [*TV station call letters*] (RBYB)
WLNZ Lansing, MI [*FM radio station call letters*]
WLO Waterloo Railroad Co. [*AAR code*]
WLO Weapons Liaison Officer (NVT)
WLO Willowair Ltd. [*British ICAO designator*] (FAAC)
WLO Wilson [*Oklahoma*] [*Seismograph station code, US Geological Survey*] (SEIS)
WLO Working Layout (SAA)
WLO World Libertarian Order (EA)
WLOB Portland, ME [*AM radio station call letters*]
WLOC Munfordville, KY [*AM radio station call letters*]
WLOC-FM Munfordville, KY [*FM radio station call letters*]
WLOD Loudon, TN [*AM radio station call letters*]
WLOE Eden, NC [*AM radio station call letters*]
WLOG Logan, WV [*AM radio station call letters*]
WLOH Lancaster, OH [*AM radio station call letters*]
WLOI La Porte, IN [*AM radio station call letters*]
WLOJ New Bern, NC [*AM radio station call letters*]
WLOK Memphis, TN [*AM radio station call letters*]
WLOL Brooklyn Park, MN [*AM radio station call letters*]
WLON Lincolnton, NC [*AM radio station call letters*]
W Lon West Longitude
W long West Longitude (BARN)
WLOP Jesup, GA [*AM radio station call letters*]
WLOQ Winter Park, FL [*FM radio station call letters*]
WLOR Huntsville, AL [*AM radio station call letters*]
WLOS Asheville, NC [*Television station call letters*]
WLOT-FM Greer, SC [*FM radio station call letters*] (RBYB)
WLOU Louisville, KY [*AM radio station call letters*]
WLOV Washington, GA [*AM radio station call letters*]
WLOV West Point, MS [*Television station call letters*]
WLOV-FM Washington, GA [*FM radio station call letters*]
WLOW Bluffton, SC [*FM radio station call letters*]
WLOW Wicklow [*County in Ireland*] (ROG)
WLOX Biloxi, MS [*Television station call letters*]
WLP Wallops Island, NASA Center (MCD)
WLP Ways of Looking at People Scale [*Psychology*] (AEBS)
WLP Wellpoint Health Networks [*NYSE symbol*] (SPSG)
WLP Wellpoint Hlth Networks [*NYSE symbol*] (TTBS)
WLP Western Legal Publications [*Database*] [*Western Legal Publications Ltd.*] [*Information service or system*] (CRD)
WLP White Light Position
WLP Women's Law Project (EA)
WLPA Lancaster, PA [*AM radio station call letters*]
WLPAPER Wallpaper
WLPB Baton Rouge, LA [*Television station call letters*]
WLPB Woodcock Language Proficiency Battery [*Achievement test*]
WL/PD Warner-Lambert/Parke-Davis [*Computer files of chemical and biological data*]
WLPE Augusta, GA [*FM radio station call letters*]
WLPF Ocilla, GA [*FM radio station call letters*]
WLPF William L. Patterson Foundation [*Defunct*] (EA)
WLPG Florence, SC [*FM radio station call letters*]
WLPH Irondale, AL [*AM radio station call letters*]
WLPI Wellington Leisure Products (EFIS)
WLPJ New Port Richey, FL [*FM radio station call letters*]
WLPM Suffolk, VA [*AM radio station call letters*]
WLPO La Salle, IL [*AM radio station call letters*]
WLPR Prichard, AL [*AM radio station call letters*]
WLPS Watermen and Lightermen's Protective Society [*A union*] [*British*]
WLPSA Wildlife Preservation Society of Australia
WLPT Jesup, GA [*FM radio station call letters*]
WLPT Wellington Properties Trust [*NASDAQ symbol*] (TTSB)
WLPW Lake Placid, NY [*FM radio station call letters*]
WLPX-FM Water Valley, MS [*FM radio station call letters*] (RBYB)
WLPZ Westbrook, ME [*AM radio station call letters*]
WLQE Moneta, VA [*AM radio station call letters*]
WLQE-FM Bedford, VA [*FM radio station call letters*] (RBYB)
WLQH Chiefland, FL [*AM radio station call letters*]
WLQH-FM Chiefland, FL [*FM radio station call letters*]
WLQI Rensselaer, IN [*FM radio station call letters*]
WLQM Franklin, VA [*AM radio station call letters*]
WLQM-FM Franklin, VA [*FM radio station call letters*]
WLQR Toledo, OH [*FM radio station call letters*]
WLQT Kettering, OH [*FM radio station call letters*]
WLQV Detroit, MI [*AM radio station call letters*]
WLQY Hollywood, FL [*AM radio station call letters*]
WLR River Buoy Tender, Large or Small [*Coast Guard symbol*] (DNAB)
WLR Wallisair Compagnie [*France ICAO designator*] (FAAC)
WLR Wampler-Longacre (EFIS)
WLR Washington Law Reporter [*District of Columbia*] [*A publication*] (DLA)
WLR Water Level Recorder
WLR Weapons Locating RADAR (AABC)
WLR Weekly Law Reports [*British*]
WLR Weighted Linear Regression [*Mathematics*]
WLR Western Law Reporter [*Canada*] [*A publication*] (DLA)
WLR West London Railway (ROG)
WLR Wilanour Resources Ltd. [*Toronto Stock Exchange symbol*]
WLR World Law Review [*A publication*] (DLA)
WLR Wrong Length Record [*Computer science*]
WLRA Lockport, IL [*FM radio station call letters*]
WLRA Wagner Labor Relations Act (OICC)
WLRA World Leisure and Recreation Association [*Formerly, IRA*] (EA)
WLRB Macomb, IL [*AM radio station call letters*]
WLRC Walnut, MS [*AM radio station call letters*]
WLRC Women's Legal Resource Centre [*Sydney, New South Wales, Australia*]
WLRD St. Pauls, NC [*FM radio station call letters*]
WLRD Warning Light Relay Driver
WLRF WLR Foods, Inc. [*NASDAQ symbol*] (NQ)
WLR Fd WLR Foods, Inc. [*Associated Press*] (SAG)
WLR Fds WLR Foods [*Associated Press*] (SAG)
WLRH Huntsville, AL [*FM radio station call letters*]
WLRI Warner-Lambert Research Institute [*New Jersey*]
WLRI-FM Westhampton, NY [*FM radio station call letters*] (RBYB)
WLRK-FM Gulfport, MS [*FM radio station call letters*] (BROA)
WLRN Miami, FL [*FM radio station call letters*]
WLRN-TV Miami, FL [*Television station call letters*]
WLRO Richmond, KY [*FM radio station call letters*] (RBYB)
WLRP San Sebastian, PR [*AM radio station call letters*]
WLRP Wandsworth's Legal Resource Project [*A publication*] (DLA)
WLRQ Cocoa, FL [*FM radio station call letters*]
WLRR Milledgeville, GA [*FM radio station call letters*]
WLRS Louisville, KY [*FM radio station call letters*]
wlrs Walrus (VRA)
WLRT Kankakee, IL [*FM radio station call letters*]
WLRV Lebanon, VA [*AM radio station call letters*]
WLRW Champaign, IL [*FM radio station call letters*]
WLRX Nappanee, IN [*FM radio station call letters*]
WLRZ Peru, IL [*FM radio station call letters*]
WLS Chicago, IL [*AM radio station call letters*]
WLS Livingston Steuben-Wyoming BOCES [*Boards of Cooperative Educational Services*], Educational Communications Center, Geneseo, NY [*OCLC symbol*] (OCLC)
WLS Wallis Island [*Wallis and Futuna Islands*] [*Airport symbol*] (OAG)
WLS Water Lily Society (EA)
WLS Weighted Least Squares [*Statistics*]
WLS Wells
WLS Welschbruch [*France*] [*Seismograph station code, US Geological Survey*] (SEIS)
WLS Welsh Language Society (EA)
WLS Westchester Library System [*Library network*]
WLS Westchester Public Library [*UTLAS symbol*]
WLS Western Launch Site [*Military*]
WLS Wet Lung Syndrome [*Medicine*] (DAVI)
WLS Williams Air, Inc. [*ICAO designator*] (FAAC)
WLS Winnefox Library System [*Library network*]
WLS World Listening Service (EA)
WLSA Louisa, VA [*FM radio station call letters*]
WLSA Wage and Labor Standards Administration (OICC)
WLSB Copperhill, TN [*AM radio station call letters*]
WLSC Loris, SC [*AM radio station call letters*]
WLSC West Liberty State College [*West Virginia*]
WLSD Big Stone Gap, VA [*AM radio station call letters*]
WLSE Wallace, NC [*AM radio station call letters*]
WLS-FM Chicago, IL [*FM radio station call letters*]
WLSH Lansford, PA [*AM radio station call letters*]
WLSI Pikeville, KY [*AM radio station call letters*]
WLSK Lebanon, KY [*FM radio station call letters*]
WLSL Walseal
WLSM Louisville, MS [*AM radio station call letters*]
WLSM-FM Louisville, MS [*FM radio station call letters*]
WLSN Greenville, OH [*FM radio station call letters*]
WLSO Sault Ste. Marie, MI [*FM radio station call letters*]
WLSP Lapeer, MI [*AM radio station call letters*]
WLSP World List of Scientific Periodicals [*A publication*] (DIT)
WLSQ Dyer, TN [*FM radio station call letters*]
WLSR Lima, OH [*FM radio station call letters*]
WLSS-FM Baton Rouge, LA [*FM radio station call letters*] (RBYB)
WLST Marinette, WI [*FM radio station call letters*]
WLS-TV Chicago, IL [*Television station call letters*]
WLSU La Crosse, WI [*FM radio station call letters*]
WLSV Wellsville, NY [*AM radio station call letters*]
WLSW Scottdale, PA [*FM radio station call letters*]
WLSY Jeffersontown, KY [*FM radio station call letters*]
WLSZ Humboldt, TN [*FM radio station call letters*]
WLT Wafer-Level Test (AAEL)
WLT Walter Industries [*NYSE symbol*]
WLT Waterload Test (DAVI)

WLT............	Weighing Less Than
WLT............	Western Law Times [1890-95] [A publication] (DLA)
WLT............	Wire Line Timing
WLT............	World Literature Today [A publication] (BRI)
WLTA..........	Plymouth, IN [FM radio station call letters]
WLTA..........	Welsh Lawn Tennis Association (DBA)
WLTAS........	Wingfoot Lighter-Than-Air Society [Later, Lighter-Than-Air Society] (EA)
WLTBU	Watermen, Lightermen, Tugmen, and Bargemen's Union [British]
WLTC..........	Gastonia, NC [AM radio station call letters]
WLTC..........	Wimbledon Lawn Tennis Championship [British]
WLTD..........	Pickens, MS [FM radio station call letters]
WLTE..........	Minneapolis, MN [FM radio station call letters]
WLTE..........	Warrant Loss to Enlisted Status [Revocation of appointment] [Navy]
WLTF..........	Cleveland, OH [FM radio station call letters]
WLTG..........	Panama City, FL [AM radio station call letters]
WLTH..........	Gary, IN [AM radio station call letters]
WLTI...........	Detroit, MI [FM radio station call letters]
WLTJ..........	Pittsburgh, PA [FM radio station call letters]
WLTK..........	Broadway, VA [FM radio station call letters]
WLTL..........	La Grange, IL [FM radio station call letters]
WLTM..........	Rantoul, IL [FM radio station call letters]
WLTN..........	Lisbon, NH [FM radio station call letters]
WLTN..........	Littleton, NH [AM radio station call letters]
WLTO..........	Nicholasville, KY [FM radio station call letters] (RBYB)
WLTP..........	Parkersburg, WV [AM radio station call letters]
WLTQ..........	Milwaukee, WI [FM radio station call letters]
WLTR..........	Columbia, SC [FM radio station call letters]
WLTR..........	Walter Industries [NASDAQ symbol] (TTSB)
WLTR..........	Walter Industries, Inc. [NASDAQ symbol] (SAG)
WLTS..........	Slidell, LA [FM radio station call letters]
WLTT..........	Shallotte, NC [FM radio station call letters]
WLTU..........	Manitowoc, WI [FM radio station call letters]
WLTV..........	Miami, FL [Television station call letters]
WLTW..........	New York, NY [FM radio station call letters]
WLTX..........	Columbia, SC [Television station call letters]
WLTY..........	Norfolk, VA [FM radio station call letters]
WLTZ..........	Columbus, GA [Television station call letters]
WLU............	Washington and Lee University [Virginia]
WLU............	Wesleyan University, Middletown, CT [OCLC symbol] (OCLC)
WLU............	Wilfrid Laurier University [Canada]
WLUA..........	Westwood, KY [FM radio station call letters]
WLUC	Marquette, MI [Television station call letters]
WLUC	Women Life Underwriters Conference (EA)
WLUJ..........	Petersburg, IL [FM radio station call letters]
WLUK..........	Green Bay, WI [Television station call letters]
WLUM..........	Milwaukee, WI [FM radio station call letters]
WLUN..........	Lumberton, MS [FM radio station call letters]
WLUP..........	Chicago, IL [FM radio station call letters]
WLUR..........	Lexington, VA [FM radio station call letters]
WLUS..........	Gainesville, FL [AM radio station call letters]
WLUS	World Land Use Survey [International Geographical Union] (BARN)
WLUV..........	Loves Park, IL [AM radio station call letters]
WLUV-FM	Loves Park, IL [FM radio station call letters]
WLUW	Chicago, IL [FM radio station call letters]
WLUX	Islip, NY [AM radio station call letters] (RBYB)
WLUZ..........	Bayamon, PR [AM radio station call letters]
WLV............	Lightship [Coast Guard symbol] (DNAB)
WLV............	Wolverine Tube [NYSE symbol] (TTSB)
WLV............	Wolverine Tube, Inc. [NYSE symbol] (SPSG)
WLVA..........	Lynchburg, VA [AM radio station call letters]
WLVB..........	Morrisville, VT [FM radio station call letters]
WLVC..........	Fort Kent, ME [AM radio station call letters]
WLVE..........	Miami Beach, FL [FM radio station call letters]
WLVF..........	Haines City, FL [AM radio station call letters]
WLVF-FM	Haines City, FL [FM radio station call letters]
WLVG-FM	Center Moriches, NY [FM radio station call letters] (BROA)
WLVH	Hardeeville, SC [FM radio station call letters]
WLVI..........	Cambridge, MA [Television station call letters]
WLVJ..........	Royal Palm Beach, FL [AM radio station call letters]
WLVK..........	Fort Knox, KY [FM radio station call letters] (RBYB)
WLVL..........	Lockport, NY [AM radio station call letters]
WLVM-AM ...	Fairview, NC [AM radio station call letters] (RBYB)
WLVO-FM ...	Live Oak, FL [FM radio station call letters] (BROA)
WLVQ..........	Columbus, OH [FM radio station call letters]
WLVR..........	Bethlehem, PA [FM radio station call letters]
WLVS..........	Lake Worth, FL [AM radio station call letters]
WLVT..........	Allentown, PA [Television station call letters]
WLVU..........	Dunedin, FL [AM radio station call letters]
WLVU..........	Holiday, FL [FM radio station call letters]
WLVV..........	Mobile, AL [AM radio station call letters]
WLVW..........	Salisbury, MD [AM radio station call letters]
WLVX-FM	Charlestown, IN [FM radio station call letters] (BROA)
WLVY..........	Elmira, NY [FM radio station call letters]
WLVZ-FM	St. Mary's, OH [FM radio station call letters] (RBYB)
WLW............	Cincinnati, OH [AM radio station call letters]
WLW............	Weldwood of Canada Ltd. [Toronto Stock Exchange symbol]
WLW............	Willows, CA [Location identifier FAA] (FAAL)
WLW............	Women Library Workers [Defunct] (EA)
WLWC-TV	New Bedford, MA [TV station call letters] (RBYB)
WLWH	Workshop Library on World Humour (EA)
WLWI-FM	Montgomery, AL [FM radio station call letters]
WLWL..........	Rockingham, NC [AM radio station call letters]
WLWT..........	Cincinnati, OH [Television station call letters]
WLWZ..........	Easley, SC [AM radio station call letters]

WLXC..........	Lexington, SC [FM radio station call letters]
WLXG..........	Lexington, KY [AM radio station call letters]
WLXI..........	Greensboro, NC [Television station call letters]
WLXN..........	Lexington, NC [AM radio station call letters]
WLXR..........	La Crosse, WI [FM radio station call letters]
WLXT..........	Petoskey, MI [FM radio station call letters]
WLXV..........	Cadillac, MI [FM radio station call letters]
WLXX..........	Chicago, IL [AM radio station call letters] (RBYB)
WLXY..........	Northport, AL [FM radio station call letters]
WLY............	Westerly
WLYC..........	Williamsport, PA [AM radio station call letters]
WLYF..........	Miami, FL [FM radio station call letters]
WLYH..........	Lancaster, PA [Television station call letters]
WLYJ..........	Clarksburg, WV [Television station call letters]
WLYK..........	Lynchburg, VA [FM radio station call letters]
WLYN..........	Lynn, MA [AM radio station call letters]
WLYR-FM	Delaware, OH [FM radio station call letters] (BROA)
WLYT..........	Haverhill, MA [FM radio station call letters]
WLYU..........	Lyons, GA [FM radio station call letters]
WLYV..........	Fort Wayne, IN [AM radio station call letters]
WLZA..........	Europa, MS [FM radio station call letters]
WLZK-FM	Paris, TN [FM radio station call letters] (BROA)
WLZQ..........	South Whitley, IN [FM radio station call letters]
WLZR..........	Milwaukee, WI [AM radio station call letters]
WLZR-FM	Milwaukee, WI [FM radio station call letters]
WLZS-FM	Beaver Springs, PA [FM radio station call letters] (RBYB)
WLZW..........	Utica, NY [FM radio station call letters]
WLZZ..........	Montpelier, OH [FM radio station call letters]
WM.............	Milwaukee Public Library, Milwaukee, WI [Library symbol Library of Congress] (LCLS)
WM.............	Multiple-Conductor Cables [JETDS nomenclature] [Military] (CET)
WM.............	Waldenstrom's Macroglobulinemia [Medicine]
WM.............	Wall Motion (MEDA)
WM.............	Ward Manager [Medicine]
WM.............	War Memorial
WM.............	Warming
WM.............	Warrant Mechanician [British military] (DMA)
W/M............	Washing Machine [Classified advertising] (ADA)
WM.............	Washington Mutual [NYSE symbol]
WM.............	Washington Mutual [NYSE symbol]
WM.............	Waste Management (NASA)
WM.............	Waste Minimization
WM.............	Watermark
WM.............	Water Meter
WM.............	Water Monitor (DS)
WM.............	Watt Meter
WM.............	Wave Meter
WM.............	Ways and Means (DLA)
WM.............	Weapon Mechanician [British military] (DMA)
WM.............	Wehrmacht-Marine [Marking on Navy vehicles] [German military - World War II]
W/M............	Weight or Measurement
WM.............	Weill-Marchesani [Syndrome] [Medicine] (DB)
WM.............	Welding Memorandum
WM.............	Wernicke-Mann [Syndrome] [Medicine] (DB)
WM.............	Wesleyan Mission [Australia]
WM.............	Western Microwave, Inc. (IAA)
WM.............	West Midlands [Metropolitan county in England]
WM.............	Wet Mount (MEDA)
WM.............	Wheel-Made (BJA)
WM.............	White Male
wm.............	White Male (STED)
WM.............	White Metal
WM.............	Whitten's Medium [for cell incubation]
WM.............	Whole Milk (MAE)
wm.............	Whole Milk (STED)
wm.............	Whole Mount [Microscopy] (STED)
WM.............	Whole Mount (AAMN)
Wm.............	William (King of England) (DLA)
WM.............	Wilson-Mikity [Syndrome] [Medicine] (DB)
WM.............	Windward Islands Airways International NV [Netherlands ICAO designator] (ICDA)
W/M............	Wing Main [Airfield] (NATG)
WM.............	Wireless Manager (ACRL)
WM.............	Wire Mesh
WM.............	Without Margin
WM.............	Woman (DAVI)
WM.............	Woman Marine (SAA)
WM.............	Women in the Mainstream [Defunct] (EA)
WM.............	Women Marines
WM.............	Word Mark (BUR)
W/M............	Words per Minute (KSC)
WM.............	Working Memory [Psychology]
WM.............	Work Measurement [Army] (AABC)
WM.............	Work of Mary [An association] (EAIO)
WM.............	World Markets [British investment firm] [Formerly, Wood Mackenzie]
WM.............	World Monitor [Television program]
WM.............	Worshipful Master [Freemasonry]
W/M............	Wound, Missile [Military] (DAVI)
WM.............	Wustite Magnetite [Geology]
W/M^2.........	Watts per Square Meter
W/(M^2 K)......	Watts per Square Meter Kelvin
W/(M^2 SR) ...	Watts per Square Meter Steradian
WMA............	Alverno College, Milwaukee, WI [Library symbol Library of Congress] (LCLS)

WMa	Madison Public Library, Madison, WI [*Library symbol Library of Congress*] (LCLS)
WMA	Mandritsara [*Madagascar*] [*Airport symbol*] (OAG)
WMA	Wallcovering Manufacturers Association (EA)
WMA	Wall Motion Abnormality [*Cardiology*] (DAVI)
WMA	Warfare Mission Area (DOMA)
WMA	War Measures Act
WMA	Washington Metropolitan Area (AFM)
WMA	Waste Management Area [*NASA*]
WMA	Waste Management Association [*Australia*]
WMA	Waste Management Authority [*New South Wales, Australia*]
WMA	Waterbed Manufacturers Association (EA)
WMA	Weather Modification Association (EA)
WMA	Welding Machine Arc
WMA	Welding Manufacturers Association [*British*] (DBA)
WMA	Wentworth Military Academy [*Lexington, MO*]
WMA	Western Music Association (NTPA)
WMA	West Mesa [*New Mexico*] [*Seismograph station code, US Geological Survey*] (SEIS)
WMA	Wheelchair Motorcycle Association (EA)
WMA	Wikalat Al-Maghreb Al-Arabi [*News agency*] [*Morocco*] (MENA)
WMA	Wildlife Management Area
WMA	Wing Main Airfield (NATG)
WMA	Women Marines Association (EA)
WMA	Workers' Music Association [*British*]
WMA	Working Mothers Association [*British*] (DBA)
WMA	World Manx Association
WMA	World Medical Association [*Ferney-Voltaire, France*]
WMA	World Modeling Association (EA)
WMAA	Bahau [*Malaysia*] [*ICAO location identifier*] (ICLI)
WMAA	Warrant Master-at-Arms [*British military*] (DMA)
WMAA	Whitney Museum of American Art [*New York, NY*]
WMAA	World Martial Arts Association (EA)
WMaAR	Wisconsin Alumni Research Foundation, Madison, WI [*Library symbol Library of Congress*] (LCLS)
WMAB	Batu Pahat [*Malaysia*] [*ICAO location identifier*] (ICLI)
WMAB	Mississippi State, MS [*FM radio station call letters*]
WMAB	Weather Modification Advisory Board
WMaBR	Wisconsin Department of Health and Social Services, Bureau of Research, Madison,WI [*Library symbol Library of Congress*] (LCLS)
WMAB-TV	Mississippi State, MS [*Television station call letters*]
WMAC	Alverno College, Milwaukee, WI [*Library symbol*] [*Library of Congress*] (LCLS)
WMAC	Benta [*Malaysia*] [*ICAO location identifier*] (ICLI)
WMaC	Central Wisconsin Colony, Staff Library, Madison, WI [*Library symbol Library of Congress*] (LCLS)
WMAC	Metter, GA [*AM radio station call letters*]
WMAC	Waste Management Advisory Council [*British*] (DCTA)
WMaCH	Wisconsin Department of Health and Social Services, Community Health Service, Madison, WI [*Library symbol Library of Congress*] (LCLS)
WMACS	AC Spark Plug Co., Electronics Division, Milwaukee, WI [*Library symbol Library of Congress*] (LCLS)
WMaCT	Children's Treatment Center, Madison, WI [*Library symbol Library of Congress*] (LCLS)
WMaCW	Central Wisconsin Colony, Staff Library, Madison, WI [*Library symbol*] [*Library of Congress*] (LCLS)
WMAD	Bentong [*Malaysia*] [*ICAO location identifier*] (ICLI)
WMAD	Sun Prairie, WI [*AM radio station call letters*]
WMAD-FM	Sun Prairie, WI [*FM radio station call letters*]
WMAE	Bidor [*Malaysia*] [*ICAO location identifier*] (ICLI)
WMAE	Booneville, MS [*FM radio station call letters*]
WMAE-TV	Booneville, MS [*Television station call letters*]
WMAF	Madison, FL [*AM radio station call letters*]
WMaF	United States Forest Products Laboratory, Madison, WI [*Library symbol Library of Congress*] (LCLS)
WMAFPH	World Medical Association for Perfect Health [*Also known as United States Association of Physicians*] (EA)
WMAG	Dungun [*Malaysia*] [*ICAO location identifier*] (ICLI)
WMAG	High Point, NC [*FM radio station call letters*]
WMaG	Madison General Hospital, Madison, WI [*Library symbol Library of Congress*] (LCLS)
WMaG-N	Madison General Hospital, School of Nursing, Madison, WI [*Library symbol Library of Congress*] (LCLS)
WMAH	Biloxi, MS [*FM radio station call letters*]
WMAH	Grik [*Malaysia*] [*ICAO location identifier*] (ICLI)
WMaH	Wisconsin Division of Health Policy and Planning Library, Madison, WI [*Library symbol Library of Congress*] (LCLS)
WMAH-TV	Biloxi, MS [*Television station call letters*]
WMAI	Gua Musang [*Malaysia*] [*ICAO location identifier*] (ICLI)
WMaJ	Jackson Clinic, Madison, WI [*Library symbol Library of Congress*] (LCLS)
WMAJ	Jendarata [*Malaysia*] [*ICAO location identifier*] (ICLI)
WMAJ	State College, PA [*AM radio station call letters*]
WMAK	London, KY [*AM radio station call letters*]
WMAL	Kuala Krai [*Malaysia*] [*ICAO location identifier*] (ICLI)
WMAL	Washington, DC [*AM radio station call letters*]
WMaLS	Wisconsin Division for Library Services, Bureau for Reference and Local Services, Madison, WI [*Library symbol Library of Congress*] (LCLS)
WMAM	Langkawi [*Malaysia*] [*ICAO location identifier*] (ICLI)
WMAM	Marinette, WI [*AM radio station call letters*]
WMaM	Methodist Hospital School of Nursing, Madison, WI [*Library symbol Library of Congress*] (LCLS)

WMaMS	Mendota Mental Health Institute, Madison, WI [*Library symbol Library of Congress*] (LCLS)
WMan	Manawa Public Library, Manawa, WI [*Library symbol Library of Congress*] (LCLS)
WMAN	Mansfield, OH [*AM radio station call letters*]
Wm & M	William and Mary (King and Queen of England) (DLA)
Wm & Mary Rev VA L	William and Mary Review of Virginia Law [*A publication*] (DLA)
WM & PHF	Waste Management and Personal Hygiene Facility [*NASA*] (KSC)
WM & S	Work Methods and Standards
WMani	Manitowoc Public Library, Manitowoc, WI [*Library symbol Library of Congress*] (LCLS)
WManiH	Holy Family Hospital, Manitowoc, WI [*Library symbol Library of Congress*] (LCLS)
WManiHN	Holy Family School of Nursing, Manitowoc, WI [*Library symbol Library of Congress*] (LCLS)
WMANT	Wissenschaftliche Monographien zum Alten und Neuen Testament [*A publication*] (BJA)
WMAO	Greenwood, MS [*FM radio station call letters*]
WMAO	Kong Kong [*Malaysia*] [*ICAO location identifier*] (ICLI)
WMAO-TV	Greenwood, MS [*Television station call letters*]
WMAP	Kluang [*Malaysia*] [*ICAO location identifier*] (ICLI)
WMAP	Monroe, NC [*AM radio station call letters*]
WMAP	Pageland, SC [*FM radio station call letters*]
WMaPI	Department of Public Instruction, Division for Library Services, Professional Library, Madison, WI [*Library symbol Library of Congress*] (LCLS)
WMaPI-CC	Department of Public Instruction, Division for Library Services, Cooperative Children's Book Center, Madison, WI [*Library symbol Library of Congress*] (LCLS)
WMaPI-PL	Department of Public Instruction, Division for Library Services, Public Library Services, Madison, WI [*Library symbol Library of Congress*] (LCLS)
WMaPI-RL	Department of Public Instruction, Division for Library Services, Reference and Loan Library, Madison, WI [*Library symbol Library of Congress*] (LCLS)
WMaPR	Wisconsin Regional Primate Research Center, Madison, WI [*Library symbol Library of Congress*] (LCLS)
WMAQ	Chicago, IL [*AM radio station call letters*]
WMAQ	Labis [*Malaysia*] [*ICAO location identifier*] (ICLI)
WMAQ-TV	Chicago, IL [*Television station call letters*]
WMAR	Baltimore, MD [*Television station call letters*]
WMaR	Raltech Scientific Services, Inc., Madison, WI [*Library symbol Library of Congress*] (LCLS)
WMAR	West Marine [*NASDAQ symbol*] (TTSB)
WMAR	West Marine, Inc. [*NASDAQ symbol*] (SAG)
WMaraS	Saint Anthony Friary, Marathon, WI [*Library symbol Library of Congress*] (LCLS)
WMarC	Marshfield Clinic, Marshfield, WI [*Library symbol Library of Congress*] (LCLS)
WMARC	World Maritime Administrative Radio Conference (DS)
WMari	Stephenson Public Library, Marinette, WI [*Library symbol*] [*Library of Congress*] (LCLS)
WMarSJ	Saint Joseph's Hospital, Marshfield, WI [*Library symbol Library of Congress*] (LCLS)
WMarW	Wood County Hospital, Marshfield, WI [*Library symbol Library of Congress*] (LCLS)
WMAS	Springfield, MA [*AM radio station call letters*]
WMaS	Student Association for the Study of Hallucinogens, Madison, WI [*Library symbol Library of Congress*] (LCLS)
WMAS-FM	Springfield, MA [*FM radio station call letters*]
WMaSM	Saint Mary's Hospital, Doctors' Library, Madison, WI [*Library symbol Library of Congress*] (LCLS)
WMaSM-N	Saint Mary's Hospital, School of Nursing, Madison, WI [*Library symbol Library of Congress*] (LCLS)
WMAT	Lima Blas [*Malaysia*] [*ICAO location identifier*] (ICLI)
WMATA	Washington Metropolitan Area Transit Authority (BARN)
WMaTC	Madison Area Technical College, Madison, WI [*Library symbol Library of Congress*] (LCLS)
WMAU	Bude, MS [*FM radio station call letters*]
WMau	Mauston Public Library, Mauston, WI [*Library symbol Library of Congress*] (LCLS)
WMAU	Mersing [*Malaysia*] [*ICAO location identifier*] (ICLI)
WMAU	Women's Martial Arts Union [*Defunct*] (EA)
WMaUCS	University of Wisconsin-Center System, Madison, WI [*Library symbol Library of Congress*] (LCLS)
WMaUEx	University of Wisconsin-Extension, Madison, WI [*Library symbol Library of Congress*] (LCLS)
WMAU-TV	Bude, MS [*Television station call letters*]
WMAV	Muar [*Malaysia*] [*ICAO location identifier*] (ICLI)
WMAV	Oxford, MS [*FM radio station call letters*]
WMaVA	United States Veterans Administration Hospital, Madison, WI [*Library symbol Library of Congress*] (LCLS)
WMAV-TV	Oxford, MS [*Television station call letters*]
WMAW	Meridian, MS [*FM radio station call letters*]
WMaW	Wisconsin Alumni Research Foundation Institute, Inc., Madison, WI [*Library symbol Library of Congress*] (LCLS)
WMAW-TV	Meridian, MS [*Television station call letters*]
WMAX	Bay City, MI [*AM radio station call letters*]
WMAX	Irondequoit, NY [*FM radio station call letters*]
WMAY	Springfield, IL [*AM radio station call letters*]
WMAZ	Macon, GA [*AM radio station call letters*]
WMAZ	Segamat [*Malaysia*] [*ICAO location identifier*] (ICLI)
WMAZ-TV	Macon, GA [*Television station call letters*]
WMB	Walnut Marketing Board (EA)

WMB............	War Mobilization Board
WMB............	Warrnambool [*Australia Airport symbol*] (OAG)
WMB............	West Merchant Bank (ECON)
WMB............	Williamsburg Technical College, Kingstree, SC [*OCLC symbol*] (OCLC)
WMB............	[*The*] Williams Companies [*NYSE symbol*] (SPSG)
WMB............	Williams Cos. [*NYSE symbol*] (TTSB)
WMBA	Ambridge, PA [*AM radio station call letters*]
WMBA	Sitiawan [*Malaysia*] [*ICAO location identifier*] (ICLI)
WMBA	Wire Machinery Builders Association [*Later, WISA*] (EA)
WMBB	Panama City, FL [*Television station call letters*]
WMBB	Sungei Patani [*Malaysia*] [*ICAO location identifier*] (ICLI)
WMBC	Columbus, MS [*FM radio station call letters*]
WMBC	Newton, NJ [*Television station call letters*]
WMBC	Wisconsin Baptist State Convention, Milwaukee, WI [*Library symbol Library of Congress*] (LCLS)
WMBD	Peoria, IL [*AM radio station call letters*]
WMBDA	Wholesale Milk Buyers and Distributors' Association [*Australia*]
WMBD-TV	Peoria, IL [*Television station call letters*]
WMBE	Chilton, WI [*AM radio station call letters*]
WMBE	Temerloh [*Malaysia*] [*ICAO location identifier*] (ICLI)
WMBF	Ulu Bernam [*Malaysia*] [*ICAO location identifier*] (ICLI)
WMBG	Williamsburg, VA [*AM radio station call letters*]
WMBH	Joplin, MO [*AM radio station call letters*]
WMBH	Kroh [*Malaysia*] [*ICAO location identifier*] (ICLI)
WMBI..........	Chicago, IL [*AM radio station call letters*]
WMBI..........	Taiping [*Malaysia*] [*ICAO location identifier*] (ICLI)
WMBI-FM	Chicago, IL [*AM radio station call letters*]
WMBL.........	Morehead City, NC [*AM radio station call letters*]
WMBL.........	Wrightsville Marine Biomedical Laboratory
WMBM........	Miami Beach, FL [*AM radio station call letters*] (RBYB)
WMBN	Petoskey, MI [*AM radio station call letters*]
WMBO	Auburn, NY [*AM radio station call letters*]
WMBP	Belpre, OH [*FM radio station call letters*]
WMBPrA......	Williams Cos. $2.21 cm Pfd [*NYSE symbol*] (TTSB)
WMBR	Cambridge, MA [*FM radio station call letters*]
WMBS	Uniontown, PA [*AM radio station call letters*]
WMBT.........	Pulau Pioman [*Malaysia*] [*ICAO location identifier*] (ICLI)
WMBT.........	Shenandoah, PA [*AM radio station call letters*]
WMBTOPCITBWTNTALI...	We May Be the Only Phone Company in Town, but We Try Not to Act Like It [*Slogan*]
WMBU	Forest, MS [*FM radio station call letters*]
WMBV	Dixon's Mills, AL [*FM radio station call letters*]
WMBW........	Chattanooga, TN [*FM radio station call letters*]
WMC............	Church of the Brethren General Board World Ministries Commission (EA)
WMC............	Concordia College, Milwaukee, WI [*Library symbol Library of Congress*] (LCLS)
WMC............	Memphis, TN [*AM radio station call letters*]
WMC............	War Manpower Commission [*Within the Office of Emergency Management*] [*World War II*]
WMC............	Waste Management Compartment [*NASA*] (KSC)
WMC............	Waste Minimization and Containment Services, Inc. (ECON)
WMC............	Watershed Management Council (WPI)
WMC............	Ways and Means Committee [*House of Representatives*] (WDAA)
WMC............	Weapons and Mobility Command [*Army*]
WMC............	Weapons Monitoring Center
WMC............	Weapons Monitoring Console
WMC............	Weight-Matched Control (STED)
WMC............	Western Maryland College [*Westminster*]
WMC............	Western Mining Corp. [*Commercial*] (EERA)
WMC............	Western Mining Corp. Holdings ADS [*NYSE symbol*] (SPSG)
WMC............	White Male Candidate [*Politics*]
WMC............	Wilmington College, Wilmington, OH [*OCLC symbol*] (OCLC)
WmC...........	Windsor Microfilming Co., Windsor, ON, Canada [*Library symbol Library of Congress*] (LCLS)
WMC............	Winnemucca, NV [*Location identifier FAA*] (FAAL)
WMC............	Wisconsin Motor Carriers Association Inc., Madison WI [*STAC*]
WMC............	WMC Ltd ADS [*NYSE symbol*] (TTSB)
WMC............	Woodfree Machine-Coated Paper (DGA)
WMC............	Wool Manufacturers Council (EA)
WMC............	Working Men's Club [*British*] (BARN)
WMC............	World Meteorological Center [*World Meteorological Organization*]
WMC............	World Methodist Council (EA)
WMC............	World Ministries Commission (EA)
WMC............	World Missions to Children [*Later, WMF*] (EA)
WMC............	World Muslim Congress (BJA)
WMCA	New York, NY [*AM radio station call letters*]
WMCA	White Metal Casting Association [*British*] (DBA)
Wm Carey C...	William Carey College (GAGS)
WMCB	Martinsville, IN [*AM radio station call letters*]
WMCC	Concordia College, Milwaukee, WI [*Library symbol*] [*Library of Congress*] (LCLS)
WMCC	Water Management Coordinating Committee [*Australia*]
WMCC-FM	Munfordville, KY [*FM radio station call letters*] (RBYB)
WMCCMEC....	Women's Missionary Council of the Christian Methodist Episcopal Church (EA)
WMCCS	Worldwide Military Command and Control System [*DoD*] (MCD)
WMCCSA	World Masters Cross-Country Ski Association (EA)
WMCD	Statesboro, GA [*FM radio station call letters*]
WMCE..........	Erie, PA [*FM radio station call letters*]
WMCF	Montgomery, AL [*Television station call letters*]
WMC-FM	Memphis, TN [*FM radio station call letters*]
WMCG	Milan, GA [*FM radio station call letters*]

WMCG	Milwaukee County General Hospital, Milwaukee, WI [*Library symbol Library of Congress*] (LCLS)
WMCH	Church Hill, TN [*AM radio station call letters*]
WMCH	Columbia Hospital School of Nursing, Milwaukee, WI [*Library symbol Library of Congress*] (LCLS)
WMCHi	Milwaukee County Historical Society, Milwaukee, WI [*Library symbol Library of Congress*] (LCLS)
WMCI..........	Mattoon, IL [*FM radio station call letters*]
WMCJ.........	Moncks Corner, SC [*AM radio station call letters*]
WMcK........	William McKinley [*US president, 1843-1901*]
WMCL........	McLeansboro, IL [*AM radio station call letters*]
WMCL........	Wideband Communications Line
WMCL........	William Mitchell College of Law [*St. Paul, MN*]
WMCM........	Milwaukee County Institutions, Mental Health Centers Libraries, Milwaukee, WI [*Library symbol Library of Congress*] (LCLS)
WMCM........	Rockland, ME [*FM radio station call letters*]
WMCN	St. Paul, MN [*FM radio station call letters*]
WMCO	New Concord, OH [*FM radio station call letters*]
WMCO	William Controls, Inc. [*NASDAQ symbol*] (NQ)
WMCO	Williams Controls [*NASDAQ symbol*] (TTSB)
WMCP	Columbia, TN [*AM radio station call letters*]
WMCP	Woman's Medical College of Pennsylvania
WMCR	Oneida, NY [*AM radio station call letters*]
WMCR-FM	Oneida, NY [*FM radio station call letters*]
WMCS	Greenfield, WI [*AM radio station call letters*]
WMCSC.......	Cardinal Stritch College, Milwaukee, WI [*Library symbol Library of Congress*] (LCLS)
WMCT	Mountain City, TN [*AM radio station call letters*]
WMC-TV	Memphis, TN [*Television station call letters*]
WMCU	Miami, FL [*FM radio station call letters*]
WMCW	Harvard, IL [*AM radio station call letters*]
WMCW	World Movement of Christian Workers [*See also MMTC*] [*Brussels, Belgium*] (EAIO)
WMCX	West Long Branch, NJ [*FM radio station call letters*]
WMCZ........	Millbrook, AL [*FM radio station call letters*]
WMD	Digital Equipment Corp., Westminster, Westminster, MA [*OCLC symbol*] (OCLC)
WMD	Doctors Hospital, Milwaukee, WI [*Library symbol Library of Congress*] (LCLS)
WMD	Mandabe [*Madagascar*] [*Airport symbol*] (OAG)
WMD	Waste Management Division [*Environmental Protection Agency*] (GFGA)
WMD	Water Management Division [*Environmental Protection Agency*] (GFGA)
WMD	Weapon Mounted Display
WMD	Weapons of Mass Destruction
WMD	Wendt Bristol Health Service [*AMEX symbol*] (SAG)
WMD	Wendt-Bristol Health Svcs [*AMEX symbol*] (TTSB)
WMD	Wind Measuring Device
WMD	Women in Marketing & Design (WDAA)
WMDA	Woodworking Machinery Distributors Association (EA)
WMDAA.......	Watch Material Distributors Association of America [*Later, WMJDA*] (EA)
WMDB	Nashville, TN [*AM radio station call letters*]
WMDB	Waste Management Database [*IAEA*] [*United Nations*] (DUND)
WMDC	Hazlehurst, MS [*AM radio station call letters*]
WMDC-FM....	Hazlehurst, MS [*FM radio station call letters*]
WMDD	Fajardo, PR [*AM radio station call letters*]
WMDe	Deaconess Hospital, Milwaukee, WI [*Library symbol Library of Congress*] (LCLS)
WMDH	New Castle, IN [*AM radio station call letters*]
WMDH-FM....	New Castle, IN [*FM radio station call letters*]
WMDI	Bar Harbor, ME [*FM radio station call letters*]
WMDio	Diocesan Library, Milwaukee, WI [*Library symbol Library of Congress Obsolete*] (LCLS)
WMDJ........	Allen, KY [*FM radio station call letters*]
WMDJ.........	Martin, KY [*AM radio station call letters*]
WMDM........	Lexington Park, MD [*FM radio station call letters*]
WMDN	Meridian, MS [*Television station call letters*]
WMDO	Wheaton, MD [*AM radio station call letters*]
WMDR	Augusta, ME [*AM radio station call letters*]
WMDR	DePaul Rehabilitation Hospital Medical Library, Milwaukee, WI [*Library symbol Library of Congress*] (LCLS)
WMDT	Salisbury, MD [*Television station call letters*]
WMDWS......	Wendt-Bristol Health Wrrt [*AMEX symbol*] (TTSB)
WME	Eaton Corp., Milwaukee, WI [*Library symbol Library of Congress*] (LCLS)
WMe	Elisha D. Smith Public Library, Menasha, WI [*Library symbol Library of Congress*] (LCLS)
WME	Waste Management International Ltd. ADS [*NYSE symbol*] (SPSG)
WME	Waste Mgmt Intl plc ADS [*NYSE symbol*] (TTSB)
WME	Williams Medium E (STED)
WME	Williams' Medium E (DB)
WME	Window Meteoroid Experiment [*NASA*] (KSC)
WME	Women and Mathematics Education (EA)
WME	Worldwide Marriage Encounter (EA)
WMEA	Biddeford, ME [*Television station call letters*]
WMEA	Portland, ME [*FM radio station call letters*]
WMEA	Welded Modules for Electronic Assemblies [*NASA*]
WMEB	Orono, ME [*FM radio station call letters*]
WMEB	West Midlands Enterprise Board [*British*] (ECON)
WMEB-TV	Orono, ME [*Television station call letters*]
WMEC..........	Eaton Corp., Milwaukee, WI [*Library symbol*] [*Library of Congress*] (LCLS)
WMEC..........	Macomb, IL [*Television station call letters*]

WMEC.......... Medium Endurance Cutter [*Coast Guard*] (NVT)
WMEC.......... Western Military Electronics Center (KSC)
WMECO........ Western Massachusetts Electric Co.
WMED.......... Calais, ME [*FM radio station call letters*]
WMed.......... Medford Free Public Library, Medford, WI [*Library symbol*] [*Library of Congress*] (LCLS)
WMED .... Waste Management and Economics Division [*Environmental Protection Agency*] (EPA)
WMED-TV .... Calais, ME [*Television station call letters*]
WMEE.......... Fort Wayne, IN [*FM radio station call letters*]
WMEF.......... Fort Kent, ME [*FM radio station call letters*]
WMEG.......... Guayama, PR [*FM radio station call letters*]
WMEH.......... Bangor, ME [*FM radio station call letters*]
WMEI.......... Arecibo, PR [*Television station call letters*]
WMEJ.......... Proctorville, OH [*FM radio station call letters*]
WMEK.......... Chase City, VA [*AM radio station call letters*]
WMEL.......... Melbourne, FL [*AM radio station call letters*]
WMEM.......... Presque Isle, ME [*FM radio station call letters*]
WMEM-TV .. Presque Isle, ME [*Television station call letters*]
WMEN.......... Knoxville, TN [*AM radio station call letters*] (RBYB)
WMen.......... Mabel Tainter Memorial Free Library, Menomonie, WI [*Library symbol Library of Congress*] (LCLS)
WMenM....... Memorial Hospital and Nursing Home, Menomonie, WI [*Library symbol Library of Congress*] (LCLS)
WMenofH .... Community Memorial Hospital, Health Science Library, Menomonee Falls, WI [*Library symbol Library of Congress*] (LCLS)
WMenU....... University of Wisconsin-Stout, Menomonie, WI [*Library symbol Library of Congress*] (LCLS)
WMeq.......... Frank L. Weyenberg Library, Mequon, WI [*Library symbol Library of Congress*] (LCLS)
WMEQ.......... Menomonie, WI [*AM radio station call letters*]
WMEQ-FM .. Menomonie, WI [*FM radio station call letters*]
WMeqW....... Wisconsin Lutheran Seminary, Mequon, WI [*Library symbol Library of Congress*] (LCLS)
WMER.......... Meridian, MS [*AM radio station call letters*]
WMer.......... T. B. Scott Free Library, Merril, WI [*Library symbol Library of Congress*] (LCLS)
WMET.......... Gaithersburg, MD [*AM radio station call letters*]
WMeU .... University of Wisconsin-Green Bay, Fox Valley Campus, Menasha, WI [*Library symbol Library of Congress*] (LCLS)
WMEV.......... Marion, VA [*AM radio station call letters*]
WMEV-FM .. Marion, VA [*FM radio station call letters*]
WMEW.......... Waterville, ME [*FM radio station call letters*]
WMEX.......... Boston, MA [*AM radio station call letters*]
WMEX-FM .. Westport, NY [*FM radio station call letters*] (RBYB)
WMEZ.......... Pensacola, FL [*FM radio station call letters*]
WMF.......... Maude Shunk Public Library, Menomonee Falls, WI [*OCLC symbol*] (OCLC)
WMF.......... White Married Female (STED)
WMF.......... White Middle-Aged Female (MAE)
WMF.......... Windows Metafile [*Vector file format*] [*Computer science*] (PCM)
WMF.......... Windows Metafile Format [*Computer science*]
WMF.......... Wire Mattress Federation
WMF.......... Women's Motorcyclist Foundation (EA)
WMF.......... Woodfree Machine-Finished Paper (DGA)
WMF.......... World Mercy Fund (EA)
WMF.......... World Missions Fellowship (EA)
WMF.......... World Monuments Fund (EA)
WMFA.......... Raeford, NC [*AM radio station call letters*]
WMFC.......... Kuala Lumpur [*Malaysia*] [*ICAO location identifier*] (ICLI)
WMFC.......... Monroeville, AL [*AM radio station call letters*]
WMFC-FM .. Monroeville, AL [*FM radio station call letters*]
WMFD.......... Mansfield, OH [*Television station call letters*]
WMFD.......... Wilmington, NC [*AM radio station call letters*]
WMFE.......... Orlando, FL [*FM radio station call letters*]
WMFE-TV .... Orlando, FL [*Television station call letters*]
WMFG.......... Hibbing, MN [*AM radio station call letters*]
WMFG-FM .. Hibbing, MN [*FM radio station call letters*]
WMFJ.......... Daytona Beach, FL [*AM radio station call letters*]
WMFL.......... Monticello, FL [*AM radio station call letters*]
WMFM.......... Petal, MS [*FM radio station call letters*]
WMFM.......... Wisconsin Scottish Rite Bodies AASR, Milwaukee, WI [*Library symbol Library of Congress*] (LCLS)
WMFN .... Zeeland, MI [*AM radio station call letters*] (RBYB)
WMFO.......... Medford, MA [*FM radio station call letters*]
WMFP.......... Lawrence, MA [*Television station call letters*]
WMFQ.......... Ocala, FL [*FM radio station call letters*]
WMFR.......... High Point, NC [*AM radio station call letters*]
WMFS.......... Bartlett, TN [*FM radio station call letters*] (RBYB)
WMFX.......... St. Andrews, SC [*FM radio station call letters*]
WMG .... Globe-Union, Inc., Milwaukee, WI [*Library symbol Library of Congress*] (LCLS)
Wmg .... Wilmington [*Delaware*] (BARN)
WMG .... Winchester Magnum (INF)
WMG .... Wire Measure Gauge
WMG .... Wire Metallizing Gun
WMG .... Working Mathematics Group (AIE)
WMGA........ Moultrie, GA [*AM radio station call letters*]
WMGa........ Wisconsin Gas Co., Milwaukee, WI [*Library symbol Library of Congress*] (LCLS)
WMGB........ Jeffersonville, GA [*FM radio station call letters*]
WMGC........ Binghamton, NY [*Television station call letters*]
WMGF........ Mount Dora, FL [*FM radio station call letters*]
WMGG........ Gallipolis, OH [*FM radio station call letters*]
WMGH........ Tamaqua, PA [*FM radio station call letters*]

WMGI .... Terre Haute, IN [*FM radio station call letters*]
WMGJ.......... Gadsden, AL [*AM radio station call letters*]
WMGK .... Philadelphia, PA [*FM radio station call letters*]
WMGL .... Ravenel, SC [*FM radio station call letters*]
WMGL .... Wilmington Marine Geological Laboratory [*North Carolina*] (NOAA)
WMGM........ Atlantic City, NJ [*FM radio station call letters*]
WMGM........ Wildwood, NJ [*Television station call letters*]
WMGN........ Madison, WI [*FM radio station call letters*]
WMGO .... Canton, MS [*AM radio station call letters*]
WMGP .... Meridian, MS [*AM radio station call letters*]
WMGQ .... New Brunswick, NJ [*FM radio station call letters*]
WMGR .... Bainbridge, GA [*AM radio station call letters*]
WMGR .... Worm Gear [*Mechanical engineering*]
WMGR-FM .. Bainbridge, GA [*FM radio station call letters*]
WMGS .... Wilkes-Barre, PA [*FM radio station call letters*]
WMGT .... Macon, GA [*Television station call letters*]
WMGV-FM .. Newport, NC [*FM radio station call letters*] (RBYB)
WMGW........ Meadville, PA [*AM radio station call letters*]
WMGX .... Portland, ME [*FM radio station call letters*]
WMGY .... Montgomery, AL [*AM radio station call letters*]
WMGZ .... Sparta, GA [*FM radio station call letters*]
WMH .... Mountain Home [*Arkansas*] [*Airport symbol*] (OAG)
WMH .... WM Helijet [*Vancouver Stock Exchange symbol*]
WMH .... Women's Market Handbook [*A publication*]
WMHB .... Waterville, ME [*FM radio station call letters*]
WMHC .... South Hadley, MA [*FM radio station call letters*]
WMHD .... Terre Haute, IN [*FM radio station call letters*]
WMHG .... Muskegon, MI [*FM radio station call letters*] (RBYB)
WMHI .... Cape Vincent, NY [*FM radio station call letters*]
WMHK .... Columbia, SC [*FM radio station call letters*]
WMHN .... Webster, NY [*AM radio station call letters*]
WMHQ .... Schenectady, NY [*Television station call letters*]
WMHR .... Syracuse, NY [*FM radio station call letters*]
WMHS .... Wall-Mounted Handling System [*AEC*]
WMHS .... World Methodist Historical Society (EA)
WMHT .... Schenectady, NY [*FM radio station call letters*]
WMHT-TV ... Schenectady, NY [*Television station call letters*]
WMHW........ Mount Pleasant, MI [*FM radio station call letters*]
WMHX-FM .. Canandaigua, NY [*FM radio station call letters*] (RBYB)
WMHY .... World Mental Health Year [*1960*]
WMI .... War Materials, Inc.
WMI .... Washington Music Institute
WMI .... Waste Management (New) [*NYSE symbol*] [*Formerly, USA Waste Services*]
WMI .... Waveguide Moisture Indicator
WMI .... Westmin Resources Ltd. [*Toronto Stock Exchange symbol Vancouver Stock Exchange symbol*]
WMI .... Wildlife Management Institute (EA)
WMI .... Wolfson Microelectronics Institute (NITA)
WMI .... Woodlands Mountain Institute (EA)
WMI .... Worker-Machine Interface
WMI .... Work Motivation Inventory [*Test*]
WMI .... World Manufacturer Identifier
WMI .... World Metal Index [*Sheffield City Libraries*] [*British Information service or system*] (IID)
WMI .... World Meteorological Intervals
WMIA.......... Arecibo, PR [*AM radio station call letters*]
WMIA.......... Woodworking Machinery Importers Association of America (EA)
WMIB.......... Waste Management Information Bureau [*Atomic Energy Authority*] [*British Information service or system*] (IID)
WMIC.......... Sandusky, MI [*AM radio station call letters*]
WMIC.......... Western Microwave, Inc. [*NASDAQ symbol*] (NQ)
WMIC/CHCC... Welsh Music Information Centre - Canolfan Hysbysrwydd Cerddoriaeth Cymru [*University College*] (CB)
WMicr.......... Western Microwave, Inc. [*Associated Press*] (SAG)
WMicTc....... Western Micro Technology, Inc. [*Associated Press*] (SAG)
WMID.......... Atlantic City, NJ [*AM radio station call letters*]
WMID .... Pleasantville, NJ [*FM radio station call letters*]
WMIE .... Cocoa, FL [*FM radio station call letters*]
WMIH.......... Cleveland, OH [*AM radio station call letters*] (RBYB)
WMIK.......... Middlesboro, KY [*AM radio station call letters*]
WMIK-FM ... Middlesboro, KY [*FM radio station call letters*]
WMIL.......... Waukesha, WI [*FM radio station call letters*]
WMiltM....... Milton College, Milton, WI [*Library symbol Library of Congress*] (LCLS)
WMIM.......... Mount Carmel, PA [*AM radio station call letters*] (RBYB)
WMIN .... Hudson, WI [*AM radio station call letters*]
WMin .... Waste Minimization [*Environmental science*] (COE)
WMIN .... Words per Minute (IAA)
WMINST...... Westminster [*England*]
WMIO .... Cabo Rojo, PR [*FM radio station call letters*]
WMIP .... Weapons Management Improvement Program [*Military*] (AABC)
WMIQ .... Iron Mountain, MI [*AM radio station call letters*]
WMIR-AM.,.. Atlantic Beach, SC [*AM radio station call letters*] (BROA)
WMIS.......... Natchez, MS [*AM radio station call letters*]
WMIS.......... Waste Management Information System
WMIT.......... Black Mountain, NC [*FM radio station call letters*]
WMIU.......... Water and Maritime Industry Union [*Australia*]
WMIW.......... Atlantic Beach, SC [*AM radio station call letters*]
WMIX.......... Mount Vernon, IL [*AM radio station call letters*]
WMIX-FM ... Mount Vernon, IL [*FM radio station call letters*]
WMIY.......... Fairview, NC [*FM radio station call letters*]
WMIZ.......... Vineland, NJ [*AM radio station call letters*]
WMJ .... Johnson Controls, Corporate Information Center, Milwaukee, WI [*Library symbol Library of Congress*] (LCLS)

WMJ............ World of Michael Jackson (EA)
WMJA........ Saginaw, MI [FM radio station call letters] (RBYB)
WMJB........ Evansville, WI [FM radio station call letters]
WMJC........ Smithtown, NY [FM radio station call letters]
WMJD........ Grundy, VA [FM radio station call letters]
WMJDA....... Watch Material and Jewelry Distributors Association [Formerly, WMDAA] (EA)
WMJE........ Clarkesville, GA [FM radio station call letters]
WMJH-AM .. Rockford, MI [AM radio station call letters] (RBYB)
WMJI......... Cleveland, OH [FM radio station call letters]
WMJJ......... Birmingham, AL [FM radio station call letters]
WMJK........ Pinconning, MI [FM radio station call letters] (RBYB)
WMJL........ Marion, KY [AM radio station call letters]
WMJL-FM... Marion, KY [FM radio station call letters]
WMJM-FM... Jeffersontown, KY [FM radio station call letters] (RBYB)
WMJQ........ Buffalo, NY [FM radio station call letters]
WMJR........ Hudson Falls, NY [FM radio station call letters]
WMJS......... Prince Frederick, MD [FM radio station call letters]
WMJT......... Moundsville, WV [AM radio station call letters]
WMJW........ Cleveland, MS [FM radio station call letters]
WMJX......... Boston, MA [FM radio station call letters]
WMJY......... Biloxi, MS [FM radio station call letters]
WMJZ......... Gaylord, MI [FM radio station call letters]
WMK.......... Watermark
wmk.......... Watermark (WDAA)
W/(M K)...... Watts per Meter Kelvin
WMK.......... Weis Markets [NYSE symbol] (TTSB)
WMK.......... Weis Markets, Inc. [NYSE symbol] (SPSG)
WMKA .... Alor Setar/Sultan Abdul Halim [Malaysia] [ICAO location identifier] (ICLI)
WMKB .... Butterworth [Malaysia] [ICAO location identifier] (ICLI)
WMKB .... Ridgebury, PA [FM radio station call letters]
WMKC .... Kota Bahru/Sultan Ismail Petra [Malaysia] [ICAO location identifier] (ICLI)
WMKC .... St. Ignace, MI [FM radio station call letters]
WMKD .... Kuantan [Malaysia] [ICAO location identifier] (ICLI)
WMKD .... Watermarked (WGA)
WMKE .... Kerteh [Malaysia] [ICAO location identifier] (ICLI)
WMKF .... Simpang [Malaysia] [ICAO location identifier] (ICLI)
WMKI.......... Ipoh [Malaysia] [ICAO location identifier] (ICLI)
WMKJ......... Johore Bahru [Malaysia] [ICAO location identifier] (ICLI)
WMKJ......... Newnan, GA [FM radio station call letters]
WMKK .... Kuala Lumpur/International [Malaysia] [ICAO location identifier] (ICLI)
WMKL-FM ... Key Largo, FL [FM radio station call letters] (BROA)
WMKM........ Inkster, MI [AM radio station call letters]
WMKM........ Malacca [Malaysia] [ICAO location identifier] (ICLI)
WMKN .... Kuala Trengganu/Sultan Mahmud [Malaysia] [ICAO location identifier] (ICLI)
WMKP .... Penang [Malaysia] [ICAO location identifier] (ICLI)
WMKR-FM... Taylorville, IL [FM radio station call letters] (RBYB)
WMKS .... Kuala Lumpur [Malaysia] [ICAO location identifier] (ICLI)
WMKS .... Macon, GA [FM radio station call letters]
WMKT......... Charlevoix, MI [AM radio station call letters]
WMKV .... Reading, OH [FM radio station call letters]
WMKW-FM... Crossville, TN [FM radio station call letters] (RBYB)
WMKX .... Brookville, PA [FM radio station call letters]
WMKY......... Morehead, KY [FM radio station call letters]
WMKZ......... Monticello, KY [FM radio station call letters]
WML........... Lakeside Laboratories, Milwaukee, WI [Library symbol Library of Congress] (LCLS)
WML........... Malaimbandy [Madagascar] [Airport symbol] (OAG)
WML........... Westar Mining Ltd. [Toronto Stock Exchange symbol Vancouver Stock Exchange symbol]
WMLB......... Cumming, GA [AM radio station call letters]
WMLC......... Monticello, MS [AM radio station call letters]
WMLC......... Way of Mountain Learning Center (EA)
WMLH .... Lutheran Hospital of Milwaukee, Milwaukee, WI [Library symbol Library of Congress] (LCLS)
WMLI-FM .... Sauk City, WI [FM radio station call letters] (RBYB)
WMLJ......... Summersville, WV [FM radio station call letters]
WMLM........ St. Louis, MI [AM radio station call letters]
WMLN......... Milton, MA [FM radio station call letters]
WMLO .... Havana, FL [FM radio station call letters]
WMLP......... Milton, PA [AM radio station call letters]
WMLQ .... Rogers City, MI [FM radio station call letters]
WMLR .... Hohenwald, TN [AM radio station call letters]
WMLT......... Dublin, GA [AM radio station call letters]
WMLV......... Ironton, OH [FM radio station call letters]
WMLX-FM ... St. Mary's, OH [FM radio station call letters] (BROA)
WMLZ......... Jupiter, FL [AM radio station call letters]
WMM.......... Marquette University, Milwaukee, WI [Library symbol Library of Congress] (LCLS)
WMM.......... Wall-Mounted Manipulator [Nuclear energy] (NRCH)
WMM.......... White Married Male (STED)
WMM.......... White Middle-Aged Male (MAE)
WMM.......... William Mitchell College of Law Library, St. Paul, MN [OCLC symbol] (OCLC)
WMM.......... Willow Mixed Media (EA)
WMM.......... Women Make Movies (EA)
WMM.......... World Medical Mission (EA)
WMM.......... World Movement of Mothers [See also MMM] [Paris, France] (EAIO)
WMMA........ Lebanon, OH [FM radio station call letters]
WMMA........ Waste Materials Management Act
WMMA........ Wood Machinery Manufacturers of America (EA)
WMMB........ Melbourne, FL [AM radio station call letters]

WMMB........ Milwaukee Blood Center, Inc., Milwaukee, WI [Library symbol Library of Congress] (LCLS)
WMMBC ...... Miller Brewing Co., Research Library, Milwaukee, WI [Library symbol Library of Congress] (LCLS)
WMMC........ Marshall, IL [AM radio station call letters]
WMMC........ Milwaukee Children's Hospital, Milwaukee, WI [Library symbol Library of Congress] (LCLS)
WMMCW ..... Medical College of Wisconsin, Medical-Dental Library, Milwaukee, WI [Library symbol Library of Congress] (LCLS)
WMME-FM ... Augusta, ME [FM radio station call letters]
WMMF........ Fond du Lac, WI [Television station call letters]
WMMG........ Brandenburg, KY [AM radio station call letters]
WMMG-FM... Brandenburg, KY [FM radio station call letters]
WMMGIC ..... MGIC Investment Corp., Milwaukee, WI [Library symbol Library of Congress] (LCLS)
WMMH .... Misericordia Hospital, Milwaukee, WI [Library symbol Library of Congress] (LCLS)
WMMI......... Shepherd, MI [AM radio station call letters]
Wm Mitchell C Law... William Mitchell College of Law (GAGS)
WMMJ......... Bethesda, MD [FM radio station call letters]
WMMK........ Destin, FL [FM radio station call letters]
WMM-L........ Marquette University, School of Law, Milwaukee, WI [Library symbol Library of Congress] (LCLS)
WMMM........ Westport, CT [AM radio station call letters]
WMMM-FM... Verona, WI [FM radio station call letters] (RBYB)
WMM/MWS... Western Material Management, Machinery, and Welding Show [Canada] (ITD)
WMMN .... Barrackville, WV [FM radio station call letters]
WMMN .... Fairmont, WV [AM radio station call letters]
WMM-N........ Marquette University, College of Nursing, Milwaukee, WI [Library symbol Library of Congress] (LCLS)
WMMO .... Orlando, FL [FM radio station call letters]
WMMP........ Wood Moulding and Millwork Producers [Later, WMMPA] (EA)
WMMPA ...... Wood Moulding and Millwork Producers Association (EA)
WMMQ .... Charlotte, MI [FM radio station call letters]
WMMR .... Philadelphia, PA [FM radio station call letters]
WMMRRI...... Wyoming Mining and Mineral Resource Research Institute [University of Wyoming] [Research center] (RCD)
WMMS........ Cleveland, OH [FM radio station call letters]
WMMS........ Mount Sinai Hospital, Milwaukee, WI [Library symbol Library of Congress] (LCLS)
WMMt......... Mount Mary College, Milwaukee, WI [Library symbol Library of Congress] (LCLS)
WMMT........ Warm Month Mean Temperature [Climatology]
WMMT........ Whitesburg, KY [FM radio station call letters]
WMMus....... Milwaukee Public Museum, Reference Library, Milwaukee, WI [Library symbol Library of Congress] (LCLS)
WMMV-AM... Cocoa, FL [AM radio station call letters] (BROA)
WMMW........ Meriden, CT [AM radio station call letters]
WMMX......... Dayton, OH [FM radio station call letters]
WMMZ........ Spartanburg, SC [AM radio station call letters]
WMN .... Maroantsetra [Madagascar] [Airport symbol] (OAG)
WMN .... Winnemucca [Nevada] [Seismograph station code, US Geological Survey Closed] (SEIS)
WMN .... Women
WMNA........ Gretna, VA [AM radio station call letters]
WMNA-FM ... Gretna, VA [FM radio station call letters]
WMNB......... North Adams, MA [FM radio station call letters]
WMNC........ Morganton, NC [AM radio station call letters]
WMNC........ Whole Mononuclear Cell [Biochemistry]
WMNC-FM ... Morgantown, NC [FM radio station call letters]
WMNF .... Tampa, FL [FM radio station call letters]
WMNG........ Northwest General Hospital, Milwaukee, WI [Library symbol Library of Congress] (LCLS)
WMNI......... Columbus, OH [AM radio station call letters]
WMNJ......... Madison, NJ [FM radio station call letters]
WMNN .... Port Henry, NY [FM radio station call letters]
WMNN .... Minneapolis, MN [AM radio station call letters] (RBYB)
WMNR .... Monroe, CT [FM radio station call letters]
WMNS........ Olean, NY [AM radio station call letters]
WMNS........ William B. McGuire Nuclear Station (NRCH)
WMNT........ Manati, PR [AM radio station call letters]
WMNV .... Rupert, VT [FM radio station call letters]
WMNX......... Wilmington, NC [FM radio station call letters]
WMNY......... Elloree-Santee, SC [AM radio station call letters]
WMNZ........ Montezuma, GA [AM radio station call letters]
WMO .... Waste Management Operations [Environmental science] (COE)
WMO .... Wausau-Mosinee Paper [NYSE symbol]
WMO .... White Mountain [Alaska] [Airport symbol] (OAG)
WMO .... White Mountain, AK [Location identifier FAA] (FAAL)
WMO .... Wichita Mountains Array [Oklahoma] [Seismograph station code, US Geological Survey Closed] (SEIS)
WMO .... Wing Maintenance Officer
WMO .... World Meteorological Office (NITA)
WMO .... World Meteorological Organization [See also OMM] [Geneva, Switzerland] [United Nations] (EAIO)
WMO .... World Monetary Organization
WMOA........ Marietta, OH [AM radio station call letters]
WMOA........ Waste Minimization Opportunity Assessment [Environmental science]
WMOB........ Mobile, AL [AM radio station call letters]
WMOD........ Bolivar, TN [FM radio station call letters]
W/MOD........ With Modification of Vertical Profile (GAVI)
WMOG........ Brunswick, GA [AM radio station call letters]
WMOH........ Hamilton, OH [AM radio station call letters]
WMOI......... Monmouth, IL [FM radio station call letters]

WMOK .... Metropolis, IL [*AM radio station call letters*]
WMoM .... Monroe Clinic, Monroe, WI [*Library symbol Library of Congress*] (LCLS)
WMON .... Montgomery, WV [*AM radio station call letters*]
WMOO .... Derby Center, VT [*FM radio station call letters*]
WMOP .... Ocala, FL [*AM radio station call letters*]
WMOQ .... Bostwick, GA [*FM radio station call letters*]
WMOR .... Morehead, KY [*AM radio station call letters*]
WmorC .... Westmoreland Coal Co. [*Associated Press*] (SAG)
WMOR-FM... Morehead, KY [*AM radio station call letters*]
WMOS .... Quincy, IL [*FM radio station call letters*] (RBYB)
WMoS .... Saint Clare Hospital, Monroe, WI [*Library symbol Library of Congress*] (LCLS)
WMOT .... Murfreesboro, TN [*FM radio station call letters*]
WMOU .... Berlin, NH [*AM radio station call letters*]
WMOV .... Ravenswood, WV [*AM radio station call letters*]
WMOX .... Meridian, MS [*AM radio station call letters*]
WMP........... Mampikony [*Malagasy*] [*Airport symbol*] (AD)
WMP........... War and Mobilization Plan [*Air Force documents*]
WMP........... Waste Management Paper [*British*] (DCTA)
WMP........... Waste Management Plan (EERA)
WMP........... Waste Minimization Plan [*Environmental science*] (COE)
WMP........... Weapon Monitor Panel (MCD)
WMP........... Weather Modification Program [*Boulder, CO*] [*Department of Commerce*]
WMP........... Weight Management Program (STED)
WMP........... Wiener Mapping Procedure
WMP........... With Much Pleasure [*Meaning, "We accept the invitation"*]
WMP........... Women and the Military Project [*An association*] (EA)
WmP........... World Microfilms Publications, London, United Kingdom [*Library symbol Library of Congress*] (LCLS)
WMPA .... Wet Maximum Power Available (SAA)
WMPA .... Women's Military Pilots Association (EA)
Wm Paterson C NJ... William Paterson College of New Jersey (GAGS)
WMPB .... Baltimore, MD [*Television station call letters*]
WMPC .... Lapeer, MI [*AM radio station call letters*]
WMPC .... War Manpower Commission [*Within the Office of Emergency Management*] [*World War II*]
WMPC .... War Materiel Procurement Capability (AFIT)
WMPCE........ World Meeting Planners Congress and Exposition [*Defunct*] (EA)
WMPCES(P)... War Manpower Commission Employment Stabilization (Plan) [*Terminated, 1945*]
WMPG .... Gorham, ME [*FM radio station call letters*]
WMPH .... Wilmington, DE [*FM radio station call letters*]
WMPI........... Scottsburg, IN [*FM radio station call letters*]
WMPI........... Women of the Motion Picture Industry, International [*Dallas, TX*]
WMPL .... Hancock, MI [*AM radio station call letters*]
WMPL........... Western Maryland Public Libraries Regional Resource Center [*Library network*]
WMPL........... World Mission Prayer League (EA)
WMPM......... Smithfield, NC [*AM radio station call letters*]
WMPN .... Jackson, MS [*FM radio station call letters*]
WMPN-TV.... Jackson, MS [*Television station call letters*]
WMPO .... Middleport-Pomeroy, OH [*AM radio station call letters*]
WMPO .... Weather Modification Program Office [*Marine science*] (MSC)
WMPO-FM... Middleport-Pomeroy, OH [*FM radio station call letters*]
WMPR .... Jackson, MS [*FM radio station call letters*]
WMPRT ...... Wartime Manpower and Personnel Readiness Team [*Military*]
WMPS .... Millington, TN [*AM radio station call letters*]
WMPT .... Annapolis, MD [*Television station call letters*]
WMPV .... Mobile, AL [*Television station call letters*]
WMPX .... Midland, MI [*AM radio station call letters*]
WMPZ........ Ringgold, GA [*FM radio station call letters*] (RBYB)
WMQ .... Quarles & Brady, Law Library, Milwaukee, WI [*Library symbol Library of Congress*] (LCLS)
WMQ .... Westmount Public Library [*UTLAS symbol*]
WMQ .... Wulumuchi [*Republic of China*] [*Seismograph station code, US Geological Survey*] (SEIS)
WMQA .... Minocqua, WI [*AM radio station call letters*]
WMQA-FM ... Minocqua, WI [*FM radio station call letters*]
WMQC .... Westover, WV [*FM radio station call letters*]
WMQQ .... Springfield, KY [*FM radio station call letters*]
WMQT .... Ishpeming, MI [*FM radio station call letters*]
WMQX-FM ... Winston-Salem, NC [*FM radio station call letters*]
WMR .... Mananara [*Madagascar*] [*Airport symbol*] (OAG)
WMR .... Reinhart, Boerner, Van Deuren, Norris and Rieselbach, Law Library, Milwaukee, WI [*Library symbol Library of Congress*] (LCLS)
WMR .... Wake Measurements RADAR [*Army*] (MCD)
WMR .... War Maintenance Reserve [*British*]
WMR .... War Materiel Requirement (AFIT)
WMR .... Water Meter
WMR .... Water-Moderated Reactor
WMR .... Wideband Multichannel Receiver
WMR .... William and Mary Review of Virginia Law [*A publication*] (DLA)
WMR .... Wonder Marine Resources [*Vancouver Stock Exchange symbol*]
WMR .... Work Metabolic Rate (MAE)
WMR .... World Medical Relief (EA)
WMRA .... Harrisonburg, VA [*FM radio station call letters*]
WMRALC .... Western Metropolitan Regional Aboriginal Land Council [*Sydney, New South Wales, Australia*]
WMRB .... Columbia, TN [*AM radio station call letters*]
WMRC .... Milford, MA [*AM radio station call letters*]
WMRC .... War Minerals Relief Commission [*Department of the Interior*] [*Abolished, 1940*] (EGAO)
WMRD-AM... Middletown, CT [*AM radio station call letters*] (RBYB)

WMREI .... Waste Management Research and Education Institute [*University of Tennessee*]
WMRF .... Lewistown, PA [*FM radio station call letters*]
WMRH .... Waupun, WI [*AM radio station call letters*]
WMRI .... Marion, IN [*FM radio station call letters*]
WMRK .... Selma, AL [*AM radio station call letters*]
WMRL .... Lexington, VA [*FM radio station call letters*]
WMRL .... Water Management Research Laboratory [*Fresno, CA*] [*Department of Agriculture*] (GRD)
WMRN .... Marion, OH [*AM radio station call letters*]
WMRN-FM... Marion, OH [*FM radio station call letters*]
WMRO .... Gallatin, TN [*AM radio station call letters*]
Wm Rob ..... William Robinson's English Admiralty Reports [*1838-52*] [*A publication*] (DLA)
Wm Rob Adm... William Robinson's English Admiralty Reports [*1838-52*] [*A publication*] (DLA)
WMRQ .... Waterbury, CT [*FM radio station call letters*] (RBYB)
WMRR .... Muskegon Heights, MI [*FM radio station call letters*]
WMRS .... Monticello, IN [*FM radio station call letters*]
WMRS .... White Mountain Research Station [*Research center*] (RCD)
WMRT .... Marietta, OH [*FM radio station call letters*]
WMRV .... Endicott, NY [*FM radio station call letters*]
WMRW .... Westhampton, NY [*FM radio station call letters*]
WMRX .... Beaverton, MI [*FM radio station call letters*]
WMRY .... Crozet, VA [*FM radio station call letters*] (RBYB)
WMS .... Wall-Motion Study (MEDA)
WMS .... Warehouse Material Stores (AAG)
WMS .... Waste Management System (MCD)
WMS .... Water Management Section [*Apollo*] [*NASA*]
WMS .... Watershed Modeling System
WMS .... Weapons Monitoring System
WMS .... Weather Mapping System
WMS .... Wechsler Memory Scale [*Neuropsychological test*]
WMS .... Wesleyan Missionary Society
WMS .... West Middle School [*South Carolina*] [*Seismograph station code, US Geological Survey*] (SEIS)
WMS .... Whaling Museum Society (EA)
WMS .... Wilderness Medical Society (EA)
WMS .... Willem Mengelberg Society (EA)
WMS .... William Morris Society [*Later, WMS/AB*] (EA)
WMS .... Wind Measuring System
WMS .... Wire Mesh Screen (OA)
WMS .... WMS Airways BV [*Netherlands ICAO designator*] (FAAC)
WMS .... WMS Industries [*Associated Press*] (SAG)
WMS .... WMS Industries, Inc. [*Formerly, Williams Electronics*] [*NYSE symbol*] (SPSG)
WMS .... Women for a Meaningful Summit (EA)
WMS .... Women in the Medical Service [*Army*]
WMS .... Women's Medical Specialist
WMS .... Women's Missionary Society, AME [*African Methodist Episcopal*] Church (EA)
WMS .... Workforce Management Staff [*Environmental Protection Agency*] (GFGA)
WMS .... Work Measurement System [*Postal Service*]
WMS .... World Magnetic Survey [*Defunct*]
WMS .... World Mariculture Society (EA)
WmS .... World Microfilms Division, Oyez Equipment Ltd., London, United Kingdom [*Library symbol Library of Congress*] (LCLS)
WMSA .... Massena, NY [*AM radio station call letters*]
WMSA .... Saint Anthony Hospital, Milwaukee, WI [*Library symbol Library of Congress*] (LCLS)
WMSA .... Woodworking Machinery Suppliers Association [*British*] (DBA)
WMS/AB ..... William Morris Society, American Branch (EA)
Wms Ann Reg... Williams' Annual Register [*New York*] [*A publication*] (DLA)
WMSC .... Upper Montclair, NJ [*FM radio station call letters*]
WMSC .... Weather Message Switching Center
WMSC .... White Mountain Scenic Railroad [*AAR code*]
WMSC .... Women's Medical Specialists Corps
WMSCMC ... Women's Missionary and Service Commission of the Mennonite Church (EA)
WMSCR........ Weather Message Switching Center Replacement (GAVI)
WMSE.......... Milwaukee School of Engineering, Walter Schroeder Library, Milwaukee, WI [*Library symbol Library of Congress*] (LCLS)
WMSE.......... Milwaukee, WI [*FM radio station call letters*]
Wms Ex....... Williams on Executors [*15th ed.*] [*1970*] [*A publication*] (DLA)
WMSF.......... Saint Francis Seminary, Milwaukee, WI [*Library symbol Library of Congress*] (LCLS)
WMSFH .... Saint Francis Hospital, Milwaukee, WI [*Library symbol Library of Congress*] (LCLS)
Wms flex ex... Williams flexion exercises [*Orthopedics*] (DAVI)
WMSFT........ Wormshaft
WMSG .... Oakland, MD [*AM radio station call letters*]
WMSH .... Sturgis, MI [*AM radio station call letters*]
WMSH-FM ... Sturgis, MI [*FM radio station call letters*]
WMSI.......... Jackson, MS [*FM radio station call letters*]
WMS-I .... Wechsler Memory Scale, Form I [*Psychology*] (DAVI)
WMSI.......... Western Management Science Institute [*University of California*] (KSC)
WMSJ .... Harpswell, ME [*FM radio station call letters*]
WMSJ.......... Saint Joseph's Hospital, Milwaukee, WI [*Library symbol Library of Congress*] (LCLS)
WMSK .... Morganfield, KY [*AM radio station call letters*]
WMSKF........ William Morris Society and Kelmscott Fellowship [*Kelmscott Fellowship and William Morris Society*] [*Formed by a merger of*] (EAIO)

WMSK-FM ... Morganfield, KY [*FM radio station call letters*]
WMSL......... Athens, GA [*FM radio station call letters*]
WMSL......... Saint Luke's Hospital, Milwaukee, WI [*Library symbol Library of Congress*] (LCLS)
WMSL......... Wet Mock Simulated Launch [*NASA*] (KSC)
WMSL......... Wichita Mountains Seismological Laboratory
WMSM........ Saint Mary's Hospital, Milwaukee, WI [*Library symbol Library of Congress*] (LCLS)
Wms Mass... Williams' Reports [*1 Massachusetts*] [*A publication*] (DLA)
WMSMi........ Saint Michael Hospital, Milwaukee, WI [*Library symbol Library of Congress*] (LCLS)
WMSMN ..... Saint Mary's School of Nursing, Milwaukee, WI [*Library symbol Library of Congress*] (LCLS)
WMSN .... Madison, WI [*Television station call letters*]
Wms Notes... Williams' Notes to Saunders' Reports [*England*] [*A publication*] (DLA)
WMSO .... Wichita Mountains Seismological Observatory
WMSP .... Montgomery, AL [*AM radio station call letters*] (RBYB)
Wms P........ Peere-Williams' English Chancery Reports [*1695-1736*] [*A publication*] (DLA)
Wms Peere... Peere-Williams' English Chancery Reports [*A publication*] (DLA)
WMSQ .... Havelock, NC [*FM radio station call letters*]
WMSR .... Manchester, TN [*AM radio station call letters*]
WMSRG....... Weather-Modification Statistical Research Groups
WMSS .... Middletown, PA [*FM radio station call letters*]
WMSS .... Westinghouse Microscan System (IAA)
WmsSon ...... Willams-Sonoma, Inc. [*Associated Press*] (SAG)
WMST .... Mount Sterling, KY [*AM radio station call letters*]
WMST-FM ... Mount Sterling, KY [*FM radio station call letters*]
WMSU .... Starkville, MS [*FM radio station call letters*]
WMSV .... Starkville, MS [*FM radio station call letters*]
Wms VT....... Williams' Vermont Reports [*27-29 Vermont*] [*A publication*] (DLA)
WMSW .... Hatillo, PR [*AM radio station call letters*]
WMSWH...... Southeastern Wisconsin Health Systems Agency, Health Science Library, Milwaukee, WI [*Library symbol Library of Congress*] (LCLS)
WMSX .... Brockton, MA [*AM radio station call letters*]
WMSY .... Marion, VA [*Television station call letters*]
WMT .... Cedar Rapids, IA [*AM radio station call letters*]
WMT .... Wal-Mart Stores [*NYSE symbol*] (TTSB)
WMT .... Wal-Mart Stores, Inc. [*NYSE symbol*] (SPSG)
WMT .... Waste Monitor Tank (IEEE)
WMT .... Weighing More Than
WMT .... Western Motor Tariff Bureau, Los Angeles CA [*STAC*]
WMT .... West Meridian Time
WMT .... Wet Metric Ton [*Waste management*]
WMT .... Windows Media Technologies [*Microsoft Corp.*]
WMTA .... Central City, KY [*AM radio station call letters*]
WMTA .... Western Maquiladora Trade Association (CROSS)
WMTB .... Emmitsburg, MD [*FM radio station call letters*]
WMTR .... Western Motor Tariff Bureau
WMTBF....... Warranty Mean Time Between Failures [*Army*]
WMTC......... Milwaukee Technical College, Milwaukee, WI [*Library symbol Library of Congress*] (LCLS)
WMTC......... Vancleve, KY [*AM radio station call letters*]
WMTC......... Waste Management Technology Center [*Oak Ridge National Laboratory*]
WMTC-FM ... Vancleve, KY [*FM radio station call letters*]
WMTC-N ..... Milwaukee Area Technical College, North Campus Center Library, Mequon, WI [*Library symbol Library of Congress*] (LCLS)
WMTC-S ..... Milwaukee Area Technical College, South Campus Center Library, Oak Creek, WI [*Library symbol Library of Congress*] (LCLS)
WMTC-W .... Milwaukee Area Technical College, West Campus Center Library, West Allis, WI [*Library symbol Library of Congress*] (LCLS)
WMTD .... Hinton, WV [*AM radio station call letters*]
WMTD-FM ... Hinton, WV [*FM radio station call letters*]
WMTE .... Manistee, MI [*AM radio station call letters*]
WMT-FM...... Cedar Rapids, IA [*FM radio station call letters*]
WMTH .... Park Ridge, IL [*FM radio station call letters*]
WMTH .... Westmeath [*County in Ireland*] (ROG)
WMTI .... Morovis, PR [*AM radio station call letters*]
WMTI Exp Stn... Manati, PR [*Radio expansion station*] (RBYB)
WMTJ......... Fajardo, PR [*Television station call letters*]
WMTK......... Littleton, NH [*FM radio station call letters*]
WMTL......... Leitchfield, KY [*AM radio station call letters*]
WMTM........ Moultrie, GA [*AM radio station call letters*]
WMTM-FM.... Moultrie, GA [*FM radio station call letters*]
WMTN .... Morristown, TN [*AM radio station call letters*]
WMTO .... Port St. Joe, FL [*FM radio station call letters*]
WMTR .... Archbold, OH [*FM radio station call letters*]
WMTR .... Morristown, NJ [*AM radio station call letters*]
WMTR .... Wheeled Mobility Test Rig [*Army*] (RDA)
WMTS......... Murfreesboro, TN [*AM radio station call letters*]
WMTS......... Western Manufacturing Technology Show and Conference (ITD)
WMTS-FM ... Murfreesboro, TN [*FM radio station call letters*] (RBYB)
WMTT......... Conklin, NY [*FM radio station call letters*] (RBYB)
WMTT......... Willamette Indus [*NASDAQ symbol*] (TTSB)
WMTT......... Willamette Industries, Inc. [*NASDAQ symbol*] (NQ)
WMTU......... Houghton, MI [*FM radio station call letters*]
WMTU......... Jackson, TN [*Television station call letters*]
WMTV......... Madison, WI [*Television station call letters*]
WMTW........ Poland Spring, ME [*Television station call letters*]
WMTX......... Clearwater, FL [*FM radio station call letters*]
WMTX......... Pinellas Park, FL [*AM radio station call letters*]
WMTY......... Greenwood, SC [*AM radio station call letters*]

WMTY-FM ... Greenwood, SC [*FM radio station call letters*]
WMTZ......... Johnston, PA [*FM radio station call letters*]
WMU .... Western Michigan University [*Kalamazoo*]
WMU .... West Mountain [*Utah*] [*Seismograph station code, US Geological Survey*] (SEIS)
WMU .... Woman's Missionary Union (EA)
WMU .... World Maritime University [*Sweden*] (DCTA)
WMUA .... Amherst, MA [*FM radio station call letters*]
WMUB .... Oxford, OH [*FM radio station call letters*]
WMUC .... College Park, MD [*FM radio station call letters*]
WMUF .... Paris, TN [*AM radio station call letters*]
WMUF .... Universal Foods Corp., Technical Information Services, Milwaukee, WI [*Library symbol Library of Congress*] (LCLS)
WMUF-FM ... Paris, TN [*FM radio station call letters*]
WMUH .... Allentown, PA [*FM radio station call letters*]
WMUK .... Kalamazoo, MI [*FM radio station call letters*]
WMUL .... Huntington, WV [*FM radio station call letters*]
WMUR .... Manchester, NH [*Television station call letters*]
WMUS .... Muskegon, MI [*AM radio station call letters*]
WMUSE .... World Markets for US Exports [*A publication*]
WMUS-FM.... Muskegon, MI [*FM radio station call letters*]
WMut .... Washington Mutual, Inc. [*Associated Press*] (SAG)
WMUU .... Greenville, SC [*AM radio station call letters*]
WMUU-FM.... Greenville, SC [*FM radio station call letters*]
WMUW .... Columbus, MS [*FM radio station call letters*]
WMUW .... University of Wisconsin-Milwaukee, Milwaukee, WI [*Library symbol Library of Congress*] (LCLS)
WMUZ .... Detroit, MI [*FM radio station call letters*]
WMV .... Madirovalo [*Malagasy*] [*Airport symbol*] (AD)
WMV .... Valuation Research Corp., Milwaukee, WI [*Library symbol Library of Congress*] (LCLS)
WMV .... War Munition Volunteers [*World War I*] [*British*]
WMV .... Watermelon Mosaic Virus
WMVA .... Martinsville, VA [*AM radio station call letters*]
WMV-E .... Watermelon Mosaic Virus E
WMVG .... Milledgeville, GA [*AM radio station call letters*]
WMVI .... Mechanicville, NY [*AM radio station call letters*]
WMVM-FM.... Mayville, WI [*FM radio station call letters*] (BROA)
WMVN .... Ishpeming, MI [*AM radio station call letters*]
WMVO .... Mount Vernon, OH [*AM radio station call letters*]
WMVP .... Chicago, IL [*AM radio station call letters*]
WMVR .... Sidney, OH [*AM radio station call letters*]
WMVR-FM ... Sidney, OH [*FM radio station call letters*]
WMVS .... Milwaukee, WI [*Television station call letters*]
WMVT .... Milwaukee, WI [*Television station call letters*]
WMVU .... Nashua, NH [*AM radio station call letters*]
WMVV .... Griffin, GA (RBYB)
WMVX-FM ... Cleveland, OH [*FM radio station call letters*] (BROA)
WMVY .... Tisbury, MA [*FM radio station call letters*]
WMW.......... Whyte & Hirschboeck, Law Library, Milwaukee, WI [*Library symbol Library of Congress*] (LCLS)
WMW.......... Women's Media Workshop [*Defunct*] (EA)
WMWA .... Glenview, IL [*FM radio station call letters*]
WMWHL ...... Wormwheel
WMWK .... Milwaukee, WI [*FM radio station call letters*]
WMWM........ Salem, MA [*FM radio station call letters*]
WMWN .... [*The*] Weatherford, Mineral Wells & Northwestern Railway Co. [*AAR code*]
WMWR-AM... Macon, GA [*AM radio station call letters*] (RBYB)
WMWV .... Conway, NH [*FM radio station call letters*]
WMX .... Wamena [*Indonesia*] [*Airport symbol*] (OAG)
WMX .... Whirlpool, Massage, Exercise [*Medicine*]
WMX .... WMX Technologies [*NYSE symbol*] (SPSG)
WMXA .... Opelika, AL [*FM radio station call letters*]
WMXB .... Richmond, VA [*FM radio station call letters*]
WMXC .... Mobile, AL [*FM radio station call letters*]
WMXD .... Detroit, MI [*FM radio station call letters*]
WMXE .... Hudson, MI [*FM radio station call letters*] (RBYB)
WMXF .... Sauk City, WI [*FM radio station call letters*]
WMXG-FM ... London, OH [*FM radio station call letters*] (BROA)
WMXH .... Olyphant, PA [*AM radio station call letters*]
WMXI-FM .... Laurel, MS [*FM radio station call letters*] (RBYB)
WMXJ......... Pompano Beach, FL [*FM radio station call letters*]
WMXK........ Morristown, TN [*FM radio station call letters*]
WMXL......... Lexington, KY [*FM radio station call letters*]
WMXM........ Lake Forest, IL [*FM radio station call letters*]
WMXN .... Stevenson, AL [*FM radio station call letters*] (RBYB)
WMXO .... Olean, NY [*FM radio station call letters*]
WMXP .... Peoria, IL [*FM radio station call letters*]
WMXQ .... Birmingham, AL [*FM radio station call letters*]
WMXR .... Woodstock, VT [*FM radio station call letters*]
WMXS .... Montgomery, AL [*FM radio station call letters*]
WMXT .... Pamplico, SC [*FM radio station call letters*]
WMX Tc...... WMX Technologies, Inc. [*Associated Press*] (SAG)
WMXU .... Starkville, MS [*FM radio station call letters*]
WMXV .... New York, NY [*FM radio station call letters*]
WMXW .... Vestal, NY [*FM radio station call letters*]
WMXX .... Jackson, TN [*FM radio station call letters*]
WMXY .... Hogansville, GA [*FM radio station call letters*]
WMXZ........ De Funiak Springs, FL [*FM radio station call letters*]
WMY .... Wakamiya [*Japan*] [*Seismograph station code, US Geological Survey Closed*] (SEIS)
WMYB .... Socastee, SC [*FM radio station call letters*]
WMYC .... Mobile, AL [*FM radio station call letters*]
WMYF .... Exeter, NH [*AM radio station call letters*]

WMYI.......... Hendersonville, NC [*FM radio station call letters*]
WMYK......... Moyock, NC [*FM radio station call letters*]
WMYL-FM... Salladasburg, PA [*FM radio station call letters*] (RBYB)
WMYM......... Cocoa, FL [*AM radio station call letters*]
WMYN......... Mayodan, NC [*AM radio station call letters*]
WMYQ......... Newton, MS [*AM radio station call letters*] (RBYB)
WMYQ-FM... Newton, MS [*FM radio station call letters*] (RBYB)
WMYR......... Fort Myers, FL [*AM radio station call letters*]
WMYS......... Indianapolis, IN [*AM radio station call letters*]
WMYT......... Carolina Beach, NC [*AM radio station call letters*]
WMYU......... Sevierville, TN [*FM radio station call letters*]
WMYX......... Milwaukee, WI [*FM radio station call letters*]
WMYY......... Schoharie, NY [*FM radio station call letters*]
WMZ........... Williams Companies [*NYSE symbol*] (SAG)
WMZ........... Williams Cos. 9.60%'QUICS' [*NYSE symbol*] (TTSB)
WMZ........... Wlliams Companies [*NYSE symbol*] (SAG)
WMZK......... Merrill, WI [*FM radio station call letters*]
WMZQ......... Arlington, VA [*AM radio station call letters*]
WMZQ......... Washington, DC [*FM radio station call letters*]
WMZX......... Owosso, MI [*FM radio station call letters*]
WN............. Calcutta Weekly Notes [*A publication*] (DLA)
WN............. Neenah Public Library, Neenah, WI [*Library symbol Library of Congress*] (LCLS)
WN............. Southwest Airlines [*ICAO designator*] (AD)
WN............. Washington [*Obsolete*] (ROG)
Wn............. Washington Reports [*A publication*] (DLA)
WN............. WAVES [*Women Accepted for Volunteer Emergency Service*] National (EA)
WN............. Weekly Notes of English Law Reports [*A publication*] (DLA)
W/N............ Weight Note [*Tea trade*] (ROG)
W-N............ Well-Nourished [*Medicine*]
wn.............. Well Nourished (STED)
WN............. Weston [*George*] Ltd. [*Toronto Stock Exchange symbol Vancouver Stock Exchange symbol*]
WN............. White-Breasted Nuthatch [*Ornithology*]
WN............. White Noise
WN............. Will Not
WN............. Winch (AAG)
WN............. Wisconsin [*Obsolete*] (ROG)
WN............. Within (ROG)
WN............. Work Notice (AAG)
WN............. World Neighbors (EA)
WN............. Wrong Number [*Telecommunications*] (TEL)
WN............. Wynn's International, Inc. [*NYSE symbol*] (SPSG)
WN............. Wynn's Intl [*NYSE symbol*] (TTSB)
Wn 2d......... Washington Reports, Second Series [*A publication*] (DLA)
WNA........... Napaskiak [*Alaska*] [*Airport symbol*] (OAG)
WNA........... Napaskiak, AK [*Location identifier FAA*] (FAAL)
WNa........... Nashotah House, Nashotah, WI [*Library symbol Library of Congress*] (LCLS)
WNA........... Wa National Army [*Myanmar*] [*Political party*] (EY)
WNA........... Washington [*DC*] National Airport [*FAA*]
WNA........... Wedge Nozzle Assembly
WNA........... Welsh Netball Association (DBA)
WNA........... Winter, North Atlantic [*Vessel load line mark*]
WNA........... Wireless Network Access
WNA........... World Nature Association (EA)
WNAA......... Greensboro, NC [*FM radio station call letters*]
WNAAA....... Women of the National Agricultural Aviation Association (EA)
WNAB......... Nashville, TN [*Television station call letters*]
WNAB......... Weekly Newspaper Advertising Bureau [*British*] (BI)
WNAC......... Providence, RI [*Television station call letters*]
WNAC......... Women Nationally Active for Christ [*An association*] (EA)
WNACFWB... Woman's National Auxiliary Convention of Free Will Baptists (EA)
WNAE......... Warren, PA [*AM radio station call letters*]
WNAF......... Women's National Aquatic Forum (EA)
WNAH......... Nashville, TN [*AM radio station call letters*]
WNAI.......... Word and Number Assessment Inventory [*Aptitude test*]
WNAK......... Nanticoke, PA [*AM radio station call letters*]
WNAL......... Gadsden, AL [*Television station call letters*]
WNAM......... Neenah-Menasha, WI [*AM radio station call letters*]
WNAP......... Indianapolis, IN [*FM radio station call letters*]
WNAP......... Norristown, PA [*AM radio station call letters*]
WNAP......... Washington [*DC*] National Airport
WNAR......... Biometric Society, Western North American Region (EA)
WNAS......... New Albany, IN [*FM radio station call letters*]
WNAT......... Natchez, MS [*AM radio station call letters*]
WNAU......... New Albany, MS [*AM radio station call letters*]
WNAV......... Annapolis, MD [*AM radio station call letters*]
WNAW......... North Adams, MA [*AM radio station call letters*]
WNAX......... Yankton, SD [*AM radio station call letters*]
WNAX-FM.... Yankton, SD [*FM radio station call letters*]
WNAZ......... Nashville, TN [*FM radio station call letters*]
WNB........... Will Not Be
WNB........... Winter Navigation Board
WNBA......... Women's National Basketball Association [*Defunct*] (EA)
WNBA......... Women's National Book Association (EA)
WNBA......... World Ninepin Bowling Association [*Germany*] (EAIO)
WNBC......... New York, NY [*Television station call letters*]
WNBF......... Binghamton, NY [*AM radio station call letters*]
WNBH......... New Bedford, MA [*AM radio station call letters*]
WNbH......... New Berlin Memorial Hospital, New Berlin, WI [*Library symbol Library of Congress*] (LCLS)
WNBI.......... Park Falls, WI [*AM radio station call letters*]
WNBN......... Meridian, MS [*AM radio station call letters*]
WNBP......... Newburyport, MA [*AM radio station call letters*]
WNBR......... Oriental, NC [*FM radio station call letters*]
WNBS......... Murray, KY [*AM radio station call letters*]
WNBT......... Wellsboro, PA [*AM radio station call letters*]
WNBT-FM.... Wellsboro, PA [*FM radio station call letters*]
WNBU......... Concord, NH [*Television station call letters*] (RBYB)
WNBX-FM.... Lebanon, NH [*FM radio station call letters*] (RBYB)
WNBY......... Newberry, MI [*AM radio station call letters*]
WNBY-FM.... Newberry, MI [*FM radio station call letters*]
WNBZ......... Saranac Lake, NY [*AM radio station call letters*]
WNC........... Naval War College, Newport, RI [*OCLC symbol*] (OCLC)
WNC........... Wabash National [*NYSE symbol*] (TTSB)
WNC........... Wabash National Corp. [*NYSE symbol*] (SPSG)
WNC........... Washington National Corp. (EFIS)
WNC........... WAVES National Corp. [*An association*] (EA)
WNC........... Weak Neutral Current [*Chemistry*]
WNC........... Weekly Notes of Cases [*Pennsylvania*] [*A publication*] (DLA)
WNC........... Wencarro Resources Ltd. [*Vancouver Stock Exchange symbol*]
WNC........... Wenic Air Services [*Singapore*] [*ICAO designator*] (FAAC)
WNC........... Wilmington [*North Carolina*] [*Seismograph station code, US Geological Survey*] (SEIS)
WNC........... Women's National Commission [*British*] (EAIO)
WNCA......... Siler City, NC [*AM radio station call letters*]
WN-CAELA... Women's Network of the Council for Adult Education in Latin America [*See also RM-CEAAL*] [*Quito, Ecuador*] (EAIO)
WN (Calc).... Calcutta Weekly Notes [*A publication*] (DLA)
WN Cas....... Weekly Notes of Cases [*Pennsylvania*] [*A publication*] (DLA)
WN Cas (PA)... Weekly Notes of Cases [*Pennsylvania*] [*A publication*] (DLA)
WNCB......... Duluth, MN [*FM radio station call letters*]
WNCC......... Barnesboro, PA [*AM radio station call letters*]
WNCCC....... Women's National Cancer Control Campaign [*British*]
WNCD......... Niles, OH [*FM radio station call letters*]
WNCE-FM.... Palmyra, PA [*FM radio station call letters*] (RBYB)
WNCG......... Clyde, OH [*FM radio station call letters*]
WNCI.......... Columbus, OH [*FM radio station call letters*]
WNCM......... Atlantic Beach, FL [*AM radio station call letters*]
WNCM......... Jacksonville, FL [*FM radio station call letters*]
WNCN......... Goldsboro, NC [*Television station call letters*]
WNCO......... Ashland, OH [*AM radio station call letters*]
WNCO-FM.... Ashland, OH [*FM radio station call letters*]
WNC (PA).... Weekly Notes of Cases [*Pennsylvania*] [*A publication*] (DLA)
WNCQ......... Morristown, NY [*FM radio station call letters*]
WNCQ......... Watertown, NY [*AM radio station call letters*]
WNCR-AM... Fair Bluff, NC [*AM radio station call letters*] (RBYB)
WNCS......... Montpelier, VT [*FM radio station call letters*]
WNCT......... Greenville, NC [*AM radio station call letters*]
WNCT-FM.... Greenville, NC [*FM radio station call letters*]
WNCT-TV..... Greenville, NC [*Television station call letters*]
WNCU......... Durham, NC [*FM radio station call letters*]
WNCV......... Niceville, FL [*FM radio station call letters*]
WNCW......... Spindale, NC [*FM radio station call letters*]
WNCX......... Cleveland, OH [*FM radio station call letters*]
WNCY-FM.... Neenah-Menasha, WI [*FM radio station call letters*] (RBYB)
WND........... Wind (KSC)
WND........... Windham [*New York*] [*Seismograph station code, US Geological Survey*] (SEIS)
WND........... Windmere Corp. [*NYSE symbol*] (SPSG)
WND........... Windmere-Durable Holdings [*NYSE symbol*] [*Formerly, Windmere Corp.*] (SG)
WND........... Wound (MSA)
WNDA......... Huntsville, AL [*FM radio station call letters*]
WNDB......... Daytona Beach, FL [*AM radio station call letters*]
WNDC......... Baton Rouge, LA [*AM radio station call letters*]
WNDC......... Woman's National Democratic Club (EA)
WNDD......... Silver Springs, FL [*FM radio station call letters*] (RBYB)
WNDE......... Indianapolis, IN [*AM radio station call letters*]
WNDH......... Napoleon, OH [*FM radio station call letters*]
WNDI.......... Sullivan, IN [*AM radio station call letters*]
WNDI-FM..... Sullivan, IN [*FM radio station call letters*]
WNDJ.......... White Stone, VA [*FM radio station call letters*]
WNDLS........ Windlass
WNDN......... Salisbury, NC [*FM radio station call letters*]
WNDO......... Weather Network Duty Officer [*Air Force*] (AFM)
WNDP......... With No Down Payment [*Business term*] (WDAA)
WNDR......... Syracuse, NY [*AM radio station call letters*]
WNDR......... Winder
WNDR......... Wonderware Corp. [*NASDAQ symbol*] (SAG)
WNDS......... Derry, NH [*Television station call letters*]
WNDT-FM.... Alachua, FL [*FM radio station call letters*] (RBYB)
WNDU......... South Bend, IN [*AM radio station call letters*]
WNDU-FM... South Bend, IN [*FM radio station call letters*]
WNDU-TV.... South Bend, IN [*Television station call letters*]
wndw.......... Window (VRA)
WNDW......... Window
WNDY......... Crawfordsville, IN [*FM radio station call letters*]
WNDY-TV.... Marion, IN [*Television station call letters*] (RBYB)
WNDZ......... Portage, IN [*AM radio station call letters*]
WNE........... Welsh National Eisteddfod (DAS)
WNE........... Western New England College, Springfield, MA [*OCLC symbol*] (OCLC)
WNE........... West Nile Encephalitis [*Medicine*] (DAVI)
WNEA......... Newnan, GA [*AM radio station call letters*]
WNEB......... Worcester, MA [*AM radio station call letters*]
WNEC......... Henniker, NH [*FM radio station call letters*]
WNEC......... Western New England College [*Springfield, MA*]

WNED .... Buffalo, NY [*AM radio station call letters*]
WNED-FM ..... Buffalo, NY [*FM radio station call letters*]
WNED-TV ..... Buffalo, NY [*Television station call letters*]
WNEG .... Toccoa, GA [*AM radio station call letters*]
WNEG-TV ..... Toccoa, GA [*Television station call letters*]
WNEH .... Greenwood, SC [*Television station call letters*]
WNEK .... Springfield, MA [*FM radio station call letters*]
WNEL .... Caguas, PR [*AM radio station call letters*]
WNeIH .... New London Community Hospital, Health Science Library, New
.... London, WI [*Library symbol Library of Congress*] (LCLS)
WNEM .... Bay City, MI [*Television station call letters*]
WN (Eng).... Weekly Notes of English Law Reports [*A publication*] (DLA)
WNEO .... Alliance, OH [*Television station call letters*]
WNEP .... Scranton, PA [*Television station call letters*]
WNEQ .... Buffalo, NY [*Television station call letters*]
WNES .... Central City, KY [*AM radio station call letters*]
WNET .... Newark, NJ [*Television station call letters*]
WNEW .... New York, NY [*FM radio station call letters*]
WNEX .... Macon, GA [*AM radio station call letters*]
WNEZ .... New Britain, CT [*AM radio station call letters*]
WNF .... Well-Nourished Female [*Medicine*]
WNF .... [*The*] Winfield Railroad Co. [*AAR code*]
WNFA .... Port Huron, MI [*FM radio station call letters*]
WNFB .... Lake City, FL [*FM radio station call letters*]
WNFC .... Willie Nelson Fan Club (EA)
WNFGA .... Woman's National Farm and Garden Association (EA)
WNFK .... Perry, FL [*FM radio station call letters*]
WNFL .... Green Bay, WI [*AM radio station call letters*]
WNFM .... Reedsburg, WI [*FM radio station call letters*]
WNFM .... World Nuclear Fuel Market (NRCH)
WNFO .... Ridgeland, SC [*AM radio station call letters*]
WNFQ .... Newberry, FL [*FM radio station call letters*]
WNFR .... Sandusky, MI [*FM radio station call letters*]
WNFR .... Winifrede Railroad Co. [*AAR code*]
WNFT .... Jacksonville, FL [*Television station call letters*]
WNFZ .... Oak Ridge, TN [*FM radio station call letters*]
WNG .... Wang Laboratories, Inc., Lowell, MA [*OCLC symbol*] (OCLC)
WNG .... Warning (AFM)
WNG .... Washington Natural Gas Co. [*NYSE symbol*] (SPSG)
WNG .... Weighing
WNG .... West New Guinea
WNG .... Wing [*of a ship*] (DS)
WNG .... Wing Airways (Pty) Ltd. [*South Africa ICAO designator*] (FAAC)
WNG .... Wingst [*Federal Republic of Germany*] [*Geomagnetic observatory
.... code*]
WNG .... Wiring (IAA)
WNGA .... Nashville, GA [*AM radio station call letters*]
WNGA .... Wholesale Nursery Growers of America (EA)
WNCC .... Athens, GA [*FM radio station call letters*]
WNGGA .... Welsh National Gymanfa Ganu Association (EA)
WNGM .... Athens, GA [*Television station call letters*]
WNGN .... Hoosick Falls, NY [*FM radio station call letters*]
WNGO .... Mayfield, KY [*AM radio station call letters*]
WNGPr .... Wash Nat'l Gas 7.45%Sr II Pfd [*NYSE symbol*] (TTSB)
WNGPrA ...... Wash Nat'l Gas 8.50%Sr III Pfd [*NYSE symbol*] (TTSB)
WNGS .... Springville, NY [*Television station call letters*]
WNGX .... Fort Ann, NY [*FM radio station call letters*]
WNGZ .... Montour Falls, NY [*FM radio station call letters*]
WNH .... Western National [*NYSE symbol*] (TTSB)
WNH .... Western National Corp. [*NYSE symbol*] (SAG)
WNH .... Whiteface [*New Hampshire*] [*Seismograph station code, US
.... Geological Survey*] (SEIS)
WNHA .... Concord, NH [*AM radio station call letters*]
WNHB .... Lake City, MI [*FM radio station call letters*] (RBYB)
WNHC .... New Haven, CT [*AM radio station call letters*]
WNHI .... Belmont, NH [*FM radio station call letters*]
WNHP.......... Washington Natural Heritage Program [*Washington State Department
.... of Natural Resources*] [*Olympia*] [*Information service or
.... system*] (IID)
WNHP.......... Wyoming Natural Heritage Program [*Wyoming State Department of
.... Environmental Quality*] [*Cheyenne*] [*Information service or
.... system*] (IID)
WNHQ .... Peterborough, NH [*FM radio station call letters*]
WNHU .... West Haven, CT [*FM radio station call letters*]
WNHV .... White River Junction, VT [*AM radio station call letters*]
WNHW .... Nags Head, NC [*FM radio station call letters*]
WNI .... Wang Institute of Graduate Studies, Tyngsboro, MA [*OCLC symbol*]
.... (OCLC)
WNI .... Weider Nutrition Intl'A' [*NYSE symbol*]
WNI .... Windkracht Nederland Information Centre [*Netherlands Wind Energy
.... Information Centre*] [*Nethergy Ltd.*] [*Database producer*] (IID)
WNI .... Women's National Institute [*Defunct*] (EA)
WNIB .... Chicago, IL [*FM radio station call letters*]
WNIC .... Dearborn, MI [*FM radio station call letters*]
WNIC .... Wide Area Network Interface Co-Processor [*Communications
.... adapter*] (PCM)
WNIE-FM ..... Freeport, IL [*FM radio station call letters*] (RBYB)
WNIJ .... Rockford, IL [*FM radio station call letters*]
WNIK .... Arecibo, PR [*AM radio station call letters*]
WNIK-FM ..... Arecibo, PR [*FM radio station call letters*]
WNIL .... Niles, MI [*AM radio station call letters*]
WNIM .... Wide-Area-Network Module [*Telecommunications*]
WNIN .... Evansville, IN [*FM radio station call letters*]
WNINTEL ..... Warning Notice: Sensitive Intelligence Sources and Methods
.... Involved (MCD)

WNIN-TV ..... Evansville, IN [*Television station call letters*]
WNIO .... Niles, OH [*AM radio station call letters*] (RBYB)
WNIQ-FM ..... Sterling, IL [*FM radio station call letters*] (RBYB)
WNIR .... Kent, OH [*FM radio station call letters*]
WNIS .... Norfolk, VA [*AM radio station call letters*]
WNIT .... South Bend, IN [*Television station call letters*]
WNIU .... De Kalb, IL [*FM radio station call letters*]
WNIV .... Atlanta, GA [*AM radio station call letters*]
WNIW-FM ..... LaSalle, IL [*FM radio station call letters*] (RBYB)
WNIX .... Greenville, MS [*AM radio station call letters*]
WNIZ .... Zion, IL [*FM radio station call letters*]
WNJA .... Jamestown, NY [*FM radio station call letters*]
WNJB .... Bridgeton, NJ [*FM radio station call letters*]
WNJB .... New Brunswick, NJ [*Television station call letters*]
WNJC .... Washington Township, NJ [*AM radio station call letters*]
WNJM-FM ..... Manahawkin, NJ [*FM radio station call letters*] (RBYB)
WNJN .... Atlantic City, NJ [*FM radio station call letters*]
WNJN .... Montclair, NJ [*Television station call letters*]
WNJP .... Sussex, NJ [*FM radio station call letters*]
WNJR .... Newark, NJ [*AM radio station call letters*]
WNJS .... Berlin, NJ [*FM radio station call letters*]
WNJS .... Camden, NJ [*Television station call letters*]
WNJT .... Trenton, NJ [*Television station call letters*]
WNJT-FM ..... Trenton, NJ [*FM radio station call letters*]
WNJU .... Linden, NJ [*Television station call letters*]
WNJW .... Franklin Lakes, NJ [*FM radio station call letters*] (RBYB)
WNJX .... Mayaguez, PR [*Television station call letters*]
WNJY .... Delphi, IN [*FM radio station call letters*]
WNJZ-FM ..... Cape May Court House, NJ [*FM radio station call letters*] (RBYB)
WNKC .... Kimberly-Clark Corp., Research and Engineering Library, Neenah, WI
.... [*Library symbol Library of Congress*] (LCLS)
WNKI .... Corning, NY [*FM radio station call letters*]
WNKJ .... Hopkinsville, KY [*FM radio station call letters*]
WNKK-FM ..... Carthage, IL [*FM radio station call letters*] (BROA)
WNKO .... Newark, OH [*FM radio station call letters*]
WNKR .... Williamstown, KY [*FM radio station call letters*]
WNKS-FM ..... Charlotte, NC [*FM radio station call letters*] (RBYB)
WNKU .... Highland Heights, KY [*FM radio station call letters*]
WNKV .... St. Johnsbury, VT [*FM radio station call letters*]
WNKX .... Centerville, TN [*AM radio station call letters*]
WNKX-FM ..... Centerville, TN [*FM radio station call letters*]
WNL .... Nicolet College, Learning Resources Center, Rhinelander, WI [*OCLC
.... symbol*] (OCLC)
WNL .... Waveguide Nitrogen Load
WNL .... Windscale Nuclear Laboratories [*British*] (NUCP)
WNL .... Within Normal Limits [*Medicine*]
WNLA .... Indianola, MS [*AM radio station call letters*]
WNLA .... Witwatersrand Native Labour Association [*Nyasaland*]
WNLA-FM ..... Indianola, MS [*FM radio station call letters*]
WNLC .... New London, CT [*AM radio station call letters*]
WNLE .... Fernadina Beach, FL [*FM radio station call letters*]
WNLK .... Norwalk, CT [*AM radio station call letters*]
WNLL .... Womens's National Loyal League [*Established by Elizabeth Cady
.... Stanton and Susan B. Anthony*]
WNLN .... Western Nigeria Legal Notice [*A publication*] (DLA)
WNLR .... Churchville, VA [*AM radio station call letters*]
WNLR .... Weighted Nonlinear Regression [*Mathematics*]
WNLR .... Western Nigeria Law Reports [*A publication*] (DLA)
WNLS .... Tallahassee, FL [*AM radio station call letters*]
WNLSC .... Women's National Land Service Corps [*World War I*] [*British*]
WNLT .... Harrison, OH [*FM radio station call letters*]
WNM .... Warm Neutral Medium [*Astrophysics*]
WNM .... Washington National Monument
WNM .... Well-Nourished Male [*Medicine*]
WNM .... White Noise Making [*Psychology*]
WNMA .... Washington National Monument Association (EA)
WNMB .... North Myrtle Beach, SC [*FM radio station call letters*]
WNMC .... Traverse City, MI [*FM radio station call letters*]
WNMC .... Weather Network Management Center [*Air Force*] (AFM)
WNMH .... Northfield, MA [*FM radio station call letters*]
WN Misc..... Weekly Notes, Miscellaneous [*A publication*] (DLA)
WNML-AM ..... Warner Robins, GA [*AM radio station call letters*] (BROA)
WNML-FM ..... Gray, GA [*FM radio station call letters*] (BROA)
WNMP .... Westwood Corp. [*NASDAQ symbol*] (SAG)
WNMT .... Garden City, GA [*AM radio station call letters*]
WNMU .... Marquette, MI [*FM radio station call letters*]
WNMU-TV .... Marquette, MI [*Television station call letters*]
WNMX-AM .... Charlotte, NC [*AM radio station call letters*] (RBYB)
WNMX-FM .... Waxhaw, NC [*FM radio station call letters*] (RBYB)
WNN .... World News Network [*In Muriel Dobbin's novel "Going Live"*]
WNNB .... Wayne Bancorp, Inc. [*NASDAQ symbol*] (SAG)
WNNC .... Newton, NC [*AM radio station call letters*]
WNND .... Fuquay Varina, NC [*FM radio station call letters*]
WNNE .... Hartford, VT [*Television station call letters*]
WNNH .... Henniker, NH [*FM radio station call letters*]
WNNI .... Christiansburg, VA [*AM radio station call letters*] (RBYB)
WNNJ .... Newton, NJ [*AM radio station call letters*]
WNNJ-FM ..... Newton, NJ [*FM radio station call letters*]
WNNK .... Harrisburg, PA [*FM radio station call letters*]
WNNN .... Canton, NJ [*FM radio station call letters*]
WNNO .... Wisconsin Dells, WI [*AM radio station call letters*]
WNNO-FM ..... Wisconsin Dells, WI [*FM radio station call letters*]
WNNR .... Sodus, NY [*FM radio station call letters*]
WNNS .... Springfield, IL [*FM radio station call letters*]
WNNT .... Warsaw, VA [*AM radio station call letters*]

WNNT-FM.... Warsaw, VA [FM radio station call letters]
WNNV.......... Aguada, PR [FM radio station call letters]
WNNW......... Salem, NH [AM radio station call letters]
WNNX.......... Atlanta, GA [FM radio station call letters]
WNNZ.......... Westfield, MA [AM radio station call letters]
WNO .... Wa National Organization [Myanmar] [Political party] (EY)
WNO .... Welsh National Opera
WNO .... Wharton & Northern Railroad Co. [Later, WHN] [AAR code]
WNO .... Wrong Number [Telecommunications] (TEL)
WNOE-FM.... New Orleans, LA [FM radio station call letters]
WNOG.......... Naples, FL [AM radio station call letters]
WNOG-FM ... Naples, FL [FM radio station call letters]
WNOI........... Flora, IL [FM radio station call letters]
WNOK.......... Columbia, SC [FM radio station call letters]
WNOL.......... New Orleans, LA [Television station call letters]
WNOO.......... Chattanooga, TN [AM radio station call letters]
WNOP.......... Newport, KY [AM radio station call letters]
WNOR.......... Norfolk, VA [AM radio station call letters]
WNOR-FM ... Norfolk, VA [FM radio station call letters]
WNOS.......... New Bern, NC [AM radio station call letters]
WNOV.......... Milwaukee, WI [AM radio station call letters]
WNOW......... Mint Hill, NC [AM radio station call letters]
WNOX.......... Loudon, TN [FM radio station call letters]
WNOZ.......... Aguadilla, PR [AM radio station call letters]
WNP .... Naga [Phillipines] [Airport symbol] (OAG)
WNP .... Washington Nuclear Plant (NRCH)
WNP .... Waste Neutralization Plant (AAEL)
WNP .... Welsh Nationalist Party (DI)
WNP .... Westland New Post [Terrorist organization] [Belgium] (EY)
WNP .... Will Not Proceed
WNP .... Will Not Process
WNP .... Wire Nonpayment
WNPA.......... Jeannette, PA [Television station call letters] (BROA)
WNPB.......... Morgantown, WV [Television station call letters]
WNPC.......... Newport, TN [AM radio station call letters]
WNPC.......... Women's National Press Club [Later, WPC] (EA)
WNPC-FM.... Newport, TN [FM radio station call letters]
WNPDL........ Windscale Nuclear Power Development Laboratories [British] (NUCP)
WNPE.......... Watertown, NY [Television station call letters]
WNPI........... Norwood, NY [Television station call letters]
WNPL-FM.... Mount Juliet, TN [FM radio station call letters] (RBYB)
WNPQ.......... New Philadelphia, OH [FM radio station call letters]
WNPR.......... Norwich, CT [AM radio station call letters]
WNPT.......... Linden, AL [FM radio station call letters]
WNPV.......... Lansdale, PA [AM radio station call letters]
WNPW......... Wide, Notched P Wave [Cardiology]
WNQM......... Nashville, TN [AM radio station call letters]
WNR .... Weapons Neutron Research Facility [Los Alamos]
WNR .... Western NORAD Region
WNR .... Windorah [Australia Airport symbol] (OAG)
WNR .... World New Religion [An association] (EA)
WNRB.......... Boston, MA [AM radio station call letters] (RBYB)
WNRC.......... Dudley, MA [FM radio station call letters]
WNRC.......... Washington National Records Center [GSA] (AABC)
WNRC.......... Women's National Republican Club (EA)
WNRCEN...... Washington National Records Center [GSA]
WNRE.......... Whiteshell Nuclear Research Establishment [Atomic Energy of Canada Ltd.] [Research center]
WNRG.......... Grundy, VA [AM radio station call letters]
WNRI........... Woonsocket, RI [AM radio station call letters]
WNRJ.......... Circleville, OH [AM radio station call letters]
WNRK.......... Newark, DE [AM radio station call letters]
WNRM......... Women in Natural Resources Management Program (EERA)
WNRN-FM ... Charlottesville, VA [FM radio station call letters] (RBYB)
WNRQ.......... Pittsburgh, PA [FM radio station call letters] (RBYB)
WNRR.......... Bellevue, OH [FM radio station call letters]
WNRS.......... Herkimer, NY [AM radio station call letters]
WNRT.......... Manati, PR [FM radio station call letters]
WNRV.......... Narrows, VA [AM radio station call letters]
WNRX.......... Tupelo, MS [AM radio station call letters] (RBYB)
WNRZ-FM.... Dickson, TN [FM radio station call letters] (RBYB)
WNS .... Nawab Shah [Pakistan] [Airport symbol] (OAG)
WNS .... Wicks'N Sticks (EFIS)
WNS .... Women's News Service
WNS .... Worldwide News Service. Jewish Telegraphic Agency (BJA)
WNS .... Wren Resources Ltd. [Vancouver Stock Exchange symbol]
WNSA.......... Woman's National Sabbath Alliance [Defunct]
WNSB.......... Norfolk, VA [FM radio station call letters]
WNSC.......... Rock Hill, SC [FM radio station call letters]
wnsct.......... Wainscot (VRA)
WNSC-TV.... Rock Hill, SC [Television station call letters]
WNSEA........ Wood Naval Stores Export Association
WNSH.......... Beverly, MA [AM radio station call letters]
WNSI-AM.... Jacksonville, AL [AM radio station call letters] (RBYB)
WNSL .... A. W. Wright Nuclear Structure Laboratory [Yale University] [Research center] (RCD)
WNSL .... Laurel, MS [FM radio station call letters]
WNSN.......... South Bend, IN [FM radio station call letters]
WNSP.......... Bay Minette, AL [FM radio station call letters]
WNSR.......... Nashville, IL [FM radio station call letters]
WNSR.......... West Nova Scotia Regiment (DMA)
WNSS-AM.... Syracuse, NY [AM radio station call letters] (RBYB)
WNST.......... Moncks Corner, SC [AM radio station call letters] (RBYB)
WNSV-FM.... Nashville, IL [FM radio station call letters] (BROA)
WNSW......... Brewer, ME [AM radio station call letters]

WNSX-FM.... Poughkeepsie, NY [FM radio station call letters] (RBYB)
WNT........... Washington National [NYSE symbol] (TTSB)
WNT........... Washington National Corp. [NYSE symbol] (SPSG)
Wn T........... Washington Territory Reports [1854-88] [A publication] (ILCA)
WNT........... Waste Neutralization Tank [Nuclear energy] (NRCH)
WNT........... What's New in Travel [CompuServe Information Service] [Information service or system] (CRD)
WNT........... World News Tonight [Television program]
WNTA.......... Rockford, IL [AM radio station call letters]
WNTC.......... Chandler, IN [FM radio station call letters]
WNTC.......... Theda Clark Memorial Hospital, Neenah, WI [Library symbol Library of Congress] (LCLS)
WNTE.......... Mansfield, PA [FM radio station call letters]
WNTF.......... Western Naval Task Force [Navy]
WNTH.......... Winnetka, IL [FM radio station call letters]
WNTI........... Hackettstown, NJ [FM radio station call letters]
WNTJ.......... Johnstown, PA [AM radio station call letters]
WNTK.......... New London, NH [FM radio station call letters]
WNTK.......... Newport, NH [AM radio station call letters]
WNTL.......... Indian Head, MD [AM radio station call letters]
WNTM......... Mobile, AL [AM radio station call letters]
WNTN......... Newton, MA [AM radio station call letters]
WNTO-TV.... Daytona Beach, FL [TV station call letters] (RBYB)
WNTPr........ Washington Natl $2.50 Cv Pfd [NYSE symbol] (TTSB)
WNTQ......... Syracuse, NY [FM radio station call letters]
WNTR.......... Cumberland, MD [AM radio station call letters]
WNTS.......... Beach Grove, IN [AM radio station call letters]
WNTT.......... Tazewell, TN [AM radio station call letters]
WNTV.......... Greenville, SC [Television station call letters]
WNTW......... Winchester, VA [AM radio station call letters]
WNTX.......... Allegan, MI [FM radio station call letters] (RBYB)
WNTY.......... Southington, CT [AM radio station call letters]
WNTZ.......... Natchez, MS [Television station call letters]
WNU .... Western Newspaper Union
WNUA.......... Chicago, IL [FM radio station call letters]
WNUB.......... Northfield, VT [FM radio station call letters]
WNUC.......... Wethersfield Township, NY [FM radio station call letters]
WNUR.......... Evanston, IL [FM radio station call letters]
WNUS.......... Belpre, OH [FM radio station call letters]
WNUT.......... Walnut Financial Services [NASDAQ symbol] (TTSB)
WNUT.......... Walnut Financial Services, Inc. [NASDAQ symbol] (SAG)
WNUU.......... Garrison, KY [FM radio station call letters]
WNUV.......... Baltimore, MD [Television station call letters]
WNUY.......... Bluffton, IN [FM radio station call letters]
WNUZ.......... Talladega, AL [AM radio station call letters]
WNV .... Wehrmachtnachrichtenverbindungen [Armed Forces Signal Communications] [German military - World War II]
WNV .... West Nile Virus
WNVA.......... Norton, VA [AM radio station call letters]
WNVA-FM.... Norton, VA [FM radio station call letters]
WNVC.......... Fairfax, VA [Television station call letters]
WNVE.......... South Bristol Township, NY [FM radio station call letters] (RBYB)
WNVL.......... Nicholasville, KY [AM radio station call letters]
WNVR.......... Vernon Hills, IL [AM radio station call letters]
WNVT.......... Goldvein, VA [Television station call letters]
WNVY.......... Cantonment, FL [AM radio station call letters]
WNVZ.......... Norfolk, VA [FM radio station call letters]
WNW .... Superior Public Library, Superior, WI [OCLC symbol] (OCLC)
WNW .... Wenatchee [Washington] [Seismograph station code, US Geological Survey] (SEIS)
WNW .... West by North West [Direction] (EERA)
WNW .... West-Northwest
WNW .... Wingwork Aviation [British ICAO designator] (FAAC)
WNWC.......... Madison, WI [FM radio station call letters]
WNWI.......... Valparaiso, IN [AM radio station call letters]
WNWK.......... Newark, NJ [FM radio station call letters]
WNWN......... Coldwater, MI [FM radio station call letters]
WNWN......... Portage, MI [AM radio station call letters] (RBYB)
WNWO......... Toledo, OH [Television station call letters]
WNWR.......... Philadelphia, PA [AM radio station call letters] (RBYB)
WNWS.......... Brownsville, TN [AM radio station call letters]
WNWS.......... Jackson, TN [FM radio station call letters]
WnWste........ Western Waste Industries [Associated Press] (SAG)
WNWV......... Elyria, OH [FM radio station call letters]
WNWWD...... West-Northwestward (FAAC)
WNWZ......... Germantown, TN [AM radio station call letters]
WNXR.......... Iron River, WI [FM radio station call letters] (RBYB)
WNXT.......... Portsmouth, OH [AM radio station call letters]
WNXT-FM .... Portsmouth, OH [FM radio station call letters]
WNY .... Burnie-Wynward [Tasmania] [Airport symbol] (AD)
WNY .... Washington [DC] Naval Yard
WNY .... Wilmington [New York] [Seismograph station code, US Geological Survey] (SEIS)
WNY .... Wynyard [Australia Airport symbol] (OAG)
WNYAC........ Western New York Athletic Conference (PSS)
WNYB.......... Buffalo, NY [Television station call letters]
WNYC.......... New York, NY [AM radio station call letters]
WNYC-FM.... New York, NY [FM radio station call letters]
WNYC-TV.... New York, NY [Television station call letters]
WNYE.......... New York, NY [FM radio station call letters]
WNYE-TV.... New York, NY [Television station call letters]
WNYG.......... Babylon, NY [AM radio station call letters]
WNYHSL...... Western New York Health Science Librarians [Library network]
WNYK.......... Nyack, NY [FM radio station call letters]

WNYLRC......	Western New York Library Resources Council [*Buffalo, NY*] [*Library network*]
WNYNRC	Western New York Nuclear Research Center Reactor (NRCH)
WNYO..........	Oswego, NY [*FM radio station call letters*]
WNYO-TV.....	Buffalo, NY [*TV station call letters*] (RBYB)
WNYQ-FM....	Queensbury, NY [*FM radio station call letters*] (RBYB)
WNYR..........	Waterloo, NY [*FM radio station call letters*]
WNYS..........	Canton, NY [*AM radio station call letters*]
WNYS..........	Syracuse, NY [*Television station call letters*]
WNYT..........	Albany, NY [*Television station call letters*]
WNYU..........	New York, NY [*FM radio station call letters*]
WNYV..........	Whitehall, NY [*FM radio station call letters*]
WNYW.........	New York, NY [*Television station call letters*]
WNZ............	Wairakei [*New Zealand*] [*Seismograph station code, US Geological Survey*] (SEIS)
WNZE..........	Largo, FL [*AM radio station call letters*]
WNZK..........	Dearborn Heights, MI [*AM radio station call letters*]
WNZN..........	Lorain, OH [*FM radio station call letters*]
WNZR..........	Mount Vernon, OH [*FM radio station call letters*]
WNZS..........	Jacksonville, FL [*AM radio station call letters*]
WNZT..........	Columbia, PA [*AM radio station call letters*]
WNZZ-AM	Montgomery, AL [*AM radio station call letters*] (RBYB)
WO..............	Wait Order
WO..............	Walkover
WO..............	Walter Owen Bentley [*Automotive engineer*] [*British*]
WO..............	Warning Order
WO..............	War Office [*British*]
WO..............	War Orientation [*Navy*]
WO..............	Warrant Officer [*Usually in combination with numbers to denote serviceman's grade*] [*Military*]
WO..............	Washington Office (FAAC)
WO..............	Wash Out [*Medicine*]
W/O............	Water-dispersed-in-Oil [*emulsion*]
W/O............	Water-in-Oil
WO..............	Water Officer (WDAA)
WO..............	Water Outlet Gasket [*Automotive engineering*]
WO..............	Weber-Osler [*Syndrome*] [*Medicine*] (DB)
w/o.............	Week Of (WDMC)
WO..............	Weeks Old [*Preceded by a number*] [*Neonatology*] (DAVI)
wo..............	Weeks Old [*Medicine*] (MEDA)
W/O............	Weight Percent (SAA)
WO..............	Welfare Officer [*British military*] (DMA)
WO..............	Welsh Office (DCTA)
WO..............	Western Operation
W/O............	West Of [*In outdoor advertising*] (WDMC)
WO..............	White Oval [*on Jupiter*]
WO..............	Wind Offset
WO..............	Wipe Out (MSA)
WO..............	Wireless Operator
WO..............	Without (AFM)
w/o.............	Without (IDOE)
wo..............	Wollastonite [*CIPW classification*] [*Geology*]
WO..............	Women
WO..............	Women Outdoors (EA)
WO..............	Women's Reserve, Ordnance Duties [*USNR officer designation*]
WO..............	Woodfree Off-Machine Paper (DGA)
W/O............	Worked Off (DGA)
WO..............	Working Overseer (ADA)
WO..............	Work Order
WO..............	World Airways [*ICAO designator*] (AD)
W/O............	Write-Off [*Accounting*]
WO..............	Write Once [*Computer science*] (CDE)
WO..............	Write Only
WO..............	Write Out
WO..............	Writer Officer [*British military*] (DMA)
WO..............	Written Off (WDAA)
W/O............	Written Order [*Medicine*]
WO1............	Warrant Officer One [*Army*]
WO3DC.......	World Ozone Data Center [*Marine science*] (OSRA)
WOA	Warrant Officers Association of the United States of America [*Defunct*] (EA)
WOA	Washington Office on Africa (EA)
WOA	Weapons Orientation Advanced (AFM)
WOA	Web Offset Association (EA)
WOA	Weight of Authority [*Legal shorthand*] (LWAP)
WOA	Work Order Authorization (MCD)
WOA	World Airways, Inc. [*ICAO designator*] (FAAC)
WOA	WorldCorp., Inc. [*NYSE symbol*] (SPSG)
WOAB.........	Ozark, AL [*FM radio station call letters*]
WOAC.........	Canton, OH [*Television station call letters*]
WOAC.........	Warrant Officer Advanced Course [*Army*] (INF)
WOAD.........	Jackson, MS [*AM radio station call letters*]
WOAD.........	World Offshore Accident Data
WOAH.........	World Organisation for Animal Health (WDAA)
WOAH.........	World Organization of Automotive Hobbyists
WOAI..........	San Antonio, TX [*AM radio station call letters*]
WOAK.........	La Grange, GA [*FM radio station call letters*]
WOAL.........	Pippa Passes, KY [*FM radio station call letters*]
WOAM........	Peoria, IL [*AM radio station call letters*]
WO & HPS...	Wall Oven and Hot Plates [*Classified advertising*] (ADA)
WOAP.........	Owosso, MI [*AM radio station call letters*]
WOA/PIA.....	Web Offset Association of Printing Industries of America (NTPA)
WOAR.........	Women Organized Against Rape
WOAS.........	Ontonagon, MI [*FM radio station call letters*]
WOAS.........	Wave-Off Advisory System [*Aircraft carrier*] [*Navy*]

WOASH........	Women Organised Against Sexual Harassment [*British*] (DI)
WOAY.........	Oak Hill, WV [*AM radio station call letters*]
WOAY-TV.....	Oak Hill, WV [*Television station call letters*]
WOAZ-FM....	Lowell, MA [*FM radio station call letters*] (RBYB)
WOB	Walter Owen Bentley [*Automotive engineer*] [*British*]
WOB	Washed Overboard [*Shipping*]
WOB	Weight on Bit [*Drilling technology*]
WOB	White on Black (DGA)
WOB	Without Optical Brightener [*Biochemistry*]
WOB	Woburn [*Parish in England*]
WOB	Work of Breathing [*Medicine*] (DAVI)
WOB	Work Order Bin (MCD)
WOBB.........	Tifton, GA [*FM radio station call letters*]
WOBC.........	Oberlin, OH [*FM radio station call letters*]
WOBC.........	Waveguide Operating below Cutoff
WOBG.........	Clarksburg, WV [*AM radio station call letters*]
WOBG.........	Salem, WV [*FM radio station call letters*]
WOBL.........	Oberlin, OH [*AM radio station call letters*]
WOBM........	Lakewood, NJ [*AM radio station call letters*]
WOBM........	Toms River, NJ [*FM radio station call letters*]
WOBN.........	Westerville, OH [*FM radio station call letters*]
W O BNDR...	Without Binder [*Freight*]
WOBO.........	Batavia, OH [*FM radio station call letters*]
W/OBO........	Without Blowout (MSA)
WOBO.........	World Bottle [*Ecology*]
WOBO.........	World Organization of Building Officials (EA)
WOBR.........	Wanchese, NC [*AM radio station call letters*]
WOBR-FM....	Wanchese, NC [*FM radio station call letters*]
WOBS-AM....	Jacksonville, FL [*AM radio station call letters*] (RBYB)
WOBT	Rhinelander, WI [*AM radio station call letters*]
WOC	Davenport, IA [*AM radio station call letters*]
WOC	Waiting on Cement
WOC	Water-Oil Contact
WOC	Wilshire Oil Co. of Texas [*NYSE symbol*] (SPSG)
WOC	Wilshire Oil Texas [*NYSE symbol*] (TTSB)
WOC	Wing Operations Center (CINC)
WOC	Win Over Communism [*A fund-raising subsidiary of the Unification Church*]
WOC	Without Compensation (ADA)
woc	Without Compensation (ODBW)
WOC	Women's Ordination Conference (EA)
WOC	Woodfree Off-Machine Coated Paper (DGA)
WOC	Woodfree Offset Cartridge Paper (DGA)
WOC	Wood's Oriental Cases [*Malaya*] [*A publication*] (DLA)
WOC	Work and Occupations [*A publication*] (BRI)
WOC	Work Order Control (MCD)
WOC	World Oceanographic Center (MSC)
WOCA.........	Ocala, FL [*AM radio station call letters*]
WOCA.........	Who Owns Corporate America [*A publication*]
WOCA.........	World Outside Centrally Planned Economic Area [*Nuclear energy*] (NUCP)
WOCA.........	World Outside Communist Areas
WOCAR.......	Aviation Warrant Officer Career Course [*Army*]
WOCC.........	Corydon, IN [*AM radio station call letters*]
WOCC.........	Worldwide Operations Control Center [*United States Information Agency*]
WOCCI........	War Office Central Card Index [*British military*] (DMA)
WOccM.......	Memorial Hospital at Oconomowoc, Oconomowoc, WI [*Library symbol Library of Congress*] (LCLS)
WOccR........	Redemptionist Seminary, Oconomowoc, WI [*Library symbol Library of Congress*] (LCLS)
WOCCU.......	World Council of Credit Unions [*Madison, WI*] (EA)
WOCD.........	Amsterdam, NY [*Television station call letters*]
WOCE	World Ocean Circulation Experiment [*World Climate Research Programme*]
WOCE-IPO ...	WOCE [*World Ocean Circulation Experiment*] International Project Office [*Marine science*] (OSRA)
WOCE-NEG...	WOCE [*World Ocean Circulation Experiment*] Numerical Experimentation Group [*Marine science*] (OSRA)
WOCE-SSG...	WOCE [*World Ocean Circulation Experiment*] Scientific Steering Group [*Marine science*] (OSRA)
WOCG.........	Huntsville, AL [*FM radio station call letters*]
WOCIT........	We Oppose Computers in Tournaments [*A chess players' group, formed in 1983*]
WOCL.........	De Land, FL [*FM radio station call letters*]
WOCL.........	War Office Casualty List [*British military*] (DMA)
WOCLS.......	World Ocean and Cruise Liner Society (EA)
WOCMDC....	Warrant Officer Candidate Military Development Course
WOCN.........	Miami, FL [*AM radio station call letters*]
WOCN.........	South Yarmouth, MA [*FM radio station call letters*]
WOCN.........	Wound, Ostomy, and Continence Nurses Society (NTPA)
WOCN.........	Wound, Ostomy and Continence Nurses Society: An Association of E.T. Nurses (EA)
WOCO.........	Oconto, WI [*AM radio station call letters*]
WOCO.........	World Council of Service Clubs [*New Zealand*] (EAIO)
WOCO.........	World Council of Young Men's Service Clubs (EA)
WOCO-FM....	Oconto, WI [*FM radio station call letters*]
WOCP.........	World Organization of China Painters (EA)
WOCPP.......	Women of Color Partnership Program (EA)
WOCQ.........	Berlin, MD [*FM radio station call letters*]
WOCR.........	Olivet, MI [*FM radio station call letters*]
WOCS.........	Work Order Control System (MCD)
WOCT.........	Baltimore, MD [*FM radio station call letters*]
WOCT.........	WAC [*Women's Army Corps*] Officer Candidate Test (AABC)
WOCU.........	War on Community Ugliness [*Program*] [*Defunct*] (EA)

WOCV .... Oneida, TN [*AM radio station call letters*]
WOCW .... Parris Island, SC [*FM radio station call letters*]
WOD .... Washington & Old Dominion R. R. [*AAR code*]
WOD .... Wind over Deck (MCD)
WOD .... Without Dependents [*Military*] (AFM)
WOD .... Woodgate Air Services [*British ICAO designator*] (FAAC)
WODA .... World Organization of Dredging Associations (EA)
WODADIBOF... Workshop on the Determination of Anti-Epileptic Drugs in Body Fluids
WODC .... Virginia Beach, VA [*FM radio station call letters*]
WODC .... Women's Olympic Distance Committee [*Later, WDC*] (EA)
WODC .... World Ozone Data Center [*Marine science*] (OSRA)
WODC .... World Ozone Data Centre (EERA)
WODCON ..... World Dredging Conference
WODCON ..... World Organization of Dredging Associations Proceedings of World Dredging Congress [*A publication*] (EAAP)
WODD .... Wave-Off Decision Device (MCD)
WODD .... World Oceanographic Data Display
WODDIN ...... Worldwide On-Line Data and Document Intelligence System
WODE .... Easton, PA [*FM radio station call letters*]
WODECO...... Western Offshore Drilling & Exploration Co.
WODI-AM .... Brookneal, VA [*AM radio station call letters*] (RBYB)
WODJ .... Greenville, MI [*FM radio station call letters*]
WODL .... Birmingham, AL [*FM radio station call letters*]
WODS .... Boston, MA [*FM radio station call letters*]
WODT .... New Orleans, LA [*AM radio station call letters*] (RBYB)
WODX .... Marco Island, FL [*AM radio station call letters*]
WODY .... Fieldale, VA [*AM radio station call letters*]
WODZ .... Rome, NY [*AM radio station call letters*]
WODZ-FM .... Rome, NY [*FM radio station call letters*]
WOE .... Warhead Output Evaluation (MCD)
WOE .... Watchdogs on Environment
WOE .... Weapon Optical Effects
WOE .... Withdrawal of Enthusiasm [*Airline pilots objection to "Welcome aboard" talks*]
WOE .... Without Enclosure (MCD)
WOE .... Without Equipment
WOE .... Wound of Entry [*Medicine*]
W/OE & SP... Without Equipment and Spare Parts
WOEC .... Warrant Officer Entry Course [*Military*] (INF)
WOEC-RC ... Warrant Office Entry Course, Reserve Component [*Army*] (INF)
WOED .... Welsh Office Education Department (DET)
WOEG-AM.... Hazlehurst, MS [*AM radio station call letters*] (BROA)
WOEI .... Union City, IN [*FM radio station call letters*]
WOEL .... Elkton, MD [*FM radio station call letters*]
Woerner Adm'n... Woerner's Treatise on the American Law of Administration [*A publication*] (DLA)
WOES .... Ovid-Elsie, MI [*FM radio station call letters*]
WOES .... Warrant Officer Education System
WOF .... Walk on Floor [*Ataxia*]
WOF .... Warmed-Over Flavor [*Food technology*]
WOF .... Widowed Oriental Female [*Classified advertising*]
WOF .... Work of Fracture [*Ceramic property*]
W of A .... [*The*] Western Railway of Alabama
WOFA .... Westinghouse Optimized Fuel Assembly [*Nuclear energy*] (NRCH)
WOFC .... Western Ohio Film Circuit [*Library network*]
WOFC .... Western Ohio Financial Corp. [*NASDAQ symbol*] (SAG)
WOFC .... Western Ohio Finl [*NASDAQ symbol*] (TTSB)
WOFE .... Rockwood, TN [*AM radio station call letters*]
WOFE-FM .... Rockwood, TN [*FM radio station call letters*]
WOFF .... Weight of Fuel Flow (MCD)
WOFI .... Wood Office Furniture Institute (EA)
WOFIWU ...... World Federation of Industrial Workers' Unions
WOFL .... Orlando, FL [*Television station call letters*]
WOFL .... Wound Fluid [*Emergency Medicine*] (DAVI)
WOFM .... Mosinee, WI [*FM radio station call letters*]
WOFN-FM .... Beach City, OH [*FM radio station call letters*] (BROA)
WOFP .... Wearout Failure Period
WOFR .... Washington Court House, OH [*AM radio station call letters*]
WOFS .... Weather Observing and Forecasting System [*Air Force*] (MCD)
WOFT .... Warrant Officer Flight Training [*Army*] (INF)
W O FTTNGS... Without Fittings [*Freight*]
WOFX .... Fairfield, OH [*FM radio station call letters*]
WOG .... Water-Oil-Gas (AAG)
WOG .... Water, Oil, Gas Rating [*Environmental science*] (COE)
WOG .... Weapon Order Generation [*Military*] (CAAL)
WOG .... Werner Oil & Gas Co. [*Vancouver Stock Exchange symbol*]
WOG .... Westernized Oriental Gentleman [*Singapore term for native following Western fashions*] [*Other translations include "Wily Oriental Gentleman" and "Wonderful Oriental Gentleman"*]
WOG .... With Other Goods [*Business term*]
wog .... With Other Goods (ODBW)
WOG .... Work Order Generator [*Military*]
WOG .... World Organization of Gastroenterology [*See also OMGE*] [*Edinburgh, Scotland*] (EAIO)
WOG .... Wrath of God [*Israeli counterterrorist group*]
WOGA .... Western Oil and Gas Association (EA)
WOGB-FM.... Kaukauna, WI [*AM radio station call letters*] (RBYB)
WOGK .... Ocala, FL [*FM radio station call letters*]
WOGL .... Philadelphia, PA [*FM radio station call letters*]
WOGO .... Hallie, WI [*AM radio station call letters*]
WOGR .... Charlotte, NC [*AM radio station call letters*]
WOGR-FM ... Salisbury, NC [*FM radio station call letters*] (RBYB)
WOGS .... Wrath of God Syndrome

WOGSC........ World Organisation of General Systems and Cybernetics [*Lytham St. Annes, Lancashiro, England*] (EAIO)
WOGT .... East Ridge, TN [*FM radio station call letters*]
WOGX .... Ocala, FL [*Television station call letters*]
WOGY .... Germantown, TN [*FM radio station call letters*]
WOH .... War on Hunger [*Program*] (EA)
WOH .... Washington Office on Haiti (EA)
WOH .... Western Oklahoma Herbarium [*Southwest Oklahoma State University*]
WOH .... Wings of Hope [*An association*] (EA)
WOH .... Work on Hand [*Insurance*]
WOHC .... Chillicothe, OH [*FM radio station call letters*]
WOHC .... Warrant Officer Hospital Corps
WOHELO ...... Work, Health, Love [*Camp Fire Girls slogan*]
WOHH .... Women's Organization of Hapoel Hamizrachi [*Later, EWA*] (EA)
WOHI .... East Liverpool, OH [*AM radio station call letters*]
WOHMA .... Waste Oil Heating Manufacturers Association (EA)
WOHP .... Portsmouth, OH [*FM radio station call letters*]
WOHP .... World Organization for Human Potential (EA)
WOHRC....... Women's Occupational Health Resource Center (EA)
WOHS .... Shelby, NC [*AM radio station call letters*]
WOHT .... Drew, MS [*FM radio station call letters*] (RBYB)
WOHZ .... Wheeling, WV [*AM radio station call letters*] (RBYB)
WOI .... Ames, IA [*AM radio station call letters*]
WOI .... Wealth of India [*A publication*]
WOI .... World of Invention [*A publication*]
WOI .... World Opportunities International (EA)
WOIC .... Columbia, SC [*AM radio station call letters*]
WOICE .... World Catalog of International Chemical Equipment [*A publication*]
WOI-FM .... Ames, IA [*FM radio station call letters*]
WOIO .... Shaker Heights, OH [*Television station call letters*]
WOIR .... Homestead, FL [*AM radio station call letters*]
WOIS .... Worn Out in Service [*Military*]
WOI-TV .... Ames, IA [*Television station call letters*]
WOIZ .... Guayanilla, PR [*AM radio station call letters*]
WOJAC .... World Organization for Jews from Arab Countries (EA)
WOJB .... Reserve, WI [*FM radio station call letters*]
WOJC .... Willys Overland Jeepster Club (EA)
WOJD .... World Organization of Jewish Deaf [*Tel Aviv, Israel*] (EAIO)
WOJG .... Bolivar, TN [*FM radio station call letters*]
WOJG .... Warrant Officer Junior Grade
WOJO .... Evanston, IL [*FM radio station call letters*]
WOJY .... Hampton, VA [*AM radio station call letters*]
WOK .... Kovar Air [*Czechoslovakia*] [*ICAO designator*] (FAAC)
WOK .... Wiener Oeffentlicher Kueche [*Viennese Open Kitchen*] [*Nonprofit temperance restaurant chain*] [*Austria*]
WOK .... Wokingham [*Municipal borough in England*]
WOK .... Wonken [*Venezuela*] [*Airport symbol*] (OAG)
WOKA .... Douglas, GA [*AM radio station call letters*]
WOKA-FM .... Douglas, GA [*FM radio station call letters*]
WOKB .... Winter Garden, FL [*AM radio station call letters*]
WOKC .... Okeechobee, FL [*AM radio station call letters*]
WOKD-FM .... Danville, VA [*FM radio station call letters*] (BROA)
WOKE-FM .... Garrison, KY [*FM radio station call letters*] (BROA)
WOKF .... Folkston, GA [*FM radio station call letters*]
WOKH .... Bardstown, KY [*FM radio station call letters*]
WOKI .... Oak Ridge, TN [*FM radio station call letters*]
WOKK .... Meridian, MS [*FM radio station call letters*]
WOKN .... Southport, NY [*FM radio station call letters*]
WOKO .... Burlington, VT [*FM radio station call letters*]
WOKQ .... Dover, NH [*FM radio station call letters*]
WOKR .... Rochester, NY [*Television station call letters*]
WOKR .... Willys-Overland-Knight Registry (EA)
WOKS .... Columbus, GA [*AM radio station call letters*]
WOKT .... Cannonsburg, KY [*AM radio station call letters*]
WOKU-AM ... Hurricane, WV [*AM radio station call letters*] (RBYB)
WOKV .... Jacksonville, FL [*AM radio station call letters*]
WOKW .... Curwensville, PA [*FM radio station call letters*]
WOKX .... High Point, NC [*AM radio station call letters*]
WOKY .... Milwaukee, WI [*AM radio station call letters*]
WOKZ-FM .... Fairfield, IL [*FM radio station call letters*] (RBYB)
WOL .... Wainoco Oil [*NYSE symbol*] (TTSB)
WOL .... Wainoco Oil Corp. [*NYSE symbol*] (SPSG)
WOL .... War-Office Letter [*An order or an instruction*] [*British*]
WOL .... Washington, DC [*AM radio station call letters*]
WOL .... Wedge Opening Load
WOL .... Wharf Owner's Liability [*Insurance*]
WOL .... Wings Aviation Ltd. [*Guyana*] [*FAA designator*] (FAAC)
WOL .... Wiretap Online Library [*Online database*]
WoI .... Wolcott's Chancery Reports [*7 Delaware*] [*A publication*] (DLA)
WoI .... Wollaston's English Bail Court Reports [*A publication*] (DLA)
WOL .... Wollongong [*Australia Airport symbol*]
wol .... Wolof [*MARC language code Library of Congress*] (LCCP)
WOL .... Wolverton [*England*] [*Seismograph station code, US Geological Survey*] (SEIS)
WOLA .... Barranquitas, PR [*AM radio station call letters*]
WOLA .... Washington Office on Latin America (EA)
WOLAP .... Workplace Optimization and Layout Planning (MHDB)
WOLB .... Baltimore, MD [*AM radio station call letters*]
WOLC .... Princess Anne, MD [*FM radio station call letters*]
WOLD .... Marion, VA [*AM radio station call letters*]
WOLD-FM .... Marion, VA [*FM radio station call letters*]
WOLE .... Aguadilla, PR [*Television station call letters*]
WOLF .... Committee for Wildlife on the Last Frontier
WOLF .... Scranton, PA [*Television station call letters*]

WOLF.......... Syracuse, NY [*AM radio station call letters*]
WOLF.......... Wash-Off Line Film (DGA)
WOLF.......... Wayne Oakland Library Federation [*Library network*]
WOLF.......... Work Order Load Forecast (MCD)
Wolf & B .... Wolferstan and Bristow's English Election Cases [*1859-65*] [*A publication*] (DLA)
Wolf & D ..... Wolferstan and Dew's English Election Cases [*1856-58*] [*A publication*] (DLA)
WolfHB ...... Wolf [*Howard B.*], Inc. [*Associated Press*] (SAG)
WOLI-FM ..... Easley, SC [*FM radio station call letters*] (RBYB)
WOLL.......... Riviera Beach, FL [*FM radio station call letters*]
Woll .... Wollaston's English Bail Court Reports, Practice Cases [*1840-41*] [*A publication*] (DLA)
Woll BC ...... Wollaston's English Bail Court Reports [*A publication*] (DLA)
WOLN .... Olean, NY [*FM radio station call letters*]
WOLO .... Columbia, SC [*Television station call letters*]
Wolohn .... Wolohan Lumber Co. [*Associated Press*] (SAG)
WOLR .... Lake City, FL [*FM radio station call letters*]
WOLS .... Florence, SC [*AM radio station call letters*]
WOLV .... Houghton, MI [*FM radio station call letters*]
WOLV .... Wolverton [*Urban district in England*]
WOLVES ...... Wireless Operationally Linked Electronic and Video Exploration System
WolvTub ..... Wolverine Tube, Inc. [*Associated Press*] (SAG)
WolvWW...... Wolverine World-Wide, Inc. [*Associated Press*] (SAG)
WOLW .... Cadillac, MI [*FM radio station call letters*]
Wolw .... Woolworth [*F.W.*] Corp. [*Wall Street slang name: "Five & Dime"*] [*Associated Press*] (SAG)
Wolwth .... Woolworth [*F.W.*] Corp. [*Wall Street slang name: "Five & Dime"*] [*Associated Press*] (SAG)
WOLX .... Baraboo, WI [*FM radio station call letters*]
WOLY .... Battle Creek, MI [*AM radio station call letters*]
WOLZ.......... Fort Myers, FL [*FM radio station call letters*]
WOM .... Weapons Output Makeup
WOM .... Wideband Optical Modulation
WOM .... Widowed Oriental Male [*Classified advertising*]
WOM .... Wireless Operator Mechanic [*British*] (DSUE)
WOM .... Wise Old Men [*Term used to refer to group of US statesmen including Dean Acheson, Charles Bohlen, Averell Harriman, George Kennan, Robert Lovett, and John McCloy*]
WOM .... Woomera [*Australia*] (BARN)
WOM .... Word-of-Mouth (WDMC)
WOM .... Write Circuit for Queuing Messages [*Computer science*] (IAA)
WOM .... Write-Only Memory [*Computer science*]
WOM .... Write Optional Memory (IEEE)
WOMAD ...... World of Music, Arts, and Dance [*Festival*] (PCM)
WOMAN...... World Organization of Mothers of All Nations
Woman Offend Rep... Woman Offender Report [*A publication*] (DLA)
Woman's J... Woman's Journal [*A publication*]
WOMB .... Courtney Foundation for the Welfare of Mother and Babies [*British*]
WOMBAT ..... Waste of Money, Brains, and Time (NHD)
WOMBAT ..... Waves on Magnetised Beams and Turbulence
WOMBAT ..... Waves on Magnetized Beams and Turbulence [*Physics*] (ADA)
WOMC .... Detroit, MI [*FM radio station call letters*]
WOMC .... Woodfree Off-Machine Coated Paper (DGA)
WOMCB ...... Woodfree Off-Machine Coated Board Paper (DGA)
WOMEN ...... Women's Organization for Mentoring, Education and Networking Unlimited, Inc.
Women Labour Conf Pap... Women and Labour Conference. Papers [*A publication*]
Women L Jour... Women's Law Journal [*A publication*] (DLA)
Women's LJ... Women's Law Journal [*A publication*] (DLA)
Women's L Rptr... Women's Law Reporter [*A publication*] (DLA)
Women's Rights L Reptr... Women's Rights Law Reporter [*A publication*] (ILCA)
WOMG-FM... Columbia, SC [*FM radio station call letters*]
WOMI .... Owensboro, KY [*AM radio station call letters*]
WOMJEP...... [*A*] Woman in Jeopardy [*Screenwriter's lexicon*]
WOMP .... Bellaire, OH [*AM radio station call letters*]
WOMP .... Western Ocean Meeting Point (DMA)
WOMP .... World Order Models Project
WOMP-FM... Bellaire, OH [*FM radio station call letters*]
WOMPI........ Women of the Motion Picture Industry, International (EA)
WOMR .... Provincetown, MA [*FM radio station call letters*]
Wom R Bks... Women's Review of Books [*A publication*] (BRI)
Womspk ...... Womanspeak [*A publication*]
WOMT .... Manitowoc, WI [*AM radio station call letters*]
WOMX-FM... Orlando, FL [*FM radio station call letters*]
WON .... Juan Air (1979) Ltd. [*Canada ICAO designator*] (FAAC)
WON .... Sports & Recreation, Inc. [*NYSE symbol*] (SAG)
WON .... Waiver of Notice [*Business term*] (MHDW)
WON .... Wondoola [*Queensland*] [*Airport symbol*] (AD)
WON .... Wool over Needle [*Knitting*]
WON .... Work Order Number (MCD)
WONA......... Winona, MS [*AM radio station call letters*]
WONAAC.... Women's National Abortion Action Coalition [*Defunct*]
WONA-FM.... Winona, MS [*FM radio station call letters*]
WONARD .... Woman's Organization of the National Association of Retail Druggists (EA)
WONB .... Ada, OH [*AM radio station call letters*]
WONC .... Naperville, IL [*FM radio station call letters*]
WONCA........ World Organization of National Colleges, Academies, and Academic Associations of General Practitioners/Family Physicians [*Australia*] (EAIO)
WOND......... Pleasantville, NJ [*AM radio station call letters*]
Wondwre ..... Wonderware Corp. [*Associated Press*] (SAG)
WONE.......... Akron, OH [*FM radio station call letters*]

WONE .... Dayton, OH [*AM radio station call letters*]
WONE .... Westwood One [*NASDAQ symbol*] (TTSB)
WONE .... Westwood One, Inc. [*Culver City, CA*] [*NASDAQ symbol*] (NQ)
WONF .... With Other Natural Flavors [*Food science*]
WONF .... Wonford [*England*]
WONG .... Canton, MS [*AM radio station call letters*]
WONG .... Weight on Nose Gear [*Aviation*] (MCD)
WONN .... Lakeland, FL [*AM radio station call letters*]
WONO .... Walterboro, SC [*FM radio station call letters*]
WONQ .... Oviedo, FL [*AM radio station call letters*]
Wont Land Reg... Wontner's Land Registry Practice [*12th ed.*] [*1975*] [*A publication*] (DLA)
WONU .... Kankakee, IL [*FM radio station call letters*]
WONW .... Defiance, OH [*AM radio station call letters*]
WONX .... Evanston, IL [*AM radio station call letters*]
WONY .... Oneonta, NY [*FM radio station call letters*]
WONZ .... Hammonton, NJ [*AM radio station call letters*]
WOO .... College of Wooster, Wooster, OH [*OCLC symbol*] (OCLC)
WOO .... Waiting on Orders
WOO .... Warrant Ordnance Officer [*Navy British*]
WOO .... Werke ohne Opuszahl [*Works without Opus Number*] [*Music*]
WOO .... Western Operations Office [*Later, WSO*] [*NASA*]
WOO .... Woodchopper, AK [*Location identifier FAA*] (FAAL)
WOO .... Woodstock [*Maryland*] [*Seismograph station code, US Geological Survey Closed*] (SEIS)
WoO.......... Work without Opus Number (WGA)
WOO .... World Oceanographic Organization
WOO .... World of Outlaws [*Auto racing*]
WOOD .... Grand Rapids, MI [*AM radio station call letters*]
Wood......... Wood on Mercantile Agreements [*A publication*] (DLA)
Wood .... Wood's English Tithe Cases, Exchequer [*4 vols.*] [*A publication*] (DLA)
Wood .... Woods' United States Circuit Court Reports [*A publication*] (DLA)
WOOD......... Write Once Optical Disk (NITA)
Wood & M... Woodbury and Minot's United States Circuit Court Reports [*A publication*] (DLA)
Wood & Minot... Woodbury and Minot's United States Circuit Court Reports [*A publication*] (DLA)
Woodb & M... Woodbury and Minot's United States Circuit Court Reports [*A publication*] (DLA)
Woodb & Min (CC)... Woodbury and Minot's United States Circuit Court Reports, First Circuit [*A publication*] (DLA)
WoodBcp ..... Wood Bancorp [*Associated Press*] (SAG)
Wood Civ L... Wood's Institutes of the Civil Law of England [*A publication*] (DLA)
Wood Com L... Wood's Institutes of the Common Law [*A publication*] (DLA)
Wood Conv... Wood on Conveyancing [*A publication*] (DLA)
Wood Decr... Wood's Tithe Cases [*England*] [*A publication*] (DLA)
Wooddesson Lect... Wooddesson's Lecture [*A publication*] (DLA)
Woodd Lect... Wooddesson's Lectures on the Laws of England [*A publication*] (DLA)
Wood El Jur... Wooddesson's Elements of Jurisprudence [*A publication*] (DLA)
Woodf... Woodfall on Landlord and Tenant [*25 eds.*] [*1802-1958*] [*A publication*] (DLA)
WOODF....... Woodford [*England*]
Woodf Cel Tr... Woodfall's Celebrated Trials [*A publication*] (DLA)
Woodf Landl & T... Woodfall on Landlord and Tenant [*25 eds.*] [*1802-1958*] [*A publication*] (DLA)
Woodf Landl & Ten... Woodfall on Landlord and Tenant [*25 eds.*] [*1802-1958*] [*A publication*] (DLA)
Woodf L & T... Woodfall on Landlord and Tenant [*28th ed.*] [*1978*] [*A publication*] (DLA)
WOOD-FM... Grand Rapids, MI [*FM radio station call letters*]
Woodf Parl Deb... Woodfall's Parliamentary Debates [*A publication*] (DLA)
Wood H .... Hutton Wood's Decrees in Tithe Cases [*England*] [*A publication*] (DLA)
Woodhd....... Woodhead Industries, Inc. [*Associated Press*] (SAG)
Wood Inst.... Wood's Institutes of English Law [*A publication*] (DLA)
Wood Inst Com Law... Wood's Institutes of the Common Law [*A publication*] (DLA)
Wood Inst Eng L... Wood's Institutes of English Law [*A publication*] (DLA)
WOODL....... Woodleigh [*England*]
Wood Land & T... Wood on Landlord and Tenant [*A publication*] (DLA)
Wood Landl & Ten... Wood on Landlord and Tenant [*A publication*] (DLA)
Wood Lect... Wooddesson's Lectures on the Laws of England [*A publication*] (DLA)
Wood Lim.... Wood on Limitation of Actions [*A publication*] (DLA)
Wood Man... Wood on Mandamus [*A publication*] (DLA)
Woodman Cr Cas... Woodman's Reports of Thacher's Criminal Cases [*Massachusetts*] [*A publication*] (DLA)
Woodm & T For Med... Woodman and Tidy on Forensic Medicine [*A publication*] (DLA)
Wood Mast & Serv... Wood on Master and Servant [*A publication*] (DLA)
Wood Mayne Dam... Wood's Mayne on Damages [*A publication*] (DLA)
WOODMEM... Leonard Wood Memorial [*Later, LWM*] [*Also known as American Leprosy Foundation*] (EA)
Wood Nuis... Wood on Nuisances [*A publication*] (DLA)
Woodr......... Woodroast Systems, Inc. [*Associated Press*] (SAG)
Wood Ry Law... Wood's Law of Railroads [*A publication*] (DLA)
Woods......... Woods' United States Circuit Court Reports [*A publication*] (DLA)
Woods CC.... Woods' United States Circuit Court Reports [*A publication*] (DLA)
Wood's Civ Law... Wood's Institutes of the Civil Law of England [*A publication*] (DLA)
Wood's Dig... Wood's Digest of Laws [*California*] [*A publication*] (DLA)
Woods Ins ... Wood on Fire Insurance [*A publication*] (DLA)
Woods Ins ... Wood's Institutes of English Law [*A publication*] (DLA)

Wood's Inst Civ L...   Wood's Institutes of the Civil Law of England [*A publication*] (DLA)

Wood's Inst Com L...   Wood's Institutes of the Common Law [*A publication*] (DLA)

Wood's R.....   Wood's Manitoba Reports [*1875-83*] [*A publication*] (DLA)

Woods St Frauds...   Wood's Treatise on the Statutes of Frauds [*A publication*] (DLA)

WOODST......   Wood Strength [*Botany*]

Wood Ti Cas...   Wood's Tithe Cases [*1650-1798*] [*A publication*] (DLA)

Wood Tit Cas...   Wood's Tithe Cases [*1650-1798*] [*A publication*] (DLA)

Wood Tr M...   Wood on Trade Marks [*1876*] [*A publication*] (DLA)

WOOD-TV ....   Grand Rapids, MI [*Television station call letters*]

Woodw ....   Woodward's Decisions [*Pennsylvania*] [*A publication*] (DLA)

Woodw Dec...   Woodward's Decisions [*1861-74*] [*Pennsylvania*] [*A publication*] (DLA)

Woodw Dec PA...   Woodward's Decisions [*1861-74*] [*Pennsylvania*] [*A publication*] (DLA)

WOODWK ....   Woodwork

woodwk ....   Woodwork (REAL)

WOODWKG...   Woodworking

WOODWT....   Wood Weight [*Botany*]

WOOF ....   Dothan, AL [*AM radio station call letters*]

Woof ....   Well-Off, Older Folks [*Lifestyle classification*]

Woof............   Well-Off, Over Fifty [*Lifestyle classification*]

WOOF-FM...   Dothan, AL [*FM radio station call letters*]

WOOL ....   Woolen

Wool...........   Woolworth's United States Circuit Court Reports [*A publication*] (DLA)

Wool CC ......   Woolworth's United States Circuit Court Reports (Miller's Decisions) [*A publication*] (DLA)

Woolf Adult...   Woolf on Adulterations [*1874*] [*A publication*] (DLA)

Wool Int ......   Woolsey's Introduction to Study of International Law [*6th ed.*] [*1888*] [*A publication*] (DLA)

Woolr Cert...   Woolrych's Certificates [*1826*] [*A publication*] (DLA)

Woolr Com...   Woolrych's Rights of Common [*2nd ed.*] [*1850*] [*A publication*] (DLA)

Woolr Cr L...   Woolrych's Criminal Law [*1862*] [*A publication*] (DLA)

Woolr LW...   Woolrych's Law of Waters [*2nd ed.*] [*1851*] [*A publication*] (DLA)

Woolr PW...   Woolrych's Party Walls [*1845*] [*A publication*] (DLA)

Woolr Sew...   Woolrych's Sewert [*3rd ed.*] [*1864*] [*A publication*] (DLA)

Woolr Waters...   Woolrych's Law of Waters [*A publication*] (DLA)

Woolr Ways...   Woolrych's Law of Ways [*2nd ed.*] [*1847*] [*A publication*] (DLA)

Woolr Wind L...   Woolrych's Window Lights [*2nd ed.*] [*1864*] [*A publication*] (DLA)

Woolsey Polit Science...   Woolsey's Political Science [*A publication*] (DLA)

Wools Int L...   Woolsey's Introduction to Study of International Law [*6th ed.*] [*1888*] [*A publication*] (DLA)

Wools Pol Science...   Woolsey's Political Science [*A publication*] (DLA)

Woolw ....   Woolworth's Reports [*1 Nebraska*] [*A publication*] (DLA)

Woolw ....   Woolworth's United States Circuit Court Reports [*A publication*] (DLA)

Woolworth ...   Woolworth's United States Circuit Court Reports [*A publication*] (DLA)

Woolworth's Cir Ct R...   Woolworth's United States Circuit Court Reports [*A publication*] (DLA)

Woolw Rep...   Woolworth's Reports [*1 Nebraska*] [*A publication*] (DLA)

Woolw Rep...   Woolworth's United States Circuit Court Reports [*A publication*] (DLA)

WOOM ....   Wives of Older Men [*An association*] (EA)

WOOMB.......   World Organization of the Ovulation Method - Billings, USA [*Later, Families of the Americas Foundation*]

WOON.........   Woonsocket, RI [*AM radio station call letters*]

WOOO.........   Shelbyville, IN [*AM radio station call letters*]

WOOOL.......   Words Out of Ordinary Language (WDAA)

Woopie........   Well-Off Older Person [*Lifestyle classification*]

WOOW ....   Greenville, NC [*AM radio station call letters*]

WOOX ....   Bedford, PA [*FM radio station call letters*]

WOOZ ....   Harrisburg, IL [*FM radio station call letters*]

WOP ....   Waiver of Premium [*Insurance*] (MHDW)

WOP ....   War on Poverty (OICC)

WOP ....   Wing Outer Panel [*Aviation*]

WOP ....   Wireless Operator [*RAF slang*] [*World War II*]

WOP ....   With Other Property (BARN)

WOP ....   Without Pain (DAVI)

WOP ....   Without Passport [*Immigration terminology*] [*Acronym often referred to early 20th century Italian immigrants*]

WOP ....   Without Payment

W/O/P ....   Without Penalty

WOP ....   Without Personnel

WOP ....   Without Preference [*Rating*]

WOP ....   Without Priorities

WOP ....   World Oil Project [*Massachusetts Institute of Technology*] [*National Science Foundation*] (IID)

WOPA ....   War Overtime Pay Act [*1943*]

WOPAG.......   Wireless Operator and Air Gunner [*British military*] (IAA)

W O PAR .....   Without Partition [*Freight*]

WOPAST......   Work Plan Analysis and Scheduling Technique (MHDB)

WOPC ....   World Oceanographic Data Processing and Services Center (MSC)

WOPD ....   Warrant Officer Professional Development [*Military*] (MCD)

WOPE ....   Without Personnel and Equipment

Wo Peo.......   Work and People [*A publication*]

WOPI ....   Bristol, VA [*AM radio station call letters*]

WOPP ....   Opp, AL [*AM radio station call letters*]

WOPR ....   War Operation Plan Response [*Pronounced "whopper"*] [*Name of NORAD computer in film "WarGames"*]

WOPR ....   Woody's Office Power Pack [*Pinecliffe International*] [*Computer science*] (PCM)

WOPR ....   Word for Windows Office Power Pack [*Computer program disk*] (PCM)

WOPTR.........   Wireless Operator [*British military*] (IAA)

WOQ ....   Wave Officers' Quarters

WOQ ....   Wooroona [*Queensland*] [*Airport symbol*] (AD)

WOQI ....   Ponce, PR [*FM radio station call letters*]

WOQT ....   Warrant Officer Qualification Test [*Military*]

WOR ....   New York, NY [*AM radio station call letters*]

WOR ....   Water-Oil Ratio

WOR ....   Wearout Rate (SAA)

WOR ....   White and Orange [*Buoy*]

WOR ....   White Owners Register (EA)

WOR ....   Worcester [*Massachusetts*] [*Seismograph station code, US Geological Survey Closed*] (SEIS)

WOR ....   Work Order Register (MCD)

WOR ....   Work Order Release (MCD)

WOR ....   Work Order Request

WOR ....   Work Outline Retrieval (MCD)

WOR ....   Worshipful

WORA ....   Mayaguez, PR [*AM radio station call letters*]

WORAM ....   Word-Oriented Random Access Memory [*Computer science*] (MCD)

WORA-TV ....   Mayaguez, PR [*Television station call letters*]

WORB ....   Farmington Hills, MI [*FM radio station call letters*]

WORBAT ....   Wartime Order of Battle (NATG)

Wor Bib Leg...   Worrall's Bibliotheca Legum [*A publication*] (DLA)

WORC.........   Washington Operations Research Council (MCD)

WORC.........   Worcester, MA [*AM radio station call letters*]

WORC.........   Worcestershire [*County in England*]

Worcest Dict...   Worcester's Dictionary [*A publication*] (DLA)

Worcester....   Worcester's Dictionary of the English Language [*A publication*] (DLA)

Worcester Poly Inst...   Worcester Polytechnic Institute (GAGS)

Worcester St C...   Worcester State College (GAGS)

WORCS.......   Worcestershire [*County in England*]

WORCS.......   Work Ordering and Reporting Communication System [*Army*]

WORD.........   Pittsburgh, PA [*FM radio station call letters*]

WORD.........   Spartanburg, SC [*AM radio station call letters*]

WORD.........   Wechsler Objective Reading Dimensions [*Test*]

WORD.........   Wind Oriented Rapid [*or Rocket*] Deployment (MCD)

Wor Dict.....   Worcester's Dictionary [*A publication*] (DLA)

Words Elect...   Wordsworth's Law of Elections [*6th ed.*] [*1868*] [*A publication*] (DLA)

Words Elect Cas...   Wordsworth's Election Cases [*England*] [*A publication*] (DLA)

Words JS....   Wordsworth's Law of Joint-Stock Companies [*A publication*] (DLA)

Words Min....   Wordsworth's Law of Mining [*A publication*] (DLA)

Words Pat ...   Wordsworth's Law of Patents [*A publication*] (DLA)

Words Ry & C...   Wordsworth's Railway and Canal Companies [*A publication*] (DLA)

WORF ....   Window Observational Research Facility [*Space technology*]

WORG.........   Elloree, SC [*FM radio station call letters*]

WORI ....   World Order Research Institute

WORK.........   Barre, VT [*FM radio station call letters*]

WORK.........   Widening Occupational Roles Kit (EDAC)

WorkCap....   Workingmens Capital Holdings, Inc. [*Associated Press*] (SAG)

WORKHO .....   Workhouse [*British*] (ROG)

Workmen's Comp L Rep...   Workmen's Compensation Law Reporter [*Commerce Clearing House*] [*A publication*] (DLA)

Workmen's Comp L Rev...   Workmen's Compensation Law Review [*A publication*] (DLA)

Works Courts...   Works on Courts and Their Jurisdiction [*A publication*] (DLA)

Works Pr .....   Works' Practice, Pleading, and Forms [*A publication*] (DLA)

WORL ....   Christmas, FL [*AM radio station call letters*]

WORLD.......   Women Organized to Respond to Life-Threatening Diseases (EA)

WorldC ....   WorldCom, Inc. [*Associated Press*] (SAG)

WorldCm .....   WorldCom, Inc. [*Associated Press*] (SAG)

WORLDDIDAC...   World Association of Manufacturers and Distributors of Educational Materials (EAIO)

World L Rev...   World Law Review [*A publication*] (DLA)

WORLDS......   Western Ohio Regional Library Development System [*Library network*]

WORLD SMART...   World Sports Medicine Association of Registered Therapists

World Trade LJ...   World Trade Law Journal [*A publication*] (DLA)

WorldV ....   WorldViews: A Quarterly Review of Resources for Education and Action [*A publication*] (BRI)

WorldWIDE...   World Women in the Environment [*Formerly, World Women in Defense of the Environment*] (EA)

WORM ....   Savannah, TN [*AM radio station call letters*]

Worm ....   White, Older Rich Man [*Lifestyle classification*]

WORM ....   Write Once, Read Mainly [*or Many Times, or Mostly*] [*Computer science*]

WORM ....   Write-Once, Read-Many [*Computer science*]

WORM ....   Write-One Read Memory

WORM CD ...   Write Once, Read Many Compact Disk (EERA)

WORM-FM...   Savannah, TN [*FM radio station call letters*]

WORMS......   Warrant Officer Personnel Management System [*Army*]

WORMS......   World Organization to Restore Male Supremacy (EA)

WORN ....   Write Once, Read Never [*Computer science*]

WORO ....   Corozal, PR [*FM radio station call letters*]

WORO ....   Weapons Operations Research Office

WOROM .....   Write-Only Read-Only Memory [*Computer science*] (MDG)

WORP ....   Word Processing [*Computer science*] (DCTA)

WORQ ....   Green Bay, WI [*FM radio station call letters*]

WORSAMS...   Worldwide Organizational Structure for Army Medical Support (AABC)

WORSE ....   Word Selection (WDAA)

WORT ....   Madison, WI [*FM radio station call letters*]

WORTAC......   Westinghouse Overall RADAR Tester and Calibrator

WortFds......	Worthington Foods, Inc. [*Associated Press*] (SAG)
WorthFd......	Worthington Foods [*Associated Press*] (SAG)
Worthgtn......	Worthington Industries [*Associated Press*] (SAG)
Worth Jur	Worthington's Power of Juries [*1825*] [*A publication*] (DLA)
Worth Prec Wills...	Worthington's General Precedent for Wills [*5th ed.*] [*1852*] [*A publication*] (DLA)
WORV.........	Hattiesburg, MS [*AM radio station call letters*]
WORW.........	Port Huron, MI [*FM radio station call letters*]
WORX.........	Madison, IN [*AM radio station call letters*]
WORX-FM....	Madison, IN [*FM radio station call letters*]
WOS	Warrant Officer Service [*Army*] (DOMA)
WOS	Web Offset Section [*Later, WOA*] (EA)
WOS	Wholly-Owned Subsidiary [*Business term*] (MHDW)
WOS	Wilson Ornithological Society (EA)
WOS	Winchester Financial [*Vancouver Stock Exchange symbol*]
WOS	Worcester [*British depot code*]
WOSA	Windows Open Services Architecture [*Microsoft Corp.*] (PCM)
WOSA	Windows Open Systems Architecture [*Computer science*]
WOSA	Workers' Organization for Socialist Action [*South Africa Political party*] (EY)
WOSAC.......	Worldwide Synchronization of Atomic Clocks
WOSAPCON...	World Safety and Accident Prevention Congress (PDAA)
WOSB	War Office Selection Board [*British*]
WOSB	Weather Observation Site Building (AABC)
WOSC	Bethany Beach, DE [*FM radio station call letters*]
WOSC	Warrant Officer Senior Course [*Army*] (DOMA)
WOSC	Western Oklahoma State College
WOSC	Western Oregon State College
WOSC	World Organisation of Systems and Cybernetics (EAIO)
WOSD	Weapons Operational Systems Development [*NORAD*]
WOSE-FM	Coshocton, OH [*FM radio station call letters*] (RBYB)
WOSF	Work Order Status File (MCD)
WOsh..........	Oshkosh Public Library, Oshkosh, WI [*Library symbol Library of Congress*] (LCLS)
WOSH	Oshkosh, WI [*AM radio station call letters*]
WOshM.......	Mercy Hospital, Nursing Library, Oshkosh, WI [*Library symbol Library of Congress*] (LCLS)
WOshM-M ...	Mercy Medical Center, Medical Library, Oshkosh, WI [*Library symbol Library of Congress*] (LCLS)
WOshU	University of Wisconsin-Oshkosh, Oshkosh, WI [*Library symbol Library of Congress*] (LCLS)
WOSIC........	Watchmakers of Switzerland Information Center (EA)
WOSIN.......	Wolters Kluwer Nv [*AM symbol*] (TTSB)
WOSL	Women's Overseas Service League (EA)
WOSM	Ocean Springs, MS [*FM radio station call letters*]
WOSN-FM....	Indian River Shores, FL [*FM radio station call letters*] (RBYB)
WOSO........	San Juan, PR [*AM radio station call letters*]
WOSP	Portsmouth, OH [*FM radio station call letters*]
WOCQ........	Eponoor, WI [*FM radio station call letters*]
WOSR	Middletown, NY [*FM radio station call letters*]
WOSS	Ossining, NY [*FM radio station call letters*]
WOSSU.......	Women on Stamps Study Unit [*American Topical Association*] [*Defunct*] (EA)
WOST	Block Island, RI [*Television station call letters*]
WOST	World's Oldest Socketed Tool [*Refers to archeological discovery of a tool dated 2500 BC*]
WOSU........	Columbus, OH [*AM radio station call letters*]
WOSU-FM....	Columbus, OH [*FM radio station call letters*]
WOSUS.......	Wang Office Systems User Society (CSR)
WOSU-TV....	Columbus, OH [*Television station call letters*]
WOSV	Mansfield, OH [*FM radio station call letters*]
WOT...........	Wide-Open Throttle
WOTAN.......	Weather Observation Through Ambient Noise [*Marine science*] (OSRA)
WOTB	Middletown, RI [*FM radio station call letters*]
WOTB	Welfare of the Blind (EA)
WOTC	Edinburg, VA [*FM radio station call letters*]
WOTCU	Wave-Off and Transition Control Unit
WOTEC	Waste Oil to Energy Converter
WOTF.........	Writers of the Future [*Science fiction writing award*]
WOTJ.........	Morehead City, NC [*FM radio station call letters*]
WOTL	Toledo, OH [*FM radio station call letters*]
WOTO	Women on Their Own [*An association*] (EA)
WOTP	World Organization of the Teaching Professions [*Switzerland*]
WOTR	Lost Creek, WV [*FM radio station call letters*]
WOTR	Wolf Trap Farm Park [*National Park Service designation*]
WOTS	Kissimmee, FL [*AM radio station call letters*]
WOTS	Warrant Officer Training System [*Military*] (INF)
WOTS	Water Operations Technical Support [*US Army Corps of Engineers*]
WOTS	Wide-Open Throttle Switch [*Automotive engineering*]
WOTS	Work Opportunities Through Self-Help (WDAA)
WOTT	Wolves on the Track [*A group of philanderers looking for girls*] [*Slang*]
WOTTCS	Warrant Officer Technical and Tactical Certification System [*Army*]
Wott Leg Wal...	Wotton. Leges Wallicae [*A publication*] (DLA)
WOTV	Battle Creek, MI [*Television station call letters*]
WOU..........	Women's Outpatient Unit (AAMN)
WOU..........	Work Opportunities Unlimited
WOUB.........	Athens, OH [*AM radio station call letters*]
WOUB-FM....	Athens, OH [*FM radio station call letters*]
WOUB-TV	Athens, OH [*Television station call letters*]
WOUC.........	Cambridge, OH [*FM radio station call letters*]
WOUC-TV	Cambridge, OH [*Television station call letters*]
WOUDE.......	Wait-on-User-Defined Event (MHDI)
WOUH.........	Chillicothe, OH [*FM radio station call letters*]
WOUI.........	Chicago, IL [*FM radio station call letters*]
WOUL........	Ironton, OH [*FM radio station call letters*]
WOUR........	Utica, NY [*FM radio station call letters*]
WOUZ........	Zanesville, OH [*FM radio station call letters*]
WOV..........	Warren & Ouachita Valley Railway Co. [*AAR code*]
WOVI.........	Novi, MI [*FM radio station call letters*]
WOVK.........	Wheeling, WV [*FM radio station call letters*]
WOVO-FM....	Glasgow, KY [*FM radio station call letters*] (RBYB)
WOVO-FM....	Horse Cave, KY [*FM radio station call letters*] (RBYB)
WOW..........	Omaha, NE [*AM radio station call letters*]
WOW..........	Waiting on Weather [*Ocean storms*]
WOW..........	War on Want [*An association*] (EAIO)
WOW..........	War on Waste [*Navy*]
WOW..........	War on Words
WOW..........	Washington Opportunities for Women
WOW..........	Water/Oil/Water [*Emulsion*] (DB)
WOW..........	Weight-on-Wheels (NASA)
WOW..........	Widening Our World [*Program sponsored by the US WEST Foundation*]
WOW..........	Widening Our World [*US West Foundation*] [*Education initiative*]
WOW..........	Wider Opportunities for Women (EA)
WOW..........	Windows on Windows [*Computer software*] (CDE)
WOW..........	Winners on Wheels [*An association*] (PAZ)
WOW..........	Without Whiskers (IAA)
WOW..........	Woman Ordnance Worker
WOW..........	Women on Wheels (EA)
WOW..........	Women on Wine (EA)
WOW..........	Women Our Wonders [*Antifeminist men's group*]
WOW..........	Women-Owned Workplaces
WOW..........	Woodmen of the World (EA)
WOW..........	Word on the Way
WOW..........	World Ocean Watch [*Marine science*] (OSRA)
WOW..........	World of Winners [*A publication*]
WOW..........	World of Work [*Career-oriented course of study*]
WOW..........	Worlds of Wonder [*Electronic toy manufacturer*]
WOW..........	Worldwide Equities Ltd. [*Toronto Stock Exchange symbol*]
WOW..........	Worn-Out Wolf [*An aging philanderer*] [*Slang*]
WOW..........	Worst-on-Worst
WOW..........	Written Order of Withdrawal [*Banking*]
WO-WA.......	Work Order-Work Authorization (SSD)
WOWAR......	Work Order and Work Accomplishment Record
WOWATE	World War II Equivalent [*Three-year and eight-month unit of time measurement proposed by former Under Secretary of the Navy R. James Woolsey*]
WOWB	Little Falls, NY [*FM radio station call letters*]
WOWC	Jasper, AL [*FM radio station call letters*]
WOWE	Vassar, MI [*FM radio station call letters*]
WOWF-FM ...	Crossville, TN [*FM radio station call letters*] (BROA)
WOW-FM.....	Omaha, NE [*FM radio station call letters*]
WOWI........	Norfolk, VA [*FM radio station call letters*]
WOWI........	Women on Words and Images (EA)
WOWK	Huntington, WV [*Television station call letters*]
WOWL	Florence, AL [*Television station call letters*]
WOWLON....	Weight-on-Wheels Lock-On [*NASA*] (NASA)
WOWM.......	Write Once, Write Mostly [*Computer science*] (IAA)
WOWN.......	Shawano, WI [*FM radio station call letters*]
WOWN.......	Without Winch
WOWO.......	Fort Wayne, IN [*AM radio station call letters*]
WOWQ.......	DuBois, PA [*FM radio station call letters*]
WOWS	Wire Obstacle Warning System (IEEE)
WOWS	Women Ordnance Workers [*A national voluntary organization*] [*World War II*]
WOWT	Omaha, NE [*Television station call letters*]
WOWW	Pensacola, FL [*FM radio station call letters*]
WOWZ	Whitesboro, NY [*FM radio station call letters*] (RBYB)
WOXD........	Oxford, MS [*FM radio station call letters*]
WOXF-FM ...	Bedford, VA [*FM radio station call letters*] (RBYB)
WOXM........	Oregon, IL [*FM radio station call letters*] (RBYB)
WOXO........	Norway, ME [*FM radio station call letters*]
WOXR........	Oxford, AL [*AM radio station call letters*]
WOXY........	Oxford, OH [*FM radio station call letters*]
WOYE........	Mayaguez, PR [*FM radio station call letters*]
WOYK........	York, PA [*AM radio station call letters*]
WOYL........	Oil City, PA [*AM radio station call letters*]
WOYL........	Women of the Year Luncheon [*British*] (DI)
WOYS........	Apalachicola, FL [*FM radio station call letters*]
WOZI.........	Presque Isle, ME [*FM radio station call letters*]
WOZK........	Ozark, AL [*AM radio station call letters*]
WOZN........	Key West, FL [*FM radio station call letters*]
WOZQ........	Northampton, MA [*FM radio station call letters*]
WOZZ........	New London, WI [*FM radio station call letters*]
WP...........	Aloha Islandair [*ICAO designator*] (AD)
WP...........	Pakistan Law Reports, West Pakistan Series [*A publication*] (DLA)
WP...........	Portage Free Public Library, Portage, WI [*Library symbol Library of Congress*] (LCLS)
WP...........	Princeville Airways [*ICAO designator*] (AD)
WP...........	Waiting Period (OICC)
WP...........	Waiver of Premium [*Insurance*]
WP...........	War and Peace Foundation (EA)
WP...........	Warming Pan [*Refers to a clergyman holding a job under a bond of resignation*] [*Obsolete Slang British*] (DSUE)
WP...........	Warm Pipe [*Nuclear energy*] (NRCH)
WP...........	Warm Pool [*Oceanography*]
WP...........	War Plans
WP...........	Warsaw Pact (NATG)

WP............	Warsaw Pact Member (WDAA)
WP............	Washington Post [A publication]
WP............	Wastepaper
WP............	Waste Pipe [Technical drawings]
WP............	Water-Dispersible Powder [Pesticide formulation]
WP............	Water Packed
WP............	Water Plane (MSA)
WP............	Water Point
W/P...........	Water/Powder [Ratio] [Pharmacology] (DAVI)
WP............	Waterproof
WP............	Water Propeller (AAG)
WP............	Water Pump (AAG)
WP............	Way-Point
WP............	Weakly Positive (MAE)
WP............	Weapons Power
WP............	Weapons Procurement (DOMA)
WP............	Weather Permitting
WP............	Weatherproof
WP............	Weekly Premium [Insurance]
WP............	Weight Penalty
WP............	Welding Procedure [Nuclear energy] (NRCH)
WP............	[The] Western Pacific Railroad Co. [AAR code]
WP............	Western Pine [Utility pole] [Telecommunications] (TEL)
WP............	Western Planner (PA)
WP............	West Point
WP............	We the People [Later, WPU] (EA)
WP............	Wet Pack [Medicine] (AAMN)
WP............	Wet Process (MSA)
WP............	Wettable Powder
W-P...........	Wheeling-Pittsburgh Steel Corp. (EFIS)
WP............	Wheel of Progress (EA)
WP............	Whirlpool [Medicine]
WP............	White Painted (BJA)
WP............	White Paper (ADA)
WP............	White Phosphorus [Military]
WP............	Wide Pore [Chromatography]
WP............	Wild Pitch [Baseball]
WP............	Will Proceed To
WP............	Will Proved [Legal] [British] (ROG)
WP............	Windfall Profit
WP............	Winning Pitcher [Baseball]
WP............	Wire Payment
WP............	Withdrawn Passing [Education] (WGA)
WP............	Without Prejudice
WP............	Wolfe Pack (EA)
WP............	Wolseley Pattern [British military] (DMA)
WP............	Women Proutists (EA)
WP............	Woodfree Printing Paper (DGA)
WP............	Woodfree Pulp Board (DGA)
WP............	Wood Pattern (MSA)
WP............	Word Processing [Movement to improve secretarial/clerical function through a managed system of people, procedures, and modern office equipment]
WP............	Word Processor (ADA)
wp............	Word Processor (ODBW)
WP............	Word Punch
WP............	Worker's Party [Ireland] [Political party]
WP............	Working Paper
W/P...........	Working Papers (AAGC)
WP............	Working Party
WP............	Working Point
WP............	Working Pressure
WP............	Work Package (NASA)
W/P...........	Work Picture [or Print] [Cinematography]
WP............	Work Preparation (AIE)
WP............	Workprint [Cinematography] (NTCM)
WP............	Work Procedure [Nuclear energy] (NRCH)
WP............	Work Program (NATG)
WP............	Workspace Pointer (MHDB)
WP............	Workspace Register Pointer [Computer science] (IAA)
WP............	World Peacemakers (EA)
WP............	World Politics [A publication] (BRI)
WP............	World Priorities (EA)
WP............	Worship
WP............	Worst Pattern (IAA)
WP............	Worthy Patriarch
WP............	Wrist Pitch (MCD)
WP............	Write Permit (NITA)
WP............	Write Protect
WP............	Writers for Peace (EA)
WP3...........	Working Party Three [Economic Policy Committee of the Organization for Economic Cooperation and Development]
WPA...........	Puerto Aysen [Chile] [Airport symbol] (AD)
WPA...........	Wagner-Peyser Act [1933] (OICC)
WPA...........	Water Jet Propulsion Assembly (MCD)
WPA...........	Water Pump Assembly
WPA...........	Webb-Pomerene Act [1918]
WPA...........	Wellhead Protection Area (GNE)
WPA...........	Well Protection Act (COE)
WPA...........	Western Pacific Airservice [Solomon Islands] [ICAO designator] (FAAC)
WPA...........	Western Pine Association [Later, WWPA] (EA)
WPA...........	Western Pistachio Association (EA)
WPA...........	Western Provident Association [British] (DI)
WPA...........	Western Psychological Association (MCD)

WPA...........	Wet-Process Phosphoric Acid [Fertilizer]
WPA...........	Whale Protection Act 1980 [Commonwealth Act] (EERA)
WPA...........	Wheelchair Pilots Association (EA)
WPA...........	Whiskey Painters of America (EA)
WPA...........	Whistleblower Protection Act of 1989 (WYGK)
WPA...........	Wildlife Production Area
WPA...........	William Penn Association [Pittsburgh, PA] (EA)
WPA...........	Wire Products Association [British] (BI)
WPA...........	With Particular Average
WPA...........	Women's Press Association (NTCM)
WPA...........	Women's Prison Association (EA)
WPA...........	Woody Point [Australia Seismograph station code, US Geological Survey Closed] (SEIS)
WPA...........	Working Party on Aquaculture [Australia]
WPA...........	Working People's Alliance [Guyana] (PD)
WPA...........	Work Package Action (MCD)
WPA...........	Work Package Address (MCD)
WPA...........	Work Performance Assessment [Test] (TMMY)
WPA...........	Workshop of the Players Art [New York City]
WPA...........	Works Progress Administration [Later, Work Projects Administration] [Part of President Franklin D. Roosevelt's New Deal]
WPA...........	World Parliament Association
WPA...........	World Pheasant Association [Reading, Berkshire, England] (EAIO)
WPA...........	World Presbyterian Alliance
WPA...........	World Psychiatric Association [Copenhagen, Denmark] (EAIO)
WPA...........	Worst Possible Accident [Nuclear safety]
WPAA.........	Andover, MA [FM radio station call letters]
WPAAS.......	Word Processing and Administrative Support System [Computer science] (HGAA)
WPAB.........	Ponce, PR [AM radio station call letters]
WPAB.........	Word Processing Aptitude Battery [Test]
WPAB.........	Word Processor Assessment Battery [Selection and placement test]
WPAC.........	Ogdensburg, NY [FM radio station call letters]
WPAC.........	Walden Pond Advisory Committee (EA)
WPAC.........	Western Pacific Airlines [NASDAQ symbol] (TTSB)
WPAC.........	Western Pacific Airlines, Inc. [NASDAQ symbol] (SAG)
WPAC.........	Working Program Advisory Committee [DoD]
W-PACC.....	Wisconsin Procedure for Appraisal of Clinical Competence (EDAC)
WPAD.........	Paducah, KY [AM radio station call letters]
WPAE-FM ...	Centreville, MS [FM radio station call letters] (RBYB)
WPAFB.......	Wright-Patterson Air Force Base [Ohio]
WPAK.........	Farmville, VA [AM radio station call letters]
WPAL.........	Charleston, SC [AM radio station call letters]
WPAL.........	Walterboro, SC [FM radio station call letters]
WPAM.........	Pottsville, PA [AM radio station call letters]
WPAN.........	Fort Walton Beach, FL [Television station call letters]
WP & T.......	War Plans and Training
WP&YR.......	White Pass & Yukon Railway [Nickname: Wait Patiently and You'll Ride]
WPAO-AM ...	Farrell, PA [AM radio station call letters] (BROA)
WPAP.........	Panama City, FL [FM radio station call letters]
WPAQ.........	Mount Airy, NC [AM radio station call letters]
WPAQ.........	Westra Preschool Assessment Questionnaire
WPAR.........	Hickory, NC [FM radio station call letters]
W PAR........	With Partition [Freight]
WP/AS	Word Processing/Administrative Support [Extension of Word Processing]
WPAT.........	Atauro [East Timor] [ICAO location identifier] (ICLI)
WPAT.........	Paterson, NJ [AM radio station call letters]
WPAT.........	Wolfe Programming Aptitude Test
WPATC.......	Western Pennsylvania Advanced Technology Center [Research center] (RCD)
WPAT-FM ...	Paterson, NJ [FM radio station call letters]
WPA-USA ...	World Pheasant Association of the USA (EA)
WPAW.........	Vero Beach, FL [FM radio station call letters] (RBYB)
WPAWA.......	World Professional Armwrestling Association [Defunct] (EA)
WPAX.........	Thomasville, GA [AM radio station call letters]
WPAY.........	Portsmouth, OH [AM radio station call letters]
WPAY-FM ...	Portsmouth, OH [FM radio station call letters]
WPAZ.........	Pottstown, PA [AM radio station call letters]
WPB...........	Gunboat [Coast Guard] (NVT)
WPB...........	Port Berge [Madagascar] [Airport symbol] (OAG)
WPB...........	Wall Plate Box
WPB...........	War Production Board [World War II]
WPB...........	Wastepaper Basket [or Bin]
WPB...........	Waste Processing Building [Nuclear energy] (NRCH)
WPB...........	Whirlpool Bath [Medicine]
WPB...........	Wide Pulse Blanking (MCD)
WPB...........	Woodfree Pulp Board (DGA)
WPB...........	World Peace Brigade (EA)
WPB...........	Write Printer Binary
WPBA.........	Atlanta, GA [Television station call letters]
WPBA.........	Women Professional Bowlers Association (EA)
WPBA.........	Women's Professional Billiard Alliance (EA)
WPBC.........	Pittsfield, ME [FM radio station call letters]
WPBC.........	Western Pacific Base Command [Marianas] [World War II]
WPBCWS....	Waste Processing Building Chilled Water System [Nuclear energy] (NRCH)
WPBEF.......	West Pakistan Bank Employees' Federation
WPBF........	Tequesta, FL [Television station call letters]
WPBGP.......	West Palm Beach Grand Prix [Automobile racing event]
WPBH.........	Port St. Joe, FL [FM radio station call letters]
WPBIC.......	Walker Problem Behavior Identification Checklist [Education]
WPBL.........	Women's Professional Basketball League [Defunct] (EA)
WPBN.........	Traverse City, MI [Television station call letters]

WPBO .... Portsmouth, OH [Television station call letters]
WPBQ .... Flowood, MS [AM radio station call letters]
WPBR .... Palm Beach, FL [AM radio station call letters]
WPBRL .... Warsaw Pact/Ballistic Research Laboratory (MCD)
WPBS .... Conyers, GA [AM radio station call letters]
WPBSA .... World Professional Billiards and Snooker Association (BARN)
WPBT......... Miami, FL [Television station call letters]
WPBX .... Southampton, NY [FM radio station call letters]
WPBY .... Huntington, WV [Television station call letters]
WPBZ .... Indiantown, FL [FM radio station call letters]
WPC........... Wafer Process Chamber (AAEL)
WPC........... Walter P. Chrysler Club (EA)
WPC........... War Pensions Committee [British military] (DMA)
WPC........... Warrior Preparation Center [Kaiserslautern, Federal Republic of Germany] [USAREUR]
WPC........... Warsaw Pact Countries
WPC........... Washington Press Club [Formerly, WNPC]
WPC........... Waste Product Costs [Solid waste management]
WPC........... Water Pollution Control
WPC........... Watt-per-Channel (IAA)
WPC........... Watts per Candle [Electricity]
Wpc .... Watts per Candle (IDOE)
WPC........... Webster's Patent Cases [1601-1855] [A publication] (DLA)
WPC........... Wedge Power Clamp
WPC........... Weldable Printed Circuit
WPC........... Wheat Protein Concentrate [Food technology]
WPC........... Whey Protein Concentrate [Food technology]
WPC........... William Paterson College [Wayne, NJ]
WPC........... William Penn College [Oskaloosa, IA]
WPC........... William Peterson College of New Jersey
WPC........... Wired Program Computer
WPC........... Wollaston's English Bail Court Reports, Practice Cases [A publication] (DLA)
WPC........... Woman Police Constable [Scotland Yard]
WPC........... Women's Political Caucus
WPC........... Wood-Plastic Combination [or Composite]
WPC........... Word Processing Center
WPC........... Workers Party of Canada
WPC........... Work Package Concept (MCD)
WP + C ...... Work Planning and Control [Computer science]
WPC........... World Peace Congress
WPC........... World Peace Council [See also CMP] (EAIO)
WPC........... World Petroleum Congresses - a Forum for Petroleum Science, Technology, Economics, and Management (EAIO)
WPC........... World Philatelic Congress of Holy Land, Israel, and Judaica Societies (EA)
WPC........... World Planning Chart [Aviation]
WPC........... World Pooling Committee (MCD)
WPC........... World Power Conference [Later, WEC]
WPC........... World Print Council (EA)
WPC........... World Pumpkin Confederation (EA)
WPCA .... Water Pollution Control Administration [Department of the Interior]
WPCA .... Wool Pullers Council of America (EA)
WPCAA ...... White Park Cattle Association of America (EA)
WP Cas....... Webster's Patent Cases [1601-1855] [A publication] (DLA)
WP Cas....... Wollaston's English Bail Court Reports, Practice Cases [A publication] (DLA)
WPCB .... Greensburg, PA [Television station call letters]
WPCB .... Western Pennsylvania Christian Broadcasting Co. [A cable TV station]
WPCC .... Clinton, SC [AM radio station call letters]
WPCC .... Western Pennsylvania Collegiate Conference (PSS)
WPCC .... Wilson Pharmaceutical & Chemical Corp.
WPCC .... World Paper Currency Collectors (EA)
WPCC .... WPC [Walter P. Chrysler] Club (EA)
WPCC .... Wright-Patterson Contracting Center [Ohio] [Air Force]
WPCD .... Champaign, IL [FM radio station call letters]
WPCE .... Portsmouth, VA [AM radio station call letters]
WPCF......... Panama City Beach, FL [FM radio station call letters]
WPCF......... Water Pollution Control Federation (EA)
WPCH......... Atlanta, GA [FM radio station call letters]
WPCHLIJS ... World Philatelic Congress of Holy Land, Israel, and Judaica Societies (EA)
WPCI .... Greenville, SC [AM radio station call letters]
WPCJ......... Pittsford, MI [FM radio station call letters]
WPCM......... Burlington, NC [FM radio station call letters]
WPCND....... Women's Patriotic Conference on National Defense (EA)
WPCO .... Mount Vernon, IN [AM radio station call letters]
WPCO .... Whiting Petroleum (EFIS)
WPcom....... Write Precompensation [Computer science] (CDE)
WPCP .... Ward's Private Companies Profiles [A publication]
WPCP .... Water Pollution Control Plant [Environmental science]
WPCR .... Plymouth, NH [FM radio station call letters]
WPCR .... Water Pollution Control Research [Environmental Protection Agency]
WPCS .... Pensacola, FL [AM radio station call letters]
WPCS .... Welsh Pony and Cob Society (DBA)
WPCSA .... Welsh Pony and Cob Society of America (EA)
WPCT......... Panama City Beach, FL [Television station call letters]
WPCTS ...... When Push Comes to Shove
WPCV .... Winter Haven, FL [FM radio station call letters]
WPCX .... Auburn, NY [FM radio station call letters]
WPD .... War Plan Division [World War II]
WPD .... Water Planning Division [Environmental Protection Agency] (EPA)
WPD .... Western Procurement Division [Marine Corps]
WPD .... Work Package Description [NASA] (NASA)

WPD .... World Pharmaceuticals Directory [A publication]
WPD .... Write Printer Decimal
WPDA .... Jeffersonville, NY [FM radio station call letters]
WPDA .... Writing Pushdown Acceptor
WPDB .... Suai [East Timor] [ICAO location identifier] (ICLI)
WPDC .... Elizabethtown, PA [AM radio station call letters]
W/PDC .... Workers'/People's Defence Committee [Ghana] [Political party]
WPDE .... Florence, SC [Television station call letters]
WPDES ...... Waste Pollution Discharge Elimination System (IEEE)
WPDF .... Wolaita People's Democratic Front [Ethiopia]
WPDH .... Poughkeepsie, NY [FM radio station call letters]
WPDJ .... Huntington, IN [AM radio station call letters]
WPDL .... Dili [East Timor] [ICAO location identifier] (ICLI)
WPDM .... Potsdam, NY [AM radio station call letters]
WPDN .... Wind Profiler Demonstration Network [Marine science] (OSRA)
WPDOS ...... WordPerfect for Disk Operating System [Computer science]
WP/DP .... Word Processing/Data Processing System (HGAA)
WPDQ .... Jacksonville, FL [AM radio station call letters]
WPDR .... Portage, WI [AM radio station call letters]
WPDT .... Johnsonville, SC [FM radio station call letters] (RBYB)
WPDX .... Clarksburg, WV [AM radio station call letters]
WPDX .... Word Processing Document Exchange Program
WPDX-FM ... Clarksburg, WV [FM radio station call letters]
WPE .... Western Pacific Energy [Vancouver Stock Exchange symbol]
WPE .... Western Plastics Exposition [HBJ Expositions and Conferences] (TSPED)
WPE .... West Pittston-Exeter Railroad Co. [AAR code]
WPE .... Workers' Party of Ethiopia
WPEA .... Exeter, NH [FM radio station call letters]
WPEARS ..... Working Papers Exhibits and Rate Schedules (AAGC)
WPEB .... Philadelphia, PA [FM radio station call letters]
WPEC .... Baucau [East Timor] [ICAO location identifier] (ICLI)
WPEC .... Weapons Production Engineering Center [Navy]
WPEC .... Western Power & Equip [NASDAQ symbol] (TTSB)
WPEC .... Western Power & Equipment Corp. [NASDAQ symbol] (SAG)
WPEC .... West Palm Beach, FL [Television station call letters]
WPEC .... World Plan Executive Council [Later, WGAE-US] (EA)
WPECC .... Western Pacific Fisheries Consultative Committee [Marine science] (OSRA)
WPEG .... Concord, NC [FM radio station call letters]
WPEH .... Louisville, GA [AM radio station call letters]
WPEH-FM ... Louisville, GA [FM radio station call letters]
WPEK .... Seneca, SC [FM radio station call letters] (RBYB)
WPEL .... Montrose, PA [AM radio station call letters]
WPEL-FM ... Montrose, PA [FM radio station call letters]
WPEN .... Philadelphia, PA [AM radio station call letters]
WPen .... West Penn Power Co. [Associated Press] (SAG)
WPen25....... West Penn Power Co. [Associated Press] (SAG)
WPEO .... Peoria, IL [AM radio station call letters]
WPEP......... Taunton, MA [AM radio station call letters]
WPER .... Asheboro, NC [FM radio station call letters] (RBYB)
WPES .... Ashland, VA [AM radio station call letters]
WPET......... Greensboro, NC [AM radio station call letters]
WPeW .... Waukesha County Technical Institute, Powaukee, WI [Library symbol Library of Congress] (LCLS)
WPEZ .... Macon, GA [FM radio station call letters]
WPF........... War and Peace Foundation (EA)
WPF........... War Production Fund [World War II]
WPF........... Watcor Purification Systems, Inc. [Vancouver Stock Exchange symbol]
WPF........... Weather Profile Facility
WPF........... Weight, Power, Fulcrum
WPF........... Whale Protection Fund (EA)
WPF........... Work Process Flow [NASA] (NASA)
WPF........... World Peace Foundation (EA)
WPF........... World Prohibition Federation
WPF........... Worldwide Pen Friends (EA)
WPF........... Wright Peak Flow [Medicine] (DAVI)
WPFA .... Wholesale Photo Finishers' Association [British] (BI)
WPFA .... William Penn Fraternal Association [Later, WPA] (EA)
WPFA .... Working Party on Feral Animals [Australia]
WPFB .... Middletown, OH [AM radio station call letters]
WPFB-FM ... Middletown, OH [FM radio station call letters]
WPFC .... Commission for Fisheries Research in the West Pacific
WPFC .... Port Allen, LA [AM radio station call letters] (RBYB)
WPFC .... Waterproof Fan Cooled (MSA)
WPFC .... Westbeth Playwrights Feminist Collective [Defunct] (EA)
WPFC .... William Perry Fan Club [Defunct] (EA)
WPFC .... World Press Freedom Committee (EA)
WPFD .... Fairview, TN [AM radio station call letters]
WPFF .... Sturgeon Bay, WI [FM radio station call letters]
WPFILD ...... West Point Fellowship in Leader Development [US Military Academy] (INF)
WPFJ .... Franklin, NC [AM radio station call letters]
WPFL .... Fuiloro [East Timor] [ICAO location identifier] (ICLI)
WPFL .... West Pakistan Federation of Labor
WPFL .... Worshipful (ROG)
WPFL-FM ... Century, FL [FM radio station call letters] (RBYB)
WPFM .... Panama City, FL [FM radio station call letters]
WPFM .... Wiping Form (AAG)
WPFM .... Wright Peak Flow Meter [Medicine] (DAVI)
WPFMC....... Western Pacific Fishery Management Council [National Oceanic and Atmospheric Administration] (GFGA)
WPFPA .... Watershed Protection and Flood Prevention Act of 1954 (COE)
WPFR-FM ... Clinton, IN [FM radio station call letters] (BROA)

WPFTA......... White Plate Flat Trackers Association (EA)
WPFUL .... Worshipful
WPFW .... Washington, DC [FM radio station call letters]
WPG .... Waterproofing (AAG)
WPG .... Weighted Pair Group
WPG .... West Point Graduate
WPG .... Wiping (MSA)
WPG .... Worcester Polytechnic Institute, Worcester, MA [OCLC symbol] (OCLC)
WPG .... WordPerfect Graphic [Novell, Inc.] [File format]
WPG .... Work Package Grouping [NASA] (NASA)
WPGA .... Perry, GA [AM radio station call letters]
WPGA-FM ... Perry, GA [FM radio station call letters]
WPGA-TV .... Perry, GA [Television station call letters]
WPGC .... Morningside, MD [AM radio station call letters]
WPGC-FM ... Morningside, MD [FM radio station call letters]
WPGD .... Hendersonville, TN [Television station call letters]
WPGDY........ WPP Group PLC [NASDAQ symbol] (SAG)
WPGG .... Evergreen, AL [FM radio station call letters]
WPGH.......... Pittsburgh, PA [FM radio station call letters]
WPGI .... Horseheads, NY [FM radio station call letters] (RBYB)
WPGI .... Western Publishing Group, Inc. [New York, NY NASDAQ symbol] (NQ)
WPGL .... Pattersonville, NY [FM radio station call letters]
WPGM .... Danville, PA [AM radio station call letters]
WPGM-FM ... Danville, PA [FM radio station call letters]
WPGR-AM ... Pittsburgh, PA [AM radio station call letters] (BROA)
WPGS .... Mims, FL [AM radio station call letters]
WPGT .... Group Fore - Women's Pro Golf Tour (EA)
WPGU .... Urbana, IL [FM radio station call letters]
WPGW .... Portland, IN [AM radio station call letters]
WPGW-FM ... Portland, IN [FM radio station call letters]
WPGX .... Panama City, FL [Television station call letters]
WPGY .... Williamsport, PA [FM radio station call letters] (RBYB)
WPH .... Wafers per Hour (AAEL)
WPH .... West Pit [Hawaii] [Seismograph station code, US Geological Survey Closed] (SEIS)
WPH .... William Penn House (EA)
WPH .... WPL Holdings [NYSE symbol] (SPSG)
WPHB.......... Philipsburg, PA [AM radio station call letters]
WPHB-FM .... Philipsburg, PA [FM radio station call letters]
WPHC.......... Waverly, TN [AM radio station call letters]
WPHD.......... Tioga, PA [FM radio station call letters]
WPHE .... Phoenixville, PA [AM radio station call letters]
WPHG-AM ... Atmore, AL [AM radio station call letters] (BROA)
WPHG-FM ... Brewton, AL [FM radio station call letters] (BROA)
WPHI .... Western Pennsylvania Horological Institute
WPHK.......... Blountstown, FL [FM radio station call letters]
WPHL .... Philadelphia, PA [Television station call letters]
WPHL .... Women's Professional Hockey League
WPHM .... Port Huron, MI [AM radio station call letters]
WPHN .... Gaylord, MI [FM radio station call letters]
WPHOA........ Women Public Health Officer's Association [British]
WPHP .... Wheeling, WV [FM radio station call letters]
WPHS .... Warren, MI [FM radio station call letters]
WPHT-AM ... Philadelphia, PA [AM radio station call letters] (RBYB)
WPI............. Wall Paper Institute [Later, Wallcovering Manufacturers Association] (EA)
WPI............. Watershed Protection Initiative (WPI)
WPI............. Watson Pharmaceuticals [NYSE symbol]
WPI............. Waxed Paper Institute [Later, FPA] (EA)
WPI............. Wedding Photographers International (EA)
WPI............. Western Personality Inventory [Psychology]
WPI............. Western Personnel Institute (AEBS)
WPI............. West Pride Industry [Vancouver Stock Exchange symbol]
WPI............. Whey Products Institute [Later, ADPI] (EA)
WPI............. Wholesale Price Index [Economics]
WPI............. Women and Priests Involved (EA)
WPI............. Women's Peace Initiative (EA)
WPI............. Worcester Polytechnic Institute [Massachusetts]
WPI............. Work Process Indicator (NASA)
WPI............. Work Progress Indicator [NASA] (NASA)
WPI............. World Patents Index [Derwent Publications Ltd.] [Database]
WPI............. World Peace Institute (EA)
WPI............. World Peace One [An association] (EA)
WPI............. World Policy Institute (EA)
WPIB .... Bluefield, WV [FM radio station call letters]
WPIC .... Sharon, PA [AM radio station call letters]
WPIC .... Water Port Identifier Code
WPIC .... Western Psychiatric Institute and Clinic [University of Pittsburgh] [Research center] (RCD)
WPIC .... WPI Group [NASDAQ symbol] (TTSB)
WPIC .... WPI Group, Inc. [NASDAQ symbol] (SAG)
WPID .... Piedmont, AL [AM radio station call letters]
WPIE .... Trumansburg, NY [AM radio station call letters]
WPIG .... Olean, NY [FM radio station call letters]
WPI Grp ...... WPI Group, Inc. [Associated Press] (SAG)
WPIK .... Summerland Key, FL [AM radio station call letters]
WPIM .... Martinsville, VA [FM radio station call letters]
WPIN .... Dublin, VA [FM radio station call letters]
WPINDEX..... Wholesale Price Index [Data File]
WPIO .... Titusville, FL [FM radio station call letters]
WPIO .... Waste Isolation Pilot Project Integration Office [Department of Energy] [Albuquerque, NM] (GAAI)

WPIP .... Winston-Salem, NC [AM radio station call letters]
WPIQ .... Brunswick, GA [AM radio station call letters]
WPIR .... Salem, VA [FM radio station call letters]
WPIS .... Wafer Parameter Identification System (IAA)
WPISC .... Western Pennsylvania Intercollegiate Soccer Conference (PSS)
WPIT........... Pittsburgh, PA [AM radio station call letters]
WPIT........... Water Pressure Integrity Test [For testing water filters]
WPIX .... New York, NY [Television station call letters]
WPJ .... Weakened Plane Joint
WPJ .... Workers' Party of Jamaica [Political party] (EY)
WPJB .... Narragansett Pier, RI [FM radio station call letters]
WPJC .... Adjuntas, PR [FM radio station call letters]
WPJK .... Orangeburg, SC [AM radio station call letters]
WPJL .... Raleigh, NC [AM radio station call letters]
WPJM .... Greer, SC [AM radio station call letters]
WPJS .... Conway, SC [AM radio station call letters]
WPK .... Air-Lift Associates, Inc. [ICAO designator] (FAAC)
WPk .... Ward's Mechanical Tissue Pack [Dentistry] (BABM)
WPk .... Wet Pack [Physical therapy] (DAVI)
WPK .... Winpak Ltd. [Toronto Stock Exchange symbol]
WPK .... Wright Peak Flow [Medicine] (DAVI)
WPKE .... Elkhorn City, KY [FM radio station call letters]
WPKE .... Pikeville, KY [AM radio station call letters]
WPKM .... Scarborough, ME [FM radio station call letters]
WPKN .... Bridgeport, CT [FM radio station call letters]
WPKO .... Bellefontaine, OH [FM radio station call letters]
WPKO .... World Professional Karate Organization (DICI)
WPKQ-FM ... Berlin, NH [FM radio station call letters] (RBYB)
WPKR .... Omro, WI [FM radio station call letters]
WPKT........... Meriden, CT [FM radio station call letters]
WPKX .... Enfield, CT [FM radio station call letters]
WPKY .... Princeton, KY [AM radio station call letters]
WPKZ .... Elkton, VA [FM radio station call letters]
WPL............. Aeronaves del Peru SA [ICAO designator] (FAAC)
WPL............. War Plan, Long-Range (CINC)
WPL............. Warren Public Library, Warren, OH [OCLC symbol] (OCLC)
WPL............. Waste Pickle Liquor [Industrial waste]
WPL............. Wave Propagation Laboratory [Boulder, CO] [National Oceanic and Atmospheric Administration]
WPL............. Windows Personal Librarian [Computer software]
WPL............. Windows Portability Libraries [Computer science]
WPL............. Winnipeg Public Library [UTLAS symbol]
WPL............. Worshipful
WPL............. Worst Path Loss
WPLA .... Callahan, FL [FM radio station call letters] (RBYB)
WPLA-FM ... Callahan, FL [FM radio station call letters] (RBYB)
WPlaU .... University of Wisconsin-Platteville, Platteville, WI [Library symbol Library of Congress] (LCLS)
WPLB.......... Greenville, MI [AM radio station call letters]
WPLB.......... Lakeview, MI [FM radio station call letters]
WPLG .... Miami, FL [Television station call letters]
WPLH .... Tifton, GA [FM radio station call letters]
WPL H .... WPL Holdings [Associated Press] (SAG)
WPLJ .... New York, NY [FM radio station call letters]
WPLJ .... White Port and Lemon Juice [Title of both song and drink]
WPLK .... Palatka, FL [AM radio station call letters]
WPLL-FM ... Fort Lauderdale, FL [FM radio station call letters] (RBYB)
WPLM .... Plymouth, MA [AM radio station call letters]
WPLM-FM ... Plymouth, MA [FM radio station call letters]
WPLN .... Nashville, TN [FM radio station call letters]
WPLO .... Grayson, GA [AM radio station call letters]
WPLO .... Water Port Liaison Office [or Officer] [Air Force] (AFM)
WPLR .... New Haven, CT [FM radio station call letters]
WPLS .... Greenville, SC [FM radio station call letters]
WPLS .... Western Plains Library System [Library network]
WPLT........... Plattsburgh, NY [FM radio station call letters]
WPLTO .... Western Plateau [NWS] (FAAC)
WPLV-AM .... West Point, GA [AM radio station call letters] (RBYB)
WPLW .... Carnegie, PA [AM radio station call letters]
WPLX .... Germantown, TN [AM radio station call letters]
WPLY .... Media, PA [FM radio station call letters]
WPlyM......... Mission House Theological Seminary, Plymouth, WI [Library symbol Library of Congress] (LCLS)
WPLZ .... Petersburg, VA [FM radio station call letters]
WPM........... War Plan, Mid-Range
WPM........... War Planning Memorandum (NATG)
WPM........... Waterproof Membrane
WPM........... Western Premium [Vancouver Stock Exchange symbol]
WPM........... West Point-Pepperell (EFIS)
WPM........... White Pine [Michigan] [Seismograph station code, US Geological Survey] (SEIS)
WPM........... Wipim [Papua New Guinea] [Airport symbol] (OAG)
WPM........... Wire-Wound Porous Material
WPM........... Wood Plastic Material
WPM........... Words per Minute
wpm........... Words per Minute (WDMC)
WPM........... Work Package Management (MCD)
WPM........... World Presbyterian Missions (EA)
WPM........... Write Program Memory [Computer science]
WPM........... Write Protect Memory
WPMA .... Wall Paper Merchants' Association of Great Britain (BI)
WPMA .... Waterproof Paper Manufacturers Association [Later, API]
WPMA .... Windows/Presentation Manager Association (EA)
WPMA .... Wood Products Manufacturers Association (EA)
WPMA .... Writing Paper Manufacturers Association [Later, API] (EA)

WPMB	Vandalia, IL [*AM radio station call letters*]
WPMC	Jellico, TN [*Television station call letters*]
WPMC	Waxed Paper Merchandising Council [*Defunct*]
WPMCP	Work Package Manpower and Cost Plan [*NASA*] (NASA)
WPME	Lewiston, ME [*Television station call letters*] (BROA)
WPME	Women for Peace in the Middle East (EA)
WPMH	Portsmouth, VA [*AM radio station call letters*]
WPMI	Mobile, AL [*Television station call letters*]
WPMN	Maliana [*East Timor*] [*ICAO location identifier*] (ICLI)
WPMR	Mount Pocono, PA [*AM radio station call letters*]
WPMRR	Work Package Milestone Progress Report (MCD)
WPMT	York, PA [*Television station call letters*]
WPMW	Mullens, WV [*FM radio station call letters*]
WPMX	Statesboro, GA [*FM radio station call letters*] (RBYB)
WPMZ	Providence, RI [*AM radio station call letters*] (RBYB)
WPN	Weapon (AAG)
Wpn	Weapon (MUSM)
WPN	Weapons Procurement, Navy (NVT)
WPN	Wolverhampton [*British depot code*]
WPN	World's Press News [*A publication*] (DGA)
WPN	Write Punch [*Computer science*] (MCD)
WPNA	Oak Park, IL [*AM radio station call letters*]
WPNA	World Proof Numismatic Association (EA)
WPNC	Plymouth, NC [*AM radio station call letters*]
WPNC-FM	Plymouth, NC [*FM radio station call letters*]
WPNE	Green Bay, WI [*FM radio station call letters*]
WPNE	White Pine Software, Inc. [*NASDAQ symbol*] (SAG)
WPNE-TV	Green Bay, WI [*Television station call letters*]
WPNFPT	Weapon Fly-to-Point (NVT)
WPNG-FM	Pearson, GA [*FM radio station call letters*] (RBYB)
WPNH	Plymouth, NH [*AM radio station call letters*]
WPNH-FM	Plymouth, NH [*FM radio station call letters*]
WPNP-AM	Mulberry, FL [*AM radio station call letters*] (BROA)
WPNR	Utica, NY [*FM radio station call letters*]
WPNSTA	Weapons Station
WPNT	Chicago, IL [*FM radio station call letters*]
WPNTS	War Plan Naval Transportation Service
WPNW	Pawtucket, RI [*AM radio station call letters*] (RBYB)
WPNX	Phenix City, AL [*AM radio station call letters*]
WPO	War Plan Orange [*World War II*]
WPO	Warsaw Pact Organization (MCD)
WPO	Washington Post'B' [*NYSE symbol*] (TTSB)
WPO	Washington Post Co. Class B [*NYSE symbol*] (SPSG)
WPO	Water for Peace Office [*Department of State*]
WPO	Water Programs Office [*Environmental Protection Agency*]
WPO	West Pacific Ocean (SAA)
WPO	Women's Project Officer
WPO	World Packaging Organization [*See also OME*] [*Paris, France*] (EAIO)
WPO	World Ploughing Organisation [*Carlisle, Cumbria, England*] (EAIO)
WPOA	Western Pacific Orthopaedic Association (EA)
WPOB	Plainview, NY [*FM radio station call letters*]
WPOC	Baltimore, MD [*FM radio station call letters*]
WPOC	Oecussi [*East Timor*] [*ICAO location identifier*] (ICLI)
WPoCC	ICA [*International Co-Operative Alliance*] Working Party on Co-Operative Communications (EAIO)
WPoCP	ICA [*International Co-Operative Alliance*] Working Party on Co-Operative Press [*Later, WPoCC*] (EAIO)
WPOD	Water Port of Debarkation (AFM)
WPOE	Water Port of Embarkation (AFM)
WPOE	Word Processing and Office Equipment (MHDI)
WPOG	Pease Oil & Gas [*NASDAQ symbol*] (TTSB)
WPOG	Pease Oil & Gas Co. [*NASDAQ symbol*] (SAG)
WPOG	Willard Pease Oil & Gas Co. [*NASDAQ symbol*] (NQ)
WPOGP	Pease Oil & Gas $1 Cv'A'Pfd [*NASDAQ symbol*] (TTSB)
WPOK	Pontiac, IL [*AM radio station call letters*]
WPOL	Winston-Salem, NC [*AM radio station call letters*] (RBYB)
WPOM	Riviera Beach, FL [*AM radio station call letters*]
WPOM	Word Processing-Output Microfilm
WPON	Walled Lake, MI [*AM radio station call letters*]
WPOP	Hartford, CT [*AM radio station call letters*]
WPOR	Portland, ME [*AM radio station call letters*]
WPOR-FM	Portland, ME [*FM radio station call letters*]
WPOS	Holland, OH [*FM radio station call letters*]
WP/OS	Word Processing/Office Systems (HGAA)
WPOW	Miami, FL [*FM radio station call letters*]
WPP	Wage Pause Program [*Business term*] (ADA)
WPP	Waterproof Paper Packing
WPP	Water Pump Package (NASA)
WPP	Weapon Position Preparation (MCD)
WPP	Weapons Production Program
WPP	Web Printing Press
WPP	Wechsler Preschool Primary Scale of Intelligence [*Education*] (DAVI)
WPP	Weibull Probability Paper [*Statistics*]
WPP	Windward Passage Patrol [*Navy*] (NVT)
WPP	Witness Protection Program (BARN)
WPP	WordPerfect Presentations [*WordPerfect Corp.*] [*Computer science*] (PCM)
WPP	Work Package Plan [*NASA*] (NASA)
WPP	World Pen Pals (EA)
WPP	Writing Proficiency Program [*Educational test*]
WPPA	Pottsville, PA [*AM radio station call letters*]
WPPA	West Point Protective Association [*Unofficial association of West Point graduates*] (VNW)
WPPB	Boca Raton, FL [*Television station call letters*]
WPPC	Penuelas, PR [*AM radio station call letters*]
WPPC	Warning Point Photocell
WPPC	Water Products Promotion Council (WPI)
WPPC	West Penn Power Co.
WPPC	West Point Parents Club (EA)
WPPD	Whole-Powder-Pattern Decomposition [*Crystallography*]
WPPDA	Welfare and Pension Plans Disclosure Act [*1958*] [*Department of Labor*]
WPPG	WPP Group PLC [*NASDAQ symbol*] (SAG)
WPP Gp	WPP Group PLC [*Associated Press*] (SAG)
WPP Grp	WPP Group PLC [*Associated Press*] (SAG)
WPPGY	WPP Group ADS [*NASDAQ symbol*] (TTSB)
WPPI	Carrollton, GA [*AM radio station call letters*]
WPPI	Wedding and Portrait Photographers International (NTPA)
WPP/IS	Writing Proficiency Program/Intermediate System [*Educational test*]
WPPL	Blue Ridge, GA [*FM radio station call letters*]
WPPM	Weight Part per Million
WPPO	Wood Products Purchasing Office [*Defense Construction Supply Center*] [*Defense Supply Agency*]
WPPR-FM	Demorest, GA [*FM radio station call letters*] (RBYB)
WPPS	Work Package Planning Sheet [*NASA*] (NASA)
WPPS	World Peace Prayer Society (EA)
WPPSI	Wechsler Preschool and Primary Scale of Intelligence [*Education*]
WPPSS	Washington Public Power Supply System [*Nicknamed "Whoops"*]
WPPW	Association of Western Pulp and Paper Workers
WPPX	Wilmington, DE [*Television station call letters*] (BROA)
WPQR	Uniontown, PA [*FM radio station call letters*]
WPQR	Welding Procedure Qualification Record [*Nuclear energy*] (NRCH)
WPR	Auckland Regional Rescue Helicopter Trust [*New Zealand*] [*FAA designator*] (FAAC)
WPR	Porvenir [*Chile*] [*Airport symbol*] (AD)
WPR	Ward Pound Ridge [*New York*] [*Seismograph station code, US Geological Survey*] (SEIS)
WPR	Wartime Personnel Requirements (NATG)
WPR	Webster's Patent Reports [*England*] [*A publication*] (DLA)
WPR	Western Planning Resources (PA)
WPR	West Pakistan Railway
WPR	White Puerto Rican
WPR	Widescope Resources Ltd. [*Vancouver Stock Exchange symbol*]
WPR	Witness Protection and Relocation [*Government agency in film "F/X"*]
WPR	Woodpecker Repellent [*In company name, WPR Co.*]
WPR	Working Party on Rationing [*Allied German Occupation Forces*]
WPR	Working Pressure
WPR	Write Permit Ring (NITA)
WPR	Written Progress Report (HCT)
WPRA	Mayaguez, PR [*AM radio station call letters*]
WPRA	Waste Paper Recovery Association Ltd. [*British*] (BI)
WPRA	Women's Professional Racquetball Association (EA)
WPRA	Women's Professional Rodeo Association (EA)
WPRB	Princeton, NJ [*FM radio station call letters*]
WPRC	Lincoln, IL [*AM radio station call letters*]
WPRC	Women Prisoners' Resource Center (WDAA)
WPRD	Winter Park, FL [*AM radio station call letters*]
WPRE	Prairie du Chien, WI [*AM radio station call letters*]
WPRE-FM	Prairie du Chien, WI [*FM radio station call letters*]
WP (REI)	Wildlife Protection (Regulations and Exports and Imports) [*Act 1982*] (EERA)
WPRG	Workers-Peasants Red Guards [*North Korea*]
WPRI	Providence, RI [*Television station call letters*]
WPRI	Wartime Pacific Routing Instructions [*Navy*]
WPRJ	Coleman, MI [*FM radio station call letters*]
WPRK	Winter Park, FL [*FM radio station call letters*]
WPRL	Lorman, MS [*FM radio station call letters*]
WPRL	Water Pollution Research Laboratory [*British*]
WPRM	San Juan, PR [*FM radio station call letters*]
WPRN	Butler, AL [*AM radio station call letters*]
WPRO	Providence, RI [*AM radio station call letters*]
WPRO	Wartime Personnel Replacement Operation [*Military*]
WPRO-FM	Providence, RI [*FM radio station call letters*]
WPRP	Ponce, PR [*AM radio station call letters*]
WPRR	Altoona, PA [*AM radio station call letters*]
WPRS	Paris, IL [*AM radio station call letters*]
WPRS	War Powers Reporting System
WPRS	Water and Power Resources Service [*Formerly, Bureau of Reclamation*] [*Department of the Interior Name changed back to Bureau of Reclamation, 1981*]
WPRS	Wittenborn Psychiatric Rating Scale
WPRT	Prestonsburg, KY [*AM radio station call letters*]
WPRT	Waypoint Report [*Aviation*] (FAAC)
WPRV	Fajardo, PR [*Television station call letters*]
WPRX	Bristol, CT [*AM radio station call letters*]
WPRY	Perry, FL [*AM radio station call letters*]
WPRZ	Warrenton, VA [*AM radio station call letters*]
WPS	International Association of Word Processing Specialists [*Formerly, NAWPS*] (EA)
WPS	Warner Publishing Services
WPS	War Planning Slate (CINC)
WPS	War Plan, Short-Range
WPS	Wartime Capability Play, Short Range (SAA)
WPS	Waste Processing System [*Nuclear energy*] (NRCH)
WPS	Watermen's Protective Society [*A union*] [*British*]
WPS	Water Phase Salt [*of smoked food*]
WPS	Water Pressure Switch
WPS	Waterproof Shroud
WPS	Water Purification System

WPS............ Watts per Steradian
WPS............ Waveform Processing System
WPS............ Wave Power Source
WPS............ Weapons Program Section
WPS............ Welding Procedure Specification [*Nuclear energy*] (NRCH)
WPS............ Western Psychological Services (DHP)
WPS............ Wet Peridotite Solidus [*Geology*]
WPS............ White Power Structure
WPS............ Wideband Packet Switch (CIST)
WPS............ Widowed Persons Service (EA)
WPS............ Wildlife Preservation Society (COE)
WPS............ Windows Printing System [*Microsoft Corp.*] (PCM)
WPS............ Wind Power System
WPS............ Wireless Preservation Society [*British*]
WPS............ Wisconsin Physicians Service [*Army*]
WPS............ With Prior Service
WPS............ Women in Public Service (EA)
WPS............ Word Processing Society
WPS............ Word Processing System (BUR)
WPS............ Words per Second
WPS............ Workplace Shell [*IBM Corp.*] [*Computer science*] (PCM)
WPS............ Work Profiling System (WDAA)
WPS............ Workstation Publishing Software
WPS............ World Photography Society (EA)
WPS............ World Politics Simulation
WPS............ World Population Society (EA)
WPS............ Worldwide Plug and Socket [*Proposed standard electrical plug for international use*] [*Pronounced "whoops"*]
WPS............ Worldwide Port System [*Army*] (RDA)
WPS............ WPS Resources [*NYSE symbol*] (TTSB)
WPS............ WPS Resources Corp. [*NYSE symbol*] (SAG)
WPSA.......... Paul Smith's, NY [*FM radio station call letters*]
WPSA.......... Welsh Pony Society of America [*Later, WPCSA*] (EA)
WPSA.......... Wildlife Preservation Society of Australia (EERA)
WPSA.......... World Professional Squash Association (EA)
WPSA.......... World's Poultry Science Association [*See also AVI*] [*Celle, Federal Republic of Germany*] (EAIO)
WPSA.......... World's Poultry Science Association, USA Branch (EA)
WPSB-FM .... Kane, PA [*FM radio station call letters*] (RBYB)
WPSC.......... Shipping Control War Plan [*Navy*]
WPSC.......... Wayne, NJ [*FM radio station call letters*]
WPSD.......... Paducah, KY [*Television station call letters*]
WPSE.......... Erie, PA [*AM radio station call letters*]
WPSG-TV .... Philadelphia, PA [*TV station call letters*] (RBYB)
WPSI.......... Wahler Physical Symptoms Inventory [*Psychiatry*] (DAVI)
WPSI.......... Word Processing Society, Inc. (EA)
WPSI.......... World Poetry Society Intercontinental (EA)
WPSK.......... Pulaski, VA [*FM radio station call letters*]
WPSL.......... Port St. Lucie, FL [*AM radio station call letters*]
WPSL.......... Western Primary Standard Laboratory
WPSM .... Fort Walton Beach, FL [*FM radio station call letters*]
WPSM .... Same [*East Timor*] [*ICAO location identifier*] (ICLI)
WPSN .... Westpoint Stevens [*NASDAQ symbol*] (SAG)
WPSO .... New Port Richey, FL [*AM radio station call letters*]
WPSP .... Royal Palm Beach, FL [*AM radio station call letters*] (RBYB)
WPSQ .... Wildlife Preservation Society of Queensland (EERA)
WPSR .... Evansville, IN [*FM radio station call letters*]
WPSR .... Weekly Performance Status Report (MCD)
WPS-RA...... World Pro Skiing-Racers Association [*Defunct*] (EA)
WPS Res ..... WPS Resources Corp. [*Associated Press*] (SAG)
WPST .... Trenton, NJ [*FM radio station call letters*]
WPSU .... State College, PA [*FM radio station call letters*]
WPSX .... Clearfield, PA [*Television station call letters*]
WPT............ Wapiti Aviation Ltd. [*Canada ICAO designator*] (FAAC)
WPT............ Warbled Pure Tone [*Speech and language therapy*] (DAVI)
WPT............ Waypoint [*ICAO*] (FAAC)
WPT............ Western Personnel Tests [*General intelligence test*]
WPT............ White Phosphorous Tracer [*Military*] (MUSM)
WPT............ Windfall Profit Tax
WPT............ With Promotion To (NOAA)
WPT............ Wolfe Screening Test for Programming Aptitude
WPT............ Word Processing Test
WPT............ Workers' Party of Turkey
WPT............ Working Point [*Technical drawings*]
WPT............ Writing Process Test (TMMY)
WPTA.......... Fort Wayne, IN [*Television station call letters*]
WPTA.......... Wooden Pail and Tub Association
WPTB.......... Statesboro, GA [*AM radio station call letters*]
WPTB.......... Wartime Prices and Trade Board
WPTD .... Dayton, OH [*Television station call letters*]
WPTE-FM .... Virginia Beach, VA [*FM radio station call letters*] (RBYB)
WPTF.......... National Council for a World Peace Tax Fund (EA)
WPTF.......... Raleigh, NC [*AM radio station call letters*]
WPTG .... West Point, VA [*FM radio station call letters*]
WPTH .... Olney, IL [*FM radio station call letters*]
WPTI.......... Wildlife Preservation Trust International (EA)
WPTL.......... Canton, NC [*AM radio station call letters*]
WPTLC........ World Peace through Law Center (EA)
WPTM.......... Roanoke Rapids, NC [*FM radio station call letters*]
WPTN.......... Cookeville, TN [*AM radio station call letters*]
WPTNG .... Weapons Training (NVT)
WPTO.......... Oxford, OH [*Television station call letters*]
WPTR-FM .... Voorheesville, NY [*FM radio station call letters*] (RBYB)
WPTS.......... Pittsburgh, PA [*FM radio station call letters*]
WPTT.......... Pittsburgh, PA [*Television station call letters*]

WPTV.......... West Palm Beach, FL [*Television station call letters*]
WPTW.......... Piqua, OH [*AM radio station call letters*]
WPTX.......... Lexington Park, MD [*AM radio station call letters*]
WPTY.......... Memphis, TN [*Television station call letters*]
WPTZ.......... North Pole, NY [*Television station call letters*]
WPU............ Puerto Williams [*Chile*] [*Airport symbol*] (AD)
WPU............ We the People, United (EA)
WPU............ Wet Pick Up (IAA)
WPU............ With Power Unit (NATG)
WPU............ Women's Protestant Union [*British*]
WPU............ Write Punch [*Computer science*]
WPUB.......... Camden, SC [*FM radio station call letters*]
WPUC.......... Waste-Paper Utilization Council [*Defunct*]
W/PUG........ Word Processing Users' Group
WPUL.......... South Daytona, FL [*AM radio station call letters*]
WPUM.......... Rensselaer, IN [*FM radio station call letters*]
WPUP.......... Royston, GA [*FM radio station call letters*]
WPUT.......... Brewster, NY [*AM radio station call letters*]
WPUV.......... Pulaski, VA [*AM radio station call letters*]
WPVA.......... Waynesboro, VA [*FM radio station call letters*]
WPVB.......... Culpeper, VA [*FM radio station call letters*]
WPVG.......... Funkstown, MD [*AM radio station call letters*]
WPVI.......... Philadelphia, PA [*Television station call letters*]
WPVL.......... Platteville, WI [*AM radio station call letters*] (RBYB)
WPVL-FM .... Platteville, WI [*FM radio station call letters*] (RBYB)
WPVO.......... Princeton, WV [*AM radio station call letters*]
WPVQ.......... Turners Falls, MA [*FM radio station call letters*]
WPVQ.......... Vieque [*East Timor*] [*ICAO location identifier*] (ICLI)
WPVR.......... Roanoke, VA [*FM radio station call letters*]
WPW .... Wolff-Parkinson-White [*Syndrome*] [*Cardiology*]
WPWA.......... Chester, PA [*AM radio station call letters*]
WPWB.......... Byron, GA [*FM radio station call letters*]
WPWC.......... Dumfries-Triangle, VA [*AM radio station call letters*]
WPWIN........ WordPerfect for Windows [*Computer science*]
WPWM.......... Wide Pulse Width Modulation
WPWOD...... Will Proceed Without Delay
WPWP......... Western Pacific Warm Pod [*Oceanography*]
WPWP......... Western Pacific Warm Pool [*Oceanography*]
WPWR......... Gary, IN [*Television station call letters*]
WPWR......... World-Wide Plantation Walker Registry (EA)
WPWRA...... Wallcovering, Fabric, and Decor Retailers Association [*British*] (EAIO)
WPWT-AM.... Colonial Heights, VA [*AM radio station call letters*] (RBYB)
WPX............ Worked All Prefixes [*Amateur radio*] (IAA)
WPXA......... Rome, GA [*Television station call letters*] (BROA)
WPXB......... Merrimack, NH [*Television station call letters*] (BROA)
WPXC......... Hyannis, MA [*FM radio station call letters*]
WPXE......... Kenosha, WI [*Television station call letters*] (BROA)
WPXG......... Suring, WI [*Television station call letters*] (BROA)
WPXH......... Gadsden, AL [*Television station call letters*] (BROA)
WPXI......... Pittsburgh, PA [*Television station call letters*]
WPXK......... Jellico, TN [*Television station call letters*] (BROA)
WPXN......... Paxton, IL [*FM radio station call letters*]
WPXR......... Roanoke, VA [*Television station call letters*] (BROA)
WPXS......... Mount Vernon, IL [*Television station call letters*] (BROA)
WPXT......... Portland, ME [*Television station call letters*]
WPXW......... Manassas, VA [*Television station call letters*] (BROA)
WPXX......... Semora, NC [*FM radio station call letters*] (RBYB)
WPXY......... Rochester, NY [*FM radio station call letters*]
WPXZ......... Punxsutawney, PA [*FM radio station call letters*]
WPY............ White Pass & Yukon Corp. Ltd. [*Toronto Stock Exchange symbol Vancouver Stock Exchange symbol AAR code*]
WPY............ World Population Year [*1974*] [*United Nations*]
WPYB.......... Benson, NC [*AM radio station call letters*]
WPYK.......... Dora, AL [*AM radio station call letters*]
WPYX.......... Albany, NY [*FM radio station call letters*]
WPZ............ Waipapa Point [*New Zealand*] [*Seismograph station code, US Geological Survey Closed*] (SEIS)
WPZ............ Western Plains Zoo [*Dubbo, New South Wales, Australia*]
WPZE-AM.... Boston, MA [*AM radio station call letters*] (BROA)
WPZM.......... Tullahoma, TN [*FM radio station call letters*] (RBYB)
WPZZ.......... Franklin, IN [*FM radio station call letters*]
WQ............ Water Quenching (OA)
WQ............ Wings Airways [*ICAO designator*] (AD)
WQ............ Wotquenne Catalog [*Used to catalog music of C.P.E Bach*] (BARN)
WQA............ Water Quality Act (GFGA)
WQA............ Water Quality Association (EA)
WQA .... Weld Quality Assurance
WQAB.......... Philippi, WV [*FM radio station call letters*]
WQAC.......... Alma, MI [*FM radio station call letters*]
WQAD.......... Moline, IL [*Television station call letters*]
WQAI.......... Fernandina Beach, FL [*AM radio station call letters*]
WQAL.......... Cleveland, OH [*FM radio station call letters*]
WQAM.......... Miami, FL [*AM radio station call letters*]
WQAQ.......... Hamden, CT [*FM radio station call letters*]
WQAU-P ..... Water Quality Analysis Unit - Purification [*Army*]
WQB............ Water Quality Based [*Environmental science*]
WQB............ Water-Quality Biological [*Survey*] [*Army*] (RDA)
WQBA.......... Miami, FL [*AM radio station call letters*]
WQBB.......... Knoxville, TN [*FM radio station call letters*]
WQBB.......... Powell, TN [*AM radio station call letters*]
WQBC.......... Vicksburg, MS [*AM radio station call letters*]
WQBE.......... Charleston, WV [*AM radio station call letters*]
WQBE-FM .... Charleston, WV [*FM radio station call letters*]
WQBEL .... Water Quality-Based Effluent Limit [*Environmental Protection Agency*]

WQBH	Detroit, MI [*AM radio station call letters*]
WQBJ	Cobleskill, NY [*FM radio station call letters*]
WQBK	Rensselaer, NY [*AM radio station call letters*]
WQBK-FM	Rensselaer, NY [*FM radio station call letters*]
WQBN	Temple Terrace, FL [*AM radio station call letters*]
WQBQ	Leesburg, FL [*AM radio station call letters*]
WQBR	Avis, PA [*FM radio station call letters*]
WQBS	San Juan, PR [*AM radio station call letters*]
WQBX	Alma, MI [*FM radio station call letters*] (RBYB)
WQBZ	Fort Valley, GA [*FM radio station call letters*]
WQC	Quinsigamond Community College, Worcester, MA [*OCLC symbol*] (OCLC)
WQC	Water Quality Certification [*Nuclear energy*] (NRCH)
WQC	Wheat Quality Council (EA)
WQCB	Brewer, ME [*FM radio station call letters*]
WQCC	La Crosse, WI [*FM radio station call letters*]
WQCD	New York, NY [*FM radio station call letters*]
WQCH	La Fayette, GA [*AM radio station call letters*]
WQCK	Clinton, LA [*FM radio station call letters*]
WQCM	Halfway, MD [*FM radio station call letters*]
WQCR	Jackson, TN [*AM radio station call letters*]
WQCS	Fort Pierce, FL [*FM radio station call letters*]
WQCT	Bryan, OH [*AM radio station call letters*]
WQCY	Quincy, IL [*FM radio station call letters*]
WQDK	Ahoskie, NC [*FM radio station call letters*]
WQDQ	Lebanon, TN [*AM radio station call letters*]
WQDR	Raleigh, NC [*FM radio station call letters*]
WQDY	Calais, ME [*AM radio station call letters*]
WQDY-FM	Calais, ME [*FM radio station call letters*]
WQEC	Quincy, IL [*Television station call letters*]
WQEC/C	Weapons Quality Engineering Center, Crane [*Indiana*]
WQED	Pittsburgh, PA [*FM radio station call letters*]
WQED-TV	Pittsburgh, PA [*Television station call letters*]
WQEJ-FM	Johnstown, PA [*FM radio station call letters*] (BROA)
WQEL	Bucyrus, OH [*FM radio station call letters*]
WQEN	Gadsden, AL [*FM radio station call letters*]
WQEQ	Freeland, PA [*FM radio station call letters*]
WQEW	New York, NY [*AM radio station call letters*]
WQEX	Pittsburgh, PA [*Television station call letters*]
WQEZ	Kennebunkport, ME [*FM radio station call letters*]
WQF	Wider Quaker Fellowship (EA)
WQFE	Brownsburg, IN [*FM radio station call letters*]
WQFL	Rockford, IL [*FM radio station call letters*]
WQFM	Milwaukee, WI [*FM radio station call letters*]
WQFN	Walker, MI [*FM radio station call letters*]
WQFS	Greensboro, NC [*FM radio station call letters*]
WQFX	Gulfport, MS [*AM radio station call letters*]
WQGL	Butler, AL [*FM radio station call letters*]
WQGN	Groton, CT [*FM radio station call letters*]
WQHA	Aquada, PR [*Television station call letters*]
WQHB	Sumter, SC [*Television station call letters*] (BROA)
WQHG	Huntingdon, PA [*FM radio station call letters*]
WQHH	Dewitt, MI [*FM radio station call letters*]
WQHK	Decatur, IN [*FM radio station call letters*]
WQHK	Fort Wayne, IN [*AM radio station call letters*]
WQHL	Live Oak, FL [*AM radio station call letters*]
WQHL-FM	Live Oak, FL [*FM radio station call letters*]
WQHQ	Ocean City-Salisbury, MD [*FM radio station call letters*]
WQHR-FM	Presque Isle, ME [*FM radio station call letters*] (RBYB)
WQHS	Cleveland, OH [*Television station call letters*]
WQHT	New York, NY [*FM radio station call letters*]
WQHY	Prestonsburg, KY [*FM radio station call letters*]
WQI	Water Quality Index
WQI	Water Quality Instrument
WQIC	Lebanon, PA [*FM radio station call letters*]
WQII	San Juan, PR [*AM radio station call letters*]
WQIK	Jacksonville, FL [*FM radio station call letters*]
WQIL	Chauncey, GA [*FM radio station call letters*]
WQIO	Mount Vernon, OH [*FM radio station call letters*]
WQIP	Water Quality Incentive Program [*Department of Agriculture*]
WQIS	Laurel, MS [*AM radio station call letters*]
WQIS	Water Quality Indicator System [*Marine science*] (GFGA)
WQIS	Water Quality Insurance Syndicate (EA)
WQIX	Horseheads, NY [*FM radio station call letters*]
WQIX-AM	Horseheads, NY [*AM radio station call letters*] (RBYB)
WQIZ	St. George, SC [*AM radio station call letters*]
WQJU	Mifflintown, PA [*FM radio station call letters*]
WQJY	West Salem, WI [*FM radio station call letters*]
WQKC	Seymour, IN [*AM radio station call letters*]
WQKE-FM	Plattsburgh, NY [*FM radio station call letters*] (BROA)
WQKI	St. Matthews, SC [*AM radio station call letters*]
WQKK	Ebensburg, PA [*FM radio station call letters*]
WQKL	Ann Arbor, MI [*FM radio station call letters*]
WQKO	Howe, IN [*FM radio station call letters*]
WQKR	Portland, TN [*AM radio station call letters*]
WQKS	Hopkinsville, KY [*AM radio station call letters*]
WQKT	Wooster, OH [*FM radio station call letters*]
WQKX	Sunbury, PA [*FM radio station call letters*]
WQKY	Emporium, PA [*FM radio station call letters*]
WQKZ-FM	Ferdinand, IN [*FM radio station call letters*] (BROA)
WQLA-FM	La Follette, TN [*FM radio station call letters*]
WQLB-FM	Tawas City, MI [*FM radio station call letters*] (BROA)
WQLC	Watertown, FL [*FM radio station call letters*]
WQLE	Kane, PA [*AM radio station call letters*]
WQLH	Green Bay, WI [*FM radio station call letters*]
WQLJ	Oxford, MS [*FM radio station call letters*]
WQLK	Richmond, IN [*FM radio station call letters*]
WQLL	Louisville, KY [*FM radio station call letters*]
WQLN	Erie, PA [*FM radio station call letters*]
WQLN-TV	Erie, PA [*Television station call letters*]
WQLR	Kalamazoo, MI [*FM radio station call letters*]
WQLS	Ozark, AL [*AM radio station call letters*]
WQLS-FM	Ozark, AL [*FM radio station call letters*]
WQLT	Florence, AL [*FM radio station call letters*]
WQLV	Millersburg, PA [*FM radio station call letters*]
WQLW	Eutaw, AL [*FM radio station call letters*]
WQLX	Galion, OH [*FM radio station call letters*]
WQLZ	Taylorville, IL [*FM radio station call letters*]
WQM	University of Massachusetts, Medical Center, Worcester, MA [*OCLC symbol*] (OCLC)
WQM	Water Quality Management
WQMA	Marks, MS [*AM radio station call letters*]
WQMC	Sumter, SC [*AM radio station call letters*]
WQMD	Water Quantity Measuring Device
WQME	Anderson, IN [*FM radio station call letters*]
WQMF	Jeffersonville, IN [*FM radio station call letters*]
WQMG	Greensboro, NC [*AM radio station call letters*]
WQMG-FM	Greensboro, NC [*FM radio station call letters*]
WQMP	Water Quality Management Project
WQMT	Chatsworth, GA [*FM radio station call letters*]
WQMU	Indiana, PA [*FM radio station call letters*]
WQMX	Medina, OH [*FM radio station call letters*]
WQMZ	Charlottesville, VA [*FM radio station call letters*]
WQNA	Springfield, IL [*FM radio station call letters*]
WQNJ	Ocean Acres, NJ [*FM radio station call letters*]
WQNN	Artesia, MS [*FM radio station call letters*]
WQNS	Waynesville, NC [*FM radio station call letters*]
WQNT-AM	Charleston, SC [*AM radio station call letters*] (RBYB)
WQNU-FM	Naples Park, FL [*FM radio station call letters*] (BROA)
WQNX	Aberdeen, NC [*AM radio station call letters*]
WQNY	Ithaca, NY [*FM radio station call letters*]
WQNZ	Natchez, MS [*FM radio station call letters*]
WQO	Water Quality Office [*Later, OWP*] [*Environmental Protection Agency*]
WQOK	South Boston, VA [*FM radio station call letters*]
WQOL	Vero Beach, FL [*FM radio station call letters*]
WQON	Roscommon, MI [*FM radio station call letters*] (RBYB)
WQOP-AM	Atlantic Beach, FL [*AM radio station call letters*] (BROA)
WQOW	Eau Claire, WI [*Television station call letters*]
WQOX	Memphis, TN [*FM radio station call letters*]
WQP	West Penn Power Co. [*NYSE symbol*] (SAG)
WQP	West Penn Pwr 8.00% 'QUIDS' [*NYSE symbol*] (TTSB)
WQPM	Princeton, MN [*AM radio station call letters*]
WQPM-FM	Princeton, MN [*FM radio station call letters*]
WQPO	Harrisonburg, VA [*FM radio station call letters*]
WQPH	Muscle Shoals, AL [*FM radio station call letters*]
WQPT	Moline, IL [*Television station call letters*]
WQPW	Valdosta, GA [*FM radio station call letters*]
WQPX	Scranton, PA [*Television station call letters*] (BROA)
WQQB-FM	Rantoul, IL [*FM radio station call letters*] (RBYB)
WQQK	Hendersonville, TN [*FM radio station call letters*]
WQQL	Springfield, IL [*FM radio station call letters*]
WQQQ	Sharon, CT [*FM radio station call letters*]
WQQW	Waterbury, CT [*AM radio station call letters*] (RBYB)
WQQZ	Quebradillas, PR [*FM radio station call letters*]
WQRA	Warrenton, VA [*FM radio station call letters*]
WQRB	Bloomer, WI [*FM radio station call letters*]
WQRC	Barnstable, MA [*FM radio station call letters*]
WQRC	Water Quality Research Council (EA)
WQRF	Rockford, IL [*Television station call letters*]
WQRI	Bristol, RI [*FM radio station call letters*]
WQRK	Bedford, IN [*FM radio station call letters*]
WQRL	Benton, IL [*FM radio station call letters*]
WQRM	Smethport, PA [*FM radio station call letters*]
WQRP	Water Quality Research Program [*US Army Corps of Engineers*]
WQRP	West Carollton, OH [*FM radio station call letters*]
WQRS	Detroit, MI [*FM radio station call letters*]
WQRT	Salamanca, NY [*FM radio station call letters*]
WQRV-FM	Avon, NY [*FM radio station call letters*] (BROA)
WQRX	Valley Head, AL [*AM radio station call letters*]
WQS	Water Quality Standards (COE)
WQS	Water Quality System [*Environmental Protection Agency*] (AEPA)
WQSA	Sarasota, FL [*AM radio station call letters*]
WQSB	Albertville, AL [*FM radio station call letters*]
WQSC	Charleston, NC [*AM radio station call letters*]
WQSE	White Bluff, TN [*AM radio station call letters*]
WQSI	Frederick, MD [*AM radio station call letters*]
WQSL	Jacksonville, NC [*FM radio station call letters*]
WQSM	Fayetteville, NC [*FM radio station call letters*]
WQSN	Kalamazoo, MI [*AM radio station call letters*]
WQSO-FM	Rochester, NH [*FM radio station call letters*] (BROA)
WQSR	Catonsville, MD [*FM radio station call letters*]
WQSS	Camden, ME [*FM radio station call letters*]
WQST	Forest, MS [*AM radio station call letters*]
WQST-FM	Forest, MS [*FM radio station call letters*]
WQSU	Selinsgrove, PA [*FM radio station call letters*]
WQSV	Ashland City, TN [*AM radio station call letters*]
WQSY	Hawkinsville, GA [*FM radio station call letters*]
WQT	Water Quench Test
WQTC	Manitowoc, WI [*FM radio station call letters*]
WQTE	Adrian, MI [*FM radio station call letters*]

WQTH-AM...	Hanover, NH [*AM radio station call letters*] (BROA)
WQTL............	Ottawa, OH [*FM radio station call letters*]
WQTM-AM...	Pine Hills, FL [*AM radio station call letters*] (RBYB)
WQTO..........	Ponce, PR [*Television station call letters*]
WQTQ..........	Hartford, CT [*FM radio station call letters*]
WQTU..........	Rome, GA [*FM radio station call letters*]
WQTW..........	Latrobe, PA [*AM radio station call letters*]
WQTY..........	Linton, IN [*FM radio station call letters*]
WQUB..........	Quincy, IL [*FM radio station call letters*]
WQUE-FM...	New Orleans, LA [*FM radio station call letters*] (RBYB)
WQUIS........	Water Quality Indicator System [*Marine science*] (MSC)
WQUL-FM...	West Frankfort, IL [*AM radio station call letters*] (RBYB)
WQUN-AM...	Hamden, CT [*AM radio station call letters*] (RBYB)
WQUT..........	Johnson City, TN [*FM radio station call letters*]
WQVE..........	Camilla, GA [*FM radio station call letters*]
WQVL-AM...	Dover, DE [*AM radio station call letters*] (BROA)
WQVR..........	Southbridge, MA [*FM radio station call letters*]
WQWK........	State College, PA [*FM radio station call letters*]
WQWQ........	Muskegon Heights, MI [*AM radio station call letters*]
WQWV-FM...	Fisher, WV [*FM radio station call letters*] (BROA)
WQXA..........	York, PA [*AM radio station call letters*]
WQXA-FM...	York, PA [*FM radio station call letters*]
WQXB..........	Grenada, MS [*FM radio station call letters*]
WQXC..........	Otsego, MI [*AM radio station call letters*]
WQXC-FM...	Otsego, MI [*FM radio station call letters*]
WQXE..........	Elizabethtown, KY [*FM radio station call letters*]
WQXI..........	Atlanta, GA [*AM radio station call letters*]
WQXJ..........	Clayton, GA [*FM radio station call letters*]
WQXK..........	Salem, OH [*FM radio station call letters*]
WQXL..........	Columbia, SC [*AM radio station call letters*]
WQXO..........	Munising, MI [*AM radio station call letters*]
WQXQ..........	Central City, KY [*FM radio station call letters*]
WQXR..........	New York, NY [*FM radio station call letters*]
WQXY..........	Hazard, KY [*AM radio station call letters*]
WQYK..........	Seffner, FL [*AM radio station call letters*]
WQYK..........	St. Petersburg, FL [*FM radio station call letters*]
WQYX..........	Clearfield, PA [*FM radio station call letters*]
WQZK..........	Keyser, WV [*FM radio station call letters*]
WQZQ..........	Dickson, TN [*FM radio station call letters*]
WQZS..........	Meyersdale, PA [*FM radio station call letters*]
WQZX..........	Greenville, AL [*FM radio station call letters*]
WQZY..........	Dublin, GA [*FM radio station call letters*]
WQZZ-FM...	Eutaw, AL [*FM radio station call letters*] (BROA)
WR...............	Sutherland's Weekly Report [*India*] [*A publication*] (DLA)
WR...............	Wagons-Restaurants [*Railroad dining cars in Europe*] [*French*]
WR...............	Wall Receptacle (MUGU)
WR...............	Wardrobe
WR...............	Wardroom [*Navy*]
wr...............	Ware (VRA)
WR...............	Warehouse Receipt [*Often negotiable*]
WR...............	Warner-Lambert Pharmaceutical Co. [*Research code symbol*]
WR...............	War Reserve (AABC)
WR...............	War Risk
WR...............	War Risk Insurance Decisions [*United States*] [*A publication*] (DLA)
WR...............	Wartime Report (MCD)
WR...............	Wartime Requirements [*Air Force document*] (AFM)
WR...............	Washout Rate
WR...............	Washroom
W/R.............	Was Received
WR...............	Wassermann Reaction [*Test for syphilis*] [*Medicine*]
WR...............	Water and Rail [*Transportation*]
WR...............	Water Repellant [*Technical drawings*]
WR...............	Water Retention (DAVI)
WR...............	Water Rinse [*Photography*] (DGA)
W/R.............	Water/Rock [*Ratio*] [*Geochemistry*]
WR...............	Waveguide, Rectangular
WR...............	Wave Retardation (DEN)
WR...............	Weakly Reactive (MAE)
WR...............	Weapon Radius (NVT)
WR...............	Weapon Range (NATG)
WR...............	Weapons Requirement [*DoD*]
WR...............	Wear Resistant
WR...............	Weather Reconnaissance
WR...............	Weather Resistant (MSA)
WR...............	Weekly Reporter [*Bengal*] [*A publication*] (DLA)
WR...............	Weekly Reporter [*England*] [*A publication*] (DLA)
WR...............	Weekly Reporter, Cape Provincial Division [*South Africa*] [*A publication*] (DLA)
WR...............	Welfare Recipient (OICC)
WR...............	Wendell's Reports [*1826-41*] [*New York*] [*A publication*] (DLA)
WR...............	Western Resources [*NYSE symbol*] (TTSB)
WR...............	Western Resources Capital I [*NYSE symbol*] (SAG)
WR...............	Western Resources Capital II [*NYSE symbol*] (SAG)
WR...............	Western Resources, Inc. [*Formerly, Kansas Power & Light Co.*] [*NYSE symbol*] (SPSG)
WR...............	West's English Chancery Reports Tempore Hardwicke [*1736-39*] [*A publication*] (DLA)
WR...............	Wet Runway [*NWS*] (FAAC)
WR...............	Wheeler Flying Service [*ICAO designator*] (AD)
W/R.............	White Room [*NASA*] (KSC)
WR...............	Whiteshell Reactor [*Canada*]
WR...............	Whole Rock [*Geology*]
WR...............	Wide Range [*Nuclear energy*] (NRCH)
WR...............	Wide Ratio [*Automotive engineering*]
WR...............	Wide Receiver [*Football*]
WR...............	Wildlife Reserve [*State*] (EERA)
WR...............	Wild Rose Resources [*Vancouver Stock Exchange symbol*]
WR...............	Willelmus Rex [*King William*]
WR...............	Wilson Repeater (IEEE)
WR...............	Wiping Reflex [*Physiology*]
WR...............	Wire Recorder (DEN)
WR...............	Wire Rope (AAG)
WR...............	Wirral Railway [*British*] (ROG)
WR...............	Wisconsin Reports [*A publication*] (DLA)
WR...............	Wissenschaftsrat [*Science Council*] [*Germany*]
WR...............	With Rights [*Securities*]
WR...............	Wolf-Raye [*Star classification*]
WR...............	Wolseley Register (EA)
WR...............	Women's Reserve [*Navy*]
WR...............	Women's Roundtable (EA)
WR...............	Woodmen Rangers (EA)
WR...............	Word Restoration
WR...............	Working Register
WR...............	Work Rate (AAMN)
WR...............	Work Request (MCD)
WR...............	Work Requirement (CAAL)
WR...............	Workshop Reporting (IAA)
WR...............	World Reporter [*World Council of Credit Unions*] [*A publication*]
WR...............	World River [*Geology*]
WR...............	Worthington Register [*Defunct*] (EA)
WR...............	Wrap
WR...............	Wreath (WGA)
WR...............	Wrench (MSA)
Wr...............	Wright [*Blood group*]
Wr...............	Wright's Reports [*37-50 Pennsylvania*] [*A publication*] (DLA)
WR...............	Wrist [*Medicine*]
WR...............	Wrist Roll (NASA)
WR...............	Write
WR...............	Writer (MSA)
wr...............	Wrong
WR2.............	Warramunga Array [*Australia Seismograph station code, US Geological Survey*] (SEIS)
WRA	Walter Reed Army Medical Center, Washington, DC [*OCLC symbol*] (OCLC)
WRA	Ward Room Attendant [*British military*] (DMA)
WRA	Warramunga Array [*Australia Seismograph station code, US Geological Survey*] (SEIS)
WRA	War Relocation Authority [*Within Office of Emergency Management*] [*To provide for the relocation of persons whose removal seemed necessary for national security, and for their maintenance and supervision*] [*World War II*]
WRA	War Reserve Allowance (CINC)
WRA	Waste Regulation Authority [*British*]
WRA	Water Research Association [*British*] (DCTA)
WRA	Weapons Replaceable [*or Replacement*] Assembly
WRA	Western Railroad Association (EA)
WRA	Western Range Association (EA)
WRA	Wetlands Resource Act (COE)
WRA	White River Air Services Ltd. [*Canada ICAO designator*] (FAAC)
WRA	Whiteware Research Association [*Defunct*] (EA)
WRA	Windarra Minerals Ltd. [*Vancouver Stock Exchange symbol Toronto Stock Exchange symbol*]
WRA	Wind Restraint Area (SAA)
WRA	With the Rule Astigmatism [*Ophthalmology*]
WRA	Women's Rabbinic Alliance [*Later, WSA*] (EA)
WRA	World Road Association [*Finland*] (EAIO)
WRA	Wrinkle Recovery Angle (IAA)
WRAA	Luray, VA [*AM radio station call letters*]
WRAAC........	Women's Royal Australian Army Corps (WDAA)
WRAAF	Women's Royal Australian Air Force (WDAA)
WRAB..........	Arab, AL [*AM radio station call letters*]
WR/ABPR	Weekly Record/American Book Publishing Record [*A publication*]
WRac..........	Racine Public Library, Racine, WI [*Library symbol Library of Congress*] (LCLS)
WRAC	Waste and Recycling Advisory Committee (EERA)
WRAC	Water Resources Advisory Committee [*Australian Environment Council*] (EERA)
WRAC	West Union, OH [*FM radio station call letters*]
WRAC	Willow Run Aeronautical Center [*Michigan*] (MCD)
WRAC	Women's Royal Army Corps [*British*]
WRacC........	Racine County Institutions Medical Library, Racine, WI [*Library symbol Library of Congress*] (LCLS)
WRacCL.......	Racine County Law Library, Racine, WI [*Library symbol Library of Congress*] (LCLS)
WRacD	DeKoven Foundation for Church Work, Racine, WI [*Library symbol Library of Congress*] (LCLS)
WRACELD....	Wounds Received in Action [*Incurred in*] Combat with the Enemy or in Line of Duty [*Army*] (AABC)
WRacGS	Girl Scouts of Racine County, Racine, WI [*Library symbol Library of Congress*] (LCLS)
WRacJ.........	S. C. Johnson & Son, Inc., Racine, WI [*Library symbol Library of Congress*] (LCLS)
WRacSD	Racine Unified School District Number One, Racine, WI [*Library symbol Library of Congress*] (LCLS)
WRacSL.......	Saint Luke's Memorial Hospital, School of Nursing, Racine, WI [*Library symbol Library of Congress*] (LCLS)
WRacSM......	Saint Mary's Hospital, Racine, WI [*Library symbol Library of Congress*] (LCLS)
WRacWa......	Walker Manufacturing Co., Racine, WI [*Library symbol Library of Congress*] (LCLS)

WRacWM..... Wustum Museum of Fine Arts, Racine, WI [*Library symbol Library of Congress*] (LCLS)

WRacWP ..... Western Publishing Co., Inc., Racine, WI [*Library symbol Library of Congress*] (LCLS)

WRacY........ Young Radiator Co., Racine, WI [*Library symbol Library of Congress*] (LCLS)

WRAD.......... Radford, VA [*AM radio station call letters*]

WRAF .... Toccoa Falls, GA [*FM radio station call letters*]

WRAF .... Women's Royal Air Force [*British*]

WRAFVR....... Women's Royal Air Force Volunteer Reserve [*British military*] (DMA)

WRAG.......... Carrollton, AL [*AM radio station call letters*]

WRAH-AM ... Easley, SC [*AM radio station call letters*] (RBYB)

WRAIN........ Walter Reed Army Institute of Nursing (AABC)

WRAIR........ Walter Reed Army Institute of Research [*Washington, DC*] (MCD)

WRAIS .... Wide Range Analog Input Subsystem

WRAJ.......... Anna, IL [*AM radio station call letters*]

WRAJ-FM .... Anna, IL [*FM radio station call letters*]

WRAK .... Williamsport, PA [*AM radio station call letters*]

WRAK-FM .... Salladasburg, PA [*FM radio station call letters*] (RBYB)

WRAL .... Raleigh, NC [*FM radio station call letters*]

WRALC .... Warner Robins Air Logistics Center [*Formerly, WRAMA*] (MCD)

WRAL-TV .... Raleigh, NC [*Television station call letters*]

WRAM .... Monmouth, IL [*AM radio station call letters*]

WRAM .... Water Resources Assessment Methodology [*Army Corps of Engineers*]

WRAM .... Wide-Range Recording and Monitoring [*System*] [*Radiation*]

WRAM .... Windows Random Access Memory (PCM)

WRAMA .... Warner Robins Air Materiel Area [*Later, WRALC*]

WRAMC .... Walter Reed Army Medical Center

WRAML .... Wide Range Assessment of Memory and Learning (TES)

WRANG....... Wrangler (ROG)

WRANS........ Women's Royal Australan Naval Service (WDAA)

WRAP .... Warfighting Rapid Acquisition Program

WRAP .... Waste Receiving and Processing Plant [*Environmental science*] (COE)

WRAP .... Waste Reduction Always Pays [*Dow Chemical Co. antipollution program*]

WRAP .... Waste Reduction Assessments Program [*Environmental Protection Agency*]

WRAP .... Waste Reduction Audit Protocol

WRAP .... Water Reactor Analysis Program [*Nuclear energy*] (NRCH)

WRAP .... Weapons Readiness Achievement Program (MUGU)

WRAP .... Weapons Readiness Analysis Program [*Navy*]

WRAP .... Weapons Reliability Assurance Program [*Navy*] (DNAB)

WRAP .... Weighter Record Analysis Program [*Computer science*] (MHDI)

WRAP .... Women's Radical Action Project [*Feminist group*]

WRAP .... Woodland Resource Analysis Program [*Tennessee Valley Authority*]

WRAP .... Worker Readjustment Program [*Department of Labor*]

WRAP .... Workpackage Risk Analysis Procedure (AAGC)

WRAP .... Workpackage Risk Assessment Procedure (AAGC)

WRAP .... World Risk Analysis Package [*S. J. Rundt & Associates*] [*Information service or system*] (IID)

WRAPS........ Workload and Repair Activity Process Simulator (PDAA)

WRAPS........ World Bank Retrieval Array Processing [*Computer science*] (CIST)

WRAQ.......... Brevard, NC [*AM radio station call letters*]

WRAR.......... Tappahannock, VA [*AM radio station call letters*]

WRAR-FM .... Tappahannock, VA [*FM radio station call letters*]

WRAS .... Atlanta, GA [*FM radio station call letters*]

WRAS .... Women's Reserve Ambulance Society [*World War I*] [*British*]

WRASPD...... World Rehabilitation Association for the Psycho-Socially Disabled (EA)

WRAT .... Wide-Range Achievement Test

WRAT-FM .... Point Pleasant, NJ [*FM radio station call letters*] (RBYB)

WRATH........ Women Refusing to Accept Tenant Harassment (EA)

Wrat-R........ Wide Range Achievement Test-Revised

WRAW .... Reading, PA [*AM radio station call letters*]

WRAWG .... Water Resource Assessment Working Group [*Australia*]

WRAX-FM .... Trussville, AL [*FM radio station call letters*] (RBYB)

WRAY .... Princeton, IN [*AM radio station call letters*]

WRAY-FM .... Princeton, IN [*FM radio station call letters*]

WRAY-TV .... Wilson, NC [*Television station call letters*] (RBYB)

WRAZ .... Raleigh, NC [*Television station call letters*] (RBYB)

WRB .... Macon/Warner Robins, GA [*Location identifier FAA*] (FAAL)

WRB .... Walter Reed Army Medical Center, Post/Patient Library, Washington, DC [*OCLC symbol*] (OCLC)

WRB .... Wardrobe (MSA)

WRB .... Warramunga Array [*Australia Seismograph station code, US Geological Survey*] (SEIS)

WRB .... War Refugee Board [*Terminated, 1945*]

WRB .... Water Resources Board [*British*] (DCTA)

WRB .... Wide-Range Burner (DNAB)

WRBA.......... Springfield, FL [*FM radio station call letters*]

WRBA.......... World Robotic Boxing Association (EA)

WRBB .... Banjarmasin/Syamsuddin Noor [*Indonesia*] [*ICAO location identifier*] (ICLI)

WRBB .... Boston, MA [*FM radio station call letters*]

WRBC .... Batu Licin [*Indonesia*] [*ICAO location identifier*] (ICLI)

WRBC .... Lewiston, ME [*AM radio station call letters*]

WRBC .... Washed Red Blood Cells [*Hematology*] (DAVI)

WRBC .... Weather Relay Broadcast Center

WRBD .... Pompano Beach, FL [*AM radio station call letters*]

WRBE.......... Lucedale, MS [*AM radio station call letters*]

WRBE-FM ... Lucedale, MS [*FM radio station call letters*]

WRBG.......... Warner Robins, GA [*FM radio station call letters*] (RBYB)

WRBH.......... New Orleans, LA [*FM radio station call letters*]

WRBI .... Batesville, IN [*FM radio station call letters*]

WRBI .... Pangkalan Bun/Iskandar [*Indonesia*] [*ICAO location identifier*] (ICLI)

WRBK .... Kotabaru/Setagen [*Indonesia*] [*ICAO location identifier*] (ICLI)

WRBL .... Columbus, GA [*Television station call letters*]

WRBM .... Muaratewe/Beringin [*Indonesia*] [*ICAO location identifier*] (ICLI)

WRBN .... Tanjung/Warukin [*Indonesia*] [*ICAO location identifier*] (ICLI)

WRBND....... Wire Bound

WRBP .... Hubbard, OH [*FM radio station call letters*]

WRBP .... Palangkaraya/Panarung [*Indonesia*] [*ICAO location identifier*] (ICLI)

WRBQ .... St. Petersburg, FL [*AM radio station call letters*]

WRBQ .... Tampa, FL [*FM radio station call letters*]

WRBR .... South Bend, IN [*FM radio station call letters*]

WRBR .... Wright Brothers National Memorial

WRBS .... Baltimore, MD [*FM radio station call letters*]

WRBS .... Sampit/H. Hasan [*Indonesia*] [*ICAO location identifier*] (ICLI)

WRBT .... Mt. Carmel, IL [*AM radio station call letters*]

WRBT .... Teluk Kepayang [*Indonesia*] [*ICAO location identifier*] (ICLI)

WRBU .... Buntok/Sanggau [*Indonesia*] [*ICAO location identifier*] (ICLI)

WRBW .... Orlando, FL [*Television station call letters*]

WRBX .... Reidsville, GA [*FM radio station call letters*]

WRBZ .... Banjarmasin Sector [*Indonesia*] [*ICAO location identifier*] (ICLI)

WRBZ .... Raleigh, NC [*AM radio station call letters*] (RBYB)

WRC .... War Resources Council [*Terminated*]

WRC .... Washed Red Cells [*Medicine*]

WRC .... Washington, DC [*Television station call letters*]

WRC .... Washington Research Council [*Research center*] (RCD)

WrC .... Water Carrier (WDAA)

WRC .... Water Research Centre [*Research center British*] (IRC)

WRC .... Water Resource Center [*Environmental Protection Agency*] (AEPA)

WRC .... Water Resources Center [*University of Illinois*]

WRC .... Water Resources Congress (EA)

WRC .... Water Resources Council [*Inactive*]

WRC .... Water-Retention Coefficient

WRC .... Watson Research Center [*IBM Corp.*]

WRC .... Weapons Release Computer [*or Controller*]

WRC .... Weather Relay Center

WRC .... Weekly Readiness Check

WRC .... Welding Research Council (EA)

WRC .... Well to Right of Course [*Aviation*] (FAAC)

WRC .... Werewolf Research Center (EA)

WRC .... Whale Rescue Centre [*Australia*]

WRC .... Wheat Research Council [*Australia*]

WRC .... Wildland Resources Center [*University of California*] [*Research center*] (RCD)

WRC .... Wildlife Rehabilitation Council (EA)

WRC .... Williams Ranch [*California*] [*Seismograph station code, US Geological Survey Closed*] (SEIS)

WRC .... Williams Research Corp.

WRC .... Women's Relief Corps

WRC .... Women's Rights Committee (EA)

WRC .... Woodchip Research Committee [*Australia*]

WRC .... World Color Press [*NYSE symbol*] (TTSB)

WRC .... World Radiocommunications Conference (TELE)

WRC .... World Rally Championship

WRC .... World Relief Canada

WRC .... World Relief Corp. (EA)

WRC .... World Romani Congress

WRC .... W. R. Carpenter Airlines [*Australia*]

WRCA .... Waltham, MA [*AM radio station call letters*]

WRCA .... Western Red Cedar Association (EA)

WRCA .... W. R. Carpenter Airlines [*Australia*]

WR Calc ..... Sutherland's Weekly Reporter, Calcutta [*India*] [*A publication*] (DLA)

WRCB .... Chattanooga, TN [*Television station call letters*]

WRCB .... War Relief Control Board [*President's*]

WRCC .... Workers' Rehabilitation and Compensation Corp. [*South Australia*]

WRCCC....... Wheeler AFB Range Communications Control Center (MCD)

WRCC-FM ... Marshall, MI [*FM radio station call letters*] (RBYB)

WRCCHE...... Western Regional Consortium, Librarians' Networking Committee [*Library network*]

WRCD .... Honeyoye Falls, NY [*FM radio station call letters*]

WRCF .... Whale Research and Conservation Fund [*Defunct*] (EA)

WRCG .... Columbus, GA [*AM radio station call letters*]

WRCGR....... Women's Reserve of the Coast Guard Reserve

WR Ch .... New Britain, CT [*FM radio station call letters*]

Wr Ch .... Wright's Ohio Reports [*1831-34*] [*A publication*] (DLA)

WRCHK....... Write Check [*Computer science*] (IAA)

WRCI .... Hillsboro, NH [*FM radio station call letters*]

WRCK .... Utica, NY [*FM radio station call letters*]

WRCKG....... Wrecking

WRCKR....... Wrecker

WRCLA .... Western Red Cedar Lumber Association (EA)

WRCM .... Wingate, NC [*FM radio station call letters*]

WRCN .... Riverhead, NY [*FM radio station call letters*]

WRCNS....... Women's Royal Canadian Naval Service [*World War II*]

WRCNSW .... Wheat Research Committee for New South Wales [*Australia*]

WRCO .... Richland Center, WI [*AM radio station call letters*]

WRCO-FM ... Richland Center, WI [*FM radio station call letters*]

WRCP .... Providence, RI [*AM radio station call letters*]

WRCPATT..... World Rabbinic Committee for the Preservation of Ancient Tombs in Tiberias (EA)

WRCQ.......... Dunn, NC [*FM radio station call letters*]

WRCQ.......... Wheat Research Committee for Queensland [*Australia*]

WRCR .... Rushville, IN [*FM radio station call letters*]

WRCR .... Wife's Restitution of Conjugal Rights [*Law suit*] [*British*] (ROG)

WRCR .... Wisconsin Railroad Commission Reports [*A publication*] (DLA)

WRCS .... Ahoskie, NC [*AM radio station call letters*]
WRCS .... Weapons Release Computer Set [*or System*] (MCD)
WRCS .... Work Ordering and Reporting Communications System [*Army*] (MCD)
WRCSA .... Wheat Research Committee for South Australia
WRCT .... Pittsburgh, PA [*FM radio station call letters*]
WRCU .... Hamilton, NY [*FM radio station call letters*]
WRCV .... Wheat Research Committee for Victoria [*Australia*]
WRCV-AM ... Grand Rapids, MI [*AM radio station call letters*] (RBYB)
WRCW .... Canton, OH [*AM radio station call letters*]
WRCWA .... Wheat Research Committee for Western Australia
WRCX .... Chicago, IL [*FM radio station call letters*]
WRCY .... Warrenton, VA [*FM radio station call letters*]
WRCZ .... Pittsfield, MA [*FM radio station call letters*]
WRD .... Warden [*Washington*] [*Seismograph station code, US Geological Survey*] (SEIS)
WRD .... Water Resources Division [*US Geological Survey*]
WRD .... Whole Rumen Digesta [*Dairy science*] (OA)
WRD .... Worm Runner's Digest [*A satirical publication*]
WRDA .... Water Resources Development Act (GFGA)
WRDB .... Reedsburg, WI [*AM radio station call letters*]
WRDB .... Worldwide Water Resources Database
WRDC .... Durham, NC [*Television station call letters*]
WRDC .... Western Rural Development Center [*Oregon State University*] [*Research center*] (RCD)
WRDC .... Westinghouse Research and Development Center (MCD)
WRDC .... White Rose Dollmakers Circle [*British*] [*An association*] (DBA)
WRDC .... Wool Research and Development Corp. [*Commonwealth*] (EERA)
WRDC .... Wright Research and Development Center [*Wright-Patterson Air Force Base*] (GRD)
WRDD .... Ebensburg, PA [*AM radio station call letters*]
WRDI .... We Remember Dean International (EA)
WRDIR .... Wrong Direction
WRDJ .... Roanoke, VA [*FM radio station call letters*]
WRDL .... Ashland, OH [*FM radio station call letters*]
WRDM .... Bloomfield, CT [*AM radio station call letters*]
WRDN .... Durand, WI [*AM radio station call letters*]
Wrdn .... Warden (PHSD)
WRDN .... Warden
WRDN-FM ... Durand, WI [*FM radio station call letters*]
WRDO .... Fitzgerald, GA [*FM radio station call letters*]
WRDR .... Egg Harbor City, NJ [*FM radio station call letters*]
WRDS-FM ... Phoenix, NY [*FM radio station call letters*] (RBYB)
WRDT-AM ... Raleigh, NC [*AM radio station call letters*] (BROA)
WRDU .... Wilson, NC [*FM radio station call letters*]
WRDV .... Warminster, PA [*FM radio station call letters*]
WRDW .... Augusta, GA [*AM radio station call letters*]
WRDW-TV ... Augusta, GA [*Television station call letters*]
WRDX-FM ... Dover, DE [*FM radio station call letters*] (BROA)
WRE .... Washington Real Estate Investment Trust [*AMEX symbol*] (SPSG)
WRE .... Washington REIT SBI [*AMEX symbol*] (TTSB)
WRE .... Weapon Research Establishment
WRE .... Whangarei [*New Zealand*] [*Airport symbol*] (OAG)
WRE .... Whole Ragweed Extract (MAE)
WRE .... Winston Resources Ltd. [*Vancouver Stock Exchange symbol*]
WREA .... Dayton, TN [*AM radio station call letters*]
WREAFS ..... Waste Reduction Evaluation at Federal Sites [*Environmental Protection Agency*]
WREB .... Greencastle, IN [*FM radio station call letters*] (RBYB)
WREC .... Memphis, TN [*AM radio station call letters*]
WREC .... Wire Rope Export Conference [*British*] (DBA)
WRECISS .... Weapons Research Establishment Camera Interception Single Shot
WRECS .... Weapon Radiation Effects on Communications Systems (MCD)
WRED .... Saco, ME [*FM radio station call letters*] (RBYB)
WREDAC ..... Weapons Research Establishment Digital Automatic Computer
WREDS .... Western Region Ethnic Disability Service [*Victoria, Australia*]
WREE .... Women for Racial and Economic Equality (EA)
WREF .... Ridgefield, CT [*AM radio station call letters*]
W REF .... With Reference To (WDAA)
WREFC .... We Remember Elvis Fan Club (EA)
WREG .... Memphis, TN [*Television station call letters*]
W/REG .... Window Regulator [*Automotive engineering*]
W REG .... With Regard To (WDAA)
WREI .... Women's Research and Education Institute (EA)
WREJ .... Richmond, VA [*AM radio station call letters*]
WREK .... Atlanta, GA [*FM radio station call letters*]
WREL .... Buena Vista, VA [*FM radio station call letters*]
WREL .... Lexington, VA [*AM radio station call letters*]
WREM-AM ... Monticello, ME [*AM radio station call letters*] (RBYB)
WREN .... Topeka, KS [*AM radio station call letters*] (RBYB)
WREN .... Washington Research and Education Network
WREN .... Women's Royal English Navy (IIA)
WRENACK .... WREN [*Women's Royal Naval Service*] Assistant Cook [*British military*] (DMA)
WRENAM ..... WREN [*Women's Royal Naval Service*] Air Mechanic [*British military*] (DMA)
WRENCINE(AB)... WREN [*Women's Royal Naval Service*] Cinema Operator (Able) [*British military*] (DMA)
WRENCINE(ORD)... WREN [*Women's Royal Naval Service*] Cinema Operator (Ordinary) [*British military*] (DMA)
WRENCK ...... WREN [*Women's Royal Naval Service*] Cook [*British military*] (DMA)
WRENDHYG... WREN [*Women's Royal Naval Service*] Dental Hygienist [*British military*] (DMA)
WRENDSA ... WREN [*Women's Royal Naval Service*] Dental Surgery Assistant [*British military*] (DMA)

WRENEDUC... WREN [*Women's Royal Naval Service*] Education Assistant [*British military*] (DMA)
WRENMET ... WREN [*Women's Royal Naval Service*] Meteorological Observer [*British military*] (DMA)
WRENMT ..... WREN [*Women's Royal Naval Service*] Motor Transport Driver [*British military*] (DMA)
WRENPHOT... WREN [*Women's Royal Naval Service*] Photographer [*British military*] (DMA)
WRENQA ..... WREN [*Women's Royal Naval Service*] Quarters Assistant [*British military*] (DMA)
WREN(R) ..... WREN [*Women's Royal Naval Service*] (RADAR) [*British military*] (DMA)
WRENREG ... WREN [*Women's Royal Naval Service*] Regulating [*British military*] (DMA)
WRENREM... WREN [*Women's Royal Naval Service*] Radio Electrical Mechanic [*British military*] (DMA)
WRENRO(M)1... WREN [*Women's Royal Naval Service*] Radio Operator (Morse) 1st Class [*British military*] (DMA)
WRENRO(M)2... WREN [*Women's Royal Naval Service*] Radio Operator (Morse) 2nd Class [*British military*] (DMA)
WRENS .... Women's Royal Naval Service [*Acronym is a phonetic reference to members of this British service branch*] [*Also, WRNS*]
WRENSA ..... WREN [*Women's Royal Naval Service*] Stores Accountant [*British military*] (DMA)
WRENS(C) ... WREN [*Women's Royal Naval Service*] Stores Assistant (Clothes) [*British military*] (DMA)
WRENS(S) ... WREN [*Women's Royal Naval Service*] Stores Assistant (Stores) [*British military*] (DMA)
WRENSTD... WREN [*Women's Royal Naval Service*] Steward [*British military*] (DMA)
WRENS(V) ... WREN [*Women's Royal Naval Service*] Stores Assistant (Victualling) [*British military*] (DMA)
WRENTEL .... WREN [*Women's Royal Naval Service*] Telephonist [*British military*] (DMA)
WRENTSA ... WREN [*Women's Royal Naval Service*] Training Support Assistant [*British military*] (DMA)
WRENWA ..... WREN [*Women's Royal Naval Service*] Weapon Analyst [*British military*] (DMA)
WRENWTR(G)... WREN [*Women's Royal Naval Service*] Writer (General) [*British military*] (DMA)
WRENWTR(P)... WREN [*Women's Royal Naval Service*] Writer (Pay) [*British military*] (DMA)
WRENWTR(S)... WREN [*Women's Royal Naval Service*] Writer (Shorthand) [*British military*] (DMA)
WREO .... Ashtabula, OH [*FM radio station call letters*]
W Rep .... West's English Chancery Reports Tempore Hardwicke [*1736-39*] [*A publication*] (DLA)
WREST .... Washington Regional Engineers, Scientists, and Technicians
WREST .... Wide Range Employability Sample Test
WRET .... Spartanburg, SC [*Television station call letters*]
WRET .... Work-Related Education and Training (AIE)
WREU .... Western Railway Employees' Union [*India*]
WREV .... Cambridge, MN [*FM radio station call letters*]
WREV .... Reidsville, NC [*AM radio station call letters*]
WREX .... Rockford, IL [*Television station call letters*]
WREX .... Wrexham [*City in Wales*]
WREY .... Millville, NJ [*AM radio station call letters*]
WREZ .... Metropolis, IL [*FM radio station call letters*]
WRF .... University of Wisconsin, River Falls, River Falls, WI [*OCLC symbol*] (OCLC)
WRF .... Weak Radial Field
WRF .... Weibull Reliability Function [*Statistics*]
WRF .... Wheat Ridge Foundation (EA)
WRF .... Wheat Ridge Ministries [*Formerly, Wheat Ridge Foundation*] (EA)
WRF .... World Rehabilitation Fund (EA)
WRF .... World Research Foundation (EA)
WRFB .... Cocoa, FL [*AM radio station call letters*]
WRFC .... Athens, GA [*AM radio station call letters*]
WRFCG .... War Reserve Functional Coordinating Group [*DoD*]
WRFD .... Columbus-Worthington, OH [*AM radio station call letters*]
WRFG .... Atlanta, GA [*FM radio station call letters*]
WRFG .... Wharfage [*Shipping*] (WGA)
WRFH .... Marietta, PA [*FM radio station call letters*]
WRFK .... California, MD [*FM radio station call letters*]
WRFL .... Lexington, KY [*FM radio station call letters*]
WRFM-FM ... Remsen, NY [*FM radio station call letters*] (RBYB)
WRFN-FM ... Warrenton, GA [*FM radio station call letters*] (BROA)
WRFQ-FM ... Mt. Pleasant, SC [*FM radio station call letters*] (RBYB)
WRFR .... Franklin, NC [*FM radio station call letters*]
WRFS .... Alexander City, AL [*AM radio station call letters*]
WRFT .... Indianapolis, IN [*FM radio station call letters*]
WRfU .... University of Wisconsin-River Falls, River Falls, WI [*Library symbol Library of Congress*] (LCLS)
WRFW .... River Falls, WI [*FM radio station call letters*]
WRFX .... Kannapolis, NC [*FM radio station call letters*]
WRFY .... Reading, PA [*FM radio station call letters*]
WRG .... Wearing (MSA)
WRG .... Weather Reconnaissance Group [*Military*]
WRG .... Westport Research Group [*Information service or system*] (IID)
WRG .... White River [*Alaska*] [*Seismograph station code, US Geological Survey*] (SEIS)
WRG .... Wire Routing Guide (MCD)
WRG .... Wiring
WRG .... Wrangell [*Alaska*] [*Airport symbol*] (OAG)
WRG .... Wrangell, AK [*Location identifier FAA*] (FAAL)

WRG .... Wrong [*Telecommunications*] (TEL)
WRGA .... Rome, GA [*AM radio station call letters*]
WRGA .... Western River Guides Association (EA)
WRGB .... Schenectady, NY [*Television station call letters*]
WRGC .... Sylva, NC [*AM radio station call letters*]
WRGG .... Endwell, NY [*FM radio station call letters*]
WRGH .... Walter Reed General Hospital (MCD)
WRGM .... Ontario, OH [*AM radio station call letters*]
WRGN .... Sweet Valley, PA [*FM radio station call letters*]
WRGO-FM .. Cedar Key, FL [*FM radio station call letters*] (RBYB)
WRGP-FM.... Homestead, FL [*FM radio station call letters*] (RBYB)
WRGR .... Tupper Lake, NY [*FM radio station call letters*]
WRGR .... Wringer
WRGS .... Rogersville, TN [*AM radio station call letters*]
WRGT .... Dayton, OH [*Television station call letters*]
WRGW .... Somersworth, NH [*FM radio station call letters*]
WRGX .... Briarcliff Manor, NY [*FM radio station call letters*]
WRh............. Rhinelander Public Library, Rhinelander, WI [*Library symbol Library of Congress*] (LCLS)
WRH .... Warnkenhagen [*German Democratic Republic*] [*Geomagnetic observatory code*]
WRH .... William Randolph Hearst [*American newspaper publisher, 1863-1951*]
WRH .... World Radio Handbook
WRHC .... Coral Gables, FL [*AM radio station call letters*]
WRHD .... Riverhead, NY [*AM radio station call letters*]
WRHI .... Rock Hill, SC [*AM radio station call letters*]
WRHL .... Rochelle, IL [*AM radio station call letters*]
WRHL .... World Roller Hockey League
WRHL-FM ... Rochelle, IL [*FM radio station call letters*]
WRHM .... Lancaster, SC [*FM radio station call letters*]
WRHN .... Rhinelander, WI [*FM radio station call letters*]
WRHO .... Oneonta, NY [*FM radio station call letters*]
WRHQ .... Richmond Hill, GA [*FM radio station call letters*]
wrhs .... Warehouse (VRA)
WRHSE .... Warehouse
WRHT .... Morehead City, NC [*FM radio station call letters*]
WRHU .... Hempstead, NY [*FM radio station call letters*]
WRHV .... Poughkeepsie, NY [*FM radio station call letters*]
WRHY .... Centre, AL [*FM radio station call letters*]
WRI .... International Water Resources Institute [*George Washington University*] [*Research center*] (RCD)
WRI .... War Resisters International [*British*]
WRI .... War Risks Insurance [*British*]
WRI .... Waterloo Research Institute [*University of Waterloo*] [*Research center*] (RCD)
WRI .... Water Research Institute [*West Virginia University*] [*Research center*] (RCD)
WRI .... Weatherstrip Research Institute
WRI .... Weingarten Realty Investors, Inc. [*NYSE symbol*] (SPSG)
WRI .... Weingarten Rlty SBI [*NYSE symbol*] (TTSB)
WRI .... Welfare Research, Inc. (EA)
WRI .... Western Research Institute [*Laramie, WY*] [*Department of Energy*] (GRD)
WRI .... Winzen Research, Inc.
WRI .... Wire Reinforcement Institute (EA)
WRI .... Wire Rope Institute
WRI .... World Research, Inc. [*San Diego, CA*] (EA)
WRI .... World Research, Inc. (EA)
WRI .... World Resources Institute (EA)
WRI .... Wrightstown, NJ [*Location identifier FAA*] (FAAL)
WRIA .... Worked Republic of India Award [*Amateur radio*] (IAA)
WRIB .... Providence, RI [*AM radio station call letters*]
WRIC .... Petersburg, VA [*Television station call letters*]
WRIC .... Richlands, VA [*AM radio station call letters*]
WRIC-FM .... Richlands, VA [*FM radio station call letters*]
WRIE .... Erie, PA [*AM radio station call letters*]
WRIF .... Detroit, MI [*FM radio station call letters*]
WRIF .... Water Resources Information File [*Terrain Analysis Center*] [*Army*]
WRIFC .... Western Regional Intercollegiate Fencing Conference (PSS)
WRIG .... Schofield, WI [*AM radio station call letters*]
Wright .... Wright's Ohio Reports [*1831-34*] [*A publication*] (DLA)
Wright .... Wright's Reports [*37-50 Pennsylvania*] [*A publication*] (DLA)
Wright Ch ... Wright's Ohio Reports [*1831-34*] [*A publication*] (DLA)
Wright Cr Cons... Wright's Criminal Conspiracies [*1873*] [*A publication*] (DLA)
Wright NP.... Wright's Ohio Nisi Prius Reports [*A publication*] (DLA)
Wright (Ohio C)... Wright's Ohio Reports [*A publication*] (DLA)
Wright R ...... Wright's Ohio Reports [*A publication*] (DLA)
Wright St L.. Wright's Advice on the Study of the Law [*A publication*] (DLA)
Wright St U.. Wright State University (GAGS)
Wright Ten... Wright on Tenures [*A publication*] (DLA)
Wrigley........ Wrigley [*Wm.*] Jr. Co. [*Associated Press*] (SAG)
WRIJ........... Masontown, PA [*FM radio station call letters*]
WRIK .... Brookport, IL [*AM radio station call letters*]
WRIK .... Metropolis, IL [*FM radio station call letters*]
WRIL .... Pineville, KY [*FM radio station call letters*]
WRIN .... Rensselaer, IN [*AM radio station call letters*]
WRINS .... Women's Royal Indian Naval Service [*British military*] (DMA)
WRIO .... Ponce, PR [*FM radio station call letters*]
WRIOT .... Wide Range Interest and Opinion Test
WRIP .... Lake City, SC [*AM radio station call letters*]
WRIpC .... Ripon College, Ripon, WI [*Library symbol Library of Congress*] (LCLS)
WRIPS .... Wave Rider Information Processing System [*Marine science*] (OSRA)

WRIPT .... Wide Range Intelligence-Personality Test [*Personality development test*] [*Psychology*]
WRIQ .... Radford, VA [*FM radio station call letters*]
WRIR-FM ..... Bethlehem, WV [*FM radio station call letters*] (RBYB)
WRIS .... Roanoke, VA [*AM radio station call letters*]
WRIS .... Water Resources Information System (NOAA)
WRISC .... Western Regional Information Service Center [*University of California*] [*Information service or system Defunct*] (IID)
WRISE .... Waste Reduction Institute for Scientists and Engineers [*Environmental Protection Agency*]
WRISE .... Wisconsin Program for the Renewal and Improvement of Secondary Education (EDAC)
WRIST .... Women's Repetition Injury Support Team [*Australia*]
WRIT .... Bamberg-Denmark, SC [*AM radio station call letters*]
WRIT .... Washington Real Estate Investment Trust [*Associated Press*] (SAG)
WRITAR....... Waste Reduction Institute for Training and Applications Research [*Environmental Protection Agency*]
WRITE .... Waste Reduction Innovative Technology Evaluation [*Environmental Protection Agency*]
WRITG .... Writing (ROG)
WRIU .... Kingston, RI [*FM radio station call letters*]
WRIU .... Weather RADAR Interface Unit (MCD)
WRIU .... Write Interface Unit
WRIV .... Riverhead, NY [*AM radio station call letters*]
WRIX .... Homeland Park, SC [*AM radio station call letters*]
WRIX .... Honea Path, SC [*FM radio station call letters*]
WRJA .... Sumter, SC [*FM radio station call letters*]
WRJA-TV .... Sumter, SC [*Television station call letters*]
WRJB .... Camden, TN [*FM radio station call letters*]
WRJC .... Mauston, WI [*AM radio station call letters*]
WRJC-FM ... Mauston, WI [*FM radio station call letters*]
WRJH .... Brandon, MS [*FM radio station call letters*]
WRJL .... Hanceville, AL [*AM radio station call letters*]
WRJM .... Geneva, AL [*FM radio station call letters*]
WRJM-TV ... Troy, AL [*Television station call letters*]
WRJN .... Racine, WI [*AM radio station call letters*]
WRJO .... Eagle River, WI [*FM radio station call letters*]
WRJQ .... Appleton, WI [*AM radio station call letters*]
WRJS .... Oil City, PA [*FM radio station call letters*]
WRJT .... Royalton, VT [*FM radio station call letters*] (RBYB)
WRJW .... Picayune, MS [*AM radio station call letters*]
WRJZ .... Knoxville, TN [*AM radio station call letters*]
WRK .... Wall & Redekop Corp. [*Toronto Stock Exchange symbol Vancouver Stock Exchange symbol*]
WRK .... Woodward's Reagent K (DB)
WRK .... Wrecker
WRKA .... Atambua/Haliwen [*Indonesia*] [*ICAO location identifier*] (ICLI)
WRKA .... St. Matthews, KY [*FM radio station call letters*]
WRKB .... Bajawa/Padhameleda [*Indonesia*] [*ICAO location identifier*] (ICLI)
WRKB .... Kannapolis, NC [*AM radio station call letters*]
WRKC .... Maumere/Wai Oti [*Indonesia*] [*ICAO location identifier*] (ICLI)
WRKC .... Wilkes-Barre, PA [*FM radio station call letters*]
WRKD .... Rockland, ME [*AM radio station call letters*]
WRKE .... Ende/Ipi [*Indonesia*] [*ICAO location identifier*] (ICLI)
WRKE .... Ocean View, DE [*FM radio station call letters*]
WRKF .... Baton Rouge, LA [*FM radio station call letters*]
WRKF .... Maskolen [*Indonesia*] [*ICAO location identifier*] (ICLI)
WRKG .... Lorain, OH [*AM radio station call letters*]
WRKG .... Ruteng/Satartacik [*Indonesia*] [*ICAO location identifier*] (ICLI)
WRKH-FM.... Mobile, AL [*FM radio station call letters*] (RBYB)
WRKI .... Brookfield, CT [*FM radio station call letters*]
WRKI .... Mbai [*Indonesia*] [*ICAO location identifier*] (ICLI)
WRKJ .... Mena [*Indonesia*] [*ICAO location identifier*] (ICLI)
WRKK .... Kupang/Eltari [*Indonesia*] [*ICAO location identifier*] (ICLI)
WRKK-AM ... Hughesville, PA [*AM radio station call letters*] (RBYB)
WRKL .... Larantuka/Gewayentana [*Indonesia*] [*ICAO location identifier*] (ICLI)
WRKL .... New City, NY [*AM radio station call letters*]
WRKM .... Carthage, TN [*AM radio station call letters*]
WRKM .... Kalabahi/Mali [*Indonesia*] [*ICAO location identifier*] (ICLI)
WRKN .... Brandon, MS [*AM radio station call letters*]
WRKN .... Naikliu [*Indonesia*] [*ICAO location identifier*] (ICLI)
WRKO .... Boston, MA [*AM radio station call letters*]
WRKP .... Moundsville, WV [*FM radio station call letters*]
WRKQ .... Madisonville, TN [*AM radio station call letters*]
WRKR .... Portage, MI [*FM radio station call letters*]
WRKR .... Rote/Lekunik [*Indonesia*] [*ICAO location identifier*] (ICLI)
WRKR .... Worker
Wrkr........... Worker (PHSD)
WRKS .... New York, NY [*FM radio station call letters*]
WRKS .... Sabu/Tardanu [*Indonesia*] [*ICAO location identifier*] (ICLI)
WRKSHP.... Workshop
WRKT .... North East, PA [*FM radio station call letters*]
WRKU .... Skarpsville, PA [*FM radio station call letters*]
WRKX .... Ottawa, IL [*FM radio station call letters*]
WRKY .... Steubenville, OH [*FM radio station call letters*]
WRKZ .... Hershey, PA [*FM radio station call letters*]
WRKZ .... Kupang Sector [*Indonesia*] [*ICAO location identifier*] (ICLI)
WRl .... Rice Lake Public Library, Rice Lake, WI [*Library symbol Library of Congress*] (LCLS)
WRL............ War Resisters League (EA)
WRL............ Wellcome Research Laboratories [*Research center British*] (IRC)
WRL............ Western Reserve Law Review [*A publication*] (ILCA)
WRL............ Westinghouse Research Laboratories (KSC)
WRL............ Wien Radiation Law [*Physics*]
WRL............ Willow Run Laboratory [*NASA*] (KSC)

WRL............ Wing Reference Line [*Aviation*]
WRL............ Worland [*Wyoming*] [*Airport symbol*] (OAG)
WRL............ Worland, WY [*Location identifier FAA*] (FAAL)
WRLA......... Sangata [*Indonesia*] [*ICAO location identifier*] (ICLI)
WRLB......... Long Bawan/Juvai Semaring [*Indonesia*] [*ICAO location identifier*] (ICLI)
WRLB-FM.... Rainelle, WV [*FM radio station call letters*] (RBYB)
WRLC......... Bontang [*Indonesia*] [*ICAO location identifier*] (ICLI)
WRLC......... Williamsport, PA [*FM radio station call letters*]
WRLD......... Batu Putih/Talisayam [*Indonesia*] [*ICAO location identifier*] (ICLI)
WRLD......... Lanett, Al [*AM radio station call letters*]
WRLD......... Valley, AL [*FM radio station call letters*]
WRLD......... World Acceptance [*NASDAQ symbol*] (TTSB)
WRLD......... World Acceptance Corp. [*NASDAQ symbol*] (SPSG)
WrldAcc..... World Access, Inc. [*Associated Press*] (SAG)
WrldCp....... World Corp. [*Associated Press*] (SAG)
WrldHrt....... World Heart Corp. [*Associated Press*] (SAG)
Wrldtalk...... Worldtalk Communication Corp. [*Associated Press*] (SAG)
WrldVl........ Worldwide Value Fund [*Associated Press*] (SAG)
WRLDWD.... Worldwide
WRLF......... Fairmont, WV [*FM radio station call letters*]
WRLG......... Smyrna, TN [*FM radio station call letters*]
WRLG......... Tanjung Selor/Tanjung Harapan [*Indonesia*] [*ICAO location identifier*] (ICLI)
WRLH......... Richmond, VA [*Television station call letters*]
WRLH......... Tanah Grogot [*Indonesia*] [*ICAO location identifier*] (ICLI)
WRLI.......... Southampton, NY [*FM radio station call letters*]
WRLI.......... Tiong Chong [*Indonesia*] [*ICAO location identifier*] (ICLI)
WRLIS........ Wessex Regional Library and Information Service (NITA)
WRLK......... Columbia, SC [*Television station call letters*]
WRLK......... Tanjung Redep/Kalimarau [*Indonesia*] [*ICAO location identifier*] (ICLI)
WRLL......... Balikpapan/Sepinggan [*Indonesia*] [*ICAO location identifier*] (ICLI)
WRLM......... Malinau [*Indonesia*] [*ICAO location identifier*] (ICLI)
WRLN......... Long Mawang [*Indonesia*] [*ICAO location identifier*] (ICLI)
WRLO......... Antigo, WI [*FM radio station call letters*]
WRLO......... Ongko Asa [*Indonesia*] [*ICAO location identifier*] (ICLI)
WRLP......... Russell, PA [*FM radio station call letters*]
WRLR......... Taraken [*Indonesia*] [*ICAO location identifier*] (ICLI)
WRLS......... Hayward, WI [*FM radio station call letters*]
WRLS......... Samarinda/Temindung [*Indonesia*] [*ICAO location identifier*] (ICLI)
WRLS......... Telular Corp. [*NASDAQ symbol*] (SAG)
WRLS......... Wireless [*Telecommunications*] (IAA)
WRLS......... Working Reference of Livestock Regulatory Establishments, Stations, and Officials [*A publication*]
WRLT.......... Franklin, TN [*FM radio station call letters*]
WRLT.......... Tanjung Santan [*Indonesia*] [*ICAO location identifier*] (ICLI)
WRLU......... Sangkulirang [*Indonesia*] [*ICAO location identifier*] (ICLI)
WRLU......... Watermen and Riverside Labourers' Union [*British*]
WRLV......... Salyersville, KY [*AM radio station call letters*]
WRLV-FM.... Salyersville, KY [*FM radio station call letters*]
WRLW......... Muara Wahau [*Indonesia*] [*ICAO location identifier*] (ICLI)
WRLX......... West Palm Beach, FL [*FM radio station call letters*]
WRLX......... World Airways, Inc. [*Air carrier designation symbol*]
WRLZ-AM.... Eatonville, FL [*AM radio station call letters*] (RBYB)
WRM.......... Wardroom (WGA)
WRM.......... Warm [*NWS*] (FAAC)
WRM.......... Warmifontaine [*Belgium*] [*Seismograph station code, US Geological Survey*] (SEIS)
WRM.......... War Readiness Materiel [*Air Force*]
WRM.......... War Reserve Mobilization (CINC)
WRM.......... War Reserve Munitions
WRM.......... Water Removal Mechanism
WRM.......... West Rim Resources, Inc. [*Vancouver Stock Exchange symbol*]
WRM.......... What Really Matters
WR(M)........ Wide Range (Monitor) [*Nuclear energy*] (NRCH)
WRM.......... William Richard Morris [*Automobile industrialist*] [*British*]
WRM.......... Worcester State College, Worcester, MA [*OCLC symbol*] (OCLC)
WRM.......... Working Reference Material [*Nuclear energy*] (NRCH)
WRM.......... World Rainforest Movement [*Penang, Malaysia*] (EAIO)
WRMA........ Fort Lauderdale, FL [*FM radio station call letters*]
WRMA........ Welded Ring Manufacturers Association [*Defunct*]
WRMAC....... Water Resources Management Advisory Committee [*Australia*]
WRMB........ Boynton Beach, FL [*FM radio station call letters*]
WRMC........ Middlebury, VT [*FM radio station call letters*]
WRMD........ St. Petersburg, FL [*AM radio station call letters*]
WRME........ Wood Raw Material Equivalent (EERA)
WRMF........ HCJB World Radio Missionary Fellowship (EA)
WRMF........ Palm Beach, FL [*FM radio station call letters*]
WRMF........ World Radio Missionary Fellowship (EA)
WRMFNT..... Warm Front [*NWS*] (FAAC)
WRMG........ Red Bay, AL [*AM radio station call letters*]
WRMJ......... Aledo, IL [*FM radio station call letters*]
WRMM........ Rochester, NY [*FM radio station call letters*]
WRMN........ Elgin, IL [*AM radio station call letters*]
WRMN........ Wireman (AABC)
WRMQ........ Orlando, FL [*AM radio station call letters*]
WRMR........ Cleveland, OH [*AM radio station call letters*]
WRMR........ War Reserve Materiel Requirement (AFIT)
WRMRATE... War Readiness Materiel Rating [*Air Force*]
WRMRB...... War Reserve Materiel Requirement Balance (AFIT)
WRMRP...... War Reserve Materiel Requirement Protectable (AFIT)
WRMRS...... War Reserve Materiel Rating System
WRMS........ Beardstown, IL [*AM radio station call letters*]
WRMS........ War Reserve Materiel Stocks
WRMS........ Watts Root-Mean-Square

WRMS-FM ... Beardstown, IL [*FM radio station call letters*]
WRMSR....... Write Machine-Specific Register [*Computer science*]
WRMSTAT ... War Readiness Materiel Status [*Air Force*]
WRMT .... Rocky Mount, NC [*AM radio station call letters*]
WRMT .... Woodcock Reading Mastery Tests [*Educational test*]
WRMU .... Alliance, OH [*FM radio station call letters*]
WRMX .... Murfreesboro, TN [*FM radio station call letters*]
WRMY .... Rocky Mount, NC [*Television station call letters*]
WRN .... Warnaco of Canada Ltd. [*Toronto Stock Exchange symbol*]
WRN .... Warning (MSA)
WRN .... War Relief for Nicaraguans (EA)
WRN .... WCI Steel [*NYSE symbol*] (TTSB)
WRN .... WCI Steel, Inc. [*NYSE symbol*] (SAG)
WRN .... Western
WRN .... Women Returners Network (AIE)
WRN .... Wool Round Needle [*Knitting*]
WRN .... Wrangler Aviation, Inc. [*ICAO designator*] (FAAC)
WRNA .... China Grove, NC [*AM radio station call letters*]
WRNB .... Warren Bancorp [*NASDAQ symbol*] (TTSB)
WRNB .... Warren Bancorp, Inc. [*NASDAQ symbol*] (NQ)
WRND .... Manchester, NH [*FM radio station call letters*]
WRNE .... Pensacola, FL [*AM radio station call letters*]
WRNG .... Warning [*NWS*] (FAAC)
WRNI .... Wide-Range Neutron Indicator (IEEE)
WRNI .... Wide-Range Nuclear Instrument (IEEE)
WrnIns........ Warner Insurance Services [*Associated Press*] (SAG)
WRNJ .... Belvidere, NJ [*FM radio station call letters*]
WRNJ .... Hackettstown, NJ [*AM radio station call letters*]
WRNL-AM .... Richmond, VA [*AM radio station call letters*] (RBYB)
WRNLR .... Western Region of Nigeria Law Reports [*A publication*] (DLA)
WRNN .... Murrell's Inlet, SC [*FM radio station call letters*]
WRNN-TV .... Kingston, NY [*Television station call letters*] (RBYB)
WRNO .... New Orleans, LA [*FM radio station call letters*]
WRNOA........ Washington Reef Net Owners Association (EA)
WRNQ .... Poughkeepsie, NY [*FM radio station call letters*]
WRNR .... Grasonville, MD [*FM radio station call letters*]
WRNR .... Martinsburg, WV [*AM radio station call letters*]
WRNR .... West Riding National Reserve [*British military*] (DMA)
WRNR .... Women's Royal Naval Reserve [*British military*] (DMA)
WRNS .... Kinston, NC [*AM radio station call letters*]
WRNS .... Women's Royal Naval Service [*Also, WRENS*] [*A member is familiarly called a "Wren"*] [*British*]
WRNS-FM..... Kinston, NC [*FM radio station call letters*]
WRNSR........ Women's Royal Naval Service Reserve [*British military*] (DMA)
WRNT .... Warrant (AABC)
wrnt .... Warrant (WDAA)
WRNT .... Warrenton Railroad Co. [*Later, WAR*] [*AAR code*]
WRNVR........ Women's Royal Naval Volunteer Reserve [*British military*] (DMA)
WRNWCA .... Western Red and Northern White Cedar Association [*Later, WRCA*] (EA)
WRNWS....... Worldwide Radio Navigation Warning System [*Intergovernmental Maritime Consultative Organization*] (GFGA)
WRNX .... Amherst, MA [*FM radio station call letters*]
WRNY .... Rome, NY [*AM radio station call letters*]
WRNZ .... Lancaster, KY [*FM radio station call letters*]
WRO .... ARC [*Agricultural Research Council*] Weed Research Organization [*Research center British*] (IRC)
WRO .... War Records Office
WRO .... War Risks Only
WRO .... Water Rights Office [*Bureau of Indian Affairs*]
WRO .... Western Regional Office
WRO .... Wichita River Oil Corp. [*AMEX symbol*] (SPSG)
WRO .... Work Release Order (MCD)
WRO .... Worship Resources Office [*An association*] (EA)
WRO .... Wroclaw [*Poland*] [*Airport symbol*] (OAG)
WROA .... Gulfport, MS [*AM radio station call letters*]
WROB .... West Point, MS [*AM radio station call letters*]
WROC .... Rochester, NY [*Television station call letters*]
WROD .... Daytona Beach, FL [*AM radio station call letters*]
WROE .... Neenah-Menasha, WI [*FM radio station call letters*]
WROG .... Cumberland, MD [*FM radio station call letters*]
Wr Ohio...... Wright's Ohio Reports [*A publication*] (DLA)
WROI.......... Rochester, IN [*FM radio station call letters*]
WROK .... Rockford, IL [*AM radio station call letters*]
WROL .... Boston, MA [*AM radio station call letters*]
WROM .... Rome, GA [*AM radio station call letters*]
WRON .... Ronceverte, WV [*AM radio station call letters*]
WRON-FM ... Ronceverte, WV [*FM radio station call letters*]
WROO .... Jacksonville, FL [*FM radio station call letters*]
WROQ .... Anderson, SC [*FM radio station call letters*]
WROR-FM .... Framingham, MA [*FM radio station call letters*] (RBYB)
WROS .... Jacksonville, FL [*AM radio station call letters*]
WROU .... West Carrollton, OH [*FM radio station call letters*]
WROV .... Martinsville, VA [*FM radio station call letters*]
WROV .... Roanoke, VA [*AM radio station call letters*]
WROW .... Albany, NY [*AM radio station call letters*]
WROX .... Cape Charles, VA [*FM radio station call letters*]
WROX .... Clarksdale, MS [*AM radio station call letters*]
WROY .... Carmi, IL [*AM radio station call letters*]
WROZ .... Lancaster, PA [*FM radio station call letters*]
WRP .... Water Resource Planning
WRP .... Water Resources Publications
WRP .... Weapons Release Programmer
WRP .... Weather Research Program [*Boulder, CO*] [*Department of Commerce*] (GRD)

WRP	Wellsford Residential Property Trust [*NYSE symbol*] (SPSG)
WRP	Wellsford Residential Prop Tr [*NYSE symbol*] (TTSB)
WRP	Wetland Reserve Program (WPI)
WRP	Wiener Random Process [*Mathematics*]
WRP	Wildlife Research Project
WRP	Wing Reference Plan [*Aviation*]
WRP	Women's Rights Project (EA)
WRP	Workers' Revolutionary Party [*British*] (PPW)
WRPA	Water Resources Planning Act [*1965*]
Wr PA	Wright's Reports [*37-50 Pennsylvania*] [*A publication*] (DLA)
WRPA-FM	Laporte, PA [*FM radio station call letters*] (RBYB)
WRPC	San German, PR [*FM radio station call letters*]
WRPC	Weather Records Processing Centers
WRPG	Warping
WRPI	Troy, NY [*FM radio station call letters*]
WRPJ	Port Jervis, NY [*FM radio station call letters*]
WRPL	Wadesboro, NC [*FM radio station call letters*]
WRPLS	Western Regional Public Library System [*Library network*]
WRPM	Poplarville, MS [*AM radio station call letters*]
WRPN	Ripon, WI [*FM radio station call letters*]
WRPPD	Wrapped
WRPPr	Wellsford Res Prop'A'Cv Pfd [*NYSE symbol*] (TTSB)
WRPPrB	Wellsford Res Prop Tr 9.65% Pfd [*NYSE symbol*] (TTSB)
WRPQ	Baraboo, WI [*AM radio station call letters*]
WRPR	Mahwah, NJ [*FM radio station call letters*]
WRPrA	Wrapper
WRPrA	Western Res Cap 7.875%'QUIPS' [*NYSE symbol*] (TTSB)
WRPS	Rockland, MA [*FM radio station call letters*]
WRPSM	War Reserve Publication Shipment Memorandum
WRPT	Write Protect [*Computer science*] (MHDB)
WRPT-AM	Peterborough, NH [*AM radio station call letters*] (RBYB)
WRQ	Westinghouse Resolver/Quantizer (IEEE)
WRQC-FM	Minneapolis, MN [*FM radio station call letters*] (BROA)
WRQK	Canton, OH [*FM radio station call letters*]
WRQM-FM	Rocky Mount, NC [*FM radio station call letters*] (RBYB)
WRQN	Bowling Green, OH [*FM radio station call letters*]
WRQO	Monticello, MS [*FM radio station call letters*]
WRQQ	Farrell, PA [*AM radio station call letters*]
WRQR	Farmville, NC [*FM radio station call letters*]
WRQV-FM	Avon, NY [*FM radio station call letters*] (RBYB)
WRQX	Washington, DC [*FM radio station call letters*]
WRR	Dallas, TX [*FM radio station call letters*]
WRR	Warm Run Record
WRR	Warrington, Inc. [*Toronto Stock Exchange symbol*]
WRR	Water Resource Region [*Water Resources Council*]
WRR	Water Resources Research [*A publication*] (NOAA)
WRR	Woodmen Rangers and Rangerettes (EA)
WRR	WRA, Inc. [*ICAO designator*] (FAAC)
WRRA	Frederiksted, VI [*AM radio station call letters*]
WRRA	Mataram/Selaparang [*Indonesia*] [*ICAO location identifier*] (ICLI)
WRRA	Water Resources Research Act [*1964*]
WRRB	Bima/Palibelo [*Indonesia*] [*ICAO location identifier*] (ICLI)
WRRC	Lawrenceville, NJ [*FM radio station call letters*]
WRRC	Water Resources Research Center [*University of Arizona*] (RCD)
WRRC	Water Resources Research Center [*Indiana University*] (RCD)
WRRC	Water Resources Research Center [*University of Minnesota of Minneapolis St. Paul*] (RCD)
WRRC	Water Resources Research Center [*Purdue University*] (RCD)
WRRC	Water Resources Research Center [*University of Hawaii*] (RCD)
WRRC	Water Resources Research Center [*University of Massachusetts*] (RCD)
WRRC	Western Rail Road Co. [*AAR code*]
WRRC	Western Regional Research Center [*Albany, CA*] [*Department of Agriculture*] (GRD)
WRRC	Western Regional Resource Center [*University of Oregon*] [*Research center*] (RCD)
WRRC	Wildlife Refuge Reform Coalition (EA)
WRRC	Willow Run Research Center [*Air Force*]
WRRC	Women's Research and Resources Centre (EAIO)
WRRE	Juncos, PR [*AM radio station call letters*]
WRRF	Washington, NC [*AM radio station call letters*]
WRRG	River Grove, IL [*FM radio station call letters*]
WRRH	Hormigueros, PR [*FM radio station call letters*] (RBYB)
WRRI	Alabama Water Resources Research Institute [*Auburn, AL*] [*Department of the Interior*] (GRD)
WRRI	Water Resources Research Institute [*New Mexico State University*] [*Research center*] (RCD)
WRRI	Water Resources Research Institute [*Oregon State University*] [*Research center*] (RCD)
WRRI	Water Resources Research Institute [*Clemson University*] [*Research center*]
WRRK	Braddock, PA [*FM radio station call letters*]
WRRL	Rainelle, WV [*AM radio station call letters*]
WRRL-FM	Rainelle, WV [*FM radio station call letters*]
WRRM	Cincinnati, OH [*FM radio station call letters*]
WRRN	Warren, PA [*FM radio station call letters*]
WRRNT	Warrant
WRRO	Warren, OH [*AM radio station call letters*]
WRRR	Bali International/Ngurah Rai [*Indonesia*] [*ICAO location identifier*] (ICLI)
WRRR	Rockford, IL [*AM radio station call letters*]
WRRR	St. Marys, WV [*FM radio station call letters*]
WRRR	Walter Reed Research Reactor [*Military*]
WRRS	Sumbawa/Sumbawa Besar [*Indonesia*] [*ICAO location identifier*] (ICLI)

WRRS	Wire Relay Radio System
WRRT	Waikabubak/Tambolaka [*Indonesia*] [*ICAO location identifier*] (ICLI)
WRRV	Middletown, NY [*FM radio station call letters*] (RBYB)
WRRW	Waingapu/Mau Hau [*Indonesia*] [*ICAO location identifier*] (ICLI)
WRRX	Micanopy, FL [*FM radio station call letters*]
WRRZ	Bali [*Indonesia*] [*ICAO location identifier*] (ICLI)
WRRZ	Clinton, NC [*AM radio station call letters*]
WRS	Walter Reed Society (EA)
WRS	Warning and Report System (CET)
WRS	War Reserve Stocks (AABC)
WRS	Warsak [*Pakistan*] [*Seismograph station code, US Geological Survey*] (SEIS)
WRS	Wasabi Resources Ltd. [*Toronto Stock Exchange symbol Vancouver Stock Exchange symbol*]
WRS	Washington Representative Services, Inc. [*Information service or system*] (IID)
WRS	Water Recirculation System
WRS	Water Recovery Subsystem [*NASA*] (KSC)
WRS	Wave Radiometer System
WRS	Weapons Recommendation Sheet (MCD)
WRS	Weather RADAR Set [*or System*]
WRS	Weather Reconnaissance Squadron [*Air Force*] (CINC)
WRS	Western Massachusetts Regional Library System, Springfield, MA [*OCLC symbol*] (OCLC)
WRS	Western Pacific Railroad Co. (MHDW)
WRS	Wide-Range Sensor
WRS	Winston Resources [*AMEX symbol*] (TTSB)
WRS	Winston Resources Ltd. [*AMEX symbol*] (SPSG)
WRS	Word Recognition System
WRS	Working Transmission Reference System [*Telecommunications*] (TEL)
WRS	Worse (FAAC)
WRS	Write Strobe
WRSA	Decatur, AL [*FM radio station call letters*]
WRSA	War Reserve Stocks for Allies (MCD)
WRSA	World Rabbit Science Association [*Cheltenham, Gloucestershire, England*] (EAIO)
WRSC	Cepu/Ngloram [*Indonesia*] [*ICAO location identifier*] (ICLI)
WRSC	State College, PA [*AM radio station call letters*]
WRSD	Folsom, PA [*FM radio station call letters*]
WRSE	Elmhurst, IL [*FM radio station call letters*]
WRSF	Columbia, NC [*FM radio station call letters*]
WRSFA	Western Reinforcing Steel Fabricators Association
WRSH	Rockingham, NC [*FM radio station call letters*]
WRSI	Greenfield, MA [*FM radio station call letters*]
WRSI	Woodroast Systems [*NASDAQ symbol*] (TTSB)
WRSI	Woodroast Systems, Inc. [*NASDAQ symbol*] (SAG)
WRSIC	Water Resources Scientific Information Center [*US Geological Survey*] [*Reston, VA Database originator*]
WRSIW	Woodroast Sys Wrrt [*NASDAQ symbol*] (TTSB)
WRSJ	Bayamon, PR [*AM radio station call letters*]
WRSJ	Surabaya/Juanda [*Indonesia*] [*ICAO location identifier*] (ICLI)
WRSK	Slippery Rock, PA [*FM radio station call letters*]
WRSK	War Readiness Spares Kit [*Air Force*] (AFM)
WRSL	Stanford, KY [*AM radio station call letters*]
WRSL-FM	Stanford, KY [*FM radio station call letters*]
WRSM	Sumiton, AL [*AM radio station call letters*]
WRSN-FM	Burlington-Graham, NC [*FM radio station call letters*] (RBYB)
WRSP	Springfield, IL [*Television station call letters*]
WRSP	Surabaya/Perak [*Indonesia*] [*ICAO location identifier*] (ICLI)
WRSP	World Register of Scientific Periodicals
WRSQ	Solo/Adi Sumarmo Wiryokusumo [*Indonesia*] [*ICAO location identifier*] (ICLI)
WRSq	Weather Reconnaissance Squadron [*Air Force*] (AFM)
WRSR	Two Harbors, MN [*FM radio station call letters*]
WRSR	Water Reactor Safety Research [*Nuclear energy*] (NRCH)
WRSS	San Sebastian, PR [*AM radio station call letters*]
WRSS	Surabaya/Gedangan [*Indonesia*] [*ICAO location identifier*] (ICLI)
WRSSR	White Russian Soviet Socialist Republic (IIA)
WRST	Oshkosh, WI [*FM radio station call letters*]
WRST	Sumenep/Trunojoyo [*Indonesia*] [*ICAO location identifier*] (ICLI)
WRSU	New Brunswick, NJ [*FM radio station call letters*]
WRSUC	Woodroast Systems, Inc. [*NASDAQ symbol*] (SAG)
WRSV	Rocky Mount, NC [*FM radio station call letters*]
WRSV	Wheat Rosette Stunt Virus [*Plant pathology*]
WRSW	Warsaw, IN [*AM radio station call letters*]
WRSW-FM	Warsaw, IN [*FM radio station call letters*]
WRT	Warrior River Terminal Co. [*AAR code*]
WRT	Water Round Torpedo (MSA)
WRT	Westerra Resources Ltd. [*Vancouver Stock Exchange symbol*]
WRT	With Reference To
WRT	With Regard To (NHD)
WRT	With Respect To (KSC)
WRT	Wright Air Lines, Inc. [*ICAO designator*] (FAAC)
WRT	Wright-Hargreaves Mines Ltd. [*Toronto Stock Exchange symbol*] (SPSG)
WRT	Wrought
wrt	Wrought (VRA)
WRT	WRT Energy Corp. [*Associated Press*] (SAG)
WRTA	Altoona, PA [*AM radio station call letters*]
WRTA	Western Railroad Traffic Association (EA)
WRTB	Wire Rope Technical Board (EA)
WRTB	Hartford, CT [*FM radio station call letters*]
WRTC	Working Reference Telephone Circuit [*Telecommunications*] (TEL)
WRTE	WRT Energy Corp. [*NASDAQ symbol*] (SAG)

WRT En	WRT Energy Corp. [*Associated Press*] (SAG)
WRTG	Garner, NC [*AM radio station call letters*]
WRTH	St. Louis, MO [*AM radio station call letters*]
WRTH	World Radio TV Handbook [*A publication*]
WRTHG	Worthing [*City in England*]
WRTI	Philadelphia, PA [*FM radio station call letters*]
WRTK	Youngstown, OH [*AM radio station call letters*] (RBYB)
WRTL	Ephrata, PA [*FM radio station call letters*]
WRTM-AM ...	Vicksburg, MS [*AM radio station call letters*] (RBYB)
WRTN	New Rochelle, NY [*FM radio station call letters*]
WRTO	Goulds, FL [*FM radio station call letters*]
WRTP	Chapel Hill, NC [*AM radio station call letters*]
WRTQ	Ocean City, NJ [*FM radio station call letters*]
WRTR	Writer
WRTS	Erie, PA [*FM radio station call letters*]
WRTTM.......	Warhead Replacement Tactical Telemetry System (DWSG)
WRTU	San Juan, PR [*FM radio station call letters*]
WRTV	Indianapolis, IN [*Television station call letters*]
WRTX	Dover, DE [*FM radio station call letters*]
WRTY	Jackson Township, PA [*FM radio station call letters*]
WRU	Watershed Research Unit [*Columbia, MO*] [*Department of Agriculture*] (GRD)
WRU	Wave Run-Up
WRU	Welsh Rugby Union [*British*] (DBA)
WRU	Western Reserve University [*Later, Case Western Reserve University*]
WRU	Who Are You [*Communication*]
WRUA	Fajardo, PR [*Television station call letters*]
WRUA	Wood Residue Utilization Act (COE)
WRUC	Schenectady, NY [*FM radio station call letters*]
WRUF	Gainesville, FL [*AM radio station call letters*]
WRUF-FM ...	Gainesville, FL [*FM radio station call letters*]
WRUL	Carmi, IL [*FM radio station call letters*]
WRUM	Rumford, ME [*AM radio station call letters*]
WRUN	Utica, NY [*AM radio station call letters*]
WRUR	Rochester, NY [*FM radio station call letters*]
WRUS	Russellville, KY [*AM radio station call letters*]
WRUSS	Western Reserve University Relay Searching Selector (SAA)
WRUV	Burlington, VT [*FM radio station call letters*]
WRUW	Cleveland, OH [*FM radio station call letters*]
WRV	Water Relief Valve
WRV	Water-Retention Value
WRV	West Riding Volunteers [*British military*] (DMA)
WRV	Winged Reentry Vehicle (IAA)
WRVA	Richmond, VA [*AM radio station call letters*]
WRVC	Huntington, WV [*AM radio station call letters*]
WRVC-FM ...	Catlettsburg, KY [*FM radio station call letters*] (RBYB)
WRVD-FM ...	Syracuse, NY [*FM radio station call letters*] (RBYB)
WRVE	Schenectady, NY [*FM radio station call letters*]
WRVF	Toledo, OH [*FM radio station call letters*] (RBYB)
WRVG	Georgetown, KY [*FM radio station call letters*]
WRVH	Richmond, VA [*AM radio station call letters*]
WRVI-FM ...	New Albany, IN [*FM radio station call letters*] (RBYB)
WRVJ	Watertown, NY [*FM radio station call letters*]
WRVK	Mount Vernon, KY [*AM radio station call letters*]
WRVL	Lynchburg, VA [*FM radio station call letters*]
WRVM	Suring, WI [*FM radio station call letters*]
WRVN	Utica, NY [*FM radio station call letters*]
WRVO	Oswego, NY [*FM radio station call letters*]
WRVP	Wedged Renal Venous Pressure [*Medicine*] (MAE)
WRVQ	Richmond, VA [*FM radio station call letters*]
WRVR	Memphis, TN [*FM radio station call letters*]
WRVS	Elizabeth City, NC [*FM radio station call letters*]
WRVS	Women's Royal Voluntary Service [*Formerly, WVS*] [*British*]
WRVT	Rutland, VT [*FM radio station call letters*]
WRVU	Nashville, TN [*FM radio station call letters*]
WRVV	Harrisburg, PA [*FM radio station call letters*]
WRVX	Mt. Carmel, TN [*AM radio station call letters*]
WRVY	Henry, IL [*FM radio station call letters*]
WRVZ	Pocatalico, WV [*FM radio station call letters*]
WR(W)	War Reserve (Weapon)
WRW	Weather Reconnaissance Wing [*Military*]
WRWA	Dothan, AL [*FM radio station call letters*]
WRWB	Harrogate, TN [*AM radio station call letters*]
WRWC	Rockton, IL [*FM radio station call letters*]
WRWD	Cornwall, NY [*AM radio station call letters*]
WRWD	Highland, NY [*FM radio station call letters*]
WRWg	Weather Reconnaissance Wing [*Air Force*] (AFM)
WRWH	Cleveland, GA [*AM radio station call letters*]
WRWJ	Murrysville, PA [*FM radio station call letters*]
WRWK	Warwick Railway Co. [*AAR code*]
WRWO	Montgomery, AL [*FM radio station call letters*] (RBYB)
WRWP	Water-Repellent Wood Preservative (DICI)
WRWR	San Juan, PR [*Television station call letters*]
WRX	Western Refrigerator Line Co. [*AAR code*]
WRXB	St. Petersburg Beach, FL [*AM radio station call letters*]
WRXC	Shelton, CT [*FM radio station call letters*]
WRXK	Bonita Springs, FL [*FM radio station call letters*]
WRXL	Richmond, VA [*FM radio station call letters*]
WRXO	Roxboro, NC [*AM radio station call letters*]
WRXQ	Olive Branch, MS [*FM radio station call letters*]
WRXR	Aiken, SC [*FM radio station call letters*]
WRXS	Ocean City, MD [*FM radio station call letters*]
WRXT	Roanoke, VA [*FM radio station call letters*]
WRXX	Centralia, IL [*FM radio station call letters*]

WRXY	Tice, FL [*Television station call letters*]
WRXZ	Sylvester, GA [*FM radio station call letters*]
WRY	Westray [*Scotland*] [*Airport symbol*] (OAG)
WRY	Wheeling Railway
WRY	World Refugee Year
WRYM	New Britain, CT [*AM radio station call letters*]
WRYT	Edwardsville, IL [*AM radio station call letters*]
WRZ	Western Rift Zone [*Geology*]
WRZA-FM ...	Kankakee, IL [*FM radio station call letters*] (RBYB)
WRZE	Nantucket, MA [*FM radio station call letters*]
WRZI	Vine Grove, KY [*FM radio station call letters*]
WRZK	Tallahassee, FL [*FM radio station call letters*]
WRZN	Hernando, FL [*AM radio station call letters*]
WRZQ	Greenburg, IN [*FM radio station call letters*]
WRZR-FM ...	Loogootee, IN [*FM radio station call letters*] (BROA)
WRZX	Indianapolis, IN [*FM radio station call letters*]
WRZZ	Ravenswood, WV [*FM radio station call letters*]
WS	Northern Wings [*ICAO designator*] (AD)
WS	Single Conductor Cable [*JETDS nomenclature*] [*Military*] (CET)
WS	Superior Public Library, Superior, WI [*Library symbol Library of Congress*] (LCLS)
WS	Waardenburg's Syndrome [*Medicine*]
WS	Wadley Southern [*Railroad*] (MHDW)
WS	Wagner's Missouri Statutes [*A publication*] (DLA)
WS	Wallops Station [*Later, WFC*] [*NASA*]
WS	Wall Street
WS	Ward Secretary [*Medicine*] (MEDA)
WS	Ware Shoals Railroad Co. [*AAR code*]
WS	Warm Shop [*Nuclear energy*] (NRCH)
WS	War Scale (ADA)
WS	War Service
WS	War Substantive [*British military*] (DMA)
WS	Warthin-Starry [*Silver impregnation stain*]
WS	Washine Chemical Corp. [*Research code symbol*]
WS	Wash Sale (MHDW)
WS	Waste Stack [*Technical drawings*]
WS	Waste System
WS	Watchman Service (LAIN)
WS	Watered Stock
WS	Water Safety
WS	Water Servicer (NASA)
WS	Water Soluble
WS	Water-Storage Cell [*Botany*]
WS	Water Supply
WS	Water Surface [*Elevation*]
WS	Water Swallow [*Medicine*] (DMAA)
WS	Water System
W S	Watt Second
w/s	Watt-Seconds
W/S	Watts per Steradian (NG)
WS	Waveform Synthesizer (IAA)
WS	Wave Soldering
WS	Weak Signals [*Radio*]
WS	Weapons Specifications (NG)
W/S	Weapons System
WS	Weapon System
WS	Weather Service
W/S	Weather Ship (NATG)
WS	Weather Squadron (MCD)
WS	Weather Station
WS	Weatherstripping (AAG)
WS	Wedgwood Society [*Defunct*] (EA)
WS	Wee Scots (EA)
WS	Weirton Steel [*NYSE symbol*] (TTSB)
WS	Weirton Steel Corp. [*NYSE symbol*] (SPSG)
WS	Welsh Society (EA)
WS	Werner's Syndrome [*Medicine*]
ws	Western Samoa [*MARC country of publication code Library of Congress*] (LCCP)
WS	Western Samoa [*ANSI two-letter standard code*] (CNC)
WS	Westphall-Struempell [*Syndrome*] [*Medicine*] (DB)
WS	West Saxon [*Dialect of Old English*] [*Language, etc.*]
WS	West Semitic (BJA)
W/S	West Side [*In outdoor advertising*] (WDMC)
WS	Wet Smoothed (BJA)
WS	Wetted Surface
WS	Wheat Straw
WS	White Sisters [*Missionary Sisters of Our Lady of Africa*] [*Roman Catholic religious order*]
WS	White Squire (MHDW)
WS	White Sucker [*Ichthyology*]
WS	White-Throated Sparrow [*Ornithology*]
WS	Wide Shot [*Photography*]
W-S	Wigner-Seitz [*Construction cell*] [*Solid state physics*]
WS	Wilderness Society (EA)
WS	[*The*] Wildlife Society
WS	Williams Syndrome [*Medicine*]
WS	Willow Society (EA)
WS	Will Ship (MCD)
WS	Winding Specification (IAA)
WS	Wind Satellite (SSD)
WS	Wind Shear [*Aviation*] (FAAC)
WS	Wind Shield (NASA)
WS	Windsonde (KSC)
WS	Wind Speed

WS..............	Wingspread (WGA)
WS..............	Wing Station [Aviation]
WS..............	Wireless Set (MCD)
WS..............	Wireless Station (IAA)
WS..............	Wire Send [Telecommunications] (TEL)
WS..............	Wire Sound
WS..............	Wirtschaft und Statistik [Germany]
Ws..............	Wisdom [Old Testament Book] (BJA)
WS..............	Withholding Statement (AAG)
W/S..............	With Stock [Business term]
WS..............	Women's Services [Military British]
WS..............	Women's Shelter [Australia]
WS..............	Women's Size
WS..............	Women's Suffrage (ROG)
WS..............	Wood-Sheathed Deck [of a ship] (DS)
WS..............	WordStar [Computer program]
WS..............	Word Sync
WS..............	Working Space
WS..............	Working Storage [Computer science] (MDG)
WS..............	Work Scope (COE)
WS..............	Worksheet (AAG)
WS..............	Work Shop [Military]
WS..............	Workshop Control (IAA)
WS..............	Work Stand (MCD)
WS..............	Work Statement (AAG)
W/S..............	Work Station [NASA] (NASA)
WS..............	Work Stoppage (AAG)
WS..............	Worldscale
WS..............	World Solidarity [Belgium] (EAIO)
WS..............	Worldwide Searches (EA)
WS..............	Worthy Sister (BJA)
WS..............	Writer to the Signet [British]
WS..............	Wrought Steel (MSA)
WSA..............	Wagner Society of America (EA)
WSA..............	War Shipping Administration [Within Office of Emergency Management] [World War II]
WSA..............	War Supplies Agency (NATG)
WSA..............	Water-Soluble Adjuvant [Immunology]
WSA..............	Water Sports Australia
WSA..............	Waveguide Slot Array
WSA..............	Weapons Systems Analysis [Army] (AABC)
WSA..............	Web Sling Association [Later, WSTDA] (EA)
WSA..............	Wedgwood Society of Australia
WSA..............	Weed Society of America [Later, WSSA] (EA)
WSA..............	Westates Airlines [ICAO designator] (FAAC)
WSA..............	Western Shoe Associates (NTPA)
WSA..............	Western Slavonic Association [Later, WSA Fraternal Life] (EA)
WSA..............	Western Surfing Association (EA)
WSA..............	Western Surgical Association (EA)
WSA..............	West Sea Development [Vancouver Stock Exchange symbol]
WSA..............	Wholesale Stationers' Association (EA)
WSA..............	Wilderness Study Area [Department of the Interior]
WSA..............	Williams-Steiger Act of 1970 (WYGK)
WSA..............	Williams Syndrome Association (EA)
WSA..............	Winter Soldier Archive [Defunct] (EA)
WSA..............	Winter Storm Watch [Telecommunications] (OTD)
WSA..............	Wisconsin Statutes Annotated [A publication] (DLA)
WSA..............	Wolverine Society of America (EA)
WSA..............	Women's Student Association (EA)
WSA..............	Workers Solidarity Alliance (EA)
WSA..............	Workplace Standards Administration [Department of Labor]
WSA..............	Work Safety Analysis [Engineering]
WSA..............	Work Sciences Association [British] (DBA)
WSA..............	World Service Authority (EA)
WSA..............	World Service Authority, District 5: Orient-Mediterranean Sea Coast [Israel] (EAIO)
WSA..............	World Sign Associates (EA)
WSA..............	Writers' Sodality of America [Defunct]
WSAA..............	Waveguide Slot Array Antenna
WSAA..............	Western States Angus Association (EA)
WSAAA..............	Western States Advertising Agencies Association (EA)
WSAAS..............	Western Sydney Area Assistance Scheme [Australia]
WSAC..............	Louisa, KY [FM radio station call letters]
WSAC..............	Washington State Apple Commission (EA)
WSAC..............	Water Space Amenity Commission [British] (DCTA)
WSAC..............	West of Scotland Agricultural College [British] (IRUK)
WSAD..............	Weapon System Analysis Division [Navy]
WSADR..............	Western States Acid Deposition Research (COE)
WSAE..............	Spring Arbor, MI [FM radio station call letters]
WSAF..............	Trion, GA [AM radio station call letters] (RBYB)
WSAG..............	Sembawang [Singapore] [ICAO location identifier] (ICLI)
WSAG..............	Washington Special Action Group [National Security Council]
WSAI..............	Cincinnati, OH [AM radio station call letters]
WSAJ..............	Grove City, PA [AM radio station call letters]
WSAJ-FM..........	Grove City, PA [FM radio station call letters]
WSAL..............	Logansport, IN [AM radio station call letters]
WSAM..............	Saginaw, MI [AM radio station call letters]
WSAM..............	Weapon Systems Acquisition Management [Navy] (MCD)
WSAM..............	Weapon Systems Acquisition Manager Program Naval Officers (AAGC)
W SAM..............	Western Samoa (WDAA)
W Sam..............	Western Samoa (VRA)
WSAN..............	Vieques, PR [FM radio station call letters]
WSAO..............	Senatobia, MS [AM radio station call letters]
WSAO..............	Weapon System Analysis Office [Navy] (MCD)
WSAP..............	Paya Lebar [Singapore] [ICAO location identifier] (ICLI)
WSAP..............	Weapon Status and Approval Panel [Military] (CAAL)
WSAP..............	Weapon System Acquisition Process (MCD)
WSAP..............	Weighted Sensitivity Analysis Program [Environmental Protection Agency]
WSAQ..............	Port Huron, MI [FM radio station call letters]
WSAR..............	Fall River, MA [AM radio station call letters]
WSAR..............	Singapore [Singapore] [ICAO location identifier] (ICLI)
WSAR..............	Weekly Significant Action Report (AFIT)
WSAS..............	Weapon System Acceptance Schedule (AAG)
WSAS..............	Weather Service Airport (DA)
WSASSA..........	Wholesale School, Art, and Stationery Supplies Association [Later, WSA] (EA)
WSAT..............	Salisbury, NC [AM radio station call letters]
WSAT..............	Tengah [Singapore] [ICAO location identifier] (ICLI)
WSAT..............	Weapon Systems Accuracy [formerly, Acceptance] Trials [Navy] (NG)
WSATO..........	War Shipping Administration Training Organization [Terminated]
WSAU..............	Wausau-Mosinee Paper [NASDAQ symbol] [Formerly, Wausau Paper Mills] (SG)
WSAU..............	Wausau Paper Mills [NASDAQ symbol] (TTSB)
WSAU..............	Wausau Paper Mills Co. [NASDAQ symbol] (NQ)
WSAU..............	Wausau, WI [AM radio station call letters]
WSAV..............	Savannah, GA [Television station call letters]
WSAVA..........	World Small Animal Veterinary Association [See also AMVPA] [Hatfield, Hertfordshire, England] (EAIO)
WSAW..............	Wausau, WI [Television station call letters]
WSAWD..........	White Sands Air Weather Detachment [New Mexico]
WSA-WGWC...	World Service Authority of the World Government of World Citizens (EA)
WSAX..............	West Saxon [Dialect of Old English] [Language, etc.]
WSAY..............	Rocky Mount, NC [FM radio station call letters]
WSAZ..............	Huntington, WV [Television station call letters]
WSB..............	Atlanta, GA [AM radio station call letters]
WSB..............	Steamboat Bay, AK [Location identifier FAA] (FAAL)
WSB..............	Wage Stabilization Board [Terminated, 1953]
WSB..............	[The] Washington Savings Bank [AMEX symbol] (SPSG)
WSB..............	Washington Service Bureau [Publisher] (AAGC)
WSB..............	Water-Soluble Base
WSB..............	Water Spray Boiler (NASA)
WSB..............	Weekly Statistical Bulletin [Database] [American Petroleum Institute] [Information service or system] (CRD)
WSB..............	Wheat-Soya Blend (EA)
WSB..............	Will Send Boat
WSB..............	World Scout Bureau [Geneva, Switzerland] (EA)
WSBA..............	York, PA [AM radio station call letters]
WSBB..............	New Smyrna Beach, FL [AM radio station call letters]
WSBC..............	Chicago, IL [AM radio station call letters]
WSBC..............	Wesbanco, Inc. [NASDAQ symbol] (NQ)
WSbD..............	Door County Library, Sturgeon Bay, WI [Library symbol Library of Congress] (LCLS)
WSBE..............	Providence, RI [Television station call letters]
WSBF..............	Clemson, SC [FM radio station call letters]
WSB-FM..........	Atlanta, GA [FM radio station call letters]
WSBG..............	Stroudsburg, PA [FM radio station call letters]
WSBI..............	Static, TN [AM radio station call letters]
WSBK..............	Boston, MA [Television station call letters]
WSBK..............	Western Bank [Coos Bay, OR] [NASDAQ symbol] (NQ)
WSBL..............	Selbyville, DE [FM radio station call letters]
WSBM..............	Florence, AL [AM radio station call letters]
WSBM..............	Wheat Soilborne Mosaic Virus
WSBMV..........	Wheat Soilborne Mosaic Virus
WSBN..............	Norton, VA [Television station call letters]
WSBP..............	Western Society of Business Publications [Defunct] (EA)
WSBR..............	Boca Raton, FL [AM radio station call letters]
WSBS..............	Great Barrington, MA [AM radio station call letters]
WSBSA..........	Weapon System Base Supply Account [Military] (AFIT)
WSBT..............	South Bend, IN [AM radio station call letters]
WSBT-TV..........	South Bend, IN [Television station call letters]
WSB-TV..........	Atlanta, GA [Television station call letters]
WSBU..............	St. Bonaventure, NY [FM radio station call letters]
WSBV..............	South Boston, VA [AM radio station call letters]
WSBW..............	Weddell Sea Bottom Water [Oceanography]
WSBY..............	Salisbury, MD [FM radio station call letters]
WSBZ..............	Miramar Beach, FL [FM radio station call letters] (RBYB)
WSC..............	Washington Science Center [Maryland] [Seismograph station code, US Geological Survey Closed] (SEIS)
WSC..............	Watered Silk Cloth (DGA)
WSC..............	Water Soluble Carbodiimide [Organic chemistry]
WSC..............	Water Studies Centre [Australia] [Chisholm Institute of Technology]
WSC..............	Water Systems Council (EA)
WSC..............	Weapons System Code
WSC..............	Weapon System Computer (MCD)
WSC..............	Weapon System Console [Military] (CAAL)
WSC..............	Weapon System Contractor
WSC..............	Weapon System Costing [Navy]
WSC..............	Weber State College [Ogden, UT]
WSC..............	Wesco Financial [AMEX symbol] (TTSB)
WSC..............	Wesco Financial Corp. [AMEX symbol] (SPSG)
WSC..............	Westech Resources Ltd. [Vancouver Stock Exchange symbol]
WSC..............	Western Sahara Campaign for Human Rights and Humanitarian Relief (EA)
WSC..............	Western Simulation Council
WSC..............	Western Snow Conference (EA)
WSC..............	Western State Conference (PSS)

WSC............ White Sisters of Charity of St. Vincent de Paul [*Roman Catholic religious order*]
WSC............ Wideband Signal Conditioner (MCD)
WSC............ Wildcat Service Corp. (EA)
WSC............ Wilkinson Sword Company [*British military*] (DMA)
WSC............ William Shatner Connection (EA)
WSC............ Wind Sounding Capability
WSC............ Wing Security Control [*Air Force*] (AFM)
WSC............ Winona State College [*Later, Winona State University*] [*Minnesota*]
WSC............ Winston Spencer Churchill [*1874-1965*] [*British statesman and prime minister*]
WSC............ Wisconsin State College [*Later, University of Wisconsin*]
WSC............ Working Security Committee [*Navy*]
WSC............ World Series Cricket
WSC............ World Spanish Congress (EA)
WSC............ World Spiritual Council (EA)
WSC............ World Sportscar Championship [*Auto racing*]
WSC............ World Straw Conference
WSC............ Wrap-Spring Clutch
WSC............ Wright State, Celina Branch, Celina, OH [*OCLC symbol*] (OCLC)
WSC............ Writing Services Center
WSC-5 .... Washington Science Center, Building 5 [*Marine science*] (OSRA)
WSCA......... Georgetown, SC [*FM radio station call letters*]
WSCA......... Weather Service Cooperating Agencies [*National Weather Service*] (NOAA)
WSCB .... Springfield, MA [*FM radio station call letters*]
WSCC .... Weapon System Configuration Control [*Navy*] (AAG)
WSCC .... Weather Service Communications Center [*National Weather Service*] (NOAA)
WSCC .... Western State College of Colorado [*Gunnison*]
WSCC .... Western Systems Coordinating Council [*Regional power council*]
WSCC .... Work Station Control Center [*NASA*] (NASA)
WSCCM ...... Weapon System Configuration Control Manual [*Navy*] (NG)
WSCD......... Duluth, MN [*FM radio station call letters*]
WSCD......... Welfare and Service Conditions Department [*British military*] (DMA)
WSCF .... Vero Beach, FL [*FM radio station call letters*]
WSCF .... Waste Sampling and Characterization Facility
WSCF .... World Student Christian Federation (EA)
WSCH .... Aurora, IN [*FM radio station call letters*]
WSCH .... Weather Service Communications Handbook [*National Weather Service*] (NOAA)
WSCI .... Charleston, SC [*FM radio station call letters*]
WSCI .... Washington Scientific [*NASDAQ symbol*] (TTSB)
WSCI .... Washington Scientific Industries, Inc. [*NASDAQ symbol*] (NQ)
WSCL......... Salisbury, MD [*FM radio station call letters*]
WSCM .... Weapon System Compatible Munition [*Military*]
WSCMB ...... Weapon System Configuration Management Board (MCD)
WSCMO ...... Weather Service Contract Meteorological Observatory (FAAC)
WSCN .... Cloquet, MN [*FM radio station call letters*]
WSCO .... Suring, WI [*Television station call letters*]
WSCO .... Weber State College [*Odgen, UT*]
WSCOC....... Wills Sainte Claire Owners Club (EA)
WSCP .... Pulaski, NY [*FM radio station call letters*]
WSCP .... Sandy Creek-Pulaski, NY [*AM radio station call letters*]
WSCP .... Weapons System Control Point
WSCP .... Weapon System Stock Control Plan (SAA)
WSCQ .... West Columbia, SC [*FM radio station call letters*]
WSCR .... Chicago, IL [*AM radio station call letters*]
WSCS .... Waste Solidification and Compaction Station [*Nuclear energy*] (NRCH)
WSCS .... Weapon System Communications System (AAG)
WSCS .... Wide Sense Cyclo-Stationary [*Telecommunications*]
WSCS-FM ... New London, NH [*FM radio station call letters*] (RBYB)
WSCSR....... Weapons System Contract Status Report [*Navy*] (NG)
WSCT.......... Springfield, IL [*FM radio station call letters*]
WSCT.......... Wainscot [*Technical drawings*]
WSCV .... Fort Lauderdale, FL [*Television station call letters*]
WSCW .... South Charleston, WV [*AM radio station call letters*]
WSCY .... Moultonborough, NH [*FM radio station call letters*]
WSCZ .... Greenwood, SC [*FM radio station call letters*]
WSD .... Sheboygan County Federated Library System, Mead Public Library, Sheboygan, WI [*OCLC symbol*] (OCLC)
WSD .... Warfare Systems Directorate (MCD)
WSD .... Water Seal Drainage [*Medicine*] (MEDA)
WSD .... Water Supply and Destination
WSD .... Weapons System Demonstration (MCD)
WSD .... Weapon Support Detachment (MCD)
WSD .... Weapon System Designator
WSD .... Weapon System Development [*Military*] (CAAL)
WSD .... Weapon System Director
WSD .... White Sands, NM [*Location identifier FAA*] (FAAL)
WSD .... Wind Speed Detector
WSD .... Working Stress Design [*Nuclear energy*] (NRCH)
WSD .... World of Scientific Discovery [*A publication*]
WSD .... World Space Directory [*A publication*]
WSD .... World Systems Division [*of Communications Satellite Corp.*] [*Telecommunications*] (TEL)
WSDA......... Water and Sewer Distributors of America (EA)
WSDB .... World Studies Data Bank (IID)
WSDC......... Weapons System Designator Code (NVT)
WSDC......... Weapon System Design Criteria (AAG)
WSDC......... Wisconsin State Data Center [*Wisconsin State Department of Administration*] [*Madison*] [*Information service or system*] (IID)
WSDD .... Weapon Status Digital Display

WSDDS .... Western Suburbs Development Disability Service [*Sydney, New South Wales, Australia*]
WSDF .... Water-Soluble Dietary Fiber [*Medicine*]
WSDH......... Sandwich, MA [*FM radio station call letters*]
WSDI .... Wall Street Deli [*Formerly, Sandwich Chef*] [*NASDAQ symbol*] (SPSG)
WSDL......... Weapons System Development Laboratory
WSDL......... Weapons Systems Data Link (MCD)
WSDM .... Brazil, IN [*AM radio station call letters*]
WSDM .... Weapon System Data Module
WSDM FM .. Brazil, IN [*FM radio station call letters*]
WSDP .... Plymouth, MI [*FM radio station call letters*]
WSDP .... Weapons System Development Plan
WSDQ .... Dunlap, TN [*AM radio station call letters*]
WSDR .... Sterling, IL [*AM radio station call letters*]
WSDS .... Salem Township, MI [*AM radio station call letters*]
WSDS .... Weighted Sum of Deviation Squared [*Statistics*]
WSDT .... Soddy-Daisy, TN [*AM radio station call letters*]
WSD/TD ..... Weapon System Demonstration Test Directive (AAG)
WSE .... National Weather Service Employees Organization
WSE .... Weapons System Evaluator (MCD)
WSE .... Weapons Systems Effectiveness
WSE .... Weapon Support Equipment [*Navy*] (NG)
WSE .... Weapon System Engineering [*Navy*] (NG)
WSE .... Western Allenbee Oil & Gas Co. Ltd. [*Vancouver Stock Exchange symbol*]
WSE .... Western Society of Engineers
WSE .... West-Southeast (ROG)
WSE .... Winnipeg Stock Exchange (HGAA)
WSE .... Work Shop Equipment (SAA)
WSE .... Wound, Skin, Enteric [*Isolation*] [*Medicine*]
WSE .... WWMCCS [*Worldwide Military Command and Control System*] Systems Engineer (MCD)
WSEA......... Pawley's Island, SC [*FM radio station call letters*]
WSEB......... Englewood, FL [*FM radio station call letters*]
WSEC .... Jacksonville, IL [*Television station call letters*]
WSEC .... Washington State Electronics Council
WSEC .... Watt-Second (AAG)
WSECL .... Weapon System Equipment Component List
WSED .... Weapons Systems Evaluation Division [*DoD*] (WDAA)
WSED .... Weapon System Electrical Diagrams
WSEE .... Erie, PA [*Television station call letters*]
WSEES .... Weapon System Electromagnetic Environment Simulator (MCD)
WSEF .... Weapons System Evaluation Facility (MCD)
WSEF .... Weapons Systems Effectiveness Factors
WSEFGT ..... Weapons System Evaluation Facility Group Test (MCD)
WSEG .... Brunswick, GA [*FM radio station call letters*]
WSEG .... Weapon System Evaluation Group [*DoD and Air Force*] (MCD)
WSEH......... Cumberland, KY [*FM radio station call letters*]
WSEI .... Olney, IL [*FM radio station call letters*]
WSEIAC ...... Weapon System Effectiveness Industry Advisory Committee
WSEK......... Somerset, KY [*FM radio station call letters*]
WSEL......... Pontotoc, MS [*AM radio station call letters*]
WSEL......... Weapon System Engineering Laboratory
WSEL-FM ... Pontotoc, MS [*FM radio station call letters*]
WSEM......... Donalsonville, GA [*AM radio station call letters*]
WSEM......... Weapon System Evaluation Missile [*Air Force*] (AFM)
WSem......... West Semitic (BJA)
WSEN......... Baldwinsville, NY [*FM radio station call letters*]
WSEO .... Nelsonville, OH [*FM radio station call letters*]
WSEO .... Weather Service Evaluation Officer [*National Weather Service*]
WSEO .... WWMCCS [*Worldwide Military Command and Control System*] System Engineering Office (MCD)
WSEP......... Waste Solidification Engineering Prototype Plant [*Nuclear energy*]
WSEP......... Weapon System Evaluation Program [*Air Force*]
WSER......... Elkton, MD [*AM radio station call letters*]
WSES .... Waterford Steam Electric Station [*Nuclear energy*] (NRCH)
WSES .... Weapons System Evaluation Squadron
WSESA .... Weapon System and Equipment Support Analysis
WSESRB ..... Weapon System Explosive Safety Review Board (COE)
WSET.......... Lynchburg, VA [*Television station call letters*]
WSET.......... Weapon System Evaluation Test [*Navy*] (NG)
WSET.......... Writers and Scholars Educational Trust [*British*] (EAIO)
WSEV......... Sevierville, TN [*AM radio station call letters*]
WSEV......... Winged Surface Effect Vehicle (PDAA)
WSEW......... Sanford, ME [*FM radio station call letters*]
WSEY......... Mount Morris, IL [*FM radio station call letters*]
WSEZ......... Paoli, IN [*AM radio station call letters*]
WSF .... Wake Shield Facility [*NASA*]
WSF .... Waste Shipping Facility [*Nuclear energy*] (NRCH)
WSF .... Water/Sand Fillable
WSF .... Water-Soluble Fraction
WSF .... Water Supply Forecast (NOAA)
WSF .... Wave Soldering Fixture (MCD)
WSF .... Weapon System File (MCD)
WSF .... Weather Support Force [*Military*] (AFM)
WSF .... Week Second Feet
WSF .... Well Spouse Foundation (EA)
WSF .... Well-Springs Foundation (EA)
WSF .... Western Sea Frontier [*Navy*]
WSF .... William Shatner Fellowship [*Defunct*] (EA)
WSF .... Women for a Secure Future (EA)
WSF .... Women's Spirituality Forum [*An association*] (EA)
WSF............ Women's Sports Foundation (EA)
WSF............ Work Station Facility

WSF............ World Salt Foundation (EA)
WSF............ World Science Fiction [France] (EAIO)
WSF............ World Scout Foundation [Geneva, Switzerland] (EAIO)
WSF............ World Sephardi Federation [See also FSM] [Geneva, Switzerland] (EAIO)
WSF............ World SF [Science Fiction] (EA)
WSF............ World Space Foundation (EA)
WSF............ World Strengthlifting Federation [India] (EAIO)
WSFA.......... Montgomery, AL [Television station call letters]
WSFB.......... Quitman, GA [AM radio station call letters]
WSFC.......... Somerset, KY [AM radio station call letters]
WSFC.......... Wallops Space Flight Center [NASA] (IAA)
WSFC.......... White Sands Field Center [New Mexico]
WSFC.......... Women's Solid Fuel Council [British] (DI)
WSFI.......... Wood and Synthetic Flooring Institute (EA)
WSFJ.......... Newark, OH [Television station call letters]
WSFL.......... Western States Football League (PSS)
WSFL-FM ... New Bern, NC [FM radio station call letters]
WSFM.......... Southport, NC [FM radio station call letters]
WSFN .... Muskegon, MI [FM radio station call letters]
WSFO .... Weather Service Forecast Office [National Weather Service]
WSFP.......... Fort Myers, FL [FM radio station call letters]
WSFP.......... World Showcase Fellowship Program [Walt Disney World]
WSFP-TV ... Fort Myers, FL [Television station call letters]
WSFQ-FM .... Reshtigo, WI [FM radio station call letters] (RBYB)
WSFR-FM .... Corydon, IN [FM radio station call letters] (RBYB)
WSFS.......... World Science Fiction Society (EA)
WSFS.......... WSFS Financial [NASDAQ symbol] (TTSB)
WSFS.......... WSFS Financial Corp. [NASDAQ symbol] (SAG)
WSFT.......... Thomaston, GA [AM radio station call letters]
WSFU-FM .... Union Springs, AL [FM radio station call letters] (RBYB)
WSFW.......... Seneca Falls, NY [AM radio station call letters]
WSFW-FM ... Seneca Falls, NY [FM radio station call letters]
WSFX.......... Nanticoke, PA [AM radio station call letters]
WSFX.......... Wilmington, NC [Television station call letters]
WSFZ-AM .... Memphis, TN [AM radio station call letters] (RBYB)
WSG .... International Wool Study Group [Defunct]
WSG .... Wasaya Airways Ltd. [Canada ICAO designator] (FAAC)
WSG .... Washington [Pennsylvania] [Airport symbol] (OAG)
WSG .... Weapons Spectrum Generator (PDAA)
WSG .... Wehrsportegruppe Hoffman Truppe [Hoffman Paramilitary Troop] [Germany]
WSG .... Wells Gold Ltd. [Vancouver Stock Exchange symbol]
WSG .... Wesleyan Service Guild [Defunct] (EA)
WSG .... Western Suburbs Greens [Political party Australia]
WSG .... White Smooth Glossy [Photographic paper] (DGA)
WSG .... Winter Study Group
WSG .... Wired Shelf Group [Telecommunications] (TEL)
WSG .... Wire Service Guild (NTPA)
WSG .... Wire Strain Gauge
WSG .... Worthiest Soldier in the Group
WSGA.......... Savannah, GA [AM radio station call letters]
WSGA.......... Water Soluble Gum Association (EA)
WSGA.......... Wine and Spirits Guild of America (EA)
WSGB.......... Sutton, WV [AM radio station call letters]
WSGC.......... Kaukauna, WI [AM radio station call letters]
WSGC.......... Ringgold, GA [FM radio station call letters]
WSGC.......... Williams-Sonoma [NASDAQ symbol] (TTSB)
WSGC.......... Williams-Sonoma, Inc. [NASDAQ symbol] (NQ)
WSGD.......... Carbondale, PA [FM radio station call letters]
WSGD.......... White Smooth Glossy Double Weight [Photographic paper] (DGA)
WSGE .... Dallas, NC [FM radio station call letters]
WSGE .... Western Society of Gear Engineers (MCD)
WSGF .... Springfield, GA [FM radio station call letters] (RBYB)
WSGH.......... Lewisville, NC [AM radio station call letters]
WSGI .... Springfield, TN [AM radio station call letters]
WSGL .... Naples, FL [FM radio station call letters]
WSGM.......... Coalmont, TN [FM radio station call letters]
WSGN.......... Gadsden, AL [FM radio station call letters]
WSGO.......... Oswego, NY [AM radio station call letters]
WSGR.......... Port Huron, MI [FM radio station call letters]
WSGS.......... Hazard, KY [FM radio station call letters]
WSGS.......... White Smooth Glossy Single Weight [Photographic paper] (DGA)
WSGT .... White Sands Ground Terminal [NASA] (MCD)
WSGT .... WWMCCS [Worldwide Military Command and Control System] Standard Graphics Terminal (DOMA)
WSGU.......... Window Sash Glaziers' Union [British]
WSGW.......... Saginaw, MI [AM radio station call letters]
Wsh .... Washington State Reports [A publication] (DLA)
WSH .... Waste Shipping Facility [Nuclear energy] (NUCP)
WSH .... Weather Service Headquarters (NOAA)
WSH .... Western Star Trucks Hldg [AMEX symbol] (TTSB)
WSH .... Western Star Trucks Holdings Ltd. [AMEX symbol] (SAG)
WsH .... William S. Hein & Co., Inc., Buffalo, NY [Library symbol Library of Congress] (LCLS)
WSH .... Wilshire Energy Resources, Inc. [Toronto Stock Exchange symbol]
WSH .... Windows Scripting Host [Computer science]
WSha.......... Bringham Memorial Library, Sharon, WI [Library symbol Library of Congress] (LCLS)
WSHA .... Raleigh, NC [FM radio station call letters]
WShawGS.... Church of Jesus Christ of Latter-Day Saints, Genealogical Society Library, Wisconsin East District Branch, Shawano, WI [Library symbol Library of Congress] (LCLS)
WSHC .... Shepherdstown, WV [FM radio station call letters]
WSHD .... Eastport, ME [FM radio station call letters]

WSHE .... Fort Lauderdale, FL [FM radio station call letters]
WShe .... Mead Public Library, Sheboygan, WI [Library symbol Library of Congress] (LCLS)
WSheL........ Lakeland College, Sheboygan, WI [Library symbol Library of Congress] (LCLS)
WSheM........ Sheboygan Memorial Hospital, Sheboygan, WI [Library symbol Library of Congress] (LCLS)
WSheSN ...... Saint Nicholas Hospital, Sheboygan, WI [Library symbol Library of Congress] (LCLS)
WSHE-TV ... Martinsburg, WV [TV station call letters] (RBYB)
WSheU .... University of Wisconsin Center-Sheboygan, Sheboygan, WI [Library symbol Library of Congress] (LCLS)
WSHF .... Wives Self-Help Foundation (EA)
WSHF-FM .... Mexico Beach, FL [FM radio station call letters] (RBYB)
WSHFT .... Wind Shift [NWS] (FAAC)
WSHG .... Ridgeland, SC [FM radio station call letters]
WSHG .... Washing (MSA)
WSHGA........ Washington State Holly Growers Association [Defunct] (EA)
WSHH .... Pittsburgh, PA [FM radio station call letters]
WSHI .... Walsh Intl [NASDAQ symbol] (TTSB)
WSHJ .... Southfield, MI [FM radio station call letters]
WSHK .... Russellville, AL [FM radio station call letters]
WSHL .... Easton, MA [AM radio station call letters]
WSHLD .... Windshield (AAG)
WSHN .... Fremont, MI [AM radio station call letters]
WshNat........ Washington National Corp. [Associated Press] (SAG)
WSHN-FM.... Fremont, MI [FM radio station call letters]
WshNt.......... Washington Natural Gas Co. [Associated Press] (SAG)
WSHO .... New Orleans, LA [AM radio station call letters]
WSHP .... Shippensburg, PA [AM radio station call letters]
WshPst.......... Washington Post Co. [Associated Press] (SAG)
WSHR .... Lake Ronkonkoma, NY [FM radio station call letters]
WSHR .... Washer (MSA)
WSHS .... Sheboygan, WI [FM radio station call letters]
WshSci .... Washington Scientific Industries, Inc. [Associated Press] (SAG)
WSHT .... Wave Superheater Hypersonic Tunnel (IAA)
WSHU .... Fairfield, CT [FM radio station call letters]
WSHV .... South Hill, VA [FM radio station call letters]
WSHW .... Frankfort, IN [FM radio station call letters]
WSHX .... Danville, VT [FM radio station call letters]
WSHY .... Shelbyville, IL [AM radio station call letters]
WSHZ-FM .... Muskegon, MI [FM radio station call letters] (RBYB)
WSI.......... Wafer-Scale Integration [Microelectronics]
WSI.......... WaferScale Integration, Inc.
WSI.......... Waingapu [Sumba Island] [Seismograph station code, US Geological Survey] (SEIS)
WSI.......... War Service Indefinite
WSI.......... War-Supporting Industry
WSI.......... Water Safety Instructor [Red Cross]
WSI.......... Water Ski Industry Association (EA)
WSI.......... Water Solubility Index [Analytical chemistry]
WSI.......... Water Stability Index [Agronomy]
WSI.......... Weapon System Integration (MCD)
WSI.......... Weather Services International Corp. [Information service or system] (IID)
WSI.......... Welfare State International [Performance group] [British]
WSI.......... Western Service, Inc. (EFIS)
WSI.......... Weston Service, Inc. (EFIS)
WSI.......... Wind Speed Indicator
WSI.......... Wind Spirit Air, Inc. [FAA designator] (FAAC)
WSI.......... World Synoptic Interval
WSI.......... Writers and Scholars International [British] (EAIO)
WSIA.......... Staten Island, NY [FM radio station call letters]
WSIA.......... Water Ski Industry Association (EA)
WSIA.......... Water Sports Industry Association (NTPA)
WSIA.......... Water Supply Improvement Association [Later, IDA] (EA)
WSIA.......... Weapons Systems Integration Agent (MCD)
WSIB.......... Selmer, TN [FM radio station call letters]
WSIC.......... Statesville, NC [AM radio station call letters]
WSIC.......... Watchmakers of Switzerland Information Center (EA)
WSIE.......... Edwardsville, IL [FM radio station call letters]
WSIF.......... Wilkesboro, NC [FM radio station call letters]
WSIG.......... Mount Jackson, VA [FM radio station call letters]
WSIG.......... Weapons Support Improvement Group [DoD] (DOMA)
WSII.......... Waste Systems International [NASDAQ symbol] [Formerly, BioSafe International] (SG)
WSIIP .... Weapons Installation Interrupted for Parts (DNAB)
WSIL.......... Harrisburg, IL [Television station call letters]
WSI/L.......... War Supporting Industries and Logistics (MCD)
WSIM.......... Water Separation Index, Modified
WSIM.......... Wooden Ships & Iron Men (PCM)
WSIP.......... Paintsville, KY [AM radio station call letters]
WSIP.......... Weapons System Improvement Program (DWSG)
WSIP-FM .... Paintsville, KY [FM radio station call letters]
WSIR.......... White Sands Integrated Range [New Mexico] (AAG)
WSIR.......... Winter Haven, FL [AM radio station call letters]
WSIT.......... Washington State Institute of Technology (KSC)
WSIT.......... Water Safety Instructor Trainer [Red Cross]
WSITC.......... Western Sydney Information Technology Centre [Australia]
WSITS.......... Weapon System Interface Trade Study [Military]
WSIU.......... Carbondale, IL [FM radio station call letters]
WSIU-TV..... Carbondale, IL [Television station call letters]
WSIV.......... East Syracuse, NY [AM radio station call letters]
WSIX.......... Nashville, TN [FM radio station call letters]
WSIY .... West Somerset Imperial Yeomanry [British military] (DMA)

WSJ............ San Juan, AK [Location identifier FAA] (FAAL)
WSJ............ Wall Street Journal [A publication] (DFIT)
WSJ............ Wall Street Journal (Eastern Edition) [A publication] (BRI)
WSJ............ Worm Screw Jack
WSJB.......... Standish, ME [FM radio station call letters]
WSJC.......... Singapore [Singapore] [ICAO location identifier] (ICLI)
WSJD.......... Princeton, IN [FM radio station call letters]
WSJI-FM ..... Cherry Hill, NJ [FM radio station call letters] (RBYB)
WSJK.......... Sneedville, TN [Television station call letters]
WSJL.......... Cape May, NJ [FM radio station call letters]
WSJM.......... St. Joseph, MI [AM radio station call letters]
WSJ-MW ..... Wall Street Journal (Midwest Edition) [A publication] (BRI)
WSJN.......... San Juan, PR [Television station call letters]
WSJP.......... Murray, KY [AM radio station call letters]
WSJR.......... Madawaska, ME [AM radio station call letters]
WSJS.......... Winston-Salem, NC [AM radio station call letters]
WSJT-FM ..... Lakeland, FL [FM radio station call letters] (RBYB)
WSJU.......... San Juan, PR [Television station call letters]
WSJV.......... Elkhart, IN [Television station call letters]
WSJW-FM ... Louisville, KY [FM radio station call letters] (RBYB)
WSJY.......... Fort Atkinson, WI [FM radio station call letters]
WSJZ-FM ..... Buffalo, NY [FM radio station call letters] (RBYB)
WSKB.......... Westfield, MA [FM radio station call letters]
WSKE.......... Everett, PA [AM radio station call letters]
WSKE-FM .... Everett, PA [FM radio station call letters]
WSKG.......... Binghamton, NY [FM radio station call letters]
WSKG-TV..... Binghamton, NY [Television station call letters]
WSKI.......... Montpelier, VT [AM radio station call letters]
WSKI.......... Winter Sports [NASDAQ symbol] (TTSB)
WSKI.......... Winter Sports, Inc. [NASDAQ symbol] (SAG)
WSKN.......... San Juan, PR [AM radio station call letters]
WSKO-AM.... Providence, RI [AM radio station call letters] (BROA)
WSKP.......... Key West, FL [FM radio station call letters]
WSKQ.......... New York, NY [FM radio station call letters]
WSKR-AM.... Denham Springs, LA [AM radio station call letters] (BROA)
WSKS.......... Rome, NY [FM radio station call letters] (RBYB)
WSKT.......... Spencer, IN [FM radio station call letters]
WSKV.......... Stanton, KY [AM radio station call letters]
WSKW.......... Skowhegan, ME [AM radio station call letters]
WSKX.......... Hinesville, GA [FM radio station call letters]
WSKY.......... Asheville, NC [AM radio station call letters]
WSKZ.......... Chattanooga, TN [FM radio station call letters]
WSL............ Warren Spring Laboratory [Research center British] (DCTA)
WSL............ War Substantive Lieutenant [British]
WSL............ Water Science Laboratories Proprietary Ltd. [Australia]
WSL............ Weather Seal (AAG)
WSL............ Windscale
WSL............ Workstation Laboratory (PCM)
WSLA.......... Slidell, LA [AM radio station call letters]
WSLB.......... Ogdensburg, NY [AM radio station call letters]
WSLBRUC... WS and LB Robinson University College [Australia]
WSLC.......... Roanoke, VA [AM radio station call letters]
WSLC.......... WOCE [World Ocean Circulation Experiment] Sea Level Center [Marine science] (OSRA)
WSLC.......... World Shortwave Listeners Club (EA)
WSLD.......... White Smooth Lustre Double Weight [Photographic paper] (DGA)
WSLD.......... Whitewater, WI [FM radio station call letters]
WSLE.......... Cairo, GA [FM radio station call letters]
WSLF.......... Western Somali Liberation Front
WSLI........... Jackson, MS [AM radio station call letters]
WSL-INT...... Weltbund zum Schutze des Lebens [World Union for the Protection of Life - WUPL-INT] (EAIO)
WSLJ.......... Watertown, NY [FM radio station call letters]
WSLK.......... Saranac Lake, NY [AM radio station call letters]
WSLL.......... Saranac Lake, NY [FM radio station call letters]
WSLM.......... Salem, IN [AM radio station call letters]
WSLM-FM.... Salem, IN [FM radio station call letters]
WSLN.......... Delaware, OH [FM radio station call letters]
WSLO.......... Malone, NY [FM radio station call letters]
WSLO.......... Weapon System Logistics Officer [Air Force] (AFM)
WSLQ.......... Roanoke, VA [FM radio station call letters]
WSLR.......... Weapon System Logistic Reviews [Navy] (NG)
WSLS.......... Roanoke, VA [Television station call letters]
WSLT.......... Clearwater, SC [FM radio station call letters]
WSLU.......... Canton, NY [FM radio station call letters]
WSLV.......... Ardmore, TN [AM radio station call letters]
WSLW.......... White Sulphur Springs, WV [AM radio station call letters]
WSLX.......... New Canaan, CT [FM radio station call letters]
WSLY.......... York, AL [FM radio station call letters]
WSM........... Nashville, TN [AM radio station call letters]
WSM........... Weapon Support Manager [Air Force]
WSM........... Weapon System Manager [Air Force] (AFM)
WSM........... Weapon System Manual
WSM........... Western Samoa [ANSI three-letter standard code] (CNC)
WSM........... Western Society of Malacologists (EA)
WSM........... West-Mar Resources Ltd. [Vancouver Stock Exchange symbol]
WSM........... Wheat-Soya-Milk
WSM........... Wheat Streak Mosaic [Plant pathology]
WSM........... White Single Male [Classified advertising]
WSM........... Wigner-Seitz Method [Solid state physics]
WSM........... Williams-Sonoma [NYSE symbol]
WSM........... Windowing System Manager [Computer science] (PCM)
WSM........... Wiseman [Alaska] [Airport symbol] (OAG)
WSM........... Wiseman, AK [Location identifier FAA] (FAAL)
WSM........... Wisman Aviation [ICAO designator] (FAAC)

WSM........... Women's Suffrage Movement (ROG)
WSM........... Wright State University, Health Sciences Library, Dayton, OH [OCLC symbol] (OCLC)
WSMA .... Western States Meat Association (EA)
WSMA .... Window Shade Manufacturers Association (EA)
WSMAC ...... Weapon System Maintenance Action Center
WSMaT .... Weapon System Management Team [Army] (RDA)
WSMB .... New Orleans, LA [AM radio station call letters]
WSMC .... Collegedale, TN [FM radio station call letters]
WSMC .... Weapons System Management Codes [Navy]
WSMC .... Western Space and Missile Center [Vandenberg Air Force Base, CA] [Air Force]
WSMC .... Western States Movers Conference
WSMD .... Mechanicsville, MD [FM radio station call letters]
WSME .... Sanford, ME [AM radio station call letters]
WSM-FM ..... Nashville, TN [FM radio station call letters]
WSMG .... Greeneville, TN [AM radio station call letters]
WSMG .... Tusculum, TN [FM radio station call letters] (RBYB)
WSMH .... Flint, MI [Television station call letters]
WSMI .... Litchfield, IL [AM radio station call letters]
WSMI-FM .... Litchfield, IL [FM radio station call letters]
WSMIS .... Weapon Systems Management Information System [Air Force] (GFGA)
WSMK .... Buchanan, MI [FM radio station call letters]
WSML .... Graham, NC [AM radio station call letters]
WSML .... Saltfree Meal [Airline notation]
WSMN .... Nashua, NH [AM radio station call letters]
WSMO .... Weapon System Materiel Officer [Air Force] (AFM)
WSMO .... Weather Service Meteorological Observatory [or Observations] [National Weather Service] (NOAA)
WSMP .... Weapons System Master Plan [Air Force] (DOMA)
WSMP .... WSMP, Inc. [Formerly, Western Steer Mom 'n' Pop's, Inc.] [NASDAQ symbol] (SPSG)
WSMPA ...... Western States Meat Association (EA)
WSMQ .... Bessemer, AL [AM radio station call letters]
WSMR .... White Sands Missile Range [New Mexico] [Army]
WSMS-FM ... Artesia, MS [FM radio station call letters] (RBYB)
WSMT .... Sparta, TN [AM radio station call letters]
WSMT .... Weapons System Maintenance Test (MCD)
WSMTC....... White Sands Missile Test Center [New Mexico]
WSMT-FM ... Sparta, TN [FM radio station call letters]
WSMTT .... White Star Mobile Training Teams [Military] (CINC)
WSMU .... North Dartmouth, MA [FM radio station call letters]
WSMV .... Nashville, TN [Television station call letters]
WSMV .... Wheat Streak Mosaic Virus
WSMX .... Winston-Salem, NC [AM radio station call letters]
WSMY .... Weldon, NC [AM radio station call letters]
WSMZ-FM ... Johnstown, Oh [FM radio station call letters] (RBYB)
WSN .... South Naknek [Alaska] [Airport symbol] (OAG)
WSN .... South Naknek, AK [Location identifier FAA] (FAAL)
WSN .... Spokane County Library, Spokane, WA [Inactive] [OCLC symbol] (OCLC)
WSN .... Wang System Networking (HGAA)
WSN .... Warm Springs [Nevada] [Seismograph station code, US Geological Survey Closed] (SEIS)
WSN .... Water-Soluble Nitrogen [Analytical chemistry]
WSN .... Western Co. of North America [NYSE symbol] (SPSG)
WSN .... Western Resources Technology [Vancouver Stock Exchange symbol]
WSN .... Western Society of Naturalists (EA)
WSNC .... Winston-Salem, NC [AM radio station call letters]
WSND .... Notre Dame, IN [FM radio station call letters]
WSNE .... Taunton, MA [FM radio station call letters]
WSNG .... Torrington, CT [AM radio station call letters]
WSNGT .... White Sands NASA Ground Terminal (MCD)
WSNI .... Thomasville, GA [FM radio station call letters]
WSNJ.......... Bridgeton, NJ [AM radio station call letters]
WSNJ-FM .... Bridgeton, NJ [FM radio station call letters]
WSNL-AM .... Flint, MI [AM radio station call letters] (BROA)
WSNN .... Potsdam, NY [FM radio station call letters]
WSNO .... Barre, VT [AM radio station call letters]
WSNP .... Water-Soluble Nonstarchy Polysaccharide [Food composition]
WSNQ .... Gaylord, MI [AM radio station call letters]
WSNR-AM .... Hartford, KY [AM radio station call letters] (RBYB)
WSNS .... Chicago, IL [Television station call letters]
WSNSCA...... Washable Suits, Novelties, and Sportswear Contractors Association (EA)
WSNT .... Sandersville, GA [AM radio station call letters]
WSNT-FM .... Sandersville, GA [FM radio station call letters]
WSNU .... Lock Haven, PA [FM radio station call letters]
WSNV .... Howland, ME [FM radio station call letters]
WSNW .... Seneca, SC [AM radio station call letters]
W/SNWS...... With Snow Tires [Automotive advertising]
WSNX .... Muskegon, MI [FM radio station call letters]
WSNY .... Columbus, OH [FM radio station call letters]
WSNY .... Wagner Society of New York (EA)
WSO .... Warrant Stores Officer [Navy British]
WSO .... Washabo [Surinam] [Airport symbol] (OAG)
WSO .... Washington Standardization Officers
WSO .... Water Service Operator (MCD)
WSO .... Watsco, Inc. [AMEX symbol] (SPSG)
WSO .... Watsco, Inc. [NYSE symbol] (SAG)
WSO .... Weapon System Officer [or Operator] [Air Force] (AFM)
WSO .... Weapon System Operator
WSO .... Weather Service Office [National Weather Service] (NOAA)
WSO .... Western Support Office [Formerly, WOO] [NASA]

WSO	White Sands Operations [*New Mexico*] [*Formerly, White Sands Missile Operations*] [*NASA*]
WSO	White Superficial Onychomycosis
WSO	Wilcox Solar Observatory
WSO	[*The*] WorkSheet Optimizer [*Laptop tool*] [*Brubaker Software*] (PCM)
WSO	World Safety Organization [*United Nations*]
WSO	World Simulation Organization
WSO	WRAF [*Women's Royal Naval Air Force*] Staff Officer [*British military*] (DMA)
WSO(AG)	Weather Service Office for Agriculture [*National Weather Service*] (NOAA)
WSO(AV)	Weather Service Office for Aviation [*National Weather Service*] (NOAA)
WSO.B	Watsco Inc. Cv CI'B' [*AMEX symbol*] (TTSB)
WSOC	Charlotte, NC [*FM radio station call letters*]
WSOC	Weapon System Operational Concept (AAG)
WSOC	Wider Share Ownership Council [*British*] (DBA)
WSOC-TV	Charlotte, NC [*Television station call letters*]
WSOE	Elon College, NC [*FM radio station call letters*]
WSOEA	Wholesale Stationery and Office Equipment Association [*Later, WSA*] (EA)
WSOF	Madisonville, KY [*FM radio station call letters*]
WSO(FW)	Weather Service Office for Fire-Weather [*National Weather Service*] (NOAA)
WSOH-FM	New Washington, IN [*FM radio station call letters*] (RBYB)
WSOJ	Petersburg, VA [*FM radio station call letters*]
WSOJ	Whole Blood Serum of a Patient with Obstructive Jaundice [*Hematology*] (DAVI)
WSOK	Savannah, GA [*AM radio station call letters*]
WSOL	San German, PR [*AM radio station call letters*]
WSOL-FM	Brunswick, GA [*AM radio station call letters*] (RBYB)
WSOM	Salem, OH [*AM radio station call letters*]
WSOM	Weather Service Operations [*NWS*] (FAAC)
WSON	Henderson, KY [*AM radio station call letters*]
WSON	Worldwide Satellite Observing Network (MCD)
WSOO	Sault Ste. Marie, MI [*AM radio station call letters*]
WSOP	White Supercalendered Offset Paper [*Publishing*]
WSOR	Naples, FL [*FM radio station call letters*]
WSOS	St. Augustine, FL [*FM radio station call letters*]
WSOT	Weapon System Operability Test [*Military*] (CAAL)
WSOU	South Orange, NJ [*FM radio station call letters*]
WSOY	Decatur, IL [*AM radio station call letters*]
WSOY	Werner Soederstroem Osakeyhtio [*Book printer*] [*Finland*]
WSOY-FM	Decatur, IL [*FM radio station call letters*]
WSP	Ward's Sales Prospector [*A publication*]
W/SP	Warheads and Special Projects Laboratory [*Picatinny Arsenal*]
WSP	Washington School of Psychiatry
WSP	Washington Square Press [*Publisher's imprint*]
WSP	Waspam [*Nicaragua*] [*Airport symbol*] (AD)
WSP	Watered Silk Paper (DGA)
WSP	Water-Soluble Polymers
WSP	Water Spray Protection [*Shipping*] (DS)
WSP	Water Supply Papers
WSP	Water Supply Point
WSP	Weapon Support Processor [*Military*] (CAAL)
WSP	Weapon System Program (SAA)
WSP	Weapon Systems Pouch (AFM)
WSP	Weibull Shape Parameter [*Statistics*]
WSP	West Penn Power Co. [*NYSE symbol*] (SPSG)
WSP	Wheel Slide Protection (PDAA)
WSP	White Star Parachute Flares [*Military*] (INF)
WSP	Wideband Signal Processor
WSP	Winspear Resources [*Vancouver Stock Exchange symbol*]
WSP	Withdrawal Seizure-Prone [*Mouse strain*]
WSP	Women Strike for Peace (EA)
WSP	Working Steam Pressure
WSP	Workshop (NATG)
WSP	Work Simplification Program [*Military*]
WSP	Work Study Program (OICC)
WSP	Work Systems Package [*Navy underwater salvage operation*] (DICI)
WSP	Worldwide Service Project
WSP	Wright State University, Piqua Branch Campus, Piqua, OH [*OCLC symbol*] (OCLC)
WSpa	Sparta Free Library, Sparta, WI [*Library symbol Library of Congress*] (LCLS)
WSPA	Spartanburg, SC [*AM radio station call letters*]
WSPA	World Society for the Protection of Animals [*WFPA and ISPA*] [*Formed by a merger of*] (EA)
WSPACS	Weapon Systems Planning [*or Programming*] and Control System
WSPA-FM	Spartanburg, SC [*FM radio station call letters*]
WSPAT	Wolfe-Spence Programming Aptitude Test
WSPA-TV	Spartanburg, SC [*Television station call letters*]
WSPB	Sarasota, FL [*AM radio station call letters*]
WSPC	Albemarle, NC [*AM radio station call letters*]
WSPC	Weapons System Partnerships Committee [*NATO*] (NATG)
WSPC	Weapons System Program Code [*Defense Supply Agency*]
WSPC	World Sports Prototype Championship [*Auto racing*]
WSPD	Toledo, OH [*AM radio station call letters*]
WSPD	Weapons System Planning Data [*Navy*]
WSPD	Weapon System Planning Document (NVT)
WSPDC	Western Sydney Planning and Development Committee [*Australia*]
WSPF	Watergate Special Prosecution Force [*Terminated, 1977*] [*Department of Justice*]
WSPG	Wall Street Planning Group (EA)
WSPG	Weapon System Phasing Group

WSPG	Weapon System Purchasing Group
WSPG	White Sands Proving Ground [*New Mexico*] [*Obsolete*]
WSPGL	Weapon System Program Guide List
WSPI	Mount Carmel, PA [*FM radio station call letters*]
WSP-I	World Socialist Party - Ireland [*Political party*] (EAIO)
WSPK	Poughkeepsie, NY [*FM radio station call letters*]
WSPL	La Crosse, WI [*FM radio station call letters*]
WSPME	Weavelength-Scanning Polarization-Modulation Ellipsometry (PDAA)
WSPN	Saratoga Springs, NY [*FM radio station call letters*]
WSPNZ	World Socialist Party of New Zealand [*Political party*] (EAIO)
WSPO	Stevens Point, WI [*AM radio station call letters*]
WSPO	Weapon System Project Office [*Air Force*]
WSPOP	Weapon System Phase-Out Procedure [*Air Force*] (AFM)
WSPPD	Weapons Systems Personnel Planning Data (MCD)
WSPPr	West Penn Pwr 4 1/2%cmPfd [*NYSE symbol*] (TTSB)
WSPQ	Springville, NY [*AM radio station call letters*]
WSPR	Springfield, MA [*AM radio station call letters*]
WSPR	Weapon System Program Review [*Army*]
WSPRD	Weapons Systems Progress Reporting Data
WSPS	Concord, NH [*FM radio station call letters*]
WSpS	Saint Michael's Hospital, Stevens Point, WI [*Library symbol Library of Congress*] (LCLS)
WSPS	Wire Strike Protection System (MCD)
WSPT	Stevens Point, WI [*FM radio station call letters*]
WSPT-AM	Stevens Point, WI [*AM radio station call letters*] (RBYB)
WSpU	University of Wisconsin-Stevens Point, Stevens Point, WI [*Library symbol Library of Congress*] (LCLS)
WSPU	Women's Social and Political Union [*British*]
WSPUS	World Socialist Party of the United States (EA)
WSP(US)	World Socialist Party of the United States (EA)
WSPW-AM	Bridgewater, NJ [*AM radio station call letters*] (BROA)
WSPX-FM	Bowman, SC [*FM radio station call letters*] (BROA)
WSPY	Plano, IL [*FM radio station call letters*]
WSPZ	Tuscaloosa, AL [*AM radio station call letters*]
WSQ	Wake Seeding and Quenching
WSq	Weather Squadron [*Air Force*] (AFM)
WSQA-FM	Hornell, NY [*FM radio station call letters*] (BROA)
WSQC	Oneonta, NY [*FM radio station call letters*]
WSQE	Corning, NY [*FM radio station call letters*]
WSQG	Ithaca, NY [*FM radio station call letters*]
WSQL-AM	Brevard, NC [*AM radio station call letters*] (BROA)
WSQN	Scranton, SC [*FM radio station call letters*]
WSQR	Sycamore, IL [*AM radio station call letters*]
WSQV	Berwick, PA [*AM radio station call letters*]
WSQX	Binghamton, NY [*FM radio station call letters*]
WSR	Canadian Helicopters [*ICAO designator*] (FAAC)
WSR	Warm Springs Repeater [*Nevada*] [*Seismograph station code, US Geological Survey Closed*] (SEIS)
WSR	Warren & Saline River Railroad Co. [*AAR code*]
WSR	War Service Regulation
WSR	Wasior [*West Irian, Indonesia*] [*Airport symbol*] (AD)
W/sr	Watts per Steradian
WSR	Weak Signal Reception
WSR	Weapons Spares Report [*Navy*]
WSR	Weapons Status Report [*Navy*] (NG)
WSR	Weapons System Review (NVT)
WSR	Weapon System Reliability [*Air Force*] (AFM)
WSR	Weapon Systems Requirement (MCD)
WSR	Weather Search RADAR (MCD)
WSR	Weather Surveillance RADAR
WSR	Weekly Summary Report
WSR	Weisenburg-Sicard-Robineau [*Syndrome*] [*Medicine*] (DB)
WSR	Wet Snow on Runway [*NWS*] (FAAC)
WSR	Wild and Scenic River (COE)
WSR	Wild and Scenic Rivers Act
WSR	Windsor Resources, Inc. [*Vancouver Stock Exchange symbol*]
WSR	Wire Shift Register
WSR	Withdrawal Seizure-Resistant [*Mouse strain*]
WSR	Wood-Shingle Roof [*Technical drawings*]
WSR	World Students Relief
WSR-88D	Weather Surveillance Radar [*Marine science*] (OSRA)
WSRA	Western Shoe Retailers Association (NTPA)
WSRA	Wild and Scenic Rivers Act
WSRA	Women's Squash Rackets Association [*British*] (BI)
WSRB	Walpole, MA [*FM radio station call letters*]
WSRC	Durham, NC [*AM radio station call letters*]
WSRC	Westinghouse Savannah River Company
WSRCC	War, Strikes, Riots, and Civil Commotions [*Insurance*] (AIA)
WSRCC	Western Suburbs Regional Chamber of Commerce [*Sydney, New South Wales, Australia*]
WSRD	Johnstown, NY [*FM radio station call letters*]
WSRE	Pensacola, FL [*Television station call letters*]
WSRF	Fort Lauderdale, FL [*AM radio station call letters*]
WSRG	Sturgeon Bay, WI [*FM radio station call letters*] (RBYB)
WSRH	Weather Service Regional Headquarters [*National Weather Service*] (NOAA)
WSRI	Rochester, NH [*FM radio station call letters*] (RBYB)
WSRI	World Safety Research Institute
WSRK	Oneonta, NY [*FM radio station call letters*]
WSRL	Water Supply Research Laboratory [*National Environmental Research Center*]
WSRL	Wisconsin Survey Research Laboratory [*University of Wisconsin*] [*Research center*] (RCD)
WSRM	Coosa, GA [*FM radio station call letters*]
WSRM	Weather Surveillance RADAR Manual (NOAA)

W/(SR-M²)... Watt per Steradian Square Meter (WDAA)
WSRN .... Swarthmore, PA [FM radio station call letters]
WSRN .... Western Satellite Research Network (PDAA)
WSRO .... Marlborough, MA [AM radio station call letters]
WSRO .... Weapon System Replacement Operations (MCD)
WSRO .... Whole System Replacement Operation [Army] (INF)
WSRO .... World Sugar Research Organisation (EAIO)
WSRP .... Weapons System Requisitioning Procedure [Military] (AABC)
WSRQ .... Queensbury, NY [FM radio station call letters] (RBYB)
WSRR .... West Shore Railroad
WSRR-FM ... Millington, TN [FM radio station call letters] (RBYB)
WSRS .... Wildlife Sound Recording Society [British]
WSRS .... Worcester, MA [FM radio station call letters]
WSRT .... Mercersburg, PA [FM radio station call letters]
WSRT .... Weapons System Reliability Test (CINC)
WSRT .... Weapon System Readiness Test
WSRT .... Westerbork Synthesis Radio Telescope
WSRV .... Smyrna, DE [FM radio station call letters]
WSRW .... Hillsboro, OH [AM radio station call letters]
WSRW-FM... Hillsboro, OH [FM radio station call letters]
WSRX .... Naples, FL [FM radio station call letters]
WSRZ .... Sarasota, FL [FM radio station call letters]
WSS .... Warfare Systems School [Air Force] (AFM)
WSS .... War Savings Staff
WSS .... Washington Strategy Seminar (EA)
WSS .... Weapon Support Systems
WSS .... Weapon System Specification (AAG)
WSS .... Weather Service Specialist [National Weather Service]
WSS .... Weekend Stress Syndrome [Psychiatry]
WSS .... Wheel Speed Sensor [Automotive engineering]
WSS .... Wheelwrights' and Smiths' Society [A union] [British]
WSS .... Wholesale Storage Site (DNAB)
WSS .... Wide Sense Stationary [Telecommunications] (IAA)
WSS .... Wind Shear Spike (SAA)
WSS .... Winston-Salem Southbound Railway Co. [AAR code]
WSS .... Women's Social Services [Salvation Army]
WSS .... Women's Studies Section [Association of College and Research Libraries]
WSS .... Workpack Scheduling System [Industrial engineering]
WSS .... Work Summarization System (MCD)
WSS .... World Ship Society [Haywards Heath, West Sussex, England]
WSS .... WWMCCS [Worldwide Military Command and Control System] Systems Specification (MCD)
WSSA .... Morrow, GA [AM radio station call letters]
WSSA .... Weapon System Support Activities (AAG)
WSSA .... Weed Science Society of America (EA)
WSSA .... Welsh Secondary Schools Association [British]
WSSA .... Western Social Science Association (EA)
WSSA .... White Sands Signal Agency [New Mexico] [Military] (MCD)
WSSA .... Wine and Spirits Shippers Association (EA)
WSSA .... World Secret Service Association [Later, WAD] (EA)
WSSAB .... Weller-Strawser Scales of Adaptive Behavior [Educational test]
WSSB .... Orangeburg, SC [FM radio station call letters]
WSSBA .... Western Single Side Band Association (EA)
WSSC .... Sumter, SC [AM radio station call letters]
WSSC .... Weapon System Support Center (AAG)
WSSC .... Weapon System Support Code [Navy] (NG)
WSSCA .... Welsh Springer Spaniel Club of America (EA)
WSSCA .... White Sands Signal Corps Agency [New Mexico] [Military] (AAG)
WSSCL .... Weapon System Stock Control List (AAG)
WSSD .... Chicago, IL [FM radio station call letters]
WSSD .... Weapon System Support Development (MCD)
WSSF .... National Weather Service Support FAcility (FAAC)
WSSF .... Weapons System Security Flight [Military]
WSSFN .... World Society for Stereotactic and Functional Neurosurgery (EA)
WSSG .... Goldsboro, NC [AM radio station call letters]
WSSG .... Weapon System Support Group (MCD)
WSSG .... WOCE [World Ocean Circulation Experiment] Scientific Steering Group [Marine science] (OSRA)
WSSH .... Lowell, MA [FM radio station call letters]
WSSI .... Carthage, MS [AM radio station call letters]
WSSI .... Re'uth Women's Social Service [An association] [Formerly, Women's Social Service for Israel] (EA)
WSSI .... Women's Social Service for Israel (EA)
WSSIB .... WWMCCS [Worldwide Military Command and Control System] Standard System Information Base (MCD)
WSSI-FM .... Carthage, MS [FM radio station call letters]
WSSJ .... Camden, NJ [AM radio station call letters]
WSSK-FM .... Saratoga Springs, NY [FM radio station call letters] (BROA)
WSSL .... Gray Court, SC [FM radio station call letters]
WSSL .... Seletar [Singapore] [ICAO location identifier] (ICLI)
WSSL .... Weapon System Stock List [Army]
WSSL .... Weapon System Stock/Support List [Air Force] (AFIT)
WSSL .... Western Secondary Standards Laboratory
WSSM .... Weapon System Staff Manager [Army] (RDA)
WSSM .... Weapon System Support Manager (AAG)
WSSMV ...... Wheat Spindle Streak Mosaic Virus
WSSN .... Weston, WV [FM radio station call letters]
WSSO .... Starkville, MS [FM radio station call letters]
WSSO .... Weapon System Support Officer [Army] (RDA)
WSSP .... Goose Creek, SC [FM radio station call letters]
WSSP .... Weapon Systems Support Program [Defense Supply Agency]
WSSPM ...... Weapons System Support Program Manager (AFIT)
WSSQ .... Sterling, IL [FM radio station call letters]
WSSR .... Georgetown, DE [AM radio station call letters]

WSSRAP...... Weldon Spring Site Remedial Action Project [Department of Energy] [Weldon Spring, MO] (GAAI)
WSSRS .... Waksman Social Skills Rating Scale
WSSS .... Charlotte, NC [FM radio station call letters]
WSSS .... Singapore Changi [Singapore] [ICAO location identifier] (ICLI)
WSSS .... Weapon System Storage Site
WSSSFAF ... Wartime Standard Support System for Foreign Armed Forces (MCD)
WSSSG....... Wide-band Spread Spectrum Signal Generator
WSSSP .... Western States Small School Project
WSST .... Cordele, GA [Television station call letters]
WSSU .... National Weather Service Support Unit (FAAC)
WSSUS .... Wide Sense Stationary Uncorrelated Scattering [Telecommunications] (IAA)
WSSX .... Charleston, SC [FM radio station call letters]
WSSY .... Talladega, AL [FM radio station call letters]
WSSZ .... Greensburg, PA [FM radio station call letters]
WSt .... D. R. Moon Memorial Library, Stanley, WI [Library symbol Library of Congress] (LCLS)
WST .... Waste
WST .... Watch Station Trainer [Military] (DWSG)
WST .... Water Supply Tank
WST .... Weapon Safety Trainer
WST .... Weapon System Test
WST .... Weapon System Trainer [Navy]
WST .... Weightlessness Simulation Test
WST .... West Aviation AS [Norway ICAO designator] (FAAC)
WST .... West Co. [NYSE symbol] (TTSB)
WST .... West Co., Inc. [NYSE symbol] (SPSG)
WST .... Westerly [Rhode Island] [Airport symbol] (OAG)
WST .... Westerly, RI [Location identifier FAA] (FAAL)
WST .... Wholesale Sales Tax
WST .... Word Synchronizing Track (NITA)
WST .... World Satellite Terminal [Telecommunications] (IAA)
WST .... World Ship Trust [Cambridge, England]
WST .... World System Teletext (NTCM)
WST .... Write Symbol Table
WSTA .... Charlotte Amalie, VI [AM radio station call letters]
WSTA .... Wall Street Telecommunications Association (CIST)
WSTA .... Weapon System Task Analysis (AAG)
WSTA .... White Slave Traffic Act
WstAmer..... WestAmerica Corp. [Associated Press] (SAG)
WstAtlas .... Western Atlas, Inc. [Associated Press] (SAG)
WSTB .... Streetsboro, OH [FM radio station call letters]
WSTB .... Water Science and Technology Board (COE)
WstBeef ..... Western Beef [Associated Press] (SAG)
WstbPR ...... Westernbank Puerto Rico [Associated Press] (SAG)
WstBrC ...... Westbridge Capital [Associated Press] (SAG)
WSTC .... Stamford, CT [AM radio station call letters]
WSTC .... Weapons System Test Card (MCD)
WSTC .... Weapon System Total Complex
WSTC .... Willimantic State Teachers College [Connecticut]
WstCstFL ... West Coast Bancorp Florida [Associated Press] (SAG)
WstCstOR ... West Coast Bancorp Oregon [Associated Press] (SAG)
WstctEg ..... Westcoast Energy, Inc. [Associated Press] (SAG)
WSTD .... Standish, MI [FM radio station call letters]
WSTDA .... Web Sling and Tiedown Association (EA)
WSTE .... Ponce, PR [Television station call letters]
WSTE .... TransAmerican Waste Indus [NASDAQ symbol] (TTSB)
WSTE .... TransAmerican Waste Industries, Inc. [NASDAQ symbol] (SAG)
WSTEA .... Weapon System Training Effectiveness Analysis
WSTE MAT... Waste Material [Freight]
W/STEP...... With Step Change in Altitude (GAVI)
WSTEW....... Transamerican Waste Inds Wrrt'A' [NASDAQ symbol] (TTSB)
WSTEZ .... Transamerican Waste Inds Wrrt'B' [NASDAQ symbol] (TTSB)
WSTF .... Andalusia, AL [FM radio station call letters] (RBYB)
WSTF .... Westaff, Inc. [Formerly, Western Staff Services] [NASDAQ symbol]
WSTF .... Western Staff Services [NASDAQ symbol] (TTSB)
WSTF .... White Sands Test Facility [New Mexico] [Military]
WSTG .... Hampton, NH [FM radio station call letters] (RBYB)
WStG .... Wehrstrafgesetz [Military Criminal Law] [German] (ILCA)
WstG .... Western Gas Resources Co. [Associated Press] (SAG)
WstgEl .... Westinghouse Electric Corp. [Associated Press] (SAG)
WstGR .... Western Gas Resources [Associated Press] (SAG)
WSTH .... Alexander City, AL [FM radio station call letters]
WSTH .... Weapon System Tactical Handbook (MCD)
WSTI .... Quitman, GA [FM radio station call letters]
WSTI .... Welded Steel Tube Institute [Later, STINA] (EA)
WSTIB .... Woolen and Silk Textiles Industries Board [New Deal]
WSTJ .... St. Johnsbury, VT [AM radio station call letters]
WSTK .... Colonial Heights, VA [AM radio station call letters]
WSTL .... South Glens Falls, NY [AM radio station call letters]
WSTL .... Weapon System Test Laboratory
WSTL .... Westell Technologies'A' [NASDAQ symbol] (TTSB)
WSTL .... Westell Technologies, Inc. [NASDAQ symbol] (SAG)
WSTL .... Whistle (MSA)
WStL & P ... Wabash, St. Louis & Pacific Railway
WSTM .... Syracuse, NY [Television station call letters]
WSTM .... Western Micro Techn'gy [NASDAQ symbol] (TTSB)
WSTM .... Western Micro Technology, Inc. [NASDAQ symbol] (NQ)
WSTM .... White Sands Missile Range Transverse Mercator [Army] (AABC)
WstMar ...... West Marine, Inc. [Associated Press] (SAG)
WstMn .... Western Mining Corp. [Associated Press] (SAG)
WstmorC.... Westmoreland Coal Co. [Associated Press] (SAG)
WstmrC...... Westmoreland Coal [Associated Press] (SAG)
Wstn .... Western (TBD)

WSTN	Western
WSTN	Weston [Roy F.], Inc. [West Chester, PA] [NASDAQ symbol] (NQ)
WSTNA	Weston(Roy F)'A' [NASDAQ symbol] (TTSB)
WSTN-AM....	Somerville, TN [AM radio station call letters] (RBYB)
WstnCC........	Western Country Clubs, Inc. [Associated Press] (SAG)
WstnGR	Western Gas Resources [Associated Press] (SAG)
WstnNat........	Western National Corp. [Associated Press] (SAG)
WstnOhF......	Western Ohio Financial Corp. [Associated Press] (SAG)
WstnPb	Western Publishing Group, Inc. [Associated Press] (SAG)
WstnPw........	Western Power & Equipment Corp. [Associated Press] (SAG)
WstnRes	Western Resources, Inc. [Associated Press] (SAG)
WstnRs	Western Resources [Associated Press] (SAG)
WSTO	Owensboro, KY [FM radio station call letters]
WSTP..........	Salisbury, NC [AM radio station call letters]
WSTP..........	Wastewater Sewage Treatment Plant (GNE)
WSTP..........	Weapon System Test Program
WstpBc	Westport Bancorp, Inc. [Associated Press] (SAG)
Wstpc	Westpac Banking Corp. [Associated Press] (SAG)
WSTPN	Wrist Pin
WstptStv	Westpoint Stevens Co. [Associated Press] (SAG)
WSTQ	Streator, IL [FM radio station call letters]
WSTR	Cincinnati, OH [Television station call letters]
WSTR	Smyrna, GA [FM radio station call letters]
WSTR	WesterFed Financial [NASDAQ symbol] (TTSB)
WSTR	Westerfed Financial Corp. [NASDAQ symbol} (SAG)
Wstrbke	Westerbeke Corp. [Associated Press] (SAG)
WstRes	Western Resources Capital II [Associated Press] (SAG)
WSTRN	Western
WSTRS	Washington State Teachers Retirement System (EDAC)
WSTS	Fairmont, NC [FM radio station call letters]
WSTS	Weapon System Training Set (AFM)
WSTS	World Semiconductor Trade Statistics [Semiconductor Industry Association] [Information service or system] (IID)
WSTSD	Westside
WSTSHD	Watershed
WstStr	Western Star Trucks Holdings Ltd. [Associated Press] (SAG)
WSTT..........	Thomasville, GA [AM radio station call letters]
WSTT..........	Weather Scenario Test Tape [Marine science] (OSRA)
WstTleS........	West TeleServices Corp. [Associated Press] (SAG)
WstTr..........	Western Transmedia, Inc. [Associated Press] (SAG)
WstTrns	Western Transmedia, Inc. [Associated Press] (SAG)
WSTTWTR ..	Wastewater
WSTU	Stuart, FL [AM radio station call letters]
WSTV..........	Steubenville, OH [AM radio station call letters]
WSTV..........	World Service Television [BBC] (ECON)
WSTW..........	Wilmington, DE [FM radio station call letters]
WstWatr	Western Water Co. [Associated Press] (SAG)
Wstwd	Westwood Corp. [Associated Press] (SAG)
WstwdF........	Westwood Financial Corp. [Associated Press] (SAG)
WstwdH........	Westwood Homestead Financial Corp. [Associated Press] (SAG)
WstWire	Western Wireless Corp. [Associated Press] (OAG)
WstwOn	Westwood One, Inc. [Associated Press] (SAG)
WSTX	Christiansted, VI [AM radio station call letters]
WSTX-FM....	Christiansted, VI [FM radio station call letters]
WSTZ..........	Vicksburg, MS [FM radio station call letters]
WSU	University of Wisconsin-Superior, Superior, WI [Library symbol Library of Congress] (LCLS)
WSU	Washington State University
WSU	Wasu [Papua New Guinea] [Airport symbol] (OAG)
WSU	Water Servicing Unit (NASA)
WSU	Wayne State University [Michigan]
WSU	Weighted Student Unit
WSU	Wichita State University [Kansas] (PDAA)
WSU	Windmill Study Unit [American Topical Association] (EA)
WSU	Women on Stamps Unit [American Topical Association] (EA)
WSU	Work Station Utility
WSU	Wright State University, Dayton, OH [OCLC symbol] (OCLC)
WSUA	Miami, FL [AM radio station call letters]
WSUB	Groton, CT [AM radio station call letters]
WSUC	Cortland, NY [FM radio station call letters]
WSUC	Wisconsin State University Conference (PSS)
WSUE	Sault Ste. Marie, MI [FM radio station call letters]
WSUF	Noyack, NY [FM radio station call letters]
WSUH..........	Oxford, MS [AM radio station call letters]
WSUI	Iowa City, IA [AM radio station call letters]
WSUI	Wisconsin Substance Use Inventory (DHP)
WSUL	Monticello, NY [FM radio station call letters]
WSUN	St. Petersburg, FL [AM radio station call letters]
WSUOPR	Washington State University, Open Pool Reactor
WSUP	Platteville, WI [FM radio station call letters]
WSUR	Ponce, PR [Television station call letters]
WSUS	Franklin, NJ [FM radio station call letters]
WSU-SDL	Washington State University Shock Dynamics Laboratory [Pullman]
WSUW	Whitewater, WI [FM radio station call letters]
WSUX	Seaford, DE [AM radio station call letters]
WSUY	Charleston, SC [FM radio station call letters]
WSV	Wall Street Ventures [Vancouver Stock Exchange symbol]
WSV	Water Solenoid Valve
WSV..........	Water-Soluble Vitamin
WSV..........	Wheelchair Sports Victoria [Australia]
WSV..........	Wooly-Monkey Sarcoma Virus [Medicine] (PDAA)
WSVA	Harrisonburg, VA [AM radio station call letters]
WSVA	Wang Software Vendors' Association [Defunct] (EA)
WSVE..........	Jacksonville, FL [AM radio station call letters]
WSVG	Mount Jackson, VA [AM radio station call letters]

WSVH..........	Savannah, GA [FM radio station call letters]
WSVI	Christiansted, VI [Television station call letters]
WSVM..........	Valdese, NC [AM radio station call letters]
WSVN..........	Miami, FL [Television station call letters]
WSVO-FM....	Staunton, VA [FM radio station call letters] (RBYB)
WSVS..........	Crewe, VA [AM radio station call letters]
WSVV-FM....	Moyock, NC [FM radio station call letters] (BROA)
WSVY..........	Portsmouth, VA [AM radio station call letters]
WSVY..........	Windsor, VA [FM radio station call letters]
WSW	Southwest Wisconsin Library System, Fennimore, WI [OCLC symbol] (OCLC)
WSW	Wall Street Week [Television program]
WSW	West by South West [Direction] (EERA)
WSW	Western Shelf Water [Oceanography]
WSW	West-Southwest
WSW	White Sidewall [Tires]
WSW	Winter Storm Warning [Telecommunications] (OTD)
WSWA	Weed Society of Australia (EERA)
WSWA	Wine and Spirits Wholesalers of America (EA)
WSWB	Scranton, PA [Television station call letters]
WSWI	Evansville, IN [AM radio station call letters]
WSWL..........	Pensacola, FL [AM radio station call letters]
WSWL..........	Warheads and Special Weapons Laboratory (MCD)
WSWMA	Water and Sewage Works Manufacturers Association [Later, WWEMA] (EA)
WSWMA	Western States Weights and Measures Association
WSWN	Belle Glade, FL [AM radio station call letters]
WSWO	Wilmington, OH [FM radio station call letters]
WSWP	Grandview, WV [Television station call letters]
WSWR	Shelby, OH [FM radio station call letters]
WSWRN	West-Southwestern (FAAC)
WSWS	Opelika, AL [Television station call letters]
WSWT	Peoria, IL [FM radio station call letters]
WSWV	Pennington Gap, VA [AM radio station call letters]
WSWV-FM....	Pennington Gap, VA [FM radio station call letters]
WSWW-AM....	Charleston, WV [AM radio station call letters] (BROA)
WSWZ	Lancaster, OH [FM radio station call letters]
WSX	Wessex Air Services Ltd. [British ICAO designator] (FAAC)
WSY..........	Airlie Beach [Australia Airport symbol]
WSY..........	MAM Aviation Ltd. [British ICAO designator] (FAAC)
WSY..........	West Somerset Yeomanry [British military] (DMA)
WSYB..........	Rutland, VT [AM radio station call letters]
WSYC..........	Shippensburg, PA [FM radio station call letters]
WSYC..........	West Somerset Yeomanry Cavalry [British military] (DMA)
WSYD..........	Mount Airy, NC [AM radio station call letters]
WSYE..........	Houston, MS [FM radio station call letters]
WSYL..........	Sylvania, GA [AM radio station call letters]
WSYM	Lansing, MI [Television station call letters]
WSYN	Georgetown, SC [FM radio station call letters]
WSYP	White Sulphur Springs & Yellowstone Park Railway Co. [AAR code]
WSYR..........	Syracuse, NY [AM radio station call letters]
WSYT..........	Syracuse, NY [Television station call letters]
WSYW	Indianapolis, IN [AM radio station call letters]
WSYW-FM....	Danville, IN [FM radio station call letters]
WSYX	Columbus, OH [Television station call letters]
WSYY	Millinocket, ME [AM radio station call letters]
WSYY-FM....	Millinocket, ME [FM radio station call letters]
WSZ..........	Westport [New Zealand] [Airport symbol] (OAG)
WSZ..........	Wheat-Sheep Zone [Agriculture]
WSZ..........	Wood Supply Zone (EERA)
WSZ..........	Wrong Signature Zero [Nuclear science] (OA)
WT..........	Nigeria Airways [ICAO designator] (AD)
WT..........	Three-Conductor Cables [JETDS nomenclature] [Military] (CET)
WT..........	WAAC Ltd. - Nigeria Airways [Nigeria] [ICAO designator] (ICDA)
WT..........	Waist Tether [NASA] (KSC)
WT..........	Wait Time [Computer order entry]
W/T..........	Walkie-Talkie
WT..........	Wall Thickness [Nuclear energy] (NRCH)
WT..........	Warm Tone [Photography]
WT..........	Warning Tag (AAG)
WT..........	Warrant
WT..........	Warrant Telegraphist [British military] (DMA)
W-T..........	Warren-Teed [Commercial firm] (DAVI)
WT..........	War Tax
WT..........	Wartime
WT..........	War Transport [British military] (DMA)
WT..........	Washington Territory [Prior to statehood]
WT..........	Washington Territory Reports [1854-88] [A publication] (DLA)
WT..........	Wash Trough
WT..........	Waste Tank
WT..........	Watchdogs of the Treasury (EA)
WT..........	Watchdog Timer (MCD)
WT..........	Watch Time
WT..........	Water Tank
WT..........	Water Tanker [British]
WT..........	Water Tender [Navy]
WT..........	Water Thermometer
WT..........	Watertight
WT..........	Water-Tube Boiler [Naval]
WT..........	Watt (IAA)
WT..........	Waveguide Transmission
WT..........	Wealth Tax (PDAA)
WT..........	Weapons Technician [Air Force] (AFM)
WT..........	Weapons Tight [Weapons will engage only objects identified as hostile]

WT	Weapon Test
WT	Weapon Training (MCD)
WT	Weight (AAG)
wt	Weight (ODBW)
WT	Weldwood Transportation Ltd. [AAR code]
WT	Wellhead Tax [Oil industry]
WT	Whiffle Tree [Structural test] (AAG)
WT	Whistletip [Catheter] [Urology] (DAVI)
WT	White (DAVI)
WT	White Pennant [Navy British]
WT	Whole-Time (WDAA)
WT	Wild Track [Cinematography]
WT	Wild Type [of a species] [Genetics]
WT	William Tell Gunnery Mate
WT	Will Talk [Telecommunications] (TEL)
WT	Wilms' Tumor [Oncology]
WT	Wind Tunnel
WT	Winterization Test (AAG)
WT	[The] Winter's Tale [Shakespearean work]
WT	Wireless Telegraphy [or Telephony]
WT	Wireless Transceiver (ACRL)
WT	Wireless Transmitter
WT	Wireless Truck [British]
WT	Wire Ticket [NASA] (NASA)
WT	Wire Transfer [Banking]
WT	Withholding Tax [IRS]
WT	Without
WT	With Tape
WT	With Title [Bibliography]
WT	Witness Terms (NITA)
WT	Wood Threshold (MSA)
WT	Word Target [Psychology]
WT	Word Terminal
WT	Word Type
WT	Workshop Trains [British]
W/T	Work Track [Cinematography]
WT	Work Type (NITA)
WT	Worldteam (EA)
WT	World Trade (IAA)
WT	Write Through [Computer science] (PCM)
WT	Written Testimony (BJA)
WT	Wyoming Territory
WTA	Tamborohano [Madagascar] [Airport symbol] (OAG)
WTA	Washington Technological Association (MCD)
WTA	Wash Rack/Treatment Area [Environmental science] (BCP)
WTA	Water Transport Association [Defunct] (EA)
WTA	Western Timber Association (EA)
WTA	Wholesale Traders' Association [British] (DBA)
WTA	Willingness-to-Accept [Market research]
WTA	Willingness to Avoid (EERA)
WTA	Window Test Apparatus
WTA	Wire Traceability and Accountability [NASA] (NASA)
WTA	Wissenschaftlich-Technischer Arbeitskreis fuer Denkmalpflege und Bauwerksanierung [International Association for the Protection of Monuments and Restoration of Buildings] (EAIO)
WTA	Women's Tennis Association [Later, WITA] (EA)
WTA	Women's Tricycle Association [British] (BI)
WTA	World Teleport Association [New York, NY] [Telecommunications] (TSSD)
WTA	Wyoming Trucking Association, Casper WY [STAC]
WTAB	Tabor City, NC [AM radio station call letters]
WTAC	Flint, MI [AM radio station call letters]
WTAC	Waste Isolation Pilot Plant Technical Assistance Contractor [Department of Energy] (GAAI)
WTAC	Water Technology Advisory Committee [Australia]
WTAD	Quincy, IL [AM radio station call letters]
WTAD	Wepman Test of Auditory Discrimination [Speech and language therapy] (DAVI)
WTAE	Pittsburgh, PA [AM radio station call letters]
WTAE-TV	Pittsburgh, PA [Television station call letters]
WTAG	Worcester, MA [AM radio station call letters]
WTAI	Melbourne, FL [AM radio station call letters]
WTAJ	Altoona, PA [Television station call letters]
WTAK	Hartselle, AL [FM radio station call letters]
WTAL	Tallahassee, FL [AM radio station call letters]
WTAM-AM	Cleveland, OH [AM radio station call letters] (RBYB)
WTAN	Clearwater, FL [AM radio station call letters]
WTAO	Murphysboro, IL [FM radio station call letters]
WTAP	Parkersburg, WV [Television station call letters]
WTAQ	La Grange, IL [AM radio station call letters]
WTAR	Norfolk, VA [AM radio station call letters]
WTAT	Charleston, SC [Television station call letters]
WTAU-AM	Zion, IL [AM radio station call letters] (RBYB)
WT Aux B	Water-Tube Auxiliary Boiler (DS)
WTAW	College Station, TX [AM radio station call letters]
WTAX	Springfield, IL [AM radio station call letters]
W/TAX	Withholding Tax [IRS] (AAG)
W/Tax	Withholding Tax (DFIT)
WTAY	Robinson, IL [AM radio station call letters]
WTAZ	Morton, IL [FM radio station call letters]
WTB	Wales Tourist Board (DCTA)
WTB	War Transportation Board [World War II]
WTB	Water-Tube Boiler [Naval]
WTB	Welttierschutzbund [Also known as WFPA, FMPA] [World Federation for the Protection of Animals]

WTB	Where's the Beef [Slogan created by the Dancer Fitzgerald Sample advertising agency for Wendy's International, Inc.]
WTB	Wilderness Trail Bike
WTB	Willamette Tariff Bureau Inc., Portland OR [STAC]
WTB	Woerterbuch [Dictionary] [German] (ROG)
WTB	Write Tape Binary [Computer science] (IAA)
WTBA	Water-Tube Boilermakers Association [British] (BI)
WTB & TS	Watch Tower Bible and Tract Society
WTBB	Bonifay, FL [FM radio station call letters]
WTBD	Work to Be Done (ADA)
WTBF	Troy, AL [AM radio station call letters]
WTBG	Brownsville, TN [FM radio station call letters]
WTBH	Chiefland, FL [FM radio station call letters]
WTBI	Greenville, SC [FM radio station call letters]
WTBI	Pickens, SC [AM radio station call letters]
WTBJ	Oxford, AL [FM radio station call letters]
WTBK	Manchester, KY [FM radio station call letters]
WTBK	Westerbeke Corp. [Avon, MA] [NASDAQ symbol] (NQ)
WTBM	Mexico, ME [FM radio station call letters]
WTBO	Cumberland, MD [AM radio station call letters]
WTBQ	Warwick, NY [AM radio station call letters]
WTBR	War Trade Board Rulings [United States] [A publication] (DLA)
WTBS	Atlanta, GA [Television station call letters]
WTBS	Water-Tube Boiler Survey (DS)
WTBT	New Port Richey, FL [FM radio station call letters] (RBYB)
WTBU	Indianapolis, IN [Television station call letters]
WTBX	Hibbing, MN [FM radio station call letters]
WTBY	Poughkeepsie, NY [Television station call letters]
WTBZ	Grafton, WV [AM radio station call letters]
WTBZ-FM	Grafton, WV [FM radio station call letters]
WTC	New York [New York] Battery Park [Airport symbol] (OAG)
WTC	Wafer Transfer Chamber (AAEL)
WTC	War Transport Council [Later, ITWC] [World War II]
WTC	Waste Water Technology Centre [Canada] (ECON)
WTC	Water Thermal and Chemical Technology Center [University of California] [Research center] (RCD)
WTC	Waterton [Colorado] [Seismograph station code, US Geological Survey Closed] (SEIS)
WTC	Well-Tempered Clavier [Compositions of J. S. Bach]
WTC	Western Telecommunications Consulting Co. [Los Angeles, CA] [Telecommunications] (TSSD)
WTC	Whole Tree Chips (PDAA)
WTC	Wind Temperature Correction
WTC	Wire Test Chamber
WTC	Women's Talent Corps [Later, CHS] (EA)
WTC	Women's Theater Council
WTC	Woodford Flight Test Center [British ICAO designator] (FAAC)
WTC	Workload Transaction Code [Navy] (NG)
WTC	World Trade Center [New York City]
WTC	World Trade Center of New Orleans [New Orleans, LA] (EA)
WTCA	Plymouth, IN [AM radio station call letters]
WTCA	Water Terminal Clearance Authority [Army] (AABC)
WTCA	Welsh Terrier Club of America (EA)
WTCA	Whole-Time Consultants' Association [British] (BI)
WTCA	Wood Truss Council of America (EA)
WTCA	World Tasar Class Association (EAIO)
WTCA	World Trade Center Arhus [Denmark] (EAIO)
WTCA	World Trade Centers Association (EA)
WTCAJ	World Trade Center of Abidjan [Ivory Coast] (EAIO)
WTCARES	Welsh Terrier Club of America Rescue Service (EA)
WTCB	Orangeburg, SC [FM radio station call letters]
WTCB	Water Tender Construction Battalion [Navy]
WTCC	Springfield, MA [FM radio station call letters]
WTCC	Water Turbine Closed Coupled (MSA)
WTCC	Wet Tropics Consultative Committee (EERA)
WTCC	Wisconsin Technical College Conference (PSS)
WTCCC	Wet Tropics Community Consultative Committee [Australia]
WTCCQ	World Trade Center Club Chongqing [China] (EAIO)
WTCCY	World Trade Centre - Cyprus (EAIO)
WTCE	Fort Pierce, FL [Television station call letters]
WTCF	Carrollton, MI [FM radio station call letters]
WTCGV	World Trade Center Geneva [Switzerland] (EAIO)
WTCH	Shawano, WI [AM radio station call letters]
WTCI	Chattanooga, TN [Television station call letters]
WTCI	Western Telecommunications, Inc. [Englewood, CO] [Telecommunications]
WTCIB	Women's Travelers Center and Information Bank [Later, WIB] (EA)
WTCIS	World Trade Center Istanbul [Turkey] (EAIO)
WTCJ	Tell City, IN [AM radio station call letters]
WTCK	World Trade Center Korea
WTCK-AM	Greensboro, NC [AM radio station call letters] (RBYB)
WTCL	Chattahoochee, FL [AM radio station call letters]
WTCM	Traverse City, MI [AM radio station call letters]
WTCM	Weld Timer Control Module
WTCM-FM	Traverse City, MI [FM radio station call letters]
WTCMM	World Trade Center Metro Manila [Philippines] (EAIO)
WTCN	World Trade Center of Nigeria (EAIO)
WTCNJ	World Trade Centre Nanjing [China] (EAIO)
WTCO	Campbellsville, KY [AM radio station call letters]
WTCO	Western Transportation Co. [AAR code]
WTCO	World Trade Center Oslo [Norway] (EAIO)
WTCQ	Vidalia, GA [FM radio station call letters]
WTCR	Huntington, WV [FM radio station call letters]
WTCR	Kenova, WV [AM radio station call letters]
WTCS	Fairmont, WV [AM radio station call letters]

WTCS........ Windshield Temperature Control Systems
WTCSS........ West Coast Off-Shore Tactical Control Surveillance System [*Navy*] (DNAB)
WTCT........ Marion, IL [*Television station call letters*]
WTCV........ Weapon and Tracked Combat Vehicle (MCD)
WTCW........ Whitesburg, KY [*AM radio station call letters*]
WTCX........ Ripon, WI [*FM radio station call letters*]
WTCY........ Harrisburg, PA [*AM radio station call letters*]
WTD........ War Trade Department [*British World War II*]
WTD........ Watertight Door
WTD........ Water Turbine Direct (MSA)
WTD........ Weapons Training Detachment [*Military*]
WTD........ Weekly Total-to-Date
WTD........ Weighted Total Demerits [*Lubricating oil test*]
WTD........ West End [*Grand Bahama Island, Bahamas*] [*Airport symbol*] (AD)
WTD........ Western Timber Co. (EFIS)
WTD........ Whitland [*British depot code*]
WTD........ Wind Tunnel Data
WTD........ World Trade Directory [*Department of Commerce*] [*A publication*]
WTD........ Write Tape Decimal (IAA)
WTD........ WTD Industries, Inc. [*Associated Press*] (SAG)
wtdb........ Water-Tube Domestic Boiler (DS)
WTDF........ Wireless Telegraph Direction Finder (IAA)
WTDI........ WTD Industries [*NASDAQ symbol*] (TTSB)
WTDI........ WTD Industries, Inc. [*Portland, OR*] [*NASDAQ symbol*] (NQ)
WTDK........ Federalsburg, MD [*FM radio station call letters*] (RBYB)
WTDR........ Statesville, NC [*FM radio station call letters*]
WTDR........ Wireless Telegraphy Direction (IAA)
WTDR........ World Trade Directory Reports [*A publication Department of Commerce*]
WTDR........ World Traders Data Report (AAGC)
WTDY........ Madison, WI [*AM radio station call letters*]
WTE........ International Symposium on Wave and Tidal Energy (PDAA)
WTE........ Waste-to-Energy [*Resource recycling*]
WTE........ Wattle Tannin Equivalent [*Chemistry*]
WTE........ Westate Resources, Inc. [*Vancouver Stock Exchange symbol*]
WTE........ World Tapes for Education [*Defunct*]
WTE........ Worse than Expected [*Politics*]
WTE........ Wotje [*Marshall Islands*] [*Airport symbol*] (OAG)
W Teach........ Western Teacher [*A publication*]
WTEB........ New Bern, NC [*FM radio station call letters*]
WTEC........ Warrantech Corp. [*New York, NY NASDAQ symbol*] (NQ)
WTEK........ Waste Technology [*NASDAQ symbol*] (TTSB)
WTEK........ Waste Technology Corp. [*New York, NY NASDAQ symbol*] (NQ)
WTEL........ Philadelphia, PA [*AM radio station call letters*]
W Tel........ Warrant Telegraphist [*British military*]
WTEM........ Bethesda, MD [*AM radio station call letters*]
WTEN........ Albany, NY [*Television station call letters*]
W Ten........ Wright's Introduction to the Law of Tenures [*A publication*] (DLA)
W TER........ Washington Territory
WTES........ West Tennessee Experiment Station [*University of Tennessee at Knoxville*] [*Research center*] (RCD)
WTEV-TV........ Jacksonville, FL [*TV station call letters*] (RBYB)
WTF........ Waste Treatment Facility [*Nuclear energy*] (IEEE)
WTF........ Waste Water Treatment Facility [*Nuclear energy*] (NRCH)
WTF........ Western Task Force [*Navy*]
WTF........ When Technology Fails [*A publication*]
WTF........ Will to Fire
WTF........ Wisconsin Test Facility [*Navy*]
WTF........ World Taekwondo Federation [*Seoul, Republic of Korea*] (EAIO)
WTF........ World Timecapsule Fund (EA)
WTFAA........ Washington Task Force on African Affairs [*Defunct*] (EA)
WTFDA........ Worldwide Television-FM DX Association (EA)
Wtff........ Waterford [*Glassware*] (BARN)
WTFM........ Kingsport, TN [*FM radio station call letters*]
WTFPA........ Wolf Trap Foundation for the Performing Arts (EA)
WTFU........ Women Teachers' Franchise Union (AIE)
WTFX........ Louisville, KY [*FM radio station call letters*]
WTG........ Waiting (MSA)
WTG........ Weighting (MSA)
WTG........ Williams Telecommunications Group [*Telecommunications service*] (TSSD)
WTG........ Wind Tape Generation
WTG........ Wind Turbine Generator
WTG........ Worker Trait Group
WTGA........ Thomaston, GA [*AM radio station call letters*]
WTGA-FM........ Thomaston, GA [*FM radio station call letters*]
WTGC........ Lewisburg, PA [*AM radio station call letters*]
WTGE........ Baton Rouge, LA [*FM radio station call letters*]
WTGF........ Milton, FL [*FM radio station call letters*]
WTGH........ Cayce, SC [*AM radio station call letters*]
WTGI........ Wilmington, DE [*Television station call letters*]
WTGL........ Cocoa, FL [*Television station call letters*]
WTGM........ Salisbury, MD [*AM radio station call letters*]
WTGN........ Lima, OH [*FM radio station call letters*]
WTGP........ Greenville, PA [*FM radio station call letters*]
Wtg P........ Writing Parchment (DGA)
WTGR........ Union City, OH [*FM radio station call letters*]
WTGS........ Hardeeville, SC [*Television station call letters*]
WTGV........ Sandusky, MI [*FM radio station call letters*]
WTGY........ Charleston, MS [*FM radio station call letters*]
WTGZ-FM........ Tuskegee, AL [*FM radio station call letters*] (RBYB)
WTH........ What the Heck [*Computer hacker terminology*] [*Bowdlerized version*] (NHD)
WTH........ Width (WGA)
WTHA-FM........ Boswell, GA [*FM radio station call letters*] (RBYB)
WTHB........ Augusta, GA [*AM radio station call letters*]
WTHC........ Seelyville, IN [*FM radio station call letters*]
WTHD........ Lagrange, IN [*FM radio station call letters*]
WTHE........ Mineola, NY [*AM radio station call letters*]
WTHE........ Workshop Test and Handling Equipment [*Military*] (CAAL)
WthfdEnt........ Weatherford Enterra [*Associated Press*] (SAG)
WTHG........ Worthington Indus [*NASDAQ symbol*] (TTSB)
WTHG........ Worthington Industries, Inc. [*NASDAQ symbol*] (NQ)
WTHI........ Terre Haute, IN [*AM radio station call letters*]
WTHI-FM........ Terre Haute, IN [*FM radio station call letters*]
WTHI-TV........ Terre Haute, IN [*Television station call letters*]
WTHK........ Hudson, NY [*FM radio station call letters*] (RBYB)
WTHL........ Somerset, KY [*FM radio station call letters*]
WTHM-FM........ Glen Arbor, MI [*FM radio station call letters*] (RBYB)
WTHN-FM........ Ellenville, NY [*FM radio station call letters*] (RBYB)
WTHO........ Thomson, GA [*FM radio station call letters*]
WTHPRF........ Weatherproof (MSA)
WTHQ........ Shelbyville, KY [*FM radio station call letters*]
WTHR........ Indianapolis, IN [*Television station call letters*]
WTHR........ Weather
WTHS........ Holland, MI [*FM radio station call letters*]
WTHT........ Lewiston, ME [*FM radio station call letters*]
WTHU........ Thurmont, MD [*AM radio station call letters*]
WTHV........ Hahira, GA [*AM radio station call letters*] (RBYB)
WTI........ Weapons Training Instruction (MCD)
WTI........ Western Telematic, Inc.
WTI........ West Texas Intermediate [*Crude oil*] (ECON)
WTI........ Wheelabrator Tech [*NYSE symbol*] (TTSB)
WTI........ Wheelabrator Technology [*NYSE symbol*] (SAG)
WTI........ Work Temperament Inventory [*Test*] (TMMY)
WTI........ Work Training in Industry
WTI........ World Trade Institute
WTI........ World Translations Index [*International Translations Centre*] [*Information service or system*]
WTIA........ Welding Technology Institute of Australia
WTIC........ Hartford, CT [*AM radio station call letters*]
WTIC........ World Trade Information Center (NITA)
WTICB........ Worldwide Travel Information Contact Book [*A publication*]
WTIC-FM........ Hartford, CT [*FM radio station call letters*]
WTIC-TV........ Hartford, CT [*Television station call letters*]
WTID........ Reform, AL [*FM radio station call letters*]
WTID........ World Travel Information Directory [*A publication*]
WTIE........ Wastewater Treatment Information Exchange [*National Small Flows Clearinghouse*]
WTIE BBS........ Wastewater Treatment and Information Exchange Bulletin Board System [*Environmental Protection Agency*] (AEPA)
WTIF........ Omega, GA [*FM radio station call letters*]
WTIF........ Tifton, GA [*AM radio station call letters*]
WTIG........ Massillon, OH [*AM radio station call letters*]
WTIK........ Durham, NC [*AM radio station call letters*]
WTIL........ Mayaguez, PR [*AM radio station call letters*]
WTIM........ Taylorville, IL [*AM radio station call letters*]
WTIN........ Ponce, PR [*Television station call letters*]
WTIP-FM........ Grand Marais, MN [*FM radio station call letters*] (BROA)
WTIQ........ Manistique, MI [*AM radio station call letters*]
WTIS........ Tampa, FL [*AM radio station call letters*]
WTIU........ Bloomington, IN [*Television station call letters*]
WTIV........ Titusville, PA [*AM radio station call letters*]
WTIX........ New Orleans, LA [*AM radio station call letters*]
WTIX-FM........ Galliano, LA [*FM radio station call letters*] (RBYB)
WTJ........ Wedge Type Jack
WTJ........ Wrin, T. J., San Francisco CA [*STAC*]
WTJA........ Jamestown, NY [*Television station call letters*]
WTJB........ Columbus, GA [*FM radio station call letters*]
WTJC........ Springfield, OH [*Television station call letters*]
WTJH........ East Point, GA [*AM radio station call letters*]
WTJP........ Gadsden, AL [*Television station call letters*]
WTJR........ Quincy, IL [*Television station call letters*]
WTJS........ Jackson, TN [*AM radio station call letters*]
WTJT........ Baker, FL [*FM radio station call letters*]
WTJU........ Charlottesville, VA [*FM radio station call letters*]
WTJX........ Charlotte Amalie, VI [*Television station call letters*]
WTJY........ Johnstown, OH [*FM radio station call letters*] (RBYB)
WTJZ........ Newport News, VA [*AM radio station call letters*]
WTK........ Noatak [*Alaska*] [*Airport symbol*] (OAG)
WTK........ Noatak, AK [*Location identifier FAA*] (FAAL)
WTKA........ Ann Arbor, MI [*AM radio station call letters*]
WTKB........ Huntingdon, TN [*FM radio station call letters*]
WTKC........ Kankakee, IL [*FM radio station call letters*]
WTKF........ Atlantic, NC [*FM radio station call letters*]
WTKG-AM........ Grand Rapids, MI [*AM radio station call letters*] (BROA)
WTKI........ Huntsville, AL [*AM radio station call letters*]
WTKL........ New Orleans, LA [*FM radio station call letters*]
WTKM........ Hartford, WI [*AM radio station call letters*]
WTKM-FM........ Hartford, WI [*FM radio station call letters*]
WTKN........ Daleville, AL [*AM radio station call letters*]
WTKO........ Ithaca, NY [*AM radio station call letters*]
WTKR........ Norfolk, VA [*Television station call letters*]
WTKS........ Cocoa Beach, FL [*FM radio station call letters*]
WTKT........ Georgetown, KY [*FM radio station call letters*]
WTKU-FM........ Ocean City, NJ [*FM radio station call letters*] (RBYB)
WTKV-FM........ Oswego, NY [*FM radio station call letters*] (RBYB)
WTKW........ Bridgeport, NY [*FM radio station call letters*]
WTKX-FM........ Pensacola, FL [*FM radio station call letters*]

WTKY............	Tompkinsville, KY [AM radio station call letters]
WTKY-FM	Tompkinsville, KY [FM radio station call letters]
WTKZ............	Allentown, PA [AM radio station call letters]
WTL..............	Tuntatuliak [Alaska] [Airport symbol] (OAG)
WTL..............	Western Canadian Land [Vancouver Stock Exchange symbol]
WTL..............	Western Trunk Line Committee, Chicago IL [STAC]
WTL..............	Wilms' Tumor Locus [Genetics] [Oncology]
WTL..............	Wyle Test Laboratories
WTLA............	North Syracuse, NY [AM radio station call letters] (RBYB)
WTLB............	Utica, NY [AM radio station call letters]
WTLC............	Indianapolis, IN [AM radio station call letters]
WTLC............	Western Trunk Line Committee
WTLC-FM	Indianapolis, IN [FM radio station call letters]
WTLG............	Starke, FL [FM radio station call letters]
WTLH............	Bainbridge, GA [Television station call letters]
WTLI-AM	Statesville, NC [AM radio station call letters] (BROA)
WTLJ............	Muskegon, MI [Television station call letters]
WTLK............	Taylorsville, NC [AM radio station call letters]
WTLK............	Worldtalk Communication Corp. [NASDAQ symbol] (SAG)
WTLK............	Worldtalk Communications [NASDAQ symbol] (TTSB)
WTLK-FM	Ponte Vedra Beach, FL [FM radio station call letters] (RBYB)
WTLK-TV	Rome, GA [Television station call letters]
WTLM-AM ...	Pepperell, AL [AM radio station call letters] (RBYB)
WTLN............	Apopka, FL [AM radio station call letters]
WTLN-FM	Apopka, FL [FM radio station call letters]
WTLO............	Somerset, KY [AM radio station call letters]
WTLQ-AM ...	Pine Island Center, FL [AM radio station call letters] (RBYB)
WTLR............	State College, PA [FM radio station call letters]
WTLS............	Tallassee, AL [AM radio station call letters]
WTLS............	West Texas Library System [Library network]
WTLT-AM	Charlotte, NC [AM radio station call letters] (BROA)
WTLV............	Jacksonville, FL [Television station call letters]
WTLW...........	Lima, OH [Television station call letters]
WTLZ............	Saginaw, MI [FM radio station call letters]
WTM.............	Waitemata Aero Club, Inc. [New Zealand] [ICAO designator] (FAAC)
WTM.............	Wind Tunnel Memorandum
WTM.............	Wind Tunnel Model
WTM.............	World Travel Market [Trade show] [British] (ITD)
WTMA...........	Charleston, SC [AM radio station call letters]
WTMA...........	Wood Tank Manufacturers Association (EA)
WTMA...........	Wool Textile Manufacturers of Australia
WTMB...........	Tomah, WI [AM radio station call letters]
WTMC...........	Ocala, FL [AM radio station call letters]
WTMC...........	Wet Tropics Ministerial Council [Australia]
WTMD...........	Towson, MD [FM radio station call letters]
WTME...........	Lewiston ME [AM radio station call letters]
WTMGE........	Wireless Telegraphy Message (IAA)
WTMH...........	Watertight Manhole (WDAA)
WTMI............	Miami, FL [FM radio station call letters]
WTMJ............	Milwaukee, WI [AM radio station call letters]
WTMJ-TV	Milwaukee, WI [Television station call letters]
WTMM..........	Richmond, VA [AM radio station call letters]
WTMN..........	Portsmouth, NH [AM radio station call letters] (RBYB)
WTMP..........	Temple Terrace, FL [AM radio station call letters]
WTMQ..........	Columbus, GA [AM radio station call letters]
WTMR..........	Camden, NJ [AM radio station call letters]
WTMS..........	World Trade in Minerals Data Base System [Computer science]
WTMT..........	Louisville, KY [AM radio station call letters]
WTMU..........	Wildlife Trade Monitoring Unit (GNE)
WTMV..........	Lakeland, FL [Television station call letters]
WTMW.........	Arlington, VA [Television station call letters]
WTMX..........	Skokie, IL [FM radio station call letters]
WTMX..........	Wang Telephone Message Exchange [Wang Laboratories, Inc.] [Telecommunications service] (TSSD)
WTMY..........	Sarasota, FL [AM radio station call letters]
WTMZ..........	Dorchester Terrace-Brentwood, SC [AM radio station call letters]
WTN.............	Warton BAE [British ICAO designator] (FAAC)
WTN.............	Western Technical Net [Air Force]
WTN.............	Wind Tunnel Note
WTN.............	Witness
WTN.............	Worldwide Television News Corp. (WDMC)
WTNA..........	Wildfowl Trust of North America (GNE)
WtnBank	Western Bank [Associated Press] (SAG)
WTNC..........	Thomasville, NC [AM radio station call letters]
WTND..........	Grifton, NC [FM radio station call letters]
WTNE..........	Trenton, TN [AM radio station call letters]
WTNH..........	New Haven, CT [Television station call letters]
WTNI...........	Hartsville, SC [AM radio station call letters]
WTNJ..........	Mount Hope, WV [FM radio station call letters]
WTNL..........	Reidsville, GA [AM radio station call letters]
WTNN..........	Farragut, TN [AM radio station call letters]
WTNP..........	Works Technical New Policy (EERA)
WTNR..........	Waynesboro, TN [AM radio station call letters]
WtnRsC.......	Western Resources Capital I [Associated Press] (SAG)
WTNS	Coshocton, OH [AM radio station call letters]
WTNS	Witness
WTNS-FM	Coshocton, OH [FM radio station call letters]
WTNSTH	Witnesseth [Legal] [British] (ROG)
WTNT..........	Tallahassee, FL [FM radio station call letters]
WTNV	Jackson, TN [FM radio station call letters]
WTNW..........	Tuscaloosa, AL [AM radio station call letters]
WTNY..........	Watertown, NY [AM radio station call letters]
WTNY	Whitney Holding [NASDAQ symbol] (TTSB)
WTNY	Whitney Holding Corp. [NASDAQ symbol] (SAG)
WTNY-FM	Watertown, NY [FM radio station call letters]

WTNZ............	Knoxville, TN [Television station call letters]
WTO.............	Warsaw Treaty Organization
WTO.............	Westam Oil Ltd. [Vancouver Stock Exchange symbol]
WTO.............	WESTPAC [Western Pacific] Transportation Office (CINC)
WTO.............	Wireless Telegraphy Officer [British military] (DMA)
WTO.............	Worked Three Oceans [Amateur radio] (IAA)
WTO.............	World Tourism Organization [Madrid, Spain]
WTO.............	World Trade Organisation (EERA)
WTO.............	World Trade Organization [Trade and tariff regulation] (ECON)
WTO.............	Wotho [Marshall Islands] [Airport symbol] (OAG)
WTO.............	Write-to-Operator [Computer science] (IBMDP)
WTOB...........	Winston-Salem, NC [AM radio station call letters]
WTOC...........	Savannah, GA [Television station call letters]
WTOD...........	Toledo, OH [AM radio station call letters]
WTOE...........	Spruce Pine, NC [AM radio station call letters]
WTOEW........	Welcome to Our Elvis World (EA)
WTOF...........	Canton, OH [FM radio station call letters]
WTOG...........	St. Petersburg, FL [Television station call letters]
WTOH...........	Mobile, AL [FM radio station call letters]
WTOH...........	Western Ohio Railroad Co. [AAR code]
WTOJ...........	Carthage, NY [FM radio station call letters]
WTOK...........	Meridian, MS [Television station call letters]
WTOL...........	Toledo, OH [Television station call letters]
WTOM...........	Cheboygan, MI [Television station call letters]
WTON...........	Staunton, VA [AM radio station call letters]
WTON-FM....	Staunton, VA [FM radio station call letters]
WTOP	Washington, DC [AM radio station call letters]
WTOR...........	Write-to-Operator with Reply [Computer science] (IBMDP)
WTOR-AM....	Youngstown, NY [AM radio station call letters] (RBYB)
WTOS...........	Skowhegan, ME [FM radio station call letters]
WTOS...........	Western Test Range Office of Safety [Air Force] (MCD)
WTOT...........	Marianna, FL [AM radio station call letters]
WTOU...........	Akron, OH [AM radio station call letters]
WTOV...........	Steubenville, OH [Television station call letters]
WToVA........	United States Veterans Administration Hospital, Tomah, WI [Library symbol Library of Congress] (LCLS)
WTOW...........	Washington, NC [AM radio station call letters]
WTOX...........	Lincoln, ME [AM radio station call letters]
WTOY...........	Salem, VA [AM radio station call letters]
WTP.............	Warrant to Pollute
WTP.............	Waste Water Treatment Plant [Also, WWTP]
WTP.............	Water Treatment Plant [Nuclear energy] (NRCH)
WTP.............	Weapons Testing Program (AAG)
WTP.............	Wiggins Teape Paper [Commercial firm British]
WTP.............	Willingness-to-Pay [Market research]
WTP.............	Woitape [Papua New Guinea] [Airport symbol] (OAG)
WTP.............	World Tape Pals (EA)
WTPA...........	Mechanicsburg, PA [FM radio station call letters]
WTPA...........	Wheelchair Tennis Players Association (EA)
WTPBC	Wool Textiles Production Board of Control [World War I] [British]
WTPC...........	Elsah, IL [FM radio station call letters]
WTPFT	Weight per Foot (IAA)
WTPI...........	Indianapolis, IN [FM radio station call letters]
WTPM..........	Aguadilla, PR [FM radio station call letters]
WTPR...........	Paris, TN [AM radio station call letters]
WTPR-FM	McKinnon, TN [FM radio station call letters] (RBYB)
WTPS...........	Quincy, FL [FM radio station call letters] (RBYB)
WTPS...........	Water, Toxics, and Pesticides Staff [Environmental Protection Agency] (GFGA)
WTPT-FM	Forest City, NC [FM radio station call letters] (BROA)
WTPX-FM	Jupiter, FL [FM radio station call letters] (RBYB)
WTQR	Winston-Salem, NC [FM radio station call letters]
WTQX	Selma, AL [AM radio station call letters]
WTR.............	Aquarion Co. [NYSE symbol] (SPSG)
WTR.............	Waiter
WTR.............	Warstar Resources, Inc. [Vancouver Stock Exchange symbol]
WTR.............	War Tax Resistance [An association Defunct] (EA)
WTR.............	Water
wtr..............	Water (VRA)
WTR.............	Waterford and Tranmore Railway [British] (ROG)
WTR.............	Waters Associates, Milford, MA [OCLC symbol] (OCLC)
WTR.............	Water Turnover Rate [Physiology]
WTR.............	Waterville [Colby College] [Maine] [Seismograph station code, US Geological Survey] (SEIS)
WTR.............	Weekly Transcript Reports [New York] [A publication] (DLA)
WTR.............	Well to Right [Aviation] (FAAC)
WTR.............	Western Test Range [Formerly, Pacific Missile Range] [Air Force]
WTR.............	Westinghouse Test Reactor
WTR.............	Winter
WTR.............	Work Transfer Record (KSC)
WTR.............	Work Transfer Request
WTR.............	Wrightsville & Tennille R. R. [AAR code]
WTR.............	Writer
WTRA...........	Mayaguez, PR [Television station call letters]
WTRB...........	Ripley, TN [AM radio station call letters]
WTRB-FM	Ripley, TN [FM radio station call letters]
WTRC...........	Elkhart, IN [AM radio station call letters]
WTRC...........	Natchez, MS [FM radio station call letters]
WTRC...........	Weapon Test Reports Committee [AEC-DoD]
WTRC...........	Women's Training and Resources Corp.
WTRE...........	Greensburg, IN [AM radio station call letters]
WTRF...........	Wheeling, WV [Television station call letters]
WTRG	Rocky Mount, NC [FM radio station call letters]
WTRG	World Trade Resources Guide [A publication]
WTRI...........	Brunswick, MD [AM radio station call letters]

WTRI-FM ..... Mount Carmel, IL [*FM radio station call letters*] (RBYB)
WTRJ .... Troy, OH [*FM radio station call letters*]
WTRK .... Bay City, MI [*FM radio station call letters*]
WTRM .... Western Test Range Manual [*Air Force*] (MCD)
WTRM .... Winchester, VA [*FM radio station call letters*]
WTRN .... Tyrone, PA [*AM radio station call letters*]
WTRO .... Dyersburg, TN [*AM radio station call letters*]
WTRP .... La Grange, GA [*AM radio station call letters*]
WTRPF .... War Tax Resister's Penalty Fund (EA)
WTRPP .... Water Pump Propeller [*on a ship*] (DS)
WTRPRF ...... Waterproof (MSA)
WTRPRFG.... Waterproofing
WTRR .... Sanford, FL [*AM radio station call letters*]
WTRS .... Dunellon, FL [*FM radio station call letters*]
WTRS .... Waters Instruments [*NASDAQ symbol*] (TTSB)
WTRS .... Waters Instruments, Inc. [*NASDAQ symbol*] (NQ)
WTRSYS ...... Water System (MCD)
WTRTT......... Watertight (MSA)
WTRV-FM .... LaCrosse, WI [*FM radio station call letters*] (RBYB)
WTRW .... Two Rivers, WI [*AM radio station call letters*]
WTRX .... Flint, MI [*AM radio station call letters*]
WTRY .... Troy, NY [*AM radio station call letters*]
WTRZ........... McMinnville, TN [*FM radio station call letters*]
WTRZ........... Winterize (AAG)
WTRZN .... Winterization (AAG)
WTS............. Tsiroanomandidy [*Madagascar*] [*Airport symbol*] (OAG)
WTS............. War Training Service [*of the Civil Aeronautics Administration*] [*Formerly Civilian Pilot Training*] [*World War II*]
WTS............. Watermen's Trade Society [*A union*] [*British*]
WTS............. Watts Industries [*NYSE symbol*] (SAG)
WTS............. Watts Industries'A' [*NYSE symbol*] (TTSB)
WTS............. Weapons Training Site [*Military*]
WTS............. Western Tariff Service Inc., Oakland CA [*STAC*]
WTS............. Westminister Theological Seminary, Philadelphia, PA [*OCLC symbol*] (OCLC)
WTS............. Whale Tumor Story [*Urban folklore term coined by Rodney Dale*]
WTS............. Windows-Based Terminal Server [*Microsoft Corp.*]
WTS............. Wind Tunnel Study
WTS............. Wing Tank Structure
WTS............. Winterswijk [*Netherlands*] [*Seismograph station code, US Geological Survey*] (SEIS)
WTS............. Wireless Telegraphy Station [*Telecommunications*] (IAA)
WTS............. Women's Transportation Seminar [*Later, WTSN*] (EA)
WTS............. Women's Transport Service [*British*]
WTS............. Word Terminal Synchronous
WT's............ Working Tools [*Freemasonry*]
WTS............. World Terminal Synchronous (IAA)
WTSA........... Brattleboro, VT [*AM radio station call letters*]
WTSA........... Wood Turners and Shapers Association [*Later, WPMA*] (EA)
WTSAC .... Wet Tropics Scientific Advisory Committee [*Australia*]
WTSA-FM .... Brattleboro, VT [*FM radio station call letters*]
WTSAP .... Wet Tropics Structural Adjustment Package (EERA)
WTSB........... Lumberton, NC [*AM radio station call letters*]
WTSB........... Wood Turners Service Bureau [*Later, WPMA*]
WTSC........... Potsdam, NY [*FM radio station call letters*]
WTSC........... West TeleServices Corp. [*NASDAQ symbol*] (SAG)
WTSC........... West Texas State College [*Later, WTSU*]
WTSC........... Wet Tantalum Slug Capacitor (NASA)
WTSDET ...... Wing Transportation Squadron Detachment [*Navy*] (DNAB)
WTSF........... Ashland, KY [*Television station call letters*]
WTSFLW...... Women's Trade Society of Fancy Leather Workers [*A union*] [*British*]
WTSG-FM..... Carlinville, IL [*FM radio station call letters*] (RBYB)
WTSH .... Rockmart, GA [*FM radio station call letters*]
WTSH .... Rome, GA [*AM radio station call letters*]
WTSHRD...... Water and Toxic Substances Health Research Division [*Environmental Protection Agency*] (GFGA)
WTSJ............ Cincinnati, OH [*AM radio station call letters*]
WTSK........... Tuscaloosa, AL [*AM radio station call letters*]
WTSL........... Hanover, NH [*AM radio station call letters*]
WTSL........... Wet Seal, Inc. [*NASDAQ symbol*] (SAG)
WTSLA......... Wet Seal Cl'A' [*NASDAQ symbol*] (TTSB)
WTSM.......... Western Transmedia [*NASDAQ symbol*] (TTSB)
WTSM.......... Western Transmedia, Inc. [*NASDAQ symbol*] (SAG)
WTSMW .... Western Transmedia Wrrt [*NASDAQ symbol*] (TTSB)
WTSN .... Dover, NH [*AM radio station call letters*]
WTSN .... Women's Transportation Seminar-National (EA)
WTSNG........ Witnessing [*Legal*] [*British*] (ROG)
WTSO .... Madison, WI [*AM radio station call letters*]
WTSP........... St. Petersburg, FL [*Television station call letters*]
WTSPT......... Waterspout
WTSR .... Trenton, NJ [*FM radio station call letters*]
WTSS........... Scranton, PA [*AM radio station call letters*] (RBYB)
WTSU........... Troy, AL [*FM radio station call letters*]
WTSU .... West Texas State University [*Formerly, WTSC*]
WTSV........... Claremont, NH [*AM radio station call letters*]
WTSX........... Port Jervis, NY [*FM radio station call letters*]
WTT............. Warfare [*Commanders*] Team Training (DOMA)
WTT............. Weapon Tactics Trainer (MCD)
WTT............. Western Tank Truck Carriers' Conference Inc., Denver CO [*STAC*]
WTT............. Westmount Resources Ltd. [*Toronto Stock Exchange symbol*]
WTT............. Wind Tunnel Test
WTT............. Wireless Telecom [*AMEX symbol*] (TTSB)
WTT............. Wireless Telecom Group [*Formerly, Noise Com, Inc.*] [*AMEX symbol*] (SAG)
WTT............. Working Timetable (DCTA)
WTT............. World Team Tennis [*League*]
WTTA........... St. Petersburg, FL [*Television station call letters*]
WTTA........... Wholesale Tobacco Trade Association of Great Britain and Northern Ireland (BI)
WTTB........... Vero Beach, FL [*AM radio station call letters*]
WTTC........... Towanda, PA [*AM radio station call letters*]
WTTC........... Western Technical Training Command [*AAFWTTC*]
WTTC-FM .... Towanda, PA [*FM radio station call letters*]
WTTE........... Columbus, OH [*Television station call letters*]
WTTELE....... World Trade Telegraph (IAA)
WTTF........... Tiffin, OH [*AM radio station call letters*]
WTTF-FM..... Tiffin, OH [*FM radio station call letters*]
WTTG........... Washington, DC [*Television station call letters*]
WTTH........... Margate City, NJ [*FM radio station call letters*]
WTTI............ Dalton, GA [*AM radio station call letters*]
WTTK........... Kokomo, IN [*Television station call letters*]
WTTL........... Madisonville, KY [*AM radio station call letters*]
WTTM.......... Trenton, NJ [*AM radio station call letters*]
WTTN........... Watertown, WI [*AM radio station call letters*]
WTTO........... Birmingham, AL [*Television station call letters*]
WTTR........... Westminster, MD [*AM radio station call letters*]
WTTS........... Bloomington, IN [*FM radio station call letters*]
WTTS........... Weak-Lined T Tauri Stars [*Astronomy*]
WTTT........... Amherst, MA [*AM radio station call letters*]
WTTU........... Cookeville, TN [*FM radio station call letters*]
WTTV........... Bloomington, IN [*Television station call letters*]
WTTW.......... Chicago, IL [*Letters stand for "Windows to the World"*] [*Television station call letters*]
WTTX-FM .... Appomattox, VA [*FM radio station call letters*]
WTTY........... World Trade Teletypewriter (CIST)
WTU............. Washington University, St. Louis, MO [*OCLC symbol*] (OCLC)
WTU............. Weekly TIF [*Taxpayer Information File*] Update [*IRS*]
WTU............. Whitetails Unlimited (EA)
WTU............. Williams Coal Seam Gas Realty [*NYSE symbol*] (SPSG)
WTU............. Williams Coal Seam Gas Rlty [*NYSE symbol*] (TTSB)
WTUA .... St. Stephen, SC [*FM radio station call letters*]
WTUC .... Tuckerton, NJ [*FM radio station call letters*]
WTUE........... Dayton, OH [*FM radio station call letters*]
WTUF........... Boston, GA [*FM radio station call letters*]
WTUG........... Tuscaloosa, AL [*FM radio station call letters*]
WTUK .... Harlan, KY [*FM radio station call letters*]
WTUL........... New Orleans, LA [*FM radio station call letters*]
WTUP .... Tupelo, MS [*AM radio station call letters*]
WTUR .... Upland, IN [*FM radio station call letters*] (RBYB)
WTURB .... Water Turbine (MSA)
WTURN........ White Turnout [*Political science*]
WTUS .... Mannington, WV [*FM radio station call letters*]
WTUX .... Meridian, MS [*FM radio station call letters*]
WTUZ........... Uhrichsville, OH [*FM radio station call letters*]
WTV............. Fowler [*Rick*] [*ICAO designator*] (FAAC)
WTV............. Water Tank Vessel [*Navy*]
WTV............. Wound Tumor Virus [*Plant pathology*]
WTVA........... Tupelo, MS [*Television station call letters*]
WTVA........... Wider Television Access [*British*]
WTVB........... Coldwater, MI [*AM radio station call letters*]
WTVC........... Chattanooga, TN [*Television station call letters*]
WTVD .... Durham, NC [*Television station call letters*]
WTVE........... Reading, PA [*Television station call letters*]
WTVF........... Nashville, TN [*Television station call letters*]
WTVG........... Toledo, OH [*Television station call letters*]
WTVH........... Syracuse, NY [*Television station call letters*]
WTVI............ Charlotte, NC [*Television station call letters*]
WTVJ............ Miami, FL [*Television station call letters*]
WTVK........... Naples, FL [*Television station call letters*] (RBYB)
WTVL........... Waterville, ME [*AM radio station call letters*]
WTVM.......... Columbus, GA [*Television station call letters*]
WTVN........... Columbus, OH [*AM radio station call letters*]
WTVO .... Rockford, IL [*Television station call letters*]
wt/vol.......... Weight per Volume [*Ratio*] [*Chemistry*] (DAVI)
WTVP........... Peoria, IL [*Television station call letters*]
WTVQ .... Lexington, KY [*Television station call letters*]
WTVR .... Richmond, VA [*AM radio station call letters*]
WTVR-FM..... Richmond, VA [*FM radio station call letters*]
WTVR-TV..... Richmond, VA [*Television station call letters*]
WTVS........... Detroit, MI [*Television station call letters*]
WTVT........... Tampa, FL [*Television station call letters*]
WTVU .... New Haven, CT [*Television station call letters*]
WTVW .... Evansville, IN [*Television station call letters*]
WTVX........... Fort Pierce, FL [*Television station call letters*]
WTVY........... Dothan, AL [*FM radio station call letters*]
WTVY-TV ..... Dothan, AL [*Television station call letters*]
WTVZ........... Norfolk, VA [*Television station call letters*]
WTw .... Joseph Mann Library, Two Rivers, WI [*Library symbol Library of Congress*] (LCLS)
WTW............ Wafer to Wafer (AAEL)
WTW............ Wall to Wall [*Technical drawings*]
WTW............ Washington Telecom Week [*A publication*]
WTW............ West Thumb [*Wyoming*] [*Seismograph station code, US Geological Survey*] (SEIS)
WTWA .... Thomson, GA [*AM radio station call letters*]
WTWA .... World Trade Writers Association [*New York, NY*] (EA)
WTWB .... Auburndale, FL [*AM radio station call letters*]
WTWB .... Johnstown, PA [*Television station call letters*]
WTWBIR....... Waste Isolation Pilot Plant Transuranic Waste Baseline Inventory Report [*Department of Energy*] (GAAI)

WTWC	Tallahassee, FL [*Television station call letters*]
WTWL.........	McKinnon, TN [*FM radio station call letters*]
WTWNU.......	Wafer to Wafer Nonuniformity (AAEL)
WTWO	Terre Haute, IN [*Television station call letters*]
WTWR	Monroe, MI [*FM radio station call letters*]
WTWS	New London, CT [*Television station call letters*]
wt/wt...........	Weight per Weight [*Ratio*] [*Chemistry*] (DAVI)
WTWX	Guntersville, AL [*FM radio station call letters*]
WTWZ	Clinton, MS [*AM radio station call letters*]
WTX	Worldtex, Inc. [*NYSE symbol*] (SPSG)
WTXF	Philadelphia, PA [*Television station call letters*]
WTXL	Tallahassee, FL [*Television station call letters*]
WTXR-FM	Toccoa Falls, GA [*FM radio station call letters*] (BROA)
WTXT	Fayette, AL [*FM radio station call letters*]
WTXX	Waterbury, CT [*Television station call letters*]
WTXY	Whiteville, NC [*AM radio station call letters*]
WTY	Westley Mines Ltd. [*Toronto Stock Exchange symbol Vancouver Stock Exchange symbol*]
WTYD	New London, CT [*FM radio station call letters*]
WTYE	Robinson, IL [*FM radio station call letters*] (RBYB)
WTYF	World Theosophical Youth Federation [*Porto Alegre, Brazil*] (EAIO)
WTYJ	Fayette, MS [*FM radio station call letters*]
WTYL	Tylertown, MS [*AM radio station call letters*]
WTYL-FM	Tylertown, MS [*FM radio station call letters*]
WTYM	Kittanning, PA [*AM radio station call letters*]
WTYR	Soddy-Daisy, TN [*AM radio station call letters*]
W Ty R	Washington Territory Reports [*1854-88*] [*A publication*] (DLA)
WTYS..........	Marianna, FL [*AM radio station call letters*]
WTYX	Jackson, MS [*FM radio station call letters*]
WTZ	Western Trinity Resource [*Vancouver Stock Exchange symbol*]
WTZ	Whakatane [*New Zealand*] [*Seismograph station code, US Geological Survey*] (SEIS)
WTZE	Tazewell, VA [*AM radio station call letters*]
WTZE-FM	Tazewell, VA [*FM radio station call letters*]
WTZQ	Hendersonville, NC [*AM radio station call letters*]
WTZR	Nanticoke, PA [*FM radio station call letters*]
WTZRA	Weitzer Homebuilders'A' [*NASDAQ symbol*] (TTSB)
WTZRA	Weitzer Homebuilders, Inc. [*NASDAQ symbol*] (SAG)
WTZX	Sparta, TN [*AM radio station call letters*]
WTZY-AM	Fairview, NC [*AM radio station call letters*] (BROA)
WU	Netherlines [*ICAO designator*] (AD)
WU	Rhine Air [*ICAO designator*] (AD)
WU	University of Wisconsin, Madison, WI [*Library symbol Library of Congress*] (LCLS)
WU	Washington University (PDAA)
WU	Wash Up [*Printing*] (DGA)
WU	Weapons and Utilities Maintenance [*Military*] (GFGA)
WU	Weather Underground (EA)
WU	Weight Unit [*Automobiles*]
WU	Wesleyan University
WU	Western European Union [*Also, WEU*] (NATG)
WU	Western Union (NITA)
WU	Western Union Telegraph Co. (TSSD)
WU	Whitetails Unlimited (EA)
WU	Window Unit (MSA)
WU	Word Understanding [*Test*] [*Hoepfner, Hendricks, and Silverman*] (TES)
WU	Workshop Unit (MSA)
WU	Work Unit [*Air Force*] (AFM)
w/u	Work-Up
WU	World Union [*Pondicherry, India*] (EA)
WU-A	University of Wisconsin, Agricultural Library, Madison, WI [*Library symbol Library of Congress*] (LCLS)
WUA	Weapon Utility Analysis
WUA	Western Underwriters Association [*Later, ISO*]
WUA	Work Unit Assignment [*Navy*] (NG)
WUAA	Wartime Unit Aircraft Activity (AFM)
WUAB	Lorain, OH [*Television station call letters*]
WUAG	Greensboro, NC [*FM radio station call letters*]
WUAL	Tuscaloosa, AL [*FM radio station call letters*]
WUAR	Women United Against Rape
WUAT	Pikeville, TN [*AM radio station call letters*]
WUAW	Erwin, NC [*FM radio station call letters*]
WUB	Woodfree Uncoated Boars [*Paper*] (DGA)
WUBE	Cincinnati, OH [*AM radio station call letters*]
WUBE-FM	Cincinnati, OH [*FM radio station call letters*]
WUBI	Baxley, GA [*Television station call letters*]
WUBJ	Jamestown, NY [*FM radio station call letters*]
WUBR-AM	Whitehall, MI [*AM radio station call letters*] (BROA)
WUBS	South Bend, IN [*FM radio station call letters*]
WUBU	South Bend, IN [*FM radio station call letters*]
WUBW	World Union of Black Writers [*See also UEMN*] (EAIO)
WUBZ-FM	Philipsburg, PA [*FM radio station call letters*] (RBYB)
WUC	Western Union Corp.
WUC	Work Unit Code
WUC	Writers Union of Canada
WUC	Wu-han [*Republic of China*] [*Seismograph station code, US Geological Survey*] (SEIS)
WU/CCM	Washington University Center for Computational Mechanics [*St. Louis, MO*]
WU/CCR.......	Washington University Center for Composites Research [*St. Louis, MO*]
WUCDU........	World Union of Christian Democratic Women [*Venezuela Political party*] (EAIO)
WUCF	Orlando, FL [*FM radio station call letters*]

WUCF	Work Unit Code File (NASA)
WUCM	University Center, MI [*Television station call letters*]
WUCM	Work Unit Code Manual
WUCO	Marysville, OH [*AM radio station call letters*]
WUCOS	Western European Union Chiefs of Staff (NATG)
WUCPS	World Union of Catholic Philosophical Societies (EA)
WUCT	World Union of Catholic Teachers
WUCU	Western Union Computer Utilities (IAA)
WUCWO	World Union of Catholic Women's Organizations [*Rosemere, PQ*] (EAIO)
WUCX	Bay City, MI [*FM radio station call letters*]
WUCX-TV	Bad Axe, MI [*Television station call letters*]
WUCZ	Carthage, TN [*FM radio station call letters*]
WUD	Would [*Amateur radio shorthand*] (WDAA)
WUDB	Work Unit Data Bank
WU-DE	University of Wisconsin, Center for Demography and Ecology, Madison, WI [*Library symbol Library of Congress*] (LCLS)
WUDO	Western European Union Defense Organization (NATG)
WU-E	University of Wisconsin, Engineering Library, Madison, WI [*Library symbol Library of Congress*] (LCLS)
WUE	Water-Use Efficiency [*Agriculture*]
WUE	Work Unit Engineer
WUEC	Eau Claire, WI [*FM radio station call letters*]
WUEMI	Western Union Electronic Mail, Inc. [*McLean, VA*] [*Telecommunications*] (TSSD)
WUEV	Evansville, IN [*FM radio station call letters*]
WUEZ	Christopher, IL [*FM radio station call letters*]
WUF	Wattle-Urea-Formaldehyde [*Adhesive component*]
WUF	Western United Front [*Fiji*] [*Political party*] (PPW)
WUF	Where Used File [*Computer science*] (IAA)
WUF	World Underwater Federation (ASF)
WUF	World Union of Free Thinkers
WUF	World University, Miami Learning Resource Center, Miami, FL [*OCLC symbol*] (OCLC)
WUFE	Baxley, GA [*AM radio station call letters*]
WUFEC	Western European Union Finance and Economic Committee (NATG)
WUFF	Eastman, GA [*AM radio station call letters*]
WUFF-FM	Eastman, GA [*FM radio station call letters*]
WUFI	World United Formosans for Independence [*Political party*] (EY)
WUFK	Fort Kent, ME [*FM radio station call letters*]
WUFL..........	Sterling Heights, MI [*AM radio station call letters*]
WUFM-FM	Columbus, OH [*FM radio station call letters*] (RBYB)
WUFN	Albion, MI [*FM radio station call letters*]
WUFO	Amherst, NY [*AM radio station call letters*]
WUFR	World Union of Free Romanians [*See also UMRL*] [*Creteil, France*] (EAIO)
WUFS	World Union of French-Speakers [*See also UMVF*] (EAIO)
WUFT..........	Gainesville, FL [*FM radio station call letters*]
WUFT-TV	Gainesville, FL [*Television station call letters*]
WUFTU	World Union of Free Trade Unions
WUFX-FM	Harriman, TN [*FM radio station call letters*] (BROA)
WUg............	Graham Public Library, Union Grove, WI [*Library symbol Library of Congress*] (LCLS)
WUG	Wau [*Papua New Guinea*] [*Airport symbol*] (OAG)
WUGA	Athens, GA [*FM radio station call letters*]
WUGN	Midland, MI [*FM radio station call letters*]
WUGNET	Windows Users Group Network
WUGO	Grayson, KY [*FM radio station call letters*]
WUgSC	Southern Wisconsin Colony and Training School, Medical Library, Union Grove, WI [*Library symbol Library of Congress*] (LCLS)
WUH	Wu-han [*Republic of China*] [*Seismograph station code, US Geological Survey*] (SEIS)
WUH	Wuhan [*China*] [*Airport symbol*] (OAG)
WUHF	Rochester, NY [*Television station call letters*]
WUHN	Pittsfield, MA [*AM radio station call letters*]
WUI	Western Union International [*Division of WUI, Inc.*]
WUI	Workers' Union of Ireland (BI)
WUIS	Springfield, IL [*FM radio station call letters*] (RBYB)
WUIS	Water Use Information System [*Westinghouse Hanford Co.*] (IID)
WUIS	Work Unit Information System [*Database*] (DTIC)
WUIV	Icard Township, NC [*AM radio station call letters*]
WUJA	Caguas, PR [*Television station call letters*]
WUJC	University Heights, OH [*FM radio station call letters*]
WUJM	Charleston, SC [*AM radio station call letters*]
WUJS	World Union of Jewish Students [*Jerusalem, Israel*]
WUKO	World Union of Karatedo Organizations [*Solna, Sweden*] (EAIO)
WUKQ-FM	Mayaguez, Puerto Rico [*FM radio station call letters*] (BROA)
WUKS-FM	St. Pauls, NC [*FM radio station call letters*] (BROA)
WUKY	Lexington, KY [*FM radio station call letters*]
WU-L	University of Wisconsin, Law Library, Madison, WI [*Library symbol Library of Congress*] (LCLS)
WUL	Washington University, Law Library, St. Louis, MO [*OCLC symbol*] (OCLC)
WUL	Workers Unity League [*Canada*]
WULA	Eufaula, AL [*AM radio station call letters*]
WULA-FM	Eufaula, AL [*FM radio station call letters*]
WULC	West Virginia Union Catalog Interlibrary Loan Network [*Library network*]
WULDS........	Western Union Long Distance Service [*Western Union Telegraph Co.*] [*Upper Saddle River, NJ*] [*Telecommunications*] (TSSD)
WULF	Hardinsburg, KY [*FM radio station call letters*] (RBYB)
WULS	Broxton, GA [*FM radio station call letters*]
WU-LT	University of Wisconsin, Land Tenure Center, Madison, WI [*Library symbol Library of Congress*] (LCLS)

WULTUO......	World Union of Liberal Trade Union Organisations [*See also WFALW*] [*Zurich, Switzerland*] (EAIO)
WU-M.........	University of Wisconsin, School of Medicine, Madison, WI [*Library symbol Library of Congress*] (LCLS)
WUM..........	Washington University, School of Medicine, St. Louis, MO [*OCLC symbol*] (OCLC)
WUM..........	Women's Universal Movement [*Defunct*] (EA)
WUM..........	Work Unit Manager
WUM..........	World Union of Mapam [*See also UMM*] (EAIO)
WUMB........	Boston, MA [*FM radio station call letters*]
WUMC-FM...	Elizabethton, TN [*FM radio station call letters*] (BROA)
WUME.........	Paoli, IN [*FM radio station call letters*]
WUMF........	Farmington, ME [*FM radio station call letters*]
WUMP........	Madison, AL [*AM radio station call letters*] (RBYB)
WUMP........	White, Urban, Middle Class, Protestant
WUMPS.......	Women Umpires [*World War II*]
WUMR.........	Memphis, TN [*FM radio station call letters*]
WUMS.........	University, MS [*FM radio station call letters*]
WUMS.........	Woman's Union Missionary Society of America [*Later, UFCS*] (EA)
WUMTPT.....	World Union of Martyred Towns, Peace Towns (EAIO)
WUMX-FM...	Charlottesville, VA [*FM radio station call letters*] (BROA)
WUN..........	Wiluna [*Australia Airport symbol*] (OAG)
WUN..........	World Union of Nigerians
WUNA.........	Ocoee, FL [*AM radio station call letters*]
WUNC........	Chapel Hill, NC [*FM radio station call letters*]
WUNC-TV ...	Chapel Hill, NC [*Television station call letters*]
WUND.........	Columbia, NC [*Television station call letters*]
WUNE.........	Linville, NC [*Television station call letters*]
WUNF.........	Asheville, NC [*Television station call letters*]
WUNG.........	Concord, NC [*Television station call letters*]
WUNH.........	Durham, NH [*FM radio station call letters*]
WUNI.........	Needham, MA [*Television station call letters*]
WUNJ.........	Wilmington, NC [*Television station call letters*]
WUNK.........	Greenville, NC [*Television station call letters*]
Wunk.........	WASP Funk [*1960's pop music*]
WUNL.........	Winston-Salem, NC [*Television station call letters*]
WUNM.........	Jacksonville, NC [*Television station call letters*]
WUNN.........	Mason, MI [*AM radio station call letters*]
WUNO.........	San Juan, PR [*AM radio station call letters*]
WUNP.........	Roanoke Rapids, NC [*Television station call letters*]
WUNR.........	Brookline, MA [*AM radio station call letters*]
WUNS.........	World Union of National Socialists (EA)
WUNT.........	Wissenschaftliche Untersuchungen zum Neuen Testament [*Tuebingen*] [*A publication*] (BJA)
WUNU.........	Lumberton, NC [*Television station call letters*] (RBYB)
WUNV.........	Albany, GA [*FM radio station call letters*]
WUNW.........	Key West, FL [*FM radio station call letters*]
WUNX.........	Harwichport, MA [*FM radio station call letters*] (RBYB)
WUNY.........	Utica, NY [*FM radio station call letters*]
WUNZ.........	Falmouth, MA [*FM radio station call letters*] (RBYB)
WUOC.........	Warm-Up Oxidation Catalyst [*Automotive engineering*]
WU/OEL.......	Washington University Optoelectronics Laboratory [*St. Louis, MO*]
WUOG.........	Athens, GA [*FM radio station call letters*]
WUOK.........	West Yarmouth, MA [*AM radio station call letters*]
WUOL.........	Louisville, KY [*FM radio station call letters*]
WUOM.........	Ann Arbor, MI [*FM radio station call letters*]
WUOSY.......	World Union of Organizations for the Safeguard of Youth [*Later, UMOSEA*]
WUOT.........	Knoxville, TN [*FM radio station call letters*]
WUOY.........	Wilmington, NC [*FM radio station call letters*]
WUP...........	Work Unit Plan [*Navy*] (NG)
WUPA.........	Wupatki National Monument
WUPA-TV.....	Atlanta, GA [*TV station call letters*] (RBYB)
WUPE.........	Pittsfield, MA [*FM radio station call letters*]
WUPI.........	Presque Isle, ME [*FM radio station call letters*]
WUPJ.........	World Union for Progressive Judaism (EA)
WUPK.........	Marquette, MI [*FM radio station call letters*]
WUPL.........	Slidell, LA [*Television station call letters*] (RBYB)
WUPL-INT....	World Union for the Protection of Life [*See also WSL-INT*] (EAIO)
WUPM.........	Ironwood, MI [*FM radio station call letters*]
WUPN.........	Mexico, NY [*FM radio station call letters*] (RBYB)
WUPN-TV ...	Greensboro, NC [*TV station call letters*] (RBYB)
WUPO.........	World Union of Pythagorean Organizations [*Ivybridge, Devonshire, England*] (EAIO)
WUPPE.......	Wisconsin Ultraviolet Photo-Polarimeter Experiment
WUPP-FM....	Warrenton, VA [*FM radio station call letters*] (BROA)
WUPR.........	Utuado, PR [*AM radio station call letters*]
WUPS.........	Houghton Lake, MI [*FM radio station call letters*]
WUPS.........	Westinghouse Uninterruptible Power System (IAA)
WUPS.........	World Union of Process Servers
WUPV.........	Ashland, VA [*Television station call letters*] (BROA)
WUPW.........	Toledo, OH [*Television station call letters*]
WUPX.........	Marquette, MI [*FM radio station call letters*]
WUPY.........	Ontonagon, MI [*FM radio station call letters*]
WUR...........	World University Roundtable
WURB.........	Western Utilization Research Branch (MCD)
WURB.........	Windsor, NC [*FM radio station call letters*]
WURC.........	Holly Springs, MS [*FM radio station call letters*]
WURD.........	Philadelphia, PA [*AM radio station call letters*]
WURL.........	Moody, AL [*AM radio station call letters*]
WURN.........	Marietta, OH [*FM radio station call letters*] (RBYB)
WUS	Woerterbuch der Ugaritischen Sprache [*A publication*] (BJA)
WUS	Word Underscore Character [*Computer science*]
WUS	World University Service [*See also EUM*] [*Geneva, Switzerland*] (EAIO)
WUSA.........	Tampa, FL [*FM radio station call letters*]
WUSA.........	Washington, DC [*Television station call letters*]
WUSA.........	Waterfowl USA (EA)
WUSB.........	Stony Brook, NY [*FM radio station call letters*]
WUSC.........	Columbia, SC [*FM radio station call letters*]
WUSC.........	Weather of US Cities [*A publication*]
WUSC.........	World University Service of Canada [*See also EUMC*]
WUSCI........	Western Union Space Communications, Inc. (MCD)
WUSF.........	Tampa, FL [*FM radio station call letters*]
WUSF-TV	Tampa, FL [*Television station call letters*]
WUSG.........	World Union Saint Gabriel [*Esher, Surrey, England*] (EAIO)
WUSI.........	Olney, IL [*FM radio station call letters*]
WUSI-TV.....	Olney, IL [*Television station call letters*]
WUSK.........	Tomah, WI [*FM radio station call letters*]
WUSL.........	Philadelphia, PA [*FM radio station call letters*]
WUSL.........	Washburn University School of Law (DLA)
WUSL.........	Women's United Service League [*British*]
WUSM.........	Hattiesburg, MS [*FM radio station call letters*]
WUSN.........	Chicago, IL [*FM radio station call letters*]
WUSO.........	Springfield, OH [*FM radio station call letters*]
WUSP.........	World Union of Stockholm Pioneers (EAIO)
WUSQ.........	Winchester, VA [*FM radio station call letters*]
WUSR.........	Scranton, PA [*FM radio station call letters*]
WU/SRL......	Washington University Semiconductor Research Laboratory [*St. Louis, MO*]
WUSS.........	Atlantic City, NJ [*AM radio station call letters*]
WUST.........	Washington, DC [*AM radio station call letters*]
WUS(UK).....	World University Service (United Kingdom) (DI)
WUS-US	World University Service/USA (EA)
WUSW.........	Oshkosh, WI [*FM radio station call letters*]
WUSX.........	Portage, WI [*FM radio station call letters*]
WUSY.........	Cleveland, TN [*FM radio station call letters*]
WUSY.........	World Union for the Safeguard of Youth
WUSZ.........	Virginia, MN [*FM radio station call letters*]
WUT...........	Warm Up Time
WUT...........	Washburn University of Topeka [*Kansas*]
WUT...........	Woman Using Television (WDMC)
WUT...........	Women Using Television (WDMC)
WUTA.........	Washington University Technology Associates
WUTB.........	Baltimore, MD [*Television station call letters*] (BROA)
WUTC.........	Chattanooga, TN [*FM radio station call letters*]
WUTC.........	Western Union Telegraph Co.
WUTELCO....	Western Union Telegraph Co.
WUTHH.......	World Union of Tnuat Haherut Hatzorar [*Tel Aviv, Israel*] (EAIO)
WUTK.........	Knoxville, TN [*AM radio station call letters*]
WUTK-FM ...	Knoxville, TN [*FM radio station call letters*]
WUTM	Martin, TN [*FM radio station call letters*]
WUTQ........	Utica, NY [*AM radio station call letters*]
WUTR.........	Utica, NY [*Television station call letters*]
WUTS.........	Sewanee, TN [*FM radio station call letters*]
WUTS	Work Unit Time Standard [*Air Force*] (AFM)
WUTS.........	Work Unit Tracking Subsystem (MCD)
WUTV.........	Buffalo, NY [*Television station call letters*]
WUTWC......	Warm Up Three-Way Catalyst [*Automotive engineering*]
WUU..........	Wau [*Sudan*] [*Airport symbol*] (OAG)
WUUA........	World Union for a Universal Alphabet (EA)
WUUC........	West Ulster Unionist Council [*Northern Ireland*]
WUUN........	Women United for United Nations (EA)
WUUS-FM....	Martinez, GA [*FM radio station call letters*] (BROA)
WUUU.........	Remsen, NY [*FM radio station call letters*]
WUV..........	Weighted Unit Value (MCD)
WUV..........	Wuvulu Island [*Papua New Guinea*] [*Airport symbol*] (OAG)
WUVA.........	Charlottesville, VA [*FM radio station call letters*]
WUVCI.......	Western Union VideoConferencing, Inc. [*Defunct*] (TSSD)
WUVR.........	Lebanon, NH [*FM radio station call letters*]
WUVT.........	Blacksburg, VA [*FM radio station call letters*]
WUW..........	Welsh Union of Writers (WDAA)
WUW..........	Wu-wei [*Republic of China*] [*Seismograph station code, US Geological Survey*] (SEIS)
WU-WA.......	University of Wisconsin, Woodman Astronomical Library, Madison, WI [*Library symbol Library of Congress*] (LCLS)
WUWF........	Pensacola, FL [*FM radio station call letters*]
WUWM........	Milwaukee, WI [*FM radio station call letters*]
WUWU........	Cordele, GA [*AM radio station call letters*]
WUX..........	Western Union Exchange [*Teleprinter*]
WUXA.........	Portsmouth, OH [*Television station call letters*]
WUXP-TV	Nashville, TN [*TV station call letters*] (RBYB)
WUZR.........	Bicknell, IN [*FM radio station call letters*]
WV...........	Diwag [*Germany*] [*Research code symbol*]
WV...........	Midwest Aviation [*ICAO designator*] (AD)
WV...........	Wall Vent [*Technical drawings*]
WV...........	Water Valve (ROG)
wv...........	Weave (VRA)
W/V..........	Weight/Volume [*Concentration*] [*Chemistry*]
WV...........	Westminster Version of the Bible [*A publication*] (BJA)
WV...........	West Virginia [*Postal code*]
Wv............	West Virginia Library Commission, Charleston, WV [*Library symbol Library of Congress*] (LCLS)
WV...........	West Virginia Reports [*A publication*] (DLA)
WV...........	Whispered Voice
W/V..........	Wind Vector [*or Velocity*] [*Navigation*]
WV...........	Wireless Van [*British*]
WV...........	Working Voltage (MSA)
WV...........	World Vision [*An association*] (EA)
wv............	Woven (VRA)

WVA............. Alderson-Broaddus College, Philippi, WV [*OCLC symbol*] (OCLC)
WVA............. Alexandria [*Virginia*] [*Airport symbol*] (AD)
WVA............. H & D Aviation [*ICAO designator*] (FAAC)
WVA............. War Veterans Administration [*Canada*]
WVA............. Watervliet Arsenal [*New York*] [*Army*]
W VA........... West Virginia (AAG)
W Va........... West Virginia Supreme Court Reports [*A publication*] (DLA)
WVA............. Wool Valuers Association [*Australia*]
WVA............. World Veterinary Association [*See also AMV*] [*Madrid, Spain*] (EAIO)
WVA............. World Vision Australia
WVAA.......... Burnettown, SC [*AM radio station call letters*]
W Va Acts.... Acts of the Legislature of West Virginia [*A publication*] (DLA)
WVAATS....... West Virginia Assessment and Tracking System (EDAC)
WVAB.......... Virginia Beach, VA [*AM radio station call letters*]
WVAB.......... War Veterans Allowance Board [*Canada*]
WVAC.......... Adrian, MI [*FM radio station call letters*]
WvAC........... Concord College, Athens, WV [*Library symbol Library of Congress*] (LCLS)
WVAC.......... Norwalk, OH [*AM radio station call letters*]
WVAC.......... Working Voltage, Alternating Current (DEN)
W Va Code... West Virginia Code [*A publication*] (DLA)
W Va Const... West Virginia Constitution [*A publication*] (DLA)
W Va Crim Just Rev... West Virginia Criminal Justice Review [*A publication*] (DLA)
WVAE.......... Fairfield, OH [*FM radio station call letters*] (RBYB)
WVAF.......... Charleston, WV [*FM radio station call letters*]
WVAH.......... Charleston, WV [*Television station call letters*]
WVAL.......... Sauk Rapids, MN [*AM radio station call letters*]
W Va Law Reports... West Virginia Reports [*A publication*] (DLA)
W Va LQ....... West Virginia Law Quarterly [*A publication*] (DLA)
WVALSA...... Whitewater Valley Area Library Services Authority [*Library network*]
WVAM......... Altoona, PA [*AM radio station call letters*]
WVAN......... Savannah, GA [*Television station call letters*]
WVAO......... Staunton, VA [*FM radio station call letters*]
WVAO......... Waynesboro, VA [*AM radio station call letters*]
W Va PSCR... West Virginia Public Service Commission Report [*A publication*] (DLA)
W Va PUR... West Virginia Public Utility Commission Reports [*A publication*] (DLA)
WVAQ.......... Morgantown, WV [*FM radio station call letters*]
WVAR.......... Richwood, WV [*AM radio station call letters*]
Wv-Ar.......... West Virginia Department of Archives and History, Charleston, WV [*Library symbol Library of Congress*] (LCLS)
W Va Reg.... West Virginia Register [*A publication*] (AAGC)
W Va Rep.... West Virginia Reports [*A publication*] (DLA)
WVAS.......... Montgomery, AL [*FM radio station call letters*]
WVAS.......... Wake Vortex Avoidance System [*FAA*]
WVAST........ Washer Visual Acuity Screening Technique [*Visual ability test*]
WVAX-AM .... Lincoln, IL [*AM radio station call letters*] (RBYB)
WVAY.......... Wilmington, VT [*FM radio station call letters*]
WVAZ.......... Oak Park, IL [*FM radio station call letters*]
WvB........... Beckley-Raleigh County Library, Beckley, WV [*Library symbol Library of Congress*] (LCLS)
WVB........... Bethany College, Bethany, WV [*OCLC symbol*] (OCLC)
WVB........... Walvis Bay [*Namibia*] [*Airport symbol*] (OAG)
Wv-B.......... West Virginia Library Commission, Book Express Unit, Charleston, WV [*Library symbol Library of Congress*] (LCLS)
WVBA.......... West Virginia Bowhunters Association
WVBA.......... Wholesale Variety Bakers Association (EA)
WvBC.......... Beckley College, Beckley, WV [*Library symbol Library of Congress*] (LCLS)
WVBC.......... Bethany, WV [*FM radio station call letters*]
WVBEA........ West Virginia Business Education Association (EDAC)
WvBeC........ Bethany College, Bethany, WV [*Library symbol Library of Congress*] (LCLS)
WVBF-AM .... Middleboro, MA [*AM radio station call letters*] (BROA)
WVBI.......... Block Island, RI [*FM radio station call letters*]
WvBl.......... Bluefield Public Library, Bluefield, WV [*Library symbol Library of Congress*] (LCLS)
WvBIS.......... Bluefield State College, Bluefield, WV [*Library symbol Library of Congress*] (LCLS)
WVBO.......... Oshkosh, WI [*FM radio station call letters*]
WVBR.......... Ithaca, NY [*FM radio station call letters*]
WvBrA.......... Appalachian Bible Institute, Bradley, WV [*Library symbol Library of Congress*] (LCLS)
WvBri.......... Benedum Civic Center Public Library, Bridgeport, WV [*Library symbol Library of Congress*] (LCLS)
WVBS.......... Burgaw, NC [*AM radio station call letters*]
WVBT-TV...... Virginia Beach, VA [*TV station call letters*] (RBYB)
WVBU.......... Lewisburg, PA [*FM radio station call letters*]
WvBu.......... Stonewall Jackson Regional Library, Buckhannon, WV [*Library symbol Library of Congress*] (LCLS)
WvBuW........ West Virginia Wesleyan College, Buckhannon, WV [*Library symbol Library of Congress*] (LCLS)
WvBV.......... United States Veterans Administration Hospital, Beckley, WV [*Library symbol Library of Congress*] (LCLS)
WvC............. Kanawha County Public Library, Charleston, WV [*Library symbol Library of Congress*] (LCLS)
WVC............. Western Veterinary Conference (EA)
WVC............. West Virginia Code [*1899*] [*A publication*] (DLA)
WvCA.......... West Virginia Department of Agriculture, Charleston, WV [*Library symbol Library of Congress*] (LCLS)
WvCAE........ Appalachian Educational Laboratory, Inc., Charleston, WV [*Library symbol Library of Congress*] (LCLS)
WvCAP........ West Virginia Air Pollution Control Commission, Charleston, WV [*Library symbol Library of Congress*] (LCLS)
WVCB .... Shallotte, NC [*AM radio station call letters*]

WVCB......... West Virginia Association of Community Bankers (TBD)
WvCBHi .... West Virginia Baptist Historical Society Deposit, Department of Archives and History, Charleston, WV [*Library symbol Library of Congress*] (LCLS)
WVCC......... Linesville, PA [*FM radio station call letters*]
WvCCD........ West Virginia Department of Civil and Defense Mobilization, Charleston, WV [*Library symbol Library of Congress*] (LCLS)
WVCF......... Welsh Venture Capital Funds
WVCF-FM..... Eau Claire, WI [*FM radio station call letters*] (RBYB)
WvCFM........ West Virginia State Fire Marshal's Department, Charleston, WV [*Library symbol Library of Congress*] (LCLS)
WVCG......... Coral Gables, FL [*AM radio station call letters*]
WvCGH........ Charleston General Hospital, Charleston, WV [*Library symbol Library of Congress*] (LCLS)
WVCH......... Chester, PA [*AM radio station call letters*]
WvCH......... West Virginia Department of Health, Charleston, WV [*Library symbol Library of Congress*] (LCLS)
WvCheC....... Consolidated Gas Supply Corp., Chelyan, WV [*Library symbol Library of Congress*] (LCLS)
WvCHi......... West Virginia Department of Highways, Charleston, WV [*Library symbol Library of Congress*] (LCLS)
WvCl.......... Clarksburg Public Library, Clarksburg, WV [*Library symbol Library of Congress*] (LCLS)
WvCIC......... Consolidated Gas Supply Corp., Clarksburg, WV [*Library symbol Library of Congress*] (LCLS)
WVCL-FM ..... Norfolk, VA [*FM radio station call letters*] (BROA)
WvCM......... Morris Harvey College, Charleston, WV [*Library symbol Library of Congress*] (LCLS)
WVCM-FM ... Carlisle, KY [*FM radio station call letters*] (BROA)
WvCMH........ West Virginia Department of Mental Health, Charleston, WV [*Library symbol Library of Congress*] (LCLS)
WvCMi......... West Virginia Department of Mines, Charleston, WV [*Library symbol Library of Congress*] (LCLS)
WvCNR........ West Virginia Department of Natural Resources, Charleston, WV [*Library symbol Library of Congress*] (LCLS)
WVCO......... Loris, SC [*FM radio station call letters*]
WVCP......... Gallatin, TN [*FM radio station call letters*]
WvCPS........ West Virginia Department of Public Safety, Charleston, WV [*Library symbol Library of Congress*] (LCLS)
WVCQ......... Brockway, PA [*AM radio station call letters*]
WVCR......... Loudonville, NY [*FM radio station call letters*]
WVCS......... California, PA [*FM radio station call letters*]
WVCT......... Keavy, KY [*FM radio station call letters*]
WvCTS........ West Virginia State Technical Services, Charleston, WV [*Library symbol Library of Congress*] (LCLS)
WVCV......... Boalsburg, PA [*FM radio station call letters*]
WvCVR........ West Virginia Division of Vocational Rehabilitation, Charleston, WV [*Library symbol Library of Congress*] (LCLS)
WVCX......... Tomah, WI [*FM radio station call letters*]
WVCY......... Milwaukee, WI [*FM radio station call letters*]
WVCY......... Oshkosh, WI [*AM radio station call letters*] (RBYB)
WVCY-TV..... Milwaukee, WI [*Television station call letters*]
WVD............. Dane County Hospital, Verona, WI [*Library symbol Library of Congress*] (LCLS)
WVD............. Davis and Elkins College, Elkins, WV [*OCLC symbol*] (OCLC)
WVD............. Waived (AABC)
WVD............. Wereldverband van Diamantbewerkers [*Worldwide Alliance of Diamond Workers*] (BARN)
WVdc.......... DC Working Voltage (IDOE)
WVDC......... Working Voltage, Direct Current
WVDF......... Wolverhampton Volunteer Defence Force [*British military*] (DMA)
WVDP......... West Valley Demonstration Project [*Department of Energy*] [*West Valley, NY*] (GAAI)
WVE............. Water Vapor Electrolysis [*Cell*]
WVE............. Wind Velocity East (MCD)
WVEC......... Hampton, VA [*Television station call letters*]
WvED......... Davis and Elkins College, Elkins, WV [*Library symbol Library of Congress*] (LCLS)
WVEE......... Atlanta, GA [*FM radio station call letters*]
WVEE......... Wheeled Vehicle Experimental Establishment [*British*]
WVEH......... Wheel Vehicle (AABC)
WVEL......... Pekin, IL [*AM radio station call letters*]
WVEM......... Water Vapor Electrolysis Module [*NASA*]
WVEO......... Aguadilla, PR [*Television station call letters*]
WVEP......... Martinsburg, WV [*FM radio station call letters*]
WVER......... Rutland, VT [*Television station call letters*]
WVES......... Accomac, VA [*FM radio station call letters*]
WVEU......... Atlanta, GA [*Television station call letters*]
WVEZ......... Louisville, KY [*FM radio station call letters*]
WVF............. Fairmont State College, Fairmont, WV [*OCLC symbol*] (OCLC)
WvF............. Marion County Public Library, Fairmont, WV [*Library symbol Library of Congress*] (LCLS)
WVF............. United States Council, World Veterans Federation (EA)
WVF............. Wave Vector Filter
WVF............. World Veterans Federation [*See also FMAC*] [*Paris, France*] (EAIO)
WVF............. World Veterans Fund [*Defunct*] (EA)
WvFa .... Fayette County Public Library, Fayetteville, WV [*Library symbol Library of Congress*] (LCLS)
WVFB......... Celina, TN [*FM radio station call letters*]
WVFC......... McConnellsburg, PA [*AM radio station call letters*]
WVFC......... WVS Financial [*NASDAQ symbol*] (TTSB)
WVFC......... WVS Financial Corp. [*NASDAQ symbol*] (SAG)
WVFG......... Uniontown, AL [*FM radio station call letters*]
WVFJ......... Manchester, GA [*FM radio station call letters*]
WVFM......... Campton, NH [*FM radio station call letters*]

WvFMHI...... Marion County Historical Society, Fairmont, WV [*Library symbol Library of Congress*] (LCLS)

WVFN .... East Lansing, MI [*AM radio station call letters*]

WvFS .... Fairmont State College, Fairmont, WV [*Library symbol Library of Congress*] (LCLS)

WVFS.......... Tallahassee, FL [*FM radio station call letters*]

WVG .... West Virginia State College/College of Graduate Studies, Institute, WV [*OCLC symbol*] (OCLC)

WVGB .... Beaufort, SC [*AM radio station call letters*]

WvGbN .... National Radio Astronomy Observatory, Green Bank, WV [*Library symbol Library of Congress*] (LCLS)

WvGIS .... Glenville State College, Glenville, WV [*Library symbol Library of Congress*] (LCLS)

WVGN.......... Charlotte Amalie, VI [*FM radio station call letters*]

WVGO.......... Richmond, VA [*FM radio station call letters*]

WVGR .... Grand Rapids, MI [*FM radio station call letters*]

WVGS .... Statesboro, GA [*FM radio station call letters*]

WVGV .... Lewisburg, WV [*Television station call letters*]

WVH .... Marshall University, Huntington, WV [*OCLC symbol*] (OCLC)

WVHA .... Wirtschaftsverwaltungshauptamt (BJA)

WvHB .... Pearl S. Buck Birthplace Museum, Hillsboro, WV [*Library symbol Library of Congress*] (LCLS)

WVHC .... Herkimer, NY [*FM radio station call letters*]

WVHF .... Clarksburg, WV [*FM radio station call letters*]

WvHfP .... United States Park Service, Harpers Ferry National Historical Park, Harpers Ferry, WV [*Library symbol Library of Congress*] (LCLS)

WVHI .... Evansville, IN [*AM radio station call letters*]

WVHL-FM .... Farmville, VA [*FM radio station call letters*] (BROA)

WVHM .... Benton, KY [*FM radio station call letters*]

WVHQ .... Dowagiac, MI [*FM radio station call letters*]

WVHR .... Huntingdon, TN [*FM radio station call letters*]

WvHu .... Cabell-Huntington Public Library [*Western Counties Regional Library*], Huntington, WV [*Library symbol Library of Congress*] (LCLS)

WvHuB........ Basic Systems, Inc., Huntington, WV [*Library symbol Library of Congress*] (LCLS)

WvHuE........ United States Army, Corps of Engineers, Huntington, WV [*Library symbol Library of Congress*] (LCLS)

WvHuG .... Huntington Galleries, Huntington, WV [*Library symbol Library of Congress*] (LCLS)

WvHuH .... Holland-Suco Color Co., Huntington, WV [*Library symbol Library of Congress*] (LCLS)

WvHuM .... Marshall University, Huntington, WV [*Library symbol Library of Congress*] (LCLS)

WvHuV........ United States Veterans Administration Hospital, Huntington, WV [*Library symbol Library of Congress*] (LCLS)

WVI............. Viroqua Public Library, Viroqua, WI [*Library symbol Library of Congress*] (LCLS)

WVI............. Watsonville, CA [*Location identifier FAA*] (FAAL)

WVI............. Work Values Inventory [*Psychometrics*]

WVI   World Vision International

WVIA .... Scranton, PA [*FM radio station call letters*]

WVIAC .... West Virginia Intercollegiate Athletic Conference (PSS)

WVIA-TV ...... Scranton, PA [*Television station call letters*]

WVIB .... Mount Kisco, NY [*FM radio station call letters*] (RBYB)

WVIC .... East Lansing, MI [*FM radio station call letters*]

WvIC........... West Virginia State College, Institute, WV [*Library symbol Library of Congress*] (LCLS)

WvICG .... West Virginia College of Graduate Studies, Institute, WV [*Library symbol Library of Congress*] (LCLS)

WVII........... Bangor, ME [*Television station call letters*]

WVIJ........... Port Charlotte, FL [*FM radio station call letters*]

WVIK .... Rock Island, IL [*FM radio station call letters*]

WVIL........... Virginia, IL [*FM radio station call letters*] (RBYB)

WVIM .... Coldwater, MS [*FM radio station call letters*]

WVIN .... Bath, NY [*FM radio station call letters*]

WVIO .... Blowing Rock, NC [*AM radio station call letters*]

WVIP .... Mount Kisco, NY [*AM radio station call letters*]

WVIQ .... Christiansted, VI [*FM radio station call letters*]

WVIR .... Charlottesville, VA [*Television station call letters*]

WVIS .... Christiansted, VI [*FM radio station call letters*]

WVIT .... New Britain, CT [*Television station call letters*]

WVIT........... West Virginia Institute of Technology

WVIV .... Pearl, MS [*FM radio station call letters*]

WVIX .... Vicksburg, MS [*AM radio station call letters*]

WVIZ .... Cleveland, OH [*Television station call letters*]

WVJC.......... Mount Carmel, IL [*FM radio station call letters*]

WVJP.......... Caguas, PR [*AM radio station call letters*]

WVJP-FM .... Caguas, PR [*FM radio station call letters*]

WVJS.......... Owensboro, KY [*AM radio station call letters*]

WVK............ Kanawha County Public Library, Charleston, WV [*OCLC symbol*] (OCLC)

WvK............ Keyser-Mineral County Public and Potomac Valley Regional Library, Keyser, WV [*Library symbol Library of Congress*] (LCLS)

WVK............ Manakara [*Madagascar*] [*Airport symbol*] (OAG)

WVKC .... Galesburg, IL [*FM radio station call letters*]

WvKeFW...... Bureau of Sport Fisheries and Wildlife, Eastern Fish Disease Laboratory, Kearneysville, WV [*Library symbol Library of Congress*] (LCLS)

WVKM .... Matewan, WV [*FM radio station call letters*]

WVKO .... Columbus, OH [*AM radio station call letters*]

WvKP.......... Potomac State College, Keyser, WV [*Library symbol Library of Congress*] (LCLS)

WVKR .... Poughkeepsie, NY [*FM radio station call letters*]

WVKS .... Toledo, OH [*FM radio station call letters*]

WVKV .... Hurricane, WV [*AM radio station call letters*]

WVKX .... Irwinton, GA [*FM radio station call letters*]

WVKY .... Louisa, KY [*AM radio station call letters*]

WVKZ .... Schenectady, NY [*AM radio station call letters*]

WVL........... Warfare Vision Laboratory [*Army*]

WVL........... Waterville [*Maine*] [*Airport symbol*] (OAG)

WVL........... Waterville, ME [*Location identifier FAA*] (FAAL)

WVL........... Wavelength [*Electronics*] (IAA)

WVL........... West Vancouver Laboratory [*Department of Fisheries and Oceans*] [*Canada*] (IRC)

Wv-L........... West Virginia State Law Library, Charleston, WV [*Library symbol Library of Congress*] (LCLS)

WVL........... Woodvale Aviation Co. Ltd. [*British ICAO designator*] (FAAC)

WVLA .... Baton Rouge, LA [*Television station call letters*]

WVLB .... Wheeled Vehicle Launched Bridge (MCD)

WVLC .... Mannsville, KY [*AM radio station call letters*] (RBYB)

WVLD .... Valdosta, GA [*AM radio station call letters*]

WvLe .... Greenbrier County Public Library, Lewisburg, WV [*Library symbol Library of Congress*] (LCLS)

WVLE .... Scottsville, KY [*FM radio station call letters*]

WvLeG .... Greenbrier College, Lewisburg, WV [*Library symbol Library of Congress*] (LCLS)

WVLI .... Kankakee, IL [*FM radio station call letters*] (RBYB)

WVLK .... Lexington, KY [*AM radio station call letters*]

WVLK-FM .... Lexington, KY [*FM radio station call letters*]

WVLN .... Olney, IL [*AM radio station call letters*]

WVLQ .... West Virginia Law Quarterly [*A publication*] (DLA)

WVLR .... Lynchburg, VA [*AM radio station call letters*]

WVLS .... Monterey, VA [*FM radio station call letters*]

Wv-LS......... West Virginia Library Commission, Library Science Department, Charleston, WV [*Library symbol Library of Congress*] (LCLS)

WVLT .... Vineland, NJ [*FM radio station call letters*]

WVLY .... Milton, PA [*FM radio station call letters*]

WvM .... Morgantown Public Library, Morgantown, WV [*Library symbol Library of Congress*] (LCLS)

WVM .... West Virginia Medical Center, Morgantown, WV [*Inactive*] [*OCLC symbol*] (OCLC)

WvMa .... Martinsburg-Berkeley County Public Library, Martinsburg, WV [*Library symbol Library of Congress*] (LCLS)

WVMA .... Women's Veterinary Medical Association [*Later, AWV*]

WvMaV....... United States Veterans Administration Center, Martinsburg, WV [*Library symbol Library of Congress*] (LCLS)

WV-MBC ..... Walking Ventilation to Maximum Breathing Capacity Ratio [*Medicine*] (MAE)

WvMBM....... United States Bureau of Mines, Morgantown, WV [*Library symbol Library of Congress*] (LCLS)

WVMC .... Mansfield, OH [*FM radio station call letters*]

WvMc .... McMechen Public Library, McMechen, WV [*Library symbol Library of Congress*] (LCLS)

WvMDOE ..... United States Department of Energy, Morgantown Energy Technology Center, Morgantown, WV [*Library symbol*] [*Library of Congress*] (LCLS)

WVMG .... Cochran, GA [*AM radio station call letters*]

WVMG-FM.... Cochran, GA [*FM radio station call letters*]

WVMH .... Mars Hill, NC [*FM radio station call letters*]

WVMI.......... Biloxi, MS [*AM radio station call letters*]

WvMIL......... Institute for Labor Studies, Appalachian Center, Morgantown, WV [*Library symbol Library of Congress*] (LCLS)

WVMJ.......... Blacksburg, VA [*FM radio station call letters*] (RBYB)

WVMM........ Grantham, PA [*FM radio station call letters*]

WVMN .... New Castle, PA [*FM radio station call letters*] (RBYB)

WvMNIO ...... United States Public Health Service, National Institute for Occupational Safety and Health, Appalachian Laboratory for Occupational Safety and Health Library, Morgantown, WV (LCLS)

WvMo .... City-County Public Library, Moundsville, WV [*Library symbol Library of Congress*] (LCLS)

WvMonI....... West Virginia Institute of Technology, Montgomery, WV [*Library symbol Library of Congress*] (LCLS)

WVMR .... Frost, WV [*AM radio station call letters*]

WVMS .... Sandusky, OH [*FM radio station call letters*]

WVMT......... Burlington, VT [*AM radio station call letters*]

WVMV .... Wisteria Vein Mosaic Virus

WVMW .... Scranton, PA [*FM radio station call letters*]

WVMX .... Stowe, VT [*FM radio station call letters*]

WVN .... Water Vapor Nitrogen [*Nuclear energy*] (NRCH)

WVN .... West Virginia Northern Railroad Co. [*AAR code*]

WVN .... Wind Velocity North (MCD)

WVN .... Woven

WVNA .... Tuscumbia, AL [*AM radio station call letters*]

WVNA-FM.... Tuscumbia, AL [*FM radio station call letters*]

WVNC .... Canton, NY [*FM radio station call letters*]

WVNE .... Leicester, MA [*AM radio station call letters*]

WVNET........ West Virginia Network for Educational Telecomputing [*Research center*] (RCD)

WVNF .... Alpharetta, GA [*AM radio station call letters*]

WVNH .... Concord, NH [*FM radio station call letters*]

WVNI .... Nashville, IN [*FM radio station call letters*]

WvNiK .... West Virginia University, Kanawha Valley Graduate Center, Nitro, WV [*Library symbol Library of Congress*] (LCLS)

WVNJ.......... Oakland, NJ [*AM radio station call letters*]

WvNmM....... Mobay Chemical Corp., Research Library, New Martinsville, WV [*Library symbol Library of Congress*] (LCLS)

WVNN .... Athens, AL [*AM radio station call letters*]

WVNO .... Mansfield, OH [*FM radio station call letters*]

WVNP .... Wheeling, WV [*FM radio station call letters*]

WVNR .... Poultney, VT [*AM radio station call letters*]
WVNS .... Claremont, VA [*AM radio station call letters*] (RBYB)
WVNS .... West Valley Nuclear Services Co. (GAAI)
WVNU .... Greenfield, OH [*FM radio station call letters*]
WVNV .... Malone, NY [*FM radio station call letters*]
WVNW .... Burnham, PA [*FM radio station call letters*]
WVNX .... Charlotte Amalie, VI [*FM radio station call letters*]
WVNY .... Burlington, VT [*Television station call letters*]
WVNY .... West Valley, New York [*Commercial waste site from 1963-81*] (GAAI)
WVNZ-AM .... Richmond, VA [*AM radio station call letters*] (RBYB)
WVOA .... DeRuyter, NY [*FM radio station call letters*]
WVOB .... Dothan, AL [*FM radio station call letters*]
WVOC .... Columbia, SC [*AM radio station call letters*]
WVOD .... Manteo, NC [*FM radio station call letters*]
WVOE .... Chadbourn, NC [*AM radio station call letters*]
WVOF .... Fairfield, CT [*FM radio station call letters*]
WVOG .... New Orleans, LA [*AM radio station call letters*]
WVOH .... Hazlehurst, GA [*AM radio station call letters*]
WVOH-FM .... Hazlehurst, GA [*FM radio station call letters*]
WVOI .... Toledo, OH [*AM radio station call letters*]
WVOJ .... Jacksonville, FL [*AM radio station call letters*]
WVOK .... Oxford, AL [*FM radio station call letters*]
WVOL .... Berry Hill, TN [*AM radio station call letters*]
WVOM .... Iuka, MS [*AM radio station call letters*]
WVON .... Cicero, IL [*AM radio station call letters*]
WVOP .... Vidalia, GA [*AM radio station call letters*]
WVOR .... Rochester, NY [*FM radio station call letters*]
WVOS .... Liberty, NY [*AM radio station call letters*]
WVOS-FM .... Liberty, NY [*FM radio station call letters*]
WVOT .... Wilson, NC [*AM radio station call letters*]
WVOV .... Danville, VA [*AM radio station call letters*]
WVOW .... Logan, WV [*AM radio station call letters*]
WVOW .... West Virginia Ordnance Works
WVOW-FM .... Logan, WV [*FM radio station call letters*]
WVOX .... New Rochelle, NY [*AM radio station call letters*]
WVOZ .... Ponce, PR [*Television station call letters*]
WvP .... Carnegie Library of Parkersburg and Wood County, Parkersburg, WV [*Library symbol Library of Congress*] (LCLS)
WVP .... Water Vapor Permeability [*Physical chemistry*]
WVP .... Windscale Vitrification Plant [*British*] (NUCP)
WVP .... Women's Vote Project [*Defunct*] (EA)
WVPA .... World Veterinary Poultry Association [*See also AMVA*] [*Huntingdon, Cambridgeshire, England*] (EAIO)
WVPB .... Beckley, WV [*FM radio station call letters*]
WvPC .... Parkersburg Community College, Parkersburg, WV [*Library symbol Library of Congress*] (LCLS)
WVPE .... Elkhart, IN [*FM radio station call letters*]
WVPG .... Parkersburg, WV [*FM radio station call letters*]
WVPH .... Piscataway, NJ [*FM radio station call letters*]
WvPhA .... Alderson-Broaddus College, Philippi, WV [*Library symbol Library of Congress*] (LCLS)
WVPM .... Morgantown, WV [*FM radio station call letters*]
WVPN .... Charleston, WV [*FM radio station call letters*]
WvPO .... Ohio Valley College, Parkersburg, WV [*Library symbol Library of Congress*] (LCLS)
WVPO .... Stroudsburg, PA [*AM radio station call letters*]
WVPR .... Windsor, VT [*FM radio station call letters*]
WVPS .... Burlington, VT [*FM radio station call letters*]
WVPT .... Staunton, VA [*Television station call letters*]
WVPW .... Buckhannon, WV [*FM radio station call letters*]
WVPX .... Akron, OH [*Television station call letters*] (BROA)
WVPY-TV .... Front Royal, VA [*TV station call letters*] (RBYB)
WVQ .... Monongahela Power Co. [*NYSE symbol*] (SAG)
WVQ .... Monongahela Pwr 8% 'QUIDS' [*NYSE symbol*] (TTSB)
WVR .... Wakefield Volunteer Rifles [*British military*] (DMA)
WVR .... Water Vapor Regained (AAEL)
WVR .... Wellington Volunteer Rifles [*British military*] (DMA)
Wv-R .... West Virginia Library Commission, Reference Department, WV [*Library symbol Library of Congress*] (LCLS)
WVR .... West Virginia Reports [*A publication*] (DLA)
WVR .... Within Visual Range [*Missile*] (MCD)
WVR .... Women's Volunteer Reserve [*World War I*] [*British*]
WVRAAM .... Within Visual Range Air-to-Air Missile
WVRB .... Wilmore, KY [*FM radio station call letters*] (RBYB)
WVRC .... Spencer, WV [*AM radio station call letters*]
WVRC .... Wabash Valley Railroad Co. [*AAR code*]
WVRC .... Wolverhampton Volunteer Rifle Corps [*British military*] (DMA)
WVRC-FM .... Spencer, WV [*FM radio station call letters*]
WVRD .... Belzoni, MS [*FM radio station call letters*]
WVRD .... World Vision Relief and Development, Inc.
WV Rep ...... West Virginia Reports [*A publication*] (DLA)
WVRK .... Columbus, GA [*FM radio station call letters*]
WVRP .... Ripley, WV [*FM radio station call letters*]
WVRQ .... Viroqua, WI [*AM radio station call letters*]
WVRQ-FM .... Viroqua, WI [*FM radio station call letters*]
WVRR-FM .... Newport, NH [*FM radio station call letters*] (BROA)
WVRRTC ...... West Virginia Rehabilitation Research and Training Center [*West Virginia University*] [*Research center*] (RCD)
WVRT .... Jersey Shore, PA [*FM radio station call letters*] (RBYB)
WVRU .... Radford, VA [*FM radio station call letters*]
WVRV .... East St. Louis, IL [*FM radio station call letters*]
WVRY .... Waverly, TN [*FM radio station call letters*]
WVS .... Water Vapor Sensor
W-V(S) .... Women's Reserve, Emergency Duties [*USNR commissioned officer designation*]

WVS .... Women's Voluntary Services [*Coordinated work of women for national service*] [*Later, WRVS*] [*British*] [*World War II*]
WVSA .... Vernon, AL [*AM radio station call letters*]
WVSA .... Water-Vapor-Saturated Air (PDAA)
WVSA .... Weidingsvereniging van Suidelike Afrika [*Grassland Society of Southern Africa-GISSA*] (EAIO)
WvSaC .... Salem College, Salem, WV [*Library symbol Library of Congress*] (LCLS)
WVSC .... Somerset, PA [*AM radio station call letters*]
WVSC .... West Virginia State College
W-V(S) (CEC)... Women's Reserve, Civil Engineering Corps Duties [*USNR commissioned officer designation*]
WVSC-FM .... Somerset, PA [*FM radio station call letters*]
WvScU .... Union Carbide Corp., South Charleston, WV [*Library symbol Library of Congress*] (LCLS)
WVSD .... Itta Bena, MS [*FM radio station call letters*]
W-V(S) (DC)... Women's Reserve, Dental Corps Duties [*USNR commissioned officer designation*]
WVS Fn .... WVS Financial Corp. [*Associated Press*] (SAG)
WVSH .... Huntington, IN [*FM radio station call letters*]
WvSh .... Shepherdstown Public Library, Shepherdstown, WV [*Library symbol Library of Congress*] (LCLS)
W-V(S) (H)... Women's Reserve, Hospital Corps Duties [*USNR commissioned officer designation*]
WvShS .... Shepherd College, Shepherdstown, WV [*Library symbol Library of Congress*] (LCLS)
WVSM .... Rainsville, AL [*AM radio station call letters*]
W-V(S) (MC)... Women's Reserve, Medical Corps Duties [*USNR commissioned officer designation*]
WVSOM .... West Virginia School of Osteopathic Medicine
WVSR .... Charleston, WV [*AM radio station call letters*]
WVSR-FM .... Charleston, WV [*FM radio station call letters*]
WVSS .... Menomonie, WI [*FM radio station call letters*]
W-V(S) (SC)... Women's Reserve, Supply Corps Duties [*USNR commissioned officer designation*]
WVST .... Petersburg, VA [*FM radio station call letters*]
WVSU .... Birmingham, AL [*FM radio station call letters*]
WVSX-TV .... Lewisburg, WV [*TV station call letters*] (RBYB)
WVSY .... Ruckersville, VA [*FM radio station call letters*]
WVSZ-FM .... Chesterfield, SC [*FM station call letters*] (RBYB)
WVT .... Water Vapor Transmission
WVT .... Watervliet Arsenal [*New York*] [*Army*]
WVT .... West Virginia Institute of Technology, Montgomery, WV [*OCLC symbol*] (OCLC)
WWTA .... Windsor, VT [*Television station call letters*]
WVTB .... St. Johnsbury, VT [*Television station call letters*]
WVTC .... Randolph Center, VT [*FM radio station call letters*]
WVTF .... Roanoke, VA [*FM radio station call letters*]
WVTF .... Western Visayan Task Force [*World War II*]
WVTI-FM .... Holland, MI [*FM radio station call letters*] (BROA)
WVTJ .... Pensacola, FL [*AM radio station call letters*]
WVTM .... Birmingham, AL [*Television station call letters*]
WVTR .... Marion, VA [*FM radio station call letters*]
WVTR .... Water Vapor Transmission Rate
WVTU .... Charlottesville, VA [*FM radio station call letters*]
WVTV .... Milwaukee, WI [*Television station call letters*]
WVTW-FM .... Charlottesville, VA [*FM radio station call letters*] (RBYB)
WVTY .... Pittsburgh, PA [*FM radio station call letters*]
wvu .... West Virginia [*MARC country of publication code Library of Congress*] (LCCP)
WVU .... West Virginia University
WVU .... West Virginia University Library, Morgantown, WV [*OCLC symbol*] (OCLC)
WvU .... West Virginia University, Morgantown, WV [*Library symbol Library of Congress*] (LCLS)
WVUA .... Tuscaloosa, AL [*FM radio station call letters*]
WvU-AE .... West Virginia University, Agricultural Engineering Library, Morgantown, WV [*Library symbol Library of Congress*] (LCLS)
WVUB .... Vincennes, IN [*FM radio station call letters*]
WVUC .... Barrackville, WV [*FM radio station call letters*] (RBYB)
WVUD .... Newark, DE [*FM radio station call letters*]
WVUE .... New Orleans, LA [*Television station call letters*]
WvU-J .... West Virginia University, School of Journalism, Morgantown, WV [*Library symbol Library of Congress*] (LCLS)
WvU-L .... West Virginia University, College of Law, Morgantown, WV [*Library symbol Library of Congress*] (LCLS)
WVUM .... Coral Gables, FL [*FM radio station call letters*]
WvU-M .... West Virginia University, Medical Center, Morgantown, WV [*Library symbol Library of Congress*] (LCLS)
WvU-Mu .... West Virginia University, Music Library, Morgantown, WV [*Library symbol Library of Congress*] (LCLS)
WvU-P .... West Virginia University, Physical Sciences Library, Morgantown, WV [*Library symbol Library of Congress*] (LCLS)
WVUR .... Valparaiso, IN [*FM radio station call letters*]
WVUT .... Vincennes, IN [*Television station call letters*]
WVUV .... Leone, AS [*AM radio station call letters*]
WVV .... Volovan [*Malagasy*] [*Airport symbol*] (AD)
WVV .... Whole Virus Vaccine [*Immunology*]
WVVA .... Bluefield, WV [*Television station call letters*]
WVVC .... Utica, NY [*FM radio station call letters*]
WVVE .... Stonington, CT [*FM radio station call letters*]
WVVI .... Manassas, VA [*Television station call letters*]
WVVI .... Willamette Valley Vineyards, Inc. [*NASDAQ symbol*] (SAG)
WVVR .... Hopkinsville, KY [*FM radio station call letters*]
WVVS .... Valdosta, GA [*FM radio station call letters*]

WVVV	St. Simons Island, GA [*FM radio station call letters*] (RBYB)
WVVW	St. Marys, WV [*AM radio station call letters*]
WVVX	Highland Park, IL [*FM radio station call letters*]
WvW	Ohio County Public Library, Wheeling, WV [*Library symbol Library of Congress*] (LCLS)
WVW	Westview Resources [*Vancouver Stock Exchange symbol*]
WvWaB	Borg-Warner Corp., Borg-Warner Chemicals Technical Center, Washington, WV [*Library symbol Library of Congress*] (LCLS)
WVWC	Buckhannon, WV [*FM radio station call letters*]
WVWC	West Virginia Wesleyan College
WvWC	Wheeling College, Wheeling, WV [*Library symbol Library of Congress*] (LCLS)
WvWelW	West Liberty State College, West Liberty, WV [*Library symbol Library of Congress*] (LCLS)
WvWEPA	United States Environmental Protection Agency, Wheeling Field Office, Wheeling, WV [*Library symbol Library of Congress*] (LCLS)
WvWH	Wheeling Hospital, Medical Library, Wheeling, WV [*Library symbol Library of Congress*] (LCLS)
WVWI	Charlotte Amalie, VI [*AM radio station call letters*]
WvWO	Oglebay Institute, Wheeling, WV [*Library symbol Library of Congress*] (LCLS)
WVWV	Huntington, WV [*FM radio station call letters*]
WVXC	Chillicothe, OH [*FM radio station call letters*]
WVXD	Chetek, WI [*FM radio station call letters*]
WVXF	Charlotte Amalie, VI [*Television station call letters*]
WVXG	Mount Gilead, OH [*FM radio station call letters*]
WVXI-FM	Crawfordsville, IN [*FM radio station call letters*] (BROA)
WVXM	Manistee, MI [*FM radio station call letters*] (RBYB)
WVXR	Richmond, IN [*FM radio station call letters*]
WVXU	Cincinnati, OH [*FM radio station call letters*]
WVXW	West Union, OH [*FM radio station call letters*] (RBYB)
WVYB	Patterson, NY [*FM radio station call letters*] (RBYB)
WVYC	York, PA [*FM radio station call letters*]
WVYE-FM ...	Port Gibson, MS [*FM radio station call letters*] (BROA)
WVYH	North Windham, ME [*FM radio station call letters*]
WVZA	Herrin, IL [*FM radio station call letters*]
WVZC	Montauk, NY [*FM radio station call letters*]
WVZD	Dennysville, ME [*FM radio station call letters*]
WVZN-AM	Columbia, PA [*AM radio station call letters*] (BROA)
WW	Israel Aircraft Industries Ltd. [*ICAO aircraft manufacturer identifier*] (ICAO)
WW	Scottish European Airways [*ICAO designator*] (AD)
WW	Severe Weather Forecast [*National Weather Service*] (FAAC)
WW	Trans-West [*ICAO designator*] (AD)
WW	Walking Wounded (ADA)
WW	Wall-to-Wall [*Carpeting*] [*Classified advertising*]
w/w	Wall to Wall (REAL)
WW	Walter Winchell [*American journalist*] (IIA)
WW	Wardroom Window [*Aerospace*] (KSC)
WW	Warehouse Warrant
WW	Warm White (DAC)
WW	Warrant Writer [*Navy British*]
WW	Waste Watch [*Defunct*] (EA)
WW	Waterwall (MSA)
WW	Water Waste (NASA)
WW	Water Watch (Program) [*Australia*]
WW	Water-White
WW	Waterworks
WW	Watson Wyatt Worldwide [*Commercial firm*] (ECON)
WW	Weather Wing (MCD)
WW	Weather Working
w/w	Weight of Solute in Weight of Solvent [*Chemistry*] (DAVI)
W/W	Weight (of Solute) per Weight (of Solvent) (STED)
w/w	Weight of Solute per Weight of Total Solution [*Chemistry*] (DAVI)
WW	Weight Watchers [*An association*]
W/W	Weight/Weight
WW	Welfare Worker [*British military*] (DMA)
WW	Well Water [*Nuclear energy*] (NRCH)
WW	Western Waste Industries [*NYSE symbol*] (SPSG)
WW	Westwater Industries Ltd. [*Toronto Stock Exchange symbol*]
WW	Wet Weight (DB)
W/W	Wheel Well (MCD)
WW	Whitewall Tire [*Automotive accessory*]
WW	White Wyandotte [*Poultry*]
WW	Wholesale Wine [*License*]
WW	Who's Who [*A publication*]
WW	Widow [*Genealogy*]
WW	Wilderness Watch (EA)
W/W	Wild Weasel [*Aerospace*]
WW	Williams & Works (EFIS)
WW	Winchester & Western Railroad Co. [*AAR code*]
W/W	Winding to Winding (MSA)
WW	Wines of Westhorpe [*Commercial firm British*]
WW	Winged Warriors/National B-Body Owners Association (EA)
WW	Wire Way [*Technical drawings*]
WW	Wire Wheel [*Automotive accessory*]
WW	Wire-Wound
ww	Wirewound (IDOE)
WW	Wire Wrap (NASA)
WW	Wirtschaftswoche-Datenbank [*Economic Week Data Bank*] [*Society for Public Economics*] [*Germany*] [*Information service or system*] (IID)
WW	Wishing Well [*An association*] (EA)
WW	With Warrants [*Stock exchange term*] (SPSG)
WW	With Warrants (EBF)
WW	With Winch
WW	Women in the Wind [*An association*] (EA)
WW	Women to the World [*An association*] (EA)
WW	Woodwind [*Instrument*] [*Music*]
ww	Woodwind (WDAA)
WW	Working Women (NTCM)
WW	Working Women, National Association of Officeworkers (EA)
WW	World War
WW	Worldwide
WW	Worldwide Equities Ltd. [*Toronto Stock Exchange symbol*]
WW	Wound Width [*Forestry*]
WW	Writers and Their Work [*British Council*]
WWA	Wallcovering Wholesalers Association [*Later, WDA*] (EA)
WWA	War Widows Association [*British*] (DBA)
WWa	Wauwatosa Public Library, Wauwatosa, WI [*Library symbol Library of Congress*] (LCLS)
WWA	Welsh Water Authority (DCTA)
WWA	Western Writers of America (EA)
WWA	Who's Wealthy in America [*A publication*]
WWA	Who's Who in America [*A publication*]
WWA	Who's Who in Art [*A publication*]
WWA	Who's Who in Australia [*A publication*]
WWA	With the Will Annexed
WWA	Woolens and Worsteds of America [*Defunct*]
WWA	World Warning Agency (MCD)
WWA	World Waterpark Association (EA)
WWA	World Watusi Association (EA)
WWA	World Wide Airlines, Inc.
WWA	Worldwide Aviation Services Ltd. [*Venezuela*] [*ICAO designator*] (FAAC)
WWAA	Westfalen Warmblood Association of America (EA)
WWAA	Who's Who Among Asian Americans [*A publication*]
WWAB	Lakeland, FL [*AM radio station call letters*]
WWABCC	World Wide Avon Bottle Collectors Club (EA)
WWABNCP ..	Worldwide Airborne Command Post [*Air Force*] (AFM)
WWABNRES...	WWMCCS [*Worldwide Military Command and Control System*] Airborne Resources (DOMA)
WWAC	Atlantic City, NJ [*Television station call letters*]
WWAC	Walk with Aid of Cane (DAVI)
WWAC	Western World Avon Club [*Defunct*] (EA)
WWAG	McKee, KY [*FM radio station call letters*]
WWal	Walworth Memorial Library, Walworth, WI [*Library symbol Library of Congress*] (LCLS)
WWalPS	Walworth Public Schools, Walworth, WI [*Library symbol Library of Congress*] (LCLS)
WWalSD	North Walworth School District Number Five, Walworth, WI [*Library symbol Library of Congress*] (LCLS)
WWAM	Jasper, TN [*AM radio station call letters*]
WWaMP	Milwaukee Psychiatric Hospital, Wauwatosa, WI [*Library symbol Library of Congress*] (LCLS)
WW & D	Willmore, Wollaston, and Davison's English Queen's Bench Reports [*1837*] [*A publication*] (DLA)
WW & H	Willmore, Wollaston, and Hodges' English Queen's Bench Reports [*1838-39*] [*A publication*] (DLA)
WW & H (Eng)...	Willmore, Wollaston, and Hodges' English Queen's Bench Reports [*1838-39*] [*A publication*] (DLA)
WW & IB	Western Weighing and Inspection Bureau
WWAP	Worldwide Asset Position [*Military*] (AABC)
WWAR	Appomattox, VA [*AM radio station call letters*] (RBYB)
WWAS	Williamsport, PA [*FM radio station call letters*]
WWAS	World-Wide Academy of Scholars [*Defunct*] (EA)
WWAS	World Wide Air Services [*Australia*]
WWaSC	Saint Camillus Hospital, Wauwatosa, WI [*Library symbol Library of Congress*] (LCLS)
WWat	Watertown Free Public Library, Watertown, WI [*Library symbol Library of Congress*] (LCLS)
WWatf	Waterford Public Library, Waterford, WI [*Library symbol Library of Congress*] (LCLS)
WWatfH	Holy Redeemer College, Waterford, WI [*Library symbol Library of Congress*] (LCLS)
WWatN	Northwestern College, Watertown, WI [*Library symbol Library of Congress*] (LCLS)
WWau	Waukesha Public Library, Waukesha, WI [*Library symbol Library of Congress*] (LCLS)
WWauC	Carroll College, Waukesha, WI [*Library symbol Library of Congress*] (LCLS)
WWauH	Waukesha Memorial Hospital, Waukesha, WI [*Library symbol Library of Congress*] (LCLS)
WWauHi	Waukesha County Historical Society, Waukesha, WI [*Library symbol Library of Congress*] (LCLS)
WWauI	Waukesha County Institution, Waukesha, WI [*Library symbol Library of Congress*] (LCLS)
WWaup	Waupun Public Library, Waupun, WI [*Library symbol*] [*Library of Congress*] (LCLS)
WWaupa	Waupaca Free Public Library, Waupaca, WI [*Library symbol Library of Congress*] (LCLS)
WWauU	University of Wisconsin Center-Waukesha County, Waukesha, WI [*Library symbol Library of Congress*] (LCLS)
WWAV	Santa Rosa Beach, FL [*FM radio station call letters*]
WWAX-FM ...	Hermantown, MN [*FM radio station call letters*] (RBYB)
WWAY	Wilmington, NC [*Television station call letters*]
WWB	Waterways Freight Bureau, Washington DC [*STAC*]
WWb	West Bend Public Library, West Bend, WI [*Library symbol Library of Congress*] (LCLS)

WWB .... Wet Weight Basis [Drying] (DICI)
WWB .... Women's World Banking [Financial organization]
WWB .... Writers War Board
WWBA .... Walt Whitman Birthplace Association (EA)
WWBA .... Western Wooden Box Association (EA)
WWBA .... Who's Who among Black Americans [A publication]
WWBB .... Providence, RI [FM radio station call letters]
WWBB .... Wire-Wrapped Breadboard
WWBC .... Cocoa, FL [AM radio station call letters]
WWBD .... Bamberg, SC [FM radio station call letters]
WWBE .... Mifflinburg, PA [FM radio station call letters]
WWBF .... Bartow, FL [AM radio station call letters]
WWBF .... Woodrow Wilson Birthplace Foundation (EA)
WWBG .... Greensboro, NC [AM radio station call letters]
WWBH .... New Smyrna Beach, FL [AM radio station call letters]
WWBK .... Fredericktown, OH [FM radio station call letters]
WWBL .... Washington, IN [FM radio station call letters]
WWBN .... Tuscola, MI [FM radio station call letters]
WWBPU .... World Wide Baraca-Philathea Union (EA)
WWBR .... Trussville, AL [FM radio station call letters]
WWBT .... Richmond, VA [Television station call letters]
WWbU .... University of Wisconsin Center-Washington County, West Bend, WI
            [Library symbol Library of Congress] (LCLS)
WWBV .... Beaver Springs, PA [FM radio station call letters]
WWBX .... Bangor, ME [FM radio station call letters] (RBYB)
WWBZ .... McClellanville, SC [FM radio station call letters] (RBYB)
WWC .... Citizen's Library, Washington, PA [OCLC symbol] (OCLC)
WWC .... Walla Walla College [Washington]
WWC .... Warren Wilson College [Swannan, NC]
WWC .... Wastewater Coalition [Environmental science]
WWC .... Wavy Walled Cylinder
WWC .... Who's Who in Consulting [A publication]
WWC .... Wilkerson/Wilkinson Clearinghouse (EA)
WWC .... William Woods College [Fulton, MO]
WWC .... World's Wristwrestling Championship (EA)
WWC .... Worldways Canada Ltd. [ICAO designator] (FAAC)
WWC .... World Wide Company (MHDW)
WWC .... Woven Wire Cloth
WWCA .... Gary, IN [AM radio station call letters]
WWCA .... Western Wireless 'A' [NASDAQ symbol] (TTSB)
WWCA .... Western Wireless Corp. [NASDAQ symbol] (SAG)
WWCA .... Women's Welsh Clubs of America (EA)
WWCB .... Corry, PA [AM radio station call letters]
WWCC .... Honesdale, PA [AM radio station call letters]
WWCC .... Western Wisconsin Communications Cooperative [Independence, WI]
            [Telecommunications] (TSSD)
WWCCIS ...... World-Wide Command and Control Information System (MCD)
WWCD .... Grove City, OH [FM radio station call letters]
WWCH .... Clarion, PA [AM radio station call letters]
WWCICS ...... Wolfe-Winrow CICS/VS Command Level Proficiency Test [Computer
            science]
WWCJ-FM ... Cape May, NJ [FM radio station call letters] (BROA)
WWCK .... Flint, MI [AM radio station call letters]
WWCK-FM.... Flint, MI [FM radio station call letters]
WWCL .... Lehigh Acres, FL [AM radio station call letters]
WWCM .... Ypsilanti, MI [AM radio station call letters]
WWCN .... North Fort Myers, FL [AM radio station call letters]
WWCO .... Waterbury, CT [AM radio station call letters]
WWCP .... Clifton Park, NY [FM radio station call letters]
WWCP .... Johnstown, PA [Television station call letters]
WWCP .... Walking Wounded Collecting Post [Military]
WWCS .... Canonsburg, PA [AM radio station call letters]
WWCT .... Peoria, IL [FM radio station call letters]
WWCT Regt... Wellington, West Coast, and Taranaki Regiment [British military]
            (DMA)
WWCTU ...... World's Woman's Christian Temperance Union [Australia] (EAIO)
WWCU .... Cullowhee, NC [FM radio station call letters]
WWCW .... Bedford, PA [FM radio station call letters]
WWD .... Cape May [New Jersey] [Airport symbol] (OAG)
WWd .... Kilbourn Public Library, Wisconsin Dells, WI [Library symbol Library
            of Congress] (LCLS)
WWD .... Weather Working Days [Construction]
WWD .... Wildwood, NJ [Location identifier FAA] (FAAL)
WWD .... Windward (KSC)
WWD .... Women's Wear Daily [A publication] (WDMC)
WWDB .... Philadelphia, PA [FM radio station call letters]
WWDC .... Washington, DC [AM radio station call letters]
WWDCFC ..... World-Wide Dave Clark Fan Club [Defunct] (EAIO)
WWDC-FM.... Washington, DC [FM radio station call letters]
WWDE .... Hampton, VA [FM radio station call letters]
WWdepSN ... Saint Norbert College, West De Pere, WI [Library symbol Library of
            Congress] (LCLS)
WWDF .... Richland, MS [AM radio station call letters] (RBYB)
wwdFHEx ... Weather Working Days, Fridays, and Holidays Excluded [Shipping]
            (DS)
WWDJ .... Hackensack, NJ [AM radio station call letters]
WWDL .... Scranton, PA [FM radio station call letters]
WWDM .... Sumter, SC [FM radio station call letters]
WWDMS ...... Worldwide Data Management System
WWDMS ...... Worldwide Standard Data Management System (MCD)
W Wdr .... Warrant Wardmaster [British military] (DMA)
WWDR-AM... Murfreesboro, NC [AM radio station call letters] (BROA)
WWDS .... Muncie, IN [FM radio station call letters]
WWDSA .... Worldwide Digital System Architecture
WWDSHEX .... Weather Working Days, Sundays, and Holidays Excluded (DS)

WWDWIIWD... When We Do What It Is We Do [Computer hacker terminology]
WWDX .... St. Johns, MI [FM radio station call letters]
WWDZ .... Danville, IL [FM radio station call letters]
WWE .... Wide World of Entertainment [TV program]
WWE .... Worldwide Energy Corp. [Toronto Stock Exchange symbol] (SPSG)
WWea .... West Allis Public Library, West Allis, WI [Library symbol Library of
            Congress] (LCLS)
WWeaJ .... Janlen Enterprises, West Allis, WI [Library symbol Library of
            Congress] (LCLS)
WWeaM ...... West Allis Memorial Hospital, West Allis, WI [Library symbol Library
            of Congress] (LCLS)
WwE & Sp ... Worldwide Entertainment & Sports Cp. [Associated Press] (SAG)
WwE & S un... Worldwide Entertainment & Sports Cp. [Associated Press] (SAG)
WWEB .... Wallingford, CT [FM radio station call letters]
WWEC .... Elizabethtown, PA [FM radio station call letters]
WWEE .... Spencer, TN [AM radio station call letters]
WWEF .... 9 to 5 Working Women Education Fund [An association] (EA)
WWEF .... Working Women Education Fund (EA)
WWEG .... Mitchell, IN [FM radio station call letters]
WWEL .... London, KY [FM radio station call letters]
WWEMA ...... Water and Wastewater Equipment Manufacturers Association (EA)
WWES .... Worldwide Entertainment & Sports Cp. [NASDAQ symbol] (SAG)
WWET .... Valdosta, GA [FM radio station call letters]
WWEV .... Cumming, GA [FM radio station call letters]
WWEZ .... Trenton, TN [FM radio station call letters]
WWF .... War/Watch Foundation (EA)
WWF .... Washington Workshops Foundation (EA)
WWF .... Welded Wire Fabric [Technical drawings]
WWF .... Whole Wheat Flour (OA)
WWF .... Widowed White Female [Classified advertising]
WWF .... Wire Wrap Fixture
WWF .... Wonder Woman Foundation [Defunct] (EA)
WWF .... WorldWide Fund for Nature (EA)
WWF .... World Wildlife Fund (EA)
WWFA .... Waterside Workers' Federation of Australia
WWFA .... World Wide Fund for Nature [Australia] (EERA)
WWFC .... Westwood Financial Corp. [NASDAQ symbol] (SAG)
WWFC .... Worldwide Fair Play for Frogs Committee
WWFD .... Key West, FL [Television station call letters]
WWFE .... Miami, FL [AM radio station call letters]
WWFG .... Ocean City, MD [FM radio station call letters]
WWFH-FM ... Freeland, PA [FM radio station call letters] (RBYB)
WWFI .... World Wildlife Fund International [Later, Worldwide Fund for
            Nature] (EAIO)
WWFL-AM ... Clermont, FL [AM radio station call letters] (BROA)
WWFM .... Trenton, NJ [FM radio station call letters]
WWFN .... Lake City, SC [FM radio station call letters]
WWFN .... World Wide Fund for Nature [Australia]
WWFNA ...... World Wide Fund for Nature Australia
WWFO .... Lafayette, FL [FM radio station call letters] (RBYB)
WWFR .... Okeechobee, FL [FM radio station call letters]
WWFS .... West Wales Field Society [British]
WWF-US ..... World Wildlife Fund - United States (EA)
WWFX .... Belfast, ME [FM radio station call letters]
WWFY-FM ... Hague, NY [FM radio station call letters] (BROA)
WWG .... HSIA [Halogenated Solvent Industry Alliance] Water Work Group
            [Defunct] (EA)
WWG .... Warhead Working Group [Military]
WWG .... Warrington Wire Gauge (BARN)
WWg .... Weather Wing [Air Force] (AFM)
WWG .... Wiederwerbgesetz (BJA)
WWGA .... Georgiana, AL [FM radio station call letters]
WWGA .... War Widows Guild of Australia
WWGB-AM ... Indian Head, MD [AM radio station call letters] (BROA)
WWGC .... Carrollton, GA [FM radio station call letters]
WWGF-FM ... Donalsonville, GA [FM radio station call letters] (BROA)
WWGL .... Lexington, TN [FM radio station call letters]
WWGM .... Alamo, TN [FM radio station call letters]
WWGN .... Ottawa, IL [FM radio station call letters]
WWGO-FM... Neoga, IL [FM radio station call letters] (RBYB)
WWGP .... Sanford, NC [AM radio station call letters]
WWGR .... Fort Myers, FL [FM radio station call letters]
WWGR .... Weil's Wyoming Government Register [A publication] (AAGC)
WWGS .... Tifton, GA [AM radio station call letters]
WWGT .... Vergennes, VT [FM radio station call letters]
WWGZ .... Lapeer, MI [FM radio station call letters]
W/WH .... With/Warhead [Nuclear]
WWH .... Women Working Home [A publication]
WWH .... W. W. Harrington's Reports [31-39 Delaware] [A publication] (DLA)
WWHA .... Welsh Women's Hockey Association (DBA)
WWHA .... Who's Who among Hispanic Americans [A publication]
WWHB .... Hampton Bays, NY [FM radio station call letters]
WWHC .... Oakland, MD [FM radio station call letters] (RBYB)
WWHE .... Woman Who Has Everything
WWHI .... Muncie, IN [FM radio station call letters]
WWhiwSD ... Whitewater Unified School District, Joint Number One, Whitewater,
            WI [Library symbol Library of Congress] (LCLS)
WWhiwU...... University of Wisconsin-Whitewater, Whitewater, WI [Library symbol
            Library of Congress] (LCLS)
WWHK .... Greenville, KY [FM radio station call letters]
WWHL .... Waterwheel
WWHN .... Joliet, IL [AM radio station call letters]
WWHO .... Chillicothe, OH [Television station call letters]
WWHP-FM ... Farmer City, IL [FM radio station call letters] (RBYB)
WWHR .... Bowling Green, KY [FM radio station call letters]

WWHRAWAC... World Wide Horse Registry for the American White and the American Creme (EA)
WWHS......... Hampden-Sydney, VA [*FM radio station call letters*]
WWHS......... Western World Haiku Society [*Defunct*] (EA)
WWHT-FM... Syracuse, NY [*FM radio station call letters*] (RBYB)
WWI............ Weight Watchers International [*Commercial firm*] (EA)
WWI............ Whirlwind I
WWI............ Working Women's Institute [*Defunct*] (EA)
WWI............ World War I
WWI............ World Watch Institute (EERA)
WWIA.......... Palm Bay, FL [*FM radio station call letters*]
WWIAC........ Wisconsin Women's Intercollegiate Athletic Conference (PSS)
WWI AERO... World War I Aeroplanes (EA)
WWIB.......... Ladysmith, WI [*FM radio station call letters*]
WWIBX........ Mgn. Stanley D. Witter Worldwide Tr. Cl.B [*Mutual fund ticker symbol*] (SG)
WWIC.......... Scottsboro, AL [*AM radio station call letters*]
WWiC.......... Winnebago County Hospital, Winnebago, WI [*Library symbol Library of Congress*] (LCLS)
WWICS........ Woodrow Wilson International Center for Scholars (EA)
WWID.......... Water & Wastewater Division (ACII)
WWidF......... White Widowed Female (STED)
WWidM........ White Widowed Male (STED)
WWIH.......... High Point, NC [*FM radio station call letters*]
WWII........... Shiremanstown, PA [*AM radio station call letters*]
WWII........... Whirlwind II (SAA)
WWII........... World War II
WWIIHSLB... World War II Honorable Service Lapel Button (AFM)
WWIII.......... World War III
WWIIVM...... World War II Victory Medal [*Military decoration*]
WWil........... Barrett Memorial Library, Williams Bay, WI [*Library symbol Library of Congress*] (LCLS)
WWIL........... Wilmington, NC [*AM radio station call letters*]
WWIL-FM.... Wilmington, NC [*FM radio station call letters*] (RBYB)
WWIMS....... Worldwide Indicators and Monitoring System (DOMA)
WWIMS....... Worldwide Integrated Management of Subsistence [*Military*] (NVT)
WWIN.......... Baltimore, MD [*AM radio station call letters*]
WWIN.......... Glen Burnie, MD [*FM radio station call letters*]
WWIO.......... Brunswick, GA [*FM radio station call letters*]
WWIO.......... Worldwide Inventory Objective (AABC)
WWiP.......... Park View Health Center, Winnebago, WI [*Library symbol Library of Congress*] (LCLS)
WWIP.......... Wabash, IN [*FM radio station call letters*]
WWIQ.......... Gray, GA [*FM radio station call letters*]
WWIS.......... Black River Falls, WI [*AM radio station call letters*]
WWiS.......... Winnebago State Hospital, Winnebago, WI [*Library symbol Library of Congress*] (LCLS)
WWIS.......... Worldwide Information Services
WWIS-FM.... Black River Falls, WI [*FM radio station call letters*]
WWIT.......... Canton, NC [*AM radio station call letters*]
WWIT.......... Who's Who in the Theatre [*A publication*]
WWITC........ Worldwide Improved Technical Control (MCD)
WWIVM....... World War I Victory Medal [*Military decoration*]
WWIZ.......... Mercer, PA [*FM radio station call letters*]
WWJ............ Detroit, MI [*AM radio station call letters*]
WWJB.......... Brooksville, FL [*AM radio station call letters*]
WWJC.......... Duluth, MN [*AM radio station call letters*]
WWJCC........ Worldwide Joint Coordinator Center [*NATO*] (NATG)
WWJD.......... What Would Jesus Do
WWJM.......... New Lexington, OH [*FM radio station call letters*]
WWJO.......... St. Cloud, MN [*FM radio station call letters*]
WWJQ.......... Zeeland, MI [*AM radio station call letters*]
WWJR.......... Sheboygan, WI [*FM radio station call letters*]
WWJ-TV...... Detroit, MI [*Television station call letters*] (RBYB)
WWJY.......... Crown Point, IN [*FM radio station call letters*]
WWJZ.......... Mount Holly, NJ [*AM radio station call letters*]
wwk............ Westwork (VRA)
WWK........... Wewak [*Papua New Guinea*] [*Airport symbol*] (OAG)
WWK........... Wilson-Westphal-Konoyalor [*Syndrome*] [*Medicine*] (DB)
WWKA......... Orlando, FL [*FM radio station call letters*]
WWKB......... Buffalo, NY [*AM radio station call letters*]
WWKC......... Caldwell, OH [*FM radio station call letters*]
WWKC......... White Wolf-Kern Canyon [*Geological fault*]
WWKF......... Fulton, KY [*FM radio station call letters*]
WWKI.......... Kokomo, IN [*FM radio station call letters*]
WWKJ-FM... Mashpee, MA [*FM radio station call letters*] (RBYB)
WWKL......... Harrisburg, PA [*FM radio station call letters*]
WWKN-AM... Battle Creek, MI [*AM radio station call letters*] (RBYB)
WWKQ......... Kissimmee, FL [*FM radio station call letters*] (RBYB)
WWKS-FM... Cruz Bay, VI [*FM radio station call letters*] (RBYB)
WWKT......... Kingstree, SC [*FM radio station call letters*]
WWKX......... Woonsocket, RI [*FM radio station call letters*]
WWKY......... Louisville, KY [*AM radio station call letters*]
WWKZ......... New Albany, MS [*FM radio station call letters*]
WWL........... New Orleans, LA [*AM radio station call letters*]
WWL2M...... Women Who Love Too Much [*Title of book by Robin Norwood*]
WWLA......... Lewiston, ME [*Television station call letters*]
WWLC-FM... Balsam Lake, WI [*FM radio station call letters*] (RBYB)
WWLD-FM... Tallahassee, FL [*FM radio station call letters*] (RBYB)
WWLE-AM... Cornwall, NY [*AM radio station call letters*] (BROA)
WWLF......... Copenhagen, NY [*FM radio station call letters*]
WWLF......... Hazleton, PA [*Television station call letters*]
WWLG......... Baltimore, MD [*AM radio station call letters*]
WWLI.......... Providence, RI [*FM radio station call letters*]
WWLI.......... Whitewing Labs [*NASDAQ symbol*] (TTSB)
WWLI.......... Whitewing Labs, Inc. [*NASDAQ symbol*] (SAG)
WWLIS........ Woodmen of the World Life Insurance Society (EA)
WWLIW....... Whitewing Labs Wrrt [*NASDAQ symbol*] (TTSB)
WWLK......... Eddyville, KY [*AM radio station call letters*]
WWLO......... Gainesville, FL [*AM radio station call letters*]
WWLODS..... Wire and Wire-Like Object Detection System [*Helicopter*] (MCD)
WWLP......... Springfield, MA [*Television station call letters*]
WWLR......... Lyndonville, VT [*FM radio station call letters*]
WWLS......... Moore, OK [*AM radio station call letters*]
WWLT......... Manchester, KY [*FM radio station call letters*]
WWLTM...... Women Who Love Too Much [*Title of book by Robin Norwood*]
WWL-TV..... New Orleans, LA [*Television station call letters*]
WWLX......... Lawrenceburg, TN [*AM radio station call letters*]
WWLZ-AM... Horseheads, NY [*AM radio station call letters*] (BROA)
WWM.......... Weizsaecker-Williams Method [*Physics*]
WWM.......... Welded Wire Matrix
WWM.......... Widowed White Male [*Classified advertising*]
WWM.......... Wire Wrap Machine
WWM.......... World-Wide Missions (EA)
WWM.......... Worldwide Monitor [*Vancouver Stock Exchange symbol*]
WWMB........ Florence, SC [*FM radio station call letters*]
WWMC........ Lynchburg, VA [*FM radio station call letters*]
WWMCCS.... Worldwide Military Command and Communications System [*Pronounced "wimex"*]
WWMCCS.... Worldwide Military Command and Control System [*DoD*]
WWMD........ Hagerstown, MD [*FM radio station call letters*]
WWME........ Worldwide Marriage Encounter (EA)
WWMG........ Shelby, NC [*FM radio station call letters*]
WWMJ......... Ellsworth, ME [*FM radio station call letters*]
WWML......... Wood, Wire, and Metal Lathers' International Union [*Later, UBC*] (EA)
WWMMP..... Western Wood Moulding and Millwork Producers [*Later, WMMPA*] (EA)
WWMMRD... Water and Waste Management Monitoring Research Division [*Environmental Protection Agency*] (EPA)
WWMO........ Eden, NC [*AM radio station call letters*]
WWMP........ Western Wood Moulding Producers [*Later, WMMPA*] (EA)
WWMR........ Rumford, ME [*FM radio station call letters*]
WWMS........ Oxford, MS [*FM radio station call letters*]
WWMS........ Waste Water Management System (NAKS)
WWMS........ Water and Waste Management Staff [*Environmental Protection Agency*] (GFGA)
WWMS........ Water and Waste Management Subsystem [*NASA*] (KSC)
W/WMS....... Water/Waste Management System (NAKS)
WWMT........ Kalamazoo, MI [*Television station call letters*]
WWMV........ Winter Wheat (Russian) Mosaic Virus [*Plant pathology*]
WWMX........ Baltimore, MD [*FM radio station call letters*]
WWN.......... Washington Women's Network [*Defunct*] (EA)
WWN.......... With Winch
WWNC........ Asheville, NC [*AM radio station call letters*]
WWNFF...... Woodrow Wilson National Fellowship Foundation (EA)
WWNH........ Madbury, NH [*AM radio station call letters*]
WWNH........ War Will Never Happen [*Philosophy attributed to the Defense Department by former Deputy Assistant Secretary of Defense John F. Ahearne*] [*1987*]
WWNJ......... Dover Township, NJ [*FM radio station call letters*]
WWNK........ Cincinnati, OH [*FM radio station call letters*]
WWNN........ Pompano Beach, FL [*AM radio station call letters*]
WWNO........ New Orleans, LA [*FM radio station call letters*]
WWNR........ Beckley, WV [*AM radio station call letters*]
WWNS........ Statesboro, GA [*AM radio station call letters*]
WWNS........ World Wide News Service (BJA)
WWNSS...... Worldwide Network of Standard Seismograph [*Stations*]
WWNSS...... Worldwide Network of Standard Seismograph Stations (PDAA)
WWNT........ Dothan, AL [*AM radio station call letters*]
WWNW....... New Wilmington, PA [*FM radio station call letters*]
WWNWS..... World-Wide Navigational Warning Service [*Marine science*] (OSRA)
WWNWS..... World Wide Navigational Weather Warning Service
WWNY........ Carthage, NY [*Television station call letters*]
WWNZ........ Orlando, FL [*AM radio station call letters*]
WWO.......... Warrant Writer Officer [*British military*] (DMA)
WW/O........ Widow Of [*Genealogy*]
WWO.......... Wing Warrant Officer [*RAF*] [*British*]
WWOCAR.... Western Wayne Oakland County Association of Realtors [*Michigan*]
WWOD........ Lynchburg, VA [*FM radio station call letters*]
WWOF........ Camp Lejeune, NC [*AM radio station call letters*]
WWOF........ Willing Workers for Organic Farms [*Australia*]
WWOG........ Cookeville, TN [*FM radio station call letters*]
WWOJ......... Avon Park, FL [*FM radio station call letters*]
WWOL........ Forest City, NC [*AM radio station call letters*]
WWON........ Fenton, MI [*AM radio station call letters*]
WWOOF...... Working Weekends on Organic Farms [*British*] [*An association*] (DBA)
WWooH....... Howard Young Medical Center, Woodruff, WI [*Library symbol Library of Congress*] (LCLS)
WWOR........ Secaucus, NJ [*Television station call letters*]
WWoVA....... United States Veterans Administration Hospital, Wood, WI [*Library symbol Library of Congress*] (LCLS)
WWOW....... Conneaut, OH [*AM radio station call letters*]
WWOZ........ New Orleans, LA [*FM radio station call letters*]
WWP.......... Walden Woods Project [*An association*] (EA)
WWP.......... Washington Water Power Co. [*NYSE symbol*] (SPSG)
WWP.......... Washington Water Pwr [*NYSE symbol*] (TTSB)
WWP.......... Watchable Wildlife Program
WWP.......... Water Wall (Peripheral Jet) (AAG)

WWP .... Weather Wing Pamphlet [*Air Force*] (MCD)
WWP .... Wire Wrap Panels (MCD)
WWP .... Workers World Party [*Political party*] (EA)
WWP .... Working Water Pressure
WWP .... World Weather Program [*National Science Foundation*]
WWP .... World Wide Peace (BUAC)
WWPA .... Western Water Polo Association (PSS)
WWPA .... Western Wood Products Association [*Australia*]
WWPA .... Williamsport, PA [*AM radio station call letters*]
WWPA .... Woven Wire Products Association (EA)
WWPB .... Hagerstown, MD [*Television station call letters*]
WWPB .... Worldwide Women Professional Bowlers (EA)
WWpC .... Central State Hospital, Waupun, WI [*Library symbol Library of Congress*] (LCLS)
WWPG .... Tuscaloosa, AL [*AM radio station call letters*]
WWPG .... Widows' War Pensions and Gratuities [*British*]
WWPH .... Princeton Junction, NJ [*FM radio station call letters*]
WWPLS ...... World Wide Pet Lovers Society [*Defunct*] (EA)
WWPMU ...... World-Wide Prayer and Missionary Union (EA)
WWPN .... Westernport, MD [*FM radio station call letters*]
WWPP .... World Women Parliamentarians for Peace (BUAC)
WWPR .... Bradenton, FL [*AM radio station call letters*] (RBYB)
W/WPR .... Windshield Wiper [*Automotive engineering*]
WWPSA ...... Western World Pet Supply Association (EA)
WWPSA ...... World Wide Pet Supply Association (NTPA)
WWPT .... Westport, CT [*FM radio station call letters*]
WWPT .... Wet-Weather Parka and Trousers [*Army*] (INF)
WWPV .... Colchester, VT [*FM radio station call letters*]
WWPX .... Martinsburg, WV [*Television station call letters*] (BROA)
WWQM .... Middleton, WI [*FM radio station call letters*]
WWQQ .... Wilmington, NC [*FM radio station call letters*]
WWr .... McMillan Memorial Library, Wisconsin Rapids, WI [*Library symbol Library of Congress*] (LCLS)
WWR .... Washington Weekly Report [*Independent Bankers Association of America*] [*A publication*]
WWR .... Washington Western [*AAR code*]
W/wr .... Watts per Steradian (IDOE)
WWR .... Western Warner Oils [*Vancouver Stock Exchange symbol*]
WWR .... Western Weekly Reports [*Carswell Co. Ltd.*] [*Canada Information service or system*] (CRD)
WWR .... Widower [*Genealogy*]
WWR .... Wire-Wound Resistor
WWR .... Wisconsin Rapids, McMillan Library, Wisconsin Rapids, WI [*OCLC symbol*] (OCLC)
WWR .... Woodill Wildfire Registry (EA)
WWR .... Woodward, OK [*Location identifier FAA*] (FAAL)
WWRC .... Washington, DC [*AM radio station call letters*]
WWRC .... Wyoming Water Research Center [*University of Wyoming*] [*Research center*] (RCD)
WWRD .... Brunswick, GA [*FM radio station call letters*] (RBYB)
WWREA ...... Wire & Wire Rope Employers' Association (BUAC)
WWREC ...... Western Washington Research and Extension Center [*Washington State University*] [*Research center*] (RCD)
WWRF .... Who's Who Resource File [*Minority Business Development Agency*] [*Database*]
WW/RGS ...... Wind Shear Warning / Recovery Guidance System (DA)
WWRI .... Worldwide Mobile Communications Routing Index (DNAB)
WWRK .... Elberton, GA [*AM radio station call letters*]
WWRK-FM ... Elberton, GA [*FM radio station call letters*]
WWRL .... New York, NY [*AM radio station call letters*]
WWRM .... Tampa, FL [*FM radio station call letters*]
WWR (NS) ... Western Weekly Reports, New Series [*Canada*] [*A publication*] (DLA)
WWRO .... Pensacola, FL [*FM radio station call letters*]
WWRQ .... Valdosta, GA [*FM radio station call letters*]
WWRR-FM ... Brunswick, GA [*FM radio station call letters*] (RBYB)
WWRS .... Mayville, WI [*Television station call letters*]
WWRS .... Wash-Water Recovery System [*in a spacecraft*] [*NASA*]
WWRT .... Scotland Neck, NC [*FM radio station call letters*]
WWRV .... New York, NY [*AM radio station call letters*]
WWRX .... Westerly, RI [*FM radio station call letters*]
WWRZ-FM ... Arcadia, FL [*FM radio station call letters*] (RBYB)
WWS .... Walker Wingsail Systems [*Shipbuilding*] [*British*]
WWS .... Wasawings AB [*Finland ICAO designator*] (FAAC)
WWS .... Water and Waste Subsystem [*Aerospace*] (MCD)
WWS .... Water Wall (Side Skegs) (AAG)
WWs .... Wausau Public Library, Wausau, WI [*Library symbol Library of Congress*] (LCLS)
WW(S) .... Well Water (System) [*Nuclear energy*] (NRCH)
WWS .... Wild Weasel Squadron [*Air Force*]
WWS .... Wind and Watermill Section [*of the Society for the Protection of Ancient Buildings*] (EA)
WWS .... Woman's Workshop [*Defunct*] (EA)
WWS .... Women's Welfare Service [*Defunct*] (EA)
WWS .... Working with Shortages (MCD)
WWS .... World Weather System
WWS .... World Wide Minerals Ltd. [*Toronto Stock Exchange symbol Vancouver Stock Exchange symbol*]
WWSA .... Walt Whitman Society of America [*Defunct*] (EA)
WWSA .... Who's Who in Saudi Arabia [*A publication*]
WWSA .... Women's War Service Auxiliary [*British military*] (DMA)
WWSB .... Sarasota, FL [*Television station call letters*]
WWSC .... Glens Falls, NY [*AM radio station call letters*]
WWSD .... Quincy, FL [*AM radio station call letters*]
WWSD .... Women's War Savings Division
WWSE .... Jamestown, NY [*FM radio station call letters*]

WWSF .... Andalusia, AL [*FM radio station call letters*] (RBYB)
WWSF .... World-Wide Stroke Foundation (EA)
WWSG .... Sylvester, GA [*FM radio station call letters*]
WWSH .... Pittston, PA [*FM radio station call letters*]
WWSJ .... St. Johns, MI [*AM radio station call letters*]
WWSK .... Mullins, SC [*FM radio station call letters*] (RBYB)
WWSL .... Philadelphia, MS [*FM radio station call letters*]
WWSM .... Annville-Cleona, PA [*AM radio station call letters*]
WWSMA ...... Wood Wool Slab Manufacturers Association [*British*] (DBA)
WWsMC ...... Marathon Health Care Center, Wausau, WI [*Library symbol Library of Congress*] (LCLS)
WWSN .... Charlotte, NC [*FM radio station call letters*] (RBYB)
WWSN .... Worldwide Seismology Net [*National Bureau of Standards*]
WWSP .... Stevens Point, WI [*FM radio station call letters*]
WWSP .... Winter Weddell Sea Project [*Marine science*] (OSRA)
WWSP .... Worldwide Surveillance Program [*Military*] (NG)
WWSR .... St. Albans, VT [*AM radio station call letters*]
WWSRA ...... Western Winter Sports Representatives Association (EA)
WWSSB ...... World-Wide Software Support Branch (MCD)
WWSSN ...... Worldwide Standardized Seismograph Network [*US Geological Survey*]
WWSSN ...... World Wide Standard Seismic Network (BUAC)
WWSSN ...... World-Wide Standard Seismograph Network [*Earthquake detection*]
WWST .... Kams, TN [*FM radio station call letters*]
WWSU .... Dayton, OH [*FM radio station call letters*]
WWSU .... World Water Ski Union [*See also UMSN*] [*Montreux, Switzerland*] (EAIO)
WWSVA ...... Worldwide Secure Voice Architecture (MCD)
WWSVCS .... World-Wide Secure Voice Communications System (MCD)
WWSVCS .... World-Wide Secure Voice Conference System (MCD)
WWSW .... Pittsburgh, PA [*AM radio station call letters*]
WWsW .... Wausau Hospitals, Inc., Wausau, WI [*Library symbol Library of Congress*] (LCLS)
WWSW-FM ... Pittsburgh, PA [*FM radio station call letters*]
WWsWV ...... Wisconsin Valley Library Service, Wausau, WI [*Library symbol Library of Congress*] (LCLS)
WWSY-FM ... Sharpsville, PA [*FM radio station call letters*] (RBYB)
WWT .... Newtok [*Alaska*] [*Airport symbol*] (OAG)
WWT .... Newtok, AK [*Location identifier FAA*] (FAAL)
WWT .... Who's Who in Technology [*A publication*]
WWT .... Wildfowl & Wetlands Trust (BUAC)
WWTA .... Marion, MA [*FM radio station call letters*]
WWTA .... Welsh Weight Training Association (BUAC)
WWTA .... Woollen and Worsted Trades Association [*British*] (BI)
WWTA .... World Welly-Throwing Association (BUAC)
WWTC .... Minneapolis, MN [*AM radio station call letters*]
WWTCA ...... World War Tank Corps Association (EA)
WWTCIP ...... Worldwide Technical Control Improvement Program (MCD)
WWTE .... Lincoln, IL [*FM radio station call letters*]
WWTF .... Wastewater Treatment Facility
WWTI .... Watertown, NY [*Television station call letters*]
WWTK .... Lake Placid, FL [*AM radio station call letters*]
WWTK .... Weitek Corp. [*NASDAQ symbol*] (CTT)
WWTL .... Walkersville, MD [*AM radio station call letters*]
WWTM .... Worcester, MA [*AM radio station call letters*]
WWTN .... Manchester, TN [*FM radio station call letters*]
WWTNC ...... West Wales Trust for Nature Conservation (BUAC)
WWTO .... La Salle, IL [*Television station call letters*]
WWTP .... Waste Water Treatment Plant [*Also, WTP*]
WWTR .... Western Water [*NASDAQ symbol*] (TTSB)
WWTR .... Western Water Co. [*NASDAQ symbol*] (SAG)
WWTS .... Waste Water Treatment System
WWTSA ...... World War Two Studies Association (NTPA)
WWTT .... Worldwide Tapetalk [*An association*] (EA)
WWTV .... Cadillac, MI [*Television station call letters*]
WWU .... Water/Wastewater Utilities [*Environmental science*]
WWU .... Western Washington University
WWU .... Wire Workers' Union (BUAC)
WWUC .... Union City, TN [*FM radio station call letters*]
WWUF .... Waycross, GA [*FM radio station call letters*]
WWUH .... West Hartford, CT [*FM radio station call letters*]
WWUI .... Working Women's United Institute [*Later, WWI*] (EA)
WWUN .... Clarksdale, MS [*FM radio station call letters*]
WWUP .... Sault Ste. Marie, MI [*Television station call letters*]
WWUS .... Big Pine Key, FL [*FM radio station call letters*]
WWV .... Walla Walla Valley Railway Co. [*AAR code*]
WWV .... Wheeling College, Wheeling, WV [*OCLC symbol*] (OCLC)
WWV .... World Wide Time [*National Bureau of Standards call letters*] (MUGU)
WWV .... World Wide Vermiculture [*An association*] (EA)
WWVA .... Wheeling, WV [*AM radio station call letters*]
WWVH .... World Wide Time Hawaii [*National Bureau of Standards call letters*] (MUGU)
WWVR .... West Terre Haute, IN [*FM radio station call letters*]
WWVR .... Wire-Wound Variable Resistor
WWVU .... Morgantown, WV [*FM radio station call letters*]
WWVY-FM ... Hampton Bays, NY [*FM radio station call letters*] (BROA)
WWVZ-FM ... Braddock Heights, MD [*FM radio station call letters*] (RBYB)
WWW .... Who Was Who [*A publication*]
WWW .... [*The*] Who, What, or Where Game [*Also, 3W's*] [*Television show*]
WWW .... Wide Whitewall Tire [*Automotive accessory*]
WWW .... Wolverine World Wide [*NYSE symbol*] (TTSB)
WWW .... Wolverine World Wide, Inc. [*NYSE symbol*] (SPSG)
WWW .... Women Welcome Women [*An association*] (BUAC)
WWW .... World Weather Watch [*World Meteorological Organization*] [*Databank*] (IID)

WWW .... World Wide Wait [*Computer science*]
WWW .... Worldwide Warranty [*Canon USA, Inc.*]
WWW .... World Wide Web [*Software*] [*Computer science*] (EERA)
WWWA-FM... Winslow, ME [*FM radio station call letters*] (BROA)
WWWB .... Greensboro, NC [*AM radio station call letters*]
WWWC .... Wilkesboro, NC [*AM radio station call letters*]
WWWC .... World without War Council (EA)
WWWCR ...... World Wide White and Creme Horse Registry (EA)
WWWD-FM... Punta Rassa, FL [*FM radio station call letters*] (BROA)
WWWE .... Cleveland, OH [*AM radio station call letters*]
WWWF .... Worldwide Wrestling Federation [*Later, WWF*]
WWWG .... Rochester, NY [*AM radio station call letters*]
WWWI .... Baxter, MN [*AM radio station call letters*]
WWWI .... Widows of World War I (EA)
WWWJ .... Who's Who in World Jewry [*A publication*] (BJA)
WWWK .... Ellenville, NY [*AM radio station call letters*]
WWWM .... Sylvania, OH [*FM radio station call letters*]
WWWN .... Vienna, GA [*AM radio station call letters*]
WWWO .... Hartford City, IN [*FM radio station call letters*]
WWWQ .... Glasgow, KY [*FM radio station call letters*]
WWWR .... Roanoke, VA [*AM radio station call letters*]
WWWS .... Buffalo, NY [*AM radio station call letters*]
WWWT .... Randolph, VT [*AM radio station call letters*]
WWWTTUTWTU... We Won't Write to Them until They Write to Us [*A servicemen's club*]
WWWV .... Charlottesville, VA [*FM radio station call letters*]
WWWV .... Women World War Veterans (EA)
WWWW .... Detroit, MI [*FM radio station call letters*]
WWWW .... Who's Who in the World of Women [*Australia A publication*]
WWWW .... Women Who Want to be Women [*An association*] (NTCM)
WWWY .... Columbus, IN [*FM radio station call letters*]
WWWZ .... Summerville, SC [*FM radio station call letters*]
WWX .... Warm White Deluxe (DAC)
WWX .... World Wide Exchange [*Commercial firm*] (EA)
WWXL .... Manchester, KY [*AM radio station call letters*]
WWXM .... Georgetown, SC [*FM radio station call letters*]
WWXQ .... Trinity, AL [*FM radio station call letters*] (RBYB)
WWXY-FM... Briarcliff Manor, NY [*FM radio station call letters*] (BROA)
WWY .... Warwickshire and Worcestershire Yeomanry [*British military*] (DMA)
WWY .... West Wyalong [*Australia Airport symbol*] (OAG)
WWY .... Wrigley [*Wm.*] Jr. Co. [*NYSE symbol*] (SPSG)
WWY .... Wrigley,(Wm) Jr [*NYSE symbol*] (TTSB)
WWYC .... Winchester, KY [*FM radio station call letters*]
WWYN .... McKenzie, TN [*FM radio station call letters*]
WWYO .... Pineville, WV [*AM radio station call letters*]
WWYZ .... Waterbury, CT [*FM radio station call letters*]
WWZ .... WIllow Resources Ltd. [*Vancouver Stock Exchange symbol*]
WWZD .... New Albany, MS [*FM radio station call letters*]
WWZN .... Pine Hills, FL [*FM radio station call letters*] (RBYB)
WWZQ .... Aberdeen, MS [*AM radio station call letters*]
WWZQ-FM... Aberdeen, MS [*FM radio station call letters*]
WWZZ-FM ... Waldorf, MD [*FM radio station call letters*] (RBYB)
WX .... Ansett Airlines of New South Wales [*ICAO designator*] (AD)
WX .... Ansett Express [*Airport symbol*]
WX .... Simplex Working [*Telecommunications*] (ADDR)
WX .... Wax
WX .... Wax (VRA)
WX .... Weather
WX .... Weather at Altitude [*Aviation*] (FAAC)
WX .... Weather Report (WDMC)
WX .... Westinghouse Elec [*NYSE symbol*] (TTSB)
WX .... Westinghouse Electric Corp. [*Wall Street slang name: "Wex"*] [*NYSE symbol*] (SPSG)
WX .... Wireless [*Communications*]
WX .... Women's Extra [*Size*]
WX .... Wound of Exit [*Medicine*] (STED)
WXAB .... McLain, MS [*FM radio station call letters*]
WXAC .... Reading, PA [*FM radio station call letters*]
WXAG .... Athens, GA [*AM radio station call letters*] (RBYB)
WXAH .... Orange Beach, AL [*FM radio station call letters*]
WXAJ .... Hillsboro, IL [*FM radio station call letters*]
WXAL .... Demopolis, AL [*AM radio station call letters*]
WXAM .... Buffalo, KY [*AM radio station call letters*]
WX-AM .... Weather and Air Movements (SAA)
WXAN .... Ava, IL [*FM radio station call letters*]
WxB .... Wax Bite [*Dentistry*]
WXBA .... Brentwood, NY [*FM radio station call letters*]
WXBB .... Kittery, ME [*FM radio station call letters*]
WXBC .... Hardinsburg, KY [*FM radio station call letters*]
WXBD .... Biloxi, MS [*AM radio station call letters*]
WXBK-AM.... Albertville, AL [*AM radio station call letters*] (BROA)
WXBM .... Milton, FL [*AM radio station call letters*]
WXBP-FM ... Hampton, NH [*FM radio station call letters*] (BROA)
WXBQ .... Bristol, VA [*AM radio station call letters*]
WXBQ-FM ... Bristol, TN [*FM radio station call letters*]
WXBX .... Rural Retreat, VA [*FM radio station call letters*]
WXC .... Westinghouse Canada, Inc. [*Toronto Stock Exchange symbol*]
WXCC .... Williamson, WV [*FM radio station call letters*]
WXCD-FM.... Chicago, IL [*FM radio station call letters*] (BROA)
WXCE .... Amery, WI [*AM radio station call letters*]
WXCF .... Clifton Forge, VA [*AM radio station call letters*]
WXCF-FM.... Clifton Forge, VA [*FM radio station call letters*]
WXCH .... Versailles, IN [*FM radio station call letters*]
WXCI .... Danbury, CT [*FM radio station call letters*]
WXCL .... Pekin, IL [*FM radio station call letters*]

WXCM-FM ... Hawesville, KY [*FM radio station call letters*] (BROA)
WXCO .... Wausau, WI [*AM radio station call letters*]
WXCON .... Weather Reconnaissance Flight Pilot Report [*Aviation*] (FAAC)
WXCR-FM.... Ballston Spa, NY [*FM radio station call letters*] (RBYB)
WXCT .... Hamden, CT [*AM radio station call letters*]
WXCV .... Homosassa Springs, FL [*FM radio station call letters*]
WXCY .... Havre de Grace, MD [*FM radio station call letters*]
WXD .... Meteorological RADAR Station [*ITU designation*] (CET)
WXD .... Waxed
WXD .... Westrex Development Corp. [*Vancouver Stock Exchange symbol*]
WXDG-FM.... Detroit, MI [*FM radio station call letters*] (BROA)
WXDJ .... Homestead, FL [*FM radio station call letters*]
WXDU .... Durham, NC [*FM radio station call letters*]
WXDX .... Beaver Falls, PA [*FM radio station call letters*] (RBYB)
WXEC .... Nekoosa, WI [*FM radio station call letters*]
WXEE .... Welch, WV [*AM radio station call letters*]
WXEF .... Effingham, IL [*FM radio station call letters*]
WXEG .... Beavercreek, OH [*FM radio station call letters*] (RBYB)
WXEL .... West Palm Beach, FL [*FM radio station call letters*]
WXEL-TV .... West Palm Beach, FL [*Television station call letters*]
WXEM .... Buford, GA [*AM radio station call letters*]
WXER .... Plymouth, WI [*FM radio station call letters*]
WXET-FM .... Arcola, IL [*FM radio station call letters*] (BROA)
WXEW .... Yabucoa, PR [*AM radio station call letters*]
WXEX-FM .... Wakefield-Peacedale, RI [*FM radio station call letters*] (BROA)
WXEZ .... Yorktown, VA [*FM radio station call letters*]
WXFL .... Florence, AL [*FM radio station call letters*]
WXFM .... Mt. Zion, IL [*FM radio station call letters*]
WXFN-AM ... Muncie, IN [*AM radio station call letters*] (BROA)
WXFX .... Prattville, AL [*FM radio station call letters*]
WXG .... Warning (MUGU)
WXGA .... Waycross, GA [*Television station call letters*]
WXGC .... Milledgeville, GA [*FM radio station call letters*]
WXGI .... Richmond, VA [*AM radio station call letters*]
WXGJ-FM .... Apalachicola, FL [*FM radio station call letters*] (RBYB)
WXGL .... Topsham, ME [*FM radio station call letters*]
WXGM .... Gloucester, VA [*AM radio station call letters*]
WXGM-FM... Gloucester, VA [*FM radio station call letters*]
WXGN-FM.... Egg Harbor Township, NJ [*FM radio station call letters*] (RBYB)
WXGO-AM ... Madison, IN [*AM radio station call letters*] (RBYB)
WXHB-FM.... Richton, MS [*FM radio station call letters*] (BROA)
WXHC .... Homer, NY [*FM radio station call letters*]
WXHD .... Mt. Hope, NY [*FM radio station call letters*]
WXHL .... Christiana, DE [*FM radio station call letters*]
WXHT-FM .... York Center, ME [*FM radio station call letters*] (RBYB)
WXIA .... Atlanta, GA [*Television station call letters*]
WXIC .... Waverly, OH [*AM radio station call letters*]
WXID .... Mayfield, KY [*FM radio station call letters*]
WXII .... Winston-Salem, NC [*Television station call letters*]
WXIK-FM .... Jackson, MI [*FM radio station call letters*] (BROA)
WXIL .... Parkersburg, WV [*FM radio station call letters*]
WXILI .... Wuxi Institute of Light Industry (BUAC)
WXIN .... Indianapolis, IN [*Television station call letters*]
WXIR .... Plainfield, IN [*FM radio station call letters*]
WXIS .... Erwin, TN [*FM radio station call letters*]
WXIT-AM .... Blowing Rock, NC [*AM radio station call letters*] (RBYB)
WXIX .... Newport, KY [*Television station call letters*]
WXIZ .... Waverly, OH [*FM radio station call letters*]
WXJB .... Harrogate, TN [*FM radio station call letters*]
WXJC .... Crystal River, FL [*FM radio station call letters*]
WXJJ .... Mt. Vernon, KY [*FM radio station call letters*]
WXJM .... Harrisonburg, VA [*FM radio station call letters*]
WXJN .... Lewes, DE [*FM radio station call letters*]
WXJX .... Washington, PA [*FM radio station call letters*]
WXJY-FM .... Georgetown, SC [*FM radio station call letters*] (BROA)
WXKB .... Cape Coral, FL [*FM radio station call letters*]
WXKC .... Erie, PA [*FM radio station call letters*]
WXKE .... Fort Wayne, IN [*FM radio station call letters*]
WXKI .... Moulton, AL [*FM radio station call letters*]
WXKL .... Sanford, NC [*AM radio station call letters*]
WXKN .... Newburg, KY [*AM radio station call letters*]
WXKO .... Fort Valley, GA [*AM radio station call letters*]
WXKO .... Pana, IL [*FM radio station call letters*]
WXKQ .... Whitesburg, KY [*FM radio station call letters*]
WXKR .... Port Clinton, OH [*FM radio station call letters*]
WXKS .... Medford, MA [*AM radio station call letters*]
WXKS-FM ... Medford, MA [*FM radio station call letters*]
WXKW .... Renovo, PA [*FM radio station call letters*] (RBYB)
WXKX .... Parkersburg, WV [*FM radio station call letters*]
WXKZ .... Prestonsburg, KY [*FM radio station call letters*]
WXL .... Wix, Inc. [*Toronto Stock Exchange symbol*]
WXLA .... Dimondale, MI [*AM radio station call letters*]
WXLC .... Waukegan, IL [*FM radio station call letters*]
WXLE .... Mechanicville, NY [*FM radio station call letters*]
WXLG .... North Creek, NY [*FM radio station call letters*]
WXLH .... Blue Mountain Lake, NY [*FM radio station call letters*]
WXLI .... Dublin, GA [*AM radio station call letters*]
WXLJ-FM .... Spangler, PA [*FM radio station call letters*] (RBYB)
WXLK .... Roanoke, VA [*FM radio station call letters*]
WXLL .... Decatur, GA [*AM radio station call letters*]
WXLM-FM ... Eminence, KY [*FM radio station call letters*] (RBYB)
WXLN .... Eminence, KY [*FM radio station call letters*]
WXLN .... New Albany, IN [*AM radio station call letters*] (RBYB)
WXLO .... Fitchburg, MA [*FM radio station call letters*]
WXLP .... Moline, IL [*FM radio station call letters*]

WXLQ .... Gorham, NH [*FM radio station call letters*]
WXLR .... Harold, KY [*FM radio station call letters*]
WXLS .... Gulfport, MS [*FM radio station call letters*]
WXLT .... Carterville, IL [*FM radio station call letters*]
WXLU .... Peru, NY [*FM radio station call letters*]
WXLV .... Schnecksville, PA [*FM radio station call letters*]
WXLV-TV .... Winston-Salem, NC [*Television station call letters*] (RBYB)
WXLW .... Indianapolis, IN [*AM radio station call letters*]
WXLX .... Newark, NJ [*AM radio station call letters*] (RBYB)
WXLY .... North Charleston, SC [*FM radio station call letters*]
WXLZ .... Lebanon, VA [*FM radio station call letters*]
WXL7 .... St. Paul, VA [*AM radio station call letters*]
WXM .... Worcester Art Museum, Worcester, MA [*OCLC symbol*] (OCLC)
WXMC .... Parsippany-Troy Hills, NJ [*AM radio station call letters*]
WXMI .... Grand Rapids, MI [*Television station call letters*]
WXMJ .... Mount Union, PA [*FM radio station call letters*]
WXMK .... Dock Junction, GA [*FM radio station call letters*]
WXML .... Upper Sandusky, OH [*FM radio station call letters*]
WXMT .... Nashville, TN [*Television station call letters*]
WXMX .... Canaan, VT [*FM radio station call letters*]
WXMY .... Saltville, VA [*AM radio station call letters*]
WXNC .... Warrenton, NC [*FM radio station call letters*] (RBYB)
WXNR-FM .... Grifton, NC [*FM radio station call letters*] (RBYB)
WXNU .... Valley Station, KY [*FM radio station call letters*] (RBYB)
WXOD .... Winchester, NH [*FM radio station call letters*]
WXOF .... Beverly Hills, FL [*FM radio station call letters*]
WXOK .... Baton Rouge, LA [*AM radio station call letters*]
WXON .... Detroit, MI [*Television station call letters*]
WXOQ .... Selmer, TN [*FM radio station call letters*]
WXOR .... Ocean Springs, MS [*FM radio station call letters*]
WXOU .... Oakland, MI [*FM radio station call letters*]
WXOW .... La Crosse, WI [*Television station call letters*]
WXOX .... Bay City, MI [*AM radio station call letters*]
WxP .... Wax Pattern [*Dentistry*]
WXPC .... Horse Cave, KY [*FM radio station call letters*]
WXPH .... Harrisburg, PA [*FM radio station call letters*] (RBYB)
WXPL .... Fitchburg, MA [*FM radio station call letters*]
WXPN .... Philadelphia, PA [*FM radio station call letters*]
WXPR .... Rhinelander, WI [*FM radio station call letters*]
WXPS-FM .... Vergennes, VT [*FM radio station call letters*] (RBYB)
WXPW .... Wausau, WI [*FM radio station call letters*] (RBYB)
WXPX .... West Hazleton, PA [*AM radio station call letters*]
WXPZ .... Milford, DE [*FM radio station call letters*]
WXQK .... Spring City, TN [*AM radio station call letters*]
WXQL .... Baldwin, FL [*FM radio station call letters*]
WXQR .... Jacksonville, NC [*FM radio station call letters*]
WXQW-FM ... Meridianville, AL [*FM radio station call letters*] (RBYB)
WXQZ .... Canton, NY [*FM radio station call letters*]
WXR .... Radiosonde Station [*ITU designation*] (CET)
WXR .... Weather RADAR
WXRA .... Eden, NC [*FM radio station call letters*]
WXRC .... Hickory, NC [*FM radio station call letters*]
WXRCNSq .... Weather Reconnaissance Squadron [*Air Force*]
WXRECCO .... Weather Reconnaissance Flight [*Navy*] (NVT)
WXRF .... Guayama, PR [*AM radio station call letters*]
WXRG .... Gulfport, MS [*FM radio station call letters*]
WXRI .... Winston-Salem, NC [*FM radio station call letters*]
WXRK .... New York, NY [*FM radio station call letters*]
WXRL .... Lancaster, NY [*AM radio station call letters*]
WXRM-FM ... Naples Park, FL [*FM radio station call letters*] (RBYB)
WXRO .... Beaver Dam, WI [*FM radio station call letters*]
WXRQ .... Mount Pleasant, TN [*AM radio station call letters*]
WXRR .... Hattiesburg, MS [*FM radio station call letters*] (RBYB)
WXRS .... Swainsboro, GA [*AM radio station call letters*]
WXRS-FM .... Swainsboro, GA [*FM radio station call letters*]
WXRT .... Chicago, IL [*FM radio station call letters*]
WXRV .... Haverhill, MA [*FM radio station call letters*] (RBYB)
WXRX .... Belvidere, IL [*FM radio station call letters*]
WXRZ .... Corinth, MS [*FM radio station call letters*]
WXSR .... Quincy, FL [*FM radio station call letters*]
WXSS .... Memphis, TN [*AM radio station call letters*]
WXST .... Loudon, TN [*FM radio station call letters*]
WXTA .... Edinboro, PA [*FM radio station call letters*]
WXTB .... Clearwater, FL [*FM radio station call letters*]
WXTC .... Charleston, SC [*AM radio station call letters*]
WXTC-FM .... Charleston, SC [*FM radio station call letters*]
WXTK .... West Yarmouth, MA [*FM radio station call letters*]
WXTL .... Jacksonville Beach, FL [*AM radio station call letters*]
WXTN .... Lexington, MS [*AM radio station call letters*]
WXTQ .... Athens, OH [*FM radio station call letters*]
WXTR .... Waldorf, MD [*FM radio station call letters*]
WXTR-AM ... Frederick, MD [*AM radio station call letters*] (RBYB)
WXTRN .... Weak External Reference [*Computer science*] (BUR)
WXTS .... Toledo, OH [*FM radio station call letters*]
WXTU .... Philadelphia, PA [*FM radio station call letters*]
WXTV .... Paterson, NJ [*Television station call letters*]
WXTX .... Columbus, GA [*Television station call letters*]
WXTZ .... Noblesville, IN [*FM radio station call letters*]
WXUR .... Herkimer, NY [*FM radio station call letters*]
WXUS .... Fort Rucker, AL [*FM radio station call letters*]
WXUT .... Toledo, OH [*FM radio station call letters*]
WXVA .... Charles Town, WV [*AM radio station call letters*]
WXVA-FM ... Charles Town, WV [*FM radio station call letters*]
WXVE .... Spangler, PA [*FM radio station call letters*]
WXVI .... Montgomery, AL [*AM radio station call letters*]

WXVL .... Crossville, TN [*FM radio station call letters*]
WXVO .... Oliver Springs, TN [*FM radio station call letters*]
WXVQ .... De Land, FL [*AM radio station call letters*]
WXVS .... Waycross, GA [*FM radio station call letters*]
WXVT .... Greenville, MS [*Television station call letters*]
WXVU .... Villanova, PA [*FM radio station call letters*]
WXVW .... Jeffersonville, IN [*AM radio station call letters*]
WXVX .... Monroeville, PA [*AM radio station call letters*]
WXWX .... Easley, SC [*FM radio station call letters*]
WXWY .... Robertsdale, AL [*AM radio station call letters*]
WXWZ .... Greer, SC [*FM radio station call letters*] (RBYB)
WXXA .... Albany, NY [*Television station call letters*]
WXXI .... Rochester, NY [*AM radio station call letters*]
WXXI-FM ..... Rochester, NY [*FM radio station call letters*]
WXXI-TV ..... Rochester, NY [*Television station call letters*]
WXXK .... Newport, NH [*FM radio station call letters*]
WXXL .... Leesburg, FL [*FM radio station call letters*]
WXXM-FM ... Philadelphia, PA [*FM radio station call letters*] (BROA)
WXXP .... Anderson, IN [*FM radio station call letters*]
WXXQ .... Freeport, IL [*FM radio station call letters*]
WXXR .... Cullman, AL [*AM radio station call letters*]
WXXU .... Cocoa Beach, FL [*AM radio station call letters*]
WXXV .... Gulfport, MS [*Television station call letters*]
WXXW .... Webster, MA [*FM radio station call letters*]
WXXX .... South Burlington, VT [*FM radio station call letters*]
WXXZ-FM .... Grand Marais, MN [*FM radio station call letters*] (RBYB)
WXYB .... Indian Rocks Beach, FL [*AM radio station call letters*]
WXYC .... Chapel Hill, NC [*FM radio station call letters*]
WXYK .... Pascagoula, MS [*FM radio station call letters*]
WXYQ .... Manistee, MI [*FM radio station call letters*]
WXYT .... Detroit, MI [*AM radio station call letters*]
WXYV .... Baltimore, MD [*FM radio station call letters*]
WXYX .... Bayamon, PR [*FM radio station call letters*]
WXYZ .... Detroit, MI [*Television station call letters*]
WXZQ-FM .... Piketon, OH [*FM radio station call letters*] (RBYB)
WXZR .... East Lyme, CT [*FM radio station call letters*]
WXZX-FM .... Culebra, PR [*FM radio station call letters*] (RBYB)
WXZZ .... Georgetown, KY [*FM radio station call letters*] (RBYB)
WY .... Indiana Airways [*ICAO designator*] (AD)
WY .... Warwickshire Yeomanry [*British military*] (DMA)
WY .... Washington Yards [*Navy*]
WY .... Way (ADA)
WY .... Western Yiddish (BJA)
WY .... Wey [*Unit of weight*]
WY .... Weyerhaeuser Co. [*NYSE symbol*] (SPSG)
WY .... Wherry (ROG)
WY .... Woman's Year
WY .... Wrist Yaw (MCD)
Wy .... Wycliffe [*English cleric, translated Bible into English, 1320-1384*] (BARN)
WY .... Wyeth Laboratories [*Research code symbol*]
WY .... Wyoming [*Postal code*]
WY .... Wyoming Reports [*A publication*] (DLA)
Wy .... Wyoming State Library, Cheyenne, WY [*Library symbol Library of Congress*] (LCLS)
Wy .... Wythe's Virginia Chancery Reports [*1788-99*] [*A publication*] (DLA)
WyA .... Lincoln County Library, Afton Branch, Afton, WY [*Library symbol Library of Congress*] (LCLS)
WYA .... Whyalla [*Australia Airport symbol*] (OAG)
WYA .... Writers for Young Adults [*A publication*]
WYA .... Wyangala [*Australia Seismograph station code, US Geological Survey Closed*] (SEIS)
WYAAA .... World Youth Action against Apartheid (BUAC)
WyAGS .... Church of Jesus Christ of Latter-Day Saints, Genealogical Society Library, AftonBranch, Afton, WY [*Library symbol Library of Congress*] (LCLS)
WYAI-FM .... Bowdon, GA [*FM radio station call letters*] (BROA)
WYAIO .... Will You Accept, If Offered, the Position Of [*Aviation*] (FAAC)
WYAJ .... Sudbury, MA [*FM radio station call letters*]
WYAK-FM ... Surfside Beach-Garden City, SC [*FM radio station call letters*]
WYAL .... Scotland Neck, NC [*AM radio station call letters*]
WYAM .... Hartselle, AL [*AM radio station call letters*]
Wy-Ar .... Wyoming State Archives and Historical Department, Cheyenne, WY [*Library symbol Library of Congress*] (LCLS)
WYAR-FM .... Yarmouth, ME [*FM radio station call letters*] (BROA)
Wyatt Prac Reg... Wyatt's Practical Register in Chancery [*1800*] [*A publication*] (DLA)
Wyatt Pr R ... Wyatt's Practical Register in Chancery [*1800*] [*A publication*] (DLA)
WYAV .... Conway, SC [*FM radio station call letters*]
WYAY .... Gainesville, GA [*FM radio station call letters*]
WYBA-FM .... Lansing, IL [*FM radio station call letters*] (BROA)
WYBB .... Folly Beach, SC [*FM radio station call letters*]
WYBC .... New Haven, CT [*FM radio station call letters*]
WYBE .... Philadelphia, PA [*Television station call letters*]
WYBF .... Radnor Township, PA [*FM radio station call letters*]
WYBG .... Massena, NY [*AM radio station call letters*]
WYBL .... Western Young Buddhist League (EA)
WYBR .... Big Rapids, MI [*FM radio station call letters*]
WYBT .... Blountstown, FL [*AM radio station call letters*]
WyBu .... Johnson County Library, Buffalo, WY [*Library symbol Library of Congress*] (LCLS)
WYBZ .... Crooksville, OH [*FM radio station call letters*]
WyC .... Laramie County Library System, Cheyenne, WY [*Library symbol Library of Congress*] (LCLS)
WYC .... Warwickshire Yeomanry Cavalry [*British military*] (DMA)

WYC............	Wiley College, Marshall, TX [*Inactive*] [*OCLC symbol*] (OCLC)
WYC............	World Youth Choir (BUAC)
WYC............	Wycombe [*England*]
WYC............	Wycombe Air Centre [*British ICAO designator*] (FAAC)
WYC............	Yes Bay [*Alaska*] [*Airport symbol*] (AD)
WYCA	Hammond, IN [*FM radio station call letters*]
WyCa	Natrona County Public Library, Casper, WY [*Library symbol Library of Congress*] (LCLS)
WyCaC.........	Casper College, Casper, WY [*Library symbol Library of Congress*] (LCLS)
WyCaCH	Wyoming State Children's Home, Casper, WY [*Library symbol Library of Congress*] (LCLS)
WyCaD.........	Wyoming School for the Deaf, Casper, WY [*Library symbol Library of Congress*] (LCLS)
WyCaGS	Church of Jesus Christ of Latter-Day Saints, Genealogical Society Library, Casper Branch, Casper, WY [*Library symbol Library of Congress*] (LCLS)
WYCB	Washington, DC [*AM radio station call letters*]
WYCC	Chicago, IL [*Television station call letters*]
WyCC..........	Laramie County Community College, Cheyenne, WY [*Library symbol Library of Congress*] (LCLS)
WYCC	Write Your Congressman Club (EA)
WYCD	Detroit, MI [*FM radio station call letters*]
WyCDA	Wyoming Department of Agriculture, Cheyenne, WY [*Library symbol Library of Congress*] (LCLS)
WyCDE.........	Wyoming Department of Education, Cheyenne, WY [*Library symbol Library of Congress*] (LCLS)
WYCE	Wyoming, MI [*FM radio station call letters*]
WYCF..........	World Youth Crusade for Freedom (EA)
WYCFD	World Youth Congress on Food and Development (EAIO)
WYCG..........	Water Valley, MS [*FM radio station call letters*]
WyCGF.........	Wyoming Game and Fish Commission, Cheyenne, WY [*Library symbol Library of Congress*] (LCLS)
WyCGS	Church of Jesus Christ of Latter-Day Saints, Genealogical Society Library, Cheyenne Branch, Cheyenne, WY [*Library symbol Library of Congress*] (LCLS)
WyCHD	Wyoming Highway Department, Cheyenne, WY [*Library symbol Library of Congress*] (LCLS)
WyCHS	Wyoming Department of Health and Social Services, Cheyenne, WY [*Library symbol Library of Congress*] (LCLS)
WYCK	Wilkes-Barre, PA [*AM radio station call letters*]
Wycl	Wycliffe [*English cleric, translated Bible into English, 1320-1384*] (BARN)
WYCL-FM	Pensacola, FL [*FM radio station call letters*] (RBYB)
WYCM	Murfreesboro, NC [*AM radio station call letters*]
WyCMS........	Laramie County Medical Society, Cheyenne, WY [*Library symbol Library of Congress*] (LCLS)
WYCO	Wausau, WI [*FM radio station call letters*]
WyCoB.........	Buffalo Bill Museum, Cody, WY [*Library symbol Library of Congress*] (LCLS)
WyCoGS	Church of Jesus Christ of Latter-Day Saints, Genealogical Society Library, Cody Branch, Cody, WY [*Library symbol Library of Congress*] (LCLS)
WYCQ	Shelbyville, TN [*FM radio station call letters*]
WYCR	York-Hanover, PA [*FM radio station call letters*]
WYCS	Yorktown, VA [*FM radio station call letters*]
WyCSE.........	State Engineer's Office, Cheyenne, WY [*Library symbol Library of Congress*] (LCLS)
WYCT..........	Kentwood, LA [*FM radio station call letters*]
WYCV	Granite Falls, NC [*AM radio station call letters*]
WyCV	United States Veterans Administration Center, Cheyenne, WY [*Library symbol Library of Congress*] (LCLS)
WYCY	Hawley, PA [*FM radio station call letters*]
WYD	Wyandotte [*Queensland*] [*Airport symbol*] (AD)
Wy-D	Wyoming State Documents, Cheyenne, WY [*Library symbol Library of Congress*] (LCLS)
WYDA-FM	Graceville, FL [*FM radio station call letters*] (RBYB)
WYDC	Corning, NY [*Television station call letters*]
WYDE	Birmingham, AL [*AM radio station call letters*]
WYDH..........	Atmore, AL [*FM radio station call letters*]
Wy Dic........	Wyatt's Dickens' Chancery Reports [*A publication*] (DLA)
Wy Dick.......	Dickens' English Chancery Reports, by Wyatt [*A publication*] (DLA)
WYDIWYG ...	What You Digitize Is What You Get
WYDN..........	Worcester, MA [*Television station call letters*]
WyDo...........	Converse County Library, Douglas, WY [*Library symbol Library of Congress*] (LCLS)
WYDO	Greenville, NC [*Television station call letters*]
WYDP-TV.....	Orange Park, FL [*TV station call letters*] (RBYB)
WYDS	Decatur, IL [*FM radio station call letters*]
WYE	Yengema [*Sierra Leone*] [*Airport symbol*] (OAG)
WYEA..........	Sylacauga, AL [*AM radio station call letters*]
WYEP..........	Pittsburgh, PA [*FM radio station call letters*]
WYER	Mount Carmel, IL [*AM radio station call letters*]
WYES..........	New Orleans, LA [*Television station call letters*]
WyEV	Unita County Library, Evanston, WY [*Library symbol*] [*Library of Congress*] (LCLS)
WyEvGS.......	Church of Jesus Christ of Latter-Day Saints, Genealogical Society Library, Evanston Branch, Evanston, WY [*Library symbol Library of Congress*] (LCLS)
WyEvSH.......	Wyoming State Hospital, Evanston, WY [*Library symbol Library of Congress*] (LCLS)
WYEZ..........	Bremen, IN [*FM radio station call letters*]
WYF	World Youth Forum [*Defunct*] (EA)
WYFA..........	Waynesboro, GA [*FM radio station call letters*]
WYFB..........	Gainesville, FL [*FM radio station call letters*]

WYFC..........	Clinton, TN [*FM radio station call letters*]
WYFD..........	Decatur, AL [*FM radio station call letters*]
WYFE	Tarpon Springs, FL [*FM radio station call letters*]
WyFEW........	United States Air Force, Francis E. Warren Air Force Base, Cheyenne, WY [*Library symbol Library of Congress*] (LCLS)
WyFEW-I......	United States Air Force Institute of Technology, Detachment 9, Francis E. WarrenAir Force Base, Cheyenne, WY [*Library symbol Library of Congress*] (LCLS)
WYFF	Greenville, SC [*Television station call letters*]
WYFG	Gaffney, SC [*FM radio station call letters*]
WYFH	North Charleston, SC [*FM radio station call letters*]
WYFI...........	Norfolk, VA [*FM radio station call letters*]
WYFJ	Ashland, VA [*FM radio station call letters*]
WYFK..........	Columbus, GA [*FM radio station call letters*]
WYFL..........	Henderson, NC [*FM radio station call letters*]
WYFL..........	World Youth Freedom League (BUAC)
WyFIL..........	Fort Laramie Historic Site, Fort Laramie, WY [*Library symbol Library of Congress*] (LCLS)
WYFM..........	Sharon, PA [*FM radio station call letters*]
WYFN	Nashville, TN [*AM radio station call letters*]
WYFO	Lakeland, FL [*FM radio station call letters*]
WYFP-FM	Harpswell, ME [*FM radio station call letters*] (BROA)
WYFQ	Charlotte, NC [*AM radio station call letters*]
WYFQ-FM	Wadesboro, NC [*FM radio station call letters*] (BROA)
WYFS..........	Savannah, GA [*FM radio station call letters*]
WYFT..........	Luray, VA [*FM radio station call letters*]
WYFV..........	Cayce, SC [*FM radio station call letters*]
WYFW	Winder, GA [*FM radio station call letters*]
WYFX..........	Boynton Beach, FL [*AM radio station call letters*]
WYFZ-FM	Keystone Heights, FL [*FM radio station call letters*] (BROA)
WyG	Campbell County Public Library, Gilete, WY [*Library symbol*] [*Library of Congress*] (LCLS)
WYG	Wyman-Gordon [*NYSE symbol*]
WYG	Wyoming Airlines Ltd. [*ICAO designator*] (FAAC)
WYGB-FM	Edinburgh, IN [*FM radio station call letters*] (BROA)
WYGC..........	Gainesville, FL [*FM radio station call letters*]
WYGE	London, KY [*FM radio station call letters*] (RBYB)
WYGH	Paris, KY [*AM radio station call letters*]
WYGINS.......	What You Get Is No Surprise [*Pronounced "wiggins"*] [*Coined by Dave Tarrant, president of Lotus Development Corp.'s graphics products group*]
WYGL..........	Elizabethville, PA [*FM radio station call letters*]
WYGL..........	Selinsgrove, PA [*AM radio station call letters*]
WYGO	Madisonville, TN [*FM radio station call letters*]
WYGR	Wyoming, MI [*AM radio station call letters*]
WYGY	Hamilton, OH [*FM radio station call letters*]
WYHC..........	Charlotte, NC [*FM radio station call letters*]
WYHK..........	Gibsonburg, OH [*FM radio station call letters*]
WYHS..........	Hollywood, FL [*Television station call letters*]
WYHT..........	Mansfield, OH [*FM radio station call letters*]
WYHY..........	Lebanon, TN [*FM radio station call letters*]
WYII...........	Williamsport, MD [*FM radio station call letters*]
WYIN	Gary, IN [*Television station call letters*]
WYIQ	Warner Robins, GA [*FM radio station call letters*]
WYIS	McRae, GA [*AM radio station call letters*]
WYJB	Albany, NY [*FM radio station call letters*]
WYJCA........	Wool Yarn Jobbers Credit Association [*Defunct*] (EA)
WYJS-FM	Pickens, MS [*FM radio station call letters*] (RBYB)
WYJZ	Pittsburgh, PA [*AM radio station call letters*]
WYKC	Grenada, MS [*AM radio station call letters*]
WyKc	Johnson County Library, Kaycee Branch, Kaycee, WY [*Library symbol Library of Congress*] (LCLS)
WyKe	Lincoln County Library, Kemmerer, WY [*Library symbol Library of Congress*] (LCLS)
WYKK..........	Quitman, MS [*FM radio station call letters*]
WYKM	Rupert, WV [*AM radio station call letters*]
WYKO	Sabana Grande, PR [*AM radio station call letters*]
WYKR	Haverhill, NH [*FM radio station call letters*]
WYKR	Wells River, VT [*AM radio station call letters*]
WYKS	Gainesville, FL [*FM radio station call letters*]
WYKT..........	Wilmington, IL [*FM radio station call letters*] (RBYB)
WYKX..........	Escanaba, MI [*FM radio station call letters*]
WYKY..........	Columbus, WI [*FM radio station call letters*]
WYKZ.........	Beaufort, SC [*FM radio station call letters*]
WYL............	Laramie County Library System, Cheyenne, WY [*OCLC symbol*] (OCLC)
WYL............	Wyle Electronics [*NYSE symbol*] (TTSB)
WYL............	Wyle Electronics Co. [*Formerly, Wyle Laboratories*] [*NYSE symbol*] (SAG)
WYLA-FM	Lacombe, LA [*FM radio station call letters*] (RBYB)
WyLan	Fremont County Library, Lander, WY [*Library symbol Library of Congress*] (LCLS)
WyLanT	Wyoming State Training School, Lander, WY [*Library symbol Library of Congress*] (LCLS)
WyLar..........	Albany County Public Library, Laramie, WY [*Library symbol Library of Congress*] (LCLS)
WyLarBM......	United States Bureau of Mines, Laramie Petroleum Research Center, Laramie, WY [*Library symbol Library of Congress*] (LCLS)
WyLarHN......	Wyoming Health Science Network, University of Wyoming, Laramie, WY [*Library symbol Library of Congress*] (LCLS)
WyLarSh......	Sherwood Hall, Laramie, WY [*Library symbol Library of Congress*] (LCLS)
WyLarSM.....	Saint Matthew's Cathedral, Laramie, WY [*Library symbol Library of Congress*] (LCLS)
WYLD	New Orleans, LA [*AM radio station call letters*]

WYLD-FM .... New Orleans, LA [*FM radio station call letters*]
WYLE .... Florence, AL [*Television station call letters*]
WyleElec ..... Wyle Electronics Co. [*Formerly, Wyle Laboratories*] [*Associated Press*] (SAG)
WYLF .... Penn Yan, NY [*AM radio station call letters*]
WYLI .... Marietta, OH [*FM radio station call letters*] (RBYB)
WYLIWYS .... Where You Look Is What You Select
WYLK-FM .... Folsom, LA [*FM radio station call letters*] (RBYB)
WYLL .... Des Plaines, IL [*FM radio station call letters*]
WyLoGS .... Church of Jesus Christ of Latter-Day Saints, Genealogical Society Library, Lovell Branch, Lovell, WY [*Library symbol Library of Congress*] (LCLS)
WYLR .... Glens Falls, NY [*FM radio station call letters*]
WYLS .... York, AL [*AM radio station call letters*]
WYLT-FM .... Bvbalia, MS [*FM radio station call letters*] (RBYB)
WyLu .... Niobrara County Library, Lusk, WY [*Library symbol Library of Congress*] (LCLS)
WYLV .... Alcoa, TN [*FM radio station call letters*]
WYLV .... Wheat Yellow Leaf Virus [*Plant pathology*]
WYM .... Wyoming Health Science Network, Laramie, WY [*OCLC symbol*] (OCLC)
Wyman .... Wyman-Gordon Co. [*Associated Press*] (SAG)
Wyman .... Wyman's Reports [*India*] [*A publication*] (DLA)
WYMB .... Manning, SC [*AM radio station call letters*]
WYMC .... Mayfield, KY [*AM radio station call letters*]
WYMG .... Jacksonville, IL [*FM radio station call letters*]
WYMJ .... Harrisburg, PA [*FM radio station call letters*] (RBYB)
WYMN .... Wyman-Gordon [*NASDAQ symbol*] (TTSB)
WYMN .... Wyman-Gordon Co. [*NASDAQ symbol*] (NQ)
WYMR .... Sebring, FL [*FM radio station call letters*] (RBYB)
WYMS .... Milwaukee, WI [*AM radio station call letters*]
WYMT .... Hazard, KY [*Television station call letters*]
WYMV .... Wheat Yellow Mosaic Virus [*Plant pathology*]
WYMX .... Greenwood, MS [*FM radio station call letters*]
WYN .... Walwyn, Inc. [*Toronto Stock Exchange symbol*]
WYN .... Wyndham [*Australia Airport symbol*]
WYN .... Wyndham Hotel [*NYSE symbol*] (TTSB)
WYNA .... Tabor City, NC [*FM radio station call letters*]
WYNC .... Yanceyville, NC [*AM radio station call letters*]
WYND .... De Land, FL [*AM radio station call letters*]
WYND .... Hatteras, NC [*FM radio station call letters*]
WYNE .... Wayne Bancorp, Inc. [*NASDAQ symbol*] (SAG)
WyNe .... Weston County Public Library, Newcastle, WY [*Library symbol Library of Congress*] (LCLS)
WyneB .... Wayne Bancorp, Inc. [*Associated Press*] (SAG)
WYNF .... Coral Cove, FL [*FM radio station call letters*]
WYNG .... Evansville, IN [*FM radio station call letters*]
WYNI .... Monroeville, AL [*AM radio station call letters*]
WYNI-FM .... Repton, AL [*FM radio station call letters*] (RBYB)
WYNK .... Baton Rouge, LA [*AM radio station call letters*]
WYNK-FM .... Baton Rouge, LA [*FM radio station call letters*]
WYNN .... Florence, SC [*AM radio station call letters*]
Wynne Bov... Wynne's Bovill's Patent Cases [*A publication*] (DLA)
Wynne Eun... Wynne's Eunomus [*A publication*] (DLA)
WYNN-FM .... Florence, SC [*FM radio station call letters*]
Wynns .... Wynn's International, Inc. [*Associated Press*] (SAG)
WYNR .... Darien, GA [*FM radio station call letters*]
WY/NRT .... Weidels Yes/No Reliability Test [*Speech and language therapy*] (DAVI)
WYNS .... Lehighton, PA [*AM radio station call letters*]
WYNT .... Upper Sandusky, OH [*FM radio station call letters*]
WYNU .... Milan, TN [*FM radio station call letters*]
WYNY .... Lake Success, NY [*FM radio station call letters*]
WYNZ .... Westbrook, ME [*FM radio station call letters*]
WYO .... Western Youth Orchestra [*Australia*]
WYO .... Write-Your-Own [*Insurance*] (MHDB)
WYO .... Wyoming (AAG)
Wyo .... Wyoming (ODBW)
WYO .... Wyoming Array [*Wyoming*] [*Seismograph station code, US Geological Survey*] (SEIS)
Wyo .... Wyoming Reports [*A publication*] (DLA)
WYOC .... High Springs, FL [*FM radio station call letters*]
WYOC .... Write-Your-Own-Company [*Insurance*] (MHDB)
WYOK .... Moss Point, MS [*FM radio station call letters*] (RBYB)
WYOM .... Wyoming (ROG)
Wyom .... Wyoming Reports [*A publication*] (DLA)
WYOO .... Springfield, FL [*FM radio station call letters*]
WYOR .... Brentwood, TN [*AM radio station call letters*]
Wyo Sess Laws... Session Laws. Wyoming [*A publication*] (DLA)
WYOS-FM .... Chenango Bridge, NY [*FM radio station call letters*] (RBYB)
WYOU .... Scranton, PA [*Television station call letters*]
WYOW-TV .... Eagle River, WI [*TV station call letters*] (RBYB)
WYOY-FM .... Gluckstadt, MS [*FM radio station call letters*] (RBYB)
WYPA-AM .... Chicago, IL [*AM radio station call letters*] (BROA)
WYPC .... Wellston, OH [*AM radio station call letters*]
WyPdS .... Sublette County Library, Pinedale, WY [*Library symbol Library of Congress*] (LCLS)
WYPL .... Memphis, TN [*FM radio station call letters*]
WyPN .... Northwest Community College, Powell, WY [*Library symbol Library of Congress*] (LCLS)
Wy Pr R .... Wyatt's Practical Register in Chancery [*England*] [*A publication*] (DLA)
WYPX .... Amsterdam, NY [*Television station call letters*] (BROA)
WYQE .... Naguabo, PR [*FM radio station call letters*]
WYR .... Waybo Resources Ltd. [*Vancouver Stock Exchange symbol*]

WYR .... [*The*] West Yorkshire Regiment [*Army British*]
WYRD-AM ... Greenville, SC [*AM radio station call letters*] (BROA)
WYRE .... Annapolis, MD [*AM radio station call letters*]
WyRi .... Fremont County Library, Riverton Branch, Riverton, WY [*Library symbol Library of Congress*] (LCLS)
WyRiC .... Central Wyoming Community College, Riverton, WY [*Library symbol Library of Congress*] (LCLS)
WYRK .... Buffalo, NY [*FM radio station call letters*]
WYRN .... Louisburg, NC [*AM radio station call letters*]
WYRQ .... Little Falls, MN [*FM radio station call letters*]
WYRS .... Manahawkin, NJ [*FM radio station call letters*]
WyRsW .... Western Wyoming College, Rock Springs, WY [*Library symbol Library of Congress*] (LCLS)
WYRU .... Red Springs, NC [*AM radio station call letters*]
WYRV .... Cedar Bluff, VA [*AM radio station call letters*]
WYRX .... Lima, OH [*AM radio station call letters*]
WYRY .... Hinsdale, NH [*FM radio station call letters*]
WYS .... West Yellowstone, MT [*Location identifier FAA*] (FAAL)
WYS .... Wyandotte Southern Railroad Co. [*AAR code*]
WYSA-FM .... Wauseon, OH [*FM radio station call letters*] (RBYB)
WYSBYGI .... What You See Before You Get It [*Computer science*]
WYSC .... McRae, GA [*FM radio station call letters*]
WYSF .... Woollen Yarn Spinners Association (BUAC)
WYSF-FM .... Birmingham, AL [*FM radio station call letters*] (BROA)
WYSH .... Clinton, TN [*AM radio station call letters*]
WyShCD ...... Wheden Cancer Detection Foundation, Sheridan, WY [*Library symbol Library of Congress*] (LCLS)
WyShF .... Sheridan County Fulmer Public Library, Sheridan, WY [*Library symbol Library of Congress*] (LCLS)
WyShGS ...... Wyoming Girls' School, Sheridan, WY [*Library symbol Library of Congress*] (LCLS)
WyShMH ...... Northern Wyoming Mental Health Center, Sheridan, WY [*Library symbol Library of Congress*] (LCLS)
WyShS .... Sheridan College, Sheridan, WY [*Library symbol Library of Congress*] (LCLS)
WyShV .... United States Veterans Administration Hospital, Sheridan, WY [*Library symbol Library of Congress*] (LCLS)
WYSIAYG .... What You See Is All You Get
WYSIMOLWYG... What You See Is More or Less What You Get [*Pronounced "wizzi-mole-wig"*]
WYSIWYG .... What You See Is What You Get [*Pronounced "wizziwig"*] [*Indicates that video display on word processor bears a high-quality resemblance to printed page that will result*]
WYSIWYP .... What You See Is What You Print [*Computer science*]
WYSK .... Spotsylvania, VA [*FM radio station call letters*]
WYSL .... Avon, NY [*AM radio station call letters*]
WYSN .... Central City, PA [*FM radio station call letters*]
WYSN-AM .... Somerset, PA [*AM radio station call letters*] (BROA)
WYSO .... Yellow Springs, OH [*FM radio station call letters*]
WYSP .... Philadelphia, PA [*FM radio station call letters*]
WYSR .... Rotterdam, NY [*FM radio station call letters*] (RBYB)
WYSS .... Sault Ste. Marie, MI [*FM radio station call letters*]
WYST .... Detroit, MI [*FM radio station call letters*]
WYSU .... Youngstown, OH [*FM radio station call letters*]
WYSY .... Aurora, IL [*FM radio station call letters*]
WYSZ .... Maumee, OH [*FM radio station call letters*]
WYT .... Wyandotte Terminal Railroad Co. [*AAR code*]
WYT .... Wyton FTU [*British ICAO designator*] (FAAC)
WYTE .... Whiting, WI [*FM radio station call letters*]
WYTH .... Madison, GA [*AM radio station call letters*]
Wythe .... Wythe's Virginia Chancery Reports [*1788-99*] [*A publication*] (DLA)
Wythe Ch (VA)... Wythe's Virginia Chancery Reports [*1788-99*] [*A publication*] (DLA)
Wythes CC... Wythe's Virginia Chancery Reports [*1788-99*] [*A publication*] (DLA)
Wythe's R... Wythe's Virginia Chancery Reports [*1788-99*] [*A publication*] (DLA)
Wythe's Rep... Wythe's Virginia Chancery Reports [*1788-99*] [*A publication*] (DLA)
Wythe (VA)... Wythe's Virginia Chancery Reports [*1788-99*] [*A publication*] (DLA)
WyThP .... Wyoming Pioneer Home, Thermopolis, WY [*Library symbol Library of Congress*] (LCLS)
WYTI .... Rocky Mount, VA [*AM radio station call letters*]
WYTL .... Harbor Tug, Small [*Coast Guard symbol*] (DNAB)
WYTM .... Buoy Tender [*Coast Guard symbol*] (DNAB)
WYTM .... Fayetteville, TN [*FM radio station call letters*]
WYTM .... Floating Workship [*Coast Guard symbol*] (DNAB)
WYTM .... Freight Ship [*Coast Guard symbol*] (DNAB)
WYTM .... Harbor Craft [*Coast Guard symbol*] (DNAB)
WYTM .... Harbor Tug, Medium [*Coast Guard symbol*] (DNAB)
WYTM .... Inshore Patrol Cutter [*Coast Guard symbol*] (DNAB)
WYTM .... Lighthouse Tender [*Coast Guard symbol*] (DNAB)
WYTM .... Patrol Boat [*Coast Guard symbol*] (DNAB)
WYTM .... Revenue Cutter [*Coast Guard symbol*] (DNAB)
WYTM .... Revenue Steamer [*Coast Guard symbol*] (DNAB)
WYTM .... Seized Boat [*Coast Guard symbol*] (DNAB)
WYTM .... Station Ship [*Coast Guard symbol*] (DNAB)
WYTM .... Steam Derrick [*Coast Guard symbol*] (DNAB)
WYTN .... Youngstown, OH [*FM radio station call letters*]
WyToE .... Eastern Wyoming College, Torrington, WY [*Library symbol Library of Congress*] (LCLS)
WyTs .... Washakie County Library, Ten Sleep Branch, Ten Sleep, WY [*Library symbol Library of Congress*] (LCLS)
WYTV .... Youngstown, OH [*Television station call letters*]
WYTZ .... Bridgman, MI [*FM radio station call letters*] (RBYB)
WyU .... University of Wyoming, Laramie, WY [*Library symbol Library of Congress*] (LCLS)
WYU .... University of Wyoming, Library, Laramie, WY [*OCLC symbol*] (OCLC)

wyu	Wyoming [*MARC country of publication code Library of Congress*] (LCCP)
WyU-Ar	University of Wyoming, Archive of Contemporary History, Laramie, WY [*Library symbol Library of Congress*] (LCLS)
WyUL	Chateaugay, NY [*FM radio station call letters*]
WyUp	Weston County Public Library, Upton Branch, Upton, WY [*Library symbol Library of Congress*] (LCLS)
WYUR-AM	Dearborn, MI [*AM radio station call letters*] (BROA)
WYUS	Milford, DE [*AM radio station call letters*]
WYUU	Safety Harbor, FL [*FM radio station call letters*]
WYVC	Camden, AL [*FM radio station call letters*]
WYVE	Wytheville, VA [*AM radio station call letters*]
WYVN	Martinsburg, WV [*Television station call letters*]
WYWCA	World Young Women's Christian Association (DI)
WyWo	Washakie County Library, Worland, WY [*Library symbol Library of Congress*] (LCLS)
WyWoI	Wyoming Industrial Institute, Worland, WY [*Library symbol Library of Congress*] (LCLS)
WYWY	Barbourville, KY [*AM radio station call letters*]
WYWY-FM	Barbourville, KY [*FM radio station call letters*]
WYXC	Cartersville, GA [*AM radio station call letters*]
WYXE	Gallatin, TN [*AM radio station call letters*] (RBYB)
WYXI	Athens, TN [*AM radio station call letters*]
WYXL	Ithaca, NY [*FM radio station call letters*]
WYXR	Philadelphia, PA [*FM radio station call letters*]
WYXY-FM	Lincoln, IL [*FM radio station call letters*] (RBYB)
WYXZ-FM	Crestline, OH [*FM radio station call letters*] (RBYB)
WYYB	Dickson, TN [*FM radio station call letters*]
WYYC	West Yorkshire Yeomanry Cavalry [*British military*] (DMA)
WYYD	Amherst, VA [*FM radio station call letters*]
WYYS	Streator, IL [*FM radio station call letters*] (RBYB)
WYYU	Dalton, GA [*FM radio station call letters*] (RBYB)
WYYY	Syracuse, NY [*FM radio station call letters*]
WYYZ	Jasper, AL [*AM radio station call letters*] (RBYB)
WYZ	Wyoming State Library, Cheyenne, WY [*OCLC symbol*] (OCLC)
WYZB	Mary Esther, FL [*FM radio station call letters*]
WYZD	Dobson, NC [*AM radio station call letters*]
WYZE	Atlanta, GA [*AM radio station call letters*]
WYZK	Valdosta, GA [*FM radio station call letters*]
WYZM	Waunakee, WI [*FM radio station call letters*]
WYZZ	Bloomington, IL [*Television station call letters*]
WZ	Berlin European [*ICAO designator*] (AD)
WZ	Trans Western Airlines of Utah [*ICAO designator*] (AD)
Wz	Warenzeichen [*Trademark*] [*German*]
WZ	War Zone
WZ	Wissenschaftliche Zeitschrift [*A publication*]
WZa	Wide Zone Alpha (MAE)
WZAC	Danville, WV [*FM radio station call letters*]
WZAC	Madison, WV [*AM radio station call letters*]
WZAD	Wurtsboro, NY [*FM radio station call letters*]
WZAK	Cleveland, OH [*FM radio station call letters*]
WZAM-AM	Ishpeming, MI [*AM radio station call letters*] (RBYB)
WZAN	Portland, ME [*AM radio station call letters*]
WZAP	Bristol, VA [*AM radio station call letters*]
WZAR	Ponce, PR [*FM radio station call letters*]
WZAT	Savannah, GA [*FM radio station call letters*]
WZAX-FM	Nashville, NC [*FM radio station call letters*] (BROA)
WZAZ	Jacksonville, FL [*AM radio station call letters*]
WZBB	Rocky Mount, VA [*FM radio station call letters*]
WZBC	Newton, MA [*FM radio station call letters*]
WZBD	Berne, IN [*FM radio station call letters*]
WZBG	Litchfield, CT [*FM radio station call letters*]
WZBH	Georgetown, DE [*FM radio station call letters*]
WZBN	Carthage, IL [*FM radio station call letters*] (RBYB)
WZBO	Edenton, NC [*AM radio station call letters*]
WZBQ	Carrollton, AL [*FM radio station call letters*] (RBYB)
WZBR	Kinston, NC [*AM radio station call letters*]
WZBS	Ponce, PR [*AM radio station call letters*]
WZBT	Gettysburg, PA [*FM radio station call letters*]
WZBU	Vineyard Haven, MA [*Television station call letters*]
WZBX	Sylvania, GA [*FM radio station call letters*]
WZBZ	Plattsburgh, NY [*AM radio station call letters*] (RBYB)
WZCH-FM	Dundee, IL [*FM radio station call letters*] (RBYB)
WZCM	Young Harris, GA [*AM radio station call letters*]
WZCO-FM	Crown Point, IN [*FM radio station call letters*] (RBYB)
WZCT	Scottsboro, AL [*AM radio station call letters*]
WZDM	Vincennes, IN [*FM radio station call letters*]
WZDQ	Humboldt, TN [*FM radio station call letters*]
WZDX	Huntsville, AL [*Television station call letters*]
WZEA-FM	Ogdensburg, NY [*FM radio station call letters*] (BROA)
WZEE	Madison, WI [*FM radio station call letters*]
WZEP	De Funiak Springs, FL [*AM radio station call letters*]
WZER	Jackson, WI [*AM radio station call letters*] (RBYB)
WZEW	East Brewton, AL [*FM radio station call letters*]
WZEZ-FM	Madisonville, KY [*FM radio station call letters*] (RBYB)
WZFM	Narrows, VA [*FM radio station call letters*]
WZFX	Whiteville, NC [*FM radio station call letters*]
WZG	Wissenschaftliche Zeitschrift fuer Juedische Geschichte [*A publication*] (BJA)
WZGC	Atlanta, GA [*FM radio station call letters*]
WZGO	Portage, PA [*AM radio station call letters*]
WZGO-FM	Portage, PA [*FM radio station call letters*]
WZGX-FM	San German, PR [*FM radio station call letters*] (RBYB)
WZHF-AM	Arlington, VA [*AM radio station call letters*] (RBYB)
WZHR	Zephyrhills, FL [*AM radio station call letters*]

WZHT	Troy, AL [*FM radio station call letters*]
WZI	Winzen International, Inc. [*Vancouver Stock Exchange symbol*]
WZID	Manchester, NH [*FM radio station call letters*]
WZIP	Akron, OH [*FM radio station call letters*]
WZIQ	Smithville, GA [*FM radio station call letters*]
WZJM	Cleveland Heights, OH [*FM radio station call letters*]
WZJN	Jackson, NH [*FM radio station call letters*]
WZJS	Banner Elk, NC [*FM radio station call letters*]
WZJT	Wissenschaftliche Zeitschrift fuer Juedische Theologie [*A publication*] (BJA)
WZJTh	Wissenschaftliche Zeitschrift fuer Juedische Theologie [*A publication*] (BJA)
WZJY	Mt. Pleasant, SC [*AM radio station call letters*]
WZJZ-FM	Richwood, OH [*AM radio station call letters*] (RBYB)
WZKB	Wallace, NC [*FM radio station call letters*]
WZKD	Orlando, FL [*AM radio station call letters*] (RBYB)
WZKL	Alliance, OH [*FM radio station call letters*]
WZKM	Montgomery, WV [*FM radio station call letters*]
WZKS	Union, MS [*FM radio station call letters*] (RBYB)
WZKX	Poplarville, MS [*FM radio station call letters*]
WZKY	Albemarle, NC [*AM radio station call letters*]
WZKZ-FM	Alfred, NY [*FM radio station call letters*] (RBYB)
WZLA	Abbeville, SC [*FM radio station call letters*]
WZLE	Lorain, OH [*FM radio station call letters*]
WZLG	Hogansville, GA [*FM radio station call letters*] (RBYB)
WZLK	Virgie, KY [*FM radio station call letters*]
WZLM	Dadeville, AL [*FM radio station call letters*]
WZLQ	Tupelo, MS [*FM radio station call letters*]
WZLR	Xenia, OH [*FM radio station call letters*]
WZLS	Biltmore Forest, NC [*FM radio station call letters*]
WZLT	Lexington, TN [*FM radio station call letters*]
WZLX	Boston, MA [*FM radio station call letters*]
WZLY	Wellesley, MA [*FM radio station call letters*]
WZMB	Greenville, NC [*FM radio station call letters*]
WZMC	Colonial Heights, TN [*AM radio station call letters*]
WZMG	Opelika, AL [*AM radio station call letters*]
WZMP	Marion, MS [*FM radio station call letters*]
WZMQ	Key Largo, FL [*FM radio station call letters*]
WZMT	Hazleton, PA [*FM radio station call letters*]
WZMX	Hartford, CT [*FM radio station call letters*]
WZNA	Moca, PR [*AM radio station call letters*]
WZNE-FM	Brighton, NY [*FM radio station call letters*] (BROA)
WZNF	Rantoul, IL [*FM radio station call letters*]
WZNG-AM	Shelbyville, TN [*AM radio station call letters*] (BROA)
WZNJ	Demopolis, AL [*FM radio station call letters*]
WZNL	Norway, MI [*FM radio station call letters*]
WZNN	Rochester, NH [*AM radio station call letters*]
WZNO	Pensacola, FL [*AM radio station call letters*] (RBYB)
WZNPS	William H. Zimmer Nuclear Power Station [*Also, ZPS*] (NRCH)
WZNS-FM	Fort Walton Beach, FL [*FM radio station call letters*] (BROA)
WZNT	San Juan, PR [*FM radio station call letters*]
WZNW-FM	Bethlehem, WV [*FM radio station call letters*] (BROA)
WZNX	Sullivan, IL [*FM radio station call letters*] (RBYB)
WZNY	Augusta, GA [*FM radio station call letters*]
WZNZ	Jacksonville, FL [*AM radio station call letters*]
WZO	Wein Zollordnung [*Wine Duty Order*] [*German*]
WZO	World Zionist Organization [*Israel*]
WZO	World Zoroastrian Organisation (BUAC)
WZOA	Women's Zionist Organization of America
WZOB	Fort Payne, AL [*AM radio station call letters*]
WZOC-FM	Plymouth, IN [*FM radio station call letters*] (RBYB)
WZOD-AM	Colonial Heights, VA [*AM radio station call letters*] (BROA)
WZOE	Princeton, IL [*AM radio station call letters*]
WZOE-FM	Princeton, IL [*FM radio station call letters*]
WZOK	Rockford, IL [*FM radio station call letters*]
WZOM	Defiance, OH [*FM radio station call letters*]
WZON	Bangor, ME [*AM radio station call letters*]
WZOO	Asheboro, NC [*AM radio station call letters*]
WZOO	Edgewood, OH [*FM radio station call letters*]
WZOQ	Wapakoneta, OH [*FM radio station call letters*]
WZOS	Oswego, NY [*FM radio station call letters*]
WZOT	Rockmart, GA [*AM radio station call letters*]
WZOU	Lewiston, ME [*AM radio station call letters*]
WZOW	Goshen, IN [*FM radio station call letters*]
WZOZ	Oneonta, NY [*FM radio station call letters*]
WZPC-FM	Shelbyville, TN [*FM radio station call letters*] (RBYB)
WZPK	Berlin, NH [*FM radio station call letters*]
WZPL	Greenfield, IN [*FM radio station call letters*]
WZPQ	Jasper, AL [*AM radio station call letters*]
WZPR	Meadville, PA [*FM radio station call letters*]
WZPT	New Kensington, PA [*FM radio station call letters*]
WZPX	Battle Creek, MI [*Television station call letters*] (BROA)
WZQK	Coeburn, VA [*FM radio station call letters*]
WZQQ	Hyden, KY [*FM radio station call letters*]
WZQR	Black Mountain, NC [*AM radio station call letters*]
WZR	Wiser Oil [*NYSE symbol*] (TTSB)
WZR	Wiser Oil Co. [*NYSE symbol*] (SAG)
WZRC	New York, NY [*AM radio station call letters*]
WZRD	Chicago, IL [*FM radio station call letters*]
WZRH	Picayune, MS [*FM radio Edition*]
WZRK	Hancock, MI [*FM radio station call letters*]
WZRQ	Ballston Spa, NY [*FM radio station call letters*]
WZRR	Birmingham, AL [*FM radio station call letters*]
WZRS	Smyrna, TN [*AM radio station call letters*]
WZRT	Rutland, VT [*FM radio station call letters*]

WZRU .... Roanoke Rapids, NC [*FM radio station call letters*]
WZRW-FM ... Marion, MS [*FM radio station call letters*]   (RBYB)
WZRX .... Jackson, MS [*AM radio station call letters*]
WZRZ-FM .... Mill Hall, PA [*FM radio station call letters*]   (RBYB)
WZS .... Widespan Zoom Stereoscope   (SAA)
WZSH-FM .... Bellows Falls, VT [*FM radio station call letters*]   (BROA)
WZSK .... Bethany Beach, DE [*FM radio station call letters*]   (RBYB)
WZSR .... Woodstock, IL [*FM radio station call letters*]
WZST .... Signal Mountain, TN [*FM radio station call letters*]
WZT .... Wartegg-Zeichentest [*Wartegg Symbol Test*] [*German Psychology*]
WZTA .... Miami Beach, FL [*FM radio station call letters*]
WZTM AM ... Largo, FL [*AM radio station call letters*]   (RBYB)
WZTR .... Milwaukee, WI [*FM radio station call letters*]
WZTU .... Bear Lake, MI [*FM radio station call letters*]
WZTV .... Nashville, TN [*Television station call letters*]
WZTY .... Hartford, MI [*FM radio station call letters*]   (RBYB)
WZTZ .... Elba, AL [*FM radio station call letters*]
WZUR-AM .... Ponce, Puerto Rico [*AM radio station call letters*]   (BROA)
WZUU-FM .... Allegan, MI [*FM radio station call letters*]   (BROA)
WZVA-FM .... Marion, VA [*FM radio station call letters*]   (BROA)
WZVN .... Lowell, IN [*FM radio station call letters*]
WZVN-TV ..... Naples, FL [*Television station call letters*]   (RBYB)
WZVU .... Long Branch, NJ [*FM radio station call letters*]
WZW .... Worcester Public Library, Worcester, MA [*OCLC symbol*]   (OCLC)
WZWW .... Bellefonte, PA [*FM radio station call letters*]
WZWY .... Orlando, FL [*Television station call letters*]
WZWZ .... Kokomo, IN [*FM radio station call letters*]
WZXA .... Sturtevant, WI [*FM radio station call letters*]
WZXI .... Buffalo Gap, VA [*FM radio station call letters*]   (RBYB)
WZXL .... Wildwood, NJ [*FM radio station call letters*]

WZXR .... South Williamsport, PA [*FM radio station call letters*]
WZXS .... Topsail Beach, NC [*FM radio station call letters*]
WZXV .... Palmyra, NY [*FM radio station call letters*]
WZY .... Nassau [*Bahamas*] [*Airport symbol*]   (OAG)
WZYP .... Athens, AL [*FM radio station call letters*]
WZYQ .... Mound Bayou, MS [*FM radio station call letters*]   (RBYB)
WZYX .... Cowan, TN [*AM radio station call letters*]
WZZA .... Tuscumbia, AL [*AM radio station call letters*]
WZZB .... Seymour, IN [*AM radio station call letters*]
WZZD .... Philadelphia, PA [*AM radio station call letters*]
WZZE .... Glen Mills, PA [*FM radio station call letters*]
WZZI-FM ...... Vinton, VA [*FM radio station call letters*]   (RBYB)
WZZJ .... Pascagoula-Moss Point, MS [*AM radio station call letters*]
WZZK .... Birmingham, AL [*AM radio station call letters*]
WZZK-FM .... Birmingham, AL [*FM radio station call letters*]
WZZL .... Reidland, KY [*FM radio station call letters*]
WZZM .... Grand Rapids, MI [*Television station call letters*]
WZZN-FM .... Mount Kisco, NY [*FM radio station call letters*]   (RBYB)
WZZO .... Bethlehem, PA [*FM radio station call letters*]
WZZQ .... Terre Haute, IN [*AM radio station call letters*]   (RBYB)
WZZQ-FM .... Terre Haute, IN [*FM radio station call letters*]
WZZR .... Stuart, FL [*FM radio station call letters*]
WZZS .... Zolfo Springs, FL [*FM radio station call letters*]
WZZT .... Morrison, IL [*FM radio station call letters*]
WZZU .... Burlington-Graham, NC [*FM radio station call letters*]
WZZU-AM .... Babylon, NY [*AM radio station call letters*]   (RBYB)
WZZW .... Milton, WV [*FM radio station call letters*]
WZZX .... Lineville, AL [*AM radio station call letters*]
WZZY .... Winchester, IN [*FM radio station call letters*]
WZZZ .... Fulton, NY [*AM radio station call letters*]

X

By Acronym

X	Abscissa (IDOE)
X	Abscissa of a Coordinate (BARN)
X	Amino Acid, Unknown or Other [*Symbol*] [*Biochemistry*]
X	Arithmetic Mean [*Statistics*]
X	Axis [*of a cylindrical lens*] [*Ophthalmology*] (DAVI)
X	By [*As in 9 x 12*]
X	Central Drug Research Institute [*India*] [*Research code symbol*]
X	Chile [*IYRU nationality code*] (IYR)
X	Christus [*Christ*] [*Latin*]
X	Closed at All Times (Except When in Actual Use) [*Ship's fittings classification*]
X	Cross [*As in X-roads*]
X	Cross [*Referring to sections*] [*Pathology*] (DAVI)
X	Crossed With (DAVI)
X	Crossmatch [*Hematology*] (DAVI)
X	Crystal Cut [*Symbol*] (DEN)
X	Decem [*Ten*] [*Latin*]
X	Drill Sergeant [*Army skill qualification identifier*] (INF)
X	Ecstasy [*Synthetic stimulant*]
X	Ethnikon Agrotikon Komma Xiton [*National Agrarian Party "X"*] [*Political party*] (PPE)
X	Examination [*Slang*]
X	Except (DAVI)
X	Exchange
X	Exclusive [*Concession in a circus or carnival*]
X	Exercise [*British military*] (DMA)
X	Exhibitions [*Trade fairs, etc.*] [*Public-performance tariff class*] [*British*]
X	Ex-Husband [*or Ex-Wife*] [*Slang*]
X	Ex-Interest [*Without the right to interest*] [*Finance*]
X	Exit [*Computer science*] [*Telecommunications*]
X	Exophoria Distance [*Ophthalmology*]
X	Experimental [*Military*] (AABC)
X	Explosion [*Military*] (CAAL)
X	Export [*Economics*]
X	Extension (AAQ)
X	Extra
X	Female Chromosome
X	Frost
X	Haploid Generation [*Biology*] (BARN)
X	Hexadecimal [*Computer science*] (IAA)
X	Horizontal Deflection [*Symbol*] (DEN)
X	Index [*Computer science*]
X	Kienboeck's Unit [*of x-ray dosage*] (AAMN)
X	Kiss [*Correspondence*]
X	Komma Xiton Ethnikis Antistasseos ["*X" National Resistance Party*] [*Political party*] (PPE)
X	Lateral [*RADAR*]
X	Location [*Symbol on map*]
X	Midweek Travel [*Airline fare code*]
X	Mistake [*or Error*] [*Symbol*]
X	Multiplication (IDOE)
X	Multiplication (IDOE)
X	No Connection (IDOE)
X	No Protest [*Banking*]
X	Number of Carriers (IDOE)
X	Parallactic Angle
%X	Percentage of the Predicted Normal Value [*Indicated by the percent sign preceding the symbol*] [*Laboratory science*] (DAVI)
X	Psychological Problem [*Classification system used by doctors on Ellis Island to detain, re-examine, and possibly deny entry to certain immigrants*]
X	Raw Score [*Psychology*]
X	Reactance [*Symbol*] [*IUPAC*] (AAG)
X	Reactance [*Measurement and physics*] (DAVI)
X	Removal of [*Surgery*] (DAVI)
X	Research [*or Experimental*] [*Designation for all US military aircraft*]
X	Respirations [*On anesthesia chart*] (DAVI)
X	Roentgen [*Ray*] [*Radiology*] (DAVI)
X	Simes [*Italy*] [*Research code symbol*]
X	St. Andrew's Cross
X	Start of Anesthesia (DAVI)
X	Strike [*Bowling symbol*]
X	Submersible Craft [*Self-propelled*] [*Navy ship symbol*]
X	Takes [*As in K x B - King Takes Bishop*] [*Chess*]
X	Ten [*Roman numeral*]
X	Times [*Multiplication sign*] [*Mathematics*]

X	Toilet [*Slang*]
X	Transistor [*Symbol*] (DEN)
X	Transmit
X	Transverse [*Referring to sections*] [*Pathology*] (DAVI)
X	Unknown Quantity (IDOE)
X	Unknown Quantity (IDOE)
X	USX Marathon [*NYSE symbol*] (SAG)
X	USX US Steel Group [*Wall Street slang name: "Steel"*] [*NYSE symbol*] (SPSG)
X	Xanthosine [*One-letter symbol; see Xao*]
X	X-Axis
X	Xenon [*Chemical element*] (IAA)
X	Xenopsylla [*A genus of fleas*] (DAVI)
X	Xerxes [*Phonetic alphabet*] [*Royal Navy World War I*] (DSUE)
X+#	Xiphoid Plus Number of Finger Breadths [*Height of fundus*] [*Obstetrics*] (DAVI)
X	X-Ray [*Phonetic alphabet*] [*Pre-World War II International*] [*World War II*] (DSUE)
X	X-Ray (KSC)
X	X-Ray Assistant [*British military*]
X	X Records [*Division of RCA-Victor*] [*Record label*]
X	Xylem [*Botany*]
x	Xylose [*As substituent on nucleoside*] [*Biochemistry*]
X₂t	Chi-Squared Test [*Statistics*] (DAVI)
X3	Times Three [*Referring to orientation to time, place, and person*] [*Neurology*] (DAVI)
XA	Auxiliary Amplifier (AAG)
Xa	Chiasma [*Genetics*] (AAMN)
xa	Christmas Island [*Indian Ocean*] [*MARC country of publication code Library of Congress*] (LCCP)
XA	Cross-Assembler [*Computer science*] (CIST)
XA	Exchange Access (ACRL)
XA	Experimental (Air Force)
XA	Extended Architecture [*Computer science*]
XA	Transmission Adapter (MDG)
Xa	Xanthine [*Biochemistry*]
XA	Xanthurenic Acid [*Clinical chemistry*]
XAA	Aeronautical Radio, Inc. [*ICAO designator*] (FAAC)
XAA	American Municipal Income Portfolio [*NYSE symbol*] (SPSG)
XAA	Amer Muni Income Portfolio [*NYSE symbol*] (TTSB)
Xaa	Unknown Amino Acid [*Laboratory science*] (DAVI)
XAAM	Experimental Air-to-Air Missile [*Air Force, NASA*]
XAAS	Xinjiang Academy of Agricultural Sciences [*China*] (BUAC)
XAC	Air Charter World [*ICAO designator*] (FAAC)
XACIC	X-Ray Attenuation Coefficient Information Center [*National Institute of Standards and Technology*]
XACT	X Automatic Code Translation (IEEE)
XAD	Certified Aircraft Dispatch, Inc. [*ICAO designator*] (FAAC)
XAD	Experimental and Development
XAES	X-Ray Auger Electron Spectroscopy (EDCT)
XAES	X-Ray Induced Auger Electron Spectroscopy
XAF	Executive Air Fleet [*ICAO designator*] (FAAC)
XAFH	X-Band Antenna Feed Horn
XAFS	X-Ray Absorption Fine Structure [*Organic chemistry*]
XAK	Cargo Ship, Merchant Marine Manned
XAL	Aerovias Xalitic SA de CV [*Mexico ICAO designator*] (FAAC)
XAL	Xenon Arc Lamp
XALC	Extended Assembler Language Coding [*Computer science*] (MHDI)
XAM	AMR Combs, Inc. [*AMR Services, Inc.*] [*ICAO designator*] (FAAC)
XAM	External Address Modifier [*Computer science*] (MHDI)
XAM	Merchant Ship Converted to a Minesweeper [*Navy symbol Obsolete*]
X-A mixture	Xylene-Alcohol [*Mixture*] [*An insecticide*] (DAVI)
Xan	Xanthine [*Biochemistry*]
X & D	Examination and Diagnosis (DAVI)
X & D	Experiment and Development [*Flotilla*] [*Landing Craft*]
X & DFLOT	Experimental and Development Flotilla [*Navy*] (DNAB)
X & O	Hug and Kiss (DAVI)
XANES	X-Ray Absorption Near Edge Spectroscopy (EDCT)
XANES	X-Ray Absorption Near-Edge Structure [*Spectroscopy*]
XANST	Xanthium strumarium [*Cocklebur*]
XANT	Xanthochromic [*Neurology*] (DAVI)
xanth	Xanthomatosis
XAO	Airline Operations Services, Inc. [*ICAO designator*] (FAAC)
Xao	Xanthosine [*Also, X*] [*A nucleoside*]
XAP	Chapeco [*Brazil*] [*Airport symbol*] (OAG)
XAP	Direct Air Inc. [*ICAO designator*] (FAAC)

XAP............	Merchant Transport [*Ship symbol*]
XAPC..........	Merchant Coastal Transport, Small [*Ship symbol*]
XAPFS........	Extended X-Ray Appearance Potential Fine Structure (EDCT)
XAPIA........	X.400 Application Program Interface Association (EA)
XAR............	Extended Attribute Record [*Computer science*] (DOM)
XARM..........	Cross Arm (AAG)
XARO..........	Artagraph Reproduction Technology [*NASDAQ symbol*] (SAG)
XAS............	Experimental Air Specification Weapons [*Navy*] (NG)
XAS............	PHH Aviation Systems, Inc. [*ICAO designator*] (FAAC)
XAS............	X-Band Antenna System
XAS............	X-Ray Absorption Spectroscopy
XASM..........	Cross Assembler [*Computer science*] (MHDI)
XASM..........	Experimental Air-to-Surface Missile [*Air Force, NASA*]
XAT............	AT & T Aviation Group [*ICAO designator*] (FAAC)
XAT............	X-Ray Analysis Trial
XATA..........	XATA Corp. [*Associated Press*] (SAG)
XATA..........	XATA Corp. [*NASDAQ symbol*] (SAG)
XATEF........	Crosswalk/Air Toxic Emission Factor [*Environmental Protection Agency*] (AEPA)
XAV............	Auxiliary Seaplane Tender [*Ship symbol*]
XAV............	Xavier University, Cincinnati, OH [*OCLC symbol*] (OCLC)
Xavier U (La)...	Xavier University (Louisiana) (GAGS)
Xavier U (Ohio)...	Xavier University (Ohio) (GAGS)
XavrCp........	Xavier Corp. [*Associated Press*] (SAG)
XAY............	Camp Atterbury, IN [*Location identifier FAA*] (FAAL)
XAY............	Xapuri [*Brazil*] [*Airport symbol*] (AD)
xb..............	Cocos [*Keeling*] Islands [*MARC country of publication code Library of Congress*] (LCCP)
XB..............	Crossbar [*Bell System*]
XB..............	Crossbar Switch (NITA)
XB..............	Experimental Bomber (MCD)
XB..............	Exploding Bridge-Wire
XB..............	International Air Transport Association (IATA) [*ICAO designator*] (ICDA)
XBAR..........	Crossbar
XBASE........	Data Base Management Software Package (MHDI)
XBASIC........	Extension of BASIC [*Computer science*]
XBB............	Berne Public Library, Berne, IN [*OCLC symbol*] (OCLC)
XBC............	"B" Corp. [*Toronto Stock Exchange symbol*]
XBC............	External Block Controller
XBC............	External Bus Controller [*Computer science*] (CIST)
XBF............	Fort Wayne, IN [*Location identifier FAA*] (FAAL)
XBG............	Bogande [*Burkina Faso*] [*Airport symbol*] (OAG)
XBG............	City of Bangor, Maine [*FAA designator*] (FAAC)
XBIOS..........	Extended BIOS [*Basic Input/Output System*] [*Operating system*]
XBK............	Xebeck [*Type of ship*] (ROG)
XBL............	Extension Bell [*Telecommunications*] (TEL)
XBLD..........	Extrabold [*Typography*]
xbld............	Extrabold [*Type*] (WDMC)
XBM............	Extended BASIC Mode [*International Computers Ltd.*]
XBM............	State University of New York, College at Brockport, Brockport, NY [*OCLC symbol*] (OCLC)
XBM............	X-Window Bitmap [*For images*]
XBN............	Biniguni [*Papua New Guinea*] [*Airport symbol*] (OAG)
XBO............	Baseops International, Inc. [*ICAO designator*] (FAAC)
XBP............	Bancshare Portfolio Corp. [*Toronto Stock Exchange symbol*]
XBP............	X-Ray Bright Point [*Astronomy*]
XBR............	Brockville [*Canada*] [*Airport symbol*] (OAG)
XBR............	Experimental Breeder Reactor
XBR............	Ozark, AL [*Location identifier FAA*] (FAAL)
XBRA..........	Cross Bracing (MSA)
Xbre............	December (BARN)
XBT............	Crossbar Tandem [*Telecommunications*] (TEL)
xbt............	Exhibit
XBT............	Expendable Bathythermograph [*Oceanography*]
XBTS..........	Extract Bit String [*Computer science*] (PCM)
Xc..............	Capacitive Reactance
XC..............	Caribbean Air Transport [*ICAO designator*] (AD)
XC..............	Cross-Clamp [*of carotid artery*]
XC..............	Cross-Continent Auto Retailers, Inc. [*NYSE symbol*] (SAG)
XC..............	Cross Country [*Also, XCY*]
xc..............	Ex Capitalisation [*Finance*]
X-C............	Ex-Coupon [*Without the right to coupons, as of a bond*] [*Finance*]
XC..............	Excretory Cystogram [*Medicine*] (MAE)
XC..............	Expandable Case
XC..............	Expendable Case (MCD)
XC..............	Experimental Cargo Aircraft
xc..............	Maldives [*MARC country of publication code Library of Congress*] (LCCP)
XC..............	Mexico [*International civil aircraft marking*] (ODBW)
XC..............	Xanthomonus Campestris [*Bacteriology*]
XC..............	X-Chromosome
XC..............	Xenotron Composer (DGA)
XC..............	Xerox Copy
XC & UC......	Exclusive of Covering and Uncovering
XCB............	Extended Core Barrel [*Drilling technology*]
XCCE..........	Extracapsular Cataract Extraction [*Ophthalmology*] (DAVI)
XCD............	Canadian Dollar [*Vancouver Stock Exchange symbol*]
XCDRI........	Xi'an Coal Design and Research Institute (BUAC)
XCE............	X-Band Cassegrain Experimental
XCED..........	Water-Jel Technologies [*NASDAQ symbol*] (SAG)
XCEL..........	Canterbury Corporate Services [*NASDAQ symbol*] (SAG)
XCEL..........	Canterbury Corporate Svcs [*NASDAQ symbol*] (TTSB)
XcelNet........	XcelleNet, Inc. [*Associated Press*] (SAG)
XCFN	External Function [*Computer science*] (DDC)

XCG	Experimental Cargo Glider
X-CGD........	X-Linked Chronic Granulomatous Disease [*Medicine*]
XCH	Christmas Island [*Airport symbol*]
XCH	Exchange (AAG)
X-chrom......	Female Sex Chromosome [*Genetics*] (DAVI)
XCI	X-Chromosome Inactivation [*Genetics*]
XCID	X-Linked Combined Immunodeficiency [*Immunology*]
XCIT	Excitation (AAG)
XCIT	Excite Inc. [*NASDAQ symbol*] (TTSB)
XCL	Armed Merchant Cruiser [*Navy symbol*]
XCL	Contel ASC [*ICAO designator*] (FAAC)
XCL	Cross Claim [*Legal shorthand*] (LWAP)
XCL	Excess Current Liabilities [*Insurance*]
XCL	Excluded from General Declassification Schedule (MCD)
XCL	Exploration Company of Louisiana, Inc. [*Later, XCL Ltd.*] [*AMEX symbol*] (SPSG)
XCL	X-Cal Resources Ltd. [*Toronto Stock Exchange symbol*]
XCL	XCL Ltd. [*Formerly, Exploration Company of Louisiana*] [*AMEX symbol*] (SAG)
XCL Ltd.	XCL Ltd. [*Formerly, Exploration Company of Louisiana*] [*Associated Press*] (SAG)
XCMD	External Command [*Computer science*] (CDE)
XCNGR......	Exchanger (AAG)
XCO............	Compuflight Operation Service, Inc. [*ICAO designator*] (FAAC)
XCO............	Cross Connection
XCOM	CrossCom Corp. [*NASDAQ symbol*] (SAG)
XCOM	CrossComm Corp. [*NASDAQ symbol*] (TTSB)
XCOM	Exterior Communications [*Military*] (CAAL)
XCONN......	Cross Connection
XCP............	Ex-Coupon [*Without the right to coupons, as of a bond*] [*Finance*]
XCP............	Executive Control Program [*Computer science*] (MCD)
XCP............	Expendable Current Profiler [*Instrumentation, oceanography*]
XCPT..........	Except (KSC)
XCR	Little Falls, MN [*Location identifier FAA*] (FAAL)
XCS............	Cape Seppings, AK [*Location identifier FAA*] (FAAL)
XCS............	CompuServe, Inc. [*ICAO designator*] (FAAC)
XCS............	Cross-Country Skiing
XCS............	Ten Call Seconds [*Telecommunications*] (TEL)
XCS............	Xerox Computer Services [*Xerox Corp.*]
XCT............	Execute (IAA)
XCT............	X-Band Communications Transponder
XCTD	Expendable Conductivity-Temperature-Depth [*Probe*] [*Marine science*] (OSRA)
XCTD	Expendable Conductivity-Temperature-Depth Probe (USDC)
XCTD	Expendable Current Temperature Density Profiler (EERA)
XCU............	Crosspoint Control Unit (NITA)
XCU............	Explosion Collapse, Underground Operations
XCU............	Extreme Close-Up [*Also, VCU*] [*Cinematography*] (NTCM)
XCVR..........	Transceiver (AAG)
XCX............	Citibank NA [*ICAO designator*] (FAAC)
XCY............	Cross Country [*Also, XC*]
XD..............	Bureau Veritas SA [*France ICAO designator*] (ICDA)
XD..............	Crossed [*Telecommunications*] (TEL)
XD..............	Examined (ROG)
XD..............	Ex-Directory [*Telecommunications*] (TEL)
X-D	Ex-Dividend [*Without the right to dividend*] [*Finance*] (SPSG)
X/D	Ex Dividendum [*Without (or Exclusive) of Dividend*] [*Finance*] (ROG)
XD..............	Executed (ROG)
XD..............	Executive Development [*Civil Service Commission*]
XD..............	Exploratory Development [*Military*] (MCD)
XD..............	Extra Dense
XD..............	X-Linked Dominant (MEDA)
XD..............	Xylem Disease [*Plant pathology*]
XDA............	Bureau Veritas SA [*France ICAO designator*] (FAAC)
XDA............	X-Band Drive Amplifier
XDC............	Xylene-Dioxane-Cellosolve [*Scintillation solvent*]
XD/CO........	Ex-Directory/Calls Offered [*Telephone service*] (DI)
XDCR	Transducer (AAG)
XDD............	Lockheed Duats [*ICAO designator*] (FAAC)
XDE............	Xylene-Dioxane-Ethanol [*Scintillation solvent*]
XDER	Transducer
XDF............	Exchange Data Format [*Computer science*] (EERA)
XDF............	Extended Distance Feature (ACRL)
XDFLD........	Secondary Index Field [*Computer science*] (MHDI)
XDH............	Xanthine Dehydrogenase [*An enzyme*]
XDI............	Xylene Diisocyanate [*Organic chemistry*]
X-Dis	Ex-Distribution
X-dis	Ex-Distribution (EBF)
X-Div	Ex-Dividend [*Without the right to dividend*] [*Finance*]
XDIVU........	Naval Experimental Diving Unit
XDM............	State University of New York, Agricultural and Technical College at Delhi, Delhi, NY [*OCLC symbol*] (OCLC)
XDM............	Xerox Dry Microfilm (NITA)
XDM............	X-Ray Density Measurement
XDMS	Experimental Data Management System [*Computer science*] (MHDI)
XD/NC........	Ex-Directory/No Connections [*Telephone service*] (DI)
XDP............	Expendable Dissipation Profiler [*Oceanography*]
XDP............	Xanthine Diphosphate [*Biochemistry*] (DAVI)
XDP............	Xanthosine Diphosphate [*Biochemistry*]
XDP............	Xeroderma Pigmentosum [*Inherited, disfiguring syndrome*]
XDP............	X-Ray Density Probe
XDP............	X-Ray Diffraction Powder
XDPC	X-Ray Diffraction Powder Camera
XDPS	X-Band Diode Phase Shifter
XDPU	Expanded Data Processing Unit (DNAB)

XDR	Crusader (ROG)
XDR	External Data Representation [Computer science]
XDR	Transducer (AAG)
XDS	Dispatch Services, Inc. [ICAO designator] (FAAC)
XDS	Exoatmospheric Defense System [DoD]
XDS	Xerox Data Systems [Formerly, SDS]
XDS	X-Ray Diffraction System
XDT	Data Transformation Corp. [ICAO designator] (FAAC)
XDT	Xenon Discharge Tube
XDUCER	Transducer
XDUP	Extended Disk Utilities Program [Computer science]
XDY	DynAir Services, Inc. [ICAO designator] (FAAC)
XDY	Valdosta Moody Air Force Base, GA [Location identifier FAA] (FAAL)
XE	Canadian Express Ltd. [Toronto Stock Exchange symbol Vancouver Stock Exchange symbol]
XE	Experimental Engine [NASA]
XE	South Central [ICAO designator] (AD)
Xe	Xenon [Chemical element]
XEB	Xylanolytic Enzyme Biodegradability [Biochemistry]
XEC	Execute
XECF	Experimental Engine - Cold Flow Configuration [NERVA]
Xechem	Xechem International [Associated Press] (SAG)
Xechm	Xechem International [Associated Press] (SAG)
XED	Medford, OK [Location identifier FAA] (FAAL)
XEDS	X-Ray Energy Dispersive System [Microparticle analysis]
XEF	Excess Ejection Fraction [Cardiology] (DAVI)
XEF	Xenon Fluoride (MCD)
XEG	Xerox Education Group
XEG	X-Ray Emission Gauge
XEIK	Xeikon NV [NASDAQ symbol] (SAG)
Xeikon	Xeikon NV [Associated Press] (SAG)
XEIKY	Xeikon N.V. ADR [NASDAQ symbol] (TTSB)
XEL	Excel Realty Trust [NYSE symbol] (TTSB)
XEL	Excel Realty Trust, Inc. [NYSE symbol] (SPSG)
XEL	Excelsior Life Insurance Co. [Toronto Stock Exchange symbol]
XEL	Helicopteros Xel-Ha SA de CV [Mexico ICAO designator] (FAAC)
XELEDOP	Transmitting Elementary Dipole with Optional Polarity (MCD)
XELFS	Extended Electron Energy Loss Fine Structure (EDCT)
Xen	De Xenophane [of Aristotle] [Classical studies] (OCD)
XEN	Xenia, OH [Location identifier FAA] (FAAL)
Xen	Xenophon [428-354BC] [Classical studies] (OCD)
Xeno	Xenometrix, Inc. [Associated Press] (SAG)
Xenomet	Xenometrix, Inc. [Associated Press] (SAG)
XENOU	Xenometrix, Inc. [NASDAQ symbol] (SAG)
Xenova	Xenova Group Ltd. [Associated Press] (SAG)
XENOW	Xenometrix Inc. Wrrt [NASDAQ symbol] (TTSB)
XEO	Experimental Engineering Orders (DNAB)
XEOS	Xerox Electro-Optical Systems
XEQ	Execute
XER	Exception Register [IBM Corp.] (CIST)
XER	Xerox Corp., Xerox Library Services, Webster, NY [OCLC symbol] (OCLC)
XER	Xerox Reproduction (AAG)
XERB	Experimental Environmental Research Buoy [Marine science] (MSC)
XERG	Xonics Electron Radiography [Medical x-ray imaging equipment]
xero	Xeromammography [Radiology] (DAVI)
Xerox	Xerox Corp. [Associated Press] (SAG)
XES	X-Ray Emission Spectra
XES	X-Ray Energy Spectrometry
XES	X-Ray Exposure Study (NUCP)
XETA	Xeta Corp. [NASDAQ symbol] (NQ)
XETRA-AM	Tijuana, Mexico [AM radio station call letters] (BROA)
XETRA-FM	Tijuana, Mexico [FM radio station call letters] (BROA)
XETV	Tijuana, Mexico [Television station call letters] (BROA)
XEWT-TV	Tijuana, Mexico [Television station call letters] (BROA)
XF	Cobden Airways [ICAO designator] (AD)
XF	Cross-Fade (WDAA)
XF	Experimental Fighter
XF	Extended Family [Unitarian Universalist program]
XF	Extra Fine
xf	Extremely Fine [Philately]
xf	Midway Islands [MARC country of publication code Library of Congress] (LCCP)
XFA	Cross-Field Acceleration
XFA	X-Ray Fluorescence Absorption
XFC	Extended Function Code
XFC	Transfer Charge [Telecommunications] (TEL)
XFC	Transferred Charge Call (NITA)
XFC	X-Band Frequency Converter
XFCN	External Function [Computer science] (CDE)
XFD	Crossfeed (NASA)
XFD	X-Ray Flow Detection
XFER	Transfer (AAG)
xfer	Transfer (CIST)
XFES	Xerox Family Education Services
XFH	X-Band Feed Horn
XfL	Cross in Front of Left Foot [Dance terminology]
XFLO	Crossflow Engine [Automotive engineering]
XFLT	Expanded Flight Line Tester
XFM	Expeditionary Force Message [Usually, EFM] [Low-rate cable or radio message selected from a list of standard wordings]
XFM	State University of New York, College at Fredonia, Fredonia, NY [OCLC symbol] (OCLC)
XFM	X-Band Ferrite Modulator
XFMI	Transformer Interface
XFMR	Transformer (AAG)
xfmr	Transformer (IDOE)
XFN	Victoria, TX [Location identifier FAA] (FAAL)
xformer	Transformer (IDOE)
XFQH	Xenon-Filled Quartz Helix
XFR	Transfer
XFRD	Transferred (ECII)
XFRMR	Transformer
XFS	American Flight Service Systems, Inc. [ICAO designator] (FAAC)
XFS	Fort Sill, OK [Location identifier FAA] (FAAL)
XFS	Xenogenic Fetal Skin [Medicine]
XFS	X-Ray Fluorescence Spectroscopy
XFSS	Auxiliary Flight Service Station [Aviation] (FAAC)
XFT	Xenon Flash Tube
XFX	Airways Corp. of New Zealand Ltd. [ICAO designator] (FAAC)
XG	Air North [ICAO designator] (AD)
XG	Crossing
XG	Xanthan Gum [Chemistry]
XGA	Extended Graphics Adapter [Computer science] (DOM)
XGA	Extended Graphics Array [IBM Corp.]
XGA	General Aviation Terminal, Inc. [Canada ICAO designator] (FAAC)
XGAM	Experimental Guided Air Missiles
XGDS	Exempt from General Declassification Schedule (MCD)
Xge	Exchange [Business term]
XGG	Gorom-Gorom [Burkina Faso] [Airport symbol] (OAG)
XGG	IMP Group Ltd. Aviation Services [Canada ICAO designator] (FAAC)
X-Gluc	X-Glucuronide
XGP	Experimental Geosynchronous Platform (SSD)
XGP	Xanthogranulomatous Pyelonephritis [Medicine]
XGP	Xerox Graphic Printer [Xerox Corp.]
XGPRT	Xanthine-Guanine Phosphoribosyltransferase [An enzyme]
XGRAPHY	Xylography [Wood engraving] (ROG)
XGS	Global Systems, Inc. [ICAO designator] (FAAC)
XGW	Global Weather Dynamics, Inc. [ICAO designator] (FAAC)
XH	Experimental Helicopter
xh	Niue [MARC country of publication code Library of Congress] (LCCP)
XH	Sign-Filled Half-Word Designator [Computer science]
XH	Special Handling Service for Aircraft [ICAO designator] (ICDA)
XHA	Special Handling Service for Aircraft [FAA designator] (FAAC)
XHAIR	Cross Hair (IEEE)
XHF	Extra-High Frequency (NVT)
XHIJ	Ciudad Juarez, Mexico [Television station call letters] (BROA)
XHM	X-Ray Hazard Meter
XHMO	Extended Hueckel Molecular Orbit [Atomic physics] (IEEE)
xho	Xhosa [MARC language code Library of Congress] (LCCP)
XHR	Extra-High Reliability
XHR	Extra-High Resolution (CIST)
XHRI	Xi'an Highway Research Institute (BUAC)
XHRM-FM	Tijuana, Mexico [FM radio station call letters] (BROA)
XHS	Indiana Historical Society, Indianapolis, IN [OCLC symbol] (OCLC)
XHST	Exhaust (AAG)
XHV	Extreme High Vacuum
XHVY	Extra Heavy
X-I	Ex-Interest [Without the right to interest] [Finance]
XI	International Aeradio Ltd. [British ICAO designator] (ICDA)
xi	St. Christopher-Nevis-Anguilla [MARC country of publication code Library of Congress] (LCCP)
XIA	Irving Oil Ltd. [Canada ICAO designator] (FAAC)
XIA	X-Band Inteferometer Antenna
Xian	Christian (VRA)
XIB	IBM Corp., Library Processing Center, White Plains, NY [OCLC symbol] (OCLC)
XIC	Convent of Immaculate Conception Sisters of St. Benedict, Ferdinand, IN [OCLC symbol] (OCLC)
XIC	Transmission Interface Converter
XIC	Xichang [China] [Airport symbol] (OAG)
XIC	X-Inactivation Centre [Genetics]
XICO	Xicor, Inc. [NASDAQ symbol] (NQ)
Xicor	Xicor, Inc. [Associated Press] (SAG)
XICS	Xerox Integrated Composition System [Xerox Corp.] [Computer typesetting system]
XICTMD	Xerox International Center for Training and Management Development [Leesburg, VA]
XID	Exchange Identification
XIE	Xieng Khouang [Laos] [Airport symbol] (AD)
XIH	Xi'an Institute of Highways (BUAC)
XII	Washington, DC [Location identifier FAA] (FAAL)
XII P	Testaments of the Twelve Patriarchs [Pseudepigrapha]
Xilinx	Xilinx, Inc. [Associated Press] (SAG)
XIM	Ithaca College, Ithaca, NY [OCLC symbol] (OCLC)
XIM	X-Ray Intensity Meter
XIN	Ex-Interest [Without the right to interest] [Finance]
XIN	Xizang Institute for Nationalities (BUAC)
XING	Crossing (MCD)
XINT	Ex-Interest [Without the right to interest] [Finance]
XI/O	Execute Input/Output (DEN)
XIO	Executive Input/Output (NITA)
XION	Xionics Document Technologies, Inc. [NASDAQ symbol] (SAG)
XionDoc	Xionics Document Technologies, Inc. [Associated Press] (SAG)
XIOX	Xiox Corp. [NASDAQ symbol] (NQ)
XIP	Execute-in-Place [Computer science]
XIP	Xerox Individualized Publishing
XIPC	Extended Interprocess Communications Facilities
XIQ	Xique-Xique [Brazil] [Airport symbol] (AD)
XIRC	Xircom, Inc. [NASDAQ symbol] (SAG)

Xircom	Xircom, Inc. [*Associated Press*] (SAG)
XIRS	Xenon Infrared Searchlight
XIS	Xenon Infrared Searchlight
XIS	Xerox Imaging System (PCM)
XIS	X^{P}RESS Information Services (IID)
XISS	Xavier Institute of Social Service [*India*] (BUAC)
XIST	Inactive Specific Transcriptase (BARN)
xistor	Transistor (IDOE)
XIT	Extra Input Terminal
XIWT	Cross Industry Working Team
XJ	Assistance Aeroportuaire de l'Aeroport de Paris [*France ICAO designator*] (ICDA)
XJ	Experimental Jaguar [*Jaguar PLC*]
XJ	Mesaba Aviation [*ICAO designator*] (AD)
xj	St. Helena [*MARC country of publication code Library of Congress*] (LCCP)
XJA	Assistance Aeroportuaire de l'Aeroport de Paris [*France*] [*FAA designator*] (FAAC)
XJM	Schenectady County Community College, Schenectady, NY [*OCLC symbol*] (OCLC)
XJN	Milwaukee, WI [*Location identifier FAA*] (FAAL)
XJP	Jasper Public Library, Jasper, IN [*OCLC symbol*] (OCLC)
XJR	Experimental Jaguar Racing
XK	Agence pour la Securite de la Navigation Aerienne en Afrique et a Madagascar (ASECNA) [*ICAO designator*] (ICDA)
XK	Experimental-Eleventh Generation [*Jaguar*] [*Automotive engineering*]
xk	St. Lucia [*MARC country of publication code Library of Congress*] (LCCP)
XK	X-Band Klystron
XKA	Kavouras, Inc. [*ICAO designator*] (FAAC)
XKO	Not Knocked Out (DAVI)
XKX	Agence pour la Securite de la Navigation Afrique-Madagascar [*France*] [*FAA designator*] (FAAC)
XL	Country Connection [*Airline code*] [*Australia*]
XL	Cross-Reference List
XL	Crystal
XL	Excess Lactate
XL	Execution Language [*Computer science*]
XL	EXEL Limited [*NYSE symbol*] (TTSB)
XL	EXEL Ltd. [*NYSE symbol*] (SPSG)
XL	Existing Light [*Photography*] (NTCM)
XL	Extra Large [*or Long*] [*Size*]
XL	Extra Load [*Automotive engineering*]
XL	Extra Long (WDMC)
X$_L$	Inductive Reactance (IDOE)
xl	St. Pierre and Miquelon [*MARC country of publication code Library of Congress*] (LCCP)
XL	Telecomunicacoes Aeronauticas Sociedada Anonima (TASA) [*Brazil ICAO designator*] (ICDA)
XL	Unmarried Lady [*Citizens band radio slang*]
XL	X-Axis of Spacelab [*NASA*] (NASA)
XL	Xylose-Lysine [*Agar base*] [*Microbiology*]
XLA	X-Band Limiter Attenuator
XLA	X-Linked Agammaglobulinaemia [*Medicine*]
X-LA	X-Linked Agammaglobulinemia (STED)
XL & UL	Exclusive of Loading and Unloading
XLATION	Translation
XLB	Xylem-Limited Bacteria [*Plant pathology*]
XLC	Extra Large Capacity
XLC	Extra Luxurious Chaparral
XLC	Indiana University, School of Medicine, Medical Education Resources Program, Indianapolis, IN [*OCLC symbol*] (OCLC)
XLC	USX Capital LLC [*NYSE symbol*] (SAG)
XLC	Xenon Lamp Collimator
XLCnnSI	XLConnect Solutions, Inc. [*Associated Press*] (SAG)
XLCPr	USX Capital LLC 'MIPS' [*NYSE symbol*] (TTSB)
XLCT	XLConnect Solutions, Inc. [*NASDAQ symbol*] (SAG)
XLD	Experimental LASER Device (MCD)
XLD	Jepenssen Data Plan, Inc. [*ICAO designator*] (FAAC)
XLD	Xylose-Lysine-Deoxycholate [*Growth medium*]
XLDT	Xenon LASER Discharge Tube
XLE	Columbus, GA [*Location identifier FAA*] (FAAL)
X-leg	Cross Leg (STED)
XLF	XL Food Systems Ltd. [*Toronto Stock Exchange symbol*]
XLF	X-Ray Luminosity Function [*Cosmology*]
XLG	Lockheed Air Terminal, Inc. [*Guam*] [*ICAO designator*] (FAAC)
XLGX	Xylogics, Inc. [*NASDAQ symbol*] (NQ)
xlh	Extra Large Hinge [*Philately*]
XLH	X-Linked Hupophosphatemia [*Medicine*] (DMAA)
XLI	Extra-Low Interstitial [*Alloy*]
XLI	X-Linked Ichthyosis (STED)
XLISP	Extension of LISP [*List Processor*] 1.5 [*Programming language*] (CSR)
XLIST	Execution List (MCD)
XLJR	X-Linked Juvenile Retinoschisis (STED)
XLL	Extra Lightly Loaded (IAA)
XLM	St. Lawrence University, Canton, NY [*OCLC symbol*] (OCLC)
XLMR	X-Linked Mental Retardation [*Genetics*]
XLNT	Excellent (WGA)
XLNX	Xilinx, Inc. [*NASDAQ symbol*] (SAG)
XLO	Ex-Cell-O Corp. (EFIS)
XL/OS	XL Operating System (NITA)
XLP	Extended-Life Protection [*Automotive engineering*]
XLP	Extra Large-Scale Packaging (MHDI)
XLP	X-Linked Lymphoproliferative Syndrome [*Medicine*]

XLPE	Cross-Linked Polyethylene [*Organic chemistry*] (NRCH)
XLPS	Xenon Lamp Power Supply
XLPS	X-Linked Lymphoproliferative Syndrome [*Medicine*]
XLR	Experimental Liquid Rocket [*Air Force, NASA*]
XLR	X-Linked, Lymphocyte-Regulated [*Genetics*]
XLR	X-Linked Recessive (STED)
XLRH	X-Linked Recessive Hypophosphataemic [*Rickets*] [*Medicine*]
XLS	Excimer LASER System (AAEL)
XLS	Extended Light Scatterer (AAEL)
XLS	Extra-Long Shot (WDMC)
XLS	St. Louis [*Senegal*] [*Airport symbol*] (OAG)
XLS	Xenon Light Source
XLS	Xerox Learning Systems
XLSS	Xenon Light Source System
XLT	Telecomunicacoes Aeronauticas SA [*Brazil*] [*ICAO designator*] (FAAC)
XLT	Xenon LASER Tube
XLTC	Excel Technology [*NASDAQ symbol*] (TTSB)
XLTCP	Excel Technology, Inc. [*NASDAQ symbol*] (SAG)
XLTCP	Excel Tech $0.40 Cv Pfd [*NASDAQ symbol*] (TTSB)
XLTCW	Excel Technology Wrrt'B' [*NASDAQ symbol*] (TTSB)
XLTN	Translation (NASA)
XLTR	Translator (MSA)
XLWB	Extra-Long Wheelbase
XM	Christmas
XM	Crossmatch (MAE)
XM	Excitation Monochromator
XM	Expanded Memory
XM	Experimental Missile [*Air Force, NASA*]
XM	Experimental Model
X$_m$	Magnetic Susceptibility [*Physics*] (DAVI)
XM	Research Missile [*NATO*]
XM	Servicios a la Navegacion en el Espacio Aereo Mexicano (SENEAM) [*Mexico ICAO designator*] (ICDA)
xm	St. Vincent [*MARC country of publication code Library of Congress*] (LCCP)
XMA	Martin Aviation Services [*ICAO designator*] (FAAC)
XMAP	Sweeper Device [*Navy symbol*]
XMAS	Christmas
XMAS	Expandable Machine Accounting System (IAA)
XMAS	Extended Mission Apollo Simulation [*NASA*] (IEEE)
X-mat	Crossmatch [*Hematology*] (DAVI)
X-match	Cross-Match (STED)
XMBA	Executive Master of Business Administration (GAGS)
X/MBR	Cross Member [*Automotive engineering*]
XMC	Borough of Manhattan Community College, New York, NY [*OCLC symbol*] (OCLC)
XMC	Malacoota [*New South Wales, Australia*] [*Airport symbol*] (AD)
XmC	Standard Microfilm Reproductions Ltd., Scarborough, ON, Canada [*Library symbol Library of Congress*] (LCLS)
XMD	Ozark, AL [*Location identifier FAA*] (FAAL)
XME	Medgar Evers College of the City University of New York, Brooklyn, NY [*OCLC symbol*] (OCLC)
XMFR	Transformer (AAG)
XMG	Mahendranagar [*Nepal*] [*Airport symbol*] (OAG)
XMH	Manihi [*French Polynesia*] [*Airport symbol*] (OAG)
XMI	Christmas Island [*Seismograph station code, US Geological Survey*] (SEIS)
XMI	Masasi [*Tanzania*] [*Airport symbol*] (OAG)
XMI	Seymour-Moss International Ltd. [*Vancouver Stock Exchange symbol*]
XMIM	Transmitter Interface Module [*Army*]
xmission	Transmission (IDOE)
xmit	Transmit (IDOE)
XMIT	Transmit [*or Transmitter*]
XMITR	Transmitter (ADDR)
XMITTER	Transmitter (NTCM)
xmitter	Transmitter (IDOE)
XML	Extensible Markup Language [*Computer science*] (IGQR)
XML	Miles Laboratories, Inc., Miles Pharmaceutical Division, West Haven, CT [*OCLC symbol*] (OCLC)
XML	Minlaton [*Australia Airport symbol Obsolete*] (OAG)
XMM	Extended Memory Manager [*Computer science*] (PCM)
XMM	Mamaia [*Romania*] [*Airport symbol*] (AD)
XMM	State University of New York, Agricultural and Technical College at Morrisville, Morrisville, NY [*OCLC symbol*] (OCLC)
XMM	Xaverian Missionary Society of Mary, Inc. (TOCD)
XMM	Xeromammography [*Radiology*] (DAVI)
XMM	X-Ray Multi-Mirror Mission [*Space observatory*]
xmn	Transmission
X (Mode)	Extraordinary Mode (MCD)
XMOS	Cross Metal Oxide Semiconductor (NITA)
XMP	Experimental Mathematical Programming System [*Computer science*] (MHDI)
XMP	Marion Public Library, Marion, IN [*OCLC symbol*] (OCLC)
XMP	Xanthosine Monophosphate [*Biochemistry*]
XMP	X/Open Management Protocol [*Computer science*]
XMP	X-Ray Micro-Probe (AAEL)
XMR	Cape Canaveral, FL [*Location identifier FAA*] (FAAL)
XMS	Experimental Development Specification [*Military*] (CAAL)
XMS	Experimental Missile Specifications
XMS	Extended Memory Specification [*Computer science*] (PCM)
XMS	Xavier Mission Sisters [*Catholic Mission Sisters of St. Francis Xavier*] [*Roman Catholic religious order*]
XMS	X-Band Microwave Source

XMS	Xerox Memory System
XMSN	Transmission (AAG)
XMT	Exempt (NVT)
XMT	Transmit (MSA)
xmt	Transmit (IDOE)
XMT	X-Band Microwave Transmitter
XMTD	Transmitted (MCD)
XMTG	Transmitting
Xmtl	Experimental (DOMA)
XMTL	Transmittal (IEEE)
XMTR	Transmitter
xmtr	Transmitter (IDOE)
XMT-REC	Transmit-Receive (AAG)
XMTR-REC	Transmitter-Receiver
XMX	Servicios a la Navegacion en el Espacio Aereo Mexicano [Mexico ICAO designator] (FAAC)
XN	Canadian National Telecommunications [Canada ICAO designator] (ICDA)
XN	Christian
XN	Ex-New [Without the right to new stocks or shares] [Stock exchange term] (SPSG)
XN	Experimental (Navy)
XNA	Xenoreactive Natural Antibody [Biology]
XNA	Xinhua News Agency [China]
XNB	X-Band Navigation Beacon
XNC	Canadian National Telecommunications [FAA designator] (FAAC)
XNC	Nazareth College of Rochester, Rochester, NY [OCLC symbol] (OCLC)
XNE	Xerox New Enterprises
XNET	XcelleNet, Inc. [NASDAQ symbol] (SAG)
XNEW	Ex New Issue [Without the right to new stocks or shares] [Stock exchange term]
XNG	Crossing [Aviation] (FAAC)
XNG	Quang Ngai [Vietnam] [Airport symbol] (AD)
XNL	NELINET [New England Library Information Network], Newton, MA [OCLC symbol] (OCLC)
XNN	Xining [China] [Airport symbol] (OAG)
XNO	North, SC [Location identifier FAA] (FAAL)
XNOS	Experimental Network Operating System
XNS	Navtech Systems Support, Inc. [Canada ICAO designator] (FAAC)
XNS	Xerox Network Services (NITA)
XNS	Xerox Network Systems [Telecommunications]
XNT	NOTAMS International, Inc. [ICAO designator] (FAAC)
XNTY	Christianity
XNU	Xinjang Norman University [China] (BUAC)
XNV	TIGIN Ltd. [ICAO designator] (FAAC)
XNVA	Xenova Group PLC [NASDAQ symbol] (SAG)
XNVAY	Xenova Group ADS [NASDAQ symbol] (TTSB)
XNX	Xenex Industries & Resources Ltd. [Vancouver Stock Exchange symbol]
XO	000 (Degrees) Communic [NYSE symbol] (TTSB)
XO	Crystal Oscillator (IEEE)
XO	Executive Officer [Military]
XO	Expenditure Order [Military] (AABC)
XO	Experimental Officer [Also, EO, ExO] [Ministry of Agriculture, Fisheries, and Food] [British]
XO	Extra Old [Designation on brandy labels]
XO	Rio Airways [ICAO designator] (AD)
XO	Xanthine Oxidase [Also, XOD] [An enzyme]
XO	X-Axis of Orbiter [NASA] (NASA)
XO	Xylenol Orange [An indicator] [Chemistry]
XOB	Xenon Optical Beacon
XOC	Experimental On-Line Capabilities [Computer science]
XOD	Xanthine Oxidase [Also, XO] [An enzyme]
XOFF	Transmitter Off (BUR)
XOGP	Xograph (VRA)
XOID	Xyloid [Woody] (ROG)
XOMA	XOMA Corp. [NASDAQ symbol] (SAG)
XOMD	Xomed Surgical Products, Inc. [NASDAQ symbol] (SAG)
XomedS	Xomen Surgical Products, Inc. [Associated Press] (SAG)
XON	Cross-Office Highway [Telecommunications] (TEL)
XON	Exxon Corp. [NYSE symbol] (SPSG)
XON	Transmitter On (BUR)
XOP	Extended Operation
XOP	X-Ray Out of Plaster [Radiology] (DAVI)
XOR	Exclusive Operating Room [Medicine] (MAE)
XOR	Exclusive Operation [Computer single-key cryptosystem] (PCM)
XOR	Exclusive Or [Gates] [Computer science]
XOS	Cross-Office Slot [Telecommunications] (TEL)
XOS	Extra Outsize [Clothing]
XOS	Xerox Operating System
XOT	Extra Output Terminal [Computer science] (MHDI)
xover	Crossover (IDOE)
XOW	Express Order Wire [Telecommunications] (TEL)
XOX C	XOX Corp. [Associated Press] (SAG)
XOXC	XOX Corp. [NASDAQ symbol] (SAG)
XP	Avior [ICAO designator] (AD)
XP	Exophoria [Medicine] (MEDA)
XP	Expandable Processor [IBM Corp.] [Computer science]
XP	Expansionist Party of the United States [Political party] (EA)
XP	Express Paid
XP	Express Parcel Systems [Europe]
XP	Extra Person (WGA)
XP	Fire Resistive Protected [Insurance classification]

XP	Radio Aeronautica Paraguaya Sociedad Anonima (RAPSA) [Paraguay] [ICAO designator] (ICDA)
xp	Spratly Islands [MARC country of publication code Library of Congress] (LCCP)
XP	X-Axis of Payload [NASA] (NASA)
XP	Xeroderma Pigmentosum [Inherited, disfiguring syndrome]
XPA	Pama [Burkina Faso] [Airport symbol] (OAG)
XPA	Pan Am Weather Systems [FAA designator] (FAAC)
XPA	X-Band Parametric Amplifier
XPA	X-Band Passive Array
XPA	X-Band Planar Array
XPA	X-Band Power Amplifier
XPAA	X-Band Planar Array Antenna
XPARS	External Research Publication and Retrieval System [Department of State]
XPC	Christus [Christ] [Latin]
XPC	Express Passenger Coach
XPC	Morgan StanGp 7%CiscoSy'PERQS' [AMEX symbol] (TTSB)
XPC	Morgan Stanley Group, Inc. [AMEX symbol] (SAG)
XPD	Cross-Polarization Discrimination [Telecommunications]
XPD	Expedient Demise [Used as title of novel by Len Deighton]
XPD	Expedite (MUGU)
XPD	X-Ray Photoelectron Diffraction
XPDR	Transponder (MUGU)
XPDU	X Protocol Data Unit (TNIG)
XPED	Xpedite Systems [NASDAQ symbol] (TTSB)
XPED	Xpedite Systems, Inc. [NASDAQ symbol] (SAG)
XPED	X-Ray Photoelectron Diffraction
Xpedite	Xpedite Systems, Inc. [Associated Press] (SAG)
XPF	Explosion Release Factor [Nuclear energy] (NUCP)
XPG	Southport Aerospace Centre [Canada] [FAA designator] (FAAC)
XPG	X/Open Portability Guide [Computer science]
XPH	Port Heiden, AK [Location identifier FAA] (FAAL)
XPHS	Xylan Polyhydrogensulfate [Antineoplastic drug]
XPI	Cross-Polarization Interference [in radio transmission]
XPI	Xinjang Petroleum Institute [China] (BUAC)
XPL	Explain [or Explanation] (IAA)
XPL	Explosive (AAG)
XPLOR	Xerox 9700 Users' Association (EA)
Xplor	Xplor Corp. [Associated Press] (SAG)
XPLOS	Explosive (FAAC)
XPLR	Xplor Corp. [NASDAQ symbol] (TTSB)
XPLT	Exploit (MUGU)
XPM	Expanded Metal [Heavy gauge]
XPM	Xerox Planning Model [A computerized representation of the Xerox Corp.'s operations]
XPN	Expansion (AAG)
XPN	External Priority Number (ECII)
XPNDR	Transponder (AAG)
XPONDER	Transponder
xponder	Transpondor (IDOE)
X-POP	X-Body Axis Perpendicular to Orbit Plane [Aerospace]
XPP	Express Paid Letter (ROG)
XPP	Xi Psi Phi [Fraternity]
XPP	Xylem Pressure Potential [Botany]
XPPA	X-Band Pseudopassive Array
XPPA	X-Band Pulsed Power Amplifier
XPR	Air-Rep [FAA designator] (FAAC)
XPR	Ex-Privileges [Without the right to privileges] [Finance]
XPrA	USX CORP 6.50% CV Pfd [NYSE symbol] (TTSB)
x pri	Ex-Privileges [Without the right to privileges] [Finance] (DS)
XPRS	US Xpress Enterprises, Inc. [NASDAQ symbol] (SAG)
XPRSA	U.S. Xpress Enterprises'A' [NASDAQ symbol] (TTSB)
XPRT	Expert Software [NASDAQ symbol] (TTSB)
XPRT	Expert Software, Inc. [NASDAQ symbol] (SAG)
XPS	Expert System [Computer science] (IAA)
XPS	X-Band Phase Shifter
XPS	XP International BV [Netherlands ICAO designator] (FAAC)
XPS	X-Ray Photoelectron Spectroscopy (RDA)
XPS	X-Ray Photoemission Spectroscopy
XPSW	External Processor Status Word
XPT	Crosspoint [Switching element] (MSA)
XPT	Export
XPT	Express Paid Telegraph
XPT	External Page Table [Computer science] (BUR)
X PT	Extra Point (WGA)
XPT	X-Band Pulse Transmitter
XPT	Xitron Portable Terminal (DGA)
XPU	West Kuparuk, AK [Location identifier FAA] (FAAL)
XPW	American Ex-Prisoners of War (EA)
XPX	Phoenix Flight Operations Ltd. [Canada ICAO designator] (FAAC)
XQ	Caribbean International [ICAO designator] (AD)
XQ	Cross-Question [Transcripts]
XQ	Experimental Target Drone [Air Force, NASA]
X/Q	Relative Concentration [Symbol] (NRCH)
XQA	Greenville, ME [Location identifier FAA] (FAAL)
XQH	Xenon Quartz Helix
XQM	Queens College, Flushing, NY [OCLC symbol] (OCLC)
XQP	Quepos [Costa Rica] [Airport symbol] (OAG)
XR	Cross Reference (MCD)
XR	Empresa de Servicios Aeronauticos [Cuba ICAO designator] (ICDA)
XR	Examiner (ROG)
XR	Exchange Rate [Economics]
XR	Export Reactor [Nuclear energy] (NRCH)
XR	Ex-Rights [Without Rights] [Investment term]

XR	Extended Range [*Film*] [*Briteline Corp.*]
XR	Extended Response (WGA)
XR	Extension Register
XR	External Reset
XR	Index Register
XR	No Returns Permitted [*Business term*]
XR	Roentgen Ray [*Radiology*] (DAVI)
XR	RY II Financial Corp. [*Toronto Stock Exchange symbol*]
XR	X-Ray
XR	X-Ray Reflectivity (AAEL)
XRA	X-Ray Assistant [*British military*] (DMA)
XRAY	Dentsply International [*NASDAQ symbol*] (SAG)
X-ray	Roentgen Beam Technology (AAEL)
XRB	X-Band RADAR Beacon
XRB	X-Ray Background [*Cosmology*]
XRC	Xerox Research Centre of Canada Library [*UTLAS symbol*]
XRC	X-Ray Centroid
XRCD	X-Ray Crystal Density
XRD	Crossroad [*Postal Service standard*] (OPSA)
XRD	X-Ray Diffraction [*or Diffractometer*]
XRDF	X-Ray Radial Distance Function [*Surface chemistry analysis*]
XRDS	Crossroads
X-REA	X-Ray Events Analyzer (KSC)
X-REF	Cross Reference (NG)
XREP	Extended Reporting (CIST)
XRF	Experimental Reproduction File [*Computer science*] (ECII)
XRF	Experimental Reproduction Film (DIT)
XRF	Explosion Release Factor [*Nuclear energy*] (NRCH)
XRF	Extended Recovery Facility (NITA)
XRF	Extended Reliability Feature (HGAA)
XRF	Rockefeller Foundation, Library, New York, NY [*OCLC symbol*] (OCLC)
XRF	X-Ray Fluorescence [*Spectrometry*] (AAEL)
XRFS	X-Ray Fluorescence Spectrometer
XRG	X-Ray Generator [*Instrumentation*]
XRGP	Extended Range Guided Projectiles (MCD)
XRI	Xenium Resources, Inc. [*Vancouver Stock Exchange symbol*]
XRII	X-Ray Image Intensifier
XRIT	X-Rite, Inc. [*NASDAQ symbol*] (NQ)
X-Rite	X-Rite, Inc. [*Associated Press*] (SAG)
XRL	Extended-Range Lance [*Missile*]
XRL	X-Ray LASER
XRM	External Relational Memory
XRM	External ROM [*Read Only Memory*] Mode [*Computer science*] (IAA)
XRM	Extra Range Multigrade [*Automotive engineering*]
XRM	X-Ray Microanalyzer [*or Microscopy*] (IEEE)
XRMD	X-Ray Microdiffraction [*Surface analysis*]
XRN	RY NT Financial Corp. [*Toronto Stock Exchange symbol*]
XRN	X-Linked Recessive Nephrolithiasis [*Medicine*]
XROAD	Crossroad
XROI	X-Ray Optical Interferometer
XRP	X-Ray and Photofluorography Technician [*Navy*]
XRP	X-Ray Polychromator
XRPM	X-Ray Projection Microscope (IEEE)
XRS	X-Ray Spectrometry
XRT	Ex-Rights [*Without Rights*] [*Investment term*] (SPSG)
XRT	Extended-Range TOW
XRT	X-Ray Technician [*Navy*]
X-RT	X-Ray Telescope (MCD)
XRT	X-Ray Therapy [*or Treatment*]
XRTOW	Extended-Range TOW [*Tube-Launched, Optically Tracked, Wire-Guided*] [*Weapon*] (MCD)
X-RTS	Ex-Rights [*Without Rights*] [*Investment term*]
X-Rts	Ex Rights (EBF)
XRW	Fort Campbell, KY [*Location identifier FAA*] (FAAL)
XRX	Xerox Corp. [*NYSE symbol*] (SPSG)
XRY	Jerez De La Frontera [*Spain*] [*Airport symbol*] (OAG)
XRY	RY Financial Corp. [*Toronto Stock Exchange symbol*]
XRY	Yakima, WA [*Location identifier FAA*] (FAAL)
XS	Across Shoulder (WDMC)
XS	Catholic Mission Sisters of St. Francis Xavier (TOCD)
XS	Christus [*Christ*] [*Latin*]
XS	Cross Section
XS	Excess
XS	Expenses
XS	Extra Small
XS	Extra Strong
XS	Extremely Severe [*Rock climbing*]
X/S	Over the Shoulder Shot [*Also, OS*] [*Cinematography*] (NTCM)
XS	Societe Internationale de Telecommunications Aeronautiques, Societe Cooperative (SITA) [*ICAO designator*] (ICDA)
XS	X-Axis of Solid Rocket Booster [*NASA*] (NASA)
XS	Xerces Society (EA)
XS	Xiphisternum [*Also called the xiphoid process*] [*Anatomy*] (DAVI)
XS3	Excess Three [*Code*]
XS-11	Excess Eleven [*1967 group of scientist-astronauts selected by NASA*]
XSA	Cross-Sectional Area [*Cardiology*]
XSA	Spectrum Air Service, Inc. [*ICAO designator*] (FAAC)
XSA	X-Band Satellite Antenna
XSAES	X-Ray Stimulated Auger Electron Spectroscopy (MCD)
XSAL	Xenon Short Arc Lamp
XSAM	Experimental Surface-to-Air Missile [*Military*] (IAA)
X-SAR	Xband-Synthetic Aperture Radar (EERA)
XSB	Smith Barney Holdings [*NYSE symbol*] (SAG)

XSB	Xavier Society for the Blind (EA)
XSC	Southampton Center of Long Island University, Southampton, NY [*OCLC symbol*] (OCLC)
XSC	South Caicos [*British West Indies*] [*Airport symbol*] (OAG)
XSCID	X-Linked Server Combined Immunodeficiency [*"Bubble Boy" disease*] [*Medicine*]
XSCR	Xscribe Corp. [*NASDAQ symbol*] (NQ)
Xscribe	Xscribe Corp. [*Associated Press*] (SAG)
XSD	Southeast Dubois County, School Corp. Library, Ferdinand, IN [*OCLC symbol*] (OCLC)
XSD	Tonopah, NV [*Location identifier FAA*] (FAAL)
XSE	Sebba [*Burkina Faso*] [*Airport symbol*] (OAG)
XSECT	Cross Section
xsect	Cross Section (VRA)
X-section	Cross Section (IDOE)
XSF	Springfield, OH [*Location identifier FAA*] (FAAL)
XSF	X-Ray Scattering Facility
X-SFA	X-Ray Surface Forces Apparatus [*Imaging technique*]
XSL	Experimental Space Laboratory
XS-LIM	Exceeds Limits of Procedure (DAVI)
XSLR	Crossed Straight Leg Raising [*Sign*] [*Neurology*] (DAVI)
XSM	Experimental Strategic Missile
XSM	Experimental Surface Missile
XSM	X-Ray Stress Measurement
XSMDC	Expanding Shielded Mild Detonating Cord (MCD)
XSN	Stepheville Aviation Services [*Canada ICAO designator*] (FAAC)
XSOA	Excess Speed of Advance Authorized [*Navy*] (NVT)
X-SONAD	Experimental Sonic Azimuth Detector (MCD)
XSP	Extended Set Processor [*Computer science*] (MHDI)
XSP	Singapore-Seletar [*Singapore*] [*Airport symbol*] (OAG)
XSP	Xi Sigma Pi [*Fraternity*]
XSP	Xylem Sap Potential [*Botany*]
XSPV	Experimental Solid Propellant Vehicle
XSR	X-Band Scatterometer RADAR
XSRG	X-Ray Standard Review Group [*Department of Health and Human Services*] (EGAO)
XSS	Experimental Space Station [*NASA*]
XSS	Xenon Solar Simulator
XSSM	Experimental Surface-to-Surface Missile [*Military*] (IAA)
XST	Experimental Stealth Tactical Demonstrator [*Air Force*]
XST	Xylem Sap Tension [*Botany*]
XSTA	X-Band Satellite Tracking Antenna
XSTD	Expendable Salinity/Temperature/Depth Probe [*Oceanography*] (MSC)
XSTD	X-Band Stripline Tunnel Diode
XSTDA	X-Band Stripline Tunnel Diode Amplifier
XSTR	Extra Strong (MSA)
XSTR	Transistor (AAG)
XSTT	Excess Transit Time
XSV	Expendable Sound Velocimeter [*Oceanography*] (MSC)
XSW	X-Ray Standing Wave [*Physics*]
XSWIS	X-Ray Standing Wave Interference Spectroscopy
XSYS	Xxsys Technologies [*NASDAQ symbol*] (SAG)
XsysTc	Xxsys Technologies [*Associated Press*] (SAG)
XSYSW	XXsys Technology Wrrt [*NASDAQ symbol*] (TTSB)
XT	Christ
XT	Cross Talk (IEEE)
XT	Executive Transportation [*ICAO designator*] (AD)
XT	Exotropia Near [*Ophthalmology*]
XT	Extended
XT	Extended Processor (NITA)
X(T)	Intermittent Exotropia [*Ophthalmology*] (DAVI)
XT	Servicos Auxiliares de Transportes Aereos (SATA) [*Brazil ICAO designator*] (ICDA)
X$_T$	Total Reactance (IDOE)
X$_t$	Total Reactance (IDOE)
XT	X-Axis of External Tank [*NASA*] (NASA)
XT	X-Ray Tube
Xta	Chiasma [*Anatomy*] (DAVI)
XTA	X-Band Tracking Antenna
XTAL	Crystal
xtal	Crystal (IDOE)
xtalk	Crosstalk (IDOE)
XTALK	Crosstalk [*Telecommunications*] (MSA)
XTASI	Exchange of Technical Apollo Simulation Information [*NASA*] (IEEE)
XTB	Experimental Test Bed [*Army*] (DOMA)
XTC	Excess Three Code (IAA)
XTC	Exco Technologies Ltd. [*Toronto Stock Exchange symbol*]
XTC	External Transmit Clock
XTE	X-Ray Timing Explorer
XTEL	Cross Tell (IEEE)
XTEL	XeTel Corp. [*NASDAQ symbol*] (TTSB)
XTEM	Cross Sectional Transmission Electron Microscopy (AAEL)
XTEN	Xerox Telecommunications Network [*Proposed*] (TSSD)
XTG	Thargomindah [*Queensland*] [*Airport symbol*] (AD)
XTIAN	Christian
XTJ	Advance Aviation Services, Inc. [*ICAO designator*] (FAAC)
XTK	Crosstrack [*Cross track error*] (GAVI)
XTLK	Cross Talk [*Aviation*] (CIST)
XTLO	Crystal Oscillator
XTM	Experimental Test Model
XTM	X-Ray Tomographic Microscope
XTN	Christian (ROG)
XTN	Qatn [*South Arabia*] [*Airport symbol*] (AD)
XTN	XTree Tools for Networks [*XTree Co.*] [*Computer science*] (PCM)

XTND	Extend [or Extended]
XTO	Cross Timbers Oil [NYSE symbol] (TTSB)
XTO	Cross Timbers Oil Co. [NYSE symbol] (SPSG)
XTO	Taroom [Queensland] [Airport symbol] (AD)
XTO	X-Band Triode Oscillator
XTON	EXECUTONE Information Systems, Inc. [NASDAQ symbol] (SPSG)
XTON	Executone Info Sys [NASDAQ symbol] (TTSB)
XTP	Express Transfer Protocol (ACRL)
XTP	Xanthosine Triphosphate [Biochemistry]
XTPA	Extended Transaction Processing Architecture [Computer science] (CIST)
XTPA	X-Band Tunable Parametric Amplifier
XTPS	Xenotron Text Processing System (DGA)
XTR	Sector Airlines [Canada ICAO designator] (FAAC)
XTR	Tara [Queensland] [Airport symbol] (AD)
XTR	X-Ray Transition Radiation
XTR	XTRA Corp. [NYSE symbol] (SPSG)
XTRA	Extra (ROG)
XTRA	XTRA Corp. [Associated Press] (SAG)
XTRAN	Experimental Translation Language (IAA)
XTRM	Brass Eagle [Stock market symbol]
XTRM	Extreme
XTRY	Extraordinary (ROG)
XTS	Cross-Tell Simulator (IEEE)
XTV	Xerox Team Vision [Xerox Business Products and Systems Group] [El Segundo, CA] (TSSD)
XTV	Xerox Technology Ventures [El Segundo, CA] (ECON)
XTWA	X-Band Traveling Wave Amplifier
XTWM	X-Band Traveling Wave MASER
XTX	New York Tax Exempt Income [AMEX symbol] (TTSB)
XTX	New York Tax Exempt Income Fund [AMEX symbol] (SAG)
XTX	X-Band Transmitter
XTY	Christianity
XU	Aerorepresentaciones Tupac Amaru [Peru] [ICAO designator] (ICDA)
XU	Excretory Urogram [Medicine]
XU	Fire Resistive Unprotected [Insurance classification]
XU	Trans Mo Airlines [ICAO designator] (AD)
XU	Xavier University [Louisiana; Ohio]
Xu	X-Ray Unit [Radiology] (DAVI)
XU	X Unit [A unit of wavelength]
XUB	Circleville, OH [Location identifier FAA] (FAAL)
XUG	Xyvision Users Group (EA)
XUM	Xenium [Gift] (ROG)
XUPS	Exide Electronics Group [NASDAQ symbol] (TTSB)
XUPS	Exide Electronics Group, Inc. [NASDAQ symbol] (SAG)
XUS	Americas Income Trust [NYSE symbol] (SPSG)
XUT	Aerorepresentaciones Tupac Amaru [Peru] [ICAO designator] (FAAC)
XUV	Extreme Ultraviolet
XV	Mississippi Valley Airways [ICAO designator] (AD)
XV	X-Ray Vision
XVA	X-Ray Vidicon Analysis
XVC	Xenotron Video Composer (DGA)
XVERS	Transverse (AAG)
xVit	Xenopus Vitellogenin
XVN	Venice, FL [Location identifier FAA] (FAAL)
XVP	Executive Vice President
XVP	Xerox Virtual Printroom
XVR	Exchange Voltage Regulator [Telecommunications] (TEL)
XVRC	Xavier Corp. [NASDAQ symbol] (SAG)
XVT	Extensible Virtual Toolkit [Computer science]
XVT	Rome, NY [Location identifier FAA] (FAAL)
XVTR	Transverter (AAG)
XW	Crosswind [Aviation] (FAAC)
XW	Experimental Warhead
XW	Extra Wide [Size]
XW	Ex-Warrants [Without Warrants] [Finance] (SPSG)
XW	Walker's Cay Air Terminal [ICAO designator] (AD)
X-Warr	Ex Warrants (EBF)
X-WARR	Ex-Warrants [Without Warrants] [Finance]
XWAVE	Extraordinary Wave (IEEE)
X-WAY	Expressway
XWB	Ozark, Fort Rucker, AL [Location identifier FAA] (FAAL)

XWC	Wabash-Carnegie Public Library, Wabash, IN [OCLC symbol] (OCLC)
XWCC	Expanded Water Column Characterization [Oceanography] (MSC)
XWS	Experimental Weapon Specification
XWS	Experimental Weapon System
XWS	WSI Corp. [ICAO designator] (FAAC)
XWW	World Weatherwatch [Canada ICAO designator] (FAAC)
XWY	West Union, IA [Location identifier FAA] (FAAL)
XX	Dos Equis [Beer] [Standard Brands, Inc.]
XX	Doublecross Committee [British military] (DMA)
XX	Double Excellent
XX	Feminine Chromosome Pair
XX	Heavy [ICAO] (FAAC)
xx	No Place [or Unknown] [MARC country of publication code Library of Congress] (LCCP)
X-X	Pitch Axis [Aerospace] (AAG)
XX	Twenty Committee [British espionage unit named after a "double-cross" operation it conducted during World War II]
XX	Valdez Airlines [ICAO designator] (AD)
XX	Without Securities or Warrants [Business term]
XX	Wrinkled Paper (BARN)
XXC	University of South Dakota, Card Reproduction Project, Vermillion, SD [OCLC symbol] (OCLC)
XXC	Xerox Canada, Inc. [Toronto Stock Exchange symbol]
XXH	Double Extra Heavy (DAC)
XXL	Extra-Extra Large [Size]
XXS	Extra-Extra Strong
XXS	Skyplan Services Ltd. [Canada ICAO designator] (FAAC)
XXSTR	Double Extra Strong
XxsysTc	Xxsys Technologies [Associated Press] (SAG)
XXV	Administracion de Aeropuertos [Bolivia] [ICAO designator] (FAAC)
XXX	Broken Paper (BARN)
XXX	International Urgency Signal
XXX	Peru, IN [Location identifier FAA] (FAAL)
XXX	Triple Excellent
XXXX	Quadruple Strength
XY	Burma [International civil aircraft marking] (ODBW)
XY	Masculine Chromosome Pair
XY	Munz Northern [ICAO designator] (AD)
XY	Myanmar [Aircraft nationality and registration mark] (FAAC)
XY	Ryan Air (GAVI)
XY	Spouse [Citizens band radio slang]
XY	Xylography [Wood engraving] (ROG)
XYA	X-Y Axis
XYA	Yandina [Solomon Islands] [Airport symbol] (OAG)
XYAT	X-Y Axis Table
XYBR	Xybernaut Corp. [NASDAQ symbol] (SAG)
Xybrnaut	Xybernaut Corp. [Associated Press] (SAG)
Xybrnt	Xybernaut Corp. [Associated Press] (SAG)
XYC	Aero Chasqui SA [Peru] [ICAO designator] (FAAC)
XYC	Irvine, KY [Location identifier FAA] (FAAL)
XYD	Daughter [Citizens band radio slang]
XYL	Ex-Young-Lady [Wife] [Amateur radio slang]
XYL	Xylocaine [Topical anesthetic] [Astra trademark for lidocaine]
XYL	Xylophone [Music]
xyl	Xylophone (WDAA)
Xyl	Xylose [Also, x] [A sugar]
XylanCp	Xylan Corp. [Associated Press] (SAG)
XYLN	Xylan Corp. [NASDAQ symbol] (SAG)
XYLO	Xylophone [Music] (ADA)
Xylogic	Xylogics, Inc. [Associated Press] (SAG)
XYM	Husband [Citizens band radio slang]
XYP	X-Y Plotter
XYR	X-Y Recorder
XYrDev	Ten-Year Device [Military decoration]
Xytron	Xytronyx, Inc. [Associated Press] (SAG)
XYX	Xytronyx, Inc. [AMEX symbol] (SPSG)
XYZ	Examine Your Zipper
XYZ	Extra Years of Zest [Gerontology]
XYZ	Island Airlines [ICAO designator] (FAAC)
XZ	Air Tasmania [ICAO designator] (AD)
XZ	Myanmar [Aircraft nationality and registration mark] (FAAC)
XZY	Philadelphia, PA [Location identifier FAA] (FAAL)

Y

By Acronym

Y................ Admittance [Symbol] [IUPAC]
Y................ Alleghany Corp. [NYSE symbol] (SPSG)
Y................ Closed at Sea (for High Degree of Emergency Readiness) [Ship's fittings classification]
Y................ Coach [Airline fare code]
Y................ Depth, Height, or Altitude [Physics] (BARN)
Y................ Doublecross [i.e., to betray] [Criminal slang]
Y................ Dry Air [Meterology] (BARN)
Y................ Except Sixth Form [For the wearing of schoolgirls' uniforms] [British]
Y................ Ex-Dividend and Sales in Full [Investment term] (DFIT)
Y................ Late Operating Contact [Symbol] (DEN)
Y................ Luminance
Y................ Male Chromosome
Y................ Nominal Gross National Product
y................ Ordinate (IDOE)
Y................ Pathfinder [Army skill qualification identifier] (INF)
Y................ Planck Function [Symbol] [IUPAC]
Y................ Prototype [Designation for all US military aircraft]
Y................ Pyrimidine [Single-letter symbol] [Genetics] (DOG)
Y................ [A] Pyrimidine Nucleoside [One-letter symbol; see Pyd]
Y................ Tanker [Army symbol]
Y................ Three-Phase Star Connection [Symbol] (DEN)
Y................ Transitional Testing [Aircraft]
Y................ Tyrosine [One-letter symbol; see Tyr]
Y................ Upsilon [Symbol] [Quantum physics]
Y................ Vertical Deflection [Symbol] (DEN)
Y................ Yacht (ADA)
Y................ Yankee [Phonetic alphabet] [International] (DSUE)
Y................ Yard [Measure]
y................ Yard (IDOE)
Y................ Yaw
Y................ Y-Axis
Y................ Yea [Vote]
Y................ Year
y................ Year (IDOE)
Y................ Yeates' Pennsylvania Reports [1791-1808] [A publication] (DLA)
Y................ Yellow [Phonetic alphabet] [Royal Navy World War I] (DSUE)
Y................ Yellow [Horticulture]
Y................ Yen [Monetary unit in Japan]
Y................ Yeoman
Y................ Yersinea [A genus of bacteria]
Y................ Yerushalmi [Palestinian Talmud] (BJA)
Y................ Yield [Agriculture] [Stock exchange term]
y................ Yocto (MEC)
Y................ Yoke [Phonetic alphabet] [World War II] (DSUE)
Y................ Yorker [Phonetic alphabet] [Pre-World War II] (DSUE)
Y................ Yoshitomi Pharmaceutical Ind. Co. Ltd. [Japan] [Research code symbol]
Y................ You
y................ You (WDAA)
Y................ Young (AAMN)
Y................ Younger [or Youngest]
Y................ Young Men's [or Women's] Christian Association [Short form of reference, especially to the group's building or specific facility, as "the Y swimming pool"]
Y................ Young's Modulus of Elasticity [Symbol] [See also E, YME]
Y................ Youngstown [Diocesan abbreviation] [Ohio] (TOCD)
Y................ Young Vic [British theatrical company]
Y................ Your
y................ Your (WDAA)
Y................ Y-Punch (IAA)
Y................ Yttrium [Preferred form, but see also Yt] [Chemical element]
Y................ Yugoslavia [IYRU nationality code] (IYR)
Y................ Yuppie [As in Y-people]
Y2K............ Year 2000
Y2Y............ Yellowstone to Canada's Yukon Territory
Y-12............ Oak Ridge Y-12 Plant [Department of Energy] [Oak Ridge, TN] (GAAI)
YA................ Ash Lighter [Navy symbol]
YA................ Government Civil Aviation Authority [ICAO designator] (ICDA)
ya................ Yarn (VRA)
YA................ Yaw Axis
YA................ Year Authorized (NITA)
YA................ Yersinia Arthritis [Medicine] (DMAA)
YA................ Yet Another [Computer hacker terminology] (NHD)
Y/A............. York-Antwerp Rules [Marine insurance]

YA............... Yosemite Association (EA)
YA............... Young Achiever [Australia]
YA............... Young Adult [Refers to books published for this market]
YA............... Young Audiences (EA)
YA............... Youth Authority Programs [Public human service program] (PHSD)
YAA............ Yachtsmen's Association of America (EA)
YAA............ Youth Ambassadors of America [Later, YAI] (EA)
YAAR.......... Yacimientos Arqueologicos [Database] [Ministerio de Cultura] [Spanish] [Information service or system] (CRD)
YAAS.......... Yunan Academy of Agricultural Sciences [China] (BUAC)
YAB............ Yet Another BASIC [Beginner's All-Purpose Symbolic Instruction Code] [Computer science]
YABA.......... Yacht Architects and Brokers Association (EA)
YABA.......... Yet Another Bloody Acronym [Computer hacker terminology] (NHD)
YABA.......... Young American Bowling Alliance (EA)
YABC.......... Yesterday's Authors of Books for Children [A publication]
YABRI......... Young Adult Book Review Index [A publication]
YAC............ Yacuiba [Bolivia] [Airport symbol] (AD)
YAC............ Yeast Artificial Chromosome [Genetics] [Biochemistry]
YAC............ Young Adult Council of National Social Welfare Assembly (EA)
YAC............ Young Astronaut Council (EA)
YAC............ Youth Affairs Council [Australia]
YACC.......... Yet Another Compiler-Compiler (MHDB)
YACC.......... Yet Another Compiler-Complier (HGAA)
YACC.......... Young Adult Conservation Corps
YACC.......... Young America's Campaign Committee [Later, FCM] (EA)
YACE.......... Yukon Alpine Centennial Expedition
Yacht.......... Yachting [A publication] (BRI)
YACHT........ Youth and Christ Hang Together
YACP.......... Young Adult Chronic Patient [Medicine] (MEDA)
YACS.......... Yugoslavia, Albania, Croatia, Serbia [Organized crime group]
YACTOFF..... Yaw Actuator Offset (KSC)
YACV.......... Youth Accommodation Coalition of Victoria [Australia]
Yad............ Yadaim (BJA)
YAU............ Young's Nova Scotia Admiralty Decisions [A publication] (DLA)
YADH.......... Yeast Alcohol Dehydrogenase [An enzyme]
YAEC.......... Yankee Atomic Electric Co.
YAF............ Asbestos Hill [Canada] [Airport symbol Obsolete] (OAG)
YAF............ Yidishe Arbeter Froyen (BJA)
YAF............ Young Americans for Freedom (EA)
YAF............ Young America's Foundation (EA)
YAF............ Yugoslavian Air Force
YAG............ Fort Frances [Canada] [Airport symbol] (OAG)
YAG............ Miscellaneous Auxiliary [Self-propelled] [Navy ship symbol]
YAG............ Yagi [Kashiwara] [Japan] [Seismograph station code, US Geological Survey] [Closed] (SEIS)
YAG............ Young Actors Guild (EA)
YAG............ Yttrium-Aluminum Garnet [LASER technology]
YAGL.......... Yttrium Aluminum Garnet LASER
Yag-laser..... Yttrium-Aluminum Garnet LASER (MED)
YAGR.......... Ocean RADAR Station Ship [Navy symbol Obsolete]
YAH............ Alfred University, Alfred, NY [OCLC symbol] (OCLC)
YAH............ Yahtse [Alaska] [Seismograph station code, US Geological Survey] (SEIS)
YAHOH........ Young Hard-of-Hearing Adults [British] (EAIO)
Yahoo.......... Yahoo, Inc. [Associated Press] (SAG)
Yahoo.......... Yet Another Hierarchically Officious Oracle [World Wide Web] (DOM)
YAI............ Young Adult Institute and Workshop (EA)
YAI............ Youth Ambassadors International (EA)
YAIC.......... Young American Indian Council
YAIG.......... Yttrium Alumnium Iron Garnet [LASER technology] (IAA)
YAK............ Yakima [Diocesan abbreviation] [Washington] (TOCD)
YAK............ Yakovlev [Russian aircraft symbol; initialism taken from name of aircraft's designer]
YAK............ Yakutat [Alaska] [Airport symbol] (OAG)
YAK............ Yakutsk [Former USSR Seismograph station code, US Geological Survey] (SEIS)
Yal............ Yalkut Shim'oni (BJA)
YAL............ Yalta [Former USSR Seismograph station code, US Geological Survey Closed] (SEIS)
YAL............ Youth Affairs Lobby (AIE)
YAL............ Yttrium Aluminum LASER
YALE.......... Spreckels Industries [NASDAQ symbol] (TTSB)
Yale L & Pol'y Rev... Yale Law and Policy Review [A publication] (DLA)
Yale Rev Law & Soc Act'n... Yale Review of Law and Social Action [A publication] (DLA)

Yale Rev of L and Soc Action... Yale Review of Law and Social Action [*A publication*] (DLA)
Yale U .... Yale University (GAGS)
YalMakh ...... Yalkut Makhiri (BJA)
YALSA .... Young Adult Library Services Association [*American Library Association*]
YAM............. American Museum of Natural History, New York, NY [*OCLC symbol*] (OCLC)
YAM............. Sault Ste. Marie [*Canada*] [*Airport symbol*] (OAG)
YAM............. Yamagata [*Japan*] [*Seismograph station code, US Geological Survey*] (SEIS)
YAM............. Yet Another MODEM [*Modulator-Demodulator*] [*Communications program*]
YAM............. Young Australian Male [*Lifestyle classification*]
YAN............. Yancey Railroad Co. [*AAR code*]
YAN .... Yangoru [*Papua New Guinea*] [*Seismograph station code, US Geological Survey*] (SEIS)
YANB .... Yardville National Bancorp [*NASDAQ symbol*] (SAG)
YANB .... Yardville Natl Banc [*NASDAQ symbol*] (TTSB)
YANCON ...... Yankee Conference [*College sports*]
Y & C .... Younge and Collyer's English Chancery Reports [*1841-43*] [*A publication*] (DLA)
Y & C .... Younge and Collyer's English Exchequer Equity Reports [*1834-42*] [*A publication*] (DLA)
Y & CCC ...... Younge and Collyer's English Chancery Cases [*62-63 English Reprint*] [*1841-43*] [*A publication*] (DLA)
Y & C Ch ..... Younge and Collyer's English Chancery Reports [*1841-43*] [*A publication*] (DLA)
Y & C Ch Cas... Younge and Collyer's English Chancery Cases [*62-63 English Reprint*] [*1841-43*] [*A publication*] (DLA)
Y & C Ex...... Younge and Collyer's English Exchequer Equity Reports [*1834-42*] [*A publication*] (DLA)
Y & C Exch... Younge and Collyer's English Exchequer Equity Reports [*1834-42*] [*A publication*] (DLA)
Y & Coll ..... Younge and Collyer's English Chancery Reports [*1841-43*] [*A publication*] (DLA)
Y & Coll ..... Younge and Collyer's English Exchequer Equity Reports [*1834-42*] [*A publication*] (DLA)
Y & D .... Bureau of Yards and Docks [*Later, NFEC*] [*Navy*]
Y & J .... Younge and Jervis' English Exchequer Reports [*1826-30*] [*A publication*] (DLA)
Y & L .... York and Lancaster Regiment [*Military unit*] [*British*] (DMA)
Y & LR .... York and Lancaster Regiment [*Military unit*] [*British*]
Y & MV........ Yazoo & Mississippi Valley Railroad Co.
Y & R .... Young & Rubicam International [*Advertising agency*]
YANGPAT..... Yangtze Patrol, Asiatic Fleet [*Navy*]
YANK .... Yankee (ROG)
YANK .... Youth of America Needs to Know
YankEnS ..... Yankee Energy Systems, Inc. [*Associated Press*] (SAG)
YANPET .... Saudi Yanbu Petrochemical Co. [*Saudi Arabia*] (BUAC)
yao.............. Yao (Bantu) [*MARC language code Library of Congress*] (LCCP)
YAO .... Yaounde [*Cameroon*] [*Airport symbol*] (OAG)
YAP............. Yap [*Caroline Islands*] [*Airport symbol*] (OAG)
YAP............. Yaw and Pitch
YAP............. Yield Analysis Pattern [*Computer science*]
YAP............. Young Americans in Prague [*Expatriot Americans in the 1990's*]
Yap.............. Young Aspiring Professional [*In book title "YAP; the Official Young Aspiring Professional's Fast-Track Handbook"*] [*Lifestyle classification*]
YAP............. Young Aspiring Professional (WDAA)
YAP............. Younger American Playwright [*Slang*]
YAPA .... Youth Action Policy Association [*Australia*]
YAPA .... Youth and Performing Arts [*Australia*]
YAPD .... Young Americans of Polish Descent [*Defunct*] (EA)
YAPLO .... Yorkshire Association of Power Loom Overlookers [*A union*] [*British*] (DCTA)
YAPLO .... Yorkshire Association of Power Loom Workers [*England*] (BUAC)
Yappie .... Young Artist Professional [*Lifestyle classification*]
YAR .... Yemen Arab Republic
YAR .... York-Antwerp Rules [*Marine insurance*]
YARA .... Young Americans for Responsible Action
Y-ARD........... Yarrow Admiralty Research Department [*Navy British*]
YARD............ Youth Associated with the Restoration of Democracy [*Kenya*] [*Political party*] (EY)
YARDS.......... Yard Activity Reporting and Decision System (PDAA)
YardvN......... Yardville National Bancorp [*Associated Press*] (SAG)
YARS .... Yugoslav Astronautical and Rocket Society (BUAC)
YARU .... Yale Arbovirus Research Unit [*Yale University*] [*Research center*] (RCD)
YAS............. Yasodhara Ashram Society (EA)
YAS............. Yaw Attitude Sensor
YASD .... Young Adult Services Division - of ALA [*American Library Association*] (EA)
YASGB .... Youth Association of Synagogues in Great Britain (BI)
YASIG .... Young Adult Special Interest Group [*Canadian Library Association*]
YASOQB....... Ye Anciente and Secret Order of Quiet Birdmen (EA)
YAT............. Attawapiskat [*Canada*] [*Airport symbol*] (OAG)
YAT............. Yaldymych [*Former USSR Seismograph station code, US Geological Survey Closed*] (SEIS)
YAT............. Yugoslavian Air Trnsport (BUAC)
Yate-Lee...... Yates-Lee on Bankruptcy [*3rd ed.*] [*1887*] [*A publication*] (DLA)
Yates Sel Cas... Yates' Select Cases [*1809*] [*New York*] [*A publication*] (DLA)
Yates Sel Cas (NY)... Yates' Select Cases [*1809*] [*New York*] [*A publication*] (DLA)
YATS .... Youth Attitude Tracking Survey [*Navy*]
YAUI .... Yet Another User Interface [*Computer science*]

YAUN .... Yet Another Unix Nerd [*Computer hacker terminology*] (NHD)
YAVIS .... Young, Attractive, Verbal, Intelligent, and Successful
YAWF .... Youth Against War and Fascism (EA)
Yawnie .... Youngish Anglophone of Westmount and Notre-Dame-De-Grace [*Canadian Yuppie identified in Keith Harrison's novel "After Six Days"*] [*Lifestyle classification*]
YAWP .... Yet Another Word Processor (BYTE)
YB................ Hyannis Aviation [*ICAO designator*] (AD)
YB................ Meteorological Operational Telecommunications Network Europe [*ICAO designator*] (ICDA)
YB................ Yard Bird [*Confined to camp*] [*Military slang*]
YB................ Yearbook
YB................ Yellowknife Bear Resources, Inc. [*Toronto Stock Exchange symbol*]
YB................ Yeshiva Benarroch. Tetuan (BJA)
YB................ Your Business [*A publication*]
YB................ Youth Brigade [*Australia*]
YB................ Youth Bureau [*Australia*]
Yb................ Ytterbium [*Chemical element*]
Yb-169-DTPA.. Ytterbium 169 Pentetate Sodium [*Chemistry*] (DAVI)
YBA............. Youth Basketball Association [*Joint program of NBA Players' Association and YMCA*]
YBAAA .... Yearbook. Association of Attenders of Alumni of the Hague Academy of Int ernational Law [*A publication*] (DLA)
YB Air & Space L... Yearbook of Air and Space Law [*A publication*] (DLA)
YB Ames....... Year Book. Ames Foundation [*A publication*] (DLA)
YBASL.......... Yearbook of Air and Space Law [*A publication*] (DLA)
YBBFC.......... Younger Brothers Band Fan Club [*Defunct*] (EA)
YBC............. Baie Comeau [*Canada*] [*Airport symbol*] (OAG)
YBC............. Yale Babylonian Collection (BJA)
YBCA .... Yearbook of Commercial Arbitration [*A publication*] (DLA)
YBCO .... Yttrium Barium Copper Oxide [*Inorganic chemistry*]
YBD .... Bowdock [*Navy symbol*]
YBD .... Yellow Band Resources [*Vancouver Stock Exchange symbol*]
YBD .... Young British Designers
YBDSA .... Yacht Brokers, Designers, and Surveyors Association (BUAC)
YBDSA .... Yacht Designers and Surveyors Association (EAIO)
YBE............. Stewart Aviation Services, Inc. [*ICAO designator*] (FAAC)
YBE............. Uranium City [*Canada*] [*Airport symbol*] (OAG)
YBE............. York Borough Board of Education, Professional Education Library [*UTLAS symbol*]
YB Ed I....... Year Books of Edward I [*A publication*] (DLA)
YB Eur Conv on Human Rights... Year Book. European Convention on Human Rights [*A publication*] (DLA)
YB Europ Conv HR... Yearbook. European Convention on Human Rights [*The Hague, Netherlands*] [*A publication*] (DLA)
YBG............. Saguenay [*Canada*] [*Airport symbol*] (OAG)
YB Human Rights... Yearbook on Human Rights [*A publication*] (DLA)
YB Hum Rts... Yearbook on Human Rights [*A publication*] (DLA)
YBIA............ Youth Business Initiative Australia
YBICJ .... Yearbook. International Court of Justice [*A publication*] (DLA)
YB Int L Comm... Yearbook. International Law Community [*A publication*] (DLA)
YB Int'l L Comm'n... Yearbook. International Law Commission [*A publication*] (DLA)
YB Int'l Org... Yearbook of International Organizations [*A publication*] (DLA)
YBJ............. Baie Johan Beetz [*Canada*] [*Airport symbol*] (OAG)
YBK............. Baker Lake [*Canada*] [*Airport symbol*] (OAG)
YBL............. Campbell River [*Canada*] [*Airport symbol*] (OAG)
YB League... Yearbook. League of Nations [*A publication*] (DLA)
YBM............. State University of New York, College at Buffalo, Buffalo, NY [*OCLC symbol*] (OCLC)
Y-BOCS........ Yale-Brown Obsessive-Compulsive Scale [*Psychology*]
Yb of Leg Stud... Year Book of Legal Studies [*Madras, India*] [*A publication*] (DLA)
Yb of the Eur Conv on Human Rights... Yearbook. European Convention on Human Rights [*The Hague, Netherlands*] [*A publication*] (DLA)
YBP............. Years before Present
YB P1 Edw II... Year Books, Part 1, Edward II [*A publication*] (DLA)
YBPC........... Young Black Programmers Coalition (EA)
YBR .... Brandon [*Canada*] [*Airport symbol*] (OAG)
YBR .... Sludge Removal Barge [*Navy*]
YBR .... Yellow Brick Road [*Intelligence test*]
YBRA .... Yellowstone-Bighorn Research Association (EA)
YBRD .... Yemen Bank for Reconstruction and Development (BUAC)
YB Rich II.... Bellewe's Les Ans du Roy Richard le Second [*1378-1400*] [*A publication*] (DLA)
YB (Rolls Ser)... Year Books, Rolls Series [*1292-1546*] [*A publication*] (DLA)
YB (RS) .... Year Books, Rolls Series [*1292-1546*] [*A publication*] (DLA)
YB (RS) .... Year Books, Rolls Series, Edited by Horwood [*1292-1307*] [*A publication*] (DLA)
YB (RS) .... Year Books, Rolls Series, Edited by Horwood and Pike [*1337-46*] [*A publication*] (DLA)
YBSC .... Year Books, Selected Cases [*A publication*] (DLA)
YB Sch L ..... Yearbook of School Law [*A publication*] (DLA)
YB (Sel Soc)... Year Books, Selden Society [*1307-19*] [*A publication*] (DLA)
YB (SS) .... Year Books, Selden Society [*1307-19*] [*A publication*] (DLA)
YBT............. Yale Oriental Series. Babylonian Texts [*New Haven, CT*] [*A publication*] (BJA)
YBT............. Youssef Ben Tachfine [*Morocco*] [*Seismograph station code, US Geological Survey*] (SEIS)
YBTV........... Young Broadcasting, Inc. [*NASDAQ symbol*] (SAG)
YBTVA .... Young Broadcasting 'A' [*NASDAQ symbol*] (TTSB)
YBUN .... Yearbook of the United Nations [*A publication*] (DLA)
YBV............. Berens River [*Canada*] [*Airport symbol*] (OAG)
YBW............ Lehman Brothers, Inc. [*AMEX symbol*] (SAG)
YB World Pol... Yearbook of World Polity [*A publication*] (DLA)
YBX............. Blanc Sablon [*Canada*] [*Airport symbol*] (OAG)

YC	Alaska Aeronautical Industries [*ICAO designator*] (AD)
Y/C	Luminance, Color
YC	Open Lighter [*Non-self-propelled*] [*Navy symbol*]
YC	Rescue Coordination Center [*ICAO designator*] (ICDA)
YC	Yacht Club
YC	Yale College (ROG)
YC	Yankee Conference [*College sports*]
YC	Yard Craft [*Navy symbol*]
YC	Yaw Channel
YC	Yaw Coupling
YC	Y-Chromosome
YC	Yeomanry Cavalry [*Military British*]
YC	Yesterday's Children (EA)
YC	Yola Clay Loam [*A soil type*]
YC	Young Conservative (WDAA)
y/c	Your Cable (DS)
YC	Youth Clubs [*Public-performance tariff class*] [*British*]
YC	Youth Conservative [*Political party*] [*British*]
YC	Youth Custody (WDAA)
YCA	Yacht Charter Association [*British*] (DBA)
YCA	Yacht Cruising Association (BUAC)
YCA	Yachting Club of America (EA)
YCA	Yale-China Association (EA)
YCA	Yearbook of Construction Articles [*A publication*] (AAGC)
YCA	Yield Component Analysis [*Botany*]
YCA	Young Concert Artists (EA)
YCA	Young Conservative Alliance of America [*Later, Campus Action Network*] (EA)
YCA	Youth Camping Association [*British*] (BI)
YCAP	Youth Committee Against Poverty
Y-CASP	City of York Community & Agency Social Planning Council (AC)
YCB	Cambridge Bay [*Canada*] [*Airport symbol*] (OAG)
YCB	Yeast Carbon Base
YCB	Yellow Creek Bluff [*Alaska*] [*Seismograph station code, US Geological Survey*] (SEIS)
YCC	Computer Center [*Yale University*] [*Research center*] (RCD)
YCC	Lightness, Color, Chromatics (TELE)
YCC	Luma Chroma Chroma [*Photo CD channels*] (PCM)
YCC	York Centre [*Vancouver Stock Exchange symbol*]
YCC	Youth Civic Center
YCC	Youth Conservation Corps (EA)
YCC	Yuma City-County Public Library, Yuma, AZ [*OCLC symbol*] (OCLC)
YCCA	National Youth Council on Civic Affairs [*Superseded by CCNYA*] (EA)
YCCA	Yorkshire Canary Club of America (EA)
YCCIP	Youth Community Conservation and Improvement Projects [*Department of Labor*]
YCD	Fueling Barge [*Navy symbol Obsolete*]
YCD	Nanaimo [*Canada*] [*Airport symbol*] (OAG)
YCD	Youth Correction Division [*Department of Justice*]
YCEE	Youth Cost per Entered Employment [*Job Training and Partnership Act*] (OICC)
YCES	Yeongnam Crop Experiment Station [*South Korea*] (BUAC)
YCF	Car Float [*Non-self-propelled*] [*Navy symbol*]
YCF	Yankee Critical Facility [*Nuclear energy*]
YCF	Young Calvinist Federation (EA)
YCF	Young Conservative Foundation [*Later, CAF*] (EA)
YCF	Youth Citizenship Fund (EA)
YCG	Castlegar [*Canada*] [*Airport symbol*] (OAG)
YCGS	York County Genealogical Society (EA)
YCH	Chatham [*Canada*] [*Airport symbol*] (OAG)
YCHT	Yacht
YCI	Year-Class Strength Index [*Pisciculture*]
YCI	Young Communist International [*Dissolved, 1943*]
YCJCYAQFTJB	Your Curiosity Just Cost You a Quarter for the Jukebox [*Tavern sign*]
YCK	Aircraft Transportation Lighter [*Navy symbol*]
YCK	Open Cargo Lighter [*Navy ship symbol*] [*Obsolete*]
YCL	Charlo [*Canada*] [*Airport symbol*] (OAG)
YCL	Yolk Cytoplasmic Layer [*Embryology*]
YCL	Young Communist League of the United States of America (EA)
YCL	Youth Counseling League (EA)
YCLA	Young Circle League of America [*Later, Workmen's Circle*] (EA)
YCM	State University of New York, College at Cortland, Cortland, NY [*OCLC symbol*] (OCLC)
YCM	Yellow, Cyan, and Magenta [*Color model*] (WDMC)
YCM	YMCA Camp [*Montana*] [*Seismograph station code, US Geological Survey Closed*] (SEIS)
YCM	Young Christian Movement [*Formerly, YCW*] [*Defunct*]
YCMD	Yaw Gimbal Command (KSC)
YCN	Cochrane [*Canada*] [*Airport symbol*] (OAG)
YCNAC	Young Conservatives National Advisory Committee (BUAC)
YCND	Youth Campaign for Nuclear Disarmament [*British*] (BI)
YCNP	Yellow Creek Nuclear Plant (NRCH)
YCO	Coppermine [*Canada*] [*Airport symbol*] (OAG)
YCP	Yaw Coupling Parameter
YCp	Yeast Centromere Plasmid [*Genetics*]
YCP	York College of Pennsylvania, York, PA [*OCLC symbol*] (OCLC)
YCP	Youth Challenge Program
YCPO	Young Children: Priority One [*Kiwanis Club*]
YCR	Cross Lake [*Canada*] [*Airport symbol*] (OAG)
YCS	High School Young Christian Students (EA)
YCS	Young Christian Student (AEBS)
YCS	Young Collector Series [*A publication*]
YCS	Youth Community Service [*ACTION project*]

YCSDS	Young Children's Social Desirability Scale (EDAC)
YCSM	Young Christian Student Movement
YCTF	Younger Chemists Task Force [*American Chemical Society*]
YCTSD	Yugoslav Center for Technical and Scientific Documentation [*Information service or system*] (IID)
YCU	Youth Clubs United
YCV	Aircraft Transportation Lighter [*Non-self-propelled*] [*Navy symbol*]
YCV	Young Citizens Volunteers [*14th (Service) Battalion, Royal Irish Rifles*] [*British military*] (DMA)
YCW	Young Christian Workers [*Later, YCM*] (EA)
YCY	Clyde River [*Canada*] [*Airport symbol*] (OAG)
YCY	Rescue Co-Ordination Center [*FAA designator*] (FAAC)
YCZ	Yellow Caution Zone [*Runway lighting*] [*Aviation*]
YD	Ama Air Express [*ICAO designator*] (AD)
YD	Authority Supervising the Aerodrome [*ICAO designator*] (ICDA)
YD	Floating Crane [*Non-self-propelled*] [*Navy symbol*]
YD	Floating Derrick [*Navy*]
YD	People's Democratic Republic of Yemen [*ANSI two-letter standard code*] (CNC)
YD	Yard [*Measure*]
YD	Yard [*Navy*]
yd	Yard [*Measure*] (ODBW)
YD	Yaw Damper [*Aviation*] (MCD)
YD	Yaw Deviation
YD	Yoreh De'ah. Shulhan 'Arukh (BJA)
YD	Yorkshire Dragoons [*British military*] (DMA)
YD	Younger Dryas [*Geoscience*]
YD	Youth Defence (BUAC)
yd²	Square Yard (CDAI)
YD³	Cubic Yard
YDA	Dawson City [*Yukon*] [*Airport symbol*] (AD)
YDA	Young Democrats of America (EA)
YDA	Youth Development Association [*British*] (DBA)
YDAW	Dawson Public Library, Yukon [*Library symbol National Library of Canada*] (NLC)
YDAY	Yesterday [*Business term*]
YDB	Yield Diffusion Bonding
YDB	Youth Development Bureau [*Department of Health and Human Services*]
YDC	Yaw Damper Computer
YDC	Yeast Extract - Dextrose Calcium Carbonate Agar [*Microbiology*]
YDC	Yellow-Dog Contract (MHDB)
YDC	Yiddish Dictionary Committee (EA)
YDC	Youth for Development and Cooperation (EAIO)
YDCA	Young Democratic Clubs of America [*Later, YDA*] (EA)
ydcw	DC Working Voltage (IDOE)
YDCW	Ymgyrch Diogelu Cymru Wledig [*Campaign for the Protection of Rural Wales*] [*See also CPRW*] (EAIO)
YDDPA	Youth Development and Delinquency Prevention Administration [*Later, Youth Development Bureau*] [*HEW*]
YDF	Deer Lake [*Canada*] [*Airport symbol*] (OAG)
YDG	District Degaussing Vessel [*Navy symbol*]
YDG	Yarding (WGA)
YDI	Yard Drain Inlet (WDAA)
YDI	Youth Development, Inc. (EA)
YDM	State University of New York, College of Ceramics at Alfred University, Alfred, NY [*OCLC symbol*] (OCLC)
YDN	Dauphin [*Canada*] [*Airport symbol*] (OAG)
YDP	Yeni Dogus Partisi [*New Dawn Party*] [*Turkish Cyprus*] [*Political party*] (EY)
YDPCK	Klondike National Historic Site, Parks Canada [*Lieu Historique National Klondike, Parcs Canada*] Dawson City, Yukon [*Library symbol National Library of Canada*] (NLC)
YDPP	Young Democratic Progressive Party [*Macedonia*] [*Political party*] (EY)
YDQ	Dawson Creek [*Canada*] [*Airport symbol*] (OAG)
YDS	Yards (MCD)
YDS	Yorkshire Dialect Society [*British*] (DBA)
YDSD	Yards and Docks Supply Depot [*Obsolete Navy*]
YDSO	Yards and Docks Supply Office [*Navy*]
YDT	Diving Tender [*Non-self-propelled*] [*Navy symbol*]
YDY	Authority Supervising the Aerodome [*FAA designator*] (FAAC)
YE	Grand Canyon Airlines [*ICAO designator*] (AD)
YE	Lighter, Ammunition [*Navy symbol*]
YE	Pearson Aircraft [*ICAO designator*] (AD)
YE	Year End
YE	Yeast Enolase [*An enzyme*]
YE	Yellow Edges
YE	Yellow Enzyme [*Biochemistry*]
ye	Yemen Arab Republic [*MARC country of publication code Library of Congress*] (LCCP)
YE	Yemen Arab Republic [*ANSI two-letter standard code*] (CNC)
YE	Yevreyskaya Entsiklopediya [*A publication*] (BJA)
YE	Youth Enterprise (AIE)
YE	Youth Entry [*British military*] (DMA)
YEA	Yanhee Electricity Authority [*Thailand*] (BUAC)
YEA	Yaw Error Amplifier
YEA	Year of Energy Action
YEA	Yeast Extract Agar [*Microbiology*]
Yea	Yeates' Pennsylvania Reports [*1791-1808*] [*A publication*] (DLA)
YEA	Youth Emotions Anonymous (EA)
YEA	Youth Evangelism Association (EA)
Yearb P7 Hen VI	Year Books, Part 7, Henry VI [*A publication*] (DLA)
Yeates	Yeates' Pennsylvania Reports [*1791-1808*] [*A publication*] (DLA)
Yeates (PA)	Yeates' Pennsylvania Reports [*1791-1808*] [*A publication*] (DLA)

Yeb	Yebamoth (BJA)
YEB	Young Engineers for Britain (ACII)
YEC	Youngest Empty Cell
YEC	Youth Employment Competency (OICC)
YEC	Youth Exchange Centre [Seymour Mews House] [British] (CB)
YECP	Yeast Extract-Casein Peptone [Medium]
YedNum	Yedi'ot Numismatiyot be-Yisrael. Jerusalem (BJA)
YEDPA	Youth Employment and Demonstration Projects Act of 1977
YEDTA	Youth Employment and Demonstration Training Act [Department of the Interior]
YEE	Youth and Environment Europe [Denmark] (BUAC)
Yeepie	Youthful Energetic Elderly Person Involved in Everything [Aging yuppie] [Lifestyle classification]
YEER	Youth Entered Employment Rate [Job Training and Partnership Act] (OICC)
Ye Et Rg Rt	Yorkshire East Riding Regiment [British military] (DMA)
YEF	Young European Federalists (BUAC)
YEF	Young Executives Forum [Automotive Service Industry Association]
YEF	Youth and Environment Europe (BUAC)
YEG	Edmonton [Canada] [Airport symbol] (OAG)
YEG	Yeast Extract - Glucose [Medium]
YEH	Yellow Enzyme, Reduced [Biochemistry]
YEI	Yellow Fever Immunization [Medicine] (DB)
YEIS	Yamaha Energy Induction System
YEK	Eskimo Point [Canada] [Airport symbol] (OAG)
YEL	Elliot Lake [Canada] [Airport symbol] (OAG)
YEL	Equitable Life Assurance Society of the United States, General Library, New York, NY [OCLC symbol] (OCLC)
YEL	Yellow (AAG)
yel	Yellow (VRA)
Yel	Yelverton's English King's Bench Reports [1603-13] [A publication] (DLA)
YEL	Young England Library [A publication]
YEL	Youth Employment Lobby [Canada]
YELD	Yeldham [England]
YELL	Yellow (DAVI)
YELL	Yellow Corp. [NASDAQ symbol] (SAG)
YELL	Yellowstone National Park
YellowCp	Yellow Corp. [Associated Press] (SAG)
yelsh	Yellowish [Philately]
Yelv	Yelverton's English King's Bench Reports [1603-13] [A publication] (DLA)
Yelv (Eng)	Yelverton's English King's Bench Reports [1603-13] [A publication] (DLA)
YEM	Empire State College, Saratoga Springs, NY [Inactive] [OCLC symbol] (OCLC)
YEM	Yemen (Sanaa) [ANSI three-letter standard code] (CNC)
YEM	Young European Movement (BUAC)
YEMINCO	Yemen Oil and Mineral Industrial Co. (BUAC)
YEN	Ammunition Lighter [Navy symbol] (DNAB)
YEN	Youth of European Nationalities (BUAC)
YEO	Yeomanry
YEO	Yeovil [British depot code]
YEO	Young Entrepreneurs Organization [Wichita, KS] (EA)
YEO	Your Eyes Only (PCM)
YEO	Youth Employment Officer [British]
YEOM	Yeomanry (WGA)
Yeomy	Yeomanry [British military] (DMA)
YEp	Yeast Episomal Plasmid [Genetics]
YEP	Young Eucalypt Program (EERA)
YEP	Your Educational Plan (AEBS)
YEPD	Yeast Extract - Peptone Dextrose [Medium]
Yer	Yerger's Tennessee Supreme Court Reports [A publication] (DLA)
YER	Yerkesik [Turkey] [Seismograph station code, US Geological Survey] (SEIS)
Yer	Yerushalmi [Palestinian Talmud] (BJA)
Yerg	Yerger's Tennessee Reports [9-18 Tennessee] [A publication] (DLA)
Yerg (Tenn)	Yerger's Tennessee Reports [9-18 Tennessee] [A publication] (DLA)
YES	Yankee Energy System [NYSE symbol] (TTSB)
YES	Yankee Energy System, Inc. [NYSE symbol] (SPSG)
YES	Years of Extra Savings
YES	Yeast Estrogen System [Biochemistry]
YES	Yeast Extract Sucrose [Cell growth medium]
YES	Yogurt Extra Smooth [Trademark of the Dannon Co., Inc.]
YES	Young Entomologists' Society (EA)
YES	Young Europeans for Security [Netherlands] (BUAC)
YES	Young Executive Society [Automotive Warehouse Distributors Association]
YES	Youth Education Services [Summer program]
YES	Youth Effectiveness Skills Program [Australia]
YES	Youth Emergency Service
YES	Youth Employment Service [Department of Employment] [British] (EA)
YES	Youth Employment Support Volunteers Program [ACTION]
YES	Youth Enquiry Service [Australia]
YES	Youth Entering Service to America [In YES Foundation, a volunteer organization proposed by the Bush administration]
YES	Youth Enterprise Scheme [British] (ODBW)
YES	Youth Exhibiting Stamps [US Postal Service]
YES	Youth for Environmental Sanity
YES	Youths for Environment and Service [Multinational association based in Turkey] (EAIO)
YesClth	Yes Clothing Co. [Associated Press] (SAG)
YesEn	Yes Entertainment, Inc. [Associated Press] (SAG)
YesEnt	Yes Entertainment, Inc. [Associated Press] (SAG)

Yeshiva U	Yeshiva University (GAGS)
YES/MVS	Yorktown Expert System for Multiple Virtual Storage Environments [Computer science] (HGAA)
YESS	Yes Entertainment [NASDAQ symbol] (TTSB)
YESS	Yes Entertainment, Inc. [NASDAQ symbol] (SAG)
YEST	Yesterday (DSUE)
YESTY	Yesterday
YET	Young Explorers Trust [British] (DBA)
YET	Youth Effectiveness Training [A course of study]
YETI	Youth Education and Training Innovators (AIE)
YETM	Yetminster [England]
YETP	Youth Employment and Training Programs [Department of Labor]
YEU	Youth for Exchange and Understanding [Germany] (BUAC)
YEV	Inuvik [Canada] [Airport symbol] (OAG)
Yev	Yevamot (BJA)
YEWF	Young Europeans for World Freedom [An association] (BUAC)
YF	Aeronautical Fixed Station [ICAO designator] (ICDA)
YF	Covered Lighter [Self-propelled] [Navy symbol]
YF	Wife [Citizens band radio slang]
yf	Yarn to Front [Knitting] (BARN)
YF	Yawmiyyaet Filastiniyya (BJA)
YF	Yellow Fever [Virus] (MAE)
YF	Yerushalmi Fragments [A publication] (BJA)
YF	Young Filmakers Foundation (EA)
YF	Youth Female [International Bowhunting Organization] [Class Equipment]
YFA	Fort Albany [Canada] [Airport symbol] (OAG)
YFB	Ferryboat or Launch [Self-propelled] [Navy symbol]
YFB	First Boston Corp., New York, NY [OCLC symbol] (OCLC)
YFB	Frobisher Bay [Canada] [Airport symbol] (OAG)
YFC	Fredericton [Canada] [Airport symbol] (OAG)
YFC	Yakima Firing Center (MCD)
YFC	Young Farmers' Club [British]
YFC	Youth for Christ [Australia]
YFCB	Yonkers Financial [NASDAQ symbol] (TTSB)
YFCI	Youth for Christ International [See also JPC] [Singapore, Singapore] (EAIO)
YFC/USA	Youth for Christ/USA (EA)
YFD	Yard Floating Dry Dock [Non-self-propelled] [Navy symbol]
YFDC	Youth Film Distribution Center (EA)
YFE	Forestville [Canada] [Airport symbol] (OAG)
YFEC	Youth Forum of the European Communities [See also FJCE] (EAIO)
YFED	York Financial [NASDAQ symbol] (TTSB)
YFED	York Financial Corp. [York, PA] [NASDAQ symbol] (NQ)
YFF	Waltham, MA [Location identifier FAA] (FAAL)
YFFC	Young Farmers Finance Council [Australia]
YFL	Youth Forum Ltd. [Australia Commercial firm]
YFM	State University of New York, Agricultural and Technical College at Farmingdale, Farmingdale, NY [OCLC symbol] (OCLC)
YFN	Covered Lighter [Non-self-propelled] [Navy symbol]
YFNA	Young Friends of North America (EA)
YFNB	Large Covered Lighter [Non-self-propelled] [Navy symbol]
YFND	Dry Dock Companion Craft [Non-self-propelled] [Navy symbol]
YFNG	Covered Lighter (Special Purpose) [Later, YFNX] [Navy symbol]
YFNX	Lighter (Special Purpose) [Non-self-propelled] [Navy symbol]
YFO	Flin Flon [Canada] [Airport symbol] (OAG)
Y-FOS	Y-Force Operations Staff [Army World War II]
YFP	Floating Power Barge [Non-self-propelled] [Navy symbol]
YFR	Refrigerated Covered Lighter [Self-propelled] [Navy symbol]
YFRI	Yellow Sea Fisheries Research Institute [China] (BUAC)
YFRN	Refrigerated Covered Lighter [Non-self-propelled] [Navy symbol]
YFRT	Covered Lighter (Range Tender) [Self-propelled] [Navy symbol]
YFS	Fort Simpson [Canada] [Airport symbol] (OAG)
YFS	Young Flying Service [ICAO designator] (FAAC)
YFT	Torpedo Transportation Lighter [Navy symbol Obsolete]
YFTU	Yugoslavia Federation of Trade Unions
YFU	Harbor Utility Craft [Self-propelled] [Navy symbol]
YFU	Why Have You Forsaken Us Letter [Fundraising]
YFU	Yard Freight Unit
YFU	Youth for Understanding (EA)
YFU	Youth for Understanding International Exchange [An association] (BUAC)
YFV	Yellow Fever Virus [Virology]
YF/VA	Young Filmakers/Video Arts [Also known as Young Filmakers Foundation] (EA)
YF(XYL)	Wife (Ex-Young-Lady) [Amateur radio slang]
YG	Garbage Lighter [Self-propelled] [Navy symbol]
YG	Yankee Group [Boston, MA] [Information service or system Telecommunications] (TSSD)
YG	Yard Gully
YG	Year Group
YG	Yellow-Green
YG	Yellow-Green Beacon [Aviation]
YGA	Gagnon [Canada] [Airport symbol] (OAG)
YGB	Gillies Bay [Canada] [Airport symbol] (OAG)
YGC	Yahweh and the Gods of Canaan [A publication] (BJA)
YGD	Corporacion Centroamericana de Dervicios de Navagacion Aerea [Mexico] [FAA designator] (FAAC)
YGEC	Yemen General Electricity Corp. (BUAC)
YGF	General Foods Technical Center, White Plains, NY [OCLC symbol] (OCLC)
YGJ	Yonago [Japan] [Airport symbol] (OAG)
YGK	Kingston [Canada] [Airport symbol] (OAG)
YGL	La Grande [Canada] [Airport symbol] (OAG)
YGL	Yttrium Garnet LASER

YGM............	State University of New York, College at Geneseo, Geneseo, NY [*OCLC symbol*] (OCLC)
YGM............	Young Grandmother
YGN............	Garbage Lighter [*Non-self-propelled*] [*Navy symbol*]
YGO............	Gods Narrows [*Canada*] [*Airport symbol*] (OAG)
YGP............	Gaspe [*Canada*] [*Airport symbol*] (OAG)
YGQ............	Geraldton [*Canada*] [*Airport symbol*] (OAG)
YGR............	Iles De La Madeleine [*Canada*] [*Airport symbol*] (OAG)
YGR............	Magdalen Island [*Quebec*] [*Airport symbol*] (AD)
ygr............	Younger (VRA)
YGRT..........	Yogurt
YGS............	Survey Craft [*Navy symbol*]
YGS............	Year of Grace Survey (DS)
YGS............	Young Guard Society [*Later, GS*] (EA)
YGT............	Target Service Task Craft [*Navy symbol*]
YGT............	Thunder Bay [*Ontario*] [*Airport symbol*] (AD)
YGTN..........	Target Barge [*Navy symbol*]
YGV............	Havre Saint Pierre [*Canada*] [*Airport symbol*] (OAG)
YGW............	Great Whale [*Canada*] [*Airport symbol*] (OAG)
YGX............	Gillam [*Canada*] [*Airport symbol*] (OAG)
YH.............	Lighter, Ambulance [*Navy symbol Obsolete*]
YH.............	RADAR Beacon [*Maps and charts*]
YH.............	Trans New York [*ICAO designator*] (AD)
YH.............	Yorkshire Hussars [*British military*] (DMA)
YH.............	Youth Hostel
YHA............	Yacht Harbour Association (BUAC)
YHA............	Youth Hostels Association
YHANI.........	Youth Hostel Association of Northern Ireland (BUAC)
YHB............	House Boat [*Navy symbol*]
YHC............	Young Herpetologist Club (BUAC)
YHCFE........	Yorkshire and Humberside Council for Further and Higher Education [*British*] (AIE)
YHD............	Dryden [*Canada*] [*Airport symbol*] (OAG)
YHI............	Holman Island [*Canada*] [*Airport symbol*] (OAG)
YHIY..........	Yorkshire Hussars Imperial Yeomanry [*British military*] (DMA)
YHJPCK.......	Kluane National Park, Parks Canada [*Parc National Kluane, Parcs Canada*] Haines Junction, Yukon [*Library symbol National Library of Canada*] (NLC)
YHK............	Gjoa Haven [*Canada*] [*Airport symbol*] (OAG)
YHLC..........	Salvage Lift Craft, Heavy [*Non-self-propelled*] [*Navy ship symbol*]
YHM............	Hamilton [*Canada*] [*Airport symbol*] (OAG)
YHM............	Hamilton College, Clinton, NY [*OCLC symbol*] (OCLC)
YHN............	Hornepayne [*Canada*] [*Airport symbol*] (OAG)
YHOO..........	Yahoo, Inc. [*NASDAQ symbol*] (SAG)
YHP............	Yokogawa Hewlett Packard Ltd. [*Japan*]
YHPA..........	Your Heritage Protection Association (EA)
YHR............	Harrington Harbour [*Canada*] [*Airport symbol*] (OAG)
YHS............	Yukuharu Haiku Society [*Superseded by Yuki Teikei Haiku Society*] (EA)
YHT............	Heating Scow [*Navy symbol*]
YHT............	Young-Helmholtz Theory [*Physics*]
YHWH..........	Yahweh [*Old Testament term for God*]
YHY............	Hay River [*Canada*] [*Airport symbol*] (OAG)
YHZ............	Halifax [*Canada*] [*Airport symbol*] (OAG)
YI.............	Intercity [*ICAO designator*] (AD)
YI.............	Young, Intact Animals [*Endocrinology*]
YIB............	Atikokan [*Canada*] [*Airport symbol*] (OAG)
YIBSV........	Yam Internal Brown Spot Virus [*Plant pathology*]
YICAM........	Societe Yoo-Hoo Industries of Cameroon (BUAC)
YICR..........	Young Israel Council of Rabbis (EA)
yid............	Yiddish [*MARC language code Library of Congress*] (LCCP)
YIE............	Young Interference Experiment [*Physics*]
YIED..........	Yunnan Provincial Institute of Epidemic Diseases Control and Research [*China*] (BUAC)
YIEPP.........	Youth Incentive Entitlement Pilot Projects [*Department of Labor*]
YIF............	St. Augustin [*Canada*] [*Airport symbol*] (OAG)
YIFCM........	Yaw Integrated Flight Control Module (MCD)
YIG............	Yttrium Iron Garnet
YIG............	Yunan Institute of Geography (BUAC)
YIGIB.........	Your Improved Group Insurance Benefits
YIH............	Yichang [*China*] [*Airport symbol*] (OAG)
YIIJS.........	Young Israel Institute for Jewish Studies [*Defunct*] (EA)
YIK............	Ivugivik [*Canada*] [*Airport symbol*] (OAG)
YIL............	Yahoo Internet Life [*Computer science*]
YIL............	Yellow Indicating Light (IEEE)
YILAG.........	Yidishe Landvirtshaftlekhe Gezelshaft [*A publication*] (BJA)
YILD..........	YieldUp International Corp. [*NASDAQ symbol*] (SAG)
YILD..........	YieldUP Intl [*NASDAQ symbol*] (TTSB)
YILDU.........	YieldUP Intl Unit [*NASDAQ symbol*] (TTSB)
YILDW.........	YieldUP Intl Wrrt'A' [*NASDAQ symbol*] (TTSB)
YILDZ.........	YieldUp Intl Wrrt'B' [*NASDAQ symbol*] (TTSB)
YIMI..........	Yunan Institute of Medical Information (BUAC)
YIN............	Niagara County Community College, Sanborn, NY [*OCLC symbol*] (OCLC)
YIN............	Yingkow [*Republic of China*] [*Seismograph station code, US Geological Survey*] (SEIS)
YIN............	Yining [*China*] [*Airport symbol*] (OAG)
YIO............	Pond Inlet [*Canada*] [*Airport symbol*] (OAG)
YIP............	Willow Run Airport [*Michigan*] [*Airport symbol*]
YIp............	Yeast Integrating Plasmid [*Genetics*]
YIP............	Youth Initiative Project (AIE)
YIP............	Youth International Party [*Members known as "yippies"*]
YIPL..........	Youth International Party Line [*Superseded by Technological American Party*]
YIPME.........	Youth Institute for Peace in the Middle East (EA)

Yippie........	Young Indicted Professional [*Lifestyle classification*]
YIR............	Yearly Infrastructure Report (NATG)
YIT............	Your Income Tax [*Computerized version of J. K. Lasser's book by the same name*]
YIT............	Youth in Transition [*Australia*]
YITB..........	Yours in the Bond [*Motto of fraternity Tau Kappa Epsilon*]
YIV............	Island Lake [*Canada*] [*Airport symbol*] (OAG)
YIVO..........	Yidisher Visnshaftlekher Institut [*Yiddish Scientific Institute*]
YIX............	Merrill Lynch & Co. [*AMEX symbol*] (SAG)
YJ.............	Commodore [*ICAO designator*] (AD)
YJ.............	RADAR Homing Beacon [*Maps and charts*]
YJ.............	Vanuatu [*Aircraft nationality and registration mark*] (FAAC)
YJ.............	Yellow Jacket [*Immunology*]
YJ.............	Yuppie Jeep
YJA............	Yachting Journalists' Association [*British*] (DBA)
YJA............	Young Journalists' Association (BUAC)
YJF............	Fort Liard [*Canada*] [*Airport symbol*] (OAG)
YJK............	Yellowjack Resources [*Vancouver Stock Exchange symbol*]
YJM............	Fulton-Montgomery Community College, Johnstown, NY [*OCLC symbol*] (OCLC)
YJS............	Yale Judaica Series [*A publication*] (BJA)
YJT............	Stephenville [*Canada*] [*Airport symbol*] (OAG)
YJV............	Yellow Jacket Venom [*Immunology*]
YK.............	Cyprus Turkish Airways [*ICAO designator*] (AD)
YK.............	RADAR Beacon [*Maps and charts*]
YK.............	Yakovlev [*Former USSR ICAO aircraft manufacturer identifier*] (ICAO)
YK.............	Yapi-Kredi Bank [*Turkey*] (ECON)
YK.............	Yom Kippur (BJA)
YK.............	York Antibodies [*Immunology*]
YKA............	Kamloops [*Canada*] [*Airport symbol*] (OAG)
YKA............	Yellowknife Array [*Northwest Territories*] [*Seismograph station code, US Geological Survey*] (SEIS)
YKB............	Yapi-Kredi Bank [*Turkey*]
YKB............	Yemen Kuwait Bank for Trade & Investment
YKB............	Yukon Bibliography [*Boreal Institute for Northern Studies*] [*Canada Information service or system Information service or system*] (CRD)
YKC............	Kingsborough Community College of the City University of New York, Brooklyn, NY [*OCLC symbol*] (OCLC)
YKC............	Yellowknife [*Northwest Territories*] [*Seismograph station code, US Geological Survey*] (SEIS)
ykc............	Yukon Territory [*MARC country of publication code Library of Congress*] (LCCP)
YKE............	Yankee Power, Inc. [*Vancouver Stock Exchange symbol*]
YKK............	Yoshido Kogyo Kabushiki-Kaishi [*Yoshida Industries Ltd.*] [*Japan*]
YKL............	Schefferville [*Canada*] [*Airport symbol*] (OAG)
YKM............	Corning Museum of Glass, Corning, NY [*OCLC symbol*] (OCLC)
YKM............	Yaak [*Montana*] [*Seismograph station code, US Geological Survey*] (SEIS)
YKM............	Yakima [*Washington*] [*Airport symbol*] (OAG)
YKM............	Young Kibbutz Movement [*Defunct*] (EA)
YKN............	Yankton [*South Dakota*] [*Airport symbol*] (OAG)
YKP............	Yeni Kibris Partisi [*New Cyprus Party*] [*Turkish Cyprus*] [*Political party*] (EY)
YKQ............	Rupert House [*Canada*] [*Airport symbol*] (OAG)
YKR............	Yukon Revenue Mines [*Vancouver Stock Exchange symbol*]
YKRI..........	Yingkou Knitting Research Institute (BUAC)
YKS............	Yakushima [*Japan*] [*Seismograph station code, US Geological Survey Closed*] (SEIS)
YKS............	Yorkshire [*County in England*]
YKT............	Yakutat [*Alaska*] [*Seismograph station code, US Geological Survey Closed*] (SEIS)
YKU............	Fort George [*Canada*] [*Airport symbol*] (OAG)
YKU............	Yakutat [*Alaska*] [*Seismograph station code, US Geological Survey*] (SEIS)
YKUF..........	Yiddisher Kultur Farband (EA)
YKW............	Yom Kippur War (BJA)
YKX............	Kirkland Lake [*Canada*] [*Airport symbol*] (OAG)
YKYBHTLW...	You Know You've Been Hacking Too Long When [*Computer science*]
YKZ............	Toronto [*Canada*] Buttonville Airport [*Airport symbol*] (OAG)
YL.............	Aircraft Accident Authority [*ICAO designator*] (ICDA)
YL.............	Long Island Airlines [*ICAO designator*] (AD)
YL.............	Montauk Caribbbean Airways and Ocean Reef Airways [*ICAO designator*] (AD)
YL.............	Yad La-Kore. La-Safran ule-Pe'ile Tarbut (BJA)
YL.............	Yawl (ROG)
YL.............	Y-Axis of Spacelab [*NASA*] (NASA)
YL.............	Yellow [*Maps and charts*]
YL.............	Yellow Lamp (IAA)
YL.............	Yield Limit (WDAA)
YL.............	Young Lady [*Amateur radio slang*]
YL.............	Young Life (EA)
YL.............	Youth Liberation Press (EA)
YLA............	Open Landing Lighter [*Navy symbol*]
YLB............	Lac La Biche [*Canada Airport symbol*]
YLC............	Clinton Community College, Plattsburgh, NY [*OCLC symbol*] (OCLC)
YLC............	Youngest Living Child [*Medicine*] (DMAA)
YLC............	Young Labour Council [*Australia*]
YLC............	Young Life Campaign (EA)
YLCC..........	Yellow Lamp Century Certificate (IAA)
YLD............	Chapleau [*Canada*] [*Airport symbol*] (OAG)
YLD............	High Income Advantage [*NYSE symbol*] (TTSB)
YLD............	High Income Advantage Trust [*NYSE symbol*] (SPSG)

YLD............ Yield [Investment term]
YLDG.......... Yielding (ROG)
YldUP......... YieldUP International Corp. [Associated Press] (SAG)
YLE............ Yule Island [New Guinea] [Airport symbol] (AD)
YLF............ Young Leadership Forum [Multinational association based in Israel] (EAIO)
YLF............ Yttrium-Lithium-Fluoride [Laser]
YLGN.......... Young Labour Green Network (BUAC)
YLH............ High Income Advantage III [NYSE symbol] (TTSB)
YLH............ High Income Advantage Trust III [NYSE symbol] (SAG)
YLI............. [The] Yorkshire Light Infantry [Military unit] [British]
YLI............. Young Ladies Institute (EA)
YLJ............. Meadow Lake [Canada] [Airport symbol Obsolete] (OAG)
YLJ............. Yale Law Journal [A publication] (BRI)
YLL............ Lederle Laboratories, Pearl River, NY [OCLC symbol] (OCLC)
YLL............ Lloydminster [Canada] [Airport symbol] (OAG)
YLLC.......... Salvage Lift Craft, Light [Self-propelled] [Navy ship symbol]
YLM........... Young Launderers' Movement [British] (BI)
YLMA.......... Young Liberal Movement of Australia
YLP............ Mingan [Canada] [Airport symbol Obsolete] (OAG)
YLR............ YAG [Yttrium Aluminum Garnet] LASER Range-Finder
YLR............ York Legal Record [Pennsylvania] [A publication] (DLA)
YLRL.......... Young Ladies Radio League
YLS............ Years of Life Saved (DB)
YLSN.......... Young Lawyers Section Newsletter [Australia A publication]
YLSTN........ Yellowstone (FAAC)
YLT............ High Income Advantage Trust II [NYSE symbol] (CTT)
YLT............ Yellow Light (MSA)
YLW........... Kelowna [Canada] [Airport symbol] (OAG)
YLW........... Yellow (ADA)
YLY............ Aircraft Accident Authority [FAA designator] (FAAC)
YM............. Dredge [Self-propelled] [Navy symbol]
YM............. Meteorological Office [ICAO designator] (ICDA)
YM............. Mountain Home Air Service [ICAO designator] (AD)
YM............. Prototype Missile (NATG)
YM............. Yacht Measurement
YM............. Yang Ming Line [Shipping] [Taiwan]
YM............. Yawing Moment (KSC)
YM............. Yearly Meetings [Quakers]
YM............. Yeast Extract - Malt Extract [Medium]
YM............. Yeast/Mannitol [Medium] (DB)
YM............. Yellow Man
YM............. Yellow Metal
YM............. Young Men's [Christian Association]
YMA........... Mayo [Canada] [Airport symbol] (OAG)
YMA........... Yarn Merchants Association [Defunct] (EA)
YMA........... Yeast Morphology Agar (BABM)
YMA........... Young Menswear Association (EA)
YMA........... Youth Music Australia
YMB........... Yeast Malt Broth
YMBA.......... Yacht and Motor Boat Association [British] (BI)
YMC........... Moore-Cottrell Subscription Agencies, Inc., North Cohocton, NY [OCLC symbol] (OCLC)
YMC........... Yeast Mold Count (OA)
YMC........... Your Marketing Consultant [An electronic publication]
YMC........... Youth and Music Canada
YMCA.......... National Counil of Young Men's Christian Associations [British] (DBA)
YMCA.......... Yesterday's Meal Cooked Again (WDAA)
YMCA.......... Young Men's Christian Association
YMCAA........ Young Men's Christian Association of Australia
YMCAIPS..... YMCA [Young Men's Christian Association] International Program Services (EA)
YMCA-USA... Young Men's Christian Associations of the United States of America (EA)
YMCF.......... Yacht Motor Club de France (BUAC)
YMCK.......... Yellow, Magenta, Cyan, Black (WDMC)
YMCU.......... Young Men's Christian Union
YMD........... People's Democratic Republic of Yemen [ANSI three-letter standard code] (CNC)
YMDZAI....... Young Men's Division - Zeirei Agudath Israel (EA)
YME........... Matane [Canada] [Airport symbol] (OAG)
Y-ME.......... Y-Me National Breast Cancer Organization (EA)
YME........... Young's Modulus of Elasticity [See also E, Y]
YMF........... Young Musicians Foundation (EA)
YMF........... Youth Male Fingers [International Bowhunting Organization] [Class Equipment]
YMFS.......... Young Men's Friendly Society [British]
YMHA.......... Young Men's Hebrew Association [Later, YM-YWHA]
YMHSI........ Yedi'ot ha-Makhon le-Heker ha-Shirah ha-'Ivrit. Jerusalem (BJA)
YMI............ Young Men's Institute (EA)
YMISIG....... Young Mensa International Special Interest Group [Defunct] (EA)
YML........... Murray Bay [Quebec] [Airport symbol] (AD)
YML........... Young Men's Lyceum
YMLC.......... Salvage Lift Craft, Medium [Non-self-propelled] [Navy ship symbol]
YMM........... Fort McMurray [Canada] [Airport symbol] (OAG)
YMM........... Yeast Minimal Medium [Microorganism growth medium]
YMM........... Youngstown and Mahoning County Public Library, Youngstown, OH [OCLC symbol] (OCLC)
YMMV.......... Your Mileage May Vary [E-Mail discussion]
YMMY.......... Yedi'ot ha-Makhon le-Mada'ei ha-Yahadut. Jerusalem (BJA)
YMO........... Moosonee [Canada] [Airport symbol] (OAG)
YMO........... Yellow Magic Orchestra [Musical group] [Japan]
YMP........... Motor Mine Planter [Navy symbol]
YMP........... Yacht Materially Prejudiced [Yacht racing] (IYR)

YMP............ Young Managing Printers [British Printing Industries Federation]
YMP............ Young Master Printer (DGA)
YMP............ Youth Mobility Program (OICC)
YMPA.......... Young Master Printers' Alliance (DGA)
YMPE.......... Year's Maximum Pensionable Earnings
YMR............ Youth Male Release [International Bowhunting Organization] [Class equipment]
YMS............ Auxiliary Motor Minesweeper [Navy symbol]
YMS............ Yanzhou Coal Mine Design & Research Institute (BUAC)
YMS............ Yaw Microwave Sensor
YMS............ Yield Measurement System
YMS............ Yurimaguas [Peru] [Airport symbol] (OAG)
YMSCO........ Yucca Mountain Site Characterization Office
YMSG.......... Your Message [Aviation] (FAAC)
YMSGD........ Your Message Date [Aviation] (FAAC)
YMT............ Chibougamau [Canada] [Airport symbol] (OAG)
YMT............ Motor Tug [Navy symbol]
YMT............ Yaba Monkey Tumour (DB)
YMU............ Yemeni Workers' Union (BUAC)
YMV............ Manicouagan [Quebec] [Airport symbol] (AD)
YMV............ Youcai Mosaic Virus [Plant pathology]
YMX............ Montreal [Canada] Mirabel International Airport [Airport symbol] (OAG)
YMY............ Meteorological Office [FAA designator] (FAAC)
YMYWHA..... Young Mens and Young Womens Hebrew Association (BUAC)
YN............. International NOTAM Office [ICAO designator] (ICDA)
YN............. Net Tender [Navy symbol Obsolete]
YN............. Nicaragua [International civil aircraft marking] (ODBW)
YN............. Night Coach [Airline fare code]
YN............. Nor-East Commuter Airlines [ICAO designator] (AD)
YN............. Yeoman [Navy rating]
YN............. Yes-No [Response prompt]
YN............. [The] Youngstown & Northern Railroad Co. [AAR code]
YN1............ Yeoman, First Class [Navy rating]
YN2............ Yeoman, Second Class [Navy rating]
YN3............ Yeoman, Third Class [Navy rating]
YNA............ Naiashquan [Canada] [Airport symbol] (OAG)
YNA............ Young Newspaper Executives Association (BUAC)
YNA............ Young Newspapermen's Association [British] (BI)
YNA............ Yugoslav National Army (BUAC)
YNB............ Yanbu [Saudi Arabia] [Airport symbol] (OAG)
YNB............ Yeast Nitrogen Base
YNC............ Paint Hills [Canada] [Airport symbol] (OAG)
YNC............ Yeoman, Chief [Navy rating]
YNC............ Yinchuan [Republic of China] [Seismograph station code, US Geological Survey] (SEIS)
YNCM.......... Yeoman, Master Chief [Navy rating]
YNCS.......... Yeoman, Senior Chief [Navy rating]
YND............ Gatineau/Hull [Canada] [Airport symbol] (OAG)
YND............ Yandina [Solomon Islands] [Airport symbol] (AD)
YNE............ Norway House [Canada] [Airport symbol] (OAG)
YNG............ Gate Craft [Non-self-propelled] [Navy symbol]
Yng............ Young (AL)
YNG............ Young
YNG............ Youngstown [Ohio] [Airport symbol] (OAG)
YNG............ Youngstown State University, Youngstown, OH [OCLC symbol] (OCLC)
YNHA.......... Yosemite Natural History Association (EA)
YNHH.......... Yale-New Haven Hospltal
YNK............ Gagnon [Quebec] [Airport symbol] (AD)
YNM............ Matagami [Canada] [Airport symbol] (OAG)
YNP............ Young National Party [Australia Political party]
YNPA.......... Young National Party of Australia [Political party]
YNPS.......... Yankee Nuclear Power Station (NRCH)
YNR............ Yorkshire, North Riding [County in England] (ROG)
YNSA.......... Seaman Apprentice, Yeoman, Striker [Navy rating]
YNSN.......... Seaman, Yeoman, Striker [Navy rating]
YNT............ Net Tender [Tug Class] [Navy symbol Obsolete]
YNT............ Yellowstone National Travelers (EA)
YNTO.......... Yugoslav National Tourist Office [Defunct] (EA)
YNV............ Yanov [Later, LVV] [Former USSR Geomagnetic observatory code]
YNW........... International Finance Corp. [AMEX symbol] (SAG)
YO............. Aeronautical Information Service Unit [ICAO designator] (ICDA)
YO............. Fuel Oil Barge [Self-propelled] [Navy symbol]
YO............. Heli-Air-Monaco [ICAO designator] (AD)
YO............. Mayotte [ANSI two-letter standard code] (CNC)
YO............. Yard Oiler [Navy symbol] (DICI)
YO............. Yarn Over [Knitting]
YO............. Y-Axis of Orbiter [NASA] (NASA)
YO............. Year-Old
Y/O............ Years Old (DAVI)
YO............. Yes [Citizens band radio slang]
Yo............. Yoma (BJA)
Yo............. Younge's English Exchequer Equity Reports [159 English Reprint] [A publication] (DLA)
YO............. Young Offender (WDAA)
YO............. Young Officer [British military] (DMA)
YOAN.......... Youth of All Nations (EA)
YOB............ Year of Birth
YOB............ Youth Opportunities Board
YoB............ Yushodo Booksellers Ltd., Tokyo, Japan [Library symbol Library of Congress] (LCLS)
YOC............ Old Crow [Canada] [Airport symbol] (OAG)
YOC............ Young Ornithologists' Club (BUAC)
YOC............ Youth Opportunity Campaign [Civil Service Commission]

YOC	Youth Opportunity Centers
YOC	Youth Opportunity Corps
YOCHINPROJ	Younger Chemists International Project [*American Chemical Society*]
YOCM	International Yogurt Co. [*NASDAQ symbol*] (NQ)
YOCM	Intl Yogurt [*NASDAQ symbol*] (TTSB)
YOD	Cold Lake [*Canada*] [*Airport symbol*] (OAG)
YOD	Year of Death
YOE	Year of Entry (MHDB)
YOG	Central Aviation, Inc. [*ICAO designator*] (FAAC)
YOG	Gasoline Barge [*Self-propelled*] [*Navy symbol*]
YOGN	Gasoline Barge [*Non-self-propelled*] [*Navy symbol*]
YOH	Oxford House [*Canada*] [*Airport symbol*] (OAG)
YOI	Young Offenders' Institution (WDAA)
YOINK	Young, One Income, No Kids [*Lifestyle classification*]
YOJ	High Level [*Canada*] [*Airport symbol*] (OAG)
YOJ	Yonagunijima [*Ryukyu Islands*] [*Seismograph station code, US Geological Survey*] (SEIS)
YOK	Yokohama [*Japan*] [*Seismograph station code, US Geological Survey*] (SEIS)
YOL	Yola [*Nigeria*] [*Airport symbol*] (OAG)
YOM	State University of New York, College at Oswego, Oswego, NY [*OCLC symbol*] (OCLC)
YOM	Year of Marriage
Yom	Yoma (BJA)
YOMINCO	Yemen Oil and Mineral Resources Corp. (BUAC)
YON	Fuel Oil Barge [*Non-self-propelled*] [*Navy symbol*]
YON	Yonago [*Japan*] [*Seismograph station code, US Geological Survey*] (SEIS)
YON	Yonkers School System, Yonkers, NY [*OCLC symbol*] (OCLC)
YONAH	Years of the North Atlantic Humpback [*Collaborative study*]
YONK	Younkers, Inc. [*NASDAQ symbol*] (SAG)
Yool Waste	Yool on Waste, Nuisance, and Trespass [*1863*] [*A publication*] (DLA)
YOP	Rainbow Lake [*Canada*] [*Airport symbol*] (OAG)
YOP	Youth Opportunities Programme [*British*] (DCTA)
YOR	Yale Oriental Research [*A publication*] (BJA)
YOR	Yoro [*Honduras*] [*Airport symbol*] (AD)
yor	Yoruba [*MARC language code Library of Congress*] (LCCP)
YORA	Younger-Onset Rheumatoid Arthritis [*Medicine*] (DAVI)
York	York Legal Record [*Pennsylvania*] [*A publication*] (DLA)
YORK	York Research [*NASDAQ symbol*] (TTSB)
YORK	York Research Corp. [*NASDAQ symbol*] (NQ)
York Ass	Clayton's English Reports, York Assizes [*A publication*] (DLA)
YorkFn	York Financial Corp. [*Associated Press*] (SAG)
YorkIn	York International [*Associated Press*] (SAG)
York Leg Rec	York Legal Record [*Pennsylvania*] [*A publication*] (DLA)
York Leg Record	York Legal Record [*Pennsylvania*] [*A publication*] (DLA)
York Leg Rec (PA)	York Legal Record [*Pennsylvania*] [*A publication*] (DLA)
YorkRs	York Research Corp. [*Associated Press*] (SAG)
YURKS	Yorkshire [*County in England*]
Yorks	Yorkshire [*County in England*] (ODBW)
YOS	Oil Storage Barge [*Non-self-propelled*] [*Navy symbol*]
YOS	Years of Service [*Army*] (INF)
YOS	Yosiwara [*Japan*] [*Seismograph station code, US Geological Survey Closed*] (SEIS)
YOSE	Yosemite National Park
YOT	Yale Oriental Texts [*A publication*] (BJA)
YOTO	Year of the Ocean [*1998*] [*United Nations*]
YOTO	Year of the Oceans [*1998*]
YOU	Young [*Australia Seismograph station code, US Geological Survey*] (SEIS)
You	Younge's English Exchequer Equity Reports [*159 English Reprint*] [*A publication*] (DLA)
YOU	Youngman Oil & Gas [*Vancouver Stock Exchange symbol*]
YOU	Young Officers' Union [*Philippines*]
YOU	Youth Opportunities Unlimited [*Project*] (EA)
YOU	Youth Organizations United
You & Coll Ch	Younge and Collyer's English Chancery Reports [*1841-43*] [*A publication*] (DLA)
You & Coll Ex	Younge and Collyer's English Exchequer Equity Reports [*1834-42*] [*A publication*] (DLA)
You & Jerv	Younge and Jervis' English Exchequer Reports [*A publication*] (DLA)
Young	Young's Reports [*21-47 Minnesota*] [*A publication*] (DLA)
Young Adm	Young's Nova Scotia Admiralty Cases [*A publication*] (DLA)
Young Adm Dec	Young's Nova Scotia Vice-Admiralty Decisions [*A publication*] (DLA)
Young Adm Dec (Nov Sc)	Young's Nova Scotia Vice-Admiralty Decisions [*A publication*] (DLA)
YoungBd	Young Broadcasting, Inc. [*Associated Press*] (SAG)
Younge	Younge's English Exchequer Equity Reports [*159 English Reprint*] [*A publication*] (DLA)
Younge & C Ch	Younge and Collyer's English Chancery Reports [*62-63 English Reprint*] [*A publication*] (DLA)
Younge & C Ch Cas (Eng)	Younge and Collyer's English Chancery Cases [*62-63 English Reprint*] [*A publication*] (DLA)
Younge & C Exch	Younge and Collyer's English Exchequer Equity Reports [*160 English Reprint*] [*A publication*] (DLA)
Younge & C Exch (Eng)	Younge and Collyer's English Exchequer Equity Reports [*160 English Reprint*] [*A publication*] (DLA)
Younge & Ch Cas	Younge and Collyer's English Chancery Cases [*62-63 English Reprint*] [*1841-43*] [*A publication*] (DLA)
Younge & Coll Ch	Younge and Collyer's English Chancery Reports [*62-63 English Reprint*] [*A publication*] (DLA)
Younge & Coll Ex	Younge and Collyer's English Exchequer Equity Reports [*160 English Reprint*] [*A publication*] (DLA)
Younge & J	Younge and Jervis' English Exchequer Reports [*148 English Reprint*] [*A publication*] (DLA)
Younge & Je	Younge and Jervis' English Exchequer Reports [*148 English Reprint*] [*A publication*] (DLA)
Younge & J (Eng)	Younge and Jervis' English Exchequer Reports [*148 English Reprint*] [*A publication*] (DLA)
Younge & Jerv	Younge and Jervis' English Exchequer Reports [*148 English Reprint*] [*A publication*] (DLA)
Younge Exch	Younge's English Exchequer Equity Reports [*159 English Reprint*] [*1830-32*] [*A publication*] (DLA)
Younge Exch (Eng)	Younge's English Exchequer Equity Reports [*159 English Reprint*] [*A publication*] (DLA)
Younge ML Cas	Younge's English Maritime Law Cases [*A publication*] (DLA)
Young ML Cas	Young's English Maritime Law Cases [*A publication*] (DLA)
Young Naut Dict	Young's Nautical Dictionary [*A publication*] (DLA)
Young VA Dec	Young's Nova Scotia Vice-Admiralty Decisions [*A publication*] (DLA)
Younker	Younkers, Inc. [*Associated Press*] (SAG)
YOUR	Your Own United Resources, Inc. (OICC)
YOUSA	Youth Organizations USA (EA)
YOUTHS	Youth Order United Toward Highway Safety (EA)
YouthSv	Youth Services International, Inc. [*Associated Press*] (SAG)
YOW	International Young Christian Workers [*Acronym is based on foreign phrase Belgium*]
YOW	Ottawa [*Canada*] [*Airport symbol*] (OAG)
YOY	Young-of-the-Year [*Conservation*]
YOYO	You're on Your Own (DOMA)
YP	Pagas Airlines [*ICAO designator*] (AD)
YP	Patrol Craft [*Self-propelled*] [*Navy symbol*]
Yp	Personal Disposable Income [*Economics*]
YP	Yard Patrol
YP	Y-Axis of Payload [*NASA*] (NASA)
YP	Year of Publication (NITA)
YP	Yeast Phase (AAMN)
YP	Yellow Pine
YP	Yield Point [*Ordinarily expressed in PSI*]
YP	Yield Pressure (MAE)
YP	Young People
YP	Young Person (AIE)
YP	Young Prisoner (WDAA)
YP	Your Problem
YPA	Port Authority of New York and New Jersey Library, New York, NY [*OCLC symbol*] (OCLC)
YPA	Prince Albert [*Canada*] [*Airport symbol*] (OAG)
YPA	Yaw Precession Amplifier
YPA	Yearbook of Procurement Articles [*A publication*] (AAGC)
YPA	Yearbook Printers Association (EA)
YPA	Yeast/Peptone/Adenine Sulphate (DB)
Y-ГAΠ	Youth Parole Service [*Public human service program*] (PHSD)
YPB	Yeast Peptone Broth [*Microbiology*]
YPBF	Yellow Sheet Price of Beef [*Business term*]
YPBYRB	Youth Parole Board and Youth Residential Board [*Victoria, Australia*]
YPC	Yangzi Petrochemical Industrial Corp. [*Commercial firm*] [*China*]
YPC	Yemen Petroleum Co. (BUAC)
YPC	Young Printers' Conference (DGA)
YPD	Floating Pile Driver [*Non-self-propelled*] [*Navy symbol*]
YPD	Parry Sound [*Canada*] [*Airport symbol*] (OAG)
YPD	Yaw Phase Detector
YPD	Yeast Extract-Peptones, Dextrose Medium [*Microbiology*]
YPD	Yellow Pages Datasystem [*National Planning Data Corp.*] [*Database*]
YPDC	Youth Policy Development Council [*Victoria, Australia*]
YPE	Peace River [*Canada*] [*Airport symbol*] (OAG)
YPE	Yoho Pitch Extractor
YPEC	Young Printing Executives Club of New York (EA)
YPF	Yacimientos Petroliferos Fiscales [*Argentinian oil company*] (ECON)
YPF	Young Playwrights Festival [*Foundation of the Dramatists Guild*]
YPF	YPF Sociedad Anonima [*NYSE symbol*] (SPSG)
YPF	YPF Sociedad Anonima ADS [*NYSE symbol*] (TTSB)
YPF Soc	YPF Sociedad Anonima [*Associated Press*] (SAG)
YPG	Yuma Proving Ground [*Arizona*] [*Army*] (AABC)
YPH	Port Harrison [*Canada*] [*Airport symbol*] (OAG)
YPI	Youth Policy Institute (EA)
YPI	Youth Pride, Inc. (EA)
YPK	Pontoon Stowage Barge [*Navy symbol Obsolete*]
YPL	Pickle Lake [*Canada*] [*Airport symbol*] (OAG)
YPL	White Plains Public Library, White Plains, NY [*OCLC symbol*] (OCLC)
YPL	York Public Library [*UTLAS symbol*]
YPL	Young People's Literature [*A publication*]
YPLA	Young People's LOGO Association (EA)
YPLB	Yellow Sheet Price of Lamb [*Business term*]
YPLL	Years of Potential Life Lost [*Epidemiology*]
YPM	Saint Pierre [*Canada*] [*Airport symbol*] (OAG)
YPM	State University of New York, College at Plattsburgh, Plattsburgh, NY [*OCLC symbol*] (OCLC)
YPM	Yale Peabody Museum
YPM	Yokefellowship Prison Ministry (EA)
YPN	Port Menier [*Canada*] [*Airport symbol*] (OAG)
YPN	Your Personal Network [*Information service or system*]
YPO	Young Presidents' Organization (EA)
YPO	Youth Programs Office [*Bureau of Indian Affairs*]
Y-POP	Y-Body Axis Perpendicular to Orbit Plane [*Aerospace*]
YPPA	Yellow Pages Publishers Association (NTPA)
YPPK	Yellow Sheet Price of Pork [*Business term*]

YPQ .... Peterborough [*Canada*] [*Airport symbol*] (OAG)
YPR .... Prince Rupert [*Canada*] [*Airport symbol*] (OAG)
YPR .... Yanks Peak Resources [*Vancouver Stock Exchange symbol*]
YPR .... Youth Population Ratio (OICC)
Y-PRO .... Youth Probation Service [*Public human service program*] (PHSD)
YPS .... Yards per Second
YPS .... Yellow Pages Service [*Telecommunications*] (TEL)
YPSCE .... Young People's Society of Christian Endeavor
YPSL .... Young Peoples Socialist League [*Later, YSD*] (EA)
YPSSRB ...... Yukon Public Service Staff Relations Board [*Canada*]
YPT .... Torpedo Retriever [*Navy symbol*] (DNAB)
YPTENC ...... Young People's Trust for the Environment and Nature Conservation
                (BUAC)
YPTES .... Young People's Trust for Endangered Species (BUAC)
YPVS .... Yamaha Power Valve System
YPW .... International Finance Corp. [*AMEX symbol*] (SAG)
YPW .... Powell River [*Canada*] [*Airport symbol*] (OAG)
YPW .... Putnam-Northern Westchester BOCES [*Boards of Cooperative
                Educational Services*], Yorktown Heights, NY [*OCLC symbol*]
                (OCLC)
YPX .... Povungnituk [*Canada*] [*Airport symbol*] (OAG)
YPY .... Collection Center [*FAA designator*] (FAAC)
YPY .... Fort Chipewyan [*Canada*] [*Airport symbol*] (OAG)
YPZ .... Young Poalei Zion (BJA)
YQ .... Lakeland [*ICAO designator*] (AD)
YQB .... Quebec [*Canada*] [*Airport symbol*] (OAG)
YQD .... The Pas, MB [*Canada*] [*Airport symbol*] (OAG)
YQF .... Red Deer [*Canada*] [*Airport symbol Obsolete*] (OAG)
YQG .... Windsor [*Canada*] [*Airport symbol*] (OAG)
YQH .... Watson Lake [*Canada*] [*Airport symbol*] (OAG)
YQI .... Yarmouth [*Canada*] [*Airport symbol*] (OAG)
YQJ .... Porquis Junction [*Ontario*] [*Airport symbol*] (AD)
YQK .... Kenora [*Canada*] [*Airport symbol*] (OAG)
YQL .... Lethbridge [*Canada*] [*Airport symbol*] (OAG)
YQM .... Moncton [*Canada*] [*Airport symbol*] (OAG)
YQQ .... Comox [*Canada*] [*Airport symbol*] (OAG)
YQR .... Regina [*Canada*] [*Airport symbol*] (OAG)
YQR .... Rochester Public Library, Rochester, NY [*OCLC symbol*] (OCLC)
YQT .... Thunder Bay [*Canada*] [*Airport symbol*] (OAG)
YQU .... Grande Prairie [*Canada*] [*Airport symbol*] (OAG)
YQV .... Yorkton [*Canada*] [*Airport symbol*] (OAG)
YQX .... Gander [*Canada*] [*Airport symbol*] (OAG)
YQY .... Sydney [*Canada*] [*Airport symbol*] (OAG)
YQZ .... Quesnel [*Canada*] [*Airport symbol*] (OAG)
YR .... Floating Workshop [*Non-self-propelled*] [*Navy symbol*]
YR .... Romania [*International civil aircraft marking*] (ODBW)
YR .... Scenic Airlines [*ICAO designator*] (AD)
YR .... Yale Review [*A publication*] (BRI)
YR .... Yaw Ring
Y-R .... Yaw-Roll (AAG)
YR .... Year [*Online database field identifier*] (EY)
yr .... Year (DAVI)
Yr. .... Yearbook (BJA)
YR .... Yemeni Riyal (BJA)
YR .... Younger
yr .... Younger (ODBW)
YR .... Young Republican
YR .... Your (AAG)
yr .... Your (ODBW)
YR .... Youth Resources (EA)
YR .... Yukon Reports [*Maritime Law Book Co. Ltd.*] [*Canada Information
                service or system*] (CRD)
YRA .... Yacht Racing Association [*British*]
YRAC .... Yacht Racing Associations Council (EA)
YRAP .... Yellow Page Rate Base Analysis Plan [*Bell System*]
YRB .... Resoluto [*Canada*] [*Airport symbol*] (OAG)
YRB .... Submarine Repair and Berthing Barge [*Non-self-propelled*] [*Navy
                symbol*]
YRB .... Yorbeau Resources, Inc. [*Toronto Stock Exchange symbol*]
YRBK .... Yearbook
YRBM .... Submarine Repair, Berthing, and Messing Barge [*Non-self-propelled*]
                [*Navy symbol*]
YRBM(L) ..... Submarine Repair, Berthing, and Messing Barge (Large) [*Navy
                symbol*]
YRBS .... Youth Risk Behavior Survey [*Medicine*]
YRC .... Submarine Rescue Chamber [*Navy symbol*]
YRC .... Yaw Ratio Controller (MCD)
YRC .... Youth Rights Campaign (BUAC)
YRDH .... Floating Dry Dock Workshop (Hull) [*Non-self-propelled*] [*Navy
                symbol*]
YRDM .... Floating Dry Dock Workshop (Machine) [*Non-self-propelled*] [*Navy
                symbol*]
YRDST .... Year-Round Daylight Saving Time
YRE .... Year Round Education (EDAC)
YRE .... Youth against Racism in Europe [*An association*] (BUAC)
YRF .... Ross Bay [*Newfoundland*] [*Airport symbol*] (AD)
YRF .... Yoga Research Foundation (EA)
YRFC .... [*The*] Young and the Restless Fan Club (EA)
YRFLN .... Year Flown (MCD)
YRG .... Air Yugoslavia [*ICAO designator*] (FAAC)
YRGB .... Yellow Red Green Blue (IAA)
YRI .... Riviere-Du-Loup [*Canada*] [*Airport symbol Obsolete*] (OAG)
YRI .... Yri-York Ltd. [*Toronto Stock Exchange symbol*]
YRINY .... Youth Research Institute of New York (EA)
YRJ .... Roberval [*Canada*] [*Airport symbol Obsolete*] (OAG)

YRK .... York International [*NYSE symbol*] (TTSB)
YRK .... York International Corp. [*NYSE symbol*] (SPSG)
YRK .... York, KY [*Location identifier FAA*] (FAAL)
YRK .... York University Library [*UTLAS symbol*]
YRKG .... York Group [*NASDAQ symbol*] (TTSB)
YRL .... Covered Lighter (Repair) [*Navy symbol Obsolete*]
YRL .... Red Lake [*Canada*] [*Airport symbol*] (OAG)
yrl .... Yearling
YRL .... York University Law Library [*UTLAS symbol*]
YRLY .... Yearly (ROG)
Yrly .... Yearly (CIST)
YRM .... Rensselaer Polytechnic Institute, Troy, NY [*OCLC symbol*] (OCLC)
YRNF .... Young Republican National Federation (EA)
YRQ .... Trois Rivieres [*Quebec*] [*Airport symbol*] (AD)
YRR .... Radiological Repair Barge [*Non-self-propelled*] [*Navy symbol*]
YRR .... Scenic Airlines, Inc. [*ICAO designator*] (FAAC)
YRS .... Red Sucker Lake [*Canada*] [*Airport symbol*] (OAG)
YRS .... Yours
YRS .... Yuen Ren Society for the Promotion of Chinese Dialect Fieldwork
                (BUAC)
YRS .... Yugoslav Relief Society
YRSI .... Yves R. Simon Institute (EA)
YRSRI .... Yangtze River Scientific Research Institute (BUAC)
YRST .... Salvage Craft Tender [*Non-self-propelled*] [*Navy ship symbol*]
YRT .... Rankin Inlet [*Canada*] [*Airport symbol*] (OAG)
YRT .... Yearly Renewable Term [*Insurance*]
YRT .... Year-Round Training [*Military*]
YRT .... Yellowroot Tea [*Folk remedy, extract of buttercup root*]
YRX .... Rimouski [*Quebec*] [*Airport symbol*] (AD)
YS .... Aeronautical Station [*ICAO designator*] (ICDA)
YS .... Nihon Aeroplane Manufacturing Co. Ltd. [*Japan ICAO aircraft
                manufacturer identifier*] (ICAO)
YS .... San Juan Airlines [*ICAO designator*] (AD)
ys .... Southern Yemen (Aden) [*MARC country of publication code Library
                of Congress*] (LCCP)
YS .... Stevedoring Barge [*Navy symbol Obsolete*]
YS .... Yacht Service [*British military*] (DMA)
YS .... Yamashita-Shinnikion Steamship Co. [*Japan*] (BUAC)
YS .... Yardstick
YS .... Yard Superintendent
YS .... Y-Axis of Solid Rocket Booster [*NASA*] (NASA)
YS .... Yellow-Bellied Sapsucker [*Ornithology*]
YS .... Yellow Spot
YS .... Yield Spread [*Investment term*]
YS .... Yield Strength [*Ordinarily expressed in PSI*]
YS .... Yield Stress
YS .... Yolk Sac (MAE)
YS .... Yoshida Sarcoma [*Medicine*]
YS .... Younger Son (ROG)
YS .... Young Soldier
YS .... Youngstown & Southern Railway Co. [*AAR code*]
YSA .... Socialist Worker Party [*Formerly, Young Socialist Alliance*] (EA)
YSA .... Young Socialist Alliance (EA)
YSA .... Youth Service America (EA)
YSAF .... Young Scientists of America Foundation [*Defunct*] (EA)
YSB .... Salomon Brothers Library, New York, NY [*OCLC symbol*] (OCLC)
YSB .... Sudbury [*Canada*] [*Airport symbol*] (OAG)
YSB .... Yacht Safety Bureau (EA)
YSB .... Yield Stress Bonding
YSC .... South Central Research Library Council, Ithaca, NY [*OCLC symbol*]
                (OCLC)
YSC .... Yearly Spares Cost (MCD)
YSC .... Yolk Sac Carcinoma [*Oncology, pathology, and pediatrics*] (DAVI)
YSCO .... Yes Clothing [*NASDAQ symbol*] (TTSB)
YSCO .... Yes Clothing Co. [*NASDAQ symbol*] (NQ)
YSD .... Seaplane Wrecking Derrick [*Self-propelled*] [*Navy symbol*]
YSD .... Young Social Democrats (EA)
YSDB .... Yield Stress Diffusion Bonding
YSDSA .... Youth Section of the Democratic Socialists of America (EA)
YSE .... Yaw Steering Error
YS/E .... Yield Strength to Elastic Modulus Ratio [*Dentistry*]
YSE .... Yield Stress Envelope [*Mechanics*]
YSF .... Stoney Rapids [*Canada*] [*Airport symbol*] (OAG)
YSF .... Yield Safety Factor (IEEE)
YSG .... Young Solicitors' Group [*British*]
YSI .... Sans Souci [*Canada*] [*Airport symbol*] (OAG)
YSI .... Yellow Springs Instrument Co.
YSICSA .... Yellow Springs Institute for Contemporary Studies and the Arts (EA)
YSII .... Youth Services International, Inc. [*NASDAQ symbol*] (SAG)
YSII .... Youth Services Int'l [*NASDAQ symbol*] (TTSB)
YSJ .... Saint John [*Canada*] [*Airport symbol*] (OAG)
YSK .... Sanikiluaq [*Canada*] [*Airport symbol*] (OAG)
YSK .... Yokosuka [*Japan*] [*Seismograph station code, US Geological Survey
                Closed*] (SEIS)
YSL .... Saint Leonard [*Canada*] [*Airport symbol*] (OAG)
YSL .... Yolk Syncytial Layer [*Embryology*]
YSL .... Young Sowers' League [*British*]
YSL .... Yves Saint Laurent [*French couturier*]
Y-SLAV .... Yugoslavia
YSLF .... Yield Strength Load Factor (CIST)
YSM .... Fort Smith [*Canada*] [*Airport symbol*] (OAG)
YSM .... State University of New York at Stony Brook, Stony Brook, NY
                [*OCLC symbol*] (OCLC)
YSM .... Yangtze Service Medal
YSM .... Young Socialist Movement

YSNC	Youth Suicide National Center (EA)
YSO	Young Stellar Object
YSP	Pontoon Salvage Vessel [Navy symbol]
YSP	Years Service for Severance Pay Purposes [Military]
YSP	Yemen Socialist Party [South Yemen] [Political party] (PD)
YSP	Youth Suicide Prevention [An association] (EA)
YSR	Nanisivik [Canada] [Airport symbol] (OAG)
YSR	Sludge Removal Barge [Non-self-propelled] [Navy symbol]
YSR	Years of Service Required
YSS	Yuzhno-Sakhalinsk [Russia] [Seismograph station code, US Geological Survey] (SEIS)
YST	Saint Therese Point [Canada] [Airport symbol] (OAG)
YST	Yeast [cells] [Laboratory science] (DAVI)
YST	Yolk Sac Tumor [Oncology]
YST	Youngest
yst	Youngest (WDAA)
YST	Yukon Standard Time (IAA)
YSTC	Yorkshire Society of Textile Craftsmen [A union] [British] (DCTA)
YSU	Summerside [Prince Edward Island] [Airport symbol] (AD)
YSV	Yooralla Society of Victoria [Australia]
YSY	Aeronautical Station [FAA designator] (FAAC)
YSY	Sachs Harbour [Canada] [Airport symbol] (OAG)
YSZ	Y-Stabilized Zirconia [Physics]
YSZ	Yttria-Stablized Zirconia [Materials science]
YT	Harbor Tug [Navy symbol]
YT	Mayotte [Internet country code]
YT	Sky West [ICAO designator] (AD)
YT	Telecommunication Authority [ICAO designator] (ICDA)
YT	Yacht (ROG)
YT	Yankee Team [Phase of the Indochina bombing operation during US military involvement in Vietnam]
YT	Yard Tug [NYSE symbol] (DICI)
YT	Yaw Trim (MCD)
YT	Y-Axis of External Tank [NASA] (NASA)
yT	Y-Matrix of Transistor (IDOE)
YT	Yom Tov (BJA)
YT	Youth Training (AIE)
Yt	Yttrium [See also Y] [Chemical element]
YT	Yukon [Canada] (ASC)
YT	Yukon Territory [Postal code] [Canada]
YTA	Pembroke [Canada] [Airport symbol] (OAG)
YTA	Yaw Trim Angle
YTA	Yiddish Theatrical Alliance (EA)
YTB	Large Harbor Tug [Self-propelled] [Navy symbol]
YTB	Yard Tug Big [Navy]
YTB	Yarn to Back [Knitting] (ADA)
YTB	Yield to Broker [Investment term]
YTB	Yuma Test Branch [Yuma, AZ] [Army]
YTC	Yield to Call [Investment term]
YTC	Yorkshire Trust Co. [Toronto Stock Exchange symbol Vancouver Stock Exchange symbol]
YTCA	Yorkshire Terrier Club of America (EA)
YTD	Year to Date (MCD)
YTD	Young Tree Decline [Plant pathology]
YTE	Cape Dorset [Canada] [Airport symbol] (OAG)
YTEC	Yarsley Technical Centre Ltd. [Research center British] (IRC)
YTEP	Youth Training and Employment Project
YTF	Yad Tikvah Foundation (EA)
YTF	Yarn to Front [Knitting] (ADA)
YTH	Thompson [Canada] [Airport symbol] (OAG)
YTH	Youth
YTHF	Yours Till Hell Freezes [Slang British] (DI)
YTHJ	Yeshivath Torah Hayim in Jerusalem (EA)
YTI	Yeshiba Toledot Isaac. Tetuan (BJA)
YTJ	Terrace Bay [Canada] [Airport symbol] (OAG)
YTL	Big Trout Lake [Canada] [Airport symbol] (OAG)
YTL	Small Harbor Tug [Self-propelled] [Navy symbol]
YTL	Youth Tennis League (EA)
YTM	Medium Harbor Tug [Self-propelled] [Navy symbol]
YTM	State University of New York, College at Utica-Rome, Utica, NY [OCLC symbol] (OCLC)
YTM	Yield to Maturity [Investment term]
YTP	Youth Training Programme [British] (AIE)
YTRC	Yokohama Technical Research Center [Mazda Motor Corp.]
YTRES	Yankee Tractor Rocket Escape System (MCD)
YTS	Timmins [Canada] [Airport symbol] (OAG)
YTS	Youth Training Scheme [British]
YTS	Yuma Test Station [Missiles]
YTT	Torpedo Testing Barge [Navy symbol Obsolete]
YTTBT	Yield Threshold Test Ban Treaty [1976]
YTTE	Yield to Total Elation
YTV	Yaw Thrust Vector
YTV	Yorkshire Television [British]
YTX	Planned District Craft [Navy symbol]
YTY	Telecommunications Authority [FAA designator] (FAAC)
YTZ	Toronto [Canada] [Airport symbol] (OAG)
YU	Aerolineas Dominicanas [ICAO designator] (AD)
YU	Yale Divinity School, New Haven, CT [Inactive] [OCLC symbol] (OCLC)
YU	Yale University
YU	Yeshiva University [New York]
YU	Yugoslavia [ANSI two-letter standard code] (CNC)
yu	Yugoslavia [MARC country of publication code Library of Congress] (LCCP)
YUA	Youth for Understanding Australia

YUB	Tuktoyaktuk [Canada] [Airport symbol] (OAG)
Yubble	Young Urban Baby [Lifestyle classification]
Yubbie	Young Urban Breadwinner [Lifestyle classification]
YuBN	Narodna Biblioteka Socijalisticke Republike Srbije, Beograd, Yugoslavia [Library symbol Library of Congress] (LCLS)
YUBO	Yucca House National Monument
YUC	Yucana Resources, Inc. [Vancouver Stock Exchange symbol]
YUC	Yucatan
yuc	Yucca (VRA)
Yuca	Young Upwardly Mobile Cuban-American [Lifestyle classification]
Yucca	Young Up-and-Coming Cuban American [Lifestyle classification]
YUCEE	Youth Unit of the Council for Environmental Education (EAIO)
YUCI	Yeshiva University Cumulative Index of Films of Jewish Interest [A publication] (BJA)
Yuckie	Young Ultimate Creative Kitscher [Lifestyle classification]
Yuckie	Young Urban Catholic [Lifestyle classification]
YUF	Pelly Bay [Canada] [Airport symbol] (OAG)
Yuffie	Young Urban Failure [Lifestyle classification]
YUG	Yugawaralite [A zeolite]
YUG	Yugoslavia [ANSI three-letter standard code] (CNC)
Yugo	Yugoslavia (VRA)
Yugo L	Yugoslav Law [A publication] (DLA)
Yugos	Yugoslavia
YUK	Youth Uncovering Krud [Antipollution organization in Schenectady, New York]
YUK	Yuzhno-Kurilsk [Former USSR Seismograph station code, US Geological Survey] (SEIS)
Yuk Ord	Yukon Ordinances [Canada] [A publication] (DLA)
Yuk Rev Ord	Yukon Revised Ordinances [Canada] [A publication] (DLA)
YUL	Montreal [Canada] [Airport symbol] (OAG)
YUL	Yale University Library
Yullie	Young Urban Laborer [Lifestyle classification]
YUM	Yale Medical School, New Haven, CT [Inactive] [OCLC symbol] (OCLC)
YUM	Yuma [Arizona] [Airport symbol] (OAG)
YUM	Yuma Gold Mines Ltd. [Vancouver Stock Exchange symbol]
YUM	Yumen [Republic of China] [Seismograph station code, US Geological Survey] (SEIS)
Yummie	Young Upwardly Mobile Marxist [Lifestyle classification]
Yummie	Young Upwardly Mobile Mountains [Rocky Mountains] [Geological take-off on the abbreviation, Yuppie] [Canada] .
Yummie	Young Urban Minister [Lifestyle classification]
Yummy	Young Upwardly Mobile Mommy [Lifestyle classification]
YUMP	Young Upwardly-Mobile Manual Person (WDAA)
Yumpie	Young Upwardly Mobile Professional [Lifestyle classification]
Yumpy	Young Upwardly Mobile Papa [Lifestyle classification]
YUN	Yearbook of the United Nations [A publication] (DLA)
YUO	Yuojima [Bonin Islands] [Seismograph station code, US Geological Survey Closed] (SEIS)
YUP	Yale University Press (DGA)
YupIls	Young Upward Professional Library Information Specialist [Lifestyle classification]
Yuppie	Young Urban Professional [In book title "The Yuppie Handbook"] [Lifestyle classification]
YUR	Yuriko Resources [Vancouver Stock Exchange symbol]
Yurpie	Young, Urban Republican Professional [Lifestyle classification]
YUS	Yale University, New Haven, CT [OCLC symbol] (OCLC)
YUS	Yushan [Mount Morrison] [Republic of China] [Seismograph station code, US Geological Survey] (SEIS)
YuSaN	Narodne Biblioteka Bosne i Hercegovine [National Library of Bosnia and Herzegovina], Sarajevo, Yugoslavia [Library symbol Library of Congress] (LCLS)
YuSkN	Nacionalna Biblioteka na Makedonija "Kliment Ohridaki", Skopje, Yugoslavia [Library symbol Library of Congress] (LCLS)
Yussie	Young Unescorted Single [Lifestyle classification]
YUX	Hall Beach [Canada] [Airport symbol] (OAG)
YUY	Rouyn-Noranda [Canada] [Airport symbol] (OAG)
YuZU	Nacionalna i Sveucilisna Biblioteka [National and University Library of Croatia], Zagreb, Yugoslavia [Library symbol Library of Congress] (LCLS)
YV	Drone Aircraft Catapult Control Craft [Navy symbol Obsolete]
YV	Mesa Aviation [ICAO designator] (AD)
YV	Venezuela [International vehicle registration and international civil aircraft marking] (ODBW)
YV	Yad Vashem [An association Israel] (EAIO)
YV	Yield Value (IAA)
yV	Y-Matrix of Vacuum Tube (IDOE)
YVA	Moroni [Comoro Islands] [Airport symbol] (OAG)
YVA	Yad Vashem Archives (BJA)
YVA	Young Volunteers in ACTION
YVB	Bonaventure [Canada] [Airport symbol] (OAG)
YVC	Catapult Lighter [Navy symbol]
YVC	Lac La Ronge [Canada] [Airport symbol] (OAG)
YVC	Yellow Varnish Cambric
YVD	Yaw Velocity Damping
YVM	Broughton [Canada] [Airport symbol] (OAG)
YVO	Onondaga Library System, Syracuse, NY [OCLC symbol] (OCLC)
YVO	Val D'Or [Canada] [Airport symbol] (OAG)
YVP	Fort Chimo [Canada] [Airport symbol] (OAG)
YVQ	Norman Wells [Canada] [Airport symbol] (OAG)
YVR	Vancouver [Canada] [Airport symbol] (OAG)
YVT	Buffalo Narrows [Canada] [Airport symbol Obsolete] (OAG)
YVT	Yakima Valley Transportation Co. [AAR code]
YVT	Youth Visiting Team [British military] (DMA)
YW	Military Flight Operational Control Center [ICAO designator] (ICDA)

YW.............. Stateswest Airlines [*ICAO designator*] (AD)
YW.............. Water Barge [*Self-propelled*] [*Navy symbol*]
YW.............. Whitehorse Public Library, Yukon [*Library symbol National Library of Canada*] (NLC)
YW.............. Yellow-White
YW.............. Yellow Wove [*Paper*] (DGA)
YW.............. Young Women of the Church of Jesus Christ of Latter-Day Saints (EA)
YW.............. Young Women's [*Christian Association*]
YW.............. Yreka Western Railroad Co. [*AAR code*]
YWA........... Yukon Archives, Whitehorse, Yukon [*Library symbol National Library of Canada*] (NLC)
YWAM .... Youth with a Mission (EA)
YWC........... Yukon College, Whitehorse, Yukon [*Library symbol National Library of Canada*] (NLC)
YWCA .... World Young Women's Christian Association (EAIO)
YWCA .... Young Women Committed to Action [*Feminist group*]
YWCAA .... Young Women's Christian Association of Australia
YWCA-USA... Young Women's Christian Association of the United States of America (EA)
YWCJCLS .... Young Women of the Church of Jesus Christ of Latter-Day Saints [*Later, YW*] (EA)
YWCTU .... Young Women's Christian Temperance Union
YWDN.......... Water Distilling Barge [*Non-self-propelled*] [*Navy symbol*]
YWED .... Department of Economic Development: Mines and Small Business, Government of the Yukon, Whitehorse, Yukon [*Library symbol National Library of Canada*] (NLC)
YWEEP........ Environmental Protection Service, Environment Canada [*Service de la Protection de l'Environnement, Environnement Canada*] Whitehorse, Yukon [*Library symbol National Library of Canada*] (NLC)
YWF........... Young World Federalists [*Later, World Federalist Youth*]
YWFD .... Young World Food and Development [*UN Food and Agriculture Organization*]
YWG .... Winnipeg [*Canada*] [*Airport symbol*] (OAG)
YWGASOYA... You Won't Get Ahead Sitting on Your Afterdeck [*Slang Bowdlerized version*]
YWH .... Victoria [*Canada*] [*Airport symbol*] (OAG)
YWH .... Whalehead [*Quebec*] [*Airport symbol*] (AD)
YWHA .... Young Women's Hebrew Association [*Later, YM-YWHA*]
YWHHR........ Department of Health and Human Resources, Government of the Yukon, Whitehorse, Yukon [*Library symbol National Library of Canada*] (NLC)
YWHS .... Whitehorse Historical Society, Yukon [*Library symbol National Library of Canada*] (NLC)
YWHS .... Young Women's Help Society [*British*]
YWIN .... Northern Program, Indian and Northern Affairs Canada [*Programme du Nord, Affaires Indiennes et du Nord Canada*] [*Library symbol National Library of Canada*] (BIB)
YWK........... Wabush [*Canada*] [*Airport symbol*] (OAG)
YWL........... Williams Lake [*Canada*] [*Airport symbol*] (OAG)
YWL........... Yawl
YWL........... Yukon Law Library, Whitehorse, Yukon [*Library symbol National Library of Canada*] (NLC)
YWLL.......... Young Workers Liberation League
YWLS.......... Library Services Branch, Government of the Yukon, Whitehorse, Yukon [*Library symbol National Library of Canada*] (NLC)
YWM........... United States Military Academy, West Point, NY [*OCLC symbol*] (OCLC)
YWM........... Youth with a Mission [*Australia*]
YWN .... Ammunition Lighter [*Navy symbol*] (DNAB)
YWN .... Ammunition Pontoon [*Navy symbol*] (DNAB)
YWN .... Farm Scow [*Navy symbol*] (DNAB)
YWN .... Floating Crane [*Non-self-propelled*] [*Navy symbol*] (DNAB)
YWN .... Floating Pile Driver [*Non-self-propelled*] [*Navy symbol*] (DNAB)
YWN .... Lighterage Pontoon [*Navy symbol*] (DNAB)
YWN .... Pontoon [*Navy symbol*] (DNAB)
YWN .... Pontoon Barge [*Navy symbol*] (DNAB)
YWN .... Prison Ship [*Navy symbol*] (DNAB)
YWN .... Receiving Ship [*Navy symbol*] (DNAB)
YWN .... Sand Scow [*Navy symbol*] (DNAB)
YWN .... School Ship [*Navy symbol*] (DNAB)
YWN .... Transfer Barge [*Navy symbol*] (DNAB)
YWN .... Water Barge [*Non-self-propelled*] [*Navy symbol*]
YWN .... Winisk [*Canada*] [*Airport symbol*] (OAG)
YWN .... Yard Tug [*Navy symbol*] (DNAB)
YWOM .... [*The*] Old Log Church Museum, Whitehorse, Yukon [*Library symbol National Library of Canada*] (NLC)
YWP............ Sir Hugh Young's Working Party for Estimation of Civilian Relief Requirements [*World War II*]

YWPCN .... National Historic Sites, Parks Canada [*Lieux Historiques Nationaux, Parcs Canada*] Whitehorse, Yukon [*Library symbol National Library of Canada*] (NLC)
YWPG .... Young World Promotion Group [*UN Food and Agriculture Organization*]
YWR .... Yorkshire, West Riding [*County in England*] (ROG)
YWRR.......... Department of Renewable Resources, Government of the Yukon, Whitehorse, Yukon [*Library symbol National Library of Canada*] (NLC)
YWS............ Young Wales Society
YWS............ Young Workers Scheme [*British*]
YWT............ Yard-Walk-Throughs [*Navy*] (NG)
YWTA.......... Department of Territorial Affairs, Government of the Yukon, Whitehorse, Yukon [*Library symbol Obsolete National Library of Canada*] (NLC)
YWU .... Yiddish Writers Union (EA)
YWU .... Youth Work Unit [*National Youth Bureau*] (AIE)
YWY............ Military Flight Operational Control Centre [*FAA designator*] (FAAC)
YWY............ Wrigley [*Canada*] [*Airport symbol*] (OAG)
YX............... Midwest Express Airlines [*ICAO designator*] (AD)
YX............... Military Service or Organization [*ICAO designator*] (ICDA)
YX............... Societe Aeronautique Jurassienne [*ICAO designator*] (AD)
YXA............ National Airports Authority of India [*FAA designator*] (FAAC)
YXC............ Cranbrook [*Canada*] [*Airport symbol*] (OAG)
YXD............ Edmonton [*Canada*] Municipal Airport [*Airport symbol*] (OAG)
YXE............ Saskatoon [*Canada*] [*Airport symbol*] (OAG)
YXF............ Four County Library System, Binghamton, NY [*OCLC symbol*] (OCLC)
YXH .... Medicine Hat [*Canada*] [*Airport symbol*] (OAG)
YXJ............. Fort St. John [*Canada*] [*Airport symbol*] (OAG)
YXK............ Rimouski [*Canada*] [*Airport symbol*] (OAG)
YXL............ Sioux Lookout [*Canada*] [*Airport symbol*] (OAG)
YXO............ Houghton College, Buffalo Campus, West Seneca, NY [*OCLC symbol*] (OCLC)
YXP............ Pangnirtung [*Canada*] [*Airport symbol*] (OAG)
YXR............ Earlton [*Canada*] [*Airport symbol*] (OAG)
YXS............ Prince George [*Canada*] [*Airport symbol*] (OAG)
YXT............. Terrace [*Canada*] [*Airport symbol*] (OAG)
YXU............ London [*Canada*] [*Airport symbol*] (OAG)
YXX............ Abbotsford [*Canada Airport symbol*]
YXY............ Military Service [*FAA designator*] (FAAC)
YXY............ Whitehorse [*Canada*] [*Airport symbol*] (OAG)
YXZ............ Wawa [*Canada*] [*Airport symbol*] (OAG)
YY............... Robert Lynd [*American author, 1892-1970*] [*Pseudonym*]
Y-Y.............. Yaw Axis (AAG)
YY............... Yedi'ot Yanai (BJA)
YYB............ North Bay [*Canada*] [*Airport symbol*] (OAG)
YYC............ Calgary [*Canada*] [*Airport symbol*] (OAG)
YYCI........... Youth-to-Youth Committee International (EA)
YYD............ Smithers [*Canada*] [*Airport symbol*] (OAG)
YYE............ Fort Nelson [*Canada*] [*Airport symbol*] (OAG)
YYF............ Penticton [*Canada*] [*Airport symbol*] (OAG)
YYG............ Charlottetown [*Canada*] [*Airport symbol*] (OAG)
YYH............ Spence Bay [*Canada*] [*Airport symbol*] (OAG)
YYJ............. Victoria [*Canada*] [*Airport symbol*] (OAG)
YYL............ Lynn Lake [*Canada*] [*Airport symbol Obsolete*] (OAG)
YYN............ Swift Current [*Saskatchewan*] [*Airport symbol*] (AD)
YYP............ Yarns of Yesteryear Project (EA)
YYP............ Yeshiva University, New York, NY [*OCLC symbol*] (OCLC)
YYQ............ Churchill [*Canada*] [*Airport symbol*] (OAG)
YYR............ Goose Bay [*Canada*] [*Airport symbol*] (OAG)
YYR............ Year of the Young Reader [*1989*] [*Library of Congress campaign*]
YYS............ Yo-Yo Stock [*Investment term*]
YYSCI......... Youth-to-Youth Sports Committee International [*Defunct*] (EA)
YYT............ St. Johns [*Canada*] [*Airport symbol*] (OAG)
YYU............ Kapuskasing [*Canada*] [*Airport symbol*] (OAG)
YYY............ Mont-Joli [*Canada*] [*Airport symbol*] (OAG)
YYY............ Organization Not Allocated Exclusive Designator [*FAA designator*] (FAAC)
YYY............ Yugntruf - Youth for Yiddish (EA)
YYZ............ Toronto [*Canada*] [*Airport symbol*] (OAG)
YZ............... Linhas Aereas da Guine-Bissau [*ICAO designator*] (AD)
YZ............... MET Databank [*ICAO designator*]
YZA............ Albany Law School, Albany, NY [*OCLC symbol*] (OCLC)
YZF............ Yellowknife [*Canada*] [*Airport symbol*] (OAG)
YZG............ Sugluk [*Canada*] [*Airport symbol*] (OAG)
YZP............ Sandspit [*Canada*] [*Airport symbol*] (OAG)
YZR............ Sarnia [*Canada*] [*Airport symbol*] (OAG)
YZS............ Coral Harbour [*Canada*] [*Airport symbol*] (OAG)
YZSZ.......... Yarlung Zangbo Suture Zone [*Geophysics*]
YZT............ Port Hardy [*Canada*] [*Airport symbol*] (OAG)
YZV............ Sept-Iles [*Canada*] [*Airport symbol*] (OAG)
YZY............ Meteorological Data Bank [*FAA designator*] (FAAC)

Z
By Acronym

Z	Administrative Aircraft [*When a suffix to Navy plane designation*]
Z	Atomic Number [*Symbol*]
Z	Aza [*As substituent on nucleoside*] [*Biochemistry*]
Z	Azimuth Angle
Z	Characteristic Impedance (IDOE)
z	Charge Number of a Cell Reaction [*Symbol*] [*Electrochemistry*]
Z	Collision Number [*Symbol*] [*IUPAC*]
Z	Compression Factor [*Symbol*] [*Thermodynamics*]
Z	Contraction [*Medicine*]
Z	Coriolis Correction
Z	Dust Haze [*Meteorology*] (WDAA)
Z	Electrochemical Equivalent (IDOE)
Z	Figure of Merit [*Symbol*] (DEN)
Z	Glutamic Acid [*or Glutamine*] [*Also, Glx Symbol An amino acid*]
Z	Haze [*Meterology*] (BARN)
Z	Impedance [*Symbol*] [*IUPAC*]
Z	Ionic Charge Number [*Chemistry*] (DAVI)
Z	Normally Open [*Ship's fittings classification*]
z	Partition Function, Particle [*Symbol*] [*IUPAC*]
Z	Partition Function, System [*Symbol*] [*IUPAC*]
Z	Planning [*Aircraft classification letter*]
Z	Stadia [*Speedways, race tracks, etc.*] [*Public-performance tariff class*] [*British*]
Z	Standardized Device (DAVI)
Z	Standard Score [*Psychology*]
Z	Switzerland [*IYRU nationality code*] (IYR)
Z	Venator Group [*NYSE symbol*] [*Formerly, Woolworth Corp.*]
Z	Weekend Travel [*Also, W*] [*Airline fare code*]
Z	Woolworth Corp. [*Wall Street slang name: "Five & Dime"*] [*NYSE symbol Toronto Stock Exchange symbol*] (SPSG)
Z	Zaire [*Monetary unit in Zaire*]
Z	Zambon [*Italy*] [*Research code symbol*]
Z	Z-Axis
Z	Zebra [*Phonetic alphabet*] [*Royal Navy World War I Pre-World War II*] [*World War II*] (DSUE)
Z	Zeitung [*Newspaper, Review*] [*German*] (ILCA)
Z	Zenith
Z	Zenith Distance [*Navigation*]
Z	Zentralblatt [*Official Gazette*] [*German*] (ILCA)
Z	Zentral-Sparkasse [*Banking Austria*] (ECON)
Z	Zentrumspartei [*Center Party*] [*German Political party*] (PPE)
z	Zepto (MEC)
Z	Zero (WDMC)
Z	Zero
Z	Zero Rate [*Valued added tax*]
Z	Zerubbabel [*Freemasonry*] (ROG)
Z	Zeta (NUCP)
Z	Zimbabwe [*Aircraft nationality and registration mark*] (FAAC)
Z	Zimmerman [*Used with a number in cataloging music of Henry Purcell*] (BARN)
Z	Zinc [*Chemical symbol is Zn*]
Z	Zionist
Z	Zircon [*CIPW classification*] [*Geology*]
Z	Zirconium [*Symbol is Zr*] [*Chemical element*] (ROG)
Z	Zloty [*Monetary unit*] [*Poland*]
Z	Zoen Tencararius [*Flourished, 13th century*] [*Authority cited in pre-1607 legal work*] (DSA)
Z	Zoll [*Customs Duty*] [*German*]
Z	Zone
z	Zone (WDMC)
Z	Zone Code (IAA)
Z	Zone Marker
Z	Zone Meridian [*Lower or upper branch*]
Z	Zuckung [*Contraction or spasm*] [*German Medicine*]
Z	Zuender [*Fuze*] [*German military*]
Z	Zuercher Bibel (BJA)
Z	Zulu [*Phonetic alphabet*] [*International*] (DSUE)
Z	Zulu Time [*Greenwich Mean Time*] (AFM)
(Z)	Zusammen [*Together*] [*Chemistry*]
Z	Zuse [*Calculator*] (HGAA)
Z	Zwischenscheibe [*Disk*] [*Also, called intermediate disk, Z band, and Z line*] [*Laboratory science*] (DAVI)
Z	Zyma AG [*Switzerland*] [*Research code symbol*]
Z8	Zilog Eight Bit One-Chip Microcomputer (HGAA)
Z80	Zilog Eight Bit Microprocessor (HGAA)
Z8000	Zilog Sixteen Bit Microprocessor (HGAA)

ZA	Alpine Aviation [*ICAO designator*] (AD)
ZA	Approach Control Office [*ICAO designator*] (ICDA)
ZA	South Africa [*ANSI two-letter standard code*] (CNC)
Za	Zabriskie's Reports [*21-24 New Jersey*] [*A publication*] (DLA)
za	Zambia [*MARC country of publication code Library of Congress*] (LCCP)
ZA	Zenith Angle [*Geophysics*]
ZA	Zentralarchiv fuer Empirische Sozialforschung [*Central Archives for Empirical Social Research*] [*University of Cologne*] [*Information service or system*] (IID)
ZA	Zero Adjuster (MSA)
ZA	Zero and Add
ZA	Zinc-Aluminum [*An alloy*]
ZA	Zone of Action
ZAA	Alice Arm/Kitsault [*Canada*] [*Airport symbol*] (OAG)
ZAA	Zartman Association of America (EA)
ZAA	Zeeman-Effect Atomic Absorption [*Spectrometry*]
ZAA	Zero Angle of Attack
ZAAP	Zero Antiaircraft Potential [*Missile*]
ZAB	Albuquerque, NM [*Location identifier FAA*] (FAAL)
Zab	Zabim (BJA)
ZAB	Zabrze [*Poland*] [*Seismograph station code, US Geological Survey*] (SEIS)
ZAB	Zinc-Air Battery
Zab Land Laws	Zabriskie on the Public Land Laws of the United States [*A publication*] (DLA)
Zab (NJ)	Zabriskie's Reports [*21-24 New Jersey*] [*A publication*] (DLA)
ZAC	Zambia Airways [*ICAO designator*] (FAAC)
ZAC	Zero Administration Client [*Computer science*]
ZAC	Zinc Aluminium Coater [*Metallurgy*]
ZAC	Zinc Ammonium Chloride [*Organic chemistry*] (WDAA)
ZACH	Zacharias [*Old Testament book*] [*Douay version*]
ZAD	Zadar [*Former Yugoslavia*] [*Airport symbol*] (OAG)
ZAD	Zenith Angle Distribution
ZADCA	Zinc Alloy Die Casters' Association [*British*] (BI)
ZADCC	Zone Air Defense Control Center (NATG)
ZADI	Zentralstelle fuer Agrardokumentation und -Information [*Center for Agricultural Documentation and Information*] [*Databank originator*] [*Information service or system*] [*Germany*] (IID)
ZAED	Zentralstelle fuer Atomkernenergie-Dokumentation beim Gmelin-Institut [*Central Agency for Atomic Energy Documentation of the Gmelin Institute*] [*Germany Database originator Also, AED*]
ZAF	South Africa [*ANSI three-letter standard code*] (CNC)
ZAF	Z-Axis Adhesive Film (AAEL)
ZAF	Zero Alignment Fixture
ZAG	Zagreb [*Croatia*] [*Airport symbol*] (OAG)
ZAGI	Zag Industries Ltd. [*NASDAQ symbol*] (SAG)
ZagIndus	Zag Industries Ltd. [*Associated Press*] (SAG)
ZAH	Zahedan [*Iran*] [*Airport symbol*] (OAG)
ZAH	Zerewitinov Active H Atom (DB)
ZAHAL	Z'va Hagana Le'Israel [*Israel Defense Forces*] [*Hebrew*]
ZAI	Zaire Aero Service [*ICAO designator*] (FAAC)
ZAI	Zeirei Agudath Israel (EA)
ZAI	Zero Address Instruction
ZAK	Zakamensk [*Former USSR Seismograph station code, US Geological Survey*] (SEIS)
ZAK	Zero Administration Kit [*Computer science*] (IGQR)
ZAL	State University of New York, Albany Library School, Albany, NY [*OCLC symbol*] (OCLC)
ZAL	Valdivia [*Chile*] [*Airport symbol*] (AD)
ZAL	Zionist Archives and Library (BJA)
ZALE	Zale Corp. [*NASDAQ symbol*] (SAG)
ZaleCp	Zale Corp. [*Associated Press*] (SAG)
ZALEW	Zale Corp. Wrrt'A' [*NASDAQ symbol*] (TTSB)
ZALIS	Zinc and Lead International Service
ZAM	State University of New York, Agricultural and Technical College at Alfred, Alfred, NY [*OCLC symbol*] (OCLC)
ZAM	Zambia (WDAA)
Zam	Zambia (VRA)
ZAM	Zamboanga [*Philippines*] [*Airport symbol*] (OAG)
ZAM	Z-Axis Modulation
ZAM	Zinc, Aluminium, Magnesium (PDAA)
Zambia LJ	Zambia Law Journal [*A publication*] (DLA)
Zam LJ	Zambia Law Journal [*A publication*] (DLA)
ZAMM	Zen and the Art of Motorcycle Maintenance [*A novel*]
ZAMS	Zero-Age Main Sequence [*Astronomy*]

ZAN............	Anchorage, AK [*Location identifier FAA*] (FAAL)
ZAN............	I am Receiving Nothing [*Amateur radio shorthand*] (WDAA)
ZAN............	Zanderij [*Surinam*] [*Airport symbol*] (AD)
ZAN............	Zante [*Greece*] [*Seismograph station code, US Geological Survey*] (SEIS)
ZAN............	Zantop International Airlines, Inc. [*ICAO designator*] (FAAC)
Zan............	Zanzibar (BARN)
ZANA...........	Zambia News Agency
ZANA...........	Zanart Entertainment [*NASDAQ symbol*] (SAG)
ZANA...........	Zanart Entmt [*NASDAQ symbol*] (TTSB)
Zanart........	Zanart Entertainment [*Associated Press*] (SAG)
ZANAU........	Zanart Entmt Unit [*NASDAQ symbol*] (TTSB)
ZANAW.......	Zanart Entmt Wrrt'A' [*NASDAQ symbol*] (TTSB)
ZANC...........	Zambia National Congress - Southern Rhodesia
Z&S............	Zero and Subtract (CIST)
Z&Z............	Zero and Add (CIST)
Zane............	Zane's Reports [*4-9 Utah*] [*A publication*] (DLA)
ZANLA........	Zimbabwe African National Liberation Army (PD)
ZANU	Zimbabwe African National Union [*Political party*] (PPW)
ZANU-PF......	Zimbabwe African National Union - Patriotic Front [*Political party*] (PD)
ZANZ...........	Zanzibar
Zanz............	Zanzibar (VRA)
Zanzib Prot LR...	Zanzibar Protectorate Law Reports [*Africa*] [*A publication*] (DLA)
ZAP............	Please Acknowledge [*Amateur radio shorthand*] (WDAA)
ZAP............	Zapata Corp. [*NYSE symbol*] (TTSB)
ZAP............	Zaporozhe [*USSR*] [*Airport symbol*] (AD)
zap............	Zapotec [*MARC language code Library of Congress*] (LCCP)
ZAP............	Zero Ability to Pay [*Real estate*]
ZAP............	Zero and Add Packed
ZAP............	Zero Antiaircraft Potential [*Missile*] (MCD)
ZAP............	Zip Code Attachment Program [*Computer science*] (WDMC)
ZAP............	Znamenity Amerikansky Pisatel [*Famous American Writer*] [*Russian*]
ZAP............	Zone Axis Pattern (MCD)
ZAP............	Zoological Action Program [*Defunct*] (EA)
ZAP............	Zymosan-Activated Plasma Rabbit [*Medicine*] (DMAA)
Zapata........	Zapata Corp. [*Associated Press*] (SAG)
ZAPAX........	Phoenix-Zweig Appreciation Cl.A [*Mutual fund ticker symbol*] (SG)
ZAPB..........	Zinc-Air Primary Battery
ZAPCX........	Phoenix-Zweig Apreciation Cl.C [*Mutual fund ticker symbol*] (SG)
ZAPO	Zimbabwe African People's Organization
ZAPP..........	Zero Assignment Parallel Processor (NITA)
ZAPS...........	Cooper Life Sciences [*NASDAQ symbol*] (TTSB)
ZAPS...........	Cooper Life Sciences, Inc. [*NASDAQ symbol*] (NQ)
ZAPU	Zimbabwe African People's Union
ZAR............	Zaire [*ANSI three-letter standard code*] (CNC)
ZAR............	Zairean Airlines [*Zaire*] [*ICAO designator*] (FAAC)
ZAR............	Zaria [*Nigeria*] [*Geomagnetic observatory code*]
ZAR............	Zaria [*Nigeria*] [*Airport symbol*] (AD)
ZAR............	Zero-G Antenna Range (SSD)
ZAR............	Zeus Acquisition RADAR [*Missile defense*]
Zaring.........	Zaring Homes, Inc. [*Associated Press*] (SAG)
ZARP	Zuid Afrikaansche Republick Politie [*South African Republic Police*] (DSUE)
ZAS............	Zaire Aero Service [*ICAO designator*] (FAAC)
ZAS............	Zarkani Air Services [*Egypt*] (EY)
ZAS............	Zas Airlines of Egypt [*FAA designator*] (FAAC)
ZAS............	Zero Access Storage
ZAS............	Zymosan-Activated Serum [*Immunology*]
ZAT............	Zantop Airways, Inc.
ZAT............	Zhaotong [*China*] [*Airport symbol*] (OAG)
ZAT............	Zinc Atmospheric Tracer
ZAT............	Zydowska Agencja Telegraficzna (BJA)
ZATW..........	Zeitschrift fuer die Alttestamentliche Wissenschaft (und die Kunde des Nachbiblischen Judentums) [*A publication*] (ODCC)
ZAU............	Chicago, IL [*Location identifier FAA*] (FAAL)
ZAV............	Zavalla [*Texas*] [*Seismograph station code, US Geological Survey Closed*] (SEIS)
Zav............	Zavim (BJA)
ZAW............	Zero Administration for Windows [*Microsoft Corp.*] [*Computer science*]
ZAW............	Zero Administration Initiative for Windows [*Microsoft Corp.*] [*Computer science*]
ZAZ............	Approach Control Office [*FAA designator*] (FAAC)
ZAZ............	Zaragoza [*Spain*] [*Airport symbol*] (OAG)
ZB..............	Air Vectors [*ICAO designator*] (AD)
ZB..............	Repetitive Flight Plan Office [*ICAO designator*] (ICDA)
ZB..............	Zebra Body [*Medicine*] (DMAA)
ZB..............	Zen Buddhism (BARN)
ZB..............	Zero-Based (IAA)
ZB..............	Zero Beat [*Radio*]
ZB..............	Zimbabwe [*IYRU nationality code*] (IYR)
ZB..............	Zimbabwe Banking Corp. Ltd.
ZB..............	Zinc Borate [*Trademark for a flame retardant compound*] [*Humphrey Chemical Co.*]
ZB..............	Zivnostenska Banka [*Czech Republic*]
ZB..............	Zoom Back [*Cinematography*] (WDMC)
ZB..............	Zuercher Bibel (BJA)
ZB..............	Zum Beispiel [*For Example*] [*German*]
ZBA............	Z. Boskovic Air Charters Ltd. [*Kenya*] [*FAA designator*] (FAAC)
ZBA............	Zero Balance Accounts (TDOB)
ZBA............	Zero-Based Analysis (ADA)
ZBA............	Zero Bias Anomaly
ZBA............	Zero Bracket Account (EBF)
ZBA............	Zero Bracket Amount [*IRS*]

ZBA............	Zoning Board of Adjustment (PA)
ZBA............	Zoning Board of Appeals (PA)
ZBA............	Zoning Board of Approval [*Generic term*] (WGA)
ZBAA...........	Beijing/Capital [*China*] [*ICAO location identifier*] (ICLI)
ZBAV...........	Association of Byelorussian American Veterans in America (EA)
ZBB............	Zero-Base Budgeting
ZBBB...........	Beijing City [*China*] [*ICAO location identifier*] (ICLI)
ZBC............	Zebec Resources [*Vancouver Stock Exchange symbol*]
ZBDC..........	Zinc Dibutyldithiocarbamate [*Organic chemistry*]
ZBE............	Zinc Battery Electrode
ZBHH..........	Huhhot [*China*] [*ICAO location identifier*] (ICLI)
ZBID...........	Zero Bit Insertion/Deletion (NITA)
ZBL............	Brooklyn Law School, Brooklyn, NY [*OCLC symbol*] (OCLC)
ZBL............	Zero-Based Linearity
ZBLAN........	Zirconium, Barium, Lanthanum, Aluminum, Sodium Fluoride [*Molar composition of glass*] [*Chemistry*]
Zbl DDR.......	Zentralblatt der Deutschen Demokratischen Republik [*A publication*] (DLA)
Zbl Soz Vers...	Zentralblatt fuer Sozialversicherung und Versorgung [*German A publication*]
ZBM............	State University of New York, College at Oneonta, Oneonta, NY [*OCLC symbol*] (OCLC)
ZBMM..........	Zenana Bible and Medical Mission [*British*] (DI)
ZBMP..........	Zero-Base Media Planning
ZBN............	Brookhaven National Laboratory, Upton, NY [*OCLC symbol*] (OCLC)
ZBO............	Bowen [*Australia Airport symbol Obsolete*] (OAG)
ZBO............	Zone of British Occupation [*Military*]
ZBOP..........	Zero-Base Operational Planning and Budgeting (MHDB)
ZBOW.........	Baotou [*China*] [*ICAO location identifier*] (ICLI)
ZBP............	Zero-Base Programming [*Military*]
ZBPE..........	Beijing [*China*] [*ICAO location identifier*] (ICLI)
ZBR............	Chah-Bahar [*Iran*] [*Airport symbol*] (OAG)
ZBR............	Zero-Base Review
ZBR............	Zero Beat Reception [*Radio*]
ZBR............	Zero Bend Radius
ZBR............	Zone-BIT [*Binary Digit*] Recording [*Computer science*]
ZBRA..........	Zebra Technologies'A' [*NASDAQ symbol*] (TTSB)
ZBRA..........	Zebra Technologies Corp. [*NASDAQ symbol*] (SPSG)
ZBS............	Zivena Beneficial Society (EA)
ZBSB..........	Zeitschriftenkatalog der Bayerischen Staatsbibliothek, Munchen [*Serials Catalogue of the Bavarian State Library, Munich*] [*Deutsches Bibliotheksinstitut*] [*Germany*] [*Information service or system*] (CRD)
ZBT............	Zeta Beta Tau [*Fraternity*]
ZBTJ...........	Zion Bemishpat Tipadeh (Isaiah 1:27) (BJA)
ZBTJ...........	Tianjin/Zhangguizhuang [*China*] [*ICAO location identifier*] (ICLI)
ZBTQM........	Zero-Based Tactical Quality Management [*Army*]
ZBTSI.........	Zero Byte Time Slot Interchange (ACRL)
ZBV............	Zoological Board of Victoria [*Australia*]
ZBW...........	Boston, MA [*Location identifier FAA*] (FAAL)
ZBY............	Sayaboury [*Laos*] [*Airport symbol*] (AD)
ZBYN..........	Taiyuan/Wusu [*China*] [*ICAO location identifier*] (ICLI)
ZBZ............	Bureau des Plans de Vol Repetitifs [*FAA designator*] (FAAC)
ZC..............	Royal Swazi National Airways [*ICAO designator*] (AD)
Z-C............	Zapalote-Chico [*Race of maize*]
Zc..............	Zechariah (BJA)
ZC..............	Ziegfeld Club (EA)
ZC..............	Zinfandel Club [*British*] (EAIO)
ZC..............	Zionist Congress [*Australia*]
ZC..............	Zone Capacity
ZC..............	Zonta Club [*Australia*]
ZCA............	Z Club of America (EA)
ZCAD..........	Zycad Corp. [*NASDAQ symbol*] (NQ)
Z/CAL..........	Zero Calibration (MCD)
ZCAV..........	Zone Constant Angular Velocity [*Computer science*]
ZCB............	Chase Manhattan Bank, New York, NY [*OCLC symbol*] (OCLC)
ZCB............	Zinc-Coated Bolt
ZCC............	Zeppelin Collectors Club (EA)
ZCC............	Zirconia-Coated Crucible
ZCCFAR	Zero Crossing Constant False Alarm Rate (IAA)
ZCCI...........	Zippy Collectors Club [*Defunct*] (EA)
ZCD............	Zero Crossing Detector
ZCD............	Zone Controlled Deposition (IAA)
ZCG............	Impedance Cardiogram (NASA)
ZChN..........	Zjednoczenie Chrzescijansko-Narodowe [*Christian National Union*] [*Poland Political party*] (EY)
ZCIC...........	Zirconia-Coated Iridium Crucible
ZCK............	Check Your Keying [*Amateur radio shorthand*] (WDAA)
ZCL............	Transmit Your Call Letters Intelligibly [*Amateur radio shorthand*] (WDAA)
ZCL............	Zacatecas [*Mexico*] [*Airport symbol*] (OAG)
ZCM............	CM Preference Corp. [*Toronto Stock Exchange symbol*]
ZCM............	State University of New York, Agricultural and Technical College at Canton, Canton, NY [*OCLC symbol*] (OCLC)
ZCMI...........	Zion's Cooperative Mercantile Institution [*Department store in Salt Lake City, UT*]
ZCN............	Zinc-Coated Nut
ZCO............	Temuco [*Chile*] [*Airport symbol*] (AD)
ZCO............	Zero Crossover (MHDB)
ZCO............	Ziegler Company, Inc. [*AMEX symbol*] (SAG)
ZCO............	Ziegler Cos. [*AMEX symbol*] (TTSB)
ZCON	Zycon Corp. [*NASDAQ symbol*] (TTSB)
ZCP............	Zinc Chloride Poisoning [*Medicine*] (DMAA)
ZCP............	Zinc Chromate Primer
ZCP............	Zonta Club of Perth [*Western Australia*]

ZCR	Zero Crossing Rate
ZCR	Zero-Temperature Coefficient Resistor
ZCR	Zone of Correct Reading (IAA)
ZCRO	Zero Cost Ration Option (TDOB)
ZCRO	Zero-Cost-Ratio Option (EBF)
ZCS	Zero Code Suppression (ACRL)
ZCS	Zero Coupon Security (EBF)
ZCS	Zinc-Coated Screw
ZCT	Zero Count Table (IAA)
ZCW	Zinc-Coated Washer
ZCZ	Cazenovia College, Witherill Learning Center, Cazenovia, NY [OCLC symbol] (OCLC)
ZD	Air Traffic Flow Control Unit [ICAO designator] (ICDA)
ZD	Ross Aviation [ICAO designator] (AD)
ZD	Zener Diode
ZD	Zenith Description (WDAA)
ZD	Zenith Distance [Navigation]
ZD	Zero Defects
ZD	Zero Discharge (DAVI)
ZD	Ziff-Davis
ZD	Zinc Deficiency (DMAA)
ZD	ZIP Code Distribution
ZD	Zone Description
ZDA	Zinc Development Association [British] (EAIO)
ZDA/LDA/CA	Zinc Development Association/Lead Development Association/Cadmium Association [Information service or system] (IID)
Z (Day)	Zero Day [The date fixed for any important military operation] [British]
ZDB	Zeitschriftendatenbank [German Union Catalog of Serials] [Deutsches Bibliotheksinstitut] [Germany] [Information service or system] (CRD)
ZDBOp	Ziff-Davis Benchmark Operation (PCM)
ZDBOP	Ziff-Davis Benchmark Operation [Computer utility tool] (PCM)
ZDBT	Zinc Dibenzyldithiocarbamate [Organic chemistry] (DICI)
ZDC	Washington, DC [Location identifier FAA] (FAAL)
ZDC	Zero Defects Council
ZDC	Zeus Defense Center [Missile defense]
ZDC	Zinc Dibenzyldithiocarbamate [Rubber accelerator]
ZDC	Zinc Die Casting
ZDCTBS	Zeus Defense Center Tape and Buffer System [Missiles] (IEEE)
ZDD	Zero Delay Device
ZDDB	Zip Code Demographic Data Base [Demographic Research Co., Inc.] [Information service or system] (CRD)
ZDDL	Zero Deletion Data Link
ZDDP	Zinc Dialkyldithiophosphate [Organic chemistry]
ZDE	Zentralstelle Dokumentation Elektrotechnik [Electrical Engineering Documentation Center] [Originator and database] [Germany Information service or system] (IID)
ZDEC	Zinc Diethyldithiocarbamate [Organic chemistry]
ZDF	Your Frequency is Drifting [Amateur radio shorthand] (WDAA)
ZDF	Zucker Diabetic Fatty [Rat strain]
ZDF	Zweites Deutsches Fernsehen [Television network] [West Germany]
ZDG	Corning Community College, Corning, NY [OCLC symbol] (OCLC)
ZDG	Zinc-Doped Germanium
ZDI	Zambian Democratic Institute
ZDI	Ziff-Davis Interactive Co. [Computer science] (PCM)
ZDI	Ziff Desktop Information [Commercial firm] (PCM)
ZDK	Zen-Do Kai Martial Arts Association, International (EA)
ZDK	Zonguldak [Turkey] [Airport symbol] (AD)
ZDM	Your Dots are Missing [Amateur radio shorthand] (WDAA)
ZDMA	Zinc Dimetylacrylate [Plastics technology]
Z DNA	Deoxyribonucleic Acid, Zigzag [DNA with left-handed helix] [Biochemistry, genetics]
ZDO	Zero Differential Overlap [Method] (DB)
ZDP	Zero Defects Program
ZDP	Zero Defects Proposal
ZDP	Zero Delivery Pressure (IEEE)
ZDP	Zimbabwe Democratic Party [Political party] (PPW)
ZDP	Zinc Dialklydithiophosphate [Automotive lubricants]
ZDPA	Zero Defects Program Audit
ZDPG	Zero Defects Program Guideline
ZDPO	Zero Defects Program Objective
ZDPR	Zero Defects Program Responsibility
ZDR	Zentraldeutsche Rundfunk [Central German Radio]
ZDR	Zeus Discrimination RADAR [Missile defense]
ZDR	Zone Data Recording [Computer science] (CIST)
ZDS	Zenith Data Systems
ZDS	Zilog Development System (NITA)
ZDS	Zinc Depletion Syndrome [Medicine] (DMAA)
ZDS	Zinc Detection System
ZDS	Zung Depression Scale [Psychiatry] (DAVI)
Zdt	Die Zoologie des Talmuds [L. Lewysohn] [A publication] (BJA)
ZDT	Zero-Ductility Transition (IEEE)
ZDTP	Zinc Dialklydithiophosphate [Automotive lubricants]
ZDV	Denver, CO [Location identifier FAA] (FAAL)
ZDV	Zero Dead Volume [Chromatography]
ZDV	Zidovudine [Antiviral]
ZDWF	Zentrale Dokumentationsstelle der Freien Wohlfahrtspflege fuer Fluechtlinge eV [Germany]
ZDX	Zoladex [Antineoplastic drug] (CDI)
ZDZ	Air Traffic Flow Control Unit [FAA designator] (FAAC)
ZE	Air Caribe International [ICAO designator] (AD)
ZE	Flight Information Database [ICAO designator] (ICDA)
ZE	Pacific National [ICAO designator] (AD)
ZE	Zenith Electronics [NYSE symbol] (TTSB)

ZE	Zenith Electronics Corp. [NYSE symbol] (SPSG)
ZE	Zero Balance Entry [Banking]
ZE	Zero Effusion
ZE	Zero Energy (BARN)
ZE	Zeros Extended (IAA)
ZE	Zollinger-Ellison [Syndrome] [Medicine]
ZE	Zone Effect
ZE	Zone Electrophoresis [Analytical biochemistry]
ZEA	Zero Energy Assembly [Nuclear energy]
ZEA	Zero Entropy Automorphism
Zeb	Zebahim (BJA)
ZEB	Zebra (ROG)
ZEB	Zero-Emissions Bus
ZEBRA	Zebra Energy Breeder Assembly
Zebra	Zebra Technologies Corp. [Associated Press] (SAG)
ZEBRA	Zero Balance, Reimbursable Account [Year-end reclassification of taxable income]
ZEBRA	Zero Coupon Eurosterling Bearer or Registered Accruing Certificates (TDOB)
ZEBRA	Zero Energy Breeder Reactor Assembly [British]
Zec.	Zechariah [Old Testament book]
ZEC	Zero Energy Coefficient
ZEC	Zinc-Electrochemical Cell
ZEC	Zinsser-Engman-Cole [Syndrome] [Medicine] (DB)
ZEC	Zone of Engineering Control [Environmental science] (COE)
ZEC	Zurich Energy Corp. [Vancouver Stock Exchange symbol]
ZECC	Zinc-Electrochemical Cell
ZECC	Zonal Electric Comfort Council [Defunct] (EA)
Zech.	Zechariah [Old Testament book]
ZECM	Zonal Elementary Circulative Mechanism
ZED	Pakatoa [New Zealand] [Airport symbol] (AD)
ZED	Zero Energy Deuterium [Type of nuclear reactor]
ZED	Zero Express Dialing
ZEDRON	Blimp Squadron [Later separated into BLIMPRON and Blimp-HEDRON] [Navy]
ZEEP	Zero End Expiratory Pressure [Medicine]
ZEEP	Zero Energy Experimental Pile [Nuclear reactor] [Canada]
ZEF	Elkin, NC [Location identifier FAA] (FAAL)
ZEF	Zero Extraction Force (EECA)
ZEG	Senggo [Indonesia] [Airport symbol] (OAG)
ZEG	Zero Economic Growth
ZEG	Zero Energy Growth
ZEI	Zeigler Coal Holding [NYSE symbol] (TTSB)
ZEI	Zeigler Coal Holding Co. [NYSE symbol] (SAG)
ZEI	Zero Environmental Impact
ZeigCoal	Zeigler Coal Holding Co. [Associated Press] (SAG)
Zeitschr Chem	Zeitschrift fuer Anorganische und Allgemeine Chemie (MEC)
ZEKE	Zero Kinetic Energy [Physics]
ZEL	Bella Bella [Canada] [Airport symbol] (OAG)
ZEL	Equitable Life Assurance Society of the United States, Medical Library, New Yor k, NY [OCLC symbol] (OCLC)
ZEL	Zelovo [Enthusiastically] [Music] (ROG)
ZEL	Zero-Length Launch [Missiles]
ZELL	Zero-Length Launch [Missiles] (MCD)
ZELMAL	Zero-Length Launch and Mat Landing [Missiles] (MCD)
ZEM	East Main [Canada] [Airport symbol] (OAG)
ZEM	Hobart and William Smith Colleges, Geneva, NY [OCLC symbol] (OCLC)
ZEM	Zero Electrophoretic Mobility [Analytical chemistry]
Zemex	Zemex Corp. [Associated Press] (SAG)
ZEMTR	Zeus Early Missile Test RADAR [Missile defense] (AABC)
ZEN	Zeitgeist, Enhancement, and Nonglare [Camera lens finish developed by Sigma]
zen	Zenaga [MARC language code Library of Congress] (LCCP)
ZEN	Zeneca Group [NYSE symbol] (SPSG)
ZEN	Zeneca Group ADR [NYSE symbol] (TTSB)
ZEN	Zenith (WDAA)
Zen	Zenzelinus de Cassanis [Deceased, 1334] [Authority cited in pre-1607 legal work] (DSA)
ZEN	Zero Effort Networking [Novell] [Computer science]
ZENCO	Zenith Electronics Corp. (EFIS)
Zeneca	Zeneca Group [Associated Press] (SAG)
ZENITH	Zero Energy Nitrogen-Heated Thermal Reactor [British] (MCD)
ZenithE	Zenith Electronics Corp. [Associated Press] (SAG)
Zenix	Zenix Income Fund [Associated Press] (SAG)
ZEN-NOH	National Federation of Agricultural Cooperative Associations [Japan] (EAIO)
ZenNtl	Zenith National Insurance Corp. [Associated Press] (SAG)
Zenz	Zenzelinus de Cassanis [Deceased, 1334] [Authority cited in pre-1607 legal work] (DSA)
ZEO	Zeolite [Chemistry]
ZEOS	Zeos International Ltd. [NASDAQ symbol] (NQ)
Zep	Zephaniah [Old Testament book]
ZEP	Zeppelin (DSUE)
Zeph	Zephaniah [Old Testament book]
ZEPHYR	Zero Energy Plutonium-Fueled Fast Reactor [British] (DEN)
ZEPI	Zonal Echo Planar Imaging (DMAA)
ZEPL	Zero Excess Propellants Line
ZEPS	Zenith Energetic Particle Spectrometer (SSD)
ZER	Pottsville, PA [Location identifier FAA] (FAAL)
Zer	Zera'im (BJA)
ZER	Zero Energy Reflection
ZERA	Zero Energy Critical Assemblies Reactor [British] (DEN)
ZERC	Zero Energy Reflection Coefficient

ZERLINA ...... Zero Energy Reactor for Lattice Investigation and New Assemblies [*India*]
Zero .... Zero Corp. [*Associated Press*] (SAG)
Z-ERS .... Zeta Erythrocyte Sedimentation Rate [*Medicine*] (DMAA)
ZERT .... Zero Reaction Tool
ZES .... Zero Energy System [*Nuclear energy*]
ZES .... Zil Elwannyen Sesel [*Formerly, Zil Eliogne Sesel, then Zil Elwagne Sesel*]
ZES .... Zollinger-Ellison Syndrome [*Medicine*]
ZES .... Zone Electrophoresis System
ZES .... Zoo Education Service [*South Australia*]
Z-ESR .... Zeta Erythrocyte Sedimentation Rate [*Hematology*] (DAVI)
ZEST .... Zinc, E-Vitamin, Siberian Ginseng, Turnera [*Health product*] [*British*]
ZET .... Zero-Emissions Truck
ZET .... Zero-Gravity Expulsion Technique
ZETA .... Zero Energy Thermonuclear Apparatus [*or Assembly*] [*AEC*]
ZETR .... Zero Energy Thermal Reactor [*British*]
ZEUS .... Olympic Steel [*NASDAQ symbol*] (TTSB)
ZEUS .... Olympic Steel, Inc. [*NASDAQ symbol*] (SAG)
ZEUS .... Zero Energy Uranium System [*British*]
ZEV .... Zero Emissions Vehicle
ZEV .... Zero-Emission Vehicle [*Automotive engineering*] (PS)
Zev .... Zevahim (BJA)
ZevE .... Zeitschrift fuer Evangelische Ethik. Gutersloh [*A publication*] (BJA)
ZEvR .... Zeitschrift fuer die Evangelischen Religionsunterricht [*A publication*] (BJA)
ZEZ .... Flight information Data Base [*FAA designator*] (FAAC)
ZF .... Berlin U.S.A. [*ICAO designator*] (AD)
ZF .... Free Balloon [*Navy symbol*]
ZF .... Zahnradfabrik Friedrichshafen AG [*West Germany*]
ZF .... Zermelo-Fraenkel [*Set theory*] [*Mathematics*]
ZF .... Zero Frequency
ZF .... Ziegfeld Follies
ZF .... Zinc Finger [*Protein*] (DMAA)
ZF .... Zionist Federation [*British*] (DBA)
ZF .... Zona Fasciculata [*Of adrenal cortex*] [*Anatomy*]
ZF .... Zone Finder [*Telecommunications*] (OA)
ZF .... Zone of Fire [*Military*] (AAG)
ZF .... Zweig Fund [*NYSE symbol*] (SPSG)
ZFAL .... Zacherley Fans at Large (EA)
ZFB .... Signals Fading Badly
ZFC .... Zero Failure Criteria (IEEE)
ZFC .... Zero-Field Cooled [*Physics*]
ZFC .... Zero Field Cooling (AAEL)
ZFC .... Zipp-Forming Cells [*Immunology*]
ZFC .... Zirconia Fuel Cell
ZFDNMR ...... Zero-Field Deuterium Nuclear Magnetic Resonance
ZFE .... Zone of Flow Establishment
ZFET .... Zionist Federation Educational Trust [*British*] (DI)
ZFF .... Zone of Fracture and Flowage [*Environmental science*] (COE)
ZfG .... Zeitschrift fuer Geschichtswissenschaft [*A publication*]
ZFGBI .... Zionist Federation of Great Britain and Ireland (DI)
ZFL .... Zeitschrift fuer Luftrecht- und Weltraumrechtsfragen [*German A publication*] (DLA)
ZFM .... Community College of the Finger Lakes, Canandaigua, NY [*OCLC symbol*] (OCLC)
ZFM .... Fort McPherson [*Canada*] [*Airport symbol*] (OAG)
ZFMA .... Zip Fastener Manufacturers Association [*British*] (DBA)
ZFNMR .... Zero-Field Nuclear Magnetic Resonance
ZFO .... Your Signals have Faded [*Amateur radio shorthand*] (WDAA)
ZfP .... Dokumentation Zerstorungsfreie Pruefung [*Nondestructive Testing Documentation*] [*Federal Institute for Materials Testing*] [*Information service or system*] (IID)
ZFP .... Zinc Finger Protein (DMAA)
ZFP .... Zyglo-Fluorescent Penetrant
ZFPT .... Zyglo-Fluorescent Penetrant Testing
ZFS .... Zero Field Splitting
ZFS .... Zone Field Selection [*Physics*] (IAA)
ZFSC .... Zero-Field Splitting Constant [*Physics*]
Z f Schweiz Recht... Zeitschrift fuer Schweizerisches Recht/Revue de Droit Suisse/ Revista di Diritto Svizzero [*Basel, Switzerland*] [*A publication*] (DLA)
Z fur die Ost Gym... Zeitschrift fuer die Oesterreichischen Gymnasien [*A publication*] (OCD)
ZFV .... Fort Severn [*Canada*] [*Airport symbol*] (OAG)
ZfV .... Zeitschrift fuer Versicherungswesen [*German A publication*] (DLA)
ZFW .... Fort Worth, TX [*Location identifier FAA*] (FAAL)
ZFW .... Zero Fuel Weight [*Aviation*]
ZG .... Air Traffic Control [*ICAO designator*] (ICDA)
ZG .... Silver State [*ICAO designator*] (AD)
Z-G .... Zapalote-Grande [*Race of maize*]
ZG .... Zap Gun
ZG .... Zero Gravity (IEEE)
ZG .... Zerstoerergeschwader [*Twin-engine fighter wing*] [*German military - World War II*]
ZG .... Zinc Gluconate [*Organic chemistry*]
ZG .... Zollgesetz [*Tariff Law*] [*German*]
ZG .... Zona Glomerulosa [*Of adrenal cortex*] [*Anatomy*]
ZG .... Zoological Gardens
Z/G .... Zoster Immune Globulin [*Immunology*] (MAH)
ZG .... Zymbal Gland [*Anatomy*]
ZGA .... Zero Grade Air
ZGB .... Zoological Gardens Board [*Western Australia*]
ZGCS .... Changsha/Datuopu [*China*] [*ICAO location identifier*] (ICLI)
ZGE .... Zero-Gravity Effect

ZGE .... Zero-Gravity Environment
ZGE .... Zero-Gravity Expulsion
ZGET .... Zero-Gravity Expulsion Technique
ZGF .... Grand Forks [*Canada*] [*Airport symbol Obsolete*] (OAG)
ZGF .... Zero Gravity Facility [*NASA*]
ZGG .... Zero-Gravity Generator
ZGGG .... Guangzhou/Baiyun [*China*] [*ICAO location identifier*] (ICLI)
ZGH .... Zonal Gravity Harmonic
ZGHK .... Haikou [*China*] [*ICAO location identifier*] (ICLI)
ZGI .... Gods River [*Canada*] [*Airport symbol*] (OAG)
ZGKL .... Guilin [*China*] [*ICAO location identifier*] (ICLI)
ZGL .... South Galway [*Queensland*] [*Airport symbol*] (AD)
ZGM .... City University of New York, Graduate School, New York, NY [*OCLC symbol*] (OCLC)
ZGM .... Ngoma [*Zambia*] [*Airport symbol*] (AD)
ZGM .... Zinc Glycinate Marker [*Immunochemistry*]
ZGMT .... Zu Gott Mein Trost [*In God My Comfort*] [*Motto of Ernst, Duke of Braunschweig-Luneburg (1564-1611)*] [*German*]
ZGN .... Zaghouan [*Tunisia*] [*Seismograph station code, US Geological Survey*] (SEIS)
ZGNN .... Nanning/Wuxu [*China*] [*ICAO location identifier*] (ICLI)
ZGOW .... Shantou [*China*] [*ICAO location identifier*] (ICLI)
ZGR .... Little Grand Rapids [*Canada*] [*Airport symbol*] (OAG)
ZGS .... Gethsemani [*Canada*] [*Airport symbol*] (OAG)
ZGS .... Your Signals are Getting Stronger [*Amateur radio shorthand*] (WDAA)
ZGS .... Zero Gradient Synchrotron [*AEC*]
ZGS .... Zero-Gravity Shower
ZGS .... Zero-Gravity Simulator
ZGS .... Zirconia Grain Stabilized [*Metal alloys*]
ZGS .... Zone Gradient Synchrotron [*Nickname: Ziggy*]
ZGT .... Zero-Gravity Trainer [*NASA*] (NASA)
ZGUA .... Guangzhou City [*China*] [*ICAO location identifier*] (ICLI)
ZGVAX .... Phoenix-Zweig Govt. Fund Cl.A [*Mutual fund ticker symbol*] (SG)
ZGW .... Your Signals are Getting Weaker [*Amateur radio shorthand*] (WDAA)
ZGWBS .... Zero-Gravity Whole Body Shower
ZGWS .... Zane Grey's West Society (EA)
ZGZ .... Air Traffic Control [*FAA designator*] (FAAC)
ZGZJ .... Zhanjiang [*China*] [*ICAO location identifier*] (ICLI)
ZGZU .... Guangzhou [*China*] [*ICAO location identifier*] (ICLI)
ZH .... Helicopter Air Traffic Control [*ICAO designator*] (ICDA)
ZH .... Royal Hawaiian Airways [*ICAO designator*] (AD)
ZH .... Zinc Heads [*Freight*]
ZH .... Zonal Harmonic
ZH .... Zone Heater
zH .... Zu Haenden [*Attention Of, Care Of, To Be Delivered To*] [*German*] (GPO)
ZHA .... Zhangjiang [*China*] [*Airport symbol*] (OAG)
ZHC .... Zajdela Hepatoma Cell (DB)
ZHCC .... Zhengzhou [*China*] [*ICAO location identifier*] (ICLI)
zHd .... Zu Haenden [*Attention Of, Care Of, To Be Delivered To*] [*German*]
ZHE .... Zero Headspace Extractor [*Environmental Protection Agency*] (ERG)
ZHF .... Zone Heat Flux
ZHHH .... Wuhan/Nanhu [*China*] [*ICAO location identifier*] (ICLI)
ZHL .... Hofstra University, Law School, Library, Hempstead, NY [*OCLC symbol*] (OCLC)
ZHM .... Hunter College of the City University of New York, New York, NY [*OCLC symbol*] (OCLC)
ZHM .... Shamshernagar [*Bangladesh*] [*Airport symbol*] (AD)
ZHN .... Honolulu, HI [*Location identifier FAA*] (FAAL)
ZHOM .... Zaring Homes [*NASDAQ symbol*] (TTSB)
ZHOM .... Zaring Homes, Inc. [*NASDAQ symbol*] (SAG)
Z HR .... Zero Hour (WDAA)
ZHR .... Zirconium Hydride Reactor
ZHSA .... Zeiss Historica Society of America (EA)
ZHU .... Houston, TX [*Location identifier FAA*] (FAAL)
ZHWH .... Wuhan [*China*] [*ICAO location identifier*] (ICLI)
ZHZ .... Helicopter Air Traffic Control [*FAA designator*] (FAAC)
ZI .... Flight Information Center [*ICAO designator*] (ICDA)
ZI .... Lucas Air Transport [*ICAO designator*] (AD)
ZI .... Zero Input
zi. .... Zinc (VRA)
ZI .... Zinc Institute [*Defunct*] (EA)
ZI .... Zonal Index
ZI .... Zone of Interior [*Military*]
ZI .... Zonta International (EA)
Z/I .... Zoom In [*Cinematography and Video*]
ZIA .... Zone of Interior Armies
ZIAX .... Zantop International Airlines, Inc. [*Air carrier designation symbol*]
ZIBF .... Zimbabwe International Book Fair
ZIC .... Victoria [*Chile*] [*Airport symbol*] (AD)
ZIC .... Zirconia-Iridium Crucible
ZICAF .... Zi Corp. [*NASDAQ symbol*] [*Formerly, Multi-Corp.*] (SG)
ZICON .... Zone of the Interior Consumers Network (MCD)
ZID .... Indianapolis, IN [*Location identifier FAA*] (FAAL)
ZID .... Zone of Initial Dilution [*Effluents*] (EG)
ZID(A) .... Zonta International Districts (Australia)
Zi de Cmo ... Ziliolus de Cremona [*Authority cited in pre-1607 legal work*] (DSA)
ZIE .... Zone Immunoelectrophoresis [*Analytical biochemistry*]
Ziegler .... Ziegler Co., Inc. [*Associated Press*] (SAG)
ZIF .... Zenix Income Fund [*NYSE symbol*] (SPSG)
ZIF .... Zero Insertion Force [*Electronics*]
ZIFT .... Zygote Intrafallopian Transfer [*Obstetrics*]
ZIFT .... Zygote Intrafallopian Tube Transfer [*Medicine*] (DMAA)
ZIG .... Zero Immune Globulin (WDAA)
zig. .... Ziggurat (VRA)

ZIG	Ziguinchor [Senegal] [Airport symbol]　(OAG)
ZIG	Zoster Immune Globulin [Immunology]
ZIGO	Zygo Corp. [NASDAQ symbol]　(NQ)
ZIH	Hofstra University, Hempstead, NY [OCLC symbol]　(OCLC)
ZIH	Zihuatanejo [Mexico] [Airport symbol]　(OAG)
ZIID	Zentralinstitut fuer Information und Dokumentation [Central Institute for Information and Documentation] [Germany Information service or system]　(IID)
ZII-ZD	Zero Intersymbol Interference - Zero Derivative　(PDAA)
ZIKO	Zion Foods Corp.　(EFIS)
ZIL	Zigzag in Line [Electronics]　(EECA)
ZIL	Zork Interactive Language [Computer science]
ZILA	Zila, Inc. [NASDAQ symbol]　(NQ)
Zilla CD	Zilla Court Decisions, Bengal, Madras, Northwest Provinces [India] [A publication]　(DLA)
Zilog	Zilog, Inc. [Associated Press]　(SAG)
Zim	Zimbabwe
ZIM	Zimchurud [Former USSR Seismograph station code, US Geological Survey Closed]　(SEIS)
ZIM	Zi Mischari [Merchant fleet] [Israel]
ZIM	Zonal Interdiction Missile　(NVT)
ZIMB	Zimbabwe　(WDAA)
ZIMBANK	Zimbabwe Banking Corp. Ltd.
ZIMCO	Zambia Industrial and Mining Corp.　(BUAC)
ZIMCO	Zimmer Homes Corp.　(EFIS)
ZIMED	Zhejiang Institute of Mechanical and Electrical Design　(BUAC)
ZIMRIGHTS	Zimbabwe Human Rights Association
ZIN	Mount Zion Church [South Carolina] [Seismograph station code, US Geological Survey Closed]　(SEIS)
zinco	Zincograph　(DGA)
ZINCOM	Zambian Industrial and Commercial Association　(BUAC)
ZinEB	Zinc Ethylenebis(dithiocarbamate) [Agricultural fungicide]
ZING	Zing Technologies [NASDAQ symbol]　(TTSB)
ZING	Zing Technologies, Inc. [NASDAQ symbol]　(SAG)
Zink	Zero Income, No Kids [Lifestyle classification]
Zinn Ca Tr	Zinn's Select Cases in the Law of Trusts [A publication]　(DLA)
ZINS	Zionist Information Service　(BUAC)
ZIO	Zinc Iodide-Osmium [Biological staining procedure]
Zion	Zionlsm　(BJA)
ZION	Zions Bancorp [NASDAQ symbol]　(TTSB)
ZION	Zions Utah Bancorp [NASDAQ symbol]　(SAG)
ZionBcP	Zions Utah Bancorp [Associated Press]　(SAG)
zip	Archiving Utility [Computer science]
ZIP	Zero Interest Payment [Banking]
ZIP	Zhengzhou Institute of Pomology [China]　(BUAC)
ZIP	Zigzag In-Line Package [Wells American] [Computer science]
ZIP	Zinc Impurity Photodetector
ZIP	Zone Improvement Plan [Postal Service code]
ZIP	Zone Information Protocol　(BYTE)
ZIP	Zoster Immune Plasma [Immunology]
ZIPA	Zimbabwe People's Army
ZIP Code	National Zoning Improvement Plan Code [US Postal Service]　(AAGC)
ZIPE	Zentralinstitut Physik der Erde [Potsdam]
Zipp	Zone of Inhibited Phage Plaques [Immunology]
ZIPRA	Zimbabwe Independent People's Revolutionary Army　(PD)
ZIR	Zero Internal Resistance
ZIS	Zone Information Socket　(ACRL)
ZISS	Zebulun Israel Seafaring Society　(EA)
ZIT	Zone Information Table [Computer science]　(PCM)
Zitel	Zitel Corp. [Associated Press]　(SAG)
ZITF	Zimbabwe International Trade Fair　(ECON)
ZITL	Zitel Corp. [NASDAQ symbol]　(NQ)
ZIZ	Flight Information Center [FAA designator]　(FAAC)
Ziz	Zizit　(BJA)
ZJ	Zipper Jacket
ZJC	State University of New York, Central Administration, Albany, NY [OCLC symbol]　(OCLC)
ZJFC	Zhejiang Forestry College　(BUAC)
ZJX	Jacksonville, FL [Location identifier FAA]　(FAAL)
ZK	Barrage Balloon [Navy symbol]
ZK	Great Lakes Aviation [ICAO designator]　(AD)
ZK	New Zealand [International civil aircraft marking]　(ODBW)
ZK	Schering AG [Germany] [Research code symbol]
ZK	Shavano Air [ICAO designator]　(AD)
ZK	Zachary Kurintner Books Ltd. [British]
ZK	Zentralkommittee [Central Committee] [of the Socialist Union Party of the German Democratic Republic]
ZK	Zera' Kodesh　(BJA)
ZK	Zuelzer-Kaplan　(DB)
ZKB	Bomber [Russian aircraft symbol]
ZKB	Kasaba Bay [Zambia] [Airport symbol]　(OAG)
ZKC	Kansas City, MO [Location identifier FAA]　(FAAL)
ZKC	Keuka College, Lightner Library, Keuka Park, NY [OCLC symbol]　(OCLC)
ZKE	Kaschechewan [Canada] [Airport symbol]　(OAG)
ZKEM	Xechem International [NASDAQ symbol]　(SAG)
ZKEM	Xechem Intl [NASDAQ symbol]　(TTSB)
ZKEMW	Xechem Intl Wrrt [NASDAQ symbol]　(TTSB)
ZKG	Kegaska [Canada] [Airport symbol]　(OAG)
ZKG	Zeitschrift fuer Kirchengeschichte [A publication]　(ODCC)
ZKHH	Hamhung [North Korea ICAO location identifier]　(ICLI)
ZKIA	Pyongyang [North Korea ICAO location identifier]　(ICLI)
ZKKC	Kimchaek [North Korea ICAO location identifier]　(ICLI)
ZKKK	Pyongyang [North Korea ICAO location identifier]　(ICLI)
ZKL	Steenkool [West Irian, Indonesia] [Airport symbol]　(AD)

ZKM	Sette Cama [Gabon] [Airport symbol]　(AD)
ZKMDRVD	Zmiesana Komisia Medzinarodnej Dohody o Rybolove vo Vodach Dunaja [International Commission for Agreement on the Danube Fishing] [Former Czechoslovakia]　(EAIO)
ZKN	Training Balloon [Navy symbol]
ZKO	Observation Balloon [Navy symbol]
ZKPY	Pyongyang/Sunan [North Korea ICAO location identifier]　(ICLI)
ZKRVD	Zmiesana Komisia o Rybolove vo Vodach Dunaja [Joint Danube Fishery Commission - JDFC] [Zilina, Czechoslovakia]　(EAIO)
ZKSC	Sunchon [North Korea ICAO location identifier]　(ICLI)
ZKSR	Sesura [North Korea ICAO location identifier]　(ICLI)
ZKT	Zeitschrift fuer Katholische Theologie [A publication]　(ODCC)
ZKUJ	Uiju [North Korea ICAO location identifier]　(ICLI)
zkW	Zero Kilowatt　(IEEE)
ZKW	Zi-ka-wei [Republic of China] [Seismograph station code, US Geological Survey]　(SEIS)
zl	Drizzle [Meteorology]
ZL	Hazelton Airlines [Airline code] [Australia]
ZL	Hazelton Air Services [ICAO designator]　(AD)
ZL	Z-Axis of Spacelab [NASA]　(NASA)
ZL	Zero Lift
ZL	Zloty [Monetary unit] [Poland]　(EY)
ZLA	Los Angeles, CA [Location identifier FAA]　(FAAL)
ZLA	Zambia Library Association　(BUAC)
ZLA	Zimbabwe Library Association　(BUAC)
ZLAN	Lanzhou City [China] [ICAO location identifier]　(ICLI)
ZLB	Balboa, Canal Zone [Location identifier FAA]　(FAAL)
ZLC	Salt Lake City, UT [Location identifier FAA]　(FAAL)
ZLC	Zero Lift Cord
ZLC	Zinc, Lead, and Cadmium Abstracts [Zinc Development Association/ Lead Development Association/Codmium Association] [British Defunct Information service or system]　(CRD)
ZLD	Zero Level Drift
ZLD	Zero Lift Drag
ZLD	Zodiacal Light Device
ZLDI	Zentralstelle fuer Luft- Raumfahrtdokumentation und Information [Center for Documentation and Information in Aeronautics and Astronautics] [West Germany] [Information service or system]
ZLE	Zaba Lee Enterprises [Vancouver Stock Exchange symbol]
Z-LEV	Zero-Level Emissions Vehicle
ZLG	La Guera [Morocco] [Airport symbol]　(AD)
ZLG	Zero Line Gap
ZLG	Zilog, Inc. [NYSE symbol]　(SAG)
ZLH	Lincoln Hospital, Bronx, NY [OCLC symbol]　(OCLC)
ZLHW	Lanzhou [China] [ICAO location identifier]　(ICLI)
ZLIC	Yinchuan [China] [ICAO location identifier]　(ICLI)
ZLISP	Zilog List Processor [Programming language] [1979]　(CSR)
ZLJ	Zambia Law Journal [A publication]　(DLA)
ZLJM	Zusters van Liefe Jezus en Maria [Sisters of Charity of Jesus and Mary - SCJM] [Belgium]　(EAIO)
ZLJQ	Jiuquan [China] [ICAO location identifier]　(ICLI)
ZLK	Zaleski, OH [Location identifier FAA]　(FAAL)
ZLL	Zero-Length Launch [Missiles]
ZLL	Zero Lot Line [Real estate]
ZLL	Zoned Lone Lamp
ZLLL	Lanzhou/Zhongchuan [China] [ICAO location identifier]　(ICLI)
ZLM	State University of New York, College at New Paltz, New Paltz, NY [OCLC symbol]　(OCLC)
ZLN	Zwiazek Ludowo-Narodowy [Populist-Nationalist Alliance] [Poland Political party]　(PPE)
ZLO	Manzanillo [Mexico] [Airport symbol]　(OAG)
ZLP	Zongo [La Paz] [Bolivia] [Seismograph station code, US Geological Survey]　(SEIS)
ZLPRI	Zhejiang Leather and Plastics Research Institute　(BUAC)
ZLR	Zanzibar Law Reports [1919-50] [A publication]　(DLA)
ZLR	Zanzibar Protectorate Law Reports [1868-1950] [A publication]　(DLA)
ZLS	Zero-Gravity Locomotion Simulator [NASA]　(PS)
ZLS	Zero Level Sparing　(MCD)
ZLSM	Zeiss Light Section Microscope
ZLSN	Xian [China] [ICAO location identifier]　(ICLI)
ZLT	La Tabatiere [Canada] [Airport symbol]　(OAG)
ZLTO	Zero-Length Takeoff　(MCD)
Z-LV	Z-Axis along Local Vertical　(MCD)
ZLV	Zero-Length Vector
ZLXN	Xining [China] [ICAO location identifier]　(ICLI)
ZLYA	Yanan [China] [ICAO location identifier]　(ICLI)
ZM	Impedance Measuring Devices [JETDS nomenclature] [Military]　(CET)
ZM	Nike-Zeus at Point Mugu [Missile defense]　(SAA)
ZM	Trans-Central [ICAO designator]　(AD)
ZM	Zambia [ANSI two-letter standard code]　(CNC)
ZM	Zero Marker　(MCD)
ZM	Zoom/MODEM [ZOOM Telephonics, Inc.]
Z-M	Zuckerman-Moloff [Sewage treatment method]
ZMA	Miami, FL [Location identifier FAA]　(FAAL)
ZMA	Zinc Metaarsenite [Insecticide, wood preservative]
ZMAAX	Phoenix-Zweig Managed Assets Cl.A [Mutual fund ticker symbol]　(SG)
ZMACX	Phoenix-Zweig Managed Assets Cl.C [Mutual fund ticker symbol]　(SG)
ZMAR	Zeus Malfunction Array RADAR [Missile defense]　(IAA)
ZMAR	Zeus Multifunction Array RADAR [Missile defense]
ZMAR	Zeus Multiple Array RADAR [Missile defense]　(IAA)
ZMAR/MAR	Zeus Multifunction Array RADAR / Multifunction Array RADAR [Missile defense]　(SAA)

ZMB .... Zambia [*ANSI three-letter standard code*] (CNC)
ZMB .... Zero Moisture Basis [*Chemical analysis*]
ZMB .... Zinc Mercaptobenzimidazole [*Organic chemistry*]
ZMBH .... Zentrum fur Moleculare Biologie Heidelberg [*Center for Molecular Biology Heidelberg*]
ZMBT .... Zinc Mercaptobenzothiazole [*Organic chemistry*]
ZMC .... Manhattan College, Library, Bronx, NY [*OCLC symbol*] (OCLC)
ZMC .... Zero-Magnetostrictive Composition (PDAA)
ZMC .... Zygomatic [*Otorhinolaryngology*] (DAVI)
ZMC .... Zygomaticomaxillary Complex [*Otorhinolaryngology*] (DAVI)
ZMD .... Sao Madureira [*Brazil*] [*Airport symbol*] (AD)
ZMD .... Zung Measurement of Depression [*Scale*]
ZMDC .... Zinc Dimethyldithiocarbamate [*Organic chemistry*]
ZME .... Memphis, TN [*Location identifier FAA*] (FAAL)
ZMIS .... Zebra Mussel Information System
ZMKR .... Zone Marker
ZML .... Medical Library Center of New York, Standardized Cataloging Service, New York, NY [*OCLC symbol*] (OCLC)
ZMM .... State University of New York, Maritime College, Bronx, NY [*OCLC symbol*] (OCLC)
ZMM .... Zone Melting Model
ZMMAS .... Zodiacal Microparticle Multiparameter Analysis System [*NASA*]
ZMMD .... Zurich, Mainz, Munich, Darmstadt [*A joint European university effort on ALGOL processors*]
ZMP .... Minneapolis, MN [*Location identifier FAA*] (FAAL)
zmphm .... Zoomorphism (VRA)
ZMR .... Zone-Melting Recrystallization [*Crystallography*]
ZMRI .... Zhejiang Mariculture Research Institute (BUAC)
ZMRI .... Zhejiang Metallurgical Research Institute (BUAC)
ZMRI .... Zinc Metals Research Institute
ZMT .... Masset [*Canada*] [*Airport symbol*] (OAG)
ZMT .... ZIP [*Zone Improvement Plan*] Mail Translator [*Postal Service*]
ZMT .... Zoom Telephonics [*Vancouver Stock Exchange symbol*]
ZMUC .... Zoologisk Museum, University of Copenhagen [*Denmark*]
ZMX .... Zemex Corp. [*NYSE symbol*] (SPSG)
ZN .... Airship (Nonrigid) [*Navy symbol*]
ZN .... Tennessee Airways [*ICAO designator*] (AD)
Zn .... True Azimuth [*Symbol*] (MUGU)
ZN .... Zenith
ZN .... Ziehl-Neelsen [*A biological stain*]
Zn .... Zinc [*Chemical element*]
ZN .... Zone
ZNA .... Nanaimo [*Canada*] Harbour Airport [*Airport symbol*] (OAG)
ZNA .... Zimbabwe National Army (BUAC)
ZNC .... New York City Technical College, Library, Brooklyn, NY [*OCLC symbol*] (OCLC)
ZNC .... Nyack, AK [*Location identifier FAA*] (FAAL)
ZNC .... Zone of Nonproliferating Cells [*Cytology*]
ZNCC .... Zimbabwe National Chambers of Commerce (BUAC)
ZND .... Zinder [*Niger*] [*Airport symbol*] (OAG)
ZNE .... Newman [*Australia Airport symbol*] (OAG)
Zn Fl .... Zinc Flocculation [*Medical test*] (MAE)
ZNFPC .... Zimbabwe National Family Planning Council (BUAC)
ZNG .... Negginan [*Canada*] [*Airport symbol*] (OAG)
ZNG .... New Glasgow [*Nova Scotia*] [*Airport symbol*] (AD)
ZnG .... Zinc Gluconate [*Organic chemistry*]
ZNG .... Zoning [*Legal shorthand*] (LWAP)
ZNGI .... Zero Net Growth Isocline [*Ecological graph*]
ZNH .... Airship, Air-Sea Rescue [*Navy symbol*]
ZNJ .... Airship, Utility [*Navy symbol*]
ZNL .... Zero Memory Non-Linear (IAA)
ZNM .... Nioga Library System, Niagara Falls, NY [*OCLC symbol*] (OCLC)
ZNN .... Nonrigid Training Airship [*Navy symbol*]
ZNO .... Nonrigid Observation Airship [*Navy symbol*]
ZNO .... North Country Community College, Saranac Lake, NY [*OCLC symbol*] (OCLC)
ZNO .... Zenco Resources, Inc. [*Vancouver Stock Exchange symbol*]
ZnO .... Zinc Oxide [*Also, called white zinc*] [*Pharmacology*] (DAVI)
ZNOE .... Zinc Oxide-Eugenol [*Dental cement*]
ZNP .... Nonrigid Patrol Airship [*Navy symbol*]
ZNP .... Zanzibar Nationalist Party
ZnP .... Zinc Protoporphyrin [*Biochemistry*]
ZNP .... Zinc Pyrithione [*Antibacterial*]
ZNP .... Zion Nuclear Plant (NRCH)
ZNR .... Zinc Oxide Non-Linear Resistance (IAA)
ZNR .... Zinc Resistor
ZNRG .... Zydeco Energy [*NASDAQ symbol*] (TTSB)
ZNRG .... Zydeco Energy, Inc. [*NASDAQ symbol*] (SAG)
ZNRGW .... Zydeco Energy Wrrt [*NASDAQ symbol*] (TTSB)
ZNS .... Nonrigid Scouting Airship [*Navy symbol*]
ZnS .... Zinc Sulfide (BYTE)
ZnSe .... Zinc Selenide (AAEL)
ZNT .... Zenith National Insurance Corp. [*NYSE symbol*] (SPSG)
ZNT .... Zenith Natl Insurance [*NYSE symbol*] (TTSB)
ZNTB .... Zambia National Tourist Bureau (BUAC)
ZnTe .... Zinc Telluride (AAEL)
ZNTW .... Zeitschrift fuer die Neutestamentliche Wissenschaft und die Kunde des Urchristentums (und der Aelteren Kirche) [*A publication*] (ODCC)
ZNU .... Namu [*Canada*] [*Airport symbol Obsolete*] (OAG)
ZNXPO .... Zeus-Nike X Program Office [*Missiles*] (MCD)
ZNXS .... Zynaxis, Inc. [*NASDAQ symbol*] (SAG)
ZNY .... New York, NY [*Location identifier FAA*] (FAAL)
ZNZ .... Zanzibar [*Tanzania*] [*Airport symbol*] (OAG)
ZO .... Oceanic Air Traffic Control [*ICAO designator*] (ICDA)

ZO .... Trans-California [*ICAO designator*] (AD)
ZO .... Z-Axis of Orbiter [*NASA*] (NASA)
ZO .... Zero Output
ZO .... Ziehen-Oppenheim [*Syndrome*] [*Medicine*] (DB)
Zo .... Zoen Tencararius [*Flourished, 13th century*] [*Authority cited in pre-1607 legal work*] (DSA)
ZO .... Zone (IAA)
ZO .... Zoning Ordinance (PA)
ZO .... Zoological Origin
Z/O .... Zoom Out [*Cinematography*]
ZO .... Zuelzer-Ogden (DB)
ZOA .... Oakland, CA [*Location identifier FAA*] (FAAL)
ZOA .... Zinc Ortho-Arsenate (LDT)
ZOA .... Zionist Organization of America (EA)
ZOA .... Zone of Aeration [*Environmental science*] (COE)
ZOA .... Zone of Avoidance [*Astronomy*]
ZOB .... Cleveland, OH [*Location identifier FAA*] (FAAL)
ZOBO .... Zongo [*La Paz*] [*Bolivia*] [*Seismograph station code, US Geological Survey*] (SEIS)
ZOC .... Zone of Cementation [*Environmental science*] (COE)
ZOC .... Zone of Contribution [*Environmental science*] (COE)
ZOC .... Zone of Convenience (ADA)
ZOC .... Zone of Convergence [*Aviation*] (DA)
ZOD .... Zero Order Detector (MCD)
ZOD .... Zodiac (ROG)
Zod .... Zodiac Records [*Record label*]
ZOD .... Zone of Deposition [*Environmental science*] (COE)
ZODIAC .... Zone Defense Integrated Active Capability (IEEE)
ZOE .... Zero Energy
ZOE .... Zinc Oxide-Eugenol [*Dental cement*]
ZOE .... Zone of Entry [*Military*] (AABC)
ZOE .... Zone of Erosion [*Environmental science*] (COE)
ZOE .... Zone of Exclusion (MCD)
ZOF .... Ocean Falls [*Canada*] [*Airport symbol Obsolete*] (OAG)
ZOF .... Zone of Fire [*Military*]
ZOF .... Zone of Flowage [*Environmental science*] (COE)
ZOF .... Zone of Fracture [*Environmental science*] (COE)
Z of C .... Zones of Communications [*Military*]
Z of I .... Zone of Interior [*Military*]
ZOG .... Paramaribo [*Suriname*] [*Airport symbol*]
ZOG .... Zeatin-O-Glucoside [*Biochemistry*]
ZOG .... Zionist Occupational Government
ZOH .... Zero Order Hold [*Telescope*]
ZOI .... Zero Order Interpolar (IAA)
ZOI .... Zone of Incorporation [*Environmental Protection Agency*] (ERG)
ZOI .... Zone of Influence [*Environmental science*] (COE)
ZOK .... I am Receiving OK [*Amateur radio shorthand*] (WDAA)
ZOL .... Zoladex (DMAA)
ZOLD .... Zeroth Order Logarithmic Distribution
ZOLL .... Zoll Medical [*NASDAQ symbol*] (TTSB)
ZOLL .... Zoll Medical Corp. [*NASDAQ symbol*] (SAG)
ZollMed .... Zoll Medical Corp. [*Associated Press*] (SAG)
ZOLT .... Zoltek Co. [*NASDAQ symbol*] (TTSB)
ZOLT .... Zoltek Companies [*NASDAQ symbol*] (SAG)
Zoltek .... Zoltek Cos. [*Associated Press*] (SAG)
ZOLZ .... Zero-Order Laue Zone (AAEL)
ZOM .... Zomba [*Malawi*] [*Airport symbol*] (AD)
ZOMO .... Zmotoryzowane Oddzialy Milicji Obywatelskiej [*Motorized Units of People's Militia*] [*Poland's riot police*]
ZOMX .... Zomax Optical Media [*NASDAQ symbol*] (TTSB)
ZOMX .... Zomax Optical Media, Inc. [*NASDAQ symbol*] (SAG)
ZomxOpt .... Zomax Optical Media, Inc. [*Associated Press*] (SAG)
ZON .... Queenstown [*New Zealand*] [*Airport symbol*] (AD)
ZON .... Zonda [*Argentina*] [*Seismograph station code, US Geological Survey*] (SEIS)
ZON .... Zone Petroleum Corp. [*Vancouver Stock Exchange symbol*]
ZONA .... Zonagen, Inc. [*NASDAQ symbol*] (SAG)
Zonagen .... Zonagen, Inc. [*Associated Press*] (SAG)
Zonar .... Zonaras [*Twelfth century AD*] [*Classical studies*] (OCD)
ZONE .... Discovery Zone, Inc. [*NASDAQ symbol*] (SAG)
ZONE .... Zeolot of Name Edification [*Computer science*]
ZOO .... Minnesota Zoological Garden, Apple Valley, MN [*OCLC symbol*] (OCLC)
ZOO .... Zero on Originality (WDMC)
ZOOACT .... Zoological Action Committee [*Defunct*] (EA)
ZOOCHEM ..... Zoochemistry (ROG)
ZOOGEOG ..... Zoogeography (ROG)
ZOOL .... Zoological [*or Zoology*]
ZOOM .... Zoom Telephonics [*NASDAQ symbol*] (TTSB)
ZOOM .... Zoom Telephonics, Inc. [*NASDAQ symbol*] (SAG)
ZoomTI .... Zoom Telephonics, Inc. [*Associated Press*] (SAG)
zoopath .... Zoopathology (BARN)
ZOOPH .... Zoophytology (ROG)
ZOP .... Zero Order Predictor
ZOP .... Zinc Oxide Pigment
ZOPA .... Zinc Oxide Producers' Association [*European Council of Chemical Manufacturers Federations*] [*Belgium*] (EAIO)
ZOPFAN .... Zone of Peace, Freedom and Neutrality [*ASEAN*]
ZOPFAN .... Zone of Peace, Freedom and Neutrality Declaration (EERA)
ZOPI .... Zero Order Polynomial Interpolator
ZOPP .... Zero Order Polynomial Predictor
ZOR .... Zinc Oxide Resistor
ZOR .... Zone of Reconnaissance
ZOR .... Zorah Media Corp. [*Vancouver Stock Exchange symbol*]
Zoran .... Zoran Corp. [*Associated Press*] (SAG)

ZORRO.........	Zero Offset Rapid Reaction Ordnance
ZOS.............	Osorno [Chile] [Airport symbol] (AD)
ZOS.............	Zapata Corp. [NYSE symbol Toronto Stock Exchange symbol]
ZOS.............	Zone of Saturation [Environmental science] (COE)
ZOS.............	Zone of Separation [United Nations] (INF)
ZOS.............	Zoom Optical System
ZOT.............	Zone of Transport [Environmental science] (COE)
ZOTS...........	Zoom Optical Target Simulator (OA)
Zouch Adm...	Zouche's Admiralty Jurisdiction [A publication] (DLA)
ZOW............	State University of New York, College at Old Westbury, Old Westbury, NY [OCLC symbol] (OCLC)
ZOW............	Zone of Weathering [Environmental science] (COE)
ZOX.............	Ground Zero [Nevada] [Seismograph station code, US Geological Survey Closed] (SEIS)
ZOZ.............	Oceanic Air Traffic Control [FAA designator] (FAAC)
ZP...............	Air Traffic Services Reporting Office [ICAO designator] (ICDA)
ZP...............	Patrol and Escort Aircraft [Lighter-than-Air] [Navy symbol] (MUGU)
ZP...............	Revlon, Inc. [Research code symbol]
ZP...............	Virgin Air [ICAO designator] (AD)
ZP...............	Zadok Perspectives [A publication] (APTA)
ZP...............	Z-Axis of Payload [NASA] (NASA)
ZP...............	Zep Energy [Vancouver Stock Exchange symbol]
Zp...............	Zephaniah (BJA)
ZP...............	Zona Pellucida [Embryology]
ZP...............	Zone Punch [Computer science] (IAA)
ZP...............	Zweeppartij [Whipping Party] [Political party Belgium]
ZPA.............	Zero Period Acceleration [Nuclear energy] (NRCH)
ZPA.............	Zeus Program Analysis [Missiles]
ZPA.............	Zone of Polarizing Activity [Embryology, genetics]
ZPapEpigr....	Zeitschrift fuer Papyrologie und Epigraphik [A publication] (BJA)
ZPAR	Zeus Phased Array RADAR [Missile defense]
ZPB.............	Z80A Processor Board [North Star Computers] (NITA)
ZPB.............	Zinc Primary Battery
ZPC.............	Zero Point of Charge
ZPC.............	Zero Print Control (IAA)
ZPC.............	Zinc-Phosphate Coating
ZPCA..........	Zugzwang Postal Chess Association (EA)
ZPD.............	Zero Path Difference
ZPDA..........	Zinc Pigment Development Association [British] (BI)
ZPE.............	Zero Point Energy
ZPE.............	Zeta Phi Eta
ZPED..........	Zeus Production Evaluation Program [Missiles] (MCD)
ZPEN..........	Zeus Project Engineer Network [Missiles]
ZPFL...........	Zanzibar and Pemba Federation of Labour
ZPG.............	Airship Group [Navy symbol]
ZPG.............	Zero Population Growth (EA)
ZPH.............	Zephyrhills, FL [Location identifier FAA] (FAAL)
ZPH.............	Zero-Phonon Hole [Spectroscopy]
ZPHGA........	Zimbabwe Professional Hunters & Guides Association
ZPI.............	New York State Psychiatric Institute, Medical Library Center of New York, New York, NY [OCLC symbol] (OCLC)
ZPI.............	Zone Position Indicator (IAA)
ZPID...........	Zentralstelle fuer Psychologische Information und Dokumentation [Center for Psychological Information and Documentation] [Database operator] [Germany Information service or system] (IID)
ZPKM..........	Kunming [China] [ICAO location identifier] (ICLI)
ZPL.............	Zero-Phonon Line [Physics]
ZPL.............	Zim Passenger Line (MHDB)
ZPLS...........	Zimmerman Preschool Language Scale (DAVI)
ZPM............	State University of New York, College at Purchase, Purchase, NY [OCLC symbol] (OCLC)
ZPM............	Zero-Point-Motion [Physics]
ZPN............	Impedance Pneumograph [Apollo] [NASA]
ZPO............	Zeus Project Office [Missiles]
ZPO............	Zinc Peroxide [Pharmacology]
ZPO............	Zone Project Officer
ZPP............	Zimbabwe Progressive Party [Political party] (PPW)
ZPP............	Zinc Protophorphyrin [Biochemistry]
ZPPP...........	Kunming/Wujiaba [China] [ICAO location identifier] (ICLI)
ZPPP...........	Zanzibar and Pemba People's Party
ZPPR	Zero Power Physics Reactor
ZPPR	Zero Power Plutonium Reactor [Nuclear energy]
ZPR............	Zero Power Reactor [Nuclear energy]
ZPrA...........	Woolworth Corp. $2.20 Cv Pfd [NYSE symbol] (TTSB)
ZPRF...........	Zero Power Reactor Facility [AEC]
ZPRON........	Patrol [Lighter-than-Air] Squadron [Navy symbol]
ZPRSN........	Zurich Provisional Relative Sunspot Number [NASA]
ZPSS..........	Zion Probabilistic Safety Study [Nuclear energy] (NRCH)
ZPT............	Zero Power Test
ZPT............	Zinc Pyridine Thione (LDT)
ZPT............	Zoxazolamine Paralysis Time [In experimental animals]
ZPV............	Zero-Point Vibration
ZPZ............	Air Traffic Services Reporting Office [FAA designator] (FAAC)
ZQ.............	Ansett New Zealand [Airline flight code] (ODBW)
ZQC............	Queensborough Community College of the City University of New York, Library, Bayside, NY [OCLC symbol] (OCLC)
ZQC............	Zero Quality Control
ZQK............	Quiksilver, Inc. [NYSE symbol]
ZQM............	State University of New York, College at Potsdam, Potsdam, NY [OCLC symbol] (OCLC)
ZQN............	Queenstown [New Zealand] [Airport symbol] (OAG)
ZQT............	Zero Quantum Transition [Physics]
ZR.............	Area Control Center [ICAO designator] (ICDA)
ZR.............	Freezing Rain [Meterology] (BARN)

ZR.............	Rigid Airship [Navy symbol]
ZR.............	Star Airways [ICAO designator] (AD)
ZR.............	Zaire [ANSI two-letter standard code] (CNC)
ZR.............	Zentralrat [Central Board] [German]
ZR.............	Zero Coupon Issue (Security) [In bond listings of newspapers]
ZR.............	Zimmerman Registry [An association] (EA)
Zr.............	Zirconium [Chemical element]
ZR.............	Zona Reticularis [Of adrenal cortex] [Anatomy]
ZR.............	Zone of Responsibility
ZR.............	Zone Refined
ZR.............	Zoological Record Online [Bio Sciences Information Service] [Information service or system] (IID)
ZRA............	Zambia Revenue Authority
ZRA............	Zero Range Approximation [Nuclear science] (OA)
ZRA............	Zero Resistance Ammeter [Instrumentation]
ZRAN..........	Zoran Corp. [NASDAQ symbol] (TTSB)
ZRBSC........	Zirconium Boride Silicon Carbide (PDAA)
ZRC............	Zenith Radio Corp.
ZRC............	Zurich Reinsurance Centre [NYSE symbol] (TTSB)
ZRC............	Zurich Reinsurance Centre Holdings [NYSE symbol] (SPSG)
ZRDI...........	Zionic Research and Development Institute [Defunct] (EA)
ZRE............	Zaire [International vehicle registration] (ODBW)
ZRE............	Zero Rate Error (MCD)
ZREC..........	Zoological Records [BioSciences Information Service]
ZRH............	Zurich [Switzerland] [Airport symbol] (OAG)
ZRI............	Serui [Indonesia] [Airport symbol] (OAG)
ZRIME.........	Zhengzhou Research Institute of Mechanical Engineering (BUAC)
ZRIO...........	Zimbabwe Rhodesian Information Office [An association] (EA)
ZRK............	Zona Receptor Kinase [An enzyme]
ZRL............	Zero Risk Level (GFGA)
ZRM............	Sarmi [Indonesia] [Airport symbol] (OAG)
ZRM............	Zone Reserved for Memory (NITA)
ZRN............	Rigid Training Airship [Navy symbol]
ZRN............	You Have a Rough Note [Amateur radio shorthand] (WDAA)
ZRN............	Zurn Indus [NYSE symbol] (TTSB)
ZRN............	Zurn Industries, Inc. [NYSE symbol] (SPSG)
ZRNO..........	Freezing Rain Information Not Available [NWS] (FAAC)
ZRO............	Zero Corp. [NYSE symbol] (SPSG)
ZRO............	Zoological Record Outline
ZRP............	Rigid Patrol Airship [Navy symbol]
ZRP............	Zero Radial Play
ZRS............	Rigid Scouting Airship [Navy symbol]
ZRS............	Russell Sage College, Troy, NY [OCLC symbol] (OCLC)
ZRT............	Zero Reaction Tool
ZRV............	Zero-Relative Velocity
ZRZ............	Area Control Centre [FAA designator] (FAAC)
ZS.............	Agrarian Party [Czech Republic] (BUAC)
ZS.............	Hispaniola Airways [ICAO designator] (AD)
Z/S............	Operational Display System
ZS.............	Z-Axis of Solid Rocket Booster [NASA] (NASA)
ZS.............	Zelena Slovenija [Greens of Slovenia] [Political party] (EY)
ZS.............	Zellweger Syndrome [Also, ZWS] [Medicine]
ZS.............	Zero and Subtract
ZS.............	Zero Shift
ZS.............	Zero State (IAA)
ZS.............	Zero Sum [Genetics]
ZS.............	Zero Suppress
ZS.............	Zoological Society [British]
ZS.............	Zoosporangia [Botany]
ZSA............	San Salvador [Bahamas] [Airport symbol] (OAG)
ZSA............	Southern Tier Library System, Corning, NY [OCLC symbol] (OCLC)
ZSA............	Zero-Set Amplifier (MSA)
ZSA............	Zululand Swaziland Association [United Kingdom] (BUAC)
ZSAM..........	Xiamen [China] [ICAO location identifier] (ICLI)
ZSAT..........	Zinc Sulfide Atmospheric Tracer
ZSB............	Zinc Storage Battery
ZSC............	Stauffer Chemical Co., Information Services, Dobbs Ferry, NY [OCLC symbol] (OCLC)
ZSC............	Zeeland Steamship Co. (MHDW)
ZSC............	Zero Subcarrier Chromaticity
ZSC............	Zinc Silicate Coat
ZSC............	Zose [Republic of China] [Seismograph station code, US Geological Survey] (SEIS)
Zschft f Ausl u Intl Privatr...	Zeitschrift fuer Auslaendisches und Internationales Privatrecht [Berlin and Tubingen, Germany] [A publication] (DLA)
Zschft Luft- u Weltr-Recht...	Zeitschrift fuer Luftrecht- und Weltraumrechtsfragen [A publication] (DLA)
Zschft Rechtsvergl...	Zeitschrift fuer Rechtsvergleichung [Vienna, Austria] [A publication] (DLA)
ZSCN..........	Nanchang [China] [ICAO location identifier] (ICLI)
ZSD............	Zebra Stripe Display
ZSD............	Zinc Sulfide Detector
ZSDS..........	Zinc Sulfide Detection System
ZSE............	Seattle, WA [Location identifier FAA] (FAAL)
ZSEV..........	Z Seven Fund [NASDAQ symbol] (TTSB)
ZSEV..........	Z-Seven Fund, Inc. [NASDAQ symbol] (NQ)
Z Sevn.......	Z-Seven Fund, Inc. [Associated Press] (SAG)
ZSF............	Zero Skip Frequency (IAA)
ZSFZ..........	Fuzhou [China] [ICAO location identifier] (ICLI)
ZSG............	Zero-Speed Generator
ZSGZ..........	Ganzhou [China] [ICAO location identifier] (ICLI)
ZSHA..........	Shanghai [China] [ICAO location identifier] (ICLI)
ZSHC..........	Hangzhou/Jianqiao [China] [ICAO location identifier] (ICLI)
ZSI............	Zero Size Image
ZSI............	Zhejiang Shipbuilding Institute (BUAC)

ZSI	Z Solar Inertial (MCD)
ZSI	Zytec Systems, Inc. [*Toronto Stock Exchange symbol Vancouver Stock Exchange symbol*]
ZSJ	St. John's University Library, Jamaica, NY [*OCLC symbol*] (OCLC)
ZSJ	Zangri, S. J., Chicago IL [*STAC*]
ZSJA	Jian [*China*] [*ICAO location identifier*] (ICLI)
ZSL	United Peasant Party [*Poland*] (BUAC)
ZSL	Zero Sight Line (DNAB)
ZSL	ZEROSLOTLAN [*Avatar Technologies, Inc.*] [*In Alliance ZSL, a PC network*]
ZSL	Zjednoczone Stronnictwo Ludowe [*United Peasants' Party*] [*Poland Political party*] (PPW)
ZSL	Zoological Society of London [*British*]
ZSM	Zoologische Staatssammlung Muenchen
ZSN	Zoological Station of Naples
ZSN	Zurich Sunspot Number [*Astrophysics*]
ZSNJ	Nanjing [*China*] [*ICAO location identifier*] (ICLI)
ZSOB	Zinc-Silver-Oxide Battery (RDA)
ZSOF	Hefei/Luogang [*China*] [*ICAO location identifier*] (ICLI)
ZSPG	Zero-Speed Pulse Generator
ZSPS	Zerex Saab Pro Series [*Auto racing*]
ZSQD	Qingdao [*China*] [*ICAO location identifier*] (ICLI)
ZSR	Zeta Sedimentation Rate [*Medicine*] (CPH)
ZSR	Zinc Sedimentation Rate (MEDA)
ZS-RDS	Zung Self-Rating Depression Scale [*Psychology*]
ZSRS	Zung Self-Rating Scale [*For depression*]
ZSS	Sassandra [*Ivory Coast*] [*Airport symbol*] (OAG)
ZSS	Zen Studies Society (EA)
ZSS	Zinc Sulfide System
ZSSA	Shanghai City [*China*] [*ICAO location identifier*] (ICLI)
ZSSA	Zoological Society of Southern Africa [*See also DUSA*] [*Port Elizabeth, South Africa*] (EAIO)
ZSSL	Shanghai/Longhua [*China*] [*ICAO location identifier*] (ICLI)
ZSSS	Shanghai/Hongqiao [*China*] [*ICAO location identifier*] (ICLI)
ZST	Bratislava [*Czechoslovakia*] [*Seismograph station code, US Geological Survey*] (SEIS)
ZST	Stewart [*Canada*] [*Airport symbol*] (OAG)
ZST	Zentralabteilung Strahlenschutz [*Central Department for Radiation Protection*] [*Germany*]
ZST	Zinc Sulfide Tracer
ZST	Zone Standard Time
ZSTAX	Phoenix-Zweig Strategy Fund Cl.A [*Mutual fund ticker symbol*] (SG)
ZSTCX	Phoenix-Zweig Strategy Fund Cl.C [*Mutual fund ticker symbol*] (SG)
ZSTN	Jinan [*China*] [*ICAO location identifier*] (ICLI)
ZSU	San Juan, PR [*Location identifier FAA*] (FAAL)
ZSU	Your Signals are Unreadable [*Amateur radio shorthand*] (WDAA)
ZSUP	Zero Suppress (IAA)
ZSW	Prince Rupert [*Canada*] [*Airport symbol Obsolete*] (OAG)
ZSZ	Sarsat Center [*FAA designator*] (FAAC)
ZT	Aerodrome Control Tower [*ICAO designator*] (ICDA)
ZT	Training Aircraft [*Lighter-than-Air*] [*Navy symbol*] (MUGU)
ZT	Zachary Taylor [*US president, 1784-1850*]
ZT	Z-Axis of External Tank [*NASA*] (NASA)
ZT	Zipper Tubing
ZT	Zone Time [*Navigation*]
ZTA	Zeta Tau Alpha [*Sorority*]
ZTAT	Zero Turn-Around Time [*Microcomputer*] [*Hitachi Ltd.*]
ZTB	Tete A La Baleine [*Canada*] [*Airport symbol*] (OAG)
ZTB	Zone Telephony Box [*Telecommunications*] (ACRL)
Ztbl	Zentralblatt [*Official Gazette*] [*German*]
ZTC	Zero-Temperature Coefficient (MSA)
ZTDC	Zimbabwe Tourist Development Corp. (BUAC)
ZTEC	Zytec Corp. [*NASDAQ symbol*] (SAG)
ZTH	Zakinthos [*Greece*] [*Airport symbol*] (OAG)
Z time	Zebra Time (MED)
ZTJWG	Zeus Target Joint Working Group [*Missiles*] (AAG)
ZTK	Stokmarknes [*Norway*] [*Airport symbol*] (AD)
ZTL	Atlanta, GA [*Location identifier FAA*] (FAAL)
ZTL	Touro Law Library, New York, NY [*OCLC symbol*] (OCLC)
ZTM	Mid-York Library System, Utica, NY [*OCLC symbol*] (OCLC)
ZTN	Zinc Tannate of Naloxone [*Opiate antagonist*]
ZTO	Zero Time Outage [*Nuclear energy*] (NRCH)
ZTO	Zone Transportation Officer [*Military*]
ZTP	Zero-Temperature Plasma
ZTR	Zweig Total Return Fd [*NYSE symbol*] (TTSB)
ZTR	Zweig Total Return Fund, Inc. [*NYSE symbol*] (CTT)
ZTRS	Zambia-Tanzania Road Services [*Zambia*] (BUAC)
ZTS	Zoom Transfer Scope (OA)
ZTS	Zymosan-Treated Serum [*Medicine*] (DMAA)
ZTSCHR	Zeitschrift [*Review*] [*German*]
Z-TSP	Zephiran-Trisodium Phosphate [*Medicine*] (DMAA)
ZTZ	Aerodrome Control Tower [*FAA designator*] (FAAC)
ZU	Upper Area Control Center [*ICAO designator*] (ICDA)
ZU	Utility Aircraft [*Lighter-than-Air*] [*Navy symbol*] (MUGU)
ZU	Zeitlich Untauglich [*Temporarily Unfit*] [*German military - World War II*]
ZU	Zia Airlines [*ICAO designator*] (AD)
ZUA	Agana, GU [*Location identifier FAA*] (FAAL)
ZUA	Central New York Union List of Serials, Syracuse, NY [*OCLC symbol*] (OCLC)
ZUB	Allied Chemical Corp., Library, Solvay, NY [*OCLC symbol*] (OCLC)
ZUC	American Foundation for Management Research, Library, Hamilton, NY [*OCLC symbol*] (OCLC)
ZUCK	Chongqing [*China*] [*ICAO location identifier*] (ICLI)
ZUD	Ancud [*Chile*] [*Airport symbol*] (AD)
ZUD	Bristol Laboratories, Library, Syracuse, NY [*OCLC symbol*] (OCLC)
ZUE	Carrier Corp., Library, Syracuse, NY [*OCLC symbol*] (OCLC)
ZUE	Zuni Energy [*Vancouver Stock Exchange symbol*]
ZUG	Community-General Hospital, Staff Library, Syracuse, NY [*OCLC symbol*] (OCLC)
ZUG	Zugdidi [*Former USSR Seismograph station code, US Geological Survey Closed*] (SEIS)
ZUGY	Guiyang [*China*] [*ICAO location identifier*] (ICLI)
ZUH	Education Opportunity Center of the State University of New York, Syracuse, NY [*OCLC symbol*] (OCLC)
ZUI	General Electric Co., Electronics Park Library, Syracuse, NY [*OCLC symbol*] (OCLC)
ZUJ	General Electric Co., Information Resources Library, Utica, NY [*OCLC symbol*] (OCLC)
ZUK	United States Veterans Administration, Hospital Library, Syracuse, NY [*OCLC symbol*] (OCLC)
ZUL	Agway, Inc., Library, Syracuse, NY [*OCLC symbol*] (OCLC)
ZUL	Silfi [*Saudi Arabia*] [*Airport symbol*] (AD)
zul	Zulu [*MARC language code Library of Congress*] (LCCP)
ZUL	Zurich-Lageren [*Switzerland*] [*Seismograph station code, US Geological Survey*] (SEIS)
ZULS	Lhasa [*China*] [*ICAO location identifier*] (ICLI)
ZUM	Churchill Falls [*Canada*] [*Airport symbol*] (OAG)
ZUM	Supreme Court, Fifth Judicial District, Law Library, Utica, NY [*OCLC symbol*] (OCLC)
ZUM	Zeitschrift fuer Urheber und Medienrecht [*Journal for Copyright and Communication*] [*NOMOS Datapool*] [*Database producer*]
ZUM	Zimbabwe Unity Movement [*Political party*] (ECON)
ZUM	Zoned Usage Messaging [*Computer science*] (CIST)
ZUM	Zone Usage Measurement (WDAA)
ZUN	Saint Joseph's Hospital, Health Center Library, Syracuse, NY [*OCLC symbol*] (OCLC)
zun	Zuni [*MARC language code Library of Congress*] (LCCP)
ZUN	Zuni Pueblo, NM [*Location identifier FAA*] (FAAL)
ZUO	Utica Mutual Insurance Co., Library, New Hartford, NY [*OCLC symbol*] (OCLC)
ZUP	Utica/Marcy Psychiatric Center, Utica Campus Library, Utica, NY [*OCLC symbol*] (OCLC)
ZUP	Zone a Urbaniser en Priorite [*Priority Urbanization Zone*] [*French*]
ZUPO	Zimbabwe United People's Organization [*Political party*] (PPW)
ZUQ	Saint Luke's Memorial Hospital Center, Medical Library, Utica, NY [*OCLC symbol*] (OCLC)
ZUR	Hancock Airbase Library, Hancock Field, NY [*OCLC symbol*] (OCLC)
ZUR	Zurfund International Ltd. [*Vancouver Stock Exchange symbol*]
ZUR	Zurich [*Switzerland*] [*Seismograph station code, US Geological Survey*] (SEIS)
ZURF	Zeus Up-Range Facility [*Missiles*] (AAG)
ZurichR	Zurich Reinsurance Centre Holdings [*Associated Press*] (SAG)
ZurnIn	Zurn Industries, Inc. [*Associated Press*] (SAG)
ZUS	Utica/Marcy Psychiatric Center, Marcy Campus Library, Utica, NY [*OCLC symbol*] (OCLC)
ZUS	Zusammen [*Together*] [*Music*]
ZUT	Maria Regina College, Library, Syracuse, NY [*OCLC symbol*] (OCLC)
ZUTRON	Airship Utility Squadron [*Navy symbol*]
ZUU	Masonic Medical Research Laboratory, Library, Utica, NY [*OCLC symbol*] (OCLC)
ZUUU	Chengdu [*China*] [*ICAO location identifier*] (ICLI)
ZUW	Munson-Williams-Proctor Institute, Library, Utica, NY [*OCLC symbol*] (OCLC)
ZUX	Mohawk Valley Learning Resource Center, Utica Library, Utica, NY [*OCLC symbol*] (OCLC)
ZUY	Special Metals Corp., Library, New Hartford, NY [*OCLC symbol*] (OCLC)
ZUZ	Crouse-Irving Hospital, School of Nursing, Library, Syracuse, NY [*OCLC symbol*] (OCLC)
ZUZ	Upper Area Control Centre [*FAA designator*] (FAAC)
ZUZZ	Zug und Zerschneidezuender [*Pull-and-Cut Igniter*] [*German military - World War II*]
ZV	Air Midwest [*ICAO designator*] (AD)
ZV	Zoomed Video [*Toshiba*] (PCM)
ZV	Zu Verfuegung [*At Disposal*] [*German*] [*Business term*]
ZVA	Jervis Public Library, Rome, NY [*OCLC symbol*] (OCLC)
ZVA	Miandrivazo [*Madagascar*] [*Airport symbol*] (OAG)
ZVA	Zero Order Variable Aperture Nonredundant Point Transmitted [*Compression algorithm*] (MCD)
ZVA	Zero-Voltage Activated [*Circuit*] [*Electronics*] (MED)
ZVB	Syracuse Research Corp., Library, Syracuse, NY [*OCLC symbol*] (OCLC)
ZVC	Utica Public Library, Utica, NY [*OCLC symbol*] (OCLC)
ZVD	Supreme Court of New York, Library, Syracuse, NY [*OCLC symbol*] (OCLC)
ZVEI	Zentralverband der Elektrotechnischen Industrie [*Electrical Equipment Industry Association*] [*Germany*] (EY)
ZVF	Zero-Velocity Fading [*Aviation*] (AIA)
ZVfD	Zionistische Vereinigung fuer Deutschaland [*Zionist Federation of Germany*]
ZVG	Springvale [*Queensland*] [*Airport symbol*] (AD)
ZVK	Savannakhet [*Laos*] [*Airport symbol*] (AD)
ZVM	Mohawk Valley Community College, Utica, NY [*OCLC symbol*] (OCLC)
ZV Port	Zoomed Video Port (PCM)
ZVR	Zener Voltage Regulator
ZVRD	Zener Voltage Regulator Diode
ZVS	Zero Voltage Switch
ZVX	Zygocactus Virus X [*Plant pathology*]

ZVZ	Zavitz Technology, Inc. [*Toronto Stock Exchange symbol*]
ZW	Air Wisconsin [*Airline code*]
ZW	Nike-Zeus at White Sands [*Missile defense*] (SAA)
ZW	Zero Wait [*Industrial engineering*]
ZW	Zero Wear
ZW	Zimbabwe [*ANSI two-letter standard code*] (CNC)
Zw	Zwischensatz [*Interpolation*] [*Music*]
ZWA	Andapa [*Madagascar*] [*Airport symbol*] (OAG)
ZWAK	Aksu [*China*] [*ICAO location identifier*] (ICLI)
ZWC	Zero Word Count
ZWC	Zone Wind Computer
ZWE	Zimbabwe [*ANSI three-letter standard code*] (CNC)
Zweig	Zweig Fund [*Associated Press*] (SAG)
ZweigTl	Zweig Total Return Fund, Inc. [*Associated Press*] (SAG)
ZWHM	Hami [*China*] [*ICAO location identifier*] (ICLI)
ZWKC	Kuqa [*China*] [*ICAO location identifier*] (ICLI)
ZWL	Wollaston Lake [*Canada*] [*Airport symbol*] (OAG)
ZWL	Zero Wavelength
ZWO	Send Words Once [*Amateur radio shorthand*] (WDAA)
ZWO	Zuiver Wentenschappelijk Orderzock [*Netherlands*]
ZWOK	Zirconium-Water Oxidation Kinetics (NRCH)
ZWP	Zone Wind Plotter
ZWS	Zellweger Syndrome [*Medicine*]
ZWS	Zentralwohlfahrtsstelle der Juden in Deutschland [*A publication*] (BJA)
ZWS	Zonal Wind Stress [*Meteorology*]
ZWSH	Kashi [*China*] [*ICAO location identifier*] (ICLI)
ZWSt	Zentralwohlfahrtsstelle der Juden in Deutschland [*A publication*] (BJA)
ZWT	Send Word Twice [*Amateur radio shorthand*] (WDAA)
ZWTN	Hotan [*China*] [*ICAO location identifier*] (ICLI)
ZWU	Union College, Schenectady, NY [*OCLC symbol*] (OCLC)
ZWUQ	Urumqi [*China*] [*ICAO location identifier*] (ICLI)
ZWV	Zero Wave Velocity
ZWW	Zonal Westerly Wind [*Climatology*]
ZWWW	Urumqi/Diwopu [*China*] [*ICAO location identifier*] (ICLI)
ZWYN	Yining [*China*] [*ICAO location identifier*] (ICLI)
ZX	Air West Airlines [*ICAO designator*] (AD)
ZXC	City College of New York, New York, NY [*OCLC symbol*] (OCLC)
ZXCFAR	Zero Crossing Constant False Alarm Rate (MSA)
ZXMP	Zero Transmission Power
ZXX	Exxon Corp., Information Center, Technical Service Coordinator, New York, NY [*OCLC symbol*] (OCLC)
ZY	Air Pennsylvania [*ICAO designator*] (AD)
Zy	Zygion (DMAA)
ZYB	Zionist Year Book [*A publication*] (BJA)
ZyC	Zymosan-Complement Reagent (DB)
Zycad	Zycad Corp. [*Associated Press*] (SAG)
ZYCC	Changchun [*China*] [*ICAO location identifier*] (ICLI)
Zycon	Zycon Corp. [*Associated Press*] (SAG)
ZydcoE	Zydeco Energy, Inc. [*Associated Press*] (SAG)
ZydecoE	Zydeco Energy, Inc. [*Associated Press*] (SAG)
ZYFV	Zucchini Yellow Fleck Virus [*Plant pathology*]
zyg	Zygotene [*Deoxyribonucleic Acid*] [*Genetics*] (DOG)
ZYG	Zygote Resources [*Vancouver Stock Exchange symbol*]
Zygo	Zygo Corp. [*Associated Press*] (SAG)
ZYHB	Harbin/Yanjiagang [*China*] [*ICAO location identifier*] (ICLI)
ZYL	Sylhet [*Bangladesh*] [*Airport symbol*] (OAG)
ZYLA	Hailar [*China*] [*ICAO location identifier*] (ICLI)
Zylo	Zyloprim [*Burroughs Wellcome Co.*] [*Pharmacology*] (DAVI)
ZYMV	Zucchini Yellow Mosaic Virus
Zynaxis	Zynaxis, Inc. [*Associated Press*] (SAG)
ZYP	Zefkrome Yarn Program [*Dow Chemical Co.*]
ZYQQ	Qiqihar [*China*] [*ICAO location identifier*] (ICLI)
ZYSH	Shenyang [*China*] [*ICAO location identifier*] (ICLI)
Zytec	Zytec Corp. [*Associated Press*] (SAG)
ZYTL	Dalian [*China*] [*ICAO location identifier*] (ICLI)
ZYU	New York University, New York, NY [*OCLC symbol*] (OCLC)
ZYYY	Shenyang/Dongta [*China*] [*ICAO location identifier*] (ICLI)
ZYZ	Aerodrome Security Services [*FAA designator*] (FAAC)
ZZ	Aircraft in Flight [*ICAO designator*] (ICDA)
ZZ	Datum Position [*Arbitrary*] [*Navy British*]
ZZ	Lighter-than-Air [*Aircraft*] [*Navy symbol*] (MUGU)
Z-Z	Roll Axis [*Aerospace*] (AAG)
ZZ	Zeitschrift fuer die Wissenschaft des Judentums [*Leopold Zunz*] [*A publication*] (BJA)
ZZ	Zig-Zag
ZZ	Zinziber [*Ginger*] [*Pharmacology*] (ROG)
ZZ	Zugzuender [*Pull Igniter*] [*German military - World War II*]
ZZ	Zu [*or Zur*] Zeit [*At This Time*] [*German*]
ZZA	Zamak Zinc Alloy
ZZB	Zanzibar [*Tanzania*]
ZZC	Zero-Zero Condition
ZZD	Zig-Zag Diagram
ZZM	Agence Nationale des Aerodromes et de la Meteorologie [*Ivory Coast*] [*ICAO designator*] (FAAC)
ZZR	Zig-Zag Rectifier
ZZR	Zigzag Riveting (MSA)
ZZT	Zu Zu [*Tennessee*] [*Seismograph station code, US Geological Survey Closed*] (SEIS)
ZZTFC	ZZ Top Fan Club (EA)
ZZU	Mzuzu [*Malawi*] [*Airport symbol*] (AD)
ZZV	Zanesville [*Ohio*] [*Airport symbol*] (AD)
ZZV	Zanesville, OH [*Location identifier FAA*] (FAAL)
ZZV	Zero-Zero Visibility
ZZW	Zero-Zero Weather
ZZZ	Aircraft in Flight [*FAA designator*] (FAAC)